Model of dictionary layout

pronunciation following headword, with stress mark (') following the accented syllable

alternative headwords with different pronunciations

abbreviation listed in text

superscripts on homographs

partial pronunciation of derivative

semicolons separating definitions

dashes separating parts of speech and derivatives

dash separating derivatives from compounds

semicolon separating compounds

cross-reference to alternative form

examples of different types of **etymology**

alternative plural forms

combined adjective and **noun** definitions

Dansker *dan'skər*, (*Shakesp*) *n* a Dane.
dant and **danton**. Earlier forms of **daunt** and **daunton**.
Dantean *dan'ti-ən* or **Dantesque** *dan-tesk'*, *adj* like (the work of) the Italian poet *Dante* Alighieri; sublime; austere. — *n* **Dan'tist** a Dante scholar. — *n* **Dantoph'-ilist** a lover of Dante.
DAP (*comput*) *abbrev*: distributed array processor.
dap[1] *dap*, *vi* to bounce; to dip gently into water; to fish with a fly bounced gently on the surface. — *n* a bait so used; a bounce. — *n* **dapp'er**. [Origin obscure]
dap[2] *dap*, (*dialect*) *n* a gym shoe, plimsoll. [Prob **dap**[1]]
daphne *daf'ni*, *n* any plant of the *Daphne* genus (family *Thymelaeaceae*) of shrubs, *incl* mezereon and spurge-laurel. [Gr *daphnē* sweet bay]
Daphnia *daf'ni-ə*, *n* a genus of water flea. — *n* **daph'nid** (*-nid*) any member of the genus. [Gr *Daphne*]
dapper[1] *dap'ər*, *adj* quick; little and active; neat; spruce. — *n* **dapp'erling** (*archaic*) a dapper little fellow. — *adv* **dapp'erly**. — *n* **dapp'erness**. [Du *dapper* brave; cf Ger *tapfer* quick, brave]
dapper[2]. See **dap**[1].
dapple *dap'l*, *adj* marked with spots or splotches; mottled. — *vt* to variegate with splotches of colour or shade. — *adj* **dapp'led**. — *adj* and *n* **dapp'le-bay'** (an animal, *esp* a horse) of bay colour, variegated with dapples; **dapp'le-grey'** (an animal, *esp* a horse) of a pale grey colour with darker spots. [Origin unknown]
dapsone *dap'sōn*, *n* a drug widely used in the treatment of leprosy, dermatitis, etc. [*di*aminodi*p*henyl*s*ulph*one*]
daquiri. See **daiquiri**.
DAR *abbrev*: Daughters of the American Revolution, a patriotic women's organization dating from 1890.
daraf *dar'af*, (*elec*) *n* a unit of elastance, the reciprocal of capacitance in farads. [*Farad* backwards]
darbies *där'biz*, (*slang*) *n pl* handcuffs. [Appar from the personal name *Darby*]
Darby and Joan *där'bi-ənd-jōn'*, *n* a devoted elderly married couple. — **Darby and Joan Club** a social club for elderly people. [Poss from characters in an 18c song]
Darbyite *där'bi-īt*, *n* a member of the Plymouth Brethren, more particularly of the Exclusive branch of the sect. [From their principal founder, J N *Darby* (1800–82)]
darcy *där'si*, (*geol*) *n* a unit used to express the permeability coefficient of a rock, for example in calculating the flow of oil, gas or water: — *pl* **dar'cys** or **dar'cies**. [From H-P-G Darcy (1803–58), Fr engineer]
Dard *därd*, *n* a person belonging to any of the peoples who speak Dardic languages. — *adj* and *n* **Dard'ic** (of or relating to) a particular Indo-European language group spoken in parts of Northern India, Pakistan and Afghanistan.

See also page x

THE CHAMBERS DICTIONARY

Managing editor
Catherine Schwarz

Chambers lexicographers
George Davidson
Elaine Higgleton
Susan Rennie
Mairi Robinson
Anne Seaton

External lexicographers
Kay Cullen
Virginia Klein
Ruth Martin
Howard Sargeant

Assistant lexicographers
Jock Graham
Rachel Hammerton
Michael Nath

We would like to acknowledge with thanks the contributions of the many members of the public who send in suggestions and comments. Such contributions are always welcome, and will be acknowledged. They should be sent to:
The Editor, *The Chambers Dictionary*, Chambers Harrap Publishers Ltd, 43-45 Annandale Street, Edinburgh, EH7 4AZ.

THE CHAMBERS DICTIONARY

Chambers

CHAMBERS
An imprint of Larousse plc
43-45 Annandale Street
Edinburgh EH7 4AZ

This edition published by Chambers Harrap Publishers Ltd 1993

Reprinted 1993, 1994 (twice)

We have made every effort to mark as such all words which we believe to be trademarks. We should also like to make it clear that the presence of a word in the dictionary, whether marked or unmarked, in no way affects its legal status as a trademark.

A CIP catalogue record for this book is available from the British Library

ISBN 0-550-10255-8 Standard
ISBN 0-550-10256-6 Thumb index
ISBN 0-550-10257-4 Gift edition
ISBN 0-550-10258-2 De luxe edition

Typeset in Great Britain at The University Press, Cambridge
Printed in England by Clays Ltd, St Ives plc

Contents

Preface

The Chambers Dictionary, the product of a long line of dictionary-making, is directly descended, through *Chambers English Dictionary*, from *Chambers's Twentieth Century Dictionary*. With the publication of each succeeding edition, editors have kept abreast of contemporary changes in the requirements of users and in language – before the 1930's few people had heard of crosswords, and in the 1950's most people were unaware of the language of computing. For this edition, careful attention has been paid to ensure that both the requirements and the language of the last decade of the century will be well served by this dictionary.

Extensively revised and updated, *The Chambers Dictionary* is *the* dictionary of its kind, a unique presentation of the English language from Chaucer to the present day, with words old and new, unusual and commonplace, treated with the accuracy, clarity and insight for which Chambers is renowned. It reflects recent developments in every sphere of life, science, sport, technology, politics, food, economics and entertainment all contributing, along with many others, to this treasury of English. Monitoring this growing language is one of the most rewarding tasks of the lexicographer; a few of the thousands of words we have scrutinized in the course of compiling this edition will make the point. Maastricht re-introduced **subsidiarity**, **crop circles** came from nowhere, **jukeboxes** moved into computing, the **fatwa** became more widely known, and **grunge** crossed the Atlantic.

With this new edition, *Chambers* continues to play its part in recording and encouraging the development of English. We hope that old friends will continue to find in it what they want, and more, and that it will bring a taste of the richness, diversity, and even humour of English to a wider public. *Chambers* is more than a dictionary to be used for finding the meaning of a word or for checking a spelling; it is a book for browsing in. At a lunch in Oxford in 1991 to celebrate the publication of the *Observer*'s AZED 1000 crossword, Richard Morse toasted *Chambers* as: '...the immensely readable book. Just as one can frequently take a short shopping list into a supermarket only to emerge with several additional purchases, so more pleasantly the checking of a single word in Chambers may lead to a more extensive acquisition of lexical items than had originally been intended.'

The comprehensiveness of its coverage commends *Chambers* as the dictionary for crosswords and other wordgames. It is the reference dictionary for the National Scrabble® Championship, the National Scrabble® Club Tournament, and the National Scrabble® Under-16 Championship. For those with competitive ambitions requiring word skills, it is the obvious choice, the width and character of its coverage being unrivalled by any other one-volume dictionary.

We are grateful to all who have played a part in making *The Chambers Dictionary* what it is – former editors, on whose firm foundations we have been able to build and extend; authors, scientists, politicians, broadcasters, in fact all who enrich the language; all readers, radio listeners and television viewers who help us in collecting this language; correspondents, spread across the world, many of whom have been assiduous in their encouragement and help over a considerable number of years. To all these, we express our acknowledgement, appreciation and thanks.

At the beginning of this century one of our predecessors, the editor of *Chambers's Twentieth Century Dictionary of the English Language*, wrote that the book 'will be found to possess many serviceable qualities'. Dr Davidson's claim, though modest in terms of today's marketing jargon, is one that we are proud still to make of *The Chambers Dictionary* 1993.

Catherine Schwarz
Managing Editor

Does grammar matter?

People often wonder where the role of the dictionary ends and the role of the grammar book begins. Dictionaries list words as individual units and explain their meanings, but what should they tell us about grammar? What *can* they tell us? Often words have many meanings, and the exact meaning of a word can only be determined from the surrounding context. The very idea of the 'word' is fraught with difficulty; linguists and philosophers (and indeed poets) have argued for centuries over what it really denotes. What matters is not individual words, but the ways in which words are assembled into utterances that convey meaning. These processes are governed by principles that together constitute what we call *grammar*, and there are important ways in which dictionaries, word-based though they are, can help explain them.

But there are problems with the concept of grammar. Grammar means different things to different people, and these differences cause much confusion. To the linguist, it means the codification of usage, and is a description of the ways in which words are *typically* used, according to carefully collected evidence. (Nowadays, computers play an important part in analysing this evidence.) Since usage changes, grammar is unstable; and since there are different varieties and dialects of English, there are many grammars.

What is ungrammatical, in this understanding of the term, is anything that does not conform to a typical pattern of usage. For example, the sentence *we promised them to stay* is ungrammatical, because (unlike *we promised to stay* and *we told them to stay*) it conforms to none of the patterns in which English is typically used. A phrase like *the green large house* is normally ungrammatical because English word-order (which is an important part of grammar) typically prefers *the large green house*. (We have to say 'normally' because we might exceptionally say *the green large house* to imply 'and not the red one'. However, we are talking about what is *typical*.) Why this should be so defies explanation and is beside the point: it is a fact of usage, and not a principle based on some objective criterion such as logic.

Other uses can be correct in one variety or dialect but not in another. For example, the second person pronoun in standard English is now invariably *you*, irrespective of the number and status of the people addressed. In some dialects this seems to be socially insufficient and alternative forms continue to exist (as in other languages, like French which has *tu* and *vous* and German which has three forms *du*, *ihr*, and *Sie*). The dialect of Liverpool, and other Irish-influenced dialects, have a plural form *youse*, as in *who are youse*? Although this is correct in the grammar of its dialect, because it is a typical usage, it is obviously not correct in the context of generally accepted standard English.

These examples of linguistic characteristics are the concern of grammar in its descriptive role. To many, grammar means something rather more restricted, namely *correct* usage. There is no doubt that language can be correct and incorrect, but what exactly does this mean? We all know that language is changing, and has been changing constantly for hundreds of years; so how do we determine what is correct and incorrect at any one time?

Clearly, uses like *we promised them to stay* and *the green large house*, that do not conform to any typical pattern, are incorrect in the sense of being ungrammatical. But what of the many uses that conform to one variety of usage but not others? For example, some dialects allow a pattern such as *she be late* instead of *she is late*; but it would usually be regarded as wrong. Then there is the question of spelling. Spellings vary from one form of English to another, and there are many variants even within one form of English. For example, we can write *judgement* or *judgment*, since both are correct. But we cannot write *accomodate* instead of *accommodate*, because it is regarded as wrong. What is the difference here?

To answer these questions, we have to consider that, although there are many varieties and dialects of English, all with their own grammars, there is a form of English that is most widely acceptable, and it is called standard English. It is not a dialect in the normal understanding of the term, because then it would be regionally located and would have words and phrases not found in other forms of the language; nor is it an accent, because standard English can be spoken in any accent. It is not even a variety, strictly speaking, because standard English exists within other varieties: there is standard British English and standard American English (more usually called General American English).

Standard English is an institutionalized form of English; that is to say, it is the form that is socially most acceptable throughout the society in which English is used. It is the form that foreign learners seek to learn, and it is the form that is most widely taught in schools. Uses that do not conform to the rules of standard English are regarded as incorrect; and they are indeed incorrect in terms of the 'standard'. This is not to say, however, that other varieties are incorrect; they are, if you like, 'non-standard'. No one would dream of questioning the validity of Scottish English, or dare to call it incorrect; and the same should be true of other varieties, the forms used for example in Northern England or in the Midlands or in East London.

On the question of spelling, it is important to

note that although English tolerates a considerable degree of variation in spelling, standard English still rejects some commonly used forms. There is very little apparent difference in principle between *judgment* (an acceptable variant) and *accomodate* (an unacceptable one), or between *advisor* (an acceptable variant of *adviser*) and *harrass* (an unacceptable variant of *harass*). In fact, there is a rule operating in the case of *judg(e)ment*, that a final unpronounced e can be dropped in certain circumstances when derivative words are formed; but it is a rule founded on usage and practicality, and is not predictable. And there are complete illogicalities: why *harass* with one *r* but *embarrass* with two, when both have similar Old French origins? All we can say is that some variants become accepted and others do not.

It is therefore an important purpose of a dictionary to inform users about which forms are correct and which are incorrect. The common spelling *despatch* is an acceptable variant because Samuel Johnson used it in his dictionary of 1755. He did so despite the fact that all his evidence – which he quotes in the dictionary – used the form *dispatch*. We do not know the reason for his choice, and it may even have been a slip of the pen. Whatever the case, its inclusion gave the new spelling an authority that seems to be based on little more than accident. No one questions it now, but people used to regard it as a suspect spelling.

Grammar matters, then, because it is the accepted way of using language, whatever one's exact interpretation of the term. Incorrect grammar hampers communication, which is the whole purpose of language. The grammar of standard English matters because it is a codification of the way of using English that most people will find acceptable. It is, of course, as much a social and political issue as a linguistic one.

The concept of good and correct usage in English is relatively recent in relation to the history of the language: it is already apparent by about 1600, when Thomas Nashe and other poets wrote about 'cleansing' English of impure uses (usually words that are not Anglo-Saxon). 18th-century grammarians – who were often also writers, including Thomas Cooke (1703–56) and more famously Bishop Robert Lowth (1710–87) – expounded it at some length. But for a language that has been in use for fifteen centuries this is indeed relatively recent. Supposedly declining standards of language are often taken as a sign – or even as a result – of social ills more generally: for example by the diarist John Evelyn in the 1660s. They are too in our own day.

In the 18th and 19th centuries, grammarians looked to Latin as the model of English grammar. Bishop Lowth was one. Another was J C Nesfield, whose *Manual of English Grammar and Composition* was published in 1898. This accounts for many principles that were adopted at the time: that a preposition should not end a sentence (because they do not in Latin sentences), that *different* should be followed by *from* (because *different* is regarded as a derivative of *differ*), and that the infinitive (eg *to be*) should not be split (eg *to really be*; because it is regarded as a unit). It is worth pointing out that no one complained about the split infinitive before about 1850. Up to that time it had been used freely and naturally, and can be found in the work of great writers and poets including Shakespeare and Lord Byron.

The traditional eight parts of speech, which are still widely current and are used in most dictionaries for native speakers (although decreasingly in those for learners of English), are based on those devised by classical grammarians who lived before the birth of Christ. These categories do not work very well in modern English; and hardly at all in the case of the adverb, which is a catch-all category of ill-matched terms as diverse in usage as *happily* and *only*, and *very* and *fast*. The terms are so well established that they are the basis of most discussion about language; but we should be aware of their shortcomings.

In our own day, the classical model is in decline. Latin is taught less and less in schools. Linguists complain, with good reason, that it is absurd to impose the grammar of one language on another, when it has a structure that is so patently different. But since this model still forms a basis – if a less sure one – of standard English, it is important that speakers and writers of English should be aware of it, and that dictionaries should advise users of its principles. In doing so, they are not propounding eternal truths, or even necessarily effectiveness of communication, but are stating the social requirements involved in the use of language. It is also important, of course, that users of a language should understand its structure and how to talk about it; and this involves knowing the special vocabulary, or *metalanguage*, of grammatical terms with which to describe it.

Most general dictionaries therefore describe words on the basis of the standard form of English, and indicate any words and uses that are well attested but deviate from the standard. Word-based grammar, where the grammatical point is determined by the word used, is within the remit of the dictionary. This includes inflection (as in *takes*, *took*, *taking*, and so on) and derivation (as in forms like *painter* and *laughable*), and processes such as government, by which one word affects the behaviour of other words used in its company (for example, the word *promise* requiring a *that* clause as in *we promised them that we'd stay*). Other aspects of syntax, which deals with the theoretically infinite juxtapositions of words, usually lie outside this remit.

Within the scope that is possible in a good dictionary, users will be guided to a better understanding and use of the standard form of English. This ability is indispensable to clear and effective communication that will find acceptance wherever English is spoken and used throughout the world.

Robert Allen
Editorial Director

Characters used in etymologies

A brief guide to the pronunciation of some of the non-English characters which appear most frequently in etymologies is given below. The pronunciations given are necessarily approximate as it is not always possible to convey the exact phonetic values intended by means of respelling symbols or verbal explanations.

Vowels

Symbol	Sound
ā, ē, ī, ū	In etymologies, these are long vowels with the sounds (or approximately the sounds) represented by the respelling symbols *a* or *ä*, *ā* or *e*, *ē*, and *o͞o* respectively.
ō	This represents a long *o* or *ö* sound or a monophthongal pronunciation of the respelling character *ō*.
ȳ	A long *ü* sound.
ǣ	A long vowel similar in sound to the RP pronunciation of respelling symbol *a*.
a, e, etc, *ă, ĕ*, etc	Short vowels corresponding to *ā, ē*, etc, with values, varying from language to language, similar to those of the corresponding long vowels or those of the short vowels of English; in Romanian, *ă* has the sound *ə*.
â, ê, î, ô, û	In some languages, eg Middle High German, these symbols are used for long vowels with the values *ä, ā, ē, ō, o͞o* respectively; in Romanian, *â* and *î* represent a sound midway between *ē* and *o͞o*.
ä, ö	These have the values of respelling symbols *e*/*ā* and *ø*/*œ* respectively.
ĩ, etc	The diacritic ˜ is used, as in the respelling, to show nasalization of vowels.

Consonants

Symbol	Sound
ḍ, ṭ, ṇ, ṣ	These are retroflex counterparts of *t, d*, etc.
ṛ	In Sanskrit, a vowel rather than a consonant; in Hindi, etc, a consonant formed by the tongue moving from a retroflex position to strike against the teeth-ridge.
ḥ	The normal *h*-sound of English.
ṁ	This marks nasalization of the preceding vowel or the following consonant in Sanskrit.
ñ	A sound similar to *ny*, as in Spanish *cañon*.
ṅ	The sound written *ng* in the respelling and in English orthography.
c	In Sanskrit, etc, a sound midway between *k* and *ch*; in Turkish, the sound of *j* as in *judge*.
ç	In French, Arabic and Portuguese, this represents the sound *s*; in Turkish, *ch*.
č, ć	In Serbo-Croat, *č* represents the sound *ch*, and *ć* represents *ty*.
ş	In Turkish, the sound *sh*.
ś	In Sanskrit, etc, a sound similar to *sh*.
q	In Arabic, a sound similar to *k* but pronounced slightly farther back in the mouth; in Chinese, a sound like *ch*; in Gothic, *kw*.
ğ	This marks a lengthening of the preceding vowel in Turkish.
gg	In Gothic, the sound *ng*.
’	In Russian words, this represents a ‘soft sign’, marking a *y*-like palatalization of the preceding consonant; in Chinese words, it is a mark of strong aspiration; in Arabic, Hebrew and Hawaiian, a glottal stop.
‘	In Arabic and Hebrew, a sound like *hh* but produced rather deeper in the throat.

Using the dictionary

(see also inside front cover)

Order of entries

All entries are listed alphabetically, each entry having as a basic pattern the following elements:

(1) Headword
(2) Pronunciation
(3) Part of speech label
(4) Definition(s)
(5) Etymology

Within this framework there are often subheads – words that are derived from the headword (*derivatives*), or *compounds* or *phrases* that include the headword or one of its derivatives. This grouping of related words within an entry preserves and explains their etymological 'family' link, while at the same time ensuring that space is used as effectively as possible.

Where, however, such grouping is felt to be less helpful to the user we have separated the words into independent entries, as at **graduate** and **society**, showing their relationships to **grade** and **social** by means of the etymologies.

Structure

The main elements of an entry are explained in greater detail below:

1. Headword

The word (in **bold** type) projecting at the head of an entry is referred to as the headword. Headwords are listed in alphabetical order.

Superscript numbers are added to headwords where necessary (see eg **cape**^{1}, **cape**^{2}) to indicate homographs (words of identical spelling but of different meaning, origin, etc).

Included in the headword list, in alphabetical order, are **cross-references**, words of which the full entry, or on which further information, is to be found elsewhere in the dictionary. Also included in the alphabetical headword sequence are **abbreviation** and **symbol** entries, which follow full-word entries of identical spelling, and which themselves are followed by **prefix**, **suffix** and **combining form** entries (see page **xi**).

2. Pronunciation

(see also inside back cover)

A respelling system (detailed on the inside back cover) has been used in this dictionary. It is a method that is intelligible to people who are not familiar with phonetic symbols, and one that allows for more than one interpretation – so that each user of the dictionary may choose a pronunciation in keeping with his or her speech.

A quick guide to some common vowel sounds is given on alternate pages of the dictionary.

Pronunciation guidance (in *italic* type) follows the headword, and is given elsewhere in an entry in parentheses where helpful. The main, current British pronunciations are given, and also significant US, etc variants if appropriate, but the numerous possible regional variations cannot be covered individually in a dictionary of this size. See pages xiv and xv for details on American English and other varieties.

Guidance on stress patterns in words of more than one syllable is given by the use of the stress mark ('), which *follows* the syllable that has the main accent, both in respelling and in subheads for which no full or partial respelling is required.

3. Part of speech label

Following the pronunciation at the head of an entry is a label to indicate the headword's part of speech (eg *adj* for adjective, *n* for noun). A further part of speech label may follow a set of definitions, to show that the preceding bold word is also used as another type of word (eg **gash**^{1} *vt* to cut deeply into. – *n* a deep, open cut).

Part of speech labels are given after all headwords except some foreign phrases, and before each direct derivative word. Compound nouns are not labelled.

Entries for prefix, suffix and combining form items treat all compound subheads as derivative items, with individual part of speech labels.

4. Definition(s)

Definitions in the dictionary entries are ordered and grouped with a view to clarity, ease of comprehension and use. Normally the most common meanings are given first, unless an earlier, perhaps more specific, sense serves to clarify or explain its subsequent use.

Definitions are separated by semicolons.

In abbreviation and symbol entries, definitions are listed alphabetically.

5. Etymology

The etymology is given in square brackets at the end of the entry. If no etymology is shown, this indicates that the origin and history of the headword is unknown or uncertain. A bold word given as an etymology directs the reader to that word entry as the derivation; other etymologies may direct the reader directly to another etymology. A bold prefix given as an etymology indicates that the headword is formed from that prefix plus the remaining word-item; both elements may be found at their separate dictionary entries.

For abbreviations used in etymologies and elsewhere in the dictionary, see pages xvi–xviii.

6. Subheads

Subheads are bold-print items not listed as separate entries, but listed and explained within an entry. Note the order in which subheads appear in an entry:

(a) *Direct derivatives*

These are words which are formed by adding a suffix or ending either to the headword or to the root word. They are given, alphabetically, immediately after the various meanings of the headword. Each is given a grammatical (part of speech) label. Their pronunciation basically follows that of the headword, with stress marks placed *after* the syllable with the main accent. Where necessary, fuller respelling guidance is given in parentheses. If the meaning of a regular, direct derivative is readily deducible, it may be undefined.

(b) *Compounds*

Compound words (ie those made up of two or more words, the first being the entry headword or one of its derivatives) follow any direct derivatives. They may be hyphenated, one-word or two-word compounds. If the compound's meaning is evident from its two parts, it may be undefined. Where no grammatical label has been given at a compound, it is to be assumed to be a noun. Those compounds which do not begin with the headword or derivative of the headword are listed under the third category, the phrases.

(c) *Phrases*

Following any direct derivatives and any compound words, all phrasal items relating to the headword are listed alphabetically. These may be phrases, phrasal verbs or idioms, or compounds which do not begin with the headword or any of its derivatives.

7. Alternative forms

Words spelt or formed in more than one way, but sharing the same meaning(s) and use, are shown in the dictionary linked by the word 'or'. Where a number of such alternatives are shown, strict alphabetical order may be waived in order to list the most commonly used form first.

At headwords, alternative forms that have different pronunciations are each followed immediately by their appropriate pronunciation(s). If the pronunciation follows both headword forms, it applies to both forms.

In hyphenated compound words, alternative forms may often be shown only by the alternative element of the compound (eg **hunt'ing=box**, **-lodge** or **-seat**).

8. Hyphenation

The symbol = at the end of a line, as in **hunting=box** above, denotes a hyphenated compound.

9. Inflections

Inflected words are shown, following a colon, after the definition(s) of a word (if any). Plural forms and verb participles, etc are shown only if they are irregular in formation, or warrant special clarification. Comparative and superlative forms of adjectives are given (again by the same criteria). Current *equivalent* feminine forms appear alongside the masculine forms, whereas distinctively or less commonly used feminine forms are shown, following a colon, after the definition(s).

10. Classification labels

A label relating to the classification (eg *colloq*, *slang*, *chem*, *elec*, *psychol*) of a word or meaning *precedes* the list of meanings where it applies to all of the meanings given.

Where a label applies to only one definition in a list, it immediately *follows* that definition.

A label which precedes the part of speech label at the head of an entry applies to *all* meanings of the word *and* to its derivatives and their meanings unless or until it is cancelled by a further classification label. This applies also where there is only one sense and one meaning of a word.

Classification labels are shown in italic print.

Foreign words A bracketed abbreviation (eg *Fr*, *Ger*) preceding the part of speech label at the head of an entry signifies that the word is still regarded as a foreign word, rather than as a naturalized English word. German nouns have been spelt with a capital letter, as they are in their country of origin.

11. Alternative pronunciations

As for alternative word forms, alternative pronunciations are shown in the dictionary linked by the word 'or', or by a comma in a string of alternatives. The main, current British pronunciations of a word are given, and also significant and commonly-encountered US, Australian, etc variants as applicable.

Alternative pronunciations at a headword are generally given in full. Elsewhere in an entry simply the syllable or syllables of a word which may be pronounced alternatively are given.

In all alternative or partial pronunciations, that part of a word not included in the respelling is to be assumed unchanged from the main pronunciation given earlier in the entry.

12. Prefix, suffix and combining forms

These entries are treated as ordinary word entries except in the respects specified below.

In the respelling given at a prefix or similar headword, often no stress pattern is specified, as it varies according to the words formed with that element.

Entries for prefix, suffix and combining form items (as already noted in **3**) show a separate part of speech label at each compound subhead 'nested' within the entry, treating them as derivatives of the headword.

Different senses within these entries are separated by semicolons. Where these senses are used for reference (eg in footers (see **12** below) or etymologies), they have been numbered.

13. Footers

These are lists, in panels at the foot of relevant pages, of words formed by the prefixes **anti-**, **non-**, **out-**, **over-**, **pre-**, **re-**, **sub-**, **super-**, **un-** and **under-** and not already listed in the dictionary.

The parts of speech and stress patterns of these words are shown; their meanings can be easily derived by referring to the numbered prefix entry, and if necessary to the word to which the prefix has been attached.

Rules of English spelling

The most important spelling rules are explained in this article; an understanding of these is assumed for all entries in the dictionary where no inflected form (plural, past tense, etc) is given. Inflected forms are given for words that have inflections with unpredictable spellings (eg *tangos* and *mangoes*), inflections with spellings that do not follow the general rules (*paid* and *laid* as opposed to *played*), or inflections that are regular but about which there is often uncertainty (eg *monkeys*, not '*monkies*').

In general, derivatives (eg nouns and adverbs based on adjectives, such as *brightness* and *brightly* from *bright*, or adjectives formed from nouns, such as *noisy* from *noise*) are spelt out in full in the dictionary, but since the rules for the formation of such derivatives are much the same as for inflections, they are covered here also.

The rules given here are those that apply in British English. See also p xiv for the rules of American spelling, where these differ from the British norm.

The basic rules of inflection and derivation:

(i) Plural **nouns** are normally formed by adding *-s* to the singular form:
cat cats *dog dogs* *horse horses*
(NB There should be no apostrophe before the *s* in a plural noun; forms like *bag's of potato's* are commonly seen but are quite wrong. *Do's* is an exception, though *dos* is also correct.)

Verbs are generally inflected by adding *-s*, *-ing* and *-ed* to the base form:
follow follows following followed

If a word ends in *s*, *z*, *x*, *sh* or *ch*, *-es* is added rather than *-s*:
kiss kisses *box boxes* *push pushes*
However, if the *ch* is pronounced [*k*] or [*hh*], *-s* alone is added:
stomachs, *lochs*, *psychs*

(ii) Comparative and superlative **adjectives** (and some adverbs) are formed by the addition of *-er* and *-est* to the base form:
black blacker blackest

(iii) **Derivatives** of nouns, verbs and adjectives are generally formed by the simple addition of a suffix to the stem:
sing singer *move movement*
red redness *cruel cruelty*
Adjectives which end in *ic* form adverbs in *-ally*: *economic economically*
(The only common exception is *publicly*.)

Inflection of nouns and verbs ending in *o*:

(i) Most **nouns** ending in *o* add *-s* to form the plural:
zoo zoos *radio radios* *Eskimo Eskimos* *albino albinos*

A small group of words add *-es*, eg *cargoes*, *echoes*, *goes*, *heroes*, *potatoes*. A number of words, such as *banjo*, *fiasco* and *halo*, may add either *-s* or *-es*. These are indicated in the dictionary.

(ii) For the 3rd person singular of the present tense of the **verb**, the rule for adding *-s* or *-es* can be stated in terms of the noun rules:
if the noun takes only *-s*, or if there is no related noun, add *-s*:
two radios → *she radios*
if the noun takes *-es* in the plural, or may take either *-s* or *-es*, add *-es* to the verb:
two echoes → *it echoes*
(The only exception to this is *do*, plural *do's* or *dos*, 3rd person singular *does*.)

Words ending in *y*:

(i) A **noun** ending in *y* preceded by a consonant generally has a plural in *-ies*:
fly flies *country countries*
Proper nouns are an exception (eg *the four Marys*), as are words in which the final *y* belongs to the adverbial part of a compound (eg *lay-bys*, *stand-bys*).
If the final *y* is preceded by a vowel, it does not change to *ie* in the plural:
day days *donkey donkeys*
(but see *money* for the exceptional plural *monies*)

(ii) The rules for **verb** inflections are much the same as for nouns. If the *y* follows a consonant, it changes to *ie* before *-s*, but if it follows a vowel, it does not:
cry cries *deny denies*
but
stay stays *enjoy enjoys* *buy buys*
Similarly, in the past tense:
cry cried *deny denied*
but
stay stayed *enjoy enjoyed*
(*Said*, *paid* and *laid* are exceptions.)

(iii) **Adjectives** ending in *y* preceded by a consonant generally change the *y* to *i* in the comparative and superlative:
happy happier happiest
The only exceptions are a few one-syllable words in which the final *y* is pronounced [*ī*]: see the dictionary entries for *dry*, *shy*, *sly*, etc.

If the final *y* is preceded by a vowel, it generally does not change in the comparative and superlative:
grey greyer greyest *coy coyer coyest*
However, a number of adjectives ending in *ey* (mostly ones based on nouns, eg

clayey from *clay*) change the *ey* to *i*:
clayey clayier clayiest

(iv) **Derivatives** follow similar rules as those for inflections, ie a *y* following a consonant changes to an *i* before a following suffix (except *-ing*), whereas one following a vowel does not:
happy happily happiness
merry merriment *deny denier*
envy enviable *comply compliant*
but
coy coyly coyness
employ employment *play player*
enjoy enjoyable *buoy buoyant*
Words which are exceptions to the inflectional rules tend to be exceptions also to the derivational rules, but the irregularities are not always predictable. See the dictionary entries for *dry*, *shy*, *sly*, etc. (Note also the spelling of *busyness*, to distinguish it from *business*.)

Words ending in *e*:
Before a suffix beginning with a vowel, the final *e* is generally dropped:
smile smiling smiled smiler
white whiter whitest whiten
pale palish *ice icy*
use usable *escape escapism*

Before a consonant, the *e* is retained:
move movement
use useful useless

There are, however, exceptions:

(i) Verbs ending in *ee*, *oe* and *ye* do not drop the *e* before *-ing*:
hoe hoeing *dye dyeing*

(ii) Verbs ending in *ie* change the *ie* to *y* before *-ing*:
die dying *tie tying*

(iii) A few verbs retain the final *e* in order to show the correct pronunciation and to be distinguishable from similar words with no *e*:
sing singing but *singe singeing*
swing swinging but *swingeing*
(Note also the adjective *holey* = full of holes, as opposed to *holy*.)

(iv) Before an *-a-* or an *-o-*, the *e* is retained after a soft *c* or *g*:
notice noticing but *noticeable*
advantage advantageous

(v) Adverbs formed from adjectives ending in *le* preceded by a consonant simply replace the final *e* with *y*:
simple simply *single singly*

(vi) Words ending in *-dge* may correctly retain or drop the final *e* in derivatives; thus *judgment* and *judgement*, *abridgment* and *abridgement* are equally correct.

(vii) Common exceptions to all the above rules are *argument*, *awful*, *daily*, *duly*, *eerily*, *gaily*, *truly* and *wholly*.

Doubling of a final consonant:
If a word ends in a single consonant which is preceded by a single vowel written with a single letter and the stress of the word is on the final syllable of the word (or if there is only one syllable), the final consonant is doubled before a suffix beginning with a vowel:
drum drumming drummed drummer
omit omitting omitted
refer referring referred referral
red redder reddest redden
ton tonnage
but
dream dreaming dreamed dreamer
profit profiting profited
enter entering entered
refer reference (note the change in stress)
green greener greenest
A few words double the final consonant contrary to the above rule:
worship worshipping worshipped worshipper
(and also *format*, *handicap*, *hobnob*, *humbug*, *kidnap*, *leapfrog* and *zigzag*)
A final *l* preceded by a single-letter vowel generally doubles regardless of the position of the stress, as in
signal signalling signalled signaller
rebel rebelling rebellion rebellious
cancel cancelling cancellation
but not before the suffixes *-ize*/*-ise*, *-ism*, *-ist* and *-ity*, as in
equal equality equalize
final finalist
though again there are exceptions, such as *medallist*, *tranquillity* and *crystallize*.
Note also *paralleling* and *paralleled* (where one would expect a double *ll* before the suffix) and *woolly* and *woollen* (where one would expect a single *l*).
A few words allow both single and double consonants: see the dictionary entries for eg *benefit*, *bias*, *bus*, *focus*, *gas*, *leaflet*, *plus* and *yes*.

Words ending in *c*:
When a suffix beginning with a vowel is added, and the consonant still has the hard [*k*] sound, the *c* becomes *ck*:
picnic picnicking picnicked picnicker
Two exceptions are *arc* and *talc*:
arcing/arcking, *arced/arcked*
talcing/talcking, *talced/talcked*
The forms without *k* are the commoner.
No *k* is added when the final *c* becomes a soft sound ([*sh*] or [*s*]) in the derivative:
magic magicking magicked but *magician*
electric electricity

***-ie-* or *-ei-*?**
The rule '*i* before *e* except after *c*' applies only to words in which the vowel has the long [*ē*] sound:
believe belief *siege* *pier*
but
deceive *deceit* *ceiling*
(Common exceptions are *seize*, *weir* and *weird*, scientific words such as *protein*, *caffeine* and *codeine*, and proper names such as *Keith*, *Neil*, *Sheila*, *Reid* and *Madeira*.)
If a word is pronounced with the sound [*ā*], *ei* is always the correct spelling:
eight *heir* *neighbour* *reign* *weight*

American English

There are many differences between the forms of English spoken and written in Britain and America. Some of these are shown below.

Spelling

Spelling differences in a number of individual words (eg *manoeuvre/maneuver*, *defence/defense*, *practise/practice*) are noted in the dictionary. Some differences involving groups of similar words are as follows:

Br	US	
-our	*-or*	American English has *-or* in words such as *color* and *humor*. *Glamour* and *saviour*, however, are generally written *-our*.
-re	*-er*	Eg *center*, *meter*, *theater*. But to show the hard sound of *c* or *g*: *acre*, *massacre*, *ogre*, etc; however, *meager* not *meagre*.
ll	*l*	In inflections and derivatives of words ending in *l* not immediately preceded by a single stressed vowel, American English does not double the *l* (cf p 18): *canceled*, *counselor*, *disheveled*, *equaled*, *marvelous*, *traveler*, etc. (Note also *woolen*.)
pp *tt*	*p* *t*	Similarly, *kidnaper*, *worshiping*, etc. And also *carburetor* (but eg *formatting*).
l	*ll*	Eg *enroll*, *fulfill*, *instill*, *skillful* and *willful*.
ae, *oe* or *e*	*e*	The tendency to replace *ae* and *oe* by *e* in words derived from Latin and Greek is more strongly developed in the US than in Britain, eg *esophagus*, *hemoglobin*.
-ize or *-ise*	*-ize*	In verbs that may be spelt *-ize* or *-ise*, the use of *-ize* is now standard in American English. Note also *analyze*, *paralyze*, etc.

As a rule, hyphens are used less frequently in American English than in British English: eg *dining room* rather than *dining-room*, *bitterroot* rather than *bitter-root*.

Pronunciation

Generally speaking American pronunciation differs from British English as follows:

Br US	
ä	In many words, eg *ask*, *dance*, *half* and *rather*, American English has a shorter, more front vowel than that of standard British English.
i	Where British English has *i* in final position in words such as *happy* and *city*, American English has *ē*.
ö	An alternative pronunciation *ä* is common in words such as *haunt*, *launch*, *saunter*, *taunt* and *vaunt*.
o	In American English, words such as *block*, *got*, *pond*, *probable* and *top* are pronounced with an *ä* sound. In words in which the vowel is followed by *f*, *s*, *th*, *r*, *g* or *ng*, eg *coffee*, *dog*, *cross*, *forest* and *long*, a longer vowel similar to *ö* is also common.
ū	After the sounds *t*, *d*, *n*, *l* and *s*, American English has *o͞o* rather than *ū*, eg in *new* and *tune*.
īl	In most words ending in *-ile*, such as *agile*, *fertile*, *fragile* and *hostile*, American English pronounces the final syllable as *-il* rather than *-īl*.
t	In words such as *latter*, *metal* and *writing*, the *-tt-/-t-* is pronounced with the same sound as that of the *-dd-/-d-* in *ladder*, *medal* and *riding*.
r	In most accents of American English *r* is pronounced at the end of a word and before a consonant.

There are a number of differences between the American pronunciation of vowels followed by *r* and the British pronunciation of the corresponding vowels:

Br	US
a	Some Americans tend to make a sound approaching *e*, so that, for example, *marry* approximates to *merry*.
ā	This is commonly pronounced as a diphthong before *r*, the first element of which is close to a lengthened *e*. The second element of the diphthong, *ə*, is sometimes not pronounced when the vowel occurs in initial or medial position; eg the usual pronunciation of *Maryland* is *mer'i-lənd*.
är spelt *-er-*	In words such as *clerk* and *Derby*, where British speech preserves an older pronunciation *är*, American speech has *ûr*.
-ə-ri	American English tends to give greater prominence than British English does to the suffixes *-ary* and *-ory*, and often also *-ery*; for example, *monetary* (Br *-tə-ri* or *-tri*, US *-te-ri*), *confectionery* (Br *-nə-ri*, US *-ne-ri*) and *obligatory* (Br *-tə-ri* or *-tri*, US *-tö-ri*).

In addition to the above, many differences between American and British English pronunciation are noted in the entries for particular words and prefixes in the dictionary. See for example *anti-*, *schedule*, *simultaneous* and *tomato*.

Lexis

Many differences between British and American usage with regard to vocabulary and meaning are noted in the dictionary, eg *bonnet/hood*, *homely* and *pavement/sidewalk*.

Some other varieties of English

British and American English are only two of the varieties of English which exist in the world today. Other forms exist elsewhere, notably in Canada, South Africa, India and Pakistan, Australia and New Zealand. Many words or meanings of words unique to these regional forms are noted in the dictionary, eg *baas*, *billabong*, *coloured*, *hartal*, *joey*. Some guidance on pronunciation and spelling is given in the following notes.

Canadian English

In spelling, Canadian usage stands midway between American English and British English. The usage is however far from uniform and varies from province to province and even from person to person. Hence spellings such as *color*, *traveler* and *center*, and *colour*, *traveller* and *centre*, are to be found alongside each other.

In pronunciation, Canadian English exhibits features found in both American and British English although it more commonly follows American English, eg speakers of Canadian English pronounce *tomato* with an *ā*.

Br	**Can**
r	Like American English, Canadian English pronounces *r* in word-final position and before a consonant.
t	In the pronunciation of many Canadians, words such as *matter* and *madder* rhyme, as in American English.
i	The sound heard in *squirrel*, etc approaches *û*.
īl	Of the words which end in *-īl* in British English, some, eg *docile*, *textile*, *fragile*, end in *-īl* as in British English, while others such as *missile* and *fertile* end in *-il* as in American English.
ī, *ow*	In Canadian English, the vowels in eg *loud* and *ride* do not rhyme with those of *lout* and *write*.

English in Australia and New Zealand

Although there are differences between the English of Australia and that of New Zealand, the two varieties are sufficiently similar to be treated together.

The spelling of Australian and New Zealand English traditionally follows that of British English but American spelling is now sometimes also found.

Features of pronunciation that can be noted are:

Br	**Austr, NZ**
r	As in British English, *r* is not pronounced before a consonant or at the end of a word, except by speakers in the southern part of the South Island of New Zealand.
i	Australian and New Zealand English have *ē* in words such as *happy* and *very*, where British English has *i*. In closed unstressed syllables, where British English has *i*, Australian and New Zealand English have *ə*, as for example in *mistake*, *defeat*, *ticket*, etc.
o͞or	The pronunciation *o͞oə* of words like *sure*, *pure*, etc has been almost entirely superseded by either *ö* or *o͞oə*.
ä	In many words in which British English has *ä*, Australian and New Zealand English have *a*. In words ending in *-ance*, New Zealand English has *ä* where Australian English has *a* or *ä*. In Australian English *lather* is pronounced with *a*, but in New Zealand with *ä*.
ō	Before *l*, this is *usu* pronounced as *o*.

English in South Africa

In spelling, South Africa follows British English. In pronunciation, notable features are:

Br	**S Africa**
r	The S African English treatment of *r* word-finally and before consonants is the same as that of British English.
i	S African English has *ē* where British English has *i* in *very*, *secretary*, etc. In other positions, *i* is pronounced more centrally than in British English, with a vowel close to *ə*.
a, *e*, *ä*, etc	There is a tendency to raise these vowels to values approaching *e*, *i*, *o*/*ö*, etc so giving *de'dē* for *daddy*, *kit'l* for *kettle*, and so on.
ār	This is normally pronounced as a long *e* or *ā* sound in words like *bear*, *fair*, etc.

English in the Indian Subcontinent

English in India, Pakistan and Bangladesh is normally learned as a second language, and is often greatly influenced by the speaker's first language. Thus no homogeneous Indian English can be described here but only a number of features about which one may make some general remarks.

Two common features of Indian English are the use of retroflex *ṭ*, *ḍ*, etc. for British English *t*, *d*, etc, and the substitution of *p*, *t*, *d* for *f*, *th*, *dh*. Speakers whose native language is Hindi or Urdu tend to insert an *i* before the initial consonant clusters in words such as *speech*, *school*, because these consonant groups do not occur in initial position in Hindi or Urdu.

Indian English pronounces word-final and pre-consonantal *r*.

Vowels in unstressed syllables are often pronounced in the way they would be in stressed syllables, where British English has *ə* or *i*.

Abbreviations used in the dictionary

The abbreviations, shown here in italic type, will also be found in the dictionary in roman type.

Many of the abbreviations are used as labels. Other, unabbreviated, labels are also found in the dictionary, all of which should be self-explanatory. It should be noted that the label *Bible*, unless it is qualified, refers to the Authorized Version.

abbrev	abbreviation
AD	Anno Domini
adj	adjective
admin	administration
adv	adverb
Afr	Africa, African
Afrik	Afrikaans
agric	agriculture
Am	America(n)
am	(L *ante meridiem*) before noon
Am football	American football
Am Ind	American Indian
Am Sp	American Spanish
anatom	anatomy, anatomically
Anglo-Fr	Anglo-French
Anglo-Ind	Anglo-Indian
Anglo-L	Anglo-Latin
anthropol	anthropology
antiq	antiquity
appar	apparently
approx	approximately
Ar	Arabic
archaeol	archaeology
archit	architecture
arith	arithmetic
Assyr	Assyrian
astrol	astrology
astron	astronomy
atomic no	atomic number
attrib	attributive(ly)
Austr	Australia(n)
autos	automobiles
AV	Authorized Version
bacteriol	bacteriology
BC	before Christ
behav	behaviourism
biochem	biochemistry
biol	biology
bot	botany, botanical
Braz	Brazilian
Bret	Breton
c	century
c.	(L *circa*) about
Can	Canada, Canadian
cap(s)	capital(s)
Caribb	Caribbean (cf **Carib** in Dictionary)
Central Am	Central America(n)
cf	(L *confer*) compare
Channel Is	Channel Islands
chem	chemistry
chem eng	chemical engineering
Chin	Chinese
Chin med	Chinese medicine
Ch of Eng	Church of England
Christian relig	Christian religion
Christian theol	Christian theology
cinematog	cinematography
civ eng	civil engineering
cm	centimetre(s)
colloq	colloquial(ly)
compar	comparative
comput	computers, computing
conj	conjunction
corresp	corresponding
crystallog	crystallography
cu	cubic
Czech	Czechoslovakian
Dan	Danish
derog	derogatorily
Dict	Dictionary
dimin	diminutive
dm	decimetre(s)
Du	Dutch
E	East, Eastern
EAfr	East Africa(n)
E Anglian	East Anglian
Eastern Ch	Eastern Church
eccles	ecclesiastical
ecol	ecology
econ	economics
educ	education
eg	(L *exempli gratia*) for example
Egyp	Egyptian
Egyp antiq	Egyptian antiquity
elec	electrical, electricity
elec eng	electrical engineering
embryol	embryology
Eng	England, English
eng	engineering
entomol	entomology
erron	erroneous(ly)
esp	especially
etc	(L *et cetera*) and so on, and the rest
ety	etymology
euphem	euphemistic(ally)
exc	except
fem	feminine
ff	following pages
fig	figurative(ly)
Finn	Finnish
fl	(L *floruit*) flourished
Flem	Flemish
foll	followed, following
fortif	fortification
FQ	*Faerie Queene*

Fr	French, France
Fr Can law	French Canadian law
Fris	Frisian
ft	foot, feet
gen	general(ly)
geog	geography
geol	geology
geom	geometry
Ger	German
Gmc	Germanic
Gr	Greek
gram	grammar
Gr Ch	Greek Church
Gr mythol	Greek mythology
Heb	Hebrew
HGer	High German
Hind(i)	Hindi
Hindu mythol	Hindu mythology
hist	history, historical
hortic	horticulture
Hung	Hungarian
hyperb	hyperbolically
Icel	Icelandic (Modern)
ie	(L *id est*) that is
image technol	image technology
imit	imitative
immunol	immunology
impers	impersonal
in	inch(es)
incl	including
Ind	India(n)
Ind admin	Indian adminis-tration
indic	indicative
infl	influenced
intens	intensive, intensifier
interj	interjection
interrog	interrogative
intrans	intransitive
Ir	Ireland, Irish
irreg	irregular(ly)
Ital	Italian, Italy
IVR	International Vehicle Registration
Jap	Japanese
Jav	Javanese
joc	jocular(ly)
kg	kilogram(s)
km	kilometre(s)
L	Latin
lb	pound(s) (weight)
LGer	Low German
linguistics	
lit and fig	literal(ly) and figurative(ly)
Lith	Lithuanian
LL	Low (or Late) Latin
masc	masculine
math	mathematics
MDu	Middle Dutch
ME	Middle English
mech	mechanics, mechanical
Med	Medieval
med	medicine
metaphys	metaphysics
meteorol	meteorology
Mex	Mexican
Mex Sp	Mexican Spanish
MFlem	Middle Flemish
MFr	Middle French
MHGer	Middle High German
microbiol	microbiology
microsc	microscopy
min ext	mineral extraction
MLGer	Middle Low German
mm	millimetre(s)
mod	modern
Mod Du	Modern Dutch
Mod Fr	Modern French
Mod L	Modern Latin (= New Latin)
mph	miles per hour
mythol	mythology
N	North, Northern
NAm	North America(n)
nat hist	natural history
naut	nautical
neg	negative
N Eng	Northern England, Northern English
New Eng	New England
New Eng Bible	New English Bible
New L	New Latin
N Irish	Northern Irish
Norw	Norwegian
n pl	noun plural
n sing	noun singular
nuc eng	nuclear engineering
NZ	New Zealand
obs	obsolete
ODu	Old Dutch
OE	Old English
OFr	Old French
OFris	Old Friesian
OHGer	Old High German
OIr	Old Irish
OLGer	Old Low German
ON	Old Norse
ONFr	Old Northern French
OPers	Old Persian
opp	opposite, opposed
orig	original(ly)
ornithol	ornithology
Orthodox Ch	Orthodox Church
OSax	Old Saxon
OSlav	Old Slavonic
OWelsh	Old Welsh
oz	ounce(s)
p	participle, participial
Pak	Pakistan(i)
palaeog	palaeography
palaeontol	palaeont-ology
pa p	past participle
pa t	past tense
pathol	pathology
perf	perfect
perh	perhaps
Pers	Persian
pers	personal, person
Peruv	Peruvian
pfx	prefix
pharm	pharmacy
pharmacol	pharmac-ology
philat	philately
philol	philology
philos	philosophy
photog	photography
phys	physics
physiol	physiology
pl	plural

pm (L *post meridiem*) after noon
Pol Polish
pol econ political economy
Port Portuguese
poss possible, possibly
pr present
prep preposition
Presbyterian Ch Presbyterian church
prev previous(ly)
priv privative
prob probably
pron pronounced, pronunciation
pr p present participle
pr t present tense
psychol psychology

qv, qqv (L *quod vide*) which see

® registered trademark
radiol radiology
RC Roman Catholic (Church)
rel related, relative
relig religion, religious
rhetoric rhetoric, rhetorical
Rom Romanian
Russ Russian
RV Revised Version

S South, Southern
SAfr South African
Sans Sanskrit
S Asia South Asia(n)
Scand Scandinavian
Sceptic philos Sceptic philosophy
Scot Scottish
Scot hist Scottish history
sculp sculpture
SE Asia South East Asia
S Eng Southern England/ English
sep separate
Serb Serbian
sfx suffix
Shakesp Shakespeare
sing singular
Sinh Sinhalese
Slav Slavonic
sociol sociology
Sp Spanish
Sp Am Spanish American
space tech space technology
specif specifically
sq square
St Saint
st stone(s)
subj subject
superl superlative
surg surgery
S US Southern United States
sv (L *sub verbo*) under the word
SW Eng South West England
Swed Swedish

t tense
technol technology
telecomm telecommunications
teleg telegraphy
theat theatre, theatrical
theat slang theatrical slang
theol theology
trans transitive
transl translation, translating, translated
trig trigonometry
Turk Turkish
TV television

UK United Kingdom
ult ultimately
US United States (of America)
USSR Union of Soviet Socialist Republics
usu usually

v verb
vet veterinary medicine
vi verb intransitive
Viet Vietnamese
vt verb transitive
vulg vulgar(ly)

W West, Western
WAfr West Africa(n)
WSax West Saxon

zool zoology

A

A[1] or **a** *ā*, *n* the first letter in the modern English alphabet as in the Roman, etc (see **aleph** and **alpha**); a musical note, the major sixth of the scale of C; something or someone of first class or order, or of a class arbitrarily designated A; one of the four blood types in the ABO blood group system; the designation of the principal series of paper sizes, ranging from A0 (841 × 1189 mm) to A10 (26 × 37 mm); in road-classification, followed by a number, the designation of a major or trunk road, as *A68*; as a medieval Roman numeral A = 50 or 500, and Ā = 5000. — **A1** (*ā wun*) the symbol for a first-class vessel in Lloyd's Register of Shipping; hence first-rate or excellent; **A'-road** a principal or trunk road; **A'-side** (*recorded music*) the side of a single which holds the principal track being marketed. — **from A to B** from one point or place to another; **from A to Z** from beginning to end; right through.

A[2] *ä* or *ə*, (*dialect*) *pronoun* a monophthongized form of **I**.

A[3] *abbrev*: absolute (temperature); Academician; Academy; ace (*cards*); acre(s); adult, formerly used to designate a motion picture at a showing of which any child under 14 should be accompanied by an adult, superseded by **PG**; advanced; alto (*music*); amateur; America; American; ammeter; ampere(s); angstrom; answer; area; argon (now *usu* **Ar**; *chem*); Associate (of a society, etc); atomic; atomic weight; Australia; Australian; Austria (IVR). — **A'-bomb** atomic bomb; **A-effect** see under **alien**; **A level** or **Advanced** (or **advanced**) **level** (a pass in) an examination generally taken after seven years of secondary education, *esp* in England and Wales (also *adj*, often with *hyphen*).

Å *symbol*: Ångström or angstrom.

a[1] *ə*, also (*esp* emphatic) *ā*, *adj* the indefinite article, a broken down form of **an**[1] used before a consonant sound. [OE *ān* one]

a[2] *ä*, *ə*, (*dialect*) *pronoun* he; she; it; they. [OE *hē* he, *hēo* she, and *hīe* they]

a[3] *abbrev*: about; absent; acceleration; accepted; acre; acreage; acting; active; adjective; advance; advanced; afternoon; alto; *anno* (*L*), in the year; *annus* (*L*), year; anonymous; answer; *ante* (*L*), before; anterior; are (metric measure); atto-.

a' *ö* or *ä*, Northern form of **all**. — *pronoun* **a''body** everybody. — *adv* **a''gate** every way. — *pronoun* **a''thing** everything. — *adv* **a''where** everywhere.

à *ə*, a form of the Latin preposition *ab* from, of, as in Thomas à Kempis (Thomas from Kempen).

ā. See **AA**.

@ *symbol*: at (a rate of); (in E-mail) at (a certain address).

a-[1] *ə*, *pfx* a reduced form of the OE preposition *an* or *on*, on, in or at, as in *a*broad, *a*fire, *a*float, *a*sleep, *a*-begging, *a*-hunting, and occasionally used separately as a preposition, as in *once a year*.

a-[2] *ə*- or *a*-, or **an-** *ən*- or *an*-, *pfx* without, not, opposite to, as in *amoral*, *anaemia* or *anodyne*. [Gr privative *a*- without or not]

AA *abbrev*: Alcoholics Anonymous; anti-aircraft; Architectural Association; Associate of Arts; Australian Army; Automobile Association; formerly used to designate a motion picture at a showing of which no child under 14 may be admitted, superseded by **15**.

AA, **āā** or **ā** *symbol*: (in prescriptions, etc) in equal quantities of each. [LL *ana*, from Gr, again]

aa *ä'ä*, *n* a type of scoriaceous volcanic rock with a rough surface and many jagged fragments. [Hawaiian]

AAA *abbrev*: Amateur Athletic Association; American Automobile Association; Australian Automobile Association.

AAAS *abbrev*: American Academy of Arts and Sciences.

AAC *abbrev*: Amateur Athletic Club; *anno ante Christum* (*L*), in the year before Christ; Army Air Corps (*US*).

AAM *abbrev*: air-to-air missile.

A and M *abbrev*: Agricultural and Mechanical; (Hymns) Ancient and Modern.

A and R *abbrev*: artists and recording; artists and repertoire.

AAQMG *abbrev*: Assistant Adjutant and Quartermaster General.

AAP *abbrev*: Australian Associated Press.

aar *abbrev*: against all risks (*commerce*); average annual rainfall.

aardvark *ärt'färk'* (*SAfr*), or *ärd'värk*, *n* the antbear, a long-nosed African edentate that feeds on termites, etc. [Du *aarde* earth, and *vark* (now *varken*) pig]

aardwolf *ärt'volf* (*SAfr*), or *ärd'wo͞olf*, *n* the earthwolf, a hyena-like African mammal that feeds mainly on termites and carrion. [Du *aarde* earth, and *wolf* wolf]

Aaronic *ā-ron'ik* or **Aaronical** *-ik-l*, *adj* pertaining to Aaron, the Jewish high-priest; pertaining to the priesthood; pontifical. — **Aaron's beard** a saxifrage, often grown dangling from pots; the great St John's wort; ivy-leaved toadflax, or a similar plant; **Aaron's rod** mullein, golden-rod, or a similar plant, with tall straight flowering stem.

AAS *abbrev*: *Academiae Americanae Socius* (*L*), Fellow of the American Academy.

A'asia *abbrev*: Australasia.

aasvogel *äs'fo͞ol* (*SAfr*), or *äs'fō-gəl*, *n* a S African vulture. [Du *aas* carrion, and *vogel* bird]

AB *ā-bē'*, *n* one of the four blood types in the ABO blood group system.

AB *abbrev*: able-bodied (seaman); Advisory Board; Alberta (Canadian province); *Artium Baccalaureus* (*L*), Bachelor of Arts (*US*); autobahn.

Ab *ab*, *n* the eleventh civil or fifth ecclesiastical month of the Jewish Calendar (parts of July and August). — Also **Av**. [Syriac]

ab-[1] *ab*-, *pfx* opposite to, from or away from, as in *abnormal* or *abreaction*. [L *ab* from]

ab-[2] *ab*-, *pfx* used to indicate a centimetre-gram-second electromagnetic unit (eg **abam'pere** and **ab'volt** equivalent respectively to 10 amperes and 10^{-8} volts). [**absolute**]

a/b *abbrev*: airborne.

ABA *abbrev*: Amateur Boxing Association; American Bar Association.

aba or **abba** *a'bə*, or **abaya** *a-bā'yə*, *n* a Syrian cloth of goat's or camel's hair, *usu* striped; an outer garment made of it; a covering outer garment, *usu* black, worn by women in some Arab countries. [Ar *'abā*, *'abāya*]

abac *ā'bak*, *n* a nomogram. [Fr *abaque*, from L *abacus*]

abaca *ä-bä-kä'*, *n* a plantain grown in the Philippine Islands; its fibre, called Manila hemp. [Tagálog]

abaci. See **abacus**.

aback *ə-bak'*, *adv* backwards; said of sails pressed backward against the mast by the wind (*naut*) — hence **taken aback** (*fig*) taken by surprise. [OE *on bæc* on back; see **a-**[1]]

abactinal *ab-ak-tī'nəl* or *ab-ak'ti-nəl*, (*zool*) *adj* remote from the actinal area; without rays. — *adv* **abactinally**. [**ab-**[1]]

abactor *ab-ak'tər*, (*obs*) *n* a cattle thief. [LL]

abacus *ab'ə-kəs*, *n* a counting-frame, consisting of horizontal rods along which movable beads can be slid; a level tablet on the capital of a column, supporting the entablature (*archit*): — *pl* **ab'aci** (*-sī*) or **ab'acuses**. [L *abacus*, from Gr *abax*, *abakos*]

Abaddon *ə-bad'ən*, *n* Apollyon; hell (*Milton*). [Heb *ābaddōn*, from *ābad* to be lost]

abaft *ə-bäft'*, (*naut*) *adv* and *prep* behind. [**a-**[1] and OE *bæftan* after, from **be-** and *æftan* (see **aft**)]

abalone *ab-a-lō'nā*, *n* an edible shellfish, the sea-ear, *esp* a richly coloured variety found on the Pacific coast of N America, a source of mother-of-pearl. [Am Sp *abulón*. Origin uncertain]

abampere *ab-am'pār*, (*elec*) *n* a unit equivalent to 10 amperes. [**ab-**[2] and **ampere**]

abandon *ə-ban'dən*, *vt* to give up; to desert; to give (oneself) without restraint; to give up all claims to; to banish (*Shakesp*). — *n* (sometimes as Fr *ä-bã-dɔ̃*) the condition of letting oneself go; careless freedom of action. — *vt* (*Spenser*) **aband'** to abandon. — *adj* **aban'doned** completely deserted; given up, as to a vice; profligate, dissolute; very wicked. — *adv* **aban'donedly**. — *n* **abandonee'** (*law*) an insurer to whom a wreck has been abandoned. — *n* **aban'donment**. — **abandon ship** the order to take to the lifeboats when a ship is in danger. [OFr *abandoner* to put at one's disposal or in one's control (*à bandon*), or to the ban; see **ban**]

à bas *a bä*, (*Fr*) *interj* down, down with!

abase *ə-bās'*, *vt* to lower, put down; to cast down; to humble; to degrade, belittle. — *adj* **abased'**. — *n* **abase'ment**. [OFr *abaissier* to bring low, from L *ad* to, and LL *bassus* low]

abash *ə-bash'*, *vt* to strike with shame or embarrassment; to disconcert; to astound (*archaic*); to confound (*archaic*). — *adj* **abashed'**. — *adv* **abash'edly**. — *adj* **abash'less** shameless; unabashed. — *n* **abash'ment**. [OFr *esbahir*, from pfx *es-* (L *ex* out), and *bahir* to astound, from interj *bah*]

abask *ə-bäsk'*, *adv* in genial warmth. [**a-**[1]]

abate[1] *ə-bāt'*, *vi* to grow less; to subside; to be abated (*law*). — *vt* to demolish (*obs*); to put an end to (*law*); to nullify, to bring down (*law*); to lessen or reduce; to deduct (with *of*); to mitigate; to blunt; to curtail (*Shakesp*); to except (*Shakesp*). — *adj* **abāt'able**. — *adj* **abāt'ed** blunted; diminished; lowered; subdued; beaten down or cut away, as the background of sculptures, etc carved in relief. — *n* **abate'ment** the act or process of abating; the sum or quantity abated; the state of being abated; the abandonment of an action, or the reduction of a legacy (*law*); a supposed mark of dishonour on a coat of arms (*heraldry*) *appar* never actually used. [OFr *abatre* to beat down, from L *ab* from, and LL *batere*, for L *batuere* to beat]

abate[2] *ə-bāt'*, *vi* and *vt* (*reflexive*) to intrude on a freehold and take possession before the heir. — *n* **abate'ment**. — *n* **abāt'or**. [OFr *enbatre* to thrust in]

abatis or **abattis** *ab'ə-tis*, *ə-bat'ē* or *-is*, (*fortif*) *n* a rampart of felled trees with branches outward; a similar arrangement of barbed wire: — *pl* **abatis** or **abattis** (*-ēz*). [Fr; see **abate**[1]]

abat-jour *a-ba-zhōōr*, (*Fr*) *n* a skylight; a screen or shutter.

abattis. See **abatis**.

abattoir *ab'ə-twär*, *n* a public slaughterhouse. [Fr; see **abate**[1]]

abattu *a-bat-ü*, (*Fr*) *adj* cast down or dejected.

abature *ab'ə-chər*, *n* in hunting, the trail through underwood beaten down by a stag. [Fr; see **abate**[1]]

abat-voix *a-ba-vwä*, (*Fr*) *n* a sounding-board.

abaxial *ab-ak'si-əl*, (*bot*) *adj* away from the axis. [**ab-**[1] and **axis**[1]]

abaya. See **aba**.

Abb. *abbrev*: Abbess; Abbey; Abbot.

abb *ab*, *n* properly, woof- or weft-yarn, but sometimes warp-yarn. [OE *āb*, *āweb*, from pfx *ā* out, and *webb* web]

ABBA *abbrev*: Amateur Basketball Association.

abba[1] *ab'ə*, *n* father (applied to God) (*Bible*); a Syriac or Coptic bishop. [Aramaic *abbā*, retained in the Greek New Testament and its translations]

abba[2]. See **aba**.

abbacy *ab'ə-si*, *n* the office or jurisdiction of an abbot; the time during which someone is abbot; an abbey. — *adj* **abbatial** (*ab-ā'shl*) pertaining to an abbey, abbot or abbess. [Appar orig Scot; LL *abbātia* abbey]

Abbasid *a-bas'id* or *ab'ə-sid*, or **Abbaside** *-sīd*, *n* any member of the later (750–1543) of the two great dynasties of caliphs, descendants of *Abbas*, uncle of Mohammed.

abbatial. See **abbacy**.

abbé *ab'ā*, *n esp* in France, a courtesy title for a priest, an ecclesiastic in minor orders, or for a tutor or holder of a benefice, even if a layman. [Fr, orig abbot]

abbess *ab'es*, *n* a woman who is head of an abbey. [LL *abbātissa*, fem of *abbās* abbot]

abbey *ab'i*, *n* a convent under an abbot or abbess, or (loosely) a prior or prioress; the church now or formerly attached to such an abbey; a name often retained by an abbatial building that has become a private house: — *pl* **abb'eys**. — **abb'ey-counter** or **abb'ey-piece** a pilgrim's token, evidence of a visit to an abbey; **abb'ey-laird** (*hist*) a debtor in sanctuary in the precincts of Holyrood Abbey; **abb'ey-lubber** a lazy monk, a term much used by the Reformers. [OFr *abaïe* (Fr *abbaye*), from LL *abbātia* (see **abba**[1] and **abbacy**)]

abbot *ab'ət*, *n* a male head of an abbey: — *fem* **abb'ess**. — *n* **abb'otship**. — **abbot of unreason** a lord of misrule or mock abbot in medieval revels. [LL *abbās*, *abbātis*, from Aramaic *abbā*; see **abba**[1]]

abbr. or **abbrev**. *abbrev*: abbreviated; abbreviation.

abbreviate *ə-brē'vi-āt*, *vt* to shorten; to contract; to abridge. — *adj* shortened. — *n* **abbrēviā'tion** an act of shortening; a shortened form; part of a word written or printed instead of the whole. — *n* **abbrē'viātor**. — *adj* **abbrē'viatory** (*-ə-tor-i*). — *n* **abbrē'viature** (*obs*) an abbreviation; an abridgement. [L *abbreviāre*, *-ātum*, from *ab* (intensive), and *brevis* short]

ABC[1] *ā-bē-sē'*, also (*obs*) **abcee** or **absey** *ab'si*, *n* the alphabet, so named from its first letters; a first reading-book; hence, the rudiments or the basics; anything arranged alphabetically, such as an acrostic or a railway guide. — **absey book** (*Shakesp*) a primer or hornbook.

ABC[2] *abbrev*: American Broadcasting Company; Arab Banking Corporation; Associated British Cinemas; Audit Bureau of Circulations; Australian Broadcasting Corporation (formerly, Commission).

ABCC *abbrev*: Association of British Chambers of Commerce.

abd *abbrev*: abdicated; abridged.

abdabs. See **habdabs**.

Abderian *ab-dē'ri-ən*, *adj* of *Abdera*, a town in Thrace, the Gotham of the ancients and birthplace of Democritus, 'the laughing philosopher'. — Also *n*. — *n* **Abderite** (*ab'dər-īt*) a native or citizen of Abdera; a simpleton or Gothamite.

abdicate *ab'di-kāt*, *vt* and *vi* formally to renounce or give up (office or dignity). — *adj* **ab'dicable**. — *adj* (*rare*) **ab'dicant**. — *n* **abdicā'tion**. — *n* **ab'dicator**. [L *ab* from or off, and *dicāre*, *-ātum* to proclaim]

abdomen *ab'də-mən* or *ab-dō'mən*, *n* the belly; in mammals, the part between diaphragm and pelvis; in arthropods, the hind-body. — *adj* **abdominal** (*-dom'*). — *adv* **abdom'inally**. — *adj* **abdom'inous** pot-bellied. [L *abdōmen*, *-inis*]

abduce *ab-dūs'*, *vt* an earlier form of **abduct**. — *adj* **abdū'cent** (*anatom*) (of a muscle) drawing back; separating. [L *abducere*, from *ab* from, and *ducere*, *ductum* to draw or lead]

abduct *ab-dukt'*, *vt* to take away by fraud or violence; to kidnap; (of a muscle) to cause abduction in (a part of the body). — *n* **abductee'** a person who is abducted. — *n* **abduction** (*-duk'shən*) the carrying away, *esp* of a person by fraud or force; separation of parts of the body after a wound or fracture (*surg*); muscular action drawing one part of the body (such as an arm or finger) away from another or away from the median axis of the body; a syllogism whose minor premise is only probable (*logic*). — *n* **abduc'tor** a person who abducts; a muscle that abducts (*anatom*). [L *abductus*, pa p of *abducere*; (see **abduce**)]

abeam *ə-bēm'*, (*naut*) *adv* in a line at right angles to a vessel's length, on the beam. [**a-**[1]]

abear *ə-bār'*, *vt* to bear, comport or behave (*obs*); (only as *infinitive*) to endure or tolerate (*dialect*): — *pa t* **abore'**; *pa p* **aborne'**. [OE *āberan*]

abecedarian *ā-bi-sē-dā'ri-ən*, *adj* pertaining to the ABC; rudimentary; arranged in the manner of an acrostic. — *n* a learner of the ABC, a beginner; a teacher of the ABC; an Anabaptist of a sect that rejected all learning. [**ABC**[1]]

abed *ə-bed'*, *adv* in bed. [**a-**[1] and **bed**[1]]

abeigh *ə-bēhh'*, (*Scot*) *adv* aloof. [Origin obscure]

abele *ə-bēl'* or *ā'bl*, *n* the white poplar-tree. [Du *abeel*, from OFr *abel* or *aubel*, from LL *albellus*, from L *albus* white]

abelia *ə-bēl'i-ə*, *n* a plant of the genus *Abelia*, shrubs of the honeysuckle family with pink or white flowers. [Clarke *Abel*, 1780–1826, English physician and botanist]

Aberdeen *ab-ər-dēn'*, sometimes *ab'*, *adj* of or originating in *Aberdeen* or Aberdeenshire. — *abbrev*: **Aber** *usu* in the designation of the Bishop of Aberdeen and Orkney. — *n* (in full **Aberdeen terrier**) a coarse-haired kind of Scottish terrier. — *adj* **Aberdō'nian** of Aberdeen; (traditionally) parsimonious (*facetious*). — Also *n*. — **Aberdeen Angus** (*ang'gəs*) a breed of polled cattle descended from Aberdeenshire humlies and Angus doddies.

aberdevine *ab-ər-di-vīn'*, *n* a bird-fancier's name for the siskin. [Ety uncertain]

Aberdonian. See **Aberdeen**.

Aberglaube *ab-ər-glow'bə*, (*Ger*) *n* superstition.

Abernethy biscuit *ab-ər-neth'i* or *-nēth'i*, also *ab'*, *bis'kit*, *n* a hard biscuit, *appar orig* with caraway seeds. [Poss after Dr John *Abernethy* (1764–1831) who was interested in diet]

aberrate *ab'ər-āt*, *vi* to wander or deviate from the right way. — *n* **aberrance** (*-er'*) or **aberr'ancy**. — *adj* **aberr'ant** wandering or straying; having characteristics not strictly in accordance with type (*bot* and *zool*). — *n* **aberrā'tion** (*-ər-*) a deviation from the usual, normal or right course, direction or behaviour; a wandering of the intellect, mental lapse; a non-convergence of rays, owing to difference in refrangibility of different colours (*chromatic aberration*) or to difference of focus of the marginal and central parts of a lens or mirror (*spherical aberration*); an apparent displacement of a star, owing to the finite ratio of the velocity of light to that of the earth (*aberration of light*; *astron*). — *adj* **aberra'tional**. [L *aberrāre*, *-ātum*, from *ab* from, and *errāre* to wander]

abessive *ab-es'iv*, (*gram*) *adj* denoting absence or lack. — *n* the abessive case. [L *abesse* to be absent]

abet *ə-bet'*, *vt* to incite by encouragement or aid (used chiefly in a bad sense; see also **aid and abet** under **aid**); to back up (*Spenser*); to make good: — *pr p* **abett'ing**; *pa p* **abett'ed**. — *n* (*Spenser*) abetting. — *n* **abet'ment** or **abett'al**. — *n* **abett'er** or (*esp law*) **abett'or**. [OFr *abeter*, from *à* (L *ad* to), and *beter* to bait; see **bait**]

ab extra *ab eks'tra*, (*L*) from the outside.

abeyance *ə-bā'əns*, *n* a state of suspension or temporary inactivity; the state of being without a claimant (eg of a peerage). — Also **abey'ancy**. — *adj* **abey'ant**. [OFr *abeance*, from *à* (L *ad* to), and *beer* or *baer* to gape or open wide; origin uncertain]

ABF *abbrev*: Actors' Benevolent Fund; Army Benevolent Fund.

ABFM *abbrev*: American Board of Foreign Missions.

ABH and **abh** *abbrev*: actual bodily harm.

abhominable. See **abominable**.

abhor *ab-hör'*, *vt* to shrink from with horror; to detest; to loathe; to protest against, to reject (*Shakesp*); to fill with horror (*Shakesp*): — *pr p* **abhorr'ing**; *pa t* and *pa p* **abhorred'**. — *n* **abhorr'ence** (*-hor'*) extreme hatred; something that is abhorred. — *n* **abhorr'ency** (*obs*). — *adj* **abhorr'ent** detesting; repugnant; strongly opposed; out of keeping; detestable; detested. — *adv* **abhorr'ently**. — *n* **abhorr'er** someone who abhors; (with *cap*; *hist*) a member of the court party in England in 1679, who abhorred the Petitioners, a Tory. — *n* **abhorr'ing** repugnance; an object of abhorrence. [L *abhorrēre*, from *ab* from, and *horrēre* to bristle or shudder]

ABI *abbrev*: Association of British Insurers.

Abib *ā'bib*, *n* earlier name for the month of **Nisan** in the Jewish calendar. [Heb *ābīb* literally an ear of corn]

abide[1] *ə-bīd'*, *vt* to bide or wait for; to meet, face or sustain; to endure; to tolerate. — *vi* to remain; to dwell or stay; to conform to, adhere to, comply with or obey (with *by*): — *pa t* **abōde'**, also **abīd'ed**, (*Spenser*) **abid'**; *pa p* **abōde'** or **abīd'ed**, also **abidd'en**. — *n* **abīd'ance**. — *adj* **abīd'ing** continual or permanent. — *n* a continuance (*archaic*). — *adv* **abīd'ingly**. [OE *ābīdan*, from pfx *ā-*, and *bīdan* to wait]

abide[2] *ə-bīd'*, (*Shakesp*; *Milton*) *vt* to aby. [**aby**, confused with **abide**[1]]

à bientôt *a byē-tō*, (*Fr*) see you again soon.

abies *āb'i-ēz*, *n* a tree of the genus *Abies*, the genus of the true firs.

abigail *ab'i-gāl*, (*archaic*) *n* a lady's-maid. [From *Abigail*, in Beaumont and Fletcher's *Scornful Lady*, or 1 Sam 25]

ability *ə-bil'i-ti*, *n* the quality or fact of being able (to); power (physical and mental); strength; skill. [OFr *ableté* (Fr *habileté*), remodelled after its source, L *habilitās*, *-ātis*, from *habēre* to have or hold; see **able**]

ab initio *ab in-ish'i-ō* or *-it'i-ō*, (*L*) from the beginning. — *abbrev* **ab init** (*ab in-it'*).

ab intra *ab in'tra*, (*L*) from the inside.

abiogenesis *ab-i-ō-jen'is-is*, or *ā-bī-*, *n* the origination of living by non-living matter, spontaneous generation. — *adj* **abiogenetic** (*-ji-net'ik*). — *adv* **abiogenet'ically**. — *n* **abiogenist** (*-oj'ə-nist*) a believer in abiogenesis. [Coined by T H Huxley in 1870; Gr *a-* (privative), *bios* life, and *genesis* birth]

abiosis *ā-bī-ō'sis*, (*med*) *n* absence of life. — *adj* **ābiot'ic** without life; inanimate. [Gr *a-* (privative), and *biotikos*, from *bios* life]

abiturient *ab-it-ū'ri-ənt*, *n* in Germany, a pupil leaving school for a university. [New L *abituriēns*, *-entis*, pr p of *abiturīre*, desiderative of L *abīre* to go away, from *ab* from, and *īre* to go]

abject *ab'jekt*, *adj* mean; worthless; grovelling; base or contemptible; cast away. — *n* an outcast; a base slave; someone in more servile subjection than a subject. — *vt* (*obs*; *ab-jekt'*) to throw or cast down or away. — *n* **abjec'tion** abjectness; casting out; forcible expulsion of spores (*bot*). — *adv* **ab'jectly**. — *n* **ab'jectness**. [L *abjicere*, *abjectum*, from *ab* from, and *jacere* to throw]

abjoint *ab-joint'*, (*bot*) *vt* to cut off by forming a septum. — *n* **abjunction** (*-jungk'shən*). [L *ab* from, and **joint** or **junction**]

abjure *ab-jōōr'*, *vt* to renounce on oath or solemnly; to recant; to repudiate. — *n* **abjurā'tion**. — *n* **abjur'er**. [L *ab* from, and *jurāre*, *-ātum* to swear]

abl. *abbrev*: ablative.

ablactation *ab-lak-tā'shən*, *n* weaning or the cessation of the production of milk; grafting by inarching (*hortic*). [L *ab* from, and *lactāre* to suckle, from *lac* milk]

ablation *ab-lā'shən*, *n* removal, *esp* surgical removal of an organ or body-tissue, etc; decrease caused by melting, evaporation, weathering or (*aerospace*) by heat friction on re-entering the atmosphere. — *vt* **ablate** (*ab-lāt'*) to remove or decrease by ablation. — *adj* **ablatitious** (*-lə-tish'əs*). — *adj* **ab'lative** (*-lə-tiv*) pertaining to ablation; in or belonging to a case which in Indo-European languages *orig* expressed *direction from* or *time when*, later extended to other functions (*gram*). — *n* the ablative case; a word in the ablative. — *adj* **ablatī'val**. — *n* **ablā'tor** a substance or material undergoing ablation, *esp* the heat shield of a spacecraft. — **ablative absolute** in Latin, a phrase generally comprising a noun or pronoun coupled with another noun, an adjective or a participle, both in the ablative case and *usu* indicating the time or cause of an event. [L *ab* from, and *lātum* used as supine of *ferre* to take]

ablaut *äp'lowt* or *ab'lowt*, (*philol*) *n* a variation in root vowel, as in s*i*ng, s*a*ng, s*o*ng, s*u*ng, explained by former accentuation, and also called gradation. [Ger *ab* off, and *Laut* sound]

ablaze *ə-blāz'*, *adv* and *adj* in a blaze or on fire; gleaming brightly. [**a-**[1] and **blaze**[1]]

able *ā'bl*, *adj* having enough strength, power or means (to do a thing); skilful: — *compar* **ā'bler**; *superl* **ā'blest**. — *vt* to enable (*obs*); to warrant (*Shakesp*). — *adj* **a'bled** able-bodied (see **differently-abled**). — *adv* **a'bly**. — *adv* **aiblins** or **ablins** (*ā'blinz*) or **yibbles** (*yib'lz*) perhaps (*Scot*). — *adj* **able-bod'ied** having a strong body; free from disability, etc; robust. — **able seaman**, **able-bodied seaman** or **able rating** (abbrev **AB**) a seaman able to perform all the duties of seamanship and having a higher rating than the ordinary sailor: — *fem* **able seawoman** or **able-bodied seawoman**. [See **ability**]

-able *-ə-bl*, *adj sfx* combining with verbs to convey any of various passive senses (now the chief use of **-able** as a living suffix), such as 'capable of being', 'able to be', 'worthy of being', 'likely to be', 'that must be'; combining with verbs to convey any of various active senses, such as 'capable of', 'able to', 'worthy of', 'suitable to', 'likely to'; combining with nouns to convey such meanings as 'worthy of', 'suitable for', 'in accordance with', 'causing'. — *n sfx* **-ability**. — *adv sfx* **-ably**. — See also **-ible**. [OFr, from L *-ābilis*, from *-bilis* as used with a 1st-conjugation verb]

ablet *ab'lit*, *n* the freshwater fish, the bleak. [Fr *ablette*, from LL *a(l)bula* dimin of *alba* white]

abloom *ə-blo͞om'*, *adv* and *adj* in a blooming state. [**a-**[1] and **bloom**[1]]

ablow *ə-blō'*, *adv* and *adj* in a blowing state. [**a-**[1] and **blow**[2,3]]

ablush *ə-blush'*, *adv* and *adj* in a blushing state. [**a-**[1]]

ablution *ə-blo͞o'shən*, *n* (often in *pl*) the act of washing, *esp* the body; ceremonial washing; (in *sing*) the wine and water used to rinse the chalice, drunk by the officiating priest (*RC relig*). — *adj* **ablu'tionary**. — *n* **ablutomane** (*ə-blo͞o'tō-mān*; Fr *-mane*, from Gr, see **mania**) a person who is obsessed with cleanliness. [L *ablūtiō*, *-ōnis*, from *ab* away, and *luere* to wash]

ably. See **able**.

ABM *abbrev*: anti-ballistic missile.

ABN *abbrev*: Aberdeen.

abnegate *ab'ni-gāt*, *vt* to deny; to renounce. — *n* **abnegā'tion**. — *n* **ab'negātor**. [L *ab* away, and *negāre* to deny]

abnormal *ab-nör'ml*, *adj* not normal. — *n* **abnor'malism**. — *n* **abnormality** (*-nör-mal'i-ti*). — *adv* **abnor'mally**. — *n* **abnor'mity**. — *adj* **abnor'mous** (*rare*). — **abnormal load** (*usu* of road transport) a larger or heavier load than is generally carried. [Fr *anormal*, from LL *anormalus*, from Gr *anōmalos* (see **anomaly**); influenced by L *norma* rule, and *ab* from]

ABO blood group system *ā-bē-ō' blud gro͞op sis'təm*, (*med*) *n* a system by which human blood is classified into four groups (O, A, B, AB) according to the antigens carried by the red blood cells.

Abo *ab'ō*, (*Austr*; *offensive*) *n* short for Aboriginal or Aborigine: — *pl* **Ab'ōs**.

aboard *ə-börd'*, *adv* or *prep* on board; in or into a ship, railway train, etc; alongside (*naut*). [**a-**[1]]

abode[1] *ə-bōd'*, *n* a dwelling-place or home; a stay. — *vt* and *vi*, *pa t* and *pa p* of **abide**. — **of no fixed abode** (*law*) having no regular or habitual address.

abode[2] *ə-bōd'*, (*obs*) *n* a presage. — *vt* (*Shakesp*) to presage. — *n* **abode'ment** (*obs*) a foreboding; an omen. [OE *ābodian* to proclaim; cf **bode**[1] and **forebode**]

a'body. See **a'**.

ab officio et beneficio *ab o-fish'i-ō* (or *-fik'*) *et ben-e-fish'i-ō* (or *-fik'*), (*LL*) literally, from office and benefice, (of a member of the clergy) suspended from office.

aboideau *ä-bwä-dō* or **aboiteau** *-tō*, *n* a tide-gate. [Canadian Fr]

aboil *ə-boil'*, *adv* and *adj* in a boiling state. [**a-**[1] and **boil**[1]]

aboiteau. See **aboideau**.

abolish *ə-bol'ish*, *vt* to put an end to. — *adj* **abol'ishable**. — *n* **abol'ishment** (*rare*). — *n* **aboli'tion**. — *adj* **aboli'tional** or **aboli'tionary**. — *n* **aboli'tionism**. — *n* **aboli'tionist** a person who seeks to abolish anything, eg slavery or capital punishment. [L *abolēre*, *-itum*, partly through Fr *abolir*]

abolla *ab-ol'ä*, (*hist*) *n* a Roman military cloak. [L]

abomasum *ab-ō-mā'səm*, *n* the fourth or true stomach of ruminants, lying close to the omasum: — *pl* **abomā'sa**. — Also **abomā'sus**. — *adj* **abomā'sal**. [L *ab* away from, and *omāsum* tripe, paunch (a Gallic word)]

abominate *ə-bom'in-āt*, *vt* to abhor; to detest. — *adj* **abom'inable** (or *obs* **abhom'inable** agreeing with an imagined derivation from *ab homine*) hateful; detestable. — *n* **abom'inableness**. — *adv* **abom'inably**. — *n* **abominā'tion** extreme aversion; anything detested or abominable. — *n* **abom'inator**. — **abominable snowman** a mythical hairy manlike creature supposed to live in the Himalayas (also called the **yeti**). [L *abōminārī*, *-ātus* to turn from as being of bad omen; see **omen**]

abondance. See **abundance**.

à bon droit *a bɔ̃ drwä*, (*Fr*) with justice.

à bon marché *a bɔ̃ mar-shā*, (*Fr*) at a good bargain, cheap.

abonnement *a-bon-mã*, (*Fr*) *n* a subscription.

aboral *ab-ö'rəl*, (*zool*) *adj* away from the mouth. [L *ab* from, and **oral**]

abord[1] *ə-börd'*, (*archaic*) *vt* to accost. — *n* approach. [Fr *aborder*, from *à bord* to the side]

abord[2] *ə-börd'*, (*Spenser*) *adv* astray. [Perh for **abroad**]

ab origine *ab ō-rij'in-ē* or *-rēg'in-e*, (*L*) from the very first, from the source.

aborigine *ab-ə-rij'i-nē* or *-ni*, *n* an original or native inhabitant of a country, *esp* (now often, and in Australia always, with *cap*) Australia. — Also (*rare*) **aborigin** or **aborigen** (*a-bor'i-jin*). — (*offensive*) *abbrev* **Abo** (*ab'ō*): — *pl* **Ab'os**. — *adj* **aborig'inal** (often with *cap*) earliest, primitive or indigenous. — *n* (now often, and in Australia always, with *cap*) an aborigine; (with *cap*) an Australian Aboriginal language. — *n* **aborig'inalism** due recognition of native peoples. — *n* **aboriginality** (*-al'i-ti*; also with *cap*) the fact of being aboriginal. — *adv* **aborig'inally**. [L (pl) *aborīginēs*, from *ab* from, and *orīgō*, *-inis* beginning; in English, **aborigines** orig had no singular form]

aborning *ə-börn'ing*, (*US*) *adv* while being born, produced, etc, as in *die aborning*. [**a-**[1] and **born**]

abort *ə-bört'*, *vi* to miscarry in birth; to fail before getting fully under way or reaching a viable stage of development; to come to nothing. — *vt* to cause to abort; to check or call off (an attack, mission, etc) at an early stage; to stop (eg the flight of a rocket) in emergency before completion of mission; to abandon (a computer activity), *usu* because an error has been made or because there has been a program or system failure. — *n* an instance of abortion (*esp* of a rocket launch). — *n* **aborticide** (*ə-bört'i-sīd*) the killing of a foetus in the womb; a drug or agent causing this, an abortifacient. — *adj* **abortifa'cient** (*-i-fā'shənt* or *-shi-ənt*) causing abortion. — *n* a means of causing abortion. — *n* **abor'tion** the premature expulsion of an embryo or a foetus, either occurring naturally (**spontaneous abortion**) or by artificial means (**induced abortion**), *esp* in the first three months of pregnancy; the procuring of an induced abortion; arrest of development; the result of such arrest; anything that fails in the course of coming into being; a misshapen being or monster. — *adj* **abor'tional** pertaining to abortion; dreadful or terrible (*colloq*). — *n* **abor'tionist** a person who performs abortions, *esp* illegally; a person who is in favour of abortion on demand. — *adj* **abor'tive** born before due time; unsuccessful; brought out or produced in an imperfect condition; abortifacient; checked in development. — *adv* **abort'ively**. — *n* **abort'iveness**. — *n*

abortuary (*ə-bört'ū-ə-ri*; from *abort*ion and mort*uary*) an anti-abortion term for an abortion clinic. — **abortion pill** a drug taken orally that brings about abortion; **contagious abortion** contagious bacterial infections of cattle and of horses, causing abortion. [L *aborīrī*, *abortus*, from **ab-**[1] (reversing the meaning), and *orīrī* to rise]

abought *ə-böt'*, *pa t* and *pa p* of **aby**.

aboulia or **abulia** *a-bōō'li-ə*, *-bow'* or *-bū'*, *n* loss of willpower; inability to make decisions. [Gr *a-* (privative), and *boulē* will]

abound *ə-bownd'*, *vi* to exist in great plenty; to be rich (in); to be filled (with). — *adj* **abound'ing**. [OFr *abunder*, from L *abundāre* to overflow, from *ab* from, and *unda* a wave]

about *ə-bowt'*, *prep* round on the outside of; around; here and there in; near in place, time, size, etc; on the person of; connected with; concerning; engaged in. — *adv* around; halfway round, in the opposite direction (eg *to face about*); nearly; here and there; on the opposite tack; in motion or activity, on the go. — *prep* **abouts'** (*Spenser*) about. — **about'-face** (*orig* used in US as a military command) the act of turning to face in the opposite direction; a complete change of opinion, attitude, etc. — Also *vi*. — Also **about'-turn**. — *vt* and *vi* **about'-ship'** to put (the ship) on the opposite tack. — **about'-sledge** a blacksmith's heavy hammer. — **about to** on the point of (doing, etc; also **just about to**); (in *neg*) not likely or keen (to do something) (*colloq*); **be about** to be up and on the go after sleep or rest; **bring about** to cause to take place; **come about** to happen in the course of time; **go about** to prepare to do; to change course or tack — literally, to steer across the direction from which the wind is blowing (*naut*); **put about** see under **put**[1]; **turn about** alternately; in rotation. [OE *onbūtan*, from *on* in (cf **a-**[1]), and *būtan* without, from *be* by, and *ūtan*, orig a locative, from *ūt* out]

above *ə-buv'*, *prep* over; in or to a position higher than that of; beyond in degree, amount, number, importance, etc; too magnanimous or proud for. — *adv* overhead; in a higher position, order or power; in an earlier passage (of text, etc); in heaven. — *adj* mentioned, stated, or given in an earlier passage. — *adj* **above'-board** open, without deception. — *adj* **above'-ground** alive; not buried. — *adj* **above'-mentioned**. — *adj* **above'-named**. — *adj* **above-the-line'** of or pertaining to the Government's expenditure and revenue allowed for in its original estimates and provided for by taxation; of or pertaining to the expenditure and revenue detailed in a company's profit and loss account. — **above-the-line advertising** advertising using conventional media such as television, radio, newspapers, cinemas and posters; **above-the-line costs, transactions**, etc (*econ*; also without *hyphens*) items in the balance of payments accounts which record total payments and receipts on visible and invisible trade and on investment and capital transactions. — **above oneself** elated; conceited; **above par** see under **par**[1]. [Late OE *ābufan*, from OE *ā-* on (cf **a-**[1]), and *bufan* above, from *be* by, and *ufan* above]

ab ovo *ab ō'vō* or *-wō*, (*L*, literally, from the egg) from the beginning.

Abp or **abp** *abbrev*: Archbishop.

ABPA *abbrev*: Australian Book Publishers' Association.

abr. *abbrev*: abridged; abridgement.

abracadabra *ab-rə-kə-dab'rə*, *n* a spell or conjuring word; gibberish; a magic word, used as a charm (*obs*). [Found in a 2c poem by Q Serenus Sammonicus]

abrade[1] *ə-brād'*, *vt* to wear down or off. — *adj* and *n* **abrā'dant** abrasive. [L *ab* from, and *rādere*, *rāsum* to scrape]

abrade[2]. See **abraid**.

Abraham-man *ā'brə-həm-man'* or **Abram-man** *ā'brəm-man'*, *n orig* a Bedlam inmate let out to beg; a sturdy beggar, *esp* one shamming insanity (*archaic*). — **sham Abraham** to feign sickness. [Said to be from an Abraham Ward in old Bedlam, London]

abraid, **abrade** *ə-brād'*, or (*Spenser*) **abray** *ə-brā'*, (*obs*) *vt* to awake or rouse. — *vi* to start; to awake. [OE *ābregdan*, from intens pfx *ā-*, and *bregdan*; see **braid**[1]]

abram *ā'brəm*, (*Shakesp*) *adj* an *obs* form of **auburn**.

abranchiate *ə-brang'ki-āt*, or **abranchial** *ə-brang'ki-əl*, (*zool*) *adj* without gills. [Gr *a-* (privative) and *branchia* gills]

abrasion *ə-brā'zhən*, *n* a wearing away; a worn-down or grazed place; a graze on the skin. — *adj* **abrā'sive** (*-ziv* or *-siv*) tending to abrade; harsh; (of a person) tending to irritate or annoy. — *n* a substance used to clean, smoothe, etc by scratching and grinding. [See **abrade**[1]]

à bras ouverts *a brä-zōō-ver*, (*Fr*) with open arms.

abraxas *ə-braks'əs*, *n* a mystic word, or a gem engraved with such a word, often bearing a mystical figure of combined human and animal form, used as a charm; (with *cap*) the genus of the gooseberry or magpie moth. [Said to have been coined by the 2c Egyptian Gnostic Basilides to express 365 by addition of the numerical values of the Greek letters]

abray. See **abraid**.

abrazo *ə-brä'sō*, *n* in Central and S America, an embrace, *esp* in greeting: — *pl* **abra'zos**. [Sp]

ABRC *abbrev*: Advisory Board for Research Councils.

abreaction *ab-rē-ak'shən*, (*psychol*) *n* the resolution of a neurosis by reviving forgotten or repressed ideas of the event first causing it. — *vi* **abreact'**. — *adj* **abreact'ive**. [L *ab* from, and **reaction**]

abreast *ə-brest'*, *adv* with fronts in line; side by side; (with *of*) keeping pace with, eg *abreast of the other car*, *abreast of the times*. [**a-**[1]]

abrégé *a-brā-zhā*, (*Fr*) *n* an abridgement.

abricock *ab'ri-kok*, an *obs* form of **apricot**.

abridge *ə-brij'*, *vt* to shorten; to epitomize; to curtail. — *adj* **abridg'able** or **abridge'able**. — *n* **abridg'er**. — *n* **abridge'ment** (sometimes **abridg'ment**) contraction; shortening; a compendium of a larger work; an epitome or synopsis; (probably) a pastime (*Shakesp*). [OFr *abregier* (Fr *abréger*), from L *abbreviāre*]

abrim *ə-brim'*, *adv* and *adj* in a brimming state, up to the brim. [**a-**[1]]

abrin. See **Abrus**.

ABRO *ab'rō*, *abbrev*: Animal Breeding Research Organization.

abroach *ə-brōch'*, (*obs*) *adv* and *adj* in a condition to let the liquor run out; in a state to be diffused, afloat or astir. [**a-**[1]]

abroad *ə-bröd'*, *adv* in or to another country; over a wide area; in full breadth; out of doors; at large; in the field; current; wide of the mark (*archaic*); astray (*archaic*). — *n* anywhere foreign, foreign places. [**a-**[1]]

abrogate *ab'rō-gāt*, *vt* to annul or rescind. — *n* **abrogā'tion**. — *adj* **ab'rogātive**. — *n* **ab'rogātor**. [L *ab* away, and *rogāre*, *-ātum* to ask, or to propose a law]

Abroma *a-brō'mə*, *n* a genus of E Indian sterculiaceous fibre-yielding trees. [Gr *a-* (privative), and *brōma* food]

abrooke *ə-brōōk'*, (*Shakesp*) *vt* to brook, bear or endure. [Pfx *a-* (intens), and **brook**[2]]

ABRSM *abbrev*: Associated Board(s) of the Royal Schools of Music.

abrupt *ə-brupt'*, *adj* truncated; as if broken off; sudden; unexpected; precipitous; steep; passing with sudden transitions; (of manners) short or rude. — *n* (*Milton*) an abyss. — *n* **abrup'tion** (*-shən*) a breaking off. — *adv* **abrupt'ly**. — *n* **abrupt'ness**. [L *abruptus*, from *ab* from, and *rumpere*, *ruptum* to break]

Abrus *a'brəs*, or *ā'*, *n* a tropical genus akin to the bean, to which crab's-eyes belong. — *n* **ā'brin** a poisonous protein contained in its seeds. [Gr *habros* graceful]

ABS *abbrev*: anti-lock braking system (*autos*); Associate of the Building Societies Institute; Association of Broadcasting Staff.

abs. *abbrev*: absence; absent; (also **absol.**) absolute; (also **absol.**) absolutely; absorbent; (also **abstr.**) abstract.

ABSA *abbrev*: Association of Business Sponsorship of the Arts.

abscess *ab'ses* or *-sis*, *n* a collection of pus in a cavity, *usu* causing an inflamed swelling. — *adj* **ab'scessed**. [L *abscessus*, from *abs* from, and *cēdere*, *cēssum* to go or retreat]

abscind *ab-sind'*, *vt* to cut off. — *n* **abscissa** (*-sis'ə*; *math*), also **absciss** or **abscisse** (*ab'sis*) the intercept between a fixed point and the foot of an ordinate; the *x*-co-ordinate in analytical geometry: — *pl* **abscissae** (*ab-sis'ē* or *-sis'ī*), **absciss'as** or **ab'scisses**. — *n* **absciss'in** same as **abscisin** (see under **abscise**). — *n* **abscission** (*-sizh'ən*) an act of cutting off, or the state of being cut off; a figure of speech in which words demanded by the sense are left unsaid, the speaker stopping short suddenly (*rhetoric*); organized shedding of a part (eg a leaf or fruit) (*bot*); liberation of a fungal spore by breakdown of part of its stalk (*bot*). — **absciss layer** or **abscission layer** (*bot*) a layer of parenchymatous cells through which a leaf, branch or bark scale separates off. [L *abscindere*, *abscissum* to cut off, from *ab* from, and *scindere* to cut]

abscise *ab-sīz'*, (*bot*) *vi* to fall off by abscission. — *vt* to cause to separate by abscission. — *n* **abscisin** (*-sis'in*) any of a number of plant hormones which promote abscission. — **abscisic acid** an abscisin that promotes abscission in leaves and dormancy in buds and seeds. [L *abscīsus*, pa p of *abscīdere*, from *abs* away, and *caedere* to cut]

abscissa, **abscissae**, **abscission**. See under **abscind**.

abscond *ab-skond'*, *vi* to hide, or get out of the way, *esp* to escape a legal process. — *n* **abscond'ence**. — *n* **abscond'er**. [L *abscondere*, from *abs* from or away, and *condere* to hide]

abseil *ap'zīl*, *ab-sīl'* or *ab'sāl*, *vi* to let oneself down a rock face using a double rope. — *n* **abseiling**. [Ger *ab* down, and *Seil* rope]

absent *ab'sənt*, *adj* being away; not present; inattentive or dreamy. — *vt* (*ab-sent'*; *usu refl*) to keep away. — *n* **ab'sence** the state of being away or not present; want or lack; non-existence; abstraction, inattention. — *n* **absentee'** a person who is absent on any occasion; a person who makes a habit of being away from his or her estate, office, school, etc. — *n* **absentee'ism** the practice of absenting oneself from duty or estate; the persistent habit of being absent from work, school, etc. — *adv* **ab'sently**. — *adj* **absent-mind'ed** inattentive to surroundings; preoccupied. — *adv* **absent-mind'edly**. — *n* **absent-mind'edness**. [L *absēns*, *-sentis*, pr p of *abesse*, from *ab* away from, and *esse* to be]

absente reo *ab-sent'ē rē'ō*, or *-te rā'ō*, (*L*; *abbrev* **abs re**) in the absence of the accused.

absey or **absey book**. See **ABC**.

absinthe or **absinth** *ab'sinth*, *n* the wormwood plant or other species of Artemisia; a bitter, green, aniseed-flavoured liqueur containing (*orig*, at least) extract of wormwood. — *adj* **absinth'iated** impregnated with absinth. — *n* **ab'sinthism** (*pathol*) illness caused by drinking too much absinthe. [Fr *absinthe*, from L *absinthium*, from Gr *apsinthion* wormwood]

absit *ab'sit*, *n* leave to pass one night away from college. — **absit invidia** (*ab'sit invid'i-a*, or *-wid'*) no offence, (literally) may there be no ill-will; **absit omen** (*ab'sit ō'mən*) touch wood, (literally) may there be no (ill) omen (as in a word just used). [L, let him, her or it be absent, from *abesse*, from *ab* away from, and *esse* to be]

absolute *ab'səl-ōōt* or *-ūt*, *adj* free from limits, restrictions or conditions; certain, positive; complete; unlimited; free from mixture, pure; independent of relation to other things; peremptory; unrestricted by constitutional checks; out of ordinary syntactic relation, standing as an independent construction, such as the Latin *ablative absolute* and Greek *genitive absolute* (*gram*); existing in and by itself without necessary relation to anything else (*philos*); capable of being conceived independently of anything else. — *n* (with *the*; often with *cap*) that which is absolute, self-existent or uncaused. — *adv* **ab'solutely** (*abbrev* **abs.** or **absol.**) separately, by itself; unconditionally; positively; completely, as a colourless but emphatic affirmative (*-lōōt'li* or *-lūt'*). — *n* **ab'soluteness**. — *n* **absolu'tion** release from punishment or guilt; acquittal; remission of sins, declared officially by a priest, or the formula by which it is expressed. — *n* **ab'solutism** government or theory of government by a ruler with unrestricted power; adherence to the doctrine of the Absolute. — *n* **ab'solutist** a supporter of absolute government, or of a philosophy of the Absolute. — Also *adj.* — *adj* **absolutory** (*ab-sol'ū-tər-i*) of, or giving, absolution. — **absolute address** (*comput*) a location within the immediate access store where an item of data can be stored; **absolute age** (*geol*) see **radiometric age**; **absolute alcohol** water-free alcohol; **absolute humidity** humidity expressed as grams of water per cubic metre of air; **absolute magnitude** the magnitude that a star would have at a standard distance of 10 parsecs; **absolute majority** a vote gained by a candidate which is greater than the total number of votes for all other candidates; **absolute monopoly** (*econ*) a situation in which a single organization has total control over the output of a product, commodity or service for which there is no substitute; **absolute music** music which does not attempt to illustrate or describe (*opp* to *programme music*); **absolute pitch** the pitch of a note as determined by the number of vibrations per second, perfect pitch; a sense of or memory for absolute pitch; **absolute privilege** (*law*) a privilege that protects members of a lawmaking body, in making (even malicious) statements from the floor, from possible charges under the laws of slander; **absolute temperature** temperature measured on the Kelvin scale or Rankine scale; **absolute undertaking** (*commerce*) a promise by a party to a contract that he or she shall take absolute responsibility for something which is necessary for the performance of the contract, eg obtaining a licence to sell the goods; **absolute units** those derived directly from fundamental units and not based on arbitrary numerical definitions; **absolute zero** the zero of the absolute scale of temperature (-273.15°C), the lowest temperature theoretically possible, at which entropy is zero. [L *absolūtus*, pa p of *absolvere*; see **absolve**]

absolve *əb-zolv'* or *-solv'*, *vt* to loose or set free from guilt; to pardon; to give absolution to or for; to acquit without blame; to discharge (from); to accomplish, finish off (*Milton*). — *n* **absolv'er**. — *n* **absolv'itor** (*L* 3*rd pers imperative passive*, let him be absolved; *Scots law*) a decision favourable to a defender. [L *absolvere*, from *ab* from, and *solvere* to loose]

absonant *ab'sən-ənt*, *adj* discordant; abhorrent; unnatural; contrary to reason (with *to* or *from*; *opp* to *consonant*). [L *ab* from, and *sonāns*, *-antis*, pr p of *sonāre* to sound]

absorb *ab-sörb'* or *-zörb'*, *vt* to suck in; to swallow up; to imbibe; to take in; to incorporate; to take up and transform (energy) instead of transmitting or reflecting (*phys*); to engage wholly or engross. — *n* **absorbabil'ity**. — *adj* **absorb'able**. — *n* **absorb'ate** an absorbed substance. — *adj* **absorbed'** swallowed or soaked up; entirely occupied or engrossed. — *adv* **absorb'edly**. — *adj* **absorbefacient** (*-i-fā'shənt* or *-shi-ənt*) causing or promoting absorption. — *n* a medicine, etc, which causes or promotes absorption. — *n* **absorb'ency**. — *adj* **absorb'ent** absorbing; able to absorb. — *n* something that absorbs. — *n* **absorb'er** something that absorbs; material for capturing neutrons without generating more neutrons (*nuc*). — *adj* **absorb'ing** engrossing the attention. — *adv* **absorb'ingly**. — *n* **absorptiometer** (*-sörp-shi-om'i-tər*) an apparatus for determining the solubility of gases in liquids. — *n* **absorp'tion** the act of absorbing; the entire occupation of the mind. — *adj* **absorp'tive** having power to absorb. — *n* **absorp'tiveness** or **absorptiv'ity**. — **absorption bands** or **lines** dark bands or lines interrupting a spectrum, due to absorption of light in the medium traversed; **absorption spectrum** a system of such lines and bands. [L *ab* from, and *sorbēre, sorptum* to suck in]

absquatulate *ab-skwot'ū-lāt*, (*facetious*; *US*) *vi* to decamp; to squat.

abstain *ab-stān'*, *vi* to hold or refrain (from, *specif* from voting or from drinking alcohol). — *vt* (*Spenser*) to restrain. — *n* **abstain'er** a person who abstains, *esp* from alcoholic drinks. — *n* **absten'tion**. — *n* **absten'tionism** the policy of not using one's vote, *esp* in a political election. — *n* and *adj* **absten'tionist**. — *adj* **absten'tious**. [Fr *abstenir*, from L *abs* from, and *tenēre* to hold]

abs re or **abse re** *abbrev*: *absente reo* (*L*), the accused being absent.

abstemious *ab-stē'mi-əs*, *adj* temperate; restrained in relation to food, drink, or other pleasures. — *adv* **abstē'miously**. — *n* **abstē'miousness**. [L *abstēmius*, from *abs* from, and *tēmētum* strong wine]

abstention, abstentious. See **abstain**.

absterge *ab-stûrj'*, (*med*) *vt* to wipe; to cleanse; to purge. — *adj* **absterg'ent** cleansing or purging. — *n* a cleansing agent. — *n* **abster'sion** a cleansing or purging process. — *adj* **abster'sive** having the quality of cleansing; purgative. — Also *n*. [L *abstergēre, -tersum* to wipe away, from *abs* from, and *tergēre* to wipe]

abstinent *ab'stin-ənt*, *adj* abstaining; temperate or self-restrained in one's appetites. — *n* **ab'stinence** an abstaining or refraining, *esp* from some indulgence (with *from*); restricting the manufacture of consumer goods so that the productive resources so released may be switched to increasing the stock of capital goods (*commerce*). — *n* **ab'stinency** the quality of being abstinent. — *adv* **ab'stinently**. [L *abstinēns, -entis*, pr p of *abstinēre*; see **abstain**]

abstract *ab-strakt'*, *vt* to draw away; to separate; to remove quietly; to purloin; to summarize; to form a general concept from consideration of particular instances. — *n* (*ab'strakt*) a summary or abridgement; in Shakesp *Antony and Cleopatra* 3. 6, explained by some as an abridgement of time of separation, while others conjecture *obstruct*; that part or thing which represents the essence; an abstraction; an abstract painting, sculpture, photograph, etc. — *adj* (*ab'strakt*) abstracted; apart from actual material instances, existing only as a mental concept (*opp* to *concrete*); away from practice, theoretical; (of terms) denoting a quality of a thing apart from the thing, eg 'redness'; representing ideas in geometric and other designs, not the forms of nature (*visual arts*); (of verse) using words primarily for their auditory and rhythmic qualities. — *adj* **abstract'ed** drawn off (with *from*); removed; absent-minded. — *adv* **abstract'edly**. — *n* **abstract'edness**. — *n* **abstrac'ter** or, formerly, in the Civil Service **abstrac'tor** a person who makes abstracts. — *n* **abstrac'tion** the act of abstracting; the state of being abstracted; abstract quality or character; withdrawal from worldly things; absent-mindedness; a purloining; the process of abstracting by the mind; a thing existing only in idea; a theory or visionary notion; an abstract term; an abstract composition (*visual arts*). — *adj* **abstrac'tional**. — *n* **abstrac'tionist** a person dealing in abstractions or unrealities. — *n* **abstrac'tionism**. — *adj* **abstrac'tive** able or tending to abstract; formed by or pertaining to abstraction. — *n* anything abstractive; an abstract. — *adv* **abstrac'tively**. — *adv* **ab'stractly**. — *n* **ab'stractness**. — **abstract expressionism** a development in art that began in America in the 1940s in which the expression of the artist's feelings informs his or her abstract representations. — **abstract of title** (*law*) a summary of facts concerning ownership; a document giving evidence, in shortened form, of the ownership of property or land; **in the abstract** as an abstraction; in theory. [L *abs* away from, and *trahere, tractum* to draw]

abstrict *ab-strikt'*, (*biol*) *vt* to set free (spores, etc), *esp* by constriction of the stalk. — *n* **abstric'tion**. [L *ab* from, and *stringere, strictum* to tie]

abstruse *ab-stro͞os'*, *adj* hidden (*archaic*); remote from apprehension; difficult to understand. — *adv* **abstruse'ly**. — *n* **abstruse'ness**. [L *abstrūsus* thrust away, from *abs* away, and *trūdere, trūsum* to thrust]

absurd *ab-sûrd'*, *adj* senseless or meaningless; opposed to reason; ridiculous. — *n* **absurd'ism** the belief that mankind lives in a world that is essentially meaningless (see **theatre of the absurd**). — *adj* and *n* **absurd'ist** (a person) following this belief. — *n* **absurd'ity** or **absurd'ness**. — *adv* **absurd'ly**. [L *absurdus*, from *ab* from, and *surdus* deaf, inaudible, indistinct, harsh, out of fashion, not to the purpose]

ABTA *ab'tə*, *abbrev*: Association of British Travel Agents.

abthane *ab'thān*, *n* a monastic territory of the Columban church. [LL *abthania*, from Gaelic *abdhaine* abbacy]

abulia. See **aboulia**.

abuna *ä-bo͞o'nə*, *n* an Ethiopian patriarch. [Ethiopian, from Arabic, our father]

abundance *ə-bund'əns*, *n* ample sufficiency; great plenty; a call of nine tricks (*solo whist*; also **abondance** (*-bund'*)); the proportion of one isotope to the total (for a specified element) (*phys*; also **abundance ratio** or **relative abundance**). — *n* **abund'ancy**. — *adj* **abund'ant**. — *adv* **abund'antly** enough; fully. [See **abound**]

abune *ə-bün'*. A Scots form of **above**.

ab urbe condita *ab ûr'be kon'di-ta* or *o͝or'be kon'di-tä*, (*L*) from the founding of the city (of Rome) 753BC (*abbrev* AUC).

aburst *ə-bûrst'*, *adv* and *adj* in a bursting condition. [**a-**[1]]

abuse *ə-būz'*, *vt* to make a bad use of; to take undue advantage of; to betray (eg a confidence); to misrepresent; to deceive; to revile or swear at; to maltreat; to violate, *esp* sexually. — *n* **abuse** (*ə-būs'*) wrong use; an evil or corrupt practice; deceit; hurt or maltreatment; undue advantage; betrayal (of confidence); ill usage, maltreatment; (*esp* sexual) violation; reviling, insulting language. — *n* **abusage** (*ə-bū'sij*) wrong use, *esp* of words or grammar. — *n* **abuser** (*ə-bū'zər*). — *n* **abū'sion** (*-zhən*; *Spenser* also *-zi-ən*; now *rare*) misuse; deception; wrong; outrage; reviling. — *adj* **abū'sive** (*-siv*) containing, giving or of the nature of, abuse; (of speech) coarse, rude or insulting; wrong; (of a word) wrongly applied, catachrestical (*archaic*). — *adv* **abū'sively**. — *n* **abū'siveness**. [L *ab* from, and *ūti, ūsus* to use]

abut *ə-but'*, *vi* to end or lean (on, upon or against). — *vt* to border: — *pr p* **abutt'ing**; *pa t* and *pa p* **abutt'ed**. — *n* **abut'ment** an endwise meeting or junction; the structure on which each side of an arch ends or rests (*archit*); a place of abutting. — *n* **abutt'al** an abutment; (in *pl*) boundaries. — *n* **abutt'er** (*law*) a person whose property abuts. — *adj* **abutt'ing** confronting. [OFr *abouter* to touch by an end, and OFr *abuter* to touch at the end; cf also Fr *aboutir* to end at, from *à* to, and *bout* or *but* end; see **butt**[4]]

abutilon *a-bū'ti-lon*, *n* a plant of the showy-flowered genus *Abutilon* of the mallow family, some species yielding fibres. [Ar *aubūtilūn*]

abutment, abuttal, etc. See **abut**.

abuzz *ə-buz'*, *adv* and *adj* in a buzz. [**a-**[1] and **buzz**[1]]

abvolt *ab'vōlt* *n* 10^{-8} volts. [**ab-**[2] and **volt**[2]]

aby or **abye** *ə-bī'*, (*archaic*) *vt* to pay the penalty for; to pay as a penalty. — *vi* to atone; to endure or continue: — *pa t* and *pa p* **abought** (*ə-böt'*). [OE *abycgan*, from pfx *a-* back, and *bycgan* to buy; merging and confused with **abide**[1]]

abysm *ə-bizm'*, *n* (*archaic* and *poetic*) an abyss. — *adj* **abys'mal** very bad (*colloq*); bottomless; unfathomable; very deep; abyssal. — *adv* **abys'mally**. [OFr *abisme*, from a LL superl of *abyssus*; see **abyss**]

abyss *ə-bis'*, *n* a bottomless gulf; primal chaos; the supposed water-filled cavity under the earth; hell; anything very deep; the depths of the sea; a measureless or apparently measureless chasm. — *adj* **abyss'al** very deep or bottomless, *esp* of ocean depths. — *adj* **abyssopelagic** (*ə-bis-ō-pi-laj'ik*) pertaining to the deepest regions of the ocean. [Gr *abyssos* bottomless, from *a-* (privative), and *byssos* depth, bottom]

Abyssinian cat *ab-i-sin'i-ən*, or *-sin'yən*, *kat*, *n* a small domestic cat of African origin, greyish or brownish marked with darker colour.

AC *abbrev*: Aero Club; air-conditioned or air-conditioning; Air Corps; aircraft(s)man; Alpine Club; alternating curent (*elec*); *ante Christum* (*L*), before Christ; appellation (d'origine) contrôlée (*Fr*); athletic club; Companion of the Order of Australia.

Ac (*chem*) *symbol*: actinium.

ac *abbrev*: alternating current (*elec*); in medical prescriptions, etc, *ante cibum* (*L*), before food.

a/c *abbrev*: account; account current.

ACA *abbrev*: Associate of the Institute of Chartered Accountants in England and Wales; Associate of the Institute of Chartered Accountants in Ireland.

acacia *ə-kā'sh(y)ə*, *n* a wattle, any plant of the genus *Acacia*, related to the sensitive plants; also applied to the *false acacia* of the genus *Robinia*: — *pl* **aca'cias** or **aca'cia**. [L, from Gr *akakiā*]

academe *ak-ə-dēm'*, (*formal* or *literary*) *n* the world of scholars; academic life; an academic, *esp* if pedantic; an academy (*poetic*). — *n* **acadēm'ia** the academic life or world. [Ety as for **academy**]

academy *ə-kad'ə-mi*, *n orig* Plato's school of philosophy; a secondary school (*esp* in Scotland), a specialized (eg military) school, or a university; a riding-school; a society for the promotion of the arts, science or fine art; the annual exhibition of the Royal Academy or of the Royal Scottish Academy. — *adj* **academic** (*-dem'ik*) *orig* of the philosophical school of Plato; of an academy or university; sceptical; scholarly; formal; theoretical only, of no practical importance or consequence. — *n orig* a Platonic philosopher; a person studying or teaching at a university, *esp* one who has scholarly tastes (sometimes *derog*); (in *pl*) academic studies (*US*). — *adj* **academ'ical** academic. — *n* in Scotland, a pupil or former pupil of an academy; (in *pl*) formal university dress, *usu* cap, gown, etc. — *n* **academ'icalism** close adherence to formal academic teaching. — *adv* **academ'ically**. — *n* **academician** (*ə-kad-ə-mish'ən*) a member of an academy, *esp* of the French Academy or the Royal Academy of Arts (London) or Royal Scottish Academy (Edinburgh). — *n* **academ'icism**, **academ'icalism** or **acad'emism**. — *n* **acad'emist** an academic; an academician. [Gr *Akadēmeia* Plato's school of philosophy, from the name of the garden outside Athens where Plato taught]

Acadian *ə-kā'di-ən*, *adj* of or pertaining to the Acadians or their dialect of French, or to Acadia, former name for part of E Canada including Nova Scotia and New Brunswick. — *n* one of the French-speaking early settlers of Acadia, or one of their descendants, including the Cajuns (qv). [Fr *Acadie* Acadia, from Micmac Ind *ākade* abundance]

acajou *ak'ə-zhōō* or *-zhōō'*, *n* the cashew tree or its fruit or gum; a kind of mahogany. [See **cashew**]

acaleph or **acalephe** *ak'ə-lef*, *-lēf* or *-le'fə*, *n* a jellyfish of the class **Acalē'pha** or **Acalē'phae**, which also includes medusas. — *n* and *adj* **acalē'phan**. [Gr *akalēphē* a nettle, sea-anemone]

acanaceous *ak-ə-nā'shəs*, (*bot*) *adj* prickly. [L *acanus* a kind of thistle, from Gr *akanos*, from *akē* a point]

acanth *ə-kanth'*, (*obs*) *n* acanthus. — *n* **acanth'a** a thorn, prickle; a spinous process. — *n pl* **Acanthā'ceae** (*ak-*) the acanthus family, related to the figworts. — *adj* **acanthā'ceous** prickly; of the Acanthaceae. — *n* **acanth'in** strontium sulphate in skeletons of Radiolaria. — *adj* **acanth'ine** of, like or ornamented with acanthus. — *n pl* **Acanthocephala** (Gr *kephalē* head) a division of parasitic worms with spiny proboscis and no mouth or alimentary canal. — *adj* **acanthoceph'alan**. — *adj* **acanth'oid** like acanthus. — *adj* **acanthopterygian** (*ak-an-thop-tər-ij'yən*; Gr *pteryx*, *-ygos* wing, fin) spiny-finned. — *adj* **acanth'ous** spiny. — *n* **acanth'us** any plant of the prickly-leaved genus *Acanthus*, *esp* *Acanthus spinosus* or *Acanthus mollis*; a conventionalized representation of an acanthus leaf, as in Corinthian capitals. [Gr *akantha* prickle, *akanthos* acanthus, from *akē* point]

acapnia *ə-kap'ni-ə*, *n* deficiency of carbon dioxide. [Gr *a-* (privative), and *kapnos* smoke]

a cappella *a ka-pel'ə* or *ä käp-pel'lä* (*music*) (of choral music) sung without accompaniment or with accompaniment merely doubling the voice parts; alla breve. — Also **alla cappella**. [Ital, in the church style]

ACARD *abbrev*: Advisory Council for Applied Research and Development.

acari, **acarian**, etc. See **acarus**.

acarpous *ā-* or *a-kär'pəs*, (*bot*) *adj* sterile, not bearing fruit. [Gr *a-* (privative), and *karpos* fruit]

acarus *ak'ə-rəs*, *n* a mite: — *pl* **ac'arī**. — *adj* **acā'rian**. — *n* **acarī'asis** disease due to or infestation by mites. — *n* **acaricide** (*a-kar'i-sīd*) a mite killer. — *n* **ac'arid** one of the Acarida. — *n pl* **Acar'ida** the order of Arachnida to which mites and ticks belong. — *adj* and *n* **acar'idan**, **acarid'ean** or **acarid'ian**. — *n pl* **Acarī'na** Acarida. — *adj* **ac'arine**. — *n* **acarodomatium** or **acaridomatium** (*-dō-mā'shyəm*) a habitat for mites provided by certain plants that benefit from their presence: — *pl* **acarodomā'tia** or **acaridoma'tia**. — *adj* **ac'aroid** mite-like. — *n* **acarol'ogist**. — *n* **acarol'ogy**. — *n* **acaroph'ily** symbiotic association of plants with mites. — **acarine disease** a disease of bees due to mites in the spiracles. [Gr *akari* a mite, from *akarēs* too short to cut, from *a-* in privative sense, and *keirein* to cut]

acarpellous or (chiefly *US*) **acarpelous** *ā-kär'pəl-əs*, (*bot*) *adj* (of flowers) having no carpels. [Gr *a-* (privative), and *karpos* fruit]

ACAS *ā'kas*, *n* Advisory, Conciliation and Arbitration Service, an independent organization set up by the British government in 1974 to help avoid or resolve industrial disputes and improve industrial relations.

acatalectic *a-kat-ə-lek'tik*, (*prosody*) *adj* (of a line of verse) having the full number of syllables. — *n* an acatalectic verse or line. [Gr *akatalēktos*, from *a-* (privative); see **catalectic**]

acatalepsy *a-kat'ə-lep-si*, (*Sceptic philos*) *n* the unknowableness to a certainty of all things. — *adj* and *n* **acatalep'tic**. [Gr *akatalēpsiā*, from *a-* (privative), *kata* thoroughly, and *lēpsis* a seizing]

acatamathesia *a-kat-ə-mə-thē'zi-ə* or *-zhə*, (*psychol*) *n* the inability to comprehend data (objects, language, etc) presented to the senses. [Gr *a-* (privative) and *katamanthanein* to observe, understand, from *kata* (intens), and *manthanein* to learn]

acates *ə-kāts'*, (*obs*) *n pl* bought provisions. — *n* **acāt'er** or **acāt'our** (*obs*) an officer who buys provisions, a caterer; a ship chandler. [OFr *acat*, from LL *accaptāre* to acquire, from L *ad* to, and *captāre* to seize; see **cate**, **cater**[1]]

acaudal *ā-kö'dl*, *adj* tailless. — Also **acau'date**. [Gr *a-* (privative) and **caudal**]

acaulescent *ak-ö-les'ənt*, *adj* having a very short stem. — *adj* **acaul'ine** (*-līn* or *-lin*) or **acaulose** (*-lōs'*) stemless. [Gr *a-* (privative), L *caulis* stem, and suffixes *-escent*, *-ine* and *-ose*]

ACC *abbrev*: Accident Compensation Corporation (*NZ*); Association of County Councils.

acc. *abbrev*: acceptance (*commerce*); accompanied; according; account (also **acct** or **a/c**); accountant; accusative (also **accus.**; *gram*).

ACCA *abbrev*: Associate of the Chartered Association of Certified Accountants.

accablé *ak-a-blā*, (*Fr*), *adj* depressed or overwhelmed.

Accadian. Same as **Akkadian**.

accede *ək-sēd'*, *vi* to come forward; to arrive (with *to*); to come to office or dignity; to join up or become a party, hence to agree or assent (with *to*). — *n* **accēd'ence**. — *n* **accēd'er**. [L *accēdere*, *accēssum* to go near, from *ad* to, and *cēdere* to go; see **cede**]

accelerando *ak-sel-ər-an'dō*, Ital *ät-chel-er-än'dō*, (*music*) *adj* and *adv* with increasing speed. — *abbrev*: **accel.** [Ital]

accelerate *ək-sel'ər-āt*, *vt* to increase the speed of; to hasten the progress or occurrence of. — *vi* to become faster. — *n* **accel'erant** an accelerating agent (also *adj*). — *n* **accelerā'tion** increase of speed; rate of change of velocity; a cumulative advance ahead of the normal or theoretical; the power or means of accelerating. — *adj* **accel'erative** quickening. — *n* **accel'erātor** any person or thing that accelerates, *esp* a substance that accelerates chemical action, a nerve or muscle that increases rate of action, an apparatus for changing the speed of a machine, or one for imparting high energies to atomic particles. Devices for accelerating charged particles include the **cyclotron** type (for accelerating the heavier particles, such as protons; used in the treatment of cancer), and modifications of this, such as the **synchrocyclotron type** and the **synchrotron** type (for accelerating electrons). Other types of accelerators are the **proton synchrotron** (of which examples are the **cosmotron** and the **bevatron**), the **betatron** (for accelerating electrons; used in medicine and industry), **linear accelerators** and **electron ring accelerators**. — *adj* **accel'eratory**. — *n* **accelerom'eter** an instrument for measuring acceleration of aircraft, etc. — **accelerated aging test** (*elec eng*) a test for the stability of cables, using twice the normal voltage; **accelerated fatigue tests** (*eng*) the mechanical application to a machine or component of simulated operating loads to find its fatigue limit before it is reached in service; **acceleration principle** the relationship between a sustained rise in the sales of a commodity and the increase in the ordering by firms of the extra factory equipment made necessary by the increased output (*commerce*). [L *accelerāre*, *-ātum*, from *ad* to, and *celer* swift]

accend *ək-send'*, (*obs*) *vt* to kindle. — *n* **accen'sion**. [L *accendere*, *accēnsum* to kindle]

accent *ak'sənt*, *n* modulation of the voice; tone of voice; stress on a syllable, word, or note; a mark used to direct this stress; a mark over a letter to indicate differences of stress, pitch, length, quality of sound, etc; intensity; any way of pronouncing speech characteristic of a region, a class or an individual; a distinguishing mark; a distinctive mode of expression, such as that of an artist; a significant word (*poetic*); a touch bringing out some particular effect (*painting*); (in *pl*) speech, language (*poetic*). — *vt* (*ək-sent'*) to express or mark the accent of; to utter; to accentuate. — *adj* **accent'ūal** according to or characterized by accent. — *n* **accentūal'ity**. — *adv* **accent'ūally**. — *vt* **accent'ūate** to mark, play or pronounce with accent; to make prominent or emphasize. — *n* **accentūā'tion** emphasis or stress; see **pre-emphasis** (*telecomm*). [L *accentus*, from *ad* to, and *cantus* song]

accentor *ak-sent'ör* or *-ər*, *n* a bird of the hedge-sparrow genus formerly called *Accentor*, but now *Prunella*. [L, one who sings with another, from *ad* to, and *cantor* singer]

accept *ək-sept'*, *vt* (*old-fashioned* or *formal*, *vi* with *of*) to take (something offered); to receive (with approbation, favour, consent, resignation or passivity); to reply to, suggesting agreement or compliance; to reply to in the affirmative, say yes to; to view favourably or to tolerate; to promise to pay (a bill of exchange); to understand, take on board. — *adj* **accept'able** worth accepting; welcome, pleasing; capable of being accepted, tolerable; satisfactory, adequate. — *n* **accept'ableness**. — *adv* **accept'ably**. — *n* **acceptabil'ity**. — *n* **accept'ance** accepting; favourable reception; favour; acceptableness; an agreeing to terms; an agreement to enter into a contract; agreement to pay a bill of exchange, *usu* by signing it; an accepted bill; acceptation. — *n* **accept'ancy**. — *n* **accept'ant** someone who accepts. — *adj* ready to receive. — *n* **acceptā'tion** a kind reception; the sense in which a word, etc, is understood. — *adj* **accept'ed** customary or usual; generally approved or agreed; established. — *adv* **accept'edly**. — *n* **accept'er**. — *adj* **accept'ive** ready to receive. — *n* **acceptiv'ity**. — *n* **accept'or** someone who accepts something, *esp* a bill of exchange; an impurity in semiconductor material which increases the conductivity of the material by attracting electrons; a horse which has its entry for a race confirmed. — **accepting house** a financial institution, such as a merchant bank, which accepts bills of exchange. [L *acceptāre*, from *accipere*, *acceptum*, from *ad* to, and *capere* to take]

acceptilation *ək-sept-il-ā'shən*, *n* the remission of a debt by fictitious payment (*Roman* and *Scots law*); Christ's atonement (on the theory that only God's acceptance made his sacrifice sufficient) (*theol*). [L *acceptīlātiō*, verbal release from debt, literally bringing of receipt]

access *ak'ses*, *n* approach; admittance; a way of opportunity, approach or entrance; addition, accession; onset or attack of illness; a fit (of illness or passion); permission to log on to a computer system, and to read and alter files held; the possibility of transferring data to and from a memory device (*comput*). — *vt* to locate or retrieve information; to retrieve information from (a computer), or from a computer in (a particular location) (*comput*); to gain access to in any sense. — *n* and *adj* **access'ary** accessory (*esp* in legal senses). — *n* **accessibil'ity**. — *adj* **access'ible** within reach; approachable; easily comprehensible. — *adv* **access'ibly**. — *n* **accession** (*ak-sesh'ən*) the act or event of acceding; a coming, *esp* to office or dignity, or as an addition or new member; that which is added; an addition by nature or industry to existing property (*law*); acquisition of such an addition by the owner of the existing property (*law*); assent; an access or fit (*obs*). — *vt* to enter in a book as an accession to a library. — *vt* **access'orize** or **-ise** to add accessories to. — *adj* **access'ory** additional; subsidiary, present along with something more important; adventitious; contributing; aiding or participating in a crime (*law*) or misdeed, but not as principal. — *n* anything, *esp* an item of equipment, that is secondary, additional or nonessential; someone who helps or allows others to commit a crime. — *adj* **accessor'ial**. — *adv* **access'orily**. — **access broadcasting** and **access television** radio and television programmes put out independently by groups of people, not professionally involved in broadcasting, who want to bring their points of view to public notice; **Access® card** a credit card issued by a group of banks; **access eye** (*building*) a plug provided in soil, waste and drain pipes that can be unscrewed for easy access to a blockage; **accessory minerals** those whose presence or absence is not considered when a type of rock is given a name; **accessory pigments** pigments found in chloroplasts and blue-green algae that transfer their absorbed energy to *chlorophyll a* (the primary pigment) during photosynthesis; **accessory shoe** same as **hot shoe**; **access road** a minor road built to give access to a house, locality, motorway, etc; **access television** see **access broadcasting**; **access time** the time needed for information stored in a computer to be retrieved. — **accessary before** (or **after**) **the fact** someone who helps a criminal before (or after) the committing of a crime; **deed of accession** (*Scots law*) one by which a bankrupt's creditors accede to a settlement privately, ie by trust-deed. [See **accede**]

acciaccatura *ät-chäk-a-too'rə*, (*music*) *n* a short appoggiatura. [Ital *acciaccare* to crush]

accidence *ak'sid-əns*, *n* the part of grammar dealing with the inflections of words. — *n* **ac'cident** anything that happens; an unforeseen or unexpected event; a chance; a mishap; an unessential quality or property; unevenness of surface. — *adj* **accidental** (*-dent'*) happening by chance; not essential. — *n* a sharp, flat, or natural not in the key-signature (*music*); (in *pl*) the strong chance effects of light (*painting*) — *n* **accident'alism** the state or quality of being accidental; chance manner; a system based on symptoms rather than on causes (*med*); use of accidentals (*painting*); the theory that events happen without a cause (*philos*). — *n* **accidental'ity**. — *adv* **accident'ally**. — *adj* **accident'ed** uneven; varied. — *adj* **ac'cident-prone** (*usu* predicative) more than normally liable to have accidents. — **a chapter of accidents** an unforeseen course of events; a series of accidents. [L *accidēns*, *-entis*, pr p of *accidere* to happen, from *ad* to, and *cadere* to fall]

accidie *ak'si-di*, *n* acedia. [OFr *accide*, from LL *acēdia* (see **acedia**)]

accinge *ak-sinj'*, (*fig*) *vt* to gird. [L *ad* to, and *cingere* to gird]

accipitrine *ak-sip'i-trīn* or *-trin*, *adj* pertaining to hawks. — *n* **accip'iter** a bird belonging to the *Accipiter* genus of hawks. [L *accipiter* a hawk]

accite *ak-sīt'*, *vt* to cite; to summon; to excite (*Shakesp*). [LL *accitāre*, from *ad* to, and *citāre* to cite or call]

acclamation *ak-lə-mā'shən*, *n* a shout of applause or assent; enthusiastic approval or welcome. — *vt* **acclaim** (*ə-klām'*) to hail or declare by acclamation; to welcome with enthusiasm. — *n* acclamation. — *adj* **acclamatory** (*ə-klam'ə-tər-i*). [L *acclāmāre*, from *ad* to, and *clāmāre*, *-ātum* to shout; see **claim**]

acclimatize or **-ise** *ə-klī'mə-tīz*, *vt* to accustom (a person, animal, plant, etc) to a new climate or environment. — Also (*US*) **acclī'mate** (or *ak'li-* or *-li-*), **clī'matize** or **-ise**. — *adj* **acclī'matīzable** or **-s-**. — *n* **acclīmatīzā'tion** or **-s-**. — Also **acclīmatā'tion** or **acclimā'tion** (*ak-lī-* or *-li-*). — *n* **acclī'matizer** or **-s-**. [Fr *acclimater*, from *à* to, and *climat* climate]

acclivity *ə-kliv'i-ti*, *n* an upward slope. — *adj* **accliv'itous** or **acclī'vous**. [L *ad* to, and *clīvus* a slope]

accloy *ə-kloi'*, (*obs*) *vt* to prick or lame with a horseshoe nail; to clog, choke or encumber (*Spenser*); to sate or cloy (*Spenser*). [See **cloy**]

accoast *ə-kōst'*. An older form of **accost**.

accoied. See **accoy**.

accoil *ə-koil'*, (*rare*) *n* reception. — *vi pa t* (*Spenser*) **accoyld'** assembled. [OFr *acoil* (Fr *accueil*)]

accolade *ak'əl-ād* or *-ād'*, also *ak-ol-äd'*, *n* an embrace; the action used in conferring knighthood, formerly an embrace or kiss, now a tap on each shoulder with the flat of a sword; high award, honour or praise publicly given; a brace or other line connecting staves (*music*; *rare*); a brace-like ornament (*archit*). [Fr, from L *ad* to, and *collum* neck]

accommodate *ə-kom'ə-dāt*, *vt* to adapt; to make suitable; to adjust; to harmonize or make consistent; to furnish or supply (with); to find or provide room, etc for; to provide with a loan; to oblige. — *vi* (*rare*) to come to terms; to make adjustment. — *adj* **accomm'odable**. — *adj* **accomm'odāting** ready to make adjustment; obliging; pliable; easily corrupted. — *adv* **accomm'odātingly**. — *n* **accommodā'tion** adaptation; adjustment, *esp* of the eye to change of distance; the adaptation or twisting of language to a sense not intended; obligingness; settlement or compromise; the supplying of needs (*esp* housing or refreshment); a help towards satisfaction of a need; a convenience; lodgings, living quarters (formerly sometimes *pl*); space for what is required; adaptation of revelation by way of compromise with human ignorance or weakness (*theol*); a loan of money. — *adj* **accomm'odātive**. — *n* **accom'modātiveness**. — *n* **accomm'odātor**. — **accommodation address** an address to which mail may be sent but which is not that of the addressee's home or office; **accommodation bill** a bill drawn, accepted or endorsed by one or more persons as security for a sum advanced to another by a third party, such as a banker; **accommodation ladder** a stairway on the outside of a ship allowing access to and from small boats, etc, alongside; **accommodation rig** an offshore oil rig with sleeping, supply, and recreational facilities; **accommodation road** a road giving access to buildings, etc, off the public road; **accommodation train** (*US*) one stopping at all or most stations on the way. [L *accommodāre*, *-ātum*, from *ad* to, and *commodus* fitting]

accompany *ə-kum'pə-ni*, *vt* to go or be in company with; to attend; to go along with; to perform an accompaniment to or for (*music*); to associate, join, or couple. — *n* **accom'panier**. — *n* **accom'paniment** something which accompanies; a subsidiary part or parts supporting a solo (*music*). — *n* **accom'panist** (also **accom'panyist**) a player who accompanies a soloist. [Fr *accompagner*; see **company**]

accomplice *ə-kom'plis*, or *-kum'*, *n* a person who helps another or others to commit a crime (*of* or *with* a person, *in* or *of* the crime); an associate (*Shakesp*). [L *complex*, *-icis* joined; pfx unexplained]

accomplish *ə-kom'plish*, or *-kum'*, *vt* to complete; to fulfil; to achieve, to equip (*obs*); to finish off, complete, in culture and acquirements. — *adj* **accom'plishable**. — *adj* **accom'plished** complete, finished or highly skilled; expert; polished. — *n* **accom'plisher**. — *n* **accom'plishment** completion; an achievement; making accomplished; an acquired skill, *esp* in matters of culture or social behaviour, sometimes superficial or merely ornamental. [OFr *acomplir*, from L *ad* to, and *complēre* to fill up; see **complete**]

accompt, accomptable or **accomptant**. Obsolescent spellings of **account**, **accountable** or **accountant** with the same pronunciation.

accorage. See **accourage**.

accord *ə-körd'*, *vi* to agree; to correspond (with). — *vt* to give or grant (to a person); to cause to agree; to reconcile. — *n* agreement; harmony; the set of notes to which an instrument is tuned; assent (*obs*). — *adj* **accord'able**. — *n* **accord'ance** or **accord'ancy** agreement; conformity; a granting. — *adj* **accord'ant** agreeing; corresponding. — *adv* **accord'antly**. — *n* **accord'er**. — *adj* **accord'ing** in accordance; agreeing; harmonious. — *adv* **accord'ingly** agreeably (*obs*); suitably; in agreement (with what precedes); therefore. — **accord and satisfaction** (*commerce*) the process by which a party agrees to release the other party from contractual obligations (the *accord*) in exchange for a consideration given for the release (the *satisfaction*); **according as** in proportion as; depending on whether; **according to** in accordance with, or agreeably to; as asserted by; **as accords** (*formal*) as may be appropriate; **of one's own accord** spontaneously; voluntarily; **with one accord** with spontaneous unanimity. [OFr *acorder*, from L *ad* to, and *cor*, *cordis* the heart]

accordion *ə-kör'di-ən*, *n* a musical instrument consisting of folding bellows, keyboard and free metal reeds. — *n* **accord'ionist**. — **accord'ion-pleating** or **accordion pleats** pleating with very narrow folds like the bellows of an accordion. [**accord**]

accost *ə-kost'*, earlier **accoast** *-kōst'*, *vt* to approach and speak (often threateningly) to; to speak first to; to solicit as a prostitute. — *vi* (*Spenser*) to lie alongside, border; to fly along near the ground. — *n* address; greeting. — *adj* **accost'able**. [OFr *acoster*, from LL *accostāre* to be side by side, from L *ad* to, and *costa* a rib, a side]

accouchement *a-kōōsh'mā* or *-mənt*, *n* delivery in childbirth. — *n* **accoucheur** (*-shœr'*), *fem* **accoucheuse** (*-shœz'*) a person who assists women in childbirth, a midwife. [Fr]

account *ə-kownt'*, *vt* to reckon; to judge, value; to recount (*obs*). — *vi* to count; to reckon; to keep accounts; to give a reason or explanation; to give a statement of money dealings; to answer as someone responsible; to have the responsibility or credit (of killing or otherwise disposing of anything or anybody; with *for*). — *n* counting; reckoning; a business relationship; a reckoning of money or other responsibilities; (in *pl*) the statement of a company's financial affairs, containing the profit and loss account and the balance sheet; a record of business transacted between two people or people and organizations; a section of a ledger in which a record is made of every transaction relating to the same activity (*bookkeeping*); a statement of money owing; a credit agreement between a customer and a supplier (eg a retail store or a financial institution) that involves the provision of goods or services in return for payment on agreed terms; money deposited in a bank, building society, etc; the period of time (*usu* a fortnight) allowed before accounts are settled (*stock exchange*); the client of an advertising agency, public relations consultancy, etc; advantage; value; estimation; consideration; sake; a descriptive report; a statement; a narrative; a performance. — *n* **accountabil'ity**. — *adj* **account'able** liable to account, responsible; explicable. — *n* **account'ableness**. — *adv* **account'ably**. — *n* **account'ancy** the office, work or profession of an accountant. — *n* **account'ant** a person whose work involves the preparation, recording, analysis and interpretation of the accounts of a company, etc. — *n* **account'antship**. — *n* **account'ing** the setting up, maintaining and analysing of financial records. — *adj* pertaining to the keeping of accounts. — **account'-book** a book for keeping accounts in; **account day** a designated day on which accounts are settled on the London Stock Exchange; **account executive** the person in an advertising agency who is responsible for looking afer a client's requirements (*abbrev* **AE**). — **bring** or **call to account** to demand of someone an explanation or justification of what they have done; to reprimand; **by all accounts** according to general opinion; **find one's account** to derive advantage; **for account of** on behalf of; **for the account** for settlement on the regular settling-day; **give a good account of oneself** to give a good performance; to do well; **go to one's (long) account** to go to the last judgement, die; **hold to account** to hold responsible; **in account with** in business relations requiring the keeping of an account with; **make account of** to set value upon; **on** or **to account** as an instalment or interim payment; **on account of** because of; **on no account** not for any reason or consideration; **on one's own account** for one's own sake; on one's own responsibility; **settle** or **square accounts** (or **an account**) **with** to complete financial transactions with; to revenge oneself against (*fig*); **take into account** or **take account of** to take into consideration; **take no account of** to overlook or fail to take into consideration; **turn to (good) account** to turn to advantage. [OFr *acconter*, from L *ad* to, and *computāre* to reckon; see **compute** and **count**[2]]

accourage *a-kur'ij* or **accorage** *ak-or-āj'*, (*Spenser*) *vt* to encourage. [OFr *acorager*, from *à* to, and *corage* courage]

accourt *ə-kört*, *vt* to entertain. [An invention of Spenser's, from **court**]

accoutre or (*US*) **accouter** *ə-ko͞o'tər*, *vt* to dress or equip (*esp* a warrior): — *pr p* **accou'tring** (or *US* **accoutering**; *ə-ko͞o'tər-ing*); *pa p* **accou'tred** (or *US* **accoutered**; *-tərd*). — *n* **accou'trement** (or *US* **accouterment**; *-tər-* or *-trə-*), also (*obs* **accustrement** or **accoustrement**) equipping; (*usu* in *pl*) dress; military equipments. [Fr *accoutrer*, earlier *accoustrer*; origin doubtful]

accoy *ə-koi'*, (*Spenser*) *vt* to still; to soothe; to subdue: — *pa p* **accoied'** or **accoyed'**. [OFr *acoyer*, from *à* to, and *coi* quiet, from L *quiētus*; see **coy**]

accoyld. See **accoil**.

accredit *ə-kred'it*, *vt* to bring into credit, show to be true or correct; to accept as true; to provide with or send with credentials; to certify as meeting official requirements; to attribute (to); to ascribe to (*with* the thing attributed); to accept (a student) for university entrance on the basis of work done in school as opposed to an examination (*NZ*). — *n* **accreditā'tion**. — *adj* **accred'ited** provided with credentials; certified officially; accepted as valid; (of livestock) certified free from a particular disease, eg brucellosis. [Fr *accréditer*, from *à* to, and *crédit* credit]

accrescent *ə-kres'ənt*, *adj* growing; ever-increasing; enlarged and persistent (*bot*). — *n* **accresc'ence**. — *vi* **accrēte'** to grow together; to become attached. — *vt* to unite; to form or gather round itself. — *n* **accrē'tion** continued growth; the growing together of parts that are usually separate; something which has grown in such a way; an extraneous addition. — *adj* **accrē'tive**. [L *accrēscere*, *accrētum*, from *ad* to, and *crēscere* to grow]

accrue (or *Spenser* **accrew**) *ə-kro͞o'*, *vi* to come as a natural result or development of something, or as an addition or product; to fall (to someone) by way of advantage; to fall due; to increase (*Spenser*). — *vt* (*Spenser*) to accumulate. — *n* **accru'al**. [OFr *acrewe* what grows up to the profit of the owner, from *acreistre*, from L *accrēscere*]

ACCT *abbrev*: Association of Cinematograph, Television and Allied Technicians.

acct *abbrev*: account.

accubation *ak-ū-bā'shən*, *n* a lying or reclining on a couch. [L *ad* to, and *cubāre* to lie down]

acculturation *ə-kul-chər-ā'shən*, *n* the process or result of assimilating, through continuous contact, features (such as customs, beliefs, etc) of another culture. — *adj* **accul'tural** — *vt* and *vi* **accul'turate**. [L *ad* to, and **culture**]

accumbent *ə-kumb'ənt*, *adj* lying down or reclining on a couch; having the radicle lying along the edges of the cotyledons (*bot*). — *n* **accumb'ency**. [L *ad* to, and *cumbere* to lie]

accumulate *ə-kūm'ūl-āt*, *vt* to heap or pile up; to amass. — *vi* to increase greatly; to go on increasing; to take university, etc degrees by accumulation, ie to take a higher degree at the same time as a lower, or at a shorter interval than usual (also *vt*). — *adj* heaped up; amassed. — *n* **accūmū'lātion** heaping up; a heap or mass. — *adj* **accūm'ūlative** heaping up or growing by progressive addition; cumulative; tending to accumulate, acquisitive. — *adv* **accum'ulatively**. — *n* **accum'ulativeness**. — *n* **accūm'ūlātor** a thing or person that accumulates; a means of storing energy, *esp* an electric battery that can be recharged by sending a reverse current through it; in a computer, etc, a device that performs arithmetical operations and stores the results. — **accumulator** or **accumulator bet** a bet on at least two, and *usu* four or more, races original stake and winnings from each race being, by previous arrangement, laid on the next race, so that the gambler either wins a large amount or loses all. [L *ad* to, and *cumulus* a heap]

accurate *ak'ū-rit*, *adj* exact. — *n* **acc'ūracy** (*-ə-si*) correctness; exactness. — *adv* **acc'ūrately**. — *n* **acc'ūrateness**. [L *accūrātus* performed with care, from *ad* to, and *cūra* care]

accurse *ə-kûrs'*, *vt* to curse; to condemn to misery or destruction. — *adj* **accurs'ed** (or *-kûrst'*), or (*poetic*) **accurst'** subjected to a curse; doomed; worthy of a curse. — *adv* **accur'sedly**. — *n* **accur'sedness**. [OE pfx *ā-*, and *cursian* to curse]

accus. *abbrev*: accusative (also **acc.**).

accuse *ə-kūz'*, *vt* to bring a charge against (with *of*). — *n* (*Shakesp*) accusation. — *adj* **accūs'able**. — *n* **accūs'al** accusation. — *n* **accūsā'tion** the act of accusing; a charge brought. — *adj* **accūs'ative** accusing; in or belonging to a grammatical case which expresses the direct object of transitive verbs, primarily expressing destination or the goal of motion. — *n* (*gram*) the accusative case; a word in the accusative case. — *adj* **accūsatī'val**. — *adv* **accus'atively**. — *adj* **accūsatō'rial** of an accuser; denoting a trial in which the judge is not the same person as the prosecutor. — *adj* **accūs'atory** containing accusation. — *adj* **accused'**. — *n* (*sing* or *pl*) the person or persons accused. — *n* **accuse'ment** (*Spenser*) a charge. — *n* **accūs'er**. — *adj* **accus'ing**. — *adv* **accus'ingly**. [L *accūsāre*, *-ātum*, from *ad* to, and *causa* cause, partly through OFr *accuser*. Accusative case (L *casus accūsātīvus*) is a mistranslation of Gr *ptōsis aitiātikē*, the case indicating what is caused or effected, from *aitiā* cause (also accusation)]

accustom *ə-kus'təm*, *vt* to make familiar by custom (with *to*); to habituate. — *adj* **accus'tomary**. — *adj* **accus'tomed** usual; frequent; habituated; in the habit. — *n* **accus'tomedness**. [OFr *acostumer* (Fr *accoutumer*), from *à* to, and *costum* or *coustume*; see **custom**]

accustrement. See **accoutre**.

AC/DC *ā'sē-dē'sē*, *abbrev*: (*elec*) alternating current/direct current. — *adj* (*slang*) bisexual.

ACE *ās*, *abbrev*: Advisory Centre for Education; Allied Command Europe; Association for the Conservation of Energy.

ace *ās*, *n* a unit; the one in dice, cards, dominoes, etc; a single point; a hole in one (see under **hole**[1]; *golf*); a winning serve, *esp* one which the opponent fails to touch (*tennis*); a jot; a person of the highest character (*Burns*); a person of distinguished achievement, an expert (*orig* an airman) (*colloq*). — *adj* (*colloq*) of highest quality; outstanding. — *vt* to serve an ace against (an opponent) (*tennis*); to play (a hole) in one stroke (*golf*). — **an ace up one's sleeve** or **an ace in the hole** a decisive but hidden advantage; **play one's ace** to use one's best weapon, resource, etc; **within an ace of** within a hair's-breadth of. [Fr *as*, from L *as* unity, from *as* Tarentine Doric form of Gr *heis* one]

-acea *-ā-sē-ə*, *n pl sfx* used in names of zoological divisions, *esp* orders or classes.

-aceae *-ā-sē-ē*, *n pl sfx* used in names of plant families.

acedia *ə-sē'di-ə*, *n* listlessness; torpor; sloth. [Gr *akēdiā*, *akēdeia*, from *a-* (privative), and *kēdos* care. See **accidie**]

acellular *ā-sel'ū-lər*, (*biol*) *adj* not containing cells; not made up of cells. [Gr *a-* (privative), and **cell**]

-aceous *-a-shəs*, *sfx* relating or related to, resembling etc.

acephalous *a-*, *ā-* or *ə-sef'ə-ləs*, *adj* headless; without a ruler, leader, etc (*fig*). [Gr *akephalos*, from *a-* (privative), and *kephalē* head]

ACER *ā'sər*, *abbrev*: Australian Council for Educational Research.

acer *ā'sər* or *ak'ər*, *n* a plant of the maple genus *Acer*, which gives its name to the family **Acerā'ceae** (*as-*). — *adj* **acerā'ceous**. [L *acer* maple]

acerate. Same as **acerose**.

acerb *a-sûrb'*, or **acerbic** *ə-sûr'bik*, *adj* bitter and sour. — *vt* **acerbate** (*as'ər-bāt*) to embitter; to irritate. — *n* **acerb'ity**. [L *acerbus*]

acerose *as'ər-ōs*, *adj* chaffy (*obs*); needle-pointed (*bot*). [L *acerosus*, from *acus*, *-eris* chaff, confused with *acus*, *-ūs* needle, or *acer* sharp]

acerous *ə-sē'rəs*, *adj* without horns, antennae or tentacles. [Gr *a-* (privative) and *keras* horn]

acervate *ə-sûr'vāt*, *adj* heaped. — *adv* **acer'vately**. — *n* **acervā'tion**. [L *acervāre*, *-ātum* to heap]

acescence *as-es'əns* or **acescency** *-i*, *n* souring; turning (of milk). — *adj* **acesc'ent**. [L *acēscere* to sour, from *acēre* to be sour]

acesulfame K *a-si-sul'fām kā*, *n* an artificial sweetener, 130 times sweeter than sugar. [*K* for *potassium*, and *sulfamic acid*]

acet- or **aceto-** *as'it-(ō-)*, *a-*, *ə-set'-(ō-)* or *a-sēt'-(ō-)*, *combining form* vinegar; acetic acid. — *n* **ac'etal** a liquid formed by oxidation of alcohol, etc; any of a class of compounds of which this is the type. — *n* **acetal'dehyde** a liquid of characteristic smell, acetic aldehyde. — *n* **acet'amide** the amide of acetic acid. — *n* **ac'etate** an ester of acetic acid; short form of **acetate rayon** an artificial fibre made from cellulose acetate; a (piece of) transparent film on which information, diagrams, etc may be written for display by overhead projector, etc. — *adj* **acetic** (*-sēt'* or *-set'*) of, of the nature of or producing acetic acid, $CH_3 \cdot COOH$, or its diluted form, vinegar. — *n* **acetificā'tion** (*-set-*). — *vt* and *vi* **acet'ify** to turn into vinegar. — *n* **ac'etone** the simplest of the ketones; any ketone. — *adj* **ac'etose** acetous. — *adj* **acē'tous** like or producing vinegar; sour. — *n* **acetyl** (*as'i-til*, *-tīl*, or *a-sē'*) the radical (CH_3CO) of acetic acid (**acetyl-salicylic acid** aspirin). — *n* **acetylchōline** (*-kō'lēn*; also *-ko'-*, *-līn* or *-lin*) a substance secreted at the ends of nerve fibres when they activate muscles. — *n* **acetylene** (*-set'*) a gas (C_2H_2), produced from calcium carbide and water, used in welding, synthesizing acetic acid, illumination, etc. — *adj* **acetylen'ic** (*-len'* or *-lēn'*). — **acetate film** film of low flammability, whose photographic emulsion is coated on cellulose acetate. — Also **non-flam film**, **safety film**. [L *acētum* vinegar]

acetabulum *as-et-ab'ū-ləm*, or *-ēt-*, (*zool*) *n* the hollow that receives the head of the thigh-bone; one of the cotyledons of the placenta of ruminants; the cavity that receives a leg in the body of insects; in various animals, a sucker: — *pl* **acetab'ūla**. — *adj* **acetab'ūlar**. [L *acētābulum* a vinegar cup]

acetate, **acetic**, etc, **acetone**, **acetyl**, **acetylene**. See under **acet-**.

ACGI *abbrev*: Associate of the City and Guilds Institute.

ach *interj*. Same as **och**.

ACGB *abbrev*: Arts Council of Great Britain.

Achaean *ə-kē'ən*, or **Achaian** *-kī'* or *-kā'*, *adj* belonging to *Achāiā* in the Peloponnese, or to Greece generally. — Also *n*.

achaenium, etc. See **achene**.

acharné *a-shär-nā*, (*Fr*) *adj* (*esp* of battles) furious or desperate. — **avec acharnement** (*a-vek a-shär-nə-mã*) obstinately, furiously, rancorously or with gusto.

acharya *ā-chär'yə*, *n* a Hindu teacher or learned man. [Hindustani *āchārya*, from Sans]

Achates *ə-kā'tēz*, *n* an intimate and trusty comrade, from Aeneas's friend in the Aeneid. — **fidus Achates** (*fē'dəs*; *L*, faithful Achates) a close and reliable friend.

achates *ə-chāts'*, (*Spenser*). Same as **acates**.

ache[1] *āk*, *n* a continued pain. — *vi* to be in or be the site of continued pain; to long (for). — *n* **ach'age** (*Tennyson*). — *n* **ach'ing**. — *adv* **ach'ingly**. — *adj* **ach'y**. [The verb was properly *ake*, the noun *ache*, as in *speak* and *speech*, from OE *acan* (verb) and *æce* (n)]

ache[2] *āch* (*Shakesp*). Same as **aitch**.

achene *a-kēn'*, **achaenium** or **achenium** *a-kē'ni-əm*, *n* a dry, indehiscent, one-seeded fruit, formed of one carpel, the seed separate from the fruit wall, as in the buttercup. — *adj* **achē'nial**. — *n* **achae'nocarp** any dry, indehiscent fruit, *esp* an achene. [From Gr *a-* (privative) and *chainein* to gape]

Achernar *ā'kər-när*, *n* a first-magnitude star in the constellation Eridanus. [Ar *ākhir al nahr* end of the river (Eridanus)]

Acheron *ak'ər-on*, (*Gr mythol*) *n* one of the rivers of Hades. — *adj* **Acheron'tic** gloomy, dark or forbidding. — **Acherontis pabulum** (*L*) (of a bad person) food for Acheron. [Gr *Acherōn*]

Acheulean or **Acheulian** *ə-shōō'li-ən*, *adj* belonging to an early Palaeolithic culture above the Chellean and below the Mousterian. [Saint *Acheul* near Amiens, France, where implements of this period are found in river deposits]

à cheval *a shə-val'*, (*Fr*) *adv* (of a bet) laid on two adjacent numbers or cards. [Literally, on horseback]

achieve (*obs* **atchieve**) *ə-chēv'*, *vt* to bring to a successful outcome; to end (*obs*); to perform; to accomplish; to win. — *adj* **achiev'able**. — *n* **achieve'ment** achieving; something achieved; an exploit; an escutcheon or armorial shield granted in memory of some achievement (*heraldry*); escutcheon, armour, etc, hung over a tomb; a hatchment. — *n* **achiev'er**. — **achievement age** the level of an individual's educational achievement as determined by comparing his or her score in a test with the average score of others of the same age; **achievement quotient** ratio of achievement age to chronological age (*usu* × 10; *abbrev*: **AQ**). [Fr *achever*, from *à chief* (*venir*), from LL *ad caput* to a head; see **chief** and **hatchment**]

achillea *a-kil'i-ə*, *n* a plant of the yarrow genus *Achillea* of perennial plants (family Compositae). [L *achillea*, *achilleos*, from Gr *achilleios*, from *Achilleus* Achilles]

Achillean *ak-il-ē'ən*, *adj* like *Achilles*, the great Greek hero in the Trojan war, invulnerable except in the heel, by which his mother held him when she dipped him in the Styx. — **Achilles' heel** or **heel of Achilles** a person's weak or most vulnerable point; **Achilles' tendon** the attachment of the soleus and gastrocnemius muscles of the calf of the leg to the heel-bone.

achimenes *a-kim'in-ēz*, or *-men'*, *n* a plant of the genus *Achimenes* of herbaceous perennial plants (family Gesneriaceae) of tropical S America: — *pl* **achimenes**. [L]

Achitophel or **Ahithophel** *ə-kit'*, or *-hit'ō-fel*, *n* a cautious person (*Shakesp*); (after Dryden's application to Shaftesbury) an able but unprincipled counsellor. [From David's counsellor who abetted the rebellion of Absalom]

achkan *äch'kən*, *n* in India, a knee-length coat with a high collar, buttoned all the way down. [Hindustani *ackan*]

achlamydeous *ak-lə-mid'i-əs*, (*bot*) *adj* without perianth. [Gr *a-* (privative), and *chlamys*, *-ydos* a mantle]

achondroplasia *ak-on-drō-plā'zhi-ə*, *n* dwarfism characterized by shortness of the arms and legs. — *adj* **achondroplastic** (*-plas'tik*). [Gr *a-* (privative), *chondros* cartilage, and *plassein* to make]

achromatic *ak-rō-mat'ik*, *adj* transmitting light without much chromatic aberration; without colour. — *n* **a'chromat** an achromatic lens. — *adv* **achromat'ically**. — *n* **achromatic'ity**. — *n* **achrō'matin** the part of a cell nucleus that does not stain with basic dyes. — *n* **achrō'matism** the state of being achromatic. — *n* **achromatiza'tion** or **-s-**. — *vt* **achrō'matize** or **-ise** to make achromatic. — *n* **achromatopsia** (*ə-krō-mə-top'si-ə*; Gr *ops* eye) total colour blindness. — *adj* **achrō'matous** having little or no colour. [Gr *a-* (privative) and *chrōma*, *-atos* colour]

achy. See **ache**[1].

acicular *as-ik'ū-lər*, *adj* needle-shaped; slender and sharp-pointed. — *adj* **acic'ulate** or **acic'ulated** marked as if with needle-scratches. [L *acicula*, dimin of *acus* a needle]

acid *as'id*, *adj* sharp; sour; (of soil) having an acid reaction; biting, keen (*fig*); ill-natured, morose (*fig*); pertaining to, of the nature of, or having the properties of an acid (*chem*); containing a large proportion of silica (*geol*); relating to acid house (qv). — *n* a substance with a sour taste; any of a class of substances which turn vegetable blues (eg litmus) red, and combine with bases, certain metals, etc, to form salts (*chem*); any of a class of substances that dissolve in water with the formation of hydrogen ions (*chem*); any of a class of substances that can transfer a proton to another substance, etc (*chem*); something harsh, biting, or sarcastic (*fig*); LSD or other hallucinogenic drug (*slang*); short form of acid house (qv). — *adj* **acid'ic**. — *adj* **acidifi'able**. — *n* **acidificā'tion**. — *n* **acid'ifier**. — *vt* **acid'ify** to make acid; to convert into an acid. — *vi* to become acid: — *pr p* **acid'ifying**; *pa t* and *pa p* **acid'ified**. — *n* **acidim'eter** an apparatus for performing acidimetry. — *n* **acidim'etry** measurement of the concentration of acids by titration with a standard solution of alkali. — *n* **acid'ity** the quality of being acid or sour; the extent to which a solution is acid (see **pH-value**). — *adv* **ac'idly**. — *n* **ac'idness**. — *n* **acidō'sis** (*med*) the presence of acids in the blood beyond normal limits. — *vt* **acid'ūlate** to make slightly acid. — *adj* **acid'ūlous** or **acid'ulent** slightly sour; subacid; (of eg mineral waters) containing carbonic acid; caustic or sharp (*fig*). — **acid drop** a sweet flavoured with tartaric acid; **acid dye** a dyestuff with acid properties; **ac'idfreak** or **ac'id-head** (*drug-taking slang*) a person who takes hallucinogenic drugs, a head (qv); **Acid House** or **acid house** a fashionable craze first apparent in the late 1980s involving large crowds of young people meeting in otherwise empty buildings (eg a warehouse) to hold **Acid House parties**, gatherings held in a hypnotic atmosphere produced by bright flashing lights and **Acid House music**, extremely loud repetitive music produced *orig* by sampling existing songs and always featuring strong complex percussion patterns, such gatherings often associated with the activities of drug-pushers; **acid rain** rain or other forms of precipitation containing sulphur and nitrogen compounds and other pollutants released by the combustion of fossil fuels in industrial processes; **acid rock** a type of rock music featuring bizarre electronic and instrumental effects supposedly influenced by, or suggestive of the effects of, hallucinogenic drugs; **acid salt** a salt in which only part of the replaceable hydrogen is replaced by a metal; **acid soil complex** (*bot*) a combination of aluminium and/or manganese toxicity with calcium deficiency which has a detrimental effect on calcicole plants; **acid test** a test for gold by acid; a searching test (*fig*). — **put the acid on** (*colloq*; *Austr* and *NZ*) to apply pressure on (a person). [L *acidus* sour, from *acēre* to be sour]

acidanthera *as-id-an'thi-rə*, also *ak-id-*, *n* a plant of the genus *Acidanthera* of white-flowered plants of NE Africa (family Iridaceae). [Gr *akis* pointed object, and *anthēra* (see **anther**)]

acierate *as'i-ər-āt*, *vt* to turn into steel. — *n* **ac'ierage** the covering of a metal plate with a film of iron. — *n* **acierā'tion**. [Fr *aciérer*, from *acier* steel, from LL *aciārium* (*ferrum*), literally edging (iron), from L *aciēs* edge]

aciform *as'i-fōrm*, *adj* needle-shaped. [L *acus* needle, and **-form**]

ACII *abbrev*: Associate of the Chartered Insurance Institute.

acinaciform *as-in-as'i-fōrm*, (*bot*) *adj* scimitar-shaped. [Gr *akīnakēs* a short sword (a Persian word), and **-form**]

acinus *as'i-nəs*, *n* one of the small fruits that make up an aggregate fruit, like the raspberry; an aggregate fruit; a pip; a racemose gland: — *pl* **ac'ini**. — *adj* **acinā'ceous** full of pips; berry-like; like a cluster of grapes. — *adj* **acin'iform** berry-like. — *adj* **ac'inous** or **ac'inose** (or *-ōs'*) consisting of acini; like a cluster of berries. [L *acinus* berry, pip]

ack-ack *ak'-ak'*, *adj* anti-aircraft. — *adv* **ack-emm'a** a.m. [Formerly military signallers' names for the letters AA and AM]

ackee. See **akee**.

ackers *ak'ərz*, (*slang*) *n pl* money. — Also **akk'as**. [Origin uncertain]

acknow *ak-nō'*, (*obs*) *vt* to recognize; to acknowledge: — *pa t* **acknew'**; *pa p* **acknown'** or **acknowne'**. — *adj* **acknowne'** (*Shakesp*) confessedly cognizant. [OE *on* in, on, and *cnāwan* to know]

acknowledge *ək-nol'ij*, *vt* to admit a knowledge or awareness of; to admit to or recognize as true, genuine, valid, or one's own; to confess; to express gratitude or thanks; to admit or intimate receipt of. — *adj* **acknowl'edgeable**. — *adv* **acknowl'edgeably**. — *n* **acknowl'edgement** (sometimes **acknowl'edgment**) recognition; admission; confession; thanks; a notification of having received something. [From **acknow**; see **knowledge**]

aclinic *ak-lin'ik*, *adj* without inclination or magnetic dip. — **aclinic line** the magnetic equator (qv). [Gr *aklinēs* horizontal, from *a-* (privative) and *klīnein* to tilt]

ACM *abbrev*: Air Chief Marshal.

ACMA *abbrev*: Associate of the Institute of Cost and Management Accountants.

acme *ak'mi*, *n* the top or highest point; the culmination or perfection in the career of anything; the crisis, eg of a disease (*archaic*). — *n* **Ac'meism** a movement in Russian poetry, active about 1910 to 1917. — *n* **Ac'meist**. — *n* **ac'mite** a soda pyroxene whose crystals often show a steep pyramid. [Gr *akmē*, from *akē* a point]

acne *ak'ni*, *n* a skin disease caused by inflammation of the sebaceous follicles, *esp* on the face, neck, and shoulders. — **acne rosacea** (*rō-zā'shi-ə*; *old-fashioned*) a chronic disease of the skin of the nose, cheeks and forehead, characterized by flushing and redness of the skin, pimples and pustules (also called **rosacea**). [Perh Gr *akmē* a point]

acock *ə-kok'*, *adv* in a cocked manner; defiantly. — *adv* **acock'-bill** (*naut*) (of an anchor ready for dropping or yards topped up (a sign of mourning)) having the end pointing upward. [**a-**[1] and **cock**[1]]

acoemeti *a-sem'i-tī*, *n pl* an Eastern order of monks (5–6c), who by alternating choirs kept divine service going on day and night. [Latinized pl of Gr *akoimētos* sleepless, from *a-* (privative), and *koimaein* to put to sleep]

acold *ə-kōld'*, (*Shakesp*) *adj* chilled. [Prob OE *ācōlod* pa p of *ācōlian*, from pfx *ā-* (intens), and *cōlian* to cool]

acolouthos *ak-ə-lo͞o'thos*, (*hist*) *n* the head of the Varangian guard of the Byzantine emperors. — *n* **acolou'thite** (*obs*) an acolyte. — *adj* **acolou'thic** or **acoluth'ic** pertaining to an after-image or sensation following upon the immediate effect of a stimulus. [Gr *akolouthos* an attendant, from *akoloutheein* to follow]

acolyte *ak'ə-līt*, or (*obs*) **acolyth** *-lith*, *n* a faithful follower; an attendant or assistant; a person in minor orders, next below subdeacon (*RC Church*); an inferior church officer. [Ety as for **acolouthos**]

à compte *a kɔ̃t*, (*Fr*) on account; in part payment.

aconite *ak'ə-nīt*, *n* any plant of the ranunculaceous genus *Aconitum*, *esp* wolf's-bane or monk's-hood; poison obtained from it, or (*poetic*) deadly poison in general (often **aconī'tum**). — *adj* **aconit'ic**. — *n* **aconitine** (*-kon'*) a poisonous alkaloid obtained from aconite. — **winter aconite** an early-flowering ranunculaceous plant (*Eranthis hyemalis*). [L *aconītum*, from Gr *akonīton*]

à contre coeur *a kɔ̃-tr' kœr*, (*Fr*) reluctantly.

ACORN *ā'körn*, *abbrev*: A Classification of Residential Neighbourhoods, a type of socio-economic classification that identifies the area and housing in which people live and can be used for direct mail or market research.

acorn *ā'körn*, *n* the fruit of the oak. — *adj* **ā'corned**. — **a'corn-cup** the woody cup-shaped part of an acorn that holds the nut; **a'corn-shell** or **a'corn-barnacle** a crustacean of the genus Balanus (*L*, acorn); **acorn worm** any of various worm-like sea-animals (enteropneusts) of the Hemichordata which have a proboscis and collar somewhat like an acorn in shape. [OE *æcern*; form influenced by confusion with **corn**[1] and perh **oak** (Northern *aik*, OE *āc*)]

à corps perdu *a kor per-dü*, (*Fr*) desperately, with might and main.

Acorus *ak'ə-rəs*, *n* the sweet-flag genus of the arum family. [Latinized from Gr *akoros*]

acosmism *ə-koz'mizm*, *n* disbelief in the existence of an eternal world, or of a world distinct from God. — *n* **acos'mist**. [Gr *a-* (privative), and *kosmos* the world]

ACOST *ā'kost*, *abbrev*: Advisory Committee on Science and Technology.

acotyledon *a-kot-i-lē'dən*, *n* a cryptogam. — *adj* **acotylē'donous**. [Gr *a-* (privative), and **cotyledon**]

acouchy or **acouchi** *ə-ko͞o'shē*, *n* a kind of small S American rodent, an agouti. [Tupí *acuchy*]

à coup sûr *a ko͞o sür*, (*Fr*) to a certainty.

acoustic *ə-ko͞os'tik* or **acoustical** *-əl*, (formerly) *-kows'*, *adj* of or relating to the sense of hearing or to the theory of sound; used in hearing, auditory; operated by sound vibrations, eg an *acoustic mine*; (of musical instruments) not electric, eg an *acoustic guitar* or *piano*; (made of material) intended to reduce the disturbance caused by excessive noise. — *n* **acous'tic** acoustic properties. — *adv* **acous'tically**. — *n* **acoustician** (*-ti'shən*) a person who studies or has studied the science of acoustics; a person who makes or repairs acoustic instruments, etc. — *n* **acous'tics** (*sing*) the science of sound; (*pl*) acoustic properties. — **acoustic coupler** a device which converts electrical pulses to sound (acoustic waves) for transmission and reception along telephone lines to and from a computer, allowing computers to be connected to a terminal by a modem and telephone handset. — *adj* **acousto-elec'tric** of or relating to electroacoustics. [Gr *akoustikos*, from *akouein* to hear]

à couvert *a ko͞o-ver*, (*Fr*) *adj* and *adv* under cover, protected.

ACP *abbrev*: African, Caribbean and Pacific.

acpt. (*commerce*) *abbrev*: acceptance.

acquaint *ə-kwānt'*, *vt* to let know; to inform. — *adj* (*Northern*) acquainted. — *n* **acquaint'ance** knowledge, *esp* when falling short of intimacy; a person (or sometimes persons) known slightly. — *n* **acquaint'anceship** slight knowledge. — *adj* **acquaint'ed** (*usu* with *with*) personally known to and on at least nodding terms with; having personal knowledge of. [OFr *acointer*, from LL *accognitāre*, from L *ad* to, and *cognitus* known]

acquest *ə-kwest'*, *n* acquisition; a thing acquired. [OFr; see **acquire**]

acquiesce *ak-wi-es'*, *vi* to rest satisfied or without making opposition; to assent (with *in*). — *n* **acquiesc'ence** quiet assent or submission. — *adj* **acquiesc'ent** acquiescing. — *n* a person who acquiesces. — *adv* **acquiesc'ently** or **acquiesc'ingly**. [L *acquiēscere*, from *ad* to, and *quiēs* rest]

acquight. See **acquit**.

acquire *ə-kwīr'*, *vt* to gain or get; to attain to, achieve. — *n* **acquīrabil'ity**. — *adj* **acquīr'able** that may be acquired. — *n* **acquīr'al**. — *adj* **acquired'**. — *n* **acquire'ment** acquisition; something learned or obtained by effort, not a gift of nature. — *n* **acquisition** (*ak-wi-zish'ən*) the act of acquiring; something which is acquired. — *adj* **acquisitive** (*ə-kwiz'*) able, desiring or eager to acquire *usu* possessions. — *adv* **acquis'itively**. — *n* **acquis'itiveness** a desire or propensity to acquire possessions. — *n* **acquist** (*ə-kwist'*) acquisition. — **acquired behaviour** or **character** behaviour or character originating in the adaptation of an organism to its environment, not inherited; **acquired immunity** (*immunol*) immunity resulting from exposure to foreign substances or micro-organisms (*opp* to *natural immunity*); **acquired taste** a liking for something that comes after some experience; a thing so liked (often *ironic*). — **Acquired Immune Deficiency Syndrome** or **Acquired Immunodeficiency Syndrome** see **AIDS**; **target acquisition** a fighter or bomber pilot's sighting of his target, either visually or by radar. [L *acquīrere*, *-quīsītum*, from *ad* to, and *quaerere* to seek]

acquit *ə-kwit'*, (*obs*) **acquite** or **acquight** *ə-kwīt'*, *vt* to free; to release; to discharge (eg a debt); to discharge (oneself of a duty); hence, to behave or conduct (oneself); to prove (oneself); to release from an accusation: — *pr p* **acquitt'ing**; *pa t* and *pa p* **acquitt'ed** or (*obs*) **acquit'**. — *n* **acquit'ment** (*obs*). — *n* **acquitt'al** a judicial discharge from an accusation. — *n* **acquitt'ance** a discharge from an obligation or debt; a receipt in evidence of such a discharge. — *vt* (*Shakesp*) to acquit or clear. [OFr *aquiter*, from L *ad* to, and *quiētāre* to quiet, settle; see **quit**]

acrawl *ə-kröl'*, *adv* crawling (with *with*). [**a-**[1] and **crawl**[1]]

acre *ā'kər*, *n* a measure of land equivalent to 4840 sq yd (approx 0.4 ha; also Scottish acre 6150.4 sq yd, Irish 7840 sq yd, both *obs*); (in *pl*) lands or estates; (in *pl*) a very large area or amount (*colloq*). — *n* **acreage** (*ā'kər-ij*) area in acres. — *adj* **acred** (*ā'kərd*) landed. — **a'cre-breadth** (*archaic*) 22 yards; **acre-foot'** a unit of volume of water equivalent to covering an acre one foot deep, ie 43 560cu ft (approx 1200cu m); **a'cre-length** (*archaic*) 220 yards. [OE *æcer* field; Ger *Acker*, L *ager*, Gr *agros*, Sans *ajra* a plain]

acrid *ak'rid*, *adj* pungent; biting. — *n* **acrid'ity**. [L *ācer*, *ācris* sharp or keen; noun sfx perh in imitation of *acid*]

acridine or **acridin** *ak'ri-dēn* or *-din*, *n* a compound found in coal-tar, a parent substance of dyes and anti-bacterial drugs. — *n* **acriflavine** (*-flā'vēn*) or **acriflavin** (*ak-ri-flā'vin*; *acri*dine and *flavin*(*e*)) an antiseptic. [**acrid**, and noun sfx *-ine*]

Acrilan® *ak'ri-lan*, *n* a type of acrylic fibre (rather like wool).

acrimony *ak'ri-mən-i*, *n* bitterness of feeling or language. — *adj* **acrimō'nious**. — *adv* **acrimō'niously**. — *n* **acrimō'niousness**. [L *ācrimōnia*, from *ācer* sharp]

acro- *ak-rō-*, *combining form* tip, point or summit. [Gr *akron* tip, end, and *akros* highest, outermost]

acroamatic *ak-rō-ə-mat'ik*, or **acroamatical** *-mat'ik-əl, adj* esoteric. [Gr *akroāmatikos*, from *akroāma* anything to be listened to, from *akroaesthai* to listen]

acrobat *ak'rō-bat, n* a performer of gymnastic feats; a person who performs balancing acts on a tightrope; a tumbler. — *adj* **acrobat'ic**. — *adv* **acrobat'ically**. — *n pl* **acrobat'ics** acrobatic performances (often *fig*). — *n sing* the art of the acrobat. — *n* **ac'robatism** the art of the acrobat. [Gr *akrobatēs* acrobat, or *akrobatos* walking on tiptoe, from *akron* point, and the root of *bainein* to go]

acrocentric *ak-rō-sen'trik*, (*biol*) *adj* (of chromosomes) having the centromere at the end. — *n* a rod-shaped chromosome. [Gr *akron* point, and **centr-**]

acrogen *ak'rō-jən, n* a non-flowering plant with the growing-point at the tip, a fern or moss. — *adj* **acrogen'ic** or **acrogenous** (*ə-kroj'i-nəs*). — *adv* **acrog'enously**. [Gr *akron* point and *-genēs* born]

acrolein *a-krō'li-in*, (*chem*) *n* the aldehyde of allyl alcohol, a pungent-smelling colourless liquid. [L *ācer, ācris* sharp, and *olēre* to smell]

acrolith *ak'rō-lith, n* a wooden statue with stone extremities. — *adj* **acrolith'ic**. [Gr *akrolithos*, from *akron* point, and *lithos* stone]

acromegaly *ak-rō-meg'ə-li, n* a disease characterized by overgrowth, *esp* of the face, hands and feet. — *adj* **acromegal'ic** suffering from acromegaly. [Gr *akron* point, and *megas, megalos* great]

acromion *ə-krō'mi-on, n* a process of the spine of the scapula (also **acromion process**): — *pl* **acromia**. — *adj* **acro'mial**. [Gr *akros* outermost, and *ōmos* shoulder]

acronychal, **acronycal** or (*US*) **acronical** *ə-kron'ik-əl, adj* (of the rising or setting of stars) occurring at nightfall. — *adv* **acron'ychally**. [Gr *akronychos* at nightfall, from *akron* point, and *nychos, -eos* night]

acronym *ak'rō-nim, n* a word formed from or based on the initial letters or syllables of other words, such as *radar*. — *n* **acronymā'nia** a craze for forming acronyms. — *adj* **acronym'ic** or **acron'ymous**. [**acro-**, and Gr *onyma* = *onoma* name]

acropetal *ə-krop'i-tl*, (*bot*) *adj* in the direction of the tip of the plant. — *adv* **acrop'etally**. [Gr *akron* tip, and L *petere* to seek]

acrophobia *ak-rō-fō'bi-ə, n* fear of heights. [Gr *akron* tip, *akros* highest, and *phobos* fear]

acrophony *ə-krof'ən-i, n* the use of a symbol (derived from an ideogram) to represent the initial sound only of the name of the object for which the ideogram stood. — *adj* **acrophonet'ic** or **acrophonic** (*-fon'*). [**acro-**, and Gr *phōnē* sound]

acropolis *a-krop'ol-is* or *ə-krop'ə-lis, n* a citadel, *esp* that of Athens. [Gr *akropolis*, from *akros* highest, and *polis* a city]

acrosome *ak'rō-sōm, n* a structure containing enzymes, found at the tip of the sperm, associated with the penetration process into the egg cell. [**acro-** and **some**[2]]

acrospire *ak'rō-spīr*, (*bot*) *n* the first leaf that sprouts from a germinating seed. [ME *akerspire*, from OE *æhher* (see **icker**) ear, and **spire**[1]]

across *ə-kros', prep* from side to side of; on or to the other side of; crosswise. — Also *adv*. — *adj* **across'-the-board'** (of wage increases, etc) applying in all cases (*adv* **across the board**). — *adj* **across'-the-ta'ble** (of a discussion, conference, etc) face to face. — **come across** to find or meet by chance; to hand over information, confession, money, etc, in answer to demand or inducement (*colloq*); **get** or **come across** to take effect (on the audience across the footlights, and so generally); **get it across** to make acceptable or to bring to a successful issue; to explain; **put it across (someone)** to deceive (him or her). [**a-**[1]]

acrostic *ə-kros'tik, n* a poem or puzzle in which the first (or last) letters of each line spell a word or sentence; an acronym. — *adv* **acros'tically**. [Gr *akros* extreme, and *stichos* a line]

acroterion *ak-rō-tē'ri-on*, (*archit*) *n* a pedestal or ornament at the top or side angle of a pediment: — *pl* **acrotē'ria**. — Also **acrote'rium** and **acrō'ter** (or *ak'*). — *adj* **acrotē'rial**. [Gr *akrōtērion* extremity, from *akros*]

acrotism *ak'rot-izm*, (*med*) *n* absence of pulsation. [Gr *a-* (privative), and *krotos* sound made by striking]

acrylic *ə-kril'ik, n* a synthetic fibre; acrylic resin. — Also *adj*. — **acrylamide gel electrophoresis** (*biol*) electrophoretic separation of proteins or RNA according to their molecular weight; **acrylic acid** a very reactive acid belonging to the series of oleic acids, obtainable from acrolein by oxidation; **acrylic resins** thermoplastic resins formed by the polymerization of esters, amides, etc, derived from acrylic acid, and used in making paints, plastics, etc. [*acro*lein, and Gr *hȳlē* matter]

acrylonitrile *ə-kril-ō-nī'trīl, n* vinyl cyanide, obtained by polymerization and used in making synthetic fibres for carpets, etc, and synthetic rubbers.

ACS *abbrev*: active control system.

ACT *abbrev*: advance corporation tax (qv); Australian Capital Territory.

act *akt, vi* to produce an effect, to do something; to behave oneself in a specified way; to perform, eg on the stage; to feign; to exert force or influence; to be suitable for performance. — *vt* to perform; to imitate or play the part of. — *n* something done or doing; an exploit; the process (of doing); a decree; a legislative enactment; a written instrument in verification; a short prayer (*RC*); a distinct main section of a play; an individual performance or turn such as in a variety show; a public disputation or lecture maintained for a degree (*archaic*). — *n* **actabil'ity**. — *adj* **act'able**. — *n* **act'ing** action; the act or art of performing an assumed or a dramatic part; feigning. — *adj* performing some duty temporarily, or for another. — *n* **act'or**, *fem* **act'ress** a person who acts on the stage, in films, etc. — *n* **act'ure** (*Shakesp*) action or performance. — **act curtain** or **act drop** a curtain for closing the proscenium arch between acts or scenes. — **act as** to perform the duties of; **act of God** a result of natural forces, unexpected and not preventable by human foresight; **act of grace** a favour, *esp* a pardon granted by a sovereign; **act of parliament** see under **parliament**; **act on** to exert an influence on; to act in accordance with; **act out** to play as an actor; **act up** (*colloq*) to behave badly; **act up to** to come in practice up to the standard of; to fulfil; **clean up one's act** (*colloq*) to regulate one's activities, put one's affairs in good or proper order; **get in on** or **get into the act** (*colloq*) to start participating in something apparently profitable already taking place in order to share in the benefits; **get one's act together** (*colloq*) to get oneself organized; **put on an act** to make a pretence; to show off. [L *āctus, -ūs* an action, doing, *āctum* a thing done, and *āctor* a doer or actor; *agere, āctum* to do or drive]

act. *abbrev*: acting; active.

acta *ak'tə, n pl* official minutes of proceedings; official proceedings or acts. — **acta sanctorum** (*ak'ta sangk-tō'rəm, -tö'*, or *-rōōm*; *L*) deeds of the saints. [L, records]

Actaeon *ak-tē'ən, n* a hunter transformed into a stag by Artemis; hence someone with horns implanted upon him, a cuckold. — *vt* to cuckold. [L *Actaeōn*, from Gr *Aktaiōn*]

acte gratuit *akt gra-twē*, (*Fr*) an impulsive act lacking motive.

actg *abbrev*: acting.

ACTH *abbrev*: adrenocorticotrophic hormone, a hormone secreted by the pituitary gland which stimulates the adrenal cortex; also produced synthetically and used as a treatment for eg rheumatoid arthritis and skin diseases.

actin *ak'tin, n* a protein found in muscle, active in muscular contraction. [**act**]

actin- or **actino-** *ak-tin-(o-), combining form* ray. — *adj* **actinal** (*ak-tī'nəl* or *ak'ti-nəl*) belonging to the radiating bands on the body of an echinoderm where the tube-like feet are, or to the region of the mouth and tentacles in Anthozoa. — *adv* **actinally**. — *n* **actinia** (*-tin'*) a sea-anemone (properly, of the genus *Actinia*): — *pl* **actin'iae** or **actin'ias**. — *n* and *adj* **actin'ian**. — *adj* **actin'ic** of or showing actinism. — *adv* **actin'ically**. — *n* **ac'tinide** or **ac'tinoid** any element of a group from atomic number 89 (actinium) upwards. — *n* **ac'tinism** the chemical action of radiant energy. — *n* **actin'ium** a radioactive metal (atomic no 89; symbol **Ac**) found in pitchblende. — *n* **actinobacillus** (*-bə-sil'əs*) a bacillus of the genus of bacteria *Actinobacillus*, one of which causes **actinobacillō'sis**, woody-tongue (qv): — *pl* **actinobacill'i**. — *n* **actin'olite** (Gr *lithos* a stone) a green amphibole. — *n* **actinom'eter** an instrument for measuring the heat-intensity or the actinic effect of light rays. — *adj* **actinomor'phic** (Gr *morphē* form; *biol*) radially symmetrical. — *n* **Actinomyces** (*-mī'sēz*; Gr *mykēs* fungus) the ray-fungus, a genus of minute fungi or filamentous bacteria with radiating mycelium. — *n* **actinomycosis** (*-kō'sis*) lumpy-jaw in cattle, etc, or other disease caused by Actinomyces. — *n* **ac'tinon** actinium emanation, an isotope of radon. — *n* **actinother'apy** the treatment of disease by exposure to rays, *esp* ultraviolet rays. — *n pl* **Actinozo'a** the Anthozoa. — **actinic glass** glass that impedes actinic rays; **actinic rays** those rays (*esp* ultraviolet) that have a marked chemical action. [Gr *aktīs*, *aktīnos* ray]

action *ak'shən*, *n* acting; activity; behaviour; a deed; an operation; a gesture; fighting; a battle; a lawsuit, or proceedings in a court; a mode of moving the legs; the movement of events in a drama, novel, etc; the mechanism, *esp* of a keyboard instrument. — *vt* to carry out or put into effect. — *adj* **ac'tionable** giving ground for a lawsuit. — *adv* **ac'tionably**. — *n* **ac'tionist** an activist. — **action committee** or **group** members of an organization who are chosen to take active measures; **action painting** an American version of tachism in which paint is dripped, spattered, smeared, etc on to the canvas; **action plan** or **sheet** a written plan detailing the various stages of a project and the length of time each will take; **action potential** (*med*) the voltage pulse(s), produced in a nerve by a stimulus or stimuli, which when rapidly repeated can lead in motor nerves to continuous muscular response; **action radius** the distance a ship or aircraft can go without running out of fuel before reaching its base or starting-point again; **action replay** on television, the repeating of a piece of film, eg the scoring of a goal in football, *usu* in slow motion; **action spectrum** (*bot*) the relationship between the rate of a light-dependent physiological process (eg photosynthesis) and the wavelength of light; **action stations** posts to be manned during or preparatory to battle (often *fig*); **ac'tion-taking** (*Shakesp*) resorting to law instead of resorting to fighting. — **a piece of the action** (*colloq*) participation in an enterprise, etc, often including a share in the profits; **industrial action** see under **industry**. [Fr, from L *āctiō*, *-ōnis*]

active *ak'tiv*, *adj* acting; in actual operation; given to action; brisk; busy; nimble; practical (*opp* to *speculative*); effective; (of a volcano) liable to erupt, not extinct; (of bacteria, etc) potent; radioactive; of that voice in which the subject of the verb represents the doer of the action (*gram*). — *vt* **ac'tivate** to make active; to increase the energy of; to increase the capacity for adsorption in (carbon); to increase the biological activity of (sewage, etc) by aeration; to stimulate; to make radioactive. — *n* **activā'tion**. — *n* **ac'tivātor** a person or thing, substance, etc that activates. — *adv* **ac'tively**. — *n* **ac'tiveness**. — *n* **ac'tivism** a philosophy of creative will, *esp* the practical idealism of Rudolf Eucken (1846–1926); a policy of direct, vigorous and sometimes militant action. — *n* **ac'tivist** a believer in the philosophy of activism; a person who supports a policy of vigorous action; a person who plays a special part in advancing a project or in strengthening the hold of political ideas. — *n* **activ'ity** quality, state, or fact of being active; occupation, *esp* recreational pursuit; a training exercise designed to teach through practical experiment, research, and discussion; (*esp* in *pl*) doings. — **activated charcoal** charcoal treated eg with acid to increase its absorptive power; **active control system** (*aeronautics*) an advanced automatic flight control system, integrating aerodynamics, structure and electronic design; **active immunity** immunity due to the making of antibodies within the organism; **active life** (*theol*) life devoted to good works as opposed to contemplation; **active list** a list of full-pay officers engaged in or available for military service; **active service** service in the battle area, or (*orig US*) in the army, navy or air force even in time of peace; **activity holiday** a holiday offering participation (and *usu* training or coaching) in a particular occupation, *esp* sport. [L *āctīvus*]

acton *ak'tən*, **hacqueton** or **haqueton** *hak'(i)tən*, *n* a stuffed jacket worn under a coat of mail. [OFr *auqueton*, from Sp, from Ar *al qūtun* the cotton]

actor, **actress**. See under **act**.

ACTS *akts*, *abbrev*: Action of Churches Together in Scotland, an ecumenical group, set up to replace the Scottish Council of Churches in 1990.

ACTT *abbrev*: Association of Cinematograph Television and Allied Technicians.

ACTU *abbrev*: Australian Council of Trade Unions.

actual *ak'tū-əl* or *ak'chōō-əl*, *adj* of the nature of an action (*Shakesp*); real; existing in fact; at the time being or current. — *n* **ac'tualist** a person who deals with or considers actual facts. — *n* **actuality** (*-al'i-ti*) the fact or state of being actual; realism; something that really exists; a newsreel or current affairs programme (also **actualités** *ak-tü-al-ē-tā*; *Fr*). — *n* **actuali'zā'tion** or **-s-**. — *vt* **ac'tualize** or **-ise** to make actual; to realize in action. — *adv* **ac'tually** as a matter of fact; truly, however little one might expect it. [Fr *actuel*, from LL *āctuālis*]

actuary *ak'tū-ər-i*, *n* a registrar or clerk (mainly *hist*; still in the Convocation of Canterbury); a person whose profession is to assess financial and business problems, *esp* insurance risks, and to calculate premiums using mathematical and statistical techniques. — *adj* **actuarial** (*-ā'ri-əl*). — *adv* **actuā'rially**. [L *āctuārius* (*scriba*) an amanuensis or a clerk]

actuate *ak'tū-āt*, *vt* to put into, or incite to, action. — *vi* to act. — *n* **actūā'tion**. — *n* **ac'tūātor**. [L *āctus* action; see **act**]

acture. See **act**.

actus reus *ak'təs rē'əs* or *ak'tōōs rā'ōōs*, (*law*) *n* the act which is necessary for the crime to be constituted: — *pl* **actus** (*-tōōs*) **rei** (*-ī* or *-ē*). [Mod L, guilty act]

acuity *ə-kū'i-ti*, *n* sharpness. [LL *acuitās*, *-ātis*, from L *acus* needle]

aculeate *ə-kū'li-āt* or **aculeated** *ə-kū'li-āt-id*, *adj* pointed; prickly; having a sting; stinging. — *n* **acu'leus** a thorn or prickle (*bot*); a sting (*zool*); an ovipositor (*zool*). [L *aculeātus*, from *aculeus* a sting or goad, dimin of *acus* needle]

acumen *ə-kū'men* or *ak'ū-mən*, *n* sharpness; quickness of perception; penetration. — *vt* **acū'minate** to sharpen; to give a point to. — *vi* (*rare*) to taper. — *adj* (*bot*) tapering in long hollow curves to a point (also **acū'minated**). — *n* **acūminā'tion**. — *adj* **acu'minous**. [L *acūmen*, *-inis* a point]

acupressure *ak-ū-presh'ər*, *n* the arrest of a haemorrhage by a needle pressing across the artery; in acupuncture or related treatments, pressure (as opposed to a needle) applied to an acupoint (qv under **acupuncture**). [L *acus* needle, and **pressure**]

acupuncture *ak'ū-pungk-chər*, *n* the science (*orig* Chinese) of puncturing the skin with needles at specified points (**ac'upoints**) in order to cure illness, relieve symptoms, or effect anaesthesia. — *n* **ac'upuncturist**. [L *acus* needle, and **point**, **puncture**]

acushla *ə-kōōsh'lə*, (*Anglo-Irish*) *n* darling. [Ir *a chuisle*, vocative of *cuisle* vein]

acute *ə-kūt*, *adj* sharp; sharp-pointed; ending in an acute angle (*bot*); keen; mentally penetrating; piercing; finely discriminating; keenly perceptive; shrewd; urgently pressing; (of a disease) coming to a crisis (*opp* to *chronic*). — *n* an acute accent. — *adv* **acute'ly**. — *n* **acute'ness**. — **acute accent** a mark (´) over a letter in ancient Greek indicating a rising pitch, now used for various purposes in indicating pronunciation in various languages; **acute angle** an angle smaller than a right angle. [L *acūtus*, pa p of *acuere* to sharpen]

ACW *abbrev*: aircraft(s)woman.

acyclic *ā-* or *a-sī'klik*, *adj* not periodic; not whorled (*bot*); with open-chain structure, aliphatic (*chem*). — *n* **acy'clovir** (*-klō-vīr*) a drug used in the treatment of forms of herpes and of HIV. [Gr *a-* (privative), and *kyklos* a wheel]

acyl *ā'sil* or *as'il*, (*chem*) *n* and *adj* (denoting) the carboxylic acid RCO-. [*A*cid and *-yl*]

AD *abbrev*: active duty (*military*); air defence; *anno domini* (*L*), in the year of the Lord, now used in numbering the years since Christ was thought to have been born (also **A.D.**); Dame of the Order of Australia.

ad[1] *ad*, (*colloq*) *n* advertisement.

ad[2] *abbrev*: after date; *ante diem* (*L*), before the day.

ad. *ad*, (*tennis*, *NAm*) *abbrev*: advantage.

-ad[1] *ad*, (*biol*) *combining form* denoting towards, as in *caudad* towards the tail, or *cephalad*, towards the head. [L *ad* to or towards]

-ad[2] *ad*, *sfx* used in (1) names for nymphs, etc (*naiad*, *dryad* or *hamadryad*); (2) titles of epic poems, etc (*Iliad* or *Dunciad*); (3) words for numerical groups (*triad*, *decad(e)*, *myriad* or *Olympiad* (qv)). [Gr *-as*, *-ados*]

ADA or **Ada** *ā'də*, *n* a computer-programming language *orig* devised for military use, one of its applications being simultaneous control of diverse operations. [Named after *Ada* Lovelace (1816–52), daughter of Byron and assistant to C Babbage]

ad absurdum. See **reductio ad absurdum**.

adactylous *ā-dak'ti-ləs*, *adj* without fingers or toes. [Gr *a-* (privative) and *daktylos* a finger]

adage *ad'ij*, *n* an old saying; a proverb. [Fr, from L *adagium*, from *ad* to, and root of *āiō* I say]

adagio *ə-dä'j(y)ō*, (*music*) *adv* slowly. — *adj* slow. — *n* a slow movement; a piece in adagio time: — *pl* **ada'gios**. [Ital, from *ad agio* at ease]

Adam *ad'əm*, *n* the first man, according to the book of Genesis; unregenerate human nature; a gaoler (*perh* as wearing buff) (*Shakesp*). — *adj* applied to a style of architecture, interior decoration and furniture designed by Robert and James *Adam* in the 18c. — *adj* **Adamic** or **Adamical** (*ə-dam'ik*, *-əl*) of or like Adam; naked. — *n* **Ad'amite** a descendant of Adam; a person who goes about naked, *esp* a member of a 2c sect in N Africa. — *adj* **Adamit'ic** or **Adamit'ical**. — *n* **Ad'amitism**. — **Adam's ale** or **wine** water; **Adam's apple** the projection of the thyroid cartilage in front of the throat, traditionally supposed to be part of the forbidden fruit stuck in Adam's throat; forbidden fruit (see **forbid**); **Adam's flannel** mullein; **Adam's needle** a species of Yucca. — **Adam and Eve** (*Cockney rhyming slang*) to believe; **not know someone from Adam** (*colloq*) not to know someone, or who someone is. [Heb *Adām*]

adamant *ad'əm-ənt* or *-ant*, *n* a name applied by the ancients to various hard substances, eg steel; an imaginary rock with fabulous properties; diamond (*obs*); lodestone (*obs*). — *adj* unyielding. — *adj* **adamantē'an** (*Milton*) hard as adamant. — *adj* **adaman'tine** unbreakable; impregnable; impenetrable; magnetically attractive (*obs*). — *adv* **ad'amantly**. — **adamantine lustre** (*mineralogy*) a lustre similar to the metallic but without opacity. [Gr *adamas*, *-antos*, prob orig steel, also diamond, from *a-* (privative), and *damaein* to tame or overcome]

Adamite, etc. See **Adam**.

Adansonia *ad-ən-sō'ni-ə*, *n* the baobab genus. [Michel *Adanson*, French botanist (1727–1806)]

ad aperturam libri *ad ap-er-tūr'am lib'rī* or *-tōōr'am lib'rē*, (*L*) as the book opens.

adapt *ə-dapt'*, *vt* to make fit or suitable; to modify; to adjust. — *n* **adaptabil'ity**. — *adj* **adapt'able**. — *n* **adapt'ableness**. — *n* **adaptation** (*ad-əp-tā'shən*) the fact, act, process or result of adapting; a character by which anything is adapted to conditions; adjustment. — *adj* **adapt'ative**. — *adj* **adapt'ed** modified to suit; suitable. — *n* **adapt'er** or **adaptor** someone who or something which adapts; an attachment or accessory enabling a piece of apparatus to be used for a purpose, or in conditions, other than that or those for which it was *orig* intended, *esp* a device that will connect two parts of different sizes, or a device that enables one to connect two electrical devices (eg a plug and socket) that have incompatible terminals, or that allows more than one electrical appliance to be powered from one socket. — *n* **adap'tion** adaptation. — *adj* **adapt'ive**. — *adv* **adapt'ively**. — *n* **adapt'iveness**. — **adaptive radiation** (*ecol*) evolutionary diversification of species from a common ancestral stock, filling available ecological niches. — Also **divergent radiation**. [Fr *adapter*, from L *adaptāre*, from *ad* to, and *aptāre* to fit]

Adar *ä'där* or *ā'där*, *n* in the Jewish calendar, the twelfth month of the ecclesiastical year, the sixth of the civil year (part of February and March). — **Adar Sheni** (*shā'nē*) Veadar, literally Adar the second. [Heb *adār*]

ad arbitrium *ad är-bit'ri-əm* or *-ōōm*, (*L*) at pleasure.

ADAS *abbrev*: Agricultural Development and Advisory Service.

ad astra *ad as'tra*, (*L*) to the stars.

ad avizandum *ad a-viz-an'dəm* or *a-vēz-än'dōōm*, (*Scots law*; *L*) for further consideration; see **avizandum**.

adaw *ə-dö'*, (*Spenser*) *vt* to daunt; to subdue. — *vi* to subside. [Appar a 16c misunderstanding of the ME adv *adaw* out of life, from OE *of dagum* from days (dative pl)]

adaxial *ad-aks'i-əl*, (*bot*) *adj* next to or towards the axis. [L *ad* next to]

adays *ə-dāz'*, (*obs*) *adv* by day; daily (*Spenser*). [OE *dæges*, genitive of *dæg* day, with prep *a* (see **a-**[1]) added later]

ADC *abbrev*: advice of duration and charge, a telephone service by which the operator advises the caller of the cost of the call he or she has just made (also **AD and C**); aide-de-camp; analogue-to-digital converter (*comput*).

ad Calendas Graecas *ad kal-en'däs grī'käs*, (*L*) at the Greek calends, ie never, as the Greeks had no calends (qv).

ad captandum (vulgus) *ad kap-tan'dəm* (*vul'gəs*), or *-dōōm* (*wōōl'gōōs*), (*L*) (used as *adv* or *adj*) with the intention of pleasing or appealing to the emotions of the crowd.

ad clerum *ad kler'əm*, or *klā'rōōm*, (*L*) to the clergy.

ad crumenam *ad krōō'mə-nam*, or *krōō-mā'nam*, (*L*) to the purse.

add *ad*, *vt* to put, join or annex (to something else); to sum up or compute the sum of; to say further. — *vi* to make an addition; to increase (with *to*); to find the total of numbers, etc. — *n* **add'er** a person who adds; a machine for adding; a basic component of a chip, consisting of a number of switches which perform addition on digital signals (*comput*). — *n* **additament** (*ə-dit'ə-mənt*, or *ad'*) something added (*archaic*); an additional ornament external to the shield, eg supporters or symbols of office (*heraldry*). — *n* **addi'tion** the act of adding; a person or thing added; the part of arithmetic or algebra that deals with adding; a person's title or designation (*Shakesp*). — *adj* **addi'tional** added. — *adv* **addi'tionally**. — *adj* **additi'tious** increasing. — *adj* **add'itive** of the nature of an addition; characterized by addition; to be added. — *n* a substance added to foodstuffs or other commodities for a special purpose, eg as a colorant or preservative. — **adding machine** an apparatus for performing basic arithmetical calculations; **addition compound** or **product** (*chem*) one formed by the direct union of two or more substances; **add'-on** (*esp comput*) an additional unit, a peripheral: — *pl* **add'-ons**; **add-to system** a hire-purchase arrangement by which a customer obtains a series of articles, making a down payment on the first only. — **add up** to amount on adding; to be consistent, or satisfactory to the mind; to point to a reasonable conclusion; **add up to** to come to as result or conclusion. [L *addere*, *additum*, from *ad* to, and *dare* to put]

add. *abbrev*: addendum; addition; additional; address.

addax *ad'aks*, *n* a large African antelope with long slightly twisted horns. [L, from an African word]

addebted *ad-et'id*, (*obs* except *Scot*) *adj* indebted; owed. [ME *endetted*, from OFr *endetter* or *endeter* to get into debt, from LL *indebitare*]

addeem *ə-dēm'*, (*obs*) *vt* to adjudge; to award. [Pfx *ad-*, and **deem**]

addend *ad'end* or *ə-dend'*, *n* a number or quantity added. [**addendum**]

addendum *ə-den'dəm*, *n* a thing to be added, such as supplementary material to a book, etc; the distance between the centre and the outer edge of a tooth on a gear or of the thread of a screw (*eng*): — *pl* **adden'da**. [L gerundive of *addere*; see **add**]

adder[1] *ad'ər*, *n* the only venomous snake found in Britain, a viper (qv). — **add'erstone** a prehistoric spindle-whorl or bead, popularly attributed to the agency of adders; **ad'der's-tongue** a genus (Ophioglossum) of ferns whose spores grow on a spike resembling a snake's tongue; **ad'der's-wort** or **add'erwort** the bistort or snakeweed, supposed to cure snake-bite. [OE *nædre* (*an adder* for *a nadder*; cf obs Ger *Atter* for *Natter*)]

adder[2]. See **add**.

addict *ə-dikt'*, *vt* (*usu* in passive with *to*) to make (someone) dependent on (*esp* a drug). — *adj* (*obs*) addicted. — *n* (*ad'ikt*) a slave to a habit or vice, *esp* a drug. — *adj* **addict'ed** inclined or given up (to); dependent on. — *n* **addict'edness**. — *n* **addic'tion** the state of being addicted; a habit that has become impossible to break. — *adj* **addict'ive** tending to cause addiction; habit-forming. — **drug of addiction** a habit-forming drug. [L *addīcere*, *addictum*, from *ad* to, and *dīcere* to declare]

addio *ad-ē'o*, *interj* good-bye: — *pl* **addi'os**. [Ital *a Dio* to God]

Addison's disease *ad'i-sənz diz-ēz'*, *n* a disease in which there is progressive destruction of the suprarenal cortex, accompanied by wasting, weakness, low blood-pressure and pigmentation of the skin (bronzed skin). [Dr Thomas *Addison* (1793–1860), who investigated it]

additament, **addition**, **additive**, etc. See **add**.

addle *ad'l*, *n* liquid filth (now *dialect*). — *adj* putrid; bad (eg of an egg); barren, empty; muddled. — *vt* and *vi* to make or become addle. — *adj* **add'led**. — *n* **add'lement**. — *adj* **add'le-brained**, **add'le-headed** or **add'le-pated** muddleheaded. [OE *adela* mud]

addoom *ə-dōōm'*, (*Spenser*) *vt* to adjudge, award. [Pfx *ad-*, and **doom**]

addorsed *ə-dörst'*, (*heraldry*) *adj* turned back to back. [L *ad* to, and *dorsum* back]

address *ə-dres'*, *vt* to arrange (*obs*); to prepare (*obs*); to dress (*obs*); to don (*archaic*); to apply or devote (oneself; with *to*); to apply oneself to; to direct; to aim; to direct one's words to or speak directly to; to send; to put a written or printed direction or indication of destination upon; to woo (*archaic*). — *vi* to direct one's words (towards) (*Shakesp*); to prepare oneself (*Shakesp*). — *n* act or mode of addressing; deportment; adroitness; preparation, a move or incipient act (*Milton*); a formal communication in writing; a speech; a direction, eg of a letter; a place to which letters, etc may be directed; a place where a person, organization, etc may be found; the place where a person lives; a name, label or number that identifies the location of a stored item of data, etc (*comput*); a location within a computer's main memory in which data is stored; (in *pl*) attentions of the nature of courtship. — *adj* **address'able**. — *n* **addressabil'ity**. — *adj* **addressed'** aimed; directed. — *adj* **addrest'** or **addressed'** (*obs*) arrayed; equipped; set up (*Spenser*); ready or prepared (*Shakesp*). — *n* **addressee'** the person to whom a letter, etc is addressed. — *n* **address'er** or **address'or**. — *n* **Addressograph**® (*ə-dres'ō-gräf*) a machine for printing addresses automatically on envelopes, etc. — **address book** a notebook, *usu* with alphabetical thumb-index, in which names and addresses can be entered; **address bus** (*comput*) the set of wires connecting the processor to the memory, used to inform the memory of the address which the processor wishes to read or write to. [Fr *adresser*, from LL *addirectiare*, from L *ad* to, and *directum* straight; see **dress** and **direct**]

adduce *ə-dūs'*, *vt* to bring forward in discussion, to cite or quote. — *adj* **addūc'ent** drawing inward or together, as a muscle does. — *n* **addūc'er**. — *adj* **addūc'ible**. — *vt* **adduct** (*ə-dukt'*) to draw inward or together. — *n* **adduc'tion** the act of adducing or of adducting. — *adj* **adduc'tive** tending to bring forward. — *n* **adduc'tor** an adducent muscle. [L *addūcere*, *adductum*, from *ad* to, and *dūcere* to bring]

adeem *ə-dēm'*, (*law*) *vt* to cancel (a bequest) by destruction or sale of the thing bequeathed, or otherwise. — *n* **ademption** (*-dem'shən*). [L *ad* to, and *emere*, *emptum* to take]

adelantado *a-de-lan-tä'dō*, (*Sp*) *n* a grandee; a provincial governor: — *pl* **adelanta'dos**.

à demi *a də-mē*, (*Fr*) by halves or half.

aden- *ad'ən-*, *combining form* denoting gland. — *n* **adenec'tomy** surgical removal of a gland. — *n* **adenine** (*ad'ən-ēn* or *ad'ən-īn*) a substance found in all glandular tissues, one of the four bases in deoxyribonucleic acids, in close association with thymine. — *n* **adenitis** (*ad-ən-ī'tis*) inflammation of glands. — *n* **adenocarcinoma** (*-ō-kär-si-nō'mə*) a malignant tumour of glandular origin or gland-like structure: — *pl* **adenocarcinō'mata** or **adenocarcinō'mas**. — *n* **adenohypophysis** (*-ō-hī-poph'i-sis*) the anterior lobe of the pituitary gland: — *pl* **adenohypoph'yses** (*-sēz*). — *adj* **ad'enoid** gland-like; glandular. — *n* (*usu* in *pl*) glandular tissue at the back of the nose. — *adj* **adenoid'al** of adenoids; affected by or as if by adenoids (such as a voice). — *n* **adenoidec'tomy** surgical removal of adenoids. — *n* **adenō'ma** a benign tumour like, or originating in, a gland: — *pl* **adenō'mata** or **adenō'mas**. — *adj* **adenō'matous**. — *n* **adenosine** (*ad'ə-nō-sin*, also *ə-den'*) a nucleoside made up of adenine and ribose, one of its compounds being **adenosine triphosphate** (*abbrev* **ATP**), which is present in all cells and stores energy for muscle contraction. — *n* **adenovī'rus** any of a group of viruses that attack the upper respiratory tract, and may produce malignancy. [Gr *adēn* gland]

Adeni *ā'di-ni*, *n* and *adj* (a citizen) of Aden.

adept *ad'ept*, *ə-dept'* or *a-dept'*, *adj* completely skilled (at or in). — *n* (*ad'ept*, *ə-dept'* or *a-dept'*) an expert; an alchemist who has attained the great secret (of the philosopher's stone) (*obs*). — *adv* **adept'ly**. — *n* **adept'ness**. [L *adeptus* (*artem*) having attained (an art), pa p of *adipīscī* to attain]

adequate *ad'i-kwit* or *-kwāt*, *adj* sufficient; competent. — *n* **ad'equacy** (*-kwə-si*). — *adv* **ad'equately**. — *n* **ad'equateness**. — *adj* **ad'equative**. [L *adaequātus* made equal, from *ad* to, and *aequus* equal]

adermin *ə-dûr'min*, *n* former name of pyridoxine. [Gr *a-* (privative), and *derma* skin, because deprivation of this vitamin was shown to cause dermatitis in rats]

Ades *ā'dēz*, (*Milton*) *n* variant of **Hades**.

adespota *ad-es'pot-a*, *n pl* anonymous works. [Gr *a-* (privative), and *despotēs* master]

à dessein *a des-ɛ̃*, (*Fr*) on purpose.

adessive *ad-es'iv*, (*gram*) *adj* (of a case, found eg in Finnish) denoting place where. — *n* the adessive case. [L *adesse* to be at a place or to be present]

ad eundem *ad ē-un'dəm* or *ā-ōōn'dem*, (*L*) to or at the same level or status (as already attained, *esp* at another university). [Short for L *ad eundem gradum*]

à deux *a dø*, (*Fr*) of two, between two, two-handed. — **à deux mains** (*mɛ̃*) with both hands; for two hands.

ad finem *ad fin'əm* or *fēn'em*, (*L*) at, to, or towards the end (*abbrev* **ad fin.**).

adharma *ə-där'mä* or *ə-dûr'mə*, *n* unrighteousness (the opposite of *dharma*). [Sans]

adhere *əd-* or *ad-hēr'*, *vi* to stick (to); to remain fixed or attached (to); to remain faithful (eg to a party, leader, or doctrine); to be consistent (*Shakesp*); to agree; to affirm a judgement (*Scots law*). — *n* **adhēr'ence** state of adhering; the growing together of unlike parts (*bot*). — *adj* **adhēr'ent** sticking; grown together and unlike. — *n* someone who adheres; a follower; a partisan; a person who is loosely associated with a body, group, party, etc without being a member. — *n* **adhēr'er**. [L *ad* to, and *haerēre*, *haesum* to stick]

adhesion *əd-hē'zhən*, *n* the act of adhering or sticking; strong, firm contact; steady attachment; growing together of unlike parts (*bot*); reunion of separated surfaces (*surg*); abnormal union of parts that have been inflamed (*pathol*); (often in *pl*) a band of fibrous tissue joining such parts. — *adj* **adhē'sive** (*-siv* or *-ziv*) sticky; likely or tending to adhere. — *n* a substance such as glue used for sticking things together. — *adv* **adhē'sively**. — *n* **adhē'siveness**. [See **adhere**]

adhibit *əd-hib'it*, *vt* to apply; to attach; to admit; to administer. — *n* **adhibi'tion**. [L *adhibēre*, *-itum*, from *ad* to, and *habēre* to hold]

ad hoc *ad hok*, (*L*) *adj* and *adv* for this special purpose. — **ad hocery** (*hok'ə-ri*; *facetious*) the use of ad hoc measures, improvisation or pragmatism.

ad hominem *ad hom'in-em*, (*L*) addressed to the feelings or prejudices of the hearer or reader; dealing with an opponent by attacking their character instead of answering their argument. [Literally, to the man]

ADI *abbrev*: approved driving instructor.

adiabatic *ad-i-ə-bat'ik*, *adj* without transference of heat. — *adv* **adiabat'ically**. [Gr *a-* (privative), *dia* through, and *batos* passable]

Adiantum *ad-i-an'təm*, *n* the maidenhair genus of ferns. [Gr *adiantos*, from *a-* (privative), and *diantos* capable of being wetted]

adiaphoron *ad-i-af'ə-ron*, (*theol* and *ethics*) *n* a matter of indifference, which is neither approved nor disapproved in the religion or ethical system; any tenet or usage considered non-essential: — *pl* **adiaph'ora**. — *n* **adiaph'orism** tolerance or indifference in regard to non-essential points in theology; latitudinarianism. — *n* **adiaph'orist**. — *adj* **adiaphoris'tic**. — *adj* **adiaph'orous**. [Gr, from *a-* (privative), and *diaphoros* differing, from *dia* apart, and *pherein* to carry]

adiathermic *ad-i-ə-thûr'mik*, *adj* impervious to radiant heat. — *n* **adiather'mancy** impermeability to radiant heat (also **ather'mancy**). — *adj* **adiather'manous**. [Gr *a-* (privative), *dia* through, and *thermē* heat]

adieu *ə-dū*, *interj* farewell, goodbye. — *n* a farewell: — *pl* **adieus** or **adieux** (*ə-dūz'*). [Fr *à Dieu* (I commend you) to God]

Adi-Granth *u-dhē'grunt'*, *n* another name for the **Granth (Sahib)**. [Hindi, the first scripture]

ad infinitum *ad in-fin-īt'əm* or *-ēt'o͞om*, (*L*) to infinity. — *abbrev* **ad inf.**

ad init. *ad in-it'*, *abbrev*: *ad initium* (*L*), at or to the beginning.

ad inquirendum *ad in-kwīr-en'dəm* or *in-kwēr-en'do͞om*, (*LL*) the name of a writ — literally, for making inquiry.

ad interim *ad in'tər-im*, (*LL*) for or in the meantime. — *abbrev* **ad int.**

adiós *ad-ē-os'*, *interj* good-bye. [Sp, literally, to God]

adipic *ə-dip'ik*, *adj* of fat, only in **adipic acid** $C_6H_{10}O_4$, an acid obtained by treating fat with nitric acid. — *adj* **adipose** (*ad'i-pōs*) fatty. — *n* **adiposity** (*-pos'i-ti*). — **adipose tissue** the vesicular structure in the animal body which contains fat. [L *adeps*, *adipis* soft fat]

adipocere *ad'i-pō-sēr*, or *-sēr'*, *n* a fatty, waxy substance resulting from the decomposition of animal bodies in moist places or under water, but not exposed to air. [L *adeps*, *adipis* soft fat, and *cēra* wax]

adipose, etc. See under **adipic**.

adit *ad'it*, *n* an opening or passage, *esp* into a mine. [L *aditus*, from *ad* to, and *ire*, *itum* to go]

adj. *abbrev*: adjective; adjourned; adjustment; adjutant (also with *cap*).

adjacent *ə-jā'sənt*, *adj* lying near or next (to). — *n* **adjā'cency**. — *adv* **adjā'cently**. [L *ad* to, and *jacēns*, *-entis*, pr p of *jacēre* to lie]

adjective *aj'ik-tiv*, *n* a word added to a noun to qualify it, or to limit its denotation by reference to quality, number or position. — *adj* added; dependent; subsidiary; (of dyes) requiring a mordant. — *adj* **adjectival** (*-tīv'l*) of an adjective; using many adjectives; used facetiously as a euphemism (eg *What adjectival nonsense!*). — *adv* **adjectī'vally**. — *adv* **ad'jectively**. [L *adjectīvum* (*nōmen*) added (word), from *adjicere*, *-jectum* to add, from *ad* to, and *jacere* to throw]

adjoin *ə-join'*, *vt* to join on; to lie next to. — *vi* to be in contact. — *adj* **adjoin'ing**. — *n* **adjoint** (*aj'oint*, *Fr ad-zhwɛ̃*) a civil officer who assists a French maire; an assistant professor in a French college. [Through Fr *adjoign-* pr p stem, and *adjoint* pa p, of *adjoindre*, from L *adjungere*, from *ad* to, and *jungere* to join]

adjourn *ə-jûrn'*, *vt* to put off to another day; to postpone; to discontinue (a meeting) in order to reconstitute it at another time or place. — *vi* to suspend proceedings and disperse, either for any time specified, or (*sine die*) without such time being specified. — *n* **adjourn'ment**. — **adjournment debate** a brief parliamentary debate, immediately before the adjournment of the House, allowing members to raise issues which would otherwise not be discussed. — **Acts of Adjournal** (*Scots law*) procedural rules of the High Court. [OFr *ajorner*, from LL *adiurnāre*, from L *ad* to, and LL *jurnus*, L *diurnus* daily; cf **journal**[1]]

Adjt or **adjt** *abbrev*: adjutant. — **Adjt-Gen.** Adjutant-General.

adjudge *ə-juj'*, *vt* to decide; to assign; to award. — *n* **adjudge'ment** (sometimes **adjudg'ment**) the act of adjudging; sentence. [OFr *ajuger*, from L *adjūdicāre*; cf **judge**]

adjudicate *ə-jo͞o'di-kāt*, *vt* to determine judicially; to pronounce; to award. — *vi* to pronounce judgement; to act as judge in a competition between amateurs in one of the arts, eg music. — *n* **adjudi'cā'tion** act or process of adjudicating; an order of the Bankruptcy Court, adjudging a debtor to be a bankrupt and transferring his or her property to a trustee (*Eng law*). — *adj* **adju'dicative**. — *n* **adju'dicātor**. [L *adjūdicāre*, *adjūdicātum*]

adjunct *aj'ung(k)t*, *adj* joined or added. — *n* a thing joined or added, but subordinate or not essentially a part; a person (*usu* subordinate) joined to another in office or service; any word or clause enlarging the subject or predicate (*gram*); any accompanying quality or non-essential attribute (*logic*). — *n* **adjunction** (*ə-jungk'-shən*). — *adj* **adjunct'ive** forming an adjunct. — *adv* **adjunct'ively**. — *adv* **ad'junctly** (or *-jungkt'-*). [L *adjunctus*, pa p of *adjungere* to join]

adjure *ə-jo͞or'*, *vt* to charge on oath; to command or request solemnly; to make swear (*obs*). — *n* **adjurā'tion** (*aj-*). — *adj* **adjur'atory**. — *adj* **adjur'ing**. [L *adjūrāre*, from *ad* to, and *jūrāre*, *-ātum* to swear]

adjust *ə-just'*, *vt* to regulate; to adapt or put in proper relation; to alter; to settle. — *vi* to adapt oneself (to). — *adj* **adjust'able**. — *adv* **adjust'ably**. — *n* **adjust'er** a person or thing that adjusts; see under **average** and **loss**. — *n* **adjust'ment**. — *n* **adjust'or** an organ or faculty that determines behaviour in response to stimuli. [Obs Fr *adjuster*, from LL *adjuxtāre* to put side by side, from L *juxtā* near; confused by association with *jūstus* right]

adjutage or **ajutage** *aj'o͞o-tij*, *n* a nozzle, as in a fountain. [Fr *ajutage*; cf **adjust**]

adjutant *aj'o͞o-tənt*, *n* an officer specially appointed to assist a commanding officer; (*usu* **adjutant bird**) a large Indian stork or crane (from its stalking gait). — *n* **ad'jutancy** the office of an adjutant; assistance (*rare*). — **adjutant-gen'eral** the head of a department of the general staff; the executive officer of a general: — *pl* **adjutants-gen'eral**. [L *adjūtāns*, *-antis*, pr p of *adjūtāre*, frequentative of *adjuvāre*, from *ad* to, and *juvāre* to assist]

adjuvant *aj'o͞o-vənt*, *adj* helping. — *n* a help; a substance added eg to a medicine, vaccine, etc to increase its effectiveness (*med*). — *n* **ad'juvancy**. [Fr, from L *ad* to, and *juvāre* to help]

adland. See under **advertise**.

ad libitum *ad lib'i-təm* or *-to͞om*, (*L*) at will, at pleasure; extempore, impromptu. — *abbrev* **ad lib**. — *adv* **ad-lib** (*ad-lib'*) spontaneously or freely. — *adj* impromptu, extemporized. — *vt* and *vi* to extemporize or speak without preparation, *esp* to fill up time. — *n* an improvised speech; a spontaneous (often humorous) remark. — *n* **ad-libb'er**. — *n* **ad-libb'ing**.

ad litem *ad lī'təm* or *lē'tem*, (*L*) (of a guardian, etc) appointed for a lawsuit.

ad loc. *abbrev*: *ad locum* (*L*), at the place.

Adm. *abbrev*: Admiral.

ad-man or **adman**. See under **advertise**.

ad manum *ad mān'əm* or *män'o͞om*, (*L*) at or to hand, ready.

ad-mass or **admass**. See under **advertise**.

admeasure *ad-mezh'ər*, *vt* to measure or measure out; to apportion. — *n* **admeas'urement**. [OFr *amesurer*, from LL *admēnsūrāre*, from L *ad* to, and *mēnsūra* measure]

admin. See under **administer**.

adminicle *əd-min'i-kl*, *n* anything that aids or supports; an auxiliary; any corroborative evidence (*law*). — *adj* **adminic'ūlar**. — *vt* and *vi* **adminic'ūlate**. [L *adminiculum* a support, from *ad* to, and *manus* hand]

administer *əd-min'is-tər*, *vt* to govern; to manage or control as a manager, steward, substitute or executor; to dispense (justice or rites); to supervise the swearing of (an oath); to give (medicine or treatment). — *vi* to minister. — *adj* **admin'istrable**. — *adj* and *n* **admin'istrant**. — *vt* **admin'istrate** to administer. — *n* **administrā'tion** (*colloq* short form **ad'min**) the act of administering; management; the organization of a business; the people whose job it is to carry out such organization; dispensation of sacraments; the government. — *adj* **admin'istrative** concerned with administration. — *adv* **admin'istratively**. — *n* **admin'istrātor** a person who manages or directs; the person to whom is committed, under a commission entitled **letters of administration**, the administration or distribution of the personal estate of a deceased person, in default of an executor; someone empowered to act for a person legally incapable of acting for themselves (*Scots law*): — *fem* **admin'istrātrix**. — *n* **admin'istrātorship**. — **administrative order** a court order allowing an administrator to freeze the debts of a company in financial difficulties. [L *administrāre*, *-ātum*, from *ad* to, and *ministrāre* to minister]

admirable, etc. See **admire**.

admiral *ad'mər-əl*, *n* the chief commander of a navy; a naval officer ranking with a general in the army (**admiral of the fleet** ranking with field marshal); an admiral's flagship; the chief ship in a fleet of merchant ships or fishing boats; a cone-shell; a butterfly of certain kinds (see **red** and **white**). — *n* **ad'miralship** the office or art of an admiral. — **Ad'miralty** (with *the*) or **the Admiralty Board** the board administering the Royal Navy (since 1964 under the British Ministry of Defence); the building where it transacts business. — **Lord High Admiral** an office dating from the 15c, William IV (when Duke of Clarence) being the last holder until the office was taken over by the Queen in 1964. [OFr *a(d)miral*, from Ar *amīr-al-bahr* a lord of the sea, confused with L *admīrābilis* (see **admire**)]

admire *əd-mīr'*, *vt* to have (or express) a high opinion of; to wonder at (*archaic*). — *vi* (*obs*) to wonder. — *adj* **admirable** (*ad'mə-rə-bl*) worthy of being admired. — *n* **ad'mirableness**. — *adv* **ad'mirably**. — *n* **admīr'a(u)nce** (*Spenser*) admiration. — *n* **admirā'tion** the act of admiring; wonder, together with esteem, love, or veneration; astonishment (*Bible*, *Shakesp* and *Milton*); admirableness (*Shakesp*); an object of admiration (*Shakesp*); a wonder (*Shakesp*). — *adj* (*archaic*) **ad'mirātive**. — *n* **admīr'er** a person who admires; a lover. — *adv* **admīr'ingly**. — **Admirable Crichton** (*krī'tən*) someone who excels in many things, from James Crichton (1560–82), Scottish athlete, Latin poet, polymath. [Fr *admirer*, from L *ad* at, and *mīrārī* to wonder]

ad misericordiam *ad mi-zer-i-kör'di-am*, (*L*) (of an argument, etc) appealing to pity.

admissible, etc. See under **admit**.

admit *əd-mit'*, *vt* to allow to enter (with *into* or *to*); to let in; to concede; to acknowledge; to confess; to be capable of (also *vi* with *of*): — *pr p* **admitt'ing**; *pa p* **admitt'ed**. — *n* **admissibil'ity** or **admiss'ibleness**. — *adj* **admiss'ible** that may be admitted or allowed (generally, or specially as legal proof). — *n* **admission** (*-mish'ən*) the act of admitting; anything admitted or conceded; permission to enter; the price charged for entry. — *adj* **admiss'ive**. — *adj* **admitt'able** that may be admitted. — *n* **admitt'ance** admission; acceptability or acceptance (*Shakesp*); the property of an electric circuit by virtue of which a current flows under the action of a potential difference (*elec*). — *adj* **admitt'ed** acknowledged or conceded; (of a law clerk) qualified to practise as a solicitor, having been admitted to the Law Society's roll of solicitors. — *adv* **admitt'edly**. [Partly through Fr, from L *admittere*, *-missum*, from *ad* to, and *mittere*, *missum* to send]

admix *ad-* or *ad-miks'*, *vt* to mix with something else. — *n* **admix'ture** the action of mixing; what is added to the chief ingredient of a mixture. [L *ad* to, and **mix**]

ad modum *ad mōd'əm* or *mod'o͞om*, (*L*) after the manner (of).

admonish *əd-mon'ish*, *vt* to warn; to reprove mildly. — *n* **admon'ishment** admonition. [OFr *amonester*, from LL *admonestāre*, from L *admonere*, from *ad* to, and *monēre* to warn]

admonition *ad-mon-ish'ən*, or *-mən-*, *n* reproof; counsel; warning; advice; ecclesiastical censure. — *adj* **admonitive** (*-mon'*) or **admon'itory** containing admonition. — *n* **admon'itor**. [L *admonitiō*, *-ōnis*; cf **admonish**]

ADN *abbrev*: People's Democratic Republic of Yemen (IVR).

adnascent *ad-nas'ənt*, *adj* growing together with or upon something else. [L *adnāscēns*, *-entis*, pr p of *adnāscī*, from *ad* to, and *nāscī* to be born]

adnate *ad'nāt* or *ad-nāt'*, (*bot*) *adj* attached (*esp* by the whole length) to another organ. — *n* **adnation** (*-nā'shən*). [L *adnātus*, usu *agnātus*, from *ad* to, and *(g)nātus* born]

ad nauseam *ad nö'zi-am*, *-shi-*, or *now'si-*, (*L*) to the point of producing disgust.

adnoun *ad'nown*, (*gram*) *n* an adjective used as a noun. — *adj* **adnom'inal**.

ado *ə-do͞o'*, *n* a to-do; bustle; trouble; difficulty; stir or fuss: — *pl* **ados'**. [**at do**, N Eng infinitive with **at** instead of **to**, borrowed from Scand]

adobe *ə-dō'bi*, *n* a sun-dried brick; a house made of such bricks; (also **adobe clay**) a name for any kind of mud which, when mixed with straw, can be sun-dried into bricks. — Also *adj*. [Sp, from *adobar* to plaster]

adolescent *ad-ō-les'ənt*, *adj* growing from childhood to maturity; between puberty and full maturity; belonging to or typical of this state; immature. — *n* a young person between childhood and adulthood. — *n* **adolesc'ence** the state or time of being adolescent. [L *adolēscēns*, *-entis*, pr p of *adolēscere* to grow up]

Adonai *ə-dōn'ī* or *ə-don-ā'ī*, *n* a name of God in the Old Testament, *usu* translated 'Lord'. — See also **Jehovah**. [Heb *adōnāi* my lord]

Adonis *ə-dō'nis*, *n* the young man beloved by Aphrodite (*Gr mythol*); a particularly handsome youth or young man; a beau or dandy; the ranunculaceous pheasant's-eye genus (*bot*). — *n pl* **Adō'nia** the festival of mourning for Adonis. — *n* **Adonic** (*ə-don'ik*; *prosody*) a verse of a dactyl and a spondee (or a trochee), said to have been used in the Adonia. — Also *adj*. — *vt* and *vi* **ad'onize** or **-ise** to adorn (oneself). [Gr *Adōnis*, from Phoenician *adōn* lord]

adoors *ə-dörz'*, (*obs*) *adv* at doors; at the door. [**a-**[1] at, and **door**]

adopt *ə-dopt'*, *vt* to take voluntarily as one's own child, with the rights of one's own child; to take into any relationship; to take as one's own; to take up; to take over; to take (a precaution, etc); to choose formally (eg a candidate); to endorse or approve (eg a resolution or minutes). — *adj* **adopt'ed** taken by adoption. — *n* **adopt'er**. — *n* **Adoptianism** or **Adoptionism** (*ə-dop'shən-izm*; often **adop'tianism**) the doctrine that Christ, as man, is the adopted son of God. — *n* **adop'tianist** or **adop'tionist**. — *n* **adop'tion**. — *adj* **adop'tious** (*-shəs*; *Shakesp*) adopted. — *adj* **adopt'ive** that adopts or is adopted. [L *adoptāre*, from *ad* to, and *optāre* to choose]

adore *ə-dör'*, *vt* to worship; to love or revere intensely; to adorn (*Spenser*). — *adj* **ador'able**. — *n* **ador'ableness**. — *adv* **ador'ably**. — *n* **adorā'tion**. — *n* **ador'er**. — *adv* **ador'ingly**. [L *ad* to, and *ōrāre* to pray]

adorn *ə-dörn'*, *vt* to deck or dress; to embellish. — *n* (*Spenser*) adornment. — *adj* (*Milton*) adorned, ornate. — *n* **adorn'ment** ornament; decoration. [OFr *äorner*, *adorner*, from L *adōrnāre*, from *ad* to, and *ōrnāre* to furnish]

adown *ə-down'*, (*archaic* or *poetic*) *adv* and *prep* same as **down**[3]. [**a-**[1]]

ADP (*comput*) *abbrev*: automatic data processing.

ad patres *ad pāt'rēz* or *pat'rās*, (*L*) (gathered) to his or her fathers, dead.

adpress *ad-pres'*, *vt* to press together. — *adj* **adpressed'** (*bot*) closely pressed together but not united. — Also **appress'**. [L *ad* to, and *premere*, *pressum* to press]

adrad *ə-drad'* or **adred** *ə-dred'*, (*Spenser*) *adj* afraid. [OE *ofdrǣd*, from pfx *of-*, and *drǣdan* to dread; see also **adread**]

adread *ə-dred'*, (*obs*) *vt* to fear. — *pa t* **adrad'** (*Spenser*). [OE *ondrǣdan*, from pfx *on-*, *and-* against, and *drǣdan* to dread]

ad referendum *ad ref-er-en'dum* or *-dōōm*, (*L*) to be further considered.

ad rem *ad rem*, (*L*) to the point; to the purpose.

adreno- or **adren-** *ə-dren(-ō-)* or *-drēn(-ō-)*, *combining form* denoting adrenal, adrenal glands, adrenalin. — *adj* **adrenal** (*ə-drē'nəl*) beside the kidneys; of or relating to the adrenal glands. — *n* an adrenal gland. — *n* **adrenaline** or **adrenalin** (*ə-dren'ə-lin*) a hormone secreted by the adrenal glands that causes constriction of the arteries, so increasing blood pressure and stimulating the heart muscle (in US **epinephrine**); also produced synthetically (as **Adrenalin®**) for this property. — *adj* **adrener'gic** (of the sympathetic nerve fibres) releasing (a substance resembling) adrenaline; activated by adrenaline; (of an agent) having the same effect as adrenaline. — *adj* **adrenocorticotrophic** or **-tropic** (*-kör'tik-ō-trof'ik* or *-trop'ik*; **cortex** and Gr *trophē* food) stimulating the activity of the adrenal cortex. — *n* **adrenoleukodys'trophy** an inherited, fatal, degenerative disease of the nervous system, affecting young boys (*abbrev* **ALD**). — **adrenal glands** the suprarenal capsules, two small ductless glands over the kidneys, which secrete adrenaline and steroids; **adrenocorticotrop(h)ic hormone** or **adrenocorticotrop(h)in** (*-trof'in*, *-trop'in*, or *-trō'*) see **ACTH**. [L *ad* to, and *rēnēs* kidneys]

Adriamycin® or **adriamycin®** *ā-dri-ə-mī'sin*, *n* an antibiotic used in the treatment of cancer.

adrift *ə-drift'*, *adj* or *adv* drifting; loose from moorings; left to one's own resources, without help, guidance or contacts; cut loose; off course or inaccurate (*colloq*). [**a-**[1]]

adroit *ə-droit'*, *adj* dexterous; skilful; ingenious. — *adv* **adroit'ly**. — *n* **adroit'ness**. [Fr *à droit* according to right, from L *directus* straight; see **direct**]

à droite *a drwät*, (*Fr*) to the right.

adry *ə-drī'*, (*archaic* or *poetic*) *adj* and *adv* in a state of thirst or dryness. [After **athirst**, **acold**, etc]

adscititious *ad-sit-ish'əs*, *adj* added or assumed; additional. — *adv* **adscitit'iously**. [L *adscīscere*, *-scītum* to take or assume, from *ad* to, and *scīscere* to inquire, from *scīre* to know]

adscript *ad'skript*, (*hist*) *adj* attached to the soil. — *n* a feudal serf so attached. — *n* **adscrip'tion**. [L *adscrīptus*, from *ad* to, and *scrībere* to write]

adsorb *ad-sörb'*, *vt* of a solid or a liquid, to accumulate on its surface a thin film of the molecules of a gas or liquid that is in contact with it (cf **absorb**). — *n* **adsorbabil'ity**. — *adj* **adsorb'able**. — *n* **adsorb'ate** the vapour or liquid absorbed. — *n* **adsorb'ent** a solid (such as charcoal) that adsorbs a gas, etc in contact with it. — *n* **adsorp'tion**. [L *ad* to, and *sorbēre* to suck in]

adsuki bean. See **adzuki bean**.

adsum *ad'sum* or *-sōōm*, (*L*) I am present; here.

ad summum *ad sum'um* or *sōōm'ōōm*, (*L*) to the highest point.

ADT (*NAm*) *abbrev*: Atlantic Daylight Time.

aduki bean. See **adzuki bean**.

adularia *ad-ū-lā'ri-ə*, (*mineralogy*) *n* a transparent orthoclase feldspar. [From the *Adula* group in the Alps]

adulate *ad'ū-lāt*, *vt* to fawn upon or flatter; to praise excessively. — *n* **adūlā'tion**. — *n* **ad'ūlātor**. — *adj* **ad'ūlatory**. [L *adūlārī*, *adūlātus* to fawn upon]

Adullamite *ə-dul'əm-īt*, *n* John Bright's name for a Whig seceder from the Liberal party (1866) (*hist*); hence someone who withdraws their allegiance from any political or intellectual group. [From the cave of *Adullam*, 1 Sam 22. 1, 2]

adult *ad'ult* or *ə-dult'*, *adj* grown-up; mature; of or for adults; suitable for the mature person only, *esp* of pornographic material. — *n* a grown-up person, animal or plant. — *n* **ad'ulthood**. [L *adultus*, pa p of *adolēscere* to grow up; see **adolescent**]

adulterate *ə-dult'ər-āt*, *vt* to debase or falsify, by mixing with something inferior or spurious; to commit adultery with (*obs*). — *vi* (*Shakesp*) to commit adultery. — *adj* defiled by adultery; spurious; corrupted by base elements. — *n* **adult'erant** something with which anything is adulterated. — *n* **adulterā'tion** the act of adulterating; the state of being adulterated. — *n* **adult'erātor** a person who adulterates a commodity. [L *adulterāre*, *-ātum*, prob from *ad* to, and *alter* another. Some forms come from Fr, remodelled later on Latin]

adulterer *ə-dult'ər-ər*, *n* a person guilty of adultery: — *fem* **adult'eress**. — *adj* **adult'erine** resulting from adultery; spurious; illegal (*hist*). — *n* the offspring of adultery. — *vi* **adult'erize** or **-ise** (*archaic*) to commit adultery. — *adj* **adult'erous** pertaining to, of the nature of, or guilty of, adultery. — *adv* **adult'erously**. — *n* **adult'ery** voluntary sexual intercourse between a married person and someone who is not their legal partner; lack of chastity generally (*Bible*); applied *esp* by theologians to marriages disapproved of, expressing reproach or scorn; image-worship; adulteration or falsification (*obs*). [**adulterate**]

adumbrate *ad'um-brāt*, or *-um'*, *vt* to give a faint shadow of; to outline faintly; to foreshadow; to overshadow. — *n* **adumbrā'tion**. — *adj* **adum'brative**. — *adv* **adum'bratively**. [L *adumbrāre*, *-ātus*, from *ad* to, and *umbra* a shadow]

adunc *ə-dungk'*, *adj* hooked. — Also **adunc'ate**, **adunc'ated** or **adunc'ous**. — *n* **aduncity** (*ə-dun'si-ti*). [L *aduncus*, *aduncātus*, from *ad* to, and *uncus* a hook]

ad unguem *ad ung'gwem*, or *ōōng'*, (*L*) to a nicety, (literally, to the nail).

ad unum omnes *ad ūn'əm om'nēz* or *ōōn'ōōm om'nās*, (*L*) all to a man.

adust *ə-dust'*, *vt* (*Milton*) to scorch. — *adj* burnt up or scorched (*obs*); browned with the sun (*obs*); sallow and melancholy (from the old notions of dryness of body) (*archaic*). [L *adūstus*, pa p of *adūrere* to burn up]

adv. *abbrev*: advent; adverb; *adversus* (*L*), against; advisory; advocate.

ad valorem *ad val-ōr'əm*, *-ōr'*, or *wal-ōr'em*, (*L*) according, in proportion, to value; depending on the value of goods, as opposed to weight, content or quantity. — *abbrev* **ad val.**

advance *əd-väns*, *vt* to put forward; to promote; to further; to raise (*Shakesp*); to extol (*obs*); to raise in price; to supply beforehand; to pay before due time; to lend, *esp* on security. — *vi* to move or go forward; to approach *esp* aggressively (with *on*); to make progress; to rise in rank or in value. — *n* a forward move; progress; an increase; a rise in price, value, or wages; payment beforehand; a loan; an approach, overture, move towards agreement, favour, etc. — *adj* forward (of position); made, given, etc ahead of time. — *adj* **advanced'** at or appropriate to a far-on stage (of education, thought, emancipation, life, etc). — *n* **advance'ment** promotion; furthering; payment in advance. — **advance copy** or **proof** one sent in advance of publication; **advance corporation tax** in UK, a tax, (currently the basic rate of income tax) deducted in advance from gross dividends and paid by the company to the Inland Revenue (*usu abbrev* **ACT**); **advanced gas-cooled reactor** (*abbrev* **AGR**) a nuclear reactor in which carbon dioxide is used as a coolant; **advanced level** see **A level** under **A**[3]; **advanced passenger train** a lightweight type of train, electrically powered, designed to run at 250km/h (156mph) and to tilt at curves (*abbrev* **APT**); **Advanced Supplementary level** see **AS-level**; **advance factory** one built to encourage development, in the belief that a firm will take it over; **advance** or **advanced guard** a guard or party in front of the main body; **advance note** an order for (generally) a month's wage given to a sailor on engaging; **advance workings** (*mining*) workings in which the whole face is carried forward, no support pillars being left. — **in advance** beforehand; in front. [OFr *avancer*, from LL *abante* (Fr *avant*), from L *ab ante* from before; the prefix refashioned later as if from *ad*]

advantage *əd-vänt'ij*, *n* superiority over another; a favourable condition or circumstance; gain or benefit; the first point after deuce (*tennis*). — *vt* and *vi* to benefit or profit. — *adj* **advan'tageable** (*rare*) profitable; convenient. — *adj* **advantageous** (*ad-vənt-ā'jəs*) of advantage; useful (with *to* and *for*). — *adv* **advantā'geously**. — *n* **advantā'geousness**. — **advantage rule** in games, a rule under which an infringement and its penalty are overlooked when this is to the advantage of the non-offending side; **advantage server** or **advantage striker** (*tennis*, etc) the server or striker who has gained the first point after deuce. — **have the advantage of** to recognize without being recognized; **take advantage of** to avail oneself of; to make undue use of an advantage over; **take at advantage** to use favourable conditions against; to take by surprise; **to advantage** so that the merits are clearly perceived. [Fr *avantage*, from *avant* before; see **advance**]

advection *ad-vek'shən*, (*meteorol*) *n* movement horizontally of air or atmospheric conditions. [L *advectio*, from *ad* to, and *vehere* to carry]

advene *ad-vēn'*, (*archaic*) *vi* to be superadded. [Ety as for **advent**]

advent *ad'vənt* or *-vent*, *n* a coming or arrival; (with *cap*) the first or the second coming of Christ; the period immediately before the Christian festival of the Nativity, including four Sundays. — *n* **Ad'ventist** someone who expects an imminent second coming of Christ; a millenarian, who expects a golden age after the second coming of Christ. — *adj* **adventive** (*-vent'*) adventitious; not permanently established (*bot*). — *n* a thing or person coming from outside. [L *advenire*, *adventum* to approach, happen, from *ad* to, and *venire* to come; *adventus* arrival]

adventitious *ad-vən-tish'əs*, *adj* accidental; additional; foreign; appearing casually; developed out of the usual order or place. — *adv* **adventi'tiously**. [L *adventīcius* extraneous]

adventure *əd-ven'chər*, *n* a chance (*obs*); a remarkable incident; an enterprise; trial of the issue (*obs*); risk; a commercial speculation; an exciting experience; the spirit of enterprise. — *vt* to risk; to dare; to venture; to put forward as a venture; to venture to say or utter. — *vi* to risk oneself; to take a risk. — *n* **adven'turer** someone who engages in hazardous enterprises; a soldier of fortune, or speculator; someone who pushes his or her fortune, *esp* by unscrupulous means: — *fem* **adven'turess** (chiefly in bad sense). — *adj* **adven'turesome** adventurous. — *n* **adven'turism** the practice of engaging in hazardous and ill-considered enterprises; in foreign policy, opportunism employed in the service of expansionism. — *n* and *adj* **adven'turist**. — *adj* **adventuris'tic**. — *adj* **adven'turous** enterprising; ready to incur risk. — *adv* **adven'turously**. — *n* **adven'turousness**. — **adventure playground** a playground with objects that can be used by children for building, to climb on, etc. [L *adventūrus* future perfect of *advenire* to approach or happen, from *ad* to, and *venire* to come; partly through Fr]

adverb *ad'vûrb*, *n* a word added to a verb, adjective or other adverb to express some modification of the meaning or an accompanying circumstance. — *adj* **adverb'ial** (*əd-*). — *vt* **adverb'ialize** or **-ise** to give the character of an adverb to. — *adv* **adverb'ially**. [L *adverbium*, from *ad* to, and *verbum* a word (transl Gr *epirrēma* literally, that which is said afterwards)]

ad verbum *ad vûr'bəm* or *wer'bŏŏm*, (*L*) word for word (literally, to a word).

adversaria *ad-vər-sā'ri-ə*, *n pl* miscellaneous notes; a commonplace book. [L *adversāria*]

adversarial *ad-vər-sār'i-əl*, *adj* combative; antagonistic; hostile, *esp* on party lines in politics. [Ety as for **adversary**]

adversary *ad'vər-sər-i*, *n* an opponent. — *adj* **adversative** (*əd-vûrs'*) denoting opposition, contrariety or variety. — *adj* **ad'verse** (*-vûrs*) contrary (with *to*); opposed; unfavourable; facing the main axis (*bot*). — *adv* **ad'versely**. — *n* **ad'verseness**. — *n* **advers'ity** adverse circumstances; misfortune; perversity (*Shakesp*). — **the Adversary** Satan. [L *adversus*, from *ad* to, and *vertere*, *versum* to turn]

advert[1] *ad-vûrt'*, *vi* (with *to*) to turn one's attention; to refer. — *n* **advert'ence** or **advert'ency** attention; heedfulness; regard. — *adj* **advert'ent** attentive; heedful. — *adv* **advert'ently**. [L *advertere*, from *ad* to, and *vertere* to turn]

advert[2]. See **advertise**.

advertise or (*esp US*) **advertize** *ad'vər-tīz* or *-tīz'*, formerly (*Shakesp*) *-vûrt'iz*, *vt* to inform or give notice to (*archaic*); to give notice of; to give public information about merits claimed for; to draw attention to; to offer for sale by public notice, printed or broadcast. — *vi* to issue advertisements; to ask (for) by means of public notice, eg in a newspaper. — *n* **advertisement** (*əd-vûr'tis-mənt* or *-tiz-*), or (*esp US*) **advertizement** (*-tiz-* or *-tīz'*) the act of advertising; a public notice, *usu* with the purpose of informing and/or changing public attitudes and behaviour (*colloq abbrev* **ad** or **ad'vert**); a short performance recorded for radio, TV, etc to advertise goods or services (*colloq abbrev* **ad** or **ad'vert**); news (*obs*). — *n* **advertiser** (*ad'*, or *-tīz'*) someone who advertises; often part of a newspaper's title. — *n* **ad'vertīsing**. — *adj* (*Shakesp*) attentive. — **ad'land** (*facetious*) the imaginary and *usu* idealized world portrayed in advertisements; the advertising industry; **ad-man** or **adman** (*ad'-man*) someone who takes part in advertising, *esp* advertising addressed to the admass; **ad'-mass** or **ad'mass** advertising intended to appeal to a mass public; the mass aimed at by such advertising; **advertising agency** an organization which helps a company to sell its products or services by undertaking market research, creating advertising material, and buying space in newspapers, TV sched-ules, etc. — **Advertising Standards Authority** (*abbrev* **ASA**) an independent group established in the UK in 1962 to ensure that the self-regulating system of advertising works effectively in the public interest. [Fr *avertir*, *avertiss-*, from L *advertere*; see **advert**[1]]

advertorial *ad-vər-tör'i-əl*, (*orig US*) *n* an advertisement presented as if it is editorial material. — Also *adj*. [*advert*isement and edit*orial*]

advew *ad-vū'*, (*Spenser*) *vt* to view. [L *ad* to, and **view**]

advice *əd-vīs'*, *n* counsel; information (*usu* in *pl*); formal official intelligence about anything; specially skilled opinion, eg of a physician or lawyer. — *adj* **advice'ful** (*obs*) (*Spenser* **avize'full**) watchful; attentive; skilled in advising. — **advice'-boat** (*obs*) a swift vessel employed in conveying despatches; **advice note** a document sent by the supplier of goods to the buyer advising that the goods ordered have been despatched. [OFr *advis* (Fr *avis*), from L *ad visum* according to what is seen or seems best]

advise *əd-vīz'*, *vt* to counsel; to recommend; to inform; to announce; to view (*obs*); to take thought of or consider (*obs*); to take to avizandum (*Scots law*). — *vi* to reflect or deliberate (*obs*); to consult (with). — *n* **advīsabil'ity**. — *adj* **advīs'able** to be recommended; expedient; open to advice. — *n* **advīs'ableness**. — *adv* **advīs'ably**. — *adj* **advīs'atory** (*rare*) advisory. — *adj* **advīsed'** having duly considered; considered; deliberate; apprised; amenable to advice. — *adv* **advīs'edly** (*-id-li*) after consideration; intentionally; wisely or prudently. — *n* **advīs'edness** deliberate consideration; prudent procedure. — *n* **advīse'ment** (*obs* or *archaic*) counsel, deliberation. — *n* **advīs'er** or **advīs'or** someone who advises; a teacher appointed by a British education authority to advise on the teaching and development of a particular subject. — *n* **advīs'ership**. — *n* **advīs'ing** (*Shakesp*) counsel, advice. — *n* **advīs'orate** the body of advisers appointed by an education authority. — *adj* **advīs'ory** having the attribute or function of advising. — **Advisory, Conciliation and Arbitration Service** see **ACAS**. [OFr *aviser*, and LL *advisāre*; cf **advice**]

ad vivum *ad vī'vum* or *wē'wŏŏm*, (*L*) to the life, lifelike.

advocaat *ad'vō-kät*, *n* a liqueur containing raw eggs and flavourings; a medicinal drink of eggs, rum or brandy, and lemon-juice. [Du *advokaatenborrel* advocate's dram, as a clearer of the throat]

advocate *ad'və-kit* or *ad'və-kāt*, *n* an intercessor or defender; someone who pleads the cause of another; in Scotland and some other countries, a person who is qualified to plead before the higher courts of law, a member of the Bar (corresponding to barrister in England); a person who recommends or urges something, eg a certain reform, method, etc; (with *cap*; New English Bible) the Holy Spirit; a solicitor (only in Aberdeen). — *vt* (*ad'və-kāt*) to plead in favour of; to recommend. — Also *vi* (with *for*). — *n* **ad'vocacy** (*-kə-si*) the function of an advocate; a pleading for; defence. — *n* **advocā'tion**. — *n* **ad'vocātor**. — *adj* **ad'vocātory**. — **advocate-dep'ute** a salaried Scottish law-officer appointed as public prosecutor by the **Lord Advocate**, the chief law-officer of the Crown and public prosecutor of crimes for Scotland. [OFr *avocat* and L *advocātus*, from *advocāre*, *-ātum* to call in, from *ad* to, and *vocāre* to call]

advocatus diaboli *ad-və-kā'təs dī-ab'ə-lī* or *ad-wō-kä'tŏŏs dē-ab'o-lē*, (*L*) *n* the devil's advocate (qv).

advoutrer *əd-vow'trər* and **advou'try**. *Obs* forms intermediate between **avoutrer** and **adulterer**, etc.

advowson *əd-vow'zən*, *n* the right of presentation to a church benefice. [OFr *avoeson*, from LL *advocātiō*, *-ōnis*, from L *advocātus*]

advt *abbrev*: advertisement.

adward (*Spenser*). Same as **award**.

adynamia *a-di-nā'mi-ə*, *n* helplessness, lack of strength accompanying a disease. — *adj* **adynamic** (*-am'*) without strength; characterized by the absence of force (*phys*). [Gr *a-* (privative), and *dynamis* strength]

adytum *ad'i-təm*, *n* the most sacred part of a temple; the chancel of a church: — *pl* **ad'yta**. [Latinized from Gr *adyton*, from *a-* (privative), and *dyein* to enter]

adze or (*US*) **adz** *adz*, *n* a cutting tool with an arched blade which is set at right angles to the handle. [OE *adesa*]

adzuki bean *ad-zŏŏ'ki bēn*, *n* a type of kidney bean grown *esp* in China and Japan. — Also **adsuki bean** (*ad-sŏŏ'ki*) and **aduki bean** (*a-dŏŏ'ki*). [Jap *azuki*]

AE *abbrev*: Air Efficiency Award.

ae *ā*, *yā* or *ye*, (*Scot*) *adj* one; very or same. — *adj* **ae'fald**, **ae'fauld**, **ā'fald** or **a'fawld** one-fold or single; single-minded; faithful; simple; sincere; honest. [Scots form of OE *ān* one, used attributively]

ae. or **aet.** *abbrev*: *aetatis* (*L*), of his or her age, aged (so many years).

AEA *abbrev*: Atomic Energy Authority.

AEB *abbrev*: Associated Examining Board.

AEC (*US*) *abbrev*: Atomic Energy Commission.

aecidium *ə-sid'i-əm* or **aecium** (*ē'si-əm*), (*bot*) *n* a cup-shaped fructification in rust fungi: — *pl* **aecid'ia** and **aec'iá**. — *n* **aecid'iospore** or **aec'iospore** spore produced in it. [Gr (dimin of) *aikiā* injury]

aedes *ā-ē'dēz*, *n* a member of the *Aedes* genus of mosquitoes, which includes *Aedes aegypti*, the species that carries yellow fever and dengue fever. [Gr *aedes* distasteful]

aedile *ē'dīl*, *n* a magistrate in ancient Rome who had the charge of public buildings, games, markets, police, etc. — *n* **ae'dileship**. [L *aedīlis*, from *aedēs*, *-is* a building]

aefald, etc. See **ae**.

aegirine *ē'jir-ēn* or **aegirite** *ē'jir-īt*, (*mineralogy*) *n* a green pleochroic pyroxene. [*Ægir* Norse sea-god or giant]

aegis *ē'jis*, *n* protection; patronage. [Gr *aigis* in Gr mythology a shield belonging to Zeus or to Pallas]

aeglogue *ēg'log*, (*archaic*) *n* an eclogue (qv). [From the mistaken belief that the word meant goat-herd discourse, from Gr *aix*, *aigos* goat, and *logos* discourse]

aegrotat *ē-grō'tat* (*archaic*) or *ē'*, *n* in universities, a medical certificate of illness, or a degree granted when illness has prevented the taking of examinations, etc. [L *aegrōtat* he or she is sick, 3rd pers sing present indicative of *aegrōtāre*, from *aeger* sick]

Aegypt. An archaic spelling of **Egypt**.

AEI *abbrev*: Associated Electrical Industries.

AELTC *abbrev*: All England Lawn Tennis Club.

aeluro-, **aelur-**. See **ailur(o)-**.

aemule *ē'mūl*, (*Spenser*) *vt* to emulate. [L *aemulārī*]

Aeneid *ē'ni-id* or *ə-nē'id*, *n* a Latin epic poem written by Virgil, the hero of which is Aeneas. [L *Aenēis*, *-idos*]

Aeneolithic *ā-ē-ni-ō-lith'ik*, *adj* belonging to a transitional stage at the end of the Neolithic age, when copper was already in use. — *adj* **aeneous** *ī'ni-əs* (*rare*) of a shining bronze colour. [L *aēneus* brazen, and Gr *lithos* stone]

Aeolian *ē-ō'li-ən*, *adj* of Aeolis or Aeolia, in NW Asia Minor, or its ancient Greek colonists. — *n* an Aeolian Greek. — *adj* **Aeolic** (*-ol'ik*) the Greek dialect of the Aeolians. — **Aeolian mode** in ancient Greek music, the same as the Hypodorian or Hyperphrygian; in old church music, the authentic (qv) mode with A for its final.

aeolian *ē-ō'li-ən*, *adj* pertaining to, acted on by, or due to the agency of, the wind; aerial. — **aeolian deposits** (*geol*) sediments deposited by wind, as desert sands, loess, etc; **aeolian** (or **Aeolian**) **harp** a sound-box with strings tuned in unison, sounding harmonics in a current of air. [L *Aeolus*, from Gr *Aiolos* god of the winds]

aeolipile or **aeolipyle** *ē'əl-i-pīl* or *ē-ol'i-pīl*, *n* a hollow ball turned by the escape of steam through valves set at a tangent. [L *Aeolus* god of the winds, and *pila* ball; or Gr *Aiolou pylai* Gates of Aeolus]

aeolotropy *ē-əl-ot'rə-pi*, *n* variation in physical properties according to direction. — *adj* **aeolotrop'ic**. [Gr *aiolos* changeful, and *tropē* a turn]

aeon or **eon** *ē'on*, *n* a vast age; eternity; the largest, or a very large division of geological time; in Gnosticism, a power emanating from the supreme deity, with its share in the creation and government of the universe. — *adj* **aeō'nian** eternal. [L *aeon*, from Gr *aiōn*]

Aepyornis *ē-pi-ör'nis*, *n* a gigantic Recent fossil wingless bird of Madagascar. [Gr *aipys* tall, and *ornis* bird]

aequo animo *ē-* or *ī-kwō an'i-mō*, (*L*) with an equable mind.

aerate *ā'ər-āt*, *vt* to put air into; to charge with air or with carbon dioxide or other gas (as in the production of **aerated waters**); to excite or perturb (*colloq*). — *n* **aerā'tion** exposure to the action of air; mixing or saturating with air or other gas; oxygenation of the blood by respiration. — *n* **ā'erātor** an apparatus for the purpose of aeration. — **aerated concrete** lightweight concrete made by a process which traps gas bubbles in the mix; **aerating root** a root that rises erect into the air, a breathing organ in mud plants. [L *āēr* air]

AERE *abbrev*: Atomic Energy Research Establishment.

aerenchyma *ā(-ə)r-eng'ki-mə*, (*bot*) *n* respiratory tissue. — *adj* **aerenchymatous** (*-kī'*). [Gr *āēr* air, *en* in, and *chyma* that which is poured]

aerial *ā-ē'ri-əl*, also *-er'*, *adj* of, in or belonging to the air; airy; unreal; lofty; (for the following meanings *usu* *ā'(ə-)ri-əl*) atmospheric; elevated; performed high above the ground, eg *aerial acrobatics*; connected with aircraft, eg used in or against aircraft; using aircraft (eg *aerial support*, *aerial reconnaissance* or *aerial warfare*); carried out from aircraft; growing in air (*biol*). — *n* (always *ā'(ə-)ri-əl*) a wire, rod, etc exposed to receive or emit electromagnetic waves; an antenna. — *n* **aer'ialist** someone who performs on the high wire or trapeze. — *n* **aeriality** (*-al'i-ti*). — *adv* **aer'ially**. — **aerial railway** or **ropeway** one for overhead conveyance; **aerial surveying** surveying by photographs taken from the air. [L *āerius*, from *āēr* air]

aerie[1]. See **eyrie**.

aerie[2]. See **aery**[1].

aeriform *ā'(ə)r-i-förm*, *adj* gaseous; unreal. [L *āēr* air, and *fōrma* form]

aero- *ā'(ə)r-ō-*, *combining form* denoting air. — *n* used as *adj* **ae'ro** of or relating to aircraft or aeronautics. — *n sing* **aerobat'ics** (Gr *bateein* to tread) the art of performing stunts in the air. — *n pl* aerial acrobatics. — *n* **a'erobe** (Gr *bios* life) an organism that requires free oxygen for respiration. — *adj* **aerobic** (*-ōb'* or *-ob'*) requiring free oxygen for respiration; biochemical change, eg effected by aerobes; involving the activity of aerobes; of or relating to aerobics. — *adv* **aerob'ically**. — *n sing* **aerob'ics** exercising by means of such rhythmic activities as walking, swimming, cycling, etc in order to improve physical fitness through increased oxygen consumption; a system intended to increase fitness and improve body-shape, consisting of fast, repeated and strenuous gymnastic exercises (also **Aerobics**®). — *adj* **aerobiolog'ical** (*-bī-ō-loj'*). — *adv* **aerobiolog'ically**. — *n* **aerobiol'ogist**. — *n* **aerobiol'ogy** the study of airborne micro-organisms. — *n* **aerobī'ont** an aerobe. — *n* **aerobīō'sis** life in the presence of oxygen. — *adj* **aerobiotic** (*-ot'ik*). — *adv* **aerobiot'ically**. — *n* **a'erobomb** a bomb for dropping from aircraft. — *n* **a'erobraking** or **aerodynamic braking** the use of a planet's atmosphere to reduce the speed of space vehicles. — *n* **a'erobus** an airbus; a passenger helicopter. — *n* **a'erodart** an arrowheaded missile of steel dropped from aircraft in warfare. — *n* **a'erodrome** (Gr *dromos* running) an area, with its buildings, etc, used for the take-off and landing of aircraft; an early flying machine (*hist*). — *adj* **aerodynam'ic** or **aerodynam'ical** (Gr *dynamis* power). — *adv* **aerodynam'ically**. — *n* **aerodynam'icist** a person concerned with aerodynamics. — *n sing* **aerodynam'ics** the dynamics of gases; the science or study of the movement of bodies in a flow of air or gas. — *n* **a'erodyne** (*-dīn*) a heavier-than-air aircraft. — *adj* **aeroelas'tic** able to be deformed by aerodynamic forces. — *n* **aeroelastic'ian** a person who studies flutter and vibration in high-speed aircraft. — *n* **aeroem'bolism** an airman's condition similar to caisson disease, caused by rapid ascent to high altitudes. — *n* **a'ero-engine** an aircraft engine. — *n* **a'erofoil** a body (eg wing or tail plane) shaped so as to produce an aerodynamic reaction (lift) normal to its direction of motion, for a small resistance (drag) in that plane. — *n* **aerogen'erator** a generator driven by wind. — *n* **a'erogram** a message by wireless telegraphy; a message sent by telegram (or telephone) and aeroplane; an aerogramme; an aerograph record. — *n* **a'erogramme** or **a'érogramme** an air letter; a sheet of thin, *usu* blue paper, with postage stamp imprinted, to be folded and sent by airmail at a special low rate. — *n* **a'erograph** a meteorograph; an airborne automatic recording instrument. — *n* **aerog'raphy** meteorology. — *n* **aerohy'droplane** a winged hydroplane or flying-boat. — *n* **a'erolite** or **a'erolith** (Gr *lithos* a stone) a meteoric stone or meteorite. — *n* **aerolithol'ogy** the science of aerolites. — *adj* **aerolit'ic**. — *adj* **aerolog'ical**. — *n* **aerol'ogist**. — *n* **aerol'ogy** the branch of science that deals with the atmosphere. — *n* **a'eromancy** (Gr *manteiā* divination) divination by atmospheric phenomena; weather forecasting. — *n* **aerom'eter** an instrument for measuring the weight or density of air and gases. — *adj* **aeromet'ric**. — *n* **aerom'etry** pneumatics. — *n* **a'eromotor** an engine for aircraft. — *n* **a'eronaut** (Gr *nautēs* a sailor) a balloonist or airman. — *adj* **aeronaut'ic** or **aeronaut'ical**. — *adv* **aeronaut'ically**. — *n sing* **aeronaut'ics** the science or art of aerial travel. — *n* **aeroneuros'is** flight fatigue, a nervous disorder of airmen, with emotional and physical symptoms. — *n* **aeron'omist**. — *n* **aeron'omy** the science of the earth's atmosphere. — *n* **a'erophobe** a person suffering from aerophobia, *esp* as fear of flying. — *n* **aerophō'bia** (Gr *phobos* fear) morbid fear of draughts; (loosely) morbid fear of flying. — *adj* **aerophob'ic** (or *-fōb'*). — *n* **a'erophone** any wind-instrument. — *n* **a'erophyte** (Gr *phyton* a plant) an epiphyte (*bot* or *pathol*). — *n* **a'eroplane** any heavier-than-air power-driven flying-machine, with fixed wings; a small plane for aerostatic experiments (see **plane**[2]). — *n* **aeroplank'ton** minute organisms carried in the air. — *n* **a'eroshell** a form of parachute enabling a spacecraft to make a soft landing. — *n* **aerosid'erite** (Gr *sidēros* iron) an iron meteorite. — *n* **a'erosol** a colloidal system, such as a mist or a fog, in which the dispersion medium is a gas; a liquid, eg insecticide, in a container under pressure; the container. — *n* **a'erospace** the earth's atmosphere together with space beyond; the branch of technology or of industry concerned with the flight of spacecraft through this. — *adj* of or belonging to, or capable of operating in, air and/or space. — *n* **a'erostat** (Gr *statos* standing) a balloon or other aircraft lighter than air; a balloonist; an air sac (*zool*). — *adj* **aerostat'ic** or **aerostat'ical**. — *n sing* **aerostat'ics** the science of the equilibrium and pressure of air and other gases; the science or art of ballooning. — *n* **aerostation** (*-stā'shən*) ballooning. — *adj* **aerotac'tic** (Gr *taxis* arrangement; adj *taktikos*) pertaining to or showing aerotaxis. — *n* **aerotax'is** (*biol*) movement towards or from oxygen. — *n* **a'erotrain** a train driven by an aircraft engine, riding on a cushion of air. — *adj* **aerotrop'ic** (Gr *tropē* turning). — *n* **aerot'ropism** (*bot*) curvature in response to concentration of oxygen. — **aerodynamic braking** see **aerobraking** above; **aerospace-plane** an aircraft-like vehicle that can take off and land on runways, manoeuvre in the atmosphere, operate in space, and re-enter the atmosphere. [Gr *āēr* air]

aeruginous *ē-rōō'ji-nəs*, or *ī-rōō'jə-*, *adj* pertaining to or like copper-rust or verdigris. [L *aerūginōsus*, from *aerūgō* rust of copper, from *aes*, *aeris* brass or copper]

aery[1] or **aerie** *ā'(ə-)ri*, (*poetic*) *adj* aerial; incorporeal; spiritual; visionary. — **aerie light** (*Milton*) light as air. [L *āerius*; see **aerial**]

aery[2]. Same as **eyrie**.

aes alienum *ēz al-i-ēn'əm* or *īs al-i-ān'ŏom*, (*L*) *n* debt, (literally) another's copper or brass.

æsc *ash, n* the rune (ᚠ) for a, used in OE for æ; the ligature æ used in OE for the same sound (that of *a* in Mod Eng RP *cat*). [OE *æsc* ashtree, the name of the rune]
Aeschna *esk'nə, n* a genus of large, *usu* colourful dragonflies.
Aesculapian *ēs-kū-lā'pi-ən,* or *es-, adj* to do with or relating to the art of healing. — Also **Escūla'pian**. [L *Aesculāpius*, Gr *Asklēpios*, the god of healing]
Aesculus *ēs'kū-ləs, n* the horse-chestnut genus of Hippocastanaceae. — *n* **aes'cūlin** a glucoside in horse-chestnut bark. [L *aesculus* a species of oak]
aesir. See **as**[2].
aesthesia or (*US*) **esthesia** *es-thēz'i-ə,* or *ēs-,* or **aesthesis** *-thē'sis, n* feeling; sensitivity. — *n* **aesthēs'iogen** something producing sensation, *esp* a stimulus or suggestion producing a sensory effect on a subject under hypnosis. — *adj* **aesthēsiogen'ic**. [Gr *aisthesis*, from *aisthanesthai* to feel or perceive]
aesthete or (*US*) **esthete**, *es'thēt* or *ēs'thēt, n* a professed disciple of aestheticism; a person who affects an extravagant love of art. — *adj* **aesthetic** (*es-thet'ik, is-* or *ēs-*) relating to possessing, or pretending to possess, a sense of beauty; artistic or affecting to be artistic; relating to perception by the senses (*obs*). — *adj* **aesthet'ical** of or relating to aesthetics. — *adv* **aesthet'ically**. — *n* **aesthetician** (*-tish'ən*) someone devoted to or knowledgeable or skilled in aesthetics; a beautician (*US*). — *n* **aesthet'icism** the principles of aesthetics; the cult of the beautiful, applied *esp* to a late 19c movement to bring art into life, which developed into affectation. — *n* **aesthet'icist**. — *vt* **aesthet'icize** or **-ise** (*-sīz*) to make aesthetic. — *n sing* **aesthet'ics** the principles of taste and art; the philosophy of the fine arts. [Gr *aisthētikos* perceptive, from *aisthanesthai* to feel or perceive]
aestival or *US* **estival** *ēs-tī'vəl,* or *es-, adj* of summer. — *vi* **aes'tivate** or (*US*) **es'tivate** (*-ti-vāt*) to pass the summer, *esp* (*usu* of animals and insects) in a state of torpor. — *n* **aestivā'tion** or (*US*) **estiva'tion** a spending of the summer; manner of folding in the flower-bud (*bot*); arrangement of foliage leaves relative to one another in the bud (*bot*); dormancy during the dry season (*zool* and *bot*). [L *aestīvus, aestīvālis* relating to summer, and *aestīvāre* to pass the summer, from *aestās* summer]
aes triplex *ēz trī'pleks* or *īs trip'leks,* (*L*) *n* a strong defence, (literally) triple brass.
aet. See **ae**.
aet *abbrev*: after extra time.
aetatis suae *ē-tat'is sū'ē* or *ī-tät'is sōō'ī,* (*L*) of his or her age.
aether *ē'thər, n.* Same as **ether** (but not generally used in the chemical sense).
Aethiopian. See **Ethiopian**.
aethrioscope *ē'thri-ō-skōp, n* an instrument for measuring the minute variations of temperature due to the condition of the sky. [Gr *aithriā* the open sky, and *skopeein* to look at]
aetiology or *US* **etiology** *ē-ti-ol'ə-ji, n* the science or philosophy of causation; an inquiry into the origin or causes of anything; the medical study of the causation of disease. — *adj* **aetiolog'ical**. [Gr *aitiologiā*, from *aitiā* cause, and *logos* discourse]
Aetnean. See **etna**.
AEU *abbrev*: Amalgamated Engineering Union.
AEW *abbrev*: airborne early warning.
AF *abbrev*: Admiral of the Fleet; Anglo-French; Associate Fellow; audio frequency.
AFA *abbrev*: Amateur Football Association.
afald, afawld. See **ae**[1].
afar *ə-fär', adv* from a far distance (*usu, from afar*); at or to a distance (*usu, afar off*). [**of** and **on**, with **far**]
afara *ə-fär'ə, n* a type of W African tree having a light-coloured, straight-grained wood. [Yoruba]
AFC *abbrev*: Air Force Cross; Association Football Club.
afear, affear or **affeare** *ə-fēr',* (*Spenser*) *vt* to frighten. — *adj* **afeard'** or **affeard'** (*Shakesp*) afraid. [Pfx *a-* (intensive), and OE *fǣran* to frighten]
affable *af'ə-bl, adj* easy to speak to; courteous, *esp* towards inferiors; pleasant or friendly. — *n* **affabil'ity**. — *adv* **aff'ably**. [Fr, from L *affābilis*, from *affārī* to speak to, from *ad* to, and *fārī* to speak]
affair *ə-fār', n* something which is to be done; business; any matter, occurrence, etc; a minor battle; a matter of intimate personal concern; a thing (*colloq*); a romantic intrigue, love affair, affaire; (in *pl*) transactions in general; (in *pl*) public concerns. [OFr *afaire* (Fr *affaire*), from *à* and *faire*, from L *ad* to, and *facere* to do; cf **ado**]
affaire *a-fer,* (*Fr*) *n* liaison or intrigue; (*usu* with name of chief person involved) an episode or incident arousing speculation and scandal. — **affaire** or **affaire d'amour** (*a-fer dam-ōōr*) a love affair; **affaire de cœur** (*a-fer də kœr*) affair of the heart; **affaire d'honneur** (*a-fer do-nœr*) affair of honour (a duel).
affear, affeare, affeard or **affear'd**. See **afear, affeer**.
affect[1] *ə-fekt', vt* to act upon; to infect or attack as or like a disease; to influence; to move the feelings of; (in *passive* only) to assign or allot. — *n* disposition of body or mind (*obs*); affection or love (*obs*); (*af'ekt*) the emotion that lies behind action (*psychol*); pleasantness or unpleasantness of, or complex of ideas involved in, an emotional state (*psychol*). — *adj* **affect'ed**. — *adj* **affect'ing** having power to move the emotions. — *adv* **affect'ingly**. — *adj* **affect'ive** of, arising from or influencing emotion. — *adv* **affect'ively**. — *n* **affectivity** (*af-ek-tiv'i-ti*). — *adj* **affect'less**. — *n* **affect'lessness**. — **affective disorders** (*psychol*) a group of disorders whose primary characteristic is a disturbance of mood. [L *afficere, affectum*, from *ad* to, and *facere* to do]
affect[2] *ə-fekt', vt* to aim at or aspire to (*obs*); to have a liking for (*archaic*); to make a show of preferring; to do, wear or inhabit by preference; to assume; to assume the character of; to make a show or pretence of. — *vi* to incline or tend. — *n* **affectā'tion** (*af-ik-*) assumption of or striving after an appearance of what is not natural or real; pretence. — *adj* **affect'ed** full of affectation; feigned. — *adv* **affect'edly**. — *n* **affect'edness**. — *n* **affect'er**. [L *affectāre, -ātum*, frequentative of *afficere*; see **affect**[1] above]
affection *ə-fek'shən, n* the act of influencing; emotion; disposition; inclination; love; attachment; affectation (*Shakesp*); an attribute or property; a disease. — *vt* (*rare*) to love. — *adj* **affec'tional**. — *adj* **affec'tionate** full of affection; loving; eager, passionate or well inclined (*obs*). — *adv* **affec'tionately**. — *n* **affec'tionateness**. — *adj* **affec'tioned** disposed (*Bible*); full of affectation (*Shakesp*). [L *affectiō, -ōnis*]
affeer *ə-fēr',* (*archaic*) *vt* to assess; to reduce to a certain fixed sum. — *adj* **affeered'** (*Shakesp* **affear'd'**) confirmed. — *n* **affeer'ment**. [OFr *affeurer*, from LL *afforāre*, from L *ad* to, and *forum* a market]
affenpinscher *af'en-pinsh-ər, n* a small dog related to the Brussels griffon, having tufts of hair on the face. [Ger, from *Affe* monkey, and *Pinscher* terrier]
afferent *af'ər-ənt,* (*physiol*) *adj* bringing inwards, as the nerves that convey impulses to the central nervous system. [L *afferēns, -entis*, from *ad* to, and *ferre* to carry]
affettuoso *äf-fet-tōō-ō'sō,* (*music*) *adj* tender. — *adv* tenderly. — Also *n.* [Ital]
affiance *ə-fī'əns, vt* to betroth. — *n* faith pledged (*obs*); contract of marriage (*archaic*); trust (*obs*); affinity (*obs*). — *adj* **affi'anced** betrothed. [OFr *afiance*; see **affy**]
affiche *af-ēsh,* (*Fr*) *n* notice or placard.
afficionado. See under **aficionado**.
affidavit *af-i-dā'vit, n* a written declaration on oath. [LL *affīdāvit*, 3rd pers sing perf of *affīdāre* to pledge one's faith; see **affy**]
affied. See **affy**.
affiliate *ə-fil'i-āt, vt* to adopt or attach as a member or branch; to attribute the paternity of; to assign the

origin of. — *vi* to become closely connected, to associate; to fraternize. — *n* (*ə-fil'i-ət*) an affiliated person, an associate; a branch, unit, or subsidiary of an organization. — *adj* **affil'iable**. — *n* **affilia'tion**. — **affiliation order** a court order requiring that the putative father of an illegitimate child should contribute to its support. [L *affīliātus* adopted, from *ad* to, and *fīlius* a son]

affine *a-fīn'*, or *a'*, *n* a relation, *esp* by marriage. — *adj* related; preserving finiteness (*math*, as in **affine geometry** the geometry associated with affine transformations, and **affine transformation** the composition of a reversible linear mapping followed by a translation). — *adj* **affined'** related; bound by some tie. [OFr *affin*, from L *affīnis* neighbouring, from *ad* to or at, and *fīnis* a boundary]

affinity *ə-fin'i-ti*, *n* nearness (*obs*); relationship by marriage; relationship of sponsor and godchild; natural or fundamental relationship, *esp* common origin; attraction; a spiritual attraction between two people; a person whose attraction for another is supposed to be of this kind; the extent to which a compound of a functional group is reactive with a given reagent (*chem*); a measure of the strength of interaction between antigen and antibody or between a receptor and its ligand (*immunol*). — *adj* **affin'itive**. — **affinity card** a credit card linked to a particular charity, to which the issuing bank pays a fee on issue and subsequent donations according to the credit level. [Ety as for **affine**]

affirm *ə-fûrm'*, *vt* to assert confidently or positively; to ratify (a judgement); to confirm or stand by (one's own statement); to declare one's commitment to; to state in the affirmative (*logic*); to declare formally, without an oath (*law*). — *vi* to make an affirmation. — *adj* **affirm'able**. — *n* **affirm'ance** affirmation; assertion; confirmation. — *adj* and *n* **affirm'ant**. — *n* **affirmation** (*af-ər-mā'shən*, or *-ûr-*) assertion; something which is affirmed; a positive judgement or proposition; a solemn declaration in lieu of an oath. — *adj* **affirm'ative** affirming or asserting; positive, not negative; (of an answer, etc) agreeing, saying 'yes'; dogmatic. — *n* the affirmative mode; an affirmative word, proposition or utterance. — *adv* **affirm'atively**. — *adj* **affirm'atory**. — *n* **affirm'er**. — *adv* **affirm'ingly**. — **affirmative action** (chiefly *US*) positive steps taken to ensure that minority groups and women are not discriminated against, *esp* as regards employment. [OFr *afermer*, from L *affirmāre*, from *ad* to, and *firmus* firm]

affix *ə-fiks'*, *vt* to fix to something; to subjoin; to attach; to append; to add (to something). — *n* (*af'iks*) an addition to a root, stem, or word, whether *prefix*, *suffix* or *infix*, to produce a derivative or an inflected form (*gram*); any appendage or addition. [L *affīgere*, *-fīxum*, from *ad* to, and *fīgere* to fix]

afflated *ə-flā'tid*, *adj* inspired. — *n* **afflā'tion** or **afflā'tus** inspiration (often divine). [L *afflāre*, *-flātum* (verb), and *afflātus*, *-ūs* (noun), from *ad* to, and *flāre* to breathe]

afflict *ə-flikt'*, *vt* to humble (*Bible*); to distress severely; to harass; to vex. — *adj* **afflict'ed** harassed by disease of body or mind (with *with*); suffering; overthrown (*Milton*); humble (*Spenser*). — *n* and *adj* **afflict'ing** distressing. — *n* **afflic'tion** state or cause of severe distress. — *adj* **afflict'ive** causing distress. [L *afflīgere*, *-flīctum* to overthrow, cast down, from *ad* to, and *flīgere* to dash to the ground]

affluent *af'lo͞o-ənt*, *adj* inflowing; abounding; wealthy. — *n* an inflowing stream. — *n* **aff'luence** inflow; abundance; wealth. — *adv* **aff'luently**. — *n* **aff'luentness**. — *n* **aff'lux** or **affluxion** (*ə-fluk'shən*) an inflow, an accession. — **affluent society** a society in which the ordinary person can afford many things once regarded as luxuries. [L *affluere*, from *ad* to, and *fluere*, *fluxum* to flow]

afforce *ə-förs'*, (*law*) *vt* to strengthen (eg a jury by addition of skilled people). — *n* **afforce'ment**. [OFr *aforcer*, from LL *exfortiāre*, from L *ex* out, and *fortis* strong]

afford *ə-förd'*, *vt* to yield, give or provide; to bear the expense, or disadvantage of (having the necessary money or other resources, or security of position); (*Spenser* **affoord**) to consent. — *n* **affordabil'ity**. — *adj* **afford'able**. [ME *aforthen*, from OE *geforthian* to further or cause to come forth]

afforest *a-* or *ə-for'ist*, *vt* to cover with forest; to convert into hunting ground (*hist*). — *adj* **affor'estable**. — *n* **afforestā'tion**. [LL *afforēstāre*, from L *ad* to, and LL *forēsta* forest]

affranchise *a-* or *ə-fran'chīz*, or *-shīz*, *vt* to free from slavery, or from some obligation. — *n* **affran'chisement** (*-chiz-* or *-shiz-*). [OFr *afranchir*, *afranchiss-*, from *à* to, and *franchir* to free, from *franc* free]

affrap *a-frap'*, (*Spenser*) *vt* and *vi* to strike. [Ital *affrappare*, from pfx *af-* (L *ad* to), and *frappare* to strike; or directly from **frap**]

affray *ə-frā'*, *n* a disturbance or breach of the peace; a brawl, fight or fray; fear (*Spenser*). — *vt* (*archaic*) to disturb or startle; to frighten; to scare away. — *adj* (*archaic*) **affrayed'** alarmed (now **afraid**). [OFr *afrayer*, *esfreer* (Fr *effrayer*), from LL *exfridāre* to break the king's peace, from L *ex* out of, and OHGer *fridu* (Ger *Friede*) peace]

affreightment *ə-frāt'mənt*, *n* the hiring of a vessel; the contract governing such a hire. [Fr *affrètement* (formerly *affrétement*), remodelled on *freight*]

affrended *a-frend'id*, (*Spenser*) *adj* reconciled. [**friend**]

affret *a-fret'*, (*Spenser*) *n* a furious onset. [Prob from Ital *affrettare* to hasten]

affricate *af'ri-kət* or *-kāt*, (*phonetics*) *n* a consonant sound beginning as a plosive and passing into the corresponding fricative. — *n* **affric'ative** affricate. — Also *adj*. — *adj* **aff'ricāted**. — *n* **affricā'tion**. [L *affricāre*, *-ātum*, to rub against, from *ad* to, and *fricāre* to rub]

affright *ə-frīt*, *vt* to frighten. — *n* sudden terror. — *adj* **affright'ed**. — *adv* **affright'edly**. — *vt* **affright'en**. — *adj* **affright'ened**. — *adj* **affright'ful** (*archaic*) frightful. — *n* **affright'ment** sudden fear. [OE *āfyrhtan*, from *ā-*, (intensive), and *fyrhtan* to frighten]

affront *ə-frunt'*, *vt* to meet face to face; to face; to confront; to throw oneself in the way of (*Shakesp*); to insult to one's face. — *n* a contemptuous treatment; an open insult; indignity. — *adj* **affronté**, **affrontée** or **affrontee** (*ä-fron'tā* or *ə-frun'tē*) facing each other; also looking frontwise, or towards the beholder (*heraldry*). — *adj* **affront'ed** insulted or offended, *esp* in public. — *n* and *adj* **affront'ing**. — *adv* **affront'ingly**. — *adj* **affront'ive**. [OFr *afronter* to slap on the forehead, from LL *affrontāre*, from L *ad* to, and *frōns*, *frontis* forehead]

affusion *ə-fū'zhən*, *n* pouring on (*esp* in baptism). [L *affūsiō*, *-ōnis*, from *affundere*, from *ad* to, and *fundere*, *fūsum* to pour]

affy *ə-fī'*, (*obs*) *vt* to trust; to assure on one's faith; to betroth; to repose or put (trust). — *vi* to trust or confide: — *pr p* **affy'ing**; *pa t* and *pa p* **affied'** (*Spenser* **affyde'**). [OFr *afier*, from LL *affīdāre*, from L *ad* to, and *fidēs* faith; cf **affiance**]

AFG *abbrev*: Afghanistan (IVR).

Afghan *af'gan*, *n* a native or citizen, or the language (Pashto), of Afghanistan; (without *cap*) a heavy knitted or crocheted woollen blanket or shawl. — **Afghan coat** a coat made of sheepskin and often embroidered, as *orig* worn in Afghanistan; **Afghan hound** an ancient hunting and sheep dog of Afghanistan and N India, kept as a pet in the West.

aficionado *a-fish-yo-nä'dō* or *a-fē-thyō-nä'dhō*, *n* an amateur; an ardent follower, fan: — *pl* **aficiona'dos**. — Also **afficiona'do**: — *pl* **afficiona'dos**. [Sp]

afield *ə-fēld'*, *adv* to, in, or on the field; to or at a distance. [**a-**[1]]

afire *ə-fīr'*, *adj* and *adv* on fire; in a state of inflammation. [**a-**[1]]

aflaj. See **falaj**.
aflame *ə-flām'*, *adj* and *adv* in a flaming or glowing state. [**a-**[1]]
aflatoxin *af-lə-toks'in*, *n* a (possibly carcinogenic) toxin produced in foodstuffs by species of the mould Aspergillus. [*A*spergillus *fla*vus, from L *aspergere* to sprinkle, and *flavus* yellow, and **toxin**]
AFL-CIO *abbrev*: American Federation of Labor and Congress of Industrial Organizations.
afloat *ə-flōt'*, *adv* and *adj* in a floating state; at sea; unfixed; in circulation. [**a-**[1]]
aflutter *ə-flut'ər*, *adv* in a flutter. [**a-**[1]]
AFM *abbrev*: Air Force Medal; audio frequency modulation.
à fond *a fɔ̃*, (*Fr*) fundamentally; thoroughly.
afoot *ə-fo͝ot'*, *adv* and *adj* on foot; astir; actively in existence. [**a-**[1]]
afore *ə-fōr'*, *prep* (*archaic* or *dialect*) before. — *combining form* denoting in front of or before. — *adv* beforehand or previously. — *adv* **afore'hand** beforehand; before the regular time for accomplishment; in advance. — *adj* **afore'mentioned** previously mentioned, aforesaid. — *adj* **afore'said** said or named before. — *adj* **afore'-thought** (*usu* after *n*) thought of or meditated before; premeditated. — *n* premeditation. — *adv* **afore'time** in former or past times. [OE *onforan*, from *on* and *foran*; see **before**]
a fortiori *ā fōr-ti-ōr'ī*, (or *-shi*) or *ä fōr-ti-ōr'ē*, (*L*) with stronger reason.
afoul *ə-fowl'*, *adj* and *adv* in entanglement; in collision (with *of*). [**a-**[1]]
AFP *abbrev*: Agence France Presse.
Afr. *abbrev*: Africa; African.
afraid *ə-frād'*, *adj* struck with fear, fearful (with *of*); timid; reluctantly inclined to think (that); regretfully admitting. [Pa p of **affray**]
afreet. See **afrit**.
afresh *ə-fresh'*, *adv* anew, once more. [Pfx *a-* of, and **fresh**]
African *af'rik-ən*, *adj* of Africa. — *n* a native of Africa; a person of black race, *esp* one whose people live now, or lived recently, in Africa. — *n* **Af'ric** (*poetic*) Africa. — *adj* African. — *n* **African'der** a S African breed of cattle. — *n* **Af'ricanism** an African characteristic. — *n* **Af'ricanist** someone who is learned in matters relating to Africa. — *n* **Africanizā'tion** or **-s-**. — *vt* **Af'ricanize** or **-ise** to make African; to exclude people of other races from, replacing them with Africans. — Also *vi*. — *adj* **Af'ricanoid** of African type. — **Af'rican-American** a Black American; **African coast fever** see **East Coast fever**; **African mahogany** a W African hardwood, from the genus *Khaya*, which seasons easily; **African violet** (also without *cap*) a plant from tropical Africa (*Saintpaulia ionantha*), commonly with violet-coloured flowers but not related to the violet. [L *Africānus*]
Afrikaans *af-ri-käns'*, *n* one of two official languages of S Africa, having developed from 17c Dutch. — *n* **Afrikan'er** (formerly **African'er**, **African'der** or **Afrikan'der**) a person born in S Africa of white parents (*esp* of Dutch descent). — Also *adj*. — *n* **Afrika'nerdom** the Afrikaners in S Africa; their nationalistic feeling or political ascendancy. — **Afrikander Bond** a S African nationalist league (1881–1911). [Du, African]
afrit or **afreet** *ä-frēt'* or *af'rēt*, (*Ar mythol*) *n* an evil demon. [Ar *'ifrīt* a demon]
Afro *af'rō*, (*colloq*, sometimes without *cap*) *adj* short for African; (of a hairstyle) characterized by thick, bushy curls standing out from the head, as worn by some Africans or people of African descent (also *n*). — **Afro-** *combining form* denoting African. — *adj* **Afro-Amer'-ican** of or relating to Black American(s). — Also *n*. — *adj* **Afro-Asian** (*-āzh'yən*) of or consisting of Africans and Asians; of Asian origin but African citizenship; of mixed Asian and African blood; (of language) belonging to a group spoken in SW Asia and N Africa. — *adj* **Afro-Caribbē'an** of or relating to (the culture, music, dance, etc of) people of African descent in or from the Caribbean area. — *adj* **Afro-cen'tric** or **Afrocen'tric** in US education, etc, of or relating to *esp* teaching which emphasizes African history and culture, with the aim of providing Black American students, etc with a sense of cultural identity. — *n* **Afrocent'rism**. — *n* **Afro-jazz'** jazz showing evidence of influence of African music. — *n* **Afro-rock'** rock music showing evidence of influence of African music.
afront *ə-frunt'*, *adv* in front (*obs*); abreast (*Shakesp*). [**a-**[1]]
afrormosia *af-rör-mō'zi-ə*, *n* a very durable W African wood used as an alternative to teak.
aft *äft*, *adj* or *adv* behind; near or towards the stern of a vessel or aircraft: — *compar* **after** (qv); *superl* **aft'ermost** or **aft'most** (qqv). [OE *æftan*]
after *äf'tər*, *prep* and *adv* behind in place; later in time than; following in search of; in imitation of; in proportion to, or in agreement with; concerning; subsequent to or subsequently, afterwards; in the manner of, in imitation of; according to; in honour of; with the name, or a name derived from the name, of. — *adj* behind in place; later in time; more towards the stern (in this sense the *compar* of **aft**). — *conj* later than the time when. — *n pl* **af'terings** (*archaic* or *dialect*) the last milk drawn in milking a cow. — *n pl* **af'ters** (*colloq*) in a meal, the dessert or other course following a main course. — *adv* **af'terward** (chiefly *US*) or **af'terwards** at a later time; subsequently. — **af'terbirth** the placenta and membranes expelled from the uterus after a birth; a posthumous birth; **af'terburner** the device used in afterburning; **af'terburning** reheat, the use of a device to inject fuel into the hot exhaust gases of a turbojet in order to obtain increased thrust; **af'tercare** care subsequent to a period of treatment, corrective training, etc; after-sales service (qv). — Also *adj*. — **af'ter-clap** (*archaic*) an unexpected sequel, after an affair is supposed to be at an end; **af'ter-crop** a second crop from the same land in the same year; **af'ter-damp** chokedamp, arising in coal-mines after an explosion of firedamp; **af'terdeck** (*naut*) the deck behind a ship's bridge; **after-dinn'er** the time following dinner. — *adj* belonging to that time, *esp* before leaving the table. — **af'ter-effect** an effect that comes after an interval. — *vt* **aftereye'** (*Shakesp*) to gaze after. — **af'tergame** a second game played in the hope of reversing the issue of the first; means employed after the first turn of affairs; **af'terglow** a glow remaining after a light source has faded, *esp* that in the sky after sunset; **af'tergrass** the grass that grows after mowing or reaping; **af'tergrowth** a later growth; an aftermath; **af'ter-guard** (*naut*) the men on the quarterdeck and poop who work the after sails, many of them unskilled; hence a drudge or person with a menial job; a merchant ship's officers; **af'terheat** (*nuc eng*) the heat from fission products in a nuclear reactor after it has been shut down; **af'ter-image** an image that persists for a time after one looks at an object; **af'ter-life** a future life; later life; a life after death; **af'ter-light** the light of later knowledge; **af'termath** later consequences (of a particular incident or occurrence), *esp* if bad; a second mowing of grass in the same season. — *adj* **af'ter-mentioned** mentioned subsequently. — **afternoon'** the time between noon and evening. — Also *adj* **af'ternoon**. — **af'terpains** the pains after childbirth, as the uterus contracts; **af'terpiece** a minor piece after a play. — *adj* **af'tersales** after a sale has been completed, *usu* with reference to servicing the goods, installation, etc. — **aftersales service** service offered by a retailer to a customer following the purchase of goods, eg repair, provision of spare parts, advice on installation; **af'tershaft** a second shaft arising from the quill of a feather; **af'tershave** a lotion for men, for use after shaving; **af'tershock** one of several minor shocks following the main shock of an earthquake; **af'tersupper** time between supper and bedtime (*obs*); *prob* a dessert at the end of a supper, *poss* a rere-supper (*Shakesp*). — *adj* in the time after supper. — **af'terswarm** a second swarm or cast (qv) of

bees; **af'tertaste** a taste that remains or comes after eating or drinking. — *adj* **af'ter-tax** (of profit) remaining after (*esp* income) tax has been paid. — **af'terthought** a thought or thing thought of after the occasion; a later thought or reflection or modification; **af'tertime** later time; **af'terword** an epilogue; **af'terworld** the world inhabited by the souls of the dead. — **after a fashion** see under **fashion**; **after all** when everything is taken into account; in spite of everything. [OE *æfter*, in origin a comparative from *af* (*æf*) off, of which **aft** is orig a superlative, but itself compared *æfter*, *æfterra*, *æftemest*, and tending to be regarded as comparative of **aft**; see **of** and **off**]

aftermost *äf'tər-mōst* or *-məst* or **aftmost** *äft'*, *adj* (*superl* of **aft**) nearest the stern; hindmost. [OE *æftemest* a double superlative]

afterward, **afterwards**. See under **after**.

AG *abbrev*: Adjutant-General; *Aktiengesellschaft* (Ger), joint stock company; (or **A-G**) Attorney-General.

Ag (*chem*) *symbol*: silver. [L *argentum*]

aga or **agha** *ä'gə* or *ä-gä'*, *n* a Turkish commander or chief officer. — **Aga Khan** (*kän*) the head of the Ismaili Muslims. [Turk *aga*, *aghā*]

agaçant *a-ga-sã*, *fem* **agaçante** *-sãt*, (*Fr*) *adj* provoking or alluring. — *n* **agacerie** (*-s(ə-)rē*) allurement, coquetry.

Agadah, **Agadic**. See under **Haggada**.

again, *ə-gen'* or *ə-gān'*, *adv* once more; in return; in response or consequence; back; further; on the other hand; to the same amount in addition; at some future time (*dialect*). — *prep* (*dialect*) against. — **again and again** repeatedly. [OE *ongēan*, *ongegn*; Ger *entgegen*]

against *ə-genst'* or *ə-gānst'*, *prep* opposite to; in opposition or resistance to; in protection from; in or into contact or collision with or pressure upon; towards the time of (*obs*); in anticipation of; in contrast or comparison with; in exchange for; instead of. — *conj* in readiness for the time that. [**again**, with genitive ending *-es*, and *-t* as in **whilst**, **betwixt** and **amongst**]

agalactia *ag-ə-lak'shi-ə*, *n* failure to secrete milk. [Gr *a-* (privative), and *gala*, *galaktos* milk]

agalloch *ə-gal'ək*, *n* eaglewood. [Gr *agallochon*, a word of Eastern origin; see **eaglewood**]

agalmatolite *ag-al-mat'ə-līt*, *n* material of various kinds (steatite, pyrophyllite, etc) from which the Chinese carve figures. [Gr *agalma*, *-atos* a statue (of a god), and *lithos* stone]

Agama *ag'ə-mə*, *n* an Old World genus of thick-tongued lizards giving name to the family **Agamidae** (*a-gam'i-dē*). — *adj* and *n* **ag'amid** (a lizard) of this family. — *adj* and *n* **ag'amoid** (a lizard) having the features of an agamid. [Carib name of another lizard]

Agamemnon *a-ga-mem'non*, *n* the leader of the Greeks in the Trojan war, king of Mycenae; generic name for a king.

agami *ag'ə-mi*, *n* the golden-breasted trumpeter, a crane-like bird of S America. [Carib name]

agamic *a-gam'ik* or **agamous** *ag'ə-məs*, *adj* asexual; parthenogenetic; cryptogamous (*obs*). — *n* **agamogenesis** (*-jen'*) reproduction without sex, as in lower animals and in plants. [Gr *a-* (privative) and *gamos* marriage]

agamid, **agamoid**. See **Agama**.

agamous. See **agamic**.

Aganippe *ag-ə-nip'ē*, *n* a fountain on Mt Helicon, sacred to the Muses (*Gr mythol*); poetic inspiration. [Gr *Aganippē*]

agapanthus *a-gə-pan'thəs*, *n* any of several plants, with clusters of blue flowers, of the *Agapanthus* genus of lily native to S Africa. [Gr *agape* love, and *anthos* flower]

agape[1] *ag'ə-pē*, *n* selfless Christian love; the love of God for man; a feast in token and celebration of such love, modelled on that held by the early Christians at communion time, when contributions were made for the poor: — *pl* **ag'apae** (*-pē*). — *n* **Agapemone** (*-pēm'* or *-pem'ə-nē*) a religious community of men and women whose 'spiritual marriages' were in some cases not strictly spiritual, founded in 1849 at Spaxton, near Bridgwater; any similar community, *esp* with reference to its delinquencies. [Gr *agapē* love, and *monē* tarrying or abode]

agape[2] *ə-gāp'*, *adj* or *adv* with gaping mouth. [**a-**[1]]

agar *ā-gär*, or **a'gar-a'gar**, *n* a jelly prepared from seaweeds of various kinds used in bacteria-culture, medicine, glue-making, silk-dressing, and cooking; any of the seaweeds concerned. [Malay]

agaric *ag'ər-ik* or *əg-ar'ik*, *n* a fungus, properly one of the mushroom family, but loosely applied. — *adj* **agar'ic**. [Gr *agarikon*]

agast. See **aghast**.

agate[1] *ag'it* or *-āt*, *n* a banded variegated chalcedony; a marble used in games, made of this material or of variegated glass; a dwarfish person (as if a figure cut in agate) (*Shakesp*); ruby type (*printing*). — *n* **ag'atewear** a form of ceramic made to look like agate. [Fr, from Gr *achātēs*, said to be so called because first found near the river *Achates* in Sicily]

agate[2] *ə-gāt'*, (*archaic* or *dialect*) *adv* agoing, on the way; astir; afoot; astray. [**a-**[1] and **gate**[2]; a Northern word]

a'gate. See **a'**.

agathodaimon *a'ga-thō-dī'mon*, (*Gr*) *n* one's good genius.

à gauche *a gōsh*, (*Fr*) to the left; on the left.

agave *a-gā'vē*, *n* a plant of the aloe-like American genus *Agave* of amaryllids, in Mexico *usu* flowering about the seventh year, in hothouse conditions requiring 40–60 (popularly 100) years. — Also called *American aloe*, *maguey* and *century plant*. [L *Agāvē*, Gr *Agauē*, daughter of Cadmus, fem of *agauos* illustrious]

agaze *ə-gāz'*, (*archaic*) *adj* and *adv* at gaze or gazing. [**a-**[1]]

agazed *ə-gāzd'*, (*Shakesp*) *adj* struck with amazement. [Prob a variant of **aghast**]

age *āj*, *n* duration of life; the time during which a person or thing has lived or existed; the time of life reached; mature years; legal maturity; the time of being old; equivalence in development to the average of an actual age; a period of time; any great division of world, human, or individual history; a generation; a century; (*esp* in *pl*) a long time, however short (*colloq*). — *vi* to grow old; to develop the characteristics of old age. — *vt* to make to seem old or to be like the old; to mature: — *pr p* **aging** or **ageing** (*āj'ing*); *pa t* and *pa p* **aged** (*ājd*). — *adj* **aged** (*āj'id*) advanced in age, old; (*ājd*) of the age of. — *n pl* (*āj'id*; *usu* with *the*) old people. — *n* **agedness** (*āj'id-nis*) the condition of being aged. — *n* **ag'ing** or **age'ing** the process of growing old or developing qualities of the old; maturing; change in properties that occurs in certain metals at atmospheric temperature after heat treatment or cold working. — *n* **age'ism** discrimination on grounds of age. — *n* and *adj* **age'ist**. — *adj* **age'less** never growing old, perpetually young; timeless. — *adj* **age'long** lasting an age. — **age'-bracket** the people between particular ages, taken as a group; **age group** a group of people of a similar age. — *adj* **age-old'** very old, ancient. — **be** or **act your age**! don't be childish; **be ages with** (*Scot*) to be the same age as; **of age** old enough to be considered legally mature (with respect to voting, crime, contracts, marriage, etc); **over age** too old; **under age** too young; not yet of age. [OFr *aäge* (Fr *âge*), from L *aetās*, *-ātis*, for *aevitās*, from L *aevum* age]

agee. See **ajee**.

agelast *aj'i-last*, *n* a person who never laughs. — *adj* **agelas'tic**. [Gr *a-*(privative), and *gelaein* to laugh]

agen (*poetic*). Same as **again**.

agency. See **agent**.

agenda *ə-* or *a-jen'də*, *n pl* (often treated as *n sing*) (a list of) things to be done; a programme of business for discussion at a meeting. — **on the agenda** requiring attention. [L neuter pl of *agendus* to be done, gerundive of *agere* to do]

agene (® in US) *ā'jēn*, *n* nitrogen trichloride, formerly widely used as a whitening agent in flour.

agent *ā'jənt*, *n* a person or thing that acts or exerts power; any natural force acting on matter; a person (or company) authorized or delegated to transact business for another; a person who acts on behalf of another in effecting a legal relationship between that other person and a third party; a sales representative for a business; formerly, a bank manager; formerly, the representative of the government in a group of Indian states; a paid political party worker; a secret agent or spy. — *vt* to conduct as a law agent (*Scot*); to act as an agent to. — *adj* acting; of an agent. — *n* **agency** (*ā'jən-si*) the operation or action of an agent; instrumentality, operation; the office or business of an agent; such a business putting employers and those requiring employment in contact with each other (eg a recruitment agency or nursing agency); formerly, a group of Indian states assigned to an agent. — *adj* **agen'tial** (*-shəl*) pertaining to an agent or agency; agentive (*gram*). — *adj* **a'gentive** (*gram*) of an affix, etc, signifying the agent of a verb, eg the suffix *-er* in *speaker*; a grammatical case denoting this. — *n* **agentiv'ity**. — **agency nurse**, **secretary**, etc, one employed through an agency; **agency shop** a shop in which the union, *usu* by agreement with the management, represents all workers whether they are members of it or not; **agent-gen'eral** a representative in England of an Australian state or Canadian province: — *pl* **agents-gen'eral**; **agentive noun** (*gram*) or (*non-technical*) **agent noun** a noun denoting the person, machine, etc doing something, eg *writer*, *accelerator*; **Agent Orange** a defoliant containing dioxin. — **law agent** (*Scot*) a solicitor; any qualified legal practitioner other than an advocate. [L *agēns*, *-entis*, pr p of *agere* to do]

agent provocateur *a-zhã prō-vo-ka-tœr*, (*Fr*) *n* a person employed to lead others, by pretending sympathy with them, into committing unlawful acts.

ageratum *ā-jər-ā'təm*, *n* any plant of the tropical American genus *Ageratum*, having clumps of long-lasting purple flowers. [New L, ult from Gr *agēraton* something which does not grow old, from *a-* (privative) and *gērat-*, stem of *gēras* old age]

agger *aj'ər* or *ag'ər*, (*Rom hist*) *n* a mound, *esp* one of wood or earth for protection or other military purpose; any elevation, *esp* artificial. [L]

aggiornamento *a-jör-na-men'tō*, (*Ital*) *n* modernizing.

agglomerate *ə-glom'ər-āt*, *vt* to make into a ball; to collect into a mass. — *vi* to grow into a mass. — *adj* (*-rət* or *-rāt*) agglomerated; clustered; gathered in a head (*bot*). — *n* (*-rət* or *-rāt*) a volcanic rock consisting of irregular fragments. — *adj* **agglom'erated**. — *n* **agglomerā'tion**. — *adj* **agglom'erative**. [L *agglomerāre*, *-ātum*, from *ad* to, and *glomus*, *glomeris* a ball]

agglutinate *ə-gloo͞t'in-āt*, *vt* to glue together; to cause to stick together or clump. — *vi* to stick as if glued; to clump. — *adj* (*-nət* or *-nāt*) agglutinated. — *adj* **agglut'inable**. — *adj* **agglut'inant**. — *n* an agglutinating agent. — *n* **agglutinā'tion** the act of agglutinating; an agglutinated mass; the clumping of bacteria, blood corpuscles, protozoa, etc (*biol*); a type of word-formation process in which words are inflected by the addition of one or more meaningful elements to a stem, each of which elements expresses one single element of meaning (*linguistics*). — *adj* **agglut'inative** tending, or having power, to agglutinate. — *n* **agglut'inin** an antibody causing agglutination of bacteria, blood-corpuscles, etc. — *n* **agglut'inogen** the substance in bacteria or in blood cells that stimulates the formation of, and unites with, agglutinin. — **agglutinating** (or **agglutinative**) **languages** languages in which words are inflected by agglutination. [L *agglūtināre*, from *ad* to, and *glūten*, *-inis* glue]

aggrace *ə-grās'*, (*Spenser*) *vt* to grace; to favour: — *pa t* **aggraced'** or **agraste'**. — *n* kindness; favour. [**grace**, after Ital *aggratiare* (now *aggraziare*)]

aggrade *ə-grād'*, (*geol*) *vt* to raise the level of (a surface) through the deposition of detritus. — *vi* to build up in this way. — *n* **aggradation** (*ag-rəd-ā'shən*). [L *ad* to, and *gradus* a step, in imitation of **degrade**]

aggrandize or **-ise** *ə-gran'dīz*, or *ag'rən-*, *vt* to make or seem to make greater. — *n* **aggrandizement** or **-s-** (*əg-ran'diz-mənt*). [Fr *agrandir*, *agrandiss-*, from L *ad* to, and *grandis* large]

aggrate *ə-grāt'*, (*obs*) *vt* to gratify or please; to thank. [Ital *aggratare*, from L *ad* to, and *grātus* pleasing]

aggravate *ag'rə-vāt*, *vt* to make more grievous or worse; to irritate or annoy (*colloq*). — *adj* **agg'ravated** (*law*) of an offence, made more serious (eg by violence). — *adj* **agg'ravating**. — *adv* **agg'ravatingly**. — *n* **aggravā'tion**. [L *aggravāre*, *-ātus*, from *ad* to, and *gravis* heavy]

aggregate *ag'ri-gāt*, *vt* to collect into a mass or whole; to assemble; to add as a member to a society; to amount to (*colloq*). — *vi* to accumulate. — *adj* (*-gət* or *-gāt*) formed of parts that combine to make a whole; gathered into a mass or whole; formed from an apocarpous gynaeceum (*bot*); formed into a single mass or cluster (*bot*). — *n* (*-gət* or *-gāt*) an assemblage; a mass; a total; any material mixed with cement to form concrete; a collection of elements having a common property that identifies the collection (*math*). — *adv* **agg'regately**. — *n* **aggregā'tion**. — *adj* **agg'regātive**. [L *aggregāre*, *-ātum* to bring together, as a flock, from *ad* to, and *grex*, *gregis* a flock]

aggress *ə-gres'*, *vi* to make a first attack; to begin a quarrel; to intrude. — *n* **aggression** (*-gresh'ən*) a first act of hostility or injury; the use of armed force by a state against the sovereignty, territorial integrity or political independence of another state; self-assertiveness, either as a good characteristic or *usu* as a sign of emotional instability. — *adj* **aggress'ive** making the first attack, or prone to do so; discourteously hostile or self-assertive, now often contrasted with *assertive*; offensive as opposed to defensive; showing energy and initiative. — *adv* **aggress'ively**. — *n* **aggress'iveness**. — *n* **aggress'or** the person who or force which attacks first. [L *aggredī*, *-gressus*, from *ad* to, and *gradī* to step]

aggri or **aggry** *ag'ri*, *adj* applied to ancient W African variegated glass beads. [Origin unknown]

aggrieve *ə-grēv'*, *vt* to press heavily upon; to cause pain or injure; to distress. — *adj* **aggrieved'** injured or distressed; having a grievance. [OFr *agrever*, from L *ad* to, and *gravis* heavy]

aggro *ag'rō*, (*slang*) *n* aggressive behaviour or trouble-making, *esp* between gangs, racial groups, etc. [Short form of **aggravation**, also associated with **aggression**]

aggry. See **aggri**.

agha. See **aga**.

aghast, earlier (or eg *Milton*) **agast**, *ə-gäst'*, *adj* stupefied with horror. [Pa p of obs *agast*, from OE intensive pfx *ā-*, and *gǣstan* to terrify]

agila *ag'i-lä*, *n* eaglewood. [Port *águila* eaglewood, or Sp *águila* eagle; see **eaglewood**]

agile *aj'īl* or (*US*) *-əl*, *adj* nimble or active; quick-moving and supple. — *adv* **ag'ilely**. — *n* **agility** (*ə-jil'i-ti*) nimbleness; swiftness and suppleness. [Fr, from L *agilis*, from *agere* to do or act]

agin *ə-gin'*, *prep* (*dialect* or *facetious*) against. — *n* **aginn'er** (*colloq*) an opponent (eg of change); a rebel, a malcontent. [**again**]

agio *aj'(i-)ō*, or *āj'*, *n* the sum payable for the convenience of exchanging one kind of money for another, eg silver for gold, paper for metal; the difference in exchange between worn or debased coinage and coinage of full value; the amount of deviation from the fixed par of exchange between the currencies of two countries; the discount on a foreign bill of exchange; money-changing, agiotage: — *pl* **ag'ios**. — *n* **agiotage** (*aj'ə-tij*) speculative manoeuvres in stocks and shares; stock-jobbing; money-changing; agio. [The word used in Ital is *aggio*, a variant of *agio* convenience]

agist *ə-jist'*, *vt* to take in to graze for payment; to charge with a public burden. — *n* **agist'ment** the action of agisting; the price paid for cattle pasturing on the land; a burden or tax. — *n* **agist'or** or **agist'er** an officer in charge of cattle agisted. [OFr *agister*, from *à* (L *ad*) to, and *giste* resting-place, from *gésir*, from a frequentative of L *jacēre* to lie]

agitate *aj'i-tāt*, *vt* to keep moving; to stir violently; to disturb; to perturb; to excite; to discuss, or keep up the discussion of. — *vi* to stir up public feeling. — *adj* **ag'itāted**. — *adv* **ag'itātedly**. — *n* **agitā'tion**. — *adj* **ag'itātive**. — *n* **ag'itātor** an agent, *esp* for the private soldiers in the Parliamentary army (*hist*); a person who excites or keeps up a social or political agitation; an apparatus for stirring. [L *agitāre*, frequentative of *agere* to put in motion]

agitato *äj-it-ä'tō*, (*music*) *adj* agitated; restless and wild. — *adv* agitatedly. [Ital, from L *agitāre* to agitate]

agitprop *aj'it-prop*, *n* (often *cap*; also **ag'it-prop**) pro-communist agitation and propaganda; (loosely) any narrow political propaganda. — Also *adj*. [Russ *Agitpropbyuro* office of *agitatsiya* agitation and *propaganda*]

Aglaia *ä-glī'a*, *n* one of the Graces. [Gr *aglaiā* splendour, triumph]

agleam *ə-glēm'*, *adj* and *adv* gleaming. [**a-**[1]]

aglee. See **agley**.

aglet, aiglet *ag'lit* or *āg'lit* or **aiguillette** *ā-gwi-let'*, *n* the metal tag of a lace or string; an ornamental tag or other metal appendage; anything dangling; (*usu* **aiguillette**) a tagged point of braid hanging from the shoulder in some uniforms. — **aglet babie** (*Shakesp*) *prob* a small figure forming the tag of a lace. [Fr *aiguillette*, dimin of *aiguille* a needle, from L *acūcula* dimin of *acus* a needle]

agley or **aglee** *ə-glī'* or *ə-glē'*, (*Scot*) *adv* askew; awry. [**a-**[1], and Scot *gley* squint]

aglimmer *ə-glim'ər*, *adj* and *adv* in a glimmering state. [**a-**[1] and **glimmer**[1]]

aglitter *ə-glit'ər*, *adj* and *adv* in a glitter. [**a-**[1]]

aglow *ə-glō'*, *adj* and *adv* in a glow. [**a-**[1]]

AGM or **agm** *abbrev*: annual general meeting.

agma *ag'mə*, *n* (the phonetic symbol ŋ for) a velar nasal consonant, as the *ng* in *thing* or the *n* in *think*. — See also **eng**. [Gr, fragment, nasalized g]

agnail *ag'nāl*, *n* a torn shred of skin beside the nail. — Also **hangnail** (*hang'*). [OE *angnægl* a corn, from *ange, enge* compressed, painful, and *nægl* nail (for driving in), confused with *hang*, and (finger-)*nail*]

agname *ag'nām*, *n* a name over and above the ordinary name and surname. — *adj* **ag'named**. [**name**; after LL *agnōmen*]

agnate *ag'nāt*, *adj* related on the father's side or (*Roman law*) through a male ancestor; related generally; allied. — *n* a person related in this way. — *adj* **agnatic** (*-nat'*) or **agnat'ical**. — *adv* **agnat'ically**. — *n* **agnā'tion**. [L *agnātus*, from *ad* to, and *(g)nāscī* to be born. See **cognate**]

agnize or **-ise** *ag-* or *əg-nīz'*, (*archaic*) *vt* to acknowledge or confess. [L *agnōscere*, from *ad* to, and *(g)nōscere* to know, modelled on **cognize**, etc]

agnomen *ag-* or *əg-nō'mən*, *n* a name added to the family name, generally on account of some great exploit, as *Africanus* to Publius Cornelius Scipio. — *adj* **agnom'inal**. [L, from *ad* to, and *(g)nōmen* a name]

agnosia *ag-nō'zi-ə* or *-zhə*, (*psychol*) *n* inability to recognize familar things or people, *esp* after brain damage. [Gr *a-* (privative) and *gnōsis* knowledge, recognition]

agnostic *ag-* or *əg-nos'tik*, *n* a person who believes that we know nothing of things beyond material phenomena, that a Creator, creative cause and an unseen world are things unknown or unknowable; loosely, a sceptic. — Also *adj*. — *n* **agnos'ticism**. [Coined by T H Huxley in 1869 from Gr *agnostos* unknown or unknowable, from *a-* (privative), *gnostos* known or knowable, and *-ic*]

agnus castus *ag'nəs kas'təs*, *n* a species of Vitex, a verbenaceous tree. [Gr *agnos*, the name of the tree, and L *castus*, a translation of Gr *hagnos* chaste, with which *agnos* was confused]

Agnus Dei or **agnus dei** *ag'nəs* or *än'yo͞os dā'ē*, *n* a part of the Roman Catholic mass beginning with these words; a musical setting of this; a figure of a lamb emblematic of Christ, bearing the banner of the cross; a cake of wax stamped with such a figure, and blessed by the Pope. [L *agnus Dēī* lamb of God]

ago *ə-gō'*, or (*archaic*) **agone** *ə-gon'*, *adv* gone; past; since. [OE *āgān*, pa p of *āgān* to pass away, from intensive pfx *ā-*, and *gān* to go]

agog *ə-gog'*, *adj* and *adv* in excited eagerness. [Perh connected with OFr *en gogues* frolicsome, of unknown origin]

agoge *a-gō'jē*, *n* in ancient Greek music, tempo; sequence in melody. — *adj* **agogic** (*a-goj'ik*) giving the effect of accent by slightly dwelling on a note. — *n sing* **agog'ics**. [Gr *agōgē* leading]

à gogo or **à go-go** *a gō-gō*, (*Fr*) in abundance, to one's heart's content; used in names of discothèques, etc. — See also **go-go**.

agoing *ə-gō'ing*, (*archaic* or *dialect*) *adj* and *adv* in motion. [**a-**[1] and **going**[2]]

agon. See **agony**.

agone. See under **ago**.

agonic *ə-gon'ik*, *adj* making no angle. — **agonic line** (*geol*) the line of no magnetic variation, along which the magnetic needle points directly north and south. [Gr *agōnos*, from *a-* (privative), and *gōniā* angle]

agonize, etc. See **agony**.

agonothetes *ə-gō-nə-thē'tēz* or *a-gō'no-thet-ās*, (*Gr*) *n* a judge or director of public games.

agony *ag'ə-ni*, *n* extreme suffering; a violent mental struggle, anguish; the death struggle; Christ's anguish in Gethsemane; conflict in games (*obs*). — *n* **ag'on** in ancient Greece, a conflict between two protagonists; a struggle. — *n* **ag'onist** (*rare*) in ancient Greece, a competitor in public games; someone engaged in a struggle, whether physical or spiritual; a chief character in a literary work; (in the following senses, a back-formation from **antagonist**) a muscle whose action is opposed by another action (the *antagonist*); a chemical substance (eg a drug) which produces an observable inhibitory or excitatory response in a body tissue (eg a muscle or nerve). — *n* **agonistes** (*a-gon-is'tēz*) someone in the grip of inner conflict. — *adj* **agonis'tic** of or relating to a chemical agonist; of or relating to a broad class of behaviour patterns including attack, threat, appeasement and flight; (also **agonist'ical**) relating to athletic contests; combative. — *adv* **agonist'ically**. — *n sing* **agonist'ics** (*archaic*) the art and theory of games and prize-fighting. — *vi* **ag'onize** or **-ise** to struggle or contend; to suffer agony; to worry intensely (*colloq*). — *vt* to subject to agony. — *adj* **ag'onized** or **-s-** suffering or expressing anguish. — *adv* **ag'onizedly** or **-s-** (*-īz-id-li*). — *adj* **ag'onizing** or **-s-** causing agony; intensely painful. — *adv* **ag'onizingly** or **-s-**. — **agony aunt** (sometimes with *caps*) a person, *usu* a woman, who gives advice in an agony column or in a radio or television programme of similar nature; **agony column** the part of a newspaper or magazine in which readers submit, and receive advice about, personal problems; the part of a newspaper containing special advertisements, eg for missing friends, etc; **agony uncle**. [Gr *agōniā* contest, agony, or *agōnistēs* competitor, from *agōn* meeting, contest]

agood *ə-go͝od'*, (*Shakesp*) *adv* in good earnest, heartily. [**a-**[1]]

agora[1] *ag'ə-rə*, *n* in ancient Greece, an assembly, place of assembly or market-place. — *n* **agoraphō'bia** morbid fear of (crossing) open places. — *adj* and *n* **agoraphō'bic** (or *-fob'*). [Gr *agorā* assembly, market-place, and *phobos* fear]

agora[2] *ag-ə-rä'*, *n* a monetary unit of Israel, worth 1/100 of an Israeli shekel: — *pl* **agorot** (*-rot'*). [Heb *agōrāh*, from *āgōr* to collect]

agouta *ə-go͞o'tə*, *n* a rat-like insectivore (*Solenodon*) of Haiti. [Taino *aguta*]

agouti, agouty or **aguti** *ə-go͞o'tē*, *n* a small S American rodent related to the guinea-pig. [Fr, from Sp *aguti*, from Guaraní *acuti*]

AGR *abbrev*: advanced gas-cooled reactor (see **advance**).

agr. or **agric.** *abbrev*: agriculture.

agraffe *ə-graf'*, *n* a hooked clasp used by stonemasons to hold blocks together. [Fr *agrafe*, from *à* to, and *grappe*, from LL *grappa*, from OHGer *krapfo* hook]

à grands frais *a grã fre*, (*Fr*) at great expense.

agranulocytosis *a-gran-ū-lō-sī-tō'sis*, *n* a blood disorder in which there is a marked decrease in granulocytes, with lesions of the mucous membrane and skin. — Also **agranulō'sis**. [Gr *ā-* (privative), **granule** or **granulocyte**, and **-osis**]

agrapha. See **agraphon**.

agraphia *a-graf'i-ə*, *n* loss of the power to write, from brain disease or injury. — *adj* **agraph'ic**. [Gr *a-* (privative) and *graphein* to write]

agraphon *a'gra-fon*, *n* a traditional utterance ascribed to Jesus, not in the canonical Gospels: — *pl* **a'grapha** (*-fa*). [Gr, unwritten]

agrarian *əg-rā'ri-ən*, *adj* relating to land, or its management or distribution. — *n* **agrā'rianism** equitable division of lands; a political movement in favour of change in conditions of property in land. [L *agrārius*, from *ager* a field]

agraste (*Spenser*), *pa t* of **aggrace**.

agravic *ə-grav'ik* or *ā-grav'*, *adj* of or relating to a condition or place where the effect of gravity is zero.

agree *ə-grē'*, *vi* to be, or come to be, of one mind (with); to suit, do well or be compatible (with); to concur (with *with* and *in*, *on* or *about*); to accede or assent (to); to be consistent (with); to harmonize; to get on together; to take the same gender, number, case, or person (with *with*; *gram*); to make friends again (*obs* or *dialect*). — *vt* to please or satisfy (*obs*); to reconcile (people; *obs*); to settle (a dispute or a difference; *obs*); to arrange with consent of all (*obs* for a time, but in recent use); to concede (that); to decide jointly (to do, that); to consent (to do): — *pr p* **agree'ing**; *pa t* and *pa p* **agreed'**. — *n* **agreeabil'ity**. — *adj* **agree'able** suitable; pleasant or affable; in harmony; conformable; willing or consenting (*colloq*). — *adv* in accordance. — *n* **agree'ableness**. — *adv* **agree'ably**. — *n* **agree'ment** concord; conformity; harmony; a compact, contract, or treaty; an embellishment (*obs*). — **agreement to agree** (*commerce*) an agreement to the effect that both parties are interested in entering into a contract at some future date. [OFr *agréer* to accept kindly, from L *ad* to, and *grātus* pleasing]

agrégé *a-grā-zhā*, (*Fr*) *n* a successful candidate in a competitive university examination for teaching posts. — *n* **agrégation** (*a-grā-ga-sjɔ̃*) the examination.

agrément *a-grā-mã*, (*Fr*) *n* the approval by a state of a diplomatic representative sent to it. — *n pl* **agréments** amenities (also **agrémens**); courtesies, charms or blandishments; embellishments, such as grace notes and trills (*music*).

agrestal, **agrestial**. See **agrestic**.

agrestic *ə-gres'tik*, *adj* of the fields; rural; unpolished. — *adj* **agrestial** (*ə-gres'ti-əl*) growing, etc in the open country; wild; growing wild in cultivated ground, such as weeds (*bot*). — Also **agres'tal**. [L *agrestis*, from *ager* a field]

agri- *ag-ri-* or **agro-** *ag-rō-*, *combining form* denoting fields, land use, or agriculture. — *n* **ag'ribusiness** or **ag'robusiness** all the operations of supplying the market with farm produce taken together, including growing, provision of farm machinery, distribution, etc. — *n* **ag'riproduct** a commodity for the use of farmers, eg fertilizer or animal feed. — *adj* **agrobiolog'ical**. — *n* **agrobiol'ogist**. — *n* **agrobiol'ogy** the study of plant nutrition and soil yields. — *n* **agrochem'ical** a chemical intended for agricultural use. — Also *adj*. — *n* **agrofor'estry** any system of land use which integrates the cultivation of trees and shrubs and the raising of agricultural crops and/or animals on the same land, whether at the same time or sequentially, taking economic, ecological and cultural factors into account. — *adj* **agroindust'rial**. — *n* **agroind'ustry** the area of production that serves the needs of both agriculture and industry. — *adj* **agrolog'ical**. — *n* **agrol'ogist**. — *n* **agrol'ogy** the study of the structure, history, etc of soils, *esp* as they affect agriculture. [L *ager*, Gr *agros* field]

agric. See **agr**.

agriculture *ag'ri-kul-chər*, *n* the art or practice of cultivating the land. — *adj* **agricult'ural**. — *adv* **agricult'urally**. — *n* **agricult'urist** someone skilled in agriculture; a farmer. — Also **agricult'uralist**. [L *ager* (Gr *agros*) field, and *cultūra* cultivation]

agrimony *ag'ri-mən-i*, *n* a perennial herb of a genus (*Agrimonia*) of the rose family, with small yellow flowers and bitter taste and a rootstock which provides a yellow dye; extended to other plants, *esp* **hemp'-agrimony** (*Eupatorium cannabinum*), a composite. [L *agrimōnia* (a blunder or misreading), from Gr *argemōnē* long prickly-headed poppy]

agrin *ə-grin'*, (*archaic*) *adv* in the act of grinning. [**a-**[1]]

agriology *ag-ri-ol'ə-ji*, *n* the comparative study of the customs found among primitive peoples. [Gr *agrios* wild, from *agros* field, and *logos* a discourse]

agrise, **agrize** or **agryze** *a-grīz'*, (*obs*) *vt* to terrify (*Spenser*); to horrify; to disfigure. — *adj* **agrised'**. [OE *āgrīsan* to dread]

agro-, **agrobiology**, etc. See under **agri-**.

agronomy *ag-ron'ə-mi*, *n* rural economy. — *adj* **agronō'mial**. — *adj* **agronom'ic** or **agronom'ical**. — *n sing* **agronom'ics** the science dealing with the management and productivity of land. — *n* **agron'omist**. [Fr *agronomie*]

agrostology *ag-ros-tol'ə-ji*, *n* the study of grasses. — *adj* **agrostological** (*-tə-loj'i-kl*). — *n* **agrostol'ogist**. [Gr *agrōstis* dog's-tooth grass]

aground *ə-grownd'*, *adv* in or to a stranded condition; on the ground. [**a-**[1]]

Agt or **agt** *abbrev*: agent; agreement.

aguacate *ä-gwä-kä'tā*, *n* the avocado pear. [Sp, from Nahuatl *ahuacatl*]

aguardiente *ä-gwär-dyen'tā*, *n* a brandy made in Spain and Portugal; any spirituous liquor. [Sp, from *agua ardiente* burning water, from L *aqua* water, and *ardēns*, *-entis*, from *ardēre* to burn]

ague *ā'gū*, *n* a burning fever (*Bible*); a fever with hot and cold fits; malaria; a shivering fit. — *adj* **agued** (*ā'gūd*) struck with ague; shivering; cold. — *adj* **ā'gūish**. — *adv* **ā'gūishly**. — **a'gūe-cake** (*obs*) a swelling on the spleen, caused by ague; **ā'gūe-fit**. — *adj* **ā'gūe-proof**. [OFr (*fièvre*) *ague*, from L (*febris*) *acūta* sharp (fever)]

aguise or **aguize** *a-gīz'*, (*obs*) *vt* to dress or equip (*Spenser*); to adorn; to fashion. [Pfx *a-*, and **guise**]

aguti. See **agouti**.

AH *abbrev*: (in dates) *anno Hegirae* (L), in the year of Hegira (ie from the flight of Mohammed in AD 622, 13 Sep).

Ah or **ah** *abbrev*: ampere hour.

ah *ä*, *interj* expressing surprise, joy, pity, complaint, objection, etc. — *vi* to make such an interjection. [Perh OFr *ah*]

AHA *abbrev*: Area Health Authority.

aha *ə-hä'*, *interj* expressing exultation, pleasure, surprise or contempt. [**ah** and **ha**]

à haute voix *a ōt vwä*, (*Fr*) aloud.

ahead *ə-hed'*, *adv* further on; in advance; forward; headlong. [**a-**[1]]

aheap *ə-hēp'*, (*obs*) *adv* in a heap. [**a-**[1]]

aheight *ə-hīt'*, (*archaic*) *adv* on high or aloft. [**a-**[1]]

ahem *ə-h(e)m'*, *interj* used to draw attention to oneself or to express a reservation, as though clearing the throat. [A lengthened form of **hem**[2]]

ahent *ə-hent'*. Northern form of **ahint**.

ahigh *ə-hī'*, (*obs*) *adv* on high. [**a-**[1]]

ahimsa *ə-him'sə*, *n* the duty of sparing animal life; non-violence. [Sans *ahiṁsā*]

ahint *ə-hint'* or **ahind** *ə-hin(d)'*, (*dialect*, *esp Scot*) *adv* and *prep* behind. [OE *æthindan*]

ahistorical *ā-his-tor'i-kəl*, *adj* not historical; taking no account of, or not related to, history. [Gr *a-* (privative) and **historical**]

Ahithophel. See **Achitophel**.
ahl *abbrev*: *ad hunc locum* (*L*), at this place.
ahold *ə-hōld'*, *adv* at or to grips, or a condition of holding; near the wind (ie so as to hold there) (*obs naut*; *Shakesp*). [**a-**[1] and **hold**[1]]
-aholic or **-oholic** *-ə-hol'ik*, (*facetious*) *adj sfx* having an addiction to (something) as in *workaholic*, *clothes-oholic*. — *n sfx* **-ahol'ism** or **-ohol'ism** (*-izm*). [By analogy, from alc*oholic* and alc*oholism*]
ahorse *ə-hörs'* or **ahorseback** *-bak*, (*archaic*) *adv* on horseback. [**a-**[1]]
ahoy *ə-hoi'*, (*naut*) *interj* used to hail another vessel, etc. [**ah** and **hoy**[2]]
AHQ *abbrev*: Army Headquarters.
Ahriman *ä'ri-män*, *n* in Zoroastrianism, the evil spirit, opposed to Ormuzd. [Pers *Ahrīman*, Zend *anro mainyus* dark spirit]
AHS *abbrev*: *anno humanae salutis* (*L*), in the year of human salvation.
à huis clos *a wē klō*, (*Fr*) with closed doors.
ahull *ə-hul'*, (*naut*) *adv* with sails furled, and helm lashed to the lee-side. [**a-**[1] and **hull**[2]]
ahungered *ə-hung'gərd* or **ahungry** *-gri*, (both *archaic*) *adj* oppressed with hunger. — Also, from confusion of prefixes, **anhung'(e)red**, **an-hung'ry** or **an hungry**. [Prob OE *of-hyngred*]
Ahura Mazda *ä'hōōr-ä maz'dä*, *n* the chief god of the ancient Persians, the creator and lord of the whole universe. [See **Ormuzd**]
ahv *abbrev*: *ad hanc vocem* (*L*), at this word.
AI *abbrev*: artificial insemination; artificial intelligence.
ai[1] *ä'ē*, *n* the three-toed sloth. [Tupí *ai*, representing the animal's cry]
ai[2]. See **ayu**.
aia. Same as **ayah**.
aiblins. See **able**.
aichmophobia *āk-mō-fō'bi-ə*, *n* abnormal fear of sharp or pointed objects. [Gr *aichmē* point of a spear, and *phobos* fear]
AID *abbrev*: Agency for International Development (*US*); artificial insemination by donor (now known as **DI**).
aid *ād*, *vt* to help. — *n* help; succour; assistance, eg in defending an action; something which helps; an auxiliary; a helper; an apparatus, etc, that gives help, eg *hearing-aid*, *navigational aid*; a feudal tax for certain purposes, eg paying the lord's ransom, the expense of knighting his son, his daughter's marriage; subsidy or money grant to the sovereign (*hist*); money, etc donated to relieve poor or disaster-stricken countries. — *n* **aid'ance** aid, help or support. — *adj* **aid'ant** (*archaic*) aiding or helping. — *adj* **aid'ed**. — *n* **aid'er**. — *adj* **aid'ful**. — *adj* **aid'ing**. — *adj* **aid'less**. — **aid and abet** (*law*) to assist and encourage, *esp* in committing a crime; **in aid of** (*colloq*) intended to achieve; in support of. [OFr *aider*, from L *adjūtāre*, frequentative of *adjuvāre*, from *juvāre*, *jūtum* to help]
aide *ād*, *n* a confidential assistant to a person of senior rank, eg an ambassador or president; an aide-de-camp. — **aide-de-camp** (*ed'-* or *ād'-də-kã'*) an officer who attends a general, governor, etc and acts as a personal assistant; an officer attending a monarch (*usu hist*): — *pl* **aides-de-camp** (*ed'-* or *ād'-*). [Fr, assistant, assistant on the field]
aide-mémoire *ād-me-mwär*, *n* an aid to the memory; a reminder; a memorandum-book; a written summary of a diplomatic document. [Fr]
aidos *ī'dōs*, (*Gr*) *n* shame, modesty.
AIDS *ādz*, *n* a condition brought about by a virus which causes the body's immune system to become deficient, leaving the sufferer very vulnerable to infection. — **AIDS-related complex** a viral condition marked *esp* by fever and swollen lymph-nodes, that may develop into AIDS. [Acronym for *a*cquired *i*mmune *d*eficiency *s*yndrome]
aiery. A variant of **eyrie**.
aiglet. Same as **aglet**.
aigre-doux *egr'-dōō* (*fem* **aigre-douce** *-dōōs*), (*Fr*) *adj* bitter-sweet, sourish.
aigrette *ā'gret* or *ā-gret'*, *n* an egret; an egret plume; any ornamental feather plume; a spray of jewels; a tuft; a pappus (*bot*); a savoury cooked in deep fat. [Fr]
aiguille *ā-gwēl'*, *n* a sharp, needle-like peak of rock; a slender boring-tool. — *n* **aiguillette'** see **aglet**. [Fr]
AIH *abbrev*: artificial insemination by husband.
aikido *ī-kē'dō*, *n* a Japanese martial art using locks and pressure against joints. [Jap, from *ai* to harmonize, *ki* breath, spirit, and *dō* way, doctrine]
aikona *ī'kon'ə*, (*Bantu*) *interj* it is not; no.
ail *āl*, *vt* (*impers*) to trouble, afflict, be the matter with; to have the matter with one. — *vi* to be sickly or indisposed. — *n* trouble; indisposition. — *adj* **ail'ing** unwell; in poor health. — *n* **ail'ment** indisposition; disease, *esp* if not very serious; pain. — **what ails him at?** (*Scot*) what is his objection to? [OE *eglan* to trouble]
ailanto *ā-lan'tō* or **ailanthus** *ā-lan'thəs*, *n* the tree of heaven (genus *Ailantus*, family *Simarubaceae*), a tall and beautiful Asiatic tree: — *pl* **ailan'tos** or **ailan'thuses**. [Amboina (Moluccas) name *aylanto* tree of the gods]
aileron *āl'* or *el'ə-rõ*, or *-ron*, *n* a flap on an aeroplane wingtip for lateral balancing; a half-gable, eg on a penthouse (*archit*). — *n* **ailette** (*ā-let'*) a plate of armour for the shoulder. [Fr diminutives of *aile*, from L *āla* a wing]
ailes de pigeon *el də pē-zhõ*, (*Fr*) *n pl* powdered side-curls of hair, known as 'pigeon's wings'.
ailette. See **aileron**.
ailment. See under **ail**.
ailuro- *ī-lōōr'ə-* or **ailur-** *ī-lōōr'-*, also **ailour(o)-** and **aelur(o)-** *ī-* or *ē-lōōr'*, *combining form* denoting cat. — *n* **ailur'ophile** or **ailour'ophile** (*-fīl*) a cat lover or fancier. — *n* **ailurophilia** or **ailourophilia** (*-fil'i-ə*) love of cats. — *adj* **ailurophil'ic** or **ailourophil'ic**. — *n* **ailur'ophobe** or **ailour'ophobe** (*-fōb*) a cat hater; someone with an abnormal fear of cats. — *n* **ailuropho'bia** or **ailouropho'bia**. — *adj* **ailuropho'bic** or **ailouropho'bic**. [Gr *ailouros* cat]
aim *ām*, *vt* to point, level or direct (a weapon or blow); to purpose or try (to do); to estimate or guess (*obs*); to place. — *vi* to direct a course; to level a weapon; to direct a blow or missile; to direct a remark with personal or special application; to direct one's intention and endeavours with a view to attaining (with *at*); to conjecture (*obs*). — *n* an act or manner of aiming; an object or purpose aimed at; design; intention; a guess or estimate (*Shakesp*); a shot (*Shakesp*). — *adj* **aim'less** without a fixed aim. — *adv* **aim'lessly**. — *n* **aim'lessness**. — **aim off** to aim slightly off the target to allow for wind or other factors (*rifle shooting*); to allow for the possible bias, exaggeration or eccentricity inherent in a statement, opinion, etc; **cry aim** (*archaic*) to encourage by calling out 'aim', hence, to applaud; **give aim** (*archaic*) to guide by reporting the result of previous shots; **take aim** to aim deliberately. [Prob partly OFr *esmer* (Picardian *amer*), from L *aestimāre*, partly OFr *aesmer*, from L *adaestimāre*; cf **esteem** and **estimate**]
ain *ān*, (*Scot*) *adj* own. [ON *eiginn* or OE *ǣgen* a variant of *āgen*]
aîné (*fem* **aînée**), *e-nā*, (*Fr*) *adj* elder or senior.
ain't *ānt*, (*colloq*) contracted form of *are not*, used also for *am* or *is not*; also for *have not* and *has not*.
Ainu *ī'nōō*, *n* a people of Japan, taller and with more abundant body hair than most Japanese; their language.
aioli or **aïoli** *ī-ō'lē*, *n* a garlic-flavoured mayonnaise. [Provençal *ai* garlic, from L *allium*, and *oli* oil, from L *oleum*]
air *ār*, *n* the gaseous mixture (chiefly nitrogen and oxygen) of which the earth's atmosphere is composed; the medium through which sound waves travel (*radio*); the medium in which aircraft operate; any gas (*obs*); a light

breeze; breath (*obs*); effluvium; the aura or atmosphere surrounding or created by anything; bearing, outward appearance, manner, look; an assumed or affected manner; (in *pl*) an affectation of superiority; exposure or publicity; a melody or tune (see also **ayre**); the chief, usually upper, part or tune (*music*). — *adj* of or pertaining to the air; affecting or regulating (the) air; by means of (the) air; operated by air; of aircraft; carried out or conveyed by aircraft. — *vt* to expose to the air; to ventilate; to warm and dry; to give an airing to, to voice; to wear openly, display; to make public knowledge, to spread. — *vi* to take an airing; to become aired; to be broadcast (*TV* and *radio*). — *n* **air'er** someone who airs; a frame on which clothes are dried. — *adv* **air'ily** in an airy manner; jauntily. — *n* **air'iness**. — *n* **air'ing** exposure to air or heat, to general notice or to open debate; a short excursion in the open air. — *adj* **air'less** without air; without free communication with the outer air; without wind; stuffy. — *n* **air'lessness**. — *adv* **air'ward** or **air'wards** up into the air. — *adj* **air'y** consisting of or relating to air; open to the air; having sufficient (fresh) air; like air; unsubstantial; sprightly, jaunty; offhand. — **air-am'bulance** an aircraft used to take patients from remote places to hospital; **air'-arm** the branch of the fighting services that uses aircraft; **air bag** a safety device in a motor-car, etc consisting of a bag that inflates to protect the occupants in a collision; an air-filled bag for another purpose, eg raising sunken craft; **air'base** a base of operations for aircraft; **air'-bath** exposure of the body to air; an apparatus for the therapeutic application of compressed or rarefied air, or for drying substances in air; **air'-bed** an inflated mattress; **air'-bell** an air-bubble; **air'-bends** aeroembolism; **air'-bladder** a sac containing gas, such as those that buoy up certain seaweeds; a fish's swim bladder, serving to regulate buoyancy, etc. — *adj* **air'borne** carried by air; borne up in the air. — **air'-brake** a brake worked by compressed air; a means of reducing the speed of an aircraft. — *adj* **air'-breathing** (of a means of propulsion) which needs to take in air for combustion. — **air'-brick** a block for ventilation; **air'-bridge** a link by air transport between two points; **air'-brush** a device for spraying paint, etc, powered by compressed air, or for touching up or toning down a photograph; a tool for achieving a similar effect in computer graphics. — Also *vt*. — *adj* **air'-brushed**. — **air'-bubble** a bubble of air, *specif* one causing a spot on a photograph. — *adj* **air'-built** built in air; having no solid foundation. — **air'burst** the explosion of a bomb, etc in the air. — *adj* designed to explode in the air. — **Air'-bus®** (also without *cap*) a very large passenger jet aircraft used for short flights; **air'-car** one made to ride on a cushion of air; **air'-cavity** or **air'-cell** (*bot*) an intercellular space containing air; **air'-chief-mar'shal** an Air Force officer of equivalent rank to an admiral or general (*abbrev* **ACM**); **air-comm'odore** an Air Force officer of equivalent rank to a commodore or brigadier; **air'-compressor** a machine which draws in air at atmospheric pressure, compresses it, and delivers it at higher pressure. — *vt* **air'-condition** to equip eg a building with devices for air-conditioning. — *adj* **air'-conditioned**. — **air'-conditioning** (devices for) the bringing of air to the desired state of purity, temperature and humidity. — *vt* **air'-cool**. — **air'-cooling** cooling by means of air. — *adj* **air'-cooled**. — **air'-corridor** in an area where flying is restricted, a narrow strip along which flying is allowed; **air'-cover** protection given by fighter aircraft to other forces during a military operation; the protecting aircraft; **air'craft** (*pl* **air'craft**) any structure or machine for travelling in the air; **air'craft-carrier** a vessel from which aircraft can take off and on which they can land; **air'craftman** or **air'craftsman** (RAF) a member of the lowest rank; **air'craftwoman** or **air'craftswoman** (someone of) the lowest rank in the WRAF; **air'-crew** the crew of an aircraft; **air curtain** a current of air directed across a doorway or other opening to prevent draughts, maintain temperature, etc; **air'-cushion** a cushion that can be inflated; a protective barrier, eg between a hovercraft and land or water, formed by down-driven air; **air dam** on a motor vehicle, a front spoiler; **air'-drain** a cavity in the external walls of a building to prevent damp from getting through to the interior. — *adj* **air'drawn** drawn in air; visionary; imaginary (*Shakesp*). — **air'drome** (chiefly *US*) an aerodrome; **air'-drop** (*military*) a landing of men or supplies by parachute. — *vt* **air'-dry** to dry by exposing to the air. — **air'-engine** an engine driven by heated or compressed air; **air'field** an open expanse where aircraft may land and take off; **air'flow** the flow of air past a moving vehicle or in a wind-tunnel; **air'foil** (*NAm*) an aerofoil; **air force** a force organized for warfare in the air, often with *caps* when referrring to a national force. — *adj* **Air Force** or **air'-force** (**air-force blue** a greyish-blue such as is used for Air Force uniforms). — **air'frame** the body of an aircraft as opposed to its engines; **air freight** transport of freight by air; the cost of this. — Also *vt*. — **air frost** (*meteorol*) an air (not ground) temperature of below 0°C; **air'gap** a gap in the magnetic circuit of a piece of electrical apparatus, eg the gap between the rotor and stator of an electric machine; **air'-gas** producer gas; **air'graph** a letter photographically reduced for sending by air; **air'-grating** a grating admitting air for ventilation; **air'-gun** a gun that discharges missiles by means of compressed air; **air'head** (*slang*) an idiot, featherbrain; **air'hole** a hole for the passage of air; a hole in ice where animals come up to breathe; an airpocket; **air'-hostess** an earlier word for a stewardess or flight attendant; **air'-house** an inflatable building of nylon or Terylene coated with polyvinyl chloride which can be used by industrial firms for storage, etc; **air'-intake** a valve or other opening through which air is drawn in, *esp* to an engine; the amount of air so drawn in; **air'-jacket** a casing containing air to reduce loss or gain of heat; a garment with airtight cavities to buoy up in water; **air'-lane** a route normally taken by aircraft because of steady winds; **air layering** the layering of shoots, not by bending them down to root in the soil but by enclosing in compost, etc at their current place of growth; **air letter** a letter sent by airmail; **air letter form** a prestamped sheet of paper used for sending correspondence by air; **air lieutenant** a rank in the Zimbabwean Air Force equivalent to a flying officer in the Royal Air Force; **air'lift** a transport operation carried out by air, *esp* in an emergency; transportation by air. — Also *vt*. — **air'line** a route or system of traffic by aircraft; a company operating such a system. — Also *adj*. — **air'liner** a large passenger aircraft; an aircraft operating in an airline; **air loadmaster** one of a team of *usu* three men in charge of winching operations on a helicopter; **air'lock** a small chamber in which the pressure of air can be raised or lowered, through which communication is made between a caisson where the air is compressed and the outer air (*civ eng*); a bubble in a pipe obstructing the flow of liquid; **air'mail** mail conveyed by air. — *vt* to send by airmail. — Also *adj*. — **air'man** a person who flies; an aircraft pilot, technician or navigator, *specif* in the Royal Air Force someone below officer rank: — *fem* **air'woman**; **air'manship** the art of handling aircraft; **air-mar'shal** an Air Force officer of equivalent rank to a vice-admiral or a lieutenant-general; **air'-mechanic** someone who tends and repairs aircraft. — *adj* **air'-minded** having one's thoughts continually and favourably directed towards flying. — **air'-miss** a near collision between aircraft; **air'-officer** an Air Force officer above the rank of air-commodore; **air'-passage** the passage by which air enters and leaves the lungs; a journey to a particular destination by air; **air-pir'acy** the hijacking of an aircraft; **air'plane** (chiefly *NAm*) an aeroplane; **air'-plant** a non-parasitic plant growing on another, an epiphyte (*bot*); **air play** the broadcasting of a song, singer, record, etc on the radio; **air'-pocket** a region of rarefied or down-flowing air, in which aircraft drop; **air'port** an aerodrome, *usu* with a custom-house, used as a station for transport of passengers and cargo; an opening for the passage of air; **air'-power** military power in terms of aircraft; **air'-pump** an instrument for pumping air out or in; **air'-raid** an attack on a place by aircraft; **air'-rail** a rail on which a road vehicle is carried overhead for part of its course; **air rifle** a rifle that discharges missiles by means of compressed air; **air'-sac** an alveolus, or the cluster of alveoli, at the termination of a bronchiole in the lungs; an outgrowth of the lung in birds, helping respiration or lightening the body; in insects, a dilatation of the trachea; **Air Scout** a member of a branch of the Scouts with special interest in air activities; **air'screw** the propeller of an aircraft; **air-sea rescue** the combined use of aircraft and high-speed launches in sea rescue; **air'shaft** a passage for air into a mine, building, etc; **air'ship** a mechanically driven dirigible aircraft, lighter than air; **air shot** in golf or cricket, a stroke that fails to connect with the ball. — *adj* **air'sick**. — **air'-sickness** nausea affecting travellers by air. — *adj, adv* and *n* **air'side** (of, in or relating to) that part of an airport having direct access to the apron, and off-limits to non-travelling public and unauthorized personnel, the area *usu* controlled by an airport authority (**go** or **pass airside** to enter this restricted area). — **air'space** the part of the atmosphere above a particular territory, state, etc; the space used or required by an aircraft in manoeuvring; cubic contents available for respirable air; an air-cell; **air'-speed** the speed of an aircraft, missile, etc in relation to the air through which it is moving; **air'-splint** a contrivance zipped up and inflated for giving temporary support to an injured limb; **air'stop** a stopping-place for helicopters; **air'stream** a flow of air; **airstream mechanism** the part(s) of the body, eg the lungs, which can produce a flow of air on which speech-sounds, etc may be produced; **air'-strike** an attack with aircraft; **air'strip** a temporary or emergency landing-place for aircraft; a runway; **air taxi** a *usu* small aeroplane or a helicopter making short trips, often to and from an airport; **air support** support given by fighter aircraft to other forces during a military operation; the supporting aircraft involved in such an operation; **air terminal** a terminus in a town to or from which passengers are conveyed from or to an airport; the terminal building(s) of an airport. — *adj* **air'tight** impermeable to air; impenetrable (*fig*). — **air'time** the amount of broadcasting time on radio or television allotted to a particular topic, type of material, commercial advertisement, etc; the time at which the broadcasting of a programme, etc is due to begin. — *adj* **air'-to-air'** from one aircraft to another. — **air-traffic control** the organized control, by visual and radio means, of the traffic into and out of aerodromes and on air routes (*abbrev* **ATC**); **air'-trap** a device to prevent the escape of foul air; **air'-umbrella** strong air-cover; **air'-vice-mar'shal** an Air Force officer of equivalent rank to a rear-admiral or major-general (*abbrev* **AVM**); **air'wave** a channel for broadcasting; **air'way** a passage for air; a radio channel; an organized route for air travel; used in *pl* to form names of airline companies; **air'woman** *fem* of airman (qv); **air'-worthiness**. — *adj* **air'worthy** in fit condition for safe flying. — *adj* **air'y-fair'y** fanciful; delicate, flimsy or insubstantial. — **give oneself airs** to put on a superior manner; **give the air** to dismiss; **go up in the air** to become excited or angry (see also below); **in the air** prevalent in a vague or indefinite form; **off the air** not broadcasting or being broadcast for a period of time; **on the air** in the act of broadcasting; broadcast by radio; **take air** to get wind or become known; **take the air** to have an airing; **up in the air** undecided; excited or angry. [OFr (and Fr) *air*, from L *āër*, *āeris*, from Gr *āēr*, *āeros* air]

Airedale *ār'dāl* or **Airedale terrier** (*ter'i-ər*), *n* a large terrier of a breed *orig* from *Airedale* in Yorkshire.

airn *ārn*, Scots form of **iron**.

airt *ārt*, (*Scot*) *n* direction, quarter. — *vt* to direct. [Perh Gaelic *aird* point (of compass)]

aisle *īl*, *n* a side division of the nave or other part of a church or similar building, generally separated off by pillars; (loosely) any division of a church, or a small building attached; a passage between rows of seats eg in an aircraft, theatre, cinema, etc; a passageway in a supermarket on either side of which products are displayed; a passageway (*NAm*); the corridor of a railway train or aircraft. — *adj* **aisled** (*īld*) having aisles. [OFr *ele* (Fr *aile*), from L *āla* a wing; confused with **isle** and **alley**]

aisling *ish'ling*, or *ash'*, *n* (a poetic description of) a vision or dream. [Ir]

ait[1] or **eyot** *āt*, *n* a small island. [Cf OE *ēgath*, *īgeoth* appar connected with *īeg* island; the phonology is obscure]

ait[2] *āt*, Scots form of **oat**.

aitch *āch*, *n* the eighth letter of the modern English alphabet (H or h). — **drop one's aitches** to fail to pronounce initial aitches on words, formerly considered a sign of lack of education. [OFr *ache*, from which LL *ahha* is inferred]

aitchbone *āch'bōn*, *n* in cattle, the bone of the rump; the cut of beef over it. [An *aitchbone* is for *a nachebone*, from OFr *nache*, from L *natis* buttock; and **bone**]

aitu *ī'tōō*, *n* in Polynesia, a demigod.

aizle. See **easle**.

Aizoon *ā-ī-zō'on*, *n* an African genus of plants giving name to the family **Aizoā'ceae**, related to the goosefoots. [Appar Gr *āei* ever, and *zōos* living]

à jamais *a zha-me*, (*Fr*) for ever.

ajar[1] *ə-jär'*, *adv* and *adj* partly open. [OE *on* on, and *cerr* a turn]

ajar[2] *ə-jär*, (*archaic*) *adj* jarring, out of tune or harmony. [**a-**[1] and **jar**[1]]

Ajax *ā'jaks*, *n* the Greek hero next to Achilles in the Trojan war; a privy, by a pun on *a jakes* (*obs*). [L from Gr *Aiās*]

ajee or **agee** *ə-jē'*, (*Scot* and *dialect*) *adv* off the straight; ajar. [**a**[1], and **gee**[3], **jee**[1]]

ajowan *aj'ō-wən* or **ajwan** *aj'wən*, *n* a plant of the caraway genus yielding ajowan oil and thymol. [Origin uncertain]

ajutage. See **adjutage**.

AK *abbrev*: Alaska (US state); Knight of (the Order of) Australia.

aka or **AKA** *abbrev*: also known as.

akaryote *ā-kar'i-ōt*, (*zool*) a cell that does not have a nucleus. [Gr *ā* (privative), and *karyon* a kernel]

ake *āk*. Old spelling of the verb **ache**.

akedah *ə-kā'dä* or *a-kā-dä*, (*Heb*) *n* the binding of Isaac in Genesis 22.

akee or **ackee** *a-kē'*, *n* a small African sapindaceous tree, now common in the W Indies; its edible fruit, often used in Caribbean cookery. [Kru *ā-kee*]

Akela *ə-kā'lə*, *n* the adult leader of a group, or pack, of Cub Scouts. [From a character in Kipling's *The Jungle Book*]

akene *a-kēn'*, *n*. Same as **achene**.

akimbo *ə-kim'bō*, *adj* and *adv* with hand on hip and elbow out. [ME *in kenebow* (possibly) in a keen (sharp) bow or bend; other suggestions are *can-bow* (ie can-handle), and ON *kengboginn* bent into a crook, from *kengr* kink, and *boginn* bowed]

akin *ə-kin'*, *adv* by kin; of nature. — *adj* related by blood; of a similar nature. [**a**[1] and **kin**[1]]

akinesia *ā-kin-ē'zi-ə* or *-ē'shə*, or **akinesis** *ā-kin-ē'sis*, (*pathol*) *n* the lack, loss, or impairment of the power of voluntary movement. [Gr *akinesia* lack of motion; *a-* (privative), and *kinein* to move]

Akkadian *ə-kād'i-ən*, *n* the Semitic language of the ancient Middle-Eastern kingdom of Akkad; a native of this kingdom. — Also *adj*. [City of *Agade*]

akkas. See **ackers**.

akolouthos, akoluthos, etc. Same as **acolouthos**, etc.
akvavit. See **aquavit**.
AL *abbrev*: Alabama (US state; also **Ala.**); Albania (IVR); Anglo-Latin.
Al *symbol*: aluminium.
à la *a la*, *prep* in the manner of, eg *à la James Joyce*; in cooking, prepared with or in the manner of (a person or place), eg *à la Dubarry* with cauliflower, *à la Florentine* with spinach, etc. [Fr, from contraction of *à la mode de*]
ala *ā'lə*, *n* a membranous outgrowth on a fruit (*bot*); a side petal in the pea family (*bot*); a large side sepal in the milkworts (*bot*); a leafy expansion running down the stem from a leaf (*bot*); any flat winglike process, *esp* of bone (*zool*): — *pl* **alae** (*ā'lē*). — *adj* **ā'lar** or **ā'lary** pertaining to a wing. — *adj* **ā'late** or **a'lated** winged, having an ala. [L *āla* wing]
Ala. See **AL**.
alaap. See **alap**.
alabamine *al-ə-bäm'ēn*, *n* a name proposed for element number 85, now called **astatine**. [*Alabama*, where its discovery in nature was claimed]
alabandine. See **almandine**. — *n* **aluband'ite** a cubic mineral, manganese sulphide.
à l'abandon *a la-bā̃-dɔ̃*, carelessly, recklessly. [Fr, neglected, uncared for]
alabaster *al'ə-bäs-tər*, or *-bäs'*, (*Spenser*, *Shakesp*, *Milton*, etc **alablaster**) *n* a soft, semi-transparent massive gypsum, widely used for ornamental purposes. — *adj* of or like alabaster. — *adj* **alabas'trine**. — **oriental alabaster** stalactitic calcite. [Gr *alabastros*, said to be from *Alabastron* a town in Egypt]
à la belle étoile *a la be-lā-twäl*, (*Fr*) in the open air.
à la bonne heure *a la bo-nœr*, (*Fr*) well done! that is right.
à l'abri *a la-brē*, (*Fr*) under shelter.
à la campagne *a la kā̃-pan-y'*, (*Fr*) in the country.
à la carte *a la kärt* or *ä lä kärt*, with each dish charged individually at the price shown on the menu; with the freedom to pick and choose (*fig*). [Fr, according to the bill of fare]
alack *ə-lak'*, *archaic interj* denoting regret. — *interj* **alack'-a-day** (*archaic*) woe be to the day; alas. [Prob **ah** and **lack**[1]]
alacrity *ə-lak'ri-ti*, *n* briskness; cheerful readiness; promptness. [L *alacritās*, *-ātis*, from *alacer*, *alacris* brisk]
Aladdin's cave *ə-lad'inz kāv*, *n* a place full of wonderful treasures (*fig*). — **Aladdin's lamp** a magic object able to grant all one's desires. [*Aladdin*, a character in *Arabian Nights*]
à la dérobée *a la dā-ro-bā*, (*Fr*) by stealth.
alae. See **ala**.
à la hauteur de *a la ō-tœr də*, (*Fr*) on a level with or abreast of; able to understand or to deal with.
alaiment. Old spelling of **allayment** (see **allay**[1]).
alalagmos *a-la-lag'mos*, (*Gr*) *n* a war-cry, cry of *alalai*.
à la lanterne *a la lā̃-tern*, (*Fr*) away with them and hang them (as in the French Revolution); literally, to the lamp(-chain).
alalia *ə-lā'li-ə*, *n* loss of speech. [Gr *a-* in privative sense, and *laleein* to talk]
à la main *a la mɛ̃*, (*Fr*) in hand or ready; by hand.
à la maître d'hôtel *a la metr' dō-tel*, in major-domo fashion; in cooking, served plain with a parsley garnish. [Fr, in the style of a house-steward or hotel-keeper]
alameda *a-la-mā'dä*, *n* a public walk, *esp* between rows of poplars. [Sp *álamo* poplar]
à la mode *a la mod(ə)*, *adv* and *adj* according to the fashion, fashionable; of beef, larded and stewed with vegetables (*cookery*); of desserts, served with ice cream (*NAm*). — Also **alamode** (*a-lə-mōd'*). — *n* **al'amode** a light glossy silk. [Fr *à la mode*]
alamort *a-lə-mört'*, *adj* half-dead; dejected. [Fr *à la mort* to the death; see also **amort**]
aland *ə-land'*, (*archaic*) *adv* ashore. [**a-**[1] and **land**[1]]
alang *ä'läng* or **a'lang-a'lang**. Same as **lalang**.
alanine *al'ə-nēn* or *-nīn*, *n* an amino acid, a common constituent of proteins. [Ger *Alanin*]
alannah *ə-län'ə*, *n* (used as term of endearment) my child. [Ir *a* O, and *leanbh* child]
alap *ə-läp'*, *n* in Indian music, the introductory section of a raga. — Also **alaap'** or **alap'a**. [Sans]
à la page *a la päzh*, (*Fr*) up to date, au courant.
à la Portugaise. See **Portugaise**.
à la poupée *a la pōō-pā*, (*Fr*) of the printing of an engraving or etching, with inks of different colours being spread on the plate with paper or cloth pads (*poupées*) before the impression is taken.
Alar *ā'lär*, *n* the chemical *daminozide*, used as a spray to prevent blemishes and to delay the ripening of apples.
alar, alary. See **ala**.
alarm *ə-lärm'*, *n* a fear-stricken state; apprehension of danger; a warning of danger; a mechanical contrivance for arousing, warning, or giving notice; the noise made by such a device; *orig* a call to arms; a din (*obs*). — *vt* to strike with fear; to arouse, startle or agitate; to give notice of danger; to call to arms (*obs*). — *adj* **alarmed'**. — *adv* **alarm'edly**. — *adj* **alarm'ing**. — *adv* **alarm'ingly**. — *n* **alarm'ism**. — *n* **alarm'ist** a scaremonger or someone who is easily alarmed. — Also *adj*. — *n* and *vt* **alarum** (*ə-la'rəm*, *-lä'*, or *-lā'*) alarm (now *archaic* except of a warning mechanism or sound). — **alarm'=bell**; **alarm call** a telephone service by which a subscriber can arrange to be called at a particular time, eg to wake him or her in the morning; **alarm'-clock** a clock that can be set to ring an alarm at a chosen time; **alarm'-radio** a clock radio. — **alarms (**or **alarums) and excursions** a stage direction for a sketchy conventionalized representation of skirmishing or the outskirts of a battle; hence, vague hostilities or confused activity; **sound the alarm** to give the signal to prepare for an emergency. [OFr *alarme*, from Ital *all'arme* to (the) arms]
alarum. See under **alarm**.
alas *ə-läs'*, *interj* (now somewhat *archaic* or *mock-heroic*) expressing grief or misfortune. — **alas the day** or **alas the while** (*archaic* or *poetic*) ah! unhappy day or time. [OFr *ha las*, *a las* (Mod Fr *hélas*); *ha* ah, and *las*, *lasse* wretched, weary, from L *lassus* wearied]
Alas. *abbrev*: Alaska (US state).
Alaskan malamute, etc. See under **malamute**.
alastrim *ə-las'trim*, *n* a mild form of smallpox or a similar disease. [Port]
alate[1] *ə-lāt'*, *adv* (*archaic*) lately. [**of** and **late**]
alate[2], **alated**. See **ala**.
a latere *ā la'tə-rē* or *ä la'tə-rā*, (*L*) (of a legate sent by the Pope) confidential, (literally) from the side.
à la volée *a la vo-lā*, (*Fr*) on the flight (said of any quick return).
alay. Old spelling of **allay**[1].
alb *alb*, *n* a priest's long white sleeved vestment. [OE *albe*, from LL *alba*, from L *albus* white]
Alb. *abbrev*: Albania.
Alba *abbrev*: Alberta (Canadian state).
albacore *al'bə-kōr* or *-kör*, *n* a large tuna with long pectoral fins; a species of mackerel (*SAfr*). — Also **al'bicore**. [Port *albacor*, from Ar *al* the, and *bukr* young camel]
Alban *al'bən*, **Albany** *-i* or **Albion** *-i-ən*, *n* ancient names for the island of Great Britain, now used poetically for Britain, England, or *esp* Scotland. — *n* **Alban** the ancient kingdom of the Picts and (Celtic) Scots, which the addition of Lothian and Strathclyde transformed into Scotland. — *n* **Albany** a Scottish dukedom first conferred in 1398. — **Albany herald** one of the Scottish heralds. [Celtic]
Alban. *öl'bən*, *abbrev*: *Albanensis* (*L*), of St Albans.
Albanian *al-bā'ni-ən*, *adj* of or pertaining to the SE European Republic of *Albania*. — *n* a native or citizen of Albania; the language of the Albanians.
albarello *al-bə-rel'ō* or *al-bar-el'lō*, *n* a majolica jar used for dry drugs: — *pl* **albarell'os** or **albarel'li** (*-lē*). [Ital]

albata *al-bā'tə*, *n* a variety of German silver. [L *albāta* (*fem*) whitened, from *albus* white]

albatross *al'bə-tros*, *n* a large, long-winged sea-bird with remarkable powers of flight; a hole in three below par (*golf*); used symbolically to mean an oppressive and inescapable fact, influence, etc (from the dead bird hung round the neck of the sailor in Coleridge's *Ancient Mariner*). [See **alcatras**; perh influenced by L *albus* white]

albe, **albee** or **all-be** *öl-bē'* or *öl'bē*, (*archaic*) *conj* albeit. [**all** and **be**]

albedo *al-bē'dō*, *n orig* whiteness; a measure of the reflecting power of an object (eg a planet), expressed as the proportion of incident light it reflects (*phys*): — *pl* **albe'dos**. [L *albēdō* whiteness, from *albus* white]

albeit *öl-bē'it*, *conj* even if, although; although it be (that). [ME *all be it*]

albergo *al-ber'gō*, (*Ital*) *n* an inn, auberge: — *pl* **alber'ghi**.

albert *al'bərt*, *n* a short kind of watch-chain. [After Queen Victoria's husband]

Alberti bass *al-bûr'ti bās*, or *-ber'*, *n* a type of bass accompaniment consisting of broken chords. [Domenico *Alberti* (1710–40), an exponent of this]

albertite *al'bər-tīt*, *n* a pitch-black solid bitumen. [Discovered at the *Albert* mine, New Brunswick, Canada]

albescent *al-bes'ənt*, *adj* becoming white; whitish. — *n* **albesc'ence**. [L *albēscēns*, *-entis*, pr p of *albēscere* to grow white, from *albus* white]

albespyne or **albespine** *al'bə-spīn*, (*archaic*) *n* hawthorn. [OFr *albespine* (Fr *aubépine*), from L *alba spīna* white thorn]

albicore. See **albacore**.

Albigensian *al-bi-jen'si-ən*, *adj* of the town of *Albi* or its district (the Albigeois), in the South of France; of a Catharist or Manichaean sect or of the 13c crusade (beginning in the Albigeois) by which, along with the Inquisition, the Catholic Church savagely suppressed it. — Also *n*. — *n pl* **Albigen'sēs**. — *n* **Albigen'sianism**. [LL *Albigēnsēs*]

albino *al-bē'nō*, or (*US*) *-bī'*, *n* a person or other animal with abnormally white skin and hair and pink irises; a plant lacking in pigment: — *pl* **albi'nos**: — *fem* **albiness** (*al'bin-es*; *archaic*). — *adj* **albin'ic** or **albinis'tic**. — *n* **al'binism** (*-bin-*) or **albinoism** (*-bē'*). — *adj* **albinotic** (*al-bin-ot'ik*). [Port *albino* white Negro or albino, from L *albus* white]

Albion. See **Alban**.

albite *al'bīt*, *n* a white plagioclase feldspar, sodium and aluminium silicate. — *adj* **albit'ic**. — *vt* **al'bītize** or **-ise** to turn into albite. [L *albus* white]

albricias *al-brē-thē'as*, (*Sp*) *n* a reward to the bearer of good news.

albugo *al-bū'gō*, *n* leucoma: — *pl* **albu'gos**. — *adj* **albugineous** (*-jin'i-əs*) like the white of an egg or of the eye. [L *albūgō*, *-inis* whiteness, from *albus* white]

album *al'bəm*, *n* a blank book for the insertion of photographs, autographs, poetical extracts, scraps, postage-stamps; a printed book of selections, *esp* of music; a book-like container for recorded discs; a long-playing disc; among the Romans, a white tablet or register on which the praetor's edicts and such public notices were recorded; a visitors' book (*US*): — *pl* **al'bums**. — **al'bum-leaf** (transl Ger *Albumblatt*) a short musical composition. [L neuter of *albus* white]

albumen *al-bū'mən*, *-min*, or *al'*, *n* the white of egg, the nutritive material surrounding the yolk in the eggs of higher animals, a mixture of proteins; any tissue within the seed-coat other than the embryo itself, endosperm and perisperm, a store of food for the young plant, no matter what its chemical nature (*bot*); an albumin (*obs*). — *vt* **albū'menize**, **albū'minize**, or **-ise** (*photog*) to cover or impregnate with albumen or an albuminous solution. — *n* **albū'min** (or *al'*) a protein of various kinds soluble in pure water, the solution coagulable by heat. — *n* **albū'minate** an alkali compound of an albumin. — *adj* **albū'minoid** like albumen. — *n* an old name for a protein in general; any one of a class of substances including keratin and chondrin. — *adj* **albū'minous** like or containing albumen or albumin; insipid. — *n* **albūminūr'ia** presence of albumin in the urine. [L *albūmen*, *-inis*, from *albus* white]

album Graecum *al'bum grē'kum* or *al'bo͝om grī'ko͝om*, (*LL*) *n* the dried dung of dogs, formerly used for inflammation of the throat.

albumin, **albuminize**, etc. See under **albumen**.

alburnum *al-bûrn'əm*, *n* sapwood, the soft wood between inner bark and heartwood. — *adj* **alburn'ous**. [L *albus* white]

alcahest. See **alkahest**.

Alcaic *al-kā'ik*, *adj* of or pertaining to the Greek lyric poet *Alcaeus* (*Alkaios*, fl. 600BC), or of the kind of verse invented by him. — *n* (*esp* in *pl*) Alcaic verses. — **Alcaic strophe** a verse form much used by Horace, consisting of two eleven-syllable Alcaics: ⏓–⏑––/–⏑⏑–⏑⏓, followed by a nine-syllable: ⏓–⏑–––⏑–⏒, and a ten-syllable: –⏑⏑–⏑⏑–⏑–⏒; imitated by Tennyson in 'O mighty-mouth'd inventor of harmonies'.

alcaicería *al-kī-the-rē'a*, (*Sp*) *n* a bazaar.

alcaide or **alcayde** *al-kād'* or *äl-kī'dhā*, or *-dā*, (*Sp*) *n* governor of a fortress; a gaoler. [Sp *alcaide*, from Ar *al-qā'īd*, from *al* the, and *qā'īd* leader, from *qāda* to lead]

alcalde *äl-käl'dā*, (*Sp*) *n* formerly, a judge or magistrate; a mayor. [Sp from Ar *al-qādī*, from *qada* to judge]

Alcan *al'kan*, *abbrev*: Aluminium Company of Canada.

alcarraza *al-ka-ra'tha*, (*Sp*) *n* a porous vessel for cooling water.

alcatras *al'kə-tras*, *n* a name applied to several large water birds, such as the pelican, gannet, frigate bird and albatross. [Sp *alcatraz* pelican]

alcayde. See **alcaide**.

alcázar *al-ka-zär'* or *-kä'thär*, (*Sp*) *n* a palace, fortress or bazaar.

Alcelaphus *al-sel'ə-fəs*. Same as **Bubalis**.

alchemy or **alchymy** *al'ki-mi*, or *-kə-*, *n* the infant stage of chemistry, aimed chiefly towards transmuting of other metals into gold, and discovering the elixir of life; a transmuting power (*fig*); a gold-like substance (eg brass) (*obs*); a trumpet made of it (*obs*). — *adj* **alchemic** (*-kem'ik*) or **alchem'ical**. — *n* **al'chemist**. — *vt* **al'chemize** or **-ise** to transmute; to change by alchemy. [Ar *al-kīmīā*, from *al* the, and *kīmīā*, from late Gr *chēmeiā*, *chymeiā*, variously explained as the Egyptian art (*Khēmiā* 'black-land' or Egypt, from the Egyptian name), the art of *Chymēs* (its supposed inventor), or the art of pouring (*chyma* fluid; cf *cheein* to pour)]

alcheringa *al-chə-ring'gə* or **alchera** *al'chə-rə*, *n* dream-time. [Australian Aboriginal words]

alchymy. See **alchemy**.

Alcidae. See **auk**.

Alcides *al-sī'dēz*, *n* a patronymic of Hercules, from Alcaeus, father of Amphitryon. [L, from Gr]

ALCM *abbrev*: air-launched cruise missile.

alcohol *al'kə-hol*, *n* a liquid generated by the fermentation of sugar or other saccharine matter and forming the intoxicating element of fermented liquors; a general term for a class of hydrocarbon compounds analogous to common (or ethyl) alcohol, in which a hydroxyl group is substituted for an atom of hydrogen; a fine powder, *esp* a sublimate (*obs*); hence (*obs*) an essence, a distillate. — *adj* **alcohol'ic** of, like, containing or due to alcohol. — *n* someone addicted to excessive drinking of alcohol. — *n* **al'coholism** alcoholic poisoning; the condition suffered by an alcoholic. — *n* **alcoholīzā'tion** or **-s-**. — *vt* **al'coholīze** or **-ise** to convert into or saturate with alcohol. — *n* **alcoholom'eter** an instrument for measuring the proportion of alcohol in solutions. — *n* **alcoholom'etry**. — **alcoholic fermentation** (*biol*) a fermentation in the absence of oxygen in which sugar is converted to alcohol and carbon dioxide. [Ar *al-koh'l*, from *al* the, and *koh'l* antimony powder used in the East to stain the eyelids]

al conto *al kon'tō*, (*Ital*) à la carte.

al contrario *al kon-trä'ri-ō*, (*Sp*) on the contrary.
Alcoran *al-ko-rän'*, (*archaic*) *n* the Koran. [Fr, from Ar *al* the, and **Koran**]
alcorza *al-kör'tha*, (*Sp*) *n* a kind of sweet; icing.
alcove *al'kōv*, *n* a recess in a room, eg for a bed, seating, shelving, etc; any recess, eg a covered outdoor shelter in a wall; a shady retreat (*archaic*). [Sp *alcoba* a place in a room railed off to hold a bed, from Ar *al* the, and *qobbah* a vault]
Alcyonium *al-si-ō'ni-əm*, *n* a genus of Anthozoa growing in masses of polyps called dead men's fingers. — *n pl* **Alcyonā'ria** the order to which Alcyonium, sea-pens, red coral and organ-pipe coral belong. — *n* and *adj* **alcyonā'rian**. [Gr *alkyoneion* an organism said to resemble a halcyon's nest, from *alkyōn* halcyon, kingfisher]
ALD *abbrev*: adrenoleukodystrophy.
Ald. *abbrev*: Alderman.
aldea *al-dā'a*, (*Sp*) *n* a village or hamlet.
Aldebaran *al-deb'ə-ran*, *n* a first-magnitude red star of the Hyades. [Ar *al-dabarān* the follower (of the Pleiades)]
aldehyde *al'di-hīd*, *n* a volatile fluid with a suffocating smell, obtained by the oxidation of alcohol; a compound differing from an alcohol in having two fewer hydrogen atoms. [Contraction of *al*cohol *dēhyd*rogenātum, alcohol deprived of hydrogen]
al dente *al den'tā*, (*cookery*) *adj* and *adv* of pasta, firm to the teeth. [Ital, to the tooth]
alder *öl'dər*, *n* any tree of the genus **Al'nus**, related to the birches, *usu* growing in moist ground; extended to various other trees or shrubs; an artificial fishing fly. — *adj* **al'dern** made of alder. — **al'der-buck'thorn** a species of buckthorn (*Rhamnus frangula*); **al'der-fly** a riverside neuropterous insect. — *adj* **al'der-leaved**. [OE *alor*; Ger *Erle*; L *alnus*]
alder-liefest *öl-dər-lēf'ist*, (*Shakesp*) *adj* most beloved of all. [OE *alra* (WSax *ealra*), genitive pl of *al* (*eal*) all, and superl of **lief**]
alderman *öl'dər-mən*, *n* in OE times a nobleman of highest rank, a governor of a shire or district, a high official; later, head of a guild; in English boroughs, a civic dignitary next in rank to the mayor, elected by fellow councillors (chiefly *hist*); a superior member of an English county council (chiefly *hist*); a member of the governing body of a borough or of its upper house, elected by popular vote (*NAm*): — *pl* **al'dermen**. — *adj* **aldermanic** (*-man'ik*). — *n* **alderman'ity**. — *adj* **al'dermanlike** or **al'dermanly** pompous and portly. — *n* **al'dermanry**. — *n* **al'dermanship**. [OE *aldorman* (WSax *ealdorman*) from *aldor* (*ealdor*) a chief, from *ald* (*eald*) old, and noun-forming suffix *-or*]
Alderney *öl'dər-ni*, *n* a small dairy-cow, formerly of a breed kept in *Alderney*, now loosely including Jersey and Guernsey. — Also *adj*.
Aldine *öl'dīn*, *adj* from the press, or named in honour, of *Aldus* Manutius of Venice and his family (15–16c).
Aldis lamp *ol'dis lamp*, *n* a portable lantern with a movable device for sending messages by Morse code. [From the inventor A C W *Aldis*]
aldose *al'dōs*, (*chem*) *n* any of a class of monosaccharide sugars which contain an aldehyde group. — **aldō-** *combining form* denoting a sugar which belongs to this class, such as glucose (an **aldohex'ose**) or ribose (an **aldopen'tose**). [*ald*ehyde]
aldrin *al'drin*, *n* a chlorinated hydrocarbon, used as a contact insecticide. [From K *Alder*, German chemist (1902–58)]
ale *āl*, *n* an alcoholic beverage made from an infusion of malt by fermentation, the name applied to beers made by a brewing process in which yeast ferments on the top of the liquid; a feast or festival, from the liquor drunk (*archaic*). — **ale'bench** (*archaic*) a bench in or before an alehouse; **ale'-berry** (*archaic*) a beverage made from ale and bread sops with flavouring; **ale'-bush**, **ale'-pole** or **ale'-stake** (*hist*) a bush, pole or stake used as an alehouse sign; **ale'-conner** a civic officer appointed to test the quality of the ale brewed (*hist*); **ale'cost** costmary (used in flavouring ale); **ale'-draper** (*obs*) a tavern-keeper; **ale'-hoof** (OE *hōfe*) ground-ivy; **ale'-house** (*colloq*) a house in which ale is sold. — *adj* (*Shakesp*) **ale'washed**. — **ale'wife** a woman who sells ale (*archaic*); a fish related to the herring, common off the NE coast of America (perhaps from its corpulent shape, but perhaps a different word): — *pl* **ale'wives**. [OE (Anglian) *alu* (WSax *ealu*); ON *öl*]
aleatory *ā'li-ə-tər-i*, *adj* depending on contingencies; used of the element of chance in poetic composition, etc; aleatoric (*music*). — *n* aleatoric music. — *adj* **aleatoric** (*ā-li-ə-tör'ik*) in which chance influences the choice of notes (*music*); aleatory. [L *āleātōrius*, from *āleātor* a dicer, from *ālea* a die]
Alec, **alec** or **Aleck**. See under **smart**.
alecost. See **ale**.
Alecto *a-lek'tō*, *n* one of the Furies. [Gr *Alēktō* (literally) unceasing]
alectryon *a-lek'tri-ōn*, (*Gr*) *n* a cock.
alee *ə-lē'*, (*naut*) *adv* on or toward the lee-side. [ON *ā* on, and *hlē* lee]
aleft *ə-left'*, *adv* on or to the left hand. [**a-**[1] and **left**[2]]
alegar *al'* or *āl'i-gər*, *n* sour ale, or vinegar made from it. [**ale**, with termination as **vinegar**]
alegge, **aleggeaunce**. See **allege**[1].
Alemaine. See **Almain**.
Alemannic *al-ə-man'ik*, *adj* of the Alemannen or their dialect. — *n* the High German dialect of Switzerland, Alsace, etc. [L *Alemanni* or *Alamanni*, an ancient people of SW Germany]
alembic *ə-lem'bik*, *n* old distilling apparatus. — *adj* **alem'bicated** over-refined. — *n* **alembica'tion**. [Ar *al* the, and *anbīq*, from Gr *ambix* cap of a still]
alembroth *ə-lem'broth*. Same as **sal alembroth**.
alength *ə-length'*, *adv* at full length. [**a-**[1]]
à l'envi *a lā-vē*, (*Fr*) emulously; in emulation.
aleph *ä'lef* or *ā'lef*, *n* the first letter of the Phoenician and Hebrew alphabets, resembling an ox's head, representing a glottal stop but adopted by the Greeks for a vowel sound. See **A** and **alpha**. [Heb *āleph* ox]
alepine *al'i-pēn*, *n* a mixed fabric of wool and silk or mohair and cotton. [Perh *Aleppo*]
à l'époque *a lā-pok*, (*Fr*) at the time.
alerce *ə-lûrs'* or *ä-ler'thā*, *n* the wood of the sandarach tree; the Chilean arbor vitae. [Sp, larch, from L *larix*, *-icis* larch, perh confused with Ar *al'arza* the cedar]
alerion or **allerion** *a-lē'ri-ən*, (*heraldry*) *n* an eagle displayed, without feet or beak. [Fr]
alert *ə-lûrt'*, *adj* watchful; wide-awake; brisk, sharp or lively. — *n* a danger warning; the time for which it lasts; a condition of readiness or expectancy; a sudden attack or suprise. — *vt* to make alert. — *adv* **alert'ly**. — *n* **alert'ness**. — **on** or **upon the alert** on the watch; wakefully attentive. [Fr *alerte*, from Ital *all'erta* on the erect, from *erto*, from L *ērēctus* erect]
Aleurites *al-ū-rī'tēz*, *n* a genus of plants of the spurge family, yielding tung oil and candle-nut. [Gr *aleuron* flour]
aleurone *a-lū'rōn*, *n* a protein found in some seeds. — Also **aleu'ron** (*-on* or *-ən*). [Gr *aleuron* flour]
alevin *al'i-vin*, *n* a young fish, *esp* a salmonid. [Fr, from OFr *alever* to rear, from L *ad* to, and *levāre* to raise]
alew *ə-lōō'* or *-lū'*, (*Spenser*) *n*. Same as **halloo**.
alewashed, **alewife**. See **ale**.
Alexander technique *al-ig-zän'dər tek-nēk'*, *n* a technique of exercise, manipulation, etc designed to improve posture and so avoid physical strain. [From its originator, the Australian actor F M *Alexander* (died 1955)]
alexanders *al-ig-zän'dərz*, *n* an umbelliferous plant (genus *Smyrnium*) the stems of which were formerly eaten as celery is now. [OE *alexandre*; L *olus atrum*, *olusatrum* literally 'black herb, vegetable', has been suggested as source]
Alexandrian *al-ig-zän'dri-ən*, *adj* relating to *Alexandria* in Egypt, its Hellenistic school of philosophy, its poetry, or the general character of its culture and taste, erudite

and critical rather than original in inspiration, sometimes with a suggestion of decadence; relating to *Alexander* the Great or any other of the same name. — Also *n*. — *n* and *adj* **Alexan'drine** Alexandrian. — *n* **alexan'drīne** a verse of six iambs (in English), or in French of 12 and 13 syllables in alternate couplets (perhaps from a poem on *Alexander* the Great by *Alexandre* Paris). — Also *adj*. — *n* **alexan'drite** a dark green mineral, a kind of chrysoberyl (discovered on the day of majority of the Cesarevich later *Alexander* II).

alexia *a-lek'si-ə*, *n* loss of power to read; word-blindness. — *adj* **alex'ic**. [New L, from Gr *a-* (privative) and *legein* to speak, confused with L *legere* to read]

alexin *a-lek'sin*, *n* a body present in the blood serum, which uniting with an anti-serum gives protection against disease. — *adj* **alexipharmic** (*-si-fär'mik*) acting against poison. — *n* **alexiphar'mic** or **alexiphar'makon** an antidote to poison. [Gr *alexein* to ward off, and *alexipharmakos*, from *pharmakon* poison]

aleye. See **allay**[1].

ALF *abbrev*: Animal Liberation Front, an organization dedicated to freeing animals from cruel or exploitative captivity.

Alf *alf*, *n* a classic example of a narrow-minded, ignorant and male-chauvinist man. — Also *adj*.

alfa. See **halfa**.

alfalfa *al-fal'fə*, *n* a variety of, or (*esp US*) another name for, the fodder plant, lucerne. [Sp *alfalfa*, from Ar *alfaçfçah*]

alfaquí *al-fa-kē'*, (*Sp*) *n* a Muslim expounder of the law.

alférez *al-fā'rāth*, (*Sp*) *n* a standard-bearer.

alforja *al-för'hha*, (*Sp*) *n* a saddle-bag; a baboon's cheek-pouch.

alfresco *al-fresk'ō*, *adv* and *adj* in the fresh or cool air; on fresh or moist plaster (*painting*). [Ital; see **fresco** and **fresh**]

Alg. *abbrev*: Algeria.

alg. *abbrev*: algebra or algebraic.

alga *al'gə*, *n* a seaweed; any member of the Algae: — *pl* **algae** (*al'jē* or *-gē*). — *n pl* **Al'gae** (*bot*) a great group of Thallophytes, the seaweeds and related forms. — *adj* **al'gal** (*-gəl*). — *n* **al'gicide** (*-ji-sīd*) a substance used to destroy algae. — *n* **al'gin** (*-jin*) sodium alginate, a gummy nitrogenous organic compound obtained from seaweeds. — *n* **al'ginate** a salt of alginic acid. — *adj* **algin'ic** (eg as in **alginic acid** an acid obtained from certain seaweeds, used in plastics, medicine, as a food-thickening agent, etc). — *adj* **al'goid** (*-goid*) of the nature of or resembling an alga. — *adj* **algolog'ical**. — *adv* **algolog'ically**. — *n* **algol'ogist**. — *n* **algol'ogy** the study of algae. — **algae poisoning** a form of often fatal poisoning affecting livestock, etc, caused by the ingestion of toxins in decomposing algae and characterized by nervous symptoms. [L *alga* seaweed]

algarroba *al-ga-rō'bə*, *n* the carob; the mesquite; the fruit of either. — Also **algarō'ba** or **algarrō'bo** (*pl* **algarro'bos**). [Sp *algarroba*, *algarrobo*, from Ar *al kharrūbah*; cf **carob**]

algate or **algates** *öl'gāt(s)*, *adv* always, at all events, nevertheless (*obs*); altogether (*Spenser*). [**all** and **gate**[2]; orig dative, with *-s* on the analogy of *always*, etc]

algebra *al'ji-brə*, *n* a method of calculating by symbols, by means of letters employed to represent quantities, and signs to represent their relations, thus forming a kind of generalized arithmetic; in modern mathematics, any of a number of systems using symbols and involving reasoning about relationships and operations. — *adj* **algebraic** (*-brā'ik*) or **algebrā'ical**. — *adv* **algebrā'ically**. — *n* **algebrā'ist** a person skilled in algebra. [Ital and Sp, from Ar *al-jebr* resetting (of anything broken), hence combination, from *jabara* to reunite]

Algerian *al-jē'ri-ən*, *adj* of Algeria or Algiers. — *n* a native of Algeria. — *n* **Algerine** (*al'jə-rēn*) an Algerian (*archaic*); (without *cap*) a pirate (*hist*).

algesia *al-jē'zi-ə*, or *-si-*, *n* sensitivity to pain. — *n* **algē'sis** the sensation of pain. [New L, from Gr *algēsis*, from *algein* to suffer]

-algia *-al'ji-ə*, *combining form* denoting pain (in a particular part or because of a particular thing). [Gr *algos* pain]

algicide. See **alga**.

algid *al'jid*, *adj* cold or chill, *esp* applied to a cold fit in disease. — *n* **algid'ity**. [L *algidus* cold]

algin, **alginate**, **algology**, etc. See **alga**.

Algol[1] *al'gol*, *n* a variable star in the constellation Perseus. [Ar *al ghūl* the ghoul]

Algol[2] *al'gol*, *n* a type of computer programming language first developed in Europe in 1950, used *esp* for scientific and mathematical applications. [*Algo*rithmic *l*anguage]

algolagnia *al-gō-lag'ni-ə*, *n* sexual pleasure obtained from inflicting or suffering pain. [Gr *algos* pain, and *lagneiā* lust]

Algonkian *al-gong'ki-ən*, or **Algonquian** also *-kwi-*, *n* a family of N American Indian languages, including Natick, Shawnee, Ojibwa, Cheyenne, etc, spoken over a wide area; a member of a tribe speaking one of these languages. — Also *adj*. [Am Eng, from **Algonquin**]

Algonquin *al-gong'kwin*, or **Algonkin** *-kin*, *n* a leading group of Indian tribes in the valley of the Ottawa and around the northern tributaries of the St Lawrence; a member of this group; their language. — Also *adj*. [Micmac Indian *algoomaking* at the place of spearing fish]

algophobia *al-gō-fō'bi-ə*, *n* obsessive fear of pain. [Gr *algos* pain, and **phobia**]

algorism *al'gə-rizm*, *n* the Arabic system of numeration; arithmetic; an algorithm. [LL *algorismus*, from Ar *al-Khwārazmi* the native of Khwārazm (Khiva), ie the 9c mathematician Abu Ja'far Mohammed ben Musa]

algorithm *al'gə-ridhm*, *n* a rule for solving a mathematical problem in a finite number of steps; a set of instructions or steps designed to provide a method of solving a problem or achieving a result (*comput*); a step-by-step method for solving a problem, often in the form of a flow chart (qv). — *adj* **algorith'mic**. — **algorithmic language** or **algorithmic orientated language** see **Algol**[2]. [**algorism**]

alguazil *al-gwa-zil'* or **alguacil** *äl-gwä-thēl'*, *n* in Spain, an officer who makes arrests, etc. [Sp (now) *alguacil*, from Ar *al-wazīr*. See **vizier**]

algum *al'gəm*, (*Bible*) *n* a wood imported into ancient Palestine, *prob* red sandalwood. — Also **al'mug**. [Heb *algūm*]

Alhagi *al-hā'jī* or *-hä'jē*, *n* a papilionaceous manna-yielding genus of desert shrubs. [Ar *al-hāj*]

Alhambra *al-ham'brə*, *n* the palace of the Moorish kings of Granada in Spain. — *adj* **Alhambresque** (*-bresk'*). [Ar *al-hamrā'* the red (house)]

alias *ā'li-əs*, *adv* otherwise known as. — *n* an assumed name: — *pl* **a'liases**. — *n* **a'liasing** (*image technol*) image imperfections resulting from limited detail in eg a raster display, resulting in a diagonal line appearing stepped. [L *aliās*, at another time, otherwise, from *alius* other]

alibi *al'i-bī*, *n* the plea in a criminal charge of having been elsewhere at the relevant time; the fact of being elsewhere; an excuse for failure (*colloq*). [L *alibī* elsewhere, orig locative, from *alius* other]

alicant *al-i-kant'*, *n* wine made near *Alicante* in Spain.

Alice *al'is*, *n* the main character in the children's fantasies *Alice's Adventures in Wonderland* (1865) and *Through the Looking-glass* (1872) by Lewis Carroll. — **Alice band** a wide hair-band of coloured ribbon or other material (as worn by Alice in Tenniel's illustrations to *Through the Looking-glass*). — *adj* **Al'ice-in-Won'derland** as if happening in a dream or fantasy; unreal.

alicyclic *al-i-sīk'lik*, *adj* having properties of aliphatic organic compounds but containing a ring of carbon atoms instead of an open chain. [**aliphatic** and **cyclic**]

alidad *al'i-dad* or *-dad'*, or **alidade** *-dād*, (*surveying*) *n* a revolving index for reading the graduations of an astrolabe, quadrant, or similar instrument, or for taking the direction of objects. [Ar *al 'idādah* the revolving radius, from *'adid* humerus]

alien *ā'li-ən* or *-lyən, adj* belonging to something else; foreign; from elsewhere; extraneous; repugnant or offensive; inconsistent (with *to*); incompatible or irreconcilable; estranged. — *n* a foreigner; a resident neither native-born nor naturalized; an outsider; an extraterrestrial; a plant introduced to a locality by man but maintaining itself. — *vt* to alienate (*archaic*); to transfer (*rare*); to estrange (*archaic*). — *n* **alienabil'ity**. — *adj* **a'lienable** (*law*) capable of being transferred to another. — *n* **a'lienage** the state of being an alien. — *vt* **a'lienate** to transfer; to estrange or to distance by taking away friendship or contact. — *adj* withdrawn; estranged. — *n* **alienā'tion** estrangement; mental or emotional detachment; the state of not being involved; the critical detachment with which, according to Bertolt Brecht, audience and actors should regard a play, considering action and dialogue and the ideas in the drama without emotional involvement. — *n* **a'lienātor**. — *adj* **al'iened** made alien; estranged. — *n* **alienee'** (*law*) a person to whom property is transferred. — *n* **al'ienism** the position of being a foreigner; the study and treatment of mental diseases. — *n* **a'lienist** a person who specially studies or treats mental diseases. — *n* **a'lienor** (*law*) a person who transfers property. — **alienation effect** or **A-effect** Brecht's theory of alienation (see above). [L *aliēnus*, from *alius* other]

aliform *ā'li-fȯrm*, or *al'*, *adj* wing-shaped. [L *āla* wing, and *forma* shape]

aligarta. See **alligator**.

alight[1] *ə-līt'*, *vi* to dismount, descend; to perch, settle; to land; to come to rest; to come by chance (upon something); to fall, strike: — *pa t* and *pa p* **alight'ed** (or **alit'**). [OE *ālīhtan* (see **light**[2])]

alight[2] *ə-līt*, *adj* on fire; lit up. [**a**[1] and **light**[1]]

align *ə-līn'*, *vt* (*NAm* **aline'**) to arrange in line; to make (eg a view or policy) fit or tally (with *with*); to regulate by a line. — *vi* to agree or fall into line; to be arranged on or in a line. — *n* **align'ment** (*NAm* **aline'ment**) setting in a line or lines; a row arranged in this way, such as of standing-stones; the ground-plan of a railway or road (*archaic*); the taking of a side, or the side taken, politically, etc. — **alignment chart** a nomogram, *esp* one comprising three scales in which a line joining values on two determines a value on the third. [Fr *aligner*, from L *ad* to, and *līneāre* to line]

alike *ə-līk'*, *adj* the same in appearance or character. — *adv* equally. [OE *gelīc*, combined with ON *ālīkr*, OE *onlīc*; see **like**[1]]

aliment *al'i-mənt*, *n* nourishment; food; provision for maintenance, alimony (*Scots law*). — *vt* to support, sustain; to provide aliment for. — *adj* **alimental** (*-ment'l*) supplying food. — *adj* **aliment'ary** pertaining to aliment; nutritive. — *n* **alimentā'tion**. — *adj* **aliment'ative**. — *n* **aliment'iveness** a phrenologist's word for the instinct to seek food or drink. — **alimentary canal** the internal passage from the mouth to the anus. [L *alimentum*, from *alere* to nourish]

alimony *al'i-mən-i*, *n* an allowance for support made by one spouse to the other pending or after their divorce or legal separation. [L *alimōnia*, from *alere* to nourish]

à l'improviste *a lɛ̃-prō-vēst*, (*Fr*) suddenly; unexpectedly; unawares.

A-line *ā'-līn*, *adj* (of clothing) narrow at the top and widening evenly to a full hem-line. [**A** and **line**[2]]

aline, alinement. See **align**.

alineation. See **allineation**.

aliped *al'i-ped*, *adj* (*zool*) having winged feet, used eg of the bat, whose toes are connected by a wing-like membrane. — *n* an animal with winged feet. [L *ālipes*, *-pedis*, from *āla* wing, and *pēs*, *pedis* foot]

aliphatic *al-i-fat'ik*, (*chem*) *adj* fatty; belonging to the open-chain class of organic compounds, or methane derivatives (*opp* to *aromatic*). [Gr *aleiphar*, *aleiphatos* oil]

aliquant *al'i-kwənt*, (*math*) *adj* such as will not divide a number without a remainder (eg 5 is an aliquant part of 12). [L *aliquantum* somewhat]

aliquot *al'i-kwot*, (*math*) *adj* such as will divide a number without a remainder. [L *aliquot* some or several]

alisma *a-liz'mə*, *n* a plant of the water-plantain genus *Alisma* of monocotyledons, giving name to the family **Alismā'ceae**. — *adj* **alismā'ceous**. [Gr *alisma* water-plantain]

alit. See **alight**[1].

aliunde *ā-li-un'de*, (*law*) *adv* from another source. — Also *adj*. [L, from elsewhere]

alive *ə-līv'*, *adj* living; vigorous; existing; lively or animated; (of a wire, etc) live; sensitive, cognizant (with *to*). — *n* **alive'ness**. — **alive and kicking** strong and active; full of vigour; **alive with** swarming with; **look alive** be brisk; hurry up. [OE *on līfe* (dative of *līf* life), in life]

aliyah or **aliya** *a-lē'yä*, *n* immigration to Israel. [Heb, literally, a going up or ascent]

alizari *al-i-zä'rē*, *n* levantine madder. — *n* **alizarin** (*a-liz'ə-rin*) or **alizarine** (*a-liz'ə-rēn*) the colouring matter of madder root ($C_{14}H_8O_{14}$) now made synthetically. [Sp and Fr, prob from Ar *al* the, and *'aҫārah* juice pressed out]

alkahest or **alcahest** *al'kə-hest*, *n* the universal solvent of the alchemists. [Appar a sham Ar coinage of Paracelsus]

alkali *al'kə-li* or *-lī*, (*chem*) *n* a substance which, dissolved in water, forms a solution containing hydroxyl ions and with a pH of more than 7: — *pl* **al'kalis** or **al'kalies**. — *adj* of, pertaining to, containing or forming an alkali. — *n* **alkalesc'ence** or **alkalesc'ency**. — *adj* **alkalesc'ent** tending to become alkaline; slightly alkaline. — *vt* and *vi* **alkalify** (*al'kəl-i-fī* or *al-kal'i-fī*). — *n* **alkalim'eter** an instrument for measuring the concentration of alkalis. — *n* **alkalim'etry**. — *adj* **al'kaline** (*-līn* or *-lin*) having the properties of an alkali; containing a high proportion of alkali. — *n* **alkalinity** (*-lin'*) the quality of being alkaline; the extent to which a substance is alkaline. — *vt* **al'kalize** or **-ise** to make alkaline. — Also **al'kalinize** or **-ise**. — *n* **al'kaloid** any of various nitrogenous organic bases found in plants, having specific physiological action. — *adj* pertaining to or resembling alkali. — *n* **alkalosis** (*al-kə-lō'sis*) an illness in which the blood or tissues of the body become too alkaline. — *n* **al'kyl** (*-kil*; Ger *Alk*ohol, alcohol and **-yl**) a general name for monovalent hydrocarbon radicals of formula C_nH_{2n+1}, often denoted R; a compound with one or more such radicals in it, such as *lead alkyl*. — **alkali metals** the univalent metals of the first group of the periodic system, lithium, sodium, potassium, rubidium, caesium, francium, forming strong basic hydroxides; **alkaline earth** an oxide of any of the alkaline earth metals; an alkaline earth metal; **alkaline earth metals** the bivalent metals of the second group of the periodic system, calcium, strontium, barium, and sometimes magnesium and radium. [Ar *alqalīy* the calcined ashes]

alkane *al'kān*, *n* the general name for a hydrocarbon of the methane series, of general formula C_nH_{2n+2}. [*alk*yd and meth*ane*]

alkanet *al'kə-net*, *n* a Mediterranean plant (genus *Alkanna*) of the borage family; a red dye obtained from its root; extended to various related plants (*Anchusa*, etc). [Sp *alcaneta*, dimin, from Ar *al-hennā* the henna]

alkene *al'kēn*, (*chem*) *n* the general name for an unsaturated hydrocarbon of the ethylene series, of general formula C_nH_{2n}. [*alk*yl and eth*ene*]

alkie or **alky** *al'ki*, (*colloq*) *n* an alcoholic.

Alkoran *n*. Same as **Alcoran**.

alkyd *al'kid*, *n* any of a group of synthetic resins used in paints and protective coatings and in adhesives. — Also **alkyd resin** (*rez'in*). [*alky*l and *acid*]

alkyl. See **alkali**.

alkyne *al'kīn*, *n* the general name for a hydrocarbon of the acetylene series, of general formula C_nH_{2n-2}. [*alk*yd and eth*yne*]

all *öl*, *adj* comprising every individual one (eg *all men, all roads, all instances*); comprising the whole extent, etc of (eg *all winter*); any whatever; (preceding 'the') as many as there are, or as much as there is (eg *all the men, all the cheese*); also used following *pl pers pronoun* or sometimes *n pl* (eg *we all laughed, the guests all came*); the greatest possible (eg *with all haste, in all sincerity*); every. — *n* the whole; everybody; everything; the totality of things; the universe; one's whole possessions or utmost efforts (formerly often in *pl*). — *adv* wholly; entirely; quite or completely; without limit, infinitely; on all sides; on each side, apiece; even or just (passing into a mere intensive, eg *all on a summer's day*, or almost into a conjunction by omission of *if* or *though*). — *combining form* denoting infinite, infinitely; universal; completely; wholly; by all; having all for object. — *n* **all'ness** the condition of being all. — Possible compounds are without limit and only a selection can be given: — *adj* **all'-Amer'ican** representative of the whole of America, *esp* in some admirable quality; typically American (in behaviour, appearance, etc); chosen to represent the United States; consisting entirely of US or American members. — **All Blacks** the New Zealand international rugby team. — *adj* **all'-building** (*Shakesp*) *poss* on which all is built, but *prob* a misprint. — **all-chang'ing-word** a spell that transforms everything. — *adj* **all-cheer'ing** giving cheerfulness to all. — **all'-clear'** a signal that the reason for sheltering, or (*fig*) for inactivity, is past. — *n pl* **all'comers** everyone who arrives or is present. — *adj* **all'-day** lasting all day. — *adj* **all-dread'ed** dreaded by all. — *adj* **all'-elec'tric** using only electricity for heating and lighting. — *adj* **all-end'ing**. — **All'-father** Woden; Zeus; God. — *adj* **all'-fired** (*colloq*, *orig US*) infernal (*perh* for hell-fired). — *adv* **all'-firedly**. — **all-fives'** a game of dominoes in which the aim is to make the end pips sum a multiple of five; **all-fours'** a card game in which there are four chances that score a point (see also **four**); **all-giv'er** (*Milton*) the giver of all, God; **all'-good** the plant good-King-Henry. — *adj* **all-good'** infinitely good. — *interj* **all-hail'** (*archaic*) a greeting (literally, all health). — *n* (*archaic*) a salutation of 'All hail'. — *vt* (*archaic*) to greet with 'All hail'. — *adj* (*orig* genitive pl of noun; *obs*) **all'hall'own, all'hall'owen, all'holl'own, all'hall'ond** (*Shakesp* **al-hallown summer** a spell of fine weather about All Hallows). — **All-hall'owmass** the feast of All Saints; **All-Hall'ows** All Saints' Day, 1 November; **All-hall'owtide** the season of All-Hallows; **all'heal** a panacea (*obs*); the great valerian or other plant thought to have healing properties, eg self-heal; **all-hid'** (*archaic*) hide-and-seek. — *adj* **all-import'ant** essential; crucial. — *adj* **all-in'** including everything (also **all-inclu'sive**; see also **all in** below); of a school, etc, comprehensive; (of wrestling) freestyle, with no restrictions on holds. — *adj* **all'night** lasting, open, etc all night. — *n* **allnight'er** any event, party, etc that lasts all night. — *adj* **all-obey'ing** (*Shakesp*) obeyed by all. — *adj* **all'-or-noth'ing** that must be gained, accepted, etc completely or not at all. — *adj* **all'-out** using maximum effort; of a strike, with everyone participating. — *adj* **all'-ov'er** over the entire surface, body, etc. — *adj* **all-ō'verish** (*colloq*) having an indefinite sense of indisposition, discomfort, or malaise. — *n* **all-ō'verishness** (*colloq*). — *adj* **all-play-all'** of a competition, in which every competitor plays against every other in turn. — *adj* **all-pow'erful** supremely powerful; omnipotent. — *adj* **all-pur'pose** that can be used for any purpose, in any circumstances, etc. — *adj* **all-red'** (*obs*) exclusively on British territory (from the conventional colouring of maps). — *adj* **all-risks'** (of insurance) covering all risks except a number specifically excluded (eg war risks, damage due to depreciation, etc). — *adj* **all'-round** including, applying to all; adequate, complete, or competent on all sides. — **all-round'er** some one who shows ability in many sports or many aspects of a particular sport, *esp* cricket; someone who shows an ability in or who has an involvement in many kinds of work, etc (also *adj*); **all-round'ness**. — *adj* **all-rul'ing**. — **all'seed** a weed (genus *Radiola*) of the flax family, or other many-seeded plant. — *adj* **all-see'ing**. — **all-sē'er** (*Shakesp*) one who sees all, ie God. — *n pl* **all'sorts** things of various odd shapes, sizes, colours, etc (also *fig*). — **all'spice** pimento or Jamaica pepper, supposed to combine the flavours of cinnamon, nutmeg and cloves (see also **Calycanthus**). — *adj* **all'-star'** having a cast or team all of whom are stars. — *adj* **all-tell'ing** (*Shakesp*). — *adv* **all'-thing** (*Shakesp*) every way. — *adj* **all'-time** of all time to date. — *n* and *adj* **all'-up** (of loaded aircraft) total (weight); (see also **all-up service** below). — *adj* **all'-weather** capable of use in all kinds of weather; weatherproof. — **all'-work** all kinds of work (*esp* domestic). — **after all** when everything has been considered; in spite of all that; nevertheless; **all along** everywhere along; all the time; **all and some** (*obs*) one and all; **all at once** suddenly; **all but** everything short of, almost; **All Fools' Day** April Fools' Day, 1 April; **all for** (*colloq*) strongly in favour of; **all found** (*usu* of a price) all in, with everything included; **All Hallows' Day** All Saints' Day; **all in** exhausted; everything included; **all in all** all things considered, all or everything together; something which someone is wholly wrapped up in; **all of** (*colloq*) as long or as far, etc as; the whole distance, time, etc of; **all out** at full power or speed; completely exhausted; **all over** everywhere; over the whole of; covered with (*colloq*); thoroughly, entirely; very characteristically; **all over the place** all awry, or in a disorganized muddle; **all over with** finished, done with, completely at an end with; **all right** unhurt, safe; adequate, suitable; acceptable (also *US colloq* **all-right**); yes, fine, ok;... you can be sure of that!; (also **a bit of all right**; *slang*) very good, or *esp* of a young woman, very attractive; **all-round camera** a camera able to make a strip picture of the whole periphery of an object revolved before it; **All Saints' Day** 1 November, a Christian festival in honour of the saints collectively; **all singing, all dancing** (*colloq*) fully functional; performing superlatively; **all's one** it is just the same; **All Souls' Day** 2 November, a RC day of prayer for souls in Purgatory; **all square** (of debts, etc) settled; (in games) having equal scores; **all systems go** everything (is) in working order, starting up, etc (also *fig*); **all that** (*usu* after a negative or a question) so, especially, as... as all that; **all the best** a phrase used to wish someone good luck, etc; **all there** completely sane; (*colloq*) of normal intelligence, not stupid; alert; **all the same** see under **same**; **all the way** a euphemistic expression for full sexual intercourse, as in *go all the way* (with someone); **all-time high** or **low** a high or low level never before reached; **all-time record** a record exceeding all others in all times; **all told** including every person, thing, etc; taking everything into account; **all to one** (*obs*) altogether; **all-up service** (*commerce*) mail destined for countries in Europe which goes by air; **all up with** at an end with; beyond any hope for; **all-wing aeroplane** an aeroplane with no fuselage, the cabin being in the wings; **and all** as well as the rest; **and all that** and all the rest of it, *et cetera*; **as all that** to that extent; **at all** in the least degree; in any way; in any circumstances; used also merely to give emphasis; **be all over someone** to be excessively and sometimes irritatingly friendly and attentive to someone; **be all things to all men** to alter one's approach, behaviour, attitude, etc to suit the person one is dealing with; to be (*usu* excessively) affable; **for all** notwithstanding; **for good and all** finally; **in all** all told; in total; **once and for all** once and once only, finally; **when all is said and done** after all; all things considered. [OE (Anglian) *all*, (WSax *eall*); Ger *all*]

alla breve *a'lə* or *äl'lä brā'vā*, or *brev*, (*music*) in quick common time; with 2 or 4 minims to the bar. [Ital, according to the breve, there being orig a breve to the bar]

alla cappella *a'lə ka-pel'ə* or *äl'lä käp-pel'lä*. See **a cappella**.

alla Franca *a'lə frang'kə* or *äl'lä frängk'ä*, (*Ital*) in the French style.

Allah *al'ä*, (*Islam*) *n* the name of God. — **Allahu akbar** (*äl-lä-hōō äk-bär*; *Ar*) God is great. [Ar *allāh*, from *alilāh*, the God]

alla marcia *a'lə mär'chə* or *äl'lä mär'chä*, (*music*) in the manner of a march. [Ital]

allantois *a-lan'tō-is*, *n* a membranous sac-like appendage for effecting oxygenation in the embryos of mammals, birds and reptiles. — *adj* **allanto'ic**. — *adj* **allan'toid** (*-toid*) sausage-shaped; pertaining to the allantois. — *n* the allantois. [Irregularly formed from Gr *allās*, *-āntos* a sausage, and *eidos* form]

alla prima *a'lə prē'mə* or *äl'lä prē'mä*, (*Ital*) a technique of painting in which only one layer of pigment is applied to the surface to complete the canvas.

allargando *a-lär-gan'dō*, (*music*) *adj* and *adv* slowing. [Ital *allargare* to broaden]

alla stoccata *a'lə sto-kat'ə* or *äl'lä sto-kä'tä*, (*Ital*) thrusting with a pointed weapon.

alla Tedesca *a'lə te-des'kə* or *äl'lä te-des'kä*, (*Ital*) in the German style.

allative *al'ə-tiv*, (*gram*) *adj* describing a case denoting movement to or towards. — *n* (a word in) the allative case. [L *allatum*, supine of *afferre*, from *ad* to, and *ferre* to bear]

alla vostra salute *äl'lä vōs'trä sa-lōō'tā*, (*Ital*) to your health.

allay[1], earlier **aleye**, **alay**, etc, *ə-lā'*, *vt* to put down; to quell; to calm; to alleviate; to abate, lessen; to reduce; to alloy or temper. — *vi* to abate. — *n* **allay'er**. — *n* **allay'ing**. — *n* **allay'ment**. [OE *ālecgan*, from pfx *ā-* (intensive), and *lecgan* to lay. This verb in ME became indistinguishable in form in some of its parts from **allay**[2] or **alloy**, and from **allege**[1], and the meanings also overlapped]

allay[2] *ə-lā'*, *vt* to alloy; to mix with something inferior; to dilute; to debase; to lessen or detract from the goodness of. — *n* alloy; alloying; dilution; lessening; impairment. [See **alloy** and the etymological note to **allay**[1]]

all-be. See **albe**.

alledge. Old spelling of **allege**[1, 2].

allée *a-lā*, (*Fr*) *n* an avenue, walk or garden path.

allege[1] (*Spenser* **allegge** or **alegge**) *ə-lej'*, (*obs*) *vt* to alleviate; to allay. — *n* **allege'ance** (*ə-lej'əns*; *Spenser* **aleggeaunce** *a-lej'i-ans*) alleviation. [OFr *aleger*, from L *alleviāre* (see **alleviate**) fused with OE *ālecgan* (see **allay**[1])]

allege[2] *ə-lej'*, *vt* to assert with a view to subsequent proof, hence without proof; to bring forward in argument or plea; to cite or quote in discussion; to declare in court upon oath (*obs*); to cite (*archaic*). — *n* **allegation** (*al-i-gā'shən*) the act of alleging; that which is alleged; an unproved or unaccepted assertion; citation. — *adj* **alleged** (*ə-lejd'*). — *adv* **allegedly** (*-lej'əd-li*). — *n* **alleg'er**. [OFr *esligier* to clear at law, from L *ex* from, and *lītigāre* to sue]

allegiance *ə-lē'jəns*, *n* the relation or obligation of liegeman to liege-lord (*hist*) or of subject to sovereign or state; loyalty (to a person or cause). — *adj* (*Shakesp*) **alle'giant**. [L *ad* to, and **liege**]

allegory *al'i-gər-i*, *n* a narrative, picture or other work of art intended to be understood symbolically; symbolical narration. — *adj* **allegoric** (*-gor'ik*) or **allegor'ical**. — *adv* **allegor'ically**. — *n* **all'egorist**. — *n* **allegorīzā'tion** or **-s-**. — *vt* **all'egorize** or **-ise** to put in the form of an allegory; to treat as allegory. — *vi* to use allegory. — *n* **all'egorizer** or **-s-**. [Gr *allēgoriā*, from *allos* other, and *agoreuein* to speak]

allegro *a-lā'grō* or *äl-lā'grō*, (*music*) *adv* and *adj* with brisk movement; lively and rather fast. — *n* an allegro piece or movement: — *pl* **alle'gros**. — *adv* and *adj* **allegret'to** somewhat brisk (less so than *allegro*). — Also *n* (*pl* **allegret'tos**). [Ital, from L *alacer* brisk]

allele or **allel** *al-ēl'*, *n* short forms of **allelomorph** (*al-ēl'ō-mörf*) any one of the two or more possible forms of a gene; a gene considered as the means of transmission of an allele. — *adj* **allelomor'phic**. — *n* **allelomor'phism**. [Gr *allēlōn* of one another, and *morphē* form]

allelopathy *al-il-op'ə-thi*, (*biol*) *n* an adverse influence exerted either by one individual plant on another for the production of a chemical inhibitor, or by one strain over another within a species. [Fr *allélopathie*, from Gr *allēlos* each other, and *pathos* suffering]

alleluia or **alleluiah** *al-i-lōō'yä*. Same as **hallelujah**.

allemande *al'(i-)mand or al-mäd*, (*music*) *n* a smooth-running movement of moderate tempo, in common time, coming after the prelude in a classical suite; a Swabian dance in triple time; a German dance in 2–4 time; a movement effecting change of position in a dance. [Fr *allemande* (fem) German]

Allen screw *a'lən skrōō*, *n* a screw with a hexagonal recess in the head, turned by an **Allen key**, an L-shaped hexagonal rod. [Orig a trademark]

allenarly *al-en'ər-li*, (*obs* except *Scots law*) *adv* solely, only. [**all** and **anerly**]

allergy *al'ər-ji*, *n* an altered or acquired state of sensitivity; an abnormal reaction of the body to substances normally harmless; hypersensitivity to certain antigens or other excitant substances; (*colloq*) antipathy, dislike or repugnance. — *n* **all'ergen** any substance that induces an allergic reaction. — *adj* **allergen'ic** causing an allergic reaction. — *adj* **allergic** (*ə-lûr'jik*) (of the body) reacting in an abnormally sensitive manner; suffering from an allergy (to). — *n* an allergic person. — *n* **all'ergist** a doctor specializing in diseases and conditions caused by allergies. [Gr *allos* other, and *ergon* work]

allerion. See **alerion**.

alleviate *ə-lēv'i-āt*, *vt* to make light; to mitigate. — *n* **allēviā'tion**. — *adj* **allēv'iative**. — *n* **allēv'iātor**. — *adj* **allēviā'tory**. [LL *alleviāre*, *-ātum*, from L *ad* to, and *levis* light]

alley[1] *al'i*, *n* a passage; a narrow lane; a back lane; a walk in a garden or shrubbery; a long narrow enclosure or rink for bowls or skittles: — *pl* **all'eys**. — *adj* **alleyed** (*al'id*) having alleys or the form of an alley. — **all'eycat** a stray cat living in alleys and back streets; **all'eyway** a narrow passage; a corridor. [OFr *alee* (Fr *allée*) a passage, from *aller* to go]

alley[2] or **ally** *al'i*, *n* a choice taw or large marble. — *n* **all'(e)y-taw'** or **all'(e)y-tor'**. [Prob orig made of **alabaster**]

allez-vous-en *a-lā-vōō-zã*, (*Fr*) away with you; begone.

allheal. See **all**.

alliaceous *al-i-ā'shəs*, *adj* garlic-like. [L *allium* garlic]

alliance. See **ally**[1].

allice or **allis** *al'is*, *n* a species of shad. — Also **allis shad**. [L *alōsa*, *alausa* shad]

allicholy or **allycholly** *al'i-kol-i*, (*Shakesp*; *joc*) *n* and *adj* melancholy.

alligarta. See **alligator**.

alligate *al'i-gāt*, (*obs*) *vt* to conjoin; to perform alligation. — *n* **alligation** (*-gā'shən*) binding together (*rare*); conjunction; calculation of values or properties of a mixture (*arith*). [L *alligāre*, *-ātum*, from *ad* to, and *ligāre* to bind]

alligator *al'i-gā-tər*, earlier **aligarta** or **alligarta** *-gär'tə*, *n* a reptile of a mainly American family related to the crocodile but with a shorter, broader snout and other distinguishing characteristics. — **alligator apple** a fruit and tree of the custard-apple genus; **alligator pear** the avocado pear. [Sp *el* the (L *ille*), and *lagarto* lizard (L *lacertus*)]

allineation or **alineation** *a-lin-i-ā'shən*, *n* position in a straight line; alignment. [L *ad* to, and *līneāre*, *-ātum* to draw a line, from *līnea* line]

allis. See **allice**.

alliteration *ə-* or *a-lit-ər-ā'shən*, *n* the recurrence of the same initial sound (not necessarily letter) in words in close succession, such as 'the low last edge of the long lone land' (Swinburne); head-rhyme, the characteristic structure of versification of OE and other Old Germanic languages, each line having three accented syllables (two in the first half) with the same initial consonant or with different initial vowels. — *vi* **allit'erate** to begin with the same sound; to constitute alliteration; to practise alliteration. — *adj* **allit'erative**. [L *ad* to, and *lītera*, *littera* a letter]

allium *al'i-əm*, *n* a plant of the *Allium* genus to which onions, leeks, garlic, etc belong. [L, garlic]

allo- *a'lō-* or *a'lə-*, *combining form* denoting other; one of a group constituting a structural unit; different; from outside. — *n* **all'ocarpy** (*bot*; Gr *karpos* fruit) fruiting after cross-fertilization. — *n* **allocheiria** or **allochiria** (*-kī'ri-ə* or *-ki'*; *bot*; Gr *cheir* hand) attribution of a sensation to the wrong part of the body, eg to the other hand when one is painful. — *adj* **allochthonous** (*al-ok'thən-əs*; *science*; Gr *chthon* ground) having moved or been moved from another environment, away from its native location. — *adj* **allog'amous**. — *n* **allog'amy** (*bot*; Gr *gamos* marriage) cross-fertilization. — *n* **all'ograft** (*immunol*) a graft from one individual to another of a different species. — *n* **all'ograph** (Gr *graphē* writing) a writing made by one person on behalf of another. — *adj* **allomet'ric**. — *n* **allom'etry** (Gr *metron* measure) (the study of) the growth of a part of the body relative to that of other parts or of the whole body, in one organism or comparatively in a number of different organisms. — *n* **all'omorph** (*-mörf*; Gr *morphē* form; *linguistics*) one of two or more forms of the same morpheme. — *adj* **allopat'ric** (*bot*; Gr *patra* fatherland) of two species or populations not growing in the same area and therefore unable to breed because of distance or geographical barrier. — *n* **all'ophone** (*-fōn*; Gr *phōnē* sound; *linguistics*) one of two or more forms of the same phoneme. — *adj* **allophonic** (*-fon'*). — *n* **all'oplasm** protoplasm differentiated to perform a special function. — *adj* **alloplas'tic** (Gr *plastikos*; see **plastic**) affected by or affecting external factors. — *n* **allopurinol** (*-pūr'in-ol*; **purin** and *-ol*, from L *oleum* oil) a drug, $C_5H_4N_4O$, used in the the treatment of gout, reducing the formation of uric acid. — *n* **all'osaur** (*-sör*; Gr *sauros* lizard) a member of the genus **Allosaur'us**, large, lizard-hipped, carnivorous dinosaurs. — *adj* **allosteric** (*-ster'* or *-stēr'*; *biol*; see **steric**) (pertaining to an enzyme the activity of which may be) influenced by a combination with another substance; pertaining to the inhibition or stimulation of activity caused by such a combination; pertaining to a protein which alters its three-dimensional structure as the result of the binding of a smaller molecule, and also often its activity. — *n* **allos'tery**. — *n* **all'otheism** (Gr *theos* god) the worship of other gods or other people's gods. — *n* **allotrope** (*al'ə-trōp*; Gr *tropos* turn, habit) an allotropic form. — *adj* **allotrop'ic**. — *n* **allot'ropism**. — *adj* **allot'ropous** having nectar accessible to all kinds of insects (*bot*); of insects, eg those that visit allotropous flowers, short-tongued. — *n* **allot'ropy** the property (*esp* in chemical elements such as carbon) of existing in more than one form. [Gr *allos* other]

allocarpy. See **allo-**.

allocate *al'ō-kāt* or *al'ə-kāt*, *vt* to place; to locate; to apportion or assign. — *adj* **all'ocable** or **allocāt'able**. — *n* **allocā'tion** the act of allocating; a share allocated; allotment; apportionment; an allowance made upon an account. [L *allocāre*, from *ad* to, and *locāre*, *-ātum* to place, from *locus* a place]

allocheiria, **allochiria**. See **allo-**.

allocution *al-ō-kū'shən*, *n* an exhortation, *esp* (*Roman hist*) of a general to his troops; a formal address, *esp* of the Pope to the cardinals. [L *allocūtiō*, *-ōnis*, from *ad* to, and *loquī*, *locūtus* to speak]

allodium or **alodium** *a-lō'di-əm*, *n* an estate not subject to a feudal superior. — Also **allod** or **alod** (*al'od*). — *adj* **allō'dial** or **alōdial** (*opp* to *feudal*). [LL *allōdium*, from a Gmc word meaning complete ownership; cf **all** and OE *ēad* wealth, prosperity]

allogamous, **allogamy**, **allograph**. See **allo-**.

alloiostrophos *a-loi-os'tro-fos*, (*Gr prosody*) *adj* irregularly divided, not in alternate strophe and antistrophe.

allometric, **allometry**, **allomorph**. See **allo-**.

allonge *al-ɔ̃zh*, *n* a piece of paper attached to a bill of exchange for further endorsement. [Fr]

allons *a-lɔ̃*, (*Fr*) *interj* let us go; come on; come.

allonym *al'ō-nim*, *n* another person's name adopted as a pseudonym by a writer. — *adj* **allon'ymous**. [Fr, from Gr *allos* other, and *onyma* = *onoma* name]

allopathy *al-op'ə-thi*, *n* orthodox medical practice, treatment of diseases by drugs, etc, whose effect on the body is the opposite of that of the disease, distinguished from *homoeopathy*. — *n* **all'ōpath**. — *adj* **allopathic** (*al-ō-path'ik*). — *adv* **allopath'ically**. — *n* **allop'athist**. [Ger *Allopathie*, coined by Hahnemann (1755–1843), from Gr *allos* other, and *pathos* suffering]

allophone ... to ... **allostery**. See **allo-**.

allot *ə-lot*, *vt* to distribute in portions; to parcel out; to assign; to divide as by lot: — *pr p* **allott'ing**; *pa t* and *pa p* **allott'ed**. — *n* **allot'ment** the act of allotting; a part or share allotted; a piece of ground let out for spare-time cultivation under a public scheme; the distribution of shares to individuals who have applied to purchase them; the number of shares distributed; a portion of a field assigned to a cottager to labour for himself (*hist*). — *n* **allottee'** someone to whom something is allotted. — *n* **allott'ery** (*Shakesp*) a share allotted. [OFr *aloter*, from *à* to, and the Gmc root of **lot**]

allotheism. See **allo-**.

allotriomorphic *a-lot-ri-ō-mör'fik*, *adj* crystalline in internal structure but not in outward form. [Gr *allotrios* alien, and *morphē* form]

allotrope, **allotropy**, etc. See **allo-**.

allow *ə-low'*, *vt* to permit; to assign; to grant or give, *esp* periodically; to concede or acknowledge; to assume as an element in calculation or as something to be taken into account; to admit or agree as due; to conclude, hence to assert (*US*); to abate; to praise (*obs*); to pass, sanction, accept (*archaic*); to indulge (*Shakesp*). — *vi* to permit; to make allowance for. — *n* **allowabil'ity**. — *adj* **allow'able** that may be allowed; permissible; excusable. — *n* **allow'ableness**. — *adv* **allow'ably**. — *n* **allow'ance** that which is allowed; a limited portion or amount allowed, allotted or granted; a ration or stint; an amount of income, etc not subject to tax; money allowed to meet expenses or in consideration of special conditions (also **allowable expense**); abatement; a sum periodically granted; a taking into account in calculation or excuse, eg in *make allowances for*; approbation (*archaic*); admission, acknowledgement or permission (*Shakesp*). — *vt* to put upon an allowance; to supply in limited quantities. — *adj* **allowed'** permitted; licensed; acknowledged. — *adv* **allow'edly**. [OFr *alouer* to praise or bestow, of double origin: (1) L *allaudāre*, from *ad* to, and *laudāre* to praise; (2) L *ad*, and *locāre* to place]

alloy *al'oi* or *ə-loi'*, *n* a mixture of metals; extended to a mixture of metal with non-metal; the baser ingredient in such a mixture (*esp* in gold or silver); anything added in a mixture that impairs or debases the main ingredient; the fineness or standard of gold or silver. — *vt* to mix (metal); to mix with a less valuable metal; to impair or debase by being present; to temper or qualify. — *vi* to become alloyed. [Fr *aloi* (n), *aloyer* (v), from OFr *alei*, *aleier*, from L *alligāre*, from *ad* to, and *ligāre* to bind; **allay**[2] is from the corresponding Norman Fr *alai*, confused with **allay**[1]]

allseed, **allspice**. See under **all**.

all-to, **alto** or **all to** *öl'to͞o*, a spurious *adv* and *pfx* arising from the wrong division of **all** and a word with the pfx *to-* asunder, such as *allto brake*, *all to brake* for *all tobrake*: hence, altogether, eg **altoruffled** (*Milton* **all to ruffld**).

allude *ə-lo͞od'* or *-lūd'*, *vi* (with *to*) to convey an indirect reference in passing; to refer without explicit mention, or with suggestion of further associations; to refer. — *n* **allu'sion** (*-zhən*) indirect reference. — *adj* **allu'sive** (*-siv*) alluding; hinting; referring indirectly; canting (*heraldry*). — *adv* **allu'sively**. — *n* **allu'siveness**. [L *allūdere*, from *ad* at, and *lūdere*, *lūsum* to play]

allure[1] *ə-lūr'* or *-lōōr'*, *vt* to entice, seduce or attract; to draw on as by a lure (*obs*). — *n* **allure'** or **allure'ment**. — *n* **allur'er**. — *adj* **allur'ing**. — *adv* **allur'ingly**. [OFr *alurer*, from *à* to, and *lurer* to lure]

allure[2] *a-lür*, (*Fr*) *n* mien, gait or air.

allusion, etc. See **allude**.

alluvia, alluvial. See **alluvium**.

alluvion *ə-lōō'vi-ən*, or *-lū'*, *n* land gradually gained from a river or the sea by the washing up of sand and earth; the formation of such land; a flood; alluvium. [L *alluviō*, *-ōnis*; see **alluvium**]

alluvium *ə-lōō'vi-əm*, or *-lū'*, *n* matter transported in suspension and deposited by rivers or floods: — *pl* **allu'via**. — *adj* **allu'vial**. [L neuter of *alluvius* washed up, from *ad* to, and *luere* to wash]

ally[1] *ə-lī'*, *vt* to join by marriage, friendship, treaty, co-operation or assimilation: — *pr p* **ally'ing**; *pa t* and *pa p* **allied'**. — *n* **a'lly** (formerly, and still by some, *ə-lī'*) a member of or party to an alliance; a state or sovereign joined in league for co-operation in a common purpose; a person that co-operates or helps, a supporter; a kinsman (*Shakesp*); anything near to another in classification or nature: — *pl* **a'llies** (or *-līz'*). — *n* **allī'ance** the state of being allied; union, or combination by marriage, treaty, etc; kinship; a group of allies or kindred; a subclass or group of families (*bot*). — *adj* **a'llied** (or *-līd'*). [OFr *alier*, from L *alligāre*; see **alligate**]

ally[2], **ally-taw**. See **alley**[2].

allycholly. See **allicholy**.

allyl *al'il*, (*chem*) *n* an organic radical (C_3H_5) whose sulphide is found in oil of garlic. [L *allium* garlic, and Gr *hȳlē* matter]

alma[1] or **almah** *al'ma*, *n* an Egyptian dancing-girl. — Also **al'me** or **al'meh** (*-me*). [Ar *'almah* learned (in dancing and music), from *'alama* to know]

alma[2] *äl'mä*, (*Ital*) *n* soul, essence.

almacantar *al-mə-kan'tər*, or **almucantar** *al-mū-kan'tər*, (*astron*) *n* a circle of altitude, parallel to the horizon; an instrument for determining a star's passage across an almacantar. [Ar *almuqantarāt* the sundials, from *al* the, and *qantarah* bridge]

Almagest *al'mə-jest*, *n* a great treatise by the Alexandrian astronomer Ptolemy (c. AD150); extended to other great medieval works on astronomy, etc. [Ar *al-majistē*, from *al* the, and Gr *megistē* (*syntaxis*), greatest (systematic treatise)]

Almain *al'mān*, (*obs*) *n* and *adj* German. — *n* **al'main** the allemande. — *n* **Al'maine**, **Al'many** or **Al'emaine** Germany. [Fr *allemand* German, and *Allemagne* Germany, from L *Alamanni* a people of SW Germany]

alma mater *al'mə mā'tər* or *al'ma mä'ter*, (*L*) *n* benign mother, applied by alumni to their university, school or college.

almanac *öl'mə-nak*, *n* a register of the days, weeks and months of the year, with astronomical events, anniversaries, etc, published annually; an annual publication containing a variety of factual information. [Appar from an Ar word *al-manākh*]

almandine *al'man-dīn* or *-dēn*, earlier **alaban'dine**, *n* precious (red iron-alumina) garnet. [LL *alabandīna*, from *Alabanda* a town in Caria, where it was found]

alme, almeh. See **alma**[1].

almery. See **ambry**.

almighty *öl-mīt'i*, *adj* omnipotent; irresistible; invincible; mighty. — Also *adv*. — **the Almighty** God; **the almighty dollar** (*Washington Irving*) money, *esp* as all-powerful. [OE *ælmihtig*]

almirah *al-mīr'ə*, *n* a cupboard, wardrobe or cabinet. [Hindi *almārī*, from Port *almario*, from L *armārium*; see **ambry**]

almond *ä'mənd*, *n* the fruit, and *esp* the kernel, of a tree related to the peach, with a dry husk instead of flesh; anything of the shape of an almond (an ellipse pointed at one end), eg a tonsil or a rock-crystal ornament. — **al'mond-blossom**. — *adj* **al'mond-eyed** with apparently almond-shaped eyes. — **al'mond-oil**; **al'mond-tree**. [OFr *almande* (Fr *amande*), from L *amygdala*, from Gr *amygdalē*]

almoner *ä'mən-ər* or *al'mən-ər*, *n* a distributor or giver of alms (*archaic*); a medical social worker attached to a hospital (no longer an official title). — *n* **al'monry** (*archaic*) a place of distribution of alms. [OFr *aumoner*, *aumonier* (Fr *aumônier*), from LL *eleēmosynārius* (adj); see **alms**]

almost *öl'mōst* or *-məst*, *adv* very nearly. [**all** and **most** (in sense of nearly)]

almous *ä'məs* or *ö'məs*, (*obs* or *dialect*) *n*. Same as **awmous**.

alms *ämz*, *n sing* and *pl* relief given out of charity to the poor; a good or charitable deed (*obs*). — **alms'-deed** (*archaic*) a charitable deed; **alms'-dish** (*archaic*) a dish for receiving alms; **alms'-drink** (*Shakesp*) leavings of drink; **alms'-fee** (*archaic*) Peter's pence; **alms'-folk** (*archaic*) people supported by alms; **alms'-house** a house endowed for the support and lodging of the poor; **alms'-man** (*archaic*) a man who lives by alms; **alms'-woman** (*archaic*). [OE *ælmysse*, through LL from Gr *eleēmosynē*, from *eleos* compassion; see also **awmous**]

almucantar. See **almacantar**.

almug *al'mug*, (*Bible*) *n* algum. [Heb *almūg*, prob for *algūm*]

alnage *öl'nij*, (*obs*) *n* measurement by the ell; inspection of cloth. — *n* **al'nager** an official inspector of cloth. [OFr *aulnage*, from *aulne* ell]

Alnus. See **alder**.

alodium, alod, alodial. Same as **allodium, allod, allodial**.

aloe *al'ō*, *n* any member of a mainly S African genus *Aloe*, consisting mostly of trees and shrubs of the lily family, extended to the so-called **American aloe** (see **Agave**), also (often in *pl*) to aloes-wood or its resin; (*usu* in *pl* form but treated as *sing*) a bitter purgative drug, condensed from the juice of the leaves of various species of Aloe. — *adj* **aloed** (*al'ōd*) planted, shaded, mixed or flavoured with aloes. — *adj* **aloet'ic** (*-ō-et'ik*). — *n* a medicine containing a great proportion of aloes. — **al'oes-wood** the heartwood of eaglewood. — **aloe vera** (*ver'a* or *vē'ra*) (also with *caps*) a variety of aloe plant or *esp* the juice of its leaves (thought to have healing and other qualities) used in cosmetics, etc. [Directly and through OE *aluwan*, *alewan* (pl), from L *aloē*, from Gr *aloē*; the application to eaglewood comes from the Septuagint translation of Heb *ahālīm*, *ahālōth* agalloch]

aloft *ə-loft'* *adv* on high; overhead; above; on the top; high up; up the mast (*naut*); in or to heaven. — *prep* (*Shakesp*) on the top of. [ON *ā lopt* (pron *loft*; of motion) and *ā lopti* (of position) in the sky, from *ā* on, in or to, and *lopt* (see **loft**)]

alogia *ə-lōj'ē-ə*, *n* inability to speak, due to brain lesion. [Gr *ā* (privative) and *logos* speech]

alogical *a-loj'i-kl*, or *ā-*, *adj* outside the domain of logic. [Gr *a-* (privative) and **logical**]

aloha *ä-lō'ə* or *-lō'hä*, *interj* greetings; farewell. [Hawaiian, love or kindness]

alone *ə-lōn'*, *adj* single; solitary; unaccompanied; without any other; by oneself; unique. — *adv* singly. — *adv* **alone'ly** (*obs* or *archaic*). — *n* **alone'ness**. — **go it alone** (*colloq*) to act on one's own, without help. [**all** and **one**]

along[1] *ə-long*, *adv* by or through the length; lengthwise; at full length; throughout; onward; together, in company or conjunction. — *prep* lengthwise by, through, or over; by the side of. — *adj* **alongshore** see **longshore**. — *n* **alongshore'man**. — *prep* and *adv* **along'side** beside; side by side (with); close to the side (of). [OE *andlang*, from pfx *and-* against, and *lang* long (see **long**[3])]

along[2] *ə-long'*, (*archaic* and *dialect*) *adj* on account (of or on). [OE *gelang*; see **long**[1]]

alongst *ə-longst*, (*obs* and *dialect*) *adv* and *prep* along; by the length (of). [OE *andlanges*, from *andlang* along, with adv genitive ending *-es* and *-t* as in **amidst**, **betwixt**, etc]

aloof *ə-lōōf'*, *adv* with avoidance or detachment; reserved and haughty; apart; some way off (from); without participation; to windward (*obs*). — *adj* distant or withdrawn. — *prep* (*Milton*) aloof from. — *adv* **aloof'ly**. — *n* **aloof'ness**. [**a-**[1] and **loof**[1]]

alopecia *al-ō-pē'si-ə* or *-shə*, *n* baldness, hair loss. — *adj* **alopecoid** (*al-ō-pē'koid* or *al-op'i-koid*) fox-like. — **alopecia areata** (*ar-ē-ä'tə* or *ar-ē-ā'tə*) baldness occurring in patches on the scalp. [Gr *alōpekiā* fox-mange or a bald spot, and *alōpekoeidēs* fox-like, from *alōpēx* fox]

aloud *ə-lowd'*, *adv* loudly; audibly. [**a-**[1]]

à l'outrance *a lōō-trãs* (*Fr*). Same as **à outrance**.

alow *ə-lō'*, (*naut*) *adv* to a lower position; in the lower part of a ship. [**a-**[1] and **low**[2]]

alow or **alowe** *ə-low'*, (*Scot*) *adv* ablaze. [**a-**[1] and **low**[4]]

ALP *abbrev*: Australian Labor Party.

alp *alp*, *n* a high mountain; a mountain pasture; (in *pl* with *cap*) the mountain ranges of Switzerland and neighbouring countries. — *adj* **Alp'ine** or **alp'ine** (*-īn*) of the Alps or other mountains; growing on mountain tops. — *n* an alpine plant; a member of the Alpine race. — *n* **alp'inism** (*-in-*) the art or practice of mountain-climbing. — *n* **alp'inist**. — **alp'enhorn** or **alp'horn** a long powerful horn made of wood and bark, used chiefly by Alpine cowherds; **alp'enstock** a mountain traveller's long spiked staff; **Alpine orogeny** (*geol*) the earth movements during the Tertiary period which led to the development of the Alps and associated mountain chains; **Alpine race** one of the principal Caucasian physical types, characterized by broad head, sallow skin and moderate stature; **Alpine skiing** competitive skiing involving downhill and slalom events. [L *Alpēs* the Alps; perh Celtic]

alpaca *al-pak'ə*, *n* a domesticated animal related to the llama; cloth made of its long silky wool. [Sp, prob from Quechua]

alpargata *äl-pär-gä'tä*, *n* a light sandal with rope or hemp sole. [Sp]

al pasto *äl päs'tō*, (*Ital*) according to a fixed rate (said of meals in a restaurant).

alpeen *al'pēn*, *n* a cudgel. [Ir *ailpín*]

alpenhorn and **alpenstock**. See **alp**.

alpha *al'fə*, *n* the first letter of the Greek alphabet (Α or α); the first or brightest star of a constellation; the beginning; in classification, the first or one of the first grade; as an ancient Greek numeral α' = 1, ͵α = 1000. — *adj* short for alphabetical (*colloq* or *comput*); in chemical classification, designating one of two or more isomeric forms of a compound. — *n* **alpha-fētōprō'tein** a protein whose presence in excessive quantities in amniotic fluid has been found to correlate with certain foetal abnormalities, eg those leading to spina bifida. — *n* **alphamet'ic** a popular mathematical puzzle in which numbers are replaced by letters forming words. — *adj* **alphanūmer'ic** or **alphanūmer'ical** consisting of, or (of a machine) using, both letters and numbers. — Also **alphamer'ic** or **alphamer'ical**. — *adv* **alphanūmer'ically** or **alphamer'ically**. — **al'pha-blocker** a drug used to make blood-vessels dilate, *esp* in muscle; **alpha-chlor'alose** a narcotic poison used in bait, eg to control vermin; **alpha particle** (*phys*) a helium nucleus given off by radioactive substances; **alpha ray** (*phys*) a stream of alpha particles; **alpha rhythm** or **wave** one of the principal slow waves recorded on electroencephalogram indicating normal relaxed brain activity. — *vt* **al'phasort** to sort, *esp* into alphabetical order (*comput*). — Also *n*. — **alpha wave** see **alpha rhythm**. — **alpha and omega** beginning and end. [Gr *alpha*, from Heb *āleph*; see **aleph** and **A**]

alphabet *al'fə-bit* or *-bet*, *n* a system of letters, *esp* when arranged in conventional set order; first elements or basics; an index (*obs*). — *vt* (*US*) to arrange alphabetically. — *n* **alphabetā'rian** someone learning the alphabet, a beginner; a student of alphabets. — *adj* **alphabet'ic** or **alphabet'ical** relating to or in the order of an alphabet. — *adv* **alphabet'ically**. — *adj* **alphabet'iform** shaped like letters. — *n* **alphabetiza'tion** or **-s-**. — *vt* **al'phabetize** or **-ise** to arrange alphabetically. — **alphabet soup** a confusing or off-putting series or mass of strings of letters, *esp* the abbreviations of names of official bodies, (after a type of soup with letter-shaped noodles in it). [Gr *alphabētos*, from *alpha* and *bēta*, the first two Greek letters]

Alphonsine *al-fon'sīn* or *-zin*, *adj* of Alphonso X (the Wise), king of Castile, or his planetary tables, completed in 1252.

alphorn, **alpine**, etc. See **alp**.

Alpini *äl-pē'nē*, *n pl* Italian troops for mountain warfare: — *sing* **Alpi'no**. [Ital, Alpine]

al più *äl pū*, (*Ital*) at most.

already *öl-red'i*, *adv* previously, or by the time in question. [**all** and **ready**]

alright *öl-rīt'*. An alternative, less acceptable, spelling of **all right**, much used in informal contexts.

als *äls* or *öls*. An obs form of **also** and **as**[1].

Alsatia *al-sā'sh(y)ə*, *n* a district long disputed by Germany and France, Alsace or Elsass; cant name for the sanctuary (till 1697) for debtors and criminals at Whitefriars, London. — *adj* **Alsa'tian** of Alsatia in either sense; a German sheepdog of wolf-like breed, often used by police and security officers because of its strength and fierceness (*usu* called **German Shepherd**, **German Shepherd dog** or **German Police dog**). — Also *n*.

alsike *al'sik*, *n* a white or pink-flowered clover. [From *Alsike*, near Uppsala, a habitat]

also *öl'sō*, *adv* likewise; further. — **al'so-ran** a horse that *also ran* in a race but did not get a 'place'; a person of a similar degree of importance. [OE *all* (WSax *eall*) *swā* all so]

alsoon or **alsoone** *al-sōōn'*, (*Spenser*) *adv* as soon. [**as**[1] and **soon**]

alstroemeria *al-strə-mē'ri-ə*, *n* a plant of the S American genus *Alstroemeria* of the amaryllis family with inverted leaves. [C *Alströmer*, 18c Swedish botanist]

alt[1] *alt*, (*music*) *n* a high tone, in voice or instrument. — **in alt** in the octave above the treble stave beginning with G; in an exalted and high-flown mood. [L *altus* high]

alt[2] *alt*, (*Milton*) *n* halt, rest. [Fr *alte* or Sp *alto*, from Ger *Halt*]

alt. *abbrev*: alternate; altitude; alto.

Alta *abbrev*: Alberta (Canadian province).

Altaic *al-tā'ik*, *n* a family of languages, forming one branch of Ural-Altaic, and consisting of Turkic, Mongolic and Tungusic. — Also *adj*.

Altair *äl-tä'ir* or *al-tār'*, *n* a first-magnitude star in the constellation Aquila. [Ar *al ta'ir* the bird]

altaltissimo *alt-al-tis'i-mō*, *n* the very highest summit. [Reduplicated compound of Ital *alto* high, and *altissimo* highest]

alta moda *äl'tä mo'dä*, (*Ital*) *n* high fashion, the art of designing and making exclusive, fashionable clothes.

altar *öl'tər*, *n* a block or table for making sacrifices on; the table used for mass or the eucharist; a place where worship or the marriage ceremony is carried out (*fig*); a ledge on a dry-dock wall. — *n* **al'tarage** offerings made upon the altar during the offertory, for the maintenance of the priest. — *adv* **al'tarwise** in the position of an altar at the east end of the chancel. — **altar boy** a boy assisting the priest at the altar, an acolyte; **al'tar-cloth** the covering of the altar, often including the frontal and the superfrontal; **al'tarpiece** a work of art placed above and behind an altar; **al'tar-rails** in a church or chapel, rails separating the presbytery from the rest of the chancel; **al'tar-stone** a stone serving as an altar; a consecrated slab forming or inserted in the top of an altar; **al'tar-tomb** a monumental memorial, in form like an altar, often with a canopy. — **family altar** the symbol or place of family worship; **high altar** the principal altar; **lead to the altar** to marry (a woman). [L *altāre*, from *altus* high]

altazimuth *alt-az'i-məth*, *n* an instrument devised by Airy for determining *al*titude and *azimuth*.

alter[1] *öl'tər*, *vt* to make different; to modify; to castrate (*archaic*). — *vi* to become different. — *n* **alterabil'ity**. — *adj* **al'terable**. — *adj* **al'terant** altering; having the power of producing changes. — *n* an alternative. — *n* **alterā'tion**. — *adj* **al'terātive** able to cause change. — *n* a medicine or treatment that changes bodily functions. — *adj* **al'tered** (of a rock) changed in mineral composition by natural forces. — *n* **alterity** (*öl-* or *al-ter'i-ti*) otherness. [L *alter* one of two or the other of two, from the root of *alius* other, and the old compar sfx *-ter*]

alter[2] *al'tər*, *adj* (*psychol*) other, distinct from oneself, used of people or things seen in contrast with the ego. — **alter ego** (*al'tər eg'ō* or *ē'gō*, *öl'tər ē'gō*, or *al'ter eg'ō*) one's second self (see **second**); a trusted, intimate friend, a confidant: — *pl* **alter egos**. [L, other]

altercate *öl'tər-kāt*, *vi* to dispute heatedly, argue. — *n* **altercā'tion**. — *adj* **al'tercātive**. [L *altercārī*, *-ātus*, from *alter* other]

altern *öl-* or *al-tûrn'*, (*archaic*) *adj* alternate. — *adv* alternately. [L *alternus*]

alternat *al-ter-na*, (*Fr*) *n* the diplomatic practice of determining precedence among powers of equal rank by lot or of otherwise avoiding the difficulty.

alternate *öl'tər-nāt*, also *al'*, formerly (eg *Milton*) *-tûr'*, *vt* to cause to follow by turns or one after the other (properly, of two things). — *vi* to follow or interchange (with each other; properly, of two things); to happen by turns, change by turns. — *n* a deputy, substitute; an alternative. — *adj* **alter'nate** (*-tûr'*; *US öl'*) arranged or coming one after the other by turns; every other or second; sometimes used with the sense 'alternative'; (of leaves) placed singly with change of side at each node; (of parts of a flower) each placed opposite the space between other parts of the flower; (of angles) placed one after the other on either side of a line (*geom*). — *n* **alter'nance** (or *al'*-) alternation, interchange or variation; training by alternate periods of theoretical and practical work. — *adj* **alter'nant** or **al'ternant** alternating. — *n* a spelling or sound variant that does not affect meaning (allomorph or allophone); a type of determinant (*math*); an alternative proposition, eg one of the components in an alternation (*logic*). — *adv* **alter'nately**. — *adj* **al'ternating**. — *n* **alternā'tion** the act of alternating; alternate succession; interchange; the type of disjunction in which 'or' is used inclusively (*logic*); reading or singing antiphonally. — *n* **al'ternātor** a generator of alternating current. — **alternate energy** see **renewable energy**; **alternate host** (*biol*) one of the two or more hosts of a parasite which has the different stages of its life-cycle in unrelated hosts (cf **alternative host**); **alternating current** an electric current that periodically reverses its direction. — **alternation of generations** (*biol*) the occurrence in a life-cycle of two or more different forms in successive generations, the offspring being unlike the parents, and commonly reproducing by a different method. [L *alternāre*, *-ātum*, from *alter* one or other of two]

alternatim *öl-tər-nā'təm*, (*music*) *adv* alternately. [L *alternātim*]

alternative *öl-tûr'nə-tiv*, *n* either of a pair, or any of a set, of possibilities; a choice between them; one of them, *esp* other than the one in question. — *adj* possible as an alternative; disjunctive; alternate (*obs*); considered by some as preferable to the existing state or form of something, very often with the connotation of being less conventional, less materialistic, more in harmony with the environment and the natural order of things, etc, as *alternative society*, *alternative technology*, *alternative energy*, *alternative medicine*, etc. — *adv* **alter'natively** with an alternative; by way of alternative. — **alternative host** (*biol*) one of two or more possible hosts in the life-cycle of a parasite (cf **alternate host**); **alternative vote** a system of voting whereby, if a voter's favourite candidate is out of the running, the vote is transferred to the candidate marked next in order of preference. — **Alternative Service Book** a modernized version of the liturgy of the Church of England, used as an alternative to the Book of Common Prayer. [**alternate**]

alterne *al-tûrn'*, (*bot*) *n* one of two or more plant communities adjoining but differing greatly. [Fr *alterne* alternate, from L *alternus*]

alternis vicibus *al-tûr'nis vi'si-bus* or *al-ter'nēs vē'ki-bōōs*, also *wē'*, (*L*) alternately.

alterum tantum *al'tə-rum tan'tum* or *al'te-rōōm tan'tōōm*, (*L*) as much more.

altesse *al-tes* (*Fr*), **alteza** *al-tā'tha* (*Sp*), or **altezza** *al-tet'sa* (*Ital*), *n* highness.

althaea or (*esp NAm*) **althea** *al-thē'ə*, *n* a plant of the marsh-mallow and hollyhock genus *Althaea* (or *Althea*), sometimes extended to the hibiscus genus and applied *esp* to the Rose of Sharon. [Gr *althaiā* marsh-mallow]

Althing *öl'thing*, *n* the Icelandic parliament. [ON and Icel]

althorn *alt'hörn*, *n* a tenor saxhorn. [**alt**[1]]

although *öl-dhō'*, *conj* though (*esp* but not necessarily, in stating matter of fact). [**all** and **though**]

altimeter *al-tim'i-tər* or *al'ti-mē-tər*, also *öl'*, *n* an instrument for measuring height, by means of differences in atmospheric pressure, or (*radio altimeter*) by means of a time taken for a radio wave from an aircraft to be reflected back. — *adj* **altimet'rical**. — *adv* **altimet'rically**. — *n* **altim'etry**. [L *altus* high, and **meter**[1]]

Altiplano *al-ti-plä'nō*, *n* a plateau in the Bolivian and Peruvian part of the Andes, containing Lake Titicaca. [Sp, plateau]

altisonant *al-tis'ən-ənt*, *adj* high-sounding. [L *altus* high, and *sonāns*, *-antis*, pr p of *sonāre* to sound]

altissimo *al-tis'(s)i-mō*, (*music*) *adj* very high. — **in altissimo** in the octave beginning on the G an octave and a fifth above middle C. [Ital, superl of *alto* high]

altitonant *al-tit'ən-ənt*, *adj* thundering on high or loudly. [L *altus* high, and *tonāns*, *-antis*, pr p of *tonāre* to thunder]

altitude *al'ti-tūd*, *n* height, *esp* above sea-level; angle of elevation of a star, etc above the horizon; length of the perpendicular from apex to base of a triangle; high rank or eminence; a high point or position; (in *pl*) exalted mood, passion or manner. — *adj* **altitūd'inal** pertaining to altitude; found at high level. — *n* **altitūdinā'rian** someone tending to loftiness in doctrine or belief. — Also *adj*. — *adj* **altitūd'inous** high. — **altitude sickness** same as **mountain sickness**. [L *altitūdō*, *-inis*, from *altus* high]

alto[1] *al'tō*, (*music*) *n* a high falsetto male voice; properly counter-tenor, the highest male voice; contralto, the lowest female voice; the part sung by a counter-tenor or contralto; an instrument of corresponding range; a person with a counter-tenor or contralto voice; a viola (*archaic*): — *pl* **al'tos**. — Also *adj*. [Ital, from L *altus* high]

alto[2]. See **all-to**.

altocumulus *al-tō-kū'mū-ləs*, *n* cumulus cloud forming at 2 400–6 000m, (8 000–20 000ft): — *pl* **altocu'muli** (*-lī*). [New L, from *altus* high, and **cumulus**.]

altogether *öl-tōō-gedh'ər*, or *-tə-*, *adv* all together (*obs* or by confusion); wholly; completely; without exception; in total; all things considered. — **for altogether** (*rare*) for all time, for good and all; **the altogether** (*colloq*) the nude. [**all** and **together**]

alto-rilievo *äl'tō-rēl-yā'vō*, (*art*) *n* high relief; figures projected by at least half their thickness from the background on which they are sculptured. — Partly anglicized as **alto-relie'vo** (*al-tō-ri-lē'vō*). [Ital. See **relief**]

altostratus *al-tō-strā'təs* or *-strä'təs*, *n* cloud forming a continuous layer at 2 400–6 000m (8 000–20 000ft): — *pl* **altostra'ti** (*-tī*). [New L, from *altus* high, and **stratus** under **stratum**]

altrices *al-trī'sēz, n pl* birds whose young are hatched very immature and have to be fed in the nest by the parents. — *adj* **altricial** (*-trish'l*). [L *altrīcēs* (pl of *altrix*) feeders or nurses]

altruism *al'troo-izm, n* the principle of living and acting for the interest of others. — *n* **al'truist**. — *adj* **altruist'ic**. — *adv* **altruist'ically**. [Fr *altruisme*, formed by Comte from Ital *altrui* someone else, from L *alterī huīc* to this other]

altum silentium *al'tum si-len'sh(y)um* or *al'tōōm si-len'ti-ōōm*, (*L*) profound silence.

ALU (*comput*) *abbrev*: arithmetic and logic unit.

aludel *al'ōō-dəl*, or *-ū-*, (*chem*) *n* a pear-shaped pot used in sublimation. [Sp, from Ar *al-uthāl*]

alula *al'ū-lə, n* in birds, the bastard-wing. [L dimin of *āla* wing]

alum *al'əm, n* double sulphate of aluminium and potassium, with 24 molecules of water, crystallizing in transparent octahedra; any similar compound of a trivalent metal (*esp* aluminium) and a univalent metal or radical. — *adj* **al'umish** having the character or taste of alum. — **al'um-root** an American plant of the saxifrage family with astringent root; **al'um-shale** or **al'um-slate** a slate consisting mainly of clay, iron pyrites and coaly matter, from which alum is obtained; **al'um-stone** alunite. [L *alūmen, -inis* alum]

aluminium *al-ū-min'i-əm* or *al-ōō-* or (*NAm*) **aluminum** *ə-loo'mi-num, n* an element (symbol **Al**; atomic no 13), a light silvery malleable and ductile metal first named (though not then isolated) by Sir Humphry Davy **alu'mium**, then (as still *NAm*) **alum'inum**. — *n* **alumina** (*ə-lū'* or *ə-lōō'mi-nə*) oxide of aluminium. — *n* **alu'minate** a salt whose acid is aluminium hydroxide. — *adj* **aluminif'erous** or **alu'minous** bearing or containing aluminium or alumina. — *vt* **alum'inize** or **-ise** to treat (a metal) so as to form an aluminium alloy on its surface; to coat (eg glass) with aluminium. — **aluminium bronze** an alloy of aluminium and copper, of lighter weight than gold, but like it in colour; **alumino-sil'icates** compounds of alumina, silica and bases. [Ety as for **alum**]

alumnus *al-um'nəs, n* a former pupil or student: — *pl* **alum'nī**: — *fem* **alum'na** (*pl* **alum'nae** *-nē*). [L, foster-son or pupil, from *alere* to nourish]

alunite *al'ū-nīt*, or *-ōō-, n* alum-stone, a hydrous sulphate of aluminium and potassium. [Fr *alun* alum]

alure *al'yər*, (*obs*) *n* a walk behind battlements; a gallery; a passage. [OFr *aleure*, from *aller* to go]

alveary *al'vi-ər-i, n* a beehive; a name given to an early dictionary of English, French, Greek and Latin; a hollow of the external ear, where wax collects (*anatom*). — *adj* **al'veated** vaulted, like a beehive. [L *alveārium* beehive, from *alveus* a hollow]

alveolus *al-vē'ə-ləs*, or *al'vi-, n* a pit, small depression or dilatation; a tooth socket; one of the clustered cells at the termination of a bronchiole in the lungs: — *pl* **alveoli**. — *adj* **alve'olar** (or *-ōl'*, or *al'*) of an alveolus; produced with the tongue against the roots of the upper teeth (*phonetics*); pitted. — *adj* **alvē'olate** (or *al'vi-*) pitted; honeycombed; inserted in an alveolus. — *n* **al'veole** an alveolus. — *n* **alveolitis** (*al-vi-ə-lī'tis*) inflammation of the alveoli in the lungs. — **alveolar arch** the part of the jaw in which the teeth are inserted. [L *alveolus*, dimin of *alveus* a hollow]

alvine *al'vīn, adj* of the belly. [L *alvīnus* from *alvus* belly]

always *öl'wāz, adv* every time; ever; continually; in any case; still (*Scot*). — *adv* **alway** (*öl'wā; archaic*) through all time; always. [**all** and **way**[2], from OE *ealne weg* (accusative) and ME *alles weis* (genitive)]

alycompaine. Same as **elecampane**.

alyssum *al'is-əm* or *ə-lis'əm, n* a plant of the *Alyssum* genus of low-growing, cruciferous plants with white, yellow or mauve flowers, grown eg in rock-gardens; a mass of such plants. — **sweet alyssum** a white scented perennial of a related genus. [Gr *alysson* a plant reputed to cure madness, from **a-**[2] and Gr *lyssa* madness]

Alzheimer's disease *alts'hī-mərz diz-ēz', n* an illness affecting the brain and causing dementia in the middle-aged or elderly. [Named after Alois *Alzheimer* (1864–1915), German neurologist]

AM *abbrev*: Albert Medal; amplitude modulation; *Anno Mundi* (*L*), in the year of the world; *Artium Magister* (*L*), Master of Arts (*US*); Associate Member; *Ave Maria* (*L*), Hail Mary; Member of the Order of Australia.

Am (*chem*) *symbol*: americium.

Am. *abbrev*: amateur; America; American.

am *am* or *əm*, used as 1st person *sing* of the verb *to be*. [OE (Anglian) *am*, *eam* (WSax *eom*), a relic of the verbs in *-mi*, from the root *es-*; cf Gr *eimi* (for *esmi*), L *sum* and Sans *asmi*]

a.m. or **am** *abbrev*: *ante meridiem* (*L*), before noon, ie in the morning.

AMA *abbrev*: American Medical Association; Association of Metropolitan Authorities; Australian Medical Association.

amabile *a-mä'bi-lā*, (*Ital*) *adj* of wines, etc, sweet.

amadavat. See **avadavat**.

amadou *am'ə-dōō, n* tinder made from fungi (genus *Polyporus*) growing on trees, used also as a styptic. [Fr, of doubtful origin]

amah *ä'mə*, (*oriental*) *n* a native maidservant or child's nurse, *esp* wet-nurse. [Port]

amain *ə-mān'*, (*archaic* or *poetic*) *adv* with main force; violently; at full speed; exceedingly. [**a-**[1] and **main**[1]]

à main armée *a mẽ-när-mā*, (*Fr*) by force of arms, with mailed fist.

a majori (ad minus) *ā mə-jö'rī* (*ad mī'nus*) or *ä mī-ōr'ē* (*ad mi'nōōs*), (*L*) from the greater (to the less).

amalgam *ə-mal'gəm, n* a mixture of mercury with other metal; any soft mixture; a mixture or blend; an ingredient. — *vt* **amal'gamate** to mix with mercury; to merge. — *vi* to unite in an amalgam; to come together as one; to blend. — *n* **amalgamā'tion** a blending or merging; a union of diverse elements; the joining together of two or more separate businesses to form one business. — *adj* **amal'gamātive**. [LL *amalgama*, perh from Gr *malagma* an emollient]

amandine *am-an'din, -dīn* or *-dēn*, or *am', n* a protein in sweet almonds; a candle or a cosmetic which is prepared from them. [Fr *amande* almond]

amanita *am-ən-ī'tə, n* a mushroom of the *Amanita* genus, including the fly agaric (qv) and other poisonous kinds. [Gr *amānītai* (pl) a kind of fungus]

amanuensis *ə-man-ū-en'sis, n* a literary assistant, *esp* one who writes to dictation or copies from manuscript: — *pl* **amanuen'sēs**. [L *āmanuēnsis*, from *ā* from, and *manus* hand]

amaracus *ə-mar'ə-kəs, n* marjoram. [L *amāracus*, from Gr *amārakos*]

amarant *am'ər-ant*, or **amaranth** *am'ər-anth, n* a fabled never-fading flower, emblem of immortality; any species of **Amarant'us** or **Amaran'thus**, the love-lies-bleeding genus, with richly coloured long-lasting spikes, giving name to the family **Amarantā'ceae** or **Amaranthā'ceae**, related to the goosefoots; (**amaranth**) a highly-nutritious S American cereal (also **grain amaranth**); a type of dye used for colouring foodstuffs. — *adj* **amarantā'ceous** or **amarantha'ceous**. — *adj* **amarant'ine** or **amaran'thine** (*-īn*). — *adj* **amarant'in** (*Milton*) of or like amaranth; fadeless; immortal; purple. [Gr *amarantos*, from *a-* (privative), and *marainein* to wither; the *th* forms from confusion with *anthos* flower]

amaretto *am-a-ret'ō, n* an Italian liqueur flavoured with almonds: — *pl* **amarett'os**. [Ital, from *amaro* bitter]

amaryllis *am-ə-ril'is, n* the belladonna lily, forming the genus *Amaryllis* which gives name to the narcissus and snowdrop family **Amaryllidā'ceae**, differing from lilies in the inferior ovary. — *n* **amaryll'id** any member of the family. — *adj* **amaryllidā'ceous**. [*Amaryllis*, a girl's name in the Gr and L poets and others]

amass *ə-mas'*, *vt* and *vi* to gather in great quantity; to accumulate. — *adj* **amass'able**. — *n* **amass'ment**. [Fr *amasser*, from L *ad* to, and *massa* a mass]

amate[1] *ə-māt'*, (*Spenser*) *vt* to match. [Pfx **a-** (intens), and **mate**[1]]

amate[2] *ə-māt'*, (*archaic*) *vt* to daunt; to dismay. [OFr *amatir* to subdue; cf **checkmate**, **mat**[2] and **mate**[2]]

amateur *am'ə-tər*, *-tūr* or *-tûr'*, *n* an enthusiast or admirer; a person who practises something for the love of it, not as a profession; someone whose understanding of, or ability in, a particular art, etc is superficial, trifling, or inexpert; a person who takes part in sport for pleasure (*opp* to *professional*); a dilettante. — Also *adj*. — *adj* **amateur'ish** (or *am'*) done imperfectly and defectively, the work of an amateur rather than a professional hand, performed without professional skill. — *adv* **amateurishly**. — *n* **amateurishness** or **am'ateurism**. — *n* **am'ateurship**. [Fr, from L *amātor*, *-ōris* a lover, from *amāre* to love]

Amati *ə-mä'tē*, *n* a violin or cello made by the *Amati* family (*c*. 1550–1700) of Cremona.

amation *a-mā'shən*, (*rare*) *n* love-making. [L *amatio*, *amationis*, from *amāre* to love]

amative *am'ə-tiv*, *adj* inclined towards love. — *n* **am'ativeness** propensity to love or to sexuality. [L *amāre*, *-ātum* to love]

amatol *am'ə-tol*, *n* a high explosive composed of *am*monium nitrate and trinitro*tol*uene.

amatory *am'ə-tər-i*, *adj* relating to or causing love; amorous. — *adj* **amato'rial** (*-tö'*). — *adv* **amato'rially**. — *adj* **amato'rian**. — *adj* **amato'rious**. [L *amātōrius*]

amaurosis *am-ö-rō'sis*, *n* blindness caused by disease of the optic nerves, *usu* without outward change in the eye. — *adj* **amaurotic** (*-rot'ik*). [Gr *amaurōsis*, from *amauros* dark]

amaze *ə-māz'*, *vt* to overwhelm with astonishment or wonder; to daze (*obs*); to bewilder (*obs*); to stun (*obs*); to strike with fear (*obs*). — *n* bewilderment (*obs*); panic (*obs*); extreme astonishment (*archaic*). — *adv* **amaz'edly**. — *n* **amaz'edness** amazement (*rare*); stupefaction (*obs*); bewilderment (*obs*); panic, terror (*obs*). — *n* **amaze'ment** astonishment mingled with wonder; incredulity; bewilderment (*rare*). — *adj* **amaz'ing**. — *adv* **amaz'ingly** (often hyperbolically). [OE *āmasian* (found in the pa p *āmasod*)]

Amazon *am'ə-zon*, *-zən*, or formerly *a-mā'zon*, *n* in Greek mythology, one of a nation of women warriors, located near the Black Sea; one of a legendary race of female warriors of S America; the great river of S America (Port *Amazonas* Amazons, *perh* based on a misunderstood Tupí-Guaraní word *amassona*, *amaçunu* tidal bore, connected with records of Amazons living on its banks); an Indian of the Amazons; (the following *usu* without *cap*) a female soldier; a strong, vigorous or aggressive woman; a tropical American green parrot; an amazon-ant. — Also *adj*. — *adj* **Amazō'nian** of or relating to the River Amazon in S America; (also without *cap*) of, relating to or resembling an Amazon. — *n* **am'azonite** amazon-stone. — *adj* and *adv* **Ama'zon-like**. — **am'azon-ant** a European and American ant (genus *Polyergus*) which enslaves the young of other species; **am'azon-stone** a green microline, said to be given by the Brazilian Amazons to the men who visited them. [Gr *Amāzōn*, *-onos*, in folk-etymology referred to *a-* (privative) and *māzos* breast, with the explanation that Amazons cut off the right breast lest it should get in the way of the bowstring]

ambages *am-bā'jēz*, *n pl* windings; roundabout ways; delays. — Also *n sing*. — Also **ambage** (*am'bij*) with *pl* **am'bages**. — *adj* **ambagious** (*-bā'jəs*) tortuous; circumlocutory. — *adj* **ambagitory** (*-baj'i-tər-i*; *Scott*). [L *ambāgēs* (pl), from *ambi-* about, and *agere* to drive or lead]

amban *am'ban*, *n* a Chinese resident official in a dependency. [Manchu, minister]

Ambarvalia *amb-är-vā'li-ə*, *n pl* an ancient Roman festival with processions round the cornfields. [L *Ambarvālia*, from *ambi* around, and *arvum* field]

ambassador *am-bas'ə-dər*, *fem* **ambassadress** *am-bas'ə-drəs*, *n* a diplomat of the highest rank, sent by one sovereign or state to another as a permanent representative; a messenger or agent. — *adj* **ambassadorial** (*-dö'ri-əl*). — *n* **ambass'adorship**. — *n* **am'bassage** (*-bəs-ij*) or **am'bassy** forms of **embassage** and **embassy**. — **ambass'ador-at-large'** an ambassador not accredited to any particular foreign government; **ambassador extraordinary** an ambassador sent on a special occasion, as distinguished from the resident ambassador. [Fr *ambassadeur*, from L *ambactus* a slave or servant, generally thought to be of Celtic origin]

ambatch *am'bach*, *n* a pith-tree. [Appar native name]

amber *am'bər*, *n* a yellowish fossil resin; the orange traffic-light, which acts as a cautionary signal between red (stop) and green (go); ambergris (*obs*). — *adj* made of amber; of the colour of amber, a clear brownish yellow. — *adj* **am'bered** (*obs*) embedded in amber; flavoured with ambergris. — *n* **am'berite** an amberlike smokeless powder. — *adj* **am'berous** or **am'bery**. — *n* **am'broid** or **am'beroid** pressed amber, a synthetic amber formed by heating and compressing pieces of natural amber too small to be of value in themselves, sometimes along with other resins. — **am'ber-fish** a golden or greenish fish (genus *Seriola*) of the horse-mackerels (Carangidae), abundant in warm seas; **am'berjack** (the species *Seriola dumerili* of) the amber-fish, a large Atlantic game-fish having golden markings when young. [Fr *ambre*, from Ar *'anbar* ambergris]

ambergris *am'bər-grēs*, *n* an ash-grey strongly-scented substance, originating in the intestines of the spermaceti whale and used in the manufacture of perfumes. [Fr *ambre gris* grey amber]

ambi- *am'bi-*, *pfx* round, both, on both sides. [L, from *ambo* both]

ambiance. See **ambient**.

ambidextrous *am-bi-deks'trəs*, (*archaic*) **ambidexterous** *am-bi-deks'tər-əs* and **ambidexter** *-deks'tər*, *adj* able to use both hands equally well; on both sides; double-dealing. — *n* **ambidex'ter** (*archaic*) someone who is ambidextrous. — *n* **ambidexterity** (*-ter'i-ti*) or **ambidex'trousness**. — *adv* **ambidex'trously**. [**ambi-** and L *dexter* right]

ambient *am'bi-ənt*, *adj* going round; (of eg air temperature) surrounding; enveloping. — *n* something which encompasses; the air or sky. — *n* **ambience** (*am'bi-əns*) or **ambiance** (*ã-bē-ãs*) environment; surrounding influence; atmosphere; the use or disposition of accessories in art. — **ambient illumination** (*image technol*) background uncontrollable light level at a location; **ambient noise** (*acoustics*) the noise existing in a room or any other environment. [L *ambiēns*, *-entis*, pr p of *ambīre*, from pfx *ambi-* about, and *īre* to go]

ambiguous *am-big'ū-əs*, *adj* doubtful; undetermined; of intermediate or doubtful nature; indistinct; wavering; having more than one possible meaning; equivocal. — *n* **ambigū'ity** doubtful or double meaning; an equivocal expression. — *adv* **ambig'uously**. — *n* **ambig'uousness**. [L *ambiguus*, from *ambigere* to go about or waver, from pfx *ambi-* both ways, and *agere* to drive]

ambilateral *am-bi-lat'ə-rəl*, *adj* relating to or involving both sides. [**ambi-** and L *latus*, *lateris* side]

ambisexual *am-bi-seks'ū-əl*, *adj* (*esp* of sexual characteristics, eg pubic hair) common to both sexes; of or relating to both sexes. [**ambi-**]

Ambisonics® *am-bi-son'iks*, *n sing* (also without *cap*) a system of high-fidelity sound reproduction using multiple channels, which electronically reproduces ambient sound as perceived by the human ear. [**ambi-**]

ambit *am'bit*, *n* circuit; scope; compass; precincts; confines. [L *ambitus* a going round, from pfx *ambi-* round, and *itus* going, from *īre*, *itum* to go]

ambition *am-bish'ən*, *n* aspiration after success or advancement; the object of aspiration. — *adj* **ambi'tionless**. — *adj* **ambitious** (*am-bish'əs*) full of ambition;

strongly desirous (of or to do); aspiring; indicating ambition; pretentious. — *adv* **ambi'tiously**. — *n* **ambi'tiousness**. [L *ambitiō*, *-ōnis* canvassing, from pfx *ambi-* about, and *īre*, *itum* to go]

ambitty *am-bit'i*, *adj* (of glass) devitrified. [Fr *ambité*, of obscure origin]

ambivalence *am-biv'ə-ləns* or **ambivalency** *-i*, *n* co-existence in one person of opposing emotional attitudes towards the same object. — *adj* **ambiv'alent**. [**ambi-** and L *valēns*, *-entis*, pr p of *valēre* to be strong]

ambivert *am'bi-vûrt*, *n* someone who is neither an extravert nor an introvert. — *n* **ambiver'sion** (*-shən*). [**ambi-** and L *vertere* to turn]

amble *am'bl*, *vi* to move, like a horse, by lifting together both legs on one side alternately with those on the other side; to move at an easy pace; to move like an ambling horse; to ride an ambling animal. — *n* an ambling pace. — *n* **am'bler**. — *n* and *adj* **am'bling**. [Fr *ambler*, from L *ambulāre* to walk about]

amblyopia *am-bli-ō'pi-ə*, *n* impaired sight without any apparent damage to the eye. [Gr *amblyōpiā*, from *amblys* dull, and *ops* eye]

Amblyopsis *am-bli-op'sis*, *n* the blindfish of the Mammoth Cave in Kentucky. [Gr *amblys* dull, and *opsis* sight]

Amblystoma. Same as **Ambystoma**.

ambo *am'bō*, *n* an early Christian raised reading-desk or pulpit: — *pl* **am'bōs** or **ambō'nes** (*-nēz*). [LL *ambō*, from Gr *ambōn*, *-ōnos* crest of a hill or pulpit]

amboceptor *am'bə-sep-tər*, (*biochem*) *n* in immunization, an antibody acting as a double receptor, linking both with the antigen and with the complement. [L *ambo* both, and **receptor**]

Amboina-wood (also **Amboyna-**) *am-boi'nə-wŏŏd*, *n* the finely coloured knotty wood of *Pterocarpus indicus*, a papilionaceous tree. — **Amboina pine** a tree (*Agathis alba*), a source of resin. [Island of *Amboina* in the Moluccas, Indonesia]

ambroid. See **amber**.

ambrosia *am-brō'z(h)i-ə* or *-z(h)ə*, *n* the food (later, the drink) of the Greek gods, which conferred everlasting youth and beauty; the anointing oil of the gods; any fragrant or delicious food or beverage; something sweet and pleasing; bee-bread; fungi cultivated for food by certain bark-beetles (**ambrosia beetles**) of the Scolytidae; (with *cap*) a genus of Compositae called in N America ragweeds. — *adj* **ambrō'sial** fragrant; delicious; immortal; heavenly. — *adv* **ambrōs'ially**. — *adj* **ambrō'sian**. [Gr *ambrosiā*, from *ambrotos* immortal, from *a-* (privative) and *brotos*, for *mbrotos* mortal; cf Sans *amṛta* immortal]

Ambrosian *am-brō'z(h)ən* or *-z(h)yən*, *adj* pertaining to St *Ambrose*, 4c bishop of Milan, to his liturgy, to the form of plainsong introduced by him, to various religious orders and to the public library at Milan (founded 1602–9 by Cardinal Federigo Borromeo) named in his honour. — *n* a member of any of these orders.

ambrotype *am'brō-tīp*, *n* an early kind of photograph made by backing a glass negative with black varnish or paper so that it appears as a positive. [Gr *ambrotos* immortal, and **type**]

ambry, **aumbry** or **almery**, (*Scot*) **awmry** or **awmrie** *am'* or *öm'(b)ri*, *n* a recess for church vessels; a cupboard; a pantry; a dresser; a safe. [OFr *almerie*, from L *armārium* a chest or safe, from *arma* arms or tools]

ambs-ace, **ames-ace** *amz'-ās* or *āmz'-ās*, *n* double ace, the lowest possible throw at dice; ill-luck; worthlessness. [OFr *ambes as*, from L *ambōs assēs* both aces]

ambulacrum *am-bū-lā'krəm*, or *-la'*, *n* a radial band in the shell of an echinoderm, bearing rows of pores through which the tube-feet protrude: — *pl* **ambulā'cra**. — *adj* **ambulā'cral**. [L *ambulācrum* a walk, from *ambulāre* to walk]

ambulance *am'bū-ləns*, *n* a vehicle or (**air ambulance**) helicopter, etc for conveying the sick or injured; a movable field hospital. — *adj* **am'bulant** walking; able to walk; moving from place to place; unfixed (*rare*); allowing or calling for walking. — *n* a walking patient. — *vi* **am'bulate** to walk. — *n* **ambulā'tion**. — *n* **am'bulātor** a walker; a wheel for road-measuring. — *adj* **am'bulatory** (*-ə-tər-i*) of or for walking; moving from place to place, not stationary; subject to change (*law*). — *n* a covered walk, eg an aisle, cloister, portico or corridor. — **ambulance broker** a broker specializing in the affairs of crashed companies; **am'bulance-chaser** a lawyer on the lookout for accidents in order to instigate actions for damages (*US*); a person or firm offering to pursue a claim on behalf of an accident-victim in return for a percentage of the sum obtained; **am'bulanceman** or **am'bulancewoman** a male or female member of the crew of an ambulance. [L *ambulāre*, *-ātum* to walk about]

ambuscade *am-bəs-kād'*, *n* an ambush. — *vt* and *vi* to ambush. — *n* **ambuscā'do** (*esp* 16–17c; would-be *Sp*) an ambuscade: — *pl* **ambuscā'dos** or **ambusca'does**. [Fr *embuscade* or Sp *emboscada*; see **ambush**]

ambush *am'bŏŏsh*, *n* a lying or laying in wait in order to attack by surprise; a place of lying in wait; a person or troop lying in wait. — *vt* and *vi* to attack from ambush. — *n* **am'bushment** (*archaic*) ambush. — **ambush bug** (*US*) any of several insects of the *Phymatidae* that prey on other insects from a place of concealment, eg within a flower. [OFr *embusche* (Fr *embûche*), from *embuscher*, from LL *imboscāre*, from *im* in, and *boscus* (see **bush**[1])]

Ambystoma *am-bis'to-mə*, *n* a genus of tailed amphibians in the gill-less or salamandroid suborder, called axolotl in the larval stage. [Irreg formed from Gr *amblys* blunt, and *stoma* mouth]

AMC *abbrev*: American Motors Corporation.

AMDG *abbrev*: *ad majorem Dei gloriam* (*L*), to the greater glory of God.

am-dram *am-dram'*, (*colloq*) *n* (*usu sing*) amateur dramatics. — Also *adj*.

amearst (*Spenser*) for **amerced**.

ameba, **amebic**, etc. US spelling of **amoeba**, **amoebic**, etc.

âme damnée *äm da-nā*, (*Fr*) a tool or agent blindly devoted to one's will (literally, a damned soul); **âme de boue** (*də bōō*) a low-minded person (literally, a soul of mud); **âme perdue** (*per-dü*) a desperate character (literally, a lost soul).

ameer. See **amir**.

ameiosis *ā-mī-ō'sis*, (*biol*) *n* non-pairing of the chromosomes in meiosis. [**a-**[2]]

Amelanchier *am-ə-lang'ki-ər*, *n* the shadbush genus of the rose family. [Fr *amélanchier*]

amelcorn *am'əl-körn*, *n* a kind of wheat, emmer. [Ger *Amelkorn*, Du *amelkorn*; cf **amylum corn**[1]]

amelia *a-mēl'i-ə*, *-mel'*, or *-yə*, *n* a congenital condition in which one or more limbs are completely absent. [**a-**[2] and Gr *melos* limb]

ameliorate *ə-mē'lyə-rāt*, *vt* to make better; to improve. — *vi* to grow better, to improve. — *n* **amēliorā'tion**. — *adj* **amē'liorātive**. [Fr *améliorer*, from L *ad* to, and *melior* better]

amen *ä-men'* or *ā-men'*, *interj* so let it be, said *esp* at the end of a prayer. — *n* an expression of assent, by saying 'amen'; the last word. — *vt* to say amen to; to ratify solemnly; to approve; to conclude. — **Amen glass** a type of drinking-glass engraved with a Jacobite inscription, *esp* 'God save the king. Amen'. [Heb *āmēn* true, truly, retained in Gr and Eng translations]

amenable *ə-mēn'ə-bl*, or (*esp US*) *ə-men'ə-bl*, *adj* ready to be led or won over; liable or subject. — *n* **amenabil'ity** or **amen'ableness**. — *adv* **amen'ably**. [Fr *amener* to lead, from *à*, from L *ad* to, and *mener* to lead, from LL *mināre* to lead or drive (eg cattle), from L *minārī* to threaten]

amenage *am'e-nāj*, (*Spenser*) *vt* to tame. [OFr *ame(s)nager*, from *à* to, and *mesnage* household]

amenaunce *am'ə-nöns*, (*Spenser*) *n* bearing. [OFr *amenance*; see **amenable**]

amend *ə-mend'*, *vt* to free from fault or error; to correct; to improve; to alter in detail, with a view to improvement, (eg a bill before parliament); to rectify; to cure; to mend. — *vi* to grow or become better; to reform; to recover. — *adj* **amend'able**. — *adj* **amend'a-tory** corrective. — *n* **amend'er**. — *n* **amend'ment** correction; improvement; an alteration or addition to a document, agreement, etc; an alteration proposed on a bill under consideration; a counter-proposal or counter-motion put before a meeting. — **make amends** to supply a loss; to compensate (for). [Fr *amender*, from L *ēmendāre*, from *ē* out of, and *mendum* a fault]

amende *am-ād*, (*Fr*) *n* a fine or penalty. — **amende honorable** (*o-nor-äbl'*) *orig*, an ignominious public confession; now, a frank admission of wrong satisfying the honour of the injured.

amenity *ə-mēn'i-ti* or *ə-men'i-ti*, *n* pleasantness, eg in situation, climate, manners or disposition; a pleasing feature, object or characteristic; a facility (*usu* in *pl*); civility. — *adj* (*rare*) **amene** (*ə-mēn'*) pleasant. — **amenity bed** a hospital bed, the occupant of which pays for amenities such as privacy while still receiving free medical treatment. [L *amoenus* pleasant]

amenorrhoea or (*esp NAm*) **amenorrhea** *a-* or *ā-men-ō-rē'ə*, *n* failure or absence of menstruation. [**a-**[2], Gr *mēn* month, and *rhoiā* a flowing]

ament *ā'mənt* or *ə-ment'*, (*psychiatry*) *n* a person who fails to develop mentally; a sufferer from amentia. — *n* **amentia** (*a-* or *ā-men'shi-ə*) mental deficiency. [L *āmēns*, *-entis*, from *ā* from, and *mēns*, *mentis* mind]

amentum *a-men'təm*, *n* a catkin: — *pl* **amen'ta**. — Also **a'ment**. — *adj* **amentā'ceous** or **amen'tal**. — *adj* **amentif'erous** catkin-bearing. [L, thong]

Amer. *abbrev*: America; American.

Amerasian *am-ər-ā'shən*, *n* a person fathered by an American serviceman in Vietnam or Korea, or, more generally, anyone of mixed American and Asian parentage. — Also *adj*. [*Amer*ican and **Asian**]

amerce *ə-mûrs'*, *vt* to fine (*esp* with a discretionary fine); to deprive; to punish. — *n* **amerce'ment** or **amerc'i-ament** infliction of a fine; a fine. — *adj* **amerc'eable** or **amerc'iable**. [Anglo-Fr *amercier*, from *à merci* at mercy]

American *ə-mer'i-kən*, *adj* pertaining to America, *esp* to the United States. — *n* a native or citizen of America; the English language as spoken in America. — *n pl* **Americana** (*ə-mer-i-kä'nə*) things characteristic of America, *esp* old books, paintings, furniture, etc. — *n* **Amer'icanism** a custom, characteristic, word, phrase or idiom characteristic of Americans; the condition of being an American citizen; (advocacy of) American policies, political attitudes, etc; devotion to American institutions. — *n* **Amer'icanist** a student of American biology, archaeology, and the like. — *n* **Americaniza'-tion** or **-s-**. — *vt* **Amer'icanize** or **-ise** to make American. — **American aloe** agave; **American blight** a plant-louse pest of apple-trees; **American bowls** tenpin bowling, a game like skittles; **American cloth** cloth with a glazed coating; **American Dream** (with **the**) the idea that the American way of life offers the possibility of unlimited economic, social, etc success to every individual; **American eagle** the bald eagle; **American Express®** **card** a type of credit card issued by a commercial company (*abbrev* **Amex**); **American football** an American game of football, somewhat resembling British Rugby football, played with an elliptical ball between teams of eleven players (unlimited substitution being allowed), scoring being by points won for touch-downs and goals; **American Indian** a member of the native race of America, thought on discovery to be Indian; **American organ** an instrument resembling the harmonium, in which air is sucked inwards to the reeds; **American pit bull terrier** an American breed of pit bull terrier (qv at **pit**[1]); **American plan** in a hotel, etc, the system of including meals in the charge for a room (see also **European plan**); **American tiger** a jaguar; **American tournament** see **round robin** under **round**. — **American standard code for information interchange** (*comput*) ASCII. [From *America*, perh so called from Richard *Ameryk*, Sheriff of Bristol, who financed John Cabot's voyage; also said to be from Amerigo (L *Americus*) Vespucci]

americium *am-ər-ish'i-əm*, *n* a radioactive metallic element (atomic no 95; symbol **Am**), obtained artificially in *America*.

Amerind *am'ər-ind*, *n* and *adj Amer*ican *Ind*ian. — Also **Amerind'ian**. — *adj* **Amerin'dic**.

à merveille *a mer-vey'*, (*Fr*) wonderfully, perfectly.

ames-ace. See **ambs-ace**.

Ameslan *a'məs-lən*, *n Am*erican *s*ign *lan*guage.

Ametabola *am-et-ab'ə-lə*, *n pl* in some classifications, the lowest insects, with little or no metamorphosis. — *n* **ametab'olism**. — *adj* **ametabol'ic** (*-ə-bol'ik*) or **ametab'-olous**. [**a-**[2] and Gr *metabolē* change]

amethyst *am'ə-thist*, *n* a bluish violet quartz used as a gemstone, anciently supposed to prevent drunkenness; its colour. — *adj* of or coloured like amethyst. — *adj* **amethyst'ine** (*-īn*). — **oriental amethyst** a purple corundum. [Gr *amethystos*, from *a-* (privative), and *methyein* to be drunken, from *methy* wine; cf **mead**[1] and Sans *madhu* sweet]

Amex *a'meks*, *abbrev*: American Express® (card); American Stock Exchange.

Amharic *am-har'ik*, *n* a Semitic language, the official language of Ethiopia. — Also *adj*. [*Amhara* district of Ethiopia]

ami *a-mē*, (*Fr*) *n* a friend: — *fem* **amie** (*a-mē*) a friend; a mistress. — **ami de cour** (*də ko͞or*) a court friend, ie an untrustworthy friend; **ami du peuple** (*dü pœpl'*) friend of the people (*esp* Marat, French revolutionist).

amiable *ām'i-ə-bl*, *adj* of sweet and friendly disposition; lovable; friendly (*Shakesp*); love-inspiring (*Shakesp*). — *n* **āmiabil'ity** or **ām'iableness**. — *adv* **ām'iably**. [OFr *amiable* friendly, from L *amīcābilis*, from *amīcus* friend; confused in meaning with OFr *amable* (Fr *aimable*), from L *amābilis*, from *amāre* to love]

amianthus *am-i-anth'əs*, or more correctly **amiantus** *-ant'əs*, *n* the finest fibrous asbestos, which can be made into cloth unaffected by fire. [Gr *amiantos* (*lithos*) undefiled (stone), from *a-* (privative), and *miainein* to soil]

amicable *am'ik-ə-bl*, *adj* in friendly spirit. — *n* **amicabil'ity** or **am'icableness**. — *adv* **am'icably**. — **amicable numbers** (*math*) see **friendly numbers**. [L *amīcābilis*, from *amīcus* a friend, from *amāre* to love]

amice[1] *am'is*, *n* a strip of fine linen, worn formerly on the head, now on the shoulders, by a priest at mass; a cloak or wrap. [OFr *amit*, from L *amictus* cloak, from *amb-* about, and *jacere* to throw]

amice[2] *am'is* or **almuce** *al-mūs'*, *n* a furred hood with long ends hanging down in front, originally a cap or covering for the head, afterwards a hood or cape with a hood and later a college hood, worn by certain religious orders. [OFr *aumuce*, of doubtful origin]

amicus curiae *a-mī'kus kū'ri-ē* or *a-mē'ko͞os ko͞o'ri-ī*, *n* formerly, in Scots law, a disinterested adviser, not a party to the case; a person or group not directly involved in a case who may be represented by request or permission of the court; counsel representing such; (wrongly) a friend in high quarters: — *pl* **amī'cī** (or *-mē'kē*). [L, a friend of the law-court]

amid *ə-mid'*, *prep* in the midst of; among. — *adv* (*archaic*) in the midst. — *adv* and *prep* **amid'most** in the very middle (of). — *adv* **amid'ships** in, near or towards, the middle of a ship lengthwise (from genitive of **ship**). — *adv* and *prep* **amidst'** amid. [OE *on middan* (dative of adj), in middle; the *s* is a later adverbial genitive ending, the *t* as in **amongst**, **betwixt**, etc]

amide *am'īd*, *n* a derivative of ammonia in which an acid radical takes the place of one or more of the three hydrogen atoms. — *n* **amido-group** (*ə-mē'dō*) the group NH_2 in such combination. [From **ammonia**]

Amidol® *am'i-dol*, *n* a colourless chemical $(C_6H_3(NH_2)_2(OH).2HCl$ used as a photographic developer.

amidships. See **amid**.

amie. See **ami**.

amigo *a-mē'gō*, (*Sp*) *n* a friend: — *pl* **ami'gos**.

amildar *am'il-där*, *n* a factor or manager in India; a collector of revenue amongst the Mahrattas. [Hindustani *'amaldār*, from Ar *'amal* work, and Pers *dār* holder]

amine *am'īn* or *-ēn*, *n* a derivative of ammonia (NH_3) in which one or more hydrocarbon radicals take the place of one or more of the three hydrogen atoms. — *n* **amino acid** (*a-mē'nō*) any of a group of organic compounds containing at least one from both the amino and the carboxyl groups (eg **amino-acetic acid**, glycine), some of which (**essential amino acids**) cannot be synthesized by the body and must be supplied in the diet; **amino group** the group NH_2 in such combination. [From **ammonia**]

aminobutene *a-mē'nō-bū'tēn*, *n* a pain-relieving drug, less addiction-forming than morphine. [**amine** and **butene**]

a minori (ad majus) *ā min-ör'ī (ad māj'us)* or *ä min-ōr'ē (ad mī'ūs)* (*L*) from the less (to the greater).

amir or **ameer** *a-mēr'* or *ə-mēr'*, *n* the title borne by certain Muslim princes. [Ar *amīr*; see **admiral** or **emir**]

amis (*Spenser*). Same as **amice**[1].

Amish *ä'mish*, or *am'*, *adj* of or belonging to a strict US Mennonite sect. — Also *n pl*. [Ger *amisch*, after the 17c Swiss bishop, J *Amman* or *Amen*]

amiss *ə-mis'*, *adv* astray; wrongly; improperly; faultily. — *adj* out of order; wrong; unsuitable; to be objected to. — *n* (*obs*) an evil; a misdeed. — **come amiss** to be unwelcome or untoward; **take amiss** to take offence at (strictly, by misinterpretation). [**a-**[1] and **miss**[1]]

amissible *ə-mis'i-bl*, *adj* liable to be lost. — *n* **amissibil'ity**. [L *āmittere*, *āmissum* to lose, from *ā* from, and *mittere* to send]

amissing *ə-mis'ing*, (*Scot*) *adj* wanting; lost. [**a-**[1]]

amitosis *am-i-tō'sis*, (*biol*) *n* cell-division without mitosis. — *adj* **amitotic** (*-tot'ik*). — *adv* **amitot'ically**. [**a-**[2] and Gr *mitos* thread]

amitryptyline *am-i-trip'tə-lēn*, *n* an antidepressant drug, also used to treat enuresis. [From *amino*, *trypt*amine (a hallucinogenic substance) and meth*yl*, with ending *-ine*]

amity *am'i-ti*, *n* friendship; goodwill; friendly relations. [Fr *amitié*, from L *amicus* a friend]

amla *äm'lə*, *n* an E Indian tree, the emblic.

AMMA *abbrev*: Assistant Masters' and Mistresses' Association.

amman. See **amtman**.

ammeter *am'i-tər*, *n* an instrument for measuring electric current *usu* in amperes. [From **ampere** and Gr *metron* measure]

ammiral. An old form (*Milton*) of **admiral**.

ammo *am'ō*, *n* a familiar contraction of **ammunition**.

Ammon *am'on*, *n* the ancient Egyptian ram-headed god *Amûn* or *Amen*, identified by the Greeks with Zeus, famous for his temple and oracle in the Libyan oasis of Siwa; (without *cap*) the Asian wild sheep, the argali (from its gigantic horns). [Gr *Ammōn*, *-ōnos*]

ammonal *am'ən-al*, *n* a high explosive made from *ammon*ium nitrate and *al*uminium.

ammonia *a-mō'ni-ə* or *ə-mō'ni-ə*, *n* a pungent compound of nitrogen and hydrogen (NH_3) first obtained in gaseous form from *sal ammoniac*; its solution in water, strictly ammonium hydroxide (*liquid ammonia*, formerly called spirits of hartshorn). — *adj* **ammō'niac** or **ammonī'acal** of ammonia; of the region of the temple of Ammon (applied only to gum ammoniac, and to sal ammoniac, which is said to have been first made in that district from camel-dung). — *n* **ammoniacum** (*am-ə-nī'ə-kəm*) gum ammoniac. — *adj* **ammō'niated** combined, impregnated, with ammonia. — *n* **ammō'nium** a univalent radical, NH_4, resembling the alkali metals in chemical behaviour. — **gum ammoniac** a gum resin used in medicine. [New L, back-formation from Eng *sal ammoniac*, from L *sal* salt, and *ammoniacus* of Ammon; see **Ammon**]

ammonite *am'ən-īt*, *n* a fossil cephalopod of many kinds, with a coiled chambered shell resembling a ram's horn. — *n* **amm'onoid** a member of the order *Ammonoidea*, to which the ammonites and related cephalopods belong. [New L *ammōnītes*, from *Ammon*]

ammophilous *am-of'i-ləs*, *adj* sand-loving. [Gr *ammos* sand, and *phileein* to love]

ammunition *am-ū-nish'ən*, *n orig* military stores generally; things used for charging fire-arms, such as missiles or propellants (*colloq* **am'mo**); explosive military devices; anything that can be used in fighting (*lit* and *fig*). — *adj* for ammunition; supplied from army stores. — *vt* to supply with ammunition. [Obs Fr *amunition*, appar from *l'amunition* for *la munition*; see **munition**]

amnesia *am-nē'zh(y)ə*, *n* loss of memory. — *n* **amne'siac** someone who suffers from amnesia. — Also *adj*. — *adj* and *n* **amne'sic**. [Gr *amnēsiā*]

amnesty *am'nəs-ti*, *n* a general pardon; a period during which offenders may admit to certain crimes or infringements without penalty; an act of oblivion. — *vt* to give amnesty to. [Gr *amnēstiā* forgetfulness]

amnion *am'ni-ən*, *n* the innermost membrane enveloping the embryo of reptiles, birds and mammals: — *pl* **am'nia**. — **amnio-** *combining form* denoting amnion; amniotic. — *n* **amniocentesis** (*am-ni-ō-sin-tē'sis*) the insertion of a hollow needle into the uterus of a pregnant woman to withdraw a sample of the amniotic fluid to test for foetal abnormalities, etc. — *adj* **amniot'ic**. — *n* **amniot'omy** surgical rupture of the amnion during, or in order to induce, labour. — **amniotic cavity** the space between the embryo and the amnion; **amniotic fluid** the fluid within the amnion in which the embryo is suspended. [Gr]

amoeba or (*US*) **ameba** *ə-mē'bə*, *n* a protozoon of ever-changing shape: — *pl* **amoe'bae** (*-bē* or *-bī*) or **amoe'bas**. — *n* **amoebī'asis** infection (*esp* of the colon) by amoebae. — *adj* **amoe'bic**. — *adj* **amoe'biform**. — *adj* **amoe'boid**. [Gr *amoibē* change]

amoebaean *ə-mē-bē'ən*, *adj* answering alternately, responsive, as often in pastoral poetry. [L *amoebaeus*, from Gr *amoibaios*, from *amoibē* alternation]

à moitié *a mwa-tyā*, (*Fr*) half; by halves.

amok *ə-mok'* or **amuck** *ə-muk'*, *adj* and *adv* in a frenzy, *esp* in the phrase **run amok**, to rush about wildly, attacking anyone in one's path (also *fig*). [Malay *amoq* frenzied]

amomum *a-mō'məm*, *n* a plant of the genus *Amomum* of the ginger family, including cardamoms and grains of Paradise. [Latinized from Gr *amōmon* prob cardamom]

à mon avis *a mo-na-vē*, (*Fr*) in my opinion.

among *ə-mung'* or **amongst** *ə-mungst'*, *prep* of the number of; amid. — *adv* **among** (*archaic*) meanwhile; all the time; betweenwhiles; here and there. [OE *on-gemang* literally in mixture or crowd, from *gemengan* to mingle; for *-st* see **against**]

amontillado *ä-mon-til-(y)ä'dō*, *n* a light medium-dry sherry *orig* from *Montilla*: — *pl* **amontilla'dos**. [Sp]

amoove (*Spenser*). Same as **amove**[1].

amoral *ā-mor'əl*, also *a-*, *adj* non-moral, outside the domain of morality. — *n* **amor'alism** refusal to recognize the validity of any system of morality. — *n* **amor'alist**. [**a-**[2] and **moral**]

amorance *am'ər-əns*, (*psychol*) *n* the state of being in love; romantic love. — *adj* **am'orant**. [L *amor* love]

amorce *ə-mörs'*, *n* a percussion cap for a toy pistol. [Fr, priming]

amoret *am'ər-et*, *n* a sweetheart (*obs*); a love-glance; a love-knot; a love sonnet or song. — *n* **amoret'to** a lover; a cupid: — *pl* **amoret'ti** (*-tē*). — *n* **amorino** (*-ē'nō*) a cupid: — *pl* **amori'ni** (*-nē*). [OFr *amorete* and Ital *amoretto* or *amorino*, diminutives from L *amor* love]

amorist *am'ər-ist*, *n* a lover; a ladies' man; one who writes of love; a seeker of sexual adventures or experiences. — *n* **am'orism**. [L *amor* love]

amornings *ə-mörn'ingz*, (*obs* or *dialect*) *adv* of a morning. [**a-**[1] and **morning**, with genitive ending added]

amoroso *am-or-ō'sō*, (*music*) *adj* tender; (of sherry) sweet, full-bodied. — Also *adv*. — *n* a lover; a ladies' man; a dark sweet sherry: — *pl* **amoro'sos**: — *fem* **amoro'sa**. [Ital and Sp]

amorous *am'ər-əs*, *adj* inclined to *esp* sexual love; in love; fond; amatory; relating to love. — *n* **amorosity** (*-os'i-ti*; *rare*). — *adv* **am'orously**. — *n* **am'orousness**. [OFr *amorous* (Fr *amoureux*), from LL *amōrōsus*, from *amor* love]

amor patriae *ā'mör pā'tri-ē* or *ä'mor pa'tri-ī*, (*L*) love of country.

amorphous *ə-mör'fəs*, *adj* without definite shape or structure; shapeless; without crystalline structure. — *n* **amor'phism** or **amor'phousness**. — *adv* **amor'phously**. [Gr *amorphos* shapeless, from *a-* (privative), and *morphē* form]

amort *ə-mört'*, (*obs* or *archaic*) *adj* spiritless, dejected. [Fr *à* to, and *mort* death; but partly from **alamort** wrongly understood as *all amort*]

amortize or **-ise** *ə-mör'tīz* or *-tiz*, (*law*) *vt* to alienate in mortmain or convey to a corporation; to pay off (a debt), *esp* through a sinking-fund. — *n* **amortizā'tion** or **-s-**. — *n* **amort'izement** or **-s-**. [LL *a(d)mortizāre*, from Fr *à* to, and *mort* death]

amor vincit omnia. See **omnia**.

amosite *am'ə-sīt*, *n* brown asbestos, a form of asbestos mined only in S Africa. [*A*sbestos *M*ines *o*f *S*outh Africa, and *-ite*]

amount *ə-mownt'*, *vi* to go up (*Spenser*); to come in total; to come in meaning or substance (with *to*). — *n* the whole sum; principal and interest together; quantity; value, import, equivalence. [OFr *amonter* to ascend, from L *ad* to, and *mōns*, *montis* a mountain]

amour *ə-mōōr'*, *n* a love affair (now *usu* discreditable); a loved one; love or friendship (*obs*); love-making (*usu* in *pl*; *archaic*). — *n* **amourette** (*a-mōō-ret'*) a petty amour; an amoretto. [Fr, from L *amor*, *amōris* love]

amour courtois *a-mōōr kōōr-twä*, (*Fr*) *n* courtly love.

amour-propre *a-mōōr-propr'*, (*Fr*) *n* self-esteem; sometimes, excessive self-esteem, as shown by readiness to take offence at slights.

amove[1] *ə-mōōv'*, *vt* to stir up (*obs*); to affect (*obs*); to rouse (*Spenser*). [OFr *amover*, from L *admovēre*, from *ad* to, and *movēre* to move]

amove[2] *ə-mōōv'*, (*law*) *vt* to remove. [L *āmovēre*, from *ā* from, and *movēre* to move]

AMP *abbrev*: adenosine monophosphate.

amp *amp*, *n* short form of **ampere** and **amplifier**.

ampassy. See **ampersand**.

ampelo- *am-pel-o-* or **ampeli-** *am-pel-i-*, *combining form* denoting of the vine, vine-like. — *n* **ampelography** (*am-pel-og'rə-fi*) the botany of the vine. [Gr *ampelos* vine]

ampelopsis *am-pi-lop'sis*, *n* a plant of the genus of climbing shrubs *Ampelopsis*; (formerly and rarely) any of certain related plants such as the Virginia creeper: — *pl* **ampelop'ses** (*-sēz*). [Gr *ampelos* vine, and *opsis* appearance]

ampere or **ampère** *am'per* or *-pēr'*, or *ã-per*, (*elec*) *n* the SI and MKSA unit of current, defined as that which, flowing in two parallel conductors, each infinitely thin and long, one metre apart in a vacuum, will produce a force between the conductors of 2×10^{-7} newtons per metre length (**international ampere** a unit formerly defined by means of the rate of deposition of silver from a solution of silver nitrate and slightly less than the practical unit in use; now the same as the unit just defined). — *n* **am'perage** current in amperes. — **ampere hour** unit of change = 3 600 coulombs, or one ampere flowing for one hour. [From A M *Ampère* (1775–1836), French physicist]

ampersand *am'pərs-and*, *n* the character & (*orig* ligatured *E* and *T*, for Latin *et*) representing *and*. — Also **am'perzand**, **am'pussy-and** and **am'passy** (*amp'ə-si*). [*and per se*, *and*, ie & by itself means 'and'; cf **a-per-se**]

Ampex® *am'peks*, *n* a system of magnetic recording of television signals. — *vt* to record by Ampex.

amphetamine *am-fet'ə-mēn*, *n* $C_9H_{13}N$, or its sulphate or phosphate, a synthetic, potentially habit-forming drug used to relieve nasal congestion or taken internally to stimulate the central nervous system. [*a*lpha *m*ethyl *phene*t*hyl *amine*]

amphi- *am'fi-*, *pfx* denoting both, on both sides (or ends) or around. [Gr]

amphibian *am-fi'bi-ən adj* amphibious; of the **Amphi'bia**, a class of cold-blooded vertebrates typically gill-breathing in the larval state and lung-breathing or skin-breathing as adults — frogs, toads, newts, salamanders, and caecilians. — *n* a member of the Amphibia; an aeroplane designed to alight on land or water; a vehicle for use on land or water. [New L *amphibia*, from Gr; see **amphibious**]

amphibious *am-fib'i-əs*, *adj* living, or adapted to life or use, both on land and in or on water; of military operations, in which troops are conveyed across the sea or other water in landing barges, assault-craft, etc, and land on enemy-held territory; of double, doubtful or ambiguous nature; leading two lives (*archaic*). [Gr *amphibios*, from *amphi* on both sides, and *bios* life]

amphibole *am'fi-bōl*, (*mineralogy*) *n* any mineral of a group of dark-coloured, rock-forming silicates differing from the pyroxenes in cleavage angle (about 56° instead of about 87°), silicates of calcium, magnesium, and other metals, including hornblende, actinolite, tremolite, etc. — *n* **amphib'olite** a rock composed essentially of amphibole. [Gr *amphibolos* ambiguous, on account of the resemblance between hornblende and tourmaline]

amphibology *am-fi-bol'ə-ji*, *n* a phrase or sentence ambiguous not in its individual words but in its construction; the use of such ambiguities. — *adj* **amphibol'ic** or **amphibolog'ical** (*-bə-loj'*). — *adj* **amphib'olous** (*-ə-ləs*). — *n* **amphib'oly** amphibology. [Gr *amphibolos*, from *amphi* on both sides, and *ballein* to throw]

amphibrach *am'fi-brak*, (*prosody*) *n* a foot of three syllables, a long between two short, or stressed between two unstressed. — *adj* **amphibrach'ic**. [L *amphibrachus*, Gr *amphibrachys* short at both ends, from *amphi* on both sides, and *brachys* short]

amphictyon *am-fik'ti-on*, (*Gr hist*) *n* a delegate to a council of an **amphic'tyony**, a league of neighbouring communities connected with a temple and cult, *esp* of Delphi. — *adj* **amphictyon'ic**. [Gr *amphiktyones*, appar for *amphiktiones* dwellers around, from *amphi* around, and *ktizein* to dwell]

amphigastrium *am-fi-gas'tri-əm*, *n* a scale-like leaf on the ventral side of some liverworts: — *pl* **amphigas'tria**. [**amphi-**, and *gastēr* belly]

amphigory *am'fi-gə-ri*, *n* nonsense verse. [Fr *amphigouri*, of unknown origin]

amphimacer *am-fim'ə-sər*, (*prosody*) *n* a foot of three syllables, a short between two long. [Gr *amphimakros*, from *amphi* on both sides, and *makros* long]

amphimixis *am-fi-mik'sis*, *n* fusion of gametes; sexual reproduction; combination of characteristics from both parents. — *adj* **amphimic'tic**. [Gr *amphi* on both sides, and *mīxis* intercourse, mixing]

Amphineura *am-fi-nū'rə*, *n pl* a class of molluscs with two ventral and two lateral nerve-cords, including Chiton. [**amphi-**, and Gr *neuron* nerve]

amphioxus *am-fi-oks'əs*, *n* a lancelet of the genus *Amphioxus* or *Branchiostoma*. [**amphi-**, and Gr *oxys* sharp]

amphipathic *am-fi-path'ik*, (*chem* and *phys*) *adj* of an unsymmetrical molecular group of which one end is hydrophilic and the other end hydrophobic. [**amphi-**, and Gr *pathos* feeling]

amphipod *am'fi-pod*, *n* one of the **Amphip'oda**, an order of small sessile-eyed crustaceans with swimming feet and jumping feet, eg sand-hoppers, etc. — *adj* **amphip'odous**. [**amphi-**, and Gr *pous*, *podos* a foot]

amphiprotic *am-fi-prō'tik*, (*chem*) *adj* having both protophilic and protogenic properties. [**amphi-** and **proto-**]

amphisbaena *am-fis-bē'nə, n* a fabulous two-headed snake; (with *cap*) a genus of snake-like lizards, chiefly tropical American, whose rounded tails give the appearance of a head at each end. — *adj* **amphisbae'nic**. [Gr *amphisbaina*, from *amphis* both ways, and *bainein* to go]

amphiscian *am-fish'i-ən, n* an inhabitant of the torrid zone, whose shadow is thrown both ways, ie northwards one part of the year, and southwards the other part. — Also *adj*. [Gr *amphiskios*, from *amphi* both ways, and *skiā* a shadow]

amphistomous *am-fis'tə-məs, adj* having a sucker at either end, as some worms. [Gr *amphistomos* with double mouth, from *amphi* on both sides, and *stoma* mouth]

amphitheatre *am'fi-thē-ə-tər, n* a building with rows of seats one above another, around an open space; a similar configuration of hill slopes; one of the galleries in a theatre. — *adj* **amphithe'atral**, **amphitheat'ric** or **amphitheatrical** (*-at'ri-kl*). — *adv* **amphitheat'rically**. [Gr *amphitheātron*, from *amphi* on both sides and *theātron* theatre]

amphitropous *am-fit'rə-pəs, (bot) adj* (of an ovule) placed T-wise on the funicle. [**amphi-** and *tropos* a turning]

Amphitryon *am-fit'ri-ən, n* in Greek mythology, the husband of Alcmene (Herakles beng the son of Alcmene and Zeus disguised as Amphitryon); a hospitable entertainer, *esp* of doubtful identity (in allusion to the line in Molière's play, 'Le véritable Amphitryon est l'Amphitryon où l'on dîne'). [Gr *Amphitryōn*]

ampholyte *am'fō-līt, n* an *amphoteric* electro*lyte*.

amphora *am'fə-rə, n* a two-handled jar used by the Greeks and Romans for holding liquids: — *pl* **am'phorae** (*-rē* or *-rī*). — *adj* **amphor'ic** (*-for'*; *med*) like the sound produced by blowing into a bottle. [L *amphora*, from Gr *amphoreus*, *amphiphoreus*, from *amphi* on both sides, and *phoreus* a bearer]

amphoteric *am-fō-ter'ik, adj* of both kinds; acting both ways, eg as acid and base, electropositive and electronegative. [Gr *amphoteros* both]

Ampicillin® *am-pi-sil'in, n* an antibiotic drug, a type of penicillin.

ample *am'pl, adj* spacious; wide; large enough; abundant; liberal; copious; full or somewhat bulky in form. — *n* **am'pleness**. — *n* **ampliā'tion** enlarging; an enlargement. — *adj* **am'pliātive** (*rare*). — *adv* **am'ply** (*-pli*). [Fr *ample*, from L *amplus*]

amplexus *am-plek'səs, n* the clasping of the female of certain amphibians by the male as part of the mating process; the period of this: — *pl* **amplexus**. — *adj* **amplexicaul** (*am-plek'si-köl*; *bot*; L *caulis* stem) clasping the stem by a dilated base. [L *amplexus*, *amplexūs* embrace or encircling]

ampliation, etc. See **ample**.

amplify *am'pli-fī, vt* to make more copious in expression; to add to; to increase loudness of (sound), strength of (current), etc. — *vi* to enlarge (*on* an utterance, etc): — *pr p* **am'plifying**; *pa p* and *pa t* **am'plified**. — *n* **amplificā'tion** enlargement. — *n* **am'plifier** someone who amplifies; a lens that enlarges the field of vision; a device for giving greater loudness. [Fr *amplifier*, from L *amplificāre*]

amplitude *am'pli-tūd, n* largeness; abundance; width; range; extent of vibratory movement (from extreme to extreme, or from mean to extreme); the angular distance from the east point of the horizon at which a heavenly body rises, or from the west point at which it sets. — **amplitude modulation** (*telecomm*) modulation in radio transmission by varying the amplitude of the carrier wave (cf *frequency modulation*). [Fr *amplitude*, from L *amplitūdō*]

amplosome *am'plə-sōm, n* the short or stocky type of human figure. [L *amplus* large, and Gr *sōma* body]

amply. See **ample**.

ampoule or (*US*) **ampule** *am'po͞ol* (also *-po͞ol'*), *n* a small sealed glass, etc container for a hypodermic dose, etc. — Also **am'pul** (*-pūl*). [Fr; see **ampulla**]

ampulla *am-po͞ol'ə, n* a small two-handled ancient Roman flask; a pilgrim's bottle; a vessel for holy oil, as at coronations; cruet for the wine and water used at the altar; any small membranous vesicle (*biol*); the dilated end of a semicircular canal in the ear: — *pl* **ampull'ae** (*-ē*). — See also **ampoule**. — *n* **ampullos'ity** (*Browning*) turgidity or bombast. [L irregular dimin of *amphora* a flagon; partly directly from L, partly through OE *ampulle*, OFr *ampo(u)le* and Ital *ampolla*]

ampussy-and. See **ampersand**.

amputate *am'pūt-āt, vt* to cut off (eg a limb). — *n* **amputā'tion**. — *n* **am'putātor**. — *n* **amputee'**. [L *amputāre*, *-ātum*, from *amb-* around, and *putāre*, *-ātum* to lop]

AMRAAM *abbrev*: advanced medium-range air-to-air missile.

amrit *am'rət, n* a sacred sweetened water used in the Sikh baptismal ceremony; the ceremony itself. [Punjabi, from Sans *amṛta* immortal]

amrita *am-rē'tä, n* the drink of the Hindu gods. — *n* **amritattva** (*am-rē-tät'vä*) immortality. [Sans *amṛta* immortal; cf Gr *ambrotos*]

amt *abbrev*: amount.

amtman *ämt'män* or **amman** *am'an, n* in Germany, Switzerland, the Netherlands and Scandinavia, a district magistrate. [Ger *Amtmann*, *Amman*, Dan and Norw *amtmand*, from *amt* office or administration (from the same root as **ambassador**) and Ger *Mann*, Dan *mand* man]

amtrack *am'trak, n* an amphibious tracked military motor landing-vehicle. [**am** for *am*phibious, and **track**[1]]

Amtrak *am'trak, n* a US corporation (the National Railroad Passenger Corporation) managing passenger rail-travel between major US cities. [*Am*erican *Tra*vel and Trac*k*]

amu *abbrev*: atomic mass unit.

amuck *ə-muk'*. See **amok**.

amulet *am'ū-let* or *-lit, n* a charm worn to ward off evil, disease, etc; a medicine supposed to operate magically. — *adj* **amulet'ic**. [L *amulētum*]

amuse *ə-mūz', vt* to occupy pleasantly; to entertain or divert; to provoke mirth in; to beguile with expectation; to occupy the attention of; to put in a muse (*obs*); to beguile (*archaic*). — *adj* **amus'able**. — *adj* **amused'**. — *adv* **amus'edly**. — *n* **amuse'ment** distraction of attention; beguiling; trifling; a pleasant feeling of the ludicrous; something which amuses; a mechanical or other device for amusement at a fairground, amusement arcade, etc; recreation; pastime. — *n* **amus'er**. — *n* **amusette** (*am-ū-zet'*) a light field gun invented by Marshal Saxe. — *adj* **amus'ing** mildly funny; diverting; entertaining. — *adv* **amus'ingly**. — *adj* **amus'ive** deceptive (*obs*); recreational (*obs*); interesting; entertaining; amusing. — *n* **amus'iveness**. — **amusement arcade** a public hall, or open area off the street with mechanical gambling machines, video games, etc; **amusement park** a public park with fairground rides, sideshows, etc. [Fr *amuser*, from *à* to, and *muser* to stare; see **muse**[1]]

amygdal *ə-mig'dəl, n* (*obs*) an almond. — *n* **amyg'dala** (*zool*) a lobe of the cerebellum; one of the palatal tonsils. — *adj* **amygdalā'ceous** related to the almond. — *n* **amyg'dale** (*-dāl*) an amygdule. — *n* **amyg'dalin** a glucoside found in cherry kernels, bitter almonds, etc, at one time thought useful in treating cancer. — *adj* **amyg'daloid** almond-shaped; having amygdules. — *n* an igneous rock in which almond-shaped steam-cavities have been filled with minerals. — *adj* **amygdaloid'al** having amygdules. — *n* **Amyg'dalus** the almond genus, or section of Prunus. — *n* **amyg'dule** a mineral-filled steam-cavity in a lava. [L *amygdala*, from Gr *amygdalē* almond]

amyl *am'il, n* an alcohol radical, C_5H_{11}. — *n* **am'ylase** (*-ās*) any of the enzymes that play a part in hydrolysis of starch and similar substances. — *n* **am'ylene** a hydrocarbon of composition C_5H_{10}. — **amyl alcohol** $C_5H_{11}OH$, the fraction of fusel-oil that distils at about

131°C; **amyl nitrate** a liquid added to diesel fuel to improve its ignition quality, also inhaled to heighten sexual pleasure; **amyl nitrite** a fruity-smelling, amber-coloured liquid, inhaled medicinally as a vasodilator. [From the first syllable of Gr *amylon* starch, fine meal, and *hȳlē* matter, from having been first obtained from fusel-oil made from starch]

amylum *am'il-əm*, (*chem*) *n* starch. — *adj* **amylā'ceous**. — *adj* **am'yloid**. — *n* in any of several pathological conditions, an intercellular deposit of starch-like material in the tissues. — *adj* **amyloid'al**. — *n* **amyloidō'sis** the condition of the body in which amyloid is deposited in the tissues. — *n* **amylop'sin** an enzyme in pancreatic juice that converts starch into sugar. [Gr *amylon* the finest flour, starch; literally, unmilled, from *a-* (privative), and *mylē* a mill]

amyotrophy *a-mi-ot'rə-fi*, *n* atrophy of the muscles. — *adj* **amyotroph'ic**. [Gr *a-* (privative), *mys* muscle, and *trophē* nourishment]

Amytal® *am'i-təl*, *n* a white crystalline powder used as a sedative. — Also without *cap*.

AN *abbrev*: Anglo-Norman.

an¹ *an* or *ən*, *adj* one; the indefinite article, used before a vowel sound, and by some (now rarely) before an unstressed syllable beginning with a sounded *h*. [OE *ān*; see **one**]

an² *an* or *ən*, (*archaic*) *conj* if. — **an'** and. [A form of **and¹**]

an³ *an* or *ən*, (*obs*) *prep* a form of **on**.

an⁴ *symbol*: actinon.

an. *abbrev*: *anno* (*L*), in the year; anonymous; *ante* (*L*), before.

an-. See **a-²**.

ana *ä'nə*, written **āā** or **ā** (in recipes and prescriptions) in equal quantities. [LL, from Gr, (literally) throughout]

-ana *-ä'nə* or *-ā'nə*, or **-iana** *-i-ä'nə* or *-ā'nə*, *sfx* denoting things belonging to or typical of (a specified person), such as sayings, anecdotes, small objects, etc, eg Johnson*iana* or Victori*ana* (the latter generally used in reference to the time of Queen Victoria rather than to Victoria herself). — **a'na** *n pl* or *collective sing* (with *pl* **a'na's** or **a'nas**) a collection of someone's table-talk or of gossip, literary anecdotes or possessions. [L neuter pl ending of adjs in *-anus*]

anabaptist *an-ə-bap'tist*, *n* a name given by opponents to a person who holds that baptism should be of adults only and therefore that those baptized in infancy must be baptized again; (with *cap*) one of a Protestant sect of German origin (1521) rejecting infant baptism and seeking establishment of a Christian communism. — *n* **anabapt'ism**. — *adj* **anabaptist'ic**. — *vt* **anabaptize'** or **-ise'** to baptize again; to rename. [Gr *ana-* again, and *baptizein* to dip]

anabas *an'a-bas*, *n* a fish of the genus *Anabas* to which belongs the climbing perch, an E Indian fish that often leaves the water. [Gr *anabās*, aorist participle of *anabainein* to climb, from *ana* up, and *bainein* to go]

anabasis *an-ab'ə-sis*, *n* a going up, ascent; a military advance up-country, such as that of Cyrus the younger (401 BC) described (with the subsequent katabasis or retreat of the 10 000) by Xenophon in his *Anabasis*. — *adj* **anabatic** (*-bat'ik*) upward-moving. [Gr, from *ana* up, and *basis* going]

anabiosis *an-ə-bī-ō'sis*, *n* returning to life after apparent death; the ability to do this; a state of suspended animation. — *adj* **anabiot'ic**. [Gr *anabiōsis*, from *ana* up or back, and *bios* life]

anableps *an'ə-bleps*, *n* a fish of the genus *Anableps* of bony fishes with open air-bladders and projecting eyes divided in two for vision in air and water. [Gr *ana* up, and *blepein* to look]

anabolism *an-ab'əl-izm*, *n* chemical building up of complex substances in living matter (*opp* to *catabolism*). — *adj* **anabolic** (*an-ə-bol'ik*). — *n* **anab'olite** a product of anabolism. — *adj* **anabolit'ic**. — **anabolic steroids** steroids used to increase the build-up of body tissue, *esp* muscle, illegally used by some athletes. [Gr *anabolē* a heaping up, from *ana* up, and *bolē* a throw]

anabranch *an'ə-bränch*, (*esp Austr*) *n* a stream that leaves a river and re-enters lower. [For *ana*stomosing *branch*]

anacardium *an-ə-kär'di-əm*, *n* a plant of the cashew-nut genus *Anacardium*, giving name to a family **Anacardiā'ceae** related to the hollies and maples. — *adj* **anacardiā'ceous**. [Gr *ana* according to, and *kardiā* heart (from the shape of the fruit)]

anacatharsis *an-ə-ka-thär'sis*, *n* vomiting. — *n* and *adj* **anacathar'tic**. [Gr *anakatharsis* clearing up, from *ana* up, throughout, and *katharsis* (see **catharsis**)]

Anacharis *ən-ak'ə-ris*, *n* a plant of the genus *Anacharis* of water-plants including *Anacharis helodea* or *Elodea canadensis*, a N American weed found in Britain in 1842, soon clogging canals and rivers by vegetative growth. [Gr *ana* up, and *charis* grace]

anachronism *ə-nak'rə-nizm*, *n* an error assigning a thing to an earlier or (less strictly) to a later age than it belongs to; anything out of keeping with chronology. — *adj* **anachron'ic**. — *adv* **anachron'ically**. — *adj* **anachronist'ic**. — *adv* **anachronist'ically**. — *adj* **anach'ronous**. — *adv* **anach'ronously**. [Gr *ana-* backwards, and *chronos* time]

anaclastic *an-ə-klas'tik*, *adj* refractive. [Gr *anaklastos* bent back, from *ana-* back, and *klaein* to break]

anacoluthia *an-ə-ko-lōō'thi-ə*, or *-lū-*, *n* a non-sequential syntactic construction in which the latter part of a sentence does not grammatically fit the earlier. — *n* **anacolu'thon** an instance of anacoluthia; anacoluthia: — *pl* **anacolu'tha**. [Gr *anakolouthiā*, *anakolouthon*, from *an-* (privative), and *akolouthos* following]

anaconda *an-ə-kon'də*, *n* a gigantic S American snake, a water-boa, *Eunectes murinus*. [Perhaps from a Sinhalese name for another snake in Sri Lanka]

anacoustic zone *an-ə-kōōst'ik zōn*, *n* a zone of absolute silence in space. [**an-** and **acoustic**]

Anacreontic *an-ak-ri-ont'ik*, *adj* after the manner of the Greek poet Anacreon, free, convivial or erotic. — *n* a poem in this vein. — *adv* **anacreont'ically**. [From the Gr poet *Anakreōn*, *fl.* 6c BC]

anacrusis *an-ə-krōō'sis*, (*prosody*) *n* one or more short syllables introductory to the normal rhythm of a line: — *pl* **anacru'ses** (*-sēz*). — *adj* **anacrustic** (*-krus'tik*). [Gr *anakrousis* a pushing back, striking up a tune, from *ana* up, back, and *krouein* to strike]

anadem *an'ə-dem*, *n* a fillet, chaplet, or wreath. [Gr *anadēma*, from *ana* up, and *deein* to bind]

anadiplosis *an-ə-di-plō'sis*, *n* rhetorical repetition of an important word (or sometimes phrase). [Gr *anadiplōsis*, from *ana* back, and *diploein* to double]

anadromous *an-ad'rə-məs*, *adj* of fish, ascending rivers periodically to spawn (*opp* to *catadromous*). [Gr *anadromos* running up, from *ana* up, and *dromos* a run]

anadyomene *a-na-dī-o'mə-nē*, *adj* coming up or emerging (*esp* of Aphrodite from the sea). [Gr *anadyomenē*]

anaemia or (*US*) **anemia** *an-ēm'i-ə*, *n* bloodlessness; lack of red blood corpuscles or of haemoglobin, a condition marked by paleness and weakness. — *adj* **anaem'ic** suffering from anaemia; sickly, spiritless, washed-out, lacking in body (*fig*). — **pernicious anaemia** a severe form of anaemia characterized by abnormalities in the red blood corpuscles, etc. [Gr *anaimiā*, from *an-* (privative), and *haima* blood]

anaerobe *an'ā(ə)r-ōb*, *n* an organism that lives in absence of free oxygen. — Also **anaero'biont**. — *adj* **anaerobic** (*-ob'ik* or *-ōb'ik*) or **anaerobiotic** (*-ō-bī-ot'ik*) living in the absence of free oxygen; of a process, etc, requiring the absence, or not requiring the presence, of free oxygen; effected by anaerobes, as a biochemical change; involving the activity of anaerobes. — *adv* **anaerob'ically** or **anaerobiot'ically**. — *n* **anaerobio'sis** life in the absence of oxygen. [Gr *an-* (privative), *āēr* air, and *bios* life]

anaesthesia or (*US*) **anesthesia** *an-əs-thē'zi-ə*, *-zyə* or *-ēs'*, also **anaesthe'sis** *-sis*, *n* loss of feeling; insensibility, general or local. — **anaesthesiol'ogy** (*usu* **anesthesiol'ogy**; *NAm*) the science of administering anaesthetics. — *n* **anaesthesiol'ogist** (*usu* **anesthesiol'ogist**; *NAm*). —

adj **anaesthetic** (*-thet'ik* or *-thēt'ik*) producing or connected with insensibility. — *n* an anaesthetic agent. — *adv* **anaesthet'ically**. — *n sing* **anaesthet'ics** the science of anaesthesia. — *n* **anaesthetist** (*-ēs'thə-tist*, or *-es'*) a person who administers anaesthetics. — *n* **anaesthetīzā'tion** or **-s-**. — *vt* **anaes'thetize** or **-ise**. — **general anaesthetic** one which produces insensibility in the whole body, *usu* causing unconsciousness; **local anaesthetic** one producing insensibility in only the relevant part of the body. [Gr *anaisthēsiā* insensibility, *anaisthētos* insensible, from *an-* (privative), and *aisthanesthai* to perceive]

anaglyph *an'ə-glif*, *n* an ornament in low relief; a picture composed of two prints, in complementary colours, seen stereoscopically through spectacles of these colours. — *adj* **anaglyph'ic**. — *n* **Anaglypta**® (*an-ə-glip'tə*) a type of plain white wallpaper that has a heavily embossed pattern. — Also *adj*. — *adj* **anaglyp'tic**. [Gr *anaglyphos*, *anaglyptos* in low relief, from *ana* up or back, and *glyphein* to engrave, carve]

anagnorisis *an-ag-nō'ri-sis*, or *-nö'*, (*literary*) *n* recognition leading to dénouement. [Gr *anagnōrisis*]

anagoge or **anagogy** *an-ə-gō'ji*, *n* mystical interpretation. — *adj* **anagogic** (*-goj'ik*) pertaining to mystical interpretation; of the strivings in the unconscious towards morally high ideals. — *adj* **anagog'ical**. — *adv* **anagog'ically**. [Gr *anagōgē* leading up, elevation, from *ana* up, and *agein* to lead]

anagram *an'ə-gram*, *n* a word or phrase formed by the letters of another in different order. — *vt* and *vi* to anagrammatize. — *adj* **anagrammat'ic** or **anagrammat'ical**. — *adv* **anagrammat'ically**. — *n* **anagramm'atism** the practice of making anagrams. — *n* **anagramm'atist** a maker of anagrams. — *vt* and *vi* **anagramm'atize** or **-ise** to transpose so as to form an anagram. [Gr *ana* back, and *gramma* letter]

anal, anally. See **anus**.

anal. *abbrev*: analogous; analogy; analysis; analytic or analytical.

analcime *an-al'sīm* or **analcite** *an-al'sīt*, *n* a cubic zeolite, a hydrated sodium aluminium silicate. [Gr *an-* (privative), and *alkimos*, *alkis* strong, because weakly electrified by friction]

analects *an'ə-lekts*, or **analecta** *-lek'tə*, *n pl* collected literary fragments. — *adj* **analec'tic**. [Gr (pl) *analekta*, from *ana* up, and *legein* to gather]

analemma *a-nə-lem'ə*, *n* a scale showing the daily declination of the sun, in the shape of a figure 8; (loosely) a sundial. [Gr, (the pedestal of) a sundial, from *ana* up, and *lambanein* to take]

analeptic *an-ə-lep'tik*, *adj* restoring vigour; restoring to consciousness, *esp* after anaesthesia; comforting. — *n* a restorative medicine. [Gr *analēptikos* restorative, from *ana* up, and *lambanein* to take]

analgesia *an-al-jē'zi-ə*, *n* painlessness; insensibility to pain. — *n* **analgesic** (*-jē'sik*) an anodyne. — *adj* producing analgesia. [Gr *analgēsiā*, from *an-* (privative), and *algeein* to feel pain]

analogue or (*US*) **analog** *an'ə-log*, *n* that which is analogous to something else, eg protein substances prepared to resemble meat; that which has a similar function (distinguished from a *homologue*) (*biol*); a variable physical quantity which is similar to some other variable in that variations in the former are in the same proportional relationship as variations in the latter, often being used to record or represent such changes (also *adj*); a device which measures continuously varying quantities, eg temperature and time; a watch with the traditional face and hands (also *adj*; *opp* to *digital*). — **analogue computer** a type of computer in which varying electrical currents or voltages, etc are used to represent proportionally other quantities (eg forces or speeds) in working out problems about these qualities; **analogue transmission** (*telecomm*) the transmission of signals and messages by means of radio waves, without first converting them to a computerized form as in *digital transmission*. — **analogue-to-digital** (**A/D**) **converter** (*comput*) an integrated circuit which enables a digital computer to accept data from an analogue device (also called **digitizer**). [Gr *analogon*, from *analogos* proportionate]

analogy *an-al'ə-ji*, *n* an agreement or correspondence in certain respects between things otherwise different; a resemblance of relations; parallelism; relation in general; a likeness; proportion, or the equality of ratios (*math*); agreement in function, as distinguished from *homology* or agreement in origin (*biol*); a resemblance by virtue of which a word may be altered on the model of another class of words, as *strove*, *striven*, remodelled upon *drove*, *driven*, *throve*, *thriven*, etc (*philol*). — *adj* **analogic** (*an-ə-loj'ik*; *rare*) or **analog'ical**. — *adv* **analog'ically**. — *n* **anal'ogist** someone who sees, follows, or uses analogies. — *vt* **anal'ogize** or **-ise** to explain or consider by analogy. — *n* **anal'ogon** (*-gon*; Gr) analogue. — *adj* **anal'ogous** (*-gəs*) having analogy; bearing some correspondence or resemblance; similar in certain circumstances or relations (with *to*); positively electrified by heating. — *adv* **anal'ogously**. — *n* **anal'ogousness**. [Gr *analogiā*, from *ana* according to, and *logos* ratio]

analphabet *an-al'fə-bet*, or **analphabete** *-bēt*, *adj* ignorant of the alphabet. — Also *n*. — *adj* **analphabet'ic** totally illiterate; not alphabetic. [Gr *analphabētos*, from *an-* (privative); see **alphabet**]

analysand. See **analysis**.

analyse or **analyze** *an'ə-līz*, *vt* to resolve or separate a thing into its elements or component parts; to ascertain those parts; to trace a thing or things to the source or cause; to discover the general principles underlying individual phenomena by doing this; to resolve a sentence into its syntactic elements (*gram*). — *adj* **an'alysable** or **-z-**. — *n* **an'alyser** or **-z-** a person who analyses; in a polariscope the nicol (or substitute) through which the polarized light passes; a device that analyses. [Gr *analȳein* to unloose, from *ana* up, and *lȳein* to loose]

analysis *ən-al'is-is*, *n* the action or process of analysing; a table or statement of the results of analysis; the examination of market research data and information (*commerce*); analytical chemistry; formerly, proof by assuming the result and reasoning back to principles (*math*); use of algebraical methods; psychoanalysis: — *pl* **anal'yses** (*-sēz*). — *Opp* to *synthesis*. — *n* **analysand** (*ən-al'i-zand*) a person undergoing psychoanalysis. — *n* **an'alyst** (*-list*) someone skilled in or practising analysis, *esp* chemical or economic; a psychoanalyst. — **analysis situs** (*sīt'əs*; *math*) older name for topology (*math* meanings). — **in the last analysis** when all inessentials are excluded from the problem or the situation. [Gr *analysis*, from *analȳein* to unloose, from *ana* up, and *lȳein* to loose]

analytic *an-ə-lit'ik*, *adj* pertaining to, performing, or inclined to analysis; resolving into first principles. — *n* (often *pl* in form) analytical logic; analytical geometry. — *adj* **analyt'ical**. — *adv* **analyt'ically**. — *n* **analytic'ity**. — **analytical chemistry** (loosely, **analysis**) chemistry concerned with determination of the constituents of chemical compounds, or mixtures of compounds; **analytical engine** a data processing machine invented by Charles Babbage in 1833, the precursor of the modern computer; **analytical geometry** co-ordinate geometry; **analytical languages** those that use separate words instead of inflexions; **analytical logic** logic which is concerned with analysis. [**analyse**]

anamnesis *an-am-nēs'is*, *n* the recalling to memory of things past; the recollection of the Platonic pre-existence; a patient's account of his or her medical history: — *pl* **anamnē'ses** (*-sēz*). — *adj* **anamnes'tic**. — *adv* **anamnes'tically**. [Gr *anamnēsis*, from *ana* up, back, and *mimnēskein* to remind, recall to memory]

anamorphosis *an-ə-mör'fə-sis*, or *-fō'*, *n* a deformed figure appearing in proportion when rightly viewed, eg in a curved mirror, or in a particular direction: — *pl* **anamorphoses** (*-fə-sēz* or *-fō'sēz*). — *adj* **anamor'phic** or

anamor'phous. [Gr *anamorphōsis* a forming anew, from *ana* back or anew, and *morphōsis* a shaping, from *morphē* shape, form]

anan *ə-nan'*, (*obs* or *dialect*) *interj* expressing failure to understand. [**anon**]

ananas *ə-nä'nas*, *n* the pineapple (*Ananas sativus*); the pinguin (*Bromelia pinguin*), or its fruit. — Also **an'ana**. [From an American Indian language]

anandrous *an-an'drəs*, (*bot*) *adj* without stamens. [Gr *anandros* lacking men, from *an-* (privative), and *anēr*, *andros* a man]

Ananias *an-ə-nī'əs*, *n* a liar. [From the story in Acts 5.1–5]

ananke *a-nangk'ē*, *n* necessity. [Gr *anankē*]

ananthous *an-an'thəs*, (*bot*) *adj* without flowers. [Gr *ananthēs*, from *an-* (privative), and *anthos* a flower]

anapaest or (*US*) **anapest** *an'ə-pēst*, (*prosody*) *n* a foot of two short (or unstressed) syllables followed by a long (or stressed) syllable, a dactyl reversed. — *adj* **anapaes'tic** or **anapaes'tical**. [Gr *anapaistos* struck back, from *ana* back, and *paiein* to strike]

anaphase *an'ə-fāz*, (*biol*) *n* the stage of mitosis at which the daughter-chromosomes move towards the poles of the spindle. [Gr *ana* up, back, and **phase**]

anaphora *ən-af'ə-rə*, *n* the rhetorical device of beginning successive sentences, lines, etc with the same word or phrase; the use of a word (such as *it* or *do*) to avoid repetition of a preceding word or group of words; the offering of the Eucharistic elements. — *adj* **anaphoric** (*an-ə-for'ik*) or **anaphor'ical** referring to a preceding word or group of words. — *adv* **anaphor'ically**. [Gr *anaphorā* a carrying back or reference, from *ana* back, and *pherein* to bear]

anaphrodisiac *an-af-rō-diz'i-ak*, *adj* tending to diminish sexual desire. — *n* an anaphrodisiac agent. [Gr *an-* (privative), and *aphrodīsiakos* sexual]

anaphylaxis *an-ə-fil-aks'is*, *n* an increased susceptibility to injected foreign material, protein or non-protein, brought about by a previous introduction of it. — Also **anaphylax'y**. — *adj* **anaphylac'tic** or **anaphylac'toid** having a resemblance to anaphylaxis. [Gr *ana* back, and *phylaxis* protection]

anaplasty *an'ə-pläs-ti*, *n* the repairing of superficial lesions by the use of adjacent healthy tissue, as by transplanting a portion of skin. — *adj* **anaplas'tic**. [Gr *ana* again, and *plassein* to form]

anaplerosis *an-ə-plē-rō'sis*, *n* the filling up of a deficiency. — *adj* **anaplerot'ic**. [Gr *anaplērōsis*, from *ana* up, and *plēroein* to fill]

anaptyxis *an-əp-tik'sis*, (*phonetics*) *n* the development of a vowel between consonants. — *adj* **anaptyc'tic**. [Gr *anaptyxis* gape, from *ana* back, and *ptyssein* to fold]

anarchy *an'ər-ki*, *n* complete absence of law or government; a harmonious condition of society in which government is abolished as unnecessary; utter lawlessness; chaos; complete disorder. — *n* **anarch** (*an'ärk*; *archaic*) an author, promoter or personification of lawlessness. — *adj* **anarchal** (*an-ärk'l*; *rare*). — *adj* **anarch'ial** (*rare*). — *adj* **anarch'ic** or **anarch'ical**. — *adv* **anarch'ically**. — *n* **an'archism** the teaching of the anarchists. — *n* **an'archist** a person whose ideal of society is one without government of any kind; a person who seeks to bring about such a condition by terrorism. — Also *adj*. — *adj* **anarchist'ic**. — *vt* **anarchize** or **-ise** (*an'ər-kīz*) to make anarchic. — *n* **anarch'o-syn'dicalism** syndicalism (qv). — *n* and *adj* **anarch'o-syn'dicalist**. [Gr *anarchiā* leaderlessness, lawlessness, from *an-* (privative), and *archē* government]

anarthrous *an-är'thrəs*, *adj* used without the article (of Greek nouns); without distinct joints (*biol*). — *adv* **anar'thrously**. — *n* **anar'throusness**. [Gr *an-* (privative), and *arthron* a joint or article]

anasarca *an-ə-sär'kə*, *n* diffused dropsy in the skin and subcutaneous tissue. [Gr phrase *ana sarka* throughout the flesh]

anastasis *an-as'tə-sis*, *n* in Byzantine art, the Harrowing of Hell; convalescence; resurrection. — *adj* **anastatic** (*an-ə-stat'ik*) of anastasis; with characters raised in relief. [Gr *anastasis* rising or raising up or again, from *ana* up, again, and *stasis* a setting or standing]

anastigmat *an-as'tig-mat*, or *-stig'*, *n* a lens specially designed to avoid the focusing defect of astigmatism. — *adj* **anastigmat'ic** (*an-ə-*) free from astigmatism. — *n* **anastig'matism**. [Gr *an-* (privative), and **astigmatic**]

anastomosis *an-as-tə-mō'sis*, *n* communication by cross-connections to form a network: — *pl* **anastomō'ses** (*-sēz*). — *vi* **anas'tomose** to intercommunicate in such a way. — *adj* **anastomot'ic**. [Gr *anastomōsis* outlet, from *ana* back, and *stoma* mouth]

anastrophe *a-* or *ə-nas'trə-fi*, (*rhetoric*) *n* inversion. [Gr *anastrophē*, from *ana* back, and *strephein* to turn]

anat. *abbrev*: anatomic; anatomy.

anatase *an'ə-tās*, *n* a mineral consisting of titanium oxide. [Gr *anatasis* a stretching, from its long crystals]

anathema *a-* or *ə-nath'i-mə*, *n* a solemn ecclesiastical curse or denunciation involving excommunication; a curse or execration; a person or thing cursed ecclesiastically or generally; an object of abhorrence: — *pl* **anath'emas**. — *adj* **anathematical** (*-mat'i-kl*). — *n* **anathematization** or **-s-** (*-mə-tī-zā'shən*). — *vt* and *vi* **anath'ematize** or **-ise**. — **anathema maranatha** (*ma-rə-na'tha*; Aramaic *māranā thā*, come, Lord) words happening to occur together in 1 Cor 16.22, wrongly understood as an intensified curse. [Gr *anathema* a thing dedicated or accursed, for *anathēma* a votive offering, from *ana* up, and the root of *tithenai* to place]

Anatolian *an-ə-tōl'i-ən*, *adj* of *Anatolia*, now the major part of Turkey; of or denoting any or all of an extinct family of languages belonging to or closely related to the Indo-European family. — *n* a native or inhabitant of Anatolia; the Anatolian family of languages.

anatomy *ə-nat'ə-mi*, *n* the art of dissecting any organized body; the science of the physical structure of an animal or plant learned by dissection; a subject for dissection (*obs*); a skeleton, a shrivelled and shrunken body, alive or dead, or mummy (*archaic*); physical frame or structure; the human body (*colloq*); dissection; analysis (*fig*). — *adj* **anatomic** (*an-ə-tom'ik*) or **anatom'ical**. — *adv* **anatom'ically**. — *n* **anat'omist** a person skilled in anatomy. — *vt* **anat'omize** or **-ise** to dissect; to lay open minutely (*fig*). [Gr *anatomē* dissection, from *ana* up, and *tomē* a cutting]

anatropous *a-* or *ə-nat'rə-pəs*, (*bot*) *adj* of an ovule, turned back and attached at the side of the funicle, which thus becomes a ridge on the ovule. — *n* **anat'ropy**. [Gr *ana* back, up, and *tropē* a turning]

anatta, **anatto**. See **annatto**.

a natura rei *ä na-tū'rə rē'ī* or *na-too'rä rā'ē*, (*L*) from the nature of the case.

anax andron *a'naks and'rōn*, (*Gr*) *n* lord of men (*esp* applied to Agamemnon).

anaxial *an-aks'i-əl*, (*zool*) *adj* asymmetrical. [**a-**[2]]

anbury *an'bər-i*, *n* a soft bloody wart on horses, etc (also **angleberry** *ang'gl-bər-i*); a disease in turnips, cabbages, etc, due to a slime-fungus. [Perh for *angberry*, from OE *ange* narrow, painful, and **berry**]

ANC *abbrev*: African National Congress.

anc. *abbrev*: anciently.

ance *āns*. Northern form of **once**.

ance-errand. See **errand**.

ancestor *an'sis-tər*, *n* someone from whom a person is descended, a forefather; a plant or animal from which another type has evolved; a person or thing regarded as the forerunner of another: — *fem* **an'cestress**. — *adj* **ances'tral** (*-ses'*) of or relating to ancestors; inherited or derived from ancestors. — *adj* **ancestorial** (*-sis-tö'ri-əl*). — *adv* **ances'trally**. — *n* **an'cestry** a line of ancestors; lineage. — **an'cestor-worship**. [OFr *ancestre*, from L *antecēssor*, from *ante* before, and *cēdere*, *cēssum* to go]

anchor *ang'kər*, *n* an implement for mooring a ship by chaining it to the bottom, for holding a balloon to the ground, or for any similar purpose; anything that gives stability or security (*fig*); a short form of anchor man.

— *vt* to fix by an anchor; to fasten. — *vi* to cast anchor; to stop or rest. — *n* **anch'orage** the act of anchoring; a place of or for anchoring; a set of anchors (*Shakesp*); rest or support to the mind (*fig*); duty imposed for anchoring. — *adj* **anch'orless**. — **Anchor Boys** the most junior section of the Boys' Brigade; **anchor buoy** a buoy indicating the position of an anchor; **anchor escapement** or **recoil escapement** a clock escapement in which the pallets push the escape-wheel slightly backwards at the end of each swing, causing a recoil of the pendulum; **anch'or-hold** the hold of an anchor upon the ground; security (*fig*); **anch'or-ice** ground ice; **anchor leg** the last stage of a relay-race; **anchor man** or **anchor** the man at the back of a team in a tug-of-war; the man who runs the last stage of a relay-race; (or **anch'or-man**) a person on whom the success of an activity depends, *esp*, on television, the person responsible for smooth running of a dialogue or discussion between or among others; **anchor plate** a heavy, *usu* steel, plate set into the ground or foundations to which bracing for a structure is fixed; **anch'or-ring** a solid generated by the revolution of a circle about an axis in its plane but not cutting it and not passing through its centre; **anch'or-stock** the cross-bar of an anchor, which causes one or other of the flukes to turn to the bottom; **anchor string** (*min ext*) a length of casing run into the top of wells and often cemented in to prevent a blow-out. — **at anchor** anchored; **cast anchor** to let down the anchor; **weigh anchor** to take up the anchor. [OE *ancor*, from L *ancora*; cf Gr *ankȳra*, from *ankos* a bend; connected with **angle**[1]]

anchorite, **anchoret** or (*Shakesp*) **anchor** *ang'kər*, *n* a man or woman who has withdrawn from the world, *esp* for religious reasons; a recluse. — *n* **anch'orage** a recluse's cell. — *n* **anch'oress** or **anc'ress** a female anchorite. — *adj* **anchorit'ic**, **anchorit'ical**, **anchoret'ic** or **anchoret'ical**. [Gr *anachōrētēs*, from *ana* apart, and *chōreein* to withdraw]

anchovy *an'chə-vi*, or *-chō-*, or *an-chō'vi*, *n* a small edible Mediterranean fish (*Engraulis encrasicholus*) of the herring family, often used for pickling, and making sauce, paste, etc. — *n* **anchoveta** (*-vet'ə*; *Am Sp*) a small Pacific anchovy, used for bait. — **an'chovy-pear** the fruit of a W Indian lecythidaceous tree (*Grias cauliflora*), often pickled. [Sp and Port *anchova*; of doubtful etymology]

anchylose, etc. See **ankylose**, etc.

ancien régime *ã-syɛ̃ rä-zhēm*, (*Fr*) the old order (*esp* before the French Revolution); **ancienne noblesse** (*ã-syen nobles*) the old nobility; the nobility of the ancien régime.

ancient[1] *ān'shənt*, *adj* very old; of former times; of long standing; belonging or relating to times long past, *esp* before the downfall of the Western Roman Empire (AD 476). — *n* an aged man; an elder or senior; someone who lived in ancient times, *usu* in *pl* and applied *esp* to the Greeks and Romans. — *adv* **an'ciently**. — *n* **an'cientness**. — *n* **an'cientry** (*archaic*) antiquity; seniority; ancestry; dignity of birth; old people (*Shakesp*). — **ancient Greek** the Greek language until the death of Alexander the Great; **ancient history** the history of Ancient Greece and Rome; information, news or gossip which, contrary to the expectations of the teller, one is already well aware of (*colloq fig*); something no longer of importance; **ancient lights** the legal right to receive in perpetuity, by certain windows, a reasonable amount of daylight; **Ancient Monument** an old and historic building, etc scheduled for preservation, *esp* if in the care of the government; **the Ancient of days** (*Bible*) the Almighty, God. [Fr *ancien*, from LL *antiānus* former, old, from L *ante* before]

ancient[2] *ān'shənt*, (*obs*) *n* a flag; a standard-bearer; an ensign. [See **ensign**]

ancile *an-sī'lē* or *an-kē'lā*, (*L*) *n* the shield that fell from heaven in the reign of Numa Pompilius, on the safety of which the prosperity of Rome depended.

ancillary *an-sil'ər-i* or *an'sil-ər-i*, *adj* auxiliary; supplementary; subsidiary; subordinate; (of computer equipment) additional in any way, not a necessary part of the computing process; subserving; ministering. — Also *n*. [L *ancilla* a maid-servant]

ancipitous *an-sip'i-təs*, or **ancipital** *an-sip'i-təl*, (*bot*) *adj* two-edged and flattened. [L *anceps*, *-cipitis* two-edged or double, from *ambi-* on both sides, and *caput*, *capitis* head]

ancle. An archaic spelling of **ankle**.

ancome *an'kəm*, (*obs* or *dialect*) *n* a sudden inflammation; a whitlow. [Cf **oncome** and **income**]

ancon *ang'kon*, *n* the elbow; a console to support a door cornice; a breed of sheep with very short legs: — *pl* **ancones** (*-kō'nēz*). [Latinized from Gr *ankōn* a bend or elbow]

Ancona *ang-kō'nə*, *n* a speckled variety of laying poultry of Mediterranean family. — Also *adj*. [*Ancona* in Italy]

ancora *ang-kō'rä*, or *-kö'*, *adv* encore. [Ital]

ancress. See under **anchorite**.

AND *and*, (*comput*) *n* a logic circuit that has two or more inputs and one output, the output signal being 1 if all its inputs are 1, and 0 if any of its inputs is 0. [**and**[1]]

AND *abbrev*: Andorra (IVR).

and[1] *and*, *ənd*, *ən* or *n*, *conj* indicating addition; also; also of another kind; used to introduce a consequence or aim; used to introduce a question expressive of surprise, realization, wonder, incredulity, etc; used to join identical words to indicate repetition, progression or continuity; sometimes *appar* meaningless ('When that I was and a little tiny boy'); as a conditional conjunction (from ME times only; often in *Shakesp*; now *archaic*; also **an**, **an if**) if; even if, although; as if. — **and all** not without; **and how** (*colloq*) I should think so indeed; **and then some** (*colloq*) and even more;. **but and** (*obs*) and also. [OE *and*, *ond*; cf Ger *und*, and L *ante* before, Gr *anti* against]

and[2] *and*, *n* the symbol ampersand; a use of the word 'and'; something added.

and[3] *ən*, (*dialect* and *Shakesp*) *conj* than. [Perh ON *an*, *en*, *enn* than]

Andalusian *an-də-lo͞o'* or *-lū'z(h)yən* or *-s(h)yən*, *n* a native of *Andalusia* (Sp *Andalucía*), in Spain; a blue variety of laying poultry, of Mediterranean family. — Also *adj*. — *n* **andalu'site** (*-sīt*) a silicate of aluminium, first found in Andalusia.

andante *an-dan'tā*, (*music*) *adv* and *adj* moving with moderately slow, even expression. — *n* a movement or piece composed in andante time. — *adj*, *adv* and *n* **andantino** (*music*; *an-dan-tē'nō*) (a movement, etc) somewhat slower than andante; now more *usu* intended for somewhat quicker: — *pl* **andanti'nos**. [Ital, pr p of *andare* to go]

Andean *an-dē'ən*, or **Andine** *an'dīn*, *adj* of or like the Andes Mountains. — *n* **andesine** (*an'diz-ēn* or *-in*; *mineralogy*) a feldspar intermediate between albite and anorthite. — *n* **an'desite** a volcanic rock with plagioclase and some ferromagnesian mineral as phenocrysts in a microlithic groundmass (both found in the Andes). — *adj* **andesitic** (*-it'ik*).

Anderson shelter *and'ər-sən shel'tər*, *n* a small air-raid shelter consisting of an arch of corrugated iron, built partially under ground, used in Britain during World War II. — Also **And'erson**. [Sir John *Anderson*, Home Secretary 1939–40]

andesine, **andesite**. See **Andean**.

andiron *and'ī-ərn*, *n* an iron bar to support the end of a log in a fire, a firedog. [OFr *andier* (Fr *landier* = *l'andier*); origin unknown; early confused with **iron**]

andouillette *ã-do͞o-yet*, *n* a small chitterling sausage. [Fr]

Andrew *an'dro͞o*, *n* one of the twelve Apostles, patron saint of Scotland. — **St Andrew's cross** a saltire, or cross of equal shafts crossed diagonally; the saltire of Scotland, white on a blue ground.

Andrew Ferrara *an'dro͞o fi-rä'rä*, *n* a make of sword-blade highly esteemed in Scotland from c.1600. — Also **An'dro** or **Andrea** (*-drā'ä* or *an'*) **Ferrara**. [According to some from *Andrea dei Ferrari* of Belluno, to others

Andrew Ferrars or *Ferrier* of Arbroath, poss as a native of Ferrara, or from L *ferrārius* smith]

andro- or **andr-** *an-dr(ō)-*, also *an-dro'*, *combining form* denoting man; male. — *adj* **androcentric** (*an-drō-sent'rik*) male-centred. — *adj* **androcephalous** (*-sef'ə-ləs*; Gr *kephalē* head) man-headed. — *adj* **androdioecious** (*-dī-ē'shəs*) having hermaphrodite and male flowers on separate plants (see **dioecious**). — *n* **androdioe'cism**. — *adj* **androecial** (*an-drē'shi-əl*). — *n* **androecium** (*an-drē'shi-əm* or *-si-əm*; Gr *oikion* house) stamens collectively; — *n* **androgen** (*an'drō-jən*) any one of the male sex hormones; a synthetic compound with similar effect. — *adj* **androgen'ic** pertaining to an androgen. — *adj* **androg'enous** having only male offspring. — *n* and *adj* **an'drogyne** (*-jīn*) (a) hermaphrodite. — *adj* **androgynous** (*an-droj'i-nəs*, or *-drog'*) having the characteristics of both male and female in one individual; hermaphrodite; having both male and female flowers (*bot*). — *n* **androg'yny** (Gr *gynē* woman) hermaphroditism. — *n* **an'droid** a robot in human form. — *n* **androl'ogy** the branch of medicine which deals with functions and diseases specific to males. — *adj* **andromonoecious** (*an-drō-mon-ē'shəs*) having hermaphrodite and male flowers on the same plant (see **monoecious**). — *n* **andromonoe'cism**. — *n* **an'drophore** (*-fōr*; Gr *phoros* a bearing) a prolongation of the receptacle carrying the stamens. — *n* **androsterone** (*ən-dros'tə-rōn* or *an-dro-stē'rōn*; from *sterol*) a male sex-hormone, found in the testes and in urine. [Gr *anēr*, *andros* man, male]

andromeda *an-drom'i-də*, *n* a plant of the genus *Andromeda* of shrubs of the heath family; a northern constellation lying between Cassiopeia and Pegasus. — *n* **andromedotoxin** (*an-drom'i-dō-tok'sin*) a vegetable drug obtained from andromeda, used in relief of high blood pressure. — **Andromeda nebula** a spiral galaxy in Andromeda, visible to the naked eye. [*Andromeda*, in Greek mythology, a maiden delivered by Perseus from a sea-monster]

andvile (*Spenser*). Same as **anvil**.

ane *yin*, *ān* (*Scot* and *obs*) *adj*, *n* and *pronoun* one; an, a. [OE *ān*]

anear *ə-nēr'*, (*archaic*) *adv* nearly; near. — *prep* near. — *vt* to approach or come near to. [**of** and **near**]

aneath *ə-nēth'*, or *Scot ə-neth'* or *ə-nāth'*, (chiefly *Scot*) *adv* and *prep* beneath. [**a-**[1] and the root of **beneath**]

anecdote *an'ik-dōt*, *n* a short narrative of an incident of private life; anecdotes collectively. — *n* **an'ecdōtage** anecdotes collectively; garrulous old age (with pun on *dotage*). — *adj* **anecdōt'al**. — *n* **anecdot'alist** a person who relates anecdotes. — *adv* **anecdot'ally**. — *adj* **anecdot'ical**. — *n* **an'ecdotist** an anecdotalist. [Gr *an-* (privative) and *ekdotos* published, from *ek* out, and *didonai* to give]

anechoic *an-ək-ō'ik*, *adj* echoless. [Gr *an-* (privative) and **echoic**]

anelace. See **anlace**.

anele *ə-nēl'*, *vt* to anoint (*archaic*); to administer extreme unction to. [OE *an* on, and *ele* oil; used in reminiscence of Shakespeare; see **unaneled**]

anemia, **anemic**. US spellings of **anaemia**, **anaemic**.

anemo- *ə-nem'ō-* or *an-i-mo'-*, *combining form* denoting wind. — *n* **anemogram** (*ə-nem'o-gram*) an anemographic record. — *n* **anem'ograph** (*-gräf*) an instrument for measuring and recording the pressure and velocity of the wind. — *adj* **anemographic** (*-graf'ik*). — *adv* **anemograph'ically**. — *n* **anemog'raphy**. — *n* **anemology** (*an-i-mol'ə-ji*) the study of the winds. — *n* **anemometer** (*-mom'i-tər*) a wind-gauge. — *adj* **anemometric** (*-mō-met'rik*) or **anemomet'rical**. — *n* **anemom'etry**. — *adj* **anemoph'ilous** wind-pollinated. — *n* **anemoph'ily**. — *n* **anemophō'bia** fear of wind or draughts. [Gr *anemos* wind; cf L *animus* and *anima*]

anemone *ə-nem'ə-ni*, *n* any member of the genus *Anemone* of the crowfoot family; a sea-anemone. [Gr *anemōnē*, from *anemos* wind]

anencephaly *an-ən-sef'ə-li*, or *-kef'*, *n* congenital absence of all or part of the brain. — Also **anencephal'ia** (*-āl'yə*). — *adj* **anencephal'ic**. [Gr *an-* (privative), and see **encephalon**]

an-end *ən-end'*, *adv* to the end, continuously (*Shakesp*); upright (*Shakesp*); straight ahead (*naut*). — **most an end** (*obs*) almost always. [**an**[3] and **end**]

anent *ə-nent'*, (mainly *Scot*) *prep* in a line with; against; towards; in regard to, concerning, about. [OE *on efen* on even]

anerly *an'ər-li*, (*archaic Scot*) *adv* only. [**ane**; *r* perh on analogy of some other word]

aneroid *an'ə-roid*, *adj* dispensing with the use of liquid. — *n* an aneroid barometer. [Fr *anéroïde*, from Gr *a-* (privative), *nēros* wet, and *eidos* form]

anesthesia, etc. US spelling of **anaesthesia**, etc.

anestrum, etc. US spelling of **anoestrum**, etc.

anetic *a-net'ik*, (*med*) *adj* soothing. [L *aneticus*, from Gr *anetikos* abating sickness]

aneuploid *an'ū-ploid*, (*biol*) *n* a cell or individual with missing or extra chromosomes or part of them. [**an-** not, and **euploid**]

aneurin *an'ū-rin* or *ə-nū'rin*, *n* vitamin B_1, deficiency of which affects the nervous system. — Also called **thiamine**. [Gr *a-* (privative), and *neuron* nerve]

aneurysm or **aneurism** *an'ūr-izm*, *n* dilatation of an artery (*pathol*); any abnormal enlargement. — *adj* **aneurys'mal** or **aneuris'mal**. [Gr *aneurysma*, from *ana* up, and *eurys* wide]

anew *ə-nū'* or (*US*) *-nōō'*, *adv* afresh; again. [**of** and **new**]

ANFO or **anfo** *abbrev*: ammonium nitrate (and) fuel oil, an explosive.

anfractuous *an-frakt'ū-əs*, *adj* winding, involved or circuitous. — *n* **anfractūosity** (*-os'i-ti*). [L *anfractuōsus*, from *ambi-* about, and *frangere* to break]

Ang. *abbrev*: *Anglice* (*L*), in English.

Angaraland *ang-gä-rä'land*, (*geol*) *n* the primitive nucleus of NE Asia. [*Angara* River]

angary *ang'gər-i*, (*law*) *n* a belligerent's right to seize and use neutral or other property (subject to compensation). [Gr *angareiā* forced service, from *angaros* a courier, from a Persian word, from Assyrian *agarru* hired labourer]

angekok or **angekkok** *ang'gi-kok*, *n* an Eskimo sorcerer or shaman. [Eskimo]

angel *ān'jl*, *n* a divine messenger; a ministering spirit; an attendant or guardian spirit; a person possessing the qualities attributed to these, ie gentleness, purity, etc; a dead person regarded as received into heaven; someone supposed to have a special commission, such as the head of the Church in Rev 2 and 3; in the Catholic Apostolic Church, someone who corresponds in a limited sense to a bishop; a messenger generally (*poetic*); a former English coin bearing the figure of an angel; a radar echo of unknown origin; a financial backer or adviser, *esp* one who finances theatrical ventures (*colloq*); a rich person who is an easy victim for those in search of money (*colloq*). — *n* **ān'gelhood**. — *adj* **angelic** (*an-jel'ik*) or **angel'ical**. — *adv* **angel'ically**. — *n* **āngelol'atry** angel-worship. — *n* **āngelol'ogy** doctrine regarding angels. — *n* **āngeloph'any** the manifestation of an angel to a human. — **an'gel-cake** or **an'gel-food** a cake made of flour, sugar, and white of egg; **angel dust** (*colloq*) the drug phencyclidine, a hallucinogen; **an'gel-fish** a kind of shark (*Squatina* or *Rhina*), with large wing-like pectoral fins; a tropical American river-fish (*Pterophyllum*) of the family *Cichlidae*, with a much-compressed, almost circular body but crescent-shaped owing to the long fin filaments, the whole banded with changing black vertical stripes; applied also to *Pomacanthus* and several other fishes of the Chaetodontidae; **Angelic Doctor** St Thomas Aquinas; **angel shot** (*hist*) cannon-balls linked by a chain, intended to destroy ships' rigging; **angels-on-horse'back** oysters and bacon on toast; **angels' share** the amount of a spirit lost in the cask through evaporation; **an'gel-water** a perfumed liquid, at first made largely from angelica, then from ambergris, rose-water, orange-flower water, etc. — **on the side of the angels** basically in sympathy with traditional virtues and virtuous aims. [Gr *angelos* a messenger]

Angeleno *an-jel-ē'nō*, *n* a native or citizen of Los Angeles: — *pl* **Angele'nos** [Am Sp *Angeleño*]

angelica *an-jel'i-kə*, *n* (with *cap*) a genus of umbelliferous plants with large leaves and double-winged fruit, once regarded as a defence against poison and pestilence; a garden plant by some included in the genus as *A. archangelica*, by others called *Archangelica officinalis*; its candied leaf-stalks and midribs, used as a decoration for cakes, etc. — **angel'ica-tree** an American aralia. [Med L *herba angelica* angelic herb]

angelus *an'ji-ləs*, (*Christian relig*) *n* a short devotional exercise in honour of the Incarnation, repeated three times daily; the bell rung in Roman Catholic countries at morning, noon, and sunset, to invite the faithful to recite the angelus. [From the introductory words, '*Angelus* domini nuntiavit Mariae']

anger *ang'gər*, *n* hot displeasure provoked by some action, incident, situation, etc, often involving hostility and a desire for retaliation; wrath; inflammation (now *dialect*); affliction (*obs*). — *vt* to make angry; to irritate. — *adj* **an'gerless**. — *adv* **an'gerly** (*archaic*) or **ang'rily**. — *n* **ang'riness**. — *adj* **ang'ry** excited with anger; feeling or directing anger towards (with *at* or *with*); (of a sore, etc) inflamed; (of the sky, or a person's facial expression, etc) of threatening or lowering aspect. — *n* an angry young man; an angry person. — **angry young man** a young man loud in disgust at what his elders have made of society (popularized by *Look Back in Anger*, play (1956) by John Osborne, one of a group of writers of the period to whom the term was subsequently applied). [ON *angr*; cf **agnail**, **anbury**, **angina**, **anguish**]

Angevin *an'ji-vin*, *adj* of *Anjou*, in France; of or relating to the Plantagenet house that reigned in England from 1154 to 1485, descended from Geoffrey V, Count of Anjou. — *n* a native of Anjou; a member of the house of Anjou (by some reckoned only down to the loss of Anjou (1204), by others, till the deposition of Richard II in 1399).

angico *an'ji-kō*, *n* a S American tree of the mimosa family (genus *Piptadenia*); its gum: — *pl* **an'gicos**. [Port, from Tupí]

angina *an-jī'nə* (or *rare* but etymologically better *an'ji-nə*), (*med*) *n* short for angina pectoris; any inflammatory affection of the throat, such as quinsy, croup, etc. — *adj* **anginal** (*an-jī'nl* or *an'ji-nl*). — **angina pectoris** a disease of the heart marked by paroxysms of intense pain, radiating from the breastbone mainly towards the left shoulder and arm. [L *angīna*; cf **anguish**]

angio- *an'ji-ō-* or sometimes *an-ji-o'-*, *combining form* denoting a case or vessel; the blood vessels (*med* and *zool*); the seed vessels (*bot*). [Gr *angeion* a case, vessel]

angiocarpous *an-ji-ō-kär'pəs*, (*bot*) *adj* having the fruit (or in fungi the hymenium) within a special covering. [Gr *angeion* a case, and *karpos* fruit]

angiogenesis *an-ji-ō-jen'ə-sis*, *n* the development of blood vessels and heart tissue in the embryo. [**angio-**]

angiogram *an'ji-ō-gram*, *n* a photograph made by angiography. — *n* **angiog'raphy** the art or process of making X-ray photographs of blood vessels by injecting the vessels with a substance opaque to the rays. [**angio-**]

angioma *an-ji-ō'mə*, (*med*) *n* a benign tumour composed of blood or lymph vessels: — *pl* **angiō'mas** or **angiō'mata**. [New L from Gr *angeion* vessel, and **-oma**]

angioplasty *an'ji-ō-plas-ti*, *n* surgery of the blood vessels; a non-surgical procedure to widen, clean out, etc the blood vessels using balloon dilatation or laser. [**angio-**]

angiosarcoma *an-ji-ō-sär-kō'mə*, (*pathol*) *n* a malignant tumour of the vascular endothelia, occurring in the liver and other sites. [**angio-**]

angiosperm *an'ji-ō-spûrm*, *n* a plant of the **Angiosperm'ae**, one of the main divisions of flowering plants, in which the seeds are in a closed ovary, not naked as in gymnosperms. — *adj* **angiosperm'al** or **angiosperm'ous**. [Gr *angeion* case, and *sperma* seed]

angiostomous *an-ji-os'təm-əs*, or **angiostomatous** *an-ji-ō-sto'mə-təs*, (*zool*) *adj* narrow-mouthed; with a mouth that is not distensible. [Gr *angeion* a vessel, case, confused with L *angere* to compress, and Gr *stoma*, *stomatos* mouth]

angklung *ang'kləng*, *n* a musical instrument of SE Asia, consisting of bamboo tubes suspended on a frame which is shaken to sound the chosen note(s). — Also **anklong** or **anklung**. [Jav *anklung*]

Angle *ang'gl*, *n* a member or descendant of the German tribe (OE *Engle*) from Schleswig that settled in Northumbria, Mercia and E Anglia during the 5c. — *adj* **Ang'lian** of the Angles. — *n* an Angle; the English dialect of the Angles. [L *Anglus*, from the Germanic name for the people of *Angul*, district of Schleswig (cf ety for **angle**[2])]

angle[1] *ang'gl*, *n* a corner; the distance or change in direction between two lines or surfaces diverging from the same point, measured in degrees (°), radians, right angles or (of angular velocity) revolutions; a measurement of such a change in direction, etc; the inclination of two straight lines, or of two curves measured by that of their tangents, or of two planes measured by that of perpendiculars to their intersection (*geom*); the spread of a cone, a number of meeting planes or the like, measured by the area on the surface of a sphere subtending it at the centre (*geom*); an outlying corner or nook (*archaic*); a point of view, a way of looking at something (*colloq*); a scheme, a plan devised for profit (*slang*); a sharply curving direction (of a shot or kick) (*sport*); a frame (*snooker*, etc); an angle shot (*squash*); an angle iron. — *vt* to move, drive, direct, turn, adjust or present at an angle; to present (news, etc) in such a way as to serve a particular end; to corner, put in a corner; to put in the jaws of a billiard pocket. — *vi* to proceed at an angle or by an angular course. — *adj* **ang'led** having angles; biased. — *adv* **ang'lewise**. — **angled deck** or (*US*) **canted deck** the flight deck of an aircraft-carrier prolonged diagonally from one side of the ship, so that aircraft may take off and land without interference from or with aircraft parked at the bows; **ang'ledozer** a bulldozer whose blade may be angled or tilted to the left or right; **angle iron** an L-shaped piece of iron or steel used in structural work, etc; **angle shot** a shot taken with a camera tilted above or below the horizontal (*cinematog*); a shot which hits first the side wall and then the front wall, without touching the floor (*squash*). — **angle of attack** (*aeronautics*) the angle between the chord line of an aerofoil and the relative airflow, normally the immediate flight path of the aircraft; **angle of division** (*phys*) the angle between the paths of a ray of light before and after passing through a prism or other optical device. [Fr, from L *angulus*, cognate with Gr *ankylos*; both from root *ank-* to bend, seen also in **anchor** and **ankle**]

angle[2] *ang'gl*, *n* a fish-hook or fishing-tackle (*obs*); an act of angling (*esp fig*). — *vi* to fish with rod and line (for); to try to gain by some artifice (with *for*). — *vt* to angle for. — *n* **ang'ler** a person who fishes with rod and line, *esp* for sport; the devil-fish or fishing-frog, a wide-mouthed voracious fish (*Lophius piscatorius*) that attracts its prey by waving filaments attached to its head; extended to related kinds, some of them remarkable for the dwarf males parasitic on the female. — *n* **ang'ling**. — **ang'leworm** any worm used as bait by anglers. [OE *angul* hook]

angleberry. See **anbury**.

anglesite *ang'gli-sīt*, *n* orthorhombic lead sulphate, a common lead ore, first found in *Anglesey*.

Anglican *ang'li-kən*, *adj* of or characteristic of the Church of England and churches in communion with it; English (*esp US*). — Also *n*. — *n* **Ang'licanism** the principles of the Church of England; attachment to

English institutions, *esp* the English Church. [Med L *Anglicanus*, from L *Anglus* Angle]

Anglice *ang'gli-sē* or *L ang'gli-kā*, (also without *cap*) *adv* in English. [Med L]

anglicize or **-ise** *ang'li-sīz*, *vt* to make English (also **ang'lify**). — *vi* to assume or conform to English ways. — *n* **ang'licism** (*-sizm*) an English idiom or peculiarity; English principles. — *n* **ang'licist** or **ang'list** a person who has a scholarly knowledge of the English language, literature and culture. — *n* **angliciza'tion** or **-s-**. — *n sing* **anglist'ics** the study of these subjects.

Anglo *ang'glō*, (*colloq*) *adj* of British extraction; (esp *US*) Anglo-American. — Also *n*: — *pl* **Ang'los**.

Anglo- *ang'lō-*, *combining form* denoting English; British; *esp* conjointly English or British and something else. — *adj* **Anglo-Amer'ican** English in origin or birth, American by settlement or citizenship; (esp *US*) having English as one's mother tongue and sharing a cultural outlook of British origin; (esp *US*) non-Hispanic; of England or Britain and America. — *n* an Anglo-American person. — *n* **Anglo-Cath'olic** a person who regards himself or herself as a Catholic of Anglican pattern; a High-Church Anglican. — Also *adj*. — *n* **Anglo-Cathol'icism**. — *adj* **Anglocen'tric** taking English or British affairs, institutions, culture, etc as a norm, focus, etc in one's outlook or behaviour. — *adj* **Anglo-French'** of England or Britain and France. — *n* the form of the French language spoken in medieval England. — *adj* **Anglo-In'dian** of England or Britain and India; of India under the British; of the English or British in India; of British birth but (formerly or presently) long resident in India; of English as spoken in India; Eurasian. — *n* a person of British birth long resident (formerly or presently) in India; an Indian Eurasian. — *n* **Anglo-I'rish** the English language as spoken in Ireland; Irish people of English descent; people of mixed English and Irish descent. — *adj* of England or Britain and Ireland; of the Anglo-Irish people or speech. — *n* **Anglo-Is'raelite** a person who believes that the British are descendants of the Jewish 'lost tribes' carried off by the Assyrians in 721BC. — Also *adj*. — *n* **angloma'nia** (also with *cap*) a craze, or indiscriminate admiration, for what is English. — *n* **angloma'niac** (also with *cap*). — *n* **Anglo-Nor'man** (the French dialect of) the Normans in England after the Norman Conquest. — Also *adj*. — (All the following also with *cap*) *n* **ang'lophile** or **ang'lophil** (Gr *philos* friend) a friend and admirer of England and things English. — Also *adj*. — *n* **anglophil'ia**. — *adj* **anglophil'ic**. — *n* **ang'lophobe** (Gr *phobos* fear) a person who fears or dislikes England and things English. — Also *adj*. — *n* **anglophō'bia**. — *adj* **anglophō'biac** or **anglophobic** (*-fōb'* or *-fob'*). — *adj* **Ang'lophone** (sometimes without *cap*) of a state, person, etc, speaking or using English (*esp* as opposed to French), in everyday affairs. — *n* an English-speaking (*esp* as opposed to French-speaking) person, *esp* in a state, etc where English is not the only language spoken. — *adj* **Anglophon'ic** (sometimes without *cap*). — *n* **Anglo-Ro'mani** a modified form of Romany with English, as used by Romanies in Britain, and also in the US, etc. — *n* **Anglo-Sax'on** Old English, the language before 1100 or 1150AD; plain English, often implying forthright use of English words that are usually taboo in ordinary conversation (*colloq*); one of the Germanic settlers in England and Scotland, including Angles, Saxons and Jutes, or one of their descendants; a Saxon of England, distinguished from the Old Saxons of the Continent; a white native speaker of English. — Also *adj*. — *n* **Anglo=Sax'ondom**. [L *Anglus*]

Angola *ang-gō'lə*, *adj* pertaining to *Angola* in Africa; (sometimes without *cap*) Angora. — *n* and *adj* **Ango'lan** (a native or inhabitant) of Angola.

angophora *ang-gof'ə-rə*, *n* any of several trees of Eastern Australia belonging to the *Angophora* genus closely related to the eucalypts. [Gr *angos* vessel, jar (from shape of fruits), and *phoros* bearing]

Angora *ang-gō'rə* or *-gö'rə*, *adj* of *Ang'ora* (Gr *Ankȳra*, in later times *Angora*, now *Ankara*) a town of ancient Galatia, now capital of Turkey; (sometimes without *cap*) of an Angora breed or yarn, etc. — *n* (in all meanings sometimes without *cap*) an Anatolian goat; its long silky wool (the true mohair); cloth made from it; a silky-haired rabbit; an Angora cat; yarn or material made partly or wholly of Angora rabbit hair. — **Angora cat** a silky-haired kind of cat similar to the Persian but with a more pointed head, longer body and full tail; a term treated by some as obsolete for Persian cat.

Angostura *ang-gos-tū'rə*, *n* a town (now Ciudad Bolívar) on the narrows (Sp *angostura*) of the Orinoco in Venezuela, giving its name to an aromatic bitter bark from certain trees of the family Rutaceae (*esp Cusparia*) formerly used in medicine. — **Angostura bitters®** a brand of aromatic bitters first made in Angostura, used as a flavouring in cocktails and other drinks, etc.

angry. See **anger**.

Angst or **angst** *ängst*, *n* anxiety, *esp* a general feeling of anxiety produced by awareness of the uncertainties and paradoxes inherent in the state of being human. — *adj* **Angst'-** (or **angst'-**) **ridden**. [Ger *Angst*, Dan *angst* fear, anxiety]

Ångström or **angstrom** *ang'* or *ong'strəm*, *n* a unit (10^{-10} metres) used in expressing wavelengths of light, ultraviolet rays, X-rays, molecular and atomic distances. — Formerly, but not now *usu*, **Ångström** (or **angstrom**) **unit**. [Anders J *Ångström* (1814–74), Swedish physicist]

Anguis *ang'gwis*, *n* the generic name not of a snake but of the blindworm. — *n* **ang'uifauna** fauna of snakes. — *adj* **ang'uiform** snake-shaped. — *n* **Anguill'a** the common eel genus. — *adj* **anguill'iform** eel-like. — *n* **Anguill'ūla** the paste-eel genus of nematode worms. — *adj* **anguine** (*ang'gwin*) of or like a snake. — *adj* **anguiped** or **anguipede** (*-ped* or *-pēd*) having feet or legs in the form of snakes, as used of mythological giants or the like. [L *anguis* snake; adj *anguīnus*; dimin *anguīlla* eel]

anguish *ang'gwish*, *n* excessive suffering of body or mind; agony. — *vt* to afflict with anguish. — *vi* to suffer anguish. — *adj* **ang'uished**. [OFr *angoisse* choking, from L *angustia* tightness, narrowness]

angular *ang'gū-lər*, *adj* having an angle or corner; measured by an angle; stiff in manner, the opposite of easy or graceful; bony and lean in figure. — *n* **angular'ity** (*-lar'i-*). — *adj* **ang'ulate** or **ang'ulated** formed with angles. — *n* **angulā'tion** the action of making angulate; an angular formation, angle; the measurement of angles. — **angular acceleration** the acceleration of a spacecraft round an axis; **angular velocity** the rate at which an object rotates round a fixed point or axis, measured as the rate of change in the angle turned through by the line between the object and the point or axis. [L *angularis*, from *angulus* **angle²**]

angusti- *ang-gus'ti-*, (*biol*) *combining form* signifying narrow. — *adj* **angustifo'liate** narrow-leaved. — *adj* **angustiros'trate** narrow-beaked. [L *angustus* narrow]

angwantibo *ang-wän'ti-bō*, *n* a small, golden brown, tailless W African lemur (*Arctocebus calabarensis*): — *pl* **angwan'tibos**. [W African word]

anharmonic *an-här-mon'ik*, (*math, phys, electronics*) *adj* not harmonic. — **anharmonic ratio** cross-ratio (harmonic when $= -1$). [Gr *an-* (privative) and *harmonikos* harmonic]

anhedonia *an-hi-dō'ni-ə*, (*psychol*) *n* the inability to feel pleasure; the loss of interest in formerly pleasurable pursuits. — *adj* **anhedon'ic**. [Gr *an-* (privative) and *hēdonē* pleasure]

anhedral *an-hē'drəl*, *adj* allotriomorphic (*chem*); having a downward (negative) dihedral angle (*aeronautics*). [Gr *an-* (privative) and adj combining form *-hedral*, ult from Gr *hedrā* seat]

an-heires (*Shakesp*) an obscure word in *Merry Wives* II.1.227, variously conjectured to be an error for **on here**, for **mynheers**, or for **ameers**.

anhelation *an-hi-lā'shən*, (*med*) *n* shortness of breath, or difficult breathing. [L *anhēlātiō*, *-ōnis*, from *anhēlāre* to gasp]

anhungered. See **ahungered**.

anhydride *an-hī'drīd*, *n* a compound representing in its composition an acid *minus* water (ie obtainable from an acid by the elimination of water, or combinable with water to form an acid). — *n* **anhy'drite** a mineral, anhydrous calcium sulphate. — *adj* **anhy'drous** free from water. [Gr *an-* (privative) and *hydōr* water]

ani *ä'nē*, *n* a tropical American bird, a black cuckoo (genus *Crotophaga*) with a curved bill and long tail: — *pl* **an'is**. [Sp or Port *aní*, from Tupí]

aniconic *an-ī-kon'ik*, *adj* symbolizing without aiming at resemblance; pertaining to aniconism. — *n* **ani'conism** (*-kən-izm*) worship or veneration of an object that represents a deity without being an image. — *n* **ani'conist**. [Gr *an-* (privative) and *eikōn* image]

anicut or **annicut** *an'i-kut*, (*Anglo-Ind*) *n* a dam. [Tamil *anaikaṭṭu* dam-building]

anigh *ə-nī'*, (*literary* or *sham-archaic*) *prep* and *adv* nigh. [*a-* as in *anear*, *afar*, and **nigh**; a modern formation]

anight *ə-nīt'*, (*Shakesp*) *adv* of nights, by night, at night. [**of** and **night**]

anil *an'il*, *n* indigo, plant or dye. [Port *anil*, from Ar *an-nīl* the indigo plant, from Sans *nīlī* indigo]

anile *an'īl* or *ān'īl*, *adj* old-womanish; imbecile. — *n* **anility** (*a-* or *ə-nil'i-ti*) old-womanishness; imbecile dotage. [L *anus*, *-ūs* an old woman]

aniline *an'il-ēn*, *-in*, or *-īn*, *n* a product of coal-tar extensively used in dyeing and other industrial and manufacturing processes, first obtained from anil. — Also *adj*. — **aniline dyes** a general term for all synthetic dyes having aniline as their base.

anima *an'i-mə*, *n* the soul, the innermost part of the personality; in Jungian psychology, the female component of the male personality. — **anima mundi** (*mun'di* or *mōōn'dē*) the soul of the world. [L]

animadvert *an-im-ad-vûrt'*, *vi* to take cognizance (*law*; *usu* with *on* or *upon*); to take note; to comment critically (on); to express censure. — *vt* to consider, to observe (*obs*). — *n* **animadver'sion**. — *n* **animadvert'er**. [L *animus* the mind, *ad* to, and *vertere* to turn]

animal *an'i-məl*, *n* an organism having life, sensation and voluntary motion (typically distinguished from a plant, which is organized and has life, but apparently not sensation or voluntary motion); often, a lower animal, ie one below man; a mammal; a brutish or sensual man; (loosely or *colloq*) a person, thing, organization, etc (as in *there's no such animal*). — *adj* of, of the nature of, derived from, or belonging to an animal or animals; brutal, sensual. — *adj* **animal'ic** (*rare*) of or pertaining to animals. — *n* **an'imalism** physicality; the state of being actuated by mere animal appetites; brutishness, sensuality; the theory that man is a mere animal being. — *n* **an'imalist** a person who practises or believes in animalism; a person who paints, carves, or writes stories about, animals. — *n* **animality** (*-al'i-ti*) animal nature or life; the status of an animal or of a lower animal. — *n* **animalizā'tion** or **-s-**. — *vt* **an'imalize** or **-ise** to represent or conceive in animal form (*rare*); to endow with animal life or the properties of animal matter; to convert into animal matter; to brutalize, sensualize. — *adv* **an'imally** physically. — **animal liberationist** a member or supporter of any body dedicated to ending the exploitation of animals by man; **animal magnetism** see under **magnet**; **animal pole** (*zool*) the apex of the upper part of a developing egg, containing little or no yolk; **animal righter** a person who believes in (and fights for) **animal rights**, the rights of animals to exist without being exploited by humans; **animal spirits** (*orig* **spirit**) formerly, a supposed principle formed in the brain out of vital spirits and conveyed to all parts of the body through the nerves; nervous force; exuberance of health and life; cheerful buoyancy of temper; the spirit or principle of volition and sensation (*Milton*); **an'imal-worship**; **an'imal-worshipper**. — **there is** (or **there ain't**) **no such animal** (*colloq*) there is no such person, creature or thing. [L *animal*, from *anima* air, breath, life, soul]

animal bipes *an'i-mal bī'pēz* or *bi'pās*, *n* (*L*) a two-footed animal, man. — **animal implume** *im-plōō'mē* or *-me*, a featherless animal; **animal rationale** *rā-shi-ō-nā'lē* or *ra-ti-ō-nä'le*, a reasoning animal; **animal risibile** *rī-si'bi-lē* or *rē-si'bi-le*, an animal able to laugh.

animalcule *an-im-al'kūl*, *n* a small animal (*obs*); a microscopic animal, one that cannot be seen by the naked eye: — *pl* **animal'cūles** or **animal'cūla**. — *adj* **animal'cūlar**. — *n* **animal'cūlist** a believer in the former biological theory (**animal'cūlism**) that the spermatozoon contains all future generations in germ. [L *animalculum*, dimin of *animal*]

animate *an'im-āt*, *vt* to give life to; to enliven; to put spirit into; to actuate; to record still drawings, etc on film or video tape in such a way that the images appear to move. — *adj* (*-mit*) living; having animal life. — *adj* **an'imated** lively; full of spirit; endowed with life; moving as if alive. — *adv* **an'imatedly**. — *n* **animat'ic** (*advertising*, *cinematog*, etc) a section of animation in or for a TV commercial, film etc; a rough simulation of a TV commercial, etc, produced from a storyboard with a voice-over. — *adj* **an'imating**. — *adv* **an'imatingly**. — *n* **animā'tion** the act of animating; the state of being alive; liveliness; vigour; the creation of the illusion of movement, *esp* in an animated cartoon; the technique or craft of this. — *n* **an'imatism** the primitive attribution of life to natural phenomena and natural objects, but not (as in *animism*) belief that spirits reside in them. — *n* **an'imātor** (also, chiefly *US*, **an'imāter**) a person who enlivens or animates something; an artist who makes drawings for animated cartoons, films, etc. — *adj* **animatron'ic** of or like something animated by animatronics. — *n sing* **animatron'ics** the art of animating a lifelike figure of a person, animal, etc by electronic means. — **animated cartoon** a motion picture produced from drawings, each successive drawing showing a very slight change of position so that a series of them gives the effect of an actual movement. [L *animāre*, *-ātum*, from *anima* air, breath, life]

animé or **anime** *an'i-mā* or *-mē*, *n* the resin of the W Indian locust-tree; extended to other gums and resins. [Said to be Fr *animé* living, from the number of insects in it; but perhaps a native name]

animism *an'im-izm*, *n* the attribution of a soul to natural objects and phenomena; G E Stahl's theory (1720) that the soul is the vital principle and source of the phenomena of animal life. — *n* **an'imist**. — *adj* **animis'tic**. [L *anima* the soul]

animo et fide *an'i-mō et fī'dē*, or *fi'dā*, (*L*) by courage and faith.

animosity *an-im-os'i-ti*, *n* strong dislike; enmity. [L *animōsitās* fullness of spirit]

animus *an'im-əs*, *n sing* intention; actuating spirit; hostility; in Jungian psychology, the male component of the female personality. [L *animus* spirit, soul]

anion *an'ī-ən*, *n* an ion that seeks the anode; an electronegative ion. — *adj* **anion'ic**. [Gr *ana* up, and *ion* going, pr p neuter of *ienai* to go]

anise *an'is*, *n* an umbelliferous plant (genus *Pimpinella*) whose aromatic seeds, of a flavour similar to liquorice, are used in making cordials, liqueurs, etc, and in baking, etc; in Matt 23 (Gr *anēthon*) believed to be dill (*Bible*). — *n* **an'iseed** the seed of anise; anisette. — *n* **anisette** (*an-i-zet'*) a cordial or liqueur prepared from anise seed. — **star-anise** see under **star**[1]. [Gr *anīson* anise]

aniso- *an-ī'sō-* or *-so'-*, *combining form* denoting unequal. — *adj* **anisocercal** (*-sûr'kl*; of fishes) with unequal tail-lobes. — *adj* **anisodac'tylous** (of birds) with three toes turned forward, one backward. — *adj* **anisom'erous** (*bot*) with unequal numbers of parts in the floral whorls. — *adj* **anisophyll'ous** (*bot*) with differently formed leaves on different sides of the shoot. — *adj* **anisotrop'ic** not isotropic, showing differences of property or of effect in different directions. — *n* **anisot'ropy**. [Gr *anisos* unequal, from *an-* (privative) and *isos* equal]

anker *angk'ər*, *n* an old measure for wines and spirits used in N Europe, varying considerably (that of Rotterdam 8½ imperial gallons). [Du]

ankerite *ang'kər-īt*, *n* a mineral, a rhombohedral carbonate of calcium, iron, magnesium and manganese. [After Professor M J *Anker* (1772–1843), Austrian mineralogist]

ankh *angk*, *n* an ansate cross, ie T-shaped with a loop above the horizontal bar, the symbol of life. [Egyp, life]

ankle or (*obs*) **ancle** *angk'l*, *n* the joint connecting the foot and leg. — *adj* **ank'led** having ankles. — *n* **ank'let** (*-lit*) an ornamental or supporting ring or chain for the ankle. — **ank'le-biter** (*Austr slang*) a child; **ank'le-boot** or **ank'le-jack** a boot reaching above the ankle; **ank'le-chain** a chain worn as decoration round the ankle; **ankle sock** a sock reaching to and covering the ankle; **ankle strap** (a shoe with) a strap which fastens round the ankle. [OE *anclēow*; cf Ger *Enkel*, and **angle**[1]]

anklong, anklung. See **angklung**.

Ankole *ang-kō'lē*, *n* a breed of large cattle with long horns. — Also *adj*. [*Ankole*, plateau region in Uganda]

ankus *ang'kəs*, *n* an elephant goad. [Hindustani]

ankylosaur *ang'kə-lə-sör*, *n* any of the **Ankylosauria** (*-sör'i-ə*), a suborder of bird-hipped plant-eating dinosaurs of the Cretaceous period, with short legs and flattened heavily-armoured bodies, including **Ankylosaur'us** which gave name to the suborder. [New L, from Gr *ankylos* crooked, and *sauros* lizard]

ankylosis or **anchylosis** *ang-ki-lō'sis*, (*pathol*) *n* the fusion of bones or skeletal parts; the fixation of a joint by fibrous bands or union of bones. — *vt* and *vi* **ank'ylose** or **anch'ylose** to stiffen or fuse, as a joint or bones. — *adj* **ank'ylosed** or **anch'ylosed**. — **ankylosing spondylitis** rheumatoid arthritis of the spine. [Gr *ankylōsis* stiffening of a joint, from *ankyloein* to crook]

ankylostomiasis or **anchylostomiasis** *ang-ki-lō-sto-mī'ə-sis*, (*pathol*) *n* hookworm disease or miner's anaemia, caused by a parasitic nematode (*Ankylostomum duodenale* or other). [Gr *ankylos* crooked, and *stoma* mouth]

ANL *abbrev*: Anti-Nazi League.

anlace or **anelace** *an'las* or *-ləs*, (*archaic*) *n* a short two-edged tapering dagger. [Ety unknown]

anlage *än'lä-gə*, (*biol*) *n* the primordium or first discernible rudiment of an organ. [Ger]

anme *abbrev*: *anonyme* (*Fr*), limited liability.

ann *an*, (*Scot*; *obs*) *n*. See **annates**.

anna *an'ə*, *n* a former coin of India, Pakistan and Bangladesh, the sixteenth part of a rupee. (Decimal coinage introduced India, 1957, Pakistan, 1961.) [Hindi *ānā*]

annabergite *an'ə-bûrg-īt*, *n* an apple-green mineral, hydrous nickel arsenate. [*Annaberg* in Saxony, eastern Germany]

annal *an'əl*, *n* a year's entry in a chronicle; (in *pl*) records of events under the years in which they happened; historical records generally; yearbooks. — *n* **ann'alist** a writer of annals. — *adj* **annalist'ic**. — *vt* **ann'alize** or **-ise** (*obs*) to record. [L *annālis* yearly, from *annus* a year]

annates *an'āts*, (*hist*) *n pl* (*obs n sing* **annat** *an'ət*), the first-fruits, or one year's income of a benefice, paid to the Pope (in England from 1535 to the crown, from 1703 to Queen Anne's bounty and extinguished or made redeemable in 1926). — *n* **ann'at** or **ann** (*Scots law*; *obs*) from 1672 to 1925 the half-year's stipend payable after a parish minister's death to his widow or next of kin. [LL *annāta*, from L *annus* a year]

annatto or **anatto** *a-* or *ə-nat'ō*, also **annatta**, **anatta** *-ə* or **arnotto** *är-not'ō*, *n* a bright orange colouring matter obtained from the fruit pulp of a tropical American tree, *Bixa orellana* (family *Bixaceae*): — *pl* **annatt'os** or **anatt'os**, etc. [Supposed to be of Carib origin]

anneal *ə-nēl'*, *vt* to heat and cool gradually (glass, metals), *esp* in order to temper or toughen; to heat (eg glass) in order to fix colours on (*archaic*); to strengthen, toughen; to reform the duplex structure of (a nucleic acid) (*biochem*). — Also *vi*. — *n* **anneal'er**. — *n* **anneal'ing**. [OE pfx *an-* on (cf **an**[3]), and *ǣlan* to burn]

annectent *ə-nek'tənt*, (*biol*) *adj* connecting, linking or having characteristics that are intermediate between those of two other species, genera, etc. [L *annectere*, from *ad* to, and *nectere* to tie]

annelid *an'ə-lid*, *n* a member of the **Annelida** (*ə-nel'i-də*), a class comprising the red-blooded worms, having a long body composed of numerous rings. [L *annellus*, *ānellus*, dimin of *ānulus* a ring]

annex *ə-neks'*, *vt* to add to the end; to join or attach; to take permanent possession of; to purloin, appropriate (*colloq*); to affix; to append. — *n* (*an'eks*) something added, now only as a documentary appendix or addendum; an annexe (*esp US*). — *n* **annexā'tion** (*an-*). — *n* and *adj* **annexā'tionist**. — *n* **annexe** a supplementary building, built as an extension to the main building. — *n* **annexion** (*ə-nek'shən*) the act of annexing (*archaic*); something annexed (*Shakesp*). — *n* **annex'ment** (*rare*) addition (*Shakesp*); the thing annexed. — *n* **annexure** (*a-nek'shər*) something added, *esp* an addition to a public document. [L *annectere*, *annexum*, from *ad* to, and *nectere* to tie]

annicut. See **anicut**.

annihilate *ə-nī'(h)il-āt*, *vt* to reduce to nothing; to put out of existence; to crush or wither by look or word (*fig*); to defeat completely (*colloq*); to cause (a subatomic particle) to undergo annihilation (*phys*). — *vi* to undergo annihilation (*phys*). — *n* **annīhilā'tion** reduction to nothing; the destruction of soul as well as body (*theol*); the process by which a particle and its corresponding antiparticle (eg an electron and a positron) combine and are spontaneously transformed into radiation (**annihilation radiation**) (*phys*). — *n* **annīhilā'tionism** the belief that the soul (*esp* of the unrepentant wicked) dies with the body. — *adj* **annī'hilātive**. — *n* **annī'hilātor**. [L *annihilāre*, *-ātum*, from *ad* to, and *nihil* nothing]

anniversary *an-i-vûrs'ə-ri*, *adj* returning, happening or commemorated about the same date every year; pertaining to annual recurrence or celebration. — *n* the day of the year on which an event happened or is celebrated as having happened in a previous year; the celebration proper to such a recurrence, *esp* a mass or religious service. [L *anniversārius*, from *annus* a year, and *vertere*, *versum* to turn]

anno *an'ō*, (*L*) in the year. — **anno Christi** (*kris'tī* or *-tē*) in the year of Christ; **anno Domini** (*an'ō dom'in-ī* or *-in-ē*) in the year of our Lord (also *n* (*colloq*) advancing old age); **anno mundi** (*mun'dī* or *mŏŏn'dē*) in the year of the world (used in reckoning dates from the supposed time of creation); **anno regni** (*reg'nī* or *-nē*) in the year of the reign; **anno salutis** (*sal-ū'tis* or *-ōō'*) in the year of redemption; **anno urbis conditae** (*ûr'bis kon'dit-ē* or *ŏŏr'bis kon'dit-ī*) in the year of the founding of the city (ie Rome, 753BC).

Annona. See **Anona**.

annotate *an'ō-tāt*, *vt* to make notes concerning (a literary work, etc). — *vi* to append notes. — *n* **annotā'tion** the making of notes; a note of explanation; comment. — *n* **ann'ōtātor**. [L *annotāre*, from *ad* to, and *notāre*, *-ātum* to mark]

announce *ə-nowns'*, *vt* to declare; to give public notice of; to make known. — *n* **announce'ment**. — *n* **announc'er** a person who announces; a person who reads the news and announces other items in the programme (*TV* and *radio*). [OFr *anoncer*, from L *annuntiāre*, from *ad* to, and *nuntiāre* to report]

annoy *ə-noi'*, *vt* and *vi* to trouble, to vex; to aggravate, irritate; to tease; to harm or injure (*esp* in military sense). — *n* **annoy**' (now *archaic* and *poetic*) or **annoy'ance** that which annoys; the act of annoying; the state of being annoyed. — *adj* **annoyed**' (with *at* or *with*). — *n* **annoy'er**. — *adj* **annoy'ing**. — *adv* **annoy'-ingly**. [OFr *anoier* (noun *anoi*, Mod Fr *ennui*), from LL *inodiāre*, from L phrase *in odiō*, hateful; Ital *annoiare*]

annual *an'ū-əl*, *adj* yearly; coming every year; lasting or living for a year; requiring to be renewed every year; performed in a year; being, or calculated as, the total for one year. — *n* a plant that lives for one year only; a publication that is produced yearly, *esp* a reference book or an illustrated gift-book; a yearbook. — *vt* **ann'ualize** or **-ise** to convert to a yearly rate, amount, etc. — *adv* **ann'ually**. — **annual accounts** a company's financial statements (*incl* profit and loss account and balance sheet), which public limited companies are legally required to publish; **annual report** the report presented by a company to its shareholders each year; **annual rings** rings, as seen in cross-section, in a branch or trunk of a tree, each representing generally a year's growth of wood. — **annual general meeting** (*abbrev* **AGM** or **agm**) a meeting of the directors and shareholders of a company, at which the annual accounts (qv) are presented and discussed, and which limited companies are legally required to hold once a year; **annual** or **annualized percentage rate** (*abbrev* **APR**) an interest percentage rate (as for hire-purchase and loan agreements) calculated and expressed on an annual basis. [LL *annuālis*, from *annus* a year]

annuity *ə-nū'i-ti*, *n* a guaranteed payment (generally of uniform amount) falling due in each year during a given term (such as a period of years or the life of an individual), *usu* purchased fron an insurance company by payment of a lump sum which is not returnable. — *n* **annū'itant** a person who receives or holds an annuity. — **annuity due** one whose first payment is due in advance; **certain annuity** one for a fixed term of years, subject to no contingency whatever; **complete annuity** one of which a proportion is payable up to the day of death; **contingent annuity** one that depends on the continuance of some status, such as the life of a person; **curtate annuity** one payable only at the end of each year survived; **deferred** or **reversionary annuity** one whose first payment is not to be made until a certain number of years have expired. [Fr *annuité*, from LL *annuitās*, *-ātis*, from L *annus* year]

annul *ə-nul'*, *vt* to make null; to reduce to nothing; to abolish: — *pr p* **annull'ing**; *pa t* and *pa p* **annulled**'. — *n* **annul'ment**. [Fr *annuler*, from LL *annūllāre*, from L *ad* to, and *nūllus* none]

annular *an'ū-lər*, *adj* ring-shaped; cutting in a ring; ring-bearing. — *n* the ring-finger. — *n* **annūlarity** (*-lar'i-ti*). — *n pl* **Annūlā'ta** (*obs*) the Annelida. — *n* **ann'ūlate** (*obs*) an annelid. — *adj* **ann'ūlate** or **ann'ūlated** ringed. — *n* **annūlā'tion** a ring- or belt-like structure; the process of forming rings; a circular formation. — *n* **ann'ūlet** a little ring; a small flat fillet encircling a column, etc (*archit*); a little circle borne as a charge (*heraldry*). — *adj* **ann'ūlose** ringed. — *n* **ann'ūlus** (*biol*) any ring-shaped structure, *esp* a ring of cells that brings about dehiscence of a moss sporogonium or a fern capsule: — *pl* **ann'ūlī**. — **annular eclipse** one in which a ring-shaped part of the sun remains visible. [L *annulāris*, for *ānulāris*, from *ānulus* a ring, dimin of *ānus* a ring]

annunciate or (now *obs*) **annuntiate** *ə-nun's(h)i-āt*, *vt* to proclaim. — *n* **annunciā'tion** (*-si-*) proclamation; *esp* (with *cap*) that of the angel to the Virgin Mary (Luke 1.26–38), or its anniversary, 25 March (**Annunciā'tion-day** Lady-day). — *adj* **annun'ciative**. — *n* **annun'ciātor** a device giving audible or visual information, eg indicating where a bell or telephone is being rung, now often operated by closed-circuit television; an announcer, someone who annunciates. — **Annunciation lily** the white lily (*Lilium candidum*) often seen in pictures of the Annunciation. [L *annuntiāre*, *-ātum*, from *ad* to, and *nuntiāre*, from *nuntius* a messenger; *c* from medieval spelling of Latin; cf **announce**]

annus mirabilis *an'əs mir-ab'il-is* or *an'ōōs mēr-äb'il-is*, (*L*) *n* literally, a year of wonders, *esp* applied to 1666 (year of plague and fire of London), or to other years of remarkable or catastrophic, etc event.

ano- *ā'nō-*, (*med*, *pathol*, etc) *combining form* denoting anus. — *adj* **anorec'tal** of or relating to the anus and rectum. [**anus**]

anoa *a-nō'ə*, *n* the sapi-utan, or wild ox of Sulawesi (formerly Celebes), like a small buffalo. [Native name]

Anobium *a-nō'bi-əm*, *n* a genus of small beetles of the family **Anobiidae** (*a-nō-bī'i-dē*), a number of species of which bore in dry wood. [New L, from Gr *ano* upwards, and *bios* life]

anode *an'ōd*, *n* the electrode by which an electric current enters an electrolyte or gas (*opp* to *cathode*); in high vacuum, the electrode to which electrons flow. — *adj* **anōd'al** (or *an'od-əl*) or **anodic** (*an-od'ik*) of an anode; upwards on the genetic spiral (*bot*). — *vt* **an'odize** or **-ise** to give a protective or decorative coat to (a metal) by using it as an anode in electrolysis. — **anodic protection** a system for protecting metal against corrosion by making it the anode (positive electrode) in a circuit (*opp* to *cathodic protection*). [Gr *anodos* way up, from *ana* up, and *hodos* way]

anodyne *an'ō-dīn*, *n* a medicine that allays pain; something that relieves mental distress; something that prevents, soothes or avoids argument, criticism or controversy. — *adj* allaying pain or mental distress; preventing, soothing or avoiding argument, criticism, or controversy; harmless, bland, innocent. [Gr *anōdynos*, from *an-* (privative) and *odynē* pain]

anoesis *a-nō-ē'sis*, *n* sensation or emotion not accompanied by understanding of it: — *pl* **anoe'ses**. — *adj* **anoet'ic**. [Gr *anoia* lack of understanding]

anoestrus or (*US*) **anestrus** *an-ēs'trəs*, (*zool*) *n* a (sometimes prolonged) period of sexual inactivity between periods of oestrus. — Also **anoes'trum**. — *adj* **anoes'trous**. [Gr *an-* (privative), and **oestrus**]

anoint *ə-noint'*, *vt* to smear with ointment or oil; to consecrate with oil; (ironically) to drub, beat thoroughly (*dialect*). — *n* **anoint'er**. — *n* **anoint'ment**. — **the Anointed** the Messiah; **the Lord's anointed** (in royalist theory) king by divine right. [Fr *enoint*, pa p of *enoindre*, from L *inungere*, *inunctum*, from *in* on, and *ung(u)ere* to smear]

anomaly *ə-nom'ə-li*, *n* irregularity; deviation from the rule, or from the strict characteristics of type, etc; something displaying such irregularity or deviation, something anomalous; the angle measured at the sun between a planet in any point of its orbit and the last perihelion (*astron*). — *adj* **anomalis'tic** or (now *rare*) **anomalis'tical** anomalous; departing from established rules; irregular. — *adv* **anomalis'tically**. — *adj* **anom'-alous** irregular; deviating from rule; (of vision) relatively insensitive to one or more colours. — **anomalistic month** and **year** see under **month** and **year**; **anomalous water** polywater. [Gr *anōmalos*, from *an-* (privative) and *homalos* even, from *homos* same]

anomie *an'ə-mē*, *n* (in society or in an individual) a condition of hopelessness caused or characterized by breakdown of rules of conduct and loss of belief and sense of purpose. — Also **an'omy**. — *adj* **anomic** (*ə-nom'ik*). [Fr, from Gr *anomia*, or *-iē* lawlessness, from *ā-* (privative) and *nomos* law]

anon *ə-non'*, (*archaic* or *literary*) *adv* in one (instant); immediately; soon; at another time; coming (in reply to a call). — *interj* expressing failure to hear or understand. [OE *on* in, and *ān* one]

anon. *abbrev*: anonymous.

Anona or **Annona** *ä-nō'nə*, *n* a tropical genus of dicotyledons, including custard-apple, sweet-sop, and other edible fruits, giving its name to the family **Anonā'ceae**, related to the magnolias. — *adj* **anonā'ceous**. [Latinized from Sp *anón*, from Taino]

anonyma *ə-non'i-mə*, (*obs*) *n* a showy woman of easy morals. [Latinized Gr]

anonymous *ə-non'i-məs*, *adj* lacking a name; without name of author, real or feigned; lacking distinctive features or individuality. — *n* **anonym** (*an'*) a person whose name is not given; a pseudonym. — *n* **anonym'ity**. — *vt* **anon'ymize** or **-ise** to remove the name(s) and any other identifying feature(s) from; to make anonymous. — *adv* **anon'ymously**. [Gr *anōnymos*, from *an-* (privative) and *onyma* = *onoma* name]

anopheles *an-of'əl-ēz*, *n* a mosquito of the *Anopheles* genus of germ-carrying mosquitoes. — *adj* **anoph'eline** relating to Anopheles. — *n* a mosquito of this genus. [Gr *anōphelēs* hurtful, from *an-* (privative) and *ophelos* help]

Anoplura *an-o-ploo'rə*, *n pl* an order or suborder of wingless insects, the bugs, and *esp* sucking lice. [Gr *anoplos* unarmed, and *ourā* tail]

anorak *an'ə-rak*, *n* a *usu* hooded waterproof outer jacket; a Greenlander's fur coat. [Greenland Eskimo word]

anorectal. See **ano-**.

anorexia *an-or-ek'si-ə*, also (formerly) **anorexy** *an'or-ek-si* (or *-ek'*), *n* lack of appetite; anorexia nervosa. — *adj* **anorec'tic** causing a lack of appetite; relating to, or suffering from, anorexia (nervosa). — *n* an anorectic substance. — Also *n* and *adj* **anoret'ic**. — *adj* **anorex'ic** relating to, or suffering from, anorexia (nervosa); relating to anorexics. — *n* a person suffering from anorexia (nervosa). — **anorexia nervosa** (*nər-vō'sə* or *-zə*; *psychol* or *med*) a condition characterized by loss of appetite and aversion to food due to emotional disturbance, normally leading to marked emaciation, etc and sometimes death. [Gr *an-* (privative), and *orexis* longing, from *oregein* to reach out]

anorthic *an-ör'thik*, (*crystallog*) *adj* triclinic, referable to three unequal oblique axes. — *n* **anor'thite** a plagioclase feldspar, calcium aluminium silicate (from the oblique angles between the prism faces). [Gr *an-* (privative), and *orthos* right]

anorthosite *an-ör'thō-sīt*, *n* a coarse-grained rock consisting almost entirely of plagioclase feldspar. [Fr *anorthose* (from Gr *an-* (privative), and *orthos* right) and **-ite**(3)]

anosmia *an-oz'mi-ə*, (*med*) *n* the partial or complete loss of sense of smell. [Gr *an-* (privative), *osmē* smell, and **-ia**(1)]

another *ə-nudh'ər*, *adj* and *pronoun* a different or distinct (thing or person); one more; a second; one more of the same kind; any other. — *adj* **anoth'erguess** (*archaic*) see **othergates**. — **one another** a compound reciprocal pronoun *usu* regarded as interchangeable with 'each other', but by some restricted to cases where more than two individuals are involved; **one with another** taken all together, taken on an average. [Orig **an other**]

anough. Same as **enough** (*singular*).

anourous. See **anurous**.

anow (*Milton*). See **enow**[1], **enough** (*pl*).

anoxia *an-ok'si-ə*, (*med*) *n* deficient supply of oxygen to the tissues. — *adj* **anox'ic**. [Gr *an-* (privative), *ox*ygen, and **-ia**(1)]

ANS *abbrev*: autonomic nervous system.

ans. *abbrev*: answer.

Ansafone® *an'sə-fōn*, *n* an answerphone (qv).

ansate *an'sāt*, or **ansated** *-id*, *adj* having a handle or handle-like shape. — **ansate cross** see **ankh**. [L *ansātus*, from *ansa* handle]

Anschauung *an-show'oong*, *n* direct perception through the senses (*psychol* or *philos*); an attitude or point of view. [Ger *Anschauung* perception, intuition, view]

Anschluss *an'shloos*, (*Ger*) *n* union, *esp* the political union of Germany and Austria in 1938.

anserine *an'sər-īn*, *adj* of the goose or the goose family; stupid. [L *anserīnus*, from *anser* goose]

ANSI *abbrev*: American National Standards Institute.

answer *än'sər*, *n* that which is said, written or done in meeting a charge, combating an argument, objection or attack; that which is called for by a question or questioning state of mind; the solution of a problem; an acknowledgement; a return in kind; anything given, sent or said in return; an immediate result or outcome in definite relation to the act it follows; a repetition or echo of a sound; restatement of a theme by another voice or instrument (*music*). — *vt* to speak, write or act in answer to or against; to say or write as an answer; to give, send, afford or be an answer to; to behave in due accordance with; to be in proportion to or in balance with; to give a conclusive or satisfactory answer to; to serve the purpose of; to fulfil; to recompense satisfactorily (*obs*); to be punished for (*colloq*). — *vi* to give an answer; to behave in answer; to be responsible (with *for*); to suffer the consequences (with *for*); to be in conformity (with *for*); to serve the purpose (with *to*), to succeed; to react (*usu* with *to*). — *adj* **an'swerable** able to be answered; accountable; suitable (*archaic*); equivalent (*archaic*); in due proportion (*archaic*). — *n* **answerabil'ity**. — *adv* **an'swerably**. — *n* **an'swerer**. — *adj* **an'swerless**. — **answerphone** (*än'sər-fōn*) or **answering machine** a device that automatically answers incoming telephone calls, plays a pre-recorded message to the callers and records their messages on audio tape; **answering service** a commercial service which answers telephone calls, takes messages, etc for its clients when they are not available. — **answer back** (*colloq*) to answer someone who expects silent submission; to answer pertly. — **answer back code** an individual set of characters by which each telex machine can identify itself and be identified. — **answer to** or **answer to the name of** to show sign of accepting as one's name; to have as one's name (*colloq*); **know all the answers** to be in complete command of the situation with no chance of being caught out (a statement *usu* made with reference to another person who is too self-confident). [OE *andswaru* (noun), *andswarian* (verb), from *and-* against, and *swerian* to swear]

ant *ant*, *n* a small, hymenopterous, scavenging (or sometimes predacious) social insect (family *Formicidae*), of proverbial industry, living in organized colonies; loosely, a termite. — *n* **ant'ing** the introduction by birds of live ants or other stimulants into their plumage, possibly as a pleasurable means of cleaning it and their skin. — **ant'bear** the great anteater, the largest species of anteaters, found in swampy regions in S America; the aardvark of S Africa; **ant'bird** a S American ant thrush; **ant cow** an aphis kept and tended by ants for its honeydew; **ant'eater** any one of a Central and South American family of edentates, adapted for feeding on ants and termites; a pangolin; an aardvark; an echidna. — *n pl* **ant'-** or **ants'-eggs** pupae of ants. — **ant'-hill** a hillock raised as a nest in wood, soil, etc by ants or by termites; anything like an ant-hill in terms of crowdedness, bustle, etc (*fig*); **ant'lion** a neuropterous insect (genus *Myrmeleon*) similar to a damselfly, whose larva traps ants in a funnel-shaped sand-hole; **ant thrush** any bird of the northern S American family *Formicariidae* which feed on insects disturbed by travelling ants, or of the long-legged thrush-like Oriental and Australian family *Pittidae*. — **have ants in one's pants** (*colloq*) to be restless, impatient, needlessly hurrying. [OE *ǣmete*; cf **emmet**]

an't *änt*, (*archaic* or *dialect*) a contraction of **are not, am not, has not**, or (*ant*) **on it, and it** (= if it).

ant-. See **anti-**.

anta[1] *an'tə*, (*archit*) *n* a square pilaster at either side of a doorway or the corner of a flank wall: — *pl* **an'tae** (*-tē*). — **in antis** (*L*) literally, between the antae; (of a portico) not framed by columns but having antae terminating the side walls; (of a portico) recessed in a façade. [L]

anta[2] *än'ta*, *n* a tapir. [Port, from Sp, elk]

Antabuse® *an'tə-būs*, *n* a drug in tablet form containing disulfiram (tetraethylthiuram disulphide, $C_{10}H_{20}N_2S_4$), which induces nausea, headaches, etc in patients ingesting alcohol, and which is therefore used in the treatment of alcoholism.

antacid *ant-as'id*, *adj* counteracting acidity of the stomach. — *n* a medicine that counteracts acidity. [**anti-**]

antagonist *an-tag'ə-nist*, *n* a person who contends or struggles with another; an opponent; a muscle that opposes the action of another; in an organism, something that has an opposite effect; a drug acting against another drug or other chemical or hormone. — Also *adj*. — *n* **antag'onism** opposition; hostility; production of opposing effects, eg in a living body; interference with the growth of another organism, eg by using up the food supply or producing an antibiotic substance. — *adj* **antagonist'ic**. — *adv* **antagonis'tically**. — *n* **antagonīzā'tion** or **-s-**. — *vt* **antag'onize** or **-ise** to struggle violently against; to counteract the action of; to arouse opposition in. [Gr *antagōnistēs*, from *anti* against, and *agōn* contest. See **agony**]

antaphrodisiac *ant-af-rō-diz'i-ak*, or *-rə-*, *adj* counteracting sexual desire. — *n* an antaphrodisiac agent. [**anti-**]

antar *an'tər*, (*Shakesp*) *n* a cave. [Fr *antre*, from L *antrum*, from Gr *antron*]

antara *an-tar'ə*, *n* a type of Andean Pan-pipes. [Am Sp, from Quechua]

Antarctic *ant-ärk'tik*, *adj* opposite the Arctic; of, near, or relating to the south pole. — *n* the south polar regions. — **Antarctic Circle** the parallel of latitude 66°32′ S, bounding the region of the earth surrounding the south terrestrial pole. [Gr *antarktikos*, from *anti* opposite, and *arktikos* (see **Arctic**)]

Antares *an-tā'rēz*, or *-tä'*, *n* a first-magnitude red star, the brightest in the Scorpius constellation. [Gr *Antarēs*, from pfx *anti-* like, and *Arēs* Mars]

antarthritic *ant-är-thrit'ik*, (*med*) *adj* counteracting arthritis. — *n* an agent that counteracts arthritis. — Also **antiarthrit'ic**. [**anti-**]

antasthmatic *ant-as(th)-mat'ik*, (*med*) *adj* counteracting asthma. — *n* an agent that counteracts asthma. — Also **antiasthmat'ic**. [**anti**]

ante *an'ti*, (*orig* and *esp US*) *n* a fixed stake put down by a poker player, *usu* before the deal; advance payment. — *vt* to stake (*poker*); to pay (*usu* with *up*). — **up** (or **raise**) **the ante** (*colloq fig*) to increase the costs or risks involved in, or the demands requiring to be met before, some action. [L, before]

ante- *an'ti-*, *pfx* signifying before. [L *ante*, old form *anti*; connected with Gr **anti-**]

ante-bellum *an'ti-bel'əm*, *n* and *adj* (happening in) the time before the war (whichever is in mind). [L phrase]

antecedent *an-ti-sē'dənt*, *adj* going before in time; prior. — *n* that which precedes in time; an ancestor; the noun or its equivalent to which a relative pronoun refers (*gram*); the conditional part of a hypothetical proposition (*logic*); the numerator term of a ratio (*math*); (in *pl*) previous principles, conduct, history, etc. — *vt* **antecēde'** to go before in time, rank, etc. — *n* **antecē'dence**. — *adv* **antecē'dently**. [L *antecēdēns*, *-entis*, from *ante* before, and *cēdere* to go]

antecessor *an'ti-ses-ər*, or *-ses'*, *n* a predecessor (*rare*); an ancestor (*obs*). [L; cf preceding word and **ancestor**]

antechamber *an'ti-chām-bər*, *n* a chamber or room leading to a more important apartment. [Fr *antichambre*, from L *ante* before, and *camera* a vault]

antechapel *an'ti-chap-l*, *n* the outer part of the west end of a college chapel. [**ante-**]

antechoir *an'ti-kwīr*, *n* the space in front of the choir in a church. [**ante-**]

antedate *an'ti-dāt*, *n* a date assigned which is earlier than the actual date. — *vt* to date before the true time; to assign to an earlier date; to bring about at an earlier date; to be of previous date to; to accelerate; to anticipate. [**ante-** and **date**[1]]

antediluvian *an-ti-di-lōō'vi-ən*, or *-lū'*, *adj* existing or happening before Noah's Flood; resembling the state of things before the Flood; very old-fashioned, primitive. — *n* an antediluvian thing or person; a person who lived before the Flood; someone who lives to be very old. — *adj* (*geol*; *rare*) **antedilu'vial**. — *adv* **antedilu'vially**. [**ante-** and L *dīlūvium* flood]

antefix *an'ti-fiks*, (*antiq*) *n* (*usu* in *pl*) an ornament concealing the ends of roofing tiles and protecting the rafters of classical temples, etc: — *pl* **an'tefixes** or **antefix'a** (*L*). — *adj* **antefix'al**. [L *ante* before, in front, and *figere*, *fixum* to fix]

antelope *an'ti-lōp*, *n* (since the 17c) any one of a group of hollow-horned, hoofed, ruminant mammals closely related to goats; a fabulous fierce horned beast (*Spenser*). [OFr *antelop*, from Med L *antalopus*, from Late Gr *antholops*, of unknown origin]

antelucan *an-ti-lū'kən*, or *-lōō'*, (*archaic*; *literary*) *adj* (of eg worship) before dawn or daylight. [L *antelūcānus*, from *ante* before, and *lūx* light]

ante lucem *an'te lū'səm* or *lōō'kəm*, (*L*) before light.

antemeridian *an-ti-mə-rid'i-ən*, *adj* before midday. [L *antemerīdiānus*, from *ante merīdiem* before noon]

ante meridiem *an'te mer-id'i-em*, or *mer-ēd'*, (*L*) before noon — *usu abbrev* **a.m.** or **am**.

ante mortem *an'te mör'tem*, (*L*) before death. — **ante-mortem inspection** an inspection of livestock by a vet immediately before slaughter, to ensure that the animal meets required standards of fitness, health, etc.

antemundane *an-ti-mun'dān*, (*archaic*; *literary*) *adj* before the existence of the world. [**ante-** and L *mundānus*, from *mundus* world]

antenatal *an-ti-nā'tl*, *adj* before birth; of, or relating to, the health and care, etc of women during pregnancy. — *n pl* **antenā'tī** (*L -nä'tē*) those born before a certain time (as opposed to *post-nati*, born after it), used of Scots born before 1603, and Americans before the Declaration of Independence (1776). — **antenatal clinic** a clinic for the purpose of treating and giving advice to pregnant women. [**ante-** and L *nātālis* natal, or *nātus* born]

ante-Nicene *an-ti-nī'sēn*, *adj* before the first council of *Nicaea* in Bithynia, AD 325.

antenna *an-ten'ə*, *n* a feeler or horn in insects, crustaceans and myriapods; in TV and radio communication, a structure for sending out or receiving electromagnetic signals; an aerial: — *pl* **antenn'ae** (*-ē*) or (*TV* and *radio*) **antenn'as**. — *adj* **antenn'al** or **antenn'ary**. — *adj* **antennif'erous** bearing or having antennae. — *adj* **antenn'iform**. — *n* **antenn'ūle** one of a first or smaller pair of antennae in crustaceans. [L *antemna*, *antenna* yard (of a mast)]

antenuptial *an-ti-nup'shəl*, *adj* before marriage. [**ante-**]

anteorbital *an-ti-ör'bit-l*, *adj* situated in front of the eyes. [L **ante**]

antepast *an'ti-päst*, (*obs*) *n* something to whet the appetite; a foretaste. [L *ante* before, and *pāscere*, *pāstum* to feed]

antependium *an-ti-pend'i-əm*, *n* a hanging for the front of an altar, a frontlet or forecloth; a frontal. [L *ante* before, and *pendēre* to hang]

antepenult *an-ti-pen-ult'*, *n* the last syllable but two (of a word). — *adj* **antepenult'imate** last but two. [L *ante* before, and **penult**]

ante-post *an'ti-pōst*, *adj* (of betting) beginning before the runners' numbers are posted; occurring during the time before the runners come under starter's orders. [**ante** and **post**[1]]

anteprandial *an-ti-prand'i-əl*, *adj* before dinner. [L *ante* before, and *prandium* dinner]

anterior *an-tē'ri-ər*, *adj* before, in time or place; in front; towards the bract or away from the axis (*bot*). — *n* **anteriority** (*-or'i-ti*). — *adv* **antē'riorly**. [L *anterior* (compar), from *ante* before]

anterograde amnesia *an'tər-ō-grād am-nē'zhə*, (*behav*) *n* loss of memory for events after injury to the brain or mental trauma, with little effect on information acquired previously. [L *anterior* previous, and *gradī*, *gressus* to go; **amnesia**]

anteroom *an'ti-rōōm*, *n* a room leading into another larger room; a waiting-room; an officers' mess sitting-room. [**ante-**; modelled on Fr *antichambre* (see **antechamber**)]

anteversion *an-ti-vûr'shən*, (*med*) *n* the tipping forward of a bodily organ. — *vt* **antevert'**. [L *ante* before, and *vertere, versum* to turn]

anthelion *an-thē'li-ən* or *-lyən*, *n* a luminous coloured ring seen on a cloud or fog-bank opposite the sun: — *pl* **anthe'lia**. [Gr *ant(h)ēlios, -on*, from *anti* opposite, and *hēlios* the sun]

anthelix. See **antihelix**.

anthelminthic *an-thel-min'thik* or **anthelmintic** *-tik, adj* destroying or expelling worms, *esp* parasitic intestinal worms. — *n* a drug used for that purpose. [Gr *anti* against, and *helmins, helminthos* a worm]

anthem *an'thəm, n* a composition for a church choir, commonly with solo passages, *usu* set to a passage from the Bible; any song of praise or gladness; loosely, an officially recognized national hymn or song (such as a *national anthem*); an antiphon (*obs*). — *vt* to praise in an anthem. — *adv* **an'themwise** (*Bacon*) in the manner of an antiphonal anthem. [OE *antefn*, from Gr *antiphōna* (pl) sounding in answer, from *anti* in return, and *phōnē* voice. See **antiphon**]

anthemion *an-thē'mi-ən, n* the so-called honeysuckle ornament in ancient art, a conventionalized plant-form more like a palmetto: — *pl* **anthē'mia**. [Gr *anthemion*, dimin of *anthos* a flower]

anther *an'thər*, (*bot*) *n* the part of a stamen that produces the pollen. — *n* **antherid'ium** the gametangium in which male gametes are produced: — *pl* **antherid'ia**. — *n* **antherozō'oid** or **antherozō'id** (Gr *zōoeidēs* like an animal, from *zōion* animal, and *eidos* shape) a motile male gamete produced in an antheridium. — **an'thersmut** a fungus (*Ustilago violacea*) causing a disease affecting plants of the carnation and pink family, in which the anthers produce the fungus spores instead of pollen. [Gr *anthēra* a medicine made from flowers, esp their inner parts, from *anthos* flower]

anthesis *an-thē'sis*, (*bot*) *n* the opening of a flower-bud; the lifetime of a flower from opening to setting of seed. [Gr *anthēsis* flowering, from *anthos* flower]

Anthesteria *an-thes-tē'ri-ə, n pl* the Athenian spring festival of Dionysos, held in the month of *Anthestērion* (February–March). [Gr *ta Anthestēria* (Feast of Flowers), *Anthestēriōn* (the month), from *anthos* flower]

antho- *an'tho-* or *an'thə-, combining form* denoting flower. — *n* **anthocarp** (*an'thō-kärp*; Gr *karpos* fruit) a fruit resulting from many flowers, such as the pineapple; a fruit of which the perianth or the torus forms part. — *adj* **anthocarp'ous**. — *n* **an'thochlore** (*-klōr* or *-klör*; Gr *chlōros* green, yellow) a yellow pigment in flowers. — *n* **anthocyan** (*-sī'ən*) or **anthocy'anin** (Gr *kyanos* blue) a glucoside plant pigment, violet in neutral, red in acid, blue in alkaline cell-sap. — *adj* **an'thoid** (Gr *eidos* shape) flower-like. — *n* **anthology**, etc see separate entry. — *n* **anthomā'nia** (Gr *maniā* madness) a craze for flowers. — *n* **anthomā'niac**. — *n* **Anthonomus** (*an-thon'ə-məs*; Gr *nomos* herbage, food) the genus of the cotton-boll weevil. — *adj* **anthophilous** (*an-thof'i-ləs*) loving, frequenting or feeding on flowers. — *n* **an'thophore** (*-thō-fōr* or *-för*; *bot*) an elongation of the receptacle between calyx and corolla. — *n* **anthophyllite** (*an-thō-fil'īt*, or *-thə-* or sometimes *-thof'*; New L *anthophyllum* clove, from Gr *phyllon* leaf) an orthorhombic amphibole, *usu* clove-brown. — *n* **anthoxan'thin** (Gr *xanthos* yellow) a yellow pigment in plants. — *n pl* **Anthozō'a** (Gr *zōia* animals) the Actinozoa, a class of coelenterates including sea anemones, corals, etc. [Gr *anthos* flower]

anthology *an-tho'lə-ji, n* a choice collection of writings, (*esp* poems), songs or paintings, etc; literally, a flower-gathering. — *n* **anthol'ogist** a person who compiles an anthology. — *vt* and *vi* **anthol'ogize** or **-ise**. [Gr, a collection of Gr epigrams, (literally), a flower-gathering, from *anthos* flower, and *-logia* gathering (from *legein* to collect)]

Anthony *an'tən-i, n* a 4c Egyptian saint, for 20 years a hermit, patron saint of swineherds, who has a pig and a bell among his symbols and who was believed to have stopped an epidemic (perhaps raphania, but commonly supposed to be erysipelas) in 1089; (also **tantony** *tan'*, **St Anthony pig** or **tantony pig**) the smallest pig in a litter; an obsequious follower. — **St Anthony's cross** a tau-cross; **St Anthony's fire** (popularly) erysipelas; **St Anthony's nut** earthnut or pignut; **tantony bell** a small bell.

anthophilous. See **antho-**.

anthracene *an'thrə-sēn, n* a product of coal-tar distillation ($C_{14}H_{10}$), a source of dyestuffs. [Ety as for **anthrax**, with sfx *-ene* (chem)]

anthracite *an'thrə-sīt, n* hard lustrous coal that burns nearly without flame or smoke, consisting almost entirely of carbon. — *adj* **anthracitic** (*-sit'ik*) of or of the nature of anthracite. [Gr *anthrakitēs* a kind of coal; cf **anthrax**]

anthracnose *an-thrak'nōs, n* any of several plant diseases caused by a fungus and characterized by the appearance of dark, sunken spots. [Ety as for **anthrax**, and Gr *nosos* disease]

anthracoid. See **anthrax**.

anthracosis *an-thrə-kō'sis, n* a diseased state of the lung due to breathing in coal-dust. [Ety as for **anthrax**, with sfx **-osis**]

anthrax *an'thraks, n* a deadly disease due to a bacillus, most common in sheep and cattle but communicable to humans (also known as *malignant pustule* or *wool-sorter's disease*); a sore caused by the disease; a carbuncle or malignant boil. — *adj* **anthracic** (*-thras'ik*). — *adj* **anthracoid** (*an'thrə-koid*) like anthrax. [Gr *anthrax, -akos* charcoal, coal, carbuncle (stone or boil)]

anthrop- or **anthropo-** *combining form* denoting man, human. — *adj* **anthropic** (*an-throp'ik*) or **anthrop'ical** human. — *n* **anthropobiol'ogy** human biology. — *adj* **anthropocentric** (*an-thrō-pō-sent'rik*; Gr *kentron* centre) regarding the human race as the centre of, or central to, the universe. — *n* **anthropogenesis** (*-jen'*). — *adj* **anthropogen'ic**. — *n* **anthropogeny** (*-poj'ən-i*; Gr *genos* race, birth) the study of man's origin. — *n* **anthrōpogeog'raphy** the geography of the races of man. — *n* **anthropogony** (*-pog'ə-ni*; Gr *gonē, gonos* birth, begetting) the study, or an account, of the origin of man. — *n* **anthropography** (*-pog'rə-fi*) study of the geographical distribution of human races. — *adj* **an'thropoid** (or *-thrōp'*; Gr *eidos* form) manlike, applied *esp* to the highest apes (gorilla, chimpanzee, orang-utan, gibbon) but also to the higher Primates generally, ie man, apes, monkeys, but not lemurs. — *n* an anthropoid ape. — *adj* **anthropoid'al**. — *n* **anthropol'atry** (Gr *latreiā* worship) man-worship, the giving of divine honours to a human being. — *adj* **anthrōpological** (*-loj'*). — *adv* **anthrōpolog'ically**. — *n* **anthropol'ogist**. — *n* **anthropol'ogy** the scientific study of human beings and their way of life, the science of man in its widest sense. — *adj* **anthropomet'ric**. — *n* **anthropometry** (*-pom'i-tri*; Gr *metreein* to measure) measurement of the human body. — *n* **anthrō'pomorph** (Gr *morphē* shape) a representation, *esp* conventionalized, of the human form in art. — *adj* **anthropomorph'ic**. — *n* **anthropomorph'ism** conception or representation of a god as having the form, personality or attributes of man; ascription of human characteristics to what is not human, *esp* an animal. — *n* **anthropomorph'ist**. — *n* **anthropomorph'ite** a person who ascribes human form, personality or attributes to God. — *adj* **anthropomorphit'ic**. — *n* **anthropomorph'itism**. — *vt* **anthropomor'phize** or **-ise** to regard as or render anthropomorphic. — *n* **anthropomorphō'sis** (or *-mörf'ə-sis*) transformation into human shape. — *adj* **anthropomorph'ous** formed like or resembling man. — *adj* **anthropopathic** (*-path'ik*). — *adv* **anthropopath'ically**. — *n* **anthropopathism** (*-pop'ə-thizm*) or **anthropop'athy** (Gr *pathos* suffering, passion) ascription of human passions and affections (to God, nature, etc). — *n pl* **anthropophagi** (*-pof'ə-jī* or *-gē*; Gr *phagein* to eat) man-eaters, cannibals. — *n* **anthropophaginian** (*-jin'i-*

ən; Shakesp) a cannibal. — *n* **anthropoph'agite** (*-ə-jīt*). — *adj* **anthropoph'agous** (*-ə-gəs*). — *n* **anthropoph'agy** (*-ə-ji*) cannibalism. — *n* **anthropophō'bia** a morbid fear of people or society. — *n* and *adj* **anthropophō'bic**. — *n* **anthropoph'ūism** (Gr *phyē* nature) the ascription of a human nature to the gods. — *n* **anthrop'ophyte** a plant introduced incidentally in the course of cultivation. — *n* **Anthropopithē'cus** (Gr *pithekos* ape) the chimpanzee. — *adj* **anthropopsy'chic** (*-sī'kik* or *-psī'kik*). — *adv* **anthropopsy'chically**. — *n* **anthropopsy'chism** (Gr *psȳchē* soul) ascription to nature or God of a soul or mind like man's. — *adj* **anthroposoph'ical**. — *n* **anthropos'ophist**. — *n* **anthropos'ophy** (Gr *sophiā* wisdom) the knowledge of the nature of men; human wisdom; *specif* the spiritualistic doctrine of Rudolf Steiner (1861–1925). — *n* **anthropot'omy** (Gr *tomē* a cut) human anatomy. [Gr *anthrōpos* man (in general sense)]

anthurium *an-thū'ri-əm*, *n* a member of the *Anthurium* genus of tropical American plants with showy leaves and flowers. [Gr *anthos* flower, and *oura* tail]

anti *an'ti*, also (*US*) *an'tī*, *prep* opposed to, against. — *n* and *adj* (a person who is) opposed to anything. [Gr *anti* against, instead of, etc]

anti- *an'ti-*, also (*US*) *an'tī-*, or often before a vowel **ant-**, *pfx* denoting (1) acting against, counteracting, resisting, resistant to; (2) opposed to; (3) opposite or reverse. [Gr *anti* against]

Words with the prefix **anti-** are listed in the following text or in the separate panels.

antiaditis *an-ti-ə-dī'tis*, (*med*) *n* tonsillitis. [Gr *antias*, *-ados* tonsil]

anti-aircraft *an'ti-ār'kräft*, *adj* intended for use against hostile aircraft. [**anti-** (1)]

antiar *an'chär* or *an'ti-är*, *n* the upas-tree; its poisonous latex. [Jav *antjar*]

antiarrhythmic *an-ti-ə-ridh'mik*, (*med*) *adj* counteracting, or capable of controlling, arrhythmia. — *n* an antiarrhythmic agent or drug. [**anti-** (1)]

antibacchius *an-ti-bə-kī'əs*, (*prosody*) *n* a foot of two long (or stressed) syllables followed by a short (or unstressed) one. [**anti-** (3) and **bacchius** (see under **bacchanal**)]

antiballistic *an-ti-bə-lis'tik*, *adj* (of a missile, etc) designed to destroy a ballistic missile. — *Abbrev* **ABM**. [**anti-** (1)]

antibarbarus *an'ti-bär'bär-us*, (*LL*) *n* a list of words and locutions to be avoided in the classical usage of a language.

antibiosis *an-ti-bī-ō'sis*, (*biol*) *n* a state of mutual antagonism between associated organisms; inhibition of growth by a substance produced by another organism. — *adj* **antibiotic** (*-ot'ik*) inimical to life; inhibiting the growth of another organism, used *esp* of a substance produced by micro-organisms which, in dilute solution, has the capacity to inhibit the growth of, or to destroy, micro-organisms causing infectious diseases; pertaining to antibiosis. — *n* an antibiotic substance. — **antibiotic resistance** (*biol*) a property of micro-organisms or cells that renders them capable of surviving high concentrations of a normally lethal agent. [**anti-** (1) and Gr noun *biosis* way of life or adj *biōtikos*, both from *bios* life]

antibody *an'ti-bod-i*, (*biol*) *n* a defensive substance produced in an organism in response to the action of a foreign body such as a bacterium, virus, or the toxin of a parasite. [**anti-** (1)]

Antiburgher *an-ti-bûrg'ər*, (*hist*) *n* a member of that section of the Scottish Secession Church which parted from the main body (the *Burghers*) in 1747, interpreting the reference in the oath administered to burgesses in Edinburgh, Glasgow and Perth, to 'the true religion presently professed within this realm' to mean the Established Church. — Also *adj*. [**anti-** (2)]

antic *ant'ik*, *adj* (*archaic*) grotesque, fantastic. — *n* (*usu* in *pl*) a fantastic action or trick, a caper; a fantastic figure or ornament (*obs*); a grotesque pageant (*Shakesp*); a buffoon, clown, mountebank (*archaic*). — *vt* (*Shakesp*) to make grotesque. — *vi* (*archaic*) to cut capers: — *pr p* **ant'icking**; *pa t* and *pa p* **ant'icked**. — Obsolete forms **ant'ick**, **ant'icke** or sometimes **ant'ique**. — *vi* **anticize** (*ant'i-sīz*; *Browning*) to play antics. — See also **antique**. [Ital *antico* ancient, from L *antīquus*; orig used of the fantastic decorations found in the remains of ancient Rome]

anticathode *an-ti-kath'ōd*, *n* the target of an X-ray tube, on which the cathode rays are focused and from which X-rays are emitted. [**anti-** (3)]

anticatholic *an-ti-kath'ə-lik*, *adj* opposed to the Catholic or the Roman Catholic Church, to Catholics, or to what is catholic. [**anti-** (2)]

anti-chip *an-ti-chip'*, *adj* (of paint, etc) resistant to chipping. [**anti-** (1)]

antichlor *an'ti-klör*, *n* any substance used in paper- or textile-making to free the pulp from the last traces of free chlorine. [**anti-** (1)]

anticholinergic *an-ti-kō-lin-ûr'jik*, (*med*) *adj* counteracting the effect of acetylcholine; blocking parasympathetic nerve impulses. — *n* a drug which blocks these impulses. [**anti-** (1)]

Antichrist *an'ti-krīst*, *n* an opponent of Christ; the great opposer of Christ and Christianity expected by the early Church, later applied by some (eg Protestant extremists) to the Pope and others. — *adj* **antichristian** (*-kris'*) relating to Antichrist; opposed to Christianity. — *n* **antichris'tianism**. — *adv* **antichris'tianly**. [Gr *Antichristos*, from *anti-* against, and *Christos* Christ]

Antichthon *an-tik'thōn*, *n* the supposed second earth thought by Pythagoreans to exist on the other side of the sun; the southern hemisphere (*obs*). — *n pl* **antich'thones** (*-thon-ēz*; *obs*) the antipodeans. [Gr *anti* opposite to, and *chthōn* earth]

anticipate *an-tis'ip-āt*, *vt* to forestall (a person or thing); to use, spend, deal with in advance or before the due time; to realize beforehand; to foresee or count upon as certain; to expect; to precede (*rare*); to advance to an earlier time, bring on sooner. — *vi* to do anything, or take action, before the appropriate, expected or due time; to be before the normal time (*obs*). — *adj* **antic'ipant** anticipating, anticipative. — Also *n*. — *n* **anticipā'tion** an act of anticipating; imagining beforehand; expectation; assignment to too early a time; the introduction of a tone or tones of a chord before the whole chord (*music*); intuition; foretaste; previous notion; presentiment; prejudice (*obs*). — *adj* **anti'cipātive** or **anti'cipatory**. — *adv* **anti'cipātively** or **anti'cipatorily**. — *n* **antic'ipātor**. [L *anticipāre*, *-ātum*, from *ante* before, and *capere* to take]

anticivic *an-ti-siv'ik*, *adj* opposed to citizenship, *esp* the conception of it engendered by the French Revolution. — *n* **anticiv'ism**. [**anti-** (2)]

Some words with **anti-** prefix; see **anti-** entry for numbered senses.

anti-abor'tion *adj* (2).	**anti-Gall'ican** *adj* and *n* (2).	**anti-mod'ernist** *adj* and *n* (1), (2).
antibactē'rial *adj* (1).	**anti-Gall'icanism** *n* (2).	**antimonarch'ical** *adj* (2).
antibil'ious *adj* (1).	**anti-inflamm'atory** *adj* (1).	**antimon'archist** *n* (2).
anticorrō'sive *adj* (1).	**anti-inflā'tionary** *adj* (1).	**anti-na'tional** *adj* (2).
antidīūret'ic *adj* and *n* (1).	**antimalā'rial** *adj* (1).	**antinoise'** *adj* (1).
antifric'tion *adj* (1).	**antimicrō'bial** *adj* (1).	**antiperistal'tic** *adj* (3).

antick, **anticke**. Obsolete forms of **antic**, **antique**.

anticlerical *an-ti-kler'i-kl*, *adj* opposed to the clergy or their power. — *n* a member of an anticlerical party. — *n* **anticler'icalism**. [**anti-** (2)]

anticlimax *an-ti-klī'maks*, *n* the opposite of climax; a ludicrous drop in impressiveness after a progressive rise; a disappointing, weak or dull outcome or follow-up, in sudden contrast to preceding events, expectations, etc. — *adj* **anticlīmac'tic**. — *adv* **anticlīmac'tically**. [**anti-** (3)]

anticline *an'ti-klīn*, (*geol*) *n* an arch-like fold dipping outwards from the fold-axis. — *adj* **anticlīn'al** sloping in opposite directions; perpendicular to the surface near the growing-point (*bot*). — *n* an anticline. — *n* **anticlinō'rium** (*-klin-* or *-klīn-*; Gr *oros* mountain) a series of folds which as a whole is anticlinal. [**anti-** (1), and Gr *klinein* to lean]

anticlockwise *an-ti-klok'wīz*, *adv* in the opposite direction to that in which the hands of a clock travel. [**anti-** (3)]

anticoagulant *an-ti-kō-ag'ū-lənt*, *n* a drug that hinders normal clotting of blood. — Also *adj*. [**anti-** (1)]

anticonvulsant *an-ti-kən-vul'sənt*, *n* a drug used to control convulsions in epilepsy, etc. — Also *adj*. — Also *n* and *adj* **anticonvul'sive**. [**anti-** (1)]

anticous *an-tī'kəs*, (*bot*) *adj* on the anterior side, or away from the axis. [L *antīcus* in front, from *ante* before]

anticyclone *an-ti-sī'klōn*, (*meteorol*) *n* a rotatory outflow of air from an area of high pressure. — *adj* **anticyclonic** (*-klon'ik*). [**anti-** (3)]

antidepressant *an-ti-di-pres'ənt*, *n* a drug used to counteract depression. — Also *adj*. [**anti-** (1)]

antidesiccant *an-ti-des'i-kənt*, *n* a chemical which prevents or inhibits the drying-out of a plant, etc. [**anti-** (1)]

anti-devolutionist *an-ti-dē-vəl-ōō'shən-ist*, *-dev-*, or *-ū'*, *n* a person who is opposed to devolution. [**anti-** (1)]

antidisestablishmentarianism *an-ti-dis-es-tab-lish-mən-tār'i-ən-izm*, *n* a movement against the removing of state recognition of an established church, *esp* the Anglican church in the 19c. — *adj* **antidisestablishmenta'rian**. [**anti-** (1)]

antidote *an'ti-dōt*, *n* something which counteracts a poison; anything that prevents an evil or something unwanted (with *against*, *for* or *to*) (*fig*). — *adj* **antido'tal**. [Gr *antidotos*, from *anti* against, and *didonai*, to give]

antidromic *an-ti-drom'ik*, (*med*) *adj* (of nerve fibres) conducting or able to conduct impulses in the opposite direction to normal. [**anti-** (1) and Gr *dromos* a course, run]

antient. An obsolete spelling of **ancient**.

anti-establishment *an-ti-es-tab'lish-mənt*, *adj* opposed to the opinions and values of the establishment in society. — *n* the people who are opposed to such opinions, etc. [**anti-** (1)]

anti-fade *an-ti-fād'*, *adj* resistant to fading. [**anti-** (1)]

anti-federal *an'ti-fed'ər-əl*, *adj* opposed to federalism; applied to the former US party afterwards called Democratic. — *n* **anti-fed'eralism**. — *n* **anti-fed'eralist**. [**anti-** (2)]

anti-feedant *an-ti-fēd'ənt*, *n* any of a number of substances present in some species of plants which make the plants resistant to insect pests. [**anti-** (1)]

anti-flash *an-ti-flash'*, *adj* protecting against the flash of explosions, etc. [**anti-** (1)]

antifouling *an-ti-fowl'ing*, *adj* intended to prevent fouling of ships' bottoms by marine growths, eg barnacles. — *n* an antifouling substance applied in paint form to ships' bottoms, etc. [**anti-** (1)]

antifreeze *an'ti-frēz*, *n* a substance (eg ethylene glycol) with low freezing point put into water to lower its freezing point, *esp* used in the radiator of an internal-combustion engine to prevent freezing up. [**anti-** (1)]

antigay *an-ti-gā'*, *adj* opposed or hostile to homosexuals or gay rights movements, activities, organizations, etc. [**anti-**]

antigen *an'ti-jen*, (*biol*) *n* any substance that stimulates the production of an antibody. — *adj* **antigen'ic**. — *adv* **antigen'ically**. — **antigenic determinant** (*immunol*) a small part of an antigen which has a structure complementary to a part of its corresponding antibody — also **epitope**; **antigenic variation** (*immunol*) the development of new antigenic determinants through genetic mutation and selection. [**anti-** (1) and Gr *gennaein* to engender]

antigropeloes or **antigropelos** *an-ti-grop'ə-lōz*, (*old*) *n pl* waterproof leggings. [Said to be from Gr *anti* against, *hygros* wet and *pēlos* mud]

antihalation *an-ti-ha-lā'shən*, (*photog*) *n* the prevention of halation by placing a layer of dye *usu* on the back of the film to absorb light which has passed through the emulsion on the film. [**anti-** (1)]

antihelix *an-ti-hē'liks*, or **anthelix** *an'thi-liks* or *an-thē'liks*, (*anatom*) *n* the inner curved ridge of the external ear: — *pl* **antihelices** (*-li-sēz*) or **anthel'ices**. [Gr *anthelix*, from *helix* a coil]

anti-hero *an'ti-hē-rō*, *n* a principal character (in a novel, play, etc) who lacks noble qualities and whose experiences are without tragic dignity: — *fem* **anti-heroine** (*-her-ō-in*). — *adj* **anti-heroic** (*-hi-rō'ik*). [**anti-** (3)]

antihistamine *an-ti-his'tə-mēn*, *n* any of a group of drugs that prevents the action of histamines in allergic conditions. [**anti-** (1)]

antihypertensive *an-ti-hī-pər-ten'siv*, *adj* (of a drug or other measure) used to lower the blood pressure. — *n* an antihypertensive drug. [**anti-** (1)]

anti-Jacobin or sometimes **antijacobin** *an'ti-jak'ə-bin*, (*hist*) *adj* opposed to the Jacobins and to the French Revolution or to democratic principles. — *n* a person opposed to the Jacobins; (with *cap*) a weekly paper started in England in 1797 by Canning and others to refute the principles of the French Revolution. — *n* **anti-Jac'obinism**. [**anti-** (2)]

antijamming *an-ti-jam'ing*, *n* a device or technique designed to prevent or reduce deliberate jamming of radio signals, radar communications, etc. — Also *adj*. [**anti-**(1)]

antiknock *an-ti-nok'*, *n* a substance that prevents knock or detonation in internal-combustion engines. — Also *adj*. [**anti-** (1)]

antilegomena *an-ti-leg-om'i-nə*, *n pl* (often with *cap*) those books of the New Testament not at first universally accepted but ultimately admitted into the Canon (2 Peter, James, Jude, Hebrews, 2 and 3 John, and the Apocalypse) — *opp* to *homologoumena*. [Gr, spoken against]

anti-lock *an-ti-lok'*, *adj* (of a braking system) designed to prevent the wheels of a vehicle locking when the brakes are applied. [**anti-** (1)]

antilogarithm *an-ti-log'ə-ridhm* or *-rithm*, *n* a number of which a particular number is the logarithm — contracted to **an'tilog**. [**anti-** (3)]

Some words with **anti-** prefix; see **anti-** entry for numbered senses.

anti-pred'ator *adj* (1).
anti-ra'cist *adj* (2).
antiri'ot *adj* (1).
anti-roll' *adj* (1).
antirust' *adj* (1).
antiship' *adj* (1).
antiskid' *adj* (1).
antisub'marine *adj* (1).
antitank' *adj* (1).
antiterr'orist *adj* (1).
antitheft' *adj* (1).
antitrinitā'rian *adj* and *n* (2).
antitrinitā'rianism *n* (2).
antivī'ral *adj* (1).
antivī'rus *adj* (2).
antiwar' *adj* (2).

antilogy *an-til'ə-ji, n* a contradiction. — *adj* **antil'ogous** (*-gəs*) of the contrary kind; negatively electrified by heating. [Gr *antilogiā* contradiction]

Antilope *an-til'ō-pē, n* the Indian antelope genus. — *adj* **antil'opine** (*-pīn*) of antelopes. [Form of **antelope**, adopted by P S Pallas, German naturalist (1741–1811)]

antilymphocyte serum *an-ti-lim'fə-sīt sē'rəm*, (*immunol*) *n* serum used to prevent defensive action of lymphocytes, eg in cases where they would reject an organ transplanted into the body. [**anti-** (1)]

antimacassar *an-ti-mə-kas'ər, n* a covering for chair-backs, etc to protect them from being soiled (*orig* from macassar oil or other grease in the hair) or for ornament. [**anti-** (1)]

anti-marketeer *an-ti-mär-ki-tēr', n* a British person who opposed Britain's entry into or opposes British membership of the European Common Market. [**anti-** (2)]

antimasque or **antimask** *an'ti-mäsk, n* a farcical interlude dividing the parts of, or preceding, the more serious masque. [**anti-** (3)]

antimatter *an'ti-mat'ər, n* hypothetical extraterrestrial matter that would consist of particles (antiparticles) similar to those of terrestrial matter but of opposite electrical charge or, in the case of the neutron, reversed magnetic polarity. [**anti-** (3)]

antimetabole *an-ti-mə-tab'ol-i*, (*rhetoric*) *n* a figure of speech in which the same words or ideas are repeated in inverse order, eg Quarles's 'Be wisely worldly, but not worldly wise'. [Gr]

antimetathesis *an-ti-mə-tath'ə-sis*, (*rhetoric*) *n* inversion of the members of an antithesis, as in Crabbe's 'A poem is a speaking picture; a picture, a mute poem'. [Gr]

antimnemonic *an-ti-ni-mon'ik, adj* tending to weaken the memory. — Also *n*. [**anti-** (1)]

antimony *an'ti-mən-i, n* a brittle, bluish-white element (atomic no 51; symbol **Sb**, for stibium) of metallic appearance; type (*obs printers' slang*). — *n* **an'timonate** (*-mən-*) or **antimō'niate** a salt of any antimonic acid. — *adj* **antimonial** (*-mō'ni-əl*) pertaining to, or containing, antimony. — *n* a drug containing antimony. — *adj* **antimonic** (*-mon'ik*) containing pentavalent antimony. — *adj* **antimō'nious** containing trivalent antimony. — *n* **an'timonide** a binary compound with antimony as one of its constituents. — *n* **an'timonite** a salt of antimonious acid; the mineral stibnite (not chemically an antimonite). [LL *antimōnium*, of unknown origin, prob from some Arabic word]

antimutagen *an-ti-mū'tə-jən*, (*biol*) *n* a compound that inhibits the action of a mutagen. [**anti-** (1)]

antinephritic *an-ti-ne-frit'ik*, (*med*) *adj* acting against diseases of the kidney. — Also *n*. [**anti-** (1)]

antineutrino *an-ti-nū-trē'nō*, (*phys*) *n* the antiparticle of the neutrino. — *n* **antineu'tron** (*-tron*) an uncharged particle that combines with the neutron with mutual annihilation and emission of energy. [**anti-** (3)]

anting. See **ant**.

antinode *an'ti-nōd*, (*phys*) *n* a point of maximum disturbance midway between nodes. — *adj* **antinōd'al**. [**anti-** (3)]

antinomian *an-ti-nō'mi-ən, n* a person who denies the obligatoriness of moral law; a person who believes that Christians are emancipated by the gospel from the obligation to keep the moral law, faith alone being necessary. — Also *adj*. — *n* **antino'mianism**. — *adj* **antinomic** (*-nom'ik*) or **antinom'ical** pertaining to, of the nature of, or involving, antinomy. — *n* **antinomy** (*an-tin'ə-mi*) a contradiction in a law; a conflict of authority; conclusions discrepant though apparently logical. [**anti-** (1) and Gr *nomos* law]

anti-novel *an'ti-nov-l* or *-nuv-l, n* a type of novel of the mid-20c which largely discards plot and character and concerns itself with tiny inner dramas on the border of consciousness. [**anti-** (3)]

Antiochene *an-tī'ō-kēn* or **Antiochian** *an-ti-ō'ki-ən, adj* of the Syrian city of *Antioch*; of the eclectic philosophy of *Antiochus* of Ascalon; of any of the Seleucid kings of that name. — *n* **Antio'chianism** a school of theology in the 4c and 5c in revolt against allegorizing of Scripture by the Alexandrian school.

antiodontalgic *an-ti-ō-dont-al'jik*, (*med*) *adj* of use against toothache. — Also *n*. [**anti-** (1), Gr *odous, odontos* tooth, and *algeein* to suffer pain]

antioxidant *an-ti-ok'si-dənt, n* a substance that prevents or inhibits oxidation. — Also *adj*. [**anti-** (1)]

antipapal *an-ti-pā'pəl, adj* opposed to the pope or the papal system. — See also **antipope**. [**anti-** (2)]

antiparallel *an-ti-par'ə-lel*, (*geom*) *adj* making with a transverse line an internal angle equal to the external angle made by another line. — Also *n*. [**anti-** (3)]

antiparticle *an'ti-pär-ti-kl, n* the 'pair' of an elementary particle, particle and antiparticle being mutually destructive, having the same mass and spin but having opposite values for their other properties (eg charge, baryon number, strangeness). [**anti-** (3)]

antipasto *an'ti-päs-tō*, (*Ital*) *n* an hors d'œuvre, an appetizer. [Cf **antepast**]

antipathy *an-tip'əth-i, n* aversion, dislike, negative feeling; repugnance; animosity, hostility; an object of antipathy; opposition in feeling (*obs*); incompatibility (*obs*); mutual opposition (*obs*). — *adj* **antipathet'ic** or **antipathet'ical**. — *adv* **antipathet'ically**. — *adj* **antipathic** (*an-ti-path'ik*) belonging to, displaying or feeling antipathy; opposite; contrary. — *n* **antip'athist** a person possessed by an antipathy. [**anti-** (1) and Gr *pathos* feeling]

antiperiodic *an-ti-pē-ri-od'ik*, (*med*) *adj* destroying the periodicity of diseases; antimalarial. — *n* a drug with such an effect. [**anti-** (1)]

antiperistalsis *an-ti-per-i-stal'sis*, (*med* and *zool*) *n* action of intestinal waves of contraction contrary to normal, from anus to mouth, forcing contents of the intestine upwards. — *adj* **antiperistal'tic**. [**anti-** (3)]

antiperistasis *an-ti-pər-ist'ə-sis*, (*archaic*) *n* opposition of circumstances; resistance or reaction. [Gr, surrounding, interchange, from *anti* against, and *peristasis* a circumstance, from *peri* around, and *stasis* a setting, stand]

anti-personnel *an'ti-pûr-sən-el', adj* intended to destroy military personnel and other persons, but not necessarily equipment, etc. [**anti-** (1)]

antiperspirant *an-ti-pûr'spi-rənt, n* a substance that helps to stop perspiration when applied to the skin. — Also *adj*. [**anti-** (1)]

antipetalous *an-ti-pet'ə-ləs*, (*bot*) *adj* opposite a petal. [**anti-** (3)]

antiphiloprogenitive *an-ti-fil-ō-prō-jen'i-tiv, adj* intended to prevent the production of offspring. [**anti-** (1)]

antiphlogistic *an-ti-flə-jist'ik, adj* acting against heat, or (*med*) inflammation. — *n* a medicine to allay inflammation. [**anti-** (1)]

antiphon *an'ti-fon, n* alternate chanting or singing; a type of church music sung by two parties each responding to the other (also called **antiph'ony** *-ən-i*). — *adj* **antiph'onal**. — *n* a book of antiphons or of anthems (also called **antiph'onary** and **antiph'oner**). — *adv* **antiph'onally**. — *adj* (*rare*) **antiphonic** (*-fon'*) or (*obs*) **antiphon'ical** mutually responsive. — *adv* **antiphon'ically**. [Gr *anti* in return, and *phōnē* voice, a doublet of **anthem**]

antiphrasis *an-tif'rə-sis*, (*rhetoric*) *n* the use of words in a sense opposite to the literal one. — *adj* **antiphrastic** (*an-ti-fras'tik*) or (*obs*) **antiphras'tical** involving antiphrasis; ironical. — *adv* **antiphras'tically**. [Gr, from *anti* against, and *phrasis* speech]

antipodes *an-tip'ə-dēz, n pl* (also *sing*; sometimes with *cap*) Australia and New Zealand, as being diametrically opposite to Great Britain or Europe on the surface of the globe; *orig* those who live on the other side of the globe, or on opposite sides (literally, standing feet to feet; *obs*); a point or place diametrically opposite to another on the surface of the earth or of any globular body or sphere; a pair of points or places so related to each other; the exact opposite of a person or a thing: — *sing* (*rare*) **antipode** (*an'ti-pōd*). — *adj* **antip'odal** or (*esp* of the Antipodes, sometimes with *cap*) **antipodē'an**. — **antipodal cells** (*bot*) in flowering plants, three cells in the embryo-sac at the end remote from the micropyle, representing the prothallus. [Gr *antipodes*, pl of *antipous* with feet opposite, from *pous*, *podos* a foot]

antipole *an'ti-pōl*, *n* the opposite pole; direct opposite. [**anti-** (3)]

antipope *an'ti-pōp*, *n* a pontiff set up in opposition to one asserted to be canonically chosen, eg one of those who resided at Avignon in the 13c and 14c. — See also **antipapal**. [**anti-** (3)]

antiproton *an-ti-prō'ton*, (*phys*) *n* a short-lived particle comparable to the proton but negatively charged. [**anti-** (3)]

antipruritic *an-ti-proo-rit'ik*, (*med*) *n* a substance that reduces itchiness. — Also *adj*. [**anti-** (1)]

antipsychotic *an-ti-sī-kot'ik*, (*med*) *adj* (of a drug) alleviating psychosis. — *n* an antipsychotic drug. [**anti-** (1)]

antipyretic *an-ti-pī-ret'ik*, (*med*) *adj* counteracting fever. — *n* an antipyretic agent. [Gr *anti-* against, and *pyretos* fever, from *pȳr* fire]

antiq. *abbrev*: antiquarian; antiques; antiquities.

antiquark *an'ti-kwärk*, (*phys*) *n* the antiparticle corresponding to the quark. [**anti-** (3)]

antiquary *an'ti-kwər-i*, *n* a person who studies, collects or deals in relics of the past, but not usually very ancient things. — *adj* (*Shakesp*) ancient. — *adj* **antiquarian** (*-kwā'ri-ən*) connected with the study of antiquities; (of books) old and rare. — *n* an antiquary; before metrication, a size of drawing-paper (53 × 31in). — *n* **antiquā'rianism**. [L *antīquārius*, from *antīquus* old]

antique *an-tēk'*, or formerly *an'tik* (and sometimes written **antick**, now *obs*), *adj* ancient; of a good old age, olden (now *archaic* or *rhetorical* in a good sense); (of articles or furniture) made in an earlier period and sought by collectors; relating to, or dealing in, antiques; old-fashioned; savouring of bygone times; after the manner of the ancients. — *n* anything very old; an old relic; a piece of old furniture or other object sought by collectors; a type of thick and bold face with lines of equal thickness (*printing*). — *vt* to alter the appearance of (wood, leather, etc) so that it seems very old. — *vi* (*US*) to collect or shop for antiques. — *vt* **antiquate** (*an'ti-kwāt*) to make antique, old or obsolete; to put out of use. — *adj* **an'tiquated**. — *n* **antiquā'tion**. — *adv* **antique'ly**. — *n* **antique'ness**. — *n* **antiquitarian** (*an-tik-wi-tā'ri-ən*) a person attached to old ways or beliefs. — *n* **antiq'uity** ancient times, *esp* the times of the ancient Greeks and Romans; great age; old age, seniority (*Shakesp*); ancient style; the people of old time; (now *usu* in *pl*) a relic of the past; (in *pl*) manners, customs, etc of ancient times. — **the antique** ancient work in art; the style of ancient art. — See also **antic**. [L *antīquus* old, ancient, from *ante* before; influenced by Fr *antique*]

antirachitic *an-ti-ra-kit'ik*, (*med*) *adj* tending to prevent or cure rickets. — Also *n*. [**anti-** (1)]

anti-racism *an-ti-rās'izm*, *n* opposition to prejudice and persecution on grounds of race, and support for policies that promote equality among and tolerance between groups of different racial origins. — *adj* and *n* **anti-ra'cist**. [**anti-** (2)]

antirrhinum *an-ti-rī'nəm*, *n* any plant of the snapdragon genus *Antirrhinum*. [Latinized from Gr *antirrīnon* snapdragon, from *anti* like, mimicking, and *rhīs*, *rhīnos* nose]

antiscian *an-tish'i-ən*, *n* a dweller on the same meridian on the other side of the equator, whose shadow at noon falls in the opposite direction. — Also *adj*. [**anti-** (3) and Gr *skiā* shadow]

antiscorbutic *an-ti-skör-būt'ik*, (*med*) *adj* acting against scurvy. — *n* a remedy or preventive for scurvy. [**anti-** (1)]

antiscriptural *an-ti-skrip'chər-əl*, *adj* opposed to the authority of the Bible. [**anti-** (2)]

anti-Semite *an-ti-sem'īt*, or *-sēm'*, *n* a hater of Semites, *esp* Jews, or of their influence. — *adj* **anti-Semitic** (*-sim-it'*). — *n* **anti-Semitism** (*-sem'* or *-sēm'*). [**anti-** (2)]

antisepalous *an-ti-sep'ə-ləs*, (*bot*) *adj* opposite a sepal. [**anti-** (3)]

antisepsis *an-ti-sep'sis*, (*med*) *n* destruction, or inhibition of growth, of bacteria by a chemical agent. — *adj* **antisep'tic**. — *n* an antiseptic agent. — *n* **antisep'ticism** (*-sizm*) antiseptic treatment. — *adv* **antisept'ically**. — *vt* **antisep'ticize** or **-ise** (*-sīz*). [Gr *anti-* against, and *sēpsis* putrefaction]

antiserum *an'ti-sēr-əm*, (*med* and *biochem*) *n* a serum which contains antibodies: — *pl* **an'tiserums** or **an'tisera**. [*anti*body and **serum**]

antisocial *an-ti-sō'shl*, *adj* opposed to the good of society, or the principles of society; disinclined to mix in society; without social instincts. — *n* **antiso'cialism**. — *n* **antiso'cialist** formerly, an unsociable person; an opponent of socialism. — *n* **antisociality** (*-shi-al'i-ti*) unsociableness; opposition to the principles of society. — *adv* **antiso'cially**. [**anti-** (2)]

antispasmodic *an-ti-spaz-mod'ik*, (*med*) *adj* preventing or alleviating spasms or convulsions. — *n* a remedy, or alleviating agent, for spasms. [**anti-** (1)]

antispast *an'ti-spast*, (*prosody*) *n* a foot composed of an iambus and a trochee. — *adj* **antispast'ic**. [Gr *antispastos*, from *antispaein* to draw back, from *spaein* to draw]

antistatic *an-ti-stat'ik*, *adj* having the property of counteracting static electricity; not attracting positively charged ions, eg dust. — Also **antistat** (*an'* or *-stat'*). — Also *n*. — **antistatic agent** (*textiles*) a substance applied to a textile to prevent its becoming charged with static electricity by friction during processing or wear; **antistatic fluid** a fluid applied to prevent the effects of static electricity on gramophone disks (dust) and sound film (scratches on the track). [**anti-** (1)]

antistrophe *an-tis'trə-fi* or *-trō-fi*, *n* the returning dance in Greek choruses, reversing the movement of the strophe (qv); the stanza answering the strophe in the same metre; repetition in reverse order (*rhetoric*); retortion of an argument (*rhetoric*); an inverse relation. — *adj* **antistrophic** (*an-ti-strof'ik*). — *adv* **antistroph'ically**. — *n* **antis'trophon** (*rhetoric*) an argument retorted on an opponent. [Gr *antistrophē*, from *strophē* a turning]

antisyzygy *an-ti-si'zi-ji*, *n* union of opposites. [Gr *antisyzygiā*, from *anti-* against, opposite, and *syzygiā* union, coupling from *sy-*, *syn-* with, together, and *zygon* a yoke]

antithalian *an-ti-thə-lī'ən*, *adj* opposed to mirth or fun. [**anti-** (1) and Gr *Thaleia*, the comic muse]

antitheism *an-ti-thē'izm*, *n* doctrine antagonistic to theism; denial of the existence of a God; opposition to God. — *n* **antithē'ist**. — *adj* **antithēist'ic**. [**anti-** (1) and Gr *theos* a god]

antithesis *an-tith'i-sis*, *n* a figure in which thoughts or words are balanced in contrast (*rhetoric*); a thesis or proposition opposing another; opposition; the direct opposite (*of* or *to*): — *pl* **antith'eses** (*-sēz*). — *n* **an'tithet** (*-thet*; *rare*) an instance of antithesis. — *adj* **antithet'ic** or **antithet'ical**. — *adv* **antithet'ically**. [Gr, from *anti-* against, opposite, and *thesis* placing]

antithrombin *an-ti-throm'bin*, (*med* and *biochem*) *n* a substance produced by the liver which prevents clotting of the blood in the veins. [**anti-** (1) and Gr *thrombos* a clot]

antitoxin *an-ti-tok'sin*, (*med* and *immunol*) *n* a substance that neutralizes toxin formed in the body. — *adj* **antitox'ic**. [**anti-** (1)]

antitrade *an'ti-trād*, *n* a wind that blows in the opposite direction to the trade wind, ie in the northern hemisphere from the north-east and in the southern hemisphere from the south-east. [**anti-** (3)]

antitragus *an-ti-trā'gəs*, (*anatom*) *n* a prominence of the external ear, opposite the tragus: — *pl* **antitrā'gī**. [**anti-** (3)]

antitrust *an-ti-trust'*, (mainly *US*) *adj* (of legislation, etc) directed against the adverse effects of trusts or other such monopolies on commerce. [**anti-** (1)]

antitussive *an-ti-tus'iv*, (*med*) *adj* tending to alleviate or suppress coughing. — *n* an antitussive agent. [**anti-** (1) and L *tussis* a cough]

antitype *an'ti-tīp*, *n* that which corresponds to the type; that which is prefigured by the type; a contrary type. — *adj* **antityp'al**, **antitypic** (*-tip'ik*) or **antityp'ical**. [**anti-** (3)]

antivaccinationist *an-ti-vak-si-nā'shən-ist*, *n* an opponent of vaccination. — *n* **antivaccinā'tionism**. [**anti-** (2)]

antivenin *an-ti-ven'in*, or **antivenene** *-ēn'*, *n* an antitoxin counteracting (*esp* snake) venom. [**anti-** (1)]

antivitamin *an'ti-vit-ə-min*, or *-vīt-*, (*med*) *n* a substance with a chemical structure very similar to a vitamin, which prevents that vitamin from having its effect. [**anti-** (1)]

antivivisection *an-ti-viv-i-sek'shən*, *n* opposition to vivisection. — *n* **antivivisec'tionism**. — *n* **antivivisec'tionist**. [**anti-** (2)]

antler *ant'lər*, *n* one of a pair of bony outgrowths from the frontal bone of a deer; *orig* the lowest branch of a stag's horn, then any branch, then the whole. — *adj* **ant'lered**. — **ant'ler-moth** a noctuid moth (*Charaeas graminis*), with antler-like markings on the wings, its larvae very destructive to pastures. [OFr *antoillier*; assumed derivation from LL *ant(e)oculāris* in front of the eyes, is unlikely]

antlia *ant'li-ə*, *n* the suctorial proboscis of insects of the Lepidoptera order (*pl* **ant'liae** *-ē*); (with *cap*) the Air Pump, a small southern constellation. — *adj* **ant'liate**. [L *antlia* a pump, from Gr *antliā* bilge-water]

antoninianus *an-tə-nin-i-ā'nəs*, (*antiq*) *n* a Roman coin equal to two denarii in value. [From 3c emperor *Antoninus*]

antonomasia *ant-on-o-mā'zi-ə*, *n* the use of an epithet, or the name of an office or attributive, for a person's proper name (eg his lordship for an earl); and conversely (eg a Napoleon for a great conqueror). [Gr, from *antonomasiā*, from *onomazein* to name, from *onoma* a name]

Anton Piller *an'ton pil'ər* or **Anton Piller order** (*ör'dər*), (*law*) *n* in English law (*esp* in copyright cases) a High Court order by which a plaintiff (or his or her representatives) may enter and search a defendant's premises, and seize material evidence. [*Anton Piller*, plaintiff to whom in 1976 such an order was granted]

antonym *ant'ə-nim*, *n* a word opposite in meaning to another. — *adj* **antonym'ic** or **anton'ymous**. — *n* **anton'ymy**. [Gr *onyma* = *onoma* a name]

antre *an'tər*, (*poetic*) *n* a cave. — Also **an'tar** (*Shakesp*). [Fr; L *antrum*, from Gr *antron* a cave]

antrorse *an-trörs'*, (*biol*) *adj* turned up or forward. [From *anterus* (hypothetical positive of L *anterior* front) and L *versus* turned]

antrum *an'trəm*, (now *esp anatom*) *n* a cavity: — *pl* **an'tra**. [L, cave]

Antrycide® *an'tri-sīd*, *n* a drug useful for cure and prevention of trypanosome diseases.

ANU *abbrev*: Australian National University (in Canberra).

Anubis *a-nū'bis*, *n* the ancient Egyptian jackal-headed god of the dead. [L, from Gr *Anoubis*, from Egyp *Anup*]

anucleate *ā-nū'kli-āt* or **anucleated** *ā-nū-kli-āt'id*, *adj* without a nucleus. [Gr *a-* (privative) and **nucleate**]

anuria *an-ū'ri-ə*, (*med*) *n* failure in secretion of urine. [Gr *an-* (privative) and *ouron* urine]

anurous *an-ū'rəs* or **anourous** *an-ōō'rəs*, (*zool*) *adj* tailless. — *n pl* **Anu'ra** or **Anou'ra** the Salientia or tailless amphibians, frogs and toads. [Gr *an-* (privative) and *ourā* tail]

anus *ā'nəs*, (*anatom* and *zool*) *n* the opening at the end of the alimentary canal by which undigested residues are excreted. — *adj* **ā'nal** of or pertaining to the anus; of or pertaining to the second stage of psychosexual development, in which the child's interest and gratification is concentrated on the excretory function (*psychol*); (of an adult) categorized as having personality traits such as obsessiveness, attention to detail, and obstinacy, thought to result from fixation at the anal stage (*psychol*). — *adv* **ā'nally**. — *adj* and *n* **anal retentive** (of or relating to) a person having anal personality traits. [L *ānus*, *-ī* a ring]

anvil *an'vil*, *n* an iron block on which smiths hammer metal into shape; the incus of the ear. — **anvil secateurs** secateurs with two straight blades, the cutting blade closing against a blunt flat blade. — **on** or **upon the anvil** in preparation, under discussion. [OE *anfilte*, *onfilti*]

anxious *ang(k)'shəs*, *adj* uneasy with fear and desire regarding something doubtful; solicitous; eager (for something, or to do something). — *n* **anxiety** (*ang(g)-zī'i-ti*) a state of being anxious; a state of chronic apprehension as a symptom of mental disorder. — *adj* **anxiolytic** (*angk-si-ō-lit'ik*; *med*) of a drug, reducing anxiety and tension. — Also *n*. — *adv* **an'xiously**. — *n* **an'xiousness**. — **the age of anxiety** now, the present time (W H Auden, 1947). [L *anxius*, from *angere* to press tightly. See **anger**, **anguish**]

any *en'i*, *adj* and *pronoun* one (unspecified); some; whichever, no matter which. — *adv* (*usu* with a *compar adj*) at all, to an appreciable extent. — *n* and *pronoun* **an'ybody** any single person; a person of any account. — *adv* **an'yhow** in any way whatever; in any case, at least; indifferently, carelessly. — *n* and *pronoun* **an'yone** (or **any one**) anybody at all; anybody whatever. — *adv* **an'yroad** (*dialect*) anyway. — *n* and *pronoun* **an'ything** a thing (unspecified), as opposed to nothing. — *adv* to any extent. — *n* **anythingā'rian** a person with no beliefs in particular. — *n* **anythingā'rianism**. — *adv* **an'ytime** at any time. — *adv* **an'yway** or (*dialect*, *esp US*) **an'yways** anyhow; in any case; in any manner (*archaic*). — *adv* **an'ywhen** (*rare* or *dialect*). — *adv* **an'ywhere** in or to any place. — *adv* **an'ywhither** (*archaic*; *rare*). — *adv* **an'ywise** (now chiefly *US*) in any manner, to any degree. — **any amount** (*colloq*) a lot; **any day** in any circumstances; **any more** any longer; **any old** any, with connotations of indifference, lack of thought, etc (**any old how** without any special care; **any old thing** anything at all); **anyone else** any other person; **anything but** certainly not, by no means; **anything goes** any sort of behaviour, dress, person, etc is tolerated or accepted; **at any rate** whatever may happen; at all events; **like anything** very much; with great vigour. [OE *ǣnig*, from *ān* one]

ANZAAS *an'zəs* or *an'zas*, *abbrev*: Australian and New Zealand Association for the Advancement of Science.

Anzac *an'zak*, *n orig* a member of the *A*ustralian and *N*ew *Z*ealand *A*rmy *C*orps during World War I; any Australian or New Zealand soldier. — Also *adj*. — **Anzac Day** April 25, a public holiday in Australia and New Zealand in memory of the Anzac landing in Gallipoli (1915).

anziani *ant-sē-än'ē*, (*Ital*) *n pl* councillors, senators.

Anzus *an'zəs*, (also **ANZUS**) *abbrev*: (the alliance between) *A*ustralia, *N*ew *Z*ealand and the *U*nited *S*tates.

AO *abbrev*: Army Order; Officer of (the Order of) Australia.

AOB or **aob** *abbrev*: any other business.

AOC *abbrev*: Air Officer Commanding; (of wine) appellation d'origine contrôlée (qv).

AOCB *abbrev*: any other competent business.

ao dai *ow dī*, *n* a traditional Vietnamese, long, high-necked tunic for women, slit to the waist at the sides, worn over trousers. [Viet]

AONB *abbrev*: Area of Outstanding Natural Beauty (protected area).

Aonian *ā-ō'ni-ən*, *adj* pertaining to *Aonia* in Boeotia in Greece, or to the Muses supposed to dwell there. — **Aonian fount** the fountain Aganippe, on a slope of Mount Helicon (the Aonian mount).

AOR *abbrev*: adult-oriented rock; album-oriented rock (or radio).

aor. *abbrev*: aorist.

aorist *ā'ər-ist*, (*gram*) *n* a tense, *esp* in Greek, expressing simple past time, with no implications of continuance, repetition or the like. — *adj* **aorist'ic**. [Gr *aoristos* indefinite, from *a-* (privative) and *horistos* limited]

aorta *ā-ör'tə*, *n* (*anatom* and *zool*) the main arterial vessel that carries blood from the heart. — *adj* **aor'tal** or **aor'tic**. — *n* **aortī'tis** (*pathol*) inflammation of the aorta. [Gr *aortē*, from *aeirein* to raise up]

aoudad *ä'o͞o-dad*, *n* a N African wild sheep. [Native name in French spelling]

à outrance *a o͞o-trãs*, (*Fr*) to the utmost; to the death; to the bitter end.

AP *abbrev*: Air Police (*US*); American plan; anti-personnel; Associated Press (*US*).

ap *abbrev*: additional premium; *ante prandium* (*L*), before a meal (on prescriptions); author's proof.

ap. *abbrev*: apothecary; apparent(ly).

apace *ə-pās'*, *adv* literally, at a quick pace; swiftly. [**a-**[1] and **pace**[1]]

Apache *ə-pa'chi*, *n* a N American Indian of a group of tribes in Arizona, New Mexico, etc; (**apache** *ə-pash'*) a lawless ruffian or hooligan in Paris or elsewhere. [Perh Zuñi *āpachu* enemy]

APACS *abbrev*: Association for Payment Clearing Services (*UK*).

apadana *ap-ə-dä'nə*, *n* the great hall or throne room of an Ancient Persian palace, free-standing, with many columns and often a portico. [OPers *apadāna* palace]

apage *ap'ə-jē* or *ap-a-ge*, or **apage Satanas** (*sat'an-as*), (*Gr*) away, depart (Satan).

apagoge *ap-ə-gō'jē*, *n* reduction to absurdity, indirect proof by showing the falsehood of the opposite. — *adj* **apagogic** (*-goj'ik*) or **apagog'ical**. — *adv* **apagog'ically**. [Gr *apagōgē* leading away, from *apagein* to lead off]

apaid. See **apay**.

apanage. See **appanage**.

apart *ə-pärt'*, *adv* separately; aside; asunder, parted; separate; out of consideration. — *n* **apart'ness**. — **set apart** to separate; to devote (to a special purpose); **take apart** (*slang*) to reprimand severely; **tell apart** to distinguish, see the difference between. [Fr *à part*, from L *ad partem* to the side]

apartheid *a-pärt'hāt* or *-pär'tīd*, *n* segregation and separate development (of races) (also *fig*, of eg segregation of the sexes). [Afrik]

apartment *ə-pärt'mənt*, *n* (now *usu* in *pl*) a separate room in a house, used or occupied by a particular person or party; a flat, a set of rooms *usu* on one floor of a building (*usu* used as a dwelling; mainly *NAm*); a compartment (*obs*). — *adj* **apartmental** (*-ment'əl*). [Fr *appartement* a suite of rooms forming a complete dwelling, from L *ad* to, and *partīre*, *partīrī* to divide, from *pars*, *partis* part]

apatetic *ap-ə-tet'ik*, (*zool*) *adj* of an animal's coloration or marking which closely resembles that of another species or of its surroundings. [Gr *apatētikos* deceitful]

apathaton *ə-path'i-tən*, *n* (*Shakesp*) for **epitheton**.

apathy *ap'əth-i*, *n* lack of feeling, passion or interest; indifference. — *adj* **apathet'ic** or **apathet'ical**. — *adv* **apathet'ically**. [Gr *apatheia*, from *a-* (privative) and *pathos* feeling]

apatite *ap'ə-tīt*, *n* a mineral consisting of calcium phosphate and fluoride (or chloride, hydroxyl or carbonate ions), a major constituent of the bones and teeth of vertebrates, and of sedimentary phosphate rocks. [Gr *apatē* deceit, from its having been confused with other minerals]

Apatosaurus *ə-pat-ə-sör'əs*, *n* the scientific name for Brontosaurus. [Gr *apatē* deceit, and *sauros* lizard]

apay or **appay** *ə-pā'*, *vt* to satisfy (*archaic*); to repay (*obs*): — *pap* and *pat* **apaid'**, **apayd'**, **appaid'** or **appayd'**. [OFr *apayer*, from L *ad*, and *pācāre*, from *pāx* peace]

APB (*NAm*) *abbrev*: all-points bulletin, ie one giving details of a wanted person, crime, etc issued by one police station and transmitted to all others in the region or state.

APC *abbrev*: armoured personnel carrier (*military*); aspirin, phenacetin and caffeine (*pharm*); automatic public convenience.

ape *āp*, *n* a monkey; *specif* an anthropoid primate; a large monkey without a tail or with a very short one; a mimic; an imitator. — *vt* to mimic; to imitate. — *n* **ape'dom**. — *n* **ape'hood**. — *n* **ap'ery** the conduct of someone who apes; any ape-like action; a colony of apes (*rare*). — *adj* **ap'ish** like an ape; imitative; foppish, silly. — *adv* **ap'ishly**. — *n* **ap'ishness** or (*Carlyle*) **ap'ism**. — **ape'man** any of several extinct primates thought to have been intermediate in development between man and the higher apes. — *adj* **ape'-shit** (*vulg US slang*) berserk; destructively crazy; extremely excited (see also **go ape**). — **go ape** (or *vulg* **ape-shit**; *US slang*) to go crazy (with *over* or *for*); **God's ape** (*obs*) a born fool; **make someone one's ape** or **put an ape in someone's hood** (*obs*) to make a fool of someone. [OE *apa*; Ger *Affe*]

apeak or **apeek** *ə-pēk*, (*naut*) *adv* vertical. [**a-**[1]]

apepsia *a-pep'si-ə*, (also **apep'sy**) (*med*) *n* failure or absence of digestive function; weakness of digestion (*obs*). [Gr *apepsiā* indigestion; *a-* (privative) and *peptein* to digest]

aperçu *a-per-sü*, *n* a summary exposition; a brief outline; a glimpse; an immediate intuitive insight. [Fr *aperçu* survey, sketch; literally (pa p of *apercevoir*), perceived]

aperient *ə-pē'ri-ənt*, *n* and *adj* (*med*) laxative. — *adj* **aperitive** (*med*; *ə-per'i-tiv*) laxative. — *n* same as **apéritif**; an aperitive medicine. [L *aperīre*, *apertum* to open]

aperiodic *ā-pē-ri-od'ik*, *adj* not periodic; coming to rest without oscillation (*phys*). — *n* **aperiodicity** (*-ə-dis'i-ti*). [Gr *a-* (privative) and **periodic**]

apéritif or **aperitif** *ə-per-i-tēf'*, *-per'*, or (*Fr*) *a-pā-rē-tēf*, *n* a drink taken as an appetizer. [Fr, from LL *aperitīvus*, from *aperīre* to open]

a-per-se *ā-pər-sē*, *n* the letter **a** by itself, making the word **a** (*archaic*); anything unique in excellence (*fig*). [L *a per sē* **a** by itself; cf **ampersand**]

apert *ə-pûrt'*, (*archaic*) *adj* open, public. — *n* **apert'ness**. [OFr, from L *apertus* open]

aperture *ap'ər-chər*, *n* an opening; a hole; the diameter of the opening through which light passes in an optical instrument such as a camera; the effective area over which an antenna extracts power from an incident wave (*radar* and *telecomm*). [L *apertura*, from *aperīre* to open]

apery. See **ape**.

apetalous *ə-pet'əl-əs*, (*bot*) *adj* without petals. — *n* **apet'aly**. [Gr *a-* (privative) and *petalon* a leaf]

à peu près, *a pø pre* (*Fr*) nearly.

APEX or **Apex** *ā'pex*, *abbrev*: (in full **Apex Trust**) Advancement of the Employment Prospects of Ex-offenders; advance purchase excursion (a reduced airline or long-distance rail fare); Association of Professional, Executive, Clerical and Computer Staff.

apex *ā'peks*, *n* the summit, tip or point; a vertex (*geom*); the culminating point or climax of anything: — *pl* **ā'pexes** or **apices** (*āp'* or *ap'i-sēz*). [L *apex*, *apicis* a tip]

apfelstrudel *ap-fəl-s(h)tro͞o'dəl*, *n* a sweet pastry containing apples, spices, etc. [Ger]

Apgar test *ap'gär test*, (*med*) *n* a system used to assess the health of a newborn baby immediately (*usu* at one and five minutes) after birth, the **Apgar score** (maximum total 10) comprising points for heart rate, muscle tone, colour, respiratory effort and response to stimulation. [After Virginia *Apgar*, US anaesthetist (1909–74)]

aphaeresis or **apheresis** *a-fē'ri-sis*, (*gram*) *n* the taking away of a sound or syllable at the beginning of a word. [Gr *aphairesis* a taking away, from *apo* away and *haireein* to take]

aphagia *ə-fā'j(i)-ə*, (*med* and *zool*) *n* inability or unwillingness to swallow or eat; (of the imago of certain insects) inability to feed. [Gr *a-* (privative) and *phagia*, from *phagein* to eat]

Aphaniptera *af-an-ip'tər-ə, n pl* the flea order (or suborder) of wingless, blood-sucking insects with well-developed hindlegs for jumping. — *adj* **aphanip'terous**. [Gr *aphanēs* invisible, and *pteron* wing]

aphanite *af'ə-nīt, n* any rock of such close texture that separate minerals contained within it cannot be distinguished by the naked eye. [Gr *aphanēs* invisible]

aphasia *a-fā'z(h)i-ə,* (*pathol*) *n* inability to express thought in words, or inability to understand thought as expressed in the spoken or written words of others, caused by brain disease or damage. — *n* and *adj* **aphā'siac**. — *adj* **aphasic** (*a-fā'zik* or *a-faz'ik*). [Gr *a-* (privative) and *phasis* speech, from *phanai* to speak]

aphelion *a-fē'li-ən,* (*astron*) *n* a planet's furthest point in its orbit from the sun: — *pl* **aphē'lia**. — *adj* (*rare*) **aphē'lian**. [Gr *apo* from, and *hēlios* sun]

apheliotropic *a-fē-li-ə-trop'ik,* (*bot,* etc) *adj* (eg of leaves, roots) turning away from the sun. — *n* **apheliot'ropism**. [Gr *apo* from, *hēlios* sun, and *tropikos* pertaining to turning]

apheresis. See **aphaeresis**.

aphesis *af'i-sis, n* the gradual and unintentional loss of an unaccented vowel at the beginning of a word (as in *squire* from *esquire*), a special form of aphaeresis. — *adj* **aphetic** (*ə-fet'ik*). — *vt* **aph'etize** or **-ise**. [Gr *aphesis* letting go, from *apo* from, and *hienai* to send]

aphis *af'is, āf'is* or **aphid** *af'id, āf'id, n* a plant-louse (eg greenfly or blackfly), a small homopterous insect that sucks plant juices: — *pl* **aph'ides** (*-i-dēz*) or **aph'ids**. — *adj* and *n* **aphid'ian**. — *adj* **aphid'ious**. — *n* **aph'icide** or **aphid'icide** (*-sīd*) a substance or agent that kills aphids. [Ety unknown]

aphonia *a-fō'ni-ə* or **aphony** *af'ə-ni, n* (*pathol*) loss of voice from hysteria, disease of larynx or vocal cords, etc. — *adj* **aphonic** (*-fon'*) non-vocal, having no sound. — *adj* **aphonous** (*af'ə-nəs*) voiceless. [Gr *a-* (privative) and *phōnē* voice]

aphorism *af'ər-izm, n* a concise statement of a principle in any science; a brief, pithy saying; an adage. — *n* **aph'orist**. — *adj* **aphoris'tic**. — *adv* **aphorist'ically**. — *vi* **aph'orize** or **-ise**. — *n* **aph'orizer** or **-s-**. [Gr *aphorizein* to define, from *apo* from, and *horos* a limit]

aphotic *a-fō'tik, adj* lightless (eg of a deep-sea region). [Gr *a-* (privative) and *phōs, phōtos* light]

aphrodisiac *af-rō-diz'i-ak,* or *-rə-, adj* exciting sexually. — *n* something that arouses sexual desire, eg a food or a drug. — *n* **aphrodis'ia** (*med*) sexual desire, *esp* violent. — *adj* **Aphrodis'ian** belonging to Aphrodite, dedicated to sexual love. [Gr *aphrodīsiakos*, from *Aphrodītē* the goddess of love]

aphtha *af'thə,* (*pathol*) *n* the disease thrush; a small whitish ulcer on the surface of a mucous membrane: — *pl* **aph'thae** (*-thē*). — *adj* **aph'thous**. — **contagious aphthae** foot-and-mouth disease. [Gr *aphtha*, mostly in pl *aphthai*]

aphyllous *a-fil'əs,* (*bot*) *adj* without foliage, leafless. — *n* **aphyll'y**. [Gr *a-* (privative) and *phyllon* a leaf]

a piacere *ä pē-a-chā'rā,* (*Ital*) at pleasure.

apian *ā'pi-ən, adj* of or relating to bees. — *adj* **āpiarian** (*-ā'ri-ən*) relating to beehives or beekeeping. — *n* **ā'piarist** a beekeeper. — *n* **ā'piary** (*-ər-i*) a place where bees are kept. — *n* **ā'piculture** beekeeping. — *n* **āpicul'turist**. — *adj* **āpiv'orous** feeding on bees. [L *apis* a bee, and *apiārium* a bee-house]

apical *ap'* or *āp'ik-l, adj* of or at the apex; denoting a sound articulated with the tip of the tongue (*phonetics*). — *adv* **ap'ically**. — *n pl* **ap'ices** see **apex**. — *adj* **apicŭlate** (*ap-ik'*; *bot*) with a short sharp point on an otherwise blunt end. — **apical meristem** (*bot*) a group of dividing cells at the tip of a stem or root. [See **apex**]

Apician *ə-pish'(y)ən, adj* relating to *Apīcius*, the Roman epicure in the time of Tiberius; (also without *cap*) luxurious and expensive in diet.

apiculture. See under **apian**.

apiece *ə-pēs', adv* for each piece, thing or person; to each individually. [**a**[1] and **piece**]

apiezon oils *a-pī'zən oilz, n pl* the residue of almost zero vapour pressure left by vacuum distillation of petroleum products. [Gr *a-* (privative), and *piezein* to press]

apiol *ā'pi-ol,* or *ap', n* an organic substance derived from parsley seeds, used (*esp* formerly) as an agent to increase menstrual flow, or to bring about abortion of a foetus. [L *apium* parsley, and *-ol*, from L *oleum*]

apish, etc. See **ape**.

apivorous. See under **apian**.

aplacental *a-plə-sen'tl, adj* without a placenta. [Gr *a-* (privative), and **placental**]

aplanatic *ap-lə-nat'ik, adj* (*esp* of a lens) free from spherical aberration. — *n* **a'planat** an aplanatic lens or instrument. — *n* **aplanatism** (*ə-plan'ə-tizm*). — *n* **aplan'ogamete** a non-motile gamete. — *n* **aplan'ospore** a non-motile spore. [Gr *a-* (privative) and *planaein* to wander]

aplasia *a-plā'z(h)i-ə,* (*med*) *n* imperfect development or absence of an organ or part. — *adj* **aplastic** (*-plas'*). — **aplastic anaemia** a form of anaemia caused by malfunctioning of the bone marrow. [Gr *a-* (privative) and New L *-plasia*, from Gr *plasis* moulding]

aplenty *ə-plen'ti, adv* in plenty. [**a-**[1] and **plenty**]

aplite *ap'līt, n* a fine-grained, light-coloured igneous rock containing mainly quartz and feldspar. [Ger *Aplit*, from Gr *haploos* simple]

aplomb *ə-plom',* or *Fr a-plɔ̃, n* literally, perpendicularity; self-possession, coolness. [Fr *aplomb*, from *à plomb* according to plummet]

aplustre *a-plus'tər,* (*antiq*) *n* the ornament on the stern of an ancient ship. [L *āplustre, aplustre*, from Gr *aphlaston*]

apnoea or (*esp NAm*) **apnea** *ap-nē'ə,* (*pathol*) *n* a cessation of breathing, asphyxia; a temporary cessation of breathing, eg (**sleep apnoea**) occurring in certain adults during sleep, or in newborn infants. [Gr *apnoia*, from *a-* (privative) and *pno(i)ē* breath]

apo. *abbrev*: apogee.

Apoc. *abbrev*: Apocalypse; Apocrypha; Apocryphal.

Apocalypse *a-pok'əl-ips, n* the last book of the New Testament, also known as the Revelation of St John; (without *cap*) any book purporting to reveal the future or last things; a revelation or disclosure. — *adj* **apocalypt'ic** pertaining to the Apocalypse; prophetic of disaster or of the end of the world. — *adj* **apocalypt'ical**. — *adv* **apocalypt'ically**. — **apocalyptic number** the number of the Beast, the mystical number 666, spoken of in the Apocalypse (13.18), supposed to be the sum of the numerical values of the Greek and Hebrew letters of a name, for which many solutions have been offered. [Gr *apokalypsis* an uncovering, from *apo* from, and *kalyptein* to cover]

apocarpous *ap-ō-kär'pəs,* (*bot*) *adj* having the carpels separate. [Gr *apo* from, and *karpos* fruit]

apocatastasis *ap'ō-kə-tas'tə-sis, n* the final restitution of all things at the appearance of the Messiah, an idea extended by Origen (185–254) to the final conversion and salvation of all created beings, the devil and his angels not excepted (*theol*); the process of return to previous or normal condition (*med*). [Gr *apokatastasis*, from *apo-* again, back, and *katastasis* establishment; cf **catastasis**]

apochromatic *ap-ə-krō-mat'ik,* (*phys* and *photog*) *adj* relatively free from chromatic and spherical aberration. — *n* **apochro'mat** an apochromatic lens or instrument. — *n* **apochro'matism**. [Gr *apo* from, and *chrōma, -atos* colour]

apocope *ə-pok'ə-pē, n* the cutting off of the last sound or syllable of a word. — *vt* **apoc'opate**. — *n* **apocopā'tion**. [Gr *apokopē*, from *apo* off, and *koptein* to cut]

apocrine *ap'ə-krīn,* (*biol*) *adj* (of a gland) whose product is formed by the breakdown of part of its active cells. [Gr *apo* off, and *krīnein* to separate]

apocrypha *ə-pok'rif-ə, n pl* (*usu* with *cap*) those books or parts of books included in the Septuagint and Vulgate translations of the Old Testament but not accepted as canonical by Jews or Protestants, and to later books

(Apocrypha of the New Testament) never accepted as canonical or authoritative by any considerable part of the Christian Church; hidden or secret things (*rare*): — *n sing* **apoc'ryphon**. — *adj* **apoc'ryphal** of the Apocrypha; of doubtful authority; spurious; fabulous. [Gr, things hidden, from *apo* from, and *kryptein* to hide]

Apocynum *a-pos'i-nəm*, *n* the dogbane genus of plants, giving name to the periwinkle family **Apocynā'ceae**, closely related to the asclepiads. — *adj* **apocynā'ceous** of that family. [Gr *apokynon* an asclepiad poisonous to dogs, from *apo* off, and *kyōn, kynos* a dog]

apod *ap'od* or **apode** *ap'ōd*, (*zool*) *n* an animal without feet or ventral fins. — *adj* **ap'od, ap'odal, ap'ode** or **ap'odous** footless. [Gr *a-* (privative) and *pous, podos* a foot]

apodictic *ap-ə-dik'tik*, or **apodeictic** *-dīk'*, *adj* necessarily true; demonstrative without demonstration; beyond contradiction. — *adj* **apodic'tical** or **apodeic'tical** (*archaic*). — *adv* **apodic'tically** or **apodeic'tically**. [Gr *apodeiktikos*, from *apodeiknynai* to demonstrate, from *apo* back, and *deiknynai*) to show]

apodosis *ə-pod'ə-sis*, (*gram*) *n* the consequent clause in a conditional sentence (*opp* to *protasis*). [Gr *apodosis*, from *apo* back, and *didonai* to give]

apodous. See **apod**.

apodyterium *ap-ə-di-tēr'i-əm*, *n* an undressing-room at an ancient bath; a dressing-room (*archaic*). [Gr *apodytērion*, from *apodyein* to undress, from *apo* from, and *dyein* to get into, put on]

apoenzyme *ap-ō-en'zīm*, (*biochem*) *n* a protein component which combines with a coenzyme (qv) to form an enzyme. [Gr *apo* from, and **enzyme**]

apogaeic. See **apogee**.

apogamy *ə-pog'ə-mi*, (*bot*) *n* omission of the sexual process in the life-history, whereby the sporophyte develops either from an unfertilized egg-cell or some other cell. — *adj* **apogam'ic** or **apog'amous**. — *adv* **apog'amously**. [Gr *apo* from, and *gamos* marriage]

apogee *ap'ō-jē*, *n* the point in the orbit of a heavenly body or an artificial satellite when it is furthest from the earth; culmination (*fig*; *opp* to *perigee*); the sun's greatest meridional altitude (*obs*). — *adj* **apogaeic** (*-jē'ik*), **apogē'al** or **apogē'an**. — *adj* **apogeotrop'ic** (*biol*) turning against the direction of gravity. — *adv* **apogeotrop'ically**. — *n* **apogeotropism** (*-ot'*). [Gr *apogaion*, from *apo* from, and *gaia* or *gē* the earth]

apograph *ap'ə-gräf*, *n* an exact copy. [Gr *apographon* a copy, from *apo* from, and *graphein* to write]

à point *a pwɛ̃*, (*Fr*) to a nicety; (of food) done to a turn, perfectly.

apolaustic *ap-ə-lö'stik*, *adj* devoted to the search of enjoyment. — *n* the philosophy of the pleasurable. [Gr *apolaustikos*, from *apolauein* to enjoy]

apolitical *a-pəl-it'ik-əl*, also *ā-*, *adj* indifferent to political affairs; uninvolved in politics. — *adv* **apolit'ically**. — *n* **apolitical'ity** or **apolit'icism**. [Gr *a-* (privative) and **political**]

Apollo *ə-pol'ō*, *n* the Greek sun-god, patron of poetry and music, medicine, archery, etc; (sometimes without *cap*) an extremely handsome young man: — *pl* **apoll'os**. — *adj* **Apollinarian** (*-i-nā'ri-ən*) sacred to Apollo; of Apollinaris, (died c.390 AD) Bishop of Laodicea in Syria, or of his doctrine that in Christ the Logos took the place of a soul; of any other Apollinaris. — *n* a follower of Apollinaris. — *n* **Apollinā'rianism**. — *n* **Apollinā'ris** (or **Apollinaris water**) a mineral water rich in sodium bicarbonate and carbon dioxide, from the Apollinaris spring in the Ahr valley of Germany. — *adj* **Apoll'ine** (*-īn*) of Apollo. — *adj* **Apollōnian** (*ap-ə-lō'ni-ən*) of Apollo; having the characteristics of Apollo, controlled, harmonious, rational (often opposed to *Dionysian*); of the mathematician Apollonius of Perga (3c BC), or another Apollonius. — *n* **apollonicon** (*-on'i-kən*) a gigantic barrel-organ, partly automatic (*music*). [Gr *Apollōn, -ōnos*, L *Apollō, -inis*]

Apollyon *a-pol'yən*, *n* the destroyer or devil (Rev 9.11). [Gr *apollyōn*, pr p of *apollyein* to destroy utterly, from *apo-* (indicating completeness) and *ollyein* or *ollynai* to destroy]

apologetic *ə-pol-ə-jet'ik*, *adj* regretfully acknowledging fault; (primarily) vindicatory, defensive. — *n* (*formal*) a defence, vindication. — *adj* **apologet'ical**. — *adv* **apologet'ically**. — *n sing* **apologet'ics** the defensive argument or method, *esp* the defence of Christianity. — *n* **apologia** (*ap-ə-lō'ji-ə*) a written defence or vindication. — *n* **apol'ogist** (*-jist*) a defender by argument. — *vi* **apologize** or **-ise** (*ə-pol'ə-jīz*) to express regret for a fault; to put forward a defence. — *n* **apologue** (*ap'ə-log*) a fable; *esp* a beast fable. — *n* **apology** (*ə-pol'ə-ji*) an explanation with expression of regret; a regretful acknowledgement of a fault; a poor specimen hardly worthy of its name; a defence, justification, apologia; an apologue (*obs*). [Gr *apologia* defence, *apologos* a tale, from *apo* off, and *logos* speaking]

apomixis *ap-ə-miks'is*, (*biol*) *n* omission of sexual fusion in reproduction, as in parthenogenesis, or in apogamy. — *adj* **apomictic** (*-mik'tik*) or **apomic'tical**. — *adv* **apomic'tically**. [Gr *apo* from, and *mixis* mingling, intercourse]

apomorphine *ap-ə-mör'fēn*, or **apomorphia** *-fi-ə*, *n* an alkaloid prepared by dehydrating morphine (morphia), a rapid and powerful emetic and expectorant. [Gr *apo* from, and **morphine**, **morphia**]

aponeurosis *ap-ō-nū-rō'sis*, (*anatom*) *n* a broad, flat, sheetlike tendon, to which a muscle attaches: — *pl* **aponeuro'ses**. — *adj* **aponeurotic** (*-rot'ik*). [Gr *aponeurōsis*, from *apo* off, and *neuron* tendon]

apoop *ə-po͞op'*, (*naut*) *adv* on the poop, astern. [**a-**[1] and **poop**]

apopemptic *ap-ə-pemp'tik*, (*rare*) *adj* valedictory. [Gr *apopemptikos*, from *apo* away from, and *pempein* to send]

apophasis *ə-pof'ə-sis*, (*rhetoric*) *n* effectively saying something by stating that you will not mention it. — *adj* **apophat'ic** (*theol*) (of a description of God) using negatives, ie saying what God is not. [L, from Gr, denial, from *apo* away from, and *phanai* to say]

apophlegmatic *ap-ō-fleg-mat'ik*, (*med*) *adj* promoting the discharge of mucus. — *n* an apophlegmatic agent. [Gr *apophlegmatikos*, from *apo* off; see **phlegm**]

apophthegm or **apothegm** *ap'ō-them*, *n* a pithy saying, more short, pointed and practical than the aphorism need be. — *adj* **apophthegmat'ic** or **apothegmat'ic**, **apophthegmat'ical** or **apothegmat'ical** (*-theg-*). — *adv* **apophthegmat'ically** or **apothegmat'ically**. — *n* **apophtheg'matist** or **apotheg'matist**. — *vi* **apophtheg'matize**, **apotheg'matize** or **-ise** to speak in apophthegms. [Gr *apophthegma*, from *apo* forth, and *phthengesthai* to utter]

apophyge *a-pof'i-jē*, (*archit*) *n* the curve where a column merges in its base or capital. [Gr *apophygē* escape]

apophyllite *a-pof'i-līt* or *ap-ō-fil'īt*, *n* a mineral, hydrated calcium potassium silicate, that exfoliates on heating. [Gr *apo* off, and *phyllon* leaf]

apophysis *a-pof'i-sis* or *-zis*, *n* an outgrowth or protuberance, *esp* on a bone, on the end of a pine-cone scale, or on a moss stalk below the capsule (*biol*); a branch from a mass of igneous rock (*geol*): — *pl* **apoph'yses** (*-sēz*). [Gr, offshoot, from *apo* off, and *phyein* to grow]

apoplectic, etc. See **apoplexy**.

apoplexy *ap'ə-pleks-i*, *n* sudden loss of sensation and motion, generally the result of haemorrhage or thrombosis in the brain (*pathol*); such a fit of infuriation that one might seem about to burst a blood-vessel (*colloq*). — *adj* **apoplec'tic** of apoplexy; infuriated (*colloq*). — Also (*archaic*) **apoplec'tical**. — *adv* **apoplec'tically**. — *n* **ap'oplex** (*archaic*) apoplexy. — *vt* (*archaic*; *Shakesp*) to affect with apoplexy. [Gr *apoplēxiā*, from *apo-* (expressing completeness) and *plēssein* to strike]

aporia *a-pōr'i-a*, or *-pör'*, (*Gr*) *n* a professed doubt of what to say or to choose (*rhetoric*); a difficulty.

aport *ə-pört*, (*naut*) *adv* on or towards the port side. [**a-**[1] and **port**[1]]

à portée *a por-tā*, (*Fr*) within reach or range.

aposematic *ap-ə-sē-mat'ik*, (*zool*) *adj* (of animal coloration) serving as a warning. [Gr *apo* away from, and *sēma*, *sēmatos* sign]

aposiopesis *ə-pos-i-ō-pē'sis*, or *ap-ō-sī-*, *n* a sudden breaking off in the midst of a sentence, eg Shakesp, *Macbeth*, I. 7. 60, 'If we should fail —'. — *adj* **aposiopetic** (*-pet'*). [Gr *aposiōpēsis*, from *apo* off, and *siōpē* silence]

apositia *ap-ō-sish'i-ə*, (*obs*; *med*) *n* an aversion to food. — *adj* **aposit'ic**. [Gr *apo* away from, and *sītos* bread, food]

apospory *ə-pos'pə-ri*, (*bot*) *n* omission of spore-formation in the life-history, when the gametophyte develops vegetatively from the sporophyte. — *adj* **apos'porous**. [Gr *apo* away from, and **spore**]

apostasy *ə-post'ə-si*, *n* abandonment of one's religion, principles or party; a revolt from ecclesiastical obedience, from a religious profession, or from holy orders (*RC*); defection. — *n* **apost'ate** (*-āt* or *-it*) a person who has abandoned their religion, principles, etc; a renegade, deserter from any allegiance. — Also *adj*. — *adj* **apostatic** (*ap-ō-stat'ik*) or **apostat'ical**. — *vi* **apostatize** or **-ise** (*ə-pos'tə-tīz*). [Gr *apostasiā* a standing away, from *apo* from, and *stasis* a standing]

a posteriori *ā pos-tē-ri-ō'rī*, *-ö'rī*, or *ä pos-ter-i-ō'rē*, *adj* (*opp* to *a priori*) applied to reasoning from experience, from effect to cause; inductive; empirical; gained from experience. — Also *adv*. [L *ā* from, and *posteriōrī*, ablative of *posterior* coming after]

apostil or **apostille** *ə-pos'til*, *n* a marginal note. [Fr *apostille*. See **postil**; origin of *a-* uncertain]

apostle *ə-pos'l*, *n* a person sent to preach the gospel; *esp* (and *usu* with *cap*) one of Christ's twelve chosen followers; a first introducer of Christianity in a country, eg Augustine, the apostle of the English; a principal champion or supporter of a new system, or of a cause; the highest in the fourfold ministry of the Catholic Apostolic Church; one of the twelve officials forming a presiding high council in the Mormon Church. — *n* **apos'tleship**. — *n* **apost'olate** (*ə-post'ə-lāt*) the office of an apostle; leadership in a propaganda (qv). — *adj* **apostolic** (*ap-əs-tol'ik*) or **apostol'ical**. — *adv* **apostol'ically**. — *n* **apostol'icism** (*-i-sizm*) or **apostolicity** (*ə-post-ə-lis'i-ti*) the quality of being apostolic. — *vi* **apos'tolize** or **-ise** to preach. — *vt* to proclaim. — **Apostles' Creed** the oldest form of Christian creed that exists, from early times ascribed to the Apostles; **apostle spoons** silver spoons with handles ending in figures of the Apostles, once a common baptismal present; **apostolical succession** the derivation of holy orders by unbroken chain of transmission from the Apostles through bishops, the theory of the Catholic Church; the assumed succession of a ministry so ordained to apostolic powers and privileges; **apostolic fathers** the immediate disciples and fellow-labourers of the Apostles, more especially those who have left writings (Barnabas, Clement of Rome, Ignatius, Hermas, Polycarp); **apostolic see** the see of Rome; **apostolic vicar** the cardinal representing the Pope in extraordinary missions. [Gr *apostolos* one sent away, from *apo* away, and *stellein* to send]

apostrophe[1] *ə-pos'trə-fi*, *n* a sudden turning away from the ordinary course of a speech to address some person or object present or absent (explained by Quintilian as addressed to a person present, but extended by modern use to the absent or inanimate); the ranging of chloroplasts along the side walls of the cell in intense light (*bot*). — *adj* **apostrophic** (*ap-ə-strof'ik*). — *vt* **apos'trophize** or **-ise** to address in or by apostrophe. [Gr *apo* from, and *strophē* a turning]

apostrophe[2] *ə-pos'trə-fi*, *n* a mark (') showing (among other uses) the omission of a letter or letters in a word; a sign of the modern English genitive or possessive case (*orig* marking the dropping of *e*). [Gr *apostrophos* turning away, elision; confused with **apostrophe**[1]]

apostrophus *ə-pos'trə-fəs*, *n* the symbol Ↄ, used in Roman numerals (IↃ = 500, IↃↃ = 5000, IↃↃↃↃ = 500000).

apothecary *ə-poth'i-kər-i*, *n* a legal description for a licentiate of the Society of Apothecaries, licensed to dispense prescribed drugs; a druggist or pharmacist (*archaic*); a medical practitioner of an inferior branch, who often kept a shop for drugs (*obs*). — **apothecaries' measure** liquid units of capacity (fluid ounce, etc) used by pharmacists before 1969; **apothecaries' weight** a pre-1969 system based on the troy ounce. [LL *apothēcarius*, from Gr *apothēkē* a storehouse, from *apo* away, and *tithenai* to place]

apothecium *ap-ə-thē's(h)i-əm*, (*bot*) *n* an open fructification in Discomycetes and lichens, often cup- or saucer-shaped: — *pl* **apothe'cia**. — *adj* **apothe'cial**. [Latinized dimin of Gr *apothēkē* a storehouse]

apothegm, etc. See **apophthegm**.

apothem *ap'ə-them*, (*math*) *n* the perpendicular from the centre to any of the sides of a regular polygon. [Gr *apo* away from, and *thema* that which is placed]

apotheosis *ə-poth-i-ō'sis*, *n* a deification; glorification; a perfect example of its type: — *pl* **apotheo'ses** (*-sēz*). — *vt* **apoth'eosize** or **-ise** (or *a-pə-thē'ə-sīz*). [Gr *apotheōsis*, from *apo-* (expressing completion) and *theos* a god]

apotropaic *ə-pot-rō-pā'ik*, or *ap'ō-trō-*, *adj* turning aside (or intended to turn aside) evil. — *n* **apotropā'ism** an apotropaic practice or custom, a superstition or magic ritual. — *adj* **apot'ropous** (*bot*) anatropous with a ventral raphe. [Gr *apo* from, and *tropē* turning]

apozem *ap'ə-zem*, (*med*) *n* a decoction. [Gr *apozema*, from *apo* off, and *zeein* to boil]

app. *abbrev*: apparent; apparently; appendix; applied; apprentice; approved; approximate.

appaid. See **apay**.

appair *ə-pār'*. An *obs* form of **impair**[1].

appal *ə-pöl'*, *vt* to horrify, dismay; to weaken, dim, fade (*obs*); to abate (*Spenser*). — *vi* to grow or become pale, flat or flavourless (*obs*); to become faint (*Spenser*): — *pr p* **appall'ing**; *pa t* and *pa p* **appalled'**. — *adj* **appall'ing**. — *adv* **appall'ingly**. [Perh from OFr *apalir*, *apallir* to become pale, make pale. See **pall**[2] and **pale**[2]]

Appaloosa *a-pə-lōō'sə*, *n* a N American breed of horse, *usu* white or grey with dark spots. [Prob the *Palouse* Indians]

appalto *a-päl'tō*, (*Ital*) *n* a contract or monopoly: — *pl* **appal'ti** (*-tē*).

appanage or **apanage** *ap'ən-ij*, *n* a provision for maintenance, *esp* of a king's younger child; dependent territory; a perquisite; an adjunct or attribute. — *adj* **app'anaged** or **ap'anaged** endowed with an appanage. [Fr *apanage*, from L *ad* and *panis* bread]

apparat *ä'pə-rät*, *n* the political machine of a Communist party. — *n* **apparatchik** (*ä-pə-räch'ik*) a member of a Communist bureaucracy or party machine; a Communist agent; a party official in any political party: — *pl* **apparat'chiks** or **apparat'chiki**. [Russ, apparatus]

apparatus *ap-ə-rā'təs* or *-ra'təs*, *n* things prepared or provided, material; a set of instruments, tools, natural organs, etc; a machine or piece of equipment with a particular purpose; materials (such as various readings) for the critical study of a document (**apparatus criticus** *ap-ə-rā'təs krit'i-kəs* or *ap-a-rä'tōōs krit'i-kōōs*); an organization or system that enables something to function: — *pl* **appara'tuses** or **appara'tus** (L *apparātūs*). [L *apparātus*, *-ūs*, from *ad* to, and *pārāre*, *-ātum* to prepare]

apparel *ə-par'əl*, *n* attire, dress (*archaic*); ecclesiastical embroidery (*archaic*); rigging (*archaic*); equipment (*obs*). — *vt* to dress, clothe (*archaic*); to adorn (*formal* or *obs*); to equip (*obs*): — *pr p* **appar'elling**; *pa t* and *pa p* **appar'elled**. — *n* **appar'elment**. [OFr *apareiller*, from L *ad* to, and *pār* equal]

apparent *ə-par'ənt*, or *-pār'*, *adj* that may be seen; obvious; conspicuous; seeming; obtained by observation without correction (distinguished from *true* or from *mean*). — *n* (*Shakesp*) heir-apparent. — *n* (*archaic*) **appar'ency** apparentness; the position of being heir-apparent. — *adv* **appar'ently**. — *n* **appar'entness**. — **apparent solar time** or **apparent time** time as measured by the apparent position of the sun in the sky (as shown eg on a sundial) as opposed to mean (solar) time. [L *appārens*, *-entis*, pr p of *appārēre*; see **appear**]

apparition *ap-ə-rish'ən*, *n* an appearing; that which appears (*esp* suddenly or unexpectedly); a phantom; a ghost; an appearance, aspect; reappearance (eg of a celestial body) after occultation. — *adj* **appari'tional**. [See **appear**]

apparitor *ə-par'i-tər*, *n* an officer in attendance on a court, to execute orders (*obs*); such an officer in an ecclesiastical court; a university beadle; someone who appears (*rare*). [L *appāritor*. See **appear**]

appartement *a-par-t(ə)-mã*, (*Fr*) *n* a set of rooms in a house for an individual or a family.

appay, appayd. See **apay**.

appeach *ə-pēch'*, (*Shakesp*) *vt* to accuse, censure or impeach. — *n* **appeach'ment**. [OFr *empechier*; see **impeach**]

appeal *ə-pēl'*, *vi* to call upon, have recourse to (with *to*); to refer (to a witness or superior authority); to make supplication or earnest request (to a person for a thing); to ask for (aid, charity, etc) by making a demand on people's feelings; to resort for verification or proof (to some principle or person); to attract one's interest or enjoyment; to demand another judgement by a higher court; to remove to another court; to ask for the umpire's decision *esp* as to whether a player is out (*cricket*). — *vt* to call on a higher court to review (a case, conviction, etc) (*esp US*); to accuse (*Spenser*, *Shakesp*); to offer up (prayers) (*Spenser*). — *n* recourse; an act of appealing; a supplication; a process by which a party may have a decision reviewed by a higher court or authority (*law*); an evocation of sympathetic feeling, interest or enjoyment; (in advertising) an element designed to meet a particular desire of consumers; an impeachment (*Shakesp*); a challenge (to defend one's honour) (*obs*). — *adj* **appeal'able** (of a decision) that can be appealed against or referred to a superior tribunal. — *adj* **appeal'ing** making an appeal; imploring; calling forth sympathy; attractive, enticing. — *adv* **appeal'ingly**. — *n* **appeal'ingness**. — **appeal court** a court of law which has jurisdiction to hear appeals on points of law from the decisions of inferior courts. — **appeal to the country** to seek approval by a general election; **Court of Appeal** a section of the English Supreme Court of Judicature that hears appeals on all High Court and most county court judgements, etc; **Court of Criminal Appeal** a (former) English Court created in 1907 for appeal in criminal cases. [OFr *apeler*, from L *appellāre*, *-ātum* to address, call by name; also to appeal to, impeach]

appear *ə-pēr'*, *vi* to become visible; to present oneself formally before an authority, court, etc; to act as the legal representative or counsel for another; to come into view, to come before the public; to perform (on stage or on film, etc); to be published; to be manifest; to seem. — *n* **appear'ance** the act of appearing, eg in court to prosecute or answer a charge; the action of seeming to be, looking like; the publication of a book, etc; the effect of appearing conspicuously, show, parade; the condition of that which appears, form, aspect; outward look or show; a naturally observable phenomenon; an apparition. — *n* **appear'er**. — **keep up appearances** to keep up an outward show, *esp* one that belies, or is intended to disguise, the inward reality; **put in an appearance** to appear in person, *esp* if only briefly; **to all appearances** so far as appears to anyone. [OFr *apareir*, from L *appārēre*, from *ad* to, and *pārēre*, *pāritum* to come forth]

appease *ə-pēz'*, *vt* to pacify; to placate by making or effecting concessions; to satisfy; to quiet; to allay. — *adj* **appeas'able**. — *n* **appease'ment** the action of appeasing; the state of being appeased. — *n* **appeas'er**. — *adv* **appeas'ingly**. — **appeasement behaviour** (*animal behaviour*) submissive behaviour of an animal in an attempt to inhibit attack by a potential aggressor. [OFr *apeser* to bring peace, from L *ad* to, and *pāx*, *pācis* peace]

appel *ə-pel'*, (*fencing*) *n* a stamp of the front foot in false attack, in order to create an opening for a hit; a sharp blow with the épée, also as a feint. [Fr, challenge, from *appeler* to call, appeal]

appel au peuple *a-pel ō pœpl'*, (*Fr*) a plebiscite.

appellant *ə-pel'ənt*, *n* a person who appeals, *specif* (*law*) against a decision of the first court or tribunal to a higher body; a person who impeaches (*obs*); a challenger to single combat (*obs*); a person who in the Jansenist controversy appealed against the bull Unigenitus (1713) to a pope 'better informed', or to a general council (*eccles hist*). — *adj* **appell'ate** relating to appeals. — *n* **appellation** (*ap-ə-lā'shən*) a name, *esp* one attached to a particular person; the act of naming. — *adj* **appellā'tional**. — *n* **appell'ative** (*ə-pel'ə-tiv*) a common noun or common name (as distinguished from a proper name); a designation. — *adj* (of nouns) common (as distinguished from proper); of or pertaining to the giving of names. — *adv* **appell'atively**. [L *appellāre*, *-ātum* to call]

appellation contrôlée *a-pel-a-syɔ̃ cɔ̃-trō-lā* or **appellation d'origine** (*dor-ē-zhēn*) **contrôlée** (*Fr*) (in the labelling of French wines) a guarantee that the wine conforms to certain specified conditions of origin, strength, etc (also *abbrev* **AOC**).

append *ə-pend'*, *vt* to hang on or attach (to something); to add. — *n* **append'age** something appended; *esp* one of the paired jointed structures (antennae, jaws or legs) of arthropods; any external outgrowth which does not appear essential to growth or reproduction of a plant (*bot*). — *adj* **append'ant** attached, annexed, consequent. — *n* (*archaic*) an adjunct, quality. [L *ad* to, and *pendere* to hang]

appendectomy *a-pen-dek'tə-mi* (*esp NAm*) or **appendicectomy** *ə-pen-di-sek'tə-mi*, *n* a surgical removal of the vermiform appendix. [Ety as for **append**, with Gr *ektomē* cutting out]

appendicitis *ə-pen-dis-ī'tis*, *n* inflammation of the vermiform appendix. [**appendix** and **-itis**]

appendicular. See **appendix**.

Appendicularia *a-pən-dik-ū-lār'i-ə*, *n* a genus of ascidians that retains the larval vertebrate characteristics which are lost in the more or less degenerate sea-squirts. — *n* and *adj* **appendiculār'ian**.

appendiculate *a-pən-dik'ū-lət*, (*biol*) *adj* having small appendages attached. [L *appendicula*, dimin of **appendix**]

appendix *ə-pen'diks*, *n* something appended or added; a supplement; an addition to a book or document, containing explanatory matter, not essential to its completeness; a process, prolongation or projection from an organ (*anatom*); *specif* the vermiform appendix (*anatom*): — *pl* **append'ixes** or **append'ices** (*-sēz*, *-siz*). — **appendix vermiformis** or **vermiform appendix** (*anatom* and *zool*) a small blind process leading off the caecum in the large intestine. [L, from *appendere* to hang, append; see **append**]

apperception *ap-ər-sep'shən*, *n* the mind's perception of itself as a conscious agent; an act of voluntary consciousness, merged with self-consciousness; the conscious assimilation of a new sense-experience to others already in the mind. — *adj* **appercep'tive**. — *adj* **appercipient** (*-sip'i-ənt*). — *vt* **apperceive** (*-sēv'*). [L *ad* to, and **perception**, **perceive**]

apperil or **apperill** *ə-per'il*, (*Shakesp*) *n* peril. [L *ad*, and **peril**]

appertain *ap-ər-tān'*, *vi* to belong (to), as a possession, a right or attribute; to pertain or relate (to). — *n* **appertain'ance** (*obs*) appurtenance. — *adj* **appertain'ing** proper, appropriate (with *to*). — *n* **appertain'ment** (*Shakesp*) appurtenance. — *adj* **apper'tinent** appertaining. — *n* (*Shakesp*) appurtenance. [OFr *apartenir*, *apertenir*, from L *ad* to, and *pertinēre* to belong]

appestat *ap'i-stat*, (*med*) *n* a neural centre in the hypothalamus believed to control (food) appetite. [*appetite*, and **-stat**]

appetent *ap'i-tənt*, *adj* eagerly desirous; craving; longing. — *n* **app'etence** or **app'etency**. [L *appetēns*, *-entis*, pr p of *appetere*, from *ad* to, and *petere* to seek]

appetite *ap'i-tīt*, *n* a strong physical desire to satisfy a bodily need (eg for food, drink or sex); natural desire; inclination, enthusiasm; desire for food; hunger (with *for*). — *adj* **app'etible** (*obs*) attractive, desirable. — *n* **appetition** (*-tish'ən*; *archaic*) direction of desire. — *adj* **app'etītive** (or *a-pet'i-tiv*) having or giving an appetite. — *vt* (*rare*) **app'etize** or **-ise** to create or whet the appetite in. — *n* **appetise'ment** (*Scott* **appeteeze'ment**). — *n* **app'etizer** or **-s-** something, *esp* food or drink, to whet the appetite. — *adj* **app'etizing** or **-s-**. — *adv* **appetiz'ingly** or **-s-** (or *ap'*). [OF *apetit*, from L *appetitus*, from *appetere*; see ety for **appetent**]

applaud *ə-plöd'*, *vt* to express approval of by clapping the hands or suchlike; to extol, praise greatly; to commend, express approval of in words. — *vi* to clap the hands or in some other way express approval. — *n* **applaud'er**. — *adj* **applaud'ing**. — *adv* **applaud'ingly**. — *n* **applause** (*-plöz'*) clapping of hands or some other sign of approval; general approbation; loud praise; acclamation. — *adj* **applausive** (*ə-plös'iv*). — *adv* **applaus'ively**. [L *applaudere*, *-plausum*, from *ad* to, and *plaudere* to clap; cf **explode**]

apple *ap'l*, *n* the firm round edible fruit of the apple-tree, with green or reddish skin and white flesh; extended to other fruits (eg pineapple, custard-apple) or even galls (oak-apple); an apple-tree; the wood of the apple-tree; the fruit of the forbidden tree in the Garden of Eden (*Bible*). — **app'le-blight** American blight, a woolly substance produced by the plant-louse that infests apple-trees; **app'le-blossom**; **apple butter** a kind of spread made from stewed apples, sugar and spices; **app'le-cart**; **app'le-jack** (*US*) apple brandy, distilled from fermented apple juice; **app'le-John** (*Shakesp*, etc) a variety of apple considered to be in perfection when shrivelled and withered (also **John-app'le**); **apple-pie'** a pie made with apples and *usu* a pastry crust. — *adj* expressing, containing, or typical of, traditionally-upheld and revered American values. — **apple-pie bed** a bed prepared as a practical joke, eg with sheets doubled up, so as to be impossible or painful to get into; **apple-pie order** perfect order; **app'le-squire** (*obs*) a prostitute's attendant; a man kept by a woman as a concubine; **apple-tart'** a tart made with apples; **app'le-tree** a tree (*Pyrus malus*) of the rose family, closely related to the pear-tree; **app'le-wife** or **app'le-woman** (*archaic*) a woman who sells apples at a stall. — **apple of discord** any cause of envy and contention, after the golden apple (in Greek mythology) inscribed 'for the fairest', thrown among the gods by Eris, goddess of discord, and claimed by Aphrodite, Pallas and Hera; **apple of Sodom** or **Dead Sea apple** a fruit described by the ancients as fair to look upon but turning to ashes when touched, variously thought to be a gall, or the fruit of an asclepiad *Calotropis procera*; by botanists applied to the poisonous green-pulped fruit of *Solanum sodomaeum*; any fair but disappointing thing; **apple of the eye** the pupil of the eye; something or someone especially dear; **apples and pears** (*rhyming slang*; often shortened to **apples**) stairs; **she's apples** (*Austr colloq*) everything is just fine, in good order; **the Big Apple** (also **the Apple**) see under **big**; **upset the apple-cart** to throw plans into confusion. [OE *æppel*, cf Ger *Apfel*; ON *epli*; Ir *ubhall*; Welsh *afal*]

appleringie *ap-əl-ring'i*, (*Scot*) *n* southernwood (*Artemisia abrotanum*). [Anglo-Fr *averoine*, from L *abrotanum*, from Gr *abrotanon*]

Appleton layer *ap'əl-tən lā'ər*, (*phys*) *n* an ionized region in the atmosphere, about 150 miles up, that acts as a reflector of radio waves. [From the British physicist Sir Edward *Appleton* (1892–1965)]

appliance ... to ... **applied**. See **apply**.

appliqué *a-plē'kā*, *-kā'* or (*Fr*) *ä-plē-kā*, *n* work applied to, or laid on, another material, either of metalwork or of lace, etc. — Also *adj*. [Pa p of Fr *appliquer* to apply]

apply *ə-plī'*, *vt* to lay or put in contact; to administer; to bring to bear; to put to use; to show the reference or relevance of; to assign; to ascribe (*obs*); to wield or ply; to direct; to devote (to a pursuit); to adapt (*obs*); to lay on as appliqué; to cover with appliqué. — *vi* to suit or agree; to have recourse; to offer oneself as a candidate; to make or lodge a request; to be relevant; to hold good; to give close attention; to betake oneself (*obs*): — *pr p* **apply'ing**; *pa t* and *pa p* **applied'**. — *adj* **applī'able** (*obs*) applicable; compliant. — *n* **applī'ance** application; an instrument or tool used for a particular purpose; apparatus; compliance (*Shakesp*). — *n* **applicability** (*ap-li-kə-bil'i-ti*). — *adj* **app'licable** (now also *-plik'* in *adj* and *adv*) that may be applied; suitable; relevant. — *adv* **app'licably**. — *n* **app'licant** a person who applies; a petitioner; a candidate for a post. — *adj* **app'licate** put to practical use, applied. — *n* **applicā'tion** the act of applying, administering or using; a thing applied; a formal request for a post, etc; an appeal or petition; diligence; close thought or attention; employment, use of anything in special regard to something else; a particular type of problem or process (*comput*); an application program (*comput colloq*); a bringing to bear; the lesson or moral of a fable; employment of a word with assignment of meaning; a kind of needlework, appliqué (*archaic*); compliance (*obs*). — *adj* **app'licātive** put into actual use in regard to anything; practical. — *n* **app'licator** a device or tool for applying something. — *adj* **app'licatory** (*-kə-tər-i*) having the property of applying. — *adj* **applied** (*ə-plīd'*) placed with a flat surface against or close to something; turned to use. — *n* **appli'er**. — **applications** (or **application**) **package**, **program** or **software** (*comput*) a package, program or software designed to cope with a particular job, as payroll-processing, vehicle-scheduling, warehouse control, etc; **applied arts** see **useful** under **use**[2]; **applied economics** economics which applies the hypotheses and analytical techniques of theoretical economics to practical problems; **applied mathematics** mathematics applied to observed facts of nature, or to practical life; **applied science** science put to use for a purpose, generally utilitarian, other than its own end (opposed to *pure*). [OFr *aplier*, and its source, L *applicāre*, *-ātum*, from *ad* to, and *plicāre* to fold]

appoggiatura *äp-pod-jä-too'rä*, (*music*) *n* a grace-note written in smaller size taking its time at the expense of the following note; a similar note with a stroke through the tail, played very quickly, ie an acciaccatura. [Ital, from *appoggiare* to lean on; same root as **appui**]

appoint *ə-point'*, *vt* to fix, settle; to select for a position, assign to a job or office; to assign, grant; to ordain, prescribe; to fix the time of (*archaic*); to engage to meet (*archaic*); to destine, devote (*archaic*); to equip (*obs* except in *pa p*); to blame, arraign (*Milton*). — *adj* **appoint'ed** fixed; furnished; equipped. — *n* **appointee'** a person appointed to a job, position or office. — *adj* **appoint'ive** (*US*) filled by appointment. — *n* **appoint'ment** an engagement, between two or more people, *esp* for a meeting, consultation, etc, at a predetermined time; an office, position, to which one is or may be nominated; direction, ordinance; nomination; (now *usu* in *pl*) equipment; an article of equipment (*archaic*); allowance paid to a public officer (*obs*). — *n* **appoint'or** a person who is given (by the owner) the power to appoint property to other persons (*law*). — **appointment book** a book in which a person's prearranged engagements are recorded. [OFr *apointer*, from *à point* to (the) point]

apport *ə-pört'*, *n* in psychical research, the (supposed) transport of material objects without material agency; (*usu* in *pl*) an object brought on the scene at a spiritualistic séance by no visible agency. [Fr, from L *apportāre* to bring]

apportion *ə-pör'shən*, *vt* to portion out; to divide into fair shares or portions; to adjust in due proportion. — *n* **appor'tionment**. [L *ad* to, and **portion**]

appose[1] *ə-pōz'*, *vt* to apply, eg a seal to a document; to place side by side. [Fr *apposer*, from L *ad* to, and *pausāre* to cease, rest; confused and blended in meaning with words from *pōnere*, *positum* to put]

appose[2] *ə-pōz'*, *vt* (*obs*) to confront; to examine, question (*Spenser*, etc). — *n* **appos'er** (*obs*). — *n* **apposition** (*ap-ə-zish'ən*) a public examination, a disputation, as on Speech Day at St Paul's School, London. [Variant of **oppose**]

apposite *ap'ə-zit*, *adj* apt; to the purpose. — *adv* **app'ositely**. — *n* **app'ositeness**. — *n* **apposition** (*-zish'ən*) application; juxtaposition; the position of a word parallel to another in syntactic relation (*gram*); growth of a cell wall by deposition on the surface (*bot*). — *adj* **apposi'tional**. — *adj* **appositive** (*ə-poz'*) placed in apposition. [L *appositus*, pa p of *appōnere* to put to, from *ad* to, and *pōnere* to put]

appraise *ə-prāz'*, *vt* to estimate the worth of; to set a price on; to value with a view to sale or (in US) payment of customs duty. — *adj* **apprais'able**. — *n* **apprais'al** or **appraise'ment** a valuation; estimation of quality. — *n* **apprais'er** a person who values property; a person who estimates quality. — *adj* **apprais'ive**. — *adv* **apprais'ively**. — **appraisal well** (*min ext*) an oil-well drilled near a discovery well to find out the size of the field. [Later form of **apprize**]

appreciate *ə-prē'shi-āt*, *vt* to estimate justly; to be fully sensible of all the good qualities in; to estimate highly; to perceive, be aware of; to raise in value, to advance the quotation or price of (as opposed to *depreciate*). — *vi* to rise in value. — *adj* **apprē'ciable** capable of being estimated or measured; considerable, significant; perceptible. — *adv* **apprē'ciably**. — *n* **apprēciā'tion** the act of setting a value, especially on a work of literature, music or art; just, and also favourable, estimation; a sympathetic critical essay; increase in value (eg of an asset or commodity). — *adj* **apprē'ciative** characterized by, expressing or implying appreciation. — *adv* **apprē'ciatively**. — *n* **apprē'ciātor** a person who appreciates, or estimates highly or justly. — *adj* **apprē'ciatory** (*-shyə-tər-i*). [LL *appretiāre*, *-ātum*, from *ad* to, and *pretium* price]

apprehend *ap-ri-hend'*, *vt* to lay hold of; to arrest; to be conscious of by the senses; to lay hold of by the intellect, recognize; to catch the meaning of, to understand; to consider, conceive; to look forward to, anticipate, *esp* with fear (*formal*). — *n* **apprehensibil'ity**. — *adj* **apprehens'ible**. — *n* **apprehen'sion** the act of apprehending or seizing; arrest; fearful anticipation, dread; conscious perception (*archaic*); conception, laying hold of by the intellect; ability to understand. — *adj* **apprehens'ive** having an apprehension or notion; fearful; anticipative of something adverse; pertaining to the laying hold of sensuous and mental impressions; intelligent, clever (*archaic*). — *adv* **apprehens'ively**. — *n* **apprehens'iveness**. [L *appraehendere*, from *ad* to, and *praehendere*, *-hēnsum* to lay hold of]

apprentice *ə-prent'is*, *n* a person bound by formal agreement to a skilled person to learn a craft or trade; a novice. — Also *adj*. — *vt* to bind by formal agreement, or to place as an apprentice. — *n* **apprent'icehood** (*Shakesp*) apprenticeship. — *n* **apprent'icement** (*rare*) or **apprent'iceship** the state of an apprentice; a time of training for a trade, or for any activity; hence, (*Hood*; *archaic*) a period of seven years. — **serve an apprenticeship** to undergo the training of an apprentice. [OFr *aprentis*, from *aprendre* to learn, from L *appraehendere*; see **apprehend**]

appress. See **adpress**.

appressorium *a-pres-ör'i-əm*, (*bot*) *n* a flattened outgrowth which attaches a parasite to its host: — *pl* **appressor'ia**. [NL, from L *appress-* (stem of *apprimere*), from *ad* and *premere* (see **adpress**)]

apprise *ə-prīz'*, *vt* to give notice to; to inform. [Fr *apprendre*, pa p *appris*; see **apprehend**]

apprize or **apprise** *ə-prīz*, (*archaic*) *vt* to put a selling price on (*Scots law*); to value, appreciate; to have sold for payment of debt (*Scots law*). — *n* **appriz'er** or **-s-** a creditor for whom property is apprized (*Scots law*). — *n* **appriz'ing** or **-s-** the sheriff's sentence directing property to be apprized (*Scott*; *archaic*). [OFr *appriser*, *aprisier*, from *à* to, and *prisier* to price, prize. See **appraise**]

appro. See under **approbation**, and **approve**[1].

approach *ə-prōch'*, *vt* to bring near; to come near to in any sense; to come into personal relations or seek communication with; to resemble. — *vi* to come near; to make an approach. — *n* a drawing near; the play or stroke by which a player puts or attempts to put the ball on to the green (also **approach'-stroke**, **-shot**, etc; *golf*); access (*archaic*); an avenue or means of access; the course or process of bringing an aircraft near to the airport, the stage prior to landing (*aeronautics*; also *adj*); approximation; attitude towards, way of dealing with; (*usu* in *pl*) advances towards personal relations; (in *pl*) trenches, etc by which besiegers strive to reach a fortress, or routes into any area of military importance. — *n* **approachabil'ity**. — *adj* **approach'able** capable of being approached, accessible; (of a person) agreeable, kind, open. [OFr *aprochier*, LL *adpropiāre*, from L *ad* to, and *prope* near]

approbation *ap-rə-bā'shən*, *n* a formal act of support or endorsement; approval; confirmation (*Shakesp*); probation, trial (*Shakesp*). — *vt* **app'robate** to approve authoritatively (*US*); to accept as valid (*Scots law*). — *adj* **app'robātive** (*archaic*) or **approbatory** (*ap'rə-bə-tər-i*, or *ə-prō'*). — **approbate and reprobate** (*Scots law*) at once to accept and reject the same deed or instrument (a forbidden practice); **on approbation** (or *colloq* **on appro** *ap'rō*) on approval. [L *approbāre*, *-ātum*; see **approve**[1]]

approof *ə-prōōf'*, (*archaic*) *n* trial, proof; sanction, approval. [OFr *approve*; see **approve**[1]]

appropinque *ap-rō-pingk'* or **appropinquate** *-wāt*, (*archaic*) *vt* and *vi* to approach. — *n* **appropinquā'tion** approach. — *n* **appropinq'uity** nearness. [L *appropinquāre* to approach, from *ad* to, and *propinquus*, from *prope* near]

appropriate *ə-prō'pri-āt*, *vt* to make the private property of someone; to take to oneself as one's own; to filch; to set apart for a purpose, assign (*formal* or *archaic*); to suit (with *to*; *archaic*). — *adj* (*-pri-ət*) suitable (with *to* or *for*); set apart for a purpose; peculiar, specific (with *to*). — *adv* **apprō'priately**. — *n* **apprō'priateness**. — *n* **apprōpriā'tion** the act of appropriating; the taking of and/or dividing of assets (*accountancy*, etc); the making over of a benefice to a monastery or other corporation; the assigning of supplies granted by parliament to particular specified objects; the sum of money allocated for spending (eg on a sales promotion); sometimes used loosely for *impropriation*. — *adj* **apprō'priative**. — *n* **apprō'priativeness**. — *n* **apprō'priātor**. — **appropriate technology** (the development, adaption or upgrading of) local or locally appropriate industries (eg spinning, weaving, pottery, etc in developing countries) as an alternative to expensive and inappropriate imported technologies; **appropriation account** an account in a partnership or company which is used to show allocation of profits; **appropriation bill** a bill stating in some detail how the revenue is to be spent. [L *appropriāre*, *-ātum*, from *ad* to, and *proprius* one's own; see **proper**]

approve[1] *ə-prōōv'*, *vt* to think well of, to be pleased with; to commend; to confirm, sanction or ratify; to show, demonstrate (*esp reflexive*; *obs*); to test (*Shakesp*); to convict (*Shakesp*). — *vi* to judge favourably, to be pleased (with *of*). — *adj* **approv'able** deserving approval. — *n* **approv'al** or (*archaic*) **approv'ance** approbation; commendation; an act of approving. — *n* **approv'er** a person who approves; an accomplice in crime admitted to give evidence against a prisoner, an informer (*Eng law*; *hist*). — *adv* **approv'ingly**. — **approved school** (between 1933 (Scotland 1937) and 1969) a state boarding school for young people who had broken the law or who were pronounced to be in need of care and protection. — **on approval** (or *colloq* **on appro** *ap'rō*) subject to approval; without obligation to buy. [OFr *aprover*, from L *approbāre*, from *ad* to, and *probāre* to test or try, from *probus* good]

approve[2] *ə-prōōv'*, (*law*) *vt* to turn to one's profit, increase the value of (*orig* and *esp* common land). [OFr *aproer*, *approuer*, from *à* to (L *ad*), and *pro*, *prou* advantage; see **prowess**; confused with **approve**[1]]

approx. *abbrev*: approximate; approximately; approximation.

approximate *ə-proks'im-it*, *adj* nearly exact, approaching correctness (**very approximate** very nearly exact; but now widely used to mean very rough); close together; nearest or next. — *vt* (*-āt*) to bring near; to come or be near to. — *vi* to come near (to), approach. — *adj* **approx'imal** (*anatom*) close together; next to. — *adv* **approx'imately** (*abbrev* **approx**.). — *n* **approximā'tion** an approach (*lit* and *fig*); an imprecise account, calculation, etc; a result in mathematics not rigorously exact, but so near the truth as to be sufficient for a given purpose. — *adj* **approx'imative** (*-i-mā-tiv* or *-i-mə-tiv*) approaching closely. [L *approximāre*, *-ātum*, from *ad* to, and *proximus* nearest, superl adj, from *prope* near]

appui *a-pwē'*, *n* support (*obs*, except *military*: defensive support); the reciprocal action between horse's mouth and rider's hand. — *vt* **appui** or **appuy** to support; *specif* to place beside a *point d'appui* (*military*): — *pr p* **appuy'ing**; *pa t* and *pa p* **appuied'** or **appuyed'**. — **point d'appui** (*pwɛ̃ da-pwē*) a position of strength or support in a line of defences (*military*); a prop; a fulcrum. [Fr, from OFr *apuyer*, from assumed LL *appodiāre*, from L *ad* to, and *podium* support]

appulse *ə-puls'*, *n* a striking against something; (of two celestial objects) an apparent coming to conjunction or to the meridian as perceived by an observer (*astron*); *specif* the close approach of a planet or asteroid to a star without the occurrence of an eclipse. [L *appulsus*, *-ūs*, from *appellere*, from *ad* towards, and *pellere* to drive]

appurtenance *ə-pûr'tən-əns*, *n* something that appertains; an appendage or accessory; a right belonging to a property (*law*). — *adj* and *n* **appur'tenant**. [Anglo-Fr *apurtenance*, from OFr *apertenance*, from *apertenir*. See ety for **appertain**]

appuy. See **appui**.

APR *abbrev*: annual percentage rate.

Apr. *abbrev*: April.

apraxia *a-praks'i-ə*, (*pathol*) *n* an inability, not due to paralysis, to perform voluntary purposeful movements of parts of the body, caused by brain lesion. [Gr, inaction]

APRC *abbrev*: *anno post Romam conditam* (*L*), in the year after the founding of Rome (753BC).

après *a-pre*, (*Fr*) *prep* after. — **après-goût** (*-gōō*) an aftertaste. — **après coup** (*kōō*) too late, after the event.

après-ski or **apres-ski** *a-pre-skē* or *-prā-*, *n* (the evening period of, or clothes, etc suitable for) amusements after the day's skiing. — Also *adj*. [Fr]

apricate *ap'ri-kāt*, (*rare*) *vi* to bask in the sun. — *vt* to expose to sunlight. — *n* **aprica'tion**. [L *aprīcārī* to bask in the sun, from *aprīcus* open to the sun]

apricot *ā'pri-kot*, *-kət*, or *a'*, formerly **apricock** *-kok*, *n* a fruit of the plum genus, roundish, orange-coloured, with a downy skin, and of a rich aromatic flavour; its colour; the tree that bears it. [Port *albricoque*, from Ar *al-birqūq*, from *al* the, Late Gr *praikokion*, from L *praecoquum* or *praecox* early ripe; the form is perh due to a fancied connection with L *aprīcus* sunny; assimilated to Fr *abricot*; see **precocious**]

April *ā'pril* or *-prəl*, *n* the fourth month of the year. — *adj* **April'ian** or **A'prilish**. — **A'pril-fish** an April fool's hoax, deception or errand (Fr *poisson d'Avril*); **April fool** a person who is hoaxed, deceived, or made a fool of on 1 April (in Scotland also called a *gowk*, as in the phrase *hunt-the-gowk* (qv under **hunt**)); a hoax or trick played on that day. — **April Fools' Day** 1 April, the day on which tricks are traditionally played and fools made. [L *Aprīlis*]

a prima vista *a prē'ma vēs'ta*, (*Ital*) at first sight.

a priori *ā prī-ō'rī*, *-ö'*, or *ä prē-ōr'ē*, the term applied to reasoning from what is prior (logically or chronologically), eg reasoning from cause to effect, from a general principle to its consequences, or even from observed fact to another fact or principle not observed, or to arguing from pre-existing knowledge, or even cherished prejudices; from the forms of cognition independent of experience (*Kant*). — *n* **apriō'rism**. — *n* **apriō'rist** a person who believes in Kant's view of a priori cognition. — *n* **apriority** (*-or'i-ti*). [L *ā* from, and *priōrī* (ablative) preceding]

apron *ā'prən*, *n* a piece of cloth, leather, etc worn in front, *esp* to protect clothes from dirt or damage; an English bishop's short cassock, or similar ceremonial or formal item of dress; anything resembling an apron in shape or use, such as a leg-covering for use in an open vehicle; a stage or part of stage in front of the proscenium arch, projecting to a greater or lesser extent into the auditorium (also **a'pron-stage**); that part of a boxing ring that extends beyond the ropes; a rim, border, etc; an area of ground surface at the entrance to a hangar, lock, airport terminal, etc; an extent of eg gravel or sand, spread outward from a source (*geol*); a flat, horizontal piece of the framework of a chair, table, etc acting to strengthen the legs; a protective plate, shielding the operator, on various machines and mechanisms; a continuous conveyor belt made up of metal, rubber, etc plates; a timber behind the stem of a ship (*shipbuilding*). — *vt* to cover with, or as if with, an apron. — *n* **ā'pronful** an amount capable of being carried in one's upturned apron. — **a'pron-man** (*Shakesp*) a man who wears an apron, a workman; **a'pron-string** a string by which an apron is tied. — **tied to a woman's apron-strings** ruled by and dependent on a woman (*esp* one's wife or mother). [ME *napron*, from OFr *naperon*, from *nappe* cloth, table-cloth, from L *mappa* a napkin (*an apron* from *a napron*; cf **adder**)]

apropos *a-prō-pō'*, or *-prə-*, *adv* to the purpose; appropriately; in reference to (with *of*); by the way, incidentally. — *adj* to the purpose, pertinent. [Fr *à propos*. See **propose** and **purpose**]

à propos de rien *a prō-pō də ryɛ̃*, (*Fr*) apropos of nothing; **à propos de bottes** (*də bot*) literally, apropos of boots, ie without real relevancy; by the way.

apsaras *up'sə-rəs*, *n* a divine water sprite (*Hindu mythol*); such a being represented as a voluptuous female figure in Hindu temple carvings, paintings, etc: — *pl* **ap'sarases** (*-sēz*). [Sans]

apse *aps*, *n* a semicircular or polygonal recess, *esp* at the east end of a church choir, and where, in the Roman basilica, the praetor's chair stood; an apsis (*astron*). — *adj* **ap'sidal** of an apse or apsis. — *n* **apsid'iole** (*archit*) a subsidiary apse. — *n* **aps'is** in an orbit, the point of greatest or least distance from the central body (*astron*); an apse: — *pl* **aps'ides** (*-dēz*; or *əp-sī'dēz*). [L *apsis*, *-īdis*, from Gr *hapsis* (*apsis*), *-īdos* a felly, wheel, arch, loop, from *haptein* to fit, connect. See **apt**]

apso. See **lhasa apso**.

APT *abbrev*: advanced passenger train.

apt *apt*, *adj* fitting; fit, suitable; apposite, appropriate; tending (to); liable, ready or prone; open to impressions, ready to learn (often with *at*); likely (to). — *vt* to fit, adapt (*obs*). — *n* **ap'titude** natural ability, readiness to learn (with *for*); tendency (with *to*); fitness. — *adv* **apt'ly**. — *n* **apt'ness**. [L *aptus* fit, suitable]

apt *abbrev*: apartment.

apterous *ap'tər-əs*, *adj* (*biol*) wingless. — *adj* **ap'teral** wingless (*zool*); without columns along the sides (*archit*). — *n* **ap'terism** (*zool*) winglessness. — *n* **apterium** (*ap-tē'ri-əm*; *ornithol*) a bare patch on a bird's skin: — *pl* **apte'ria**. [Gr *a-* (privative) and *pteron* feather, wing, side-wall]

apteryx *ap'tər-iks*, *n* a member of the flightless genus of birds, *Apteryx*, the kiwis, found in New Zealand, having vestigial wings, no tail, reddish-brown feathers that lack aftershafts, and being about the size of a large hen: — *pl* **ap'teryxes**. — *adj* **apterygial** (*-tər-ij'i-əl*; *zool*) lacking paired fins or other limbs. — *n pl* **Apterygota** (*ap-ter-i-gō'tə*) a class of primitive insects, wingless, without metamorphosis (ie bristle-tails, springtails, but see **Collembola**). [Gr *a-* (privative) and *pteryx*, *-ygos* wing]

aptitude, **aptly**, **aptness**. See **apt**.

aptote *ap'tōt*, (*gram*) *n* an indeclinable noun. — *adj* **aptotic** (*-tot'ik*) uninflected. [Gr *aptōtos*, from *a-* (privative) and *ptōsis* case]

apyrexia *ap-i-reks'i-ə*, (*med*) *n* absence or intermission of fever. — *adj* **apyret'ic**. [Gr *apyrexiā*, from *a-* (privative) and *pyressein* to be feverish]

AQ *abbrev*: achievement quotient.

aq. *abbrev*: *aqua* (*L*), water, solution, liquid (*chem* and *pharm*); aqueous.

AQPS (*horse-racing*) *abbrev*: *autre que pur sang* (*Fr*), other than pure blood, non-thoroughbred.

aqua *ak'wə*, (*L*) *n* water. — **aqua caelestis** (*sē-les'tis*, or *kī-*) rain water; rectified spirits; cordial (L *caelestis* coming from heaven); **aqua fontana** (*fon-tän'ə*; L *fontānus*, *-a*, *-um* of a spring) spring water; **aqua fortis** or **aquafor'tis** (L *fortis*, strong) (ancient name for) concentrated nitric acid; etching with nitric acid; **aquafor'tist** an etcher or engraver who uses aquafortis; **aqua mirabilis** (*obs*; L *mīrābilis* wonderful) a preparation distilled from cloves, nutmeg, ginger, and spirit of wine; **aqua pura** (*pū'ra*) pure water; **aqua regia** (*rē'jyə* or *rā'gi-a*; L *rēgius*, *-a*, *-um* royal) a mixture of nitric and hydrochloric acids, which dissolves the royal metal, gold; **aqua Tofana** (*tō-fä'nə*) a secret poison (probably arsenical) made by a 17c Sicilian woman Tofana; **aqua vitae** (*vī'tē* or *wē'tī*; L, of life) alcohol; brandy, whisky, etc. [L *aqua* water]

aqua- *ak'wə-* or *ak'wa-*, also **aqui-**, *combining form* denoting water. — *adj* **aquabat'ic**. — *n sing* or *n pl* **aquabat'ics** spectacular feats in water. — *n* **a'quaboard** a board for riding on the surface of water. — *n* **a'quacade** (*NAm*) an exhibition of swimming, diving, etc, *usu* accompanied by music. — *n* **a'quaculture** or **a'quiculture** the practice of using the sea, lakes, rivers, etc for fish-farming, shellfish cultivation, the growing of plants, etc. — *n* **a'quadrome** a centre with facilities for water-skiing competitions; **aquafer** see **aquifer** entry. — *n* **a'qualung** a lightweight, self-contained diving apparatus with compressed-air supply carried on the back. — *n* **a'quanaut** a skin-diver; someone who explores and/or lives in the sea at considerable depth. — *n sing* or *n pl* **aquanaut'ics**. — *n* **a'quaphobe** a person suffering from an extreme fear of water. — *n* **a'quaphobia**. — *adj* and *n* **aquaphō'bic**. — *n* **a'quaplane** a board on which a person stands and is towed behind a motorboat. — *vi* to ride on an aquaplane; (of a car, etc) to travel or skid on a film of water which has built up between the tyres and the road surface. — *n* **a'quaplaner**. — *n* **a'quaplaning**. [L *aqua* water]

aquamanile *ak-wə-mə-nī'lē*, *-nē'lā* or **aquamanale** *-nā'lē*, *n* a medieval ewer, often in the form of a human or animal figure; a basin in which the priest washes his hands during the celebration of mass (*eccles*). [Through LL, from L *aquae* of water, and *mānālis* flowing, or *manus* hand]

aquamarine *ak-wə-mə-rēn'*, *n* a pale bluish-green variety of beryl, a gemstone; its colour. — *adj* bluish-green. [L *aqua marīna* sea water, from *mare* the sea]

aquanaut, **aquaphobe**, **aquaplane**, etc. See under **aqua-**.

aquarelle *ak-wə-rel'*, *n* watercolour painting; a painting in (transparent) watercolours. — *n* **aquarell'ist**. [Fr, from Ital *acquerella*, *acquarella*, from *acqua*, from L *aqua* water]

aquarium *ə-kwā'ri-əm*, *n* a tank or (a building containing) a series of tanks for keeping aquatic animals or plants: — *pl* **aquā'riums** or **aquā'ria**. — *adj* **aquā'rian**. — *n* (*archaic*) an aquarist. — *n* **aquā'rist** (or *ak'wə-*) a person who keeps, or is curator of, an aquarium (also (now *obs*) **aquār'iist**). [Ety as for **Aquarius**]

Aquarius *ə-kwār'i-əs*, *n* the Water-bearer, a sign of the zodiac, and the constellation with which it formerly coincided, between Capricorn and Pisces; a person born between 20 January and 19 February, under the sign of Aquarius. [L *aquārius*, *-a*, *-um*, adj from *aqua* water]

aquarobics *ak-wə-rō'biks*, *n sing* a system, or the practice, of aerobic-style exercises performed in chest-high water and to music. — *adj* **aquarō'bic**. [**aqua-** and aer**obics**]

aquatic *ə-kwat'ik*, or *-kwot'*, *adj* living, growing, practising sports, or taking place, in or on water. — *n* an aquatic plant, animal or sportsperson. — *n sing* or *n pl* **aquat'ics** water sports. [L *aquāticus*, from *aqua* water]

aquatint *ak'wə-tint*, *n* a method of etching on copper by the use of resin and nitric acid; a print produced by such a method. — Also **aquatint'a**. — *vt* and *vi* **a'quatint** to engrave in aquatint. [Ital *acqua tinta* dyed water, from L *aqua* water, and *tingere*, *tinctum* to dye]

à quatre *a katr'*, (*Fr*) of or between four; four together; **à quatre mains** (*mɛ̃*) for four hands.

a quattr' occhi *a kwat-ro'kē*, (*Ital*) face to face, tête-à-tête.

aquavit *äk'wə-vēt*, or *ak'*, *n* a Scandinavian spirit made from potatoes or grain, flavoured with caraway seeds. — Also **ak'vavit**. [Dan, Swed and Norw *akvavit*, from Med L *aqua vītae*]

aqueduct *ak'wi-dukt*, *n* an artificial channel or pipe for conveying water, most commonly understood to mean a bridge across a valley; a bridge carrying a canal; a small passage in an animal body (*zool*). [L *aqua* water, and *dūcere*, *ductum* to lead]

aqueous *ā'kwi-əs*, *adj* of water; watery; deposited by water. — **aqueous humour** (*med* and *zool*) the watery fluid between the cornea and the lens in the eye. [L *aqua* water]

aqui-. See **aqua-**.

aquiculture. See **aquaculture** under **aqua-**.

aquifer *ak'wi-fûr*, (*geol*) *n* any rock formation containing water in recoverable quantities (sufficient to supply wells, etc). — Also **a'quafer**. [New L, from L *aqua* water, and *ferre* to carry]

Aquifoliaceae *ak-wi-fō-li-ā'si-ē*, *n pl* the holly family. — *adj* **aquifoliā'ceous** (*-shəs*). [L *aquifolium* holly, from *acus*, *-ūs* needle, and *folium* leaf]

Aquila *ak'wi-lə*, *n* the golden eagle genus; the Eagle, a constellation N of Sagittarius. — *adj* **aq'uiline** (*-līn*) of the eagle; hooked like an eagle's beak. [L *aquila* eagle]

aquilegia *ak-wi-lē'jyə*, *n* a plant of the columbine genus, *Aquilegia*, *usu* blue-flowered perennials, native to Europe, N Africa and Asia. [Prob L *aquila* eagle]

aquiline. See under **Aquila**.

Aquilon *ak'wi-lon*, (*Shakesp*; also without *cap*) *n* the north wind. [L *aquilō*, *-ōnis*]

aquiver *ə-kwiv'ər*, *adv* or *predicative adj* in a quivering state. [**a-**[1]]

a quoi bon? *a kwa bɔ̃*, (*Fr*) what's the good of it?

AR *abbrev*: airman recruit (*US*); annual return (*finance*); Arkansas (US state); army regulation; autonomous region (or republic).

Ar (*chem*) *symbol*: argon.

ar *är*, *n* the eighteenth letter of the modern English alphabet (R or r).

Ar. *abbrev*: Arab; Arabia; Arabian; Arabic; Aramaic.

ARA *abbrev*: Aircraft Research Association; Amateur Rowing Association; Associate of the Royal Academy; Association of the River Authorities.

Arab *ar'əb*, *n* one of the Semitic people inhabiting Arabia and neighbouring countries; a horse of a native Arabian breed popular for its grace and speed; a neglected or homeless boy or girl (*usu* **street** or **city Arab**). — *adj* Arabian. — *adj* **Arabian** (*ə-rā'bi-ən* or *-byən*) of or belonging to Arabia or the Arabs. — *n* a native of Arabia; an Arabian horse (see **Arab**). — *adj* **Arabic** (*ar'əb-ik*) relating to Arabia, or to its language, numerals or script. — *n* the language or script of the Arabs; see also **gum arabic** under **gum**[2]. — *n* **Ar'abism** an Arabic idiom. — *n* **Ar'abist** a person learned in, or studying, Arabic culture, history, language, etc. — *n* **arabizā'tion** or **-s-**. — *vt* **ar'abize** or **-ise** to make Arab. — *n* **Ar'aby** a poetical form of *Arabia*. — **Arabian camel** a one-humped camel; **Arabic** (or **Arabian**) **numerals** the numerals in ordinary use in arithmetic, eg 1,2,3,4, (as opposed to *Roman numerals*), transmitted from India to Europe by the Arabs. [L *Arabs*, *Arabis*, from Gr *Araps*, *Arabos*]

Arab. *abbrev*: Arabia; Arabian; Arabic.

araba *är-ä'bä*, *n* a heavy screened wagon used by the Tatars and others. — Also **ar'ba** or **arō'ba**. [Ar and Pers *'arābah*]

arabesque *ar-ə-besk'*, *adj* after the manner of Arabian designs; of or in the style of an arabesque. — *n* painted, sculptured or metalwork ornament, known *esp* from Islamic art and that of the Spanish Moors, consisting of foliage and other plant forms curiously and intricately intertwined; a piece of such artwork; a short musical composition with analogous decorative qualities; a posture in ballet dancing in which one leg is stretched out backwards parallel with the ground and the body is bent forward from the hips. — *adj* **arabesqued'** ornamented with arabesques. [Fr, from Ital *arabesco*; *-esco* corresponding to Eng *-ish*]

Arabian, **Arabic**. See **Arab**.

arabica *ə-rab'i-kə*, *n* coffee produced from the shrub *Coffea arabica*, grown *esp* in Brazil and other S American countries.

arabin *ar'əb-in*, (*chem*) *n* the essential principle of gum arabic (qv under **gum**[2]). — *n* **ar'abinose** (or *-ab'*) a sugar produced from arabin, used as a culture medium for certain bacteria. [*Arab*ic and **-in**]

arabis *ar'ə-bis*, *n* any member of a large genus, *Arabis*, of trailing plants (family Cruciferae), including rockcress, wall-cress, etc. [LL *Arabis* Arabian, perh from its dry habitats]

Arabism, **arabize**, etc. See **Arab**.

arable *ar'ə-bl*, *adj* (of land) fit for ploughing or crop production; relating to the use of such land. [L *arābilis*, from *arāre*, cognate with Gr *aroein* to plough, OE *erian*, Eng **ear** (vt), and Ir *araim*]

Araby. See **Arab**.

Araceae, **araceous**. See **Arum**.

arachis *ar'ə-kis*, *n* any plant of the Brazilian genus *Arachis* of the pea family, including the monkey-nut, ground-nut, or peanut, which ripens its pods underground. — **arachis oil** peanut oil. [Gr *arachos* and *arakis*, names of leguminous plants]

Arachnida *a-rak'ni-də*, *n pl* the large class of arthropods that includes spiders, scorpions, mites, etc. — *n* **arach'nid** any member of the class. — *n* and *adj* **arach'nidan**. — *adj* **arach'noid** of or like the Arachnida; like a cobweb, formed of or covered with fine interwoven hairs or fibres (*bot* and *zool*). — *n* (*anatom* and *zool*) the arachnoid membrane. — *adj* **arachnoi'dal**. — *n* **arachnoidi'tis** (*med*) inflammation of the arachnoid membrane. — *adj* **arachnolog'ical**. — *n* **arachnol'ogist** a person who studies the Arachnida. — *n* **arachnol'ogy**. — *n* **arach'nophobe** a person suffering from an extreme fear of spiders. — *n* **arachnophō'bia**. — **arachnoid membrane** (*anatom* and *zool*) one of the three coverings of the brain and spinal cord, between the dura mater and pia mater, non-vascular, transparent and thin. [Gr *arachnē* spider]

araeometer or **areometer** *ar-i-om'i-tər*, (*hist*) *n* an instrument for determining specific gravity, a hydrometer. — *adj* **araeometric** or **araeometrical** (*-met'*). — *n* **araeom'etry** the measuring of specific gravity. [Gr *araios* thin, and *metron* measure]

araeostyle or **areostyle** *a-rē'ō-stīl*, (*archit*) *adj* having columns four diameters or more apart. — *n* a building or colonnade so built. — *adj* **araeosystyle** or **areosystile** (*-sis'tīl*) alternately araeostyle and systyle. — Also *n*. [Gr *araios* thin, sparse, and *stȳlos* column]

aragonite *ar'ə-gə-nīt* or *ə-rag'ə-nīt*, *n* an orthorhombic mineral composed of calcium carbonate. [*Aragon*, in Spain]

araise or **arayse** *ə-rāz'*, (*obs*) *vt* to raise; to raise from the dead (*Shakesp*). [Pfx *a-* (intens) and **raise**]

arak. Once *obs*, now the more usual spelling of **arrack**.

Araldite® *a'rəl-dīt*, *n* an epoxy resin used as a strong glue.

aralia *ə-rā'li-ə*, *n* a plant of the *Aralia* genus of the ivy family, **Araliā'ceae**, much grown as decorative plants. — *adj* **araliā'ceous**. [Perh Am Ind origin]

Aramaic *ar-ə-mā'ik*, *adj* relating to *Aramaea*, or Aram (roughly, modern Syria), or to its language. — Also **Aramaean** (*-mē'ən*). — *n* any of a group of Semitic languages (including that spoken by Christ) once used in this and neighbouring areas, *esp* in commerce and government, still spoken by some small communities in Syria and Lebanon. — *n* **Aramā'ism** an Aramaic idiom. [Gr *Aramaios*]

arame *ə-rä'mi*, *n* a type of edible seaweed, looking like black bootlaces. [Jap]

aramid fibre *ar'ə-mid fī'bər*, *n* an exceptionally strong lightweight synthetic fibre much used in composite materials. [*ar*omatic poly*amid*e **fibre**]

Aran *a'rən*, *adj* (of knitwear) made in a style or with a pattern that originated in the *Aran* Islands, off the west of Ireland.

Aranea *a-rā'ni-ə*, *n* the garden-spider genus (also called Epeira): — *n pl* **Arā'neae** (*-ē*), **Araneida** (*ar-ə-nē'i-də*) or **Araneidae** (*-dē*) spiders as a class or order. — *n* **arā'neid** (*-ni-id*) a spider. — *adj* **arā'neous** cobwebby. [L *arānea* spider]

arapaima *ar-ə-pī'mə*, *n* a gigantic S American river-fish, chief food-fish of the Amazon, reaching sometimes 200kg (4cwt), the pirarucu (*Arapaima*, or *Sudis*, *gigas*; family Osteoglossidae). [Of Tupí origin]

arapunga *ar-ə-pung'gə*, or **araponga** *-pong'gə*, *n* the campanero or S American bell-bird. [Tupí *araponga*]

arar *är'är*, *n* the sandarac tree. [Moroccan name]

araroba *ä-rä-rō'bə*, *n* Goa powder, a bitter yellow powder obtained from cavities in a papilionaceous Brazilian tree (*Andira*, or *Vataireopsis*, *araroba*), and introduced to Goa from Brazil, yielding chrysarobin; the tree itself. [Prob Tupí]

araucaria *a-rö-kā'ri-ə*, *n* a tree of the monkey-puzzle genus, *Araucaria*, evergreen coniferous trees of S America and Australasia. [*Arauco*, in S Chile]

à ravir *a ra-vēr*, (*Fr*) ravishingly.

arayse. See **araise**.

arb *ärb*, (*colloq*; *stock exchange*) *n* short form of **arbitrageur**.

arba. See **araba**.

arbalest *är'bəl-est*, (esp *hist*) *n* a medieval crossbow; a cross-staff; an arbalester. — Also **ar'balist**, **ar'blast** or **ar'cubalist**. — *n* **ar'balester**, **ar'balister** or **ar'blaster** a crossbowman. [L *arcuballista*, from *arcus* bow, and *ballista* (see **ballista**); partly through OE *arblast*, from OFr *arbaleste*]

arbiter *är'bi-tər*, *n* a judge; an umpire, or a person chosen by parties to decide between them; a person who has absolute control, or right to judge. — Also *fem* **ar'bitress**. — *adj* **ar'bitrable**. — *n* **ar'bitrage** (*-trij*) arbitration; buying stocks and shares in one country or market and selling them in another to profit by the price differences, or by price changes due to mergers, takeovers, etc (also *vi*). — *n* **ar'bitrager** or *usu* **arbitrageur** (*-tra-zhœr'*) a person who carries out arbitrage (*colloq* short form **arb**). — *adj* **ar'bitral** (mainly *Scots law*). — *n* **arbit'rament** (now less *usu* **arbit'rement**) the decision of an arbiter; determination; power of decision. — *vi* and *vt* **ar'bitrate** to decide, determine (*archaic*); to refer to arbitration; to judge as arbiter or arbitrator. — *n* **arbitrā'tion** (submission to) the decision of an arbiter; in industrial relations and law, a method of settling a dispute by referring it to an independent body or arbitrator, both parties having agreed beforehand to abide by its decision. — *n* **ar'bitrātor** an arbiter; a person who is appointed to determine a dispute or difference (*law*, etc): — *fem* **ar'bitrātrix** (*archaic*). — **Arbitration Court** (*Austr* and *NZ*) a tribunal for the settlement of industrial disputes. [L]

arbiter elegantiarum *ar'bit-er el-e-gan-shi-ār'əm* or *el-e-gan-ti-är'ŏŏm*, (*L*) *n* a judge on matters of taste.

arbitrary *är'bi-trər-i*, *adj* arising from accident rather than from rule; capricious; not bound by rules; (of a penalty, etc) dependent upon the discretion of an arbiter, judge or court (rather than upon a set law or statute); (of a ruler or power) despotic, absolute. — *adv* **ar'bitrarily**. — *n* **ar'bitrariness**. [L *arbitrārius*, from *arbiter*]

arbitrate, arbitration, etc. See under **arbiter**.

arbitrium *ar-bit'ri-əm* or *-ŏŏm*, (*L*) *n* power of decision.

arblast. See **arbalest**.

arbor[1] *är'bər*, (*bot* and *chem*) *n* a tree. — *adj* **arborā'ceous** tree-like; wooded. — *adj* **arboreal** (*är-bö'ri-əl*) of, or of the nature of, trees; tree-dwelling. — *adj* **arbo'reous** of or belonging to trees; tree-like; in the form of a tree; wooded. — *n* **arboresc'ence** a tree-like growth; a tree-like crystalline formation. — *adj* **arboresc'ent** growing, formed or branched like a tree. — *n* **ar'boret** a shrubbery (*obs*); an arboretum (*obs*); a little tree, shrub (*Milton*). — *n* **arborē'tum** (or *är-bor-ā'tŏŏm*) a botanic garden of trees: — *pl* **arborē'ta**. — *adj* **arboricul'tural**. — *n* **ar'boriculture** the culture of trees, *esp* for ornamental and scientific purposes. — *n* **arboricul'turist**. — *n* **ar'borist** a person who studies trees. — *n* **arborīzā'tion** or **-s-** an arborescence. — *adj* **ar'borous** of, or formed by, trees. — **Arbor Day** in US, Canada, Australia and New Zealand, a day yearly set apart for the general planting of trees; **arbor vitae** (*vī'tē* or *wē'tī*; L, tree of life) an evergreen coniferous tree of the genus *Thuja*, related to cypress; the tree-like branching in the vertical cross-section of the human cerebellum (*anatom*). [L *arbor* tree]

arbor[2] *n* a cylindrical or conical shaft, beam, spindle or axis in a mechanical device. [**arbor**[1]]

arbor[3]. See **arbour**.

arbour or (now *NAm*) **arbor** *är'bər*, *n* a grass-plot, garden, herb-garden or orchard (*obs*); a grassy seat (*obs*); a retreat or bower of trees or climbing plants; a pergola (*esp NAm*); a shaded walk (*Milton*). — *adj* **ar'boured** having, or in, an arbour. [Anglo-Fr *herber*, from L *herbārium*, from *herba* grass, herb; meaning changed through confusion with L *arbor* tree]

arbutus *är-bū'təs*, or *är'*, *n* a shrub or tree of the strawberry-tree genus *Arbutus*, ornamental evergreens native to S Europe; a N American creeping plant of the heath family (also known as *trailing arbutus* or *mayflower*), with fragrant pink or white flower clusters (*NAm*). — *n* **ar'bute** (*archaic*) the strawberry-tree or other arbutus. [L]

ARC *abbrev*: Aeronautical Research Council; (formerly) Agricultural Research Council (now **AFRC**); AIDS-related complex.

arc *ärk*, *n* a part of the circumference of a circle or other curve (*math*, *astron*, etc); a luminous discharge of electricity (of low voltage and high current) across a gap between two conductors or terminals; an arch (*Milton*). — *adj* (*math*) denoting an inverse hyberbolic or trigonometrical function (as in **arc sine** (or **arcsin**), **arc cosine** (or **arccos**) and **arc tangent** (or **arctan**)). — *vi* to form an arc: — *prp* **arc'ing** or **arck'ing**; *pat* and *pap* **arced'** or **arcked'**. — *n* **arc'ing** or **arck'ing**. — **arc'-lamp** or **arc'-light** a lamp whose source of light is an electric arc between carbon electrodes; **arc'second** (*astron*) a unit of angle measurement, $\frac{1}{3600}$ of a degree; **arc-welding** see **weld**[2]. [L *arcus* a bow]

arcade *är-kād'*, *n* a row of arches, open or closed, on columns or pilasters; a walk with an arch over it; a covered passageway lined with shops. — *adj* **arcād'ed**. — *n* **arcād'ing**. [Fr, from LL *arcāta* arched; see **arch**[1]]

Arcadian *är-kād'i-ən*, *adj* of *Arcadia* (or poetically **Arcady** *är'kə-di*), a district in Greece whose people were traditionally idealized as having a simple rural lifestyle, with much music and dancing; pastoral; simple, innocent. — Also *n*. — *n* **Arcād'ianism**.

arcane *är-kān'*, *adj* secret; mysterious. — *adv* **arcane'ly**. — *n* **arcane'ness**. — *n* **arcan'ist** (*-kān'*) a person who has knowledge of a secret manufacturing process (*esp* in ceramics). [L *arcānus* secret, from *arca* a chest]

arcanum *är-kā'nəm*, *n* a secret or mystery; a secret remedy or elixir: — *pl* **arca'na**. [L, neuter of *arcānus* (see ety for **arcane**)]

arccos *abbrev*: arc cosine (see **arc**).

arc de triomphe *ärk də trē-ōf*, (*Fr*) *n* triumphal arch.

arc-en-ciel *ärk-ā-syel*, (*Fr*) *n* a rainbow.

arch[1] *ärch*, *n* a structure of wedge-shaped stones or other pieces supporting each other by mutual pressure and able to sustain an overlying weight; anything of a similar form; an archway; an arched gateway; the bony structure of the foot between the heel and toes, normally having an upward curve; a curved or arch-shaped skeletal structure supporting, covering or enclosing an organ or organs (*anatom* and *zool*); (*usu* in *pl*) with various *adjs* (grey, dark, silvery, etc), collectors' names for moths of different kinds, with markings like arcading. — *vt* to cover or provide with an arch. — *vt* and *vi* to bend in the form of an arch. — *adj* **arched** having the form of an arch; covered with an arch. — *n* **arch'let** a little arch. — *adv* **arch'wise** in the manner of an arch. — **arch'-stone** see **voussoir**; **arch'way** an arched or vaulted passage or entrance. — **Court of Arches** (also known as **the Arches**) the ecclesiastical court of appeal for the province of Canterbury, formerly held at the church of St Mary-le-Bow (so called from the arches that support its steeple). — **dropped** or **fallen arch** a flattened foot arch. [OFr *arche*, from L *arcus* bow (as if *arca*)]

arch[2] *ärch*, *adj* chief, principal (now *esp* in compounds; see **arch-**); waggish, mischievous; roguish; cunning, shrewd; finished, accomplished, pre-eminent, *esp* in evil (*Bunyan*). — *n* (*Shakesp*) chief. — *adv* **arch'ly**. — *n* **arch'ness**. [From pfx **arch-**, in words such as *arch-rogue*, etc]

arch. *abbrev*: archaic; archaism; archery; archipelago; architect; architectural; architecture.

arch- *ärch-* (or *ärk-* in direct borrowings from Greek), *pfx* first or chief, often used to give further emphasis to an already critical or disparaging epithet. — *n* **arch'-druid** a chief or presiding druid. — *n* **arch-en'emy** a chief enemy; Satan (also **arch-fel'on**, **arch-fiend'**, **arch-foe'**). — *n* **arch-fla'men** a chief flamen or priest. — *n* **arch-her'etic** a leader of heresy. — *n* **arch-mock'** (*Shakesp*) the height of mockery. — *n* **arch-pi'rate** a chief pirate. — *n* **arch-po'et** a chief poet; a poet-laureate (*obs*). — *n* **arch-prel'ate** a chief prelate. — *n* **arch-priest'** a chief priest; in early times, a kind of vicar to the bishop; later, a rural dean; a superior appointed by the Pope to govern the secular priests sent into England from the foreign seminaries during the period 1598–1621; in the Eastern Orthodox Church, the highest title among the secular clergy. — **arch-trait'or** a chief traitor, greatest of traitors, sometimes applied *esp* to the devil, or to Judas. — *n* **arch-vill'ain** a supremely villainous person. [OE *arce-*, *ærce-*, through L from Gr *archi*, from *archos* chief]

-arch *-ärk* or *-ərk*, *combining form* denoting chief, ruler, as in *matriarch*, *monarch*. [Gr *archē* rule]

archae- *combining form*. See **archaeo-**.

Archaean *är-kē'ən*, (*geol*) *adj* and *n* (of or relating to) the oldest geological period, early Pre-Cambrian. [Gr *archaios* ancient, from *archē* beginning]

archaeo- or (*esp NAm*) **archeo-** *är-ki-ō-* or *-o-*, **archae-** or (*esp NAm*) **arche-** *är-ki-*, *combining form* denoting ancient, primitive; pertaining to archaeology. — *n* **archaeoastron'omy** the study of prehistoric (eg megalithic) monuments with a view to establishing their possible astronomical significance. — *n* **archaeomag'netism** the process of ascertaining magnetic intensity and direction in a prehistoric object (the date at which there was a corresponding intensity and direction in the earth's magnetic field being the date also of the object). — *n* **archaeometall'urgy** the study of archaeological metal objects and methods of metal production, etc. — *n* **archaeozool'ogist**. — *n* **archaeozool'ogy** the study of zoological remains in archaeology. [Gr *archaios* ancient, from *archē* beginning]

archaeol. *abbrev*: archaeology.

archaeology or (*esp NAm*) **archeology**, *är-ki-ol'ə-ji, n* the study of human antiquities, *usu* as discovered by excavation of material remains. — *adj* **archaeolog'ical**. — *adv* **archaeolog'ically**. — *n* **archaeol'ogist**. [LL, from Gr *archaiologia* the study of antiquity]

archaeometry *är-ki-om'ə-tri, n* the use of scientific methods in archaeology. — *adj* **archaeomet'ric**. — *n* **archaeom'etrist**. — Also **archeom'etry**, etc. [**archaeo-**]

archaeopteryx *är-ki-op'tə-riks, n* a Jurassic fossil bird of the *Archaeopteryx* genus, with a long bony tail, sharp-toothed jaws, and wings bearing three clawed digits. [**archaeo-** and Gr *pteryx* wing]

Archaeornithes *är-ki-ör'ni-thēz, n pl* a subclass of primitive reptile-like fossil birds, the Saururae, including the archaeopteryx and similar birds. [**archaeo-** and Gr *ornithes*, pl of *ornīs*, *ornīthos* bird]

Archaeus. See **Archeus**.

archaic *är-kā'ik, adj* not absolutely obsolete but no longer in general use; antiquated, savouring of the past; old-fashioned. — *adv* **archā'ically**. — *n* **archā'icism** (an) archaic quality or style. — *n* **ar'chāism** an archaic word or phrase; a tendency to archaize. — *n* **ar'chāist**. — *adj* **archāist'ic** affectedly or imitatively archaic. — *vi* **ar'chaize** or **-ise** to imitate the archaic; to use archaisms. — *n* **ar'chaizer** or **-s-**. [Gr *archaikos*, from *archaios* ancient, from *archē* beginning]

archangel *ärk'ān-jl*, or *-ān'*, *n* an angel of the highest order; garden angelica; dead-nettle; a kind of pigeon. — *adj* **archangelic** (*-an-jel'*). [Gr *archangelos*, from *archos* chief, and *angelos* messenger]

archbishop *ärch-bish'əp*, or *ärch'*, *n* a metropolitan bishop who superintends the bishops in his province, and also exercises episcopal authority in his own diocese. — *n* **archbish'opric** the office or jurisdiction of, or area governed by, an archbishop. [OE *ærcebiscop*; see **arch-** and **bishop**[1]]

arch-chimic *ärch-kim'ik*, (*Milton*) *adj* supreme in alchemy. [See **arch-** and **chemic**]

Archd. *abbrev*: Archdeacon; Archduke.

archdeacon *ärch-dē'kən*, or *ärch'*, *n* a chief deacon; the ecclesiastical dignitary having the chief supervision of a diocese or part of it, next under the bishop. — *n* **archdeac'onry** the office, jurisdiction or residence of an archdeacon. [OE *ærcedīacon*; see **arch-** and **deacon**]

archdiocese *ärch-dī'ə-sis* or *-sēs*, *n* an archbishop's diocese or jurisdiction. [**arch-** chief, and **diocese**]

archduke *ärch'dūk* or *ärch-dūk'*, (*hist*) *n* the title of certain early reigning dukes of importance, and of princes of the imperial house of Austria: — *fem* **archduchess** (*ärch-duch'is*) a princess of the imperial house of Austria; a wife or widow of an archduke. — *adj* **archdū'cal**. — *n* **archduch'y** or **archduke'dom**. [**arch-** chief, and **duke**]

arche- *combining form*. See **archaeo-**.

archegonium *ärk-i-gō'ni-əm*, (*bot*) *n* the flask-shaped female reproductive organ of mosses and ferns, and (in a reduced form) of flowering plants: — *pl* **archego'nia**. — *adj* **archego'nial**. — *adj* **archego'niate** having archegonia. — *n pl* **Archegoniā'tae** a main division of the vegetable kingdom, bryophytes and pteridophytes. [Gr *archegonos* founder of a race]

archenteron *ärk-en'tər-on*, (*zool*) *n* in the developing embryo, the primitive gut. [Gr pfx *arch-*, and *enteron* gut]

archeology, etc. See **archaeology**, etc.

archer *ärch'ər*, *n* a person who shoots with a bow and arrows: — also *fem* (*archaic*) **arch'eress**. — *n* **arch'ery** the art or sport of shooting with the bow; a company of archers; a collection of bows and arrows, etc. — **arch'erfish** a small spiny-finned fish of (*esp* SE) Asia and Australia that catches insects by shooting water at them from its mouth. — **the Archer** the constellation and sign of the zodiac Sagittarius. [OFr *archier*, from L *arcārius*, from *arcus* a bow]

archetype *ärk'i-tīp*, *n* the original pattern or model, prototype. — *adj* **archetȳp'al** or **archetyp'ical**. [Gr *archetypon*, from *arche-*, *archi-*, and *typos* a model]

Archeus or **Archaeus** *är-kē'əs*, (*hist*; also without *cap*) *n* the personification of a spirit supposed by Paracelsus to dwell in and control all living things and processes, residing primarily in the stomach. [New L *archaeus*, from Gr *archaios* original]

archgenethliac *ärch-je-neth'li-ak*, (*Browning*; in derogatory sense) *n* the greatest of genethliacs or astrologers. [**arch-**]

Archibald *är'chi-bəld* or in short form **Archie** *är'chi*, (*military slang*, *esp* from World War I and II) *n* an anti-aircraft gun. [Arbitrary name]

Archichlamydeae *är-ki-klə-mid'i-ē*, (*bot*) *n pl* one of the main divisions of the dicotyledons, in which the petals, if present, are in general not united. — *adj* **archichlamyd'eous**. [Gr pfx *archi-* denoting primitiveness, and *chlamys*, *-ydos* mantle]

archidiaconal *är-ki-dī-ak'ə-nəl*, *adj* of an archdeacon, his office or his jurisdiction. [Gr *archidiākonos*; see **deacon**]

archiepiscopal *är-ki-i-pis'kə-pəl*, *adj* of an archbishop. — *n* **archiepis'copacy** or **archiepis'copate** the dignity or province of an archbishop. — **archiepiscopal cross** a patriarchal cross. [Gr *archiepiskopos* archbishop]

archil *är'chil* or *-kil*, *n* a red or violet dye made from various lichens; a lichen that yields it, *esp* a species of Roccella. — Also called **orchel** (*ör'chəl*), **orchella** (*-chel'ə*), **or'chil** or **orchill'a**. — **orchill'a-weed** an archil lichen. [OFr *orchel*, *orseil* (Fr *orseille*), from Ital *orcello* (origin undetermined)]

Archilochian *är-ki-lō'ki-ən*, *adj* of, relating to or derived from *Archilochus* (Gr *Archilochos*) of Paros (c. 714–676BC), Greek lyric poet and lampooner, reputed originator of iambic metre, and proverbially bitter and satirical. — *n* an Archilochian verse, ie dactylic tetrameter catalectic, dactylic trimeter catalectic (*lesser Archilochian*), or dactylic tetrameter combined with trochaic tripody (*greater Archilochian*).

archilowe *är'hhi-lō*, (*obs Scot*) *n* a treat in return. [Origin unknown]

archimage *är'ki-māj*, *n* a chief magician or enchanter. [Gr pfx *archi-* chief, and *magos* a magician; older than Spenser's Archimago]

archimandrite *är-ki-man'drīt*, *n* in the Greek Church, an abbot, the head of a monastery or convent. [Late Gr *archimandrītēs*, from pfx *archi-* first, and *mandrā* an enclosure, a monastery]

Archimedean *ärk-i-mē-dē'ən* or *-mē'di-ən*, *adj* pertaining to *Archimedes*, a celebrated Greek mathematician of Syracuse (c.287–212BC). — **Archimedean drill** a drill in which to-and-fro movement of a nut on a helix causes an alternatory rotary motion of the bit; **Archimedean screw** a machine for raising water, etc, in its simplest form a tube bent spirally turning on its axis; **Archimedean spiral** the curve described by a point moving uniformly along a uniformly revolving radius vector, its polar equation being $r = a\theta$; **principle of Archimedes** or **Archimedes' principle** that a body weighed when immersed wholly or partly in a fluid shows a loss of weight equal to the weight of fluid it displaces.

archipelago *ärk-i-pel'ə-gō*, *n orig* (with *cap*) the Aegean Sea; a sea abounding in islands, such as the Aegean, hence a group of islands: — *pl* **archipel'agoes** or **archipel'agos**. — *adj* **archipelagic** (*-pi-laj'ik*). [An Italian compound *arcipelago* from Gr pfx *archi-* chief, and *pelagos* sea, with pfx restored to Gr form]

archit. *abbrev*: architect; architectural; architecture.

architect *ärk'i-tekt*, *n* a designer of buildings, *specif* someone professionally qualified as such; a designer of ships (*naval archit*); a maker or planner (of something).

— *vt* to plan or design as an architect. — *adj* **architecton'ic** pertaining to architecture; constructive; controlling, directing; pertaining to the arrangement of knowledge (*metaphys*). — *n* (often in *pl* form) the science of architecture; the systematic arrangement of knowledge (*metaphys*). — *adj* **architec'tural** (*-chər-əl*). — *adv* **architec'turally**. — *n* **arch'itecture** the art or science of building; structure; *specif* one of the fine arts, the art of designing buildings; style of building; structures or buildings collectively; the overall design of the software and *esp* the hardware of a computer, or of a local network; organization, framework, structure. [Gr *architektōn* master-builder, from pfx *archi-* chief, and *tektōn* a builder]

architrave *ärk'i-trāv*, (*archit*) *n* the lowest division of the entablature resting immediately on the abacus of the column; the collective name for the various parts, jambs, lintels, etc, that surround a door or window; the moulding round an arch. — *adj* **arch'itraved**. [Ital *architrave*, from Gr pfx *archi-* chief, and L *trabs*, *trabis* a beam]

architype *ärk'i-tīp*, (*zool*) *n* a primitive type from which others may be derived [Gr pfx *archi-* first, and **type**]

archive *är'kīv*, *n* (*usu* in *pl*) a repository of public records or of records generally; public records; (*rare* in *sing*) a historical document; files of data stored on tape or disk (*comput*). — *vi* and *vt* to keep archives or store in archives. — *adj* **archī'v'al** (or *ärk'i-vəl*). — *n* **archivist** (*ärk'i-vist*) a keeper of archives or records. [Fr, from LL *archī(v)um*, from Gr *archeion* office of chief magistrates, from *archē* government]

archivolt *är'ki-vōlt*, (*archit*) *n* the under-curve of an arch, intrados; an ornamental moulding on it. [Ital *archivolto*, from *arco* (L *arcus* an arch) and *volta* vault]

archlute *ärch'lo͞ot* or *-lūt*, *n* a large double-necked bass lute, popular *esp* in the 17c. [**arch-** and **lute**[1]]

archology *ärk-ol'ə-ji*, (*rare*) *n* doctrine of the origin of things; the science of government. [Gr *archē* beginning, rule, and *logos* discourse]

archon *är'kon*, *-ōn* or *-ən*, (*hist*) *n* one of nine chief magistrates of ancient Athens. — *n* **arch'onship** the office of an archon. — *n* **arch'ontate** an archon's tenure of office. — *adj* **archontic** (*-ont'ik*). [Gr *archōn*, *-ontos*, pr p of *archein* to be first, to rule]

-archy *-ärk-i* or *-ərk-i*, *combining form* denoting government of a particular type, as in *oligarchy*, *monarchy*. [Gr *archē* rule]

ARCIC *abbrev*: Anglican-Roman Catholic International Commission.

arco saltando *är'kō säl-tän'dō*, (*music*) with rebounding bow. — *n* a quick staccato. — **arco** or **coll'arco** (*music*) with the bow (a direction marking the end of a pizzicato passage). [Ital]

arcsin *abbrev*: arcsine (see **arc**).

arctan *abbrev*: arc tangent (see **arc**).

Arctic or **arctic** *ärk'tik*, *adj* relating to the Arctic, north pole or to the north; extremely cold (*colloq*); *orig*, of or relating to the (Great) Bear. — *n* (*usu* **the Arctic**) the area lying north of the Arctic Circle or north of the timber line; (**arctic**) a waterproof overshoe (*NAm*). — **Arctic Circle** the parallel of latitude 66°32′N, bounding the region of the earth surrounding the north terrestrial pole; **arctic fox** a small fox (*Alopex lagopus*) of Arctic regions; **Arctic Ocean** the world's smallest ocean, lying north of the Arctic Circle. [L *arcticus* north, of or relating to (the northern constellation) the Great Bear, from Gr *arktikos*, from Gr *arktos* a bear]

Arctiidae *ärk-tī'id-ē*, *n pl* the family of medium-sized nocturnal moths, the tiger-moths, whose hairy caterpillars are known as woolly-bears. — *n* **arc'tiid** (*-ti-*) a moth of this family. [New L, ult from Gr *arktos* bear]

Arctogaea *ärk-tō-jē'ə*, *n* a zoological region including all lands outside of Notogaea and Neogaea. — *adj* **Arctogae'an** or **Arctogae'ic**. [Gr *arktos* bear, and *gaia* earth]

arctoid *ärk'toid*, *adj* bear-like. [Gr *arktos* a bear]

arctophile *ärk'tə-fīl*, *n* a lover or collector of teddy-bears (also **arc'tophil**). — *n* **arctoph'ilist**. — *n* **arctophil'ia**. — *n* **arctoph'ily**. [Gr *arktos* bear, and **-phile**]

Arctostaphylos. See **bear-berry**.

Arcturus *ärk-tū'rəs*, or *-to͞o'*, *n* the brightest star in the northern sky, a red giant in the constellation Boötes. [Gr *Arktouros*, from *arktos* bear, and *ouros* guard]

arcuate *är'kū-āt* or **arcuated** *-id*, *adj* arched, bow-shaped (*esp* in scientific use). — *n* **arcuā'tion**. [L *arcuātus*, pa p of *arcuāre* to bend like a bow, from *arcus* a bow]

arcubalist *är'kū-bə-list*, *n*. See **arbalest**.

ARCUK *abbrev*: Architects' Registration Council of the United Kingdom.

arcus *är'kəs* or **arcus senilis** (*sē-nī'lis*), (*pathol*) *n* a bow-shaped or ring-shaped greyish fatty deposit in the cornea (*esp* common in old people). [L *arcus* a bow, and *senilis* of old people]

ARD (*med*) *abbrev*: acute respiratory disease (of any type).

ard *ärd*, (*archaeol*) *n* a primitive type of plough, used to scratch the top layer of soil. [ME, from ON *arthr* plough]

Ardas *ur-das'*, *n* in the Sikh religion, a short direct prayer to God (similar in status to the Lord's Prayer in Christianity). [Punjabi, supplication]

Ardea *är'di-ə*, *n* the heron and bittern genus. [L *ardea* heron]

ardeb *är'deb*, *n* an Egyptian dry measure of $5\frac{1}{2}$ bushels. [Ar *irdab*]

ardent *ärd'ənt*, *adj* burning, fiery; zealous, burning with emotion; combustible, inflammable (*obs* except in **ardent spirits**, distilled alcoholic liquors, whisky, brandy, etc). — *n* **ard'ency**. — *adv* **ard'ently**. — *n* **ard'our** or (*NAm*) **ard'or** warmth of passion or feeling; eagerness; enthusiasm (with *for*). [L *ardēns*, *-entis*, pr p of *ardēre* to burn]

ardentia verba *ar-den'shi-ə* (or *-ti-a*) *vûr'bə* (or *wer'ba*), (*L*) words that burn, glowing language.

ardor, **ardour**. See **ardent**.

ard-ri, **ard-righ**, **ardri** or **ardrigh** *örd'rē*, or *-rē'*, (*Ir hist*) *n* a head king. [Ir *ārd* noble, and *rī* king]

arduous *ärd'ū-əs*, *adj* steep, difficult to climb; difficult to accomplish; laborious. — *adv* **ard'uously**. — *n* **ard'uousness**. [L *arduus* steep, high]

are[1] *är*, *n* the unit of the metric land measure, 100 sq m. [Fr, from L *ārea* a site, space, court]

are[2] *är*, used as plural of the present indicative of the verb *to be*. [Old Northumbrian *aron*, which ousted the usual OE *sind*, *sindon*; both from the root *es-*]

area *ā'ri-ə*, *n* a space or piece of ground; a portion of surface; a region (*lit* and *fig*); part of a building, city, etc designated a special purpose or character; the floor of a theatre, etc; a sunken space around or alongside the basement of a building (*NAm* **a'reaway**, *esp* as a passageway); the superficial extent (of a specified ground surface). — *adj* **ā'real**. — **area code** (*US*) a three-digit number used before the local telephone number when dialling long-distance telephone calls; **area sampling** a marketing technique in which a number of people or organizations within particular geographical areas are sampled at random; **ā'rea-sneak** a thief who sneaks in by area doors; **areaway** see **area**. [L *ārea* an open empty place, etc]

areach *a-rēch'*, (*obs*) *vt* to reach, get at; to seize: — *pa t* (*Spenser*) **arraught** (*a-röt'*). [OE *ārǣcan*, from *ā-* (intensive) and *rǣcan* to reach]

aread, **arede** or **arreede** *a-rēd'*, *vt* to declare, utter (*obs*); to guess (*archaic*); to interpret, explain (*archaic*); to adjudge (*obs*); to decide (*obs*); to counsel (*Milton* and *Spenser*): — *pa t* and *pa p* **ared'** or **aredd'**. [OE *ārǣdan*; see **read**]

areal. See **area**.

arear, **arere**. Spenserian spellings of **arrear** (*adv*).

à rebours *a rə-bo͞or*, (*Fr*) against the grain; contrarily.

areca *ar'i-kə* or *ə-rē'kə*, *n* a tree of the betel-nut genus of palms, *Areca*, native to SE Asia and the Indian subcontinent. — **areca-nut** betel-nut, the nut of *Areca catechu*, chewed by the Malays, southern Indians, etc, for its intoxicating effects, staining the teeth and gums bright red. [Port, from Malayalam *adekka*]

ared, aredd, arede. See **aread**.

arefaction *ar-i-fak'shən*, (*obs*) *n* drying. — *vt* and *vi* **ar'efy** to dry up, wither. [L *ārefacere* to make dry, from *ārēre* to dry, and *facere* to make]

areg. See **erg**[2].

arena *ə-rē'nə*, *n orig*, part of the ancient amphitheatre strewed with sand for combats; an area enclosed by seating, in which public sporting contests or entertainments take place; any sphere of action. — *adj* **arenaceous** (*ar-i-nā'shəs*) sandy; composed of sand or quartz grains (*geol*); with shell(s) composed of agglutinated sand-grains (*zool*); sand-growing (*bot*). — *n* **Arenā'ria** the sandwort genus, related to chickweed; a genus of birds, the turnstones. — *n* **arenā'tion** remedial application of (hot) sand. — *adj* **arenic'olous** (*zool*) sand-dwelling. — **arena stage** a stage which can have audience all round it (see **theatre-in-the-round** under **theatre**). [L *arēna* sand]

aren't *ärnt*. Contraction of **are not** or (*colloq*, as interrogative) **am not**.

areography *ar-i-og'rə-fi*, *n* description of the physical features of the planet Mars. — *adj* **areograph'ic**. [Gr *Arēs* Mars, and *graphein* to write]

areola *a-rē'ō-lə*, *n* a small space marked off by lines, or a slightly sunken spot (*biol*); an interstice in a tissue (*physiol*); any circular pigmented area such as that around the nipple (*physiol*); the part of the iris of the eye bordering on the pupil (*physiol*): — *pl* **arē'olae** (*-lē*). — *adj* **arē'olar**. — *adj* **arē'olate** or **arē'olated** divided into small areas. — *n* **areolā'tion** division into areolae. — *n* **areole** (*ar'i-ōl*; *bot*) an areola; a spiny or hairy spot on a cactus. [L *āreola*, dimin of *ārea* (see **area**)]

areometer. See **araeometer**.

Areopagus *ar-i-op'əg-əs*, *n* the Hill of **Arēs** (Greek god of war), on which the supreme court of ancient Athens was held; the court itself; any important tribunal. — *n* **Areop'agite** (*-gīt* or *-jīt*) a member of the Areopagus. — *adj* **Areopagitic** (*-git'* or *-jit'*) pertaining to the Areopagus. [Latinized from Gr *Areios pagos* hill of Arēs (identified with Roman Mars)]

areostyle, areosystile. See **araeostyle**.

arere. See **arear**.

aret or **arett** *a-ret'*, (*obs*) *vt* to entrust, commit (*Spenser*); to assign, allot; to adjudge, award. [OFr *areter*, from *a-* to, and *reter*, from L *reputāre* to reckon]

arête *a-ret'*, *n* a sharp ridge; *esp* in French Switzerland, a rocky edge on a mountain. [Fr, from L *arista* an ear of corn, fish-bone, spine]

Aretinian *ar-i-tin'i-ən*, *adj* pertaining to Guido of Arezzo (died 1050). — **Aretinian syllables** (*music*) the initial syllables of the half-lines of a hymn to John the Baptist, which, falling on successive notes of the diatonic scale, were used (apparently by Guido, and still in Italy and France) as names for the notes: — *Ut* queant laxis *re*sonare fibris *Mi*ra gestorum *fa*muli tuorum, *Sol*ve polluti *la*bii reatum, Sancte Ioannes. Thus C in the bass is *C fa ut*, being the fourth note (fa) of the first hexachord (on G) and the first note (ut) of the second hexachord (on C). See **gamut**. [L *Arētīnus*, *Arrētinus* of Arrētium or Arezzo]

arett. See **aret**.

arew *a-rōō'*, (*Spenser*) *adv* arow, in a row.

arfvedsonite *är'ved-sən-īt*, (*mineralogy*) *n* a sodium-rich amphibole. [After J A *Arfvedson* (1792–1841), Swedish mineralogist]

Arg (*chem*) *symbol*: arginine.

argal *är'gl*, *adv* Shakespeare's gravedigger's bungled attempt to say the Latin word *ergō* therefore.

argala *är'gə-lə*, *n* the adjutant stork of India. [Hindustani *hargīla*]

argali *är'gə-li*, *n* the great wild sheep (*Ovis ammon*) of Asia. [Mongol]

argan *är'gan*, *n* a Moroccan timber-tree of the family Sapotaceae; its oil-bearing seed. [N African pronunciation of Ar *arjān*]

argand *är'gand*, *n* a gas- or oil-lamp admitting air to both the inside and outside of the flame. — Also *adj*. [Invented by Aimé *Argand* (1755–1803)]

Argathelian *är-gə-thē'li-ən*, (*hist*) *adj* of the party in 18c Scotland that approved of the political influence of the house of Argyle. [LL *Argathelia* Argyle]

argemone *är-jem-ō'nē*, *n* a plant of the prickly poppy genus *Argemone*, with showy white or yellow flowers and prickly leaves. [Gr *argemōnē* a kind of poppy]

argent *ärj'ənt*, *adj* and *n* silver (*archaic* or *poetic*); silvery-white or white (*heraldry*). — *adj* **argentif'erous** (*geol*) silver-bearing. — *adj* **ar'gentine** (*-īn*) of or like silver. — *n* white metal coated with silver; spongy tin; a small marine fish (family **Argentin'idae**) with silvery sides. — *n* **ar'gentite** silver-glance, native sulphide of silver. [Fr, from L *argentum* silver]

argent comptant *ar-zhã kɔ̃-tã*, (*Fr*) *n* ready money.

Argentine *är'jən-tīn* or **Argentinian** *är-jən-tin'i-ən*, *adj* of or belonging to Argentina (a republic in S America), or its people. — *n* a native or citizen of Argentina (also **Argentino** *-tē'nō*). [*Argentina* the republic named from the Rio de la Plata (silver river)]

argentine, argentite. See **argent**.

Argestes *är-jes'tēz*, (*Milton*) *n* the NW wind personified. [Gr *Argestēs*]

arghan *är'gan*, *n* pita fibre, or the plant yielding it. [Origin unknown]

Argie *är'jē*, (*colloq*; *derog*) *n* and *adj* (an) Argentine, *esp* at or following the time of the Falkland Islands conflict of 1982. [Abbreviated form]

argie-bargie. See under **argue**.

argil *är'jil*, *n* potter's clay; pure clay or alumina. — *adj* **argillā'ceous** (*geol*) clayey. — *n* **ar'gillite** (*geol*) an indurated clay rock. [L *argilla*, Gr *argillos* white clay, from *argēs* white]

arginine *ar'ji-nīn*, *n* one of the essential amino-acids. [Origin obscure]

Argive *är'gīv* or *-jīv*, *adj* belonging to the ancient Greek city of *Argos* (*hist*); Greek (*literary*). — Also *n*.

argle-bargle. See under **argue**.

Argo *är'gō*, *n* a large southern constellation consisting of four separate constellations.

argol[1] *är'gol*, *n* dried dung used as fuel. [Mongolian]

argol[2] *är'gol*, *n* a hard crust (*gen* reddish) formed on the sides of wine-vessels, from which cream of tartar and tartaric acid are obtainable. [Prob connected with Gr *argos* white]

argon *är'gon*, *n* a colourless, odourless inert gas (atomic no 18; symbol **Ar**) discovered in the atmosphere in 1894 by Rayleigh and Ramsay. It constitutes about 1% by volume of the atmosphere from which it is obtained by fractionation of liquid air, and is used in gas-filled electric lamps, radiation counters and fluorescent tubes. — **argon laser** a laser using argon, which gives strong emission at 488.0, 514.5, and 496.5 nm. [Gr *ārgon* (neuter) inactive, from *a-* (privative) and *ergon* work]

Argonaut *är'gō-nöt*, *n* one of those who sailed in the ship *Argo* in search of the golden fleece (*Gr mythol*); (without *cap*) the paper nautilus (genus *Argonauta*). — *adj* **argonaut'ic**. [Gr *Argō*, and *nautēs* a sailor]

argosy *är'gə-si*, (*hist*; also *fig* and *poetic*) *n* a great merchant ship, *esp* of Ragusa (modern Dubrovnik) or Venice. [Ital *Ragusea* Ragusan (ship)]

argot *är'gō*, *n* slang, *orig* that of thieves and vagabonds; cant. [Fr; of unknown origin]

argue *ärg'ū*, *vt* to discuss with reasoning; to persuade or bring by reasoning (into or out of a course of action); to seek to show by reasoning; to give reason to believe; to prove or indicate; to accurse (*obs*). — *vi* to contend with reasoning; to contradict, dispute; to offer reasons. — *adj* **arg'ūable** capable of being disputed; capable of being maintained. — *adv* **ar'gūably**. — *n* **arg'ūer**. — *n* **ar'gufier**. — *vi* **ar'gūfy** (*colloq*) to bandy arguments; to wrangle. — *vt* to harass with arguments or wrangling. — *n* **ar'gūment** a reason or series of reasons offered as or possible towards proof or inducement (with *for* or *against*); exchange of such reasons; debate; matter of debate or contention; a summary of subject-matter; hence contents (*Shakesp*); proof, evidence (*archaic*); a variable upon which another depends, or a quantity or element to which a function, operation, etc applies (*math*, *comput*, *logic*); the angle between a vector and its axis of reference (*math*). — *n* **argūmentā'tion** reasoning; sequence or exchange of arguments. — *adj* **argūment'ative** fond of, prone to or addicted to arguing; controversial. — *adv* **argūment'atively**. — *n* **argūment'ativeness**. — *vi* **ar'gy-bar'gy**, **ar'gie-bar'gie** or **ar'gle-bar'gle** (*orig Scot*) to argue tediously or vexatiously. — *n* a bandying of argument. [Fr *arguer*, from L *argūtāre* (frequentative of *arguere* to show, accuse); *argūmentum* proof, accusation, summary of contents]

argulus *är'gū-ləs*, *n* a fish louse of the *Argulus* genus, extremely destructive to fish life: — *pl* **ar'gulī**. [Dimin of **argus** (qv)]

argument, etc. See **argue**.

argumentum *är-gū-men'tum* or *är-gōō-men'tōōm*, (*L*; *rhetoric* and *logic*) *n* argument, proof. — **argumentum ad baculum** see **argumentum baculinum**; **argumentum ad crumenam** (*ad krōō'mən-əm* or *-mān-am*) argument addressed to the purse (ie to the desire for money); **argumentum ad hominem** (*hom'in-em*) an appeal to the known prejudices and preferences or previous admissions of an opponent; argument relying upon personal abuse, or attack upon the opponent's character, rather than his or her viewpoint; **argumentum ad ignorantiam** (*ig-nör-an'shi-əm* or *ig-nōr-an'ti-am*) argument founded on the ignorance of an opponent; **argumentum ad invidiam** (*in-vid'i-am*, or *-wid'*) an appeal to prejudices; **argumentum ad judicium** (*jōō-dish'i-əm* or *ū-dik'i-ōōm*) an appeal to commonsense or judgement; **argumentum ad rem** (*rem*) argument to the purpose, directed at the real issue; **argumentum ad verecundiam** (*ve-re-kun'di-am*, or *-kōōn'*) an appeal to awe or reverence (towards a prestigious or authoritative name or figure); **argumentum baculinum** (*ba-kūl-īn'um* or *ba-kōōl-ēn'ōōm*) or **argumentum ad baculum** the argument of the stick or rod, ie of force; **argumentum per impossibile** (*per im-po-sib'il-ē* or *-ā*) the proof from the absurdity of a contradictory supposition; **argumenti causa** (*är-gū-men'tī kö'zə* or *ar-gōō-men'tē kow'za*) for the sake of argument.

argus *är'gəs*, *n* (with *cap*) in Greek mythology, Io's guardian, whose hundred eyes Hera transferred to the peacock's tail; (with *cap*) a vigilant watcher; an East Indian pheasant (**argus pheasant**) of the genus *Argusianus*, with a long colourful tail with eye-spots; a butterfly with many eye-spots on the wings (as some *Lycaenidae* and *Satyridae*); an ophiuroid with much-divided coiling arms: — *pl* **ar'guses**. — *adj* **Ar'gus-eyed**. — **argus tortoise beetle** a black-spotted, reddish, tortoise-shaped beetle that feeds on plants of the convolvulus family. [Gr *Argos*, *literally* bright]

argute *är-gūt'*, *adj* shrill; keen; shrewd. — *adv* **argute'ly**. — *n* **argute'ness**. [L *argūtus*]

argy-bargy. See under **argue**.

argyle or **Argyll** *är-gīl'*, *n* a vessel for containing gravy and keeping it hot, designed by John, 4th Duke of *Argyll*, in early 1770s; (a sock knitted in) a lozenge pattern adapted from Campbell of Argyll tartan (also *adj*).

argyria *är-jir'i-ə*, *n* (*med*) skin pigmentation caused by long exposure to or use of preparations of silver. — *n* **ar'gyrite** same as **argentite**. — *n* **ar'gyrodite** a mineral composed of silver, germanium and sulphur. [Gr *argyros* silver]

arhythmia, arhythmic. See **arrhythmic**.

aria *ä'ri-ə*, (*music*) *n* an air or melody, *esp* an accompanied vocal solo in a cantata, oratorio or opera; a regular strain of melody followed by another in contrast and complement, and then repeated *da capo*. [Ital, from root of **air**]

Arian *ā'ri-ən*, *adj* of, pertaining to, or following, *Arius* of Alexandria (died 336), or Arianism. — *n* a person who adheres to the doctrines of Arius; a Unitarian. — *n* **A'rianism** the heretical doctrine of Arius, that Christ was not consubstantial (qv) with God the Father, but only the first and highest of all finite beings. — *vt* and *vi* **A'rianize** or **-ise**.

arid *ar'id*, *adj* dry; parched; barren; (of a region or climate) having so little rainfall as to support only desert or semi-desert vegetation (see **arid zone** below); meagre, lifeless. — *n* **arid'ity** or **ar'idness**. — *adv* **ar'idly**. — **arid zone** (*ecol*) a zone of latitude 15°–30°N and S in which the rainfall is so low that only desert and semi-desert vegetation occur. [L *aridus*]

Ariel *ā'ri-əl*, *n* a man's name in the Old Testament; in later demonology, a water-spirit; an angel; a spirit of the air (such as Shakespeare's Ariel, also a sylph in Pope); (without *cap*) species of swallow, petrel and toucan. [Heb *Ariel*, with meaning influenced by **air**]

ariel *ā'ri-əl*, *n* a kind of mountain gazelle native to Arabia. [Ar *aryil*]

Aries *ā'ri-ēz*, *n* the Ram, a constellation giving name to, and formerly coinciding with, a sign of the zodiac; a person born between 22 March and 20 April, under the sign of Aries (*astrol*). — **first point of Aries** the intersection of equator and ecliptic passed by the sun in (the northern) spring, now actually in Pisces. [L *ariēs*, *-etis* ram]

arietta *ar-i-et'ə*, (*music*) *n* a little aria or air. — Also (*Fr*) **ariette** (*-et'*). [Ital *arietta*, dimin of *aria*]

aright *ə-rīt'*, *adv* in a right way; rightly; on or to the right (*archaic*). — **a-rights'** (*Spenser*) rightly. [**a-**[1] and **right**[1]]

aril *är'il*, (*bot*) *n* a covering or appendage of some seeds, an outgrowth of the funicle; sometimes, a caruncle (*false aril*). — Also (*New L*) **arill'us**: — *pl* **arill'ī**. — *adj* **ar'illary**, **ar'illate** or **ar'illated** having an aril. — *n* **ar'illode** a caruncle or false aril, from near the micropyle. — *adj* **ar'illoid**. [LL *arillus* raisin]

Arimaspian *ar-i-mas'pi-ən*, (*Gr mythol*) *adj* pertaining to the *Arimaspi*, described by Herodotus as a one-eyed people of the extreme north, warring perpetually with griffins for gold hoards. — Also *n*. — Also *adj* and *n* **Ar'imasp**.

arioso *a-ri-ō'sō*, (*music*) *adj* and *adv* in the melodious manner of an aria, or between aria and recitative. — Also *n*: — *pl* **ario'sos** or **ariosi** (*-sē*). [Ital *aria*]

ariot *ə-rī'ət*, *adv* in riot, riotously. [**a-**[1]]

aripple *ə-rip'l*, *adv* in a ripple. [**a-**[1]]

aris *ar'is*, (*Cockney slang*) *n* arse. [Short for 'Aristotle', rhyming slang for 'bottle', which is in turn short for 'bottle and glass', rhyming slang for 'arse']

arise *ə-rīz'*, *vi* to rise up; to take rise, originate (with *from* or *out of*); to come into being, view, or activity: — *pa t* **arose** (*ə-rōz'*); *pa p* **arisen** (*ə-riz'n*). [Pfx *a-* up, out, and **rise**]

arish. See **arrish**.

arista *ə-ris'tə*, (*biol*) *n* a bristly process from the glume of certain grasses, an awn; a bristle-like appendage on some insects' antennae. — *adj* **aris'tate** (or *ar'*) awned. [L, an awn]

Aristarch *ar'is-tärk*, *n* a severe critic. [*Aristarchus*, Alexandrian grammarian (c.160 BC)]

aristate. See **arista**.

Aristides *ar-is-tī'dēz*, *n* an embodiment of justice. [L, from Gr *Aristeidēs*, Athenian statesman (5c BC]

Aristippus *ar-is-tip'əs*, *n* an embodiment of self-indulgence. [L, from Gr *Aristippos*, the founder of the Cyrenaic school of philosophy (c.435–c.356BC]

aristocracy *ar-is-tok'rə-si*, *n* government by, or political power of, a privileged order; a state governed in this way; a nobility or privileged class; a class of people holding privileged status in any field. — *n* **aristocrat** (*ar'is-tə-krat*, or *ə-ris'*; sometimes (*colloq*) shortened to **aristo** (*a'ris-tō* or *ə-ris'tō*): — *pl* **aristos**) a member of the or an aristocracy; a person who has the characteristics of or attributed to an aristocracy; a haughty person; one of the best (or the best) of its kind. — *adj* **aristocrat'ic** belonging to aristocracy; having the character that belongs to, or is thought to befit, aristocracy. — Also **aristocrat'ical**. — *adv* **aristocrat'i-cally**. — *n* **aristocratism** (*-tok'rə-tizm*) the spirit of, practices of, or belief in, aristocracy. [Gr *aristokratiā*, from *aristos* best, and *kratos* power]

aristolochia *ar-is-tō-lō'ki-ə*, *n* any plant of the the birthwort genus *Aristolochia*, herbs and climbers, specially abundant in tropical S America, giving name to the family **Aristolochiā'ceae**. [Gr *aristolocheia*, from *aristos* best, and *locheiā* child-birth, from the former reputation of birthwort]

aristology *ar-is-tol'ə-ji*, (*rare*) *n* the science or art of dining. [Gr *ariston* breakfast, luncheon, and **-logy**]

ariston metron *ar-is'ton met'ron*, (*Gr*) *n* the middle (or moderate) course is the best; the golden mean.

Aristophanic *ar-is-to-fan'ik*, *adj* relating to or characteristic of the Greek comic dramatist *Aristophanes* (c.448–c.388BC).

Aristotelian *ar-is-to-tē'li-ən*, or **Aristotelean** *ar-is-tot-i-lē'ən*, *adj* relating to Aristotle (Gr *Aristotelēs*) or to his philosophy. — *n* a follower of Aristotle. — *n* **Aristotē'-lianism** or **Aristot'elism**. — **Aristotle's lantern** a chewing apparatus in sea-urchins, the framework of muscles and ossicles supporting the teeth and enclosing the lower oesophagus (compared by Aristotle to a ship's lantern).

Arita *a-rē'tə*, *n* a Japanese porcelain manufactured from the early 17c at *Arita* near Nagasaki.

arith. *abbrev*: arithmetic; arithmetical.

arithmetic *ə-rith'mə-tik*, *n* the science of numbers, *incl* addition, subtraction, multiplication, division; the art of calculating by numbers; a treatise on calculation by numbers (*obs*). — *adj* **arithmetic** (*ar-ith-met'ik*) or **arithmet'ical**. — *adv* **arithmet'ically**. — *n* **arithmetician** (*-mə-tish'n*, or *ar'*) a person skilled in arithmetic. — **arithmetical progression** or **sequence** a series increasing or diminishing by a common difference, eg 7, 10, 13, 16, 19, 22, or 12, $10\frac{1}{2}$, 9, $7\frac{1}{2}$, 6; **arithmetic** (or **arithmetical**) **mean** see **mean**[2]. — **arithmetic and logic unit** (*comput*; *abbrev* **ALU**) the part of a central processing unit that carries out arithmetic and logical operations required by an input command. [Gr *arithmētikē* (*technē* art) of numbers, from *arithmos* number]

arithmo- *ar-ith-mo-*, *combining form* denoting number or numbers. — *n* **arithmomā'nia** (*psychiatry*) an obsessive preoccupation with numbers, characterized by a compulsion to count people or objects. — *n* **arithmom'eter** (*hist*) a calculating machine. — *n* **arithmophō'bia** fear of numbers. [Gr *arithmos* number]

Ariz. *abbrev*: Arizona (US state).

Ark. *abbrev*: Arkansas (US state).

ark *ärk*, *n* a chest or coffer; in Jewish history, the wooden coffer in which the Tables of the Law were kept; a large floating vessel, as *esp* (*usu* with *cap*) Noah's in the biblical Flood (Gen 6–8); a toy representing Noah's ark. — *vt* (*obs*) to put in an ark. — *adj* and *n* **ark'ite**. — **ark'-shell** a boxlike bivalve mollusc shell (genus *Arca*). — **out of the Ark** (*colloq*) utterly old-fashioned, antediluvian. [OE *arc* (*earc*), from L *arca* a chest, from *arcēre* to guard]

arkose *är-kōs'*, *n* a sandstone rich in feldspar grains, formed from granite, etc. [Fr]

arles *ärlz*, also *ārlz*, (*archaic*; *dialect*) *n pl* an earnest, *esp* in confirmation of a bargain, or an engagement of a servant. — *vt* **arle** to give earnest-money to or for. — **arle'-penny** or **arles'-penny**. [Northern; ME *erles*, appar through OFr from a dimin of L *arrha*]

arm[1] *ärm*, *n* the human forelimb from shoulder to hand; an upper limb in other bipedal mammals; a similar member in other animals, eg a tentacle; a narrow projecting part; an inlet; a branch; a subdivison of a large company, organization, etc, *esp* one specializing in a certain area, service, resource; a rail or support for the arm, eg on a chair; (in clothing) a sleeve; power (*fig*). — *vt* (*obs*) to take in the arms; to conduct arm-in-arm. — *adj* **armed** (*usu* in compounds) having an arm or arms, as in *one-armed*. — *n* **arm'ful**: — *pl* **arm'fuls**. — *adj* **arm'less**. — *n* **arm'let** a little arm; a ring or band round the arm. — **arm'band** a band of cloth worn round the sleeve; an inflatable plastic cuff worn on the upper arm as a buoyancy aid; **arm'chair** a chair with arms. — *adj* amateur; stay-at-home; doctrinaire, theoretical; conducted from (the security or comfort of) home; comfortable. — *n* and *adj* **arm'-chancing** see **chance one's arm** under **chance**. — **arm'hole** the hole in a garment through which the arm is put. — *adv* **arm-in-arm'** with arms interlinked. — **arm'lock** (in wrestling, etc; also *fig*) a hold by the arms (also *vt*); **arm'pit** the hollow under the shoulder; **arm'-rest** the arm (qv) of a chair. — **at arm's length** at a distance (*lit* and *fig*); not showing friendliness or familiarity but careful detachment; (of negotiations, etc) in which each party preserves its independent ability to bargain (*adj* **arms'-length**, eg in shareholding, having broad and ultimate control, without involvement in policy decisions, etc); **in arms** carried as a child; (of a child) young enough for this; **right arm** someone's main support or assistant; **secular arm** the civil authority (*opp* to the spiritual or ecclesiastical); **the long arm of the law** the far-reaching power and influence of the law, *esp* the police force; **within** (or **in**) **arm's reach** able to be reached easily, ie from where one is sitting; **with open arms** with a hearty welcome. [OE *arm* (*earm*); cognate with L *armus* the shoulder-joint, and with Gr *harmos* a joint]

arm[2] *ärm*, *n* a weapon; a branch of the fighting forces; (in *pl*) weapons of offence and defence; (in *pl*) hostilities; (in *pl*) fighting, soldiering; (in *pl*) heraldic insignia, coat-of-arms. — *vt* to provide with weapons, means of protection, armature, or (*fig*) equipment; to make (a bomb, etc) ready to explode; to strengthen (a vehicle, etc) with a metal plate or similar. — *vi* to take arms. — *adj* **armed** supplied with arms; provided with means of defence; (of an animal, etc) having a protective armour; (of a plant) thorny, prickly, barbed; with beak, claws, etc, of a particular tincture (*heraldry*). — **armed eye** the eye aided eg with a magnifying glass (*opp* to *naked eye*); **arms race** competition among nations in building up armaments. — **bear arms** to serve as a soldier; (also **give arms** (*obs*)) to show or have armorial bearings (*heraldry*); **in arms** armed; ready to fight; quartered (*heraldry*); **lay down one's arms** to surrender, submit; **of all arms** of every kind of troops; **take arms** or **take up arms** to resort to fighting; **under arms** armed; **up in arms** in readiness to resist; protesting hotly. [Fr *armes*, from L *arma* (pl)]

Arm. *abbrev*: Armenian; Armoric.

armada *är-mä'də*, (sometimes, *esp* formerly, *-mā'*), *n* a fleet of armed ships, *esp* that sent by Philip II of Spain against England in 1588. [Sp, fem pa p of *armar*, from L *armāre* to arm]

armadillo *ärm-ə-dil'ō*, *n* an American mammal with long snout, tubular ears and large front claws, an edentate whose body is covered with bands of bony plates: — *pl* **armadill'os**. [Sp, dimin of *armado* armed; see **armada**]

Armageddon *är-mə-ged'n*, *n* the great symbolical battlefield of the Apocalypse, scene of the final struggle between the powers of good and evil (*Bible*); a great, or *esp* the ultimate, war or battle of nations. [*Harmagedōn* or *Armageddōn* given as Heb name in Rev 16.16; perh suggested by the famous battlefield of *Megiddo*, in the plain of Esdraelon]

Armagnac *är-mä-nyak*, *n* a dry brandy distilled in SW France. [Name of district]

Armalite® *ar'mə-līt*, *n* a low-calibre, high-velocity assault rifle with an automatic and semi-automatic facility.

armament *är'mə-mənt*, *n* a force equipped for war; total means of making war; munitions, *esp* for warships; defensive equipment. [L *armāmenta* tackle, equipment]

armamentarium *är-mə-men-tā'ri-əm*, *n* the collective equipment, medicines, etc available to a doctor or other medical practitioner: — *pl* **armamenta'ria** or **armamenta'riums**. [L, arsenal, armoury]

armature *är'mə-chūr, n* armour; any defensive apparatus; a wooden or wire support around which a sculpture, model, etc, is constructed; a piece of ferromagnetic material, eg an iron bar, set across the poles of a magnet; a moving part in a magnetic circuit to indicate the presence of electric current; a rotor, the metal part (wound with current-carrying wire) that, in a generator, turns to produce a current, and in a motor, provides the current that produces torque. [L *armātūra* armour]

Armenian *är-mē'nyən, adj* belonging to *Armenia*, in western Asia, or its people or language, or their branch of the Christian Church. — *n* a native of Armenia; one of the Armenian people; the language of the Armenians. — *adj* **Armē'noid** of the eastern branch of the Alpine race. — Also *n.*

armes parlantes *ärm par-lãt, (Fr)* used of arms that indicate the name of the family that bears them, such as a press and a tun for Preston. [Literally, talking arms]

armet *är'mit, (hist) n* a helmet introduced about 1450 in place of the basinet, consisting of an iron cap, spreading over the back of the neck, having in front the visor, beaver and gorget. [Fr]

armgaunt *ärm'gönt, (Shakesp) adj perh* with gaunt limbs, or *perh* worn with armour, but *prob* an error.

armiger *är'mi-jər, (heraldry* or *hist) n* a person entitled to a coat-of-arms; an esquire. — Also **armi'gero** (*Shakesp*; Slender's blunder in *Merry Wives*). — *adj* **armi'geral**. — *adj* **armi'gerous** bearing, or entitled to bear arms. [L, an armour-bearer, from *arma* arms, and *gerere* to bear]

armilla *är-mil'ə, n* a bracelet (*archaeol*; also **ar'mil**); a frill on a mushroom stalk (*bot*). — *adj* **armill'ary** (or *är'*) of bracelets or hoops. — **armillary sphere** (*astron*) a skeleton sphere made up of hoops to show the motions of the celestial bodies. [L *armilla* an armlet, dimin of *armus* the upper arm, the shoulder]

armillaria *är-mil-ār'i-ə, n* any fungus of the genus *Armillaria*, *esp* the honey fungus (qv), also known as shoestring fungus or bootlace fungus.

Arminian *är-min'i-ən, n* a follower of *Arminius* (1560–1609), who denied the Calvinistic doctrine of absolute predestination, as well as that of irresistible grace. — Also *adj.* — *n* **Armin'ianism**.

armipotent *är-mip'ə-tənt, (archaic* or *literary) adj* powerful in arms. [L *arma* arms, and *potēns, -entis* powerful]

armistice *är'mi-stis, n* a suspension of hostilities; a truce. — **Armistice Day** 11 Nov 1918, the day fighting ended in World War I, kept since as an anniversary, from 1946 as Remembrance Sunday (qv). [Fr, from LL *armistitium*, from L *arma* arms, and *sistere* to stop]

armlet. See **arm**[1].

armoire *är-mwär', (antiques*, etc) *n* a large, decorative wardrobe or cupboard. [Fr]

armorial. See **armour**.

Armoric *är-mor'ik, adj* of *Armorica* (Brittany), or its people. — *n* the Breton language. — *n* and *adj* **Armor'ican**. [L *Armoricus*, from Gallic *are-morici* dwellers by the sea]

armour or (*NAm*) **armor** *är'mər, n* defensive clothing, *esp* of metal, chain-mail, etc; protective covering; armoured vehicles; heraldic insignia. — *adj* **armō'rial** of heraldic arms. — *n* a book of coats-of-arms. — *n* **ar'morist** a person skilled in heraldry. — *n* **ar'mory** heraldry; armorial bearings (*archaic*); armoury (*US*); a drill hall and headquarters of an army unit (*US*); an arsenal (*US*). — *adj* **ar'moured** protected by armour, armour plate, etc; (of glass, etc) strengthened, protective. — *n* **ar'mourer** a maker, repairer or custodian of arms and armour. — *adj* **ar'mourless**. — *n* **ar'moury** a collection of arms and armour; a place where arms are kept; a place where arms are manufactured (*US*); armour collectively (*archaic*). — **armorial bearings** the design in a coat of arms; **ar'mour-bearer** a person who carries another's armour, a squire. — *adj* **ar'mour-clad** clad in armour. — *n* an armoured ship. — **armoured-car'**, **-crui'ser** and **-train'**; **ar'mour-plate** a defensive metal plate for a ship, tank, etc. — *adj* **ar'mour-plated**. [OFr *armure*, from L *armātūra*, from *arma* arms]

armozeen or **armozine** *är-mō-zēn', n* a kind of taffeta or plain silk (*usu* black), used for clerical gowns. [Fr *armoisin*]

armure *är'mūr, n* a type of fabric with a pebbled surface. [Fr]

army *ärm'i, n* a large body of people armed for war and under military command; a body of people banded together in a special cause, sometimes (eg the 'Salvation Army') in imitation of military methods; a host, multitude (eg of people, insects, etc); a great number. — **army ant** any of several kinds of stinging ants which move about in vast numbers; **army corps** (*kör*) a miniature army comprising all arms of the service; **army list** a list of all commissioned officers; **army worm** the larva of a small fly (*Sciara*) that collects in vast armies and can move in multitudes from field to field destroying crops; the larva of any of several (*esp* N American and E African) types of moth that can move in multitudes from field to field destroying crops. [Fr *armée*, pa p fem of *armer*, from L *armāre, -ātum* to arm]

arna *är'nä, n* the Indian water-buffalo (*Bubalus bubalis*). [Hindi]

Arnaut or **Arnaout** *är-nowt', n* an Albanian, *esp* one in the Turkish army. [Turk]

arnica *är'ni-kə, n* a tincture of the flowers of a composite plant (*Arnica montana* or mountain tobacco) which is applied to sprains and bruises (but not to open wounds). [Origin unknown]

arnotto. See **annatto**.

arnut *är'nət*. Same as **earth-nut**.

aroba. See **araba**.

aroid. See **arum**.

aroint or **aroynt** *ə-roint', (archaic)* apparently *vt*, used twice by Shakespeare in the phrase, '*Aroint* thee, witch', meaning away, begone; to drive or frighten away (*Browning*). [Origin unknown]

arolla *a-rol'ə, n* the Swiss stone-pine or Siberian cedar (*Pinus cembra*). [Fr *arolle*]

aroma *ə-rō'mə, n* a spicy or distinctive fragrance; flavour or peculiar charm (*fig*). — *adj* **aromatic** (*ar-ō-mat'ik*) fragrant; spicy; belonging to the closed-chain class of organic compounds, or benzene derivatives (*opp* to *fatty* or *aliphatic*; *chem*). — Also *n.* — *vt* **arō'matize** or **-ise** to render aromatic; to perfume. — **aromather'apy** a method of treating bodily ailments using essential plant oils, *esp* in combination with massage; **aromather'apist**. [L, from Gr *arōma, -atos* spice]

arose. See **arise**.

around *ə-rownd', prep* on all sides of; round or round about; somewhere near; in existence or circulation (*colloq*). — *adv* on every side; in a circle; round about, on the move. — **get around to** (*colloq*) to reach the point of (doing something); **have been around** (*colloq*) to be experienced or sophisticated. [**a-**[1] and **round**[2]]

arouse *ə-rowz', vt* and *vi* to rouse; to stimulate. — *n* (*rare*) an act of arousing, an alarm. — *n* **arous'al**. — *n* **arous'er**. [Pfx *a-* (intensive) and **rouse**[1]]

a-row or **arow** *ə-rō', adv* in a row; one following the other (*obs*). [**a-**[1] and **row**[1]]

aroynt. See **aroint**.

ARP *abbrev*: air raid precautions.

arpeggio *är-ped'j(y)ō, (music) n* a chord of which the notes are performed, not simultaneously, but in rapid (normally upward) succession; the notes of a chord played or sung, *esp* as an exercise, in rapid ascending or descending progression, according to a set pattern: — *pl* **arpegg'ios**. — *vt* **arpegg'iate** (*-ji-āt*) to perform or write in arpeggios. — *n* **arpeggiā'tion**. — *n* **arpeggione** (*är-pej-i-ōn'ā*) an early 19c bowed stringed instrument. [Ital *arpeggiare* to play the harp, from *arpa* harp]

arpent *är'pənt* or *är-pã, n* an old French measure for land (still used in Quebec and Louisiana) varying from about 50 to 35 ares ($1\frac{1}{4}$ acres to $\frac{5}{6}$ of an acre). [Fr, from L *arepennis*, said to be a Gallic word]

arpillera *ar-pil-yä'rə*, *n* a pictorial Peruvian wall decoration consisting of colourful threads and scraps stitched on to a sackcloth backing. [Sp, sackcloth]

arquebus *är'kwi-bus* or **harquebus** (*här'*), (*hist*) *n* an old-fashioned handgun. — *n* **arquebusade'** a lotion for shot-wounds. — *n* **arquebusier** (*-bus-ēr'*) a soldier armed with an arquebus. [Fr *arquebuse*, from Du *haakbus*, from *haak* hook, and *bus* box, barrel of a gun; Ger *Hakenbüchse*]

ARR *abbrev*: *anno regni regis* (or *reginae*) (*L*), in the year of the king's (or queen's) reign.

arr. *abbrev*: arranged (by); arranger; arrival; arrived, arrives, arriving, etc.

arracacha *ar-a-käch'ə*, *n* an umbelliferous plant (genus *Arracacia*) of northern S America, with edible tubers. [Quechua *aracacha*]

arrack or now *usu* **arak** *ar'ək*, *n* an ardent spirit made in Eastern countries from toddy, or the fermented juice of the coco and other palms, as well as from rice and jaggery sugar. [Ar *'araq* juice]

arragonite. Another spelling of **aragonite**.

arrah *ar'ə*, *interj* Anglo-Irish expression of emotion, wonder, mild expostulation, etc.

arraign *ə-rān'*, *vt* to call to account (*obs*); to put on trial; to accuse publicly. — *n* **arraign'er**. — *n* **arraign'ing**. — *n* **arraign'ment**. [OFr *aresnier*, from LL *arratiōnāre*, from L *ad* to, and *ratiō*, *-ōnis* reason]

arrange *ə-rānj'*, *vt* to set in a rank or row; to put in order; to settle or work out; to adapt for other instruments or voices, or for a different setting or style (*music*). — *vi* to come to an agreement (with *to*); to make plans (with *to* or *for*). — *n* **arrange'ment**. — *n* **arrang'er**. [OFr *arangier*, from *à* to, and *rangier*, *rengier*; see **range**]

arrant *ar'ənt*, *adj* downright, unmitigated, out-and-out; notorious; rascally. — *adv* **arr'antly**. [A variant of **errant**]

arras *ar'əs*, *n* rich tapestry (as formerly made at *Arras* in France); a hanging screen of tapestry for a wall. — *adj* **arr'ased** covered with arras. — *n* **arr'asene** an embroidery material, of wool and silk.

arraught. See **areach**.

array *ə-rā'*, *n* order, arrangement; an imposing, purposeful or significant arrangement; an arrangement of terms in rows and columns, (*esp* if square) a matrix (*math*); a set of storage locations, etc referenced by a single identifier (*comput*); dress or equipage (*archaic* or *poetic*). — *vt* to empanel (jurors) (*law*); to dress, adorn or equip (*archaic* or *poetic*); to put in order, arrange (*obs*). — *n* **array'al**. — *n* **array'er**. — *n* **array'ment** the act of arraying; clothing (*obs*). [Anglo-Fr *arai*, OFr *arei*, array, equipage, from L *ad*, and the Gmc root found in Eng **ready**, Ger *bereit*]

arrear *ə-rēr'*, *n* that which is in the rear or behind (*archaic*); (*usu* in *pl*) that which remains unpaid or undone; (in *pl*) total unpaid debt, debts not paid by the due date; (in *sing* or now *usu pl*) the condition of being behindhand. — *adv* (*obs*) backward, behind. — *n* **arrear'age** arrear, arrears. — **in arrears** behindhand, *esp* in the payment of debts, rent, etc. [OFr *arere*, *ariere* (Fr *arrière*), from L *ad* to, and *retrō* back, behind]

arrect *a-rekt'*, *adj* (of an animal's ears) upright, pricked up; on the alert. [L *arrēctus*]

arrectis auribus *ar-ek'tēs ow'ri-bŏŏs*, (*L*) with ears pricked up.

arreede. See **aread**.

arrest *ə-rest'*, *vt* to bring to a standstill, check; to seize; to catch, fix (eg the attention); to apprehend and take into custody (a person) by legal authority; to seize by warrant; to take as security (*Shakesp*). — *n* the act of arresting; seizure by warrant; stoppage, failure (eg of an organ or mechanism). — *adj* **arrest'able** (of an offence) such that the offender may be arrested without warrant; liable to arrest. — *n* **arrestation** (*ar-es-tā'shən*) the act of arresting; arrest. — *n* **arrestee'** (*Scots law*) a person prevented by arrestment from making payment or delivery to another until the arrester's claim upon that other is secured or satisfied. — *n* **arrest'er** a person who, or thing which, arrests; a lightning-arrester (qv under **lighten**[1]); a person who makes an arrestment (*Scots law*; also **arrest'or**). — *adj* **arrest'ive** tending to arrest. — *n* **arrest'ment** a checking, stopping; detention of a person arrested till liberated on bail, or by security (*law*); a process which prohibits a debtor from handing over to his or her creditor money or property until a debt due by that creditor to a third party, the arrester, is paid or secured (*Scots law*). — **arrester gear** shock-absorbing transverse cables on an aircraft-carrier's deck for the arrester hook of an alighting aircraft to catch on; **arrester hook** a hook put out from an aircraft alighting on an aircraft-carrier, to catch on the arrester gear. — **arrest of judgement** (*law*) a delay between conviction and sentence because of possible error; **cardiac arrest** a heart attack; heart failure; **under arrest** having been apprehended by legal authority, held in custody. [OFr *arester*, from L *ad* to, and *restāre* to stand still]

arrêt *a-ret'*, *ä're'* or *ä-rā'*, *n* a decision; the judgement of a tribunal. [Fr, from OFr *arester*; see **arrest**]

arrhenotoky *ar-ən-ot'ə-ki*, (*biol*) *n* parthenogenetic production of males alone, by virgin females. [Gr *arrēn* male, and *tokos* offspring]

arrhythmic or **arhythmic** *ā-rith'mik*, or *-ridh'*, *adj* having an irregular or interrupted rhythm. — *n* **arrhyth'mia** or **arhyth'mia** (*med*) irregularity of the heartbeat. [Gr *a-* (privative)]

arriage *ar'ij*, (*hist*) *n* a former feudal service in Scotland, said to have been rendered by the tenant with his beasts of burden. [See **average** and **aver**[2]]

arride *ə-rīd'*, (*archaic*) *vt* to please, gratify. [L *arrīdēre*]

arriéré *ar-ē-ār-ā*, (*Fr*) *adj* backward, old-fashioned.

arrière-ban *ar'ē-er-ban* or *-bã*, (*hist*) *n* a feudal sovereign's summons to all freemen to take the field; the army thus collected. [OFr *ariereban*, from OHGer *hari* army, and *ban* public proclamation; confused with Fr *arrière*]

arrière-garde *ar-ē-er-gärd*, (*Fr*) *n* rearguard.

arrière-pensée *ar-ē-er-pã-sā*, (*Fr*) *n* a mental reservation; a subsidiary or concealed aim.

arriero *ar-i-ā'rō*, (*Sp*) *n* a muleteer: — *pl* **arrie'ros**.

arris *ar'is*, (*building*, etc) *n* a sharp edge on stone, metal, etc at the meeting of two surfaces. — **arris gutter** a V-shaped gutter *usu* of wood; **arris rail** a wooden, etc rail of triangular section; **arris tile** an angular roof-tile for use where hips or ridges intersect. [See **arête**]

arrish or **arish** *är'ish*, (*dialect*) *n* a stubble field. [OE *ersc* (in compounds)]

arrive *ə-rīv'*, *vi* to reach any place; to attain to any object (with *at*); to achieve success or recognition; to happen, come about (*obs*); to reach shore or port (*obs*). — *vt* (*obs*) to reach. — *n* **arriv'al** the act of arriving; a person or thing that arrives; the attainment of a position or state. — *n* **arriv'ance** or **arriv'ancy** (*Shakesp*) company arriving. [OFr *ariver* to reach shore, from LL *adrīpāre*, from L *ad* to, and *rīpa* shore]

arrivederci or **a rivederci** *är-ē-vəd-er'chē*, (*Ital*) *interj* goodbye until we meet again.

arriviste *a'rē-vēst*, *n* a person 'on the make'; a parvenu, upstart; a self-seeker. — *n* **arr'ivisme**. [Fr]

arroba *a-rō'bə* or *ä-ro'bä*, *n* a (regionally variable) weight of 25 pounds (11·35kg) or more, used in Spanish, Portuguese and Spanish American regions. [Sp and Port from Ar *ar-rub'* the quarter]

arrogance *ar'ə-gəns*, *n* undue assumption of importance; conceit, self-importance. — *adj* **arr'ogant** claiming too much; overbearing; conceited, self-important. — *adv* **arr'ogantly**. [Fr, from L *arrogāntia*; see **arrogate**]

arrogate *ar'ə-gāt*, *vt* to claim as one's own; to claim proudly or unduly; to ascribe, attribute or assign (to another). — *n* **arrogā'tion** act of arrogating; undue assumption. [L *arrogāre*, from *ad* to, and *rogāre*, *-ātum* to ask, to claim]

arrondissement *ä-rɔ̃-dēs'mã*, *n* in France, a subdivision of a department, or a municipal subdivision of some large cities, *esp* Paris. [Fr, from *arrondir* to make round]

arrow[1] *ar'ō*, *n* a straight, pointed missile, made to be shot from a bow; any arrow-shaped mark or object; (in *pl*) darts (*colloq*); the chief shoot of a plant (*obs*); *specif* the flowering stem of the sugar-cane. — *vt* to indicate or show the position of, by an arrow. — *adj* **arr'owy** of or like arrows. — **arr'ow-grass** a grass of the genus of marsh plants (*Triglochin*) whose burst capsule is like an arrow-head; **arr'ow-head** the head or pointed part of an arrow; an aquatic plant (*Sagittaria sagittifolia*) of the Alismaceae, with arrow-shaped leaves. — *adj* **arr'ow-headed** shaped like the head of an arrow. — **arr'ow-poison** poison smeared on arrow-heads; **arr'owroot** a West Indian plant, *Maranta arundinacea* or other species; its rhizome, *orig* used in S America as an antidote to arrow-poison; a nutritious starch from the rhizome, now *esp* in powdered form used as a thickener, etc; extended to other plants and their starch (see **Portland**); **arr'ow-shot** the range of an arrow; **arr'owwood** species of Viburnum (*esp V. dentatum*) or other shrubs or trees formerly used by American Indians to make arrows. [OE *arwe*; prob cognate with L *arcus* bow]

arrow[2]. See **ary**.

arroyo *ə-roi'ō*, (*US*) *n* a rocky ravine; a dry watercourse: — *pl* **arroy'os**. [Sp]

'Arry *ar'i*, (*old colloq*) *n* a jovial vulgar Cockney: — *fem* **'Arr'iet**. — *adj* **'Arr'yish**. [Cockney pronunciation of *Harry*, *Harriet*]

arse *ärs* or (*NAm*) **ass** *as*, (now *vulg*) *n* the buttocks; impudence, cheek (*Austr*). — *n* **arse'hole** (*NAm* **ass'-hole**) the anus (*vulg*); a worthless, contemptible, etc person (*vulg slang*). — **arse licker** or **arse'-licker** (*vulg slang*) an extremely obsequious person; **arse'-licking**. — *adv* and *adj* **ars'y-vers'y** (*slang*) backside foremost, contrary. — **arse around** or **about** (*vulg slang*) to mess around, do nothing in particular or nothing of any value. [OE *ærs* (*ears*); Ger *Arsch*, Swed *ars*; cognate with Gr *orros* (for *orsos*)]

arsenal *ärs'(i-)nl*, *n* a dockyard (*hist*); a magazine or factory for naval and military weapons and ammunition; a stock of anything considered of analogous power or potential; a storehouse (*fig*). [Ital *arzenale*, *arsenale* (Sp, Fr *arsenal*), from Ar *dār aççināʻah* workshop, from (*dār* house), *al* the, and *çināʻah* art]

arsenic *ärs'(ə-)nik*, *n* the chemical element (symbol **As**; atomic no 33); a poison, the trioxide of the element (As_2O_3; **white arsenic**). — *n* **ar'senate** or **arseniate** (*-sē'ni-āt*) a salt of arsenic acid. — *adj* **arsenic** (*-sen'ik*), **arsen'ical** or **arsē'nious** composed of or containing arsenic. — In chemistry **arsenic** is applied to compounds in which arsenic is pentavalent, **arsenious** to those in which it is trivalent. — *n* **ar'senide** a compound of arsenic with a metal. — *n* **ar'senite** a salt of arsenious acid. — *n* **arsenopyrī'tēs** mispickel, a mineral composed of iron, arsenic and sulphur. — *n* **arsine** (*är'sēn*, *-sin* or *-sīn*) the poisonous gas, hydride of arsenic (AsH_3); a compound in which one or more hydrogen atoms of AsH_3 are replaced by an alkyl radical, etc. [Gr *arsenikon* yellow orpiment, fancifully associated with Gr *arsēn* male, and the alchemists' notion that metals have sex]

arses. See **arse** and **arsis**.

arshin, **arshine** or **arsheen** *är-shēn'*, *n* an old measure of length, about 28in (71cm) in Russia, about 30in (76cm, but legally a metre) in Turkey. [Turkish]

arsine. See under **arsenic**.

arsis *är'sis*, (*Gr prosody* and *music*) *n* literally, a lift, an up-beat; hence the weak position in a bar or foot; understood by the Romans as the strong position; used in English in both senses; elevation of the voice to higher pitch: — *opp* to *thesis*: — *pl* **ar'sēs**. [L, from Gr *arsis*, from *airein* to lift]

arsmetrick *ärz-met'rik*, *n* an *obs* form of **arithmetic** founded on the false etymology *ars metrica* (*L*), art of measuring.

arson[1] *är'sn*, *n* the crime of maliciously and feloniously setting fire to houses, haystacks, ships, forests, or similar property. — *n* **ar'sonist** or (*rare*) **ar'sonite**. [OFr *arson*, from L *arsiō*, *-ōnis*, from *ardēre*, *arsum* to burn]

arson[2] *är'sn*, (*obs*) *n* a saddlebow. [OFr *arçun*, from L *arcus* a bow]

arsphenamine *ärs-fen'ə-mēn* or *-mīn*, *n* salvarsan (qv), a synthetic compound of arsenic. [*ars*enic, *phen*e and *amine*]

arsy-versy. See under **arse**.

art[1] *ärt*, (*archaic*, *esp liturgical*, *formal* or *poetic*) used as *2nd pers sing* present indicative of the verb *to be*. [OE (WSax) *eart*, (Mercian) *earth*, (Northumbrian) *arth*; from the root *es-* seen in **is**, **are**]

art[2] *ärt*, *n* practical skill, or its application, guided by principles; human skill and agency (*opp* to *nature*); application of skill to production of beauty (*esp* visible beauty) and works of creative imagination, as in the fine arts; (in general use) the visual arts, drawing and painting, and *usu* sculpture; a branch of learning, *esp* one of the *liberal* arts (see **trivium**, **quadrivium**), as in *faculty of arts*, *master of arts*; skill or knowledge in a particular department; a skilled profession or trade, craft, or branch of activity; magic or occult knowledge or influence; a method or knack of doing a thing; cunning, artifice, crafty conduct; a wile, trick. — *adj* of, for or concerned with painting, sculpture, etc (as in *art gallery*, *art historian*); intended to be decorative or artistic; produced with studied artistry, not arising spontaneously or by chance. — *adj* **art'ful** cunning; skilful, masterly; produced by art; dexterous, clever (*archaic*). — *adv* **art'fully**. — *n* **art'fulness**. — *n* **art'iness** the quality or state of being arty. — *adj* **art'less** simple; guileless, unaffected; inartistic (*rare*). — *adv* **art'lessly**. — *n* **art'lessness**. — *adj* **art'y** (*colloq*), or less commonly **art'sy**, artistic, or aspiring to be. — *n* (*colloq*) an arty person. — **art autre** (*är-tō-tr'*) a post-World War II movement in painting, including tachisme; **art brut** the primitive (literally, raw), unrefined or naïve art of non-professional or untrained artists (eg children, mental patients, prisoners, etc); **art deco** (*ärt dek'ō*) the style of decorative art characteristic of the 1920s and 1930s, developing the curvilinearity of art nouveau into more streamlined geometrical forms; **art form** a set form or arrangement in poetry or music; an accepted medium of artistic expression; **art house** a cinema that shows films regarded as artistic as distinct from popular, *incl* cult and foreign, subtitled films. — *adj* **art'-house**. — **art nouveau** (*är nōō-vō'*) a decorative form of art (c.1890–1910) in which curvilinear forms are important and fundamentally unrelated images are often combined in a single design; **art paper** a type of paper for illustrations, coated with a composition containing china clay; **arts'man** a craftsman (*obs*); a scholar (*obs*); **art'-song** a song whose words and music are the product of conscious art, the music reflecting every turn of meaning (distinguished from a *folk-song*); **arts student** a student in the faculty of arts; **art student** a student of painting, sculpture, etc; **art therapy** art used as a means of communication, or a creative activity, to assist personal development, diagnosis and rehabilitation; **art union** (*Austr* and *NZ*) a lottery; **art'work** the illustrations and other decorative material in a publication; production of or work in creating, artistic objects; work(s) of art. — *adj* **arty-craft'y** to do with, or *esp* involved in, arts and crafts; self-consciously artistic. — *adj* **arty-fart'y** (*derog colloq*) arty, arty-crafty. — **art and part** (*orig law*, etc) concerned in either by *art* in contriving or by *part* in actual execution, now loosely used in the sense of participating, sharing; **fine art** the aesthetically significant forms of art (now *usu* defined as architecture, painting, sculpture and some graphic arts) as distinct from *applied* and *decorative* art; loosely, (a college course combining) art history and practical art tuition; sometimes, the fine arts (see below); an operation or practice requiring special skill or craftsmanship (*colloq*); **get something down to a fine art** to become very skilled at something through practice; **soft art** (and **soft sculpture**) works of art (and sculpture) constructed from textiles or other soft materials; **term of art** a technical word; **the fine arts** painting, poetry, music, etc. [L *ars, artis*]

art. *abbrev*: article; artificial; (also **arty**) artillery.

artal. See **rotl**.

artefact or **artifact** *är'ti-fakt, n* (*esp archaeol*) a thing made by human workmanship. — *adj* **artefac'tual**. [L *arte*, by art (ablative of *ars*), and *factum* made]

artel *är-tel', n* a Russian workers' guild. [Russ]

artemisia *är-te-miz'i-ə, n* any plant of the *Artemisia* genus of composites including wormwood, southernwood, mugwort, sagebrush, etc. [Gr *artemisiā*]

artery *är'tər-i, n* a tube or vessel that conveys blood from the heart to the body (*anatom* and *zool*); any main channel of communication or movement. — *adj* **arterial** (*-tē'ri-əl*). — *n* **artērializā'tion** or **-s-**. — *vt* **artēr'ialize** or **-ise** to make arterial. — *n* **arteriog'raphy** (*radiol*) the radiological examination of arteries following direct injection of a contrast medium. — *n* (*anatom* and *zool*) **artē'riole** a very small artery. — *n* **artēriosclerō'sis** (*med*; Gr *sklērōsis* hardening) hardening of the arteries. — *adj* **artēriosclerotic** (*-ot'ik*). — *n* **artēriot'omy** (*obs med*; Gr *tomē* a cut) the cutting or opening of an artery, to let blood. — *n* (*med*) **arterī'tis** inflammation of an artery. — **arterial road** a main traffic road from which lesser routes branch. [L *artēria*, from Gr *artēriā* windpipe, artery]

artesian *är-tē'zyən* or *-zh(y)ən, adj* (sometimes with *cap*) a type of well in which water rises in a borehole by hydrostatic pressure from a basin whose outcrop is at a higher level. [*Artesian* of Artois (LL *Artesium*) in N France where such wells were in early use]

artful. See **art**[2].

arthralgia *är-thral'j(i-)ə*, (*pathol*) *n* pain in a joint. — *adj* **arthral'gic**. — *adj* **arthritic** (*-thrit'ik*) of, pertaining to, or of the nature of, arthritis. — *n* a person suffering from arthritis; a gouty person. — *n* **arthritis** (*är-thrī'tis*) inflammation of a joint, associated with swelling, pain, stiffness, etc; (such inflammation caused by) gout. [Gr *arthron* a joint, and *algos* pain]

arthrodesis *är-thrō-dē'sis*, (*med*) *n* the immobilizing of a joint in the body by the surgical fusion of the bones. [Gr *arthron* joint, and *desis* binding together]

arthromere *är'thrō-mēr*, (*zool*) *n* a body segment of an articulated animal, a somite. [Gr *arthron* a joint, and *meros* part]

arthropathy *är-throp'ə-thi*, (*med*) *n* a disease of the joints. [Gr *arthron* joint, and *patheia* suffering]

arthroplasty *är'thrō-plas-ti*, (*med*) *n* surgical repair of a joint; replacement of a joint by an artificial joint. [Gr *arthron* joint, and *plastos* moulded]

arthropod *är'thrō-pod, n* any member of the **Arthropoda** (*är-throp'od-ə*), a major division of the animal kingdom, with segmented bodies and jointed appendages (crustacea, arachnids, peripatuses, millipedes, centipedes, insects, tardigrades, etc). — *adj* **arthrop'odal**. [Gr *arthron* joint, and *pous, podos* a foot]

arthroscopy *är-thros'ko-pi*, (*med*) *n* examination of a joint with an endoscope. [Gr *arthron* joint, and *skopeein* to look]

arthrosis *är-thrōs'is*, (*med*) *n* connection by a joint, articulation; degenerative, non-inflammatory, disease of the joints. [Gr *arthrōsis*, from *arthron* a joint]

arthrospore *är'thrō-spör*, (*bot*) *n* a conidium; (inappropriately) a vegetative cell that has passed into a resting state. [Gr *arthron* joint, and *sporā* seed]

Arthurian *är-thū'ri-ən, adj* relating to King *Arthur*, a 6c ruler of the Britons, whose court is the centre of many legends, but who himself probably had real existence; pertaining to the legends. — *npl* **Arthurian'a** stories, etc connected with the court of King Arthur.

artic. See **articulated lorry** under **article**.

artichoke *är'ti-chōk, n* a thistlelike perennial plant (*Cynara scolymus*) with fleshy large scaly head and bracts and edible receptacle; the grey-green flower-head of the artichoke, served as a vegetable. — **Jerusalem artichoke** a totally different plant, a species of sunflower with edible tubers like potatoes (Jerusalem being a corruption of Ital *girasole* sunflower); the white-fleshed tuber with knobbly brownish or reddish skin, served as a vegetable. [N Ital *articiocco* (Ital *carciofo*), from OSp *alcarchofa*, from Ar *al-kharshōfa, al-kharshūf*]

article *är'ti-kl, n* a separate element, member or part of anything; a particular object or commodity; an item; a single clause or term; a distinct point in an agreement, or (in *pl*) an agreement regarded as made up of such (as in *articles of apprenticeship*, etc); (in *pl*) rules or conditions generally; a section, paragraph or head; a literary composition in a newspaper, periodical, encyclopedia, etc, dealing with a subject distinctly and independently; the adjective *the* (*definite article*), *a* or *an* (*indefinite article*) or the equivalent in another language (*gram*); a joint, segment (*obs*); a juncture, critical moment, nick of time (*obs*). — *vt* to bind by articles of apprenticeship; to set forth as a charge (that); to indict; to stipulate (*obs*); to arrange by agreement, etc (*obs*). — *vi* to bring specific charges (against; *obs*). — *adj* **ar'ticled** bound as apprentice (eg in a legal office). — *adj* **artic'ūlable** that can be articulated. — *n* **artic'ulacy** articulateness. — *adj* **artic'ūlar** belonging to the joints; at or near a joint. — *n pl* **Articūlā'ta** in Cuvier's classification, the arthropods and higher worms. — *adj* **artic'ūlate** jointed; composed of distinct parts; (eg of human speech) composed of recognizably distinct sounds; clear; able to express one's thoughts with ease. — *vt* to attach by a joint; to connect by joints; to form into distinct sounds, syllables or words. — *vi* to form a joint (with; *lit* and *fig*); to speak distinctly; to come to terms (*Shakesp*). — *adj* **artic'ūlated**. — *adv* **artic'ūlately**. — *n* **artic'ūlateness**. — *n* **articūlā'tion** jointing; a joint; a segment; distinctness, or distinct utterance; a consonant. — *n* **artic'ūlātor** a person who articulates or speaks; a person who articulates bones and mounts skeletons; an apparatus, etc that articulates. — *adj* **artic'ūlatory**. — **articulated lorry** etc, a lorry, etc made easier to manœuvre by having its (sometimes detachable) front section flexibly attached to the rear section so that it can move at an angle to it (*colloq* shortening **artic'** (or *är'*)). — **articles of association** (a document containing) the internal regulations and conditions for the business of a joint-stock company registered under the Companies Acts; **articles of faith** the binding statement of points of belief of a Church, etc; **articles of war** the code of regulations for the government and discipline of armed services; **in the article of death** (*archaic*; L *in articulō mortis*) at the point of death; **Lords of the Articles** (*hist*) a standing committee of the Scottish parliament who drafted the measures to be submitted; **of great article** (*Shakesp*) of great importance; **Thirty-nine Articles** the articles of religious belief finally agreed upon by the bishops and clergy of the Church of England in 1562. [L *articulus* a little joint, *articulāre, -ātum* to provide with joints, to utter distinctly, from *artus* joint]

artifact. See **artefact**.

artifice *är'ti-fis, n* contrivance or trickery; an ingenious expedient; a crafty trick, machination; skill, craft, resource; handicraft (*Milton*); workmanship (*obs*). — *n* **artif'icer** a mechanic (*esp army* and *navy*); a person who creates skilfully; a craftsman; a contriver; (with *cap*) the Creator; a trickster (*obs*). [L *artificium*, from *artifex, -ficis* an artificer, from *ars, artis* art, and *facere* to make]

artificial *är-ti-fish'əl, adj* contrived (*opp* to *spontaneous*); made by man; synthetic (*opp* to *natural*); fictitious, factitious, feigned, made in imitation (*opp* to *real*); affected in manners; (of classifications) based on superficial structural features rather than on natural relationships (*biol*); ingenious (*obs*); *perh* creative, playing the artificer, or *perh* merely skilful (*Shakesp*); technical (*obs*). — *n* **artificiality** (*-fish-i-al'i-ti*). — *vt*

artific'ialize or **-ise**. — *adv* **artific'ially**. — *n* **artific'ialness**. — **artificial horizon** a gyroscopic device indicating an aircraft's altitude in relation to the horizontal; **artificial insemination** the injection of semen into the uterus or vagina by other means than sexual union; **artificial intelligence** the use of computers in such a way that they perform functions normally associated with human intelligence, such as learning, adapting, self-correction and decision-taking; **artificial kidney** a kidney machine; **artificial language** an invented language functioning not as the native speech of its users but as a computer language or means of international communication; **artificial porcelain** soft-paste porcelain; **artificial radioactivity** radiation from isotopes after high-energy bombardment in an accelerator by alpha particles, protons, or neutrons; **artificial respiration** stimulation of respiration manually or mechanically by forcing air in and out of the lungs; **artificial selection** (*biol*) see **select**; **artificial silk** see **silk**; **artificial sunlight** light from lamps rich in ultraviolet rays. — **artificial insemination by donor** former name for **donor insemination** (discontinued because of the similarity of its commonly used *abbrev* **AID** to **AIDS**). [ME, from L *artificialis*, from *artificium* (see **artifice**)]

artillery *är-til'ər-i*, *n* offensive weapons of war, formerly in general, now the heavier kinds (ancient ballistas, catapults, modern cannon, etc); a branch of the military service using these; the science of handling guns, gunnery; missiles (*obs*). — *n* **artill'erist** a person skilled in artillery; a gunner. — **artill'eryman** a soldier of the artillery; **artill'ery-plant** a tropical American plant (genus *Pilea*) of the nettle family that ejects its pollen in puffs. [OFr *artillerie*, from *artiller* to arm, of doubtful origin]

artiness. See **art**[2].

artiodactyl *är-ti-ō-dak'til*, (*zool*) *adj* even-toed. — *n* a member of the **Artiodac'tyla** or even-toed ungulates, in which the third and fourth digit form a symmetrical pair and the hindfoot bears an even number of digits (cf **perissodactyl**). [Gr *artios* even in number, and *daktylos* finger or toe]

artisan *ärt-i-zan'*, or *ärt'*, *n* a handicraftsman or mechanic, a skilled manual worker. — *adj* **artis'anal** (or *ärt'*). [Fr, from Ital *artigiano*, ult from L *artitus* skilled, from *ars, artis* art]

artist *ärt'ist*, *n* a person who practises or is skilled in an art, now *esp* a fine art; a person who has the qualities of imagination and taste required in art; a painter or draughtsman; a performer, *esp* in music; a person good at, or given to, a particular activity, such as *booze artist* (*esp Austr* and *US slang*); a learned man (*obs*); someone who professes magic, astrology, alchemy, etc, or chemistry (*obs*). — *adj* **artist'ic** or (now *rare*) **artist'ical**. — *adv* **artist'ically**. — *n* **art'istry** artistic pursuits; artistic workmanship, quality or ability. — **artistic temperament** the emotional and capricious temperament ascribed to artists; **artist's proof** an unnumbered proof (now *esp* a first impression) of a print made and/or kept for the artist's own use or record. [Fr *artiste*, from L *ars, artis* art]

artiste *är-tēst'*, *n* a public performer, entertainer; someone adept in a manual art. [Fr]

Artium Baccalaureus *är'shi-um* (or *-ti-o͝om*) *bak-a-lö'rē-us* (or *-low'rā-o͝os*), (*L*) *n* Bachelor of Arts. — **Artium Magister** (*ma-jis'tər* or *-gis'ter*) or **Magister Artium** Master of Arts.

artless. See **art**[2].

artocarpus *är-tō-kär'pəs*, *n* a plant of the genus *Artocarpus* of the mulberry family, that includes breadfruit and jack. [Gr *artos* bread, and *karpos* fruit]

artsy, arty, arty-farty. See **art**[2].

arugula *ə-ro͞o'gə-lə*, *n* rocket, a Mediterranean herb used in salads. [Ital dialect, ult from L *eruca* a colewort]

arum *ā'rəm*, *n* a perennial plant of the cuckoo-pint or wake-robin genus, *Arum*; any of several related plants, *esp* the **arum lily** with large leaves, fleshy stem, large ornamental white spathe with yellow spadix (also **calla lily**). — *n pl* **Arā'ceae** (*a-*) the family of spadicifloral monocotyledons to which they belong. — *adj* **araceous** (*a-rā'shəs*) or **aroid** (*ā'roid*) of the Araceae; like an arum. — *n* **ā'roid** any plant of the family. — **arum lily** (see **arum** above) Zantedeschia. [L *arum*, from Gr *aron*]

arundinaceous *ə-run-di-nā'shəs*, (*bot*) *adj* of or like a reed. [L *arundināceus*, from *arundō, -inis* a reed]

arval *är'vəl*, *adj* pertaining to ploughed land. — **Arval Brethren** in ancient Rome, a college of priests who sacrificed to the field deities. [L *arvālis*, from *arāre* to plough]

Arvicola *är-vik'ō-lə*, *n* the water-rat genus of voles. — *n* **ar'vicole** a member of the genus. — *adj* **arvic'oline**. [L *arvum* a field, and *colere* to inhabit]

arvo *är'vō*, (*Austr colloq*) *n* short form of afternoon: — *pl* **ar'vos**.

ary *ä'ri* or *e'ri*, or (*obs*) **arrow** *ar'ō*, (*dialect*) *adj* any. [From **e'er a**, **ever a**; cf **nary**]

Aryan *ā'ri-ən* or *ä'*, *adj* Indo-Germanic, Indo-European; of the Indian, or Indian and Iranian, branch of the Indo-European languages; speaking one of these languages; (in Nazi politics) Caucasian, *esp* of northern European type and *esp* as *opp* to *Jewish*. — *n* a member of the prehistoric people belonging to the Indo-European language family, or a descendant; the parent Indo-European language; a speaker of an Aryan language; (in Nazi politics) a person of Aryan descent. — *vt* **Ar'yanize** or **-ise**. [Sans *ārya* noble]

Arya Samaj *är'yä sä-mäj'*, *n* a reformed Hindu religious body or school, founded by Dayananda Saraswati (1824–83), based on the Vedas, and opposing idolatry, caste, and child-marriage. [Hindi *ārya samāj* noble association]

aryballos *ar-i-bal'os*, (*antiq*) *n* a globular oil-flask with a neck. — *adj* **aryball'oid**. [Gr]

aryl *ar'il*, (*chem*) *n* any aromatic univalent hydrocarbon radical. [**aromatic**, and Gr *hȳlē* matter]

arytaenoid or **arytenoid** *ar-i-tē'noid*, (*anatom* and *zool*) *adj* pitcher-shaped. — *n* one of a pair of cartilages or muscles of the larynx. [Gr *arytainoeidēs*, from *arytaina* a cup, and *eidos* form]

AS *abbrev*: Advanced Supplementary (examination); air speed; air staff; all sections (*insurance*); Anglo-Saxon; *anno salutis* (*L*), in the year of salvation; anti-submarine; Assistant Secretary.

As (*chem*) *symbol*: arsenic.

as[1] *az* or *əz*, *adv* in whatever degree, proportion or manner; to whatever extent; in that degree; to that extent; so far; (passing into *conj* or almost *prep*) for instance; in the manner, character, part, aspect, of; in so far as; whereas. — *conj* because, since; while, when; as if; that (consequence) (*Milton*); than (*illiterate* or *dialect*). — *pronoun* who, which, that (after *such, so, same*, or where a statement is treated as antecedent; in *Shakesp* after a demonstrative pronoun; otherwise *dialect* or *illiterate*). — **as also** likewise; **as**... **as** or... **as** no matter how...; **as concerning**, **as for**, **as regards** or **as to** for the matter of; **as from** or **as of** from (a specified time); **as how** that (with noun clause) (*illiterate* or *dialect*); introducing a question (similarly **as why**) (*obs*); **as if** or **as though** as it would be if; **as is** (*colloq*) as it stands; unaltered; **as it were** so to speak; in a kind of way; **as many as** all who; **as much** the same; just that; **as now** or **as then** just as at this or that time; **as was** formerly; in a former state; **as well** also; in addition; equally well, suitably, happily, etc; **as yet** up to the moment; until now (also **as-yet**); **as you were** a military order to return to the former position; in general use, countermanding an instruction; **so as to** with the purpose or consequence specified; **when as** (*archaic*) at what time. [OE *all-swā* (*eall-swā*) all so, wholly so]

as[2] *äs*, (*Scand mythol*) *n* a Norse god, an inhabitant of Asgard: — *pl* **aesir** (*es'ir*). [ON *āss* a god (pl *æsir*); cf OE *ōs*, seen in such proper names as *Os*wald, *Os*ric]

as[3] *as*, (*Roman antiq*) *n* a Roman unit of weight, a pound of 12 ounces; a Roman copper coin, *orig* a pound in weight, ultimately half an ounce: — *pl* **ass'es**. [L *ās*, *assis*]
ås *ōs*, (*geol*) *n* a kame or esker: — *pl* **åsar** (*ōs'är*). [Sw]
ASA *abbrev*: Advertising Standards Authority; Amateur Swimming Association; American Standards Association, used eg to label photographic film speeds.
asafoetida *as-ə-fet'i-də*, or *-fēt'*, *n* a foul-smelling gum resin, obtained from the root latex of some species of *Ferula*, and formerly used medicinally. — Also **asafet'ida**, **assafoet'ida** or **assafet'ida**. [Pers *azā* mastic, and L *fētida* (*fem*) stinking]
a salti *ä säl'tē*, (*Ital* literally, in jumps) by fits and starts.
asana *ä'sə-nə*, *n* any of the positions taught in yoga. [Sans *āsana*]
ASAP or **asap** *abbrev*: as soon as possible.
åsar. See **ås**.
asarum *as'ə-rəm*, *n* the dried root of the wild ginger (*Asarum canadense*). — *n* **asarabacca** (*as-ə-rə-bak'ə*; L *bacca* berry) a plant (*Asarum europaeum*), of the birthwort family, formerly used in medicine. [L *asarum* (from Gr *asaron*) asarabacca]
asbestos *az-bes'tos*, *n* a fine fibrous form of certain minerals capable of being woven into incombustible cloth or felted sheets for insulation, etc; (commercially) chrysotile, a fibrous serpentine. — *adj* of or like asbestos. — *adj* **asbes'tic**, **asbes'tiform**, **asbes'tine** or **asbes'tous** of or like asbestos. — *n* **asbestō'sis** a lung disease with scarring and carcinoma caused by inhaling asbestos dust over long periods. — **asbestos cement** cement containing asbestos fibres, used to make thin slabs for various purposes in building. [Gr, (literally) unquenchable, from *a-* (privative) and *sbestos* extinguished]
ASBM *abbrev*: air-to-surface ballistic missile.
ascarid *as'kə-rid*, *n* any nematode worm of the parasitic genus *Ascaris* (family **Ascar'idae**), infesting the small intestines. — Also **as'caris** (*-kə-ris*): — *pl* **ascarides** (*-kar'i-dēz*). — *n* **ascariasis** (*as-kə-rī'ə-sis*) infestation with, or disease caused by, ascarids (*esp Ascaris lumbricoides*). [Gr *askaris*, pl *askarides*]
ascaunt. See **askance**.
ascend *ə-send'* or *a-send'*, *vi* to go up, mount, rise; to go back in time or ancestry. — *vt* to go up, mount, climb; to trace back in time or ancestry; to go up to (*Shakesp*). — *n* **ascend'ance** or **ascend'ence** (both *rare*), now *usu* **ascend'ancy** or **ascend'ency**, dominating influence. — *n* **ascend'ant** or less commonly **ascend'ent** the part of the ecliptic just risen or about to rise above the horizon at any instant (a planet in the ascendant is supposed to influence a person born at the time) (*astrol*); a position of pre-eminence; an ancestor or relative in the ascending line; a person who rises or mounts (*obs*); a rise, up-slope (*obs*). — *adj* rising; just risen above the horizon; predominant. — *n* **ascend'er** a person or thing that ascends; (the upper part of) a letter such as b, d, h, k (*printing*, etc). — *adj* **ascend'ible** (also **ascend'able**) scalable. — *adj* **ascend'ing** rising; curving up from a prostrate to an erect position (*bot*). — *n* **ascension** (*-sen'shən*) ascent (a Gallicism when used of a mountain ascent); an ascent to heaven, *esp* Christ's. — *adj* **ascen'sional**. — *adj* **ascen'sive** moving or tending upwards. — *n* **ascent'** a going up; advancement; a going back in time or ancestry; a way up; an up-slope. — **Ascen'sion-day** or **Ascension Day** (*Christian relig*) Holy Thursday, ten days before Whitsunday, commemorating Christ's Ascension; **Ascen'siontide** Ascension-day to Whitsunday. — **ascend the throne** to become king or queen; **right ascension** (*astron*) a co-ordinate of the position of a celestial body measured (*usu* in terms of time) eastwards along the celestial equator from the First Point of Aries, the other co-ordinate being the declination. [L *ascendere*, *ascēnsum*, from *ad* to, and *scandere* to climb]
ascertain *as-ər-tān'*, *vt* to find out for certain; to verify, prove; to apprise (*obs*); to assure (*obs*); to make certain, prove (*obs*). — *adj* **ascertain'able**. — *n* **ascertain'ment**. — **ascertained goods** (*business law*) goods which are identified and agreed upon after the contract is made. [OFr *acertener* to make certain, from *à* to, and *certain* certain]
ascesis *ə-sē'sis*, *n* the practice of disciplining oneself; asceticism. [Gr *askēsis* exercise, training]
ascetic *a-* or *ə-set'ik*, *n* a person who rigidly abstains from ordinary bodily gratifications for conscience's sake; a person who aims to achieve holiness through mortification of the flesh; a strict hermit; a person who lives a life of austerity. — *adj* **ascet'ic** or **ascet'ical** rigorous in mortifying the flesh; of asceticism; austere. — *adv* **ascet'ically**. — *n* **ascet'icism** (*-sizm*). [Gr *askētikos*, from *askētēs*, a person in training, from *askeein* to work, exercise, train]
asci. See **ascus**.
ascian *ash'i-ən*, *n* an inhabitant of the torrid zone, shadowless when the sun is right overhead. [Gr *askios* shadowless, from *a-* (privative) and *skiā* a shadow]
ascidium *a-sid'i-əm*, *n* (*bot*) a pitcher-shaped leaf or part of a leaf, such as the pitcher of the pitcher plants, the bladder of the bladderwort: — *pl* **ascid'ia**. — *n* **ascid'ian** (*zool*) a sea-squirt, or tunicate, a degenerate survivor of the ancestors of the vertebrates, shaped like a double-mouthed flask. [Gr *askidion*, dimin of *askos* a leather bag, wine-skin]
ASCII *as'ki*, (*comput*) *abbrev*: American Standard Code for Information Interchange, a binary code representing characters and used by VDUs, printers, etc.
ascites *a-sī'tēz*, (*pathol*) *n* dropsy of the abdomen. — *adj* **ascit'ic** (*-sit'ik*) or **ascit'ical**. [Gr *askītēs*, from *askos* belly]
ascititious. Same as **adscititious**.
Asclepius or **Asclepios** *as-klē'pi-əs*, *n* (*Gr mythol*) a mortal who became the god of healing (L *Aesculapius*). — *n* **asclē'piad** a plant of the genus Asclepias; a verse used by the Greek poet *Asclepiades* (*Asklēpiadēs*; 3c BC) made up of a spondee, two (in the *Greater Asclepiad* three) choriambi, and an iambus (– –/– ⏑ ⏑ –/– ⏑ ⏑ –/⏑ –). — *n pl* **Asclepiadā'ceae** the milk-weed and swallow-wort family, closely related to the periwinkle family. — *adj* **asclepiadaceous** (*-ā'shəs*; *bot*). — *n* and *adj* **Asclepiadē'an** or **Asclepiad'ic** (*prosody*). — *n* **asclē'pias** a plant of the chiefly American genus *Asclepias* of the swallow-wort family, milk-weed. [Gr *Asklēpios* the god, *Asklēpiadēs* the poet, *asklēpias*, *-ados* swallow-wort]
ascomycete, **ascospore**. See under **ascus**.
asconce or (*Shakesp*) **a sconce**, *obs* forms of **askance**.
ascorbic *ə-skör'bik*, *adj* antiscorbutic, only in **ascorbic acid** vitamin C ($C_6H_8O_6$). — *n* **ascor'bate** a salt of ascorbic acid. [Gr *a-* (privative) and **scorbutic**]
ascot *as'kot*, *n* a type of necktie with broad ends that are tied to lie one across the other. [The race-course at *Ascot*, England, well-known for the fashionable dress of spectators]
ascribe *ə-* or *a-skrīb'*, *vt* to attribute, impute or assign. — *adj* **ascrīb'able**. — *n* **ascription** (*-skrip'shən*) the act, expression or formula of ascribing or imputing, eg that ascribing glory to God at the end of a Christian sermon. [L *ascrībere*, from *ad* to, and *scrībere*, *scrīptum* to write]
ascus *as'kəs*, (*bot*) *n* an enlarged cell, commonly elongated, in which usually eight spores are formed: — *pl* **asci** (*as'ī*). — *n* **ascomycete** (*as-kō-mī'sēt*) any one of the **Ascomycetes** (*-sē'tēz*), one of the main divisions of the fungi, characterized by formation of asci. — *n* **as'cospore** a spore formed in an ascus. [Gr *askos* bag]
Asda *abbrev*: Associated Dairies.
Asdic *as'dik*, *n* an apparatus for detecting and locating a submarine or other underwater object by means of ultrasonic waves echoed back from the submarine, etc. [*A*llied (or *A*nti-) *S*ubmarine *D*etection *I*nvestigation *C*ommittee]
ASE *abbrev*: Association for Science Education.

-ase *-āz* or *-ās*, (*chem*) *sfx* denoting an enzyme, *specif* one that hydrolyses the prefixed substance (thus *fructase*, *amylase*, *protease*). [diast*ase*, from Gr *diastasis* separation]

ASEAN or **Asean** *a'si-ən*, *abbrev*: Association of South East Asian Nations.

aseismic *a-*, *ā-* or *ə-sīz'mik*, *adj* free from earthquakes. [Gr *a-* (privative) and **seismic**]

aseity *a-* or *ā-sē'i-ti*, (*philos*) *n* self-origination. [L *ā* from, and *sē* (*ablative*) oneself]

asepalous *a-*, *ā-* or *ə-sep'ə-ləs*, (*bot*) *adj* without sepals. [Gr *a-* (privative) and **sepal**]

asepsis. See **aseptic**.

aseptate *a-*, *ā-* or *ə-sep'tāt*, (*bot*) *adj* not partitioned by septa. [Gr *a-* (privative) and **septum**]

aseptic *a-*, *ā-* or *ə-sep'tik*, *adj* not liable to, or preventing, decay or putrefaction; involving or accompanied by measures to exclude micro-organisms. — *n* an aseptic substance. — *n* **asep'sis** freedom from sepsis or blood-poisoning; the process of rendering, or condition of being, aseptic; exclusion of micro-organisms: — *pl* **asep'ses**. — *n* **asep'ticism** (*-sizm*) aseptic treatment. — *vt* **asep'ticize** or **-ise** (*-ti-sīz*) to make aseptic; to treat with aseptics. [Gr *asēptos*, from *a-* (privative) and *sēpein* to cause to decay]

asexual *a-*, *ā-* or *ə-seks'ū-əl*, *adj* without sex; not involving sexual activity; vegetative. — *n* **asexūality** (*-al'i-ti*). — *adv* **asex'ūally**. [Gr *a-* (privative) and **sexual**]

Asgard *äs'gärd*, *n* the heaven of Norse mythology, abode of the twelve gods and twenty-six goddesses, and of heroes slain in battle. [ON *Āsgarthr*, from *āss* a god, and *garthr* an enclosure]

ASH *abbrev*: Action on Smoking and Health.

ash[1] *ash*, *n* a well-known timber tree (*Fraxinus excelsior*, or other species) of the olive family; its white, tough, hard wood; an ashen spear-shaft or spear (*obs*). — *adj* **ash'en** made of, or relating to, the ash tree. — **ash'-key** the winged fruit of the ash; **ash'-plant** an ash sapling; a whip, staff or walking-stick made from an ash sapling. [OE *æsc*; Ger *Esche*, ON *askr*]

ash[2] *ash*, *n* (often in *pl*) the dust or remains of anything burnt; (also **volcanic ash** or **ashes**) volcanic dust, or a rock composed of it; (in *pl*) the remains of a human body when burnt; (in *pl*) a dead body (*fig*; *poetic*). — *adj* **ash'en** of the colour of ash; (of the face) very pale. — *n* **ash'ery** a place where potash or pearl-ash is made. — *adj* **ash'y**. — **ash'-bin, -bucket** or **-can** a receptacle for ashes and other household refuse. — *adj* **ash-blond'** (of hair) of a pale, silvery blond colour; having hair of this colour: — *fem* (also *n*) **ash-blonde'**. — *adj* **ash'en-grey** of the colour of wood ashes. — **ash'-heap** a heap of ashes and household refuse; **ash'-hole** or **-pit** a hollow, *esp* under a fireplace, to receive ashes; **ash'-leach** a tub in which alkaline salts are dissolved from wood ashes; **ash'-pan** a tray fitted underneath a grate to receive the ashes; **ash'-stand** or **ash'-tray** a small tray or saucer for tobacco ash; **Ash Wednesday** (*Christian relig*) the first day of Lent, named from the custom of sprinkling ashes on the head to show penance and mourning. — *adj* **ash'y-grey**. — **the Ashes** a term applied by the *Sporting Times* (in a mock 'In Memoriam' notice) to the loss of prestige in English cricket after the Australians' successful visit in 1882, after which English teams strove to 'bring back the ashes', or mortal remains; hence, the test-match series between England and Australia or the trophy which they vie to 'bring back' or retain respectively. [OE *asce*; ON *aska*]

ashake *ə-shāk'*, (*archaic*) *adv* or predicative *adj* in a shaking state. [**a-**[1]]

ashamed *ə-shāmd'*, *adj* feeling or affected with shame (with *of* an action or person; with *for*, meaning on behalf of, a person; also with *to do*, or *that*). — *vi* **ashame'** (*obs*) to feel shame. — *vt* (*archaic*) to put to shame. — *adv* **ashamed'ly** (or *-id-li*). — *n* **ashamed'ness** (or *-id-nes*). — *adj* (*archaic*) **asham'ing**. [Pfx *a-* (intensive), and OE *sc(e)amian* to shame]

ashen, etc. See **ash**[1,2].

ashet *ash'it*, (now chiefly *Scot*; also *NEng*) *n* a large meat-plate or flat serving-dish. [Fr *assiette*]

ashine *ə-shīn'*, (*archaic* or *poetic*) *adv* or predicative *adj* in a shining state. [**a-**[1]]

ashiver *ə-shiv'ər*, (*archaic* or *poetic*) *adv* or predicative *adj* in a shivering or quivering state. [**a-**[1] and **shiver**[2]]

Ashkenazim *äsh-kə-näz'im*, *n pl* the Polish and German Jews (as distinguished from the *Sephardim*, the Spanish and Portuguese Jews). [Heb *Ashkenaz* a northern people (Gen 10) by later Jews identified with Germany]

ashlar or **ashler** *ash'lər*, *n* a squared or dressed stone used in building or facing a wall; finely-jointed masonry of such stones. — Also *adj*. — *vt* to face with ashlar. — *n* **ash'laring** or **ash'lering** ashlar masonry or facing; a vertical timber between floor-joist and rafter. — **ash'lar-work** ashlar masonry. [OFr *aiseler*, from L *axillāris*, from *axilla*, dimin of *axis* axle, plank]

ashore *ə-shör*, *adv* on, or on to, the shore or land (from the sea). [**a-**[1] and **shore**[1]]

ashram *äsh'rəm*, (*Hinduism*) *n usu* in India, a hermitage for a holy man, or a place of retreat for a religious community; such a community. — *n* **ash'rama** any one of the four stages of life which a man of the upper three castes should ideally pass through: pupil, householder, hermitage-dweller, and wanderer who has renounced the world. — *n* **ash'ramite** a person living in an ashram. [Sans *āśrama*]

Ashtaroth, Ashtoreth. See **Astarte**.

Ashura *ash'ōō-rä*, (*Islam*) *n* a fast day observed on the tenth day of Moharram (qv), *esp* among Shiite Muslims, in commemoration of the death of Imam Hosain. [Ar *'Ashūrā*]

Asian *ā'sh(i)ən*, *ā'shyən*, *-zh-*, or **Asiatic** *-i-at'ik*, *adj* belonging to *Asia* (*esp* Asia Minor); formerly in literature or art, florid. — *n* a native of Asia, or person of Asian descent. — *adj* **Asianic** (*-an'ik*) Asian, *esp* of a group of non-Indo-European languages of Asia and Europe. — *n* **Asiat'icism** (*-i-sizm*) imitation of Asiatic or Eastern manners.

aside *ə-sīd'*, *adv* on or to one side; privately; apart. — *n* words spoken in an undertone, so as not to be heard by some person present; words spoken by an actor which the other persons on the stage are supposed not to hear; an indirect effort of any kind. — *adj* (*US*) private, apart. — *prep* (now only *Scot*) beside. — **aside from** apart from; **set aside** to quash (a judgement); to put to one side (*lit* and *fig*). [**a-**[1] and **side**[1]]

asinico *as-i-nē'kō*, (*Shakesp*) *n* a stupid fellow. [Sp *asnico*, dimin of *asno*, from L *asinus* ass]

asinine *as'in-īn*, *adj* of or like an ass; idiotic. — *n* **asininity** (*-in'i-ti*). [L *asinīnus*, from *asinus* ass]

ASIO *āz'* or *az'i-ō*, *abbrev*: Australian Security Intelligence Organization.

ask[1] *äsk*, *vt* to beg, request, seek; to make a request of; to inquire; to inquire of; to invite; to proclaim (*archaic*). — *vi* to make a request (for); to inquire (*after* a person or their welfare, etc, *about* a matter, etc). — *n* **ask'er**. — **asking price** the price set by the seller of an article before bargaining has begun; the asking rate. — **ask for it** (*colloq*) to behave in a way likely to bring trouble on oneself; **I ask you**! would you believe it, don't you agree (*usu* expressing criticism); **if you ask me** in my opinion. [OE *ascian*, *acsian*; Ger *heischen*, ON *æskja*]

ask[2] *ask*, (*dialect*) *n* a newt. — Also **ask'er**. [Appar OE *āthexe*; cf Ger *Eidechse* lizard]

askance *ə-skans'*, *adv* sideways; awry; obliquely; quizzically, sceptically. — Also **askant'**. — *vt* (*Shakesp*) to turn aside. — *prep* (*Shakesp*) **ascaunt'** (folio reading **aslant**) slantwise across. — **look, eye** or **view askance** to look (at) with disdain, disapproval, envy, or (now *usu*) suspicion. [Ety very obscure]

askari *äs'kä-rē* or *äs-kä'rē*, *n* an E African soldier or policeman: — *pl* **askaris**. [Ar *'askarī* soldier]

asker. See **ask**[1,2].

askesis. Same as **ascesis**.
askew *ə-skū'*, *adv* or *adj* at or to an oblique angle; awry. [Appar **a-**[1] and **skew**[1]]
asklent. See **aslant**.
ASL *abbrev*: American Sign Language, the sign language (qv) used in N America.
aslake *ə-slāk'*, *vt* to slake (*obs*); to mitigate (*archaic*); to appease (*obs*). [OE *āslacian*; see **slake**[1]]
aslant *ə-slänt'*, *adv* or *adj* on the slant, slantwise. — *prep* slantwise across, athwart. — Also **asklent'** (*Scot*). [**a-**[1] and **slant**[1]]
asleep *ə-slēp'*, *adv* or *adj* in or to a sleeping state; dead (*euphem*); (of limbs) numbed, sometimes with tingling or prickly feeling. [**a-**[1]]
ASLEF *az'lef*, *abbrev*: Associated Society of Locomotive Engineers and Firemen.
AS-level *ā-es'-lev-əl*, *n* (a pass in) an Advanced Supplementary level GCSE examination, one which covers a smaller syllabus than the corresponding Advanced level, designed to provide supplementary A-level study for full-time A-level students. — Also *adj*. [Abbrev]
ASLIB or **Aslib** *abbrev*: (formerly) Association of Special Libraries and Information Bureaux, now the Association for Information Management.
aslope *ə-slōp'*, (*archaic*) *adv* or *adj* on the slope. [OE *āslopen*, pa p of *āslūpan* to slip away]
ASM *abbrev*: air-to-surface missile.
-asm. See **-ism**.
asmear *ə-smēr'*, (*archaic*) *adj* smeared over. [**a-**[1]]
Asmodeus *as-* or *az-mə-dē'əs* or **Asmoday** *-dā'*, *n* an evil spirit of Semitic mythology. [L, from Gr *Asmodaios*, from Heb *Ashmadai*]
asmoulder *ə-smōl'dər*, (*archaic*) *adv* in a smouldering state. [**a-**[1]]
asocial *a-* or *ā-sō'shl*, *adj* not social; antisocial. [Gr *a-* (privative)]
asp[1] *asp* or *äsp*, (*archaic*) *n* an aspen.
asp[2] *asp* or *äsp*, *n* a venomous snake of various kinds, including *Vipera aspis* of southern Europe, Cleopatra's asp (*prob* the horned viper), the biblical asp (*prob* the Egyptian juggler's snake, *Naja haje*), and the cobra de capello. — Also (*archaic* and *poetic*) **asp'ic** or **asp'ick**. [L, from Gr *aspis*]
asparagus *əs-par'ə-gəs*, *n* any plant of the *Asparagus* genus of Liliaceae, with leaves reduced to scales, some cultivated as ornamental plants, and one species (*A. officinalis*) for its young shoots eaten as a delicacy. — *n* **asparag'inase** (*-aj'*) an enzyme that causes asparagine to hydrolyse to aspartic acid and ammonia. — *n* **aspar'agine** (*-jin* or *-jēn*) an amino acid found in asparagus and other vegetables. — **asparagus bean** a tropical American bean (*Vigna sesquipedalis*) with very long pods; **asparagus pea** the Goa bean; **aspar'agus-stone** a pale yellowish green apatite. [L, from Gr *asp(h)aragos*]
aspartic acid *as-pär'tik as'id*, *n* an amino acid found in young sugar-cane, etc, and formed by the hydrolysis of asparagine. — *n* **aspartame** (*ə-spär'tām*) an artificial sweetener, 200 times sweeter than sucrose, derived from aspartic acid and phenylalamine. [Irreg coinage from *aspar*agine, and **acid**]
Aspasia *as-pā'zyə* or *as-pä'zi-a*, *n* a gifted Athenian courtesan, mistress of Pericles (*Gr hist*); any charming and accomplished woman of easy morals.
aspect *as'pekt* (in *Spenser*, *Shakesp*, *Milton*, etc, *as-pekt'*), *n* a look, a glance (*obs*); a view in a specific direction; a direction of facing; an appearance presented; way of viewing; a surface facing a particular direction, face, side, elevation; the situation of one planet with respect to another, as seen from the earth (*astrol*); in some languages, a verbal form expressing such features as simple action, repetition, beginning, duration, etc (*gram*); attitude (*aeronautics*). — *vt* **aspect'** (*obs*) to look at or for. — *adj* **as'pectable** (*archaic*) visible; worth looking at. — *adj* **aspec'tual** (*gram* and *astrol*) of or relating to aspect. — **aspect ratio** the ratio of the width to the height of a reproduced image (*TV*; also **picture ratio**); the ratio of the span of an aerofoil to its mean chord. [L *aspectus*]
aspen *asp'ən*, also *äsp'*, or *-in* (or *Spenser* **aspine**) *n* the trembling poplar. — *adj* made of, or like, the aspen; tremulous; timorous. — *adj* **as'pen-like**. [OE *æspe*; Ger *Espe*]
asper[1] *as'pər*, *n* a Turkish monetary unit, worth 1/120 of a piastre, formerly a silver coin, now only money of account. [Gr *aspron* rough, later white]
asper[2] *as'pər*, *adj* (*obs*) rough, harsh. — *n* the Greek rough breathing (L *spīritus asper*). — *vt* **as'perate** to roughen. — *n* **asperity** (*-per'*) roughness; harshness; bitter coldness; (in *pl*) excrescences, rough places. — *adj* **as'perous** rough with short hairs. [L *asper*]
asperge *as-pûrj'*, *vt* to sprinkle. — *n* an aspergillum for holy water. — *n* **aspergation** (*-gā'*). — *n* **asper'ger** (*-jər*). — *n* **asper'ges** (*RC*) a short service introductory to the mass, so called from the words *Asperges me, Domine, hyssopo et mundabor* (Psalm 51). — *n* **aspergill** (*as'pər-jil*) a holy-water sprinkler. — Also **aspergillum** (*-jil'əm*): — *pl* **aspergill'a** or **aspergill'ums**. — *n* **aspergillō'sis** a disease, fatal to birds and also occurring in domestic animals and man, caused by any of various moulds, *esp* species of Aspergillus. — *n* **Aspergill'um** a genus of boring Lamellibranchs in which the shell forms an elongated cone, ending in a disc pierced with numerous small tubular holes. — *n* **Aspergill'us** a genus of minute moulds occurring on decaying substances. [L *aspergere*, from *ad* to, and *spargere* to sprinkle]
asperity, **asperous**. See under **asper**[2].
asperse *as-pûrs'*, *vt* to slander or accuse falsely; to bespatter. — *n* **asper'sion** calumny; slander; a shower or spray (*Shakesp*); sprinkling with holy water (*RC*). — *adj* **aspers'ive**. — *n* **aspersoir** (*äs-per-swär*; *Fr*) an aspergillum. — *n* **aspersō'rium** (*-ri-əm*; *L*) a holy-water vessel. — *adj* **aspers'ory** (*rare*) tending to asperse; defamatory. — *n* an aspergillum; an aspersorium. [L *aspergere*, *aspersum*, from *ad* to, and *spargere* to sprinkle]
asphalt *as'falt*, *n* a black or dark-brown, hard, bituminous substance, occurring naturally, and obtained as a residue in petroleum distillation, etc, anciently used as a cement; a mixture of this with rock chips or other material, used for paving, roofing, etc. — Also **asphal'tum**. — *vt* **as'phalt** to lay, cover or impregnate with asphalt. — *n* **as'phalter** a person who lays asphalt. — *adj* **asphalt'ic**. [Gr *asphaltos*, from an Eastern word]
aspheric *ə-* or *ā-sfer'ik*, *adj* not spherical; (of a surface) not forming part of a sphere. [**a-**[2]]
aspheterism *as-fet'ər-izm*, *n* (*Southey*) denial of the right of private property. — *vi* **asphet'erize** or **-ise** (*Coleridge*). [Gr *a-* (privative) and *spheteros* one's own]
asphodel *as'fə-del*, or *-fo-*, *n* a plant of the lily family with spikes of clustered flowers and narrow grasslike leaves (in Greek mythology, the plant of the dead); applied to other plants, *esp* **bog-asphodel**. [Gr *asphodelos*; cf **daffodil**]
asphyxia *as-fik'si-ə*, (*med*) *n* (literally) stoppage of the pulse; stoppage or suspension of the vital functions owing to any cause which interferes with respiration and prevents oxygen from reaching the body tissue. — Also (formerly) **asphyx'y**. — *adj* **asphyx'ial**. — *n* and *adj* **asphyx'iant** (a chemical substance) producing asphyxia. — *vt* **asphyx'iate** to produce asphyxia in. — *adj* **asphyx'iāted**. — *n* **asphyxiā'tion** the action of asphyxiating or condition of being asphyxiated. — *n* **asphyx'iātor**. [Gr *asphyxiā*, from *a-* (privative) and *sphyxis* pulse]
aspic[1], **aspick**. See **asp**[2].
aspic[2] *as'pik*, *n* a clear savoury meat- or fish-jelly used as a glaze or a mould for fish, game, hard-boiled eggs, etc. [Fr, perh from *aspic* (asp) because it is 'cold as an aspic' (French proverb)]
aspic[3] *as'pik*, *n* the broad-leaved lavender (*Lavandula spica* or *latifolia*). [Fr, from L *spīca* spike]

aspidistra *as-pid-ist'rə*, *n* an evergreen plant of the *Aspidistra* genus of the Liliaceae family, often grown indoors, having long, tough leaves and brownish-purple flowers. [Perh Gr *aspis* a shield]

aspidium *as-pid'i-əm*, (*bot*) *n* any one of the shield-fern genus (*Aspidium*) of ferns (including those *usu* divided between the genera *Dryopteris*, *Polystichum* and *Tectaria*), having a shield-shaped or kidney-shaped indusium: — *pl* **aspid'ia**. — *adj* **aspid'ioid**. [Gr *aspidion*, dimin of *aspis* shield]

aspine. See **aspen**.

aspire *əs-* or *as-pīr'*, *vi* (with *to*, *after*, or an infinitive) to desire eagerly; to aim at, or strive for, high things; to tower up. — *n* **aspīr'ant** (or *as'pir-*) a person who aspires (with *after* or *for*); a candidate. — *adj* (*rare*) ambitious; mounting up. — *vt* **aspirate** (*as'pir-āt*) to pronounce with a full breathing, ie the sound of *h*, as in *house* (*phonetics*); to follow (a stop) by an audible breath (*phonetics*); to replace (a consonant) by another sound, normally a fricative, when there is a combination with the sound *h* or the letter *h* (*gram*, *phonetics*, etc); to draw (gas, fluid, etc) out of a cavity, eg (*med*) a body cavity, by suction. — Also *vi*. — *n* (*-it* or *-ət*) the sound represented by the letter *h*; a consonant sound, a stop followed by an audible breath, such as *bh* in Sanskrit; sometimes extended to a fricative; a mark of aspiration, the rough breathing (ʻ) in Greek; a letter representing an aspirate sound. — Also *adj*. — In French '*h* aspirate', no longer sounded, still affects the junction with the preceding word. — *n* **aspirā'tion** eager desire; (usu in *pl*) lofty hopes or aims; pronunciation of a sound with a full breathing; an aspirated sound; drawing a gas, liquid or solid, in, out or through; breathing (*obs*). — *n* **as'pirātor** an apparatus for drawing air or other gases through bottles or other vessels; an instrument for removing fluids or solids from cavities of the body (*med*). — *adj* **aspirā'tional** relating to the aspirations or aims of a person or of people. — *adj* **aspīr'atory** (*-ə-tə-ri* or *as'pir-*) relating to breathing. — *adj* **aspīr'ing** desiring, aiming at, etc. — *adv* **aspīr'ingly**. — *n* **aspīr'ingness**. — **drop one's aspirates** to omit to pronounce the sound of *h*. [L *aspīrāre*, *-ātum*, from *ad* to, and *spīrāre* to breathe]

aspirin *as'pər-in*, *n* a drug (acetyl-salicylic acid) used for relieving rheumatic pains, neuralgia, etc. [Ger, from *A(cetyl)* and *Spir(säure)* spiraeic (now salicylic) acid, and **-in** (3)]

asplenium *as-plē'ni-əm*, *n* spleenwort, any fern of a widely-distributed genus of ferns, *Asplenium*, with long or linear sori, with indusium arising from a vein (eg wall-rue). [Gr *asplēnon*, (literally) spleenless, from *a-* (privative) and *splēn* spleen, reputedly a cure for spleen]

asport *as-pört*, (*rare*) *vt* to carry away, *esp* wrongfully. — *n* **asportā'tion**. [L *asportāre*, from *abs* away, and *portāre* to carry]

aspout *ə-spowt'*, (*archaic*) *adv* spoutingly. [**a-**[1]]

asprawl *ə-spröl'*, (*archaic*) *adv* in a sprawl. [**a-**[1]]

aspread *ə-spred'*, (*archaic*) *adv* in or into a spreading state. [**a-**[1]]

asprout *ə-sprowt'*, (*archaic*) *adv* in a sprouting state. [**a-**[1]]

asquat *ə-skwot'*, (*archaic*) *adv* squattingly. [**a-**[1]]

asquint *ə-skwint'*, *adv* and *adj* towards the corner of the eye; obliquely. [Appar **a-**[1], and some such word as Du *schuinte* slant]

ASR *abbrev*: airport surveillance radar; air-sea rescue; automatic send and receive (or answer, send and receive), a teletypewriter and receiver used in conjunction with a computer.

Ass. or **Assoc.** *abbrev*: Associate; Associated; Association.

ass[1] *as* or *äs*, *n* a small, *usu* grey, long-eared animal of the horse genus; a dull, stupid fellow, a fool (*colloq*). — **asses' bridge** the *pons asinorum*, or fifth proposition in the first book of Euclid's *Elements* of geometry, as being for some an impassable barrier to further progress. [OE *assa*, from L *asinus*; cf Gr *onos* ass]

ass[2]. See **arse**.

assafetida. See **asafoetida**.

assagai. See **assegai**.

assai[1] *äs-sä'ē*, (*music*) *adv* very. [Ital, from L *ad* to, and *satis* enough]

assai[2] *ä-sä'ē*, *n* a S American palm (*esp Euterpe edulis*); its small, fleshy, dark purple fruit; a drink made from its fruit. [Tupí]

assail *ə-sāl'*, *vt* to attack. — *adj* **assail'able**. — *n* **assail'ant** a person who attacks. — *n* **assail'er**. — *n* **assail'ment**. [OFr *asaillir*, from L *assilīre*, from *ad* upon, and *salīre* to leap]

assart *as-ärt'*, (*hist law*) *vt* to reclaim for agriculture by grubbing. — *n* a forest clearing; asserted land; the grubbing up of trees and bushes. [Anglo-Fr *assarter*, from LL *exsartāre*, from L *ex* out, and *sar(r)īre* to hoe, weed]

assassin *ə-* or *a-sas'in*, *n orig* a follower of the Old Man of the Mountains, a member of his military and religious order in Persia and Syria (11c–13c), notorious for secret murders; a person who, *usu* for a fee or reward, or for political reasons, kills by surprise or secretly. — *vt* **assass'inate** to murder by surprise or secret assault; to murder (*esp* a prominent person) violently, often publicly; to destroy (eg a person's reputation) by treacherous means; to maltreat (*Milton*). — *n* (*obs*) a person who assassinates. — *n* **assassinā'tion**. — *n* **assass'inātor**. [Through Fr or Ital from Ar *hashshāshīn* hashish-eaters]

assault *ə-sölt'*, *n* a sudden violent attack; a storming, eg of a town; rape, attempted rape, indecent attack; in English law, unlawful attempt to apply force to the person of another (when force is actually applied, the act amounts to *battery*); an attack of any sort by arguments, appeals, abuse, etc. — *vt* to make an assault or attack upon; to attack indecently, rape, or attempt to rape. — *adj* used in attack; preparing, or prepared, for attack. — *n* **assault'er**. — **assault boat** a portable boat for landing on beaches or crossing rivers; **assault course** a course laid out with obstacles that must be negotiated, used for training soldiers, etc (also *fig*). — **assault at** or **of arms** a display of attack and defence in fencing. [OFr *asaut*, from L *ad* upon, and *saltus* a leap, from *salīre* to leap. See **assail**]

assay *a-* or *ə-sā'*, *vt* to put to the proof, to make trial of; to test; to determine the proportion of a metal, or other component, in; to give or yield as result; to test fatness of (a killed stag) by a trial cut (*obs*); to taste before presenting to a dignitary, etc (as guarantee against poison) (*hist*); to put to proof in action; to afflict (*Spenser*); to tempt (*obs*); to affect (*Spenser*); to experience (*Shakesp*); to endeavour (now *usu* **essay**); to assail (*Spenser* and *Shakesp*); to challenge (*Shakesp*); to accost (*Shakesp*). — *vi* to venture, make an attempt; to carry out assaying (of ores, etc). — *n* (sometimes *as'ā*) a test, trial; a determination of proportion of metal in an ore, or of a certain constituent in a substance; a specimen used for the purpose; the quality or standard of a metal as found by assaying; determination of the fatness of a stag (*obs*); experiment (*obs*); experience (*obs*); endeavour, attempt, tentative effort (*usu* **essay**); an assault (*Spenser* and *Shakesp*, etc); proof, temper, quality or standard, such as might be found by assaying (*obs*; *Spenser* and *Shakesp*). — *adj* **assay'able**. — *n* **assay'er** a person who assays metals. — *n* **assay'ing**. — **assay'-master** an officer who determines the amount of gold or silver in coin or bullion; **assay office** (often with *caps*) a (government) department in which gold and silver articles are assayed and hallmarks assigned; **assay'-piece** a sample chosen for assay; an example of excellence. — **cup of assay** (*hist*) a small cup for trial tasting before offering to a dignitary, etc. [OFr *assayer* and *assai*; see **essay**]

assegai or **assagai** (*Afrik* **assegaai**) *as'ə-gī*, *n* a slender spear of hard wood tipped with iron, either for hurling or for thrusting with, used in S Africa. — *vt* to kill or wound with an assegai. [Through Fr or Port from Ar *azzaghāyah*, from *az* = *al* the, and *zaghāyah*, a Berber word]

assemble *ə-sem'bl*, *vt* to call or bring together; to collect; to put together the parts of; to convert (a program) to machine code from assembly language (*comput*). — *vi* to meet together. — *n* **assem'blage** a collection of persons or things; the whole collection of remains found on an archaeological site; all the flora and fauna of one type in an ecosystem (*biol*); the putting together of parts (*technical*); (also *a-sã-bläzh*), (putting together) a sculptural or other work of art consisting in whole or in part of selected objects, *usu* objects made for another purpose. — *n* **assem'blance** or **assem'blaunce** (*Spenser*) an assembling. — *n* **assem'bler** someone who or or something that assembles; a program that converts a program in assembly language into one in machine code (*comput*). — *n* **assem'bly** the act of assembling; the putting together of parts; a company assembled; a formal ball or meeting for dancing and social intercourse (*hist*); a reception or at-home (*hist*); a meeting for religious worship or the like; a deliberative or legislative body, *esp* in some legislatures a lower house; a drumbeat, *esp* a signal for striking tents (*military*). — **assembly hall** a hall, eg in a school, in which assemblies are held; **assembly language** (*comput*) a low-level program language using mnemonics, in which each statement corresponds to a machine-code instruction; **assembly line** a serial arrangement of workers and apparatus for passing on work from stage to stage in assembling a product; **assem'blyman** or **assem'blywoman** a member of an assembly or lower house; **assembly room** a public ballroom or room for entertainments or formal gatherings. — **General Assembly** in Scotland, Ireland and the United States, the highest court of the Presbyterian Church; in England and Wales, the highest court of the United Reformed Church; **Legislative Assembly** or **House of Assembly** the lower or only house of some legislatures; **National Assembly** (also **Constituent Assembly**) the first of the revolutionary assemblies in France (1789–91); (also **Church Assembly**) a body set up in 1920 'to deliberate on all matters concerning the Church of England and to make provision in respect thereof', consisting of houses of Bishops, Clergy, and Laity, superseded in 1970 by the **General Synod** (see **synod**). [Fr *assembler*, from LL *assimulāre* to bring together, from *ad* to, and *simul* together]

assemblé *ä-sã-blā*, (*ballet*) *n* a leap with extended leg followed by a landing with both legs together. [Fr *assembler* to bring together]

assembly. See **assemble**.

assent *a-* or *ə-sent'*, *vi* to express agreement or acquiescence (with *to*). — *n* an agreeing or acquiescence; compliance. — *adj* **assentaneous** (*rare*; *as-ən-tā'ni-əs*) ready to agree. — *n* **assentā'tion** obsequious assent, adulation. — *n* **ass'entātor** (*obs*). — *n* **assent'er**. — *adj* **assentient** (*ə-sen'shənt*) or **assent'ive**. — *adv* **assent'ingly**. — *n* **assent'iveness**. — *n* **assent'or** a person who subscribes a candidate's nomination paper in addition to proposer and seconder. — **royal assent** the sovereign's formal acquiescence in a measure which has passed the Houses of Parliament. [L *assentīrī* to assent, agree and also its frequentative *assentārī* to flatter]

assert *ə-sûrt'*, *vt* to declare positively; to lay claim to; to insist upon; to affirm; to vindicate or defend by arguments or measures (now used only with cause as object, or reflexively); to bear evidence of (*obs*; *rare*). — *adj* **assert'able**. — *n* **assert'er** or **assert'or** a champion, defender; a person who makes a positive statement. — *n* **asser'tion** (*-shən*) affirmation, averment; a positive statement or declaration; that which is averred or declared; the act of claiming one's rights; vindication or championship (*archaic*). — *adj* **assert'ive** asserting or confirming confidently; positive, dogmatic; self-assertive. — *adv* **assert'ively**. — *n* **assert'iveness**. — *adj* **assert'ory** affirmative. — **assert oneself** to defend one's rights or opinions, sometimes with unnecessary zeal; to thrust oneself forward. [L *asserere*, *assertum* to lay hands on, claim, from *ad* to, and *serere* to join]

assess *ə-ses'*, *vt* to fix the amount of (eg a tax); to tax or fine; to fix the value or profits of, for taxation (with *at*); to estimate, judge, evaluate (eg a person's work, performance, character). — *adj* **assess'able**. — *n* **assess'ment** the act of assessing; the examining of income and profit to calculate the amount of tax to be paid; the valuing of property to calculate the amount to be paid in rates; (the amount of) a tax or charge assessed. — *n* **assess'or** a person who assesses; a legal adviser who sits beside a magistrate; a person appointed as an associate in office with another; a person who assesses taxes, or value of property, income, etc for taxation; someone who shares another's dignity (*archaic*). — *adj* **assessō'rial** (*as-*). — *n* **assess'orship**. — **assessment centre** a place where young offenders are detained so that their individual needs can be assessed and recommendations formulated about their future. [L *assidēre*, *assessum* to sit beside (esp of judges in a court) from *ad* to, at, and *sedēre* to sit]

assets *as'ets*, *n pl* (*orig sing*) the property of a deceased or insolvent person, considered as chargeable for all debts, etc; the entire property of all sorts belonging to a merchant or to a trading association. — *false sing* **ass'et** an item of property; something advantageous or well worth having; an item of monetary value belonging to a business or organization (categorized for accounting purposes as *current*, *fictitious*, *fixed*, *intangible* or *tangible*). — **ass'et-stripper**; **ass'et-stripping** (now *usu derog*) the practice of acquiring control of a company and selling off its assets for financial gain. [From the Anglo-Fr law phrase *aver assetz* to have enough, from OFr *asez* enough, from L *ad* to, and *satis* enough]

asseverate *ə-*, *a-sev'ər-āt*, *vt* to declare solemnly (formerly, now *archaic*, **assev'er**). — *adj* **assev'erating**. — *adv* **assev'eratingly**. — *n* **asseverā'tion**. [L *asseverāre*, *-ātum*, from *ad* to, and *sevērus* serious; see **severe**]

assez bien *a-sā byẽ*, (*Fr*) pretty well.

asshole. See **arse**.

assibilate *a-* or *ə-sib'i-lāt*, (*phonetics*) *vt* to sound as a sibilant. — *n* **assibilā'tion**. [L *ad* to, and *sībilāre* to hiss]

assiduity *as-id-ū'i-ti*, *n* persistent application or diligence; (in *pl*) constant attentions. — *adj* **assiduous** (*ə-sid'ū-əs*) constant or unwearied in application; unflagging, unremitting. — *adv* **assid'ūously** unremittingly. — *n* **assid'ūousness**. [L *assiduus*, from *ad* to, at, and *sedēre* to sit]

assiege *ə-sēj'*, (*Spenser*) *vt* to besiege. [See **siege**]

assiento *as-ē-en'tō*, (*hist*) *n* a treaty (*esp* that between Spain and Britain, 1713) for the supply of African slaves for Spanish American dominions: — *pl* **assien'tos**. [Sp (now *asiento*) seat, seat in a court, treaty]

assign *ə-sīn'*, *vt* to allot, share out; to designate, appoint; to put forward, adduce; to make over, transfer; to ascribe, refer; to specify; to fix, determine. — *n* a person to whom any property or right is made over, an assignee (*law*); (in *pl*; *Shakesp*) appendages. — *adj* **assign'able** that may be assigned. — *n* **assignation** (*as-ig-nā'shən*) an appointment to meet, used chiefly of secret, clandestine meetings between lovers and mostly with disapproval; the making over of any right to another (*Scots law*). — *n* **assignee** (*as-īn-ē'*) a person to whom any right or property is assigned; a person who receives a contractual right or liability under an assignment; a trustee of a sequestrated estate. — *n* **assignment** (*-sīn'*) the act of assigning; anything assigned; a legal process whereby contractual rights and liabilities may be transferred from an original contracting party to a third person; the writing by which such a transfer is made; a task, piece of work, etc allotted; (*Spenser* altered in 1596 to **dessignment**) design, enterprise. — *n* **assignor** (*law*; *as-i-nör'*) a person who transfers a contractual right or liability under an assignment. — **assigning authority** a national body authorized to assign load-lines to ships. [Fr *assigner*, from L *assignāre* to mark out, from *ad* to, and *signum* a mark or sign]

assignat *as'ig-nat* or *a-sēn-yä'*, (*hist*) *n* one of the paper bonds first issued in 1789 by the French government on the security of the appropriated church lands, and later (1790–97) accepted as notes of currency. [Fr]

assignation, assignee, assignment, assignor. See **assign**.

assimilate *ə-sim'il-āt*, *vt* to make similar or like (with *to* or *with*); to convert into a substance similar to itself, as the body does to food; to take fully into the mind, experience effects of (eg knowledge); to receive and accept fully within a group, absorb; to modify (a speech sound), making it more like a neighbouring sound in a word or sentence (*phonetics*). — *vi* to become like (with *to*); to be incorporated or absorbed (into). — *adj* **assim'ilable**. — *n* **assimilā'tion**. — *n* **assimilā'tionist** a person who advocates a policy of assimilation, *esp* of racial groups (also *adj*). — *adj* **assim'ilātive** having the power or tendency to assimilate. [L *assimilāre*, *-ātum*, from *ad* to, and *similis* like]

assist *ə-sist'*, *vt* to help (*with* work, etc, *in* a matter, etc); to work as an assistant to; to accompany or attend (*Shakesp*). — *vi* to help (with *with* or *in*); to be present at a ceremony, etc (now a Gallicism). — *n* (*NAm*) an act that assists; help; a play that makes it possible for a batter or runner to be put out (*baseball*); a play that helps to make a goal-score possible (*ice-hockey*). — *n* **assis'tance** help; relief. — *adj* **assis'tant** helping. — *n* a person who assists; a helper. — *n* **assis'tantship** the post of assistant. — *adj* **assis'ted** for which help (eg financial aid, additional power) is supplied. — **assisted take-off** a take-off in which the full power of an aircraft's normal engines is supplemented by eg turbo-jet, rocket motor units, or liquid rockets. [Fr *assister*, from L *assistere* to stand by, from *ad* to, and *sistere* to set, take one's stand]

assize *ə-sīz'*, *n* (in *pl*) periodical sittings of judges on circuit, in England and Wales, with a jury (until 1972, when Crown Courts replaced them); a legislative sitting (*hist*); a statute settling the weight, measure, or price of anything (*hist*); a trial by jury (*Scot*); a jury (*Scot*); judgement, sentence (*obs*). — *vt* (*obs*) to assess; to set or fix the quantity or price of. — *n* **assiz'er** an officer with oversight of weights and measures; a juror (*hist*; *Scots law*). [OFr *assise* assembly of judges, set rate, from *asseoir*, from L *assidēre*, from *ad* to, and *sedēre* to sit]

Assoc. See **Ass.**

associate *ə-sō'shi-āt*, or *-si-*, *vt* to join, connect, link; to connect in one's mind; to make a colleague or partner; to accompany (*Shakesp*). — *vi* to consort, keep company (with *with*); to combine or unite. — *adj* (*-ət* or *-āt*) associated; connected; confederate; joined as colleague or junior colleague. — *n* (*-ət* or *-āt*) a person joined or connected with another; a colleague, companion, friend, partner or ally; a person admitted to a society without full membership. — *n* **associabil'ity**. — *adj* **asso'ciable** (*-shi-ə-bl* or *-shə-bl*) capable of being associated. — *n* **assō'ciateship**. — *n* **associā'tion** (*-si-* or *-shi-*) an act of associating; union or combination; a society of persons joined to promote some object; a set of species of plants or animals characteristic of a certain habitat (*biol*); loose aggregation of molecules (*chem*); (also **association football**, *colloq* **soccer**) the game as formulated by the Football Association (formed 1863), with eleven players a side (*opp* to *Rugby*); connection of thoughts or of feelings; (*usu* in *pl*) thought, feeling or memory, more or less permanently connected with eg a place, an occurrence, or something said; a relationship between the EEC and certain other countries, eg in Africa and the Caribbean, being more than just a trade agreement but with the associated members not enjoying membership of the EEC. — *n* **associa'tionism** (*psychol*) the theory which considers association of ideas to be the basis of all mental activity. — *adj* **assō'ciātive** tending to association; such that $(a * b) * c = a * (b * c)$, where * denotes a binary operation (*math*). — *n* **associativity** (*-ə-tiv'*). — **associate professor** in N America, Australia and New Zealand, a university or college teacher immediately below professor in rank; **association copy** a copy of a book deriving additional interest from some association, eg a copy inscribed as given to or by some person of note; **associative learning** learning based on association of ideas (qv). — **association of ideas** mental linkage that facilitates recollection, eg by similarity, contiguity or repetition. [L *associāre*, *-ātum*, from *ad* to, and *socius* a companion]

assoil[1] *ə-soil'*, *vt* to absolve, acquit (with *of* or *from*; *archaic*); to discharge, release (with *of* or *from*; *archaic*); to solve (*obs*); to dispel (*obs*); to determine (*obs*). — *n* **assoil'ment** (*archaic*) absolution. — *vt* **assoilzie** (*ə-soil'i* or *-yi*) to absolve (*obs Scot*); to free (defender or accused) of a claim or charge (*Scots law*). [Anglo-Fr *assoilier*, from L *ab* from, and *solvere* to loose]

assoil[2] *ə-soil'*, (*archaic*; *erron*) *vt* to soil, sully, dirty.

assonance *as'ən-əns*, *n* a correspondence in sound; vowel-rhyme, coincidence of vowel sound without regard to consonants, as in *mate* and *shape*, *feel* and *need*; extended to correspondence of consonants with different vowels; resemblance, correspondence. — *adj* **ass'onant**. — *adj* **assonantal** (*-ant'əl*). — *vi* **ass'onate** to correspond in vowel sound; to practise assonance. [L *assonāre*, *-ātum*, from *ad* to, and *sonāre* to sound]

assort *ə-sört'*, *vt* to distribute in classes, classify; to class, rank. — *vi* to agree or be in accordance; to suit well; to keep company (*archaic*). — *adj* **assort'ative** (*-ə-tiv*). — *adj* **assort'ed** classified, arranged in sorts; made up of various sorts. — *n* **assort'edness**. — *n* **assort'er**. — *n* **assort'ment** the act of assorting; a quantity or number of things assorted; a variety. — **assortative mating** (*bot*) non-random mating, resulting from eg pollinating insects. [Fr *assortir*, from L *ad* to, and *sors*, *sortis* a lot]

assot *ə-sot'*, (*obs*) *vt* to befool, or besot. — *adj* **assott'** or **assott'ed** (*Spenser* etc) infatuated. [OFr *asoter*, from *à* to, and *sot* fool; see **sot**[1]]

ASSR *abbrev*: Autonomous Soviet Socialist Republic (an administrative division within the former Soviet Union).

Asst or **asst** *abbrev*: Assistant or assistant.

assuage *ə-swāj'*, *vt* to soften, mitigate or allay. — *vi* (*archaic*) to abate or subside; to diminish. — *n* **assuage'ment**. — *n* and *adj* **assuag'ing**. — *adj* **assuā'sive** (*-siv*) soothing; mitigating. [OFr *assouager*, from L *ad* to, and *suāvis* mild]

assubjugate *a-sub'jōō-gāt*, (*Shakesp*) *vt* to reduce to subjection. [*a-*, intensive pfx, and **subjugate**]

assuefaction *as-wi-fak'shən*, (*obs*) *n* habituation. [L *assuēfacere*, from *assuētus* accustomed, and *facere* to make]

assuetude *as'wi-tūd*, *n* accustomedness; habit. [L *assuētūdo*]

assume *ə-sūm'* or *-sōōm'*, *vt* to adopt, take in; to take up, take upon oneself; to take for granted; to arrogate; to pretend to possess. — *vi* to make undue claims; to be arrogant. — *adj* **assum'able**. — *adv* **assum'ably**. — *adj* **assumed'** appropriated, usurped; pretended, simulated; taken as the basis of argument. — *adv* **assum'edly**. — *adj* **assum'ing** haughty; arrogant. — *n* assumption; arrogance; presumption. — *conj* (often with *that*) if it can be taken for granted that. — *adv* **assum'ingly**. — *n* **assumpsit** (*ə-sump'sit*) an action at common law, the historical basis of the modern law of contract, in which the plaintiff asserts that the defendant undertook (L *assūmpsit*) to perform a certain act and failed to fulfil his or her promise. — *n* **assumption** (*-sum'* or *-sump'*) an act of assuming; taking upon oneself; arrogance; taking for granted; supposition; that which is taken for granted or supposed; the minor premise in a syllogism (*logic*); a taking up bodily into heaven, *esp* the **Assumption of the Virgin**, celebrated on 15 August (declared a dogma of the Roman Catholic Church on the 1 November 1950); reception, incorporation (*archaic*). — *n* **Assump'tionist** a member of the Roman Catholic congregation (*Augustinians of the Assumption*) founded at Nîmes in 1843. — Also *adj*. — *adj* **assump'tive** of the nature of an assumption; gratuitously assumed; apt, or too apt, to assume. — **deed of assumption** (*Scots law*) a deed executed by trustees under a trust-deed assuming a new trustee or settlement. [L *assūmere*, *assūmptum*, from *ad* to, and *sūmere* to take]

assure *ə-shōōr'*, *vt* to make sure or secure; to give confidence; to tell positively; to insure; to betroth (*obs*). — *adj* **assur'able**. — *n* **assur'ance** confidence; feeling of certainty; subjective certainty of one's salvation (*theol*); composure; self-confidence; unabashedness; audacity; a positive, confidence-giving declaration; insurance which provides for a future certainty rather than a possibility, now *esp* life insurance; security; the securing of a title to property (*law*); a promise; a surety, warrant; a betrothal (*obs*). — *adj* **assured'** certain; confident; beyond doubt; insured; self-confident; over-bold; brazen-faced; secured; pledged; betrothed (*obs*). — *n* a person whose life or property is insured; the beneficiary of an insurance policy. — *adv* **assur'edly** certainly, in truth, undoubtedly (also *interj*); confidently (*archaic*). — *n* **assur'edness**. — *n* **assur'er** a person who gives assurance; an insurer or underwriter; a person who insures his or her life. [OFr *aseürer* (Fr *assurer*), from LL *adsēcūrāre*, from *ad* to, and *sēcūrus* safe; see **sure**[1]]

assurgent *ə-sûr'jənt*, *adj* rising, ascending; rising in a curve to an erect position (*bot*); depicted as rising from the sea (*heraldry*). — *n* **assur'gency** the tendency to rise. [L *ad* to, and *surgere* to rise]

asswage. An obsolete spelling of **assuage**.

Assyrian *a-* or *ə-sir'i-ən*, *adj* of or relating to the vast, ancient empire of Assyria, or the civilization, art, culture or language of the Assyrians. — *n* an inhabitant or native of Assyria; the Semitic language of ancient Assyria; a modern form of an Aramaic dialect still spoken, Syriac. — *n* **Assyriol'ogist**. — *n* **Assyriol'ogy** the science of Assyrian antiquities. [Gr *Assyrios* from *Assyriā*]

assythment *ə-sīth'mənt*, (*Scots law*; now *hist*) *n* indemnification, or reparation, by someone who has caused a death, etc. [ME *aseth* amends, from OFr *aset*, adv mistaken for objective of nominative *asez*; see **assets**]

AST *abbrev*: advanced supersonic transport; Atlantic Standard Time, one of the standard time zones in N America, and the time in it; automatic station tuning (*radio*).

astable *ā-stā'bl*, *adj* not stable; oscillating between two states (*elec*). [Gr *a-* (privative) and **stable**[1]]

astacology *as-tə-kol'ə-ji*, *n* the science of the crayfish or of breeding it. — *adj* **astacological** (*-loj'*). — *n* **astacol'ogist**. [Gr *astakos* lobster, crayfish, and **-logy**]

astarboard *ə-stär'bōrd*, (*naut*) *adv* on or towards the starboard. [**a-**[1]]

astare *ə-stār'*, (*archaic*) *adv* in a state of staring. [**a-**[1] and **stare**[1]]

astart *ə-stärt'*, (*Spenser*) *vi* to start up; to befall. — *adv* with a start, suddenly. [Pfx *a-* up, and **start**]

Astarte *as-tär'ti*, (*mythol*) *n* the Phoenician goddess of love, whose attributes symbolize the notion of productive power, identified with the Semitic goddess **Ashtaroth** (*ash'tar-oth*) or **Ash'toreth** (*Bible*, etc) and the Assyrian and Babylonian **Ish'tar**, goddess of love and war. [L and Gr form of the name, from Phoenician *'strt*, rel to Heb *'Ashtoreth*]

astatic *a-stat'ik*, *adj* having no tendency to stand in a fixed position; without polarity, as a pair of magnetic needles set in opposite directions (*phys*). — *n* **astatine** (*as'tə-tēn*) a radioactive chemical element (atomic no 85; symbol **At**) of the halogen series. [Gr *astatos* unstable, from *a-* (privative) and *statos*, verbal adj of *histanai* to make to stand]

astatki *as-tat'kē*, *n* the residue of petroleum-distillation, used as fuel. [Russ *ostatki*, *pl* of *ostatok* residue]

asteism *as'tē-izm*, (*rhetoric*) *n* refined irony. [Gr *asty*, *asteōs* a town; seen as a place of refinement]

astely *a-stē'li*, (*bot*) *n* absence of a central cylinder or stele. — *adj* **astē'lic**. [Gr *a-* (privative) and *stēlē* column]

aster *as'tər*, *n* a star (*obs*); a starlike figure, as in mitotic cell-division (*biol*); a plant of the *Aster* genus of Compositae, with showy radiated heads, white to lilac-blue or purple, flowering in late summer and autumn (hence often called Michaelmas daisies), or a related form; extended to the similar **China aster** (*Callistephus hortensis*) brought from China to France by a missionary in the 18c. [Gr *astēr* star]

-aster *-ast-ər*, *combining form* denoting a poor imitation of; a person who has pretensions to being, as in *criticaster*, *poetaster*, *politicaster*. [L]

asteria. See **asterism**.

Asterias *ə-stēr'i-as*, *n* the common crossfish or five-fingers genus of sea urchins. — *n* **as'terid** or **asterid'ian** a starfish. [New L, from Gr, starred, from *astēr* star]

asterisk *as'tə-risk*, *n* a star-shaped mark (*) used as a reference to a note, as a mark of omission, as a mark of a word or root inferred to have existed but not recorded, and for other purposes. — *vt* to mark with an asterisk. — *adj* **as'terisked**. [LL *asteriscus* a small star, from Gr *asteriskos*, dimin of *astēr* a star]

asterism *as'tə-rizm*, *n* a group of stars; three asterisks placed to direct attention to a passage; in some gemstones and minerals, the property of showing by reflected or transmitted light a star-shaped luminous figure due to inclusions or tubular cavities. — *n* **asteria** (*as-tēr'i-ə*) a precious stone that shows asterism when cut *en cabochon*. — *adj* **astēriated** (*mineralogy*) showing asterism. [Gr *asterismos* a constellation]

astern *ə-stûrn'*, (*naut*) *adv* in or towards the stern; behind. [**a-**[1]]

asteroid *as'tə-roid*, *n* any of the thousands of rocky objects found generally in orbits between those of Mars and Jupiter (also, *esp* formerly, called a **minor planet**); a starfish, a member of the Asteroidea. — *adj* resembling a star, star-shaped; of the Asteroidea. — *adj* **asteroid'al**. — *n pl* **Asteroid'ea** a class of echinoderms, the starfishes. [Gr *asteroeidēs* star-like]

astert *ə-stûrt'*, (*obs*) *vi* same as **astart**.

asthenia *as-thē'ni-ə* or *-thi-nī'ə*, *n* (*med*) debility, loss of muscular strength. — *adj* **asthenic** (*-then'ik*) of or relating to asthenia; lacking strength; of a slender body type, narrow-chested, with slight muscular development (*anthropol*); (of, or characteristic of, a person) belonging to a type thought prone to schizophrenia, having a small, light trunk and disproportionately long limbs (*psychol*). — *n* a person of asthenic type. — *n* **asthenosphere** (*-then'ə-sfēr*; *geol*) the upper mantle of the earth, a shell lying below, and softer and more readily able to yield to persistent stress than, the lithosphere. [Gr *astheneia*, from *a-* (privative) and *sthenos* strength]

asthma *as'mə*, also *asth'*, *ast'*, and in US *usu az'*, *n* a chronic disorder of the organs of respiration, characterized by difficulty of breathing, wheezing, and a tightness in the chest. — *adj* **asthmatic** (*-mat'*) or (*old*) **asthmat'ical**. — *adv* **asthmat'ically**. [Gr *asthma*, *-atos*, from *aazein* to breathe with open mouth]

asthore *as-thōr'*, (*Anglo-Ir*) *n* darling. [Ir *a stóir*, vocative of *stór* treasure]

Asti *as'tē*, *n* an Italian white wine made round about *Asti* in the Monferrato hills in Piedmont.

astichous *as'ti-kəs*, (*bot*) *adj* not in rows.. [Gr *a-* (privative) and *stichos* a row]

astigmatism *ə-stig'mə-tizm*, *n* a defect in an eye, lens or mirror, by which rays from a single point are not focused at a single point. — Also **astig'mia** (*-mi-ə*). — *adj* **astigmatic** (*a-stig-mat'ik*). — *adv* **astigmat'ically**. [Gr *a-* (privative) and *stigma*, *-atos* a point]

astilbe *as-til'bi*, *n* a plant of the *Astilbe* genus of perennial plants of the family Saxifragaceae, with clusters of red or white flowers. [Gr *a-* (privative) and *stilbos* glittering]

astir *ə-stûr'*, *adv* on the move; out of bed, up and about; excited, roused; in motion. [**a-**[1] and **stir**[1]]

ASTM *abbrev*: American Society for Testing and Materials.

ASTMS (sometimes *as'təmz*) *abbrev*: Association of Scientific, Technical and Managerial Staffs (now part of MSF after amalgamation with TASS in 1988).

astomatous *a-stom'ə-təs*, or *-stōm'*, (*bot* and *zool*) *adj* mouthless, or without a mouthlike opening. — Also **astomous** (*as'tə-məs*). [Gr *a-* (privative) and *stoma*, *-atos* mouth]

astonish *əs-ton'ish*, *vt* to impress with sudden surprise or wonder; to amaze or shock; to daze or stun (*Shakesp*). — Earlier forms **astone** (*ə-stun'*), **astun'** and **astony** (*-ston'i*). — *adj* **aston'ied** (*obs*). — *adj* **aston'ished** amazed; dazed, stunned (*obs*). — *adj* **aston'ishing** very wonderful, amazing; very surprising, extraordinary. — *adv* **aston'ishingly**. — *n* **aston'ishment** amazement; wonder; a cause for astonishment. [Ultimately from L *ex* out, and *tonāre* to thunder]

astoop *ə-stōōp'*, (*archaic*) *adv* in a stooping position. [**a-**[1] and **stoop**[1]]

astound *əs-townd'*, *vt* to amaze, to strike dumb with astonishment. — *adj* **astound'** (*archaic*) or **astound'ed** stunned; dazed; amazed. — *adj* **astound'ing**. — *adv* **astound'ingly**. — *n* **astound'ment** (*archaic*). [From the pa p **astoned**; see **astonish**]

astr. or **astron.** *abbrev*: astronomical; astronomy.

astraddle *ə-strad'l*, *adv* with legs wide apart and *usu* on each side of something. [**a-**[1]]

astragal *as'trə-gəl*, *n* a small semicircular moulding (often a beading) round a column or elsewhere (*archit*); a round moulding near the mouth of a cannon; a glazing bar in a window (*archit*; *Scot*); (in *pl*) dice (*obs*). — *n* **astragalus** (*as-trag'əl-əs*) the ankle bone (*zool*); (with *cap*) the tragacanth and milk-vetch genus. [Gr *astragalos* a vertebra, ankle bone, moulding, milk-vetch, in *pl* (knucklebones used as) dice]

astrakhan *as-trə-kan'*, *n* lambskin with curled wool from the Middle East; a rough fabric made in imitation of it. — *adj* made of astrakhan; (of a lamb) of the type suitable for astrakhan production. [*Astrakhan*, a city on the Caspian Sea]

astral *as'trəl*, *adj* belonging to the stars; starry; star-shaped; belonging to a mitotic aster (*biol*); in theosophy, of a supersensible substance supposed to pervade all space and enter into all bodies. — **astral body** (*theosophy*) an astral counterpart of the physical body; a ghost or wraith; **astral spirits** spirits supposed to animate the heavenly bodies, forming, as it were, their souls. [L *astrālis*, from *astrum* a star]

astrand *ə-strand'*, *adv* on the strand. [**a-**[1] and **strand**[1]]

astrantia *as-tran'shi-ə*, *n* a plant of the *Astrantia* genus of hardy, perennial umbelliferous plants with showy petal-like bracts. [Gr *astron* star]

astraphobia *as-trə-fō'bi-ə* or **astrapophobia** *-tra-pə-fō'bi-ə*, *n* a morbid fear of (thunder and) lightning. [Gr *astrapē* lightning, and *phobos* fear]

astray *ə-strā'*, *adv* out of the right way, off course; out of the correct place; away from correct behaviour, wrong; in a lost state. [**a-**[1]]

Astrex (rabbit). See **Rex**.

astrict *ə-strikt'*, (*archaic*) *vt* to bind, to compress; to constipate (*med*); to restrict (*Scots law*). — *n* **astric'tion** (*-shən*) constipation (*med*); obligation, binding (*obs*). — *adj* **astric'tive** astringent (*med*); binding (*obs*). [L *astringere*, *astrictum*, from *ad* to, and *stringere* to draw tight]

astride *ə-strīd'*, *adv* in a striding position; with a leg on each side. — *prep* astride of; on either side of. [**a-**[1]]

astringe *ə-strinj'*, *vt* to draw together or tight, to compress (*med*); to constipate (*med*); to bind, oblige (*obs*). — *n* **atrin'gency**. — *adj* **astrin'gent** having power to contract organic tissues (*med*); styptic (*med*); contracting, drawing together; (of eg manner) sharp, austere, severe; (of eg words, criticism) caustic, biting. — *n* an astringent agent, eg a medical preparation, or a cosmetic lotion to tone the skin. — *adv* **astrin'gently**. [Ety as for **astrict**]

astringer. See **austringer**.

astro- *as'trō-* or *-tro'*, *combining form* denoting: star; celestial body; outer space; star-shaped; astrology. [Gr, from *astron* a star]

astrocyte *as'trə-sīt*, (*anatom* and *zool*) *n* a much-branched, star-shaped neuroglia cell. — *n* **astrocytō'ma** a tumour of the central nervous system, composed largely of astrocytes: — *pl* **astrocytō'mas** or **astrocytō'mata**. [**astro-**]

astrodome *as'trə-dōm*, *n* a small transparent observation dome on the top of the fuselage of an aeroplane, for astronomical observations; a sports centre covered by a huge translucent dome, *orig* one at Houston, Texas. [**astro-**]

astrodynamics *as-trō-dī-nam'iks*, *n sing* the science of the motion of bodies in outer space and the forces that act on them. — *n* **astrodynam'icist**. [**astro-**]

astrofell. See **astrophel**.

astrogeology *as-trō-jē-ol'ə-ji*, *n* the study of the geology of the moon, etc. — *n* **astrogeol'ogist**. [**astro-**]

astroid *as'troid*, (*math*) *n* a hypocycloid with four cusps. [**astro-** and **-oid**]

astrol. *abbrev*: astrological; astrology.

astrolabe *as'trə-lāb*, *n* an ancient instrument for showing the positions of the sun and bright stars at any given time, or for taking altitudes above the horizon. [**astro-** and *-labe*, from *lab-*, root of Gr *lambanein* to take]

astrolatry *ə-strol'ə-tri*, *n* star-worship. [**astro-** and Gr *latreia* worship]

astrology *ə-strol'ə-ji*, *n* the study of the supposed influence of the movements and positions of the stars and planets on human and terrestrial affairs (formerly called *judicial astrology*); *orig* practical astronomy (*obs*). — *n* **astrol'oger**. — *adj* **astrolog'ic** or **astrolog'ical**. — *adv* **astrolog'ically**. [L *astrologia* (early) astronomy, from Gr *astron* star, and *logos* discourse]

astrometeorology *as'trō-mēt-i-ər-ol'ə-ji* or *-mēt-yər-*, *n* the study of the influence, or supposed influence, of the stars, planets, etc on climate and weather. [**astro-**]

astrometry *as-trom'ə-tri*, *n* the precise measurement of position in astronomy. [**astro-**]

astron. See **astr**.

astronaut *as'trə-nöt*, *n* a person engaged in space travel. — *n sing* **astronaut'ics** the science of travel in space. [**astro-** and *-naut*, from Gr *nautes* a sailor]

astronavigation *as-trō-nav-i-gā'shən*, *n* the navigation of aircraft, spacecraft or sailing craft by means of observation of the stars. [**astro-**]

astronomy *ə-stron'ə-mi*, *n* the study of the celestial bodies and the heavens in all scientific aspects. — *n* **astron'omer**. — *adj* **astronom'ical** or **astronom'ic** relating to astronomy; prodigiously great, like the distance of the stars (*colloq*). — *adv* **astronom'ically**. — *vi* **astron'omize** or **-ise** to study astronomy. — **astronomical unit** the earth's mean distance from the sun, about 92.9 million miles, used as a measure of distance within the solar system; **astronomical year** see under **year**. [*astronomia*, from Gr *astron* star, and *nomos* law]

astrophel or **astrofell** *as'trō-fel*, (*Spenser*) *n* an unidentified bitter starlike plant — the seaside aster has been suggested. [Poss Gr *astron* star, and *phyllon* leaf]

astrophysics *as-trō-fiz'iks*, *n sing* the branch of astronomy which applies the laws of physics to the study of the stars and interstellar matter. — *adj* **astrophys'ical**. — *n* **astrophys'icist**. [**astro-**]

Astroturf® *as'trō-tûrf*, *n* an artificial surface for sports pitches, etc, having a woven, grass-like pile on a rubber base (used *esp* for American or Association football). — Also *adj*.

astrut *ə-strut'*, (*archaic*) *adv* protrudingly; distendedly. — *adj* protruding; distended. [**a-**[1] and **strut**[1]]

astucious, astuciously, astucity. See **astute**.

astun. See **astonish**.

astute *as-* or *əs-tūt'*, or (in US) *-tōōt'*, *adj* shrewd; perceptive, sagacious; wily. — Also (*Scott*) **astucious** (*-tū'shəs*). — *adv* **astu'ciously** (*Scott*). — *n* **astucity** (*-tū'si-ti*). — *adv* **astute'ly**. — *n* **astute'ness**. [L *astūtus*, from *astus* craft]

astylar *a-stī'lər*, (*archit*) *adj* without columns. [Gr *a-* (privative) and *stȳlos* a column]

asudden *ə-sud'ən*, (*archaic*) *adv* suddenly. [**a-**[1]]

asunder *ə-sun'dər*, *adv* apart; into parts; separately. [**a-**[1]]

ASW *abbrev*: antisubmarine warfare.

aswarm *ə-swörm'*, *adv* in swarms. [**a-**[1], and **swarm**[1]]

asway *ə-swā'*, *adv* swayingly. [**a-**[1]]

aswim *ə-swim'*, (*archaic*) *adv* afloat. [**a-**[1]]

aswing *ə-swing'*, (*archaic*) *adv* swingingly; in a swing. [**a-**[1]]

aswirl *ə-swûrl'*, *adv* in a swirl. [**a-**[1]]

aswoon *ə-swōōn'*, (*archaic*) *adv* in a swoon. [Poss for *on* or *in swoon*; or orig a pa p, ME *iswowen*, from OE *geswōgen* swooned (not known in other parts of speech)]

asylum *ə-sī'ləm*, *n* a place of refuge for debtors and for those accused of crime; an institution for the care or relief of the unfortunate, such as the blind or (*old-fashioned*) mentally ill; (any place of) refuge or protection: — *pl* **asy'lums**. — **political asylum** protection given to a person by one country from arrest in another; refuge provided by a country to a person leaving his or her own without the permission of its government. [L *asȳlum*, from Gr *asȳlon* (neuter) inviolate, from *a-* (privative) and *sȳlon*, *sȳlē* right of seizure]

asymmetry *a-sim'ə-tri*, or *ā-*, *n* lack of symmetry, irregularity of form or arrangement. — *adj* **asymmetric** (*-et'rik*) or **asymmet'rical**. — *adv* **asymmet'rically**. — *n* **Asymmetron** (*-sim'ə-tron*) one of the genera of marine organisms making up the lancelets. [Gr *asymmetriā*, from *a-* (privative) and *symmetriā* symmetry]

asymptomatic *a-sim(p)'tə-mat-ik*, or *ā-*, *adj* having, displaying or producing no symptoms. — *adv* **asymptomat'ically**. [**a-**[2]]

asymptote *a'sim(p)-tōt*, (*math*) *n* a line (*usu* straight) that continually approaches a curve but never meets it. — *adj* **asymptotic** (*-tot'ik*) or **asymptot'ical**. — *adv* **asymptot'ically**. [Gr *asymptōtos*, from *a-* (privative), *syn* together, *ptōtos* apt to fall, and *piptein* to fall]

asynartete *a-sin'är-tēt*, (*prosody*) *adj* not connected, consisting of two members having different rhythms. — *n* a verse of such a kind. — Also **asynartetic** (*-tet'ik*). [Gr *asynartētos*, from *a-* (privative), *syn* together, and *artaein* to knit]

asynchronism *a-sing'krə-nizm*, or *ā-*, *n* lack of synchronism or correspondence in time. — Also **asyn'chrony**. — *adj* **asyn'chronous**. — *adv* **asyn'chronously**. — **asynchronous transmission** transmission of electronic data along communication lines, in which time intervals between characters vary and data is transmitted when available. [Gr *a-* (privative), *syn* together, and *chronos* time]

asyndeton *a-sin'də-ton*, (*rhetoric*; *gram*) *n* a sentence or construction in which the conjunctions are omitted. — *adj* **asyndet'ic**. [Gr *asyndeton*, from *a-* (privative) and *syndetos* bound together, from *syn* together, and *deein* to bind]

asynergy *a-* or *ā-sin-ûr'ji*, (*med*) *n* lack of co-ordination in action, eg of muscles. — Also **asyner'gia**. [Gr *a-* (privative), *syn* together, and *ergon* work]

asyntactic *a-sin-tak'tik*, or *ā-*, *adj* loosely put together, irregular, ungrammatical. [Gr *asyntaktikos*, from *a-* (privative) and *syntaktos*, from *syntassein* to put in order together]

asystole *a-sis'to-lē*, or *ā-*, (*med*) *n* inability of the heart to empty itself. — Also **asys'tolism**. [Gr *a-* (privative) and *systolē* contraction]

AT *abbrev*: administrative trainee; alternative technology; antitank; appropriate technology.

At (*chem*) *symbol*: astatine.

at *at* or *ət*, *prep* denoting (precise) position in space or time, or some similar relation, such as amount, response, occupation, aim, activity. — **at it** occupied in a particular way, doing a particular thing; up to some criminal activity (*colloq*); having sexual intercourse (*colloq*); **at that** see under **that**; **get someone at it** to make someone excited, worked up or agitated; **where it's at** see under **where**. [OE *æt*; cf Gothic and ON *at*, L *ad*, Sans *adhi*]

ATA *abbrev*: Air Transport Association (*US*); Air Transport Auxiliary.

atabal *at'ə-bal* or *ä-tä-bäl'*, *n* a Moorish kettledrum. [Sp, from Ar *at-tabl* the drum]

atabeg *ät-ä-beg'* or **atabek** *-bek'*, *n* a Turkish ruler or high official. [Turk *atabeg*, from *ata* father, and *beg* prince]

atabrin or **atebrin** *at'ə-brin*, *n* mepacrine.

atacamite *a-tak'ə-mīt*, *n* a mineral, a basic chloride of copper. [*Atacama*, in Chile]

atactic. See **ataxia**.

ataghan. Same as **yataghan**.

Atalanta *a-tə-lan'tə*, (*Gr mythol*) *n* a fleet-footed Arcadian (or Boeotian) maiden who raced against her suitors, and was defeated by Milanion (or Hippomenes), who dropped golden apples on the course to delay her.

atalaya *ä-tä-lä'yä*, *n* a watchtower. [Sp, from Ar]

ataman *at'a-man*, *n* a Cossack headman or general, a hetman: — *pl* **at'amans**. [Russ, from Ger *Hauptmann*, from *Haupt* head, and *Mann* man]

atap or **attap** *at'ap*, *n* the nipa palm; its leaves used for thatching. [Malay]

ataraxia *at-ə-rak'si-ə* or **ataraxy** *at'ə-rak-si*, *n* tranquillity, the freedom from anxiety *orig* aspired to by the Epicureans, Stoics and Sceptics; a state of calmness, tranquillity (*med*). — *adj* and *n* **atarac'tic** or **atarax'ic** (a) tranquillizing (drug). [Gr *ataraxiā*, from *a-* (privative) and *tarassein* to disturb]

à tâtons *a tä-tɔ̃*, (*Fr*) gropingly.

atavism *at'əv-izm*, *n* the reappearance of ancestral, but not parental, characteristics; reversion to an ancestral, or to a primitive, type. — *adj* **atavist'ic**. [L *atavus* a great-great-great-grandfather, an ancestor, from *avus* a grandfather]

ataxia *a-tak'si-ə*, or **ataxy** *a-tak'si* or *at'aks-i*, *n* inability to co-ordinate voluntary movements (*med*; see **locomotor ataxy** under **locomotive**); lack of order (*obs*). — *adj* **atact'ic** or **atax'ic**. [Gr *ataxiā* disorder, from *a-* (privative) and *taxis* order]

ATC *abbrev*: air-traffic control; Air Training Corps; automatic train control.

atchieve. See **achieve**.

Ate *ā'tē*, *ä'tē* or *ä'tā*, *n* the Greek goddess of mischief and of all rash actions and their results. [Gr *Ātē*]

ate *et* or *āt*, *pa t* of **eat**.

atebrin. See **atabrin**.

atelectasis *a-tel-ek'tə-sis*, (*med*) *n* incomplete inflation of a lung at birth; the collapse of a lung in an adult. — *adj* **atelectatic** (*-tat'ik*). [Gr *atelēs* incomplete, and *ektasis* stretching out]

ateleiosis *a-tel-ī-ō'sis*, *-i-*, or *a-tēl-*, (*med*) *n* dwarfism without disproportion. [Gr *ateleiōtos* insufficient, from *a-* (privative) and *telos*, an end]

atelier *at'əl-yā*, *n* a workshop, *esp* an artist's studio. [Fr]

a tempo *ä tem'pō*, (*music*) in time, ie revert to the previous or original tempo. [Ital]

à terre *a ter*, (*Fr*) on the ground; with the foot (*usu* both feet) flat on the ground (*ballet*).

Athanasian *ath-ə-nā'sh(y)ən* or *-z(h)yən*, *adj* relating to *Athanasius* (c.296–373), or to the Christian creed erroneously attributed to him.

athanasy *ə-than'ə-si*, *n* deathlessness. [Gr *athanasiā*, from *a-* (privative) and *thanatos* death]

athanor *ath'ə-nör*, (*hist*) *n* an alchemist's self-feeding digesting furnace. [Ar *at-tannūr*, from *al* the, and *tannūr* furnace, from *nūr* fire]

Atharvaveda *ä-tär'vä-vā'dä*, (*Hinduism*) *n* one of the Vedas, comprising spells, charms and exorcistic chants. [Sans, from *atharvan* fire-priest, and *veda* knowledge]

atheism *ā'thi-izm*, *n* disbelief in the existence of a god. — *n* **a'theist**. — *adj* **atheist'ic** or **atheist'ical**. — *adv* **atheist'ically**. — *vi* **a'theize** or **-ise** to talk or write as an atheist. — *vt* to render godless; to make an atheist of. — *adj* **a'theous** (*Milton*) atheistic; godless. [Gr *atheos*, from *a-* (privative) and *theos* god]

atheling *ath'əl-ing*, (*hist*) *n* a member of a noble family; later, a prince of the blood royal, or the heir-apparent. [OE *ætheling*, from *æthele* noble; cf Ger *Adel*]

athematic *ath-i-mat'ik*, *adj* without a thematic vowel (*gram* and *linguistics*); not using themes as a basis (*music*). — *adv* **athemat'ically**. [**a-**[2]]

Athene *a-thē'nē* or **Athena** *-nə*, *n* the Greek goddess of wisdom, born from the head of Zeus, tutelary goddess of Athens, identified by the Romans with Minerva. — *n* **Athenaeum** (*ath-ə-nē'əm*) a temple of Athene; an ancient institution of learning, or literary university; a name sometimes taken by a literary institution, library, or periodical. — *adj* **Athenian** (*a-thē'ni-ən*) of Athens. — *n* a native or citizen of Athens or Attica.

atheology *ā-thi-ol'ə-ji*, *n* opposition to theology. — *adj* **atheological** (*-ə-loj'i-kl*). [**a-**[2]]

atherine *ath'ər-īn*, *adj* belonging or pertaining to a genus (*Atherī'na*) of small fishes of a family (**Atherinidae**; *-in'i-dē*) similar to the grey mullets, sometimes sold as smelt. — *n* an atherine fish. [Gr *atherīnē*]

athermancy *ath-ûr'mən-si*, (*phys*) *n* impermeability to radiant heat. — *adj* **ather'manous**. [Gr *a-* (privative) and *thermainein* to heat]

atheroma *ath-ər-ō'mə*, (*pathol*) *n* a cyst with contents of a porridge-like consistency; atherosclerosis. — *adj* **atherōm'atous**. — *n* **atherosclero'sis** (*-ō'sis*) the thickening of the inner coat of arteries by deposition of cholesterol and other substances, the most significant form of arteriosclerosis. — *n* and *adj* **atherosclerotic** (*-ot'ik*). [Gr *athērōma*, from *athērē* or *atharē* porridge]

athetesis *ath-i-tē'sis*, *n* rejection (of a passage of text) as spurious. — *vt* **ath'etize** or **-ise** to reject. [Gr *athetēsis* rejection, from *a-* (privative) and the root of *tithenai* to set]

athetosis *ath-i-tō'sis*, (*pathol*) *n* slow, involuntary writhing movement of fingers and toes due to a lesion of the brain. — *adj* **ath'etoid**. — *adj* **athetos'ic** or **athetot'ic**. [Gr *athetos* without position, set aside, and **-osis** (2)]

a'thing. See **a'**.

athirst *ə-thûrst'*, *adj* thirsty; (with *for*) eager, avid. [OE *ofthyrst*; see **thirst**]

athlete *ath'lēt*, *n* a person who takes part in vigorous physical exercise, *orig* and *esp* in contests of strength, speed, endurance or agility; a person who is active and vigorous in body or mind. — Also **athlē'ta** (*obs*). — *adj* **athletic** (*-let'ik*) relating to athletics; of, like or suitable for an athlete; strong, vigorous; of a long-limbed, large-chested muscular type of body (*anthropol*). — *adv* **athlet'ically**. — *n* **athlet'icism** (*-i-sizm*) practice of, training in, or devotion to, athletics. — *n pl* or *n sing* **athlet'ics** athletic sports. — *n sing* the practice of athletic sports. — **athlete's foot** a contagious disease of the foot, caused by a fungus. — **sexual athlete** see under **sex**. [Gr *athlētēs*, from *athlos* contest]

at-home. See under **home**.

-athon *-ə-thon* or **-thon**, *combining form* denoting something long in terms of time and endurance, *usu* a prolonged fund-raising event, eg *telethon*, *talkathon*, *walkathon*. [After mar*athon*]

athrill *ə-thril'*, (*archaic*) *adv* in a thrill, thrilling. [**a-**[1]]

athrob *ə-throb'*, *adj* and *adv* with throbs, throbbing. [**a-**[1]]

athrocyte *ath'ro-sīt*, (*biol*) *n* a cell having the ability to absorb and store foreign matter. — *n* **athrocyto'sis**: — *pl* **athrocytō'sēs**. [Gr *athroos* in a group, crowded, and **-cyte**]

athwart *ə-thwört'*, *prep* across. — *adv* sideways; transversely; awry; wrongly; perplexingly. [**a-**[1]]

atilt *ə-tilt'*, *adv* on a tilt; as a tilter (*hist*). [**a-**[1] and **tilt**[2]]

atimy *at'i-mi*, *n* loss of honour; in ancient Athens, loss of civil rights, public disgrace. [Gr *atimiā*, from *a-* (privative) and *timē* honour]

atingle *ə-ting'gl*, *adj* and *adv* in a tingle. [**a-**[1] and **tingle**[1]]

a-tishoo or **atishoo** *ə-tish'ōō*, *interj* and *n* (*colloq*) (an imitation of) the sound of a sneeze.

Ativan® *at'i-van*, *n* a proprietary name for lorazepam, a drug used to treat anxiety or insomnia, a tranquillizer for short-term use.

Atkins. See **Tommy Atkins**.

Atlantean, **Atlantes**. See **Atlas**.

Atlantic *ət-* or *at-lan'tik*, *adj* of, bordering on or relating to the Atlantic Ocean; of o pertaining to Atlas, Atlantean (*obs*). — *n* the Atlantic Ocean, extending from the Arctic to the Antarctic, separating the continents of Europe and Africa from North and South America. — *n* **Atlan'ticism** the policy of close co-operation between N America and W Europe. — *n* **Atlan'ticist**. — *n* **Atlan'tis** a legendary vanished island in the Atlantic Ocean. — **Atlantic Charter** an Anglo-American declaration during the Second World War of eight common principles of right in future peace; **Atlantic (Standard) Time** the standard time used in the easternmost time zone of Canada, four hours behind Greenwich time. [L *atlanticus*, from Gr *atlantikos* of Atlas (see **Atlas**)]

Atlantosaurus *ət-lan'tə-sö-rəs*, *n* a gigantic lizard-hipped, four-footed, herbivorous Jurassic dinosaur of Colorado and Wyoming. [New L, from Gr *Atlas*, *Atlantos* (see **Atlas**) and *sauros* lizard]

ATLAS *at'ləs*, *abbrev*: automated telephone line address system, a memory store in which the operator can store programmed telephone numbers for calls required later in the day; automatic tabulating, listing and sorting package, a software package for these purposes.

Atlas *at'ləs*, *n* the Titan who held up the heavens on his shoulders (*Gr mythol*); the African mountain range into which Atlas was transformed (*Gr mythol*); (*pl* **Atlantes** *at-lan'tēz*) a figure of a man serving as a column in a building. — *adj* **Atlantē'an** of Atlas; gigantic; of Atlantis. [Gr *Atlas*, *Atlantos*]

atlas[1] *at'ləs*, *n* a book of maps, plates or the like, and often geographical information; the first cervical vertebra, supporting the skull (*anatom*); before metrication, a size of drawing-paper: — *pl* **at'lases**. [From **Atlas**, whose figure used to appear on title pages of atlases]

atlas[2] *at'ləs*, (*obs*) *n* a satin manufactured in the East. [Ar]

atlatl *at'əl-āt-əl* or *at'l-at-l*, *n* an American Indian throwing-stick; an ancient Mexican spear-thrower. [Nahuatl, spear-thrower]

ATM *abbrev*: automated (or automatic) teller machine.

atm. *abbrev*: atmosphere (unit of pressure); atmospheric.

atman *ät'mən*, (*Hinduism*) *n* the divine within the self, the essential self. [Sans *ātman* self, soul]

atmology *at-mol'ə-ji*, (*phys*) *n* the science of the phenomena of aqueous vapour. — *n* **atmol'ogist**. [Gr *atmos* vapour, and *logos* discourse]

atmolysis *at-mol'i-sis*, (*phys* and *chem*) *n* a method of separating mixed gases by their different rates of passage through a porous septum. — *vt* **at'molyse** or **-yze** (*-līz*). [Gr *atmos* vapour, and *lysis* loosing, from *lyein* to loose]

atmometer *at-mom'i-tər*, (*phys* and *bot*) *n* an instrument for measuring the rate of evaporation from a moist surface. [Gr *atmos* vapour, and *metron* measure]

atmosphere *at'məs-fēr*, *n* the gaseous envelope that surrounds the earth or any of the celestial bodies; any gaseous medium; a unit of atmospheric pressure equal to the pressure exerted by a column of mercury 760 millimetres in height at 0°C, practically the same as standard atmosphere (see under **standard**); a feeling of space and distance in a picture; any surrounding influence or pervading feeling (*fig*). — *adj* **atmospher'ic** (*-fer'ik*), or **atmospher'ical** of or depending on the atmosphere; having a perceptible atmosphere (eg of a place, music, etc). — *adv* **atmospher'ically**. — *npl* **atmospher'ics** noises interfering with radio reception, due to electric disturbances in the ether. — **atmospheric engine** an early variety of steam engine in which the steam is admitted only to the underside of the piston; **atmospheric hammer** a hammer driven by compressed air; **atmospheric pollution** harmful concentrations of gases and aerosols in the atmosphere; **atmospheric pressure** the pressure exerted by the atmosphere at the surface of the earth due to the weight of the air. [Gr *atmos* vapour, and *sphaira* a sphere]

at. no. or **at. numb.** *abbrev*: atomic number.

atoc. See **atok**.

atocia *a-tō'shi-ə*, (*zool*) *n* (*rare*) sterility in a female. — *n* **atoke** (*at'ōk*) the sexless part in certain polychaete worms. — *adj* **atokous** (*at'ək-əs*) or **at'okal** without offspring. [Gr *atokiā*, from *a-* (privative) and *tokos* birth, offspring]

atok or **atoc** *a-tok'*, *n* a species of skunk. [Peruv]

atoke, etc. See **atocia**.

atoll *at'ol* or *ə-tol'*, *n* a coral island consisting of a circular belt of coral enclosing a central lagoon. [Name in Maldive Islands]

atom *at'əm*, *n* the smallest particle in an element which can take part in a chemical reaction, consisting of a nucleus and one or more orbiting electrons (*chem*); a hypothetical particle of matter so small as to be incapable of further division, according to atomic philosophy (qv); anything very small. — *adj* **atomic** (*ə-tom'ik*) pertaining to atoms; obtained by means of atomic fission, as **atomic energy** or **atomic power**; driven by atomic power, as **atomic aircraft-carrier**, **icebreaker**, **merchantman**, **submarine**, etc; heated by atomic power, as **atomic radiator**. — *adj* **atom'ical**. — *n* **atomicity** (*at-əm-is'i-ti*; *chem*) the state or fact of being composed of atoms; the number of atoms in a molecule; valency. — *n* **at'omism** the doctrine that atoms arranged themselves into the universe; atomic philosophy; the atomic theory; a theory that mental processes and psychological states can be analysed into simple elements (*psychol*). — *n* **at'omist** a person who believes in atomism. — *adj* **atomis'tic**. — *adv* **atomist'ically**. — *n* **atomizā'tion** or **-s-** the reduction of liquids to the form of spray; reduction into small units, splintering, fragmentation. — *vt* **at'omize** or **-ise** to reduce to atoms; to reduce (a liquid or solid) to a fine spray or minute particles; to destroy by atomic weapons. — *n* **atomī'zer** or **-s-** an instrument for discharging liquids in a fine spray. — *n* **at'omy** (*archaic*) an atom, or mote; a pygmy (*Shakesp*). — **atom** (or **atomic**) **bomb** a bomb in which the nuclei of uranium or plutonium atoms bombarded by neutrons split with explosive transformation of part of their mass into energy; **atomic clock** a clock in which, to achieve greater accuracy, the oscillations of a quartz crystal (see **quartz clock**) are regulated by the vibration of certain atoms such as a caesium atom; **atomic energy** nuclear energy; **atomic mass unit** 1/12 of the mass of an atom of C-12; **atomic number** the number of units of charge of positive electricity on the nucleus of an atom of an element; **atomic philosophy** a system of philosophy enunciated by Democritus, which taught that the ultimate constituents of all things are indivisible particles, differing in form and in their relations to each other; **atomic pile** a device for the controlled release of nuclear energy, eg a lattice of small rods of natural uranium embedded in a mass of pure graphite which serves to slow down neutrons; **atomic power**, **atomic radiator** see **atomic** above; **atomic second** a time interval whose measurement uses the frequency of radiation emitted or absorbed during transition from one energy state to another of a chosen atom; **atomic theory** the hypothesis that all atoms of the same element are alike and that a compound is formed by union of atoms of different elements in some simple ratio; **atomic time** time whose unit is the atomic second; **atomic transmutation** the change of one type of atom to another as a result of a nuclear reaction; **atomic warfare** warfare using atomic weapons; **atomic weight** relative atomic mass (qv); **a'tom-smasher** (*colloq*) an apparatus for breaking up the atom, an accelerator. — **Atomic Energy Authority** and **Atomic Energy Commission** the respective bodies in Britain and the USA responsible for the development and control of atomic energy; **primeval atom** a hypothetical dense conglomerate from whose explosion 60 thousand million years ago the universe was (according to one theory) gradually formed. [Gr *atomos*, from *a-* (privative) and *tomos*, verbal adj of *temnein* to cut]

atomy[1] *at'əm-i*, (*Shakesp*) *n* a skeleton or walking skeleton. [Formerly also *atamy* and *natomy*, for **anatomy**, mistakenly divided *an atomy*]

atomy[2]. See under **atom**.

atonal, etc. See **atony**.

atone (or *obs* **attone**) *ə-tōn'*, *adv* (*obs*) at one, at once, together. — *vi orig* to make *at one*, to reconcile (*obs*); to give satisfaction or make reparation (*for*); to make up for deficiencies; to agree, be in accordance (*Shakesp*). — *vt* to appease, to expiate; to harmonize, or reconcile (*obs*). — *n* **atone'ment** the act of atoning; expiation; reparations; the reconciliation of God and man by means of the incarnation and death of Christ (*Christian theol*); reconciliation (*obs*). — *n* **aton'er**. — *adv* **aton'ingly**. — **attonce** (*ə-tons'*) or **attones** (*ə-tōnz'*; both *Spenser*) at once; together. [**at one**]

atony *at'ən-i*, *n* lack of muscle tone, energy or strength, debility (*med*); lack of stress or accent (*prosody*). — *adj* **atonal** (*ā-tō'nl*, or *a-*; *music*) not referred to any scale or tonic. — *n* **atō'nalism**. — *n* **atō'nalist**. — *n* **atonality** (*at-ə-nal'i-ti*). — *adj* **atonic** (*a-ton'ik*) without tone (*prosody*); unaccented (*prosody*); (of a muscle) relaxed, lacking tone (*med*); debilitated (*med*). — *n* **atonic'ity** (*-is'*) atony. [Gr *atoniā*, from *a-* (privative) and *tonos* tone, strength]

atop *ə-top'*, *adv* on or at the top. — *prep* on top of. [**a-**[1] and **top**[1]]

atopy *at'ə-pi*, or *ā'*, (*med*) *n* hypersensitivity with an inherited tendency to acute allergic reaction, but without predisposition to any particular type of allergic reaction. — *adj* **atopic** (*-top'*). [Gr *atopia* strangeness, from *a-* (privative) and *topos* place]

à tort et à travers *a tor ā a tra-ver*, (*Fr*) at random; **à toute force** *a to͞ot fors*, (*Fr*) by all means, absolutely; **à tout hasard** *a to͞o a-zär*, (*Fr*) at all hazards; **à tout prix** *a to͞o prē*, (*Fr*) at any price; **à tout propos** *a to͞o prō-pō*, (*Fr*) on every occasion.

ATP *abbrev*: adenosine triphosphate; advanced turboprop; Automatic Train Protection.

atrabilious *at-rə-bil'yəs*, (*archaic*) *adj* of a melancholy temperament; hypochondriac; splenetic, acrimonious. [L *āter*, *ātra* black, and *bīlis* gall, bile]

atracurium *a-trə-kū'ri-əm*, *n* a muscle-relaxing drug used in surgery.

atrament *a'trə-ment*, (*archaic*) *n* blacking; ink; any black fluid, such as that emitted by the octopus. — *adj* **atrament'al** or **atrament'ous**. [From L *ātrāmentum* ink, from *āter* black]

à travers *a tra-ver*, (*Fr*) across, through.

atrazine *at'rə-zēn*, *n* a widely used chemical weedkiller ($C_8H_{14}N_5Cl$), a white crystalline compound. [*a*mino *triazine*]

atremble *ə-trem'bl*, (*archaic* or *poetic*) *adv* in a tremble. [**a-**[1]]

atresia *ə-trēzh'*(*y*)*ə*, (*anatom*) *n* absence of, or closure of, a passage in the body. [Formed from Gr *trēsis* perforation]

atrip *ə-trip'*, (*naut*) *adv* (of an anchor when it is just drawn out of the ground) in a perpendicular position; (of a sail) when it is hoisted from the cap, sheeted home and ready for trimming. [**a-**[1]]

atrium *ā'* or *ā'tri-əm*, or *ät'ri-o͝om*, *n* the entrance hall or chief apartment of an ancient Roman house; a church forecourt or vestibule; a central courtyard (*mod archit*); a cavity or entrance (*zool* and *anatom*); *specif* either of the two upper cavities of the heart into which blood passes from the veins: — *pl* **a'tria** or sometimes **a'triums**. — *adj* **a'trial**. [L *ātrium*]

atrocious *ə-trō'shəs, adj* extremely cruel or wicked; awful, heinous; very grievous; appalling, execrable. — *adv* **atrō'ciously**. — *n* **atrō'ciousness**. — *n* **atrocity** (*ə-tros'i-ti*) atrociousness; an atrocious act. [L *ātrōx* or *atrōx*,

Atropa. See **Atropos**.

atrophy *at'rəf-i, n* wasting away; degeneration; diminution of size and functional activity by disuse; emaciation. — *vt* and *vi* (*lit* and *fig*) to (cause to) suffer atrophy; to starve, to waste away. — *adj* **at'rophied**. [Gr *a-* (privative) and *trophē* nourishment]

atropin *at'ro-pin* or **atropine** (also *-pīn*), *n* a poisonous alkaloid found in deadly nightshade, used in medicine eg for premedication. — Also **atropia**. — *n* **at'ropism**. [New L *Atropa belladonna*, from **Atropos**; see also **belladonna**]

Atropos *at'rō-pos*, (*Gr mythol*) *n* the Fate that cuts the thread of life. — *n* **At'ropa** the deadly nightshade genus of the potato family. [Gr]

atropous *at'rō-pəs*, (*bot*) *adj* (of an ovule) orthotropous. [Gr *a-* (privative) and *tropos* turning]

ATS *abbrev*: anti-tetanus serum; Auxiliary Territorial Service (superseded by **WRAC**, 1949). — *n pl* **Ats** (*ats*) women of the Auxiliary Territorial Service.

ats (*law*) *abbrev*: at the suit of.

Att. *abbrev*: Attorney (also **Atty**).

attaboy *at'ə-boi*, (*colloq*) *interj* expressing encouragement or approval. [Poss corruption of *that's the boy*]

attach *ə-tach'*, *vt* to bind or fasten; to connect or associate; to join in action, function or affection; to seize or arrest (*law*); to seize, lay hold of (*obs*). — *vi* to adhere, to be fastened; to be attributable or incident (to); to come into effect (*rare*). — *adj* **attach'able**. — *adj* **attached'**. — *n* **attach'ment** an act or means of fastening; a bond of fidelity or affection; seizure of goods or person by virtue of a legal process; a piece, etc that is to be attached. — **attachment order** (*law*) a court order prohibiting a debtor from selling off his or her assets until a particular claim has been settled; **attachment theory** (*behav*) a theory which proposes that the emotional bond between human infants and their parents has an evolutionary history and that various attachment behaviours enhance survival. [OFr *atachier*, from *a* (from L *ad* to), and perhaps the root of **tack**[1]]

attaché *ə-tash'ā, n* a junior member of an ambassador's staff; an attaché-case. — **atta'ché-case** a small rigid rectangular case for documents, etc. [Fr, attached]

attack *ə-tak'*, *vt* to act against with violence; to assault; to criticize severely; to begin (a task or activity) vigorously; to begin to affect or act destructively upon. — *vi* to take the initiative in attempting to score (*sport*); to launch an attack. — *vt* and *vi* (*music*) to begin (a phrase or piece) or to go on to (the next section) without break or repeat; to perform sharply and vigorously. — *n* an assault or onset; the offensive part in any contest; the beginning of active operations on anything, even dinner; severe criticism or calumny; a sudden onset or episode of illness; a performer's approach to a piece, dance, etc, or their style of beginning in terms of crispness, verve, and precision (*music, ballet*, etc); used collectively (with *the*) to designate the players in a team who are in attacking positions, eg the forwards in football or hockey; in lacrosse, the name of certain positions between centre and the opponents' goal. — *adj* **attack'able**. — *n* **attack'er**. [Fr *attaquer*; a doublet of **attach**]

attain *ə-tān'*, *vt* to reach or gain by effort; to accomplish; to reach, arrive at (*archaic*). — *vi* (*archaic*) to come or arrive. — *n* **attainabil'ity** or **attain'ableness**. — *adj* **attain'able** that may be reached, achievable. — *n* **attain'ment** an act of attaining; the thing attained; acquisition; (in *pl*) acquirements in learning. [OFr *ataindre*, from L *attingere*, from *ad* to, and *tangere* to touch]

attainder *ə-tān'dər, n* the action of attainting; the loss of civil rights through conviction for high treason (*hist; law*). — *vt* **attaint'** to convict (*obs*); to deprive of rights by conviction for treason (*hist; law*); to accuse (*archaic*); to disgrace, stain (from a fancied connection with *taint; archaic*). — *n* the act of touching, *esp* a hit (in tilting) (*archaic*); infection (*Shakesp*); attainder; a stain, disgrace. — Older *pap* **attaint'** (*Shakesp*) corrupted, tainted. — *n* **attaint'ment** or **attaint'ure**. [OFr *ataindre* (see **attain**)]

attaint. See **attainder**.

attap. See **atap**.

attar *at'ər, n* a very fragrant essential oil made in Bulgaria and elsewhere, chiefly from the damask rose. — Also **ott'o**, **ott'ar**. [Pers *atar*]

attask *ə-täsk'*, (*obs*) *vt* to take to task (only in the *pap* **attaskt'** a doubtful reading in Shakespeare's *King Lear*). [Pfx *a-* (intensive)]

attemper *ə-tem'pər*, (*archaic*) *vt* to mix in due proportion; to modify or moderate; to adapt. — *adj* **attem'pered**. [L *attemperāre* from *ad* to, and *temperāre* to regulate]

attempt *ə-temt'*, *vt* to try, endeavour (to do, or with *n* of action); to try to obtain (*obs*); to tempt, entice (*archaic*); to make an attack upon (*archaic* or *obs*). — *vi* to make an attempt or trial. — *n* an effort; a personal assault (now *usu on* someone's life); any intentional act that can fairly be described as one of a series which, if uninterrupted and successful, would constitute a crime (*law*); temptation (*Milton*). — *n* **attemptabil'ity**. — *adj* **attempt'able** that may be attempted. — *n* **attempt'er** a person who attempts; a tempter (*Milton*). [OFr *atempter*, from L *attentāre*, from *ad* to, and *temptāre, tentāre* to try, from *tendere* to stretch]

attend *ə-tend'*, *vt* to wait on; to accompany (*archaic*); to be present at (a meeting, etc); to go regularly to (a school, etc); to wait for (*obs*); to give attention to (*obs*). — *vi* to listen (to); to apply oneself, direct one's mind and efforts (with *to*); to act as an attendant or companion (with *on* or *upon*; *archaic*); to wait, be consequent (with *on* or *upon*; *archaic*). — *n* **attend'ance** the act of attending; presence; number of persons attending; attention, careful regard (*Bible*). — *n* (*obs*) **attend'ancy** attendance, a retinue; relative position. — *adj* **attend'ant** giving attendance; accompanying. — *n* a person who attends or accompanies; a servant; (with *on* or *upon*) what accompanies or follows, a consequence; a person who owes a duty or service to another (*law*). — *n* **attendee'** used in the sense of 'attender', of a person attending a conference, attendance centre, etc. — *n* **attend'er** a person who pays attention or is attentive; a person who attends; a companion (*archaic*). — *n* **attend'ment** (*obs rare*) accompaniments; (*Spenser* **atten'dement**) intention. — **attendance allowance** a non-contributory benefit paid to an invalid who requires constant attendance or supervision; **attendance centre** a non-residential centre where a young offender may be required to attend regularly, instead of serving a prison sentence. [L *attendere, attentum*]

attent. See under **attention**.

attentat *a-tã-tä*, (*Fr*) *n* an (*esp* unsuccessful) attempt at an (*esp* political) crime of violence.

attention *ə-ten'shən, n* the act of attending; steady application of the mind; care, consideration; civility, courtesy; the position of standing rigidly erect with hands by the sides and heels together (*military*); (in *pl*) courtship (*archaic*). — *interj* used in calling for someone's, or *esp* a crowd's, attention; an order to come to attention, in readiness to execute a command (*military*). — *adj* **attent'** (*Spenser* and *Shakesp*) giving attention. — *n* (*Spenser*) attention. — *adj* **atten'tional** (*psychol*, etc) relating to attention or concentration. — *adj* **attent'ive** full of attention; courteous, mindful; alert, observant. — *adv* **attent'ively**. — *n* **attent'iveness**. — **attention line** a line in a letter used to indicate the particular employee of an organization to whom the document is addressed; **attention span** the length of time for which a person can concentrate; **attention value** (*advertising*) the degree to which an advertisement has been noticed or remembered by a reader or viewer. — **draw (someone's) attention to** to direct (someone's) notice towards; **selective attention** (*behav*) the aspect of perception that implies a readiness to respond to a particular stimulus or aspects of it. [L *attentiō*, *-ōnis*]

attenuate *ə-ten'ū-āt*, *vt* to make thin or lean; to break down into finer parts; to reduce in density; to reduce in strength or value. — *vi* to become thin or fine; to grow less. — *n* **atten'uant** anything that attenuates. — Also *adj*. — *adj* **atten'uate** or **atten'uated** thin; thinned; dilute, rarefied; tapering. — *n* **attenuā'tion** the process of making slender; reduction of intensity, density, force, or (of bacteria) virulence; in homoeopathy, the reduction of the active principles of medicines to minute doses; reduction in magnitude, amplitude or intensity, arising from absorption or scattering (*nuclear* and *telecomm*). — *n* **atten'uator**. — **attenuated vaccine** (*immunol*) live bacterial or virus vaccine in which the microbes have a greatly diminished capacity to cause disease but are still able to evoke protective immunity. [L *attenuāre*, *-ātum*, from *ad* to, and *tenuis* thin]

attercop *at'ər-kop*, (*obs* or *dialect*) *n* a spider; an ill-natured person. [OE *attorcoppa*, from *attor*, *ātor* poison and perh *cop* head, or *copp* cup]

attest *ə-test'*, *vt* to testify or bear witness to; to affirm by signature or oath; to give proof of, to manifest; to call to witness (*obs*). — *vt* and *vi* (*old*) to enrol for military service. — *vi* to bear witness (to). — *n* (*Shakesp*) witness, testimony. — *adj* **attest'able**. — *adj* **attest'ative**. — *n* **attestā'tion** (*at-*) an act of attesting; administration of an oath. — *adj* **attest'ed** vouched for; certified free from disease, *specif* the tubercle bacillus. — *n* **attest'er** or **attest'or**. [L *attestārī*, from *ad* to, and *testis* a witness]

Att.-Gen. *abbrev*: Attorney-General (also **AG**, **A-G**, **Atty-Gen.**)

Attic *at'ik*, *adj* of Attica or Athens; refined, classical, pure (in taste, language, etc). — *n* the dialect of Ancient Greek used in Athens. — *n* **Att'icism** (*-sizm*). — *vt* **Atticize** or **-ise** (*at'i-sīz*) to make conformable to the language or idiom of Attica. — *vi* to use the idioms of the Athenians; to side with the Athenians; to affect Attic or Greek style or manners. — **Attic salt** wit of a dry, delicate and refined quality. [Gr *Attikos*, from *Attikē* Attica]

attic *at'ik*, (*archit*) *n* a low storey or structure above the cornice of the main part of an elevation, *usu* of the so-called **Attic order**, ie with square columns or pilasters instead of pillars; a room in the roof of a house. [The structure was supposed to be in the Athenian manner; see **Attic**]

attire *ə-tīr'*, *vt* to dress, array or adorn; to prepare. — *n* dress, clothing; any kind of covering (*obs*). — *n* **attire'ment** (*obs*). — *n* **attir'ing**. [OFr *atirer* to put in order, from *à tire* in a row, from *à* (L *ad*) to, and *tire*, *tiere* order, dress; see **tier**]

attitude *at'i-tūd*, *n* posture, or position; a posture or position expressing some thought or feeling; a habitual mode of thought or feeling; a studied or affected posture; a position on one leg with the other leg extended behind, modelled on the position of the *Flying Mercury* of Giovanni Bologna (1524–1608) (*ballet*); of an aircraft in flight, or on the ground, the angles made by its axes with the relative airflow, or with the ground, respectively; the tilt of a vehicle measured in relation to the surface of the earth as horizontal plane (*space flight*); a personal viewpoint of or to a product or organization (*marketing*); antagonistically insolent manner, posture, and *esp* style and tone of speech, lip (*US slang*). — *adj* **attitud'inal**. — *n* **attitudinā'rian** a person who studies attitudes. — *vi* **attitud'inize** or **-ise** to assume affected attitudes. — *n* **attitud'inizer** or **-s-**. — *n* **attitud'inizing** or **-s-**. — **attitude angle** in a cornering motor vehicle, the slight angle between the track of the vehicle and the direction in which the tyres are pointing. — **strike an attitude** to assume a position or figure indicative of a feeling or emotion not really felt. [Fr *attitude* or Ital *attitudine*, from L *aptitūdō*, *-inis*, from *aptus* fit]

atto- *at-ō-*, *pfx* denoting one million million millionth, 10^{-18}. [Dan and Norw *atten*, eighteen]

attollent *ə-tol'ənt*, *adj* lifting up, raising; (*usu* **attoll'ens**; of a muscle) involved in raising or lifting up (*med*, *anatom*). — *n* (*usu* **attoll'ens**) a muscle that raises. [L *attollēns*, *-entis*, pr p of *attollere* to lift up, from *ad* to, and *tollere* to lift]

attonce, **attone**. See **atone**.

attorn *ə-tûrn'*, (*law*) *vt* to transfer to another. — *vi* to accept tenancy under a new landlord. — *n* **attorn'ey** (OFr pa p *atorné*) a person legally authorized to act for another; a person legally qualified to manage cases in a court of law (esp *NAm*); a solicitor, lawyer, attorney at law (esp *NAm*): — *pl* **attor'neys**. — *vt* (*Shakesp*) to perform by proxy; to employ as a proxy. — *n* **attor'neydom**. — *n* **attor'neyism**. — *n* **attor'neyship**. — *n* **attorn'ment** acknowledgement of a new landlord. — **Attorney-Gen'eral** the chief law officer for England, the Republic of Ireland, a dominion, colony, etc, the English one being a member of the government, representing the Crown in important civil and criminal matters, and leader of the English Bar; the Crown's attorney in the duchies of Lancaster and Cornwall, and the county palatine of Durham; in the United States, one of the seven officials who constitute the president's cabinet, the head of the Department of Justice; also (without *caps*) the legal adviser of a State governor. — **attorney at law** or **public attorney** a professional and duly qualified legal agent; **attorney in fact** or **private attorney** a person duly appointed by power of attorney to act for another in matters of contract, money payments, and the like; **letter**, **warrant** or **power of attorney** a formal instrument by which one person authorizes another to perform specific acts on his or her behalf. [LL *attornāre* to assign; see **turn**]

attract *ə-trakt'*, *vt* to cause to approach by means of unseen forces; to draw (a crowd, attention, financial investment, etc); to allure or entice; to be attractive to; to be liable to (tax) (*law*, etc). — *adj* **attract'able** that may be attracted. — *n* **attract'ant** something that attracts, *esp* that effects communication in insects and animals. — *adj* **attract'ing**. — *adv* **attract'ingly**. — *n* **attrac'tion** the act of attracting; an attracting force; that which attracts. — *adj* **attract'ive** having the power of attracting; alluring or appealing. — *adv* **attract'ively**. — *n* **attract'iveness**. — *n* **attract'or**. — **Great Attractor** a powerful gravitational force of uncertain origin pulling certain galaxies, including our own, towards its source. [L *attrahere*, *attractum*, from *ad* to, and *trahere* to draw]

attrahent *at'rə-hənt* or *ə-trā'ənt*, *adj* attracting or drawing; (*usu* **att'rahens**; eg of a muscle) that draws towards (*med* or *anatom*); (of a substance) acting as an attractant (*biol*). — *n* that which attracts. [L *attrahēns*, *-entis*, pr p of *attrahere*; see **attract**]

attrap *ə-trap'*, (*Spenser*) *vt* to adorn with trappings; to dress or array. [L *ad* to, and **trap**[4]]

attrib. *abbrev*: attributed; attributive; attributively.

attribute *ə-trib'ūt* (or *Milton at'ri-būt*), *vt* to ascribe, assign, or consider as belonging. — *n* (*at'*) that which is attributed; that which is inherent in, or inseparable from, anything; that which can be predicated of anything; a quality or property; a virtue; an accessory; (in art) a conventional symbol; a word added to another to denote an attribute (*gram*). — *adj* **attrib'utable**. — *n* **attribution** (*at-ri-bū'shən*) the or an act of attributing; that which is attributed. — *adj* **attrib'utive** expressing an attribute; (of an adjective) placed immediately before or immediately after the noun it qualifies (*gram*). — *n* a word added to another to denote an attribute (*gram*). — *adv* **attrib'utively**. [L *attribuere*, *-tribūtum*, from *ad* to, and *tribuere* to give]

attrist *ə-trist'*, (*obs*) *vt* to sadden. [Fr *attrister*, from L *ad* to, and *tristis* sad]

attrite *ə-trīt'*, *adj* worn by rubbing or friction (*obs*); repentant through fear of punishment, not yet from the love of God (*theol*). — *vt* **attrite'** or **attrit'** (*US military*) to wear down, gradually diminish (enemy forces, strength, morale or resources); to destroy, kill (*euphem*). — *n* **attrit'** (*euphem*) the wearing down of enemy forces; a death (among enemy personnel). — *n* **attrition** (*a-* or *ə-trish'ən*) rubbing together; wearing down; a defective or imperfect sorrow for sin (*theol*); the wearing down of an adversary, resistance, resources, etc (*fig, esp military*). — *adj* **attrit'ional**. [L *attrītus*, from *atterere*, from *ad* to, and *terere*, *trītum* to rub]

attuition *at-ū-ish'ən*, (*psychol*) *n* a mental operation intermediate between sensation and perception. — *adj* **attui'tional**. — *adj* **att'uent** performing the function of attuition. — *vt* **att'uite** (*-īt*) to be conscious of by attuition. — *adj* **attu'itive**. — *adv* **attu'itively**. [L *ad* to, and *tuērī* to attend to]

attune *ə-tūn'* (or in US *-tōōn*), *vt* to put in tune; to make (one's voice, song, etc) tuneful; to make (something) harmonize or accord; to accustom or acclimatize. — *n* **attune'ment**. [L *ad* to, and **tune**]

Atty *abbrev*: Attorney.

ATV *abbrev*: all-terrain vehicle; Associated Television.

atwain *ə-twān'*, (*archaic*) *adv* in twain, in(to) two parts; asunder. [**a-**[1]]

atweel *ə-twēl'*, (*Scot*) *adv* or *interj* well; indeed. [**wat weel**, ie wot well]

atween *ə-twēn'*, (*archaic* or *dialect*) *adv* betweenwhiles. — *prep* between. — *adv* and *prep* **atwixt'** betwixt.

atwitter *ə-twit'ər*, *adv* in a state of twittering. [**a-**[1] and **twitter**[1]]

at. wt. *abbrev*: atomic weight.

atypical *a-* or *ā-tip'i-kl*, *adj* not typical. [**a-**[2] and **typical**]

AU *abbrev*: (or **ÅU**) Ångström unit (now *usu* called Ångström, abbrev **Å**); astronomical unit.

Au (*chem*) *symbol*: gold. [L *aurum*]

aubade *ō-bäd'*, *n* a musical announcement of dawn; a sunrise song. [Fr, from *aube* dawn, from Provençal *alba* dawn]

auberge *ō-berzh'*, *n* an inn. — *n* **aubergiste** (*ō-ber-zhēst'*) an innkeeper. [Fr, of Gmc origin; see **harbour**]

aubergine *ō'ber-jēn* or *-zhēn*, *n* the fruit of the egg-plant, the brinjal; its purple colour. — *adj* of this colour. [Fr dimin of *auberge* a kind of peach, from Sp *alberchigo*, from Ar *al* the, and Sp *pérsigo*, from L *persicum* a peach]

Aubrey holes *ö'bri hōlz*, *n pl* the 56 circular pits surrounding the stone circle of Stonehenge in Wiltshire. [John *Aubrey* (1626–97) who discovered them]

aubrieta, **aubrietia** or (*popularly*) **aubretia** *ö-brē'* or *ö-bri-ē'sh(y)ə*, *n* a plant of the purple-flowered Mediterranean genus *Aubrieta* of trailing cruciferous plants, much grown in rock-gardens, etc. [After Claude *Aubriet* (c.1665–1742), naturalist-painter]

auburn *ö'bûrn*, *adj orig* light yellow; reddish brown. [LL *alburnus* whitish, from L *albus* white]

AUC *abbrev*: *anno urbis conditae* (or *ab urbe condita*) (*L*) in the year from the building of the city, ie Rome (753BC).

auceps *ö'seps*, (*Walton*) *n* a hawker. [L, bird-catcher, fowler, from *avis* bird, and *capere* to catch]

au contraire *ō kɔ̃-trer*, (*Fr*) on the contrary.

au courant *ō kōō-rã*, (*Fr*) well-informed; well up in the facts or situation. [Literally, in the current or stream]

auction *ök'shən*, *n* a public sale at which goods are sold to the highest bidder; a method of selling goods or property by inviting bids; auction bridge. — *vt* to sell by auction. — *adj* **auc'tionary**. — *n* **auctioneer'** a person who sells or is licensed to sell by public auction. — *vt* to sell by auction. — **auction bridge** a development of the game of bridge in which the players bid for the privilege of choosing trump suit or no-trumps and the declarer of trumps plays his or her partner's hand as a dummy. — **auction by reserve** an auction in which the auctioneer may not withdraw the lot once the first bid is made, and the lot is sold to the highest bidder; **Dutch auction** a kind of auction at which the salesperson starts at a high price, and comes down till a bid is made; any of several other unconventional or informal types of auction. [L *auctiō*, *-ōnis* an increasing, from *augēre*, *auctum* to increase]

auctorial *ök-tō'ri-əl*, or *-tö'*, *adj* of an author or his or her trade. [L *auctor*, *-ōris* author]

aucuba *ö'kū-bə*, *n* any plant of the Japan laurel genus *Aucuba*. [Jap]

audacious *ö-dā'shəs*, *adj* daring; bold; impudent. — *adv* **audā'ciously**. — *n* **audā'ciousness** or **audacity** (*ö-das'i-ti*). [Fr *audacieux*, from L *audāx*, from *audēre* to dare]

audax et cautus *ö'daks et kö'təs* or *ow'daks et kow'tōōs*, (*L*) bold and cautious.

au désespoir *ō dā-zes-pwär*, (*Fr*) in despair.

audible *öd'i-bl*, *adj* able to be heard. — *n* (*Am football*) a tactic or game plan called out in coded form by the quarterback at the line of scrimmage. — *n* **audibil'ity** or **aud'ibleness**. — *adv* **aud'ibly**. [Med L *audibilis*, from L *audire* to hear]

audience *ö'di-əns*, *n* the act of hearing; a ceremonial interview; an assembly of hearers or spectators; the listeners to a radio programme, viewers of a television programme, or even readers of a book, magazine, author, etc; the people exposed to a particular medium (*esp* TV, radio or cinema); a judicial hearing (*archaic*); admittance to a hearing; (or **audiencia** *ow-di-en-tchē'ə* or *-sē'ə*) a court of government or justice in the Spanish-American Empire; the territory administered by it. — *adj* **aud'ient** listening; paying attention. — *n* (*formal, esp eccles hist*) a hearer. — **audience participation** involvement by members of the audience in a theatrical performance, television or radio programme, etc *esp* by direct appeals to them from performers; **audience research** the discovery of facts about an audience (*esp* of radio or TV programmes) such as age and behaviour patterns. [L *audientia*, from *audire* to hear]

audile *ö'dil* or *-dīl*, *adj* pertaining to hearing. — *n* a person inclined to think in terms of sound. [*aud*itory and sfx *-ile*, following **agile**, **fragile**, etc]

audio- *ö'di-ō-*, *combining form* denoting sound, *esp* denoting recorded and broadcast sound; pertaining to, using, or involving, audio-frequencies. — *n* **aud'io** reproduction of recorded or broadcast sounds (also *adj*); sound (*opp* to *vision*; *colloq*); an acoustic device by which a pilot returning to an aircraft-carrier knows when the aircraft is at a proper speed for landing; short for **audiotypist** or **audiotyping**: — *pl* **aud'ios**. — **audio book** a book in recorded form, eg on audio cassette. — **audio cassette** a cassette of audiotape. — **audio disc** (or **disk**) a disc on which sound is recorded. — *n* **aud'io-engineer'** a person whose job concerns the transmission and reception of broadcast sound. — *n* **audio-frequency** (*ö'di-ō-frē'kwən-si*) a frequency of oscillation which, when the oscillatory power is converted into a sound pressure, is perceptible by the ear. — *n* **aud'iogram** a tracing produced by an audiograph. — *n* **aud'iograph** a machine used to test a patient's hearing by transmitting sound waves directly to the inner ear. — *n* **audio-loca'tion** echo location. — *adj* **audiolog'ical**. — *n* **audiol'ogist**. — *n* **audiol'ogy** the science of hearing, *esp* with reference to the diagnosis and treatment of hearing defects. — *n* **audiom'eter** an instrument for measuring differences in hearing; one for measuring minimum intensities of sounds which, for specified frequencies, are perceivable by the ear. — *adj* **audiomet'ric**. — *n* **audiometrician** (*-mi-trish'ən*). — *n* **aud'iophil** (*-fil*) or **audiophile** (*-fīl*) an enthusiast for the true reproduction of recorded or broadcast sound. — *n* **aud'iotape** magnetic tape for recording and reproducing sound; a sound recording on tape, an audio-cassette. — *n* **aud'iotyping**. — *n* **aud'iotyp'ist** a typist able to type directly material reproduced by a dictating machine. — *adj* **audiovis'ual** concerned simultaneously with seeing and hearing; of a device or method that uses both sound and vision (eg a cassette and filmstrip or slides). — *adv* **audiovis'ually**. — *n* **aud'iphone** an instrument which, pressed against the teeth, communicates sounds through the bones to the ears. — **audiovisual aids** material such as pictures, closed-circuit TV, teaching machines, etc used in the classroom. [1st pers sing of pr t of L *audīre* to hear]

audit *ö'dit, n* an examination of accounts by an authorized person or persons; a statement of account; a check or examination; an evaluation of a specified quantity or quality, as in *energy audit, efficiency audit*; a calling to account generally; a periodical settlement of accounts (*obs*); audience, hearing (*obs*). — *vt* to examine and officially verify, etc (the accounts of a company); to attend (a course or class) without intending to take any examination (*NAm*). — *n* **aud'itor** a person who audits accounts; a hearer (*fem* **aud'itress**); a person who audits a course or class (*NAm*). — *n* **aud'itorship**. — **audit ale** an ale of special quality brewed for some Oxford and Cambridge colleges (*orig* for use on the day of audit); **Audit Commission** the body responsible for the auditing of local authorities and NHS bodies in England and Wales; **audit trail** (*comput*) the record of the file updating that takes place during a specific transaction. [L *audītus* a hearing, from *audīre* to hear]

audita querela *ö-dī'tə kwə-rē'lə* or *ow-dē'tä kwe-rā'lä*, (*L*; *law*) the name of a writ giving leave to appeal (literally, the suit having been heard).

audition *ö-dish'ən, n* a trial performance by an applicant for an acting, musical, etc part, place or position (also *vt* and *vi* with *for*); the sense, or an act, of hearing; mode of hearing; something heard (*rare*). — *adj* **aud'itive** of, or related to, hearing. [L *audītiō, -iōnis* a hearing, from *audīre* to hear]

auditor, etc. See **audit**.

auditorium *ö-di-tö'ri-əm, n* in a theatre or the like, the space allotted to the audience; a public hall, for concerts, meetings, etc (*NAm*); the reception room of a monastery: — *pl* **audito'riums** or **audito'ria**. [L *audītōrium*, from *audītōrius* concerning hearing or hearers]

auditory *ö'di-tər-i, adj* relating to the sense, process or organs of hearing. — *n* (*archaic*) an audience; a place where lectures, etc are heard. [L *auditōrius*]

AUEW *abbrev*: Amalgamated Union of Engineering Workers. — **AUEW-TASS** (*-tas*) *abbrev*: Amalgamated Union of Engineering Workers Technical, Administrative and Supervisory Section.

auf *öf*, (*obs*) *n* an elf's child, an oaf. [ON *älfr* elf]

au fait *ō fe*, (*Fr*) well-acquainted with a matter; well-informed, expert (with *with*).

aufgabe *owf'gä-bə*, (*psychol*) *n* a task set as an experiment, etc. [Ger]

Aufklärung *owf-kle'rŏŏng*, (*Ger*) *n* enlightenment, *esp* the 18c intellectual movement.

Aufl. *abbrev*: *Auflage* (*Ger*) edition.

au fond *ō fɔ̃*, (*Fr*) at bottom.

au fromage *ō fro-mäzh*, (*Fr*) with cheese.

auf Wiedersehen *owf vē'dər-zā-ən*, (*Ger*) goodbye till we meet again.

Aug. *abbrev*: August; Augustine.

aug. *abbrev*: augmentative.

Augean *ö-* or *ow-jē'ən, adj* filthy; difficult. [From *Augeas*, in Greek legend the king of Elis whose filthy oxstalls Herakles cleaned by diverting the river Alpheus through them]

auger *ö'gər, n* a carpenter's boring tool; an instrument for boring holes in the ground. — **au'ger-bit** an auger that fits into a carpenter's brace; **au'ger-hole**; **au'ger-shell** Terebra; **au'ger-worm** the goat-moth larva, which bores trees. [From *nauger* (*an auger* for *a nauger*), from OE *nafugār*, from *nafu* a nave of a wheel, and *gār* a piercer; see **nave**[2] and **gore**[2]]

Auger effect *ō-zhā i-fekt'*, (*phys*) *n* the non-radiative transition of an atom from an excited state to one of lower energy with emission of an electron (**Auger electron**). [Pierre *Auger*, French physicist (born 1899)]

aught *öt, n* anything, anything at all; a whit, jot. [OE *ā-wiht* contracted to *āht* (whence **ought**), and shortened to *aht* (whence **aught**); *ā-wiht* is from *ā, ō* ever, and *wiht* creature, whit, wight]

augite *ö-jīt* or *-gīt, n* one of the pyroxene group of minerals, very similar to hornblende, *usu* greenish, an essential component of many igneous rocks. — *adj* **augitic** (*-jit'* or *-git'*). [Gr *augē* brightness]

augm. *abbrev*: augmentative; *augmenté* (*Fr*), enlarged.

augment *ög-ment', vt* to increase; to make larger. — *vi* to grow larger. — *n* **aug'ment** (*-mənt*) increase (*obs*); the prefixed vowel or initial vowel-lengthening in some past tenses of the verb in Sanskrit and Greek; sometimes applied also to such inflectional prefixes as the *ge-* of the German perfect participle. — *adj* **augment'able**. — *n* **augmentā'tion** increase; addition; an additional charge in a coat-of-arms bestowed as a mark of honour (*heraldry*); the repetition of a melody in notes of greater length than the original (*music*); an increase of stipend obtained by a parish minister by an action raised in the Court of Teinds against the titular and heritors, or an increase in a feu-duty, rent, etc (*Scots law*). — *adj* **augment'ative** having the quality or power of augmenting; (of an affix or derivative) increasing the force of the original word (*gram*; also *n*). — *adj* **augment'ed**. — *n* **augment'er**. — *n* **augment'or** (*biol*) a nerve that increases the rate of activity of an organ. — **augmented interval** (*music*) an interval increased by a semitone. — **Augmented Roman Alphabet** earlier name for Initial Teaching Alphabet. [L *augēre* to increase]

Augmentin® *ög-men'tin, n* a drug administered along with an antibiotic such as Ampicillin® that prevents the antibiotic from being metabolized, and thus ensures its potency.

au grand sérieux *ō grã sā-ryø*, (*Fr*; now **très au sérieux** *tre-zō*) in all seriousness.

au gratin *ō gra-tɛ̃*, (*Fr*) cooked covered with breadcrumbs or grated cheese, or with both.

augur *ö'gər, n* among the ancient Romans, a person who sought knowledge of secret or future things by observing the flight and the cries of birds; a diviner; a soothsayer; *appar* an augury or portent (*Shakesp*). — *vt* to foretell from signs. — *vi* to guess or conjecture; to bode or protend. — *adj* **au'gural** (*-ū-rəl* or *-yər-əl*). — *n* **au'gūrer** (*Shakesp*) an augur. — *n* **au'gurship**. — *n* **au'gūry** the art or practice of auguring; an omen. — **augur well** (or **ill**) **for** to be an encouraging (or discouraging) sign with respect to. [L; prob from *avis* bird]

August *ö'gəst, n* the eighth month of the year. [After the Roman emperor *Augustus*]

august[1] *ö-gust', adj* venerable; imposing; sublime; majestic. — *adv* **august'ly**. — *n* **august'ness**. [L *augustus*, from *augēre* to increase, honour]

august[2] or *usu* **auguste** *ow-gŏŏst', n* (also with *cap*) a circus clown of the white-faced, bungling type. [Ger, Augustus]

Augustan *ö-gust'ən, adj* pertaining to the Emperor *Augustus*, or to the brilliant literature of his reign (31 BC–AD 14); hence pertaining to any similar age, such as the reign of Anne in English, and that of Louis XIV in French, literature; classic; refined.

auguste. See **august**[2].

Augustine *ö'gəst-in, ö-gust'in*, or **Augustinian** *-tin'i-ən, n* a person belonging to any order of monks or nuns whose rule is based on the writings of St Augustine; a person who holds the opinions of St Augustine, *esp* on predestination and irresistible grace (*theol*). — *adj* **Augustin'ian** of or relating to St Augustine. — *n* **Augustin'ianism**. — **Augustinian** (or **Austin**) **canons** see **canon**; **Augustinian** (or **Austin**) **friars** or **hermits** the fourth order of mendicant friars, wearing a black habit, but not to be confused with the Black Friars or Dominicans.

Aujeszky's disease *ow-yes'kiz di-zēz', n* a notifiable disease of pigs, cattle, sheep, dogs, cats and rats, caused by a herpes virus, with symptoms similar to those of rabies.

[*Aujeszky*, a Hungarian scientist (died 1933), who identified it]

au jour le jour *ō zhōōr lə zhōōr*, (*Fr*) from hand to mouth (literally, from day to day).

auk *ök*, *n* a short-winged, black-and-white, heavy-bodied seabird of the family **Alcidae** (*al'si-dē*). — *n* **auk'let** one of the smaller birds of the family. — **great auk** a large, flightless auk, the garefowl (extinct c.1844); **little auk** an auk (*Plautus alle*) of the N Atlantic and Arctic Oceans, the rotche or dovekie. [ON *ālka*]

aula *ö'lə*, *n* (*L*) a hall. — *adj* **aulā'rian** relating to a hall, *esp* one in a collegiate university. — *n* at Oxford University, a member of a hall, as distinguished from a collegian. — *adj* **au'lic** (*formal* or *archaic*) of or relating to a royal court; courtly. — **Aula Regis**, or *Curia Regis*, (*hist*) a feudal assembly of tenants-in-chief; the Privy Council; the Court of King's Bench; **Aulic Council** (*hist*; Ger *Reichshofrat*) a court or personal council of the Holy Roman Empire, established in 1501 by Maximilian I, and co-ordinate with the Imperial Chamber (*Reichskammergericht*). [L *aula*, Gr *aulē* court, courtyard, hall]

auld *öld*, (*Scot*) *adj* old. — *adj* **auld-farr'ant** (ie old-favouring) old-fashioned (*archaic*); precocious. — *adj* **auld'-warld** (*archaic*) old-world, ancient. — **the Auld Kirk** (*archaic*) the Church of Scotland; whisky; **auld lang syne** long ago (literally, old long since); **Auld Reekie** old smoky, ie Edinburgh. [OE *ald*]

aulic. See **aula**.

aulnage, **aulnager**. Variant spellings of **alnage**, **alnager**.

aulos *ö'los* or *ow'los*, *n* an ancient Greek wind instrument, a double pipe with double reeds: — *pl* **aul'oi** (*-oi* or *-ē*). [Gr]

aumail *ö-māl'*, (*archaic*; *rare*) *vt* to enamel; to figure or variegate (*Spenser*). [See **enamel**]

aumbry *öm'bri*, *n*. Same as **ambry**.

au mieux *ō myø*, (*Fr*) on the best of terms (literally, at the best).

aumil *ö'mil* or *ä'mil*, *n* an amildar.

au naturel *ō na-tü-rel*, (*Fr*) cooked plainly, or uncooked; served without dressing (*cookery*). [Literally, in the natural state]

aune *ōn*, (*obs*) *n* an old French measure of length (*esp* of fabric), *approx* 119cm (47in). [OFr *aulne*; rel to **alnage**, **ell**[1]]

aunt *änt*, *n* a father's or mother's sister, or an uncle's wife or a great-aunt (used with *cap* as a title either before a woman's first name or independently); a woman to whom one can turn for advice, sympathy, practical help, etc (*fig*); (*usu* in *dimin* **Aunt'ie**) a title sometimes used by children for female friends of their parents; (in *dimin* **Aunt'ie**) a facetious name for the BBC; an old woman (*obs*); a gossip (*obs*); a procuress (*obs*). — *n* **auntie** or **aunty** *dimin* for **aunt**. — *adj* **aunt'ly**. — **Aunt Sally** a fairground or pub game, in which sticks or balls are thrown to smash a pipe in the mouth of a wooden figure; any of various variant versions of the game; a target for abuse (*fig*). [OFr *ante*, from L *amita* a father's sister]

aunter *ön'tər*, (*obs*) *n* adventure. [OFr *aventure*]

au pair *ō per*, *adj* used of an arrangement whereby girls come from abroad (*esp* to learn the language) and perform light domestic duties, babysitting, etc for a family in exchange for board and lodging and pocket-money; *orig* meaning by mutual service without payment. — *n* an au pair girl. [Fr]

au pied de la lettre *ō pyā də la letr'*, (*Fr*) exactly, literally. [Literally, to the foot of the letter]

au pis aller *ō pē-za-lā*, (*Fr*) at the worst; as a last resort.

au poids de l'or *ō pwa də lor*, (*Fr*) very dear (literally, at its weight in gold).

au premier *ō prə-myā*, (*Fr*) on the first (floor).

aura *ö'rə*, *n* a supposed subtle emanation, *esp* that essence which is claimed to emanate from all living things and to provide an atmosphere for occult phenomena, invisible to most people but *appar* seen by some as a luminous or coloured glow surrounding other living forms; air, distinctive character (*fig*); the peculiar sensations that precede an attack of epilepsy, hysteria, or certain other ailments (*pathol*): — *pl* **aur'ae** (*-ē*) or **aur'as**. — *adj* **aur'al** pertaining to the air, or to the aura. [L *aura* a breeze]

aural[1] *ö'rəl*, *adj* of, pertaining to, or received by, the ear. — *adv* **aur'ally**. — *adj* **aur'iform** ear-shaped. — *n* **aur'iscope** (*med*) an instrument for examining the ear, an otoscope. — *n* **aur'ist** a specialist in diseases of the ear, an otologist. [L *auris* ear]

aural[2]. See **aura**.

aura popularis *ö'rə po-pū-la'ris* or *ow-ra po-pōō-lä'ris*, (*L*) *n* the breeze of popular favour (literally, the popular breeze).

aurate *ö'rāt*, *n* a salt of auric acid. — *adj* **au'rated** compounded with auric acid (*obs*); gold-coloured. — *adj* **aureate** (*ö'ri-ət*) gilded; golden; floridly rhetorical. — *n* **aurē'ity** the peculiar properties of gold. — *n* **au'reus** (*ö'ri-əs* or *ow'rā-ōōs*) a gold coin of the Roman empire: — *pl* **au'rei** (*-ī* or *-ē*). — *adj* **au'ric** pertaining to gold; containing trivalent gold (*chem*). — *adj* **aurous** (*ö'rəs*) containing univalent gold. — **auric acid** a hypothetical acid of composition $HAuO_2$, *usu* applied to auric hydroxide ($Au(OH)_3$) or *esp* auric oxide (Au_2O_3). [L *aurum* gold]

aurea mediocritas *ö'rē-a mē-dē-o'kri-tas* or *ow'rā-a me-di-o'kri-täs*, (*L*) *n* the golden (or happy) mean.

aureate, **aureity**. See **aurate**.

aurelia *ö-rē'li-ə*, *n* a jellyfish of the large *Aurelia* genus of common jellyfishes, or of a related genus; formerly, a chrysalis or pupa (from its golden colour). — *adj* **aurē'lian** golden; of an aurelia. — *n* (*obs*) a lepidopterist. [New L, from L *aurum* gold]

aureola *ö-rē'ə-lə* or **aureole** *ö'rē-ōl*, *n* a crown, or an increment to the ordinary blessedness of heaven, gained by virgins, martyrs, and doctors (*hist* and *RC theol*); the gold or coloured disc or ring represented around the head in a religious picture, symbolizing glory; a glorifying halo (*fig*); a halo or corona around the sun or moon, or the clear space within it (*meteorol*); the coloured rings around the spectre of the Brocken (*meteorol*); (*appar erron*) a halo surrounding the whole figure (eg a *vesica piscis*); any halo-like appearance. — *adj* **au'reoled** encircled with an aureole. [L, fem of *aureolus* golden, dimin of *aureus* of gold]

Aureomycin® *ö-rē-ō-mī'sin*, *n* a tradename for *chlortetracycline*, an antibiotic used against typhus and other diseases, obtained from Strepto*myces aureo*faciens.

au reste *ō rest*, (*Fr*) as for the rest; besides.

au revoir *ō rə-vwär*, (*Fr*) goodbye until we meet again.

auric. See **aurate**.

auricle *ör'i-kl*, *n* the external ear (*zool*); an earlike appendage to an atrium in the heart, or the atrium itself (*anatom*); an earlike lobe of a leaf, etc (*bot*). — *adj* **aur'icled** having appendages like ears. — *n* **auric'ūla** a species of primula (also called bear's ear, or dusty-miller); (with *cap*) a genus of gasteropod molluscs. — *adj* **auric'ūlar** pertaining to the ear; known by hearing, or by report; told privately. — *adv* **auric'ūlarly**. — *adj* **auric'ūlate** (*-lət*) or **auric'ūlated** ear-shaped; having auricles or appendages like ears. — **auricular confession** confession to a priest. [L *auricula*, dimin of *auris* the ear]

auriferous *ör-if'ər-əs*, *adj* bearing or yielding gold. — *vt* and *vi* **au'rify** to turn into gold. [L *aurifer* from *aurum* gold, and *ferre* to bear; *facere* to make]

auriform. See under **aural**.

aurify. See **auriferous**.

Auriga *ö-rī'gə*, *n* a prominent northern constellation. [L *auriga* charioteer]

Aurignacian *ö-rig-nā'sh(y)ən*, *adj* belonging to an upper Palaeolithic culture that succeeded the Mousterian and preceded the Solutrean. [*Aurignac*, in Haute-Garonne, SW France, where objects of this culture have been found]

auriscope, **aurist**. See under **aural**.

aurochs *ör'* or *owr'oks*, *n* the urus or wild ox (extinct 1627); (*formerly* and *erron*) the European bison. [OHGer *ûr-ohso*, from *ûr* (adopted into L as *ūrus*, into Gr as *ouros* wild ox), and *ohso* ox]

aurora *ö-rö'rə*, *n* (often with *cap*) the dawn; (with *cap*) the (Roman) goddess of dawn (*poetic*); a rich orange colour; a luminous atmospheric phenomenon of electrical character seen in and towards the Polar regions, with a tremulous motion, and streamers of light: — *pl* **auro'ras** or **auro'rae**. — *adj* **auro'ral** of or pertaining to the aurora. — *adj* **auro'ral** or **auro'rean** pertaining to the dawn; rosy; fresh and beautiful. — *adv* **auro'rally**. — **aurora borealis** (*bō-ri-ā'lis*, *-ä'lis* or *bö-*) or (*rare*) **septentrionalis** (*sep-ten-tri-on-ā'lis* or *-ä'lis*) the northern aurora or northern lights (also with *caps*); **aurora australis** (*ös-trā'lis* or *os-* or *-ä'lis*) the southern lights, a similar phenomenon in the southern hemisphere (also with *caps*); **auroral zones** the two regions (around the north and south geomagnetic poles) in which the aurora is most and most frequently seen, and electrical disturbances occur. [L *Aurōra*]

aurous. See **aurate**.

aurum potabile *ö'rum po-tab'i-lē* or *ow'room pō-täb'i-le*, (*L*) *n* a former medicine or cordial containing a small quantity of gold, (literally, potable gold).

AUS *abbrev*: Australia, including Papua New Guinea (IVR).

auscultation *ös-kəl-tā'shən*, *n* listening to internal bodily sounds (eg of the heart, lungs, abdomen, foetal heart, etc) as an aid to diagnosis, *usu* with a stethoscope. — *vt* and *vi* **aus'cultate** to examine by auscultation. — *n* **aus'cultātor** a person who practises auscultation; an instrument for the purpose; formerly in Germany, a person who had passed their first public examination in law, and who was merely retained, not yet employed or paid by government. — *adj* **auscultatory** (*-kul'tə-tə-ri*). [L *auscultāre* to listen]

au second *ō sə-gɔ̃*, (*Fr*) on the second (floor).

au secours *ō sə-ko͞or*, (*Fr*) a call for help.

au sérieux *ō sā-ryø*, (*Fr*) seriously.

Ausgleich *ows'glīhh*, (*Ger*) *n* a settlement; an arrangement; the agreement between Austria and Hungary in 1867.

Ausländer *ows'len-dər*, (*Ger*) *n* a foreigner.

Auslese *ows'lā-zə*, (*Ger*) *n* choice, selection; wine made from selected bunches of grapes.

Ausonian *ö-sō'ni-ən*, (*poetic*) *adj* Italian. [L *Ausonia* a poetical name for Italy]

auspice *ös'pis*, *n orig* an omen drawn from observing birds; an omen, *esp* a good one, a prognostic; augury; (in *pl*) patronage. — *vt* **auspicate** (*ös'pi-kāt*) to foreshow; to initiate or inaugurate with hopes of good luck. — *vi* to augur. — *adj* **auspicious** (*-pish'əs*) having good auspices or omens of success; favourable, fortunate, propitious. — *adv* **auspi'ciously**. — *n* **auspi'ciousness**. [Fr, from L *auspicium*, from *auspex*, *auspicis* a bird-seer, from *avis* bird, and *specere* to look, to observe]

Aussichtspunkt *ows'zihhts-po͝ongkt*, (*Ger*) *n* a selected position for admiring scenery, a vantage point: — *pl* **Aussichtspunkte** (*-tə*).

Aussie *oz'i* or *os'i*, (*slang*) *n* and *adj* Australian.

Aussiedler *ows'zēd-lər*, (*Ger*) *n* an immigrant. [Literally, out-settler]

austenite *ös'tə-nīt*, (*chem*) *n* a solid solution of carbon or other substance in one of the forms of iron. — *adj* **austenit'ic** (of stainless steels) composed chiefly of austenite. [W C Roberts-*Austen* (1843–1902), English metallurgist]

Auster *ös'tər*, (*literary*) *n* the south wind. [L]

austere *ös-tēr'*, *adj* sour and astringent; harsh; severe, stern; grave; severe in self-discipline; severely simple, without luxury. — *adv* **austere'ly**. — *n* **austere'ness** or **austerity** (*-ter'*) the quality of being austere; severity of manners or life; harshness; asceticism; severe simplicity of style, dress or habits. — *adj* evincing or adopted in austerity. [L *austērus*, from Gr *austēros*, from *auein* to dry]

Austin. See **Augustine**.

Austr. *abbrev*: Australia; Australian.

austral *ös'trəl*, *adj* (also with *cap*) southern. — *n* the unit of currency in Argentina (100 centavos): — *pl* **austral'es** (*-trä'lāz*). [L *austrālis* southern, from *Auster* the south wind]

Australasian *os-trə-lā'zhən* or *-zi-ən*, *adj* pertaining to Australasia, or the lands that lie south-east of Asia. — *n* a native or colonist of one of these lands. [L *austrālis* southern, and **Asian**]

Australian *ös-trā'li-ən*, *adj* of, or pertaining to, *Australia*, the largest island in the world and the smallest continent, an independent member of the Commonwealth (formerly a British colony). — *n* a person native to or resident in Australia. — *n* **Austrā'lianism** an Australian idiom; a characteristically Australian attitude. — *n* **aus'tralite** a tektite found in the interior of Australia. — *n* **Aus'tralorp** an Australian breed of black hen (*Austral*ian and *Orp*ington). — **Australia Day** (a public holiday celebrating) the anniversary of the founding of the colony of New South Wales on 26 January 1788; **Australian crane** see **brolga**; **Australian rules football** or **Australian rules** an Australian version of football played by eighteen a side with an oval ball (also *Austr colloq* **Rules**). [L *austrālis* southern, from *Auster* the south wind]

Australopithecus *os-trəl-ō-pith'i-kəs*, or *-trāl-*, *n* a genus of extinct human-like primates, known from fossil skulls, etc, found in southern Africa, and belonging to the subfamily **Aus'tralopithecī'nae**. — *adj* and *n* **australopith'ecine** (*-sēn*). — **Australopithecus robustus** a proto-human species that lived between two and three million years ago. [New L, from L *austrālis* southern, and Gr *pithēkos* ape]

Austrian *ös'tri-ən*, *adj* of or pertaining to *Austria*, a federal republic in central Europe. — *n* a native or citizen of Austria. — **Austrian blind** a fabric window blind with several vertical lines of shirring, giving a decorative gathered effect, *esp* when the blind is raised.

Austric *ös'trik*, *adj* belonging to a family of languages divided into **Austrōāsiat'ic** (in India and Indo-China, including the Munda or Kolarian, Mon-Khmer and Khasi groups, and the languages of the Semang and Sakai) and **Austrōnē'sian** (including the Indonesian, or Malay, Polynesian, Micronesian and Melanesian groups). [L *Auster* south wind, **Asiatic**, and Gr *nēsos* island]

austringer *ö'strin-jər*, *n* a keeper of goshawks. — Also **a'stringer** or **ostreger** (*os'tri-jər*; *Shakesp*). [OFr *ostruchier*]

Austroasiatic, **Austronesian**. See **Austric**.

AUT *abbrev*: Association of University Teachers.

aut-. See **auto-**.

autacoid *ö'tə-koid*, (*med*) *n* an internal secretion that excites or inhibits action in various tissues; a hormone or chalone. [Gr *autos* self, and *akos* drug]

autarchy *öt'är-ki*, *n* absolute power. — *adj* **autar'chic** or **autar'chical**. — *n* **aut'archist**. [Gr *autos* self, and *archein* to rule]

autarky *öt'är-ki*, *n* self-sufficiency; the economic situation of a country which is a closed economy conducting no international trade (*econ*). — *adj* **autar'kic** or **autar'kical**. — *n* **aut'arkist**. [Gr *autarkeia*, from *autos* self, and *arkeein* to suffice]

autecology *ö-tek-ol'ə-ji*, *n* (study of) the ecology of an individual organism or species. — *adj* **autecolog'ic** or **autecolog'ical**. [**auto-** (1)]

auteur *ō-tœr*, *n* a film-director, *esp* thought of as the creator of a particular genre, and showing a unique personal stamp. [Fr, (literally) author]

authentic *ö-then'tik*, *adj* genuine; authoritative; true, entitled to acceptance, of established credibility; (of writing) trustworthy, as setting forth real facts; own, proper (*Milton*); applied in music to medieval modes (eg Gregorian chants) having their sounds within the octave above the final (qv; *opp* to *plagal*); in existentialism, used to describe the way of living of someone who takes full cognizance of the meaninglessness of the world yet deliberately follows a consistent course of action. — Also (*archaic*) **authent'ical**. — *adv* **authent'ically**. — *vt* **authen'ticate** to make authentic; to prove genuine; to give legal validity to; to certify the authorship of. — *n* **authenticā'tion**. — *n* **authen'ticātor**. — *n* **authenticity** (*ö-thən-tis'i-ti*) the quality of being authentic; the state of being true or in accordance with fact; genuineness. — **authentic cadence** (*music*) a perfect cadence. [Gr *authentikos* warranted, from *autos* self]

author *öth'ər*, *n* a person who brings anything into being; a beginner of any action or state of things; the original writer of a book, article, etc (also *fem* **auth'oress**); elliptically, an author's writings; one's authority for something (*obs*). — Also (*esp NAm*) *vt*. — *n* **auth'orcraft**. — *adj* **authorial** (*-thō'* or *-thö'*). — *adj* **auth'orish**. — *adj* **authorīz'able** or **-s-**. — *n* **authorizā'tion** or **-s-**. — *vt* **auth'orize** or **-ise** to give authority to; to sanction; to justify; to establish by authority. — *adj* **auth'orless** anonymous. — *n* **auth'oring**. — *n* **auth'orism** the state or quality of being an author. — *n* **auth'orship**. — **authorized capital** the maximum amount of money that a company is allowed to raise by issuing shares to the public if it desires to do so; **Authorized Version** the English translation of the Bible completed in 1611 (also called **King James Bible** or **Version**). [Through Fr from L *auctor*, from *augēre*, *auctum* to increase, to produce]

authority *ö-thor'it-i*, *n* legal power or right; power derived from office or character or prestige; weight of testimony; permission; a person or body holding power; an expert; a passage or book referred to in witness of a statement; the original bestower of a name (*biol*). — *adj* **authoritā'rian** setting authority above freedom; relating to, governed by, or stressing the importance and power of authority, or of a small group representing it; domineering, disciplinarian. — Also *n*. — *n* **authoritā'rianism**. — *adj* **authoritative** (*ö-thor'it-āt-iv* or *ö-thor'it-ət-iv*) having the sanction or weight of authority; accepted, approved; definitive, reliable; dictatorial. — *adv* **author'itatively**. — *n* **author'itativeness**. [L *auctōritas*, *-ātis*, from *auctor* (see **author**)]

authorizable, **authorization**, **authorize**. See under **author**.

autism *öt'izm*, (*psychiatry*) *n* absorption in imaginative activity directed by the thinker's wishes, with loss of contact with reality; an abnormality of childhood development affecting language and social communication. — *adj* and *n* **autis'tic**. — *adv* **autis'tically**. [Gr *autos* self]

auto- *ö-tō-*, or sometimes before a vowel **aut-** *öt-*, *combining form* denoting (1) self; (2) same; (3) self-caused; (4) automobile; (5) automatic. [Gr *autos* self, same]

auto[1] *ö'tō*, *n* (chiefly *NAm*) short form of **automobile**: — *pl* **au'tos**.

auto[2] *ä'ōō-tō*, *n* a drama, *esp* a short religious one; an auto-da-fé: — *pl* **au'tos**. [Sp and Port, from L *actus* an act]

autoantibody *ö-tō-an'ti-bod-i*, (*med*) *n* an antibody produced in reaction to an antigenic constituent of the body's own tissues. [**auto-** (1)]

Autobahn or **autobahn** *ow'tō-bän*, or *ö'tə-*, (*Ger*) *n* a highway with dual carriageway for motor traffic only, a motorway.

autobiography *ö-tō-bi-og'rə-fi*, *n* a person's life written by the subject. — *n* **autobiog'rapher**. — *adj* **autobiographic** (*-ō-graf'ik*) of the nature of autobiography. — *adj* **autobiograph'ical** of, or relating to, autobiography; autobiographic. — *adv* **autobiograph'ically**. [Gr *autos* self, *bios* life, and *graphein* to write]

autobus *ö'tō-bus*, *n* a motor-bus. [**auto-** (4)]

autocade. Same as **motorcade**. [**auto-** (4)]

autocar *ö'tō-kär*, *n* a motor car. [**auto-** (4)]

autocarp *ö'tō-kärp*, *n* a fruit produced by self-fertilization. [Gr *autos* self, and *karpos* fruit]

autocatalysis *ö-tō-kə-tal'is-is*, *n* the catalysis of a reaction by a product of that reaction (*chem*); reaction or disintegration of a cell or tissue due to the influence of one of its own products (*zool*). — *vt* **autocatalyse** or **-yze** (*-kat'ə-līz*). — *adj* **autocatalytic** (*-lit'ik*). [**auto-** (1, 3)]

autocephalous *ö-tō-sef'ə-ləs*, *adj* having its own head; independent. — *n* **autoceph'aly** condition of being autocephalous. [Gr *autos* self, and *kephalē* head]

autochanger *ö'tō-chān-jər*, *n* (a record-player having) a device by means of which records are dropped from a stack one at a time on to the turntable. [**auto-** (5)]

autochthon *ö-tok'thon*, *n* one of the primitive inhabitants of a country; an aboriginal: — *pl* **autoch'thons** or **autoch'thonēs**. — *adj* **autoch'thonous** (of flora, fauna) indigenous; formed in the region where found (*geol*); originating in the organ in which it is found (*pathol*); (of an idea) coming into the mind with no apparent connection to the subject's train of thought (*psychol*). — *n* **autoch'thonism** or **autoch'thony** the condition of being autochthonous. [Gr *autochthōn* sprung from the soil, from *autos* self, and *chthōn*, *chthonos* soil: the Athenians claiming to have actually sprung from the soil]

autoclave *ö'tō-klāv*, *n* a strong, sealed vessel for carrying out chemical reactions under pressure and at high temperatures, or one in which super-heated steam under pressure is used for sterilizing or cooking. — *vt* and *vi* to sterilize in an autoclave. [Fr, self-fastening apparatus, from Gr *autos* self, and perhaps L *clāvis* key or *clāvus* nail]

autocoprophagy *ö-tō-ko-prof'ə-ji*, (*zool*) *n* refection. [**auto-** (1) and **coprophagy**]

autocrat *ö'tō-krat*, *n* a person who rules by his or her own power; an absolute sovereign; a dictatorial person. — *n* **autocracy** (*-tok'rə-si*) an absolute government by one person; despotism. — *adj* **autocrat'ic**. — *adv* **autocrat'ically**. [Gr *autokratēs*, from *autos* self, and *kratos* power]

autocrime *ö'tō-crīm*, *n* theft of, or from, a motor vehicle. [**auto-** (4)]

autocritique *ō-tō-krē-tēk*, (*Fr*) *n* self-criticism, *esp* political.

autocross *ö'tō-kros*, *n* motor racing round a rough grass track. [**auto-** (4)]

autocue *ö'tō-kū*, *n* a device showing a television speaker the text of what he or she has arranged to say. [**auto-** (5)]

autocycle *ö'tō-sī'kl*, *n* a motorcycle. [**auto-** (4)]

auto-da-fé *ö'tō-da-fā'*, *n* the public declaration of the judgement passed on heretics in Spain and Portugal by the Inquisition; the infliction of the punishment that immediately followed, *esp* the public burning of the victims: — *pl* **autos-da-fé**. [Port *auto da fé* (Sp *auto de fe*); *auto*, from L *actum* act; *da* of the, from L *de* of; and *fé*, from L *fidēs* faith]

autodestruct *ö-tō-di-strukt'*, *adj* (of a craft, missile, etc) capable of destroying itself; pertaining to the function of self-destruction. — *vi* (of a missile, machine, etc) to destroy itself. [**auto-** (1)]

autodidact *ö-tō-dī'dakt* or *ö'tō-di-dakt*, *n* a self-taught person. — *adj* **autodidact'ic**. — *adv* **autodidact'ically**. — *n* **autodidact'icism**. [Gr *autodidaktos*, from *autos* self, and *didaktos* taught]

auto-digestion *ö-tō-dī-jest'yən* or *-di-*, *n* autolysis. [**auto-** (1)]

autodyne *ö'tō-dīn*, *adj* in radio, of an electrical circuit in which the same elements and valves are used both as oscillator and detector. [**auto-** (2) and **(hetero)dyne**]

autoerotic *ö-tō-ə-rot'ik*, *adj* relating to sexual excitement or gratification gained from one's own body, with or without external stimulation. — *n* **autoerot'icism** or **autoer'otism**. [**auto-** (1)]

autoexposure *ö-tō-eks-pō'zhər*, *n* a system for automatically adjusting the aperture and/or shutter speed of a camera according to the lighting conditions. [**auto-** (5)]

autoflare *ö'tō-flār*, *n* an aircraft automatic landing system operating from an altitude of 50 feet and dependent on a very accurate radio altimeter. [**auto-** (5)]

autofocus *ö'tō-fō-kəs*, *n* a device which automatically focuses a camera lens on the subject being photographed. — Also *adj*. [**auto-** (5)]

autogamy *ö-tog'ə-mi*, (*bot* and *zool*) *n* self-fertilization. — *adj* **autog'amous** or **autogamic** (*ö-tō-gam'ik*). [Gr *autogamos* breeding alone, from *autos* self, and *gamos* marriage]

autogenous *ö-toj'ə-nəs*, *adj* self-generated; independent; (of a graft or vaccine) produced from tissue, bacteria, from the patient's own body (*med*); (of a joint) made without flux, etc, by melting edges together (*metalwork*); capable of autogenesis (*zool*). — *n* **autogen'esis** spontaneous generation. — *adj* **autogen'ic** self-generated or produced from the subject's own body, autogenous. — *n sing* **autogen'ics** (also **autogenic training**) a system of relaxation teaching voluntary control of bodily tension, etc. — *n* **autog'eny** autogenesis. [Gr *autogenēs*, from *genos* offspring]

autogiro or **autogyro** *ö-tō-jī'rō*, *n* a rotating-wing aircraft whose chief support in flight is derived from the reaction of the air upon freely-revolving rotors: — *pl* **autogi'ros** or **autogy'ros**. [Orig trademark; invented by Juan de la Cierva in 1923; Sp, from Gr *autos* self, and *gyros* circle]

autograft *ö'tō-gräft*, (*surg*) *n* a graft from one part to another of the same body. — Also *vt*. [**auto-** (2) and **graft**[1]]

autograph *ö'tō-gräf*, *n* one's own handwriting; a signature, *usu specif* that of a famous person, kept as a collector's item; an original manuscript, handwritten by the author. — *vt* to write with one's own hand; to write one's signature in or on, to sign. — *adj* handwritten by the author; (of painting, sculpture, etc) done by the artist, not by a pupil or follower. — *adj* **autographic** (*-graf'ik*). — *adv* **autograph'ically**. — *n* **autography** (*ö-tog'rə-fi*) the act of writing with one's own hand; reproduction of the outline of a writing or drawing by facsimile. — **autograph album** or **book** one in which to collect signatures (of friends, famous personalities, etc) and often rhymes or epigrams, etc. [Gr *autographos* written with one's own hand, from *autos* self, and *graphein* to write]

autogravure *ö-tō-grav-ūr'*, or *ö'*, *n* a process of photo-engraving similar to autotype. [**auto-** (2)]

autoguide *ö'tō-gīd*, *adj* and *n* (of) a system whereby information on traffic conditions is collected by roadside sensors and relayed to drivers via receivers in their vehicles. [**auto-** (4) or (5)]

autogyro. See **autogiro**.

autoharp *ö'tō-härp*, *n* a kind of zither, with button-controlled dampers, which produces chords. [**auto-** (5)]

autohypnosis *ö-tō-hip-nō'sis*, *n* a self-induced hypnotic state, or the process of bringing it on. [**auto-** (1)]

auto-immunity *ö-tō-im-ūn'i-ti*, *n* the production by a living body of antibodies which attack constituents of its own tissues, the cause of certain serious diseases (**auto-immune diseases**). — *n* **auto-immuniza'tion** or -s-. [**auto-** (1)]

auto-intoxication *ö'tō-in-toks-i-kā'shən*, *n* poisoning by substances produced within the body. — *n* and *adj* **auto-intox'icant**. [**auto-** (1, 3)]

autokinesis *ö-tō-kin-ē'sis*, *n* spontaneous motion, *esp* the apparent movement of a stationary object. — *adj* **autokinet'ic**. [Gr *autokinesis* self-motion]

autolatry *ö-tol'ə-tri*, *n* worship of oneself. [Gr *autos* self, and *latreiā* worship]

autologous *ö-tol'ə-gəs*, *adj* making use of blood or tissue obtained from (and stored for re-use in the treatment of) the same patient, prior to or during an operation or transfusion; derived from the same individual. [**auto-** (2) and *-logous* (on the model of *homologous*)]

autology *ö-tol'ə-ji*, *n* scientific study of oneself. [**auto-** (1)]

Autolycus *ö-tol'i-kəs*, *n* a thief; a plagiarist. [From the character in Shakespeare's *Winter's Tale*, or in Greek mythology]

autolysis *ö-tol'is-is*, *n* the breaking down of dead tissue by enzymes produced in the organism's own cells. — *vt* and *vi* **aut'olyse** or **-yze** (*-līz*) to (cause to) undergo autolysis. — *adj* **autolyt'ic**. — **autolysed yeast powder** a flavour-enhancer derived from yeast. [Gr *autos* self, and *lysis* loosening]

automat *ö'tə-mat*, *n* a restaurant or shop where dishes, hot or cold, are obtained from slot machines (chiefly *US*); a vending machine, *esp* for food and drink; an automaton (*archaic*). [From trademark; after **automatic**]

automate. See **automation**.

automatic *ö-tə-mat'ik*, *adj* working by itself without direct and continuing human operation; (of a firearm) reloading itself from an internal magazine, or able to continue firing as long as there is pressure on the trigger; (of a motor vehicle or its gears) operated by automatic transmission; (of a telephone system) worked by automatic switches; (of behaviour, reactions, etc) done, etc without thinking, mechanical; (of a process) carried out by an automatic machine; occurring as a matter of course. — *n* an automatic firearm, machine, etc; the position of the switches, etc on a machine, etc that allows it to operate automatically. — *adj* **automat'ical** (*archaic*). — *adv* **automat'ically**. — *n* **automaticity** (*-tis'i-ti*). — *n* **autom'atism** automatic or involuntary action; the power of initiating vital processes from within the cell, organ or organism, independently of any direct or immediate stimulus from without (*biol*); the self-acting power of the muscular and nervous systems, by which movement is effected without intelligent determination (*med* and *zool*); action without conscious volition; the doctrine that animals are automata, their movements, etc being the result of mechanical laws; suspension of control by the conscious mind, so that ideas may be released from the unconscious, a technique of surrealism (*art*). — *n* **autom'atist** a person who holds the doctrine of automatism; a person who acts automatically. — **automatic defibrillator** a small battery-powered device implanted in the body which senses and corrects abnormal heart rhythms; **automatic drive** automatic transmission; **automatic gain control** a system in amplifiers that compensates for a wide range of input signals to give a more uniform level of output; **automatic pilot** (also **au'topilot**) a device which can be set to guide and control an aircraft or a ship on a chosen course; used *fig* of an automatism that takes over one's actions or behaviour in fatigue, abstraction, etc; **automatic teller** or **automatic teller machine** (*abbrev* **ATM**) an electronic panel set into the exterior wall of a bank, etc from which (on the insertion of one's cash card and the keying of one's personal identification number) to obtain cash or information about one's account, etc; **Automatic Train Protection** (*abbrev* **ATP**) a system which automatically stops or slows down a train in response to a signal or speed restriction; **automatic transmission** (in a motor vehicle) power transmission by fluid drive, allowing gears to change automatically; the transmission of (*usu*) computer data between two points via a telephone system; **Automatic Vehicle Identification** (*abbrev* **AVI**) a system for toll roads which recognizes electronically-tagged vehicles and automatically charges the owner's account; **automatic vending** the sale of products (eg cigarettes, confectionery) by means of coin-operated slot-machines; **automatic writing** writing performed without the volition of the writer. [Gr *automatos* self-moving, from *autos* self]

automation *ö-tə-mā'shən*, *n* a high degree of mechanization in manufacture, the handling of material between processes being automatic and the whole system being automatically controlled. — *vt* **aut'omate** to apply automation to. [Irreg formation from **automatic**]

automaton *ö-tom'ə-tən*, *n* a machine that imitates the movement of a living creature, activated by a concealed mechanism such as clockwork; such a machine as a toy, amusement or decoration; a living being regarded as without consciousness; a person who acts by routine, without intelligence or feeling: — *pl* **autom'atons** or **autom'ata**. [Gr, neuter of *automatos* (see **automatic**]

automobile *ö-tō-mō-bēl'*, or *ö'*, or *-mō'*, *adj* self-moving. — *n* a motor car. — *n pl* **automobil'ia** collector's items of motoring interest. — *n* **automō'bilism**. — *n* **automō'bilist**. [Gr *autos* self, and L *mōbilis* mobile]

automorphism *ö-tō-mör'fizm*, *n* ascription to others of one's own characteristics; isomorphism of an algebraic system with itself (*math*). — *adj* **automor'phic** marked by automorphism; idiomorphic. — *adv* **automor'phically**. [Gr *autos* self, and *morphē* form]

automotive *ö-tō-mō'tiv*, *adj* self-propelling; of or pertaining to automobiles; of or pertaining to the motor car trade. [Gr *autos* self, and LL *motivus* causing to move]

autonomy *ö-ton'əm-i*, *n* the power or right of self-government, *esp* partial self-government; the Kantian doctrine that the human will carries its guiding principle within itself (*philos*). — *adj* **autonomic** (*ö-tō-nom'ik*), self-governing; pertaining to the autonomic nervous system (*zool*); spontaneous (*bot* and *zool*). — *adj* **autonom'ical**. — *n sing* **autonom'ics** the study of self-regulating systems for process control. — *n* **auton'omist**. — *adj* **auton'omous** (of a country, region, etc) (partially) self-governing; independent; (of the will) guided by its own principles (*philos*); autonomic (*bot* and *zool*). — **autonomic nervous system** (*zool* and *med*) a system of nerve fibres, innervating muscles, glands, etc, whose actions are automatic. [Gr *autonomos*, from *autos* self, and *nomos* law]

autonym *ö'to-nim*, or *-tə-*, *n* a writing published under the author's real name; an author's real name. — Also *adj*. [Gr *autos* self, and *onyma* (= *onoma*) name]

autophagous *ö-tof'ə-gəs*, *adj* self-devouring; (of a bird) capable of feeding itself from the moment of hatching. — *n* **autophā'gia** or **autophagy** (*-ə-ji*) sustenance by self-absorption of the tissues of the body, eg during starvation (*med*); in a lysosome, the intracellular digestion of material of the cell (*biochem*); eating or biting of part of one's own body (*psychiatry*). [Gr *autos* self, and *phagein* to eat]

autophanous *ö-tof'ə-nəs*, *adj* self-luminous. [Gr *autos* self, and *phānos* bright]

autophoby *ö-tof'əb-i*, *n* (*rare*) a shrinking from making any reference to oneself. — *n* **autophōbia** fear of (being by) oneself. [Gr *autos* self, and *phobos* fear]

autophony *ö-tof'ən-i*, (*med*) *n* in the diagnosis of thoracic disease, observation of the resonance of one's own voice by speaking with the ear on the patient's chest; a condition in which the patient is aware of increased resonance of his or her voice, pulse, etc in the head, as in certain diseases of the middle ear, etc. [Gr *autos* self, and *phōnē* sound]

autopilot. See **automatic pilot** under **automatic**.

autopista *ow'tō-pēs-ta*, (*Sp*) *n* a highway for motor traffic only; a motorway.

autoplasty *ö'tō-plas-ti*, (*surg*) *n* grafting of healthy tissue from another part of the same body. — *adj* **autoplas'tic**. [Gr *autos* self, and *plastos* formed]

autopoint *ö'tō-point*, *n* a point-to-point (qv) over rough country in motor vehicles. [**auto-** (4)]

autopsy *ö'top-si*, or *-top'*, or **autopsia** *ö-top'si-ə*, *n* a post-mortem examination of a corpse; personal inspection (*obs*). — *vt* **autopsy**. — *adj* **autopt'ic** or **autopt'ical**. — *adv* **autopt'ically**. [Gr *autos* self, and *opsis* sight]

autoradiography *ö-tō-rā-di-og'rə-fi*, *n* a technique used to show the distribution of radioactively labelled molecules in cells or tissues. — *n* **autora'diograph** an autoradiographic record. — *adj* **autoradiograph'ic**. [**auto-** (1)]

auto-reverse *ö-tō-ri-vûrs'*, *n* and *adj* (a facility provided in a cassette player for) reversing the tape direction so as to play the following side on completion of the first, without turning the tape over manually. [**auto-** (5), (1)]

autorickshaw *ö-tō-rik'shö*, *n* a light, three-wheeled vehicle powered by a motorcycle engine, used in India, etc. [**auto-** (4)]

autoroute *ō-tō-rōōt*, (*Fr*) *n* a highway for motor traffic only; a motorway.

autoschediasm *ö-tō-sked'i-azm*, or *-skēd'*, *n* anything extemporized. — *adj* **autoschedias'tic**. — *vt* **autosched'iaze** (*-āz*). [Gr *autoschediasma* improvisation, *autoschediazein* to extemporize, from *autoschedon* on the spot, from *autos* self, and *schedios* off-hand]

autoscopy *ö-tos'kə-pi*, (*psychol*) *n* hallucination of an image of one's body. — *adj* **autoscop'ic**. [Gr *autos* self, and *skopeein* to see]

autosome *ö'tō-sōm*, (*biol*) *n* a chromosome other than a sex-chromosome. — *adj* **autosom'al**. [Gr *autos* self, and *sōma* body]

autostrada *ä'ōō-tō-strä-da*, (*Ital*) *n* a highway for motor traffic only, a motorway.

auto-suggestion *ö'tō-sə-jes'chən*, (*psychol*) *n* a mental process similar to suggestion, but originating in a belief in the subject's own mind. [**auto-** (3)]

autotelic *ö-tō-tel'ik*, *adj* being an end in itself, or its own justification. [Gr *autotelēs*, from *autos* self, and *telos* end]

autoteller *ö'tō-tel-ər*, *n* an automatic telling machine (qv under **automatic**). [**auto-** (5)]

autotheism *ö-tō-thē'izm*, *n* assumption of divine powers; the doctrine of the self-subsistence of God, *esp* (in *Christian theol*) of the second person in the Trinity. — *n* **autothe'ist**. [Gr *autos* self, and *theos* a god]

autotimer *ö'tō-tīm-ər*, *n* a device on a cooker, etc that can be adjusted in advance to turn the apparatus on or off at a desired time. [**auto-** (5)]

autotomy *ö-tot'ə-mi*, (*zool*) *n* the reflex casting off of part of its body by an animal attempting to escape. [Gr *autos* self, and *tomē* cut]

autotoxin *ö-tō-tok'sin*, *n* a poisonous substance formed within the organism against which it acts. [**auto-** (1)]

autotransplantation *ö-tō-trans-plän-tā'shən* (or *-plan-*), (*zool*) *n* the reinsertion of a transplant or graft from a particular individual in the same individual. [**auto-** (1)]

autotrophic *ö-tō-trof'ik*, (*biol*) *adj* capable of building up food materials from inorganic matter. — *n* **au'totroph** an autotrophic organism. [Gr *autos* self, and *trophē* food]

autotype *ö'tō-tīp*, *n* a true impress or copy of the original; a process of printing from a photographic negative in a permanent pigment. — *vt* to reproduce by such a process. — *n* **autotypog'raphy** a process by which drawings made on gelatine are transferred to a plate from which impressions may be taken. [**auto-** (2)]

autovac *ö'tō-vak*, *n* a vacuum mechanism in a motor car for raising petrol to a higher tank so that it may flow by gravity to the carburettor. [**auto-** (4)]

autrefois acquit, **attaint** or **convict** *ōt-rə-fwä a-kē*, *a-tẽ*, or *kɔ̃-vē*, (*law*) three defence pleas, arguing that a defendant cannot be charged a second time with an offence of which he or she has been acquitted, or a (capital) offence of which he or she has been found guilty. [Fr]

autre temps, autre moeurs *ot-rə tã*, *ot-rə mœr*, (*Fr*) other times, other manners (or customs).

autumn *ö'təm*, *n* the third season of the year, when fruits are gathered in, generally (in the N hemisphere) from August or September to October or November; astronomically, from the autumnal equinox to the winter solstice; a period of harvest or of maturity. — *adj* **autum'nal** (*ö-tum'nəl*) pertaining to autumn; blooming in autumn; beyond the prime (*fig*); withering or withered (*fig*). — *adv* **autum'nally**. — *adj* **au'tumny**

(*-tə-mi*; *colloq*) autumn-like. — **autumn crocus** a species of *Colchicum*, meadow-saffron. [L *autumnus*]

autunite *ö'tun-īt*, *n* a mineral composed of a hydrous phosphate of uranium and calcium. [*Autun* in France, one of its localities]

au voleur *ō vo-lœr*, (*Fr*) stop thief!

auxanometer *öks-ən-om'it-ər*, *n* an instrument for measuring plant-growth. [Gr *auxanein* to grow, and *metron* measure]

aux armes *ö-zärm*, (*Fr*) to arms.

auxesis *ök-sē'sis*, *n* increase in size; hyperbole; growth resulting from an increase in cell size (*biol*). — *adj* **auxet'ic**. — *n* something that promotes auxesis. [Gr *auxēsis* increase]

auxiliary *ög-zil'yər-i*, *adj* helping; subsidiary; peripheral (*comput*). — *n* a helper; a subordinate or assistant person or thing; an auxiliary verb (*gram*); (*esp* in *pl*) a soldier serving with another, allied, nation; a naval vessel not used for combat. — *n* and *adj* **auxil'iar** (*archaic*) (an) auxiliary. — **auxiliary verb** (*gram*) a verb that helps to form the mood, tense or voice of another verb. [L *auxiliāris*, from *auxilium* help, from *augēre* to increase]

auxin *öks'in*, (*bot*) *n* any of a number of growth-promoting substances present in minute quantities in plants. [Gr *auxein* to increase]

auxometer *öks-om'it-ər*, (*optics*) *n* an instrument for measuring magnifying power. [Gr *auxein* to increase, and *metron* measure]

AV *abbrev*: audio-visual; (or **A.V.**) Authorized Version.

Av. A variant spelling of **Ab**.

Av. *abbrev*: Avenue (in street names); *Avocat* (*Fr*), lawyer; *Avril* (*Fr*), April.

av *abbrev*: *annos vixit* (*L*), lived (so many) years.

av. See **ave.**

ava¹ or **ava'** *ə-vö'*, (*Scot*) *adv* at all. [For **of all**]

ava² *ä'vä*. Same as **kava**.

avadavat *av-ə-də-vat'* or **amadavat** *am-ə-*, *n* an Indian songbird related to the weaver birds. [From *Ahmadabad*, whence they were sent to Europe as cagebirds]

avail¹ *ə-vāl'*, *vt* to be of value or service to; to benefit; (reflexively with *of*) to make use, take advantage; to give (someone) the benefit (of), inform (someone of) (*esp US*; *archaic*). — *vi* to be of use; to answer the purpose; to draw advantage, be the better (*Shakesp*). — *n* effectual advantage (*archaic* except in phrases such as *of* or *to no avail*, *of any avail*); (in *pl*) profits, proceeds (*obs*). — *adj* **avail'ful** (*obs*) of avail; serviceable. — *adj* **avail'ing**. — *adv* **avail'ingly**. [L *ad* to, and *valēre* to be worth, to be strong; appar modelled on **vail³**]

avail², **availe**. See **avale**.

available *ə-vāl'ə-bl*, *adj* at one's disposal, that one may avail oneself of; accessible; within reach; obtainable; to be had or drawn upon; valid (*law*); profitable (*obs*). — *n* **availabil'ity** quality of being available; power of effecting or promoting an end; the possession of qualities, other than merit, which predispose a candidate to success in an election (*esp US politics*; *archaic*). — *n* **avail'ableness**. — *adv* **avail'ably**. — **available market** (*business law*) a market where goods can be sold and bought freely, the price being fixed by the law of supply and demand. [**avail¹** and **-able**]

aval *āv'əl*, *adj* pertaining to a grandparent. [L *avus* grandfather]

avalanche *av'ə-länsh*, *-länch*, *-la-* or *-lö-*, *n* a hurtling mass of snow, with ice and rock, descending a mountain side; a landslip; a snowslip, eg from a roof; an overwhelming influx (*fig*); a shower of particles resulting from the collision of a high-energy particle with matter (*nucleonics*). — *vt* and *vi* to carry or come down as or like an avalanche. [Fr dialect, from *avaler*; see **avale**]

avale, **avail** or **availe** *ə-vāl'*, (*obs*) *vt* to lower (*Spenser*); to doff. — *vi* (*Spenser*) to come down; to alight. [Fr *avaler* to descend, from *à* (L *ad*) to, and *val* (L *vallis*) valley]

avant *a-vã*, (*Fr*) before. — *n* **avant-goût** (*-goo*) a foretaste; **avant-propos** (*-prō-pō*) preliminary matter; preface.

avant-courier *av-ã-koor'i-ər* or *-koo-ryā*, *n* a person who runs or is sent ahead; (in *pl*) scouts or advance guard (*hist*). [Fr *avant-coureur* forerunner, scout; *avant-courrier* forerunner]

avant-garde *av-ã-gärd'*, *n* those who create or support the newest ideas and techniques in an art, etc. — *adj* of or relating to the avant-garde; daringly innovative or unconventional. — *n* **avant-gard'ism** avant-garde theory or practice, or support of these. — *n* **avant-gard'ist** or **avant-gard'iste** a member of the avant-garde. [Fr, vanguard]

avanti *a-vän'tē*, (*Ital*) *interj* forward.

avanturine. See **aventurine**.

avarice *av'ər is*, *n* eager desire for wealth; covetousness. — *adj* **avaricious** (*-ish'əs*) extremely covetous, grasping, mercenary; greedy of gain. — *adv* **avari'ciously**. — *n* **avari'ciousness**. [Fr, from L *avāritia*, from *avārus* greedy, from *avēre* to pant after]

avascular *ə-vas'kū-lər* or *ā-*, (*med*) *adj* not having blood vessels. [Gr *a-* (privative), and **vascular**]

avast *ə-väst'*, (*naut*) *interj* hold fast! stop! [Prob Du *houd vast* hold fast]

avatar *a-və-tär'*, *n* the manifestation of a Hindu deity in a visible form; incarnation; supreme glorification of any principle (*fig*). [Sans *ava* away, down, and root *tar-* to pass over]

avaunt¹ *ə-vönt'*, *interj* (*archaic*) move on; begone. — *n* (*Shakesp*) dismissal. — *vi* (*obs*) to advance (*Spenser*); to depart. [Fr *avant* before, from L *ab* from, and *ante* before]

avaunt² *ə-vönt'*, (*obs*) *vt* and *vi* to boast. — *n* a boast. [OFr *avanter*, from LL *vānitāre* to boast, from L *vānus* vain]

AVC *abbrev*: additional voluntary contribution (to a pension scheme); automatic volume control.

avdp. or **avoir.** *abbrev*: avoirdupois.

ave *ā'vē*, *ä'vi* or *ä'vā*, (*formal archaic*, or *esp RC liturgical*) *interj* be well and happy; hail. — *n* (*RC*) a recitation of the address or prayer to the Virgin Mary, in full, **ave Maria** (*ä'vā mə-rē'ə*) or **ave Mary**, the Hail Mary, or angelic salutation (Luke 1.28). — **ave atque vale** *ā'vē at'kwi vā'lē*, *ä'vā* (*-wā*) *at'kwe vä'lā* (*-wä'*), (*L*) hail and farewell. [Imperative of L *avēre* to be well. See **angelus**]

ave. or **av.** *av*, *abbrev*: avenue; average.

avec plaisir *a-vek ple-zēr*, (*Fr*) with pleasure.

Avena *a-vē'nə*, *n* the oat genus of grasses. — *adj* **avenaceous** (*av-i-nā'shəs*) of the nature of oats; belonging to the Avena genus. [L *avēna* oats]

avenge *ə-venj'* or *-venzh'*, *vt* to take vengeance on someone on account of; to requite or repay. — *n* (*obs*) revenge. — *adj* **avenge'ful**. — *n* **avenge'ment** (*archaic*). — *n* **aveng'er**: — *fem* (*rare*) **aveng'eress**. — *adj* **aveng'ing**. [OFr *avengier*, from L *ad* to, and *vindicāre* to claim. See **vengeance**]

avenir *av-ə-nēr*, (*Fr*) *n* future.

avens *av'ənz*, *n* any plant of the hardy rosaceous genus *Geum* (eg **water avens** *Geum rivale* with pinkish flowers; **wood avens** herb-bennet, with yellow flowers); also the related sub-alpine **mountain avens** (*Dryas octopetala*), an evergreen dwarf shrub that bears white flowers. [OFr *avence*]

aventail or **aventaile** *av'ən-tāl*, (*hist*) *n* the flap or movable part of a helmet in front, for admitting air. [OFr *esventail* air-hole, from L *ex* out, and *ventus* wind]

aventre *a-ven'tr*, (*Spenser*) *vt* (*appar*) to thrust, direct. [Origin unknown]

aventure *ə-ven'chər*. Obsolete form of **adventure**.

aventurine *a-ven'chə-rin* or **avanturine** *-van'*, *n* a brown, spangled kind of Venetian glass; a kind of quartz enclosing spangles of mica or haematite (also **gold'-stone**). — *adj* shimmering or spangled, eg of certain kinds of feldspar or sealing-wax. [Ital *avventura* chance, because of the accidental discovery of the glass]

avenue *av'ən-ū*, in US *-oo*, *n* the principal approach to a country-house, *usu* bordered by trees; a double row of trees, with or without a road; a wide and handsome street, with or without trees; (with *cap*) used in street names generally; any passage or entrance into a place; means of access or attainment (*fig*). [Fr, from L *ad* to, and *venīre* to come]

aver[1] *ə-vûr'*, *vt* to declare to be true; to affirm or declare positively; to prove or justify (*law*): — *pr p* **averr'ing**; *pa p* **averred'**. — *n* **aver'ment** positive assertion; a formal offer to prove a plea (*law*); the proof offered (*law*). [Fr *avérer*, from L *ad* and *vērus* true]

aver[2] *ā'vər*, (*obs*) *n* possessions; cattle; a draught animal, *esp* an old or worthless cart-horse (*Scot*). [OFr *aveir*, *aver* (Fr *avoir*) possessions, stock, from L *habēre* to have]

average *av'ər-ij*, *n* the arithmetical mean value of any quantities (see under **mean**[2]); estimation of such a mean; loosely, an ordinary or typical value, common run; *orig* a customs duty or similar charge (*obs*); any expense other than freight payable by the owner of shipped goods; expense or loss by damage of ship or cargo; equitable distribution of expense or loss; assessment of compensation in the same proportion as amount insured bears to actual worth. — *adj* mean, medial; prevailing, typical, ordinary. — *vt* to obtain the average of; to amount to on an average; to do or achieve on an average. — *vt* and *vi* to even out to an average. — **average adjuster** an assessor employed by an insurance company in marine claims. — **average cost pricing** (*business*) a method of fixing the price of a product by adding a gross profit margin on to its average variable costs so as to cover its average total cost of production; **law of averages** popularly, a proposition stating that the mean of a situation is maintained by the averaging of its extremes. [Cf Fr *avarie*, Ital *avaria* duty on goods, from Ar *'awārīyah* damaged goods; poss connected with **aver**[2]]

Avernus *a-vûr'nəs* or *a-ver'nŏŏs*, or *-wer'*, (*poetic*) *n* the (entrance to the) infernal regions (*Roman mythol*); any abyss (after Lake Avernus in Campania). [L, from Gr *aornos* (*limnē*) birdless (lake), from the tradition that birds were killed by the lake's poisonous exhalations]

Averroism or **Averrhoism** *av-ər-ō'izm*, *n* the doctrine of the Arab philosopher *Averrhoës* (1126–98), that the soul is perishable, the only immortal soul being the world-soul from which individual souls went forth, and to which they return. — *n* **Averrō'ist** or **Averrhō'ist**.

averruncate *av'ər-ung-kāt*, (*rare*; *archaic*, *perh obs*) *vt* to ward off; (wrongly) to uproot. — *n* **averruncā'tion**. — *n* **av'erruncātor** an instrument for cutting off branches of trees. [L *āverruncāre* to avert, perh confused with *ēruncāre* to weed out]

averse *ə-vûrs'*, *adj* disinclined (with *to* or sometimes pedantically *from*); reluctant; turned away or backward (*obs*); turned away from the main axis (*bot*). — *adv* **averse'ly**. — *n* **averse'ness**. — *n* **aver'sion** turning aside; dislike; hatred; the object of dislike. — *adj* **aver'sive** showing aversion; with the purpose, or result, of averting. — *vt* **avert'** to turn aside; to prevent; to ward off. — *adj* **avert'ed**. — *adv* **avert'edly**. — *adj* **avert'ible** or *rarely* **avert'able** capable of being averted. — **aversion therapy** treatment of a person suffering from an undesirable habit or a compulsive form of behaviour by associating his or her thoughts about it with something unpleasant such as the administration of an electric shock. [L *āvertere*, *āversus*, from *ab* from, and *vertere* to turn]

avert. See under **averse**.

avertiment *a-vûr'ti-ment*, (*Milton*) *n* advertisement.

Avertin® *ə-vûr'tin*, *n* tradename of the anaesthetic *tribromoethanol*.

Aves *ā'vēz* or *ä'vās*, or *-wās*, *n pl* birds as a class of vertebrates. — *adj* **ā'vian** or **avine** (*ā'vīn*) of or pertaining to birds. — *n* **ā'viarist** a person who keeps an aviary. — *n* **ā'viary** a large cage or enclosure, etc for keeping birds. — *n* **ā'viculture** (or *av'*) bird-rearing; bird-fancying. — *n* **āvifau'na** (or *av-*) the bird-life found in a region. — *adj* **ā'viform** (or *av'*) bird-like in form or structure. — *adj* **ā'vine** avian. [L *avis* bird]

Avesta *ə-ves'tä*, *n* the Zoroastrian holy Scriptures. — *adj* **Aves'tan** or **Aves'tic** of the Avesta or its East Iranian language. — *n* the language of the Avesta, also called Zend. [Pehlevi *Avîstâk* lore]

avgas *av'gas*, (*US*) *n* any kind of *av*iation *gas*oline.

avgolemono *av-gə-le'mə-nō*, (*Gr*) *n* a soup or sauce made from chicken stock, lemon juice and egg yolks. [Mod Gr *avgo* egg, and *lemono* lemon]

AVI *abbrev*: Automatic Vehicle Identification.

avian, **aviary**, etc. See **Aves**.

aviate *ā'vi-āt*, *vi* to fly mechanically, navigate the air, a back-formation from **aviation**. — *n* **āviā'tion** the art or practice of mechanical flight; the production, design, operation, etc of aircraft; the aircraft industry; (*usu* military) aircraft collectively (*US*). — *n* **ā'viātor** a pilot who flies aircraft, an airman or airwoman. — *n* **ā'viatress** or **aviatrix** (*ā-vi-ā'triks*) a female pilot. — **aviation spirit** a motor fuel with a low initial boiling-point and complying with a certain specification, for use in aeroplanes. [L *avis* a bird]

Avicula *ə-vik'ū-lə*, *n* a genus of pearl oysters, so named from their winglike shape, giving the name to the family **Avicū̆l'idae**. [New L, from L *avicula* little bird]

Avicularia *ə-vik-ū-lār'i-ə*, *n* the bird-catching spider genus, giving the name to the family **Aviculārī'idae**. [New L, from L *aviculārius* bird-keeper]

aviculture. See under **Aves**.

avid *av'id*, *adj* greedy; eagerly desirous. — *n* **avid'ity** greed; desire, eagerness; a measure of the strength of binding between an antigen and an antibody (*immunol*). — *adv* **av'idly**. — *n* **av'idness**. [L *avidus*]

avidin *a'vi-din*, *n* a protein found in egg-white which combines with biotin and prevents its absorption. [From **avid** and biot*in*]

aviette *ā-vi-et'*, (*hist*) *n* an aeroplane driven by man-power; a type of glider. [Fr, from **avi(on)** and dimin sfx *-ette*]

avifauna, **aviform**, **avine**. See under **Aves**.

avion *av-yɔ̃*, (*Fr*) *n* an aeroplane. — **par avion** (*par av-yɔ̃*) by air; by airmail.

avionics *ā-vi-on'iks*, *n sing* the science concerned with the development and use of electronic and electrical devices for aircraft and spacecraft. — *adj* **avion'ic**. [*av*iation and electr*onics*]

avisandum. See **avizandum**.

avis au lecteur *a-vē ō lek-tœr*, (*Fr*) notice to the reader.

avise, **avize** or **avyze** *a-vīz'*, obsolete forms (*Spenser*, etc) of **advise**. — *n* **avise'ment** (*obs*). — *adj* **avize'full** (*Spenser*) watchful.

avised. See **black-a-vised** under **black**.

aviso *ə-vī'zō*, *n* an advice-boat (*hist*); a notification (*obs*): — *pl* **avi'sos**. [Sp, advice, advice-boat, from L *ad visum* (see **advice**]

avital *ə-vī'tl* or *av'i-tl*, (*obs*) *adj* of a grandfather; ancestral. [L *avītus*, from *avus* a grandfather]

avitaminosis *ā-vit-ə-min-ōs'is* or *ə-* or *-vīt-*, (*med*) *n* lack of vitamins or a condition due to this. [**a-**[2], **vitamin** and = **osis**]

avizandum *av-iz-an'dəm*, (*Scots law*) *n* private consideration of a case by a judge before giving judgement. — Also **avisan'dum**. [Gerund of LL *avizāre*, *avisāre* to advise]

avize, **avizefull**. See **avise**.

AVM *abbrev*: Air Vice-Marshal; automatic vending machine.

avocado *a-və-kä'dō*, *n* a tropical evergreen tree of the laurel family; (also **avocado pear** (*pār*)) its pear-shaped fruit, with buttery-textured, bland-flavoured flesh around a single large stone (also **alligator pear**); the colour of the skin of the fruit, blackish-green; the colour of the flesh of the fruit, yellowish-green: — *pl* **avoca'dos**. — Also *adj*. [Sp *aguacate*, from Aztec *ahuacatl*]

avocat consultant *a-vō-kä kɔ̃-sül-tã*, (*Fr*) *n* consulting lawyer, chamber counsel.

avocation *av-ə-kā'shən*, *n* properly, a diversion or distraction from one's regular employment; improperly used for **vocation**, business which calls for one's time and attention; diversion of the thoughts from any employment (*archaic*); the calling of a case to a higher court (*law*). [L *āvocātiō, -ōnis* a calling away, from *ab* from, and *vocāre* to call]

avocet or **avoset** *av'ə-set*, *n* a wading bird (genus *Recurvirostra*) with webbed feet and long, slender, curved, elastic bill. [Fr *avocette*, Ital *avosetta*]

Avogadro's constant or **number** *a-və-gä'drōz kon'stant*, or *num'bər*, (*phys*) *n* the number of specified elementary units (eg molecules, atoms, ions) in a mole of any substance. — **Avogadro's law**, **rule** or **hypothesis** the law that at equal temperature and pressure equal volumes of gases contain the same number of molecules. [A *Avogadro* (1776–1856), Italian physicist]

avoid *ə-void'*, *vt* to evade, escape; to shun, shirk; to empty (*obs*); to invalidate (*law*); to leave, quit (*Shakesp*); to dismount from (*obs*). — *vi* (*obs*) to take oneself off. — *adj* **avoid'able**. — *n* **avoid'ance** the act of avoiding or shunning; an act of annulling (*law*); the shunning of certain relatives among primitive peoples (*anthropol*). — **avoidable costs** (*econ*) costs which arise exclusively from the production process and which would not be incurred if no output took place. [Anglo-Fr *avoider*, OFr *esvuidier*, from L *ex* out, and root of **void**]

avoirdupois *av-ər-də-poiz'* or *av'*, or *av-wär-dū-pwä'*, *n* (*abbrev* **avdp**. or **avoir**.) a system of weights in which the pound (lb) equals 16 ounces (oz); (*esp facetious*) weight, *esp* heaviness or stoutness (*NAm colloq*). — *adj* of the system of weights. [OFr *aveir de pes* to have weight, from L *habēre* to have, *dē* from, and *pēnsum* that which is weighed]

avoision *ə-voi'zhən*, *n* a portmanteau-word coined by the Institution of Economic Affairs in 1979 to represent a compromise, and blurring of the moral distinction, between tax *avoi*dance (which is legal) and tax eva*sion* (which is illegal).

à volonté *a vo-lɔ̃-tā*, (*Fr*) at pleasure.

avoset. See **avocet**.

a vostro beneplacito *a vos'trō bā-nā-plä'chē-tō*, (*Ital*) at your pleasure, at your will.

à votre santé *a votr' sã-tā*, (*Fr*) to your health.

avouch *ə-vowch'*, (*archaic*) *vt* to avow or to acknowledge; to vouch for; to assert positively, to maintain; to guarantee; to own to; to appeal to (*obs*). — *vi* to give assurance. — *n* (*Shakesp*) evidence. — *adj* **avouch'able**. — *n* **avouch'ment**. [OFr *avochier*, from L *advocāre* to call to one's aid. See **vouch**, **advocate**]

avoure *a-vowr'*, (*Spenser*) *n* avowal. [See **avow**]

avouterer *a-vōō'tər-ər* or **avoutrer** *-trər* and **avoutry** *-tri*. Obsolete forms of **adulterer** and **adultery**.

avow *ə-vow'*, *vt* to declare; to acknowledge, own to; to maintain or affirm. — *vi* (*law*) to justify an act done. — *n* (*archaic*) a solemn promise; a vow. — *adj* **avow'able**. — *n* **avow'ableness**. — *n* **avow'al** a positive declaration; an acknowledgement; a frank confession. — *adj* **avowed'**. — *adv* **avow'edly**. — *n* **avow'er**. — *n* **avow'ry** the act of avowing and justifying in one's own right the distraining of goods (*law*); advocacy considered as personified in a patron saint (*obs*). [OFr *avouer*, orig to swear fealty to, from L *ad* to, and LL *vōtāre*, from L *vōtum* a vow: with sense affected by L *advocāre*. See **vow**, **avouch**]

avoyer *a-vwa-yā*, (*Fr*) *n* formerly, the chief magistrate in some Swiss cantons.

AVR *abbrev*: Army Volunteer Reserve.

a vuestra salud *a vōō-äs'tra sä-lōōdh'*, (*Sp*) to your health.

avulse *ə-vuls'*, *vt* to pluck or tear away by force. — *n* **avul'sion** forcible separation; a tearing away, out of or off (eg *med*, of part of the body); the sudden removal of land by change of a river's course or flooding, whereby it remains the property of the original owner (*opp* to *alluvion*). [L *āvellere*, *āvulsum*]

avuncular *ə-vung'kū-lər*, *adj* of or suitable to an uncle; benign, kindly. [L *avunculus* an uncle]

avvogadore *a-vō-ga-dō'rā*, (*Ital*) *n* an official criminal prosecutor in Venice.

avyze. See **avise**.

aw *ö*, (chiefly *Scot* and *US*) *interj* expressing disappointment, sympathy, disgust, etc.

awa or **awa'** *ə-wö'* or *-wä'*, (*Scot*) *adj* away.

AWACS *ā'waks*, *abbrev*: airborne warning and control system (a radar system mounted on an aircraft, used to detect enemy planes, and to control weapons or planes directed against them).

await *ə-wāt'*, *vt* to wait or look for; to be in store for; to attend (*obs*); to lie in wait for, to watch for (*obs*). — *n* (*Spenser*) an ambush, watch. [ONFr *awaitier*, from *à* to and *waitier* (see **wait**[1])]

awake *ə-wāk'*, *vt* to rouse from sleep; to rouse from inaction, cause to be active or alert. — *vi* to cease sleeping; to rouse oneself from sleep, inattention or indifference: — *pa t usu* **awoke'**, sometimes **awaked'**; *pa p* **awōk'en**, also (*archaic*) **awaked'** or **awoke'**. — *adj* not asleep; vigilant; alert, aware, cognizant (with *to*). — *vt* **awak'en** to awake; to rouse into interest or attention; to call to a sense of sin (*theol*). — *vi* to awake; to spring into being. — *adj* **awak'ening** becoming awake; rousing; revivifying, reanimating. — *n* a becoming awake, aware or active; a throwing off of indifference or ignorance; a rousing. — *n* and *adj* **awak'ing**. — **be awake to** to be fully aware of. [OE *āwæcnan* (pa t *āwōc*, pa p *āwacen*), confused with *āwacian* (pa t *āwacode*). See **wake**[1], **watch**]

awanting *ə-wont'ing*, (chiefly *Scot*; *archaic*) *adj* wanting; missing. [**a-**[1], and the gerund of **want**]

award *ə-wörd'*, *vt* to give officially as a payment or prize; to determine such payment, etc; to adjudge; to grant. — *n* that which is awarded; a prize; judgement or final decision, *esp* of arbitrators. [OFr *ewarder*, *eswarder* to determine or ordain after examination, from L *ex* thoroughly, and the root of **ward** and **guard**]

aware *ə-wār'*, *adj* informed or conscious (with *of*); wary (*obs*). — *n* **aware'ness** state of being aware; consciousness, *esp* a vague or indistinct form. [OE *gewær* wary, watchful, from *wær* cautious. See **ware**[3]]

awarn *a-wörn'*, (*Spenser*) *vt* to warn. [Pfx *a-* (intensive) and **warn**[1]]

awash *ə-wosh'*, *adv* on a level with the surface of the water; afloat at the mercy of the waves. — *adj* having the surface covered with water; full of (with *with*). [**a-**[1]]

awatch *ə-woch'*, (*archaic*) *adv* on the watch. [**a-**[1]]

awave *ə-wāv'*, (*archaic*) *adv* in a wave; in waves. [**a-**[1]]

away *ə-wā'*, *adv* onward; continuously; without hesitation, stop or delay; forthwith; out of the place in question; not at home; on the opponents' ground (*sport*; also *adj*); at or to a distance; off; in or into an averted direction; out of existence, life or consciousness; with effect of removal or elimination; far; about (after *here*, *there* or *where*; now *dialect*); (with omission of verb; *usu* acting as an *imper*) = go away or (with *with*) take away; (with omission of verb; *usu* acting as an *infin* after *can*, *may*, etc) to endure (with *with*; *archaic*). — *n* a match won by a team playing on the opponents' ground (*football pools*). — *interj* begone; get out. — *adv* **aways'** (*obs*, *Spenser* **awayes'**) away. — **away from it all** in or into a place which is remote from the bustle of life; **make away with** to steal, run off with; to destroy (*archaic*). [OE *aweg*, *onweg*, from *on* on, and *weg* way]

awdl *owdl*, (*Welsh*) *n* a Welsh ode conforming to the strict metrical, alliterative and internal rhyming conventions of traditional bardic verse.

awe *ö*, *n* reverential wonder or fear; dread; power to inspire awe (*archaic*). — *vt* to strike with or influence by awe or fear. — *adj* **awed** (*öd*) awe-stricken; expressive of awe. — *adj* **awe'less** without awe; fearless; regarded without awe (*Shakesp*). — *n* **awe'lessness**. — *adj* **awe'some** (or *obs* **aw'some**) awed; awe-inspiring; dreadful; amazing, great, impressive (*slang*). — *adv* **awe'somely**. — *n* **awe'someness**. — *adj* **awe'-inspiring** causing a sense of awe; astonishing, breathtaking. —

adj **awe'-stricken** or **awe'struck** struck with awe (*vt* **awe'strike**). [ON *agi*; cf OE *ege* fear; Gr *achos* distress]

aweary *ə-wē'ri*, (*archaic*) *adj* weary. — *adj* **awea'ried** weary. [Pfx *a-* (intensive) and **weary**[1]]

a-weather *ə-wedh'ər*, (*naut*) *adv* towards the weather or windward side (*opp* to *alee*). [**a-**[1]]

a-week *ə-wēk'*, *adv* in the week. [**a-**[1]]

aweel *ə-wēl'*, (*Scot*) *interj* well; well then. [**ah well**]

aweigh *ə-wā'*, (*naut*) *adv* in the process of being weighed, as an anchor just raised from the bottom. [**a-**[1] and **weigh**[1]]

aweto *ä-wā'tō*, or (*Maori*) *ä-fe'tō*, *n* the so-called vegetable caterpillar, the body of the caterpillar filled with a parasitic fungus, used to obtain a pigment: — *pl* **awe'tos**. [Maori *awheto*]

awful *ö'fəl*, *adj* very bad, thoroughly unpleasant; tiresomely great (*colloq*); inspiring awe, causing dread (*archaic*); filled with awe (*obs*). — *adv* (*colloq*) very. — *adv* **aw'fully** very, thoroughly (*colloq*); badly, dreadfully; so as to fill with awe or terror, in an awe-inspiring manner (*archaic*); in an awe-struck manner (*archaic*). — *n* **aw'fulness**. [**awe**, with sfx *-ful*]

awhape *ə-(h)wāp'*, (*Spenser*) *vt* to confound or amaze. [Cf Gothic *af-hwapjan* to choke]

awheel *ə-(h)wēl'* (*obs* **awheels'**), *adv* on wheels, *esp* on a bicycle. [**a-**[1]]

a'where. See **a'**.

awhile *ə-(h)wīl'*, *adv* for some time; for a short time. [OE *āne hwīle* a while (dative); combined as early as 13c]

a-wing *ə-wing'*, *adv* on the wing. [**a-**[1] and **wing**[1]]

awkward *ök'wərd*, *adj* clumsy; ungraceful; embarrassed; difficult to deal with; embarrassing; oblique, inverted, backhanded (*obs*); froward (*obs*); adverse (*Shakesp*). — *adj* **awk'wardish**. — *adv* **awk'wardly**. — *n* **awk'wardness** clumsiness; embarrassing or inharmonious quality or condition. [Prob ON *afug* turned the wrong way, and sfx *-ward*]

awl *öl*, *n* a pointed instrument for boring small holes. — **awl'bird** (*dialect*) the green woodpecker; the avocet. [OE *æl*; ON *alr*, Ger *Ahle*]

awmous *ö'məs*, (*Scot*) *n* alms. [ON *almusa*; cf OE *ælmysse* alms]

awmrie, awmry. See **ambry**.

awn *ön*, *n* the beard of barley, or similar bristly growth or structure from a glume, etc. — *adj* **awned**. — *n* **awn'er** a machine for removing the awns from grain. — *adj* **awn'less**. — *adj* **awn'y**. [ON *ögn* or a lost OE cognate; Ger *Ahne*]

awning *ön'ing*, *n* a covering (*esp* of canvas) to shelter eg a window, door or patio from the sun or weather. — *vt* **awn** to shelter with an awning. [Origin unknown; Fr *auvent* window-shade, may be connected]

awny. See **awn**.

awoke *ə-wōk'*, *pa t* of **awake**.

AWOL *ā'wol*, (*military*) *abbrev*: absent (or absence) without official leave.

awork *ə-wûrk'*, (*archaic*) *adv* at work. [**a-**[1]]

awrack *ə-rak'*, (*obs*) *adv* in a state of wreck. [**a-**[1], and **wrack**[1,2]]

AWRE *abbrev*: Atomic Weapons Research Establishment.

awrong *ə-rong'*, (*obs*) *adv* wrongly. [**a-**[1]]

awry *ə-rī'*, *adj* twisted to one side; distorted, crooked; wrong, amiss. — *adv* askew; unevenly; perversely; erroneously. — **look awry** to look askance at anything; **walk awry** (*archaic*) to go wrong. [**a-**[1]]

AWU *ā'wōō*, *abbrev*: atomic weight unit.

ax. *abbrev*: axiom.

axe or (*NAm*) **ax** *aks*, *n* a tool for hewing or chopping, having its edge and handle in the same plane; a pointed stone-dressing hammer (*building*); the ruthless cutting down of expenditure (*fig*); dismissal from one's job (with *the*; *colloq*); a musical instrument, eg (*jazz*) a saxophone or (*esp rock music*) a guitar (*slang*): — *pl* **ax'es**. — *vt* to hew or strike with an axe; to dismiss as superfluous (*colloq*); to cut down, reduce (*fig*); to dispense with (*fig*). — **axe'-breaker** (*Austr*) any of several kinds of hard-wooded tree; **axe'-head**; **axe'man** (*US usu* **ax'man**) a man who carries or uses an axe; a man who plays a guitar or (*esp jazz*) other musical instrument (*slang*); **axe'-stone** a kind of jade used for making axes. — **axe to grind** a personal reason for getting involved. [OE *æx*; cf Gr *axīnē*]

axel *aks'l*, (*figure skating*) *n* a jump from one skate to the other, incorporating one and a half or (**double axel**) two and a half turns in the air. [*Axel* Paulsen (1855–1938), a Norwegian skater]

axerophthol *aks-ər-of'thol*, *n* vitamin A, a pale yellow crystalline substance, deficiency of which causes xerophthalmia. [**a-**[2] and *xerophthalmia*]

axes. See under **axe** and **axis**[1].

axial, axile. See under **axis**[1].

axilla *ak-sil'ə*, *n* the armpit (*anatom*); the axil (*bot*): — *pl* **axill'ae** (*-ē*). — *n* **ax'il** (*bot*) the upper angle between leaf and stem or branch and trunk. — *adj* **ax'illar** or **ax'illary**. [L *āxilla* the armpit]

axinite *aks'in-īt*, *n* a brilliant brown mineral with axe-shaped crystals, containing calcium, aluminium, boron, silicon, etc. — *n* **axin'omancy** (Gr *manteiā* divination) divination from the motions of an axe poised upon a stake, or of an agate placed upon a red-hot axe. [Gr *axīnē* an axe]

axiology *aks-i-ol'ə-ji*, (*philos*) *n* the science of the ultimate nature, reality and significance of values. — *adj* **axiological** (*-ə-loj'i-kl*). — *n* **axiologist** (*-ol'ə-jist*). [Gr *axia* worth, value, from *axios* worthy, and **-logy**]

axiom *aks'i-əm*, *n* a self-evident truth; a universally received principle; an assumption made for the purpose of argument. — *adj* **axiomat'ic** or **axiomat'ical**. — *adv* **axiomat'ically**. — *n sing* **axiomat'ics** the study of axioms and axiom systems. [Gr. *axiōma*, *-atos*, from *axioein* to think worthy, to take for granted, from *axios* worthy]

axioma medium *ak-si-ōm'a mē'di-əm* or *me'di-ōōm*, (*L*) *n* a generalization from experience.

axis[1] *ak'sis*, *n* a line about which a body rotates, or about which a figure is conceived to revolve; a straight line about which the parts of a figure, body or system are symmetrically or systematically arranged; a fixed line adopted for reference in co-ordinate geometry, curve-plotting, crystallography, etc; an axle (*obs*); the second vertebra of the neck in higher vertebrates (*zool*); the main stem or root, or a branch in relation to its own branches and appendages (*bot*); an alliance of powers, as if forming together an axis of rotation, *esp* the political alliance of Germany and Italy (1936): — *pl* **axes** (*ak'sēz*). — *adj* **ax'ial** relating to, or of the nature of, an axis. — *n* **axial'ity**. — *adv* **ax'ially**. — *adj* **ax'ile** (*ak'sīl*; *bot*) coinciding with an axis. — *n* **ax'oid** a curve generated by the revolution of a point round an advancing axis. — **axis cylinder** (*anatom*) the excitable core of a medullated nerve-fibre. — **axis of incidence** the line passing through the point of incidence of a ray perpendicularly to the refracting surface; **axis of refraction** the continuation of the same line through the refracting medium; **axis of the equator** the polar diameter of the earth which is also the axis of rotation. [L *axis* an axle; cf Gr *axōn*, Sans *aksa*, OE *eax*]

axis[2] *ak'sis*, *n* a white-spotted deer of India: — *pl* **ax'ises**. [L *axis*, Pliny's name for an Indian animal]

axle *aks'l*, *n* the pin or rod in the nave of a wheel on or by means of which the wheel turns; a rounded spindle end of an axle-tree; a pivot or support of any kind (*fig*); an axis (*obs*). — **ax'le-box** the box (eg on a railway carriage) in which the axle end turns; **ax'le-guard** a pedestal (qv) or pillow-block; **ax'le-tree** a crossbar or shaft fixed across the underside of a cart or similar vehicle, on each rounded end of which a wheel rotates; an axle (*obs*). [More prob ON *öxull* than a dimin from OE *eax*]

Axminster *aks'min-stər*, *n* a variety of cut-pile carpet, the tufts of pile each being inserted separately into the backing during its weaving. — Also *adj*. [*Axminster* in Devon, where it originated]

axoid. See under **axis**[1].

axolotl *aks'ə-lot-l*, *n* a type of Mexican salamander (genus *Ambystoma*) commonly retaining its larval character throughout life, though capable of breeding. [Aztec]

axon *aks'on*, (*anatom* and *zool*) *n* an extension of a nerve cell or neuron which in most cases transmits impulses away from the cell. — *n* **ax'oplasm** the cytoplasm of an axon. [New L, from Gr *axōn* axis]

axonometric *aks-ən-ō-met'rik*, *adj* of an architectural or other projection in which a drawing of a three-dimensional object has all lines to exact scale, with all parallel lines remaining parallel, so that it appears distorted. [Gr *axōn* (see **axon**), *-o-* and **-metric** (see **-meter**)]

ay[1] *ā*, *interj* ah, oh; alas, *esp* in *ay me*. [ME *ey*, *ei*, perh from Fr *ahi*, *aï*; cf Sp *ay de mí*]

ay[2]. See **aye**[2].

ay[3]. See **aye**[1].

ayah *ī'ə*, *n* an Indian or S African waiting-maid or nursemaid. — Also **aia**. [Hind *āyā*; from Port *aia* nurse]

ayahuasco *a-yə-(h)was'kō*, *n* a S American vine of the family Malpighiaceae; a drink made from the roots of the vine, having hallucinatory effects: — *pl* **ayahuas'cos**. [Am Sp *ayahuasca*, from Quechua *ayawáskha*]

ayatollah *a-yə-tol'ə*, or *-tō'*, *n* (sometimes with *cap*) a Muslim religious leader of the Shiah sect; (loosely) an ideological leader or policy maker. [Pers, from Ar, sign of God, from *āyat* sign, and *allāh* God]

aye[1] or **ay** *ā*, (now *Northern* or *archaic*) *adv* ever; always; for ever. — **for aye** or **for ever and aye** for ever, to all eternity. — *combining form* denoting ever, as in Shakespeare's **aye'-remaining**, etc. [ON *ei* ever; OE *ā*; connected with **age** and **ever**]

aye[2] or **ay** *ī*, *adv* yea; yes; indeed. — *n* (in parliamentary use and generally **aye**) a vote in the affirmative; a person who votes in the affirmative. — *interj* (*naut*; *usu* **aye aye**) expressing affirmation, agreement, compliance with an order. — **the ayes have it** (in parliament) affirmative votes are in the majority. [Perh a dialect form of **aye**[1]; perh a variant of **yea**]

aye-aye *ī'-ī*, *n* an aberrant squirrel-like nocturnal lemur of Madagascar, with very long thin fingers. [Malagasy *aiay*]

ayelp *ə-yelp'*, *adv* in a state of yelping. [**a-**[1]]

ayenbite *ä-yen'bīt*, (*obs*) *n* remorse, as in the book-title *Ayenbite of Inwyt* (remorse of conscience). [ME *ayen* again, and **bite**]

aygre *ā'gər*, (*Shakesp*). Same as **eager**[1].

Aylesbury *ālz'bər-i*, *n* a breed of ducks much valued as food. — Also *adj*. [A market town in Bucks]

Aymara *ī-mə-rä'*, *n* an Indian people of S America; a member of the Aymara people; their language (of the Andean-Equatorial family), now confined to Bolivia, Peru and parts of northern Chile: — *pl* **Aymaras'** or (collectively) **Aymara'**. — *adj* and *n* **Aymaran'**. [Sp *aimará*]

ayont *ə-yont'*, (*Northern*) *adv* and *prep* beyond. [Pfx *a-*, and **yond**]

ayre *ār*, *n* an old spelling of **air**, *esp* as a tune or song, in particular an Elizabethan or Jacobean song for solo voice.

ayrie. Same as **eyrie**.

Ayrshire *ār'shər*, *n* a breed of reddish-brown and white dairy cattle. — Also *adj*. [The former Scottish county, where they originated]

ayu *ä'ū*, *ī'(y)o͞o* or **ai** *ī*, *n* a small edible Japanese fish (*Plecoglossus altevis*). — Also called **sweet'fish**. [Jap]

ayuntamiento *a-yo͞on-ta-mē-än'tō*, (*Sp*) *n* a municipal council: — *pl* **ayuntamien'tos**.

Ayurveda *ä-yo͞or-vā'də*, *n* the body of classical Indian medical teaching. — *adj* (also with *cap*) **ayurve'dic**. [Sans, knowledge of long life]

ayword *ā'wûrd*, (*Shakesp*) *n* a byword, proverbial reproach. [Origin obscure]

AZ *abbrev*: Arizona (US state).

azalea *a-zā'li-ə*, *n* a plant of the group of deciduous shrubs, *Azalea*, (formerly a separate genus, now a subgenus of Rhododendron with five stamens and annual leaves) popular for their many showy flowers. [Gr *azaleos* dry; reason for name uncertain]

azan *ä-zän'*, *n* the Muslim call to public prayer made five times a day by a muezzin. [Ar *'adhan* invitation]

Azania *a-zā'ni-ə* or *-zä'ni-ə*, *n* a name given by some Black activists to S Africa. — *n* and *adj* **Aza'nian**.

Azapo *a-za'pō*, *abbrev*: Azanian People's Organization.

azathioprine *az-ə-thī'ə-prēn*, *n* a synthetic drug used in transplant surgery to suppress the body's immune system. [**azo-**, **thio-** and **purin**]

azeotrope *ə-zē'ə-trōp*, (*chem*) *n* any liquid mixture which distils without a change in the proportion(s) of its components at a boiling-point which *usu* differs from that of any component. — *adj* **azeotrop'ic** (*-trop'*). [Gr *a-* (privative), *zeein* to boil, and *tropos* a turn]

Azerbaijani *a-zər-bī-jä'ni* or *-zhä'ni*, *n* a native or inhabitant of *Azerbaijan*; the Turkic language of Azerbaijan; a speaker of Azerbaijani in the neighbouring state of Iran: — *pl* **Azerbaija'ni** or **Azerbaija'nis**. — *n* **Azer'i** an Azerbaijani (short form).

azide *ā'zīd*, or *a'*, (*chem*) *n* a salt or an ester derived from hydrazoic acid. — *n* **azidothy'midine** AZT (qv), a derivative of thymidine. [**az(o)-** and chem sfx *-ide*]

Azilian *a-zil'i-ən*, (*archaeol*) *adj* belonging to a period of transition between Palaeolithic and Neolithic. [Mas d'*Azil*, Ariège, where objects of this culture have been found in a cave]

azimuth *az'im-əth*, (*astron*, *surveying*, etc) *n* the arc of the horizon between the meridian of a place and a vertical circle passing through any celestial body. — *adj* **az'imuthal** (or *-mūdh'* or *-mūth'*) of or pertaining to the azimuth. [Ar *as-sumūt*, from *as* = *al* the, and *sumūt*, pl of *samt* direction. See **zenith**]

azine *ā'zēn* or *-zin*, (*chem*) *n* any six-membered organic compound containing one or more nitrogen atoms. [**azo-**]

azione *a-tsi-ō'nā* or **azione sacra** (*sak'ra*) (*music*) *n* a composition, like an oratorio in form, but performed as a drama. [Ital]

azo- *āz-ō-* or *az-ō*, also **az-** *combining form* denoting nitrogen. — *n* **azo-com'pound** a compound in which two nitrogen atoms are each attached to (*usu*) a carbon atom, eg **azoben'zene** $C_6H_5N{:}NC_6H_5$. — *n* **azo dye** a dye (*usu* yellow, red or brown) containing an azo-compound. [**azote**]

Azobacter. See under **azote**.

azoic *a-zō'ik*, *adj* without life; before the existence of animal life; (of rocks, etc) formed when there was no animal life on the Earth, containing no organic traces. [Gr *a-* privative and *zōē* life]

azolla *a-zol'ə*, *n* a tiny water fern of the genus *Azolla* native to tropical or subtropical areas. [New L, appar formed from Gr *azein* to dry, and *ollynai* to destroy]

azonal *a-zōn'əl*, or *ā-*, *adj* not arranged in zones or regions. — *adj* **azonic** (*a-zon'ik*) not limited to a zone, not local. [Gr *a-* (privative) and *zōnē* a belt]

azote *a-zōt'*, *n* an old name for nitrogen, so called because it does not sustain animal life. — *adj* **azot'ic** (*a-zot'ik*) nitric. — *vt* **az'otize** or **-ise** to combine with nitrogen. — *adj* **azō'tous** nitrous. — *n* **Azōtobac'ter** a genus of nitrogen-fixing bacteria. — *n* **azotur'ia** an excess of urea or other nitrogenous substances in the urine (*med*); muscle weakness occurring in horses during or after training (*vet*). [Gr *a-* (privative) and *zaein* to live]

azoth *äz'oth*, *n* the alchemist's name for mercury; Paracelsus's universal remedy. [From Ar *az-zāūg*, from *al* the, and *zāūg*, from Pers *zhīwah* quicksilver]

Azrael *az'rā-el*, (*Jewish* and *Muslim mythol*) *n* the angel of death.

AZT *abbrev*: azidothymidine, a drug used in the treatment of AIDS.

Aztec *az'tek*, *n* one of a people dominant in Mexico before the Spanish conquest; the Aztec language,

Nahuatl. — Also *adj.* — **Aztec two-step** (*slang*) Montezuma's revenge, diarrhoea.

azulejo *a-thōō-lā'hhō*, (*Sp*) *n* a painted and glazed pottery tile: — *pl* **azule'jos**.

azure *azh'ər*, *āzh'ər* or *ā'zhūr*, *adj* of a faint blue; sky-coloured; blue (represented in engraving, etc by horizontal lines) (*heraldry*). — *n* a delicate blue colour; the sky. — *adj* **azurē'an** or **az'urine** (*-īn*) azure. — *n* **az'urine** a blue-black aniline dye; a freshwater fish, the blue roach. — *n* **az'urite** blue basic carbonate of copper, chessylite. — *adj* **az'urn** (*Milton*) azure. — *adj* **az'ury** bluish. [OFr *azur*, from LL *azura*, from Ar *al* the, and *lazward*, Pers *lājward* lapis lazuli, blue colour]

azygous *az'i-gəs*, *adj* not yoked or joined with another (*biol*); unpaired (*anatom*). — *n* **az'ygos** (*biol*) an unpaired structure. — *n* **azygy** (*az'i-ji*). [Gr *azygos*, from *a-* (privative) and *zygon* a yoke]

azymous *az'i-məs*, *adj* unfermented; unleavened. — *n* **az'ym** (*-im*), or more usually **az'yme** (*-īm* or *-im*) unleavened bread. — *n* (also with *cap*) **az'ymite** a member of any church using unleavened bread in the Eucharist. [Gr *azȳmos*, from *a-* (privative) and *zȳmē* leaven]

B

B or **b** *bē*, *n* the second letter in the modern English alphabet, called by the Phoenicians *beth*, the house, corresponding to the Greek *β*, beta; the second in a series; something of a second class or order (such as a road of secondary importance), or of a class arbitrarily designated B; see **blood-group**; a designation indicating lesser importance, secondary billing, etc such as the **B'-side** of a record, a **B'-movie**, or **B'-Special** a member of an auxiliary, part-time, mainly Protestant police force operating in Northern Ireland until 1970; the seventh note of the diatonic scale of C major (H in German notation, B being used for B flat) (*music*); the subsidiary series of paper sizes, ranging from B0 (1000 × 1414 mm) to B10 (31 × 44mm); in hexadecimal numbering, 11; as a medieval Roman numeral B = 300, B̄ = 3000. — **B** or **B flat** a 19c euphemism for domestic bedbug; **B lymphocyte** a type of lymphocyte or cell, originating (in mammals) in the bone marrow, which manufactures antibody in response to stimulation by an antigen; in old music **B quadratum**, **quadrate B** or **square B** is B natural, **B rotundum**, **round B** is B flat. — **not know a B from a battledore**, **broomstick** or **bull's foot** (*old slang*) to be very ignorant; **the three B's** Bach, Beethoven and Brahms.

B or **B.** *abbrev*: Bachelor; Baron; bass (*music*); Belgium (IVR); bishop (*chess*); Britain; British.

B *symbol*: baryon number (*phys*); black (on lead pencils to indicate softness); boron (*chem*).

B *symbol*: magnetic flux density.

B- (*aeronautics*) *pfx* used to designate a bomber plane.

b or **b.** *abbrev*: barrel(s); billion; book; born; bowled (*cricket*).

b *abbrev*: breadth.

BA *abbrev*: Bachelor of Arts; Booksellers' Association (of Great Britain and Ireland); British Academy, a body promoting literary and social studies; British Airways.

Ba (*chem*) *symbol*: barium.

ba *bä*, *n* in ancient Egyptian religion, the soul, represented as a bird with a human head. [Egyp]

ba' *bö*, *n* Scots form of **ball**[1,2]. — *n* **ba'ing** and **ba'spiel** see under **ball**[1].

BAA *abbrev*: British Airports Authority.

baa *bä*, *n* the cry of a sheep. — *vi* to bleat. — *n* **baa'ing**. [Imit]

Baal *bā'əl*, *n* a god of the Phoenicians, *orig* probably a fusion of many local gods; a false god generally: — *pl* **Bā'alim**. — *n* **Bā'alism**. — *n* **Bā'alite**. [Heb]

BAAS *abbrev*: British Academy for the Advancement of Science.

baas *bäs*, (*SAfr*) *n* master, overseer, sir (*esp* as used by a black or coloured S African addressing a white). — *n* **baas'skap** the condition in which one section of the population is treated as a master race; the theory used to justify this. [Afrik, from Du]

Baathist or **Ba'athist** *bä'thist*, *n* a member of the socialist or reformist party of various Arab countries, *esp* Syria and Iraq. — Also *adj*. — *n* **Baa'thism** or **Ba'a'thism**. [Ar *baath* renaissance]

baba *bä'bä*, *n* a small cake, leavened with yeast, with or without fruit, soaked in a rum syrup. — Also **rum baba** or **baba au rhum** (*ō rom*). [Fr, from Pol *baba* old woman]

babaco *bə-bak'ō*, *n* a subtropical five-sided fruit related to papaya, *orig* from Ecuador.

babacoote *bab'ə-kōōt*, *n* a large lemur, the indri or a closely related species. [Malagasy *babakoto*]

babassu *bab-ə-sōō'*, *n* a Brazilian palm (Attalea) or its oil-yielding nut. [Prob Tupí]

Babbitt *bab'it*, *n* a conventional middle-class businessman (or other person) who esteems success and has no use for art or intellectual pursuits. — *n* **Babb'ittry**, **Babb'itry** or **Babb'ittism**. [Eponymous hero of novel (1922) by Sinclair Lewis]

babbitt *bab'it*, *vt* to fit with **Babbitt**, **Babbit** or **Babbitt's metal**, a soft anti-friction alloy (tin, with copper antimony, and *usu* lead). [Isaac *Babbitt* (1799–1862), the Massachusetts inventor]

babble *bab'l*, *vi* to speak like a baby; to make a continuous murmuring sound like a brook, etc; to talk incoherently or irrelevantly; to talk incessantly; to divulge secrets. — *vt* to say in a confused, uncontrolled or unthinking way; to divulge by foolish talk. — *n* idle senseless talk; disturbance caused by interference from other conversations (*telephony*); confused murmuring, as of a stream. — *adj* **babb'lative**. — *n* **babb'lement**. — *n* **babb'ler** someone who babbles; a cook (*Austr rhyming slang*; also **babbling brook**); any of a large group of noisy, chattering, thrush-like birds (also **babbling thrush**). — *n* and *adj* **babb'ling**. — *adj* **babb'ly**. [Prob imit, from the repeated syllable *ba*; cf Du *babbelen*, Ger *pappelen*, Fr *babiller*, perh influenced by *Babel*]

babe *bāb*, *n* a form of **baby**.

Babee. See **Babi**.

Babel *bā'bl*, *n* (also without *cap*) a confused sound of voices; (also without *cap*) a scene of confusion; a foolishly conceived lofty structure. — *n* **bā'beldom**. — *adj* **bā'belish** or **bab'elesque**. — *n* **bā'belism**. [Heb *Bābel*, prob Assyr *bāb-ili*, gate of God, associated in Gen 11.9 with confusion]

babesiasis *bab-i-zī-'ə-sis* or **babesiosis** *ba-bē-zē-ō'sis*, *n* redwater, a cattle infection caused by the parasite **Babesia** (*ba-bē'zh(y)ə*). [Victor *Babes* (died 1926), Romanian bacteriologist]

Babi or **Babee** *bä'bē*, *n* a member of an eclectic Persian sect, followers of *Bab*-ed-Din 'the Gate of Righteousness' (Mirza Ali Mohammed, 1819/20–50), who claimed to be a prophet bringing a new revelation from God. — Also **Ba'bist**. — *n* **Ba'bism**, **Ba'biism** or **Ba'beeism**.

babiche *ba-bēsh'*, *n* thongs or laces made of rawhide. [Fr-Can, from Algonquian]

babingtonite *bab'ing-tən-īt*, *n* a pyroxene, ferrous silicate with admixtures, sometimes worked as an iron ore. [After William *Babington* (1756–1833), mineralogist]

Babinski effect or **reflex** *bə-bin'ski i-fekt'* or *rē'fleks*, (*physiol*) *n* a reflex curling upwards of the toes when the side of the foot is stroked, normal in babies but abnormal in others. [After Joseph *Babinski* (1857–1932), the French neurologist]

babiroussa, **babirusa** or **babirussa** *bä-bi-rōō'sə*, *n* a wild hog found *esp* in Sulawesi, Indonesia, with great upturned tusks in the male. [Malay *bābi* hog, and *rūsa* deer]

Babism. See **Babi**.

bablah *bab'lə* or **babul** *bä'bōōl* or *-bōōl'*, *n* a species of acacia (*A. arabica*) from which gum arabic is obtained; the pods of that and other species, used for tanning. [Hind and Pers *babūl*]

baboo. See **babu**.

baboon *bə-bōōn'*, *n* large monkey of various species, with long muzzle, dog-like tusks, large lips, a tail, and buttock-callosities; a clumsy, uncouth person of low intelligence. — *n* **baboon'ery**. — *adj* **baboon'ish**. [ME *babewyn* grotesque figure, baboon, from OFr *babuin*, poss from *baboue* grimace]

babouche, **babuche** or **baboosh** *bə-bōōsh'*, *n* an Oriental heelless slipper. [Fr, from Ar *bābūsh*, from Pers *pā* foot, and *pūsh* covering]

babu or **baboo** *bä'bōō*, *n* a title for Hindus in some parts of India corresponding to Mr; an Indian clerk; an Indian with a superficial English education (*esp hist*). — Also *adj*. — *n* **ba'budom**. — *n* **ba'buism**. [Hindi *bābū*]

babuche. See **babouche**.

babul. See **bablah**.

babushka *bə-bōōsh'kə*, *n* a triangular headscarf tied under the chin; a grandmother, granny, elderly woman. [Russ *bábushka* grandmother, dimin of *baba* old woman]

baby *bā'bi*, *n* an infant, young child; an unborn child; the youngest or smallest member of a family or group; a young animal; a babyish person; a thing small of its kind, as varieties of grand piano, car, etc; a small incandescent spotlight used in film and television production (*image technol*); a girl, girlfriend, often as an affectionate term of address (*colloq*); an inexperienced person; one's pet project, invention, machine, etc; one's own responsibility; a doll (*obs*); the reflection of oneself in the pupil of another's eye (*obs*). — *vt* to treat like a baby; to pamper. — Also *adj*. — *n* **ba'byhood**. — *adj* **ba'byish**. — **ba'by-batterer** a person who indulges in **ba'by-battering** in instances of the **battered baby syndrome** (qv under **batter**); **baby beef** beef from calves which are fattened for slaughter on a diet of roughage and high protein concentrates; **baby bond** (*colloq*) a special savings scheme for children; **baby bonus** (*Can colloq*) family allowance; **baby boom** (*colloq*) a sudden sharp increase in the birth-rate; **baby boomer** a person born during a baby boom, *esp* that which followed World War II; **ba'by-bouncer** (*UK*) or **ba'by-jumper** (*US*) a harness or seat suspended from springs, elastic straps, etc in which a young baby can amuse itself; **Baby Buggy®** a light, collapsible push-chair for a baby or toddler; **baby carriage** (*NAm*) a baby's pram; **baby doll** a doll in the form of a baby; a woman with an innocent childlike appearance and personality; **baby-doll pyjamas** women's pyjamas with a loose top and very short bottoms with elasticated legs; **baby face** a young-looking face, *esp* one plump and smooth like a baby's; someone with such a face; **ba'by-farming** (*obs*) looking after infants for pay; **ba'byfood** any of various foods specially prepared, eg by straining, blending, etc, for babies; **baby grand** a small grand piano, about 5 feet in length; **Ba'bygro®** an all-in-one stretch-fabric suit for a baby: — *pl* **Ba'bygros**; **baby house** a doll's-house; **ba'by-minder** a person who takes in young children to look after for pay; **ba'by-ribbon** a very narrow ribbon. — *vi* and (*esp NAm*) *vt* **ba'by-sit** to act as baby-sitter (to). — **ba'by-sitter** a person who looks after a baby, child or children to relieve the usual carer; **ba'by-sitting**; **ba'by-snatcher** a person marrying or having as a lover someone who is much younger (*usu derog*; also **cradle-snatcher**); a person who steals a baby, eg from its pram (*colloq*); **ba'by-snatching**; **ba'by-talk** the speech of babies learning to talk, or an adult's imitation of it; **ba'by-tooth** a milk tooth; **ba'by-walker** a wheeled frame with a canvas, etc seat for supporting a baby learning to walk. — **be left holding the baby** to be left in the lurch with an irksome responsibility; **throw out the baby with the bathwater** to get rid of the essential along with the superfluous. [Prob imit. See **babble**]

Babylon *bab'i-lon*, *n* a place of sorrowful exile; a place, etc of luxury and decadence, used (*derog*) formerly by Protestants in reference to the Roman Catholic Church, more recently by Rastafarians of western culture, or generally by one group of another group which they consider to be corrupt. — *adj* **Babylō'nian** of Babylon; huge, gigantic; Romish, popish (*obs*; from the identification with Rome of the scarlet woman of Rev 17); Babel-like, confused in language; luxurious, decadent. — *n* an inhabitant of Babylon; the ancient language of Babylonia, Akkadian. — *adj* **Babylon'ish**. — **Babylonian** or **Babylonish captivity** the exile of the Jews deported to Babylon in 597 and 586 BC, lasting till *c*.538; the exile of the popes at Avignon, 1309–77. [*Babylon*, city of ancient Mesopotamia]

BAC *abbrev*: British Aircraft Corporation.

bacca *bak'ə*, (*bot*) *n* a berry. — *adj* **bacc'ate** having berries; berry-like; pulpy. — *adj* **bacciferous** (*bak-sif'ər-əs*) bearing berries. — *adj* **bac'ciform** of the shape of a berry. — *adj* **bacciv'orous** living on berries. [L *bacca* a berry]

baccalaureate *bak-ə-lö'ri-āt*, *n* the university degree of bachelor, or a diploma of lesser status awarded by a college, etc. — *adj* **baccalau'rean**. [LL *baccalaureus*, altered from *baccalārius*. See **bachelor**]

baccarat or **baccara** *bak'ə-rä*, *n* a French card game played by betters and a banker; a type of crystal made at *Baccarat*, France. [Fr]

baccare. See **backare**.

baccate. See **bacca**.

Bacchus *bak'əs*, *n* the (chiefly Roman) god of wine. — *n* **Bacchae** (*bak'ē*) priestesses or female followers of Bacchus. — *n* **bacchanal** (*bak'ə-nəl*) a worshipper, priest or priestess of Bacchus; a drunken reveller; a dance, song or revel in honour of Bacchus. — *adj* relating to drinking or drunken revels. — *n pl* **bacchanā'lia** or **bacch'anals** orgiastic feasts in honour of Bacchus; drunken revels. — *n* **bacchanalian** (*-nā'li-ən*) a drunken reveller. — *adj* bacchanal. — *n* **bacchanā'lianism**. — *n* and *adj* **bacchant** (*bak'ant*) a priest, priestess or votary of Bacchus; a reveller; a drunkard: — *pl* **bacch'ants** or **bacchant'es**. — *n* **bacchante** (*bə-kant'* or *bak'ant*, or after Italian *baccante*, *ba-kant'i*) a priestess of Bacchus; a female bacchanal. — *adj* **bacchiac** (*bak-ī'ək*) relating to the bacchius. — *adj* **Bacch'ian** (*bak'i-ən*) or **Bacchic** (*bak'ik*) relating to Bacchus; (often without *cap*) jovial; (often without *cap*) drunken. — *n* **bacchī'us** (*Gr* and *L prosody*) a foot of two long syllables preceded by one short: — *pl* **bacchī'ī**. [L *Bacchus*, Gr *Bakchos*]

bacciferous, etc. See **bacca**.

baccy *bak'i*, or **bacco** *-ō*, *colloq* short forms of **tobacco**.

bach *bähh*, (*Welsh*) *n* affectionate term of address (chiefly used after a person's name).

Bach. or **bach**. *abbrev*: Bachelor or bachelor.

bacharach *bak'ər-ak* or *bähh'ə-rähh*, *n* a wine from *Bacharach*, on the Rhine.

bachelor *bach'əl-ər*, *n* an unmarried man; one who has taken his or her first degree at a university; a young knight who follows the banner of another, as too young to display his own (*hist*); a young unmated bull-seal or other male animal. — *n* **bach** or **batch** (*Austr* or *NZ colloq*) a bachelor. — *vi* to live as a bachelor; to do for oneself. — Also *vt* with *it*. — *n* **bach'elordom** or **bach'elorhood**. — *n* **bach'elorism** habit or condition of a bachelor. — *n* **bach'elorship** the degree of bachelor. — **bachelor flat** or (*slang*) **pad** a flat or other residence for an unmarried person; **bach'elor-girl** a young unmarried woman who supports herself; **bachelor's-butt'ons** a double-flowered yellow or white buttercup; also applied to double feverfew, species of Centaurea, and many other plants; **bachelor's wife** an ideal woman with none of the shortcomings of married men's wives. — **Bachelor of Arts** (*abbrev* **BA**) or **Bachelor of Science** (*abbrev* **BSc**) a university or college degree conferred upon a student who has successfully completed an undergraduate course in the arts/humanities or the sciences/social sciences respectively; a man or woman who has received such a degree. — **knight-bachelor** see **knight**. [OFr *bacheler*, from LL *baccalārius*; of doubtful origin]

Bach trumpet *bähh trum'pit*, *n* a small modern trumpet for playing the complex high-pitched parts in Bach and other baroque music. [After Johann Sebastian *Bach*, German composer (1685–1750)]

bacillus *bə-sil'əs*, *n* (with *cap*) a genus of aerobic rod-shaped bacteria (family Bacillaceae); a member of the genus; (loosely) any rod-shaped bacterium; (popularly) any disease-causing bacterium: — *pl* **bacill'ī**. — *n pl* **Bacillā'ceae** a family (order Eubacteriales) of endospore-producing bacteria. — *n* **bacillaemia** or (*US*) **bacillemia** (*-ē'mi-ə*; *med*) the presence of bacilli in the blood. — *adj* **bacill'ar** or **bacill'ary** (also *bas'*) of the shape or nature of a bacillus, rodlike. — *n* **bacill'icide** something which destroys bacilli. — *adj* **bacill'iform**. [LL *bacillus*, dimin of *baculus* a rod]

bacitracin *bas-i-trā'sin*, *n* an antibiotic obtained from a certain bacterium and used against Gram-positive bacteria, *esp* in skin infections. [LL *bacillus*, and Margaret *Tracy*, an American child in whom the substance was found]

back[1] *bak*, *n* the rear part of the body in man (*specif* between the neck and buttocks), and the upper part in other creatures; the rear part, the side opposite to the front, or the side remote from that *usu* presented or seen; the underside of a leaf or of a violin; part of the upper surface of the tongue opposite the soft palate; the convex side of a book, opposite to the opening of the leaves; the thick edge of a knife, etc; the upright rear part of a chair, bench, etc; something added to the rear or far side; the surface of the sea, or of a river; the keel and keelson of a ship; one of the players behind the forwards, eg the *full back* (who guards the goal), *halfbacks* and *three-quarter backs* (*football*, etc); the side of a sloping vein nearest the surface (*mining*); the earth between one level and the one above (*mining*). — In *pl* with *cap* **the Backs** the grounds of Cambridge colleges backing on to the river Cam. — *adj* rearward, situated at or towards the back of; (of a road) not main, not direct; remote; reversed; made by raising the back of the tongue (*phonetics*); belonging to the past. — *adv* to or towards the back; to or towards the place from which one came; to a former state or condition; behind; behind in time; in return, reply or retaliation; in check; again; ago. — *vt* to help or support; to support (a horse, an opinion, etc) by placing a wager or bet; to countersign or endorse; to provide a back or backing for; to lie at the back of; to form the back of; to cause to move backward or in the opposite direction; to write or print at the back of (a parliamentary bill, etc); to mount or ride (now *rare*). — *vi* to move or go back or backwards; (with *on* or *on to*) to have the back facing; (of the wind) to change counter-clockwise. — *adj* **backed** having a back. — *n* **back'er**. — *n* **back'ing** support at the back; support for an enterprise; musical accompaniment, *esp* of a popular song; the action of putting or going back; a body of helpers; anything used to form a back or line the back; counter-clockwise change of wind. — *adj* **back'most** farthest to the back. — *adj* and *adv* **backward** (*bak'wərd*) towards the back; on the back; towards the past; from a better to a worse state; in a direction opposite to the normal; (of a fielder in cricket) standing slightly behind the usual for that position, eg *backward point*. — *adj* keeping back; shy, bashful; unwilling; retarded, slow in development; dull or stupid (*colloq*); late. — *n* the past portion of time (*poetic*). — *n* **backwardā'tion** (*stock exchange*) the percentage paid by a seller of stock for keeping back its delivery till the following account; the postponement of delivery of the stock. — *adv* **back'wardly**. — *n* **back'wardness**. — *adv* **back'wards** backward. — **back'-ache** pain in the back; **back'band** a rope, strap or chain passing over a horse's back and holding up the shafts of a vehicle (also **back'-chain** and **back'-rope**); **back'beat** (*music*, *orig jazz*) one of the normally unstressed beats in a bar, used as a secondary syncopated beat. — *adj* **back'-bench** of or sitting on the **back benches**, the seats in parliament occupied by members who do not hold office. — **back'bench'er**. — *vt* **back'bite** to speak ill of or unkindly of (someone) in their absence (also *vi*). — **back'biter**; **back'biting** (also *adj*). — *adj* **back'-block** of the back-blocks. — **back'-blocker**. — *n pl* **back'-blocks** (*Austr* and *NZ*) remote, sparsely populated country; the back part of a station, far from water. — **back'-board** a board at the back of a cart, boat, etc; a board fastened across the back to straighten the body; a board laid under a mattress, to support the back while sleeping; a rigid vertical panel placed above and behind the basket to deflect the ball (*basketball*); **back'bond** a deed attaching a qualification or condition to the terms of a conveyance or other instrument (*Scots law*); **back'bone** the spinal column; a main support or axis; something similar to the spinal column in appearance and function; the keel and keelson; the spine of a book (chiefly *US*); firmness of character. — *adj* **back'boned**. — *adj* **back'boneless**. — **back'breaker** a very heavy job; a hold in which one's opponent is pressed down on his back over one's knee or shoulder (*wrestling*); **back burner** the rear burner on a stove, used *esp* for keeping a pot simmering that needs no immediate attention; (*fig*, *orig US*) low-priority or pending status. — Also *adj*. — *adj* **back'-breaking** exhausting. — *vi* and *vt* **back'-cal'culate** to make a calculation as to an earlier condition, situation, etc (*esp* as to the level of person's intoxication) based on data recorded at a later time. — **back'-calcula'tion**; **back-chain** see **backband**; **back'chat** answering back; impertinence, repartee. — Also *vi*. — **back'-cloth** or **back'drop** the painted cloth or curtain at the back of the stage; the background to any situation, activity, etc. — *vi* and *vt* **back'-comb** to give (the hair) a puffed-out appearance by combing the underlying hairs towards the roots and smoothing the outer hairs over them. — **back'-country** remote, thinly-populated districts. — Also *adj*. — **back'court** (*lawn tennis*) that part of the court lying behind the service-line (also *adj*); in other games, that part of the court nearest the baseline; **back'-crawl** (*swimming*) the crawl stroke, performed on the back. Now *usu* called **back-stroke**; **back'-cross** a cross between a hybrid and a parent; the process or act of back-crossing. — *vt* to cross (a hybrid) with a parent. — *vt* **back-date'** to put an earlier date on; to count as valid retrospectively from a certain date. — **back door** a door in the back part of a building. — *adj* **back'-door** unworthily secret; clandestine. — **back-down** see **back down** below; **back'-draught** a backward current; **backdrop** see **back-cloth**; **back'-end'** the rear end; the later part of a season (*dialect*); the late autumn (*dialect*); **back'fall** an obsolete term for an acciaccatura (*music*); a fall on the back as in wrestling (often *fig*); a lever in the coupler of an organ. — *adj* **back'field** (*football*, etc) of or in the position of a back or the backs. — **back'file** the back numbers of a newspaper, journal, etc; **back'fill** the material used in backfilling. — *vt* and *vi* to refill (eg foundations or an excavation) with earth or other material. — **back'fire** ignition of gas in an internal-combustion engine's cylinder at the wrong time, or inside eg a bunsen-burner instead of at the outlet; a controlled forest or prairie fire started in order to create a bare space, to stop a major fire spreading further (*NAm*). — *vi* (*bak-fīr'*) to have a backfire; to start a backfire (*NAm*); to go wrong (*colloq*). — **back'fitting** (*nuc eng*) making changes to nuclear (and other) plants already designed or built eg to cater for changes in safety criteria; **back foot** (*cricket*) the batsman's foot farthest from the bowler (**off the back foot** (of a stroke) played with the weight on the back foot, defensive in stance; also *adj* **back'-foot**); **back-formā'tion** the making of a word from another that is, wrongly or humorously, taken to be a derivative, as the verb *sidle* from the adverb *sideling* treated as if it were a participle; **back'-friend** a pretended friend (*obs*); a backer, a friend who stands at one's back. — *adj* **back'-ganging** (*Scot*) in arrears. — **back garden** or (*Scot*) **back green** a garden or green at the back of a house; **back'ground** the space behind the principal figures of a picture; that against which anything is, or ought to be, seen (*fig*); upbringing and previous history; environment; an inconspicuous or obscure position, the shadows; ground at the back. — *adj* in the background (*lit* or *fig*); (of music, light, etc) complementary to and unobtrusively accompanying something else such as a film or social activity; **background heating** heating which provides a low level of warmth but requires supplementing for complete comfort; **background processing** (*comput*) processing carried out non-interactively, when work placed in a **background queue** is attended to as computing resources become available; **background radiation** low-level radiation from substances present in the environment; **background tasks** (*comput*) tasks such as printing which a computer can carry out simultaneously with foreground tasks such as data input; **back'hair** the hair at the back of the head; **back'hand** a stroke made with the back of hand turned in the direction of the stroke (*tennis*, etc); the part of the court to the left of a right-handed player, or the right of a left-handed (*tennis*); handwriting with the letters sloping backwards. — Also *adj*. — *adj* **back'-handed** backhand; (of a blow) carried out with the back of the hand; (of a compliment, etc) indirect, dubious, sarcastic, insincere. — **back'-hander** a blow with the back of the hand; a backhand stroke; a bribe (*colloq*); an extra glass of wine out of turn, the bottle being passed back. — *vt* **back'-heel** (*football*) to kick (the ball) backwards with the heel. — Also *n*. — **back'hoe** (also **backhoe loader**) (a tractor equipped with) a shovel at the end of a mechanical arm, for making minor excavations; **back'ing-down** shirking; **backing storage** (*comput*) the storage of data externally from the computer in backing store; **backing store** (*comput*) a large-capacity computer data store supplementary to a computer's main memory; **back'land** a piece of land at the back of an established property, *specif* when viewed or used as an area for building development; back-country; **back lane** a lane to the rear of a building or buildings; **back'lash** reaction or consequence, *esp* if violent; the jarring or recoiling motion of ill-fitting machinery; **back'lift** (*cricket* or *football*, etc) a backward lifting of the bat (or leg) before the stroke is played (or ball is kicked); **back'-light** (*photog*) light falling on a subject from the rear; **back'-lighting**; **back'-lill** (*Scot*) sometimes (*erron*) **-lilt** the left-hand thumb-hole at the back of a bagpipe chanter; **back'list** books previously published which a publisher keeps in print, as opposed to newly published books; **back'-load** a load taken on by a lorry for a return journey. — *vi* to obtain a back-load. — **back'-loading**; **back'log** a reserve or accumulation of business, stock, work, etc that will keep one going for some time (*colloq*); a log at the back of a fire (chiefly *NAm*); **back'lot** (*films*, *TV*) the outdoor area, often next to the studio, used for exterior scenes; **back'marker** a person who starts a race with the least advantageous handicap; a competitor at the back of the field; **back-mutā'tion** (*biol*) see **reversion**; **back'number** a copy or issue of a newspaper or magazine of a previous date; a person or thing out of date, old-fashioned or no longer useful. — *adj* **back'-office** of staff, etc who work in banks, the Civil Service, etc, behind the scenes out of the public view. — **back'pack** a pack carried on the back, a rucksack. — *vi* to carry a pack on the back, *esp* as a hiker. — **back'packer**; **back'packing**; **back passage** a passageway at or towards the rear of a building; the rectum (*colloq*); **back'pay** pay that is overdue; pay for work that was done in the past, often resulting from a back-dated pay increase. — *vi* **back-ped'al** to push the pedals backwards, as in slowing a fixed-wheel bicycle; to hold back; to reverse one's course of action; to retreat from an opponent while still facing him (*boxing*). — **back-ped'alling**; **back'piece** or **back'-plate** a piece or plate of armour for the back; **back pressure** (*eng*) the pressure opposing the motion of the piston of an engine on its exhaust stroke; the exhaust pressure of a turbine; **back'-projection** the projection of film on to the back of a special screen so as to be seen from the other side as a background to action taking place in front of the screen. — *adj* **back'room** (of people) doing important work behind the scenes, *esp* in secret (*colloq*). — **back-rope** see **backband**; **back row** (*Rugby football*) the last line of forwards in a scrum. — *adj* **back'-row**. — **back'saw** a saw stiffened by a thickened back; **back'scatter** (*phys*) the deflection of radiation or particles by scattering through angles greater than 90° with reference to the original direction of travel. — *vt* to scatter in this way. — *vi* **back'scratch**. — **back'scratcher** a long-handled instrument for scratching the back; a person who practises backscratching; **back'scratching** doing favours in return for favours, for the advantage of both parties; servile flattery; **back-seat driver** someone free of responsibility but full of advice; someone controlling from a position from which he or she ought not to control; **back'set** a setting back, reverse; an eddy or counter-current; **back'sey'** (-*sī*; *Scot*) sirloin; **back'shift** a group of workers whose time of working overlaps or comes between the day-shift and the night-shift; the time this group is on duty; **back'side** the back or rear side or part of anything; the rear part of an animal; the buttocks (*colloq*); the premises at the rear of a house (*Scot*); **back'sight** a sight taken back towards a previous fixed point (*surveying*); the sight of a rifle nearer the stock; **back'-slang** slang in which every word is pronounced as if spelt backwards. — *adj* **back'slapping** vigorously and demonstratively cheery. — *n* such an approach, manner or behaviour towards associates. — *vi* **back'slide** to slide or fall back in faith, morals or work, etc. — **back'slider**; **back'sliding**. — *vi* **back'space** (or -*spās'*) to move the carriage of a typewriter one or more spaces back by means of a particular key. — *n* the key used for backspacing (also **back'spacer** or **backspace key**); the act of backspacing. — **back'-spaul** or **-spauld** (*Scot*) the back of the shoulder; the hindleg. — *vt* and *vi* **backspeir'** or **-speer'** (*Scot*) to cross-question. — **back'spin** (*sport*) a rotary movement against the direction of travel of a ball imparted to reduce its momentum on impact. — *adj* and *adv* **backstage'** (*lit* and *fig*) behind the scenes, unobserved by the public. — **back'stairs** servants' or private stairs of a house. — *adj* secret or underhand. — **back'stall** a garrotter's confederate on the look-out behind. — *vi*: — *pr p* only, **backstart'ing** (*Spenser*) starting back. — **back'stays** ropes or stays extending from the topmast-heads to the sides of a ship, and slanting a little backward (*naut*); any stay or support at the back; **back'stitch** (*needlework*) a stitch in which the needle enters behind, and comes out in front of, the end of the previous stitch. — Also *vi* and *vt*. — **back'stop** a screen, wall, etc acting as a barrier in various sports or games, eg shooting, baseball, etc; (the position of) a player, eg in baseball, who stops the ball; something providing additional support, protection, etc; something preventing excessive backward movement; **back straight** (*athletics*) the straight part of the track farthest from the finish; **back street** a street away from the main road in a town or city, *esp* as part of a poorer, less fashionable area; a back lane; **back-street abortion** an abortion performed by an unqualified person operating illicitly; **back'-stroke** a blow or stroke in return; back-crawl (*swimming*), a stroke with alternate backward circular movements of each arm and scissors movements of the legs, performed on the back; formerly a stroke with simultaneous backwards circular movements of both arms, and the breaststroke kick, performed on the back (also called **English back-stroke**); **back'swing** (*sport*) (in a swing of a club, racket, etc) the first stage, in which it is swung back and away from the ball; **back'sword** a sword with a back or with only one edge; a fencing stick with a basket-hilt, a singlestick; **backsword'man**. — *adj* **back-to-back'** with backs facing and *usu* close up against each other; (of houses) built thus (also *n*); following in close sequence (*colloq*). — *vi* **back'track** to go back on one's course. — *n* a return track to the starting point; a retracing of steps. —

back'tracking; **back'-up** a standby, support or reserve; a copy taken of data being worked on, stored on another disk against the possibility of damage to or loss of the working disk (*comput*); the overflow from an obstructed pipe, etc; **back-up file** (*comput*) a copy of a computer file to be used in the event of the original file being lost or corrupted; **back'veld** (*-felt*; *SAfr*) country remote from towns. — *adj* remote, rustic, primitive. — **backvel'der** (*-dər*); **back'wash** a receding wave; a backward current; a reaction, repercussion or aftermath. — *vt* to affect with backwash; to clean the oil from (wool) after combing. — **back'water** a pool or belt of water connected with a river but not in the line of its present course or current; a place unaffected by the movements of the day; water held back by a dam; water thrown back by the turning of a water-wheel; a backward current of water; swell of the sea caused by a passing ship; **back'woods** the forest beyond the cleared country; **backwoods'man** a person who lives in the backwoods; a person of uncouth manners; a peer who seldom attends the House of Lords; **back'word** a withdrawal of a promise, etc; a retort; **back'work** (*mining*) work done underground but not at the coal-face; **back'worker**. — *adj* **back'-wounding** (*Shakesp*) backbiting. — **backyard'** a yard behind a house. — *adj* (of a person) operating a small business from domestic premises, as *backyard mechanic*, or practising unofficially or illegally. — **back and fill** (*naut*) to trim sails so that the wind alternately presses them back and fills them; to vacillate; **back and forth** to and fro; **back down** (*n* **back'down**) to abandon one's opinion or position; to move (a boat) backwards by pushing the oars (*rowing*); **back of** (*US*) behind; **back out** to move out backwards; to evade an obligation or undertaking; **back to front** the wrong way round, with the back where the front should be; reversed, in mirror image; in the wrong order, with matters that should be deferred being discussed or dealt with first; completely, thoroughly; **back to nature** back to a simple way of life (also often **back'-to-nat'ure** as *adj*); **back up** to give support to; (of water) to accumulate behind an obstruction; to make a back-up of (data) (*comput*); **backward and forward** to and fro; **back water** to row or turn the paddle-wheels backward; **bend**, **fall** or **lean over backwards** (*colloq*) to go even to the point of personal discomfort so as to be accommodating or to please; **break the back of** to overburden; to accomplish the hardest part of; **get off someone's back** to stop pestering or bothering someone; **get someone's back up** (*colloq*) to annoy or irritate someone; **give** or **make a back** to take up position for leap-frog; **keep**, **place** or **put on the back burner** to set aside, postpone work on, or keep in reserve for later consideration or action; **know something backwards** to have a thorough knowledge of something; **on the back of** close behind; just after (*Scot*); **put one's back into** to put great effort into; **ring bells backward** to begin with the bass bell, in order to raise the alarm; **set one's** or **put someone's back up** to show or arouse resentment, irritation or anger; **take a back seat** to withdraw into an inconspicuous or subordinate position; **talk through the back of one's neck** see under **neck**; **to the backbone** through and through. [OE *bæc*; Swed *bak*, Dan *bag*]

back[2] *bak*, *n* a large vat or tub. — *n* **back'et** (*Scot*) a shallow wooden trough for carrying ashes, coals, etc. [Fr *bac* trough, dimin *baquet*, perh partly through Du *bak*]

backare or **baccare** *bak'ār* or *bak'ā'ri*, (*Shakesp*) *interj* back; stand back. [Perh for *back there*; or sham Latin]

backfisch *bäk'fish*, (*obs*) *n* a young girl, a flapper. [Ger *Backfisch* fish for frying, perhaps in allusion to immaturity]

backgammon *bak-gam'ən* or *bak'*, *n* a board-game for two players with dice and fifteen men or pieces each; a triple game scored by the winner bearing off all 15 men while the loser still has a stone in the winner's inner table. — *vt* to defeat in such a way. [**back**, because the pieces are sometimes taken up and obliged to go *back*, that is, re-enter at the table, and ME *gamen* play]

backra *bak'* or *buk'rə*, (*Caribbean*) *n* a white man or woman; white people. [Ibo, Efik *mbakára* white man]

backsheesh, **backshish**. See **baksheesh**.

backward, **backwards**, etc. See **back**[1].

baclava. See **baklava**.

bacon *bā'kn*, *n* pig's flesh (now the back and sides) salted or pickled and dried, and used as food; a rustic (*Shakesp*). — *n* **ba'coner** a pig suitable for bacon production. — **bring home the bacon** (*colloq*) to achieve an object, successfully accomplish a task; to provide material support; **save (some)one's bacon** (*colloq*) (to enable someone) to come off unscathed from a difficult situation. [OFr *bacon*, of Gmc origin; cf OHGer *bahho*, *bacho*; Ger *Bache*]

Baconian *bā-kō'ni-ən*, *adj* pertaining to Francis *Bacon* (1561–1626), or his inductive philosophy, or to Roger *Bacon* (died *c*. 1292) or his teaching, or to the theory that Francis Bacon wrote Shakespeare's plays. — Also *n*. — *n* **Bacō'nianism**.

bacteria *bak-tē'ri-ə*, *n pl* the Schizomycetes, a class of unicellular or filamentous micro-organisms, saprophytic, parasitic or autotrophic, agents in putrefaction, nitrogen fixation, etc, and the cause of many diseases. — Also used erroneously as *sing*. — *sing* **bactē'rium** any member of the class, *esp* a rod-shaped one. — *n* **bacteraemia** or (*US*) **bacteremia** (*-ē'mi-ə*) the presence of bacteria in the blood. — *adj* **bactē'rial**, **bactē'rian** or **bacteric** (*-ter'ik*). — *adj* **bactēricī'dal**. — *n* **bactē'ricide** a substance that destroys bacteria. — *n* **bactērio-chlorophyll** (*-klor'* or *-klōr'ō-fil*) in some bacteria, a substance related to the chlorophyll of green plants. — *combining form* **bacterio-** or **bacteri-** pertaining to bacteria. — *n* **bactē'rioid** or **bac'teroid** a swollen bacterium living symbiotically in the root-nodules of beans and other plants. — *adj* **bactēriolog'ical**. — *n* **bactēriol'ogist**. — *n* **bactēriol'ogy** the scientific study of bacteria. — *n* **bactēriolȳ'sin** (or *-ol'i-*) an antibody that destroys bacteria. — *n* **bactēriol'ysis** destruction of bacteria by an antibody (Gr *lysis* dissolution). — *adj* **bactēriolyt'ic**. — *n* **bacteriophage** (*bak-tē'ri-ō-fāj* or *-fäzh*) any of a large number of virus-like agents, present in the atmosphere, soil, water, living things, etc, whose function is to destroy bacteria (Gr *phagein* to eat). — *n* **bactēriō'sis** any bacterial plant-disease. — *n* **bactērios'tasis** inhibition of the growth of bacteria (Gr *stasis* standing). — *n* **bactē'riostat** an agent that inhibits their growth. — *adj* **bactēriostat'ic**. — *vt* **bac'terize** or **-ise** to treat with bacteria. — **bacteroid** see **bacterioid**. — **bacteria bed** a filter bed; **bacterial leaching** (*min ext*) see **leaching**; **bacterial recovery** (*min ext*) see **microbiological mining**. [Gr *baktērion*, dimin of *baktron* a stick]

Bactrian *bak'tri-ən*, *adj* belonging to *Bactria* (now nearly corresponding to Balkh, a district of N Afghanistan), *esp* applied to a two-humped camel. — *n* a two-humped camel.

baculiform *bə-kū'li-förm* or *bak'ū-li-*, (*biol*) *adj* rod-shaped. [L *baculum* a stick, and **-form**]

baculine *bak'ū-līn*, *adj* pertaining to the stick or cane, or to punishment by flogging. [L *baculum* a stick]

baculite *bak'ū-līt*, *n* a fossil of the genus **Baculites** (*-īt'ēz*), allied to the ammonites, with a straight, tapering shell. [L *baculum* a stick]

baculovirus *bak'ū-lō-vī-rəs*, *n* a type of virus only found to attack insects. [L *baculus* a rod, and **virus**]

baculum *bak'ū-ləm*, *n* the bone in the penis of certain mammals. [L *baculum* a stick]

bad *bad*, *adj* (*compar* **worse**, *superl* **worst**) ill or evil; wicked, naughty; hurtful; incorrect, faulty; rotten; poor; unskilful; worthless; unfavourable; painful; unwell; spurious; severe; harmful; offensive, disagreeable; having serious effects; good, attractive (*slang*, *orig US*). — *n* something evil, wicked, hurtful, etc. — *n* **badd'ie** or **badd'y** (*colloq*) a criminal person or villain, *esp* as portrayed in films, television or radio shows. —

adj **badd'ish** somewhat bad; not very good. — *adv* **bad'ly** in a bad way; severely; to a marked extent, very much. — *n* **bad'ness**. — *adj* **bad'ass** (*US slang*) touchy, difficult; tough, intimidating. — Also **bad'assed**. — **bad'ass** a difficult person; **bad blood** angry or hostile feeling; **bad debt** a debt that cannot be recovered and is therefore written off as a loss; **bad lands** greatly eroded wasteland in South Dakota; (*usu* **bad'lands**) any similar eroded region; **bad language** swearing. — *adj* **bad'ly-off** poorly provided *esp* with money. — **bad'man** (chiefly *US*) an outlaw. — *vt* **bad'mouth** (*colloq*) to criticize, malign. — **bad news** any unwelcome, upsetting or irritating event, or a report of such; someone or something troublesome, irritating, etc (*slang*); **bad shot** a wrong guess. — *adj* **bad-tem'pered**. — **bad trip** (*colloq*) an episode of terrifying hallucinations and physical discomfort resulting from taking a drug, *esp* LSD. — **feel bad about** (*colloq*) to be sorry about, regret; **from bad to worse** into an even worse situation; **go bad** to decay, become mouldy or putrid; **go to the bad** to go to moral ruin; **in a bad way** (*colloq*) ill; in trouble; **in someone's bad books** unpopular with someone; **make the best of a bad job** (*colloq*) to do the best one can in unfavourable circumstances; **not bad** fairly good; **not half bad** (*colloq*) pretty good, excellent; **too bad** (*colloq*) what a pity!; regrettable, a shame; **to the bad** in deficit; **with a bad grace** ungraciously. [Ety very obscure. The ME *badde* is perh from OE *bæddel* a hermaphrodite, *bædling* an effeminate fellow]

baddeleyite *bad'li-īt*, *n* a mineral yielding zirconium, consisting of 90% zirconium dioxide found in beach sands, in Sri Lanka and Brazil. [Joseph *Baddeley*, who brought specimens to Europe in 19c]

badderlock *bad'ər-lok*, (*Scot*) *n* an edible seaweed (*Alaria*) resembling tangle. — Also **balderlocks** (*böl'dər-loks*). [Poss for **Balder's locks**]

bade *bad* (*poetic bād*), *pa t* of **bid** (both verbs).

badge *baj*, *n* a mark or emblem showing rank, membership of a society, etc; any distinguishing mark or symbol. — *vt* to call by a distinguishing name, mark or symbol. — **badge engineering** (*autos*) the bringing out of a new model that is only marginally, if at all, different from one already existing under a different marque. [ME *bage*. Origin obscure]

badger *baj'ər*, *n* a burrowing, nocturnal, hibernating animal of the otter and weasel family; applied to other animals, such as hyrax, wombat, ratel; a paint-brush or other brush (made of badger's hair); (with *cap*) a member of the junior section of the St John's ambulance brigade. — *vt* to pester or worry. — *adj* **badg'erly** like a badger; greyish-haired, elderly. — **badg'er-baiting** or **-drawing** the sport of setting dogs to draw out a badger from a barrel or artificial earth, etc; **badg'er-dog** the dachshund, a long-bodied and short-legged dog used in drawing the badger. — *adj* **badg'er-legged** having legs of unequal length, as the badger was commonly supposed to have. [Prob from **badge** and the noun-forming suffix *-ard*, in reference to the white mark like a badge on its forehead]

badging-hook. See **bagging-hook**.

badinage *bad'in-äzh*, *n* light playful talk; banter. [Fr *badinage*, from *badin* playful or bantering]

badious *bā'di-əs*, (*bot*) *adj* chestnut-coloured. [L *badius*]

badmash or **budmash** *bud'mash*, (*Ind*) *n* an evil-doer. [Pers]

badminton *bad'min-tən*, *n* a game played with rackets and a shuttlecock on a court with a high net, with the object of making the shuttlecock strike the ground in the opponent's court; a cooling summer drink of claret, sugar and soda-water. [*Badminton* in Gloucestershire, a seat of the Dukes of Beaufort]

BAe *abbrev*: British Aerospace.

Baedeker *bā'di-kər*, *n* any of the series of travellers' guidebooks published by Karl *Baedeker* (1801–59) or his successors; any similar guidebook; any handbook or vade-mecum. — **Baedeker raid** one of the series of raids by the Luftwaffe in 1942 on places in Britain listed in Baedeker.

bael, **bel** or **bhel** *bel*, *n* a thorny Indian rutaceous tree (*Aegle marmelos*); its edible fruit, the Bengal quince. [Hind]

baetyl *bē'til*, *n* a magical or holy meteoric stone. [Gr *baitȳlos*]

BAF *abbrev*: British Athletics Federation.

baff *baf*, (*golf*) *vt* to strike the ground with the sole of the club, and so to send the ball up in the air. — *n* **baffy** (*baf'i*) a club like a brassy, but with a slightly shorter shaft and a more sloping face.

baffle *baf'l*, *vt* to frustrate, confound, bewilder, or impede perplexingly; to regulate or divert (liquid, gas, sound waves, etc); to provide with a baffle; to cheat, hoodwink (*obs*); to disgrace publicly (*obs*). — *n* a plate or similar device for regulating or diverting the flow of liquid, gas, sound waves, etc (also **baff'le-board**, **baff'le-plate** or **baff'ler**); confusion, check (*obs*). — *n* **baff'lement**. — *n* **baff'ler** a baffle. — *adj* **baff'ling**. — *adv* **baff'lingly**. — **baff'legab** (*slang*) the professional logorrhoea of many politicians, officials and salespeople, characterized by prolix abstract circumlocution and/or a profusion of abstruse technical terminology, used as a means of persuasion, pacification or obfuscation; **baffle wall** a wall that acts as a baffle, *esp* for sound. [Perh Scot and connected with *bauchle* to treat contemptuously; but cf Fr *bafouer*, or earlier *beffler*, from OFr *befe* mockery]

baft[1] *bäft*, *n* a coarse fabric, *orig* Oriental, later made in and shipped from England. [Pers *baft* woven]

baft[2] *bäft*, (*archaic*) *adv* and *prep* behind; abaft, astern (*naut*). [OE *beæftan*, from *be* by, and *æftan* behind]

BAFTA *baf'tə*, *abbrev*: British Academy of Film and Television Arts.

bag *bag*, *n* a sack, pouch, receptacle for carrying or containing; a handbag; a bagful; a measure of various quantities; a game-bag, hence the quantity of fish or game secured, however great; an udder; an unattractive, slovenly or immoral woman (*slang*); a person's line or vocation (*slang*); (in *pl*) trousers (*colloq*); a quantity of drugs, *esp* heroin in a paper or other container (*drug-taking slang*). — *vi* to bulge, swell out; to sag; to drop away from the right course (*naut*). — *vt* to put (*esp* game) into a bag; hence to kill (game); to cram full; to seize, secure or steal; to claim or reserve for oneself (*colloq*); to denigrate or criticize (*Austr* and *US*): — *pr p* **bagg'ing**; *pa p* **bagged**. — *n* **bag'ful** as much as a bag will hold: — *pl* **bag'fuls**. — *adj* **bagged** (*bagd*) in a bag; hanging slackly or in bags. — *n pl* **bagg'ies** (*orig Austr*) baggy shorts. — *adv* **bagg'ily**. — *n* **bagg'iness**. — *n* **bagg'ing** cloth or material for bags. — *adj* **bagg'it** (*Scot*) bagged; full of spawn, etc. — *n* a ripe female salmon that has failed to shed her eggs. — *adj* **bagg'y** loose like a bag; bulged. — **bag lady** a homeless female derelict who carries her possessions, accumulated scavengings, etc around with her in a shopping bag (or *usu* several); **bag'man** a man who carries a bag; an old-fashioned name for a commercial traveller; a man who collects or distributes money as part of racketeering (*US*); a swagman (*Austr*); **bag'-net** a bag-shaped net for catching fish; **bag'wash** (a laundry offering) a laundry service in which only basic washing is done; **bag'wig** an 18c wig with back-hair enclosed in an ornamental bag. — **bag and baggage** with all one's belongings, completely, as in *to clear out bag and baggage*; **bag of bones** an emaciated living being; **bag of tricks** the whole outfit; **bags (I)** (*slang, orig children's*) I lay claim to; **bags of** (*slang*) plenty of; **in the bag** secured or as good as secured; **let the cat out of the bag** to disclose a secret. [ME *bagge*, from ON *baggi* a bundle]

bagarre *ba-gär*, (*Fr*) *n* a scuffle, brawl, rumpus.

bagasse *bə-gas'*, *n* dry refuse in sugar-making. — *n* **bagassō'sis** an industrial disease caused by inhaling bagasse. [Fr; Sp *bagazo* husks of grapes or olives after pressing]

bagatelle *bag-ə-tel'*, *n* a trifle, trinket; a piece of music in a light style; a game played on a board with balls, *usu* nine, and a cue or spring, the object being to put the balls into numbered holes or sections. [Fr, from Ital *bagatella* a conjuror's trick, a trifle]

bagel *bā'gəl*, *n* a hard leavened ring-shaped roll. [Yiddish *beygel*, from Ger *Beugel*, from Gmc root *bug-* to bend]

baggage *bag'ij*, *n* travellers' luggage; the tents, provisions, etc of an army; an immoral woman; a cheeky young woman. — **bagg'age-animal**; **bagg'age-car** (*US*) a railway luggage-van; **baggage reclaim** the process whereby (*esp* long-distance) travellers collect their baggage on arrival at their destination; the area in an airport terminal, etc where travellers collect their baggage after arrival; **bagg'age-train** a train of baggage-animals, wagons, etc. [OFr *bagage*, from *baguer* to bind up]

bagging-hook *bag'ing-hŏŏk*, (*dialect*) *n* a type of sickle. — Also **badging-hook** (*baj'-*). [Ety uncertain]

bagnio *ban'yō*, *n* an Oriental prison; a brothel; a bathing-house, *esp* one with hot baths (*obs*): — *pl* **bagn'ios**. [Ital *bagno*, from L *balneum* a bath]

bagpipes *bag'pīps*, *n pl* (also *n sing* **bag'pipe**) a wind-instrument consisting of a *bag* fitted with *pipes*, *usu* consisting of a chanter and some drones. — *n* **bag'piper**. — *n* **bag'piping**.

BAgr or **BAgric** *abbrev*: Bachelor of Agriculture.

baguette *bag-et'*, *n* a long narrow French loaf of white bread with a thick crust; a precious stone cut in the shape of a long rectangle; a small moulding like an astragal (*archit*). [Fr dimin, from L *baculum* rod]

baguio *bä-gē'ō*, *n* a hurricane: — *pl* **bagui'os**. [Philippine Islands Sp]

bah *bä*, *interj* expressing disgust or contempt. [Fr]

bahada. See **bajada**.

Bahadur *bə-hä'dər* or *-hö'*, (*Ind*) *n* a title of respect often added to the names of officers and officials. [Hindi *bahādur* hero]

Bahai or **Baha'i** *bə-* or *bä-hä'ē*, *n* an adherent of an *orig* Persian religion, a development of Babism (see **Babi**), following the teaching of *Baha*-Ullah, 'the Glory of God' (Mirza Husain Ali, 1817–92), and emphasizing world unity and peace; the religion itself. — Also *adj*. — *n* **Baha'ism**. — *n* **Baha'ist** or **Baha'ite**.

Bahamian *bə-hā'mi-ən* or *-hä'mi-ən*, *n* a native or inhabitant of the *Bahamas*; a descendant of such. — Also *adj*.

Bahasa Indonesia *bə-hä'sə in-də-nē'zi-ə*, *-zhi-ə* or *-zhyə*, *n* the Indonesian language. — **Bahasa Malaysia** Malay. [Malay, Indonesian *bahasa* language]

baht *bät*, *n* the monetary unit of Thailand (100 satang). [Thai *bāt*]

bahut *ba-hŏŏt'*, *bä-ü*, *n* an ornamented, *usu* round-topped, chest or cabinet. [Fr]

bahuvrihi *bä-hŏŏ-vrē'hē*, *n* a class of compound words in which the first element governs or describes the second, but the qualified element cannot be substituted for the whole eg *turncoat*, *hunchback*, *blue-stocking*). — Also *adj*. [Sans, from *bahu* much and *vrihi* rice, together forming such a compound]

BAI *abbrev*: *Baccalaureus in Arte Ingeniaria* (*L*) Bachelor of Engineering.

baignoire *ben-wär*, *n* a theatre box on a level with the stalls. [Fr, bath]

bail[1] *bāl*, *n* the (*usu* monetary) security given to procure the release of an accused person by assuring his or her subsequent appearance in court; release from custody on the strength of such security; the person or persons giving or becoming that security; jurisdiction, custody (*Spenser*). — *vt* to set (someone) free by giving security for them; to release on such security being given; to deliver (goods) in trust upon a contract (*law*). — *adj* **bail'able**. — *n* **bailee'** (*law*) a person to whom goods are bailed. — *n* **bail'er** (*US*) a variant spelling of **bailor**. — *n* **bail'ment** (*law*) a delivery of goods in trust; the action of bailing a prisoner. — *n* **bail'or** (*law*) a person who bails goods to a bailee. — **bail'bond** a bond given by a prisoner and his or her surety upon being bailed; **bail'-dock** or **bale'-dock** a room at the Old Bailey, London, in which prisoners were formerly kept during the trials; **bail-out** see **bail out** below; **bails'man** a person who gives bail for another. — **accept**, **admit to** or **allow bail** are all said of the magistrate; the prisoner **offers** or **surrenders to bail**; **bail out** (*colloq*) to stand bail for (a prisoner); to assist out of (financial) difficulties (*n* **bail'-out**); **forfeit** or (*colloq*) **jump bail** to fail to reappear in court at the designated time after being released on bail; **give leg bail** to run for it; **stand**, **go** or **give bail** to provide the bail (for a prisoner). [OFr *bail* custody, handing over, *baillier* to control, guard, hand over, from L *bājulāre* to bear a burden, carry, carry on]

bail[2] or **bayle** *bāl*, *n* a barrier; a pole separating horses in an open stable; a frame for holding a cow's head during milking (*Austr* and *NZ*). — *vt* **bail** (*Shakesp* **bale**) to confine. — **bail up** to secure (a cow's head) in a bail (*Austr* and *NZ*); to stop and disarm in order to rob (*Austr*); to put one's hands up in surrender (*Austr*); to bring or be brought to bay, to corner or be cornered (*Austr*). [OFr *baile*, perh from *baillier* to enclose; or L *baculum* a stick]

bail[3] *bāl*, (*cricket*) *n* one of the cross-pieces on the top of the wicket. — *n* **bail'-ball** or **bail'er** a bowled ball that hits or removes a bail without disturbing the stumps. [Prob connected with **bail**[2]]

bail[4] *bāl*, *n* on a typewriter, teleprinter, etc, a hinged bar that holds the paper against the platen. [Prob connected with **bail**[2]]

bail[5] (also **bale**) *bāl*, *n* a bucket or other container for ladling out water from a boat. — *vt* to clear (a boat, etc) of water with bails; to ladle (water)(often with *out*; see also **bail out**). — *n* **bail'er**. — **bail** (*usu* **bale**) **out** to escape from an aeroplane by parachute; to escape from a potentially difficult situation; see also under **bail**[1]. [Fr *baille* bucket, perh from LL *bacula*, dimin of *baca* a basin]

bail[6] *bāl*, *n* a hoop; a semicircular handle, as of a kettle, etc. [Prob ON *beygla* hoop, from the Gmc root *bug-* to bend]

bailey *bāl'i*, *n* the outer wall of a feudal castle; hence the outer court, or any court within the walls. — **motte and bailey** see under **motte**[2]. — **the Old Bailey** the Central Criminal Court in London in what was the ancient bailey between Ludgate and Newgate. [Fr *baille* palisade, enclosure, from LL *ballium*]

Bailey bridge *bā'li brij*, *n* a prefabricated bridge constructed speedily for emergency use. [Designed during World War II by Sir Donald *Bailey*]

bailie *bāl'i*, *n* in Scotland, the title of a magistrate who presides in a burgh court and is elected by the town council from among the councillors (now *hist*); a sheriff's officer (*obs*; cf **water-bailie**); the chief magistrate of a Scottish barony or part of a county (*obs*); a land-steward (*obs*). — *n* **bail'ieship**. — Also **baill'ie** and **baill'ieship**. [OFr *bailli* and *baillif*; see **bailiff**]

bailiff *bāl'if*, *n* an agent or land-steward; a sheriff's officer; the first civil officer in Jersey and in Guernsey; a court official (chiefly *US*); formerly any king's officer, eg sheriff, mayor, etc, *esp* the chief officer of a hundred (county division), surviving in certain cases as a formal title; a foreign magistrate (*hist*). — *n* **bail'iwick** the jurisdiction of a bailiff (*law*); jurisdiction in general (*law*); someone's area of interest (*joc*). [OFr *baillif*, from LL *bājulivus*, from *bājulus* carrier, administrator. See **bail**[1]]

bailli *bī-yē*, (*Fr*) *n* a magistrate. — *n* **bailliage** (*-äzh*) his jurisdiction.

baillie. See **bailie**.

Baily's beads *bā'liz bēds*, (*astron*) *n pl* bright spots, resembling a string of beads, visible during the last seconds before a total eclipse of the sun. [Detected in 1836 by the astronomer F *Baily*]

bainin *bä-nēn'*, *n* a type of wool produced in Ireland that is only partially scoured and therefore retains some natural oil. — Also *adj*. [Ir *báinín* homespun]

bainite *bā'nīt*, *n* a constituent of a certain stage in the heat treatment of steel. [From E C *Bain* (1891–1971), US metallurgist]

bain-marie *ban-ma-rē'* or *bẽ-ma-rē*, *n* a vessel of hot or boiling water into which another vessel is placed to cook slowly or keep hot (*cookery*); a water-bath (*chem*). [Fr *bain-marie* bath of Mary, from L *balneum Mariae*; origin uncertain, perh from *Mary* or Miriam, sister of Moses, who reputedly wrote a book on alchemy]

Bairam *bī'räm* or *bī-räm'*, *n* the name of two Muslim festivals, the *Lesser Bairam* lasting three days, after the feast of Ramadan, and the *Greater*, seventy days later, lasting four days. [Pers]

bairn *bārn*, (*Scot* and *NEng*) *n* a child. — *adj* **bairn'like** or **bairn'ly**. — **bairn's'-part** see **legitim**; **bairn'-team** or **bairn'-time** a brood of children. [OE *bearn*, from *beran* to bear]

Baisaki *bī-sak'i*, *n* a Sikh festival commemorating the founding of the Khalsa brotherhood, held at the Hindu New Year. [Hindi *Baisakh* the month April, from Sans *Vais'ākha*]

baisemain *bāz'mẽ*, (*obs*) *n* chiefly in *pl*, a compliment paid by kissing the hand. [Fr *baiser* to kiss, and *main* hand]

bait *bāt*, *n* food put on a hook to attract fish or make them bite; any allurement or temptation; a rage (*slang*); a refreshment, *esp* on a journey (*archaic* or *dialect*); a stop for that purpose (*archaic*). — *vt* to set (a trap, etc) with food; to tempt; to feed (a horse, etc), *esp* on a journey (*archaic*); to set dogs on (a bear, bull, etc); to persecute, harass; to exasperate, *esp* with malice, tease. — *vi* to take, or stop for, refreshment on a journey (*archaic*). — *n* **bait'er**. — *n* **bait'ing**. — **bait'fish** fish used as bait; fish that may be caught with bait. — **bait and switch** another name for **switch selling**. [ME *beyten*, from ON *beita* to cause to bite, from *bita* to bite]

baize *bāz*, *n* a coarse, *usu* green, woollen cloth with a long nap, used mainly for coverings, linings, etc; a table cover of such cloth, *esp* the covering of card- and snooker-tables, etc. — *vt* to cover or line with baize. [Fr *baies*, pl (fem) of *bai*, from L *badius* bay-coloured]

bajada or **bahada** *ba-hä'də*, (*geol*) *n* a slope formed by aggradation, consisting of rock debris. [Sp *bajada* a slope]

Bajan *bā'jən*, (*colloq*) *adj* Barbadian. [Variant short form]

bajan *bā'jən* (*Aberdeen*) or **bejant** *bē'jənt* (*St Andrews*), *n* a freshman (so formerly at several continental universities). [Fr *béjaune* novice, from *bec jaune* yellow bill, unfledged bird]

Bajau *bə-jow'*, *adj* of or relating to a people of Sabah, a state of E Malaysia. — *n* a member of this people.

Bajocian *ba-jō'si-ən*, (*geol*) *adj* of a division of the Middle Jurassic. [L *Bajocassēs* a people living in Bayeux]

bajra, *bäj'rə* or *-rä*, also **bajri** or **bajree** *bäj'rē*, *n* a kind of Indian millet. [Hindi]

baju *bä'jōō*, *n* a short jacket worn in Malaya. [Malay]

bake *bāk*, *vt* to dry, harden or cook by the heat of the sun or fire; to make or cook in an oven; to harden by cold (*Shakesp*); to cake (*Shakesp*). — *vi* to cook or become firm through heat; (of persons, weather, etc) to be very hot (*colloq*); to work as a baker: — *pa p* **baked** (*bākt*), **bāk'en** (*archaic*); *pr p* **bāk'ing**. — *n* a baking; a party at which the food is baked (*NAm*); a kind of biscuit (*Scot*). — *n* **bāk'er** a person who bakes or sells bread, etc; an artificial fly used in salmon-fishing. — *n* **bāk'ery** a bakehouse; a baker's shop. — *n* **bāk'ing** the process by which bread (or cake, etc) is baked; a quantity baked at one time. — **bake'apple** (*Can*) the fruit of the cloudberry; **bake'board** (*Scot*) a board for kneading dough on; **baked Alaska** a pudding consisting of ice cream, and *usu* cake, covered with meringue, baked rapidly; **baked beans** beans boiled and baked, now generally applied to a variety tinned in tomato sauce; **bake'house** a house or place used for baking in; **bake'meat** (*Bible*) pastry, pies; **baker's dozen** see **dozen**; **bake'stone** a flat stone or plate of iron on which cakes are baked in the oven; **bake'ware** heat-resistant dishes suitable for use in baking; **bak'ing-powder** a mixture (eg tartaric acid and sodium bicarbonate) giving off carbon dioxide, used as a raising agent in baking; **bak'ing-soda** sodium bicarbonate. [OE *bacan*; cognate with Ger *backen* to bake, Gr *phōgein* to roast]

Bakelite® *bā'kəl-īt*, *n* a synthetic resin with high chemical and electrical resistance, made by condensation of cresol or phenol with formaldehyde. [From its inventor, L H *Baekeland* (1863–1944)]

Baker day *bā'kər dāy*, (*colloq*) *n* a periodic in-service training day for teachers, on which students do not attend school. [Kenneth *Baker*, Secretary of State for Education, 1986–9]

Bakewell pudding or **tart** *bāk'wel pŏŏd'ing* or *tärt*, *n* a flan consisting of a pastry base spread with jam and a filling made of eggs, sugar, butter and ground almonds. [*Bakewell*, Derbyshire]

baklava or **baclava** *bak'lə-və*, *n* a Middle-Eastern dessert made of layers of filo pastry, honey, nuts, etc. [Turk]

baksheesh, **bakhshish**, **backsheesh** or **backshish** *bak'* or *buk'shēsh*, *n* a gift or present of money in various Eastern or N African countries, a gratuity or tip. — *vt* to give money to, tip. [Pers *bakhshīsh*]

bal. (*bookkeeping*) *abbrev*: balance.

Balaam *bā'lam*, *n* a prophet who strives to mislead, like *Balaam* in Num 22. 24; unimportant paragraphs kept in readiness to fill up a newspaper (*journalistic slang*). — *n* **Bā'laamite**. — *adj* **Bālaamit'ical**. — **Ba'laam-box** or **-basket** a place in which such paragraphs are kept in readiness.

Balaclava, **Balaclava cap** or **helmet** *bal-ə-klä'və* (*kap* or *hel'mit*), *n* (also without *cap*) a knitted hood covering the head and neck, with an opening for the face. [*Balaklava* in Crimea]

baladin *ba-la-dẽ*, (*Fr*) *n* a theatrical dancer: — *fem* **baladine** (*-dēn*).

balalaika *ba-lə-lī'kə*, *n* a Russian musical instrument, like a guitar, with triangular body and *usu* three strings. [Russ]

balance *bal'əns*, *n* equilibrium; what is needed to produce equilibrium, a counterpoise; harmony among the parts of anything; stability of body or mind; equality or just proportion of weight or power; the sum required to make the two sides of an account equal, hence the surplus, or the sum due (*bookkeeping*); the process of balancing an account, or the tabular representation of this (*bookkeeping*); the remainder; the act of weighing two things; an instrument for weighing, *usu* formed of two dishes or scales hanging from a beam supported in the middle; (with *cap*) Libra, sign of the Zodiac; a contrivance that regulates the speed of a clock or watch. — *vt* to set or keep in equilibrium; to counterpoise; to compare; to weigh in a balance; to settle (eg an account); to examine and test so as to make the debtor and creditor sides of an account agree (*bookkeeping*). — *vi* to have equal weight or power, etc; to be or come to be in equilibrium; to hesitate or fluctuate; in dancing, to match one's partner's steps to and fro; (of accounts) to have the credit and debit sides equal (*bookkeeping*). — *adj* **bal'anced** poised so as to preserve equilibrium; stable, well-adjusted; fair, unbiased; (of a meal, diet, etc) containing a combination of the types of food necessary for good health. — *n* **bal'ancer** a person who, or that which, balances; an acrobat; a fly's rudimentary hindwing (see also **halteres**). — **balanced flue** a sealed unit which both takes its air for combustion from outside the building and discharges the gases produced to the outside; **balanced pair** (*telecomm*) two wires which are electrically balanced to each other and earth; **bal'ance-sheet** a statement which shows the assets and liabilities of a company on a specified date; a summary and balance of accounts; **bal'ance-wheel** a wheel in a watch or chronometer which regulates the beat or rate. — **balance of mind** sanity; **balance of nature** ecological equilibrium caused by interdependence; **balance of payments** the difference over a stated period between a nation's total receipts (in all forms) from foreign countries and its total payments to foreign countries; **balance of power** a state of equilibrium of forces in which no nation or group of nations has the resources to go to war with another or others with likelihood of success; potentially decisive power held by a third party when two others are in equilibrium; **balance of trade** the difference in value between a country's imports and exports; **in the balance** unsettled; undecided; **off balance** unstable, *esp* mentally or emotionally; in a state of unreadiness to respond to an attack, challenge, etc; **on balance** having taken everything into consideration; **strike a balance** to choose a middle-of-the-road decision. [Fr, from L *bilanx* having two scales, from *bis* double, and *lanx*, *lancis* a dish or scale]

balancé *bal-ã-sā*, (*Fr*; *ballet*) *n* a rocking step taking the weight from one foot to the other.

Balanus *bal'ə-nəs*, *n* the acorn-shell genus. — *n* **balanitis** (*bal-ə-nī'tis*) inflammation of the glans penis in mammals. — *n* **Balanogloss'us** (Gr *glōssa* tongue) a genus of wormlike animals of the Hemichordata. [Gr *balanos* acorn, glans penis]

balas *bal'as*, *n* a rose-red spinel (*usu* **balas ruby**). [OFr *balais* (Ital *balascio*), from LL *balascus*, from Pers *Badakhshān*, a place near Samarkand where they are found]

balata *bal'ə-tə*, *n* the gum of the bully-tree of S America, used as a substitute for rubber and gutta-percha. [Prob Tupí]

balboa *bäl-bō'ə*, *n* the monetary unit of Panama (100 centésimos). [Vasco Nuñez de *Balboa*, *c*. 1475–1517]

Balbriggan *bal-brig'ən*, *n* a knitted cotton fabric like that *orig* made at *Balbriggan*, Ireland; underclothing made of it.

balbutient *bal-bū'sh(y)ənt*, *adj* stammering. [L *balbūtiēns*, *-entis*, from *balbūtīre* to stutter]

balcony *balk'ə-ni* (or 18c *bal-kō'ni*), *n* a platform, with a balustrade or railing, projecting from the wall of a building, supported by pillars or consoles, and with access *usu* from a door or window; in theatres, *usu* the gallery immediately above the dress circle (*NAm* the dress circle itself). — *n* **balconet** or **balconette** (*bal-kə-net'*) a miniature balcony. — *adj* **bal'conied**. [Ital *balcone*, from *balco*, of Gmc origin; OHGer *balcho* (Ger *Balken*), Eng **balk**]

bald *böld*, *adj* without hair, feathers, etc on the head (or on other parts of the body); (of a bird or animal) having white markings on the face; bare, unadorned; (of a tyre) having a worn tread (*colloq*); lacking in grace or charm, blunt; undisguised, obvious; paltry, trivial (*archaic*). — *adj* **bald'ing** going bald. — *adj* **bald'ish** somewhat bald. — *adv* **bald'ly** plainly, without tactful circumlocution. — *n* **bald'ness**. — *n* **bald'y** (*colloq*) a bald-headed person (also *adj*); an over-short haircut (*Scot*). — **bald'-coot** or **bald'icoot** the coot, from its pure white wide frontal plate; **bald'-eagle** the American white-headed eagle, used as the national emblem. — *adj* **bald'-faced** (of a bird or animal) having white markings on the face. — **bald'-head** a person with a bald head. — *adj* **bald'-headed** having a bald head. — *adj* and *adv* (*slang*) **bald'-headed** without restraint, without regard for the consequences; out and out. — **baldicoot** see **bald-coot**; **bald'pate** a person destitute of hair; a kind of wild duck. — *adj* **bald'pate** or **bald'pated**. — **bald as a coot** see under **coot**. [Perh **balled** rounded]

baldachin or **baldaquin** *böl'də-kin*, *n* silk brocade; a canopy over a throne, pulpit, altar, etc; in RC processions, a canopy carried over the priest who carries the host. [Ital *baldacchino*, Fr *baldaquin* a canopy, from Ital *Baldacco* Baghdad, from where the material of which they were made came]

balderdash *böl'dər-dash*, *n* senseless talk; anything jumbled together without judgment; obscene language or writing (*dialect*); a jumbled mixture of liquids (*obs*). [Origin unknown]

balderlocks. See **badderlocks**.

baldicoot. See under **bald**.

baldmoney *böld'mun-i*, *n* spignel; gentian of various kinds. [Ety unknown]

baldric or **baldrick** *böld'rik*, *n* a warrior's belt or shoulder sash, for supporting a sword, etc; (*Spenser* **baudricke**) the zodiac. [Cf MHGer *balderich* girdle]

Baldwin *böld'win*, (*US*) *n* a variety of apple. [Personal name]

bale[1] *bāl*, *n* a bundle, or package of goods; a measure, *esp* (*US*) 500lb of cotton; a group (of turtles); the set of dice for any special game (*obs*). — *vt* to make into bales. — *n* **bal'er** a machine for baling hay, etc. [ME *bale*, perh from OFr *bale*, from OHGer *balla*, *palla* ball. See **ball**[1]]

bale[2]. See **bail**[5].

bale[3] *bāl*, *n* evil, injury, mischief (*archaic*); misery, woe (*archaic*). — *adj* **bale'ful** malignant, hurtful, of evil influence; painful (*obs*); sorrowful, lugubrious (*archaic*). — *adv* **bale'fully**. — *n* **bale'fulness**. [OE *bealu*; OHGer *balo*; ON *böl*]

balection. See **bolection**.

baleen *bə-* or *ba-lēn'*, *n* whalebone, horny plates growing from the palate of certain whales. — Also *adj*. [OFr *baleine*, from L *balaena* whale]

bale-fire *bāl'-fīr*, *n* a bonfire; a beacon-fire (*Scot*); a funeral pyre (*obs*). [OE *bǣl*; cf ON *bāl* bale, and Gr *phalos* bright, white]

Balfour declaration *bal'fər dek-lə-rā'shən*, *n* the statement made in November 1917 by Arthur *Balfour*, the then British Foreign Secretary, that the British Government was in favour of the establishment of a national home for the Jewish people in Palestine.

balibuntal *bal-i-bun'tl*, *n* (a hat made of) fine, closely-woven straw. [From *Baliuag* in the Philippines, and *buntal*, Tagálog for the straw of the talipot palm]

Balinese *bä-lə-nēz'*, *adj* pertaining to the island of Bali (east of Java), its people, or their language. — Also *n*.

balista. See **ballista**.

balk or **baulk** *bö(l)k*, *vi* to pull up or stop short; to refuse a jump, etc; to jib (at something) (*fig*); to lie out of the way (*Spenser*); to bandy words (*obs*). — *vt* to shirk, avoid; to decline; to ignore, pass over; to let slip; to put a stumbling-block in the way of, to thwart, frustrate, foil, check; to chop (logic) (*Shakesp*). — *n* a check, frustration; a disappointment; a failure to take a jump or the like; the part of a billiard table marked off by the balkline; a forbidden action by the pitcher (*baseball*); a squared timber; a tie-beam of a house, stretching from wall to wall, *esp* when laid so as to form a loft (**the balks**); an unploughed ridge; a place overlooked, an omission (*obs*); a ridge (*obs*); the beam of a balance (*obs*); a rope to connect fishing-nets. — *adj* **balk'd** (*Shakesp*) *prob* heaped in balks. — *n* **balk'er**. — *n* **balk'iness**. — *n* and *adj* **balk'ing**. — *adv* **balk'ingly**. — *adj* **balk'y** apt to balk; perverse, refractory. — **balk'line** a line drawn across a billiard table; a boundary line for the preliminary run in a jumping competition. [OE *balca* ridge; OHGer *balcho* beam]

Balkanize or **-ise** (also without *cap*) *böl'kən-īz*, *vt* to reduce to the condition of the *Balkan* peninsula, which was divided in the late 19th and early 20th centuries into a number of mutually hostile territories. — *n* **Balkanizā'tion**, **balkanizā'tion** (or **-s-**).

ball[1] *böl*, *n* anything spherical or nearly so; a rounded or matted mass; any rounded protuberant part of the body, eg the ball of the foot; a round or oval object used in sports (of varying size, shape and composition according to the sport); a throw or delivery of the ball at cricket, etc; a game played with a ball, *esp* (*US*) baseball or football; a bullet or solid missile projected from a gun, cannon, etc; a spherical mass of wound yarn, string, etc; the eyeball; a bolus for a horse; a spherical cake of soap (*obs*); (in *pl*) testicles (*vulg*); (in *pl*) nonsense (also *interj*; *vulg*); (in *pl*) guts, courage (*slang*, *esp US*). — *vt* to form into a ball; to clog; to entangle; (of swarming bees) to cluster round (the queen); (*usu* of a man) to have sexual intercourse with (*vulg slang*, *orig US*). — *vi* to gather into a ball; to clog. — *adj* **balled** formed into a ball. — *n* **ball'ing** forming into a ball; snowballing; (*Scot* **ba'ing** *bö'ing*, also **ba'spiel** *bö'spēl*) a periodical game of football played by the population of a town in the streets and sometimes in the river. — *n* **ball'siness**. — *adj* **ballsy** (*böl'zi*; *slang*, *esp US*) gutsy, tough and courageous. — *adj* **ball'-and-claw'** see **claw-and-ball** under **claw**. — **ball'barrow** a wheelbarrow with a ball-shaped wheel; **ballbear'ing** a device for lessening friction by making a revolving part turn on loose steel balls; one of the balls so used; **ball'-boy** or **ball'-girl** (*tennis*) a boy or girl who collects balls that are out of play, supplies balls to the server, etc; **ball'-breaker** or (*US*) **ball'-buster** (*vulg slang*) a person, task or job, etc that is excessively demanding; a woman who is ruthless, demanding or demoralizing in her treatment of men. — *n* and *adj* **ball'-breaking** or **-busting**. — **ball'clay** (*geol*) a fine-textured highly plastic clay used for ceramics; **ball'cock** the stopcock of a cistern regulated by a floating ball that rises and falls with the water; **ball'-flower** (*archit*) an ornament in Decorated Gothic, resembling a ball within a globular flower; **ball'-game** any game played with a ball, *esp* (*US*) baseball or football; a situation, as in *a new ball-game* (*colloq*); **ball lightning** a slowly-moving luminous ball occasionally seen during a thunderstorm; **ball mill** (*eng*) a horizontal cylindrical container in which a substance is ground by rotation with steel or ceramic balls; **ball park** (chiefly *US*) a baseball field; the area designated for the landing of a spacecraft; **in the right ball park** (*colloq* and *fig*) more or less correct. — *adj* (*orig US*) **ball'park** approximate (*esp* in the phrase *ballpark figures*). — **ball'-player** a player (*esp* of football) with outstanding ball-control skills; a baseball-player (*NAm*); **ball'point** or **ballpoint pen** a fountain-pen with a tiny ball rotating against an inking cartridge as its writing tip. — *adj* **ball'-proof** proof against balls discharged from firearms. — *adj* **balls'-aching** (*slang*) tedious. — **ballsed-up**, **balls-up** see **balls up** below. — **ball and socket** (*physiol* and *eng*) a joint formed of a ball partly enclosed in a cup-shaped cavity, allowing rotation on various axes; **ball of fire** a lively, dynamic person; a glass of brandy (*colloq*); **balls up** (*vulg*) to make a muddle or mess of; to throw into confusion (*n* **balls'-up**; *adj* **ballsed'-up**); **ball up** to clog; to make a mess of (*slang*; *n* **ball'up** (*US*); *adj* **balled'-up**); **by the balls** (*vulg*) at someone's mercy, in a helpless state; **keep the ball rolling** to keep things going; **make a balls** or **balls-up of** (*vulg*) to do badly, make a thorough mess of; **no ball** (*cricket*, etc) a delivery of the ball adjudged contrary to rule; **on the ball** (*colloq*) properly in touch with the situation; on the alert; **play ball** see under **play**; **set, start** or **get the ball rolling** to make the first move; to start things going; **the ball at one's feet** success within one's grasp; an opportunity ready to be taken; **the ball's in your court** the responsibility for the next move is yours; **three balls** the sign of a pawnbroker. [ME *bal*, from ON *böllr*; OHGer *ballo*, *pallo*]

ball[2] *böl*, *n* a (*usu* formal) gathering for dancing. — *vi* (*NAm slang*) to enjoy oneself, have a ball (*n* **ball'ing**). — **ball'-dress**; **ball-gown**; **ball'room**; **ballroom dancing** recreational formal dancing. — **ball the jack** (*US slang*) to hurry; **have a ball** to enjoy oneself very much (*colloq*); **open the ball** to begin operations. [OFr *bal*, from *baller* to dance, from LL *ballāre*, perh from Gr *ballizein* to dance]

ballabile *bal-ä'bi-lā*, *n* a part of a ballet danced by the whole corps de ballet, with or without the principal dancers: — *pl* **balla'biles** or **balla'bili** (*-lē*). [Ital, fit to be danced, from *ballare* to dance, from LL *ballāre*]

ballad *bal'əd* (*hist* **ballet** *-ət*, *archaic Scot* **ballat** *-ət* or **ballant** *bal'ənt*), *n* a slow, sentimental song; a simple narrative poem in short stanzas (*usu* of four lines, of eight and six syllables alternately); a popular song, often scurrilous, referring to contemporary persons or events (chiefly *hist*); formerly a drawing-room song, *usu* sentimental, in several verses sung to the same melody; *orig* a song accompanying a dance; (**ballet** *bal'ət*) a form of madrigal (*hist*). — (*obs*) *vt* to make ballads about. — *n* **balladeer'** a person who sings ballads (also *vi*). — *n* **ball'adist** a writer or singer of ballads. — *n* **ball'adry** ballads collectively; ballad-making. — **ballad concert** a concert of drawing-room ballads; **ball'admonger** a dealer in, or composer of, ballads; **ballad opera** (*hist*) an opera with spoken dialogue, and songs set to existing popular tunes. [OFr *ballade*, from LL *ballāre* to dance; see **ball**[2]]

ballade *ba-läd'*, *n* a poem of one or more triplets of stanzas, each of seven, eight or ten lines, including refrain, followed by an envoy, the whole on three (or four) rhymes; sometimes (loosely) any poem in stanzas of equal length; an ill-defined form of instrumental music, often in six-eight or six-four time. — **ballade royal** rhyme royal (James VI and I's **ballat royal** has an additional line and rhymes *ababbcbc*). [An earlier spelling of **ballad**, with old pronunciation restored]

balladin(e). Same as **baladin(e)**.

ballan *bal'ən*, *n* a species of wrasse. — Also **ball'anwrasse**. [Perh Irish *ball* spot]

ballant. A Scots form of **ballad**.

ballast *bal'əst*, *n* heavy material used to weigh down and steady a ship or balloon; broken stone or other material used as the bed of a road or railway; anything which provides steadiness or stability; something which maintains or stabilizes the current in a circuit (*electronics*). — *vt* to load with ballast; to make or keep steady; to load (*Shakesp*): — *pa p* **ball'asted** (*Shakesp* **ball'ast**). — **ball'ast-heaver**. — **in ballast** carrying ballast only. [Prob Old Swed *barlast*, from *bar* bare, and *last* load]

ballat. See **ballad, ballade**.

ballerina *bal-ə-rē'nə*, *n* a female ballet-dancer: — *pl* **balleri'nas**; formerly also **balleri'ne** (*-nā*). [Ital]

ballet[1] *bal'ā* or *bal-ā'*, *n* a theatrical performance of formalized dancing with set steps, mime and fluid graceful movements; the art or activity of dancing in this way; (a suite of) music for it; a troupe giving such performances; in skiing, skating, etc, a balletic performance; a dance (*obs*). — *adj* **balletic** (*bal-et'ik*) of the art of ballet; in or similar to the style of ballet. — *adv* **ballet'ically**. — *n* **balletomane** (*-et'ō-mān*) an enthusiast for ballet. — *n* **balletomā'nia**. — **ball'et-dancer**; **ball'et-dancing**; **ball'et-girl**; **ball'et-master** or **ball'et-mistress** a man or woman who directs or teaches ballet. [Fr, from dimin of *bal* a dance]

ballet[2]. See **ballad**.

ballista or **balista** *ba-lis'tə*, *n* a Roman military engine in the form of a crossbow for projecting heavy missiles. [L, from Gr *ballein* to throw]

ballistic *ba-lis'tik*, *adj* projectile; relating to projectiles. — *n sing* **ballis'tics** the science of projectiles. — *n* **ballis'tite** a smokeless powder composed of guncotton and nitroglycerine. — *n* **ballistōcar'diogram** a record produced by a **ballistōcar'diograph**, an instrument for detecting the movements in the body caused by each heartbeat. — *n* **ballistōcardiog'raphy**. — **ballistic missile** a guided missile that ends in a ballistic descent, the guidance being only over part of its course; **ballistic pendulum** a suspended block for finding the velocity of projectiles. [**ballista**]

ballium *bal'i-əm*, *n* the LL form of **bailey**.

ballocks. See **bollocks**.

ballon *ba-lɔ̃*, (*dance*) *n* bounciness of step. [Fr, ball]

ballon d'essai *ba-lɔ̃ de-sā*, (*Fr*) *n* an experimental balloon; a feeler or preliminary sounding of opinion.

balloon *bə-lōōn'*, *n* an apparatus for travel in the air, or for carrying weather-recording instruments, etc, supported by buoyancy rather than mechanically driven, consisting of a large bag that is filled with gas, and a cabin or basket beneath; a toy consisting of an inflatable rubber bag; something inflated or hollow, *usu* coloured (*fig*); a large globular wine-glass; a round-bottomed flask (*chem*); an ornamental ball on a pillar, etc (*archit*); a balloon-shaped outline enclosing the words or thoughts of a strip cartoon character; a balloon-shaped outline enclosing words, etc for insertion into text (*proofreading*, etc); a game played with a large inflated ball, or the ball itself (*obs*; also **ballon** *ba-lɔ̃* or *ba-lōn'*). — *adj* of or like a balloon. — *vt* to inflate; to send high in the air. — *vi* to ascend or travel in, or as if in, a balloon; to puff out like a balloon; (of an aeroplane) to rise up in the air (as a result of landing on a firm surface, or increased airspeed, etc). — *n* **ballonet** (*bal-o-net'*) in a balloon or dirigible, a small bag from which air is allowed to escape, and into which air is forced, to compensate for changes of pressure in the gas-bag. — *n* **balloon'ing**. — *n* **balloon'ist**. — *adj* **balloon'-back'** (of a dining-room chair) having a circular or oval-shaped back-support. — **balloon barrage** a system of balloons attached to each other and to the ground, as a protection against hostile aircraft; **balloon tyre** a large pneumatic tyre of low pressure; **balloon'-vine'** heartseed, a tropical American climber with bladdery pods. — **when the balloon goes up** when the trouble starts; when proceedings begin. [Ital *ballone*, augmentative of *balla* ball]

ballot *bal'ət*, *n* a ticket or paper (formerly a small ball) used in registering a secret vote; a secret vote registered or method of voting by putting a ballot into a box; in US extended to open voting. — *vi* to vote by ballot; to draw lots: — *pr p* **ball'oting**; *pa t* and *pa p* **ball'oted**. — *n* **ballotee'**. — **ball'ot-box** a box into which ballots are put in voting; **ball'ot-paper** a paper on which a ballot vote is recorded; **ball'ot-rigging** dishonest manipulation of a ballot. [Ital *ballotta*, dimin of *balla* ball. See **ball**[1]]

ballow *bal'ō*, (*Shakesp*) *n* a cudgel. — Other readings are **bat** and **battero**. [Perh a misprint for **baton**]

ballsy. See **ball**[1].

bally *bal'i*, (*slang*) *adj* a euphemism for **bloody**, but almost meaningless.

ballyhoo *bal-i-hōō'*, (*slang*) *n* noisy propaganda; fuss, commotion. — *vt* to create loud publicity, make a ballyhoo, about: — *pr p* **ballyhoo'ing**; *pa t* and *pa p* **ballyhoo'ed**.

ballyrag. See **bullyrag**.

balm *bäm*, *n* an aromatic substance; a fragrant and healing ointment; aromatic fragrance; anything that heals or soothes pain; a tree yielding balm; a labiate plant, *Melissa officinalis*, with an aroma similar to that of lemon; extended to *Melittis* (*bastard balm*) and other garden herbs. — *vt* to embalm (*archaic*); to anoint with fragrant oil (*Shakesp*); to soothe (*archaic*). — *adv* **balm'ily**. — *n* **balm'iness**. — *adj* **balm'y** fragrant; mild and soothing; bearing balm. — **balm** (or **balsam**) **of Gilead** the resinous exudation of trees of the genus *Commiphora* or *Balsamodendron*, from the belief that it is the substance mentioned in the Bible (Jer 8.22) as found in Gilead; the balsam fir. [OFr *basme*, from L *balsamum*. See **balsam**]

balmacaan *bal-mə'kän*, *n* a man's loose overcoat with raglan sleeves. [From *Balmacaan*, near Inverness, Scotland]

bal masqué *bal mas-kā*, (*Fr*) *n* a masked ball.

balm-cricket *bäm-krik'it*, (*Tennyson*) *n* a cicada. [Ger *Baum* tree, and **cricket**[1]]

Balmer series *bal'mər sē'rēz* or *-riz*, (*phys*) *n* a group of lines in the hydrogen spectrum named after the discoverer. [J J *Balmer* (1825–98), Swiss mathematician]

balmoral *bal-mor'əl*, *n* a round flat Scottish bonnet with a pompom; a figured woollen petticoat; a kind of boot lacing in front. — *n* **balmorality** (*bal-mər-al'i-ti*; also with *cap*; *joc*) enthusiasm for the superficial trappings of Scottish culture. [*Balmoral*, royal residence in Aberdeenshire (Grampian Region) built in Queen Victoria's reign]

balmy[1]. A variant of **barmy**.

balmy[2]. See under **balm**.

balneal *bal'ni-əl*, *adj* of baths or bathing. — *n* **bal'neary** a bath; a bathing-place; a medicinal spring. — *adj* of or for bathing. — *n* **balneā'tion** bathing: — *n* **balneol'ogist**. — *n* **balneol'ogy** the scientific medical study of bathing and mineral springs. — *n* **balneother'apy** treatment of disease by baths. [L *balneum*, from Gr *balaneion* bath]

balneum Mariae *bal'ni-əm ma-rī'ē* or *bal'ne-ŏŏm ma-rē'ī*, (*L*) *n* a bain-marie.

baloney or **boloney** *ba-* or *bə-lō'ni*, (*slang*) *n* deceptive talk; nonsense; (chiefly *US*) Bologna sausage. [Thought to be from **Bologna sausage**]

baloo or **balu** *bä'lōō*, *n* in India, a bear. [Hindi *bhālū*]

bal paré *bal pa-rā*, (*Fr*) *n* a dress ball.

balsa *böl'sə* or *bäl'sə*, *n* corkwood, a tropical American tree (*Ochroma lagopus*) of the silk-cotton family, with very light wood (also **bal'sawood**); a raft or float. [Sp, raft]

balsam *böl'səm*, *n* a plant of the genus *Impatiens* (family Balsaminaceae); a liquid resin or resinous oily substance, *esp* balm of Gilead; any healing agent (*fig*). — *vt* to heal; to embalm (*rare*). — *adj* **balsamic** (*-sam'ik*). — *adj* **balsamif'erous** producing balsam. — *n* **Balsamī'na** a discarded synonym of Impatiens, giving name to the balsam family **Balsaminaceae** (*-in-ā'si-ē*), closely related to the geraniums. — *adj* **bal'samy** fragrant. — **balsam fir** an American fir (*Abies balsamea*); **balsam of Peru** and **of Tolu** see **Peru** and **Tolu**; **balsam poplar** an American species of poplar; **Canada balsam** a turpentine from the balsam fir. [L *balsamum*, from Gr *balsamon*; prob of Semitic origin]

Balt *bölt*, *n* a native or inhabitant of the Baltic provinces or states; a speaker of a Baltic language; a member of the former land-owning class (of German origin) in the Baltic provinces or states; an immigrant to Australia from the Baltic or (loosely) Europe generally (*Austr colloq*). — *adj* **Balt'ic** of the sea separating Scandinavia from Germany and Russia; of, denoting or relating to a Balt or Balts. — *n* the Baltic languages, Lithuanian, Latvian and (extinct) Old Prussian. — *n* **Balt'oslav**. — *adj* **Balt'oslav**, **Balt'oslavic** or **Baltoslavon'ic** of a family of Indo-European languages comprising the Slavonic and Baltic languages. [From the *Baltic Sea*, from L *Baltia* Scandinavia]

balthazar or **balthasar** *bal'thə-zär*, *n* a very large wine-bottle, in capacity *usu* taken to equal 16 ordinary bottles (12·80 litres or 2·75 gallons). — Also **belshazzar** (*bel-shaz'ər*). — All forms also with *cap*. [Coined in reference to Daniel 5.1]

Baltimore *böl'tim-ör*, *n* a common orange and black N American bird of the hangnest family, called also *firebird*, *Baltimore oriole*, etc. [From Lord *Baltimore*, whose livery was orange and black]

balu. See **baloo**.

Baluch or **Baluchi** *ba-lōōch'* or *ba-lōō'chi*, *n* a native or inhabitant of Baluchistan; the language of the people of this region. — *adj* of this region or its people. — *n* **Baluchitherium** (*-thē'ri-əm*; Gr *therion* wild beast) a gigantic Tertiary fossil rhinoceros found in this region. [Pers *Balūchī*]

baluster *bal'əs-tər*, *n* a small pillar supporting a stair rail or a parapet coping, often circular in section and curvaceous in outline; a balustrade (*archaic*). — *adj* (of a vessel, its stem or handle) like a baluster in shape. — *adj* **bal'ustered**. — *n* **bal'ustrade** a row of balusters joined by a rail or coping. [Fr *balustre*, from LL *balaustium*, from Gr *balaustion* pomegranate flower; from its shape]

balzarine *bal'zə-rēn*, *n* a light dress material of mixed cotton and worsted. [Fr *balzorine*]

bam *bam*, (*colloq*) *n* a hoax; a false tale. — *vt* to cheat or hoax. [See **bamboozle**]

bambino *bam-bē'nō*, *n* a child; a picture or image of the child Jesus: — *pl* **bambi'nos** or **bambi'ni** (*-nē*). [Ital]

bamboo *bam-bōō'*, *n* a gigantic tropical and subtropical grass (genus *Bambusa*) with hollow-jointed woody stem; the stem, used *esp* for making furniture; bamboo-coloured bisque porcelain. — **bamboo curtain** the impenetrable political barrier of Asiatic, *esp* Chinese, communism (after **iron curtain**). [Perh Malay *bambu*]

bamboozle *bam-bōō'zl*, (*colloq*) *vt* to deceive; to confound or mystify. — *n* **bamboo'zlement**. [Origin unknown; first appears about 1700]

bampot *bam'pot*, (*Scot colloq*) *n* an idiot, fool. — Also **bamm'er**. [Ety uncertain]

Ban *ban*, (*hist*) *n* the governor of a **Ban'at** (also **Ban'ate** or **Bann'at**), a military district on the boundaries of the Hungarian kingdom. [Pers *bān* lord]

ban[1] *ban*, *n* a prohibition; sentence of banishment; outlawry; anathematization; a denunciation; a curse; a condemnation by society, etc; a proclamation (*obs*). — *vt* to forbid or prohibit; to curse (*archaic* and *dialect*); to anathematize. — *vi* to curse (*archaic*). [OE *gebann* proclamation, *bannan* to summon: cf **ban**[3] and **banns**]

ban[2] *ban*, *n* a Romanian coin, one hundredth part of a leu: — *pl* **bani** (*bany*). [Rom]

ban[3] (*hist*) *n* in feudal England, the calling of the younger vassals for military service; those so called; in the Prussian army, each of two divisions of the army reserve. — **arrière-ban** (*ar-i-ār-ban'* or (*Fr*) *ar-yer-bã*) in feudal England, the reserve or older vassals liable for military service. [OFr, of Gmc origin; cf **ban**[1]]

banal *bən-äl'*, *adj* commonplace, trivial, flat. — *n* **banal'ity** cliché, triviality, triteness. — *vt* **banal'ize** or **-ise** to make banal. — *n* **banaliza'tion** or **-s-**. — *adv* **banal'ly**. [Fr]

banana *bə-* or *ba-nä'nə*, *n* a gigantic tree-like herbaceous plant (*Musa sapientum*) or its nutritious yellow fruit which grows in hanging bunches. — **bana'na-bender** (*Austr colloq*) a Queenslander. — *adj* **bana'na-fingered** clumsy, all thumbs. — **Bana'naland** (*Austr*) Queensland; **Banan'alander** (*Austr*) a Queenslander; **banana liquid**, **oil** or **solution** a solution with the odour of bananas, used for various purposes, eg in photography, as a solvent for paint, etc; **banana plug** (*elec eng*) an electrical plug with one conductor, with a spring metal tip in the shape of a banana; **banana republic** (*derog*) any of the small republics in the tropics which depend on exports of fruit and on foreign investment; hence any small country dependent on foreign capital; **banana skin** (*fig*) something which causes a slip-up or a downfall; **banana split** a dish composed of a banana halved lengthways, ice cream, and other ingredients. — **be** or **go bananas** (*slang*) to be or go crazy; **top banana** the star entertainer in a line-up (*esp* of comedians); the most important person in a group, organization, etc (*colloq*). [Sp or Port, from the native name in Guinea]

banausic *ban-ö'sik*, *adj* merely mechanical; really or apparently appropriate to an artisan; vulgar; materialistic. — Also **banau'sian**. [Gr *banausikos*, from *banausos* a handicraftsman]

Banbury cake *ban'bər-i kāk*, *n* a kind of mince-pie made in *Banbury*, Oxfordshire.

banc *bangk*, (*law*) *n* the judges' bench. — **in banc** or **in banco** in full court. [Fr]

banco *bang'kō*, *n* the standard money in which a bank keeps its accounts, as distinguished from the current money of the place. [Ital; see **bank**[1,3]]

Band *bant*, (*Ger*) *n* a volume of a book or journal: — *pl* **Bände** (*ben'də*).

band[1] *band*, *n* that by which loose things are held together; a moral bond of restraint or of obligation (*fig*); a tie or connecting piece; (in *pl*) shackles, bonds, fetters; an agreement or promise given (*archaic*); security given (*archaic*); a banding together, a confederacy (*Scot*); a pledge (*Spenser*). — *n* **band'ster** (*hist*) a binder of the sheaves after the reapers. — **band'-stone** a stone set transversely in a wall to bind the structure. [ME *band*, *bond*, from ON *band*. See **band**[2], **bind**, **bond**[1]]

band[2] *band*, *n* a flat strip (of cloth, rubber, metal, etc) to bind round or reinforce anything, as a hat-band, waistband, rubber band, etc; a stripe of contrasting colour, texture, etc; a flat strip between mouldings, or dividing a wall surface; a finger-ring; a belt for driving machinery; the neck-band or collar of a shirt, also the collar or ruff worn in the 17c (termed a *falling-band* when turned down); (in *pl*) the pair of linen strips hanging down in front from the collar, worn by some Protestant clergymen and by barristers and advocates, formerly by others; a group or range of frequencies or wavelengths between two specified limits (*radio*, *electronics*); in sound reproduction, a separately recorded section of a record or tape; a track on a record; one or more tracks on a magnetic storage disk, etc (*comput*); a group of close-set lines *esp* in a molecular spectrum (*phys*); a particular range, between an upper and lower limit, of eg intelligence, wealth, etc. — *vt* to mark with a band; to ring (a bird) (*NAm*). — *adj* **band'ed** fastened as with a band; striped with bands; arranged in or into bands. — *n* **band'ing** the division of children in the final year of primary school into three groups according to ability, in order to obtain an even spread in the mixed-ability classes usual in comprehensive schools. — **band'-box** (or *ban'boks*) a light kind of box for holding (*orig*) bands, caps, millinery, etc. — *adj* (*esp US*) very neat and tidy, spruce; delicate, flimsy. — **band'brake** or **band'-clutch** a brake or clutch in the form of a flexible band that can be tightened about a wheel or drum; **band'-fish** a bright red Mediterranean fish (*Cepola*), or other ribbon-shaped fish; **band'-saw** an endless saw, a toothed steel belt; **band'-string** an ornamental string for fastening bands or a collar; **band'-wheel** a wheel on which a strap or band runs; **band'width** the width of a band of radio frequencies; the range of frequencies in a communications channel. [ME *bande*, from OFr *bande*, of Gmc origin; cf OE *bindan*; Ger *Binde* a band; Eng **band**[1], **bind**]

band[3] *band*, *n* a group of people bound together for any common purpose; a troop of conspirators, confederates, etc; a group of instrumentalists, *esp* brass, wind and percussion players, often attached to a regiment; a group of players providing dance-music; an orchestra (*colloq*); a group of reservation Indians with elected chiefs (*Can*); a herd or flock (*NAm*). — *vt* to form into a band. — *vi* to associate, assemble, confederate. — **band'-call** a rehearsal; **band'master** the conductor of a band; **band-pass filter** (*telecomm*) a filter which freely passes currents having frequencies within specified nominal limits, and highly attenuates currents with frequencies outside these limits; **bands'man** a member of a band of musicians; **band'stand** a structure for accommodating a band of musicians; **band'wagon** the car that carries the band in a circus procession; a fashionable movement, a trend enjoying current success. — **Band of Hope** an association of young people pledged to lifelong abstinence from alcoholic drinks, founded about 1847; **beat the band** (*colloq*) to be the tops; (in the phrase **to beat the band**) so as to beat everything, fit to bust; **jump** or **leap on the bandwagon** to join in any popular and currently successful movement in the hope of gaining advantage from it; **then the band played** that was the end of it. [Fr *bande*, of Gmc origin, with changed sense; cf **band**[1,2], **bend**[1], **bind**]

band[4] *band*, (*Spenser*) *vt* to ban or banish.

band[5]. An obsolete *pa t* of **bind**.

banda *ban'də*, (*Afr*) *n* a thatched hut. [Native word]

bandage *n* a strip of cloth for winding round an injured part of the body; an adhesive plaster for protecting a wound or cut; a piece of cloth used to blindfold the eyes. — *vt* to bind with a bandage. [MFr *bandage*; see also ety at **band**[2]]

Band-aid® *band'-ād*, *n* a type of sticking-plaster for covering minor wounds. — *adj* (*usu* without *cap*; of policies, etc) makeshift, temporary.

bandalore *ban'də-lör*, (*obs*) *n* an 18c toy resembling a yo-yo (qv) which, through the action of a coiled spring, returned to the hand when thrown down. [Origin unknown]

bandana or **bandanna** *ban-dan'ə*, *n* a silk or cotton coloured handkerchief, with spots or diamond prints, *orig* from India. [Hind *badhnū* a mode of dyeing]

bandar *bun'där, n* a rhesus monkey. [Hindi]

B and B, b. and b., B & B or **b & b** *abbrev*: bed and breakfast (see under **bed**).

bandeau *ban'dō* or *ban-dō', n* a band to bind the hair, worn around the head; a band inside a hat; a bandage for the eyes: — *pl* **bandeaux** (*ban'dōz* or *-dōz'*). [Fr]

bandeirante *bɔ̃-dā-ē-rɔ̃t', (Port) n* a pioneer, explorer or adventurer, *esp* one who took part in expeditions (*bandeiras*) in search of gold and slaves in 17c Brazil.

bandelet *band'ə-let, (archit) n* a small flat moulding around a column. [Fr *bandelette*]

bandelier *ban-də-lēr'*. A form of **bandoleer**.

banderilla *ban-* or *bän-dā-rēl'yä, n* a dart with a streamer, stuck by bullfighters in the bull's neck. — *n* **banderillero** (*ban-* or *bän-dā-rēl-yā'rō*) a bullfighter who uses banderillas: — *pl* **banderille'ros**.

banderol, banderole *ban'də-rōl*, **bandrol** *ban'drōl* or **bannerol** *ban'ə-rōl* (*Spenser* **bannerall** *-röl*) *n* a small banner or streamer, like that on a masthead; a flat band with an inscription, common in Renaissance buildings (*archit*). [Fr]

bandersnatch *ban'dər-snach, n* a monster invented by Lewis Carroll.

bandicoot *ban'di-ko͞ot, n* the largest species of rat, found in India and Sri Lanka, called also *Malabar-rat* and *pig-rat*; a member of the genus *Perameles* of small marsupials. — *vt* (*Austr*) to remove (potatoes) from the ground leaving the tops undisturbed. [Telugu *pandi-kokku* pig-rat]

bandit *ban'dit, n* an outlaw; a brigand; an enemy plane (*airmen's slang*): — *pl* **ban'dits** or **banditti** (*ban-dit'ē*; also loosely used as *sing*, a body of bandits). — *n* **ban'ditry**. — **one-armed bandit** a fruit-machine, so called from the similarity to an arm of the lever pulled to operate it, and the heavy odds against the user. [Ital *bandito*, pl *banditi*, from LL *bannīre*, *bandīre* to proclaim. See **ban**]

bandmaster. See under **band**[3].

bandobast or **bundobust** *bun'dō-bust, (Ind) n* an arrangement, settlement. [Hindi and Pers *band-o-bast* tying and binding]

bandog *ban'dog, n* an aggressive dog kept chained or tied up; a cross between an American pit bull terrier and a mastiff, rottweiler or Rhodesian ridgeback, bred for exceptional ferocity. [ME *band-dogge*; **band**[1] and **dog**]

bandoleer or **bandolier** *ban-dō-lēr', n* a shoulder belt, *esp* for carrying ammunition. — *adj* **bandoleer'ed** or **bandolier'ed** wearing a bandoleer. [OFr *bandouillere*, from Ital *bandoliera*, from *banda* a band]

bandoleon. See **bandoneon**.

bandolero *ban-dō-lā'rō, n* a highwayman: — *pl* **bandole'ros**. [Sp]

bandoline *ban'dō-lēn, n* a gummy substance formerly used for stiffening the hair. — *vt* to stiffen (the hair) with bandoline. [Prob from **band**[1]]

bandoneon *ban-dō'nē-ən* or *ban-don'i-ən, n* a kind of button accordion popular in S America, *esp* for playing tango music. — Also **bandon'ion, bandol'eon**. [S Am Sp, from H *Band*, its German inventor]

bandook. See **bundook**.

bandore *ban-dōr, n* an Elizabethan wire-stringed instrument like a cittern. — Also **bando'ra**. [Sp *bandurria*, Fr *mandore*; L *pandura*, Gr *pandourā* a three-stringed lute]

bandrol. See **banderol**.

bandsman, bandstand. See under **band**[3].

bandura *ban-do͞o'rə, n* a Ukrainian twelve-stringed instrument of the lute family. [Ukrainian, from Pol, from Ital, from L *pandura* (cf **bandore**)]

bandwagon. See under **band**[3].

bandwidth. See under **band**[2].

bandy[1] *ban'di, n* a club bent at the end for striking a ball; a ball-game played with such a club, an early form of hockey (also **ban'dy-ball**); a game played on ice, similar to ice-hockey but played with a ball and curved sticks; a version of tennis (*obs*); a tennis stroke (*obs*). [Origin obscure]

bandy[2] *ban'di, vt* to beat to and fro; to toss from one to another (eg words *with* someone); to pass (a story, information, etc) from mouth to mouth (with *about*); to give and take (blows or reproaches); to fight, strive (*Shakesp*): — *pr p* **ban'dying**; *pa t* and *pa p* **ban'died**. — *n* **ban'dying**. [Origin obscure]

bandy[3] *ban'di, adj* bent wide apart at the knee; having such legs or crooked legs. — *adj* **ban'dy-legged'**. [Poss **bandy**[1]]

bandy[4] *ban'di, (Ind) n* a carriage or (bullock) cart. — **ban'dyman**. [Telugu *bandi*]

bane *bān, n* a source or cause of evil, misery, etc; poison; destruction, death; mischief, harm (*archaic*). — *vt* to harm (*archaic*); to poison (*Shakesp*). — *adj* **bane'ful** destructive; pernicious; poisonous. — *adv* **bane'fully**. — *n* **bane'fulness**. — **bane'berry** a black poisonous berry, the fruit of the ranunculaceous plant *Actaea spicata*; the plant itself. — **the bane of one's life** something which causes one enormous trouble or misery. [OE *bana* a murderer; ON *bani* death]

bang[1] *bang, n* a heavy blow; a sudden loud noise; an explosion; a thrill, burst of activity, sudden success (*fig*); an act of sexual intercourse (*slang*); an injection of a drug (*slang*). — *vt* to beat; to strike violently; to slam (eg a door); to push down, depress (prices, the market) (*stock exchange slang*); to have sexual intercourse with (*slang*); to beat or surpass. — *vi* to make a loud noise; to slam; to inject a drug (*slang*); to dash, bounce (*dialect*). — *adv* with a bang; abruptly; absolutely (as in *bang up-to-date*, *bang in the middle*). — *adj* complete, total (used for emphasis, as in *the whole bang lot*). — *n* **bang'er** something that bangs; an explosive firework; a decrepit old car (*colloq*); a sausage (*slang*). — *adj* **bang'ing** dealing blows; overwhelming, very great (*colloq*). — *n* **bang'ing**. — *n* **bang'ster** (*obs Scot*) a violent person; a braggart; a victor. — *adj* **bang'-up** (*archaic slang*) in the height of excellence or fashion. — **bang goes** (*colloq*) that's the end of; **bang off** (*colloq*) immediately; **bang on** (*colloq*) right on the mark; to speak at length, *esp* assertively and repetitiously; **bang one's head against a brick wall** to waste one's time in unproductive effort; **bang out** to produce in a hurry (eg a piece of typing); of printers, to mark someone's retirement or the end of someone's apprenticeship by banging tables, etc with mallets, etc; **bang to rights** *orig*, caught red-handed (*criminals' slang*); certainly, absolutely, no doubt (*colloq*); **bang up** (*slang*) to imprison, *specif* to shut up in a cell; to knock about, beat up (*US*); **Big Bang** see under **big**[1]; **go with a bang** to go well, be a success. [ON *banga* to hammer; cf Ger *Bengel* a cudgel]

bang[2] *bang, n* a fringe, hair cut square across the brow (often in *pl*). — *vt* to cut (hair) square across. — *adj* **banged** wearing the hair in such a way. — **bang'-tail** a tail with the end tuft squared; an animal whose tail-hair is banged; **bang-tail muster** (*Austr*) a cattle round-up in which the tail-hair is banged as each animal is counted. [Orig an Americanism, poss from the phrase *bang off* (see under **bang**[1])]

bang[3]. Same as **bhang**.

Bangalore torpedo *bang'gə-lör tör-pē'dō, n* an explosive device for blowing gaps in barbed-wire obstacles, etc, invented by sappers and miners of the Indian army at *Bangalore*.

bangle *bang'gl, n* a circular bracelet worn on the arm or leg. — *adj* **ban'gled** wearing bangles. [Hindi *baṅgrī*, *baṅglī*]

bangsring. See **banxring**.

bani. See **ban**[2].

banian, banyan, *ban'yən* or *-yan* or **bania** *ban'yə, n* an Indian fig-tree with vast rooting branches; (also with *cap*) a Hindu trader, *esp* from Gujarat; loosely, outside India, any Hindu; an Indian broker or financier; a loose jacket, gown, or undergarment worn in India. — **banian days** (*obs*) days on which no meat was served, hence days of short commons generally, from the abstinence from flesh of the Banian merchants.

[Port *banian*, perh through Ar *banyān*, from Hindi *baniyā*, from Sans *vāṇija*, from *vaṇij* a merchant]

banish *ban'ish*, *vt* to condemn to exile; to drive away; to expel. — *n* **ban'ishment** exile. [Fr *bannir*, *baniss-*, from LL *bannīre* to proclaim]

banister or **bannister** *ban'is-tər*, *n* a stair-rail with its supports (often in *pl*). [**baluster**]

banjax *ban-jaks'* or *ban'*, (*slang*) *vt* to ruin, destroy. [Anglo-Irish; poss combination of **bang**[1] and **smash**]

banjo *ban'jō* or *ban-jō'*, *n* a musical instrument played with the fingers or with a plectrum, having a long neck, a circular body of stretched parchment like a drum, and *usu* five strings of catgut and wire; applied to various tools or devices shaped like a banjo: — *pl* **ban'jos** or **ban'joes**. — *n* **ban'joist** (*-ist*). [S US black pronunciation of **bandore**]

banjulele *ban-jōō-lā'li*, *n* a small banjo with gut strings. [*banjo* and *ukulele*]

bank[1] *bangk*, *n* a mound or ridge; an upward slope; the edge of a river, lake, etc; the raised border of a road, railway cutting, etc; the surface at a pit-mouth; the coal-face in a mine; a shoal or shallow; a bed of shellfish; a mass of cloud or mist; the tilt of an aircraft. — *vt* to enclose with a bank; to deposit or pile (up); to cover (a fire) with ashes, etc, so as to make it burn more slowly (often with *up* or *down*); (usu with *down*) to restrain (passions etc likely to erupt at any moment). — *vt* and *vi* (of aircraft) to tilt in turning. — *n* **bank'er** a locomotive used to help pull a heavy load up a steep slope (also **bank(ing) engine**); a fishing vessel on the Bank of Newfoundland, or a fisherman in such a vessel; a river full to the top of its banks (*Austr*). — *adj* **bank'erly** like a banker. — *n* **bank'ing** the building up of the outside of bends in a road, railway or sports track; an embankment. — *adv* **bank'-high** up to the top of the bank. — **banks'man** an overseer at a pit-mouth. — **from bank to bank** from the time the collier begins to descend for his spell of work till he reaches the top again. [ME *banke*, prob Scand; cognate with **bank**[2,3], **bench**]

bank[2] *bangk*, *n* a tier or rank, eg of oars, keys on a typewriter, etc; a bench for the rowers in a galley; the bench on which judges sat; a set of apparatus or equipment laid out together; a working table in various crafts; a pottery. — *n* **bank'er** a mason's bench; a builder's board on which cement, etc is mixed. — **bank'er-mark** a mason's mark on a stone. [OFr *banc*, of Gmc origin; cognate with **bank**[1,3]]

bank[3] *bangk*, *n* an institution for the keeping, lending and exchanging, etc of money; a moneybox for savings; a stock of money, fund or capital; in games of hazard, the money held by the proprietor or the person who plays against all; in card games, etc, a pool to draw cards, tokens, etc from; the person who holds this supply; any store of material or information, eg **blood bank** and **databank**; any supply, reserve or pool (of workers, resources, etc); bank paper. — *vt* to deposit in a bank. — *vi* to have a bank account; to count, rely (on) (*colloq*). — *n* **bank'ability**. — *adj* **bank'able** able to be received by a bank; reliable; *esp* of a film star, likely to ensure profitability (*US*). — *n* **bank'er** a person who keeps a bank; a person employed in banking business; a betting card game; a certainty, something that can be banked on or betted on; a result forecast the same in all the entries as being a certainty (*football pools*). — Also *adj*. — *n* **bank'ing** the business of the banker. — *adj* pertaining to a bank. — **bank account** an account set up by a customer depositing money in a bank; the business record of the money deposited in a bank; **bank'-āgent** formerly in Scotland, the head of a branch bank (now **bank'-manager**); **bank balance** the amount of money by which a bank account is in credit; **bank'-bill** (formerly) a bank-note; a bank draft; **bank'-book** or **bank pass book** a book in which a record is kept of money deposited in or withdrawn from a bank; **bank card** see **banker's card**; **bank'-cheque** an order to pay issued upon a bank; **bank draft** a bill drawn by one bank upon another; **banker's card** a card issued by a bank guaranteeing the honouring of any cheque up to a specified value (also **bank card**); **banker's draft** a bill of exchange obtained from a bank by one of its customers, enabling the purchase of goods, etc by the presentation of the draft to the seller, the bank debiting the customer's account with that amount; **banker's envelope** an envelope with the flap on the long edge, and *usu* approximately the same width as A4 paper; **banker's order** a standing order (qv); **bank giro** a credit clearing system which enables transfer of money between accounts in UK banks; **bank-hol'iday** a weekday on which banks are legally closed, bills falling due on these being payable the following day, in England and Wales observed as a general holiday; **bank interest** an amount paid by a bank to a depositor; an amount charged by a bank to a borrower; **bank loan** an amount lent by a bank to a borrower for a specific period at an agreed rate of interest; **bank'-note** a note issued by a bank, which passes as money, being payable to the bearer on demand; **bank'-paper** bank-notes in circulation; **bank paper** a thin strong paper similar to but lighter than bond paper; **bank pass book** see **bank-book** above; **bank'-rate** until 1972 the rate at which the Bank of England was prepared to discount bills, replaced by minimum lending rate (qv), itself replaced in 1981 by the base rate; **bank reserves** the cash reserve kept readily available by a bank for ordinary demands; **bank'roll** money resources. — *vt* to finance. — **bank statement** a summary, provided by the bank, of the transactions on a customer's account; **bank'-stock** a share or shares in the capital stock of a bank. — **bank of issue** one that issues its own notes or promises to pay; **break the bank** in gambling, to win from the management the sum fixed as the limit it is willing to lose on any one day; **central bank** a national bank (eg in UK the Bank of England), which deals mainly with its own government and with other banks, eg regulating interest rates and managing the national debt; **clearing bank** a bank which is a member of the London Clearing-House; **joint-stock bank** one whose capital is subscribed by a large number of shareholders; **laugh** (or **cry**) **all the way to the bank** to be delighted (or (*ironic*) sorry) to be making a lot of money, *esp* undeservedly or as a result of sharp practice; **merchant bank** one whose functions include financing transit of goods and providing financial and commercial advice; **private bank** one carried on by fewer than ten persons. [Fr *banque*, from Ital *banca*; of Gmc origin, cognate with **bank**[1,2]]

banket *bang-ket'*, (*SAfr*; *geol*) *n* a gold-bearing pebbly conglomerate. [Du *banketje* almond rock]

bankrupt *bangk'rupt*, *n* a person who fails in business; an insolvent person; a person who is or becomes deficient or lacking in a specified quality (eg *a moral bankrupt*). — *adj* insolvent; destitute (with *of*); deficient or lacking in a specified quality (eg *spiritually bankrupt*). — *vt* to make bankrupt; to have (a person) declared bankrupt; to ruin or impoverish (*fig*). — *n* **bank'ruptcy** (*-si*) the state of being or act of becoming bankrupt. [Fr *banque-route*, Ital *banca rotta*, from *banca* bank, and *rotto*, *-a*, from L *ruptus* broken]

Banksia *bangk'si-ə*, *n* a genus of Australian Proteaceae; (without *cap*) a shrub or tree of the genus. [After Sir Joseph *Banks* (1744–1820)]

banlieue *bã-lyø*, (*Fr*) *n* a suburb.

Bannat. See **Ban**.

banner *ban'ər*, *n* strictly, a square flag bearing a coat of arms; a military standard; a flag bearing some device, often carried on two poles, used in processions, etc; something which represents one's beliefs; a military subdivision, *esp* in the Manchu army (*hist*). — *adj* **bann'ered** furnished with banners. — **banner cloud** a stationary cloud that forms on the lee side of some mountains; **banner headline** a large-type headline running right across a newspaper page. [OFr *banere*, from LL *bandum*, *bannum*; cognate with **band**[1] and **bind**]

banneret *ban'ər-et*, (*hist*) *n* a knight of higher grade, *orig* one bringing vassals under his own banner, later, one dubbed on the field of battle (often confused with **baronet**). [OFr *baneret* literally bannered]

bannerol, **bannerall**. See **banderol**.

bannister. See **banister**.

bannock *ban'ək*, (chiefly *Scot*) *n* a flat (*orig* home-made) cake of oatmeal, barley or pease-meal, *usu* baked on a griddle. [OE *bannuc*]

banns *banz*, *n pl* a proclamation of intended marriage. — **forbid the banns** to make formal objection to a projected marriage. [**ban**[1]]

banoffee pie *bə-nof'ē pī*, *n* a dessert consisting of a sweet pastry case filled with bananas and soft toffee or caramel and topped with cream. [*ban*ana and t*offee*]

banquet *bangk'wit*, *n* a feast; now *esp* a lavish formal meal followed by speeches; a course of sweetmeats, fruit and wine, separate, or after a meal (*obs*). — *vt* to give a feast to or in honour of. — *vi* to feast: — *pr p* **banq'ueting**; *pa t* and *pa p* **banq'ueted**. — *n* **banq'ueter**. — *n* **banqueteer'**. — *n* **banq'ueting**. — **banq'ueting-hall**; **banq'ueting-house**. [Fr, from *banc* bench]

banquette *bang-ket'*, *n* a raised way inside a parapet; a footway, *esp* on a bridge; a built-in wall-sofa used instead of individual seats, eg in a restaurant; the long seat behind the driver in a French diligence. [Fr; Ital *banchetta*, dimin of *banca* seat]

banshee *ban'shē*, (*orig Ir folklore*) *n* a female spirit who wails and shrieks before a death in the family to which she is attached. [Ir *bean sídhe*, Old Ir *ben síde* woman of the fairies]

bant[1]. See **banting**[1].

bant[2] *bant*, (*dialect*) *n* vigour, strength, springiness. [Cf **bent**[1] and MDu **bant** power, force]

bantam *ban'təm*, *n* a small variety of the common domestic fowl; a small man, *esp* a soldier. — *adj* of bantam breed; little and combative. — **ban'tamweight** a weight category applied variously in boxing and wrestling; a sportsman of the specified weight for the category (eg in professional boxing above flyweight, **jun'ior-bantamweight** maximum 52 kg/115 lb), **ban'tamweight** (maximum 54 kg/118 lb) and **su'per-bantamweight** maximum 55 kg/122 lb). [Prob *Bantam* in Java]

banteng *ban'teng* or **banting** *-ting*, *n* an East Indian wild ox. [Malay]

banter *ban'tər*, *vt* to make fun of; to joke at; to impose upon, trick (*archaic*). — *n* humorous ridicule; joking; a joke (*archaic*). — *n* **bant'erer**. — *n* and *adj* **bant'ering**. — *adv* **bant'eringly**. [Ety unknown]

Banthine® *ban'thēn*, *n* a synthetic drug used against peptic ulcers.

banting[1] *bant'ing*, (*obs*) *n* weight-reduction by avoiding fat, sugar and starch. — *vi* **bant** (back-formation) to diet. — *n* **bant'ingism**. [From W *Banting* (1797–1878), a London cabinetmaker, who recommended it to the public in 1863]

banting[2]. See **banteng**.

bantling *bant'ling*, (*archaic* and *derog*) *n* a young child, a brat. [Prob Ger *Bänkling* bastard, from *Bank* bench]

Bantu *ban'tōō*, (also without *cap*) *n* a name given to a large group of African languages and the peoples speaking them in S and Central Africa; the official name for the African peoples of S Africa. — Also *adj*. — *n* **Ban'tustan** the coined name for a semi-independent region, or homeland, of S Africa populated and administered by Bantus; a region of similar status elsewhere. [Bantu, people]

banxring or **bangsring** *bangks'ring*, *n* a tree-shrew. [Jav *bangsring*]

banyan. See **banian**.

banzai *bän'zä-ē*, *n* a Japanese battle-cry and salute to the emperor; a Japanese exclamation of joy. — *adj* (of Japanese parties) rollicking; (of Japanese military attacks) kamikaze. [Jap *banzai* 10 000 years, forever]

baobab *bā'ō-bab*, *n* a gigantic tropical W African tree, the monkey-bread tree (*Adansonia digitata*; family Bombacaceae). [Prob African]

BAOR *abbrev*: British Army of the Rhine.

Bap. or **Bapt.** *abbrev*: Baptist.

bap *bap*, (*Scot* and *N Eng*) *n* a large, flat, elliptical breakfast roll. [Ety uncertain]

bap. or **bapt.** *abbrev*: baptized.

Baphomet *baf'ō-met*, *n* a mysterious idol the Templars were accused of worshipping. — *adj* **baphomet'ic**. [For *Mahomet*]

Bapt. See **Bap.**

baptize or **-ise** *bapt-īz'*, *vt* to administer baptism to; to christen, give a name to; to name at launching and break a bottle of wine on the bow of (a ship). — *n* **bapt'ism** (*-izm*) immersion in or sprinkling with water as a religious ceremony; an experience regarded as initiating one into a society, group, etc. — *adj* **baptis'mal**. — *adv* **baptis'mally**. — *n* **bapt'ist** a person who baptizes; (with *cap*) a member of a Christian sect which approves only of baptizing by immersion, and that only of persons who profess their faith in Christ. — *n* **bap'tistery** or **bap'tistry** a place for administration of baptism, whether a separate building or part of a church. — **baptismal name** one given at baptism, a Christian name; **baptismal regeneration** the doctrine of the remission of sin original and actual, and of the new birth into the life of sanctifying grace, in and through the sacrament of baptism. — **baptism by desire** the grace held to be given to a believer who ardently desires baptism, but dies before receiving it; **baptism for the dead** the vicarious baptism of a living for an unbaptized dead Christian; **baptism of blood** martyrdom of the unbaptized Christian; **baptism of fire** the gift of the Holy Spirit; martyrdom by fire regarded as an equivalent to baptism; any trying ordeal, such as a first experience of being under fire; **clinical baptism** baptism administered to the sick; **conditional** (or **hypothetical**) **baptism** baptism administered conditionally when it is doubtful whether the person was previously baptized validly or at all; **private baptism** baptism elsewhere than in church. [Gr *baptizein*, from *baptein* to dip]

bapu *bä'pōō*, (*Ind*) *n* spiritual father. [Hindi]

Bar. *abbrev*: Barrister.

bar[1] *bär*, *n* a rod, strip or oblong block of any solid substance; formerly, any of various standards of weight or value; a pound, sovereign (esp *half a bar* ten shillings) (*obs slang*); a strong rod or long piece used as a lever, door fastening, barrier, part of a gate or grate, etc; a crossbar; a bolt; a barrier; an obstruction or impediment; that which completely puts an end to an action or claim; in salary statements, a level beyond which one cannot rise unless certain conditions, concerning eg the amount of advanced work one does, are met; a bank or shoal as at the mouth of a river or harbour; a counter across which liquor or food is served; (one room in) a public-house; a counter at which one particular article of food, clothing, etc, is sold, or one particular service is given; a rail or similar structure marking off a space, as in a house of parliament, or that at which prisoners are arraigned in court; (*usu* with *cap*) barristers or advocates collectively, or (loosely) the legal profession; a court; an authority appealed to; a ballet-dancer's exercise rail (*usu* **barre**); an addition to a medal, a strip of metal below the clasp; a ridge between a horse's teeth; a stripe, *esp* transverse; a horizontal band across a shield (*heraldry*); a rhythmic unit in music, consisting of a certain number of beats in either simple or compound time, marked by the time signature; a bar line (*music*) (see also **double-bar**); (in *pl*) the game of (prisoners'-) base (but see **base**[1]). — *vt* to fasten, secure, shut (out or in), furnish or mark with a bar or bars; to hinder; to obstruct; to exclude the possibility or validity of; to preclude; to divide into bars: — *pr p* **barr'ing**; *pa t* and *pa p* **barred**. — *prep* except, but for. — *n* **barr'ing**. — *prep* except for; leaving out of consideration. — *adj*

bar'ful (*Shakesp* **barre'full**) full of obstructions. — **bar'-bell** a bar weighted at the ends for gymnastic exercises; **bar billiards** a small-scale version of billiards played in bars; **bar'-chart** or **bar'-graph** a graph showing comparative quantities by means of rectangular blocks of varying proportional height; **bar code** an arrangement, readable by computer, of thick and thin parallel lines, eg printed on, and giving coded details of, goods at a point of sale, library books, etc. — *adj* **bar'-coded**. — **bar code reader** or **scanner** an optical device which can read bar code data and translate them into digital signals for processing; **Bar Council** the governing professional body of English barristers; **bar'fly** (*old-fashioned colloq*) a drinker who spends his or her time in bars; **bar-graph** see **bar-chart**; **bar'-iron** iron in malleable bars; **bar'keeper** keeper of a refreshment bar or toll-bar; **bar line** a vertical line across the staff between each bar (*music*); **bar lunch** or **bar meal** a light meal or snack available in a bar; **bar'-magnet** a permanent magnet in the form of a straight bar; **bar'maid**, **bar'man** or **bar'person** a woman, man or person who serves at a bar in a public-house, etc; **bar'-parlour** a small room adjoining a bar in a public house; **barred code** (*telecomm*) any dialled code that automatic exchange apparatus is primed to reject by connecting the caller no further than the number unobtainable tone; **barring-out'** (*obs*) the shutting out of a schoolmaster from school by the pupils, to enforce demands; **bar'-room** (chiefly *US*) a room in which there is a bar, taproom (also *adj*); **bar-sin'ister** see **baton sinister**; **bar slide** a bar-shaped hair ornament; **bar stool** a high stool suitable for sitting at a bar; **bar supper** a bar meal available in the evening; **bar'tender** a barman or barmaid; **bar'wood** a red dyewood imported in bars from Africa. — **at the bar** in court; in practice as a barrister or advocate; **bar none** (*colloq*) with no exceptions; **behind bars** in prison; **called to the bar** admitted as barrister or advocate; **called within the bar** made Queen's (or King's) Counsel in the UK. [OFr *barre*, from LL *barra*]

bar[2] *bär*, (*meteorol*) *n* a unit used in expressing atmospheric pressure (1 bar = $10^5 N/m^2$; 1 **mill'ibar**, used for barometric purposes, = $10^2 N/m^2$): — *pl* **bar**. — *adj* **bar'ic** barometric. [Gr *baros* weight]

bar[3] *bär*, **baur** or **bawr** *bör*, (*Scot*) *n* a joke; an amusing incident or story. [Poss Scot *bar* (the game of tossing the) caber]

bar[4] *bär*, *n* a fish, the maigre. [Fr]

bar. *abbrev*: baritone.

baracan. See **barracan**.

baragouin *bä-rä-gwẽ* or *-gwin'*, *n* any jargon or unintelligible language. [Fr; from Bret *bara* bread, and *gwenn* white, said to have originated in the Breton soldiers' astonishment at white bread]

barasingha or **barasinga** *ba-ra-sing'gə*, (*Ind*) *n* the swamp deer, *Cervus duvauceli*. [Hindi *bārah singā*, literally twelve horn]

barathea *bar-ə-thē'ə*, *n* a soft fabric of worsted, or of worsted and silk, etc. [Origin unknown]

barathrum *ba-rath'ro͝om*, *n* an abyss; an insatiable person. [L, from Gr *barathron*]

baraza *ba-ra'za* (*EAfr*) *n* a public meeting-place; a meeting. [Swahili]

BARB or **Barb** *bärb*, *abbrev*: Broadcasters' Audience Research Board.

barb[1] *bärb*, *n* a subsidiary backward-facing projection near the point of an arrow, fish-hook, etc; one of the filaments of a feather's web; a sting (*fig*); a wounding or wittily-pointed remark; a woven linen covering for the throat and breast (and sometimes the lower part of the face) worn by women in the Middle Ages, still part of the habit of certain orders of nuns. — *vt* to arm with barbs; to pierce, as with a barb; to shave, trim, mow (*obs*). — *adj* **barb'ate** bearing a hairy tuft. — *adj* **barb'ated** barbed; bearded. — *n* **barbe** a Waldensian teacher. — *adj* **barbed** having a barb or barbs (eg **barbed'-wire**, used for fences); (by confusion) barded. — *n* **barb'el** a freshwater fish of the carp family with beard-like appendages at its mouth; such an appendage. — *adj* **barb'ellate** (*bot*) having barbed or bearded bristles. — *n* **barb'et** a tropical bird with bristly beak; a kind of poodle. — *n* **barbicel** (*bär'bi-sel*) a tiny hook on the barbule of a feather. — *n* **barb'ule** a small barb; a fish's barbel; a hair-like structure on the barb of a feather. [L *barba* a beard]

barb[2] *bärb*, *n* a horse of a racing breed related to the Arab; a dark-coloured fancy pigeon. [From *Barbary*, where the breeds originated]

Barbados or **Barbadoes** *bär-bā'dōs*, *-dos* or *-dōz*, *adj* of the West Indian island of Barbados. — *n* and *adj* **Barbā'-dian**. — **Barbados cherry** the cherry-like fruit of West Indian trees of the genus Malpighia; **Barbados earth** an earthy marl found in Barbados; **Barbados gooseberry** the edible fruit of a West Indian climbing cactus (*Pereskia aculeata*); **Barbados leg** elephantiasis; **Barbados pride** a West Indian shrub, peacock-flower (*Caesalpinia* or *Poinciana pulcherrima*); an Asiatic ornamental tree (*Adenanthera pavonina*) naturalized in the West Indies, also called red sandalwood.

barbarous *bär'bər-əs*, *adj* falling short of the standard of correctness, classical purity, and good taste; unscholarly; corrupt, ungrammatical or unidiomatic; uncultured; uncivilized; brutal; harsh. — *n* **barbār'ian** someone without taste or refinement; a somewhat uncivilized man; a cruel man; *orig* someone who was not a Greek, later neither a Greek nor a Roman; a foreigner. — Also *adj*. — *adj* **barbar'ic** (*bär-bar'ik*) uncivilized; characteristic of barbarians; rude; tastelessly ornate and ostentatious; wild and harsh; foreign. — *n* **barbarization** or **-s-** (*bär-bər-ī-zā'shən*). — *vt* **bar'barize** or **-ise** to make barbarous; to corrupt, as a language. — *n* **bar'barism** savagery, brutal or uncivilized behaviour; rudeness of manners; a form of speech offensive to scholarly taste. — *n* **barbar'ity** (*bär-bar'i-ti*) savageness; cruelty. — *adv* **bar'barously**. — *n* **bar'barousness**. [Gr *barbaros* foreign, literally stammering, from the unfamiliar sound of foreign tongues]

Barbary *bär'bər-i*, *n* the country of the *Berbers*, in N Africa. — *adj* **barbaresque** (*-esk'*). — **Barbary ape** the magot, a kind of macaque, the only European monkey; **Barbary coast** the N African coast in the Mediterranean; **Barbary sheep** a N African wild sheep. **[Berber]**

barbasco *bär-bas'co*, *n* any of a variety of S American plants, the juice of whose roots is used in the preparation of fish-poisons, synthetic hormones, etc: — *pl* **barbas'cos**. [Sp]

barbastelle or **barbastel** *bär-bəs-tel'*, or *bär'*, *n* a hairy-lipped bat. [Fr]

barbe. See **barb**[1].

barbecue, **barbeque** or (*informal*) **bar-b-q** *bär'bi-kū*, *vt* to grill over an open fire, *usu* of charcoal, often adding a highly seasoned sauce to the food; to roast whole (*obs*); to cure on a barbecue (*obs*). — *n* a framework for barbecuing food over an open fire; a portable grill for cooking thus; food cooked in this way; a party, *esp* held out of doors, where food is so cooked; an open floor on which coffee-beans and the like are spread out to dry. [Sp *barbacoa*, from Haitian *barbacòa* a framework of sticks set upon posts]

barbel, **barbellate**. See **barb**[1].

barber *bär'bər*, *n* a person who shaves beards, cuts and styles men's hair, etc. — *vt* to shave or cut the hair of. — **barb'er-monger** (*Shakesp*) a man decked out by his barber, a fop; **barber's block** a round block on which wigs are made; **bar'ber-shop** or **bar'bershop** a type of music originating in the US, played, or *esp* sung, in close chromatic harmony, *usu* in quartets. — Also *adj*. — **barber's pole** the barber's sign, a pole striped spirally, *gen* red and white; **barber's rash** or **itch** an infection by the fungus *Tinea barbae*, causing a scaly rash in the bearded area as well as sycosis; **barb'er-surgeon** (*hist*) one who let blood and drew teeth as well as shaved. [OFr *barbour*, from L *barba* a beard]

barberry *bär'bər-i, n* a thorny shrub (*Berberis*) of various species, most with yellow flowers and red berries, common in ornamental hedges. [LL *berberis*; the Ar *barbārīs* is borrowed; not connected with **berry**]

Barberton daisy *bär'bər-tən dā'zi, n* (a plant of) the Gerbera genus of composites native to South Africa, flourishing *esp* in the *Barberton* district of Transvaal.

barbet. See **barb**[1].

barbette *bär-bet', n* an earthen terrace inside the parapet of a rampart, serving as a platform for heavy guns; a fixed cylinder which encloses and protects the rotating part of an armoured turret in a warship. [Fr]

barbican *bär'bi-kən, n* a projecting watchtower over the gate of a castle or fortified town; *esp* the outwork intended to defend the drawbridge. [OFr *barbacane*; origin unknown]

barbicel. See **barb**[1].

barbie *bär'bi*, (*Austr colloq*) *n* a barbecue.

Barbie doll® *bär'bi dol, n* a glamorous teenage doll with separately purchasable clothing and accessories appropriate to fantasy versions of an exciting modern lifestyle.

barbituric *bärb-it-ū'rik*, (*chem*) *adj* applied to an acid got from malonic acid and urea, source of important sedatives. — *n* **barb'itone** (also *US* **barb'ital**) a derivative of barbituric acid used as a sedative and hypnotic. — *n* **barbit'urate** (or *-tūr'*) a salt or ester of barbituric acid. [From the lichen Usnea *barbata* and *uric* acid]

Barbizon School *bär'bi-zon skōōl*, (*art*) *n* a mid-19th-century group of French painters. [From *Barbizon* a village near Paris]

barbola *bär-bō'lə* or **barbola work** (*wûrk*), *n* ornamentation with small flowers, fruit, etc made of plastic paste and coloured. [Orig proprietary term, from **barbotine**]

barbotine *bär'bə-tin, n* a fine clay used for ornamenting pottery; pottery ornamented with this. — Also *adj*. [Fr, from *barboter* to dabble about noisily]

Barbour® *bär'bər* or **Barbour**® **jacket** (*jak'ət*) (also **Bar'-bour**® **coat** (*kōt*)), *n* a strong waterproof jacket (or coat), *esp* one made of waxed cotton.

bar-b-q. See **barbecue**.

barbs *barbz*, (*slang*) *n pl* short for **barbiturates**.

barbule. See **barb**[1].

barca *bär'ka*, (*Ital*) *n* a boat, barge.

barcarolle or **barcarole** *bär'kə-rōl, -rōl'* or *-rol'*, *n* a gondolier's song; a musical composition of a similar character. [Ital *barcarola* a boat-song, from *barca* a boat]

Barcelona nut *bär-sə-lō'nə nut, n* a type of hazelnut exported from Spain, *usu* kiln-dried to retain its flavour.

BArch *abbrev*: Bachelor of Architecture.

barchan(e). See **barkhan**.

Barclaycard *bär'kli-kärd, n* a cheque guarantee and credit card issued by *Barclays* Bank.

bard[1] *bärd, n* one of the ancient Celtic order of formal poets and singers; a strolling minstrel (*archaic*; *Scot*); a poet (*literary*); a poet whose work has won a competition at the Eisteddfod. — *adj* **bard'ic**. — *n* **bard'ling** a poetaster. — *adj* **bardol'atrous**. — *n* **bardol'atry** Shakespeare-worship (Gr *latreiā* worship). — *n* **bard'ship**. — *adj* **bard'y** (*Scot*) insolent; impudent. — **bard'-craft**. — **the Bard** the poet regarded by a country as its national poet, eg Shakespeare, Burns. [Scot Gaelic and Ir *bard*]

bard[2] *bärd, n* piece of bacon or pork fat used to cover meat or game during cooking to prevent drying-out; (in *pl*) a protective or ornamental covering for a war-horse (*obs*). — *vt* to cover (a piece of meat or game) with bards; to provide (a horse) with bards (*obs*). — *adj* **bard'ed** caparisoned. [Fr *barde*, from Sp *albarda* pack-saddle, perh from Ar *al-barda'ah*, from *al* the, and *barda'ah* mule's pack-saddle]

bard[3]. An old spelling of **barred**; also short for **barded**.

bardash *bar-dash'*, (*obs*) *n* a homosexual male, a catamite. [Fr *bardache*]

bardo *bär'dō*, (*Tibetan Buddhism*) *n* the intermediate stage between death and rebirth. [Tibetan, between two]

bare[1] *bār, adj* naked; open to view; uncovered, bare-headed (*obs*); without the usual covering; unarmed (*obs*); unfurnished, empty; threadbare, worn; unprovided or scantily provided; poor; scanty; mere; unadorned, unpolished (*obs*); paltry (*Shakesp*); laid waste (*Shakesp*; *Milton*). — *vt* to strip or uncover. — *adv* **bare'ly** hardly, scarcely; just and no more; not quite; nakedly (*obs*); plainly, explicitly, openly (*obs*). — *n* **bare'ness**. — *adj* **bār'ish** somewhat bare. — *adj* and *adv* **bare'back** without a saddle. — *adj* **bare'backed** with bare back; unsaddled. — *adj* **bare'boat** in shipping, used of a charter or hire in which the chartering company is totally responsible for manning, supplies, maintenance and insurance. — **bare'bone** (*Shakesp*) a very lean person; **bare bones** the barest essentials or facts. — *adj* **bare'-breached** (*Scot*) trouserless. — *adj* **bare'faced** with the face uncovered; beardless; avowed (*Shakesp*); impudent. — *adv* **barefacedly** (*-fāst'li* or *-fās'id-li*). — **bare'facedness**. — *adj* and *adv* **bare'foot** or **barefoot'ed** having the feet bare; discalced. — **barefoot doctor** *orig* in China, an agricultural worker trained in the basic principles of health, hygiene and first-aid in order to treat fellow-workers. — *adj* and *adv* **bare-hand'ed** with no weapon. — *adj* and *adv* **barehead'ed** without a hat. — *adj* and *adv* **bare-knuck'le** or **bare-knuck'led** without boxing gloves on; fiercely aggressive. — **bareland croft** a croft with no croft house. — *adj* and *adv* **bare'legged**. — **with one's bare hands** with no weapon or tool. [OE *bær*; Ger *baar, bar*; ON *berr*]

bare[2] *bār*. Old *pa t* of **bear**[1].

barege or **barège** *bä-rezh'*, *n* a light, silky dress-fabric. — *n* **baregine** (*bar'i-jēn*) a gelatinous mass of bacteria and sulphur found in mineral waters. [*Barèges* in Hautes-Pyrénées]

baresark. Erroneous form of **berserk**.

barf *bärf*, (*NAm slang*) *vi* to vomit. [Ety unknown]

bargain *bär'gən, n* a contract or agreement; any transaction or deal (*stock exchange*); something acquired by bargaining; something for sale at an advantageously low price; haggling, discussion about terms of purchase, etc (*Shakesp*); strife, struggle (*obs*; *Northern*). — *vi* to make a contract or agreement; to haggle; to count on; to strive (*obs*; *Scot*). — *vt* to lose by bad bargaining (with *away*). — *n* **bar'gainer**. — **bar'gain-basement** or **-counter** places in a shop where bargains are sold; **bar'gain-hunter** a person who goes shopping for bargains. — **bargain and sale** in law, a mode of conveyance whereby property may be assigned or transferred for valuable consideration; **bargain for** to count on, make allowance for, expect; **bargaining chip** (*US*) or **counter** (*UK*) an advantage or asset possessed by one party which can be used to extract a concession in negotiations; **into the bargain** as well, in addition; **make the best of a bad bargain** to do one's best in an adverse situation; **sell someone a bargain** (*Shakesp*) to make a fool of someone; **strike a bargain** to agree on terms. [OFr *bargaine*]

bargander. See **bergander**.

barge *bärj, n* a flat-bottomed freight boat, with or without sails, used on rivers and canals; a lighter; a large pleasure-boat; the second boat of a man-of-war; a small sailing vessel (*obs*). — *vi* to move clumsily; to bump (*into*); to push one's way rudely. — *n* **barg'ee** a bargeman. — **barge'man** manager of a barge; **barge'-master** proprietor of a barge; **barge'pole** a pole for propelling a barge. — **barge in** to intrude; to interfere; **not touch with a bargepole** to refuse to have anything to do with. [OFr *barge*, from LL *barga*; cf **bark**[2]]

barge-board *bärj'bōrd, n* a board along the edge of a gable to cover the rafters and keep out rain. — **barge'-couples** gable rafters; **barge'-stones** those making up the sloping edge of a gable. [Perh LL *bargus* a gallows]

bargello *bär'je-lō, n* a type of needlepoint or tapestry stitch that produces a zigzag pattern: — *pl* **bar'gellos**. [The *Bargello*, a Florentine museum, having examples of this stitch]

barghest, **bargest** or **barghaist** *bär'gest* or *-gāst, n* a dog-like goblin portending death. [Perh connected with Ger *Berggeist* mountain-spirit]

bargoose *bär'gōōs*, (*S Eng dialect*) *n* the barnacle goose; the shelduck: — *pl* **bar'geese**. [First sense a contraction; second sense poss from the band of brown on its shoulders, and its goose-like movement]

baric. See **bar**[2], **barium**.

barilla *bar-il'ə, n* an impure sodium carbonate produced by burning certain seaside plants; a seaside plant (*Salsola soda*) common in Spain and Sicily. [Sp]

barite. See **barium**, **baryta**.

baritone or **barytone** *bar'i-tōn, n* a deep-toned male voice between bass and tenor; a singer with such a voice (in these senses now *usu* **bar'itone**); any of several low-pitched musical instruments, *esp* the baritone saxaphone; (**barytone**, also **bar'yton**) a musical instrument like the viola da gamba with sympathetic strings added. — *adj* of the pitch and compass of a baritone or barytone; (**barytone**) (*classical Gr gram*) not having an acute accent on the last syllable. [Gr *barytonos* deep-sounding, not accented, from *barys* heavy, deep, and *tonos* a tone]

barium *bā'ri-əm, n* a metallic element (atomic no 56; symbol **Ba**) present in baryta. — *adj* **bā'ric**. — *n* **bā'rite** (*NAm*) barytes. — **barium meal** a mixture of barium sulphate administered to render the alimentary canal opaque to X-rays. [See **baryta**]

bark[1] *bärk, n* the abrupt cry of a dog, wolf, etc; the report of a gun; a cough (*colloq*). — *vi* to utter a bark; to clamour; to advertise wares noisily; to cough (*colloq*). — *vt* to utter with a bark (*Spenser*); to utter abruptly and peremptorily; to advertise (wares) noisily. — *n* **bark'er** a dog; a barking dog; a tout advertising wares, a show, etc in a loud voice to attract custom; a pistol or cannon (*obs slang*). — *adj* **bark'ing** barking mad. — **barking deer** the muntjac; **barking iron** (*slang*) a pistol; **barking mad** (*slang*) crazy, raving mad. — **bark up the wrong tree** (*fig*) to act, speak, proceed, etc under a misapprehension, mistakenly to take inappropriate action; **chief barker** the title of the president of the Variety Club of Great Britain; **his bark is worse than his bite** his words may be bad-tempered or fierce, but his actual deeds are not so bad. [OE *beorcan*]

bark[2] or **barque** *bärk, n* a ship of small size, square-sterned, without head-rails; technically, a three-masted vessel whose mizzen-mast is fore-and-aft-rigged (instead of being square-rigged like the fore and main masts); any boat or sailing ship (*poetic*). — *n* **bark'entine** or **barqu'entine** (*-ən-tēn*) a three-masted vessel, with the fore-mast square-rigged, and the main-mast and mizzen-mast fore-and-aft-rigged. [Fr *barque*, from LL *barca*; poss from Gr *bāris* a Nile barge]

bark[3] *bärk, n* the rind or covering of the trunk and branches of a tree; that used in tanning or dyeing; that used in medicine (cinchona); an outer covering or skin. — *vt* to strip or peel bark or skin from; to tan (leather); to cover with or as if with bark, encrust. — *vi* to form a bark (*obs*). — *vt* and *vi* **bark'en** to dry up into a barky crust. — *adj* (*poetic*) made or composed of bark. — *adj* **bark'less**. — *adj* **bark'y**. — **bark'-bed** a hotbed of spent bark; **bark'-beetle** any beetle of the family Scolytidae, tunnellers in and under bark. — *adj* **bark'-bound** prevented from growing by failure to shed the bark. — **bark'-cloth** a thin papery kind of cloth made by soaking and beating the inner bark of some trees, *esp* tapa; **bark'-louse** any of various aphids that infest the bark of trees. [ON *börkr*; Dan *bark*]

Barker's mill *bärk'ərz mil, n* a device rotated by water, invented by a 17c Dr *Barker*.

barkhan, **barkan**, **barchan** or **barchane** *bär-kän', n* a crescent-shaped sand-dune, of the type found in the Turkestan deserts. [Native word in Turkestan]

barley[1] *bär'li, n* a hardy grass (*Hordeum vulgare* and other species); its grain used for food, and for making malt liquors and spirits. — **bar'ley-bree**, **-broo** or **-broth** (*Scot*) strong ale; whisky; **bar'leycorn** (personified as *John Barleycorn*) the grain from which malt is made; a single grain of barley; a measure of length = $\frac{1}{3}$ of an inch (*obs*); a V-shaped sight on a gun; **barley sugar** a sweet made by melting and cooling sugar (formerly by boiling it with a decoction of barley). — *adj* **bar'ley-sugar** *usu* (eg of furniture legs, etc) referring to the twisted spiral shape of a barley-sugar stick. — **barley water** a liquid produced by boiling down pearl barley in water, *usu* sweetened and flavoured as a cold drink; **barley wine** a strong English beer; **pearl barley** the grain stripped of husk and pellicle, and completely rounded by grinding; **pot barley** the grain deprived by milling of its outer husk, used in making broth, etc. [OE *bærlic* of barley, from root of **bear**[3], and suffix *-līc*]

barley[2] *bär'li*, (*Scot* and *N Eng dialect*) *interj* in games, a call for truce. — *n* a truce; a breathing-space. [Perh **parley**]

barley-brake or **-break** *bär'li-brāk, n* an old country game, *orig* played by three couples, in which one pair had to catch the others. [Perh because often played in a *barley*-field; or perh from the previous word]

barm *bärm, n* froth of fermenting liquor; yeast. — *adj* **barm'y** frothy; fermenting; mentally unsound (*slang*; also **balmy** *bä'mi*). — *n* **barm'iness**. — *adj* **barm'y-brained**. — **barm cake** (*Eng dialect*) a soft round bread roll. [OE *beorma*, Dan *bärme*, Ger *Bärme*]

barmbrack *bärm'brak*, (*Ir*) *n* a currant bun. [Ir *bairigen* or *bairśin*, and *breac* speckled cake]

barm-cloth *bärm'-kloth*, (*archaic*) *n* an apron. [OE *barm* (WSax *bearm*) bosom, and **cloth**]

Barmecide *bär'mi-sīd, n* a person who offers an imaginary or pretended banquet or other benefit. — *adj* **Bar'mecide** or **Barmecī'dal**. [From an imaginary feast given to a beggar in the *Arabian Nights*, by one of the *Barmecide* family]

bar mitzvah, **bar mizvah** or **bar mitsvah** *bär mits'və, n* (sometimes *caps*; also hyphenated or as one word) in the Jewish religion, a boy attaining the age (*usu* 13 years) of religious responsibility; the festivities held in recognition of this event. [Heb, son of the law]

barmkin *bärm'kin*, (*archaic*; *Northern*) *n* a battlement, or a turret, on the outer wall of a castle; the wall itself. [Origin obscure]

barn[1] *bärn, n* a building in which grain, hay, etc are stored; a stable or cattle shed (*NAm*); a large garage for buses, trucks, etc (*NAm*). — *vt* to store in a barn. — **barn dance** a social gathering at which square-dances and other traditional country-dances are danced; a progressive dance; **barn'-door** the door of a barn; an adjustable flap in front of a light source, eg a studio lamp for controlling the light; in cricket, a player who blocks every ball (*old-fashioned*; *facetious*); humorously, a target too broad to be missed; **barn owl** a species of owl, generally buff-coloured above and white below; **barns'breaking** (*Scot*) a boisterous frolic; an injurious or mischievous activity. — *vi* **barn'storm** to tour *usu* country areas giving theatrical performances; to travel about speaking at meetings, *usu* for election purposes. — Also *vt*. — **barn'stormer**; **barn'storming**; **barn'yard**. — Also *adj* as in **barnyard fowl**. [OE *bereern*, contracted *bern*, from *bere* barley, and *ern* a house]

barn[2] *bärn*, (*nuc phys*) *n* unit of effective cross-sectional area of nucleus, $10^{-28}m^2$. [Appar from 'as big as a *barn*']

Barnaby *bärn'ə-bi, n* a form of *Barnabas*. — *n* **Bar'nabite** a member of the Congregation of Regular Clerics of St Paul, founded at Milan in 1530, so called from their church of St Barnabas there. — **Barnaby Day**, **Barnaby Bright** or **Long Barnaby** St Barnabas' Day, 11 June, in Old Style reckoned the longest day.

barnacle[1] *bär'nə-kl, n* a barnacle-goose; a cirripede crustacean that adheres to rocks and ship bottoms; a companion not easily shaken off. — **bar'nacle-goose** or

ber'nicle-goose a wild black and white goose of N Europe (*Branta leucopsis*) once believed to develop from a barnacle (the **goose'-bar'nacle**) that attaches itself, *esp* to floating wood, by a thick stalk. [OFr *bernaque*, from LL *bernaca*]

barnacle[2] *bär'nə-kl*, *n* an instrument put on a restless horse's nose to keep him quiet; (in *pl*) spectacles (*obs colloq*). — *adj* **bar'nacled**. [OFr *bernac*]

barney *bär'ni*, (*colloq*) *n* a rough noisy quarrel; humbug; a prize-fight.

barocco, barock. See **baroque**.

barodynamics *bar-o-dī-nam'iks*, *n sing* mechanics applied to heavy structures, such as dams and bridges, which may collapse under their own weight. [Gr *baros* weight, and **dynamics**]

barogram *bar'ō-gram*, *n* a tracing produced by a barograph. [Gr *baros* weight, and **-gram**]

barograph *bar'ō-gräf*, *n* a recording barometer. [Gr *baros* weight, and **-graph**]

barometer *bə-rom'i-tər*, *n* an instrument for measuring atmospheric pressure; a weather-glass; an indicator of change (eg in public opinion; *fig*; also *adj*). — *adj* **barometric** (*bar-ō-met'rik*) or **barometrical** (*-met'ri-kl*). — *adv* **baromet'rically**. — *n* **barometry** (*ba-rom'ət-ri*). [Gr *baros* weight, and *metron* measure]

barometz *bar'ō-mets*, *n* the Scythian lamb, a plant at one time supposed to be also animal, growing on a stalk but eating grass like a lamb, near the Caspian Sea; a fern (*Cibotium* or *Dicksonia barometz*), of the East Indies and Pacific islands, whose woolly rootstock and leaf bases looked somewhat like a lamb. [Russ *baranets* club-moss, dimin of *baran* ram]

baron *bar'ən*, *n* a title of rank, the lowest in the British peerage; a foreign noble of similar grade; the head of any organization or institution who is regarded as wielding despotic power (eg a *press baron*); formerly a title of the judges of the Court of Exchequer; in feudal times a tenant-in-chief of the crown; later a peer or great lord of the realm generally; the owner of a freehold estate, whether titled or not (*Scot hist*); a husband (opposed to *feme* wife; *heraldry* and *Eng law*); till 1832, the name for the parliamentary representatives of the Cinque Ports. — *n* **bar'onage** the whole body of barons; a list or book of barons. — *n* **bar'oness** a baron's wife, or a woman holding a baronial title in her own right. — *adj* **baronial** (*bə-rō'ni-əl*) pertaining to a baron or barony; applied to a turreted style of architecture popular in Scotland. — *n* **baronne** (*Fr*; *ba-ron*) a baroness. — *n* **bar'ony** the territory of a baron; in Ireland, a division of a county; in Scotland, a large freehold estate, or manor; the rank of baron; the sphere of influence of a press baron, etc. — **baron bailie** (*Scot hist*) a magistrate appointed by the lord superior in a burgh of barony; **bar'on-off'icer** (*Scott*) an estate official. — **baron of beef** a joint consisting of two sirloins left uncut at the backbone. [OFr *barun*, *-on*, from LL *barō*, *-ōnis* man]

baronet *bar'ən-et*, *n* now the lowest British hereditary title (*of England*, now *of Great Britain*, since 1611; *of Scotland*, or *of Nova Scotia*, since 1625; *of Ireland*, since 1619); a lesser baron (*obs*; confused with **banneret**); a baron's substitute (*obs*). — *n* **bar'onetage** the whole body of baronets; a list or book of baronets. — *n* **bar'onetcy** the rank or title of baronet. — *n* **bar'onetess** the wife of a baronet. — *adj* **baronet'ical**. [Dimin of **baron**]

barong *ba-rong'*, *n* a broad-bladed Philippine knife. [Moro]

barony. See under **baron**.

baroque *bə-rok'* or *-rōk'*, *n* a bold, vigorous, exuberant style in architecture, decoration, and art generally, that arose with the Counter-Reformation and prevailed in Louis XIV's time, degenerating into tasteless extravagance in ornament; a comparable style in music, or literature; *orig* a jeweller's term applied to a rough pearl. — Also **barok'** or **barocco** (*bə-rok'ō*; *pl* **barocc'os**). — *adj* in baroque style; whimsical; flamboyant; rococo. [Fr from Port and Sp; of architecture, from Ital]

baroreceptor *bar'ō-rə-sep-tər*, (*med*) *n* a sensory receptor sensitive to a pressure stimulus. [Gr *baros* weight, and **receptor**]

baroscope *bar'ō-skōp*, *n* an instrument for indicating changes in the density of the air. [Gr *baros* weight, and *skopeein* to look at]

barostat *bar'ō-stat*, *n* an automatic device for regulating pressure, eg in an aircraft. [Gr *baros* weight, and **-stat**]

Barotse *bə-rot'si*, *n* a member of a Negroid, mainly Zambian, African people; their language.

barouche *ba-* or *bə-ro͞osh'*, *n* a four-wheeled carriage with two bench-seats and a retractable hood. [Ger *Barutsche*, from Ital *baroccio*, from L *bis* twice, and *rota* a wheel]

barp *bärp*, (*Scot dialect*) *n* a mound or cairn. [Gaelic *barpa* a burial cairn]

barque, barquentine. See **bark**[2].

barracan or **baracan** *bar'ə-kan*, (*obs*) *n* a thick, strong fabric resembling camlet. [Fr *barracan*, from Ar *barrakān* camlet, Pers *barak* a fabric made of camel's hair]

barrace *bar'as*, (*obs*) *n* the lists in a tournament. [OFr *barras*, from *barre* bar]

barrack[1] *bar'ək*, *n* (*usu* in *pl*, often behaving as in *sing*) a building for soldiers, *esp* in a garrison; a huge, plain, often bleak, building, *esp* for housing many persons. — *vt* and *vi* to lodge in barracks. — *adj* **barr'ack-room** (of humour, etc) somewhat coarse. — **barrack-room lawyer** an argumentative soldier given to disputing military procedure; hence any insistent but unqualified giver of advice; **barrack square** a military drilling yard; strictness, rigorous training. — *adj* strict, rigorous. — **confined to barracks** of soldiers, not allowed out of the barracks when off duty, as a punishment; extended to general use, *esp* of children, confined to the house or school as a punishment. [Fr *baraque*, from Ital *baracca*, or Sp *barraca* tent]

barrack[2] *bar'ək*, *vt* and *vi* to make a hostile demonstration (against), *esp* by cheering ironically, at a cricket-match, etc. — *vi* (with *for*; *Austr* and *NZ*) to support, shout encouragement to. — *n* **barr'acker**. — *n* and *adj* **barr'acking**. [Prob N Ir dialect *barrack* to brag]

barracoon *bar-ə-ko͞on'*, *n* a depot for slaves. [Sp *barracón*, augmentative of *barraca* tent]

barracouta *bar-ə-ko͞o'tə*, *n* an edible fish (*Thyrsites*) of the hairtail family, from the Southern hemisphere, called snoek in S Africa and elsewhere; (also **barracoo'ta** or **barracu'da** *-də*) a voracious W Indian fish (*Sphyraena*) similar to the grey mullets. [Sp *baracuta*]

barrage *bar'ij*, or (*military*) *bar-äzh'* or *bar'äzh*, *n* an artificial bar across a river; the forming of such a bar; a barrier formed by a continuous shower of projectiles along a fixed or a moving line (curtain-fire), or by captive balloons, or mines, or otherwise; a heavy or continuous fire, as of questions, criticisms, etc; in sport, a heat or round to select contestants, or decide a dead-heat. — **barr'age-balloon**; **barr'age-fire** curtain-fire. [Fr, from *barre* bar]

barramundi *bar-ə-mun'di*, *n* any of several Australian river-fish (eg *Lates calcarifer*) valued as a food, a fish of the genus *Scleropages* (family Osteoglossidae), and the Australian lung-fish of the *Neoceratodus* genus. — Formerly also **barramun'da**. [Aboriginal]

barranca *bar-ang'kə*, (*US*) *n* a deep gorge. — Also **barran'co** (*pl* **barran'cos**). [Sp *barranco*]

barrat *bar'ət*, *n* (*obs*) deceit, strife or trouble. — *n* **barr'ator** a person who vexatiously stirs up lawsuits, quarrels, etc. — *adj* **barr'atrous**. — *adv* **barr'atrously**. — *n* **barr'atry** fraudulent practices on the part of the master or mariners of a ship to the prejudice of the owners (*maritime law*); the stirring up of suits and quarrels, forbidden under penalties to lawyers; the purchase or sale of offices of church or state. [OFr *barat* deceit; traced by some to Gr *prattein* to do, by others to a Celtic or a Scand origin]

barre *bär, n* a horizontal rail fixed to the wall at waist level, which ballet-dancers use to balance themselves while exercising (sometimes **bar**); a capo on a guitar, lute, etc; the placing of the left forefinger across the strings of a guitar, etc to act as a capo. — *adj* **barré** (*ba-rā*) of a chord on a guitar, etc, played with the left forefinger laid across the strings. [Fr]

barrefull. See **barful** under **bar**[1].

barrel *bar'əl, n* a wooden container made of curved staves bound with hoops; its contents or its capacity (36 imperial gallons of ale and beer; 35 imperial gallons, 42 US gallons, of oil; various weights or quantities of other goods); a revolving drum; a cylinder eg of a capstan; a hollow cylinder eg of a pen or quill; a tube eg of a gun; a toggle-button; the trunk of a horse, etc; a roly-poly person (*colloq*); a large quantity, a lot (eg of fun) (*colloq*). — *vt* to put in barrels. — *vi* to travel or move very quickly, drive very fast (*NAm*). — *n* **barr'elage**. — *n* **barr'elful** (*pl* **barr'elfuls**) as much as a barrel will hold. — *adj* **barr'elled** having a barrel or barrels; put in barrels. — **barr'el-bulk** a measure of capacity of five cubic feet. — *adj* **barrel-chest'ed** having a large, rounded, projecting ribcage. — **barr'el-house** a cheap saloon (*adj* of jazz, crude and rough in style); **barr'el-organ** a mechanical instrument for playing tunes by means of a revolving drum set with pins and turned by a handle; **barrel roll** (*aerobatics*) a complete revolution on the longitudinal axis; **barrel vault** a vault with a simple semi-cylindrical roof (*adj* **barr'el-vaulted**). — **have someone over a barrel** to be in a position to get whatever one wants from someone. [OFr *baril*; perh connected with **bar**[1]]

barren *bar'ən, adj* incapable of bearing offspring; not producing fruit, seed, crops, vegetation, etc; infertile; unproductive, unfruitful (*lit* and *fig*); arid, jejune; lacking in, devoid of (with *of*); dull, stupid (*Shakesp*). — *n* (in *pl* with *cap*) in N America, plateaux with shrubs, etc but no timber. — *n* **barr'enness**. — **barren strawberry** a plant (*Potentilla fragariastrum*) very like the wild strawberry, but with inedible fruit; **barr'enwort** a herb (*Epimedium*) of the barberry family. [OFr *barain, brahain, brehaing*]

barret *bar'it, n* a flat cap; a biretta. — **barr'et-cap**. [Fr *barette*; cf **beret, biretta**]

barrette *ba-ret', n* a bar-shaped hair-clip or hair ornament. [Dimin of Fr *barre* bar]

barretter *bə-ret'ər*, (*electronics*) *n* a resistor capable of variation and used for a number of purposes such as detecting radio waves or stabilizing electric current. [Perh from OFr *barateor* exchanger]

barricade *bar'ik-ād, n* a temporary defensive barrier, eg to block a street; a barrier. — *vt* to block; to close or enclose with a barricade. — *n* (earlier form) **barricā'do**: — *pl* **barricā'dos** or **barricā'does**. — Also *vt*. [Fr *barricade* or Sp *barricada*, perh from Fr *barrique* or Sp *barrica* cask, the first street barricades being casks filled with stones, etc; or from LL *barra* bar]

barrico *bar-ē'kō, n* a small cask: — *pl* **barri'cos** or **barri'coes**. [Sp *barrica*]

barrier *bar'i-ər, n* a defensive stockade or palisade; a fence or other structure to bar passage or prevent access; a separating or restraining obstacle; (in *pl*) lists; (in *pl*) a martial exercise of the 15th and 16th centuries in which the combatants were on opposite sides of a low fence. — *vt* to shut by means of a barrier. — **Barrier Act** an act of the General Assembly of the Church of Scotland (1697) decreeing that changes in the law of the Church, even when approved by the Assembly, should not become law until approved by a majority of presbyteries; **barrier contraception** the method of contraception in which a physical barrier is placed between the sperm and the ovum, such as a condom or diaphragm; **barrier cream** a dressing for the skin, *esp* of the hands, used as a protection against dirt, oils and solvents; **barrier layer** (*electronics*) see **depletion layer**; **barrier nursing** the nursing of patients in isolation from other patients for fear of cross-infection; **barrier reef** a coral-reef fringing a coast with a navigable channel inside. [OFr *barriere*, from LL *barrāria*, from *barra*]

barrio *bar'i-ō, n* (*esp US*) a Spanish-speaking, *usu* poor, community or district: — *pl* **barr'ios**. [Sp, district, quarter]

barrister *bar'is-tər, n* a person who is qualified to plead at the bar in a law-court (in Scotland called *advocate*). — *adj* **barristerial** (*-tē'ri-əl*). — *n* **barr'istership**. — **barrister-at-law**. — **revising barrister** a barrister formerly appointed to revise the voters' lists. [From LL *barra* bar (ie orig of the Inns of Court)]

barrow[1] *bar'ō, n* a small *usu* hand-propelled cart for carrying a load; a similar structure without any wheels, to be carried by two people. — **barr'ow-boy** a street-trader with wares displayed on a barrow; **barr'ow-tram** the shaft of a barrow. [OE *bearwe*, from *beran* to bear]

barrow[2] *bar'ō, n* a hill or hillock (*obs* except in place names); an ancient earth-built grave-mound, tumulus. [OE *beorg*; cf Ger *Berg*]

barrow[3] *bar'ō*, (now only *dialect*) *n* a castrated boar. [OE *bearg*]

barrulet *bar'ū-lit*, (*heraldry*) *n* a horizontal band one-quarter the width of a bar. [Dimin of *barrule*, assumed dimin of OFr *barre*; cf **bar**[1]]

Bart *abbrev*: Baronet.

bartender. See under **bar**[1].

barter *bär'tər, vt* to give in exchange (with *for* or *away*). — *vi* to trade by exchange of commodities; to bargain over the terms of such an exchange. — *n* trade by direct exchange of goods. — *n* **bar'terer**. — **barter trading**. [Prob OFr *barat*; see **barrat**]

Bartholin's glands *bär'tə-linz glandz*, (*physiol*) *n pl* a pair of mucus-secreting glands in the vagina. [Discovered by Caspar *Bartholin* (1655–1738), a Danish anatomist]

Bartholomew *bär-thol'ə-mū*, or (*obs*) **Bartholmew, Bartlemew** *-t(h)l-mū*, or **Bartlemy** *-tl-mi, adj* relating to the Apostle *Bartholomew*, his day (24 August), or the fair held about that time at West Smithfield, London (1133–1855); sold at Bartholomew Fair. — **Barthol'omew-tide** the time about St Bartholomew's Day. — **Black Bartholomew** 24 August 1662, when the Act of Uniformity came into force in England.

bartizan or **bartisan** *bär'ti-zan* or *-zan', n* a parapet or battlement; a projecting gallery on a wall-face; (*erron*) a corbelled corner turret. — *adj* **bar'tizaned** (or *bar-ti-zand'*). [Appar first used by Scott, who found a reading *bertisene*, for **bratticing**; see **brattice**]

barton *bär'tən, n* a farmyard. [OE *bere-tūn* yard, from *bere* barley, and *tūn* enclosure]

Bart's *bärts, abbrev*: St Bartholomews's Hospital, London.

barycentric *bar-i-sen'trik, adj* pertaining to the centre of gravity. [Gr *barys* heavy, and *kentron* centre]

barye *bär'ē*. Same as **microbar**.

baryon *bar'i-on, n* any one of the heavier class of subatomic particles, which includes protons and neutrons (*opp* to *lepton*). — **baryon number** the number of baryons minus the number of antibaryons (antiparticles of baryons) in a system. [Gr *barys* heavy]

barysphere *bar'is-fēr, n* the heavy core of the earth within the lithosphere. [Gr *barys* heavy, and *sphaira* sphere]

baryta *bə-rī'tə, n* barium monoxide. — *n* **bary'tes** (*bə-rī'tēz*) heavy spar, barium sulphate (also **barite** *bā'rīt*); (loosely) baryta. — *adj* **barytic** (*ba-rit'ik*) of or containing baryta or barium. — **baryta paper** paper coated on one side with an emulsion of barium sulphate and gelatine, used in moving-pointer recording apparatus and for photographic printing papers. [Gr *barys* heavy]

baryton, barytone. See **baritone**.

BAS *abbrev*: Bachelor of Agricultural Science; British Antarctic Survey.

basal. See under **base**[1].

basalt *bas'ölt* or *bas-ölt', n* a dark-coloured igneous rock composed essentially of plagioclase and pyroxene, and commonly olivine and magnetite or titaniferous iron;

esp a compact rock of this kind; a type of pottery similar in appearance to the rock. — *adj* **basalt'ic**. [L *basaltēs*, from Gr *basanītēs* (*lithos*) touchstone]

basan *ba'zən*, *n* a sheepskin roughly tanned and undressed. [Ar *bitanah* lining]

basanite *bas'ən-īt*, *n* a black jasper that serves as a touchstone; a variety of basalt containing nepheline, leucite, or analcime. [Gr *basanos* touchstone]

bas-bleu *bä-blø*, (*Fr*) *n* a bluestocking.

bascule *bas'kūl*, *n* an apparatus one end of which rises as the other sinks. — **bascule bridge** a bridge with one or more sections that rise when a counterpoise sinks in a pit. [Fr *bascule* seesaw]

base[1] *bās*, *n* that on which something rests; the foot, bottom; a foundation, support; the part, eg of an organ of a plant or animal, nearest the place of attachment; the foot of a pillar, on which the shaft rests (*archit*); the side or face on which a geometrical figure is regarded as standing; the lower part of a shield (*heraldry*); (in *pl*) a knee-length pleated skirt worn by medieval knights (*Spenser*); a horse's housing (*Milton*); a number on which a system of numeration or of logarithms is founded; the chief ingredient; an ingredient of a mixture that plays a subsidiary but important part, such as giving bulk; in dyeing, a mordant; a starting-point; a standard against which comparisons can be made; in make-up, the foundation or first layer of colour applied to the skin; a base-line; a fixed station in games such as baseball; an old game of which prisoners'-base and rounders are forms, and baseball a development (possibly a different word; see **bar**[1]); a place from which operations are conducted or on which they depend; home or headquarters eg of a fleet; a compound that reacts with an acid to form a salt, or dissolves in water forming hydroxyl ions (*chem*); the region between the emitter and collector of a transistor, into which minority carriers are injected (*electronics*); that element in words to which suffixes and prefixes are added, the stem (*philol*). — *vt* to found or place on a base: — *pr p* **bās'ing**; *pa p* **based** (*bāst*). — *adj* **bās'al** pertaining to or situated at the base; at the lowest level; (loosely) fundamental. — *adj* **base'less** without a base or foundation. — *n* **base'lessness**. — *n* **base'ment** the storey of a building beneath the ground floor; an underlying support; a complex of igneous and metamorphic rocks beneath sedimentary rock (*geol*). — *adj* **basilar** (*bas'il-ər*) situated at the base, *esp* of the skull. — **basal anaesthesia** anaesthesia acting as a basis for further and deeper anaesthesia; **basal ganglia** in vertebrates, ganglia connecting the cerebrum with other nerve centres; **basal metabolic rate** the output of calories per square metre of body surface per hour by a fasting and resting individual; **basal metabolism** the amount of energy required by a fasting and resting individual; **basal plane** (*crystallog*) a crystal face or form parallel to the lateral or horizontal axes; **base'ball** a team game, played nine-a-side with bat and ball, the players on the batting side making a circuit of four bases on the field; a ball for the game; **base'baller**. — *adj* **base'band** (*telecomm*) applied to a device capable of operating only over a narrow range of frequencies. — **base'board** a board which forms a base for something; a skirting-board (*NAm*); **base'-burner** (*NAm*) a stove in which fuel is fed automatically from a hopper; **base'-level** (*geog*) the level to which land can be or is eroded by water. — *adj* **base'-levelled**. — **base'-line** an accurately measured line used as a base for triangulation; each of the lines at the back of the court (*tennis*); a line joining bases (*baseball*); the line on which the type stands, below which the descenders hang (*printing*); a starting-point against which to measure something, a standard of comparison; **base'liner** a player whose main game is from the base-line (*tennis*); **base'-load** (*elec eng*) the minimum demand of electricity on a power-station (cf **peak-load**); **base'man** (*baseball*) any of the three fielders stationed near first, second and third base (hence *first baseman*, etc); **base'plate** the foundation plate of a piece of heavy machinery; **base rate** the rate, determined by a bank, on which it bases its lending rates of interest; **base ring** a strengthening band of metal round the breech of a muzzle-loading cannon; **base'runner** a baseball player in course of performing his circuit of bases; **base substitution** (*biol*) a mutation in which a base or bases in the DNA are replaced by different bases (cf **deletion mutation**). — **base out** (*US*) to bottom out; **get to** or **make first base** (*NAm colloq*) to complete the first stage in a process; **off base** (*NAm colloq*) wrong, mistaken. [Fr *base*, from L *basis*, from Gr *basis*, from root of *bainein* to go]

base[2] *bās*, *adj* low in place, value, estimation or principle; low in morals, reprehensible, vile; worthless; debased; counterfeit; servile as opposed to *free* (*law*); lowly, humble (*Bible* and *Shakesp*); illegitimate (*obs*); bass (*obs*). — *adv* **base'ly**. — *n* **base'ness**. — *adj* **base'-born** (*archaic*) low-born; illegitimate. — **base coin** spurious coin; **base metal** any metal other than the precious metals; any metal that alters on exposure to air (*opp* to *noble metal*). — *adj* **base'-minded** of a low mind or spirit; mean. — *adj* **base'-spirited** mean-spirited. [Fr *bas*, from LL *bassus* thick, squat]

base[3] *bās*, *vt*. A form of **abase**.

base[4] *bās*: **base jumping** the recreational practice of parachuting from low-level objects and structures (*esp* landmarks), including specifically a *b*uilding, an *a*erial, a *s*pan and an *e*arthbound object (eg a mountain); **base jumper**. [Acronymic]

baseball. See **base**[1].

base-court *bās'-kört*, (*hist*) *n* the outer court of a castle or mansion; an inferior court of justice. [Fr *basse-court* (now *basse-cour*)]

baselard *bas'ə-lärd*, (*obs*) *n* a dagger or hanger. [Anglo-Fr]

basement. See under **base**[1].

basen. See **basin**.

basenji *bə-sen'jē*, *n* a smallish, erect-eared, curly-tailed African hunting dog that rarely barks. [Bantu, *pl* of *mosenji, musengi* native]

bases. *Pl* of **base**[1] and **basis**.

BASF *abbrev*: *Badische Anilin und Soda-Fabrik* (a German chemical company).

bash *bash*, *vt* to beat, batter; to smash; to dent; to attack harshly or maliciously, physically or verbally. — *vi* to crash (into) (*colloq*); to become dented; to solicit as a prostitute (*slang*). — *n* a heavy blow; the mark of a blow; a dent; a party (*colloq*). — *n* **bash'er** a person who, or thing that, bashes (sometimes used as *sfx*); a straw hat (*slang*). — *n* **bash'ing** (often used as *sfx*, as in *queer-bashing, union-bashing*) the activity of making harsh or malicious physical or verbal attacks on individuals or (members of) groups one dislikes. — **bash on** (*colloq*) to persevere, carry on; **have a bash** (*colloq*) to have a try; to make an attempt (at); **on the bash** (*slang*) on the spree; on the streets as a prostitute. [Prob Scand]

bashaw *ba-shö'*, *n* a pasha (*archaic*); a haughty person. — *n* **bashaw'ism**. — *n* **bashaw'ship**. [Turk *başa*; cf **pasha**]

bashful *bash'fŏŏl*, *adj* modest; shy, lacking confidence; resulting from or indicating modesty or shyness. — *vi* **bash** (*Spenser*) to be abashed. — *adv* **bash'fully**. — *n* **bash'fulness**. — *adj* **bash'less** (*obs*) unashamed. [See **abash**]

Bashi-Bazouk *bash-ē-bə-zōōk'*, *n* a Turkish irregular soldier. — *n* **Ba'shi-Bazouk'ery**. [Turk *başi-bozuk* wild head]

bashlik *bash'lik*, *n* a Russian hood with long ends. [Russ *bashlyk* a Caucasian hood, from Turk *baş* a head]

basho *bash'ō*, *n* in sumo wrestling, a tournament: — *pl* **bash'o**. [Jap]

Basic or **BASIC** *bā'sik*, *n* a computer language using a combination of simple English and algebra. [*B*eginners' *A*ll-purpose *S*ymbolic *I*nstruction *C*ode]

basic *bās'ik*, *adj* belonging to or of the nature of a base; fundamental; simple, plain, without extras; containing excess of a base (*chem, dyeing, steel-making*, etc); poor in silica — opp to *acid* (*geol*). — *n* (in *pl*) fundamental principles. — *adv* **bās'ically** with reference to what is basic; fundamentally, essentially. — *n* **bāsicity** (*bās-is'it-i*). — **Basic English** a reduced English vocabulary of 850 words for teaching foreigners or for use as an auxiliary language; (without *cap*) English using few and simple words; **basic process** a steel-making process with a furnace lined with material rich in metallic oxides; **basic salt** a salt having one or more hydroxyl groups in place of an acid radical or radicals; **basic slag** a by-product of the basic process, rich in lime and used as manure. [**base**[1]]

basidium *bas-id'i-əm*, (*bot*) *n* a fungal fructification from which spores (*usu* four) are released: — *pl* **basid'ia**. — *adj* **basid'ial**. — *n pl* **Basidiomycetes** (*ba-sid-i-ō-mī-sē'tēz*) one of the main groups of fungi, characterized by the possession of basidia, including the familiar toadstools as well as rusts and smuts. — *adj* **basidiomycē'tous**. — *n* **basid'iospore** a spore produced by a basidium. [Gr *basis* basis, and Gr dimin ending *-idion*]

basifixed *bā'si-fikst*, (*bot*) *adj* attached by the base. [**base**[1] and **fixed**]

basifugal *bās-* or *bas-if'ū-gl*, (*bot*) *adj* developing in a direction away from the base. [**base**[1] and L *fugere* to flee]

basil[1] *baz'il*, *n* an aromatic labiate plant (*Ocimum*; also called *sweet basil*); extended to calamint and other labiates. [OFr *basile*, from L *basilisca*, representing Gr *basilikon* literally royal, perh with reference to *basiliskos* basilisk, cobra, as a reputed cure for snake-bite]

basil[2] *baz'il*. Same as **basan**.

basil[3]. See **bezel**.

basilar. See under **base**[1].

Basilian *ba-* or *bə-zil'i-ən*, or *-sil'*, *adj* of St *Basil* (*c*. 329–79). — *n* a monk or nun following his rule.

basilica *bə-sil'i-kə*, *n* a large oblong hall, with double colonnades and commonly a semicircular apse, used for judicial and commercial purposes; a magnificent church formed out of such a hall, or built after its plan; a Roman Catholic church with honorific privileges; *orig* a royal palace. — *adj* **basil'ical** royal. — *adj* **basil'ican** of a basilica. — *n* **basil'icon** an ointment of various kinds, as being of sovereign virtue. — **basilic vein** the large vein in the upper part of the arm (*physiol*). [Gr *basilikos, -ē, -on* royal, from *basileus* king]

basilisk *bas'* or *baz'il-isk*, *n* a mythical serpent which could kill with a glance or breath, so named, according to Pliny, from its crown-like crest; a harmless crested lizard of tropical America; a brass cannon throwing a shot of about 200lb (*hist*). [Gr *basiliskos*, dimin of *basileus* a king]

basin *bā'sn*, (*archaic* **ba'son**) *n* a wide open container or dish; a sink, washbasin; a basinful; any hollow place containing water, such as a dock; the area drained by a river and its tributaries; a region of synclinal structure (*geol*). — *n* **ba'sinful** as much as fills a basin: — *pl* **ba'sinfuls**. — *adj* **ba'sin-wide** (*Spenser* **basen wide**) wide as a basin. — **have a basinful** (*colloq*) to have more than enough (of). [OFr *bacin*, from LL *bachinus*, perh from *bacca* a vessel]

basinet *bas'i-net*, or **basnet** *bas'net*, *n* a light close-fitting steel helmet worn alone with a visor, or with the great helm over it. [Dimin of **basin**]

basipetal *bās-* or *bas-ip'i-tl*, (*bot*) *adj* proceeding or developing in the direction of the base. [**base**[1] and L *petere* to seek]

basis *bās'is*, *n* the foundation, or that on which a thing rests; the groundwork or first principle; the fundamental ingredient; a pedestal: — *pl* **bas'es** (*bās'ēz*). [See **base**[1]]

bask *bäsk*, *vi* to lie in the warmth or sunshine (often *fig*). — **basking shark** a large but harmless shark that shows its great dorsal fin as it basks. [ON *bathask* to bathe]

Baskerville *bas'kər-vil*, *n* a printing type-style. [From the originator, J *Baskerville*, 18c printer]

basket *bäs'kit*, *n* a container made of plaited or interwoven twigs, rushes, canes or other flexible material; a basketful; the hoop with an open net attached, used as a goal at basketball; a goal scored in basketball; a collection of similar or related ideas or things; a group, collection (of currencies, *esp* those of the participating members of the EMS on which the ECU is based) (*econ*); a bastard (*euphem*); the back part of a stage-coach outside; a basket-hilt. — *n* **bas'ketful** as much as fills a basket: — *pl* **bas'ketfuls**. — *n* **bas'ketry** basketwork. — **bas'ketball** a team game in which goals are scored by throwing a ball into a raised horizontal net (*orig* a basket); the ball used in the game; **bas'ket-case** (*orig NAm*, now *gen slang*) a person with all four limbs amputated (*obs*); a nervous wreck, someone unable to cope; a country that cannot cope economically; **bas'ket-chair** a wicker chair; **basket clause** (*NAm*) a comprehensive clause in a contract; **bas'ket-hilt** a sword hilt with a protective covering like basketwork; **bas'ket-maker** (with *caps*; *archaeol*) a member of an early American culture of SW US, known for their basketwork; **bas'ket-making**; **bas'ket-stitch** (*knitting*) groups of plain and purl stitches alternating vertically and horizontally, resembling basketwork in effect; **bas'ketweave** a form of weaving using two or more strands in the warp and weft; **bas'ketwork** articles made of interlaced twigs, canes, etc (also *adj*); the art of making these. [Origin obscure]

basmati rice *bas-mat'i rīs*, *n* a long-grain, naturally perfumed rice.

bas mitzvah, etc. See **bath mitzvah**.

basnet. See **basinet**.

basoche *ba-sosh*, (*Fr*) *n* a medieval guild of clerks of the parliament of Paris, performers of mystery plays.

bason. See **basin**.

basophil *bās'ə-fil*, *adj* of *esp* white blood cells having an affinity for basic stains. — *n* a cell of this kind. — *adj* **basophil'ic** basophil. [*bas*ic and **-phil**]

ba'spiel. See **balling** under **ball**[1].

Basque *bäsk*, *n* a member of a people (in their own tongue *Euscara, Eskuara*) inhabiting the western Pyrenees, in Spain and France; their agglutinative non-Indo-European language; (without *cap*) a short-skirted jacket, or a continuation of a bodice a little below the waist; (without *cap*) on a skirt, a similar area extending shortly below the waist, to which pleats or gathers are often attached; (without *cap*) a close-fitting (under-)bodice. — *adj* **Basque** of the Basques or their language or country. — *adj* **basqued** (*bäskt*) furnished with a basque. — *n* **basquine** (*-kēn'*) an outer petticoat worn by Basque and Spanish women. [Fr *Basque*, from L *Vascōnēs* a people of Gascony]

bas-relief *bas-ri-lēf'* or *ba'-ri-lēf*, or (*Ital*) **basso-rilievo** *bäs'sō-rēl-yā'vō*, popularly **-relievo** *bas'ō-ri-lē'vō*, *n* sculpture in which the figures do not stand far out from the ground on which they are formed. [Fr and Ital. See **base**[2] and **relief**]

bass[1] *bās*, *n* the lowest part in music; a bass singer, often in *Ital* form **basso** (*bäs'sō*), *pl* **bas'sos, bas'si** (*-si*); a bass instrument, *esp* (*colloq*) a bass guitar or double-bass; low-frequency sound as output from an amplifier, etc. — *adj* low, deep; (of a musical instrument or voice) low in pitch and compass. — *vt* (*Shakesp*) to utter in a deep tone. — *n* **bass'ist** a person who plays a double-bass or a bass guitar. — *adj* **bass'y** somewhat bass; predominantly bass. — **bass'-bar** a strip of wood on the belly of a violin, etc, under the bass foot of the bridge, to distribute the vibrations; **bass clef** (*music*) the F clef, in which the F a fifth below middle C is written on the fourth line of the stave; **bass compensation** differential attenuation introduced into a sound-reproducing system to emphasize bass frequencies (*acoustics*); **bass drum** the large drum of an orchestra or band; **bass fiddle** (*colloq*) a double-bass; **bass guitar** an electric guitar similar in sound and range to the double-bass;

bass horn an old wind instrument, a modification of the serpent; **bass tuba** the lowest instrument of the saxhorn class — the bombardon; **bass viol** a six-stringed instrument, used for playing the lowest part in early music, the viola da gamba; the double-bass (*colloq*, *esp US*). [See **base**²]

bass² or **basse** *bas*, *n* a European sea-fish of the sea-perch family (*Labrax lupus* or *Morone labrax*); extended to other sea and freshwater fishes. — *vt* to fish for bass. [OE *bærs*; cf Ger *Bars* the perch]

bass³ *bas*, *n* bast; any article made of bast or some similar material. — **bass'wood** an American lime-tree or its wood. [See **bast**]

basset *bas'it*, *n* a low-set, smooth-coated hound with long ears (also **bass'et-hound** or **basset hound**); an old Venetian card-game, resembling faro, widely popular in the 18c; an outcrop (*geol*). — *vi* (of strata) to crop out (*geol*). — **basset horn** (Ital *corno di bassetto*) a low-pitched instrument of the clarinet family. — **bass'et-hornist**. [Fr, from *bas* low]

bassinet *bas'i-net*, *n* a kind of basket with a hood, used as a cradle; a similarly shaped perambulator; a bed in hospital, with necessary equipment, for care of a baby. [Fr dimin of *bassin* a basin]

basso. See **bass**¹.

bassoon *bə-soon'* or *-zoon'*, *n* (Ital *fagotto*) a woodwind instrument important in the modern orchestra, with a compass from B flat below the bass stave to C or F in the treble. The **double bassoon** (Ital *contrafagotto*) sounds an octave lower. — *n* **bassoon'ist**. [Ital *bassone*, augmentative of *basso* low, from root of **base**², **bass**¹]

basso profundo or **basso profondo** *bä'sō prō-fun'dō* or (*Ital*) *prō-fōōn'do* (*Ital*; *music*, *esp opera*) *n* an extremely deep bass voice or singer: — *pl* **basso profundos**.

basso-rilievo. See **bas-relief**.

basswood. See **bass**³.

bast *bast*, *n* phloem, the conductive material in a plant; inner bark, *esp* of lime; fibre; matting. — Also **bass** (*bas*). See **bass**³. [OE *bæst*; Ger *Bast*]

basta *bas'tə*, (*Shakesp*) *interj* enough. [Ital and Sp]

bastard¹ *bas'tərd* or *bäs'tərd*, *n* a child born of parents not married to each other; a difficult or unpleasant person or thing, an unfortunate person, or neutrally, a chap (*vulg*); a sweet Spanish wine (*Shakesp*). — *adj* born out of wedlock; not genuine; resembling, but not identical with, the species bearing the name (*science*, *esp bot*); of abnormal shape or size; false. — *n* **bast'ardism** bastardy. — *n* **bastardizā'tion** or **-s-**. — *vt* **bas'tardize** or **-ise** to debase, corrupt; to pronounce to be or prove to be a bastard. — *vi* to beget bastards (*Shakesp*); to degenerate. — *adj* **bas'tardly**. — *n* **bas'tardy** the state of being a bastard. — **bas'tard-bar** an inaccurate name for the baton-sinister in heraldry; **bastard file** a file with teeth of a medium degree of coarseness; **bastard title** an abbreviated title of a book on an otherwise blank page preceding the full title-page; **bastard types** (*printing*) types cast with an extra deep bevel to avoid the use of leads, such as longprimer face on pica body; **bas'tard=wing** three, four, or five feathers on the first digit (corresponding to the thumb) of a bird's wing. [OF *bastard* (Fr *bâtard*) child of the pack-saddle (OFr *bast*)]

bastard² *bas'tərd*, (*SAfr hist*) *n* a person of mixed white and Hottentot parentage. — Also *Afrik* **baster** (*bas'tər*). [Du *bastaard* bastard]

baste¹ *bāst*, *vt* to beat with a stick. — *n* **bāst'ing**. [Prob connected with ON *beysta*, Dan *böste* to beat]

baste² *bāst*, *vt* to keep (meat) moist when roasting by drizzling melted fat or butter over. [Ety unknown]

baste³ *bāst*, (*needlework*) *vt* to tack. [OFr *bastir*, from OHGer *bestan* to sew]

bastel-house (*Northern*) *n* a fortified house, *usu* with vaulted ground-floor. [**bastille**]

baster. See **bastard**².

bastide *bas-tēd*, (*Fr*) *n* a French country-house.

bastille *bas-tēl'*, *n* (with *cap*) an old fortress and state prison in Paris, demolished in the Revolution (July 1789); hence any prison, *esp* as a symbol of tyranny; a tower for the defence of a fortress (*hist*); a movable tower used by besiegers. — **Bastille Day** 14 July, a French national holiday. [Fr, from OFr *bastir* (Fr *bâtir*) to build]

bastinado *bast-in-ād'ō* or **bastinade** *bast-in-ād'*, *vt* to beat with a baton or stick, *esp* on the soles of the feet (an Eastern punishment): — *pr p* **bastinād'oing** or **bastinād'ing**; *pa p* **bastinād'oed** or **bastinād'ed**. — *n* **bastinād'o** or **bastinade'**: — *pl* **bastinā'does**. [Sp *bastonada*, Fr *bastonnade*, from *baston* baton; cf **baton**, **batten**]

bastion *bast'yən*, *n* a kind of tower at the angle of a fortification; a defence (*fig*). — *adj* **bast'ioned**. [Fr, from Ital *bastione*, from *bastire* to build]

bastle, **bastle-house**. Same as **bastel-house**.

bastnäsite or **bastnaesite** *bast-nā'sīt*, *n* a yellow to reddish-brown fluocarbonate of cerium, the heaviest element yet found to occur naturally. [Swed *bastnäsit*, from *Bastnäs* where it was found]

basto *bäs'tō*, *n* in quadrille, the ace of clubs: — *pl* **bas'tos**. [Sp, club]

Basuto *ba-soo'tō*, *n* the Bantu people of Lesotho (formerly Basutoland); one of these people (*pl* **Basu'tos**); their language (also **Sotho**). — Also **Basu'tu** (*-too*).

BASW *abbrev*: British Association of Social Workers.

bat¹ *bat*, *n* a flattish club for striking the ball in cricket; a club for baseball; in tennis, etc, a racket (*colloq*); something shaped like a bat, eg the signalling devices used by a batman to guide aircraft; a batsman; a heavy stick; the clown or harlequin's lath; a piece of brick; speed, rate (*slang*); a drunken spree (*slang*); a blow; a sheet of batting (also **batt**); a layer of felt used in hat-making (also **batt**). — *vt* and *vi* to hit with a bat in cricket, etc; to hit as with a bat: — *pr p* **batt'ing**; *pa t* and *pa p* **batt'ed**. — *n* **batt'er**. — *n* **batt'ing** the management of a bat in playing games; cotton wadding prepared in sheets, for quilts, etc. — **bat'fish** any of several groups of fish with wing-like projections, *esp* the *Ogocephalidae* or the Pacific *Epippidae*; **bat'fowling** catching birds at night by confusing them with lights; **bat'man** a man on an airfield or aircraft carrier who assists planes to taxi to position using a pair of lightweight bats (also **bats'man**); **bat printing** a method of printing in which designs are transferred by means of a sheet of gelatine; **bats'man** or **bats'woman** a person who wields the bat at cricket, etc; (**batsman**) see also **batman**; **bats'manship**. — **bat around** (*slang*) to wander; to go on a bat; **carry** or **carry out one's bat** (*cricket*) to be not-out at the end of an innings, *esp* when one has gone in first and when all ten wickets have fallen; **off one's own bat** by one's own efforts; on one's own initiative; **right off the bat** (*NAm colloq*) straightaway; **take out one's bat** (*cricket*) to be not-out at the end of an innings, *esp* when one has gone in later than first and when all ten wickets have fallen. [Perh from OE *bat* (a doubtful form), prob Celtic *bat* staff]

bat² *bat*, *n* a flying mammal with wings attached mainly to its arms and hands, but extending along its sides to the hind-feet and tail. — *adj* **bats** (*colloq*) crazy. — *adj* **batt'y** batlike; bat-infested; crazy (*colloq*). — *adj* **bats'wing** shaped like a bat's wing, eg of the flame of a gas burner. — **batwing sleeve** a sleeve that is very wide at the armhole and tight at the wrist. — **blind as a bat** completely blind; **have** (or **be**) **bats in the belfry** (*colloq*) to be crazy or slightly mad; **like a bat out of hell** (*colloq*) very quickly. [ME *bakke*, appar from Scand; cf Dan *aftenbakke* evening-bat]

bat³ *bat*, *vt* to flutter (*esp* an eyelid). — **not bat an eye** or **eyelid** to show no surprise or emotion; not to sleep a wink. [Cf **bate**³]

bat⁴ *bat*, *n* the *colloq* speech of a foreign language, lingo. — **sling the bat** to speak such a language. [Hindi, speech, word]

bat. or **batt.** *abbrev*: battalion; battery.

batable *bāt'ə-bl*, *adj* short for **debatable**.

batata *bə-tä'tə*, *n* the sweet-potato. [Sp from Haitian]

Batavian *bə-tā'vi-ən, adj* pertaining to the ancient *Batāvi* in the Low Countries, or to the modern Dutch, or to Batavia (Jakarta). — Also *n*.

batch *bach, n* the quantity of bread baked, or of anything made or got ready, at one time; a set; quantity of material required for one operation; a group of similar objects or people; a collection of computer transactions which are processed as a single unit. — *vt* to collect into, or treat in, batches. — *adj* and *n* **batch'ing**. — **batch loaf** a loaf baked touching others and pulled apart after baking, having hard top and bottom crusts and soft sides; **batch processing** (*comput*) a method of processing data in which similar items of data are collected together for processing at one time; **batch production** a type of production in which identical items are manufactured and processed in groups rather than singly. [From the root of **bake**]

bate[1] *bāt, vt* and *vi* to abate; to lessen, diminish; to blunt. — *adj* **bate'less** that cannot be blunted (*Shakesp*); not bated (*obs*). — *n* **bate'ment** (*obs*) reduction. — **batement light** a window whose sill is not horizontal. — **with bated breath** (holding one's breath) in fear or suspense. [Aphetic form of **abate**[1]]

bate[2] *bāt, n* (*Spenser*) strife, contention. — *adj* **bate'-breed'ing** (*Shakesp*). [Aphetic form of **debate**]

bate[3] *bāt, vi* to beat the wings impatiently, to try to fly from the fist or perch when still attached by leash or jesses (*falconry*); to be impatient (*obs*). [OFr *batre*, from LL *batere*]

bate[4]. Same as **bait**, a rage (*slang*).

bateau *bä-tō', n* a light river-boat, *esp* on Canadian rivers: — *pl* **bateaux** (*-tōz'*). [Fr]

bateleur *bat'lər, n* a short-tailed African eagle. [Fr, mountebank, appar from its characteristic movements]

BATF *abbrev*: Bureau of Alcohol, Tobacco and Firearms (US).

Bath *bäth, n* a famous city in Somerset, with Roman *baths*. — *n* **Bathō'nian** (*geol*) a division of the Middle Jurassic (also *adj*). — **Bath bun** a rich sweet bun; **Bath chair** (also without *cap*) a large wheelchair for invalids; **Bath Oliver** a plain biscuit invented by Dr W Oliver of Bath; **Bath stone** a building-stone quarried at Bath.

bath[1] *bäth, n* water for immersing the body; an act of bathing; a receptacle or a house for bathing; (in *pl*) a building containing baths for the use of the public, and a swimming pool; a place for undergoing medical treatment by means of bathing; the act of exposing the body to vapour, mud, sunlight, etc; a liquid or other material (eg sand), or a receptacle, in which anything is immersed for heating, washing or steeping (*chem*): — *pl* **baths** (*bädhz*, also *bäths*). — *vt* to give a bath to; to wash (oneself) in a bath. — *vi* to take a bath. — **bath'cube** bath-salts in the form of a solid cube; **bath'house** or **bath-house**; **bath'robe** (*orig US*) a towelling loose-fitting garment worn *esp* before and after bathing or swimming; **bath'room** a room containing a bath, and *usu* a washbasin and lavatory; (*esp NAm*) a lavatory; **bath'-salts** a *usu* sweet-smelling substance used to soften and perfume bath water; **bath'-sheet** an extra-large bath-towel; **bath'-towel** a large towel; **bath'tub** a bath, in UK often a moveable tub, but in N America the permanent bathroom fixture. — **Order of the Bath** a British order of knighthood, so named from the bath taken before installation. [OE *bæth*; Ger *Bad*]

bath[2] *bäth, n* the largest Jewish liquid measure, containing about eight imperial gallons. [Heb]

bath-brick *bäth'brik, n* a preparation of siliceous silt, manufactured at Bridgwater in the form of blocks and used in cleaning knives. [Traditionally said to be named after the first maker, one *Bath*, or from its resemblance to *Bath stone*]

bathe *bādh, vt* to wash as in a bath; to wash or moisten, with any liquid; to moisten, suffuse, encompass. — *vi* to take a dip or swim; to bask. — *n* the act of bathing; a swim or dip. — *n* **bāth'er** someone who bathes; (in *pl*; *Austr* and *NZ*) a swimming costume. — **bathing beauty** or (*old-fashioned*) **bathing belle** an attractive woman in a swimsuit, *esp* when competing in a beauty contest; **bāth'ing-box** or **-hut** a small structure for bathers to change in; **bāth'ing-costume** or **-dress** (*old-fashioned*) a swimsuit; **bāth'ing-machine** (*hist*) a wheeled bathing-hut for transporting a bather into the sea; **bāth'ing-suit** (*old-fashioned* or *US*) a swimsuit. [OE *bathian*]

bathetic. See **bathos**.

bathmism *bath'mizm, n* a supposed directive force in evolution or an inherent tendency to develop along divergent lines. — *adj* **bath'mic**. [Gr *bathmos* step]

bath mitzvah, **bath mizvah** or **bath mitsvah** *bäth mits'və* (also **bas mitzvah**, etc *bäs* or **bat mitzvah**, etc *bät*; sometimes with *caps*; also hyphenated or as one word; *esp US*) a girl of the Jewish religion attaining the age (*usu* 12 years) of religious responsibility; the festivities held in recognition of this event. [Heb, daughter of the law]

batholite *bath'ō-līt, n* a mass of igneous rock that has risen from a great depth. — Also **bath'olith**, **bath'ylite** or **bath'ylith**. — *adj* **batholitic**, **batholithic**, **bathylitic** or **bathylithic** (*-lit'*, *-lith'*). [Gr *bathos* depth, or *bathys* deep, and *lithos* a stone]

bathometer *bath-om'it-ər, n* a bathymeter. [Gr *bathos* depth, and *metron* measure]

Bathonian. See **Bath**.

bathophobia *bath'ō-fō-bi-ə, n* morbid fear of falling from a high place. [Gr *bathos* depth, and *phobos* fear]

bathorse *bat'hörs, bät'* or formerly *bä'hörs*, (*hist*) *n* a pack-horse carrying an officer's baggage. [Fr *bât* pack-saddle]

bathos *bā'thos, n* a ludicrous descent from the elevated to the ordinary in writing or speech. — *adj* **bathetic** (*bə-thet'ik*; irregularly formed on the analogy of *pathos*, *pathetic*). [Gr *bathos* depth]

bathy- *bath'i-* or *bath-i'-*, *combining form* denoting deep. — *adj* **bath'yal** (*bath'i-əl*) of ocean depths of between 200 and 2000 metres. — *n* **bathyb'ius** (Gr *bios* life) a substance on the sea bottom formerly thought to be living matter. — *adj* **bathygraph'ical** (Gr *graphein* to write) of maps, representing the contours of the sea bed. — **bathylite** or **bathylith** see **batholite**. — *n* **bathymeter** (*bath-im'ət-ər*; Gr *metron* measure) a sounding instrument. — *adj* **bathymet'ric** or **bathymet'rical**. — *n* **bathym'etry** the science of sounding seas and lakes. — *adj* **bathyorograph'ical** (Gr *oros* mountain) of maps representing the contours of land height and water depth. — *adj* **bathypelagic** (*-aj'ik*; Gr *pelagos* sea) found in the depths of the sea, down to 4000m below sea-level. — *n* **bath'ysphere** (Gr *sphaira* sphere) a submersible observation chamber (**bath'yscaphe** or **bath'yscape** are later types). [Gr *bathys* deep]

batik *bat'ik* or *ba-tēk', n* an *orig* Indonesian method of producing designs on cloth by covering with wax, for each successive dipping, those parts that are to be protected from the dye; fabric patterned by this method. [Malay]

bating *bāt'ing, prep* excepting, except. [**bate**[1]]

batiste *ba-tēst', n* a fine fabric of linen, cotton or wool. [Fr, cambric, from *Baptiste*, the reputed original maker or from its use in wiping the heads of children after baptism]

batler *bat'lər*, (*Shakesp*) *n* a beetle for beating clothes. — Altered by some editors to **bat'let**. [**bat**[1]]

batman[1] *bat'mən*, formerly *bä'mən, n* an officer's personal attendant; a person in charge of a bathorse (*hist*). — **batwoman** (*bat'*) an officer's female personal attendant. [Fr *bât* pack-saddle, and **man**[1]]

batman[2]. See **bat**[1].

bat mitzvah, etc. See **bath mitzvah**.

batology *ba-tol'ə-ji, n* the study of brambles. — *adj* **batological** (*-loj'*). — *n* **batol'ogist**. [Gr *batos* bramble]

baton *bat'ən* or *bat'n*, also (*archaic*) **batoon** *bə-tōōn', n* a staff of office, eg that of a marshal; a policeman's truncheon; a short stick passed on from one runner to the next in a relay-race; a light wand used by the conductor of an orchestra; a knobbed staff carried, tossed and twirled by a drum major, etc at the head of a marching band, etc; a baton round. — *vt* to strike with a baton. — **baton charge** a swift forward movement of police against a hostile crowd, with truncheons drawn for use. — *vt* **bat'on-charge**. — **baton gun** a gun which fires **baton rounds**, plastic bullets, used in riot-control; **baton-sin'ister** a heraldic indication of illegitimacy, improperly called *bar-sinister*, a diminutive of a bend-sinister, not extending to the sides of the shield, so as to resemble a marshal's baton laid diagonally over the family arms from sinister to dexter. — **under the baton of** (of choirs and orchestras) conducted by. [Fr *bâton*]

batrachia *bə-trā'ki-ə*, (sometimes with *cap*) *n pl* the Amphibia; the Salientia, tailless amphibia, or frogs and toads. — *adj* and *n* **batrā'chian**. — *n* **batrachopho'bia** an aversion to frogs, toads and newts. — *adj* **batrachopho'-bic**. [Gr *batrachos* a frog]

batsman. See under **bat**[1].

batswing. See under **bat**[2].

batswoman. See under **bat**[1].

batt. See **bat**[1] or **bat**. (*abbrev*).

batta *bat'ə*, (*Anglo-Ind*) *n* an allowance in addition to ordinary pay; subsistence money. [Prob Kanarese *bhatta* rice]

battailous *bat'ā-ləs*, (*Spenser*) *adj* warlike. [OFr *batail-los*; see **battle**[1]]

battalia *bət-äl'yə* or *-āl'*, *n* order of battle (*archaic*); the main body of an army in array (*obs*). [Ital *battaglia*; see **battle**[1]]

battalia pie *bət-al'yə pī*, *n* articles such as pin-cushions, embroidered by nuns in convents with scenes from the Bible; a pie containing sweetbreads, etc. [Fr *béatilles*, dimin from L *beātus* blessed, and perh L *pius* pious]

battalion *bə-tal'yən*, *n* a body of soldiers consisting of several companies; a body of men drawn up in battle array. [Fr *bataillon*, from Ital *battaglione*; see **battle**[1]]

batteilant *bat'ā-lənt*, (*Spenser*) *adj* combatant. [Fr *batail-lant*]

battels *bat'lz*, (*Oxford*) *n pl* accounts for provisions received from college kitchens and butteries; sums charged in college accounts generally. — *vi* **batt'el** to have such an account. — *n* **batt'eler** someone who battels; a student of rank below a commoner (*obs*). [Poss connected with **battle**[2]]

battement *bat-mã*, (*ballet*) *n* a movement in which one leg is extended to the front, side or back. [Fr, beating, from *battre* to beat]

batten[1] *bat'n*, *vi* to thrive at the expense of (with *on*); to grow fat; to feed abundantly (on; *lit* and *fig*). — *vt* (*obs*) to fatten. [ON *batna* to grow better, from *bati* advantage; cf Du *baten* to avail]

batten[2] *bat'n*, *n* a piece of sawn timber used for flooring, support of laths, etc; a strip of wood fastened across parallel boards, or used to fasten down hatches aboard ship, etc; a row of electric lamps or a strip of wood carrying them. — *vt* to fasten or furnish with battens. — *n* **batt'ening** battens forming a structure. — **batten down the hatches** to prepare for a crisis; *orig* to secure the hatches on a ship against bad weather. [**baton**]

Battenberg, **Battenburg** or **Battonberg**, etc **cake** *bat'ən-bûrg* (*kāk*), *n* a kind of cake *usu* made in pink and yellow squares and covered with marzipan. [Perh from *Battenberg* a village in Germany]

batter[1] *bat'ər*, *vt* to hit with repeated blows; to damage or wear with beating or by use; to attack with artillery; to attack (people or ideas) (*fig*). — *n* ingredients (*usu* flour and eggs) beaten along with some liquid (eg milk) into a paste (*cookery*); paste for sticking; a damaged piece of type (*printing*). — *adj* **batt'ered** suffering frequent violent assaults; in particular **battered baby** (or **child**) a baby (or child) suffering such attacks at the hands of its parents, or **battered wife** a woman who suffers such attacks by her spouse; covered or treated with batter. — **batt'ering-ram** a large beam used for battering down walls. — **battered baby** (or **child**) **syndrome** a collection of symptoms found in a baby or young child, caused by violence on the part of the parent or other adult suffering from social and psychological disturbance; **on the batter** (*slang*) on the bat, on a spree. [OFr *batre* (Fr *battre*), from LL *battere* (L *ba*(*t*)*tuere*) to beat]

batter[2] *bat'ər*, (*building*) *n* slope (eg of the face of a structure) upwards and backwards. — *vi* to slope in this way. [Origin doubtful]

batter[3]. See **bat**[1].

batterie *bat-*(*ə-*)*rē*, (*ballet*) *n* a jump in which the dancer beats the calves together. — **batterie de cuisine** (*də kwē-zēn*; *Fr*) a set of cooking utensils. [Fr, from *battre* to beat; see **batter**[1]]

battero. See **ballow**.

battery *bat'ər-i*, *n* the act of battering; a wound (*Shakesp*); a number of cannon or other offensive weapons with their equipment; the place on which cannon are mounted; a unit of artillery or its personnel; a collection or set of equipment; a combination of Leyden jars, lenses, or other apparatus; a battery of tests; a series (of questions); a series of two or more electric cells arranged to produce, or store, electricity; a single voltaic or solar cell; an attack against a person, beating, wounding, or threatening by touching clothes or body (*law*); an arrangement of tiers of cages in which hens are kept, the eggs they lay running down into wire containers outside the cages; an arrangement of similarly restrictive compartments for rearing pigs or cattle intensively; utensils for preparing or serving meals (cf **batterie de cuisine**); the pitcher and catcher (*baseball*); the percussion section of an orchestra. — **battery of tests** (*psychol*) a set of tests covering various factors relevant to some end purpose, eg job selection; **cross batteries** two batteries commanding the same spot from different directions; **masked battery** a battery out of the enemy's view. [OFr *batterie*]

battill. Old spelling of **battle**[2].

batting. See **bat**[1].

battle[1] *bat'l*, *n* a contest between opposing armies; a fight or encounter; conflict, struggle (*fig*); a battalion (*archaic*). — *vi* to fight; to struggle; to contend (with *against* or *with*). — *vt* to contest; to dispose in battalions (*archaic*). — *n* **batt'ler** someone who struggles, *esp* (*Austr* and *NZ*) unsuccessfully or to make a living. — **batt'le-axe** or **-ax** a kind of axe once used in battle; a domineering, *usu* older woman (*colloq*); **battle-axe block** or **section** (*Austr* and *NZ*) a plot of land without a street frontage, with access to and from the street via a drive or lane; **batt'le-cruiser** a large cruiser with battleship qualities; **batt'le-cry** a war-cry; a slogan; **batt'ledress** a soldier's ordinary uniform; **battle fatigue** (*psychol*) a psychological disorder caused by stress of combat (also *fig*); **batt'lefield** or **batt'le-ground** (*lit* and *fig*) the place on which a battle is or was fought; **batt'le-piece** a picture or description of a battle; **batt'leplane** (*obs*) a large fighting aeroplane; **battle royal** a general mêlée; a fierce fight (also *fig*). — *adj* **batt'le-scarred** scarred in battle; well worn, looking well used. — **batt'leship** a warship of the first class. — **do battle** (often *fig*) to fight; **half the battle** anything that brings one well on the way to success; **join battle** to engage in fighting. [Fr *bataille*, from L *battuālia* fighting]

battle[2] *bat'l*, *adj* (*dialect*) nourishing; fertile. — *vt* and *vi* (*archaic*) to feed; to fatten; to make or become fertile. [Perh connected with ON *bati* improvement; see **batten**[1]]

battle[3] *bat'l*, (*obs*) *vt* to furnish with battlements (*esp* in *pa p*). [OFr *batailler* movable defences]

battledore or **battledoor** *bat'l-dör*, (*obs* or *archaic*) *n* a light bat for striking a shuttlecock; the game played with this; a wooden bat used for washing, etc; a hornbook. — **not to know a B from a battledore** to be thoroughly ignorant. [Perhaps Sp *batidor* a beater, a washing beetle]

battlement *n* a wall or parapet with embrasures. — *adj* **batt'lemented**. [Same as **battle**[3]]

battology *bat-ol'ə-ji, n* futile repetition in speech or writing. — *adj* **battolog'ical**. [Gr *battologiā* stuttering, said to be from *Battos*, who consulted the Delphic oracle about his defect of speech (Herodotus 4.155), and *legein* to speak]

battre la campagne *batr' la kā-pan-y'*, (*Fr*) to scour the country, to beat the bush.

batts. See **bot**.

battue *ba-tōō', ba-tū'* or *bä-tü, n* a hunt in which animals are driven into some place for the convenience of the shooters; indiscriminate slaughter. [Fr, from *battre* to beat]

battuta *bät-tōō'tä*, (*Ital*) *n* a beat. — **a battuta** in strict time.

batty, batwing. See under **bat**[2].

batwoman. See **batman**[1].

bauble *bö'bl, n* a trifling piece of finery; a child's plaything; a jester's sceptre, a stick surmounted by a head with ass's ears; a piece of childish fooling; a foolish person (*Shakesp*). — *adj* **bau'bling** (*Shakesp*) trifling. [OFr *babel, baubel* toy, trinket]

bauchle *böhh'l*, (*Scot*) *n* a loose, down-at-heel, or badly worn, shoe; a worn-out, useless or clumsy person or thing. — *vi* to shamble. — *vt* to make shapeless; to bungle or spoil. [Origin obscure]

baud[1] *böd*, (*teleg*) *n* a unit of signalling speed, given as the number of signal events per second; the speed at which computers pass information (eg by telephone line) to other computers etc, given in bits per second (*comput*). [Fr inventor J M E *Baud*ot (died 1903)]

baud[2]. See **bawd**[2].

baudekin *böd'i-kin*. Same as **baldachin**.

baudric, baudrick or **baudricke** *böd'rik*. Same as **baldric**.

baudrons *böd'rəns*, (*Scot*) *n* quasi-proper name for the cat; also for the hare. — Also with *cap*. [Origin obscure]

bauera *bow'ə-rə, n* a plant of the *Bauera* genus of evergreen shrubs with pink flowers (family Saxifragaceae) found in Australia. [F and F A *Bauer*, 19c Austrian botanical painters]

Bauhaus *bow'hows, n* a German school of art and architecture (1919–33) having as its aim the integration of art and technology in design. [Literally building-house]

bauhinia *bō-hin'i-ə, n* a plant of the *Bauhinia* genus of tropical trees of the family Caesalpinaceae. [J and G *Bauhin*, 17c Swiss botanists]

bauk, baulk. Same as **balk**.

baur. See **bar**[3].

bausond *bös'ənd*, (*obs Northern*) *adj* of animals, having white spots, *esp* on the forehead, or a white stripe down the face. — *adj* **baus'on-faced**. [OFr *bausant* black and white spotted]

bauxite or **beauxite** *bök'sīt* or *-zīt*, or *bō'zīt, n* a clay compound containing aluminium. — *adj* **bauxitic** (*-it'ik*). [From Les *Baux*, near Arles, and *-ite*]

bavardage *bäv-är-däzh', n* chattering, prattle. [Fr *bavard* garrulous, from *bave* drivel]

bavin *bav'in, n* a bundle of brushwood. — **bavin wits** (*Shakesp*) wits that blaze and die like bavins. [Origin unknown]

bawbee *bö-bē'*, (*Scot*) *n* a halfpenny; *orig* a silver coin worth three Scots pennies; (*usu* in *pl*) money. [Prob from a Scottish mint-master (1538), Alexander Orrok of Sillebawbe]

bawble. Same as **bauble**.

bawcock *bö'kok*, (*Shakesp*) *n* a fine fellow. [From Fr *beau* fine, and *coq* a cock]

bawd[1] *böd, n* a female brothel-keeper or procuress; formerly a male pander. — *adv* **bawd'ily**. — *n* **bawd'iness**. — *n* **bawd'ry** procuring (*obs*); unchastity (*archaic*); lewd talk (*archaic*). — *adj* **bawd'y** lewd, sexually explicit. — *n* bawdy talk. — *adj* **bawd'-born** (*Shakesp*) born of a bawd. — **bawd'y-house** (*archaic*) a brothel. [Prob ME *bawdstrot* pander, from OFr *baldestrot*, prob from *bald* bold, gay, and the root of **strut**]

bawd[2] (*Shakesp* **baud**) *böd, n* a hare. [Perh **baudrons**]

bawdkin. Same as **baldachin**.

bawl *böl, vt* and *vi* to shout or cry out very loudly. — *n* a loud cry or shout. — *n* **bawl'er**. — *n* **bawl'ing**. — **bawl out** (*colloq*) to reprimand loudly and bullyingly. [Perh LL *baulāre* to bark, but cf Icel *baula* to low like a cow, from ON *baula* a cow]

bawley *bö'li*, (*Essex* and *Kent*) *n* a small fishing-smack. [Origin obscure]

bawn *bön, n* a fortification round a house; an enclosure for cattle. [Ir *bábhun* enclosure]

bawr. See **bar**[3].

baxter *bak'stər*, (*obs*) *n* a baker. [**bake**]

bay[1] *bā, adj* reddish brown inclining to chestnut (of horses, *usu* with a black mane and tail). — *n* a bay horse. [Fr *bai*, from L *badius* chestnut-coloured]

bay[2] *bā, n* an inlet of the sea with a wider opening than a gulf; an inward bend of the shore; a similar recess in a land form, eg in a mountain range. — **bay salt** coarse-grained salt, *orig* from sea-water. — **the Bay State** Massachusetts. [Fr *baie*, from LL *baia* a harbour]

bay[3] *bā, n* the space between two columns, timbers, walls, etc; any recess or stall; a space for a vehicle to park; a space where vehicles can be loaded and unloaded (also **loading bay**); a passing-place in a military trench; a side-line in a railway station (also **bay'-line**); a compartment or section of an aircraft (eg bomb bay) or ship (eg sick bay); the space under one house gable (*Shakesp*). — **bay window** any window forming a recess. — *adj* **bay-win'dowed**. [OFr *baée*, from *baer* to gape, be open; prob connected with **bay**[2]]

bay[4] *bā, n* the laurel tree; extended to other trees and shrubs, species of *Magnolia, Myrica*, etc; (in *pl*) an honorary garland or crown of victory, *orig* of laurel; hence (in *pl*), literary renown (*archaic*). — **bay'berry** the berry of the bay tree, or of candle-berry; a tree (*Pimenta acris*) related to allspice; **bay leaf** the dried leaf of the laurel tree (*Laurus nobilis*) used as a flavouring agent in cooking; **bay rum** an aromatic liquid prepared from the leaves of *Pimenta acris*, used medicinally and cosmetically; this liquid mixed with certain other substances. [OFr *baie* a berry, from L *bāca*]

bay[5] *bā, n* barking, baying (*esp* of a dog in pursuit); the combined cry of hounds in conflict with a hunted animal; the last stand of a hunted animal when it faces the hounds at close quarters (also *fig*). — *vi* to bark or howl (*esp* of large dogs). — *vt* to bark or howl at; to utter by baying; to chase with barking; to bring to bay. — **bay (at) the moon** to make a futile gesture; **bring to bay** to force to make a stand; **keep at bay** to prevent from coming closer; **stand** (or **be**) **at bay** to face the dogs at close quarters; to face one's pursuers. [Partly OFr *abai* barking, *bayer* to bark, partly OFr *bay* open-mouthed suspense, from LL *badāre* to open the mouth]

bay[6] *bā*, or **bez** *bā* or *bāz, n* (in full **bay'-antler** or **-tine**) the second tine of a deer's horn. [OFr *besantlier*, from *bes-* secondary (from L *bis* twice), and *antlier* antler]

bay[7] or **baye** *bā*, (*Spenser*) *vt* to bathe.

bayadère *bä-yä-der', n* a Hindu dancing-girl; a horizontally-striped woven fabric. [Fr, from Port *bailadeira*]

Bayard[1] *bā'är(d)*, or Fr *bä-yär, n* a type of knight 'without fear and without reproach'. [From the French knight *Bayard* (*c.* 1473–1524)]

Bayard[2] *bā'ärd* or *-ərd, n* a horse famous in medieval legend; (without *cap*) a bay horse or a horse generally (*archaic*); a type of blind recklessness or bold ignorance.

baye. See **bay**[7].

bayle. See **bail**[2].

bayonet *bā'ə-nit, n* a stabbing blade of steel that may be fixed to the muzzle of a firearm; military force; (in *pl*) soldiers armed with bayonets; (also **bayonet fitting**) a type of fitting for a light bulb, camera lens, etc, in which prongs on its side fit into slots to hold it in place. — *vt* to stab with a bayonet; to force at the point of the bayonet. — *adj* **bay'oneted** armed with a bayonet. —

bayonet joint, socket, etc one with, or for, a bayonet fitting. [Fr *baïonnette*, perh from *Bayonne* in France; or from OFr *bayon* arrow]

bayou *bī'ōō*, (*US*) *n* the marshy offshoot of a lake or river. [Perh Fr *boyau* gut, or Choctaw *bāyuk* little river]

bayt. A Spenserian spelling of **bate**[1]; also of **bait**.

bazaar or **bazar** *bə-zär'*, *n* an Eastern market-place or exchange; a fair in imitation of an Eastern bazaar, often selling goods in aid of charity; a big shop. [Pers *bāzār* a market]

bazazz. See **bezzazz**.

bazooka *bə-zōō'kə*, *n* a crude wind instrument with a slide, used for humorous purposes; an anti-tank gun for rocket-driven projectiles; a rocket launcher situated on the wing of an aeroplane. [Invented name]

bazouki. See **bouzouki**.

bazzazz. See **bezzazz**.

BB *abbrev*: Boys' Brigade. — *symbol*: very black (on lead pencils).

bb *abbrev*: books.

BBB *symbol*: (on a pencil) blacker than a BB pencil.

BBBC *abbrev*: British Boxing Board of Control.

BBC *abbrev*: British Broadcasting Corporation.

BBFC *abbrev*: British Board of Film Censors.

BC *abbrev*: Battery Commander; (or **B.C.**) before Christ (used in dating to indicate the number of years before the year once thought to be that of Christ's birth); Board of Control; British Columbia (Canadian Province); British Council.

BCC *abbrev*: British Council of Churches.

BCD. See **binary coded decimal** under **binary**.

BCG or **bcg** *abbrev*: bacillus of Calmette and Guérin, a strain of tubercle bacillus, used for inoculation.

BCh *abbrev*: *Baccalaureus Chirurgiae* (*L*), Bachelor of Surgery.

BCL *abbrev*: Bachelor of Civil Law.

BCom or **BComm** *abbrev*: Bachelor of Commerce.

BCS *abbrev*: British Computer Society.

BD *abbrev*: Bachelor of Divinity; bank draft; bills discounted.

bd *abbrev*: board; bond; bound.

BDA *abbrev*: British Dental Association.

Bde *abbrev*: Brigade.

bdellium *del'i-əm*, *n* a gum from *Commiphora* trees; used to translate, but *prob* unconnected with, Heb *b'dōlakh* (Gen 2.12; meaning unknown). [L, from Gr *bdellion*]

BDH *abbrev*: British Drug Houses.

BDI *abbrev*: *Bundesverband der Deutschen Industrie* (*Ger*), Federation of German Industry.

BDS *abbrev*: Bachelor of Dental Surgery; Barbados (IVR).

bds *abbrev*: boards.

BE *abbrev*: Bachelor of Engineering; Board of Education.

Be (*chem*) *symbol*: beryllium.

be *bē*, *vi infin* to live; to exist; to happen, take place; to have the state or quality mentioned; (with *infin*) must, need (to); 'be' also helps form some compound tenses, such as continuous and passive: — *pr p* **bē'ing**; *pa p* **been** (*bēn* or *bin*); *present subjunctive* **be**; *archaic* and *dialect present indicative* **be** (see **am, art, is, are**); for *pa t* see **was, wast, were, wert**. — *n* **be'-all** (*Shakesp*) all that is to be (**be-all and end-all** the supreme aim or issue). [OE *bēon*; Ger *bin* (1st pers); Gaelic *bi* exist; Welsh *byw* live; Gr *phyein* produce, grow; L *fuī* I was, *fīō* I become; Sans *bhavati* he is; orig to grow]

b e *abbrev*: bill of exchange.

be- *bi-*, *pfx* used (1) to form words with the sense of around, on all sides, in all directions, thoroughly, as in *besiege*; (2) to form verbs from adjectives and nouns (often in facetious modern coinages, eg *bejerseyed*); (3) formerly, to make intransitive verbs transitive, as in *bespeak*. [OE *bi-*, weak form of *bī* (see **by**[1])]

BEA (*old*) *abbrev*: British European Airways.

BEAB *abbrev*: British Electrical Approvals Board.

beach *bēch*, *n* the shore of a sea or of a lake, *esp* when sandy or pebbly; a marginal terrace formed by waves; the strand. — *vt* to drive or haul up on a beach. — *adj* **beached** having a beach; driven on a beach. — *adj* **beach'y** pebbly. — **beach'-ball** a large, *usu* inflatable, colourful ball for playing games on a beach; **beach boy** a male beach attendant; a beach bum; **beach buggy** an open vehicle with huge tyres, used for driving on beaches; **beach bum** a young man who loafs about on the beach; **beach'comber** (*-kōm-*) a long rolling wave; a loafer about the wharfs in Pacific seaports; a settler on a Pacific island who maintains himself by pearl-fishery; someone who gathers jetsam, etc on beaches; **beach'-combing**. — *adj* **beach'front** of property, facing the beach. — **beach'head** an area held on an enemy's shore for the purpose of landing; **beach'-master** an officer in charge of disembarking troops. [Orig a dialect word for shingle]

beach-la-mar *bēch-lä-mär'*, *n* a SW Pacific creole. [Port *bicho do mar* sea-slug, *bêche-de-mer*, the chief product of the area]

beacon *bē'kən*, *n* a fire on high ground lit as a signal, eg to warn of danger; a hill on which it could be lit; a buoy, lighthouse etc marking a rock or shoal in navigable waters; a light or other signal to guide aircraft; a sign marking a street crossing, eg a **Belisha** (*bə-lē'shə* or *bə-lish'ə*) **beacon** (Leslie Hore-*Belisha*, British minister of transport who introduced it in 1934); a wireless transmitter in which the radiation is concentrated in one or more narrow beams, so as to act as a guide to shipping or aircraft; anything that warns of danger. — *vt* to act as a beacon to; to light up; to mark by beacons. — *vi* to shine like a beacon. — **floating beacon** a lightship. [OE *bēacen* a beacon, a sign]

bead *bēd*, *n* a prayer (*obs*); a little ball strung with others in a rosary, for counting prayers; a similar ball or the like pierced for stringing to form a necklace, etc; a beadlike drop; the front-sight of a gun; a narrow moulding *orig* of semicircular section, sometimes broken into beadlike parts, now in various shapes, used *esp* for edging, covering small gaps, etc; the flange of a tyre. — *vt* to provide with beads or beading. — *vi* to form a bead or beads. — *adj* **bead'ed** having beads or a bead; in beadlike form. — *n* **bead'ing** bead moulding; work in beads. — *adj* **bead'y** beadlike, small and bright (as eyes); covered with beads or bubbles. — **bead'-house** *orig* a chapel; an almshouse whose inmates were required to pray for the founder's soul. — *adj* **bead'-proof** of such proof or strength as to carry beads or bubbles after shaking, as alcoholic liquors. — **bead'-roll** *orig* a list of the dead to be prayed for, hence a list of names, a long series; a rosary; **beads'man** or **bedes'man** a man bound or endowed to pray for others; a licensed beggar (*Scot*): — *fem* **beads'woman**; **beady eye** used to suggest distrustful attentiveness to another's behaviour. — **draw a bead on** (*US*) to take aim at; **tell one's beads** to say one's prayers. [OE *gebed* prayer; see **bid**[2]]

beadle *bēd'l*, *n* a mace-bearer, *esp* (Oxford and Cambridge Universities **bedel** or **bedell** *-del'*, or *bēd'*) a vice-chancellor's; a minor official of a church, college, etc; a parish officer with the power of punishing minor offenders; in Scotland, the church-officer attending on the minister; a messenger or crier of a court (*obs*). — *n* **bead'ledom** or **bead'lehood** stupid officiousness. — *n* **bead'leship, bed'elship** or **bed'ellship** the office of beadle or bedel. [OE *bydel*, from *bēodan* to proclaim, to bid; affected by OFr form *bedel*]

beadman, bedeman. Old forms of **beadsman** (see under **bead**).

beady. See **bead**.

beagle *bē'gl*, *n* a small hound; sometimes, a harrier (dog); a bailiff; a small kind of shark; a spy (*obs*). — *vi* to hunt with beagles. — *n* **bea'gler**. — *n* **bea'gling** hunting with beagles. [Ety unknown; poss OFr *beegueulle* clamourer, from *beer* to gape, and *gueule* throat]

beak *bēk*, *n* a bird's bill; a hard or sharp snout; a nose (*joc*); a pointed projection; in the ancient galley an iron point projecting from the bow for piercing the enemy's vessel; a magistrate, schoolmaster or schoolmistress (*slang*). — *adj* **beaked** (*bēkt*). — *adj* **beak'y**. — **beak'-iron** same as **bick-iron**. [OFr *bec*, from L *beccus* (recorded by Suetonius) a cock's bill]

beaker *bēk'ər*, *n* a large drinking-bowl or cup, or its contents; a deep glass or other vessel used by chemists, generally with a lip for pouring; a *usu* plastic tumbler; one of a set of similar cylindrical-shaped objects, a child's toy. — **Beaker Folk** a round-headed, heavy-browed, square-jawed people that appeared in Britain at the dawn of the Bronze Age, makers of round barrows in which bell-shaped pottery beakers are often found. [ON *bikarr*, prob from LL *bicārium*, or *bīcārium*, appar from Gr *bīkos* a drinking bowl]

beam *bēm*, *n* a large and straight piece of timber or iron forming one of the main structural members of a building, etc; any of the transverse pieces of framing extending across a ship's hull; the part of a balance from which the scales hang; the stem, or main part of a deerhorn, an anchor or a plough; either of the two wooden cylinders in a loom; a raised horizontal bar on which gymnasts perform balancing exercises (*gymnastics*); a great fault (*fig*; from the metaphor of the mote and the beam in Matt 7.3); a tree (*obs* except in *hornbeam*, *whitebeam*, etc); the greatest width of a ship or boat; breadth; a shaft or ray of light or other radiations; a gleam; a broad smile, lighting up the face. — *vt* to send forth; to place on a beam; to transmit or direct, eg by beam system. — *vi* to shine; to smile radiantly. — *n* **beam'er** a workman or machine that puts yarn on the beam of a loom; a fast, head-high ball (*cricket*); a beam trawler. — *adv* **beam'ily** radiantly. — *n* **beam'iness** radiance; breadth. — *n* and *adj* **beam'ing**. — *adv* **beam'ingly**. — *adj* **beam'ish** radiant. — *adj* **beam'less** without beams; emitting no rays. — *n* **beam'let** a little beam. — *adj* **beam'y** shining; radiant; massive like a weaver's beam; broad. — **beam compass** an instrument consisting of a beam and adjustable legs, for drawing extra-large circles; **beam'-ends** the ends of the transverse beams of a ship; **beam'-engine** a steam-engine with a beam connecting the piston-rod and the crank of the wheel-shaft; **beam sea** one rolling against the ship's side; **beam system** a system whereby, with the aid of reflectors, short wireless waves are projected (like a lighthouse beam) in a particular direction, not radiated in all directions; **beam trawl** a trawling net kept open by a beam along its upper lip, resting on runners; **beam trawler**; **beam trawling**; **beam tree** a pleonastic name for the whitebeam; **beam weapon** any weapon whose destructive force consists of a beam of energy such as subatomic particles. — **abaft** or **before the beam** behind or before a line across the greatest width of a ship; **broad in the beam** wide-hipped; **fly** or **ride the beam** to fly an aircraft in the direction shown by a radio beam; **lee** or **weather beam** the side away from, or towards, the wind; **off** (or **on**) **the beam** off (or on) the course shown by a radio beam; off (or on) the right track (*fig*); **on her beam-ends** of a ship, so much inclined to one side that the beams become nearly vertical; **on one's beam-ends** in acute distress, destitute; **on the beam** in the direction of a ship's beams, at right angles to her course; see **off the beam**; **on the port** (or **starboard**) **beam** applied to any distant point out at sea, at right angles to the keel, and on the left (or right) side; **ride the beam** see **fly the beam**; **weather beam** see **lee beam**. [OE *bēam* tree, stock of a tree, ray of light; Ger *Baum* tree; perh related to Gr *phȳma* a growth, from *phyein* to grow]

BEAMA *abbrev*: British Electrical and Allied Manufacturers' Association.

bean *bēn*, *n* the name of several kinds of leguminous plants and their seeds, *esp* the common or broad bean (*Vicia faba*) and the French, kidney or haricot bean (*Phaseolus vulgaris*); applied also to the seeds of other plants, from their beanlike form, such as coffee; a coin (*obs* except in **not a bean** (*colloq*) not a cent, no money at all); the head (*colloq*). — *vt* (*colloq*) to hit on the head. — *n* **bean'ery** (*US slang*) a cheap restaurant. — *n* **bean'ie** (*colloq*) a small, close-fitting hat. — *n* **bean'o** (*colloq*) a beanfeast, a rowdy jollification; bingo: — *pl* **bean'os**. — **bean'bag** a small cloth bag containing dried beans or the like, used in games, etc; a large cushion filled eg with chips or balls of plastic foam, used as seating (also **beanbag chair**); **bean caper** a shrub (*Zygophyllum*) of steppe and desert whose flower-buds are used as capers; **bean curd** a soft paste made from soya-beans, used in Chinese and vegetarian cookery; **bean'feast** an annual dinner given by employers to their workers; a jollification; **bean'-king** the king of the festivities on Twelfth Night, finder of a bean hidden in the Twelfth-cake; **bean'pole** a supporting pole up which a bean plant climbs; a tall, very thin person (*colloq*); **bean sprout** the young shoot of the mung bean or certain other beans, used as a vegetable *esp* in Chinese cookery; **bean'stalk** the stem of a bean plant; **bean tree** a name given to several trees, as Moreton Bay chestnut, carob tree, and catalpa. — **full of beans** in high spirits; **give someone beans** (*archaic*) to treat someone severely; **know how many beans make five** (*colloq*) to be fully alert, know what's what; **old bean** see under **old**; **spill the beans** see under **spill**[1]. [OE *bēan*, Ger *Bohne*]

bear[1] *bār*, *vt* to carry; to have; to convey; to remove from the board in the final stage of the game (*backgammon*); to sustain or support; to thrust or drive; to endure, tolerate; to admit of; to purport; to behave or conduct (oneself); to bring forth, give birth to (*pap* **born** (*börn*) in passive uses except with *by*); to display on one's heraldic shield, to be entitled to (*heraldry*). — *vi* to suffer; to be patient; (with *on* or *upon*) to have reference to; to press (*on* or *upon*); to lie in, or take, a direction; to be capable of sustaining weight; to be productive: — *pr p* **bear'ing**; *pa t* **bore** (*archaic* **bare**); *pa p* **borne** (*börn*). — *n* (*Spenser* **beare** *bēr*) a burden; also (*Spenser*) a bier (see **bier**). — *adj* **bear'able** able to be borne or endured. — *n* **bear'ableness**. — *adv* **bear'ably**. — *n* **bear'er** a person who or that which bears; the actual holder of a cheque, etc; a person who helps to carry the coffin at a funeral, a pall-bearer; a carrier or messenger; formerly in India, a personal, household or hotel servant. — *n* **bear'ing** demeanour; direction; a supporting surface; relation, relevance; a heraldic device or coat of arms; the part of a machine that bears friction, *esp* part of a shaft or axle and its support (sometimes in *pl*; see **ball-bearing**). — Also *adj*. — **bearer bill**, **bond**, **security**, etc a bond, etc which has been made out to be payable to the person in possession of it; **bearing cloth** (*hist*) a gown worn at a child's baptism; **bearing rein** a fixed rein between the bit and the saddle, by which a horse's head is held up and its neck made to arch. — **bear a hand** see under **hand**; **bear away** to sail away; to carry away; **bear down** to overthrow; to press downwards; in childbirth, to exert downward muscular pressure; (with *upon* or *towards*) to sail with the wind (towards); (with *upon*) to approach (someone or something) rapidly and purposefully; **bear hard** (*Shakesp*) to have ill-will to; **bear hard** or **heavily upon** (*lit* and *fig*) to press heavily on; to oppress, afflict; **bear in hand** to make out, maintain (*archaic*); to keep in expectation, to flatter someone's hopes (*Shakesp*); **bear in mind** to remember (that); to think of, take into consideration; **bear in upon** (*usu* in *passive*) to impress upon, or to make realize, *esp* by degrees; **bear out** to corroborate; **bear up** to keep up one's spirits; **bear up for** to sail towards (a place); **bear with** to make allowance for; **bear witness** see **witness**; **bring to bear** to bring into operation (*against* or *upon*); **find**, **get** (or **lose**) **one's bearings** to ascertain (or to become uncertain of) one's position or orientation. [OE *beran*; Gothic *bairan*, L *ferre*, Gr *pherein*; Sans *bharati* he carries]

bear[2] *bār*, *n* a heavy carnivorous animal with long shaggy hair and hooked claws; also applied to other unrelated animals, such as the koala; a teddy bear; a person who sells stocks for delivery at a future date, anticipating a fall in price (*stock exchange*; *opp* to *bull*; the old phrase *a bearskin jobber* suggests an origin in the proverbial phrase, to sell the bearskin before one has caught the bear); the name of two constellations, the Great and Little Bear (Ursa major and minor); any rude, rough or ill-mannered fellow. — *vi* (*stock exchange*) to act as a bear. — *vt* (*stock exchange*) to lower the price of (a stock) or depress (a market) by selling speculatively. — *adj* **bear'ish** like a bear in manners; inclining towards, anticipating, a fall in price (*stock exchange*). — *adv* **bear'ishly**. — *n* **bear'ishness**. — **bear-animal'cule** a tardigrade, a kind of arthropod; **bear'-baiting** the former sport of setting dogs to attack a bear; **bear'berry** a trailing plant (*Arctostaphylos*) of the heath family; extended to various plants; **bear'bine** a bindweed; **bear'-cat** a panda; **bear garden** an enclosure for bear-baiting or for exhibiting bears; a turbulent assembly; **bear hug** a hold in which one wraps one's arms tightly around one's opponent's arms and upper body (*wrestling*); a similar tight hug; **bear'-lead** to lead about eg a performing bear, but also more *gen* to supervise, act as tutor to; **bear pit** an enclosure for bears; **bear's'-breech** acanthus; **bear's'-ear** auricula; **bear's'-foot** black hellebore; **bear'skin** the pelt of a bear; a shaggy woollen cloth for overcoats; the high fur cap worn by the Guards in the UK; **bear'ward** a warden or keeper of bears. [OE *bera*; Ger *Bär*; Du *beer*; apparently from an Indo-European root *bhero-* brown]

bear[3] or **bere** *bēr*, *n* barley; in Scotland now the little-grown four-rowed (really six-rowed) variety. [OE *bere*]

bear[4]. See **bere**[2].

bearbine. See **bear**[2].

beard *bērd*, *n* the hair that grows on the chin and cheeks of a man's face; the tuft on the lower jaw of a goat, seal, etc; a fish's barbel; an awn or threadlike spike as on the ears of barley (*bot*); a tuft of hairs; a barb of a hook, an arrow, etc; the gills of an oyster, etc. — *vt* to oppose resolutely or with effrontery; to take by the beard. — *adj* **beard'ed** having a beard; prickly; awned; barbed. — *n* **beard'ie** (*colloq*) a bearded person. — *adj* **beard'less** having no beard; young, immature. — **beard'-grass** a kind of bearded grass (*Polypogon*). [OE; Ger *Bart*, Russ *boroda*]

beare. See under **bear**[1].

béarnaise *bā-ar-nez* or **béarnaise sauce** (*sös*) *n* (also with *cap*) a sauce made from egg yolks, butter, shallots, tarragon, chervil and wine vinegar. [Fr *béarnaise* (fem of *béarnais*) of Béarn, region of SW France]

bearward. See under **bear**[2].

beast *bēst*, *n* an irrational animal, as opposed to man; a four-footed animal; a brutal person; anything beastly (*colloq*); a police officer (*slang*). — *n* **beast'hood** the state or nature of a beast. — *n* **beast'ie** (*orig Scot*) a *dimin* form of **beast**, the four-footed animal; an insect, spider, etc (*colloq*). — *adv* **beast'ily** (*Shelley*) bestially. — *n* **beast'liness**. — *adj* **beast'like** (also *adv*). — *adj* **beast'ly** vile, disagreeable (*colloq*); like a beast in actions or behaviour, bestial. — *adv* abominably, frightfully (*colloq*); brutishly. — **beast fable** a story in which animals behave like humans; **beast'ly-head** (*Spenser*) personality or self of a beast. — **beast of burden** an animal, eg a donkey or bullock, used to carry or pull loads; **the beast with two backs** a man and a woman in the act of having sexual intercourse; **mark of the Beast** a stamp on the forehead or right hand of a worshipper of **the Beast** (Antichrist) as in Revelation 13; hence a sign of whatever was considered to be of Antichrist, or (loosely) evil or even bad manners; **number of the beast** the apocalyptic number. [OFr *beste* (Fr *bête*), from L *bestia*]

beastings. Same as **beestings**.

beat *bēt*, *vt* to strike repeatedly; to pound; to form (a path, track, etc) by frequent use of the same route; to batter; to whip up or switch; to flap; to strike (bushes, undergrowth, etc) in order to rouse game; to thrash; to defeat, to frustrate; to forestall; to be too difficult for; to outdo, excel; to drive or thrust (back, down, off, etc); to spread (eg gold) flat and thin by beating with a tool; to mark (time) with a baton, etc; to break or bruise (*Bible*). — *vi* to give strokes repeatedly; to flap; to pulsate; to impinge; to mark time in music; to swindle (*US*); to sail as close as possible to directly into the wind: — *prp* **beat'ing**; *pa t* **beat**; *pa p* **beat'en** or now rarely **beat**. — *n* a recurrent stroke, its sound, or its moment, eg of a watch, verse, the pulse, or a conductor's baton; the rhythmic base unit in music, *usu* grouped into bars; pulsation, *esp* that heard when two notes nearly in tune are sounded together; a round or course, such as a policeman's; an area of land or stretch of riverbank on which sportsmen hunt or fish; a place of resort; the act of beating in order to rouse game. — *adj* worn out, exhausted (*colloq*); relating to beatniks (*colloq*); affected with bursitis (eg *beat elbow* or *knee*). — *adj* **beat'able**. — *adj* **beat'en** made smooth or hard by beating or treading; trite; worn by use; exhausted (*Austr* and *NZ colloq*). — *n* **beat'er** a person or thing which beats or strikes; a person who rouses or beats up game; a crushing or mixing instrument. — *n* **beat'ing** the act of striking; a thrashing; a defeat; pulsation or throbbing; the rousing of game. — *n* **beatnik** (*bēt'nik*) one of the **beat generation** (*orig* in *US*), bohemian poets, etc who, in the 1950s, dissociated themselves from the aims of contemporary society; a young person whose behaviour, dress, etc is unconventional. — **beat music** popular music with a very pronounced rhythm. — *adj* **beat'-up** dilapidated through excessive use. — **beat about the bush** see under **bush**; **beat a retreat** to retreat, *orig* to beat the drum as a signal for retreat (**beat the retreat** to perform the military ceremony (**beating the retreat**) consisting of marching and military music *usu* performed at dusk (*orig* marking the recall of troops to their quarters)); **beat down** of a buyer, to try to reduce (the price of goods), to persuade (the seller) to settle for less; **beat it** (*slang*) to make off hastily or furtively; (often as *imperative*) go away!; **beat one's brains** or **beat one's brains out** to puzzle about something; **beat one's breast** to show extravagant signs of grief; **beat out** to flatten or reduce in thickness by beating; **beat someone's brains out** to kill by hitting repeatedly on the head; to subject to a vicious beating; **beat someone to it** to manage to do something before someone else can; **beat the air** to fight to no purpose, or against an imaginary enemy; **beat the bounds** to trace out boundaries in a perambulation, certain objects in the line of journey being formally struck; **beat the clock** to do or finish something within the time allowed; **beat the retreat** see **beat a retreat** above; **beat up** to pound or whip into froth, paste, a mixture, etc; to put up game, by beating the bushes, etc; to alarm by a sudden attack; to thrash, to subject to a violent and brutal attack (*colloq*; also in US **beat up on**); to disturb; to arouse; to go about in quest of anything; to make way against wind or tide; **take a beating** to suffer physical or verbal chastisement; **take some** (or **a lot**) **of beating** (*colloq*) to be of very high quality, ie to be difficult to surpass. [OE *bēatan*, pa t *bēot*]

beatae memoriae *bi-ā'tē me-mō'ri-ē*, also *-mö'*, or *be-ä'tī me-mo'ri-ī*, (*L*) of blessed memory.

beath *bēdh*, (*Spenser*) *vt* to bathe, heat. [OE *bethian* to foment]

beatify *bi-at'i-fī*, *vt* to make blessed or happy; to declare to be in the enjoyment of eternal happiness in heaven, and therefore entitled to public reverence (*RC*). — *adj* **beatific** (*bē-ə-tif'ik*) or **beatif'ical** making supremely happy; revealing supreme happiness. — *adv* **beatif'ically**. — *n* **beatificā'tion** the act of beatifying; a declaration by the Pope that a person is blessed in heaven, authorizing a certain definite form of public reverence payable to them, the first step to canonization (*RC*). — **beatific vision** a glimpse of the glory of heaven. [L *beātus* blessed, and *facere* to make]

beati pacifici *bi-ā'tī pa-sif'i-sī* or *be-ä'tē pa-kif'i-kē*, (*L*) blessed are the peacemakers.

beatitude *bi-at'i-tūd*, *n* heavenly happiness; happiness of the highest kind; a title given to patriarchs in the

Orthodox Churches; (in *pl*) the sayings of Christ in Matt 5, declaring certain classes of person to be blessed (*Christian relig*). [L *beātitūdō*, from *beātus* blessed]

beatnik. See under **beat**.

beatus ille *bē-ā'to͞os* or *bā-ä'to͞os il'ā*, (*L*) happy the man (*literally* he).

beau *bō*, *n* a man attentive to dress or fashion; a fop or dandy; a lover: — *pl* **beaux** (*bōz*): — *fem* **belle** (*bel*). — *adj* **beau'ish**. — **beau garçon** (*gär-sɔ̃*) a handsome man; a dandy; **beau geste** (*zhest*) a gracious gesture; **beau-ideal** (*bō-ī-dē'əl* or *bō-ē-dā-äl*) ideal beauty; a type or embodiment of the highest excellence; **beau jour** (*zho͞or*) a fine day, good times; **beau monde** (*mɔ̃d*) the world of fashion and high society; **beau-pere** (*bū-pēr'*; *obs*; Fr *père* father) a term of courtesy for father, used *esp* of ecclesiastical persons; (*Spenser*; OFr *per* equal, peer) a companion; **beaux arts** (*bō-zär*) the fine arts; **beaux esprits** (*-zes-prē*) see **bel esprit**; **beaux yeux** (*-zyø*) fine eyes; a pretty woman. [Fr *beau, bel*, from L *bellus* fine, gay]

beaufet or **beauffet** *buf-et'*, *n obs* forms of **buffet**[2] sideboard, cupboard.

beaufin. An over-sophisticated spelling of **biffin**.

Beaufort scale *bō'fərt skāl*, *n* a scale of wind velocity, with 0 for calm, 12 for hurricane. [Devised by Sir Francis *Beaufort* (1774–1857) English admiral and hydrographer]

Beaujolais *bō-zho-lā*, *n* a red or white wine of east central France. [From *Beaujolais*, a subdivision of Lyonnais]

beaumontague or **beaumontage** *bō-mon-tāg'* or *-mon'tij*, *n* a composition for hiding cracks and holes in wood or iron, varying in make-up. [Perh from Elie de *Beaumont* (1798–1874), French geologist]

Beaune *bōn*, *n* a red or white wine from *Beaune* in eastern France.

beauté du diable *bō-tā dü dyäbl'*, (*Fr*) *n* an irresistible or overpowering beauty; an attractiveness which the charm and sparkle of youth give to an otherwise unattractive person.

beauty *bū'ti*, *n* the quality that gives pleasure to the sight, or aesthetic pleasure generally; a particular grace or excellence; a beautiful person (often *ironic*), *esp* a woman; the beautiful women as a group (*obs*); a very fine specimen of its kind (*colloq*); the good feature (of) (*colloq*); (in *pl*) beautiful passages or extracts; see **bottomness** (*phys*). — *vt* (*Shakesp*) to make beautiful. — *interj* (*Austr* and *NZ*) an enthusiastic expression of approval (also *Austr*, *NZ* and *Scot* **you beauty**). — *n* **beaut** (*slang*) someone or something exceptionally beautiful or remarkable. — *adj* and *interj* (*esp Austr*) excellent, fine. — *adj* **beau'teous** (*bū'ti-əs*) a bookish word for beautiful. — *adv* **beau'teously**. — *n* **beau'teousness**. — *n* **beautician** (*bū-tish'ən*) a person engaged in women's hairdressing, facial make-up, manicuring, etc. — *n* **beautificā'tion**. — *n* **beau'tifier** a person who or something which beautifies or makes beautiful. — *adj* **beau'tiful** good-looking, attractive; with qualities that give pleasure or delight to the senses, *esp* the eye and ear, or which awaken admiration in the mind. — *adv* **beau'tifully**. — *vt* **beau'tify** to make beautiful; to grace; to adorn. — *vi* (*rare*) to become beautiful, or more beautiful. — **beauty contest** a competition held for the selection of a beauty queen; **beauty parlour** or **salon** an establishment for the hairdressing, manicuring, face-massaging, etc of women; **beauty queen** a girl who is voted the most attractive or best-proportioned in a competition; **beauty sleep** sleep, *esp* the sleep before midnight, considered the most refreshing; **beauty spot** a patch placed on the face to heighten beauty; a birthmark resembling such a patch; a foil to set off something else; a scene of outstanding beauty. — **the beautiful people** (also with *caps*) the rich and fashionable members of the international social set. [OFr *biaute* (Fr *beauté*), from LL *bellitās, -ātis*, from L *bellus*]

beaux. See **beau**.

beauxite. See **bauxite**.

beaver[1] *bēv'ər*, *n* an amphibious rodent (*Castor*); its valuable fur; a hat of beaver fur or a substitute material; a glove of beaver fur; a heavy woollen cloth; a boy belonging to the most junior branch of the scout movement (also **Beaver Scout**). — *n* **beav'ery** a place where beavers are kept. — **beav'erboard** (® with *cap* in US) a building board of wood-fibre; **beaver lamb** lambskin dyed to look like beaver fur; **beaver rat** the coypu; the musquash; the Australian water-rat, *Hydromys*; **beav'er-tree** or **beav'er-wood** a species of magnolia whose bark beavers eat. — **beaver away** (*colloq*) to work very hard (at); **mountain beaver** the sewellel. [OE *befer*, *beofor*; Du *bever*, Ger *Biber*, Gaelic *beaghar*, L *fiber*]

beaver[2] *bēv'ər*, *n* in medieval armour, the covering for the lower part of the face, the visor being that for the upper part (later the movable beaver was confused with the visor); a beard or bearded man (*slang*); the female pubic area or genitalia (*orig US*). — *adj* **beav'ered**. [OFr *bavière* child's bib, from *bave* slaver]

bebeeru *bi-bē'ro͞o*, *n* the greenheart tree of Guyana. — *n* **bebee'rine** (*-rin* or *-rēn*) an alkaloid yielded by its bark, a substitute for quinine. [Native name]

beblubbered *bi-blub'ərd*, *adj* disfigured by weeping. [**be-** (1)]

bebop *bē'bop*, *n* a variety of jazz music, from about 1940, which added new harmonies, melodic patterns, and rhythms to accepted jazz characteristics. — Also *vi*. [Imit of two quavers in the rhythm; see also **bop**[1]]

bebung *bā'bo͝ong*, (*music*) *n* a tremolo effect produced on the clavichord by fluctuating the pressure of the finger on the key. [Ger]

becall *bi-köl'*, *vt* to call names. [**be-** (1)]

becalm *bi-käm'*, *vt* to make calm, still or quiet. — *adj* **becalmed'** motionless from lack of wind. [**be-** (2)]

became *bi-kām'*, *pa t* of **become**.

bécasse *bā-käs*, (*Fr*) *n* a woodcock.

because *bi-koz'* or *bi-köz'*, *adv* and *conj* for the reason that; on account (of). [**by** and **cause**]

beccaccia *bāk-kä'chä*, (*Ital*) *n* a woodcock.

beccafico *bek-a-fē'kō*, *n* a garden warbler or related bird, considered a delicacy *esp* by the Italians: — *pl* **beccafi'cos**. [Ital, from *beccare* to peck, and *fico* a fig]

béchamel, béchamel sauce or **bechamel** *bā-shə-mel* (*sös*) or *besh'ə-mel*, *n* a white sauce flavoured with onion and herbs and sometimes enriched with cream. [Fr; from the name of a steward of Louis XIV]

bechance *bi-chäns'*, (*archaic*) *vi* to happen by chance (to); to befall. — *adv* by chance; accidentally. [**be-** (1) and **chance**, *vi*]

becharm *bi-chärm'*, *vt* to charm; to enchant. [**be-** (1)]

béche-de-mer *besh'də-mer*, *n* the trepang or sea-slug, a species of Holothuria, much esteemed in China as a food delicacy; beach-la-mar (qv). [Fr, from Port *bicho do mar* 'sea-worm', the sea-slug]

Becher's Brook *bē'cherz bro͝ok*, *n* a notoriously difficult jump in the Grand National steeplechase; a particularly difficult or critical obstacle, problem or possible stumbling-block.

beck[1] *bek*, (*N Eng dialect*) *n* a stream. [ON *bekkr*; Ger *Bach*]

beck[2] *bek*, *n* a sign with the finger or head; a nod; a bow or curtsey (*Scot*). — *vi* to make such a sign. — *vt* to call by a nod. — **at someone's beck (and call)** subject to someone's will. [A contraction of **beckon**]

becke *bek*, (*Spenser*) *n*. Same as **beak**.

becket *bek'it*, (*naut*) *n* a loop of rope having a knot at one end and an eye at the other; a large hook, or a wooden bracket used to keep loose tackle or spars in a convenient place. [Perh Du *bogt*, *bocht* a bend of rope]

beck-iron. Same as **bick-iron**.

beckon *bek'n*, *vt* and *vi* to nod or (now *usu*) make a summoning sign (to). [OE *bīecnan*, from *bēacen* a sign. See **beacon**]

becloud *bi-klowd'*, *vt* to obscure by clouds; to dim, obscure. [**be-** (2)]

become *bi-kum'*, *vi* to come to be; to be the fate of; to arrive, have got (to a place) (*obs*). — *vt* to suit or befit; to grace or adorn fittingly; to look well in: — *pa t* **became'**; *pa p* **become'**. — *adj* **becom'ing**. — *adv* **becom'ingly**. — *n* **becom'ingness**. [OE *becuman*; see **come**]

becquerel *bek'ə-rel*, *-rəl* or *-rel'*, *n* the derived SI unit of radioactivity, symbol **Bq**, equal to one disintegration per second. [A H *Becquerel* (1852–1908), French physicist]

becurl *bi-kûrl'*, *vt* to curl. [**be-** (1)]

BEd *abbrev*: Bachelor of Education.

bed[1] *bed*, *n* a couch or place to sleep on; a mattress; a bedstead; a garden plot; a layer of oysters, etc; a place in which anything rests; conjugal union, sexual intercourse, the marriage-bed, matrimonial rights and duties; the channel of a river; a sea or lake bottom; a layer or stratum; the underside of something; an underlying surface; a flat surface on which something can be laid. — *vt* to put to bed; to provide, or make, a bed for; to have sexual intercourse with; to plant in a bed; to lay in layers or on a surface; to embed. — *vi* to go to bed; to cohabit: — *pr p* **bedd'ing**; *pa p* **bedd'ed**. — *adj* **bedd'able** sexually attractive. — *n* **bedd'er** a plant suitable for a flower bed; a bedmaker in a Cambridge college (*colloq*). — *n* **bedd'ing** bedclothes, etc, with or without the mattress; litter for cattle; stratification (*geol*; **false bedding** see **false**). — *adv* **bed'ward** or **bed'wards** in the direction of bed; towards bedtime. — **bed'-bath** the washing of a sick person in their bed, a blanket bath; **bed'-bottle** a bottle for bedridden males to urinate in; **bed'bug** the common bug (*Cimex lectularius*); **bed'chamber** (*archaic*) a bedroom; **bed'-closet** a closet serving as a bedroom; **bed'clothes** sheets, blankets, etc for a bed; **bed'cover** an upper covering for a bed; **bedding plant** a plant sufficiently well-grown for planting in a bed; **bedd'y-bye** or **-byes** bed, as a place to sleep (used in speaking to children or *facetious*). — *adj* **bed'fast** (*Northern*) confined to bed. — **bed'fellow** a sharer of a bed; a colleague; something or someone that associates with another; **bed'-jacket** a light jacket worn when sitting up in bed; **bed'-key** a tool for tightening a bedstead; **bed'-linen** sheets and pillow-cases; **bed'maker** a person who makes the beds and cleans college rooms at Oxford, etc; **bed'pan** a utensil into which a person confined to bed can urinate and defecate; a warming-pan; **bed'-plate** (*mech*) the metal base to which the frame of a machine, engine, etc is attached; **bed'post** a corner support of a bedstead; **bed'presser** (*Shakesp*) a heavy, lazy fellow; **bed'-rest** confinement to bed, *usu* on medical orders; a support for someone sitting up in bed. — *adj* **bed'ridden** (also *obs* **bed'rid**) confined to bed by age or sickness; worn out. — **bed'right** or **bed'-rite** (*Shakesp*) the privilege or due of the marriage-bed; **bed'rock** the solid rock underneath superficial formations; fundamental principles; the lowest state. — *adj* bottom, lowest; basic, fundamental. — **bed'-roll** a sleeping-bag or bedclothes rolled up so as to be easily carried by a camper, etc; **bed'room** a room with a bed; a sleeping apartment; room in bed, sleeping space. — *adj* (*esp* of a comedy or farce) involving or hinting at sexual activity between people in a bedroom, in night-clothes, etc. — **bed'-settee** a sofa that converts into a bed; **bed'-sheet** a cotton, nylon, etc sheet for a bed; **bed'side** the space beside a bed. — Also *adj*. — **bedside book** one *esp* suitable for reading in bed; **bedside manner** that assumed by a doctor, etc at a sickbed; **bed-sitt'ing-room** a combined bedroom and sitting-room, eg in lodgings (shortened to **bed'-sit'** or **bed'-sitt'er**); **bed'-socks** warm socks for wearing in bed; **bed'sore** an ulcer, *esp* over the bony prominences, arising from long confinement to bed; **bed'spread** a coverlet put over a bed by day; **bed'-staff** a staff or lath formerly used for various purposes in connection with beds; a handy weapon; **bed'stead** a frame for supporting a bed; **bed'straw** any plant of the genus *Galium*, *esp* (Our) Lady's bedstraw (*Galium verum*), once used as stuffing for mattresses; **bed'-swerver** (*Shakesp*) a person false to their marriage vow; **bed'-table** a table for use by a person in bed; **bed'tick** (*old*) the case into which stuffing is put to make a mattress; **bed'time** the time for going to bed. — *adj* to do with, or suitable for, bedtime. — **bed'-wetting** the accidental passing of urine in bed; **bed'-work** (*Shakesp*) work easily performed, as if done in bed. — *adj* **bed'-worthy** sexually attractive. — **be brought to bed (of)** (*archaic*) to give birth (to); **bed and board** food and lodging; full connubial relations; **bed and breakfast** overnight accommodation with breakfast at a hotel, etc (*adj* **bed'-and-break'fast** (*stock exchange*) of deals in which shares standing at a loss are sold one day and rebought the next to establish a loss for tax purposes); **bed down** to (cause to) settle down, *esp* in a makeshift bed, for sleep; **bed of down** a bed of roses; **bed of honour** the grave of a soldier who has fallen in battle; **bed of justice** (Fr *lit de justice*) the king's throne in the Parlement of Paris; a sitting at which the king was present, chiefly for the registration of his own decrees; **bed of nails** the board studded with nails on which fakirs lie; an extremely difficult and uncomfortable situation; **bed of roses** any easy or comfortable place; **bed out** to plant out in a flower-bed, etc; **get out of bed on the wrong side** to start the day in a bad mood; **go** or **put to bed** (of newspapers, magazines, etc) to go to or send to press; **go to bed with** to have sexual intercourse with; **keep one's bed** to remain in bed; **lie in the bed one has made** to have to accept the consequences of one's own acts; **Lords** or **Ladies of the Bedchamber** officers in the royal household who wait upon a king or queen; **make a bed** to tidy and put in order the bedclothes on a bed; **take to one's bed** to go to bed because of illness, grief, age, etc. [OE *bed(d)*; Ger *Bett*, ON *bethr*; prob related to L *fodere* to dig (as orig a hole)]

bed[2] *bed*, (*Spenser*). Same as **bid**[2].

bedabble *bi-dab'l*, *vt* to dabble or wet. [**be-** (1)]

bedad *bi-dad'*, (*Ir*) *interj* an oath, = by God. [Variant of **begad**]

bedaggle *bi-dag'l*, *vt* to dirty by dragging along the wet ground. [**be-** (1)]

bedarken *bi-därk'ən*, *vt* to cover with darkness. [**be-** (1)]

bedash *bi-dash'*, *vt* to bespatter, splash. [**be-** (1)]

bedaub *bi-döb'*, *vt* to daub over or smear. [**be-** (1)]

Bedawin. Same as **Bedouin**.

bedazzle *bi-daz'l* or **bedaze** *bi-dāz'*, *vt* to dazzle or overpower by any strong light: — *pa p* **bedazz'led** or **bedazed'** stupefied, besotted. — *n* **bedazz'lement**. [**be-** (1)]

beddable. See **bed**[1].

bede (*obs*). Same as **bead** a prayer.

bedeafen *bi-def'n*, *vt* to make deaf; to stun. [**be-** (1)]

bedeck *bi-dek'*, *vt* to deck or ornament. [**be-** (1)]

bedeguar *bed'i-gär*, *n* a soft spongy gall found on the branches of sweet-brier and other roses, also called the sweet-brier sponge. [Fr *bédeguar*, from Pers and Ar *bādā-war* literally wind-brought]

bedel[1] or **bedell**. Old spellings of **beadle**, still used at Oxford and Cambridge Universities.

bedel[2] *bē'dl*, (*Bridges*) *n appar* for **bevel**, ie bevel-wheel.

bedeman, **bedesman**. Same as **beadsman**.

bederal. See **bedral**.

bedevil *bi-dev'l*, *vt* to throw into confusion; to torment; to play the devil, make havoc, with; to treat with devilish malignity; to possess as a devil would: — *pr p* **bedev'illing**; *pa t* and *pa p* **bedev'illed**. — *n* **bedev'ilment**. [**be-** (2)]

bedew *bi-dū'*, *vt* to moisten gently, as with dew. [**be-** (2)]

bedide *bi-dīd'*, (*Spenser*). Same as **bedyed**.

bedight *bi-dīt'*, (*archaic* or *poetic*) *vt* to equip, array, furnish; to adorn: — *pa t* and *pa p* **bedight'**. [**be-** (1)]

bedim *bi-dim'*, *vt* to make dim or dark: — *pr p* **bedimm'ing**; *pa t* and *pa p* **bedimmed'**. — *n* and *adj* **bedimm'ing**. [**be-** (2)]

bedizen *bi-dīz'ən* or *bi-diz'ən*, *vt* to dress gaudily. — *adj* **bediz'ened**. — *n* **bediz'enment**. [**be-** (1)]

bedlam *bed'ləm*, *n* a place of uproar, a madhouse; pandemonium; an asylum for lunatics (*archaic*); a madman (*obs*). — *adj* fit for a madhouse. — *n* **bed'lamism** anything characteristic of madness. — *n* **bed'lamite** a madman. [From the priory St Mary of *Bethlehem*, in London, afterwards a madhouse (Bethlehem Royal Hospital)]

Bedlington *bed'ling-tən* or **Bedlington terrier** (*ter'i-ər*), *n* a long-bodied lightly-built terrier, swiftest of its kind. [*Bedlington*, near Morpeth, where it was first bred]

Bedouin or **Beduin** *bed'ōō-in*, *-ēn* or *bed'win*, *n* (also without *cap*) a tent-dwelling nomad Arab (*orig pl*): — *pl* **Bed'ouin** or **Bed'ouins**. — Also *adj*. — *n* and *adj* **Bedu** (*bed'ōō*) (a) Bedouin. [Fr *bédouin*, from Ar *badāwin* dwellers in the desert]

bedraggle *bi-drag'l*, *vt* to soil by dragging in the wet or dirt. — *adj* **bedragg'led**. [**be-** (1)]

bedral or **bederal** *bed'(ə)rəl*, (*Scot*) *n* a beadle, church-officer, or minister's attendant; a grave-digger. [**beadle**]

bedrench *bi-drench'* or *-drensh'*, *vt* to drench or wet thoroughly. [**be-** (1)]

bedrop *bi-drop'*, *vt* to drop upon. — *adj* **bedropped'** or **bedropt'** sprinkled as with drops; strewn. [**be-** (3)]

Beds. *abbrev*: Bedfordshire.

Bedu. See **Bedouin**.

beduck *bi-duk'*, *vt* to duck or plunge under water. [**be-** (1)]

Beduin. Same as **Bedouin**.

bedung *bi-dung'*, *vt* to manure; to befoul with dung. [**be-** (2)]

bedust *bi-dust'*, *vt* to cover with dust. [**be-** (2)]

bedwarf *bi-dwörf'*, *vt* to make dwarfish. [**be-** (2)]

bedye *bi-dī'*, *vt* to dye or stain: — *pa t* and *pa p* **bedyed'** (*Spenser* **bedide'** or **bedyde'**). [**be-** (1)]

bee[1] *bē*, *n* a four-winged insect that makes honey; a gathering of persons to unite their labour for the benefit of one individual or family, or for some joint amusement, exercise or competition (as *quilting-bee*, *husking-bee*, *spelling-bee*); a busy person; (*usu* in *pl*) a lump of a type of yeast. — **bee balm** a species of Monarda or other sweet-smelling plant; **bee'-bread** the pollen and honey mixture fed by bees to their young; **bee'-eater** any bird of a brightly-plumaged family (Meropidae) closely related to the kingfishers, which feed on bees; **bee'-flower** a flower pollinated by bees; **bee'-fly** a nectar-eating fly of the Bombyliidae family; **bee'-glue** propolis; **bee'hive** a case or box in which bees are kept, made of straw-work, wood, etc (*adj* dome-shaped, like an old-fashioned beehive, as **beehive hairstyle**, **beehive tomb**); a place bustling with activity; a beehive hairstyle; **bee'-house**; **bee'keeper**; **bee'-keeping**; **bee'-kite** the honey-buzzard; **bee'line** the most direct route from one point to another (*esp* in **make a beeline for**; see below); **bee'-master** a beekeeper; **bee'-moth** a moth whose larvae are very destructive to young bees; **bee'-orchis** an orchid whose flower resembles a bee; **bee'-skep** a beehive, properly of straw; **beesting lips** or **beestung lips** pouting lips; **bees'wax** the wax secreted by bees and used by them in constructing their cells; this wax as used for various purposes, eg for polish, candles or cosmetics. — *vt* to polish with beeswax. — **bees'wing** a filmy crust of tartar formed in port and some other wines after long keeping. — *adj* **bees'winged** (of wine) so old as to show beeswing. — **a bee in one's bonnet** an obsession; a whimsical or crazy fancy on some point; **make a beeline for** to take the most direct way towards (like the honey-laden bee's way home); **the bee's knees** (*colloq*) someone or something particularly good, admirable, etc. [OE *bēo*; Ger *Biene*]

bee[2] *bē*, *n* the second letter of the alphabet (B, b).

Beeb *bēb*, (*colloq*) *n* the BBC; a BBC microcomputer.

beech *bēch*, *n* a common forest tree of the genus *Fagus* with smooth grey bark; extended to the related genus *Nothofagus* and to many trees not related; the wood of such a tree. — *adj* **beech'en** (*archaic*). — **beech'-drops** cancer-root, an American orobanchaceous plant parasitic on beech roots; **beech'-fern** a fern of the polypody family (a mistranslation of Phegopteris; from Gr *phēgos*, a kind of oak); **beech'-marten** the stone-marten; **beech'-mast** the mast or nuts of the beech tree, which yield a valuable oil, **beech'-oil**; **beech'-wood** a wood of beech trees; beech timber. [OE *boece*, *bēce*; Ger *Buche*, L *fāgus*, Gr *phēgos* (oak)]

beef *bēf*, *n* the flesh of adult domestic cattle as food; extended to that of some other animals, such as the horse; muscle; vigorous muscular force; a steer or cow, *esp* one fattened for the butcher (*archaic*; *pl* in this sense **beefs** or **beeves** *bēvz*); a complaint; an argument or quarrel. — *adj* of beef. — *vi* to grumble. — *adj* **beef'y** like beef; fleshy, muscular; stolid. — *adj* **beef'-brained** stupid. — **beef'-brewis** (*obs*) or **beef broth** broth made from beef; **beef'burger** a round flat cake of minced meat, *usu* fried or grilled; **beef'cake** a muscle-man or muscle-men; photographs of such; brawn as distinct from brain; **beef cattle** cattle reared mainly for their meat, as opposed to *dairy cattle* reared mainly for milk production; **beef'eater** the ox-bird or ox-pecker; a consumer of beef; a yeoman of the guard; a warder of the Tower of London; **beef'-ham** beef cured like ham; **beef olive** a thin slice of beef rolled round a savoury stuffing and *usu* stewed; **beef'steak** a thick lean slice of beef for grilling or frying; **beefsteak fungus** an edible fungus *Fistulina hepatica*, which looks rather like beefsteak; **beef-tea'** a drink make from beef stock, often given to invalids supposedly to stimulate their appetite; **beef tomato** a particularly large variety of tomato. — *adj* **beef'-witted** stupid. — **beef'-wood** the wood of Casuarina and other trees. — **beef up** (*colloq*) to add strength to, to reinforce. [OFr *boef* (Fr *bœuf*), from L *bōs*, *bovis*; cf Gr *bous*, Gaelic *bò*, Sans *go*, OE *cū*]

beefalo *bēf'ə-lō*, *n* a cross between a cow and a N American buffalo: — *pl* **beef'aloes** or **beef'alos**. [*beef*, and buff*alo*]

beegah. Same as **bigha**.

Beelzebub *bi-el'zi-bub*, *n* a form of Baal worshipped by the Philistines at Ekron; the prince of the fallen angels; a devil or the Devil. [Heb *ba'al z'būb* fly-lord]

been *bēn*, sometimes *bin*, *pa p* of **be**; *present infinitive* and *pl present indicative* of **be** (*archaic*).

beenah *bē'nä*, *n* a form of marriage (in Sri Lanka, etc) in which the man goes to live with his wife's relatives and the children belong to her group. [Ar *bīnah* separate]

beep *bēp*, *n* the sound made by the horn of a car, etc, or by a pager or other electronic device. — *vi* and *vt* to (cause to) make such a sound. — *n* **beep'er**. [Imit]

beer[1] *bēr*, *n* an alcoholic drink made by fermentation, in which the yeast settles to the bottom (cf **ale**), from malted barley flavoured with hops; the generic name of malt liquor, including ale and porter; a glassful, etc of this to drink; applied to other fermented liquors such as ginger beer. — *n* **beer'age** brewers collectively, the brewing industry. — *adj* **beer'y** affected by beer; smelling or tasting of beer; in the habit of drinking beer. — *n* **beer'iness**. — **beer'-barrel**; **beer belly** a protuberant belly caused, or considered so, by excessive beer-drinking; **beer'-bottle**; **beer'-engine** or **beer'-pump** a machine for drawing beer up from the casks to the bar; **beer'-garden** a garden with tables where beer and other refreshments may be purchased; **beer'hall** (*SAfr*) a large public drinking-place for non-whites; **beer'-house** a house where beer is sold; **beer'-mat** a small, *usu* cardboard table-mat for a beer-glass, etc; **beer'-money** money given in lieu of beer and spirits; a gratuity; **beer'-parlor** or **-parlour** (*Can*) a public room in a hotel, etc, where beer is served; **beer'-up** (*Austr slang*) a drinking-bout. — **beer and skittles** idle enjoyment; **bitter beer** pale ale, a highly hopped beer made from the very finest selected malt and hops (**mild** or **sweet** ale being comparatively lightly hopped); **black beer** a kind of beer made at Danzig, black and syrupy; **dry beer** see under **dry**; **small beer** weak beer; something trifling or unimportant, *esp* when compared with something else. [OE *bēor*; Ger *Bier*, Du *bier*, ON *bjorr*]

beer[2]. See **bere**[2].

beesome *bē'səm*, (*Shakesp*) *adj* supposed to be for **bisson**.

beestings *bēst'ingz*, *n* the first milk drawn from a cow after calving. [OE *bȳsting*, *bēost*; Ger *Biest*, Du *biest*]

beet[1] *bēt*, *n* a plant (genus *Beta*; esp *Beta vulgaris*) of the goosefoot family, with a red or white succulent root, used as food (red; see **beetroot** below) and as a source of sugar (white). — **beet'-fly** a fly whose larvae are injurious to beet and mangel-wurzel; **beet'root** the dark red root of the beet plant cooked and eaten as a vegetable; **beet sugar**. [OE *bēte*, from L *bēta*]

beet[2] or **bete** *bēt*, (*obs* except *dialect*) *vt* to improve; to mend (*esp* a fire); to relieve, assuage. — *n* **beet'mister** (*Scott* **-master**) a help in need. [OE *bētan*; cf *bōt*, **boot**[2]]

beetle[1] *bē'tl*, *n* any insect of the Coleoptera, an order in which the forewings are reduced to hard and horny covers for the hindwings; a game in which a drawing of a beetle is made up gradually from its component parts, body, head, etc, according to the throw of dice, the object being to produce a completed drawing; (*esp* with *cap*) a particular variety of small Volkswagen car with rounded roof and bonnet, resembling a beetle (*colloq*). — *vi* to jut, to overhang (first found in *Shakesp*); to scurry (*colloq*). — *adj* (always applied to brows) overhanging, scowling. — *adj* **beet'ling** jutting; prominent; overhanging. — *adj* **beet'le-browed** with overhanging or prominent brows. — **beetle brows**; **beet'le-crusher** (*slang*) a big heavy foot or boot; a policeman; an infantryman; **beetle drive** a progressive series of games of beetle. — *adj* **beet'le-eyed** blind. — **beetle off** to hurry away like a beetle, scurry (*colloq*); to fly (*airmen's slang*); **black beetle** the cockroach (properly not a beetle). [ME *bityl*, from OE *bitula*, *bitela*, from *bītan* to bite; the connection of beetle brows with the insect is not accepted by all]

beetle[2] *bē'tl*, *n* a heavy wooden mallet used for driving wedges, crushing or beating down paving-stones, or the like; a wooden pestle-shaped utensil for mashing potatoes, beating linen, clothes, etc. — **beet'lehead** or **beet'lebrain** a heavy stupid person. — *adj* **bee'tleheaded** or **beet'lebrained**. [OE *bīetl*, from *bēatan* to beat]

beetroot. See **beet**[1].

beeves *bēvz*, *n pl* cattle, oxen. [See **beef**]

BEF *abbrev*: British Expeditionary Force.

bef. *abbrev*: before.

befall *bi-fōl'*, (*archaic*) *vt* (or *vi* with *dative*) to fall or happen to; to occur to. — *vi* to happen or come to pass; to befit; to fall in one's way (*Spenser*): — *pr p* **befall'ing**; *pa t* **befell'**; *pa p* **befall'en** (*Spenser* **befeld'**). [OE *bef(e)allan*; see **fall**]

befana or **beffana** *be-fä'nə*, *n* an Epiphany gift. [Ital *La Befana*, a toy-bringing old woman, a personification of Epiphany, Gr *epiphaneia*]

befinned *bi-find'*, *adj* having fins. [**be-** (2)]

befit *bi-fit'*, *vt* to be fitting, or suitable to or for; to beseem. — *vi* to be right: — *pr p* **befitt'ing**; *pa p* **befitt'ed**. — *adj* **befitt'ing**. — *adv* **befitt'ingly**. [**be-** (1)]

beflower *bi-flow'ər*, *vt* to cover or sprinkle all over with flowers. [**be-** (2)]

beflum *bi-flum'*, (*Scott*) *vt* to befool, cajole. [Cf **flummery**]

befoam *bi-fōm*, (*archaic*) *vt* to bespatter or cover with foam. [**be-** (2)]

befog *bi-fog'*, *vt* to envelop in fog; to obscure. [**be-** (2)]

befool *bi-fo͞ol'*, *vt* to make a fool of or deceive; to treat as a fool. [**be-** (2)]

before *bi-fōr'*, *prep* in front of; ahead of; in the presence or sight of; under the consideration or cognizance of; previous to; previous to the expiration of; in preference to; superior to. — *adv* in front; sooner; earlier; in the past; formerly. — *conj* previous to the time when (sometimes with *that*); rather than that. — *adj* (*Shakesp*) previous. — *adv* **before'hand** before a particular time; in advance or anticipation; by way of preparation; in advance of one's needs; in credit, comfortably off (*archaic*). — *adj* **before'-men'tioned**. — *adv* **before'time** (*archaic*) in former time. — **be beforehand with** to forestall (a person); **before Christ** see **BC**; **before the mast** serving as an ordinary sailor; **before the wind** in the direction in which the wind is blowing, and hence helped along by it. [OE *beforan*. See **fore**]

befortune *bi-fōr'tūn*, (*Shakesp*) *vi* with *dative* to happen to, to befall. [**be-** (3)]

befoul *bi-fowl'*, *vt* to make foul; to soil. [**be-** (2)]

befriend *bi-frend'*, *vt* to commence a friendship with; to act as a friend to; to favour. — *n* **befriend'er**. [**be-** (2)]

befringe *bi-frinj'*, *vt* to adorn with fringes. [**be-** (2)]

befuddle *bi-fud'l*, *vt* to reduce to a confused condition (*esp* through drink). [**be-** (1)]

beg[1]. Same as **bey**.

beg[2] *beg*, *vi* to ask for alms or charity, *esp* habitually; (of a dog) to sit up on the hindquarters for a reward. — *vt* to ask for earnestly; to beseech; to pray; to fail to answer or resolve: — *pr p* **begg'ing**; *pa t* and *pa p* **begged** (*begd*). — *n* **beggar** (*beg'ər*) a person who begs; a person who lives by begging; (hyperbolically) a person who is in need, *esp* of money; an impoverished person; often used playfully and even affectionately. — *vt* to reduce to beggary; to exhaust or impoverish; to go beyond the resources of eg description or imagination (*fig*). — *n* **begg'ardom** the fraternity of beggars. — *n* **begg'arliness**. — *adj* **begg'arly** poor; mean; worthless. — *adv* meanly. — *n* **begg'ary** extreme poverty. — *n* and *adj* **begg'ing**. — *adv* **begg'ingly**. — **begg'ar-man**; **begg'ar-my-neigh'bour** a game that goes on till one player has gained all the others' cards; profit-making at the expense of others (also *adj*); **beggar's lice**, **beggar's ticks** or **beggar ticks** any of various plants with burrs; the burrs themselves; **begg'ing-bowl** a bowl carried by beggars, *esp* certain orders of monks, to receive food, money, etc (often *fig*); **begg'ing-letter** a letter soliciting charity, *esp* money. — **beg for a fool** (*obs*) to sue for the guardianship of, and administration of the estate of, on grounds of mental deficiency; **beggar belief** to be impossible to believe; **beg off** to obtain another's release through entreaty; to seek remission of some penalty or liability; **beg the question** to avoid giving an answer; to assume that the thing to be proved is already true in one of the premisses, or in part of the proof (*logic*); **go begging** or **a-begging** to lack a purchaser, occupant, etc. [Perh from **beghard** (qv), the verb being a back-formation]

begad *bi-gad'* and **begar** *bi-gär'*, (*Shakesp*) *interjs* by God! [Euphem alterations of]

began *bi-gan'*, *pa t* of **begin**.

begar[1] *bā'gär*, (*Ind*) *n* forced labour. [Hindi *begār*]

begar[2]. See **begad**.

begat. See **beget**.

begem *bi-jem'*, *vt* to adorn, as with gems. [**be-** (2)]

beget *bi-get'*, *vt* to produce or cause; (of humans, and commonly of the father) to produce (offspring); to produce as an effect, to cause: — *pr p* **begett'ing**; *pa t* **begot'** (or *archaic*, *esp Bible* **begat'**); *pa p* **begott'en** (or **begot'**). — *n* **begett'er** someone who begets; a father; the agent that occasions or originates anything (now often **only begetter**). [OE *begitan* to acquire; see **get**]

beggar. See **beg**[2].

beghard *beg'ärd*, *n* in Flanders or elsewhere from the 13c, a man living a monastic life without vows and with power to return to the world. [Flem *beggaert*; origin doubtful; cf **béguine**]

begift *bi-gift'*, *vt* to present with gifts. [**be-** (2)]

begild *bi-gild'*, *vt* to gild; to cover or overlay with gold-leaf. [**be-** (1)]

begin *bi-gin'*, *vi* to come into being; to originate; to perform the first act; to open or commence; to have an opening or commencement. — *vt* to perform the first act of; to enter on; to start: — *pr p* **beginn'ing**; *pa t* **began'** (now rarely **begun'**); *pa p* **begun**. — *n* **beginne'** (*Spenser*) beginning. — *n* **beginn'er** someone who begins; a person who is in the early stages of learning or doing anything. — *n* **beginn'ing** origin; a start; an entering upon action; an opening or first part; a rudiment. — *adj* **beginn'ingless.** — **to begin with** firstly; at first. [OE *beginnan* (less usual than *onginnan*), from pfx *be-* and *ginnan* to begin]

begird *bi-gûrd'*, (*archaic* or *poetic*) *vt* to gird or bind with a girdle; to surround or encompass: — *pa t* and *pa p* **begirt'** (or **begird'ed**). [OE *begyrdan*; **be-** (1) and **gird**]

beglamour *bi-glam'ər*, *vt* to invest with glamour; to bedazzle, infatuate or impress with glamour. [**be-** (2)]

beglerbeg *beg'lər-beg*, *n* formerly the governor of a Turkish province, in rank next to the grand vizier. [Turk, literally bey of beys]

begloom *bi-gloōm'*, *vt* to render gloomy. [**be-** (2)]

begnaw *bi-nö'*, *vt* to gnaw or bite, to eat away. [**be-** (1)]

bego *bi-gō'*, *vt* to beset (*obs* except in compound **woe-begone**). [OE *begān* to beset, surround]

begone *bi-gon'*, *interj* be gone; be off; get away.

begonia *bi-gō'ni-ə*, *n* a plant of the genus *Begonia* (giving name to a family **Begoniā'ceae**) of tropical, *esp* American, plants cultivated for their waxy, brightly-coloured flowers and their remarkable unequal-sided and often coloured leaves. [Named after Michel Bégon (1638–1710), French patron of botanical science]

begored *bi-görd'*, (*Spenser*) *adj* besmeared with gore. [**be-** (2)]

begorra or **begorrah** *bi-gor'ə*, *interj* (*esp facetious*; attributed to Irish speakers) by God! [Euphem alteration]

begot, begotten. See **beget.**

begrime *bi-grīm'*, *vt* to soil with grime. [**be-** (2)]

begrudge *bi-gruj'*, *vt* to grudge; to envy the possession of. [**be-** (1)]

beguile *bi-gīl'*, *vt* to charm; to cheat or deceive; to spend (time) pleasantly; to trick into some course of action. — *n* **beguile'ment.** — *n* **beguil'er.** — *adv* **beguil'ingly.** [**be-** (1), and obs transitive verb **guile**]

beguine[1] *bə-gēn'*, *n* a dance of French W Indian origin or its music, in bolero rhythm. [Fr]

beguine[2] or **béguine** *bāg'ēn* or *beg'in*, *n* a member of a sisterhood living as nuns but without vows, and with power to return to the world: — *masc* **beguin** or **béguin** (*bāg-ẽ* or *beg'in*) a beghard. — *n* **béguinage** (*bāg'ēn-äzh* or *beg'in-ij*) an establishment for béguines. [Fr *béguine*; cf **beghard**]

begum *bā'gəm* or *bē'gəm*, *n* a Muslim princess or lady of rank; a deferential title given to any Muslim lady. [Urdu *begam*; cf **beg**[1], **bey**]

begun *bi-gun'*, *pa p* (sometimes *pa t*) of **begin.**

begunk *bi-gungk'*, (*Scot*) *vt* to trick; to play a trick on; to cheat; to jilt. — *n* a trick; a jilting. [Origin uncertain; Scot *gunk* jilt, trick, recorded later]

behalf *bi-häf'*, *n* interest, benefit; sake, account; part. — **on** (*NAm* **in**) **behalf of,** or **on** (*NAm* **in**) **someone's behalf** speaking, acting, etc for (someone). [ME *behalve*, from OE *be healfe* by the side. See **half**]

behappen *bi-hap'n*, (*Spenser*) *vt* to happen to. [**be-** (1)]

behatted *bi-hat'id*, *adj* wearing a hat. [**be-** (2)]

behave *bi-hāv'*, *vt* to conduct (oneself) well; to manage, conduct (often *oneself*) in a specified manner. — *vi* to conduct oneself in a specified manner (often *towards*); to conduct oneself well; (of things) to function, handle, respond: — *pa t* and *pa p* **behaved'.** — *n* **behaviour** or (*NAm*) **behavior** (*bi-hāv'yər*) conduct; manners or deportment, *esp* good manners; general course of life; treatment of others; manner of action; the activity of an organism, *esp* as measurable for its effects; response to stimulus (*physiol* and *psychol*); the functioning, response or activity of an object or substance. — *adj* **behāv'ioural** or (*NAm*) **behāv'ioral** of or relating to behaviour or behaviourism. — *adv* **behāv'iourally** or (*NAm*) **behāv'iorally.** — *n* **behāv'iourism** or (*NAm*) **behāv'iorism** a psychological method which uses the objective observation of the conduct of organisms under certain stimuli as the basis for all its theories and conclusions. — *n* **behāv'iourist** or (*NAm*) **behāv'iorist** an upholder of behaviourism. — **behavioural enrichment** the creation of a mentally stimulating environment for a captive animal, eg in a zoo, with provision of objects for the animal to investigate and play with; **behavioural science** a science which studies the behaviour of human beings or other organisms (eg psychology, sociology); **behaviour therapy** a means of treating a neurotic symptom (eg a phobia) by training the patient in new behaviour and gradually conditioning him or her to react normally. — **on** or **upon one's best behaviour** consciously trying to be as well-behaved as possible. [**be-** (1) and **have**; OE had *behabban* to detain, restrain]

behead *bi-hed'*, *vt* to cut off the head of. — *n* **behead'al** (*rare*). — *n* **behead'ing.** [**be-** (1) meaning off or away]

beheld *bi-held'*, *pa t* and *pa p* of **behold.**

behemoth *bē'i-moth* or *bi-hē'moth*, *n* an animal described in Job 40.15, usually taken to be the hippopotamus; a great beast; something huge or gigantic. [Heb *b'hēmōth*, pl of *b'hēmāh* beast, or a Hebraistic form of the Egyptian *p-ehe-mout* water-ox]

behest *bi-hest'*, *n* a command; a request; a promise (*obs*). [OE *behǣs* a promise; see **hest**]

behight *bi-hīt'* or **behote** *bi-hōt'*, (*obs*) *vt* to vow; to promise; to warrant, to command, to name (*Spenser*): — *pa t* and *pa p* **behight'** or **behote'.** [OE *behātan* to vow, from *be-* and *hātan* to be called, to call, to command. For the confusion of tenses and voices and for reduplication, see **hight**]

behind *bi-hīnd'*, *prep* in, to or at the back of (in position, or as a support); at the far side of; in the place or state left by; after (in time, rank or order); in the past compared with; later than; causing; supporting; inferior to, or less far advanced than. — *adv* at the back, in or to the rear; backward, less advanced; past; remaining after someone's departure; in arrears. — *n* the rump, the buttocks (*euphem*); a score worth one point made in a number of ways (also *adj*) (*Austr rules football*). — *adj* **behind'-door'** surreptitious, clandestine. — *adj* and *adv* **behind'hand** tardy, late; in arrears; out of date, behind the times; less well prepared or provided than others. — **behind someone's back** without someone knowing (when they might feel entitled to know); **come from behind** to progress from the rear of a field of contestants into a winning position (also *fig*); **put something behind one** to resign something (*usu* unpleasant) to the past and consider it finished. [OE *behindan*; Ger *hinten*; see **hind**[3]]

behold *bi-hōld'*, *vt* (*literary* or *Bible*) to look at; to view, see; to contemplate; perhaps, to restrain (*Spenser*). — *vi* (*literary* or *Bible*) to look: — *pa t* and *pa p* **beheld'.** — *imperative* or *interj* (*archaic*) see; lo; observe. — *adj* **behold'en** bound in gratitude (to); under an obligation (to). — *n* **behold'er** a person who beholds; an onlooker. — *adj* **behold'ing** (*Shakesp*) beholden. — *n* (*Shakesp*) sight, contemplation. [OE *behaldan* (WSax *behealdan*) to hold, observe, from *be-* and *h(e)aldan* to hold]

behoof *bi-hoōf'*, *n* benefit; convenience. [OE *behōf*]

behote. See **behight.**

behove or (*esp US*) **behoove** *bi-hoōv'* (unhistorically *bi-hōv'*), *vt* and *vi* (now only used impersonally with *it*) to be fit, right or necessary. — *adj* **behove'ful** (*archaic*). — *adj* **behove'ly** (*obs*) useful; profitable. [OE *be hōfian* to be fit, to stand in need of]

behowl *bi-howl'*, *vt* to howl at (Warburton's emendation for 'beholds' in *Midsummer Night's Dream*, V.2.2). [**be-** (3)]

beige *bāzh*, *adj* greyish buff with a slight hint of pink. — *n* a woollen fabric of undyed wool. [Fr]

beigel *bā'gəl*, *n* an alternative spelling of **bagel.**

beignet *ben'yā*, *n* a fritter; a deep-fried ball of choux pastry. [Fr]

bein *bēn*, *adj* and *adv* comfortable (*Scot*); well off (*Scot*); good (*thieves' slang*). — Also **bien.** — *n* (*Scot*) **bein'ness.** [ME *bene*, of dubious origin; ON *beinn*, L *bene*, and Fr *bien*, all offer difficulties]

being *bē'ing*, *n* existence; substance; essence; any person or living thing that exists or may exist; anything material or immaterial that can be conceived as existing (*philos*). — *adj* existing or present. — *adj* **bē'ingless**. — *n* **bē'ingness**. — **the Supreme Being** God. [Verbal noun and *pr p* of **be**]

beinked *bē-ingkt'*, *adj* smeared with ink. [**be-** (2)]

bejabers *bi-jā'bərs*, *interj* (*esp facetious*; attributed to Irish speakers) by Jesus! [Euphem alteration]

bejade *bi-jād'*, (*obs*) *vt* to tire out. [**be-** (1)]

bejant. See **bajan**.

bejesuit *bi-jez'ū-it*, *vt* to initiate or seduce into Jesuitism. [**be-** (2)]

bejewel *bi-jōō'əl*, *vt* to adorn with or as if with jewels. — *adj* **bejew'elled**. [**be-** (2)]

bekah *bē'kä*, (*Bible*) *n* a half-shekel. [Heb]

bekiss *bi-kis'*, *vt* to cover with kisses. [**be-** (1)]

beknave *bi-nāv'*, *vt* to call or treat as a knave. [**be-** (2)]

beknown *bi-nōn'*, (*archaic* or *dialect*) *adj* known. [**be-** (1)]

bel[1] *bel*, *n* a measure for comparing intensity of noises, electric currents, etc, the number of bels being the logarithm to the base 10 of the ratio of one to the other; cf **decibel**. [From Alexander Graham *Bell* (1847–1922), telephone inventor]

bel[2]. See **bael**.

belabour or (*US*) **belabor** *bi-lā'bər*, *vt* to beat soundly; to assail verbally. [**be-** (1)]

bel-accoyle *bel-a-koil'*, (*Spenser*) *n* favourable or kind reception. [OFr *bel acoil* fair welcome. See **accoil**]

belace *bi-lās'*, *vt* to adorn with lace. [**be-** (2)]

belah *bē'lä*, *n* an Australian tree of the Casuarina genus. [Aboriginal]

bel air *be-ler*, (*Fr*) *n* fine deportment.

belamoure or **bellamoure** *bel-a-mowr'*, (*Spenser*) *n* a beloved one; some kind of flower. [Fr *bel amour* fair love]

belamy *bel'a-mē*, (*Spenser*) *n* a good or intimate friend. [Fr *bel ami* fair friend]

Bel & Dr. (*Bible*) *abbrev*: (the Apocryphal Book of) Bel and the Dragon.

belate *bi-lāt'*, *vt* (*archaic*) to make late; to retard. — *adj* **belāt'ed** coming too late; out of date; benighted (*obs*). — *adv* **belat'edly**. — *n* **belāt'edness**. [**be-** (2)]

belaud *bi-löd'*, *vt* to praise up. [**be-** (1)]

belay *bi-lā'*, *vt* to make fast; to secure by a turn (of a rope) around a cleat, belaying pin, point of rock, etc (*naut* and *mountaineering*); to set or overlay, (*with* ornament) (*Spencer*); to beset, to besiege (*obs*); to waylay (*obs*): — *pa t* and *pa p* **belayed'**. — *interj* enough; hold. — *n* (*mountaineering*) a turn of a rope in belaying; the rock etc around which a belay is made. — **belaying pin** (*naut*) a pin for belaying ropes around. [OE *belecgan*; Ger *belegen*, Du *beleggen*. See **lay**[3]]

bel canto *bel kän'tō*, (*Ital*) *n* a manner of operatic singing that cultivates beauty of tone. — Also *adv*.

belch *belch* or *belsh*, *vt* and *vi* to void (wind) from the stomach by the mouth; to eject violently; to pour forth, as the smoke from a volcano, chimney, etc. — *n* an act of belching. [OE *bealcian*; Du *balken*]

belcher *bel'chər*, *n* a dark-blue neckerchief with blue-centred white spots. [From Jim *Belcher*, a famous English boxer]

beldam or **beldame** *bel'dəm*, *n* an old woman (formerly a term of address); a hag; a furious woman; a grandmother or remoter ancestress (*obs*). [Formed from **dam** mother, and *bel-*, used like *grand-*, from Fr *bel*, *belle*, but not a French use]

beleaguer *bi-lēg'ər*, *vt* to lay siege to; to pester. — *n* **beleag'uerment**. [Du *belegeren* to besiege, from *be-*, and *leger* camp. See **leaguer**[1]]

belee *bi-lē'*, (*Shakesp*) *vt* to place on the lee side of something. [**be-** (2)]

belemnite *bel'əm-nīt*, *n* a fossil pointed like a dart, being the internal shell of a cephalopod mollusc, formerly known as *thunderbolt*, *thunder-stone*, *elf-bolt*. [Gr *belemnitēs*, from *belemnon* a dart]

bel esprit *be-les-prē*, (*Fr*) *n* a wit or genius: — *pl* **beaux esprits** (*bō-zes-prē*).

bel étage *be-lā-täzh*, (*German Fr*) *n* the best storey, the first floor.

belfry *bel'fri*, *n* the part of a steeple or tower in which bells are hung; a bell-tower, sometimes a separate building; a movable wooden tower, used in the Middle Ages in attacking a fortification. — *adj* **bel'fried** having a belfry. [Orig and properly a watchtower, from OFr *berfroi*, from MHGer *berchfrit*, from *bergan* to protect and *frid*, *frit* a tower]

Belg. *abbrev*: Belgian; Belgium.

belga *bel'gə*, *n* a former currency unit of Belgium used in foreign exchange (from 1926 till the end of World War II), value five paper francs. [L *Belga* a Belgian]

belgard *bel-gärd'*, (*Spenser*) *n* a fair or kind look. [Ital *bel guardo* lovely look]

Belgian *bel'jən*, *adj* of *Belgium*, a country of Europe. — *n* a native or citizen of Belgium. — *adj* **Bel'gic** of the *Belgae*, a Celtic tribe which inhabited Belgium in Roman times, or of Belgium. — **Belgian Blue** a variety of cattle; **Belgian hare** a hare-like breed of domestic rabbit. [L *Belga*, *Belgicus*]

Belgravian *bel-grā'vi-ən*, *adj* belonging to *Belgravia* (a fashionable part of London), or to fashionable life.

Belial *bēl'yəl*, *n* the devil; in Milton, one of the fallen angels. Not a proper name in Old Testament. [Heb *b'li-ya'al*, from *b'li* not, and *ya'al* use]

belie *bi-lī'*, *vt* to show the untruth of; to present falsely, misrepresent or falsify; to contradict or reject as false or a lie; to be false to; to fill with lies (*Shakesp*); to fail to fulfil or justify: — *pr p* **bely'ing**; *pa t* and *pa p* **belied'**. — *n* **belī'er**. [**be-** (3)]

belief *bə-lēf'*, *n* conviction of the truth of anything; faith; confidence or trust in a person, etc; an opinion or doctrine believed; intuition, natural judgment (as used by some philosophers). — *adj* **belief'less**. — **the belief** (*archaic*) the Apostles' Creed; **to the best of my belief** as far as I know. [Noun use of ME *bileven*; see ety at **believe**]

believe *bi-lēv'*, *vt* to regard as true; to accept as true what is said by (someone); to think (followed by a noun clause). — *vi* to be firmly convinced; to have *esp* religious faith (*in* or *on*); to judge. — *adj* **believ'able**. — *n* **believ'er** a person who believes; a person who is an adherent of Christianity, Islam, or any other religion. — *adj* **believ'ing** trustful; having belief. — *adv* **believ'ingly**. — **believe something of someone** to think someone capable of something; **be unable** or **hardly able to believe one's eyes** or **ears** to receive with incredulity what one has just seen or heard; **I (don't) believe so** I (don't) think so; **make believe** see under **make**. [ME *bileven*, from *bi-*, *be*, and *leven*, superseding OE *gelēfan*]

belike *bi-līk'*, (*archaic*) *adv* probably; perhaps. [OE pfx *be-* and **like**[1]]

Belisha beacon. See **beacon**.

belittle *bi-lit'l*, *vt* to make small; to make (something or someone) out to be insignificant or unimportant; to disparage. — *n* **belitt'lement**. — *adj* **belitt'ling**. [**be-** (2)]

belive *bi-līv'*, (*archaic* and *Scot*) *adv* with speed; immediately. [ME *bi life* from *bī* by and *līfe* dative of *līf* life]

bell[1] *bel*, *n* an instrument for giving a ringing sound, typically a hollow vessel of metal with flared mouth struck by a tongue or clapper, but taking many other forms; anything bell-shaped, as in diving-bell, bell-glass, the open end of some wind-instruments, etc; a flower corolla shaped like a bell; the body of a Corinthian or Composite capital, without the surrounding foliage (*archit*); the sound of a bell; a signal or intimation by bell; a stroke or double stroke of a bell to indicate the number of half-hours of the watch that have elapsed, 'two bells', 'three bells', etc, meaning that two, three, etc half-hours have passed, the end of the watch of four hours being eight bells (*naut*). — *vi* to ring. — *vt* to furnish with a bell, *esp* in **bell the cat** (qv below). — *adj* **belled** shaped like a bell. — *vt* and *vi* to (cause to) flare out in the shape of a bell. — **bell beaker** the distinctive wide-necked pottery vessel found (sometimes inverted) in the graves of Beaker Folk; **bell'bind** (*dialect*) hedge or field bindweed; **bell'-bird** the S American campanero; any of several Australian and NZ birds with a bell-like call, such as either of the two species of honey-eater (*Manorina melanophrys* and *Anthornis melanura*) or the thickhead (*Oreoica gutturalis*); elsewhere, other birds with bell-like notes. — *adj* **bell'-bottomed** (of trousers) widening greatly towards the ankle. — **bell'-boy** (chiefly *NAm*) a bellhop; **bell'-buoy** a buoy carrying a bell, rung by the movement of the waves; **bell'cote** (*archit*) an ornamental structure made to contain one or two bells, and often crowned by a small spire; **bell crank** a lever with two arms, *usu* at right angles, and a common fulcrum at their junction; **bell end** a rounded end, *esp* to the back of a tent; **bell'-flower** a campanula; **bell'-founder** a person who casts bells; **bell'-foundry**; **bell'-glass** a bell-jar; **bell'hanger** a person who hangs and repairs bells; **bell'-heather** a variety of erica with bell-shaped flowers; **bell'hop** a hotel porter or page; **bell'-housing** a tapered outer casing of part of a vehicle's transmission; **bell'-jar** a bell-shaped glass cover, in laboratories placed over apparatus to confine gases, etc, or used to protect ornaments or flower arrangements; **bell magpie** (*Austr*) the currawong; **bell'man** a person who rings a bell, *esp* on the streets, before making public announcements; a town-crier; **bell'-metal** the metal of which bells are made, an alloy of copper and tin; **bell'-pull** a cord or handle used in ringing a bell; **bell'-punch** a ticket punch containing a signal-bell; **bell'push** a button used in ringing an electric or spring bell; **bell'-ringer** a person who rings a bell on stated occasions; a performer on church bells or musical hand-bells; **bell'=ringing**; **bell'-rope** the rope by which a bell is rung. — *adj* **bell'-shaped**. — **bell'-siller** (*-sil'ər*; *Scott*) a fee for bell-ringing at a funeral; **bell'-tent** a bell-shaped tent; **bell'-tower** a tower built to contain one or more bells, a campanile; **bell'-turret** a turret containing a chamber for a bell, *usu* crowned with a spire; **bell'-wether** the leading sheep of a flock, on whose neck a bell is hung; a ringleader; a setter of a standard, pattern or trend, a leader (*econ*, etc); **bell'wort** any plant of the Campanulaceae; the liliaceous genus *Uvularia* (*US*). — **bear** or **carry off** (or **away**) **the bell** to have or gain the first place; **bell, book and candle** a phrase popularly used in reference to a form of excommunication ending, 'Do to (ie shut) the book, quench the candle, ring the bell'; **bells and whistles** (*slang*) additional, largely decorative rather than functional features; **bells of Ireland** an annual plant (*Moluccella laevis*) with white flowers and green bell-shaped calyxes, sometimes used in dried-flower arrangements; **bell the cat** to undertake the leading part in any hazardous enterprise, from the fable of the mice who proposed to hang a warning bell round the cat's neck; **clear as a bell** (of a sound) distinct and pure in tone; **give someone a bell** (*slang*) to telephone someone; **sound as a bell** in perfect condition, health, etc. [OE *belle* cognate with Du *bel*]

bell[2] *bel*, *n* a bubble formed in a liquid. [Ety doubtful; cf Du *bel* perh from L *bulla* a bubble in water]

bell[3] *bel*, *vi* to bellow, roar; to utter loudly. — *n* the cry of a stag at rutting-time. [OE *bellan* to roar; cf Ger *bellen*]

belladonna *bel-ə-don'ə*, *n* the deadly nightshade or dwale (*Atropa belladonna*), all parts of which are narcotic and poisonous from the presence of atropine; the drug prepared from it. — **belladonna lily** a pink-flowered S African amaryllis. [Ital *bella donna* fair lady; one property of belladonna is to enlarge the pupil of the eye]

bella figura *bel-a fi-gōōr'ə*, *n* good impression or appearance. [Ital]

bellamoure. See **belamoure**.

bellarmine *bel'är-mēn*, *n* a greybeard, or large jug with a big belly, decorated with a bearded face, said to represent Cardinal *Bellarmine* (1542–1621), made in mockery by Dutch Protestants.

Bellatrix *bel-ā'triks* (L *-ä'trēks*), *n* a second-magnitude star in Orion, one of the corners of the quadrilateral. [L *bellātrix* female warrior]

belle *bel*, *adj fem* of **beau**. — *n* a beautiful woman or girl; the chief beauty of a place or occasion. — **belle amie** (*be-la-mē*) a female friend or mistress; **belle assemblée** (*be-la-sã-blā*) a fashionable gathering; **belle-de-nuit** (*-də-nwē*; *Fr*, night beauty) marvel of Peru (qv); **belle laide** (*bel led*) a jolie laide. — Also *adj*. — **belle-mère** (*bel-mer*) a mother-in-law; **belle passion** (*pa-syɔ̃*) the tender passion, love; **belle peinture** (*pɛ̃-tür*) naturalistic painting; **belle vue** (*vü*) a fine prospect. — **la belle époque** (*la-bel-ā-pok*; also with *caps*) 'the fine period', the time of security and gracious living for the well-to-do, ended by World War I. [Fr *belle* (*fem*), from L *bellus, -a, -um*]

belles-lettres *bel-let'r'*, *n pl* polite or elegant literature, including poetry, fiction, criticism, aesthetics, etc. — *n* **bellett'rist** or **bellet'rist**. — *adj* **belletris'tic** or **belletris'tical**. [Fr, literally fine letters]

belleter *bel'ə-tər*, *n* a bell-founder. [For *bellyetter*, from **bell** and OE *gēotan* to pour]

bellibone *bel'i-bōn*, (*Spenser*) *n* a beautiful and good woman. [Appar Fr *belle* (*et*) *bonne*]

bellicose *bel'ik-ōs*, *adj* contentious, warlike. — *adv* **bell'icosely**. — *n* **bellicosity** (*-kos'i-ti*). [L *bellicōsus*]

bellied. See **belly**.

belligerent *bel-ij'ər-ənt*, *adj* aggressive; waging war; recognized legally as waging war. — *n* a country, person, etc waging war; one recognized as so doing. — *n* **bellig'erence**. — *n* **bellig'erency**. — *adv* **bellig'erently**. [L *belligerāre* to wage war, from *bellum* war, and *gerere* to wage]

Bellona *bel-ō'na*, *n* the Roman goddess of war; a woman of great spirit and vigour.

bellow *bel'ō*, *vi* to roar like a bull; to make any violent outcry. — *vt* to roar out. — *n* the roar of a bull; any deep loud sound or cry. — *n* **bell'ower**. [ME *belwen*; OE *bylgian* to roar; cf **bell**[3]]

bellows *bel'ōz*, or (*old-fashioned*) *bel'us*, *n pl* or *n sing* an instrument for producing a current of air to blow up a fire, or sound an organ, accordion, etc (also **pair of bellows**); a telescopic sleeve connected between a camera body and lens, used when focusing on small close objects; something which fans the fire of hatred, jealousy, etc; the lungs. — *adj* in the form of a bellows, allowing for expansion, as in a gusseted tongue of a boot, etc. — **bell'ows-fish** the trumpet-fish. — **bellows to mend** (*esp* in sporting parlance) shortness of breath, eg in a horse. [Ety as for **belly**; the singular form did not survive the 15c]

bellum internecinum *bel'əm* or *-ōōm in-tər-nes-īn'əm* or *-ter-nek-ēn'ōōm*, (*L*) *n* a war of extermination.

belly *bel'i*, *n* the part of the body between the breast and the thighs, containing the intestines, etc; the stomach, as the receptacle of the food; the bowels; the womb or uterus (*archaic*); the deep interior of anything; the bulging part of anything, as of a bottle, or any concave or hollow surface, as of a sail; the front or under surface, as opposed to the *back*; in a violin or a leaf, the upper surface; a sound-board on a piano (*music*). — *adj* ventral, abdominal; belonging to the flesh, carnal (*theol*). — *vi* to swell or bulge out (often with *out*): — *pa t* and *pa p* **bellied** (*bel'id*). — *adj* **bell'ied** with a belly, *esp* a big belly, pot-bellied; bulging; puffed out. — *n* **bell'yful** a sufficiency; more than enough. — *n* and *adj* **bell'ying**. — **bell'y-ache** a pain in the belly; a persistent complaint or whine (*slang*). — *vi* (*slang*) to complain whiningly. — **bell'y-band** a saddle-girth; a band fastened to the shafts of a vehicle, and passing under the belly of the horse drawing it; **bell'y-button** (*colloq*) the navel; **bell'y-dance** a sensuous Eastern dance, performed by a woman, with very pronounced movement of the abdomen and hips. — *vi* to perform such a dance. — **bell'y-dancer**; **bell'y-flop** an inexpert dive in which one lands face down, flat on the water; a belly-landing. — Also *vi*. — **bell'y-god** a person who makes a god of his belly, a glutton; **bell'y-landing** (of an aircraft) a landing without using the landing-wheels; **bell'y-laugh** a deep unrestrained laugh; **belly tank** (*aeronautics*) see **ventral tank**; **bell'y-timber** (*archaic*) provisions, food. — **belly up to** (*US slang*) to go directly or purposefully towards; **go belly up** (*US slang*) to die, fail (as a dead fish, floating belly upwards); of a business, etc, to fail. [ME *bali*, *bely*, from OE *bælig*, *belig*, *bælg*, *belg* bag]

belomancy *bel'ō-man-si*, *n* divination by means of arrows. [Gr *belos* a dart, and *manteiā* divination]

Belone *bel'ə-ni*, *n* a genus of needle-fish of the family **Belon'idae**, including the garfish. [Gr *belone* a needle, from *belos* a dart]

belong *bi-long'*, *vi* (in all senses *usu* with *to*) to pertain (to); to be the property (of; with *to*); to be a part or appendage (of), or in any way connected (with) (with *with* or *to*); to have a proper place (in); to be entirely suitable; to be a native or inhabitant, or member (of). — *n* **belong'er** (*sociol*) a person of conservative, middle-class values and lifestyle, conforming to social norms. — *npl* **belong'ings** possessions; personal effects; matters connected with any person (*obs*); persons connected, relatives (*obs*). [ME *bi-*, *belongen*, intensive of *longen*. See **long**²]

Belorussian or **Byelorussian** *byel-ə-rush'ən*, *adj* White Russian, of Belorussia or Byelorussia, a region to the west of Moscow (*hist*); of Belorussia or Byelorussia, a member state of the CIS; of their language or people. — Also *n*. [Russ *Belorussiya*, from *beliy* white]

belove *bi-luv'*, *vt* (*obs* except in *pap* **beloved** *bi-luvd'*) to love. — *adj* **beloved** (*bi-luv'id*) much loved, very dear, often compounded with *well-*, *best-*, etc. — *n* (*bi-luv'id*) a person who is much loved. — *adj* **belov'ing** (*Shakesp*) loving. [**be-** (1)]

below *bi-lō'*, *prep* beneath in place, rank or quality; underneath; not worthy of. — *adv* in a lower place; farther on in a text; downstairs; on earth, or in hell. — *adj* and *adv* **belowstairs'** downstairs; in or belonging to the servants' quarters. — *adj* **below-the-line'** of or pertaining to that part of the government's spending and revenue not allowed for in its original estimates; of or pertaining to business spending or income which, because of its unusual nature, is listed separately from the normal financial details on a company's accounts. [ME *bilooghe*, from *bi* by, and *looghe* low]

bel paese *bel pä-ā'zē*, *n* a mild Italian cheese. [Formerly a trademark; Ital, literally beautiful country]

bel sangue *bel sän'gwā*, (*Ital*) n gentle blood.

belshazzar. See **balthasar**.

belt *belt*, *n* a band of leather or other material, *esp* one worn around the waist; a band of flexible material used to transmit motion in machinery; a broad stripe of anything, different in colour or material from whatever surrounds it; something which confines or restrains; a zone of country, a district (*geog*); a strait; a band for the waist awarded in recognition of a specific (grade of) achievement (see **black**, **Lonsdale**); a sharp blow, impact or shock (*colloq*). — *vt* to award a belt, or to invest formally with one, as in conferring knighthood; to encircle with a belt; to thrash with a belt; to hit hard (*colloq*). — *vi* (*slang*) to hurry. — *adj* **belt'ed** wearing a belt, eg of a knight; marked with a band or bands of different colours. — *n* **belt'er** (*colloq*) something outstanding or strikingly good or bad; a song for belting out. — *n* **belt'ing** belts collectively; material for making belts; a beating. — *adj* **belt-and-bra'ces** giving double security or double the chances of success. — **belt'man** (*Austr*) the member of the lifesaving team who swims out to the rescue, with a line tied to his belt; **belt'way** (*US*) a ring-road. — **belt out** (*colloq*) to sing, play or send out vigorously or with great enthusiasm; **belt up** (*slang*) to be quiet; **hit**, etc, **below the belt** to hit, etc, an opponent's body lower than the waist (forbidden in some sports); hence (*fig*) to deliver a mean blow, attack unfairly; **hold the belt** to hold the championship in wrestling, boxing, or the like; **tighten one's belt** to reduce one's demands or expenditure, to economize (*n* **belt'-tightening**); **under one's belt** (*fig*) firmly and irrevocably secured or in one's possession. [OE *belt*, from L *balteus*]

Beltane *bel'tān*, *n* an ancient Celtic festival, held at the beginning of May, when bonfires were lighted on the hills; the first day of May (*Old Style*), one of the four old quarter-days of Scotland, the others being Lammas, Hallowmas and Candlemas. — Also *adj*. [Gaelic *bealltainn*, *beilteine*, appar bright fire. It has nothing to do with **Baal**]

beluga *bi-lōō'gə*, *n* the white whale, one of the dolphin family, closely allied to the narwhal, found in Arctic seas; the great Russian sturgeon, a source of caviare, *Acipenser huso*. [Russ *beliy* white]

belvedere *bel'vi-dēr* or *bel-vi-dēr'*, *n* a pavilion or raised turret or lantern on the top of a house, built to provide a view, or to admit the breeze; a summer-house on high ground. [Ital *belvedere*, from *bel* beautiful, and *vedere* to see]

belying. See **belie**.

BEM *abbrev*: British Empire Medal.

bema *bē'mə*, *n* the tribune or rostrum from which Athenian orators made their speeches; hence the apse or chancel of a basilica; a raised platform in a synagogue (*Judaism*). [Gr *bēma* a step]

bemad *bi-mad'*, (*archaic*) *vt* to madden. [**be-** (1)]

bemaul *bi-möl'*, (*archaic*) *vt* to maul thoroughly. [**be-** (1)]

bemazed *bi-māzd'*, (*archaic*) *adj* stupefied, bewildered. [**be-** (1)]

Bembex *bem'beks*, or **Bembix** *-iks*, *n* a genus of sand-wasps, noted for their loud buzz; (without *cap*) a member of the genus. [Gr *bembix* a buzzing insect]

bemean¹ *bi-mēn*, (*archaic*) *vt* to make mean, to lower or debase. [**be-** (2)]

bemean² *bi-mēn'*, (*obs*) *vi* to signify. [**be-** (1)]

bemedal *bi-med'əl*, (*archaic*) *vt* to cover with medals. [**be-** (2)]

bemete *bi-mēt'*, (*archaic*) *vt* to measure. [**be-** (1)]

bemire *bi-mīr'*, (*archaic*) *vt* to soil with mire; (in *passive*) to be stuck in the mire. — *adj* **bemired'**. [**be-** (2)]

bemoan *bi-mōn'*, *vt* to lament, bewail; to pity. — *vi* to grieve. — *n* **bemoan'er**. — *n* **bemoan'ing**. [**be-** (1)]

bemock *bi-mok*, (*archaic*) *vt* to mock at, deride. [**be-** (1)]

bemoil *bi-moil'* (*Shakesp*) *vt* to bemire, bedraggle. [**be-** (1)]

bemonster *bi-mon'stər*, (*archaic*) *vt* to make monstrous; to regard or treat as a monster. [**be-** (2)]

bemouth *bi-mowdh'*, (*archaic*) *vt* to mouth about. [**be-** (1)]

bemud *bi-mud'*, (*archaic*) *vt* to bespatter with mud; to confuse. [**be-** (2)]

bemuddle *bi-mud'l*, (*archaic*) *vt* to confuse or muddle completely. [**be-** (1)]

bemuffle *bi-muf'l*, (*archaic*) *vt* to wrap or muffle up completely. [**be-** (1)]

bemuse *bi-mūz'*, *vt* to put in confusion; to puzzle; to stupefy. — *adj* **bemused'**. [**be-** (1)]

ben¹ *ben*, (*Scot* and *Ir*) *n* a mountain peak. [Gaelic *beinn*, oblique case of *beann*]

ben² *ben*, (*Scot*) *prep* and *adv* in or toward the inner or better room or rooms (of). — *n* the inner or better room or rooms of a house (as opposed to the *but*) or kitchen through which formerly one had to pass first). — **a but and ben** a two-roomed house; **but and ben** backwards and forwards in the house (also *fig*); out and in; at opposite ends of a house or passage; **far ben** on terms of great intimacy or favour. [ME *binne*, from OE *binnan* within]

ben³ *ben*, *n* any of several tropical trees of the Moringa genus, *esp* the horseradish tree (*Moringa oleifera*), its seed (**ben'-nut**) yielding **ben'-oil** or **oil of ben**, used as a lubricant and in the preparation of perfumes and cosmetics. [Ar *bān*]

bename *bi-nām'*, *vt* to name, mention; to vow: — *pa t* and *pa p* **benamed'** (*archaic* **benempt'**). [OE *benemnan*, from *nemnan* to name]

bench *bench* or *bensh*, *n* a long (*usu* wooden) seat with or without a back; a seat in a boat; a work-table or working-place; a judge's seat; the body or assembly of judges; a tribunal; a seat for officials and reserve players at a match (*football*, *baseball*, etc); a level ledge in the slope of masonry or earthwork; a level tract between a river and nearby hills (*US*); a terrace (*geol*); in a greenhouse or conservatory, a raised bed or a platform with sides, for holding potted plants; a platform on which dogs are shown. — *vt* to place on or provide with benches; to take (a player) out of a game; to put (plants) on greenhouse benches; to show (dogs). — *combining form* used to denote the particular area in Parliament where MPs sit, and their respective prominence (as in *front bench*, *back bench*). — *n* **bench'er** a senior member of an inn of court. — *n* **bench'ership**. — **bench fees** laboratory fees paid by scientific, medical and technical students; **bench'-hole** (*Shakesp*) a latrine; **bench'mark** a surveyor's mark cut on a rock, etc indicating a point of reference in levelling; something taken or used as a point of reference or comparison, a standard, criterion, etc (also *adj*); a standard program, used to compare the performance of different makes of computer (*computing*); **bench'-warrant** one issued by a judge rather than a justice or magistrate. — **on the bench** holding the office of a judge or bishop; officiating as judge; **raise to the bench** to make a judge or bishop. [OE *benc*; cognate with Ger *Bank* and Du *bank*]

bend[1] *bend*, *vt* to force into (or out of) a curved or angled form; to curve; to bow, turn (the body) downwards; to dispose or incline to a point of view; to aim or direct (one's attention, etc); to alter or disregard (rules) for one's own purposes; to subject (to one's will, etc); to fasten (*naut*); to drink hard at (*Scot*); to subject to tension (*obs*); to brace or bring to tension (*obs*; also *fig*). — *vi* to curve; to stoop; to bow (down) the body; to give way, yield, or show flexibility; to turn in a given direction; to incline to a point of view; to drink hard (*Scot*): — *pa t* and *pa p* **bent**; also **bend'ed**. — *n* a knot by which a line is tied to another, or to itself after passing through a ring, etc; a band, strip; a parallel band crossing a shield diagonally from top left to bottom right (a **bend-sin'ister** a mark of illegitimacy, runs from top right to bottom left; *heraldry*); an act of bending; state of being bent; a bent thing; a place of bending; a bow or stoop; half a butt of leather cut lengthwise; a directing of the eye (*Shakesp*); a strengthening band (*Spenser*); a pull of liquor, or a drinking bout (*Scot*). — *adj* **bend'ed** (only in **on bended knee**). — *adj* **bend'ee** (*heraldry*) bendy. — *n* **bend'er** a person or machine which bends; a (drunken) spree (*slang*); a temporary shelter consisting of a shell of woven branches covered with tarpaulins or plastic sheeting (*colloq*); a sixpence (*obs slang*); a thing very large or fine of its kind (*dialect*). — *n* and *adj* **bend'ing**. — *adv* **bend'ingly**. — *n* **bend'let** (*heraldry*) a half-width bend. — *adv* **bend'wise** (*heraldry*) diagonally. — *adj* **bend'y** divided into bends (*heraldry*); full of or characterized by curves or bends; flexible (*colloq*). — *n* and *adj* **bent** see **bent**[1]. — **bent'wood** wood artificially curved for chair-making, etc. — Also *adj*. — **bend over backwards** see under **back**[1]; **round the bend** (*colloq*) crazy, mad; **the bends** decompression sickness, also known as *caisson disease*; aeroembolism. [OE *bendan* to constrain, bind, fetter, string (as a bow), *bend* bond, fetter]

bend[2] *bend*, (*Spenser*) *n*. Same as **band**[3].

bene[1] *bēn*, (*archaic*; *Wordsworth*) *n* a prayer; a boon. [OE *bēn*]

bene[2]. An old spelling of **been**.

beneath *bi-nēth'*, *adv* and *prep* below; in a lower position so as to be under, or nearly so, or to be covered (by); inside, behind or at the back (of); at a lower level relative to. — *prep* in a manner or of a type not worthy of the dignity of or unbecoming to. — *adj* (*Shakesp*) lower. [OE *beneothan*]

bene decessit *be'ne di-se'sit* or *dā-kā'sit*, (*LL*) *n* a leaving certificate given to a schoolboy, curate, etc, *literally* he has left well.

benedicite *ben-i-dīs'i-ti* or *-dis'* (L *-dēk'i-te*), *interj* bless you (an old form of greeting). — *n* a blessing; a grace at table; (with *cap*) the canticle beginning *Benedicite omnia opera* (All ye works of the Lord, bless ye) from *The Song of the Three Holy Children*. [L *benedīcite*, pl imperative of *benedīcere* to bless, from *bene* well, and *dīcere* to say, speak]

Benedick *ben'i-dik* or **Benedict** *-dikt*, *n* a name for a newly married man, *esp* if formerly a confirmed bachelor. [From *Benedick* in Shakespeare's *Much Ado about Nothing*]

Benedict. See **eggs Benedict** under **egg**[1].

benedict *ben'i-dikt*, (*obs*) *adj* blessed; benign. — *n* **benedic'tion** (*-shən*) a blessing; a solemn invocation of the divine blessing on men or things; a blessing pronounced at the end of a religious service; a brief and popular service in the Roman Catholic Church; grace before or after a meal; blessedness. — *adj* **benedic'tional**. — *adj* **benedict'ive**. — *adj* **benedict'ory**. — *n* **Benedict'us** the canticle of Zacharias (Luke 1. 68–79: Blessed be the Lord God of Israel), used in the Roman and Anglican services; the fifth movement of the Mass — Blessed is he that cometh in the name of the Lord. — *adj* **benedight** (*-dīt'*; *Longfellow*) blessed. — **apostolic benediction** that at the end of 2 Cor. [L *benedīcere*, *benedictum*, from *bene* well, and *dicere* to say, speak]

Benedictine *ben-i-dik'tin* or *-tīn*, *adj* pertaining to St *Benedict* of Nursia (480–547), or his monastic rule. — *n* a monk or nun of the order founded by him at Monte Cassino; (*-tēn*) a cordial or liqueur resembling Chartreuse, distilled at Fécamp in Normandy, formerly by Benedictine monks.

Benedictus. See under **benedict**.

benefaction *ben-i-fak'shən*, *n* the act of doing good; a good deed done or benefit conferred; a grant or endowment. — *vt* **ben'efact** to confer a benefit on. — *n* **ben'efactor** (or *-fak'*) a person who confers a benefit; a person who aids eg an institution financially, a patron: — *fem* **ben'efactress** (or *-fak'*). — *adj* **benefac'tory**. [L *benefactiō*, *-ōnis*; cf following entries]

benefic *bi-nef'ik*, *adj* kindly; benign; beneficent; favourable (*astrol*). — *n* **benefice** (*ben'i-fis*) a church living, an area from which an income is obtained, *esp* in return for the spiritual care of its inhabitants; the income so obtained; a fief (*hist*). — *adj* **ben'eficed** possessing a benefice. — *n* **beneficence** (*bi-nef'i-səns*) active goodness; kindness; charity; a beneficent gift. — *adj* **benef'icent**. — *adj* **beneficential** (*-sen'shl*). — *adv* **benef'icently**. — *adj* **beneficial** (*ben-i-fish'l*) useful; advantageous; enjoying the use of and profits from property (*law*). — *n* (*Spenser*) *appar* a letter of presentation to a benefice. — *adv* **benefic'ially**. — *n* **benefi'cialness**. — *n* **benefi'ciary** a holder of a benefice or a fief; a person who receives a gift or advantage; a person who enjoys, or has the prospect of enjoying, any interest or estate held in trust by others, eg under a will or insurance policy (*law*). — Also *adj*. [L *beneficus* kindly, beneficent, *beneficium* a service, benefit, from *bene* well, and *facere* to do]

beneficiate *be-ni-fish'i-āt*, *vt* to treat (ores, etc) to get rid of impurities. — *n* **beneficiā'tion** treatment of ores, etc to get rid of impurities. [Sp *beneficiar* to benefit, from L *beneficium* a service, benefit]

benefit *ben'i-fit*, *n* any advantage, natural or other; a performance, match, etc whose proceeds go to one of the company, a player, or other particular person or cause (also *adj*); a right in the form of money or services enjoyed under social security or insurance schemes; a kindness; a favour. — *vt* to do good to; to be to the advantage of. — *vi* to obtain advantage or good (with *from* or *by*): — *pr p* **ben'efiting** (also **ben'efitting**); *pa t* and *pa p* **ben'efited** (also **ben'efitted**).

— **benefit of clergy** see under **clergy**; **benefit of inventory** (*Scots law*; *hist*) an heir's privilege of securing himself against unlimited liability for his ancestor, by producing within a year an inventory of his heritage or real estate, to the extent of which alone he was liable; **benefit of the doubt** presumption of innocence when culpability is uncertain; **benefit society** a friendly society. [ME *benfet*, from Anglo-Fr *benfet*, from L *benefactum*]

Benelux *ben'ə-luks*, *n* a name for (the economic union between) *Be*lgium, the *Ne*therlands and *Lux*embourg.

bene merentibus *be'ne mer-ent'ib-us* or *-ōōs*, (*L*) to the well-deserving.

benempt. See **bename**.

beneplacito *be-ne-plä'chē-tō*, (*Ital*) *interj* good pleasure; by your leave.

Benesh *ben'esh*, *n* a system of notation for detailing movements in dancing, introduced in 1955 by Joan and Rudolf *Benesh*.

benet[1] *bi-net'*, *vt* to catch in a net, to ensnare. [**be-** (1) or (2)]

benet[2] *ben'it*, *n* an exorcist, the third of the four lesser orders in the Roman Catholic church. [OFr *beneit*, from L *benedictus* blessed]

bene vobis *be'ne vō'bis* or *wō'bēs*, (*L*) *interj* health to you.

benevolence *bi-nev'ə-ləns*, *n* disposition to do good; an act of kindness; generosity; a gift of money, *esp* for support of the poor; a kind of forced loan or contribution, levied by kings without legal authority, first so called under Edward IV in 1473 (*Eng hist*). — *adj* **benev'olent** charitable, generous; kindly, well disposed. — *adv* **benev'olently**. [OFr *benivolence* and L *benevolentia*]

BEng *abbrev*: Bachelor of Engineering.

Bengal *ben-göl'* or *beng-göl'*, *n* a striped cotton woven in the *Bengal* region, or an imitation of it. — *adj* from Bengal, modern Bangladesh and the Indian state of West Bengal; made of Bengal. — *n* and *adj* **Bengalese** (*ben-gə-lēz'* or *beng-*) a person from Bengal: — *pl* **Bengalese'**. — *adj* **Bengali** (*ben-gö'li* or *beng-*) of or belonging to Bengal or Bengalis. — *n* a person from Bengal; the language of Bengal, the official language of Bangladesh. — *n* **bengaline** (*beng'gə-lēn*) a fabric *usu* of silk and cotton or silk and wool, with a crosswise rib. — **Bengal fire** or **Bengal light** a brilliant, steady, blue light, used as a shipwreck signal, to illuminate country at night, and in fireworks.

beni, beniseed. See **benne**.

benight *bi-nīt*, *vt* (chiefly in *passive*) to be overtaken by night (ie before reaching one's destination); (*active*) to cover with darkness; to darken, cloud (*fig*; of sorrow, disappointment, etc). — *adj* **benight'ed** overtaken by night; lost in intellectual or moral darkness; ignorant. — *vt* **benight'en** (*rare*) to benight. — *n* **benight'ening**. — *n* **benight'er**. — *n* **benight'ing** (also *adj*). — *n* **benight'ment**. [**be-** (2)]

benign *bi-nīn'*, *adj* favourable, *esp* in astrology (as opposed to *malign*); gracious and kindly; of a mild type (as opposed to *malignant*; *med*); (of weather or climate) mild, salubrious. — *n* **benignancy** (*bi-nig'nən-si*) benignant quality. — *adj* **benig'nant** kind and gracious; beneficial, favourable; not malignant. — *adv* **benig'nantly**. — *n* **benig'nity** goodness or kindliness of disposition; a kindness, a kindly act; favourable circumstances, propitiousness, of climate, weather, disease, planets. — *adv* **benign'ly** (*-nīn'*). [OFr *benigne*, from L *benīgnus*, prob from *bene* well, and root of *genus* birth, type]

Benioff zone *ben'i-əf zōn*, (*tectonics*) *n* a seismic zone generated by collision between plates. [From its discoverer Hugo *Benioff* (1899–1968), American geophysicist]

benison *ben'i-zən* or *-sən*, *n* a benediction, blessing. [OFr *beneiçun*, from L *benedictiō*, *-ōnis*]

bénitier *bā-nē'tyā*, *n* a holy-water font, or stoup. [Fr, from LL *benedictārium*, from L *benedictus*]

benj *benj*, *n* bhang. [Ar]

Benjamin *ben'jə-min*, *n* a youngest son; a favourite child. [As in Gen 42]

benjamin[1] *ben'jə-min*, *n* a kind of 19c overcoat. [Perh alluding to **Joseph** (qv); or a tailor's name]

benjamin[2] *ben'jə-min*, *n* gum benzoin. — Also **gum benjamin**. — **ben'jamin-tree** Styrax; the American spice-bush; a kind of fig-tree. [**benzoin**]

benne *ben'ē*, **benni** or **beni** *ben'i*, *n* sesame. — **benn'e-seed**, **benn'i-seed** or **ben'iseed** sesame seed. [From (Sierra Leone) Mende *bene*]

bennet[1] *ben'it*. See **herb-bennet** under **herb**.

bennet[2] *ben'it*, (*S Eng*) *n* a dry grass stalk. [**bent**[2]]

benny[1] *ben'i*, (*slang*) *n* an overcoat. [Prob abbrev of **benjamin**[1]]

benny[2] *ben'i*, (*slang*) *n* an amphetamine tablet. [Abbrev of **Benzedrine**]

bent[1] *bent*, *pa t* and *pa p* of **bend**. — *adj* curved; having a bend; intent, determined (*on* or *upon* doing something); morally crooked, or criminal (*colloq*); homosexual, or otherwise sexually deviant (*slang*); stolen (*slang*); obedient, governed (*Spenser*). — *n* tendency, trend, inclination; direction; leaning or bias, natural inclination of the mind; the extent to which a bow may be bent or a spring wound; capacity of endurance; a piece of framework (*building*); curvature, curve (*obs*). — **to the top of one's bent** to the full measure of one's inclination. [**bend**[1]]

bent[2] *bent*, *n* any stiff or wiry grass; the old dried stalks of grasses; a genus (*Agrostis*) of grasses, slender and delicate in appearance, some useful as pasture-grasses and for hay (also **bent'-grass**); a place covered with bents, a heath (*Northern*); a hillside. — *adj* **bent'y**. — **take the bent** (*Scot*) to take flight. [OE *beonet*, found in place names, as *Beonetlēah* Bentley]

Benthamism *ben'thəm-izm*, *n* the social and political teaching of Jeremy *Bentham* (1748–1832), the philosophical doctrine of utilitarianism. — *n* **Ben'thamite**.

benthos *ben'thos*, *n* the flora and fauna of the sea bottom or lake bottom (opposed to *plankton* and *nekton*). — *adj* **ben'thic**. — *adj* **benthon'ic** or **benthoal** (*ben-thō'əl*) living on the sea bottom. — *adj* **benthopelagic** (*-thō-pi-laj'ik*) (of marine fauna) living just above the sea bed. — *n* **ben'thoscope** a submersible sphere from which to study deep-sea life. [Gr *benthos* depth]

bentonite *ben'tən-īt*, *n* a valuable clay, consisting mainly of montmorillonite, widely used in industry as a bond, filler, etc. [Fort *Benton*, Montana, where it was found]

ben trovato *ben trō-vä'tō*, (*Ital*) *adj* apt but untrue.

bentwood. See **bend**[1].

benumb *bi-num'*, *vt* to make insensible or powerless; to stupefy (now chiefly with cold); to deaden the feelings of; to paralyse generally. — *adj* **benumbed'**. — *n* **benumbed'ness**. — *n* **benumb'ment**. [**be-** (2)]

ben venuto *ben ven-ōōt'ō*, (*Ital*) *interj* welcome.

Benzedrine® *ben'zi-drēn*, *n* a tradename for amphetamine.

benzene *ben'zēn*, *n* the simplest of the aromatic series of hydrocarbons, discovered by Faraday in 1825, now mostly prepared by destructive distillation of coal-tar, its molecule consisting of a ring or closed chain of six carbon atoms each with a hydrogen atom attached, formerly called benzine or benzol, names now used differently (see below). — *n* **ben'zal** or **benzyl'idine** a radical whose oxide is **benzal'dehyde** or oil of bitter almonds. — *n* **benz'idine** a base used in preparing azo-dyes. — *n* **ben'zil** a double benzoyl radical. — *n* **benzine** (*ben'zēn*) a mixture of hydrocarbons obtained by destructive distillation of petroleum, used as a solvent, motor fuel, etc; improperly, benzene. — *n* **ben'zoate** (*-zō-āt*) a salt of benzoic acid. — *n* **benzocaine** (*ben-zō-kā'in* or *ben'zō-kān*) a drug used as a local anaesthetic and in the treatment of gastritis (**benzine** and **cocaine**). — *n* **benzodiazepine** (*ben-zō-dī-az'ə-pēn*, *-pin* or *-pīn*) one of a group of tranquillizing and soporific drugs. — *n* **ben'zol** or **ben'zole** crude benzene, used as a motor-spirit; improperly, benzene. — *n* **ben'zoline** benzine; impure benzene. — *n* **benzoyl** (*ben'zō-il*) the radical C_6H_5:CO. — *n* **benzpyrene** (*benz-pī'rēn*) a cancer-inducing hydrocarbon ($C_{20}H_{12}$) found in coal-tar and present in small quantities in smoke, including tobacco smoke (**benzene** and **pyrene**). — *n* **ben'zyl** (*-zil*) the radical $C_6H_5CH_2$. — *n* **benzylidine** see **benzal** above. — **benzene hexachloride** (known as **BHC**) a chlorinated hydrocarbon, a very toxic insecticide. [From **benzoin**]

benzoin *ben'zō-in* or *-zoin*, *n* gum benjamin, the aromatic and resinous juice of *Styrax benzoin*, a tree of Java and Sumatra, used in perfumery, in pastilles, for incense and court-plaster, and friar's balsam. — *adj* **benzo'ic** pertaining to benzoin, as **benzoic acid**, an acid, C_6H_5·COOH, found in benzoin and other gums. [In the 16c, *benjoin*, most prob through Ital from Ar *lubān jāwī* frankincense of Jawa (ie Sumatra)]

bepaint *bi-pānt'*, (*archaic*) *vt* to paint over; to colour. [**be-** (1)]

bepat *bi-pat'*, (*archaic*) *vt* to pat frequently, to beat. [**be-** (1)]

bepatched *bi-pacht'*, (*archaic*) *adj* mended with patches; wearing patches on the face by way of adornment. [**be-** (1)]

bepearl *bi-pûrl'*, (*archaic*) *vt* to cover over with pearls. [**be-** (1)]

bepelt *bi-pelt'*, (*archaic*) *vt* to pelt vigorously. [**be-** (1)]

bepepper *bi-pep'ər*, (*archaic*) *vt* to pelt with a rain of shot or blows. [**be-** (1)]

bepester *bi-pest'ər*, (*archaic*) *vt* to vex or pester greatly. [**be-** (1)]

bepity *bi-pit'i*, (*archaic*) *vt* to pity greatly. [**be-** (1)]

beplaster *bi-pläs'tər*, (*archaic*) *vt* to plaster thickly; to daub. [**be-** (1)]

beplumed *bi-plo͞omd'*, (*archaic*) *adj* adorned with feathers. [**be-** (2)]

bepommel *bi-pum'l*, (*archaic*) *vt* to pommel soundly. [**be-** (1)]

bepowder *bi-pow'dər*, (*archaic*) *vt* to powder over. [**be-** (1)]

bepraise *bi-prāz'*, (*archaic*) *vt* to lavish praise on. [**be-** (1)]

beprose *bi-prōz'*, (*archaic*) *vt* to reduce to prose; to discuss in prose and tediously. [**be-** (2)]

bepuff *bi-puf'*, (*archaic*) *vt* to puff out; to praise greatly. [**be-** (1)]

bequeath *bi-kwēdh*, *vt* to leave by will to another person (strictly, personal property); to pass on to posterity, to leave behind; to commit or entrust to anyone (*obs*). — *adj* **bequeath'able**. — *n* **bequeath'al**. — *n* **bequeath'ment**. [OE *becwethan*, from pfx *bi-*, *be-* and *cwethan* to say; see **quoth**]

bequest *bi-kwest'*, *n* the act of bequeathing; that which is bequeathed, a legacy. [ME *biqueste*, from OE pfx *bi-*, *be-* and *cwethan* to say; see **quoth**]

berate *bi-rāt'*, *vt* to scold or chide severely. [**be-** (1)]

beray *bi-rā'*, (*obs*) *vt* to befoul. — Also (*erron*) **bewray'**. [**be-** (1) and **ray**[1]]

Berber *bûr'bər*, *n* a member of one of the Muslim peoples of N Africa; the language of the Berbers. — Also *adj*. [Ar *barbar*; connection with Gr *barbaros* is doubtful]

berberis *bûr'bər-is*, *n* any shrub of the barberry genus (*Berberis*), giving name to the family **Berberidā'ceae**, related to the buttercup family. — *adj* **berberidā'ceous**. — *n* **ber'berine** an alkaloid obtained from barberry roots. [Ety as **barberry**]

Berbice chair *bə-bēs' chār*, *n* an armchair whose arms extend to form leg-rests. [From *Berbice* a river and county in Guyana]

berceau *ber-sō*, (*Fr*) *n* a cradle; a covered walk: — *pl* **berceaux** (*-sōz* or *-sō*).

berceuse *ber-søz'*, *n* a lullaby or cradle song; a musical composition in similar rhythm. [Fr]

berdache or **berdash** *bər-dash'*, *n* an American Indian transvestite, *usu* male, adopting not only the dress but also the status and role of the opposite sex. [Fr *bardache* male homosexual]

bere[1]. Another spelling of **bear**[3] barley.

bere[2], **beer** or **bear** *bēr*, *n* a pillow-case (*usu* **pill'ow-bere**). [Origin obscure; cf Ger *Bühre*]

Berean *be-rē'ən*, *n* a member of an 18c Scottish presbyterian sect. — Also *adj*. [*Beroea*, Gr *Beroia* in Macedonia, where the people searched the scriptures daily (Acts 17.11)]

bereave *bi-rēv'*, *vt* to widow, orphan, or deprive by death of some dear relative or friend; to deprive or rob of anything valued; to snatch away (*obs*): — *pa t* and *pa p* **bereaved'** (*usu* by death), **bereft'** (*usu* in general sense); *archaic pa p* **bereav'en**. — *adj* **bereaved'**. — *n* **bereave'ment** loss by death of a relative or friend. [OE *berēafian* to plunder; see **reave**]

beret *ber'i* or **berret** *ber'et*, *n* a flat, round, woollen or felt cap worn by Basques and others. [Fr *béret*]

berg[1] *bûrg* or *berhh*, *n* (*SAfr*) a hill or mountain. — **berg'-adder** a venomous S African viper, living on hillsides; **berg'-cedar** a rare conifer (*Widdringtonia juniperoides*) of the Cedarbergen in South Africa; **bergfall** (*bûrg'föl* or *berk'fäl*; Ger, mountain fall) a fall of mountain rock; **berghaan** (*berhh'hän* or *bûrg'hän*; Du, mountain cock; *SAfr*) the bateleur eagle; **bergmehl** (*berk'māl*, or *bûrg'*; Ger, mountain flour) a powdery deposit of diatom frustules; **bergschrund** (*berk'shro͝ont*; Ger, mountain cleft) a crevasse formed where a glacier or snowfield moves away from a mountain wall; **berg wind** in S Africa, a hot, dry wind blowing from the mountains towards the coastal regions. [Ger *Berg*, Du *berg* hill; cognate with **barrow**]

berg[2] *bûrg*, *n* short for **iceberg**.

bergamask *bûr'gə-mäsk*, *n* (also with *cap*) a native of *Bergamo* in Italy; a rustic dance associated with that district. — Also **ber'gomask**.

bergamot[1] *bûr'gə-mot*, *n* a kind of citron or orange, whose aromatic rind yields oil of bergamot, used in perfumery; the essence so extracted; a mint of similar smell; a kind of woven tapestry made in Bergamo; a kind of rug made in Bergama (also **ber'gama**). [Said to be from *Bergamo* in Italy; or *Bergama* (Pergamum) in Asia Minor; or as next word]

bergamot[2] *bûr'gə-mot*, *n* a fine pear. [Fr, from Ital, from Turk *begarmudi* prince's pear]

bergander or **bargander** *bər-gan'dər*, *n* the shelduck. [Perh from **burrow** and **gander**]

bergenia *bər-gē'ni-ə*, *n* a plant of the *Bergenia* genus of perennial plants of the family Saxifragaceae, having red, purple or pink flowers. [K A von *Bergen*, an 18c botanist and physician]

bergère *ber-zher*, *n* a type of easy chair or sofa with cane back and arms. — Also *adj*. [Fr, shepherdess]

berghaan, **bergmehl**. See **ber**.

bergomask. See **bergamask**.

bergshrund. See under **berg**[1].

Bergsonian *bûrg-sō'ni-ən*, *adj* pertaining to Henri *Bergson* (1859–1941) and his philosophy of creative evolution. — *n* a follower of Bergson. — *n* **Berg'sonism** (*-sən-izm*).

bergylt *bûr'gilt*, *n* a red northern sea-fish of the Scorpaenidae. [Norw *berggylta* rock-pig]

beribboned *bi-rib'ənd*, *participial adj* decorated with ribbons. [**be-** (2)]

beriberi *ber'i-ber-i*, *n* an Eastern disease caused by lack of vitamin B_1. [Sinh *beri* weakness]

berk or **burk** *bûrk*, (*slang*) *n* a fool. [Short for Cockney rhyming slang *Berkeley Hunt*, for *cunt*]

Berkeleian *bärk'lē'ən*, *bärk'li-ən*, or *US bûrk'-*, *adj* pertaining to Bishop *Berkeley* (1685–1753), who maintained that the world we see and touch depends for its existence on being perceived. — *n* a follower of Berkeley. — *n* **Berkelei'anism** (or *bärk'*).

berkelium *bər-kē'li-əm* (earlier *bûrk'li-əm*), *n* a metallic radioactive element (atomic no 97; symbol **Bk**), prepared in a cyclotron at *Berkeley*, California.

Berks. *bärks*, *abbrev*: Berkshire.

berley or **burley** *bûr'li*, (*Austr*) *n* bait, groundbait; leg-pulling, humbug (*colloq*). [Origin unknown]

berlin *bûr'lin*, *bər-lēn'* or *-lin'*, *n* an old four-wheeled covered carriage, with a seat at the rear covered with a hood (also **ber'line**); a closed motor car with the driver's seat partitioned off. — **Berlin blue** Prussian blue; **Berlin wool** a fine dyed wool for worsted work, knitting, etc. [From the city of *Berlin*]

berm *bûrm*, *n* a wall of sand built as a defence in desert warfare; a narrow ledge or path beside a road, etc; the area of level ground between the raised mound of a barrow or other earthwork and the ditch surrounding it (*archaeol*). [Fr *berme*; Ger *Berme*]

Bermudan *bər-mū'dən* or **Bermudian** *-mū'di-ən*, *adj* and *n* (a native or inhabitant) of Bermuda. — **Bermuda grass** (*bər-mū'də*) a type of grass native to Southern Europe, now growing widely in warm countries, with wiry rootstock, used in lawns and for binding sand-dunes; **Bermuda rig** a sailing rig in which there is a large fore-and-aft sail fixed directly to a tall mainmast. — *adj* **Bermuda rigged**. — **Bermuda shorts** shorts, for men or women, reaching almost to the knee. — Also **Bermu'das**; **Bermuda Triangle** the area between Florida, the Bahamas and Cuba where ships and aeroplanes are alleged to have mysteriously disappeared.

Bernardine *bûr'nər-din* or *-dēn*, *adj* Cistercian. — Also *n*. [From *Bernard* of Clairvaux, founder of the order]

bernicle-goose. Same as **barnacle-goose**.

berob *bi-rob'*, (*Spenser*) *vt* to rob or plunder. [**be-** (1)]

berret. See **beret**.

berry[1] *ber'i*, *n* any small succulent fruit; a simple fruit with pericarp succulent throughout (thus excluding strawberry, raspberry and blackberry, which are aggregate fruits) (*bot*); a coffee-bean; a cereal grain; a lobster's or crayfish's egg; a knob on a swan's bill. — *vi* to produce berries, to swell; to gather berries. — *adj* **berr'ied** bearing berries; of lobsters, etc, having eggs. — *n* **berr'ying**. — **berry bug** the harvest-mite or chigger, of the genus *Trombicula*. [OE *berie*]

berry[2] *ber'i*, *n* a pottage or sop (as in **ale-berry**, **bread-berry**). [OE *brīw* pottage, porridge]

bersaglieri *ber-säl-yä'rē*, *n pl* the riflemen or sharp-shooters of the Italian army, first organized in the Sardinian army in 1836. [Ital; pl of *bersagliere*, from *bersaglio* a target]

berserk or **berserker** *ber-sûrk'(ər)*, *-zûrk'(ər)*, *n* a Norse warrior who on the battlefield was filled with a frenzied and irresistible fury. — *adj* **berserk'** violently frenzied or angry (*usu* with *go*; *rare* **berserk'er**). — *adv* **berserk'ly**. [ON *berserkr*, literally prob bear-sark]

berth *bûrth*, *n* a sleeping-place in a ship or train, *usu* a narrow fixed bunk; a place allotted to a ship at anchor or at a wharf; room for a ship to manoeuvre; any allotted or assigned place; a situation or place of employment, *usu* a comfortable one. — *vt* and *vi* to moor or dock (a ship). — *vt* to provide with a berth. — *n* **berth'age** accommodation, or dues paid, for mooring or anchoring. — **give a wide berth to** to keep well away from, avoid. [Ety obscure]

bertha *bûr'thə*, *n* a woman's deep (*usu* lace) collar worn to cover a low neckline (also **berthe**); (with *cap*; often **Big Bertha**) a big German gun (from Frau *Berta* Krupp of the Krupp steelworks), first used of guns shelling Paris 1918. — **bertha army worm** a type of cutworm of north central US and Canada, destructive to crops. [Woman's name]

Bertholletia *bûrth-ō-lē'sh(y)ə*, *n* the brazil-nut genus of Lecythidaceae. [Named in honour of the chemist C L *Berthollet* (1748–1822)]

Berthon-boat *bûr'thon-bōt*, *n* a type of collapsible boat. [Edward L *Berthon* (1813–99), its inventor]

bertillonage *ber-tē-yon-äzh*, (*Fr*) *n* a system of criminal identification by detailed measurement, worked out by Alphonse *Bertillon* (1853–1914), a Paris police officer.

Berufsverbot *bə-ro͞ofs'fər-bōt*, (*Ger*) *n* in Germany, the policy of excluding political extremists from public service.

beryl *ber'il*, *n* a precious stone occurring in hexagonal crystals, of which emerald and aquamarine are varieties, a silicate of beryllium and aluminium, green, colourless, yellow or blue, once thought to have magic properties. — *adj* pale greenish. — *n* **beryll'ia** the oxide of **beryll'ium**, a metallic element (atomic no 4; symbol **Be**), used for windows in X-ray tubes, and industrially to harden alloys, etc. — *n* **berylliō'sis** a disease caused by exposure to the fumes or dust from beryllium salts, in which granulomata are formed *esp* in the lungs. [OFr *beryl*, from L *bēryllus*, from Gr *bēryllos*]

BES *abbrev*: Business Expansion Scheme.

besaint *bi-sānt'*, (*archaic*) *vt* to make a saint of: — *pa p* **besaint'ed** canonized; haunted with saints. [**be-** (2)]

bescatter *bi-skat'ər*, (*archaic*) *vt* to scatter over. [**be-** (1)]

bescrawl *bi-scröl'*, (*archaic*) *vt* to scrawl or scribble over. [**be-** (1)]

bescreen *bi-skrēn'*, (*archaic*) *vt* to screen; to overshadow. [**be-** (1)]

bescribble *bi-skrib'l*, (*archaic*) *vt* to write in a scribbling hand; to scribble about, over, or upon. [**be-** (3)]

besee *bi-sē'* (*obs*) *vt* to look to; to provide for; to treat; to provide, furnish, apparel, adorn: — *pa p* **beseen'**. — *adj* **beseen'** of (specified) appearance; (well etc) furnished. [OE *besēon*, from *be-* (pfx) and *sēon* to see]

beseech *bi-sēch'* (*Spenser* **beseeke** *bi-sēk'*), *vt* to entreat, to implore; to ask or pray earnestly to (God, etc); to beg: — *pa t* and *pa p* **besought** (*bi-söt'*) or **beseeched'**. — *n* (*Shakesp*) entreaty. — *n* **beseech'er**. — *n* and *adj* **beseech'ing**. — *adv* **beseech'ingly**. — *n* **beseech'ingness**. [**be-** (1) and ME *sechen*; see **seek**]

beseem *bi-sēm'*, *vi* to seem (*obs*); to be fitting or becoming. — *vt* to be seemly for; to become; to be fit for or worthy of. — *n* and *adj* **beseem'ing**. — *adv* **beseem'ingly**. — *n* **beseem'ingness**. — *adj* **beseem'ly** (*rare*). [**be-** (1)]

beseen. See **besee**.

beset *bi-set'*, *vt* to surround with hostile intentions, to besiege; to assail mentally, perplex, endanger, with problems, temptations, obstacles, etc; to surround or set round with anything (now *esp* jewels; now only in *pa p*); to occupy so as to allow no-one to go out or in: — *pr p* **besett'ing**; *pa t* and *pa p* **beset'**. — *n* **beset'ment**. — *n* **besett'er**. — *adj* **besett'ing** constantly assailing; dominant. [OE *besettan*, from *settan* to set]

beshadow *bi-shad'ō*, (*archaic*) *vt* to cast a shadow over. [**be-** (1)]

beshame *bi-shām'*, (*archaic*) *vt* to put to shame. [**be-** (1)]

beshine *bi-shīn'*, (*archaic*) *vt* to light up. — *adj* **beshone** (*-shon'*). [**be-** (1)]

beshrew *bi-shro͞o'*, (*archaic*) *vt* to wish evil on, to curse (latterly only in oaths). [**be-** (1) and obs vt **shrew** to curse]

beside *bi-sīd'*, *prep* by or to the side of, next to, near; outside of; away from; as distinct from, compared with; over and above, besides (*rare*). — *adv* nearby; besides; apart; to the side. — *adv* **besides'** in addition; moreover; otherwise, else. — *prep* over and above; other than, with the exception of; apart from; beside (*obs*); away from (*obs*). — **beside oneself** having lost self-control, irrational (with worry, anger, etc); **beside the mark**, **point** or **question** irrelevant (and therefore inconsequential). [OE *besīdan* by the side (dative); the *-s* in *besides* is of the adverbial genitive]

besiege *bi-sēj'*, *vt* to lay siege to, to attack violently and surround with the intent of capturing; to attack and surround with armed forces; to throng round in large numbers; to importune; to pester (*colloq*). — *n* **besiege'ment**. — *n* **besieg'er**. — *n* and *adj* **besieg'ing**. — *adv* **besieg'ingly** (*rare*) urgently. [**be-** (1)]

besigh *bi-sī'*, (*archaic*) *vt* to sigh over. [**be-** (3)]

besing *bi-sing'*, (*archaic*) *vt* to celebrate in song. — *adj* **besung'**. [**be-** (3)]

besit *bi-sit'*, (*archaic*) *vt* to besiege; to sit well on, to suit. — *adj* **besitt'ing** (*Spenser*) becoming. [OE *besittan*, from *sittan* to sit]

B ès L (*Fr*) *abbrev*: *Bachelier ès Lettres* Bachelor of Letters.

beslave *bi-slāv'*, *vt* to make a slave of; to call slave. [**be-** (2)]

beslaver *bi-slav'ər*, (*archaic*) *vt* to slaver or slobber upon; to cover with fulsome flattery. [**be-** (1)]

beslobber *bi-slob'ər*, *vt* to besmear with the spittle running from one's mouth; to cover with drivelling kisses; to flatter fulsomely. [**be-** (1)]

beslubber *bi-slub'ər*, *vt* to bedaub or besmear. [**be-** (1)]

besmear *bi-smēr'*, *vt* to smear over; to bedaub; to pollute, besmirch. [**be-** (1)]

besmirch *bi-smûrch'*, *vt* to soil, eg with smoke or dirt; to sully (a reputation, etc). [**be-** (1)]

besmut *bi-smut'*, *vt* to blacken with soot. — *adj* **besmutt'ed**. [**be-** (1)]

besmutch *bi-smuch'*, (*archaic*) *vt* to besmirch. [**be-** (1)]

besognio *bi-zōn'yō*, *n* a beggar: — *pl* **besogn'ios**. [Ital; see **bezonian**]

besoin *bə-zwɛ̃*, (*Fr*) *n* need, want, desire.

beso las manos *bā'sō läs mä'nōs*, (*Sp*) *interj* I kiss your hands.

besom[1] *bē'zəm*, *n* a bunch of twigs for sweeping or a broom made of twigs tied to a handle; (*Scot biz'əm* or *buz'əm*) any broom; any cleansing or purifying agent. — *vt* to sweep (often with *away* or *out*): — *pr p* **be'soming**; *pa t* and *pa p* **be'somed**. — **be'som-head** a blockhead; **be'som-rider** a witch. — **jump the besom** see under **broom**. [OE *besema*; Ger *Bezen*, Du *bezem*]

besom[2] *biz'əm* or *bē'zəm*, (*Northern*) *n* a term of reproach for a woman, *gen* implying slatternliness, laziness, impudence, or unscrupulous energy. [Perh the same word as the preceding; or perh connected with OE *bysn*, *bisn* example, or ON *bȳsn* wonder]

besonian. See **bezonian**.

besort *bi-sört'*, (*Shakesp*) *vt* to match, befit, become. — *n* suitable company. [**be-** (1)]

besot *bi-sot'*, *vt* to make sottish, dull, or stupid; to make a sot of; to cause to dote; to infatuate: — *pr p* **besott'ing**; *pa p* **besott'ed**. — *adj* **besott'ed** infatuated; stupefied, stupid; intoxicated. — *adv* **besott'edly**. — *n* **besott'edness**. [**be-** (2)]

besought *bi-söt'*, *pa t* and *pa p* of **beseech**.

besouled *bi-sōld'*, (*archaic*) *adj* endowed with a soul. [**be-** (2)]

bespangle *bi-spang'gl*, *vt* to adorn with spangles, or with anything sparkling or shining. [**be-** (2)]

bespatter *bi-spat'ər*, *vt* to spatter or sprinkle with dirt or anything wet; to defame. — *adj* **bespatt'ered**. [**be-** (1)]

bespeak *bi-spēk'*, *vt* to engage in advance, to order or apply for; to request or ask for; to betoken, be evidence for; to foretell; to address (*poetic*). — *vi* (*obs*) to speak, speak out: — *pa t* **bespoke'** (or *archaic* **bespake'**); *pa p* **bespōk'en**, also **bespoke'** (see also **bespoke**, below). — *n* an actor's benefit, so called because his friends and patrons choose the piece to be performed; an application in advance. [**be-** (3)]

bespeckle *bi-spek'l*, *vt* to mark with speckles or spots. — *adj* **bespeck'led**. [**be-** (1)]

bespectacled *bi-spek'tə-kəld*, *adj* wearing, or as if wearing, spectacles. [**be-** (2)]

bespeed *bi-spēd'*, (*archaic*) *vt* to help on: — *pa t* **besped'**; *pa p* **besped'** having got on (well, etc). [**be-** (1)]

bespice *bi-spīs'*, (*Shakesp*) *vt* to season with spice. [**be-** (2)]

bespit *bi-spit'*, (*archaic*) *vt* to spit upon, defile with spittle: — *pa t* and *pa p* **bespit'** or **bespat'**; *pa p* (*Browning*) **bespate'**. [**be-** (1)]

bespoke *bi-spōk'*, (*esp* of clothes) specially tailored or designed to the client's measurements, requirements, etc; (of a tailor, etc) making clothes, etc, to order. [Pa p of **bespeak**]

besport *bi-spört'*, *vt* to disport (oneself). [**be-** (1)]

bespot *bi-spot'*, *vt* to cover with spots. — *adj* **bespott'ed**. — *n* **bespott'edness**. [**be-** (1)]

bespout *bi-spowt'*, *vt* to spout over; to declaim pompously. [**be-** (1)]

bespread *bi-spred'*, *vt* to spread over; to cover: — *pr p* **bespread'ing**; *pa t* and *pa p* **bespread'**. [**be-** (3)]

besprent *bi-sprent'*, (*obs*) *pa p* sprinkled over; scattered. [OE *besprengan*; see **sprinkle**]

besprinkle *bi-spring'kl*, *vt* to sprinkle over. [**be-** (1)]

B ès S (*Fr*) *abbrev*: *Bachelier ès Sciences* Bachelor of Sciences.

Bessarabian *bes-ə-rā'bi-ən*, *adj* of *Bessarabia*, a region in the south-west of the former USSR. — *n* a native or citizen of Bessarabia; a type of carpet from this region.

Bessemer *bēs'əm-ər*, *adj* pertaining to the steel-making process invented by Sir Henry *Bessemer* (1813–98). — **Bessemer converter** a type of furnace used in the Bessemer process; **Bessemer iron** or **pig** pig-iron suitable for making Bessemer steel; **Bessemer process** a process for making steel from molten pig-iron.

Besserwisser *bes'ər-vis-ər*, (*Ger*; often *facetious*) *n* someone who (thinks he or she) always knows better or more than anyone else.

best *best*, *adj* (serving as *superl* of **good**) good in the highest degree; first; highest; most excellent in any way. — *n* one's utmost endeavour, the limit of one's ability; the highest perfection; the most outstanding or finest example; the most advantageous or largest share, part, success or lot (as in the *best of the bargain*, *the best of three*, of tosses, games, etc); best wishes (*colloq*); one's smartest clothing. — *adv* (*superl* of **well**) to the highest degree of quality, excellence, etc; better than anyone else. — *vt* (*colloq*) to win against, to outdo or outwit. — *adj* **best'-ball** (*golf*) applied to foursomes, etc in which it is the lowest score at individual holes that is counted. — **best-before date** the date (stamped, etc on a package *esp* with the wording 'best before (eg) 15 August') up to which a manufacturer can guarantee the good quality of a consumer (*usu* food) product; **best boy** (*esp NAm*) the chief assistant to the head lighting electrician on a film or television production crew; **best boy** or **girl** (*colloq*) a favourite friend of the opposite sex, a boyfriend or girlfriend; **best buy** the most highly recommended purchase from those available; **best end** a cut of lamb, etc from the part of the neck nearest the ribs; **best maid** (*Scot*) a bridesmaid; **best man** the groom's (male) attendant and ring-keeper at a wedding; **best part** the larger part; **bestsell'er** a book that has sold many copies, overall or in a given season; the writer of such a book; **bestsell'erdom** bestsellers collectively, popular publishing. — *adj* **bestsell'ing** of a book or author that is a bestseller. — **(all) for the best** likely to have the best ultimate outcome; **all the best** see under **all**; **at best** assuming the most favourable conditions; **for the best** done with the best of intentions or outcome; see **(all) for the best** above; **get** or **have the best of it** to gain the advantage in a contest; **give someone best** to concede the victory to someone; **had best** see under **have**; **make the best of** to obtain the best results from (a poor, unpromising, etc situation); **make the best of one's way** to go as fast as one can; **put one's best foot forward** see under **foot**; **six of the best** see under **six**; **with the best (of them)** as successfully as anyone. [OE *betst*, *betest*; see **better**]

bestad(de). See **bestead**[2].

bestain *bi-stān'*, (*archaic*) *vt* to stain all over. [**be-** (1)]

bestar *bi-stär'*, (*archaic*) *vt* to cover with stars. [**be-** (2)]

bestead[1] *bi-sted'*, *vt* to help, relieve; to be of use to, avail. — *vi* to profit, be advantageous: — *pa t* **bestead'ed**; *pa p* **bestead'** or **bested'**. [**be-** (1) and obs *vt* **stead**]

bestead[2] or **bested** *bi-sted'* (*Spenser* **bestad** or **bestadde** *bi-stad'*), *adj* set about (*with*); beset (with *by*, of foes; with *with*, of dangers, etc); situated (*usu* with *ill*, *hard*, etc). [**be-** (2) and **stead** placed]

bestial *best'i-əl*, *adj* like an animal; sexually depraved; rude, unrefined. — *n* (*Scot*) a collective name for cattle. — *vt* **best'ialize** or **-ise** to make bestial. — *n* **best'ialism** lack of the human capacity for reasoning. — *n* **bestiality** (*-al'i-ti*) behavioural likeness to animals; disgusting vice; copulation between a person and an animal. [L *bestiālis*, from *bestia* beast]

bestiary *best'i-ər-i*, *n* a book of a type popular in the Middle Ages, describing animals, both real and fabled, allegorized for moral teaching purposes. [LL *bestiārium* a menagerie, from *bestia* a beast]

bestick *bi-stik'*, *vt* to cover all over; to transfix; to adorn: — *pa t* and *pa p* **bestuck'**. [**be-** (1)]
bestill *bi-stil'*, (*archaic*) *vt* to make quiet, to hush. [**be-** (1)]
bestir *bi-stûr'*, *vt* to cause to begin lively action; to arouse into activity. [**be-** (1)]
bestorm *bi-störm'*, (*archaic*) *vt* to assail with storms or tumult. [**be-** (1)]
bestow *bi-stō'*, *vt* to give or confer (a reward, distinction, etc); to endow with (a particular quality); to stow, place, or put by (*archaic*); to provide accommodation for (*archaic*); to apply, employ (resources, etc); to acquit (oneself) (*Shakesp*). — *n* **bestow'al** act of bestowing; disposal. — *n* **bestow'er**. — *n* **bestow'ment**. [**be-** (1)]
bestraddle *bi-strad'l*, *vt* to bestride. [**be-** (3)]
bestraught *bi-ströt'*, (*obs*) *adj* distraught; distracted; mad. [**distraught**, with change of pfx to **be-** (1)]
bestreak *bi-strēk'*, *vt* to overspread with streaks. [**be-** (1)]
bestrew *bi-stro͞o'*, *vt* to cover loosely with something strewn or scattered over: — *pa p* **bestrewed'** or **bestrown** (*-strōn'*), or **bestrewn'**. [**be-** (1)]
bestride *bi-strīd'*, *vt* to stand or sit across in an imposing manner; to defend or protect; to stride over: — *pa t* **bestrode'** or (*archaic*) **bestrid'**; *pa p* **bestridd'en** or (*archaic*) **bestrid'**. — *adj* **bestrīd'able**. [**be-** (3)]
bestuck *pa t* and *pa p* of **bestick**.
bestud *bi-stud'*, *vt* to adorn as with studs, as the sky with stars. [**be-** (1)]
besuited *bi-so͞o'tid*, *adj* wearing a suit. [**be-** (2)]
bet *bet*, *n* a prediction of the result of anything yet to be decided, often gambled on with money or other stakes; the stakes to be lost or won on the result of a doubtful outcome. — *vt* and *vi* to lay or stake (money, etc) as a bet; to predict: — *pr p* **bett'ing**; *pa t* and *pa p* **bet** or **bett'ed**. — *n* **bett'er** a person who bets. — Also **bett'or**. — *n* **bett'ing**. — **betting shop** premises, not on a racecourse, licensed for the placing of bets and payment of winnings. — **an even bet** an equal chance; **a good (better** or **best) bet** a (more or most) hopeful proposition or possibility; **you bet** (*slang*) certainly. [Poss shortened from the noun **abet**]
bet. *abbrev*: between.
beta *bē'tə*, *n* the second letter (B, β) of the Greek alphabet; in the ancient Greek alphabetic numbering system β′ = 2, ͵β = 2000; in classification, the second or one of the second grade, the grade below alpha; in a constellation, a star second in brightness. — *adj* in chemical classification, designating one of two or more isomeric forms of a compound; relating to electrons. — *n* **be'tacism** (*-sizm*) pronunciation of the sound of b as that of v. — *n* **be'tatron** (Gr *-tron* agent suffix) see **accelerator** under **accelerate**. — **be'ta-blocker** a drug that reduces heart-rate and interferes with the action of stress hormones such as adrenaline, used to treat eg high blood-pressure and angina; **beta-carotene** (*-kar'ə-tēn*) a nutrient found in yellow and orange fruits and vegetables; **beta decay** radioactive decay with the emission of an electron or positron; **Beta fibre** a high-fibre product of sugar-beet used as a dietary supplement to aid the absorption of cholesterol; **beta rays** streams of **beta particles** or electrons, given off by radium and other radioactive substances; **beta-thalassemia** (*-tha-lə-sē'mi-ə*) a genetic disorder of the haemoglobin. [Gr *bēta*; see **B**, **beth**]
betaine *bē'tə-in* or *-ēn*, *n* a crystalline, sweet-tasting alkaloid occurring in sugar beet and other plants, also found in animals. [L *bēta* beet, and *-ine*]
betake *bi-tāk'*, (*literary*) *v reflexive* to take oneself to, to go; to apply or have recourse to: — *pa t* **betook'**; *pa p* **betāk'en**. [**be-** (1)]
bete. See **beet**[2].
bête *bet*, (*Fr*) *n* a brute, a stupid person. — *n* **bêtise** (*bet-ēz*) stupidity; a blunder. — **bête noire** (*nwär*) *literally* black beast; a bugbear; a person or thing that one especially dislikes or fears.
beteem or **beteeme** *bi-tēm'*, (*Spenser* and *Shakesp*) *vt* to grant, vouchsafe, allow. [Perh from a lost OE word corresp to Du *betamen* to beseem]
betel *bē'tl*, *n* the leaf of the **be'tel-pepper** (*Piper betle*) which is chewed in the East along with the areca-nut and lime. — **be'tel-nut** the areca-nut. [Through Port from Malayalam *vettila*]
Betelgeuse or **Betelgeuz** *bet'əl-jo͞oz*, *n* a reddish first-magnitude star in Orion's shoulder. [Fr, from Ar *bayt-al-jawzā'* Orion]
beth *beth* or *bāth*, *n* the second letter of the Hebrew and Phoenician alphabets, resembling a house. [Heb *bēth* house; see **B**, **beta**]
bethankit *bi-thangk'it*, (*Scot*) *interj* elliptical for *God be thanked*. — *n* a grace.
Beth Din *bāt dēn* or *beth din*, *n* a Jewish court, in London presided over by the Chief Rabbi. [Heb *bēth* house, and *dīn* judgement]
bethel *beth'əl*, *n* a Methodist or Baptist church; an old ship fitted as a place of worship for sailors. [Heb *Bēth-ēl* house of God]
Bethesda *be-thez'də*, (*Heb*) *n* a healing pool at Jerusalem; (*usu* without *cap*) a Nonconformist church building.
bethink *bi-thingk'*, (*literary*) *vt* to think about or call to mind; to recollect (*usu* in the phrase *bethink oneself of*); to propose to (oneself). — *vi* to consider: — *pa t* and *pa p* **bethought** (*bi-thöt'*). [OE *bithencan*; cf Ger *bedenken*. See **think**]
bethrall *bi-thröl'*, (*Spenser*) *vt* to enslave. [**be-** (2)]
bethumb *bi-thum'*, *vt* to mark with the thumbs: — *pa p* **bethumbed'**. [**be-** (1)]
bethump *bi-thump'*, *vt* to thump or beat soundly. [**be-** (1)]
bethwack *bi-thwak'*, *vt* to thrash soundly. [**be-** (1)]
betide *bi-tīd'*, *vt* to befall, happen to (*orig* with *dative* and formerly sometimes followed by *to* or *unto*); (*erroneous* and *rare*) to betoken: — *pa t* **betī'ded** or **betid** (*-tid'*); *pa p* **betid'** (*Spenser* **betight** *bi-tīt'*). [**be-** (1); see **tide**[2]]
betime *bi-tīm'*, (*Shakesp*) *vi* to betide. [**be-** (2)]
betimes *bi-tīmz'*, (*literary*) *adv* in good time; early; speedily, soon. [**be-** (1) and **time**, with adverbial genitive *-s*]
bêtise. See **bête**.
betitle *bi-tī'tl*, *vt* to give a name to. [**be-** (2)]
betoil *bi-toil'*, *vt* to weary with toil. [**be-** (1)]
betoken *bi-tō'kən*, *vt* to show by a sign; to be an omen of; to mean, to symbolize (*archaic*). [**be-** (1)]
béton *bā'tɔ̃*, (*Fr*) *n* lime concrete; concrete.
betony *bet'ən-i*, *n* a common labiate plant (*Stachys* or *Betonica officinalis*) growing in woods, of great repute in ancient and medieval medicine; extended to various labiate and scrophulariaceous plants. [Fr *bétoine*, from L *betonica, vettonica*]
betook *bi-to͝ok'*, *pa t* of **betake**.
betoss *bi-tos'*, (*Shakesp*) *vt* to agitate. [**be-** (1)]
betray *bi-trā'*, *vt* to give information about treacherously (to an enemy); to disclose in breach of trust; to deceive (someone innocent and trustful), to seduce; to disappoint the hopes of; to reveal or show unintentionally; to show signs of. — *n* **betray'al** the or an act of betraying. — *n* **betray'er** a traitor; the seducer of a trustful female. [**be-** (1) and OFr *trair* (Fr *trahir*), from L *tradere* to deliver up]
betread *bi-tred'*, *vt* to tread over or walk upon: — *pa t* **betrod'**; *pa p* **betrodd'en**. [**be-** (1)]
betrim *bi-trim'*, *vt* to trim or set in order, to deck, to dress. [**be-** (1)]
betroth *bi-trōdh'* or *-trōth'*, *vt* to contract or promise to marry (a woman); to affiance (one person to another); to pledge (oneself) to (*obs*). — *n* **betroth'al** or **betroth'ment** an engagement to marry; a ceremonious declaration of such an engagement. — *adj* and *n* **betrothed'** (a person) promised in marriage. [**be-** (2), and **troth** or **truth**]
better *bet'ər*, *adj* (serving as *compar* of **good**) good in a greater degree; preferable; improved; more suitable; larger; kinder; stronger in health; completely recovered from illness, etc (*Northern*). — *adv* (*compar* of **well**) well to a greater degree or extent; more fully,

completely, expertly, etc; over or more. — *n* a person superior in quality or rank (*esp* in *pl*). — *vt* to make better; to surpass, to do better than. — *vi* (*rare*) to grow better. — *adj* **bett'ered**. — *adj* **bett'ering**. — *n* **bett'ering** amelioration; improvement. — *n* **bett'erment** improvement, *esp* in standard of life, status or value of property. — *adj* **bett'ermost** best. — *n* **bett'erness**. — **bett'er-ball** a form of stroke-play golf in which all players play a drive but thereafter each player plays only one ball alternately, a four-ball; **better half** a jocular or patronizing term for a spouse, formerly applied seriously to wife or husband, intimate friend, and even the soul as opposed to the body. — **be better than one's word** to do more than one had promised; **be (all) the better for** to be improved as a result of; **better off** in superior circumstances; more fortunate; richer; **for better (or) for worse** whatever the result may be; **for the better** in the way of improvement; **get the better of** to gain the advantage over, overcome; **had better** see under **have**; **have seen** or **known better days** to be worse off or in worse condition now than formerly; **the better part of** more than half of; **think better of** to revise one's decision about, *esp* to decide against; to have a higher opinion of. [OE *bet* (adv), *betera* (adj) better; Gothic *batiza*, Ger *besser*; prob cognate with **boot**[2]]

betty *bet'i*, *n* a man who occupies himself with housework; a burglar's jemmy (*old slang*). — **Betty Martin** an expression of disbelief (*usu* in the phrase *all my eye and Betty Martin*). [Dimin of *Elizabeth*]

Betula *bet'ū-lə*, *n* the birch genus, giving name to the family **Betulā'ceae**, which includes hazel and hornbeam. [L *betula*]

betumbled *bi-tum'bəld*, (*Shakesp*) *participial adj* tumbled or disordered. [**be-** (1)]

between *bi-twēn'*, *prep* in, to, through or across the space that separates; intermediate to; indicating a choice of alternatives; indicating that both alternatives apply; by combined action or influence of; from one to another of; in joint possession of (*gen* of two). — *adv* in or to an intermediate place; at spatial or temporal intervals. — *n* an interval (*Shakesp*); an intermediate size of needle. — *n* **between'ity** (*playful*) intermediateness. — *n* **between'ness** the state or fact of being between. — **between'-decks** the space between any two decks of a ship (also *adv*); **between'-maid** a servant subsidiary to two others (*esp* cook and housemaid), a tweeny. — *adv* **between'time**, **between'times** or **between'-whiles** at intervals. — **between ourselves** or **between you and me** (*slang* **and the cat** or **post** or **bedpost**, etc), **between the two of us**, or **between us two** in confidence; **between the devil and the deep blue sea** in a desperate dilemma, faced with two undesirable alternatives; **go between** to act as a mediator (*n* **go'-between**). [OE *betwēonum* and *betwēon*, from *be* by, and *twēgen*, *twā* twain, two]

betwixt *bi-twikst'*, *prep* and *adv* (*archaic*) between. — **betwixt and between** in a middling, undecided, or intermediate position. [OE *betweox*, from *twā* two, and the suffix *-ix* -ish, with added *-t*, as in *against* and *amidst*]

Beulah *bū'lə*, *n* a name for the land of Israel in Isaiah 52. 4; a Nonconformist chapel. [Heb, literally married woman]

beurre *bœr*, (*Fr*) *n* butter. — **beurre manié** (*ma-nyā*) a butter and flour mixture for thickening sauces; **beurre noir** (*nwär*) butter heated until it browns.

beurré or **beurre** *bœ-rā*, *adj* of delicate flavour and texture, applied to several varieties of pear. — Also *n*. [Fr, buttery]

BeV *abbrev*: billion electron-volts, where billion = one thousand million.

bevatron *bev'ə-tron*, *n* a type of proton accelerator (see under **accelerate**). [From **BeV** and Gr agent suffix *-tron*]

bevel *bev'l*, *n* a slant or inclination of a surface; a tool opening like a pair of compasses, and adjustable for measuring angles. — *adj* having the form of a bevel; slanting. — *vt* to form so as to have a bevel or slant. — *vi* to slant: — *pr p* **bev'elling**; *pa t* and *pa p* **bev'elled**. — *adj* **bev'elled** cut to an oblique angle, sloped off. — *n* **bev'eller**. — *n* **bev'elling**. — *n* **bev'elment**. — **bev'el-gear** or **bev'el-wheels** (*mech*) wheels working on each other in different planes, the cogs of the wheels being bevelled or at oblique angles to the shafts. [From the (unattested) older form of Fr *beveau* bevel (tool)]

bever[1]. See **beverage**.

bever[2]. An obsolete form of **beaver**[1] and **beaver**[2].

beverage *bev'ər-ij*, *n* any liquid for drinking, *esp* tea, coffee, milk, etc; a mixture of cider and water (*obs*); a drink or drink-money to celebrate an occasion (*dialect*). — *n* **bever** (*bēv'ər*) a small snack between meals (*dialect*); a time for drinking (*obs*). — *adj* **bevv'ied** (*slang*) drunk. — *n* **bevv'y** or **bev'y** (*colloq*) an alcoholic drink; a drinking session. — **beverage room** (*Can*) a beer parlour. [OFr *bevrage* (Fr *breuvage*), *beivre*, from L *bibere* to drink]

Bevin boy *bev'in boi*, *n* a young man in the UK in World War II selected to work in a coalmine instead of doing the normal military service. [After Ernest *Bevin* (1881–1951), Minister of Labour and National Service during the war]

bevue *bā-vü*, *n* a blunder. [Fr *bévue*]

bevy[1] *bev'i*, *n* a company or flock (of larks, quails, swans, roes or ladies). [Origin obscure]

bevy[2]. See under **beverage**.

bewail *bi-wāl'*, *vt* to lament; to mourn loudly over (*esp* the dead). — *vi* to lament. — *adj* **bewailed'**. — *n* and *adj* **bewail'ing**. [**be-** (1)]

beware *bi-wār'*, *vi* (*usu* with *of*, or with *that* or *lest*) to be on one's guard (against); to be careful (of); to take heed; to take care (of) (*obs*); to take warning (by) (*obs*). — *vt* to be on one's guard against; to take care of (*obs*); to take care (with *infin* or clause) (*archaic*). Used normally only in infinitive and imperative; old writers have *was ware*, etc. [**be** and **ware**]

beweep *bi-wēp'*, *vt* to weep over, lament; to wet or disfigure by weeping: — *pa t* and *pa p* **bewept'**. [**be-** (1)]

beweltered *bi-wel'tərd*, (*archaic*) *participial adj* besmeared by weltering in blood. [**be-** (1)]

bewet *bi-wet'*, (*Shakesp*) *vt* to wet or moisten: — *pa t* and *pa p* **bewett'ed** or **bewet'**. [**be-** (1)]

bewhiskered *bi-wis'kərd* or *-hwis'kərd*, *adj* having whiskers on the face. [**be-** (2)]

bewhore *bi-hōr'*, (*Shakesp*) *vt* to call a whore; to make a whore of. [**be-** (2)]

Bewick's swan *bū'iks swon*, *n* a small white swan (*Cygnus bewickii*) native to N Asia and NE Europe, that winters occasionally in W Europe. [T *Bewick* (died 1828), Eng wood-engraver, illustrator of *History of British Birds*]

bewig *bi-wig'*, *vt* to cover or dress in a wig. — *adj* **bewigged'**. [**be-** (2)]

bewilder *bi-wil'dər*, *vt* to perplex, confuse; to cause to get lost (*archaic*). — *adj* **bewil'dered** confused in mind; lost (*archaic*); trackless, pathless (*archaic*); confused, mixed up (*archaic*). — *adj* **bewil'dering**. — *adv* **bewil'deringly**. — *n* **bewil'derment**. [**be-** (1) and obs Eng *wildern*, from OE *wilddēoren* wilderness, from *wild* wild, and *dēor* beast]

bewitch *bi-wich'*, *vt* to affect by witchcraft (mostly malignantly); to fascinate or charm. — *n* **bewitch'ery**. — *adj* **bewitch'ing** charming; enchanting. — *adv* **bewitch'ingly**. — *n* **bewitch'ment**. [**be-** (1)]

bewray[1] *bi-rā'*, (*archaic*) *vt* to reveal, *esp* inadvertently; to betray; to divulge; to show up; to reveal the existence, presence or whereabouts of. [ME *bewreien*, from *be-*, and OE *wrēgan* to accuse]

bewray[2]. See **beray**.

bey *bā*, *n* a Turkish governor (*hist*); a Turkish title of rank (*hist*); in *mod* Turkey, the usual term of address to adult males, *corresp* to Mr. [Turk]

beyond *bi-yond'*, *prep* on the farther side of; farther on in comparison with; out of reach of; above, superior to, better than; apart from, in addition to. — *adv* farther away; into the hereafter. — *n* (with *the*) the unknown;

the hereafter. — **beyond measure** too great to be measured; excessively; **beyond one** more than one is able to do; outside one's comprehension; **beyond seas** abroad; **go beyond** to surpass, go further than; to circumvent; to overreach (*Bible*; *Shakesp*); **the back of beyond** a place of extreme remoteness; **the (Great) Beyond** the afterlife. [OE *begeondan*, from pfx *be-*, and *geond* across, beyond; see **yon**]

bez, bez-antler, -tine. See **bay**[6].

bezant *bez'ənt* or *biz-ant'*, *n* a gold coin first struck at Byzantium or Constantinople; a small yellow circle like a gold coin (*heraldry*).

bezazz. See **bezzazz**.

bezel *bez'l*, *n* the part of the setting of a precious stone which encloses it; an oblique side or face of a cut gem; the grooved rim in which a watch-glass, etc is set; a sloped cutting edge (eg of a chisel; *usu* **basil** *baz'l*); an indicator light on a car dashboard. [From an OFr word represented by mod Fr *biseau*; ultimate origin uncertain]

bezique *bi-zēk'*, *n* a card-game for two, three or four people, played with two packs, from which all cards below the seven have been removed; the winning combination at this game of the knave of diamonds and queen of spades. [Fr *besigue*, of obscure origin]

bezoar *bē'zör*, *n* a stony concretion found in the stomachs of goats, antelopes, llamas, etc, formerly thought to be an antidote to all poisons. — *adj* **bezoardic** (*bez-ō-ärd'ik*). [Through Sp *bezoar* and Ar *bāzahr*, from Pers *pādzahr* antidote, from *zahr* poison]

bezonian or **besonian** *bi-zō'nyən*, (*Shakesp*) *n* a beggar. [Ital *bisogno* need]

bezzazz, bezaz, bazzazz, bazazz, bizzazz or **bizazz** *bə-zaz'*, (*colloq*) *n* variants of **pizzazz**.

bezzle *bez'l*, (*obs*) *vi* to drink hard. — *vt* to squander; to despoil; to consume. [OFr *besiler*. See **embezzle**]

bf *abbrev*: brought forward (as in accounts, etc); bloody fool (*vulg*).

BFPO *abbrev*: British Forces Post Office (abroad).

BG *abbrev*: Bulgaria (IVR).

BH *abbrev*: British Honduras (IVR).

Bhagavad Gita *bäg'ə-vəd gē'tə*, or *bug'ə-*, *n* a sacred Hindu text, part of the Mahabharata. [Sans, song of the blessed one]

bhajan *buj'ən*, *n* a Hindu religious song. [Sans]

bhajee or **bhagee** *bä'jē*, *n* (in Indian cookery) an appetizer consisting of vegetables cooked in batter.

bhakti *buk'ti*, *n* (in Hinduism) devotion to a god, as a path to salvation; a form of yoga. [Sans, portion]

bhang *bang*, *n* a narcotic and intoxicant, the leaves and shoots of hemp. [Hindi *bhā̃g*; Pers *bang*; Sans *bhaṅga*]

bhangra *bung'ru* or *bang'rə*, *n* a combination of traditional Punjabi and Western pop music. — Also *adj*.

bharal *bur'əl*, *n* the blue sheep of the Himalaya, *Pseudois nayaur*. — Also **burrel, burrell, burrhel** or **burhel**. [Hindi]

Bharat *bu'rut*, *n* Hindi name of the Republic of India. — *adj* **Bha'rati**. [*Bharata* legendary monarch]

Bharata Natyam *bur'ə-tə nat'yəm*, *n* a form of Hindu temple dance originating in the Madras region, first described by the sage *Bharata*.

BHC *abbrev*: benzene hexachloride.

bhel. See **bael**.

bhindi *bin'di*, *n* okra as used in Indian cookery. [Hindi]

bhisti, bheesty, bheestie or **bhistee** *bēs'tē*, *n* an Indian water carrier. [Urdu *bhīstī*, from Pers *behistī*, from *bihisht* paradise]

bhp *abbrev*: brake horse-power.

Bhs or (formerly) **BHS** *abbrev*: British Home Stores (a department store).

Bi (*chem*) *symbol*: bismuth.

bi *bī*, (*colloq*) *adj* short for **bisexual**. — Also *n*: — *pl* **bi's**.

bi- *bī-*, sometimes **bin-** *bin-* before a vowel, *pfx* two, twice, double. [L *bis* twice, two-, *bīnī* two by two, for *duis*, *duīnī*]

biannual *bī-an'ū-əl*, *adj* happening, etc twice a year, half-yearly. — *n* (rarely) a biennial. — *adv* **biann'ually**. [L *bi-* twice, two-, and *annus* year]

bias *bī'əs*, *n* a one-sided mental inclination; a prejudice; any special influence that sways one's thinking; an unevenness or imbalance, *esp* in distribution or sampling of statistics; (in the game of bowls) a bulge or greater weight on one side of a bowl making it turn to one side; a turning to one side by a bowl; a slanting line or cut diagonally across the grain of a fabric; the voltage applied to certain electronic components to cause them to function in a given direction only. — *adj* cut slantwise. — *adv* slantwise. — *vt* to prejudice or influence, *esp* unfairly; to affect so as to cause movement etc in one direction rather than another; to cut on the slant: — *pr p* **bī'asing** (also **bī'assing**); *pa t* and *pa p* **bī'ased** (also **bī'assed**). — *n* **bī'asing**. — **bias binding** (a long narrow folded piece of) material cut slantwise to provide stretch and used for binding *esp* curved edges in sewing; **bī'as-drawing** (*Shakesp*) a turning awry. [Fr *biais* slant; of unknown origin]

biathlon *bī-ath'lon*, (*sport*) *n* a competition in cross-country skiing and shooting. — *n* **biath'lete**. [L *bi-* two-, and Gr *athlon* a contest]

biaxial *bī-aks'i-əl*, *adj* having two (optic, etc) axes. — Also **biax'al**. [**bi-**]

Bib. *abbrev*: Bible.

bib *bib*, *n* a cloth or plastic shield put under a young child's chin; (of an apron, overalls, etc) the front part above the waist; a vest bearing their number worn by competing athletes, etc; the pout, a fish of the cod and haddock genus with a large chin barbel. — *vt* and *vi* to drink, to tipple. — *adj* **bibā'cious**. — *n* **bibā'tion** tippling. — *n* **bibb'er** a tippler; chiefly used as a combining form, eg (*Bible*) *wine-bibber*. — *n* **bib'ful** see **spill a bibful** below. — **bib'cock** a tap with downturned nozzle. — **best bib and tucker** (*colloq*) best clothes; **bib and brace** applied to overalls with a front bib and straps over the shoulders; **spill a bibful** (*slang*) to give away a secret, make an embarrassing revelation. [Prob from L *bibere* to drink; perh partly imit]

bibble-babble *bib'l-bab'l*, (*Shakesp*) *n* idle talk. [Reduplication of **babble**]

Bibby *bib'i*, *n* a stateroom on a passageway in a ship. [Name of a shipping line]

bibelot *bēb'lō*, *n* a knick-knack. [Fr]

bibl. *abbrev*: biblical; bibliographical; bibliography.

bible *bī'bl*, *n* (*usu* with *cap*) (the book containing) the Scriptures of the Old and New Testaments; (*usu* with *cap*) a comprehensive book regarded as the ultimate authority on its subject; the third stomach of a ruminant, with many folds like the leaves of a book. — *adj* **biblical** (*bib'li-kəl*) of, like or relating to the Bible. — *adv* **bib'lically**. — *n* **bib'licism** (*-sizm*) biblical doctrine, learning or literature; literal interpretation and acceptance of the Bible. — *n* **bib'licist** or **bib'list** a person skilled in biblical learning; a person who makes the Bible the sole rule of faith (*obs*); a person who interprets and accepts the Bible literally. — **Bible belt** those areas of the Southern USA of predominantly fundamentalist and puritanical Christian religious dogma; **Bible paper** very thin strong paper for printing; **Bi'ble-pounder** or **-thumper** a vigorous, aggressive or dogmatic Christian preacher. — *n* and *adj* **Bī'ble-pounding** or **-thumping**. [Fr, from LL *biblia*, fem sing (earlier neuter pl) from Gr *biblia* books, esp the canonical books (sing *biblion* a book, dimin of *biblos* papyrus, paper)]

bibli- *bib'li-*, *combining form* denoting book or books. — *n* **bibliographer** (*-og'rə-fər*) a person versed in bibliography; the compiler of a bibliography. — *adj* **bibliographic** (*-ə-graf'ik*) or **bibliograph'ical** (*-əl*). — *n* **bibliog'raphy** the study, description or knowledge of books, in regard to their outward form, authors, subjects, editions and history; a list of books on a particular subject or by a single author; a list of the works referred to in the process of writing a book, article, etc. — *n* **bibliolater** (*-ol'ə-tər*) or **bibliol'atrist** a person given to bibliolatry. — *adj* **bibliol'atrous**. — *n* **bibliol'atry** (Gr *latreiā* worship) a superstitious reverence for a book, *esp* the Bible. — *adj* **bibliological** (*-ō-loj'i-kəl*). — *n* **bibliologist** (*-ol'ə-jist*). — *n* **bibliol'ogy** bibliography; book-lore. — *n* **bib'liomancy** (*-man-si*; Gr *manteiā* divination) divination by opening the Bible or other book at random. — *n* **bib'liomane**. — *n* **bibliomā'nia** (Gr *maniā*, madness) a mania for collecting or possessing books; love of books. — *adj* **bibliomā'niac**. — *adj* **bibliomaniacal** (*-mə-nī'ə-kəl*). — *adj* **bibliopegic** (*-pej'ik*; Gr *pēgnynai* to fix). — *n* **bibliopegist** (*-op'i-jist*) a bookbinder; a fancier of bindings. — *n* **bibliop'egy** the fine art of bookbinding. — *n* **bibliophagist** (*-of'ə-jist*; Gr *phagein* to eat) a voracious reader. — *n* **bib'liophil** or **bibliophile** (*-fil, -fīl*; Gr *philos* friend) a lover or collector of books. — Also *adj*. — *n* **biblioph'ilism**. — *n* **biblioph'ilist**. — *n* **biblioph'ily**. — *n* **bibliophō'bia** (Gr *phobeein* to fear) hatred of books. — *n* **bib'liopole** (Gr *pōlēs* seller) a bookseller. — *adj* **bibliopolic** (*-pol'ik*) or **bibliopol'ical** (*-əl*). — *n* **bibliop'olist**. — *n* **bibliop'oly** bookselling. — *n* **bibliothē'ca** (Gr *bibliothēkē* from *thēkē* repository) a library; a bibliography; a series of books. — *n* **biblioth'ecary** (*rare*) a librarian. [Gr *biblion* book; cf **Bible**]

biblio. or **bibliog.** *abbrev*: bibliography.

bibulous *bib'ū-ləs*, *adj* addicted to strong drink; absorbent of liquid. — *adv* **bib'ulously**. — *n* **bib'ulousness**. [L *bibulus*, from *bibere* to drink]

bicameral *bī-kam'ər-əl*, *adj* (of a legislative body) having two chambers. — *n* **bicam'eralism**. — *n* **bicam'eralist** an advocate of the bicameral parliamentary system. [L *bi*-two-, and *camera* chamber]

bicarbonate *bī-kär'bən-āt*, *n* an acid salt of carbonic acid; sodium bicarbonate, used in baking-powder or as an antacid digestive remedy (*colloq* short form **bicarb**'). [**bi-** twice, and **carbonate**]

BICC *abbrev*: British Insulated Callender's Cables.

biccy *bik'i*, (*colloq*) *n* short form of biscuit: — *pl* **bicc'ies**.

bice *bīs*, *n* a pale blue or green paint. [Fr *bis*]

bicentenary *bi-sen-tēn'ər-i* or *-ten'ər-i*, or (*esp NAm*) **bicentennial** *bī-sen-ten'i-əl*, *adj* happening every two hundred years; pertaining to a two-hundredth anniversary. — *n* a two-hundredth anniversary. [L *bi-* two-, and *centēnārius* pertaining to a hundred, from *centum* a hundred; or *bi-*, *centum* and *annus* a year]

biceps *bī'seps*, *n* a muscle with two heads, *esp* that at the front of the upper arm or that at the back of the thigh. — *adj* **bicipital** (*-sip'*) of or relating to the biceps; two-headed. [L *biceps* two-headed, from *bi-* two-, and *caput* head]

bichon frise *bē'shɔ̃ frē-zā'*, *n* a modern breed of small dog with curly white coat. [Fr *bichon* a breed of lapdog, and *frisé* curly]

bichord *bī'körd*, *adj* (of a musical instrument) having paired strings in unison for each note. [L *bi-* two-, and **chord**[2]]

bichromate *bī-krō'māt*, *n* a dichromate, or salt of dichromic acid. [**bi-**]

bicipital. See **biceps**.

bicker[1] *bik'ər*, *vi* to argue in a petty way, squabble; to quiver; to glitter; (of running water) to run quickly and noisily; to patter. — *n* a fight, a quarrel; a clattering noise; a rapid, noisy, short run (*Scot*). [Of unknown origin]

bicker[2] *bik'ər*, (*Scot*) *n* a bowl, *esp* of wood, for holding liquor; a vessel of wooden staves for porridge. [Scot form of **beaker**]

bick-iron *bik'-ī-ərn*, *n* a small anvil with two horns; the tapered end of an anvil. [From earlier *bickern*, a two-horned anvil, from Fr *bigorne*, from L *bicornis* two-horned]

biconcave *bī-kon'kāv*, *adj* concave on both sides. [**bi-**]

biconvex *bi-kon'veks*, *adj* convex on both sides. [**bi-**]

bicorn or **bicorne** *bī'kōrn*, *adj* two-horned; two-cornered. — *n* (*military, formal* or *hist*) a hat with brim folded up on both sides, forming two corners (worn either front-to-back or side-to-side). [L *bicornis* two-horned, from *bi-* two-, and *cornū* a horn]

bicorporate *bī-kör'pər-āt*, (*heraldry*) *adj* double-bodied, as the head of a lion to which two bodies are attached. [**bi-**]

bicultural *bī-kul'chə-rəl*, *adj* of, having, containing or consisting of two distinct cultures. — *n* **bicul'turalism**. [**bi-**]

bicuspid *bī-kus'pid*, *adj* having two cusps. — *n* a tooth located between the molars and the canine teeth, a premolar. — *adj* **bicusp'idate**. [**bi-**]

bicycle *bī'si-kl*, *n* a vehicle with two wheels, one directly in front of the other, driven by pedals or (**mo'tor-bicycle**) a motor. — Now commonly in short form **bike**. — *vi* to ride a bicycle. — *n* **bī'cyclist**. — **bicycle chain** the chain transmitting motion from the pedals to the wheels of a bicycle; **bicycle clip** a metal clip for holding a cyclist's trousers closely to his or her leg to avoid fouling the wheels, etc; **bicycle polo** see under **polo**[1]; **bicycle pump** a hand pump for inflating bicycle tyres. [L *bi-* two-, and Gr *kyklos* a circle or wheel]

bid[1] *bid*, *vt* to offer, *esp* to offer to pay at an auction; to propose (how many tricks one will win, eg in bridge); to proclaim (eg the banns of marriage). — *vi* to make an offer or proposal: — *pr p* **bidd'ing**; *pa t* **bade** (*bad*; also, *esp poetic*, *bād*) or **bid**; *pa p* **bidd'en** or **bid**. — *n* an offer of a price; the amount offered; an attempt to win or achieve something (*journalism*); a call (*cards*). — *adj* **bidd'able** tractable, easily persuaded or controlled; capable of or fit for bidding (*cards*). — *n* **bidd'er**. — *n* **bidd'ing** an offer, the offering of a price; the act or process of making bids (*cards*); the bids made (*cards*). — **bid price** the price investors have to pay when buying shares. — **bid fair** to seem likely; **bid in** (of an owner or his or her agent) in an auction, to overbid the highest offer; **bid/offer spread** the overall cost (expressed as a percentage) of investing in unit trusts, including the difference in price for buying and selling, the initial charge, and dealing costs; **bid up** to raise the market price of (something) artificially, by means of specious bids, etc. [OE *bēodan*; Gothic *biudan*, Ger *bieten* to offer]

bid[2] *bid*, *vt* to invite; to command; to ask for (*archaic*); to pray (*obs*); to greet with, to say as a greeting. — Tenses are as in the preceding verb, with which it has been confused. — *n* **bidd'ing** a command; an invitation. — **bidd'ing-prayer** *orig* the praying, or saying, of a prayer, then by confusion with **bid**[1] taken to mean enjoining or inviting of prayer; a petitionary prayer said just before the sermon; a prayer of intercession for the living and the dead, said in English churches until the Reformation. [OE *biddan*; Gothic *bidjan*; Ger *bitten*. See **bead**]

bidarka *bī-där'kə*, *n* an Alaskan Eskimo kayak. [Russ *baidarka*, dimin of *baidara* an umiak]

biddy *bid'i*, *n* a chicken, a hen (*dialect*); in *Shakesp* applied to Malvolio; an old woman (*slang* and *derog*). — **red biddy** see **red**. [Poss the woman's name *Biddy* (short for *Bridget*), but perh the first meaning is another word]

bide *bīd*, *vi* (*archaic* or *Scot*) to wait; to dwell; to remain. — *vt* to await (*obs* except in *bide one's time* to await a favourable moment); to face unflinchingly (*poetic*); to endure: — *pa t* **bīd'ed**, **bode**, (*Shakesp*) **bid**, or (*Scot*) **bade** (*bād*); *pa p* **bīd'ed** or (*obs* and *Scot*) **bidd'en**. — *n* **bīd'ing** (*Shakesp*) residence, habitation. — **bī'die-in** (*Scot, colloq*) a resident lover. [OE *bīdan*; but sometimes for **abide**]

bident *bī'dənt*, *n* a two-pronged tool; a two-year-old sheep. — *adj* **bidental** (*bī-dent'l*) two-pronged; two-toothed. — *n* (*Roman antiq*) a place struck by lightning (possibly consecrated by sacrifice of a sheep). — *adj* **bīdent'āte** or **bīdentāt'ed** two-toothed. [L *bi-* two, and *dēns*, *dentis* a tooth]

bidet *bē'dā* or *bi-det'*, *n* a basin on a low pedestal, for washing the genital and anal areas, etc; a small horse (*archaic*). [Fr, pony]

bidirectional *bī-dī-rek'shə-nəl, adj* operating in two directions; printing the lines of a text alternately left to right and right to left (*comput*, etc).

bidon *bē'dɔ̃, n* a container for liquids, such as a wooden cup, water bottle, tin-can or oil-drum. — *n* **bidonville** (*bē'don-vēl* or *bē-dɔ̃-*) in a French-speaking country, a shanty town with dwellings made from oil-drums. [Fr]

Biedermeier *bē'dər-mī-ər, adj* of a style of furniture derived from the French empire style, common in Germany in the first half of the 19c; (of German painting) of the Romantic Revival; bourgeois, hidebound (*derog*). [Name of a fictitious German poet]

bield *bēld*, (chiefly *Scot*) *n* shelter; protection. — *vt* (*Scott*) to shelter. — *adj* **bield'y**. [Northern; OE *beldo* (WSax *bieldo*) courage; related to **bold**]

bien[1]. Another spelling of **bein**.

bien[2] *byɛ̃*, (*Fr*) *adv* well. — **bien-aimé** (*byɛ̃-ne-mā*) well-beloved; **bien chaussé** (*shō-sā*) well-shod; **bien élevé** (*-nā-ləv-ā*) well brought up, well-mannered; **bien entendu** (*-nã-tã-dü*) of course; it goes without saying; **bien-être** (*-netr*) a sense of wellbeing; **bien pensant** (*pã-sã*) right-thinking; orthodox; **bienséance** (*-sā-ãs*) propriety; (in *pl*) the proprieties.

Biennale *bē-ə-nä'lā, n* an international art festival held regularly in Venice since 1895. [Ital, biennial]

biennial *bī-en'i-əl* or *-en'yəl, adj* lasting two years; happening or appearing once in two years. — *n* a plant that flowers and fruits only in its second year, then dies. — *adv* **bienn'ially**. [L *biennium* two years, from *bi-* two, and *annus* a year]

bier *bēr, n* a stand or frame of wood for carrying a dead person to the grave. — **bier right** (*hist*) the ordeal of appearing before the corpse one was believed to have murdered (which was expected to bleed in the presence of the murderer). [OE *bǣr*; cf Ger *Bahre*, L *feretrum*. From root of verb **bear**[1]]

bierkeller *bēr'kel-ər, n* a German or German-style bar, selling beer. [Ger, beer cellar]

biestings. Same as **beestings**.

bifacial *bī-fā'shl, adj* having two-faces; having two dissimilar sides. [**bi-**]

bifarious *bī-fā'ri-əs, adj* in two rows (*bot*); double (*obs*). — *adv* **bifār'iously**. [L *bifārius* double]

biff *bif*, (*colloq*) *n* a blow. — *vt* to strike hard.

biffin *bif'in, n* a variety of red cooking apple; such an apple slowly dried and flattened into a cake. [For *beefing*, from its colour of raw beef]

bifid *bif'id* or *bī'fid, adj* divided into two parts by a deep split. [L *bifidus*, from *bi-* two, and *findere* to cleave or split]

bifilar *bī-fī'lər, adj* having two threads. [L *bi-* two, and *fīlum* thread]

bifocal *bī-fō'kəl, adj* having two different focal lengths. — *n pl* **bifō'cals** spectacles with bifocal lenses, for far and near vision. [**bi-**]

bifold *bī'fōld, adj* twofold; of two kinds (*Shakesp*). [**bi-**]

bifoliate *bī-fō'li-āt, adj* having two leaves or leaflets. — *adj* **bifō'liolate** having two leaflets. [L *bi-* two-, and *folium* leaf]

biform *bī'fōrm, adj* having two forms. [L *biformis*, from *bi-* two-, and *fōrma* form]

bifurcate *bī'fûr-kāt* or *-fûr', adj* having two prongs or branches. — *vi* to divide into two branches. — *adj* **bī'furcated**. — *n* **bifurcā'tion**. [L *bifurcus*, from *bi-* two-, and *furca* a fork]

big[1] *big, adj* (*compar* **bigg'er**, *superl* **bigg'est**) large or great; grown-up; older (as in *big sister, big brother*); magnanimous, generous (*usu facetious*); loud; pompous, pretentious, boastful; very important, as the *Big Three, Big Four*, etc, leaders, countries, organizations, etc; (of things) significant, considerable; advanced in pregnancy (*obs*). — *adv* (*colloq*) boastfully or ambitiously, as in *talk big*; greatly or impressively; on a grand scale, as in *think big*. — *adj* **bigg'ish**. — *n* **bigg'y** or **bigg'ie** (*colloq*) a large or important person or thing. — *n* **big'ness** bulk, size. — **big band** a large jazz- or dance-band. — Also (with *hyphen*) as *adj*. — **Big Bang** or **big bang** the explosion of a small dense mass which some scientists believe to have been the origin of the universe; the changes in the system and rules of the British Stock Exchange instituted on 27 October 1986, in effect deregulating many of its practices and abolishing the distinction between jobbers and brokers. — *adj* **big-bell'ied** having a big belly; pregnant (with). — **Big Ben** the bell in the clock tower of the Houses of Parliament, London; the tower itself; the clock itself; **Big Blue** a nickname for the IBM computer company; **Big Board** (*US colloq*; also without *caps*) the New York Stock Exchange; **Big Brother** a dictator, as in George Orwell's *Nineteen Eighty-four* (1949); a powerful leader or organization, regarded as ubiquitous and sinister; **Big Brotherism**; **big bucks** or **big money** (*slang*) large amounts of money; **big'-bud** a swelling of currant buds owing to a gall-mite; **big business** large business enterprises and organizations, *esp* collectively; **Big C** (*colloq*) cancer; **big cat** see under **cat**[1]; **big cheese** (*old-fashioned slang*) an important person; **big deal** (*colloq*) used as a scornful response to an offer, boast, etc; **big Daddy** or **big White Chief** (*colloq*; both also **Big**) a paternalistic or domineering head of an organization, etc; **big dipper** a roller-coaster at an amusement park (*orig US*); (with *caps*) the constellation Great Bear (*esp NAm*); **big end** in an internal-combustion engine, the larger end of the connecting rod; **Big-endian** see **Little-endian** under **little**; **big fish** a powerful person; such a person in a criminal organization thought worthy of capture; **big'foot** in the US and Canada, a hairy primate reputed to inhabit wilderness areas, and said to be between 6 and 15 feet tall; **Big Four** a collective name for the four largest UK clearing banks, The Midland, Lloyds, Barclays and the National Westminster; **big guns** (*colloq*) the important, powerful persons in an organization, etc; **big'-head** (*colloq*) a conceited person; conceit (*NAm*). — *adj* **big'headed**. — *adj* **big-heart'ed** generous. — **big'horn** the Rocky Mountain goat or sheep; **big house** prison (*US slang*); the house of the local landowner, a wealthy citizen, or the like; **big money** see **big bucks** above; **big'mouth** (*slang*) a talkative and often boastful or indiscreet person. — *adj* **big'mouthed**. — **big name** (*colloq*) a celebrity; **big noise** (*colloq*) an important person. — *vt* **big'-note** (*Austr colloq*) to boast about oneself, try to make oneself seem important. — **big science** scientific and technical research that requires large financial resources; **big screen** the cinema (as opposed to TV). — Also often (with *hyphen*) as *adj*. — **big shot** see **bigwig** below; **big stick** (*colloq*) a display of force, as threat or means of persuasion. — *adj* **big-tick'et** (*US colloq*) expensive. — **big'-time** (*colloq*) the top level in any pursuit, *esp* show-business. — *adj* at the top level; important. — **big toe** see under **toe**; **big top** a large circular tent used for circus performances; **big wheel** a Ferris wheel; **big White Chief** see **big Daddy** above; an important person (*colloq*); **big'wig** or **big shot** (*colloq*) a powerful person, a person of some importance. — **be big on** (*colloq*) to do a lot of, be strong in (a particular area of work, etc); **go over big (with)** (*colloq*) to impress greatly; **in a big way** to a large extent; vigorously, enthusiastically; **that's big of him** etc (*usu ironic*) that action, etc is generous on his, etc part; **the Big Apple** (also **the Apple**) (*colloq*) New York City; **too big for one's boots** or **breeches** conceited, self-important; **what's the big idea**? what on earth is going on? [ME *big*; origin obscure]

big[2] *big*, (*Scot*) *vt* to build, to pile up. — *n* **bigg'in** anything built, a house. [ON *byggja*, cognate with OE *būian*]

biga *bī'gə* or *bē'ga*, (*Roman antiq*) *n* a two-horse chariot: — *pl* **bi'gae**. [L, earlier in pl, from **bi-** and **jugum** yoke]

bigamy *big'ə-mi, n* the custom, crime or fact of having two wives or husbands at once; a second marriage (*eccles law*). — *n* **big'amist** a person who has committed bigamy. — *adj* **big'amous**. — *adv* **big'amously**. [L *bi-*, two- and Gr *gamos* marriage]

bigarade *bē'ga-räd*, *n* a bitter Seville orange. — **bigarade sauce** a sauce flavoured with these oranges. [Fr]

bigener *bī'jin-ər*, (*bot*) *n* a hybrid between different genera. — *adj* **bigeneric** (*-er'ik*). — **bigeneric hybrid** a hybrid resulting from a cross between individuals from two different genera. [L *bigener* a hybrid]

bigg *big*, *n* four-rowed barley. [ON *bygg*]

biggin[1] *big'in*, (*archaic*) *n* a child's cap or hood; a nightcap; a serjeant-at-law's coif. [Fr *béguin* béguine's cap]

biggin[2]. See **big**[2].

bigha *bē'gə*, *n* a land measure in India, locally $\frac{1}{3}$ to $\frac{2}{3}$ of an acre. [Hindi]

bight *bīt*, *n* a wide bay; a bend or coil (in a rope, etc). [OE *byht*; cf Dan and Swed *bugt*, Du *bocht*]

bignonia *big-nō'ni-ə*, *n* any member of the *Bignonia* genus of tropical plants with trumpet-shaped flowers, giving name to the family **Bignoniā'ceae**. — *adj* **bignoniā'ceous**. [Named after the Abbé *Bignon*, Louis XIV's librarian]

bigot *big'ət*, *n* a person blindly and obstinately devoted to a particular set of ideas, creed or political party, and dismissive towards others. — *adj* **big'oted** having the qualities of a bigot. — *n* **big'otry** blind or excessive zeal, *esp* in religious, political or racial matters. [OFr; origin disputed]

biguanide *bī-gwä'nīd*, *n* one of a group of drugs used in the treatment of late onset diabetes. [**bi-** and *guan*idine and **-ide**]

Bihari *bi-hä'ri*, *n* an inhabitant or native of Bihar in NE India; the language of this people. — *adj* of or relating to Bihar, its people or language. [Hindi].

bijection *bī-jek'shən*, (*math*) *n* a mapping function that is both an injection and a surjection. [**bi-**, and *-jection* from L *jacere* to throw]

bijou *bē'zhōō*, *n* a trinket; a jewel: — *pl* **bijoux** (*bē'zhōōz*). — *adj* small and elegant. — *n* **bijouterie** (*bē-zhōōt'ər-ē*) jewellery, *esp* trinkets. [Fr]

bijwoner. Same as **bywoner**.

bike[1] *bīk*, (*colloq*) *n* and *vi* short form of **bicycle** or **motorbike**. — *n* **bī'ker** or (*Austr* and *NZ colloq*) **bī'kie** a member of a gang of motorcycle riders. — *n* **bī'king**. — **bike'way** (*NAm*) a lane, road, etc exclusively for pedal cycles. — **get off one's bike** (*Austr slang*) to lose control of oneself; **on your bike** (*slang*) a contemptuous expression of dismissal.

bike[2] or **byke** *bīk*, (*Scot*) *n* a nest of wasps, wild bees, etc; a swarm of people. — *vi* to swarm. [Origin unknown]

bikini *bi-kē'ni*, *n* a brief swimming-costume, in two separate parts. [From *Bikini*, an atoll of the Marshall Islands, scene of atom-bomb experiments in the late 1940s; the bikini's effects on men were reputed to be similar]

bilabial *bī-lā'bi-əl*, (*phonetics*) *adj* produced by contact or approximation of the two lips, eg b or w. — *n* a bilabial consonant. — *adj* **bīlā'biate** (*bot*) two-lipped, like some corollas. [L *bi-* two- and *labium* a lip]

bilander *bī'land-ər*, *n* a two-masted cargo vessel used in Holland. — Also **by'lander**. [Du *bijlander*]

bilateral *bī-lat'ər-əl*, *adj* having or involving two sides; affecting two parties or participants mutually. — *n* **bilat'eralism** two-sidedness; equality in value of trade between two countries. — *adv* **bilat'erally**. [L *bi-* two, and *latus*, *lateris* side]

bilberry *bil'bər-i*, *n* a whortleberry shrub; its dark-blue berry. [Cf Dan *böllebær*]

bilbo *bil'bō*, *n* a rapier or sword: — *pl* **bil'boes** or **bil'bos**. [From *Bilbao*, in Spain]

bilboes *bil'bōz*, *n pl* a bar with sliding shackles for confining prisoners' ankles. [Perh connected with **bilbo**]

Bildungsroman *bil'dōōngs-rō-män* or *-dōōngz-*, (*Ger*) *n* a novel concerning the early emotional or spiritual development or education of its hero.

bile *bīl*, *n* a thick bitter fluid secreted by the liver as an aid to digestion; excess or disturbance of its secretion; either of two (out of the four) humours of early physiology, of which **yellow bile** (also known as *choler*) was associated with anger, and **black bile** with melancholy; irritability, ill-temper. — *adj* **biliary** (*bil'yər-i*) of the bile, the bile-ducts or the gall bladder. — *n* short form of **biliary fever**, infectious canine jaundice. — *adj* **bilious** (*bil'yəs*) pertaining to or affected by bile; irritable, bad-tempered; (of colours) very unpleasant, sickly. — *adv* **bil'iously**. — *n* **bil'iousness**. — **bile'-ducts** the ducts that convey the bile to the small intestine. [Fr, from L *bīlis*]

bilge *bilj*, *n* the bulging part of a cask; the broadest part of a ship's bottom; the lowest internal part of the hull, below the floorboards (also in *pl*); filth, dirty water, etc such as collects there; rubbish, drivel (*slang*). — *vi* (of a ship) to spring a leak in the bilge. — *adj* **bilg'y** having the appearance and disagreeable smell of bilge-water. — **bilge'-keel** a ridge along the bilge of a ship to prevent or reduce rolling; **bilge'-pump**; **bilge'-water**. [Perh altered from **bulge**]

Bilharzia *bil-här'zi-ə* or *-tsi-ə*, *n* a genus of parasitic worms with adhesive suckers, infesting human and other blood, with two larval stages, first in water-snails and then in man. — *n* **bilharz'ia**, **bilharzī'asis** or **bilharziō'sis** a disease (also known as schistosomiasis) caused by these worms, common in tropical countries, *esp* Egypt and other parts of Africa. [From Theodor *Bilharz* (1825–62), a German parasitologist]

bilian *bil'i-an*, *n* a heavy ant-proof lauraceous timber tree of Borneo. [Malay]

biliary. See **bile**.

bilimbi *bil-im'bi*, *n* an East Indian tree of the wood-sorrel family; its acid fruit. — Also **bilim'bing**, **blim'bing**. [Dravidian and Malay]

bilingual *bī-ling'gwəl*, *adj* expressed in two languages; speaking two languages, *esp* as mother tongues or with similar fluency. — *n* **bīling'ualism**. — *adv* **biling'ually**. — *n* **bīling'uist**. [L *bilinguis*, from *bi-* two-, and *lingua* tongue]

bilious. See **bile**.

bilirubin *bil-i-rōō'bin*, *n* an orange pigment in bile. — *n* **biliver'din** a green pigment in bile. [L *bīlis* bile, and *ruber* red, or *verd* as in *verdure*]

biliteral *bī-lit'ər-əl*, *adj* of or involving two letters; written in two scripts. [L *bi-* two-, and *lītera*, *littera* a letter]

biliverdin. See **bilirubin**.

bilk *bilk*, *vt* to elude; to cheat; to avoid paying someone what is due. — *n* **bilk'er**. [Perh a form of **balk**; orig a term in cribbage]

Bill *bil*, (*slang*) *n* (with *the*) (members of) the police force. [**Old Bill**, qv under **old**]

bill[1] *bil*, *n* a concave battle-axe with a long wooden handle; a billhook. — **bill'hook** a cutting tool with a long blade and wooden handle in the same line with it, often with a hooked tip, used in eg pruning; **bill'man** a soldier armed with a bill. [OE *bil*]

bill[2] *bil*, *n* the beak of a bird, or anything similar in shape or function; a sharp promontory; the point of an anchor fluke (*naut*). — *vi* to touch bills as doves do; hence, to caress or talk fondly. — *combining form* **-billed** (*-bild*) having a bill of the stated type. — *n* and *adj* **bill'ing**. — **bill'board** (*naut*) a board used to protect a ship's planking from damage by the bills when the anchor is weighed; **bill'-fish** (*NAm*) any of a number of fish with elongated jaws. [OE *bile*, related to **bill**[1]]

bill[3] *bil*, *n* a written account of money owed; a draft of a proposed law; a bill of exchange, a promissory note; a bank-note (*NAm*); a poster advertising an event, product, etc (often as a *combining form*, as in *playbill*, *handbill*); a slip of paper serving as an advertisement; a list of performers, etc in order of importance; a programme of entertainment; any written statement of particulars; a written accusation of serious crime (*Eng criminal law*). — *vt* to send an invoice to; to announce or advertise; to enter (items) on a statement (*obs*). — *adj* **billed** (*bild*) named in a list or advertisement. — *n* **bill'ing** the making out or sending of bills or invoices; the (total amount of) money received from customers or clients; advertising by poster; precedence of naming in an announcement or poster, eg *top billing*, *second billing*, etc. — **bill'board** (chiefly *NAm*) a board on which large advertising posters are stuck, a hoarding; **bill'book** a book used in commerce in which an entry is made of all bills accepted and received; **bill'-broker** a person who deals in bills of exchange and promissory notes; **bill'-chamber** a department of the Scottish Court of Session dealing with summary business; **bill'-discounter** a person who discounts or advances the amount of bills of exchange and notes which have some time to run; **bill'fold** (*NAm*) a soft case or wallet for paper money; **bill'head** a form used for business accounts, with name and address printed at the top; **bill'poster** or **bill'sticker** a person who sticks up bills or posters. — **bill of adventure** a document produced by a merchant stating that goods shipped by him, and in his name, are the property of another, whose adventure or chance the transaction is; **bill of costs** an account of a solicitor's charges and outgoings in the conduct of the client's business; **bill of exceptions** a statement of objections by way of appeal against the ruling or direction of a judge; **bill of exchange** a document promising payment of a certain sum on a certain date by one party or another; a document employed by the parties to a business transaction whereby payment is made through a mutually convenient third party, thereby avoiding the cost and complications of foreign exchange; **bill of fare** a list of dishes or articles of food, a menu; **bill of health** an official certificate of the state of health on board ship before sailing; **bill of indictment** a statement of a charge made against a person; **bill of lading** a document signed by the shipowner or his master or agent, stating that specified goods have been shipped or received for shipment, and specifying the terms and conditions under which they are being transported; **bill of mortality** (*hist*) an official return of births and deaths in the London area (hence **within the bills of mortality** within the London district for which such returns were made); **bill of quantities** a list of items giving the quantities of material and brief descriptions of work comprised in an engineering or building works contract (*building*, *civ eng*); **bill of rights** see under **right**[1]; **bill of sale** (*Eng law*) a formal deed transferring the ownership (but not the possession) of goods; **bill of sight** permission to land imported goods of which the merchant does not know the quantity or the quality; **bill of store** a licence from the customs authorities to reimport British goods formerly exported; **bill of victualling** a victualling-bill (qv); **clean bill of health** a certificate stating that there is no illness on board a ship; a statement that a person is healthy; a statement that an organization, etc is in a good condition; **double** (or **triple**) **bill** a programme of entertainment consisting of two (or three) main items, *esp* films; **fill the bill** see under **fill**[1]; **top the bill** to head the list of performers, be the star attraction. [LL *billa*, from L *bulla* a knob, a seal, hence a document bearing a seal, etc; cf **bull**[2]]

billabong *bil'ə-bong*, (*Austr*) *n* a cut-off loop of a river, replenished only by floods; an offshoot from a river (strictly one that does not rejoin it). [Aboriginal *billa* river, and *bung* dead]

billboard. See **bill**[2,3].

billet[1] *bil'it*, *n* a note or letter assigning quarters to soldiers or others; the quarters requisitioned; an allocated sleeping- or resting-place; a job or occupation; a little note or document. — *vt* to quarter or accommodate (eg soldiers): — *pr p* **bill'eting**; *pa t* and *pa p* **bill'eted**. [OFr *billette*, dimin of *bille*; see **bill**[3]]

billet[2] *bil'it*, *n* a small log of wood used as fuel; a piece of timber sawn on three sides and rounded on the fourth; a bar of metal; an ornament in Norman architecture in the form of short cylinders with spaces between; a bearing in the form of an upright rectangle (*heraldry*). — **bill'et-head** a piece of wood round which the harpoon-line runs. [Fr *billette*, from *bille* the young trunk of a tree; origin unknown]

billet-doux *bil-i-do͞o'* or *bē-yä-do͞o'*, *n* a love-letter: — *pl* **billets-doux'** (same pronunciation as the *sing*). [Fr *billet* letter, and *doux* sweet]

billiards *bil'yərdz*, *n sing* any of various games played with a cue and balls on a rectangular table, the table in the most common version having pockets at the sides and corners, into which the balls can be struck. — *adj* **bill'iard**. — **bill'iard-ball**; **bill'iard-cloth** a green cloth for covering a billiard-table; **bill'iard-marker** a person who marks the points made by the players; **bill'iard-cue**; **bill'iard-table**. [Fr *billard*, from *bille* a stick, hence a cue]

billie. See **billy**.

billingsgate *bil'ingz-gāt*, *n* foul and abusive language. [From *Billingsgate* the former London fish-market]

Billings method *bil'ingz meth'əd*, *n* a rhythm method of contraception involving the examination of the discharge from the cervix. [Dr Evelyn *Billings*, an Australian physician]

billion *bil'yən*, *n* in Britain, France (since 1948), etc, a million millions (unit and twelve zeros); in NAm, and often now in Britain, one thousand millions (unit and nine zeros), a milliard. — *n* **billionaire'** a person who is worth a billion pounds, dollars, etc. — *adj* and *n* **bill'ionth**. [**bi-** and **million**]

billon *bil'ən*, *n* base metal; *esp* an alloy of silver with copper, tin, or the like. [Fr, from same root as **billet**[2]]

billow *bil'ō*, *n* a great wave; a wave, the sea (*poetic*). — *vi* to roll or swell in great waves or clouds; to bulge (out), as a sail in the wind. — *adj* **bill'owed**. — *adj* **bill'owing**. — *adj* **bill'owy**. [Appar ON *bylgja*; Swed *bölja*, Dan *bölge* wave]

billy or **billie** *bil'i*, *n* a cylindrical container with a wire handle and lid for boiling water, cooking, etc out of doors (also **bill'y-can**); a brother (*Scot*); a comrade, a companion-in-arms (*Scot*); a truncheon (*NAm*): — *pl* **bill'ies**. — **bill'y-goat** a he-goat. [Prob from *Bill*, a familiar abbrev of William]

billyboy *bil'i-boi*, *n* a cargo boat. [Prob connected with **bilander**]

Billy Bunter *bil'i bun'tər*, *n* the type of a fat, greedy, clumsy schoolboy. [Name of a character in stories by Frank Richards (pseudonym of Charles Hamilton, 1875–1961)]

billy-can. See **billy**.

billycock *bil'i-kok*, *n* a hard felt hat. [Poss from *William Coke*, nephew of Earl (1837) of Leicester, or from 19c Cornish hatter *William Cock*]

billy-oh or **billy-o** *bil'i-ō*, *n* in phrase **like billy-oh** or **billy-o** vigorously, fiercely. [Origin obscure]

bilobar *bī-lō'bər*, **bilobate** *bī-lō'bāt* or **bilobed** *bī'lōbd*, *adj* having two lobes. — *adj* **bilobular** (*bī-lob'ū-lər*) having two lobules. [L *bi-* two-, and **lobe** or **lobule**]

bilocation *bī-lō-kā'shən*, *n* the power of being in two places at the same time. [Coined from L *bi-* two-, and **location**]

bilocular *bī-lok'ū-lər*, *adj* divided into two cells. [L *bi-* two-, and *loculus*, dimin of *locus* place]

biltong *bil'tong* (*SAfr*) *n* sun-dried lean meat. [Du *bil* buttock, and *tong* tongue]

BIM *abbrev*: British Institute of Management.

Bim *bim*, (*slang*) *n* an inhabitant of Barbados.

Bimana *bim'ə-nə* or *bī-mā'nə*, *n pl* two-handed animals, an obsolete name for mankind. — *adj* **bim'anal** or **bim'anous**. [L *bi-* two- , and *manus* hand]

bimanual *adj* using or performed with both hands. — *adv* **biman'ually**. [**bi-**]

bimbashi *bim-bä'shē*, *n* a military officer (in Turkey or Egypt). [Turk *bin* thousand, and *baş* head]

bimbo *bim'bō*, (*slang*, *usu contemptuous*) *n* a person, now *usu* a woman, *esp* one who is young and physically very attractive but dim, naive or superficial; a youngster: — *pl* **bim'bos**. — *n* **bimbette'** (*slang*) a particularly dim, etc female bimbo. [Ital, child]

bimestrial *bī-mes'tri-əl*, *adj* of two months' duration. [L *bimestris*, from *bi-*, and *mēnsis* a month]

bimetallic *bī-mi-tal'ik, adj* composed of, or using, two metals; (of a monetary system) in which gold and silver are used in fixed relative values. — *n* **bimetallism** (*bī-met'əl-izm*) such a system. — *n* and *adj* **bimet'allist**. — **bimetallic strip** a strip formed by bonding two metals one of which expands more than the other, so that it bends with change of temperature, used in thermostatic switches, etc.

bimillenary *bī-mil'in-ər-i, n* a period of two thousand years; a two thousandth anniversary. — Also *adj*. [**bi-**]

bimillennium *bī-mil-en'i-əm, n*. Same as **bimillenary**: — *pl* **bimillen'iums** or **bimillen'ia**. [**bi-**]

bimodal *bī-mō'dəl, (statistics) adj* having two modes. — *n* **bimodal'ity**. [**bi-** and **mode**]

bimolecular *bī-mə-lek'ū-lər, (chem) adj* involving two molecules. [**bi-** and **molecule**]

bimonthly *bī-munth'li, adj* or *adv* (happening, etc) once in two months; (happening, etc) twice a month. [**bi-** and **month**]

bin[1] *bin, n* a container for rubbish; a container for storing or displaying goods; a stand or case with compartments in which to store bottled wine in a wine-cellar; the wine contained in it; short for **loon'y-bin**, a lunatic asylum (*slang*); gaol (*slang*); a pocket (*slang*). — *vt* to put (eg bottled wine) into a bin: — *pr p* **binn'ing**; *pa t* and *pa p* **binned**. — **bin'-bag** (*colloq*) a bin-liner; **bin card** a record card detailing the stock level in a storage bin; **bin'-liner** a *usu* plastic bag for lining a rubbish bin or dustbin; **bin'man** a dustman. [OE *binn* a manger]

bin[2] *bin, (Shakesp)* used for **be** and **been**.

bin-. See **bi-**.

binary *bī'nər-i, adj* composed of or relating to two; twofold; expressed in binary notation; relating to two terms (*math, logic*); describing the two-way division of British higher education into universities and the other institutions. — *n* binary notation; a binary star. — **binary code** (*comput*) the encoding of information as a unique set of bits, eg characters as ASCII; **binary coded decimal** (*comput*) a decimal number written in binary code in groups of four bits, with each group representing a single digit of the decimal number (also *abbrev* as **BCD**); **binary digit** (*comput, telecomm*) either of the two digits 0 and 1; the smallest unit of information (*usu abbrev* as **bit**[2]); **binary fission** (*biol*) the division of an organism or cell into two parts; **binary form** (*music*) a form of a movement founded on two themes; **binary notation** a system of numerical notation using the base 2 (instead of 10 as in the decimal system) in which numbers are expressed using only the binary digits; **binary number** a number expressed in binary notation; **binary pulsar** (*astron*) a system consisting of a pulsar and a small companion star rotating round each other; **binary star** (*astron*) a double star revolving about its common centre of gravity; **binary system** a system using binary notation; **binary weapon, munition**, etc a bomb or shell loaded with two separate canisters of non-toxic chemicals, the chemicals combining at the time of firing to produce a lethal compound. [L *bīnārius*, from compound *bīnī* two by two]

binate *bī'nāt, (bot) adj* growing in pairs; double; consisting of two leaflets. [New L *bīnātus*, from L *bīnī* two by two]

binaural *bīn-ö'rəl, adj* having, employing, or relating to two ears; (of sound reproduction) using two sound channels. — *adv* **binaur'ally**. — **binaural effect** the ability to tell the direction from which a sound is coming, as a result of the different arrival times of the sound at a person's two ears. [**bin-** (under **bi-**)]

Binca® *bing'kə, n* an open-weave canvas fabric used for embroidery, etc.

bind *bīnd, vt* to tie or fasten together; to pass or put something round; to restrain; to fix; to sew a border on; to bandage or tie (*up*); to fasten the sections together and put a cover on (a book); to impose an obligation on; to oblige by oath or promise; to contract as an apprentice; to hold or cement firmly; to cause (dry ingredients) to cohere by adding a small amount of liquid (*cookery*); (of frost) to make (the earth) stiff and hard; to constipate; to bore (*old-fashioned slang*). — *vi* to become bound; to chafe, restrict free movement; to complain (*old-fashioned slang*): — *pa t* and *pa p* **bound** (*bownd*). — *n* a tie (*music*); a difficult or annoying situation, a bore (*slang*); the indurated clay between layers of coal; capacity, measure (*Scot*); a stem of the hop or other twiner. — *n* **bind'er** a person who binds (books, sheaves, etc); anything that binds, such as a rope, a bandage, a cementing agent, a tie-beam, a header in masonry, or a case or file for binding loose papers in; an attachment to a reaping-machine for tying the bundles of grain cut and thrown off; a reaping-machine provided with such an attachment. — *n* **bind'ery** a workplace where books are bound. — *adj* **bind'ing** restraining; obligatory; (of specific foods, etc) likely to cause constipation. — *n* the act of someone who binds; anything that binds; the covering of a book. — **binder twine** twine used in a binder; **bind'weed** any of various weeds that trail along the ground and twine themselves around other plants, trees, etc (*esp* one of the genus *Convolvulus*); also (**black bindweed**) a species of *Polygonum*. — **be bound up in** to be wholly devoted to or occupied with; **be bound up with** to be intimately or indissolubly connected with; **bind over** to subject to legal constraint (*esp* not to disturb the peace); **I'll be bound** I'll bet, I'm certain. See also **bound**[1] and **bounden**. [OE *bindan*; cf Ger *binden*, Sans *badhnōti* he binds]

bindi-eye *bin'di-ī, n* an Australian herbaceous plant, *esp* of the genus *Calotis*, with burr-like fruits. [Aboriginal]

bine *bīn, n* the flexible stem of a climbing plant; the stem of the hop. [Orig dialect form of **bind**]

binervate *bī-nûrv'āt, adj* with two ribs or nerves. [**bi-** and **nerve**]

bing[1] *bing, (dialect) n* a heap or pile (*esp* of waste from a coal-mine); a bin. [ON *bingr*]

bing[2] *bing, (obs slang; Scott) vi* to go. [Perh Gipsy]

binge *binj* or *binzh, (colloq) n* a bout of overindulgence, *esp* in eating and drinking. — *vi* to overindulge in this way. — *n* **bin'ger**. [Perh from dialect *binge* to soak]

Binghi *bing'gi, n* (also without *cap*; *Austr slang, usu derog*) an Aboriginal; the archetypal Aboriginal. [Aboriginal, brother]

bingle *bing'gl, n* a hairstyle midway between bob and shingle. — Also *vt*.

bingo[1] *bing'gō, n* a familiar name for brandy. [Prob B, for **brandy**, and **stingo**]

bingo[2] *bing'gō, n* a game in which numbers are called at random which may then be covered on players' cards, prizes being won by the first to cover all or certain of the numbers displayed on a card (cf **housey-housey** under **house**, **lotto** under **lottery**, **tombola**). — *interj* the exclamation made by the first player to finish in this game; an exclamation expressing a sudden discovery, unexpectedness, etc: — *pl* **bing'os**. — **bingo hall**. [Origin uncertain]

bingy *bin'ji (Austr colloq) n* the stomach. [Aboriginal]

bink *bingk, (Scot) n* a bench, a bank, a shelf; a plate-rack; a wasps' or bees' nest. [Northern form of **bench**]

binnacle *bin'ə-kl, (naut) n* the casing in which a ship's compass is kept. [Formerly *bittacle*, from Port *bitācola*, from L *habitāculum* a dwelling-place, from *habitāre* to dwell]

binocle *bin'o-kl* or *-ə-kl, n* a telescope for use with both eyes at once, binoculars. [Ety as for **binocular**]

binocular *bī-* or *bi-nok'ū-lər, n* (*usu* **binoculars**) a binocular telescope; a binocular microscope. — *adj* with two eyes; suitable for use with two eyes; stereoscopic. — *adv* **binoc'ularly**. [L *bīnī* two by two, and *oculus* an eye]

binomial *bī-nōm'i-əl, adj* consisting of two terms, as *a* + *b* (*math*); binominal. — *n* a binomial expression; the two-part Linnaean name of an animal or plant. — **binomial distribution** (*statistics*) the probability distribution of the total number of specified outcomes in a predetermined number of independent trials, each having a constant probability of outcome; **binomial theorem** Newton's theorem giving any power of a binomial. [L *binōmius*]

binominal *bī-nom'in-əl*, *adj* making use of two names, as the Linnaean nomenclature which names every species by giving first the generic and then the specific name. [L *binōmin-*, from *bi-* two- and *nomin-* name]

bint *bint*, (*colloq*, *usu derog*) *n* a girl, woman, girlfriend. [Ar, daughter]

binturong *bin'tū-rong*, *n* a SE Asian prehensile-tailed carnivore, related to the civet. [Malay]

bio *bī'ō* (*pl* **bī'os**) or **biog** *bī'og* or *-og'*, *n* short forms of **biography**.

bio- *bī-ō-*, *combining form* signifying: life; living organisms; life or living organisms in relation to their biological environment; living tissue, as in eg the following. — *n* **bioassay** (*bī-ō-ə-sā'* or *-as'ā*) the assessment of the strength and effect of a drug or other substance by testing it on a living organism and comparing the results with the known results of another drug, etc. — *n sing* **bio-astronaut'ics** the science dealing with the effects of travel in space on living organisms. — *n* **bioavailabil'ity** the extent to which a drug, etc, after administration (eg by mouth), is available to the tissue it is intended to act on. — *adj* **bioavail'able**. — *adj* **biobibliograph'ical** dealing with the life and writings of someone. — *n* **bi'oblast** (Gr *blastos* germ) a hypothetical unit of living matter; a minute granule in protoplasm. — *n* **biocat'alyst** a substance, eg an enzyme, that produces or speeds up a biochemical reaction. — *adj* and *n* **biochem'ical**. — *adv* **biochem'ically**. — *n* **biochem'ist**. — *n* **biochem'istry** the chemistry of living things, physiological chemistry. — *adj* **biocidal** (*-sīd'*) killing living material, pesticidal. — *n* **bi'ocide**. — *n* **bioclimatol'ogy** another name for **biometeorology**. — *n* **biocoenology** (*bī-ō-sēn-ol'ə-ji*) the study of biocoenoses. — *n* **biocoenosis** (*bī-ō-sēn-ō'sis*; Gr *koinos* common) an association of organisms ecologically interdependent: — *pl* **biocoenoses** (*-nō'-sēz*). — *adj* **biocoenotic** (*-not'ik*) ecological. — *n* **bioconver'sion** the conversion of organic matter into usable energy, now *esp* by means of biological processes. — *n pl* **biodā'ta** (*esp US* and *Anglo-Ind*) biographical information, curriculum or curricula vitae. — *adj* **biodegrād'able** (of substances) able to be broken down by bacteria. — *n* **biodegradā'tion** (also **biodeteriorā'tion**). — *adj* **biodestruct'ible** biodegradable. — *n* **biodiver'sity** the diversity of the natural world, ecological variety and richness. — *adj* **biodynam'ic** dealing with the activities of living organisms; (of a system of land cultivation) fertilizing with organic materials only. — *n sing* **biodynam'ics**. — *n* **bioecol'ogy** the branch of ecology dealing with the interrelationship of living organisms and the environment. — *n* **bioelectric'ity** electrical phenomena in plants and animals. — *n sing* **bioenerget'ics** the biology of energy relationships in living organisms or energy changes produced by them. — *n* **bioengineer'**. — *n* **bioengineer'ing** see **biological engineering** under **biology**. — *n sing* **bioeth'ics** the study of the ethical problems produced by medical and biological research, etc. — *n* **biofeed'back** a technique for learning control of autonomic body functions in response to monitoring by electronic instruments such as an electrocardiograph. — *n* **bioflā'vonoid** (also called **citrin**) a vitamin that regulates the permeability of the capillary walls, found in citrus fruit, blackcurrants and rose-hips. — *n* **bi'ogas** domestic or commercial gas obtained by bioconversion. — *n* **bi'ogen** (*-jen*; Gr *genos* race, offspring) a hypothetical unit of protoplasm. — *n* **biogen'esis** (Gr *genesis* production) the derivation of living things from living things only; biogeny. — *adj* **biogenet'ic** or **biogen'ic** relating to biogens, biogeny, or biogenesis. — *n* **biogenous** (*-oj'*) parasitic; biogenic. — *n* **biog'eny** the course of organic evolution or development of living organisms. — *adj* **biogeochem'ical**. — *n* **biogeochem'istry** the science of plants and animals in relation to chemicals in the soil. — *n* **biogeog'rapher**. — *adj* **biogeograph'ical**. — *n* **biogeog'raphy** the geographical distribution of plants and animals. — *n* **bi'ograph** (Gr *graphein* to write) a biography; a bioscope. — *vt* (*colloq*) to write a biography of. — *n* **biohaz'ard** a danger of disease or pollution from living organisms, encountered eg during biological research. — *n* **bioluminesc'ence** the emission of light by living organisms, such as certain insects, marine animals, bacteria, fungi. — *adj* **bioluminesc'ent**. — *n* **biolysis** (*bī-ol'i-sis*) the disintegration of organic matter under the influence of bacteria. — *n* **bi'omass** the quantity or weight of living material (animals, plants, etc) in a unit of area; living material as a source of energy. — *n* **biomatē'rial** suitable synthetic material from which to produce artificial body parts that are to be in direct contact with living tissue. — *n* **biomathemati'cian**. — *n sing* **biomathemat'ics** mathematics as applied to the biological sciences. — *n* **bi'ome** an extensive ecological community, *usu* with a dominant vegetation. — *n sing* **biomechan'ics** the mechanics of movements in living creatures. — *adj* **biomed'ical** of or pertaining to both biology and medicine; applied to the study of the effects of stress, *esp* space travel, on living organisms. — *n* **biomed'icine**. — *adj* **biometeorolog'ical**. — *n* **biometeorol'ogy** the effect of weather and climate on plants, animals and man. — *adj* **biomet'ric**. — *n* **biometrician** (*-trish'ən*). — *n* **biom'etry** (Gr *metron* measure) the statistical or quantitative study of biology (also *n sing* **biomet'rics**). — *n* **bi'omining** (*min ext*) same as **microbiological mining**. — *n* **bi'omorph** (Gr *morphē* form) a representation of a living thing as decoration. — *adj* **biomorph'ic**. — *adj* **bionom'ic**. — *n sing* **bionom'ics** (Gr *nomos* law) the study of the relations between the organism and its environment, ecology. — *n* **bi'oparent** a biological parent, not a step-parent or guardian. — *n* **biophor** or **biophore** (*bī'ō-för*; Gr *phoros*, carrying) Weismann's hypothetical unit of living matter. — *adj* **biophys'ical**. — *n* **biophys'icist**. — *n sing* **biophys'ics** a form of biology dealing with biological structures and processes in terms of physics. — *n* **bi'oplasm** (Gr *plasma* form) protoplasm. — *adj* **bioplas'mic**. — *n* **bi'oplast** (Gr *plastos* moulded) a minute portion of protoplasm. — *n* **biopoiesis** (*-poi-ēs'is*) the creation of living from non-living material as an evolutionary process. — *adj* **biopsycholog'ical**. — *n* **biopsychol'ogy** the branch of psychology, or of biology, which deals with the interaction of mind and body, and the effects of this interaction. — *n sing* **biorhyth'mics** the study of biorhythms. — *n pl* **bi'orhythms** physiological, emotional and intellectual rhythms or cycles, supposed to cause variations in mood or performance. — *n* **biosat'ellite** an artificial satellite containing living organisms to be studied during flight. — *n* **biosci'ence** any one of the biological sciences. — *adj* **bioscientif'ic**. — *n* **biosci'entist**. — *n* **bi'oscope** (Gr *skopeein* to look at) a cinematographic apparatus or theatre; a cinema (*SAfr*); the cinema (*SAfr colloq*). — *n* **bi'osphere** the part of the earth and its atmosphere in which living things are found. — *adj* **biospher'ic**. — *adj* **biostā'ble** not affected by the biological environment. — *adj* **biostratigraph'ic** or **biostratigraph'ical**. — *n* **biostratig'raphy** the stratigraphy of sedimentary rocks. — *n* **biosyn'thesis** the production of complex molecules by a living organism. — *adj* **biosynthet'ic**. — *adj* **biosystemat'ic**. — *n sing* **biosystemat'ics** the study of relationships of organisms and of laws of classification. — *n* **biō'ta** the flora and fauna of a region. — *adj* **biotechnolog'ical**. — *n* **biotechnol'ogist**. — *n* **biotechnol'ogy** the utilization of living organisms (eg bacteria) in industry, etc, eg in the creation of energy, destruction of waste, and the manufacture of various products; ergonomics (*NAm*). — *n* **bi'otype** within a species, a distinct sub-group. — **biochemical oxygen demand** a measure of the amount of oxygen required by micro-organisms in a volume of water, used as a guide to the state of pollution of the water; **biogenetic law** the theory of recapitulation of the history of the race in the development of the individual. [Gr *bios* life]

biog. See **bio**.

biography *bī-og'rə-fi*, *n* a written account or history of the life of an individual; such accounts collectively; the art of writing such accounts. — *n* **biographee'** the subject of biography. — *n* **biog'rapher** a person who writes biography. — *adj* **biograph'ic** or **biograph'ical**. — *adv* **biograph'ically**. [**bio-** and Gr *graphein* to write]

biohazard. See under **bio-**.

biol. *abbrev*: biology.

biology *bī-ol'ə-ji*, *n* the science of living things; the life sciences collectively, including botany, anatomy and physiology, zoology, etc. — *adj* **biological** (*-loj'*) of or pertaining to biology; physiological; produced by physiological means; effected by living organisms or by enzymes; (of washing powder, etc) using enzymes to clean clothes. — *adv* **biolog'ically**. — *n* **biol'ogist**. — **biological clock** an in-built mechanism which regulates the physiological rhythms and cycles of living organisms; **biological control** a method of reducing the numbers of a pest (plant, animal or parasite) by introducing or encouraging one of its enemies; **biological engineering** the provision of (electrical, electronic, etc) aids for bodily functions, eg artificial limbs and joints, hearing aids, etc (also **bioengineering**); the engineering required in biosynthesis of animal and plant products, eg for fermentation processes (also **bioengineering**); the manipulation of living cells so as to promote their growth in a desired way; **biological warfare** methods of warfare involving the use of disease bacteria or toxic substances. [**bio-** and **-logy**]

bioluminescence ... to ... **biomorphic**. See under **bio-**.

bionic *bī-on'ik*, *adj* relating to or using bionics; superhuman, *esp* with parts of the body replaced with electronic devices (*colloq*). — *n sing* **bion'ics** the study of methods of working of living creatures and the application of the principles observed to the design of computers and other machines; (loosely) the replacement of parts of the body by electronic or mechanical devices, such as powered limbs, heart valves, etc. [**bio-** and (**electr**)**onic**]

bionomic(s). See under **bio-**.

biont *bī'ont*, *n* a living organism. — *adj* **bion'tic**. — *combining form* **-biont** signifying an organism belonging to a specified habitat or environment. — *adj combining form* **-bion'tic**. [Gr *bios* life, and *ōn* (stem *ont-*) from *einai* to be]

biopic *bī'ō-pik*, *n* a film, *usu* an uncritically admiring one, telling the life-story of a celebrity. [*bio*graphical *pic*ture]

biopsy *bī'op-si*, *n* the surgical removal of tissue or fluid from a living body for diagnostic examination; such examination. [Fr *biopsie*, from Gr *bios* life, and *opsis* sight]

-biosis *-bi-ō'sis*, *combining form* signifying a (specified) way of living. — *adj combining form* **-biotic** (*-bī-ot'ik*). [Gr *biōsis* way of life; adj *biōtikos*]

biotic *bī-ot'tik*, *adj* pertaining to living organisms. — *adv* **biot'ically**. [Gr *biōtikos*]

biotin *bī'ō-tin*, *n* one of the members of the vitamin B complex (also known as vitamin H). [Gr *biotos* means of living]

biotite *bī'ō-tīt*, *n* a black or dark ferromagnesian mica. [From J B *Biot* (1774–1862), French physicist and astronomer]

biparous *bip'ər-əs*, *adj* producing offspring in twos; dichasial. [**bi-** and L *parere* to bring forth]

bipartisan *bī-pärt-i-zan*, *adj* pertaining to, supported by, or consisting of members of, two parties. [**bi-**]

bipartite *bī-pärt'īt*, *adj* divided into two parts; (of eg a document) having two corresponding parts; (of eg an agreement) affecting two parties. — *n* **bipartition** (*-tish'ən*) division into two parts. [L *bi-* two-, and *partītus* divided, from *partīre*, *-īrī* to divide]

biped *bī'ped*, *n* an animal with two feet. — *adj* **bī'ped** or **bī'pedal** (*bī-ped'əl* or *-pē'dəl*) having two feet; using two feet for walking. — *n* **biped'alism**. [L *bipēs*, *-pedis*, from *bi-* two-, and *pēs*, *pedis* foot]

bipetalous *bī-pet'əl-əs*, *adj* having two petals. [L *bi-* two-, and **petal**]

biphasic *bī-fā'zik*, *adj* having two phases. [**bi** and **phase**[1]]

biphenyl *bī-fē'nīl*, *n* and *adj*. Same as **diphenyl**.

bipinnaria *bī-pin-ā'ri-ə*, *n* a starfish larva with two ciliated bands. [L *bi-* two-, and *pinna* a feather]

bipinnate *bī-pin'āt*, (*bot*) *adj* pinnate with each pinna itself pinnate. [**bi-**]

biplane *bī'plān*, *n* an aeroplane or glider with two sets of wings, one above the other. [L *bi-* two-, and **plane**[2]]

bipod *bī'pod*, *n* a two-legged stand. [L *bi-* two-, and Gr *pous*, *podos* a foot]

bipolar *bī-pō'lər*, *adj* having two poles, extremities or extremes (*lit* and *fig*); pertaining to or occurring at both North and South Poles; (of a transistor) using both positive and negative charge carriers (*electronics*). — *n* **bipolar'ity**. [**bi-**]

bipropellant *bī-prop-el'ənt*, *n* rocket propellant made up of two liquids, the fuel and the oxidizer, kept separate prior to combustion. [**bi-**]

bipyramid *bī-pir'ə-mid*, *n* a crystal form of two pyramids base to base.

biquadratic *bī-kwəd-rat'ik*, *n* a quantity twice squared, or raised to the fourth power. — **biquadratic equation** an equation involving the fourth, and no higher, power of the unknown quantity; **biquadratic root** the square root of the square root. [L *bi-* twice, and *quadrātus* squared]

biquintile *bi-kwin'tīl*, *n* the aspect of planets when they are twice the fifth part of a great circle (ie 144 degrees) from each other. [L *bi-* twice, and *quintus* the fifth]

biramous *bī'rə-məs*, *adj* forked, with two branches, as some crustacean limbs. [**bi-**]

birch *bûrch*, *n* a hardy forest-tree (*Betula*), with smooth white bark and very durable wood; a rod for punishment, consisting of a birch twig or twigs. — *vt* to flog. — *adj* **birch** or **birch'en** made of birch. — **birch fly** see **black fly**; **birch rod** a birch for punishment. [OE *berc*, *bierce*; ON *björk*, Sans *bhūrja*]

bird *bûrd*, *n* a warm-blooded, egg-laying, feathered vertebrate of the class *Aves*, having forelimbs modified into wings; a general name for a feathered animal (*orig* applied to the young); a person (*slang*; *usu* with *adj*, eg *rare bird*, *odd bird*); a prison sentence, prison (*slang*; from **bird-lime**, rhyming slang for 'time'); a girl, *esp* one's girlfriend (now *slang*; *orig* confused with **bride** or **burd**[1]). — *vi* to shoot at or seek to catch or snare birds. — *n* **bird'er** (*colloq*) a bird-watcher. — *n* **bird'ie** (*dimin*) a little bird; the achievement of a hole in golf in one stroke less than par (also *vi* and *vt*). — *n* **bird'ing** the hunting or snaring of birds; bird-watching. — *adj* **bird'like**. — **bird-alane** see **burd**[2]; **bird'bath** a basin set up for birds to bathe in; **bird'-bolt** (*Shakesp*) a short thick blunted bolt or arrow for killing birds without piercing. — *adj* **bird'-brained** (*colloq*) flighty, silly. — **bird'cage** a cage of wire or wicker for holding birds; the paddock at a race-course (*orig* that at Newmarket, now *Austr* and *NZ colloq*); **bird'call** a bird's song; an instrument for imitating birdsong; **bird'-catcher** a professional catcher of birds. — *n* and *adj* **bird'-catching**. — **bird-catching spider** a bird-spider; **bird'-cherry** a small wild cherry tree (*Prunus padus*); its astringent fruit; **bird'-dog** (*NAm*) a dog trained to find or retrieve birds for hunters. — *vt* to watch closely. — *adj* **bird'-eyed** quick-sighted. — **bird'-fancier** a person who breeds cagebirds, or keeps them for sale. — *adj* **bird'-hipped** (of dinosaurs) having a pelvis slightly similar to a bird's, the pubis extending backwards to lie parallel with the upper pelvis, ornithischian. — **bird'-house** (*US*) a nesting-box; an aviary; **bird impact** bird strike; **bird'ing-piece** a fowling-piece; **bird'-life** birds collectively; **bird'-lime** a sticky substance for catching birds; see also **bird** *n*, above; **bird'-louse** a louse-like insect of the Mallophaga, parasitical on birds and mammals (*pl* **bird'-lice**); **bird'-lover** a person who likes birds and (often) who promotes their welfare; **bird'man**

an ornithologist or a person otherwise concerned with birds; a man who flies (or attempts flight) using his own muscle power (*usu science fiction*); an airman (*obs colloq*); **bird-nesting** see **bird's-nesting** below; **bird-of-par'adise** see under **paradise**; **bird-of-paradise flower** any of various plants of the genus *Strelitzia*, found in S America and Southern Africa, with flowers resembling birds' heads; **bird'-pepper** a species of capsicum; **bird'-scarer** a mechanical device for scaring birds away from growing crops; **bird'seed** seed (hemp, etc) for feeding cagebirds; a thing trifling in amount, chicken feed (*slang*); **bird's'eye** a kind of primrose, of speedwell, or of tobacco. — *adj* such as might be seen by a flying bird; having markings like birds' eyes. — **bird's'-foot** a papilionaceous genus (*Ornithopus*) with clawlike pods; **bird'shot** pellets suitable for shooting birds; **bird'-skiing** water-skiing with a winglike device that enables the skier to rise off the water; **bird's'-nest** the nest in which a bird lays and hatches her eggs; a name given to several plants from their appearance, *esp Monotropa* and *Neottia* (bird's-nest orchid); **bird's'-nesting** or **bird'-nesting** seeking and robbing birds' nests; **bird's-nest soup** (*Chinese cookery*) a soup made from swallows' nests; **bird'song** a bird's or birds' musical vocalization; **bird'-spider** any of various large spiders (*Mygale*) preying on small birds, found in tropical America; extended to others of the *Aviculariidae*; **bird strike** the collision of a bird or birds with an aircraft resulting in aircraft damage; **bird'-table** a table, inaccessible to cats, for wild birds to feed on; **bird'-watcher**; **bird'-watching** the observation of birds in their natural habitat; **bird'wing** or **birdwing butterfly** any of various very large brightly coloured butterflies of SE Asia. — *adj* **bird'-witted** flighty; incapable of sustained attention. — **a bird in the hand is worth two in the bush** a certainty is not to be thrown away for a poor chance of something better; **a little bird told me** I heard from a source I will not reveal; **bird's-eye view** a general view from above; a general view of a subject; **bird's-foot trefoil** a papilionaceous genus (*Lotus*) with clustered pods like birds' feet; **birds of a feather** see under **feather**; **do bird** (*slang*; see **bird** *n*, above) to serve a prison sentence; **(strictly) for the birds** (*slang*) not to be taken seriously, of little value; **get** (or **give someone**) **the bird** (ie the goose; *orig stage slang*) to be hissed (or to hiss someone); hence to be dismissed (or to dismiss someone); **in bird** (*slang*; see **bird** *n*, above) in prison; **like a bird** with alacrity. [OE *brid* the young of a bird, a bird]

birefringent *bī-rə-frin'jənt*, (*mineralogy*) *adj* doubly refracting, as Iceland spar is. — *n* **birefrin'gence**. **[bi-]**

bireme *bī'rēm*, *n* an ancient vessel with two banks of oars. [L *birēmis*, from *bi-* two-, and *rēmus* an oar]

biretta *bir-et'ə*, *n* the square cap with three or four projections on the crown worn by RC clergy, black for priests, purple for bishops, and red for cardinals. [Ital *berretta*, from LL *birretum* cap]

biriyani or **biryani** *bir-yä'ni* or *bi-ri-yä'ni*, *n* a spicy rice dish. [From Urdu]

birk *birk* or *bûrk*, (*Northern*) *n* birch. — *adj* **birk'en** birchen.

birkie *birk'i*, (*Scot*) *n* a strutting or swaggering fellow; a fellow generally. — *adj* active. [Perh connected with ON *berkia*, OE *beorcan* to bark]

birl[1] *birl*, *vt* and *vi* to spin round (*Scot*); to make a log spin by treading on it (*NAm*); to toss a coin or coins (*Scot*). [Appar onomatopoeic]

birl[2] or **birle** *birl*, (*Northern*) *vt* and *vi* to pour out; to ply with drink; to carouse. — *n* **birl'er**. — *n* **birl'ing** the act of drawing liquor. [OE *byrelian*, from *byrele* a cup-bearer, from *beran* to bear]

birlieman *bir'li-mən*, (*Scott*) *n*. Same as **byrlaw-man**.

birlinn *bir'lin*, *n* a chief's barge or galley in the Western Isles (*hist*). [Gaelic *birlinn*, from ON *byrthingr*, from *byrthr* burden]

Birminghamize or **-ise** *bûr'ming-əm-iz*, *vt* to make up artificially. [From *Birmingham* the industrial city in the English Midlands]

Biro® *bī'rō*, *n* a kind of ballpoint pen: — *pl* **Bi'ros**. [L *Biró*, Hungarian inventor]

birostrate *bī-ros'trāt*, *adj* double-beaked. [L *bi-* twice, and *rōstrātus* beaked, from *rōstrum* a beak]

birr[1] *bir*, (*esp Scot* and *US*) *n* impetus, force, vigour; a violent push (*Scot*); emphasis, stress in speaking; any sharp whirring sound. — *vi* to whirr. [ON *byrr* a favourable wind]

birr[2] *bûr* or *bēr*, *n* the monetary unit of Ethiopia. [Amharic]

birse *birs*, (*Scot*) *n* bristle. — *adj* **bir'sy**. — **lick the birse** to draw a hog's bristle through the mouth, as in admission as a burgess (*souter*) in Selkirk; **set up someone's birse** to rouse the wrath of someone, from the bristling up of enraged animals. [OE *byrst*]

birsle *birs'l*, (*Scot*) *vt* to scorch, to toast. [Origin unknown]

birth[1] *bûrth*, *n* a place allotted to a ship at anchor. [Same as **berth]**

birth[2] *bûrth*, *n* the process of being born; the act of bearing young; coming into the world; dignity of family; origin; the offspring born (*archaic*). — *vt* (*US*) to give birth to. — *n* **birth'dom** (*Shakesp*) birthright. — *n* **birth'ing** (*esp* natural) childbirth. — Also as *adj*. — **birth certificate** an official document giving the date and place of one's birth and the names of one's parents; **birth control** the control of reproduction by contraceptives; **birth'mark** a mark, eg a pigmented area or spot, on one's body at birth; a distinguishing quality; **birth mother** the mother who gives birth to the child (as contrasted with an adoptive or a genetic mother); **birth'night** the night on which one is born, or the anniversary of that night; the evening of the sovereign's birthday (*obs*); **birth parent** a natural parent (as contrasted with an adoptive parent); a birth mother or her partner (as contrasted with a genetic parent); **birth pill** a contraceptive pill; **birth'place** the place of one's birth; **birth'-rate** the proportion of live births to population; **birth'right** the right or privilege to which one is entitled by birth; native rights; **birth sign** the sign of the zodiac under which one was born; **birth'stone** a gemstone associated with one's birth sign. — *adj* **birth'-strangled** (*Shakesp*) strangled at birth. — **birth'-weight** a baby's weight at birth; **birth'wort** a plant (*Aristolochia clematitis*) formerly reputed to help parturition. [Prob ON *byrthr*]

birthday *bûrth'dā*, *n* the day on which one is born; its anniversary, or a day officially held instead. — *adj* relating to the day or anniversary of one's birth. — **birth'day-book** a book in which to record the birthdays of one's friends; **birthday honours** titles, etc, conferred on the sovereign's official birthday; **birth'day-suit** complete nakedness. — **official birthday** a day on which a sovereign's or ruler's birthday is officially celebrated. **[birth**[2] and **day]**

biryani. See **biriyani**.

BIS *abbrev*: Bank for International Settlements.

bis *bis*, *adv* twice; a direction indicating that a section is to be repeated (*music*). [L]

biscacha. Same as **viscacha**.

Biscayan *bis'kā-ən* or *-kā'*, *adj* of or pertaining to *Biscay* in Spain, its people, or their language; Basque generally. — *n* a native of Biscay; a long heavy musket, or its bullet (*obs*).

biscuit *bis'kit*, *n* a small, thin, crisp cake made of unleavened dough (*UK*); an unsweetened scone eaten with meat or gravy (*NAm*); pottery that has been fired but not yet glazed; a square mattress (*military slang*). — *adj* pale brown in colour. — *adj* **bis'cuity** like a biscuit in flavour or texture. — **bis'cuit-root** camass. — **take the biscuit** (*ironic*) to surpass everything else. [OFr *bescoit* (Mod Fr *biscuit*), from L *bis* twice, and *coquere*, *coctum* to cook or bake]

bise *bēz*, *n* a cold N or NE wind prevalent at certain seasons in and near Switzerland. [Fr]

bisect *bī-sekt'*, *vt* and *vi* to divide into two (*usu* equal) parts. — *n* **bisec'tion**. — *n* **bisec'tor** a line that divides an angle or line into two equal parts. [L *bi-* two-, and *secāre*, *sectum* to cut]

biserial *bī-sē'ri-əl*, (*biol*) *adj* arranged in two series or rows. [**bi-**]

biserrate *bī-ser'āt*, (*biol*) *adj* doubly serrated. [**bi-**]

bisexual *bī-seks'ū-əl*, *adj* hermaphrodite; attracted sexually to both sexes. — Also *n*. — *n* **bisexual'ity**. — *adv* **bisex'ually**. [**bi-**]

bish *bish*, (*colloq*) *n* a blunder, mistake. [Origin obscure]

bishop[1] *bish'əp*, *n* in the Roman Catholic and Orthodox churches and in the Anglican Communion, a senior clergyman consecrated for the spiritual direction of a diocese, *usu* under an archbishop; in the early Christian, and certain modern Protestant, churches, a spiritual overseer of a local church or group of churches; a chessman which moves diagonally over any number of empty squares; a hot drink of mulled red wine flavoured with bitter oranges; any of several kinds of colourful African weaver bird (also **bish'op-bird**). — *vt* to confirm (*joc*); to appoint to the office of bishop; to supply with bishops (*rare*); to let (milk etc) burn while cooking (*N Eng dialect*). — *n* **bish'opdom** episcopal order; bishops collectively. — *n* **bish'opess** a bishop's wife; a female bishop (*joc*). — *n* **bish'opric** the office and jurisdiction of a bishop; a diocese. — **bishop's cap** a genus (*Mitella*) of the saxifrage family, with one-sided inflorescences; **bishop's court** the court of a diocesan bishop; the Commissary Court (*Scots law*); **bishop sleeve** a full sleeve drawn in tightly at the wrist; **bish'opweed** or **bishop's weed** goutweed. — **the bishop has put his foot in it** (*obs*) it has burnt while cooking. [OE *biscop*, from L *episcopus*, from Gr *episkopos* overseer, from *epi* upon, and *skopeein* to view]

bishop[2] *bish'əp*, *vt* to fill, or otherwise tamper with, the teeth of (a horse, to make it seem younger). [From a person of the name]

bisk. See **bisque**[1].

bismar *bis'* or *biz'mər*, (*Orkney* and *Shetland*) *n* a kind of steelyard. [ON *bismari*]

bismillah *bis-mil'a*, *interj* in the name of Allah. [Ar]

bismuth *bis'* or *biz'məth*, *n* a brittle reddish-white element (atomic no 83; symbol **Bi**). [Ger *Bismuth*, *Wissmuth* (now *Wismut*), origin unknown]

bisociation *bī-sō-si-ā'shən* or *-shi-*, *n* the simultaneous association of an idea or object with two quite different sets of facts or ideas, eg in a pun. — *adj* **bisō'ciative**. [**bi-** and **association**]

bison *bī'sn* or *-zn*, *n* a large wild ox with shaggy hair and a fatty hump, the European bison, almost extinct except in parks, and the American, commonly called buffalo in America. [From L *bisōn*, *-ontis*, prob of Gmc origin; cf OHGer *wisunt*, OE *wesend*]

Bispa *bis'pə*, *abbrev*: British Independent Steel Producers' Association.

bisque[1] or **bisk** *bisk*, *n* a rich shellfish soup, made with wine and cream. [Fr]

bisque[2] *bisk*, *n* a kind of unglazed white porcelain; pottery that has undergone the first firing before being glazed. [See **biscuit**]

bisque[3] *bisk*, *n* a term at tennis, golf, etc for the handicap whereby a player allows a weaker opponent (at latter's choice of time) to score a point in a set, deduct a stroke at a hole, take an extra turn in croquet, etc. [Fr]

bissextile *bis-ekst'īl*, *adj* having an intercalary day. — *n* leap year. [L *bisextilis*, from *bis* twice, and *sextus* sixth, the sixth day before the kalends of March (24th February) being doubled]

bisson *bis'ən*, *adj* (*Shakesp* **bee'some**) blind, purblind; (*Shakesp* **biss'on**) *perh* blinding. [OE *bisene* blind]

bistable *bī'stā-bl*, *adj* (of a valve or transistor circuit) having two stable states.

bistort *bis'tört*, *n* adderwort or snakeweed, a plant (*Polygonum bistorta*) of the dock family with twisted rootstock. Also called **snakeweed**. [L *bistorta*, from *bis* twice, and *tortus*, *-a*, *-um* twisted]

bistoury *bis'tər-i*, *n* a narrow surgical knife for making incisions. [Fr *bistouri*]

bistre or **bister** *bis'tər*, *n* a pigment of a warm brown colour made from the soot of wood, *esp* beechwood, used for ink and paint. — *adj* **bis'tred**. [Fr *bistre*; origin unknown]

bistro *bē'strō*, *n* a small bar or restaurant: — *pl* **bis'tros**. [Fr slang, poss from Russ *bystro* quickly]

bisulcate *bī-sul'kāt*, *adj* cleft in two (*zool*); cloven-footed (*zool*); with two furrows (*bot*). [L *bi-* two-, and *sulcus* a furrow]

bisulphate *bī-sul'fāt*, *n* an acid sulphate. — *n* **bīsulph'ide** a disulphide.

bit[1] *bit*, *n* a bite, a morsel; a small piece, a little; a coin; $12\frac{1}{2}$ cents (*NAm*) (used only in **two**, **four** or **six bits**, ie a quarter, a half or three-quarters of a dollar); the smallest degree; a brief space of time; a small tool for boring (see **brace**); the boring-piece of a drilling-machine; the cutting or biting part of various tools; the part of the bridle that the horse holds in its mouth; the part of a key that engages the lever of the lock; used with the effect of a diminutive as in *a bit of a laddie* (*pl bits o' laddies*), *a bit laddie* (*dialect*, *esp Scot*); a girl, young woman (*slang*); an (area of) activity, an act, a role (*slang*). — *vt* to put the bit in the mouth of; to curb or restrain: — *pr p* **bitt'ing**; *pa p* **bitt'ed**. — *adj* **bit'less** without a bit. — *adj* **bit'sy** (*colloq*) prettily small. — *n* **bitt'ie** (*Scot*) a small piece, short distance, or short time. — *n* **bitt'ock** (*Scot*) a little bit. — *adj* **bitt'y** scrappy, disjointed, made up of odds and ends; not forming an artistic whole. — **bit'-part** a small part in acting; **bit player** an actor who plays bit-parts. — **a bit** or **a bit of** somewhat, rather, as in *a bit of a fool*, *a bit stupid*; **a bit of all right** (*slang*) a person or thing highly approved of; **a bit off** (*colloq*) in bad taste; **a bit on the side** (*slang*) (one's partner in) extramarital sexual relations; **bit by bit** piecemeal; gradually; **bits and bobs** or **bits and pieces** odds and ends; **do one's bit** to do one's due share; **every bit** just as much; **not a bit** or **not a bit of it** not at all; **off the bit** on a loose rein; **on the bit** on a tight rein; **take** (or **get**) **the bit in** (or **between**) **one's teeth** to throw off control; to take up or have a tenacious or keen interest (in) or occupation (with something); **to bits** (to fall, etc) apart. [From **bite**]

bit[2] *bit*, (*comput*) *n* a binary digit (see under **binary**). — **bit'map** (*comput*) a method of organizing the screen display whereby each pixel is assigned to one or more bits in memory, depending on the level of shading or number of colours required. — *adj* **bit'-mapped**. — **bit'-mapping**; **bit'-rate** the rate of transmission of bits, *usu* given as **bits per second** (also *abbrev* as **bps**); **bit'-slice** a simple but high-performance microprocessor of either 2, 4 or 8 bits, individually programmed and combined to form a customized CPU of any desired word size. — **bits per inch** a measurement for the density of data on a storage medium (also *abbrev* as **bpi**).

bit[3] *bit*, *pa t* and *pa p* of **bite**.

bitch *bich*, *n* the female of the dog, wolf, and fox; a woman, very rarely a man (*abusive*); a malicious or arrogant woman (*slang*); an extremely difficult or unpleasant situation or problem (*slang*); an act of grumbling or complaining (*slang*). — *vi* (*slang*) to complain, talk bitchily. — *vt* (*slang*) to mess up, spoil (often *bitch up*); to behave bitchily towards. — *n* **bitch'ery** ill-tempered, malicious behaviour or talk. — *adv* **bitch'ily**. — *n* **bitch'iness**. — *adj* **bitch'y** catty, malicious; resembling or characteristic of a bitch. — **the bitch goddess** material success as an object of worship. [OE *bicce*; ON *bikkja*]

bite *bīt*, *vt* and *vi* to seize or tear with the teeth; to puncture with the mouthparts, as an insect does; to cut or penetrate; to eat into chemically; to smart or cause to smart; to take effect; to grip, to take firm hold (of); to deceive, to take in (now only in *passive*); to accept something offered as bait (also *fig*); to speak harshly against (*archaic*): — *pa t* **bit**; *pa p* **bitt'en** or (*archaic*) **bit**. — *n* a grasp by the teeth; the manner or configuration in which the teeth come together; a puncture by an insect; the wound or sore caused by this; a nibble at the bait (*angling*); something bitten off; a mouthful; a snack; biting quality; grip; pungency; incisiveness; corroding action; a playful imposition, a swindling (*obs slang*). — *n* **bīt'er** a person or thing that bites; an animal with a habit of biting; a fish apt to take the bait; a cheat (*obs* except in **the biter bit** the cheater cheated; the wrongdoer paid back). — *n* **bit'ing**. — *adj* which bites; sharp, cold; sarcastic. — **bīt'ing-louse** a bird-louse. — **bite and** (or **or**) **sup** something to eat and (or) drink; **bite back** to refrain from saying; **bite in** (*etching*) to eat out the lines of with acid; **bite off more than one can chew** to overestimate one's capacities; to undertake something one cannot achieve; **bite one's lip** to restrain one's anger or mirth; **bite someone's head off** to speak to someone unnecessarily angrily; **bite** or **bite on the bullet** to submit bravely to something unpleasant; to face up to an unpalatable fact or situation; **bite the dust** to fall down dead; (of plans, etc) to come to nothing; **bite the hand that feeds one** to show ingratitude, often with the likely result of losing the help one is receiving; **bite the thumb** (*obs*) to express defiance by knocking the thumb-nail against the teeth; **bitten off** abruptly cut short; **once bitten, twice shy** a bad experience makes one cautious on a second occasion; **put the bite on** to extort money from; **sound bite** see under **sound**; **what's biting you**, etc? what is the matter with you, etc, what is annoying you, etc? [OE *bītan*; Gothic *beitan*, ON *bīta*, Ger *beissen*]

bito *bē'tō*, *n* a tree (*Balanites aegyptiaca*; family Zygophyllaceae) of dry tropical Africa and Asia; its oil-yielding fruit: — *pl* **bi'tos**.

bitonal *bī-tōn'əl*, *adj* using two musical keys simultaneously. — *n* **bitonal'ity**. [**bi-**]

bitt *bit*, (*naut*) *n* a post for fastening cables, etc (*usu* in *pl*). — *vt* to fasten (a cable, etc) round the bitts. — *n* **bitt'er** the turn of cable round the bitts, hence *perh* **the bitter end** the end of the rope; the end of a task, however long-drawn-out or difficult; final conclusive defeat or death. [Perh ON *biti* a cross-beam]

bittacle. Same as **binnacle**.

bitte *bit'ə*, (*Ger*) *interj* please; don't mention it; I beg your pardon.

bitter[1] *bit'ər*, *adj* having a taste like that of quinine or hops; sharp; painful; acrimonious; broodingly resentful. — *n* any substance having a bitter taste, *esp* a type of ale. — *adj* **bitt'erish**. — *adv* **bitt'erly**. — *n* **bitt'erness**. — *n pl* **bitt'ers** a liquid prepared from bitter herbs or roots, and used to aid digestion or stimulate appetite, or to flavour drinks. — **bitt'er-apple** a type of cucumber, the colocynth; **bitt'er-cress** cardamine; **bitt'er-earth** magnesia; **bitt'er-king** an intensely bitter shrub of the quassia family, growing in the Eastern Archipelago; **bitter lemon** a lemon-flavoured soft drink; **bitter orange** the Seville orange, bitter when ripe, used for making marmalade, etc; **bitt'er-pit** a disease of apples, etc, characterized by brown spots and depressions; **bitt'er-root** an American xerophytic plant of the purslane family; **bitt'er-spar** dolomite; **bitt'ersweet** the woody nightshade (*Solanum dulcamara*), whose stems when chewed taste first bitter, then sweet; an apple that tastes both sweet and bitter (*Shakesp*); a mixture of sweet and bitter (also *fig*; also *adj*); **bitter vetch** see **vetch**; **bitt'erwood** any of various trees, *esp* of the Simarubaceae. — **a bitter pill to swallow** something which is difficult or unpleasant to accept, such as an unwelcome fact; **the bitter end** see **bitt**. [OE *biter*, from *bītan* to bite]

bitter[2]. See **bitt**.

bitterling *bit'ər-ling*, *n* a small brightly coloured fish (*Rhodeus amarus*).

bittern[1] *bit'ərn*, *n* a marsh bird of the heron family. [ME *bittour*, *botor*, from OFr *butor*]

bittern[2] *bit'ərn*, *n* a bitter oily liquid remaining in salt-works after crystallization of the salt. [**bitter**[1]]

bittock, **bitty**. See **bit**[1].

bittor, **bittour** or **bittur** *bit'ər*, (*Spenser*, *Dryden*) *n* the bittern.

bitumen *bit'ū-mən* or *bi-tū'*, *n* the name applied to various inflammable impure mixtures of hydrocarbons, such as naphtha, petroleum, asphalt; one of these, a tarry substance used to surface roads and roofs. — *vt* **bitū'minate** to mix with or make into bitumen (also **bitū'minize** or **-ise**). — *n* **bituminizā'tion** or **-s-**. — *adj* **bitū'minous** or **bitūmed'** (or *bit'*; *Shakesp*) impregnated with bitumen. — **bituminous coal** coal that flames in burning, being rich in volatile hydrocarbons. [L *bitūmen*, *-inis*]

bivalent *bī-vā'lənt* or *biv'ə-lənt*, *adj* having a valency of two (*chem*); pertaining to one of a pair of homologous chromosomes (also *n*). — *n* **bivalence** or **bivalency**. [**bi-** and **-valent**]

bivalve *bī'valv*, *n* an animal, *esp* a lamellibranch, having a shell in two valves or parts, such as the oyster; a seed vessel of a similar kind. — *adj* having two valves. — *adj* **bivalv'ular**. [L *bi* two-, and *valva* a folding-door]

bivariate *bī-vā'ri-āt*, *adj* (*statistics*) involving two variables. — Also **bivā'riant** (*chem*). — Also *n*.

bivious *biv'i-əs*, *adj* (*obs*) leading two, or different, ways. — *n* **biv'ium** in echinoderms, the two rays enclosing the madreporite. [L *bivius*, from *bi-* two-, and *via* a way]

bivouac *biv'ōō-wak*, *n* a makeshift camp or camping place; the making of or staying in this. — *vi* to pass the night in the open air or in a makeshift camp; to make such a camp: — *pr p* **biv'ouacking**; *pa p* **biv'ouacked**. — Also (*slang*) *n* and *vi* **bivv'y**. [Fr, from Ger *Beiwacht* additional watch]

bi-weekly *bī-wēk'li*, *adj* occurring or appearing once every two weeks, or twice a week. — Also *adv*. — *n* a periodical issued twice a week, or once every two weeks.

Bixa *bik'sə*, *n* a tropical American genus of plants yielding anatta, giving name to the **Bixā'ceae**, a family of parietal Archichlamydeae. [Sp *bixa*, from Taino *bixa*]

bi-yearly *bī-yēr'li*, *adj* and *adv* (happening, issued, etc) twice a year, or every two years.

biz *biz*. Slang for **business**.

bizarre *bi-zär'*, *adj* odd; fantastic; extravagant. — *n* **bizarr'erie**. [Fr, from Sp *bizarro* gallant, brave, poss from Basque *bizarra* beard]

bizazz. See **bezzazz**.

bizcacha. See **viscacha**.

bizone *bī'zōn*, *n* a unit or country formed of two zones, eg that comprising the British and US occupation zones in Germany after 1945. — *adj* **bīzō'nal**.

bizzazz. See **bezzazz**.

Bk (*chem*) *symbol*: berkelium.

bk *abbrev*: bank; book.

bkg *abbrev*: banking.

bkpg *abbrev*: bookkeeping.

bks *abbrev*: barracks; books.

BL *abbrev*: Bachelor of Law; Bachelor of Letters; British Legion; British Leyland; British Library.

bl *abbrev*: bale; barrel; bill of lading.

blab[1] *blab*, *vi* to talk idly; to tell tales. — *vt* to let out (a secret): — *pr p* **blabb'ing**; *pa p* **blabbed**. — *n* a person who lets out secrets; a tattler (*Milton*); tattling. — *n* **blabb'er** or **blabber'mouth** a person who blabs, *esp* one who reveals secrets. — *n* and *adj* **blabb'ing**. [ME *blabbe*; cf ON *blabbra*, Ger *plappern*]

blab[2] *blab*, *n* (*obs*) a blister. — *vt* to swell. — *adj* **blabb'er** swollen. [**bleb**]

black *blak*, *adj* of the darkest colour; reflecting no light; used as a classification of pencil-leads to indicate softness in quality and darkness in use; obscure; dismal; sullen; bad-tempered, angry; horrible; grotesque, grimly humorous, making a joke of tragic or unpleasant aspects of life, as in **black comedy** or **black humour**; dusky; dirty; malignant; unlucky; dark-haired; wearing dark armour or clothes; (of coffee or tea) without milk or cream; illicit; (of income) not reported in tax returns; unofficial; under trade-union ban; (the following senses often with *cap*) dark-skinned, of African, West Indian or Australian Aboriginal descent; of African, Asian or mixed descent (*esp SAfr*); (of an area or state) inhabited or controlled by Black people; of, belonging to, or relating to, Black people. — *n* black colour or absence of colour; a dark-skinned person, *esp* of African, West Indian or Australian Aboriginal descent; a black pigment; (*usu* with *cap*) the player with the black pieces (*chess*, *draughts*); a smut; smut fungus; black clothes (formerly, still in Scotland, in *pl*). — *vt* to make black; to punch (someone's eye) so as to produce a black eye; to soil or stain; to draw in black; to blackmail (*slang*); to put under trade-union ban, to boycott, ban. — *vt* **black'en** to make black; to defame. — *vi* to become black. — *n* **black'ing** a substance used for blacking leather, metal etc. — *adj* **black'ish**. — *adv* **black'ly**. — *n* **black'ness**. — **black'amoor** (*archaic*) a Negro or other dark-skinned person. — *adj* **black-and-blue'** livid in colour because of bruising. — *adj* and *n* **black-and-tan'** (a dog) having black hair on the back, and tan or yellowish-brown elsewhere; (*usu* **Black-and-Tan'**) (of) an armed auxiliary policeman in Ireland in the 1920s (from his khaki uniform with black cap and armlet). — *n* a drink that is a mixture of ale and stout or porter. — *adj* **black'-and-white'** partly black, partly white; drawing or drawn in black on a white ground; not in colour (*cinematog*, *photog*, *TV*); consisting of extremes, not admitting any middle ground. — **black art** magic (*perh* a translation of L *nigromantia*, erroneously used for Gr *nekromanteiā*, see **necromancy**). — *adj* **black-a-vised** (*blak'ə-vīst* or *-vīzd*; *perh* Fr *à vis* in the face) swarthy. — *vt* **black'ball** to vote against (someone) by putting a black ball into a ballot-box; to ostracize; to vote against, veto (a proposal). — **black'balling**; **black'band** iron ore containing enough coal to calcine it; **black bass** a N American freshwater fish (*Micropterus*); **black bean** an Australian tree, *Castanospermum australe*, with attractive wood; the wood of this tree; any black bean of the genus *Phaseolus*; a soy bean, the seed of the plant *Glycine max*, used in Asiatic cookery; **black-bee'tle** a cockroach; **black belt** a belt showing the highest grade of proficiency in various martial arts; a person who has attained this grade; an area with rich dark soil (*US*); a region of the Southern US in which Blacks outnumber Whites (*US*); **black'berry** the bramble or its fruit; in some districts, the blackcurrant or the bilberry; **black'berrying** gathering blackberries; **black'-bird** a species of thrush, the male of which is black; a grackle or other bird of the *Icteridae* (*NAm*); a Negro or Polynesian recruited or kidnapped for labour (*archaic slang*); **black'birder** a person or ship engaged in slave-trading; **black'birding**; **black'board** a board painted black, for writing on with chalk; a similar board of any colour. — *adj* **black'-boding** of evil omen. — **black body** a body or surface that absorbs all incident radiation, reflecting none; **black body radiation** that emitted by a black body; **black body temperature** that at which a black body would emit the same radiation as is emitted by a given radiator at a given temperature; **black book** an important book bound in black; a book recording the names of persons deserving punishment (see also **in someone's black books** below); **black bottom** an American dance of the late 1920s; **black box** a type of seismograph for registering underground explosions; a unit of electronic equipment which records all the flight details in an aircraft; a device or unit, *esp* electronic, whose internal workings need not be understood by the user (*comput*, etc); **black'boy** an Australian grass-tree; **black bread** dark, coarse rye-bread. — *adj* **black'-browed** having black eyebrows; sullen, scowling. — **black'buck** an Indian antelope, the male of which is dark-coloured; **black'-bull'y** sapodilla; **black bun** (*Scot*) a rich dark fruit-cake in a pastry case, traditionally eaten at New Year; **black butt** any of several Australian trees of the genus Eucalyptus, used for timber; **black'cap** a warbler, the male of which has a black crown; an apple baked with a caramelized sugar coating; a black American raspberry; **black cap** the cap put on by English judges to pronounce sentence of death (*hist*); **black'-cat** the pekan; **black cattle** (*archaic*) cattle of any colour, *orig* from Wales or Scotland; **black chalk** bluish-black clay-slate, used for drawing, and for making black paint. — *adj* **black'-coated** wearing a black coat; of the professional class. — **black'cock** the male of the **black grouse**; **Black Consciousness** (also without *caps*) a Black movement promoting and publicizing the separate cultural traditions of Black society; **Black Country** the industrial Midland counties of England; **blackcurr'ant** the small black berry of the garden shrub *Ribes nigrum* of the gooseberry genus; **black damp** air in a mine in which the oxygen has been displaced by carbon dioxide; **black death** (with *the* and usu with *caps*) a deadly epidemic of bubonic plague that swept over Asia and Europe, reaching England in 1348; **black diamond** same as **carbonado**[2]; (in *pl*) coal; **black dog** (with *the*) depression, melancholy; **black draught** a purgative medicine, chiefly senna and Epsom salts; **black drop** a liquid preparation of opium, vinegar, and sugar; **black earth** a fertile deposit covering wide regions in S Russia and in Central India; **black economy** economic activity involving payment in kind or cash not declared for tax purposes; **Black English** (*orig US*) any of the varieties of English spoken by (*esp* urban) Blacks; **black eye** an eye of which the iris is dark; bruising around the eye due to a blow or fall; **black-eye(d) bean** or **pea** the cow-pea (qv); **black-eyed Susan** a N American composite plant of the Rudbeckia genus, whose flowers have dark centres and yellow or orange rays; a tropical African climbing plant (*Thunburgia alata*) that has yellow flowers with purple centres; **black'face** a breed of sheep with a black face; stage make-up for a white performer playing a negro; such a performer. — *adj* **black'faced**. — **black'-fellow** an Australian Aborigine. — *adj* **black'-figure** or **black'-figured** (*ancient Gr pottery*) having black painted figures on a plain (*usu* red) clay ground (cf **red-figure(d)**); **black'fish** a name given to several kinds of fish, eg the black ruff, a kind of perch; the pilot whale; a salmon after spawning; **black'-fisher** a poacher of fish by night; **black'-fishing**; **black flag** the flag of a pirate; the banner of anarchism; the flag hoisted at the execution of a criminal; the flag waved to call a driver in from a racing circuit (also *vt*); **black fly** a thrips or aphid that infests beans, etc; these insects collectively; any of several black- or grey-bodied insects of the *Simuliidae*, hump-backed blood-suckers (also known as **birch fly** and **buffalo gnat**) some of which carry the nematode that causes onchocerciasis; **Black'foot** a member of a tribe of Algonquin American Indians: — *pl* **Black'foot** or **Black'feet**. — Also *adj*. — **Black Forest gateau** or **cake** an elaborate rich chocolate cake filled and topped with cherries and cream; **black'-fox** the pekan; **Black Friar** (also without *caps*) a Dominican, from his black mantle (over a white woollen habit); **black Friday** Good Friday; an unlucky Friday; **black frost** frost without rime or snow; **black'game** blackgrouse; **black gold** (*colloq*) oil; **black gram** same as **urd**; **black grouse** a large N European grouse, the male of which (*black-cock*) is black with a lyre-shaped tail, and the female of which is called a **greyhen**; **blackguard** (*blag'gärd*; somewhat *old-fashioned*) a contemptible scoundrel. — Also *adj*. — *vt* to vituperate. — *vi* to play the blackguard. — **black'guardism**. — *adj* and *adv* **black'-guardly**. — **black hand** (*usu* with *caps*) a secret society or underground influence; **black'head** an accumulation of sebum in a pore or hair follicle, a comedo; a bird of various kinds, such as the blackheaded gull; an infectious disease of turkeys, pheasants and other fowl. — *adj* **black'headed** having a black head. — **black'heart** a dark kind of cherry. — *adj* **black-heart'ed** having an evil disposition. — **black hole** a punishment cell, *esp* (with *caps*) that at Calcutta in which 123 of 146 British prisoners were alleged to have died of suffocation in 1756; a field of such strong gravitational pull that matter and energy cannot escape from it, presumed to exist where a massive star has collapsed (*astron*); **black house** an obsolete type of house in the Scottish highlands and islands, built of turf; **black ice** a thin layer of transparent ice on a road; **black'jack** vingt-et-un, or a game like it; a combination of an ace and a face-card in the game of blackjack; a large jug for holding drink, *orig* made of leather; a pirate flag; zinc-blende; a short leather-covered club with weighted head (*NAm*). — Also *vt* to hit with a blackjack (*NAm*). — **black knight** a company making an unwelcome bid to take over another; **black'lead** a black mineral (plumbago, not lead) used in making pencils, blacking grates, etc; **black'leg** black-quarter; any of a number of diseases of vegetables; a swindler, *esp* at a racecourse; a worker continuing to work during a strike or one taking a striker's place. — *vi* to work as a blackleg. — **black letter** the Old English (also called Gothic) typeface (𝔅𝔩𝔞𝔠𝔨-𝔩𝔢𝔱𝔱𝔢𝔯); **black light** invisible infrared or ultraviolet electromagnetic radiation; **black'list** a list of defaulters or persons against whom a warning is necessary, or who are liable to loss of employment or lack of full recognition because of their (*usu* political) views. — *vt* **black'list** to put on a blacklist. — **black'listing**; **black lung** a lung disease of miners, pneumoconiosis; **black magic** see under **magic**; **black Maria** (*mə-rī'ə*) a prison van; a shell that emits dense black smoke or a gun discharging it (*obs military slang*); **black mark** something known or noted to one's discredit; **black market** buying and selling (*esp* of scarce products) that is against the law or official regulations; **black-marketeer'** a person who operates on the black market; **black mass** a travesty of the mass practised in devil-worship; **black Monday** Easter Monday; (the day of) the international stock-market crash in October 1987; the day of return to school; **black money** income not reported for tax purposes; **Black Monk** a Benedictine (also without *caps*); **black nationalism** (also with *caps*) a movement aimed at increasing Black self-determination and reducing White influence in all areas with a Black population; **black nationalist**; **black'out** total extinction or concealment of lights; a failure or cut in electrical power; a sudden loss of consciousness, or failure of the mind to work; a complete stoppage or suppression (of news, communications, etc); a stoppage in the transmission of radio or television programmes; a break in radio communication. — *adj* for blacking out windows, etc with. — (See also **black out** below). — **Black Panther** a member of a militant Black American organization; **black paper** an unofficial document similar in form to a government white paper, criticizing official policy; **Black Pope** (*disparagingly*) the head of the Jesuits; **black powder** gunpowder used in quarry work; **Black Power** (also without *caps*) a militant movement to increase the influence of Black people, *esp* in predominantly White countries; **black-pudd'ing** a blood-pudding (qv); **black-quart'er** an apoplectic disease of cattle; **black rat** the smaller of the two British rats (*usu* brown); **black robin** an extremely rare NZ bird, *Petroica traversi*; **Black Rod** the usher of the chapter of the Garter and of the House of Lords, who summons the Commons at the opening of the UK Parliament; a similar officer in Commonwealth parliaments; **black sheep** a disreputable member of a family or group; **Black'shirt** a member of a Fascist organization, *esp* in the Nazi SS and in Italy during World War II; **black'smith** a smith who works in iron; **black snake** a large agile non-poisonous snake (*Coluber constrictor*) (*US*); a very venomous snake (*Pseudechis porphyriacus*), closely related to the cobra (*Austr*); a long whip; **black spot** the name given to disease of various plants, eg roses; a small area which has bad conditions or a bad record; **Black Stone** a piece of black basalt sacred to Muslims; **black stump** (*Austr* and *NZ*) a mythical distance-marker on the edge of civilization (*esp* in **beyond the black stump** in the far outback); **black swan** a swan with black plumage and red beak, native to Australia; something rare or non-existent; **black'thorn** a dark-coloured thornbush bearing sloes, with white flowers that appear before its leaves in March and April; a walking-stick made from its stem; **black tie** a man's black bow tie worn with a dinner-jacket. — *adj* (of an occasion) formal, at which a dinner-jacket should be worn. — **black'top** (*esp NAm*) bituminous material used for surfacing roads, etc; a road so surfaced; **black velvet** champagne and stout. — *adj* **black'-visaged** having a black visage or appearance. — **black vomit** vomit containing blood, *usu* being a sign of some disease, eg yellow fever; **black'wash** a lotion of calomel and lime-water; anything that blackens; **Black Watch** see under **watch**; **blackwater** a cattle disease (see **redwater**); (also **blackwater fever**) a fever in which the urine is dark-coloured; **black widow** a very venomous American and Far Eastern spider, the female with a black body and the habit of eating her mate; **black'-wood** the dark-coloured timber of several trees, including the American logwood, an Australian acacia, and the East Indian *Dalbergia labifolia*; any one of the trees themselves; (with *cap*) a bidding convention in bridge named after its American inventor. — **black in the face** purple through strangulation, passion, or effort; **black out** to obliterate with black; to extinguish or cover all lights; suddenly to lose consciousness; to suppress (news or radio communication); **in black and white** in writing or in print; (in art, etc) in no colours but black and white; (to see a situation, etc) only as one extreme or the other; **in someone's black books** (*colloq*) having incurred someone's displeasure; in trouble or disgrace (in a certain person's eyes); **in the black** solvent, out of debt; making a profit; **put the black on** (*slang*) to blackmail. [OE *blæc* black]

blackmail *blak'māl*, *n* payment made to robbers for protection (*hist*); hush-money extorted under threat of exposure, often baseless; such extortion. — *vt* to extort money from (a person); to force by threats (into doing something). — *n* **black'mailer**. — **blackmail selling** the practice of refusing to further the sale of property unless the purchaser fulfils certain conditions, such as arranging the mortgage with a given company. [**black** and *mail*, an obsolete term for payment of money]

blad[1] *blad*, *n* a sample of a book produced as promotional material. [Poss ety as **blaud**; or *bl*urb and *ad*vertisement]

blad[2]. See **blaud**.

bladder *blad'ər*, *n* a thin distended or distensible bag; any such bag in the animal body, *esp* the receptacle for urine. — *adj* **bladd'ered**. — *adj* **bladd'ery**. — **bladd'er-campion** a species of silene with inflated calyx; **bladd'er-cherry** the winter-cherry or strawberry tomato; **bladd'er-nut** a genus (*Staphylea*) of shrubs with inflated capsule; **bladd'er-worm** the asexual state of a tapeworm or cestode; **bladd'erwort** a genus (*Utricularia*) of floating plants with bladders that catch small animals; **bladd'erwrack** a common brown seaweed with air bladders. [OE *blǣdre*, from *blāwan* to blow; OHGer *blā(h)en*, *blājen* to blow; Ger *Blatter*, from *blähen*; cf L *flātus* breath]

blade *blād*, *n* the flat or expanded part of a leaf or petal, *esp* a leaf of grass or corn; the cutting part of a knife, sword, etc; a sword; (in *pl*) hand-shears for shearing sheep (*Austr* and *NZ*); the flat part of an implement, not necessarily having a cutting edge; the flat part of an oar; an oar; the paddle-like part of a propeller; the free outer part of the tongue behind the tip; a dashing fellow (*archaic*). — *adj* **blad'ed**. — **blade'-bone** the flat bone at the back of the shoulder, the scapula; **blade'-work** (*rowing*) management of the oars. [OE *blæd*; cf ON *blath*, Ger *Blatt*]

blae *blā*, (*Scot*) *adj* blackish or dark bluish; livid; bleak. — *n sing* or *pl* **blaes**, **blaize** or **blaise** (*blāz*) hardened clay or somewhat carbonaceous shale, often blae (also red) in colour. — **blae'berry** the whortleberry or bilberry. [ON *blār* livid]

blag *blag*, (*slang*) *vt* and *vi* to rob, steal; to scrounge, wheedle. — *n* a theft, robbery; a scrounge. — *n* **blagg'er**. [Ety uncertain]

blague *blăg*, *n* humbug, pretentious nonsense. — *n* **blagueur** (*blă-gœr*) a person who talks pretentious nonsense. [Fr]

blah *blä*, (*slang*) *n* bunkum; pretentious nonsense. — Also **blah'-blah'**. — *vi* to talk stupidly or insipidly. — *adj* **blah** dull, insipid. [Poss imit]

blain[1] *blān*, *n* a boil or blister. [OE *blegen*]

blain[2] *blān*, *n* a fish (*Gadus luscus*), the bib or pout.

BLAISE *blāz*, *abbrev*: British Library Automated Information Service.

blaise, **blaize**. See **blae**.

blame *blām*, *vt* to find fault with; to censure; to impute fault to; to accuse of causing; to bring discredit upon (*Spenser*, *Bible*). — *n* the imputation of a fault; culpability; responsibility for what is wrong, not as it should be; injury (*Spenser*). — *adj* (*US*) confounded (also *adv*). — *adj* **blā'mable** or **blame'able**. — *n* **blā'mableness** or **blame'ableness**. — *adv* **blā'mably** or **blame'ably**. — *adj* **blamed** (*US slang*) damned, confounded (also *adv*). — *adj* **blame'ful** deserving blame. — *adv* **blame'fully**. — *n* **blame'fulness**. — *adj* **blame'less** without blame; guiltless; innocent. — *adv* **blame'lessly**. — *n* **blame'worthiness**. — *adj* **blame'worthy** deserving blame; culpable. — **be to blame** to be the cause of something bad. [Fr *blâmer*, OFr *blasmer*, from Gr *blasphēmeein* to speak ill; see **blaspheme**]

blanc-de-Chine *blã-də-shēn*, *n* a white porcelain made at Te-hua under the Ming dynasty. [Fr, white of China]

blanch *blänch* or *blänsh*, *vt* to whiten; to remove colour from; to prevent (celery, etc) from turning green by growing it in the dark; to immerse (fruit, vegetables, etc) briefly in boiling water (*cookery*). — *vi* to grow white; to fade; to become pale. — *adj* and *adv* see **blench**[2]. [Fr *blanchir*, from *blanc* white; see **blank**]

blanchisseuse *blã-shē-sœz*, (*Fr*) *n* a laundress.

blancmange *blə-mäzh'* or *-mönzh'*, *n* a flavoured milk dessert thickened with cornflour or gelatine and set in a mould; *orig* fowl or other meat mixed with cream, etc (*obs*). [Fr *blancmanger*, from *blanc* white, and *manger* food]

blanco *blangk'ō*, (*military*) *n* an opaque white or khaki substance for treating uniform belts, etc. — *vt* to treat with blanco. [*Blanco*, a trademark, from Fr *blanc* white]

bland[1] *bland*, *adj* gentle; mild; without distinctive characteristics, dull; not irritating or stimulating; polite, suave; unemotional, impassive; ironical. — *adv* **bland'ly**. — *n* **bland'ness**. [L *blandus*]

bland[2] *bland*, *n* in Orkney and Shetland, buttermilk and water. [ON *blanda*]

blandish *bland'ish*, *vt* to flatter and coax, to cajole. — *n* **bland'ishment** flattery, cajolery; (in *pl*) winning expressions or actions, attractions. [Fr *blandir*, *blandiss-*, from L *blandīrī*]

blank *blangk*, *adj* (of writing paper, etc) not written on; (of a questionnaire, etc) printed with empty spaces for information to be inserted, or with these spaces still unfilled; empty; featureless; expressionless; nonplussed; sheer; unproductive; (of verse) unrhymed. — *n* a blank space in a document; a card, sheet of paper, game tile, etc with no mark or writing on it; a lottery-ticket that brings no prize; emptiness, a void or vacancy; a lapse of memory or concentration; the white mark in the centre of a target (*archery*); a type of document with blank spaces to be filled up (*archaic* except in *US*); a roughly shaped piece to be fashioned into a manufactured article; a dash in place of an omitted (*esp* taboo) word; a blank cartridge. — *vt* to make blank; *euphem* used for 'damn', from the former convention of printing 'd — '; (*esp* with *off*) to seal (an opening) with a plug, etc; (*esp* with *out*) to blot out, cover up; to prevent (one's opponent in a game) from making any score (*NAm*); to make pale (*obs*); to disconcert (*Milton*). — *vt* and *vi* to produce blanks during a manufacturing process. — *n* **blank'ing**. — *adv* **blank'ly**. — *n* **blank'ness**. — **blank cartridge** one without a bullet; **blank cheque** a signed cheque in which the sum is not filled in; complete freedom to act as one thinks best; **blank door** or **window** a recess imitating a doorway or window. — *n*, *adj* or *adv* **blank'ety-blank'**, **blank'ety**, **blank'y** or **blankety blank blank** *colloq* for 'damned' as in **blank** *vt* above. — **blank verse** unrhymed verse *esp* of five feet. — **draw a blank** (*colloq*) to get no result, to fail; **go blank** or **go a complete**, etc **blank** (*colloq*) to be unable to think of any response. [Fr *blanc*, from root of Ger *blinken* to glitter, from OHGer *blichen*; cf Gr *phlegein* to shine]

blanket *blangk'it*, *n* a covering, *usu* of wool or a similar synthetic fabric, for a bed, or used as a garment by American Indians, etc; a covering generally; fertile material put round a nuclear reactor core to breed new fuel; a rubber or plastic sheet used in offset printing to transfer the image from the plate to the paper; coverage; something that conceals or obscures. — *vt* to cover, obstruct, or extinguish with, or as if with, a blanket (*lit* and *fig*); to toss in a blanket; to cover (an area) totally, eg with publicity. — *adj* applying generally or covering all cases; applied to American Indians or Black S Africans who retain the traditional tribal way of life. — *n* **blank'eting** cloth for blankets; tossing in a blanket. — **blanket bath** the washing of a sick person in bed; **blanket coverage** advertising, etc that is directed at the public in general rather than a particular target audience; **blanket finish** a very close finish to a race; **blanket mire** or **bog** a continuous area of peat bog over a wide extent; **blanket spray** a spray of pesticide, etc covering everything in a given area; **blanket stitch** a stitch used *esp* for the edges of a blanket; **blank'etweed** a rapidly-spreading green filamentous alga that forms in ponds. — **on the blanket** applied to IRA prisoners in jail who wear blankets instead of prison clothes as a protest against their having criminal rather than political status; **on the wrong side of the blanket** illegitimately; **wet blanket** a damper of spirits; a killjoy. [OFr *blankete*, dimin of *blanc* white]

blanquet *blã-ke*, (*Fr*) *n* a variety of pear.

blanquette *blã-ket*, (*Fr*) *n* a ragout of eg chicken or veal made with a white sauce.

blare *blār*, *vi* to roar; to sound loudly and *usu* harshly, as eg a trumpet does. — *n* a loud harsh noise. [ME *blaren*, from MDu *blaren*]

blarney *blär'ni*, *n* flattery or cajoling talk. — *vt* to cajole. — **blar'ney-land** Ireland. [*Blarney* Castle, near Cork, where a stone difficult to reach is said to confer the gift of persuasive talk on those who kiss it]

blasé *blä'zā*, *adj* indifferent to pleasure, etc because of familiarity; surfeited with enjoyments. [Fr pa p of *blaser* to cloy]

blash *blash*, (*Scot*) *n* a dash or splash of liquid or semi-liquid; battering rain; watery stuff. — *adj* **blash'y**. [Imit]

blaspheme *blas-fēm'*, *vt* to speak impiously or contemptuously of God or sacred things. — *vi* to speak profanely or impiously; to curse and swear. — *n* **blasphem'er**. — *adj* **blasphemous** (*blas'fi-məs*; *Spenser* and *Milton* *-fē'*). — *adv* **blas'phemously** (*Spenser* *-fē'*). — *n* **blas'phemy** (*Spenser* also *-fē'*) impious or profane speaking or behaviour; contempt or indignity offered to God. — **blasphemous libel** (*law*) blasphemy against the Christian faith. [Gr *blasphēmiā*; see **blame**]

blast *bläst*, *n* a blowing or gust of wind; a forcible stream of air; a sound of a wind instrument, car horn, etc; an explosion or detonation; a shock-wave of air caused by this; a violent verbal outpouring; any scorching, withering or pernicious influence; a blight. — *vi* to emit blasts; to use explosives; to swell (*dialect*); to wither (*obs*); to curse; to smoke marijuana (*slang*). — *vt* to blow up, destroy or damage with explosives; to create (a cavity, etc) with explosives; to inflate (*dialect*); to strike with a blast; to blight, wither or scorch (crops, etc; also *fig*); to strike with a curse, to curse, to attack vituperatively. — *interj expletive* expressing irritation or annoyance. — *adj* **blast'ed** blighted; cursed, damned (often as intensifier). — *n* **blast'er** a person or thing that blasts; a sand-wedge (*golf*). — *n* and *adj* **blast'ing**. — *n* **blast'ment** (*Shakesp*) blight. — **blast'-furnace** a smelting furnace into which hot air is blown; **blast'-furnaceman**; **blast'-hole** a hole in the bottom of a pump through which water enters; **blast'-off** the (moment of) launching of a rocket-propelled missile or space capsule (*vt* and *vi* **blast off**); **blast'-pipe** a pipe in a steam-engine, to convey the waste steam up the chimney. — **in** or **at full blast** in a state of maximum activity. [OE *blǣst*; cf ON *blāsa*, Ger *blasen*]

-blast *-blast* (*biol*) *combining form* denoting: developing; budding; immature. [Gr *blastos* bud]

blastema *bla-stē'mə*, *n* primordial material; the primordium of an organ; the protoplasmic part of an ovum, distinguished from the yolk; the axial part of a plant embryo. [Gr *blastēma* sprout]

blasto- *blas'tō-*, (*biol, esp embryol*) *combining form* denoting sprout, bud, germ. — *n* **blas'tocoel** or **blas'tocoele** (*-sēl*) the cavity inside a blastula. — *n* **blas'tocyst** the blastula in mammals. — *n* **blas'toderm** (Gr *derma* skin; *embryol*) the layer or layers of cells arising from the germinal disc, or the portion of a partially segmenting egg which undergoes division. — *n* **blastogenesis** (*-jen'*) transmission of hereditary characteristics by the germ-plasm; reproduction by budding. — *adj* **blastogen'ic** pertaining to the germ-plasm. — *adj* and *n* **blast'oid**. — *n pl* **Blastoid'ea** (Gr *eidos* form) a group of bud-like calcareous fossil echinoderms. — *n* **blas'tomere** (Gr *meros* part) one of the cells formed in an early stage of the cleavage of a fertilized ovum. — *n* **blas'topore** (Gr *poros* a passage) the orifice of a gastrula. — *n* **blas'tosphere** (Gr *sphaira* a sphere) a blastula. [Ety as for **-blast**]

blastula *blas'tū-lə*, *n* a hollow sphere of cells, one cell thick, formed in the cleavage of a fertilized ovum. — *adj* **blast'ūlar**. — *n* **blastulā'tion**. [Ety as for **-blast**]

blat[1] *blat*, (*NAm*) *vi* to cry like a sheep or calf; to make a lot of noise; to blab: — *pr p* **blatt'ing**; *pa p* **blatt'ed**. — *vt* to blurt out. [Imit]

blat[2]. See **blatt**.

blatant *blā'tənt*, (*Spenser* also **blattant**, prob *blat'ənt*), *adj* clamorous, offensively noisy; offensively obtrusive; glaringly obvious; flagrant. — *adv* **blat'antly**. [Prob a coinage of Spenser: for the *blatant beast*, see *Faerie Queene* V.12.37 onward]

blate *blāt*, (*Scot*) *adj* bashful, timidly awkward. [Perh OE *blā* pale]

blather, **blatherskite**. See **blether**.

blatt or **blat** *blat*, (*slang*) *n* a newspaper. [Ger]

blatter *blat'ər* (chiefly *Scot*) *n* a clattering rainy blast; a clatter or torrent of words. — *vi* to beat with clattering, like rain on a window. — *vt* to utter volubly. [L *blaterāre* to babble, with sense prob modified by sound]

blaubok *blow'bok*, or *Afrik* **bloubok** *blō'bok*, *n* a small Southern African antelope; a large extinct species of Southern African antelope. [Du *blauw* blue, and *bok* goat]

blaud or **blad** *blöd*, (*Scot*) *n* a fragment; a broken-off slab; a screed or selection (of verse, etc). — *vt* to strike; to disfigure. [Perh connected with OE *blāwan* to blow]

Blaue Reiter *blow'ə rī'tər*, *n* (with *Der*) the name given to an important art book published by two artists in Munich and transferred (1911) to the group of Expressionist painters formed round them. [Ger, The Blue Rider]

blawort *blä'* or *blä'wûrt*, (*Scot*) *n* the harebell; the corn bluebottle. — Also **blewart** (*bloo'ərt*). [**blae** and OE *wyrt* herb]

blay or **bley** *blā*, *n* the bleak, a small fish. [OE *blǣge*]

blaze[1] *blāz*, *n* a burst of light or of flame; a fire; an area of brilliant light or colour; a bursting out or active display (of a quality or feeling). — *vi* to burn with a strong flame; to throw out a brilliant light; to be furious (*colloq*). — *n pl* **blaz'es** the fires of hell, in imprecations like **to blazes**; also **like blazes** furiously, frenziedly. — **blazing star** (*NAm*) any of several star-shaped flowers such as *Chamaelirium luteum* or *Liatris squarrosa*. — **blaze away** to fire a rapid and repeated stream of bullets; to work very hard (*colloq*); **blaze up** to burst into flames; to become furious or very excited (*colloq*). [OE *blæse* torch]

blaze[2] *blāz*, *n* a white mark on an animal's face; a mark on a tree made by chipping the bark or otherwise. — *vt* to mark (a tree or a track) with a blaze. — *adj* **blazed'**. — **blaze a** (or **the**) **trail** (*lit* and *fig*) to show the way as a pioneer. [Perh Du *bles* or ON *blesi*; or **blaze**[1]]

blaze[3] *blāz*, *vt* (with *abroad*) to proclaim, to spread (news). — *n* **blaz'er** (*Spenser*) a person who spreads or proclaims. [MDu *blāsen*; cognate with ON *blāsa* to blow; confused with **blazon**]

blazer[1] *blā'zər*, *n* a light jacket, often in the colours or with the badge of a club, school, etc. — *adj* **blaz'ered**. [**blaze**[1]]

blazer[2]. See **blaze**[3].

blazon *blā'zn*, also (*heraldry*) *blaz'n*, *vt* to make public; to display ostentatiously; to depict or to explain in heraldic terms (*heraldry*). — *n* a coat-of-arms, heraldic bearings (also *fig*); the science or rules of coats-of-arms; a description or representation (of good qualities). — *n* **blaz'oner** a person who blazons; a herald. — *n* **blaz'onry** the art of drawing or of deciphering coats-of-arms; heraldry. [Fr *blason* a shield, confused with **blaze**[3]]

bldg *abbrev*: building.

bleach *blēch*, *vt* to make pale or white; to whiten (eg textile fabrics); to clean or disinfect with bleach. — *vi* to grow white. — *n* a process or act of bleaching; a bleaching agent. — *n* **bleach'er** a person or thing that bleaches. — *n pl* **bleach'ers** (*esp US*) cheap, open-air seats for spectators at a sports ground, etc; the people occupying such seats. — *n sing* a tier of such seats. — *n* **bleach'ery** a place for bleaching cloth. — *n* and *adj* **bleach'ing**. — **bleach'-field** a place for bleaching cloth; a bleacher's office or works; **bleaching green** a green for bleaching clothes on; **bleaching powder** a compound of calcium, chlorine and oxygen ($CaOCl_2$). [OE *blǣcan*]

bleak[1] *blēk*, *adj* dull and cheerless; cold, unsheltered; barren, desolate; colourless (now only *dialect*). — *adv* **bleak'ly**. — *n* **bleak'ness**. — *adj* **bleak'y** (*obs*) bleak. [Appar ON *bleikr*, cognate with OE *blǣc*, *blāc* pale, shining, black; cf **bleach**]

bleak[2] *blēk*, *n* a small silvery river-fish whose scales yield a pigment used in making artificial pearls. [ON *bleikja*, or a lost equivalent OE word]

blear *blēr*, *adj* (of the eyes) dim, watery; blurred as with inflammation; dim, indistinct. — *vt* to dim (the eyes); to dim the sight of; to blur (the face); to hoodwink. — *adj* **bleared**. — *n* **blear'iness**. — *adj* **blear'y** (of the eyes) blurred, dim, watery; dull with sleep, drowsy. — *adj* **blear'eyed** or **blear'y-eyed**. [Cf Ger *Blerr* soreness of the eyes]

bleat *blēt*, *vi* to cry like a sheep; to complain, whine; to talk nonsense. — *n* a sheep's cry or similar quavering sound; a complaint, grumble. — *n* **bleat'er** (*colloq*) a complainer. — *n* and *adj* **bleat'ing**. [OE *blǣtan*; imit; cf L *bālāre* to bleat; Gr *blēchē* a bleating]

bleb *bleb*, *n* a transparent blister of the cuticle; a bubble, as in water. [Variant of **blob**]

bled *bled*, *pa t* and *pa p* of **bleed**.

blee *blē*, (*archaic*) *n* complexion, colour. [OE *blēo*]

bleed *blēd*, *vi* to exude blood or sap; to be severely wounded or die in battle (*archaic*); to ooze or drop like blood; (of paint or dye) to run; (of printed matter) to overrun the edge of the page; to have money, etc extorted from one; to feel great pity. — *vt* to draw blood from, *esp* therapeutically (*hist*); to draw sap from; to print or to trim (the printed sheet) so that the text, etc runs off the page; to extort or extract from; to draw off (liquid or gas) from any closed system or container, eg hydraulic brakes or central heating radiators: — *pa t* and *pa p* **bled**. — *n* (*printing*) an illustration deliberately extended beyond the trimmed page. — *n* **bleed'er** a person who bleeds; a haemophiliac (*colloq*); an extortioner (*US slang*); a (nasty) person (*slang*). — *n* **bleed'ing** a discharge of blood or sap; the act or process of drawing off blood; the diffusion or running of colouring matter; traces of copper showing through worn silver-plate; the drawing off of liquid or gas from a closed system. — *adj* emitting blood, sap or other liquid; terribly weakened by war; full of compassion; bloody (*literally* in *Shakesp*, *fig* as *mod colloq expletive*). — **bleeding heart** a name given to various plants of the genera *Dicentra*, *Colocasia*, etc; a contemptuous name for a do-gooder; **bleed nipple** or **valve** a valve to enable liquid or gas to be drawn from a closed system or tank. — **bleed like a pig** or **a stuck pig** to bleed copiously; **my heart bleeds for you**, etc (*often ironic*) I am very sorry. [OE *blēdan*. See **blood**]

bleep *blēp*, *vi* to give out a short high sound or radio signal. — *vt* to contact (a person) by activating his or her bleeper. — *n* a sound or signal given out by a bleeper; a bleeper. — *n* **bleep'er** a device that bleeps on receiving a certain radio or other signal; such a device, carried by eg a doctor, policeman, etc, by which he or she can be contacted. [Imit]

blemish *blem'ish*, *n* (*lit* and *fig*) a stain, defect or flaw. — *vt* (*archaic*) to disfigure, damage, spoil; to tarnish; to defame; to disrupt (the peace) (*law*). — *n* **blem'ishment** (*Spenser*). [OFr *blesmir*, *blemir*, pr p *blemissant* to stain, of dubious origin]

blench[1] *blench* or *blensh*, *vi* to shrink or start back, to flinch. — *n* (*Shakesp*) a sideways look. [OE *blencan*]

blench[2] *blench* or *blensh*, (*Scot hist*) *adj* or *adv* (of feudal tenure) on the basis of payment of a merely nominal yearly duty. — Also **blanch**. [See **blanch**]

blend[1] *blend*, *vt* to mix (components) together, *esp* so as to lose their individual identity; to pollute, vitiate (*Spenser*). — *vi* to be mingled; to harmonize; to shade off: — *pa t* and *pa p usu* **blend'ed**, also (*esp poetic*) **blent**. — *n* a mixture; a portmanteau word. — *n* **blend'er**. — *n* **blend'ing**. [ME *blenden*; cf OE *blandan*, ON *blanda*]

blend[2] *blend*, (*obs*) *vt* to blind; to dazzle; to delude, beguile: — *pa p* **blent'** or **yblent'**. [OE *blendan*]

blende *blend*, *n* a mineral, zinc sulphide. [Ger *Blende*, from *blenden* to deceive, from its confusible resemblance to galena]

Blenheim *blen'əm*, *n* a kind of spaniel named after the Duke of Marlborough's country house in Oxfordshire.

blennorrhoea *blen-ō-rē'ə*, *n* a discharge of mucus. [Gr *blennos* mucus, and *rhoiā* flow]

blenny *blen'i*, *n* a member of the genus *Blennius* of acanthopterygian fishes, *usu* slimy. [Gr *blennos* mucus]

blent *blent*, *pa t* and *pa p* of **blend**[1,2].

blepharism *blef'ər-izm*, *n* spasm of the eyelid. — *n* **blepharī'tis** inflammation of the eyelid. — *n* **blepharoplas'ty** plastic surgery of the eyelids. — *n* **blepharospa'sm** blepharism. [Gr *blepharon* eyelid]

blesbok *bles'bok*, *n* a S African antelope with a blaze on its forehead. [Du *bles* blaze, and *bok* goat]

bless[1] *bles*, *vt* to consecrate; to make the sign of the cross over (*Christian relig*); to extol as holy, to pronounce holy or happy; to invoke divine favour upon; to wish happiness to; to make joyous, happy or prosperous; to glorify; to approve officially: — *pa p* **blessed** (*blest*) or **blest**. — *adj* **bless'ed** or **blest** happy; prosperous; in heaven; beatified; accursed, confounded (*euphem* for *blasted*). — *adv* **bless'edly**. — *n* **bless'edness**. — *n* **bless'ing** a wish or prayer for happiness or success; any means or cause of happiness; a gift from God (*Bible*); a prayer invoking the favour of God at a meal; official approval. — **blessed sacrament** (*Christian relig*) the consecrated Host; **Blessed Virgin** (*RC*) the Virgin Mary (also **BVM**). — **a blessing in disguise** something proving unexpectedly advantageous; **be blessed with** to have the good fortune to possess; **bless me!** or **bless my soul!** (*old-fashioned*) an exclamation of surprise; **bless you** for **God bless you**, used superstitiously to someone who has just sneezed; **single blessedness** the unmarried state. [OE *blēdsian*, *blētsian*, *bletsian* to bless, prob from *blōd* blood]

bless[2] *bles*, (*Spenser*) *vt* to brandish: — *pa t* **blest** or **blist**. [Perh from **bless**[1] as if to make the sign of the cross; or from **bless**[3]; or poss connected with **blaze**[1]]

bless[3] *bles*, *vt* to wound; to thrash. [Fr *blesser* to wound]

blest *blest*, *pa p* of **bless**[1]. — Also *adj*.

blet *blet*, *n* incipient internal decay in fruit without external sign; a part affected with this. — *vi* (of fruit) to become soft or sleepy: — *pr p* **blett'ing**; *pa t* and *pa p* **blett'ed**. [Fr]

blether (*Scot*) *bledh'ər* or **blather** (*US* and *dialect*) *bladh'ər*, *vi* to talk garrulous nonsense; to chat, gossip. — *n* a person who blethers; (often in *pl*) garrulous nonsense; a chat. — *n* **bletherā'tion**. — *n* **bleth'erer** or **blath'erer**. — *n* and *adj* **bleth'ering**. — **bleth'erskate** or **bleth'eranskate** (*Scot*), or **blath'erskite** (*dialect*) a garrulous talker of nonsense. [ME *blather* from ON *blathra* talk foolishly, *blathr* nonsense; prob *skate* the fish]

bleuâtre *blø-ätr'*, (*Fr*) *adj* bluish.

blew[1] *bloo̅*, *pa t* of **blow**.

blew[2] an old spelling (*Spenser*, *Milton*) of **blue**[1].

blewart. See **blawort**.

blewits *blū'its*, *n* a kind of edible mushroom of the *Tricholoma* family, lilac-coloured when young. [Perh from **blue**]

bley *blā*, *n*. Same as **blay**.

blight *blīt*, *n* a disease in plants which shrivels or withers them; a fungus, insect, or other cause of blight; anything that injures, destroys, depresses or frustrates; a blighted state, decay, a setback, a check. — *vt* to affect with blight; to shrivel; to frustrate. — *adj* **blight'ed** affected with blight; spoiled, ruined; (of a *usu* urban area) becoming a slum. — *n* **blight'er** a term of (*usu* playful) abuse, scamp, beggar, wretch (*slang*); a cause of blighting. — *n* and *adj* **blight'ing**. — *adv* **blight'ingly**. — **planning blight** a fall in value, and consequent neglect, of property in an area, caused by uncertainty about its planned future. [Origin obscure; perh connected with **bleach**, **bleak**[1]]

blighty *blī'ti*, (*military slang*) *n* home; the home country; a wound necessitating return home (*World War I*). [Hindi *bilāyatī* foreign, European, from Ar *wilāyat* province, country. Cf **vilayet**]

blimbing. Same as **bilimbi**.

blimey or **blimy** *blī'mi*, (*slang*) *interj* expressing surprise or annoyance. — Also **cor blimey** or **gorbli'mey**. [Corruption of *God blind me*]

blimp[1] *blimp*, *n* a small type of airship-like, heavier-than-air, craft for observing, advertising, etc; a soundproof housing for a sound-film camera. [Ety uncertain]

blimp[2] *blimp*, *n* an incurably conservative elderly military officer, as Colonel *Blimp* of the cartoonist David Low (1891–1963), or any other person of similar views. — *adj* **blimp'ish** like Colonel Blimp. — *n* **blimp'ishness**.

blimy. See **blimey**.

blin *blin*, (*Spenser*) *vt* and *vi* to cease (from). — *n* cessation; stoppage. [OE *blinnan* to cease, from **be-** (1) and *linnan* to cease]

blind *blīnd*, *adj* without sight; dark; obscure; invisible, hidden from view; not directed, or affording no possibility of being directed, by sight or by foresight; without previous or adequate knowledge; ignorant or undiscerning; unobserving; voluntarily overlooking; without an exit; (in flying) using instruments only, without seeing one's course or receiving radio directions; (of plants) failing to produce expected growth or flowers; of or intended for the blind, eg **blind school**; extremely drunk (*colloq*). — *n* (with *the*) people without sight collectively; something intended to blind one to the facts; a window-screen, either on a roller or made of slats; an awning; something which obstructs the light or the view; a screen behind which hunters hide (*NAm*); a stake put up without seeing one's cards (*poker*); a drinking spree, a binge (*slang*). — *vt* to make blind; to darken, obscure or deceive; to dazzle; to make matt; to fill in cracks on (a newly made road) with grit, to scatter grit on (a tarry surface). — *vi* to curse, swear (*slang*); to drive extremely fast and recklessly (*slang*). — *n* **blind'age** (*military*) a temporary wooden screen faced with earth as a protection against splinters of shell, etc. — *adj* **blind'ed** deprived of sight; without intellectual discernment. — *n* **blind'er** a person or thing that blinds; (*usu* in *pl*) a horse's blinkers (*NAm*); a spectacular sporting performance (*colloq*); a drinking spree (*colloq*). — *n* and *adj* **blind'ing**. — *adj* **blind'less**. — *adv* **blind'ly**. — *n* **blind'ness**. — **blind alley** a cul-de-sac; a situation, job, etc, which does not offer any prospect of improvement or advancement (also *adj* **blind-all'ey**); **blind'-coal** anthracite (as burning without flame); coal partly carbonized by an igneous intrusion; **blind date** a social meeting with someone of the opposite sex one has not met before; the partner (to be) met in this way. — *adj* **blind-drunk'** so drunk as to be like a blind man. — **blind'fish** an eyeless fish (Amblyopsis) of the Kentucky Mammoth Cave. — *adj* **blind'fold** (earlier **blind'-felled** struck blind) having the eyes bandaged so as not to be able to see; (of chess, etc) played without seeing the board; thoughtless; reckless. — Also *adv*. — *vt* to cover the eyes of; to mislead. — *n* a piece of fabric, handkerchief, etc used for covering up the eyes. — **blind'-gut** the caecum; **blindman's-buff'** (ie *buffet*) a game in which a blindfold player tries to catch the others; **blind road** a grassy track invisible to those that are on it; **blind'-side** the side on which a person is blind to danger; (one's) weak point; (*usu* **blind side**) the part of the field between the scrum, etc and the touch-line nearer it (*Rugby football*); **blind spot** the spot on the retina where the optic nerve joins and where there are no visual cells; a point within the normal range of a transmitter at which the field strength is abnormally small (*radio*); a point on a road which is obscured from vision; an area in an auditorium where one cannot see or hear properly; a region of understanding in which one's intuition and judgment always fail. — *adj* **blind'-stamped**. — **blind stamping** or **tooling** (*bookbinding*) making impressions on the covers without gilding; **blind'-storey** a triforium; **blind summit** a summit on a road whose slope is such as to prevent one from seeing approaching traffic; **blind trust** (chiefly *NAm*) a trust which manages a political public figure's private capital, so as to prevent conflict of interest; **blind'worm** a slow-worm. — **bake blind** to bake (a pastry case) without a filling; **blind (someone) with science** to confuse (someone) with too much detail; **not a blind bit of** (*colloq*) not any; **the blind leading the blind** the ignorant trying to instruct the ignorant; **turn a blind eye** to pretend not to have seen. [OE *blind*; ON *blindr*]

blindman's buff. See under **blind**.

blini *blē'ni*, *n* a small buckwheat pancake, *esp* as eaten with caviar and sour cream: — *pl* **bli'ni** or **bli'nis**. [Russ; see **blintz**]

blink *blingk*, *vi* to close both eyes momentarily; to wink; to glance, peep; to look with the eyes half-closed; to look with amazement (*at*); to shine unsteadily or intermittently. — *vt* to open and close (the eyes) rapidly; to flash (a light) off and on; to shut out of sight, to ignore or evade (*rare*). — *n* a glimpse, glance or wink; a gleam, *esp* momentary. — *n* **blink'ard** (*archaic*) a person who blinks or has bad eyes. — *adj* **blinked** affected with blinking. — *n* **blink'er** (*usu* in *pl*) leather flaps to prevent a horse from seeing sideways or backwards; an intermittent flashing light. — *vt* to obscure or limit the vision of (*lit* and *fig*); to put blinkers on (a horse). — *adj* **blink'ered**. — *adj* or *adv* **blink'ing** (*slang*) used as intensifier, *prob* as a substitute for *bloody*. — *n* **blinks** a mud or water weed (*Montia*) of the purslane family, with minute half-closed flowers. — **on the blink** (of an electrical or electronic device) (going) out of order. [Cf **blench**[1]]

blintz or **blintze** *blints*, *n* a thin filled pancake. [Yiddish *blintse*, from Russ *blin* (pl *blini*) pancake; cf **blini**]

blip *blip*, *n* a sharp tap or blow; the image of an object on a radar screen, *usu* a bright spot or sudden sharp peak on a line; an unforeseen phenomenon claimed or expected to be temporary (chiefly *econ*); the short, high sound made by a radar instrument. — *vi* to produce a blip. — *vt* to tap or hit sharply.

bliss *blis*, *n* the highest happiness; the special happiness of heaven. — *adj* **bliss'ful**. — *adv* **bliss'fully**. — *n* **bliss'fulness**. — *adj* **bliss'less**. [OE *blīths*, from *blīthe* blithe]

blist *blist*, (*Spenser*) *pa t* and *pa p* of **bless**[1,2].

blister *blis'tər*, *n* a thin bubble or bladder on the skin, often containing watery matter; a similar spot elsewhere (eg on a leaf, metal or paint); a medication applied to raise a blister; the protective bulging outer hull of a double-hulled ship, to lessen risk of sinking (*naut*); a transparent bulge on the fuselage of an aeroplane, eg for observation; an irritating person, a pest (*slang*). — *vt* to raise a blister or blisters on; to attack with scathing words; to ornament with puffs (*Shakesp*). — *vi* to develop blisters. — *adj* **blis'tery**. — *adj* **blis'tering** (of criticism) virulent, cruel; painfully intense or strenuous; (of the weather) very hot; (of an action, pace, etc) hard, fast. — **blis'ter-beetle** or **blis'ter-fly** an insect used for blistering, *esp* Spanish fly (Cantharis); **blister card** or **pack** a bubble pack; **blister copper** copper at an intermediate stage of production, about 98% pure; **blis'ter-plaster** a plaster made of Spanish flies, used to raise a blister; **blis'ter-steel** or **blis'tered-steel** steel made from wrought-iron with a blistered surface. [ME; most prob OFr *blestre*, connected with ON *blāstr*, *blāsa* to blow; Ger *Blase*]

BLit. See **BLitt**.

blite *blīt*, *n* a name for several plants of the goosefoot family. [Gr *bliton*]

blithe *blīdh*, *adj* cheerful; merry; joyfully heedless. — *adv* **blithe'ly**. — *n* **blithe'ness**. — *adj* **blithe'some** joyous. — *adv* **blithe'somely**. — *n* **blithe'someness**. [OE *blīthe* joyful. See **bliss**]

blither *blidh'ər*, *vi* to blether (qv). — *adj* **blith'ering** used to express contempt.

BLitt or **BLit** *bē-lit'*, *abbrev*: *Baccalaureus Litterarum* (*L*), Bachelor of Literature; Bachelor of Letters.

blitz *blits*, *n* an attack or bombing from the air (also **blitzkrieg** *blits'krēg*); any sudden, overwhelming attack (also **blitzkrieg**); an intensive campaign (*colloq*); a burst of intense activity, in order to achieve something (*colloq*). — *vt* to attack or damage (as if) by an air-raid; to deal with or complete by a burst of intense activity. [Ger *Blitzkrieg* lightning war, the German method first used in Poland in 1939, from *Blitz* lightning and *Krieg* war]

blive *blīv*, (*Spenser*) *adv*. Same as **belive**.

blizzard *bliz'ərd*, *n* a blinding storm of wind and snow. — *adj* **blizz'ardly**. — *adj* **blizz'ardy**. [A 19c coinage, most prob onomatopoeic, on the analogy of *blow*, *blast*, etc]

BLLD *abbrev*: British Library Lending Division.

bloat *blōt*, *vt* to swell or puff out; to dry (fish) partially by smoke. — *vi* to swell or grow turgid. — *n* the cattle and sheep disease hoove (also **bloat'ing**); bloatedness; a drunkard. — *adj* puffed up, swollen, *esp* with self-indulgence. — *adj* **bloat'ed** having been bloated; swollen (often as a result of gluttony); swollen with riches (*fig*). — *n* **bloat'edness**. — *n* **bloat'er** a herring partially dried in smoke, *esp* at Yarmouth. — **bloated capitalists** a political catch-phrase used by Marxists and other socialists (and also (*joc*) by others) to describe the ruling or managerial class. [Cf ON *blautr* soft]

blob *blob*, *n* a drop or globule; anything soft and round; a round spot; a score of zero, a duck (*cricket slang*). — *vi* to make a blob or blobs, to form into a blob or blobs. [Imit]

bloc *blok*, *n* a combination of parties, nations or other units to achieve a common purpose. [Fr]

block *blok*, *n* a mass of wood or stone, etc, *usu* flat-sided; a piece of wood or other material used as a support (eg for chopping, beheading), shaped as a mould, engraved, etc for printing from, or used as a toy; (in *pl*) starting-blocks (qv; often in *fig* phrases describing speed in starting on an enterprise); a pulley with its framework or the framework alone; a compact mass, group or set; a group of buildings bounded by intersecting streets; such a group regarded as a measure of distance (*NAm*); a large building containing individual units of accommodation, etc; a building lot (*esp Austr*); an extensive area of land for settlement, etc (*Austr* and *NZ*); an obstruction; the head (*esp* in phrase *knock someone's block off*); an impassive person; a psychological barrier preventing intellectual development, progress, etc; an instance of, or a cause of, blockage or blocking; an administrative unit in India; a bloc; a group of records or information units treated as a complete unit during the transfer of data (*comput*); (also **license block**) a section of sea within which a company is licensed to explore for and extract oil or gas; a brake-block; a cylinder-block; a chopping-block; a pad of writing or drawing paper. — *adj* in a block or lump; comprising a number grouped and dealt with together. — *vt* to close or obstruct (a place) with obstacles; to obstruct (a person); to impede or prevent; to make inactive, bring to a standstill, interrupt; to shape as on a block, or to sketch out roughly (often with *in* or *out*); to stop (a ball) with one's bat resting upright on the ground (*cricket*); to hinder the play or the action of an opposing player (*sport*); to print (*usu* a fabric) from a block; to stamp a pattern, etc on (leather, a book cover, etc); (also with *out*) to plan or rehearse the movements of the actors in (a scene, etc) (*theat*). — *n* **blockade'** a cutting off of a place by surrounding it with troops or ships (*military*); obstruction. — *vt* to block up by troops or ships. — *n* **block'age** an act or instance of obstructing, or the state of being obstructed; resistance to understanding, learning, etc set up by existing habits of thought and action. — *adj* **blocked**. — *n* **block'er** a player who blocks (*sport*); a substance, used as a drug, that prevents the production, or the operation, of some other substance in the body (*med*). — *n* **block'ing** the interruption of a train of thought, *esp* by unpleasant thoughts rising in the mind; the cut-off of anode current in a valve because of high negative voltage in the grid (*electronics*). — *adj* **block'ish** like a block; stupid, dull. — *adj* **block'y** block-shaped; in blocks; stocky, chunky. — **blockade'-runner** a person or ship that passes through a blockading force; **block'board** plywood board made up of veneer enclosing thin strips of wood; **block'-book** a book printed from engraved blocks, not movable types; **block'buster** a bomb or explosive charge able to destroy a number of buildings simultaneously; a forceful or powerful thing or person; an expensively produced and commercially successful film, novel, etc. — *n* and *adj* **block'busting**. — **block capital** a capital letter written in san serif; **block'-chain** an endless chain of blocks and links; **block'-coal** coal that breaks into cuboidal blocks; **block diagram** one made up of squares and rectangles representing different hardware and software components, with lines showing their interconnections (*comput*); **blocked shoe** a ballerina's dancing pump with a stiffened toe-piece, enabling her to dance on points; **blocked style** (*typing*) the display style, with all text beginning at the left margin without centring, indenting or underscoring; **block gauge** a block of hardened steel with its opposite faces accurately ground and polished flat and parallel, used to check the accuracy of other gauges; **block grant** a general grant made by the central government to a local authority for all its services; **block'head** a stupid person; a wooden head; **block'hole** (*cricket*) the place where a batsman rests his bat; **block'house** a small temporary fort; a house constructed of squared logs; a shelter of reinforced concrete, etc used as an observation post and control centre for rocket launches, etc; **blocking motion** notice of intention to bring up a certain matter at a future date, thus preventing (or blocking) raising of the subject on a motion for adjournment; **block letter** a block capital; block type; **block plane** a small very acute-angled plane for cutting across the grain at the end of a piece of wood; **block printing** printing from hand-carved or engraved blocks, now used for specialist books, wallpaper and textiles; **block release** release from employment for a period of weeks or more in order to follow a course of study; **block'-ship** a warship too old for action, but useful in port defence; **block'-system** (*railways*) a system in which no train is allowed on to a section of line so long as any other is on it; **block'-tin** tin in the form of blocks or ingots; **block type** a heavy-letter type, without serifs; **block vote** a vote by a delegate at a conference, counted as the number of people he or she represents; **block'-work** hollow blocks of precast concrete used for building. — **do one's block** (*Austr* and *NZ colloq*) to be very angry; **on the block** up for auction. [Fr *bloc*, prob Gmc in origin]

bloke *blōk*, *n* a man, chap (*colloq*); the commander (*naut slang*). — *adj* **blok'eish** matey, hearty, like one of the blokes. [Origin obscure]

bloncket *blongk'et*, (*Spenser*) *adj* grey. [Fr *blanquet*, *blanchet* whitish, dimin of *blanc* white]

blond (*usu* in *fem* **blonde**) *blond*, *n* a person of fair complexion and light-coloured hair (*opp* of *brunette*). — *adj* (of hair) between pale gold and light chestnut in colour; having fair hair and *usu* a fair complexion; light-coloured. — **blond beast** (also with *caps*) a blond type of N European man, admired, eg by Nietzsche, for his physical splendour; any predatory type of man; **blonde bombshell** an extremely attractive blonde woman; **blond'-** or **blonde'-lace** lace made of silk, *orig* raw silk. [Fr]

blonde *n* see under **blond**; (**blonde®**) a floodlight with a variable beam for studio use (*image technol*). [**blond**]

blood *blud*, *n* the oxygenating fluid (red in the higher animals) circulating in the body; descent, birth; relationship, kinship; (elliptically) a blood-horse, one of good pedigree; a swaggering dandy about town; the blood-royal (as in *princes of the blood*); temperament; bloodshed or murder; the juice of anything, *esp* if red; the supposed seat of passion, hence temper, anger (as *his blood is up*), etc; the sensual nature of man; a sensational or melodramatic tale, a penny-dreadful (*slang*). — *vt* to bleed; to smear with blood; to initiate into blood sports or to war (also *fig*). — *adj* **blood'ed** having blood; of pure blood, pedigreed; initiated. — *combining form* **-blood'ed** having blood or temperament of the specified kind. — *adj* **blood'less** without blood; dead; anaemic, pale; happening without bloodshed; spiritless, lifeless; unemotional. — *n* **blood'lessness**. — **blood agar** agar-agar for growing bacteria, to which blood has been added before the jelly set. — *adj* **blood-and-thund'er** (of fiction, etc) sensational, melodramatic. — **blood bank** a supply of blood plasma, or the place where it is kept; **blood'-bath** a bath in warm blood; a massacre (also *fig*). — *adj* **blood'-bespotted** spotted or sprinkled with blood. — **blood'-bird** an Australian honey-eater, the male of which has scarlet plumage; **blood blister** a blister with blood in it, caused eg by a bruise. — *adj* **blood'-boltered** clotted or matted with blood. — *adj* **blood'-bought** (*Shakesp*) bought at the expense of blood or life. — **blood'-brother** a brother by birth; a person who has entered a close and binding friendship with another, in some cultures by ceremonies involving the mixing of blood; **blood cell** any of the cells that circulate in the blood. — *adj* **blood'-consuming** (*Shakesp*). — **blood corpuscle** a cell normally contained in suspension in the blood; **blood count** the number of red or white corpuscles in the blood. — *adj* **blood'-curdling** exciting horror with a physical feeling as if the blood had curdled. — *adv* **blood'curdlingly**. — **blood donor** a person who gives blood for use in transfusion; **blood doping** or **packing** the practice of temporarily increasing the oxygen-carrying capacity of an athlete's blood by reinjecting red blood cells previously drawn off; **blood'-dust** haemoconia; **blood'-feud** a family feud arising out of an act of bloodshed, a vendetta; **blood'-fine** a fine paid in compensation for a murder; **blood'-flower** Haemanthus; a species of *Asclepias*. — *adj* **blood'-frozen** (*Spenser*) having the blood frozen or chilled. — **blood'-group** any of various types of blood identified and defined by their antigenetic structures, *esp* one of the four types of human blood (designated O, A, B, AB); **blood'-guilt** or **blood'-guiltiness** the guilt of shedding blood, eg in murder. — *adj* **blood'-guilty**. — **blood'heat** the normal temperature of human blood (37°C or 98·4°F); **blood'-horse** a horse of the purest and most highly prized blood, origin or stock, a thoroughbred. — *adj* **blood'-hot** as hot or warm as blood. — **blood'hound** a large hound, noted for its powers of following a scent; a detective (*colloq*); **blood'letter**; **blood'letting** drawing off blood by opening a vein (also *fig*); bloodshed; **blood'-line** (of animals, etc) all the individuals in a family line over a number of generations, *esp* as considered with regard to some characteristic or other; **blood'lust** desire for bloodshed; **blood'-money** money earned by laying or supporting a capital charge against anyone, *esp* if the charge is false or made by an accomplice; money paid to a hired assassin; money paid or accepted for doing something shameful; compensation formerly paid to the next of kin of a victim who has been killed; **blood oath** (*Austr*) an interjection expressing surprise or anger; **blood orange** a variety of orange with red or red-streaked pulp; **blood packing** see **blood doping**; **blood plasma** the almost colourless liquid left after the blood cells and platelets have been removed from blood; **blood'-plate** a platelet; **blood'-poisoning** a name popularly, but loosely, used of pyaemia and septicaemia; **blood pressure** the pressure of the blood on the walls of the blood vessels, varying with age and physical condition; **blood'-pudding** a pudding made with blood and other materials; **blood purge** the massacre or execution of large numbers believed by a government or ruler to be disloyal; **blood'-rain** rain coloured by red dust from the desert. — *adj* **blood'-red** of the colour of blood. — **blood'-relation** or **-relative** a person related by common ancestry; **blood'root** a N American plant (*Sanguinaria canadensis*) of the poppy family with red rootstock and sap; **blood-roy'al** royal descent; **blood'-sacrifice** (*Shakesp*) a sacrifice made with bloodshed; **blood sausage** a blood-pudding; **blood'shed** the shedding of blood; slaughter. — *adj* **blood'shot** (of the eye) red or inflamed with blood. — *adj* **blood'-sized** sized or smeared with blood. — **blood'-spavin** a disease of horses consisting of the swelling of a vein on the inside of the hock, from a checking of the blood; **blood sports** those involving the killing of animals, fox-hunting and the like. — *adj* **blood'sprent** sprinkled with blood. — **blood'stain**. — *adj* **blood'stained** stained with blood; guilty of murder. — **blood'stock** pedigree horses collectively; young men available as dance partners; **blood'stone** a green chalcedony with blood-like spots of red jasper; haematite; **blood'stream** the blood flowing through the body (also *fig*); **blood'sucker** an animal that sucks blood, *esp* a leech; an extortioner; a person who sponges on another. — *adj* **blood'sucking** that sucks or draws blood (also *fig*). — **blood'-tax** (*derog*) conscription or universal military service; **blood test** an analysis of a small specimen of blood. — *adv* **blood'-thirstily**. — **blood'thirstiness** eager desire to shed blood. — *adj* **blood'thirsty**. — **blood transfusion** the taking of blood from the veins of one person and subsequent injection of it into those of another; **blood type** blood group; **blood'-typing** the classification of blood according to blood groups, or the identification of the blood group to which a sample of blood belongs; **blood vessel** a vein or artery; **blood'-wagon** (*slang*) an ambulance; **blood'-wite** or **blood'-wit** (*OE law*) a fine for shedding blood; the right to levy it; **blood'wood** a name for various trees with red wood or juice, or their timber, eg a lythraceous tree of the East Indies (*Lagerstroemia*), eucalyptus of different kinds, or logwood; **blood'-worm** a red aquatic midge larva (*Chironomus*). — **after** or **out for (someone's) blood** having murderous intentions (towards someone) (*lit* and *fig*); **avenger of blood** the next of kin to a murdered person whose duty it was thought to be to avenge his death; **blood and iron** see **Blut**; **blood is thicker than water** family obligations take precedence over other ties; **first blood** the first drawing of blood in a fight (also *fig*); **fresh**, **new** (or **young**) **blood** new (or young) members in any association of people, to add vitality and new ideas; **in blood** in full vigour; **in hot** (or **cold**) **blood** in (or free from) excitement or sudden passion; **in one's blood** in one's character, inborn; **make someone's blood boil** (or **run cold**) to arouse someone's fury (or to horrify someone). [OE *blōd*; cf OFris *blōd* and Ger *Blut*]

bloody *blud'i*, *adj* of the nature of blood; stained with blood; like or consisting of blood; marked by considerable bloodshed; murderous, cruel. — *adj* or *adv* as an intensifier, sometimes expressing anger, but often almost meaningless. — *vt* to make bloody: — *pr p* **blood'ying**; *pa t* and *pa p* **blood'ied**. — *adv* **blood'ily**. — *n* **blood'iness**. — **blood'y-bones** see **rawhead**. — *adj* **blood'y-eyed**. — *adj* **blood'y-faced**. — **bloody flux** dysentery, in which the discharges from the bowels are mixed with blood; **bloody hand** see under **hand**; **bloody Mary** a cocktail consisting of vodka, tomato juice and seasoning. — *adj* **bloody-mind'ed** liking bloodshed, cruel; in a mood of, or inclined to show, aggressive obstinacy (*colloq*). — **bloody-mind'edness**; **blood'y-nose** (or **blood'y-nosed**) **beetle** a beetle (*Timarcha*) that exudes red liquid when disturbed; **blood'y-sweat** a sweat accompanied by the discharge of blood.

bloom[1] *blōōm*, *n* a blossom or flower (also *collectively*); the state of being in flower; the prime or highest perfection of anything; the first freshness of beauty of anything; rosy colour; the glow on the cheek; a powdery, waxy or cloudy surface or appearance; a sudden rapid seasonal multiplication of phytoplankton, algae, etc. (*bot*) — *vi* to bear flowers; to come into flower; to be in a state of beauty or vigour; to flourish. — *vt* to give a bloom to. — *adj* **bloom'ing** flowering; flourishing; fresh and youthful; bright; (as an intensifier) bloody (*euphem colloq*). — *adj* **bloom'less** without bloom. — *adj* **bloom'y** flowery; flourishing; covered with bloom. [ON *blōm*; cf Gothic *blōma*, Ger *Blume*]

bloom[2] *blōōm*, *n* a mass or bar of iron or steel in an intermediate stage of manufacture, *esp* one thicker than a *billet*. — *n* **bloom'ery** a furnace for making iron ore or iron into blooms. [OE *blōma*]

bloomer[1] *blōōm'ər*, *n* and *adj* an outfit for women, advocated by Mrs *Bloomer* of New York about 1849 (although not devised by her), consisting of a jacket with close sleeves, a skirt falling a little below the knee, and long (or short), loose, baggy trousers gathered at the ankle (or below the knee); (in *pl*) bloomer trousers; (in *pl*) a loose undergarment similar to knickers, with legs gathered above the knee.

bloomer[2] *blōōm'ər*, *n* an absurd and embarrassing blunder (*colloq*); a longish crusty loaf of white bread with rounded ends and a number of slashes across the top; a plant that blooms in a specified way, eg *perennial bloomer*; a floriated initial letter. [**bloom**[1]]

bloomery. See **bloom**[2].

Bloomsbury Group *blōōmz'bər-i grōōp*, *n* a group of literary and artistic friends, some living in Bloomsbury, who wrote during and after World War I, including Virginia Woolf, Lytton Strachey and E M Forster. — *n* **Blooms'buryite** a member of the Bloomsbury Group.

bloop *bloop*, (*esp NAm*) *n* a howling sound on a soundtrack or made by a radio. — *vi* to make such a sound. — *n* **bloo'per** a radio that makes such a sound; a stupid mistake (*slang*). [Imit]

bloosme *bloom*, *n* and *vi* Spenser's form of **blossom**, modified by **bloom**[1].

blore *blōr* or *blör*, (*archaic*) *n* a violent gust of wind. [Prob related to **blare** and **blow**[3]]

blossom *blos'əm*, *n* a flower or bloom, *esp* one that precedes edible fruit (also *collectively*); the state of being in flower (*lit* or *fig*). — *vi* (often with *out*) to produce blossoms or flowers; to flourish and prosper. — *n* **bloss'oming**. — *adj* **bloss'omy** covered with flowers, flowery. [OE *blōstm*, *blōstma*, from the same root as **bloom**[1], and L *flōs*]

blot[1] *blot*, *n* a spot, as of a drop of ink; an obliteration; a stain in reputation; a blemish; see **blotting** below (*biol*). — *vt* to obliterate, destroy (*lit* and *fig*; often with *out*); to spot or smudge; to disgrace; to blemish; to remove excess (ink, lipstick, etc) with blotting-paper, paper tissue, etc: — *pr p* **blott'ing**; *pa t* and *pa p* **blott'ed**. — *n* **blott'er** a person who blots; a sheet, pad or book of blotting-paper; a record of police-station activity (*US*). — *adj* **blottesque** (*-esk'*; of painting) executed with heavy blot-like touches (also *n* a daub); (of writing) vigorously descriptive. — *n* **blott'ing** spotting as with ink; obliterating; smudging; drying with blotting-paper, etc; blotting-paper; the method for transferring biological molecules *usu* from a gel to a filter (also **blot**; *biol*). — *adj* **blott'o** (*slang*) helplessly drunk. — *adj* **blott'y** blotted; smudged. — **blott'ing-pad** a pad of blotting-paper; **blott'ing-paper** unsized paper, used for absorbing ink. — **blot one's copybook** to blemish one's record, *esp* by an indiscretion. [Origin obscure]

blot[2] *blot*, *n* a piece liable to be taken at backgammon; exposure of a piece; a weak point in anything. [Cf Dan *blot*, Du *bloot* naked, exposed]

blot[3] *blot*, (*Spenser*) *n* spawn. [Perh connected with **blow**[3]]

blotch *bloch*, *n* an irregular discoloration; a pustule; any plant disease characterized by blotching. — *vt* to mark or cover with blotches. — *adj* **blotched**. — *n* **blotch'iness**. — *n* and *adj* **blotch'ing**. — *adj* **blotch'y**. [Prob formed on **blot**[1]]

bloubok. See **blaubok**.

blouse *blowz*, *n* a shirt-like garment for women; a short, loose jacket gathered into a waistband, part of a soldier's or airman's battledress; a loose belted outer garment worn by (*esp* French) workmen. — *vt* to arrange in loose folds. — *vi* to puff out loosely. [Fr]

blouson *bloo'zon*, *n* a loose outer garment gathered into a waistband. — **blouson noir** (*bloo-zõ nwär'*) a rebellious young man, *usu* one of a group, so called from the black windcheaters worn by many of them. [Fr]

blow[1] *blō*, *n* a firm stroke or knock, *esp* with the fist or a striking tool; a sudden misfortune or calamity. — *adj* **blow'-by-blow** (of a story or description) very detailed. — **at a blow** by a single action, suddenly; **come to blows** (of people quarrelling) to start fighting. [Found from the 15c; perh from **blow**[3] or connected with Ger *bläuen* to beat]

blow[2] *blō*, *vi* to bloom or blossom. — *vt* (*Milton*) to put forth (eg flowers): — *pr p* **blow'ing**; *pa t* **blew** (*bloo*); *pa p* **blown** (*blōn*). — *n* blossom, bloom; a display of blossom. [OE *blōwan*; Ger *blühen*; cf **bloom**[1], **blossom**]

blow[3] *blō*, *vi* to produce a current of air; (of air or wind) to move (often *impers*); to be carried along by air, etc; to breathe hard; (of a whistle or other signal, or a brass instrument) to sound; to take part in a jazz session; to spout, as whales do; to boast; to act as an informer (*slang*); (of insects) to deposit eggs; to explode, collapse (often with *up*, *down*, *in*, etc); of an electric fuse, to melt (also *vt*). — *vt* to force air on or into; to force air down (one's nose) in order to clear it; to shape (glass, etc) by blowing air into it; to make (air, etc) move; to drive by a current of air; to sound (eg a brass instrument); to destroy or force by explosive; to spread by report; to inform on; to fan or kindle; (of insects) to deposit eggs on; (in imprecations) to curse, confound, blast (*usu* with *me*, *it*); to squander (*slang*); to fail to succeed with or in when one has the chance (*slang*; *usu* with *it*): — *pa t* **blew** (*bloo*); *pa p* **blown** (*blōn*), in imprecations **blowed** (*blōd*). — *n* a blast; a breath of fresh air; an insect egg; cannabis (*UK slang*); cocaine (*US slang*). — *n* **blow'er** a person who blows; a mechanical device for producing a blast of air, etc; an escape of gas through a crack (*mining*); a speaking-tube, telephone, or similar means of sending messages (*colloq*); a communication system (*colloq*). — *n* **blow'ie** (*Austr* and *NZ colloq*) a blowfly. — *adj* **blown** out of breath, tired; swelled; stale, worthless. — *adj* **blow'y** windy; gusty. — **blow'back** backward pressure of gases, eg in a boiler, engine or firearm; **blow'ball** the downy head of a dandelion in seed; **blow'down** an accident in a nuclear reactor. — *vt* **blow'-dry** to arrange (hair) by simultaneously brushing and drying it with a hand-held hair-drier. — Also *n*. — **blow'fish** any globe-fish; **blow'fly** a flesh-fly (*Sarcophaga*); a bluebottle (*Calliphora*); **blow'gun** a blowpipe (weapon); **blow'hard** a boastful person. — Also *adj*. — **blow'hole** a whale's nostril; a hole in ice to which seals, etc come to breathe; a vent for escape of gas, etc; a bubble in metal; a natural vent from the roof of a cave up to the ground surface, through which air and water are forced by rising tides; **blow'job** (*slang*) an act of fellatio; **blow'lamp** a portable lamp producing a jet of very hot flame; **blow'-moulding** a process used in manufacturing plastic objects, the molten thermoplastic being blown against the sides of the mould; **blow'-off** see **blow off** below; **blow'-out** a lavish meal or entertainment (*slang*); a tyre-burst (*colloq*); a violent escape of oil and gas from an oil well; **blow-out preventer** a stack of heavy-duty valves fitted in the wellhead of an oil well to prevent blow-outs; **blow'pipe** a pipe through which air is blown on to a flame, to increase its heat, used in *blowpipe analysis*, etc; a long straight tube from which an arrow, pellet, etc is blown by the breath; a glass-blower's tube; **blow'torch** (*NAm*) a blowlamp; **blow'-up** an explosion; an enlargement of (part of) a photograph, illustration, etc; **blow'-valve** a snifting-valve. — **blow away** (*slang*) to kill, murder; **blow a well** temporarily to remove pressure at a wellhead to allow tubings and casings to be blown free of debris, water, etc (*min ext*); **blow hot and cold** to be favourable and unfavourable by turns, to be irresolute; **blow in** to turn up unexpectedly; **blow off** to allow (steam, etc) to escape; (of steam, etc) to escape forcibly. — Also (with *hyphen*) *n* and *adj*. — **blow on** or **upon** to take the bloom, freshness, or the interest off; to bring into discredit; to inform upon; **blow one's** (or **someone's**) **mind** (*slang*) to go (or cause to go) into a state of ecstasy under the influence of a drug or of an exhilarating experience; **blow one's stack** or **top** (*colloq*) to explode in anger; **blow out** to extinguish by blowing; to become extinguished; to force outwards by an explosion; (of a tyre) to burst suddenly (*colloq*); (of an oil well) to emit an uncontrolled jet of oil and gas; **blow over** to pass away or die down, as a storm, a danger or a scandal; **blow** (**someone's** or) **one's brains out** to kill (someone or) oneself by shooting (them or) oneself in the head; **blow someone's cover** (*slang*) to reveal someone's identity; **blow the whistle on** (*slang*) to inform on (a person); **blow up** to come suddenly into prominence; to destroy by explosion; to explode; to finish in disaster; to inflate (*lit* and *fig*); to scold; to lose one's temper; to enlarge (eg an illustration); to go to pieces (*US slang*); **blow upon** see **blow on** above. [OE *blāwan*; Ger *blähen*, *blasen*; L *flāre*]

blowze or **blowse** *blowz*, *n* a ruddy, fat-faced young woman; a beggar girl (*obs*). — *adj* **blowzed** or **blowsed** blowzy. [Perh related to **blush** or **blow**, or of cant origin]

blowzy or **blowsy** *blow'zi*, *adj* fat and ruddy, or flushed with exercise; dishevelled; coarse, rowdy. [**blowze**]

BLRD *abbrev*: British Library Reference Division.

blub *blub*, (*colloq*) *vi* to weep, sob: — *pr p* **blubb'ing**; *pa t* and *pa p* **blubbed'**. [Short for **blubber**]

blubber *blub'ər*, *n* the fat of whales and other sea animals; excessive fat; a jellyfish; a bout of weeping. — *vi* to weep effusively. — *adj* **blubb'ered** of a face, swollen with weeping. [ME *blober*, *bluber*; prob imit]

blucher properly *blühh'ər*, often *blo͞ok'ər* or *blo͞och'ər*, (*obs*) *n* a strong leather half-boot or high shoe. [Marshal *Blücher*, the Prussian general at Waterloo]

blude *blüd*, *n* a Scots form of **blood**. — *adj* **blud'y** or **blud'ie**.

bludge *bluj*, (*slang*, *esp Austr* and *NZ*) *n* an easy job. — *vi* and *vt* to scrounge. — *vi* to loaf about; to evade work or other responsibility. — *n* **bludg'er**.

bludgeon *bluj'n*, *n* a short stick with a heavy striking end; something or someone that is effective but heavy-handed. — *vt* to beat with a bludgeon; to assail heavily (*fig*); to coerce (*colloq*). [First in 18c; origin very obscure]

blue[1] *blo͞o*, *adj* of the colour of the unclouded sky; livid; greyish; dismal; depressed; (of women) intellectual, pedantic (*obs*); indecent or obscene; dressed in blue; symbolized by blue; politically conservative or right-wing. — *n* the colour of blue things; a blue object; the sky; the sea; a blue pigment; (also **wash'ing-blue**) a blue powder or liquid (indigo, Prussian blue, etc) used in laundries; a member of a party whose colour is blue (eg *hist* the opponents of the Greens in ancient Constantinople, or the 17th-century Presbyterians, later (and currently) the Conservatives); a present or past representative of Oxford or Harrow (dark blue), Cambridge or Eton (light blue), in sports; a similar representative of any university; the badge awarded to him or her, or the honour of wearing it; blue clothes; a bluestocking (*obs*); a butterfly of the family *Lycaenidae*; a former squadron of the British fleet; an argument or fight (*Austr* and *NZ slang*). — *vt* to make blue; to treat with blue. — *vi* to turn blue. — *n* **blue'ing** or **blu'ing** the process of imparting a blue colour, *esp* to metal, or of neutralizing yellow laundry; blue-rot in wood; washing blue (*US*). — *adv* **blue'ly**. — *n* **blue'ness**. — *adj* **blues'y** like the blues. — *adj* **bluey** (*blo͞o'i*) inclined towards blue (*esp* in compounds, eg **bluey-green'**). — *n* (*colloq*) an aerogramme. — *n* (*Austr*) a bundle or swag, often in a blue cloth; a summons, *usu* for a traffic offence; someone with ginger hair (*slang*). — *adj* **blu'ish**. — **blue asbestos** crocidolite; **blue baby** a baby with congenital cyanosis; **blue'back** the sockeye, chief salmon of the N Pacific; **blue bag** a barrister's bag; a small bag of washing-blue; **Blue'beard** a villainous character in European folklore, who murdered his wives in succession; (also without *cap*) any similar wife-murderer; **blue'bell** in S England the wood-hyacinth; (*blo͞o'bel'*) in Scotland and N England the harebell; **blue'berry** the fruit of *Vaccinium vacillans* and other American species; **blue'bird** a small American bird (*Sialia sialis*) related to the warblers. — *n* and *adj* **blue'-black** black with a tinge of blue; blue changing eventually to black. — **Blue Blanket** the banner of the Edinburgh craftsmen; **blue blood** aristocratic blood (Sp *sangre azul*). — *adj* **blue'-blooded**. — **blue-bonn'et** a round flat blue woollen cap; a Scottish peasant, a Scotsman; **blue book** a report or other paper printed by parliament (from its blue paper wrapper); **blue'bottle** a large fly (*Calliphora*) with metallic blue abdomen, a blowfly; the blue cornflower; a policeman or beadle (*slang*); the Portuguese man-of-war (*Austr* and *NZ*); **bluebreast** see **bluethroat**; **blue'buck** the blaubok; **blue'cap** a one-year-old salmon, with blue-spotted head; the blue titmouse; a Scotsman (*Shakesp*); **blue'-cheese** blue-veined cheese, eg Gorgonzola; **blue'-chip** a term applied to the most reliable industrial shares, or to anything of high value or prestige. — Also *adj*. — **blue'coat** a serving-man, almsman, or other wearing a blue coat (*archaic*); a pupil of Christ's Hospital or other *Bluecoat school*, whose uniform is a blue coat. — Also *adj*. — *adj* **blue'-collar** relating to manual work or workers. — **blue devil** an evil demon; (in *pl*) the apparitions seen in delirium tremens, hence deep despondency; **blue duck** a species of duck (*Hymenolaimus malacorhynchus*) found in the mountains of New Zealand; **blue ear disease** (*vet*) a viral disease of pigs, affecting their respiratory and reproductive systems; **Blue Ensign** a blue flag with the Union Jack in one corner, till 1864 the flag of the Blue squadron, now flown by the Naval Reserve and certain yachts and merchant vessels; **blue'-eye** the Australian blue-faced honey-eater, a bird with blue eye-patches; **blue-eyed boy** a favourite who can do no wrong; **blue film** or **movie** a pornographic film; **blue'fish** a large voracious fish (*Pomatomus saltatrix*) of the Serranidae, on the US Atlantic coast; **blue flag** one awarded to beaches meeting European Community standards of cleanness; **blue fox** an arctic fox; its fur; **blue funk** (*slang*) a state of great terror; **blue'gown** one of a former class of licensed beggars in Scotland, a King's Bedesman; **blue'grass** a slightly glaucous permanent grass (*Poa pratensis*, etc) of Europe and N America, *esp* Kentucky; a simple style of country music, originating in Kentucky and popular in the Southern US. — *adj* **blue'-green** or **blue'-grey** between blue and green or grey. — **blue-green algae** the *Cyanophyceae*; **blue ground** a greyish-blue decomposed agglomerate in which diamonds are found; **blue gum** any of several species of Eucalyptus (*esp E. globulus*); **blue hare** the mountain hare; **blue'jacket** a seaman in the navy; **blue jay** a N American jay (*Cyanocitta cristata*); **blue john** ornamental fluorspar; **blue laws** (*US hist*) puritanical 18c laws in Connecticut; **Blue Mantle** one of the pursuivants of the English College of Arms; **blue mould** a fungus that turns bread, cheese, etc blue; **blue movie** see **blue film**; **blue murder** (*colloq*) used in phrases describing a terrible din or commotion; **blue'nose** (*NAm*) a straitlaced or puritanical person (*colloq*); (with *cap*) a nickname for a Nova Scotian; **blue note** a flattened note, *usu* third or seventh, characteristic of the blues; **blue pencil** a pencil of the colour traditionally used for correcting, emending, etc. — *vt* **blue-pen'cil** to correct, edit or censor. — **Blue Peter** a blue flag with a white rectangle hoisted when a ship is about to sail; a call for trumps in whist; **blue pointer** a large voracious shark found off the coast of Australia, the mako shark; **blue'print** a photographic print, white on blue, on paper sensitized with ferric salts produced from a photographic negative or a drawing on transparent paper (also called cyanotype, ferroprussiate print); a detailed plan of work to be done, or a guide or model provided by agreed principles or rules or by conclusions from earlier experiment. — Also *vt*. — **blue ribbon** or **riband** the ribbon of the Order of the Garter; any very high distinction or prize (also *adj*); the badge of the teetotal Blue Ribbon Army, founded in America in 1878; **blue rinse** (*hairdressing*) a bluish colouring for white or grey hair. — *adj* **blue-'rinse** or **blue-'rinsed** applied, *usu* disparagingly, to the supposed type of well-groomed, *usu* middle-class, older women (**blue rinsers**). — **blue'-rot** a blue discoloration in coniferous wood, caused by a fungus, *Ceratostomella*; **blue ruin** (*slang*) gin; **blue sheep** the bharal. — *adj* **blue sky** or **skies** (of research, etc) having no immediate practical application; (of stocks, securities) financially unsound or fraudulent. — **blue-sky laws** (*US*) laws to prevent fraud in the sale of stocks (against capitalizing of the blue skies stocks); **blue'stocking** an intellectual woman; **blue'stone** or **blue vitriol** hydrated copper sulphate; **blue streak** something as rapidly moving and dramatic as lightning, *esp* applied to speech (often as **talk a blue streak**); **blue'throat** or **blue'breast** a songbird of Europe and Asia, the male of which has a blue throat; **blue tit** a small bird (*Parus caeruleus*) with blue wings and tail and a blue-topped head; **blue tongue** a viral disease of sheep and cattle transmitted by mosquitoes; **blue'-tongue** (*Austr*) a rouseabout; a lizard of the genus

Tiliqua; **blue water** open sea; **blue water-gas** see under **water**; **blue'weed** viper's bugloss (also **blue thistle**); **blue whale** Sibbald's rorqual, the biggest living animal; **blue whiting** a fish of the cod family, found in northern seas; **blue'wing** an American teal. — **burn blue** (of candles) to burn with a blue flame (eg as an omen of death or signifying the presence of the Devil); **full blues** full formal naval uniform (*Navy slang*); **into the blue** into the unknown; **once in a blue moon** very rarely (from the rare occasions when the moon appears to be blue because of dust particles in the atmosphere; **out of the blue** from the cloudless sky; entirely unexpectedly; **shout**, **scream** or **cry blue murder** to shout loudly in pain, alarm or rage; **the Blues** the Royal Horse Guards; **the blues** depression; (*usu* construed as *sing*) a slow sad song, *orig* an American Negro folksong, characteristically with three four-bar lines and blue notes, or any similar composition (sometimes neither slow nor sad); **true blue** a person unswervingly faithful, *esp* to political party of blue persuasion, *orig* used of Covenanters (see above under **blue** *n* above; *adj* **true'-blue**); **washing-blue** see under **blue** *n* above. [ME *blew*, from OFr *bleu*, of Gmc origin; ON *blā* gave ME *bla*, *blo* and **blae**]

blue[2] *bloō*, *vt* to squander. [Prob for **blow**[3]]

bluette *blü-et*, (*Fr*) *n* a spark, flash; a short playful piece of music.

bluff[1] *bluf*, *adj* steep or upright in front; rough and hearty in a good-natured way; outspoken; (of the shape of a body) such that, when it moves through air or other fluid, it leaves behind it a large disorderly wake and experiences a large drag (*opp* of *streamlined*); blustering, surly (*dialect*). — *n* a high steep bank, *esp* of a river; a clump of trees (*Can dialect*). — *adv* **bluff'ly**. — *n* **bluff'ness**. [Perh Du *blaf* broad, flat; or MLGer *blaff* even, smooth]

bluff[2] *bluf*, *vt* or *vi* to deceive or seek to deceive by concealment of weakness or show of self-confidence or threats (*orig poker* to conceal poor cards). — *n* a bluffing act or behaviour; a horse's blinker. — *n* **bluff'er**. — **call someone's bluff** to expose or challenge someone's show of strength, confidence, etc. [Perh Du *bluffen* to brag, boast]

bluggy *blug'i* (*joc*) *adj* bloody.

bluid *blüd*, *n* a Scots form of **blood**. — *adj* **bluid'y**.

blunder *blun'dər*, *vi* to make a gross mistake; to flounder about. — *vt* to utter thoughtlessly; to mismanage, bungle; to achieve, put or make by blundering. — *n* a gross mistake. — *n* **blun'derer**. — *n* and *adj* **blun'dering**. — *adv* **blun'deringly**. [ME *blondren*; prob connected with **blend**[2]]

blunderbuss *blun'dər-bus*, (*hist*) *n* a short handgun with a wide bore. [Du *donderbus*, from *donder* thunder, *bus* a box, gun-barrel, gun; Ger *Donnerbüchse*]

blunge *blunj*, (*pottery*) *vt* to mix (clay or the like) with water. — *n* **blung'er** a machine or person that blunges. [From *bl*end and pl*unge*]

blunk *blungk*, (*Scot*) *vt* to spoil; to bungle. — *n* **blunk'er** (*Scott*) a bungler, or according to Jamieson, someone who prints cloth.

blunt *blunt*, *adj* not having a sharp edge or point; rough, unrefined, ordinary; outspoken, abrupt, direct; dull; barren (*Spenser*). — *vt* to make dull. — *vi* to become dull. — *n* (*obs slang*) money, *esp* cash. — *adj* **blunt'ish**. — *adv* **blunt'ly**. — *n* **blunt'ness**. — **blunt instrument** any heavy object used as a weapon. — *adj* **blunt'-witt'ed** (*Shakesp*) dull, stupid. [Origin unknown]

blur *blûr*, *n* an ill-defined spot or smear; a confused impression. — *vt* to blot; to make indistinct in outline; to blemish, disfigure (*obs*). — *vi* to make blurs: — *pr p* **blurr'ing**; *pa t* and *pa p* **blurred**. [Perh a variant of **blear**]

blurb *blûrb*, *n* a publisher's commendatory description of a book, *usu* printed on the jacket; any brief commendatory advertisement. — *vt* (*esp US colloq*) to praise, describe, state, etc in a blurb. [Attributed to Gelett Burgess (1866–1951), American author]

blurt *blûrt*, *vt* to utter suddenly or unadvisedly (with *out*). — *vi* (*Shakesp*) to snort or puff in scorn. — *n* an abrupt outburst (*rare*). — *adv* with a blurt. — *n* and *adj* **blurt'ing**. [Prob imit]

blush *blush*, *n* a red glow on the skin caused by shame, modesty, etc; any reddish colour or suffusion. — *adj* pinkish. — *vi* to grow red as a result of shame, modesty, etc; to grow red. — *vt* to make red. — *n* **blush'er** a person who blushes; a cosmetic, *usu* pinkish, applied to the cheeks, etc to add colour to them. — *n* **blush'et** (*Ben Jonson*) a blushing girl. — *adj* **blush'ful**. — *n* and *adj* **blush'ing**. — *adv* **blush'ingly**. — *adj* **blush'less**. — *adv* **blush'lessly**. — **blush'-rose** a pink variety of rose. — **at (the) first blush** at the first glance or sight; offhand; **put to the blush** (*archaic*) to cause to blush. [Cf OE *blyscan* to shine]

bluster *blus'tər*, *vi* to blow boisterously; to storm, rage; to bully or swagger. — *vt* to utter loudly or boastfully; to bully by a show of temper. — *n* a blast or roaring eg of the wind; bullying or boasting language; a storm of anger. — *n* **blust'erer**. — *n* and *adj* **blus'tering**. — *adv* **blus'teringly**. — *adj* **blus'terous** (*Shakesp* **blus'trous**) noisy; boastful. — *adj* **blus'tery** stormy; swaggering. [Cf E Frisian *blüstern* to bluster]

Blut *bloōt*, (*Ger*) *n* blood. — **Blut und Boden** (*oōnt bō'dən*) blood and earth, and **Blut und Ehre** (*ā'rə*) blood and honour (Nazi party slogans); **Blut und Eisen** or **Eisen und Blut** (*ī'zən*) blood and iron (Bismarck), relentless force.

blutwurst *bloōt'voōrst*, *n* blood-pudding. [Ger]

Blvd *abbrev*: Boulevard.

BM *abbrev*: Bachelor of Medicine; British Museum.

BMA *abbrev*: British Medical Association; British Midland Airways.

BMATT (sometimes *bē'mat*) *abbrev*: British Military Advisory and Training Team.

BMEWS (sometimes *bē'mūz*) *abbrev*: ballistic missile early warning system.

BMJ *abbrev*: British Medical Journal.

BML *abbrev*: British Museum Library.

BMus *abbrev*: Bachelor of Music.

BMW *abbrev*: *Bayerische Motoren Werke* (*Ger*), Bavarian motor works.

BMX *bē'em-eks*, *n* cycle racing on a rough artificial track; a BMX bike. — **BMX bike** a small bicycle designed for BMX racing, also used for stunt-riding. [Abbrev for *bicycle motocross*]

Bn *abbrev*: Baron.

bn *abbrev*: battalion; billion.

BNB *abbrev*: British National Bibliography.

BNC *abbrev*: Brasenose College, Oxford.

BNEC *abbrev*: British National Export Council.

BNFL *abbrev*: British Nuclear Fuels Limited.

BNOC (sometimes *bē'nok*) *abbrev*: British National Oil Corporation.

bo[1] (*pl* **bos**), **boh** *bō* or **boo** *boō*, *interj* an exclamation used in fun to startle someone. — **not be able to say boo to a goose** to be extremely timid.

bo[2]. See **bo tree**.

bo[3] *bō*, (*US slang*) *n* a familiar term of address for a man: — *pl* **bos**.

b.o. *abbrev*: body odour (also **B.O.**); branch office; buyer's option.

boa *bō'ə*, *n* (with *cap*) a genus, mainly S American, of large snakes that kill their prey by squeezing; popularly any large constricting snake; a long, serpent-like coil of fur, feathers or the like worn round the neck by women. — **boa constrictor** properly the name of one species; popularly any boa, python or similar snake. [L *boa* a kind of snake]

BOAC (*old*) *abbrev*: British Overseas Airways Corporation.

boak. See **boke**.

Boanerges *bō-ən-ûr'jēz*, *n* a noisy preacher or shouting orator (*sing* and *pl*). [Sons of thunder, from Mark 3. 17]

boar *bōr*, *bör*, *n* the male pig or its flesh. — *adj* **boar'ish** swinish; brutal. — **boar'fish** a fish (*Capros*) of the horse-mackerel family with hoglike snout; **boar'-hound** a powerful dog used for hunting the wild boar, *esp* the great Dane or German mastiff; **boar'-spear** a spear used in boar-hunting. — **wild boar** the wild pig of Europe and Asia, having prominent tusks. [OE *bār*; Du *beer*]

board (*Spenser*, etc **bord, borde, boord** or **boorde**) *bōrd* or *börd*, *n* a long and wide, comparatively thin, strip of timber; a table; provision of meals (with or without lodging); a table around which committee meetings are held; a formal group or committee, *esp* one that administers a company, etc; a slab, etc prepared for playing a game (such as a chessboard) or other special purpose (such as a notice-board, blackboard, surf-board); the side of a ship (*naut*); (in *pl*) the stage; a sheet of stiff or laminated paper; a flat sheet of composite material, such as *chipboard, plasterboard*, etc; a rectangular piece forming the side of a book-binding; the Stock Exchange (*US*); (in duplicate bridge) a set of hands, or the board or set of pockets into which the set of hands is placed for passing on to the next group of players; conversation (*Spenser*); coast (*Spenser*). — *vt* to cover with boards (often with *up*); to supply with food (and bed) at fixed terms; to place in lodgings; to go on board (a ship) with hostile intent; to enter (a ship or (*orig US*) a train, bus, etc); to accost, to attack (*Shakesp*). — *vi* to receive food (with or without lodging); to live as a boarder (*with*); to border (*Spenser*). — *n* **board'er** a person who receives board; a pupil at a boarding-school; a person who boards a ship. — *n* **board'ing** the act of covering with boards; a structure or collection of boards; the act of boarding a ship, aircraft, etc; the provision of board. — **board'-foot** a unit of **board'-measure** for timber, a piece one inch thick by 12 inches square; **board'-game** a game (eg chess, snakes-and-ladders) which is played with pieces, counters, etc on a specially designed board; **boarding card** or **pass** a card allowing one to board an aircraft, ship, etc; **board'ing-house** a house where boarders are kept; **boarding party** a group of people who go on board a ship; **boarding pass** see **boarding card**; **board'ing-pike** a pike used in boarding a ship, or in defending it when attacked; **board'ing-school** a school in which board and lodging are provided for pupils; **board-measure** see **board-foot**; **board meeting** a meeting of the board of directors of an organization; **board'room** a room for meetings of a board of directors. — *adj* taking place in a boardroom. — **board'sailing** sailboarding; **board'sailor**; **board'-school** (formerly) a school under control of a school-board; **board-wa'ges** payment to a servant in lieu of food; **board'walk** (*NAm*) a footpath made of boards. — **above board** openly; **board of directors** a group of individual directors appointed by a company and collectively responsible for the management of that company; **Board of Trade** (*UK*) a ministry within the DTI; (without *caps*; *NAm*) a chamber of commerce; **Board of Trade unit** (*elec*) a kilowatt-hour (*abbrev* **BTU**); **board out** to have one's meals elsewhere than where one lives; to place in lodgings; **go by the board** to go over the side of a ship; to be discarded or ignored; to meet disaster; **on board** aboard; see also **take on board** below; **sweep the board** to win everything; to take all the cards; **take on board** to receive or accept (suggestions, new ideas, additional responsibilities, etc). [OE *bord* board, the side of a ship; ON *borth*, connected either with **bear**[1] or with **broad**]

boart. See **bort**.

boast[1] *bōst*, *vi* to talk conceitedly; to brag (with *of*). — *vt* to brag of; to speak proudly or confidently of, *esp* justifiably; to possess with pride. — *n* an expression of pride; a brag; the cause of boasting. — *n* **boast'er**. — *adj* **boast'ful** given to bragging. — *adv* **boast'fully**. — *n* **boast'fulness**. — *n* **boast'ing**. — *adj* **boast'less** without boasting; simple, unostentatious. [ME *bōst*; origin unknown; appar Welsh *bostio* and Gaelic *bòsd* a bragging, are borrowed from English]

boast[2] *bōst*, *vt* (in stone-cutting) to shape roughly. — *n* **boast'er** a broad steel chisel used for boasting. [Origin unknown]

boast[3] *bōst*, (*squash*) *vt* to (make the ball) first hit one of the side walls and then the end wall. — *n* such a stroke. — *adj* **boast'ed**. — *n* **boast'ing**. [Perh Fr *bosse* the place where the ball hits the wall]

boat *bōt*, *n* a small rowing, sailing or motor vessel; a ship; a boat-shaped utensil (as *sauce-boat*). — *vi* to sail about in a boat. — *vt* to put or convey in a boat; to ship (oars); (with *it*) to go in a boat. — *n* **boat'er** a person who boats; a straw hat. — *n* **boat'ie** (*Austr* and *NZ*) a boating enthusiast; (*UK university slang*) a rowing enthusiast. — *n* **boat'ing**. — **boat'bill** a bird of the heron family (from the shape of its bill); **boat'-builder** a person or firm that constructs boats; **boat'-deck** a ship's top deck, on which the lifeboats are carried; **boat'-fly** a water-bug (Notonecta), with boat-shaped body, that swims on its back; **boat'-hook** a hook fixed to a pole used for pulling or pushing off a boat; **boat'house** a house or shed for a boat; **boat'-load**; **boat'man** a man who is in charge of a boat; a rower; **boat neck** a high slit-shaped neckline extending on to the shoulders. — *adj* **boat'-necked**. — **boat people** refugees, *esp* from Vietnam, who set off in boats to find a country that will admit them; **boat'race** a race between rowing-boats; (with *the* and *cap*) the annual boatrace between Oxford and Cambridge universities; **boat'-racing**; **boat'-song** a song sung by a boatman; **boat'tail** a grackle; **boat'-train** a train run to connect with a ship. — **have an oar in another's boat** to meddle with someone else's affairs; **in the same boat** (of people) in the same unfavourable circumstances; **push the boat out** (*colloq*) to entertain, celebrate, etc lavishly; **take to the boats** to escape in lifeboats from a sinking ship (also *fig*). [OE *bāt*, cognate with ON *beit*]

boatel. See **botel**.

boatswain (often **bosun, bo'sun, bo's'n** or **bos'n**) *bō'sn*, *n* the foreman of a crew (warrant-officer in the navy) who looks after a ship's boats, rigging, flags, etc; the skua (*prob* from its aggressiveness). — **boat'swain-bird** the tropic-bird; **boatswain's call, pipe** or **whistle** see under **whistle**; **boatswain's chair** (*naut*) a wooden seat slung from ropes, for a man working on a ship's side, rigging, etc; **boatswain's mate** boatswain's assistant. [**boat** and **swain**]

bob[1] *bob*, *vi* to move quickly up and down or to and fro; to curtsy or bow quickly; (with *for*) to try to catch (a swinging or floating apple, etc) with one's teeth as a game; to ride a bobsled; to fish with a bob. — *vt* to move in a short jerking manner; to tap; to perform, measure, do etc (something) with a bob; to make a curtsy; to cut (hair) square across; to dock, to bobtail: — *prp* **bobb'ing**; *pa t* and *pa p* **bobbed**. — *n* a short jerking motion; a quick curtsy; anything that moves with a bob or swing; the weight of a pendulum, plumb-line, etc; a pendant (*archaic*); a knot of hair; a short straight haircut for women and girls; a bunch or cluster (eg of cherries) (*dialect*); a bunch of lobworms, used in catching eels; a bob-fly; any small roundish body; the refrain or burden of a song (*archaic*); a short line at or near the end of the stanza (*poetry*); a bobsled; (in *pl*) the runners for a bobsled (*NAm*); a dance (*Scot*); a slight blow (*obs*); a jibe (*obs*); (also **plain bob** (*bell-ringing*)) a term in change-ringing, eg **bob minor** is rung on six bells, **bob major** on eight, **bob royal** on ten, **bob maximus** on twelve. — *adj* **bobb'ish** in good spirits. — **bob'-apple** the game of trying to catch a swinging or floating apple with one's teeth; **bob'cat** a kind of lynx; **bob'-cherry** the game of trying to catch a swinging cherry with one's teeth; **bob'-fly** (*angling*) the top dropfly; **bob'sled** or **bob'sleigh** a short sledge; a sleigh made up of two of these; a racing sledge for two or more people, with a continuous seat, steering mechanism, and brakes; **bob'tail** a short or cut tail; an animal with a bobbed tail (also *adj*); applied in contempt to the rabble, as in *rag-tag and bobtail*. —

Also *vt*. — *adj* **bob'tailed** with tail cut short. — **bob'wheel** (*poetry*) the bob with the lines following it; **bob'wig** a wig with the ends turned up into short curls. — **bob up** to appear suddenly. [Poss Gaelic *baban*, *babag* tassel, cluster]

bob[2] *bob*, (*obs*) *vt* to make a fool of; to take by cheating (*Shakesp*); to cheat (out of) (*Shakesp*). [OFr *bober*]

bob[3] *bob*, (*old-fashioned slang*) *n* a shilling: — *pl* **bob**. [Prob not OFr *bobe* = $1\frac{1}{2}$d]

boba *bō'bə*, *n* another name for **yaws**.

bobac. See **bobak**.

Bobadil *bob'ə-dil*, *n* a swaggering boaster. [From the soldier in Ben Jonson's *Every Man in his Humour*]

bobak or **bobac** *bō'bak*, *n* a species of marmot. [Polish *bobak*]

bobbery *bob'ər-i*, (*obs slang*) *n* a noisy row. [Perh Hindi *bāp re* O father]

bobbin *bob'in*, *n* a reel or spool for winding yarn, wire, etc; narrow cord. — **bobb'in-lace** pillow-lace; **bobb'in-net** or **bobb'inet** a fine machine-made netted lace. [Fr *bobine*]

bobbish. See **bob**[1].

bobble *bob'l*, *n* a bobbing action; the movement of disturbed water; a woolly ball for trimming clothes, etc; (*usu* in *pl*) pilling on the surface of cloth. — *vt* and *vi* to bob rapidly or continuously; to fumble or bungle (*orig US*). — *adj* **bobb'ly** (of cloth) pilled. — **bobble hat** a *usu* knitted tapering hat with a bobble at the top. [**bob**[1]]

bobby *bob'i*, (*slang*) *n* a policeman. [Familiar form of *Robert*, from Sir Robert Peel, Home Secretary at the passing of the Metropolitan Police Act, 1828; cf **peeler**]

bobby calf *bob'i käf*, *n* a calf slaughtered before it has been weaned.

bobby-dazzler *bob'i-daz-lər*, (*colloq*) *n* anything overwhelmingly excellent, striking or showy, *esp* a woman; a young girl who sets out to make an impression.

bobby-pin *bob'i-pin*, *n* a hairgrip.

bobbysock *bob'i-sok*, (*colloq*, *esp formerly*) *n* an ankle-sock, *esp* as worn by teenage girls. — *n* **bobb'ysoxer** an adolescent girl, teenager.

bobcat. See **bob**[1].

bobolink *bob'ō-lingk*, *n* a N American songbird. [*Bob Lincoln*, imit of its note]

bobsled, bobsleigh. See **bob**[1].

bobstays *bob'stāz*, (*naut*) *n pl* ropes used to hold the bowsprit down to the stem, and counteract the strain of the foremast-stays.

bobtail. See **bob**[1].

bob-white *bob-(h)wīt'*, *n* an American quail. [Imit]

bocage. Same as **boscage**.

bocca *bok'ka*, (*Ital*) *n* mouth.

boche or **bosche** *bosh*, (*derog World War I slang*; *orig Fr*) *n* a German, *esp* a German soldier. — Also with *cap*.

bock[1] *bok*, (*Fr*, from *Ger*) *n* a strong German beer; now often a glass or mug of beer (holding a quarter of a litre). [From *Einbocker bier*, *Eimbockbier* beer from Einbeck (Eimbeck)]

bock[2]. See **boke**.

BOD *abbrev*: biochemical oxygen demand.

bod *bod*, (*orig services slang*) *n* a person. [Contraction of **body**]

bodach *bōd'əhh*, *bod'*, or *Gaelic bot'əhh*, (*Scot*) *n* an old man, a churl; a goblin or spectre. [Gaelic]

boddle. See **bodle**.

bode[1] *bōd*, *vt* to portend; to be a prediction of; to foretell; to have a presentiment of. — *vi* to be a (good or bad) omen. — *n* (*Scot*) a bid, offer. — *adj* **bode'ful** boding, ominous. — *n* **bode'ment** an omen, presentiment. — *adj* **bod'ing** presaging. — *n* an omen or portent. [OE *bodian* to announce, from (*ge*)*bod* a message; related to **bid**]

bode[2] *bōd*. See **bide**.

bodega *bo-dē'gə* or *Sp bō-dā'ga*, *n* a wine-shop; a warehouse for storing and maturing wine. — *n* **bodeguero** (*-gā'rō*; *Sp*) a man who owns or runs a bodega: — *pl* **bodeguer'os**. [Sp, from L, from Gr *apothēkē* a storehouse]

bodge *boj*, (*colloq*) variant of **botch** (*vt* and *vi*); (*Shakesp vi*) *prob* variant of **budge**[1]. — *n* (*colloq*) a piece of poor or clumsy workmanship; a clumsy worker (also **bodg'er**).

bodger *boj'ər*, (*dialect*) *n* a travelling pedlar who turns beechwood to make chairs, etc; see also under **bodge**. [Origin uncertain]

bodgie *boj'i*, (*Austr* and *NZ*) *n* a young Australian male of the 1950s, similar in dress and behaviour to the British Teddy boy; something that is a fake, useless, or fraudulent (also *adj*). [Perh from *bodge* to botch]

Bodhisattva *bō-di-sat'wə* or *-və*, or *bo-*, (*Buddhism*) *n* a person who postpones entry into nirvana in order to help others; a future Buddha. [Sans *bodhi* enlightenment, and *sattva* existence]

bodhi tree. See **bo tree**.

bodhrán *bow-rän'* or *bō'rən*, *n* a shallow one-sided drum, common in Irish and Scottish folk music. [Irish Gaelic]

bodice *bod'is*, *n* a woman's tight-fitting outer waistcoat; the close-fitting upper part, from shoulder to waist, of a woman's dress; a stiffened inner garment (*orig pl* of **body**) (*archaic*). — **bod'ice-ripp'er** a romantic (historical) novel involving sex and violence.

bodikin *bod'i-kin*, *n dimin* of **body**, in *Od's bodikins* God's little body.

bodily. See **body**.

bodkin *bod'kin*, *n* a small pointed tool for pricking holes, for dressing the hair, for correcting type, etc; a large blunt needle for threading tape, etc; a small dagger (*obs*). — **sit** or **ride bodkin** to be wedged in tight between two others. [Poss connected with Welsh *bidog* dagger]

bodle or **boddle** *bod'l* or *bōd'l*, *n* a former Scottish copper coin, in the 17c worth about one-sixth of an English penny, the smallest coin. [Origin unknown]

bodrag *bod'rag*, (*Spenser*) *n* a hostile attack, a raid. — Also **bord'raging**. [Perh Ir *buaidhreadh* a disturbance]

body *bod'i*, *n* the whole frame of a human or a lower animal; the main part of an animal, as distinguished from the limbs; the main part of anything; the main text of a letter, advertisement, etc, excluding eg headings, address, etc; the part of a vehicle which carries the load or passengers; a garment or part of a garment covering the trunk, a bodice; a legless close-fitting garment fastening at the crotch; a corpse; matter, as opposed to spirit; substance or substantial quality; fullness, as of flavour in a wine; solidity; a three-dimensional figure (*obs math*); opacity of a paint or pigment; a mass; a person (*colloq*); a number of persons united by something they have in common; size of type: — *pl* **bod'ies**. — *vt* (*usu* with *forth*) to give form to; to embody: — *pr p* **bod'ying**; *pa t* and *pa p* **bod'ied**. — *adj combining form* **-bod'ied**. — *adj* **bod'iless** without a body; incorporeal. — *adj* **bod'ily** of the body, *esp* as opposed to the mind; actual, real (*Shakesp*). — *adv* in the flesh; as a whole. — **bodily function** any of the processes or activities performed by or connected with the body, such as breathing, hearing and digesting; **body armour** protective covering or clothing for the body; **bod'y-bag** a bag made of heavy material in which a dead body (*esp* that of a war casualty or accident victim) is transported; **body blow** in boxing, a blow to the body; a serious setback; **bod'y-builder** a person who by an exercise and dietary regime builds up the size and strength of the muscles; an apparatus for exercising muscles; a nutritious food; a person who makes vehicle bodies. — *n* and *adj* **bod'y-building**. — **body carpet** or **carpetting** carpet manufactured in strips that are joined together to form the required size; **bod'y-cavity** the cavity in which the viscera of the higher animals lie, the coelom; **bod'y-check** (*sport*) a deliberate obstruction of an opposing player's movements, permitted in eg lacrosse and ice-hockey, not in soccer (also *vt*); **bod'y-checking**; **body clock** the biological clock; **body colour** the degree of consistency, substance and tingeing power of a paint; watercolour mixed with zinc or other white to give it body; **bod'y-curer** (*Shakesp*) a doctor; **bod'yguard** a guard consisting of one person or several people, to accompany and give physical protection to someone; **body image** (*psychol*) a person's subjective picture of his or her own body; **body language** communication of information by means of conscious or unconscious gestures, attitudes, facial expressions, etc; **bod'yline, body-line bowling** or **bodyline bowling** (*cricket*) fast bowling delivered at the batsman's body; **body packer** (*slang*) someone who smuggles drugs by swallowing them or otherwise hiding them in their body; **body politic** the collective body of the people in its political capacity; **bod'y-popper**; **bod'y-popping** a form of dancing with robot-like movements; **body servant** a personal attendant; **bod'yshell** bodywork; **body shop** a vehicle body repair or construction shop; **bod'y-snatcher** (*hist*) a person who secretly disinters dead bodies (*usu* to sell them) for dissection; **body stocking** a one-piece, skin-tight undergarment for women; **bod'ysuit** a close-fitting one-piece garment for women; **bod'y-warmer** a padded sleeveless jacket; **bod'ywork** the metal outer shell of a motor vehicle. — **body and soul** one's entire self; **in a body** (acting) all together. [OE *bodig*]

Boeotian *bi-ō'sh(y)ən*, *adj* of *Boeotia* in Greece, proverbial for the dullness of its inhabitants; hence, stupid, dull. — Also *n*.

Boer *bōōr*, (chiefly *hist*) *n* a S African of Dutch descent, *orig* one engaged in farming. — Also *adj*. — **boerewors** (*bōōr'ə-vörs*; *SAfr*; *Afrik boere-* farmers', country style, and *wors* sausage) a traditional S African sausage, *usu* containing a mixture of beef and pork; **Boer War** either of two wars (1880–81 and 1899–1902) fought between Britain and S Africa. [Du; see **boor** and **bower**[2]]

boeuf bourguignon *bøf bōōr-gē-nyɔ̃*, *n* a beef and vegetable casserole cooked in red wine. [Fr, burgundy beef]

boff *bof*, (*slang*; *esp US*) *n* a punch; a hearty laugh; an entertainment. — *vi* and *vt* to hit, slug. — *vi* to copulate. [Ety uncertain; perh in part imit]

boffin *bof'in*, (*orig services slang*) *n* a research scientist, *esp* one employed by the armed forces or government.

Bofors gun *bō'förz* or *-förs gun*, *n* a single- or double-barrelled, quick-firing anti-aircraft gun. [From *Bofors*, Sweden, where orig made]

bog *bog*, *n* spongy, *usu* peaty, ground; a marsh; a type of vegetation growing on peat deficient in lime; a lavatory (*slang*). — *vt* to sink. — Also *vi*. — *n* **bogg'iness**. — *adj* **bogg'y**. — **bog'-asphodel** a yellow-flowered liliaceous bog-plant (*Narthecium ossifragum*); **bog'bean** buckbean, a marsh plant; **bog'-butter** a butter-like substance found in Irish peat-bogs; **bog'-cotton** cotton-grass; **bog-iron** see **bog-ore**; **bog'land**; **bog'-Latin** Shelta; **bog'-moss** sphagnum; **bog'-myrtle** sweet-gale (*Myrica gale*), a bog plant; **bog'oak** trunks of oak embedded in bogs and preserved from decay; **bog'-ore** or **bog'-iron** an iron ore found in boggy land, limonite; **bog spavin** see **spavin**; **bog'trotter** (*slang*, often *derog*) an Irishman. — *n* and *adj* **bog'trotting**. — **bog down** to encumber or be encumbered with an overwhelming amount of work, a difficult task, etc. [Ir and Scot Gaelic *bogach*, from *bog* soft]

bogan *bō'gən*, (*NAm*) *n* a quiet tributary or backwater. [Algonquian *pokelogan*]

bogbean. See **buckbean**.

bogey[1] *bō'gi*, *n* in golf, the score, for a given hole or for the whole course, of an imaginary good player, Colonel *Bogey*, fixed as a standard: the bogey can be higher than par or sometimes equivalent to it, now *usu* a score of one stroke above the par for any hole. — **double bogey** (*golf*) a score of two above par for any hole. [Perh **bogy**]

bogey[2]. See **bogie**, **bogy**.

boggard *bog'ərd*, **boggart** *-ərt* or **boggle** *bog'l*. See **bogle**.

boggle *bog'l*, *vi* to start, draw back with fright; to hesitate, demur; to equivocate; (of one's mind, *esp* in *the mind boggles*) to be unable to imagine or grasp something, to be astounded by something (*colloq*). — *n* a scruple, objection; a bungle. — *n* **bogg'ler**. [**bogle**]

bogie or **bogey** *bō'gi*, *n* a low heavy truck, a trolley; a small railway freight truck; a pivoted undercarriage, as in a railway locomotive or vehicle; a child's home-made racing cart (*Scot*). [Ety unknown; perh connected with **bogy**]

bogle *bō'gl*, *n* a spectre or goblin; a scarecrow (*Scot*; also **tattie-bogle**); a bugbear, or source of terror. — **bogg'le**, **bogg'ard** and **bogg'art** are *N Eng* forms. — **bogle about the bush** or **stacks** a kind of hide-and-seek. [Scot; poss connected with **bug**[1]]

bogong *bō'gong*, *n* a noctuid moth eaten by Australian Aborigines. — Also **bugong** (*bōō'-*). [Aboriginal]

bogus *bō'gəs*, *adj* counterfeit, spurious. [An American cant word, of very uncertain origin, possibly ult related to **bogy**]

bogy or **bogey** *bō'gi*, *n* a goblin; a bugbear or special object of dread; the devil; a policeman (*slang*); a piece of nasal mucus (*slang*): — *pl* **bō'gies** or **bō'geys**. — *n* **bō'gyism** or **bō'geyism**. — **bo'gy-man** or **bo'gey-man** the Devil or other frightening being with whom to threaten children. [Perh a form of **bogle**]

boh. See **bo**[1].

bohea *bō-hē'*, *n* the lowest quality of black tea; black tea generally. [From the *Wu-i* hills in China]

Bohemian *bō-hē'mi-ən*, *n* a native or inhabitant of Bohemia, formerly a kingdom, later part of Czechoslovakia; a gypsy; an artist or writer, or anyone, who sets social conventions aside; the Czech language. — Also *adj*. — *n* **Bohē'mianism** (also without *cap*). — **Bohemian ruby** rose quartz; **Bohemian topaz** citrine. [Fr *bohémien* a gypsy, from the belief that these wanderers came from *Bohemia*]

bohunk *bō'hungk*, (*NAm slang*, *esp US*) *n* a Slav or Hungarian, *esp* an unskilled labourer; the language of such a labourer. [Perh *Bo*hemian *Hung*arian]

boil[1] *boil*, *vi* to pass rapidly from liquid into vapour with violent and copious production of bubbles; to reach boiling-point; (of a vessel) to contain boiling liquid; to bubble up as if from the action of heat; to be heated in boiling liquid; to be hot; to be very excited or angry. — *vt* to heat to a boiling state; to cook, dress, clean or otherwise treat by boiling. — *n* the act or condition of boiling; a swirling disturbance made at the surface of the water by a fish coming to the fly. — *n* **boil'er** a person who boils; that in which anything is boiled; a vessel in which steam is generated; a vessel in which water is heated for circulation; a (*usu* old) fowl, best cooked by boiling. — *n* **boil'ery** a place for boiling, *esp* for obtaining salt. — *n* **boil'ing** the act of causing to boil; the condition of being boiled or at boiling-point; a quantity boiled at once; a boiled sweet (*Scot*); a collection, set (*colloq*). — *adj* at boiling-point; very hot; bubbling; extremely angry. — **boiled shirt** a dress shirt; **boiled sweet** a sweet of boiled sugar, flavouring, and often colouring; **boil'er-maker** an industrial metal-worker; a drink consisting of whisky with a beer chaser (*US slang*); **boiler suit** a one-piece overall with trousers, and *usu* long sleeves; **boil'ing-point** the temperature at which a liquid, *esp* water, boils, *esp* at atmospheric pressure; the point of emotion, *esp* anger, where control is lost; **boiling-water reactor** a light-water reactor in which steam drives the turbines directly (see also **light-water reactor**, **pressurized water reactor**); **boil away** to evaporate (completely) by boiling; **boil down** to reduce in bulk by boiling; to extract the substance of (*lit* and *fig*); **boil down to** (*fig*) to mean, to signify when reduced to essentials; **boil off** to remove (impurities, etc) by boiling; **boil over** to bubble over the sides of the containing vessel; to break out into unrestrained indignation. — **come to the boil** to reach boiling-point; to reach a critical state; **on the boil** boiling; active. [OFr *boillir*, from L *bullīre*, from *bulla* a bubble]

boil[2] *boil*, *n* an inflamed swelling, *esp* one caused by infection of a hair follicle. [OE *bȳl*; Ger *Beule*]

boing *boing* or **boink** *boink*, *n* the sound of a bouncing impact. — *interj* imitating this sound. — *vi* to bounce or hit with such a sound. [Imit]

boisterous *bois'tər-əs*, *adj* noisy and exuberant; wild; turbulent; stormy. — *adv* **bois'terously**. — *n* **bois'-terousness**. [ME *boistous*]

boîte de nuit *bwät də nwē*, (*Fr*) *n* a nightclub.

bok *bok*, (*SAfr*) *n* a goat; an antelope (used both of male and female). [Du, goat]

boke or **boak** *bōk*, (*Northern*) *vi* to belch; to retch, vomit; to gush, spurt. — *vt* to vomit; (of a volcano, etc) to emit. — *n* the act of boking; vomit. — Also (*Scot*) **bock** (*bōk* or *bok*). [Prob imit but compare Older Scot *bolk*, ME *bolken*, and **belch**]

Bokmål *bo͞okmōl*, *n* one of the two official written varieties of modern Norwegian (the other being Nynorsk), based on the written Danish introduced when Norway and Denmark were united (formerly called Riksmål). [Norw, book language]

boko *bō'kō*, (*slang*) *n* the nose: — *pl* **bō'kos**. [Origin unknown]

bolas *bō'läs*, *n* (properly *pl*) a S American missile, consisting of two or more balls or stones strung together, swung round the head and hurled so as to entangle an animal. — **bolas spider** a spider that catches its prey with a sticky drop on the end of a line thrown like a bolas. [Sp, balls]

bold *bōld*, *adj* daring; actively courageous; forward or impudent; presumptuous; executed vigorously; striking, noticeable, well marked; steep or abrupt; (of eg currants) full-flavoured, mature, plump; (of type) bold-faced. — *n* bold-faced type. — *vt* **bold'en** (*obs*) to make bold. — *adv* **bold'ly**. — *n* **bold'ness**. — **bold face** bold-faced type. — *adj* **bold'-face**. — *adj* **bold'-faced** impudent; (of type) having a black heavy face. — **be so bold (as to)** to venture (to), take the liberty (of); **bold as brass** utterly unabashed; **make bold** to venture, take the liberty. [OE *bald*; OHGer *bald*, ON *ballr*]

bold-beating *bōld'-bēt'ing*, (*Shakesp*) *adj* possibly for 'bowl-beating' ie tub-thumping, or a conflation of **bold** and **browbeating**.

bole[1] *bōl*, *n* the trunk of a tree. [ON *bolr*; Ger *Bohle* a plank]

bole[2] *bōl*, *n* a friable earthy clay, *usu* red. [Gr *bolos* a clod]

bole[3] *bōl*, (*Scot*) *n* a recess in a wall; an opening to admit light and air (also **win'dow-bole**). [Origin unknown]

bolection or **balection** *bō-* or *bə-lek'shən*, (*archit*) *n* a moulding around a panel, projecting beyond the surface of the framing. [Origin unknown]

bolero *bə-lā'rō*, *n* Spanish national dance; a tune to which it may be danced; (*usu bol'ə-rō*) a jacket or waistcoat not reaching the waist nor meeting in front: — *pl* **boleros**. [Sp]

Boletus *bol-ē'təs*, *n* a genus of fungi, both edible and poisonous, with a pore-like surface instead of gills; (without *cap*) a fungus of this genus: — *pl* **bole'tuses** or **bole'tī**. [L *bōlētus*, from Gr *bōlītēs* mushroom]

bolide *bō'līd*, *n* a large meteor, *esp* one that bursts; a fireball. [Fr, from L *bolis*, *-idis*, from Gr *bolis* missile]

bolivar *bol-ē'vär*, *n* the standard monetary unit of Venezuela (100 céntimos). [From Simón *Bolívar* (1783–1830)]

boliviano *bol-ē-vi-ä'nō*, *n* a Bolivian dollar (100 centavos): — *pl* **bolivia'nos**.

bolix. See **bollocks**.

boll[1] *bōl*, *n* a swelling; a knob; a round seed-capsule, as in cotton, flax, poppy, etc. — *vi* to swell, to form bolls. — *adj* **bolled** (*bōld*) swollen, podded. — *adj* **bollen** (*bō'lən*, *Shakesp* *bōln*; *obs*) swollen. — **boll'-weevil** a weevil (*Anthonomus grandis*) whose larvae infest cotton-bolls; **boll'-worm** a moth caterpillar that destroys cotton-bolls, maize, tomatoes, etc, in US *Chloridea obsoleta*, in Egypt and India *Earias insulana* and *E. fabia*. [A form of **bowl**[2], from OE *bolla*]

boll[2] *bōl*, *n* a measure of capacity for grain, etc, used in Scotland and N England, in Scotland *usu* = 6 imperial bushels, in England varying from 2 to 6 bushels; also a measure of weight, containing, for flour, 140 lb. [Prob ON *bolli*]

Bollandist *bol'ən-dist*, *n* any of the Jesuit writers who continued the *Acta Sanctorum* by John *Bolland* (1596–1665).

bollard *bol'ərd*, *n* a short post on a wharf or ship, etc, round which ropes are secured; one of a line of short posts preventing the passage of motor vehicles. [Prob **bole**[1]]

bollen. See **boll**[1].

bolletrie *bol'ə-trē*. Same as **bully-tree**.

bollix. See **bollocks**.

bollock *bol'ək*, (*slang*) *vt* to reprimand severely. — *n* **boll'ocking**. [From **bollocks**]

bollocks *bol'əks*, **ballocks**, **bollix** or **bolix** *bol'* or *bal'əks*, *n pl* (now generally considered *vulg*) testicles. — *n sing* (*slang*) nonsense; a muddle, mess. — *vt* (*US slang*) (*usu* with *up*) to make a botch of. — **boll'ock-naked** (*vulg slang*) completely naked. [OE *beallucas* testicles]

bolo[1] *bō'lō*, (*esp US*) *n* in boxing, a long sweeping uppercut: — *pl* **bo'los**. — Also **bolo punch**. [Ety uncertain]

bolo[2] *bō'lō*, *n* a traditional long-bladed Philippine knife: — *pl* **bo'los**. [Sp]

Bologna *bol-ōn'yä*, *adj* of the town of *Bologna* in Italy. — *adj* and *n* **Bologn'ese** (or *-āz'*). — **Bologna phial** an unannealed bottle that shatters on scratching; **Bologna phosphorus** barium sulphide; **Bologna sausage** a large sausage made of mixed meats; **Bologna stone** fibrous barytes. — **spaghetti (alla) bolognese** see **spaghetti**. [L *Bonōnia*]

bolometer *bō-lom'i-tər*, *n* an instrument for measuring radiant energy. — *adj* **bolomet'ric**. — *n* **bolom'etry**. [Gr *bolē* stroke, ray (from *ballein* to throw), and *metron* a measure]

boloney. See **baloney**.

Bolshevik (or **bolshevik**) *bol'shə-vik*, *n* a member of the Russian Majority (or Extreme) Socialist party (*opp* to *Menshevik*) (*hist*); a violent revolutionary Marxist communist; an anarchist, agitator, causer of trouble (used loosely as a term of disapproval). — Also *adj*. — *adj* colloquially contracted **bol'shie** or **bol'shy** awkward, intractable; left-wing. — Also *n*. — *n* **bol'-shevism**. — *n* **bol'shevist** a Bolshevik. — Also *adj*. — *vt* **bol'shevize** or **-ise**. [Russ, from *bolshe* greater, from its more thoroughgoing programme, or from its being in a majority (ie at the Russian Social Democratic Congress in 1903), and *-vik*, agent suffix]

bolster *bōl'stər*, *or bol'*, *n* a long, sometimes cylindrical, pillow or cushion; a pad; anything resembling it in form or use, *esp* any piece of a mechanism acting as a support against pressure; a form of cold chisel; the jutting-out part of a knife which abuts on the handle. — *vt* (also with *up*) to support as with a bolster; to hold up; to pad (*out*, etc). — *adj* **bol'stered** supported; swelled out. — *n* and *adj* **bol'stering** propping up or supporting. [OE *bolster*]

bolt[1] *bōlt* or *bolt*, *n* a bar or rod that slides into a hole or socket to fasten a door, etc; a heavy screw or pin with a head; an arrow, *esp* for a crossbow; a thunderbolt; a roll of a definite measure (of cloth, etc); the uncut edge of a sheet folded for a book; a rush, a sudden dash. — *vt* to fasten with a bolt; to utter precipitately; to swallow hastily; to cause to rush out, run away or take flight; to connect or join (*fig*); to break away from, withhold support from (*US*); to make up (cloth) into bolts. — *vi* to spring, dart; to run away, escape; (of a horse) to run out of control; to withhold support from one's party, its policy or nominee (*US*); (of a plant) to flower and run to seed. — *adv* like a bolt. — *n* **bolt'er**. — **bolt'head** the head of a bolt; **bolt'hole** a hole into which a bolt slides; a secret passage or way of escape; a refuge from danger; a secluded, private place. — *adj* **bolt'-on** additional, supplementary. — **bolt'-rope** a rope sewn round the edge of a sail to prevent it from tearing. — **a bolt from the blue** an unexpected event; **a fool's bolt is soon shot** a fool soon gives away the initiative, leaving himself or herself unprotected; **bolt upright** upright, and straight as an arrow; **have shot one's bolt** to be unable to do more than one has done. [OE *bolt*; OHGer *bolz*]

bolt[2], **bolter**, **bolting**. See **boult**.

Boltzmann constant *bōlts'mən kon'stənt*, (*phys*) *n* the ratio of the gas constant to Avogadro's constant. [Ludwig *Boltzmann* (1844–1906), Austrian physicist]

bolus *bō'ləs*, *n* a rounded mass; a large pill: — *pl* **bo'luses**. [L *bōlus*, from Gr *bōlos* a lump]

boma[1] *bō'mə*, (*EAfr*) *n* a fenced enclosure. [Swahili]

boma[2] *bō'mə*, *n* a boa or anaconda. [Congo; thence carried by Portuguese to Brazil]

bomb *bom* or (*old-fashioned*) *bum*, *n* a hollow case containing explosive, incendiary, smoke-producing, poisonous, or other offensive material; (with *the*) nuclear weapons collectively; a piece of programming, inserted into software, that can be activated to sabotage the system (*comput*); (also **volcanic bomb**) a rounded mass of lava thrown out by a volcano; an old worn-out car (*Austr* and *NZ colloq*); (of a play, etc) a fiasco, a flop (*NAm slang*). — *vi* to throw, discharge, or drop bombs; (sometimes with *out*) to be a flop, fail (*NAm slang*); to move very quickly, *esp* in a vehicle (*colloq*). — *vt* to attack, injure or destroy with bombs. — *n* **bomber** (*bom'ər*) a person who bombs or plants bombs; a bombing aeroplane. — Also *adj*. — *n* **bomb'let** a small bomb; a part of a larger complex weapon. — **bomb'-calorim'eter** an apparatus for determining the calorific value of fuels by ignition in a thick-walled steel vessel; **bomb'-disposal** the act of removing and detonating previously unexploded bombs; **bomber jacket** a short jacket with zipped front and elasticated waist. — *adj* **bomb'-happy** in a state of mind for discharging bombs without compunction; with nerves shattered by exposure to bombing. — **bomb-ketch** see **bomb-vessel**. — *adj* **bomb'-proof** proof or secure against the force of bombs. — *n* (*obs*) a bomb-proof structure. — **bomb'shell** a bomb; (now only *fig*) a sudden and surprising piece of news; **bomb'-sight** a device for aiming and releasing bombs from a bomber; **bomb'site** an area which has been laid waste by air-raid(s); **bomb'-squad** a group of soldiers or police trained in bomb-disposal; **bomb'-vessel** or **-ketch** (*hist*) a vessel for carrying mortars used in bombarding from the sea. — **bombed out of one's mind** or **skull** (*slang*) stoned; **cost a bomb** (*colloq*) to be very expensive; **go like a bomb** to go very well or very quickly; **make a bomb** (*colloq*) to make or earn a great deal of money. [Fr *bombe*, prob from L *bombus*, from Gr *bombos* humming sound]

bombacaceous. See **bombax**.

bombard *bom-bärd'* *vt* to attack with artillery; to batter or pelt; to subject to a succession of blows or impingements; to assail, eg with questions (*fig*); to subject (eg an atom) to a stream of particles at high speed (*phys*). — *n* (*bom'bärd*) an early cannon for throwing stones, etc; a large liquor-jug, a black-jack (*Shakesp*); an old form of bassoon. — *n* **bombardier** (*bom-* or *bum-bər-dēr'*) the lowest non-commissioned officer in the British artillery; the person in a bomber who aims and releases the bombs. — *n* **bombardment** (*bom-bärd'mənt*). — *n* **bombar'don** (or *bom'*) the bass tuba; a bass reed stop on the organ. — **bombardier beetle** a beetle that explosively discharges an acrid volatile fluid. [OFr *bombard* an old cannon for firing stones or shot; see also ety of **bomb**]

bombasine or **bombazine** *bom'bə-zēn* or formerly *bum'*, *n* a twilled or corded fabric of silk and worsted, or of cotton and worsted. [Fr *bombasin*, from LL *bombȳcinus*, from Gr *bombȳkinos* silken, from *bombȳx* silkworm]

bombast *bom'bast*, *n* pompously inflated language; cotton-wool, padding, stuffing (*obs*). — *adj* (*Shakesp*) inflated. — *vt* (*-bast'*, also *bom'*) (*archaic*) to pad, stuff; to inflate, make grandiose. — *adj* **bombas'tic** pompous; inflated. — *adv* **bombas'tically**. [Variant of obs *bombace*, from OFr, from as **bombax**]

bombax *bom'baks*, *n* any tree of the *Bombax* genus of tropical, chiefly S American trees, giving name to the silk-cotton family, **Bombacā'ceae**. — *adj* **bombacā'ceous**. [LL *bombax* cotton, from Gr *bombȳx* silk]

Bombay duck *bom'bā duk*, *n* a fish, the bummalo.

bombazine. See **bombasine**.

bombe *bom* or *bɔ̃b*, *n* a dessert, *usu* ice cream frozen in a round or melon-shaped mould. [Fr]

bombé *bom'bā* or *bɔ̃-bā*, *adj* (of furniture) having a rounded, convex front. [Fr, bulging, convex]

bomber. See **bomb**.

bombilate *bom'bil-āt* or **bombinate** *bom'bin-āt*, *vi* to hum, buzz, drone, boom. — *n* **bombilā'tion** or **bombinā'tion**. [L *bombilāre*, *bombināre*]

bombo *bom'bō*, (*Austr colloq*) *n* cheap wine, plonk: — *pl* **bom'bos**. [Ety uncertain]

bombora *bom-bō'rə* or *-bö'rə*, (*Austr*) *n* a submerged reef; a dangerous current or rough sea over such a reef. [Aboriginal]

Bombyx *bom'biks*, *n* the silkworm moth genus, giving name to the family **Bombycidae** (*-bis'i-dē*). — *n* **bom'bycid** an insect of the family. — Also *adj*. [Gr *bombȳx*]

bon *bɔ̃*, (*Fr*) *adj* good. — **bon accueil** (*bo-na-kœy*) good reception, due honour; **bon ami** (*fem* **bonne amie**) (*bo-na-mē*) good friend; lover; **bon appetit** (*bo-na-pə-tē*) good appetite, said politely to those who are (about to start) eating; **bon camarade** (*ka-ma-rad*) good comrade; **bon chrétien** (*krā-tyɛ̃*) *literally* 'good Christian', a kind of pear, the William; **bon diable** (*dē-äbl'*) a good-natured fellow; **bon goût** (*gōō*) good taste; **bon gré, mal gré** (*grā*, *mal grā*) willing or unwilling, willy-nilly; **bonjour** (*-zhōōr*) good day; good morning; **bon marché** (*mar-shā*) a bargain; cheapness; cheap; cheaply; **bon mot** (*pl* **bons mots**) (*mō*) a witty saying; **bonsoir** (*-swär*) good evening; **bon ton** (*tɔ̃*) the height of fashion; **bon vivant** (*vē-vã*) a jovial companion; a person who lives well, *esp* one who enjoys fine food (*fem* **bonne vivante** is not used in Fr); **bon viveur** (*vē-vœr*; not used in Fr) a bon vivant, *esp* a man-about-town; **bon voyage** (*vwä-yäzh*) may you have a good journey. [Fr, from L *bonus* good]

bona *bō'nə* or *bo'na* (*L*) *n pl* goods. — **bona mobilia** (*mō-bi'li-ə* or *-a*) (*law*) movable goods; **bona peritura** (*per-i-tū'rə* or *-tōō'ra*) (*law*) perishable goods; **bona vacantia** (*va-kan'shi-ə* or *wa-kan'ti-a*) (*law*) unclaimed goods.

bona fide *bō'nə fīd*, *fī'də*, *-di*, or *bo'nä fi'dā*, *adj* genuine; done or carried out in good faith. — *n* (*Ir colloq*) a public house legally open outside normal licensing hours to serve travellers. — **bona fides** (*fī'dēz* or *fid'ās*) good faith; genuineness; also (treated as *pl*) proofs of trustworthiness. [L, (in) good faith]

bonamano. See **buonamano**.

bonamia *bon-ā'mi-ə*, *n* a parasite that causes bonamiasis. — *n* **bonami'asis** a fatal disease of oysters, attacking their immunological system.

bonanza *bon-an'zə*, *n* a rich mine or vein of precious ore (*NAm*); a large amount of (*usu*) silver; any source of wealth or stroke of luck. — *adj* very prosperous. [Sp, good weather (at sea)]

Bonapartean *bō-nə-pärt'i-ən*, *adj* of Napoleon *Bonaparte* or his family. — *n* **Bō'napartism** attachment to his dynasty or policy. — *n* and *adj* **Bō'napartist**.

bona-roba *bō'nə-rō'bə*, (*Shakesp*) *n* a prostitute, courtesan. [Ital *buona roba*, literally good stuff (or dress)]

bonasus or **bonassus** *bon-as'əs*, *n* a bison. [L from Gr *bonasos*, *bonassos*]

bonbon *bon'bon* or *bɔ̃-bɔ̃*, *n* a confection, a sweet; a cracker (for pulling) (*obs*). — *n* **bonbonnière** (*bɔ̃-bon-yer'*) a fancy box for holding sweets. [Fr, reduplication of *bon* good]

bonce *bons*, *n* a large marble; the head (*slang*). [Origin obscure]

bond[1] *bond*, *n* something that binds; a link, connection, union or (*chem*) attraction; a written obligation to pay a sum or to perform a contract; a debenture, a security issued by the government or a company when borrowing money; a mortgage (*Scots law*); any adhesive or cementing force or material; in building, the overlapping connection of one course of stones or bricks with another, as in **English bond** or **Flemish bond**; (in *pl*) imprisonment, captivity; the status of goods retained in a **bonded warehouse** or **store** until duties are paid or the goods are exported; bond paper. — *vt* to connect, secure or bind with a bond; to put in a bonded warehouse; to put in a condition of bond; to cause to adhere (to) (eg metal to glass or plastic). — *vi* to adhere together securely; to form an emotional bond. — *adj* **bond'ed** secured by bond. — *n* **bond'er** a bondstone or header. — *n* **bond'ing** an act of bonding; the forming of a close emotional attachment, *esp* between a mother and her newborn child (*psychol*). — **bonded debt** the debt of a corporation represented by the bonds it has issued, as contrasted with its floating debt; **bonded warehouse** see under *n* above; **bond energy** the energy, in joules, released on the formation of a chemical bond between atoms and absorbed on its breaking; **bond'-holder** a person who holds bonds of a private person or public company; **bond paper** a superior kind of paper, used *esp* as stationery, *orig* intended for bonds; **bonds'man** a surety; **bond'stone** a stone that reaches a considerable distance into or entirely through a wall, binding it together; **bond'-timber** timber built into a wall for the purpose of binding it together lengthwise; **bond'-washing** an illegal series of deals in bonds designed to avoid payment of tax. [A variant of **band**, from OE *bindan* to bind]

bond[2] *bond, adj* in a state of servitude. — *n* **bond'age** captivity; slavery, serfdom, villeinage; a sexual practice in which the partners derive additional pleasure through, or by applying, physical restraint or binding. — *adj* (of *usu* black leather clothes or accessories) aggressive-looking, with chains, metal studs, buckles, etc. — *n* **bond'ager** a female outworker in the Borders and N England, one of whom every male farm worker had to provide for the farm work. — **bond'maid, bond'-woman** or **bonds'woman** a female slave or serf; **bond'-man** or **bonds'man** a male slave or serf; **bond'manship**; **bond'servant** a slave; **bond'-service** the condition of a bondservant; slavery; **bond'-slave** a slave; **bonds'man, bonds'woman** see **bondman, bondwoman** above. [OE *bonda* a farmer, a householder, from ON *bōndi, būandi* a tiller, a husbandman, from *būa* to till, cognate with OE *buan*, the meaning having been affected by association with **bond**[1]]

bondsman. See **bond**[1,2].

bonduc *bon'duk, n* the nicker seed. [Ar *bonduq* a kind of nut]

bone *bōn, n* a hard substance forming the skeleton of the higher animals; a separate piece of the skeleton; a piece of whalebone or other material used for stiffening corsets, etc; a bobbin for lace-making; (in *pl*) the skeleton or anything resembling it in any way; (in *pl*) mortal remains; (in *pl*) pieces of bone or something similar held between the fingers of the hand and rattled together to keep time to music; (in *pl*) dice; (in *pl*) a nickname for a doctor (*colloq*). — *vt* to take the bones out of (eg meat); to provide (a corset, etc) with bones; to seize, to nab (*slang*). — *adj* **boned** having bones; having the bones removed. — *adj* **bone'less** lacking bones; spineless (*fig*). — *n* **bō'ner** (*slang*) a howler, a blunder. — *n* **bō'niness**. — *adj* **bō'ny** full of, consisting of, or like bones; thin. — **bone'-ache** pain in the bones; **bone'-ash** or **bone'-earth** the remains of bones burned in air; **bone'-bed** a deposit of fossil bones; **bone'-brecc'ia** rock formed of broken fossil bones; **bone'-black** the carbonaceous remains of bones heated in the absence of air; **bone'-cave'** a cave containing deposits of fossil bones of animals that lived in it or their prey; **bone china** china in the making of which bone-ash is used. — *adj* **bone-dry'** as dry as a bone; under total prohibition of alcohol. — **bone'-dust** ground or pulverized bones, used in agriculture; **bone-earth** see **bone-ash**; **bone'head** a blockhead. — *adj* **bone'-headed**. — *adj* **bone-i'dle** utterly idle, idle to the bone. — **bone'-lace** lace woven with bobbins, formerly often made of bones; **bone marrow grafting** (*med*) grafting or transplantation of bone marrow to patients with bone marrow failure (used in aplastic anaemia or after therapeutic destruction of the bone marrow in leukaemia); **bone'-meal** ground bones used as fertilizer and as animal feed; **bone'-mill** a mill where bones are ground; **bone'-oil** a liquid produced by the destructive distillation of bones; **bone'set** a N American species of hemp agrimony; **bone'setter** a person who treats broken or dislocated bones, *esp* when not surgically qualified; **bone'shaker** a *colloq* name for earlier forms of bicycle; any uncertainly reliable, crazy vehicle; **bone spavin** see **spavin**; **bone'-tur'quoise** a blue fossil bone or tooth used as turquoise. — *adj* **bone'-weary** utterly exhausted. — **bone'yard** (*slang*) a cemetery; **bony fishes** the Teleostei, an order of fishes including most of the living forms; **bony pike** the American (and fossil) garfish. — **a bone to pick** a difference to be cleared up (with somebody); something to occupy one (*archaic*); **bare bones** the essentials (of a subject); **bone of contention** something that causes strife; **bone up on** (*slang*) to study or collect information about (a subject); **close to the bone** see **near the bone** below; **feel in one's bones** to know instinctively, without proof; **make no bones of** or **about** to have no scruples about; to make no fuss or difficulty about; to be quite open about; **near** (or **close to**) **the bone** on the verge of being indecent; offensively pointed; mean; hard up, poor; **(never) make old bones** (not) to live to old age; **to the bone** to the inmost part; to the minimum; **work one's fingers to the bone** to work until one is exhausted. [OE *bān*; Ger *Bein* leg]

bonfire *bon'fīr, n* a large fire in the open air on occasions of public celebration for consuming garden refuse, etc, *orig* a fire in which bones were burnt. — **Bonfire night** November 5, Guy Fawkes night (see **guy**). [**bone** and **fire**]

bong *bong, n* a deep hollow or ringing sound. — *vi* to make such a sound. — Also *vt*. [Imit]

bongo[1] *bong'gō, n* a Central African bushbuck: — *pl* **bong'os**. [Native name]

bongo[2] *bong'gō* or **bongo drum** (*drum*), *n* a small Cuban drum, generally used in pairs, played with the fingers: — *pl* **bon'gos** or **bongo drums**. [Am Sp *bongó*]

bongrace *bon'grās, n* a shade against the sun worn on the front of women's hats in the Middle Ages; a broad-brimmed hat or bonnet. [Fr *bonne* (fem) good, and *grâce* grace]

bonheur-du-jour *bo-nœr-dü-zhōōr, n* a small desk or writing-table popular *esp* in 18c France. [Fr, happiness of the day]

bonhomie or **bonhommie** *bon'o-mē, n* easy good nature. — *adj* **bon'homous**. [Fr]

bonibell. See **bonnibell**.

bonie. See **bonny**.

boniface *bon'i-fās, n* an innkeeper. [From the hearty *Boniface* of Farquhar's *Beaux' Stratagem*, or the *Bonifazio* of Ariosto's *La Scolastica*]

bonilasse. See **bonnilasse**.

boning *bōn'ing, n* the process of estimating straightness by looking along a row of poles, as in **bo'ning-rod** or **-telescope**.

bonism *bon'izm, n* the doctrine that the world is good, but not the best possible. — *n* **bon'ist**. [L *bonus* good]

bonito *bo-nē'tō, n* any of several large fish of the mackerel family, somewhat smaller than the tunas: — *pl* **boni'tos**. [Sp]

bonk *bongk*, (*colloq*) *n* a blow or thump, or its sound; an act of sexual intercourse (*vulg*). — *vt* to hit or thump; to have sexual intercourse with (*vulg*). [Imit]

bonkers *bong'kərz*, (*slang*) *adj* crazy; slightly drunk.

bonne *bon*, fem of **bon**, (*Fr*) *adj* good. — *n* a French maid or nursemaid. — **bonne chance** (*shãs*) good luck; **bonne compagnie** (*kɔ̃-pa-nyē*) good society; **bonne femme**

(*fam*; *cookery*) of a dish, cooked simply and garnished with fresh vegetables and herbs; **bonne foi** (*fwa*) good faith; **bonne grace** (*gräs*) good grace, gracefulness; (in *pl*) favour; **bonne mine** (*mēn*) good appearance, pleasant looks.

bonne-bouche *bon-bo͞osh'*, *n* a delicious morsel. [Fr, pleasant taste, from *bonne* (fem) good, and *bouche* mouth]

bonnet *bon'it*, *n* a woman's head-covering, tied on by ribbons, etc; a man's soft cap (now *Scot*); an additional part laced to the foot of jibs, or other fore-and-aft sails, to gather more wind (*naut*); a wire cowl over a chimney-top; the cover of a motor car engine, or of various parts of machinery, etc; the second stomach of a ruminant; a raised portion between guns at a salient (*fortif*); a decoy or pretended player or bidder at a gaming-table or an auction, the accomplice of a thimble-rigger or other petty swindler. — *vt* to put a bonnet on; to crush someone's own hat over the eyes of (someone). — *adj* **bonn'eted**. — **bonnet laird** (*Scot*) a small landowner (who wore a bonnet, not the hat of the gentry); **bonn'et-monkey** an Indian macaque (from the appearance of the head); **bonn'et-piece** a gold coin of James V of Scotland, on which the king wears a bonnet; **bonnet-rouge** (*Fr*; *bon-ā-ro͞ozh*) the red cap of liberty of the French Revolution, in the form of a Phrygian cap. [OFr, from LL *bonnetum*, orig the name of a material]

bonnibell or **bonibell** *bon-i-bel'*, (*Spenser*) *n* a good and fair maid. [Fr *bonne et belle* good and fair; or for *bonny belle*]

bonnilasse or **bonilasse** *bon'i-läs*, *n* (*Spenser*) for **bonny lass**.

bonny or **bonnie** *bon'i* (*Scot* also *bō'ni*; *Burns* (*adj* only) **bonie**), *adj* comely, pretty; plump; healthy-looking; as a general term expressing appreciation, fine, splendid, considerable, etc (often *ironic*); smiling, cheerful (*obs*); big and strong (*Shakesp*). — *n* a sweetheart. — Also *adv*. — *adv* **bonn'ily**. — *n* **bonn'iness**. [Origin obscure]

bonny-clabber *bon'i-klab'ər*, (*Anglo-Ir*) *n* milk naturally clotted on souring. [Ir *bainne* milk, and *claba* thick]

bonsai *bon'sī* or *bōn'sī*, *n* a dwarf tree growing in a pot, produced by special methods of cultivation (*pl* **bon'sai**); the art of growing such trees. [Jap *bon* tray, bowl, and *sai* cultivation]

bonsella *bon-sel'ə*, (*SAfr*) *n* a gratuity to a Black African. [Zulu *ibhanselo* a gift]

bonspiel *bon'spēl*, *n* a curling match. [Appar from a Du compound of *spel* play; cf **ba'spiel** under **ball**[1]]

bontebok *bon'tə-bok*, *n* a S African antelope. [Du *bont* particoloured, and *bok* goat]

bonus *bō'nəs*, *n* something good or desirable gained or given with something else; a premium beyond the usual interest for a loan; an extra dividend to shareholders; a policy-holder's share of profits; an extra payment to a workforce, salesmen, etc, eg for reaching specified targets or at special times of year such as Christmas; a bribe. — **bonus issue** an issue of additional shares (**bonus shares**) to a company's shareholders in proportion to their existing shareholding, representing a capitalization of reserves. [L *bonus* good]

bonxie *bongks'i*, (*Shetland*) *n* the great skua. [ON *bunkie* heap]

bonze *bonz*, *n* a Buddhist priest. [Jap *bonzô* or *bonzi* a priest]

bonzer or **bonza** *bon'zə*, (*Austr colloq*) *adj* very good. [Perh from Fr *bon* good, influenced by US *bonanza*]

boo[1] or **booh** *bo͞o*, *n* and *interj* a sound expressing disapproval or contempt. — *vt* and *vi* to show disapproval (of) by making such a sound. — **boo-hoo** (*-ho͞o'*) the sound of noisy weeping. — *vi* to weep noisily. — **boo'-word** a word denoting something disliked, disapproved of, or feared.

boo[2]. See **bo**[1].

boob[1] *bo͞ob*, (*colloq*) *vt* to bungle. — *vi* to blunder. — *n* a blunder (also **booboo** *bo͞o'bo͞o*) a stupid fellow (*US*). — **boob tube** (*NAm slang*) a television set. [**booby**[1]]

boob[2] *bo͞ob*, (*slang*) *n* (*usu* in *pl*) a female breast. — **boob'-tube** (*slang*) a woman's garment of stretch fabric covering the torso from midriff to armpit. [**booby**[2]]

booboo. See **boob**[1].

boobook *bo͞o'bo͝ok*, *n* an Australian owl (*Ninox boobook*). [Aboriginal; from its cuckoo-like cry]

booby[1] *bo͞o'bi*, *n* a stupid person; a pupil at the bottom of the class; a name for various kinds of gannet. — *adj* **boo'byish** like a booby; stupid. — *n* **boo'byism**. — **boo'by-prize** a prize for the least successful in a competition, etc; **boo'by-trap** a harmless-looking object which on being touched sets off an explosion; a form of practical joke, by which something is made to fall upon someone entering a door, or the like. — *vt* to set up a booby-trap in or on. [Perh Sp *bobo* a dolt]

booby[2] *bo͞o'bi*, (*slang*) *n* a female breast. [Obs Eng *bubby*]

boodie or **boodie-rat** *bo͞o'di-(rat)*, *n* a now rare species of rat-kangaroo, found in the islands off W Australia. [Aboriginal]

boodle[1] *bo͞od'l*, *n* counterfeit money; money obtained by political or official corruption; spoil; caboodle. [Perh Du *boedel* property]

boodle[2] *bo͞od'l*, (*slang*) *n* a stupid person.

boody *bo͞od'i*, *vi* to sulk or mope: — *pr p* **bood'ying**; *pa t* and *pa p* **bood'ied**. [Fr *bouder* to pout]

boogie-woogie *bo͞og'i-wo͞og'i*, *n* a jazz piano style with a repeated strongly rhythmic bass and melodic variations above. — *n* **boog'ie** boogie-woogie; dancing to pop music. — *vi* to dance to pop music: — *pr p* **boog'ieing**; *pa t* and *pa p* **boog'ied**. [Reduplicated from US slang *boogie* a Negro performer]

booh. See **boo**[1].

book *bo͝ok*, *n* a collection of sheets of paper, etc, bound or otherwise fastened together, either printed, written on, or blank; a large-scale literary composition; a division of a volume or composition; (with *the* and sometimes *cap*) the Bible; a record of bets made with different people; any source of information or knowledge; a set of rules; a libretto; a script; the first six tricks gained by a side in whist, etc; a structure resembling a book; (in *pl*) formal accounts of transactions, eg minutes of meetings, records kept of a business. — *vt* to engage or reserve in advance; (of the police, a traffic warden, etc) to take the name of, for an alleged offence; hence, to arrest; (of a referee) to enter a player's name in a notebook for an offence (*football*); to write or enter in a book (*archaic*). — *vi* to make a reservation in advance. — *adj* **book'able**. — *adj* **book'ful** full of information gathered from books. — *n* **book'ie** (*colloq*) a bookmaker. — *n* **book'ing** a reservation of eg a room in a hotel, a theatre seat, a seat on a plane, train, etc; an engagement for the services of someone, *usu* a performer; the taking of a name for an offence. — *adj* **book'ish** relating to books; fond of books, studious; acquainted only with, and experienced only through books. — *n* **book'ishness**. — *adj* **book'less** without books; unlearned. — *n* **book'let** a little book, *esp* one of only a few pages, saddle-stitched, with paper covers. — *adj* **book'sie** or **book'sy** by way of being literary. — *adj* **book'y** bookish. — **book'-account** an account of debt or credit in a book; **book'binder** a person who binds books; **book'bindery** (*US*) a place where books are bound; **book'binding**; **book'-canvasser** a person who goes around soliciting orders for a book (*obs*); **book'-case** a piece of furniture with shelves for books; **book club** a society that buys, circulates on loan, or prints books for its members; **book'-debt** a sum owing to a seller, as shown in the seller's business-books. — *adj* **booked-out'** or **booked-up'** full up; unable to accept further reservations, bookings or appointments. — **book'-end** one of a pair of props for the end of a row of books; **book'-hand** (*hist*) one of the writing styles used to produce copies of books in manuscript before the invention of printing; **book'-holder** a prompter in the theatre; **book'ing-clerk** a person who sells tickets; **book'ing-hall**; **book'ing-off'ice** an office where reservations are made or tickets sold; **book'keeper**; **book'-**

keeping the keeping of accounts in a regular and systematic manner; the record of the financial transactions of a business; **book'land** (OE *bōcland*) land taken from the *folcland* or common land, and granted by *bōc* or written charter to a private owner. — *adj* **book'-learned** (*-lûrn'id*). — **book'-learning** learning acquired from books, as opposed to practical knowledge; **book'lore** (*Scot* **book'-lear** or **buik'-lear** *-lār*) book-learning; bibliographical lore; **book'louse** a wingless insect of the Corrodentia, which damages books: — *pl* **book'lice**; **book'maker** a person who accepts bets at race-courses, etc, and pays out the winnings; a person who makes up books from the writings of others, a compiler; **book'making**; **book'man** a scholar, student; **book'mark** or **book'marker** a (decorative) strip of leather, fabric, paper, etc, or other object, for marking a particular opening or one's current place in a book; **book'-mate** (*Shakesp*) a companion in study, a schoolfellow; **book'-mindedness** habitual direction of the mind towards books; **book'mobile** (*NAm*) a mobile library; **book'-muslin** muslin used in book-binding; **book'-oath** (*Shakesp*) an oath made on the Book or Bible; **book'plate** a label usually pasted inside the cover of a book, bearing the owner's name or other distinguishing information; **book'-post** an arrangement for the transmission of books by post, including special charges, etc; **book price** or **value** the officially-recorded value, not necessarily the market value, of a commodity, etc; **book'rest** a support for a book, a bookstand; **book'-scorpion** a scorpion-like arachnid found in libraries, probably feeding on booklice; **book'seller** a person who sells books; formerly a publisher; **book'selling**; **book'shelf** a shelf for books; **book'shop** a shop where books are sold; **book'stall** a stall or stand where books are sold; **book'stand** a bookstall; a stand or support for holding up a book in reading; **book'store** (*US*) a bookshop; **book'-token** a voucher to be exchanged for books of a stated price, given as a gift; **book trade** the trade of dealing in books; **book value** see **book price**; **book'work** study from books, theoretical as opposed to practical work; work on account books, etc; **book'worm** a grub that eats holes in books, *esp* a beetle larva (*Anobium*); a person who is devoted to reading. — **an open** (or **closed**) **book** a person or subject that is well known or clearly understood (or not known or understood at all); **be on the books** to have one's name in an official list; to be a member; **book in** to reserve a place or room; to register at a hotel; **book of original** (or **first**) **entry** (*bookkeeping*) a book in which the first record of transactions is made, eg before entry in a ledger; **book of words** (*colloq*) directions for use; **book out** to leave a hotel formally, by settling one's bill, handing in one's key, etc; **book through** to book as a whole a journey to be made in parts; **bring to book** to bring to account; **closed book** see **an open book** above; **get one's books** to be dismissed; **in anyone's book** indeed, without any doubt; **in my** (etc) **book** in my (etc) view; **in someone's good** (or **bad**) **books** favourably (or unfavourably) regarded by someone; **read (someone) like a book** to understand thoroughly (*usu* a person's character or motives); **suit one's book** to be agreeable to or favourable to one; **take a leaf out of someone's book** to profit by someone's example; **talk like a book** to talk pedantically, or with precision and readiness; **throw the book at** (*colloq*) to administer a lengthy and detailed reproof to; to punish severely; **without book** from memory; unauthorizedly. [OE *bōc* book, beech; cf Ger *Buche* beech, and *Buch* book, supposed to be from early Germanic use of beech boards]

Boolean algebra *bōō'lē-ən al'ji-brə*, (*logic*) *n* a logical system which makes the algebraic manipulation of sets possible. — **Boolean expression** an expression containing the logical operators 'and', 'or', 'not', used extensively in computing. [Named after George *Boole* (1815–64)]

boom[1] *bōōm*, *n* a pole which controls the position of a sail; a chain or bar stretched across a harbour; a barrier of floating logs; an inflatable barrier used to contain oil from spillages, etc; a long beam; a movable and *usu* extendable beam which holds an overhead camera or microphone in a TV studio or film set; a tree (as *combining form*, eg *kaffir-boom*, etc; *SAfr*). — **boom'-iron** a ring in which a ship's boom slides; **boom'slang** (*S* and *EAfr*) a venomous tree-snake. [Du *boom* beam, tree]

boom[2] *bōōm*, *vt* to make a hollow sound or roar. — *n* a hollow roar. — **boom'-box** (*slang*) powerful portable radio and cassette recorder with built-in speakers, a ghetto-blaster. [From a LGer root found in OE *byme* a trumpet, Du *bommen* to drum; like **bomb**, of imit origin]

boom[3] *bōōm*, *vi* to become active or busy suddenly; to become suddenly prosperous; to increase sharply in value. — *vt* to push into sudden prominence; to boost by advertising. — *n* a sudden increase of activity in business, etc, a period of expansion of the economy; a sudden rise in price or value. — *n* and *adj* **boom'ing**. — *n* **boom'let** a minor economic boom. — **boom town** one which has expanded rapidly and prospered because of eg the arrival of a valuable new industry. — **boom and bust** alternate periods of economic expansion and recession. [Prob from **boom**[2]]

boomer *bōōm'ər*, (*Austr* and *NZ*) *n* a large male kangaroo, *esp* of the great grey species; anything large or very successful (*colloq*). [Partly from **boom**[2], partly from Eng dialect *boomer* anything very large of its type]

boomerang *bōōm'ə-rang*, *n* a curved missile used by the Australian Aborigines, sometimes so balanced that it returns towards the thrower; an act that recoils upon the agent. — *vi* to recoil in such a way, backfire. [Aboriginal]

boomps-a-daisy. See under **bump**[1].

boon[1] *bōōn*, *n* a gift, favour; something to be thankful for, a blessing; a petition, request (*obs*). [ON *bōn* prayer, cognate with OE *bēn*]

boon[2] *bōōn*, *adj* jovial, convivial, or intimate (as a *boon companion*). [Fr *bon*, from L *bonus* good]

boondocks *bōōn'doks*, (*US colloq*) *n pl* (with *the*) wild or remote country; a dull provincial place. — Also **the boo'nies**. [Tagálog *bundok* mountain]

boondoggle *bōōn'dog-l*, (*US*) *n* a Scout's plaited cord of varicoloured leather strips; an article of simple handcraft; work, or a task, of little or no practical value, *esp* work officially provided as a palliative for unemployment. — *vi* to do such work. [Scout coinage]

boong *bōōng*, (*Austr offensive*) *n* an Aborigine; a New Guinea native; any coloured person. [Aboriginal]

boonies *bōō'niz*. See under **boondocks**.

boor *bōōr*, *n* a coarse, ill-mannered person; a Dutch colonist in S Africa (*hist*); a countryman, a peasant (*obs*). — *adj* **boor'ish** awkward or rude. — *adv* **boor'ishly**. — *n* **boor'ishness**. [Du *boer*; perh partly OE *būr*, *gebūr* farmer]

boord or **boorde** *bōrd* or *bōrd*, old spellings of **board** (*Spenser*, etc).

boorka. See **burka**.

boortree. See **bourtree**.

boose. See **booze**.

boost *bōōst*, *vt* to push up; to raise (eg price, morale); to advertise or promote; to supplement or increase (eg voltage or air supply); to increase the pressure of; to push (a spacecraft) into orbit by means of a booster. — *vi* (*US*) to shoplift; to steal. — Also *n*. — *n* **boost'er** a person or thing which boosts; a keen supporter (*US*); an auxiliary motor in a rocket, *usu* breaking away after delivery of its impulse; any device to increase the effect of another mechanism; an additional dose of a vaccine to increase or renew the effect of the original dose; a shoplifter (*US*). [Orig US; ety unknown]

boot[1] *bōōt*, *n* a covering for the foot and at least the ankle, often the calf or even higher up the leg, made of leather, rubber, etc; a compartment in a motor car for luggage, etc; a kick (*colloq*); an instrument of torture for the leg

(*Scot hist*); a box or receptacle in a coach (*obs*). — *vt* to put boots on; to kick; to turn out, dismiss (with *out*; *colloq*); to start up the initial programs on (a computer), to bootstrap, *usu* by transferring the disk-operating system program from its storage on the disk into the computer's working memory (often with *up*). — *adj* **boot'ed** having boots on, equipped for riding; (of birds, *esp* poultry) having feathered legs. — *n* **bootee** (*bōō'tē* or *-tē'*) a short boot; an infant's knitted boot; (*bōō'tē*) a Royal Marine (*services slang*). — *n* **boot'ikin** (*obs*) the boot for torture (*Scot*); a boot or mitten for the gouty; an infant's legging. — *n* **boots** a hotel servant who cleans boots, runs messages, etc. — **boot'black** a person whose job is to clean and polish shoes; a shoeblack; **boot boy** same as **bovver boy**; **boot'-catcher** an inn servant who helped to pull off guests' boots. — *adj* **boot'-faced** with an unsmiling, expressionless face. — **boot'-hook** an instrument for pulling on long boots; **boot'hose** (*Shakesp*) a long over-stocking which covers the leg like a boot: — *pl* **boot'hose**; **boot'-jack** a device for pulling off boots; **boot'lace** a lace for fastening boots; **bootlace tie** a very thin stringlike necktie; **boot'last** or **boot'-tree** the last or foot-like mould on which boots or shoes are made or stretched to keep their shape; **boot'leg** the leg of a high boot. — *vt* to smuggle (alcoholic drink); to make or deal in (illicit goods such as alcoholic drink or illegally made recordings). — Also *vi*. — *adj* made or sold illicitly. — **boot'legger**; **boot'legging**. — *adj* **boot'less** without boots. — **boot'licker** a toady (*US* **boot'lick**; also *vt*); **boot'licking**; **boot'maker**; **boot'making**; **boot sale** same as **car boot sale**; **boot'strap** a bootlace; a strap on the back of a boot to help in pulling it on; (*comput*) the piece of software that boots up. — Also *adj*. — Also *vt* (*comput*) to input initial data so as to enable the subsequent loading of a computer program. — **boot'-topping** the part of a ship's hull between the load-line and the water-line when the ship is without cargo; the act of coating this; paint, etc, for the purpose; **boot-tree** see **bootlast**; **boot virus** (*comput*) a computer virus in the sector of a floppy disk used in booting up. — **bet one's boots** to be quite certain; **boot and saddle** (altered from Fr *boute-selle* place saddle) the signal for mounting (**boots and saddles** the bugle call which formerly called the US cavalry to mount); **boots and all** (*Austr* and *NZ*) without reservation; **die in one's boots** or **with one's boots on** to die while still working, still in harness; **get the boot** (*slang*) to be dismissed; **have one's heart in one's boots** to have lost courage; **lick someone's boots** to try to ingratiate oneself with someone by obsequious behaviour; **like old boots** (*slang*) vigorously; **pull oneself up by one's (own) bootstraps** to get on by one's own efforts; **put the boot in** or **put in the boot** (*slang*) to resort to physical or verbal bullying; to attack unfairly; to bring a situation to an end brutally; **the boot is on the other leg** (*obs*) or **foot** responsibility (now) lies the other way, the situation is reversed; **too big for one's boots** conceited, bumptious; **tough as old boots** robust; indestructible. [OFr *bote* (Mod Fr *botte*), from LL *botta, bota*, of doubtful origin]

boot[2] *bōōt*, *vt* to give profit or advantage to. — *n* (*obs*) advantage; profit; any reparation or compensation paid (*OE law*); booty (*Shakesp*). — *adj* **boot'less** unprofitable, useless. — *adv* **boot'lessly**. — *n* **boot'lessness**. — **to boot** in addition. [OE *bōt* compensation, amends, whence *bētan* to amend (see **beet**[2])]

Boötes *bō-ō'tēz*, *n* a constellation beside the Great Bear, containing the bright star Arcturus. [Gr *Boōtēs* literally an ox-driver]

booth *bōōdh* or *bōōth*, *n* a hut or small shop of simple construction; a stall at a fair or market; a partly-enclosed compartment, such as one in which to vote, telephone, or eat in a restaurant. [ON *būth*, or a cognate word; cf Ger *Bude*]

booty *bōōt'i*, *n* spoil taken in war or by force; plunder, a prize. — **play booty** to join with others in order to cheat one player; to play a game with the intention of losing. [MLGer *bute*; cognate with ON *bȳti* share, from *bȳta* to divide]

booze, (*obs*) **boose** *bōōz*, or (*archaic*) **bouse** *bowz*, (*colloq*) *vi* to drink alcohol, *esp* to excess. — *n* intoxicating liquor; a drinking bout. — *adj* **boozed**. — *n* **booz'er** a person who boozes; a public house (*slang*). — *adv* **booz'ily**. — *n* **booz'iness**. — *adj* **booz'ing** drinking; for drinking. — *adj* **booz'y** or **booz'ey** inclined to booze; drunken. — **booze'-up** a drinking bout. [Variant of **bouse**[1]]

bop[1] *bop*, *n* short for **bebop**, of which it was a development in the 1950s. — *vi* (*colloq*) to dance to pop music. — *n* **bopp'er**.

bop[2] *bop*, (*slang*) *n* a blow. — *vt* to strike. [Imit]

bo-peep *bō-pēp'*, *n* a children's game in which one peeps from behind something and cries 'Bo'.

bor *bö(r)*, *n* neighbour, an E Anglian form of address to man or woman. [OE *būr*, usu *gebūr* farmer; cf **neighbour**]

bor. *abbrev*: borough.

bora[1] *bö'rə*, *n* a strong NE wind in the upper Adriatic. [Venetian variant of Ital *borea*, from L *boreas*]

bora[2] *bö'rə*, *n* an Australian Aboriginal initiation rite. [Aboriginal]

borachio *bor-ach'(i-)ō*, *n* a Spanish wine-skin; a drunken fellow: — *pl* **borach'ios**. [Sp *borracha, borracho*]

boracic, boracite. See **borax**[1].

borage *bur'ij* or *bor'ij*, *n* a blue-flowered, bristly, aromatic herb, *Borago officinalis*, (family **Boraginā'ceae**), the leaves of which have a cucumber-like flavour and are used in salads and to flavour drinks. — *adj* **boraginā'ceous**. [LL *borrāgō*]

borak *bör'ək* or **borax** *bör'aks*, (*Austr* and *NZ slang*) *n* nonsense, banter. — **poke borak at** to make fun of, jeer at. [Aboriginal]

borane. See **boron**.

borax[1] *bö'raks*, *n* a mineral, hydrated sodium tetraborate, found on alkaline lake shores. — *adj* **bo'ric** or **boracic** (*bo-ras'ik*) of or relating to borax or boron; penniless, skint (*colloq*; rhyming slang for *boracic lint*). — *n* **bo'racite** (*-rə-sīt*) a mineral composed of magnesium borate and chloride. — *n* **bo'rate** a salt of boric acid. — **boric, boracic** or **orthoboracic acid** an acid (H_3BO_3) obtained from borax, and also found native in mineral springs in Italy. [Fr and LL *borax*, from Ar *būraq*]

borax[2]. See **borak**.

borazon. See **boron**.

borborygmus *bör-bə-rig'məs*, *n* the sound of flatulence in the intestines. — *adj* **borboryg'mic**. [Gr *borborygmos*]

bord, borde. *Obs* spellings of **board**.

bordar *börd'ər*, (*hist*) *n* a villein who held his cottage at his lord's pleasure. [LL *bordārius* of Gmc origin. See **board**]

Bordeaux *bör-dō'*, *n* claret, wine of the *Bordeaux* region of SW France. — **Bordeaux mixture** a mixture of lime and copper sulphate, used to kill fungus and insect parasites on plants.

bordel *bör'dəl*, (*archaic*) *n* a brothel. — Also **bordello** (*-del'ō*; *Ital*): — *pl* **bordell'os**. [OFr *bordel* a cabin, from LL *borda*]

border *börd'ər*, *n* the edge or margin of anything; the boundary of a country, etc, *esp* (with *cap*) that between England and Scotland; (in *pl* with *cap* and *the*) the area of Scotland bordering on England, *esp* between the Border and Lothian; a flower-bed in a garden; a piece of ornamental edging or trimming. — *adj* of or on the border. — *vi* to come near or to be adjacent (with *on*, *upon*, *with*); to verge on, be nearly the same as (with *on*). — *vt* to provide with a border; to form a border to, be adjacent to. — *adj* **bord'ered**. — *n* **bord'erer** a person who lives or was born on the border of a country. — *adj* **bord'erless**. — **Border collie** a breed of medium-sized, *usu* black and white, collie dog; **bordered pit** (*bot*) a thin area in the secondary wall of a cell, surrounded by a thickened arched border; **border effect** (*image technol*) a faint dark line on the denser side of a boundary between a lightly exposed and a heavily exposed region on a developed emulsion (also **edge effect** or **fringe effect**); **bord'erland** a border region; the undefined margin between two things (also *adj*); **Border Leicester** a sheep of a breed developed by cross-breeding Leicesters and Cheviots. — *adj* **bord'erline** marginal, doubtfully or just coming within the definition of a quality, condition, etc. — Also *n.* — **Borders Region** a local administrative area of Scotland, comprising Tweeddale, Ettrick and Lauderdale, Berwickshire and Roxburgh; **Border terrier** a small rough-haired terrier, *orig* from the Borders. [OFr *bordure*; from root of **board**]

bordereau *bor-d(ə-)rō*, (*Fr*) *n* a memorandum or detailed statement.

bordraging *börd'rag-ing*, *n.* See **bodrag**.

bordure *bör'dūr* or *-jo͞or*, (*heraldry*) *n* a border surrounding a shield. [Ety as for **border**]

bore[1] *bör*, *vt* to pierce (something) so as to form a hole; to produce (a hole) by drilling, etc; to weary or annoy with tediousness (*perh* a different word: not known before mid-18c). — *vi* to form a hole or borehole by drilling or piercing; (of a racehorse or athlete) to push against other competitors (to gain advantage in a race) (also *vt*). — *n* a hole made by boring; the cavity of a tube; the diameter of the cavity of a tube; an artesian well (*Austr*); a person, thing or activity that wearies; something that causes annoyance, a nuisance (*colloq*). — *n* **bore'dom** tedium. — *n* **bor'er** a person or thing that bores; a name common to many animals, *esp* insects that pierce wood, rocks, etc. — *adj* **bor'ing** causing boredom, tedious. — *n* the act of making a hole in anything; a hole made by boring; (in *pl*) the chips produced by boring. — *adv* **bor'ingly**. — **bore'hole** a bore made in the earth's crust for investigation or for water, oil, etc. [OE *borian* to bore; cf Ger *bohren*; cognate with L *forāre* to bore, Gr *pharynx* the gullet]

bore[2] *bör*, *pa t* of **bear**[1].

bore[3] *bör*, *n* a tidal flood that rushes with great violence up the estuaries of certain rivers, an eagre. [ON *bāra* a wave or swell]

Boreas *bor'* or *bör'i-as*, *n* the North Wind. — *adj* **bo'real** (*bo'* or *bö'*) of the North Wind or the North; (with *cap*) of a biogeographical region consisting of the northern and mountainous parts of the Northern hemisphere; (with *cap*) of a post-glacial period when the climate of Europe and N America resembled that of the present Boreal region. [L, from Gr]

borecole *bör'kōl*, *n* kale. [Du *boerenkool* literally peasant's cabbage]

boree *bö'rē*, (*Austr*) *n* any of several species of acacia. [Aboriginal]

boreen *bō-rēn'*, *n* a lane. [Ir *bóithrín*]

borel. See **borrel**.

borgo *bör'gō*, (*Ital*) *n* a borough, a market-town: — *pl* **bor'gos**. — *n* **borghetto** (*bor-get'tō*) a big village: — *pl* **borghet'tos**.

boric. Same as **boracic** under **borax**[1].

boride. See **boron**.

born *börn*, *pa p* of **bear**[1]. — **born again** having received new spiritual life, converted (*adj* (also *fig*) **born'-again**); **born fool**, **born mimic**, etc, someone whose folly, mimic ability, etc, is innate; **born to be** destined to be; **in (all) one's born days** in one's whole lifetime; **not born yesterday** not young in experience, not a fool.

borne *börn*, *pa p* of **bear**[1]. — **be borne in on** to be realized or grasped by.

borné *bor'nā*, *adj* limited, narrow-minded. [Fr pa p of *borner* to limit]

Bornholm disease *börn'hōm diz-ēz'*, *n* epidemic pleurodynia, a rare infectious disease caused by a virus. [From the Baltic island *Bornholm* where it was first described]

bornite *börn'īt*, *n* a copper ore, sulphide of copper and iron. [I von *Born* (1742–91), Austrian mineralogist]

boron *bö'ron*, *n* a non-metallic element (atomic no 5; symbol **B**), present in borax and boric acid, obtained as an amorphous powder or impure in diamond-like crystals. — *n* **borane** (*bör'ān*) any boron hydride, efficient as high-energy fuel. — *n* **borazon** (*bör'a-zon*) a man-made substance, a compound of boron and nitrogen, hard as diamond. — *n* **boride** (*bör'īd*) any of a class of substances made by combining boron chemically with a metal, some of which are extremely hard and heat-resistant. — *n* **borosil'icate** a salt of boric and silicic acids, used in making heat- and chemical-resistant glass. [See **borax**[1]]

boronia *bo-rō'ni-ə*, *n* an Australian scented shrub of the genus *Boronia*. [F *Borone* (1769–94), Italian botanist]

borough *bur'ə*, *n* a town with a corporation and special privileges granted by royal charter; a town that sends representatives to parliament; one of the local government divisions of London or New York. — **borough court** formerly, an inferior court dealing with minor offences, etc, presided over by local magistrates; **bor'ough-English** a former custom in some S English boroughs (till 1925), by which estates descended to the youngest son; **bor'ough-monger** a buyer or seller of the parliamentary seats of boroughs; **bor'ough-reeve** the chief municipal official in some unincorporated English towns prior to 1835; **close** or **pocket borough** a borough whose parliamentary representation was in the nomination of some person — common before 1832; **county borough** a borough (by Acts of 1888, 1926, 1958, respectively above 50 000, 75 000 and 100 000 inhabitants) with some of the attributes of a county — abolished 1974; **rotten borough** one of the boroughs which still returned members to parliament although the constituency had disappeared — all abolished in 1832. — The Scottish terms are grouped under **burgh**. [OE *burg*, *burh* a city, from *beorgan*, cognate with Ger *bergen* to protect]

borrel, **borrell** or **borel** *bor'əl*, (*archaic*) *adj* rustic, boorish. [OFr *burel* coarse cloth]

borrow *bor'ō*, *vt* and *vi* to obtain (money, etc) on loan or trust; to adopt (words, etc) from a foreign source; to derive from another (with *from*, *of*). — *vi* (*golf*) to allow for slope or wind, *esp* by putting the ball uphill of the hole. — *n* a pledge or surety (*archaic*); a borrowing (*Shakesp*); the allowance to be made for a slope on a green (*golf*). — *adj* **borr'owed** taken on loan; counterfeit; assumed. — *n* **borr'ower**. — *n* and *adj* **borr'owing**. — **borrowed time** an unexpected extension of life, or of the time allowed for some activity; **borrow hole** or **pit** (*civ eng*) a pit formed by the excavation of material to be used elsewhere for embanking, etc; **borrowing days** the last three days of March (*Old Style*), supposed in Scottish folklore to have been borrowed by March from April, and to be especially stormy. — **to borrow** (*obs*) for a pledge or surety. [OE *borgian*, from *borg*, *borh* a pledge, security]

borsch or **borscht** *börsh(t)*, *n* a Russian and Polish beetroot soup. — Also **bortsch** (*börch*), etc. [Russ *borshch*]

borstal or **borstall** *bör'stəl*, *n* formerly an establishment for the detention of young adult delinquents, now replaced by a range of more or less similar detention systems. [From the first reformatory of the kind at *Borstal*, a suburb of Rochester, Kent]

bort or **boart** *bört*, *n* diamond fragments or dust; a coarse diamond or crystalline form of carbon, used industrially for cutting or as an abrasive. [Ety doubtful]

bortsch. See **borsch**.

borzoi *bör'zoi*, *n* a dog like a huge greyhound, but with a long soft coat. [Russ *borzii* swift]

bosbok. See **bush-buck** under **bush**[1].

boscage or **boskage** *bosk'ij*, *n* thick foliage; woodland. [Fr *boscage*, *bocage*, from LL *boscus*, cognate with Ger *Busch*, Eng **bush**]

boschbok, **boschveld**. See **bush-buck**, **bushveld** under **bush**[1].

bosche. See **boche**.

Bosé-Einstein statistics. See **boson**.

bosh *bosh*, (*colloq*) *n* nonsense; foolish talk. — Also *interj*. [Turk *bosh* worthless]

boshta *bosh'tə* or **boshter** *-tər*, (*obs Austr colloq*) *adj* very good. [Perh a variant of **bonzer**]

bosk *bosk*, (*literary*) *n* a thicket, a little wood. — *n* **bosk'et** or **bos'quet** (*obs*) a thicket; a plantation. — *n* **bosk'iness**. — *adj* **bosk'y** woody or bushy; shady; somewhat tipsy (*colloq*). [Cf **bush**[1] and **boscage**]

boskage. See **boscage**.

bosker *bos'kər*, (*obs Austr colloq*) *adj* very good. [Perh a variant of **bonzer**]

bo's'n, bos'n. See **boatswain**.

bosom *bŏŏz'əm*, *n* the breast of a human being; the part of the dress that covers it; (sometimes in *pl*) a woman's breasts; the imagined seat of the passions and feelings, the heart; desire (*Shakesp*); one's embrace, clasp; any close or secret receptacle. — *adj* (*attributively*) confidential; intimate. — *vt* to enclose in the bosom; to carry in the bosom. — *adj* **bos'omed** having a bosom; enclosed. — *combining form* **-bos'omed** having a bosom of a specified kind. — *adj* **bos'omy** (of a woman) having large breasts. — **Abraham's bosom** the abode of the blessed dead. [OE *bōsm*; cf Ger *Busen*]

boson *bō'son*, (*phys*) *n* any of a class of subatomic particles whose behaviour is governed by **Bose-Einstein statistics**, according to which, under certain conditions, particles of the same kind will accumulate in each low-energy quantum mechanical state. [S N *Bose* (1894–1974), Indian physicist]

bosquet. See under **bosk**.

boss[1] *bos*, *n* a knob or stud; a thickened part of a shaft, for strengthening or to allow attachment of other parts (*mech*); a wheel or propeller hub; a raised ornament in wood or leatherwork or (*archit*) at the intersection of ribs in a vault; a dome-shaped protuberance of igneous rock exposed by erosion. — *vt* to ornament with bosses. — *adj* **bossed** embossed. — *adj* **boss'y** having bosses. [OFr *boce* (Fr *bosse*) from OHGer *bôzan* to beat]

boss[2] *bos*, (*colloq*) *n* a chief or leader; a master, manager or foreman; the person who pulls the wires in political intrigues. — *adj* chief; excellent. — *vt* to manage or control; to domineer over (sometimes with *about* or *around*). — *adv* **boss'ily**. — *n* **boss'iness**. — *adj* **boss'y**. — *n sing* **boss'yboots** (*colloq*) a person who enjoys telling others what to do. [New York Dutch *baas* master]

boss[3] *bos*, (*Scot*) *adj* hollow; empty. [Obscure]

boss[4] *bos*, *vi* (*dialect* and *slang*) to make a mess of. — *n* a mistake. — *adj* **boss'-eyed** with one good eye; squint-eyed; out of true. — **boss shot** a bungled shot or attempt. [Origin unknown]

bossa nova *bos'ə nō'və*, *n* a style of dancing originating in Brazil, or the music for it. [Port *bossa* trend, tendency, and *nova* new]

bostangi *bos-tan'ji*, (*hist*) *n* a Turkish palace guard. [Turk *bostanji*]

boston *bost'ən*, *n* a game of cards, somewhat similar to whist; a kind of waltz. — **Boston terrier** a breed of dog arising from cross-breeding between a bulldog and a bull-terrier. [From *Boston*, USA]

bostryx *bos'triks*, (*bot*) *n* a cymose inflorescence in which each lateral axis arises on the same side (cyclically) of its parent axis. [Gr, curl]

bosun, bo'sun. See **boatswain**.

Boswellian *boz-wel'i-ən*, *adj* after the hero-worshipping, detailed and intimate manner of James Boswell in his biography of Samuel Johnson. — *n* **Bos'wellism**. — *vi* **Bos'wellize** or **-ise** (*-wəl-īz*) to write like Boswell.

bot or **bott** *bot*, *n* the maggot of a botfly, parasitic in the intestines of the horse and other animals; (in *pl*) the diseased condition caused by this; (*Scot* **batts**) colic; (only **bot**) a cadger (*Austr colloq*). — *vi* and *vt* (only **bot**) to cadge (*Austr colloq*). — **bot'fly** a name for various flies of the family Oestridae that lay their eggs on horses, etc; **bot'hole** a hole in a hide due to boring by a bot. [Origin unknown]

bot. *abbrev*: botanical; botany; bottle.

botany *bot'ən-i*, *n* the science of plants; the plants of an area; fine wool, *orig* from Botany Bay (sometimes with *cap*; also *adj*). — *adj* **botan'ic** or **botan'ical**. — *n* **botan'ical** a drug made from vegetable matter. — *adv* **botan'ically**. — *n* **bot'anist** a person skilled in botany. — *vi* **bot'anize** or **-ise** to seek for and collect plants for study. — *n* **bot'anomancy** (*obs*) divination by means of plants, *esp* the leaves of sage and fig. — **Botany Bay** an early convict settlement near what is now Sydney; a general name for a convict settlement. [Gr *botanē* grass, fodder]

botargo *bot-är'gō*, *n* a relish made of mullet or tunny roe: — *pl* **botar'gos** or **botar'goes**. [Ital, from Ar *butarkhah*]

BOTB *abbrev*: British Overseas Trade Board.

botch *boch*, *n* a clumsy patch; badly finished work; a bungle; a swelling on the skin; a boil, pimple, or sore (*Milton*); a blemish. — *vt* to patch or mend clumsily; to put together unsuitably or unskilfully; to bungle (often with *up*). — *vi* to do repairs; to bungle. — *n* **botch'er** a bungler; a repairer. — *n* **botch'ery**. — *n* and *adj* **botch'ing**. — *adj* **botch'y** marked with or full of botches. [Partly perh from ONFr *boche* (OFr *boce*) ulcer; verb prob from ME *bocchen* to bungle]

botel or **boatel** *bō-tel'*, (*orig US*) *n* a waterside hotel catering especially for boat-owners; a boat or ship which functions as a hotel. [From *boat* and *hotel*]

botfly. See **bot**.

both *bōth*, *adj* and *pronoun* the two; the one and the other. — *adv* or *conj* as well (sometimes of more than two). [ON *bāthar* (superseding OE *bēgen, bā*); Ger *beide*; cf L *ambō*, Gr *amphō*, Sans *ubhau*, orig *ambha*]

bothan *bo'han*, (*Scot*) *n* a booth, hut; an illegal drinking den. [Gaelic]

bother *bodh'ər*, *vt* to perplex or tease; to worry or concern; to fluster; to pester; to give pain or trouble to. — *vi* to stir oneself; to worry or be concerned (about). — *n* petty trouble, difficulty, or perplexity. — *interj* expressing irritation. — *interj* **botherā'tion** (*colloq*). — *adj* **both'ersome**. — **bother one's head about** to trouble oneself about; **I** or **they** etc **cannot be bothered** I or they etc consider it too much trouble (to do something); I or they etc find (someone or something) annoying (with *with*). [First found in 18c Irish-born writers; poss Anglo-Ir for **pother** or from Ir *bodhair* to annoy or deafen]

bothy or **bothie** *both'i*, (chiefly *Scot*) *n* a humble cottage or hut; a one-roomed hut or temporary dwelling, often built as a shelter in a mountain; a barely furnished dwelling for farm-servants. — **bothy ballad** a folk-song dealing with country matters, *usu* bawdy; **both'yman**. [Cf **booth**]

botoné or **bottony** *bot'ən-i*, (*heraldry*) *adj* having buds or knobs at the extremity, applied to a cross having each arm terminated in three buds, like trefoil. [OFr; see **button**]

bo tree *bō trē* or **bodhi tree** (*bōd'i*), *n* in India and Sri Lanka the pipal (*Ficus religiosa*), holy tree of the Buddhists, under which Buddha found enlightenment, planted close by every temple. [Sinh *bo*, from Pali *bodhi* perfect knowledge]

botryoid *bot'ri-oid* or **botryoidal** *-oid'əl*, *adj* like a bunch of grapes. — *adj* **bot'ryose** botryoidal; racemose (*bot*). — *n* **Botrytis** (*bə-trī'tis*) a genus of fungi (family *Moniliaceae*), several of which cause plant diseases, and one of which (*Botrytis cinerea*) causes noble rot (see under **noble**). [Gr *botrys* a bunch of grapes]

bott. See **bot**.

botte *bot*, (*Fr*) *n* a pass or thrust in fencing.

bottega *bot-tā'gä*, (*Ital*) *n* a wine shop; the studio of an artist and his assistants or apprentices.

bottine *bot-ēn'*, *n* a high boot; a half-boot; a lady's boot; a small boot. [Fr, dimin of *botte* boot]

bottle[1] *bot'l*, *n* a bundle (of hay). [OFr *botel*]

bottle[2] *bot'l*, *n* a narrow-necked hollow vessel, *esp* of glass or plastic, for holding liquids; a bottleful; liquor or drinking; a glass or plastic container with a teat for feeding milk to a baby; a hot-water bottle; (chiefly with *the*) alcoholic drink or drinking, a drinking bout;

money collected from busking, the takings (*slang*); courage, firmness of resolve (*slang*). — *vt* to enclose in a bottle or bottles; to preserve in bottles or jars. — *vi* to collect money from busking (*slang*). — *adj* **bott'led** enclosed or preserved in bottles or jars; shaped or protuberant like a bottle; kept in restraint; drunk (*slang*). — *n* **bott'leful** as much as fills a bottle: — *pl* **bott'lefuls**. — *n* **bott'ler** a person or machine that bottles; an excellent person or thing (*Austr colloq*). — **bottle bank** a purpose-built skip in which empty glass bottles, jars, etc may be deposited for collection for recycling; **bott'le-blond** or (*fem*) **bott'le-blonde** someone whose blond(e) hair-colouring came out of a bottle (ie is artificial, not natural); **bott'le-brush** a brush for cleaning bottles, with bristles standing out from a central axis; a name for various plants of similar appearance, such as horse-tail, mare's-tail, Banksia, and Callistemon; **bott'le-chart** a chart showing currents from evidence of bottles thrown into the sea; **bott'le-coaster** a bottle-slider. — *vt* **bott'le-feed** to feed milk to from a bottle rather than the breast. — **bott'le-fish** a fish (*Saccopharynx ampullaceus*) that can blow its body out like a bottle; **bott'le-gas** or **bottled gas** liquefied butane or propane gas in containers for use in lighting, cooking, heating, etc; **bott'le-glass** a coarse green glass used in the making of bottles; **bott'le-gourd** or *false calabash* a climbing, musky-scented Indian cucurbitaceous annual, with bottle-shaped fruit. — *adj* and *n* **bott'le-green** dark green, like bottle-glass. — **bott'le-head** a bottle-nosed whale; **bott'le-holder** a boxer's attendant; a backer or supporter generally; **bott'le-imp** an imp confined in a bottle; **bott'le-neck** a narrow place in a road where traffic is apt to be congested (often *fig*); a traffic hold-up; a style of guitar playing in which a glissando effect is produced by sliding (*orig*) a bottle-neck or (now *usu*) a tube fitted on to a finger along the strings (also **bottleneck guitar**); **bott'le-nose** a large swollen nose; a bottle-nosed toothed whale (*Hyperoodon planifrons*) or dolphin (*Tursicops truneatus* and others). — *adj* **bott'le-nosed** with a nose or snout shaped like a bottle. — **bott'le-o** or **-oh** (*Austr*) a dealer in used bottles (from his cry); **bott'le-opener** a device for opening bottles; **bott'le-party** a more or less improvised drinking party where each person brings a bottle. — *adj* **bott'le-shouldered** with sloping shoulders like a champagne bottle. — **bott'le-slider** a tray for passing a decanter round the table; **bott'le-tree** an Australian sterculiaceous tree with swollen trunk; **bott'le-washer** a person or machine that washes bottles; a factotum, dogsbody. — **bottle off** to draw from the cask and put into bottles; **bottle out** (*slang*) to lose one's nerve and withdraw (from eg a contest); **bottle up** to enclose (as) in a bottle; to confine, keep contained (an army, etc); to hold back, restrain (emotions); **bring up on the bottle** to rear by bottle-feeding rather than by breast-feeding; **pass the bottle of smoke** (*Dickens*) to acquiesce in some falsehood; to make pretence; **three-bottle man** a man able to drink three bottles of wine without seeming the worse for it. [OFr *bouteille*, dimin of *botte* a vessel for liquids, from LL *butis* a vessel]

bottom *bot'əm*, *n* the lowest part or surface of anything; that on which anything rests or is founded; the part of the body one sits on, buttocks; the bed of the sea, a river, etc; the seat of a chair; the less dignified or important end (of a table, class, etc); the foot of a page, hill, etc; low land, eg by a river; the lower part of a ship, hence the ship itself; groundwork, foundation; the fundamental character or ingredient; staying power, stamina; solidity of character; financial resources; the portion of a wig hanging down over the shoulder; (*usu* in *pl*) the dregs or sediment resulting from various industrial processes; a ball of thread (*Shakesp*). — *adj* undermost, lowest; fundamental; of a quark, having bottomness (*phys*). — *vt* to ground or base (*esp* with *on* or *upon*); to get to the bottom of, understand fully; to get to the bottom of (a mine, etc; *Austr*; also *vi*); to wind (*Shakesp*). — *vi* to find bottom; to found, rest. — *adj* **bott'omed**. — *adj* **bott'omless** having no bottom; very deep; limitless. — *adj* **bott'ommost** (*-mōst* or *-məst*) nearest the bottom. — *n* **bott'omness** a property that characterizes quarks and hadrons, conserved in strong and electromagnetic interactions between particles (*also* **beauty**). — *n* **bott'omry** (*law*) the practice of obtaining a loan (to finance a sea voyage) using the ship as security. — **bottom dead-centre** see **outer dead-centre**; **bottom drawer** the drawer or any supposed place in which a young woman keeps articles for use after her marriage; **bottom end** the big end in a vertical internal combustion engine; **bott'om-fish** a fish that feeds on the bed of the sea, a lake, etc (also *collectively*); **bott'om-glade** (*Milton*) a glade or open space in a bottom or valley; **bott'om-grass** (*Shakesp*) grass growing on low ground. — *adj* **bott'om-heav'y** having the lower part too heavy or large in proportion to the upper. — **bottom-hole assembly** the drilling string attached to the bottom of the drilling pipe, comprising the drill bit and collars to maintain direction (*min ext*); **bott'om-land** (*US*) alluvial deposits; **bottomless pit** hell; **bottom line** the final line of a financial statement, showing net profit or loss; the essential factor in a situation; **bott'om-sawyer** the sawyer who works at the bottom of the saw-pit; **bott'om-up** (of eg business strategy, computer programming, etc) based on the requirements or desires of the users rather than on a centralized decision taken by the business managers or computer programmers. — **at bottom** fundamentally; **at the bottom of** the real origin or cause of; **bet one's bottom dollar on** to bet all one has on, be absolutely certain about; **bottom out** (*US* **base out**) of prices, etc, to reach and settle at the lowest level, *esp* just before a rise; **from the bottom of one's heart** with heartfelt sincerity; **get to the bottom of** to investigate exhaustively; **stand on one's own bottom** (*obs*) to be independent; **the bottom has fallen out of the market** there has been a sudden reduction in the market demand (for something); **touch** or **hit bottom** to reach the lowest point. [OE *botm*; Ger *Boden*; cognate with L *fundus* bottom, Gaelic *bonn* the sole]

bottony. See **botoné**.

botty *bot'i*, *n* a child's or slang word for (a person's) **bottom**.

botulism *bot'ū-lizm*, *n* severe, often fatal, poisoning by tinned or other food carrying a **botulinum toxin**, a powerful bacterial poison produced by the *Bacillus botulinus* (or *Clostridium botulinum*) organism. [L *botulus* sausage, from the shape of the bacteria]

bouche *bōōsh*, (*Fr*) *n* the staff of cooks in a large house.

bouché *bōō-shā*, (*Fr*) *adj* stoppered; corked while still fermenting.

bouchée *bōō-shā*, (*Fr*) *n* a small patty.

bouclé *bōō'klā*, *n* a yarn having the threads looped to give a bulky effect; a fabric made of such a yarn. — Also *adj*. [Fr, curled, looped]

bouderie *bōō-d(ə-)rē*, (*Fr*) *n* pouting, sulking.

boudoir *bōōd'wär*, *n* a woman's private room. — **boudoir grand** a small grand piano, slightly bigger than a baby grand (see under **baby**). [Fr, from *bouder* to pout, to be sulky]

bouffant *bōō-fã*, *adj* (of a hairstyle or the style of an article of clothing) puffed out, full, bulging.

bouffe. See **opera bouffe**.

bougainvillaea or **bougainvillea** *bōōg-ən-vil'i-ə* or *-vil-ē'ə*, *n* any member of a tropical American genus (*Bougainvillea*) of Nyctaginaceae, frequently trained over trellises, its triplets of flowers almost concealed by rosy or purple bracts (also **bougainvil'ia**). [From the first French circumnavigator of the globe, Louis Antoine de *Bougainville* (1729–1811)]

bouge. A Shakespearian form of **budge**[1].

bouget. A Spenserian form of **budget**[1].

bough *bow*, *n* a branch of a tree; the gallows. — **bough'pot** or **bow'pot** (*archaic*) a pot for boughs as an ornament; a flower-pot; a bunch of flowers. [OE *bōg*, *bōh* an arm, the shoulder; Ger *Bug* shoulder, the bow of a ship, from OE *būgan* to bend]

bought[1], **boughten**. See **buy**.

bought[2] *bowt*, (*obs*) *n* a bend or curve; a twist or coil (*Spenser*). [See **bight**]

bougie *bōō'zhē*, *n* a wax candle; a medical instrument (*orig* of waxed linen) for distending contracted body passages, or for calibration, applying medication, etc. [Fr, a wax candle, from *Bougie* in Algeria]

bouillabaisse *bōō-yä-bes'*, *n* a Provençal thick, spiced soup made of fish and vegetables. [Fr]

bouilli *bōō'yē*, *n* boiled or stewed meat. — *n* **bouillon** (*bōō'yɔ̃*) a strong broth. [Fr; see **boil**[1]]

bouillotte *bōō-yot'*, *n* a gambling card game resembling poker. [Fr]

bouk *bōōk*, (*Scot*) *n* body; bulk. [OE *būc* belly, ON *būkr*, coalescing with **bulk**[2]]

Boul. *abbrev*: Boulevard.

boulder *bōld'ər*, *n* a large stone rounded by the action of water; a mass of rock transported by natural agencies from its native bed (*geol*). — *adj* containing boulders. — **bould'er-clay** a stiff stony mass of finely ground rock, *usu* containing boulders and pebbles, deposited as a ground moraine under land-ice. [Origin obscure; Swed dialect *bullersten*, large stone in a stream, has been compared]

boule[1]. See **buhl**.

boule[2] *bōō'lē*, *n* the parliament of modern Greece; a council or senate in ancient Greece. [Gr *boulē*]

boules *bōōl*, *n pl* a French form of bowls played on rough surfaces, pétanque. [Fr]

boulevard *bōōl'(ə-)vär(d)*, *n* a broad road, walk, or promenade bordered with trees; a broad main road; a strip of grass between pavement and road or the centre strip between two carriageways (chiefly *Can*). — *n* **boulevardier** (*bōōl-vär-dyā*) a frequenter of boulevards or promenades, chiefly of Paris; a man-about-town. [Fr (orig applied to a road built on demolished town fortifications), from MDu *bollewerc*; see **bulwark**]

bouleversement *bōōl-vers-mã*, *n* an overturning; overthrow, ruin. [Fr]

boulle. See **buhl**.

boult or **bolt** *bōlt*, *vt* to sift through coarse cloth; to examine by sifting. — *n* **boult'er** or **bolt'er** a sieve; a machine for separating bran from flour. — *n* **boult'ing** or **bolt'ing**. — **boulting** or **bolting cloth** a firm silk or nylon fabric with various mesh sizes used for boulting meal or flour, for embroidery, or for photographic enlargements; **boult'ing-hutch** or **bolt'ing-hutch** a hutch or large box into which flour falls when it is boulted. [OFr *bulter*, from *buleter*, appar from *bure*, from LL *burra* a coarse reddish-brown cloth, from Gr *pyrrhos* reddish]

boun or **bowne** *bōōn* or *bown*, *vt* (used *reflexively*) and *vi* to prepare; to get ready; to dress; to set out. — *adj* ready. [See **bound**[4]; revived by Sir Walter Scott]

bounce[1] *bowns*, *vi* to jump or spring suddenly; to spring up or back like a ball; to burst (into or out of a room, etc); (of a cheque) to come back to the payee unredeemed because of lack of funds in the drawer's account; to boast, to exaggerate. — *vt* to cause to rebound; (of a bank) to return (a cheque) to the payee unredeemed; to turn out, eject, dismiss; to hustle, force; to reprimand, to bring to book (*slang*); to beat (*obs*). — *n* a thud; a leap or spring; springiness; resilience, vitality; boasting, a bold lie; dismissal (*US colloq*). — *adv* and *interj* expressing sudden or bouncing movement or (formerly) the noise of a gun. — *n* **bounc'er** a person or thing that bounces; a cheque that bounces (*colloq*); a ball bowled so as to bounce and rise sharply off the ground (*cricket*); a person employed to eject undesirable people from a club, dance-hall, etc, or to prevent them from entering; something big; a bully; a liar. — *adv* **boun'cily**. — *n* **boun'ciness**. — *adj* **bounc'ing** large and heavy; energetic; hearty. — *adj* **bounc'y** prone to bouncing or full of bounce; lively, cocky; vigorous, resilient. — **bounce back** to recover quickly and easily. [Du *bonzen* to strike, from *bons* a blow]

bounce[2] *bowns*, *n* the lesser spotted dogfish.

bound[1] *bownd*, *pa t* and *pa p* of **bind**. — *adj* tied, fastened; (of books) provided with a binding; in linguistics, of a morpheme that cannot stand alone but only occurs as part of a word, eg the plural marker *-s*. — *combining form* restricted to, or by, something specified, eg *housebound, stormbound*. — **bound'-bailiff** a sheriff's officer, so called from his bond given to the sheriff for the discharge of his duty. — **bound to** obliged to (a person, etc); certain to (do something) (*perh* partly from **bound**[4]).

bound[2] *bownd*, *n* a limit; (in *pl*) the limit of that which is reasonable or permitted; (in *pl*) a borderland, land generally within certain understood limits, the district. — *vt* to set bounds to, to limit or restrain; to surround or form the boundary of. — *adj* **bound'ed** restricted, cramped; surrounded. — *adj* **bound'less** having no limit; vast. — *n* **bound'lessness**. — **bound water** water held by colloidal interaction and capillary forces (*bot*). — **out of bounds** not to be visited, entered, etc; in such a prohibited place. [OFr *bonne*, from LL *bodina*; cf Bret *bonn*, a boundary]

bound[3] *bownd*, *vi* to spring or leap. — *n* a spring or leap. — *n* **bound'er** a person who bounds; a person whose moral conduct is objectionable (*old-fashioned slang*). — *adj* **bound'ing**. — **by leaps and bounds** by startlingly rapid stages. [Fr *bondir* to spring, in OFr to resound, from L *bombitāre*]

bound[4] *bownd*, *adj* ready, prepared (*obs*); ready to start (for); on the way to (with *for*, or following an *adv*, eg *homeward bound*; also as *combining form*, eg in *southbound*). — See also **bound**[1]. [ON *būinn*, pa p of *būa* to prepare; cf **boun**]

boundary *bownd'ə-ri* or *bownd'ri*, *n* a limit; a border; termination, final limit; a hit to the limit of the ground (*cricket*); a score for such a hit (four or six runs). — **boundary layer** the very thin layer of air on the surface of an aircraft whose viscosity affects the aircraft's velocity, causing turbulence to build up and thereby increasing drag (**boundary-layer control** the removal of the boundary layer by a suction system or other means); **bound'ary-rider** (*Austr*) a person who is responsible for the maintenance of fences on a station. [**bound**[2]]

bounden *bownd'n*, *adj* obligatory. [Archaic pa p of **bind**]

bountree *bōōn'tri*. See **bourtree**.

bounty *bown'ti*, *n* generosity in bestowing gifts; the gift bestowed; money offered as an inducement to enter the army, or as a reward or premium in general, or (**king's** or **queen's bounty**) to a mother who has three or more children at a birth. — *adj* **boun'teous** or **boun'tiful** generous in giving. — *adv* **boun'teously** or **boun'tifully**. — *n* **boun'teousness** or **boun'tifulness**. — *n* **boun'tyhed** (*Spenser*). — **bounty hunter** a person who hunts down wanted criminals, or anything for which a reward has been offered. — **Lady Bountiful** the charitable great lady of a district; ironic name for a patronizingly generous female do-gooder. [OFr *bontet* (Mod Fr *bonté*) goodness, from L *bonitās*, *-ātis*, from *bonus* good]

bouquet *bōōk'ā* or *-ā'*, *n* a bunch of flowers; the perfume given off by wine; a compliment, praise. — *n* **bouquetière** (*bōō-k(ə)-tyer*) a flower-girl. — **bouquet garni** (*bōō'kā gär-nē'*) a bunch or sachet of herbs used as flavouring, removed before the dish is served (*Fr*, garnished bouquet). [Fr *bouquet*, dimin of *bois* a wood; cf Ital *bosco*; see **boscage**, **bush**[1]]

bourasque *bōō-rask'*, *n* a tempest. [Fr *bourrasque*; Ital *borasco* a storm]

Bourbon *bōōr'bon*, *n* a member of the European royal family which ruled in France and elsewhere between the 16th and 20th centuries; a political reactionary (*US*); a hybrid variety of rose; (without *cap*; *usu bûr'bən*) maize whiskey (*orig* made in *Bourbon* County, Kentucky). — *n* **Bour'bonism**. — *n* **Bour'bonist** an adherent of the Bourbons. — **Bourbon biscuit** two chocolate-flavoured pieces of biscuit with chocolate cream between.

bourd *bōōrd*, (*obs*) *n* a jest, fun. — *n* **bourd'er** (*obs*) a jester. [OFr *bourde*, of unknown origin]

Bourdon gauge *bōr'* or *bōōr'dən gāj*, *n* a type of gauge for measuring the pressure of gases or liquids. [E *Bourdon*, French engineer (1808–84)]

bourdon[1] *bōōr'dən*, *n* a drone bass of a bagpipe; a bass stop in an organ or harmonium; the bass accompaniment to a melody (*obs*). [See **burden**[2]]

bourdon[2] *bōōr'dən*, (*obs*) *n* a pilgrim's staff; a club. [Fr, from LL *burdō*, *-ōnis* a mule]

bourg *bōōrg*, *n* a town, *esp* beside a castle; a market-town. [Fr]

bourgeois[1] *bûr-jois'*, *n* an old type size, larger than brevier and smaller than longprimer, approximately 9-point. [Fr; perh from the name of the type-founder]

bourgeois[2] *bōōrzh'wä*, *n* a member of the middle class; a merchant or shopkeeper; a person with capitalist, materialistic or conventional values: — *fem* **bourg'eoise**. — *pl* **bourg'eois**. — *adj* middle-class; conventional; humdrum; conservative; capitalist; materialistic. — *n* **bourgeoisie** (*bōōr'zhwä-zē* or *-zē'*) the middle class of citizens, *esp* seen as capitalistic, materialistic, etc. — *n* **bourgeoisifica'tion**. — *vt* **bourgeois'ify** to convert to a bourgeois way of thinking or living. [Fr *bourgeois* a citizen]

bourgeon. See **burgeon**.

bourguignon *bōōr-gē-nyɔ̃*, (*cookery*) *adj* (of meat dishes) stewed with onion, mushrooms and Burgundy wine. [Fr, Burgundian]

Bourignian *bōōr-in'yən*, *adj* of or pertaining to Antoinette *Bourignon* (1616–80), a religious visionary for whom religion consisted in inward emotion, not in knowledge or practice.

bourkha. Same as **burka**.

bourlaw. See **byrlaw**.

bourn[1] or **bourne** *bōōrn*, *bōrn* or *börn*, (*archaic*) *n* a boundary, limit or goal; domain (*Keats*). [Fr *borne* a limit]

bourn[2], **bourne**. *S Eng* variants of **burn**[1].

bourrée *bōōr'ā* or *-ā'*, *n* a brisk dance in duple time, from the Auvergne or the Basque provinces; a musical composition in the same rhythm. [Fr]

bourse *bōōrs*, *n* an exchange where merchants meet for business; any European stock exchange, *esp* (with *cap*) that in Paris. [Fr; see **purse**]

boursier *bōōr-syā*, (*Fr*) *n* a foundation-scholar; a speculator on the exchange.

bourtree or **boortree** *bōōr'tri*, (*Scot*) *n* the elder-tree. — Also **bountree** (*bōōn'tri*). — **bour'tree-gun** a pop-gun made of an elder twig. [Ety unknown]

bouse[1] *bōōz* or *bowz*, *vi* and *n* archaic form of **booze**. — *adj* **bous'ing** or **bous'y**. — *n* **bous'ingken** (*obs thieves' slang*) a low drinking-shop. [ME *busen*, appar from MDu *būsen* to drink excessively]

bouse[2] or **bowse** *bows*, (chiefly *naut*) *vt* and *vi* to haul with tackle. [Origin unknown]

boustrophedon *bōō-* or *bow-strof-ē'don*, *adj* and *adv* (of ancient writing) alternately from right to left and from left to right. [Gr *boustrophēdon* turning like ploughing oxen, from *bous* ox, and *strophē* a turning]

bout *bowt*, *n* a turn or period of time doing something; a stint; in boxing or wrestling, a contest; a fit or attack (of an illness). [**bought**[2]]

boutade *bōō-täd'*, *n* a sudden outburst (*fig*). [Fr, from *bouter* to thrust]

boutique *bōō-tēk'*, *n* a small shop; a department in a shop; in the 1960s, used *esp* for a small, expensive, exclusive dress shop for women; now, a small shop, or a department in a shop, selling fashionable clothes, etc; a small specialist business or agency operating within a larger business sphere, *esp* advertising, accountancy or investment services. — *adj* small, specialist, exclusive. [Fr]

bouton *bōō-tɔ̃*, *n* an enlargement of the end of a nerve fibre in contact with part of another nerve fibre. — *adj* **boutonné** or **boutonnée** (*-ton-ā*) reticent, buttoned-up. — *n* **boutonnière** (*-to-nyer*) a flower for the buttonhole, etc. [Fr, button]

bouts rimés *bōō rē-mā'*, *n pl* rhyming words given out by someone as the line-endings of a stanza, for others to fill up the lines. [Fr, rhymed ends]

bouzouki *bōō-zōō'ki*, *n* a plucked metal-stringed instrument, used *esp* in Greece. — Also **bazou'ki** (*bə-*) [Mod Gr]

bovate *bō'vāt*, (*hist*) *n* an oxgang. [LL *bovāta*, from *bōs*, *bovis* an ox]

bovid *bō'vid*, *adj* belonging to the family **Bo'vidae**, which includes not only cattle but also other ruminants such as sheep and goats. — Also *n*. [New L *Bovidae*, from L *bōs*, *bovis* an ox]

bovine *bō'vīn*, *adj* of or pertaining to cattle; stupid, dull. — *n* an animal of the cattle family. — *adv* **bo'vinely**. — **bovine somatotrophin** a hormone drug that increases milk production in cattle; **bovine spongiform encephalopathy** an infectious degenerative brain disease of cattle, *orig* caused by cattle feed processed from scrapie-infected sheep remains, *usu abbrev* **BSE**. [L *bōs*, *bovis* an ox or cow]

Bovril® *bov'ril*, *n* a concentrated beef extract used to make drinks, to flavour meat dishes, etc. [L *bōs*, *bovis* ox, cow]

bovver *bov'ər*, (*slang*) *n* rowdy or violent behaviour by street gangs. — Also *adj*. — **bovver boy** a member of a gang of hooligans in the habit of engaging in street fights using heavy, hobnailed boots (**bovver boots**) to kick their opponents; a troublemaker, *esp* one who uses rough methods. [Prob Cockney pron of **bother**]

bow[1] *bow*, *vi* to bend; to bend the neck or body in greeting, acknowledging a compliment, etc; to submit (to). — *vt* to bend or incline downwards; to crush down; to usher with a bow; to express by a bow. — *n* a bending of the neck or body as a formal or respectful greeting, or to acknowledge applause, etc. — *adj* **bowed** (*bowd*) bent forward. — **a bowing acquaintance** a slight acquaintance; **bow and scrape** to kowtow, to ingratiate oneself sycophantically; **bow in** to make a first appearance in public; **bow out** to withdraw or retire from a place, situation, etc; **make one's bow** to retire ceremoniously; to leave the stage; **take a bow** to acknowledge applause or recognition. [OE *būgan* to bend; cognate with L *fugere* to flee, to yield]

bow[2] *bō*, *n* a piece of flexible wood or other material for shooting arrows, bent by means of a string stretched between its ends; anything of a bent or curved shape, such as the rainbow; a bow-shaped strip for collecting current from an overhead wire (*elec eng*); a yoke (*Shakesp*); a rod (*orig* curved but now nearly straight) strung with horsehair, by which the strings of a violin, etc are played; a ring of metal forming a handle; the frame surrounding the lenses, or the curved end of the leg of spectacles (*US*); a bowknot; a looped knot of ribbons; a bow tie; a single movement (up or down) or stroke of the bow in playing an instrument. — *vi* to handle the bow in playing. — *vt* to play (an instrument) with a bow; to mark (for stringed instruments) which notes should be played downbow and which upbow. — *n* **bow'ing** the technique of playing a stringed instrument with a bow; the marking of the up- and down-bows. — *n* **bow'yer** a bowman; a maker of bows for archery. — *adj* **bow'-backed** with bent back. — *adj* **bow'bent** (*Milton*) bent like a bow. — **bow'-boy** a boy archer; Cupid (*Shakesp*). — *n pl* **bow'-compasses** a small pair of compasses, often with a bow-shaped spring instead of a hinge. — **bow'fin** a N American freshwater fish (*Amia*) of the Holostei. — *adj* **bow'=fronted** having a convex front. — **bow'-hand** the hand in which the bow is held, normally in archery, the left, in stringed instrument-playing, the right; **bow'head** the right whale, of the Arctic, with a large head and arched jaw; **bow'knot** a (*usu* decorative) knot with one or two loops; **bow'-leg** a bandy leg like a bow. — *adj* **bow'=**

legged (*-legd* or *-leg-id*). — **bow'man** an archer; **bow'saw** a saw with a narrow blade stretched like a bowstring in a strong bow-shaped frame (also **log'saw**); a saw with a narrow blade stretched in an H-shaped frame and held taut by tightening a cord at the opposite end of the frame; **bow'shot** the distance to which an arrow can be shot from a bow; **bow'string** the string by which a bow is drawn; a string with which the Turks strangled offenders (*hist*); a horizontal tie on a bridge or girder. — *vt* to strangle with a bowstring (*pa t* and *pa p* **bow'stringed**, sometimes **bow'strung**). — *adj* of, for or having a bowstring. — **bow'string-hemp** the genus Sansevieria or its fibre; **bow tie** a necktie tied in a two-looped bowknot, often for formal wear. — *adj* **bow'-tied** wearing a bow tie. — **bow-win'dow** a window projecting in a curve; a pot-belly (*obs slang*). — *adj* **bow-win'dowed**. — **draw the long bow** to make extravagant statements; **on the bow hand** wide of the mark; **two strings to one's bow** an alternative in reserve. [OE *boga*; cognate with Ger *Bogen*]

bow[3] *bow*, *n* the forepart of a ship or boat, often used in *pl*, the ship, etc being considered to have starboard and port bows, meeting at the stem; the rower nearest the bow (*rowing*). — *n* **bow'er** or **bow'er-anchor** an anchor at the bow (*best-bower* and *small-bower*). — **bow'-oar** the oar nearest the bow; **bow'-side** (*rowing*) the rowers on the same side as bow; **bow'-wave** the wave created by the bow of a moving vessel; a shock wave (*fig*). — **bold** or **bluff bow** a broad bow; **lean bow** a narrow bow; **on the (port** or **starboard) bow** within 45° (to port or starboard) of the point right ahead. [From a LGer, Du or Scand word for shoulder; see **bough**]

bowat, **bowet** or **buat** *bōō'ət*, (*Scot*) *n* a lantern. — **MacFarlane's buat** (*Scott*) the moon. [LL *boeta* box]

bowdlerize or **-ise** *bowd'lər-īz*, *vt* to expurgate a book or writing, by removing whatever might be considered indelicate, *esp* to do so unnecessarily. — *n* **bowdleriza'tion** or **-s-**. — *n* **bowd'lerizer** or **-s-**. [From Dr T *Bowdler* (1754–1825), who published an expurgated Shakespeare in ten volumes in 1818]

bowel *bow'əl*, *n* an interior part of the body, now *esp* the large intestine; (in *pl*) the entrails, intestines; (in *pl*) the innermost, interior part of anything; (in *pl*) feelings of pity, tenderness (*obs*, *Bible* and *Shakesp*). — *vt* (*obs*) to take out the bowels of: — *pr p* **bow'elling**; *pa p* and *pa t* **bow'elled**. — **bowel movement** an instance or act of excretion or defecation; faeces, excrement. [OFr *boel*, from L *botellus* a sausage, an intestine]

bower[1] *bow'ər*, *n* a shady enclosure or recess in a garden, an arbour; an inner apartment (*archaic*); a lady's private room, boudoir (*poetic*); a dwelling (*poetic*). — *vt* to enclose; to embower (*Shakesp*). — *vi* (*Spenser*) to lodge. — *adj* **bow'ery** leafy, shady. — **bow'er-bird** an Australian bird that makes a bower adorned with colourful feathers, shells, etc; a person who collects useless bits and pieces (*Austr colloq*); **bow'erwoman** (*archaic*) a chambermaid, lady's maid. [OE *būr* a chamber, from root of *būan* to dwell]

bower[2] *bow'ər*, *n* the name in euchre for the two highest cards, the knave of trumps, and the other knave of the same colour, the *right* and *left bower* respectively. [Ger *Bauer* peasant, knave at cards]

bower[3], **bower-anchor**. See **bow**[3].

bowery *bow'ə-ri*, *n* (*US archaic*) a farm. — **the Bowery** a street in New York frequented by tramps and drunks. [Du *bouwerij*]

bowes. A Miltonic spelling of **boughs**.

bowet. Same as **bowat**.

bowget. *Obs* variant of **budget**[1].

bowie knife *bō'i*, (or *US bōō'i*) *nīf*, *n* a strong, one-edged dagger-knife with a blade about twelve inches long. [From Colonel *Bowie*, died 1836, who popularized it, and perhaps invented it]

bowl[1] *bōl*, *n* a ball (*obs*); a heavy wooden ball with a bias (qv); (in *pl*) a game played by rolling such balls on a green towards a jack; (in *pl*) sometimes the game of skittles (ninepins) or American bowls (tenpins); (*Scot* **bool**) a marble; (in *pl*) the game of marbles. — *vi* to play at bowls or ninepins or tenpins; to roll or trundle (*esp* with *on* or *along*); to travel swiftly and smoothly in a wheeled vehicle (*usu* with *along*); to pitch the ball to the batsman at the wicket (*cricket*); to be bowler. — *vt* to roll or trundle; to deliver by bowling (*cricket*); to put out by hitting the wicket with a bowled ball (also with *out*; *fig* to overcome): — *pa p* **bowled'** (*cricket*) put out (by being bowled or caught) when a specified person was bowler. — *n* **bowl'er** person who plays at bowls or who bowls in cricket. — *n* and *adj* **bowl'ing**. — **bowl'ing-alley** a long narrow covered place for ninepin- or tenpin-bowling; **bowl'ing-crease** see **crease**; **bowl'ing-green** a smooth grassy plot for bowls. — **bowl over** to knock down; to overwhelm, thoroughly impress or delight. [Fr *boule*, from L *bulla*]

bowl[2] *bōl*, *n* a vessel, characteristically of approximately hemispherical shape, for domestic use; a round drinking-cup, more wide than deep; drink, alcohol; a bowlful; the round hollow part of anything; a large bowl-shaped structure, stadium, etc. — *n* **bowl'ful** as much as fills a bowl. [OE *bolla*]

bowlder *bōld'ər*, *n*. Same as **boulder**.

bowler[1] *bō'lər*, *n* a stiff felt hat with a round crown and narrow brim. — **bowler hat** a bowler. — *vt* (with *hyphen*; *orig services slang*) to discharge, dismiss. [Said to be name of a hatter who made it in 1850]

bowler[2]. See **bowl**[1].

bowline *bō'lin*, *n* a rope from the weather side of the square sails to the larboard or starboard bow, to keep the sail close to the wind (*naut*); (also **bowline knot**) a simple knot which makes a loop that will not slip at the end of a rope. [MLGer *bōlīne*, MDu *boechlijne*]

bowne. See **boun**.

bowpot. Same as **boughpot**.

bowr *bowr*, (*Spenser*) *n* a muscle. [**bow**[1] to bend]

bowse. See **bouse**[2].

bowser *bow'zər*, *n* a light tanker used for refuelling aircraft on an airfield (also with *cap*); a petrol pump (*old*; now *Austr* and *NZ*). [Orig tradename]

bowsprit *bō'sprit*, (*naut*) *n* a strong spar projecting over the bows of a ship. [MLGer *bōgsprēt*, MDu *boechspriet*]

bowwow *bow'wow'*, *n* a dog (*childish* or *facetious*); (*bow-wow'*) a dog's bark. [Imit]

bowyang *bō'yang* (*Austr colloq*) *n* (*usu* in *pl*) straps or strings tied round each trouser-leg below the knee by outdoor labourers. — *adj* limited in outlook, hick. [UK dialect variations may derive from the Austr; origin unknown]

bowyer. See under **bow**[2].

box[1] *boks*, *n* an evergreen shrub or small tree (*Buxus sempervirens*) with hard smooth yellowish wood, often used to border garden-walks and flower-beds (also **box'-tree** or **box'wood**); its wood (also **box'wood**); extended to various other plants, *esp* the Eucalyptus. — Also *adj*. — *adj* **box'en** made of or like boxwood. [OE *box*, from L *buxus*, from Gr *pyxos* the box-tree]

box[2] *boks*, *n* a case or receptacle (*usu* with four sides and a lid) for holding anything; a compartment or cubicle; a small house or lodge, such as a *shooting-box*, etc; in a theatre, a small enclosure with several seats; an old square pew or similar enclosure, such as a *sentry-box*, *signal-box*, *witness-box*, etc; the pitcher's or the batter's standing-place (*baseball*); the penalty box (*football*); the driver's seat on a carriage; a case for protecting machinery, etc; a gearbox; the case of a ship's compass; a predicament; an accidental mixing of flocks of sheep (*Austr* and *NZ*); a light, padded shield covering the genitals (*sport*, *esp cricket*); part of a printed page enclosed within lines, etc; the contents of a box; a fund; a (Christmas) present; a stock or package of units put together for unit trusts (*finance*). — *vt* to put into or provide with a box or boxes; to enclose, confine (often with *in* or *up*); to overturn (a watchman) in his box (*obs slang*); to mix (eg flocks of sheep) (*Austr* and *NZ*); to make a cut in the trunk of (a tree) to collect the sap. — *n* **box'ful** as much as a box will hold: — *pl* **box'fuls**. — *n* **box'iness**. — *adj* **box'y** shaped like a box; (of clothes) having a square appearance; (of reproduced music) sounding as if recorded in a box. — **box'-bed** a kind of bed formerly common in Scotland, often in a living-room or kitchen, with its ends, sides and roof of wood, and sometimes capable of being closed in front by two sliding panels; **box-cam'era** a simple box-shaped camera; **box canyon** (*NAm*) a narrow canyon with almost vertical sides; **box'car** (*NAm*) a box-wagon; **box'-cloth** a heavy cloth for riding garments; **box'-coat** a short loose coat; a heavy overcoat worn by those travelling on the outside of a coach (*obs*); **box'-day** one of the Court of Session vacation days when papers ordered to be deposited in court must be lodged; **box file** a box-shaped container with a spring clip for holding documents steady, capable of holding many or *esp* bulky items; **box'-frame** a box-shaped framework of a building; **box'-girder** a hollow, square or rectangular girder, often used in bridge construction. — *vt* **box'-haul** to veer (a square-rigged ship) hard round. — **Boxing Day** the day after Christmas, when boxes or presents were traditionally given to employees, etc; the first weekday after Christmas, observed as a public holiday; **box'-iron** a hollow smoothing-iron in which a heater is placed; **box jellyfish** (*Austr*) any of several tropical jellyfish with venomous tentacles; **box junction** an area at a crossroads or other road-junction, marked with yellow criss-crossed lines, into which a vehicle may not move unless its exit is clear; **box'keeper** an attendant who opens the doors of boxes at theatres, etc (*obs*); **box'-kite** a kite composed of open-ended boxes; **box'-lobby** the lobby leading to the boxes in a theatre; **box number** a number to which replies eg to advertisements may be sent either at a post office or a newspaper; **box'-office** in a theatre, etc, the office at which seats may be booked; receipts from a play, etc; ability to draw an audience; an attraction as judged by the box-office. — Also *adj*. — **box'-pleat** a type of double pleat formed by folding the cloth under in both directions. — *adj* **box'-pleated**. — **box profits** profits made by financial managers when buying and selling units for unit trusts; **box'room** a room (*esp* a small room without an outside window) in which boxes, etc, are stored; **box'-seat** a driver's seat on a coach; a seat in a box in a theatre, etc; a commanding or favourable position (*Austr colloq*); **box'-spanner** a spanner consisting of a cylindrical piece of steel shaped at one or both ends into a hexagon to fit over the appropriate nut, and turned by a rod inserted through a hole at the opposite end; **box'-spring** one of a set of spiral springs in an open box-shaped frame as part of a mattress; **box van** a motor van with a box-shaped goods compartment; **box'-wagon** a closed railway wagon; **box'wallah** (*Ind*) (see **wallah**) a pedlar; a businessman or shopkeeper (*derog*). — **box the compass** to name the 32 compass points in order in either or both directions; to make a complete turnaround in any opinion; **in the wrong box** in a false position, in a scrape; **the box** (*colloq*) the television set; television; **the whole box and dice** (*Austr* and *NZ*) the whole lot. [OE *box*, from L *buxem*, accusative of *buxis* from Gr *pyxis* a box]

box[3] *boks*, *n* a blow on the head or ear with the hand. — *vt* to strike with the hand or fist, *esp* in a boxing match. — *vi* to fight with the fists, *esp* in a boxing match. — *vt* and *vi* (*Scot*) to butt. — *n* **box'er** a person who boxes or is skilled in boxing; a medium-sized, smooth-haired dog of a breed, with bulldog blood, developed in Germany; (*hist*; with *cap*) a member of a Chinese society hostile to foreigners, the name arising from a Chinese phrase literally meaning 'righteous harmonious fist'. — *n* **box'ing** the act or art of fighting with the fists, *esp* now as a sport; a fight with the fists. — **boxer shorts** loose shorts as worn by boxers; loose-fitting underpants for men, with an elasticated waistband and front opening; **box'ing-glove** a padded glove worn in boxing. — **box clever** to act in a clever or cunning way. [Poss connected with Gr *pyx* with the fist]

Box and Cox *boks and koks*, *n pl* two people who never meet, or who alternate in a place, job, etc. — *adj* and *adv* alternating. [From the play *Cox and Box* in which two men rent the same room by night and day respectively; adapted (1847) by J M Morton from French farce, and made into a comic opera (1867) by F C Burnand and A S Sullivan]

box-calf *boks'-käf*, *n* a chrome-tanned calfskin with rectangular markings made by rolling. [Said to be named after Joseph *Box*, a shoemaker]

boy *boi*, *n* a male child; a lad; a son; a young man generally; (in Ireland and elsewhere) a man; in some countries a native or coloured servant or labourer (as a form of address *offensive* in S Africa); a slave (*obs*); (in *pl*) a group of men with whom a man is friendly or familiar (*colloq*); a man with a particular function, skill, etc, as in *backroom boy*; a camp-follower (*Shakesp*); knave (*obs*). — *vt* (*Shakesp*) to play (a female part) as a boy. — *interj* same as **oh boy** below. — *n* **boy'hood**. — *adj* **boy'ish**. — *adv* **boy'ishly**. — *n* **boy'ishness**. — **boy bishop** a mock bishop formerly elected by choirboys or schoolboys, in office from St Nicholas' to Holy Innocents' Day (6–28 December); **boy'friend** a girl's favourite boy for the time being; a male lover in a romantic or sexual relationship. — *adj* **boy'-girl** of a romantic relationship between a young boy and girl; romantically sentimental. — *adj* **boy'-meets-girl'** (often of love stories) following the normal romantic pattern. — **Boys' Brigade** an organization of boys for the promotion of habits of obedience, reverence, discipline, and self-respect; **Boy Scout** see **Scout**; **boy's love** southernwood; **boy's play** trifling. — **boys will be boys** one must expect and put up with foolish or childish behaviour; **oh boy** an expression of pleasure, enthusiasm, etc; **the boy next door** an ordinary young man, *esp* when regarded as a romantic partner; **the boys in blue** (*facetious*) the police. [ME *boi* boy; Fris *boi*; Du *boef*, Ger *Bube*]

boyar *bo-yär'* or *boi'är*, *n* a member of the old Russian aristocracy next in rank to the ruling princes, before the reforms of Peter the Great. [Russ *boyarin*]

boyau *bwo'yō*, *bwä'yō* or *boi'ō*, (*fortif*) *n* a communication trench: — *pl* **bo'yaux**. [Fr, bowel]

boycott *boi'kot*, *vt* to refuse to take part in, deal with, handle by way of trade, etc; to shut out from all social and commercial intercourse. — *n* an act of boycotting. — *n* **boy'cotter**. [From Captain *Boycott* of County Mayo, who was so treated by his neighbours in Dec 1880]

boyg *boig*, *n* an ogre; an obstacle or problem difficult to get to grips with. [Norw *bøig*]

Boyle's law. See under **law**.

boyo *boi'ō*, (*slang*; *orig Ir* and *Welsh*) *n* a boy, young man. [**boy**]

boysenberry *boi'sən-ber-i*, *n* a fruit growing on a bramble, a hybrid of certain raspberries and blackberries. [Rudolph *Boysen*, 20c US horticulturalist]

bozo *bō'zō*, (*slang*, *orig US*) *n* a man, fellow, now *esp* a rather dim-witted one. [Prob Sp dialect *boso*, from Sp *vosotros* you (pl)]

bozzetto *bot-set'tō*, (*Ital*) *n* a small model or sketch of a projected sculpture: — *pl* **bozzet'ti** (*-tē*).

BP *abbrev*: (used in radiocarbon dating, with 1950 as 'present') before present; (also **B/P**) bills payable; blood pressure; British Petroleum; British Pharmacopoeia.

Bp *abbrev*: Bishop.

bp *abbrev*: (also **b/p**) bills payable; birthplace; bishop; boiling point.

BPC *abbrev*: British Pharmaceutical Codex.

BPharm *abbrev*: Bachelor of Pharmacy.

BPhil *abbrev*: *Baccalaureus Philosophiae* (*L*), Bachelor of Philosophy.

bpi (*comput*) *abbrev*: bits per inch.

b.pl. *abbrev*: birthplace.

bps (*comput*) *abbrev*: bits per second.

Bq *symbol*: becquerel.

BR *abbrev*: (also **B/R**) bills receivable; Brazil (IVR); British Rail.

Br (*chem*) *symbol*: bromine.

Br. *abbrev*: Britain; British; Brother.

br *abbrev*: bank rate; bedroom; (also **b/r**) bills receivable.

br. *abbrev*: branch; bridge; brother; brown.

bra *brä*, *n* short for **brassière**. — *adj* **bra'less** not wearing a brassière.

braaivleis *brī'flās*, (*SAfr*) *n* a barbecue party. [Afrik *braai* to grill, and *vlies* meat]

brabble *brab'l*, (*archaic*) *vi* to babble or clamour; to brawl or wrangle. — *n* a clamorous contest, a brawl (*Shakesp*); a quibble. — *n* **brabb'lement**. [Du *brabbelen* to stammer, to jabber]

braccate *brak'āt*, *adj* having feathered legs or feet. [L *brācātus* wearing breeches]

braccio *brät'chō*, *n* an obsolete Italian measure of length, more than half a metre: — *pl* **braccia** (*brät'chä*). [Ital, literally arm]

brace *brās*, *n* anything that draws together and holds tightly; an instrument of wood or iron used by carpenters and metal-workers for turning boring tools; a type of bracket ({ or }) connecting words, lines, staves of music, indicating that they are taken together, and also used as a third level of bracket in algebra, after round and square brackets; a pair or couple (*esp* of game shot); (in *pl*) straps worn over the shoulders for supporting the trousers; (often in *pl*) an appliance made of wire fitted over the teeth to straighten them; (in *pl*) ropes for squaring or traversing horizontally the yards of a ship; armour for the arm (*Shakesp*). — *vt* to tighten or strengthen, to give firmness to; to steady and make (oneself) ready for a blow, etc; to tone up; to embrace, encompass (*Spenser*). — *n* **brāc'er**. — *adj* **brāc'ing** giving strength or tone. — **brace-and-bit'** a brace with the drilling bit in place. [OFr *brace* (Fr *bras*) the arm, power, from L *brāchum*, *bracchium*, Gr *brachīōn*]

bracelet *brās'lit*, *n* an ornament for the wrist; a handcuff (*colloq*). [Fr dimin, from L *brāchiāle*, from *brāchium*; *see* **brace**]

brach *brach*, *n* a dog for the chase, a bitch hound. — *n* **brach'et** or **bratch'et** a brach; a whelp; a brat. [OFr *brachet*, pl *brachès*, dimin of *brac*, from LL *braccō*, of Gmc origin]

brachial, brachiate. See **brachium**.

brachiopod *brak'i-ō-pod*, *n* a member of a class **Brachiopoda** (*-op'o-də*) of shelled sea creatures related to worms and Polyzoa, having usually two long arm-like processes serving to waft food particles to the mouth. [Gr *brachīōn* an arm, and *pous*, *podos* a foot]

Brachiosaurus *brak-i-ō-sö'rəs*, *n* a genus of huge lizard-hipped plant-eating dinosaurs, unusual in that their front legs were longer than their back legs; (without *cap*) a member of the genus. [Gr *brachīōn* an arm, and *sauros* a lizard]

brachistochrone *bra-kis'tō-krōn*, (*math*) *n* the curve along which a particle acted on by a force (eg gravity) will pass in the shortest time from one given point to another. [Gr *brachistos*, superl of *brachys* short, and *chronos* time]

brachium *brā'kē-əm* or *bräk'i-ōōm*, *n* (*anatom*) the upper part of the arm or fore-limb. — *adj* **brachial** (*brāk'* or *brak'i-əl*) of the arm. — *adj* **brach'iāte** (*bot*) having branches in pairs at right angles to the stem. — *vi* (*zool*) to use the arms as a supplementary means of locomotion. — *n* **brachiā'tion**. — **brachial artery** the great arterial trunk supplying the arm between the armpit and the elbow, direct continuation of the axillary artery; **brachium civile** (*si-vī'lē*) (*L*) the civil arm; **brachium seculare** (*sek-ū-lā'rē* or *sā-kōō-lä're*) the secular arm. [L *brāchium*; see **brace**]

brachy- *brak'i-* or *-i'-*, *combining form* signifying short. — *n* **brachyax'is** (*crystallog*) brachydiagonal. — *n* **brachycephal** (*-sef'əl*; Gr *kephalē* a head) a short-headed person. — *adj* **brachycephalic** (*-si-fal'ik*) or **brachycephalous** (*-sef'ə-ləs*) short-headed, *esp* having a skull whose breadth is 80 per cent or more of its length. — *n* **brachyceph'aly** short-headedness (*opp* to *dolichocephaly*). — *adj* **brachydac'tyl, brachydactyl'ic** or **brachydac'tylous**. — *n* **brachydac'tyly** (Gr *daktylos* finger, toe) abnormal shortness of fingers and toes. — *n* **brachydiag'onal** (*crystallog*) the shorter lateral axis. — *n* **brach'ydome** a dome parallel to the brachydiagonal. — *n* **brachyg'raphy** certain old systems of shorthand. — *n* **brachyl'ogy** condensed expression. — *n* **brachypin'akoid** or **brach'yprism** a pinakoid or prism parallel to the brachydiagonal. — *adj* **brachyp'terous** (Gr *pteron* wing) short-winged; short-finned. — *n pl* **Brachyura** (*-ū'rə*; Gr *ourā* a tail) a group of decapod crustaceans having the abdomen reduced and bent forward under the thorax, the crabs. — *adj* **brachyū'ral** or **brachyū'rous**. [Gr *brachys* short]

brack *brak*, *n* a flaw in cloth. [Related to **break**[1]]

bracken *brak'ən*, *n* fern, especially *Pteridium aquilinum*, the commonest British fern, abundant on hillsides, etc. [Ety obscure]

bracket *brak'it*, *n* a projecting support; a small shelf fastened to a wall; a gas-pipe projecting from a wall (*hist*); either of a pair of symbols used to enclose words or mathematical symbols, such as **round brackets** or parentheses, **square brackets**, and braces; one of the side pieces of a gun-carriage, supporting the trunnions; the space intervening between overestimated and underestimated shots at a target in range-finding (*artillery*); a bracketed group; a group or category defined and demarcated by certain limiting parameters, as in *income bracket*. — *vt* to support by brackets; to enclose by brackets; to group together. — *vt* and *vi* to find the range (*artillery*). — **bracket clock** a rectangular clock with an internal pendulum designed to stand on a table or wall-bracket; **brack'et-creep** an inflationary phenomenon whereby a salary rise makes a taxpayer less well off by pushing him or her into a higher tax bracket. [Fr *braguette*, from Sp *bragueta*, from L *brāca*, sing of *brācae* breeches]

brackish *brak'ish*, *adj* saltish, rather salt. — *n* **brack'ishness**. [Du *brak* brackish]

bract *brakt*, *n* a leaf (often modified) that bears a flower in its axil. — *adj* **bract'eal**. — *n* **bract'eate** (*archaeol*) a thin-beaten plate of gold or silver. — *adj* made of metal beaten thin; having bracts. — *adj* **bract'eolate** having bracteoles. — *n* **bract'eole** a small leaf on the axis of a flower. — *adj* **bract'less**. — *n* **bract'let** a bracteole. [L *bractea* a thin plate of metal, gold-leaf]

brad *brad*, *n* a small tapering nail with a side projection instead of a head. — **brad'awl** a small boring tool. [ON *broddr* spike]

Bradbury *brad'bə-ri*, *n* a name for a £1 note (*hist*): — *pl* **Brad'burys** or **Brad'bury's**. [From J S *Bradbury*, Secretary to the Treasury 1913–19]

Bradshaw *brad'shö*, *n* a noted railway-guide, 1839–1961, first published by George *Bradshaw*.

brady' *brad-i-*, *combining form* signifying slow. — *n* **bradycard'ia** (Gr *kardiā* heart) slowness of heartbeat. — *adj* **bradypept'ic** (Gr *peptikos* digesting) slow of digestion. — Also *n*. — *n* **brad'yseism** (*-sīzm*; Gr *seismos* a shake) a slow up-and-down movement of the earth's crust. [Gr *bradys* slow]

brae *brā*, (*Scot*) *n* a sloping bank of a river or sea-shore; a hill-slope. [ON *brā* eyelid; cf **brow**]

brag *brag*, *vi* and *vt* to boast or bluster: — *pr p* **bragg'ing**; *pa t* and *pa p* **bragged**. — *n* a boast or boasting; a thing one boasts of or is proud of; a card game like poker. — *adj* or *adv* (*Spenser*) proud, proudly. — *adv* **bragg'ingly**. — *adv* **brag'ly** (*Spenser*). [Origin doubtful]

bragadisme. See under **braggart**.

braggadocio *brag-ə-dō'shi-ō* or *-chiō*, *n* a braggart or boaster (also with *cap*); empty boasting: — *pl* **braggado'cios**. [From *Braggadochio* (prob *-dok'yō*) in Spenser's *Faerie Queene*]

braggart *brag'ərt, adj* boastful. — *n* a vain boaster. — *n* **bragg'artism** (*Shakesp* **brag'adisme**) boastfulness. — *adj* **bragg'artly**. [Fr *bragard* vain, bragging]

Brahma[1] *brä'mə, n* a large, *orig* Chinese breed of fowl, modified in Europe and America, having feathered legs. — Also *adj.* [*Brahmaputra*, whence it is said to have been brought]

Brahma[2] *brä'mə* (*brä-mä'*), *n* the first god of the Hindu triad, the creator of the Universe. — *n* **Brah'man** (*-mən*) or **Brah'min** one of the highest or priestly caste (*Hinduism*); (**Brahmin**; *derog, esp US*) a highly cultured or socially snobbish person, *esp* of the Boston upper class. — *adj* **Brahmanic** (*-man'*), **Brahman'ical**, **Brahmin'ic**, **Brahmin'ical** or **Brah'minee** appropriated to the Brahmans. — *n* **Brah'manism** or **Brah'minism** one of the religions of India, worship of Brahma; the religion and practices of the Brahmans. — *n* **Brahmi** (*brä'mē*) an ancient Indian alphabet. — **Brahma Samaj** (*su-mäj'*) or **Brahmo Somaj** a reformed Hindu theistic society or church, founded in 1830; **brahmin** (*US* **Brahman**) **bull** or **cow** the zebu, or a zebu cross.

Brahms and Liszt *brämz ənd list*, (*rhyming slang*) *adj* pissed, drunk.

braid[1] *brād, vt* to plait, intertwine; to arrange in plaits; to thread, wind about or through; to trim, bind, or outline with braid; to jerk, whip out (*obs*). — *vi* (*obs*) to start; to change colour or appearance. — *n* a plait, *esp* of hair (now chiefly *NAm*); a band for the hair; a fabric woven in a narrow band; an interweaving, plaiting; embroidery; a sudden movement, start (*obs*). — *adj* **braid'ed** plaited; entwined; trimmed with braid; tarnished, faded (*obs*). — *n* **braid'ing** plaiting; manufacture of braid; work in braid; embroidery; braids collectively. [OE *bregdan* to move quickly, flash, change colour, plait, weave; ON *bregtha*]

braid[2] *brād*, (*Shakesp*) *vt* to upbraid, to reproach. [Prob from **upbraid** or another meaning of **braid**[1] as in ON]

braid[3] *brād, adj* Scots form of **broad**.

braide *brād*, (*Shakesp*) *adj* dissembling, deceitful. [OE *brægd* falsehood, from *bregdan* to weave]

Braidism *brād'izm*, (*archaic*) *n* hypnotism. [From Dr James *Braid*, who practised it *c.* 1842]

brail *brāl, n* one of the ropes used to truss up a sail (*naut*); a piece of leather to bind up a hawk's wing; (in *pl*) the feathers about a hawk's rump. — *vt* to haul in (eg a sail) by pulling upon the brails. [OFr *brail*, from L *brācāle* a waist-belt, from *brācae* breeches]

Braille *brāl, n* a kind of raised type in relief for the blind, having arbitrary signs consisting of varying combinations of six dots on the following basic arrangement (⁚⁚). — Also *adj.* — *vt* to transcribe, print or mark in Braille. — *n* **braill'er** a machine for writing in Braille. — *n* **Braill'ist** a person who can transcribe Braille. [From Louis *Braille* (1809–52), the inventor]

brain *brān, n* (sometimes in *pl*) in vertebrates, that part of the central nervous system that is contained within the skull; in invertebrates, the nervous ganglia near the head end of the body; the seat of the intellect and of sensation; the intellect; (in *pl*) intelligence, common sense (*colloq*); a person of exceptional intelligence (*colloq*); (in *pl*) a person or persons planning and controlling an enterprise; the controlling mechanism in an electronic device. — *vt* to dash out the brains of; to hit hard over the head (*colloq*); to conceive of (*Shakesp*). — *adj* **brained** having brains (*esp* in *combining form* **-brained**). — *n* **brain'iness**. — adj **brain'ish** (*Shakesp*) brainsick; hot-headed; furious. — *adj* **brain'less** without brains or understanding; silly. — *adv* **brain'lessly**. — *n* **brain'lessness**. — *adj* **brain'y** (*colloq*) well endowed with brains; intellectual. — **brain'box** (*colloq*) the cranium; a very clever person; **brain'case** the cranium; **brain'child** an original thought or work: — *pl* **brain'children**; **brain coral** a coral with brain-like convolutions; **brain damage** a general term covering all injury or disease of the brain, temporary or permanent. — *adj* **brain'-dead**. — **brain death** the cessation of function of the brain, thought by some doctors to be the true indication of death, rather than the cessation of the heartbeat (also called **cerebral death**); **brain drain** the continuing loss of citizens of high intelligence and creativity through emigration; **brain fag** extreme tiredness of the nerves or brain (*obs*); **brain fever** encephalitis, inflammation of the brain; **brain-fever bird** an Indian cuckoo (*Cuculus varius*) that sings repetitively in the night; **brain'pan** the cranium; **brain'-power** intellectual ability. — *adj* **brain'sick** diseased in the understanding, deranged. — *adv* **brain'sickly** (*Shakesp*). — **brain'sickness**; **brain stem** the stemlike part of the brain connecting the spinal cord with the cerebral hemispheres, and controlling certain major functions, eg the operation of the heart and lungs and the ability to be conscious; **brain'storm** a sudden disturbance of the mind; a sudden inspiration; **brain'-storming** (*orig US*) the practice of thrashing out a problem, developing a strategy, etc by intensive group discussion in which ideas are put forward in an extempore manner; **brains trust** a committee of experts; a number of reputedly well-informed persons chosen to answer questions of general interest in public and without preparation, *usu* on radio or television; **brain'-teaser** (*colloq*) a difficult puzzle or problem; **brain'-washing** the subjection of a person to systematic indoctrination or mental pressure to make them change their views or confess to a crime, etc. — *vt* **brain'wash**. — **brain'-wave** an electrical impulse produced by the brain; a sudden bright idea. — **on the brain** as an obsession; **pick someone's brains** see under **pick**[1]. [OE *brægen*; Du *brein*, dialect Ger *Bregen*]

braird *brārd* or **breer** *brēr, n* (*orig Scot*) the first shoots of corn or other crop. — *vi* (of crops) to appear above ground. [OE *brerd* edge]

braise[1] *brāz, vt* to stew (*usu* portion-sized pieces of meat, whole vegetables, etc) in a closed pan. [Fr *braiser*]

braise[2] or **braize** *brāz, n* a sea-bream or porgy. [Perh connected with **bream**[1], or with **bass**[2]]

brake[1] *brāk*, archaic *pa t* of **break**[1].

brake[2] *brāk, n* fern; bracken. [Perh **bracken**]

brake[3] *brāk, n* a thicket. — *adj* **brāk'y**. [Ety obscure]

brake[4] *brāk, n* a device for applying resistance to the motion of a body either to slow it down (eg a vehicle brake) or to absorb and measure the power developed by an engine, etc; any means of stopping or slowing down (*fig*); an instrument for breaking flax or hemp; a harrow; a kind of vehicle (see **break**[2]). — *vt* to slow down or stop with, or as if with, a brake. — *vi* to apply or operate a brake, *esp* on a vehicle; to be slowed down or stopped by a brake. — *adj* **brake'less**. — **brake'-block** a block pressed against a wheel as brake; **brake drum** a metal drum attached to a wheel or shaft so as to retard motion by the application of brake shoes; **brake'-fade** a decrease of efficiency in a brake sometimes resulting in complete absence of stopping-power; **brake horsepower** the effective or useful power of a motor, measured by brake applied to the driving shaft; **brake light** a red light at the rear of motor vehicles to warn following drivers when the brakes are applied; **brake lining** asbestos-base friction fabric riveted to brake shoes; **brake pads** the friction material in a disc brake, corresponding to the brake shoes in a drum brake; **brake parachute** a parachute attached to the tail of some high-performance aircraft, used as a brake for landing; **brake'-shoe** the rubbing part of a brake; **brakes'-man** (*US* **brake'man**) the man whose business it is to manage the brake of a railway train; **brake'-van** (*railways*) the carriage in which the brake is worked; **brake'-wheel** the wheel to which a brake is applied. [From root of **break**[1]; cf Du *braak* a flax-brake]

brake[5] *brāk, n* a handle, as of a pump; a lever for working a machine. [Prob through OFr *brac*, from L *brāchium* an arm]

brake[6] *brāk*, (*Shakesp*) *n* an obscure word in *Measure for Measure*, II.1.39 (not made clearer by emendation of *ice* to *vice*).

Bramah-press *bräm'ə-pres*, *n* a hydraulic press invented by Joseph *Bramah* (*c.* 1748–1814), inventor also of the **Bram'ah-lock**, etc.

bramble *bram'bl*, *n* the blackberry bush, a wild prickly shrub of the raspberry genus (*Rubus*); any rough prickly shrub; a blackberry (*Scot*). — *vi* to gather blackberries. — *n* **bram'bling** a bird closely related to the chaffinch. — *adj* **bram'bly**. — **bram'ble-berry**; **bram'ble-bush** a blackberry bush or thicket; **bram'ble-finch** the brambling. [OE *brēmel*; Du *braam*, Ger *Brombeere*]

brame *brām*, (*Spenser*) *n* fierce passion, longing. [Prob Ital *brama*]

bran *bran*, *n* the husks of grain sifted from the flour; the coarsest part of the ground husks, formerly prescribed medically, now eaten generally as a health food; the coarser part or refuse of anything. — *n* **bran'fulness**. — *adj* **brann'y**. — **bran'-mash**; **bran'-pie'** (*obs*) or **bran'-tub** a tub of bran from which small presents, etc, are drawn eg at parties. [OFr *bran*, perh of Celtic origin]

brancard *brangk'ərd*, (*obs*) *n* a horse-litter. [Fr]

branch *bränch* or *bränsh*, *n* a shoot or arm-like limb of a tree; anything like a limb of a tree; any offshoot from a main trunk, such as a minor road, railway line, etc (also *adj*); a subdivision, a section or department of a subject; any subordinate division of a business, subsidiary factory, shop, office, etc (also *adj*); a tributary or (*rare*) brook (*US*); a departure from the sequential ordering of instructions into a different section of the program, eg because of a GOTO or an IF ... THEN statement (*comput*). — *vt* to divide into branches; to adorn with figures of branches, by embroidery or otherwise (*Spenser*, etc). — *vi* to spread out as a branch or in branches (with *off* or *from*). — *adj* **branched**. — *n* **branch'er** a young hawk or other bird when it leaves the nest and begins to take to the branches. — *n* **branch'ery** branches collectively (*lit* and *fig*). — *n* and *adj* **branch'ing**. — *adj* **branch'less**. — *n* **branch'let** a little branch. — *adj* **branch'y**. — **branch'-line** a subsidiary railway line; **branch'-officer** (*navy*) since 1949, any officer holding warrant; **branch'-pilot** one who holds the Trinity House certificate; **branch'-work** ornamental figured patterns. — **branch out** (of a business, etc) to expand, diversify. [Fr *branche*, from LL *branca* an animal's paw]

branchia *brangk'i-ə*, *n* a gill: — *pl* **branch'iae** (*ē-ē*). — *adj* **branch'ial**. — *adj* **branch'iate**. [L *branchia*, from Gr *branchion* (pl *-a*)]

Branchiopoda *brangk-i-op'o-də*, *n pl* a class or subclass of Crustacea with numerous flattened, leaf-shaped, lobed swimming-feet that serve also as breathing organs. — *n* and *adj* **branch'iopod**. [Gr *branchia* gills, and *pous*, *podos* foot]

brand *brand*, *n* a piece of wood burning or partly burned; an instrument for branding; a mark burned into anything with a hot iron; a trademark, tradename, design, etc by which a product or group of products is identified; a particular product or class of products; in general, a particular type or kind; a flaming torch (*poetic*); a sword, from its glitter; a mark of infamy, stigma; a general name for the fungoid diseases or blights of grain crops (*bunt*, *mildew*, *rust* and *smut*). — *vt* to burn or mark with a hot iron, or otherwise; to fix a mark of infamy upon, to stigmatize (sometimes with *as*); to fix indelibly in the memory. — *adj* **brand'ed**. — *n* **brand'er** (*Scot*) a gridiron. — *vt* to cook on the gridiron. — *adj* **brand'ered**. — *n* **brandise** (*brand'is*; OE *isen* iron) a trivet. — *n* **brand'ling** a salmon-parr; a type of worm, reddish with lighter bands, used eg as bait for fishing. — *n* **brand'reth** (ON *brandreith*, from *reith* carriage) a stand of wood for a cask or hayrick; a gridiron (*dialect*); a rail round a well. — **brand awareness** the level of public familiarity with a branded product; **branded goods** goods sold under the proprietary name of their manufacturer; **brand'-image** the impression that the public has of a product or (*fig*) a person; **brand'ing-iron**; **brand'-iron** a gridiron; an iron to brand with; a trivet or tripod to set a pot or kettle upon; (*Spenser* **brond'yron**, etc) a sword; **brand leader** the brand of product with the largest share of the market; **brand loyalty** continued support by consumers of a particular brand rather than its competitors; **brand'-name** a tradename identifying a particular manufacturer's products. — *adj* **brand'-new** quite new (as if newly from the fire) (also *obs* **bran'-new**). — **a brand from the burning** a person snatched out of a pressing danger (from Amos 4.11). [OE *brand*, *brond*, ON *brandr*, from root of **burn**[2]]

brandade *brã-däd*, *n* a Provençal dish made of salt fish cooked with olive oil, garlic and cream. [Fr]

brandise. See **brand**.

brandish *brand'ish*, *vt* to wave or flourish (eg a brand or weapon). — *n* a waving or flourish. [Fr *brandir*, *brandiss-*, from root of **brand**]

brandling, brandreth. See **brand**.

brandy *brand'i*, *n* an alcoholic spirit distilled from grape wine; a glass of this; (with modifier) an alcoholic spirit distilled from wine made from other fruits, or a liqueur made by steeping fruit in brandy, eg *peach brandy*, *cherry brandy*. — *adj* **bran'died** heartened or strengthened with brandy. — **brand'y-ball** a kind of sweet; **brand'y-bottle** (*dialect*) candock; **brandy butter** butter with brandy and sugar beaten in; **bran'dy-glass** a short-stemmed drinking-glass with a globular bowl; **brand'y-pawnee** (Hindi *pānī* water) brandy and water; **brand'y-snap** a thin crisp biscuit flavoured with ginger and *orig* brandy. [Formerly *brand-wine*, from Du *brandewijn*, from *branden* to burn, to distil, and *wijn* wine; cf Ger *Branntwein*]

brangle *brang'gl*, (*archaic*) *vi* to wrangle. — *n* a brawl. — *n* **brang'ling** disputing. [Fr *branler*]

brank[1] *brangk*, *n* buckwheat. [Pliny says *brance* (doubtful reading, perh *brace*) is the Gallic name of a kind of corn]

brank[2] *brangk*, *vi* to prance, toss the head; to strut or swagger. — *adj* **brank'y** (*Scot*) showy. [Prob a variant of **prank**]

branks *brangks*, (*Scot*) *n pl*, rarely in *sing*, a bridle; a scold's bridle, with a hinged iron framework to enclose the head and a bit or gag. [Ety very obscure; OFr *bernac* (see **barnacle**[2]); Ger *Pranger* pillory, Du *prang* fetter, have been compared]

brankursine *brangk'ər-sin* or *-ûr'*, *n* acanthus, or bear's-breech. [LL *branca ursīna* a bear's paw]

branle. See **brawl**[2].

bran-new. See **brand-new** under **brand**.

bransle. See **brawl**[2].

brant-goose. See **brent-goose**.

brantle. See **brawl**[2].

bras. A Spenserian spelling of **brass** (*n*).

brasero *brä-sä'rō*, *n* a brazier; a place for burning criminals or heretics: — *pl* **braser'os**. [Sp, from *brasa* a live coal]

brash[1] *brash*, *n* angular fragments of rock, which occasionally form the basement bed of alluvial deposits; fragments of crushed ice; clippings of hedges or trees. — *adj* **brash'y**. [Prob Fr *brèche*]

brash[2] *brash*, *n* heartburn, water-brash; a sudden burst of rain; a slight attack of illness (*Scot*); an attack or bout (*obs Northern*). — *vt* (*obs*) to attack. [Prob onomatopoeic]

brash[3] *brash*, *adj* forward, bumptious; crude, flashy; reckless, impetuous (*US*); (of wood) brittle (*US*).

brasier. Same as **brazier**.

brass *bräs* or (*Spenser*) **bras**, *n* an alloy of copper and zinc; bronze (*obs*); effrontery (*slang*); money (*slang*); an article or fixture of brass; a renewable sleeve for a bearing (*eng*); a memorial plate of brass in a church; (*collectively*) the brass wind-instruments or their players in an orchestra or band; a prostitute (*slang*). — *adj* made of brass. — *adv* **brass'ily**. — *n* **brass'iness**. — *n* **brass'y** a former name for (a stroke with) a brass-soled wooden golf club (also **brass'ie**; also *adj*); a bronze-coloured fish, the bib or pout. — *adj* like brass in appearance, hardness, sound, or otherwise; brazen-faced. — **brass band** a band of players of (mainly) brass wind-instruments; a small military band; **brass'-bounder** (*obs*) a midshipman; a privileged apprentice on a ship for whom a premium is paid (so called from his gold braid). — *adj* **brass'-faced** (*colloq*) impudent, shameless. — **brass farthing** something of very little or no value; **brass'founder** a person who casts objects in brass; **brass'founding**; **brass hat** (*military slang*) a staff officer (with gold braid on his hat); **brass monkey** (*slang*) a term used variously to refer to extremely cold weather (in allusion to the expression *cold enough to freeze the balls off a brass monkey*, ie cannon; **brass neck** (*colloq*) effrontery; **brass plate** a name plate on a professional person's office door, *usu* made of brass, *usu* a symbol of membership of the professional class; **brass'-rubber**; **brass'-rubbing** the process of copying the design on a church memorial brass, etc on to paper by laying the paper over the brass and rubbing it with coloured wax, chalk, etc; the copy so obtained; **brass tacks** details of practical business. — **brass (someone) off** (*slang*) to make (someone) annoyed or fed up; **top brass** brass hats; those in authority at the top (also **the brass**). [OE *bræs*]

brassard *bras'ärd*, *n* a piece of armour for the arm (*hist*; also **brassart** *bras'ärt* or **brass'et**); an armband or armlet. [Fr, from *bras* arm]

brasserie *bras'(ə-)rē*, *n* a bar serving food; a simple restaurant. [Fr, brewery]

brassica *bras'i-kə*, *n* a plant of the turnip and cabbage genus (*Brassica*) of Cruciferae. [L, cabbage]

brassière or **brassiere** *bras'i-er*, *braz'* or in US sometimes *brə-zēr'*, *n* a woman's undergarment to support or cover the breasts, now *usu* shortened to **bra**. [Fr]

brast *obs* and *Northern* for **burst** (*pr t*, *pa t*, and *pa p*).

brat *brat*, *n* a contemptuous name for a child; a badly-behaved child or (now) young person; any over-garment of coarse cloth (*obs* or *dialect*); a child's pinafore (*obs* or *dialect*); an apron (*obs* or *dialect*). — *n* **brat'ling** a little brat. — *adj* **bratt'ish**. — *adj* **bratt'y**. — **brat pack** (*colloq derog*) a group of successful and popular young (*usu* teenage male) stars working in a creative field, *esp* cinema, with a rowdy, high-spirited image (also *adj* with *hyphen* or as one word); **brat packer** a member of the brat pack. [OE *bratt*, prob cognate with OIr *brat* plaid, Gaelic *brat* apron]

bratchet *brach'it*. See **brach**.

brattice *brat'is*, **brattish** *brat'ish* or **brettice** *bret'is*, *n* in medieval siege operations, a fixed tower of wood; a covered gallery on a castle wall, commanding the wall-face below (in these senses also **bretesse** *bri-tes'* or **bretasche** *bri-tash'*); a wooden partition; a wooden lining; a partition to control ventilation in a mine. — *vt* to provide with a brattice. — *n* **bratt'icing** or **bratt'-ishing** work in the form of brattices; cresting or ornamental work along a ridge, cornice or coping (*archit*). — **bratt'ice-cloth** strong tarred cloth used for mine brattices. [OFr *breteshe*, from LL *bretachia*; cf **bartisan**]

brattle *brat'l*, (chiefly *Scot*) *n* a clattering noise; a quarrel; tumult. — *vi* to make a clattering noise. — *n* and *adj* **bratt'ling**. [Imit]

bratwurst *brat'vo͞orst*, *n* a type of German sausage. [Ger]

braunch. An old spelling of **branch**.

braunite *brow'nīt*, *n* an ore of manganese. [From A E *Braun*, a German treasury official]

brava. See **bravo**.

bravado *brav-ä'dō*, *n* a display of bravery; boastful threatening; a swaggerer (*obs*): — *pl* **brava'dos** or **brava'does**. — *vi* to display bravado. [Sp *bravada*; see **brave**]

Bravais lattice *brav'ā* or *brə-vā' lat'is*, (*crystallog*) *n* one of the 14 different lattices formed by the points of crystals. [From A *Bravais*, 19c French physicist]

brave *brāv*, *adj* daring, courageous; noble; making a fine appearance; finely dressed, showy, handsome; excellent. — *vt* to meet boldly; to defy; to face (out). — *n* a brave soldier, *esp* a N American Indian warrior; a bully, a bravo (*archaic*); bravado (*archaic*). — *adv* bravely (*poetic*). — *adv* **brave'ly**. — *n* **brav'ery** courage; heroism; finery, showy dress; bravado (*obs*). — **brave new world** a desirable or perfect future society (from Shakesp, *Tempest*, V.1.183), *usu* used sardonically, specifically by Aldous Huxley as the title of his novel (1932) portraying a society where scientific, etc progress has produced a repressive, totalitarian regime rather than a utopia. [Fr *brave*; Ital and Sp *bravo*; origin unknown; cf **braw**]

bravo *brä'vō*, *interj* (also *brä'vō'*) well done; excellent (also **bra'va** when addressed to a woman, **bra'vi** *-vē*, to a number of persons). — *n* a daring villain; a hired assassin: — *pl* **bra'vos** or **bra'voes**. [Sp and Ital]

bravura *brä-vo͞o'rə*, *n* spirit and dash in execution (*music*); a florid air with difficult and rapid passages (*music*); a brilliant or daring display. — Also *adj*. [Ital]

braw *brö*, (*Scot*) *adj* fine, splendid; dressed finely. — *adv* **braw'ly**. — *predicative adj* very well. — *n pl* **braws** fine clothes. [Scot variant of **brave**]

brawl[1] *bröl*, *n* an unruly, rowdy punch-up. — *vi* to fight rowdily; to make a disturbance; (of a stream) to murmur or gurgle. — *n* **brawl'er**. — *n* and *adj* **brawl'ing**. [ME *bralle*, of doubtful origin; perh connected with Du *brallen*, Ger *prahlen* to boast]

brawl[2] *bröl*, *n* an old French dance or dance-tune. — Also **branle**, **bransle** (*bran'l*) or **brantle** (*brant'l*). [Fr *branle*]

brawn *brön*, *n* muscle, *esp* of the arm or calf of the leg; thick flesh; muscular strength; a boar (*dialect*); a preparation of meat made from pig's head and ox-feet, cut up, boiled and pickled. — *adj* **brawned**. — *n* **brawn'iness** quality of being brawny; muscularity. — *adj* **brawn'y** fleshy; muscular; strong. [OFr *braon* flesh (for roasting); of Gmc origin, cf Ger *braten* to roast]

braxy *brak'si*, (*Scot*) *n* a bacterial disease of sheep; applied loosely to various diseases of sheep; a sheep so infected; its flesh. — Also *adj*. — **braxy mutton** the flesh of a braxy sheep or generally of a sheep that has died of disease or accident. [Prob orig pl of *brack*, variant of **break**[1]]

bray[1] *brā*, *vt* to break, pound, or grind small, as in a mortar. — *n* **bray'er** an instrument for grinding or spreading ink in printing. [OFr *breier* (Fr *broyer*)]

bray[2] *brā*, *n* the cry of the ass, a heehaw; any harsh grating sound. — *vi* to make a sound like an ass, to heehaw; to give out harsh sounds. — *n* **bray'er**. [OFr *brai*, *brait*; *braire*, from LL *bragīre*, perh of Celtic origin]

Braz. *abbrev*: Brazil; Brazilian.

braze[1] *brāz*, *vt* to cover with, or make like, brass. — *adj* **brā'zen** of or belonging to brass; impudent. — *vt* to face (out) impudently. — *adv* **brā'zenly**. — *n* **brā'zenness** or **brā'zenry** effrontery. — *n* **brazier** (*brāz'yər* or *brāzh'(y)ər*) a worker in brass. — **bra'zen-face** a shameless, impudent person. — *adj* **bra'zen-faced**. [**brass**]

braze[2] *brāz*, *vt* to join with hard solder. — *adj* **braze'-less** without soldering. — *n* **brazier** (*brāz'yər* or *brāzh'(y)ər*) a container or tray for hot coals. [OFr *braser* to burn; perh influenced by **brass**. Cf **braise**[1], **brasero**]

brazier. See **braze**[1,2].

brazil *brə-zil'*, *n usu* **brazil'-wood**, the hard reddish wood of the East Indian sappan tree or *esp* tropical American species of *Caesalpinia*, used in dyeing. — *n* **brazilein** (*-zil'i-in*) a dyestuff obtained by the oxidation of brazilin. — *n* **Brazil'ian** a native or citizen of Brazil, in S America. — *adj* of or from Brazil. — *n* **braz'ilin** a dyestuff obtained from brazil-wood. — **Brazilian ruby** not a true ruby, used for pink topaz (topaz that has become red after heating) or red tourmaline; **Brazilian wax** carnauba; **Brazil nut** the white, oily, edible, hard-shelled seed of a large Brazilian tree (*Bertholletia*); the tree itself. [OFr *bresil* (Sp *brasil*, Ital *brasile*), from LL *brasilium* a red dyewood brought from the East. When a similar wood was discovered in S America the country became known as *terra de brasil*, land of red dyewood]

BRCS *abbrev*: British Red Cross Society (see **Red Cross**).

BRE *abbrev*: Bachelor of Religious Education (chiefly *US*); Building Research Establishment.

breach *brēch*, *n* a break; an act of breaking; an opening or discontinuity; a breaking of a law, contract, covenant, promise, etc; a quarrel; a broken condition or part of anything; a gap made in a fortification; breakers (*obs*). — *vt* to make a breach or opening in. — *vi* (of a whale) to leap clear of the water. — **breach of promise** failure to carry out a promise to marry; **breach of the peace** a violation of the public peace by riot, etc. [ME *breche*, partly from OE *bryce*, but influenced by OFr *bresche* (Mod Fr **brèche**)]

bread *bred*, *n* food made of a baked dough of flour or meal, *usu* with yeast or other raising agent; food; livelihood; money (*slang*). — *vt* to cover (a cutlet, etc) with breadcrumbs before cooking. — *adj* **bread'ed**. — **bread'-and-butt'er** bread sliced and buttered; livelihood. — *adj* connected with making a living or with the consumption of bread-and-butter; materialistic, practical; youthful, naive; ordinary, routine. — **bread-and-butter letter** a letter of thanks for hospitality; **bread'-basket** a basket for holding bread; the stomach (*slang*; also *fig*); **bread'berry** bread steeped in hot milk; **bread'board** a board on which bread is cut or dough kneaded; a board on which temporary or experimental electronic circuits may be laid out; **bread'-chipper** (*Shakesp*) a person who cuts the crusts off bread, an under-butler; **bread'-corn** grain of which bread is made; **bread'crumb** the inner parts of a loaf; (*usu* in *pl*) bread crumbled down, eg as a dressing (when commercially produced *usu* coloured orange) for fish, etc. — *vt* to cover with breadcrumbs. — **bread'fruit** the fruit of a moraceous tree (*Artocarpus incisa*) of the South Sea Islands, which when roasted forms a good substitute for bread; **bread'head** (*slang*) a drug dealer who is not an addict; someone motivated by money alone ; **bread knife** a large serrated knife for cutting bread; **bread'line** see **on the breadline** below; **bread'nut** the fruit of a tropical American tree (*Brosimum alicastrum*) related to the breadfruit tree, used as bread when boiled or roasted; **bread pudding** a baked pudding made with bread, milk, sugar, eggs and dried fruit; **bread'room** an apartment in a ship's hold where the bread is kept; **bread'root** the prairie-turnip, a N American papilionaceous plant (*Psoralea esculenta*) with an edible root; the yam; **bread sauce** a thick milk-based sauce made with bread(crumbs); **bread'-stick** a long, thin stick of bread dough baked until crisp; **bread study** any branch of study taken up as a means of gaining a living; **bread'stuff** bread in any form; any material of which bread is made; **bread tree** a name for various trees whose seeds or pith yield a substitute for bread, eg *Kaffir-bread*; **bread'winner** the person who earns a living for a family. — **bread and circuses** translation of the Roman satirist Juvenal's *panem et circenses* (food and amusements at public expense); **bread buttered on both sides** very fortunate circumstances; **cast one's bread upon the waters** to be generous or charitable without expecting earthly reward; **know which side one's bread is buttered on** to know how to act for one's own best interests; **on the breadline** at subsistence level, with just enough to make ends meet (from **breadline**, a queue of poor or down-and-out people waiting for free food, *esp* from government sources); **take the bread out of someone's mouth** to deprive someone of the means of living. [OE *brēad*, prob from a Gmc root meaning a fragment; cf Scot use of **piece**]

breaded[1]. See **bread**.

breaded[2]. See **brede**.

breadth *bredth*, *n* extent from side to side, width; an area or extent considered for its width; liberality of mind; in art, subordination of details to the harmony of the whole. — *adv* **breadth'ways** or **breadth'wise** in terms of breadth; broadside on. [OE *brǣdu*, from *brād* broad]

break[1] *brāk*, *vt* to divide, part or sever, wholly or partially; to rupture, burst; to shatter, crush; to destroy the continuity or integrity of; to damage (something) so that it fails to work; to interrupt (a fall, journey, etc); to escape forcibly from (*colloq*); to make a forced entry to; to bruise or penetrate the surface of; to break a bone in, or separate the bones of; to overcome or wear out; to tame or habituate to obedience (see also **break in** below); to crush the spirit of; to cure (of a habit); to violate (eg a law, promise, bounds or prison); to set aside (eg a will); to cut up (an animal's body); to unfurl; to decipher (a code); to impart (*esp* with delicacy); to make bankrupt; to demote or cashier; to improve on (a particular time, number of strokes, etc for a course or distance); to arpeggiate (*music*); to cause to change from a simple vowel to a diphthong (*linguistics*). — *vi* to separate; to come apart, or go to pieces, *esp* suddenly; to give way; to start away, to make a sudden burst of speed; to disperse; to burst forth (*usu* with *out*); to force a passage (with *out* or *through*); to pass suddenly into a condition or action (eg into laughter, revolt, sweat, spots; with *out*); (of flowers) in plant-breeding, to become variegated or striped; to pause for rest or refreshment; (of eg day, hope, a scene) to come into view, appear suddenly; (of news) suddenly to become generally known; to become bankrupt; (of a boy's voice at puberty) to change suddenly; to collapse; (of a wave) to burst into foam; to sever a connection, friendship (*with*); (of a ball) to change direction (*cricket*, *golf*); to break the balls (*billiards* etc; see below); to change from a simple vowel to a diphthong under influence of a neighbouring sound (*linguistics*); (of the weather) to change suddenly, *esp* after a settled period; (of cloud, etc) to disperse: — *pa t* **broke**, *archaic* **brake**; *pa p* **brō'ken** or, less *usu*, **broke**. — *n* an act of breaking; the state of being broken; an opening or crack; a discontinuity; a breach in a relationship; a pause, interval or interruption; a pause for rest or refreshment; a consecutive series of successful strokes (*billiards*, *croquet*); the number of points so scored at billiards; a continuous run of anything; the opening shot (*billiards*); the start of a horse-race; the deviation of a ball on striking the pitch (*cricket*); an instance of breaking service (*tennis*); onset (of the monsoon); a social blunder (*US*); a chance (as in *an even break* a fair or equal chance); a good chance, an opportunity. — *adj* **break'able**. — Also *n*, in *pl* items that can be (easily) broken. — *n* **break'ableness**. — *n* **break'age** the act of breaking or its consequences; the article or quantity broken. — *n* **break'er** a person or machine that breaks something; a wave broken on rocks or shore; someone who broadcasts on Citizen's Band radio (*slang*). — *n* and *adj* **break'ing**. — **break'away** revolt, defection; withdrawal, secession; an escape; a sudden attacking movement in various sports; an escape; a stampede or stampeding animal (*Austr*). — *adj* having seceded, defected, etc. — *adj* **break'back** crushing. — **breakbone fever** dengue; **break crop** (*agric*) a crop grown in rotation with cereals; **break'dance** or **break'dancing** a form of dance to rock or disco music using some routines drawn from gymnastics. — *vi* **break'dance**. — **break'dancer**; **break'down** a stoppage through accident; collapse; a nervous breakdown; disintegration; a vigorous and noisy American dance; the sudden passage of current through an insulating material at **breakdown voltage** (*elec eng*); an analysis, investigation of data under different headings. — *adj* assisting after a breakdown, etc, eg **breakdown truck** or **breakdown gang** a vehicle or gang that clears and tows away a vehicle after a breakdown or wreckage after an accident. — *n* and *adj* **break'-even** see **break even** below. — *n* and *adj* **break'-front** (a bookcase, wardrobe, etc) having a centre section projecting beyond the two end sections. — **break'-in** an illegal (and sometimes violent) entering of a building; **break'ing-point** the point at which a person, relationship, situation, etc breaks down under stress; **breaking stress** the stress necessary to break a material, either in tension or compression (*eng*). — *adj* **break'-jaw** very difficult to pronounce accurately. — *adj* **break'neck** headlong, very fast, *usu* dangerously so. — **break-out** see **break out** below; **break point** a point giving a player the opportunity to break service (*tennis*); (also **break'point**) a point at which a computer program will stop running to allow checking, etc; **break'-promise** or **break'-vow** (both *Shakesp*) a person who habitually breaks promises or vows; **break'through** a forcible passage through a barrier; the solving of a problem, *esp* scientific, after much effort, opening the way to further developments; any comparable success; **break'time** (at school, etc) recess, break between work periods; **break'-up** dissolution; dispersal; **break-vow** see **break-promise** above; **break'water** a barrier against the force of the waves; **break'-wind** a wind-break. — **break a jest** to make a jest, crack a joke; **break a lance with** to enter into a contest with; **break a record** see under **record**; **break a strike** see under **strike**; **break away** to make a breakaway; to be scattered, as clouds after a storm; **break bread** to have a meal (*with*); to administer or take part in Holy Communion (*Christian relig*); **break bulk** to open the hold and take out a portion of the cargo; to begin to use goods supplied in bulk; **break camp** to dismantle and pack one's tents, etc; **break cover** (of eg a fox) to burst out from concealment; **break down** to demolish; to crush; to collapse; to be overwhelmed by one's emotions; to suffer a nervous breakdown; to fail completely; to analyse; **break even** to avoid making a loss but fail to make a profit; to reach the point at which revenue equals costs (*n* and *adj* **break'-even**). — **break forth** to burst out, issue; **break ground** see under **ground**[2]; **break in** (also **break**) to tame or accustom (an animal) to obedience; to make (shoes, etc) less stiff by use; **break in, in on** or **into** to enter violently; to interpose abruptly; **breaking and entering** house-breaking, illegal entry into property; **break into** to begin to use up or spend (something held in reserve, a large denomination note, etc); **break it down** (*Austr colloq*) stop it!; **break loose** to extricate oneself forcibly; to break through all restraint; **break no squares** to make no difference, do no harm, matter little; **break of day** dawn; **break off** to detach by breaking; to put an abrupt end to; to leave off or stop abruptly; **break one's mind** (*obs*) to communicate one's thoughts to somebody; **break out** to appear suddenly; to break through all restraint; to escape (*n* **break'-out**); to become active suddenly; to become covered with (a rash, etc; with *in*); **break service** or **break someone's serve** (*tennis*, etc) to win a game in which one's opponent is serving; **break sheer** (of a ship riding at anchor) to be forced by wind or tide out of a position clear of the anchor; **break someone's heart** to crush someone emotionally, *esp* by failing them in love; **break the balls** (or simply **break**) to open the game by striking the red ball or giving a miss, or to continue the game this way when a similar position occurs (*billiards*); to open the game by striking one of the red balls (*snooker*); **break the ice** (*fig*) to get through first difficulties, *esp* restraint on first meeting; **break through** to make a breakthrough; **break up** to break open; to break in pieces; to go to pieces; to put an end to; to disperse, to part; (of a school) to close for the holidays; to dig or plough up; to disconcert or upset (*colloq*); to make helpless with laughter (*colloq*); **break upon the wheel** (*hist*) to punish by stretching on a wheel and breaking the bones; **break wind** to let out flatulence from the bowels; **break with** to cease relations with, *esp* to quarrel with; to cease adherence to (tradition, a habit). [OE *brecan*; Ger *brechen*]

break[2] or **brake** *brāk*, *n* a long wagonette; a carriage frame that is all wheels and no body, used in breaking in horses; an estate car. [**break**[1], perh by way of **brake**[4] *vt*]

breaker[1]. See **break**[1].

breaker[2] *brāk'ər*, *n* a small water-cask, used on shipboard. [Prob Sp *bareca* barrel]

breakfast *brek'fəst*, *n* the first meal of the day (also *adj*); a break or breaking of fast. — *vi* to take breakfast. — *vt* to provide with breakfast. — **break'fast-room**; **break'fast-set** the crockery used at breakfast; **break'fast-table**; **breakfast TV** television programmes broadcast in the early morning.

bream[1] *brēm*, *n* a freshwater fish of the carp family, with high-arched back; a fish of the family Sparidae (sea-bream); a fish (Ray's bream, *Brama raii*) related to the mackerel; extended to other fishes. [OFr *bresme* (Fr *brême*), from OHGer *brahsema* (Mod Ger *Brassen*)]

bream[2] *brēm*, *vt* to clean (eg a ship's bottom) by burning off seaweed, shells, etc. [Prob connected with **broom**, Du *brem*]

breare *brēr*, (*Spenser*) *n*. Same as **brier**.

breaskit. See **brisket**.

breast *brest*, *n* the front of the human body between the neck and the belly; one of the two mammary glands in women (or rudimentary in men), forming soft protuberances on the chest; the corresponding part of any animal; the part of a jacket, etc which covers the breast; a swelling slope; (the source of) the emotions, affections; singing voice (*obs*). — *vt* to set the breast against, to push forward with the breast against; to surmount; to oppose manfully. — *adj* (*usu* as *combining form*) **breast'ed** having (a certain type of) breast(s). — **breast'bone** the sternum, the bone running down the middle of the breast, to which the first seven ribs are attached; **breast cancer** a malignant tumour of the breast. — *adv* **breast-deep'** as deep to reach to the breast. — *adj* **breast'-fed**. — *vt* **breast'-feed** to give milk to (a baby) from the breasts rather than from a bottle. — **breast'-feeding**. — *adv* **breast-high'** high as the breast; breast-deep. — **breast'-knot** a knot of ribbons worn on the breast; **breast'pin** an ornamental pin for the breast; **breast'plate** a plate or piece of armour for the breast; an embroidered square of linen with precious stones, worn on the breast of the Jewish high-priest (*Bible*); **breast'plough** a kind of spade for cutting turf, with a cross-bar against which the breast is pressed; **breast'-pump** a pump for removing milk from the breasts; **breast'rail** the upper rail of a breastwork; **breast screening** mammography, as a diagnostic tool for breast cancer; **breast'stroke** a swimming-stroke performed breast-down, with circling movements of the arms and a frog-like movement of the legs; **breastsummer** or **bressummer** (*bres'ə-mər*) a summer or beam supporting the whole, or a great part, of the front of a building in the manner of a lintel; **breast wall** a retaining wall; **breast wheel** a water-wheel turned by water delivered upon it at about half its height; **breast'work** (*fortif*) a hastily constructed earthwork. — **double-** and **single-breasted** see under **double** and **single**; **make a clean breast** to make a full confession. [OE *brēost*; Ger *Brust*, Du *borst*]

breath *breth*, *n* the air drawn into and then expelled from the lungs; exhaled air as smell or vapour; power of breathing; life; a single act of breathing; breathing without vibrating the vocal cords (*phonetics*); a sound so produced; a whisper; the time occupied by a single act of breathing; a very slight breeze; a slight suspicion. — *adj* produced by breath without voice. — *vt* **breath'alyze** (in UK *usu* **breath'alyse**) to test with a breathalyzer. — *n* **breath'alyzer** (in UK *usu* **breath'-alyser**) a device which indicates the amount of alcohol in a person's breath, by means of a plastic bag containing alcohol-sensitive crystals which change colour when a certain concentration of alcohol vapour is blown through them. — *adj* **breathed** (*bretht*) having a breath (*esp* as *combining form*, eg **long-breathed**, and see also under **breathe**). — *adj* **breath'ful** (*Spenser*) full of breath or air, also full of scent or odour. — *adv* **breath'ily**. — *n* **breath'iness**. — *adj* **breath'less** out of breath; with the breath held or taken away, from excitement, interest, etc; breezeless, airless; dead. — *adv* **breath'lessly**. — *n* **breath'lessness**. — *adj* **breath'y** (of a speaking voice) accompanied by much unvocalized breath; (of a singer or instrument-player) without proper breath control, causing impure sound. — *adj* **breath'taking** astounding. — **breath'-test** a test carried out on a person's breath, by breathalyser or other device, to determine how much alcohol that person has consumed. — **below** or **under one's breath** in a low voice; **catch one's breath** to rest until one is no longer out of breath; to stop breathing for an instant; **in the same breath** at the same time; **out of breath** having difficulty in breathing; panting from exertion, etc; **save one's breath** to refrain from pointless talk; **spend** or **waste one's breath** to talk to no avail or profitlessly; **take (one's) breath** to recover freedom of breathing; to stop for breath, rest, or refreshment; **take someone's breath away** to make someone breathless with astonishment, delight, etc; **with bated breath** with breath restrained out of suspense, fear or reverence. [OE *brǣth*; Ger *Brodem* steam, breath]

breathe *brēdh*, *vi* to draw in or expel breath or air to or from the lungs or other respiratory organs; to respire; (of wind) to blow lightly; (of wine) to be exposed to the air so as to improve in flavour; (of fabric, leather, etc) to allow air, moisture, etc to pass through; to take breath, to rest or pause; to live, continue to draw breath. — *vt* to draw into or expel from the lungs; to instil, imbue; to breathe out (fire, etc); to utter unvoiced (*phonetics*); to utter softly, whisper; to express, display; to give breathing-space to, allow to rest; to tire by some brisk exercise. — *adj* **breathable** (*brēdh'ə-bl*). — *adj* **breathed** (*brēdhd*; *phonetics*) pronounced without voice (see also under **breath**). — *n* **breath'er** someone who breathes or lives; a spell of exercise; a rest to recover breath; a vent to release pressure or for ventilation. — *n* **breath'ing** the act of breathing; an instance of breathing; aspiration, longing; respite; either of two signs (traditionally open and close single quotes respectively) used in Greek to signify presence (rough breathing) or absence (smooth breathing) of the aspirate. — *adj* lifelike. — **breath'ing-hole** (*Can*) an opening in the ice for a submerged animal to breathe; **breath'ing-space** or (*obs*) **breath'ing-time** space or time in which to breathe or rest; a brief respite; **breath'ing-while** time sufficient for drawing breath; any very short period. — **breathe again** to be relieved after an anxious moment or time; **breathe down someone's neck** to keep too insistently close to someone, *esp* by way of supervision; **breathe easily** or **freely** to be at ease; **breathe one's last** to die; **breathe (up)on** (*obs*) to tarnish the name of. [From **breath**]

breccia *brech'yə*, (*geol*) *n* a rock composed of angular fragments. — *adj* **brecciated** (*brech'i-ā-tid*) reduced to or composed of breccia. [Ital]

brecham *brehh'əm*, (*Scot*) *n* a horse-collar. [OE *beorgan* to protect, and *hama* covering]

Brechtian *brehht'i-ən*, *adj* pertaining to or suggestive of the writings or dramatic theories and techniques of the German playwright, Bertolt *Brecht* (1898–1956).

bred *bred*, *pa t* and *pa p* of **breed**.

brede *brēd*, *n* and *vt* an archaic form of **braid**[1]. — *pa t* and *adj* (*Spenser*) **bread'ed**.

bree[1] *brē*, (*Scot*) *n* the eyebrow. [OE *brǣw*, *brēaw*; cf Ger (*Augen*)*braue*; and **brae**]

bree[2] *brē*, (*Scot*) *n* the liquor in which anything has been boiled. [Perh OE *brīw*; cf **berry**[2], Ger *Brei*]

breech *brēch*, *n* (almost always in *pl*, **breeches** *brich'iz*; in NAm, etc also **britches**) a garment worn by men on the lower parts of the body: strictly, as distinguished from trousers, coming to just below the knee, but often used generally for trousers; (in *sing*) the lower back part of the body, the buttocks; breech birth or delivery (*obstetrics*); the lower or back part of anything, *esp* of a gun (*pl* in these senses *pronounced brēch'iz*). — *vt* (*brich*, *brēch*; *obs*) to put into breeches; to flog. — *adj* **breeched**. — *n* **breeching** (*brich'ing*) a part of a horse's harness attached to the saddle, coming round the breech and hooked to the shafts; a strong rope attached to the breech of a gun to secure it to a ship's side. — *adj* (*Shakesp*) subject to whipping. — *adj* **breech'less** trouserless. — **breech birth** or **delivery** one in which the buttocks, and sometimes also the feet, of the baby come first; **Breeches Bible** the Geneva Bible (qv), with 'breeches' for 'aprons' in Gen 3.7; **breech'es-buoy** a life-saving apparatus enclosing the person like a pair of breeches; **breeches part** or **role** (*theat*, *opera*) a part in which a woman plays a man or boy; **breech'-loader** a firearm loaded by introducing the charge at the breech instead of the muzzle. — *adj* **breech'-loading**. — **wear the breeches** (of the female in a (*usu* marital) relationship) to be in charge. [OE *brēc*, *pl* of *brōc*; cf Ger *Bruch*, Du *broek*]

breed *brēd*, *vt* to generate or bring forth; to cause or promote the generation of, or the production of breeds of; to train or bring up; to cause or occasion. — *vi* to be pregnant (now *dialect*); to produce offspring; to be produced or brought forth; to be in training, to be educated (*Scott*): — *pa t* and *pa p* **bred**. — *n* that which is bred, progeny or offspring; a strain, variety or race; a kind, type. — *n* **breed'er** a person or thing that breeds; a breeder reactor. — *n* **breed'ing** the act or process of producing; ancestry, pedigree; upbringing; manners. — Also *adj*. — **breed'-bate** (*Shakesp*) a person who foments trouble or strife; **breeder reactor** a nuclear reactor which creates more fissile material than it consumes; **breed'ing-ground** a place where animals, etc go to breed; an attitude, environment, etc which fosters or creates *esp* something considered undesirable. [OE *brēdan* to cherish, keep warm; Ger *brüten* to hatch]

breeks *brēks*, *n pl* Scots form of **breeches** trousers.

breem. See **breme**.

breer. See **braird**.

breese. See **breeze**[2].

breeze[1] *brēz*, *n* a light wind; a disturbance or quarrel (*colloq*); a whispered rumour (*colloq*); something delightfully easy (*slang*). — *vi* to blow as or like a breeze; to go briskly and cheerily (*slang*); to do, achieve, etc something with ease (with *through*). — *adj* **breeze'less**. — *adv* **breez'ily**. — *n* **breez'iness**. — *adj* **breez'y** fanned with or subject to breezes; bright, lively, exhilarating. — **breez'eway** a roofed passage, *usu* open at the sides, connecting two buildings. — **breeze up** to freshen into a breeze; **breeze up sale** (*horse-racing*) a horse sale at which prospective purchasers can watch (*usu* young, untried) horses go through their paces over a short distance; **get the breeze up** to get the wind up (see **wind**[1]). [OSp *briz* NE wind]

breeze[2], **breese** or **brize** *brēz*, (*archaic* or *dialect*) *n* a gadfly, botfly, or other dipterous pest of horses and cattle. [OE *briosa*]

breeze[3] *brēz*, *n* furnace refuse used in making **breeze brick**, **breeze blocks** or **breeze concrete** for building. [Perh OFr *brese*]

bregma *breg'mə*, (*anatom*) *n* the part of the skull where the frontal and the two parietal bones join, sometimes divided into the right and left bregmata: — *pl* **breg'mata**. — *adj* **bregmat'ic**. [Gr]

brehon *brē'hən*, (*Ir hist*) *n* a judge in medieval Ireland. — **Brehon Law** or **Laws** the system of jurisprudence in use among the Irish until near the middle of the 17c. [Ir *breitheamh*, pl *breitheamhuin*]

breloque *brə-lok'*, *n* an ornament attached to a watch-chain. [Fr]

breme or **breem** *brēm*, (*Spenser*) *adj* fierce, keen. [Perh related to OE *brēman* to rage]

bremsstrahlung *bremz'shträ-lo͝ong*, (*phys*) *n* electromagnetic radiation produced when an electron collides with, or is deflected by, a positively charged nucleus. [Ger *bremsen* to brake and *Strahlung* radiation]

Bren *bren* or **Bren gun** (*gun*), *n* (also without *cap*) a light machine-gun. [First manufactured in *Br*no, in Czechoslovakia, and then in *En*field, in England]

bren or **brenne** *bren*, (*obs*) *vt* and *vi* to burn: — *pa t* and *pa p* **brent**. — *adj* **brent**. [See ety for **burn**[2]]

brent *brent*, (*Scot*) *adj* lofty; steep; smooth, unwrinkled. [OE *brant* steep; ON *brattr*]

brent-goose *brent'-gōōs*, *n* a small wild goose, having the head, neck, long wing feathers, and tail black, the belly white, the rest slaty-grey, often confused with the barnacle goose. — Also **brant'-goose** or **brent barnacle**. [Prob *branded* brindled]

brer *brûr* or *brär*, (*Southern US dialect*) *n* brother (*usu* followed by a name).

brere *brēr*, (*Spenser*) *n* a form of **brier**.

bressummer. See **breastsummer** under **breast**.

Bret. *abbrev*: Breton.

bretasche, bretesse. See **brattice**.

brethren *bredh'rən*. See **brother**.

Breton *bret'ən*, *n* a native of Brittany (*Bretagne*), France; the Celtic tongue of Brittany, Brezonek; (also without *cap*; also **Breton hat**) a hat with a rounded crown and turned-up brim. — *adj* of Brittany; Armoric. [Fr]

brettice. See **brattice**.

Bretwalda *bret-wöl'də*, (*hist*) *n* a title of certain kings of Old English kingdoms, whose superiority over the others was more or less acknowledged. [Prob Lord of the *Britons*, or of *Britain*, from OE *walda* ruler]

breve *brēv*, *n* the mark of a short vowel (as in ĕ), *opp* to *macron*; an obsolescent note, ‖𝅜‖, twice as long as the longest now generally used (the semibreve), but half (or in perfect time one-third) as long as the obsolete long (*music*); a papal brief (see under **brief**). [L *brevis* short]

brevet *brev'it*, *n* a military commission entitling an officer to take rank above that for which he receives pay. — *vt* to confer such rank on: — *pr p* **brev'eting**; *pa t* and *pa p* **brev'eted** (those who pronounce it *bri-vet'* write **brevett'ing** and **brevett'ed**). [Fr, from L *brevis* short]

brevet d'invention *brə-ve dɛ̃-vã-syɔ̃*, (*Fr*) *n* a patent.

breveté *brəv-tā*, (*Fr*) *adj* patented.

breviary *brēv'i-ər-i*, *n* a book containing the daily service of the RC Church. [L *breviārium*, from *brevis* short]

breviate *brē'vi-āt*, *n* a short compendium; a lawyer's brief. [L *breviātus*, from *breviāre* to shorten]

brevier *brə-vēr'*, *n* an old type size (*approx* 8-point) between bourgeois and minion, said (doubtfully) to have been used for breviaries.

brevi manu *brē'vī mān'ū* or *bre'wē man'ōō*, (*L*) *adv* off-hand, *literally* with a short hand.

brevipennate *brev-i-pen'ət*, *adj* of birds, having short wings. [L *brevis* short, and *penna* wing]

brevity *brev'it-i*, *n* shortness; conciseness. — **brevity code** a code in which a single symbol is substituted for a group of words. [Poss Anglo-Fr *breveté* shortness, infl by L *brevitās*, *brevitātis*, from L *brevis* short]

brew *brōō*, *vt* to prepare by infusion, boiling and fermentation, as beer from malt and other materials, or by infusion, mixing or boiling, without fermentation, as for tea or punch; to contrive or plot. — *vi* to perform the operation of brewing ale or beer, etc; (*esp* of tea) to be in the process of being brewed; to be in preparation, gathering or forming. — *n* a brewing; a brewage; a variety of making of a brewed beverage; a concoction, mixture. — *n* **brew'age** something brewed; the process of brewing. — *n* **brew'er** a person who brews. — *n* **brew'ery** a place used for brewing. — *n* **brew'ing** the act or an instance of making liquor from malt; the quantity brewed at once. — *n* **brew'ster** (now mainly *Scot*; *orig fem*) a brewer. — **brewer's droop** (*colloq*) in a man, inability to get an erection when drunk; **brewers'** or **brewer's yeast** a yeast used in brewing, especially *Saccharomyces cerevisiae*, also used medically as a source of the vitamin B complex vitamins; **brew'-house** a brewery; **brew'master** the supervisor of the brewing in a brewery; **brew'pub** a combined pub and small-scale brewery, serving its own real ale. — **brew up** to make tea. — Also *n* **brew'-up**. [OE *brēowan*; cf Ger *brauen*]

brewis *brōō'is*, (*archaic* and *dialect*) *n* broth, *esp* beef broth; bread soaked in broth, fat, gravy, or the like. [OFr *broez*, infl by OE *brīw* bree]

Brezhnev Doctrine *brezh'nev dok'trin*, *n* the Soviet doctrine which arose during the leadership of Leonid *Brezhnev* (died 1982), that the Soviet Union had the right to intervene in the internal affairs of another communist country to counter a supposed threat to socialism.

Brezonek *brez'ə-nek*, *n*. See **Breton**.

briar. See **brier**[1,2].

Briard *brē-är(d)*, *n* a large, heavy, hairy dog of a French breed. [*Brie*, district in NE France]

Briarean *brī-ā'ri-ən*, *adj* relating to *Briareus* (Gr *Briareōs*), a hundred-handed giant; many-handed. [Gr *briaros* strong]

bribe *brīb*, *n* something offered to someone to influence their judgement unduly or to persuade them to behave in a certain way; spoil, booty (*obs*). — *vt* to influence by offering a bribe; to gain over or win over by bribery; to steal (*obs*). — *vi* to practise bribery. — *n* **brīb'er**. — *n* **brīb'ery** the act of giving or taking bribes. — **brib'ery-oath** an oath taken by an elector that he had not been bribed. [OFr *bribe* a lump of bread; origin doubtful]

bric-à-brac or **bricabrac** *brik'ə-brak*, *n* old curiosities, knick-knacks, or other treasured odds and ends. [Fr]

brick *brik*, *n* baked clay; a shaped block of baked clay, generally rectangular (the standard dimensions being about 23cm × 11.5cm × 6.5cm (9 × 4$\frac{1}{2}$ × 3in)); a brick-shaped block of other material, often compressed; a child's building-block of wood, etc; a loaf or a bun more or less in the shape of a brick; the colour of brick, brick-red; a helpful, supportive, kind person (*colloq*). — *adj* made of brick or bricks; of the colour of brick, brick-red. — *vt* to fill or wall (in, up, etc) with brick; to cover with brick or an appearance of brick. — *adj* **brick'en** (*obs*) made of brick. — *n* **brick'ie** (*colloq*) a bricklayer. — *n* **brick'ing** brickwork; imitation brick-work. — *adj* **brick'y** like or of brick. — **brick'bat** a piece of brick, *esp* if used as a missile; a critical remark; **brick'clay** a clay containing sand and a good deal of iron; any clay, loam or earth used for brick-making; **brick'-dust** powdered brick; the colour of powdered red brick; **brick'-earth** a clayey silt or loam used for brick-making; **brick'field** a place where bricks are made; **brick'fielder** (*Austr*) a hot dry wind (*orig* one bringing dust from the brickfields of Sydney suburbs); **brick'-kiln** a kiln in which bricks are made; **brick'layer** in the building trade, a person who lays and builds with bricks; **brick'laying**; **brick'maker**; **brick'making**; **brick'-nog** or **brick'-nogging** see **nog**[2]. — *adj* **brick-red'** of the colour of an ordinary red brick. — *adj* **brick'shaped** of the shape of a standard brick. — **brick'-tea** tea pressed into cakes; **brick'work** work constructed in brick; bricklaying; **brick'works** a factory producing bricks; **brick'yard** a brickfield. — **a brick short of a load** (*colloq*) not quite all there; **drop a brick** to say or do something horrifyingly tactless or indiscreet; **like a ton of bricks** heavily and promptly; **like banging** (or **knocking**) **one's head against a brick wall** said of a laborious but unrewarding attempt, eg to persuade, inform, etc; **make bricks without straw** to try to do a piece of work without the materials necessary for it; to make something that will not last; **see through a brick wall** to be unusually perspicacious. [Fr *brique*, from the same root as **break**[1]]

brickle *brik'l*, (*Spenser* and *Scot*) *adj* apt to break; weak; troublesome. [Cf **bruckle**]

brickwall *brik'wöl*, a corruption of **bricole**.

bricole *brik'əl*, *-ōl* or *brik-ōl'*, *n* a medieval military catapult for hurling stones; the rebound of a ball from the wall of a real tennis court; a similar stroke in billiards; a rebound (*fig*). [Fr, from LL *briccola*]

bridal *brīd'əl*, *n* (*poetic* or *archaic*) a marriage feast; a wedding. — *adj* belonging to or relating to a bride or a wedding; nuptial. — **bridal suite** a set of hotel rooms intended for a newly married couple; **bridal wreath** any of various shrubs of the genus *Spiraea*, having sprays of white flowers. [OE *brȳdealo*, literally bride-ale; see **bride** and **ale** (feast)]

bride *brīd*, *n* a woman about to be married or newly married. — *vi* and *vt* (with *it*; *Shakesp*) to act the bride. — **bride'-ale** (*archaic*) the ale-drinking at a marriage feast (see **bridal**); **bride'-bed** (*archaic*) the marriage bed;

bride'cake or **bride's'-cake** wedding cake; **bride'-chamber** (*archaic*) a nuptial apartment; the room in which a wedding is performed; **bride'groom** a man about to be married or newly married; **bride'maid** or **bride'maiden**, **bride's'-maid**, **brides'maid**, **bride'man**, **bride's'-man**, **brides'man** (all except *bridesmaid obs* or *dialect*) young unmarried people who attend the bride and bridegroom at a wedding; **bridesmaid** see **bride-maid**; a team or individual that is always runner-up or never quite makes it to the top (*sport slang*); **bride'-wealth** or **bride'-price** in tribal societies, etc, a price paid (*usu* in kind) to a bride's family by the bridegroom. [OE *brȳd*; ON *brūthr*, Ger *Braut*]

bridewell *brīd'wəl*, *n* a house of correction; a gaol. [From a palace near *St Bride's Well* in London]

bridge[1] *brij*, *n* a structure spanning a river, road, etc giving communication across it by foot, road, rail, etc; the narrow raised platform from which the captain of a ship gives directions; a thin upright piece of wood supporting the strings in a violin or similar instrument; the bony upper part of the nose; a support for a billiard cue; bridge-work; in the theatre, a platform (for stagehands) that rises above the stage; anything that connects across a gap (*lit* and *fig*); a type of electrical circuit for measuring resistance, etc. — *vt* to be or to build a bridge over; to connect the extremities of (a gap) (*fig*); to make an electrical connection between. — *adj* **bridge'able** or **bridg'able**. — *adj* **bridge'less**. — *n* **bridg'ing** the process of making, or the construction forming, a bridge; a brace or braces fixed between joists to strengthen them; provision of credit necessary for a business transaction; a method of climbing a rock chimney by straddling it. — Also *adj*. — **bridge'board** a notch-board; **bridge'-builder** a person who builds bridges; a person who tries to reconcile hostile parties, etc, *esp* in diplomacy; **bridge'-building**; **bridge'head** a fortification covering the end of a bridge nearest to the enemy's position; a place suitable for such fortification; any advanced position seized in enemy territory; **bridge'-house** a house at the end of a bridge; **bridge'-work** (*dentistry*) a bridge-like structure by which false teeth are attached to natural teeth or roots; **bridging loan** a short-term loan, *usu* for a fairly large sum and at a relatively high rate of interest, providing bridging for a business transaction, *esp* house purchase. — **bridge of boats** a bridge resting on boats moored abreast across a piece of water; **cross a bridge when one comes to it** to bother about a future problem only when it affects one. [OE *bryg*; Ger *Brücke*, ON *bryggja*]

bridge[2] *brij*, *n* any of various card-games, for two pairs of players, developed from whist (see **auction bridge** and **contract bridge**); *orig* a variety (**bridge whist**) in which the dealer or dealer's partner chose the trump suit, or no-trumps, and the dealer played his or her partner's hand as a dummy. — **Bridgera'ma** an apparatus which shows on large electronically-lit boards the steps of a bridge game in progress in another room. — **bridge'-drive** a tournament of bridge-playing. [Earlier known as *bridge whist*, *biritch*; ety unknown]

bridie *brī'di*, (*Scot*) *n* a meat and onion turnover.

bridle *brīd'l*, *n* an apparatus on a horse's head by which to control it; any curb or restraint; a movement expressing resentment, scorn or vanity, a tossing back of the head, like a horse pulled up by the bridle; a mechanical device that limits movement between parts of a component. — *vt* to put a bridle on; to manage by a bridle; to check or restrain. — *vi* to toss the head (*up at* the thing taken amiss). — *adj* **brī'dled** wearing a bridle; (of a bird) with markings similar to a bridle. — *n* **brī'dler** a person who governs or restrains with or as with a bridle. — **bri'dle-hand** the hand that holds the bridle in riding, the left hand; **bri'dle-path** or **-road** a path or way for those riding or leading horses; **bri'dle-rein** the strap of a bridle. — *adj* **bridle'-wise** (*US*; of a horse) obedient without requiring the use of the bridle. — **bite on the bridle** to be impatient, like a restive horse. [OE *brīdel*; OHGer *brittel*]

bridoon *brid-ōōn'*, *n* the light snaffle usual in a military bridle in addition to the ordinary bit, controlled by a separate rein. [Fr *bridon*, from *bride* a bridle]

Brie *brē*, *n* a white, soft cheese made in *Brie*, NE France.

brief *brēf*, *n* a summary of a client's case by a solicitor for the instruction of a barrister or counsel (*law*); a writ; a papal brief (see below); a short statement of any kind; a statement of the aims of an advertising campaign, etc; instructions; a lawyer, *esp* a barrister (*slang*); (in *pl*) close-fitting legless underpants for men or women. — *adj* short in duration; (now *usu* of clothing) short in length or extent, scanty, skimpy; concise; brusque in manner. — *vt* to give information or issue instructions to; to instruct or retain (a barrister). — *n* **brief'ing** the action, or an instance, of making or giving a brief; instructions or information imparted. — *adj* **brief'less**. — *adv* **brief'ly**. — *n* **brief'ness**. — **brief'-bag** the bag in which a barrister carries his or her briefs to and from court; **brief'-case** a small case for carrying briefs, or for documents in general. — **hold a brief** (*law*) to be retained as counsel; (with *for*) to argue for, to champion; **hold no brief for** not to support or advocate; **in brief** in few words; **king's brief** a royal mandate ordering collections to be made in churches for specified charitable purposes; **papal brief** a less formal papal document than a bull; **take a brief** to undertake a case; **the brief and the long** (*Shakesp*) the short and the long; **to be brief** in order to speak in few words. [Fr *bref*, from L *brevis* short]

brier[1] or **briar** *brīr* or *brī'ər*, *n* a prickly shrub; a wild rose bush. — Also (*Spenser*, etc) **brere** (*brēr*). — *adj* **briered** or **briared** caught in or covered with briers. — *adj* **brier'y** thorny; full of briers. — **sweet brier** eglantine, a wild rose (*Rosa rubiginosa*) with scented leaves. [OE (Anglian) *brēr* (WSax *brǣr*)]

brier[2] or **briar** *brī'ər*, *n* the white heath (*Erica arborea*), a S European shrub; a tobacco-pipe made out of its root. — Also **bri'er-root** or **bri'er-wood**. — Also *adj*. [Fr *bruyère* heath]

Brig. *abbrev*: Brigadier.

brig[1] *brig*, *n* a two-masted, square-rigged vessel; a place of detention on board ship (*US navy*); a prison (*US slang*). [Short form of **brigantine**[1]]

brig[2] *brig*, *n* Northern form of **bridge**[1]. [ON *bryggja*]

brigade *brig-ād'*, *n* a body of troops consisting of a group of regiments, battalions or batteries commanded by a general officer; a band of people more or less organized for a specific purpose. — *vt* to form into brigades; to group (people) together, *esp* oppressively. — *n* **brigadier** (*brig-ə-dēr'*) a general officer (in the British Army and Royal Marines) between colonel and major-general in rank, having command of a brigade; a brigadier general (*US colloq*); (*brē-gä-dyā*) in the French army, a corporal. — **brigade'-ma'jor** a staff-officer attached to a brigade as assistant to the brigadier; **brigadier general** an officer ranking above colonel and below major general (*US army*); a former name for a brigadier (*British army*). [Fr *brigade*, from Ital *brigata*, from LL *briga* strife]

brigalow *brig'ə-lō*, (*Austr*) *n* any of several species of acacia. [Aboriginal]

brigand *brig'ənd*, *n* a bandit or highway robber, *esp* a member of a gang. — *n* **brig'andage** or **brig'andry**. — *n* **brigandine** or **brigantine** (*brig'ən-dēn*, *-tēn*) a coat-of-mail of steel rings or plates sewed on to linen or leather. [Fr, from Ital *brigante*, from LL *briga* strife]

brigantine[1] *brig'ən-tēn*, *n* a two-masted vessel, with the main mast of a schooner and the foremast of a brig. [Fr *brigantin*, from Ital *brigantino* pirate ship]

brigantine[2]. See under **brigand**.

Brig. Gen. *abbrev*: Brigadier General.

bright *brīt*, *adj* shining; full of light; vivid; clear; cheerful; vivacious; clever; illustrious; hopeful, having good prospects; beautiful (*archaic*). — *adv* brightly; clearly. — *vt* and *vi* **bright'en** to make or grow bright or brighter; to clear up; to cheer up. — *adv* **bright'ly**. — *n* **bright'ness**. — *adj* **bright'some** bright; brilliant. —

brightening agent a compound that increases the brightness of a white or coloured textile by converting some of the ultraviolet radiation into visible light; **bright-field illumination** a method of illumination in microscopy in which the specimen appears dark on a bright background; **bright'-work** polished metal on cars, etc. — **bright and early** very early; in good time; **bright-eyed and bushy-tailed** eager and alert; **bright young thing** a member of the young and fashionable social set in the 1920s and 1930s; **the bright lights** the places of entertainment in a city centre; city life, *esp* as compared with the quiet life of the countryside. [OE *byrht*, *beorht*; cognate with Gothic *bairhts* clear]

Bright's disease *brīts diz-ēz'*, *n* a generic name for diseases of the kidneys with albumen in the urine. [From Dr Richard *Bright* (1789–1858)]

brigue *brēg*, *vi* to intrigue. — *n* strife; intrigue. — *n* **briguing** (*brēg'ing*) canvassing. [Fr]

brill[1] *bril*, *n* a fish related to the turbot, spotted with white. [Ety unknown]

brill[2] *bril*, (*colloq*) *adj* short form of **brilliant**, excellent.

brilliant *bril'yənt*, *adj* sparkling; glittering; splendid; superlatively bright, having a dazzling hard lustre; of outstanding or conspicuous ability or intelligence; performing or performed in a showy manner or with great display of technical skill; (of musical tone) bright and clear, without many high harmonies; very good, excellent (*colloq*); brilliant-cut. — *n* a brilliant-cut diamond or other gem; a very small type (about 4-point). — *vt* and *vi* to cut and polish the smaller triangular facets on a diamond. — *n* **brill'iance** or **brill'iancy**. — *adv* **brill'iantly**. — *n* **brill'iantness**. — *adj* **brill'iant-cut** (of gems) cut in a many-faceted form resembling two pyramids base to base, the upper one cut off square. [Fr *brillant*, pr p of *briller* to shine, which like Ger *Brille* eyeglass is from LL *beryllus* a beryl]

brilliantine *bril'yən-tēn*, *n* perfumed hair oil for making the hair glossy. [Fr, from *brillant* shining]

brim *brim*, *n* the upper edge of a vessel or of a similarly-shaped cavity; the margin or brink of a river or lake; the rim of a hat. — *vt* to fill to the brim. — *vi* to be or become full to the brim: — *pr p* **brimm'ing**; *pa t* and *pa p* **brimmed**. — *adj* **brim'ful** or **brim-full'** full to the brim; brimming with tears. — *n* **brimful'ness** or **brimfull'-ness**. — *adj* **brim'less** without a brim. — *adj* **brimmed** brim-full; having a brim (also as *combining form* eg *wide-brimmed*). — *n* **brimm'er** a bowl, glass, etc full to the brim. — *adv* and *adj* **brimm'ing**. [ME *brymme*]

briming *brē'ming* or *bri'ming*, (*Cornwall*) *n* phosphorescence of the sea. [Origin unknown]

brimstone *brim'stən*, *n* sulphur (*archaic*); a virago, a scold (*obs*); (in full, **brimstone butterfly**) a common yellow butterfly of the cabbage-white genus (*Gonepteryx rhamni*). — *adj* **brim'stony**. [Literally burning stone; from OE *brȳne* a burning, from *byrnan* to burn, and **stone**; cf Ger *Bernstein*]

brinded *brin'did*, **brindled** *brin'dld* or **brindle** *brin'dl*, *adj* marked with spots or streaks. — *n* **brin'dle** the state of being brindled. [See **brand**]

brindisi *brin'di-zi* or *brēn-dē'zē*, (*Ital*) *n* a toast; a drinking-song.

brine *brīn*, *n* very salt water; the sea; any saline solution. — *vt* to treat with brine. — *n* **brin'iness**. — *adj* **brīn'ish** like brine; somewhat salt. — *adj* **brīn'y** pertaining to brine or to the sea; salt. — **brine'-pan** or **-pit** a pan or pit in which brine is evaporated to obtain salt; a salt spring; **brine'-shrimp** a small phyllopod crustacean of salt-lakes and brine pools. — **the briny** (*colloq*) the sea. [OE *brȳne* a burning]

Brinell hardness test or **Brinell test** *bri-nel'* (*härd'nis*) *test*, (*metallurgy*, etc) *n* a test to determine the hardness (**Brinell hardness**) of a substance, expressed in terms of its **Brinell (hardness) number**, by pressing a steel ball into the substance being tested under a given pressure. [From the Swedish engineer, J A *Brinell* (1849–1925), who devised the test]

bring *bring*, *vt* to fetch; to cause to come; to persuade or force (oneself); to bring forward, cite or institute (eg an argument, charge, action): — *pa t* and *pa p* **brought** (*bröt*). — *n* **bring'er**. — *n* **bring'ing**. — **bring about** to bring to pass or effect; to turn round; **bring and buy sale** a charity sale at which those who attend both bring items to be sold, and buy other items; **bring down** to overthrow; to lower; to humble; to shoot; **bring forth** to give birth to or produce; **bring forward** to advance; to present or suggest (an idea, etc); **bring home** to prove; to impress, convince; **bring home the bacon** see under **bacon**; **bring in** to introduce; to yield as income; to pronounce (a verdict); **bringings forth** (*Shakesp*) the fruits of one's own actions; **bringing up** upbringing, rearing, training; **bring off** to bring away, eg by a boat from a ship; to rescue; to achieve, bring to a successful conclusion; to induce an orgasm in (*vulg*); **bring on** to induce; to cause to advance; to advance the growth of (plants); **bring oneself to** to persuade or steel oneself to (do something unpleasant); **bring out** to make clear or prominent; to put (eg a book, play or singer) before the public; to introduce (a young woman) formally into society as a debutante; to encourage (a shy person) to be more outgoing; to cause (workers) to come out on strike; (of an allergy, etc) to make (a person) covered in (spots, etc); **bring over** to convert; **bring round** to restore from illness or unconsciousness; to win over; **bring the house down** to provoke or receive a general, enthusiastic burst of applause; **bring to** to restore to consciousness; to bring to a standstill (*naut*); **bring to bear** see under **bear**[1]; **bring under** to subdue; **bring up** to rear or educate; to introduce to notice; to make prominent; to vomit; **bring up the rear** to come last; **brought forward** (*bookkeeping*) (of a partial sum) transferred to the head of the next column. [OE *bringan* to carry, bring; perh related to **bear**[1]]

brinjal *brin'jäl* or *-jöl*, *n* in India, the aubergine. [Sans *vātiṅgaṇa*, through Pers, Ar and Port]

brinjarry *brin-jär'i*, *n* a travelling dealer in grain and salt in S India. [Hindi *banjārā*]

brink *bringk*, *n* the edge or border of a steep place or of a river (often *fig*). — **brink'man** a person who practises **brink'manship** or **brinks'manship**, the action or art of going to the very edge of, but not into, war or other disaster in pursuit of a policy. — **on the brink of** on the point of, very near. [Prob Dan *brink* declivity]

brio *brē'ō*, *n* liveliness, vivacity, spirit. [Ital]

brioche *brē-osh'*, *n* a type of light, soft loaf or roll rich with butter and eggs. [Fr]

briony. Same as **bryony**.

briquette or **briquet** *bri-ket'*, *n* a brick-shaped block made of compressed coal-dust, charcoal, etc; a small brick-shaped slab. — *vt* to form into briquettes. [Fr *briquette*, dimin of *brique*, **brick**]

brisé *brē-zā*, (*ballet*) *n* a movement in which the dancer jumps off one foot, strikes the feet or legs together and lands on two feet. — **brisé volé** (*vol-ā*; Fr pa p of *voler* to fly) a brisé performed with each leg alternately, completed by landing on one foot: — *pl* **brisés volés** (*brē-zā volā* or *vol-āz*). [Fr pa p of *briser* to break]

brise-soleil *brēz-sol-āy*, (*Fr*) *n* a louvred screen to keep sunlight from walls and windows of buildings. [Literally, sun-break]

brisk *brisk*, *adj* full of life and spirit, lively; promptly active; invigorating; sharp, effervescing; pert (*obs*); spruce (*obs*). — *vt* and *vi* to make or become brisk; to move briskly. — *vt* and *vi* **brisk'en** to make or become brisk. — *adj* **brisk'ish**. — *adj* **brisk'y** (*Shakesp*). — *adv* **brisk'ly**. — *n* **brisk'ness**. [First found in Shakespeare's time; poss Welsh *brysg* brisk of foot; perh Fr *brusque*]

brisket *bris'kit* (*Scott* **breaskit** *bres'kit*), *n* the breast (*Scot*); the breast of an animal, *esp* the part next to the ribs; meat from this part of an animal. [Perh connected with Fr *brechet*, *brichet*]

brisling *bris'ling*, *n* a Norwegian sprat. [Norw, sprat]

brissel-cock *bris'l-kok*, (*obs Scot*) *n* a fowl conjectured to be the turkey. [Ety uncertain]

bristle *bris'l*, *n* a short stiff hair. — *vi* to stand erect (like bristles); to be copiously provided, be full (with *with*); to have or set bristles erect; to show rage or resistance. — *vt* to cover (as with bristles); to make bristly; to make (eg bristles) erect: — *pr p* **brist'ling**; *pa t* and *pa p* **brist'led**. — *adj* **brist'led** having or fitted with bristles. — *n* **brist'liness**. — *adj* **brist'ly**. — **bristlecone pine** or **brist'lecone** a western American pine (*Pinus aristata*) with bristle-like prickles on its cones, used in radiocarbon dating; **brist'le-fern** a filmy fern (*Trichomanes radicans*) with a bristle on the receptacle; **bris'tle-grass** a grass of the genus *Setaria*; **brist'le-tail** any insect of the Thysanura; **brist'le-worm** a chaetopod. — **set up one's bristles** to show resistance. [Connected with OE *byrst*; Scot *birse*; cognate with Ger *Borste*, ON *burst*]

Bristol *bris'tl*, *n* a city in the county of Avon, England. — *npl* **bris'tols** breasts (*Cockney rhyming slang* from *Bristol city*, **titty**[1]). — **Bristol board** a smooth cardboard; **Bristol-brick'** an earthy material for scouring cutlery, like bath-brick; **Bristol-di'amond** a kind of quartz crystal found near Bristol; **Bristol-milk'** sherry (17c joke). — **Bristol fashion** in good order.

brisure *brizh'yər* or *brē-zür'*, *n* any part of a rampart or parapet which breaks off at an angle from the general direction (*fortif*); a variation of a coat-of-arms showing the relation of a younger to the main line (*heraldry*). [Fr, from *briser* to break]

Brit *brit*, *n* (*colloq* short form of **British**) a British person.

Brit. *abbrev*: Britain; Britannia; British; Briton.

brit *brit*, *n* a young herring, sprat, or other fish. [Ety unknown]

Britannia *bri-tan'yə* or *-i-ə*, *n* a seated female figure with a trident and helmet, representing Britain or the British Commonwealth; the ancient Roman province occupying the south of what is now Great Britain. — **Britannia metal** an alloy, mainly tin with copper, antimony, lead or zinc or a mixture of these, similar to pewter. [L *Britannia*, *Brittan(n)ia*, Great Britain or the British Islands]

Britannic *brit-an'ik*, *adj* pertaining to Britannia or Britain (*archaic*, but surviving officially in *Britannic majesty*). [See **Britannia**]

britches. See **breech**.

British *brit'ish*, *adj* pertaining to Britain, to its former or present inhabitants or citizens, or to its empire or commonwealth of nations; relating to the variety of English used in Britain; relating to the ancient Britons. — *n* the British people; the language of the ancient Britons; Welsh (*obs*). — *vt* and *vi* **Brit'icize** or **-ise** to make or become British or like the British. — *n* **Brit'isher** (*orig US*) a native or citizen of Britain. — *n* **Brit'ishism** or **Brit'icism** (*-sizm*) an expression characteristic of the English spoken in Britain. — *n* **Brit'ishness**. — **British bulldog** a team-game of chasing in which as the members of one team are caught, they join the other team; **British disease** extreme militancy in industrial relations, *esp* excessive use of strikes; **British gum** dextrin; **British plate** a kind of German silver; **British Standards Institution** see **BSI**; **British Standard Time** the time, one hour ahead of Greenwich Mean Time, used in Britain throughout the year from 1968 to 1971; **British Summer Time** the time adopted in Britain during the summer, one hour ahead of Greenwich Mean Time (to give extra daylight in the evenings); **British thermal unit** the amount of heat required to raise the temperature of 1lb of water by 1°F, equivalent to 1055.06 joules; **British warm** see **warm**. [OE *Brettisc*, from *Bret* a Briton, Welshman]

Briton *brit'ən*, *n* a native or citizen of the United Kingdom; one of the Brythonic inhabitants of Britain before and after the coming of the English, or one of their present representatives the Welsh; a Breton (*obs*): — *fem* (*Spenser*) **Brit'oness**. — *adj* **Britton'ic** Brythonic. [L *Brittō*, *-onis*, or *-ōnis*; see **Brythonic**]

brittle *brit'l*, *adj* apt to break, easily broken; frail; curt, edgy, sensitive; unstable. — *n* a type of hard toffee made with caramelized sugar and nuts. — *adv* **britt'ley** or **britt'ly**. — *n* **britt'leness**. — **brittle bones** an inherited disease, *osteogenesis imperfecta*, characterized by abnormal fragility of the bones; **britt'le-star** a member of a class of echinoderms like starfish with long, snaky, sharply differentiated arms. [OE *brēotan* to break]

britzka, **britzska**, **britska** *brits'kə* or **britschka** *brich'kə*, *n* an open four-wheeled carriage with a folding top. [Polish *bryczka*]

Brix Scale *briks skāl*, *n* a scale used in measuring the density of sugar in a solution at a given temperature. [From A F W *Brix* (1798–1890), German scientist]

brize. See **breeze**[2].

BRN *abbrev*: Bahrain (IVR).

Bro. *abbrev*: Brother: — *pl* **Bros**.

bro *brō*, *n* a place for which one feels great affinity because of birth, upbringing, long residence, etc there. [Welsh, locality]

broach *brōch*, *vt* to pierce (eg a cask), to tap; to open up or begin; to start to speak about. — *vi* and *vt* to (cause a sailing-ship to) veer dangerously when running downwind, so as to lie beam on to the waves (also *n*). — *n* a tapering, pointed instrument, used chiefly for boring or rounding holes; a spit; (also **broach'-spire**) a church spire, now restricted to one without parapets, consisting of a tall octagonal and a low square pyramid interpenetrating each other; a visible corner of the square pyramid in such a spire. — *n* **broach'er** a broach or spit; a person who broaches or utters. — **broach the admiral** to steal some liquor from a cask in transit or in store; **broach to** (*naut*) to turn to windward. [Fr *broche*; cf **brooch**]

broad *bröd*, *adj* wide; large, spacious, free or open; widely diffused; covering a wide range, spectrum, etc; giving prominence to main elements, or harmony of the whole, without insisting on detail; slow and full-toned; strongly marked in pronunciation or dialect; (of a vowel) open (*phonetics*); outspoken, obvious, unsubtle; coarse, vulgar; having liberal mind or outlook; (of money) denoting the less liquid categories (eg M2, M3: see under **M**), such as that in an account, etc, realizable only with several months' notice. — *n* the broad part; (in East Anglia) a lake-like expansion of a river; a broadpiece; a woman or, sometimes, a prostitute (*NAm slang*). Also *adv*. — *vt* and *vi* **broad'en** to make or grow broad or broader. — *adj* **broad'ish**. — *adv* **broad'ly**. — *n* **broad'ness**. — **broad'-arrow** a mark (⍏) used on government property, or generally. — *adj* **broad'band** across, involving, or designed to operate across, a wide range of frequencies (*telecomm*); capable of accommodating data from a variety of input-sources, as voice, telephone, television, etc (*comput*); **broad'-based** including a wide range of opinions, subjects, political groups, etc. — **broad bean** a plant (*Vicia faba*) of the pea family, or one of its large flat edible seeds which grow in pods; **broad'bill** any of several birds with a broad bill, such as the spoonbill, the scoup (*US*), or a member of the tropical Eurylaimidae; **broad'-brim** a hat with a broad brim, such as those once worn by Quakers; a Quaker (*colloq*). — *adj* **broad'brush** rough; not worked out in detail (*colloq*). — **Broad Church** a party within the Church of England favouring a broad and liberal interpretation of dogmatic definitions and creed subscription; (*esp* without *cap*) a political or other group, party, etc that is similarly liberal-minded or all-inclusive. — *adj* **broad'-church**. — **broad'cloth** a fine, fulled woollen or worsted cloth; **broad day** or **daylight** clear, open daylight. — *adj* **broad'-gauge** see **gauge**. — **broad jump** (*NAm*) long jump; **broad'-leaf** any tobacco plant with broad leaves. — *adj* **broad'-leaved** (*esp* in classifying types of tree) having broad leaves, not needles; deciduous, hardwood. — *adj* **broad'loom** (of carpet) woven on a wide loom. — *adj* **broadmind'ed** liberal; tolerant. — *adv* **broadmind'edly**. — **broadmind'edness**; **broad'-piece** a 17c 20-shilling coin; **Broad Scots** (also *formerly* **Scotch**) older or dialect forms of the Scottish tongue, a development of Old English; **broad'sheet** any standard sheet of paper, unfolded and uncut; a large sheet of paper printed *usu* on one side only, containing eg an advertisement or (*hist*) a proclamation, ballad, popular song, etc; a newspaper of large format, measuring *approx* 40 × 60cm (about 16 × 24in); a quality newspaper; **broad'side** the side of a ship; all the guns on one side of a ship of war; their simultaneous discharge; a strongly critical verbal attack; a broadsheet. — *adj* **broad'-spectrum** wide-spectrum. — **broad'sword** a cutting sword with a broad blade; a man armed with such a sword; **broad'tail** fur prepared from the skin of very young Karakul lambs; **broad'way** a broad road, often the name of the chief thoroughfare of a town or district. — *adv* **broad'ways** or **broad'wise** breadthwise. — **as broad as it is long** six of one and half-a-dozen of the other. [OE *brād*, Gothic *braiths*]

broadcast *bröd'käst*, *n* a radio or TV programme; the transmission of material by radio or TV for reception by the public; sowing by broadcasting; general dissemination. — *vt* to scatter, send out or disseminate freely by any means, *esp* by radio or TV transmission. — *vi* to transmit a broadcast; to take part in a broadcast: — *pa t* and *pap* **broad'cast** or (now *rare*) **broad'casted.** — *adj* scattered or sown over the general surface; dispersed widely; communicated generally, by word of mouth, pamphlets, radio, TV, or any other means; by means of broadcast. — *adv* in all directions. — *n* **broad'caster.** — *n* **broad'casting.** — **Broadcasters' Audience Research Board** the group that commissions and publishes data on British TV audience research; **broadcast videotex** teletext. [Ety as for **broad**, and **cast** to throw]

Brobdingnagian *brob-ding-nag'i-ən*, *n* an inhabitant of the fabled region of *Brobdingnag* in Swift's *Gulliver's Travels*, where everything was gigantic. — *adj* of Brobdingnag; (*usu* without *cap*) immense. — *adj* **Brob'dingnag** immense. — Also (*erron*) **Brobdignag'ian** and **Brob'dignag.**

brocade *brōk-ād'*, *n* a heavy silky fabric with a raised (or apparently raised) design on it. — *adj* **brocād'ed** woven or worked in the manner of brocade; dressed in brocade. [Ital *broccato*, Fr *brocart*, from Ital *broccare*, Fr *brocher* to prick, stitch; from same root as **broach**]

brocage. See **brokerage** under **broker.**

brocard *brōk'ärd* or *-ərd*, *n* an elementary law or principle; a canon; (*bro-kar*) a gibe (*Fr*). [Fr *brocard*, LL *brocarda*, from *Brocard* or *Burchard*, Bishop of Worms, who published a book of ecclesiastical rules]

brocatelle or (now *NAm*) **brocatel** *brok-ə-tel'*, *n* a stiff, *orig* silk-and-linen, heavy-figured fabric like brocade. [Fr, from Ital *brocatello* gold tinsel, from *broccato* brocade]

broccoli *brok'ə-li*, *n* a hardy variety of cauliflower; (also **sprouting broccoli**) a variety of this with purple or green floret buds, also eaten as a vegetable. [Ital; pl of *broccolo* a sprout, dimin of *brocco* a skewer, a shoot]

broch[1] *brohh*, *n* a dry-built circular tower of the late Iron Age with galleries in the thickness of the wall, common in Scotland, very rare elsewhere; a luminous ring around the moon. Also **brogh** and **brough.** [Scot, from ON *borg*; OE *burh*]

broch[2] *brōch.* Obsolete spelling of **broach, brooch.**

brochan *brohh'ən*, (*Scot*) *n* gruel; sometimes porridge. [Gaelic]

broché *brō'shā*, *adj* of fabrics, woven with a pattern like brocade. — *n* such a fabric. [Fr pa p of *brocher* to stitch]

brochette *bro-shet'*, *n* a small metal or wooden skewer for holding food together or steady while cooking. [Fr]

brochure *brō'shōōr* or *-shōōr'*, also *bro'*, *n* a pamphlet, information or publicity booklet. [Fr, from *brocher* to stitch, from *broche* a needle. See **broach**]

brock[1] *brok*, *n* a badger; a dirty, stinking fellow. — *adj* **brocked** or **brock'it** (*Scot*) variegated, *esp* black and white. [OE *brocc*, from Celtic (eg Gaelic *broc*)]

brock[2] *brok*, (*Scot*) *n* food scraps; pigswill; rubbish. — *n* **brock'age** fragments of crockery, furniture, etc (*Scot*); a mis-struck coin. [OE (*ge*)*broc* fragment, from *brecan* to break]

Brocken spectre *brok'ən spek'tər*, *n* the shadow of an observer, enlarged and often surrounded by coloured lights, thrown on to a bank of cloud, a phenomenon sometimes encountered on mountain-tops. [*Brocken*, a peak in the Harz mountains]

brocket *brok'it*, *n* a stag in its second year, with its first, dagger-shaped, horns; a small S American deer with short unbranched horns. [Fr *brocard*, from *broque* a spike]

brockit. See **brock**[1].

brockram *brok'rəm*, (*N Eng*) *n* breccia.

brod[1] *brod*, *n* a Scots form of **board.**

brod[2] *brod*, (*dialect*) *n* a goad; a spike; a kind of nail; a prick. — *vt* to prod: — *pr p* **brodd'ing**; *pa t* **brodd'ed.** [OE *brord*; ON *broddr*; cf OIr *brot* and Gaelic *brod* a goad, sting]

brodekin or **brodkin** *brōd'kin*, (*obs*) *n* a buskin. [Fr *brodequin*]

broderie anglaise *brod-rē ã-glez* or *brō'də-ri ä'gläz*, *n* openwork embroidery. [Fr, English embroidery]

Broederbond *brōō'-* or *brōō'dər-bont*, (*SAfr*) *n* an organization of Nationalist Afrikaners, highly secret until recent years, with membership in key public and professional positions, etc. [Afrik from Du *broeder* brother, and *bond* band, fellowship]

brog *brog*, (*Scot*) *n* an awl. — *vt* to prick: — *pr p* **brogging**; *pa t* **brogged.** [Origin obscure]

brogh. See **broch**[1].

brogue[1] *brōg*, *n* a stout shoe, *usu* with a decorative pattern of holes (also **brō'gan**); a rough shoe of untanned leather formerly worn in parts of Scotland and Ireland. [Ir *brōg*, dimin *brògan* and Gaelic *bròg* a shoe]

brogue[2] *brōg*, *n* a lilting Irish accent. — *adj* **brog'uish** or **brogu'eish** having a slight brogue. [Perh **brogue**[1], but Ir *barróg* hold, grip, speech impediment, is also suggested]

broider *broid'ər*, (*archaic*) *vt* and *vi* to embroider. — *n* **broid'erer.** — *n* **broid'ering.** — *n* **broid'ery.** [OFr *brouder*, *broder*; see **embroider**]

broil[1] *broil*, *n* a noisy quarrel; a confused disturbance. — Also (*Scot*) **brulyie, bruilzie** or **brulzie** (*brōōl'(y)i* or *brül'yi*). — *n* **broil'er** a person who stirs up broils. [Fr *brouillier* to trouble]

broil[2] *broil*, *vt* to cook over hot coals; (*esp NAm*) to grill. — *vi* to be extremely hot, or (*NAm*) enraged. — *n* **broil'er** a very hot day; a quickly-reared young chicken sold ready for broiling (also *adj*). [OFr *bruillir* or *bruller* to burn]

brokage. See **broker.**

broke *brōk*, *pa t* and old *pap* of **break**[1], the latter surviving as *adj* (*colloq*) bankrupt, without money; hard up. — **go for broke** to make an all-out bid or supreme effort, or to gamble everything (in order to gain something).

broken *brō'kən*, *pap* of **break**[1]. — *adj* smashed, in pieces; incomplete, fragmentary; interrupted; altered in direction; (of flowers) in plant-breeding, variegated; with surface interrupted; intermittent; humbled or crushed; shattered in health, spirit, estate or position; bankrupt; thrown into disorder; dispersed, routed; trained to saddle or bridle (also **broken-in'**); outlawed (*obs*); infringed, violated; (of a chord) played as an arpeggio (*music*); (of a language) spoken badly or haltingly, as by a learner. — *adv* **brōk'enly.** — *n* **brōk'enness.** — *adj* **brok'en-backed** having the back dislocated; (of a ship) so loosened in her frame as to droop at both ends. — *adj* **brok'en-down** worn-out; ill; no longer functional; ruined in character or strength. — *adj* **broken-heart'ed** crushed emotionally; greatly depressed or hurt, *esp* by disappointment in love. — *adv* **broken-heart'edly.** — *n* **broken-heart'edness.** — **broken home** the home of children whose parents are divorced or have separated; **broken man** a man whose life is completely shattered; a man under outlawry, *esp* in the Highlands and Border country (*hist*); **broken meats** the leavings of a banquet;

broken music (*Shakesp*) part-music. — *adj* **broken-wind'ed** (of eg a horse) having short breath or disordered respiration.

broker *brōk'ər*, *n* a person employed to buy and sell for others; a secondhand dealer; a go-between, negotiator or intermediary; a stockbroker; a pander, pimp (*obs*). — *vi* **broke** or (*US*) **brok'er** to bargain, negotiate; to act as broker. — *n* **brōk'erage** or **brōk'age**, (*obs*) **brōc'age**, the business of a broker; commission for transacting business for others; procuring, pimping (*obs*). — *n* **brōk'ery** (*obs*) the business of a broker; broker's wares. — *n* **brōk'ing**. — **brō'ker-dealer** (*stock exchange*) since 27 Oct 1986, a firm or person officially combining the jobs of stockbroker and stockjobber, but only acting as one or the other in any single deal. [ME *brocour*, from Anglo-Fr *brocour*. The original meaning seems to be tapster; cf **broach**]

brolga *brol'gə*, *n* a large grey Australian crane. — Also **Australian crane** or **native companion**. [Aboriginal]

brolly *brol'i*, (*colloq*) *n* an umbrella.

bromate. See **bromine**.

brome-grass *brōm'-gräs*, *n* a grass (*Bromus*) strongly resembling oats. [Gr *bromos* a kind of oats]

bromelain *brom'ə-lān* or **bromelin** *-lin*, *n* an enzyme, obtained from the juice of the pineapple plant, that breaks down proteins, used medically and in skin care products, etc. [**bromelia**]

bromelia *brə-mēl'yə*, *n* any plant of the genus *Bromelia*, giving name to the pineapple family, **Bromēliā'ceae**, mainly epiphytic and xerophytic monocotyledons, with stiff leaves in rosettes. — *adj* **bromēliā'ceous**. — *n* **bromēl'iad** any plant of the family. [Named in honour of the Swedish botanist Olaus *Bromel* (1639–1705)]

bromine *brō'mēn*, *-min* or *-mīn*, *n* a non-metallic chemical element (atomic no 35; symbol **Br**), a red liquid giving off an irritating, poisonous brown vapour. — *n* **brō'mate** a salt of bromic acid. — *adj* **brō'mic**. — *n* **brō'mide** a salt of hydrobromic acid, HBr; a platitude; a dull platitudinous person (from the use of bromides as sedatives); a type of monochrome photographic print, loosely applied to other types. — *adj* **brōmid'ic** conventionally commonplace. — *n* **brōmidrō'sis** or **brōmhidrō'sis** osmidrosis. — *n* **brominā'tion** the substitution by bromine in or the addition of bromine to organic compounds. — *n* **brō'mism** or **brō'minism** poisoning by an overdose of bromine. — *n* **brō'moform** a bromine compound analogous to chloroform. — **bromic acid** a compound of hydrogen, bromine and oxygen, $HBrO_3$; **bromide paper** a paper with a sensitive surface containing silver bromide, used in printing from a negative (*photog*). [Gr *bromos* stink]

brommer *brom'ər*, (*SAfr*) *n* the bluebottle fly. [Afrik; onomatopoeic]

bromo- *brō'mō-*, or before a vowel **brom-** *brōm-*, *combining form* denoting bromine.

bronchi, **bronchia**, etc. See **bronchus**.

broncho. See **bronco**.

broncho- *brong'kō-*, *combining form* relating to the bronchi. — *n* **bron'cho-constrictor** or **bron'cho-dilator** any drug that causes the bronchi to narrow or expand. — *n* **bronchog'raphy** radiological examination of the trachea or bronchi. — *n* **bronch'oscope** an instrument which, when passed down into the bronchi, allows their examination, the removal of foreign bodies, etc. — *adj* **bronchoscop'ic** or **bronchoscop'ical**. — *adv* **bronchoscop'ically**. — *n* **bronchos'copy**.

bronchus *brong'kəs*, *n* (*anatom*) either of the main forks of the windpipe: — *pl* **bronch'i** (*-ī*). — *n pl* **bronch'ia** (erroneously *bronchiae*) the small branches of the bronchi. — *adj* **bronch'ial** pertaining to the bronchi, or to the bronchia. — *n* **bronchiectasis** (*-ek'tə-sis*) a chronic disease caused by dilated bronchi. — *n* **bronch'iole** (*-ōl*) any of the minute branches of the bronchi. — *adj* **bronchitic** (*-it'ik*) pertaining to or suffering from bronchitis. — *n* a person suffering from bronchitis. — *n* **bronchitis** (*-ī'tis*) inflammation of the lining of the bronchial tubes. [Gr *bronchos* windpipe, and *bronchia* bronchia]

bronco or **broncho** *brong'kō*, (*NAm*) *n* a wild or half-tamed horse: — *pl* **bron'cos** or **bron'chos**. — **bronc'o-buster** a person who breaks in broncos; a cowboy. [Sp *bronco* rough, sturdy]

brond. An obsolete form of **brand**.

brondyron, etc. See under **brand**.

brontosaurus *bron-tə-sör'əs*, *n* a member of the *Brontosaurus* genus, the popular (and formerly the technical) name for the Apatosaurus genus, lizard-hipped, quadripedal, herbivorous dinosaurs, found as fossils in Wyoming and Colorado. — Also **bront'osaur**. [Gr *brontē* thunder, and *sauros* lizard]

Bronx cheer *brongks chēr*, (*US*) *n* a vulgar sound of disapproval, a raspberry. [From the *Bronx* borough of New York City]

bronze *bronz*, *n* an alloy of copper and tin; now also applied to a copper alloy without tin; anything cast in bronze; the colour of bronze; a bronze medal; impudence (*obs*). — *adj* made of bronze; coloured like bronze. — *vt* and *vi* to make or become bronze-like; to harden (*fig*, *obs*). — *adj* **bronzed** coated with bronze; bronze-coloured, sunburned; hardened (*fig*, *obs*). — *adj* **bronz'en** (*rare*). — *n* **bronz'er**. — *vt* **bronz'ify** (*rare*) to make into bronze. — *n* **bronz'ing** the process of giving or assuming the appearance of bronze. — *n* **bronz'ite** an enstatite with bronze-like lustre. — *adj* **bronz'y**. — **Bronze Age** (*archaeol*) a prehistoric condition or stage of culture coming between the Stone Age and the Iron Age marked by the use of bronze as the material for tools and weapons; **bronzed skin** Addison's disease; **bronze medal** in athletics competitions, etc, the medal awarded as third prize; **bronze'-wing**, **bronze-wing pigeon** or **bronzed-wing(ed) pigeon** any of various species of Australian pigeon with lustrous bronze markings on the wings. [Fr, from Ital *bronzo*, *bronzino*, perh from L (*aes*) *Brundusīnum* (brass) from Brindisi; or perh from Pers *birinj*, *pirinj* copper]

broo[1] *broo͞* or *brü*, (*Scot*) *n* liquor that comes off from anything or in which anything has been boiled. [Prob OFr *bro*, *breu* broth]

broo[2] or **brow** *broo͞*, (*Scot*) *n* brow in any sense; (*perh* a different word) liking, good opinion (with *of*). [**brow**]

broo[3]. See **buroo**.

brooch *brōch*, *n* an ornamental clasp with a joined pin fitting into a hook. — *vt* (*Shakesp*) to adorn as with a brooch. [Fr *broche* a spit; see **broach**]

brood *broo͞d*, *n* something bred; offspring, children, or family; the number hatched, produced or cherished at once; the condition of breeding or brooding; a race, kind, breed; parentage, extraction (*archaic*). — *adj* for breeding (as in *brood mare*, etc). — *vt* to sit on or cover in order to breed or hatch; to hatch; to cover, eg with wings; to cherish with care; to meditate moodily on. — *vi* to sit as a hen on eggs; to hang envelopingly (over); to think anxiously for some time; to meditate silently (with *on* or *over*). — *n* **brood'er** a person or animal that broods; a heated building or enclosure for rearing young chicks. — *n* **brood'iness**. — *adv* **brood'ingly**. — *adj* **brood'y** (of a hen) inclined to sit or incubate; (of a woman) wanting to have a baby (*colloq*); prolific, fertile (*obs*); apt to brood, sullen, moody. — **brood'-pouch** or **brood'-sac** a body-cavity eg in viviparous cockroaches in which eggs or embryos are received and developed. [OE *brōd*; Du *broed*; cf **breed**]

brook[1] *broo͝k*, *n* a small stream. — *n* **brook'let** a little brook. — **brook'lime** a speedwell that grows in brooks and ditches; **brook'weed** water pimpernel (*Samolus*), a water-plant of the primrose family superficially like a crucifer. [OE *brōc*; Du *broek*, Ger *Bruch*]

brook[2] *broo͝k*, *vt* to enjoy (now chiefly *Scot law* or *archaic*); to bear or endure. [OE *brūcan* to use, enjoy; Ger *brauchen*, L *fruī*, *fruct-*]

brookite *brŏŏk'īt*, *n* a mineral, titanium oxide. [After Henry James *Brooke* (1771–1857), English mineralogist]

brool *brōōl*, *n* a deep murmur. [Ger *Brüll* a roar]

broom *brōōm*, *n* a yellow-flowered papilionaceous shrub, *Cytisus scoparius*, or a related plant; a besom made of its twigs or of anything similar; a long-handled domestic sweeping brush. — *vt* to sweep with a broom. — *adj* **broom'y** covered with or consisting of broom. — **broom'ball** a team game played on ice, *orig* by British diplomatic staff in Moscow, using brooms and a plastic ball; **broom'-corn** a kind of millet of whose stalks brooms are made; **broom'rape** (L *rapum* a knob) a genus (*Orobanche*) of plants, parasitic on broom and other roots; **broom'staff** (*archaic*) or **broom'stick** the handle of a broom. — **marry over the broomstick** or **jump the besom** or **broomstick** to go through an irregular form of marriage in which both jump over a broomstick; **new brooms sweep clean** people newly appointed to a position work very conscientiously, or try to sweep away abuses, old attitudes, old methods, etc; **not know a B from a broomstick** to be very ignorant. [OE *brōm*]

broose (*Scott* **brouze**), *brōōz* or *brüz*, (*Scot*) *n* a race at a wedding. [Origin unknown]

Bros. (sometimes pronounced *bros*), (*commerce*) *abbrev*: Brothers.

brose *brōz*, *n* a food made by pouring boiling water or milk on oatmeal or peasemeal, seasoned with salt and butter. — **Athole brose** a mixture of whisky and honey and sometimes oatmeal; **brose and bannock day** Shrove Tuesday. [Scot; perh connected with **brewis, broo**[1]]

broth *broth*, *n* water in which vegetables and meat, etc have been boiled, used as soup or (in *med science* often with other substances added) as a medium for culture of bacteria. — **a broth of a boy** (*Ir*) the quintessence of a good fellow. [OE *broth*, from *brēowan* to brew; see **brew**]

brothel *broth'l*, *n* a house or establishment where prostitution is practised. — **brothel creeper** (*colloq*) a man's soft, *usu* suede, shoe with thick crêpe sole. [ME *brothel* worthless person, from OE *brothen* ruined, from *brēothan* to go to ruin; influenced in meaning by **bordel**]

brother *brudh'ər*, *n* a male in relation to another person of either sex born of the same parents or (*half-brother*) parent; anyone closely united with or resembling another who is associated in common interests, occupation, etc; a fellow-member of a religious order, a trade union, etc; a fellow-creature; a fellow-citizen; someone of the same religion as another; a lay member of a male religious order; a kinsman (*Bible*); as a form of address to (*usu*) a stranger (*esp US dialect* or *archaic*, or, now also *UK*, *facetious*): — *pl* **broth'ers** or **breth'ren**, the latter *esp* used in the sense of fellow-members and in the names of certain bodies, such as *Christian Brethren*, *Moravian Brethren*, *Plymouth Brethren*, etc. — *adj* associated in any relation (also as a *combining form*, as in **brother-man'**). — *interj* expressing surprise, disgust, etc. — *n* **broth'erhood** the state of being a brother; an association of men for any purpose. — *adj* **broth'erlike**. — *n* **broth'erliness**. — *adj* **broth'erly** like a brother; kind or affectionate. — **brother-ger'man** a full brother, one with whom one has both parents in common (as opposed to a *half-brother*); **broth'er-in-law** the brother of a husband or wife; a sister's husband; a husband's or wife's sister's husband: — *pl* **broth'ers-in-law**. [OE *brōthor*, pl *brēther*; cognate with Ger *Bruder*, Gaelic *brathair*, L *frāter*, Sans *bhrātr*; Gr *phrātēr* fellow-clansman]

Brotstudien *brōt'shtōō-dē-ən*, (*Ger*) *n pl* studies by which one earns one's living, *literally* bread studies.

brough. See **broch**[1].

brougham *brōō'əm*, *brō'əm* or *brōōm*, *n* a one-horse closed carriage, named after Lord *Brougham* (1778–1868); an early motor car with uncovered driver's seat.

brought *bröt*, *pa t* and *pa p* of **bring**.

brouhaha *brōō-hä'hä* or *brōō'hä-hä*, *n* fuss, excitement, clamour, or an instance of this. [Fr; perh from Heb]

brouze. See **broose**.

brow *brow*, *n* the eyebrow; the ridge over the eyes; the forehead; a person's aspect, appearance; the edge of a hill; a gallery in a coalmine running across the face of the coal; a ship's gangway (*navy*); a pit-head. — *adj* **brow'less** without eyebrows; without shame. — **brow'-antler** or **brow'-tine** the first tine of a deer's horn; **brow'band** the bridle strap that goes over a horse's forehead. — *vt* **brow'beat** to bear down on with stern looks or speech; to bully. — **brow'beater**; **brow'beating**. — *adj* **brow'-bound** crowned. [OE *brū*]

brown *brown*, *adj* of a dark, woody or dusky colour, tending towards red or yellow; dark-complexioned; tanned or sunburnt; formerly conventionally applied to a sword, *perh* burnished, *perh* rusty, *perh* blood-stained. — *n* a dark-reddish earthy or woody colour; a brown pigment; a brown object or thing; a copper coin (*obs slang*); a close-flying number of game birds, *esp* (*lit* and *fig*) **fire into the brown** to shoot into an area without aiming at a particular target. — *vt* to give a brown colour to; to roast until brown. — *vi* to become brown. — *n* **brown'ie** a drudging domestic goblin (*folklore*); (with *cap*; in full **Brownie Guide**) a member of the junior section of the Girl Guides, having a brown (since 1990 yellow) uniform; (a square piece of) a kind of rich, chewy chocolate cake containing nuts (*US*); a simple, early, mass-produced make of box camera (also **Brown'ie**®); a kind of currant bread (*Austr* and *NZ*). — *n* **brown'ing** the process of making or becoming brown; a product for making gravy, etc brown. — *adj* **brown'ish**. — *n* **brown'ness**. — *adj* **brown'y** of a brownish colour. — **brown algae** or **brown seaweeds** the Phaeophyceae, one of the main divisions of the algae. — *vt* and *vi* **brown-bag'** (*US*) to bring (one's lunch, or alcohol) in a brown paper bag or something similar. — **brown bear** the common bear of Europe and Asia; **brown Bess** the old British flintlock musket (from its brown walnut stock); **brown bill** a foot-soldier's or watchman's halberd, painted brown; **brown bread** any dark-coloured bread, *esp* that made of unbolted flour, eg wholemeal. — *adj* (*rhyming slang*) dead. — **brown coal** lignite; **brown dwarf** see **dwarf**; **brown earth** a type of soil with a rich brown surface layer, formed under deciduous forest in temperate humid regions; **brown fat** heat-producing fat cells of a brownish colour, found in various parts of the body, eg between the shoulder-blades, thought to be activated by overeating and thus to have a bearing on weight-gain. — *n* and *adj* **brown'field (site)** (a site) having previously undergone semi-rural or agricultural development (as opposed to **greenfield**). — **brown George** a hard biscuit; a brown earthenware vessel; **brown goods** (*commercial jargon*) a term covering types of electrical equipment *orig* wooden-cased, such as audio and TV (as opposed to traditionally white kitchen appliances such as refrigerators and washing-machines); **Brownie Guide** see **Brownie** above; **Brownie Guider** see **Brown Owl** below; **brownie point** (sometimes *ironic*, *usu* in *pl*) a good mark or commendation for doing well; **brown lung (disease)** byssinosis. — *vt* and *vi* **brown'-nose** (*vulg slang*; *esp US*) to act obsequiously (towards), curry favour (with). — **brown'-noser**; **brown'out** (*esp US*) a reduction in electrical power, etc, a partial blackout; **brown owl** the tawny owl; (with *caps*; now correctly **Brownie Guider**) the former official, now the popular, name for a woman who has charge of a group of Brownies; **brown paper** coarse strong paper used chiefly for wrapping; **brown rat** the larger and commoner of the two British rats (often black); **brown rice** rice hulled but not polished; **brown rot** any of several plant diseases causing browning; **brown sauce** any brown-coloured savoury sauce, now *esp* a sharp-flavoured commercially bottled variety; **Brown'shirt** a member of Hitler's organization of storm-troopers; a Nazi; a fascist; **brown spar** a brownish variety of dolomite; **brown'stone**

(*US*) a dark brown sandstone, regarded as the favourite building material of the prosperous classes; a building made of this; **brown stout** a kind of dark ale; **brown study** a reverie; absent-mindedness; **brown sugar** unrefined or partially refined sugar; **brown trout** a kind of trout common in Europe, dark-coloured on the back and lighter underneath. — **browned off** (*colloq*) fed up; bored; downhearted, dispirited; **do brown** (*slang*) to deceive or take in completely. [OE *brūn*; Du *bruin*, Ger *braun*]

Brownian *brown'i-ən*, (*phys*) *adj* pertaining to Robert *Brown* (1773–1858), who drew attention to **Brownian movement** or **motion**, an agitation of particles in a colloid solution caused by the impact of molecules in the surrounding medium.

Brownist *brown'ist*, *n* a person holding the church principles of Robert *Browne* (c. 1550–1633), which were taken up and modified by the Independents or Congregationalists of England. — *n* **Brown'ism**.

brown jolly *brown jol'i*, *n* a corruption of **brinjal**.

browse *browz*, *vi* to feed on the rough shoots of plants; to read or look round a shop in a casual or haphazard way. — *vt* to browse on. — *n* young twigs and shoots; an act of browsing. — *n* **brows'er**. — *n* **brows'ing** the shoots and leaves of plants; fodder; the action of the verb browse. — *adj* **brows'y**. [OFr *brouster* (Fr *brouter*), from *broust* a sprout]

browst *browst*, (*Scot*) *n* a brewing. **[brew]**

brrr *interj* imitative of shivering with cold.

BRS *abbrev*: British Road Services.

BRU *abbrev*: Brunei (IVR).

brucellosis *brōō-səl-ō'sis*, *n* a disease of animals, also called **contagious abortion** (see **abortion**), communicable to man as undulant fever. [Sir David *Bruce* (1855–1931), Australian-born bacteriologist, New L *-ella*, and **-osis**]

bruchid *brōō'kid*, *adj* and *n* (a beetle) of the family **Bru'chidae** whose larvae live on peas, beans, etc. [Gr *brouchos* locust]

brucine *brōōs'ēn*, *n* an alkaloid, less physiologically active than strychnine, obtained from nux vomica. [Wrongly thought to come from the simarubaceous genus *Brucea*, named after James *Bruce* (1730–94), Scottish African traveller]

brucite *brōōs'īt*, *n* a mineral, magnesium hydroxide. [Named after A *Bruce*, American mineralogist]

Brücke *brü'kə*, *n* (with **Die** *dē*) a group of expressionist painters formed in Dresden in 1905. [Ger, the bridge]

bruckle *bruk'l*, (*Scot*) *adj* liable to break, brittle and unstable. [OE *brucol*, from *brecan* to break]

Bruges group *brōōzh grōōp*, *n* a group of British politicians opposed to the creation of a federal Europe. [From *Bruges*, Belgium, where Margaret Thatcher made a famous anti-federalist speech]

bruhaha. A spelling of **brouhaha**.

Bruin *brōō'in*, *n* a name for a bear, *esp* in children's stories; the name of the bear in the epic *Reynard the Fox*. [Du, brown]

bruise *brōōz*, *vt* to crush by beating or pounding without breaking the surface; to pound; to pulverize by pounding; to mark and discolour part of the surface of (eg the skin of a person, fruit, etc); to hurt by unkind words. — *vi* to be marked with bruising; to be injured physically or in feelings; to ride recklessly along (*hunting slang*). — *n* an injury with discoloration of the human skin made by anything blunt and heavy; a similar injury to fruit or plants. — *n* **bruis'er** a person or thing that bruises; a prize-fighter, or a big, strong, aggressive person generally (*colloq*). — *n* and *adj* **bruis'ing**. [OE *brȳsan* to crush, combined with OFr *brisier*, *bruiser*, *bruser* to break]

bruit *brōōt*, *n* something rumoured widely; a rumour or report; a murmur heard in auscultation (*med*); noise (*archaic*). — *vt* to spread by rumour; to report; to make famous. [Fr *bruit*, from Fr *bruire*; cf LL *brugītus*; prob imit]

brûlé *brü-lā*, (*cookery*) *adj* with a coating of caramelized sugar. [Fr, burnt]

brulzie, bruilzie or **brulyie** *n*. Scots forms of **broil**[1].

Brum *brum*, (*colloq*) *n* Birmingham. — *n* **Brumm'ie** a person from Birmingham. [Contraction of **Brummagem**]

Brumaire *brü-mer'*, *n* the second month in the French revolutionary calendar, about 22 Oct to 20 Nov. [Fr *brume* fog, from L *brūma* winter]

brumby *brum'bi*, (*Austr*) *n* a wild horse. [Origin unknown]

brume *brōōm*, *n* fog. — *adj* **brum'al** relating to winter. — *adj* **brum'ous** foggy, wintry. [L *brūma* winter, contracted from *brevima* (not attested) the shortest day, from *brevis* short]

Brummagem *brum'ə-jəm*, (*colloq*) *n* (without *cap*) Birmingham; a thing made in Birmingham, *esp* something showy and worthless. — *adj* showy and worthless, sham, counterfeit. [Old form of the name]

brummer *brōōm'ər*, (*SAfr*) *n* older form of **brommer**.

brumous. See **brume**.

brunch *brunch* or *brunsh*, *n* a meal combining *br*eakfast and l*unch*. [Portmanteau word]

Brunella. See **prunella**.

brunette *brōōn-et'*, *n* a woman or girl with brown or dark hair. — *adj* (of hair-colour) dark brown. — Also (*esp anthropol*) in *masc* **brunet'**. [Fr dimin of *brun* brown]

Brunonian *brōō-nō'ni-ən*, *adj* relating to the system of medicine founded by Dr John *Brown* of Edinburgh (*c.* 1736–88) in which all diseases are categorized as *sthenic* or *asthenic*, depending on excess or deficiency of excitement. [*Brūnō*, *-ōnis*, Latinization of *Brown*]

brunt *brunt*, *n* the force of a blow; the chief stress or crisis of anything; the shock of an onset or contest. — *vt* (*rare*) to bear the brunt of. [Origin obscure]

brush *brush*, *n* an implement set with bristles or similar for grooming, cleansing, painting, applying friction or beating a soft rhythm; a tuft; a bushy tail, *esp* of the fox; a bundle of wires, strips, etc, making electrical contact between surfaces in relative motion; a brush-like electrical discharge of sparks or luminosity; any brushlike effect; an application of a brush; a grazing contact; a fleeting encounter; a skirmish, a clash; lopped or broken twigs; an area of shrubs and small trees, a thicket; thick forest (*Austr*); the backwoods; a brisk run or race (*US*). — *vt* to pass a brush over, groom, sweep, paint, etc with a brush; to touch or rub as if with a brush; to apply or remove by a sweeping motion (with *on*, *off* or *away*). — *vi* to use a brush; to pass with light contact; to move off abruptly, make off. — *adj* **brushed** smoothed, rubbed, straightened, etc with a brush; (of cloth) with the surface roughened or raised. — *n* **brush'er**. — *n* **brush'ing**. — *adj* lively, brisk. — *adj* **brush'y** like a brush; covered with brush. — **brush'-fire** a fire of dry bushes, etc, which usually spreads quickly and dangerously (also *fig* and as *adj*); **brush kangaroo** (*Austr*) a wallaby (*esp* large); **brush'-off** (*colloq*) a curt or discourteous dismissal or act of ignoring; a rebuff; **brush turkey** an E Australian mound-bird; **brush-up** see **brush up** below; **brush'wheel** a revolving brush; a friction wheel with bristles on the rubbing surface; **brush'wood** loppings and broken branches; underwood or stunted wood; **brush'work** work done with a brush; a painter's individual manner of using the brush. — **brush aside** or **off** to ignore or dismiss, *esp* brusquely; **brush up** to freshen one's appearance; to clean and tidy; to renew one's knowledge of (a subject; sometimes with *on*) (*n* **brush'-up**). [OFr *brosse* brushwood; prob connected with **bristle**]

brusque *brōōsk* or *brusk*, *adj* blunt and abrupt in manner. — *adv* **brusque'ly**. — *n* **brusque'ness**. — *n* **brusquerie** (*brōōs'kə-rē*). [Fr]

Brussels *brus'əlz*, *n* the capital of Belgium; (in full **Brussels carpet**) a kind of worsted carpet with heavy uncut pile on a linen backing. — **Brussels lace** a fine lace with appliqué sprigs on a net ground; **Brussels sprout** (also without *cap*) a variety of the common cabbage with many heads, each like a miniature cabbage; an individual head from this.

brust *brust*, (*Spenser*). Same as **burst**.

brut *brōōt*, (*Fr*) *adj* (of wines) unsweetened, dry.

brute *brōōt*, *adj* belonging to the lower animals; irrational; stupid; coarse; grossly sensual; lacking in sophistication, crude; (of a thing) merely physical; unworked, in its natural or raw state. — *n* one of the lower animals, *esp* the larger mammals; a brutal person; a large articulated goods trolley used on railway stations; a very large high-intensity spotlight. — *vt* see **bruting** below. — *adj* **brut'al** like a brute; unfeeling; coarse; inhuman, senselessly cruel; grossly sensual. — *n* **brut'alism** deliberate crudeness of style in art, architecture, literature, etc. — *n* and *adj* **brut'alist**. — *n* **brutal'ity**. — *n* **brutalizā'tion** or **-s-**. — *vt* **brut'alize** or **-ise** to make like a brute, to degrade; to treat with brutality. — *vi* to become like a brute. — *adv* **brut'ally**. — *adj* **brute'like**. — *n* **brute'ness** a brutelike state; brutality; stupidity (*Spenser*). — *vt* **brut'ify** to make brutal, stupid or uncivilized: — *pr p* **brut'ifying**; *pa t* and *pa p* **brut'ified**. — *n* **brut'ing** the process of shaping a diamond by rubbing it with another (also *vt* **brute** and *n* **brut'er**). — *adj* **brut'ish** brutal. — *adv* **brut'ishly**. — *n* **brut'ishness**. — **brute fact** a fact alone, presented without explanation; **brute force** sheer physical strength. [Fr *brut* rough, crude, from L *brūtus* dull, irrational]

brutum fulmen *brōō'tum* (or *-tōōm*) *ful'men* (or *fōōl'*) (*L*), *n* an ineffectual threat, *literally* random thunderbolt.

Brutus *brōō'təs*, *n* a kind of wig; a way of wearing the hair brushed back from the forehead, popular at the time of the French Revolution, when it was fashionable to admire the old Romans, such as *Brutus*.

bruxism *bruks'izm*, *n* habitual grinding of the teeth. [Gr *brychein* to gnash]

bry- or **bryo-** *brī(-ō)-*, *combining form* denoting moss. [Gr *bryon* moss, liverwort]

bryology *brī-ol'ə-ji*, *n* the study of mosses. — *adj* **bryological** (*-ə-loj'i-kl*). — *n* **bryol'ogist**. [Gr *bryon* moss, liverwort, and *logos* discourse]

bryony *brī'ə-ni*, *n* a wild climbing plant (*Bryonia dioica*, **white bryony**) of the gourd family, common in English hedgerows. — **black bryony** a climbing plant (*Tamus communis*) of the yam family, similar to bryony in habit and disposition. [L *bryōnia*, from Late Gr *bryōniā*]

bryophyte *brī'ō-fīt*, *n* a member of the **Bryophyta** (*-of'i-tə*), one of the main groups of the vegetable kingdom, mosses and liverworts. [Gr *bryon* moss, liverwort, and *phyton* plant]

Bryozoa *brī-ō-zō'ə*, *n pl* an old name for the Polyzoa, from their resemblance to mosses. [Gr *bryon* moss, and *zōia* living things]

Brython *brith'on*, *n* a Celt of the group to which Welsh, Cornish and Bretons belong, distinguished from Goidel. — *adj* **Brython'ic**. [Welsh *Brython* Briton, introduced in philological use by Sir John Rhys (1840–1915)]

BS *abbrev*: Bachelor of Science (*US*); Bachelor of Surgery; Bahamas (IVR); British Standard(s); Building Society; bullshit (*US slang*).

bs *abbrev*: balance sheet; bill of sale; bullshit (*US slang*).

BSB *abbrev*: British Satellite Broadcasting, a company licensed to broadcast programmes by satellite.

BSC *abbrev*: British Steel Corporation; Broadcasting Standards Council.

BSc *abbrev*: Bachelor of Science.

BSE *abbrev*: bovine spongiform encephalopathy.

BSI *abbrev*: British Standards Institution, an organization which lays down minimum standards of quality and issues standard specifications for a wide range of manufactured goods.

BSL *abbrev*: British Sign Language, the sign language (qv) used in Britain.

BSM *abbrev*: British School of Motoring.

B-Special. See **B**.

BST *abbrev*: bovine somatotrophin; British Standard Time; British Summer Time.

BT *abbrev*: British Telecom.

Bt *abbrev*: Baronet.

BTA *abbrev*: British Tourist Authority.

BTCV *abbrev*: British Trust for Conservation Volunteers.

BTEC *abbrev*: Business and Technician Education Council.

BTU *abbrev*: Board of Trade unit (1kWh); British thermal unit (also **Btu** or **btu**).

bu. *abbrev*: bushel(s).

buat. See **bowat**.

buaze or **bwazi** *bū'āz* or *bwä'zi*, *n* an African fibre-yielding polygalaceous shrub (*Securidaca*). [Native name]

bub[1] *bub* or **bubby** *bub'i*, *n* boy (as term of address) (*US*); a baby (*Austr* and *NZ colloq*). [Cf Ger *Bube* boy]

bub[2] *bub*, (*archaic slang*) *n* strong drink. [Origin unknown]

buba *bōō'bə*, (*med*) *n* another name for **yaws**.

bubalis *bū'bə-lis*, *n* a member of the *Bubalis* genus (also called *Alcelaphus*) of antelopes, including the hartebeest. — Also **bubal** (*bū'bəl*). — *adj* **bū'baline**. — *n* **Bū'balus** the buffalo genus. [Gr *boubalis*, *boubalos* African antelope, Late Gr *boubalos* buffalo, from *bous* ox]

bubble *bub'l*, *n* a globule of liquid or solidified liquid blown out with gas; anything empty and insubstantial; an unsound or fraudulent scheme; a bubbling noise. — *adj* insubstantial; deceptive; fleeting, transient; like a bubble in shape and lightness. — *vi* to rise in bubbles; to give off bubbles; to make sounds as of rising and bursting bubbles; (with *with*) to show (great joy, rage, etc); to blubber (*Scot*). — *vt* to cheat with bubble schemes (*archaic*). — *adj* **bubb'ly** (*lit* and *fig*). — *n* (*colloq*) champagne. — **bubble bath** a cosmetic preparation that makes foam in bath-water; **bubb'le-car** a midget motor car resembling a bubble in its rounded line and windowed top; **bubb'le-chamber** (*phys*) a device for showing the path of a charged particle by the string of bubbles left in its track, a variant of the cloud-chamber; **bubb'le-gum** a kind of chewing-gum that can be blown into large bubbles. — *adj* **bubb'le-headed** frivolous, flighty. — **bubble memory** (*comput*) a memory composed of minute moving pockets of magnetism that represent, by their presence or absence in relation to fixed points, bits (qv) of digital information; **bubble pack** a type of packaging in which goods are enclosed in a transparent bubble of plastic, etc backed by card; **bubb'le-shell** a gasteropod (*Bulla*) with thin globose shell; **bubble sort** (*comput*) a method of sorting items of data in a list by repeatedly scanning the list and putting adjacent pairs of items in order; **bubb'ly-jock** (*Scot*) a turkey-cock. — **bubble and squeak** a British dish of leftover boiled potatoes and cabbage mashed together and fried, sometimes together with other leftovers; **bubble over** to show uncontrolled anger, mirth, etc; **bubble under** to hover just below a significant point or division, as on a scale. [Cf Swed *bubbla*, Du *bobbel*]

bubinga *bōō'bing-ə*, *n* a species of W African tree (*esp Didelotia africana*) or its hard wood, used in furniture-making. [Bantu]

Bubo *bū'bō*, *n* a genus of large horned owls, including the eagle owl. [L *bubo*, *-onis* a horned owl]

bubo *bū'bō*, (*med*) *n* an inflammatory swelling of the lymph nodes, *esp* in the groin or armpit: — *pl* **bū'boes**. — *adj* **bubonic** (*-bon'ik*) relating to or characterized by buboes. — *n* **bubonocele** (*bū-bon'ō-sēl*; Gr *kēlē* tumour) a hernia in the groin, with related swelling. — *n* **bū'bukle** (*Shakesp*) a ridiculous word of Fluellen's (*Henry V*, III.6.108) for a red pimple, made up from *bubo* and *carbuncle*. — **bubonic plague** a form of plague characterized by buboes. [L *būbō*, from Gr *boubōn* the groin, a bubo]

buccal *buk'əl*, *adj* of, towards or pertaining to the cheek; pertaining to the mouth, oral. [L *bucca* cheek]

buccaneer or **buccanier** *buk-ən-ēr'*, *n* one of the piratical adventurers in the W Indies during the 17c, who plundered chiefly Spanish ships. — *vi* to act as a buccaneer. — *n* and *adj* **buccaneer'ing**. — *adj* **buccaneer'ish**. [Fr *boucanier*, from *boucan* a Carib wooden gridiron (used by French settlers in the West Indies)]

buccina *buk'sin-ə*, *n* a Roman curved trumpet. — *n* **buc'cinātor** (*anatom*) a flat cheek muscle used in chewing and blowing. — *adj* **buc'cinatory**. — *n* **Buc'cinum** the whelk genus of molluscs, with trumpetlike shell. [L *būcina* trumpet, *būcinātor* trumpeter]

bucellas *bōō-sel'əs*, or *bū-*, *n* a white wine from *Bucellas* near Lisbon.

Bucentaur *bū-sen'tör*, *n* the Venetian state barge used formerly in an Ascension-Day ceremony in which the doge dropped a ring into the sea, symbolizing the marriage of Venice with the Adriatic. [Ital *bucentoro*, *bucintoro*, of uncertain origin]

Bucephalus *bū-sef'ə-ləs*, *n* Alexander the Great's famous war-horse; any horse (*familiar* or *facetious*). [Gr *Boukephalos*, from *bous* ox, and *kephalē* head]

Buchmanism *bōōhh'mən-izm*, *n* the Oxford Group movement. — *adj* and *n* **Buch'manite** (*-īt*). [See **Oxford**]

buchu or **bucku** *bōō'hhōō*, *-chōō* or *-kōō*, (*SAfr*) *n* a rutaceous genus (*Barosma*) with leaves of medicinal value. [Hottentot]

buck[1] *buk*, *n* the body of a cart. — **buck'board** a light horse-drawn vehicle consisting of a flexible board on four wheels, with a two-person seat (*NAm*); **buck'wagon** (*SAfr*, *archaic*) a large canvas-covered trek wagon. [OE *būc* body]

buck[2] *buk*, *n* the male of eg the deer, goat, hare or rabbit (cf *doe*); a bok (qv); a lively young man (*archaic*); a dandy (*archaic*); a male Negro, American Indian, Aborigine, etc (*offensive*; often *adj*); a counter or marker (*cards*); a dollar (*NAm* and *Austr colloq*); an act of bucking. — *vi* (of a horse etc) to jump repeatedly into the air, coming down with the back arched, head down, and forelegs stiff. — *vt* to throw (a rider) by bucking; to resist, be in opposition to; to cheer, invigorate, tone up (*slang*; *usu* with *up*). — *n* **buckeen'** an impoverished youthful member of the minor Irish aristocracy, or one aspiring to their way of life without the means to support it. — *n* **buck'er** an animal that bucks. — *adj* **buck'ish** lively, frisky; dandified; like a goat. — *adv* **buck'ishly**. — **buck'-eye** the American horse-chestnut (genus *Aesculus*); a native of the state of Ohio (*US*). — *adj* (*US*) flashy, showy; corny. — **buck'horn** or **buck's'-horn** the material of a buck's horn as used for handles, etc; a British plantain with leaves shaped like buck's horn (also **buck's horn plantain**); **buck'hound** a small kind of staghound used for hunting bucks; **buck'-jumper** an animal that bucks; **buck-passing** see **pass the buck** below; **buck'-rabbit** a male rabbit; Welsh rarebit with poached egg; **buck'rake** a large agricultural rake, often attached to a tractor; **buck'saw** a large saw consisting of a blade set in an H-shaped frame tightened by a cord, used with a saw-horse; **buck'shot** a large kind of shot, used in shooting deer; **buck'skin** a soft leather made of deerskin or sheepskin; a strong twilled woollen cloth, cropped of nap; a horse of buckskin (greyish-yellow) colour; a backwoods American; (in *pl*) breeches or a suit of buckskin. — *adj* made of or like the skin of a buck. — **buck's**, **bucks'** or **bucks party** (*Austr colloq*) a stag-party for a man about to be married; **buck'thorn** a genus (*Rhamnus*) of shrubs whose berry supplies the sap-green used by painters; see also **sea-buckthorn**; **buck'-tooth** a projecting front tooth. — **buck up** (*slang*) to hurry up, to get going; to cheer up; to improve; to stimulate; to dress up (*dialect*); **make a fast buck** (*colloq*) to earn some money quickly or easily but not necessarily honestly; **pass the buck** (*slang*) to shift the responsibility to someone else (from the practice of passing the marker to the next dealer in some forms of poker) (*n* **buck'-passing**); **the buck stops here** the final responsibility rests here. [OE *buc*, *bucca*; Du *bok*, Ger *Bock* a he-goat]

buck[3] *buk*, (*archaic* or *dialect*) *vt* to soak or steep in lye, a process in bleaching. — *n* lye in which clothes were steeped before bleaching. — *n* **buck'ing**. — **buck'basket** a basket in which clothes were carried to be bucked; **buck'-wash** or **-washing**. [Ety obscure: ME *bouken*; cognate words are Ger *bäuchen*, *beuchen*]

buckaroo or **buckeroo** *buk'ə-rōō*, or *-rōō'*, (*US*) *n* a cowboy. — Also **buckay'ro**: — *pl* **buckay'ros**. [Sp *vaquero*]

buckbean *buk'bēn*, *n* a marsh plant (*Menyanthes trifoliata*) of the gentian family. — Also called **bog'bean**. [Flem *bocks boonen* goat's beans]

buckeen. See **buck**[2].

bucket *buk'it*, *n* a vessel for drawing or holding water, etc; one of the compartments on the circumference of a water-wheel; one of the scoops of a dredging-machine; a wastepaper bin (*colloq*); a subdivision of a data file, used to locate data (*comput*); something shaped like a bucket; an ice cream tub (*Austr colloq*); (a glass of) alcoholic drink (*Scot colloq*); a bucketful. — *vt* to lift in a bucket. — *vt* and *vi* to drive or ride very hard or bumpily; to push forward mercilessly; to swindle (*archaic*). — *vi* (of rain) to pour heavily (*colloq*). — *n* **buck'etful** as much as a bucket will hold: — *pl* **buck'etfuls**. — *n* **buck'eting**. — **bucket seat** a round-backed, often forward-tipping, seat in a car, aeroplane, etc; **bucket shop** (*colloq*) the office of an unregistered stockbroker, a mere agent for bets on the rise or fall of prices of stock, etc (*orig US*); any not wholly reliable agency, eg one dealing in unsold airline tickets; **buck'et-wheel** a contrivance for raising water by means of buckets attached to the circumference of a wheel. — **bucket and spade** a child's beach toy, comprising a small bucket and spade for playing with sand and water; **give the bucket** to dismiss; **kick the bucket** (*slang*) to die (*perh* from dialect *bucket* a beam from which slaughtered animals are hung). [Prob connected with OE *būc* a pitcher, or OFr *buket* a pail. Not Gaelic *bucaid* a bucket]

buckhorn, **buckhound**. See under **buck**[2].

buckie *buk'i*, (*Scot*) *n* a shellfish such as the whelk; an obstinate, awkward person. [Prob related to L *buccinum* a shellfish]

buckle *buk'l*, *n* a (*usu* metal or plastic) fastening for a strap or band, consisting of a rim and a tongue; a crisped, curled or warped condition. — *vt* and *vi* to connect or fasten with a buckle; to bend or warp; to prepare (*esp* oneself) for action; to join closely eg in fight or marriage (*obs* or *dialect*). — *n* **buck'ler** a small shield used in parrying; a protector, protection. — *vt* (*Shakesp*) to protect, shield. — **buck'le-beggar** (*Scot hist*) a person who performed marriages without a licence. — **buckle down** to apply oneself zealously (to); **buckle to** to buckle down to; **buckle under** to give in or collapse under strain. [Fr *boucle* the boss of a shield, a ring, from LL *buccula*, dimin of *bucca* a cheek]

Buckley's *buk'liz* or **Buckley's chance** (*chäns*), (*Austr colloq*) no chance at all. [Origin doubtful]

buckling *buk'ling*, *n* a smoked Baltic herring. [Ger *Bückling*]

buckminsterfullerene *buk-min-stər-fōōl'ər-ēn*, *n* a ball-shaped molecule containing 60 carbon atoms, the first discovered fullerene. — Also **buck'yball**. [From *Buckminster Fuller*, US engineer (1895–1983), who designed a geodesic dome for the 1967 Montreal Expo]

bucko *buk'ō*, *n* a swaggerer, a domineering bully (*orig naut slang*); a young lad, chap (chiefly *Ir*): — *pl* **buck'oes**. [**buck**[2]]

buckra *buk'rə*, *n* (used by W Indian and Southern US Blacks) a white man. [Calabar Efik *mbākara* a European]

buckram *buk'rəm*, *n* a coarse open-weave fabric of jute, cotton or linen made very stiff with size; stiffness in manners and appearance. — *adj* made of buckram; stiff; precise. — *vt* to give the quality of buckram to. [OFr *boquerant*]

Bucks. *abbrev*: Buckinghamshire.
bucksaw. See under **buck**[2].
Buck's fizz or **buck's fizz** *buks fiz*, *n* champagne (or sparkling white wine) and orange juice. [*Buck's* Club (in London) and **fizz**]
buckshish *buk'shēsh*. Same as **baksheesh**. — *adj* **buckshee'** free, gratuitous; spare, extra. [See **baksheesh, bukshi**]
buckshot, buckskin. See under **buck**[2].
bucksom. A Miltonic spelling of **buxom**.
buckthorn, bucktooth. See under **buck**[2].
bucku. See **buchu**.
buckwheat *buk'(h)wēt*, *n* a plant (*Polygonum* or *Fagopyrum*), its seed used *esp* in Europe for feeding horses, cattle and poultry, in America for making into cakes for the breakfast table, etc. [Prob Du *boekweit*, or Ger *Buchweizen* beech-wheat, from the shape of the seeds]
buckyball. See **buckminsterfullerene**.
bucolic *bū-kol'ik* or (less often) **bucolical** *-əl*, *adj* pertaining to the tending of cattle; pastoral; rustic, rural. — *n* **bucol'ic** a pastoral poem or poet; a rustic. — *adv* **bucol'ically**. [L *būcolicus*, from Gr *boukolikos*, from *boukolos* a herdsman]
bud[1] *bud*, *n* a rudimentary shoot of a plant; a flower while still not opened; in simple organisms, a protuberance that develops asexually into a new individual (*biol*); the first visible rudiment of a limb, horn, etc; something undeveloped or immature; a term of endearment to a young person (*obs*); a débutante (*obs US*). — *vt* to put forth as buds; to graft by inserting (a bud) under the bark of another tree. — *vi* to put forth buds; to come as a bud; to be in or issue from the bud; to begin to develop: — *pr p* **budd'ing**; *pa t* and *pa p* **budd'ed**. — *n* **budd'ing**. — *adj* in bud; beginning to develop or show talent in a particular way (as *a budding poet*). — *adj* **budd'y**. — *adj* **bud'less**. — **bud'-scale** a leaf specialized as a scale protecting a bud; **bud'worm** a larva that feeds on plant or tree buds. — **in bud** putting forth buds; **nip in the bud** to destroy or put a stop to (something) at its very beginning. [ME *budde*; perh related to Du *bot* a bud]
bud[2]. See **buddy**[1].
Buddha *bŏŏd'ə* or *bōōd'ə*, *n* a title applied to Sakyamuni or Gautama, the N Indian founder (5c BC) of a religion of spiritual purity; a general name for any one of a series of teachers of whom he is one; (*usu* without *cap*) a statue or picture of the Buddha. — *n* **Budd'hism** the religion founded by the Buddha. — *n* **Budd'hist** a believer in Buddhism. — *adj* **Budd'hist** or **Buddhist'ic**. — **Buddhist cross** the swastika. [Sans *buddha* wise, from *bodhati* he understands]
buddle *bud'l*, *n* a sloping container for washing ore. — *vt* to wash in a buddle. [Origin unknown]
buddleia *bud'li-ə* or *bud-lē'ə*, *n* a plant of the Loganiaceae, of the genus *Buddleia*, shrubs and trees with opposite leaves and showy clusters of purple or orange flowers. [Named in honour of Adam *Buddle* (died 1715), Eng botanist]
buddy[1] *bud'i*, (*orig US*) *n* brother, friend (as term of address); a pal, one's most constant companion; someone who volunteers to help and care for a person suffering from AIDS. — Also (*esp* as term of address) **bud**. — **budd'y-budd'y** a friend, pal; **buddy movie** a film on the theme of male camaraderie. [Prob from same root as **butty**[1]]
buddy[2]. See **bud**[1].
budge[1] *buj*, *vi* and *vt* to move or stir. — *n* **budg'er**. — **budge up** (*colloq*) to move closer together (eg along a bench) *usu* so as to make room for others. [Fr *bouger*, from L *bullīre* to bubble]
budge[2] *buj*, *n* lambskin fur. — *adj* pompous; stiff. [Origin obscure]
budge[3]. See **budgerigar**.
budgeree *buj'ər-ē*, (*Austr obs colloq*) *adj* good. [Aboriginal *budgeri*]
budgerigar *buj'ər-i-gär* or *-gär'*, *n* a small cage and aviary bird, an Australian parrakeet: — *familiarly* **budge** or **budgie** (*buj'i*). [Aboriginal]
budgerow or **budgero** (*pl* **budgeros**) *buj'ər-ō*, (*Anglo-Ind*) *n* a heavy keel-less barge. [Hindi *bajrā*]
budget[1] *buj'it*, *n* (often with *cap*) a financial statement and programme put before parliament by the Chancellor of the Exchequer; a plan of domestic or business expenditure; a restricted spending allowance; the overall expenditure allowed for a specific period or occasion; a sack or its contents (*obs*); a compact collection of things; news; a socket in which the end of a cavalry carbine rests (*archaic*). — *adj* cheap, economical, inexpensive. — *vi* to prepare a budget. — *vt* to provide for in a budget; to organize the spending of (money, etc): — *pr p* **budg'eting**; *pa t* and *pa p* **budg'eted**. — *adj* **bud'getary**. — **budget account** a special bank account, into which money is paid regularly by the bank from a customer's main account and from which payment of previously agreed recurring expenses, eg fuel bills, TV licence, is made; an account with a shop, into which the customer makes regular payments to cover purchases at the shop; **budgetary control** a system of financial control of a business by constantly monitoring the activities of the various departments in terms of the individual budgets assigned to each; **budget deficit financing** a deliberate budgeted excess of government expenditure over income, with the object of stimulating economic growth, financed by borrowing. — **budget for** to allow for, when planning one's expenditure. [Fr *bougette*, dimin of *bouge* a pouch, from L *bulga*]
budget[2] *buj'it*, *n* a fixed rudder on a barge. [Ety uncertain]
budgie. See **budgerigar**.
budmash. See **badmash**.
budo *bōō'dō*, *n* the system or philosophy of the martial art: — *pl* **bu'dos**. [Jap, the way of the warrior]
buenas noches *bwen'as noch'es*, (*Sp*) goodnight; **buenas tardes** (*tar'dhes*) good afternoon; **buenos dias** (*bwen'os dē'as*) good day, good morning.
buff[1] *buf*, *n orig* buffalo-hide; now white leather from which the grain surface has been removed, used for army accoutrements; a military coat; the colour of buff, a dull light yellow; the bare skin; a buff-stick or buff-wheel; (in *pl*) certain regiments in the British army, from their former buff-coloured facings (eg East Kent Regiment, Ross-shire Buffs); a member of a party whose colour is buff; an enthusiast, fan, expert (*orig* a keen attender at fires, so called from the buff uniform of the former New York volunteer firemen) (*colloq*). — Also *adj*. — *vt* to polish with a buff. — *n* **buff'er** a person or thing that buffs or polishes. — *n* **buff'ing** the act or process of polishing. — **buff'-coat** or **buff'-jerkin** a strong, military coat; a soldier; **buff'-leather**; **buff'-stick, buff'-wheel** or **buff'ing-wheel** a stick or wheel covered with buff-leather or the like, and impregnated with an abrasive for polishing. — **in the buff** naked. [Fr *buffle* a buffalo]
buff[2] *buf*, *n* a dull blow or its sound; a buffet, blow or stroke (*obs*). — *vt* to strike, *esp* with a dull sound; to burst out. — **blindman's buff** see under **blind**. [OFr *buffe* a blow]
buffa. See **buffo**.
buffalo *buf'ə-lō*, *n* a name for certain large animals of the cattle family, *esp* the tame, often domesticated, Asiatic buffalo, and the entirely wild and fierce Cape buffalo of Southern Africa; the American bison (*NAm*): — *pl* **buff'aloes**. — *vt* (*NAm colloq*) to bewilder; to overawe. — **buff'alo-berry** a N American shrub of the Elaeagnaceae, or its edible fruit; **buff'alo-bird** an ox-pecker; **buffalo chips** dried buffalo dung used as fuel; **buffalo gnat** see **black fly** under **black**; **buff'alo-grass** a short grass (*Buchloe dactyloides*) growing on the western prairies of the US; any of various other American or African grasses; **buff'alo-nut** a N American shrub of the sandalwood family; its oil-yielding nut; **buff'alo-robe** a bison-hide rug or cloak. [Ital *buffalo*, through L from Gr *boubalos*]
buffe. See **buffo**.
buffer[1] *buf'ər*, *n* a mechanical apparatus for deadening the force of a concussion, as in railway carriages or at the

end of a railway line; a ship's fender; something or someone that acts as a protection against impact, shock or damage; a fellow, *esp* a dull or ineffectual fellow (as in *old buffer*); a boatswain's mate (*naut*); a substance or mixture which opposes change of hydrogen-ion concentration in a solution (*chem*); a temporary store into which data can go while awaiting transfer eg from computer to printer, acting as an adjusting mechanism between processes of different speeds (*comput*). — *vt* to protect against shock (*lit* and *fig*); to add a buffer to (*chem*). — *vi* to use, or be used as, a buffer. — *adj* **buff'ered**. — **buffer state** or **zone** a neutral country or zone lying between two others whose relations are or may become strained; **buffer stock** stock held in reserve to minimize the effect of price fluctuations or unreliable deliveries. [**buff**[2]]

buffer[2]. See under **buff**[1].

buffet[1] *buf'it*, *n* a blow with the fist; a slap; a stroke, *esp* heavy and repeated, eg of the wind, fortune, etc. — *vt* to strike with the hand or fist; to knock or push about roughly, to batter; to struggle against, beat back. — *vi* to deal heavy blows, to battle. — *n* **buff'eting** a striking with the hand, boxing; repeated blows; irregular oscillation of any part of an aircraft, caused and maintained by an eddying wake from some other part. [OFr *buffet*, from *buffe* a blow, esp on the cheek]

buffet[2] *bo͞of'ā*, *n* a refreshment counter or bar; a meal set out on a table, etc, from which the diners serve themselves; (*buf'it*) a sideboard, an ornamental side-table for the display of china; a low (*esp* rectangular) stool (*Northern*). — Also *adj*. — **buffet car** (*bo͞of'ā kär*) a railway coach with light meal or snack service. [Fr *buffet*; origin unknown]

buffi. See **buffo**.

bufflehead *buf'l-hed*, *n* a N American diving duck resembling the golden-eye; a stupid fellow. [From **buffalo** and **head**]

buffo *bo͞of'fō*, *adj* comic. — *n* a comic actor in an opera: — *pl* **buf'fi** (*-fē*); *fem* **buf'fa**; *pl* **buf'fe** (*-fā*). [Ital]

buffoon *buf-o͞on'*, *n* a person who sets out to amuse others by jests, grimaces, etc; a fool. — *n* **buffoon'ery**. [Fr *bouffon*, from Ital *buffone*; *buffare* to jest]

bufo *bū'fō*, (*Ben Jonson*) *n* a black tincture in alchemy. [L *būfō* toad]

bufotenine *bū-fō-ten'ēn* or *-ten'in*, *n* a poisonous paralysing hallucinogenic drug. [Fr, from L *bufo* toad (from the skin of which it is obtained), *ten-* hold, and **-ine**[1] (1)]

bug[1] *bug*, *n* (*obs*) a bogy, or object of terror. — *n* **bug'aboo** a bogy, or object of terror; a cause of anxiety. — **bug'bear** an object of terror, dislike or annoyance; **bug'-word** (*obs*) a terrifying or threatening word. [ME *bugge*, poss from Welsh *bwg* a hobgoblin]

bug[2] *bug*, *n* a name applied loosely to certain insects, *esp* of the Hemiptera (Heteroptera), and *specif* to one (*Cimex lectularius*) that infests houses and beds; any insect or small animal (*NAm*); a disease-germ; a viral disease (*colloq*); a craze, obsession; an enthusiast; a crazy person; an important person (**big bug**); a snag, a defect, a fault, now *esp* in a computer system or program (*colloq*); a hidden microphone; a light vehicle stripped of everything inessential; a lunar excursion module (see **module**); the weight allowance given to an apprentice jockey (*US racing*). — *vt* to plant a concealed listening device in; to annoy, irritate, pester (*slang*): — *pr p* **bugg'ing**; *pa t* and *pa p* **bugged**. — *adj* **bugged**. — *n* and *adj* **bugg'ing**. — *adj* **bugg'y** infested with bugs; crazy, batty (*US colloq*). — **bug'bane** or **bug'wort** a ranunculaceous plant (*Cimifuga foetida*) related to baneberry, reputed to drive away insects; **bug'house** a mental hospital (*US*); a cinema (*slang*). — *adj* insane. — **bug'-hunter** a collecting entomologist. [Perh OE *budda* beetle; perh same as **bug**[1]]

bug[3] *bug*, (*US colloq*) *vi* (of the eyes) to start or bulge. — *adj* **bug'-eyed** with eyes protruding in astonishment, etc.

bug[4] *bug*, (*US*) *vi* (with *out*) to desert or retreat, *esp* in panic. — *n* **bug'-out** desertion; a deserter. [Perh from **bugger (off)**]

bugbear. See under **bug**[1].

buggan *bug'ən*, **buggane** *-ān* or **buggin** *-in*, (*dialect*) *n* an evil spirit, a hobgoblin. [**bug**[1]; cf **bogle**]

bugger *bug'ər*, *n* (with *cap*) a Bulgarian heretic, believed capable of any crime (*obs*); someone guilty of buggery; a term of abuse for a man or child, often quite colourless or even kindly (*vulg colloq*); a rogue, scamp, applied inoffensively to child or animal (*US*); a difficult or unpleasant task, etc (*vulg colloq*). — *vt* to practise buggery with; (the following all *vulg colloq*) to exhaust; to frustrate, ruin the plans of; to spoil, prevent success in (also with *up*). — *vi* (with *off*; *vulg colloq*) to go away quickly. — *interj* (*vulg colloq*) used to express annoyance. — *n* **bugg'ery** (*law*) anal intercourse between a man and another man, a woman, a child or an animal. — (The following all *vulg colloq*) **bugger all** none, nothing. — *adj* **bugg'er-all** no. — **bugger about** or **around** to potter about, do nothing useful; to mess (someone) about; **don't** or **couldn't give a bugger** couldn't care less. [Fr *bougre*, from *Bulgarus* Bulgarian]

Buggins's turn *bug'inz-əz tûrn*, *n* the assigning of promotion, etc in accordance with seniority, by rotation, etc. [Origin unknown]

buggy[1] *bug'i*, *n* a light carriage or gig of several kinds; in N America, a one-horse, four-wheeled vehicle with one seat, in England, two-wheeled, in India, hooded; a beach buggy (qv); a baby buggy (qv); a light, very basic vehicle. [Ety unknown]

buggy[2]. See under **bug**[2].

bugle[1] *bū'gl*, *n orig* a buffalo or wild ox; a bugle-horn, the musical instrument. — *vi* to play or sound on a bugle; to make a sound like a bugle. — *n* **bū'gler** a person who plays the bugle. — *n* **bū'glet** a small bugle. — **bū'gle-band**; **bū'gle-call**; **bū'gle-horn** a horn used as a drinking vessel or hunting horn; a treble instrument with or without keys, *usu* made of copper, similar to the trumpet, but having the bell less expanded and the tube shorter and more conical, used more for signalling than music. [OFr *bugle*, from L *būculus*, dimin of *bōs* an ox]

bugle[2] *bū'gl*, *n* a slender elongated bead, *usu* black, used as a decoration on clothing. — *adj* (*Shakesp*) like bugles. [Poss connected with LL *bugulus* hair-pad, or with Du *beugel* ring]

bugle[3] *bū'gl*, *n* a member of the genus (*Ajuga*) of labiate plants without upper-lip. — **bū'gle-weed** (*US*) a mint of the genus *Lycopus* of the labiate family. [Fr, Ital *bugola*, from LL *bugula*, *būgillō*]

bugler, **buglet**. See under **bugle**[1].

bugloss *bū'glos*, *n* a name for several plants of the borage family, especially *Lycopsis arvensis*, a common cornfield weed, and viper's bugloss (qv). [Fr *buglosse*, from L *būglōssa*, from Gr *bouglōssos*, from *bous* ox, and *glōssa* tongue]

bugong. See **bogong**.

bugwort. See under **bug**[2].

buhl *bo͞ol*, *n* a complicated form of marquetry, with one or more of gold, silver, brass, pewter, ivory or mother-of-pearl inlaid in tortoiseshell, etc, forming panels for furniture decoration; furniture decorated with such marquetry. — Also **boulle**, **boule**. [From Charles André *Boulle* (1642–1732), a cabinetmaker in the service of Louis XIV]

buhrstone *bûr'stōn*, *n* a variety of quartz, containing many small empty cells, which give it a roughness of surface particularly adapted for millstones; a millstone made of this. — Also **burr'stone**. [Perh connected with **burr**[1], from its roughness]

buik or **buke** *buk*, *bük* or *būk*, (*Scot*) *n* variants of **book** and of **bouk**.

build *bild*, *vt* to erect (eg a house, bridge, etc); to construct (eg a railway, etc); to control the building of, to have built; to establish (*fig*); to base (eg hopes) (on); to form (combinations) (*cards*). — *vi* to construct a building or buildings, to be a builder; to increase gradually; to depend (*on* or *upon*): — *pa t* and *pa p* **built** or (*archaic*) **build'ed**. — *n* physical form; make, style of construction. — *n* **build'er** a person who builds, or controls the work of building; a substance added to soap, etc to increase its effectiveness. — *n* **build'ing** the art, occupation or process of erecting houses, etc; a substantial structure for giving shelter, eg a house, office-block; used as a collective noun for a gathering of rooks. — *adj* **built** formed or shaped; constituted, naturally disposed. — **builders' merchant** a trader who supplies building materials; **build'ing-block** a hollow or solid block made of concrete or other material, larger than a brick; a child's toy made of wood, etc; a component part (*fig*); **build'ing-board** an artificial material made in panels for lining walls; **building line** the line, fixed by a local authority, beyond which buildings must not project; **building paper** any of several types of heavy-duty waterproof paper consisting of bitumen sandwiched between layers of kraft paper, and used for insulation and damp proofing of various kinds; **building society** a society that advances money to its members as mortgages for homes, and provides interest-bearing accounts for savers; **build'-up** a building up, increasing or strengthening; the amount of this; a working up of favourable publicity; preliminaries leading up to a climax in a story, speech, etc. — *adj* **built'-in** formed as part of a main structure, *esp* if recessed; present as part of one's genetic inheritance; inherent; included (as part of a deal, etc); very firmly fixed. — **built-in obsolescence** the deliberate inclusion in a product of features which lead to deterioration or out-of-dateness before the end of the product's useful life. — *adj* **built'-up** (of an area) covered with buildings; raised by adding something to the underside. — **build in** to enclose or fix by building; to incorporate at the initial stage (*lit* and *fig*); **build up** to close up (eg a doorway) by building work; to cover with buildings; to raise the height of by adding something; to create, be created, or increase, gradually (eg a concentration of troops, a reputation, voltage, tension); to put together from parts already made; to strengthen (someone) physically; to edify spiritually (*obs*). [OE *gebyld*, pa p of (not attested) *byldan* to build, from *bold* a dwelling]

buirdly *bûrd'li*, (*Scot*) *adj* stalwart, large and well made. [Poss a variant of **burly**]

buist *büst*, (*Scot*) *n* a box; a tar-box; an owner's mark on sheep or cattle. — *vt* to mark thus. [OFr *boiste* (Fr *boîte*) box]

buke. See **buik**.

bukshi or **bukshee** *buk'shē*, *n* a paymaster. See **buckshish**. [Pers *bakhshī*]

bulb *bulb*, *n* a subterranean bud with swollen leaf-bases in which reserve materials are stored; a flowering plant that grows from such; a protuberance or swelling; a bulb-shaped object; the medulla oblongata; a dilatation or expansion of a glass tube; a light bulb; a bulb-shaped rubber device for squeezing, as eg in an eye-dropper or bicycle horn. — *vi* to form bulbs; to bulge out or swell. — *adj* **bulb'ar**. — *adj* **bulbed**. — *adj* **bulbif'erous** (of a plant) producing bulbs. — *n* **bulb'il** or **bulb'el** a small bud that may grow into an independent plant. — *n* **bulbos'ity**. — *adj* **bulb'ous** bulging; swollen. — *adv* **bulb'ously**. — *n* **bulb'ousness**. — **bulb of percussion** a raised cone on a worked flint, marking where a blow was struck. [L *bulbus*, from Gr *bolbos* an onion]

bulbul *bŏŏl'bŏŏl*, *n* any bird of the family *Pycnotidae* of Africa and Asia; in Persian poetry, the nightingale; a sweet singer. [Ar]

Bulg. *abbrev*: Bulgaria or Bulgarian.

Bulgarian *bul-gā'ri-ən*, *adj* of Bulgaria or its language. — *n* a native or citizen of Bulgaria; the Slavonic language of Bulgaria. — *n* **Bul'gar** (*-gär*) a member of an ancient Finno-Ugrian tribe that settled in what is now Bulgaria and adopted the Slavonic language; a Bulgarian. — Also *adj*. — *adj* **Bulgaric** (*-gar'ik*). — *n* the ancient language of the Bulgars. — *vt* **Bul'garize** or **-s-** to make Bulgarian.

bulge *bulj*, *n* a protuberance, swelling; a salient (*military*); a temporary increase. — *vi* and *vt* to swell out. — *n* **bul'ger** a wooden golf club with a convex face (*hist*). — *n* **bul'giness**. — *adj* **bul'ging** swelling out; overfull. — *adv* **bul'gingly**. — *adj* **bul'gy**. — **have** or **get the bulge on someone** (*old-fashioned slang*) to have or get a decided advantage over someone. [OFr *boulge*, prob from L *bulga* a leather knapsack: a Gallic word; cf **bilge**]

bulgine. See **bullgine**.

bulgur or **bulghur** *bŏŏl'-* or *bul'gər*, *n* a form of cooked, broken wheat. — Also **bulg(h)ur wheat**. [Turk]

bulimia *bū-lim'i-ə*, (*med*) *n* abnormal hunger or appetite (also *fig*); bulimia nervosa. — Earlier forms **būl'imy**, **bulī'mus**. — *adj* and *n* **bulim'ic**. — **bulimia nervosa** (*nər-vō'sə* or *-zə*) a pathological condition, an eating disorder in which binge eating is followed by depression and guilt, self-induced vomiting and purging, etc. [Gr *boulīmiā*, from *bous* ox, and *līmos* hunger]

bulk[1] *bulk*, *n* a stall or framework built in front of a shop. — *n* **bulk'er** (*archaic*) a street thief or prostitute. [Ety doubtful; cf ON *bālkr* beam, OE *bolca* gangway of a ship]

bulk[2] *bulk*, *n* a cargo; the belly, trunk or body; a hull or hold; volume or size; great size; the greater part; any huge body or structure; a mass; a heap (now only of tobacco); the thickness of paper; the thickness of a book without its covers. — *vi* to have bulk; to fill out (with *out* or *up*); to be of weight or importance; (of paper, etc) to be of (specified) bulk. — *vt* to put or hold in bulk; to transport (several different consignments) together as a single load; (often with *out* but also with *up*) to cause to swell, make greater in size. — *adv* **bulk'ily**. — *n* **bulk'iness**. — *adj* **bulk'y** having bulk; filling much space; unwieldy. — **bulk buying** large-scale purchase of a commodity, *esp* on preferential terms and by a single buyer, sometimes on behalf of a body of consumers; guaranteed purchase by one country of all or most of another's output of a commodity; **bulk cargo** cargo such as coal or wheat that is not packed in containers but loaded in bulk; **bulk carrier** a vessel carrying bulk cargo; **bulk discount** a reduction in a unit price when large quantities are purchased. — **break bulk** see under **break**[1]; **bulk large** to be prominent or intrusive; to seem important; **load in bulk** to put cargo in loose; **sell in bulk** to sell cargo as it is in the hold; to sell in large quantities. [Prob ON *bulki* heap or cargo, confused with OE *buc* belly; see **bouk**]

bulkhead *bulk'hed*, *n* any of the partitions separating one part of the interior of a ship, aircraft, etc from another; a protecting barrier or structure; the roof of a **bulk** (**bulk**[1]); the bulk itself. — **collision bulkhead** that nearest the bow. [**bulk**[1] and **bulk**[2]]

bull[1] *bŏŏl*, *n* an uncastrated male of the cattle family; a male whale, walrus, elephant, moose, etc; (with *cap*) Taurus (*astrol*); a person who seeks to raise the price of stocks, and speculates on a rise (*opp* to *bear*); a bull's-eye, (a shot that hits) the centre of a target; nonsense (*slang*); tediously excessive discipline, eg too much drill, polishing of kit, etc (*military slang*); a policeman (*US obs slang*). — *adj* male; massive, strong; (of the stock market), rising. — *vt* to try to raise the price of; to polish over-zealously (*military slang*); (of a bull) to copulate with (a cow). — *vi* to brag (*slang*); to talk rubbish (*slang*); (of a cow) to be on heat, take the bull. — *n* **bull'ing** the mounting of cows by other cows, indicative of their being on heat. — *adj* **bull'ish** like a bull; obstinate, aggressive; inclining towards rising prices (*stock exchange*); optimistic, upbeat (*colloq*). — *adv* **bull'ishly**. — *n* **bull'ishness**. — *n* **bull'ock** an ox or castrated bull. — *vi* (*Austr* and *NZ*) to work very hard. — *vt* to force (one's way). — *n* **bull'ocky** (*Austr* and *NZ*) a bullock-driver. — **bull ant** short for **bulldog ant**; **bull'-baiting** the former sport of baiting or exciting bulls with dogs; **bull'bar** (*Austr*) a strong metal bar on the front of a vehicle to protect it from damage if struck by an animal; **bull'bat** (*US*) the night-hawk; **bull'-beef** an ox fattened for slaughter (*obs*); (*Shakesp* in *pl*) **bull'-beeves**; **bull'-beggar** (*dialect*) a hobgoblin, etc; **bull'-calf** a male calf; a stupid fellow, a lout; **bull'-dance** a dance of men only; **bull'dog** a breed of sturdy muscular dogs of great courage, formerly used for baiting bulls; a person of obstinate courage; a short-barrelled revolver of large calibre; a proctor's attendant at Oxford; (with *cap*; ®) a bulldog clip. — *vt* to attack like a bulldog; to wrestle with and throw (a steer, etc) (*US*). — **bulldog ant** a black or red Australian ant with a vicious sting; **bulldog clip** a clip with a spring, used for holding papers, etc together or to a board; **bull'dust** *euphem* for **bullshit** (*Austr* and *NZ*); fine dust, as on outback roads (*Austr*); **bull fiddle** (*US colloq*) a double-bass; **bull'fight** a popular spectacle in Spain, Portugal, S France, and Latin America, in which a bull is goaded to fury by mounted men (picadors) armed with lances, and killed by a specially skilful unmounted swordsman (matador); **bull'fighter**; **bull'fighting**; **bull'finch** a common European finch with red breast and thick neck; (*perh* for *bull-fence*) a kind of high, thick hedge hard to jump; **bull'frog** a large frog. — *adj* **bull'-fronted** having a forehead like a bull. — **bull'head** the miller's thumb, a small river fish with a large, flat head; extended to various similar fishes, eg the pogge (*armed bullhead*); a stupid person. — *adj* **bull-head'ed** impetuous and obstinate. — **bull-head'edness**; **bull'-hoof** a West Indian passion-flower (from the shape of its leaf); **bull'-horn** (*NAm*) a loudhailer; **bull'-mastiff** a cross between a bulldog and a mastiff, the mastiff strain predominating. — *adj* **bull'-necked** thick-necked. — *adj* and *n* **bull'nose** (something) with a blunt nose or rounded edge. — *adj* **bull'-nosed**. — **bull'ock's-heart** the custard-apple; **bull'-of-the-bog'** (*Scot*) the bittern; **bull'-pen** a pen for a bull; a similar enclosure for prisoners (*US*); a part of the ground where pitchers warm up (*baseball*); **bull point** (*colloq*) a key point, a salient point; **bull'-pup** a young bulldog; **bull'-ring** the enclosure for bull-fighting or bull-baiting; a ring for a bull's nose; **bull'-roarer** an oblong slip of wood, whirled at the end of a string to give a loud whirring noise; a similar artefact used in an Australian Aboriginal ceremonial, the *turndun*; the similar *rhombos* of the Greek mysteries; **bull session** (*esp NAm*) an informal discussion *esp* between men; **bull's'-eye** the central boss formed in making a sheet of spun glass; a thick lens, or round piece of glass, as in a lantern; a lantern; a round opening or window; the centre of a target; a shot that hits it; a big, round, hard peppermint sweet; **bull'shit** (*vulg slang*) nonsense; deceptive humbug; bull (*military slang*). — *vi* and *vt* to talk nonsense (to), often with the intention of deceiving; to polish over-zealously (*military slang*). — **bull'shitter**; **bull'shitting**; **bull's wool** (*Austr colloq*) any fibrous bark; *euphem* for **bullshit**; **bull-terr'ier** a breed of dog with a smooth, short-haired coat, *orig* a cross between a bulldog and a terrier; **bull'-trout** a large variety of sea-trout (*Salmo trutto eriox*); a salmon that has re-entered fresh water after spawning; **bull'whip** or **bull'whack** a heavy short-handled whip. — *vt* to lash with a bullwhip. — **a bull in a china shop** a person who lacks the delicacy that the situation calls for; **bull into** to plunge hastily into; **not know a B from a bull's foot** to be very ignorant; **take the bull by the horns** to grapple boldly with a danger or difficulty. [ME *bole*, prob ON *bole*, *boli*; most prob related to **bellow**]

bull[2] *bŏŏl*, *n* an edict of the pope with his seal affixed. — *n* **bull'ary** a collection of papal bulls. [L *bulla* a knob, a lead seal]

bull[3] *bŏŏl*, *n* a ludicrous self-contradiction. [Prob OFr *boul* cheat]

bull[4] *bŏŏl*, *n* drink made by pouring water into a cask that formerly held alcohol. [Origin unknown]

bull[5] *bŏŏl*, *n* a deck game in which pads are thrown at an inclined board, the **bull'-board**. [Origin unknown]

bulla *bŏŏl'ə*, *n* a seal attached to a papal document; a round metal ornament worn by children in ancient Rome; a blister; (with *cap*) the bubble-shell genus of molluscs: — *pl* **bull'ae**. — *adj* **bull'ate** blistered or puckered, bubble-like, inflated. [L *bulla*]

bullace *bŏŏl'is*, *n* the fruit or tree of the wild plum (*Prunus insititia*), closely related to the damson. [Cf OFr *beloce*]

bullary. See under **bull**[2].

bullate. See under **bulla**.

bull-board. See **bull**[5].

bulldoze *bŏŏl'dōz*, *vt* to intimidate, to bully; to level and clear by bulldozer; to demolish as if by bulldozer; to force or push through against opposition (*fig*). — *n* **bull'dozer** a person who bulldozes; a powerful, heavy tractor with a vertical blade at the front, used for levelling and clearing land. [Origin obscure]

buller *bŏŏl'ər*, (*Scot*) *n* turbulence in water; a bubbling; a bellow. — *vi* to seethe; to gurgle; to bellow. [Cf Dan *bulder*, Swed *buller* rumble, noise, roar; prob partly from or influenced by OFr *bullir*, Icel *bulla* to boil]

bullet *bŏŏl'it*, *n* a little ball; a projectile, now *esp* a round or conical one fired from any kind of small-arm; a plumb or sinker in fishing; a solid dot used to highlight items in a list (*printing*). — **bull'et-head** a round head; an obstinate fellow (*US*). — *adj* **bull'et-headed**. — *adj* **bull'et-proof** proof against bullets. [Fr *boulette*, dimin of *boule* a ball, from L *bulla*]

bulletin *bŏŏl'i-tin*, *n* an official report of public news, or of a patient's progress; a periodical publication of a society, etc. — **bulletin board** a noticeboard containing messages, advertisements, and interchange of information, *esp* (*comput*) an electronic one containing also programs and databases. [Fr, from Ital *bullettino*]

bullet-tree, **bulletrie**. Same as **bully-tree**.

bullgine or **bulgine** *bŏŏl'jīn*, (*US colloq*) *n* a steam locomotive. [Said to be **bull**[1] and eng*ine*]

bullion *bŏŏl'yən*, *n* gold or silver in the mass and uncoined; gold or silver in general; a heavy twisted cord fringe, often covered with gold or silver wire. — *n* **bull'ionist** one in favour of metallic currency. [Perh connected with LL *bulliō*, *-ōnis* a boiling]

bullock. See under **bull**[1].

bully[1] *bŏŏl'i*, *n* a person, often of superior strength or size, who distresses or persecutes others, eg with threats, cruel teasing, etc; a blustering, noisy, overbearing fellow; a ruffian hired to beat or intimidate anyone (*archaic*); a man who lives on the earnings of a prostitute (*obs*); a term of genial familiarity, *esp* to a man (*obs*). — *adj* excellent, great (*colloq*); blustering (*archaic*). — *vi* to bluster. — *vt* to oppress cruelly; to threaten in a noisy way: — *pr p* **bull'ying**; *pa t* and *pa p* **bull'ied**. — *interj* good. — *n* **bull'yism**. — **bull'y-boy** a ruffian hired to beat or intimidate someone. — Also *adj*. — **bull'y-rook** (*obs*) a hired ruffian; a comrade. — **bully for you**, etc (often *ironic*) good for you, etc. [Perh Du *boel* a lover; cf Ger *Buhle*]

bully[2] *bŏŏl'i*, *n* a miner's hammer.

bully[3] *bŏŏl'i*, *n* a scrimmage (*Eton football*); formerly in hockey, the opening or re-starting move, where one player from each team struck the ground and the opponent's stick alternately three times in quick succession, before attempting to be the first to strike the ball lying between them (also **bull'y-off**). — *vt* and *vi* **bull'y** or **bully off**. [Origin uncertain]

bully[4] *bŏŏl'i* or **bully-beef** *bŏŏl'i-bēf*, *n* tinned or pickled beef. [Prob Fr *bouilli* boiled beef, influenced by **bull**[1]]

bullyrag *bŏŏl'i-rag* or **ballyrag** *bal'i-rag*, *vt* to assail with abusive language or horseplay; to badger, intimidate. [Origin unknown; perh from **rag**[2]]

bully-tree *bŏŏl'i-trē*, *n* a name for several W Indian sapotaceous trees yielding good timber, edible fruits and balata, *esp Mimusops balata*. — Also **bull'et-tree**, **bull'etrie** or **boll'etrie**. [Perh from **bullace** or **balata**]

buln-buln *bŏŏl'n-bŏŏl'n*, (*Austr*) *n* a lyre-bird. [Aboriginal]

bulrush *bŏŏl'rush*, *n* a name given to two distinct tall marsh or water plants, the reed-mace or cat's-tail, and club-rush, a plant of the sedge family; in the Bible, the plant papyrus. — *adj* **bul'rushy**. — **bulrush millet** pearl millet. [Perh **bole**[1], or **bull**[1] in sense of massive or coarse, and **rush**[2]]

bulse *buls, n* a small bag for or of diamonds, gold dust, etc. [Port *bolsa*, from LL *bursa* a purse. See **purse**]

bulwark *bŏŏl'wərk, n* a fortification or rampart; a breakwater or sea-wall; the side of a ship projecting above the deck; any means of defence or security. — *vt* to defend; to fortify. [Cf Ger *Bollwerk*]

bum[1] *bum, n* the buttocks (*colloq*); the anus (*vulg*). — *vt* (*vulg*) to have anal intercourse with: — *pr p* **bumm'ing**; *pa t* or *pa p* **bummed**. — **bum bag** or **bum'bag** a small bag, *usu* worn on a belt round the waist, *orig* used by skiers, etc; **bum'bai'liff** (*obs*; *Shakesp* **bum'-bay'lie**) a bailiff who comes behind to make arrests; a sheriff's officer; **bum'freezer** (*slang*) an Eton jacket; a waist-length jacket; **bum roll** a shaped pad or cushion worn below the waist to make a skirt stand out from the body; **bum'sucker** (*vulg*) a toady; **bum'sucking**. — **bums on seats** (*theat*) audiences, good houses. [Cf **bump** in sense of swelling]

bum[2] *bum, vi* to hum or make a murmuring sound, like a bee. — *vt* (*Scot*) to toss, hurl: — *pr p* **bum'ming**; *pa t* and *pa p* **bummed**. — *n* a humming sound. — *n* **bumm'er** a person or thing that bums. — **bum'-bee** (*dialect*) a bumble-bee; **bum'-clock** (*Scot*) a flying beetle that drones. — **head'-bummer** (*hĕd'*-; *Scot*) a manager or person in authority. [Imit]

bum[3] *bum*, (chiefly *NAm slang*) *n* a (drunken) spree; a dissolute fellow, a tramp; a sponger; a devotee of a (specified) sport, etc to such an extent as to neglect other responsibilities. — *adj* worthless; despicable; dud; wrong, false. — *vi* to loaf; to sponge; to live dissolutely. — *vt* to cadge: — *pr p* **bumm'ing**; *pa t* and *pa p* **bummed**. — *n* **bumm'er** a plundering straggler or camp-follower (during the American Civil War); a dissolute fellow, a loafer, a sponger; a dismal failure (*colloq*); something worthless (*colloq*); a disappointment (*colloq*); a bad trip on drugs (*colloq*); a nasty experience (*colloq*). — **bum steer** (*slang*) something misleading, false or worthless, a dud. — **give someone the bum's rush** (*slang*) to eject someone by force; to dismiss someone summarily, *esp* from one's employment. [Cf **bummel**]

bumalo. See **bummalo**.

bumbaze *bum-bāz'*, (*Scot*) *vt* to perplex, bamboozle. [Origin obscure]

bumbershoot *bum'bər-shŏŏt*, (*US facetious*) *n* an umbrella. [Alteration of *umbrella*, with para*chute*]

Bumble *bum'bl, n* a beadle; a self-important minor official. — *n* **Bum'bledom**. [From Mr *Bumble* in Dickens's *Oliver Twist*]

bumble or (*Scot*) **bummle** *bum'(b)l, vi* to utter indistinctly; to bungle; to make a buzzing sound, to drone; to bustle about blunderingly. — *n* confusion; indistinct utterance; a bungler; an idler. — *n* **bum'bler** a bungler. — *n* **bum'bling**. — **bum'ble-bee** a large wild loud-humming bee, a humble bee; **bum'ble-foot** cellulitis in a bird's foot, due to pus-forming organisms; club-foot; **bum'ble-puppy** the old game of nine-holes; unscientific whist or bridge; a racket game in which a string is wound round a post by hitting a slung ball or bag. [Frequentative of **bum**[2]]

bumbo *bum'bō, n* a mixture of rum or gin, water, sugar and nutmeg, or similar drink: — *pl* **bum'bos**. [Perh Ital *bombo*, a child's word for drink]

bum-boat *bum'bōt, n* a Thames scavenger's boat (*obs*); a boat bringing vegetables, etc for sale to ships. [Origin doubtful]

bumf or **bumph** *bumf*, (*colloq*) *n* lavatory paper; papers, official papers, documents (*disparagingly*). [Short for *bum-fodder*, from **bum**[1] and **fodder**]

bumkin or **bumpkin** *bum'kin, n* a short beam of timber projecting from each bow of a ship, for the purpose of extending the lower corner of the foresail to windward; a small outrigger over the stern of a boat, usually serving to extend the mizzen. [From **boom**[1] and dimin termination *-kin*]

bummalo or **bumalo** *bum'ə-lō, n* the Bombay duck, a small Indian fish of a family (*Scopelidae*) related to the salmon, dried and eaten as a relish: — *pl* **bumm'alo** or **bum'alo**. — Also **bummalō'ti** or **bumalō'ti**. [Marathi *bombīl*]

bummaree *bum-ər-ē', n orig* a middleman in Billingsgate fish-market; a porter at Smithfield meat-market. [Ety unknown]

bummel *bŏŏm'əl, n* a stroll; a leisurely journey. [Ger *Bummel*]

bummer. See under **bum**[2,3].

bummle. See **bumble**.

bummock *bum'ək*, (*Orkney*) *n* a brewing of ale for a feast. [Ety unknown]

bump[1] *bump, vi* to make a heavy or loud noise; to knock dully; to jolt; to move joltingly; (of a cricket-ball) to bound high on striking the pitch. — *vt* to strike with a dull sound; to strike against; to dislodge, knock, shove; in bumping races (*esp* Oxford and Cambridge), to catch up with and touch (the boat in front), and consequently move up one place; (with *out*) to spread out (text) in printing so as to fill any desired number of pages (*printing*); to turn away (a passenger who holds a valid reservation for a seat on a flight) because the airline has allowed too many seats to be booked. — *n* a dull heavy blow; a thump; (in *pl*) a customary series of thumps (administered in various ways in various parts of the country) *esp* to a child celebrating his or her birthday; a high rebound of a cricket-ball; the act of bumping in a bumping race; a jolt; a lump or swelling; a protuberance on the head associated by phrenologists with specific qualities or propensities of mind; hence (*colloq*) faculty. — *n* **bump'er** any thing or person that bumps; a bar on the front and back of a motor vehicle to lessen the shock of collision; a railway buffer (*US*); a pad fitted round the inside of a cot to stop a baby bumping himself or herself; a bumping race; a cup or glass filled to the brim for drinking a toast; anything large or generous in measure; a crowded house at a theatre or concert. — *adj* full to overflowing; unusually large or plentiful. — *vi* to drink bumpers. — *adv* **bump'ily**. — *n* **bump'iness**. — *n* **bump'ing**. — *n* **bumpol'ogy** (*joc*) phrenology. — *interj* **bumps'adaisy** or **boomps'-a-daisy** exclamation on bumping into someone or something, or to a child on falling. — *adj* **bump'y**. — **bumping race** a boat-race in which the boats start at fixed intervals, and seek to bump, not to pass the boat in front. — **bump and grind** to dance erotically with exaggerated movements of the hips; **bump into** to happen to meet (someone); **bump off** (*slang*) to kill, murder; **bump start** to start a car by pushing it and engaging the gears while it is moving (*n* **bump'-start**); **bump up** (*colloq*) to raise (prices); to increase the size of; **with a bump** with an unpleasant suddenness. [Imit]

bump[2] *bump*, (*obs*) *n* the booming cry of the bittern. — *vi* to utter that cry. [Imit]

bumper[1] *bump'ər*, (*Austr colloq*) *n* a cigarette butt. [Perh a conflation of **butt**[4] and **stump**]

bumper[2]. See under **bump**[1].

bumph. See **bumf**.

bumpkin[1] *bump'kin, n* an awkward, clumsy rustic; a clown. — *adj* **bump'kinish**. [Prob Du *boomken* a log]

bumpkin[2]. See **bumkin**.

bumptious *bump'shəs, adj* offensively self-important. — *adv* **bump'tiously**. — *n* **bump'tiousness**. [Prob formed from **bump**[1]]

bun[1] *bun, n* a kind of sweet roll or cake; hair formed into a rounded mass. — **bun'-fight** (*colloq*) a tea-party; a noisy occasion or assembly. [Perh from OFr *bugne* a swelling]

bun[2] *bun, n* a dry stalk (*dialect*); a hare's scut (*Northern*). [Possibly Gaelic *bun* a root, a stump]

bun[3] *bun, n* a playful name for a rabbit or a squirrel. [Origin unknown]

buna *bōō'nə*, *n* an artificial rubber made by the polymerization of butadiene. [Orig a trademark]

BUNAC *bū'nak*, *abbrev*: British Universities North America Club.

Bunbury *bun'bə-ri*, *n* the name of an invented person used as an excuse for sudden departures. — *vi* to make such an excuse or departure. [From the invented character in Wilde's *The Importance of Being Earnest*]

bunce *buns*, (*slang*) *n* profit or gain. — *vi* to ring up wrongfully on every customer's bill the price of an item kept beside the till of a supermarket, etc, in order to defray losses by theft, etc. [Ety uncertain, perh altered from *bonus*]

bunch *bunch* or *bunsh*, *n* a number of things aggregated or fastened together; a definite quantity fastened together, as of linen yarn (180 000 yards), etc; a cluster; a handful, eg of flowers; a group (*colloq*); something in the form of a tuft or knot; (in *pl*) a hairstyle in which the hair is pulled to both sides at the back of the head, and each tuft secured with a ribbon, etc; a lump, hump, swelling (*obs*). — *vi* to swell out in a bunch; to cluster, form a tight group. — *vt* to make a bunch of; to concentrate. — *adj* **bunched** gathered into a bunch; humped, protuberant; lumpy. — *n* **bunch'iness**. — *n* **bunch'ing** the act of drawing together into a bunch; too close grouping together of cars on a motorway, etc (*esp* after a long gap), of ships arriving in port, etc. — *adj* **bunch'y** growing in bunches or like a bunch; bulging. — *adj* **bunch'-backed** (*Shakesp*) hump-backed. — **bunch'-grass** any of several clumped W American grasses. — **bunch of fives** see under **five**. [Origin unknown]

bunco. See **bunko**.

buncombe. See **bunkum**.

Bund *bōōnt*, (*Ger*) *n* a league or confederacy. — **Bundesbank** (*bōōn'des-bangk*) the state bank of Germany; **Bundesrat** or formerly **Bundesrath** (*-rät*) the upper house of the parliaments of Germany and of Austria; the executive council of the federal republic of Switzerland; **Bun'destag** (*-tähh*) the lower house of the parliament of Germany; **Bun'deswehr** (*-vār*) the German armed forces.

bund *bund*, *n* (*orig* in India, etc) a man-made embankment or dam. — *vt* to embank. [Hindi *band* from Pers]

bundle *bun'dl*, *n* a number of things loosely bound together; a bunch; a loose parcel; a strand of conducting vessels, fibres, etc (*biol*, *fibre optics*, etc); a definite measure or quantity, such as two reams of paper, twenty hanks of linen yarn, etc; a lot of money, *esp* **make a bundle** (*slang*). — *vt* to make into a bundle or bundles; (*usu* with *up*) to wrap up warmly; to put hastily or unceremoniously (away, etc); to hustle; to sell (*esp* specific computer software along with hardware) as a single package. — *vi* to pack up one's things for a journey; to go hurriedly or in confusion (with *away*, *off* or *out*); to lie in bed together fully clad (an old custom in Wales, New England and parts of Scotland for sweethearts and others) (*n* **bund'ling**). — **bundle of fun** an exuberant and entertaining person (sometimes *ironic* of one who is not); **bundle of laughs** (*orig US*) an entertaining person or situation (often *ironic*); **bundle of nerves** see under **nerve**; **drop one's bundle** (*Austr slang*) to lose one's nerve, to give up; **go a bundle on** (*slang*) to like or be enthusiastic about. [Related to **bind** and **bond**[1]]

bundobust. See **bandobast**.

bundook or **bandook** *bun'dōōk*, (*military slang*) *n* a rifle. [Hindi *bandūq*]

bundu *bōōn'dōō*, (*Southern Afr*) *n* a remote uncultivated region. [Bantu]

Bundy® *bun'di*, (*Austr*) *n* a time-clock in a factory, etc.

bung[1] *bung*, *n* the stopper of the hole in a barrel; a large cork. — *vt* to stop (up) or enclose with a bung (also *fig*). — **bung'hole** a hole for a bung; **bung'-vent** a small hole in a bung to let gases escape, etc. [Ety uncertain]

bung[2] *bung*, *n* a purse (*obs thieves' cant*); a cutpurse, pickpocket (*Shakesp*). — **nip a bung** to pick a pocket. [Cf OE *pung* purse]

bung[3] *bung*, (*slang*) *vt* to throw or shove carelessly and hurriedly. [Imit]

bung[4] *bung*, (*Austr colloq*) *adj* dead; bankrupt; useless. — **go bung** to die; to fail, go bust; to go phut. [Aboriginal]

bung[5] (*criminals' slang*) *n* a bribe, tip. — *vt* to bribe, pay. [Ety unknown]

bungalow *bung'gə-lō*, *n* a lightly-built house, properly with a veranda and one storey; (loosely) a one-storey house; in some parts of Australia, a separate living structure in the garden. — *adj* and *n* **bung'aloid** (*facetious, usu derog*). — **dak bungalow** see **dak**. [Hindi *banglā* (house) in the style of Bengal]

bungee or **bungey** *bunj'i*, *n* a tension device using springs, elastic cable or rubber in such a way as to facilitate the movement of the controls in aircraft, etc; also **bun'gie**, **bun'gy**, **bun'je**, **bun'jee**, **bun'jie** or **bun'jy** (*slang*) *n* india-rubber, a rubber or eraser. — **bungee jumping** the sport of jumping from a height with strong rubber ropes or cables attached to the ankles to ensure that the jumper bounces up before reaching the ground or other surface. [Ety unknown]

bungle *bung'gl*, *n* anything clumsily done; a gross mismanagement. — *vi* to act in a clumsy manner. — *vt* to make or mend clumsily; to mismanage grossly; to make a failure of because of a lack of skill. — *n* **bung'ler**. — *adj* **bung'ling** clumsy, awkward; unskilfully or badly done. — Also *n*. — *adv* **bung'lingly**. [Ety doubtful; cf Swed dialect *bangla* to work ineffectually]

bunia. See **bunnia**.

bunion *bun'yən*, *n* a lump or inflamed swelling on the first joint of the big toe. [Ety unknown; poss Ital *bugnone* a botch]

bunje, **bunjee**, **bunjie**, **bunjy**. See **bungee**.

bunk[1] *bungk*, *n* a box or recess in a ship's cabin; a sleeping-berth anywhere; one of a pair of single beds one above the other (also **bunk bed**). — *vi* to occupy a bunk. — *n* **bunk'er** a compartment for fuel on shipboard; the fuel-oil carried by a ship for its own use; a large bin or chest, *esp* for coal (*Scot*); a sand-pit or sandy gap in turf, *esp* as a hazard in a golf course; a window-seat and chest (*Scot*); a turf seat (*Scot*); a slab beside a sink (*Scot*). — *vt* to fuel; to play into a bunker. — *vi* to fuel. — *adj* **bunk'ered** in a bunker; in difficulties. — **bunk'house** a building containing sleeping accommodation for labourers on a ranch, etc. [Cf ON *bunki*, Scand *bunke* heap]

bunk[2] *bungk*, (*slang*) *n* fleeing, running away (*esp* in phrase **do a bunk**). — *vi* to flee; (with *off*) to do a bunk, to play truant.

bunk[3]. See **bunkum**.

bunker[1] *bung'kər*, *n* an underground bombproof shelter. — **bunker mentality** a belief that one is secure and that one's world will survive unchanged in spite of evidence to the contrary. [Ger]

bunker[2]. See under **bunk**[1].

bunko or **bunco** *bung'kō*, (*US*) *n* a form of confidence-trick in which the victim is swindled or taken somewhere and robbed: — *pl* **bunk'os** or **bunc'os**. — *vt* to rob or swindle in such a way. — **bunk'o-steerer** a con-man. [Perh from Sp *banca* a kind of card-game]

bunkum or (*esp US*) **buncombe** *bung'kəm*, also **bunk** *bungk*, *n* bombastic speechmaking intended for the newspapers rather than to persuade the audience; humbug, claptrap. [From *Buncombe*, a county in N Carolina, whose representative is said to have gone on talking in Congress, explaining apologetically that he was 'only talking for Buncombe']

bunnia or **bunia** *bun'i-ə*, *n* a Hindu merchant. [Hindi]

bunny *bun'i*, *n* a young rabbit, *esp* a pet name for one (also **bunny rabbit**); a simpleton, a scapegoat (*Austr colloq*). — **bunn'y-girl** (sometimes with *caps*) a nightclub hostess provocatively dressed in a brief, tight-fitting costume with a white fluffy tail, and wearing rabbit-like ears; **bunny hop** a rocking jump from a squatting position, with both feet kicked backwards together;

bunn'y-hug a 20c American dance. — Also *vi*. [Ety unknown; cf **bun**[3]]

bunodont *bū'nō-dont*, *adj* having tuberculate molars (*opp* to *lophodont*). [Gr *bounos* a rounded hill, and *odous*, *odontos* a tooth]

bunraku *bōōn-rä'kōō*, *n* a Japanese form of puppet theatre in which the puppets, *usu* about 3ft (1m) high, are each manipulated by three men who remain visible throughout the performance. [Jap]

Bunsen burner or **Bunsen** (also without *cap*) *bun'sən* or, *bōōn'sən* (*bûrn'ər*), *n* a gas-burner, used in laboratories, in which a good supply of air is caused to mingle with the gas before ignition, to produce a smokeless flame of low luminosity but great heating power. [From the inventor R W *Bunsen* (1811–99), a German chemist]

bunt[1] *bunt*, *n* stink-brand, a disease of wheat; the fungus (*Tilletia*) that causes it. — *adj* **bunt'ed**. — *adj* **bunt'y**. [Ety unknown]

bunt[2] *bunt*, *n* the bagging part of a fishing-net, a sail, etc. — *vi* (of a sail, etc) to belly. — **bunt'line** a rope passing from the foot-rope of a square sail to prevent bellying in furling. [Ety unknown]

bunt[3] *bunt*, *vi* to push with the horns, butt; to block a ball with the bat (*baseball*; also *vt* and *n*). — *n* a push. — *n* **bunt'ing** pushing; a boys' game, played with sticks and a small piece of wood; a strong timber, a stout prop.

buntal *bunt'əl*, *n* the straw of the talipot palm. [Tagálog]

Bunter *bōōn'tər*, (*geol*) *n* the lowest division of the Trias. [From Ger *bunt* mottled]

bunter *bunt'ər*, (*dialect*) *n* a female rag-picker; a low woman.

bunting[1] *bunt'ing*, *n* a thin worsted fabric for ships' colours; flags; small strips of coloured cloth or paper hung from strings as decorations for a boat, street, etc. [Ety uncertain]

bunting[2] *bunt'ing*, *n* any of the small finch-like birds of the subfamily *Emberizinae* (family *Emberizidae* or perhaps *Fringillidae*). [Ety uncertain]

bunting[3]. See **bunt**[3].

buntline. See **bunt**[2].

bunya *bun'yə* or **bun'ya-bun'ya**, *n* an Australian tree (*Araucaria bidwillii*), the cones of which contain large edible seeds. [Aboriginal]

bunyip *bun'yip*, *n* a fabulous monster of Australian Aboriginal legend; an impostor. [Aboriginal]

buonamano *bwō-na-mä'nō* or **bonamano** *bo'na-*, (*Ital*) *n* a tip: — *pl* **buonama'ni** or **bonama'ni** (*-nē*).

buona sera *bwō'na sā'ra*, (*Ital*) good evening.

buon giorno *bwōn jor'nō*, (*Ital*) good day.

buoy *boi* (in US often *bōō'ē* and in derivatives below *bōō'y-*), *n* a floating secured mark, serving (by its shape, colour, light, sound, etc) as a guide or as a warning. — *vt* to provide or mark with buoys or marks; to keep afloat, bear up, or sustain (*usu* with *up*); to raise, lift (the spirits, etc; *usu* with *up*). — *vi* to rise. — *n* **buoy'age** a series of buoys or floating beacons to mark the course for vessels; the provision, or system, of buoys. — *n* **buoy'ance** (*rare*) or **buoy'ancy** the capacity for floating or causing to float lightly on water or in the air; loss of weight owing to immersion in a fluid; lightness of spirit, cheerfulness, resilience. — *adj* **buoy'ant** tending to float or to buoy up; (of spirits, etc) light, cheerful and resilient; (of share prices, sales, profits, etc) tending to rise; (of a firm) with rising profits, etc. — *n* **buoy'antness**. — **buoyancy aid** an inflated support for *esp* children learning to swim; **buoyant density** the density of molecules, particles or viruses as determined by flotation in a suitable liquid. [Du *boei* buoy, fetter, through Romance forms (Norman Fr *boie*), from LL *boia* a collar of leather]

BUPA *bōō'pə* or *bū'pə*, *abbrev*: British United Provident Association, a private medical insurance organization.

Buphaga *bū'fä-gə*, *n* a small genus of African birds, closely related to the starlings, which feed on the larvae of gadflies, etc, parasitic on the backs of cattle, camels, etc. — Also **beefeater** and **ox-pecker**. [Gr *bous* an ox, and *phagein* to eat]

buplever *bū-plev'ər*, *n* the plant hare's-ear (*Bupleurum*). [Fr *buplèvre*, from L *būpleurum*, from Gr *bous* ox, and *pleuron* rib]

buppy *bup'i*, (*colloq*) *n* a black urban professional. [Cf **yuppie**]

Buprestis *bū-pres'tis*, *n* a genus of beetles of a large family, **Bupres'tidae**, those occurring in warmer countries having brilliant colour and metallic sheen, some of which are known as golden beetles. — *n* and *adj* **bupres'tid**. [Gr *bouprēstis* a kind of poisonous beetle, from *bous* ox, and *prēthein* to swell]

BUR *abbrev*: Burma, now called Myanma (IVR).

bur. See **burr**[1,2].

Burakumin *boor'ə-kōō-min*, (*Jap*) *n pl* members of the lowest feudal caste in Japan, officially abolished in 1871 but in fact still regarded as untouchables, who perform the most menial tasks.

buran *bōō-rän'*, *n* a violent blizzard blowing from the NE in Siberia and Central Asia. [Russ]

Burberry *bûr'bər-i*, *n* a good-quality raincoat. — *adj* characteristic of clothing made by Burberrys. [From *Burberrys*, trademark of Burberrys Ltd]

burble[1] *bûrb'l*, (*Scot*) *n* a tangle. — *vt* to confuse. [Prob connected with OFr *barbouiller* to jumble]

burble[2] *bûrb'l*, *n* a murmur. — *vt* and *vi* to murmur; to gurgle; to talk excitedly and rather incoherently (*colloq*). — *n* **burb'ler**. — *n* **burb'ling** separation of the flow of air from the upper surface of a moving aerofoil. — **burble point** or **burbling point** (*aerodynamics*) the angle of attack at which the sharp drop in the ratio of lift to drag (an effect of burbling too near the leading edge) first appears. [Prob onomatopoeic]

burbot *bûr'bət*, *n* a freshwater fish, like the ling, with a longish barbel on its lower jaw. [Fr *bourbotte*, *barbotte*, from LL *borba* mud, or L *barba* a beard]

burd[1] *bûrd*, (*obs*) *n* a maiden; a lady. [OE *byrde* well-born (or perh *brȳd* bride), prob combined or confused with ON *byrthr*, OE *byrd* birth, offspring]

burd[2] *bûrd*, (*Scot*) *n* a bird; a young bird; a young animal of any kind; offspring, progeny; a term of endearment. — *n* **burd'ie** (*dimin*). — **burd'-alane** or **bird'-alane** the last remaining of a family. — *adj* and *adv* (*Morris* **bird'=alone**) quite alone.

burdash *bûr-dash'*, *n* a fringed sash worn by gentlemen in the time of Anne and George I. [Origin unknown]

burden[1] *bûr'dən* (*archaic* **burthen** *bûr'dhən*), *n* a load; a ship's carrying capacity (still often **burthen**); something grievous, oppressive, or difficult to bear; an obligation; any restriction, limitation or encumbrance affecting person or property (*Scots law*); a child in the womb (*obs*); a birth, confinement (*obs*); (in *pl*) a boat's floorboards. — *vt* to load; to oppress; to encumber. — *adj* **bur'denous** or **bur'densome** heavy; oppressive. — **burden of proof** the obligation to prove one's contention. [OE *byrthen*, from *beran* to bear]

burden[2] *bûr'dən* (*archaic* **burthen** *bûr'dhən*), *n* a bourdon or bass; the part of a song repeated at the end of every stanza, a refrain; the main theme of anything. [Fr *bourdon* a humming tone in music, from LL *burdō* a drone bee; confused with **burden**[1]]

burden[3] *bûr'dən*, *n* a pilgrim's staff. [See **bourdon**[2]]

burdock. See under **burr**[1].

bureau *bū'rō* or *bū-rō'*, *n* a writing-table combined with a chest of drawers; a chest of drawers (*US*); a room or office where a writing-table is used; a department or office for the transacting of business, such as collecting and supplying information; a government department: — *pl* **bureaux** or **bureaus** (*-ōz*). [Fr from OFr *burel* coarse russet cloth, from L *burrus* red]

bureaucracy *bū-rok'rə-si*, *n* a system of government or administration by officials, responsible only to their departmental chiefs; any system of administration in which matters are hindered by excessive adherence to minor rules and procedures; officials as a group. — *n* **bur'eaucrat** a government official; a bureaucratist. — *adj* **bureaucrat'ic**. — *adv* **bureaucrat'ically**. — *n* **bureau'cratist** someone who practises or favours bureaucracy.

— *n* **bureaucratizā'tion** or **-s-**. — *vt* **bureauc'ratize** or **-ise** to form into a bureaucracy; to make bureaucratic. [**bureau**, and Gr *kratos* power]

bureau de change *bü-rō də shãzh*, (*Fr*) *n* an office where currency can be exchanged.

burette *bū-ret'*, *n* (also *US* **buret**) a graduated glass tube with a tap, for measuring liquids run off; a cruet for religious ceremonies. [Fr]

burg *bŏŏrg* or *bûrg*, *n* a fortress or a walled town (*hist*); a town (*US colloq*; *bûrg*). [W Gmc *burg*; OE *burh*; cf **burgh** and **borough**]

burgage *bûr'gij*, *n* a tenure in socage for a yearly rent; a tenure in Scotland in royal burghs under nominal service of watching. [LL *burgāgium*, from the root of **borough**, **burgh**]

burganet or **burgonet** *bûr'gə-net*, *n* a light 16c helmet with cheek-pieces. [Fr *bourguignotte*, literally Burgundian]

burgee *bûr'jē*, *n* a triangular or swallow-tailed flag or pennant; a kind of small coal for furnaces. [Origin uncertain]

burgeon or (*obs*) **bourgeon** *bûr'jən*, *vi* to produce sprouts or buds; to grow. [Fr *bourgeon* a bud, shoot]

burger *bûr'gər*, (*colloq*) *n* short form of **hamburger**, **cheeseburger**, etc. — Also *adj*. — **-burger** used as a *combining form* as in *beefburger*, *cheeseburger*, to denote (a bread roll containing) a fried or grilled cake of meat, etc made of, or accompanied by, the particular food mentioned.

burgess *bûr'jis*, *n* a freeman or citizen of a borough or burgh (*technically*, cf **burgher**); a member of a privileged class in a town; a member of parliament for a borough (*hist*); an elected member of the American colonial assembly (*hist*); a borough magistrate or town councillor (*hist*). — **burgess oath** see **Antiburgher**. [OFr *burgeis*]

burgh *bûr'ə*, spelling of **borough**, used for Scottish burghs, otherwise *archaic*. — *adj* **burghal** (*bûrg'l*). — *n* **burgher** (*bûrg'ər*) a freeman or citizen of a borough (used non-technically of British towns, in technical sense chiefly of continental towns, cf **burgess**); a townsman; (with *cap*) a Seceder who felt free to take the burgess oath (see **Antiburgher**) (*Scot*); a citizen of one of the S African Boer republics (*hist*); in Sri Lanka, a Eurasian of Dutch or Portuguese extraction, or a person of European race assimilated to the native population (*hist*). — **burgh court** formerly in Scotland, an inferior court of summary jurisdiction presided over by a bailie. — **parliamentary burgh** a burgh whose boundaries, as first fixed in 1832 for parliamentary representation, were adopted later for municipal purposes; a burgh which by itself or in combination elected a member of parliament; **police burgh** a burgh constituted by the sheriff for purposes of improvement and police; **royal burgh** a corporate body deriving its existence, constitution and rights from a royal charter, actual or presumed to have existed. — **burgh of barony** a corporation under a feudal superior or baron, who sometimes nominated the magistrates; **burgh of regality** a burgh of barony enfranchised by crown charter, with regal or exclusive criminal jurisdiction within its territory. [See **borough**]

burghul *bŏŏr'gŏŏl*, *n* bulgur. [Pers]

burglar *bûrg'lər*, *n* a person who enters a building as a trespasser (before 1969, by night) to commit a felony, eg to steal. — Also (*obs*) *vi* and *vt*. — *adj* **burglarious** (*-lā'ri-əs*). — *adv* **burglā'riously**. — *vt* **burg'larize** or **-ise** (*NAm colloq*). — *n* **burg'lary**. — *vi* **burgle** (*bûr'gl*; a back-formation from **burglar**) to commit burglary. — *vt* to enter as a burglar. — **aggravated burglary** burglary involving the use of weapons or explosives. [Ety uncertain]

burgomaster *bûr'gō-mäs-tər*, *n* the chief magistrate of an Austrian, Dutch, Flemish or German town. [Du *burgemeester*; Ger *Bürgermeister*, literally borough-master]

burgonet. See **burganet**.

burgoo *bûr-gŏŏ'* or *bûr'gŏŏ*, *n* a sailor's dish of boiled oatmeal with salt, butter and sugar; a stew or thick soup for American picnics. [Ety prob ult same as **bulgur**]

burgrave *bûr'grāv*, (*hist*) *n* the governor or hereditary ruler of a German town or castle. [Ger *Burggraf*]

burgundy *bûr'gən-di*, *n* (*usu* with *cap*) a French wine (red unless specified otherwise), made in *Burgundy*; a similar wine made elsewhere; the purplish-red or dark red colour of red Burgundy. — **Burgundy mixture** a fungicide composed of copper sulphate, sodium carbonate and water; **Burgundy pitch** a resin properly prepared by melting and straining the exudation from Norway spruce (now obtained mainly elsewhere).

burhel. Same as **bharal**.

burial *ber'i-əl*, *n* the act of burying; a funeral; a tomb (*archaic*). — **bur'ial-ground** a ground set apart for burials; **bur'ial-place** a burial-ground; the place where anyone is buried; **burial society** an insurance society for providing the expenses of burial. [OE *byrgels* a tomb; see **bury**]

Buridan's ass *bū'ri-danz as* or *äs*, *n* in the sophism doubtfully attributed to the French 14c schoolman Jean *Buridan*, an ass dying of starvation through inability to choose between two equidistant and equally desirable sources of food.

burin *būr'in*, *n* a kind of chisel of tempered steel, used in copper engraving; the distinctive style of an engraver; a palaeolithic flint tool. — *n* **bur'inist** an engraver. [Fr; from root of **bore**[1]]

buriti *bŏŏ-ri-tē'*, *n* the miriti palm. [Tupí]

burk. See **berk**.

burka or **boorka** *bŏŏr'kə*, *n* a loose garment, with veiled eyeholes, covering the whole body, worn in public by Muslim women. [Urdu *burqa'*, from Ar]

burke *bûrk*, *vt* to murder, *esp* by smothering; to put an end to quietly, to silence, suppress; to evade. [From *Burke*, an Edinburgh Irishman (hanged 1829), who committed murder in order to sell the bodies of his victims for dissection]

Burkitt lymphoma *bûr'kit lim-fō'mə* or **Burkitt's lymphoma** (*bûr'kitz*), *n* a malignant tumour of the immune system, chiefly affecting children in Africa and associated with Epstein-Barr virus. [Denis *Burkitt*, British surgeon, who first described the condition in 1957]

burl[1] *bûrl*, *n* a small knot in thread or wool; a knot in wood. — *vt* to pick knots, etc from (cloth) in finishing. — *n* **bur'ler**. — *adj* **bur'ly**. — **bur'ling-iron**; **bur'ling-machine**. [OFr *bourle* tuft of wool]

burl[2] *bûrl*, (*Austr* and *NZ colloq*) *n* an attempt, shot. [Prob Scots *birl*, *burl* a twist, turn]

burlap *bûr'lap*, *n* a coarse canvas of jute or hemp for wrappings, or a lighter material, eg of flax, for wall-coverings, etc, sometimes in *pl*. [Origin uncertain]

burlesque *bûr-lesk'*, *n* a ludicrous imitation; a piece of literature, of acting, or other performance that mocks its original by grotesque exaggeration or by combining the dignified with the low or the familiar; an entertainment combining often coarse jokes, striptease, songs and dancing (*NAm*); a playful or jocular composition (*music*). — *adj* of the nature of burlesque; practising burlesque. — *vt* to mock by burlesque; to make a burlesque of. [Ital *burlesco*; prob from LL *burra* a flock of wool, a trifle]

burletta *bûr-let'ə*, *n* a musical farce; comic opera. [Ital; dimin of *burla* a jest]

burley[1] *bûr'lē*, *n* an American thin-leaved tobacco. [Prob from a personal name]

burley[2]. See **berley**.

burly[1] *bûr'li*, *adj* big and sturdy. — *n* **bur'liness**. [ME *borlich*; perh the same as OHGer *burlīh* high, from *bōr* a height]

burly[2]. See under **burl**[1].

Burman *bûrm'ən*, *adj* relating to *Burma* (since 1989, the Republic of Myanma). — *n* a person belonging to the majority ethnic group of Myanma. — *adj* **Burmese** (*bûr'mēz* or *-mēz'*) Burman. — *n* the official language of Myanma; (until 1989) a native or citizen of Burma. —

Burmese cat a breed of short-haired domestic cat, similar to the Siamese, typically dark brown in colour, with golden eyes; **Burmese glass** a kind of unpolished semi-opaque coloured glass, popular in Victorian times.

burn[1] *bûrn*, (now chiefly *Scot*) *n* a small stream or brook. — **burn'side** the ground beside a burn. [OE *burna* brook, spring; cf Du *born*, Ger *Born*]

burn[2] *bûrn*, *vt* to consume or injure by fire or great heat; to produce an effect of heat on (as to bake pottery, produce charcoal, calcine lime, scorch food, wither grass); to brand; to oxidize; to use (up), eg uranium, in a nuclear reactor (*usu* with *up*); to corrode; to sting; to make (a hole, etc) by fire or analogous means. — *vi* to be burnt; to be on fire; to give out heat or light; to glow; to feel very hot; to sting; to be inflamed with passion: — *pa t* and *pa p* **burnt** or **burned**. — *n* a hurt or mark due to burning; a controlled fire to reduce vegetation, or the area so cleared (*NAm*, *Austr*, *NZ*); the firing of a rocket engine in order to produce thrust; tobacco, a smoke, a cigarette (*slang*); a very fast ride, etc on a motorcycle, in a speed-boat, etc; pain felt in a muscle, experienced during demanding exercise. — *n* **burn'er** a person or thing that burns; a fixture or part of a lamp, gas-jet or gas cooker from which a flame comes. — *n* **burn'ing** the act of consuming by fire; conflagration; inflammation; a quantity burned at one time; controlled expenditure of rocket propellant for course adjustment purposes. — *adj* very hot; scorching; ardent; excessive. — Also *adv*. — *adv* **burn'ingly**. — **burning bush** the emblem of the Church of Scotland and other Presbyterian churches with the motto 'Nec tamen consumebatur', adopted from Exod 3.2, in memory of the unconquerable courage of the Covenanters under the cruel persecutions of the 17c; applied to various plants, such as dittany, whose volatile oil may catch fire in the air, some American species of spindle-tree with bright red fruits, artillery plant, etc; **burn'ing-glass** a convex lens concentrating the sun's rays at its focus to produce fire or heat; **burn'ing-house** a kiln; **burn'ing-mirror** a concave mirror for producing fire or heat by concentrating the sun's rays; **burning mountain** a volcano; **burn'ing-point** the temperature at which a volatile oil in an open vessel will take fire from a match held close to its surface; **burning question** or **issue** one keenly discussed; **burn-out** see **burn out** below; **burnt almonds** almonds in burnt sugar; **burnt cork** charred cork used for blacking the face. — Also (with *hyphen*) *vt*. — **burnt cream** crème brûlée; **burnt'-ear** smut in oats, wheat, etc; **burn'-the-wind** (*Scot*) a blacksmith; **burnt-off'ering** something offered and burned on an altar as a sacrifice (also *facetious*); **burnt-sienn'a** see under **sienna**; **burn'-up** the using up of fuel in a nuclear reactor. — **burn a hole in one's pocket** said of money when one is eager to spend it; **burn blue** see under **blue**[1]; **burn daylight** (*Shakesp*) to waste time; **burn down** to burn to the ground; **burned out** ineffective, exhausted; **burned up** (*US slang*) angry; **burn in** to fix and make durable by intense heat; to imprint indelibly; **burn one's boats** or **bridges** to cut oneself off from all chance of retreat; to stake everything on success; **burn one's fingers** or **get one's fingers burnt** to suffer as a result of interfering, speculating, etc; **burn out** to destroy or drive out by burning; to burn till the fire dies down from want of fuel; to (cause to) break down or fail to work as a result of overheating; to (cause to) become ineffective through overwork, exhaustion, etc (*n* **burn'-out**); **burn the candle at both ends** see under **candle**; **burn the midnight oil** to study late into the night; **burn the water** (*Scot*) to spear salmon by torchlight; **burn up** to consume completely by fire; to be burned completely; to increase in activity of burning; to make short or easy work of; to become or make angry (*US slang*); **(money) to burn** (money) in great abundance. [In OE the transitive weak verb *bærnan*, *bærnde*, *bærned* has been confused with the intransitive strong verb *beornan*, *byrnan*, *barn*, *bornen*; cf Ger *brennen* to burn]

burnet *bûr'nit*, *adj* (*obs*) dark brown. — *n* a fine dark woollen cloth of the Middle Ages; the name of two closely related rosaceous plants, the great burnet (*Sanguisorba officinalis* or *Poterium officinale*), a meadow-plant, and common or salad burnet (*Sanguisorba minor*) sometimes used in salads, both with close aggregates of brownish-purple flowers; the burnet moth. — **burnet moth** a moth of the Zygaenidae, *esp* of the genus *Arthrocera*, with red-spotted or red-streaked forewings; **burnet rose** or **burnet-leaved rose** a wild rose (*Rosa spinosissima*) with leaves like burnet, the Scotch rose; **burnet saxifrage** a plant (*Pimpinella saxifraga*) related to anise, with burnet-like leaves. [OFr *burnete*, *brunette*; see **brunette**]

burnettize or **-ise** *bûr'nit-īz*, *vt* to treat with Burnett's fluid, a solution of zinc chloride, a preservative for timber, etc against dry-rot and insects, patented by Sir William *Burnett* (1779–1861).

burnish *bûrn'ish*, *vt* to polish; to make bright by rubbing. — *n* polish; lustre. — *n* **burn'isher**. — *n* **burn'ishing**. — *n* **burn'ishment**. [Fr *brunir*, *bruniss-* to burnish, from *brun* brown]

burnous *bûr-nōōs'* or **burnouse** *-nōōz'*, *n* a cape with a hood much worn by the Arabs. [Fr, from Ar *burnus*]

Burnsian *bûrnz'i-ən*, *adj* pertaining to Robert *Burns* (1759–96), the Scottish poet. — *n* a student or admirer of Burns. — *n* **Burns'ite** a devotee of Burns.

burnt *pa t* and *pa p* of **burn**[2]. — Also *adj*.

buroo *bə-rōō'* or **broo** *brōō*, (*Scot* and *Ir*) *n* the office at which people receive unemployment benefit; unemployment benefit. — **on the buroo** or **broo** unemployed and receiving unemployment benefit. [**bureau**]

burp *bûrp*, *vi* (*colloq*) to belch. — Also *n*. — *vt* to rub or pat a baby's back after it has been fed, thought to help it to belch. [Imit]

burqa *bûr'kə*. Same as **burka**.

burr[1] or **bur** *bûr*, *n* the prickly seed-case or head of certain plants, which sticks to clothes or animals; any impediment or inconvenient adherent; any lump, ridge, etc, more or less sharp, an excrescence on a tree, or markings representing it in wood (as in **burr-wal'nut**); a knot in thread; a knob at the base of a deer's horn; the rough edge to a line made by an engraving tool, which, when the plate is inked, gives a further quality to the line; waste raw silk; the sweetbread or pancreas; club-moss (*Scot*); the name for various tools and appliances, such as the triangular chisel for clearing the corners of mortises, etc; the blank driven out of a piece of sheet-metal by a punch; burrstone; a partly vitrified brick. — *adj* **burr'y**. — **bur'dock** a composite plant (*Arctium lappa*) with hooked involucral bracts and docklike leaves; any species of *Xanthium*; **bur-mar'igold** any plant of the composite genus *Bidens*, with barbed pappus; a species of *Xanthium*; **bur'-reed** a reedlike genus (*Sparganium*) of water-plants with globular flower-heads; **burrstone** see **buhrstone**; **bur'-thistle** spear-thistle; **bur'weed** any of various burry plants such as burdock, bur-reed, clot-bur (*Xanthium*), etc. — **burr in the throat** something seeming to stick in the throat, producing a choking sensation. [Cognate with Dan *borre* a bur]

burr[2] or **bur** *bûr*, *n* the rough sound of *r* pronounced in the throat, as by many Northumberland people. — *vi* to whisper hoarsely, to murmur. [Usu associated with **burr**[1] but perh imit]

burramundi *bur-ə-mun'di*, an *obs* variant of **barramundi**.

burra sahib *bur'ə sä'ib*, *n* in India, a title of respect for the head of a family, a superior officer, etc. [Hindi *bara* great, and **sahib**]

burrawang *bur'ə-wang*, (*Austr*) *n* any of various palm-like plants of the genus *Macrozaemia* or *Cycas*, having edible nuts. [From Mount *Budawang*, New South Wales]

burrel[1] *bur'əl*, *n* a coarse russet cloth of medieval times. [See ety for **bureau**]

burrel[2], **burrell** or **burrhel**. Same as **bharal**.

burrito *bŏŏ-rē'tō*, *n* a Mexican dish consisting of a flour tortilla, filled with meat, beans, chilli, etc and folded: — *pl* **burri'tos**. [Mex Sp, a young donkey, from Sp *burro* a donkey, and dimin suffix]

burro *bŏŏr'ō*, *n* a donkey: — *pl* **burr'os**. [Sp]

burrow *bur'ō*, *n* a hole in the ground dug *esp* by certain animals for shelter or defence; a passage, hole or gallery dug or eaten through wood, stone, etc; a refuge. — *vi* to make holes underground as rabbits do; to work one's way deeply under the surface; to live or hide in a concealed place. — *vt* to make a burrow in; to make by burrowing. — **burr'ow-duck** the shelduck or bergander; **burr'owing-owl** a small long-legged diurnal American owl nesting in burrows. [Prob a variant of **borough**, from OE *beorgan* to protect]

burrowstown *bur'əs-tōōn*, (*Scot*) *n* a town that is a burgh. [**burgh**]

burrstone. See **buhrstone**.

bursa *bûr'sə*, *n* a pouch or sac, *esp* one containing viscid lubricating fluid at points of friction (*zool*): — *pl* **bur'sae** (*-sē*). — *adj* **bur'sal** relating to a bursa. — *adj* **bursic'ūlate** resembling a small pouch. — *adj* **burs'iform** pouch-shaped. — *n* **bursī'tis** inflammation of a bursa. [LL *bursa* a purse, from Gr *byrsa* skin or leather]

bursal. See under **bursa** and **bursar**.

bursar *bûr'sər*, *n* a person who keeps the purse, a treasurer; in Scotland and New Zealand, a student or pupil maintained at a university or school by funds derived from endowment. — *adj* **bur'sal** fiscal. — *adj* **bursarial** (*-sā'ri-əl*). — *n* **bur'sarship** the office of a bursar. — *n* **bur'sary** the treasury of a college or monastery; the bursar's room in a college; in Scotland and New Zealand, a scholarship. — *n* **burse** (*bûrs*) a purse; a case for holding the corporal (chiefly *RC*); a scholarship (*obs Scot*); an obsolete form of **bourse**. [**bursa**]

Bursch *bŏŏrsh*, *n* a student in a German university: — *pl* **Bursch'en**. — *n* **Bursch'enism**. — *n* **Bursch'enschaft** (*-shäft*) a students' association. [Ger *Bursch* a companion, student]

burse. See under **bursar**.

Bursera *bûr'sər-ə*, *n* a tropical American genus of trees yielding elemi and timber, giving name to the family **Burserā'ceae**, related to the rue family. — *adj* **burserā'ceous**. [Joachim *Burser* (1593–1649), German botanist]

bursiculate, bursiform, bursitis. See under **bursa**.

burst *bûrst*, *vt* to break into pieces; to break open or cause to give way suddenly or by violence; to make or have something burst; to tear apart the perforated sheets of (continuous stationery). — *vi* to fly open or into pieces, *esp* owing to a force from within; to give way suddenly; to break forth or away; to force a way (through, etc); to break suddenly into being, or into some condition, activity, or expression of feeling: — *pa t* and *pa p* **burst**, *archaic*, *dialect* and *US* **burst'ed** or **bust'ed**; *obs pa p* **burst'en**. — *n* an act, occasion or result of bursting; a sudden outbreak; a hard gallop; a spurt; a drunken bout (*obs colloq*); a measure of the strength of an envelope. — *adj* **burst** ruptured. — *n* **burst'er** a person or thing that bursts; *specif* a machine that separates continuous stationery. — **burst binding** an unsewn bookbinding in which the gathered sections are perforated at the fold and glue is made to penetrate through the perforations; **burst'-up** a complete break; disruption; commotion; collapse; failure. [OE *berstan*; Ger *bersten*; see also **bust**[2]]

burthen *bûr'dhən*, *n* and *vt*. See **burden**[1,2].

Burton *bûr'tn*, *n* a drink. — **gone for a Burton** drowned, dead (*airmen's slang*); absent; missing; no longer in existence. [A town in Staffordshire famous for its beer]

burton *bûr'tn*, (*naut*) *n* a tackle of two or three blocks. [Ety unknown]

burweed. See under **burr**[1].

bury *ber'i* or *bûr'i*, *vt* to hide in the ground; to cover, hide, put (something) deep inside something else; to consign (a dead body) to the grave, the sea, etc; to hide or blot out of remembrance; (in *passive*) to be deeply engrossed (in): — *pr p* **bur'ying**; *pa t* and *pa p* **bur'ied**. — *n* (*dialect*) a burrow. — **bur'ying-beetle** a beetle (*Necrophorus* or a related genus) that buries small animals as food for its larvae; **bur'ying-ground** a plot of ground set apart for burying the dead; a graveyard; **bur'ying-place**. — **bury one's head in the sand** to refuse to face the facts; **bury the hatchet** to renounce enmity, to become reconciled. [OE *byrgan* to bury; Ger *bergen* to hide]

bus (now *rare* **'bus**; *obs* **buss**) *bus*, *n* a road vehicle with one (*single-decker*) or two (*double-decker*) decks for transporting a considerable number of passengers, *usu* on a regular or prearranged route; a car, aeroplane, etc (as a term of affection; *slang*); a number of conductors forming a circuit or route along which data or power may be transmitted (also **highway** or **trunk**; *comput*); the part of the payload of a space exploration vehicle (or a missile) which contains the atmospheric (re-)entry probes (or warheads): — *pl* **bus'es** or (less commonly) **buss'es**. — *vt* to transport by bus, sometimes *specif* as in **busing** below. — *vi* to go by bus; in a restaurant, etc, to clear dirty dishes from tables, replenish supplies of needed items, and otherwise assist the waiting staff (*NAm*). — *adj* of or relating to a bus or buses. — *n* **bus'ing** or (less commonly) **buss'ing** the transporting by bus of people from one district to another, *esp* children to school, to achieve a more even racial, etc balance, for economic reasons, etc (chiefly *NAm*). — **bus'-bar** an electric conductor connecting with a number of circuits (*electronics*, etc); **bus'boy** or **bus'girl** (*NAm*) an assistant waiter or waitress, a person who buses; **bus'-conductor**; **bus'-driver**; **bus lane** a traffic lane restricted to buses for all or part of the day; **bus'-fare**; **bus'man** the driver or conductor of a bus; **bus pass** a pass entitling its holder to travel on services run by specified bus companies without (further) payment or at a reduced fare; **bus shelter** an open-sided structure at a bus stop, giving some protection against the weather; **bus stop** a halting-place for a bus, for passengers to board it or alight; the post or sign *usu* marking such a place. — **busman's holiday** a holiday spent in activities similar to one's work; **miss the bus** to lose an opportunity. [Short form of **omnibus**]

bus. *abbrev*: business.

busby *buz'bi*, *n* a fur hat with a bag hanging on its right side, worn *esp* by hussars; a bearskin hat (*colloq*). [Prob Hung]

bush[1] *bŏŏsh*, *n* a woody plant, between a tree and an undershrub in size; a shrub thick with branches; anything of bushy tuftlike shape, eg a bushy head of hair or the pubic hair; forest; wild uncultivated country covered with bushes, trees, etc; such country even though treeless; the wild; a bunch of ivy hung up as a tavern sign (*obs*); a tavern (*obs*). — *vi* to grow thick or bushy. — *vt* to set bushes round; to support with bushes; to cover (seeds) by means of the bush-harrow. — *adj* **bushed** lost in or as in the bush (*Austr* and *NZ*); suffering mental disturbance as a result of living in isolation (*Can*); tired (*slang*). — *n* **bush'iness**. — *adj* **bush'y** full of or like bushes; thick and spreading. — *n* (*Austr* and *NZ colloq*) someone who lives in the bush. — **bush'-baby** any of several, nocturnal, small African lemur-like primates, such as *Galago maholi*, also called **night-ape**; **bush'-buck** a small S African antelope, or any other of the same genus (Tragelaphus). — Also (*Du*) **boschbok** (*bos'bok*), (*Afrik*) **bosbok** (*bos'bok*). — **bush'-cat** the serval; **bush'craft** practical knowledge of the bush and skill in its ways; **bush'fire** (*esp Austr* and *NZ*) a fire in forest or scrub; **bush'-fly** a small black Australian fly (*Musca vetustissima* or other species); **bush'-fruit** a fruit growing on a bush, such as gooseberry or raspberry; **bush'-harrow** a light harrow for covering grass-seeds, formed of a barred frame interwoven with bushes or branches; **bush'-house** (*Austr*) a house or hut in the bush or in a garden; **bush jacket** see **bush shirt** below; **bush'-lawyer** (*Austr*) any of several prickly climbing plants, *esp* of the genus *Calamus*; someone who pretends a knowledge of law; **bush'man** a settler, or traveller, in the bush (*Austr* and *NZ*); (with *cap*) one of a now almost extinct nomadic, short-statured, yellowish-brown, aboriginal race of huntsmen in S Africa (Cape Du *Bos(jes)man*); (with *cap*) any of the languages of this people. — Also *adj*. — **bush'manship** bushcraft; **bush'master** a venomous S American snake (*Lachesis muta*); **bush pig** a wild pig of S Africa and Madagascar; **bush pilot** an airline pilot operating over uninhabited country; **bush'ranger** a lawless person, often an escaped criminal, who takes to the bush and lives by robbery (*Austr*); a backwoodsman; a rapacious person; **bush'-rope** a liana; **bush shirt** or **bush jacket** a cotton, etc garment with four patch pockets and a belt; **bush'-shrike** any bird belonging to certain genera of an African subfamily of the shrikes, applied collectively to the subfamily as a whole; an ant-thrush (Formicariidae family); **bush sickness** a disease of cattle, sheep and goats, caused by a mineral deficiency in pastures (*Austr* and *NZ*); **bush tea** tea made from the leaves of various S African shrubs; **bush telegraph** the rapid transmission of news among primitive communities by drum-beating, etc; gossip, rumour (*facetious*); **bush'-tit** a small long-tailed titmouse of W America, which builds a large hanging nest; **bush'veld** or **bosch'veld** (*bos'*) veld made up largely of woodland. — *vi* **bush'walk** to walk or hike through the bush as a leisure activity (*Austr*). — Also *n*. — **bush'walker**; **bush'walking**. — *vi* **bush'whack** (chiefly *NAm*) to range through the bush; to fight in guerrilla warfare; to travel through woods, *esp* by clearing a way to do so; to work in the bush, *esp* as an unskilled labourer felling timber (*Austr* and *NZ*). — *vt* (*NAm*) to ambush. — **bush'whacker** a guerrilla fighter; a backwoodsman, country dweller, often (*derog*) a country bumpkin or lout (*NAm* and *Austr*); a short heavy scythe for cutting bushes; a person who clears a way in the bush; a sniper; **bush'whacking** the habits or practices of bushwhackers; the process of forcing a way for a boat by pulling at the bushes overhanging a stream; **bush'woman** a woman living in the African or Australian bush. — **beat about the bush** prevaricate, to avoid coming to the point; **go bush** (*Austr colloq*) to go off into the bush; to leave town or one's usual haunts; to abandon civilized life. [ME *busk*, *busch*, from ON *buskr*, from a Gmc root found in Ger *Busch*, LL *boscus*, Fr *bois*. Some uses are from the corresponding Du *bosch*]

bush[2] *bŏŏsh*, *n* a cylindrical sleeve which forms a bearing surface or a guide for drilling. — *vt* to provide with a bush. — *n* **bush'ing** a bush; an insulator which enables a live conductor to pass through an earthed wall (*elec eng*). — **bush'-metal** hard brass, gunmetal, a composition of copper and tin, used for journals, bearings, etc. [MDu *busse*, from L *buxis* a box]

bushel[1] *bŏŏsh'əl*, *n* a dry measure of 8 gallons, in UK no longer official, for grain, fruit, etc (**imperial bushel** 2219·36cu in); a container for this quantity; a large amount or number (now *US colloq*). — **hide one's light under a bushel** to keep quiet about or conceal one's talents or abilities. [OFr *boissiel*, from root of **box**[2]]

bushel[2] *bŏŏsh'əl*, (*US*) *vt* and *vi* to mend or alter (eg men's clothes). — *n* **bush'eller**. — *n* **bush'elling**. — **bush'elman** or **bush'elwoman**. [Cf Ger *bosseln*]

bushido *bŏŏ'shi-dō*, *n* a Japanese code of chivalry. [Jap *bushi* warrior, and *dō* doctrine]

business *biz'nis*, *n* employment; a trade, profession or occupation; a task or errand incumbent or undertaken; a matter requiring attention; dealings, commercial activity; a commercial or industrial operation; a commercial or industrial concern; the level of commercial activity; one's concerns or affairs; a matter or affair; a complex, difficult or awkward matter or affair; action as distinguished from dialogue (*theat*); thing, used quite indefinitely, sort of thing (*colloq*); (*biz'i-nis*, also written **busyness**) the state of being busy. — Also *adj* (*biz'nis*). — *adj* **bus'inesslike** methodical, systematic, practical; (of clothing, appearance, etc) severe. — **business card** a card carried by business people, with their name and designation, and the name, address, telephone number and description, etc of their firm; **business cycle** (*NAm*) trade cycle; **business end** (*colloq*) the end or part of something that actually functions or does the work (as *business end of a fork*); **bus'inessman** or *fem* **bus'inesswoman** someone engaged in commercial or industrial business, *esp* as a manager; **business park** an area, landscaped and provided with infrastructure, set aside for business use and intended to attract new industry; **business reply service** a postal service allowing replies to correspondence to be sent at the expense of the business addressee; **business suit** a formal suit appropriate for office wear. — **do one's business** (*euphem*) to defecate; **do the business for** to settle, make an end of; to ruin; **genteel business** (*theat*) such parts as require good dressing; **get down to business** to set to work seriously; **like nobody's business** (*colloq*) keenly, energetically; **make it one's business** to undertake to accomplish something or see it done; **man of business** a law agent who conducts one's affairs; **mean business** to be in earnest; **mind one's own business** to confine oneself to one's own affairs; **place of business** a workplace; **send someone about their business** to dismiss someone unceremoniously; **the business** (*slang*) exactly what is required, the right person, etc for the job. [**busy**]

busk[1] *busk*, *vt* or *vi* to prepare; to dress. [ON *būa* to prepare, and *-sk*, contraction of *sik* oneself]

busk[2] *busk*, *n* a piece of bone, wood or steel in the front of a corset; a corset. — *adj* **busked**. [Fr *busc*]

busk[3] *busk*, *vi* to cruise along a shore, to beat about (*naut*); (with *for* or *after*) to seek; to play an instrument, sing, dance, display paintings, etc in the street or other public place for money. — *n* **busk'er** a street musician, actor or artist. — *n* **busk'ing**. [Prob Sp *buscar* to seek]

busket *busk'ət*, (*Spenser*) *n* a little bush. [See **bush**]

buskin *busk'in*, *n* a high thick-soled boot worn in ancient times by actors in tragedy; a calf- or knee-length boot (*obs*); tragedy as a dramatic genre. — *adj* **busk'ined** wearing buskins; tragic. [Ety uncertain; cf OFr *brousequin*; Du *broosken*; Sp *borceguí*]

busky *busk'i*, (*Shakesp*) *adj*. Same as **bosky**.

buss[1] *bus*, *n* a rude or playful kiss, a smacker. — *vt* to kiss, *esp* in a rude or playful manner. [Cf Ger dialect *buss*, Welsh and Gaelic *bus*, L *bāsium*]

buss[2] *bus*, *n* a small two-masted Dutch vessel, used in the herring and mackerel fisheries. [OFr *busse*, LL *bussa*; cf Ger *Büse*]

buss[3]. See **bus**.

bussu *bŏŏs'ōō*, *n* a tropical American palm (*Manicaria*) with gigantic leaves and netted spathes that serve as cloth. [Port, from Tupí *bussú*]

bust[1] *bust*, *n* a sculpture representing the head and breast of a person; the upper front part of the human body, *esp* a woman's. — *adj* **bust'ed** breasted; adorned with busts. — *adj* **bust'y** (*colloq*) of a woman having a large bust. [Fr *buste* Ital and Sp *busto*]

bust[2] *bust*, (*colloq*) *vt* and *vi* to break, shatter; to make or become bankrupt. — *vi* (*cards*, *darts*) to exceed the required score. — *vt* (*NAm*) to arrest; to raid; to punch; to demote (*military*): — *pa t* and *pa p* **bust'ed** or **bust**. — *n* a drinking bout, a spree; a police raid (*slang*); a sudden collapse of the economy; a bad hand at cards; a punch (*NAm*). — *adj* ruined, penniless. — *n* **bust'er** (*colloq*) something large; a frolic (*old slang*); a roisterer (*old slang*); a horse-breaker; a form of address to a man or boy; a strong south wind (*Austr*); someone or something that destroys or shatters, *esp* as *combining form*, as in *blockbuster*. — *n* (*esp* as *combining form*) **bust'ing**. — **busted flush** see under **flush**[4]; **bust'-up** a quarrel or disruption; a disturbance or brawl. — **bust up** to part after a quarrel or disagreement; to break up (a meeting); **go bust** to become bankrupt; to exceed the required score (*darts*, *cards*). [Orig a colloq form of **burst**]

bustard *bust'ərd*, *n* any bird of the genus *Otis*, *usu* ranked with cranes. [Fr *bistard*, from L *avis tarda* slow bird (a misnomer)]

busted. See under **burst**.

bustee *bus'tē*, *n* in India, a settlement or a collection of huts. [Hindi *bastī*]

bustier *bü-styā*, (*Fr*) *n* a strapless long-line brassière or tight-fitting bodice.

bustle[1] *bus'l*, *vi* to busy oneself noisily or fussily (often with *about*); to be full of or busy with (with *with*). — *n* hurried activity; stir; tumult. — *n* **bust'ler**. [ME *bustelen*, of uncertain ety]

bustle[2] *bus'l*, *n* a frame or pad for causing a skirt to stand out from the hips. [Origin uncertain]

busy *biz'i*, *adj* fully employed; active; diligent; meddling; fussily active; (of a telephone line or room) engaged; (of a picture or design) unrestful because it has too much detail. — *n* (*slang*) a detective. — *vt* to make busy; to occupy: — *pr p* **bus'ying**; *pa t* and *pa p* **bus'ied**. — *adv* **bus'ily**. — *n* **bus'yness** the state of being busy (see **business**). — **bus'ybody** a person who meddles in others' affairs; a mirror at a window arranged to show the street below. — *vi* to behave like a busybody. — **busy Lizzie** a popular fast-growing pot-plant of the *Impatiens* genus, *usu* with pink or white flowers. [OE *bysig*]

but[1] *but*, *prep* except; without (*obs*); in or toward the outer room of (*Scot*). — *conj* on the other hand; in contrast; nevertheless; unless, if not (*archaic*); other than (that); without it being the case that; introducing emphasis, as in *nobody, but nobody, must go*; except that (merging in *prep*); that not (developing into a negative *rel pronoun*); than, sooner than (*archaic*). — *adv* only, merely; however (*dialect*); in or to the outer room, outwards (*Scot*). — *n* an objection; an outer room (*Scot*). — Also *adj*. — *vt* to put forward as an objection. — **anything but** certainly not; **but and** (*obs*) and also; **but and ben** see **ben**[2]; **but for** or **but that** were it not for, or that; **but if** (*obs*) unless. [OE *be-ūtan*, *būtan* without, from *be* by, and *ūtan* out, near and yet outside]

but[2] *but*, *n*. Another spelling of **butt**[2,3,4].

butadiene *bū-tə-dī'ēn*, *n* a hydrocarbon, C_4H_6, used in making synthetic rubber. [*buta*ne, **di-** and chem sfx *-ene*]

butane *bū'tān*, *n* a hydrocarbon of the alkane series, C_4H_{10}, widely used as a fuel (see **bottle-gas**). — *n* **bu'tanol** (*-tə-nol*) the name of two of the isomers of butyl alcohol one of which exists in two enantiomeric forms. [**butyl**]

Butazolidin ® *bū-ta-zol'i-din*, *n* phenylbutazone (qv). — Sometimes shortened to **bute** (*būt*; *slang*; also with *cap*).

butch *bŏŏch*, *n* a very short haircut for men or women; an aggressively tough man (*slang*); the 'male' partner in a homosexual or lesbian relationship (*slang*). — *adj* tough; aggressively masculine. [NAm boy's nickname]

butcher *bŏŏch'ər*, *n* a person whose business is to slaughter animals for food, or who deals in their meat; a person who delights in bloody deeds; a vendor of sweets, newspapers, etc on a railway train (*US*). — *vt* to slaughter and prepare (animals) for sale as food; to put to a bloody death, to kill cruelly; to spoil, botch. — *n* **butch'ering** or **butch'ing** (back-formation) the act of killing for food, or cruelly. — *adj* **butch'erly** butcher-like, cruel, murderous (formerly also *adv*). — *n* **butch'er's** (*orig* **butcher's hook**; *Cockney rhyming slang*) a look. — *n* **butch'ery** great or cruel slaughter; a slaughterhouse. — **butch'er-bird** a shrike; a bird of the genus *Cracticus* (*Austr*); **butcher meat** or **butcher's meat** the flesh of animals slaughtered by butchers, as distinguished from fish, fowls and game; **butch'er's-broom** an evergreen shrub (*Ruscus aculeatus*) of the lily family, with phyllodes, formerly used by butchers for sweeping their blocks. [OFr *bochier*, *bouchier* a person who kills he-goats, from *boc* a he-goat; cf **buck**[2]]

bute or **Bute**. See **Butazolidin**.

Butea *būt'i-ə*, *n* a genus of papilionaceous trees, including the dhak, yielding Bengal kino. [Named after Lord *Bute* (1713–92), prime minister and botanist]

but-end. Same as **butt-end** under **butt**[4].

butene *bū'tēn*, *n* butylene.

butler *but'lər*, *n* a male servant in charge of liquors, plate, etc; an officer in a royal household. — *vi* to act as butler. — Also **butt'le** (back-formation). — *n* **but'lerage** the department of a domestic butler; duty on imported wine once paid to the king's butler (*obs*); the office of king's butler (*obs*). — *n* **but'lership**. — *n* **but'lery** the butler's pantry. — **butler's pantry** the pantry where the plate and glassware are kept. [Norman Fr *butuiller*, from LL *buticulārius*. Cf **bottle**]

butment. Same as **abutment**.

butt[1] *but*, *vt* to strike with the head, as a goat, etc does. — *vi* to strike with the head (also with *at* or *against*); to go or drive head first; to jut out. — *n* a push or blow with the head. — *n* **butt'er** an animal that butts. — **butt in** to interfere, thrust oneself into a conversation, etc. [OFr *boter* to push, strike]

butt[2] *but*, *n* a large cask of varying capacity; a wine butt properly = 126 gallons (*approx* 573 litres), a beer and sherry butt properly = 108 gallons (*approx* 491 litres). [Cf Fr *botte*, Sp *bota*, LL *butta*]

butt[3] *but*, *n* a mark or mound for archery or shooting practice; a mound behind targets; someone who is made an object of ridicule; a hiding place for grouse-shooters. — **butt'-shaft** (*Shakesp*) an arrow. [Fr *but* goal]

butt[4] *but*, *n* the thick and heavy end; the stump; a tree-trunk; the part of a hide from or towards the rear of an animal; thick leather; the fag-end of a cigar or cigarette; the buttocks (*NAm colloq*); the wooden, etc handle or steadying shoulder-part of a pistol or rifle; a remnant; a butt-end. — *vi* to abut; to meet end to end. — **butted joint** a joint formed between the squared ends of the two jointing pieces, which come together but do not overlap; **butt'-end** the square end of a plank meeting another end to end; **butt welding** welding the seam formed by joining two butt-ends. [Ety uncertain; poss connected with **butt**[3] and **abut**]

butt[5] *but*, *n* a flatfish of various kinds. [Poss connected with **butt**[4]; cf Swed *butta* turbot, Du *bot*, Ger *Butt* flounder; cf **halibut**, **turbot**]

butte *būt*, (*NAm*) *n* a conspicuous and isolated hill, cliff-sided, often flat-topped, in the western US and Canada. [Fr]

butter[1] *but'ər*, *n* an edible fatty solid obtained from cream by churning; extended to various substances resembling or containing it; an old chemical name for certain oily chlorides (butter of *antimony*, of *tin*, etc); flattery. — *vt* to spread over with butter, mortar, or other soft substance; to flatter (*usu* with *up*); to fail to catch, drop (*archaic*). — *n* **butt'erine** (*-ēn*) a margarine made partly from milk. — *n* **butt'eriness**. — *adj* **butt'ery** like butter; smeared with butter or the like. — **butt'er-and-eggs** any of various plants with two-toned yellow flowers; **butt'er-bake** (*Scot*) or **butt'er-biscuit** a cake like a biscuit but softer; **butt'er-ball** a single portion of butter rolled into a ball; a bufflehead (*US*); a chubby, roly-poly person (chiefly *US colloq*); **butt'er-bean** any of several varieties of lima bean; **butt'er-bird** in Jamaica, the bobolink; **butt'er-boat** a container for melted butter at table; **butt'er-box** a box for butter; an old nickname for a Dutchman; **butt'erbur** or **butt'erdock** a plant related to coltsfoot with knobbed masses of flower heads and great rhubarb-like leaves; **butt'er-cloth** or **-muslin** a loose-woven cloth formerly used for wrapping butter; **butt'er-cooler** a dish for keeping butter in water at table; **butter cream** butter and sugar beaten together with flavouring and sometimes colouring and used to fill and top cakes, etc; **butt'ercup** a crowfoot (*Ranunculus*), *esp* of one of those species that have golden-yellow cup-shaped flowers; **butt'er-dish** or **-plate** a dish or plate for holding butter at table; **butterdock** see **butterbur** above; **buttered eggs** (*archaic*) scrambled eggs; **butt'er-fat** the fat contained in butter, chiefly glycerides of palmitic and oleic acids. — *adj* **butt'er-fingered** (*colloq*). — **butt'er-fingers** (*sing*; *colloq*) someone who lets a ball, etc they ought to catch slip through their fingers; **butt'er-fish** a name for various slimy fishes, *esp* the gunnel; **butt'erfly** a general name for any of the daylight Lepidoptera, roughly distinguished from moths by their clubbed antennae; a frivolous, flighty person; butterfly stroke (often *abbrev* **fly**); (in *pl*) butterflies in the stomach: — *pl* **butt'erflies**. — *adj* light, flighty, like a butterfly. — **butt'erfly-bow** a bow whose loops and ends are spread like butterfly's wings; **butterfly bush** buddleia; **butterfly clip** or **plaster** a lightweight adhesive plaster, with broadened ends, used in place of a suture to draw together the edges of superficial wounds; **butterfly effect** (*phys*, *meteorol*) the theory that a small variation in calculation at the beginning of a process can lead to a huge variation at a later stage; **butt'erfly-fish** a blenny with an eye-spot on the dorsal fin; any fish of the family Chaetodontidae; **butt'erfly-flower** one adapted for pollination by butterflies; **butterfly kiss** a caress consisting of fluttering the eyelashes against one's partner's skin; **butterfly net** a small-meshed conical net with a wide round open end on a hoop attached to a handle, used for catching butterflies; **butt'erfly-orchis** or **-orchid** any of various orchids with flowers resembling a butterfly; **butterfly plaster** see **butterfly clip**; **butt'erfly-screw** or **-nut** a screw or nut turned by winged finger-grips; **butterfly stroke** (*swimming*) a stroke performed lying on one's front, the arms working simultaneously with an overarm action, and with an undulating movement of both legs together from the hips; **butterfly valve** a disc-shaped valve in a carburettor, etc; a valve consisting of two hinged plates; **butt'erfly-weed** pleurisy-root; **butterhead lettuce** a kind of soft-leaved yellow-hearted lettuce; **butter icing** butter cream; **butt'er-knife** a blunt knife for taking butter from a butter-dish; **butt'er-milk** the liquid that remains after butter has been separated from cream by churning; **butter-muslin** see **butter-cloth** above; **butt'ernut** the oily nut of the N American white walnut; the tree itself; its light-coloured close-grained wood; a brownish-grey; an edible nut of the souari (*Caryocar*) tree of Guiana (also called **souari-nut**); **butter oil** a dairy product consisting almost entirely of milk fat; **butt'er-paper** a translucent greaseproof paper suitable for wrapping butter; **butt'er-pat** a pat of butter; each of a pair of wooden bats for working butter into shape; **butter-plate** see **butter-dish**; **butt'er-print** a mould for shaping butter; a child (*obs slang*); **butt'erscotch** a kind of toffee containing much butter; a flavouring made from or similar to this; **butt'er-tree** any of various trees that yield a buttery substance, *esp* of the genera *Bassia, Butyrospermum, Caryocar, Pentadesma*; **butt'er-wife** or **butt'er-woman** (*obs*) a woman who makes and sells butter; **butt'erwort** any species of Pinguicula, a genus of insectivorous bog-plants, (family *Lentibulariaceae*) with glistening leaves. — *adj* **buttery fingered** butter-fingered. — **buttery fingers** butter fingers. — **butterflies in the stomach** (*colloq*) nervous tremors in the stomach; **butter up** to flatter; **look as if butter wouldn't melt in one's mouth** to look speciously innocent or well-behaved. [OE *butere*; Ger *Butter*; both from L *būtȳrum*, from Gr *boutȳron*, appar from *bous* ox, and *tȳros* cheese]

butter[2]. See under **butt**[1].

butter-bump *but'ər-bump*, *n* the bittern. See **bittern**[1] and **bump**[2].

butterfly, **butterine**, etc. See under **butter**[1].

buttery[1] *but'ər-i*, *n* a storeroom for provisions, *esp* liquors; a room in *esp* an Oxford or Cambridge college where food and drink are supplied to students. — **butt'ery-bar** the ledge for holding tankards in the buttery; **butt'ery-hatch** a half-door over which provisions are handed from the buttery. [Fr *bouteillerie*, literally place for bottles; cf **butler**, **bottle**[2]]

buttery[2]. See under **butter**[1].

buttle. See **butler**.

buttock *but'ək*, *n* either side of the rump or protuberant part at the back of the body above the legs; a cut of meat from the buttock, eg silverside; a throw by use of the buttock (*wrestling*). — *vt* to throw in this way. — **butt'ock-mail** (*Scot*) the fine formerly exacted by the church in commutation of sitting on the stool of repentance; **buttock planes** sectional planes drawn longitudinally through a ship, used in calculating volumes, etc. [Dimin of **butt**[4]]

button *but'n*, *n* a knob or disc, used as a fastening, ornament or badge; a knob, eg that at the end of a foil, that for winding a watch, that to which a violin tailpiece is looped; a bud; the knob which is the beginning of a horn on a stag's head; a projection on the loom of an oar to keep it inside the gate; the head of an unexpanded mushroom (also **button mushroom**); a pimple; the push-button of an electric bell, a vending machine, etc; anything of little value; a person who acts as a decoy or accomplice (*obs slang*); (in *pl*) sheep's dung. — *adj* like a button, used eg of small varieties of vegetables, blooms, etc of a compact, globular shape. — *vt* to fasten by means of buttons; to close up tightly. — *vi* to be capable of being fastened with buttons. — *n sing* **butt'ons** a page in a hotel, etc (also **boy in buttons** (*obs*)). — *adj* **butt'ony** set with buttons; like a button or buttons. — **button accordion** an accordion played by means of buttons. — *adj* **butt'on-back** (of chairs, etc) decorated with buttons pressed into the upholstery at regular intervals on the back and sometimes elsewhere. — **button-ball** see **button-wood**; **butt'on-bush** a N American shrub (*Cephalanthus*) of the madder family, with globular flower-heads; **button cell** or **button cell battery** a small, flat, circular battery, used to power a watch, etc; **button chrysanthemum** a kind of chrysanthemum with small round flowers. — *adj* **butt'oned-up** (*slang*) uncommunicative. — **butt'onhole** the slit through which a button is passed; a flower or flowers for wearing in the buttonhole of a lapel. — *vt* to make buttonholes in; to sew with a stitch suitable to reinforce (*esp* cut) edges (**buttonhole-stitch**); to detain in talk (*orig* **butt'onhold**). — **butt'onholer** a person or sewing-machine attachment that makes buttonholes; **butt'on-hook** a hook for pulling buttons through buttonholes in boots, gloves, etc; **butt'on-mould** the wooden, plastic etc base for leather- or cloth-covered buttons; **button mushroom** see under *n* above; **button quail** any of several ground-living birds of genus *Turnix* inhabiting warm grasslands; **button scurvy** yaws. — *adj* **butt'on-through** (of a woman's dress or skirt) buttoning in front from top to bottom. — **butt'on-wood** a small tropical Atlantic coast evergreen tree (*Conocarpus erecta*) of the myrobalan family; a plane-tree (*US*; also **butt'on-ball**). — **buttoned up** (*slang*) successfully fixed up; safe in hand; ready for action; see also **buttoned-up** above; **button up** or **button your lip** (*colloq*) be quiet; **have all one's buttons (on)** to be all there; **have one's finger on the button** to be poised for action; **in his buttons** a conjectural reading in *Merry Wives* where the quarto has *betmes*, probably a misprint for *talons*; **on the button** (*colloq*) precisely, exactly, punctually; **press the button** to set in motion some momentous action, *esp* the launching of nuclear weapons against an enemy target. [Fr *bouton* any small projection, from *bouter* to push]

buttress *but'rəs*, *n* a projecting support built on to the outside of a wall; any support or prop; something that looks like a buttress, eg a projection from a hill. — *vt* to prop or support with, or as if with, a buttress. — **butt'ress-root** a root, often growing from the trunk, that helps to keep a tree upright; **butt'ress-thread** an asymmetric screw thread with one face at right angles to and the other inclined to the shaft. [OFr *bouterez*, from *bouter* to push, bear against]

butty[1] *but'i*, (*dialect*) *n* a chum, comrade, work-fellow, partner, *esp* in a coalmine (also **butt'yman**); someone who takes a contract for work in a coalmine (*obs*); a barge towed by another. — **butt'y-collier**; **butt'y-gang**. [Appar dimin of dialect *buttar* a companion]

butty[2] *but'i*, (*NEng*) *n* a sandwich, snack. [**butter**[1] and **-y**[2]]

butyl *bū'til*, or *US -təl*, *n* a radical C_4H_9. — *n* **bū'tylene** (also **bū'tene**) an olefine hydrocarbon (C_4H_8) in three isomers. — **butyl alcohol** any of four isomeric alcohols of formula $C_4H_9{\cdot}OH$ used as solvents, etc. [See **butter**[1], and Gr *hȳlē* matter]

butyric *bū-tir'ik*, *adj* pertaining to or derived from butter. — *adj* **butyrā'ceous** buttery, containing butter. — *n* **bū'tyrate** a salt of butyric acid. — **butyric acid** a volatile fatty acid ($C_3H_7{\cdot}COOH$), one isomer of which gives rancid butter its smell. [See **butter**[1]]

buvette *bü-vet*, (*obs Fr*) *n* a small refreshment bar eg at a roadside or in a station.

buxom *buks'əm*, *adj* (of a woman) plump and comely; lively, jolly; yielding, elastic (*obs*). — *n* **bux'omness**. [ME *buhsum* pliable, obedient, from OE *būgan* to bow, yield, and **-some**[1]]

buy *bī*, *vt* to purchase for money; to bribe; to obtain in exchange for something; to redeem (*theol*); to accept, believe (*slang*). — *vi* to be or act as a buyer: — *pr p* **buy'ing**; *pa t* and *pa p* **bought** (*böt*), *archaic pa p* **bought'en**. — *n* something purchased. — *adj* and *n* **buy'able**. — *n* **buy'er** a person who buys; a person employed to buy goods (eg for a store or company) . — **buy'-back** (*commerce*) the optional or obligatory buying back by the seller of all or part of what was sold, eg shares; **buyers'** (or **buyer's**) **market** one in which buyers control the price, because supply exceeds demand; **buy'-in** the purchase of a company by an individual or group from outside the company (see also under **buy in** below). — **a good buy** (*colloq*) a wise purchase, a bargain; **buy and sell** (*Shakesp*) to traffic in; **buy in** to collect a stock (of) by buying; to buy shares; to buy into; to buy back for the owner at an auction when the reserve price is not reached (*n* **buy'-in**); **buy into** to pay for a share or interest in; **buy off** to buy exemption or release for; to get rid of by paying; **buy out** to dispossess or take over possession from by payment (*n* **buy'-out**), *specif* the purchase of a company by its own staff or managers; to buy off; **buy over** to win over by payment; to bribe; **buy up** to purchase the whole available stock of; **have bought it** (*slang*) to have been killed; **I'll buy that** I'll accept that explanation though it seems surprising. [OE *bycgan*, *bohte*, *boht*; Gothic *bugjan*]

buzz[1] *buz*, *vi* to make a noise like that of insects' wings; to murmur; to talk excitedly; to move quickly, bustle (*slang*). — *vt* to utter with a buzzing sound; to whisper or spread secretly; to transmit by Morse over a telephone wire by means of a key; to summon with a buzzer; to make a telephone call to (*colloq*); to throw (*slang*); to fly very low over or very close to; to interfere with in flight by flying very near to (*aeronautics*). — *n* the noise of bees or flies in flight; a humming sound; a voiced hiss; a whispered report; a telephone call (*colloq*); a pleasant or excited feeling, a kick (*colloq*); enthusiasm (*colloq*); a craze, fad (*colloq*). — *n* **buzz'er** an apparatus that makes a buzzing sound; a person who buzzes; a whisperer or tell-tale (*Shakesp*). — *n* and *adj* **buzz'ing**. — *adv* **buzz'ingly**. — *adj* **buzz'y**. — **buzz bomb** a flying bomb; **buzz'-saw** (*NAm*) a circular saw; **buzz'-wig** a great bushy wig; **buzz word** or **buzz'word**, **buzz phrase** or **buzz term** (*colloq*) a well-established term in the jargon of a particular subject, science, etc, its use by other individuals or groups conveying the impression of specialized knowledge and of being very up-to-date. — **buzz off** (*slang*) to go away. [From the sound]

buzz[2] *buz*, *vt* to drain (a bottle) to the last drop of wine. [Origin uncertain]

buzzard[1] *buz'ərd*, *n* a large bird of prey of the genus *Buteo*, despised by falconers; extended to some others, such as the *honey-buzzard*, *turkey-buzzard*; a form of abuse for a person, sometimes *euphem* for **bastard**. [Fr *busard*]

buzzard[2] *buz'ərd*, *n* a blundering insect, such as a cockchafer or night-flying moth. — **buzz'ard-clock** (*dialect*) cockchafer. [**buzz**[1]]

BV *abbrev*: *Beata Virgo* (*L*), Blessed Virgin; *Bene vale* (*L*), farewell; *Besloten Vennootschap* (*Du*), limited company.

BVM *abbrev*: *Beata Virgo Maria* (*L*), Blessed Virgin Mary.

BVM & S *abbrev*: Bachelor of Veterinary Medicine and Surgery.

b/w or **B/W** *abbrev*: black and white.

bwana *bwä'nä*, (*EAfr obs*) *n* master; sir. [Swahili]

bwazi. See **buaze**.

BWB *abbrev*: British Waterways Board.

BWR *abbrev*: boiling-water reactor.

BWV *abbrev*: *Bach Werke Verzeichnis* (*Ger*), catalogue of Bach's works.

by[1] *bī*, *prep* at the side of; near to; along a route passing through, via; past; (in oaths) in the presence of, or with the witness of; through (denoting the agent, cause, means, etc); to the extent of; in quantity measurable in terms of; in accordance with; in respect of; (of time) not after; during (day, night, etc); multiplied into, or combined with another dimension of; in succession to; (of horses, etc) sired by; besides (*Scot*); in comparison with (*Scot*). — *conj* by the time that (*archaic* and *Scot*); than (*Scot*). — *adv* near; aside; away; past; in reserve. — *n* and *adj* see **bye**[1]. — *prefix* **by-** or **bye-** near; aside; past; side, subsidiary; indirect; incidental. — **by-and-by'** (*NAm*) the future, a future occasion. — *adv* see under **by and by** below. — **by'-blow** a side blow; an illegitimate child (*archaic*); **by'catch** immature fish, etc caught along with the desired catch; **by'-corner** an out-of-the-way place; **by'-drinking** (*Shakesp*) drinking between meals; **by'-election** a parliamentary election for a seat during the sitting of parliament; **by'-end** a subsidiary aim; **by'-form** a subsidiary form; a form varying from the usual one; **by'-going** the action of passing by (*esp* in **in the by-going**, in passing). — *adj* **by'gone** (*-gon*) former, past. — *npl* **by'gones** past happenings or grievances; ornaments, household articles, etc of former times which are not fine enough, or not old enough, to be valued as antiques (also in *sing*). — **by'-lane** a side lane or passage out of the common road; **bylaw** and **bye-law** see separate entry; **by'line** a line at the head of a newspaper or magazine article or photograph naming the author or photographer; the touch-line (*football*); **by'-mōtive** an unavowed motive; **by'-name** or **by'name** a nickname; another name by which a person is known. — *adj* **by'-ordinar** (*Scot*) extraordinary. — **by'pass** a road, route or passage for carrying traffic, fluids, electricity, etc round an obstruction, congested place, etc (**cardiopulmonary bypass** a method whereby (in cardiac surgery) circulation and oxygenation of blood is maintained artificially, bypassing the heart and lungs; **coronary bypass** a surgical operation to bypass a blocked coronary artery with a grafted blood vessel from eg the patient's leg). — *vt* to supply with a bypass; to direct (eg fluid) along a bypass; to go round and beyond by a bypass; to ignore, leave out; to evade. — **by'-passage** a side passage. — *adj* **by'-past** (*Shakesp*) past; gone by. — **by'path** a secluded or indirect path; **by'place** a secluded place; **by'-play** action subordinate to and apart from the main action, *esp* in a play; **by'-plot** a subsidiary plot; **by'-product** a product created incidentally in the process of making something else; an unintended side effect; **by'road** a minor or side road; **by'room** (*Shakesp*) a side or private room; **by'-speech** (*obs*) an incidental speech, an aside; **by'stander** someone who stands by or near one; an onlooker; **by'-street** an obscure street; **by'-thing** (*archaic*) a thing of minor importance; **by'-time** (*archaic*) leisure time; **by'way** a side-road, a private, secluded or obscure way; an obscure or minor area of interest; **by'word** a common saying, proverb;

an object of scorn; someone or something noted for a specified characteristic; **by'-work** (*obs*) work done in leisure time. — **by and by** at some future time; before long, presently; in the course of time; in succession, in order of succession (*obs*; *Spenser* **by-and-by'**); **by and large** speaking generally; on the whole; whether close-hauled or before the wind (*naut*); **by oneself** alone; **by the by** (or **bye**) or **by the way** in passing, incidentally; **cardiopulmonary bypass** and **coronary bypass** see **bypass** above; **let bygones be bygones** let past quarrels be ignored; **without (so much as) a by-your-leave** without (even) asking permission. — See also **bye**[1]. [OE *bī, bi, big*; Ger *bei*, L *ambi-*]

by[2]. See **bye**[1].

by-. See under **by**[1].

by-blow, **bycatch**. See under **by**[1].

bycoket *bī'kok-it*, *n* an ornamental cap with peaks at both front and back worn in the 15c. [OFr *bicoquet*, prob *bi-* (L *bis*) double, and *coque* a shell]

by-corner, **by-drinking**. See under **by**[1].

bye[1] or **by** *bī*, *n* anything of minor importance, a side issue, a thing not directly aimed at; (in games) the state of a player or team that has not drawn an opponent, and passes without contest to the next round; (in golf) the holes remaining after the match is decided, played as a subsidiary game (*obs*); (in cricket) a run made from a ball bowled but not struck or touched by the batsman; (in cockfighting) a battle not forming part of a main (*obs*): — *pl* **byes**. — *adj* subsidiary; part; indirect. — See also **by**[1]. [See **by**[1]]

bye[2] *bī* or **bye-bye** *bī-bī'* or *bə-bī'*, *colloq* forms of **goodbye**.

bye-. See under **by**[1].

bye-byes *bī'-bīz*, (*colloq*) *n* (used to children) sleep, *esp* as **go to bye-byes**. [Prob **bye-bye**, perh with influence from **beddy-byes**]

bye-law. See **bylaw**.

by-election. See under **by**[1].

Byelorussian. See **Belorussian**.

by-end . . . to . . . **bygones**. See under **by**[1].

byke. See **bike**[2].

bylander. Same as **bilander**.

by-lane. See under **by**[1].

bylaw or **bye-law** *bī'lö*, *n* a law of a local authority or private corporation; a supplementary law or an inferred regulation. [The same as **byrlaw**, from ON *bȳjar-lög*; Dan *by-lov* town-law; from ON *būa* to dwell. Cf **bower**[1]]

byline. See under **by**[1].

bylive (*Spenser*). Same as **belive**.

by-motive, **by-name**. See under **by**[1].

bynempt. *Obs pa t* of **bename**.

BYO *abbrev*: bring your own, *esp* bring your own alcohol.

BYOB *abbrev*: bring your own bottle, beer or (*colloq*) booze.

by-ordinar . . . to . . . **by-product**. See under **by**[1].

byre *bīr*, (mainly *Scot*) *n* a cowhouse. — **byre'man** or **byre'woman** a farm-servant who looks after cows. [OE *bȳre*]

byrlady *bər-lā'di* and **byrlakin** *bər-lā'kin*, (*archaic*) *interj* short forms of *By Our Lady* or *Ladykin*.

byrlaw *bir'lö*, (*archaic Northern*) *n* local law, surviving longest in rural areas, and dealing with local customs and civil disputes. — Also **bourlaw** (*bōōr'*). — *n* **byr'law-man** (*Scott* **bir'lieman**) an arbiter, oddsman or umpire in such matters. [See **bylaw**]

byrnie *bir'ni*, (*Scot hist*) *n* a mail-coat; a breastplate. [ON *brynja*; OE *byrne*]

byroad. See under **by**[1].

Byronic *bī-ron'ik*, *adj* possessing the characteristics of Lord *Byron* (1788–1824), or of his poetry, overstrained in sentiment or passion, cynical and libertine. — *adv* **Byron'ically**. — *n* **By'ronism**.

byroom, **by-speech**. See under **by**[1].

byssus *bis'əs*, *n* a fine yellowish flax; linen made from it (the 'fine linen' of the Bible); the bundle of filaments by which some shellfish attach themselves. — *adj* **byssā'ceous** composed of a mass of fine threads; delicately filamentous. — *adj* **byss'al** pertaining to a mollusc's byssus. — *adj* **byss'ine** made of fine linen. — *n* **byssinō'sis** a lung disease of textile workers. — *adj* **byss'oid** byssaceous. [L, from Gr *byssos* a fine flaxen substance]

bystander, **by-street**. See under **by**[1].

byte *bīt*, (*comput*) *n* a set of *usu* eight binary digits (bits) considered as a unit; the amount of storage space occupied by such a unit. [Poss from *binary digit eight*, or from **bit**[2] and **bite**]

by-thing, **by-time**. See under **by**[1].

bytownite *bī'town-īt*, (*mineralogy*) *n* a plagioclase intermediate between anorthite and labradorite. [*Bytown*, former name of Ottawa, where it occurs]

byway. See under **by**[1].

bywoner *bī'wōn-ər* or *bī'vōn-ər*, (*SAfr*) *n* an authorized squatter on another's farm; a landless poor white. [Du *bijwonen* to be present]

byword, **by-work**. See under **by**[1].

byzant *biz'ənt* or *biz-ant'*. Same as **bezant**.

Byzantine *biz-an'tīn*, *bīz-an'tīn* or *-tin*, or *biz'ən-*, *adj* relating to *Byzantium* (later Constantinople, now Istanbul), the Byzantine Empire or Church; designating the variety of Greek spoken and written in the Byzantine Empire; rigidly hierarchic; intricate, tortuous. — *n* an inhabitant of Byzantium. — *n* **Byzan'tinism** the manifestation of Byzantine characteristics. — *n* **Byzan'tinist** a person who studies, or is expert in, Byzantine history, affairs, etc. — **Byzantine architecture** the style prevalent in the Eastern Roman Empire down to 1453, marked by the round arch springing from columns or piers, the dome supported upon pendentives, capitals elaborately sculptured, mosaic or other incrustations, etc; **Byzantine Church** the Eastern or Greek Orthodox Church; **Byzantine Empire** the Eastern or Greek Empire from AD 330 to 1453. [Gr *Bȳzantion*]

C

C or **c** *sē*, *n* the third letter in the modern English alphabet, in origin a rounded form of the Greek *gamma*; a written or spoken representation of this; one of the notes of the musical scale, the sound on which the system is founded, being the keynote of the natural scale, C major, which has neither flats nor sharps; a grade rating a student's work as fair or average; the third highest in a category or range; something shaped like the letter C. — **C1** an official term indicating (a member of) the social class or group categorized as supervisory and clerical (*UK*); **C2** an official term indicating (a member of) the social class or group categorized as skilled or manual (*UK*); **C3** in a poor state of physical fitness (see also **A1**); **C'-horizon** (*geol*) the layer of soil beneath the B-horizon (qv) and above the bedrock, consisting mainly of weathered rock; **c-spring** see **cee-spring**.

C or **C.** *abbrev*: Calorie, a kilocalorie; *esp* in place names on maps, Cape; castle (*chess*); Catholic; clubs (*cards*); cocaine (*slang*); Coloured (*SAfr*); Conservative; Corps; Cuba (IVR); the sum of × 100 (*NAm slang*). — **C'-section** (*colloq*) Caesarean section; **C3** (*esp US*; *military*) *abbrev*: communications, command and control (also **C-cubed'**).

C *symbol*: carbon (*chem*); century (preceding numeral, eg C20, twentieth century); common time, four crotchets in a bar (*music*); coulomb(s); (as a Roman numeral) 100.

C *symbol*: compliance (*physics*); electrical capacitance.

C̄ *symbol*: 100 000.

°C *symbol*: degree(s) Celsius; degree(s) Centigrade.

C- (*esp US*) *abbrev*: in designation of military aircraft, cargo transport.

c or **c.** *abbrev*: canine (*dentistry*); *caput* (L), chapter (*pl* **cc**); carat; caught by (*cricket*); cent(s); centi-; centimes; century (following numeral, eg 20c, twentieth century); *circa* (*L*), about; cloudy (*meteorol*); cold (water); college; colt; constant (*math*); contralto; cubic.

c (*math* and *phys*) *symbol*: the speed of light.

¢ *symbol*: cent(s).

© *symbol*: copyright.

c/- (*Austr* & *NZ*) *symbol*: in addresses, care of.

CA *abbrev*: California (US state); Central America; Chartered Accountant (Scotland and Canada); chief accountant; consular agent; Consumers' Association; County Alderman.

Ca (*chem*) *symbol*: calcium.

ca *abbrev*: cases; *circa* (L), about.

c/a (*banking* and *commerce*) *abbrev*: capital account; credit account; current account.

CAA *abbrev*: Civil Aviation Authority.

CAB *abbrev*: Citizens' Advice Bureau; Civil Aeronautics Board (*US*).

ca' or **caa'** *kö*, (*Scot*) *vt* and *vi* to call; to drive, urge on or propel; to knock or push (with *down*, *off*, *over*, etc). — *n* **ca''ing-** or **caa'ing-whale** a pilot whale, often taken by ca'ing or driving ashore. — **ca' canny** to go easy; to proceed warily; deliberately to restrict output or effort. [**call**[1]]

Caaba. See **Kaaba**.

caatinga *kä-ting'gə*, *n* in Brazil, open, comparatively low forest, on white sandy soil derived from granite. [Tupí, white forest]

cab[1] *kab*, *n* a taxi-cab; a compartment for the driver or operator of a lorry, railway locomotive, crane, etc; a light *usu* two-wheeled, horse-drawn carriage for public hire (*hist*). — See also **hansom-cab**. — *n* **cabb'y** or **cabb'ie** a familiar *dimin* of **cab'-driver** a taxi driver, or of **cab'man** a person who drives a horse-drawn cab. — **cab'-rank** or **cab'-stand** a place where cabs stand for hire; **cab'-runner** or **cab'-tout** a person whose business it is to call cabs. [Shortened from **cabriolet**]

cab[2] *kab*, *n* an ancient Hebrew measure of capacity equal to approx 1.6 litres (about three pints). [Heb *qab*]

caba. US form of **cabas**, having **cabas** as *pl*.

cabal *kə-bal'*, *n* a small group or council united for some secret purpose, *esp* political intrigue; a secret plot or intrigue; a name in English history given to the King's inner group of advisors, *esp* five unpopular ministers (1667–73) of Charles II, whose initials happened to make up the word. — *vi* to form such a group or council for a secret purpose; to intrigue: — *pr p* **caball'ing**; *pa t* and *pa p* **caballed'**. — *n* **caball'er**. [Fr *cabale*; from Heb *qabbālāh*; see **cabbala**]

cabala, etc. See **cabbala**.

cabaletta *ka-bə-let'ə*, *n* a simple operatic song or instrumental melody in rondo form, characterized by a continuously repeated rhythm; *esp* in 19c Italian opera, the lively final section of an aria or duet: — *pl* **cabalett'as** or **cabalett'e** (-ə). [Ital, prob from *cobo-letta*, dimin of *cobola* a couplet, stanza, from Old Provençal *cobla*, from L *copula*; perh influenced by Ital *cavallo* horse, from being thought to be rhythmically similar to a horse's canter]

caballero *kab-al-yār'ō*, *n* a Spanish gentleman; *esp* in south-west US, a horseman: — *pl* **caballer'os**. [Sp, from L *caballārius* horseman, from *caballus* horse]

caballine *kab'ə-lin*, *adj* pertaining or suited to a horse. [L *caballīnus*, from *caballus* a horse]

cabana *kə-ban'(y)ə*, (*esp US*) *n* a small tentlike cabin, *esp* used as a changing hut on the beach or by a swimming-pool; a cabin or chalet. [Sp *cabaña*]

cabaret *kab'ə-rā*, *n* an entertainment, at a nightclub or restaurant, made up of performances by singers, dancers, comedians, etc; a nightclub or restaurant where such entertainment is provided (*orig Fr*; now chiefly *US*). [Fr, tavern; prob for *cabaneret*, from *cabane* a hut]

cabas *kab'ä*, *n* a woman's work-basket, shopping bag or handbag. — See also **caba**. [Fr, flat basket]

cabbage[1] *kab'ij*, *n* a vegetable (*Brassica oleracea*) of the Cruciferae family, having several cultivated varieties with large green or dark red leaves forming a central, rounded edible head; the edible leaf bud of certain palms; a brain-damaged or mentally subnormal person (*colloq*); a dull, inactive person (*colloq derog*); bank-notes or paper money (*NAm slang*). — *adj* **cabb'agy**. — **cabbage-butt'erfly** or **cabbage-white'** a large white butterfly (*Pieris*) whose larvae feed on the leaves of cabbage and similar plants; **cabb'age-fly** see **cabbage-root fly** below; **cabb'age-lettuce** a type of lettuce with a cabbage-like head; **cabb'age-moth** a moth (*Mamestra brassicae*) whose larvae feed on cabbage; **cabb'age-palm** any of several palms having leaf buds that are eaten like cabbage, *esp Oreodoxa oleracea* of the W Indies, and including the **cabbage palmetto** (*Sabal palmetto*) of tropical America; **cabb'age-rose** a rose with a rounded, cabbage-like form; **cabb'agetown** (*Can*) a city slum (from an area in Toronto whose inhabitants were believed to exist on a diet of cabbage); **cabb'age-tree** a New Zealand plant (*Cordyline australis*), the largest of the lily family, with bushy heads of grass-shaped leaves; **cabb'age-worm** the larva of the cabbage-butterfly or of the cabbage-moth. — **cabbage-root fly** a fly (*Erioischia brassicae*) whose maggots damage cabbage roots; **cabbage-tree hat** (*Austr*) a broad-brimmed hat made from the leaves of the cabbage-tree. [Fr *caboche* head, poss from L *caput*]

cabbage[2] *kab'ij*, (*archaic slang*) *vt* and *vi* to steal or purloin, *orig* of tailors who took small pieces of a customer's cloth as a perquisite. — *n* cloth so appropriated. [Origin uncertain; perh from MFr *cabas* cheating, theft]

cabbala or **cabala** *kab'ə-lə* or *kə-bä'lə*, *n* a secret mystical tradition of Jewish rabbis, who read hidden meanings into the Old Testament and other texts; any secret, esoteric, occult or mystic doctrine or lore. — Also **kabala**, **kabbala**, **kabbalah** or **qabalah**. — *n* **cabb'alism** or **cab'alism** the science of the cabbala. — *n* **cabb'alist** or **cab'alist** someone versed in the cabbala. — *adj* **cabbalist'ic**, **cabbalist'ical**, **cabalistic** or **cabalist'ical** relating to the cabbala; having a hidden meaning. [Med L, from Heb *qabbālāh* tradition, from *qibbēl* to receive]

cabbie, **cabby**. See **cab**[1].

caber *kāb'ər*, *n* a heavy pole, generally the trimmed trunk of a tree, which is held upright and tossed or hurled by athletes at Highland games. [Gaelic *cabar*]

cabernet *n* a type of black grape used to produce a dry red wine, *orig* grown in Bordeaux and now in many other wine-producing regions in California, Australia, S America, etc. — Also **cabernet sauvignon**. [Fr]

CABG (*surg*) *abbrev*: coronary artery bypass graft.

cabin *kab'in*, *n* a hut or small, simple dwelling-house, often constructed of wood; (in a ship) a room used for living accommodation or as an office; (on a small boat) a compartment used as a shelter by the crew and passengers; (in an airliner) the section of the aircraft for carrying passengers and luggage; a railway signal-box. — *vt* to shut up in a cabin or in a cramped space; to hamper in action (*fig*). — *vi* to live in a cabin. — **cabin altitude** the nominal pressure maintained in the cabin of a pressurized aircraft; **cab'in-boy** a boy who waits on the officers or cabin passengers of a ship; **cabin class** the class of accommodation, *esp* on a passenger ship, between tourist and first class; **cabin crew** the members of an aircraft crew who look after passengers; **cabin cruiser** a power-driven boat with living accommodation on board; **cabin fever** (*Can*) a state of severe depression brought on by living for long periods in isolated places and in cramped conditions, eg in a small cabin during the long winter months; **cabin passenger** formerly, a passenger entitled to superior accommodation; a passenger having cabin accommodation. [Fr *cabane*, from LL *capanna*]

cabinet *kab'(i-)nit*, *n* a cupboard, or piece of furniture, with doors, shelves and drawers, for storing or displaying articles; the outer case housing a radio, television, etc; *orig* a private room, *esp* one in which a sovereign's advisors met for consultation; hence (*usu* with *cap*) the committee made up of a group of senior ministers who together formulate policy in the government of a country; in UK, a meeting of this group of ministers; in US, the president's advisory council, consisting of heads of government departments; the bed or nest of a beast or bird (*Shakesp*). — **Cabinet Council** an earlier name for the Cabinet; **cab'inet-edition** one less in size and price than a library edition, but elegant enough in format to be suitable for display; **cab'inetmaker** a craftsman skilled in making cabinets and other fine furniture; **cab'inetmaking** the occupation or art of the cabinetmaker; the getting together of a new set of cabinet ministers; **cabinet minister** a member of a cabinet; **cab'inet-photograph** one of about 15 by 10cm (6 by 4 inches) in size; **cabinet-pudd'ing** a steamed pudding containing dried fruit; **cab'inetwork** an example of the fine craftsmanship of a cabinetmaker. [Dimin of **cabin**; cf Fr *cabinet*]

Cabiri *ka-bī'rī* (or L *kä-bē'rē*), *npl* a group of ancient deities, protectors of seafarers, whose cult spread from Lemnos, Samothrace and Imbros. — Also **Cabei'ri**. — *adj* **Cabir'ian** or **Cabir'ic**. [Latinized from Gr *Kabeiroi*]

cable *kā'bl*, *n* a strong rope or chain for hauling or tying anything, *esp* a ship's anchor; a cable-laid rope; a cable-length; a cable-stitch, or the pattern formed by a series of these; a line of submarine telegraph wires embedded in gutta-percha and encased in coiled strands of iron wire; a bundle of insulated wires encased in a sheath for transmitting electricity or electrical signals and *usu* laid underground; a cabled message or cablegram; cable television. — Also *adj*. — *vt* and *vi* to provide with or fasten with a cable; to tie up; to telegraph or send by cable; to provide with cable television. — *n* **cablet** (*kā'blət*) a cable or cable-laid rope with a circumference of less than 25cm (10 inches). — *n* **cā'bling** a bead or moulding like a thick rope. — **ca'ble-car** a car suspended from a moving overhead cable, used as a method of transport up mountains, across valleys, etc; a car on a cable-railway; **ca'blegram** a telegram sent by cable. — *adj* **ca'ble-laid** (of a rope) composed of three strands or ropes with a right-handed twist, twisted together in a left-handed direction. — **ca'ble-length** or **ca'ble's-length** a tenth of a nautical mile, *approx* 183 metres (200 yards) or 100 fathoms (in US, approx 219 metres (720 feet) or 120 fathoms); **ca'ble-moulding** a bead or moulding carved in imitation of a thick rope; **cable release** (*image technol*) a device, a length of stiff wire cable in a flexible tube, for releasing a camera shutter; **ca'ble-stitch** (a series of stitches producing) a pattern or design resembling a twisted rope; **cable television** the transmission of television programmes by cable to individual subscribers; **ca'ble-tram'way** or **cable-rail'way** one along which cars or carriages are drawn by a cable operated by a stationary motor; **ca'blevision** cable television; **cā'bleway** a structure for transport of material in cars suspended from a cable. [OFr, from LL *capulum* a halter, from L *capĕre* to hold]

cabob. Same as **kebab**.

caboc *ka'bək*, *n* a double cream cheese rolled in oatmeal. [Ety as for **kebbock**]

caboceer *kab-ō-sēr'*, *n* a W African headman. [Port *cabeceira*, from *cabo*, from L *caput* head]

caboched or **caboshed** *kə-bosht'*, (*heraldry*) *adj* in full face with no neck showing. [Fr *caboché*, from L *caput* head]

cabochon *ka-bō-shɔ̃*, *n* a precious stone polished but uncut, or cut **en** (*ã*) **cabochon**, ie rounded on top and flat on the back, without facets. — Also *adj*. [Fr *caboche*, from L *caput* head]

caboodle *kə-bo͞o'dl*, (*informal*) *n* a crowd or collection. [Origin unknown]

caboose *kə-bo͞os'*, *n* a ship's kitchen; a cooking stove on a ship's deck; a car, *usu* at the rear of a goods or construction train for the train crew or workmen (*NAm*); someone bringing up the rear (*US*); a mobile hut equipped with a stove (*NAm*). [Du *kabuis*; cf Ger *Kabuse*]

caboshed. See **caboched**.

cabotage *kab'o-tij*, *n* the right of control, exercised by a particular country, over air traffic within its own territory; coastal navigation and trading (*naut*). [Fr]

cabré *kä'brā*, *adj* rearing (*heraldry*); (of an aeroplane) flying upturned with tail down. [Fr *cabrer* to caper]

cabretta *kə-bret'ə* *n* a soft leather made from the skins of a hairy S American sheep. [From Sp *cabra* a nanny-goat]

cabrie *kab'rē*, *n* a pronghorn. — Also **cab'rit**. [Sp *cabrito* kid]

cabriole *kab'ri-ōl*, (*ballet*) *n* a leap with one leg outstretched and the other struck against it. — *adj* (of furniture legs) curved, often ending in an ornamental foot like an animal's paw. — *n* **cabriolet** (-*lā'*) a light horse-drawn carriage with two wheels and a folding hood; formerly, a motor car like a coupé, with a folding top; a small 18c armchair of curved design. [Fr, from L *capra* a goat]

cacafogo *kak-ə-fō'gō* or **cacafuego** -*fū'gō* (Sp *kä-kä-fwā'gō*), (*obs*) *n* a spitfire, blusterer: — *pl* **cacafog'os** or

-fueg'os. [Sp and Port *cagar* to void excrement, and Port *fogo*, Sp *fuego* fire]

ca' canny. See under **ca'**.

cacao *kə-kä'ō* or *kə-kā'ō*, *n* the tropical American tree *Theobroma cacao* or its edible seeds from which cocoa and chocolate are made. — **cacao bean** same as **cocoa bean**; **cacao butter** same as **cocoa butter**. [Mex, from Nahuatl *cacahuatl* cacao tree]

cachaemia *ka-kē'mi-ə*, (*archaic*) *n* an abnormal and chronic condition of the blood. — *adj* **cachae'mic**. [Gr *kakos* bad, and *haima* blood]

cacciatore *kach-ə-tö'ri* or **cacciatora** *-tö'rə*, (*cookery*) *adj* of meat, *esp* chicken or veal, cooked with tomatoes, mushrooms, onions and herbs. [Ital, hunter]

cachalot *kash'ə-lot* or *-lō*, *n* the sperm-whale. [Fr]

cache *kash*, *n* a hiding-place for treasure, provisions, ammunition, etc; a collection of stores hidden away; a hoard. — *vt* to hide. — **cache memory** (*comput*) an extremely fast part of the main store; **cachepot** (*kash'pō* or *-pot*) an ornamental container used to hold and conceal a flowerpot; **cache-sexe** (*kash-seks'*) a piece of fabric, etc covering only the genitals. [Fr *cacher* to hide]

cachet *kash'ā*, *n* a private seal, *esp* affixed to a letter or document; any distinctive stamp or distinguishing characteristic (*fig*), *esp* something showing or conferring prestige; a thin wafer-like case enclosing an unpleasant-tasting medicine; a design or mark stamped on mail to commemorate an event, or for advertising purposes. [MFr, from *cacher* to press]

cachexy *ka-kek'si* or **cachexia** *ka-kek'si-ə*, (*med*) *n* a condition of profound physical weakness and wasting of the body associated with severe starvation or chronic disease, eg tuberculosis or cancer. — *adj* **cachec'tic** or **cachec'tical**. [L, from Gr *kachexiā*, from *kakos* bad and *hexis* condition, from the root of *echein* to have]

cachinnate *kak'in-āt*, (*formal*; *esp literary*) *vi* to laugh loudly. — *n* **cachinnā'tion**. — *adj* **cachinn'atory** (or *kak'*). [L *cachinnāre* to laugh loudly]

cacholong *kach'o-long*, *n* a variety of quartz or of opal, generally of a milky colour. [Fr, from Kalmuck]

cacholot. Same as **cachalot**.

cachou *ka-shōō'*, *n* a pill or lozenge, used to sweeten the breath; a variant of **catechu**. [Fr]

cachucha *kə-chōō'chə*, *n* a lively Spanish solo dance in 3–4 time, with a rhythm like the bolero; music for this dance. [Sp]

cacique *ka-sēk'*, *n* a W Indian or American Indian chief; in Spain or Latin America, a local political boss. — Also **cazique'**. — *n* **caciqu'ism** *esp* in W Indies and Latin America, government by a cacique. [Haitian]

cack-handed *kak'-hand'id*, (*colloq*) *adj* left-handed; clumsy. — Also **kack'-hand'ed**. — *n* **cack'-hand'edness**. [Dialect *cack* excrement, from L *cacāre* to defecate]

cackle *kak'l*, *n* a loud, squawking or clucking sound made by a hen or goose; noisy or raucous talk or laughter. — *vi* to make such a sound; to chatter or laugh noisily or raucously. — *vt* to utter in a cackling manner. — *n* **cack'ler**. — **cut the cackle** (*colloq*) to stop the aimless chattering (and come to the point). [ME *cakelen*; cognate with MDu *kākelen*]

caco- *kak-ō-* or sometimes *kak-o'-*, *combining form* denoting bad or incorrect. [Gr *kakos* bad].

cacodemon or **cacodemon** *kak-ō-dē'mən*, *n* an evil spirit or devil; a nightmare (*Shakesp*). [Gr *kakos* bad, and *daimōn* spirit]

cacodoxy *kak'ō-dok-si*, *n* a bad doctrine or wrong opinion. [Gr *kakos* bad, and *doxa* an opinion]

cacodyl *kak'ō-dil*, *n* a colourless, poisonous, foul-smelling liquid, composed of arsenic, carbon and hydrogen. — *adj* **cacodyl'ic**. [Gr *kakōdēs* stinking, and *hȳlē* matter]

cacoepy *kak-ō'ə-pi*, *n* bad or wrong pronunciation. [Gr *kakos* bad, and *epos* word]

cacoethes *kak-ō-ē'thēz*, *n* a bad habit or itch; an uncontrollable urge or desire; an itch or intense longing. — **cacoethes loquendi** (*kak-ō-ē'thēz* or *ka-kō-āth'ās lō-kwen'dī* or *lo-kwen'dē*) (*L*) a mania for talking, *esp* for giving speeches, literally an itch for speaking; **cacoethes scribendi** (*skrī-ben'dī* or *skrē-ben'dē*) a mania for writing or getting things into print, literally an itch for writing. [Gr *kakoēthēs*, *-es* ill-disposed, from *kakos* bad, and *ēthos* habit]

cacogastric *kak-ō-gas'trik*, *adj* of or pertaining to an upset stomach; dyspeptic. [Gr *kakos* bad, and *gastēr* the belly]

cacogenics *kak-ō-jen'iks*, *n sing* dysgenics. [Gr *kakos* bad, and *genos* race]

cacography *kak-og'rə-fi*, *n* bad handwriting or spelling. — *n* **cacog'rapher**. — *adj* **cacographic** (*-ō-graf'ik*) or **cacograph'ical**. [Gr *kakos* bad, and *graphē* writing]

cacolet *kak'ō-lā*, *n* a double pannier; a military mule litter. [Fr, prob from Basque]

cacology *ka-kol'ə-ji*, *n* a bad choice of words or faulty pronunciation. [Gr *kakos* bad, and *logos* speech]

cacomistle or **cacomixl** *ka'kə-mi(k)s-əl*, *n* a small carnivorous mammal (*Bassariscus*) related to the raccoon and found in south-west US and Central America. — Also **ringtail** or **ringtailed cat**. [Mex Sp, from Nahuatl *tlaco* half, and *miztli* cougar]

cacoon *ka-kōōn'*, *n* the large seed of a tropical climber (*Entada scandens*) of the mimosa family, used for making scent-bottles, snuff-boxes, etc; the purgative and emetic seed of a tropical American climber (*Fevillea cordifolia*) of the gourd family. [Origin uncertain]

cacophony *ka-kof'ə-ni*, *n* a harsh or disagreeable sound; a discordant mixture of sounds; dissonance. — *adj* **cacoph'onous**, **cacophonic** (*-ō-fon'ik*), **cacophon'ical** or **cacophonious** (*-fō'ni-əs*) harsh-sounding. [Gr *kakos* bad, and *phōnē* sound]

cacotopia *kak-ō-tō'pi-ə*, *n* a state, imaginary or otherwise, in which everything is as bad as it can possibly be (*opp* of *Utopia*). — *adj* **cacotō'pian**. [Gr *kakos* bad, and *topos* a place]

cacotrophy *ka-kot'rə-fi*, *n* bad or inadequate diet. [Gr *kakos* bad, and *trophē* nourishment]

cactus *kak'tus* or *-təs*, *n* a general name for any plant of the family **Cactā'ceae** (now divided into several genera) of desert regions of America, having thick fleshy stems that store water, and leaves reduced to spines or scales; (also **cactus dahlia**) a variety of double-flowered dahlia with grill-like petals: — *pl* **cac'tī** or **cac'tuses**. — *adj* **cactā'ceous**. — *adj* **cac'tiform**. [L, from Gr *kaktos* cardoon, a prickly plant of S Europe]

cacuminal *ka-kū'min-əl*, (*phonetics*) *adj* produced by turning the tip of the tongue up and back towards the hard palate; retroflex. — *n* a cacuminal sound. [L *cacūmen*, *-inis* top, point, tip]

CAD or **Cad** (often *kad*) *abbrev*: computer-aided design (or draughting); compact audio disc.

cad *kad*, *n* an inferior assistant (*obs*); a person who runs errands (*obs*); a man who lacks the instincts of a gentleman or who behaves dishonourably (*old-fashioned* or *facetious*). — *adj* **cadd'ish**. — *n* **cadd'-ishness**. [Shortened from **cadet**; see also ety at **caddie**]

cadastral *ka-das'trəl*, *adj* of, or as recorded in, a **cadastre** (*ka-das'tər*), the official public register of the ownership, boundaries and value of landed property of a country for taxation purposes; applied also to a survey on a large scale. [Fr, from Ital *catastro*, from late Gr *katastikhon* a register]

cadaver *kə-dav'ər*, (*surg* and *anatom*) *n* a human corpse, *esp* one used for organ transplant or dissection. — *adj* **cadav'eric**. — *adj* **cadav'erous** (*-rəs*) corpselike; sickly-looking; gaunt or haggard. — *n* **cadav'erousness**. [L *cadāver* a dead body, from *cadere* to fall (dead)]

CADCAM *kad'kam*, *abbrev*: computer-aided design and (computer-aided) manufacture.

caddice. See **caddis**[1].

caddie or **caddy** *kad'i*, *n* someone who assists a golfer at play, carrying the clubs; an 18c messenger or errand porter in some large Scottish towns (also **cad'ie** or **cad'ee**). — *vi* to act as a caddie; to carry clubs. — **caddie car** or **caddy car** a light, two-wheeled trolley for carrying a bag of golf clubs round the course. — Also **caddie** (or **caddy**) **cart**. [Ety as for **cadet**, through Scots use]

caddis[1] or **caddice** *kad'is*, *n* worsted ribbon or braid. — Also (*Shakesp*) **cadd'yss**. [OFr *cadaz*, *cadas* tow]

caddis[2] *kad'is*, *n* the larva of the caddis-fly, which lives in water in a **cadd'is-case**, a silken sheath covered with fragments of wood, stone, shell, leaves, etc, open at both ends. — Also **cadd'is-worm**. — **cadd'is-fly** any small mothlike insect of the order Trichoptera that lives near, and lays its eggs in, water. [Origin obscure]

caddy[1] *kad'i*, *n* a small box for holding tea; any storage container (*US*). [Malay *kati*, the weight of a small packet of tea]

caddy[2]. See **caddie**.

caddyss. See **caddis**[1].

cade *kād*, *n* a lamb or colt left by its mother and brought up by hand, a pet lamb. — Also *adj*. [Ety unknown]

-cade *-kād*, *combining form* denoting a procession or show, as in *motorcade*. [See **cavalcade**]

cadeau *ka-dō*, (*Fr*) *n* a gift or present: — *pl* **cadeaux** (*-ō*).

cadee. See **caddie**.

cadelle *n* a small black beetle (*Tenebroides mauritanicus*) found worldwide, that lives on stored food, eg grain. [Fr, from Provençal *cadello*, from L *catellus* little dog]

cadence *kā'dəns*, *n* the fall in pitch of the voice, as at the end of a sentence; rise and fall of sound, modulation or intonation; rhythm; a succession of chords closing a musical phrase or at the end of a complete melody (*music*; see **imperfect**, **perfect**, **plagal**, **cadence**); falling, sinking (*Milton*). — *adj* **cā'denced** rhythmical. — *n* **cā'dency** rhythm; the relative status of the branch of a family descended from a younger son (*heraldry*). — *adj* **cā'dent** (*Shakesp*) falling. — *adj* **cadential** (*kə-den'shəl*). [Fr, from L *cadere* to fall]

cadential. See **cadence** and **cadenza**.

cadenza *kä-dent'sa* or *kə-den'zə*, (*music*) *n* an outstanding virtuoso passage or flourish, sometimes improvised, given by a solo instrument or voice towards the end, or at some important stage, of a movement, concerto or aria. — *adj* **cadential** (*kə-den'shəl*). [Ital *cadenza*, from L *cadere* to fall]

cadet *kə-* or *ka-det'*, *n* a person undergoing training for the armed forces or the police; in New Zealand, an apprentice or trainee gaining experience in sheep-farming; a younger son or a member of a **cadet branch** of a family, descended from a younger son. — *n* **cadet'ship**. — **cadet corps** an organized body undergoing basic military training, *esp* schoolboys. [Historically, a younger son or brother sent away to be trained for a commission in the army, from Fr *cadet*, from Gascon dialect *capdet*, from dimin of L *caput* the head]

cadge[1] *kaj*, *vt* and *vi* to sponge (money, etc); to beg or go about begging. — *n* **cadg'er** a sponger; *orig* a dealer who travelled around remote country areas, buying and selling farm produce; a hawker or pedlar. [Prob connected with **catch**]

cadge[2] *kaj*, (*falconry*) *n* a padded wooden frame on which a number of hawks may be carried. [Prob **cage**; perh **cadge**[1]]

cadgy *kaj'i*, (*NE Scot dialect*) *adj* cheerful, friendly and hospitable; wanton. — Also **kidg'ie**. [Cf Dan *kaad* wanton, from ON *kātr* merry]

cadi or **kadi** *kä'di* or *kā'di*, *n* a magistrate in Muslim countries. [Ar *qādī* a judge]

cadie. See **caddie**.

CADMAT *kad'mat*, *abbrev*: computer-aided design, manufacture and test(ing).

Cadmean *kad-mē'ən*, *adj* relating to *Cadmus* (Gr *Kadmos*), who, according to legend, introduced the **Cadmean letters**, sixteen simple letters that formed the original Greek alphabet. — **Cadmean victory** one very costly to both sides. [From *Cadmus*, in Gr mythology, who sowed a dragon's teeth from which sprang an army of soldiers who fought amongst themselves until only five were left]

cadmium *kad'mi-əm*, *n* an element (atomic no 48; symbol **Cd**), a bluish-white metal, occurring in zinc ores, used in alloys, magnets, metal-plating and as a control in nuclear reactors. — **cadmium yellow** a vivid orange or yellow pigment of cadmium sulphide used in paints, etc. [Gr *kadmiā*, *kadmeiā* (*gē*) Cadmean (earth), calamine]

cadrans *kad'rənz*, *n* an instrument by which a gem is adjusted while being cut. [Fr *cadran* a quadrant, dialect]

cadre *kad'r'*, *käd'ri* or *kad'ər*, also *käd'*, *n* a basic structure, *esp* the nucleus of a military unit, the commissioned and non-commissioned officers, etc, around whom the rank and file may be quickly grouped; any nucleus of key personnel; (*prob* from *Fr* through *Russ*) a group of activists in a revolutionary, *orig* Communist, party; a member of such a group. [Fr, from L *quadrum* square]

caduac *kad'ū-ak*, (*obs*) *n* a casualty or windfall. [Scot, from L *cadūcum*]

caduceus *ka-dū'si-us*, (*Gr* and *Roman mythol*) *n* the rod of Hermes (Mercury), messenger of the gods, generally represented as a wand surmounted with two wings and entwined by two serpents; a symbol resembling this rod, used as an emblem by the medical profession: — *pl* **cadū'ceī**. — *adj* **cadū'cean**. [L, from Gr *kārȳkeion* a herald's wand, from *kēryx*, *-ykos* a herald]

caducibranchiate *ka-dū-si-brang'ki-āt*, (*biol*) *adj* (of amphibians) losing the gills on attaining maturity. [L *cadūcus* caducous, and *branchiae* gills]

caducous *ka-dū'kəs*, (*biol*) *adj* (of parts of a plant or animal) shed or falling at an early stage; easily detached. — *n* **caducity** (*ka-dū'si-ti*) the quality of being perishable or transitory; senility. [L *cadūcus*, from *cadere* to fall]

CAE *abbrev*: College of Advanced Education (*Austr*); computer-aided engineering (also **Cae**).

caecilian *sē-sil'i-ən*, *n* any wormlike, burrowing amphibian of the order Apoda (or Gymnophiona), having sightless eyes, and living in moist earth in tropical regions. [L *caecus* blind]

caecum or (*NAm*) **cecum** *sē'kəm*, (*biol*; *anatom*) *n* (in plants and animals) any structure or protusion that ends in a sac or pouch; *specif* a blind-ending sac between the large and small intestines in an animal: — *pl* **cae'ca**. — *adj* **cae'cal**. — *n* **caecitis** or (*NAm*) **cecitis** (*sē-sī'tis*) inflammation of the caecum. [L, neuter of *caecus* blind]

caeono- *sē-nō-* or **caino-** *kī-nō-*, *combining form* denoting recent. — *n* **caenogen'esis** (*zool*) a phenomenon whereby features that are adaptations to the needs of the young stages develop early, and disappear in the adult stage.

Caenozoic *sē-nō-zō'ik*. Same as **Cainozoic**.

caen-stone *kā'ən-stōn*, *n* a cream-coloured limestone from Caen (*kâ*) in France.

Caerns. *abbrev*: Caernarvonshire (formerly a county in Wales).

Caerphilly *kär-fil'i*, *n* a mild white cheese, *orig* made in *Caerphilly*, a town in S Wales.

caerule, **caerulean**. See **cerulean**.

caesalpiniaceous *ses-* or *sēz-al-pi-ni-ā'shəs*, *adj* of, or belonging to, the **Caesalpiniā'ceae**, a family of tropical leguminous plants, including brazil-wood, cassia and dividivi. [Named after Andrea *Cesalpino* (1519–1603), Ital botanist]

Caesar *sē'zər*, *n* an absolute monarch, an autocrat, from the Roman dictator Gaius Julius *Caesar* (100–44 BC); (also without *cap*) a Caesarean section (*colloq*). — *adj* **Caesarean** or **Caesarian** (*-ā'ri-ən*) relating to Julius Caesar; relating to (a) birth carried out by Caesarean section. — *n* a Caesarian section; an adherent of Caesar, an imperialist. — *n* **Cae'sarism**. — *n* **Cae'sarist**. — *n* **Cae'sarship**. — **caesaropapism** (also with *cap*; LL *pāpa* pope; *sē-zə-rō-pā'pizm*) control of the church by a secular ruler or by the state. — **Caesarean section** or **operation** delivery of a child by cutting through the walls of the abdomen. [Perh from L *caedere* to cut, from the tradition that the first bearer of the cognomen *Caesar* was delivered in this way]

caese. See **sessa**.

caesious *sēz'i-əs, adj* bluish or greyish green. [L *caesius* bluish grey]

caesium or (*NAm*) **cesium** *sēz'i-əm, n* an element (atomic no 55; symbol **Cs**), a silver-white, soft, alkaline metal; used in the form of compounds or alloys in photo-electric cells, etc. — **caesium clock** an atomic clock regulated by the natural resonance frequency of excited caesium atoms. [Ety as for **caesious**]

caespitose or (*NAm*) **cespitose** *sēs'pi-tōs,* (*bot*) *adj* tufted, growing in tufts; turf-like. [L *caespes, -itis* turf]

caestus. Variant of **cestus**[2], or, less often, **cestus**[1].

caesura or (*NAm*) **cesura**, *si-zū'rə,* (*prosody*) *n* division of a metrical foot between two words; a pause or natural breathing space occurring anywhere in a line of verse (*usu* near the middle): — *pl* **caesu'ras** or **caesu'rae**. — *adj* **caesū'ral** or (*NAm*) **cesū'ral**. [L *caesūra*, from *caedere, caesum* to cut off]

CAF (*US*) *abbrev*: cost and freight.

cafard *ka-fär',* *n* depression, the blues. [Fr, literally, a cockroach, hypocrite]

cafe or **café** *kaf'ā* or *ka'fi, n* a coffee-house or a small, inexpensive restaurant. — **café au lait** (*ō lē*) coffee made with milk; the light brown colour of this; **café-chantant** or **café-concert** a cafe providing musical entertainment; **café filtre** strong black filtered coffee; **café noir** black coffee (ie without milk); **café society** fashionable society. [Fr *café* coffee-house)]

cafeteria *ka-fi-tē'ri-ə, n* a restaurant where customers serve themselves, or are served from, and *usu* pay at, a counter before sitting down to eat. [Cuban Sp, a tent in which coffee is sold]

caff. Slang term for **café** or **cafeteria**.

caffeine or **caffein** *kaf'ēn* or *kaf-ē'in, n* an alkaloid that occurs naturally in coffee, tea, cocoa, and cola nuts, acting as a mild stimulant to the nervous system. — *adj* **caff'einated** containing caffeine (cf **decaffeinated**). — *n* **caff'einism** or **caffeism** an unhealthy condition caused by taking excessive amounts of caffeine; an addiction to caffeine. [Fr *caféine*; see **coffee**]

Caffre. See **Kaffir, Kafir**.

cafila, caffila or **kafila** *ka'fēl-a, kä', -fil-* or *-ä, n* a caravan, caravan train. [Ar *qāfilah*]

CAFOD *käf'od, abbrev*: Catholic Fund for Overseas Development.

caftan *kaf'tən* or *kaf-tan', n* a long-sleeved Persian or Turkish garment, reaching to the ankles and often tied with a sash; any loose shirt or dress with wide sleeves made in imitation of this. — Also **kaftan**. [Turk *qaftān*]

cage *kāj, n* a compartment or enclosure, *usu* made from bars and wires, for confining captive animals and birds; a prison; a frame with a platform or platforms used in hoisting in a vertical shaft, eg in a mine or lift; a framework that encloses, protects or supports; any structure resembling a cage in function; a structure of steel supports and netting to protect garden fruit and vegetables from birds; a squirrel's nest (*dialect*); a goal, consisting of a frame with a net attached, as in ice hockey; in baseball, a protective screen used in batting practice (*US informal*). — *vt* to imprison in a cage: — *pr p* **cag'ing**; *pa t* and *pa p* **caged**. — *adj* **caged** confined. — *n* **cage'ling** a bird that is or has been kept in a cage. — **cage'bird** a bird of a kind habitually kept in a cage; **cage'-cup** a kind of glass bowl of late Roman times, with a filigree-type glass decoration attached to the bowl by tiny struts (also **diatrē'tum**); **cage'work** open-work like the bars of a cage. — **cage in** (*usu fig*) to imprison; **rattle someone's** (or **the**) **cage** (*colloq*) to stir (someone) up, provoke (someone's) anger or irritation. [Fr, from L *cavea* a hollow place]

cagey or **cagy** *kāj'i,* (*colloq*) *adj* not frank, secretive; artfully shy, wary, chary. — *adv* **cag'ily**. — *n* **cag'iness**, **cag'yness** or **cag'eyness**. [Origin unknown]

cagot *käg'ō, n* one of an outcast class found scattered in the western Pyrenees, supposed to be the descendants of lepers. [Fr; origin unknown]

cagoul, **cagoule** or **kagoule** *kə-go͞ol', n* a lightweight, weatherproof anorak, often knee-length. [Fr *cagoule* a monk's hood]

cagy. See **cagey**.

cahier *ka-yā,* (*Fr*) *n* a notebook; a report, *esp* of the proceedings of a meeting; in bookbinding, a section ready for binding.

cahoots *kə-ho͞ots, n pl esp* in the phrase **in cahoots** (*colloq*) in collusion (with). [Ety uncertain]

CAI *abbrev*: computer-aided (or -assisted) instruction.

caille *ka'y,* (*Fr cookery*) *n* quail.

cailleach *kal'yəhh,* (*Scot*) *n* an old woman. — Also **caill'ach** or **caill'iach**. [Gaelic *cailleach*]

caimac or **caimacam**. Same as **kaimakam**.

caiman. See **cayman**.

Cain *kān, n* in the Bible, Adam's son, murderer of Abel (Gen 4), hence (allusively) a murderer. — *n* **Cain'ite** a descendant of Cain; a member of a 2c sect of Gnostics who revered Cain and Judas. — *adj* **Cain'-coloured** (*Shakesp*) of the traditional colour of Cain's beard and hair, red. — **raise Cain** to make a determined or angry fuss.

cain or **kain** *kān,* (*hist*) *n* in Scotland and Ireland, rent paid in kind, *esp* in produce from a tenanted farm; tribute. — **pay (the) cain** to pay the penalty. [Sc and Ir Gaelic *càin* rent, tax]

ca'ing-whale. See **ca'**.

cainogenesis. See **caenogensis**.

Cainozoic *kī-nō-zō'ik,* (*geol*) *adj* and *n* Tertiary. [Gr *kainos* new, and *zōē* life]

caique or **caïque** *kä-ēk', n* a light narrow boat as used on the Bosporus; the skiff of a galley. [Fr, from Turk *kaik* a boat]

caird *kārd,* (*Scot*) *n* an itinerant tramping tinker, a gypsy, a vagrant. [Sc and Ir Gaelic *ceard*]

Cairene *kī'rēn* or *kī-rēn', adj* relating to Cairo. — *n* a native or citizen of Cairo.

cairn *kārn, n* a heap of stones, *esp* one raised over a grave, or as a landmark on a mountain-top or path; a small variety of Scottish terrier (in full **cairn terrier**) *orig* bred for driving foxes from their earths among cairns. — *adj* **cairned** marked with cairns. — *n* **cairngorm'** or **cairngorm'-stone** a semi-precious stone, a brown or yellow quartz found in the Cairngorm Mountains in Scotland. [Gaelic *càrn*]

caisson *kā'sən* or *kə-so͞on', n* a tumbril or ammunition wagon; a strong case for keeping out the water while the foundations of a bridge are being built; an apparatus for lifting a vessel out of the water for repairs or inspection; the pontoon or floating gate used to close a dry-dock. — **caisson disease** see **decompression sickness** under **decompress**. [Fr, from *caisse* a case or chest. See **case**[1]]

caitiff *kā'tif, n* a mean despicable fellow. — *adj* mean, base. — *n* **cai'tive** (*Spenser*) captive, subject. [OFr *caitif* (Fr *chétif*), from L *captīvus* a captive, from *capere* to take]

cajeput. See **cajuput**.

cajole *kə-jōl', vt* to coax (into); to cheat by flattery (into or out of). — *n* **cajole'ment** coaxing in order to delude; wheedling, flattery. — *n* **cajol'er**. — *n* **cajol'ery**. [Fr *cajoler* to chatter; ety doubtful]

Cajun *kā'jən, n* a descendant of the French-speaking Acadians deported to Louisiana in 1755; the language of the Cajuns. — *adj* (sometimes without *cap*) of or pertaining to Cajun or the Cajuns; belonging to or characteristic of Cajun traditions (*esp* in reference to their lively syncopated music or spicy cookery). [Corruption of **Acadian**]

cajuput *kaj'ə-put, n* a pungent, volatile aromatic oil, distilled from leaves of an Indo-Malayan and Australian myrtaceous tree (*Melaleuca leucodendron*) used in the treatment of skin disorders. — Also **caj'eput**. [Malay]

cake *kāk*, *n* a breadlike composition enriched with additions such as sugar, eggs, spices, currants, peel, etc; a separately made mass of such composition; a piece of dough that is baked; a small loaf of fine bread; any flattened mass baked, as *oatcake*, or formed by pressure or drying, as of soap, clay, snow, blood; cattle cake; a madcap or fool (*archaic slang*). — *vt* and *vi* to form into a cake or hard mass. — *n* and *adj* **cāk'ing**. — *adj* **cāk'y** or **cak'ey**. — **cake hole** (*slang*) mouth; **cake'walk** a dance developed from a prancing movement once performed by Black Americans in competition for a cake; something accomplished with supreme ease. — *vi* to perform a cakewalk or execute similar movements. — **caking coal** a bituminous coal that fuses into a mass in burning. — **a piece of cake** (*colloq*) something very easy to do; **cakes and ale** *vaguely* all the good things of life; **go** or **sell like hot cakes** see **hot**[1]; **have one's cake and eat it** or **eat one's cake and have it** to have the advantage of both alternatives; **take the cake** (*slang*) to carry off the honours; to be the ultimate in idiocy or intolerable behaviour (*ironic*); to top it all. [ON *kaka*]

CAL (often *kal*), *abbrev*: computer-aided (or -assisted) learning.

Cal. *abbrev*: (great or large) calorie, kilocalorie; California (US state).

cal. *abbrev*: calendar; calibre; (small or gram-)calorie.

Calabar-bean *kal-ə-bär'-bēn*, or *kal'-*, *n* the dark-brown extremely poisonous seed of the tropical African climbing plant (*Physostigma venenosum*), a source of the drug, physostigmine, used to treat glaucoma.

calabash *kal'ə-bash*, *n* a gourd, or its shell used as a vessel, tobacco-pipe, etc; the fruit of the calabash tree or its shell similarly used. — **calabash nutmeg** the fruit of a tropical anonaceous tree (*Monodora myristica*) whose seeds are used as nutmegs; **calabash tree** a tropical American tree (*Crescentia cujete*) with large melonlike fruit. [Fr *calebasse*, from Sp *calabaza*, from Pers *kharbuz* melon]

calaboose *kal'ə-bo͞os* or *-bo͞os'*, (*US slang*) *n* a prison. [Sp *calabozo*]

calabrese *kal-ə-brā'zā* or *kal-ə-bree'zi*, *n* a variety of green sprouting broccoli. [Ital Calabrian]

caladium *kal-ā'di-əm*, *n* any tropical plant of the genus *Caladium*, of the arum family, the plants of which are grown for their attractive foliage. [Latinized from Malay *kélādy*, a related plant]

calamanco *kal-ə-mangk'ō*, *n* a satin-twilled woollen fabric, with a chequered or brocaded design woven into the warp; a garment made of this: — *pl* **calamanc'os** or **calamanc'oes**. [Du *kalamink*, Ger *Kalmank*, Fr *calmande*; origin unknown]

calamander *kal-ə-man'dər*, *n* a hard valuable wood of the ebony genus, brownish with black stripes, used in making furniture and imported from India and Sri Lanka. [Prob Sinh]

calamari *kä-lä-mär'ē* or *kal-ə-mär'ē*, (*Mediterranean cookery*) *n pl* squid. [Ital, pl of *calamaro*, squid; see ety for **calamary**]

calamary *kal'ə-mər-i*, *n* any of various species of squid. [L *calamārius*, from *calamus*, from Gr *kalamos* pen, from the shape of their internal shell]

calamine *kal'ə-mīn*, *-min*, *n* zinc carbonate (smithsonite); in US, a major ore of zinc (hemimorphite). — **calamine lotion, ointment** or **powder** a soothing lotion, ointment or powder for the skin, containing zinc carbonate mixed with ferric oxide. [Fr, from LL *calamīna*, prob from L *cadmia*; see **cadmium**]

calamint *kal'ə-mint*, *n* a genus (*Calamintha*) of labiate aromatic plants allied to mint and thyme. [Fr, from Gr *kalaminthē*]

calamite *kal'ə-mīt*, *n* a general name for an extinct family of treelike plants from Carboniferous times, thought to be related to horsetails. [L *calamus* a reed]

calamity *kə-lam'i-ti*, *n* a great misfortune; a disaster, *esp* a sudden one; affliction. — *adj* **calam'itous** disastrous, tragic or dreadful. — *adv* **calam'itously**. — *n* **calam'itousness**. [Fr *calamité*, from L *calamitās*, *-ātis*]

calamus *kal'ə-məs*, *n* (with *cap*) a genus of palms whose stems make canes or rattans; the hollow shaft at the base of a bird's feather, a quill (*zool*); the reed pen used in ancient times; the traditional name of the sweet-flag or its aromatic root: — *pl* **cal'amī**. [L, from Gr *kalamos* reed, cane, pen]

calando *kä-län'dō*, (*music*) *adj* and *adv* gradually slowing with diminishing volume. [Ital, lowering, letting down]

calandria *kal-an'dri-ə*, *n* a sealed vessel through which tubes pass, used in the core of certain types of nuclear reactor as a heat exchanger. [Sp, lark]

calanthe *kal-an'thi*, *n* an orchid of the genus *Calanthe*, having tall spikes of long-lasting flowers. [Gr *kalos* beautiful, and *anthē* blossom]

Calanus *ka-lā'nəs* or *kal'ə-nəs*, *n* a genus of copepods, swimming in plankton, important as whale and fish food.

calash *kə-lash'*, *n* a light low-wheeled carriage with a folding top; a large hood with a framework of hoops fashionably worn by ladies in the 18c. [Fr *calèche*; of Slav origin]

calathea *kal-ə-thē'ə*, *n* a plant of the S American genus *Calathea*, many of which have variegated leaves, often grown as houseplants, eg the zebra plant. [L, from Gr *kalathos* basket]

calathus *kal'ə-thəs*, *n* a symbol of fruitfulness in classical art, a fruit basket with a wide top carried on the head: — *pl* **cal'athi**. [Gr *kalathos* basket]

calavance *kal'ə-vans*, *n* a name for certain varieties of pulse. — Also **car'avance**. [Sp *garbanzo* chick-pea, said to be Basque *garbantzu*]

calcaneum *kal-kā'ni-əm* or **calcaneus** *-ni-əs*, (*anatom*) *n* the heel-bone: — *pl* **cal'canea** or **cal'canei**. — *adj* **calca'neal** or **calca'nean**. [L *calcāneum* the heel, from *calx* the heel]

calcar[1] *kal'kär*, *n* a spur-like projection, *esp* from the base of a petal (*bot*); a spur on a bird's leg (*zool*): — *pl* **calcār'ia**. — *adj* **calcarif'erous** having a spur or spurs (*bot* and *zool*). — *adj* **calcar'iform** spur-shaped. — *adj* **cal'carine** spurlike. — **calcar avis** (*zool* and *anatom*) the hippocampus minor in the brain (literally bird's spur). [L, a spur, from *calx* the heel]

calcar[2] *kal'kär*, *n* an oven or furnace for calcining the materials of frit before melting; a furnace or oven for annealing. [L *calcāria* a lime-kiln]

calcareous *kal-kā'ri-əs*, *adj* chalky; limy; of, or containing, calcium carbonate. — **calcareous tufa** see **tufa**. [L *calcārius*, from *calx* lime]

calceamentum *kal-si-ə-men'təm*, *n* a red silk embroidered sandal forming part of the insignia of the Holy Roman Empire. [L *calceāmentum* a shoe]

calced *kalst*, *adj* (*rare*) of Carmelites, wearing shoes, (*opp* to *discalced*). — *vt* **cal'ceate** to shoe. — *adj* **cal'ceate** or **cal'ceated** shod. — *adj* **cal'ceiform** or **cal'ceolate** (*bot*) slipper-shaped. [LL *calceus* a shoe]

calcedonio *kal-che-don'i-ō*, *n* a type of Venetian coloured glass resembling natural stones like chalcedony. [Ital, chalcedony]

calcedony. A variant form of **chalcedony**.

calceolaria *kal-si-ō-lā'ri-ə*, *n* any plant of the S American genus *Calceolaria*, the plants of which are largely cultivated for the beauty of their slipperlike flowers; slipperwort. [L *calceolus*, dimin of *calceus* a shoe]

calces. See **calx**.

calci- *kal'si-* or **calc-** *kals-*, *combining form* denoting calcium or limestone. [See **calcium**]

calcicole *kal'si-kōl*, *n* any plant that thrives on soil containing lime or chalk — Also *adj*. — *adj* **calcic'olous**. [L *calx*, *calcis* lime, limestone, and *colere* to dwell]

calciferol *kal-si'fer-əl*, *n* vitamin D_2. [*calcif*erous and ergoster*ol*]

calciferous *kal-si'fer-əs*, *adj* containing lime. — **Calciferous Sandstone** the lowest group of carboniferous rocks in Scotland. [L *calx*, *calcis* lime, limestone, and *ferre* to bear]

calcifuge *kal'si-fūj*, *n* any plant that will not tolerate limy or chalky soil. — Also *adj*. — *adj* **calcifugous** (*-sif'ū-gəs*). [L *calx*, *calcis* lime, limestone, and *fugere* to flee]

calcify *kal'si-fī*, *vt* and *vi* to convert or become converted into lime; to harden or become hard by the deposition of calcium salts or compounds, as in body tissue; to make or become rigid and inflexible (*fig*). — *adj* **calcif'ic** calcifying or calcified. — *n* **calcificātion** the process of calcifying or becoming calcified, a conversion into lime. [**calcium**]

calcine *kal'sin* or *kal'sīn*, *vt* to reduce (*esp* a metal ore or mineral) to a calx by heating; to subject to prolonged heating, *esp* so as to oxidize, or so as to drive out water and carbon dioxide. — *adj* **cal'cinable**. — *n* **calcinātion**. [Med L *calcināre*, from L *calx*, *calcis* lime]

calcite *kal'sīt*, *n* a mineral, calcium carbonate crystallized in the hexagonal system, the main constituent of limestone and many marbles. — Also **calcspar** (*kalk'-spär*).

calcitonin *kal-si-tō'nin*, *n* a hormone, produced in the thyroid gland, which regulates the amount of calcium in the blood and inhibits loss of calcium from the bones of the skeleton. [*cal*cium and *tone* with suffix *-in*]

calcium *kal'si-əm*, *n* a soft greyish-white metallic element (atomic no 20, symbol **Ca**) of the alkaline earth group, present in limestone, chalk and gypsum and *usu* occurring in the form of one of its compounds. — *adj* **cal'cic** containing calcium. — **calcium carbide** a grey solid chemical compound, CaC_2, used in the production of acetylene; **calcium carbonate** an insoluble chemical compound, $CaCo_3$, found naturally in limestone and chalk, and used in the production of lime and cement; **calcium hydroxide** a white powder made by adding water to lime and used in the production of plaster and cement, slaked lime; **calcium oxide** a white chemical compound, CaO, used in producing other calcium compounds and in agriculture to reduce acidity in soil (also **calx**, **lime** or **quicklime**); **calcium phosphate** a mineral salt essential in the formation of bones and teeth in animals, and for the healthy growth of plants. [L *calx*, *calcis* lime, limestone]

calcrete *kal'-krēt*, (*geol*) *n* a composite rock made up of sand and gravel cemented with calcium carbonate. [*cal*ci- and con*crete*]

calc-sinter *kalk'-sin-tər*, *n* travertine. [Ger *kalk-sinter*, from *kalk* lime, and *sinter* slag]

calcspar. See **calcite**.

calc-tuff or **calc-tufa**. Same as **tuff** or **tufa**.

calculate *kal'kū-lāt*, *vt* to count or reckon; to think out, *esp* mathematically; to think, intend, purpose or suppose (*US*). — *vi* to make a calculation; to estimate. — *adj* **cal'culable**. — *adv* **cal'culably**. — *adj* **cal'culāted** thought out; reckoned; computed; fitted, likely, of such a nature as probably (to). — *adj* **cal'culāting** deliberately selfish and scheming; shrewd, circumspect; tending to think or plan ahead. — *n* **calculā'tion** the art or process of calculating; an estimate; a forecast or projection. — *adj* **calculā'tional** or **cal'culātive** relating to calculation. — *n* **cal'culātor** a person who or thing that calculates; an electronic device that performs arithmetical calculations; a book, set of tables, etc for obtaining arithmetical results. — **calculated risk** a possibility of failure, the degree of which has been estimated and taken into account before a venture is undertaken; **calculating machine** any machine for speedily obtaining arithmetical results, eg a pocket calculator, computer, etc. [L *calculāre*, *-ātum* to count using little stones, from *calculus*, dimin of *calx* a stone]

calculus *kal'kū-ləs*, *n* a system of computation or calculation used in higher branches of mathematics permitting the manipulation of continually varying quantities (*pl* **cal'culuses**); a stone-like concretion which forms in certain vessels or organs of the body, eg the kidney or gall bladder (*pl* **cal'culī**); the mixture of plaque and saliva that forms a hard brownish-yellow layer on the teeth, tartar. — *adj* **cal'cular** pertaining to the mathematical calculus. — *adj* **cal'culary**, **cal'culose** or **cal'culous** pertaining to or affected with stone or with gravel. — **differential calculus** a branch of calculus which enables calculation of the rate at which one quantity changes in relation to another, used to find velocities, slopes of curves, etc; **integral calculus** a branch of calculus concerned with finding integrals and applying them to find eg the areas enclosed by curves, the solution of differential equations, etc. [For ety see **calculate**]

caldarium *kal-där'i-əm* or *kal-där'i-ōōm*, (*L*) *n* a hot room in Roman baths: — *pl* **caldar'ia**.

caldera *käl-dā'rə*, (*geol*) *n* a large crater formed by the collapse of the central part of a volcano after eruption. [Sp, cauldron]

caldron. Same as **cauldron**.

Caledonian *kal-i-dō'ni-ən*, *adj* of or pertaining to ancient *Caledonia*, to the Highlands of Scotland, or to Scotland generally (*esp poetic*); pertaining to a mountain-forming movement of Silurian and Old Red Sandstone times, well developed in Scotland (*geol*). — *n* (*literary*) a Scot. [L *Calēdonia* northern Britain]

calefaction *kal-i-fak'shən*, *n* the act of heating; the state of being heated. — *adj* **calefacient** (*-fā'shənt*) warming. — *n* anything that warms; a medicinal preparation that warms the area it is applied to. — *adj* **calefac'tive** communicating heat. — *n* **calefac'tor** a small stove. — *adj* **calefac'tory** warming. — *n* (*hist*) a room in which monks warmed themselves; a warming-pan, or priest's pome or hand-warmer: — *pl* **calefac'tories**. — *vt* and *vi* **cal'efy** to make or grow warm. [L *calefacere*, from *calēre* to grow hot, and *facere*, *factum* to make]

calembour *kal-ã-bōōr*, (*Fr*) *n* a pun.

calendar *kal'ən-dər*, *n* the way in which the natural divisions of time are arranged with respect to each other for the purposes of civil life; an almanac or table of months, days, and seasons, or of facts about specific days, etc; a list of documents arranged chronologically with summaries of contents; a list of canonized saints, or of prisoners awaiting trial; a list of events, appointments, etc; any list or record. — *vt* to place in a list or enter in a calendar; to analyse and index. — *n* **cal'endarer**. — *n* **calendariza'tion** or **-s-**. — *vt* **cal'endarize** or **-ise** in accounting, to divide (something, eg a budget) into equal units of time within a year (*usu* months). — *n* **cal'endarist**. — *adj* **calen'dric** or **calen'drical** of, pertaining to, or like a calendar in some way. — **cal'endar-line** the date-line; **calendar month** and **calendar year** see under **month** and **year**; **perpetual calendar** see under **perpetual**. [L *calendārium* an account-book, from *kalendae* calends]

calender[1] *kal'ən-dər*, *n* a machine with rollers for finishing or glazing the surface of cloth, paper, etc, using a combination of moisture, heat, and pressure. — *vt* to press in a calender. — *n* **cal'endering**. — *n* **cal'endrer**. — *n* **cal'endry** a place where calendering is done: — *pl* **cal'endries**. [Fr *calandre*, from L *cylindrus*, from Gr *kylindros* roller]

calender[2] *kal'ən-dər*, *n* a member of a mendicant order of wandering dervishes in Persia and Turkey. [Pers *qalandar*]

calendrer, **calendring**. See under **calender**[1].

calendric, **calendrical**. See under **calendar**.

calends or **kalends** *kal'əndz*, *n pl* the first day of each month in the ancient Roman calendar. [L *kalendae*, from *calāre*, from Gr *kaleein* to call (because the order of the days was proclaimed at the beginning of each month)]

calendula *ka-len'dū-lə*, *n* any plant of the genus *Calendula*, the marigold genus; a preparation of marigold flowers formerly used in plasters, etc, for the healing of wounds. [L *kalendae* calends (but the connection is obscure)]

calenture *kal'ən-chər*, (*hist*) *n* a tropical fever or delirium caused by heat; heatstroke. [Fr, from Sp *calentura*, from L *calēns*, *-entis*, from *calēre* to be hot]

calescence *kal-es'əns*, *n* increase in heat. [L *calēscĕre*, inchoative of *calēre* to be hot]

calf[1] *käf*, *n* the young of any bovine animal, *esp* the cow; the young of the elephant, whale, and certain other mammals; calfskin leather; an iceberg that has broken off a glacier or larger iceberg; a stupid or loutish person (*slang*): — *pl* **calves** (*kävz*), or (of calfskin) **calfs**. — *vt* and *vi* **calve** (*käv*) to give birth to a calf; to detach (a glacier or iceberg). — *adj* **calf'-bound** bound in calfskin. — **calf'-country** or **calf'-ground** (*Scot*) the place where one spent one's youth; **calf'dozer** a small bulldozer; **calf'-love** immature or youthful amorous attachment or affection; **calf's'-foot** or **calves''-foot jelly** a savoury jelly made from the gelatine produced by boiling the foot of a calf; **calf'skin** the skin of the calf, making a fine leather suitable for bookbinding and shoes; **calf'-time** youth. — **divinity calf** a dark-brown calf bookbinding with blind stamping, and without gilding, used on theological books; **golden calf** the image set up by Aaron and worshipped by the Israelites during the absence of Moses on Sinai; wealth or money as an object of worship; **half'-calf** a bookbinding in which the back and corners are in calfskin; **in** or **with calf** (of cows) pregnant; **kill the fatted calf** to celebrate or welcome lavishly or extravagantly; **mottled calf** a light-coloured bookbinding, decorated by sprinkling drops of acid on its surface; **smooth calf** a binding in plain or undecorated calf leather; **tree calf** a bright brown calf bookbinding, stained by acids with a pattern resembling the trunk and branches of a tree. [OE (Anglian) *cælf* (WSaxon *cealf*)]

calf[2] *käf*, *n* the thick fleshy part at the back of the leg below the knee: — *pl* **calves** (*kävz*). — *adj* **calf'less** (*archaic*) having a thin leg. [ON *kālfi*]

caliature-wood *kal'i-ə-chər-wŏŏd*, *n* an old term for a tropical dye-wood, perhaps red-sanders. — Also **caliatour**, **calliature**, etc.

Caliban *kal'i-ban*, *n* a man of brutish or uncouth nature, from the character of that name in Shakespeare's *Tempest*.

calibre or (*esp NAm*) **caliber** *kal'i-bər*, *n* the diameter of a bullet or shell; the diameter of the bore of a gun or tube; character or capacity, degree of suitability or excellence (*fig*). — *vt* **cal'ibrāte** to determine the diameter of a gun barrel or tube; to determine true values by comparison with an accurate standard; to mark or adjust gradations or positions on. — *n* **calibrā'tion** the act of calibrating; one of a series of marks or gradations that indicate values or positions. — *n* **cal'ibrātor**. — *adj* **cal'ibred** or **cal'ibered**. [Fr *calibre* the bore of a gun, perh from L *quā librā* of what weight, or from Ar *qālib* a mould]

caliche *kä-lē'chā*, *n* sand containing Chile saltpetre; a crust of calcium carbonate that forms on the surface of the soil in arid regions. [Sp]

calico *kal'i-kō*, *n* a cotton cloth first imported from *Calicut* in India; plain white unprinted cotton cloth, bleached or unbleached; coarse brightly-coloured printed cotton cloth (*esp NAm*); a spotted or piebald animal, *esp* a horse (*NAm*): — *pl* **cal'icos** or **cal'icoes**. — *adj* made of calico; with a brightly-coloured design (*NAm*); spotted (*NAm*). — **cal'ico-bush**, **cal'ico-flower** or **cal'ico-tree** kalmia; **cal'ico-printing** the process of printing coloured patterns on cloth, eg calico. **cal'ico-wood** the snowdrop-tree.

calid *kal'id*, *adj* warm. — *n* **calid'ity**. [L *calidus* hot]

Calif. *abbrev*: California (US state).

calif. See **caliph**.

Califont® *kal'i-font*, (*NZ*) *n* a gas-fuelled water-heater.

California poppy *kal-i-förn'yə pop'i*, *n* an annual poppy-like plant (*Escholtzia californica*) of W America, having bright yellow or orange flowers.

californium *kal-i-för'ni-əm*, *n* a radioactive chemical element (atomic no 98; symbol **Cf**), artificially produced from curium. [First produced at the University of *California*]

caligo *kal-ī'gō*, *n* reduced vision, dimness of sight (*med*). — *adj* **caliginous** (*kal-ij'i-nəs*) (*archaic*) dim, obscure, dark. — *n* **caliginos'ity**. [L *cālīgō*, *-inis* fog]

caligraphy. A faulty spelling of **calligraphy**.

Caligulism *kal-ig'-yŏŏl-ism*, *n* an example of debauched or excessive behaviour, eg sexual depravity, extreme cruelty, etc. [From the Roman emperor *Caligula*, who often exhibited such behaviour]

calima *kal'i-mə*, *n* a dust storm or cloud that spreads over southern Europe from the Sahara desert, causing heatwaves. [Sp, haze]

caliology *kal-i-ol'ə-ji*, *n* the science and study of birds' nests. [Gr *kaliā*, *kalīā* a nest, and *logos* discourse]

calipash *kal'i-pash*, *n* the edible flesh of a turtle close to the upper shell, a dull greenish fatty gelatinous substance. — *n* **cal'ipee** the edible light-yellowish flesh from around the turtle's lower shell. [Prob from W Indian words]

calipers. See **callipers**.

caliph *kal'if* or *kā'lif*, *n esp* formerly (the title given to) a spiritual leader of Islam regarded as a successor of Mohammed. — Also **calif**, **kalif** or **khalif**. — *adj* **cal'iphal**. — *n* **cal'iphate** the office, rank, government or empire of a caliph. [Fr *calife*, from Ar *khalīfah* a successor]

Calippic or **Callippic Period** *ka-lip'ik*, *pēr'i-əd*, *n* the cycle discovered by the Athenian astronomer *Kal(l)ippos* (c. 350 BC) equalling four Metonic cycles less one day, or a period of seventy-six years, when the new moons fall on the same days of the year.

calisaya *kal-i-sā'yə*, *n* a variety of Peruvian bark.

calisthenics. See **callisthenics**.

caliver *kal'i-vər*, (*Shakesp*) *n* a kind of light musket. [Same as **calibre**]

calix *kā'liks* or *kal'iks*, *n* a cup, chalice: — *pl* **cal'ices** (*-sēz*). — Cf **calyx**. [L *calix* a cup]

Calixtin[1] or **Calixtine** *kal-iks'tin*, *n* a member of the 15c Bohemian sect of Hussites, an Utraquist. — Also *adj*. [From their demanding the chalice (L *calix*) as well as the bread for the laity in communion]

Calixtin[2] or **Calixtine** *kal-iks'tin*, *n* a follower of the syncretist Lutheran divine, Georg *Calixtus* (1586–1656).

calk[1]. See **caulk**.

calk[2] *kök*, *n* a pointed piece on a horseshoe to prevent slipping. — Also **calk'in** or **calk'er**, **caulk'er**. — *vt* to provide with a calk. [OE *calc* shoe, from L *calx* a heel]

calk[3] or **calque** *kök*, *kalk*, *vt* to transfer (a design, etc) by rubbing the back with colouring matter and then tracing with a blunt point on to a surface placed beneath. — *n* (*usu* **calque**; *kalk*) a loan-translation (see under **loan**[2]). [L *calcāre* to tread, from *calx* the heel]

calker, **calkin**. See **calk**[2].

call[1] *köl*, *vi* to cry aloud, speak loudly, shout (often with *out*); of an animal or bird, to utter a cry or characteristic sound; to make a short visit (with *on*, *for*, *at*); to make a telephone call; to demand that a player show his hand after repeated raising of stakes (*poker*); to try to predict the result of tossing a coin; to make a bid (*bridge*). — *vt* and *vi* (*cards*) to declare (trump suit, etc). — *vt* to name; to summon or request to be present; to rouse from sleep or from bed; to designate or reckon; to select for a special office, eg to the Bar; to telephone; to read out the names in (a roll); to demand the repayment of (a debt, loan, redeemable bonds, etc); to give the order for (a strike); to make a call (*sport*); to demand the playing of (an exposed card) (*poker*); to apply (an offensive name) to (*colloq*); to broadcast a commentary on (a race, etc) (*Austr* and *NZ*). — *n* a summons or invitation (to the witness-box, the telephone, the stage or rehearsal, etc); a sense of vocation; a demand; a short visit; a signal by trumpet, bell, etc; a telephone connection or conversation, or a request for one; occasion, cause (*colloq*); a declaration or undertaking, or the right to make it in turn (*cards*); a decision on the status of a shot, articulated by an umpire or (*esp tennis*) a line judge (*sport*); a cry, *esp* of a bird; admission to the rank of barrister; an invitation to the pastorate of a congregation; an option of buying within a certain time certain securities or commodities at a stipulated price (*stock exchange*; also **call option**); the money paid to secure such an option; one instalment of the payment for newly-issued securities. — *n* **call'er**. — *n* **call'ing** vocation, an occupation or profession. — **call alarm** a small radio transmitter used, *esp* by elderly people living alone, to summon help in an emergency; **call'-at-large** a form of pastoral call sometimes adopted by a presbytery where a congregation is not unanimous, in which the name of the person to be called is not inscribed beforehand, and the names cannot be adhibited by mandate; **call'-barring** the ability to restrict outgoing telephone calls to certain numbers (*telecomm*); **call'-bird** a bird trained to lure others into snares by its call; **call'-box** a public telephone-box; **call'-boy** a boy who calls the actors when they are required on stage; **call'-girl** a prostitute who arranges appointments with clients by telephone; **call house** a house of prostitution; **calling card** a visiting card; **call'ing-crab** the fiddler-crab, which waves its larger claw when disturbed; **call'-money** (*finance*) money called in for repayment; **call'-note** the note by which a bird or animal calls to its own kind; **call option** (*stock exchange*) see **call** above; **call-out** see **call out** below; **call sign** or **call signal** (*communications*) a combination of letters and numbers, identifying a particular ship, aircraft, transmitter, etc; **call'-up** an act of calling up, *esp* conscription into the armed forces; **call waiting** the ability to accept an incoming telephone call routed by another number while holding a call on one's own number (*telecomm*). — **call attention to** to point out; **call back** to recall; to visit again; to telephone again; **call by** (*colloq*) to visit in passing; **call down** to invoke; to rebuke, reprove sharply and angrily (*esp US colloq*); **call for** to come for and take away with one; to ask loudly for; to demand; to require (**called'-for** required, necessary; **not called for** uncalled-for); **call forth** to evoke; **call for trumps** (*cards*) to play a card as a signal to a partner to lead a trump; **call in** to bring in from public use old currency notes, etc (*banking*); to demand repayment of (a debt, etc); to call to one's help (eg a doctor, the police); to withdraw from circulation; to withdraw (eg an application); **call in** (or **into**) **question** to challenge, cast doubt on; **call off** to order to come away; to withdraw or back out; to cancel or abandon; **call of nature** (*euphem*) a need to urinate or defecate; **call on** or **upon** to invoke, appeal to; to make a short visit to; **call out** to challenge to fight, eg a duel; to summon to service, bring into operation; to instruct (members of a trade union) to come out on strike; to request or arrange a visit (eg of a repairman, service engineer; *n* and *adj* **call'-out**); **call over** to read aloud (a list); **call the shots** (*orig US*) or **call the tune** to say what is to happen, to order, or to be in command; **call to account** see under **account**; **call to mind** to recollect, or cause to recollect; **call to order** to call upon (participants) to observe the rules of debate; (of a chairman) to announce that a formal meeting is starting; **call up** to summon, to a tribunal, to *esp* military service, to memory; to display (information, data, etc on a computer screen); **on call** available if required; ready to answer summons; **pay a call** (*colloq euphem*) to go to the lavatory, respond to a call of nature; **within call** within calling distance. [OE *ceallian* and ON *kalla*]

call[2] *köl*, (*Spenser*) *n* a caul or cap.

calla *kal'ə*, *n* a poisonous marsh plant (*Calla palustris*) of the arum family; (also **calla lily**) any African lily of the genus *Zantedeschia* having showy brightly-coloured flowers. [Origin doubtful]

callant *käl'ənt* or **callan** *käl'ən*, (*Scot*) *n* a lad or fellow. [Du *kalant*]

caller *käl'ər* or *köl'ər*, (*Scot*) *adj* (of fish, vegetables, etc) fresh; (of wind, water, etc) cool and refreshing. [Prob the same as **calver**]

callet *kal'it*, (*Shakesp*) *n* a scold, a woman of bad character, a prostitute. [Origin doubtful]

calliature. See **caliature-wood**.

Callicarpa *kal-i-kär'pə*, *n* a genus of deciduous Japanese and Chinese shrubs and small trees, grown for their attractive berries and autumn foliage. [Gr *kalos* beautiful, and *karpos* fruit]

callid *kal'id*, (*rare*) *adj* shrewd. — *n* **callid'ity** shrewdness. [L *callidus* expert]

calligram or **calligramme** *kal'igram*, *n* a design using the letters of a word. [*calli*graphy and *-gram*]

calligraphy *kə-lig'rə-fi*, *n* fine handwriting or penmanship; artistic script produced with a brush; a line or lines in art suggesting this; loosely, a characteristic style of writing. — *n* **callig'rapher**. — *adj* **calligraphic** (*kal-i-graf'ik*) or **calligraph'ical**. — *n* **callig'raphist**. [Gr *kallos* beauty, and *graphein* to write]

Calliope *kə-lī'ə-pi* or *kal-ī'o-pē*, (*Gr mythol*) *n* the Muse of epic poetry; (without *cap*) a keyboard musical instrument similar to an organ, with a set of whistles operated by steam or compressed air. [Gr *Kalliopē*]

callipers or (*esp US*) **calipers** *kal'i-pərz*, *n pl* compasses with legs suitable for measuring the inside or outside diameter of bodies; a calliper splint. — Sometimes in *sing*. — Also **call'iper-compasses**. — *n* **call'iper** in papermaking, a measure of the thickness of a single sheet of paper, *usu* expressed in microns or millimetres. — *vt* to measure with callipers. — **calliper splint** a metal splint fitted to the leg to provide support. [**calibre**]

Callippic. See **Calippic**.

callipygous *kal-i-pī'gəs*, *adj* having beautiful buttocks. — Also **callipygean** (*-pij'i-ən*). [Gr *kallipȳgos* an epithet of Aphrodite, from *kallos* beauty, and *pȳgē* buttock]

Callistemon *kal-i-stē'mon*, *n* an Australian genus of the myrtle family, bottle-brush shrubs. [Gr *kallos* beauty, and *stēmōn* a thread (stamen)]

callisthenics or (*esp US*) **calisthenics** *kal-is-then'iks*, *n pl* exercises designed to achieve gracefulness, fitness and strength. — *adj* **callisthen'ic** or **calisthen'ic**. [Gr *kallos* beauty, and *sthenos* strength]

Callitriche *kal-it'ri-kē*, *n* the water-starwort genus, constituting the **Callitrichā'ceae** a family of widely-distributed aquatic plants. [Gr *kallos* beauty, and *thrix*, *trichos* hair]

callous *kal'əs*, *adj* (*esp* of the skin) hardened; unfeeling, unsympathetic, cruel. — *n* **callos'ity** a thickening of the skin; callousness. — *adv* **call'ously**. — *n* **call'ousness** lack of feeling, brutality. [L *callōsus*, from *callus* hard skin]

callow[1] *kal'ō*, *adj* unfledged, unbearded; inexperienced. [OE *calu*; Ger *kahl* bald]

callow[2] *kal'ō*, *adj* low-lying and liable to be submerged. — *n* an alluvial flat. [Perh Ir *calad* a riverside meadow]

calluna *kə-lū'nə*, *n* a plant of the heather genus *Calluna*. [Gr *kallȳnein* to beautify, to sweep, from *kalos* beautiful]

callus *kal'əs*, *n* an area of thickened or hardened skin; new material by which fractured bones are consolidated (*pathol*); soft tissue that forms over a cut surface (*bot*). [L]

calm[1] *käm*, *adj* still or quiet; of the weather, not windy; (of a person or an action) serene, tranquil, assured; cool, impudent (*colloq*). — *n* absence of wind (also in *pl*); repose; serenity of feelings or actions. — *vt* and *vi* (also **calm down**) to make or become calm; to quiet. — *vt* to becalm. — *n* and *adj* (*med*) **calmant** or **calmative** (both *kal'*, *kä'*). — *adj* **calmed** (*kämd*). — *adv* **calm'ly**. — *n* **calm'ness**. — *adj* **calm'y** (*Spenser*) characterized by calm. [Fr *calme* (Ital *calma*), from LL *cauma*, from Gr *kauma* noonday heat, from *kaiein* to burn]

calm[2], **calmstone**. See **cam**[3].

calmodulin *kal-mod'ū-lin*, (*biochem*) *n* a protein found in plant and animal cells that is a receptor of calcium and affects many processes involving calcium within cells. [**calcium**, **modul**(**ate**) and sfx *-in*]

Calmuck. See **Kalmuck**.

calmy[1]. See **calm**[1].
calmy[2]. See **cam**[3].
calo *abbrev*: (*music*) calando.
calomel *kal'ō-mel*, *n* mercurous chloride, used in medicine as a purgative. [Fr *calomel*, appar from Gr *kalos* beautiful and *melās* black.
calorie or **calory** *kal'ər-i*, *n* the amount of heat needed to raise one gram of water 1° centigrade in temperature, *usu* from 14.5°C to 15.5°C (*small* or *gram-calorie*) (in 1950 it was recommended that this should be superseded as a unit of heat and internal energy by the *joule*); an *international table calorie* (cal_{IT}) = 4.1868 joules, a *thermochemical calorie* = 4.1840 joules; (sometimes with *cap*) the amount of heat needed to raise one kilogram of water 1° centigrade in temperature (*great*, *large*, or *kilogram-calorie*, *kilocalorie*; = 1000 small calories) (used in expressing the heat- or energy-producing value of foods); the hundredth part of the heat required to raise a gram from 0° to 100° (*mean calorie*; equal to 4.1897 joules) — *adj* **caloric** *ka-lor'ik*, of or pertaining to heat or calories. — *n* the nature of heat as a subtle, self-repellant fluid, according to a principle, **caloric theory**, widely held up to c. 1850 (*archaic*). — *n* **caloric'ity**. — *adj* **calorif'ic** of, pertaining to, or causing heat; heating. — *n* **calorificā'tion**. — *n* **calor'ifier** an apparatus for heating water in a tank, the source of heat being a coil of heated pipes immersed in the water. — *n* **calorim'eter** an instrument or apparatus for measuring heat capacities, latent heats, thermal constants, etc. — *n* **calorim'etry**. — *n* **cal'orist** a person who believes the caloric theory (see above under **caloric**). — **calor gas**® (sometimes with *caps*) a type of gas for cooking, heating, etc, *usu* sold in large metal containers for use where there is no permanent supply of gas; **caloric test** (*med*) a test (used to determine whether a patient with hearing loss has a diseased inner ear) in which the outer ear is flooded with water at temperatures above and below body temperature and the consequent effect on the inner ear is apparent in reflex flickering of the eye; **calorie conscious** being aware of the number of calories in food, *esp* in order to lose weight. — *adj* **calorie controlled** of a diet in which consumption of calories is strictly controlled in order to lose weight. — **calorie** (or **Calorie**) **counter** a person or device that counts calories, *esp* as part of a weight-reducing diet; **calorific value** of a food or fuel, the number of heat units produced by complete combustion of unit mass. [L *calor* heat]
calotte *kal-ot'*, *n* a plain skullcap as worn by RC clergy. [Fr]
calotype *kal'ō-tīp*, *n* an early kind of photography (invented c. 1834 by W H Fox Talbot) in which a positive was produced from a negative image laid down on paper treated with silver iodide. — *n* **cal'otȳpist**. [Gr *kalos* beautiful and *typos* an image]
caloyer *kal'o-yər*, *n* a Greek Orthodox monk, *esp* of the order of St Basil. [Fr, from Ital, from Late Gr *kalogēros*, from Gr *kalos* beautiful, and *gēras* old age]
calp *kalp*, *n* in Ireland, a dark shaly limestone occurring in the middle of the Carboniferous Limestone.
calpa. Same as **kalpa**.
calpac, **calpack**. See **kalpak**.
calque. See **calk**[3].
Caltech *kal'tek*, *abbrev*: California Institute of Technology.
caltha *kal'thə*, *n* a plant of the *Caltha* genus of flowers to which the marsh marigold belongs. [L]
caltrop *kal'*, *köl'trop*, *n* an old military weapon, an iron ball with four spikes, so arranged that when it is laid on the ground one spike always stands upright, used to obstruct an enemy; a name for several plants with fruits so shaped, eg (*esp* in *pl*) water chestnut. — Also **cal'trap** or **cal'throp**. [OE *coltetræppe*, *calcatrippe*, from L *calx* heel, and the root of **trap**[1]]
calumba *ka-lum'bə*, *n* the root of an E African plant (*Jateorhiza columba*) used as a stomachic and tonic. [Perh from *Colombo* in Sri Lanka]
calumet *kal'ū-met*, *n* the peace-pipe of the N American Indians, a tobacco-pipe smoked in token of peace. [Norman Fr *calumet* shepherd's pipe (Fr *chalumet*), from L *calamus* reed]
calumny *kal'əm-ni*, *n* false accusation or statement; slander, defamation. — *vt* **calumniate** (*kə-lum'ni-āt*) to accuse falsely; to slander. — *vi* to spread false or slanderous reports. — *n* **calumniā'tion**. — *n* **calum'niātor**. — *adj* **calum'niātory** or **calum'nious** of the nature of calumny; slanderous. — *adv* **calum'niously**. [L *calumnia*, prob connected with *calvī* to deceive]
calutron *kal'ū-tron*, *n* a mass spectrometer used in the separation of isotopes. [*Cal*ifornia *U*niversity and **-tron**]
Calvados *kal'və-dos*, or *-dos'*, *n* a brandy made from cider or apple-pulp, *esp* in the Calvados department of Normandy.
calvaria *kal-vā'ri-ə*, *n* the upper part of skull enclosing the brain in vertebrates. [L, skull]
Calvary *kal'və-ri*, *n* the name of the place near Jerusalem where Jesus was crucified; (sometimes without *cap*) a representation of Christ's crucifixion, or a series of scenes connected with it (*Christian relig*); an experience of intense mental suffering. — **Calvary cross** (*heraldry*) a Latin cross mounted on three steps. [LL *calvāria* skull, from *calvus* bald; also used to translate Aramaic *gogulthō* or *gogolthā* (Heb *gulgōleth*, Grecized as *golgotha*)]
calve, **calves**. See **calf**.
calver *kal'vər*, *vt* to prepare (salmon or other fish) when alive or freshly caught. — *adj* **cal'vered**. [Cf **caller**]
Calvinism *kal'vin-izm*, *n* the Christian doctrines as interpreted by the French protestant theologian and religious reformer, John *Calvin* (1509–1564) in his *Institutes of the Christian Religion*, and as adopted by the Reformed and Presbyterian Churches, *esp* the scriptures and the Holy Spirit as the sole authority and truth, predestination of particular election, the incapacity for true faith and repentance of the natural man, efficacious grace, and final perseverance (continuance of the saints in a state of grace until the final state of glory). — *n* **Cal'vinist**. — *adj* **Calvinist'ic** or **Calvinist'ical**.
calvities *kal-vish'i-ēz*, (*med*) *n* baldness. [L *calvitiēs*, from *calvus* bald]
calx *kalks*, *n* the substance of a metal ore or mineral that remains after it has been subjected to intense heat; see also **calcium oxide**: — *pl* **calxes** (*kalk'siz*) or **calces** (*kal'sēz*). [L *calx*, *calcis* lime]
calycanthus *kal-i-kan'thəs*, *n* a shrub of the N American genus *Calycanthus*, including Carolina allspice or strawberry shrub. [New L]
calyciform. . . to . . . **calycoideous**. See **calyx**.
calypso *ka-lip'sō*, *n* a W Indian ballad, *usu* dealing with topical events, *usu* made up as the singer goes along and sung in syncopated rhythm to an accompaniment of simple percussion instruments: — *pl* **calyp'sos**. — *n* **calypso'nian** a writer or singer of calypsos. [Poss from 17c-18c W African *kaiso* ceremonial song]
calyptra *ka-lip'trə* or **calyptera** *-lip'terə*, (*bot*) *n* a hood or hoodlike structure, *esp* that covering the spore capsule of mosses and liverworts; a root-cap. — *adj* **calyp'trate** capped or hooded. — *n* **calyp'trogen** the layer of cells on the growing tip of a root giving rise to the root cap. [Gr *kalyptrā* a veil]
calyx *kā'liks* or *kal'iks*, *n* the outer covering of a flower, its modified leaves termed sepals that protect the developing flower (*bot*); any cuplike structure in the body, *esp* any of the cavities of the kidney: — *pl* **ca'lyxes** or **ca'lyces** (*-sēz*). — *n* **calycanthemy** (*kal-ik-an'thi-mi*; Gr *anthemon* flower) the condition of having the calyx like a corolla. — *n pl* **Calyciflorae** (*-is-i-flō'rē* or *-flō'*; L *flōs*, *flōris* flower) a subclass of dicotyledons with a corolla of distinct petals. — *adj* **calyciform** (*kal-is'*) having the form of a calyx. — *adj* **calyc'inal** or **calycine** (*kal'i-sīn*) pertaining to or resembling a calyx. — *n* **cal'ycle**, **cal'icle** or **cal'ycule** a whorl of bracts,

epicalyx or involucre (*bot*); a cuplike structure, such as the cup of a coral (*zool*). — *adj* **cal'ycled** having a calycle. — *adj* **cal'ycoid** or **calycoi'deous** like a calyx. — *adj* **calyculate** (*kə-lik'ū-lāt*) having a calyculus. — *n* **calyculus** (*-lik'ū-*) a cuplike structure. [Gr *kalyx* a covering, from *kalyptein* to cover]

calzone *kal-tsō'ne*, *n* a folded over pizza: — *pl* **calzo'ni** or **calzo'nes**. [Ital]

CAM often *kam*, *abbrev*: computer-aided manufacturing, or manufacture.

cam[1] *kam*, (*mech*) *n* an irregular projection on a revolving shaft or rotating cylinder, shaped so as to transmit regular movement to another part, eg to open the cylinder valves of a car engine. — **cam'shaft** or **cam'wheel** a shaft or wheel, bearing a cam or cams. [Du *kam* cam or comb; cf **comb**, **kame**]

cam[2] *adj* and *adv*. See **kam**.

cam[3], **caum** or **calm** *käm* or *köm*, (*Scot*) *n* pale bluish-grey clay or soft slate; a slate pencil; pipeclay; limestone (*obs*). — *vt* to whiten with camstone. — *adj* **calm'y** clayey. — **cam'stone**, **caum'stone**, **calm'stone** or **cam'-stane** a white argillaceous stone used for whitening hearthstones and doorsteps. [Origin unknown]

Cama. See **Kama**.

camaïeu *kam-a-yø'*, *n orig* a cameo; a painting in monochrome, or in simple colours not imitating nature; a style of printing pictures producing the effect of pencil-drawing; a literary work or play that is monotonous or lacks interest: — *pl* **camaïeux** (*-yø'*). [Fr; see **cameo**]

Camaldolite *kam-al'dō-līt*, *n* a member of a religious order founded by St Romuald at *Camaldoli* early in the 11c. — Also *adj*. — *n* and *adj* **Camal'dolese**.

caman *kam'an*, *n* a shinty stick. — *n* **camanachd** (*kam'an-ahh(k)*) shinty. [Gaelic]

camaraderie *kam-ə-räd'ə-rē*, *n* good fellowship; the intimacy of comradeship. [Fr]

camarilla *kam-ə-ril'ə*, *n* a band of secret intriguers, *esp* against legitimate ministers at court; a cabal or coterie; *orig* a small room. [Sp, dimin of *cámara* a chamber]

camaron *kam-ar-ōn'* or *kam'ə-ron*, *n* a kind of freshwater crustacean similar to a crayfish. — Also **maron** (*esp Austr*). [Sp *camarón* a shrimp, from L *cam(m)arus* a sea crab, from Gr *kammaros*]

camass, **camas**, **camash** or **quamash** *kam'as*, *-ash*, *kwom'-ash* or *kwam-ash'*, *n* any of several N American plants of the genus *Camassia* of the lily family, *esp* the variety found in the north-western US having a sweet edible bulb; the bulb of this plant. — **cam'ass-rat** a small gopher-like rodent that feeds on the bulbs of the camass. [Chinook *kámass*]

Camb. *abbrev*: Cambridge; Cambridgeshire (also **Cambs**.).

camber *kam'bər*, *n* a slight convexity on an upper surface (as on a road, a beam, the deck of a ship, the wing section of an aeroplane, etc). — *vt* to form a camber on or give a camber to. — *vi* to arch slightly. — *n* **cam'bering** (*geol*) a type of rock-folding that forms rounded hills and valleys. [Fr *cambre*, from L *camerāre* to vault]

Camberwell beauty *kam'bər-wəl bū'ti*, *n* a large butterfly (*Nymphalis antiopa*) having deep maroon wings with a row of blue spots and an edging of cream, so called because first recorded in England in 1748 at *Camberwell*.

cambist *kam'bist*, *n* a person skilled in the science of financial exchange; a manual or listing of currency exchange rates. — *n* **cam'bism** or **cam'bistry**. [Ital *cambista*, from L *cambīre* to exchange]

cambium *kam'bi-əm*, (*bot*) *n* a layer or cylinder of meristem in roots and stems, by whose differentiation into xylem and phloem lateral growth or girth is added: — *pl* **cam'biums** or **cam'bia**. — *adj* **cam'bial**. — *adj* **cam'biform**. [LL, from L *cambīre* to change]

Cambodian *kam-bōdi-ən*, *adj* of or pertaining to *Cambodia* (officially called *Kampuchea*), a country of SE Asia. — *n* a native of Cambodia; its language.

camboge. Obsolete form of **gamboge**.

cambrel. See **gambrel**.

Cambrian *kam'bri-ən*, *adj* pertaining to *Cambria* or Wales; Welsh; of the geological system (well represented in Wales) of the older or Lower Palaeozoic period, next above the Archaean or Pre-Cambrian. — *n* an inhabitant of Cambria, or Wales; the Cambrian system. [Latinized from Welsh *Cymry* Welshmen, and *Cymru* Wales]

cambric *kām'brik*, *n* a fine white linen, *orig* manufactured at *Kamerijk* (Cambrai) in French Flanders; a cotton imitation of this. — **cambric tea** a beverage made of hot water, milk, sugar and sometimes a small amount of tea.

Cambridge *kām'brij*, *adj* of or pertaining to *Cambridge*, an English university town. — **Cambridge blue** a light blue (see also **blue**); **Cambridge ring** (*comput*) a computer network facility, developed at Cambridge University, in which several users within one geographical location may communicate with each other; **Cambridge roller** a ring roller (qv).

Cambs. See **Camb**.

camcorder *kam'kör'dər*, *n* a portable video *cam*era and sound re*corder* combined in one unit.

came[1] *kām*, *pa t* of **come**.

came[2] *kām* or **calm** *käm*, *n* a lead rod for framing a pane in a leaded or stained-glass window. [Origin unknown]

camel *kam'əl*, *n* either of two large ruminant mammals of Asia and Africa, having a single hump on the back (**dromedary** or **Arabian camel**), or two humps (**Bactrian camel**), used as beasts of burden or for riding in desert regions because of their ability to survive for long periods without food and water; a watertight float attached to a vessel to increase its buoyancy; a humped type of early aeroplane, used in World War I; a light yellowish-brown colour. — *adj* of the colour camel. — *n* **cameleer'** someone who drives or rides a camel. — *n* **cam'elid** an animal of the **Camel'idae**, the family of artiodactyls which includes camels and llamas. — Also *adj*. — *n* **cam'eline** a material made from camel hair. — *adj* of the nature of a camel. — *adj* **cam'elish** like a camel, obstinate. — *adj* **cam'eloid** of the camel family. — Also *n*. — *n* **cam'elry** troops mounted on camels. — **cam'elback** an inferior grade of rubber, made from reclaimed or synthetic rubber, used for retreading tyres. — *adj* **cam'el-backed** hump-backed. — **cam'el-corps** troops mounted on camels; **camel hair** or **camel's hair** the hair of the camel, used for making a soft cloth; the hair of the squirrel's tail used for making artists' paint-brushes; **camel spin** (*skating*) a type of spin in which one leg is extended horizontally behind the skater; **camel's thorn** a papilionaceous manna-yielding desert plant (*Alhagi maurorum*) on which camels graze. [L *camēlus*, from Gr *kamēlos*, from Phoenician or Heb *gāmāl*]

cameleon. Same as **chameleon**.

camellia *ka-mēl'yə* or *-mel'yə*, *n* any shrub of the *Camellia* genus of evergreen shrubs closely related to tea, native to eastern Asia, and grown for their beautiful rose-like flowers. [Named from *Kamel*, Latinized as *Camellus*, a Moravian Jesuit who collected plants in the Philippine Islands]

camelopard *kam-el'ō-pärd* or *kam'əl-ō-pärd*, *n* an obsolete term for the giraffe. — Also **cameleopard** (*kam-ə-lep'ərd*). — *n* **Camelopardalis** (*kə-mel-ə-pär'də-lis*) a northern constellation close to Ursa Minor. [L *camēlopardus*, from Gr *kamēlopardalis* from Gr *kamēlos* the camel, and *pardalis* the panther]

camelot *kam'lot*, (*Fr*) *n* a hawker, pedlar; a newspaper vendor.

Camembert *kam'əm-ber* or Fr *kam-ã-ber*, *n* a soft rich cheese made near *Camembert*, in Normandy.

cameo *kam'i-ō*, *n* a gem with figure (*usu* a head or bust in profile) carved in relief, *esp* one in which a differently coloured lower layer serves as ground; a short literary piece; a small rôle in a play or film, often giving scope for character acting: — *pl* **cam'eos**. — *adj* miniature, small and perfect of its kind. — **cam'eo-part** or **cam'eo-rôle**; see **cameo** above; **cam'eo-shell** a helmet-shell; **cameo ware** pottery with relief dcoration on a ground of a different colour. [Ital *cammeo*, from LL *cammaeus*, of uncertain origin]

camera *kam'ər-ə*, *n* the photographer's apparatus, for recording an image on a light-sensitive plate or film; the apparatus that receives the image of the scene and converts it into electrical impulses for transmission (*TV*); a judge's private chamber (*pl* **camerae**); a legislative chamber; a vaulted room; the papal treasury; a cavity or chamber, *esp* in mollusc shells (*biol*): — *pl* **cam'eras**. — *adj* **cam'eral** of or pertaining to a judge's or a legislative chamber. — *adj* **cam'erāted** chambered; vaulted. — *n* **camerā'tion**. — **camera lucida** (*lū'sid-ə*; L, light chamber) a device by which the image of the object under a microscope is made to appear by reflection on a piece of paper so that it may be viewed and drawn simultaneously; **cam'eraman** a person who operates a television or film camera; **camera obscura** (*ob-skūr'ə*; L, dark chamber) a dark chamber in which an image of outside objects is projected on a screen; **camera-ready copy** (*printing*) finished text and/or illustrations ready for conversion to film from which printing plates will be made. — *adj* **cam'era-shy** (*colloq*) not liking or unwilling to be photographed. — **camera tube** the transducer device in a television or video camera that converts an optical image of a scene into electrical signals; **cam'erawork** the process or technique of filming or taking photographs. — **in camera** in a judge's private room; in secret; in private; **on camera** in front of a camera, being filmed; **to camera** (of a person) facing or addressing a TV or film camera. [L *camera*, Gr *kamarā* vault]

camerlengo *kam-ər-leng'gō* or **camerlingo** *-ling'gō*, *n* a papal treasurer: — *pl* **camerleng'os** or **camerling'os**. [Ital; connected with **chamberlain**]

Cameronian *kam-ə-rōn'i-ən*, *n* a follower of the Covenanter Richard *Cameron*, a member of the Reformed Presbyterian Church, a body that refused to accept the Revolution settlement (most of whom united with the Free Church in 1876); a soldier of the Cameronian regiment (the 26th and 90th Foot, later First Battalion of Scottish Rifles, disbanded in 1968), formed from a body of Cameronians (1689). — Also *adj*.

camese. See **camise**.

cami- *kam'i-*, *combining form* denoting camisole. — *n pl* **cam'iknickers** a woman's undergarment combining a camisole and knickers. — *n* **cam'i-top**.

camino real *kä-mē'nō rā-äl'*, (*Sp*) *n* a highway. [Literally royal road]

camion *kam'i-ən*, *n* a heavy lorry or wagon. [Fr]

camis *kam'is* or **camus** *kam'əs*, *n* (*Spenser*) a loose light robe. [Sp and Provençal *camisa* shirt, from L *camisia*]

camisade *kam'is-ad* or **camisado** *-ä'dō*, *n* a night attack, probably because shirts were often put on over armour for identification: — *pl* **cam'isades** or **camisa'dos**. [Sp *camisada*]

Camisard *kam'i-sär* or *-zär*, *n* an insurgent Huguenot of the Cevennes who fought against the French king's forces from 1685 to 1705, so called from the *camise* or blouse worn by the peasants.

camisole *kam'i-sōl*, *n* a loose underbodice with thin shoulder straps rather than sleeves; a sleeved jacket, a woman's loose negligée or jacket. [Fr]

camise or **camese** *kam-ēs'*, *n* a loose shirt or tunic, as worn by Arabs. [Ar *qamīç*, perh L *camisia*]

camlet *kam'lit*, *n* a cloth perhaps *orig* of camel's hair, but now chiefly of wool and goat's hair; a strong waterproof cloth. [Fr, from LL *camelotum*, from L *camēlus*; or perh Ar *khamlat* nap]

camogie *kamō'gē*, *n* in Ireland, a game, a form of hurling, played by women. [Anglicized from Ir Gaelic *camógaíocht*, from *camóg* a crooked stick]

camomile or **chamomile** *kam'ō-mīl*, *n* a name for several plants related to chrysanthemum, or their dried flowers, used medicinally for the stomach, as a tonic, etc, *esp Anthemis nobilis* (common camomile) and *Matricaria chamomilla* (wild camomile). — **camomile** (or **chamomile**) **tea** medicinal tea made with dried camomile flowers. [Fr *camomille*, from L *chamomilla*, from Gr *chamaimēlon*, literally earth-apple, from the apple-like smell of its blossoms, from *chamai* on the ground, and *mēlon* an apple]

Camorra *kam-or'ə*, *n* a Neapolitan secret society formed c. 1820, similar to the Mafia; (without *cap*) any similar society or organization. — *n* **Camorr'ism**. — *n* **Camorr'ist** or **Camorris'ta**. [Ital]

camote *kamō'tā*, *n esp* in W Indies, a yam or sweet potato. [Sp]

camouflet *kä-mōō-flā*, (*military*) *n* a mine used to destroy an underground enemy gun emplacement. [Fr, a whiff of smoke intentionally blown in the face, an affront]

camouflage *kam'ōōfläzh* or *kam'ə-fläzh*, *n* any device or means for disguising or concealing, or for deceiving an adversary, *esp* by adopting the colour, texture, etc of natural surroundings or backgrounds; the use of such a device or means. — *vt* and *vi* to deceive, counterfeit or disguise. — *n* **cam'oufleur** (*Fr*) a person or animal skilled in the art of camouflage. [Fr *camoufler* (verb); see also **camouflet**]

camp[1] *kamp*, *n* a place on which a tent or tents or the like are pitched; a collection of temporary dwellings, or their inhabitants collectively; temporary quarters of an army, tribe, travellers, holiday-makers, or others; an old fortified site; a permanent military station, depot or training school; a settlement that has grown up rapidly, as a mining town; a place where prisoners of war are detained; military service or life; an area of pasture that has been fenced off (*SAfr*); a place where sheep or cattle assemble (*Austr* and *NZ*); a party or group supporting a certain set of beliefs or doctrine. — *vi* to encamp, or pitch tents; to live in a tent or in temporary or makeshift accommodation (often with *out*, ie in the open); (of sheep or cattle) to gather in a group (*Austr* and *NZ*). — *n* **camp'er** a person who camps; a motor vehicle purpose-built, or which can be converted, for use as temporary living accommodation (also **camper van**). — **camp'-bed**, **-chair** or **-stool** a portable folding bed, chair or stool; **camp'-drafting** (*Austr*) a competition in which stockmen on horseback display their skill in drafting cattle; **camp'-fever** typhus, typhoid, or other fever tending to occur in camps with poor sanitary conditions; **camp'fire** the outdoor fire of an encampment; a reunion, lodge, or section, of certain organizations; **camp-foll'ower** a civilian who follows behind an army or works in a military camp, providing services for the military personnel; a person associated with a (political, etc) group without actually being a member; **camp'ground** (*US*) a campsite; **camp-meet'ing** a religious gathering in the open air or in a temporary encampment; **camp oven** (*Austr* and *NZ*) a metal box used for baking over a campfire; **camp-preach'er** a person who preaches at camp-meetings; **camp'site** ground suitable, or specially laid out, for camping. — **break camp** to pack up tents, equipment, etc and leave a camp; **camp on** (*telecomm*) to put (a telephone call) through to an engaged extension, to be connected automatically when the extension is free; **camp out** to live temporarily in a tent or in the open air; to stay temporarily in improvised accommodation; **go camping** to spend a holiday living in a tent or tents in the countryside. [Fr *camp* camp, from L *campus* a plain]

camp[2] *kamp*, (*obs*) *n* conflict; an old form of the game of football. — *vi* to fight, struggle. — *vi* **cam'ple** to wrangle. [OE *camp* battle; cf Ger *Kampf*]

camp[3] *kamp*, *adj* theatrical, affected, exaggerated; effeminately homosexual; characteristic of homosexuals. — *n* absurd and vulgar extravagance in manner, deliberate (**high camp**) or without full awareness of the effect. — Also *vi*. — *adj* **camp'y**. — *adv* **camp'ly**. — *n* **camp'ness**. — **camp it up** to show camp qualities ostentatiously; **camp up** to make exaggerated, etc. [Ety unknown]

campagna *käm-pän'yä*, (*Ital*) *n* once equivalent to **champaign**, now only a geographical proper name.

campaign *kam-pān'*, *n* a series of co-ordinated operations designed to achieve a military objective, in or at a certain time, and influenced by factors such as geography, position and strength of the enemy, etc; military service in the field; an organized series of activities aimed at achieving some goal or object, as in advertising or in politics, *esp* before an election or in order to influence policy. — *vi* to serve in or conduct a campaign. — *n* **campaign'er** a person actively involved in a political or other campaign; one who has served in several campaigns, a veteran (also **old campaigner**). [Fr *campagne*, from L *campania*, from *campus* a field]

campana *kam-pä'nə*, a bell-shaped object, such as the core of a Corinthian capital; a flower, perhaps the pasque-flower. [LL, a bell]

campanero *kam-pa-nā'rō*, *n* the S American bellbird or arapunga, having snowy-white plumage and a call like the peal of a church bell: — *pl* **campane'ros**. [Sp, bellman]

campaniform *kam-pan'i-förm*, (*biol*) *adj* bell-shaped. [LL *campana* a bell, and **-form**]

campanile *kam-pan-ē'lā*, *n* a bell-tower, *esp* a tall one detached from a church: — *pl* **campani'les**, or sometimes (*Ital*) **campani'li** (*-lē*). [Ital from *campana* a bell]

campanist *kam'pən-ist*, *n* a person with an expert knowledge of bells. [Ety as for **campana**]

campanology *kam-pən-ol'ə-ji*, *n* the study of bells; the art of bell-ringing. — *adj* **campanolog'ical**. — *n* **campanol'ogist**. [LL *campana* a bell, and **-ology**]

campanula *kam-pan'ū-lə*, *n* a plant of the *Campanula* genus (giving its name to a family **Campanulā'ceae**) commonly known as bell-flowers or bells, the best-known being the harebell or Scottish bluebell. — *adj* **campanūlā'ceous**. — *adj* **campan'ūlar**. [New L, from LL *campana* a bell]

Campanularia *kam-panū-lār'ia*, *n* a common genus of Hydrozoa with simple or branched stems and polyps surrounded by bell-shaped sheaths. [Ety as for **campanula**]

campanulate *kam-pan'ū-lāt*, *adj* bell-shaped. [LL *campana* a bell]

Campari *kam-pä'ri*, *n* a bitter-tasting, bright-red Italian apéritif flavoured with herbs. [Name of manufacturers; trade name in US]

Campbellite *kam'bəl-īt*, *n* a member of the US sect known as Disciples of Christ, founded by Alexander *Campbell* (1788–1866).

campeachy wood *kam-pēch'i wŏŏd*, *n* logwood, first exported from Campeachy (*Campeche*, in SE Mexico).

campeador *kam-pi-ə-dör'*, *n* a champion, *esp* the Cid. [Sp]

campesino *kam-pə-sē'nō*, *n* a Latin-American peasant farmer: — *pl* **campesin'os**. [Sp, from *campo* country, field, from L *campus* field]

campestral *kam-pes'trəl*, *adj* of or pertaining to fields or open country. — Also **campes'trian**. [L *campester*, from *campus* field]

camphire *kam'fīr*, *n* an old name for camphor; henna (*Bible*). [**camphor**]

camphor *kam'fər*, *n* a solid essential oil, derived from the camphor laurel (a species of cinnamon tree) of Taiwan, etc, or synthetically manufactured, having an aromatic smell and bitter taste, used as a liniment in medicine, and as a plasticizer, and as an insect repellent; any similar compound of the terpene series. — *n* **camphane** (*kam'fān*) a terpene hydrocarbon ($C_{10}H_{18}$), parent substance of the camphor group. — *n* **camphene** (*kam'fēn* or *-fēn'*) a camphor-like terpene hydrocarbon ($C_{10}H_{16}$) used in insecticides. — *n* **camphine** (*kam'fēn* or *-fīn*) an old name for rectified oil of turpentine. — *adj* **camphorā'ceous** like camphor. — *vt* **cam'phorate** to impregnate or treat with camphor. — *adj* **camphoric** (*-for'ik*) of or pertaining to camphor. — **cam'phorated oil** a liniment containing camphor, used to relieve irritation of the skin. [Fr *camphre*, from LL *camphora*, from Ar *kāfūr*]

campion *kam'pi-ən*, *n* any plant of the genera *Lychnis* (or *Melandryum*) and *Silene* having *usu* pink or white star- or salver-shaped flowers with notched petals. [Origin obscure; poss from obs *campion* champion]

cample. See **camp**[2].

campo *kam'pō*, *n* an area of open grassland in S America, *esp* in Brazil: — *pl* **cam'pos**. [Sp, from L *campus* a field]

campodeid *kam-pō'dē-id*, *n* a primitive wingless insect of the order Diplura having an elongated body and mouth parts hidden in the head. — *adj* **campodē'iform** of or resembling the **Campodē'idae**, like certain six-legged, hard-bodied active insect larvae. [Gr *kampē* caterpillar, and *eidos* form]

campo santo *kam'pō san'tō*, (*Ital*) *n* a cemetery, literally sacred field.

camporee *kam-pō-rē'*, *n* a local meeting of Scouts. [**camp** and (jamb)*oree*]

camp-sheathing *kamp'shē'dhing*, **camp-shedding** *-shed'ing* or **camp-sheeting** *-shēt'ing*, **camp-shot** *-shot*, *n* piles and boarding protecting a river bank, etc. [Origin unknown]

Camptonite *kamp'tən-īt*, *n* an igneous rock, a lamprophyre composed essentially of plagioclase and hornblende. [*Campton* in New Hampshire]

campus *kam'pəs*, *n* university or college grounds; a self-contained division of a university; a university or college, *esp* one in which all the buildings are on a single site; the academic world: — *pl* **cam'puses**. [L, field]

Campus Martius *kam'pəs mär'shəs*, *kam'pŏŏs mär'ti-ŏŏs*, (*L*) *n* a grassy plain used by the ancient Romans for athletic games, military drill, etc. [Field of Mars]

campylobacter *kam'pil-ō-bak-tər*, *n* a bacterium that is a common cause of gastroenteritis in humans, and also of abortion in cattle and sheep. — *n* **campylobactēriō'sis** infection with campylobacter. [Gr *kampylos* bent, and *bacterion* a little rod (from its shape)]

campylotropous *kam-pil-ot'rə-pəs*, (*bot*) *adj* (of an ovule) curved over so that the funicle appears to be attached to the side between the micropyle and the chalaza. [Gr *kampylos* curved, and *tropē* turning]

CAMRA *kam'rə*, *abbrev*: Campaign for Real Ale.

camsho *kam'shō* **camshoch** or **camsheugh** *kam'shuhh*, (*Scot*) *adj* crooked or deformed. [Cf **cam**[1], and OE *sceolh* awry]

camstairy, **camsteerie** or **camsteary** *kam-stār'i* or *-stēr'i*, (chiefly *Scot*) *adj* perverse, unruly, quarrelsome. [Ety dubious]

camstone. See **cam**[3].

camus[1] *kam'əs*, *adj* flat-nosed. [Prob Fr *camus*]

camus[2]. See **camis**.

camwood *kam'wŏŏd*, *n* the wood of a W African tree (*Baphia nitida*) used in making a red dye. [Perh from Afr name *kambi*]

Can. *abbrev*: Canada; Canadian; Canal; Canberra (*Austr*).

can. *abbrev*: canon (*music*); canto (*music*); canton.

can[1] *kan*, *vt* (*obs* in *infinitive* except in Scots) to be able; to have sufficient power; to have skill in: — 3rd *pers* **can**, *obs* 2nd *pers sing* **canst**; *participle obs* except **could** in Scots; *pa t* **could**. — **can** is used for *gan* in ME and in Spenser. — **can do** (*colloq*) I (or we) can do it, it can be done; **no can do** (*colloq*) I (or we) can't do it, it can't be done. [OE *cunnan* to know (how to do a thing), to be able; present indicative *can*; Gothic *kunnan*, Ger *können* to be able. See **con**[2], **ken**[1], **know**; also **cannot**, **can't**, **couth**.]

can[2] *kan*, *n* a tin, a container of tin-plate in which meat, fruit, etc, are sealed up to preserve them; a container for holding or carrying liquids, generally of tinned iron, with a handle over the top; the amount that a can holds (see also **canful** below); a container for various things, such as ashes or rubbish (*US*); a drinking-mug; a chimney-pot; a cylindrical container for storing film;

a jacket in which a fuel rod is sealed in an atomic reactor; a depth charge (*naval slang*); (with *the*) jail (*slang*); a lavatory (*slang*); the buttocks (*NAm slang*); (in *pl*) headphones (*slang*). — *vt* to put into tins in order to preserve; to store in containers; to stop, put an end to (*NAm slang*; see also **can it** below); to dismiss or sack from a job (*NAm slang*); to record (music, etc) in advance: — *pr p* **cann'ing**; *pa t* and *pa p* **canned**. — *adj* **canned** packed in tins; (of music, etc) recorded in advance for reproduction on a sound track or video, prerecorded; drunk (*slang*). — *n* **can'ful** the amount that a can holds: — *pl* **can'fuls**. — *n* **cann'er** a person whose job it is to put foodstuffs in cans. — *n* **cann'ery** a place where provisions are tinned. — **can'bank** the equivalent of a bottle bank (qv) for cans; **can buoy** a cylindrical navagational buoy, painted black, that marks the port, or left side, of a channel (cf **nun buoy**); **can'-opener** a tin-opener. — **can it** (*slang*) stop talking about, doing, etc that; **can of worms** an unpredictable and potentially difficult situation or problem; **carry the can** (*slang*) to take the blame or responsibility; **in the can** (of a motion picture, piece of music, etc) having been satisfactorily recorded, completed, etc, and ready for release; (of radio or TV material), recorded and stored for future use. [OE *canne*]

cañada *kän-yä'dä, n* a small narrow canyon, *esp* in western US. [Sp]

Canadian *kə-nā'di-ən, adj* of or pertaining to *Canada*. — *n* a native or citizen of Canada. — **Canada balsam** a transparent resin obtained from the balsam fir, used, when cured, as a mounting medium for microscopic specimens; **Canada Day** a Canadian public holiday, the anniversary of the union of the provinces, 1 July 1867 (formerly called **Dominion Day**); **Canada goose** a common wild goose (*Branta canadensis*) of N America; **Canada lily** a N American lily (*Lilium canadense*), with small yellow or orange bell-shaped flowers; **Canada rice** see **Zizania**; **Canadian canoe** a long narrow canoe, pointed at both ends, that is propelled by hand-held single-bladed paddles; **Canadian French** French as spoken in Canada (also *adj*); **Canadian pondweed** a N American aquatic plant (*Anacharis* or *Elodea canadensis*), introduced into Europe and commonly used in ponds as an oxygenator.

canaigre *kə-nā'gər* or *kə-nī'grē, n* a large Texan dock (*Rumex hymenosepalus*), whose root is used in tanning. [Mex Sp]

canaille *kan-äy'*, *kan-ī'* or *kən-āl'*, *n* the mob, the vulgar rabble, the masses. [Fr, from L *canis* a dog]

Canajan *kan'a-jan*, (*Can informal*) *n* Canadian English.

canakin. See **cannikin**.

canal *kə-nal'*, *n* an artificial watercourse, *esp* for navigation; a duct or passage that conveys fluids (*biol*); a groove; any of the indistinct channel-like markings apparent on the surface of Mars when viewed through a telescope (*astron*). — *adj* **canalicular** (*kan-ə-lik'ū-lər*) like or pertaining to a canaliculus. — *adj* **canalic'ulate** or **canalic'ulated** channelled, grooved or having furrows. — *n* **canalic'ulus** (*biol* and *anatom*) a small furrow or channel, eg one that occurs in bone: — *pl* **canalic'ulī**. — *n* **canalization** or **-s-** (*kan-əl-ī-zā'shən*) the construction of canals; the formation of an artificial channel; conversion into a canal; direction into a fixed channel (*lit* and *fig*). — *vt* **can'alize** or **-ise** to make a canal through; to convert into a canal; to direct into a fixed channel (*lit* and *fig*). — **canal'-boat** a boat for canal traffic; **canal'-cell** (*bot*) a cell in the neck of an archegonium; **canal'-rays** (*phys*) positive rays, a stream of positively electrified particles through a perforation in the cathode of a vacuum-tube. [L *canālis* a water-pipe]

canapé *ka'nə-pi* or *ka-na-pā, n* a small biscuit or piece of pastry or bread, etc with a savoury filling or spread, *usu* served with drinks; a sofa; a method of bidding in contract bridge in which a player bids a weak suit first, then rebids in his strongest suit. [Fr]

canard ka-när(*d*)', *n* a false rumour, a hoax; a second wing fitted near the nose of an aircraft, *esp* one smaller than the main wing and acting as the horizontal stabilizer; an aircraft with such a wing. — *adj* denoting such a wing, aircraft configuration, etc. [Fr, literally duck]

Canarese. See **Kanarese**.

canary *kə-nā'ri, n* a song-bird (finch) found in the Canary Islands, bright yellow in domestic breeds; a bright yellow colour (also **canary yellow**); a light sweet wine from the *Canary* Islands; a lively dance said to have originated in the Canary Islands (often in pl); an informer (*slang*); a convict (*Austr slang*); a guinea or sovereign (*obs slang*). — *adj* canary-coloured, bright yellow. — *vi* to dance the canary; to prance about. — **canā'ry-bird** a canary; a jail-bird or convict (*slang*); a mistress; **canā'ry-creeper** a S American climbing plant (*Tropaeolum peregrinum* or *canariense*), cultivated for its rapid growth and bright yellow flowers; **canā'ry-grass** a grass (*Phalaris canariensis*) whose seed (**canā'ry-seed**) is used as bird seed; **canā'ry-wood** the timber of two species of *Persea* or *Laurus* of the Canary Islands, Azores and Madeira.

canasta *kə-nas'tə, n* a card game similar to rummy, played with two full packs of cards, in which up to six players amass points by declaring sets of cards of the same rank; a set of seven or more cards of the same rank in canasta (also **meld**). [Sp, basket]

canaster *kə-nas'tər, n* a roughly broken kind of tobacco (so called from the rush basket in which it was *orig* imported from Spanish America). [Sp *canastra, canasta*, from Gr *kanastron*]

canc. *abbrev*: cancellation; cancelled.

cancan *kan'kan, n* an uproarious dance of French origin, *usu* performed on stage by women of the chorus and *orig* considered very improper because of the high kicking and raising of skirts. [Fr *cancan* chatter, scandal, the cancan; usu referred to L *quamquam*, the pronunciation of which was long hotly disputed in the French schools; Littré quotes OFr *caquehan* a noisy assembly]

cancel *kan'sl, vt* to annul or suppress; to revoke or discontinue; to abolish or call off; to counterbalance, compensate for or offset; to cross out or delete; (often with *out*) to eliminate as balancing each other, eg equal quantities from opposite sides of an equation, common factors from numerator and denominator of a fraction; to mark or stamp (eg a postage stamp) to prevent reuse. — *vi* (with *out*) to neutralize each other: — *pr p* **can'celling**; *pa t* and *pa p* **can'celled**. — *n* the process of correcting a serious error in a book, etc by removing a printed leaf or sheet; the part so cancelled, or (*usu*) the new one substituted. — *adj* **can'cellate** or **can'cellated** marked with a lattice-like pattern, reticulate; porous or spongy (*anatom*). — *n* **cancellā'tion** cancelling; cross-wise marking. — *n pl* **cancelli** (*kan-sel'ī*; L *kang-kel'ē*) cross-pieces forming a lattice-work or grating, as in the division between the choir and the body of a church; reticulations (*anatom*). — *adj* **can'cellous** (*anatom*) of bone, etc, having a spongy or porous structure. [L *cancellāre* to cross out, *cancellī* lattice-work, dimin of *cancer* a lattice]

cancelier or **canceleer** *kan-si-lēr'*, (*Scott*) *vi* (of a hawk) to turn on the wing before stopping. — Also *n*.

cancellarial *kan-səl-ār'i-əl*, or **cancellarian** *-i-ən, adj* relating to a chancellor. — *n* **cancellā'riate** chancellorship. [L *cancellārius*; see **chancellor**]

Cancer *kan'sər, n* the genus to which the edible crab belongs; a constellation (the Crab) between Gemini and Leo, and a sign of the zodiac (once coincident with it) whose first point marks the limits of the sun's course northward in summer; someone born under this sign. — *n* or *adj* **Cancer'ian**. — See also **tropic**. [L, crab]

cancer *kan'sər, n* loosely, any malignant new growth or tumour; properly, a carcinoma or disorderly growth of epithelial cells which invade adjacent tissue and are frequently spread by the lymphatics and blood-vessels to other parts of the body; any corroding evil or evil influence (*fig*). — *vi* **can'cerate** to become cancerous. — *n* **cancerā'tion**. — *adj* **can'cerous** of, like or affected with cancer. — *n* **cancerphobia** or **cancerophobia** (*-fō'bi-ə*) excessive fear of contracting, or that one may have, cancer. — **cancer root** beech-drops; **cancer stick** (*slang*) a cigarette. [L, crab, poss from the crab-like blood vessels that radiate from a cancerous tumour]

cancionero *kän-thyō-nā'rō*, *n* a collection of songs or poems, a songbook: — *pl* **cancione'ros**. [Sp]

cancriform *kang'kri-förm*, *adj* crab-shaped; like cancer. [**cancer** and **-form**]

cancrine *kang'krīn*, *adj* crab-wise; (of verses, etc) reading both ways, palindromic. [L *cancer* crab (from the false notion that a crab walks backwards)]

cancrizans *kang'kri-zanz*, (*music*) *adj* of a canon, having the imitating vocal part repeating the theme backwards (see also **crab canon**). [L *cancrizāre* to move backwards (like a crab)]

cancroid *kang'kroid*, *adj* crab-like; cancer-like. — *n* a type of slow-growing skin cancer. [**Cancer**, **cancer** and **-oid**]

CAND *abbrev*: Campaign Against Nuclear Dumping.

c and b (*cricket*) *abbrev*: caught and bowled (by).

candela *kan-del'ə* or *-dē'lə*, *n* the SI unit of luminous intensity (symbol **cd**); the luminous intensity in a given direction of a source that emits monochromatic radiation of frequency 540×10^{12} hertz and that has a radiant intensity in that direction of (1/683) watt per steradian. [L *candēla* candle]

candelabrum *kan-di-lā'brəm*, or *-lä'*, *n* a branched and ornamented candlestick or lampstand: — *pl* **candela'bra** — also used as a false *sing* with *pl* **candela'bras**. — **candelabrum tree** any of several African trees with branches arranged like a candelabrum. [L *candēlābrum*, from *candēla* candle]

candelilla *kän-dā-lēl'yə*, *n* a Mexican wax-yielding spurge. [Sp, dimin of *candela* candle]

candescent *kan-des'ənt*, *adj* glowing; white-hot. — Also (*archaic*) **candent** (*kan'dənt*). — *n* **candescence** (*kan-des'əns*) a white heat. [L *candēre* to glow (inceptive *candēscere*)]

c and f *abbrev*: cost and freight.

C and G *abbrev*: City and Guilds (of London Institute).

candid *kan'did*, *adj* frank, ingenuous; unposed, unrehearsed, informal; free from prejudice, unbiased; fair, impartial; white (*obs*); shining, clear (*obs*). — *adv* **can'didly**. — *n* **can'didness**. — **candid camera** a camera used for taking unposed photographs or films of people (*usu* without their knowledge) engaged in the normal activities of their daily life; this style of photography. [L *candidus* white]

candida *kan'did-ə*, *n* one of the genus *Candida* of parasitic, yeastlike imperfect fungi. — *adj* **can'didal**. — *n* **candidiasis** (*kan-di-dī'ə-sis*) an infection of the skin or mucous membranes caused by a candida (*usu C. albicans* which causes thrush). [L *candida*, fem of *candidus* white]

candidate *kan'di-dāt*, *n* a person who seeks or is nominated for any office or honour or who applies for a job, promotion, etc; a person or thing apparently suitable for a particular end; an examinee. — *n* **can'didature**, **can'didateship** or **can'didacy** (*-də-si*). [L *candidātus* dressed in white (because in Ancient Rome, candidates for election wore white togas), from *candidus* white]

candie. See **candy**[2].

candied. See **candy**[1].

candle *kan'dl*, *n* a cylinder of wax, tallow or the like surrounding a wick, burned to give light; something resembling this in appearance or function; a photometric unit; (or **new candle**) candela; (**international candle** or **standard candle**) a former unit of luminous intensity; a jet in a gas-stove; a luminary (*literary*). — *vt* to test (an egg) for freshness by holding up before a candle or other light. — **can'dleberry** wax myrtle or bayberry (*Myrica cerifera*) of the spurge family, or its fruit; **candle bomb** a small glass bomb filled with water, exploding in a candle flame; **can'dle coal** same as **cannel coal**; **can'dle-dipping** the method of making candles by dipping instead of moulding; **can'dle-doup** see **doup**; **can'dlefish** see **eulachon**; a W American fish, *Anaplopoma fimbria*, a cheek-armoured acanthopterygian, the *black candle-fish*; **can'dle-holder** a candlestick or candelabrum; a person who holds a candle to provide light for another while working or reading — hence someone who abets, connives or assists; **can'dlelight** the light of a candle; illumination by candles; the time when candles are lighted; **can'dle-lighter** a person whose job it is to light the candles; a spill; **can'dlenut** the oil-yielding fruit of a species of a tropical tree (*Aleurites mollucana*) of the Pacific Islands. — *adj* **can'dle-paring** miserly, stingy or parsimonious. — **can'dle-power** the illuminating power of a source of light; a former name for luminous intensity; **can'dle-snuffer** a person or device that snuffs out candles (see **snuff**[2]; also *fig*); **can'dlestick** a portable stand for a candle, *orig* a stick or piece of wood; **can'dle-tree** a tropical American tree (*Parmentiera cerifera*) with candle-like pods; **can'dle-waster** (*old slang*) someone who studies late; **can'dlewick** a soft cotton tufted material used for bedspreads, etc; the wick of a candle; **can'dlewood** the wood of various W Indian and Mexican resinous trees. — **burn the candle at both ends** to exhaust oneself by attempting to do too much, *usu* by going to bed late and getting up early for work; **do a candle** of a parachute, to fail to open out properly; **not fit to hold a candle to** (*derog*) not to be compared with; to be very inferior to; **sell by the candle** (*hist*) to offer for sale by auction as long as a small piece of candle burns, the bid made just before it goes out being successful; **the game is not worth the candle** the thing is not worth the effort or expense required. [OE *candel*, from L *candēla*, from *candēre* to glow]

Candlemas *kan'dl-məs*, (*Christian relig*) *n* the church festival of the purification of the Virgin Mary, on 2 February, when candles are blessed; a quarter-day in Scotland. [**candle** and **mass**]

candock *kan'dok*, *n* the yellow water-lily. [**can**[2] and **dock**[1]]

candour or (*NAm*) **candor** *kan'dər*, *n* frankness and openness; sincerity; freedom from prejudice, impartiality; purity (*obs*); kindness (*obs*); whiteness (now *rare*). [Fr *candeur*, from L *candor* whiteness, from *candēre* to shine]

CANDU or **Candu** *kan'doo*, (*nuc eng*) *n* a type of thermal nuclear power reactor developed by and widely used in Canada. [*Ca*nada, *d*euterium and *u*ranium]

C and **W** *abbrev*: country and western (music).

candy[1] *kan'di*, *n* a sweet of sugar boiled and crystallized (also also **su'gar-can'dy**); any form of confectionery (*NAm*; *pl* **can'dies**); cocaine (*drug-taking slang*). — *vt* to preserve or coat with sugar; to crystallize (sugar, etc); to encrust. — *vi* to crystallize; to become encrusted. — *adj* **can'died** encrusted or preserved with candy or sugar; sugared, flattering (*obs*). — **candy floss** or (*NAm*) **cotton candy** a fluffy ball of spun sugar, coloured and flavoured, sold on the end of a stick; something insubstantial or ephemeral. — Also *adj*. — **candy store** (*NAm*) a sweet shop or confectioners'; **candy stripe** a textile fabric pattern, consisting of narrow coloured stripes on a white background at intervals equal or nearly equal to the width of the stripe. [Fr *candi*, from Ar *qandah* candy]

candy[2] *kan'di*, *n* a S Indian weight, generally containing 20 maunds, approx 500 lb Imperial. — Also **can'die** or **kan'dy**. [Tamil]

candytuft *kan'di-tuft*, *n* a cruciferous plant of the genus *Iberis*, with flowers in tufts or corymbs, the outer petals larger than the inner. [From *Candia* Crete, where a species was found, and **tuft**]

cane *kān*, *n* the stem of one of the small palms (eg calamus or rattan) or the larger grasses (eg bamboo or sugar-cane), or raspberry or the like; wicker, rattan, etc used to weave baskets or light furniture; a slender stick used as a support for plants, etc; a slender, flexible rod used for beating, eg as a school punishment; a walking-stick. — *vt* to beat with a cane; to make or weave (eg chairs) with canes. — *n* **can'ing** a thrashing with a cane; a severe beating or defeat (*colloq*). — *adj* **can'y** like, made of, or abounding in cane. — *adj* **cane'-bottomed** (of a chair, etc) having a seat of interwoven cane strips. — **cane'brake** a thicket of canes, *esp* (in Southern US) of a giant reed; **cane'-chair** a chair made of rattan; **cane'fruit** fruit borne upon canes, such as raspberries and blackberries; **cane grass** (*Austr*) any of several long-stemmed grasses growing in swamps and marshes; **cane'-mill** a mill for crushing sugar-cane; **cane piece** (*W Indies*) a field of sugar cane, *esp* one belonging to a peasant farmer; **cane'-sugar** sucrose, *esp* that obtained from the sugar-cane; **cane'-toad** (*Austr*) the large toad (*Bufo marinus*) introduced to, and now abundant in, Queensland; **cane'-trash** refuse of sugar-cane used for fuel when boiling the juice. [Fr *canne*, from L *canna*, from Gr *kannē* a reed]

caneh. See **kaneh**.

canella *kan-el'ə*, *n* cinnamon (*obs*); any of the low aromatic trees of the genus *Canella*, of the family **Canellā'ceae** (*-si-ē*), *esp C. winterana* of the W Indies which yields white cinnamon or *canella bark*. [LL, dimin of *canna* reed]

canellini. See **cannellini**.

canephor *kan'i-fōr*, *-fór*, (*archit*) *n* a female (or male) sculptured figure carrying a basket on the head. — Also **cane'phora**, **can'ephore** or **canephorus** (*ka-nē'for-əs*). [Gr *kanēphoros* a basket bearer, as at the Panathenaic festival, from *kaneon* basket and *phoros* bearing]

Canes Venatici *kä'nēz və-nat'i-sī*, *n* a faint constellation in the northern hemisphere close to Ursa Major. [L, hunting dogs]

canescent *ka-nes'ənt*, *adj* tending to or becoming white or grey; hoary. — *n* **canesc'ence**. [L *cānēscēns*, from *cānēre*, from *cānus* hoary]

canfield *kan'fēld*, (*cards*) *n* a game adapted from patience in which money is gambled on the turn of each card. [R A Canfield, US gambler (1855–1914)]

cang. See **cangue**.

cangle *kang'l*, (*Scot*) *n* noise or disturbance; a dispute. — *vi* to argue or wrangle. [Cf Norw *kjangle* to quarrel]

cangue or **cang** *kang*, *n* formerly a Chinese portable pillory carried on the shoulders by petty offenders. [Fr *cangue*, from Port *cango* a yoke]

canicular *ka-nik'ū-lər*, *adj* pertaining to the Dog Star (**Canic'ula**) or **Sirius**. — **canicular days** the dog days; **canicular year** and **canicular period** or **cycle** see **Sothic year** and **Sothic period** or **cycle**. [L *canīculāris*, adj, and *canīcula*, dimin of *canis* a dog]

canid *kan'id*, (*zool*) *n* a member of the genus *Canis*, or of the family **Can'idae** (*-i-dē*), including dogs, wolves, foxes and jackals. [New L *Canidae*, from L *canis* dog]

canikin. See **cannikin**.

canine *kan'īn* or *kān'īn*, *adj* like or pertaining to the dog or related species. — *n* any animal of the dog family; a canine tooth. — *n* **caninity** (*kə-* or *kā-nin'i-ti*). — **canine appetite** a huge appetite; **canine distemper** see **distemper**; **canine letter** R (from its growling sound); **canine tooth** one of four sharp-pointed teeth between the incisors and the pre-molars. [L *canīnus*, from *canis* a dog]

Canis *kan'is*, *n* the dog genus, typical of the family Canidae. [L, dog]

Canis Major *kan'is mā'jər*, *n* a constellation in the S hemisphere containing Sirius, the Dog Star. — *genitive* (*L*) **Canis Majoris** (*mə-jö'ris*). [L, greater dog]

Canis Minor *kan'is mī'nər*, *n* a constellation in the N hemisphere near Gemini and Orion. — *genitive* (*L*) **Canis Minoris** (*mi-nö'ris*). [L, lesser dog]

canister *kan'is-tər*, *n* a box or case, *usu* of metal, for holding tea, shot, etc. — *vt* **can'ister**, **can'isterize** or **-ise** to put into, pack in, canister(s). — *n* **canisterizā'tion** or **-s-**. — **canister shot** case-shot. [L *canistrum* a wicker-basket; Gr *kanastron*, from *kannē* a reed]

canities *ka-nish'i-ēz*, *n* whiteness of the hair. [L]

canker *kang'kər*, *n* an ulcer; ulceration; a fungus disease in trees and shrubs, *esp* one due to Nectria; inflammation in horses' feet; irritation and ulceration in dogs' and cats' ears; an abscess or ulcer in birds; anything that corrupts, consumes, irritates or decays; a cankerworm; a dog-rose (*Shakesp*). — *vt* to eat into; corrupt or destroy; to infect or pollute; to make sour and ill-conditioned. — *vi* to grow corrupt; to decay. — *adj* **cank'ered** malignant, soured, crabbed; corroded (*obs*); polluted (*obs*). — *adv* **cank'eredly**. — *n* **cank'eredness**. — *adj* **cank'erous** corroding like a canker. — *adj* **cank'ery** affected with canker; crabbed (*Scot*). — **cank'erworm** a larva that feeds on and destroys plants, *esp* fruit. [L *cancer* a crab]

cann. Same as **con**[3].

canna[1] *kan'ə*, *n* a tropical or subtropical plant of the genus *Canna*, several species being cultivated for their showy reddish-orange flowers. [L, a reed]

canna[2]. See **cannot**.

canna[3] *kan'ə* or **cannach** *kan'əhh*, (*Scot*) *n* cotton-grass. [Gaelic *canach*]

cannabis *kan'ə-bis*, *n* hemp, a plant of the *Cannabis* genus, *esp Cannabis sativa* (common hemp) and *C. indica* (Indian hemp); a narcotic or mood-altering drug, variously known as hashish, bhang, marihuana, etc, obtained from the cannabis plant. — *adj* **cann'abic**. — *n* **cann'abin** a resin obtained from the dried leaves and flowers of the cannabis plant, containing the active principle of the drug (also **cannabis resin**). — *n* **cann'abinoid** any of a number of substances found in canabin, having narcotic or mood-altering properties. — *n* **cann'abinol** a crystalline phenol obtained from cannabin. [Gr *kannabis*; cf OE *hænep*]

cannel *kan'l*, *n* a bituminous coal that burns with a bright flame, used for making oils and gas. — Also **cann'el-coal** or **can'dle-coal**. [Prob form of **candle**]

cannellini or **canellini** *kan-ə-lē'nē*, *n pl* the white haricot beans used in French and Italian cooking. — Also **cannellini beans**. [Ital]

cannelloni *kan-ə-lō'nē*, *n pl* hollow tubes of pasta, stuffed with cheese, meat, etc. [Ital *cannelloni*, augmentative of *cannello* small tube]

cannelure *kan'i-lūr*, *n* a groove or a fluting; a groove round the cylindrical part of a bullet. [Fr]

cannibal *kan'i-bl*, *n* any eater of the flesh of its own species. — *adj* relating to or practising cannibalism. — *n* **cann'ibalism** the practice of eating one's own kind. — *adj* **cannibalist'ic**. — *n* **cannibaliza'tion** or **-s-**. — *vt* **cann'ibalize** or **-ise** to repair (a vehicle, aircraft, machine, etc) with parts taken from other vehicles, etc; to take (parts), or take parts from (vehicles, aircraft, machines), for such repairs. — *adv* **cann'ibally** (*Shakesp*). [Sp *Caníbal*, *Caríbal* Carib]

cannikin *kan'i-kin*, *n* a small can. — Also **can'akin** or **can'ikin**. [Dimin of **can**]

cannon *kan'ən*, *n* a great gun *usu* mounted on wheels (*hist*; *pl* **cann'ons** or **cann'on**); a rapid-firing, large-calibre gun fitted to an aeroplane, ship or helicopter gunship (*pl* **cann'ons** or **cann'on**); a cannon bone; a cannon bit; a stroke in which the cue-ball hits both the red and the opponent's ball (*billiards*; also *esp NAm* **carom**); a similar stroke in certain other games; the metal loop at the top of a bell. — *vi* to cannonade; to make a cannon (*billiards*); to strike on the rebound; to collide. — *vt* to collide with. — *n* **cannonade'** an attack with heavy artillery. — *vt* to attack or batter with heavy artillery. — *n* **cannoneer'** or **cannonier'** a soldier who managed and fired a cannon (*hist*); an artilleryman. — *n* **cann'onry** an attack or volley of heavy artillery fire; artillery. — **cann'onball** a ball to be shot from a cannon (*hist*); something resembling this in appearance, weight or force, eg a fast low shot in tennis. — *vi* to move rapidly with great force. — **can'nonball-tree** a S American tree (*Couroupita guianensis*) with a large woody fruit; **cannon bit** a smooth round bit; **cannon bone** a bone below the knee or hock in hoofed mammals, formed by the fusion of the persisting metacarpals or metatarsals; (in birds) the tarsometatarsus; **cann'on-fodder** men in a (*usu*) large army, regarded merely as material to be expended in war; **cann'on-game** a form of billiards in which, the table having no pockets, the game consists in making a series of cannons; **cann'on-metal** gun-metal. — *adj* **cann'on-proof** able to withstand cannon-shot. — **cann'on-shot** a cannonball; the distance to which a cannon will throw a cannonball. [Fr *canon*, augmentative, from L *canna* a reed]

cannot *kan'ət*, *v* can not (contracted to **can't** *känt*, *Scot* **canna** *kan'ā* or *kan'ə*, or **cannae** *kan'ā*). [**can**[1] and **not**]

cannula or **canula** *kan'ū-lə*, (*surg*) *n* a narrow tube, *esp* one for removing fluid from bodily cavities, or the breathing-tube inserted in the windpipe after tracheotomy: — *pl* **cann'ulae** (*-ū-lē*) or **cann'ulas**. — *adj* **cann'ular** or **cann'ulate**. [Dimin of *canna* a reed]

canny *kan'i*, *adj* knowing; skilful; shrewd, *esp* in business; sparing in money matters; lucky or fortunate (*Scot*); gentle; innocent; good or nice (*Northern*); sly or pawky. — Also *adv*. — *adv* **cann'ily**. — *n* **cann'iness**. — **ca' canny** see **ca'**; **no' canny** preternatural; dangerous. [Appar connected with **can**[1]]

canoe *kə-nōō'*, *n* a light, narrow, flat-bottomed boat, propelled by one or more paddles (*orig* made of a hollowed tree-trunk, or of bark or skins): — *vi* to paddle a canoe; to travel in a canoe. — *n* **canoe'ing**. — *n* **canoe'ist**. — **in the same canoe** (*NZ*) of, or belonging to, the same tribe; **paddle one's own canoe** see under **paddle**. [Sp *canoa*, from Haitian *canoa*]

cañon. See **canyon**.

canon[1] *kan'ən*, *n* a law or rule, *esp* in ecclesiastical matters; a generally accepted rule or principle, eg in morals; a standard or criterion; the books of the Bible accepted as the standard or rule of faith by the Jewish or Christian faiths; works forming any similar standard; a series of prayers in the Mass during which the Host is consecrated (*RC*); the recognized genuine works of any author; a type of vocal or instrumental musical composition in which the melody is repeated by one part following another in imitation; a list of the canonized saints; formerly a large size of type (*printing*). — *adj* **canonic** (*kə-non'ik*) or **canon'ical** of the nature of, according to, or included in a canon; regular; orthodox or accepted; ecclesiastical. — *adv* **canon'ically**. — *n pl* **canon'icals** the official dress of the clergy, regulated by the church canons. — *n* **canonicity** (*kan-ən-is'i-ti*) the state of belonging to the canon. — *n* **can'onist** a person learned in canon law. — *adj* **canonist'ic**. — *n* **canonizā'tion** or **-s-**. — *vt* **can'onize** or **-ise** (*Shakesp -non'*) to enrol in the canon or list of saints; to recognize as canonical. — **canonical hours** set hours for prayer or the services prescribed for these times; any time between 8am and 6pm, when marriages may take place in an English parish church (*Ch of Eng*); **canon law** a digest of the formal decrees of councils, ecumenical, general and local, of diocesan and national synods, and of patriarchal decisions concerning religious doctrine and discipline; **canon lawyer** a canonist. [OE *canon*, from L *canōn*, from Gr *kanōn* a straight rod, from *kannē* a reed]

canon[2] *kan'ən*, *n* a member of a body of clergymen serving a cathedral or other church and living under a rule; a clerical dignitary belonging *esp* to a cathedral, enjoying special emoluments, and obliged to reside there part of the year. — *n* **can'oness** a member of a community of women living under a religious rule but not under a vow; a woman holding a prebend or canonry, often living in the secular world. — *n* **canon'icate** the rank or office of a canon. — *n* **can'onry** the office or benefice of a canon; canons collectively; (often with *cap*) a building in which a canon resides. — **canon regular** a member of either of two religious orders (Augustinian or Black Canons, and Premonstratensian or White Canons) who live in communities as monks but perform the duties of secular clergy; **canon residentiary** a canon obliged to reside at a cathedral and take a share in the duty; **canon secular** a canon who is not a canon regular; **honorary canon** a person with the titular rank of canon in a cathedral, but without duties or emoluments; **minor canon** a person who conducts cathedral services but is not a member of the chapter. [OE *canonic*, from L *canonicus*, from *canōn*; see **canon**[1]]

canoodle *kə-nōōd'l*, (*slang*) *vi* to kiss and cuddle. [Origin obscure]

canophilist *kə-nof'i-list* or **cynophilist** *si-* or *sī-*, (often *facetious*) *n* a lover of dogs. — *n* **canophilia** (*kan-ō-fil'i-ə*) or **cynophilia** (*sin-* or *sīn-*) love of dogs. [L *canis* a dog and Gr *phileein* to love]

canophobia *kan-ō-fō'bi-ə* or **cynophobia** *sin-* or *sīn-ō-*, *n* morbid fear of dogs. [L *canis*, from Gr *kyon*, *kynos* dog, and Gr *phobos* fear]

Canopus *kə-nō'pəs*, *n* the brightest star in the southern constellation *Carina*; an ancient Egyptian vase with a carved top or stopper in the form of a human or animal head, for holding the entrails taken from a body during the embalming process (also **Canopic jar**, **vase** or **urn**). — *adj* **Cano'pic**. [L, from Gr *Kanōpos*, Menelaus's steersman who died at Canopus in Egypt, was stellified as Canopus, and identified with an Egyptian god worshipped in the form of a jar with human head]

canopy *kan'ə-pi*, *n* a covering hung over a throne or bed; a ceremonial covering held over the head; any overhanging covering, such as the sky; the topmost layer of branches and foliage in a forest; a rooflike projection over a niche, tomb, statue, stall, altar, etc; the transparent cover over the cockpit of an aircraft; the overhead fabric part of a parachute. — *vt* to cover with a canopy: — *pr p* **can'opying**; *pa t* and *pa p* **can'opied**. [Fr *canapé*, from L *cōnōpium*, *cōnōpēum*, from Gr *kōnōpion* a couch with a mosquito curtain, from *kōnōps* a mosquito]

canorous *kan-ō'rəs*, *-ö'*, or *kan'*, (*formal*) *adj* musical; singing; resonant. — *adv* **cano'rously** (or *kan'*). — *n* **cano'rousness** (or *kan'*). [L *canōrus*, from *canor* melody, from *canere* to sing]

canst. See **can**[1].

canstick *kan'stik*, (*Shakesp*) *n* a candlestick. [Contraction]

Cant. *abbrev*: Canterbury; Canticles.

cant[1] *kant*, *vi* to speak in a whining or wheedling manner; to use language whose meaning has evaporated from continued repetition; to use the specialized vocabulary or jargon of thieves, politicians, lawyers, etc; to talk in an affectedly solemn or hypocritical way. — *n* a hypocritical, affected or perfunctory style of speech or thought; the vocabulary or language peculiar to a particular group or sect; odd or peculiar talk of any kind; slang; a common saying or stock phrase; affected use of religious phrases or moral sentiments. — Also *adj*. — *n* **cant'er** a person who cants, *esp* a beggar; a person who makes hypocritical or affected statements. — *adj* **cant'ing** whining, pretending to piety. — **canting arms** (*heraldry*) a coat of arms in the form of a rebus, or a visual pun on the bearer's surname. [L *cantāre*, frequentative of *canere* to sing]

cant[2] *kant*, *n* an inclination from the vertical or horizontal plane; a toss or jerk which tilts or turns anything; a sloping or tilted position or face; one of the segments forming a side-piece in the head of a cask; a ship's timber lying obliquely to the line of the keel. — *vt* and *vi* to turn on the edge or corner; to tilt or toss suddenly; to tilt or slope. — Also **kant**. — *adj* **cant'ed** tilted, sloping. — *n* **cant'ing** tilting. — **cant'-board** a sloping board; **cant'dog** or **cant'hook** (*forestry*) a metal hook on a long handle, for rolling logs; **canted deck** (*aeronautics*) see **angled deck**; **cant'ing-coin** a piece of wood to prevent casks rolling; **cant'ing-wheel** a wheel with bevelled cogs; **cant'-rail** a timber supporting the roof of a railway carriage. [Prob connected with Du *kant*; Ger *Kante* corner]

cant[3] *kant*, *n* sale by auction. — *vt* to sell by auction. [OFr *encant* auction; origin uncertain, cf LL *incantāre* to put up to auction]

cant[4] *kant*, (*Northern*) *adj* brisk; lively; merry. [Cf LGer *kant*, and **canty**]

can't contraction of **cannot**.

Cantab. *kan'tab*, *abbrev*: *Cantabrigiensis* (*L*), of Cambridge.

cantabank *kan'tə-bangk*, *n* a strolling singer. [Ital *cantambanco*]

cantabile *kan-tä'bē-lā*, (*music*) *adj* flowing and melodious, like singing. — Also *n*. [Ital, suitable for singing]

Cantal *kan'tal*, or *kã'tal*, *n* a hard, full-fat French cheese made from cow's milk, from the *Cantal* department of the Auvergne.

cantala *kan'talə*, *n* a coarse fibre used in making strong thread or twine, obtained from a tropical American plant (*Agave cantala*). [Origin unknown]

cantaloupe or **cantaloup** *kan'tə-lōōp*, *n* a small musk melon with a ribbed skin; in the US any of several varieties of cultivated melon. [Fr, from Ital *Cantalupo*, near Rome, where it was first grown in Europe]

cantankerous *kən-tang'kər-əs*, *adj* irascible; contrary, quarrelsome or stubborn. — *adv* **cantan'kerously**. — *n* **cantan'kerousness**. [Perh ME *contek* strife]

cantar. Same as **kantar**.

cantata *kan-tä'tə*, *n orig* the name applied to a sort of musical narrative by one person, accompanied by a single instrument; since the later introduction of an air, the modern concert aria; now also a choral work, a short oratorio or opera intended for concert performance only. — *n* **cantatrice** (*kan-ta-trē'chā* or *kan'tə-trēs*) a female singer. [Ital, from L *cantāre*, frequentative of *canere* to sing]

cantate *kan-tä'tā* or *kan-tā'tē*, *n* the 98th Psalm, from its opening words in Latin, 'Cantate Domino'.

canteen *kan-tēn'*, *n* a flask for carrying liquids, used by soldiers, etc; a set of cooking utensils for soldiers, campers, etc; a box containing a set of knives, forks and spoons; a set of cutlery; a cafeteria or small shop for soldiers; a restaurant attached to an office, factory, etc; a public house (*SAfr*). [Fr *cantine*, from Ital *cantina* a cellar]

cante jondo or **cante hondo** *kän'tā hhon'dō*, (*Sp*) *n* an emotional and melancholy type of song sung *esp* by Andalusian gypsies. [Sp, intense song]

canter *kan'tər*, *n* an easy gallop. — *vi* to move at an easy gallop. — *vt* to make (a horse, etc) canter. [Orig *Canterbury-gallop*, from the easy pace at which the pilgrims rode to Canterbury]

canterbury *kan'tər-bər-i*, *n* a stand with divisions in it for holding books, music, etc: — *pl* **can'terburys** or **can'terburies**. — **Canterbury bell** *orig* the nettle-leaved bellflower, or throatwort; now applied to a cultivated biennial plant (*Campanula medium*) with large blue, white, or pink bell-like flowers; loosely applied to other large-flowered bellflowers; **Canterbury lamb** frozen or chilled New Zealand lamb imported by the UK.

cantharis *kan'thər-is*, *n* a blisterbeetle or Spanish fly (*Lytta* or *Cantharis*); in *pl* **cantharides** (*kan-thar'i-dēz*) a blistering agent and stimulant made from their dried bodies, formerly also used as an aphrodisiac. — *n* **can'tharid** a member of the genus Cantharis or Lytta. — *adj* **canthar'idal**, **cantharid'ian** or **cantharid'ic**. — *n* **canthar'idine** the active principle of blisterflies. [L *cantharis*, from Gr *kantharis* (a blisterbeetle), pl *kantharides*]

cantharus *kan'thə-rəs*, *n* a large two-handled drinking-cup; a laver in the atrium before ancient churches: — *pl* **can'tharī**. [L, from Gr *kantharos*]

canthaxanthin *kan-thə-zan'thin* or **canthaxanthine** *kan'-thə-zan'thēn*, (*chem*) *n* an orange dye, formerly widely used as a food additive in salmon and eggs to enhance colour, now banned in many countries because of its link with certain cancers.

canthus *kan'thəs*, *n* the angle where the upper and lower eyelids meet: — *pl* **can'thī**. [L, from Gr *kanthos*]

canticle *kan'ti-kl*, *n* a song; a non-metrical hymn, *esp* one used in church service as the benedicite; a canto (*Spenser*); a short canto; (in *pl*; *usu* with *cap*) the Song of Solomon (also **Canticle of Canticles**). — *n* **can'ticum** a canticle; a part-song in an ancient play. [L *canticum*, dimin *canticulum*]

cantico, **canticoy**. See **kantikoy**.

cantilena *kan-ti-lē'nə*, *n* a ballad or light song; a vocal or instrumental melody; a cantus firmus or melody for church use; a singing exercise or solfeggio. [L *cantilēna*]

cantilever *kan'ti-lēv-ər*, or *-lēv'*, *n* a support or beam fixed at one end and free at the other; a large bracket for supporting cornices, balconies, and stairs. — *vt* to construct (a support or beam) so that it is fixed at one end only. — *vi* to project or support like a cantilever. — *adj* **can'tilevered**. — **cantilever bridge** a bridge constructed of beams or cantilevers built into piers at each end of the span and connected together in the middle of the span. [Perh **cant** angle, and **lever**]

cantillate *kan'ti-lāt*, *vt* and *vi* to chant or intone, *esp* Hebrew scriptures in the Jewish liturgical service. — *n* **cantillā'tion**. — *adj* **can'tillatory**. [L *cantillāre* to sing softly, from *cantāre* to sing]

cantina *kan-tē'nə*, *n* a bar or saloon; a wine-shop. [Sp and Ital]

cantion *kan'shən*, (*Spenser*) *n* a song. [L *cantiō*, *-ōnis*]

cantle *kan'tl*, *n* a corner, edge or slice of anything; the raised hind part of a saddle; the crown of the head (*Scot*). — *vt* to cut or break a piece from; to divide. — *n* **cant'let** a fragment. [**cant**[2] edge]

canto *kan'tō*, *n* a division of a long poem; the part in a piece of music that carries the melody; the highest part in a piece of choral music (also **cant'us**): — *pl* **can'tos**. — Also (*Shakesp*) **can'ton**. — **canto fermo** (*fûr'mō*) plainsong, the unornamented melody used in the Western Church from the earliest times, to which later other parts in counterpoint were added. [Ital, from L *cantus*, from *canere* to sing]

canton[1] *kan'tən* or *kan-ton'*, *n* a corner (*obs*); a division or space (*obs*); a division of territory, constituting in Switzerland a separate government, in France a subdivision of an arrondissement; a pilastered or quoined corner of a building (*archit*); (on a shield) an ordinary, ie a square occupying generally the dexter, sometimes the sinister, chief of the field (*heraldry*). — *vt* to divide into cantons; (*military kən-tōōn'*) to allot quarters to (military personnel): — *pr p* **can'toning**; *pa t* and *pa p* **can'toned**. — *adj* **can'tonal** pertaining to or divided into cantons. — *adj* **can'toned** ornamented at the corners with projecting pilasters (*archit*); placed amongst charges occupying the corners of a shield (*heraldry*). — *n* **cantoniza'tion** or **-s-**. — *vt* **can'tonize** or **-ise** to divide (a town, etc) into separate areas according to the religions, ethnic origins, etc of the inhabitants. — *n* **canton'ment** (military *kən-tōōn'mənt*) the temporary quarters of troops taking part in manoeuvres or active operations; in British India, a permanent military town (*hist*). [OFr *canton*; Ital *cantone* corner, district, from *canto* a corner; cf **cant**[2]]

canton[2]. See **canto**.

Canton crepe *kan-ton' crāp* *n* a fine crinkled silk or crepe, *orig* made in *Canton* in China.

Cantonese *kan-ton-ēz'*, *adj* belonging to or typical of *Canton*, a city in S China; of a style of cooking originating there. — *n* a native of Canton; the dialect of Canton: — *pl* **Cantonese'**.

cantor *kan'tör*, *n* the leader of the singing in a church, a precentor; in a synagogue, the person who chants the liturgy and leads the congregation in prayer (also **chazan**). — *adj* **cantorial** (*-tō'ri-əl*, or *-tö'*) of or pertaining to a precentor or his position on the north side of a cathedral (cf **decanal**). — *adj* **cantō'ris** (*genitive* of L *cantor* of the cantor) to be sung on the cantorial or north side of a choir (cf **decani**). [L, singer, from *canere* to sing]

cantred *kan'tred*, or **cantref** *kan'trev*, (*hist*) *n* a division of a county, a hundred. [Welsh *cantref*, from *cant* hundred, and *tref* town]

cantrip *kan'trip*, (*Scot*) *n* a wilful piece of trickery or mischief; a witch's spell. — Also *adj*. [Ety unknown]

Cantuar. *kan-tū-är*, *abbrev*: *Cantuaria* (*L*), Canterbury (as the archiepiscopal see of the primate of the Church of England).

cantus *kan'təs*, *n* a melody or chant, *esp* in medieval ecclesiastical music; the highest part in a piece of choral music (also **canto**): — *pl* **can'tus**. — **cantus firmus** (*fûr'məs*) canto fermo. [L, song, from *canere* to sing]

canty *kan'ti*, (*Scot*) *adj* cheerful, lively. — *n* **can'tiness**. [**cant**[4]; cf LGer *kantig*]

Canuck *kə-nuk'*, (*informal*; often *derog*) *n* a Canadian (*NAm*); a French-Canadian or the French-Canadian language (*Can*); a small Canadian horse or pony. — *adj* relating to Canada or to Canadians. [Ety uncertain]

canula. See **cannula**.

canvas *kan'vəs*, *n* a coarse cloth made of cotton, hemp or other material, used for sails, tents, etc, and for painting on; the sails of a vessel collectively (*naut*); a tent or tents; a piece of stretched canvas, painted or to be painted; the covered front or back of a racing-boat (whence **a canvas-length, a win by a canvas** (*rowing*)); open-weave material on which embroidery or tapestry is worked; the floor of a boxing or wrestling ring; the background against which events occur (*lit* and *fig*). — *vt* to cover or line with canvas. — **can'vasback** a N American duck (*Aythyra valisineria*), with an ashy white back crossed by dark zigzag lines, closely related to the pochard; **can'vas-climber** (*Shakesp*) a sailor; **can'vas-stretcher** a wooden frame on which canvas is stretched for oil-painting; **can'vas-work** embroidery on canvas, or on cloth over which canvas has been laid to guide the stitches. — **under canvas** having the sails unfurled, under sail; in a tent or tents. [OFr *canevas*, from L *cannabis*, from Gr *kannabis* hemp]

canvass *kan'vəs*, *vt* to toss in a canvas blanket (*obs*); hence, to criticize roughly; to examine; to discuss thoroughly; to solicit votes, orders, contributions, etc from; to scrutinize (votes, etc) in order to establish their validity (chiefly *NAm*). — *vi* to solicit votes, etc (with *for*); to go from person to person seeking information. — *n* close examination; a seeking or solicitation of votes, information, etc; a scrutiny of votes (chiefly *NAm*). — *n* **can'vasser**. [**canvas**]

cany. See **cane**.

canyon or **cañon** *kan'yən*, *n* a deep gorge or ravine. [Sp *cañón* a hollow, from root of **cannon**]

canzone *kant-sō'nā* or **canzona** *kan-zō'nə*, *n* a song or air resembling, but less elaborate than, a madrigal; an instrumental piece of similar character; a Provençal or Italian form of lyric poetry, consisting of a series of stanzas without a refrain: — *pl* **canzo'ni** (*-nē*) or **canzo'nas**. — *n* (*dimin*) **canzonet** (*kan-zō-net'*) or **canzonetta** (*kan-tsō-net'ə*: *pl* **canzonet'te** *-tā*). [Ital, a song, from L *cantiō*, *-ōnis*, from *canere* to sing]

caoutchouc *kow'chŏŏk*, *n* raw rubber, gum-elastic; the latex of rubber trees. [Fr, from Carib *cahuchu*]

CAP (sometimes *kap*) *abbrev*: Common Agricultural Policy (of the EEC).

cap[1] *kap*, *n* formerly, a woman's light head covering, *usu* worn indoors and made from lace, fine linen, etc; a flat brimless hat, *usu* with a peak; an official or symbolic headdress or one appropriated to a special class or use, academic, athletic, etc; an occasion of being selected for *esp* a national team, symbolized by a cap; a person so selected; the enamel which covers a tooth (*anatom*); an artificial covering for a tooth, replacing the natural enamel; a caplike covering of any kind; the top of a toadstool; the uppermost or terminal part of anything; a percussion cap (qv) for a toy gun, etc; a collection of money taken at a fox hunt (*orig* in a cap) for hunt servants, charity, etc; (also **Dutch cap**) a contraceptive diaphragm. — *vt* to cover the end or top of; to touch with a cap in conferring a degree (chiefly *Scot* and *NZ*); to select as a member of a team; to outdo or surpass by following with something better, more significant, etc; to seal off and halt the flow from (an oil or gas well); to set a limit to (*esp* local authority budgets). — *vt* and *vi* to salute by raising the cap: — *pr p* **capp'ing**; *pa p* and *pa t* **capped** (*kapt*). — *n* **capp'er**. — *n* **capp'ing** the action of the verb *cap*; a covering, eg a hard crust that forms on soil during dry weather; a graduation ceremony (*informal*). — **cap'-case** (*obs*) a small travelling-case, a chest; **cap'-paper** a kind of wrapping paper; a size of writing paper; **cap pistol** a toy gun using a percussion cap; **cap rock** a stratum of (*usu* impervious) rock overlying oil- or gas-bearing strata; **cap screw** a bolt with a threaded shaft and cylindrical head with a hexagonal indentation for turning it; **cap sleeve** a short sleeve, just covering the shoulder; **cap'stone** a coping stone; the top or finishing stone of a structure; a stone slab laid flat over the top of a cist (*archaeol*); the horizontal stone of a dolmen (*archaeol*); a flat stone acting as a cap, eg to a shaft or chimney. — **black cap** see under **black**; **cap and bells** the insignia of a professional jester; **cap and collar mortgage** one having a minimum (*collar*) and maximum (*cap*) rate of interest; **cap in hand** submissively; supplicatingly; **cap of liberty** the conical cap, *usu* made of red material, given to a Roman slave on enfranchisement, and adopted during the French revolution as an emblem of freedom, now the symbol of republicanism; **cap of maintenance** see under **maintain**; **cap verses** to quote verses in turn, according to rule; **college cap** a mortarboard or trencher-cap; **set one's cap at** (of a woman) to set oneself to captivate (a man); **the cap fits** the allusion is felt to apply; **throw up one's cap** to make this gesture (*lit* or *fig*) in token of immoderate joy; **to cap it all** as a (often unpleasant) climax. [OE *cæppe*, from LL *cappa* a cape or cope]

cap[2] *kap*, or **caup** *köp* (*Scot*) *n* a wooden drinking-bowl, with two handles. [OE *copp* a cup; or Scand *koppr*]

cap. (sometimes *kap*) *abbrev*: capacity; *capiat* (*L*), let him or her take; capital; capitalize; capital letter; *caput* (*L*), chapter.

capa *kä'pə*, *n* a Spanish cloak; fine Cuban tobacco for the outer layers of cigars. [Sp]

capable *kā'pə-bl*, *adj* comprehensive (*Shakesp*); having (*esp* legal) right, or (with *of*) right to (*obs*); having practical ability; able (often with *of*); qualified. — *n* **capabil'ity** the quality or state of being capable; (*usu* in *pl*) a feature capable of being used or developed; ability for the action indicated, because provision and preparation have been made; manufacturing facilities, such as factories or plant. — *n* **cā'pableness**. — **capable of** able to take in, contain, understand, etc (*archaic*); sufficiently able, good, well-made, etc to, or sufficiently bad, foolish, etc, to (followed by verbal noun or other action noun); susceptible of. [Fr, from LL *capābilis*, from L *capere* to hold, take]

capacious. See under **capacity**.

capacitance *kə-pas'i-təns*, *n* the property that allows a system to store an electric charge; the value of this expressed in farads (qv). — *n* **capac'itor** an electrical device capable of storing electric charge, *usu* consisting of conductors separated by an insulator. [**capacity**]

capacity *kə-pas'i-ti*, *n* the power of holding, containing, absorbing or grasping; the maximum amount that may be contained, held, absorbed, etc; volume; an ability or talent; mental power; the position or function in which one does something; legal competence; maximum possible output or performance; formerly capacitance (*electronics*); possession of industrial plant, technology, etc, with resulting ability to produce goods. — *adj* attaining or containing the maximum number possible. — *adj* **capacious** (*kə-pā'shəs*) able to hold much; roomy; wide; extensive. — *adv* **capā'ciously**. — *n* **capā'ciousness**. — *vt* **capac'itate** to make legally competent; to make or render capable; to qualify; to cause (a sperm) to undergo changes while in the female reproductive tract enabling it to fertilize an egg. — *n* **capacitā'tion**. — **capacity for heat** power of absorbing heat; **legal capacity** the power to alter one's rights or duties by the exercise of free will, or responsibility for one's acts; **to capacity** to the utmost capacity, the fullest extent possible. [Fr *capacité*, from L *capāx*, *-ācis* able to receive, from *capere* to hold]

cap-à-pie or **cap-a-pie** *kap-ə-pē*, (*archaic* or *facetious*) *adv* (dressed) from head to foot, eg of a knight in armour. [OFr *cap a pie* (Mod Fr *de pied en cap*), from L *caput* head, *ad* to and *pēs* foot]

caparison *kə-par'i-sən*, *n* an ornamented covering for a horse, *esp* a rich cloth laid over a warhorse; rich clothing and ornaments generally. — *vt* to cover (a horse or other animal) with a caparison; to dress very richly. — *adj* **capar'isoned**. [Fr *caparaçon*, from Sp *caparazón*, augmentative of *capa* cap, cover, from LL *cappa* cape]

cape[1] *kāp*, *n* a covering for the shoulders attached as a tippet to a coat or cloak; a sleeveless cloak. — *n* **cape'let** a small cape. — **cape'work** the skill or technique of a bullfighter in making the bull follow the cape. [OFr *cape*, from LL *cappa*]

cape[2] *kāp*, *n* a head or point of land jutting into the sea or a lake; (with *cap*) see **the Cape** (below). — *vi* (*naut*) to keep a course. — **Cape cart** (*SAfr*) a two-wheeled horse-drawn vehicle with a hood; **Cape Coloured** a person of mixed race, in the Cape Province of S Africa; **Cape doctor** (*SAfr*) a strong SE wind in the Cape, so named because it was believed to blow away germs; **Cape Dutch** a former name for Afrikaans (qv); an architectural style of the Cape, characterized by white-washed, gabled, thatched-roof, single-storey houses; **Cape gooseberry** the strawberry tomato (*Physalis peruviana*), a S American solanaceous plant with bladdery calyx, naturalized in S Africa; its edible, soft, yellow fruit; **Cape hyacinth** see **hyacinth**; **Cape nightingale** a frog; **Cape pigeon** a species of petrel (*Daption capensis*), a common winter visitor to the Cape area of S Africa; **Cape smoke** (*SAfr slang*) S African brandy, dop; **Cape sparrow** see under **mossie**[2]. — **the Cape** the Cape of Good Hope; Cape Province, Capetown and Cape Peninsula. [Fr *cap*, from L *caput* the head]

capelet. See **cape**[1].

capelin *kap'ə-lin* or **caplin** *kap'lin*, *n* a small fish (*Mallotus villosus*) of the smelt family, abundant off Newfoundland, much used as bait. [Fr *capelan*]

capeline or **capelline** *kap'ə-lin*, *n* a small iron skullcap worn by archers; a light woollen hood for evening wear; a surgical bandage for the head. [Fr, from LL *capella*, from *capa* a cap]

Capella *ka-pel'ə*, *n* a first-magnitude star in the northern constellation Auriga. [L, literally she-goat]

capellet or **capelet** *kap'ə-lit*, (*vet*) *n* a cyst-like swelling on a horse's elbow, or on the back part of the hock. [Fr, from LL *capella*, from *capa* a cap]

capellmeister. Same as **kapellmeister**.

caper[1] *kā'pər*, *n* a thorny S European shrub (*Capparis spinosa*), with edible flower-buds (also **cap'er-bush**); a flower-bud of this shrub, pickled and used in cooking as a flavouring or garnish. — **cā'per-sauce** a sauce for boiled mutton, etc, made with capers; **cā'per-spurge** a kind of spurge whose capsules are sometimes pickled; **cā'per-tea** a black tea with a knotty curled leaf. [L *capparis*, from Gr *kapparis*]

caper[2] *kā'pər*, *vi* to leap or skip like a goat; to dance playfully; to frolic. — *n* a leap; a gambol; an escapade; any activity or pursuit (*colloq*); an illegal or questionable act, a crime (*slang*). — *n* **cā'perer**. — **cut a caper** or **cut capers** to gambol; to attempt to attract attention by one's behaviour. [L *caper* (masc), *capra* (fem) a goat]

caper[3]. See **capercailzie**.

capercailzie or **capercaillie** *kap-ər-kā'lyi*, *-li* or (*erron*) *-lzi*, also *kā'pər-* *n* a large European woodland grouse (*Tetrao urogallus*), the male of which has dark plumage and a fan-shaped tail. — Also **cap'er**. [Gaelic *capull coille* horse of the wood]

Capernaite *ka-* or *kə-pûr'ni-īt*, *n* an inhabitant of *Capernaum* in Galilee; (*polemically*) a believer in transubstantiation (John 6. 35, 51). — *adj* **Capernaitic** (*-it'ik*). — *adv* **Capernait'ically**.

capernoity, **capernoitie** or **cappernoity** *kap-ər-noi'ti*, (*Scot*) *n* the head, noddle. — *adj* peevish; irritable; capricious; drunk, giddy. — *adj* **capernoit'ed** capernoity. [Origin unknown]

capeskin *kāp'skin*, *n* a type of soft leather made from the skins of long-haired sheep or lambs. [Cape of Good Hope]

capias *kā'pi-as*, or *ka'*, (*law*) *n* a writ which authorizes the arrest of the person named in it. [L, you should seize, from *capere* to take]

capillaceous *kap-i-lā'shəs*, *adj* hairlike; having numerous fine filaments. [L *capillāceus* resembling hair, from *capillus* hair]

capillaire *kap-i-lār'*, *n* a syrup, an infusion of maidenhair fern flavoured with orange-flower water. [Fr]

capillary *kə-pil'ə-ri*, sometimes *kap'*, *adj* pertaining to hair; hairlike; of very small bore; relating to capillary action. — *n* a fine-bored tube; a minute thin-walled blood vessel that forms a network connecting arteries with veins (*anatom*). — *n* **capillarity** (*-lar'i-ti*) capillary quality; an obsolete term for capillary action. — *n* **capillitium** (*kap-i-lish'i-əm*) a mass of threads. — **capillary action** the force that causes a liquid in contact with a solid to rise (as in a capillary tube), or to spread (as through blotting-paper), caused by surface tension; **capillary electrometer** an electrolytic cell, consisting of a capillary tube joining two electrodes that contain mercury, used as a measuring device for small voltages; **capillary matting** highly absorbent matting made of fine filaments, used in watering greenhouse, etc plants; **capillary tube** a glass tube with a fine bore used in medicine, thermometers, etc. [L *capillus* hair]

capita. See **caput**.

capital[1] *kap'it-l*, *adj* relating to the head; involving or punishable by the death penalty; placed at the head; main, principal, most important; excellent (*colloq*); relating to capital; (of a letter) of the form or size which begins a sentence or name, upper-case. — *n* the chief or most important thing; the chief town or seat of government; a capital letter; the property and equipment and/or money used for carrying on a business; money invested or lent at interest; capitalists collectively, or their political and economic influence and interests; any advantage used as a means of gaining further advantages. — *interj* excellent. — *n* **cap'italism** the condition of possessing capital or wealth; the economic system which is driven by the profit-motive and depends on investment of private capital to provide the means of production, distribution and exchange. — *n* **cap'italist** a person who owns capital, *esp* when invested for profit in business; a person who advocates capitalism as an economic system. — Also *adj*. — *adj* **capitalist'ic**. — *n* **capitalīzā'tion** or **-s-**. — *vt* **cap'italize** or **-ise** to provide with capital; to convert into capital or money; to turn to account; to print or write with capital letters or an initial capital letter. — *vi* to turn to one's advantage, to profit from (with *on*). — *adv* **cap'itally** chiefly; principally; excellently (*colloq*); by capital punishment. — **capital account** a financial statement showing the value of a company, calculated by deducting total liabilities from total assets to give a net value; an account of fixed assets (*US*); **capital assets** fixed assets; **capital cross** a Greek cross with terminations like Tuscan capitals; **capital expenditure** spending on capital assets; expenditure from which benefits may be expected in the long term; **capital gains** profits from the sale of bonds or other assets; **capital gains tax** a tax levied on the profit made on the sale of certain assets; **capital goods** goods to be used in production of other goods, not for sale to consumers. — *adj* **capital-intens'ive** requiring a comparatively large amount of capital relative to the amount of labour involved. — **capitalization issue** an issue of shares given free by a company to its shareholders (in proportion to the size of their holdings) in order to capitalize reserves, a bonus issue; **capital levy** a tax on capital or the profit derived from the sale of property, etc, as opposed to a tax on earned income; **capital offence** a crime, eg treason or murder, punishable by the death penalty; **capital punishment** the death penalty; **capital ship** a warship of the largest and most heavily armoured class in a fleet; **capital sin** (*obs*) deadly sin; **capital sum** a lump sum payable on an insurance policy; **capital territory** the part of a country in which the capital city is situated; **capital transfer tax** a tax payable on gifts of money or property over a certain value, made either during the lifetime of the giver or after his or her death. — **circulating** or **floating capital** that which constantly changes hands, as wages paid to workmen, raw material used; **fixed capital** buildings, machines, tools, etc; **make capital (out) of** to turn to advantage; **working capital** capital needed to carry on a business; liquid capital (see under **liquid**); assets after debts have been paid. [OFr *capitel*, from L *capitālis*, from *caput* the head]

capital² *kap'it-l*, *n* the head or top part of a column, that supports the entablature (*archit*); a chapter of a book (*rare*). [L *capitellum*, dimin of *caput* head]

capitalism, etc. See **capital¹**.

capitan *käp-i-tän'* or *kap'i-tan*, (*hist*) *n* the chief admiral of the Turkish fleet. — *n* **capitan'o** a head-man: — *pl* **capitan'os** or **capitan'ī** (*-ē*). [Sp *capitán*, and Ital *capitano*; see **captain**.]

capitate *kap'it-āt*, (*bot and zool*) *adj* having a head, knob or capitulum; shaped like a head. [L *capitātus*, from *caput* head]

capitation *kap-i-tā'shən*, *n* a numbering of heads or individuals; a poll-tax; the levying of this. — **capitation allowance** or **grant** an allowance or grant of so much a head; **capitation fee** a payment made to a general practitioner for each patient on his or her list. [L *capitātus* headed, and *capitātiō*, *-ōnis* poll-tax, from *caput* head]

capitayn *kap-i-tān'*, (*Spenser*) *n* a captain.

capitellum. See **capitulum**.

Capitol *kap'it-ol* or *-əl*, *n* the temple of Jupiter at Rome, built on the *Capitoline* hill; the building where Congress or a state legislature meets (*US*). — *adj* **capitō'lian** or **capit'oline**. [L *Capitōlium*, from *caput* the head]

capitular¹ *kə-pit'ūl-ər*, *n* a statute passed in a chapter or ecclesiastical court; a member of a chapter. — *adj* relating or belonging to a chapter in a cathedral. — *adv* **capit'ularly**. — *n* **capit'ulary** a collection of ordinances of Charlemagne, etc; a heading. — *adj* of a chapter. [See ety for **chapter**]

capitular². See **capitulum**.

capitulate¹ *kə-pit'ūl-āt*, *vi* to draw up terms of agreement (*obs*); to yield or surrender, *esp* on certain stated conditions. — *n* **capit'ulant** a person who capitulates. — *n* **capitulā'tion**. — *adj* **capit'ulatory**. [LL *capitulātus*, pa p of *capitulāre* to arrange under heads, from *capitulum* a chapter]

capitulate². See **capitulum**.

capitulum *kə-pit'ū-ləm*, *n* a close head of sessile flowers, as in the Compositae family of daisies and related flowers (*bot*); the head or enlarged knob-like part at the end of a long bone, eg a rib (also **capitell'um**) (*anatom*): — *pl* **capit'ula** or **capitell'a**. — *adj* **capit'ular**. — *adj* **capit'ulate**. [L, dimin of *caput* head]

capiz *kap'iz*, *n* the translucent shell of a bivalve mollusc, (*Placuna placenta*), used in making jewellery, etc. [Tagálog]

caple or **capul** *kā'pl*, *n* a horse. [ME *capel*; cf ON *kapall*; Irish *capall*; LL *caballus* a horse]

caplet *kap'lət*, *n* a solid medicinal tablet with a hard coating (of a soluble material as used to make capsules), *usu* in an elongated oval form to ease swallowing. [*cap*sule and tab*let*]

caplin. See **capelin**.

capnomancy *kap'nō-man-si*, *n* divination by smoke. [Gr *kapnos* smoke, and *manteiā* divination]

capo¹ *kap'ō*, *n* the head of a branch of the Mafia; by extension, the leader of any band or organization, criminal or otherwise: — *pl* **cap'os** or **capi**. [Ital *capo*, from L *caput* head]

capo² *cap'ō* (*pl* **cap'os**), in full **capotasto** *kapō-tas'tō* (*pl* **capotastos**) or **capodastro** *kapō-das'trō* (*pl* **capodas'tros**), *n* a movable bridge secured over the fingerboard and strings of a lute or guitar, to alter the pitch of all the strings together. [Ital *capo tasto* or *dastro* head stop]

capocchia *kä-pok'kyə*, (*Shakesp*; also **chipo'chia**) *n* a fool. [Ital]

capodastro. See **capo²**.

capoeira or **capuera** *kap-ōō-ā'rə*, *n* a martial art and dance combination developed by African slaves in 19c Brazil. [Port]

capon *kā'pn*, *n* a castrated cock fattened for eating; a humorous name for certain fish, variously a herring, haddock or sole; a love-letter (*Shakesp*). — *vt* **cā'ponize** or **-ise** to make (a cock) into a capon by castration. [OE *capun*; L *capō*, *-ōnis*, Gr *kapōn*, from *koptein* to cut]

caponier or **caponiere** *kap-ō-nēr'*, *n* a covered passage across the ditch around a fortified place. [Fr *caponnière*, Sp *caponera* capon-coop]

caporal *kap-or-äl'*, *n* a kind of strong, dark, shag tobacco. [Fr]

capot *kə-pot'*, (*cards*) *n* the winning of all the tricks by one player at the game of piquet, and scoring forty. — *vt* to score capot against. [Fr]

capotasto. See **capo²**.

capote *kə-pōt'*, *n* a long, *usu* hooded, cloak or mantle. [Fr, dimin of *cape* a cloak; see **cape**]

Cappagh-brown *kap'ä-brown*, *n* a brown bituminous earth pigment, stained with oxide of manganese and iron from *Cappagh* near Cork. — Also **Capp'ah-brown**.

capparidaceous *ka-pə-ri-dā'shəs*, *adj* of the **Capparidā'ceae** family of plants, related to the crucifers, and including **capparis** (*kap'ər-is*) the caper genus of shrubs. [See **caper**]

cappuccino *ka-pōō-chē'nō*, *n* black coffee with a little milk; white coffee made frothy with pressurized steam and often served topped with powdered or grated chocolate: — *pl* **cappuccin'os**. [Ital, Capuchin, perh from the colour of a Capuchin's gown]

capreolate *kap'ri-ō-lāt*, (chiefly *bot*) *adj* having or resembling tendrils. [L *capreolus* a tendril]

capric *kap'rik*, **caproic** *kəp-rō'ik* and **caprylic** *kəp-ril'ik*, *adj* applied to three fatty acids obtained from butter, etc, having a goatlike smell. — *n* **cap'rate**, **cap'roate** and **cap'rylate** salts respectively of these acids; **caprolactam** (*kap-rō-lak'tam*) a crystalline amide used in the production of nylon. [L *caper* a goat]

capriccio *kä-prē'cho* or *kə-prē'chi-ō*, (*music*) *n* a kind of free composition, not keeping to the rules of any particular form: — *pl* **capri'ccios** or **capricci** (*-prē'chē*). — *adv* **capriccioso** (*-ō'sō*) in a free style. [Ital, perh from L *caper*; see **caper²**]

caprice *kə-prēs'*, *n* an unpredictable or unaccountable change of mind, opinion or behaviour; a whim; changeableness; a capriccio (*music*). — *adj* **capricious** (*kə-prish'əs*) humorous (*Shakesp*); full of caprice; changeable. — *adv* **capri'ciously**. — *n* **capri'ciousness**. [Fr *caprice* and Ital *capriccio*; perh from L *caper* (masc), *capra* (fem) a goat]

Capricorn *kap'ri-körn*, *n* in astrology, the tenth sign of the zodiac represented as a horned goat or monster; a person born between 23 December and 19 January, under the sign of Capricorn; the constellation Capricornus. — *adj* **Capricorn'ian** pertaining to, or characteristic of, a person born under the sign of Capricorn (also *n*). — See also under **tropic**. [L *capricornus*, from *caper* a goat, and *cornū* a horn]

caprid *kap'rid*, (*zool*) *n* a member of the goat family, Capridae. — Also *adj*. — *n pl* **Capridae** (*kap'ri-dē*) in former classifications, the family of Artiodactyla comprising sheep, goats, etc. — *n pl* **Cap'rinae** in modern classification, the family which includes goats and ibex. [L *caper*, a goat]

caprifig *kap'ri-fig*, *n* the goat-fig, a species of wild fig of Europe and Asia. — *n* **caprificā'tion** a method of promoting the fertilization of cultivated edible figs (which are mainly dioecious) by hanging branches of caprifig flowers (which have both male and female flowers) on the edible fig trees so that the parasitic gall-wasps living on the female (or gall) flowers carry pollen to the flowers of the cultivated fig. — *vt* **cap'rify**. [L *caprīcus* the wild fig, from *caper* a goat, and *fīcus* a fig]

caprifole *kap'ri-fōl* or (*Spenser*) **caprifoil** *-foil*, *n* an old name for honeysuckle. — *n pl* **Caprifoliā'ceae** (*-si-ē*) the honeysuckle family or plants. — *adj* **caprifoliā'ceous**. [L *caper* goat, and *folium*, leaf]

capriform *kap'ri-förm*, *adj* goatlike. [L *caper* goat, and *fōrma* form]

caprify. See **caprifig**.

caprine *kap'rīn*, *adj* of or like a goat. [L *caprīnus*, from caper a goat]

capriole *kap'ri-ōl*, *n* a high leap made from bent knees (*ballet*); an upward leap without advancing, in which the horse has all four feet off the ground and kicks its back legs at the height of the jump (*dressage*). — *vi* to perform a capriole; to caper. [OFr *capriole*, from Ital *capriola*, from L *caper* (masc), *capra* (fem) a goat]

Capri pants *kə-prē' pants*, *n pl* women's tapering trousers ending above the ankle, with a short slit on the outside leg. — Also **Capris'**. [*Capri*, island in the Bay of Naples]

caproic, **caprolactam**, **caprylic**, etc. See **capric**.

caps *kaps*, *abbrev*: capitals, capital letters (in printing and writing).

capsaicin. See **capsicum**.

Capsian *kap'si-ən*, *n* a Mesolithic culture (of the period 8c–3c BC) of N Africa, distinguished by its microlithic and geometrically-shaped tools. — *adj* of, or characteristic of, this culture. [Latinized *Capsa* Gafsa, in Tunisia]

capsicum *kap'si-kəm*, *n* a tropical American shrubby plant of the genus *Capsicum*, of the potato family, yielding a fleshy, many-seeded fruit; the fruit of one species, eaten as a vegetable (also called *green* or *red pepper*); the dried seeds of other species, yielding paprika and cayenne pepper. — *n* **capsaicin** (*kap-sā'i-sin*) the hot-tasting principle of certain species of capsicum. [Perh L *capsa* a case]

capsid[1] *kap'sid*, *n* the outer protein shell of a virus. [L *capsa* case]

capsid[2] *kap'sid*, *n* any of several small active bugs of the order Heteroptera, that feed on plants, a common pest of fruit and other crops. — Also **capsid bug**. [Gr *kapsis* gulping, from *kaptein* to gulp down]

capsize *kap-sīz'*, *vt* to overturn (*esp* a boat). — *vi* to be overturned. — *n* an overturning. — *adj* **capsiz'able**. — *n* **capsiz'al**. [Origin unknown]

capstan *kap'stən*, *n* an upright mechanical device turned by bars, levers or a motor, used for winding in heavy ropes or cables, *esp* on a ship; the revolving shaft which engages with and draws a tape through a tape-recorder, etc; (also **capstan lathe**) a lathe with a revolving turret holding several tools which can be used in succession. — **capstan table** a round-topped, often revolving table. [Fr *cabestan*, *capestan*, through LL forms from L *capere* to take, hold]

capsule *kap'sūl*, *n* a dry seed-case which splits to release seeds (*bot*); the spore-bearing part of a moss (*bot*); a fibrous or membranous covering (*zool*); an envelope of protein or polysaccharides surrounding the cell walls of certain bacteria; a gelatine case for holding a dose of medicine; a small container; a metallic cap or covering, as on a wine cork; a spacecraft or aircraft, or a part of one, that houses the instruments and crew in a self-contained unit; a similar craft, to be used on or under water. — *adj* **cap'sular** in the form of or resembling, a capsule; brief, condensed. — *adj* **cap'sulary**. — *adj* **cap'sulate** contained in or made into a capsule. — *vt* **cap'sulize** or **-ise** to condense; to enclose in a capsule. [Fr, from L *capsula*, dimin of *capsa* a case, from *capere* to hold]

Capt. *abbrev*: Captain (in titles).

captain *kap'tin*, *n* a head or chief officer; the commander of a ship; the commander of a company of troops (*obs*); in the navy, an officer of the rank below commodore and above commander; in the army (in US also the Air Force), an officer of the rank below major and above lieutenant; the senior pilot of a civil aircraft; a senior police or fire officer (*NAm*); the overseer of a mine; the leader of a team or club; a person in charge of waiters and bellboys in a hotel (*NAm*); the head boy or head girl of a school. — *vt* to lead or act as captain. — *n* **cap'taincy** the rank or commission of a captain; the period of office of a captain; the leadership or rule of a captain. — *n* **cap'tainship** or (*obs*) **cap'tainry** the rank or condition of a captain; skill in commanding. — **captain-gen'eral** the commander of an army; **captain's biscuit** a fancy kind of hard biscuit; **captain's chair** a wooden armchair with back and arms in one semicircular piece supported on vertical spindles. — **captain of industry** a leading industrial figure or the head of a large industry. [OFr *capitaine*, from LL *capitāneus* chief, from L *caput* head]

Captain Cooker *kap'tin kŏŏk'ər*, (*NZ*) *n* a wild pig. [After Captain James Cook (1728–79), who is thought to have released pigs in the New Zealand bush]

captan *kap'tən*, *n* a type of agricultural fungicide produced from mercaptan. [From **mercaptan**]

caption *kap'shən*, *n* a heading, legend or accompanying wording of an article, chapter, illustration or cinematograph picture, etc; the act of taking (*formal*); an arrest (*legal*); the formal title of an indictment or deposition which shows the authority under which it is executed or taken (*Eng law*); in Scotland, before 1837, a formal warrant to apprehend a debtor or other defaulting obligant, given in the Bill Chamber after letters of horning had been executed. — *vt* to give a caption (heading, etc) to. [L *captiō*, *-ōnis*, from *capere* to take]

captious *cap'shəs*, *adj* ready to find *esp* trivial faults or take offence; carping; peevish. — *adv* **cap'tiously**. — *n* **cap'tiousness**. [L *captiōsus*, from *captiō*; see **caption**]

captive *kap'tiv*, *n* a prisoner; a person or animal kept in confinement. — *adj* confined; kept in bondage; of an animal, living its whole life in a zoo or other controlled habitat; restrained by a line (as a balloon); charmed or subdued by anything (*fig*); pertaining to captivity; that cannot refuse what is offered (as a *captive audience*, *market*, etc). — *vt* (*kap'tiv*; also in *Spenser*, *Milton*, *kap-tiv'*) to make captive or to captivate. — *n* **cap'tivance** or **cap'tivaunce** (*Spenser*) captivity. — *vt* **cap'tivate** to charm; to fascinate or engage the affections of. — *adj* **cap'tivating**. — *n* **captiv'ity** the condition or period of being captive or imprisoned. — **captive bolt** or **captive bolt pistol** a gunlike device which fires a rod, used in slaughtering animals; **captive time** time during which a person is not working but must be available at the place of work. [L *captīvus*, from *capere*, *captum* to take]

capture *kap'chər*, *n* the act of taking; the thing taken; an arrest; transference of a tributary to another river by erosion (*geol*). — *vt* to take as a prize; to win control or possession of; to take by force; to succeed in representing (something intangible or elusive) in a fixed or permanent form; of an atomic or nuclear system, to acquire an additional particle (*phys*); (of a star or planet) to bring another body into orbit round it (*astron*). — *n* **cap'tor** or **cap'turer**. [L *captura*, *captor*, from *capere*, *captum* to take]

capuche or **capouch** *kə-pŏŏsh'* or *-pŏŏch'*, *n* a hood or cowl, *esp* that worn by the *Capuchins*. [Ital *cappuccio*, from LL *cappa*]

Capuchin *kap'ū-chin* or *kap-o͞o-shēn'*, *n* a friar of a strict branch of the Franciscan order, which became a separate order in 1619, so called from the pointed hood worn; (without *cap*) a hooded cloak like a Capuchin's; (*usu* without *cap*) a hooded pigeon; (without *cap*) a capuchin monkey. — **capuchin cross** a cross with each arm terminated by a ball; **capuchin monkey** a S American monkey of the genus *Cebus*, with thick hair like a monk's cowl. [Fr, cowl, from LL *cappa*; see **cap**, **cape**]

capul. See **caple**.

caput *kap'ut* or *-ət*, *n* the head (*anatom*); a head; a bony protuberance (*anatom*): — *pl* **cap'ita** (see also **per capita**). — **caput mortuum** (*mör'tū-əm*) the residuum after distillation or chemical analysis, literally dead head; worthless residue. [L]

capybara *kap-i-bä'rə*, *n* the largest living rodent, a native of S America, resembling a large guinea-pig. [Port, from Tupí]

CAR *abbrev*: compound or compounded annual rate.

Car. *abbrev*: *Carolus* (*L*), Charles.

car *kär*, *n* a self-propelled wheeled vehicle designed to carry passengers (also **motor car**); a wheeled vehicle of a specified type (as *jaunting-car*, *tramcar*, etc); a railway carriage, *esp* of a specified type (as *dining-car*, *sleeping-car*, etc); any railway carriage, wagon or truck (*NAm*); the part of a balloon, cable-car, or airship that carries passengers and load; a chariot or cart (*poetic*). — **car bomb** an explosive device concealed beneath or inside a car, detonated by remote control or when the car engine is started; **car'-coat** a short coat designed for wearing in a car; **car'fare** (*NAm*) the fare on a bus, tram, etc; **car ferry** a ferry boat on which cars can be transported; **car'load** as much as a car will carry; **car'man** (*archaic*) a man who drives a car or cart; a carter; **car'park** an open space or a building for parking cars; **car phone** a radio-operated telephone for use in a car; **car pool** an arrangement by which several car owners take turns in giving lifts to each other; a number of cars owned by a business for use by employees; **car'port** a covered parking space, *esp* a space under a roof projecting from a building. — *adj* **car'-sick** affected with nausea by the movement of a car. — **car'-sickness**; **car'-wash** a place specially equipped for the automatic washing of cars. — **car boot sale** a sale at which goods are sold direct from the boots of the owners' cars. [OFr *carre*, from LL *carra*, a Celtic word, seen in Irish *carr*, Breton *karr*]

carabao *kä'rə-bä-o*, *n* the domesticated Asiatic buffalo. [Philippine Sp, from Visayan *karaba'aw*]

carabid *kar'ə-bid*, *n* a beetle of the genus *Carabus*, of the ground-beetle family **Carabidae** (*kə-rab'i-dē*). — *adj* of, or characteristic of, the Carabidae. [Gr *kārabos* a kind of beetle]

carabine. See **carbine**.

carabineer, **carabinier**. See **carbine**.

carabiniere *kä-rä-bē-nyā'rā*, (*Ital*) *n* a member of the Italian national police force: — *pl* **carabinie'ri** (*-rē*).

caracal *kar'ə-kal*, *n* the desert lynx of N Africa and S Asia, having long legs and black-tipped ears; its fur. [Fr, prob from Turk *qara-qulaq* black ear]

caracara *kä-rä-kä-rä'*, or *kä-rä-kä'rä*, *n* a name for several S American carrion-eating birds of prey. [Imitative]

carack. See **carrack**.

caracol or **caracole** *kar'ə-kōl*, *n* a half-turn or wheel (*dressage*); a spiral staircase. — *vi* to turn half-round; to prance about. [Fr *caracole*, from Ital *caracollo*, from Sp *caracol* a spiral snail shell]

caract *kar'əkt*, (*Shakesp*) *n* a mark; a sign. [Appar Gr *charaktos* marked]

caracul. See **karakul**.

carafe *kə-raf'*, *n* a water-bottle or wine-flask for the table; the amount contained in a carafe. [Fr *carafe*, prob from Ar *gharafa* to draw water]

caramba *kär-äm'bə*, (*Sp*) *interj* expressing admiration, annoyance or surprise.

carambola *ka-rəm-bō'lə*, *n* a small E Indian tree (*Averrhoa carambola*) of the wood-sorrel family; its acrid yellow pulpy fruit used for making tarts, preserves, etc. [Port]

carambole. See under **carom**.

caramel *kar'ə-mel*, *n* a dark-brown substance produced from sugar by loss of water on heating, used in colouring and flavouring food and drink; a chewy sweet made with sugar, butter, etc. — *adj* made of or containing caramel; of the colour of caramel. — *vt* and *vi* to turn into caramel. — *n* **caramelizā'tion** or **-s-**. — *vt* and *vi* **car'amelize** or **-ise**. — Also (*rare*) **car'omel**. [Fr, from Sp *caramelo*]

carangid *kə-rang'gid* or *-jid*, or **carangoid** *-goid*, *n* any spiny-finned marine fish of the genus *Caranx*, of the family **Carangidae** (*kar-an'ji-dē*), which includes the scads, jacks, pilot fish, etc. — Also *adj*. [Origin obscure]

caranna *kar-an'ə* or **carauna** *-ön'ə*, *n* a resinous substance yielded by various S American burseraceous trees. [Sp *caraña*, from Tupí]

carap *kar'ap* or *kə-rap'*, *n* any tree of the genus *Carapa*, tropical trees of the mahogany family yielding **car'ap-nuts**, **car'ap-oil** or **car'ap-wood** (or **crab'-nuts**, **-oil** or **-wood**). [*caraipi*, the native Guiana name]

carapace *kar'ə-pās*, *n* the thick hard shell, made of bone or chitin, of the crab, tortoise, turtle, etc; an inpenetrable outer shell, eg a reserved manner used as a protection against outside influences. — *adj* **carapā'cial** (*-shl*). [Fr, from Sp *carapacho*]

carat *kar'ət*, *n* a unit of weight (metric carat = 200mg) used for gems; (also *esp NAm* **karat**) a unit used in expressing the proportion of gold in an alloy, 24-carat gold being pure gold; worth, estimate (*obs*). [Fr, from Ar *qīrāt*, perh from Gr *keration* a carob-seed used as a weight]

carauna. See **caranna**.

caravan *kar'ə-van*, or *-van'*, *n* a company travelling together for security, *esp* in crossing the desert; a company of people; a fleet with convoy; a covered van; a house on wheels. — *vi* to travel in a caravan: — *pr p* **car'avaning** or **caravann'ing**; *pa t* and *pa p* **car'avaned** or **caravanned'**. — *n* **caravaneer'** the leader of a caravan. — *n* **caravan'er** or **caravann'er** a caravaneer; someone who stays in a caravan, *esp* for holidays. — *n* **caravanette'** a motorized mobile home. — *n* **caravanserai** (*-van'sə-rī*) *esp* formerly in some Eastern countries, a kind of unfurnished inn or extensive enclosed courtyard where caravans stop. Also **caravan'sarai** or **caravan'sary**. — **caravan site** or **caravan park** an open space laid out for caravans. [Pers *kārwān* caravan, and *kārwānsarāī* from (*sarāī* inn)]

caravance. See **calavance**.

caravel *kar'ə-vel*, *n* a light Mediterranean sailing-ship. [Fr *caravelle*, *from* Ital *caravella*; cf LL *cārabus*, Gr *kārabos* a light ship]

caraway *kar'ə-wā*, *n* an umbelliferous plant (*Carum carvi*) with aromatic fruits (**caraway seeds**) used as a tonic and condiment. [Prob Sp *alcaravea* (*carvi*), Ar *karwiyā*, from Gr *karon*]

carb *kärb*, (*colloq*) *n* short for **carburettor**.

carbachol *kär'bə-kol* or *-kōl*, *n* a synthetic drug used to disperse fluids, eg urine, retained in the body. [**car**bamic acid and *cho*line]

carbamate *kär'bə-māt* or *kär-bam'āt*, *n* a salt or ester of carbamic acid, used *esp* as a pesticide. — *n* **carbamide** (*kär'bə-mīd*, *kär-bam'īd*) urea. — *n* **car'baryl** (*-bə-ril*) a carbamate insecticide. — **carbamic acid** an acid, CH_3NO_2, a half amide of carbonic acid. [**carbon**, **amide** and **aryl**]

carbanion *kär-ban'ī-ən*, (*chem*) *n* an ion carrying a negative electric charge at the carbon position.

carbaryl. See under **carbamate**.

carbazole *kär'bə-zōl*, *n* a chemical compound derived from coal tar and used in making dyes.

carbide *kär'bīd*, *n* a compound of carbon with another element, *esp* calcium carbide. — **carbide tool** (*eng*) a cutting and forming tool used for hard materials or at high temperatures. [**carbon**]

carbine *kär'bīn, n* a short light rifle. — Also (*esp* formerly) **car'abin** or **car'abine**. — *n* **carbineer'**, **carabineer'**, **carbinier'** or **carabinier'** a soldier armed with a carbine; a light cavalryman; a soldier of the 6th Dragoon Guards (from 1939, 3rd Carabineers). [Fr *carabine*]

carbo- *kär-bō-*, sometimes *kärbo'-*, or before a vowel **carb-** *combining form* denoting carbon.

carbocyclic *kär-bō-sīk'lik, adj* homocyclic. [**carbon** and **cyclic**]

carbohydrate *kär-bō-hī'drāt, n* a compound of carbon, hydrogen and oxygen, the last two being in the same proportion as in water; extended to similar compounds, the sugars and starches which form the main source of energy in food. [See **carbon** and **hydrate**]

carbolic *kär-bol'ik, n* (in full **carbolic acid**) phenol. [L *carbō* coal, and *oleum* oil]

carbon *kär'bən, n* a non-metallic element (atomic no 6; symbol **C**), widely diffused, occurring uncombined as diamond, graphite and buckminsterfullerene; a piece of carbon (*esp* an electrode or a lamp-filament), or of carbon paper; a carbon copy; a carbonado diamond. — Also *adj*. — *adj* **carbonā'ceous** coaly; containing much carbon; like carbon. — *n* **carbon'alite** an intrusive carbonate rock. — *n* **car'bonate** a salt of carbonic acid. — *vt* to combine or impregnate with carbon dioxide; to carbonize. — *n* **carbonā'tion**. — *adj* **carbonic** (*-bon'ik*) pertaining to carbon. — *adj* **carbonif'erous** producing carbon or coal; (with *cap*; *geol*) belonging to the Carboniferous system (see below). — *n* **carbonizā'tion** or **-s-**. — *vt* **car'bonize** or **-ise** to reduce to carbon; to char or coke; to cover with carbon. — *vi* to become carbonized. — **carbon anhydrase** an enzyme in living tissues that helps to transport carbon dioxide from the tissues to the lungs by acting as a catalyst in the reaction between carbon dioxide and water; **carbon arc** an arc between two carbon electrodes, used for high-intensity lighting; **carbon black** a form of finely divided carbon produced by partial combustion of hydrocarbons, used in making inks and rubber; **carbon copy** a duplicate of writing or typed matter made by interleaving **carbon paper**, a paper coated with a pigment made of carbon or other material; any exact duplicate. — *vt* **car'bon-cop'y** to copy exactly. — **carbon cycle** the circulation and transfer of carbon between animals, plants and the atmosphere; the function of carbon in various nuclear reactions in stars; **carbon dating** estimating the date of death of prehistoric organic material from the amount of carbon-14 still present in it; **carbon dioxide** an oxide of carbon (CO_2), a colourless, odourless, incombustible gas, present in the atmosphere, formerly called *carbonic-acid gas*, which in solution in water forms **carbonic acid**; **carbon dioxide snow** dry ice (see **ice**); **carbonic acid** (H_2CO_3), a weak acid; **carbon disulphide** (CS_2), a colourless, flammable liquid with an unpleasant smell, used in the manufacture of man-made fibres and solvents; **carbon fibres** very fine filaments of carbon used in bundles, bound together by resins, to form strong lightweight materials; **car'bon-14** a radioactive isotope of carbon, used eg as a tracer element in biological studies or in dating archaeological material; **carbon microphone** a microphone in which variations in sound pressure produced in a diaphragm are detected in a current passing through carbon granules which register a decrease of contact resistance as the sound pressure increases; **carbon monoxide** (CO) a colourless, odourless, very poisonous gas which burns with a blue flame to form carbon dioxide; **carbon process** (*photog*) a printing process using paper sensitized with potassium bichromate and coated with gelatine and a pigment; **carbon steel** steel containing carbon, with different properties according to the quantity of carbon used; **carbon tax** a tax imposed on industry, and on the users of motor vehicles, to try to limit the amount of carbon being released into the atmosphere from the burning of fossil fuels; **carbon tetrachloride** (CCl_4) a solvent made from chlorine and carbon disulphide; **car'bon-12** an isotope of carbon with a mass of 12, used as a standard in determining relative atomic and molecular weight. — **the Carboniferous** or **the Carboniferous System** one of the main divisions of the Palaeozoic rocks, formed between the Devonian and Permian, and including the Mountain or Carboniferous Limestone, the Millstone Grit, and the Coal Measures. [Fr *carbone*, from L *carbō*, *-ōnis* coal, charcoal]

carbonado[1] *kär-bən-ā'dō, n* a piece of meat cut crossways for broiling on coals (*obs*); (also **carbonnade'** or **carbonade'**) a beef stew made with beer: — *pl* **carbona'does** or **carbona'dos**. — *vt* to cut crossways for broiling (*obs*); to slash (*obs*). [Sp *carbonada*]

carbonado[2] *kär-bən-ā'dō, n* a variety of black, opaque, crystalline carbon, harder than diamond, used in industry for drilling, etc. — Also called **black diamond** or **black carbon**. [Port, carbonated]

Carbonari *kär-bon-är'ē, n pl* members of a secret society in Italy at the beginning of the 19c, founded to help forward a republican government. — *n* **Carbonar'ism**. [Ital, literally charcoal burners]

carbonyl *kär'bə-nil, (chem) n* the radical CO. — *vt* **carbonylate** (*kär-bon'i-lāt*) to introduce the carbonyl group into. — *n* **carbonylā'tion**. [**carbon**, **oxygen** and Gr *hȳlē* matter]

Carborundum® *kär-bər-un'dum, n* a silicon carbide, used as a substitute for corundum in grinding, etc. [**carbon** and **corundum**; a trademark in some countries]

carboxyl *kär-boks'il, n* the radical COOH. — *adj* **carboxylic** (*-bok-sil'ik*). [**carbon**, **oxygen** and Gr *hȳlē* matter]

carboy *kär'boi, n* a large glass or plastic bottle, with basketwork or other casing, used for containing or transporting dangerous chemicals. [Pers *qarābah*]

carbuncle *kär'bung-kl, n* a mythical self-luminous gem; a fiery-red precious stone (almandine or precious garnet); a large pimple *esp* on the face or neck; a local inflammation of the skin and subcutaneous tissues, caused by bacterial infection; an architectural monstrosity or eyesore. — *adj* **car'buncled** set with the gem carbuncle; afflicted with carbuncles; having red inflamed spots. — *adj* **carbun'cular** belonging to or like a carbuncle; red; inflamed; unsightly. [L *carbunculus*, dimin of *carbō* a coal]

carburet *kär'bū-ret*, or *-ret'*, *n* a carbide (*obs*). — *n* **carburā'tion**, **carburetion** (*-rāsh'ən, -resh'ən*) or **carburīzā'tion** or **-s-**. — *vt* **carburet**, **car'burate** or **car'burize** or **-ise** to combine with carbon; to charge with carbon compounds. — *adj* **car'buretted** (or *-ret'id*). — *n* **car'burettor**, **carburett'er**, or *US* **car'buretor** or **car'bureter** (also *-ret'ər*) an apparatus for charging a gas with carbon compounds, *esp* part of an internal-combustion engine in which air is mixed with volatile fuel in the desired proportion. — **carburetted gas** a mixed illuminant obtained by passing water-gas over hot hydrocarbons; **carburetted hydrogen** a compound of carbon and hydrogen such as marsh-gas or olefiant gas. [Fr *carbure*, from L *carbō* coal]

carby *kär'bi, n* (*Austr*) short for carburettor.

carcajou *kär'kə-jōō, n* the glutton or wolverene. [Can Fr, prob from an Indian name]

carcake *kär'kāk, (Scot) n* a kind of cake for Shrove Tuesday. [OE *caru* grief, and **cake**]

carcanet *kär'kə-net, (obs) n* a collar of jewels; a jewelled head-ornament. [Fr (and obs Eng) *carcan* an iron collar used for punishment, from LL *carcannum*, from Gmc]

carcase or **carcass** *kär'kəs, n* a dead body of an animal *esp* one to be used as meat; a live human body (*disrespectful* or *facetious*); the framework of anything; a ruin; an incendiary shell; the body of a tyre as distinct from the tread. — *vt* to put up the framework of; to make a carcase of. — **carcase meat** or **carcass meat** raw meat as prepared for the butcher's shop, not tinned. [OFr *carquois* (Fr *carcasse*) a skeleton]

carceral *kär'sə-rəl, adj* of or pertaining to prison or a prison. [L *carcerālis*, from *carcer* prison]

carcinogen, carcinogenic. See **carcinoma**.

carcinology *kär-si-nol'ə-ji, n* the study of crustaceans. — *adj* **carcinological** (*-ə-loj'i-kl*). — *n* **carcinol'ogist**. [Gr *karkinos* a crab, and *logos* discourse]

carcinoma *kär-si-nō'mə, n* a cancer: — *pl* **carcinō'mata** or **carcinō'mas**. — *adj* **carcinō'matous**. — *n* **carcin'ogen** (*-jen*) a substance that encourages the growth of cancer. — *n* **carcinogen'esis**. — *adj* **carcinogen'ic**. — *n* **carcino-genic'ity**. — *n* **carcinō'sis** or **carcinōmatō'sis** spread of cancer in the body. [Gr *karkinōma*, from *karkinos* crab]

CARD sometimes *kärd, abbrev*: Campaign Against Racial Discrimination.

Card. *abbrev*: Cardinal.

card[1] *kärd*, a small, *usu* rectangular piece of cardboard or stiff paper; one with figures or symbols for playing a game; one with a person's name and address, with a greeting, invitation, message, etc (*calling card, visiting card, Christmas card, birthday card*, etc); a small piece of cardboard or plastic carrying information, showing membership or proof of identity, etc, either in print or on a magnetic strip (*identity card, membership card, credit card*, etc); a domino; the dial of a mariner's compass (also **compass card**); a map; a perforated plate used as a guide in weaving; a personal announcement in a newspaper or elsewhere (*NAm*); the programme of races at a race-meeting; a printed circuit board (*comput*); a punched card (*comput*); a person (*old slang*); a comical or eccentric person; (in *pl*) a game played with cards. — *vt* to return on a scoring-card (*golf*); to enter in a card index. — *adj* **card'-carrying** openly expressing membership of or support for a party or group; *orig* holding a membership card of a party, etc, *esp* the Communist party. — **card'-case** *esp* formerly, a case for carrying visiting cards; **card'castle** a structure of playing cards built one upon the other in storeys; any flimsy or precarious structure; **card catalogue** a card index; **card column** (*comput*) one of the eighty or ninety columns of a punched card with lines parallel to the short edge of the card (cf **card row**); **card file** a card index; **card'-game** any game played with playing-cards; **card'-holder** someone who has a membership card; hence a member of a club, organization, etc; **card index** one with entries on separate cards. — *vt* **card'-in'dex**. — **card mechanic** see under **mechanic**; **card'phone** a public telephone from which calls are made using a pre-paid plastic card rather than money; **card'punch** (*comput*) a machine which perforates cards to record data; **card reader** (*comput*) a device which reads the data represented by holes on a punched card and converts them to a form suitable for storage or processing; **card row** (*comput*) one of the rows of a punched card with lines parallel to the long edge of the card (*cf* **card column**); **card'-sharp** or **card'-sharper** a person who cheats at cards; **card'-table** a table for playing cards on; **card'-vote** a voting system that gives each delegate's vote a value in proportion to the number he represents. — **a card up one's sleeve** an advantageous factor or argument kept in reserve; **cards in one's hands** everything under one's control; **cards on the table** one's resources and moves freely laid open; **cooling card** (*Shakesp*) anything that discourages, or dashes hopes; **get one's cards** to be dismissed from one's employment; **house of cards** a card-castle, cards built up into storeys; any flimsy or precarious structure, scheme, etc; **leading card** a strong point in one's case; **make a card** to win a trick in a card-game; **on the cards** not improbable; likely to happen; **play one's cards well** (or **badly**) to make (or not to make) the best of one's chances; to act (or not to act) in a way that will bring one benefit or advantage; **show (all) one's cards** to expose one's secrets or designs, *esp* when giving an advantage to someone else by so doing; **speak by the card** to speak with precision and to the point; **the cards are stacked against (someone** or **something)** the circumstances, or facts, are ranged against (a person, an argument, etc); **throw up** (or **in**) **the cards** to give in; to admit defeat. [Fr *carte*, from L *c(h)arta*, from Gr *chartēs* paper; cf **carte**[2]]

card[2] *kärd, n* an instrument for combing wool, flax, etc, before spinning. — *vt* to comb (wool, etc); to mix, adulterate (*Shakesp*). — *n* **card'er**. — **carding wool** short-stapled wool. [Fr *carde*, from L *carduus* a thistle]

cardamine *kär-dam'i-nē, n* a plant of the genus of cress (*Cardamine*) including the cuckoo-flower or lady's smock. [Gr *kardaminē*, from *kardamon* cress]

cardamom or **cardamum** *kär'də-məm, n* the seed capsules of several tropical plants of the ginger family, used as an aromatic, pungent spice. — Also **card'amon**. [L *cardamōmum*, from Gr *kardamōmon*]

cardan joint *kär'dan joint, n* a type of universal joint which can rotate out of alignment within its shaft. [Invented by Geronimo *Cardano* (1501–76), Italian mathematician]

cardboard *kärd'bōrd, n* a thin, stiff, finely-finished paste-board; a rougher, thicker material made from paper pulp and used to make cartons or boxes. — *adj* made of cardboard; flimsy, insubstantial; stiff. — *adj* **card'-boardy**. — **cardboard city** an area in which homeless people live or sleep, using cardboard boxes, etc, as shelter. **[card**[1] and **board]**

cardecu or **cardecue** *kär'di-kū*, (*obs*) *n* an old French silver coin. [Fr *quart d'écu* quarter of a crown]

cardi or **cardy** *kär'di*, (*colloq*) *n* short for **cardigan**.

cardiac *kär'di-ak, adj* belonging to the heart or to the upper end of the stomach. — *n* a cordial or heart stimulant; a person with cardiac disease. — *adj* **cardiacal** (*-dī'ə-kl*) cardiac. — **cardiac arrest** stopping of the heartbeat; **cardiac failure** heart-failure; **cardiac massage** rhythmic manual massage of the heart, either directly or by pressure on the chest wall, to restart or maintain blood-circulation after heart-failure. [L *cardiacus*, from Gr *kardiakos*, from *kardiā* heart, the upper end of the stomach]

cardialgia *kär-di-al'ji-ə*, or **cardialgy** *kär'di-al-ji, n* discomfort or a burning pain at the upper orifice of the stomach, apparently at the heart; heartburn. [Gr *kardia* heart, and *algos* pain]

cardigan *kär'di-gən, n* a knitted woollen jacket with buttons up the front, named after Lord *Cardigan* (1797–1868). — *adj* **car'diganed** wearing a cardigan.

cardinal *kär'di-nl, adj* of fundamental importance, chief; pertaining to a hinge; on which a thing hinges; of a deep scarlet colour, like a cardinal's cassock or hat. — *n* (with *cap* in titles) one of the leading dignitaries of the church constituting the Sacred College at Rome, to whom pertains the right of electing a new pope (*RC*); a cardinal number; a short cloak, worn by ladies in the 17c and 18c; a cardinal bird; a S European butterfly (*Pandoriana pandora*). — *n* **car'dinalate** or **car'dinalship** the office or dignity of cardinal. — *adj* **cardinalā'tial** or **cardinali'tial** pertaining to a cardinal or to the office of cardinal. — *adv* **car'dinally** fundamentally. — **cardinal beetle** any of various large, red-coloured, beetles of the family *Pyrochroidae*; **car'dinal-bird, cardinal grosbeak** or (*US*) **redbird** a large American seed-eating finch (*Richmondena cardinalis*), the male bright red with a crest, the female brown; **car'dinal-bishop, car'dinal-priest** and **car'dinal-deacon** the three orders of cardinal in the Sacred College; **cardinal flower** a N American plant (*Lobelia cardinalis*) with bright scarlet lobed flowers; **cardinal number** a number expressing quantity (1, 2, 3, etc) as distinct from an ordinal (first, second, third, etc); **cardinal point** any of the four chief points of the compass, north, south, east, or west; **cardinal virtue** one of the chief moral qualities, justice, prudence, temperance, fortitude, upon which the whole of human nature was supposed to hinge. [L *cardinālis*, from *cardō, cardinis* a hinge]

cardio- *kär-di-ō-*, or before a vowel **cardi-**, *combining form* denoting heart. — *n* **car'diogram** a tracing obtained from a cardiograph. — *n* **car'diograph** an instrument for recording movements of the heart. — *n* **cardiog'-rapher** a person who uses a cardiograph. — *n* **cardiog'-**

raphy. — *adj* **cardiological** (*-loj'i-kl*). — *n* **cardiol'ogist**. — *n* **cardiology** (*-ol'ə-ji*) the science that deals with the structure, function and diseases of the heart. — *adj* **cardiomō'tor** pertaining to the action of the heart. — *n* **cardiomyop'athy** myocardiopathy. — *adj* **cardiopul'-monary** pertaining to the heart and lungs. — *adj* **cardiorespir'atory** relating to the action of the heart and lungs. — *adj* **cardiothoracic** (*-thöra'sik*) relating to the heart and chest. — *adj* **cardiovascular** (*-vas'kū-*) pertaining to or involving the heart and blood-vessels. — *n* **cardī'tis** inflammation of the heart. [Gr *kardiā* heart]

cardioid *kär'di-oid*, *adj* heart-shaped. — *n* a heart-shaped curve traced by a fixed point on the circumference of a circle rolling around another circle of equal radius. [Gr *kardiā* heart]

cardoon *kär-dōōn'*, *n* a Mediterranean plant (*Cynara cardunculus*) closely related to the true artichoke, its leafstalks and ribs eaten like celery. [Obs Fr *cardon*, from L *carduus* a thistle]

cardophagus *kär-dof'ə-gəs*, (*obs*) *n* a thistle-eater, a donkey. [Latinized from Gr *kardos* thistle, and *phagos* eater, glutton]

Cards. *abbrev*: Cardiganshire, a former county of Wales (now part of Dyfed).

carduus *kär'dū-əs*, (*Shakesp*) *n* a thistle. [L]

cardy. See **cardi**.

CARE *kār*, *abbrev*: Cooperative for American Relief Everywhere.

care *kār*, *n* affliction; anxiety; heedfulness; heed; charge, oversight; residential or non-residential medical or social welfare services; an object of anxiety or watchfulness. — *vi* to be anxious; to be inclined; to be concerned; to mind; to have affection, fondness or regard for (with *for* or about); to provide for, look after, watch over (with *for*). — *adj* **care'ful** full of care; heedful; painstaking, thorough; anxious (*Bible*); grievous (*Spenser*); sorrowful (*Spenser*). — *adv* **care'fully**. — *n* **care'fulness**. — *adj* **care'less** without care; heedless, unconcerned. — *adv* **care'lessly**. — *n* **care'lessness**. — *n* **car'er** a person who cares; a person who takes responsibility for another, dependent, person. — *adj* **car'ing** compassionate; concerned professionally with social, medical, etc welfare (as the *caring professions*, ie social workers, nurses, etc). — **care assistant** a person employed to look after children or old or disabled people in a home, hospital, etc; **care attendant** a person employed by social services to care for physically or mentally handicapped people in day centres or residential homes; **care card** a plastic card with an inbuilt memory chip used for storing an individual's medical records. — *adj* **care'-crazed** (*Shakesp*) crazed or broken with care and solicitude. — *adj* **care'free** free from anxiety, worry or responsibility. — **care label** a label on a garment giving washing, dry-cleaning, etc, instructions. — *vt* and *vi* **care'take** to act as caretaker (for a property, etc). — **care'taker** someone put in charge of a place, *esp* a building. — *adj* exercising temporary supervision or control, as *caretaker government*. — **care'worker** a person employed to help look after dependent people in their own homes. — *adj* **care'worn** showing signs of stress, anxiety, etc. — **care and maintenance** the keeping of an industrial plant, shipyard, etc in sound condition at times when production has been discontinued so that it may be restarted immediately new orders are received; **care (and protection) order** an order by a magistrate placing a child in care; **care of** to be delivered to the custody of, or at the address of (*usu abbrev* **c/o**); **for all I** (or **you**, etc) **care** it is a matter of indifference to me (or you, etc); **have a care** to take care; **I**, etc, **couldn't care less** I, etc, do not care in the least; **in care** (of a child) in the guardianship of a local authority or other official organization; (of an elderly person) in an old people's home or geriatric ward; **in care of** (*US*) care of (see above); **take care** to be careful or cautious; **take care of** to look after with care; to make the necessary arrangements regarding (*colloq*). [OE *caru*; Gothic *kara* sorrow; ON *kæra*, to lament]

careen *kə-rēn'*, *vt* and *vi* to tilt or cause to tilt to one side. — *vt* to turn (a vessel) over on the side, *esp* for repairing or cleaning (*naut*). — *n* an upturned position. — *n* **careen'age** a place where ships are careened; the cost of careening. [L *carīna* keel]

career *kə-rēr* or (*obs*) **cariere** (*kar'*; *Spenser*), *n* a rush; progress through life; one's profession or occupation; progress or advancement in one's profession or occupation. — *adj* having a career; dedicated to a career. — *vi* to gallop; to rush wildly; to move or run rapidly. — *n* **career'ism**. — *n* **career'ist** a person intent on his or her own advancement. — Also *adj*. — **career break** a period away from one's occupation or profession for study, childcare, etc; **career diplomat** one who has risen through the profession, rather than a political appointee; **careers master** or **mistress** a schoolteacher who advises pupils on their choice of career; **career woman** or **career girl** a woman who follows a career. [Obs Fr *carrière* a racecourse, from LL *carrāria* carriage-road, from *carrus* wagon]

carême *ka-rem*, (*Fr*) *n* Lent. — Also with *cap*.

caress *kə-res'*, *vt* to touch affectionately or lovingly; to fondle. — *n* a gentle, loving or affectionate touch. — *n* and *adj* **caress'ing**. — *adv* **caress'ingly**. — *adj* **caress'ive**. [Fr *caresser*, from Ital *carezza* an endearment, from L *cārus* dear]

caret *kar'ət*, *n* (in proofreading, etc) a mark, ‸, to show where to insert something omitted. [L, literally, there is missing]

carex *kā'reks*, *n* a plant of the genus of sedges *Carex*: — *pl* **cā'rices** (*-ris-ēz*). [L]

Carey Street *kā'ri strēt*, (*euphem*) *n* the state of bankruptcy. [The street in London where the bankruptcy court was formerly situated]

carfax *kär'faks* or **carfox** *-foks*, *n* a place where four roads meet, *esp* an intersection of main roads in the centre of a town. [L *quadrifurcus* four-forked]

carfuffle or **curfuffle** *kər-fuf'l*, (*orig Scot*) *n* commotion, agitation. — *vt* to disorder or agitate. — Also **kerfuff'le** or **kefuff'le**. [Gaelic pfx *car-* , and Scot *fuffle* to disorder]

cargo *kär'gō*, *n* the goods carried by a ship or aeroplane; any load to be carried: — *pl* **car'goes**. — *vt* to load, weigh down (with *with*). — **cargo cult** a type of religion in certain S Pacific islands based on the belief that ancestors or supernatural beings will return bringing products of modern civilization and thus make the islanders rich and independent; any setting of too high a value on material possessions; **cargo cultist**. [Sp, from root of **car**]

cargoose *kär'gōōs*, *n* the crested grebe: — *pl* **car'geese**. [ON *kjarr* copsewood, and **goose**]

cariacou *kar'i-ə-kōō* or **carjacou** *kär'jə-kōō*, *n* any deer of the American genus or subgenus *Cariacus*, including the Virginian deer. [Tupí, *cariacu*]

cariama *kä-ri-ä'mə*, *n*. Same as **seriema**.

Carib *kar'ib*, *n* a member of a race of American Indians inhabiting parts of C America and northern S America; their language. — Also *adj*. — *adj* **Car'iban**. [Sp *Caribe*]

Caribb. *abbrev*: Caribbean.

Caribbean *kar-i-bē'ən* or (*esp NAm*) *kər-ib'iən*, *adj* of or pertaining to the Caribbean Sea and the islands of the West Indies, their inhabitants or their culture; of or pertaining to the Caribs or their language. — Also *n*.

Caribbee bark *kar-i-bē' bärk*, *n* the bark of several W Indian rubiaceous trees of the genus *Exostema* used as a substitute for cinchona. [**Carib**]

caribe *kä-rē'bā*, *n* the S American piranha fish. [Sp, cannibal]

caribou *kar-i-bōō'* or *kar'i-bōō*, *n* the N American reindeer. [Can Fr]

Carica *kar'i-kə*, *n* the papaw genus of plants of the family **Caricā'ceae**, related to the passion-flowers. [L *Carica* (*fīcus*) a dried fig from Caria, an ancient region in Asia Minor]

caricature *kar'i-kə-tūr, -tūr', -cho͝or* or *-cho͞or', n* a likeness or representation of anything so exaggerated or distorted as to appear ridiculous or comical; an absurd or ludicrous imitation or version of something. — *vt* to ridicule by representing an exaggerated or distorted likeness; to burlesque. — *adj* **caricatūr'al**. — *n* **caricatūr'ist**. [Ital *caricatura*, from *caricare* to load, from root of **car**]

carices. See **carex**.

CARICOM or **Caricom** *kar'i-kom, abbrev*: *Car*ibbean *Com*munity, a Caribbean Common Market.

cariere. An obsolete form of **career**.

caries *kā'ri-ēz, n* decay, *esp* of teeth. — *adj* **cariogenic** (*-ri-ō-jen'ik*) tending to give rise to caries. — *adj* **cā'rious** decayed. [L *cariēs*]

CARIFTA *kar-if'tə, abbrev*: *Car*ibbean *F*ree *T*rade *A*rea.

carillon *kə-ril'yən* or *kar'il-yən, n* a set of bells for playing tunes; a mechanism for playing them; a melody played on them; an instrument or organ-stop imitating a peal of bells. — *vi* to play a carillon. — *n* **carill'onneur** (also *-nûr'*) or **carill'onist** (also *kar'*). [Fr, from LL *quadriliō, -ōnis* a quaternary, as formerly rung on four bells]

carina *kə-rī'nə*, (*biol*) *n* a keel or keel-like ridge as in a bird's breastbone; the boat-shaped structure formed by the two lower petals in the pea family; (with *cap*) a constellation in the S hemisphere containing Canopus, the second brightest star. — *adj* **carinate** (*kar'i-nāt*) keeled. [L *carīna* a keel]

carioca *kar-ē-ō'kə, n* a Brazilian dance or its tune, a maxixe or variety of it; (with *cap*) a native of Rio de Janeiro. — Also *adj*. [Port]

cariogenic. See **caries**.

cariole or **carriole** *kar'i-ōl, n* a small open carriage; a light cart. [Fr *carriole*, from root of **car**]

caritas *ka'ri-tas* or *kä'ri-täs*, (*L*) *n* (Christian) charity.

carious. See **caries**.

carjacou. See **cariacou**.

cark[1] *kärk*, (*archaic*) *n* care, anxiety or solicitude. — *vt* to burden or harass. — *vi* to be anxious. — *adj* **cark'ing**. [Norman Fr *kark(e)*, from LL *carcāre*, from *carricāre* to load; see also **charge**]

cark[2] *kärk*, (*Austr slang*) *vi* to break down; to die. [Origin uncertain]

carl *kärl, n* a husbandman (*obs*); a churl (*archaic*); a miser (*Scot*). — *n* **car'line** (*-lin*; *Scot*) an old woman; a witch. — *adj* **carl'ish** (*archaic*) churlish; clownish. — *n* **car'lot** (*Shakesp*; *As You Like It*) a churl or peasant. — **carl'-hemp** the female plant of hemp (literally male-hemp, as stronger than fimble, the true male). [ON *karl* a man, a male; see **churl**]

Carley float *kär'li flōt, n* an emergency rubber raft. [From the inventor's name]

carline[1] *kär'lin, n* any plant of the genus *Carlina* closely related to the true thistles, *esp* the **carline thistle** (*C. vulgaris*). [From a legend that an angel showed the root to *Carolus*, ie Charlemagne, as a remedy for a plague]

carline[2], **carlish**. See **carl**.

carling *kär'ling*, (*naut*) *n* a strong beam used for supporting the deck in a ship, etc.

Carlist *kär'list, n* a supporter of the claims of the Spanish pretender Don *Carlos* de Borbón (1788–1855), second son of Charles IV, and his representatives. — Also *adj*. — *n* **Car'lism**.

carlock *kär'lok, n* Russian isinglass. [Russ *karluk*]

carlot. See **carl**.

Carlovingian. See **Carolingian**.

Carlylese *kär-līl-ēz', n* the vigorous, irregular phraseology and vocabulary of the essayist and historian Thomas *Carlyle* (1795–1881). — *adj* **Carlylesque'** or **Carlyl'ean**. — *n* **Car'lylism** (or *-līl'*).

carmagnole *kär-man-yōl', n* a popular song and dance of the French Revolution; a kind of short jacket worn by revolutionaries at that time with a broad collar and lapels and several rows of buttons. [Prob from *Carmagnola* in Piedmont]

Carmelite *kär'mi-līt, n* a White Friar, or friar of the order of Our Lady of Mount *Carmel*, in Palestine (now Israel), which was founded there c. 1156, becoming a mendicant order in 1247; a member of a contemplative order of nuns founded in 1452 (also *adj*); (without *cap*) a fine woollen fabric of beige or similar colour.

carminative *kär'min-ə-tiv*, or *-min', adj* expelling or relieving flatulence. — *n* a medicine with that effect. [L *cārmināre* to card, comb out, from *cārmen* a card for wool]

carmine *kär'mīn* or *-min, n* the bright red pigment obtained from the cochineal insect; its colour. — *adj* of that colour. [Fr *carmin* or Sp *carmín*, from Sp *carmesí* crimson, from Ar *qirmazī* crimson, from same root as **crimson**]

carnage *kär'nij, n* extensive or indiscriminate slaughter, *esp* of people. [Fr, from Ital *carnaggio* carnage, from L *carō, carnis* flesh]

carnahuba. See **carnauba**.

carnal *kär'nl, adj* fleshly; sensual; unspiritual; bodily; sexual; murderous, flesh-eating (*Shakesp*). — *vi* (*obs*) to act carnally. — *vt* **car'nalize** or **-ise** to sensualize. — *n* **car'nalism**. — *n* **car'nalist** a sensualist. — *n* **carnality** (*-nal'i-ti*) the state of being carnal. — *adv* **car'nally**. — **carnal knowledge** (*law*) sexual intercourse. — *adj* **carnal-mind'ed** worldly-minded. [L *carō, carnis* flesh]

carnallite *kär'nəl-īt, n* a milk-white or pinkish hydrous chloride of potassium and magnesium. [Named after the mineralogist Rudolf Von *Carnall* (1804–74)]

carnaptious *kär-nap'shəs* or **curnaptious** *kər-*, (*Scot* and *Irish*) *adj* bad-tempered, cantankerous. [Origin obscure]

carnassial *kär-nas'i-əl, adj* adapted for flesh-eating. — *n* one of the teeth of carnivores specially adapted for tearing flesh, being the last premolar of the upper jaw and first molar of the lower jaw (also **carnassial tooth**). [Fr *carnassier* flesh-eating, from L *carō, carnis* flesh]

carnation *kär-nā'shən, n* a double-flowering cultivated variety of the clove pink, *Dianthus caryophyllus*; a colour ranging from light pink to deep crimson; a flesh colour in painting. — *adj* of the colour carnation. — *adj* **carnā'tioned** ruddy. [L *carnātiō, -ōnis* fleshiness]

carnauba or **carnahuba** *kär-nä-o͞o'bə*, or *-now', n* a Brazilian palm (*Copernicia cerifera*); the yellowish wax obtained from its leaves (also **Brazilian wax** or **carnauba wax**). [Braz]

carnelian. See **cornelian**[1].

carneous. See **carnose**.

carnet *kär'nā, n* a customs or other permit; a book of tickets, vouchers, or coupons. [Fr]

carney. See **carny**.

carnifex *kär'ni-feks*, (*L*) *n* an executioner.

carnify *kär'ni-fī*, (*pathol*) *vt* and *vi* of soft tissue, *esp* in the lungs, to alter and become like muscle, as a result of disease. — *adj* **carnific'ial**. — *n* **carnifica'tion**. [L *carō* flesh, and *facere* to make]

carnival *kär'ni-vl, n* a festive occasion, often with a procession, sideshows, etc; a feast observed by Roman Catholics just before the fast of Lent; riotous feasting, merriment or amusement; an entertainment similar to a fair. — *adj* **carnivalesque'** characteristic of or appropriate to a carnival. [Ital *carnevale*, from LL *carnelevārium*, appar from L *carnem levāre* to put away meat]

Carnivora *kär-niv'ə-rə, n pl* an order of flesh-eating mammals, including dogs, cats, bears, weasels, etc. — *n* **car'nivore** (*-vōr* or *-vör*) an animal or plant that feeds on flesh. — *adj* **carniv'orous** flesh-eating. — *adv* **carniv'orously**. — *n* **carniv'orousness**. [L *carō, carnis* flesh, and *vorāre* to devour]

carnose *kär'nōs* or **carneous** *kär'ni-əs, adj* fleshy; of or like flesh. — *n* **carnos'ity** (*pathol*) a fleshy excrescence growing in and obstructing any part of the body. [See **carnal**]

Carnot cycle *kär'nō sī'kl*, *n* an ideal heat engine cycle of maximum thermal efficiency. [Nicolas *Carnot*, French physicist (1796–1832)]

carnotite *kär'nō-tīt*, *n* a yellow mineral (hydrated vanadate of uranium and potassium) important as a source of radium, vanadium and uranium. [Adolphe *Carnot*, French mine inspector, died 1920]

carny[1] or **carney** *kär'ni*, (*dialect*) *vt* and *vi* to coax, wheedle. — *n* flattery; a flatterer. — *adj* cunning, sly. [Origin unknown]

carny[2] or **carney** *kär'ni*, (*NAm slang*) *n* a carnival; a person who works in a carnival: — *pl* **car'neys**.

carob *kar'ob* or *-əb*, *n* the algarroba or locust-tree (*Ceratonia siliqua*), a caesalpiniaceous Mediterranean tree; its edible fruit; a substitute for chocolate prepared from its fruit. [Fr *carobe*, from Ar *kharrūbah*; cf **algarroba**]

caroche *kä-rosh'*, (*hist*) *n* a stately carriage used on ceremonial occasions. [Fr, from Ital *caroccio*, *carro*, from L *carrus* car]

carol *kar'əl*, *n* a song of joy or praise; a Christmas song or hymn; a ring-dance or the song accompanying it (*archaic*); an enclosure for a study in a cloister, etc (see also **carrel**). — *vi* to dance or sing a carol; to sing or warble. — *vt* to praise or celebrate in song: — *pr p* **car'olling**; *pa p* and *pa t* **car'olled**. — *n* **car'oller**. [OFr *carole*; Ital *carola* orig a ring-dance, perh from L *chorus*, Gr *choros*, or L or Gr *choraulēs*, a fluteplayer who accompanies a chorus]

Carolina *kar-ə-lī'nə*, *n* either of two states (North and South) of the United States. — Also *adj*. — *adj* **Carolinian** (*-lin'i-ən*). — **Carolina allspice** see **calycanthus**; **Carolina pink** an American species of Silene (bladder-campion); pinkroot (see **pink**[3]).

Caroline *kar'ə-līn* or **Carolean** *kar-ə-lē'ən*, *adj* of, belonging to, or characteristic of the British kings Charles I or II, or the periods of their reign (also **Carolin'ian**); of, belonging to, or characteristic of, the reign of any other king named Charles. — **Caroline minuscule** see **Carolingian**. [L *Carolus* Charles]

Carolingian *kar-ə-lin'ji-ən* or **Carlovingian** *kär-lō-vin'ji-ən*, *adj* relating to a dynasty of Frankish kings, so called from *Karl* (L *Carolus*) the Great or Charlemagne (742–814). — **Carolingian** (or **Caroline**) **minuscule** a script developed in France at the time of Charlemagne.

carolus *kar'ə-ləs*, *n* a gold coin of the time of Charles I; any gold coin of the reigns of various kings named Charles: — *pl* **car'oluses** or **car'oli** (*-lī*). [L *Carolus* Charles]

carom *kar'əm*, *n* and *vi* short form of **carambole** (*kar'əm-bōl*), a cannon in billiards. [Fr *carombole*, from Sp *carambola* the red ball in billiards]

caromel. See **caramel**.

carotene *kar'ō-tēn* or **carotin** *-tin*, *n* any of a number of reddish-yellow pigments widely distributed in plants that are converted to vitamin A in the body. — *n* **carotenoid** or **carotinoid** (*kar-ot'in-oid*) any of a group of pigments similar to carotenes, found in plant and some animal tissues. [L *carōta* carrot, and sfx *-ene*]

carotid *kə-rot'id*, *adj* relating to the two great arteries that supply blood to the head and neck. [Gr *karōtides* (pl), from *karos* sleep, so named because compression of them caused unconsciousness]

carouse *kə-rowz'*, *vi* to hold a drinking-bout; to drink freely and noisily. — *n* a drinking bout or party; a noisy revel. — *n* **carous'al** a carouse; a feast. — *n* **carous'er**. — *adv* **carous'ingly**. [OFr *carous*, Fr *carrousse*, from Ger *gar aus* quite out, ie empty the glass]

carousel or (*NAm*) **carrousel** *kar-ōō-zel'* or *-ə-sel'*, *n* a merry-go-round (*NAm*); a circular magazine for a slide projector that rotates as each slide is shown; a rotating conveyor, eg for luggage at an airport or air terminal; a tilting match or tournament, to which were added games, shows and allegorical representations (*hist*). [Fr *carrousel*]

carp[1] *kärp*, *vi* to find fault (with *at*); to nag about trivialities. — *n* **carp'er**. — *n* and *adj* **carp'ing** cavilling; fault-finding. — *adv* **carp'ingly**. [Most prob Scand, ON *karpa* to boast, modified in meaning through likeness to L *carpere* to pluck, deride]

carp[2] *kärp*, *n* an edible freshwater fish of the family *Cyprinidae*. [OFr *carpe*, from LL *carpa*; poss Gmc]

-carp *-kärp*, (*bot*) *combining form* denoting a fruit or fruiting body.

carpal. See **carpus**.

carpe diem *kär'pē dī'em* or *kär'pe dē'em*, (*L*) enjoy the present, literally seize the day.

carpel *kär'pl*, (*bot*) *n* the female organ of a flower, a modified leaf comprising ovary, stigma and style and forming, singly or with others, the gynaeceum (qv). — *adj* **car'pellary**. — *adj* **car'pellate** (of a flower) female. — *n* a flower containing carpels. — *n* **carpogō'nium** the female organ in red seaweeds, indirectly producing **carp'ospores**. — *n* **carpo'logy** the study of fruit and seeds. — *adj* **carpoph'agous** (*zool*) fruit-eating. — *n* **carp'ophore** a prolongation of a flower axis below or between the carpels. [Gr *karpos* fruit]

carpentaria *kär-pən-tā'ri-ə*, *n* an evergreen shrub of the hydrangea family, cultivated for its glossy foliage and yellow-centred white flowers.

carpenter *kär'pint-ər*, *n* a person skilled in woodwork as used in building houses, ships, etc. — *vi* to do the work of a carpenter. — *vt* to make by carpentry; to put together or construct. — *n* **car'pentry** the trade or work of a carpenter. — **car'penter-bee** or **-ant** a bee or ant that excavates its nest in wood. [OFr *carpentier*, from LL *carpentārius*, from *carpentum* a car, from root of **car**]

carpet *kär'pit*, *n* a woven, felted or tufted covering for floors, stairs, etc; a smooth, or thin, surface or covering; the surface of the ground (*cricket*); a prison sentence of three months (*slang*); odds of three to one (*bookmakers' slang*); 300 (*salesmen's slang*); a carpet-moth; a tablecloth (*Shakesp*). — *vt* to cover with or as if with a carpet; to have up for reprimand: — *pr p* **car'peting**; *pa p* and *pa t* **car'peted**. — *n* **car'peting** material of which carpets are made; carpet, or carpets. — **car'petbag** a travelling-bag made of carpeting; **car'petbagger** (*derog*) a person who comes to a place with which he has no previous connection for political or other ends; in the US, an adventurer from the northern states who sought a political career in the South after the end of the Civil War, whose only property qualification for office was his carpetbag of personal belongings; **carpet-bag steak** a beefsteak stuffed with oysters; **car'pet-bed** or **car'pet-bedding** a system of horticulture in which plants are arranged in mosaic or geometrical designs; **carpet beetle** or (*NAm*) **carpet bug** any of several beetles or their larvae which are harmful to carpets and fabrics; **carpet biter** a person prone to violent fits of rage; **car'pet-bombing** systematic bombing of a whole area; the delivery of unsolicited mail, *esp* advertising matter; **car'pet-knight** a knight dubbed at court by favour, not on account of his military exploits; hence an effeminate person; **car'petmonger** (*Shakesp*) an effeminate person; **car'pet-moth** any of the larger moths of the geometrid family Larentidae; **carpet plot** (*math*) the function of more than one variable represented as values on a graph, the shape of which resembles a flying carpet; **car'pet-rod** one of the rods used to keep a stair carpet in its place; **carpet shark** a shark of the genus *Orectolobus*, with a spotted back like a patterned carpet; **car'pet-slipper** a slipper with an upper *orig* made of carpeting; **car'pet-snake** a variegated python of Australia (*Morelia variegata*); **car'pet-sweeper** an apparatus with a revolving brush and a dust-pan, for sweeping carpets; **carpet tile** one of a number of squares of carpeting which are laid together in such a way as to form an area of carpet. — **brush** or **sweep under the carpet** to hide from someone's notice, put out of one's mind (unpleasant problems or facts); **on the carpet** under discussion (jocular transl of Fr *sur le tapis*); up before someone in authority for reprimand; at or near ground level (*airmen's slang*). [OFr *carpite*, from LL *carpeta*, *-pita* coarse fabric made from rags pulled to pieces, from L *carpere* to pluck]

carphology *kär-fol'ə-ji*, (*rare*) *n* floccillation, fitful plucking movements as in delirium. [Gr *karphos* straw, and *logeiā* gathering]

carpogonium, **carpology**, **carpophagous**. See **carpel**.

carpus *kär'pəs*, (*anatom*) *n* the wrist, or corresponding part of the forelimb: — *pl* **carpi** (*kär'pī*). — *adj* **car'pal** pertaining to the carpus. — *n* a bone of the carpus. — *n* **carpometacar'pus** in birds, a bone of the wing formed by fusion of some of the carpals with the metacarpals. — **carpal tunnel syndrome** numbness and pain in the fingers caused by compression of the nerve as it passes through the **carpal tunnel** (between the bones of the wrist and the tendons). [Latinized from Gr *karpos* wrist]

carr *kär*, *n* (a copse, *esp* of willow, in) boggy ground. [ON *kjarr*]

carrack *kar'ək*, (*hist*) *n* a large Mediterranean galleon, used for transporting goods. — Also **car'ack**, **carr'act** or **carr'ect**. [OFr *carraque*, from LL *carraca*; ety dubious]

carrageen or **carragheen** *kar-ə-gēn'*, *n* a purplish-red North Atlantic seaweed (*Chondrus crispus*) and a related species (*Gigartina mamillosa*), used for making soup and a kind of blancmange, and as an emulsifying and gelling agent (also called **Irish moss**). — *n* **carragee'nan**, **carraghee'nin** or **carragee'nin** a colloid prepared from red algae, used in food processing, pharmaceuticals, etc. [Prob Irish *carraigín* little rock, from *carraig* rock]

carrat, **carraway**. Same as **carat**, **caraway**.

carrect. See **carrack**.

carrel or **carrell** *kar'əl*, *n* a carol (*hist*); a desk or alcove in a library for private study. [See **carol**]

carriage *kar'ij*, *n* the act or cost of carrying; a four-wheeled horse-drawn vehicle for passengers; a railway passenger-coach; a wheeled support of a gun; the structures on which an aeroplane lands; a carrying part of a machine; bearing, deportment; the loop of a sword-belt (*Shakesp*); behaviour (*archaic*); a burden (*Shakesp*); baggage (*Bible*). — *adj* **carr'iageable** that may be conveyed or transported in carriages. — **carriage bolt** a *NAm* name for **coach bolt**; **carriage clock** a small portable clock, *usu* with a case with a handle on top; **carriage dog** a coachdog; another name for **Dalmatian**; **carr'iage-drive** a road for carriages through parks, etc; **carriage driving** the competitive sport of driving a carriage and horse(s); **carriage line** another name for **coach line**. — *adv* **carriage-free'** without charge for transport. — *adv* **carriage-for'ward** without prepayment of charges for carriage. — **carriage horse** a horse that draws a carriage. — *adv* **carriage-paid'** with prepayment of charges for carriage. — **carriage trade** trade from the wealthy; **carr'iageway** a road, or part of a road, used by vehicles. — **carriage and pair** a carriage drawn by two horses. [See **carry**]

carrick bend *kar'ik bend*, (*naut*) *n* a knot for joining two ropes, formed by looping and interlacing the ends together. [Perh connected with **carrack**, and the root of **bind**]

carrick bitt *kar'ik bit*, (*naut*) *n* one of two posts used to support a windlass. [**carrick** (see ety for **carrick bend**) and **bitt**]

carrier. See **carry**.

carriole. See **cariole**.

carrion *kar'i-ən*, *n* the dead and rotting body or flesh of any animal; anything vile or rotten. — *adj* relating to, or feeding on, putrid flesh. — **carrion beetle** a beetle of the family *Silphidae*, which feeds on carrion; **carr'ion-crow** the common crow (*Corvus corone*); the black vulture (*US*); **carr'ion-flower** a N American climbing plant (*Similax herbacea*), with flowers that smell like putrid flesh; a S African asclepiad plant (*Stapelia*) with fleshy stem and stinking flowers. [Fr *charogne*, from LL *carōnia*, from L *carō*, *carnis* flesh]

carritch *kar'ich*, (*Scot*) *n* a catechism. [Fr *catéchèse*, taken to be a plural]

carriwitchet *kar-i-wich'it*, *n* a quip; a quibble. [Origin unknown]

carronade *kar-ən-ād'*, (*hist*) *n* a short naval cannon of large bore. [From *Carron*, a town in the Central Region of Scotland with ironworks]

carron oil *kar'ən oil*, *n* a liniment *orig* of linseed-oil and limewater. [Formerly used for burns by workers at *Carron* (see **carronade**) ironworks]

carrot *kar'ət*, *n* a plant of the *Umbelliferae* family, having a tapering root of a reddish or yellowish colour; the root itself, which is edible and sweet; an incentive, enticement. — *adj* **carr'oty** carrot-coloured (*esp* of the hair). — **carrot fly** an insect, *psila rosae*, whose larvae are a serious pest of carrots. — **carrot and stick** incentive and punishment, as alternative methods of persuasion. [Fr *carotte*, from L *carōta*]

carrousel. A *NAm* spelling of **carousel**.

carry *kar'i*, *vt* to convey; to bear; to lead or transport; to take by force or capture; to effect; to gain; to behave or conduct oneself; to pass or win, by a majority; to add to another column (*arith*); (of a newspaper, television or radio programme, etc) to publish or include (eg an item of news), or to publish or include as a regular feature; to do the work of, or perform in sport or entertainment well enough to cover up the deficiencies of (another); to keep (merchandise, etc) in stock; (of money) to be sufficient for; to maintain; to be sufficient to maintain; to be pregnant with; to hold in saluting position (*military*). — *vi* (of a sound) to reach or be transmitted; (of a gun) to have (a specified) range; to be pregnant; to have drugs or an illegal weapon on one's person (*slang*): — *pr p* **carr'ying**; *pa p* and *pa t* **carr'ied**. — *n* the distance a golf ball goes when struck till it touches the ground; range; an act of carrying; the portage of a boat; land across which a boat has to be carried between one navigable stream or stretch and another (*chiefly NAm*); the position of 'carry arms' (*military*); the sky, movement of clouds (*Scot*); the digit carried to the next digit position when the base number is exceeded (*comput*). — *n* **carr'ier** a person who or an organization that carries, *esp* for hire; anything that carries; an instrument for carrying; a passenger aircraft; a basket, framework, etc for carrying luggage, as on a bicycle; a person who or animal that transmits disease (without suffering from it) by harbouring germs, or a virus; a vehicle for communicating a signal in cases where the medium cannot convey the actual signal (as speech, etc, in radio transmission); (also **carrier wave**) a constant frequency in an amplitude-modulation transmission (*telecomm*); non-active material mixed with, and chemically identical to, a radioactive compound (*nuc phys*); a carrier-pigeon; a carrier bag; an aircraft carrier. — **carrier bag** a strong paper or plastic bag with handles, for carrying shopping, etc; **carrier gas** a gas, eg helium, mixed with oxygen, used in providing an air supply to divers when at great depths; **carr'ier-pigeon** a pigeon with homing instincts, used for carrying messages; a pigeon of a fancy breed no longer so used; **carrier rocket** a rocket used to carry, eg a satellite into orbit; **carr'ycot** a small portable cot for a baby; **carrying charge** (*accounting*) the notional cost of unproductive assets; **carr'y-on** a book published in the style of, and marketed in connection with, an established and lucrative writer; see also **carry on** below; **carr'y-out** (chiefly *Scot*) a meal or (*esp* alcoholic) drink bought and taken away to be consumed elsewhere; **carr'ytale** (*Shakesp*) a tale-bearer. — **carry all before one** to bear down all obstacles; to be very successful in a competition or endeavour; **carry away** to carry off; to deprive of self-control by exciting the feelings; to transport; **carry back** (*accounting*) to set (a loss) against the previous year's profit, in order to lessen the total tax liability (*n*

carr'y-back); **carry both ends of the log** (*Austr*) to do all the work that should be shared by two people; **carry forward** to transfer written or printed matter to the next page, or figures to the next column; **carry it** to behave, demean oneself; to gain the advantage, carry the day (also **carry it away**); **carry off** to cause the death of; to kidnap, abduct; to gain or to win, as a prize; to cause to pass muster, to make to pass by assurance or dissimulation; **carry on** to manage; to continue; to proceed; to complain or behave unrestrainedly (*n* **carr'y-on'** or **carrying-on'**: — *pl* **carr'y-ons'** or **carryings-on'**); to flirt (*with*); **carry one's bat** see under **bat**; **carry one's point** to overrule, or overcome by argument, objections to one's plan or view; **carry out** to accomplish; to carry out for burial (*old-fashioned*); **carry over** to bring into the other (political, etc) party; to take (eg an account) to a new page; to postpone to the next occasion; to postpone payment of (an account) to the next accounting period; **carry the can** to accept responsibility for a misdemeanour or error; **carry the day** to be successful; to win the day; **carry through** to support through difficulties; to succeed in putting into effect, to accomplish; **carry too far** to continue beyond reasonable or acceptable limits; **carry up** to continue a building upward; to trace back; **carry weight** to possess authority; to have force. [OFr *carier*, from LL *carricāre* to cart, from L *carrus* a car]

carryall[1] *kar'i-öl*, *n* a light four-wheeled one-horse carriage; a type of motor vehicle with bench seats facing sideways, for carrying several passengers (*NAm*). [**cariole**, changed by folk-etymology]

carryall[2] or **carry-all** *kar'i-öl*, *n* (*NAm*) an overnight bag, a holdall.

carse *kärs*, (*Scot*), *n* an alluvial riverside plain. [Perh **carr**]

carsey. See **karzy**.

cart *kärt*, *n* a two-wheeled vehicle without springs, used for farm purposes, or for conveying heavy loads; a light two-wheeled horse-drawn vehicle with springs; any small vehicle drawn by an animal, eg an ox or donkey, or pushed or pulled by hand. — *vt* to convey in a cart; to carry, *esp* with difficulty or effort (often with *around*); to carry and display (a person) publicly in a cart as a punishment (*hist*). — *n* **cart'age** the act or cost of carting. — *n* **cart'er** a person who drives a cart. — **cart'-horse** a horse suitable for drawing heavy loads; **cart'-house** a shed for keeping carts; **cart'load** as much as a cart can carry; **cart'road, cart'-track** or **cart'way** a road or way used by or suitable for carts; **cart's'-tail** the rear of a cart, *esp* when used as a place of punishment (*hist*); **cart'wheel** the wheel of a cart; a sideways somersault with arms and legs extended. — *vi* to make a sideways somersault. — **cart'wright** a carpenter who makes carts. — **cart off** (*colloq*) to remove; to take away; **in the cart** (*slang*) in an awkward predicament; in trouble; **put the cart before the horse** to reverse the natural or sensible order of things; **village cart** an uncovered two-wheeled carriage for one horse, with a low body and one seat; **Whitechapel cart** or **chapel cart** a light two-wheeled spring-cart used in delivering shop goods. — See also **dogcart, mail-cart, tax-cart**, etc. [Ety doubtful; OE *cræt*, or ON *kartr*]

carta. See **charta**.

carte[1]. See **quart**[1].

carte[2] *kärt*, *n* a card, *esp* one of pasteboard; a bill of fare; a ticket; a playing card (*Scot*); a carte-de-visite. — **carte'-blanche'** (*-blâsh*) a blank paper, *esp* one bearing a signature, to be filled up at the recipient's discretion; unlimited authority, freedom of action (*pl* **cartes blanches**); **carte des vins** wine list; **carte-de-visite** (*-də-vē-zēt'*) a visiting card; a small photographic portrait pasted on a card; **carte du jour** (*dü zhōōr*) menu (of the day); **carte du pays** lay of the land, literally map of the country. [Fr, from L *c(h)arta*; see **card**]

carte-blanche. See **carte**[2].

cartel *kär-tel'*, *n* a combination of independent firms or enterprises formed to control a market, eg by keeping up prices, monopolizing production, etc; a political alliance or bloc; a written challenge (*obs*); an agreement for exchange of prisoners (*obs*); a card with writing on it. — *n* **car'telism**. — *n* **car'telist** a member of a cartel; a supporter of cartels. — *n* **carteliza'tion** or **-s-**. — *vt* and *vi* **car'telize** or **-ise**. — **cartel clock** a hanging wallclock with the case *usu* of metal. [Fr, from L *c(h)arta*; see **card**]

Cartesian *kär-tē'zi-ən* or *-zhyən*, *adj* relating to the French philosopher René *Descartes* (1596–1650), or his philosophy, or mathematical methods. — *n* a follower of Descartes. — *n* **Cartēs'ianism**. — **Cartesian co-ordinates** (*math*) co-ordinates in which the position of a point in a plane or in space is specified by its distances from two lines or three planes respectively; **Cartesian devil, diver**, or **bottle-imp** a scientific toy named after Descartes, a glass container with a floating figure that sinks when the top of the container is pressed.

carthamine *kär'thə-min*, *n* a dye obtained from safflower. [LL *carthamus*, from Ar *qartum* saffron]

Carthusian *kär-thū'zi-ən* or *-thōō'*, *n* a monk or (since 1229) a nun of an order founded by St Bruno in 1086, noted for its strictness; a scholar of the Charterhouse School, founded on the site of a Carthusian monastery in London, now in Godalming. — *adj* of or pertaining to the order or the school. [L *Cartusiānus*, from *Catorissium* Chatrousse, a village in Dauphiné, near which their first monastery, La Grande Chartreuse, was founded]

cartilage *kär'ti-lij*, *n* gristle, a firm pearly white substance forming the embryonic skeleton of vertebrates (*temporary cartilage*) converted into bone in adults. — *adj* **cartilaginous** (*-laj'*). — **cartilaginous fishes** fishes with a cartilaginous skeleton, including the sharks, rays and chimaeras. [Fr, from L *cartilāgō, -inis*; cognate with *crātis* wickerwork, and Gr *kartallos* a basket]

cartography *kär-tog'rə-fi*, *n* the skill or practice of making maps and charts. — *n* **cartog'rapher**. — *adj* **cartographic** (*-tō-graf'ik*) or **cartograph'ical**. — *n* **car'togram** a map presenting statistical information in diagrammatic form. — *n* **cartol'ogy** the science of maps and charts. — *adj* **cartolog'ical**. [L *c(h)arta*, from Gr *chartēs* a sheet of paper, and Gr *graphein* to write]

cartomancy *kär'tō-mən-si*, *n* divination or the telling of fortunes using playing cards. [LL *carta* a card, and Gr *manteiā* divination]

carton *kär'tən*, *n* a container made of cardboard, or (for holding liquids) of waxed paper or plastic; a small white disc within the bull's-eye of the target; a shot that strikes it. — *vt* to put into a carton. — *n* **car'tonage** or **car'tonnage** pasteboard or cardboard; the outer covering of a mummy. — **carton-pierre** (*kär'tɔ̃-pyer*) a kind of papier-mâché, imitating stone. [Fr; see **cartoon**]

cartoon *kär-tōōn'*, *n* a comic or satirical drawing commenting on topical events or politics; a strip cartoon; a cinematograph film made by photographing a succession of drawings (also **animated cartoon**); a preparatory drawing on strong paper to be reproduced in fresco, tapestry, etc; any large sketch or design on paper. — *vt* to make a cartoon or working design of; to caricature by a cartoon. — *adj* **cartoon'ish** exaggerated in design or brightly coloured like a strip or film cartoon. — *n* **cartoon'ist** a person who draws or makes cartoons. [Fr *carton* or Ital *cartone*, augmentative of *carta*]

cartophily *kär-tof'i-li*, *n* the hobby of collecting cigarette-cards. — *n* **cartophile** (*kär'tō-fīl*) or **cartoph'ilist**. — *adj* **cartophil'ic**. [L *c(h)arta*, from Gr *chartēs* a sheet of paper, and Gr *philiā* a liking]

cartouche *kär-tōōsh'*, *n* a scroll-like ornament or decorative border with rolled ends (*archit*); in hieroglyphics, an ancient Egyptian oval figure enclosing royal or divine names; an oval shield used for women or ecclesiastics (*heraldry*); in certain fireworks, a paper case containing combustible materials; a case for cartridges or mortar bullets (*hist*). — Also **cartouch'**.

[Fr, from Ital *cartoccio*, from L *c(h)arta*, from Gr *chartēs* paper]

cartridge *kär'trij*, *n* a case containing the charge for a gun (**blank'-car'tridge** with powder only; **ball'-car'tridge** with a bullet as well); a small container which can easily be inserted into and removed from a machine, holding eg film for a camera, ink for a pen, a typewriter ribbon, part of the pick-up head of a record player; a type of cassette of magnetic tape. — **car'tridge-belt** a belt having pockets for cartridges; **cartridge clip** a metal container holding cartridges for loading an automatic firearm; **car'tridge-pāper** a light-coloured, strong paper for drawing or printing on, *orig* manufactured for making cartridges; **cartridge pen** a pen with a removable container for ink which may be replaced when empty; **cartridge starter** (*aeronautics*) a device for starting aero-engines in which a slow-burning cartridge is used to operate a piston or turbine unit geared to the engine shaft. [A corruption of **cartouche**]

cartulary *kär'tū-lər-i*, *n* a register-book of a monastery, etc; the person who kept the records; the place where the register is kept. [LL *chartulārium*, from L *chartula* a document, from *charta* paper]

carucate *kar'ū-kāt*, (*hist*) *n* as much land as a team of oxen could plough in a season. — *n* **car'ucage** a tax on the carucate, first imposed by Richard I in 1198. [LL *carrūcāta* ploughland, from *carrūca* plough, from root of **car**]

caruncle *ka-* or *kə-rung'kl*, *n* a small fleshy outgrowth on the heads of certain birds, eg a cock's comb; an outgrowth near the micropyle on some seeds; any fleshy growth in or on the body. — *adj* **carun'cular**, **carun'culate** or **carun'culous**. [Fr, from L *caruncula*]

carvacrol *kär'və-krol*, (*chem*) *n* an isomer of and substitute for thymol, obtained from camphor by heating with iodine, present in origanum, etc. [Fr *carvi* caraway, and L *acer* sharp, with *oleum* oil]

carve *kärv*, *vt* to cut (wood, stone, ivory, etc) into forms, patterns, etc; to make or shape by cutting; to cut up (meat) into slices or pieces; to apportion or distribute. — *vi* to exercise the art or perform the act of carving; to make affected gestures or amorous advances (*Shakesp*): — *infinitive* (*Spenser*) **carv'en**; *pa p* **carved** or *archaic* **carv'en**. — *adj* **carv'en** carved. — *n* **carv'er** a person who carves; a wood-carver; a sculptor; a carving-knife (or fork); a tree used for carving (*Spenser*); a dining chair with arms. — *n* **carv'ery** a type of buffet-service restaurant where the main course meat is served from the joint on request. — *n* **carv'ing** the act or art of sculpture, *esp* in wood or ivory; a carved form, shape or figure; the act or art of cutting up meat at table. — **carv'ing-knife** a large sharp knife for carving meat. — **carve out** to hew out; to make or create by one's own efforts (*fig*); **carve up** (*slang*) to divide, *esp* booty; to injure a person, *esp* by slashing with a knife or razor (*n* **carve'-up**); **to cut and carve** to refine. [OE *ceorfan* to cut; Du *kerven*; Ger *kerben* to notch]

carvel *kär'vəl*, *n* an old form of **caravel**. — *adj* **car'vel-built** (of boats) built without overlap of planks (distinguished from *clinker-built*).

carvy *kär'vi*, (*Scot*) *n* caraway; a caraway seed, *esp* one coated with sugar. [Fr *carvi*; see **caraway**]

caryatid *kar-i-at'id*, *n* a female figure used instead of a column to support an entablature: — *pl* **caryat'ids** or **caryat'ides** (*-i-dēz*). — *adj* **caryat'ic**. — *adj* **caryat'idal**. — *adj* **caryatidē'an**. — *adj* **caryatid'ic**. [Gr *Karyātis* a priestess of Artemis at *Karyai* (*Caryae*), pl *Karyātides*]

Caryocar *kär'i-ō-kär*, *n* the butternut genus of plants, giving name to the family **Caryocarā'ceae** (*-si-ē*). [Gr *karyon* nut, and *karā* head]

caryophyllaceous *kar-i-ō-fi-lā'shəs*, *adj* of or belonging to the **Caryophyllā'ceae**, a family of plants including the pink, carnation and sweet william. [*Caryophyllus*, early botanical name for clove-pink, from Gr *karyophyllon* clove-tree (from similar smell)]

caryopsis *kar-i-op'sis*, *n* a dry indehiscent fruit in which the pericarp is united with the testa, characteristic of the grasses: — *pl* **caryop'ses** (*-sēz*) or **caryop'sides** (*-si-dēz*). [Gr *karyon* a nut, and *opsis* appearance]

caryopteris *kar-i-op'tər-is*, *n* any of several deciduous subshrubs of the genus *Caryopteris*, of the Verbenaceae, having small, blue flowers.

casa *kä'zä*, (*Ital* and *Sp*) *n* a house, mansion.

Casanova *kas-ə-nō'və*, *n* a man conspicuous for his amorous adventures, as was Giovanni Jacopo *Casanova* de Seingalt (1725–98).

casbah. Same as **kasba(h)**.

cascabel *kas'kə-bel*, *n* the part behind the base-ring of a cannon. [Sp]

cascade *kas-kād'*, *n* a waterfall; a trimming of lace or other material in loose waves like a waterfall; apparatus connected in series, each piece operating the next one in turn or acting on the output of the preceding one. — *vi* to fall in cascades; to form a cascade. [Fr, from Ital *cascata*, from L *cadere* to fall]

cascadura *kas-kə-doo'rə*, *n* a type of catfish of the family *Callichthyidae*, having an armoured scaly skin.

cascara *kas-kä'rə*, *-kā'rə* or *kas'kə-rə*, *n* a Californian buckthorn, *Rhamnus purshiana*, also known as the **cascara buckthorn**; the bark of the cascara, also known as **cascara sagrada** (*sə-grä'də* or *-grā'*; *Sp*, sacred) used as a tonic and laxative. — *n* **cascarill'a** the aromatic bitter bark of a W Indian shrub, *Croton eluteria*, also known as **cascarilla bark**; the shrub itself. — **cascara amarga** (*ə-mär'gə*; *Sp*, bitter) the bitter bark of a tropical American tree of the quassia family, formerly used to treat syphilis and skin diseases. [Sp *cáscara* bark]

caschrom *kas'krōm*, *n* a sort of spade with a bent handle, formerly used in the Scottish Highlands for tilling the ground. — Also **cas crom**. [Gaelic *cas* foot, handle, and *chrom* fem of *crom* bent, crooked]

casco *kas'kō*, *n* a Philippine cargo barge: — *pl* **cas'cos**. [Sp]

Case *kās*, *abbrev*: computer-aided software (or systems) engineering.

case[1] *kās*, *n* a covering, box or sheath containing something; the contents of such a box, etc, as in *a case of wine*; a set, eg of pistols; a facing for walls; the boards and back of a hardback book; a tray with many compartments in which a compositor keeps types of different sizes and styles (*printing*). — *vt* to enclose in a case. — *n* **cās'ing** the act of putting on a case; an outside covering of any kind, as of boards, plaster, etc; a strong rigid pipe or tube lining a well, shaft, etc; the outer covering of a tyre; the outer deck of a submarine; cleaned animal intestines, or a substitute, used to case sausage meat, etc. — **case'-bottle** a bottle made to fit into a case with others, a bottle with a covering. — *adj* **case'-bound** (of a book) with a hard cover. — **cased glass** or **case glass** a type of 19c glass consisting of one or more layers of coloured glass laid on clear glass and cut away to form various patterns. — *vt* **case'-harden** to harden on the surface, as by carbonizing iron (*metallurgy*); to make callous or insensitive through previous experience. — **case'-hardening**; **case'-knife** a large knife kept in a sheath; **case'maker** a person who makes covers for books; **case'man** a compositor; **case'-shot** canister-shot, an artillery projectile for use at close quarters; **case'-worm** a caddis-worm; **cas'inghead** (*mineral ext*) the part of the well that is above the surface and to which the pipelines and control valves are attached. [ONFr *casse* (mod Fr *châsse* and *caisse*), from L *capsa*, from *capere* to take]

case[2] *kās*, *n* that which happens, an event or occurrence; state or condition; subject of question, investigation or inquiry; (an instance of) a person or animal having a disease; (records relating to) a person under medical treatment or being dealt with by a social worker, etc; an odd or humorous character (*slang*); a legal statement of facts either in total or as presented by the defence or the prosecution; a lawsuit; a plausible contention, something to be said for a position or action, a point; (any of the specific types of) grammatical relation of a noun, pronoun, or (in some languages) adjective to another word in the sentence, and/or its variation in form to express that relation. — *vt* (*slang*) to reconnoitre or examine, *usu* with a view to burglary. — **case'book** formerly, a book in which a doctor records the history of his cases; a book recording medical, legal, etc cases which are valuable as examples for reference; **case history** a record of ancestry, environment, personal history, etc, for use in diagnosis and treatment, or for some other purpose; **case'-law** law established by judicial decisons made in previous cases; **case'-load** the number of cases a doctor, social worker, etc has to deal with at a particular time; **case'-study** a study based on the analysis of one or more cases or case histories; (the gathering and organizing of information for) a case history; **case'-work** (*social work*) the study of maladjusted individuals or of families, their environment and personal history, often together with supervision and guidance; **case'-worker**.— **as the case may be** depending on or in accordance with the particular circumstances; **case in point** an example or illustration of what is under discussion; **in any case** anyway, however; whatever happens; **in case** in the event that; in order to make safe, make sure, etc; **in case to** in fit condition for; **make out one's case** to give reasons for one's statements or position; **put (the) case** to suppose an instance; to take for example; **the case** the fact, the reality. [OFr *cas*, from L *cāsus*, from *cadere* to fall]

casein *kā'sēn* or *-si-in*, *n* a protein obtained from milk, forming the basis of cheese. [From L *cāseus* cheese, and sfx *-in*]

casemate *kās'māt*, *n* any bombproof vaulted chamber or an armoured compartment, eg in a ship; *orig* a loopholed gallery, from which the garrison of a fort could fire upon an enemy who had obtained possession of the ditch. — *adj* **case'mated**. [Fr; derivation uncertain]

casement *kās'mənt*, *n* the case or frame of a window; a window that opens on vertical hinges (also **casement window**); a hollow moulding. — *adj* **case'mented** having casements. — **casement cloth** a plain cotton fabric, suitable for casement curtains; **casement curtain** a curtain hung from a window-sash; **casement window**. [For **encasement** (Fr *enchassement*), or LL *casamentum* house-frame, or directly from **case**[1]]

caseous *kā'si-əs*, *adj* cheeselike. — *n* **cāseā'tion** the formation of cheese through casein. [L *cāseus*, cheese; see **casein**]

casern or **caserne** *kə-zûrn'*, (*hist*) *n* a barrack or billet for soldiers. [Fr, from Sp *caserna*]

cash[1] *kash*, *n* coins or paper money; available or ready money. — *adj* using cash; paid by cash. — *vt* to turn into or exchange for money. — *n* **cashi'er** a person who has charge of the receiving and paying of money. — *adj* **cash'less** operated, paid for, conducted, performed, etc using credit cards or computer transfers, without the use of cash. — **cash'-account** an account which shows cash transactions (*bookkeeping*); a form of account with a bank, by which a person is entitled to draw out sums by way of loan — also called **cash'-cred'it**. — *adj* **cash-and-carr'y** of or denoting a business, method of trading, etc which involves *cash and carry* (see below). — **cash'-book** a book of account in which a record of all receipts and disbursements is kept (*bookkeeping*); **cash'-box**; **cash card** a coded plastic card issued by a bank that allows the holder to obtain money from a bank account via a cash dispenser; **cash cow** a well-established business or other enterprise that produces cash with a minimum of maintenance or management; **cash-credit** see **cash-account**; **cash crop** a crop intended for sale, not for consumption by the producer; **cash desk** a table, etc, with a till where money is taken for goods purchased; **cash dispenser** a machine, *usu* in or outside a bank, which dispenses bank notes on the insertion of a special coded plastic card; **cash flow** the movement of money in and out of a business; **cash'-keeper** cashier; **cash limit** a limit set on the total amount of money a company, institution, local authority, etc may spend; **cash machine** a cash dispenser; **cash payment** payment in ready money; **cash point** the place in a shop, supermarket, etc where money is taken for goods purchased; an automatic teller machine, a cash dispenser; **cash'-railway** formerly, a mechanical device for interchange of cash between counter and cashdesk in a shop; **cash'-register** a till that automatically and visibly records the net amount put in. — **cash and carry** sale for cash, with uplift and delivery of goods to be performed by the buyer; a *usu* large shop which trades in this way, often at wholesale prices; **cash down** with payment at the time of purchase; **cash in** to exchange for money; to seize an advantage; **cash in on** to turn to one's advantage; **cash in (one's checks** or **chips)** to exchange counters for money on leaving a gaming-table or gambling house; to die (*slang*); **cash up** to count the total amount of money taken in a shop, department, etc, *usu* at the end of the day; **hard cash** see under **hard**; **out of cash**, **in cash** without, or with, money; out of, or in, pocket. [A doublet of **case** a box, from OFr *casse* a box]

cash[2] *kash*, *n* a small Eastern coin. [Port *caixa*, from Sinh *kāsi* coin, from Tamil *kāsu*]

cashaw *kə-shö'*, *n* a kind of pumpkin (*US*; also **cushaw**); a W Indian mesquite. [Algonquian]

cashew *kə-shōō'* or *kash'ōō*, *n* a spreading tropical American tree (*Anacardium occidentale*) with kidney-shaped nuts (**cash'ew-nuts**) whose kernels (edible only when roasted) and fleshy stalks (**cash'ew-apples**) are used as food. [Tupí *caju*; cf **acajou**]

cashier[1] *kash-ēr'*, *vt* to dismiss from a post *esp* in the armed forces, in disgrace; to discard or put away; to annul. — *n* **cashier'er**. — *n* **cashier'ing** or **cashier'ment** dismissal; a punishment for army and naval officers, more severe than dismissal, in that it disqualifies from entry into public service in any capacity (abolished 1970). [Du *casseren* (*kasseren*) to cashier, from Fr *casser*, from L *cassāre*, from *cassus* void, empty]

cashier[2]. See **cash**[1].

cashmere *kash'mēr*, *n* (a fabric made from) fine soft *Kashmir* goats' hair; any (product made from) similar wool. — Also *adj*.

casino *kə-sē'nō*, *n* an establishment for gambling, *usu* with roulette and card and dice games; a card-game in which players match cards in hand with others on the table (also **cassi'no**); formerly, a building with public dance halls, gaming tables, etc, or a room for public dancing: — *pl* **casi'nos**. [Ital, dimin of L *casa* a house]

cask *käsk*, *n* a hollow round container for holding liquor, made of wooden staves bound with hoops; a quantity contained in such a vessel; a casque (*obs*); a flask (*nuc eng*). — *vt* to put in a cask. [Fr *casque*, from Sp *casco* skull, helmet, cask]

casket *käsk'it*, *n* a little cask or case; a small case for holding jewels, etc; a coffin (*esp NAm*). [Ety uncertain]

Caslon *kaz'lən*, *n* a style of printing type designed by William *Caslon* (1692–1766); a typeface imitating this style.

casque *käsk*, *n* a cover for the head (*obs* **cask**); a helmet (*obs* **cask**); a helmet-like horny protuberance, as on the beak or head of some birds (*zool*). [A doublet of **cask**]

Cassandra *kəs-an'drə*, (*Gr mythol*) *n* a daughter of Priam, king of Troy, loved by Apollo, who gave her the gift of prophecy, but not of being believed; hence, anyone who expresses pessimistic views of the political or social future and is not listened to.

cassareep or **cassaripe** *kas'ə-rēp*, *n* the juice of the bitter cassava root, a potent antiseptic, made into syrup and used in sauces, *esp* in W Indian cookery. [From Tupí]

cassata *ka-sä'tə*, *n* an (*orig* Italian) ice-cream containing candied fruit and nuts. [Ital]

cassation *ka-sā'shən*, *n* annulment; in French law, the quashing of a decision of a court; hence **court of**

cassation the supreme tribunal or higher court of appeal; an 18c instrumental suite similar to a serenade or divertimento (*music*). [LL *cassātiō, -ōnis*, from *cassāre* to bring to nought]

cassava *kə-sä'və, n* a tropical American plant of the *Manihot* genus whose roots yield a nourishing starch. — Also **manioc** or **tapioca**. [From a Taino (language of extinct W Indian tribe) name]

Cassegrain(ian) telescope *kas-ə-grān'(i-ən) tel'i-skōp, n* a type of reflecting telescope devised by, and named after, a 17c Frenchman, N *Cassegrain*.

casserole *kas'ə-rōl, n* a stew-pan; a covered pot in which food is both cooked and served; the dish of food or stew cooked in this way. — *vt* to cook in a casserole. — **casserole cookery** cooking in the dish in which the food is to be served. [Fr]

cassette *kas-et', n* a small casket; a light-tight container for an X-ray film, or one for film that facilitates loading in a camera, projector, microfilm-reader, etc; a plastic case containing a reel of magnetic tape, often with pre-recorded material on it. — **cassette recorder** or **player** a machine which records on to or plays magnetic tape cassettes; **cassette single** or **cassing'le** a pre-recorded tape cassette of a single disc. [Fr, dimin of *casse* case]

cassia *kas(h)'yə, n* a coarser kind of cinnamon (**cass'ia-bark**); the tropical Asian tree (*Cinnamomum cassia*) that yields it; (often with *cap*) a genus of shrubs of the Caesalpinia family whose pods yield senna and the drug cassia fistula or purging cassia. [L *casia*, from Gr *kasiā* (also *kassiā*), from Heb *qetsīʿāh*]

cassimere or **casimere** *kas'i-mēr, n* a twilled cloth of the finest wools. — Also **ker'seymere**. [Corruption of **cashmere**]

cassino *kə-sē'nō, n* a card game in which players match cards in hand with others exposed on the table: — *pl* **cassi'nos**. [See **casino**]

Cassiopeia *kas-i-ō-pē'(y)ə, n* a northern constellation named after the mother of Andromeda. — *n* **cassiopē'-ium** a former name for **lutetium**.

cassis *ka-sēs', n* a syrupy blackcurrant drink or flavouring. [Fr]

cassiterite *ka-sit'ə-rīt, n* a brown or black mineral, SnO_2, a dioxide of tin, found in alluvial deposits and acid igneous rocks. — Also called **tinstone**. [Gr *kassiteros* tin]

cassock *kas'ək, n* a long robe or outer coat worn by clergy and choristers; a shorter garment, *usu* of black silk, worn under the Geneva gown by Scottish ministers. — *adj* **cass'ocked**. [Fr *casaque*, from Ital *casacca*]

cassolette *kas'ō-let, n* a censer; a perfume-box with perforated lid. [Fr, from Sp *cazoleta*, from *cazo* a saucepan]

cassonade *kas-o-nād', n* unrefined sugar. [Fr]

cassone *kä-sō'nā, (Ital) n* a large chest, elaborately carved and painted.

cassoulet *ka-sōō-lā, (Fr) n* a stew consisting of haricot beans, onions, herbs and various kinds of meat.

cassowary *kas'ə-wər-i, n* any member of a genus (*Casuarius*) of flightless birds, found *esp* in New Guinea, closely related to the emu. [Malay *kasuārī* or *kasavārī*]

cassumunar *kas-ōō-mū'nər, n* an E Indian ginger. [Origin unknown]

cast *käst, vt* to throw or fling, *esp* violently; to throw (a fishing-line or net) into the water; to throw off, get rid of, drop or discard; (of animals) to shed or moult (hair, etc); to project or create (a shadow); to throw out or give out (light, heat, etc); to mould or shape (metal, plastic, etc, or artefacts from it); to appoint (an actor *for* a part, or *as* a character in a play, etc); to assign (the parts in a play, etc); to voice, express or create (doubts, etc); to reject, condemn, dismiss or decide against; to purpose, devise or consider (*archaic*); to calculate, computate or add up (*now rare*); to direct (a glance, thoughts, etc); to formulate, or to arrange in a suitable order or form; to register (a vote); to predict or calculate (a horoscope) (*astrol*); (of animals) to give birth, *esp* prematurely; to make (printing plates) in stereotype or electrotype (*printing*); to dig and cut (peat) (*Scot*). — *vi* to throw a fishing-line into the water; (of wood) to warp; (of sailing vessels) to veer; to look or seek; (of animals) to moult: — *pa t* and *pa p* **cast**. — *n* the act of casting; a throw of anything, eg the sounding-lead, a fishing-line, etc; the thing thrown, *esp* in angling; the distance thrown; a twist or squint, eg of the eye; a turn or sample performance; a good turn, eg a lift or conveyance in a vehicle (*Scot*); indigestible matter ejected by a bird, earthworm, etc; a throw or turn of fortune, a chance; a mould; a rigid casing, *usu* of plaster of Paris and, often, gauze, for holding a broken bone in place while it sets; form, manner, stamp or quality (*esp* of a person); an overall shade or tinge of colour; the assignment of the various parts of a play, etc to the several actors, etc; the company of actors playing roles in a given play, film, etc; a pair of hawks (*falconry*); a second swarm of bees leaving a hive after the first swarm. — *adj* moulded; rejected, cast off; defeated at law; (of an animal) on its back and unable to get up. — *adj* **cast'ed** (*Shakesp*) cast off. — *n* **cast'ing** the act of casting or moulding; that which is cast; a mould. — **cast'away** a person shipwrecked in a desolate or isolated place; an outcast. — *adj* worthless, rejected. — **casting couch** (*facetious*) a couch on which actresses are said to be seduced with the promise of a part in a film, play, etc; **casting director** a person responsible for casting actors for all the parts in a film, TV production, play, etc; **cast'ing-net** a species of net for fishing; **cast'ing-vote** a chairman's deciding vote in case of deadlock; **cast'ing-weight** the weight that makes the balance cast or turn when exactly poised; **cast-i'ron** an iron-carbon alloy distinguished from steel by its containing substantial amounts of cementite or graphite, meaning it is unsuitable for working and must be cast. — *adj* hard, rigid; unarguable, incontestable. — *adj* **cast'-off** rejected, laid aside, given away, no longer wanted, etc. — *n* anything, *esp* clothing, given or thrown away, no longer wanted, etc; the act or result of casting off manuscript or typewritten copy. — **cast-steel'** steel that has been cast, not shaped by mechanical working. — **cast about** to look about, to search (for) literally or in one's mind; to turn, to go round (*Bible*); **cast a horoscope** or **nativity** to make an astrological calculation of someone's future or character; **cast anchor** to anchor a ship; **cast an eye** or **a glance** to look briefly and informally; **cast a spell (upon)** to utter or perform an enchantment or to put under an enchantment; **cast a vote** to record or make a vote; **cast away** to wreck; to waste; **cast back** to direct one's thoughts to the past; **cast down** to deject or depress mentally; to turn downward; **cast loose** to set loose or adrift; **cast lots** see under **lot**; **cast off** to reject; to release (hawks or hounds) in order to hunt or pick up a scent; to release (a boat) from its moorings; (in knitting, etc) to eliminate stitches by looping them together and removing them from the pins; to calculate the amount of printed matter that manuscript or typewritten copy will make when typeset; **cast on** (in knitting, etc) to make stitches; **cast out** (*Scot*) to quarrel; **cast up** to throw up; to bring up or mention (a past error, wrongdoing, etc) as a reproach; to turn up, appear or emerge (*Scot*); **cast water** (*archaic*) to inspect or test urine in medical diagnosis; **the last cast** extremities. [ON *kasta* to throw]

Castalian *kas-tā'li-ən, adj* pertaining to *Castalia*, a fountain on Parnassus, sacred to Apollo and the Muses and thought to be a source of poetic inspiration.

Castanea *kas-tān'i-ə, n* the chestnut genus, of the beech family (*Fagaceae*). — *n* **Castanospermum** (*kas-tan-ō-spûr'məm*; Gr *sperma* a seed) an Australian papilionaceous tree, the Moreton Bay chestnut, so called from the taste of its nuts. — *n* **castanospermine** (*-mēn*) an alkaloid obtained from the seeds of the Moreton Bay chestnut, used to make drugs for the treatment of AIDS. [Gr *kastanon* chestnut]

castanet *kas'tə-net* or *-net'*, *n* either of a pair of hollow shell-shaped pieces of ivory or hard wood, bound by a band on the thumb, and struck by the finger to produce a clicking sound used as an accompaniment to Spanish dances and guitars. [Sp *castañeta*, from L *castanea* a chestnut]

caste *käst*, *n* a social class amongst Hindus in India; an exclusive or hereditary social class; a type of individual in some polymorphic social insects. — *adj* **caste'less** having no caste. — **caste'-mark** a mark indicating a person's caste, worn on the forehead (also *fig*). — **lose caste** to descend in social rank. [Port *casta* breed, race, from L *castus* pure, unmixed]

castellan, **castellated** and **castellum**. See **castle**.

caster. See **castor**[1].

castigate *kas'tig-āt*, *vt* to punish or scold; to criticize severely; to emend (*obs*). — *n* **castigā'tion**. — *n* **cas'tigātor**. — *adj* **cas'tigatory** (*-ə-tər-i*). [L *castīgāre*, *-ātum*, from *castus* pure]

Castilian *kas-til'yən*, *adj* of, or typical of, Castile. — *n* a person born or living in Castile; the language of Castile, standard Spanish. — **Castile soap** a hard soap made with olive oil and soda. [Sp *Castellano*]

castle *käs'l*, *n* a fortified house or fortress; the residence of a prince or nobleman, or a large country mansion generally; a rook in chess; a defensive tower borne on an elephant's back (*hist*); a large ship, *esp* of war (*hist*). — *vt* to enclose or fortify with a castle. — *vi* (*chess*) to move the king two squares towards the castle and place the castle on the square the king has passed over. — *n* **castellan** (*kas'təl-an*) the governor or keeper of a castle. — *adj* **castellated** (*kas'tel-āt-id*) having turrets and battlements like a castle. — *n* **castell'um** a small Roman fort; a mile-castle. — *adj* **cas'tled** provided with or having castles. — **cas'tle-building** the act of building castles in the air or forming visionary projects; **cas'tle-guard** the guard for the defence of a castle; **castle nut** a six-sided nut with six radial slots, two of which line up with a hole in the bolt or screw, a split pin preventing turning. — **castles in the air** or **in Spain** imaginary or unrealistic plans, project or hopes. [OE *castel*, from L *castellum*, dimin of *castrum* a fortified place]

castock *kas'tək* or **custock** *kus'tək*, (*Scot*) *n* a cabbage stock. [**kale** and **stock**[1]]

Castor *kas'tor* or *-tər*, *n* one of the Dioscuri, twin brother of Pollux, son of Leda, renowned for his skill in horse-taming (*Gr mythol*); a bright star in the constellation Gemini (the Twins). [L, from Gr *Kastōr*]

castor[1] or **caster** *käst'ər*, *n* a small solid swivelling wheel attached to furniture enabling it to be easily moved; a vessel with perforated top for sprinkling sugar, etc. — **castor action** or **caster action** (*autos*) the use of king-pins to give the steearable front wheels fore-and-aft stability and a self-centring tendency after angular deflection; **castor sugar** or **caster sugar** white granulated sugar crushed to form fine grains. [Ety as for **cast**]

castor[2] *käs'tər*, *n* the beaver (genus *Castor*); castoreum; a hat of beaver or similar fur. — *n* **castoreum** (*-tō'ri-əm* or *-tö'*) the dried perineal sacs of the beaver, or a brown unctuous strong-smelling substance obtained from them, formerly used in medicine and perfumery. — *n* **cas'tory** (*Spenser*) a red or pink colour got from castoreum. [L *castōr*, *-oris*, from Gr *kastōr*, *-oros* beaver]

castor[3] *käs'tər*, (*Austr slang*) *adj* good; excellent.

castor-oil *käs'tər-oil'*, *n* a medicinal and lubricating oil obtained from the seeds of a tropical African euphorbiaceous plant, *Ricinus communis*, the **castor-oil plant**. [Perh from use as substitute for **castor(eum)**]

castral *kas'trəl*, *adj* belonging to the camp. [L *castra*]

castrametation *kas-trə-me-tā'shən*, *n* the art of designing a camp. [L *castra* a camp and *mētārī*, *-ātus* to measure off, from *mēta* a boundary]

castrate *kas-trāt'*, *vt* to deprive of the power of generation; to remove the testicles from, to geld or emasculate; to render powerless, lacking in impact, etc. — *adj* **castrat'ed** gelded; rendered ineffective, expurgated. — *n* **castrā'tion**. — *n* **castrato** (*käs-trä'tō*; from *Ital*) a male singer castrated in boyhood so as to preserve a soprano or alto voice: — *pl* **castra'ti** (*-tē*). [L *castrāre*, *-ātum*]

casual *kaz(h)'ū-əl*, *adj* accidental; unforeseen; occasional; off-hand; (of sexual relations) lacking in depth of feeling or commitment; negligent; careless; unceremonious, relaxed, free and easy; (of a worker) employed only according to demand, without permanent employment. — *n* an occasional employee; (also with *cap*) a member of a gang of hooligans who frequent football matches and deliberately start fights, cause disturbances, etc. — *n* **casualīza'tion** or **-s-**. — *n* **cas'ualism** the belief that chance governs all things; the employment of casual labour. — *vt* **cas'ualize** or **-ise** to turn (regular workers) into casual workers. — *adv* **cas'ually**. — *n* **cas'ualness**. — *n pl* **cas'uals** slip-on flat-heeled shoes; loose-fitting, comfortable and informal clothing. — **casual clothes** informal clothing; **casual labour** (*usu* seasonal) workers without permanent employment; **casual labourer** a worker employed for short periods as required; **casual ward** a workhouse department providing temporary accommodation for labourers, paupers, etc (*hist*). [L *cāsuālis*, from *cāsus*; see **case**[2]]

casualty *kazh'ū-əl-ti*, *n* a person injured or killed; an accident; a misfortune; a person lost to one side in a conflict by wounds, death, desertion, etc (*military*); a thing damaged or destroyed; the casualty department of a hospital; an incidental charge or payment. — **casualties of superiority** in the feudal law of Scotland, payments to the superior in certain contingencies (eg death), ultimately redeemed or extinguished by the Act of 1914; **casualty department** or **ward** a hospital department or ward, in which accident and emergency patients are treated. [Ety as for **casual**]

casuarina *kas-ū-ə-rī'nə*, *n* any tree of the genus *Casuarina*, including the she-oak and beefwood of Australia and S Asia, constituting a family **Casūarinā'ceae**. [Named from its resemblance to *Cassowary* plumage]

casuist *kaz'ū-ist*, *n* a person who studies and resolves cases of conscience (*philos*); often, someone who argues plausibly but falsely in such cases. — *adj* **casūist'ic** or **casūist'ical**. — *adv* **casūist'ically**. — *n* **cas'ūistry** the science or doctrine of cases concerned with moral conscience (*philos*); the reasoning which enables a person to decide in a particular case between apparently conflicting duties; plausible but flawed reasoning. [Fr *casuiste*, from L *cāsus*; see **case**[2]]

casus belli *kā'səs be'lī* or *be'lē*, *n* something that causes, involves or justifies war. [L]

casus conscientiae *kā'səs kon-shi-en'shi-ē* or *kōn-skē-en'tē-ī*, *n* a case of conscience. [L]

casus foederis *kā'səs fē'də-ris* or *foi'de-ris*, *n* a case clearly coming within the provisions of a treaty. [L]

CAT *kat*, *abbrev*: College of Advanced Technology; computer-aided (or computer-assisted) or computed axial tomography. — **CAT scanner** or **CT scanner** see separate entry.

cat[1] *kat*, *n* a carnivore of genus *Felis*, *esp* the domesticated kind or any of the smaller wild species; a spiteful or malicious woman (*derog*); a piece of wood tapering at each end, struck with the **cat'-stick** in the game of tipcat; the game of tipcat; short for the **cat-o'-nine'-tails**, a whip with nine knotted tails or lashes, once used in the army and navy; a heavy tackle for raising the anchor to the cat head (*naut*); a movable penthouse to protect besiegers (*hist*); a double tripod with six legs; a showily dressed man (*old slang*); a man, chap (*slang*); a jazz fan (*slang*); a coward or timid animal (*Austr slang*); short for caterpillar (tractor). — *vt* to lash with a cat-o'-nine-tails; to raise the anchor to the cathead (*naut*); to vomit. — *n* **cat'hood** the state of being a cat or having the nature of a cat. — *n* **cat'kin** a crowded spike or tuft of small unisexual flowers with reduced scalelike bracts, as in the willow, hazel, etc. — *adj*

cat'like like a cat; noiseless, stealthy. — *n* **cat'ling** a surgical knife used in amputations; a little cat, a kitten (*archaic*); a catgut string (*Shakesp*). — *n* **catt'ery** a place where cats are bred, or cared for in their owners' absence. — *adj* **catt'ish** or **catt'y** like a cat; spiteful; back-biting. — *adv* **catt'ishly** or **catt'ily**. — *n* **catt'ishness** or **catt'iness**. — **cat'amount** any of various large wild cats, applied *esp* to the puma and the lynx; **catamoun'tain** or **cat o' mountain** any of various large wild cats, applied *esp* to the leopard, panther or ocelot. — *adj* ferocious, savage. — *adj* **cat-and-dog'** constantly quarrelling. — *adj* **cat-and-mouse'** used of harassing or toying with an opponent, victim, etc before finally killing, defeating or otherwise disposing of them; also of waiting and watching for the right moment to attack and dispose of one's opponent. — **cat'bird** an American bird of the thrush family with a mewing note; any Australian bowerbird having a catlike call; **cat'-burglar** a burglar who performs nimble climbing feats or employs stealth and agility to gain access to premises; **cat'call** formerly, a squeaking instrument used in theatres to express disapprobation; a shrill whistle or cry expressing disapproval or derision, *esp* at an artiste's performance. — *vi* to make a catcall. — *vt* to direct catcalls at. — **cat-cracker** see separate entry; **cat door** a cat-flap. — *adj* **cat'-eyed** having eyes like a cat; able to see in the dark. — **cat'fish** a fish with catlike whiskers near its mouth; the wolf-fish; **cat'-flap** a small door set in a larger door to allow a cat entry and exit; **cat'gut** a kind of cord made from the intestines of sheep and other animals used for violin strings, surgical ligatures, etc; the violin or other stringed instrument (*old-fashioned* or *facetious*); a coarse corded cloth. — *adj* **cat'-hammed** with thin hams like a cat's. — **cat'head** (*naut*) one of two strong beams projecting from the bow of a ship through which passes the tackle by which the anchor is raised; a spider tool, a lathe accessory consisting of a turned sleeve with four or more radial screws at each end (*eng*); **cat'hole** (*naut*) one of two holes in the after part of a ship through which hawsers may pass for steadying the ship or for heaving astern; **cat'house** a brothel (*esp NAm slang*); a place where cats are cared for; **cat'-lap** any thin or unappetizing drink; **cat litter** a granular absorbent material used to line a tray, on which a domestic cat may urinate and defecate indoors; **cat'-mint**, **cat'nep** or **cat'nip** a mint-like labiate plant (*Nepeta cataria*) attractive to cats; **cat'nap** a brief sleep, *esp* without lying down; **cat o' mountain** see **catamountain** above; **cat-o'-nine-tails** see **cat**; **cat's'-brains** (*archaic*) a geological formation of sandstone veined with chalk; **cat's-cra'dle** a pastime in which a string looped about the fingers and passed from player to player is transformed from one symmetrical pattern to another; an impenetrably intricate set of regulations, instructions, etc; **cat's'-ear** any plant of the European compositous genus *Hypochoeris*, having yellow dandelion-like flowers; **cat's'-eye** a name for various chatoyant minerals that resemble a cat's eye when polished, *esp* a greenish-yellow variety of chrysoberyl; (®) a small reflector set in a frame fixed in a road surface to indicate traffic lanes; **cat's'-foot** a European compositious plant (*Antennaria dioica*) having woolly leaves and white flowers (also called **mountain-everlasting**); ground ivy; **cat'-silver** a variety of silvery mica; **cat'skin**; **cat's'-meat** horse's flesh, or the like, sold for cats; any rather unappetizing food; **cat's'-paw** a person who is used by another (from the fable of the monkey who used the paws of the cat to draw chestnuts out of the fire); a hitch in a rope providing two loops for a hook; a light breeze forming ripples on the water's surface (*naut*); **cat's'-tail** a catkin; timothy-grass; the reed-mace or bulrush; **cat'suit** a type of one-piece trouser suit; **cat's-whisk'er** (*radio*) a delicate wire brought into contact with a crystal to rectify the current in some forms of crystal detector and produce audibility; **cat'-walk** a narrow footway, eg on a bridge, above the stage in a theatre, or for the models in a fashion show; **cat'worm** a polychaete worm (*Nephthys hombergi*) frequently used as a fishing bait (also called **white worm**). — *adj* **cat'-witted** small-minded, conceited and spiteful. — **cat'works** (*min ext*) the assemblage of motors and catheads providing power for secondary activities on drilling platforms, eg pipe-hoisting. — **bell the cat** see under **bell**; **big cats** see **the big cats** below; **catted and fished** (of an anchor) raised to the cathead and secured to the ship's side; **care killed the** (or **a**) **cat** worry killed the cat, even with his proverbial nine lives; **Cheshire cat** (*chesh'ər kat* or *chesh'ēr'*) a cat renowned for grinning, like the Cheshire cat in Lewis Carroll's *Alice's Adventures in Wonderland*; **enough to make a cat laugh** ie even the least inclined; **in the catbird seat** (*NAm*) in an advantageous position; **Kilkenny cats** proverbial cats who fight till each destroys the other; **let the cat out of the bag** see under **bag**; **like a cat on hot bricks** or **on a hot tin roof** (*colloq*) uneasy, restive; very nervous; **like something the cat brought in** or **dragged in** bedraggled, slovenly in dress, scruffy, etc; **not have a cat in hell's chance** (*slang*) to have no chance at all; **play cat-and-mouse with** to deal with in a cat-and-mouse way; **put the cat among the pigeons** to stir up a great deal of trouble; **rain cats and dogs** (*colloq*) to rain very heavily; **room to swing a cat** a minimum of space; **see which way the cat jumps** to see how things are going to turn out before committing oneself; **the big cats** lions, tigers, leopards, etc; **the cat's pyjamas** or **the cat's whiskers** (*slang*) the very thing that is wanted, the ideal thing; anyone or anything considered to be the best or greatest; **turn (the) cat in (the) pan** to change sides with dexterity; **wait for the cat to jump** see **see which way the cat jumps**; **whip the cat** see under **whip**. [OE *cat*; found also in Celtic, Slav, Ar, Finn, etc]

cat² *kat*, *n* an old name for a coal and timber vessel on the north-east coast of England. — *n* **cat'boat** a cat-rigged boat. — *adj* **cat'-rigged** having one great fore-and-aft mainsail spread by a gaff at the head and a boom at the foot, for smooth water only. [Obscurely connected with **cat¹**]

cat³ *kat*, *n* short for **catamaran** and **catalytic converter**.

cat. *abbrev*: catalogue; catechism.

catabasis *kə-tab'ə-sis*, *n* a downward movement; the decline of a disease in a population.

catabolism or **katabolism** *kat-ab'ə-lizm*, (*biol*) *n* the disruptive processes of chemical change in organisms — destructive metabolism, opposed to *anabolism*. — *adj* **catabolic** (*kat-ə-bol'ik*). [Gr *katabolē*, from *kataballein* to throw down, from *kata* down, and *ballein* to throw]

catacaustic *kat-ə-kös'tik*, (*math* and *phys*) *adj* pertaining to or denoting a caustic curve or caustic surface formed by reflection. — *n* a catacaustic curve or surface. [Gr *kata* against, and **caustic**]

catachresis *kat-ə-krē'sis*, (*rhetoric*) *n* misapplication or incorrect usage of a word. — *adj* **catachrestic** (*-kres'tik*, or *-krēs'tik*) or **catachres'tical**. — *adv* **catachres'tically**. [Gr *katachrēsis* misuse, from *chrēsis* use]

cataclasm *kat'ə-klazm*, *n* a disruption, a breaking down. — *adj* **cataclas'mic** pertaining to or of the nature of a cataclasm. — *adj* **cataclas'tic** (*geol*) (of rocks) mylonitic, or granular as a result of crushing. [Gr *kataklasma*, from *kata* down, and *klaein* to break]

cataclysm *kat'ə-klizm*, *n* a great flood or other major disaster; a debacle; a great revolution or change, *esp* one that affects an entire political or social system. — *adj* **cataclys'mic**. — *adv* **cataclys'mically**. [Gr *kataklysmos*, from *kata* downward, and *klyzein* to wash]

catacomb *kat'ə-kōm*, or *-kōōm*, *n* a subterranean excavation used as a burial-place, *esp* near Rome, where many of the early Christian victims of persecution were buried; any place built with crypt-like recesses for storing books, wine, etc. — *adj* **catacumbal** (*-kum'bl*). [Ital *catacomba*, from LL *Catacumbas*, perh in some way from Gr *kata* down, and *kymbē* a cup]

catacoustics *kat-ə-kōōs'tiks* or (*esp* formerly) *-kows'tiks*, *n sing* the area of the science of acoustics that deals with echoes or reflected sounds. [Gr *kata* back, and **acoustics**]

catacumbal. See **catacomb**.

catadioptric *kat-ə-dī-op'trik* or **catadioptrical** *-kl*, *adj* pertaining to or employing both reflection and refraction, as in the construction of some long-focal-length photographic lenses. [See **catoptric** and **dioptric**]

catadromous *kət-ad'rəm-əs*, *adj* (of fishes) descending periodically for spawning to the lower parts of a river or to the sea (*opp* to *anadromous*). [Gr *kata* down, and *dromos* a run]

catafalque *kat'ə-falk*, *n* a temporary tomb-like structure used in funeral ceremonies and processions. — Also **catafal'co**: — *pl* **catafal'coes**. [Fr, from Ital *catafalco*]

Cataian or **Catayan** *kə-tā'ən*, (*Shakesp*) *n* a Cathayan or Chinese, used as a vague term of reproach. [*Cathay* poetical name for China]

Catalan *kat'ə-lan*, *adj* of or belonging to *Catalonia*; of or concerning Catalan. — *n* a person born or living in Catalonia; the Romance language spoken *esp* in Catalonia, Andorra and the Balearic Islands.

catalase. See **catalysis**.

catalectic *kat-ə-lek'tik*, *adj* incomplete; lacking one syllable in the last foot (*prosody*). — *n* **catalex'is**. [Gr *katalēktikos* incomplete, from *katalēgein* to stop]

catalepsy *kat'ə-lep-si*, *n* a state where one is more or less completely incapacitated, with bodily rigidity, as in hypnotic trances and sometimes in schizophrenia; cataplexy in animals. — *adj* and *n* **catalep'tic**. [Gr *katalēpsis* seizure, catalepsy, from *kata* down, and *lēpsis* taking, seizure]

catalexis. See **catalectic**.

catallactic *kat-ə-lak'tik*, *adj* pertaining to exchange. — *adv* **catallac'tically**. — *n sing* **catallac'tics** political economy. [Gr *katallaktēs* a money-changer]

catalo. Same as **cattalo**.

catalogue *kat'ə-log*, in NAm often **catalog**, *n* a systematic list of names, books, pictures, etc; a list of university courses and descriptions, *usu* including a calendar (*US*). — *vt* to put in a catalogue; to make a catalogue of. — *n* **cat'aloguer**, in NAm often **cat'aloger**. — *vt* **cat'aloguize** or **-ise**, in NAm often **cat'alogize**. [Gr *katalogos*, from *kata* in order, and *legein* to reckon]

catalogue raisonné *ka-ta-log re-zon-ā*, (*Fr*) *n* a classified descriptive catalogue.

catalpa *kət-al'pə*, *n* a low bignoniaceous tree of the American and Japanese genus *Catalpa* with profuse blossoms and long cigar-like pendent pods. [American Indian (Creek) *kutuhlpa*]

catalysis *kə-tal'i-sis*, *n* the chemical influence of a substance which is not itself permanently changed. — *n* **cat'alase** an enzyme that reduces hydrogen peroxide. — *n* **cat'alyst** a catalyzing agent; a catalytic converter; a person who causes or promotes change by their presence in a situation or their input into it (*fig*). — *adj* **catalytic** (*-lit'ik*) or **catalyt'ical**. — *adv* **catalyt'ically**. — *vt* **cat'alyze** or **-yse** (*-līz*) to subject to catalysis; to act as a catalyst for. — *n* **cat'alyzer** or **-yser** a catalyzing agent; a catalytic converter. — **catalytic converter** a device fitted to the exhaust of a motor vehicle which converts harmful impurities in the exhaust gases to carbon dioxide, nitrogen and water by oxidation. [Gr *katalysis*, from *kata* down, and *lyein* to loosen]

catamaran *katə-mə-ran'*, or *kat-am'ə-ran*, *n orig* a raft of logs lashed together; a boat, *esp* a sailing boat with two hulls; an old kind of fire-ship, long superseded; a bad-tempered woman (*rare*). [Tamil *kaṭṭu-maram* tied wood]

catamenia *kat-ə-mē'ni-ə*, (*physiol*) *n pl* the menstrual discharge or menses. — *adj* **catamē'nial**. [Neuter pl of Gr *katamēnios* monthly, from *kata* against, and *mēn* a month]

catamite *kat'ə-mīt*, *n* a boy kept for homosexual purposes. [L *catamītus*, from Gr *Ganymēdēs* Ganymede]

catamount, **catamountain**. See **cat**[1].

catapan *kat'ə-pan*, *n* the governor of Calabria and Apulia for the Byzantine emperor. [According to Littré, from Gr *katepanō tōn axiōmatōn* one placed over the dignities]

cataphonics *kat-ə-fon'iks*, *n sing* catacoustics. — *adj* **cataphon'ic**. [Gr *kata* back, and *phōnē* sound]

cataphoresis *kat-ə-fə-rē'sis*, *n* electrophoresis; the introduction into the body of medicinal substances by means of an electric current. [Gr *kata* down, and *phorēsis* a carrying]

cataphract *kat'ə-frakt*, *n* a suit of mail; a soldier in full armour (*old military*). — *adj* **cataphrac'tic**. [Gr *kataphraktēs* a coat-of-mail, from *kata* (intens), and *phrassein* to enclose, protect]

cataphyll *kat'ə-fil*, *n* a rudimentary or simplified leaf. — *adj* **cataphyll'ary**. [Gr *kata* down, and *phyllon* leaf]

cataphysical *kat-ə-fiz'i-kl*, (*rare*) *adj* unnatural. [Gr *kata* down, against, and *physis* nature]

cataplasm *kat'ə-plazm*, *n* a plaster or poultice. [Gr *kataplasma*]

cataplexy *kat'ə-plek-si*, *n* a condition of immobility induced by extreme emotion, eg shock (*med*); a physical state resembling death, adopted by some animals to discourage predators. — *adj* **cataplec'tic**. [Gr *kataplēxis* amazement, from *kata* down, and *plēssein* to strike]

catapult *kat'ə-pult*, *n* (in ancient history) a war machine for throwing boulders, etc; a small forked stick having an elastic string fixed to the two prongs, used for firing small stones; any similar device, eg for launching aeroplanes from an aircraft carrier. — *vt* and *vi* to shoot out from, or as if from, a catapult. — *adj* **catapul'tic**. — *n* **catapultier** (*-tēr'*). — **catapult fruit** a fruit that shoots out its seeds. [L *catapulta*, from Gr *katapeltēs*]

cataract *kat'ə-rakt*, *n* a waterfall; a water-spout, etc; an opaque condition of the lens of the eye, painless, unaccompanied by inflammation; the area rendered opaque, which is surgically removeable; a portcullis (*obs*); a floodgate (*Milton*). [L *cataracta*, from Gr *kataraktēs* portcullis, waterfall]

catarrh *kat-är'*, *n* a discharge of fluid resulting from the inflammation of a mucous membrane, *esp* of the nose; a cold in the head. — *adj* **catarrh'al** or **catarrh'ous**. [L *catarrhus*, from Gr *katarrhous*, from *kata* down, and *rheein* to flow]

catarrhine or **catarhine** *kat'ə-rīn*, *adj* of or pertaining to one of the two divisions of Primates, including all the Old World monkeys, having a narrow partition between the nostrils. [Gr *katarrīs* with hanging nose, from *kata* down, and *rhīs*, *rhīnos* nose]

catasta *kət-as'tə*, *n* a block on which slaves were exposed for sale; a stage, scaffold or place for torture. [L]

catastasis *kə-tas'tə-sis*, *n* the part of a drama in which the action has reached its height. [Gr *katastasis* settlement]

catastrophe *kət-as'trə-fi*, *n* a sudden disaster or misfortune; an unfortunate conclusion, outcome, etc; a final event; the climax of the action of the plot in a play or novel; a sudden and violent upheaval in some part of the surface of the earth (*geol*); in catastrophe theory (see below), a discontinuous change (*math*); rear (*Shakesp*). — *adj* **catastrophic** (*kat-ə-strof'ik*). — *adv* **catastroph'ically**. — *n* **catas'trophism** the old theory of geological change by vast, unconnected catastrophes and new creations (*opp* to *uniformitarianism*). — *n* **catas'trophist**. — **catastrophe theory** the branch of mathematics dealing with continuous changes in the input of a system which cause a discontinuous change (ie a catastrophe) in the output of the system. [Gr *kata* down, and *strophē* a turning]

catatonia *kat-ə-tō'ni-ə*, *n* a type of schizophrenia characterized by periodic states of rigidity or immobility. — *adj* and *n* **catatonic** (*-ton'*). [Gr *kata* down, and *tonos* stretching, straining, from *teinein* to stretch]

catawba *kə-tö'bə*, *n* an American variety of grape (*Vitis labrusca*); a red wine made from it. [*Catawba* River in Carolina]

catbird, **catcall**, **etc**. See **cat**[1].

catch *kach*, *vt* to take hold of, *esp* of a thing in motion; to take hold of (the ball) after the batsman has hit it and before it touches the ground (*cricket*); to dismiss (a batsman) thus; to hear (*colloq*); to understand or comprehend; to seize (a person, etc) after pursuit; to trap or ensnare when hunting, fishing, etc; to entangle or fasten on (to); to come upon, to happen to see; to meet or contact (a person) (*colloq*); to be in time for; to take (a train, bus, etc) as a means of transport; to strike, hit; to get (a disease) by infection or contagion; to attract (a person's attention, notice, etc); to succeed in reproducing (someone's qualities or likeness, etc) by painting, photography or imitation; to take (fire). — *vi* to be contagious; to be entangled or fastened; (of a fire, or of anything to be burned) to catch light: — *infinitive* in *Spenser* sometimes **catch'en** or **ketch**; *pa t* and *pa p* **caught** (*köt*), also *obs* and *dialect* **catched** or **catcht**; *pa t* in *Spenser* also **keight** *kīt*). — *n* seizure; an act of catching, *esp* the ball at cricket, etc; a clasp, or anything that fastens or holds; that which is caught; a person who is considered worth catching as a marriage partner; a sudden advantage taken; a concealed difficulty or disadvantage; in someone's voice, an indistinctness caused by strong emotion; a children's game in which a ball, etc is thrown and caught in turn; a round for three or more voices, often deriving comic effect from the interweaving of the words (*music*). — *adj* **catch'able** capable of being caught. — *n* **catch'er**. — *n* **catch'ing** the action of the verb; a nervous or spasmodic twitching. — *adj* infectious (*med* or *fig*); captivating, attractive. — *n* **catch'ment** the act of collecting water; the water collected from a river, etc; a catchment area; the pupils collected from a school catchment area. — *adj* **catch'y** attractive; deceptive; (of a tune, etc) readily taking hold in the mind, memorable; fitful. — *adj* **catch'-all** covering or dealing with a number of instances, eventualities or problems, *esp* ones not covered or dealt with by other provisions. — **catch-as-catch-can'** a style of wrestling in which any hold is allowed. — Also (*esp NAm*) *adj* and *adv* using any method that is available. — **catch'-basin** or **catch'-pit** a trap for dirt in a drain; **catch'-crop** a secondary crop grown before, after, or at the same time as, and on the same piece of ground as, a main crop; **catch'-drain** a drain on a hillside to catch the surface-water; **catch'fly** a name for a species of campion (*Lychnis viscaria*) and several bladder-campion (*Silene*) with sticky stems; **catching pen** (*Austr* and *NZ*) a pen for holding sheep awaiting shearing; **catchment area** the area from which a river or reservoir is fed (also **catchment basin**); the area from which the pupils for a school are drawn, or the locality served by some other public facility such as a library or a hospital; **Catchment board** (*NZ*) a public body responsible for water supply from a catchment area; **catch'penny** a worthless thing made only for profit. — Also *adj*. — **catch'-phrase** a phrase that becomes popular and is much repeated; a slogan; **catch-pit** see **catch-basin**; **catch points** railway points which can derail a train to prevent it accidentally running on to a main line; **catch-the-ten'** a card game in which the aim is to capture the ten of trumps. — *adj* **Catch 22** (title of novel by J Heller, 1961) denoting an absurd situation in which one can never win, being constantly balked by a clause, rule, etc which itself can alter to block any change in one's course of action, or being faced with a choice of courses of action, both or all of which would have undesirable consequences. — *n* such a situation. — **catch'weed** goosegrass or cleavers; **catch'word** the word at the head of the page in a dictionary or encyclopaedia; (in typed correspondence) the first word of a page given at the bottom of the preceding page; any word or phrase taken up and repeated, *esp* as the watchword or slogan of a political party; an actor's cue. — **catch at** to make a hasty attempt to catch; **catch cold (at)** to suffer a financial or other misfortune (as a result of making an unwise investment, etc); **catch fire** or **light** to become ignited; to become inspired by passion or enthusiasm; **catch hold of** to seize; **catch it** (*colloq*) to get a scolding or reprimand; **catch me** or **him**, etc, an emphatic colloquial phrase implying that there is not the remotest possibility of my or his, etc doing the thing mentioned; **catch on** to comprehend; to become fashionable, to catch the popular imagination; **catch one's breath** see under **breath**; **catch one's death** see under **death**; **catch out** to detect in error or deceit; to put (a batsman) out by catching the ball after it has been hit and before it touches the ground (*cricket*); **catch sight of** to get a glimpse of; **catch someone's drift** to follow and understand what someone is talking about; **catch up** to draw level (with) and sometimes overtake; **catch up** or **away** to snatch or seize hastily. [From OFr *cachier*, from LL *captiāre* from *captāre*, intens of *capere* to take; see **chase**]

catchpole or **catchpoll** *kach'pōl*, (*hist*) *n* a constable, a sheriff's officer. [Through OFr from LL *cachepolus*, *chassipullus* someone who chases fowls; see **chase** and **pullet**]

catchup or **catsup**. See **ketchup**.

cat-cracker *kat'-krak-ər*, *n* (in full, **catalytic cracker**) an industrial plant in which the chemical cracking of crude petroleum is speeded up by the use of a catalyst. — *n* **cat'-cracking** (in full, **catalytic cracking**).

cate *kāt*, (*archaic*) *n* (nearly always in *pl*) a viand; a dainty, a delicacy. [Aphetic; see **acates**; cf **cater**[1]]

catechize or **-ise** *kat'i-kīz*, *vt* to instruct, *esp* in the Christian faith, by question and answer; to question as to belief; to examine systematically by questioning. — *adj* **catechetic** (*-ket'ik*) or **catechet'ical** relating to catechism or oral instruction in the first principles, *esp* of Christianity. — *adv* **catechet'ically**. — *n sing* **catechet'ics** the art or practice of teaching by question and answer; that part of theology which deals with **catechesis** (*-kē'sis*), or primary oral instruction, as that given to catechumens. — *n* **cat'echism** any comprehensive system of teaching drawn up in form of question and answer; a set of questions; a thorough examination by questions. — **cat'echist** a person who catechizes; a teacher of catechumens; an indigenous teacher in a mission church. — *adj* **catechis'tic**, **catechis'tical** or **catechis'mal** pertaining to a catechist or catechism. — *n* **cat'echizer** or **-s-**. — *n* **cat'echīzing** or **-s-**. [L *catēchismus*, formed from Gr *katēchizein*, *katēcheein* to din into the ears, from *kata* back, and *ēchē* a sound]

catechu *kat'i-choo* or *-shoo*, *n* a dark extract of Indian plants (acacia, betel-nut, etc) which are rich in tannin. — *n* **cat'echol** (*-kōl* or *-chōl*) a white crystalline phenol-alcohol derived from catechu. — *n* **catechō'lamine** (*-kō'lə-mēn* or *-chō'*) any of several compounds (eg adrenaline and noradrenaline) that are derivatives of catechol. [Cf Malay *cachu*]

catechumen *kat-i-kū'mən*, *n* a person who is being taught the rudiments of Christianity; in the early Christian Church, a converted Jew or heathen undergoing instruction preparatory to baptism. — *n* **catechū'menate**. — *adj* **catechūmen'ical**. — *adv* **catechūmen'ically**. — *n* **catechū'menism** or **catechū'menship**. [Gr *katēchoumenos* being taught, pr p passive of *katēcheein* to teach; cf **catechize**]

category *kat'i-gər-i*, *n* what may be affirmed of a class; a class or order of things, people, etc possessing similar characteristics; (in *pl*) the highest classes under which objects of philosophy can be systematically arranged, understood as an attempt at a comprehensive classification of all that exists (*philos*); (in *pl*) in Kant's system, the root-notions of the understanding, the specific forms of the *a priori* or formal element in rational cognition (*quantity*, *quality*, *relation*, *modality*, etc) (*philos*). — *adj* **categorematic** (*-gor-i-mat'ik*) capable of being used by itself as a term. — *adj* **categorial** (*ka-tə-gör'i-əl* or *-gör'*) of or pertaining to a category. — *adv* **categor'ially**. — *adj* **categorical** or **categoric** (*-gor'*) positive; absolute; unconditional; without exception. — *adv* **categor'ically** absolutely; without qualification, unconditionally; expressly. — *n* **categor'icalness** the quality of being absolute and unqualified. — *n* **cat'egorist** a person who categorizes. — *n* **categoriza'tion** or **-s-**. — *vt* **cat'egorize** or **-ise** to place in a category or list; to class. — **categorical imperative** in the ethics of Kant, the absolute unconditional command of the moral law, irrespective of every ulterior end or aim, obliging people to act responsibly (*philos*). [Gr *katēgoriā* assertion, predication, accusation, from *katēgoros* an accuser, *kata* down, against, and *agorā* assembly]

catelog. An obsolete spelling of **catalogue**.

catena *kə-tē'nə*, *n* a chain or connected series, as in **catena patrum**, a chronological series of extracts from the Fathers on any doctrine of theology: — *pl* **cate'nae** (*-nē*) or **cate'nas**. — *n* **cat'enane** (*chem*) a compound having molecules linked like a chain. — *adj* **catenarian** (*kat-i-nā'ri-ən*) of, or of the nature of, a chain or a catenary. — *n* **catē'nary** (or *US kat'*) the curve formed by a flexible cord, hanging freely between two points of support, and acted on by no other force than gravity; the arrangement of pylons and cables through which electricity is supplied on some electrified railway lines. — *adj* relating to, or like, a chain. — *vt* **catenate** (*kat'i-nāt*) to connect as in or by a chain. — *adj* linked as in a chain. — *n* **catenā'tion**. [L *catēna* chain]

cater[1] *kā'tər*, *vi* to provide food, entertainment, etc (for); to provide the requirements of (a person, occasion, etc; with *to* or *for*). — *vt* (*NAm*) to provide food, entertainments, etc for (an occasion). — *n* (*obs*) an acater; a person who supplies provisions (sometimes *fig*). — *n* **cā'terer**. — *n* **cā'teress**. — *n* **cā'tering**. [Ult from L *captāre* to seize]

cater[2] *kā'tər*, *n* (*obs*) the four in dice. — *vt* and *vi* (*dialect*) to move diagonally. — Also *adj* and *adv*. — *adj* **catercor'ner** or **catercor'nered** diagonal. — Also *adv*. [MFr *quatre* four, from L *quattuor*]

cateran *kat'ər-ən*, (*esp lit*) *n* a Highland reiver or free-booter; a robber or brigand generally. [Old Gaelic *ceatharn*, *ceithern* a band of soldiers (Irish *ceithern* foot-soldiers; see **kern(e)**)]

cater-cousin *kā'tər-kuz'n*, (*Shakesp*) *n* a person allied by familiarity, affection or sympathy, rather than kindred; an intimate friend. [More prob connected with **cater** to provide food, than *quatre* or *quarter*]

caterpillar *kat'ər-pil-ər*, *n* a butterfly or moth grub; extended to other insect larvae; an unproductive consumer (*archaic*); **Caterpillar®** a tractor or other (*esp* earth-moving) vehicle running on endless articulated tracks made up of a series of flat metal plates. [Prob OFr *chatepelose* hairy cat; see also **cat**[1] and **pile**[1]]

caterwaul *kat'ər-wöl*, *n* the shriek or cry emitted by a domestic cat, *esp* when in heat. — *vi* to make such a noise; to make any discordant sound similar to this, *esp* loud and tuneless singing; to behave lasciviously (*archaic*); to quarrel like cats. — *n* **cat'erwauling**. [**cat**[1]; the second part prob imitative]

cates. See **cate**.

catfish and **catgut**. See **cat**[1].

Cath. *abbrev*: Catholic.

cath. *abbrev*: cathedral; cathode.

Cathaian. See **Cathayan**.

Cathar *kath'ər*, *n* a member of a medieval Manichaean sect, chiefly in S France and N Italy, the Albigensians: — *pl* **Cath'arī** or **Cath'ars**. — *n* **Cath'arism**. — *n* **Cath'arist**. [Gr *katharos* pure]

cathartic *kath-ärt'ik* or **cathartical** *-kl*, *adj* cleansing, purifying; having the power or effect of cleansing the bowels (*med*); purgative; causing emotional or psychological catharsis. — *n* **cathart'ic** a purgative medicine. — *vt* **cath'arize** or **-ise** to render absolutely clean; to purge. — *n* **cathar'sis** purification; evacuation of the bowels; purification of the emotions, achieved, according to Aristotle, through the witnessing of theatrical tragedy; the purging of the effects of a pent-up emotion and repressed thoughts, by bringing them to the surface of consciousness (*psychol*): — *pl* **cathar'ses** (*-sēz*). [Gr *kathartikos* fit for cleansing, from *katharos* clean]

Cathayan or **Cathaian** *ka-thā'ən*, *n* and *adj* Chinese. [See **Cataian**]

cathead. See **cat**[1].

cathectic. See **cathexis**.

cathedral *kə-thē'drəl*, *n* the principal church of a diocese, containing the bishop's throne. — *adj* belonging to a seat of authority or a cathedral; having a cathedral. — *n* **cathedra** (*-thē'drə* or *-thed'rə*) a bishop's throne; the episcopal dignity; see also **ex cathedra**. — *adj* **cathedrat'ic** promulgated *ex cathedra*, authoritative. [L *cathēdra*, *cathedra*, from Gr *kathedrā* a seat]

Catherine pear *kath'(ə)rin pār*, *n* a small and early variety of pear.

Catherine-wheel *kath'(ə-)rin-(h)wēl*, *n* a rotating firework; a rose-window (*archit*); a wheel set round with teeth (*heraldry*); a sidewise somersault. [From St *Catherine* of Alexandria (4th century), who miraculously escaped torture on a wheel]

catheter *kath'i-tər*, *n* a tube for admitting or removing gases or liquids through channels of the body, *esp* for removing urine from the bladder. — *n* **cath'eterism** the use of the catheter. — *n* **catheterizā'tion** or **-s-** insertion of a catheter. — *n* **cath'etus** a straight line perpendicular to another straight line or surface. [Gr *kathetos* perpendicular, *kathetēr* a catheter, from *kathienai* to send down, from *kata* down, and *hienai* to send]

cathetometer *kath-i-tom'ə-tər*, *n* an instrument for measuring vertical distances not exceeding a few decimetres. — Also called **reading telescope** or **reading microscope**. [Gr *kathetos*, perpendicular, and **-meter**]

cathexis *kə-thek'sis*, (*psychol*) *n* a charge of mental energy attached to any particular idea or object: — *pl* **cathex'es** (*-sēz*). — *adj* **cathec'tic**. [Gr *kathexis* holding]

cathisma *kə-thiz'mə*, *n* in Greek use, a section of the psalter; a troparion or short hymn used as a response. [Gr, from *kathizein* to sit down]

cathode *kath'ōd*, *n* the electrode of an electrolytic cell at which positively charged ions are discharged into the exterior electric circuit; the positive terminal or electrode of a dry battery; in valves and tubes, the source of electrons. See **anode**. — *adj* **cath'odal**. — *adj* **cathod'ic**. — *n* **cathod'ograph** a photograph by X-rays. — *n* **cathodog'rapher**. — *n* **cathodog'raphy**. — **cathode-ray oscillograph** the complete equipment for registering transient wave-forms on a photographic plate within the vacuum of a cathode-ray tube; **cathode-ray oscilloscope** see **oscilloscope**; **cathode rays** streams of negatively charged particles (electrons) proceeding from the cathode of a vacuum tube; **cathode-ray tube** a device in which a narrow beam of electrons, which can be deflected by magnetic and/or electrostatic fields, acts on a fluorescent screen or photographic surface, used in television sets, etc; **cathodic protection** protection of a metal structure underground or under water against electrolytic corrosion by making it the cathode in an electrolytic cell. [Gr *kathodos* a going down, from *kata* down, and *hodos* a way]

catholic *kath'ə-lik*, *adj* (with *cap*) belonging to the Christian Church before the great schism between East and West, or to any church claiming to be historically related to it, *esp* after the schism the Western church, and after the Reformation the Church of Rome (Roman Catholic), but applied also eg to Anglicans; (with *cap*) relating to the Roman Catholics; liberal (*opp* of *exclusive*); universal; general, embracing the whole body of Christians; orthodox, as opposed to *heterodox* and *sectarian*. — *n* (with *cap*) an adherent of the RC Church. — *n* **Cathol'icism** the tenets of the RC Church; (without *cap*) catholicity (*rare*). — *n* **catholicity** (*-is'i-ti*) universality; liberality or breadth of view; Catholicism (*rare*). — *n* **catholiciza'tion** or **-s-** (also with *cap*). — *vt* and *vi* **cathol'icize** or **-ise** (also with *cap*) to make or become Catholic. — *n* **cathol'icon** (*-kon*) a universal remedy, a panacea; (sometimes with *cap*) a comprehensive work, eg an encyclopaedic dictionary. — *n* **Cathol'icos** the Patriarch of Armenia. — **Catholic (and) Apostolic Church** a body formed in England about 1835, having an elaborate, symbolic ritual and a complex ecclesiastical hierarchy, and emphasizing the existence in the present day of miracles and prophecy, and the imminent second coming of Christ; **catholic creditor** (*Scots law*) a creditor whose debt is secured over two or more subjects belonging to the debtor, eg over two or more heritable estates; **Catholic emancipation** the relief of the Roman Catholics from certain vexatious penal regulations and restrictions, granted in 1829; **catholic** or **general epistles** certain epistles in the canon addressed to the Church universal or to a large and indefinite circle of readers; **Catholic King** (*hist*) a title given to the king of Spain; **German Catholics** a body that broke away from the Roman Catholic Church in Germany in 1844 on the occasion of the exhibition of the Holy Coat at Trier; **Old Catholics** a body that broke away from the Roman Catholic church in Germany in opposition to the dogma of papal infallibility proclaimed by the Vatican Council in 1870. [Gr *katholikos* universal, from *kata* throughout, and *holos* the whole]

Catiline *kat'i-līn*, *n* a daring and reckless conspirator (L Sergius *Catilina*, whose plot to destroy the senate in Rome was foiled by Cicero, 63 BC). — *adj* **catilinarian** (*-li-nā'ri-ən*).

cation or **kation** *kat'ī-ən*, *n* an ion that travels towards the cathode; a positively-charged ion. [Gr *kata* down, and *ion*, neuter, from pr p of *ienai* to go]

catkin, **catling**, **catmint**, **catnep** and **catnip**, etc. See **cat**[1].

Catonian *kə-tō'ni-ən*, *adj* resembling or relating to *Cato*, the Roman censor (234–149 BC), or *Cato* Uticensis (95–46 BC), both noted for gravity of manners; hence grave, severe, unbending.

catoptric *kat-op'trik*, *adj* relating to reflection. — *n sing* **catop'trics** the branch of optics which is concerned with reflected light. [Gr *katoptron* a mirror, from *kata* back, and the root of *opsomai* I shall see]

CAT scanner *kat skan'ər*, or **CT scanner** (*sē-tē'*), short for **computer-assisted** or **computed axial tomography scanner**, an X-ray machine that produces three-dimensional images built up from a sequential series of X-ray sections of (a part of) the body (qqv under **compute**).

catsup. See **ketchup**.

cattabu *kat'ə-bū*, *n* a cross between domestic cattle and zebu. [From *catt*le and ze*bu*]

cattalo or **catalo** *kat'ə-lō*, *n* a cross between the bison ('buffalo') and the domestic cow: — *pl* **catt'alo(e)s**. [From *catt*le and buff*alo*]

cattle *kat'l*, *n pl* bovine mammals of the genus *Bos*, *esp* oxen, bulls and cows; domesticated mammals including oxen, etc and also horses, sheep, etc (*archaic*). — **cattle cake** a concentrated, processed food for cattle, in the form of blocks or cakes; **cattle grid** or (*NAm*) **cattle guard**, (*NZ*) **cattle stop**, a frame of spaced bars covering a trench or depression in a road where it passes through a fence, crossable by motor vehicles or pedestrians but not by hoofed animals; **catt'le-lifter** a stealer of cattle; **catt'le-lifting**; **catt'leman** a person who tends cattle, or who rears them on a ranch; **catt'le-plague** a term applied to certain disease of domestic cattle, *esp* rinderpest or steppe murrain; **cattle prod** a rod or goad, often capable of delivering low-voltage electric shocks, for driving cattle, etc; **cattle show** an exhibition of cattle or other domestic animals in competition for prizes. [OFr *catel*, *chatel*, from LL *captāle*, L *capitāle*, from *caput* the head]

cattleya *kat-lē'ə*, *n* any American orchid of the genus *Cattleya*, grown for their large pink or white flowers. [New L, from William *Cattley*, English botanist]

catty *kat'i*, *n* a unit of measurement used in SE Asia and China, equal to about 1·3 lb avoirdupois in SE Asia and Hong Kong, and about 1·1 lb avoirdupois (500 grammes) in China. — Also **kat'i** or **katt'i**. [Malay *kati*]

Caucasian *kö-kā'z(h)i-ən*, *n* a person belonging to that one of the main ethnological divisions of mankind which is native to Europe, North Africa and western and central Asia; a member of the white race; a white person; a native of the *Caucasus* or the country around it. — *adj* of or pertaining to a Caucasian or Caucasians in any of the above senses; pertaining to the Caucasus or the country around it; of or pertaining to the languages spoken in the Caucasus which do not belong to the Indo-European, Semitic or Ural-Altaic groups (*linguistics*).

Caucasoid *kö'kə-zoid*, *adj* of or pertaining to the ethnic group of light-complexioned people indigenous to Europe, northern Africa, SW Asia and the Indian subcontinent; Caucasian. — *n* a member of this group.

cauchemar *kōsh-mär*, (*Fr*) *n* a nightmare.

caucus *kö'kəs*, *n* a meeting or group of members of a political party formed to nominate candidates or delegates or to decide how to vote on any question in a legislative assembly, its decision binding on those who attend (*esp NAm*); the members of such a group; any small group which acts as a (semi-)autonomous body within a larger group or organization, *esp* (*derog*) one which is excessively influential. — *vi* to hold a caucus; to control by means of a caucus. [Ety doubtful; perh John Smith's Algonkian word *Caw-cawaassough*, an adviser; perh a corruption of '*caulkers*' meetings']

caudal *kö'dl*, *adj* pertaining to the tail. — *adj* **cau'dad** (*esp zool* and *anatom*) towards the tail. — *adj* **cau'dāte** or **cau'dated** having a tail or tail-like appendage. — **caudal anaesthesia** a form of epidural anaesthesia. [L *cauda* tail]

caudex *kö'deks*, (*bot*) *n* the stem of a tree, *esp* of a palm or tree-fern: — *pl* **caud'icēs** (*-i-sēz*) or **caud'exes**. — *n* **caud'icle** the stalk of the pollen-masses of certain orchids. [L]

caudillo *kow-dēl'yō*, *n* in Spanish-speaking countries, a military or political leader; the head of the state: — *pl* **caudil'los**. [Sp]

caudle *kö'dl*, *n* a warm drink, sweetened and spiced, formerly given to the sick. — *vt* to give a caudle to; to mix. — **caudle cup** a two-handled cup, *usu* of silver, with a bulbous or cylindrical body and *usu* a lid. — **hempen caudle** (*Shakesp*) the hangman's noose. [ONFr *caudel*, from L *calidus* hot]

caudron *kö'drən*. A Spenserian form of **cauldron**.

cauf. See **corf**.

caught *köt*, *pa t* and *pa p* of **catch**.

cauk or **cawk** *kök*, *n* chalk (*dialect*); barytes in platy crystals. [A form of **chalk**]

cauker. See **caulk**.

caul *köl*, *n* a net or covering for the head (*hist*); the membrane covering the head of some infants at birth, being part of the inner membrane of the foetal sac; *the great omentum*. [OFr *cale* a little cap, prob Celtic; cf Irish *calla* a veil, hood]

cauld[1] *köld*, (*Scot*) *n* a dam in a stream, a weir. [Origin obscure]

cauld[2] *köld*, (*Scot*) *adj* and *n* cold. — *adj* **cauldrife** (*köld'rif*) apt to feel chilly; chilling, lifeless, without vigour.

cauldron or **caldron** *köl'drən*, *n* a large kettle for boiling or heating liquids. — **cauldron subsidence** (*geol*) the subsidence of a cylindrical mass of the Earth's crust, bounded by a circular fault up which the lava has *usu* risen to fill the cauldron. [OFr *caudron*, from L *caldārium*, from *calidus* hot, from *calēre* to be hot]

cauliflower *ko'* or *kö'li-flowr*, *n* a variety of cabbage (*Brassica oleracea botrytis*) with a white, closely-packed, flower-head, eaten as a vegetable. — **cauliflower cheese** boiled or steamed cauliflower with a cheese sauce; **cauliflower ear** an ear permanently swollen and misshapen by injury, *esp* from boxing.

[Earlier *cole-florye*, *colie-florie*, from LL *cauliflōra*, from L *caulis* cabbage; see **cole** and **flower**]

caulis *kö'lis* (*L kow'lis*), *n* the stem of a plant; one of the main stems at the angles of the Corinthian capital (*archit*): — *pl* **cau'les** (*-lēz* or *-lās*). — *adj* **caulesc'ent** (of plants) having a stem rising above the ground. — *n* **cau'licle** (*bot*) a rudimentary stem. — *adj* **caulic'olous** growing on a stem (*bot*). — *adj* **caulic'ūlāte**. — *n* **caulic'ūlus** one of the slender stems springing from the *caules* or main stalks supporting the volutes in the Corinthian capital (*archit*). — *n* **cauliflo'ry** (*bot*) production of flowers on old stems from dormant buds. — *adj* **caul'iform** having the form of a stem. — *adj* **caulig'enous** borne on the stem. — *adj* **caul'inary** or **cau'line** belonging to or growing from a stem. — *n* **cau'lōme** a plant's stem structure as a whole. [L *caulis* a stalk]

caulk or **calk** *kök*, *vt* to render (planks, etc of a boat) watertight by pressing oakum or another suitable material into the seams. — *vi* (*sailors' slang*) to snooze. — *n* **caulk'er** a person who caulks; a dram; a big lie (also **cauk'er**). — *n* **caulk'ing**. — **caulk'ing-iron** an instrument like a chisel used for pressing oakum (tarred rope) into the seams of ships. [OFr *cauquer* to press, from L *calcāre* to tread, from *calx* heel]

caulker. See under **caulk** and **calk**[2].

caum or **caumstane**. See **cam**[3].

caup. See **cap**[2].

causa *kow'zə*, (*L*) *n* cause. — **causa causans** (*kow'zanz*; *legal*) *n* the immediate cause; the cause in action. — **causa sine qua non** (*sī'nē kwā non* or *si'ne kwä nōn*; *legal*) an indispensable cause or condition allowing something, eg the causa causans, to be operative, but not itself a causa causans.

cause *köz*, *n* that which produces an effect; that by or through which anything happens; a motive; an inducement; a legal action between contending parties; sake, advantage; an ideal, principle or belief in the name of which people band together to do something; an accusation (*Shakesp*); a matter, affair in general (*Shakesp*). — *vt* to produce; to bring about the existence of; to bring about the occurrence of; to give excuses for (*Spenser*; *infinitive* **caus'en**). — *conj* (*dialect* or *colloq*) because (*usu* **'cause**). — *adj* **caus'al** being the cause, that causes; relating to a cause or causes. — *n* **causal'ity** the relationship between cause and effect; the mechanics of the cause of something. — *adv* **caus'ally**. — *n* **causā'tion** the act of causing; the bringing about of an effect; causality. — *n* **causā'tionism** the principle of universal causation. — *n* **causā'tionist**. — *adj* **caus'ative** causal; of the nature of, or expressing, causation. — *n* (*gram*) a form or class of verb expressing causation. — *adv* **caus'atively**. — *adj* **cause'less** without cause; without just cause. — *adv* **cause'lessly**. — *n* **cause'lessness**. — *n* **caus'er**. — **cause list** (*legal*) a list of cases awaiting trial. — **efficient cause** the means by which a thing took its present form; **final cause** see under **final**; **first cause** the original cause or creator of all, God; **formal cause** the essence or idea of a thing; **have** or **show cause** to have to give reasons for a certain line of action; **hour of cause** (*Scots law*) hour or time of trial; **make common cause** (often with *with*) to unite for a common object; **material cause** that out of which a thing is framed; **natural causes** causes (of death) such as old age or disease, as opposed to violence or accident; **occasional causes** see under **occasion**; **secondary causes** causes derived from a primary or first cause; **show cause** (*Eng law*) to argue against the confirmation of a provisional order or judgment. [Fr, from L *causa*]

cause célèbre *kōz sā-lebr'*, (*Fr*) *n* a very notable or famous trial; a notorious controversy or highly controversial person: — *pl* **causes célèbres** (*kōz*).

causerie *kōz'ər-ē*, *n* a chat or gossip; a conversational paragraph about literature or art; a short and informal essay on any subject in a newspaper or magazine. [Fr]

causeway *köz'wā*, *n* a raised road or path through a marsh or across water; a pathway raised and paved with stone; a paved or cobblestoned road. — *adj* **cause'-wayed**. [ME *causee*, from OFr *caucie*, from LL (*via*) *calciāta* a trodden way, from L *calx* heel]

causey *köz'i*, *n* a causeway (*dialect*); a paved road or street, formerly of cobblestones (*Scot*).

caustic *kös'tik*, *adj* burning; corroding; pertaining to, or of the shape of, a caustic (*math* and *phys*); (of remarks, etc) bitter, severe, cutting (*fig*). — *n* a chemical substance that has a corroding or burning action; an envelope of light rays proceeding from a fixed point and reflected (*catacaustic*) or refracted (*diacaustic*) by a curve (*math*); a caustic curve or caustic surface (*phys*). — *adv* **caus'tically**. — *n* **causticity** (*-tis'i-ti*) quality of being caustic. — *n* **caus'ticness**. — **caustic ammonia** ammonia as a gas, or in solution; **caustic curve** a curve in the shape of a caustic, the form of a plane section through a caustic surface (*phys*); **caustic lime** quicklime; **caustic potash** potassium hydroxide; **caustic soda** sodium hydroxide, used in making soap; **caustic surface** a caustic-shaped surface, the envelope of rays of light reflected or refracted by a curved surface (*phys*). — **common caustic** potash; also silver nitrate; **lunar caustic** silver nitrate in sticks for surgical use. [L *causticus*, from Gr *kaustikos*, from *kaiein* future and *kausein* to burn]

cautel *kö'tl*, *n* cunning, craft (*Shakesp*); insidious purpose (*Shakesp*); caution (*obs*); wariness (*obs*); a traditionary caution or written direction about the proper manner of administering the sacraments (*obs*). — *adj* **cau'telous** cautious (*obs*); insidious (*Shakesp*); artful (*Shakesp*). [Fr *cautèle*, from L *cautēla*, from *cavēre*, *cautum* to guard against]

cauterize or **-ise** *kö'tər-īz*, *vt* to burn or destroy with a caustic substance, a hot metal implement, etc, *esp* to destroy infected tissue in a wound; to sear (*fig*). — *n* **cau'ter** or **cau'tery** burning or destroying with caustics, a hot metal implement, etc; a burning, caustic substance, etc for burning or destroying tissue. — *n* **cau'terant** a cauterizing substance. — *n* **cau'terism**. — *n* **cauterīzā'tion** or **-s-**. — *adj* **cauterīzing** or **-s-**. [Fr *cautériser*, from LL *cautērizāre*, from Gr *kautēr* a hot iron, from *kaiein* to burn]

caution *kö'shən*, *n* heedfulness, carefulness; a warning; a warning that what a person says may be used as evidence (*law*); an alarming, amusing or astonishing person or thing (*colloq*); (also *kā'*) security, surety, bail (*Scots law*). — *vt* to warn to take care; to give (someone) a caution (*law*). — *adj* **cau'tionary** containing caution or cautions; given as a pledge. — *n* **cau'tioner** a person who cautions or advises; (also *kā'*) a surety (*Scots law*). — *n* **cautionry** (*kā'*) the act of giving security for another (*Scots law*). — *adj* **cautious** (*kö'shəs*) possessing or using caution; watchful, heedful; prudent. — *adv* **cau'tiously**. — *n* **cau'tiousness**. — **caution money** money paid in advance as security for good conduct. [Fr, from L *cautiō*, *-ōnis*, from *cavēre* to beware]

cavalcade *kav-əl-kād'*, or *kav'*, *n* a procession of people on horseback or in vehicles; a parade. — *vi* to proceed in a cavalcade. [Fr, through Ital and LL, from L *caballus* a horse]

cavalier *kav-əl-ēr'*, *n* a knight; (with *cap*) a Royalist in the English Civil War; a swaggering fellow; a gallant or gentleman in attendance upon a lady, as her escort or partner in a dance or the like; (in military fortification) a raised work so situated as to command the neighbouring country. — *adj* like a cavalier; war-like; haughty, supercilious, devil-may-care, incautious. — *vi* to act as cavalier to a lady. — *adj* **cavalier'ish** like, or characteristic of, a cavalier. — *n* **cavalier'ism**. — *adv* **cavalier'ly** off-hand; haughty, with supercilious disregard or curtness. — *adj* cavalierish. — **Cavalier King Charles spaniel** see **spaniel**. [Fr, from Ital *cavallo*; see **cavalcade**]

cavaliere servente *kä-vä-lē-er'e ser-ven'te*, (*Ital*) *n* a gallant or lover of a married woman; a lady's man.

cavalla *kə-val'ə* or **cavally** *kə-val'i*, *n* an American fish of the scad family, or any of several related carangoid fish. [Sp *caballa* and Port *cavalla* mackerel]

cavalry *kav'əl-ri*, *n* the part of an army made up of soldiers on horseback; (a troop of) mounted soldiers. — *n* **cav'alryman**. — **cavalry twill** see **twill**[1]. [Fr *cavallerie*, from Ital *cavalleria*, from L *caballārius* horseman, from *caballus* horse]

cavass. See **kavass**.

cavatina *kav-ät-ē'nə*, (*music*) *n* a melody with no second part or da capo; loosely, a short operatic air, of a smooth and melodious character, often part of a grand scena. [Ital]

cave[1] *kāv*, *n* a hollow in a rock, a cliff or underground; a small faction of seceders from a political party (from the Cave of Adullam, *Bible*: 1 *Samuel* 22. 1–2); the ash-pit under the furnace in glassworks. — *vt* to hollow out. — *vi* to inhabit a cave. — *n* **ca'ver** a person who explores caves. — *n* **ca'ving** the sport or pastime of cave-exploration. — **cave'-bear** (*Ursus spelaeus*) a bear of the Pleistocene period of which fossil remains have been found in caves; **cave'-dweller** a person who lives in a cave, *esp* one of the Stone Age people of prehistoric times; **cave'-earth** a fine deposit on cave floors; **cave-in** see **cave in** below; **cave'man** a cave-dweller; a modern male of primitive and chauvinistic attitudes and ways (*colloq*). — **cave in** to slip, to subside, to collapse inwards (*n* **cave'-in**); to yield to outside pressure, to give way, to collapse (*fig*). [Fr *cave*, from L *cavus* hollow]

cave[2] *kav'i* or *kāv'i*, *interj* (*schoolboy slang*) beware. — **cave canem** (*kā'vi*, *ka'vā*, *-wā*, *kā'nəm*, *ka'nem*) (*L*) beware of the dog, a frequent inscription on Roman thresholds; **keep cave** to keep watch. [L *cavē*, imperative sing of *cavēre* to take care]

caveat *kā'vi-at*, *n* a notice or warning; a formal warning, entered in the books of a court or public office, that no step be taken in a particular matter without notice to the person lodging the caveat. — **caveat actor** (*kā'vi-at*, *ka've-at*, *-we-*, *ak'tör*) let the doer beware; **caveat emptor** (*emp'tör*) it is the buyer's responsibility. [L, 3rd person sing subjunctive of *cavēre* to take care]

cavel *kāv'l*, (*Scot*) *n* a piece of wood, etc used in casting lots; a lot cast; fate, chance (*fig*). [Du *kavel*]

cavendish *kav'ən-dish*, *n* tobacco moistened and pressed into rectangular cakes. [Poss from the name of the orig manufacturer]

cavendo tutus *kā-*, *ka-ven'dō*, *-wen' tū'təs*, *tōō'tōōs*, (*L*) safe by taking heed.

cavern *kav'ərn*, *n* a large cave or a large underground chamber. — *vt* to put in a cavern; to hollow out. — *adj* **cav'erned** made up of or full of caverns; inhabiting a cavern. — *adj* **cav'ernous** like a cavern in size, huge and dark; containing or full of caverns. — *adv* **cav'ernously**. — *adj* **caver'nūlous** full of little cavities, porous. [Fr *caverne*, from L *caverna*, from *cavus* hollow]

cavesson *kav'əs-ən*, *n* a noseband for a horse. [Fr *caveçon*, from Ital *cavezzone*, from L *capitia*, *capitium* a head-covering]

cavetto *ka-vet'ō*, (*archit*) *n* a hollowed moulding whose curvature is the quarter of a circle, used chiefly in cornices: — *pl* **cavett'i** (*-i*). [Ital dimin of *cavo*, from L *cavus* hollow]

caviare or **caviar** *kav'i-är* or *kav-i-är'*, *n* salted roe of the sturgeon fish; something whose flavour is too fine for the common taste (*fig*). [Prob 16c Ital *caviale*, from Turk *khāvyār*]

cavicorn *kav'i-körn*, *adj* hollow-horned, as a ruminant is. — *n* an animal of the **Cavicor'nia** or Bovidae. [L *cavus* hollow, and *cornū* a horn]

cavie or **keavie** *kāv'i*, (*Scot*) *n* a hen-coop or cage. [Cf Du *kevie*, Ger *Käfig*, from L *cavus*]

cavil *kav'il*, *vi* to make petty, trifling objections (with *at* or *about*); to quibble: — *pr p* **cav'illing**; *pa t* and *pa p* **cav'illed**. — *n* a trifling objection. — *n* **cavillā'tion**. — *n* and *adj* **cav'illing**. — *n* **cav'iller**. [OFr *caviller*, from L *cavillārī* to practise jesting]

cavity *kav'it-i*, *n* a hollow; a hollow space or hole; a decayed hollow in a tooth. — *vi* **cav'itate** to form hollows. — *n* **cavitā'tion** the formation of cavities in a structure, or of gas bubbles in a liquid, or of a vacuum, or of a partial vacuum as between a body moving in a fluid and the fluid; a cavity. — *adj* **cav'itied**. — **cavity radiation** (*phys*) the radiation emerging from a small hole leading to a constant temperature enclosure; **cavity wall** a wall consisting of two layers with an air-space between. [L *cavitās*, from *cavus* hollow]

cavo-rilievo *kä'vō-rē-lyā'vō*, *n* a kind of relief sculpture in which the highest surface is below the level of the original stone, which is left round the outlines of the design. [Ital *cavo* hollow, and *rilievo* relief; see **cave** and **relief**]

cavort *kə-vört'*, *vi* to frolic, bound about joyfully. [Perh corruption of **curvet**]

cavy *kāv'i*, *n* a member of the guinea-pig genus (*Cavia*) of rodents. [*Cabiai*, native name in French Guiana]

caw *kö*, *vi* to cry as a crow. — *n* the cry of a crow. — Also **kaw**. — *n* **caw'ing**. [Imitative]

cawk. See **cauk**.

cawker. Same as **calker**.

caxon *kak'sən*, *n* a kind of wig (*hist*). [Origin obscure]

Caxton *kaks'tən*, *n* a book printed by William *Caxton* (1422–91), the first English printer; a kind of printing-type in imitation of Caxton's.

cay *kā*, *n* a low islet, the same as **key**[3]. [Sp *cayo*]

cayenne *kā-en'*, *n* a very strong, pungent red pepper (**cayenne pepper**) made from several species of capsicum. — *adj* **cayenned'** seasoned with cayenne. [Usu referred to *Cayenne* in French Guiana; but prob from Tupí]

cayman or **caiman** *kā'mən*, *n* any of the Central and South American crocodilian animals of the genus *Caiman* and related genera, similar to alligators: — *pl* **cay'mans**. [Sp *caimán*, most prob Carib]

cayuse *kī-ūs'*, (*NAm*) *n* a small American Indian pony; a small or poor horse. [Am Ind]

cazique. A form of **cacique**.

CB *abbrev*: Citizens' Band (radio); Companion of the (Order of the) Bath; confined (or confinement) to barracks; County Borough.

Cb (*chem*) *symbol*: columbium (now niobium).

cb *abbrev*: centre of buoyancy (of a boat, etc).

CBC *abbrev*: Canadian Broadcasting Corporation.

cbd *abbrev*: cash before delivery.

CBE *abbrev*: Commander of the (Order of the) British Empire.

CBer *sē-bē'ər*, *n* short for Citizens' Band radio user.

CBI *abbrev*: Confederation of British Industry.

CBIS *abbrev*: computer-based information system.

CBS *abbrev*: Columbia Broadcasting System.

CBSO *abbrev*: City of Birmingham Symphony Orchestra.

CC *abbrev*: Cape Colony (*SAfr*); Cape Coloured (see **cape**[2]); closed circuit (transmission); confined to camp (*military*); County Council or County Councillor; Cricket Club; Croquet Club.

cc *abbrev*: *capita* (*L*), chapters; carbon copy or copies; cubic centimetre(s).

CCCP. See **USSR**.

CCD *abbrev*: charge coupled device.

CCF *abbrev*: Central Control Function; chronic heart failure (*med*); Combined Cadet Force.

C clef *sē klef*, (*music*) *n* a symbol, an ornamental form of the letter C, used to indicate middle C on the stave.

CCR *abbrev*: critical compression ratio.

CCT *abbrev*: compulsory competitive tendering.

CCTV *abbrev*: closed circuit television.

CCU *abbrev*: coronary care unit.

CD *abbrev*: Civil Defence; compact disc; contagious disease(s); *Corps Diplomatique* (*Fr*), Diplomatic Corps.

Cd *abbrev*: coefficient of drag.

Cd (*chem*) *symbol*: cadmium.

cd *abbrev*: cash discount.

cd *symbol*: candela.
c/d (*bookkeeping*) *abbrev*: carried down.
CDI *abbrev*: Compact Disk Interactive.
CDN *abbrev*: Canada (IVR).
Cdn *abbrev*: Canadian.
Cdr *abbrev*: Commander.
Cdre *abbrev*: Commodore.
CD-ROM *abbrev*: compact disk read-only memory.
CDSO *abbrev*: Companion of the Distinguished Service Order.
CDT *abbrev*: Central Daylight Time (*NAm*); craft, design, technology.
CDU *abbrev*: *Chrislich-Demokratische Union* (*Ger*), Christian Democratic Union.
CDV *abbrev*: canine distemper virus (*vet*); Civil Defence Volunteers.
CE *abbrev*: Chancellor of the Exchequer; chemical or chief engineer; Church of England; civil engineer; Common Entrance; Common Era; *Communauté européene* (*Fr*), the mark showing that toys conform with EC toy safety standards since Jan 1990; Council of Europe.
Ce (*chem*) *symbol*: cerium.
ceanothus *sē-ə-nō'thəs*, *n* any shrub of the American genus *Ceanothus*, of the buckthorn family. [Gr *keanōthos* corn-thistle]
ceas(e). See **sessa**.
cease *sēs*, *vt* and *vi* to desist from; to stop; to end. — *n* an end; cessation. — *adj* **cease'less** without stop, continuous; incessant. — *adv* **cease'lessly**. — *n* **ceas'ing**. — **cease-fire'** an order to cease firing; an agreed end of active hostilities. [Fr *cesser*, from L *cēssāre* to give over, from *cēdere* to yield]
ceaze. An obsolete spelling of **seize**.
cebadilla. See **sabadilla**.
Cebus *sē'bəs*, *n* the generic name of the capuchin monkeys. — *n pl* **Cebidae** (*seb'i-dē*) a family including all the New World monkeys except the marmosets. [Gr *kēbos* a kind of monkey]
ceca, **cecal**, **cecum**. See **caecum**.
Cecidomyia *ses-id-o-mī'i-ə*, *n* a gall-midge, a genus of flies destructive to vegetation. [Gr *kēkis*, *-idos* a gall, and *myia* a fly]
cecils *ses'* or *sēs'ilz*, *n pl* minced meat, breadcrumbs, onions, etc made into balls and fried. [Ety doubtful]
cecitis. *NAm* spelling of **caecitis**.
cecity *sē'si-ti*, *n* blindness. — *n* **cecutiency** (*si-kū'shyən-si*) a tendency to blindness. [L *caecus* blind]
cecropia *si-krō'pi-ə*, *n* any tree of the tropical American genus *Cecropia*, of the mulberry family, some with hollow stems that give food and housing to a protective garrison of ants. — **cecropia moth** a large brightly-coloured American moth. [Named after the mythical Attic King *Cecrops* (Gr *Kekrōps*) represented as half-dragon, half-human]
cecum. *NAm* spelling of **caecum**.
cecutiency. See **cecity**.
cedar *sē'dər*, *n* a large evergreen coniferous tree (*Cedrus*, including *Cedar of Lebanon*, *Atlantic cedar*, and *deodar*) remarkable for the durability and fragrance of its wood; applied also to many more or less similar trees, as the Barbados cedar, properly a juniper, and the Bastard Barbados cedar, a tree of the genus *Cedrela*; the wood of these trees, cedarwood. — *adj* made of cedar. — *adj* **cē'dared** covered with cedars. — *adj* **cē'darn** (*poetic*) of cedar. — *adj* **cē'drine** belonging to the cedar-tree. — **ce'dar-bird** an American waxwing; **ce'dar-nut** the seed of the cembra pine; **ce'darwood** (also *adj*). [L *cedrus*, from Gr *kedros*]
cede *sēd*, *vt* to yield or give up to another person, country, etc. — *vi* to give way, yield. [L *cēdere*, *cēssum* to yield, to give up]
cedi *sed'i*, *n* the standard unit of decimal currency of Ghana, equal to 100 pesewas: — *pl* **ced'is**.
cedilla *si-dil'ə*, *n* a mark, *orig* a subscript Z, placed under the letter c (thus ç), formerly used in Spanish to indicate that the letter had the sound of (Spanish) *z* where that of *k* would be expected, still used *esp* in French and Portuguese to indicate an *s*-sound as before *a*, *o*, *u*, and in other languages used to denote other sounds, eg Turkish ş (*sh*) and ç (*ch*). [Sp (Fr *cédille*, Ital *zediglia*), all dimins from *zēta*, the Greek name of *z*; see **z**]
CEDO *abbrev*: Centre for Education Development Overseas.
cedrate *sē'drāt*, *n* citron. [Fr *cédrat*, from L *citrus*]
Cedrela *sed-rē'lə*, *n* a tropical genus of Meliaceae, allied to mahogany. — *adj* **cedrelā'ceous**. [Sp dimin of *cedro*, *cedra* cedar; see **cedar**]
cedrine. See **cedar**.
cedula *sed'ū-lə*, *n* a S American promissory-note or mortgage-bond on lands. [Sp; cf **schedule**]
cee *cē*, *n* the third letter of the alphabet (C or c); anything shaped like it. — **cee-spring** or **c-spring** (*sē'spring*) a spring in the shape of a C to support the frame of a carriage.
Ceefax® *sē'faks*, *n* the teletext service of the British Broadcasting Corporation. [**see** and **facts**]
CEGB *abbrev*: Central Electricity Generating Board (privatized in January 1990 and split into three companies: *Powergen*, *National Grid* and *National Power*).
CEI *abbrev*: Council of Engineering Institutions.
ceil *sēl*, *vt* to overlay the inner roof of (*obs*); to overlay or line; to provide with a ceiling. — *adj* **ceiled**. — *n* **ceil'ing** the inner roof of a room; the highest altitude at which an aircraft can fly; the height above the ground of the base of the cloud-layer; an upper limit. — *adj* **ceil'inged** having a ceiling. — *n* **ceilom'eter** (*meteorol*) an instrument for measuring the cloud ceiling. [Prob connected with Fr *ciel*, Ital *cielo*, LL *caelum* a canopy]
ceilidh *kā'li*, *n* in Scotland and Ireland, an informal evening of song, story and dancing. — Also (*Irish*) **ceil'i**. [Gaelic, a visit]
ceinture *sē-tür*, (*Fr*) *n* a girdle, belt.
cel *n*. See **celluloid**.
cel. *abbrev*: celebrated.
celadon *sel'ə-don*, *n* a pale-green colour; a Chinese pottery glaze of the colour; the pottery so glazed. [Fr, perh after a character in D'Urfé's *Astrée*]
celandine *sel'ən-dīn*, *n* either of two plants (**greater celandine**, *Chelidonium majus* and **lesser celandine**, *Ranunculus ficaria*) supposed to flower when the swallows came, and to perish when they went. [OFr *celidoine*, from Gr *chelīdonion*, from *chelīdōn* a swallow]
celebrate *sel'i-brāt*, *vt* to mark by solemn ceremonies, as a festival or an event; to perform with proper rites and ceremonies, such as a mass, the eucharist, marriage, etc; to publish the praises of; to make famous. — *vi* to do something enjoyable because of a feeling of pleasure at some event, achievement, etc. — *n* **cel'ebrant** a person who celebrates; the principal person officiating at a rite or ceremony. — *adj* **cel'ebrated** distinguished; famous. — *n* **celebrā'tion** the act of celebrating; any solemn or joyous ceremony. — *n* **cel'ebrātor**. — *adj* **cel'ebratory**. — *n* **celebrity** (*si-leb'ri-ti*) fame; notoriety; a person of distinction or fame (*slang abbrev* **celeb'**). [L *celebrāre*, *-ātum*, from *celeber* frequented]
celerity *si-ler'i-ti*, *n* quickness, speed; rapidity of motion or thought. [Fr *célérité*, from L *celeritās*, from *celer* quick]
celery *sel'ər-i*, *n* an umbelliferous plant (*Apium graveolens*) whose blanched leafstalks are eaten cooked or uncooked as a vegetable. — *n* **celeriac** (*si-ler'i-ak*) a variety of celery with a swollen stem-base like a turnip. [Fr *céleri*, from Gr *selīnon* parsley]
celesta *si-les'tə* or **celeste** *si-lest'*, *n* a keyboard instrument in which bell-like sounds are produced by hammers striking steel plates suspended over wooden resonators. [Fr *céleste* heavenly]
celeste *si-lest'*, *adj* sky-blue. — *n* voix céleste; a kind of soft pedal on a piano. [Fr *céleste*]
celestial *si-lest'yəl*, *adj* heavenly, divine, sublime; living in heaven; of or in the visible heavens (*esp astron*);

Chinese (*old colloq*; usu *humorously*). — *n* an inhabitant of heaven, a celestial being; a Chinese (*old colloq*). — *adv* **celest'ially**. — **Celestial Empire** (*hist*) China, the Chinese Empire; **celestial equator** (*astron*) a great circle in which the plane of the earth's equator cuts the celestial sphere; **celestial globe** a model of the celestial sphere showing the relative positions of stars, etc; **celestial horizon** see **horizon**; **celestial mechanics** (*astron*) the study of the motions of celestial objects in gravitational fields, *esp*, as by Newton, satellite and planetary motion in the solar system; **celestial navigation** navigation by the stars, etc (also **astronavigation**); **celestial poles** (*astron*) the two points at which the earth's axis, extended indefinitely, cut the celestial sphere; **celestial sphere** (*astron*) an imaginary sphere of infinite radius, of which the observer is the centre, onto which stars and other celestial bodies are projected. [Through Fr from L *caelestis*, from *caelum* heaven]

Celestine *sel'is-tīn* or *sil-es'tin*, *n* a monk of an order founded in 1264 by Pietro da Morrone, afterwards Pope *Celestine* V.

celestite *sel'əs-tīt* or *sə-les'tīt*, or **celestine** *sel'əs-tin* or *-tīn*, *n* a sky-blue, red or white mineral, strontium sulphate, crystallized in the orthorhombic system, and occurring in rock salt and gypsum. [Through Ger, from L *caelestis* celestial].

celiac. *NAm* spelling of **coeliac**.

celibacy *sel'i-bəs-i*, *n* the unmarried state, *esp* as adhered to under a religious vow; abstention from sexual relations. — *adj* **celibatā'rian** favouring or advocating celibacy. — *adj* **cel'ibate** (*-it*) living as a single person; abstaining from sexual relations. — *n* a person who is unmarried, or bound by a vow not to marry. [L *caelebs* single]

cell[1] *sel*, *n* a unit-mass of living matter, the smallest capable of independent existence, consisting of a nucleus surrounded by cytoplasm and bounded by a cell membrane and sometimes a cell wall, as in plants; the whole bacterium or yeast, the *bacterial cell*; a small room in a prison, monastery, etc; a vessel with electrodes and an electrolyte for electrolysis, or an apparatus for generating an electric current by chemical action, *esp* a dry battery; a unit group, *esp* of espionage personnel, political activists or terrorists; a small monastery or nunnery dependent on another; one compartment of a honeycomb; a hermit's one-roomed dwelling; a small enclosed cavity (*biol*); the cavity containing pollen in an anther lobe (*bot*); one chamber in an ovary (*bot*); one of the spaces into which the wing of an insect is divided (*zool*); (a radio transmitter serving) one of the geographical areas into which Britain is divided for the coverage of cellular radio (qv); a part of the atmosphere that behaves as a unit (*meteorol*); a unit of homogenous reactivity in a nuclear reactor core; a unit or area of storage in computing, eg the smallest unit capable of storing a single bit. — *adj* **celled** having cells, cellular. — *adj* **cellif'erous** having or producing cells. — *adj* **cell'ūlar** consisting of, characterized by or containing cells or compartments; relating to or involving cells in the body; consisting of a number of separate rooms, as in *cellular office*; composed of ordinary cells without vessels (as the lower cryptogams); porous; of open texture. — *adj* **cell'ūlāted**. — *n* **cell'ule** a little cell. — *adj* **cellūlif'erous** having or producing little cells. — *n* **cell'ūlite** deposits of fat cells, not responsive to dieting or exercise, which give the skin a dimpled, pitted appearance. — *n* **cellūlī'tis** inflammation of the subcutaneous body tissue caused by pyogenic bacteria. — *n* **celluloid** see separate entry. — *adj* **cell'ulose** see separate entry. — **cell cycle** (*biol*) the complete series of processes undergone in cell division; **cell division** (*biol*) the process in which cells each split into two new cells, so increasing in number during growth or reproduction; **cell-free transcription** (*biol*) in vitro transcription; **cell-free translation** (*biol*) in vitro translation; **cell membrane** (*biol*) the surface membrane surrounding a cell; a cell wall; **cell'phone** a portable telephone for use in a cellular radio system; **cellular immunity** or **cell-mediated immunity** an acquired immunity in which white corpuscles from the lymph glands play a major part; **cellular radio** a system of radio communication based on a network of roughly hexagonal geographical cells each served by a transmitter, the receiving equipment automatically tuning in to each in turn as it moves across the cells' borders. [OFr *celle*, from L *cella*, connected with *celāre* to cover]

cell[2]. See **celluloid**.

cella *sel'ə*, *n* the naos, or inner chamber of a classical temple: — *pl* **cell'ae** (*-ē*). [L, shrine]

cellar[1] *sel'ər*, *n* any underground room or vault; a room for storing wine, beer, coal, etc, often below ground level; a stock of wine. — *vt* to store in a cellar. — *n* **cell'arage** (a quantity of) cellar space; a charge for storing in cellars. — *n* **cell'arer** or **cell'arist** a person who is in charge of the cellar; an officer in a monastery who looks after the provisions. — *n* **cell'aret** a case, cupboard or drawer for holding bottles of wine, etc. — *adj* **cell'arous** (*Dickens*) belonging to a cellar; excavated; sunken. — **cell'ar-book** a record of wines kept in a cellar; **cell'ar-flap** a plate covering an entrance to a cellar; **cell'arman** a person responsible for a cellar. [OFr *celier*, from L *cellārium*, from *cella*]

cellar[2]. See **salt-cellar**.

Cellnet® *sel'net*, *n* in UK, a system of mobile telecommunications using cellular radio.

cello *chel'ō*, *n* short for violoncello (sometimes written **'cello**): — *pl* **cell'os**. — *n* **cell'ist** or **'cell'ist** violoncellist.

cellobiose *sel-ō-bī'ōz* or *-ōs*, (*biol*) *n* a dissaccharide, $C_{12}H_{22}O_{11}$, obtained by complete hydrolysis of cellulose. — Also **cellose**. [From *cell*ulose, pfx **bi-**, and sfx **-ose**]

cellophane® *sel'ō-fān*, *n* a tough, transparent, paperlike wrapping material made from viscose. [*cell*ul*o*se and Gr *phainein* to show]

cellose. See **cellobiose**.

cellphone, **cellular**, **cellulite**. See **cell**[1].

cellulase *sel'ū-lāz* or *-lās*, *n* an enzyme that can split cellulose into glucose, present in organisms in the guts of animals and in the leaf stalks of higher plants.

celluloid® *sel'ū-loid*, *n* (with *cap* in US) a thermoplastic, made from nitrocellulose, camphor and alcohol, which is elastic, very strong and often transparent or translucent; (often shortened to **cel** or **cell**) a sheet of this material; cinematographic film generally; the world of film and cinema.

cellulose *sel'ū-lōz* or *-lōs*, *n* a carbohydrate forming the chief component of cell walls in plants and in wood (cotton-down, linen fibre and wood pulp being almost pure cellulose). — *adj* containing cells. — *adj* **cellulosic** (*-lōz'ik*) containing or derived from cellulose. — **cellulose acetate** a chemical compound obtained by the action of acetate and sulphuric acid on cellulose, used in the manufacture of textiles, varnish and photographic film; **cellulose nitrate** a chemical compound obtained by the action of nitric acid on cellulose, used in the manufacture of textiles, explosives, plastics, etc. [Fr, from *cellule* a living cell]

celom. See **coelom**.

celsitude *sels'i-tūd*, *n* loftiness. [L *celsitūdō*, from *celsus* lofty]

Celsius *sel'si-əs*, *adj* pertaining to the centigrade scale used in the thermometer constructed by Anders *Celsius* (1701–44), in which the freezing-point of water is 0° and the boiling-point is 100°.

celt *selt*, (*archaeol*) *n* a prehistoric axe-like implement with a bevelled edge. [From a supposed L word *celtes* a chisel]

Celt *kelt* or *selt*, also **Kelt**, etc *kelt*, *n* a Gaul (*hist*); extended to include members of other Celtic-speaking or recently Celtic-speaking peoples, *esp* the inhabitants of parts of Britain, Ireland and NW France. — *adj* **Celt'ic** pertaining to the Celts; of a branch of the Indo-European family of languages including Breton,

Welsh, Cornish, Irish, Gaelic, Manx. — Also *n*. — *n* **Celt'icism** a Celtic idiom or custom. — *n* **Celt'icist** an expert or specialist in Celtic language and/or culture. — *n* **Celtomā'nia**. — **Celtic cross** a Latin cross, carved in the style common to the Celts, Scandinavians, and Northumbrian Angles and used conventionally for Christian memorials, etc, with a broad circle around the point of intersection of the crossbar and the upright, sometimes miscalled Runic cross; **Celtic fringe** an offensive term applied to Wales, Ireland and the Highlands and Islands of Scotland, which have different cultural, social and political characteristics from the rest of the British Isles; **Celtic Sea** the area of sea to the south of Ireland and west of Cornwall. — **P'-Celt'**; **Q'-Celt'**. — *adj* and *n* **P'-Celt'ic** and **Q'-Celt'ic** (pertaining to) respectively, one of the Celtic languages in which Indo-European *qu* became *p* and one in which *qu* became *k* (written *c*). [L *Celtae*; Gr *Keltoi* or *Keltai*]

Celt. *abbrev*: Celtic.

cembalo *chem'bä-lō*, *n* a musical instrument with strings struck by hammers, a dulcimer; a similar instrument with a keyboard, such as a harpsichord or pianoforte: — *pl* **cem'balos** or **cembali**. — *n* **cem'balist** a person who plays a cembalo; (also *sem'*) a person who plays the pianoforte in an orchestra (*rare*). [Ital; see **cymbal**]

cembra *sem'brə*, *n* the Swiss stonepine. — Also **cembra pine**. [New L, from Ger dialect *zember* timber; cf Ger *Zimmer* room]

cement *si-ment'*, formerly *sem'ənt*, *n* anything that makes two substances or objects stick together; a fine powder made of clay and calcined limestone, mixed with water and sand to make mortar or mixed with water, sand and aggregate to make concrete; a bond or union; glue or adhesive; material used for dental fixings; cementum. — *vt* to unite or bond with cement; to join firmly. — *n* **cementation** (*sem-ən-tā'shən*) the act of cementing; the process of impregnating the surface of one substance with another by surrounding it with powder and heating, as in steel-making, case-hardening, turning glass into porcelain; precipitation; the process of injecting fluid cement mixture for strengthening purposes. — *adj* **cemen'tatory** or **cementi'tious** having the quality of cementing or uniting firmly. — *n* **cemen'ter**. — *n* **cemen'tite** compound of iron and carbon Fe_3C, found in cast iron, etc. — *n* **cemen'tum** the bony outer covering of the root of a tooth. — **cement'-copper** copper obtained by precipitation; **cement gun** an apparatus for spraying fine concrete or cement mortar; **cement mixer** a machine with a revolving drum for mixing concrete; **cement'-stone** a clayey limestone, suitable for making hydraulic cement; **cement'-water** water containing copper salts, as in copper mines. [OFr *ciment*, from L *caementum* chip of stone used to fill up in building a wall, short for *caedimentum*, from *caedere* to cut]

cemetery *sem'i-tri*, *n* a burial-ground for the dead. [LL *coemētērium*, from Gr *koimētērion* sleeping-place]

cemitare. Spenser's spelling of **scimitar**.

CEN. See **CENELEC**.

cen. *abbrev*: central; century.

cenacle *sen'ə-kl*, *n* a supper room or guest room, *esp* that in which the Last Supper was eaten by Christ and the apostles; a group with common interests; a literary coterie, or its meeting-place. [Fr *cénacle*, from L *cēnāculum*, from *cēna* supper]

cendré *sã-drā*, (*Fr*) *adj* ash-blond.

-cene *-sēn*, *combining form* denoting a recent division of geological time in the Tertiary System, eg Eocene, Pliocene. [*Gr kainos* new]

CENELEC (sometimes *abbrev* **CEN**) *abbrev*: *Commission Européene de Normalisation Electrique*, European Electrical Standards Co-ordinating Committee.

CEng *sē-eng' abbrev*: Chartered Engineer.

cenesthesis. Same as **coenaesthesis**.

cenobite. Same as **coenobite**.

cenogenesis. *NAm* spelling of **caenogenesis**.

cenospecies *sēn'ō-spē-shēz*, (*biol*) *n* all members of an ecospecies related to each other by the ability to interbreed or hybridize. [Gr *koinos* common, and **species**]

cenotaph *sen'ə-täf*, *n* an empty tomb; a sepulchral monument in honour of one or more people buried elsewhere. [Gr *kenotaphion*, from *kenos* empty, and *taphos* a tomb]

cenote *si-nō'ti*, *n* a deep, natural hole in the ground with a pool at the bottom of it, *esp* in the Yucatán peninsula, often used by the Mayas as a place of sacrifice. [MexSp, from Maya *conot*, *tyonot*]

Cenozoic *sē-nō-zō'ik*. Same as **Cainozoic**.

cens *sãs*, (*Fr Can law*) *n* a nominal annual payment given to the owner of an estate or property in recognition of his or her title. [Fr L *cēnsēre* to estimate]

cense[1] *sens*, *vt* to burn incense in front of (an altar, etc). [**incense**[2]]

cense[2] *sens*, (*obs*) *vt* to think; to assess. — *n* a public rate of tax; rank or condition. [L *cēnsēre* to estimate]

censer *sens'ər*, *n* a ceremonial container in which incense is burned. [OFr *censier*, *encensier* (Fr *encensoir*), from LL *incēnsorium*, from L *incendere*, *incēnsum* to burn]

censor *sen'sör*, or *-sər*, *n* a magistrate who kept account of the property of Roman citizens, imposed taxes, and watched over their morals (*hist*); an official with similar functions elsewhere; any of various officials in certain universities; an official who examines books, papers, telegrams, letters, films, etc, with powers to delete material, or to forbid publication, delivery or showing; an unconscious inhibitive mechanism in the mind, that prevents what is painful to the conscious from emerging from the subconscious (*psychol*); a person who censures or blames. — *vt* to subject to censorship or to censorial examination or condemnation. — *adj* **censorial** (*-ō'ri-əl*, *-ö'*) pertaining to a censor, or to the correction of public morals. — *adj* **censo'rian** censorial. — *adj* **censo'rious** expressing censure; fault-finding. — *adv* **censo'riously**. — *n* **censo'riousness**. — *n* **cen'sorship** the work of a censor, censoring; the office of censor; the time during which a censor holds office. — **censor morum** (*sen'sər mör'əm* or *kān'sor mō'rōōm*; *L*) censor of morals. [L *cēnsor*, *-ōris*)

censure *sen'shər*, *n* an unfavourable opinion or judgement; blame; reproof. — *vt* to form or give an unfavourable opinion or judgement of; to blame; to condemn as wrong; to sentence (*Shakesp*). — *adj* **cen'surable** deserving censure; blamable. — *n* **cen'surableness**. — *adv* **cen'surably**. [L *cēnsūra*, from *cēnsēre* to estimate]

census *sen'səs*, *n* an official enumeration of inhabitants with statistics relating to them. — *adj* **cen'sual** (*-sū-əl*) relating to or containing a census. — *vt* to carry out a census of. [L *cēnsus*, *-ūs* a register]

cent *sent*, *n* a hundredth part of various monetary units, *esp* of a dollar; a coin of that value. — *n* **cent'age** rate by the hundred. — *n* **cent'al** a unit of weight equal to 100 lb (45.3kg), formerly used for measuring grain. — **per cent** by the hundred (symbol %). [L *centum* a hundred]

cent. *abbrev*: central; *centum* (*L*), a hundred; century.

centare. See **centiare**.

centaur *sen'tör*, *n* a mythical creature, half man and half horse. — *adj* **centau'rian**. [Gr *kentauros*]

centaurea *sen-tö'ri-ə* or *-tö-rē'ə*, *n* a plant of the genus *Centaurea* including knapweed, cornflower, etc. See also **centaury**.

Centaurus *sen-tö'rəs*, *n* a constellation in the S hemisphere containing Alpha Centauri and Beta Centauri. [Gr *kentauros* centaur]

centaury *sen'tö-ri*, *n* a name applied to plants of the gentianaceous genera *Erythraea* and *Chlora*, and to the composite genus *Centaurea*. [According to Gr mythol the *centaur* Chiron healed a wound with *kentaurion*, one of these plants]

centavo *sen-tä'vō, n* a Portuguese and Spanish American coin and monetary unit, one hundredth of the standard unit of currency: — *pl* **centa'vos**. [Sp and Port]

centenary *sen-tēn'ər-i* (also *-ten'* or *sen'*), *n* a hundred; a century or hundred years; a hundredth anniversary. — *adj* pertaining to a hundred or to a centennial. — *n* **centenā'rian** a person who is a hundred years old or more. — *n* **centenā'rianism**. — *n* **centenier** (*sen'tən-ēr*) a centurion; in Jersey, an honorary part-time police officer with judicial powers. [L *centēnārius*, from *centēnī* a hundred each, from *centum*]

centennial *sen-ten'yəl, adj* happening once in a hundred years; lasting a hundred years. — *n* (*NAm*) a hundredth anniversary, a centenary. [L *centum* a hundred, and *annus* a year]

center[1]. The *NAm* spelling of **centre**.

center[2] *sen'tər*, (*Shakesp*) *n* a cincture, waist-belt.

centering. See **centring**.

centesimal *sen-tes'i-məl, adj* hundredth; having divisions of a hundredth, as a centigrade thermometer has. — *adv* **centes'imally**. [L *centēsimus*, from *centum*]

centesimo *chen-tez'i-mō* or *sen-tes'i-mō, n* a coin and monetary unit of Italy, Chile, Uruguay and Panama, one hundredth of the standard unit of currency. [Ital and Sp]

centesis *sen-tē'sis*, (*surg*) *n* and *combining form* a puncture, as in *amniocentesis*: — *pl* **centeses** (*sen-tē'sēz*). [Gr *kentēsis*, from *kentein* to prick]

centi- *sen'ti-* or **cent-** *combining form* denoting 1/100 of the unit named. [L *centum* a hundred]

centiare *sen'ti-är* or **centare** *sen'tär, n* a unit of area, the hundredth part of an are, 1sq m (1·196sq yd). [L *centum* a hundred, and *ārea* area]

centigrade *sen'ti-grād, adj* of a scale, *esp* the **Celsius** temperature scale, having a hundred degrees between the freezing and boiling points of water. [L *centum* a hundred, and *gradus* a step, a degree]

centigram or **centigramme** *sen'ti-gram, n* the hundredth part of a gram. [Fr, from L *centum* a hundred, and **gram**]

centilitre or (*NAm*) **centiliter** *sen'ti-lē-tər, n* the hundredth part of a litre, 10 cubic centimetres. [Fr, from L *centum* a hundred, and **litre**]

centillion *sen-til'yən, n* in UK and Germany, the hundredth power of a million, ie 1 followed by 600 zeros; in N America and France, the hundred-and-first power of a thousand, ie 1 followed by 303 zeros. — *n* **centill'ionth**. [L *centum* a hundred, and the ending of **million**]

centime *sã'tēm* or *sã-tēm', n* a French coin, 1/100 of a franc; any of several coins of various countries, 1/100 of their standard unit of currency. [Fr, from L *centesimum* a hundredth]

centimetre or (*NAm*) **centimeter** *sen'ti-mē-tər, n* a linear measure, the hundredth part of a metre. — *adj* **centimet'ric** having a wavelength of between one and ten centimetres. — **centimetre-gram-second** (*abbrev* **CGS** or **cgs**) formerly applied to a system of scientific measurement with the centimetre, gram and second as units of length, mass and time. [Fr, from L *centum* a hundred, and **metre**[2]]

centimo *sen'ti-mō* or *then'ti-mō, n* a coin and monetary unit of Spain, Venezuela, Paraguay and Costa Rica, one hundredth of the standard unit of currency. [Sp]

centi Morgan *sen'ti mör'gen*, (*genetics*) *n* a measure of the distance between the loci of two genes on the same chromosome obtained from the cross-over frequency and used in genetic mapping. [**centi-** and T H Morgan (1866–1945), US biologist]

centinel or **centinell** *sen'ti-nl*, obs spellings of **sentinel**. — **centinel** (**private**) a private soldier.

centipede *sen'ti-pēd, n* any myriapod of the class Chilopoda, carnivorous flattened animals with many segments, each bearing one pair of legs. [L *centum* a hundred, and *pēs, pedis* a foot]

centner *sent'nər, n* a unit of weight in Germany and Scandinavia equal to 50kg (110·23lb), or in Russia 100kg (220·46lb); a unit of weight equal to 100lb (45·3kg) (also called in US **short hundredweight**). [Ger, from L *centēnārius*; cf **centenary**]

CENTO *sen'tō, abbrev*: Central Treaty Organization (formed 1959 to foster economic and military co-operation between UK, Iran, Turkey and Pakistan; disbanded 1979).

cento *sen'tō, n* a poem manufactured by putting together lines or passages of one author or of several authors; a composition formed by joining bits and pieces from various authors; a string of commonplace phrases and quotations: — *pl* **cen'tos** or **centones**. — *adj* **cen'tonate** (*bot*) blotched, patchy. — *n* **cen'toist** or **cen'tonist**. [L *centō, -ōnis*, Gr *kentrōn* patchwork]

central, etc. See **centre**.

centre or (*NAm*) **center**, etc *sen'tər, n* the middle point of anything, *esp* a circle or sphere; the middle area of anything; a person or thing in the middle; a fixed point of reference; the point toward which all things move or are drawn; a nucleus or focal point; a resort; a stronghold; a meeting place; a place, institution, etc devoted to a specified activity; a part or area of the brain or nervous system that controls a specified action or function (*physiol*); a player in a central position (*Rugby football, etc*); a centre-forward (*soccer, hockey*, etc); the player in the centre of the offensive line, who starts the play by passing the ball through his legs to a backfield player (*Am football*); (a shot that hits) the ring around the bull's eye (*archery*); a political party, or its members, having moderate opinions; of a conic, the point through which all diameters pass (*math*); a rod with a conical tip for supporting a workpiece in a lathe or other machine tool (*machinery*). — *vt* to place on or connect to a centre. — *vi* to be placed in the middle; to have a centre; to lie or move in relation to a centre (often with *on*, or *upon, round* or *around*): — *pr p* **cen'tring**; *pa t* and *pa p* **cen'tred**. — *adj* pertaining to the political centre. — *adj* **cen'tral** belonging to, in, or near, the centre; principal, dominant, most important, essential. — *n* **cen'tralism** the tendency or policy of administering by the sovereign or central government matters which would be otherwise under local management. — *n* **cen'tralist** (also *adj*). — *n* **centrality** (*-tral'i-ti*) central position; dominance, the quality of being essential or principal. — *n* **centralizā'tion** or **-s-** the act or process of moving or drawing towards a centre; centralism. — *vt* and *vi* **cen'tralize** or **-ise** to move to, draw to, or concentrate at a centre. — *adv* **cen'trally**. — *adj* **cen'tred** positioned in the centre. — *n* **cen'treing** see separate article **centring**. — *adj* **cen'tric** relating to, placed in, or containing the centre; (of plants) cylindrical and tapering, terete. — *combining form* **-cen'tric** having a specified type of centre. — *adj* **cen'trical**. — *adv* **cen'trically**. — *n* **cen'tricalness**. — *n* **centricity** (*-tris'i-ti*). — *n* **cen'trism** the practice of sticking to the middle ground in politics; the holding of moderate, non-extreme political opinions. — *adj* and *n* **cen'trist**. — **central angle** (*math*) an angle bounded by two radii of a circle; **central bank** a state-owned or state-controlled bank which carries out government financial policy, regulates the money supply, influences interest rates and acts as a link between the government and the banking system; **central dogma** the principle that the transfer of genetic information from DNA to the protein sequence is irreversible, ie it cannot flow from protein to DNA; **central fire** a cartridge having the fulminate in the centre of the base (also *adj* **cen'tre-fire**); **central force** (*phys*) the force on a moving body that is always directed towards or from a fixed point, the centre of force; **central heating** a system of heating a building by water, steam or warm air conducted throughout the building from one point; **central locking** in a motor vehicle, the automatic locking of all the doors as the driver's door is locked; **Central Powers** in and before the war of 1914–18, the German Empire and Austria-Hungary; **central processor** see phrases below; **central reservation** a *usu* tarred or paved area in the centre of a motorway or major road acting as a division between traffic travelling in opposite directions; **centre-back** (*soccer*) the central player in the middle of the defence; the position of this player; **centre bit** a joiner's tool, turning on a centre, for boring circular holes in wood; **cen'treboard** a rectractable keel fitted to small racing yachts and dinghies; **cen'trefold** or **centre spread** the two facing centre pages of a newspaper, magazine, etc; an article, design or set of photographs printed on these; a photograph of a nude woman or man printed on these; **centre-for'ward** (*soccer, hockey*, etc) the central player in the line of forwards; the position of this player; **centre-half'** (*soccer, hockey*, etc) the central player in the line of half-backs; the position of this player; **centre lathe** (*eng*) a machine tool for cutting metal in which the tool is held steady and the workpiece rotates; **cen'treline** an often imaginary line that divides a body or shape into two equal halves; **cen'trepiece** something placed at the centre, *esp* an ornament for the middle of a table, ceiling, etc; a central character or feature in a story, film, etc; **centre punch** a tool, a steel bar with a conical point, used for marking the centre of holes to be drilled; **cen'tre-rail** a rail between the ordinary rails on a railway track; **centre spread** see **centrefold**. — *adj* and *adv* **centre stage** in or to the centre of a theatre stage; at or to the position where (eg political, media, etc) attention is focused. — **centre-three-quar'ter** (*rugby*) one of the two players positioned in the middle of the three-quarter-back line; the position of these players. — **Central European Time** (*abbrev* **CET**) the standard time in W European countries, equivalent of British Summer Time, one hour ahead of Greewich Mean Time; **central nervous system** (*zool*) the main ganglia of the nervous system with their associated nerve cords, in vertebrates consisting of the brain and spinal cord; **central processor** or **central processing unit** (*abbrev* **CPU**) the part of a computer which performs the logical and arithmetical operations on the data and which controls other units of the computer system; **central to** essential,most important for the understanding or working of; **centre of attraction** the point to which bodies tend by the force of gravity or the like; **centre of buoyancy** or **displacement** the centre of gravity of the immersed portion of a floating body; **centre of excellence** a focal point, *esp* a university (or one of its departments), for work at the highest level (in a particular subject); **centre of gravity** the single point at which the resultant gravitational forces of a body act; **centre of inertia** or **mass** the point through which any plane divides a body into two parts of equal mass; **centre of oscillation** the point in a pendulum such that, if all the matter were concentrated there, the pendulum would have the same period; **centre of percussion** the point where the direction of a blow meets the plane in which lie the centre of inertia and a possible axis of rotation such that the blow imparts a rotation without pressure on the axis; **centre of pressure** the point on a surface immersed in fluid at which the resultant pressure may be taken to act (*phys*); the point at which the resultant of aerodynamic forces intersects the chord line of an aerofoil; **centre of symmetry** a point in a figure such that any straight line through it meets the figure in two points at equal distances on either side. [Fr, from L *centrum*, from Gr *kentron* a sharp point]

centri- *sen-tri'-*, *sen'tri-*, **centr-** or **centro-** *sen'tro-*, *combining form* denoting centre.

centric, etc. See **centre**.

centrifugal *sen-trif'ū-gəl*, *sen'* or *-fū'*, *adj* tending away from a centre; conducting or carrying outwards from the centre, efferent (*biol*); using, or produced by centrifugal force; proceeding in development from the apex towards the base (*bot*). — *vt* **centrif'ugalize** or **-ise** (or *sen'*, *-fū'*) to subject to centrifugal force. — *adv* **centrifugally**. — *n* **cen'trifuge** (*-fūj*; also **centrifugal machine**) any machine which, using rapid rotation, separates substances of different densities by centrifugal force; any rotating device used for studying the effects of gravitational force and varying accelerations on humans and animals. — *vt* to subject to such rotation. — *n* **centrifugation** (*-fū-gā'shən*) or **centrifugence** (*-trif'ū-jəns*, *sen'* or *-fū'*) centrifugal tendency or force; (**centrifugation**) centrifuge separation. — **centrifugal force** the resistance of a revolving body, by virtue of its inertia, to an acceleration towards the centre, equal and opposite to centripetal force; **centrifugal machine** a centrifuge; **centrifuge separation** the technique of isotope separation applied to the enrichment of ^{235}U in uranium (sometimes called **centrifugation**). [Ety as for **centre**, and L *fugere* to flee]

centring or (*NAm*) **centering** *sen'tər-ing* or *sen'tring*, (*building*) *n* the framework upon which an arch or vault of stone, brick or iron is supported during its construction. — Also **cen'treing**.

centriole *sen'trē-ōl*, (*zool*) *n* a rodlike body (*usu* one of a pair) in animal cells that forms the centre of polymerization of the microtubules in certain thread-like structures, eg in sperm flagelli and the mitotic spindle. [New L *centriolum*, dimin of L *centrum*]

centripetal *sen-trip'ə-tl*, *adj* tending towards a centre; conducting or carrying towards the centre, afferent (*biol*); proceeding in development from the base towards the apex (*bot*). — *n* **centrip'etalism**. — **centripetal force** a force acting on a revolving body, causing it to tend inward towards the centre, equal and opposite to centrifugal force. [Ety as for **centre** and L *petere* to seek]

centrobaric *sen-trō-bar'ik*, *adj* relating to the centre of gravity. [Ety as for **centre**, and Gr *baros* weight]

centroclinal *sen-trō-klī'nl*, (*geol*) *adj* dipping towards a centre from all directions. [Ety as for **centre**, and Gr *klīnein* to lean]

centrode *sen'trōd*, (*math*) *n* a locus traced out by the successive positions of an instantaneous centre of pure rotation. [Ety as for **centre**, and Gr *hodos* a path]

centroid *sen'troid*, (*math*) *n* the point where the medians of a triangle intersect; the centre of mass. — *adj* **centroid'al**. [Ety as for **centre**, and Gr *eidos* form]

centromere *sen'trə-mēr*, (*biol*) *n* the portion of DNA that attaches a chromosome to the spindle during cell division. [Ety as for **centre**, and Gr *meros* part]

centrosome *sen'trə-sōm*, (*biol*) *n* a small body found in the protoplasm of a cell, forming by division the two poles of the mitotic spindle. [Ety as for **centre**, and Gr *sōma* a body]

centrosphere *sen'trə-sfēr*, (*geol*) *n* the central part of the earth below the crust, the barysphere.

centrum *sen'trəm*, (*anatom*) *n* the main part of a vertebra: — *pl* **cen'trums** or **cen'tra**. [L]

centry[1] *sen'tri*, *n* centre (*Shakesp*); centering (*obs*).

centry[2]. An *obs* spelling of **sentry**.

centum *sen'təm* or *ken'to͝om*, *n* a hundred. — **centum languages** the group of Indo-European languages in which an original palatal consonant appears as a guttural sound, as in L *centum* hundred in which the 'c' is sounded 'k'' (cf **satem languages**); **centumvir** (*sentum'vir*; L *vir* a man) one of the Roman judges chosen annually for civil suits, *orig* 105 in number (three from each of the thirty-five tribes): — *pl* **centum'virī**. — *n* **centum'virate**. [L *centum* a hundred]

centuple *sen'tū-pl*, *adj* hundredfold. — *vt* to multiply or increase a hundred times. — *n* **centuplicā'tion**. — *adj* **centū'plicate**. — *n* one of a hundred like things or copies. — *vt* to centuple. [L *centuplus* and *centuplex*, from *centum* hundred, and *plicāre* to fold]

century *sen'tū-ri*, *n* a set or series of a hundred, as of Roman soldiers, runs at cricket, or consecutive years (*esp* reckoned from the conventionally accepted date of Christ's birth). — *adj* **centūrial**. — *n* **centuriā'tion** division into hundreds. — *n* **centū'riātor** one of a group of 16c Reformed divines of Magdeburg who compiled a church history in 13 volumes, each volume covering a century. — *n* **centū'rion** in the ancient Roman army, an officer who had the command of a hundred men; a person who has scored or achieved a hundred in any way. — **century plant** an agave (*Agave american*) of Mexico and southern US which flowers only once in many years. [L *centuria* a century, from *centum* a hundred]

CEO *abbrev*: Chief Executive Officer.

ceòl mór *kyol mōr* or *mör*. Same as **pibroch**. [Gaelic, great music]

ceorl *chā'örl* or *kā'örl*, *n* in England before the Norman Conquest, an ordinary freeman of the lowest rank. [OE *ceorl*; see **churl**]

cep *sep*, *n* a type of edible mushroom of the Boletus genus with a brown shiny cap and white underside. [Fr *cèpe*, from L *cippus* a stake]

cepaceous *si-pā'shəs*, (*bot*) *adj* smelling or tasing of onion or garlic. [From the species name of the onion, *Allium cepa*]

cephal- *sef'əl-*, *si-fal'-*, *kef'al-* or *ki-fal'-*, or **cephalo-** *combining form* denoting head. — *adj* **ceph'alad** (*zool* and *anatom*) situated near, facing towards, or passing to the head. — *adj* **ceph'alate** having a head. — *adj* **cephal'ic** of or belonging to the head. — *n* a remedy for headache. — **-cephal'ic** and **-ceph'alous** *adjectival combining forms*. — *adj* **ceph'alous** having a head. — *n* **cephalag'ra** (Gr *agrā* a catching) gout in the head. — *n* **cephalal'gia** (Gr *algos* pain; *med*) headache. — *adj* **cephalal'gic**. — *n* **Cephalas'pis** (Gr *aspis* shield) an Upper Silurian and Old Red Sandstone genus of extinct fishes or fishlike animals (ostracoderms) with a head-shield. — *n* **cephalin** (*biochem*) a compound of phosphorus found in the brain and nervous tissue (also **kephalin**). — *n* **cephalī'tis** inflammation of the brain. — *n* **cephalizā'tion** or **-s-** in animal evolution, the specialization of the anterior end or head as the site of the mouthparts, sensory organs and principal ganglia of the central nervous system. — *n* **cephalocele** (*sef'əl-ə-sēl*; *med*) the protrusion of the membranes of the brain through a hole in the skull. — *n* **cephalochordate** (*-ō-kör'dāt*; Gr *chordē* cord) a member of the subphyllum *Cephalochordata*, of chordate fishlike animals (including the lancelets and amphioxus), having a persisting notochord projecting beyond the nerve cord to the end of the snout. — *n* **cephalom'etry** (*med*) the measurement of the foetal head in the uterus, by ultrasound or radiology; the measurement of the head by x-ray, *esp* in orthodontics. — *n* **ceph'alopod** (*-pod*; Gr *pous*, *podos* foot) a member of the **Cephalopoda** (*-op'od-ə*), the highest class of molluscs, *usu* large, exclusively marine animals (including cuttlefish, squid, octopus, etc), with the foot modified into arms or tentacles surrounding the mouth. — *n* **cephalospō'rin** any of a group of wide-spectrum antibiotics derived from the fungus *Cephalosporium*. — *n* **cephalōtho'rax** the fused head and thorax in some arthropods. — *n* **cephalotomy** (*kef-al-ot'ə-mi*; Gr *tomē* a cut) the dissection of the head. — **cephalic index** the ratio of the breadth to the length of the skull expressed as a percentage; **cephalic presentation** the usual position of a child in the womb just before birth, head downwards. [Gr *kephalē* head]

Cepheus *sē'fūs* or *-fē-əs*, *n* a northern constellation named after Andromeda's father, a mythical king of Ethiopia. — **Cepheid variable** (*sē'fi-id*; *astron*) any star of the type of the star *δ* Cephei ('classical' cepheid) or of a similar short-period star of the 'cluster type', from whose rhythmically varying brightness its distance can be inferred, this characteristic being important for the determination of distance scale in the universe. [Gr *Kēpheus*]

ceraceous. See **cere**.

ceramic *se-* or *ke-ram'ik*, *adj* pertaining to a ceramic or to ceramics; made of a ceramic. — *n* **ceram'ic** any product that is first shaped and then hardened by means of heat, or the material from which it is formed (*esp* traditional potter's clay, but also a large range of modern materials of quite different composition; (in *pl*) articles made of ceramic material. — *n sing* **ceram'ics** the potter's art; the science or study of ceramic materials. — *n* **cer'amal** a cermet. — *n* **ceram'ist** or **ceram'icist** a person who makes a scientific study of clays and other ceramic materials, or who puts them to practical use. — *n* **ceramog'raphy** the description or study of pottery. — *n* **cer'met** a material made from a combination of *cer*amic particles and a *met*al matrix, used in aeronautics and engineering; a type of electronic resistor made of such material. — **ceramic hob** a type of cooking surface on an elecric cooker, consisting of a flat ceramic plate with heating elements on the underside; **ceramic oxide** a combination of an inorganic material with oxygen having superconducting qualities at high temperature. [Gr *keramos* potter's earth]

cerargyrite *ser-är'jər-īt*, *n* a mineral consisting of silver chloride in crystalline form, horn silver. [Gr *keras* horn, and *argyros* silver]

cerasin *ser'ə-sin*, *n* the insoluble portion of cherry-tree gum. [L *cerasus*, Gr *kerasos* the cherry-tree]

cerastes *se-ras'tēz*, *n* any venomous viper of the genus *Cerastes*, *esp* the N African horned viper, with a horny process over each eye: — *pl* **ceras'tes**. — *n* **ceras'tium** any low ground-covering plant of the genus *Cerastium*, including the alpine mouse-ear chickweed, with horn-shaped capsules, and *Cerastium tomentosum*, snow-in-summer. [Gr *kerastēs*, from *keras* a horn]

cerat- *ser-ət-*, or **cerato-** *ser-ət-ō-*, *combining form* denoting horn. — See also **kerat-** or **kerato-**. [Gr *keras*, *-atos* horn]

cerate, **cerated**. See **cere**.

ceratitis. Same as **keratitis** (see under **keratin**).

ceratodus *ser-at'ō-dəs*, *n* (a fossil of) any extinct lungfish of the genus *Ceratodus*, of the Cretaceous and Triassic periods; the barramunda, an Australian lungfish, formerly included in the genus, but now classified *Neoceratodus*. [Gr *keras*, *-atos* horn, and *odous* tooth]

ceratoid *ser'ə-toid*, (*anatom*) *adj* having the form or texture of a horn. [Gr *keratoeidēs*, from *keras* horn, and *eidos* form]

ceratopsian *ser-ə-top'si-ən*, or **ceratopsid** *-top'sid*, *n* a member of a large group of bird-hipped, plant-eating dinosaurs of the late Cretaceous, having armoured neck-frills and horns or beaks, the best known example being *Triceratops*. — Also *adj*. [Gr *keras* horn, and *ops* face]

Ceratosaurus *ser-ə-tō-sö'rəs*, *n* a flesh-eating dinosaur of the Jurassic period. [Gr *keras* horn, and *sauros* lizard]

Cerberus *sûr'bər-əs*, *n* the monster that guarded the entrance to Hades, a dog with three heads (*mythol*); a grim, dangerous and watchful guardian. — *adj* **cerbē'rian** or more correctly **cerbē'rean**. — **a sop to Cerberus** see under **sop**. [L, from Gr *Kerberos*]

cercal. See **cercus**.

cercaria *sər-kā'ri-ə*, (*zool*) *n* the final larval stage of many trematode worms: — *pl* **cercariae**. — *adj* **cercā'rian**. [Gr *kerkos* a tail]

cercopid. See **froghopper**.

cercopithecid *sûr-kō-pith'ə-sid* or **cercopithecoid** *-koid*, *n* any of several Old World long-tailed monkeys of the genus *Cercopithecus*, including the Diana monkey, vervet, and moustached monkey. [Gr *kerkos* tail, and *pithēkos* monkey]

cercus *sûr'kəs*, *n* a tail-like appendage, *esp* a flexible sensory organ at the tip of the abdomen in certain arthropods: — *pl* **cerci'** (*-sē*). — *adj* **cer'cal** pertaining to a tail. [Gr *kerkos* tail]

cere *sēr*, *vt* to cover with wax; to wrap (a dead body) in cerecloth. — *n* the bare waxlike patch at the base of the upper part of a bird's beak. — *adj* **cērā'ceous** waxy. — *n* **cēr'ate** a medicated paste or stiff ointment containing wax (*med*). — *adj* **cēr'ated** (of a bird) having a cere. — *adj* **cēr'eous** waxy. — *adj* **cerif'erous** (*biol*) producing wax. — **cere'cloth** or **cerement** (*sēr'mənt*) a cloth dipped in melted wax formerly used to wrap a dead body in; any burial clothes. [L *cēra* wax]

cereal *sē'ri-əl*, *adj* of crops, etc, relating to edible grain. — *n* a grain used as food, such as wheat, barley, oats, etc;

a food prepared from such grain, *esp* any of the various breakfast foods. [L *cereālis* of grain or agriculture, from *Cerēs* Roman goddess of corn]

cerebellum *ser-i-bel'əm*, *n* the lower posterior part of the brain, whose function is to coordinate voluntary movements and maintain balance: — *pl* **cerebell'a** or **cerebell'ums**. — *adj* **cerebell'ar**, **cerebell'ic** or **cerebell'-ous**. [L, little brain, dimin of *cerebrum*]

cerebrum *ser'i-brəm*, *n* the front and larger part of the brain; loosely, the whole brain: — *pl* **cer'ebrums** or **cer'ebra**. — *adj* **cer'ebral** (also *sə-rē'brəl*) pertaining to the brain or the cerebrum; intellectual, as opposed to practical; of consonant sounds, produced by inverting the tip of the tongue on the palate (*phonetics*). — *n* **cer'ebralism** the theory that all mental operations originate in the brain. — *n* **cer'ebralist**. — *vi* **cer'ebrate** to think, to use the brain. — *n* **cerebrā'tion** action of the brain, *esp* unconscious. — *adj* **cer'ebric** (or *sər-eb'rik*) cerebral. — *adj* **cereb'riform** brain-shaped. — *n* **cerebrī'tis** inflammation of the cerebrum. — *n* **cer'e-broside** any of various lipids found in nerve tissue. — *adj* **cerebrōspīn'al** relating to the brain and spinal cord together. — *n* **cerebrotonia** (*-tō'ni-ə*; L *tonus* tone) the temperament associated with ectomorphic body type characterized by introversion and hypersensitivity. — *adj* **cerebrōton'ic**. — *adj* **cer'ebrōvas'cūlar** relating to the cerebrum and its blood vessels. — **cerebral cortex** the outer layers of the cerebral hemispheres associated with higher function of the nervous system; **cerebral death** see **brain death** under **brain**; **cerebral dominance** the tendency of one side of the brain to dominate certain functions, eg the left side of the cerebum produces right-handedness in the majority of people; **cerebral haemorrhage** haemorrhage of a blood vessel or blood vessels in the brain, *esp* the rupture of an artery; **cerebral hemisphere** one of the two lateral halves of the cerebrum; **cerebral palsy** a form of congenital paralysis marked by lack of muscular coordination, etc; **cer-ebrospinal fever** meningitis; **cerebrospinal fluid** the clear colourless fluid that surrounds the spinal cord and ventricles in the brain; **cerebrovascular accident** a sudden interruption of the blood supply to the brain, as in a cerebral haemorrhage. [L *cerebrum* the brain; prob cognate with Gr *karā* the head, and *krānion* the cranium]

cerement, **cereous**. See **cere**.

ceremony *ser'i-mə-ni*, *n* a rite; a formal act, custom, convention, etc; such rites, acts, etc regarded collectively; pomp, formality, etc. — *adj* **ceremonial** (*-mō'ni-əl*) relating to or of the nature of ceremony or a ceremony. — *n* an act that conforms with custom or convention; a set of formal rituals or actions; (a book containing) a prescribed order of service or ritual (*Christian relig*). — *n* **ceremō'nialism** adherence to formality or custom — *adv* **ceremō'nially**. — *adj* **ceremō'nious** given to ceremony; particular in observing formalities; precise, punctilious. — *adv* **ceremō'-niously**. — *n* **ceremō'niousness**. — **master of ceremonies** the person who directs the form and order of the ceremonies to be observed on some public occasion, eg a banquet; a compère; **stand on ceremony** to be punctilious about formalities; **without ceremony** informally; without adhering to conventions, customs, etc. [L *caerimōnia* sanctity]

Cerenkov radiation *cher-en'kof* (or *-yen'kof*) *rā-di-ā'shən*, (*phys*) *n* the bluish light emitted by a beam of charged particles passing through a transparent medium at a speed greater than the speed of light through that medium. [From P A *Cerenkov* (born 1904), Russian physicist]

Ceres *sē'rēz*, *n* the Roman name for the Greek Demeter, goddess of agriculture and corn; the largest asteroid (minor planet). [L *Cerēs*, *-eris*, prob from root of *creāre* to create]

ceresin or **ceresine** *ser'ə-sin* or *-sēn*, *n* a kind of hard, whitish wax prepared from ozokerite and used as a stubsitute for beeswax. [L *cera* wax]

cereus *sē'ri-əs*, *n* any of several species of columnar American cacti of the genus *Cereus*, having spiny stems with pronounced ribs, and including some species that grow to 9m (30ft) in height. [L *cēreus* waxen, wax-taper (from their stiff form)]

cerge *sûrj*, *n* a large wax candle burned before the altar. — Also **cierge** or **serge**. [OFr, from L *cēreus*, from *cēra* wax]

ceria, **ceric**. See **cerium**.

ceriferous. See **cere**.

Cerinthian *sər-in'thi-ən*, *adj* pertaining to *Cerinthus*, one of the earliest heretics in the Christian Church, against whose crude Gnosticism the Gospel of John was written, according to Irenaeus.

ceriph. See **serif**.

cerise *sər-ēz'*, also *-ēs'*, *n* and *adj* (a) light and clear purplish red. [Fr, cherry]

cerium *sē'ri-əm*, *n* a metallic chemical element (atomic no 58; symbol **Ce**), one of the rare-earth metals. — *n* **cē'ria** its oxide. — *adj* **cē'ric** or **ce'rous** of or containing cerium. — *n* **cē'rite** a mineral, its hydrous silicate. — **cerium metals** a group of rare-earth metals including cerium, lanthanum, neodymium, samarium, promethium and praseodymium. [Named from the asteroid *Ceres* discovered about the same time]

cermet. See under **ceramic**.

CERN *sûrn*, *abbrev*: *Conseil Européen pour la Recherche Nucléaire* (*Fr*), European Organization for Nuclear Research, now known as the European Laboratory for Particle Physics.

cerne *sûrn*, (*Shakesp*) a shortened form of **concern**.

cernuous *sûr'nū-əs*, (*bot*) *adj* (of flowers and buds) nodding, bowing down, drooping. [L *cernuus* inclined forwards]

cerograph *sē'rō-gräf*, *n* a writing on wax; an encaustic painting; printing by means of engraving on a plate spread with wax. — *adj* **cērographic** (*-graf'ik*) or **cērograph'ical**. — *n* **cērographist** (*-rog'rə-fist*). — *n* **cērog'raphy**. [Gr *kēros* wax, and *graphein* to write]

ceromancy *sē'rō-man-si*, *n* divination by dropping melted wax in water. [Gr *kēros* wax, and *manteiā* divination]

ceroon. A *NAm* spelling of **seron**.

ceroplastic *sē-rō-plas'tik*, *adj* pertaining to wax modelling; modelled in wax. — *n sing* **ceroplas'tics** the art of wax modelling. [Gr *kēros* wax, and *plastikos* plastic, from *plassein* to mould]

cerotic acid *si-rot'ik as'id*, *n* a fatty acid ($C_{26}H_{52}O_2$) found in beeswax and certain fats. [Gr *kēros* wax]

cerotype *sēr'ō-tīp*, (*printing*) *n* an engraving on a copper plate coated with wax used as a mould for preparing an electrotype printing plate. [Gr *kēros* wax, and **type**]

cerous. See **cerium**.

cerris *ser'is*, *n* the turkey oak (*Quercus cerris*). — *adj* **cerr'ial**. [L *cerreus*]

cert *n*. See **certain**.

cert. or **certif**. *abbrev*: certificate; certificated; certify.

certain *sûr'tn*, *adj* sure, confident; not to be doubted, indisputable; resolved; fixed, decided, determined; reliable, dependable; regular; inevitable; named or specified but not known; some (indeterminate number or quantity of). — *adv* **cer'tainly** without doubt, undoubtedly; in a resolved, fixed, etc manner. — *interj* yes, of course. — *n* **cer'tainty** (*slang abbrev* **cert**, sometimes in the phrase **dead cert**). — *n* **cer'titude** (a) certainty. — **a certain person** a person known but not specifically named, implying some degree of contempt; **a lady of a certain age** a woman who is no longer young; **for certain** assuredly, certainly; **in a certain condition** (*euphem*) pregnant; **make certain** see under **make**; **moral certainty** see under **moral**. [OFr, from L *certus*, from *cernere* to decide]

certes *sûr'tiz*, (*archaic*) *adv* certainly; truly. — **(by) my cer'tie** or **cer'ty** (*Scot*) assuredly. [Fr]

certif. See **cert**. (*abbrev*).

certificate *sər-tif'i-kāt* or *-kət*, *n* a written declaration, official or formal, of some fact; a printed statement of qualification(s) or recognized professional status. — *vt* to give a certificate to. — *adj* **cer'tifiable** (*-fī-ə-bl*) capable of being certified (*esp* as insane). — *adv* **cer'tifīably**. — *adj* **certif'icated** (of eg a teacher) holding a certificate of training and fitness. — *n* **certificā'tion**. — *n* **certif'icātory** a certificate. — Also *adj*. — *n* **cer'tifier** a person who certifies. — *vt* **cer'tify** to declare as true; to inform; to declare or confirm in writing; to declare (someone) insane; to refer by certiorari (*law*): — *pr p* **cer'tifying**; *pa p* **cer'tified**. — **certified cheque** a cheque on which a bank has guaranteed payment; **certified milk** milk certified as yielded by tuberculin-tested herds, fulfilling required conditions as to bacterial content, etc. [Fr *certificat*, from L *certificāre*, from *certus* certain, and *facere* to make]

certiorari *sûr-shi-ō-rā'rī*, (*law*) *n* a writ to call up the records of a lower court for consideration in the High Court of Justice. [LL *certiōrārī* to be informed of, from *certior*, compar of *certus* certain]

certitude. See **certain**.

certy. See **certes**.

cerulean or **caerulean** *si-rōō'li-ən*, *adj* sky-blue; dark-blue; sea-green. — *adj* **cerule** or (*Spenser*) **caerule** (*sēr'ūl*) sky-blue. — *adj* **cerū'leous**. — *n* **cerū'lein** (*-lē-in*) a coal-tar dyestuff, producing fast olive greens. [L *caeruleus* dark blue or green]

ceruloplasmin *si-rōō-lō-plaz'min*, *n* a protein in the blood that facilitates the storage and transport of copper. [L *caeruleus* dark blue and **plasmin**]

cerumen *si-rōō'men*, *n* the brownish-yellow secretion produced by glands in the outer ear, ear wax. — *adj* **ceru'minous**. [L *cēra* wax]

ceruse *sē'rōōs*, or *si-rōōs'*, *n* white lead used as a pigment. — *n* **cē'rusite** or **cē'russite** naturally-occurring lead carbonate. [Fr, from L *cērussa*, connected with *cēra*, Gr *kēros* wax]

cervelat *ser've-lä*, *n* a kind of smoked sausage, made of pork. [Fr, from Ital *cervellata*]

cervid *sûr'vid*, *n* and *adj* (of or relating to) one of the true deer of the family *Cervidae*, in which all the members (except the water deer) have antlers in the male animal. [L *cervus* a stag, and **-id**[1]]

cervine *sûr'vīn*, *adj* relating to deer; resembling deer; fawn-coloured. [L *cervīnus*, from *cervus* a stag]

cervix *sûr'viks*, *n* a technical name for the (back of the) neck; a necklike narrowing of an organ, *esp* the lower part of the uterus: — *pl* **cer'vixes** or **cer'vices** (*-sēz*). — *adj* **cervical** (*sûr'vi-kl*, *sər-vī'kl*). — *n* **cervici'tis** inflammation of the neck of the womb. — *n* **cervicography** the photographing of the neck of the womb to identify early signs of cancer. — **cervical screening** the routine and regular examination of women to facilitate the early identification of cancer of the cervix; **cervical smear** the collection of a sample of cells from the neck of the womb and the examination of these cells (**cervical cytology**) under a microscope, as an early test for cancer. [L *cervīx*, *cervīcis* neck]

Cesarean. A spelling (*esp NAm*) of **Caesarean**.

cesarevitch, **cesarewitch**, **cesarevna**. See **tsar**.

cesium. *NAm* spelling of **caesium**.

cespitose. See **caespitose**.

cess *ses*, (*obs*) *n* in UK, a tax, a local rate; in Ireland, the obligation by a local population to provide food, lodgings and supplies for the soldiers of the lord deputy. — *vt* to impose (a tax) or billet (soldiers) in this way. — **bad cess to** (*Anglo-Ir*) bad luck to. [Shortened from **assess**]

cessation *ses-ā'shən*, *n* a ceasing or stopping; a rest; a pause. [L *cessātiō*, *-ōnis*. See **cease**]

cesse *ses*, (*Spenser*) *vi*. Same as **cease**.

cesser *ses'ər*, (*law*) *n* the cessation of a term or liability when an obligation is fulfilled. [Fr *cesser* to cease]

cession *sesh'ən*, *n* a yielding up, ceding. — *n* **cess'ionary** someone to whom an assignment (of eg property) has been legally made. — **cessio** (*ses'i-ō* or *sesh'i-ō*) **bonō'rum** (*Scots law*) a debtor's surrender of his estate to his creditors in return for a judicial protection from imprisonment in respect of his debt, from 1880 a summary process in small bankruptcies, finally abolished 1913. [L *cēssiō bonōrum* the surrender of one's goods]

cesspit *ses'pit* or **cesspool** *-pōōl*, *n* a pit or pool for collecting sewage or filthy water. [Origin obscure]

c'est-à-dire *set-a-dēr* or *sāt*, (*Fr*) that is to say.

c'est la vie *se la vē* or *sā*, (*Fr*) that's life.

cestode *ses'tōd*, *n* any parasitic worm of the subclass *Cestoda*, including the tapeworm or bladderworm. — *n* **ces'toid** a ribbon-like cestode. — Also *adj*. — *n* and *adj* **cestoid'ean**. [Gr *kestos* a girdle, a strap, and *eidos* form]

cestos. See **cestus**[1].

Cestracion *ses-trā'si-on*, *n* a primitive type of shark represented by the Australian Port Jackson shark. [Perh Gr *kestrā* a kind of fish, or *kestros* sharp, and *akē* point]

cestui *set-ē'* or *sest'wē*, (esp *law*) *n* he, that one, used in such phrases as **cestui que trust** (*ki-trust*) a person entitled to the benefit of a trust, and **cestui que use** a person for whose benefit property is granted in trust to another. [OFr, dative of *cest* that]

cestus[1] or **cestos** *ses'təs*, *n* a girdle, *esp* that of Aphrodite (Venus) in classical mythology. [L, from Gr *kestos* girdle]

cestus[2] or **caestus** *ses'təs*, *n* an ancient Roman boxing glove loaded with metal. [L *caestus*]

cesura. See **caesura**.

cesure *sē'zūr*, (*Spenser*) *n* a break; interruption. [**caesura**]

CET *abbrev*: Central European Time.

cetacean *si-tā'shi-ən* or *-shyən*, *n pl* a member of the order Cetacea of aquatic mammals having streamlined fish-like form, including the toothed whales, or *Odontoceti* (sperm whales, bottle-noses, dolphins, etc) and the baleen whales, or *Mystacoceti* (right whale, hump-backs, rorquals). — Also *adj*. — *adj* **cetā'ceous**. — *n* **cete** (*sēt*) a whale or sea-monster. — *n* **cetol'ogy** the study of whales. [Gr *kētos* a sea-monster]

cetane *sē'tān*, (*chem*) *n* a colourless liquid hydrocarbon found in petroleum, used in determining the cetane number of diesel fuel. — **cetane number** or **cetane rating** a measure of the ignition quality of diesel engine fuel. [Gr *kētos* a sea-monster]

cete[1] *sēt*, *n* a collective noun for a group of badgers. [Poss L *coetus*, assembly]

cete[2]. See under **cetacean**.

ceterach *set'ər-ak*, *n* a member of the scale-fern genus *Ceterach*, including *C. officinarium*, the rusty-back fern. [Med L *ceterach*, from Ar *shītarakh*]

cetera desunt *set'ə-rə dē'sunt* or *kā'te-ra dā'sōōnt*, (*L*) the rest are missing.

ceteris paribus *set'ər-is par'i-bus* or *kā'te-rēs pa'ri-bōōs*, (*L*) other things being equal.

cetology. See **cetacean**.

cet. par. *abbrev*: ceteris paribus.

cetyl *sē'til*, (*chem*) *n* the univalent radical $C_{16}H_{33}$. — **cetyl alcohol** a waxy crystalline solid used in detergents and pharmaceuticals, so-called because compounds of it occur in spermaceti. [Gr *kētos* a sea-monster, and *hȳle* matter]

cetywall. See **setwall**.

cevadilla. See **sabadilla**.

cevapcici *che-vap-chi'chi*, *n pl* Yugoslavian kebabs of minced beef and pork flavoured with mint and paprika, formed into small sausages.

ceviche *sə-vē'chi*, (*Mexican*, etc *cookery*) *n* raw fish marinated in lime juice and served as an hors d'oeuvre. [Am Sp]

cevitamic acid *sē-vi-tam'ik a'sid*, *n* ascorbic acid, vitamin C. [The letter *c* and *vitamin*]

Ceylon *si-lon'*, *n* the name (until 1972) of the island of Sri Lanka. — *adj* and *n* **Ceylonese** (*se-* or *sē-lə-nēz'*). — *n* **cey'lonite** or **cey'lanite** see **pleonaste**. — **Ceylon moss** a red seaweed (*Gracilaria lichenoides*) of the E Indian Ocean.

CF *abbrev*: Chaplain to the Forces.

CF, **cf** or **c and f** *abbrev*: cost and freight.
Cf (*chem*) *symbol*: californium.
cf *abbrev*: *confer* (*L*), compare.
c.f. *abbrev*: centre-forward (*sport*).
c/f or **c.f.** (*bookkeeping*) *abbrev*: carried forward.
CFA *abbrev*: *Colonies Françaises d'Afrique*, French African Colonies; *Communauté financière africaine*, as in **CFA franc** (*abbrev* **CFAFr**) standard montary unit of various (former) French territories in Africa.
CFC *abbrev*: chlorofluorocarbon.
CFD *abbrev*: computational fluid dynamics.
CFE *abbrev*: College of Further Education; Conventional Forces in Europe (the subject of arms reduction talks held between the US, European nations and the Soviet bloc).
cfg *abbrev*: cubic feet of gas.
CFI, **cfi** or **cf and i** *abbrev*: cost, freight (and) insurance.
CFO *abbrev*: Chief Fire Officer.
CFOD. See **CAFOD**.
CFP *abbrev*: *Colonies Françaises du Pacifique*, French Pacific Colonies; Common Fisheries Policy (of the EEC); *Comptoirs français du Pacifique*, as in **CFP franc** (*abbrev* **CFPFr**) standard monetary unit of various French Pacific territories.
CFR *abbrev*: commercial fast reactor (in the nuclear industry).
cft *abbrev*: cubic feet (or foot).
CG *abbrev*: captain-general; Captain of the Guard; coastguard; Coldstream Guards; commanding general; consul general; *Croix de Guerre* (*Fr*), war decoration.
cg *abbrev*: centigram(s) or centigramme(s); centre of gravity.
CGBR *abbrev*: central government borrowing requirement.
cge *abbrev*: carriage. — **cge fwd** cariage forward; **cge pd** carriage paid.
CGI or **CGLI** *abbrev*: City and Guilds (of London) Institute.
CGM *abbrev*: Conspicuous Gallantry Medal.
CGPM *abbrev*: *Conférence Générale des Poids et Mesures* (*Fr*), General Conference on Weights and Measures.
CGS *abbrev*: centimetre-gram-second (also **cgs**); Chief of the General Staff.
CGT *abbrev*: capital gains tax (also **cgt**); *Confédération Général du Travail* (*Fr*), General Confederation of Labour (the largest French trade union).
CH *abbrev*: Companion of Honour; Switzerland (IVR; from L *Confederatio Helvetica*).
Ch. *abbrev*: Champion; Chaplain; Chapter; Chief; China; Chinese; Christ; Chronicles (*Bible*); Church.
ch *ch*, (*obs*) *pronoun* SW English dialect for **ich** I, fused with the verb, as **cham** I am, **chave** I have, **chill** I will. [ME *ich*, from OE *ic*]
ch. *abbrev*: chain (linear measure); chapter; chart; check (*chess*); chestnut; child; children; chirurgeon (*archaic*), surgeon; choir; church.
c.h. *abbrev*: central heating; centre half (*sport*); clearing house; club house; court house; customs house.
cha *chä*, *n* tea; char. [Chin *ch'a*; see **char**[4]]
chabazite *kab'ə-zīt*, *n* a mineral of the zeolite group, a white or colourless hydrated silicate of aluminium and calcium, found in rhombohedral crystals. [From a misreading of Gr *chalazios* a kind of stone, from *chalaza* hailstone]
Chablis *shablē'*, *n* a very dry white Burgundy wine made at *Chablis*, department of Yonne, in France.
chabouk *chä'bo͝ok*, *n* a horse-whip. [Pers *chābuk*]
chace. See **chase**[1].
cha-cha or **cha-cha-cha** *chä'-chä'* (*-chä'*), *n* a dance of Latin American origin, consisting of a series of short steps followed by a rhythmic hip-swaying shuffling movement; music for this dance.
chack *chak* or *chäk*, *n* (*Scot*) a snack; a snapping shut or pinching, as by a door or window. — *vt* to pinch or nip in such a way. [Imit]
chacma *chak'mə*, *n* a large baboon (*Papio ursinus*) of S and E Africa. [From Hottentot]
chaco. Same as **shako**.
chaconne *sha-* or *shə-kon'*, *n* an old Spanish dance *prob* originating in Mexico, with slow stately movement; its musical form, a series of variations on a ground bass, in triple time, appearing in vocal and instrumental music as well as in ballets. — Cf **passacaglia**. [Fr, from Sp *chacona*, from Basque *chucun* pretty]
chacun à son goût *shak-œ̃ a sɔ̃ go͞o*, (*Fr*) each person to his own taste. — Also **à chacun son goût**.
chad[1] *shad*, *n* a kind of fish. [See **shad**]
chad[2] *chad*, (*comput*) *n* the little bits of paper or cardboard punched out of paper tape or cards. [Origin uncertain]
Chad[1] *chad* or **Chadic** *chad'ik*, *n* a branch of the Afro-Asiatic language spoken in West and Central Africa. — *adj* **Chad'ic**. [Lake *Chad*]
Chad[2] *chad*, *n* (*usu* **Mr Chad**) a character in facetious sketches *esp* of the 1940s, portrayed as a bald head peering over a wall, with a caption beginning 'Wot no ...?', in protest at wartime shortages, etc. [Origin uncertain]
chadar, **chaddar**, **chaador chador**, **chuddah** or **chuddar** *chud'ə(r)*, *n* the large veil worn by Muslim and Hindu women, covering head and body; a cloth spread over a Muslim tomb. [Pers *chaddar*, Hindi *caddar* a square cloth]
chaenomeles *n* a shrub of the *Chaenomeles* genus of flowering shrubs, such as the japonica and flowering quince.
chaeta *kē'tə*, *n* a chitinous bristle on the body of the earthworm and other invertebrates: — *pl* **chaetae** (*kē'tē*). — *adj* **chaetif'erous** (*zool*) having bristles. — *n* **chaetodon** (*kē'tō-don*; Gr *odous*, *odontos* tooth) any fish of the tropical genus *Chaetodon* having slender teeth and making up the family **Chaetodon'tidae**. — *n* **chaetognath** (*kē'təg-nath*; Gr *gnathos* jaw) a coelomate, wormlike marine invertebrate, including the arrow-worm, having bristles round the mouth. — *n* **chaetopod** (*kē'tō-pod*; Gr *pous*, *podos* foot) a worm (such as the earthworm, lobworm, sea-mouse, etc) of the class **Chaetop'oda**, that moves with the help of bristles. [Gr *chaitē* hair, spine; cf **seta**]
chafe *chāf*, *vt* to heat, fret, irritate or wear by rubbing; to cause to fret or rage. — *vi* to heat, irritate, etc, by rubbing; to fret or rage (with *against* or *at*). — *n* irritation caused by rubbing. — *n* **chaf'er** (*obs*) a chafing-dish, a saucepan. — **chaf'ing-dish** a vessel for heating by hot coals, etc; a dish for cooking on the table; **chaf'ing-gear** mats, spun-yarn, battens, etc used on the rigging and spars of a ship to prevent damage by rubbing or chafing. [Fr *chauffer*, from L *calefacere*, from *calēre* to be hot, and *facere* to make]
chafer *chāf'ər*, *n* any of several kinds of beetle, *esp* of the Scarabaeidae, eg the cockchafer. [OE *cefer*; Du *kever*; Ger *Käfer*]
chaff *chäf* or *chaf*, *n* husks from corn that has been threshed or winnowed; chopped hay and straw used as animal feed or bedding; strips of metallic foil, bits of wire, etc, fired into or dropped through the air to deflect radar signals and so interfere with detection; rubbish, or worthless material; the dry bracts enclosing the flowers of some members of the daisy family; light banter, badinage. — *vt* to tease; to banter with. — *n* and *adj* **chaff'ing**. — *adv* **chaffingly**. — **chaff'-cutter** or **chaff'-engine** a machine for cutting up straw or hay. [OE *ceaf*; cf Du *kaf*]
chaffer *chaf'ər*, *vi* to bargain; to haggle about price; to sell, exchange, or bandy (*obs*). — *n* **chaff'erer** a haggler. — *n* **chaff'ery** buying and selling; haggling (*obs*). [ME *chapfare* a bargain, from OE *cēap* price, and *faru* way]
chaffinch *chaf'inch* or *-insh*, *n* a little songbird of the finch family, the male having a pinkish body and grey head with black and white markings. [**chaff** and **finch**]
chaffron. See **chamfrain**.
chaft *chaft* or *chäft*, (*Scot*) *n* (*usu* in *pl*) the jaw; the cheek. [ON *kjaptr*; cf Swed *kaft*, Dan *kieft*]

chagan *kä-gän'*, *n* an early form of **khan**.

Chagas' disease *shä'gəs di-zēz*, *n* a tropical disease transmitted by the parasitic microorganism *Trypanosoma cruzi*, and characterized by high fever and inflammation and swelling of the heart muscles, spleen, liver, etc. [From Carlos *Chagas* (1879–1934), Brazilian physician]

chagrin *shag'rin* or *shə-grēn'*, *n* a feeling of vexation, annoyance or embarrassment. — *vt* to vex, annoy or embarrass. — *adj* **chagrined'**. [Fr *chagrin* shagreen, rough skin, ill-humour]

chai or **chi** *chī*, fem of **chal**.

chain *chān*, *n* a series of links or rings passing through one another, used to restrain, support, pull, etc, or in jewellery; a number of things connected in series; a linked series, eg of house-buyers and -sellers; a mountain range; a string of islands; something that binds; a connected course or train (of events); a measure of 100 links, or 66 feet (see **Gunter's chain** under **gunter**); a measure of 100 feet (see **engineer's chain** at **engineer**); a series of shops, hotels, restaurants, etc under the same ownership or management; a number of atoms linked in succession (*chem*); a routine consisting of segments each of which uses the output of the preceding segment as input (*comput*); (in *pl*) fetters, bonds, confinement or restriction generally; (in *pl*) circular apparatus of metal links fitted to the wheels of a car to provide traction in icy conditions. — *vt* to fasten (also **chain up** or **down**); to fetter; to restrain; to measure, with chain or tape (*surveying*). — *adj* **chained** bound or fastened, as with a chain; fitted with a chain. — *adj* **chain'less** without chains; unfettered; unrestricted. — *n* **chain'let** a small chain. — **chain armour** chain mail; **chain bolt** a large bolt used to secure the chain-plates to the ship's side; **chain'brake** a cut-off safety device on a chainsaw, activated automatically if the chainsaw kicks back; **chain'-breaker** a method or device for resolving or avoiding the difficulties created by a chain of house-buyers and -sellers each awaiting action on the part of others earlier or later in the sequence; **chain bridge** a bridge suspended on chains; a suspension bridge; **chain cable** a cable made up of iron links; **chain drive** transmission of power by chain-gear. — *adj* **chain'-driven**. — **chain gang** a gang of convicts wearing leg-irons, *esp* chained together on an outside working party; **chain'-gear** or **chain'-gearing** gearing consisting of an endless chain and (generally) sprocket-wheels; **chain grate** a device for stoking a (*usu* industrial) furnace in which fuel is drawn into the furnace by means of a rotating chain; **chain harrow** a harrow made up of chainwork; **chain letter** a letter soliciting (among other things) the sending, by the recipient, of similar letters with or without a limit to other people; **chain lightning** forked or zigzag lightning; a strong or harsh-tasting whisky (*slang*); **chain locker** (*naut*) a compartment at the forward end of a ship for storing the anchor chain when the anchor is not in use; **chain mail** armour of small connected metal links, much used in Europe in the 12c and 13c; **chain'man** (*surveying*) an assistant to a surveyor who takes measurements with a chain; **chain moulding** (*archit*) moulding in the form of a chain; **chain pier** a pier supported by chains like a chain bridge. — *n pl* **chain'plates** (*naut*) iron plates bolted below the channels on a ship, to serve as attachments for the dead-eyes, through which the standing rigging or shrouds and backstays are secured. — **chain printer** (*comput*) a type of line printer with the characters mounted on a metal or plastic chain, forming a continuous loop; **chain pump** a pump consisting of an endless chain, *usu* with discs; **chain reaction** a process in which each reaction is in turn the stimulus of a further reaction; **chain reactor** a nuclear reactor; **chain rule** an arithmetical rule, so called from the terms of the problem being stated as equations, and connected, as if by a chain, so as to obtain by one operation the same result as would be obtained by a number of different operations in simple proportion; the rule for solving problems by compound proportion; **chain'saw** a power saw with cutting teeth linked in an endless chain; **chain'shot** two bullets or half-bullets fastened together by a chain, used formerly to destroy ships' rigging. — *vt* and *vi* **chain'-smoke** to smoke (cigarettes, etc) non-stop, often lighting each from the previous one. — **chain'-smoker**; **chain'stitch** a stitch in knitting or sewing resembling the links of a chain; **chain store** one of a series of shops, *esp* department stores, under the same ownership or management and located in different places; **chain'wheel** a toothed wheel, as on a bicycle, which meshes with a chain to transmit motion; **chain'work** work looped or linked like a chain; network. — **chain of command** a series of military or civic functionaries, each taking orders from the one immediately senior to himself. [OFr *chaeine*, from L *catēna*]

chaîné *shen-ā*, (*ballet*) *n* a series of small fast turns, often with the arms extended, used to cross a floor or stage. [Fr]

chair *chār*, *n* a movable seat for one person, with a back, *usu* four legs, and sometimes arms; the seat or office of someone in authority, eg a judge, a bishop, or the person presiding over any meeting; a chairperson; *orig* the seat from which a professor delivered his or her lectures; a professorship; the instrument or the punishment of death by electrocution (*informal*; with *the*); a support for a railway rail securing it to a sleeper. — *vt* to conduct (a meeting, etc) as chairperson; to carry publicly in triumph; to place in a seat of authority. — **chair'-bed** a chair capable of being turned into a bed. — *adj* **chair'borne** (*colloq*) working at a desk. — *adj* **chair'bound** unable to walk; confined to a wheelchair. — **chair'lift** a set of seats suspended from cables used to carry skiers, etc uphill; **chair'man** a person (male or female) who takes the chair, or presides at an assembly or meeting (also **chair'person**; *fem* **chair'woman**); **chair'manship**; **chair'-organ** a choir-organ (perhaps because it sometimes formed the back of the organist's seat); **chairperson**, **chairwoman** see under **chairman**. [Fr *chaire*, from L, from Gr *kathedrā*]

chaise *shāz*, *n* a light open carriage for one or more persons; a travelling carriage (see **post-chaise**); a chaise-longue. — **chaise'-longue'** (*-lɔ̃g'*) a couch with back at one end only and short armrest, designed for lying on. [Fr, a form of *chaire*; see **chair**]

chakra *chak'ra*, *n* amongst the Sikhs, a disc-shaped knife used as a missile; a discus representing the sun, as in portrayals of Hindu Gods; in yoga, a centre of spiritual power in the body. [Sans *cakra* wheel]

chal *chal*, *n* fellow; person: — *fem* **chai** or **chi** (*chī*). [Romany]

chalan or **challan** *chul'ən*, (*Ind*) *n* a way-bill; a pass; the sending up of an accused person before a magistrate; a form used when money due to a government department is paid, not to the department itself, but to the government Treasury. — Also *vt*. [Hindi *calan*]

chalaza *ka-lā'zə*, *n* in a bird's egg, one of two spiral chords of albumen that hold the yolk sac in position (*zool*); the base of the ovule (*bot*): — *pl* **chala'zas** or **chala'zae**. [Gr *chalaza* hail, lump]

chalazion *kə-lā'zi-ən*, (*med*) *n* a round painless cyst or swelling in the eyelid resulting from the blocking of a gland. — Also **meibomian cyst**. [Gr *chalaza* lump]

chalazogamy *kal-az-og'ə-mi*, (*bot*) *n* the entry of the pollen tube through the chalaza (opp to *porogamy*). — *adj* **chalazogamic** (*kəl-az-ō-gam'ik*). [See **chalaza** and **-gamy**]

chalcanthite *kal-kan'thīt*, *n* a blue mineral, $CuSo_4 5H_2O$, hydrated copper sulphate in crystalline form. [Gr *chalkos* copper, and *anthos* flower]

chalcedony *kal-sed'ə-ni*, or *kal'*, *n* a microcrystalline, white or bluish-white mineral composed of silica, *usu* of banded and translucent appearance and having a waxy lustre, a variety of quartz found in sedimentary rocks. — *adj* **chalcedonic** (*-si-don'ik*). — *n* **chalced'onyx** (or *-on'*) an agate of alternating white opaque and greyish translucent chalcedony. [Gr *chalkēdōn*, poss from *Chalcedon*, in Asia Minor]

chalcid *kal'sid*, *n* any small parasitic insect of the family Chalcididae, that lay their eggs inside the bodies of other insects, or, as with the **chalcid wasp**, within the seeds of plants. [Gr *chalkos* copper, from the metallic colouring of their bodies]

Chalcidian *kal-sid'i-ən*, *adj* pertaining to *Chalcis* in Euboea, or its people. — **Chalcidian alphabet** the alphabet used by Chalcidian settlers in S Italy and Sicily, from which the Latin alphabet developed.

chalco- *kal-kō*, *combining form* pertaining to or containing copper.

chalcocite *kal'kə-sīt*, *n* a greyish-black mineral, Cu_2S, sulphide of copper of orthorhombic crystalline structure. [Gr *chalkos* copper, and **-ite**]

chalcography *kal-kog'rə-fi*, *n* the art of engraving on copper or brass. — *n* **chalcog'rapher** or **chalcog'raphist**. — *adj* **chalcograph'ic** or **chacograph'ical**. [Gr *chalkos* copper, and *graphein* to write]

Chalcolithic *kal-kō-lith'ik*. Same as **Aeneolithic**. [Gr *chalkos* copper, and *lithos* stone]

chalcopyrite *kal-kō-pī'rīt*, *n* copper pyrites, $CuFeS_2$, a yellow double sulphide of copper and iron, the commonest ore of copper. [Gr *chalkos* copper, and **pyrite**]

Chaldaic *kal-dā'ik* or **Chaldee** *kal'dē*, *adj* relating to *Chaldaea*, an ancient region of S Babylonia. — *n* the language of the Chaldaeans; an inhabitant of the ancient region of Chaldaea; a soothsayer (*rare*); a member of the Chaldaean church. — *n* **chal'dāism** a Chaldaic idiom. — *adj* **Chaldae'an** or **Chalde'an** (*-dē'ən*) Chaldaic. — *n* a native of Chaldaea.

chalder *chöl'dər*, *n* an old Scottish dry measure, containing 16 bolls. [Prob a form of **chaldron**]

chaldron *chöl'drən*, *n* an old unit of capacity, equal to 36 heaped bushels (= $25\frac{1}{2}$cwt). [Fr *chaudron*; see **cauldron**]

chalet *shal'ā* (the spelling **châlet** is wrong), *n* a summer hut used by Swiss herdsmen in the Alps; a wooden villa; a small house, *usu* of wood, built for use by holidaymakers, etc. [Fr]

chalice *chal'is*, *n* a drinking cup or bowl; a (*usu* gold or silver) communion-cup; a cup-shaped flower (*bot*). — *adj* **chal'iced** (*bot*) (of flowers) cup-like. [OFr *chalice*, from L *calix*, *calicis*; cf Gr *kylix* a cup; **calyx** is a different word]

chalicothere *kal'i-kō-thēr*, *n* a member of an extinct group of large odd-toed animals of the Tertiary period, typically having a horse-like head and feet bearing three large claws. [New L, small stone beast, from Gr *chalix* pebble, and *thērion*, dimin of *thēr* beast]

chalk *chök*, *n* a white soft rock, composed of finely-grained calcium carbonate, chiefly minute fragments of fossil shells and organic remains; a substitute for this used for writing, etc; a piece of this. — *vt* to write, rub or mark with chalk; to fertilize (land) with chalk. — *vi* of paint, to become chalky. — *n* **chalk'iness**. — *adj* **chalk'y**. — **chalk'board** (*esp NAm*) a blackboard; **chalk'face** (*colloq*, *usu* in the phrase **at the chalkface**) in the classroom, as the centre of a teacher's activities; **chalk'pit** a pit from which chalk is quarried; **chalk'stone** a stone or piece of chalk; one of the white concretions that form round the joints in chronic gout, a tophus; **chalk talk** (*NAm*) an informal talk or lecture using explanatory notes and diagrams on a blackboard. — **as like** (or **as different**) **as chalk and cheese** completely unalike; **by a long chalk** by a considerable distance or degree; **chalk and talk** the formal, traditional teaching method that relies on oral instruction and use of the blackboard; **chalking the door** (*hist*) in Scotland, a form of warning tenants to remove from burghal tenements; a method of giving tenants notice to quit; **chalk out** to trace out, as with chalk, to outline (a plan, etc); **chalk up** to make a special (*esp* mental) note of; to record (a score, etc); to charge or ascribe to (a person or to a person's account, etc); **not know** (or **can't tell**) **chalk from cheese** (*usu derog*) to be incapable of seeing, or unable to distinguish between, important differences because of lack of knowledge or judgement; **the Chalk** (*geol*) the uppermost part of the Cretaceous system in England. [OE *cealc*, from L *calx* limestone]

challah *hä'lə*, *n* Jewish bread, *usu* in the form of a plaited loaf, eaten to celebrate the Sabbath. [Heb *hallāh*]

chalan. See **challan**.

challenge *chal'inj*, *vt* to summon (someone) to settle a matter by fighting or by any kind of contest; to subject to stress, examination or test; to stimulate; to accuse; to object to; to dispute (a statement, judgement, etc); to administer a challenge to (*med*). — *vi* (of a hunting dog or hound) to show that a scent has been picked up by emitting a howl or cry. — *n* a summons to a contest of any kind; a calling into question of anyone or anything; an objection to a juror; the demand for identification and authority made by a sentry; an accusation or charge; a claim; a difficulty which stimulates interest or effort; a task, undertaking, etc to test one's powers and capabilities to the full; the administration to an immunized person or animal of a substance which causes allergic reaction or infection, in order to test the effectiveness of immunization (*med*). — *adj* **chall'engeable** that may be challenged. — *adj* **challenged** (*esp NAm*) handicapped or impaired, as in *physically challenged*. — *n* **chall'enger** a person who challenges to a combat or contest of any kind; a claimant; a person who objects or calls someone or something into question. — *adj* **chall'enging**. — *adv* **chall'engingly**. — **challenge to the polls** (*law*) an objection to a person or persons selected to serve on a jury, or **challenge to the array**, to the whole body of jurors. [OFr *chalenge* a dispute, claim, from L *calumnia* a false accusation, from *calvī* or *calvere* to deceive]

challis *chal'is*, *shal'is* or shal'i, or **challie** *shal'i*, *n* a soft glossless silk or lightweight fabric made of wool, cotton or synthetic fibres. — Also **shall'i**. [Origin uncertain]

chalone *kāl'* or *kal'ōn*, *n* one of a group of chemicals occurring in animal tissues, whose action inhibits the growth and differentiation of cells in the tissue. — *adj* **chalon'ic**. [Gr *chalaein* to relax]

chalumeau *shal-ū-mō'* or *shal-ü-mō'*, *n* an early rustic reed instrument that developed into the clarinet; now applied to the lowest register of the clarinet: — *pl* **chalumeaux** (*-mōz'*). [Fr, from OFr *chalemel*, from LL *calamellus*, dimin of *calamus* a pipe, a reed]

chalutz *hä'lo͞ots*, *n* a member of the early group of immigrants to Israel that established and worked the first kibbutzim (agricultural settlements). [Heb *halutz* pioneer]

chalybean *kal-ib-ē'ən*, or *ka-lib'i-ən*, (*metallurgy*) *adj* tempered. — *adj* **chalyb'eate** containing iron compounds. — *n* a water or other liquid, *esp* a drug, containing iron salts. — *n* **cha'lybite** siderite (qv). [Gr *chalyps*, *chalybos* steel, or *Chalyps* one of the *Chalybes*, a nation in Pontus famous for steel-making]

cham[1] *kam*, *n* an *obs* form of **khan**; an autocrat.

cham[2]. See **ch**.

chamade *shə-mäd'*, (*military hist*) *n* a drum or trumpet call inviting an enemy to parley or surrender. [Fr]

chamaeleon. See **chameleon**.

chamaephyte *kam'i-fīt*, (*bot*) *n* a woody or herbaceous plant that produces buds close to the ground. [Gr *chamai* on the ground, and **-phyte**]

Chamb. *abbrev*: Chamberlain.

chamber *chām'bər*, *n* a room; the place where an assembly meets; a house of a legislature, eg the French Chamber of Deputies; an assembly or body of people met for some purpose, such as a chamber of commerce; a hall of justice; a compartment, an enclosed space; a cavity; a chamber pot; a compartment in a gun where the bullet or cartridge is placed prior to firing; a small cannon (*archaic*); (in *pl*) a suite of rooms occupied separately, *esp* by lawyers; (in *pl*) a judge's room for hearing cases not taken into court. — *vt* to put in a chamber; to confine. — *vi* to be wanton (*archaic*). — *adj*

cham'bered confined; having rooms or space separated by a succession of walls; (of a shell) having partitions that form a chamber or chambers. — *n* **cham'berer** a person who plots or intrigues (*archaic*); a gallant, a lover (*archaic*). — *n* **cham'bering** (*Bible*) lewd or wanton behaviour. — **chamber concert** a concert of chamber music; **chamber council** (*Shakesp*) a private or secret council; **chamber counsel** or **chamber counsellor** a counsel who gives his advice privately, but does not plead in court; **chambered nautilus** see **pearly nautilus**; **cham'ber-lye** (*archaic*) urine; **cham'bermaid** a girl or woman employed to clean bedrooms in hotels, etc; formerly, and still in US, a housemaid; **chamber music** music, performed by a small group such as a quartet, suitable for a room rather than a theatre or a large hall; **chamber of commerce** (sometimes with *caps*) a group of businesspeople working together to promote local trade; **chamber orchestra** a small orchestra for the performance of chamber music; **chamber organ** a small organ suitable for a room; **cham'berpot** a container for urine, etc, used in a bedroom; **chamber practice** the business of a chamber counsel. [Fr *chambre*, from L *camera*, from Gr *kamarā* a vault, a room]

chamberlain *chām'bər-lin*, *n* an officer appointed by a monarch, nobleman or corporation, to perform domestic and ceremonial duties or to act as factor, steward or treasurer. — *n* **cham'berlainship**. — **Lord Chamberlain** an officer of high standing in the royal household, having control over all the officers and servants 'above stairs', except those of the bedchamber, over the establishment attached to the Chapel Royal, and the physicians, surgeons, and apothecaries of the household; **Lord Great Chamberlain** a hereditary officer who is in in charge of the palace of Westminster and to whom on solemn occasion the keys of Westminster Hall and of the Court of Requests are delivered. [OFr *chambrelenc*; OHGer *chamerling*, from L *camera* a chamber, and **-ling**]

Chambertin *shā-ber-tẽ*, *n* a dry red Burgundy from the vineyard of that name near Dijon.

chambranle *shā-brāl*, (*archit*) *n* a decoration around the frame of a doorway, fireplace or other opening. [Fr]

chambray *shŏm'brā*, *n* a fine cotton or linen fabric, with interwoven white and coloured threads. [Orig US; related to **cambric**]

chambré *shā-brā*, (*Fr*) *adj* (of wine) at, or brought to, room temperature.

chameleon or **chamaeleon** *kə-mēl'yən*, *n* a small African lizard with a prehensile tail and tongue, eyes capable of independent movement and the ability to change colour to blend with its surroundings; an inconstant, changeable, or readily adaptable person (*fig*). — Also *adj*. — *adj* **chameleonic** (*-i-on'ik*) and **chamel'eon-like**. [L *chamaeleōn*, from Gr *chamaileōn*, from *chamai* (cf L *humī*) on the ground (ie dwarf), and *leōn* a lion]

chamelot *cham'* or *kam'e-lot*, (*Spenser*) *n*. Same as **camlet**.

chamfer *cham'fər*, *n* a bevel or slope made by paring off the edge or corner of a *usu* right-angled surface; a groove, channel or furrow. — *vt* to cut or grind off bevel-wise (eg a corner); to channel or make furrows upon; to flute (eg a column). — *adj* **cham'fered** bevelled; furrowed, grooved, wrinkled. [Fr *chanfrein*, from OFr *chanfraindre*, appar from *chant fraindre*, from L *cantum frangere* to break the edge or side]

chamfrain *cham'frən*, *n* a piece of leather or plate of steel to protect the face of a horse in battle. — Also **cham'fron** or **chaf'fron**. [Fr *chanfrein*; origin unknown]

chamiso *shə-mē'sō* or **chamise** *shə-mēz'*, *n* a rosaceous shrub (*Adenostoma fasciculatum*) of California: — *pl* **chami'sos** or **chamis'es**. — *n* **chamisal'** a dense thicket of chamisos. [Am Sp *chamiza* cane]

chamlet *cham'* or *kam'let*, *n*. Same as **camlet**.

chammy. See **chamois**.

chamois *sham'wä*, *n* a goatlike antelope (*Rupicapra rupicapra*) inhabiting high mountains in southern and central Europe (*pl* **cham'ois**); a pale greyish brown colour; (*sham'i*) a soft pliant leather *orig* made from its skin (also **chammy**, **shammy** or **chamois** etc **leather**). [Fr, perh from Swiss Romanic; cf Ger *Gemse* a chamois]

chamomile. See **camomile**.

champ[1] *champ*, *vi* to make a snapping or munching noise with the jaws while chewing. — *vt* to bite or chew; to munch; to crush; to mash. — *n* the act of champing; (*esp* in N Ireland) a dish made of potatoes, leeks and spring onions. — **champ at the bit** (of a horse) to gnaw at the bit nervously or impatiently; to show signs of impatience while waiting for something to begin. [Poss onomatopoeic; connected with **jam**[2]]

champ[2] *champ*, (*heraldry*) *n* field. [Fr]

champ[3] *champ*, (*slang*) *n* short form of **champion**.

champac. See **champak**.

champagne *sham-pān'*, *n* a white sparkling wine, strictly from *Champagne* in France (sometimes coloured pink); the pale yellowish-white colour of white champagne; loosely, a wine similar to that from Champagne. — **champagne socialist** (*disparagingly*) a person whose comfortable or extravagant standard of living belies his or her professed socialist politics.

champaign *cham'pān'* or *sham-pān'*, *adj* level, open. — *n* an expanse of open level country. [Doublet of **campaign**, from OFr *champaigne*, from L *campānia* a plain]

champak or **champac** *chum'puk* or *cham'pak*, *n* an E Indian tree (*Michelia champaca*) of the magnolia family, with oppressively scented yellow flowers, regarded as sacred by Hindus. [Hindi]

champart *shā-pär*, *n* the division of the produce of land, the right of the feudal lord. [Norman Fr, from L *campī pars* part of the field]

champers *sham'pərz*, (*colloq*) *n* champagne.

champerty *cham'pər-ti*, (*law*) *n* a contract, unenforceable in law but not a criminal offence, in which an outside party agrees to finance a litigant's action in return for a share of the proceeds. — *adj* **cham'pertous**. [See **champart**]

champignon *sham'pin-yɔ̃*, *n* a mushroom or other edible fungus, *esp* the fairy-ring champignon (*Marasmius oreades*). [Fr]

champion *cham'pi-ən*, *n* someone who defends a cause; a successful combatant; a person who fights in single combat for himself or for another (*hist* or *archaic*); (in sports) a competitor who has excelled all others; anything, eg an animal or cultivated plant, that wins first place in a show; a hero. — *adj* acting or ranking as champion, first; excellent (*colloq*). — *adv* (*dialect*) excellently. — *vt* to challenge (*obs*); to defend; to support. — *n* **cham'pioness** (*rare*). — *n* **cham'pionship** the position of honour gained by being champion; a contest held to decide who is the champion; the act of championing a cause. [Fr, from LL *campiō*, *-ōnis*, from L *campus* a plain, a place for games]

champlevé *shā-lə-vā*, *n* a type of enamel work in which vitreous powders are laid in channels cut in a metal base. — Also *adj*. [Fr]

Champs Elysées *shā-zā-lē-zā*, (*Fr*) Elysian Fields (Elysium); also a famous open space and avenue in Paris.

Chanc. *abbrev*: Chancellor; Chancery.

chance *chäns*, *n* that which happens or results fortuitously, or without assignable cause; fortune; an unexpected event; risk; opportunity; possibility of something happening; (sometimes in *pl*) probability; (in *pl*) misfortunes (*archaic*). — *vt* to risk. — *vi* to happen; (with *up* or *on*) to happen to find or meet. — *adj* happening by chance. — *adv* perchance. — *adj* **chance'ful** full of risk or danger (*archaic*); full of chance(s). — *adj* **chance'less** without an opportunity. — *n* **chanc'er** (*colloq*) an unscrupulous person prepared to seize any opportunity to make money or for his or her own advancement, an opportunist. — *adj* **chanc'y** or **chanc'ey** risky, uncertain; lucky, safe (*Scot*). — **chance'-comer** someone who arrives by chance or unexpectedly. — **by chance** accidentally; **chance one's**

arm to take a chance, often recklessly or with little hope of success; **chance upon** or **on** to find or come across by chance; **chance would be a fine thing** (*colloq*) some hope!; **even chance** equal probability for or against; **how chance?** (*Shakesp*) how does it happen that?; **no chance** or **not a chance** (*colloq*) that will not happen or succeed; **stand a good chance** to have a reasonable expectation; **take one's chance** to accept what happens; to risk an undertaking; **the chances are** it is probable or likely; **the main chance** the chief object or best opportunity (*esp* in the phrase **have an eye to the main chance** to be aware of opportunity for self-enrichment). [OFr *cheance*, from LL *cadentia*, from L *cadere* to fall]

chancel *chän'sl*, *n* the eastern part of a church, *orig* separated from the nave by a screen of latticework to prevent general access to the altar, sanctuary and choir. [OFr, from L *cancellī* lattices]

chancellor *chän'səl-ər*, *n* a court secretary (*hist*); a chief minister; the president, or a judge, of a court of chancery or other court; the official who keeps the registers of an order of knighthood; the titular or (*US*) active head of a university; the foreman of a jury (*Scot*). — *n* **chan'cellorship**. — *n* **chan'cellery** or **chan'cellory** the position, department, etc of a chancellor; the office attached to an embassy or consulate. — **chancellor of a cathedral** an officer who had charge of the chapter library, custody of the common seal, superintendence of the choir practices, and headship of the cathedral schools; **chancellor of a diocese** an ecclesiastical judge uniting the functions of vicar-general and official principal, appointed to assist the bishop in questions of ecclesiastical law, and hold his courts for him; **Chancellor of the Exchequer** the chief minister of finance in the British government; **Lord Chancellor** or **Lord High Chancellor** the Speaker of the House of Lords, head of the judiciary of England and Wales, and keeper of the Great Seal. [Fr *chancelier*, from LL *cancellārius* orig an officer that had charge of records, and stood near the *cancelli* (L), cross-bars surrounding the judgement seat]

chance-medley *chäns-med'li*, *n* unintentional homicide, *usu* resulting from a sudden violent dispute, in which the killer is not entirely without blame (*law*); action with an element of chance. [OFr *chance medlée* mingled chance]

Chancery *chän'sər-i*, *n* formerly, the highest court of justice next to the House of Lords, presided over by the Lord High Chancellor, *now* a division of the High Court of Justice; a court of public record generally; the office of a chancellor; (without *cap*) the political office in an embassy or legation (*UK diplomatic*). — **Chancery Office** in Scotland, an office in the General Register House at Edinburgh, managed by a director, in which all royal charters of novodamus, patents of dignities, gifts of offices, remissions, legitimations, presentations, commissions, and other writs appointed to pass the Great and Quarter Seals are recorded; **in chancery** (of an estate, etc) in litigation; (of a wrestler's or boxer's head) held firmly under his adversary's arm (*slang*); hence, in an awkward or helpless predicament (*slang*). [Fr *chancellerie*]

chancre *shang'kər*, (*med*) *n* the hard nodular swelling that develops in the primary stage of syphilis. — *n* **chanc'roid** a sexually transmitted disease characterized by ulceration of the genital organs and enlarged lymph nodes in the groin. — Also called **soft chancre**. — *adj* **chanc'roidal**. — *adj* **chanc'rous**. [Fr; a form of **canker**]

chancy. See **chance**.

chandelier *shan-di-lēr'*, *n* an ornamental lighting fixture, suspended from the ceiling and often branched, for holding several lights. [Fr, from LL *candēlāria* a candlestick, from L *candēla* a candle]

chandelle *shan-del'* or (*Fr*) *shã-del*, *n* a sharp upward turn of an aircraft using momentum to achieve the maximum rate of climb. — *vi* to perform this manoeuvre. [Fr, candle]

chandler *chand'lər*, *n* a maker of candles; a dealer in candles, oil, soap, etc; a dealer in a specified type of goods (as in *corn-chandler*, *ship-chandler*). — *n* **chand'lering**. — *adj* **chand'lerly**. — *n* **chand'lery** the business of, premises of, or goods sold by a chandler. [Fr, from LL *candēlārius* a candle-maker, from L *candēla* a candle]

Chandler's wobble *chand'lər(z) wob'l*, *n* the very small displacement of the earth's axis of rotation which causes variation in latitude and longitude. [S C *Chandler* (1846–1913), American astronomer]

Chandrasekhar limit *chan-drə-sē'kər lim'it*, (*astron*) *n* the upper limit of mass for a White Dwarf. [S *Chandrasekhar* (born 1910), Indian-American astrophysicist]

change *chānj*, *vt* to alter or make different; to give or receive for another or for an equivalent; to cause to move or to pass from one state to another; to exchange or replace. — *vi* to undergo change; to change one's clothes or transfer from (one bus, train, etc) to another. — *n* the act of changing; alteration or variation of any kind; exchange (*archaic*); fickleness (*archaic*); a shift; variety; money given for money of a different kind, or in adjustment of a payment; coins of low value (*collectively*); satisfaction (*colloq*); an exchange (now *usu* **'change**). — *n* **changeabil'ity** or **change'ableness** fickleness; the power of being changed. — *adj* **change'able** subject or prone to change; fickle; inconstant; able to or capable of change; showing variation of colour. — *adv* **change'ably**. — *adj* **change'ful** full of change; changeable. — *adv* **change'fully**. — *n* **change'fulness**. — *adj* **change'less** without change; constant. — *n* **change'ling** a surreptitious substitute; a child substituted for another, *esp* one supposed to be left by the fairies; hence, an undersized crabbed child; a half-witted person (*archaic*); a person apt to change (*archaic*). — *n* **chāng'er** someone or something that changes the form of anything; a person employed in changing or discounting money (*obs*). — **change'-house** (*Scot*) a small inn or alehouse; **change'over** transition to a new system, position or condition; the act or process of passing over, exchanging or transferring from one to another; **change point** (*surveying*) a staff station to which two sights are taken, a foresight and a backsight (also called **turning point**); **change-ringing** see **ring the changes** below. — **change colour** to blush or turn pale; **change down** (*autos*) to change to a lower gear; **change face** (*surveying*) to rotate a theodolite telescope about its horizontal axis so as to change the sighting from left to right or vice versa; **change front** (*military*) to change the direction of fire of (troops, artillery, etc); to alter one's opinion; **change gear** to select a higher or lower gear (*autos*); to increase or decrease the pace of activity (*fig*); **change hands** to be transferred from one owner to another; **change of heart** a change of attitude, viewpoint or opinion, often resulting in the reversal of a decision; **change of life** the time of a woman's life at which menstruation is about to cease, the menopause; **change of state** (*phys*) any change in the state of matter, eg from solid to liquid, liquid to gas, etc; **change oneself** (now only *Scot*) to change one's clothes; **change one's mind** to form a different opinion; **change one's tune** to change one's attitudes or opinions; to change one's manner of speaking; **change up** (*autos*) to change to a higher gear; **get no change out of** (*colloq*) to be unsuccessful in attempts to obtain concessions, information, cooperation, etc from (a person or organization); **put the change on** (*old* and *dialect*) to delude or trick; **ring the changes** to go through all the possible permutations in ringing a peal of bells (*n* **change'-ringing**); to perform a repeated action or actions in varying ways, order, etc; **small change** (*collectively*) coins of low value; a petty thing (*colloq*). [Fr *changer*, from L *cambīre* to barter]

chank *changk* or **chank-shell** *changk'-shel*, *n* the shell of several species of Turbinella, gasteropod molluscs of the E Indian seas, sliced into bangles for Hindu women. [Hindi *chankh*; cf **conch**]

channel[1] *chan'l*, *n* the bed of a stream of water; a strait or narrow sea; a navigable passage through a body of water; a passage for conveying a liquid; a groove or furrow; a gutter; means of passing or conveying; a spiritual medium (also **chann'eler**); gravel, shingle (*Scot*; also **channer**); (in *pl*) means of communication; a one-way path for a signal; a physical path for data, eg between a central processing unit and a peripheral device (*comput*); a narrow range of frequencies, part of a frequency band, for the transmission of radio and television signals without interference from other channels. — *vt* to make a channel; to furrow; to convey (through); to direct (into a particular course; *lit* and *fig*): — *pr p* **chann'elling**; *pa t* and *pa p* **chann'elled**. — *vt* **chann'elize** or **-ise** to create or provide a channel for; to direct or convey through a channel. — *adj* **chann'elled**. — **channel seam** a seam on clothing outlined by stitching running along both sides; **channel seaming**; **channel stone** or **channel stane** (*Scot*) a curling-stone; **channel surfing** (*colloq*) moving rapidly from one TV channel to another by using the remote control, zapping. — **channel of distribution** (*marketing*) the means by which a product reaches the consumer from the producer, eg through wholesalers, retailers, etc (also **distribution channel**); **the Channel** the English Channel. [OFr *chanel*, *canel*, from L *canālis* a canal]

channel[2] *chan'l*, (*naut*) *n* a flat piece of wood or iron projecting horizontally from a ship's side to spread the various shrouds (*fore*, *main*, and *mizzen* channels) and keep them clear of the bulwarks. [For *chain-wale*]

chanoyu *chä'no-ū*, *n* a Japanese tea ceremony. [Jap, hot water for tea]

chanson *shã'sɔ̃*, *n* a song. — *n* **chansonette** (*-son-et'*) a little song, a ditty. — *n* **chansonnier** (*-son'ē-ā*) a collection of songs, *esp* old French; a cabaret performer of, *esp* satirical, songs. — **chanson de geste** (*də zhest*) an old French epic poem, *usu* celebrating the exploits of knights. [Fr]

chant or (*rare*) **chaunt** *chänt*, *vt* to recite in a singing manner; to intone repetitiously or rhythmically; to sing; to celebrate in song. — *n* song; melody; a kind of church music, in which prose is sung; a slogan spoken or sung in a repetitious or rhythmic manner. — *n* **chant'er**, **chaunt'er** or **chant'or** a singer; a precentor; (in a bagpipe) the pipe with fingerholes, on which the melody is played. — *n* **chant'ress** or **chaunt'ress**. — *n* **chant'ry** or **chaunt'ry** an endowment, or chapel, for the chanting of masses. — *n* **chanty** see **shanty**[2]. [Fr *chanter*, from L *cantāre*, from *canere* to sing]

chantage *shã-täzh'*, *n* blackmail, *esp* the extortion of money so as not to make scandalous facts public. [Fr]

chanterelle[1] *shan-* or *shã-tər-el'*, *n* the treble string of a musical instrument, such as a violin or lute. [Fr, from L *cantāre* to sing]

chanterelle[2] or **chantarelle** *chan-tər-el'*, *n* a yellowish edible fungus (*Cantharellus cibarius*). [Fr, dimin from Gr *kantharos* cup]

chanteuse *shan'to͞os* or *-to͞oz*, also *shã-tøz*, *n* a female nightclub singer. [Fr]

chantey. See **shanty**[2].

chanticleer *chant'i-klēr* or *-klēr'*, *n* a cock. [From the name of the cock in the old fable of *Reynard the Fox*, from OFr *chanter* to sing, and *cler* clear]

chantie. See **shanty**[2].

Chantilly *shan-ti'li* or *shã-tē-yē*, *n* a silk or linen ornamental lace, black or white, having a delicate floral or scrolled pattern. — Also **Chantilly lace** (*lās*). — *adj* (of cream) sweetened and whipped, and *usu* flavoured with vanilla; prepared or served with such cream. [From *Chantilly*, France, where the lace was first made]

chantor, **chantress**, **chantry**. See **chant**.

chanty[1]. See **shanty**[2].

chanty[2] *chan'ti*, (*Scot slang*) *n* a chamber pot. [Origin unknown]

Chanukah or **Chanukkah**. See **Hanukkah**.

chaos *kā'os*, *n* the state of matter before the universe was reduced to order; disorder; shapeless mass. — *n* **chaol'ogy** the study of chaos or of chaos theory. — *adj* **chaot'ic** confused. — *adv* **chaot'ically**. — **chaos theory** the theory that apparently random phenomena observed in various branches of science result from complex dynamic underlying principles. [Gr]

chap[1] *chap*, *vi* to crack; to strike, of a clock, etc, or to knock at a door (*Scot*). — *vt* to cause to crack or divide. — *n* a crack; an open crack or split in the skin, caused by exposure to cold; a knock (*Scot*). — *adj* **chap'less**. — *adj* **chapped** cracked, of a heavy soil in dry weather, or of the skin in cold weather; cut short. — *adj* **chapp'y**. — **chap'stick** a small stick of a substance for soothing chapped lips. [ME *chappen*; cognate with Du and Ger *kappen*]

chap[2] *chap*, (*colloq*) *n* a man or boy, a fellow: — *fem* (*facetious*) **chap'ess** or **chapp'ess**. — *n* **chapp'ie** a familiar *dimin* of **chap**. — **chap'book** a book or pamphlet of popular stories, etc, such as was formerly hawked by chapmen or pedlars; **chap'man** a person who buys or sells (*archaic*); an itinerant dealer; a pedlar. [OE *cēap* trade, *cēapman* trader; cf **cheap**; Ger *kaufen*, *Kaufmann*]

chap[3] *chap*, *n* a chop or jaw; a cheek. — *adj* **chap'fallen** same as **chopfallen** (qv under **chop**[3]). — *adj* **chap'less** without a lower jaw. [Cf **chop**[3]; from N Eng and Scot *chaft*, ON *kjaptr* jaw]

chap. *abbrev*: chaplain; chapter.

chaparajos *shap-ə-rā'ōs* or *chä-pä-rä'hhos*, or **chaparejos** *-rā'* or *-rē'*, *n pl* cowboy's leather riding leggings (*abbrev* **chaps** or **shaps**). [Mex Sp]

chaparral *shap-ə-ral'* or *chäp-ä-räl'*, *n* a thicket of dense tangled brushwood. — **chaparral cock** a type of cuckoo of the Californian and Mexican chaparral that is capable of running at great speed, the roadrunner. [Sp, from *chaparro* dwarf evergreen oak, one of the plants growing there]

chapati or **chapatti** *chəp-ät'i*, (*Indian cookery*) *n* a thin flat piece of unleavened bread. [Hindustani]

chapbook. See **chap**[2].

chape *chāp*, *n* the plate of metal at the point of a scabbard; the catch or hook by which the sheath of a weapon was attached to the belt; the metal spike of a buckle. — *adj* **chape'less**. [Fr, from LL *capa* a cap]

chapeau *shä-pō*, *n* a hat: — *pl* **chapeaux**. — **chapeau-bras** (*brä*; *hist*) a compressible three-cornered hat designed to be carried under the arm. [Fr]

chapel *chap'l*, *n* a place of Christian worship inferior or subordinate to a regular church, or attached to a house or institution; an oratory in a mausoleum, etc; a cell of a church containing its own altar; a dissenters' place of worship, as of Nonconformists in England, Roman Catholics or Episcopalians in Scotland, etc; a chapel service; a body of musicians, such as a choir, an orchestra, or both, whether connected with a chapel or not; a newspaper or printing office, or an association or trade union of printing workers or journalists. — *adj* Nonconformist. — *n* **chap'elry** the jurisdiction of a chapel. — **chapel cart** see under **cart**; **chap'el master** (Ger *Kapellmeister*) a director of music; **chapel royal** the oratory of a royal palace. — **chapel of ease** a chapel for worshippers living at some distance from the parish church; **father** or **mother of the chapel** the president of a printing office or chairperson of a printers' or journalists' association or trade union branch; **lady chapel** see under **lady**; **proprietary chapel** a chapel that is private property. [OFr *capele*, from LL *cappella*, dimin of *cappa* a cloak or cope; orig from the cloak of St Martin]

chapelle ardente *sha-pel är-dãt*, (*Fr*) *n* a chapel or chamber in which a corpse lies in state before burial, surrounded by lighted candles.

chaperon or **chaperone** *shap'ə-rōn*, *n* formerly, a kind of hood or cap; a person (*esp* an older woman) who accompanies a girl or young woman to social events for protection, restraint, or appearance's sake; someone who supervises a group of children or young people, eg on school outings, etc. — *vt* to attend in such a capacity. — *n* **chap'eronage**. [Fr, a large hood, from *chape* a hooded cloak, from LL *cappa*; see **cape**[1]]

chapiter *chap'i-tər*, (*archit*) *n* the head or capital of a column. [Fr *chapitre*, from L *capitulum*, dimin of *caput* the head]

chapka or **czapka** *chap'kə*, *n* a military cap of a shape adapted from the traditional Polish peasant cap, worn by lancer regiments. — Also **schapska** (*shaps'kə*). [Pol *czapka* a cap]

chaplain *chap'lin*, *n* a Christian clergyman attached to an institution, establishment, organization or family. — *n* **chap'laincy**, **chap'lainry** or **chap'lainship**. [OFr *chapelain*, from LL *cappellānus*, from *cappella*; see **chapel**]

chaplet *chap'lit*, *n* a garland or wreath for the head; a circlet of gold, etc; a string of beads used in counting prayers, one-third of a rosary in length; the prayers counted on this string; anything forming a string or in the shape of a string of beads; a metal support of a cylindrical pipe. — *adj* **chap'leted**. [OFr *chapelet*, from *chape* a headdress]

Chaplinesque *chap-lin-esk'*, *adj* of or similar to the style of comedy of Charles Chaplin, a combination of anarchic humour and endearing pathos.

chapman, **chappess**, **chappie**. See **chap**[2].

chappal *chup'l* or *chap'l*, *n* a type of open sandal worn in India, having a single strap of leather attached to the sole between the first and second toes. [Hindi]

chaprassi, **chaprassy** or **chuprassy** *chu-präs'i*, *n* an office messenger; a household attendant; an orderly. [Hindi *chaprāsi* badge-wearer, messenger, from *chaprās* a badge]

CHAPS or **Chaps** *chaps*, (*banking*) *abbrev*: clearing house automated payment system.

chaps. See **chaparajos**.

chapstick. See **chap**[1].

chaptalize or **-ise** *chap'tə-līz*, *vt* to add extra sugar to wine during its fermentation to increase its alcohol content, *usu* a prohibited or closely controlled practice. — *n* **chaptalīzā'tion** or **-s-**. [From the originator, J A *Chaptal*, a late 19c French chemist]

chapter *chap'tər*, *n* a main division of a book, or of any written work; a subject or category generally; a period in history, of a person's life, etc; a numbered division of the Acts of Parliament of a session; an assembly of the canons of a cathedral or collegiate church, or the members of a religious or military order (from the custom of reading a chapter of the rule or of the Bible); the members of any of these collectively; an organized branch of a society, club or fraternity; a Roman numeral on a clock or watch face; a chapiter (*Spenser*). — *vt* to put or divide into chapters; to take to task. — **chap'terhouse** a building used for meetings of the chapter of a cathedral or church; the meeting place of a society or college fraternity (*esp US*). — **chapter and verse** exact reference to, or a complete specification of, the source or sources of one's information; **chapter of accidents** see under **accident**. [OFr *chapitre*, from L *capitulum*, dimin of *caput* the head]

chaptrel *chap'trəl*, (*archit*) *n* the capital of a pillar which supports an arch. [Dimin of **chapiter**]

char[1] or **charr** *chär*, *n* any small fish of the genus *Salvelinus*, of the salmon family, found in mountain lakes and rivers. [Prob Celtic; cf Gaelic *ceara* red, blood-coloured]

char[2] *chär*, *vt* to reduce (wood) to carbon. — *vt* and *vi* to scorch: — *pr p* **charr'ing**; *pa t* and *pa p* **charred'**. — *n* a substance, eg charcoal, resulting from charring. — *adj* **charr'y** pertaining to charcoal. [Origin obscure]

char[3] *chär* or **chare** *chār*, *n* an occasional piece of work, an odd job; (in *pl*) household work; a charwoman. — *vi* to do odd jobs of work; to do house-cleaning. — *vt* (*Scott*) to do, accomplish: — *pr p* **charr'ing** or **chār'ing**; *pa t* and *pa p* **charred'** or **chāred'**. — **char'woman** or **char'lady** a woman employed to do rough cleaning. [OE *cerran*, *cierran* to turn; see also **jar**[3], **ajar**]

char[4] *chär*, (*slang*) *n* tea. [Cockney spelling of **cha**]

char[5] *chär*, *n* (on the Indian subcontinent) a newly-formed island created by the deposition of silt in the channel of a large river, eg the Ganges.

chara *kā'rə*, *n* any plant of the genus *Chara*, freshwater algae of a family and class, including the stoneworts, **Charā'ceae** and **Charoph'yta**, having stems encrusted with calcareous matter and whorled branches. [L, some plant]

charabanc or **char-à-banc** *shar'ə-bang* or *-bã*, *n* formerly, a long open vehicle with rows of transverse seats; more recently, a tourist coach. — (*colloq*) *abbrev* **cha'ra**: — *pl* **char'abancs**, **char'-à-bancs** or **chars'-à-bancs**. [Fr *char à bancs* carriage with benches]

characid *ka-ras'id*, or **characin** *kar'ə-sin*, *n* any carnivorous freshwater fish of the family **Charac'idae**, *usu* small and brightly-coloured, including the piranha. — *adj* **char'acin**. — *adj* **chara'cinoid**. [Gr *charax* a fish of some kind]

character *kar'ək-tər* (*Spenser*, *Shakesp*, etc *-ak'*), *n* a letter, sign, figure, stamp or distinctive mark; a mark of any kind, a symbol in writing, etc; writing generally, handwriting; a secret cipher (*obs*); one of a set of symbols, eg letters of the alphabet, numbers, punctuation marks, that can be arranged in groups to represent data for processing (*comput*); any essential or distinguishing feature; a quality; nature; personal appearance (*obs*); the aggregate of peculiar qualities which constitutes personal or national individuality; moral qualities collectively; the reputation of possessing these; the variant or abnormality in structure, appearance or function in any organism that is attributed to the presence of a specific gene or set of genes (*genetics*); a formal statement of the qualities of a person who has been in one's service or employment, a testimonial; position, rank or status, or a person who has filled it; a person, *esp* one noted for eccentricity or distinctive personality; a personality as created in a play or novel or appearing in history; a literary genre, consisting in a description in prose or verse of a human type, or of a place or object on that model, a dominant form of literature in the 17c under the influence of Theophrastus and the theory of humours; a person (*slang*). — *vt* (*archaic*) to engrave, imprint or write; to represent, delineate or describe. — *adj* **char'acterful**. — *n* **char'acterism** a characteristic; a characterization. — *n* **characteris'tic** that which marks or constitutes the character; the integral part of a logarithm (*math*). — *adj* **characteris'tic** or **characteris'tical**. — *adv* **characteris'tically**. — *n* **characterīzā'tion** or **-s-**. — *vt* **char'acterize** or **-ise** to describe by distinctive qualities; to be a distinguishing mark or quality of. — *adj* **char'acterless** without character or distinctive qualities. — *n* **char'acterlessness**. — *n* **characterol'ogy** the science or study of the variety and development of character. — *n* **characterol'ogist**. — *n* **char'actery** (also *Shakesp -ak'*; *archaic*) writing; a system of symbols or letters used to express thoughts; the symbols so used. — **character actor** an actor who plays character parts; **character assassination** the destruction of a person's reputation by slander, rumour, etc; **characteristic curve** (*image technol*) a graph used to plot the relationship of the density of a photographic material and the logarithm of the exposure producing this density; **characteristic radiation** (*phys*) the wavelength of radiation that characterizes the atom of a particular substance; **characteristic spectrum** (*phys*) the ordered arrangement of frequency of radiation characteristic of the underlying atomic structure; **characteristic X-rays** see under **X**; **character literature**; **character part** a stage or film role portraying an unusual or eccentric personality type; **character recognition** (*comput*) a process used to recognize individual printed or written characters; **character sketch** a short description of the main traits in a person's character; **character witness** a person who makes a statement or gives evidence providing details of eg an accused person's character and past behaviour to a court of law. — **in character** in harmony with the part assumed, appropriate; in keeping with the person's usual conduct or attitudes; dressed for the part; **out of character** not in character, unlike that which one would expect from the person concerned. [Fr *caractère*, from L *charactēr*, from Gr *charaktēr*, from *charassein* to cut, engrave]

charade *shə-räd'* or (*NAm*) usu *-rād'*, *n* a type of riddle, the subject of which is a word proposed for solution from an enigmatical description of its component syllables and of the whole; an acted riddle in which the syllables and the whole are uttered or represented in successive scenes; a piece of ridiculous pretence or absurd behaviour. [Fr, perh from Provençal *charrada* chatter, or Sp *charrada* clownishness]

Charadrius *kar-ad'ri-əs*, *n* the plover genus, giving name to the family **Charad'riidae**. [Gr *charadrios* a bird, prob the thick-knee]

charango *chə-rang'gō*, *n* a small S American stringed instrument, with a sound-box made from an armadillo shell, that produces a sound similar to a mandolin.

charas, *chär'əs* or **churrus** *chur'əs*, *n* the resinous exudation of hashish, a narcotic and intoxicant. [Hindustani]

charcoal *chär'kōl*, *n* charred wood, or fuel made by charring wood; the carbonaceous residue of wood or animal matter that has undergone combustion with exclusion of air; a stick of charcoal used for drawing; a drawing made in charcoal. — *n* and *adj* (also **charcoal grey**) (of) a dark grey colour. — *vt* to draw with or blacken with charcoal. — **charcoal burner** a person whose job is to burn wood to produce charcoal. [**char**[2] and **coal**]

charcuterie *shär-küt-rē*, *n* a pork butcher's shop or wares; a delicatessen, or the meats sold in it. [Fr]

chard *chärd*, *n* the edible leafstalk of a variety of white beet, *Beta vulgaris cicla*. — Also called **Swiss chard** or **leaf beet**. [L *carduus* thistle]

chardonnay *shär-do-nā'*, *n* a type of grape, *orig* from the Burgundy region of France but now grown in all the major wine-growing regions of the world, used in making dry white wine; the wine made from this grape. [Fr]

chare. See **char**[3].

Charentais *shar-ã-tā*, *n* a type of small, round greenish-yellow melon with sweetly-scented orange flesh. [Fr, from *Charente*, a department of France]

charet *char'et*, (*Spenser*) *n* same as **chariot**.

charge *chärj*, *vt* to exact or demand from, to ask as the price; to set down as a liability or debt against; to accuse; to deliver an official injunction, exhortation or exposition to; to advance in accusation (that); to give a task to, to order or command; to load, to put something into, to fill; to load heavily, to burden; to fill completely; to cause to accumulate electricity; to place a bearing upon (with *with*; *heraldry*); to attack at a rush. — *vi* to make an attack. — *n* cost or price; a financial liability, a debt; an accusation (*law*); an attack or onset; care or custody; the person or thing in one's care or custody; a command; an order; that which is laid on; a load or burden; the load of powder, fuel, etc, for a gun, furnace, etc; an accumulation of electricity; a device borne on a shield (*heraldry*); a thrill, an agreeable sensation (*esp drug-taking slang*); (in *pl*) expenses. — *adj* **charge'able** liable to be charged; open to accusation; blamable; burdensome (*Bible*). — *n* **charge'ableness**. — *adv* **charge'ably**. — *adj* **charged** (*phys*) (of a capacitor, battery, conductor, etc) holding, storing or receiving electrical charge or energy. — *adj* **charge'ful** (*archaic*) burdensome or expensive. — *adj* **charge'less**. — *n* **char'ger** a flat dish capable of holding a large joint of meat, a platter; a warhorse; a battery charger. — **charge account** an account in which goods obtained are entered to be paid for later. — *vt* **charge'cap**. — **charge'-capping** the imposition, by central government, of an upper limit on the amount that may be levied by local government in respect of community charges on individuals; **charge'-card** a card issued by a store, shop, etc which authorizes a customer to obtain goods on credit; **charge-coupled device** (*comput*) a unit of memory in which information is stored using charged particles that circulate continuously through cells printed on a semiconductor; **charge (-discharge) machine** (*nuc eng*) a device for inserting or removing fuel without escape of radiation and often without reactor shutdown. — Also called **(re)fuelling machine**; **charge'-hand** or **charge'-man** the leader of a group of workmen, but lower in rank than foreman; **charge'house** (*Shakesp*) a school; **charge'nurse** a nurse in charge of a ward in a hosptial; **charge'sheet** a police document listing details of an accused person and the charges against him or her. — **bring a charge** (*law*) to accuse (with *against*); **charge down** (*rugby football*) to run towards (a kicked ball) and block it; **give in charge** to hand over to the police; **in charge** in control or authority, responsible (often with *of*); **take charge of** to assume the care or control of. [Fr *charger*, from LL *carricāre* to load, from L *carrus* a wagon; see **car**, **cargo**]

chargé-d'affaires *shär'zhā-dä-fer'*, *n* a diplomatic agent of lesser rank, accredited to the department for foreign affairs and holding his credentials from the minister; the person in charge of a diplomatic mission in the absence of the ambassador: — *pl* **chargés-d'affaires** (*shär'zhā-*). — Also short form **chargé**. [Fr]

charily, **chariness**. See **chary**.

chariot *char'i-ət*, *n* a horse-drawn, two-wheeled vehicle used in ancient warfare or racing; a light four-wheeled carriage with back seats and box; any ceremonial vehicle or carriage. — *vt* (*archaic*) to carry in a chariot. — *vi* (*archaic*) to ride in a chariot. — *n* **charioteer'** someone who drives a chariot. — *vt* and *vi* (*archaic*) to drive or to ride in a chariot or similar vehicle. [Fr, dimin of *char* a car]

Charis *kar'is* (Gr *hhär'is*), *n* any one of the three **Char'ites** (*-tēz*, Gr *-tes'*), the Graces (Aglaia, Euphrosyne and Thalia), Greek goddesses of all that imparts graciousness to life.

charisma *kə-riz'mə* or **charism** *kar'izm*, *n* personal quality or gift that enables an individual to impress and influence many of his or her fellows; a similar quality felt to reside in an office or position; a spiritual power given by God. — *adj* **charismat'ic** of, pertaining to, or having charisma or charism. — **charismatic movement** a non-denominational religious movement based on a belief in the divinely-inspired gifts of speaking in tongues, healing, prophecy, etc. [Gr *charis*, *-itos* grace]

charity *char'i-ti*, *n* the disposition to think favourably of others, and do them good; the donation of goods, money, etc to those in need; alms or almsgiving; a *usu* non-profit-making foundation, institution or cause, devoted to caring for those in need of help, etc; universal love (*New Testament*); (in *pl*; *archaic*) affections. — *adj* **char'itable** of or relating to, showing, inspired by charity; (of an institution, etc) having the status of, being in the nature of, a charity. — *n* **char'itableness**. — *adv* **char'itably**. — **char'ity-boy** or **cha'rity-girl** a pupil in a **char'ity-school**, a school for the poor supported by endowments or gifts. — **charity begins at home** help, support, etc should first be given to one's own family, countrymen, etc before others, *usu* an excuse for not helping others; **cold as charity** see under **cold**. [Fr *charité*, from L *cāritās*, *-ātis*, from *cārus* dear]

charivari *shär-i-vär'i*, *n* a cacophonous mock serenade, *orig* to newly-weds, using kettles, pans, lids, etc; a cacophony of sound, din. — Also (*NAm*) **shivar'ee** or **chivar'ee** (also *shiv'*). [Fr, from LL *caribaria* a headache]

chark *chärk*, *vt* to burn (wood, etc) to charcoal. — *n* charcoal, coke. [**charcoal**]

charka or **charkha** *chär'kə*, *n* a spinning wheel used in Indian households for spinning cotton. [Hindi]

charlady. See **char**[3].

charlatan *shär'lə-tən*, *n* someone who pretends to have special knowledge or ability, *esp* one who claims to have medical knowedge; a quack; a fraud. — *adj* **charlatanic** (*-tan'ik*) or **charlatan'ical**. — *n* **char'latanism**. — *n* **char'latanry**. [Fr, from Ital *ciarlatano*, from *ciarlare* to chatter; imit]

Charles' law *chärl'ziz lö*, (*phys*) *n* the principle (only approximately true) that all gases have the same coefficient of expansion at constant pressure. — Also called **Guy-Lussac's law**. [From J A C *Charles* (1746–1823) French chemist who originated it]

Charles's Wain *chärlz'iz wān*, (*old*) *n* the seven bright stars that make up the Plough (Ursa Major). [OE *Carles wægn*, Carl being Charlemagne]

charleston *chärls'tən*, *n* a lively 20c dance characterized by spasmodic kicking with the knees turned inwards. — *vi* to dance the Charleston. [*Charleston* in S Carolina]

Charlie[1] or **Charley** *chär'li*, (also without *cap*) *n* a credulous person; an inefficient, ineffectual person, a fool (often in the phrase *a proper Charlie*); (a member of) the Vietcong (*US military slang*); a night-watchman (*obs*); the small triangular beard familiar in the portraits of *Charles* I; a small moustache, resembling that worn by *Charlie* Chaplin; a name for a fox. — **charley horse** (*NAm slang*) muscle strain as a result of strenuous exercise; **Char'ley-pitcher** (*slang*) a thimble-rigger. [From the name *Charles*]

Charlie[2] *chär'li*, *n* a communications code word for the letter *c*; cocaine (*drug-taking slang*).

charlock *chär'lək*, *n* wild mustard (*Sinapis arvensis*), a common yellow-flowered cornfield weed. [OE *cerlic*]

charlotte *shär'lət*, *n* a kind of deep tart containing fruit and covered with sponge or bread. — **charlotte russe** (*rüs*) a dessert of custard or cream enclosed in a kind of sponge-cake. [From the name *Charlotte*]

charm[1] *chärm*, *n* a spell; something thought to possess occult power, *esp* that brings good luck, such as an amulet, a metrical form of words, etc; a talisman, amulet, etc; a trinket, *esp* one worn on a bracelet; power of fascination; attractiveness; (in *pl*) personal attractions; that which can please irresistibly; in particle physics, (the quantum number used to account for) the unusual properties and behaviour of certain elementary particles. — *vt* to influence by a charm; to subdue by secret influence; to enchant; to delight; to allure. — *adj* **charmed** bewitched; delighted; protected as by a special or magic charm; (in particle physics) having charm. — *n* **charm'er**. — *adj* **charm'ful** abounding in charms. — *adj* **charm'ing** highly pleasing; delightful; fascinating. — *adv* **charm'ingly**. — *adj* **charm'less** devoid of charm. — *adv* **charm'lessly**. — **charm offensive** a method of trying to get what one wants by overwhelming with reasonableness, attractive offers, etc. — **like a charm** having the desired result as if influenced by a magic spell, perfectly. [Fr *charme*, from L *carmen* a song]

charm[2]. Same as **chirm**.

charmeuse *shär'mōōz* or Fr *shar-møz*, *n* a soft satin material made *orig* of silk, but now also of synthetic fibres. [Orig a tradename]

charneco *chär'ni-kō*, (*Shakesp*) *n* a kind of sweet wine. [Prob from a village near Lisbon]

charnel *chär'nəl*, *n* a burial place (*obs*); a charnel house. — *adj* sepulchral; death-like. — **char'nel house** a place where bodies or bones are deposited (also *fig*). [OFr *charnel*, from LL *carnāle*, from L *carnālis*, from *carō*, *carnis* flesh]

Charolais or **Charollais** *shar'ō-lā*, *n* a breed of beef cattle and, more recently, of sheep named after an old district of France (Charolais) of which Charolles was the capital.

Charon *kā'rən*, *n* the ferryman who rowed the spirits of the dead across the river Styx and Acheron in the lower world (*Gr mythol*); a satellite of the planet Pluto. [Gr *Charōn*]

charoset(h). See **haroset(h)**.

charpie *shär'pē* or *-pē'*, *n* lint shredded down to form a soft material for dressing wounds. [OFr *charpir*, from L *carpere* to pluck]

charpoy *chär'poi*, *n* a lightweight Indian bedstead or cot, made up of webbing stretched on a four-legged frame. [Hindustani *chārpāī*, from Pers *chahār-pāī* four feet]

charqui *chär'kē*, *n* beef cut into long strips and dried in the sun, jerked beef. [Quechua]

charr. Same as **char**[1].

chart *chärt*, *n* a marine or hydrographical map, showing part of a sea or other water, with the islands, contiguous coasts, soundings, currents, etc; an outline map, diagram, or a tabular statement giving information of any kind; (*usu* in *pl*) the lists of the ten, twenty, etc most popular records, ie those which have sold the most copies, each week. — *vt* to map; to make a chart. — *vi* (of a popular recording) to enter the pop charts — *n* **chart'ist** a person who makes and/or studies charts of past performances, *esp* of stocks and shares, with a view to forecasting future trends. — *n* **chart'ism**. — *adj* **chart'less** not mapped, uncharted. — **chart'-buster**. — *adj* **chart'-busting** (*slang*) *esp* of recording artists or their music, very successful. — **chart'house** or **chart'-room** the room in a ship where charts are kept. [OFr *charte*, from L *c(h)arta* a paper, from Gr *chartēs*]

charta or **carta** *kär'tə*, *n* a charter. — *adj* **chartā'ceous** papery. [L *c(h)arta*, from Gr *chartēs* a sheet of paper]

charter *chärt'ər*, *n* any formal writing in evidence of a grant, contract, or other transactions, conferring or confirming titles, rights or privileges, etc; the formal deed by which a sovereign guarantees the rights and privileges of his or her subjects; a document creating a borough or other corporation; any instrument by which powers and privileges are conferred by the state on a body of persons for a special object; a set of principles that form the constitution of an organization; (an agreement or contract for) the let or hire of eg a ship or aircraft; a patent; a grant; an allowance. — *vt* to establish by charter; to let or hire (eg a ship or aircraft) on contract. — *adj* hired (as in *charter plane*); made in a hired aircraft (as in *charter flight*). — *adj* **chart'ered** granted or protected by a charter; privileged; licensed; hired by contract. — *n* **chart'erer**. — **chart'er-chest** a box in which charters are preserved; **chartered accountant, engineer** or **surveyor**, etc a person qualified under the regulations of the relevant institute or professional body which has a royal charter; **chartered company** a trading company acting under a charter from the crown; **charter mayor** the mayor of a borough at the time of its charter; **charter member** an original member of an incorporation; **chart'erparty** see separate entry below. [OFr *chartre*, from L *cartula*, *c(h)arta*, from Gr *chartēs* a sheet of paper]

Charterhouse *chärt'ər-hows*, *n* a Carthusian monastery; the famous hospital and school instituted in London in 1611, on the site of a Carthusian monastery. [See **Carthusian**]

charterparty *chärt'ər-pär-ti*, *n* the common written form in which a contract of affreightment is expressed, as in the hiring of the whole or part of a ship for the conveyance of goods. — Also **charter party**. [Fr *charte partie*, literally a divided charter, as the practice was to divide it in two and give a half to each person, from L *c(h)arta partīta*; see **charta**]

Chartism *chärt'izm*, *n* (the programme and principles of) a 19c reform movement in Great Britain that campaigned for the extension of political power to the working classes, whose aims as included in the People's Charter (1838) have since been achieved, except annual parliaments. — *n* **Chart'ist**. — Also *adj*. [See **charter**]

chartism, chartist. See **chart**.

chartography *kär-tog'rə-fi*. Same as **cartography**.

Chartreuse *shär-trœz*, *n* a Carthusian monastery, *esp* the original one, La Grande Chartreuse near Grenoble in France; (sometimes without *cap*) a green or yellow liqueur, manufactured there by the monks from aromatic herbs, flowers and brandy; (without *cap*) a greenish-yellow colour. — *adj* of this colour. [See **Carthusian**]

chartulary *kär'tū-lər-i*. Same as **cartulary**.

charwoman. See **char**[3].

chary *chā'ri*, *adj* cautious; wary (of doing, saying, giving, etc); careful (of) (*archaic*); fastidious, shy; precious (*obs*). — *adv* **chār'ily**. — *n* **chār'iness**. [OE *cearig*, from *cearu* care]

Charybdis *kə-rib'dis*, *n* (in the *Odyssey*) a dangerous monster that dwelt under a fig-tree on a rock opposite to Scylla (qv), and three times a day swallowed and threw up the waters of the sea, later identified with a current or a whirlpool on the Sicilian side of the Straits of Messina. — *adj* **Charyb'dian**.

chase[1] *chās*, *vt* to pursue; to hunt; to seek; to drive away; to put to flight; to follow with a chaser or chasse. — Also (*obs*) **chace**. — *vi* (*colloq*) to hurry (about, around or after). — *n* pursuit; a hunting; (with *the*) the sport of hunting; the object of a hunt, quarry; an unenclosed private game preserve; a steeplechase; the second impact of an unreturned ball, for which the player scored unless his opponent bettered it (and scored) by a similar impact nearer the end wall (*real tennis*). — *n* **chas'er** a pursuer; a hunter; a horse for steeplechasing; a drink of a different, *usu* complementary or contrasting, type, drunk immediately after another (*colloq*); a woman over-assiduous in pursuit of men (*old slang*); an aeroplane for pursuing hostile aircraft (*airforce slang*); a chasse. — **chase'port** the porthole at the bow or stern of a naval ship (through which a gun is fired during pursuit). — **beasts of chase** (*archaic*) properly the buck, doe, fox, marten and roe; wild animals that are hunted generally; **chase rainbows** see **rainbow-chaser** under **rain**[1]; **chase the dragon** (*drug-taking slang*) to inhale the fumes of melting powdered heroin; **give chase** to set off in pursuit; **go and chase yourself** (*slang*) go away, clear out; **wild-goose chase** a chase hither and thither; any foolish or profitless pursuit of the unattainable. [OFr *chacier*, *chasser*, from L *captāre*, frequentative of *capere* to take]

chase[2] *chās*, *vt* to enchase, to decorate (metal) by engraving. — *n* **chās'er** a person who engraves metal; a tool for engraving metal or for cutting threads on screws. — *n* **chās'ing** the art of engraving on the outside of raised metalwork; the art of cutting the threads of screws. [Short for **enchase**]

chase[3] *chās*, *n* a case or frame for holding printing type making up a page; a groove. [Fr *châsse*, a setting, from L *capsa* a chest; see **case**[1]]

Chasid, **Chasidic**, etc. See **Hasid**.

chasm *kaz'əm*, *n* a yawning or gaping hollow; a gap or opening; a void space. — *adj* **chas'med**. — *adj* **chasmic** (*kaz'mik*) or **chas'mal**. — *adj* **chas'my**. [Gr *chasma*, from *chainein* to gape; cf **chaos**]

chasmogamy *kaz-mog'ə-mi*, (*bot*) *n* the condition of having flowers that open, allowing cross-pollination. Cf **cleistogamy**. — *adj* **chasmogamic** (*-mō-gam'ik*). [Gr *chasma* a gape, and *gameein* to marry]

chasse *shas*, *n* a dram or liqueur taken after coffee. — Also **chasse-café'**. [Fr *chasser* to chase]

chassé *shas'ā*, *n* a gliding step in dancing. — *vi* to make such a step. — *vt* (*slang*) to dismiss. — **chassé-croisé** (*-krwä'zā*) a dance movement in which partners change places by means of a chassé. [Fr]

chassepot *shas'pō*, *n* a breech-loading rifle used by the French army between 1866 and 1874. [From A A *Chassepot* who invented it]

chasseur *shas-œr'*, *n* a hunter or huntsman; a member of a body of French light infantry or cavalry; a liveried attendant, *esp* in hotels. — *adj* (*cookery*) of or cooked in a sauce containing mushrooms, shallots, white wine and herbs. [Fr, from *chasser* to hunt; see **chase**[1]]

Chassid, **Chassidic**, etc. See **Hasid**.

chassis *shas'ē* or *-i*, *n* the structural framework of a motor car to which the movable working parts and body may be attached; the framework of a radio, television, etc; an aeroplane's landing-carriage; a casemate gun carriage; a wooden frame or sash for eg a window (*obs*); a woman's body (*joc slang*): — *pl* **chassis** (*shas'ēz* or *-iz*). [Fr *chassis* frame]

chaste *chāst*, *adj* sexually virtuous; modest; decent and pure in taste and style; restrained. — *adv* **chaste'ly**. — *vt* **chasten** (*chās'n*) to free from faults by punishing; hence, to discipline or punish; to purify or refine; to restrain, subdue, moderate, or temper. — *adj* **chās'tened** purified; modest; tempered. — *n* **chās'tener**. — *n* **chaste'ness**. — *n* **chās'tenment**. — *vt* **chastise** (*chas-tīz'*) to inflict *esp* physical punishment upon for the purpose of correction; to subdue to a state of order or obedience; to refine, purify, correct (*obs*); to moderate, restrain (*archaic*). — *adj* **chastīs'able**. — *n* **chastisement** (*chas'tiz-mənt*). — *n* **chastity** (*chas'ti-ti*) sexual purity; virginity or celibacy; refinement of style; moderation. — **chaste tree** a small European and Asian tree (*Vitex agnus-castus*) with upright panciles of violet-blue, fragrant flowers; **chastity belt** a device said to have been worn by eg wives of absent crusaders, to prevent their having sexual intercourse; a device made in modern times according to its supposed design. — Also *fig*. [OFr *chaste*, from L *castus* pure]

chasuble *chaz'* or *chas'ū-bl*, *n* a sleeveless vestment worn over the alb by the priest while celebrating Mass. [Fr, from LL *casubula*, from L *casula*, dimin of L *casa* a hut]

chat[1] *chat*, *vi* to talk easily or familiarly. — *vt* (often with *up*) to talk to informally and often flirtatiously in order to gain something, eg to cajole or seduce: — *pr p* **chatt'ing**; *pa t* and *pa p* **chatt'ed**. — *n* familiar, informal talk. — *n* **chatt'iness**. — *adj* **chatt'y** given or inclined to chat; of the nature of chat. — **chat'-line** or **chat'line** a telephone service in which callers contact each other through a monitored central switchboard, to engage in informal conversation. — Also *adj*. — **chat show** (*colloq*) a radio or television programme in which invited personalities talk informally with their host. — Also **talk show**. [From **chatter**]

chat[2] *chat*, *n* any small songbird of a subfamily (*Turdinae*) of thrushes, including the stonechat and the whinchat; any of various Australian wrens. [Imit]

chat[3] *chat*, (*dialect*) *n* a small potato of poor quality.

chat[4] *chat*, (*obs slang* and *Austr* and *NZ colloq*) *n* a louse. — *adj* **chatt'y** lousy, flea-infested; dirty (*Austr* and *NZ colloq*). [Orig cant *chat(t)s*, lice]

château *shä'tō*, *n* a castle or large country house, *esp* in France; a vineyard estate around a castle, house, etc, *esp* in Bordeaux (common in names of wines associated with specific estates, eg *Château Lafite*, *Château Margaux*): — *pl* **chât'eaux** (*-tōz*). — *n* **châtelain** (*shat'ə-lɛ̃*) a castellan, lord of the manor. — *n* **chât'elaine** (*-len*) a female keeper or mistress of a castle or a large household; formerly, an ornamental bunch of short chains bearing keys, scissors, etc, attached to a waist-belt and worn by women; a similar thing in miniature attached to a watch-chain. — **château bottled** of wine, bottled on the estate in which it has been produced; **châteaux en Espagne** (*shä-tō-zã-nes-päny'*) (*Fr*) castles in Spain, castles in the air. [Fr *château* (OFr *chastel*), from L *castellum*, dimin of *castrum* a fort]

Chateaubriand *shä-tō-brē-ã'*, (*cookery*) *n* (also without *cap*) a thick steak cut from grilled fillet of beef, *usu* served with fried potatoes and mushrooms. [François René, Vicomte de *Chateaubriand* (1768–1848), French author and statesman]

chaton *shä-tɔ̃'*, *n* the setting or stone of a finger-ring. [Fr]

chatoyant *shat-wä-yã* or *shat-oi'ənt*, *adj* (eg of gems, birds' plumage, etc) with a changing lustre, iridescent, shimmering. — *n* **chatoyance** (*shat-wä-yãs* or *shat-oi'əns*) or **chatoy'ancy**. [Fr]

chatta *chät'ä*, *n* an umbrella. [Hindi]

chattel *chat'l*, *n* (*law*) any kind of property which is not freehold, distinguished further into *chattels-real* and *chattels-personal*, the latter being personal moveables (plate, furniture, etc), the former including leasehold interests. — **chattel house** (in the West Indies) a movable wooden house; **chattel mortgage** (*NAm*) a mortgage on moveable personal property; **goods and chattels** all personal moveable possessions. [OFr *chatel*, from LL *captāle*, from L *capitāle*, etc, property, goods]

chatter *chat'ər*, *vi* to talk idly or rapidly; (of some birds and animals) to utter a rapid succession of short notes or sounds; (of the teeth when one shivers) to make a series of rapid clicking sounds. — *n* a noise like that made by a magpie, or by the teeth striking together; idle talk. — *n* **chatt'erer** someone who or something that chatters; an idle or rapid talker; a name applied to two families of birds, the waxwings and the cotingas. — *n* **chatt'ering**. — **chatt'erbox** (*informal*) someone who talks or chatters incessantly; **chattering classes** (*derog*) the section of society, *usu* the educated or well-informed, who are in the habit of discussing and commenting on social, economic, political, etc issues. [From the sound]

chatty[1]. See **chat**[1].

chatty[2] or **chatti** *chat'i*, (*Anglo-Ind*) *n* an earthenware water-pot. [Hindi *chāṭī*, from Dravidian]

chatty[3]. See **chat**[4].

Chaucerian *chö-sē'ri-ən*, *adj* like or pertaining to the writings of *Chaucer*. — *n* a student, imitator or follower of Chaucer. — *n* **Chau'cerism** anything characteristic of Chaucer.

chaudfroid *shō-frwä*, *n* a jellied sauce, or a dish, eg of chicken, including it. [Fr, literally, hot-cold]

chaud-mellé *shōd-mel'ā*, (*esp Scots law*) *n* a fight arising in the heat of passion; the killing of a person in such a fight. [OFr *chaude-mellee* hot fight; see **mêlée**]

chaufe or **chauff** (*Spenser*) *chöf*. Forms of **chafe**.

chauffer or **chaufer** *chö'fər*, *n* a small portable furnace or stove. [See **chafer** under **chafe**]

chauffeur *shō'fər* or *-fœr'*, *n* a person employed to drive a motor car: — *fem* **chauffeuse** (*-føz'*). — *vi* and *vt* to drive or act as a chauffeur (for): — (*facetious*; of women) **chauffeuse'**. [Fr, stoker]

chaulmoogra or **chaulmugra** *chöl-mōō'grə*, *n* a name for various Asian trees of the family Flacourtiaceae, yielding **chaulmoogra oil**, used, *esp* formerly, in the treatment of leprosy. [Bengali]

chaumer *chö'mər*, (*Scot*) *n* formerly, a room or building in which male farmworkers sleep. [**chamber**]

chaunce, chaunge. Old forms of **chance, change**.

chaunt, chaunter, chauntress, chauntry. See **chant**.

chausses *shōs*, or *shō'zis*, *n pl* medieval closely fitting breeches, hose generally; the protective pieces for the legs in armour. — *n pl* **chaussures** (*-ür'*) a general name for boots and shoes, footgear. [OFr *chauces*, from L *calcia* hose]

Chautauqua *shə-tök'wə*, *n* a village and lake in US where summer educational meetings were instituted in the late 19c; (also without *cap*) a *usu* outdoor meeting of this type, with lectures, etc. — *adj* **Chautauquan** (*shə-tö'kwən*) pertaining to a system of instruction for adults by home reading and study under guidance, evolved from the *Chautauqua* (New York State) Literary and Scientific Circle, organized in 1878.

chauvinism *shō'vin-izm*, *n* an exaggerated or fanatical pride in one's country, with a corresponding contempt for foreign nations; fanatical or extravagant attachment to any group, place, cause, etc. — *n* **chau'vin**. — *n* and *adj* **chau'vinist**. — *adj* **chauvinist'ic**. — **male chauvinist (pig)** see under **male**. [From Nicolas *Chauvin*, an ardent veteran of Napoleon's, who figures in Cogniard's *La Cocarde tricolore*]

chave. See **ch**.

chavender *chav'ən-dər*, *n* another name for the chub. [Cf **cheven**]

chaw[1] *chö*, (*Spenser*) *n* a jaw. [See **jaw**[1]]

chaw[2] *chö*, *vt* to chew (tobacco; also *dialect*). — *n* a quantity for chewing (*esp* of tobacco). — **chaw'bācon** (*contemptuous*) a country fellow, an uncouth rustic. — **chawed up** (*dialect* or *old US slang*) destroyed; defeated; crushed; reprimanded. [By-form of **chew**]

chawdron *chö'drən*, (*Shakesp*) *n* the entrails of an animal. [OFr *chaudun*]

chay[1]. A *colloq* form of **chaise**.

chay[2] *chī* or *chā*, **chaya** *chī'ə*, or **shaya** *shī'ə*, *n* an Indian plant (*Oldenlandia*) of the madder family whose root (**chay'root**) yields a red dye. [Cf Tamil *saya*]

chayote *chä-yō'tē* or *chī-ō'tē*, *n* a tropical American cucurbitaceous climbing plant (*Sechium edule*); its edible fruit eaten as a vegetable. — Also **chō'chō**. [Sp, from Nahuatl *chayotli*]

chazan. See **hazan**.

ChB *abbrev*: *Chirurgiae Baccalaureus* (*L*), Bachelor of Surgery.

CHD *abbrev*: coronary heart disease.

ChE *abbrev*: Chemical Engineer.

che *chə*, (*Shakesp*) *pronoun* a SW English dialect form of I. [OE *ic*; cf **ch**]

cheap *chēp*, *adj* low in price or cost; charging low prices; of a low price in relation to the real or market value; easily obtained; obtained or gained using unworthy, low or contemptible means; of little value, or considered to be so; paltry; inferior; having low moral standards; vulgar. — Also *adv*. — *n* (*obs*) bargain, buyer's advantage. — *vt* **cheap'en** to make cheap, to lower the price of; to lower the reputation of; to make vulgar or tawdry; to beat down the price of, to bargain; to ask the price of (*archaic*). — *n* **cheap'ener**. — *n* **cheap'ie** or **cheapy** (*colloq*) something which is low in price or cost. — Also *adj*. — *adv* **cheap'ly**. — *n* **cheap'ness**. — *adj* **cheap'o** (*colloq*; *usu derog*) cheap, *esp* with connotations of inferiority or tawdriness. — **cheap'-jack** (*orig* **cheap Jack** or **John**) a travelling hawker who professes to give great bargains. — *adj* inferior, of bad quality, worthless. — **cheap labour** labour paid at a poor rate; **cheap'skate** (*informal*) a miserly person. — **cheap and nasty** offensively inferior and of low value; **dirt cheap** extremely or ridiculously cheap; **feel cheap** to have a sense of inferiority and humiliation, *esp* relating to one's moral standards; **on the cheap** cheap or cheaply. [OE *cēap* price, a bargain, and *ceapian* to buy; ON *kaupa*, Ger *kaufen* to buy]

cheat[1] *chēt*, *n* a person who cheats; a fraud; a deception; a card-game in which deception is allowed; an escheat, a forfeit (*obs*); a piece of plunder, a stolen thing (*obs*); a thing in general, *esp* the gallows (*thieves' slang*; see also **nubbing-cheat**). — *vt* to deceive, defraud or impose upon. — *vi* to be deceitful. — *n* **cheat'er** a person who cheats; an officer who collected the fines and taxes to be paid into the Exchequer (*hist*); (in *pl*) spectacles (*NAm slang*); (in *pl*) falsies (*slang*). — *n* **cheat'ery** (*colloq*) cheating. — *n* **cheat'ing**. — **cheat on** (*colloq*) to deceive, *esp* to be unfaithful to (one's wife, husband, lover, etc); **put a cheat upon** to deceive; **tame cheater** (*Shakesp*) a decoy. [**escheat**]

cheat[2] *chēt*, *n* a US *name* for **rye-brome**. — Also called **chess**. — **cheat bread** (*obs*) bread of a lower quality than manchet, made of a somewhat coarser wheat flour. [Origin uncertain]

chechako, chechaqua, chechaquo. See **cheechako**.

Chechen *chech'ən* or *chə-chen'*, *n* a member of the majority population of the N Caucasian Chechen-Ingush ASSR of the Russian Republic, or their Caucasian language.

chéchia *shā'shya*, *n* a cylindrical skullcap, worn by Arabs and adopted by French troops in Africa. [Fr, from Berber *tashashit*, pl *tishushai* skullcap]

check *chek*, *vt* to bring to a stop; to restrain or hinder; to rebuke; to verify, often by comparison; to punch (eg a ticket); to tick (*NAm*); to nip, pinch, crush, as by biting or shutting (*Scot*; also **chack**); to deposit or receive in exchange for a check; to send (baggage) on a passenger's ticket (*NAm*); to place in check (*chess*); to mark with a pattern of crossing lines. — *vi* to make investigations; to come to a stop; to forsake the quarry for some other bird (with *at*; *falconry*). — *n* anything that checks; a sudden stop, repulse or rebuff; a position when a player's king is exposed to attack unless it is protected or moved (*chess*); in certain games, a stopping of an opposing player's forward progress; restraint; control; a rebuke, a reprimand (*obs*); a mark put against items in a list; a tick (*NAm*); an order for money (*usu* written **cheque** except *NAm*); a means of verification or testing, eg to evaluate the standard of something; any token or ticket used as security, to indicate ownership, etc, a counterfoil; a ticket or token, given to show that a person has paid, eg for admission (see also **raincheck** under **rain**[1]); a restaurant bill; a counter used in games at cards (hence **pass in one's checks** to die); a pattern of cross lines forming small squares, as in a chessboard; any fabric woven with such a pattern; a mechanism that holds a piano hammer after striking. — *adj* divided into small squares by crossing lines. — *n* **check'er** someone who hinders, rebukes or scrutinizes; a cashier; a cloakroom attendant (*NAm*); (in *pl*; *NAm*) the game of draughts. — *adj* **check'y** or **che'quy** (*heraldry*) chequered. — **check action** piano action with checks; **check'book** (*NAm*) a cheque book; **check'clerk** a clerk who checks accounts, etc; **check digit** (*comput*) a digit carried in computer processes to discover errors, check accuracy, etc; **checked square** a square in a crossword that belongs to the solution of two clues; **check'erboard** a checked board on which checkers or draughts is played; **check'-in** see **check in** below; **checking account** (*NAm*) a current account; **check'-key** a latch-key; **check'list** a list for verification purposes; a comprehensive list; an inventory; **checkmate** see separate entry; **check'-off** see **check off** below; **check'out** the cash desk where goods bought in a supermarket, etc are paid for; the act of checking out (see below); **check'point** a place where an official check of documents, etc is made; **check'rail** an inner rail on a railway track that prevents a train from being derailed, *esp* when going round corners (also **guardrail**); **check'rein** a bearing rein, a strap hindering a horse from lowering its head; **check'room** or **check'ing-room** (*NAm*) a cloakroom, luggage room or room where goods are checked; **check'-string** a string by which the occupant of a carriage may attract the driver's notice; **check'-till** a till that records sums received; **check'-up** a testing scrutiny; a medical examination, *esp* one of a series of regular examinations; **check'weigher** or **checkweigh man** a colliery worker who, on behalf of the miners, checks the weight of coal sent up to the pit-mouth. — **check in** to record one's arrival at work; to register one's arrival at a hotel, airport, etc (*n* **check'-in**); **check off** to mark off on a list, *usu* with a tick, as having arrived, been completed, etc; to deduct (trade union dues) from a worker's pay before he or she receives it (*NAm*; *n* **check'-off**); **check out** to record one's departure from work; to depart, having paid one's bill, etc, from a hotel, etc; to investigate, examine or test; to look at or inspect (*slang*; *n* **check'-out** or **check'out**); **check up** to investigate; to examine and test (often with *on*); **hold** or **keep in check** to restrain, control or keep back. [OFr *eschec*, *eschac*, through Ar from Pers *shāh*, king]

checker. See under **check** and **cheque**.

checkerberry *chek'ər-ber-i*, *n* the fruit of various American plants, *esp* the wintergreen (*Gaultheria*).

checklaton *chek-lat'ən*, *n* understood and explained by Spenser as gilded leather used for making embroidered jacks. — Also **schecklaton** or **shecklaton**. [**ciclaton**, perh by association with **latten**]

checkmate *chek'māt*, *n* (a move resulting in) a position where one's adversary's king can neither be protected nor move to escape, ending the game (*chess*); a complete check, defeat or winning manoeuvre. — *vt* to put (one's adversary's king) in checkmate (*chess*); to defeat or render incapable of counter attack. — *interj* (*chess*) a call made to indicate that an adversary's king has been placed in checkmate. [OF *eschec mat*, from Ar *shāh māt*(*a*) the king is dead]

checky. See **check**.

Cheddar *ched'ər*, *n* a kind of hard cheese *orig* made at *Cheddar* in Somerset. — **Cheddar pink** a species of pink (*Dianthus gratianopolitanus*) found on the limestone cliffs at Cheddar.

cheddite *ched'īt*, (*chem*) a mixture of castor oil, ammonium perchlorate and a solvent, used as an explosive. [Fr *Chedde*, town in France where first manufactured]

cheechako *chē-chä'kō*, (*Can* and *Alaska*) *n* a tenderfoot: — *pl* **cheecha'kos** or **cheecha'koes**. — Also **checha'ko**, **cheechal'ko**, **checha'qua** or **checha'quo**. [Chinook jargon, new-come]

chee-chee. See **chi-chi**.

cheek *chēk*, *n* the side of the face below the eye, the fleshy lateral wall of the mouth; effrontery, impudence (*colloq*); a side-post of a door, window, etc; the cheek strap of a horse's bridle; the ring at the end of a bit; any of various things arranged in lateral or opposite pairs, such as one of the jaws of a vice; a buttock (*colloq*). — *vt* (*colloq*) to address insolently. — *adv* **cheek'ily**.— *n* **cheek'iness**. — *adj* **cheek'y** (*colloq*) rude; saucy. — **cheek'bone** the bone above the cheek; **cheek'piece** the part of a helmet, bridle, etc that covers the cheek; **cheek'pouch** a dilatation of the cheek, forming a bag, as in rodents, monkeys, etc, used for storing food; **cheek'tooth** a molar tooth. — **cheek by jowl** side by side, in close proximity; **tongue in cheek** see under **tongue**; **turn the other cheek** see under **turn**. [OE *cēce*, *cēace* cheek, jaw; cf Du *kaak*]

cheep *chēp*, *vi* to chirp, as a young bird. — *n* a sound of cheeping. — *n* **cheep'er** a young bird, *esp* a young gamebird or chicken. [Imit]

cheer *chēr*, *n* face (*archaic*); disposition, frame of mind (with *good*, etc); joy; a shout of approval or welcome; kind treatment (*obs*); entertainment; fare, food. — *vt* to comfort; to encourage; to applaud; to inspirit. — *vi* to shout encouragement or applause; to take comfort (*obs*); to be of good cheer (*obs*). — *n* **cheer'er**. — *adj* **cheer'ful** in, of, resulting in, or accompanied by good spirits; pleasant, bright, gay. — *adv* **cheer'fully**. — *n* **cheer'fulness**. — *adv* **cheer'ily**. — *n* **cheer'iness**. — *interj* **cheerio**! goodbye!; good health! (used when drinking a toast). — *n* a bright informal goodbye; a kind of small frankfurter (*Austr* and *NZ*): — *pl* **cheerios'**. — *n* **cheer'ishness** (*obs*) cheerfulness. — *adj* **cheer'less** dreary, without comfort, gloomy. — *n* **cheer'lessness**. — *adj* **cheer'ly** (*archaic*) cheerful. — *adv* (*archaic*) in a cheery manner; heartily. — *interj* **cheers**! (*colloq*) good health! (used when drinking a toast); thank you!; cheerio, goodbye! — *adj* **cheer'y** cheerful; promoting or resulting in cheerfulness. — **cheer'leader** (*esp NAm*) a person who directs organized cheering, as at team games. — **cheer up** (*colloq*) to make or become more cheerful; **what cheer**? (*archaic*) how are you? [OFr *chiere* face, from LL *cara* the face]

cheerio. See **cheer**.

cheese[1] *chēz*, *n* a kind of food made from the curd of milk coagulated by rennet, separated from the whey, of a soft creamy consistency or pressed into a solid or semi-solid mass, traditionally and usually wheel-shaped; a solid mass of this; a flavoured kind of food, with the consistency of soft cheese, eg *lemon cheese*; anything of the shape of a whole cheese; the receptacle of a thistle-head; the cheese-shaped disc used in skittles. — *n* **chees'iness**. — *adj* **chees'y** having the nature of cheese; (of a smile) broad (*colloq*); artifical, insincere (*colloq*). — **cheese'board** a flat wooden board on which cheese is cut and served; a collection of cheeses served on such a board; **cheese'burger** a hamburger with melted cheese on top of it; **cheese'cake** a kind of cake having a base of pastry or biscuit crumbs, with a filling of cream cheese, sugar, eggs, flavouring, etc; women with sex appeal, *esp* when photographically displayed in magazines, etc (*slang*; cf **beefcake**); **cheese'cloth** a loose-woven light gauze used for wrapping cheeses; a stronger type of loosely-woven cotton cloth used for making shirts, etc; **cheese'cutter** (*naut*) a movable keel that may be drawn up inside a boat; a square-peaked cap. — *adj* **cheese'-head** (of bolts and screws) having a short thick cylindrical head. — **cheese'hopper** or **cheese skipper** a small fly (*Piophila casei*) whose larvae feed on cheese and move by jumping; **cheese'mite** a very small arachnid (*Tyroglyphus longior*) that breeds in cheese; **cheese'monger** a dealer in cheese; **cheese'parer** a mean or stingy person, a skinflint; **cheese'paring** *orig* a paring of cheese rind; parsimony, stinginess. — *adj* mean and parsimonious. — **cheese'press** a machine or device in which curds for cheese are pressed; **cheese'-rennet** the plant lady's bedstraw, said to have been used formerly as rennet in curdling milk; **cheese straw** a long thin piece of pastry flavoured with cheese; **cheese'taster** a long hollow tool for taking a sample from the inside of a cheese; **cheese'vat** a vat or wooden case in which curds are separated or pressed in cheese making; **cheese'wire** a thin wire used for cutting cheese; **cheese'-wood** (*Austr*) the yellow wood of various Australian trees of the genus *Pittosporum*; **cheese'wring** another name for a cheesepress. — **green cheese** unripe or unmatured cheese; **hard cheese** (*slang*) hard luck; **make cheeses** (*archaic*) to whirl round and then sink down suddenly so as to make the skirt stand out like a cheese. [OE *cēse*, *cȳse* curdled milk (cf Ger *Käse* cheese), from L *cāseus*]

cheese[2] *chēz*, *n* the correct thing (*obs slang*); anything of excellent quality. — **big cheese** (*slang*) a person of importance, a boss. [Prob Pers and Hindi *chīz* thing]

cheese[3] *chēz*, *vt* (*slang*; usu *imperative*) in the phrases **cheese it** to stop it; run away, clear off, make oneself scarce (*esp thieves' slang*); **cheesed off** (also **cheesed**) fed up, disgusted, disgruntled. — *vi* (*slang*) to grovel.

cheetah or **chetah** *chē'tə*, *n* a large animal of the cat family, found in Africa and SW Asia, the fastest land animal, having long legs, a spotted coat and claws that cannot be retracted. [Hindi *cītā*, from Sans *citraka*, *citrakāya* having a speckled body]

cheewink. Same as **chewink**.

chef *shef*, *n* a *usu* male cook, *esp* a head cook (in full **chef de cuisine** (*də kwē-zēn*) the head of a kitchen), *esp* in a hotel or restaurant; a medieval reliquary in the shape of a head. — **chef d'oeuvre** (*shā-dœ-vr'*) a masterpiece: — *pl* **chefs d'oeuvre** (*shā-*). [Fr, head, chief; see **chief**]

cheilitis *kī-lī'tis*, (*med*) *n* inflammation, dryness and cracking of the lips or the corners of the mouth.

cheiro-. See **chiro-**.

cheka *chā'kə*, *n* (also with *cap*) the Russian secret police of 1917–22. — *n* **chek'ist** a member of the cheka. [Russ *che ka*, names of the initial letters of the words for extraordinary commission]

Chekhovian or **Chekovian** *che-kō'vi-ən*, *adj* pertaining to the Russian writer Anton *Chekhov* (1860–1904), or to (the style of) his stories and plays.

chela[1] *kē'lə*, *n* (*zool*) the prehensile claw of an arthropod such as the crab: — *pl* **chē'lae** (*-ē*). — *adj* **chē'late**. — *n* (*chem*) a coordination compound (eg haemoglobin) in which a central metallic ion is attached to an organic molecule at two or more positions. — *vi* (*chem*) to form a chelate. — *n* **chēlā'tion**. — *n* **chēlā'tor**. — *adj* **chēlif'erous** (*zool*) having a chela or chelae. — *adj* **chēliform** (*zool*) shaped like a chela or pincer. — *n* **chē'liped** one of the pair of legs carrying the chelae in arthropods. — **chelation therapy** the treatment of heavy metal (eg lead) poisoning or certain other diseases by a substance (**chelating agent**) which combines chemically with the toxic substances and renders them harmless. [Latinized from Gr *chēlē* claw]

chela[2] *chā'lə*, *n* a novice in Buddhism; a disciple of a religious teacher or leader. — *n* **che'laship**. [Hindi *celā* servant, disciple]

chelate, chelating agent, chelation therapy. See **chela**[1].

chelicera *kē-lis'ə-rə*, *n* one of a pair of biting appendages on the heads of arachnids: — *pl* **chēlic'erae** (*-rē*). — *adj* and *n* **chelic'erate** (*zool*) (of or like) a member of the subphylum *Chelicerata*, including arachnids and the horsehoe crab. [Gr *chēlē* a crab's claw, and *keras* horn]

cheliferous, cheliped. See **chela**[1].

Chellean *shel'i-ən*, (*old archaeol*) *adj* belonging to an early Palaeolithic culture, older than Acheulean. [*Chelles*, near Paris, where flints of this stage are found]

cheloid. See **keloid**.

chelone *kə-lō'nē*, *n* any perennial N American plant of the genus *Chelone*, *esp* varieties cultivated for their lilac, pink or white flowers, the turtle-head. [Gr *chelōnē* tortoise]

chelonian *ki-lō'ni-ən*, *n* a reptile of the order *Chelonia*, with a horny shell and horny beak, including tortoises and turtles. — Also *adj*. [Gr *chelōnē* a tortoise]

Chelsea *chel'sē*, *n* a district of London formerly noted as an artists' quarter. — **Chelsea bun** a rolled bun filled with currants and raisins; **Chelsea pensioner** an elderly, often disabled, ex-soldier, connected with the Chelsea Royal Hospital; **Chelsea ware** a variety of china made in the 18c.

cheluviation *kē-lōō-vi-ā'shən*, (*bot*) *n* the leaching of iron and aluminium oxides from soils, *esp* those planted with conifers and heaths.

chem. *abbrev*: chemical; chemistry.

chem- *kem-*, **chemi-** *kem-i-* or **chemo-** *kēmō-*, *combining forms* denoting chemicals or indicating the involvement of chemical reactions. — *adj* **chemiat'ric** iatrochemical, of medicine and physicians. — *n* **chemiluminesc'ence** luminescence arising from chemical processes, eg that of the glow-worm. — *n* **chem'itype** any chemical process for obtaining impressions from an engraving. — *n* **chem'itȳpy**. — *n* **chemoattrac'tant** a chemical which provokes a chemotactic movement of eg cells or bacteria towards its area of highest concentration. — *n* **chemoautotroph** (*kemöt'ə-trof*) (*biol*) any organism, eg bacteria, that produces energy by a process of oxidation of inorganic compounds, such as iron, ammonia and hydrogen sulphate. — *n* **chem'ōnasty** (*bot*) plant movement provoked, but not orientated by a chemical stimulus. — *n* **chemoprophylaxis** the prevention of infectious disease by drugs. — *n* **chemōpsychī'atry** treatment of mental illness by drugs. — *adj* **chemōpsychiat'ric**. — *adj* **chemōrecep'tive**. — *n* **chemōrecep'tor** a sensory nerve-ending that responds to a chemical stimulus. — *n* **chemosphere** (*meteorol*) the thermosphere. — *n* **chem'ōstat** an apparatus for growing cultures of bacteria, fungi, tissue, etc. — *n* **chemōsyn'thesis** (*bot*) the formation of organic molecules by some bacteria by means of energy derived from chemical changes. — *adj* **chemōtac'tic** pertaining to chemotaxis. — *n* **chemōtax'is** movement of cells or a whole organism in a definite direction in response to chemical stimulus. — *n sing* **chemōtherapeu'tics** or more commonly **chemōther'apy** treatment of infectious diseases or cancer by means of chemical compounds selectively directed against invading microorganisms or cancerous tissue. — *n* **chemot'ropism** (*bot* and *zool*) orientation by differential growth in response to chemical stimulus. — *adj* **chemōtrop'ic**. — *n* **chemurgy** (*kem'ər-ji*) a branch of applied chemistry concerned with the use of agricultural products, or other organic raw materials, for industry. — *adj* **chemur'gic** or **chemur'gical**. [New L, from Late Gr *chēmeiā* (see **alchemy**)]

chemic, chemical, etc. See under **chemistry**.

chemico- *kem-i-kō*, *combining form* signifying a combination with chemistry or chemicals.

chemin de fer *shə-mɛ̃ -də fer'*, (*cards*) *n* a variety of baccarat (*familiar* short form **chemmy** *shem'i*). [Fr, railway]

chemise *shə-mēz'*, *n* a woman's shirt-like undergarment; a straight dress, a smock. — *n* **chemisette'** a kind of bodice worn by women; formerly, a piece of lace or muslin filling up the open front of a woman's dress. [Fr *chemise*, from LL *camisia* a nightgown, surplice]

chemistry *kem'is-tri*, *n* the physical science of the properties of elementary and compound substances, and the laws of their combination and action one upon another (also *archaic* **chymistry** *kim'is-tri*); loosely, the elements contained in or making up any complex structure or phenomenon; an indefinable or instinctual quality that causes an interaction between two people, as in *sexual chemistry*. — *adj* **chem'ic** alchemical (*obs*); iatrochemical (*obs*); chemical. — *n* an alchemist or a chemist (*obs*); bleaching powder (*archaic*). — *vt* to treat with bleaching powder: — *pr p* **chem'icking**; *pa t* and *pa p* **chem'icked**. — *adj* **chem'ical** relating to chemistry; versed in or studying chemistry; alchemical (*obs*); iatrochemical (*obs*). — *n* a substance obtained by chemical means or used in chemical operations. — *adv* **chem'ically**. — *n* **chem'ism** (*obs*) chemical action. — *n* **chem'ist** a person skilled in chemistry; a manufacturer of or dealer in chemicals and drugs; a pharmacist; an alchemist (*obs*). — **chemical abuse** the act or process of taking, smoking or sniffing harmful drugs, chemical solvents, etc; **chemical affinity** the tendency to combine with one another exhibited by many substances, or the force by which the substances constituting a compound are held together; **chemical closet** or **toilet** a kind of toilet containing deodorizing and liquefying chemicals, used when running water is not available; **chemical dependency** addiction to alcohol and/or drugs; **chemical engineering** engineering applied to the design, construction and operational processes of (*esp* industrial) chemical plant and works; **chemical reaction** a process in which the structure of a chemical is changed to form another substance which retains the nuclei of the original chemical or chemicals but with a different configuration or content of atoms, energy, etc; **chemical warfare** warfare involving the use of irritating or asphyxiating gases, oil flames, etc; **chemical wood** wood pulp broken down by the action of chemicals, used in the manufacture of synthetic fibres, paper, etc. [See ety for **alchemy**]

chemmy. See **chemin de fer**.

chenar *chē-när'*, *n* the oriental plane tree (*Platanus orientalis*). [Pers *chinār*]

chenet *shə-ne*, (*Fr*) *n* an andiron.

chenille *shə-nēl'*, *n* a thick, velvety cord or yarn of silk or wool resembling a woolly caterpillar; a velvet-like material used for table covers, etc. [Fr *chenille* hairy caterpillar, from L *canicula* a little dog, from *canis* a dog]

chenix. See **choenix**.

chenopod *ken'ō-pod*, *n* any dicotyledonous flowering plant of the family **Chenopodiā'ceae** including leaf beet, sugar beet, beetroot, mangelwurzel, spinach and goosefoot. — *adj* **chenopodiā'ceous**. [Gr *chēn* goose, and *pous*, *podos* foot]

cheongsam *chongsam'*, *n* a tight-fitting high-necked dress with slits at the sides, as worn by Chinese women. [Chin (Cantonese), long dress]

cheque or (*NAm*) **check** *chek*, *n* a money order on a bank; a counterfoil (*obs*). — **cheque book** or (*NAm*) **check'-book** a book of cheque forms; **cheque card** a card issued by a bank to a client, guaranteeing payment of cheques up to a certain limit. — **blank cheque** a cheque signed by the drawer without having the amount indicated; concession of power without limit (*fig*); **cheque-book diplomacy** negotiations where financial considerations are the most important element; **cheque-book journalism** news, articles, etc based on information bought, *usu* at a high price; **crossed cheque** an ordinary cheque with two transverse lines drawn across it, which have the effect of making it payable only through a bank account. [See **check**]

chequer *chek'ər*, *n* a chessboard, also a chessman (*archaic*); alternation of colours, as on a chessboard (see also **checker**). — *vt* to mark in squares of different colours; to variegate; to interrupt. — *adj* **cheq'uered** or **check'ered** variegated, like a chessboard; varying in character; eventful, with alternations of good and bad fortune, as in *a chequered career*. — *adv* **cheq'uerwise**. — **chequered flag** the black and white flag shown to the winner and subsequent finishers in a motor race; **chequered skipper** a rare British butterfly (*Carterocephalus palaemon*) having dark brown wings with light gold markings resembling those on a chessboard; **cheq'uerwork** any pattern having alternating squares of different colours. [See **check**]

chequy. See under **check**.

cher or *fem* **chère** *sher*, (*Fr*) *adj* dear.

cheralite *cher'ə-līt*, *n* a radioactive mineral rich in thorium and uranium. [*Chera*, ancient name of Travancore, where discovered, and Gr *lithos* a stone]

cherchef't. A Miltonic spelling of **kerchiefed**.

Cherenkov radiation. A variant spelling of **Cerenkov radiation**.

cherimoya *cher-i-moi'ə* or **cherimoyer** *-ər*, *n* a Peruvian fruit (*Anona cherimolia*) resembling the custard apple. [Quechua]

cherish *cher'ish*, *vt* to protect and treat with great care and affection; to treasure; to nurture, nurse; to entertain in the mind. — *adj* **cher'ished** (of number plates) with a combination of letters and numbers specially chosen by the owner of the vehicle. — *n* **cher'ishment**. [Fr *chérir*, *chérissant*, from *cher* dear, from L *cārus*]

Cherkess *chər-kes'*, *n* a Circassian; the Caucasian language of the Cherkesses: — *pl* **cherkess'es**. [Russ]

chernozem *chûr'nō-zem*, *n* a very fertile soil of sub-humid steppe, consisting of a dark topsoil over a lighter calcareous layer. — Also **tscher'nosem**. [Russ, black earth]

Cherokee *cher'ə-kē*, *n* (a member of) a tribe of Iroquoian Indians of N America, now mainly living in Oklahoma; the Iroquoian language of the Cherokee.

cheroot *shə-ro͞ot'*, *n* a cigar cut square at either end. [Fr *cheroute*, representing the Tamil name *shuruttu* a roll]

cherry[1] *cher'i*, *n* a small fleshy fruit having a large hard stone; the tree (*Cerasus*, a subgenus of *Prunus*) that bears it; any tree bearing similar fruits; the wood of any of these trees; a bright red colour, cherry-red; the new ball, taken after a certain number of runs have been scored or overs bowled (*cricket slang*); virginity or the hymen (*slang*). — *adj* like a cherry in colour, *usu* bright red; ruddy. — **cherry bean** another name for the cowpea; **cherr'y-bob** in children's games, two cherries joined by the stalks; **cherry bounce** cherry brandy; brandy and sugar; **cherry brandy** a liqueur made by steeping Morello cherries in brandy; **cherr'y-coal** a soft shining coal; **cherry laurel** a species of cherry with evergreen laurel-like leaves; **cherr'y-pepper** a W Indian capsicum; **cherry picker** a type of crane consisting of a jointed or telescopic hydraulic arm ending in a platform which is raised to enable work or inspection to be carried out at heights; **cherry-pie'** a pie made of cherries; the common garden heliotrope; **cherr'y-pit** (*obs*) a game in which cherry-stones are thrown into a small hole; **cherry plum** a plum that has a flavour similar to a cherry; **cherr'y-stone** the hard endocarp of the cherry, the stone; **cherry tomato** a small cherry-sized red or yellow tomato. — **have** (or **take**) **two bites** (or **a second bite**) **at the cherry** (*colloq*) to have (or take) a second chance or opportunity. [OE *ciris*, from L *cerasus*, from Gr *kerasos* a cherry-tree; it is said to have been introduced from *Kerasous* (*Cerasus*) in Pontus, by Lucullus, but was known in Europe long before his time]

cherry[2] *cher'i*, (*Spenser*) *vt* to cheer. [See **cherish**]

chersonese *kûr'sə-nēz* or *-nēs*, (*esp poetic*) *n* a peninsula. [Gr *chersonēsos*, from *chersos* land, dry land, and *nēsos* an island]

chert *chûrt*, (*geol*) *n* a siliceous rock of cryptocrystalline silica occurring as bands or concretions in sedimentary rock, eg limestone. — *adj* **chert'y**. [Ety doubtful]

cherub *cher'əb*, *n* a winged being with human face, an attendant of God (*Bible*); an angelic being of the second order of celestial spirits, ranking above thrones and below seraphim; a sweet innocent-looking chubby-faced person, *esp* a child: — *pl* **cher'ubs**, **cher'ubim** (*-ə* or *-ū-bim*) or **cher'ubims**. — *adj* **cherubic** (*-o͞o'bik*),

cheru'bical or **cherubim'ic** angelic. — *adv* **cheru'bically**. — *n* **cher'ubin** (*Shakesp*) a cherub. [Heb *k'rub*, pl *k'rubim*]

cherup *cher'up*. Same as **chirrup**.

chervil *chûr'vil*, *n* an umbelliferous plant (*Anthriscus cerefolium*) cultivated as an aromatic pot-herb; also other species of Anthriscus (*common*, *wild* and *rough chervil*); extended to sweet cicely (*sweet chervil*). [OE *cerfille*, from L *caerefolium*, from Gr *chairephyllon*, from *chairein* to enjoy, and *phyllon* a leaf]

Ches. *abbrev*: Cheshire.

Cheshire *chesh'ər* or *-ēr*, *n* a type of mild cheese, *orig* made in the county of Cheshire. — Also **Cheshire cheese**.

Cheshire cat. See under **cat**[1].

Cheshvan. See **Hesvan**.

chesil *chez'il*, *n* gravel, shingle (*obs*); bran (*dialect*). — Also **chis'el**. [OE *cisil*]

chesnut. See **chestnut**.

chess[1] *ches*, *n* a game of skill for two players, in which figures or men of different kinds are moved on a chequered board. — **chess'board** the board on which chess is played; a chequered design; **chess'man** any of the sixteen figures used by each player in a game of chess. [OFr *eschès* (Fr *échecs*; Ital *scacchi*; Ger *Schach*), from Pers *shāh* a king]

chess[2] *ches*, *n* one of the parallel planks forming the deck of a pontoon-bridge (*usu* in *pl*).

chess[3] a *US* name for **rye-brome**.

chessel *ches'l*, *n* a cheese mould. [**cheese**[1]]

chessylite *ches'i-līt*, *n* basic carbonate of copper, vivid blue in colour, azurite. [*Chessy*, near Lyons in France, where it occurs]

chest *chest*, *n* a large strong box; the part of the body between the neck and the abdomen, the non-technical name for the thorax; a treasury; a chestful. — *vt* (*esp* in football) to hit or direct (the ball) with one's chest. — *adj* **chest'ed** having a chest; placed in a chest. — *n* **chest'ful** enough to fill a chest. — *adj* **chest'y** of the quality of the chest-voice; suggestive of disease of the chest (*colloq*); having a large chest or bosom; self-important (*slang*). — **chest freezer** a long, low freezer which opens at the top; **chest'-note** in singing or speaking, a deep note; **chest protector** a covering to keep the chest warm; **chest register**, **chest tone** or **chest voice** the lowest register of the voice (cf **head voice**). — **chest of drawers** a piece of furniture consisting of a case in which a number of drawers slide; **chest of viols** (*archaic*) a set of viols (*usu* two trebles, two tenors, two basses) for ensemble playing; **get (something) off one's chest** (*colloq*) to get (something) off one's mind by admitting, stating or declaring (it) openly. [OE *cyst*, from L *cista*, from Gr *kistē*; Scot *kist*]

chesterfield *chest'ər-fēld*, *n* a heavily padded sofa; formerly, a long overcoat. [Lord *Chesterfield* (1694–1773), English statesman and author]

chestnut (now rarely **chesnut**) *ches'nut*, *n* a tree of genus *Castanea*, *esp* the *Spanish* or *sweet chestnut*; its edible nut, encased (three together) in a prickly husk; its hard timber; the **horse chestnut** (*Aesculus hippocastanum*), its fruit, nut or timber; a chestnut horse; a horny knob on the inner surface of a horse's foreleg; a stale joke or cliché. — *adj* of chestnut colour, reddish-brown. — **pull the chestnuts out of the fire** to take control and rescue someone or something from a difficult situation, *esp* one that seems hopeless. [OFr *chastaigne*, from L *castanea*, perh from *Castana*, in Thessaly]

Chesvan. See **Hesvan**.

chetah. See **cheetah**.

chetnik *chet'nik*, *n* a Serbian resistance fighter involved in guerilla warfare against Turkish rule in the 19c and against occupying forces in both World Wars. [Serb *cetnik*, from *ceta* a troop]

cheval de bataille *shə-val də bä-tä-y*, (*Fr*) *n* a favourite topic or subject, a hobby, literally warhorse.

cheval-de-frise *shə-val-də-frēz'*, *n* a defensive structure of iron spikes set in wood, used *esp* to stop cavalry: — *pl* **chevaux-de-frise** (*shə-vō-*). [Fr *cheval* horse, *de* of, and *Frise* Friesland]

chevalet *shə-va'lā* or *she'*, (*music*) *n* the bridge of a stringed instrument. [Fr, dimin of *cheval*, a horse]

cheval-glass *shə-val'-gläs*, *n* a large glass or mirror supported on a frame and able to swivel. — Also **cheval mirror**. [Fr *cheval* horse, stand]

chevalier *shev-ə-lēr'*, *n* a cavalier; a knight; a gallant. — **chevalier d'industrie** (*shə-va-lyā dɛ̃-düs-trē*; *Fr*) an adventurer, a person who lives by his wits, literally a knight of industry. [Fr, from LL *caballārius*, from L *caballus*, a horse]

chevelure *shev'(ə-)lür*, *n* a head of hair or arrangement of the hair; a periwig; the nebulous part of a comet (*astron*). [Fr, from L *capillātūra*, from *capillus* hair]

cheven *chev'ən*, *n* the chub. — Also **chev'in**. [Fr *chevin*, *chevanne*]

cheverel or **cheveril** *chev'ər-əl*, *n* a kid; soft, flexible kidskin leather. — *adj* like kid leather, soft and pliable. — *n* **chevrette** (*shəv-ret'*) a thin kind of goatskin. — *n* **chevron** or **cheveron** (*shev'*; *obs*) a kid glove. [Fr *chevreau*, *chevrette* a kid, from *chèvre*; L *capra* a she-goat]

cheverye (*Spenser*). See **chiefery** under **chief**.

chevesaile *chev'ə-sāl*, *n* an ornamental collar of a coat. [OFr *chevesaile*, from *chevece* the neck]

chevet *shə-vā'*, (*archit*) *n* the eastern end of a Christian church comprising the apse and chapels. [Fr]

cheville *shə-vē'*, *n* the peg of a stringed instrument (*music*); a redundant word or expression used in a verse or sentence for purposes of metre or balance only. [Fr, peg, from L *clāvicula*, dimin of *clāvis* a key]

chevin. See **cheven**.

Cheviot *chē'vi-ət* or *chev'i-ət*, *n* a hardy breed of short-woolled sheep reared on the *Cheviot* Hills; a cloth made from their wool.

chevisance *chev'i-zəns*, *n* (*obs*) achievement; resource; gain; money dealings; performance (*Spenser*); an unidentified flower. [Fr, from *chevir* to accomplish; *chef* the head, the end]

chèvre *shevr'*, (*Fr*) *n* cheese made from goat's milk.

chevrette. See **cheverel**.

chevron[1] *shev'rən*, *n* a rafter; the representation, *usu* on a shield, of two rafters of a house meeting at the top (*heraldry*); a V-shaped band on the sleeve, a mark of non-commissioned rank or (in army and RAF, inverted) of long service and good conduct; a pattern consisting of a line of horizontal black and white V-shapes on a board (**chevron board**) used as a road sign to indicate a sharp bend. — *adj* **chev'roned**. — *adj* **chev'rony** (*heraldry*). [Fr *chevron* rafter, from L *capreolus*, dimin of *caper* a goat]

chevron[2]. See under **cheverel**.

chevrotain *shev'rō-tān* or *-tən*, *n* a mouse deer, a member of the family *Tragulidae*, an Old World primitive group of tropical forest-dwelling small, deerlike animals intermediate in form between true deer and other ungulates such as pigs, including the water chevrotain (*Hyemoschus aquatcus*) of C Africa, and three species of the genus *Tragulus* found in SE Asia. [Fr, dimin of *chèvre*, from L *capra* she-goat]

chevy. See **chivvy**.

chew *chōō*, *vt* to bruise and grind with the teeth; to masticate; to meditate, reflect. — *n* the action of chewing; something that is chewed, *esp* a quid of tobacco. — *adj* **chew'able**. — *n* **chew'er**. — *n* **chew'ie** (*esp Austr slang*) chewing-gum. — *adj* **chew'y** soft and sticky, able or requiring to be chewed, like toffee. — **chew'ing-gum** a preparation made from chicle gum, produced by the sapodilla plum tree, sweetened and flavoured, or a substitute for this. — **chew out** (*colloq*) to tell off, reprimand; **chew the cud** (of cows, etc) to masticate for a second time food that has already been swallowed and partly digested in the first stomach; to ruminate in thought (also **chew over**); **chew the rag** or **chew the fat** (*slang*) to keep on arguing the point; to converse, gossip; **chew up** to destroy, damage or disfigure (something) by a biting or grinding action like chewing; to cause (someone) to be upset or nervous (*colloq*). [OE *cēowan*; Ger *kauen*; cf **jaw**[1]]

chewet[1] *chōō'it*, *n* a chough (*obs*); a chatterer (*Shakesp*). [Fr *chouette* chough (now owl)]

chewet[2] *chōō'it*, (*obs*) *n* a pie or pudding of miscellaneous chopped meats.

chewink *chə-wingk'*, *n* a large finch of eastern N America, the red-eyed towhee. [Imit]

Cheyenne *shī-an'* or *-en'*, *n* (a member of) a tribe of N American Indians now living in Montana and Oklahoma; the Algonquian language of this tribe. [Can Fr, from Siouan (Dakota) *Shahiyena* people who speak unintelligibly]

chez *shā*, (*Fr*) *prep* at the home or establishment of.

chg. *abbrev*: charge.

chi[1] *kī* or *hhē*, *n* the twenty-second letter (X or χ) of the Greek alphabet, representing an aspirated *k* sound; as numeral χ' = 600, $_{\prime}\chi$ = 600 000; in inscriptions χ = 1000 (for **chilīoi**). [Gr *chei*, *chī*]

chi[2] *chī*. Same as **chai**.

chi[3], **ch'i**. See **qi**.

chiack *chī'ak*, (*Austr colloq*) *vt* to tease, deride, jeer at. — Also *n*. — Also **chy'ack**. — *n* **chī'acking**. [UK obs slang, to greet, salute]

Chian *kī'ən*, *adj* pertaining to *Chios*, an island in the Aegean Sea. — *n* an inhabitant of Chios.

Chianti *kē-an'ti* or *-än'*, or *Ital kyän'tē*, *n* a dry red (or white) wine of Tuscany. [*Chianti* Mountains]

chiao *jow*, *n* a coin of the People's Republic of China, one-tenth of 1 yuan: — *pl* **chiao**. [Chin]

chiarezza *kya-ret'za*, (*music*) *n* purity, clarity, brightness. [Ital]

chiaroscuro *kyär-ō-skōō'rō*, (*esp painting*) *n* management or disposition of light and shade in a picture; a painting in black and white; the effect of light and shade or variety and contrast (also *fig*): — *pl* **chiaroscu'ros**. [Ital, literally bright dark, from *chiaro* clear, and *oscuro* obscure, dark]

chiasma *kī-az'mə*, or **chiasm** *kī'azm*, *n* the cross-shaped connection formed by the crossing over of Chromatids during meiosis (*biol*); a decussation or intersection, *esp* that of the optic nerves (*anatom*): — *pl* **chias'mas**, **chias'mata** or **chi'asms**. — *n* **chīas'mus** (*rhetoric*) contrast by parallelism in reverse order, as *Do not live to eat, but eat to live*: — *pl* **chias'mi**. — *adj* **chīas'tic**. — *n* **chīas'tolite** (Gr *lithos* a stone; *mineralogy*) a variety of andalusite with black cruciform inclusions of carbonaceous matter. [Gr *chiasma* a cross-shaped mark, *chiastos* laid crosswise, like the Greek letter X (*chi*, *chei*)]

chiaus *chows*. Same as **chouse**.

chibol. See **cibol**.

chibouk or **chibouque** *chi-bŏŏk'*, *n* a long straight-stemmed Turkish tobacco pipe. [Turk *chibūk*]

chic *shēk*, *n* style, elegance; artistic skill. — *adj* having chic; smart, elegant and fashionable. — *adv* **chic'ly**. [Fr]

chica, **chicha** or **chico** *chē'kə*, *n* an orange-red dye-stuff, used by S American Indians as a stain for the skin, and obtained by boiling the leaves of bignonia. [From a native name]

Chicago *shi-kä'gō*, *n* a form of contract bridge played in sets of four deals, not in rubbers. [The US city]

chicane *shi-kān'*, *vi* (*archaic*) to use tricks and artifice. — *vt* (*archaic*) to deceive. — *n* a trick or artifice; a series of sharp bends on a motor-racing track; a bridge hand without trumps, for which a score above the line used to be allowed. — *n* **chicā'ner** a person who chicanes; a quibbler. — *n* **chicā'nery** trickery or sharp practice, *esp* in legal proceedings; quibbling, deception. — *n* **chicā'ning** quibbling, deception. [Fr *chicane* sharp practice at law, from Late Gr *tzykanion* a game at mall, *tzykanizein* to play at mall, from Pers *tchugagan* a crooked mallet]

chicano *chi-kä'nō* or *shi-*, *n* (*US*, sometimes considered *derog*; also with *cap*) an American of Mexican descent: — *pl* **chica'nos**. — *fem* **chica'na**: — *pl* **chica'nas**. — Also *adj*. [Sp *mejicano* Mexican]

chiccory. See **chicory**.

chich *chich*. Same as **chickpea**.

chicha[1] *chēch'ə*, *n* a S American liquor fermented from maize or cane sugar, etc; a S American tree with edible nut-like seeds. [Am Sp]

chicha[2]. See **chica**.

chichi or **chi-chi** *shē'shē* or *chē'chē*, *adj* pretentious; fussy, precious, affected; stylish, chic, self-consciously fashionable. — *n* something that is, or the quality of being, chichi; red tape; fuss. [Fr]

chi-chi *chē'chē*, (*disparagingly*) *n* formerly in British India, a Eurasian; affected or mincing Eurasian English. — Also *adj*. — Also **chee'-chee**. [Perh Hindi *chī-chī* nasty, fie!, as characterizing the manner of their speech]

chick[1] *chik*, *n* the young of fowls, *esp* of the hen; a child, as a term of endearment; a girl or young woman (*slang*). — *n* **chick'en** the young of birds, *esp* of the domestic fowl; the domestic fowl; the flesh of a fowl (not always very young); a prairie chicken; a youthful person, *esp* a girl; a faint-hearted person (*colloq*); a type of game, challenge or competition in which physically dangerous or forbidden activities are undertaken until one of the participants loses their nerve (*colloq*). — *adj* (*colloq*) cowardly, frightened, scared. — *vi* (*colloq*) to show fear. — *n* **chick'ling** a little chicken. — **chick'-a-biddy** or **chick'-a-diddle** terms of endearment addressed to children; **chick'en-feed** poultry food; small change or a trifling sum of money (*colloq*); something of little value (*colloq*); **chicken hawk** (*esp* (*US*) any hawk that preys on domestic chickens; **chick'en-hazard** a game at hazard for low stakes. — *adj* **chick'en-hearted** or **chick'en-livered** timid, cowardly. — **chick'enpox** a contagious febrile disease, chiefly affecting children, not unlike a mild form of smallpox; **chicken run** an enclosure for hens; **chicken wire** wire-netting having a small hexagonal mesh; **chick'pea** see separate entry; **chick'weed** any plant of the genus *Stellaria*, *esp S. media*, one of the commonest of weeds, much relished by fowls and cagebirds; a similar related plant, **mouse-ear chickweed**, of the genus *Cerastium*; **chickweed-wintergreen** see **wintergreen** under **winter**. — **chicken-and-egg situation** one in which it is impossible to tell which is the cause and which the effect; **chicken out** (*colloq*; often with *of*) to desert, quit, through losing one's nerve or cowardice; **count one's chickens before they are hatched** to plan or act on the basis of expectations or future results without conclusive evidence that they will be fulfilled; **no (spring) chicken** (*derog* or *facetious*) no longer young; **the chickens have come home to roost** see under **roost**[1]. [OE *cicen*; cf Du *kieken*, Ger *Küken*]

chick[2] *chik*, (*Anglo-Ind*) *n* a hanging door screen or sun blind of narrow strips of bamboo laced together or fastended loosely with string. [Hindi *ciq*]

chickadee *chik-ə-dē'*, *n* a N American songbird of the titmouse family (*Paridae*). [Imit, from its note]

chickaree *chik-ə-rē'*, *n* another name for the American red squirrel, *Sciurus hudsonicus*. [Imit, from its cry]

chickling[1] *chik'ling*, *n* a species of pea (also **chickling vetch** *Lathyrus sativus*). [Earlier *chich*, *chichling*, from Fr *chiche*, from L *cicer* chickpea]

chickling[2]. See **chick**[1].

chickpea *n* gram, a plant of the pea family (*Cicer arietinum*); its edible pea-like seed. [Earlier *chick-pease*, with ety as **chickling**].

chicle *chik'l* or *chik'li*, *n* the gum of the sapodilla tree, the main ingredient in chewing-gum. [Sp, from Nahuatl]

chicly. See **chic**.

chico. See **chica**.

chicory or **chiccory** *chik'ə-ri*, *n* succory, a blue-flowered composite plant (*Cichorium intybus*); its carrot-like root (roasted and ground and used as a coffee substitute). — *n* **chic'on** (*-ən*) the shoot of the chicory plant, eaten like lettuce. [Fr *chicorée*, from L *cichorēum*, from Gr *kichorion*]

chide *chīd*, *vt* to scold, rebuke, reprove by words. — *vi* to make a snarling, murmuring sound, as a dog or trumpet does: — *pr p* **chīd'ing**; *pa t* **chid** or sometimes **chīd'ed** or **chode** (*archaic*); *pa p* **chid** or **chidd'en** or sometimes **chīd'ed**. — *n* **chīd'er** (*Shakesp*) a quarrelsome person. — *n* **chīd'ing** scolding. [OE *cīdan* (a weak verb)]

chidlings. See **chitterling**.

chief *chēf*, *adj* head; principal, highest, first; outstanding, important (with *compar* **chief'er**, *superl* **chief'est**); intimate (*Scot*). — *adv* chiefly. — *n* a head or principal person; a leader; the principal part or top of anything; the greater part; the upper part of the field cut off by a horizontal line, generally occupying the upper third of the area of the shield (*heraldry*). — *n* **chief'dom** or **chief'ship** the state of being chief; sovereignty. — *n* **chief'ery** or **chief'ry** (*Spenser* **chev'erye**) an Irish chieftaincy; the dues paid to a chief or the supreme lord; a chief's lands. — *n* **chief'ess** a female chief. — *adj* **chief'less** without a chief or leader. — *n* **chief'ling**. — *adv* **chief'ly** in the first place; principally; for the most part. — *n* **chief'tain** the head of a clan; a leader or commander: — *fem* **chief'tainess**. — *n* **chief'taincy**. — *n* — **chief'tainry**. — *n* **chief'tainship**. — **chief-bar'on** the President of the Court of Exchequer; **Chief Constable** (in UK) an officer commanding the police force in an administrative area; **chief justice** see under **justice**. — **-in-chief** *combining form* denoting at the head, first in rank, as *commander-in-chief*. — **chief of staff** (*military*) a senior staff officer; (with *cap*) the senior officer of each of the armed forces (in the US of the army and air force); **in chief** borne in the upper part of the shield (*heraldry*); (of a tenure) held directly from the sovereign; most importantly. [Fr *chef*, from L *caput* the head]

chield *chēld*, (*Scot*) *n* a lad, a man. — Also **chiel**. [Appar a form of **child**]

chiffchaff *chif'chaf*, *n* a small European warbler, *Phylloscopus collybita*. [Imit of its call]

chiffon *shif'on* or *shē'fɔ̃*, *n* a thin fine clothing fabric of silk, nylon, etc; (in *pl*) trimmings, or other adornments. — *n* **chiffonier** or **chiffonnier** (*shif-ən-ēr'*) an ornamental cabinet; a chest of drawers. [Fr, rag, adornment, from *chiffe* rag]

chigger. See **chigoe**.

chignon *shē'nyɔ̃*, *n* a knot or roll of hair worn at the back of the head and neck. [Fr, the nape of the neck (jointed like a chain), from *chânon* link of a chain, from *chaîne* a chain]

chigoe *chig'ō*, **chigre** or **chigger** *chig'ər*, *n* a tropical American, African and Indian sand flea (*Tunga penetrans*), the pregnant female of which buries itself in the skin of its host, *esp* beneath the toenails; the parasitic larva of a harvest-mite (*Trombicula*) of America, Europe and Asia, that burrows in the skin. — Also **jigg'er**. [W Indian name; cf Carib *chigo*, and Wolof (W African language) *jiga* an insect]

chihuahua *chi-wä'wä*, *n* a breed of very small dog, *orig* from Mexico, weighing around 1kg (2lb), with big eyes and pointed ears. [*Chihuahua* in Mexico]

chik. Same as **chick**[2].

chikara[1] *chi-kä'rə*, *n* a four-horned Indian antelope; an Indian gazelle (also **chinka'ra**). [Hindi]

chikara[2] *chik'ə-rə*, *n* an Indian instrument of the violin class. [Hindi *cikārā*]

chikhor or **chikor**. See **chukor**.

chilblain *chil'blān*, *n* a painful red swelling, *esp* on hands and feet, caused by constriction of small blood vessels in cold weather. [**chill**[1] and **blain**[1]]

child *chīld*, *n* a very young person (up to the age of sixteen for the purpose of some acts of parliament, under fourteen in criminal law); a female infant (*dialect and archaic*); a son or daughter; a childish person; a person strongly influenced by, associated with, or a product of (another person, or group of people, an age or environment, etc); a disciple or adherent; a youth of gentle birth, *esp* in ballads, etc (*archaic*; also **childe** or **chylde**); an offspring; a descendant; an inhabitant: — *pl* **children** (*chil'drən*); double *pl* from (*old* and *dialect*) **chil'der**. — *vt* and *vi* (*archaic*) to bring forth. — *adj* **child'ed** (*Shakesp*) possessed of a child. — *n* **child'hood** the state of being a child; the time of being a child. — *adj* **child'ing** (*Shakesp*) fruiting, teeming. — *adj* **child'ish** of or like a child; silly; trifling. — *adv* **child'ishly**. — *n* **child'ishness** that which is suitable or natural to a child; puerility. — *adj* **child'less** without children. — *adj* **child'like** like a child; becoming a child; docile; innocent. — *adj* **child'ly** (*archaic*) natural or becoming to a child. — *n* **child'ness** (*Shakesp*) the nature or character of a child. — **child abuse** any form of physical or mental cruelty to or neglect of a child by a parent or guardian; **child'bearing** the act or condition of carrying and giving birth to children. — *adj* **child'-bearing**. — **child'bed** (*archaic*) the state or condition of a woman giving birth to a child; **childbed fever** an old name for puerperal fever; **child benefit** (*UK* and *NZ*) an allowance granted by the government to parents for children; **child'birth** the giving birth to a child; parturition; **child care** the provision of residental care by local authorities or other organizations for children whose parents are unable to care for them; the provision of part-time care for children while their parents are at work; **child'crowing** a nervous affection with spasm of the muscles closing the glottis; **child endowment** (*Austr*) child benefit; **child guidance** professional counselling of disturbed or disruptive children; **child'minder** a person, *usu* untrained but often listed on an official register as being fit, who looks after other people's children. — *adj* **child'proof** or **child'-resistant** not able to be damaged, opened, worked, etc by a child. — **Children's Panel** (in the Scottish legal system) a panel of people drawn from social services, the community and other relevant agencies that hear (in private) cases of child crime or child abuse that occur in a locality (in 1970 Children's Panels took over most of the functions of the juvenile courts); **child's play** something very easy to do; **child'-study** the psychology and physiology of children; **child welfare** the health and well-being of young children as an object of systematic social work; **child-wife'** a very young wife. — **second childhood** the childishness of old age; **with child** (*archaic* or *literary*) pregnant. [OE *cild*, pl *cild*, later *cildru*, *cildra*]

Childermas *chil'dər-məs*, (*archaic*) *n* Holy Innocents' Day, a festival (28 Dec) to commemorate the slaying of the children by Herod. [OE *cildra*, genitive pl of *cild* child, and *mæsse* mass]

Chile *chil'i*, *adj* of Chile. — *n* and *adj* **Chil'ean** or *obs* **Chil'ian**. — **Chile** (or **Chilean**) **pine** the monkey puzzle; **Chile saltpetre** impure naturally-occurring sodium nitrate.

chile *chīl*. Variant form of **child**.

chili[1] or **chile** *chil'i*. Variant forms of **chilli**.

chili[2] *shil'ē*, *n* a hot dry wind of N Africa. [Berber]

chiliad *kil'i-ad*, *n* the number 1000; 1000 of anything; a period of 1000 years, a millenium. — *n* **chil'iagon** a plane figure with 1000 angles. — *n* **chiliahē'dron** a solid figure with 1000 plane faces. — *n* **chiliarch** (*kil'i-ärk*) a leader or commander of a thousand men. — *n* **chil'iarchy** the position of chiliarch. — *n* **chil'iasm** the doctrine that at some future time Christ will reign bodily upon the earth for 1000 years. — *n* **chil'iast** a person who holds this belief; a person who believes in a coming happier time on earth. — *adj* **chilias'tic**. [Gr *chīlias*, *-ados*, from *chīlioi* 1000]

chill[1] *chil*, *n* coldness; a cold that causes shivering; an attack of shivering with chattering teeth, pale skin and a sensation of coldness, often preceding a fever (*med*); anything that disheartens or damps the spirits; a type of foundry mould that accelerates cooling. — *adj* shivering with cold; slightly cold; unfriendly, aloof. — *vi* to grow cold; (of a metal) to become hardened by cooling. — *vt* to make chill or cold; to cool; to preserve by cold; to injure with cold; to discourage or dishearten; to fill with dread; to cloud or bloom the surface of (by cold air); to harden (a metal) by cooling; to take the chill off (*dialect*). — *adj* **chilled** made cold; hardened by chilling, as iron; preserved by cold, as beef. — *n* **chill'er**. — *adv* **chill'ily**. — *n* **chill'iness**. — *n* and *adj* **chill'ing**. — *n* **chill'ness**. — *adj* **chill'y** cold; chilling; sensitive to cold; unfriendly, aloof. — **chill cabinet** a refrigerated cabinet for displaying perishable foods in shops, supermarkets, etc; **chilled meal** a ready-prepared dish kept at a low temperature but not frozen, and sold from a chill cabinet; **chill factor** the degree by which weather conditions, eg wind (as in **wind-chill factor**), increase the effect of low temperatures; **chilly bin** (*NZ*) an insulated container for transporting food and drink packed in ice, eg for picnics, etc. — **chill out** (*slang*) to relax, eg after a period of hard work or strenuous exercise; **take the chill off** to warm slightly; to make lukewarm. [OE *cele, ciele* cold; see **cold, cool**]

chill[2]. See **ch**.

chillada *chil-äd'ə, n* in Mexican cookery, a spiced fried cake made from pureed vegetables and lentils, flavoured with green peppers.

chilli *chil'i, n* the pod of one of the varieties of capsicum, extremely pungent and stimulant, used in sauces, pickles, etc, and dried and ground to form cayenne pepper; chilli con carne (*colloq*): — *pl* **chill'is** or **chill'ies**. — Also **chil'i** or **chil'e**. — **chilli con carne** (*kon kär'nē*) a spicy dish of minced meat, chillis or chilli powder, and often kidney beans, tomatoes, etc, originating in Mexico. [Nahuatl]

Chillingham cattle *chil'ing-əm kat'l, n* an ancient breed of wild, white-coated cattle, now confined to a single herd which roams the *Chillingham* estate in Northumberland.

chillum *chil'um, n* the part of a hookah containing the tobacco and charcoal balls; a hookah itself; the act of smoking it. [Hindi *chilam*]

Chilognatha *kī-log'nä-thə, n pl* the order which contains the millipedes. [Gr *cheilos* lip, and *gnathos* jaw]

chilopod *kī'lə-pod* or **chilopodan** *kī-lop'ə-dən, n* a member of the order *Chilopoda* which contains the centipedes. [Gr *cheilos* lip, and *pous, podos* foot]

Chiltern hundreds. See under **hundred**.

chimaera. Older spelling of **chimera**.

chimb. See **chime[2]**.

chime[1] *chīm, n* a set of bells tuned in a scale; (often in *pl*) the ringing of such bells in succession; a definite sequence of bell-like notes sounded as by a clock; the harmonious sound of bells or other musical instruments; agreement of sound or of relation; harmony; rhyme; jingle. — *vi* to sound a chime or in chime; to accord or agree; to jingle; to rhyme; to say words or recite in a rhythmic or mechanical manner. — *vt* to strike, or cause to sound in chime; to indicate by chiming. — **chime in** (*informal*) to join in, in agreement. [ME *chimbe*, perh from OFr *cymbale*, from L *cymbalum* a cymbal]

chime[2] or **chimb** *chīm, n* the rim formed by the ends of the staves of a cask; a hollowed or bevelled channel in the waterway of a ship's deck (*naut*). — Also **chine**. [Cognate with Du *kim*, Ger *Kimme* edge]

chimer *chim'ər* or **chimere** *chi-mēr', n* a long sleeveless tabard; the upper robe worn by a bishop. [OFr *chamarre*; cf **cymar**; Sp *zamarra, chamarra* sheepskin]

chimera or **chimaera** *kī-* or *ki-mē'rə, n* (sometimes with *cap*) any idle or wild fancy; an organism (plant or animal) made up of two genetically distinct tissues or created by combining genetic material from two distinct species (*biol*); a fabled fire-spouting monster, with a lion's head, a serpent's tail, and a goat's body (*Gr mythol*); a picture or representation of an animal having its parts made up of various animals. — *n* **chimer'id** a fish of the genus *Chimaera* or related genera of the family **Chimaer'idae** (*-i-dē*). — *adj* **chimeric** (*-mer'ik*) or **chimer'ical** of the nature of a chimera; wild; fanciful; pertaining to an organism made up of, or created by combining, genetic material from two distinct species. — *adv* **chimer'ically**. — *n* **chimer'ism** the state of being, or the process of creating, a genetic chimera. [L, from Gr *chimaira* a she-goat]

chimere. See **chimer**.

chimney *chim'ni, n* a passage for the escape of fumes, smoke or heated air from a fireplace, engine or furnace; a chimney stack; a glass tube surrounding a lamp flame; a volcanic vent; a steeply-inclined part of a lode or one that branches from the main lode (*mining*); a cleft in a rock-face just large enough for a mountaineer to enter and climb. — Also (*dialect*) **chim'ley** or **chum'ley**. — *vt* (*mountaineering*) to climb (a narrow crevice) with one's back against one wall and feet against the other. — **chim'neybreast** the part of a wall that projects into a room and contains the fireplace and chimney; **chimney can** a chimney pot; **chim'ney-corner** or **chim'ney-nook** (*Scot* **-nuik**) in old chimneys, (a seat in) the space between the fire and the side wall of the fireplace; the fireside, commonly spoken of as the place for the aged and infirm; **chim'ney piece** a shelf over the fireplace, a mantelpiece; **chimney pot** a cylindrical pipe of earthenware or other material at the top of a chimney; a top-hat (in full **chimneypot hat**); **chimney shaft** the part of a chimney which rises above the roof, or a chimney standing isolated, such as a factory chimney; **chimney stack** a group of chimneys or flues contained within a single unit; a chimney stalk; **chimney stalk** a very tall chimney, *usu* serving a factory or power station; **chimney swallow** the common swallow; a species of N American swift (also **chimney swift**); **chim'ney-sweep** or **chim'ney-sweeper** a person who sweeps or cleans chimneys; **chim'ney top** the top of a chimney. [Fr *cheminée*, from L *camīnus* a furnace]

chimo *chē'mō*, (*Can*) *interj* a word used as a greeting. [From Eskimo-Aleut]

Chimonanthus *kī-mō-nan'thəs, n* a genus of shrubs native to China, *esp C. praecox*, the wintersweet, a deciduous species cultivated for its yellow spicy-scented flowers which appear in winter. [New L, from Gr *cheimon* winter, and *anthos* flower]

chimpanzee *chim-pən-zē', n* an intelligent anthropoid ape (*Pan troglodytes*) inhabiting the tropical C African forests, *usu* living as part of a group of four to twenty individuals and considered to be the primate that most closely resembles man in intelligence and social behaviour: — often shortened to **chimp**. [West African dialect]

Chin. *abbrev*: China; Chinese.

chin *chin, n* the jutting part of the face below the mouth, the front of the lower jaw. — *adj* **chin'less** having a receding chin; ineffectual and not very clever, *esp* applied to an upper-class person, as in *chinless wonder* (*facetious*). — *vt* to question or tackle aggressively or impertinently (*slang*). — **chin'strap** the strap on a helmet, etc that goes under the chin. — *n* and *vi* **chin'wag** (*slang*) talk. — **keep one's chin up** to keep cheerful in a difficult situation (*usu* shortened to **chin up**! used as an encouragement); **take it on the chin** to face misfortune, defeat, criticism, etc courageously and without flinching. [OE *cin*; Ger *Kinn*, Gr *genys* (jaw)]

china[1] *chī'nə, n* (*orig* **chi'naware**) articles of porcelain brought from China in the 16c; Chinese porcelain or *esp* any Western imitation or version of it; mate (from *china plate*; *Cockney rhyming slang*). — *adj* made of china; (with *cap*) of, from, etc China. — *n* **Chinese** (*chī-nēz'*) a native or citizen of China (*pl* **Chīnese'** — *archaic colloq sing* **Chīnee'**); the language of China; a meal of Chinese food (*colloq*). — *adj* (in names of commodities, sometimes without *cap*) of, concerning or relating, etc to China, its language or its people. — **China aster** see under **aster**; **china bark** see **cinchona**; **china clay** kaolin (qv), fine white clay used in making porcelain, etc; **China goose** the Chinese goose; **China grass** rami; **China ink** see under **ink**; **China jute** a species of Abutilon; **Chi'naman** a Chinese person (*derog*); an off-break bowled by a left-handed bowler to a right-handed batsman (*cricket*); **chi'naroot** root-stock of

Smilax china; **China rose** any of several garden roses, *esp Rosa chinensis*, a shrub rose, ancestor of many cultivated varieties; **china stone** partly decomposed granite; **China tea** a kind of tea grown in China and smoke-cured; **Chi'natown** a Chinese quarter in a city or town; **Chinese block** a Chinese temple block; **Chinese boxes** a set of boxes nesting one inside another, so that when one box is opened, yet another is found to be opened inside it; **Chinese burn** the burning pain caused by gripping another person's lower arm with two hands and deliberately twisting the flesh in opposite directions; **Chinese cabbage** either of two kinds of plant, *Brassica chinensis* or *Brassica pekinensis*, with edible leaves; **Chinese checkers** or **chequers** a board game similar to draughts for two, four or six players; **Chinese copy** an exact copy, including all the defects in the original; **Chinese goose** the largest living goose, *Anser* (or *Cygnopsis*) *cygnoides*, domesticated in E Asia; **Chinese gooseberry** a subtropical vine (*Actinidia chinensis*) with edible fruit, commonly called **kiwi fruit**; **Chinese lantern** a collapsible paper lantern; same as **winter-cherry**; **Chinese leaves** the edible leaves of Chinese cabbage; **Chinese paper** a fine soft brownish paper-like material made from bamboo bark, used in making fine impressions of engravings; also the so-called rice paper; **Chinese pavilion** see **pavilion**; **Chinese puzzle** a very difficult puzzle or problem; **Chinese radish** mooli (also **white radish, daikon**); **Chinese red** a bright red colour or pigment; **Chinese restaurant syndrome** a short-lived illness with symptoms including chest pain, dizziness and flushing, attributed to the consumption of too much monosodium glutamate, common in Chinese food; **Chinese sugarcane** see under **sorghum**; **Chinese temple block** a percussion instrument consisting of a hollow wooden block that is struck with a hammer; **Chinese wall** or **walls** the strict demarcation barriers which must exist between eg the corporate finance and investment advisory departments of a bank, etc in order to ensure that privileged information available to one department is not available to the other and so prevent conflicts of interest from arising; **Chinese water deer** a small deer (*Hydropotes inermis*) of swampland in China and Korea, having tusks and no antlers; **Chinese whispers** a game in which a message is passed in a whisper from one to another of a group of people, with the result that the final version is different from the original, often amazingly or humorously so; **Chinese white** a zinc oxide pigment. [Prob from the *Ch'in* dynasty, third century BC]

china[2] *kī'nə, kēn'ə*. See **quina**.

chinampa *chin-am'pə, n* a 'floating garden' of earth piled on floating mats of twigs. [Sp, from Nahuatl *chinamitl*]

Chinagraph® *chī'nə-gräf, n* a kind of pencil that writes on glass, porcelain, etc. [**china**, and Gr *graphein* to write]

chinar. Same as **chenar**.

chincapin. See **chinkapin**.

chinch *chinch*, (*Southern US*) *n* the bedbug. — **chinch bug** a heteropterous insect (*Blissus leucopterus*), a serious pest of cereal crops in the US. [Sp *chinche*, from L *cimex*]

chincherinchee or **chinkerinchee** *ching'kə-rin-chē* or *chin-kə-rin'chē, n* a lilaceous S African plant (*Ornithogalum thyrsoides*), with dense, conical spikes of cup-shaped white flowers. — Also (*colloq*) **chinks**. [Said to be imit of the flower-stalks rubbing together in the wind]

chinchilla *chin-chil'ə, n* a small rodent of S America valued for its soft grey fur; the fur itself; (with *cap*) a breed of rabbits, or of cats, with soft grey fur. [Sp]

chin-chin *chin'chin'*, (*colloq*) *interj* hello; good-bye; good health (as a toast). [Anglo-Chin, from Chin *ts'ing ts'ing*]

chincough *chin'kof*, (*dialect*) *n* whooping-cough. [For *chink-cough*; cf Scot *kink-hoast*, Du *kinkhoest*; see **chink**[3] and **cough**]

chindit *chin'dit, n* (also with *cap*) a member of General Orde Wingate's Allied commando force in Burma during World War II. [Burmese *chinthey* a griffin, the force's badge]

chine[1] *chīn, n* the spine or backbone (*archaic*); a piece of the backbone and adjoining parts of an animal (*esp* of a pig) for cooking; anything resembling a backbone; the crest of a ridge; the extreme outside longitudinal member of the planing bottom of a flying-boat hull or a seaplane float, running parallel with the hull (*aeronautics*). — *vt* to break the back of. [OFr *eschine*, prob from OHGer *scina* pin, thorn]

chine[2] *chīn, n* a ravine. [OE *cinu* a cleft]

chine[3]. See under **chime**[2].

chiné *shē-nā', adj* (of fabric) mottled, with the pattern printed on the warp. [Fr, dyed in a (supposedly) Chinese way]

Chinee, Chinese. See **China**.

Chink *chingk*, **Chinkie** or **Chinky** *ching'ki*, (*colloq* and *offensive*) *n* and *adj* Chinese. — *n* **chink'ie** or **chink'y** (*colloq*) a meal of Chinese food. **[China]**

chink[1] *chingk, n* a cleft, a narrow opening. — *vi* to crack. — *vt* to fill up cracks. — *adj* **chink'y** full of chinks. — **chink in someone's armour** a significant weakness or vulnerable point in someone's personality. [Appar formed upon ME *chine* a crack, from OE *cinu* a cleft]

chink[2] *chingk, n* a clinking sound, as of coins or glasses; money (in *Shakesp* **chinks**) (*slang*). — *vi* to emit a sharp ringing sound. — *vt* to cause (coins, glasses, etc) to make a sharp ringing by clinking together. [Imit]

chink[3] *chingk* (*Northern* **kink** *kingk*), (*dialect*) *n* a gasp for breath. — *vi* to gasp. [Cf Du *kinken* to cough; Ger *keichen* to gasp]

chinkapin, chincapin or **chinquapin** *ching'kə-pin, n* the dwarf chestnut of the US. [Algonquian]

chinkara. See **chikara**[1].

chinkerinchee, chinks. See **chincherinchee**.

chino *chē'nō*, (*orig US*) *n* a strong cloth of twilled cotton; (in *pl*) trousers made from this cloth: — *pl* **chi'nos**. [Am, from Sp]

Chino- *chīnō-, combining form* denoting of or relating to China. See also **Sino-**.

chinoiserie *shē-nwä-z(ə)rē, (Fr) n* (a decorative or fine art object in) a style of design or decoration that uses or copies Chinese motifs or methods.

Chinook *chin-o͞ok', n* (a member of) a tribe of N American Indians of the NW Pacific coast; their Penutian language; a pidgin language, consisting of words from French, English, Chinook, and other American-Indian tongues, formerly used by fur traders and settlers in NW US (also **Chinook Jargon**); (without *cap*) a warm dry wind blowing down the eastern side of the Rocky Mountains, making winter grazing possible; also, a warm moist wind blowing on to the NW coast of the US from the Pacific. — **Chinook salmon** a Pacific salmon valued as a food fish.

chinovnik *chin-ov'nik, n* a high official in the Russian civil service; a bureaucrat. [Russ, from *chin* rank]

chinquapin. See **chinkapin**.

chintz *chints, n* a glazed fabric cotton, *usu* printed in several colours on a white or light ground. — *adj* **chintz'y** covered with, or like, chintz; (of decor) flowery, like chintz (often *derog*); cheap, tawdry; mean, miserly. [Orig pl, from Hindi *chīṭ* spotted cotton cloth]

chionodoxa *kī-ō-nō-dok'sə, n* any plant of the liliaceous genus *Chionodoxa*, commonly called glory-of-the-snow, having early-blooming star-shaped flowers. [Gr *chiōn* snow, and *doxa* glory]

chip *chip, vt* to strike with small sharp cutting blows; to strike or break small pieces off the surface of (also with *at*); to remove by chipping (often with *away* or *off*); to slice or pare; to cut as with an adze; to chaff, tease (*colloq*). — *vi* to become chipped; to play a chip shot: — *pr p* **chipp'ing**; *pa t* and *pa p* **chipped**. — *n* an act of chipping; a piece chipped off, *esp* a flattish fragment; a small fragment of stone (also **chipp'ing**); a surface flaw or mark left when a small piece has been broken off; a thin slice or small piece of food, eg fruit; a potato-chip;

a potato crisp (*NAm*); a thin strip of wood, used for making boxes, baskets, etc; a basket or container made in this way; a small, flat piece of wood, plastic, etc used to represent money in certain games; a minute piece of silicon or other semiconducting material on which one or more microcircuits can be formed (also **microchip** or **silicon chip**); a piece of money (*slang*); a piece of dried dung of cow or bison; a hit or kick which sends a ball high into the air over a short distance (*sport*); a key on a musical instrument (*archaic*). — *n* **chipp'er** (*Irish colloq*) a chip shop. — *n* **chipp'ie** (*NZ*) a potato crisp. — *n* **chipp'ing**. — *adj* **chipp'y** abounding in chips; dry as a chip; seedy from taking too much alcohol; touchy, quarrelsome, aggressive (*Can colloq*); having a chip on one's shoulder (see below; *colloq*). — *n* (a meal from) a chip-shop (*colloq*; also **chipp'ie**): see also **chips** and separate entry **chippy**. — *n* **chips** (*slang*) a carpenter (also **chipp'y**); a regimental pioneer sergeant, *usu* a carpenter; money. — *n pl* fried potato-chips (*colloq*). — *adj* **chip'-based** (*electronics*) (of parts or equipment) using, controlled by or incorporating microchips. — **chip basket** a fruit basket of interwoven chips; a metal basket in which potato-chips are placed for frying; **chip'board** reconstructed wood made by consolidation of chips from woodland trimmings, workshop waste, etc, with added resin; a wastepaper cardboard used in box-making; **chip carving** wood carving by removal of small splinters; **chip hat** a hat of palm-leaf strips; **chip heater** (*Austr* and *NZ*) a type of water heater that is fuelled by burning chips of wood; **chip'-shop** a restaurant selling takeaway meals of fish and chips, etc; **chip shot** (*golf*) a short lofted approach to a green. — **chip in** to enter the game by putting chips on the table (*gambling*); to interpose; to pay part of the cost of something (*colloq*); **chip off** (or *orig* **of**) **the old block** someone with the characteristics of their father; **chip on one's shoulder** an aggressively defiant manner, as if daring anyone to knock it off; sensitivity or readiness to take offence, *usu* about a supposed fault or weakness in one's personality or background; bitterness, grievance; **have had one's chips** to have died; to have had and lost one's chance; to have been beaten; **when the chips are down** at a moment of crisis or critically important time. [ME *chippen*; MLGer, MDu *kippen* to hatch by chipping shell]

chipmunk *chip'mungk*, or **chipmuck** *-muk*, *n* any mainly terrestrial squirrel (*Tamias* or *Eutamias*) of N America and parts of Asia, with dark stripes on the back and cheek pouches for storing and carrying food. [From NAm Indian name]

chipochia. See **capocchia**.

chipolata *chip-ə-lä'tə*, *n* a small sausage, used as a garnish, etc. [Fr, from Ital *cipolla* onion]

Chippendale *chip'ən-dāl*, *adj* applied to a style of furniture, made by, designed by, or after the style of Thomas Chippendale, an 18c cabinetmaker; also applied to a style of book-plates.

chipper[1] *chip'ər*, (*informal* and *colloq*) *adj* briskly cheerful; well, fit. [Perh same word as Northern dialect *kipper* lively]

chipper[2]. See under **chip**.

chippy[1] *chip'i*, (*NAm*) *n* a flirtatious or promiscuous woman. [**chip**, variant of **cheep**]

chippy[2]. See under **chip**.

chiquichiqui *chē-kē-chē'kē*, *n* a piassava palm (*Leopoldinia*). [Tupí]

chiragra *kī-rag'rə*, *n* gout in the hand. — *adj* **chirag'ric** or **chirag'rical**. [Gr *cheiragrā*, from *cheir* hand, and *agrā* a catching]

chirality *kī-ral'i-ti*, *n* the property of a chemical, *esp* a crystal, of existing in left-handed and right-handed structural forms; the handedness of such a chemical. — *adj* **chī'ral**. [Gr *cheir* hand]

chi-rho *kī'rō'*, (*Christian relig*) *n* (also *cap*) a monogram of XP (*chī*, *rhō*, ch, r), the first letters of the Greek *Chr*istos (Christ).

chirimoya. Same as **cherimoya**.

chirk *chûrk*, *vi* to chirp or squeak; to grate (*Scot*). [OE *cearcian* to creak]

chirl *chirl*, (*Scot*) *vi* to emit a low sound; to warble. — *n* a kind of musical warble. [Imit]

chirm *chûrm*, *vi* to cry out; to chirp. — *n* noise, din, hum of voices; a flock of goldfinches (also **charm**). [OE *cirman* to cry out; cf Du *kermen*]

chiro- or **cheiro-**, etc *kī'rō-* or *kī-ro'-*, *combining form* denoting hand. — *n* **chirog'nomy** (Gr *gnōmē* understanding) palmistry. — *n* **chi'rōgraph** (Gr *graphein* to write) a written or signed document. — *n* **chirog'rapher** (*obs*) an official of the Court of Common Pleas. — *n* **chirog'raphist** an expert in handwriting; a palmist (*Pope*). — *n* **chiorog'raphy** handwriting, penmanship; calligraphy. — *n* **chirol'ogist**. — *n* **chirol'ogy** the language of gesture; the study of the hand. — *n* **chi'rōmancy** (*-man-si*; Gr *manteiā* divination) fortune-telling by reading the hand. — *adj* **chirōmant'ic** or **chirōromant'ical**. — *n* **chiron'omer** (Gr *nomos* law) a gesticulator. — *adj* **chirōnom'ic**. — *n* **chironomid** (*kī-ron'ō-mid*) a member of a large genus of common midges (*Chironomus*) of the family **Chironomidae** (*kī-rō-nom'i-dē*). — *n* **chiron'omy** the art of gesticulation or of mime. — *n* **chirop'teran** (Gr *pteron* wing) a member of the **Chirop'tera**, an order of mammals comprising the bats. — adj **chiropteroph'ilous** (Gr *phileein* to love) (of flowers) pollinated by bats. — *adj* **chirop'terous**. — *n* **Cheirōthē'rium** (Gr *thērion* beast) a Triassic labyrinthodont with hand-like footprints. [Gr *cheir* hand]

Chiron *kī'rən*, *n* a body *orig* thought to be a minor planet with an orbit between Saturn and Uranus, but now reckoned to be a very large comet. [Gr, name of mythological teacher]

chiropodist *ki-rop'ə-dist* (older *kī-*, also *shi-*), *n* a person who treats minor ailments of the feet, eg corns, verrucas. — *adj* **chiropō'dial**. — *n* **chirop'ody**. [Appar Gr *cheir* hand, and *pous*, *podos* foot; but *cheiropodēs* means having chapped feet]

chiropractic *kī-rə-prak'tik*, *n* a method of treating disorders of the locomotor system, which relies upon the removal of abnormal nerve functioning by manipulation of the spinal column; a chiropractor. — *n* **chīroprac'tor** a person who practises chiropractic. [Gr *cheir* hand, and *praktikos* concerned with action, from *prattein* to do]

chirp *chûrp*, *n* the sharp thin sound of certain birds and insects. — *vi* to make such a sound; to talk in a cheerful and lively fashion. — *vt* to urge by chirping. — *n* **chirp'er** a little bird. — *adv* **chirp'ily**. — *n* **chirp'iness**. — *adj* **chirp'ing**. — *adj* **chirp'y** lively; merry. [Imit]

chirr or **chirre** *chûr*, *vi* to chirp like a cricket or grasshopper. [Imit]

chirrup *chir'əp*, *vi* to chirp; to make a clucking sound with the mouth, as when urging on a horse; to cheer up. — *adj* **chirr'upy** cheerful. [Lengthened form of **chirp**, associated with **cheer up**]

chirt *chûrt*, *n* a squeeze; a squirt. — *vt* to squeeze; to squirt. [Connected with **chirr**]

chirurgeon *kīr-ûr'jən*, **chirurgery** *-jər-i*, and **chirurgical** *-ji-kl*, old forms of **surgeon**, **surgery** and **surgical**, with pronunciation readjusted to the ultimate Greek etymology. — *adv* **chirur'geonly** (*obs*) in a manner becoming a surgeon. [Fr *chirurgien*, from Gr *cheirourgos*, from *cheir* hand, and *ergon* a work]

chisel[1] *chiz'l*, *n* a hand tool consisting of a steel blade with the end bevelled to a cutting edge, used for shaping or working wood, stone or metal. — *vt* to cut, carve, etc with a chisel; to cheat (*slang*): — *pr p* **chis'elling**; *pa t* and *pa p* **chis'elled**. — *adj* **chis'elled** cut or shaped with a chisel; having sharp outlines, as if cut by a chisel (*fig*). — *n* **chis'eller** a person who uses a chisel; a cheat or swindler (*slang*). — *n* **chis'elling**. — **chisel tooth** a rodent's chisel-shaped incisor. [OFr *cisel*, from L *caedere* to cut]

chisel[2] *chiz'l*, *n*. See **chesil**.

Chislev. Same as **Kislev**.

chit[1] *chit*, *n* a short informal letter or note; a bill which one signs and pays at a later date, *esp* in a club, service mess, etc; a voucher or receipt; an order or pass; a testimonial, *esp* a character reference given to a servant. — Also **chitt'y**. [Anglo-Ind, from Hindi *citthī*]

chit[2] *chit*, *n* a child; a girl (*disparagingly*). — *adj* **chitt'y**. — *adj* **chitt'y-faced**. [*kit*, contraction of **kitten**]

chit[3] *chit*, (*dialect*) *n* a shoot. — *vi* to sprout. — *vt* to cause or encourage (seeds, *esp* seed potatoes) to sprout. [Perh OE *cīth* a shoot]

chital *chē'təl*, *n* the axis deer. [Hindi]

chitarrone *kēt-ə-rō'nā*, *n* a large lute-like instrument with a long double neck: — *pl* **chittaro'ni**. [Ital]

chitchat *chit'chat*, *n* chatting or idle talk; prattle; gossip. — *vi* to chat, gossip. [A reduplication of **chat**[1]]

chitin *kī'tin*, *n* the substance consisting of polysaccharide which forms most of the hard outer skeletons of arthropods and of the cell-walls of fungi. — *adj* **chī'tinous** or **chit'inoid**. [Fr *chitine*, from Gr *chitōn* a tunic]

chitlings. See **chitterling**.

chiton *kī'ton*, *n* the loose tunic worn in ancient Greece; any primitive marine mollusc of the genus *Chiton*, with an elongated body covered with a shell of movable plates. [Gr *chitōn* a tunic]

chittagong *chit'ə-gong*, *n* an Indian variety of domestic fowl. — **chittagong wood** a cabinetmaker's wood, *usu* that of *Chickrassia tabularis* of the mahogany family. [*Chittagong* in Bangladesh]

chitter *chit'ər*, *vi* to shiver or (of the teeth) to chatter (*dialect*); to chirp or twitter (*NAm*). — *n* **chitt'ering**. [Cf **chatter**]

chitterling *chit'ər-ling*, *n* (also in *pl*) the smaller intestines of a pig or other edible animal, prepared as a dish; a frill (*obs*). — Also (*dialect*) **chid'lings** or **chit'lings**. [Ety uncertain]

chiv *chiv* or *shiv*, (*slang*) *n* and *vt* knife. — Also **shiv**. [From older *chive* knife (*thieves' slang*) or perh Romany *chiv* blade]

chivalry *shiv'əl-ri* (*orig chiv'*), *n* the usages and qualifications of chevaliers or knights; bravery and courtesy; the system of knighthood in feudal times and its social code; a body of knights; noblemen, knights collectively. — *adj* **chivalric** (*-al'*) or **chiv'alrous** pertaining to chivalry; bold; gallant. — *adv* **chiv'alrously**. — *n* **chiv'alrousness**. [Fr *chevalerie*, from *cheval*, from LL *caballus* a horse]

chivaree. See **charivari**.

chive[1] *chīv*, *n* a herb of the onion family, with tufts of hollow leaves (used in cooking) and clustered bulbs; a small bulb (*archaic*). — Also **cive** (*sīv*). [Fr *cive*, from L *cēpa* an onion]

chive[2], *chiv*. Same as **chiv**.

chivvy, **chivy** *chi'vi* or **chevy** *che'vi*, *vt* to harass, pester or urge; to hunt or chase. — *n* (*obs*) a hunting cry, a pursuit or hunt. [Perh from the Border ballad of battle, *Chevy Chase*]

chiyogami *chi-yō-gäm'i*, *n* hand-printed patterned Japanese paper. [Jap]

chizz or **chiz** *chiz*, (*schoolboy slang*) a cheat, swindle; a nuisance. — *vi* to cheat. [**chisel**[1]]

Ch.J. *abbrev*: Chief Justice.

Chladni figures. Same as **sonorous figures**.

chlamys *klam'is*, *n* a short cloak worn by men in ancient Greece; a purple cope: — *pl* **chlam'yses** or **chlam'ydes** (*-i-dēz*). — *adj* **chlam'ydate** (*zool*) (of molluscs) having a mantle. — *adj* **chlamyd'eous** (*bot*) having a perianth. — *n* **chlamydia** (*klə-mid'i-ə*) any microorganisms of the genus *Chlamydia*, resembling viruses and bacteria, which cause various diseases in man and birds and abortion (**chlamydial abortion**) in animals; a sexually transmitted disease caused by *Chlamydia trachomatis*. — *adj* **chlamyd'ial**. — *n* **chlamydomō'nas** a member of the genus *Chlamydomonas* of (mainly freshwater) green algae. — *n* **chlam'ydospore** a thick-walled spore of certain fungi. [Gr *chlamys*, pl *chlamydes*]

chloanthite *klō-an'thīt*, *n* a valuable nickel ore, nickel arsenide occurring in the cubic system. [From Gr *chloanthēs* sprouting]

chloasma *klō-az'mə*, (*med*) *n* a condition in which the skin becomes marked by yellowish-brown patches, sometimes occurring during pregnancy or at the time of the menopause. [Gr *chloasma* greenness, yellowness, from *chloē* verdure]

chloracne *klör-ak'ni*, *n* a type of disfiguring skin disease resembling acne in appearance, caused by contact with or exposure to chlorinated hydrocarbons.

chlor- *klör-* or **chloro-** *-ō-* or *-ə-*, *combining form* denoting chlorine; green. — *n* **chlor'al** (or *-al'*) a limpid, colourless, oily liquid (CCl_3CHO), of penetrating odour, formed when anhydrous alcohol is acted on by dry chlorine gas; (loosely) **chloral hydrate**, a white crystalline substance used as a hypnotic and sedative. — *n* **chlo'ralism** the habit, or the morbid effects, of using chloral hydrate. — *n* **chlo'ralose** a hypnotic drug mainly used for anaesthetizing animals in laboratory experiments. — *n* **chloram'bucil** (*-byōō-sil*) an oral drug used to treat some cancers, eg cancer of the ovary and leukaemia. — *n* **chloramphen'icol** an antibiotic drug used to treat serious infections such as typhoid and cerebrospinal meningitis, and (in the form of eye drops) for bacterial conjunctivitis. — *n* **chlorargyrite** (*klō-rär'ji-rīt*; Gr *argyros* silver) horn silver. — *n* **chlo'rate** a salt of chloric acid used in defoliant weedkillers, etc. — *n* **chlor'dan** or **chlordane** (*-dan* or *-dān*) a highly poisonous liquid insecticide. — *n* **chlorella** (*klo-rel'ə*) a member of the genus *Chlorella* of green freshwater algae. — *adj* **chlo'ric** or **chlo'rous** of, containing or derived from chlorine. — *n* **chlo'rīde** a compound of chlorine with another element or radical; bleaching powder (**chloride of lime**), not a true chloride. — *vt* **chlo'ridize** or **-ise** to convert into a chloride; to cover with chloride of silver (*photog*). — Also **chlo'ridate**. — *n* **chlorim'eter** same as **chlorometer**. — *adj* **chlorimet'ric**. — *n* **chlorim'etry**. — *vt* **chlor'inate** to treat or cause to combine with chlorine (as in sterilization of water, extraction of gold from ore). — *n* **chlorinā'tion**. — *n* **chlor'inator**. — *n* **chlorine** (*klō'*, *klö'rēn* or *-rīn*), or **chlorin** (*klörin*) a yellowish-green halogen gas (atomic no 17; symbol **Cl**) with a peculiar and suffocating odour, used in bleaching, disinfecting, and poison gas warfare. — *vt* **chlo'rinize** or **-ise** to chlorinate. — *n* **chlorin'ity** (*esp* in seawater) a measure of the amounts of chlorine, iodine, bromine and fluorine present. — *n* **chlo'rite** a salt of chlorous acid combined with a metal or other chemical (*chem*); a general name for a group of minerals, hydrated silicates of magnesia, iron and alumina, typically dark green and rather soft, resembling mica but not elastic. — *adj* **chloritic** pertaining to, of the nature of, or containing, the mineral chlorite. — *n* **chloritīzā'tion** or **-s-** (*geol*) the alteration of ferromagnesian minerals into chlorite or similar material. — *n* **chlorobrō'mide** a compound of chlorine and bromine with a metal or organic radical; a photograph taken on paper coated with this. — *n* **chlorocru'orin** a green respiratory pigment found in some Polychaeta. — *n* **chlo'rodyne** a patent medicine of anodyne and hypnotic effect, containing chloroform. — *n* **chlorofluorocar'bon** an alkane in which chlorine and fluorine atoms have been substituted for hydrogen atoms, used in aerosols, refrigerants, etc, some of which are thought to break down ozone in the earth's atmosphere (*usu abbrev* **CFC**). — *n* **chloroform** (*klor'ō-förm*) a limpid, mobile, colourless, volatile liquid ($CHCl_3$) with a characteristic odour and a strong sweetish taste, used as an anaesthetic, and as a solvent for oils, resins and various other substances. — *vt* to administer chloroform to, in order to render unconscious. — *n* **chlor'oformer** or **chlor'oformist**. — *n* **chlorom'eter** an apparatus for measuring available chlorine in bleaching powder, etc. — *adj* **chloromet'ric**. — *n* **chlorom'etry**. — *n* **Chloromy'cetin** ® (*-mī-sēt'in*) a brand name for the drug chloramphenicol. — *n pl* **Chlorophyceae** (*-fis'i-ē*; Gr *phȳkos* seaweed) the green, mainly freshwater, seaweeds, one of the main divisions of the Algae. — *n* **chlorophyll** or **chlorophyl** (*klor'ə-fil*, or *klö'rō-fil*; Gr *phyllon* leaf) the green pigment present in all plants and algae, involved in the process of photosynthesis. — *n* **chlo'roplast** (Gr *plastos* moulded) a chlorophyll-bearing plastid in plants and algae. — *adj* **chloroplast'al**. — *n* **chlor'oprene** a colourless liquid derived from acetylene and hydrochloric acid and used in the production of neoprene. — *n* **chlo'roquin** or **chlor'oquine** a drug used to suppress malaria and as an anti-rheumatic. — *n* **chlorō'sis** formerly, a wasting disease (**green sickness**) typically affecting young women, characterized by anaemia, extreme lassitude and a greenish tinge of the skin, caused by deficiency of iron; blanching of the green parts of a plant in which production of chlorophyll has been affected by mineral deficiency, lack of light, etc (*bot*). — *adj* **chlorot'ic** pertaining to or affected by chlorosis. — *n* **chlorprō'mazine** an antipsychotic drug widely used in the treatment of schizophrenia and mania. — **chloric acid** a monobasic acid ($HClO_3$), a vigorous oxidizing agent; **chlorine water** an aqueous solution of chlorine; **chlorite-schist'** a schistose rock composed of chlorite, *usu* with quartz, epidote, etc; **chloritic marl** a marl at the base of the English Chalk stained green with glauconite (not chlorite); **chlorous acid** a hypothetical acid ($HClO_2$), known in solution and by its salts; **chlorprom'azine hydrochloride** a drug which induces a feeling of well-being. [Gr *chlōros* pale green]

ChM *abbrev*: *Chirurgiae Magister* (*L*), Master of Surgery.

Chm *abbrev*: chairman (also **chmn.**); checkmate.

CHO *abbrev*: Confederation of Healing Organizations.

choano- *kō-ə-nō-* or **choan-** *combining form* denoting pertaining to a funnel. — *n* **choana** (*kō'ə-nə*; *zool*) a funnel-shaped aperture; (*usu* in *pl*) one of the internal nostrils which open into the roof of the mouth in air-breathing vertebrates: — *pl* **cho'anae**. — *n* **cho'anocyte** (*zool*) a cell in which the flagellum is surrounded by a sheath of protoplasm, found in sponges and stalked protozoa (also **collar cell**). [Gr *choanē* funnel]

chobdar *chōb'där*, *n* in India, an usher. [Pers]

choc *chok* and **choccy** *chok'i*, (*colloq*) *n* and *adj* short forms of **chocolate**. — **choc'-ice** or **choc'-bar** a bar of ice cream with a chocolate covering.

chocaholic or **chocoholic** *chok-ə-hol'ik*, *n* a person who is addicted to chocolate. [*choc*olate, and **-aholic** or **-oholic**]

chocho. See **chayote**.

chock *chok*, *vt* to fasten or secure with or as if with a block or wedge. — *n* a wedge to prevent movement; a log. — *adj* **chock'-a-block**, **chock-full'** or **choke-full'** quite full. — *adj* **chock'er** full up (*slang*; *orig Austr* and *NZ*); annoyed, fed up (*slang*). — **chock'stone** (*mountaineering*) stone jammed in a mountain crack, chimney or crevice. — *adj* **chock'-tight** very tight. [See **choke**]

chocko or **choco** *chok'ō*, (*Austr old slang*) *n* a militiaman or member of the conscript army (as opposed to professional soldiers) in World War II. [From *chocolate soldier*]

chocoholic. See **chocaholic**.

chocolate *chok'(ə-)lit*, *n* a paste made of the ground seeds of *Theobroma cacao* (cocoa), with sugar and flour or similar material, *usu* hardened into slabs; a sweet made of, or covered with, the paste; a beverage made by dissolving the paste (or a powder prepared from it) in hot water or milk. — *adj* chocolate-coloured, dark reddish-brown; made of or flavoured with chocolate. — *n* **chocolatier'** a person who makes, or a manufacturer of, chocolate sweets. — *adj* **choc'olaty** or **choc'olatey**. — *adj* **choc'olate-box** (*esp* of a picture or painting) pretty or charming in an overly sentimental manner. [Sp *chocolate*; from Nahuatl *chocólatl* a mixture containing chocolate]

Choctaw *chok'tö*, *n* a N American Indian of a tribe formerly chiefly in Mississippi; the tribe, or its language; (without *cap*) a skating movement, forward on the edge of one foot, then backward on the opposite edge of the other (cf **Mohawk**). [Choctaw *Chahta*]

chode *chōd*, an archaic *pa t* of **chide**.

choenix or **chenix** *kē'niks*, *n* in ancient Greece, a dry measure equivalent to rather more than a quart. [Gr, in Rev 6. 6]

Chogyal *chog'yäl*, *n* the title of the ruler of Sikkim.

choice *chois*, *n* the act or power of choosing; the thing chosen; an alternative; a preference; the preferable or best part; variety from which to choose. — *adj* worthy of being chosen; select; of superior quality; appropriate. — *adj* **choice'ful** (*archaic*) making many choices, fickle. — *adv* **choice'ly** with discrimination or care. — *n* **choice'ness** particular value; excellence; nicety. — *adj* **choice'-drawn** (*Shakesp*) selected with care. — **by, for** or **from choice** by preference; **Hobson's choice** the choice of the thing offered or nothing (from *Hobson*, a Cambridge horsekeeper, who let out the horse nearest the stable door, or none at all); **make choice of** to select; **take one's choice** to take what one wishes or prefers. [Fr *choix*, from *choisir*; cf **choose**]

choir *kwīr*, *n* a chorus or band of singers, eg those belonging to a church; the part of a church appropriated to the singers; the part of a church, cathedral, etc in front of the altar, often separated from the nave by a rail or screen; a group of instruments of the same class playing together. — *vi* (*Shakesp*) to sing in chorus. — **choir'boy**, **choir'-girl** or **choir'man** a boy, girl or man who sings in a choir; **choir loft** a gallery in a church, cathedral, etc used by the choir; **choir'master** the director of a choir; **choir organ** *orig* a small organ separate from, but played with, a 'great organ', now a section of a large organ played on the lowest manual and suitable for accompanying a choir; **choir school** a school, *usu* maintained by a cathedral, to educate boys who also sing in the choir; **choir'screen** a screen of latticework, separating the choir from the nave. — *n pl* **choir'stalls** fixed seats in the choir of a church, generally of carved wood. [Fr *chœur*, from L *chorus*, from Gr *choros*; see **chorus**]

choke[1] *chōk*, *vt* to stop or interfere with the breathing of (whether by compression, blocking, fumes, emotion, or otherwise); to injure or suppress by obstruction, overshadowing, or deprivation of air, etc; to constrict; to block; to clog; to obstruct. — *vi* to be choked; to die (*slang*); to lose one's nerve when facing an important challenge. — *n* a complete or partial stoppage of breath; the sound of choking; a constriction; a valve in a carburettor which reduces the air supply and thus enriches the petrol/air mixture; a choking coil. — *adj* **choked** (*colloq*) angry; disappointed; upset. — *n* **chōk'er** something or someone that chokes; formerly, a large neck-cloth; a very high collar, *esp* as worn by the clergy; a close-fitting necklace or jewelled collar. — *n* **chokey** or **choky** see separate entry **choky**. — *adj* **chōk'y** tending to, or inclined to, choke. — **choke'berry** a small astringent fruit of various N American shrubs related to the apple; **choke'bore** a gun-bore narrowed at the muzzle; a shotgun so bored; **choke chain** a collar and lead for a dog consisting of a looped chain which tightens around the dog's neck when it pulls on the lead; **choke'cherry** an astringent American cherry; **choke'coil** a choking coil; **choke'damp** carbon dioxide or other suffocating gas in mines. — *adj* **choke-full** see **chock-full** under **chock**. — **choke line** see **kill line** under **kill**[1]; **choke'-pear** an astringent pear; anything that reduces one to silence; **choking coil** a coil of thick wire of high impedance, used to limit the flow of alternating electric current. — **choke back** or **choke down** to suppress (emotion) as if by a choking action; **choke off** to get rid of; to deter by force, to discourage; **choke up** to fill completely; to block up; (*usu* in passive) to overcome with emotion. [Ety dubious]

choke[2] *chōk*, *n* the inedible central part of a globe artichoke.

choko *chō'kō*, *n* the fruit of a tropical vine (*Sechium edule*), similar to cucumber and eaten as a vegetable in the W Indies. [From a S American Ind name]

chokra *chō'krə*, *n* a boy; a boy or young man employed as a servant in a household or regiment: — *fem* **chok'ri**. [Anglo-Ind, from Hindi *chhokrā*, *chhokrī*]

choky or **chokey** *chō'ki*, *n* a prison (*slang*); a toll-station; a lock-up; a chokidar. — *n* **chokidar** or **chowkidar** (*chō'* or *chow'ki-där*) a watchman. [Anglo-Ind, from Hindi *caukī*, *caukīdār*]

chol-. See **chole-**.

cholaemia or **cholemia** *ko-lē'mi-ə*, (*med*) *n* an accumulation of bile pigments in the blood. — *adj* **cholae'mic**. [Gr *cholē* bile, and *haima* blood]

cholagogue *kol'ə-gog*, *n* a purgative causing evacuations of bile from the gall bladder into the duodenum. — *adj* **cholagog'ic** (*-gog'ik* or *-goj'ik*). [Gr *cholē* bile, and *agōgos* leading]

cholangiography *kol-an-ji-og'rə-fi*, *n* the examination by X-ray of bile ducts. [Gr *cholē* bile, and *angeion* case, vessel]

chole- *kol-* or *kōl-i-* or *-ə-*, or **chol-** *combining form* denoting bile or gall. [Gr *cholē* bile]

cholecalciferol *kō-li-kal-sif'ə-rol*, *n* vitamin D_3, a substance found in oily fish and liver which regulates the balance of calcium and phosphate in the body.

cholecyst *kō'li-sist*, *n* the gall bladder. — *n* **cholecystec'tomy** surgery to remove the gall bladder. — *n* **cholecystī'tis** inflammation of the gall-bladder. — *n* **cholecystog'raphy** the examination of the gall bladder and common bile duct by X-ray. — *n* **cholecystos'tomy** (Gr *stoma* mouth) or **cholecystot'omy** (Gr *tomē* a cut) the surgical formation of an opening in the wall of the gall bladder. [Gr *cholē* bile, and *kystis* a bladder]

cholelith *ko'lə-lith*, *n* a gallstone. — *n* **cholelithiasis** (*ko-lə-li-thī'ə-sis*) the presence of stones in the gall bladder and bile ducts. [Gr *cholē* bile, and *lithos* stone]

cholent *cho'lənt*, *n* (in Judaism) a stew, prepared on Friday and cooked slowly overnight for serving at lunch on the Sabbath, consisting of meat, beans, potatoes and dumplings. [Yiddish]

choler *kol'ər*, *n* anger, irascibility; yellow bile, one of the four bodily humours, an imbalance of which was thought to produce irritability (*archaic*); the bile (*obs*); biliousness (*obs*). — *adj* **chol'eric** full of choler; passionate; angry, bad-tempered. — *adv* **chol'erically** (also *-er'*). [Gr *cholerā*, from *cholē* bile, partly through Fr]

cholera *kol'ər-ə*, *n* an acute and frequently fatal infection of the small intestine, characterized by bilious vomiting and severe diarrhoea, acquired by ingesting food or water contaminated by the bacterium *Vibrio cholerae*. — *adj* **choleraic** (*kol-ər-ā'ik*). — **British cholera** an acute gastro-intestinal infection formerly common in summer. [Gr *cholerā*, from *cholē* bile]

choleric. See **choler**.

cholestasis *kō-lə-stā'sis*, *n* a condition in which stagnation of bile in the liver results in jaundice and/or liver disease. [Gr *cholē* bile, and *stasis* stoppage, stationariness]

cholesterol *ko-les'tər-ol*, *n* a sterol ($C_{27}H_{45}OH$), occurring in all body cells and involved in the transport of fats through the bloodstream to tissues throughout the body, and in the formation of bile salts and hormones. High levels of cholesterol in the blood are thought to increase the risk of arteriosclerosis (formerly called **choles'terin**). — *adj* **cholester'ic**. — *n* **cholesterolae'mi** or **cholesterole'mia** (*med*) the presence of comparatively high levels of cholesterol in the blood. [Gr *cholē* bile, and *stereos* solid]

choli *chō'lē*, *n* a short, short-sleeved bodice as worn by Indian women under a sari. [Hindi *colī*; from Sans but prob of Dravidian origin]

choliamb *kō'li-amb*, (*prosody*) *n* a variety of iambic trimeter having a spondee for an iambus as the sixth foot. — *n* and *adj* **choliam'bic**. [Gr *chōliambos*, from *chōlos* lame, and *iambos* iambus]

cholic *kol'ik* or *kōl'ik*, *adj* pertaining to bile. — **cholic acid** an acid ($C_{24}H_{40}O_5$) obtained from bile and used as an emulsifier. [Gr *cholē* bile]

chol'ine *kō'lin*, *-lēn'*, *n* $[HOCH_2CH_2N(CH_3)_3]^+OH^-$ an alcohol found in bile, used in the synthesis of lecithin, etc, and in preventing accumulation of fat in the liver. [Gr *chiolē* bile and sfx **-ine**]

cholinergic *kol-in-ûr'jik*, *adj* (of nerve fibres) releasing acetylcholine; activated or transmitted by acetylcholine; (of an agent) having the same effect as acetylcholine. [From acetyl*choline* and Gr *ergon* work]

cholinesterase *kol-in-est'ər-āz*, *n* an enzyme which breaks down a choline ester into choline and an acid, *esp* acetylcholine into choline and acetic acid. [**choline**, **ester** and sfx **-ase**]

choltry *chōl'tri*, *n* a caravanserai; a shed used as a place of assembly. — Also **choul'try**. [From Malayalam]

chomp *chomp*, (*colloq*) *vt* and *vi* to munch with noisy enjoyment. — *n* the act or sound of munching thus. [Variant of **champ**[1]]

chon *chōn*, *n* a Korean unit of currency, one hundredth of a won.

chondrus *kon'drəs*, *n* a cartilage; a chondrule; (with *cap*) a genus of cartilaginous red seaweeds to which carrageen belongs: — *pl* **chondrī**. — *adj* **chon'dral**. — *n* **chondre** (*kon'dər*) a chondrule. — *n* **chondrificā'tion** formation of chondrin, or development of or change into cartilage. — *vt* and *vi* **chon'drify** to change into cartilage. — *n* **chon'drin** a firm, elastic, translucent, bluish-white gelatinous substance, the matrix of cartilage. — *n* **chon'driosome** a mitochondrion, a minute body in the cytoplasm of a cell. — *n* **chon'drite** a meteorite containing chondrules; a fossil resembling *Chondrus*. — *adj* **chondrit'ic**. — *n* **chondrītis** (*med*) inflammation of a cartilage. — *combining form* **chondro-**, **chondri-** or **chondr-** of or relating to cartilage; granular. — *n* **chon'droblast** a cell that forms cartilage. — *n* **chondrocrān'ium** a cartilaginous skull, as in embryos, fishes, etc. — *n* **chondrogen'esis** chondrification. — *adj* **chon'droid** like cartilage. — *n* **chondromato'sis** (*med*) a condition in which benign tumours (**chondro'mas**) made up of cartilage cells form in the bones, *esp* of the hand. — *n* **chondroph'orine** (*zool*) a member of the Chondrophora, a suborder of hydrozoans similar to medusae but with a different internal structure. — *n* **chondrostian** (*kon-dros'ti-ən*; Gr *osteon* bone) a member of the Chondrostei, an order of bony fishes including the sturgeon, bichir and paddlefish. — *n* **chon'drule** a rounded granule found in meteorites and in deep-sea deposits. [Gr *chondros* a grain, grit, cartilage]

choo-choo *chōō'chōō*, *n* a child's word for a railway train. [Imit]

choof *chōōf*, (*esp Austr slang*) *vi* and *interj* (*usu* with *off*) to go away.

chook *chŏŏk*, (*colloq*, *esp Austr* and *NZ*) *n* a hen, chicken. — Also **chook'ie** (also *Scot*). [Imit]

choom *chŏŏm*, (*Austr colloq*) *n* (often with *cap*) an Englishman.

choose *chōōz*, *vt* to take or pick out in preference to another thing; to select; to will or determine; to think fit. — *vi* to make a choice (between, from, etc): — *pa t* **chose** *chōz*; *pa p* **chos'en**. — *n* **choos'er**. — *adj* **choos'y** or **choos'ey** (*colloq*) difficult to please, fastidious. — **cannot choose but** (*archaic*) can have no alternative but; **choosers of the slain** the Valkyries; **not much to choose between** each about equally good or bad; **pick and choose** to select with care or at leisure; **the chosen people** the Israelites (1 Chron 6, 13). [OE *cēosan*, Du *kiesen*]

chop[1] *chop*, *vt* to cut with a sudden blow (away, down, off, etc); to cut into small pieces; to strike with a sharp blow (*karate*; also *vi*); to thrust or clap (*archaic*); to reduce greatly or abolish (*colloq*). — *vi* to hack; to come suddenly or accidentally (*archaic*); to thrust (*archaic*); to crack or fissure; to take a direction (meaning converging with **chop**[2]): — *pr p* **chopp'ing**;

pa t and *pa p* **chopped**. — *n* an act of chopping; chopped food; a piece cut off; a slice of mutton, lamb or pork, *usu* containing a rib; food (*WAfr colloq*); a share (*Austr* and *NZ slang*); a crack; a sharp downward blow; (with *the*) dismissal (*colloq*). — *n* **chopp'er** a person or thing that chops; a cleaver; a helicopter (*slang*); the penis (*slang*); a type of motorcycle or bicycle with very high handlebars and a low saddle; a submachine-gun (*slang*); (in *pl*) teeth (*slang*). — *n* and *adj* **chopp'ing**. — *adj* **chopp'y** full of chops or cracks; (of the sea, etc) running in irregular waves, rough (also **chopp'ing**). — **chop'-house** *esp* formerly, a house where mutton-chops and beefsteaks are served; an eating-house; **chopp'ing-block** or **chopp'ing-board** one on which material to be chopped is placed; **chopp'ing-knife** a knife for chopping or mincing meat. — **chop at** to aim a blow at; **chop in** to break in, interrupt; **chop up** to cut into small pieces; **for the chop** (*slang*) about to get the chop; **get the chop** (*slang*) to be dismissed from one's job, etc; to be killed; **not much chop** (*Austr* and *NZ colloq*) not much good. [A form of **chap**[1]]

chop[2] *chop*, *vt* and *vi* to buy and sell, barter, or exchange (*Milton*); to change direction (meaning converging with **chop**[1]): — *pr p* **chopp'ing**; *pa t* and *pa p* **chopped**. — *n* an exchange; a change. — **chop'logic** false reasoning, illogicalness, sophistry; a person who chops logic. — **chop and change** to buy and sell; to change about; **chop logic** to argue contentiously or fallaciously; **chops and changes** vicissitudes. [Connection with **chop**[1] and with **chap**[2] is not clear]

chop[3] *chop*, *n* the chap or jaw; (in *pl*) a person with fat cheeks; the mouth or jaws of anything, such as a cannon or a vice. — *vt* to eat. — *vi* to snap: — *pr p* **chopp'ing**; *pa t* and *pa p* **chopped**. — *adj* **chop'fallen** literally, having the chop or lower jaw fallen down; cast-down; dejected. — **lick one's chops** (*colloq*) to wait eagerly or greedily. [See **chap**[3]]

chop[4] *chop*, *n* in China and India, a seal; a brand; a sealed document. — *n* **chop'house** in China, a customs house. — **first chop** best quality; **no chop** no good. [Hindi *chāp* seal, impression]

chop-chop *chop-chop'*, *adv* promptly. [Pidgin English, from Chin]

chopin[1] *chop'in*, *n* an old French liquid measure containing nearly an English imperial pint; an old Scottish measure containing about an English quart. [OFr *chopine*, MDu *schoppe*; Scot *chappin*, Ger *Schoppen* a pint]

chopin[2] or **chopine** *chop-ēn'* or *chop'in*, *n* a high clog or patten introduced into England from Venice during the reign of Elizabeth I. [Sp *chapin*]

chopping *chop'ing*, *adj* stout, strapping, plump. [Perh **chop**[1]; cf **thumping**]

chopstick *chop'stik*, *n* (*usu* in *pl*) either of two small sticks used by the Chinese instead of a fork. [**chop-chop**, and **stick**[2]]

chop suey *chop-so͞o'i*, *n* a miscellaneous Chinese-style dish made up of chopped meat, bean sprouts, etc fried in sesame oil. [Chin, mixed bits]

choragus *ko-rā'gəs* or **choregus** *-rē'gəs*, *n* (in ancient Greek drama) the organizer, sponsor or leader of a chorus; the leader of a choir or organizer of musical activities, festivals, etc. — *adj* **choragic** (*-raj'* or *-rāj*) or **choregic** (*-rēj'ik*). [Gr *chorāgos*, *chorēgos*, from *choros* chorus, and *agein* to lead]

choral, **chorale**. See **chorus**.

chord[1] *körd*, (*music*) *n* the simultaneous combination of notes of a different pitch. — *adj* **chord'al**. — *n* **chord'ing** the distribution of chords in a piece of harmony. — **common chord** a note combined with its third, perfect fifth and octave; **chord symbol** any symbol used to indicate a chord in musical notation. [From **accord**]

chord[2] *körd*, *n* a string of a musical instrument (*archaic* and *poetic*); a sensitive area of the emotions, feelings, etc (*fig*); a straight line joining any two points on a curve (*geom*); an old spelling of cord (see under **spinal** and **vocal**); the straight line joining the leading and the trailing edges of an aerofoil section (*aeronautics*). — *n* **chor'da** (*zool*) any stringlike structure in the body; the notochord: — *pl* **chor'dae**. — *adj* **chord'al**. — *n* **chordames'oderm** (*anatom*; *zool*) the layer of specialized cells in the middle of a developing embryo which forms the notochord and structures of the central nervous system. — *n* **chor'date** a member of the **Chordāta**, a phylum of the animal kingdom, including the vertebrates and protochordates, animals possessing a notochord at some stage of their development. — Also *adj*. — *n* **chordophone** (*kör'dō-fōn*; *music*) any instrument in which a string vibrates to produce a sound, including the zither, piano, lute, lyre and harp. — *adj* **chordophonic** (*-fon'ik*). — *n* **chordotomy** see **cord**. — **strike a chord** to prompt a feeling of recognition, familiarity, empathy, etc. [Gr *chordē* a string, intestine]

chordee *kör'dē*, (*med*) *n* a condition, *usu* of infant boys, in which there is an abnormal downward curvature of the penis.

chore *chōr* or *chör*, *n* a routine, *esp* household, task; an unpleasant or tedious task. [Form (orig US) of **char**[3]]

-chore *-kör*, (*bot*) *combining form* denoting a plant distributed by a specified means or agency, eg *zoochore*. [Gr *chōrein* to go, move]

chorea *ko-rē'ə*, *n* a nervous condition, characterized by irregular involuntary movements of the limbs or face, a feature of *Huntingdon's chorea* and *Sydenham's chorea*. [L, from Gr *choreiā* a dance]

choree *kō'rē* or *kö'*, (*prosody*) *n* a trochee. — Also **chorē'us**. — *adj* **chorē'ic**. [Gr *choreios*]

choregus. See **choragus**.

choreography *kor-ē-og'rə-fi*, *n* the art, or the notation, of dancing, *esp* ballet dancing; the art of arranging or composing dances, *esp* ballets; the arrangement or composition of a ballet. — *vt* **chor'eograph** to arrange or compose (a dance, dances, etc). — *vi* to practise choreography. — *n* **choreog'rapher** or **chor'eograph**. — *adj* **choreograph'ic**. — Also **choreg'raphy**, **chor'egraph**, etc. [Gr *choros* dance, and **-graphy**]

chorepiscopal *kō-ri-pis'kə-pl* or *kö-*, *adj* pertaining to a local or suffragan bishop of the early church. [Gr *chōrā* place, country]

choria. See **chorion**.

choriamb *kor'i-amb* or **choriambus** *-am'bəs*, (*prosody*) *n* a foot of four syllables, the first and last long, the others short. — *adj* and *n* **choriam'bic**. [Gr *choriambos*, from *choreios* a trochee, and *iambos* iambus]

choric, **chorine**. See under **chorus**.

chorion *kō'ri-on* or *kö'*, (*anatom*) *n* one of the two membranes that surround an embryo and which in mammals develops into the placenta as the embryo develops in the uterus: — *pl* **cho'ria**. — *adj* **cho'rioid** or **cho'roid** of or resembling a chorion. — *n* the vascular tunic of the eyeball, between the retina and the sclera. — *n* **choroidītis** (*med*) inflammation of the choroid. — *adj* **chorion'ic** or **cho'rial** of or pertaining to the chorion. — *n* **choriocarcinō'ma** a malignant tumour that develops from the placenta in the uterus. — **chorionic gonadotrophin** a hormone produced in mammals when an embryo begins to form in the uterus, its presence in the urine being an indication of pregnancy; **chorionic villus sampling** a method of diagnosing abnormalities in a foetus by removing a tiny sample of chorionic tissue from the edge of the placenta for laboratory analysis. [Gr *chorion*]

chorisis *kō'ris-is* or *kö'*, (*bot*) *n* multiplication of parts, organs, etc by branching or splitting. — *n* **chō'rism**. — *n* **chōrizā'tion** or **-s-**. [Gr *chōrisis* separation]

chorist, etc. See **chorus**.

chorizo *cho-rē'zō*, *n* a dry, highly-seasoned sausage, made from pork. [Sp]

chorizont *kō'ri-zont* or **chorizontist** *-zont'ist*, *n* a person who disputes identity of authorship, *esp* one who ascribes the *Iliad* and *Odyssey* to different authors. [Gr *chōrizōn*, *-ontos* separating]

chorography *kō-rog'rə-fi, kö-, (geog) n* the process or technique of mapping or describing particular districts or regions (cf **topography**). — *n* **chorog'rapher**. — *adj* **chorographic** (*-ro-graf'ik*) or **chorograph'ical**. [Gr *chōrā* region, country, and **-graphy**]

choroid. See **chorion**.

chorology *ko-rol'ə-ji, n* the science or study of the geographical distribution of anything. — *adj* **chorolog'ical**. — *n* **chorol'ogist**. [Gr *chōrā* region, country, and **-logy**]

chortle *chört'l, vi* to chuckle; to utter a gurgling, gleeful laugh. — Also *n*. [Coined by Lewis Carroll in 1872]

chorus *kō'rəs* or *kö', n* a band of singers and dancers; in Greek tragic drama, a group of people who, between the episodes, danced and chanted counsel and comment on the action; in later drama, a person who performs similar functions alone, including speaking the prologue; a company of singers, a choir; a composition which is sung by a chorus; the combination of voices in one simultaneous utterance; a refrain, in which the company or audience may join with the soloist or choir. — *vt* to sing or say together: — *pr p* **cho'rusing**; *pa t* and *pa p* **cho'rused**. — *adj* **chor'al** pertaining to or sung by a chorus or a choir. — *n* (*ko-räl'*; often altered to **chorale'**) a simple harmonized composition with slow rhythm; a psalm or hymn tune; any part of the service sung by the whole choir (*RC*); a choir or chorus (*esp NAm*). — *adv* **chor'ally** in the manner of a chorus; suitable for a choir. — *adj* **choric** (*kor'ik* or *kō'rik*). — *n* **chorine** (*kōr'ēn* or *kör'*; *esp US slang*) a chorus-girl. — *n* **chorist** (*kor'ist, kō'rist*), **chor'alist**, **chor'ister** or (*obs*) **quirister** (*kwir'istər*) a member of a choir. — **choral prelude** a composition, *usu* for organ, in the manner of a chorale; **chorus girl** a woman who dances and sings in a chorus on the stage; **chorus master** the director of a choir or chorus. [L, from Gr *choros* dance; see also **choir**]

chose[1], **chosen**. See **choose**.

chose[2] *shōz, (law) n* a thing; a piece of personal property, a chattel. — **chose jugée** (*shōz zhü-zhā*) something already decided and profitless to discuss, a settled matter. — **chose in action** a personal right of property which can only be claimed by a court action and not by taking physical possession. [Fr, from L *causa* thing]

chota *chō'tə, (Anglo-Ind) adj* small, little; younger, junior. — **chota hazri** (*haz'ri* or *häz'ri*) early light breakfast of tea, toast and *usu* fruit; **chota peg** a small drink, *usu* whisky with soda or water. [Hindi *chhotā*]

chott. See **shott**.

chou *shōō, n* a cabbage; an ornamental soft rosette; a cream bun; dear, pet (*colloq*): — *pl* **choux** (*shōō*). — **choux pastry** very light, rich pastry made with flour, butter and eggs. [Fr]

chough[1] *chuf, n* a passerine bird (*Pyrrhocorax pyrrhocorax*), of the crow family, inhabiting sea-cliffs and mountains and having glossy black plumage, red legs and a red down-curved bill (also called **red-legged crow**, **Cornish chough**); a related bird, the Alpine chough (*Pyrrhocorax graculus*), of Europe and Asia. [Perh imit of its cry]

chough[2]. See **chuff**.

choultry. See **choltry**.

chounter. See **chunter**.

chouse *chows, n* a cheat, a swindler; a person who is easily cheated, a dupe (*obs*); a trick or swindle. — *vt* to cheat, swindle. [Prob from Turk *chaush* a messenger or envoy]

chout *chowt, n* in India, one-fourth part of the revenue, extorted by the Mahrattas as blackmail; hence, blackmail, extortion. [Hindi *chauth* the fourth part]

choux. See **chou**.

chow *chow, n* food; (also with *cap*) a Chinese person (*Austr, NZ* and *archaic slang*). — *adj* mixed, miscellaneous. — *n* **chow'-chow** a Chinese mixed condiment; a mixed fruit preserve; a breed of long-haired dog with a curly tail, originating in China (also **chow**). [Pidgin Eng, food]

chowder *chow'dər, (esp NAm) n* a stew or thick soup made of fish or clams with vegetables; a similar soup made with other main ingredients. [Fr *chaudière* a pot]

chowkidar. See **choky**.

chow mein *chow mēn* or *-män, n* fried noodles; a Chinese-style dish of seasoned shredded meat and vegetables, served with fried noodles. [Chin, fried noodles]

chowry or **chowri** *chow'ri, n* a hand-held device used for driving away flies. [Hindi *caurī*]

choy-root. Same as **chay**[2].

CHP *abbrev*: combined heat and power.

Chr. *abbrev*: Christ; Christian.

chrematist *krē'mə-tist, n* a political economist. — *adj* **chrematis'tic** pertaining to finance, money-making, or political economy. — *n sing* **chrematis'tics** the science or study of wealth; political economy. [Gr *chrēmatistēs* a money-getter, from *chrēma, -atos* a thing, possession, money]

chrestomathy *kres-tom'ə-thi, n* an anthology of choice or literary passages, *usu* used by students in the learning of a foreign language. — *adj* **chrestomathic** (*-tō-math'ik*) or **chrestomath'ical**. [Gr *chrēstos* useful, and *mathein* (aorist) to know]

chrism *krizm, n* consecrated or holy oil; a sacramental anointing, unction; confirmation; chrisom. — *adj* **chris'mal** pertaining to chrism. — *n* a case for containing chrism; a pyx; a veil used in christening. — *n* **chris'matory** a vessel for holding chrism. — *n* **chris'om** or **christ'om** a white cloth or robe (also **chris'om-cloth** or **chris'om-robe**) put on a child newly anointed with chrism at its baptism; the child itself. — **chrisom child** (*archaic*) a child still wearing the chrisom-cloth; a child that died in its first month after baptism, buried in its chrisom-cloth; an innocent child. [OFr *chresme* (Fr *chrême*), from Gr *chrīsma*, from *chrīein* to anoint]

Chrissie *kris'i, (esp Austr slang) n* Christmas.

Christ *krīst, n* the Anointed, a name given to Jesus of Nazareth; the Messiah. — *interj* (*taboo slang*) an expression of irritation, surprise, anger, etc. — *vt* **christen** (*kris'n*) to baptize in the name of Christ; to give a name to; to use for the first time (*colloq*). — *n* **Christendom** (*kris'n-dəm*) that part of the world in which Christianity is the received religion; the whole body of Christians. — *n* **christening** (*kris'ning*) the ceremony of baptism. — *n* **Christ'hood** the condition of being the Christ or Messiah. — *n* **Christian** (*kris'chən*) a believer in the religion based on the teachings of Christ, or one so classified; a follower of Christ; a person whose behaviour is considered becoming to a follower of Christ; often a vague term of approbation, a decent, respectable, kindly, charitably-minded person; a human being (*colloq*). — *adj* relating to Christ or his religion; in the spirit of Christ. — *n* **Christ'ianism**. — *n* **Christianity** (*kris-ti-an'i-ti*) the religion based on the teachings of Christ; the spirit of this religion. — *n* **christianīzā'tion** or **-s-**. — *vt* **christ'ianize** or **-ise** to make Christian; to convert to Christianity. — *n* **christ'ianizer** or **-s-**. — *adj* **Christ'ianlike**. — *adj* **Christ'ianly**. — Also *adv*. — *n* **Christ'ianness**. — *n* **christ'ingle** (*krist'ing-gəl*) a Christmas symbol for children, *usu* consisting of an orange containing a candle, with fruit and nuts and red paper or ribbon, representing Christ as the light of the world, its creation and his passion. — *n* **Chrīst'liness**. — *adj* **Chrīst'less**. — *adj* **Chrīst'like**. — *adj* **Chrīst'ly** like Christ. — **Christ-cross-row** or **criss-cross-row** (*kris'kros-rō*; *archaic* and *dialect*) the alphabet, from hornbooks in which the alphabet was preceded by the figure of a cross (**Christ-cross** or **criss-cross**); **Christian era** the era counted from the traditionally accepted date of the birth of Christ; **Christian name** the name given at one's christening; the personal name as distinguished from the surname; **Christian Science** a religion based on spiritual or divine healing with rejection of orthodox medicine, founded in 1866 by Mary Baker Eddy; **Christian Scientist**; **Christian Socialism** a mid-19c movement for applying Christian ethics to social reform; the principles of a pre-World War II Austrian Roman Catholic political party; **Christ's'-thorn** any of several prickly shrubs, eg *Paliurus spina-christi* of the buckthorn family common in the Mediterranean region, or a kind of jujube tree (*Zizyphus spina-christi*), from which Christ's crown of thorns is thought to have been made. [OE *Crīst*, from Gr *Chrīstos*, from *chrīein* to anoint]

Christadelphian *kris-tə-del'fi-ən, n* a member of a small religious sect, founded in the US, which believes that only the righteous will achieve eternal life, the wicked and sinners will be utterly destroyed, and which bases its teaching and practice on literal interpretation of the Bible. [Gr *Chrīstos* Christ, and *adelphos* brother]

Christe eleison. See **Kyrie eleison**.

Christiania *kris-ti-än'i-ə*, also **Chris'tie** or **Chris'ty** (*skiing*) *n* (also without *caps*) a turn with skis parallel executed when descending at speed. [Former name of Oslo]

christingle. See under **Christ**.

Christmas *kris'məs, n* an annual festival, *orig* a mass, in celebration of the birth of Christ, held on 25 December (**Christmas Day**); the season at which it occurs; evergreens, *esp* holly, for Christmas decoration (*archaic* and *dialect*). — Also *adj*. — *adj* **Christ'massy** or **Christ'masy** of or suitable for Christmas. — **Christmas beetle** any of various Australian scarab beetles; **Christmas box** a box containing Christmas presents; a Christmas gift, often of money, to tradesmen, etc; **Christmas cactus** a S American cactus with showy red flowers; **Christmas cake** a rich fruit cake, *usu* iced, made for Christmas; **Christmas card** a greeting card sent at Christmas; **Christmas daisy** the aster; **Christmas disease** a genetically acquired bleeding disorder similar to haemophilia, in which absence of a protein (factor IX) affects the proper coagulation of the blood; **Christmas eve** 24 December; **Christmas pudding** a rich, spicy fruit pudding, eaten at Christmas; **Christmas rose** or **flower** an evergreen plant (*Helleborus niger*) that bears cup-shaped white flowers in winter or early spring; **Christmas stocking** a stocking that children hang up on Christmas eve to be filled with presents by Santa Claus; **Christ'mas-tide** or **Christ'mas-time** the season of Christmas; **Christmas tree** a tree, *usu* fir, set up in a room or a public place at Christmas time and decorated with lights, gifts, etc; an apparatus fitted to the outlet of an oilwell to control the flow of oil or gas. [**Christ** and **mass**[2]]

Christocentric *kris-tō-sen'trik, adj* (of theology, religion, etc) centring on Christ.

Christogram *kris'tōgram, n* a symbol representing Christ, *esp* the monogram chi-rho.

Christolatry *kris-tol'ə-tri, n* worship of Christ. [Gr *Chrīstos* Christ, and *latreiā*, worship]

Christology *kris-tol'ə-ji, n* that branch of theology which is concerned with the nature and person of Christ. — *adj* **Christolog'ical**. — *n* **Christol'ogist**. [Gr *Chrīstos*, and *logos* discourse]

christom *kriz'əm*. See **chrisom** under **chrism**.

christophany *kris-tof'ə-ni, n* an appearance of Christ to men. [Gr *Chrīstos*, and *phainesthai* to appear]

Christy[1]. See **Christiania**.

Christy[2] or **Christie** *kris'ti*, (*Can*) *n* (also without *cap*) a bowler hat. [An English manufacturer)

Christy-minstrel *krist'i-min'strəl, n* one of a troupe of entertainers with blackened faces.. [Instituted by George *Christy*, in New York]

chroma *krō'mə, n* quality of colour; a hue; (in colour television) the colour component of a signal. — *n* **chrō'mate** a salt of chromic acid. — *adj* **chrōmat'ic** pertaining to, or consisting of, colours; coloured; relating to notes in a melodic progression, which are raised or lowered by accidentals, without changing the key of the passage, and also to chords in which such notes occur (*music*). — *adv* **chrōmat'ically**. — *n* **chrōmat'icism** (*music*) the state of being chromatic; the use of chromatic tones. — *n* **chrōmaticity** (*-tis'*) the colour quality of light, one method of defining it being by its purity (saturation) and dominant wavelength. — *n sing* **chrōmat'ics** the science of colours. — *n* **chrō'matid** one of the two thread-like structures formed by the longitudinal divison of a chromosome. — *n* **chrō'matin** a readily stained substance in the nucleus of a cell made up of DNA, RNA and proteins. — *adj* **chrōmatograph'ic**. — *n* **chrōmatog'raphy** methods of separating substances in a mixture which depend on selective adsorption, partition between non-mixing solvents, etc, using a **chrōmat'ograph**, and which present the substances as a **chrōmat'ogram**, such as a series of visible bands in a vertical tube. — *n* **chrōmat'ophore** (*biol*) a pigment cell, or a pigment-bearing body in protoplasm or photosynthetic bacteria. — *n* **chrōmatop'sia** (Gr *opsis* sight) coloured vision. — *n* **chromatosphere** see **chromosphere** below. — *n* **chrō'matype** or **chrō'motype** a photographic process that uses chromium salts; a photograph in colours; a sheet printed in colour. — *n* **chrome** chromium or a chromium compound. — Also *adj*. — *vt* (in dyeing) to treat with a chromium solution; to plate with chromium. — *n* **chrō'mel** an alloy of nickel and chromium, used in heating elements. — *n* **chrōmene** a chemical compound produced by certain plants that acts as an insecticide. — *adj* **chrō'mic** pertaining to trivalent chromium. — *n* **chrōmid'ium** an algal cell in a lichen; a free fragment of chromatin: — *pl* **chrōmid'ia**. — *n* **chrō'minance** (*TV*) the difference between any colour and a reference colour (*usu* a white of specified chromaticity) of equal luminance. — *n* **chrō'mite** a mineral, a double oxide of chromium and iron. — *n* **chrō'mium** a metallic element (atomic no 24; symbol **Cr**) remarkable for the beautiful colour of its compounds. — *n* **chrō'mō** a chromolithograph: — *pl* **chrō'mos**. — *n* **chrōmogen** a substance that can be made into a dye; a coloured compound containing a chromatophore. — *n* **chrō'mōgram** a combination of photographs in different colours to give an image in natural colours. — *n* **chrōmōlith'ograph** (*abbrev* **chromo**) a lithograph printed in colours. — *n* **chrōmōlithog'raphy**. — *n* **chrō'momere** (*biol*) one of the characteristic granules of compacted chromatin which appear on a chromosome during the early stages of meiosis. — *adj* **chrōmophil** or **chrōmophil'ic** staining heavily in certain microscopic techniques (*biol*). — *n* **chrō'mophore** the group of atoms in a chemical compound responsible for its colour. — *adj* **chrōmophon'ic**. — *n* — **chrō'mōplast** (*bot*) a chromatophore. — *n* **chrō'mōscope** an apparatus for combining coloured images. — *adj* **chrōmosō'mal**. — *n* **chrō'mōsome** a rod-like portion of the chromatin of a cell nucleus, performing an important part in mitotic cell division, and in the transmission of hereditary characters. — *n* **chrō'mōsphere** a layer of incandescent gas surrounding the sun through which the light of the photosphere passes (also **chrō'matosphere**). — *n* **chromotype** see **chromatype** above. — *n* **chrōmōtypog'raphy** printing in colours. — *n* **chrōmōxy'lograph** (Gr *xylon* wood) a picture printed in colours from wooden blocks. — *n* **chrōmōxylog'raphy**. — **chrō'makey** (*TV*) a special effect in which a coloured background can be removed from a picture and a different background substituted; **chromatic aberration** the blurring of an optical image, with colouring of the edges, caused by light of different wavelengths being focused at different distances; **chromatic adaption** (*bot*) differences in amount or proportion of photosynthetic pigments in plants in response to the amount and colour of available light; **chromaticity coordinates** (*phys*) numbers whose values are used to specify a colour; **chromaticity diagram** (*phys*) a diagram on which the chromaticity of a colour is plotted; **chromatic scale** (*music*) a scale proceeding by semitones; **chrome alum** a violet-coloured crystalline substance, used as a mordant in dyeing; **chrome leather** leather prepared by chrome tanning; **chrome plating** electroplating with chromium; **chrome spinel** picolite; **chrome steel** an alloy steel containing chromium; **chrome tanning** tanning with salts of chromium; **chrome**

tape magnetic tape coated with chrome dioxide; **chrome yellow** a pigment of lead chromate; **chromic acid** an acid of chromium (H_2CrO_4), of an orange-red colour, much used in dyeing and bleaching; **chromosomal aberration** any visible abnormality in chromosome number or structure; **chromosome mapping** the assigning of genes to chromosomes and the determination of their exact position on the chromosome; **chromosome number** the number of chromosomes in a cell nucleus, constant for any given species. [Gr *chrōma, -atos* colour]

Chron. (*Bible*) *abbrev*: Chronicles.

chron. *abbrev*: chronicle; chronological; chronology.

chron- *kron'* or *krən-* or **chrono-** *-ō-*, *-ə-* or *kron-o'*, *combining form* denoting time. — *n* **chrōn'axie** (*med*) a time constant in the excitation of a nerve or muscle which equals the smallest time required to produce a response when the stimulus is double the minimum intensity required to produce a basic response. — *adj* **chron'ic** relating to time (*obs*); lasting a long time; of a disease, deep seated or long continued (as opposed to *acute*); deplorable (*slang*). — *n* a chronic invalid; a student who repeatedly fails in examinations (*old slang*). — *adj* **chron'ical** chronic. — *adv* **chron'ically**. — *n* **chronic'ity**. — *n* **chronobiol'ogy** the science of biological rhythms, *esp* where the properties of the rhythms are measured. — *n* **chron'ogram** (Gr *gramma* letter) an inscription or phrase in which letters form a date in Roman numerals. — *n* **chron'ograph** (Gr *graphein* to write) a chronogram; an instrument for taking exact measurements of time, or for recording graphically the moment or duration of an event. — *n* **chronog'rapher** a chronicler. — *n* **chronog'raphy** chronology. — *n* **chronol'oger**. — *adj* **chronolog'ic** or **chronolog'ical**. — *adv* **chronolog'ically**. — *n* **chronol'ogist**. — *vt* **chronol'ogize** or **-ise** to arrange in chronological order or establish the order in time of (events, etc). — *n* **chronol'ogy** (Gr *logos* discourse) the science of computing time; a scheme of time; order of time. — *n* **chronom'eter** (Gr *metron* measure) an instrument for accurate measurement of time. — *adj* **chronomet'ric** or **chronomet'rical**. — *n* **chronom'etry** the art of measuring time accurately by means of instruments; measurement of time. — *n* **chrō'non** (*phys*) a unit of time, ie that required for a photon to travel the diameter of an electron, 10^{-24} seconds. — *n* **chron'oscope** (Gr *skopeein* to look) an instrument used for measuring extremely short intervals of time, *esp* in determining the velocity of projectiles. — *n* **chron'otron** a device which measures very small time intervals by comparing the distance between electric pulses from different sources. — **chronological age** age in years, etc (opposed eg to *mental age*). [Gr *chronos* time; adj *chronikos*]

chronicle *kron'-i-kl*, *n* a continuous record of events in order of time; a history; a story, account; (in *pl*, with *cap* the name of two of the Old Testament books. — *vt* to record as a chronicle. — *n* **chron'icler** a writer of a chronicle. — **chronicle play** a drama which depicts or portrays historical events or characters (also **history play**). [Anglo-Fr *cronicle*, from L *chronica*, from Gr *khronika* annals]

chronique scandaleuse *kro-nēk skā-da-lœz*, (*Fr*) *n* a story full of scandalous events or details; unsavoury gossip or tittle-tattle.

chrys- *kris-*, or **chryso-** *kris'ō-*, *-ə-* or *kris-ō'*, *combining form* denoting gold. — *n* **chrys'alid** or **chrys'alis** (Gr *chrȳsallis*) *orig* a golden-coloured butterfly pupa; a pupa generally; a pupa case: — *pl* **chrysalides** (*kris-al'i-dēz*), **chrys'alises** or **chrys'alids**. — *n* **chrysan'themum** (*kris-* or *kriz-*; Gr *anthemon flower*) a plant of the *Chrysanthemum* genus of composite plants, eg the corn marigold and ox-eye daisy; any of several cultivated plants of the genus, with colourful double flowerheads (often shortened to **chrysanth'**). — *n* **chrysarō'bin** (see **araroba**) a yellow crystalline mixture obtained from the wood of a S American tree, *Andira araroba*; a derivative of this used medicinally as a purgative and in the treatment of skin disease. — *adj* **chryselephant'ine** (Gr *elephantinos*, from *elephas, -antos* ivory) (*esp* of ancient Greek sculpture) made of or overlaid with gold and ivory. — *n* **chrysober'yl** a mineral, beryllium aluminate, of various shades of greenish-yellow or gold colour. — *n* **chrysocoll'a** (Gr *chrȳsokolla* gold-solder, *perh* applied to this mineral, from *kolla* glue) a silicate of copper, bluish-green in colour. — *n* **chrysoc'racy** (Gr *krateein* to rule) the rule of wealth, plutocracy. — *n* **chrys'olite** (Gr *lithos* stone) olivine, *esp* yellow or green precious olivine; olivine used as a gemstone. — *n* **chrys'ophan** (Gr *phainesthai* to appear) an old name for chrysarobin. — *n* **chrysoph'ilite** (Gr *phileein* to love) a lover of gold. — *n* **chrys'oprase** (*-prāz*; Gr *prason* a leek) a green variety of chalcedony used as a gemstone. — *n* **chrys'otile** (Gr *tilos* a shred) a fibrous variety of serpentine, a form of asbestos. — **chrysophantic acid** an oxidation product of chrysarobin used against skin diseases. [Gr *chrȳsos* gold]

chs. *abbrev*: chapters.

chthonian *thō'ni-ən*, or **chtonic** *thon'ik*, *adj* pertaining to the earth or the underworld and the deities inhabiting it; ghostly. [Gr *chthōn, chthonos* the ground]

chub *chub*, *n* a small fat European river fish (*Squalius* or *Leuciscus cephalus* of the carp family; any of several N American fishes, eg the black bass. [Origin unknown]

Chubb® *chub*, *n* a type of lock which cannot be picked, invented by Charles *Chubb* (1772–1846), a locksmith in London. — Also **chubb'-lock**.

chubby *chub'i*, *adj* plump. — *n* **chubb'iness**. [Perh from **chub**]

chuck¹ *chuk*, *n* the call of a hen; a clucking noise; a chicken (*dimin* **chuck'ie**); a term of endearment. — *vi* to make the noise of a hen. [A variant of **cluck**]

chuck² *chuk*, *n* a gentle stroke or tap under the chin; a toss or throw, hence dismissal (*colloq*); a pebble or small stone (more *usu* **chuck'ie**, **chuck'ie-stone** or **chuckie-stane** *Scot*); (in *pl*) a game with such stones (often called **chuck'ies**); any game of pitch and toss. — *vt* to stroke or tap lightly under the chin; to toss; to pitch; to abandon or dismiss. — **chucker-out'** (*colloq*) a person who expels undesirable people, eg from a public house, a meeting, etc, a bouncer; **chuck-far'thing** formerly, a game in which a farthing was chucked into a hole; **chuck'hole** (*NAm*) a pothole. — **chuck in** (*colloq*) to give up; to abandon; to make a contribution to the cost of (*Austr*); **chuck it** (*colloq*) to stop, give over; **chuck off** (*Austr* and *NZ slang*; *usu* with *at*) to abuse; **chuck out** (*colloq*) to expel (a person); to throw away, get rid of; **chuck up** (*colloq*) to give up; to give in; to vomit. [Fr *choquer* to jolt; allied to **shock**]

chuck³ *chuk*, *n* a lump or chunk; an instrument for holding an object so that it can be rotated, as on the mandrel of a lathe; food (*slang*); a cut of beef extending from the neck to the shoulder blade. — **chuck wagon** a wagon carrying food, cooking apparatus, etc, for cattle herders, etc. [Origin uncertain; cf Ital *cioco* a block, stump]

chuck⁴ *chuk*, (*Can*) *n* any large body of water. See also **saltchuck**. [NAm Ind *chauk*]

chuck-full. Same as **chock-full** (qv under **chock**).

chuckle¹ *chuk'l*, *n* a quiet or suppressed laugh. — *vt* to call, as a hen does her chickens. — *vi* to laugh in a quiet or suppressed manner. — *n* **chuck'ling**. [Cf **chuck¹**]

chuckle² *chuk'l*, *adj* clumsy. — **chuck'le-head** a stupid loutish fellow; a blockhead, dolt. — *adj* **chuck'le-headed** stupid; awkward, clumsy. [Prob **chock** a log]

chuddah, **chuddar**. Variants of **chadar**.

chuddy *chud'i*, (*Austr* and *NZ colloq*) *n* chewing gum.

chufa *chōō'fə*, *n* a sedge (*Cyperus esculentus*), with edible nut-like tubers. [Sp]

chuff¹ or chough *chuf*, (*dialect*) *n* a clown; a surly or boorish fellow. — *n* **chuff'iness** boorishness. — *adj* **chuffed** disgruntled. — *adj* **chuff'y** coarse and surly. [ME *chuffe, choffe*, a boor, of obscure origin]

chuff *chuf* or **chuff-chuff** *chuf'-chuf*, *vi* to make a series of puffing sounds, as a steam locomotive does; to move while making such sounds. [Imit]

chuffed *chuft*, (*colloq*) *adj* very pleased. [Dialect *chuff* happy, chubby]

chug *chug*, *n* a short, dull explosive noise, as of an internal-combustion engine. — *adj* **chugg'ing**. — *vi* **chug** to make a chugging noise; (of a vehicle) to move while making such a noise. [Imit]

chukker or **chukka** *chuk'ər* or *-ə*, *n* a period of play, being one of the divisions in a game of polo. — **chukka boot** an ankle-length leather or rubber boot, like those worn for polo. [Hindi *cakkar* a round]

chukor *chu-kör'*, **chukar** *-kär'*, **chikhor** or **chikor** *chi-kör'*, *n* an Indian partridge (*Alectoris chukar* or *graeca*), having light plumage with black markings. [Hindi *cakor*]

chum[1] *chum*, *n orig* a person who shares a room or rooms with another; a friend or associate. — *vi* to share a room; to be or become a chum. — *vt* to assign as a chum (with *on*); to be or become a chum to; to accompany (*dialect*). — *n* **chumm'age** the quartering of two or more persons in one room; a fee demanded from a new chum. — *adj* **chumm'y** sociable. — *n* a chum. — **chum up with** to become friendly or intimate with. [Perh a corruption of **chamber-fellow**]

chum[2] *chum*, *n* a type of salmon (*Oncorhynchus keta*), of the Pacific. [Chinook Jargon *tsum* spots]

chum[3] *chum*, (*esp NAm*) *n* a groundbait of chopped fish, etc used by anglers. [Origin uncertain]

chumley. See **chimney**.

chummy *chum'i*, *n* a chimney sweeper's boy (*old slang*); a criminal, *esp* a thief (*police slang*). — See also **chum**[1]. [**chimney**]

chump *chump*, *n* an end lump of wood, mutton, etc; a thick lump; a blockhead; the head. — *n* **chump'ing** (*NEng dialect*) collecting wood for Guy Fawkes bonfires. — **off one's chump** (*slang*) out of one's mind, mad. [Perh related to **chunk**]

chunder *chun'dər*, (*Austr slang*) *vi* to vomit. — Also *n*. — *adj* **chun'derous** sick-making, nauseating.

chunk *chungk*, *n* a thick piece of anything, eg wood or bread. — *n* **chunk'ing** (*psychol*) the association of a number of items so that they are retained in the memory as a single entity. — *adj* **chunk'y** in chunks; short and broad; (of sweaters, etc) thick and heavy. [Perh related to **chuck**[3]]

Chunnel *chun'l*, (*colloq*) *n* (also without *cap*) the tunnel underneath the English Channel, connecting England and France. [*C*hannel *t*u*nnel*]

chunter *chun'tər*, (*colloq*) *vi* (often with *on*) to mutter; to grumble; to chatter unceasingly and meaninglessly. — Also (*obs* or *dialect*) **choun'ter**, **chun'der** or **chunn'er**. [Imit]

chupati, **chupatti**. Same as **chapati**, **chapatti**.

chuppah or **huppah** *hūp'-ə*, *n* the canopy under which a Jewish marriage ceremony is performed; the wedding ceremony. [Heb]

chuprassy *chup-räs'i*. See **chaprassi**.

church *chûrch*, *n* a building set apart for public worship, *esp* that of a parish, and *esp* that of an established or once established form of the Christian religion; a church service; the whole body of Christians; the Christian clergy; any particular sect or denomination of Christians; any body professing a common creed. — *adj* of the church; ecclesiastical; belonging to the established church (*colloq*). — *vt* to perform a service in church with (eg a woman after childbirth, a newly-married couple, etc). — *n* **churchian'ity** devotion to the church rather than to Christ. — *n* **church'ing**. — *n* **church'ism** adherence to the form of principles of some church; ecclesiasticism. — *adj* **church'less** not belonging to a church; without church approval or blessing. — *adj* **church'ly** concerned with the church; ecclesiastical. — *adv* **church'ward** or **church'wards**. — *adj* **church'y** obtrusively devoted to the church; like or savouring of the church or church life. — **church'-ale** a church festival; **Church Army** an organization of the Church of England, resembling the Salvation Army; **Church Commissioners** a group of churchmen, government and legal representatives, who act as trustees in administering the property of the Church of England; **church court** a court for deciding ecclesiastical causes; a kirk session; a presbytery, synod, or general assembly; **church'goer** a person on the way to, or who regularly goes to, church; **church'going** the act or habit of going to church; **church key** (*US*) a pointed lever-like tool for making pouring- or drinking-holes in tin cans; **church'man** a clergyman or ecclesiastic; a member or upholder of the established church; **church'manship** the beliefs, practices, etc, of a clergyman or practising church member, *esp* high or low church attitudes to Anglican doctrine; **church militant** the church on earth in its struggle against the powers of evil; **church mouse** a mouse inhabiting a church, a proverbial example of poverty; **church-off'icer** a church attendant or beadle; **church-parade'** a uniformed parade of a military or other body for the purpose of churchgoing; **church'-people**; **church'-rate** an assessment for the sustentation of the fabric, etc of the parish church; **church school** a school controlled or run by a church; an organization for religious education run by a church (*NAm*); **church-ser'vice** a religious service in a church; the form followed; a book containing it; **church' text** a thin and tall form of black-letter Gothic print; **church triumphant** the portion of the church which has overcome this world and entered into glory; **church'-warden** an elected lay officer who represents the interests of a parish or church; a long-stemmed clay pipe; **church'way** the public way or road that leads to the church; **church'woman** a female member or upholder of a church, *esp* the Anglican Church; **church'-yard** a burial ground round a church. [OE *cirice*, *circe*, from Gr *kȳriakon* belonging to the Lord, from *kȳrios* lord]

Churchillian *chûr-chil'iən*, *adj* of, in the manner of, or resembling (*esp* the rhetorical style or statesmanlike qualities of) Sir Winston *Churchill* (1874–1965), British prime minister.

churidars *chōō'ri-därz*, *n pl* tight-fitting trousers as worn by Indian men and women. [Hindi]

churinga *chōō-ring'gə*, *n* a sacred amulet of the Australian Aborigines. [Aboriginal]

churl *chûrl*, *n* a rustic, an agricultural labourer (*hist*); an ill-bred, surly fellow. — *adj* **churl'ish** rude; surly; ungracious. — *adv* **churl'ishly**. — *n* **churl'ishness**. [OE *ceorl* a countryman; ON *karl*, Ger *Kerl* a man; Scot *carl*]

churn *chûrn*, *n* an apparatus used for making butter in which cream or whole milk is repeatedly stirred and turned until the fat is separated from the liquid; a large milk-can suggestive of an upright churn; anything that mixes, turns over or agitates. — *vt* to agitate so as to obtain butter; to stir or agitate violently (often with *up*); to turn over persistently (eg ideas in the mind). — *vi* to perform the act of churning; to move restlessly or in an agitated manner; (of brokers, financial advisers, etc) to encourage clients to surrender existing endowment insurance policies and buy new ones or to invest in loss-making share deals; (of a government) to pay state benefits to a certain category of people from funds obtained by taxing others, eg those with higher incomes. — *n* **churn'ing** the act of making butter; the quantity of butter made at a churning; the practice of encouraging mortgagees and investors to cash in existing endowment policies and buy new ones or to invest in loss-making share deals, in order to generate commissions (*finance*). — **churn'-drill** a drill worked by hand, not struck with the hammer, a jumper; **churn'-milk** buttermilk; **churn'-staff** the plunger which agitates the milk in an upright churn; the sun-spurge. — **churn out** to produce rapidly, continuously or mechanically. [OE *cyrin*; ON *kirna* a churn, Du *karnen*, and Ger *kernen* to churn]

churn-owl *chûrn'-owl*, *n* a dialect name for the nightjar. [Appar **churr** and **owl**]
churr *chûr*, *n* a low trilling sound made by certain birds and insects. — *vi* to make this sound. — **churr'-worm** the fen-cricket. [Prob imit]
churrigueresque *chōō-ri-gə-resk'*, (*archit*) *adj* of an extravagant style of architecture and ornament of the baroque period in Spain and Spanish America. [From José de *Churriguera* (1665–1725), Spanish architect]
churrus. See **charas**.
chuse *chōōz*, an *obs* spelling of **choose**.
chut *chut*, *interj* an expression of impatience.
chute[1] or **shute** *shōōt*, *n* a waterfall, rapid; a passage or sloping trough for sending down goods, water, logs, coal, rubbish, etc; a slide in a park, etc; a narrow passage for controlling cattle. — Also *shoot*. [Fr *chute* fall, combined with **shoot**]
chute[2] *shōōt*, (*colloq*) short for **parachute**. — *n* **chut'ist** a parachutist.
chutney *chut'ni*, *n* a condiment (*orig* E Indian) of mangoes, chillies, etc; an imitation made with various alternative ingredients, such as apples. [Hindi *catnī*]
chutzpah or **hutzpah** *hhōōt'spə*, *n* effrontery, brazenness, impudence. [Heb and Yiddish]
chyack. See **chiack**.
chylde. See **child**.
chyle *kīl*, (*med*, *zool*) *n* a white fluid, mainly lymph mixed with fats derived from food in the body, formed in the small intestine during digestion. — *adj* **chylā'ceous**. — *adj* **chylif'erous** containing chyle. — *n* **chylifica'tion** the production of chyle. — *vt* **chyl'ify** to turn into or produce chyle. — *n* **chylū'ria** (Gr *ouron* urine) the presence of chyle in the urine. — *n* **chylomicron** a tiny globule of fat, the form in which fat is carried in blood and chyle. [Gr *chȳlos* juice, from *cheein* to pour]
chyme *kīm*, *n* the pulp to which food is reduced in the stomach before entering the small intestine. — *adj* **chymif'erous**. — *n* **chymificā'tion** the act of being formed into chyme. — *vt* **chym'ify** to form into chyme. — *n* **chymotryp'sin** an enzyme produced in the pancreas, active in the hydrolysis of proteins during digestion. — *adj* **chym'ous**. [Gr *chȳmos* chyme, juice, from *cheein* to pour]
chymistry. See **chemistry**.
chymous. See **chyme**.
chynd *chīnd*, (*Spenser*) *adj* cut into chines.
chypre *shē'pr'*, *n* a perfume made from sandalwood, *orig* from Cyprus. [Fr, Cyprus]
CI *abbrev*: Channel Islands; *Côte d'Ivoire* (*Fr*), Ivory Coast (IVR).
Ci *symbol*: curie.
CIA *abbrev*: Central Intelligence Agency (*US*).
Cia. *abbrev*: *Compagnia* (*Ital*) *Compañía* (*Sp*), Company.
ciao *chä'ō* or (*Eng*) *chow*, *interj* an informal greeting used on meeting or parting: — *pl* **ciaos**. [Ital]
CIB *abbrev*: Chartered Institute of Bankers; Criminal Investigation Branch (of the police force) (*NZ*).
cibachrome *sē'ba-krōm*, (*photog*) *n* a type of colour print made directly from a colour transparency without first making a negative.
cibation *si-bā'shən*, (*obs*) *n* the seventh of the twelve processes employed by alchemists in the search for the philosopher's stone, 'feeding the matter'; taking food, feeding. [L *cibātiō*, *-ōnis* feeding]
cibol *sib'əl* or **chibol** *chib'əl*, *n* a variety of onion (*Allium fistulosum*); a spring onion. [Fr *ciboule*, Sp *cebolla*, from LL *cēpola*, dimin of L *cēpa* an onion; see **sybo**]
ciborium *si-bō'ri-əm* or *-bö'*, *n* a vessel closely resembling a chalice, *usu* with an arched cover, in which the host is deposited (*Christian relig*); a free-standing structure consisting of a canopy supported on four pillars over the high altar (*archit*): — *pl* **cibo'ria**. [L, a drinking-cup, from Gr *kibōrion* the seed-vessel of the Egyptian waterlily]
CIBS *abbrev*: Chartered Institute of Building Societies (*UK*).
CIC *abbrev*: Commander-in-Chief.
cicada *si-kä'də* or *-kā'də* or **cicala** *-kä'lə*, *n* a homopterous insect of warm regions, having a broad body and large transparent wings, the male of which makes a loud chirping sound. — *n* **cicadell'id** any homopterous insect of the genus *Cicadella*, the leaf-hoppers, which feed by sucking plant tissue, some species being a serious pest of crops. [L *cicāda*; Ital *cicala*]
cicatrice *sik'ə-tris*, *n* a scar over a healed wound; a scar in the bark of a tree; the scar-like mark left where a leaf, etc has been attached; a mark, impression (*Shakesp*): — *pl* **cicatrī'cēs**. — Also **cicatrix** (*sik-ā'-triks* or *sik'ə-triks*): — *pl* **cic'atrixes**. — *n* **cicatric'ula**, **cicat'richule** or **cicat'ricle** a white spot, the germinating point in the yolk of an egg; the hilum of grains (*bot*); a small scar. — *n* **cicatrīzā'tion** or **-s-** the process of healing over to form a cicatrice. — *vt* **cic'atrīze** or **-ise** to promote the formation of a cicatrix on; to scar. — *vi* to heal. [L *cicātrīx*, *-īcis* a scar]
CICB *abbrev*: Criminal Injuries Compensation Board.
cicely *sis'ə-li*, *n* a name for several umbelliferous plants related to chervil, *esp Myrrhis odorata* (sweet cicely). [L and Gr *seseli*]
Cicero *sis'ə-rō* (*L kik-e-rō*), *n* a famous Roman orator; (without *cap*) a measure of type between pica and English. — *n* **cicerone** (*chich-ə-rō'ni*, also *sis-ə-rō'ni*) a person who shows and explains the curiosities of a place to visitors and sightseers; a guide: — *pl* **cicerō'ni** (*-nē*) or **cicerō'nes**. — *vi* to act as cicerone. — *n* **Cicerō'nian** (*sis-*) an imitator or admirer of Cicero's Latin diction and style. — Also *adj*. — *adj* **Ciceronic** (*-ron'ik*). — *n* **Cicerō'nianism** the character of Cicero's Latin style or an imitation of this in literature, etc. [L *Cicerō*, *-ōnis*; Ital *Cicerone*]
cichlid *sik'lid*, *n* any teleost fish of the family **Cich'lidae**, which carries its young in its mouth, including the angel fish of the Amazon. — *adj* **cich'loid**. [Gr *kichlē* a kind of wrasse]
cichoraceous *sik-ə-rā'shəs*, (*bot*) *adj* of or belonging to the *Cichoraceae*, a sub-order of plants including the chicory, endive, dandelion, etc. [New L *cichorāceae*, from *cichorium* chicory, from Gr *kichorion*]
Cicindelidae *si-sin-dē'li-dē*, *n* a family of carnivorous beetles, the tiger beetles, that hunt their insect prey on the run. [L *cicindēla* glow-worm, from *candēla* a candle]
cicinnus *si-sin'əs*, *n* a cincinnus. [Latinized from Gr *kinkinnos* a ringlet]
cicisbeo *chē-chēz-bā'ō*, or *chi-chiz-*, *n esp* formerly, a married woman's gallant or *cavaliere servente* in Italy; the acknowledged lover of a married woman: — *pl* **cicisbe'i** (*-ē*). — *n* **cicisbē'ism**. [Ital]
ciclaton *sik'lə-tən* or **ciclatoun** *-tōōn*, (*obs*) *n esp* in medieval times, cloth of gold or other rich material. [OFr *ciclaton*, from Ar, perh from the root of **scarlet**]
cicuta *si-kū'tə*, *n* a plant of the genus *Cicuta* of poisonous umbelliferous plants including waterhemlock and cowbane. [L *cicūta* hemlock]
CID *abbrev*: Council of Industrial Design; Criminal Investigation Department (of the police force).
cid *sid* or *sēd*, *n* a chief, captain or hero; (with *cap*) the title given to the 11c Castilian champion Rodrigo (or Ruy) Diaz. [Sp, from Ar *sayyid* lord]
cidaris *sid'ə-ris*, *n* a Persian royal tiara; (with *cap*) a genus of sea urchins, mostly fossil. [Gr *kidaris*]
-cide *-sīd*, *combining form* denoting (1) killing, murder; (2) killer, murderer. — *adj combining form* **-cī'dal**. [L *caedere* to kill]
cider or **cyder** *sī'dər*, *n* an alcoholic drink made from apples. — *n* **cī'derkin** a type of weak cider. — *adj* **cī'dery**. — **ci'der-and** a mixture of cider and spirits; **ci'der-cup** a drink of sweetened cider, with other ingredients; **ci'der-press** an apparatus for pressing the juice from apples in cider-making. [Fr *cidre*, from L *sīcera*, from Gr *sikera* strong drink, from Heb *shēkār*]
ci-devant *sē-də-vã*, (*Fr*) *adj* and *adv* before this, former, formerly. — *n* a formerly important person.

CIE *abbrev*: Companion of the (Order of the) Indian Empire; Córas Iompair Éireann (*Ir*), Transport Organization of Ireland.
Cie. *abbrev*: *Compagnie* (*Fr*), Company.
ciel, cieling. Variants of **ceil, ceiling**.
cierge. See **cerge**.
cif *abbrev*: cost, insurance, freight.
cig, etc. See **cigar**.
cigar *si-gär'*, *n* a roll of tobacco leaves (*usu* with a tapered end) for smoking. — *n* **cigarette** (*sig-ə-ret'*) finely-cut tobacco rolled in thin paper (*colloq* shortened forms **cig, cigg'ie** and **cigg'y**). — *n* **cigarillo** (*sig-ə-ril'ō*) a small cigar: — *pl* **cigarill'os**. — **cigarette card** a picture card formerly given away with a packet of cigarettes, valued by cartophilists; **cigarette case** or **cigar case** a small case for carrying cigarettes or cigars; **cigarette end** or **cigarette butt** the unsmoked remnant of a cigarette; **cigarette holder** and **cigar'-holder** a holder with a mouthpiece for smoking a cigarette or cigar; **cigarette lighter** a mechanical device which produces a flame for lighting cigarettes; **cigarette paper** thin paper for making cigarettes. — *adj* **cigar'-shaped** cylindrical with tapered ends. — **cigar tree** a species of Catalpa with long cigar-like pods. [Sp *cigarro*]
ci-gît *sē-zhē*, (*Fr*) here lies.
CIGS *abbrev*: Chief of the Imperial General Staff (*UK hist*).
CII *abbrev*: Chartered Insurance Institute.
cilice *sil'is*, *n* haircloth; a penitential garment made of haircloth. — *adj* **cilicious** (*-ish'əs*). [L, from Gr *kilikion* a cloth made of Cilician goat's hair]
cilium *sil'i-əm*, (*biol*) *n* one of the fine hair-like structures that are borne on the surface of a cell, that move liquid over the surface of the cell or act as locomotor organs in eg protozoons and flatworms: — *pl* **cil'ia**. — *adj* **cil'iary**. — *adj* **cil'iate** bearing a cilium or cilia; fringed with hairs; of or relating to *Ciliata*, a subclass of Protozoa, having cilia for locomotion. — *n* a member of the subclass *Ciliata*. — *adj* **cil'iolate** fringed with very short fine hairs. — *n pl* **Cilioph'ora** (Gr *phoros* bearing) a subphylum of Protozoa, including the ciliates, that possess cilia at some time in the life cycle. — **ciliary body** (*anatom*) the circular muscle ring attached by fibres to the lens of the eye, which by contracting can alter the shape of the lens to increase focussing power. [L *cilium* eyelash]
cill *sil*, (*building*) *n* a variant of **sill**, sometimes used in the trade.
CIM *abbrev*: Commission on Industry and Manpower; computer input on microfilm; computer integrated manufacture.
cimar. See **cymar**.
cimbalom *sim'bə-ləm*, *n* a Hungarian form of the dulcimer. [Hung, from Ital *cembala* cymbal]
cimelia *sī-mē'li-ə*, *n pl* treasures in storage. [Gr *keimēlia*]
ciment fondu *si-mã fɔ̃-dōō*, (*building*) *n* (also with *caps*) a type of rapid-hardening cement with a high aluminium content. [Fr, melted cement]
cimetidine *sī-met'i-dēn*, *n* a generic drug that reduces the secretion of hydrochloric acid in the stomach and thus promotes the healing of gastric and duodenal ulcers.
cimex *sī-meks*, *n* any heteropterous insect such as the bed bug, of the genus *Cimex*, which gives name to the family **Cimicidae** (*sī-* or *si-mis'i-dē*): — *pl* **cimices** (*sim'i-sēz*). [L, bug]
cimier *sē-myā'*, *n* the crest of a helmet. [Fr]
ciminite *sim'in-īt*, *n* a rock intermediate between trachyte and andesite, containing olivine. [Monte *Cimini*, in Italy]
Cimmerian *sim-ē'ri-ən*, *adj* relating to the Cimmerii, a tribe fabled to have lived in perpetual darkness; hence, extremely dark or gloomy.
cimolite *sim'ō-līt*, *n* a type of clay, or hydrous silicate of aluminium, similar to fuller's earth. [Gr *kimōliā*, prob from *Kimōlos* an island of the Cyclades]
C-in-C *abbrev*: Commander-in-chief.
cinch *sinch*, *n* a saddle girth (*US*); a secure hold (*colloq*); a certainty (*colloq*); something easy (*colloq*); a card game in which the five of trumps ranks highest. — *vi* (*esp NAm*) to tighten the cinch; to tighten one's grip on (*fig*). — *vt* to bind firmly, *esp* with a belt around the waist; to make sure of (*colloq*); to pull (clothing) in tightly at the waist. — *n* **cinch'ing** distortion of magnetic tape caused by low winding tension resulting in slippage of the layers of tape on the spindles. [Sp *cincha*, from L *cingula*]
cinchona *sing-kō'nə*, *n* any rubiaceous tree of the *Cinchona* genus of trees, which yield the bark from which quinine and related by-products are obtained; the dried bark of these trees (also called **Peruvian bark, china bark**); a drug obtained from the bark. — *adj* **cinchonaceous** (*-kən-ā'shəs*) or **cinchonic** (*-kon'ik*). — *n* **cinch'onine** an alkaloid obtained from cinchona bark and used as a substitute for quinine. — *adj* **cinchoninic** (*-nin'ik*). — *n* **cinch'onism** a condition resulting from overdoses of cinchona or quinine. — *n* **cinchonīzā'tion** or **-s-**. — *vt* **cinch'onize** or **-ise** to treat with cinchona or quinine. [Said to be so named from the Countess of *Chinchón*, who was cured of a fever by it in 1638]
cincinnus *sin-sin'əs*, (*bot*) *n* a uniparous cymose inflorescence in which the plane of each daughter axis is at right angles, alternately to right and left, with that of its parent axis. — *adj* **cincinn'ate**. [L, a curl]
cincture *singk'chər*, *n* a girdle or belt; a moulding around the top or bottom of a column (*archit*). — *vt* to gird, encompass, surround. — *adj* **cinct** (*rare*) surrounded, encircled. — *adj* **cinc'tured** having a cincture. [L *cinctūra*, from *cingere*, *cinctum* to gird]
cinder *sin'dər*, *n* the refuse of burned coals; an ember; anything charred by fire; a scoriaceous fragment of lava; a strong stimulant such as whisky put in tea, soda-water, etc (*old slang*). — *vi* and *vt* to turn to cinder(s). — *n* **Cinderell'a** a scullery-maid, a drudge; a despised and neglected person or thing; a girl from poor or obscure origins who achieves success or fame. — Also *adj*. — *adj* **cin'dery**. — **cinder block** (*NAm*) breeze block; **cinder cone** a hill of loose volcanic materials; **Cinderella dance** a dancing-party ending at midnight; **cinder path** or **cinder track** a path or racing-track laid with cinders. [OE *sinder* slag; cf Ger *Sinter*; not connected with Fr *cendre*]
cine- or **ciné-** *sin'i-*, *combining form* denoting cinema or cinematograph. — *n* **cineangiog'raphy** the recording of the movement of blood in the blood vessels by photographing a series of X-ray images to create a moving picture. — *n* **cin'e-bīol'ogy** or **ciné-biol'ogy** the study of biological phenomena by means of cinematographic records. — *n* **cinemicrog'raphy** cinematographic recording of changes under the microscope. — *n* **cin'eplex** a multiple-cinema complex. — *n* **Cinerama®** (*-ə-rä'mə*) a method of film projection on a wide curved screen to give a three-dimensional effect (being the picture photographed with three **cineram'ic** cameras). — **cine camera** or **ciné camera** a camera for taking moving photographs; **cine film** film suitable for use in a cine camera; **cine projector** or **ciné projector**; **ciné vérité** cinéma vérité.
cinéaste, cineaste or **cineast** *sin'ē-ast*, *n* a person who takes an artistic interest in, or who makes, motion pictures. [Fr]
cinema *sin'ə-mə* or *-mä*, *n* a cinematograph; a building in which motion pictures are shown; (with *the*) motion pictures collectively, or as an art; material or method judged by its suitability for the cinema. — Also (*old*) **kin'ema**. — *n* **cin'emathèque** or **cin'ematheque** (*-tek*) a small, intimate cinema; a film archive. — *adj* **cinemat'ic** pertaining to, suitable for, or characteristic of, the cinema. — **cin'ema-goer** a person who goes (regularly) to the cinema; **cin'ema-organ** an organ with showier effects than a church organ; **Cin'emaScope®** a method of film projection on a wide screen using film that has photographed the image at twice the normal width; **cinéma vérité** realism in films by portraying scenes that have the appearance of real life. [**cinematograph**]

cinematograph *sin-ə-mat'ə-gräf*, *n* apparatus for filming, printing and projecting a series of instantaneous photographs so as to give a moving representation of a scene, with or without reproduction of sound; an exhibition of such photographs. — Also (*old*) **kinemat'ograph**. — *n* **cinematog'rapher**. — *adj* **cinematograph'ic** or **cinematograph'ical**. — *n* **cinematog'raphist**. — *n* **cinematog'raphy** the art of making motion pictures; motion picture photography. [Fr *cinématographe*, from Gr *kīnēma*, *-atos* motion, and *graphein* to write, represent]

cineol or **cineole** *sin'i-ol* or *-ōl*, *n* eucalyptol, a camphor-smelling disinfectant liquid ($C_{10}H_{18}O$), obtained from several essential oils, such as eucalyptus, wormwood and cajeput. [From *Artemisia cīna* a species of wormwood, and L *oleum* oil]

cineplex, **cine-projector**, **Cinerama**®. See under **cine-**.

cineraria[1] *sin-ə-rā'ri-ə*, *n* a composite plant, a member of the genus *Senecio*, *esp S. cruentus* a brightly-flowered cultivated variety with ashy down on the leaves. [L *cinerārius* ashy, from *cinis*, *cineris* ash]

cineraria[2]. See **cinerarium** under **cinerary**.

cinerary *sin'ə-rə-ri*, *adj* pertaining to ashes; for containing ashes of the dead. — *n* **cinerā'rium** a place for depositing the ashes of the dead after cremation: — *pl* **cinerā'ria**. — *n* **cinerā'tion**. — *n* **cinerā'tor**. — *n* **cinē'rea** the grey matter of the brain. — *adj* **cinē'real** ashy; cinerary. — *adj* **cinē'reous** ashy-grey; ashy. — *adj* **cineri'tious** ashy-grey; pertaining to the grey matter of the brain. [L *cinereus* ashy, from *cinis*, *cineris* ash]

cinerin *sin'ər-in*, *n* either of two compounds derived from pyrethrum and used as insecticides. [L *ciner*, *cineris* ash, and chem sfx **-in**]

Cingalese. See **Sinhalese**.

cingulum *sing'gū-ləm*, *n* a girdle, as of a priest's alb; a girdle-like structure, such as the band round the base of the crown of a tooth. [L *cingere* to gird]

cingulum Veneris *sing'gū-ləm ve'nə-ris* or *king'gŏŏ-lŏŏm we'ne-ris*, (*L*) the girdle of Venus.

cinnabar *sin'ə-bär*, *n* a mineral, sulphide of mercury, called vermilion when used as a pigment. — *adj* vermilion-coloured. — *adj* **cinnabaric** (*- bär'ik*). — *adj* **cinn'abarine** (*-bə-rēn*). — **cinnabar moth** a large red European moth whose black and yellow caterpillars feed on ragwort. [Gr *kinnabari*, from Pers]

cinnamon *sin'ə-mən*, *n* the spicy bark of a lauraceous tree of Sri Lanka; the tree; a light yellowish brown. — Also *adj*. — *adj* **cinnamic** (*-am'ik*) or **cinnamonic** (*-ə-mon'ik*) obtained from, or consisting of, cinnamon. — **cinnamic acid** weak white organic acid found in cinnamon oil and used in perfumery; **cinnamon bear** a cinnamon-coloured variety of the American black bear; **cinnamon stone** a yellowish grossular garnet, hessonite. [Gr *kinnamōmon*, later *kinnamon*, from Heb *qinnāmōn*]

cinnarizine *sin-ar'i-zēn*, *n* a generic antihistamine drug used to relieve nausea and travel sickness, and, in higher doses, in the treatment of certain vascular diseases.

cinquain *sing'kān*, *n* a poetic form consisting of five lines of two, four, six, eight and two syllables respectively. [Fr]

cinque *singk*, *n* the number five, as on dice. — **cinque'foil** a common bearing representing a flower with five petals borne full-faced and without a stalk (*heraldry*); a similar figure formed by cusps in a circular window or the head of a pointed arch (*archit*); the plant *Potentilla reptans* (*bot*); the five-bladed clover (*bot*); **cinque'pace** formerly, a lively dance, the pace or movement of which is characterized by five beats; **Cinque Ports** the five ancient ports on the south coast of England lying opposite to France, *orig* Sandwich, Dover, Hythe, Romney and Hastings, and later including Winchelsea, Rye, and a number of subordinate ports. — *adj* **cinque'-spotted** (*Shakesp*) having five spots. [Fr]

cinquecento *ching'kwe-chen-tō*, *n* the 16th century, *esp* in reference to Italian art and architecture of the Renaissance period. [Ital, five hundred (*mil-*, one thousand, being understood)]

Cinzano® *chin-zä'nō*, *n* an Italian vermouth. [Manufacturers' name]

CIO. See AFL-CIO.

CIOB *abbrev*: Chartered Institute of Building.

cion. A spelling of **scion** still used in US.

CIPA *abbrev*: Chartered Institute of Patent Agents.

CIPFA *abbrev*: Chartered Institute of Public Finance and Accountancy.

cipher (sometimes **cypher**) *sī'fər*, *n* a secret code; an interweaving of the initials of a name; any person or thing of little value, a nonentity; any of the Arabic numerals; formerly, the character 0 (*arith*); in an organ, continuous sounding of a note not played, due to a mechanical defect. — *vi* to work at arithmetic; of an organ, to sound a note continuously when it is not played. — *vt* to write in cipher; to calculate; to decipher (*Shakesp*). — *n* **cī'phering**. — **cīpher key** a key to a cipher or piece of secret writing. [OFr *cyfre*, Fr *chiffre*, from Ar *sifr* zero, empty]

CIPM *abbrev*: *Comité International des Poids et Mesures* (*Fr*), International Committee of Weights and Measures.

cipollino *chē-pol-lē'nō* or **cipolin** *sip'ō-lin*, *n* a marble with green and white bands in which calcite is interfoliated with mica or talc, the chief source of which is the island of Euboea: — *pl* **cipolli'nos**. [Ital *cipolla* an onion]

cippus *sip'əs*, *n* the stocks; a monumental pillar (*archit*): — *pl* **cipp'ī**. [L *cippus* a post]

CIR *abbrev*: Commission on Industrial Relations.

cir. or **circ.** *abbrev*: *circa*, *circiter* or *circum* (*L*), about.

circa *sûr'kə*, *prep* and *adv* about, around. [L]

circadian *sûr-kā'di-ən*, *adj esp* (in **circadian rhythm**) pertaining to any biological cycle (eg of varying intensity of metabolic or physiological process, or of some feature of behaviour) which is repeated, *usu approx* every 24 hours. [From L *circa* about, *di(em)* day, and sfx **-an**]

Circaean *sûr-sē'ən*, *adj* relating to the beautiful sorceress *Circe*, who transformed the companions of Ulysses into swine by a magic beverage (*Gr mythol*); infatuating and degrading. — Also **Circe'an**. — *n* **Circae'a** the enchanter's nightshade genus. [L *Circē*, from Gr *Kirkē*]

circar. Same as **sircar**.

Circassian *sûr-kas(h)'yən*, *adj* belonging to *Circassia*, the country of the Cherkesses in the western Caucasus. — *n* a Cherkess; the language of the Cherkesses; (without *cap*) a kind of light cashmere (also **circassienne'**). — **Circassian circle** a progressive dance in reel time.

circensian *sûr-sen'shi-ən*, *adj* relating to the Circus Maximus, Rome, where games were held. — Also **circen'sial** (*obs*). [L *circēnsis*, from *circus*]

circinate *sûr'sin-āt*, *adj* ring-shaped; rolled inwards (*bot*). [L *circināre*, *-ātum* to make round]

circiter *sûr'si-tər*, *prep* (formerly used with dates) about, around. [L]

circle *sûr'kl*, *n* a plane figure bounded by one line every point of which is equally distant from a fixed point called the centre; the circumference of the figure so defined; a circular object; a ring; a planet's orbit; a parallel of latitude; a series ending where it began; a figure in magic; a group of things in a circle; an area of seating in a theatre or cinema above the stalls, such as the *dress circle* or *upper circle*; a company surrounding or associating with the principal person; those of a certain class or group; an administrative unit. — *vt* to move round; to encompass; to draw a circle around. — *vi* (often with *round* or *around*) to move in a circle; to stand in a circle. — *adj* **cir'cled** circular; encircled. — *n* **cir'cler**. — *n* **cir'clet** a little circle; a little circular band or hoop, *esp* a metal headband. — *n* and *adj* **cir'cling** moving in a circle. — **cir'cle-rider** a person who rides in circles to round up cattle; **cir'cle-riding**. — **come full circle** to return to the beginning; to regain or turn out to be in a former state; **dress circle** see under **dress**; **go**

round in circles to get no results in spite of effort; not to get anywhere; **great** (or **small**) **circle** a circular section of a sphere whose centre is (or is not) the centre of the sphere; **reasoning in a circle** assuming what is to be proved as the basis of the argument; **run round in circles** to act in too frenzied a way to achieve anything useful. [OE *circul*, from L *circulus*, dimin of *circus*; allied to OE *hring* a ring]

circlip *sûr'klip*, (*eng*) *n* a spring washer in the form of an incomplete circle, used as a retaining ring.

circs *sûrks*, (*slang*) *n pl* a shortened form of **circumstances**.

circuit *sûr'kit*, *n* a journey round; a way round; perimeter; a roundabout way; an area enclosed; the path, complete or partial, of an electric current; a round made in the exercise of a calling, *esp* in England (till 1972) by judges; the judges making the round; a district in which such a round is made, as by Methodist preachers, commercial travellers, etc; a group of theatres, cinemas, etc under common control, through which an entertainment circulates; the venues visited in turn and regularly by sports competitors, performers, etc; a series of exercises to be carried out consecutively and repeated; a motor-racing track; a diadem (*Shakesp*). — *vt* to go round. — *n* **circuiteer**' a judge who goes on a circuit. — *adj* **circuitous** (*-kū'i-təs*) indirect, roundabout. — *adv* **circū'itously**. — *n* **circū'itousness**. — *n* **circuitry** (*sûr'kit-ri*) the detailed plan of a circuit, as in radio or television, or its components. — *n* **circū'ity** motion in a circle; an indirect or roundabout course. — **circuit board** a printed circuit board (qv under **print**); **circuit breaker** a switch or other device for interrupting an electric circuit; anything which halts or interrupts a process temporarily; **circuit judge** a judge in a county or crown court; **circuit rider** (*hist*) a preacher who goes on a circuit; **circuit training** a form of athletic training consisting of repeated series of exercises. [Fr, from L *circuitus*, from *circuīre*, from *circum* round, and *īre* to go]

circuitus verborum *sûr-kū'it-əs vûr-bō'rəm*, *-bö'* or *kir-kōō'it-ōōs wer-bō'rōōm*, (*L*) a circumlocution.

circular *sûr'kū-lər*, *adj* of or pertaining to a circle; in the form of a circle; round; ending in itself; recurring in a cycle; addressed to a circle of persons. — *n* a letter or notice sent to a number of persons. — *n* **circularity** (*-lar'i-ti*). — *vt* **cir'cularize** or **-ise** to make circular; to send circulars to. — *adv* **cir'cularly**. — **circular breathing** a technique used in playing a wind instrument, in which a phrase is sustained by forcing air out of the mouth while breathing through the nose; **circular file** (*comput*) a file in which each item has a pointer to the next, the last leading back to the first; **circular function** any of the trigonometrical functions with argument in radians; **circular letter** a letter of which copies are sent to several persons; **circular measure** the reckoning of angles in radians; **circular note** a former letter of bank credit addressed to foreign bankers for the use of a traveller, being a kind of bill personal to the bearer; **circular polarization** (*telecomm*) an electromagnetic wave for which either the electric or magnetic field vector describes a circle at the wave frequency, used in satellite communications; **circular saw** a power-driven saw in the shape of a flat disc with a serrated edge; **circular velocity** the horizontal velocity of a body required to keep it in orbit, at a given altitude, around a planet. [L *circulāris*]

circulate *sûr'kū-lāt*, *vt* to cause to go round as in a circle; to spread. — *vi* to move round; to be spread about; to repeat in definite order (of decimals). — *adj* **cir'culable** capable of being circulated. — *n* and *adj* **cir'culating**. — *n* **circulā'tion** the act of moving in a circle or in a closed path (as the blood); spreading or moving about; dissemination; the sale of a periodical; the money in use at any time in a country. — *adj* **cir'culative** or **cir'culatory** circulating. — *n* **cir'culātor**. — **circulating capital** working capital; **circulating library** a small library that moves around a group of schools, hospitals, etc; one from which books are circulated among subscribers; **circulating medium** (*finance*) currency as a means of exchange; **circulatory system** the system of blood and lymph vessels, including the heart. — **in** or **out of circulation** in or out of general use, activity, etc. [L *circulāre*, *-ātum*]

circum- *sûr'kəm-*, *sər-kum'-* or *sûr-kəm-*, *combining form* denoting around. [L *circum*]

circumambages *sûr-kəm-am-bā'jēz* or *-am'bi-jiz*, *n sing* and *n pl* roundabout methods of speech. — *adj* **circumambā'gious** (*-jəs*) roundabout in speech. [L *circum* around, and *ambāgēs* a winding]

circumambient *sûr-kəm-am'bi-ənt*, *adj* going round about, encompassing. — *n* **circumam'bience** or **circumam'biency**. [L *circum* around, and *ambīre* to go round]

circumambulate *sûr-kəm-am'bū-lāt*, *vi* to walk round about. — *n* **circumambulā'tion**. [L *circum* around, and *ambulāre*, *-ātum* to walk]

circumbendibus *sûr-kəm-ben'di-bəs*, *n* a roundabout way, method or expression. [Joc formation from L *circum* round, **bend**, and L ablative pl ending *-ibus*]

circumcentre *sûr'kem-sen-tər*, *n* the centre of the circumscribed circle or sphere. [**circum-**]

circumcise *sûr'kəm-sīz*, *vt* to cut or cut off all or part of the foreskin (of a male) or all or part of the clitoris (of a female), often as a religious rite; to purify (*fig*). — *n* **cir'cumciser**. — *n* **circumcision** (*-sizh'n*) the act of circumcising; the state of being circumcised; those who are circumcised, *esp* the Jews (*archaic*). [L *circumcīdere*, *-cīsum*, from *caedere* to cut]

circumdenudation *sûr-kəm-den-ū-dā'shən*, (*geol*) *n* denudation or erosion of surroundings, leaving an isolated elevation. [**circum-**]

circumduct *sûr'kəm-dukt*, *vt* to lead around or about, to cause to revolve round an imaginary axis so as to describe a cone. — *vt* **circumduce** (*-dūs'*; *Scots law*) to declare to be at an end (the term for leading proof). — *n* **circumduc'tion**. — *adj* **circumduct'ory**. [L *circum* round, and *dūcere*, *ductum* to lead]

circumference *sər-kum'fər-əns*, *n* the boundary line, *esp* of a circle; compass; distance round. — *adj* **circumferential** (*-en'shl*). — *n* **circum'ferentor** (*-en-tər*) an instrument for measuring horizontal angles, consisting of a graduated circle, sights, and a magnetic needle; a graduated wheel for measuring the circumference of wheels. [L *circum* around, and *ferre* to carry]

circumflect *sûr-kəm-flekt'*, *vt* to bend round; to mark with a circumflex. — *n* **cir'cumflex** an accent (ˆ) *orig* denoting a rising and falling of the voice on a vowel or syllable. — Also *adj*. — *n* **circumflexion** (*-flek-shən*) a bending round. [L *circum* around, and *flectere*, *flexum* to bend]

circumfluence *sər-kum'flōō-əns*, *n* all flowing around; the engulfing of food by surrounding it (eg by protozoa, etc). — *adj* **circum'fluent** or **circum'fluous**. [L *circum* around, and *fluere* to flow]

circumforaneous *sûr-kəm-fō-rā'ni-əs* or *-fö-*, or **circumforanean** *-ni-ən*, *adj* wandering about as from market to market, vagrant. [L *circum* around, and *forum* the forum, market-place]

circumfuse *sûr-kəm-fūz'*, *vt* to pour around or about. — *adj* **circumfused'**. — *adj* **circumfus'ile** molten; poured around or about. — *n* **circumfusion** (*-fū'zhən*). [L *circum* around, and *fundere*, *fūsum* to pour]

circumgyrate *sûr-kəm-ji-rāt'*, *vi* to whirl or roll round. — *n* **circumgyrā'tion**. — *adj* **circumgy'ratory**. [L *circum* around, and *gȳrāre*, *-ātum* to turn]

circumincession or **circuminsession** *sûr-kəm-in-sesh'ən*, (*theol*) *n* the reciprocity of existence in one another of the three persons of the Trinity. [L *circum* around, and *incessus*, pa p of *incēdere* to go, proceed]

circumjacent *sûr-kəm-jā'sənt*, *adj* lying round; bordering on every side. — *n* **circumjā'cency**. [L *circum* around, and *jacēns*, *-entis* lying, from *jacēre* to lie]

circumlittoral *sûr-kəm-lit'ə-rəl*, *adj* adjacent to or bordering the shoreline. [L *circum* around, and *littus*, for *lītus*, *-oris* shore]

circumlocution *sûr'kəm-lə-kū'shən*, *n* expressing an idea in more words than are necessary; an instance of this;

evasive talk. — *vi* **circumlocūte'** to use circumlocution. — *adj* **circumlocū'tional** or **circumlocū'tionary**. — *n* **circumlocū'tionist** a person who uses circumlocution. — *adj* **circumlocutory** (*-lok'ū-tər-i*). [L *circum* around, and *loquī, locūtus* to speak]

circumlunar *sûr-kəm-lo͞o'nər, -lū', adj* situated or moving round the moon. [L *circum* around, and *lūna* the moon]

circummure *sûr-kəm-mūr'*, (*Shakesp*) *vt* to wall around. [L *circum* around, and *mūrus* a wall]

circumnavigate *sûr-kəm-nav'i-gāt, vt* to sail or fly right round. — *adj* **circumnav'igable**. — *n* **circumnavigā'tion**. — *n* **circumnav'igātor**. [**circum-**]

circumnutation *sûr-kəm-nū-tā'shən*, (*bot*) *n* rotation in a nodding position, as the spiral path described by the growing point of a plant. — *vi* **circumnū'tate**. — *adj* **circumnū'tatory**. [L *circum* around, and *nūtāre, -ātum* to nod]

circumpolar *sûr-kəm-pō'lər, adj* situated or ranging round the pole. — **circumpolar stars** stars so near the pole of the heavens that (for places at the latitude in question) they never set but merely revolve round the pole. [**circum-**]

circumpose *sûr-kəm-pōz', vt* to place round. — *n* **circumposi'tion** the act of placing round. [L *circumpōnere* by analogy with *impose*, etc]

circumscissile *sûr-kəm-sis'il*, (*bot*) *adj* (of a seed vessel) opening by a circular transverse line. [L *circum* around, and *scissilis* cleavable]

circumscribe *sûr-kəm-skrīb', vt* to draw a line round; to describe a curve or figure touching externally; to enclose within certain limits, to curtail, abridge. — *adj* **circumscrīb'able**. — *n* **circumscrīb'er** a person who circumscribes. — *n* **circumscription** (*-skrip'shən*) limitation; the line that limits; the act of circumscribing; an inscription running round; a defined district. — *adj* **circumscrip'tive** marking the external form or outline. [L *circum* around, and *scrībere, scrīptum* to write]

circumsolar *sûrkəm-sō'lar, adj* situated or moving round the sun. [L *circum* around, and *sōl* the sun]

circumspect *sûr'kəm-spekt, adj* looking round on all sides watchfully; cautious; prudent. — *n* **circumspec'tion** watchfulness; caution; examining. — *adj* **circumspec'-tive** looking around; wary. — *adv* **cir'cumspectly**. — *n* **cir'cumspectness**. [L *circum* around, and *specere, spicere, spectum* to look]

circumstance *sûr'kəm-stəns, n* the logical surroundings of an action; an attendant fact; an accident or event; ceremony; detail; (in *pl*) the state of one's affairs. — *vt* to place in particular circumstances. — *adj* **circumstantial** (*-stan'shl*) consisting of details; minute. — *n* **circumstantiality** (*-stan-shi-al'i-ti*) the quality of being circumstantial; minuteness in details; a detail. — *adv* **circumstan'tially**. — *n pl* **circumstan'tials** incidentals; details. — *vt* **circumstan'tiate** to prove by circumstances; to describe exactly. — **circumstantial evidence** evidence which is not positive nor direct, but which is gathered inferentially from the circumstances in the case. — **in good** (or **bad**) **circumstances** prosperous (or unprosperous); **in** or **under no circumstances** never; **in** or **under the circumstances** conditions being what they are; **not a circumstance to** (*old US colloq*) nothing in comparison to. [L *circum* around, and *stāns, stantis* standing, from *stāre* to stand]

circumterrestrial *sûr-kəm-ti-res'tri-əl, adj* situated or moving round the earth. [L *circum* around, and *terrestris*, from *terra* the earth]

circumvallate *sûr-kəm-val'āt, vt* to surround with a rampart. — *n* **circumvallā'tion** a surrounding with a wall; a wall or fortification surrounding a town or fort; engulfing of food by surrounding it (eg by protozoa) (*zool*). [L *circum* around, and *vallum* rampart]

circumvent *sûr-kəm-vent', vt* to go round; to encompass; to surround so as to intercept or capture; to get round, or to outwit. — *n* **circumven'tion**. — *adj* **circumvent'ive** deceiving by artifices. [L *circum* around, and *venīre, ventum* to come]

circumvolve *sûr-kəm-volv', vt* to roll round. — *vi* to revolve. — *n* **circumvolution** (*-lo͞o'* or *-lū'*) a turning or rolling round; anything winding or sinuous. [L *circum* around, and *volvere, volūtum* to roll]

circus *sûr'kəs, n* a circular or oval building for public entertainments (*Roman antiq*); a place, building or tent for entertainment by acrobats, clowns, performing animals, etc; a show of this kind or the company of performers (also *fig*); a group of houses arranged in the form of a circle; an open place at a street junction; a natural amphitheatre; a group of people who travel around putting on a display (such as a *flying circus*), often in the form of a competition (such as a *tennis circus*); a noisy entertainment or scene. — *adj* **cir'cussy** or **cir'cusy**. [L *circus*, from Gr *kirkos*]

ciré *sē'rā, n* (a fabric with) a highly glazed finish. [Fr pa p of *cirer* to wax]

cire perdue *sēr per-dü*, (*Fr*) *n* a method of casting in metal, the mould being formed round a wax model which is then melted away, literally lost wax.

cirl *sûrl* or **cirl bunting** (*bun'ting*), *n* a species of bunting (*Emberiza cirlus*). [Ital *cirlo*]

cirque *sûrk, n* a circus; a ring (*poetic*); a deep round hollow, a natural amphitheatre, formed by glaciation (*geog*). [Fr]

cirrate, **cirriform**, etc. See **cirrus**.

cirrhopod *sir'ə-pod* and **Cirrhopoda** *si-ro'pə-də*, older forms of **cirripede** and **Cirripedia** (as if from Gr *kirrhos* tawny, and *pous, podos* foot).

cirrhosis *si-rō'sis, n* a wasting of the proper tissue of the liver, accompanied by abnormal growth of connective tissue. — *adj* **cirrhot'ic**. [Gr *kirrhos* tawny, from the colour of the liver so diseased]

cirripede *sir'i-pēd* or **cirreped** *-ped, n* one of the **Cirripē'dia**, a subclass of marine Crustacea, including the barnacles. — Also **cirrh'ipede** and **Cirrhipē'dia**. [L *cirrus* a curl, and *pēs, pedis* foot]

cirrus *sir'əs, n* the highest form of clouds, consisting of curling fibres; a tendril (*bot*); any curled filament (*zool*): — *pl* **cirr'ī**. — *adj* **cirr'ate** or **cirr'iform** like a cirrus. — *adj* **cirr'igrade** moving by cirri. — *adj* **cirr'ose** with tendrils. — *adj* **cirr'ous** having a cirrus. — **cirr'o=cū'mūlus** a cloud of small white flakes or ripples (also called *mackerel sky*); **cirr'o-strā'tus** a high thin sheet of haze-like cloud. [L, a curl, tuft; the common *erron* spellings cirrhus, etc are due to confusion with Gr *kirrhos* tawny]

cirsoid *sûr'soid*, (*med*) *adj* of or resembling a dilated vein or varix. [Gr *kirsos* swollen vein]

CIS *abbrev*: Chartered Institute of Secretaries; Commonwealth of Independent States.

cis- *sis-, combining form* denoting on this side. — *adj* **cisalpine** (*sis-alp'in* or *-īn*), on this (ie the Roman) side of the Alps. — *adj* **cislu'nar** on this side of the moon, ie between the moon and the earth. — *adj* **cismon'tane** on this side of the mountains (as opposed to *ultramontane*). — *adj* **cispadane** (*-pā'dān* or *sis'pa-dān*; L *Padus* the river Po) on this (the Roman) side of the Po. — *adj* **cispon'tine** on this side of the bridges, ie in London, north of the Thames. [L *cis* on this side]

cisco *sis'kō, n* any of several salmonoid fish of the genus *Coregonus, esp C. artedi*, found in the Great Lakes of N America (also called **lake herring**): — *pl* **cis'coes** or **cis'cos**. [Fr Can *cisco(ette)*, from Ojibwa *pemitewiskawet* that which has oily flesh]

ciselure *sēz'lo͞or, n* the art or operation of chasing; the chasing upon a piece of metalwork. — *n* **cis'eleur** (*-lər*), a chaser. [Fr]

cislunar, **cispadane**. See under **cis-**.

cisplatin *sis-plat'in, n* a generic anticancer drug, used *esp* in the treament of cancer of the ovary and testis. [**cis-** and *platin*um]

cispontine. See under **cis-**.

cissoid *sis'oid*, (*math*) *n* a plane curve consisting of two infinite branches symmetrically placed with reference to the diameter of a circle, so that at one of its extremities they form a cusp, while the tangent to the circle at the other extremity is an asymptote. [Gr *kissoeidēs* ivy-like, from *kissos* ivy, and *eidos* form]

cissus *sis'əs*, *n* any climbing plant of the genus *Cissus*, including the kangaroo vine. [New L, from Gr *kissos* ivy]

cissy *sis'i*, (*slang*) *n* an effeminate man; a timid, nervous boy; a cry-baby. — Also *adj*. [Partly from the name *Cecily*, partly from **sister**; cf **sis**]

cist *sist* or *kist*, (*archaeol*) *n* a tomb consisting of a stone chest covered with stone slabs. — Also **kist**. — *adj* **cist'ed** containing cists. — *adj* **cist'ic** like a cist. [See **chest**]

Cistercian *sis-tûr'shən*, *n* a member of the order of monks established in 1098 in the forest of Cîteaux (*Cistercium*), in France, an offshoot of the Benedictines. — Also *adj*.

cistern *sis'tərn*, *n* an artificial reservoir or tank for holding water or other liquid; a natural reservoir. — *n* **cistern'a** (*anatom*) a sac or space containing eg cerebrospinal or lymph fluid: — *pl* **cistern'ae**. [L *cisterna*, from *cista* a chest]

cistic. See **cist**.

cistron *sis'trən*, (*genetics*) *n* a section of a chromosome which controls a single function. [*cis-trans* test, one defining the unit of genetic function]

cistus *sis'təs*, *n* any plant of the rockrose genus (*Cistus*) of shrubby plants, giving name to the family **Cistāceae**, cultivated for the beauty of their flowers: — *pl* **cis'tuses**. — *adj* **cistaceous** (*-ā'shəs*). [Gr *kistos* rockrose]

cistvaen. See **kistvaen**.

CIT *abbrev*: Chartered Institute of Transport.

cit. *abbrev*: citation; citizen.

cit *sit*, (*archaic slang*) *n* a term of contempt for a townsman, not a gentleman: — *fem* **cit'ess**. — *n pl* **cits** (*US slang*) civilian clothes. [**citizen**]

citadel *sit'ə-dəl*, *n* a fortress in or near a city; the place where the guns are kept in a warship; in the Salvation Army, the hall in which meetings are held. [Ital *cittadella*, dimin of *città* a city; see **city**]

cite *sīt*, *vt* to call or summon; to summon to appear in court; to quote; to name; to adduce as proof. — *adj* **cit'able** or **cite'able** that can be cited. — *n* **cīt'al** summons to appear. — *n* **citā'tion** (*sī-* or *si-*) an official summons to appear; a document containing the summons; the act of quoting; the passage or name quoted; mention in dispatches; official recognition of achievement. — *adj* **cit'atory** having to do with citation; addicted to citation. — *n* **cīt'er**. [L *citāre*, *-ātum* to call, intens of *ciēre*, *cīre* to make to go]

CITES *abbrev*: Convention on International Trade in Endangered Species (of Wild Fauna and Flora).

cithara *sith'ə-rə*, *n* an ancient Greek musical instrument differing from the lyre in its flat shallow sound chest. — *n* **cith'arist** a player on it. — *adj* **citharist'ic**. — *n* **cith'er**, **cith'ern** or **citt'ern** an early modern metal-stringed musical instrument similar to the lute, played either with a plectrum or with the fingers; the Tirolese zither. [L, from Gr *kitharā*; cf **guitar**, **zither**]

citify. See **city**.

citigrade *sit'i-grād*, *adj* moving quickly, applied to the Lycosidae or wolf-spiders that run down their prey. [L *citus* quick, and *gradus* a step]

citizen *sit'i-z(ə)n*, *n* an inhabitant of a city; a member of a state; a townsman; a freeman; a civilian (*US*): — *fem* **cit'izeness**. — *vt* **cit'izenize** or **-ise** to make a citizen of. — *n* **cit'izenry** the general body of citizens. — *n* **cit'izenship** the state of being, or of having rights and duties of, a citizen; conduct in relation to these duties. — **citizen's arrest** an arrest, legally allowable, made by a member of the public; **Citizens' Band** (*orig US*) a band of radio frequencies on which the public are permitted to broadcast personal messages, etc; **Citizens' Band radio** (also **CB radio**). [ME *citesein*, from OFr *citeain*; see **city**]

cito *sī'* or *ki'tō*, (*L*) *adv* quickly.

citole *sit'ōl* or *sit-ōl'*, *n* a medieval stringed instrument, probably an early form of the cither (qv under **cithara**).

citron *sit'rən*, *n* the fruit of the citron tree, resembling a lemon. — *n* **cit'range** (*-rənj*) a hybrid between citron and orange. — *n* **cit'rate** a salt of citric acid. — *adj* **cit'reous** citrine. — *adj* **cit'ric** derived from the citron. — *n* **cit'rin** the water-soluble vitamin P, found in citrus fruits, etc. — *adj* **cit'rine** (*-rin*) dark and greenish yellow, like a citron or lemon. — *n* citrine colour; a rock crystal of this colour, false topaz. — *n* **citronell'a** a Ceylon grass (**citronella grass**, *Cymbopogon nardus*) yielding **citronella oil**, a yellow oil used in perfumery. — *n* **citronell'al** a colourless aldehyde with a lemon scent, present in citronella and other essential oils, used as a flavouring and in perfumery. — *adj* **cit'rous**. — *n* **cit'rus** a citron tree; (with *cap*) a genus of Rutaceae including the citron, lemon, orange, etc. — **citric acid** the acid to which lemon and lime juice owe their sourness, $C_6H_8O_7$; **citron tree** the tree that bears the citron fruit (*Citrus medica*), considered to be the ancestor of the lemon and lime; **citron wood** or **citrus wood** the most costly furniture wood of the ancient Romans (perhaps sandarach); the wood of the citron tree; **citrus fruits** citrons, lemons, limes, oranges, grapefruit, and their hybrids. — **citric acid cycle** a cycle of chemical changes in living material (eg muscle), in the course of which citric acid is oxidized, and by which acetic acid or acetyl is converted to carbon dioxide and water, the chemicals released in the process being important to the tissue (also called **Krebs cycle**). [L *citrus*, from which comes also Gr *kitron* a citron]

citrulline *sit-rul'ēn* or *sit'rə-lēn*, *n* an amino-acid formed as an intermediate in the production of urea. [L *citrullus* a type of watermelon (in which it is found), from *citron*]

cittern. Same as **cither**. [See under **cithara**]

city *sit'i*, *n* a large town; an incorporated town that has or had a cathedral; a town on which the dignity has been conferred by tradition or grant; in various countries a municipality of higher rank, variously defined; the business centre or original area of a large town; (with *the* and often with *cap*) the centre of British financial affairs, most banks, etc, being in the City of London. — *n* **citificā'tion** or **cityficātion** — *adj* **cit'ified** or **cit'yfied**. — *vt* **cit'ify** or **cityfy** to give the characteristics or attitudes of the city, or city culture, to (a person, etc). — **city article** in a newspaper, a financial or commercial article; **City Company** a London corporation representing any of the medieval trade guilds; **city desk** the desk or (*fig*) the department or field of work of a city editor; **city editor** the financial editor of a newspaper; the editor in charge of local news, etc of a newspaper (*US*); **city farm** an area established within an urban area in order that city children may learn something about farming, *esp* animal husbandry; **city fathers** the magistrates; the town or city council; **city hall** a town hall; (the officials of) municipal government (*NAm*); city bureaucracy (*NAm*); **city man** a man engaged in commercial or financial work in a city; **city manager** a person appointed by an elected body to manage the administrative affairs of a city; **city mission** a mission for evangelizing the poor classes in the large cities; **city planning** (*NAm*) town planning; **cit'yscape** a drawing, painting or picture of a city (modelled on *landscape*); **city slicker** a city dweller regarded as over-sophisticated and untrustworthy; **city state** a sovereign state consisting of a city with a small surrounding territory. — **city of God**, **heavenly city**, etc, the ideal of the Church of Christ in glory; **city of refuge** by Mosaic law, any of six cities on the River Jordan where the perpetrator of an accidental homicide might flee for refuge; **city technology college** a secondary school set up in an inner city district, funded by central government and (local) industry, specializing in teaching scientific and technological subjects; **Eternal City** Rome; **Holy City** Jerusalem. [Fr *cité* a city, from L *civitās*, *-ātis* the state, from *cīvis* a citizen]

civ. *abbrev*: civil; civilian.
cive. See under **chive**.
civet *siv'it*, *n* a small cat-like carnivore of the genus *Viverra*, of Africa and S Asia, that secretes a musky fluid from anal glands (also **civet cat**); the fur of this animal; a fatty yellowish musk obtained from this animal and used in perfumery. [Fr *civette*, from Ar *zabād*]
civic *siv'ik*, *adj* pertaining to a city or citizen. — *adv* **civ'ically**. — *n sing* **civ'ics** the science of citizenship; the study of government and its business (*NAm*). — **civic centre** a place in which the chief public buildings of a town are grouped; **civic crown** an oak wreath awarded to a Roman soldier for saving a citizen's life in battle. [L *cīvicus*, from *cīvis* citizen]
civil *siv'il*, *adj* pertaining to the community; polite (in any degree short of discourtesy); pertaining to ordinary life, not military; lay, secular, temporal, not ecclesiastical; pertaining to the individual citizen; relating to private relations amongst citizens, and such suits as arise out of these (as opposed to *criminal*) (*law*); naturally good, as opposed to good through regeneration (*theol*). — *n* **civil'ian** a person engaged in civil as distinguished from military and naval pursuits; a professor or student of civil law (not canon law). — Also *adj*. — *vt* **civil'ianize** or **-ise** to convert from military to civilian use; to replace military personnel in (a factory, etc) by civilians. — *n* **civ'ilist** (*archaic*) a person versed in civil law. — *n* **civil'ity** civilization (*archaic*); good breeding (*obs*); politeness; (often in *pl*) an act of politeness. — *adv* **civ'illy**. — *n* **civ'ism** good citizenship; the state of being favourably inclined to French Revolution principles. — **civil aviation** non-military flying, *esp* commercial airlines and their operation; **civil commotion** a term used in insurance policies denoting a state of civil unrest between riot and civil war; **civil day**, **year** or **time** the day, year or time, as reckoned for ordinary purposes; **civil death** (*law*) formerly, the loss of all civil and legal privileges; **civil defence** a civilian service for the wartime protection of the civilian population against enemy attack; **civil disobedience** refusal to obey laws and regulations, pay taxes, etc, used as non-violent means of forcing concessions from government; **civil engineer** a person who plans and builds railways, roads, bridges, docks, etc, as opposed to a military engineer, or to a mechanical engineer; **civil engineering**; **civil law** (as opposed to *criminal law*) the law laid down by a state regarding the rights of the inhabitants, *esp* that founded on Roman law; **civil liberty** (often in *pl*) personal freedom of thought, word, action, etc; **civil list** formerly, a list of charges for civil government purposes; now the expenses of the sovereign's household (**civil list pensions** those granted by royal favour); **civil marriage** a marriage performed by an official who is not a clergyman and involving a civil contract without religious ceremony and vows; **civil rights** (often with *caps*) the rights of a citizen to personal freedom, ie political, racial, legal, social, etc. — Also *adj*. — **civil servant** a person who works in the **civil service**, the paid service of the state chiefly in public administration (other than military, naval, legislative and judicial); **civil twilight** the interval of time during which the sun is between the horizon and 6° below the horizon, morning and evening (*astron*); **civil war** a war between citizens of the same state. [L *cīvīlis*, from *cīvis* citizen]
civilize or **-ise** *siv'il-īz*, *vt* to reclaim from barbarism; to instruct in arts and refinements. — *adj* **civilīz'able** or **-s-**. — *n* **civilīzā'tion** or **-s-** the state of being civilized; culture; cultural condition or complex. — *adj* **civ'ilized** or **-s-** (having) advanced beyond the primitive savage state; refined in interests and tastes; sophisticated, self-controlled and well-spoken. — *n* **civ'ilīzer** or **-s-**. [See **civil**]
civvy *siv'i*, (*slang*) *n* and *adj* civilian; (in *pl* **civv'ies**) civilian clothes. — **civvy street** (*colloq*) civilian life after a period of service in the armed forces, police, etc.
CJ *abbrev*: Civil Justice.
CJD *abbrev*: Creutzfeldt-Jakob disease.
CL *abbrev*: Ceylon (IVR).
Cl (*chem*) *symbol*: chlorine.
cl. *abbrev*: centilitre.
clabber *klab'ər*, (*esp Scot* and *Irish*) *n* mud. [Irish *clabar* mud]
clabby-doo. See **clappy-doo**.
clachan *klä'* or *kla'hhən*, (*Scot*) *n* a small village. [Gaelic *clachan*, from *clach* stone]
clack *klak*, *vi* to make a noise as of a hard, flat thing flapping; to chatter; to cackle. — *n* a noise of this kind; an instrument making it; the sound of chattering voices; the tongue (*colloq*). — *n* **clack'er**. — **clack'box** the box containing the clack valve of an engine; **clack'dish** (*archaic*) a wooden dish carried by beggars, having a movable cover which they clacked to attract attention; **clack valve** a valve consisting of a hinged flap or other device that falls back with a clacking noise. [Prob imit]
Clactonian *klak-tō'ni-ən*, (*archaeol*) *adj* of or relating to a palaeolithic culture characterized by tools of flaked stone used as chopping and hewing implements. — Also *n*. [From *Clacton*-on-Sea, where the tools were first found]
clad *klad*, *pa t* and *pa p* of **clothe**. — *adj* clothed, or covered. — *vt* to cover one material with another, eg one metal with another (as in a nuclear reactor), or brick or stonework with a different material (in building). — *n* **cladd'er**. — *n* **cladd'ing**.
clade *klād*, (*biol*) *n* a group of organisms that have evolved from a common ancestor. — *n* **clād'ism** adherence to cladistic theories. — *n* **clād'ist**. — *adj* **cladist'ic**. — *n* **cladist'ics** a taxonomic theory which classifies organisms according to the shared characteristics which distinguish a group from other groups. — *n* **cladogen'esis** evolution of clades as if by branching from a common ancestor. — *n* **clād'ogram** a branching diagram showing the development of a clade. [Gr *klados* branch]
cladode *klad'ōd*, (*bot*) *n* a branch or stem with the appearance and functions of a leaf. [Gr *klados* a shoot]
cladosporium *klad-ō-spör'i-əm*, (*bot*) *n* a fungus affecting the leaves of plants, particularly those cultivated in greenhouses.
claes *klāz*, (*Scot*) *n pl* clothes.
clag *klag*, (*dialect*) *vi* to stick. — *vt* to bedaub: — *pr p* **clagg'ing**; *pa t* and *pa p* **clagged**. — *n* a sticky mass or clot of dirt, etc. — *adj* **clagg'y** tenacious, sticky. [Prob Scand; Dan *klag* mud; cf **clay**]
claim *klām*, *vt* to demand or assert as a right; to maintain or assert; to call for; to take (life). — *vi* to make a claim (*on* one's insurance policy, etc). — *n* a demand for something supposed due; an assertion that something is a fact; a right or ground for demanding; the thing claimed, *esp* a piece of land appropriated by a miner; (*Spenser* **clame**) a call, shout. — *adj* **claim'able** that can be claimed. — *n* **claim'ant** or **claim'er** a person who makes a claim. — **claiming race** (*US*) a race in which any horse having taken part in the race may be bought at a previously fixed price by anyone starting a horse at the meeting (cf *selling race*); **claim'-jumper** a person who takes possession of another's mining claim; **claims assessor** an assessor employed by an insurance company, *usu* in motor accident claims. — **lay claim to** to assert a right to; **stake a claim** see under **stake**[1]. [OFr *claimer*, from L *clāmāre* to call out]
clairaudience *klār-öd'i-əns*, *n* the alleged power of hearing things beyond the range of the normal sense of hearing. — *n* and *adj* **clairaud'ient**. [Fr *clair*, from L *clārus* clear, and **audience**]
claircolle. See **clearcole**.
clair de lune *klār də loon'*, *n* a bluish colour, *esp* that of a certain kind of porcelain glaze; porcelain glazed in this way; a kind of shiny bluish glass. [Fr, moonlight]

clair-obscure or **clare-obscure** *klār-ob-skūr'*, *n* chiaroscuro (qv). [Fr *clair*, from L *clārus* clear, and Fr *obscur*, from L *obscūrus* obscure]

clairschach *klār'shähh*. A variant spelling of **clarsach**.

clairvoyance *klār-voi'əns*, *n* the alleged power of discerning things beyond the normal range of sense or perception. — Also **clairvoy'ancy**. — *n* and *adj* **clairvoy'ant**. [Fr *clair*, from L *clārus* clear, and Fr *voir*, from L *vidēre* to see]

clam[1] *klam*, *n* a gripping instrument. [OE *clam* fetter]

clam[2] *klam*, *n* an edible shellfish of various kinds, *esp* the round clam or quahog (*Venus mercenaria*) and the long clam (*Mya arenaria*); a scallop or scallop-shell; a very reticent person (*colloq*). — *vi* to gather clams: — *pr p* **clamm'ing**; *pa t* and *pa p* **clammed**. — **clam'bake** a baking of clams on hot stones, with layers of potatoes, fish, sweetcorn, etc, popular at picnic parties in US; such a party; any informal party; **clam-chow'der** chowder made with clams; **clam'shell** a cockpit canopy hinged at front and rear (*aeronautics*); a hinged part of the thrust reverser in a gas turbine; (an excavating machine with) a bucket with two hinged jaws (*NAm*). — **clam up** (*colloq*) to become silent. [**clam**[1]]

clam[3] *klam*, *n* noise produced by ringing two or more bells together. — Also *vt* and *vi*. [Prob onomatopoeic]

clamant *klam'ənt* or *klām'ənt*, *adj* calling aloud or earnestly. — *n* **clam'ancy** urgency. — *adv* **clam'antly**. [L *clāmāre* to cry out]

clamber *klam'bər*, *vi* and *vt* to climb with difficulty, grasping with hands and feet (often with *up* or *over*). — *n* the act of clambering. [From the root of **climb**; cf Ger *klammern*, from *klemmen* to squeeze or hold tightly]

clame. See under **claim**.

clamjamphrie, **clamjamfry** *klam-jam'fri*, or **clanjamfray** *klan-*, (*Scot*) *n* rubbish; nonsense; rabble. [Derivation uncertain]

clammed, **clamming**. See **clam**[2].

clammy *klam'i*, *adj* sticky; moist and adhesive; unpleasantly damp, and often warm. — *adv* **clamm'ily**. — *n* **clamm'iness**. [Dialect *clam* dampness, from OE *clæman* to anoint]

clamour[1] or (*NAm*) **clamor** *klam'ər*, *n* a loud continuous outcry; uproar; any loud noise; persistent expression of dissatisfaction. — *vi* to cry aloud in demand (often with *for*); to make a loud continuous outcry. — *adj* **clam'orous** noisy, boisterous. — *adv* **clam'orously**. — *n* **clam'orousness**. — *n* **clam'ourer**. [L *clāmor*, *-ōris*]

clamour[2] *klam'ər*, (*Shakesp*) *vt* to silence, check the ringing of. [Perh connected with **clam**[3]]

clamp[1] *klamp*, *n* a piece of timber, iron, etc used to fasten things together or to strengthen any framework; any instrument for holding; a wheel clamp. — *vt* to bind with a clamp; to grasp or press firmly; to put (on) authoritatively, impose; to fit a wheel clamp to (a car). — *n* **clamp'er** someone or something that clamps. — **clamp down on** to suppress, or suppress the activities of, firmly (*n* **clamp'down**). [From a root seen in OE *clam* fetter; Du *klamp* a clamp; related to **clip**, **climb**]

clamp[2] *klamp*, *n* a heavy tread. — *vi* to tread heavily. [Prob imit]

clamp[3] *klamp*, *n* a stack, as of bricks for burning, peats, etc; a heap; a heap of root vegetables covered with earth or straw to protect it in cold weather. — *vt* to put in clamps. [Prob Du *klamp* heap]

clamper *klam'pər*, (*Scot*) *vt* to botch up. [Origin unknown; prob connected with **clamp**[1]]

clan *klan*, *n* a tribe or collection of families subject to a single chieftain, commonly bearing the same surname, and supposed to have a common ancestor; a clique, sect; a collective name for a number of persons or things. — *adj* **clann'ish** closely united and holding aloof from others, like the members of a clan. — *adv* **clann'ishly**. — *n* **clann'ishness**. — *n* **clan'ship** association of families under a chieftain; feeling of loyalty to a clan. — **clans'man** and **clans'woman** a member of a clan. [Gaelic *clann* offspring, tribe, from L *planta* a shoot]

clandestine *klan-des'tin*, *adj* concealed or hidden; private; sly. — *adv* **clandes'tinely**. — *n* **clandes'tineness** or **clandestin'ity**. [L *clandestīnus*, from *clam* secretly]

clang[1] *klang*, *vi* to produce a loud deep ringing sound. — *vt* to cause to clang. — *n* a ringing sound, like that made by striking large pieces of metal, or that of a trumpet; the sonorous cry of some birds, such as cranes or geese. — *n* **clang'er** a tactless or ill-timed remark or comment; a stupid mistake. — *n* and *adj* **clang'ing**. — *adj* **clangorous** (*klang'gər-əs*). — *adv* **clang'orously**. — *n* **clang'our** or (*NAm*) **clang'or** a clang; a loud ringing noise. — *vi* to make a clangour. — **clang'box** a deflector fitted to a jet engine to divert gas flow for eg VTOL or STOL operation. — **drop a clanger** (*colloq*) to say something tactless; to make a stupid blunder. [L *clangere* to sound; *clangor* noise of birds or wind instruments]

clang[2]. See **klang**.

clanjamfray. See **clamjamphrie**.

clank *klangk*, *n* a metallic sound, less prolonged than a clang, such as is made by chains hitting together. — *vi* or *vt* to make or cause to make a clank. — *n* **clank'ing**. [Prob formed under the influence of **clink**[1] and **clang**[1]]

clap[1] *klap*, *n* the noise made by the sudden striking together of two things, *esp* the hands; a slap; a pat (*Scot*); a sudden blow or stroke (*lit* or *fig*); a burst of sound, *esp* thunder. — *vt* to strike together so as to make a noise; to applaud with the hands; to bang; to pat (*Scot*); to thrust or drive together suddenly; to fasten or close promptly; to put suddenly or throw (eg in prison). — *vi* to strike the palms of the hands together; to strike or slam with a noise; to applaud; to come or go suddenly (*archaic*): — *pr p* **clapp'ing**; *pa t* and *pa p* **clapped**. — *n* **clapp'er** a person who claps; a thing that claps, eg the tongue of a bell; a device for shaking a mill hopper; an instrument for making a striking noise, such as a rattle; the tongue (*slang*). — *vi* to make a noise like a clapper. — *vt* to ring by pulling on a clapper. — *n* and *adj* **clapp'ering**. — *n* **clapp'ing** applause; the noise of striking. — **clap'board** (or *klab'ərd*) wood for barrel staves, wainscot (*archaic*); a thin board used in covering wooden houses (*esp NAm*); **clap'bread** a kind of hard-baked oatmeal cake; **clap'-dish** same as **clackdish**; **clap'net** a net made to clap together suddenly by pulling a string; **clapo'meter** (*colloq*) a device for gauging the level of audience appreciation in talent contests, etc by measuring the volume of noise generated by their applause. — *adj* **clapped'-out'** (*colloq*) tired, exhausted; worn out, of no more use. — **clapp'erboard** or **clapp'erboards** a hinged board (or a set of hinged boards) clapped together in front of camera before or after shooting a piece of film, to help synchronize sound and vision; **clapp'erboy** the person who works the clapperboards. — *vt* **clapp'erclaw** (*archaic*) to claw or scratch; to scold or abuse. — **clapp'erclawer**; **clap'-sill** a lock-sill, the bottom part of the frame on which lock-gates shut; **clap'trap** a trick to gain applause (*archaic*); flashy but insincere or empty words; meaningless nonsense. — Also *adj*. — **claptrapp'ery**. — **clap eyes on** to catch sight of, to see; **clap hands** to applaud with the hands; to make an agreement (*archaic*); **clap hold of** to seize roughly or firmly; **clap on** (*colloq*) to put on (clothes) quickly; **clap up** (*archaic*) to conclude suddenly; **like the clappers** (*colloq*) at top speed. [ON *klappa* to pat; Du and Ger *klappen*]

clap[2] *klap*, (*slang*) *n* (with *the*) gonorrhoea. — *vt* to infect with gonorrhoea. [Cf Du *klapoor*]

clapper[1] *klap'ər*, *n* a simple bridge of slabs or planks laid across supports, *usu* piles of stone (*dialect*; also **clapper bridge**); a raised footpath (*dialect*); a rabbit hole (*obs*). [LL *claperium* heap of stones, rabbit hole]

clapper[2]. See under **clap**[1].

clappy-do *klap'i-dōō* or **clabby-do** *klab'-i-*, (*Scot*) *n* a type of large black mussel. [Gaelic *clab* large mouth, and *dubh* black]

claque *klak*, *n* a group of hired applauders; sycophantic supporters. — *n* **claqueur** (*kla-kûr'*) a member of a claque. [Fr, from *claquer* to clap]

clarabella *klar-ə-bel'ə*, *n* an organ stop having a sweet, fluty tone. [L *clārus* clear, and *bellus*, beautiful]

clarain *klar'ān*, (*mineralogy*) *n* lustrous, brightly-coloured bands in coal.

Clare *klār*, *n* a nun of a Franciscan order founded by St *Clare* (1212). — Also **Poor Clare**.

clarence *klar'əns*, *n* a four-wheeled carriage, having interior seating for two or more persons. [Named after the Duke of *Clarence* (William IV)]

Clarenceux or **Clarencieux** *klar'ən-sū*, (*heraldry*) *n* the second king-of-arms in England, so named from the Duke of *Clarence*, son of Edward III.

clarendon *klar'ən-dən*, (*printing*) *n* a form of condensed roman type having a heavy face.

clare-obscure. See **clair-obscure**.

claret *klar'ət*, *n orig* applied to wines of a light-red colour, but now used in UK for the dark-red wines of Bordeaux; a dark red colour (also *adj*); blood (*old slang*). — *vi* to drink claret. — **clar'et-cup** a drink made up of iced claret, brandy, sugar, etc; **claret jug** a fancy jug for holding claret. [Fr *clairet*, from *clair*, from L *clārus* clear]

clarichord *klar'i-körd*, *n* a clavichord. [As if from L *clārus* clear; see **clavichord**]

clarify *klar'i-fī*, *vt* to make clear or easily understood; to make (*esp* butter) clear or pure: — *vi* to become clear: — *pr p* **clar'ifying**; *pa t* and *pa p* **clar'ified**. — *n* **clarificā'tion**. — *n* **clar'ifier**. [L *clārus* clear, and *facere* to make]

clarinet, *klar-in-et'* or *klar'*, or (*archaic*) **clarionet** *-i-ən-*, *n* a wind instrument, *usu* of wood, in which the sound is produced by a single thin reed, the range of pitch being approximately that of the violin. — *n* **clarinett'ist**. — **bass clarinet** one pitched an octave lower than the ordinary clarinet. [Fr, from L *clārus* clear]

clarino *kla-rē'nō*, *n* the highest register of the trumpet in baroque music; an organ stop imitating this; a trumpet, a clarion: — *pl* **clari'ni** or **clarin'os**. — *adj* relating to the trumpet's highest register [Ital]

clarion *klar'i-ən*, *n* a kind of trumpet whose note is clear and shrill; the sound of a trumpet, or a sound resembling that of a trumpet. — **clarion call** (*fig*) a stirring summons (to duty, etc). [Fr *clairon*, from *clair*, from L *clārus* clear]

clarionet. See **clarinet**.

clarity *klar'i-ti*, *n* clearness. [ME *clarte*, from L *clāritās*, *-ātis*]

clarkia *klärk'i-ə*, *n* any plant of the N American genus *Clarkia* (family *Onagraceae*), a favourite border plant. [Named in honour of Captain *Clark*, of Lewis and Clark's expedition]

claro *klä'rō*, *n* a light-coloured mild cigar: — *pl* **cla'ros** or **cla'roes**. [Sp, light, from L *clarus*]

clarsach *klär'səhh*, *n* the old Celtic harp strung with wire. [Gaelic *clàrsach* and Irish *cláirseach* a harp]

clart *klärt*, (*Scot* and *N Eng*) *n* (often in *pl*) mud; dirt. — *vt* to dirty. — *adj* **clart'y** sticky and dirty. [Origin unknown]

clary *klā'ri*, *n* any plant of the genus *Salvia sclarea*, sometimes used as a culinary herb, with pale-blue flowers and aromatic leaves, wild sage. [LL *sclarea*; origin unknown]

clash *klash*, *n* a loud noise, such as is caused by the striking together of sheets of metal; noisy opposition or contradiction; an outbreak of fighting; chatter, gossip (*Scot*). — *vi* to dash noisily together; to meet in opposition; to act in a contrary direction; to disagree; of events, to coincide disturbingly or inconveniently; (of colours) to jar visually when placed together; to gossip (*Scot*). — *vt* to strike noisily against; to bang, slam (*dialect*). — *n* **clash'er**. — *n* **clash'ing** a striking against; opposition, conflict, disagreement. — **clash'-ma-clā'vers** (*Scot*, modelled on **clishmaclaver**) idle chat, gossip. [Imit; cf Ger *Klatsch* and Swed *klatsch*]

clasp *kläsp*, *n* a fastening, eg for a piece of jewellery; an embrace; a grasp. — *vt* to fasten with a clasp; to enclose and hold in the hand or arms; to embrace. — *n* **clas'per** that which clasps; the tendril of a plant; (*usu* in *pl*) a clasping organ (*zool*). — *n* **clasp'ing**. — **clasp knife** a knife whose blade folds into the handle. [ME *clapse*]

class *kläs*, *n* a rank or order of persons or things; high rank or social standing; the system or situation in any community in which there is division of people into different social ranks; a number of schoolchildren or students who are taught together, or are in the same year of school or of their course; a group of students graduating together (in a certain year, eg *class of 1989*) (*NAm*); a scientific division or arrangement in biological classification, a division above an order; a grade, (of merit in examination, accommodation in a ship or railway train, etc); a section of a Methodist congregation; style, quality (*colloq*). — *vt* to form into a class or classes; to arrange methodically. — *vi* to take rank. — *adj* (*slang*) of high class. — *adj* **class'able** or **class'ible** capable of being classed. — *adj* **classed**. — *n* **class'iness** (*colloq*) the quality of being classy. — *n* **class'ism** prejuduce or discrimination on grounds of social class. — *adj* **class'ist** motivated or influenced by classism. — *adj* **class'less** having no class distinctions; not belonging to any social class; not confined to any particular category; pertaining to sports with events of this sort. — *adj* **class'y** (*colloq*) of or characteristic of high or upper class. — **class action** (*US law*) in US, an action taken by one or more persons on their own behalf and on that of all others adduced as having the same grievance; **class'-book** a book used in class teaching. — *adj* **class'-conscious** clearly or acutely conscious of membership of a social class. — **class-con'sciousness**; **class-distinc'tion**; **class'-fellow** or **class'mate** a pupil in the same class at school or college; **class'-leader** the leader of a class in a Methodist church; **class legislation** legislation in the interests of a class; **class list** a list grouping students according to the class of their honours degree; **class'man** a person who has gained honours of a certain class at the Oxford examinations (as opposed to *passman*); **class'room** a room in which a class is held; **class war** or **class struggle** (*esp* in Marxist theory) hostility or conflict that arises between different social ranks or classes, *esp* between the proletariat and the combined middle and upper classes in a capitalist society. — **in a class of** or **on its own** so good as to be without an equal; **take a class** to take honours in an examination, as opposed to the mere pass. [L *classis* a division of the Roman people]

class. *abbrev*: classical; classification.

classes aisées *klas e-zā*, (*Fr*) *n pl* the well-off classes.

classic *klas'ik*, *n* any great writer, composer or work; a student of the ancient classics; a standard work; something of established excellence; something quintessentially typical or definitive; any of five flat races (eg the Derby) for three-year-olds, or other established sporting event; something delightful of its kind, such as a good story (*colloq*); (in *pl*) Greek and Latin studies. — *adj* **class'ic** or **class'ical** (*usu* **classic**) of the highest class or rank, *esp* in literature or art; (**classical**) of orchestral and chamber music, etc, as opposed to jazz, folk music, etc; (**classical**) of theories based on concepts established before relativity and quantum mechanics (*phys*); (*usu* **classical**) relating to or characteristic of the best Greek and Roman writers; (*usu* **classical**) pertaining to Greek and Latin studies; (*usu* **classical**; ie opposed to *romantic*) resembling or in the style of the authors of Greece and Rome or the old masters in music; chaste, refined, restrained, in keeping with classical art; (*usu* **classic**) having literary or historical associations; traditionally accepted, long or well established; (*usu* **classic**) excellent, definitive (*slang*); (*usu* **classic**) of clothes, made in simple tailored style that does not soon go out of fashion; (**classical** or **classic** (*Milton*)) Presbyterian, of a classis. — *n* **classical'ity**. — *adv* **class'ically**. — *n* **class'icalness**. — *n* **class'icism** (*-sizm*) or **class'icalism** a classical idiom; (in literature, music, etc) a principle, character or tendency such as is seen in Greek classical literature, marked by beauty of form, good taste, restraint and clarity (as opposed to *romanticism*). — *n* **class'icist** or (*rare*) **class'icalist** a person versed in the classics, or devoted to their being used in education; someone who is for classicism rather than romanticism. — *vt* **class'icize** or **-ise** to make classic or classical. — *vi* to imitate a classical style in literature, music, etc. — **classic car** a motor car of classic design, *esp* one manufactured between 1925 and 1942; **classic races** the five chief annual horseraces, the Two Thousand Guineas, One Thousand Guineas, Derby, Oaks, and St Leger. [L *classicus* of the first class, from *classis* class]

classify *klas'i-fī*, *vt* to arrange in classes or categories; to make secret for security reasons: — *pr p* **class'ifying**; *pa p* **class'ified**. — *adj* **class'ifiable** (or *-fī'*) capable of being classified. — *adj* **classif'ic** denoting classes. — *n* **classificā'tion** the act or a system of arranging in classes or categories. — *adj* **classificā'tory**. — *adj* **class'ified** arranged in classes or categories; of a road, categorized as being in a class entitled to receive a government grant; of information, secret. — *n* **class'ifier**. — **classification schedule** (in library science) the printed schedule detailing a system of classification; **classified advertisements** advertisements in a newspaper or periodical grouped according to the goods or services offered. [L *classis* class, and *facere* to make]

classis *klas'is*, *n* a group; (in certain churches) a presbytery; a bay of a library (*obs*). [L]

clastic *klas'tik*, *adj* (of sedimentary rock) composed of fragments (**clasts**) of older rock, fragmental (*geol*); divided or divisible into parts (*biol*). [Gr *klastos*, from *klaein* to break]

clat. See **claut**.

clatch *klach* or *kläch*, (*Scot*), *n* a splashy slapping sound; a slap; anything sloppy and pasty; anything lumbering or clumsy, *esp* an old carriage; an ungainly person; a slut; a botched piece of work. — *vi* to dabble or work in miry matter. — *vt* to daub, plaster; to work up into a pasty mess; to botch. [Cf Ger *Klatsch* slap]

clathrate *klath'rit* or *-rāt*, *adj* shaped like a net or lattice (*bot*); (of a molecular compound) having one component enclosed in the cavities of the crystals of another component (*chem*). [L *clāthrāre* to provide with a lattice]

clatter *klat'ər*, *n* a repeated rattling noise; a repetition of abrupt, sharp sounds; noisy talk; gossip (*Scot*, often in *pl*). — *vi* to make rattling sounds; to chatter. — *vt* to cause to rattle. — *n* **clatt'erer**. — *adv* **clatt'eringly**. — *adj* **clatt'ery**. [OE *clatrung* clattering (verbal noun)]

claucht. See **claught**.

Claude Lorraine glass *klöd lor-ān' gläs*, (*art*) *n* a convex mirror, *usu* coloured, employed for viewing landscape. [Named after the painter *Claude Gelée*, known as *le Lorrain* (1600–82)]

Claudian *klö'di-ən*, *adj* pertaining to the Romans of the name of *Claudius*, *esp* the emperors of that gens (Tiberius, Caligula, Claudius, Nero), or to their period (AD 14–68).

claudication *klö-di-kā'shən*, (*med*) *n* a limp, lameness; a cramp-like pain in one or both legs that develops on walking, caused by eg atherosclerosis. [L *claudicātio*, *-ōnis*, from *claudus* lame]

claught[1] or **claucht** *klöhht*, (*Scot*) *vt* and *vi* to snatch; to clutch. — *n* a hold; a snatch; a clutch. [From the pa t of **cleek**]

claught[2]. See **cleek**.

clause *klöz*, *n* a group of words that contains a subject and its finite verb (*gram*); an article or part of a contract, will, act of parliament, etc. — *adj* **claus'al**. — *adj* **claus'ūlar** pertaining to, or consisting of, a clause or clauses. — **dependent clause** a part of a sentence which cannot stand in isolation as a sentence in itself (as opposed to **independent clause**). [Fr *clause*, from L *claudere* to shut]

claustral *klös'trəl*, *adj* cloistral, secluded; pertaining to a claustrum; narrow-minded. — *n* **claustrā'tion** the act of shutting in a cloister. — *n* **claus'trum** (*anatom*) a thin layer of grey matter in the brain hemispheres: — *pl* **claus'tra**. [L *claustrum* an enclosed space]

claustrophobia *klö-strə-fō'bi-ə* or *klos-trə-*, *n* a pathological dread of confined spaces. — *n* **claus'trophōbe** a sufferer from claustrophobia. — *adj* **claustrophō'bic** (or *-fob'*). [L *claustrum* an enclosed space, and **phobia**]

clausula *klö'zhə-lə* or *klow'sōō-la*, *n* a short clause ending a period in Latin prose: — *pl* **clau'sulae** (*-ē* or *-ī*). [L]

clausular. See **clause**.

claut *klöt* or **clat** *klat* or *klät*, (*Scot*) *n* a claw; a scratch; a blow; a grasp; a scraping hoe; something scraped together, a lump. — *vt* to scratch, claw; to scrape; to hoe. [Perh connected with **claw**]

clave[1] *klāv*, *n* (*biol*) a club-shaped organ or club-shaped end of an organ. — **clavate** (*klā'vāt* or *klav'āt*) or **clav'ated** (*-id*) club-shaped. — *n* **clavā'tion** articulation in a socket. — *adj* **clav'iform** in the form of a club. — *n* **clav'iger** (*-i-jər*) a club-bearer. — *adj* **clavigerous** (*-ij'ər-əs*) club-bearing. — *adj* **clav'ūlate** somewhat club-shaped. [L *clāva* a club]

clave[2] *klāv*, (*archaic*) *pa t* of **cleave**[1,2].

clave[3] *klä'vā*, *n* one of a pair of small wooden cylinders held in the hands and struck together to mark S American dance rhythms. [Sp, key to code, etc, clef, from L *clāvis* key]

clavecin *klav'ə-sin*, *n* a harpsichord. — *n* **clav'ecinist**. [Fr *clavecin*, from L *clāvis* a key]

claver *klā'vər*, (*Scot*) *n* idle talk, gossip. — *vi* to talk idly. [Origin uncertain; cf Gaelic *clabair* a prater]

clavicembalo *klav-i-chem'bə-lō*, *n* a cembalo with keys, a harpsichord: — *pl* **clavicem'balos**. [Ital, from L *clāvis* key, and **cembalo**]

clavichord *klav'i-körd*, *n* an old keyboard stringed instrument in which the tangent striking the string and producing the sound also determines the vibrating length. [L *clāvis* a key, and *chorda* a string]

clavicle *klav'i-kl* or **clavicula** *klə-vik'ū-lə*, *n* the collarbone; the wishbone in birds. — *adj* **clavic'ūlar**. [Fr *clavicule*, from L *clāvicula*, dimin of *clāvis* a key]

clavicorn *klav'i-körn*, (*zool*) *adj* having clavate antennae. — *n* any beetle of the group **Clavicorn'ia**, including the ladybirds. [L *clāva* a club, and *cornū* a horn]

clavicytherium *klav-i-sī-thēr'i-əm*, *n* an upright form of spinet. [L *clāvis* key, and *cytherium*, from *cithara*]

clavie *klā'vi*, (*Scot*) *n* tar barrel burnt for luck at Burghead on Hogmanay. [Unknown]

clavier *klä-vēr'* or *klav'i-ər*, *n* the keyboard of a musical instrument; a stringed keyboard instrument, *esp* the clavichord or the pianoforte. [Fr, (or Ger *Klavier*, from Fr), from L *clāvis* a key]

claviform. See under **clave**[1].

claviger, **clavigerous**. See under **clave**[1], **clavis**.

clavis *klā'vis* (L *klä'wis*), *n* a key, hence a clue or aid for solving problems, interpreting a cipher, etc, a glossary: — *pl* **clā'ves** (*-vēz*; L *klä'wās*). — *n* **claviger** (*klav'i-jər*) someone who keeps a key, a custodian. — *adj* **clavig'erous** keeping keys. [L *clāvis* a key]

clavulate. See under **clavate**.

claw *klö*, *n* the hooked nail of a bird, mammal or reptile, or the creature's foot with a number of such nails; the leg of a crab, insect, etc, or its pointed end or pincer; the narrow basal part of a petal (*bot*); anything shaped or used like a claw. — *vt* to scratch, tear, scrape, seize (with or as if with a claw or claws); to flatter, fawn on (*obs*). — *adj* **clawed** having claws. — *adj* **claw'less**. — *adj* **claw'-and-ball** (of furniture) having feet carved to represent an animal's claw holding a ball (also **ball'-and-claw**). — **claw'back** an arrangement by which the financial benefit from allowances, etc is partially recouped by the government in extra taxation; extended to other situations where financial outlay is recovered by taxation or penalty; **claw'-foot** (*med*) pes cavus, a deformity of the foot in which the toes are turned under and the arch is exaggerated; **claw hammer** a hammer with one part of the head divided into two claws, for pulling out nails. — **claw back** to recoup (money) by means of taxation, etc; **claw off** (*naut*) (of sailing vessels) to move away from (a hazard) by beating; **claw me and I'll claw thee** (*obs*) you scratch my back and I'll scratch yours. [OE *clawu*; cognate with Ger *Klaue* and related to **cleave**[2]]

clay *klā*, *n* earth in very fine particles, tenacious and impervious (*agric*); a tenacious ductile earthy material, hydrated aluminium silicates more or less impure (*chem* and *mineralogy*); earth in general; the human body; a clay pigeon; (in full **clay'-pipe'**) a tobacco-pipe of baked clay. — *vt* to purify (eg sugar) with clay. — *adj* **clayed** clay-like. — *adj* **clay'ey** made of clay; covered with clay; like clay. — *adj* **clay'ish** of the nature of clay. — *n* **claymāt'ion** (*films*) the animation of clay or plasticine® figures. — *adj* **clay'-bank** (*US*) brownish yellow. — *n* (*US*) a horse of this colour. — *adj* **clay'-brained** (*Shakesp*) stupid. — *adj* **clay'-cold** cold as clay, lifeless. — **clay court** a type of hard-surfaced tennis court; **clay eater** a person addicted to chewing a fatty clay in Brazil and elsewhere; **clay-ir'onstone** a clayey chalybite; **clay'-marl** a whitish chalky clay; **clay mineral** any of a group of water-soluble aluminium silicates that are the chief constituents of clay; **clay'pan** a compacted layer of subsoil that retains water; a shallow depression in clay soil, holding water after rain (*Austr*); **clay pigeon** (often shortened to **clay**) a saucer-shaped disc (*usu* made of pitch and powdered limestone) thrown from a spring-loaded trap and shot at as a substitute for various types of gamebird; **clay'-pit** a pit from which clay is dug; **clay road** (*NZ*) an unmetalled road; **clay'-slate** hard, fissile argillaceous rock. — **feet of clay** (*fig*) faults and weaknesses of character not at first apparent or suspected; **wet one's clay** to drink. [OE *clæg*; cf Dan *klæg and* Ger *Klei*]

claymore *klā-mōr'* or *-mör'*, *n* a large sword formerly used by the Scottish Highlanders; the old Celtic one-handed, two-edged longsword; now applied inaccurately to the basket-hilted sword of the officers of Highland regiments; (also **claymore mine**) a type of explosive mine. [Gaelic *claidheamh mór*, from Gaelic and Irish *claidheamh* sword, and *mór* great]

claytonia *klā-tō'ni-ə*, *n* a N American plant of the genus *Claytonia*, related to *Lewisia*, having succulent leaves and small cup-shaped flowers. [From J *Clayton* (1693–1773), US botanist]

clean *klēn*, *adj* free from dirt, stain, or anything that contaminates; pure, fresh; guiltless; honest, uncorrupted; neat in execution, unerring; clear-cut, sharply defined; even; having nothing of an incriminating nature, such as a weapon, illegal drugs, etc on one's person (*slang*); (of a driving licence) without any endorsements for motoring offences; (of an athlete) clear of drugs when tested; complete; without a catch (*angling*); free of radioactive fall-out; of a design that causes little turbulent wake (*aerodynamics*). — *adv* quite, entirely; smoothly; without mishap. — *vt* to make clean, or free from dirt, corruption, contamination, etc. — *n* an act of cleaning; a lift of the weight to the shoulders, where it is held with arms bent (*weight-lifting*; **clean and jerk** such a lift followed immediately by a jerk (qv)). — *n* **clean'er** a person or thing that cleans. — *n* and *adj* **clean'ing** (the act of) making clean. — *n* **cleanliness** (*klen'li-nis* or *-nes*) habitual cleanness or purity. — *adj* **cleanly** (*klen'li*) clean in habits and person; pure; neat. — *adv* (*klēn'li*) in a clean manner. — *n* **cleanness** (*klēn'nis* or *-nes*). — *adj* **clean-cut'** neat, well-shaped or well-formed; uncluttered, without blemish or unnecessary ornament; with a neat, respectable appearance. — **clean hands** freedom from guilt or corruption; **cleaning lady** or **cleaning woman** a woman employed to clean a house, office, etc. — *adj* **clean-limb'ed** with shapely limbs; trim. — *adj* **clean-liv'ing** morally upright; respectable. — **clean room** (in the manufacture of computer and precision components) an area in a factory, etc where rigorous standards of cleanliness are maintained; a special facility for handling material, destined for space activities, in a sterile and dust-free environment. — *adj* **clean-shav'en** with all facial hair shaved off. — **clean'-skin** (*Austr*) an unbranded animal (also **clear'skin**); a person with a clean police record (*colloq*); **clean'-tim'bered** (*Shakesp*) well-proportioned; **clean'-up** an act of thorough cleaning; the stamping out of an evil or illegal activity (see also **clean up** below). — **a clean sheet** or **slate** a fresh start; **a clean sweep** a complete change; the winning or gaining of all the prizes, votes, etc (*usu* with *of*); **clean as a whistle** very clean or cleanly; completely emptied; **clean bowled** (*cricket*) bowled out by a ball which hits the stumps without hitting the bat; **clean out** to clean the inside of; to take away all someone's money from (someone) (*colloq*); **clean up** to make clean; to free from vice, corruption, etc; to make (large profits) (*n* and *adj* **clean'-up**); **clean up one's act** (colloq) to reform one's behaviour or bad practices; **come clean** (*slang*) to confess or divulge everything; **make a clean break** to sever a relationship, etc completely; **show a clean pair of heels** to run away; **take (someone) to the cleaners** (*slang*) to take all, or a great deal of, a person's money, etc; to beat or criticize (someone) severely. [OE *clæne*; Ger *klein* small]

cleanse *klenz*, *vt* to make clean or pure. — *adj* **cleans'able**. — *n* **cleans'er** a person who, or that which, cleanses; cleansing-cream, lotion or the like. — *n* **cleans'ing** cleaning, purification. — **cleans'ing-cream** a type of cream used to remove make-up or dirt from the face; **cleansing department** the section of local administration that deals with the collecting and disposing of refuse and the cleaning of streets. [OE *clænsian*]

CLEAR *klēr*, *abbrev*: Campaign for Lead-free Air.

clear *klēr*, *adj* pure, bright, undimmed, unclouded, undulled; free from obstruction, difficulty, complication, contents, blame or accusation; disengaged; plain, obvious; distinct; without blemish, defect, drawback, or diminution; lucid; transparent; not coded; not blocked. — *adv* in a clear manner; plainly; wholly; quite; out of the way (of). — *vt* to make clear; to empty; to free from obscurity, obstruction or guilt; to free, acquit or vindicate; to leap, or pass by or over; to make as profit; to settle (eg a bill); to decode; to unscramble; to declare free from security, etc restrictions; to remove (data) from memory so that fresh data can be recorded (*comput*); to pass (a cheque, etc) through a clearing bank; to pass through (customs, etc). — *vi* to become clear; to grow free, bright, transparent; to sail after satisfying all demands and obtaining permission. — *n* **clear'age** a piece of land cleared. — *n* **clear'ance** the act of clearing; general removal or emptying; eviction from lands; removal of hindrances; intervening space; play between parts, as of a machine; a certificate that a ship has been cleared at the custom house; a declaration of freedom from restrictions. — *n* **clear'er** someone or something that clears; a clearing bank. — *n* **clear'ing** the act of making clear; an area with no trees within a forest or woodland; the tract of land cleared of wood, etc for cultivation; the method by which bankers change cheques and drafts, and arrange the differences; the method or process by which the final remaining university and college places are allocated to hitherto unsuccessful applicants shortly before the courses start (*UK educ*). — *adv* **clear'ly** in a clear manner; distinctly; obviously. — *n* **clear'ness**. — **clearance cairn** (*archeol*) a heap of stones cleared from agricultural land, as distinct from a burial cairn; **clearance sale** a sale of goods at reduced prices in order to make room for new stock. — *adj* **clear-cut'** sharp in outline, definite; free from obscurity. — *adj* **clear-eyed'** clear-sighted, discerning. — **clear felling** the wholesale felling of all the trees in a particular area. — *adj* **clear-head'ed** having a clear understanding. — **clearing bank** a bank that is a member of the London Bankers' Clearing House, through which it makes credit and cheque transfers to and from other banks; **clearing house** an office where financial clearing business is done; a central source or pool of information, etc; **clearing sale** (*Austr*) the sale of moveable property and stock from a farm or similar property, *esp* following the sale of the land and buildings; **clear-obscure'** same as **chiaroscuro**. — *adj* **clear-sight'ed** having clearness of sight; discerning. — **clear-sight'edness**; **clear'skin** see **cleanskin** under **clean**; **clear-starch'ing** the act of stiffening linen with clear starch; **clear'story** see **clerestory**; **clear'way** a stretch of road on which motorists are not allowed to stop; **clear'wing** a transparent-winged moth of the family *Sesiidae*, often resembling wasps. — **clear as a bell** see under **bell**; **clear away** to remove (crockery, uneaten food, etc) after a meal; **clear off** to get rid of, dispose of; to go away, *esp* in order to avoid something (*colloq*); **clear one's throat** to give a slight cough; **clear out** to get rid of; to empty; to empty out, sort through, tidy up (eg a room or cupboard), throwing away unwanted material (*n* **clear-out**); (of a ship) to clear and leave port; to take oneself off; **clear the air** to simplify the situation and relieve tension; **clear the decks** (*fig*) to clear away everything surplus, so as to prepare for action; **clear the way** to make the way open; **clear up** to make or to become clear; (of weather) to become fine after cloudiness, rain or snow; to explain (a mystery, misunderstanding, etc); to tidy up; **in the clear** free of suspicion; out of a difficulty; solvent. [Fr *clair*, from L *clārus* clear]

clearcole *klēr'kōl*, *n* a priming coat consisting of size or glue with whiting. — Also **clere'cole** or **claircolle** (*klār'*). [Fr *claire colle* clear glue]

cleat *klēt*, *n* a wedge; one of several pieces attached to the sole of a shoe for protection or grip; a piece of wood, etc nailed across anything to keep it in its place or give it an additional strength; a piece attached to parts of a ship for fastening ropes. — *vt* to strengthen with a cleat; to fasten to or by a cleat. [From a supposed OE *clēat*; cf Du *kloot*; Dan *klode*; Ger *Kloss*]

cleavage. See under **cleave**[1].

cleave[1] *klēv*, *vt* to divide or to split; to separate with violence; to go or cut through; to pierce. — *vi* to split apart; to crack: — *pr p* **cleav'ing**; *pa t* **clōve** or **cleft**, (*archaic*) **clāve**; *pa p* **clōv'en** or **cleft**. — *adj* **cleav'able** capable of being cleft. — *n* **cleav'ableness**. — *n* **cleav'age** a split; a tendency to split, *esp* (in rocks and minerals) in certain directions; mitotic cell division (*biol*); the hollow between a woman's breasts, *esp* as shown by a low-cut dress. — *n* **cleav'er** a person or thing that cleaves; a butcher's chopper. — *adj* **cleav'ing** splitting. — *n* a cleft. — **cleft palate** see **palate**. — **in a cleft stick** (*fig*) in a difficult situation; in a dilemma. [OE *clēofan*, cognate with Ger *klieben*]

cleave[2] *klēv*, *vi* to stick or adhere; to unite: — *pa t* **cleaved** or (*archaic*) **clāve**; *pa p* **cleaved**. — *n* **cleav'ers** or **clivers** (*kliv'ərz*) goose-grass (*Galium aparine*) which cleaves to fur or clothes by its hooks. — *n* **cleav'ing** the act of adhering. — Also *adj*. [OE *clifian*; cognate with Ger *kleben*]

cleché *klech'ā*, *klesh'ā*, (*heraldry*) *adj* voided or hollowed throughout, showing only a narrow border. [Fr]

cleck *klek*, (*Scot*) *vt* to hatch. — *n* **cleck'ing** a brood. [ON *klekia*; cf Dan *klække* to hatch]

cleek *klēk*, *n* a large hook (*Scot*); formerly, a narrow-faced iron-headed golf club. — *vt* to seize, to hook. — *vi* (*Scot*) to go arm in arm; to link; to marry: — *pa t* and *pa p* **cleeked**, **cleek'it** or **claught** (*klöhht*). [Northern, perh related to **clutch**]

cleep. See **clepe**.

cleeve. See **cleve**.

clef *klef*, (*music*) *n* a character placed on the stave by which the absolute pitch of the following notes is fixed. [Fr *clef* key, from L *clāvis*; Gr *kleis* a key]

cleft[1] *kleft*, *pa t* and *pa p* of **cleave**[1]. — **cleft palate** see under **palate**.

cleft[2] *kleft*, *n* an opening made by cleaving or splitting; a crack, fissure, or chink. — Also **clift** (*Bible*). — *adj* split, divided. [Cf Ger *Kluft*, and Dan *klyft* a hole]

cleg *kleg*, *n* a gadfly, horse-fly. [ON *kleggi*]

cleidoic *klī-dō'ik*, (*zool*) *adj* (of a bird's or insect's egg) enclosed in a more or less impervious shell and thus isolated from the environment. [Gr *kleidoun* to lock up, from *kleis*, *kleidos* key]

cleistogamy or **clistogamy** *klīs-tog'ə-mi*, (*bot*) *n* production of small flowers, often simplified and inconspicuous, which do not open, and in which self-pollination occurs. — *adj* **cleistogamic** (*-tə-gam'ik*) or **cleistog'amous**. [Gr *kleistos* closed, and *gamos* marriage]

cleithral or **clithral** *klī'thrəl*, *adj* completely roofed over. [Gr *kleithron* a bar]

clem *klem*, *vi* and *vt* to starve. [Eng dialect *clam*; Ger *klemmen* to pinch]

clematis *klem'ə-tis* or *klə-mā'tis*, *n* any ranunculaceous temperate climbing plant of the genus *Clematis*, cultivated for their colourful flowers, including traveller's joy. [L, from Gr *klēmatis* a plant, prob periwinkle, from *klēma* a twig]

clement *klem'ənt*, *adj* (*esp* of weather) mild; gentle; kind; merciful. — *n* **clem'ency** the quality of being clement; mildness; readiness to forgive. — *adv* **clem'ently**. [Fr, from L *clēmēns*, *-entis*]

clementine *klem'ən-tēn* or *-tīn*, *n* a type of orange, either a variety of tangerine or a hybrid of orange and tangerine.

Clementine *klem'ən-tēn* or *-tīn*, *adj* relating to any of the popes named *Clement*, *esp* Clement I or Clement V.

clenbuterol *klen-bū'tər-ol*, *n* a drug which mimics the hormone adrenaline.

clench *klench* or *klensh*, *vt* to close tightly; to grasp; to clinch. — *adj* **clench-built** (of boats) clinker-built. [Same as **clinch**]

clepe or **cleep** *klēp*, (*archaic*) *vt* to call; to name: — *pa p* **yclept** (*i-klept'*), also **ycleped'** or (*Milton*) **ycleap'd** (*i-klēp'id* or *i-klēpt'*). [OE *clipian* to call]

clepsydra *klep'si-drə*, *n* an instrument for measuring time by the trickling of water, a waterclock. [L, from Gr *klepsydrā*, from *kleptein* to steal, and *hydōr* water]

cleptomania. See **kleptomania**.

clerecole. See **clearcole**.

clerestory or **clearstory** *clēr'stō-ri* or *-stö-*, (*archit*) *n* an upper storey or part with its own row of windows, *esp* the storey above the triforium in a church. [**clear** (prob in sense of lighted) and **storey**]

clergy *klûr'ji*, *n* the ministers of the Christian or other religion collectively, as holders of an allotted office (as opposed to the laity); learning, education (*archaic*). — *adj* **cler'gyable** or **cler'giable** entitled to or admitting of the benefit of clergy. — **cler'gyman** one of the clergy, a regularly ordained minister; **cler'gywoman** a woman who is a minister of religion; a woman belonging to a clergyman's family (*facetious.*). — **benefit of clergy** originally an exemption of clergymen, in certain cases, from criminal process before a secular judge, but later covering the first offence of all who could read; **black clergy** in Russia, all the regular or monastic, as distinct from the secular or parochial, clergy; **clergyman's knee** inflammation of the bursa above the bony prominence below the knee caused by prolonged kneeling; **clergyman's sore throat** chronic pharyngitis. [Fr *clergé*, from L *clēricus*, from Gr *klērikos*, from *klēros* a lot, a heritage, then the clergy]

cleric *kler'ik*, *n* a clergyman. — *adj* **cler'ical** belonging to the clergy; of, done by or relating to a clerk, office worker, or to general office work. — *n* **cler'icalism** undue influence of the clergy, sacerdotalism. — *n* **cler'icalist**. — *n pl* **cler'icals** clerical garb. — *n* **cler'icate** the position of a clergyman; clerical position. — *n* **clericity** (*klər-is'i-ti*). — **clerical collar** the white collar worn by many Christian clergy, fastened behind the neck. [LL *clēricus* a priest, clerk]

clerihew *kler'i-hū, n* a jingle that humorously sums up the life and character of some notable person in two short couplets. [Started by E *Clerihew* (Bentley) in his *Biography for Beginners* (1905)]

clerisy *kler'i-si, n* scholars, educated people as a class. [Ger *Klerisei*, from LL *clēricia*]

clerk *klärk* or (*NAm*) *klûrk, n* a person employed to deal with correspondence, accounts, records, etc in an office; a record-keeper or account-keeper, *esp* for a law court or legislative body; a shop-assistant (*NAm*); a hotel receptionist (*NAm*); a lay minister (*Ch of Eng*); a clergyman or priest; a scholar (*archaic*). — *vi* to act as clerk. — *n* **clerk'dom**. — *n* **clerk'ess** a female clerk. — *adj* **clerk'ish** like a clerk. — *adj* **clerk'ly** (*obs*) scholarly. — *adv* in a scholarly or learned manner. — *n* **clerk'ship**. — **clerk of the course** (in horse- or motor-racing) an official in charge of administration; **clerk of the weather** an imaginary functionary facetiously supposed to govern the weather; **clerk of works** or **clerk of the works** a person who superintends building work or the maintenance of a building, etc; **Lord Clerk-Register** see under **register**; **St Nicholas's clerks** (*archaic*) thieves; **town clerk** see under **town**. [OE *clerc* a priest, from LL *clēricus*; see **clergy**]

cleruch *kler'ōōk* or *-uk*, (*Gr hist*) *n* a citizen of Athens granted an allotment of land in foreign territory while retaining his Athenian citizenship. — *n* **cler'uchy** or **cleruch'ia**. [Gr *klērouchos*, from *klēros*, allotment and *echein* to have]

cleuch and **cleugh** *klōōhh*. Scots forms of **clough**.

cleve or **cleeve** *klēv*, (*dialect*) *n* a cliff; a hillside. [ME *cleof*, a variant of **cliff**[1]]

cleveite *klē'vīt* or *klā'və-īt*, (*mineralogy*) *n* a pitchblende in octahedral crystals containing helium, a variety of uranitite. [P T *Cleve* (1840–1905), Swedish chemist]

clever *klev'ər, adj* dexterous, deft; able; bright, intelligent; ingenious; skilful; good-natured (*US dialect*). — *n* **cleveral'ity** (*Scot*). — *n* **clev'erness**. — *adj* **clev'erish** somewhat clever. — *adv* **clev'erly**. — *adj* **clev'er-clev'er** flaunting a superficial knowledgeableness; too clever. — **clever dick** (*slang*) a person who thinks himself or herself clever. [Orig dialect; poss connected with ME *clivers* claws]

clevis *klev'is, n* a U-shaped piece of metal through which tackle may pass, fixed at the end of a beam. [Ety uncertain]

clew or **clue** *klōō, n* a ball of thread, or the thread in it (*archaic*); a thread that guides through a labyrinth; the lower corner of a sail (*naut*); one of the cords by which a hammock is suspended. — *vt* to coil up into a clew or ball; to tie up to the yards (*usu* with *up*); to fix up (*fig*). — **clew'-garnet** (*naut*) a tackle for clewing up the smaller square sails for furling. — *n pl* **clew'-lines** (*naut*) ropes attached to the clews on square sails by which they are clewed up for furling. — **clew up** to draw up the lower edges of a square sail ready for furling (*naut*); to tie up loose ends (*fig*). [OE *cliwen*; cf Du *kluwen*; Ger *Knäuel*]

clianthus *kli-an'thəs, n* any climbing shrub or subshrub of the genus *Clianthus*, of Australia and New Zealand, with red or white flowers, including the parrot's bill and glory pea. [L, from Gr *kleos* glory, and *anthos* flower]

cliché *klē'shā, n* a stereotyped phrase, or literary tag; something hackneyed as idea, plot, situation; an electrotype or stereotype plate (*printing*); the impression made by a die in any soft metal. — *adj* **cli'ché-ridden, cli'chéed** or **cli'ché'd** filled with clichés. [Fr]

click *klik, n* a short, sharp ticking sound; anything that makes such a sound, such as a latch for a gate; a clucking sound produced by sudden retraction of the tongue from the upper teeth, palate, or elsewhere, characteristic of certain S African native languages, represented, eg in Zulu, by C (dental), Q (retroflex), and X (lateral). — *vi* to make a light, sharp sound; to fit into place opportunely or successfully, *esp* to be naturally compatible, either socially or sexually, with another person (*slang*). — *vt* (*dialect*) to fasten the latch of (a gate). — *n* **click'er** the compositor who distributes the copy among a companionship of printers, makes up pages, etc; a person who cuts up leather for the uppers and soles of boots. — *n* **click'ing** the action of the verb. — **click beetle** any of various beetles of the family *Elateridae*, which can flip over with a clicking sound if on their back; **click'-clack** a persistent clicking noise; **click'ety-click** or **click'ety-clack'** a continuous, *usu* regular, clicking sound. [Dimin of **clack**]

clicket *klik'ət, n* a latch. — *vi* to make a clicking sound. [OFr (and Fr) *cliquet*]

client *klī'ənt, n* a person who employs a lawyer or other professional adviser; a customer; a vassal, dependant or hanger-on. — *n* **clī'entage** the whole number of one's clients; the client's relation to the patron. — *adj* **clīental** (*-ent'l*). — *n* **clientèle** (*klē-ā-tel'*) or **clientele** (*klī'ən-tēl*) a following; all the clients of a lawyer, shopkeeper, etc. — *n* **clī'entship**. — **client-centred therapy** (*psychol*) a method of psychotherapy in which clients are encouraged to learn to resolve their own problems by developing their ability to interpret and take responsibility for their own actions; **client state** a state which depends on another for protection, economic aid, etc. [L *cliēns, -entis* a dependant upon a *patrōnus* (protector)]

cliff[1] *klif, n* a high steep rock face or, *esp* bordering the sea, side of a mountain. — *adj* **cliffed** or **cliff'y** having cliffs; craggy. — **cliff'-face** the sheer or steep front of a cliff; **cliff'hanger** a tense, exciting adventure or contest; an ending line of an episode of a serial, etc that leaves one in suspense; a serial, film, etc that keeps one in suspense. — *vi* **cliff'hang**. — *n* and *adj* **cliff'hanging**. [OE *clif*; Du *clif*; ON *klif*]

cliff[2] *klif*, (*music*) *n*. Same as **clef**.

clift[1]. See **cleft**[2].

clift[2] *klift, n* same as **cliff**[1] (through the influence of **cleft**). — *adj* **clift'ed** or **clift'y** broken into cliffs.

climacteric *klī-mak'tər-ik* or *klī-mak-ter'ik, n* a critical period in human life, in which some great bodily change takes place, *esp* the menopause, or the equivalent in men; any critical time. — *adj* pertaining to such a period; critical. — *adj* **climacter'ical**. — **climacteric phase** (*bot*) (in certain fruits) the period when full growth has been achieved and an increased respiration rate promotes rapid ripening. — **the grand climacteric** (generally) the sixty-third year, supposed to be a critical period for men. [Gr *klīmaktēr*, from *klīmax* a ladder]

climatic, climatial. See **climax**.

climate *klī'mit* or *-māt, n* the condition of a country or place with regard to temperature, moisture, etc (also *fig*); the character of something (*fig*); a region (*Shakesp*). — *vi* (*Shakesp*) to remain in a certain place. — *adj* **clī'matal**. — *adj* **clīmatic** (*-mat'ik*) or **clīmat'ical**. — *vt* **clī'matize** or **-ise** see **acclimatize**. — *adj* **clīmatograph'ical**. — *n* **clīmatog'raphy** a description of climates. — *adj* **clīmatolog'ical**. — *n* **clīmatol'ogist**. — *n* **clīmatol'ogy** the science of climates, or an investigation of the causes on which the climate of a place depends. — *n* **clī'mature** (*Shakesp*) a region. — **climate of opinion** the critical atmosphere or complex of opinions prevalent at a particular time or in a particular place. [Fr *climat*, from L *clima*, from Gr *klima, -atos* slope, from *klīnein* to slope]

climax *klī'maks, n* (of a story, play, piece of music, etc) the most interesting and important or exciting part; a culmination; sexual orgasm; the arranging of discourse in order of increasing strength (*rhetoric*); loosely, the last term of the rhetorical arrangement; the relatively stable culmination of a series of plant and animal communities developing in an area (also **climax community**). — *vi* to ascend in a climax; to culminate (in); to experience sexual orgasm. — *adj* **climact'ic** or **climact'ical** pertaining to a climax. — *adv* **climac-**

t'ically. [Gr *klīmax*, *-akos* a ladder, from *klīnein* to slope]

climb *klīm*, *vi* or *vt* to ascend or mount by clutching with the hands and feet; to ascend with difficulty; to mount; (of plants) to ascend by clinging to other objects, by means of hooks, tendrils, twining stems, or otherwise; extended to similar downward movement (to *climb down*): — *pa t* and *pa p* **climbed**. — *n* an act of climbing; an ascent. — *adj* **climb'able**. — *n* **climb'er** someone or something that climbs; a person who is intent upon his or her own social advancement; an old-fashioned name for a bird whose feet are mainly adapted for climbing; a climbing plant (*bot*). — *n* and *adj* **climb'ing**. — **climbing boy** formerly, a small boy employed by a chimney-sweep to climb chimneys; **climb'ing-frame** a wooden or metal structure on or through which children can climb; **climbing iron** a metal frame with a horizontal spike, worn strapped to the feet as an aid in climbing trees, telegraph poles, etc; **climbing wall** a wall, specially constructed with hand and foot holds for practising mountaineering and rock-climbing techniques. — **climb down** to become more humble; to abandon a firmly stated opinion or resolve, or an excessive or overweening demand, position or attitude (*n* **climb'-down**). [OE *climban*; cf Ger *klimmen*; **clamber**, **cleave**[2]]

clime *klīm*, (chiefly *poetic*) *n* a country, region, tract. [**climate**]

clinamen *klin-ā'mən*, *n* inclination. [L *clīnāmen*]

clinch *klinch* or *klinsh*, *vt* to drive home (an argument); to settle or confirm; to fasten or rivet a nail by bending and beating down the point; to fasten (a rope) by means of a half hitch with the end turned back and secured (*naut*); to clench (*obs*). — *vi* to grapple. — *n* an act of clinching; an embrace (*colloq*); a holding grapple (*boxing*); the fastening of a nail by beating it back; a pun; a punning retort. — *n* **clinch'er** someone that clinches; a decisive argument. — *adj* **clinch'er-built** clinker-built. — **clinch'er-work** the disposition of the side planks of a vessel, when the lower edge of one row overlaps the row next under it. [Same as **clench**; causal form of **clink**[4]]

clindamycin *klin-də-mī'sin*, *n* an antibiotic drug used for serious infections that do not respond to other antibiotics.

cline *klīn*, (*biol*) *n* a gradation of differences of form, etc seen eg within one species over a specified area of the world. [See **clino-**]

cling *kling*, *vi* to stick close by adhesive surface or by clasp; to adhere in interest or affection; to hold to an opinion; (of wood) to shrink. — *vt* (*archaic*) to attach; to shrivel: — *pa t* and *pa p* **clung**. — *n* adherence. — *adj* **cling** or **cling'stone** (of peaches, etc) having the pulp adhering firmly to the stone (opposed to *freestone*). — *n* **cling'er**. — *n* **cling'iness**. — *adj* **cling'y** tending to cling; sticky. — **cling'film** a type of transparent plastic film used to wrap food, seal food containers, etc. — *adj* **clingstone** see **cling** (*adj*) above. — *n* a clingstone fruit. [OE *clingan*]

clinic *klin'ik*, *n* a private hospital or nursing-home; an institution, or a department of one, or a group of doctors, for treating patients or for diagnosis or giving advice; any group meeting for instruction, often remedial, in a particular field; the instruction of medicine or surgery at the bedside of hospital patients; a session of such instruction; a person confined to bed by sickness (*archaic*). — Also *adj*. — Also **clinique** (*klin-ēk'*). — *adj* **clin'ical** hospital-like; concerned with or based on observation; strictly objective; analytical; plain, functional in appearance. — *adv* **clin'ically**. — *n* **clinician** (*-ish'ən*) a doctor, etc who works directly with patients; a doctor, etc who runs, or works in, a clinic. — **clinical baptism** baptism administered to persons on their sickbed; **clinical convert** a person converted on his or her deathbed; **clinical death** a state of the body in which the brain has entirely ceased to function, though artificial means can be used to maintain the action of the heart, lungs, etc; **clinical lecture** one given to students at the bedside of the sick; **clinical medicine** or **surgery** medicine or surgery as taught by clinics; **clinical thermometer** a finely-calibrated thermometer in which the temperature taken continues to be indicated until reset by shaking; **clinical trial** the study of existing data or the obtaining of new data on human patients directly in order to test the efficacy of a treatment or a hypothesis related to the cause of a disease. [Gr *klīnikos*, from *klīnē* a bed]

clink[1] *klingk*, *n* a ringing sound made by striking metal, glass, etc. — *vt* to cause to make a short, soft, ringing sound. — *vi* to make a short, soft, ringing sound; to go with a clink. — **clink'stone** phonolite (from its metallic clink when struck). [A form of **click** and **clank**]

clink[2] *klingk*, *n* (*slang*) prison. [Appar orig *Clink* prison in Southwark]

clink[3] *klingk*, (*Spenser*) *n* said to mean a keyhole, or a latch. [Cf Du *klink* latch]

clink[4] *klingk*, *vt* to clinch; to rivet. — *adj* (*slang*) **clink'ing** excellent. [Northern form of **clinch**]

clinker[1] *kling'kər*, *n* the incombustible residue of fused ash raked out of furnaces; furnace slag; the cindery crust of some lava flows; a hard brick (also **klink'er**). [Du *klinker* (the brick); **clink**[1]]

clink'er[2] *kling'kər*, *n* a nail used as a protective stud in footwear, *esp* in climbing boots. — *adj* **clink'er-built** (*esp* of ships' and boats' hulls) made of planks which overlap those below (as distinguished from carvel-built) and fastened with clinched nails. [**clink**[3]]

clinker[3] *kling'kər*, (*slang*) *n* someone or something that is popular, well-liked or exceedingly good. [**clink**[1]]

clino- *klī'nō-*, *combining form* signifying oblique, reclining. — *n* **clī'nōaxis** (*crystallog*) the clinodiagonal. — *n* **clīnōdiag'onal** in a monoclinic crystal, that lateral axis which is not perpendicular to the vertical axis (also *adj*). — *n* **clinometer** (*klīn-* or *klin-om'i-tər*) any of various instruments for measuring slope, elevation, or inclination. — *adj* **clinomet'ric**. — *n* **clinom'etry**. — *n* **clīnōpin'acoid** or **clinopin'akoid** a form consisting of two faces parallel to the clinoaxis and the vertical axis. [Gr *klīnein* to lean and *klīnē* a bed]

clinochlore *klī'nō-klōr* or *-klör*, *n* a green mineral, a distinctly mono*clinic* variety of *chlor*ite.

clinquant *klingk'ənt*, *adj* tinselly; glittering with gold or tinsel. — *n* tinsel; imitation gold leaf. [Fr, from Du *klinken* to clink]

clint *klint*, (*geol* and *dialect*) *n* (*usu* in *pl*) one of a series of limestone blocks or ridges divided by fissures orgrikes; any exposed outcrop of flinty rock on a hillside or stream bed. [ME, cliff, connected with Swed, Dan and MLGer *klint* crag, cliff; cf ON *klettr* rock]

Clio[1] *klī'ō*, (*Gr mythol*) *n* the Muse of history. [Gr *Kleiō* proclaimer]

Clio[2] *klī'ō*, *n* a genus of shell-less pteropods, 'whales' food'. [Gr *Kleiō*, a sea-nymph]

cliometrics *klī-ō-met'riks*, *n sing* the application of statistical analysis of data in economic history. [**Clio**[1] and econo*metrics*]

clip[1] *klip*, *vt* to cut with shears; to cut off; to trim or cut off the hair, twigs, ends, edges, etc of; to cut out (a magazine article, etc); to excerpt a section from (a film, etc); to pare down; to reduce or curtail; to shorten (a speech sound); to abbreviate (a word) *esp* in speech, as 'sec' for 'second'; to punch a piece from (a ticket, etc); to cheat, overcharge (*colloq*); to hit with a sharp blow. — *vi* to go at a high speed, *esp* when this is sustained over a distance: — *pr p* **clipp'ing**; *pa p* **clipped** or **clipt**. — *n* an act of clipping; the thing removed by clipping; the yield of wool from a number of sheep, goats, etc; a sharp, stinging blow; a high speed; a piece taken from a film for separate showing. — *adj* **clipped** or (*archaic*) **clipt**. — *n* **clipp'er** a person who clips; a clipping instrument; a swift mover, *specif* a fast sailing vessel; a showy spirited person or anything admired (*old slang*). — *n* **clipp'ie** (*colloq*) a woman bus or tram conductor. — *n* **clipp'ing** the act of clipping, *esp* the edges of coins;

a small piece clipped off, a shred or paring; a newspaper cutting; an act of obtaining money by deception or cheating. — *adj* superb (*old slang*); fast in movement. — **clip joint** a place of entertainment, eg a night-club, where customers are overcharged or cheated. — **clip coin** to pare the edges of coins; **clip (someone's) wings** (*fig*) to restrain or thwart (someone's) ambition; to cramp (someone's) freedom of action. [Prob from ON *klippa* to cut; Dan *klippe*]

clip[2] *klip*, *vt* to encircle, hold firmly or embrace. — *n* a device for gripping, clasping, fastening or holding things together; a piece of jewellery that clips on to clothing, etc; a container for ammunition which is clipped on to, and from which the bullets pass directly into, a pistol, rifle, etc. — **clip'board** a portable board with a spring clip for holding papers. — *adj* **clip'-fed** (of firearms) loaded automatically from an ammunition clip. — *adj* **clip'-on** fastening on to something or fastened by means of a clip. — *n* a clip-on tie; (in *pl*) ear-rings that clip on to the ear-lobes; (in *pl*) sunglasses that clip on to ordinary spectacles. [OE *clyppan* to embrace; Ger *Kluppe* pincers]

clip-clop. See **clop**.

clipe. See **clype**.

clipt. See **clip**[1].

clique *klēk*, *n* an exclusive group of persons; a faction; a coterie (*usu derog*). — *adj* **cliqu'ey**, **cliqu'y** or **cliqu'ish** relating to a clique; exclusive. — *n* **cliqu'iness**. — *n* **cliqu'ishness**. — *n* **cliqu'ism** the tendency to form cliques. [Fr, orig in sense of claque; prob connected with **click**]

clish-clash *klish'klash* or **clishmaclaver** *klishmə-klāv'ər*, (*Scot*) *n* gossip. [See **clash and claver**]

clistogamy. See **cleistogamy**.

clitellum *kli-* or *klī-tel'əm*, (*zool*) *n* a saddle-like structure around the anterior part of some annelid worms, having glands which secrete mucus to form a sheath around a copulating pair and a cocoon around the eggs: — *pl* **clitell'a**. — *adj* **clitell'ar**. [L *clītellae* pack-saddle]

clithral. Same as **cleithral**.

clitic *klit'ik*, (*linguistics*) *adj* (of a word, eg French 'me', 'te', 'le') not capable of being pronounced with full word-stress, but dependent on, and pronounced as though part of the preceding or following word. — Also *n*. [Back-formation from **proclitic**, **enclitic**]

clitoris *kli'* or *klī'tə-ris*, *n* a small elongated erectile structure at the front of the vulva in female mammals, homologous with the male penis. — *adj* **clit'oral**. — *n* **clitoridec'tomy** surgical removal of part or all of the clitoris, female circumcision. [Gr *kleitoris*]

CLit. *abbrev*: Companion of Literature (awarded by the Royal Society of Literature, London).

clitter *klit'ər*, *vt* and *vi* to make, or cause to make, a shrill rattling noise. — **clitt'er-clatt'er** idle talk, chatter. [Related to **clatter**]

clivers. Same as **cleavers**.

clivia *klīvi-ə*, *n* any of the leek-like S African plants of the genus *Clivia*, with strap-shaped leaves and flower stems which produce many orange flowers in terminal umbels. [From Lady Charlotte *Clive* (died 1866)]

Cllr. *abbrev*: Councillor.

Clo. *abbrev*: Close (in street names).

cloaca *klō-ā'kə* (*L -ä'ka*), *n* (in most vertebrates excluding higher mammals) the terminal part of the gut into which the urinary and reproductive ducts open forming a single posterior opening; a sewer, a privy; a sink of moral filth: — *pl* **cloacae** (*klō-ā'sē* or *ä'kī*). — *adj* **clōā'cal** or **cloacinal** (*klō-ə-sī'nl*). — *adj* **clōā'calin** or **clōā'caline**. [L *cloāca*, from *cluēre* to purge]

cloak *klōk*, *n* a loose outer garment; a covering; that which conceals; a disguise, pretext. — *vt* to clothe with a cloak; to cover; to conceal (*usu* with *with* or *in*). — Also (*archaic*) **cloke**. — *adj* **cloak and dagger** concerned with plot and intrigue, *esp* espionage; **cloak-and-sword** concerned with fighting, intrigue and romance. — **cloak'room** a room for keeping coats and hats; a room in a public place, eg a theatre, in which outer garments and luggage may be temporarily deposited; a lavatory. [OFr *cloke*, *cloque*, from LL *cloca* a bell, horseman's bell-shaped cape; see **clock**[1]]

cloam *klōm*, (*dialect*) *n* and *adj* (made of) earthenware or clay. [OE *clām* mud]

clobber[1] *klob'ər*, *n* a paste used by shoemakers to hide the cracks in leather. — *vt* to overpaint a piece of porcelain and enamelled decoration. [Origin uncertain]

clobber[2] *klob'ər*, (*slang*) *n* clothing, equipment. [Origin uncertain]

clobber[3] *klob'ər*, (*slang*) *vt* to strike very hard; to attack, cause to suffer (*fig*); to defeat overwhelmingly. [Origin unknown]

clochard *klo-shär*, (*Fr*) *n* a tramp.

cloche *klosh*, *n* a glass or plastic cover (*orig* bell-shaped) under which plants are forced or protected from frost, etc; a lady's close-fitting hat. [Fr, from LL *cloca*, *clocca* a bell]

clock[1] *klok*, *n* an instrument for measuring time, operated mechanically, electronically or by some other means, on which the hours, minutes, etc are indicated by means of pointers on a dial face, or displayed digitally; any device or instrument for recording, measuring, etc, either operated by similar means or which may be read like a clock; a speedometer or mileometer (*colloq*); an electrical circuit that generates a regular stream of pulses, used eg to synchronize the operations in a computer; the downy seed-head of a dandelion. — *vt* to time by a clock or stopwatch; to achieve (a certain officially attested time for a race); to hit (*slang*); to observe, notice (*slang*); to turn back the mileometer of (a car, etc), so that it registers a lower figure than the actual mileage (*n* **clock'ing** this (illegal) practice). — *vi* to register a time by a recording clock. — *n* **clock'er**. — *adv* **clock'wise** in the direction in which the hands of a clock move. — **clock card** a card on which the hours worked by an employee are recorded by a time clock; **clock-golf'** a putting game on a green marked like a clock dial, in which the player putts from the position of each hour figure to a hole near the centre; **clock-'maker**; **clock-ra'dio** an electronic apparatus combining the functions of alarm-clock and radio, *esp* for bedside use (also **alarm-radio** or **radio-alarm**); **clock tower** a *usu* square tower having a clock at the top with a face on each exterior wall; **clock-watcher**, **clock-watching** see **watch the clock** below; **clock'work** the works or machinery of a clock; steady, regular machinery like that of a clock (see also **like clockwork** below). — *adj* automatic. — **against the clock** making an effort to overcome shortage of time or achieve the shortest time; **beat the clock** to finish a job, task, etc before the time limit runs out; **clock in, out, on** or **off** to register time of coming or going, in or out, or on or off duty; **clock up** (*colloq*) to reach or record (a certain speed, score, etc); **know what o'clock it is** to be wide awake, to know how things are; **like clockwork** as smoothly as if driven by clockwork; **o'clock** (for earlier **of the clock**) as reckoned or shown by the clock; in a direction corresponding to that which would be taken by the hour-hand of a horizontal clock relative to a person standing at the centre and facing twelve; **put back the clock** or **put the clock back** to return to earlier time and its conditions; to take a retrograde step; **put the clock** (or **clocks**) **back** or **forward** to alter the clocks to allow for the change from or to summer time; **round the clock** for the whole of a twenty-four hour period; **watch the clock** to keep watch on the passage of time, eagerly waiting for one's work-time to finish and *usu* doing only the minimum amount of work required (*n* **clock'-watcher**; *n* **clock'-watching**). [ME *clokke*, prob through OFr from LL *cloca*, *clocca* a bell; Mod Fr *cloche* bell, Du *klok* bell, clock, Ger *Glocke* bell]

clock[2] *klok*, *n* an ornament on the side of a stocking. — *adj* **clocked** ornamented with such clocks. [Ety uncertain]

clock[3] *klok* or *klōk*, (*Scot* and *dialect*) *n* a beetle. — *n* **clock'er** a large beetle. [Origin unknown; cf Swed dialect *klocka* beetle, earwig]

clock[4] *klok*, (*Scot*) *vi* to cluck; to brood or sit. — *n* a brooding hen's cry; a cluck. — *n* **clock'er** a clocking hen. [OE *cloccian*; Du *klokken*]

clod *klod*, *n* a thick round mass or lump that sticks together, *esp* of earth or turf; a concreted mass; the ground; a bed of fireclay in a coalmine; the body of a man, as formed of clay; a stupid person. — *vt* to pelt (*archaic*); to throw (*Scot*). — *vi* (*archaic*) to throw clods: — *pr p* **clodd'ing**; *pa t* and *pa p* **clodd'ed**. — *adj* **clodd'ish**. — *n* **clodd'ishness**. — *adj* **clodd'y** earthy. — *adv* **clod'ly**. — **clod'hopper** a countryman; a peasant; a clumsy dolt; a heavy, clumsy shoe or boot (*slang*). — *adj* **clod'hopping** boorish. — **clod'poll**, **clod'pole** or **clod'pate** a stupid fellow, a bumpkin. — *adj* **clod'pated**. [A later form of **clot**]

cloff[1] *klof*, (*Scot*) *n* a cleft. [Cf ON *klof*]

cloff[2] *klof*, (*commerce*) *n* an allowance given on buying certain goods wholesale, of 2 lb in every 3cwt, after tare and tret have been deducted. [Origin obscure]

clofibrate *klō-fib'rāt* or *-fīb'rāt*, *n* a lipid-lowering drug that is used to reduce high levels of fats and cholesterol in the blood.

clog *klog*, *n* a wooden shoe; a shoe with a wooden sole; a block or log of wood; a heavy block of wood fastened to a man or animal to restrict movement; anything hindering motion, an impediment; an obstruction.. — *vt* to choke up with an accumulation (often with *up*); to obstruct, impede; to fasten a clog to; to sole with wood. — *adj* **clogged** choked up, blocked; encumbered. — *n* **clogg'er** a person who makes clogs. — *n* **clogg'iness**. — *adj* **clogg'y** lumpy, sticky. — **clog'al'manac** an early form of almanac or calendar having characters notched on wood, horn, etc to indicate the weeks, months, festivals, etc; **clog box** a Chinese temple block; **clog'dance** a dance performed with clogs, the clatter keeping time to the music; **clog dancer**; **clog dancing**. [Ety dubious]

cloison *klwä-zɔ̃* or *kloi'zn*, *n* a partition, dividing fillet or band. — *n* **cloisonnage** (*klwäz-on-äzh'*) cloisonné work or process. — *adj* **cloisonné** (*klwäz-on-ā*, *kloi-zon'ā*, or *-ā'*) decorated with enamel which is inlaid in compartments formed by small fillets of metal. — *n* enamelwork of this kind. [Fr]

cloister *klois'tər*, *n* a covered arcade forming part of a monastic or collegiate establishment; a place of religious retirement, a monastery or nunnery; an enclosed place; monastic life. — *vt* to confine in a cloister; to confine within walls. — *adj* **clois'tered** dwelling in or enclosed by cloisters; sheltered from reality and the full experience of life. — *n* **clois'terer** a person belonging to a cloister. — *adj* **clois'tral** claustral, pertaining or confined to a cloister; secluded. — *n* **clois'tress** (*Shakesp*) a nun. — **clois'ter-garth** the court or yard enclosed by a cloister. [OFr *cloistre* (OE *clauster*), from L *claustrum*, from *claudere*, *clausum* to shut]

cloke. See **cloak**.

clomb *klōm*, (*archaic*) *pa t* and *pa p* of **climb**.

clomiphene *klom'i-fēn*, *n* a synthetic drug used to stimulate ovulation in apparently infertile women. [Coined from *chloramine* and **-phene**]

clomp *klomp*, *n* a heavy tread or similar sound. — *vi* to walk with a heavy tread. [Variant form of **clump**].

clonazepam *klō-naz'i-pam*, *n* a sedative drug used as an anticonvulsant in the prevention of epileptic fits.

clone *klōn*, (*biol*) *n* a group of two or more individuals with identical genetic makeup derived, by asexual reproduction, from a single common parent or ancestor, *orig* applied to plants, but later applied much more widely; any of such individuals; a person or thing closely similar to another, a copy or replica (*colloq*). — *vt* to reproduce as a clone; to produce a clone or clones of. — *adj* **clō'nal**. — *adv* **clō'nally**. — **clonal selection** a hypothesis which explains an immune response as being due to proliferation, in response to stimulation by a particular antigen, of a clone of lymphocytes that produce the antibody corresponding to that antigen. [Gr *klōn* shoot]

clonic. See **clonus**.

clonk *klongk*, *n* the dull sound of something heavy falling on to a surface. — *vi* to make such a sound. — *vt* to hit. [Imit]

clonus *klō'nəs*, *n* a type of spasm in which a muscle undergoes a series of rapid contractions and relaxations, *usu* a sign of damage to nerve fibres in the motor cortex of the brain or a characteristic featrure of grand mal epilepsy. — *adj* **clonic** (*klon'ik*). — *n* **clonicity** (*-nis'*). [Latinized from Gr *klonos* tumult]

cloop *kloo͝p*, *n* the sound of drawing a cork from a bottle. [Imit]

cloot[1] *kloo͝t*, Scot *klüt* or *klit*, *n* a division of a cloven hoof; loosely, a hoof. — *n* **Cloot'ie** or **Cloots** the devil. [Scot; ety uncertain]

cloot[2] *kloo͝t*, *klüt* or *klit*, (*Scot*) *n* a cloth. — **clootie dumpling** a suet pudding, containing currants, raisins, etc, steamed or boiled in a cloth. [**clout**]

clop *klop*, *n* the sound of a horse's hoof-tread against a hard surface. — *adv* with a clop. — *vi* to make or go with such a sound. — Also **clip'-clop'** and **clop'-clop'**. [Imit]

cloqué *klo-kā'*, *n* an embossed fabric. — Also *adj*. [Fr]

close[1] *klōs*, *adj* near, in time or place (often with *to* or *by*); shut up or shut tight with no opening; stictly confined; narrow; nearly equal or even; near the surface, short; tight in fit; compact; crowded, dense; stifling, unventilated, airless; intimate; stingy, miserly; (of money, finance, etc) difficult to obtain; private, restricted to a certain class or group; reserved; hidden or secluded; secret; thorough, detailed; rigorous, careful; (of a vowel) pronounced with slight opening, or with the tongue tense. — *adv* in a close manner or position; tightly; nearly; densely; secretly. — *n* an enclosed place; a small enclosed field; a small, quiet, *esp* dead-end road; a narrow passage off a street, *esp* leading to a tenement stairway or courtyard; the precinct of a cathedral. — *adv* **close'ly**. — *n* **close'ness**. — *adj* **close-band'ed** closely united. — *adj* **close'-barred** firmly closed. — *adj* **close-bod'ied** fitting close to the body. — **Close Brethren** the Exclusive Brethren, a branch of the Plymouth Brethren whose members will not associate with (eg eat in company with) people outside their group; **close call** a narrow escape; **close company** a firm controlled by five, or fewer, people who own a majority of the shares; **close corporation** a corporation which fills up its own vacancies, without outside interference. — *adj* **close'-cropped** (of hair) cut very short; (of grass, etc) cut, or eaten by animals, down to the level of the ground. — *adj* **close-fist'ed** and **close-hand'ed** penurious, covetous. — *adj* **close'-fitting** (of clothes) designed to fit tightly. — *adj* **close'-grained** with the particles, fibres, etc close together, compact. — *adj* **close-in'** positioned or operating at a small distance. — **close harmony** (*music*) harmony in which the notes of chords lie close together. — *adj* **close'-hauled** (*naut*) (in trim for) sailing as near as possible towards where the wind is coming from. — **close'head** (*Scot*) the entrance to a close, or the gossips that congregate there. — *adj* **close'-knit** (of communities, etc) closely connected, bound together. — *adj* **close-lipped'** or **close-mouthed'** reticent, saying little. — **close quarters** see **at close quarters** below. — *adj* **close'-reefed** (*naut*) having all reefs taken in. — **close season** or **closed season** a time of the year when it is illegal to kill certain game or fish, *usu* the breeding season; a prohibited or inactive period; **close shave** or **close thing** a close call; **close'-stool** a chamberpot enclosed in a box or stool; **close tennis** real tennis, distinguished from lawn-tennis. — *adj* **close'-tongued** (*archaic*) cautious in speaking, reticent. — **close'-up** a photograph or film taken near at hand and thus detailed and big in scale; a close scrutiny. — **at close quarters** (of fighting) hand-to-hand or at close range; in close proximity; **close on** almost, nearly; **close to the chest** without revealing one's intentions. [Fr *clos* shut, from L *claudere*, *clausum* to close, shut up]

close[2] *klōz*, *vt* to complete, conclude; to end, terminate; to block, make impassable or impenetrable; to forbid access to; to place (a door, etc) so as to cover an opening, to shut; to put an end to discussion of; to cease operating or trading; to make close, draw or bring together, narrow; to unite; to approach or pass near to. — *vi* to come to an end; to cease operating or trading; to come together; to unite; to narrow; to grapple; to agree (with); (of currency, a financial index, etc) to measure or be worth (a specified figure) at the end of the day's business (with *at*). — *n* the manner or time of closing; a pause or stop; a cadence; the end; a junction, union; an encounter, a conflict (*Shakesp*). — *adj* **closed** shut; blocked; not open to traffic; with permanent sides and top; having a lid, cover, etc; exclusive, having few contacts outside itself, eg *a closed community*; not open to all, restricted; continuous and finishing where it began. — *n* **clos'er** someone or something that concludes; any portion of a brick used to close up the bond next to the end brick of a course (*building*). — *n* **clos'ing** enclosing; ending; coming together, agreement. — *n* **clos'ure** the act of closing; something that closes or fastens; the end; the ending of a parliamentary debate by a member calling for a vote. — *vt* to apply the closure to (a parliamentary debate). — **closed book** (*fig*) a mystery, something about which one knows or understands nothing; a subject or matter that has been concluded and which is no longer for consideration, discussion, etc. — *adj* **closed chain** (*chem*) having a molecule in which the atoms are linked ringwise, like a chain with the ends united. — **closed circuit** an electrical circuit in which current flows when voltage is applied; a television system in which the transmission is restricted to a limited number of screens connected to the television camera by cables, etc (also **closed circuit television**); **closed community** (*ecol*) a plant community that is so dense that no new species can colonize; **closed couplet** (*prosody*) two metrical lines whose grammatical structure and sense concludes at the end of the second line. — *adj* **closed-door** see **behind closed doors** below. — **close-down** see **close down** below; **closed population** (*biol*) a population in which there is no new gene input from outside and in which genetic change is possible only by mutation; **closed scholarship** a scholarship open only to those candidates able to fulfil certain criteria, such as attendance at a particular school, etc; **closed set** (*math*) a set in which the result of combining any two members of the set using a given operation always results in a member of the original set; **closed shop** an establishment in which only members of a trade union, or of a particular trade union, will be employed; the principle or policy implied in such a regulation; in the development of computer programs, a situation where only specialist operating personnel have access to a computer (opposed to *open shop*); **closed syllable** (*phonetics*) one ending in a consonant; **closing price** the value of shares on the stockmarket when business stops for the day; **closing time** the time at which business stops, *esp* in public houses. — **behind** (or **with**) **closed doors** in private, the public being excluded, as in court cases, committee meetings, etc (*adj* **closed-door'**); **close a bargain** to come to an agreement; **close down** to come to a standstill or stoppage of work; (*esp* in team games, eg football) to slow the pace of a game and prevent the oppositon from making any attacking manoeuvres; (of a television or radio station) to end a period of broadcasting; (of a business) to cease trading (*n* **close'down**); **close in upon** to surround and draw near to; **close on** to catch up with; **close one's eyes** (*euphem*) to die; **close one's eyes to** to ignore or disregard purposely; **close ranks** (of soldiers drawn up in line) to stand closer together in order to present a more solid front to the enemy; to unite, make a show of solidarity in order to protect a member or all the members of a group from attack; **close with** to accede to; to grapple or engage in combat with; **with closed doors** see **behind closed doors** above. [Fr *clore*, *clos*, from L *claudere*, *clausum*]

closet *kloz'it*, *n* a recess or cupboard off a room, *esp* in N America, a clothes cupboard or wardrobe; a small private room, formerly the private chamber of the sovereign; a privy; a horizontal band one-half the width of a bar (*heraldry*). — *adj* secret, private. — *vt* to shut up in or as if in, or take into, a closet; to conceal: — *pr p* **clos'eting**; *pa t* and *pa p* **clos'eted**. — **closet play** or **closet drama** a play to be read rather than acted; **closet queen** (*slang*) a male homosexual who does not openly admit his homosexuality; **closet strategist** a mere theorist in strategy. — **come out of the closet** openly to admit a practice, tendency, habit, etc previously kept a close secret (*esp* homosexuality). [OFr *closet*, dimin of *clos* an enclosure; see **close**]

clostridium *klos-trid'i-əm*, *n* any of several species of ovoid or spindle-shaped bacteria including those causing botulism and tetanus: — *pl* **clostrid'ia**. — *adj* **clostrid'ial**. [New L, from Gr *klōstēr* a spindle]

closure. See under **close**[2].

clot *klot*, *n* a mass of soft or fluid matter solidified, such as blood; a fool. — *vt* and *vi* to form into clots: — *pr p* **clott'ing**; *pa t* and *pa p* **clott'ed**. — *vt* **clott'er** to coagulate. — *n* **clott'iness**. — *n* **clott'ing** coagulation. — *adj* **clott'y**. — **clotted cream** a famous Devonshire delicacy, thick cream made from scalded milk (also called **clouted cream**); **clotting factor** any of a group of proteins in the blood essential in the process of blood clotting (also called **coagulation factor**). [OE *clott*, a clod of earth; cf Du *klos* block; Dan *klods*; Ger *Klotz*]

clote *klōt*, *n* the burdock; extended to other plants with hooks or burs. — **clotbur** (*klot'bər*) or **clote'bur** same as **cocklebur**. [OE *clāte*]

cloth *kloth* or *klöth*, *n* woven material from which garments or coverings are made; a piece of this material for a particular use, such as a floorcloth or tablecloth; clothing (*archaic*); (with *the*) the clerical profession, the clergy; sails; a theatre curtain: — *pl* **cloths** (*kloths* or *klödhz*). — **cloth cap** a flat cap. — *adj* **cloth-cap'** symbolic of the working-class. — *adj* **cloth'-eared** (*slang*) deaf, *usu* because inattentive. — **cloth'-hall** an exchange building or market for the cloth trade; **cloth'-yard** the yard by which cloth was measured, formerly 37 inches; **cloth of gold** cloth woven of threads of gold and silk or wool; **cloth of state** a canopy; **cloth-yard shaft** an arrow a cloth-yard long. [OE *clāth* cloth; Ger *Kleid* a garment]

clothe *klōdh*, *vt* to cover with a garment; to provide with clothes; to invest, equip; to cover: — *pr p* **clothing** (*klōdh'ing*); *pa t* and *pa p* **clothed** (*klōdhd*) or **clad**. — *n pl* **clothes** (*klōdhz*; *colloq klōz*) garments or articles of dress; blankets, sheets, etc, bedclothes. — *n* **clothier** (*klō'dhi-ər*) a person who makes or sells cloth or clothes. — *n* **clothing** (*klō'dhing*) clothes, garments; covering. — **clothes'-basket** a large basket for holding and carrying clothes for washing; **clothes'-brush** a brush for removing dirt, fluff, etc from clothes. — *adj* **clothes'-conscious** concerned about one's clothes and appearance. — **clothes'-horse** a frame for hanging laundry on to air or to dry; **clothes'-line** a rope or wire, etc for hanging washing on to dry; **clothes moth** any of various tineid moths whose larvae feed on wool or fur; **clothes'-peg** or **clothes'-pin** a wooden or plastic clip to hold washing on a clothes-line; **clothes'-pole** a pole from which clothes-lines are hung; a clothes prop; **clothes'-press** a cupboard, often with drawers, for storing clothes; an apparatus for pressing clothes; **clothes'-prop** a movable notched pole for raising or supporting a clothes-line; **clothes'-sense** dress-sense. [OE *clāthian*, from *clāth* cloth]

Clotho *klō'thō*, (*Gr mythol*) *n* the Fate that holds the distaff from which Lachesis spins the thread of life. [Gr *klōthō*]

cloture *klō'chər* or Fr *klō-tür*, *n* closure; a method of ending a debate in a legislative assembly, *usu* by calling for an immediate vote (*esp US*). — Also *vt*. [Fr *clôture*; see **closure**]

clou *kloo*, (*fig*) *n* the main point of interest, the centre of attraction; a dominant idea. [Fr, nail]

cloud *klowd*, *n* a mass of fog, consisting of minute particles of water, often in a frozen state, floating in the atmosphere; anything unsubstantial (*fig*); a great number of things; anything that obscures as a cloud does; a dullness; a dark or dull spot; a great volume of dust or smoke; anything gloomy, overhanging or ominous. — *vt* to overspread with clouds; to darken; to defame; to stain with dark spots or streaks; to dull. — *vi* to become clouded or darkened. — *n* **cloud'age**. — *adj* **cloud'ed** hidden by clouds; darkened, indistinct, dull (*fig*); variegated with spots. — *adv* **cloud'ily**. — *n* **cloud'iness**. — *n* **cloud'ing** a cloudy appearance. — *adj* growing dim. — *adj* **cloud'less** unclouded, clear. — *adv* **cloud'lessly**. — *n* **cloud'let** a little cloud. — *n* **cloud'-scape** a view or picture of clouds. — *adj* **cloud'y** darkened with, or consisting of, clouds; obscure; gloomy; stained with dark spots; (of liquid) lacking (proper or expected) clarity or limpidity. — **cloud base** the under-surface of a cloud or clouds; the height of this above sea level; **cloud'berry** a low plant of N America and N Europe, related to the bramble, *usu* found on high open moorland, with an orange-red sweet-flavoured berry. — *adj* **cloud'-built** made of clouds, unsubstantial. — **cloud'burst** a sudden downpour of rain over a small area. — *adj* **cloud'-capt** (*Shakesp*) capped with or touching the clouds. — **cloud-cuck'oo-land** or **cloud'land** an imaginary situation or land, *esp* as the product of impractical or wishful thinking; **cloud ceiling** the height of the cloud base above the ground; **cloud chamber** (*phys*) an apparatus in which the path of high-energy charged particles is made visible by means of droplets condensed on gas ions; **clouded leopard** an arboreal cat (*Felis nebulosa*) smaller than a leopard. — *adj* **cloud'-kissing** (*Shakesp*) touching the clouds. — **cloud'-seeding** the induction of rainfall by scattering particles, eg dry ice, silver iodide, on clouds from aircraft. — *adj* **cloud'-topped** covered with or touching the clouds. — **on cloud nine** (*colloq*) intensely happy; **under a cloud** in trouble, disgrace or disfavour; **with one's head in the clouds** in a dreamy impractical way or state. [OE *clūd* a hill, then a cloud; cf **clod, clot**]

clough *kluf*, or *klow*, (*dialect*) *n* a ravine; a valley. [OE would be *clōh*; Scot *cleuch*]

clour *kloor*, (*Scot*) *n* a knock; a swelling caused by a knock, a bruise. — *vt* to knock; to raise a bump. [Origin doubtful]

clout *klowt*, *n* influence, power (*colloq*); a blow or cuff; (in archery) the mark or target, *usu* in long-distance shooting; a shot that hits its mark; a piece of cloth, *esp* used for mending, a patch; a garment; a protective plate or nail. — *vt* to hit with great force. to cuff; to cover with a cloth; to mend with a patch; to protect with a plate or with nails. — *adj* **clout'ed** (*Shakesp*) heavy and patched or having nails in the soles, as shoes; covered with a clout. — *n* **clout'er**. — **clout'-nail** a large-headed nail; **clout'-shoe** a shoe with clout-nails. [OE *clūt*; cf ON *klūtr* a kerchief; Dan *klud* rag]

clouted *klowt'id*, *adj* clotted. [See **clot**]

clove[1] *klōv*, *pa t* of **cleave**[1]. — **clove'-hitch** a kind of hitch knot, used to connect a rope to another rope of greater thickness or to secure a rope to a post, etc.

clove[2] *klōv*, *n* a division of a bulb, as in garlic. [OE *clufu*; cf **cleave**[1]]

clove[3] *klōv*, *n* an old weight (7, 8, or 10 pounds) for wool and cheese. [Fr *clou*, from L *clāvus* nail]

clove[4] *klōv*, *n* the flower-bud of the **clove'-tree** (*Eugenia caryophyllus*), dried as a spice, and yielding an essential oil, **oil of cloves**, used in medicine to relieve abdominal pain or as a remedy for toothache; (in *pl*) a flavouring obtained from it. — **clove-gill'yflower** or **clove'pink** a variety of pink, smelling of cloves. [Fr *clou* nail, from its shape, from L *clāvus* a nail]

cloven *klōv'n*, *adj* split; divided. — *adj* **cloven-foot'ed** or **cloven-hoofed'** having the hoof divided, as does the ox or sheep. — **the cloven hoof** applied to any indication of devilish agency or temptation, from the early representation of the devil with cloven hoofs, probably from Pan, some of whose characteristics he shares. [*Pa p* of **cleave** to divide]

clover *klō'vər*, *n* any papilionaceous plant of the genus *Trifolium*, with heads of small flowers and trifoliate leaves, affording rich pasturage. — *adj* **clov'ered** covered with clover. — *adj* **clov'ery** abounding in clover. — **clov'ergrass** clover as pasturage; **clov'erleaf** a traffic arrangement in which one road passes over the top of another and the roads connecting the two are in the pattern of a four-leafed clover; any interlinked arrangement of this shape. — Also *adj*. — **live in clover** to live luxuriously or in abundance. [OE *clāfre* (usu *clǣfre*); Du *klaver*; Dan *klöver*; Ger *Klee*]

clow *klow*, *n* a Scots form of **clove**[4]. — **clow-gill'ieflower**.

clowder *klow'dər*, (*rare*) *n* a collective name for a number of cats. [Variant of **clutter**]

clown *klown*, *n* a comic entertainer, *esp* in the circus, with colourful clothes and make-up; a person who behaves in a comical way; a stupid person (*colloq*); a rude, clumsy or boorish person. — *vi* to play the clown. — *n* **clown'ery** a clown's performance. — *n* **clown'ing**. — *adj* **clown'ish** of or like a clown; coarse and awkward; rustic. — *adv* **clown'ishly**. — *n* **clown'ishness**. [Perh from LGer, cf Fris *klönne*, *klünne*]

cloxacillin *kloks-ə-sil'in*, *n* a pencillin-type antibiotic used to treat infections by staphylococcal bacteria.

cloy *kloi*, *vt* to block up (*archaic*); to satiate to the point of disgust; to disgust, weary; to prick (a horse in shoeing) (*obs*); to gore (*Spenser*); to spike (a cannon) (*archaic*). — *vi* to become distasteful from excess; to cause distaste, *esp* by being too sweet or rich. — *adj* **cloyed**. — *adj* **cloy'ing**. — *adj* **cloy'less** (*Shakesp*) that cannot cloy. — *n* **cloy'ment** (*Shakesp*) satiety, surfeit. — *adj* **cloy'some** satiating. [Aphetized from *accloy*, from OFr *encloyer* (Fr *enclouer*), from LL *inclāvāre* to drive in a nail, from *in* in, and *clāvus* a nail]

cloze *klōz*, (*educ*) *adj* denoting a type of exercise in which the reader is required to supply words that have been deleted from a text, as a test of comprehension in reading (**cloze test**). [Formed from **closure**]

CLP *abbrev*: Constituency Labour Party.

CLR *abbrev*: computer language recorder.

CLT *abbrev*: computer language translator.

club *klub*, *n* a heavy tapering stick, knobby or thick at one end, used to strike with; a cudgel; a bat used in certain games; an instrument for playing golf, with a wooden, iron or aluminium head, or a wooden head with brass sole; a playing card with black trefoil pips; a combination, bunch; a clique, set; an association of persons for social, political, athletic or other ends; an association of persons who possess premises or facilities which all members may use; a clubhouse, or the premises occupied by a club; a nightclub. — *vt* to beat with a club; to use a heavy object as a club; to throw into confusion (*military*); to gather into a bunch; to combine. — *vi* (*esp* with *together*) to join together for some common end; to combine together; to share in a common expense; to visit nightclubs. — *adj* **club'bable** or **club'able** sociable. — *n* **clubbabil'ity** or **clubabil'ity**. — *adj* **clubbed** enlarged at the end like a club. — *n* **clubb'er** a person who frequents nightclubs. — *n* **clubb'ing** beating; combination; a thickening, as of finger-ends, or of cabbage-stems attacked by insect larvae; the frequenting of nightclubs. — *adj* **clubb'ish** given to clubs. — *n* **clubb'ism** the club system. — *n* **clubb'ist** a clubman. — *adj* **clubb'y** characteristic of a club; sociable; exclusive, cliquey. — *n sing* **clubs** see **clumps**. — **club class** a class of seat on an aircraft between tourist class and first class; **club'-face** the face of a golf club; **club-foot'** a deformed foot. — *adj* **club-**

foot'ed. — *vt* **club'-haul** (*naut*) to tack, *esp* in an emergency, by dropping the lee anchor and hauling in the anchor cable to bring the stern of the boat to windward. — **club'-head** the head of a golf club. — *adj* **club'-head'ed** having a thick head. — **club'house** a house for the accommodation of a club; **club'land** the area around St James's in London, where many of the old-established clubs are; an area or region containing a large number of nightclubs or working-men's clubs; **club'-law** government by violence; **club'-line** (*printing*) a short line at the end of a paragraph; **club'man** a member of a club or clubs; a frequenter of clubs, man-about-town; **club'manship**; **club'master** the manager of, or purveyor for, a club; **club moss** any primitive mosslike plant of the order Lycopodiales, typically having small overlapping leaves and creeping stems, eg *Lycopodium* and *Selaginella*; **club'room** the room in which a club meets; **club'root** a fungal disease which attacks the roots of plants of the Cruciferae; **club'rush** any sedge of the genus *Scirpus*; **club sandwich** a sandwich of three slices of bread or toast, containing two fillings; **club soda** soda water; **club'woman**. — **in the club** or **in the pudding club** (*slang*) pregnant; **join the club** (*colloq*) we are all in the same position; me too; **on the club** (*slang*) certified unfit to work. [ON and Swed *klubba*; same root as **clump**]

cluck *kluk*, *n* the call of a hen to her chickens; any similar sound; a fool (*NAm*; now also **dumb'-cluck**). — *vi* to make such a sound. — *adj* **cluck'y** (*Austr slang*) obsessed with babies, broody. [Imit; cf Du *klokken*, Ger *glucken*, Dan *klukke*, and **clock**[4]]

cludgie *klud'ji*, (*Scot slang*) *n* a lavatory, *esp* a communal one. [Origin uncertain]

clue[1] *klōō*, *n* anything that points to the solution of a mystery. — *adj* **clue'less** (*colloq*) ignorant, stupid; helpless. — *adj* **clued-up'** (*colloq*) (well-)informed. — **clue in** (*colloq*) to inform; **not have a clue** to have no information; to have no idea, no notion at all; to be without the necessary skills to do something. [See **clew**]

clue[2]. See **clew**.

clumber *klumb'ər*, *n* a kind of thickset spaniel, *orig* bred at *Clumber*, in Nottinghamshire.

clump *klump*, *n* a shapeless mass of anything; a cluster; a clot; a thick additional sole; a heavy tread; a blow. — *vi* to walk heavily; to clot; to cluster. — *vt* to put in a clump; to beat. — *n* **clump'er**. — *n* **clump'iness**. — *adj* **clump'ing** (*colloq*) heavy and clumsy. — *n sing* **clumps** a parlour game of question and answer (also called **clubs**). — *adj* **clump'y** having many clumps; heavy. [Prob Scand; Dan *klump* a lump. Cf Ger *Klump*, and **club**]

clumsy *klum'zi*, *adj* badly made; unwieldy; awkward; ungainly; unskilfully executed; lacking manual dexterity or coordination. — *adv* **clum'sily**. — *n* **clum'siness**. [ME *clumsen* to be stiff or benumbed]

clunch *klunch* or *klunsh*, *n* a tough clay. [Prob related to **clump**]

clung *klung*, *pa t* and *pa p* of **cling**.

Cluniac *klōōn'i-ak*, *n* a monk or nun of a branch of the Benedictine order originating at *Cluny* in France in AD 910. — Also *adj*.

clunk *klungk*, *n* a dull metallic noise; a thump or thud; a dolt (*NAm*). — *vi* to fall with a dull metallic sound. — *vt* (*dialect*) to gurgle while swallowing. [Imit]

clupeoid *klōō'pē-oid* or **clupeid** *klōōpē-id*, *n* any fish of the family **Clupē'idae**, including the herring genus *Clupea*, typically having forked tails and slim, flattened bodies. — Also *adj*. [L *clupea* a kind of river fish]

clusia *klōō's(h)i-ə*, *n* any plant of the American genus *Clusia*, evergreen climbing plants, shrubs and trees, including the pitch apple. [After the French botanist Charles de Lécluse (L *Clusius*)]

cluster *klus'tər*, *n* a number of things of the same kind growing or joined together; a bunch; a mass; a crowd; a statistically significant number of people within a sample, who have given characteristics. — *vi* to grow in or gather into clusters. — *vt* to collect into clusters; to cover with clusters. — *adj* **clus'tered** grouped. — *adj* **clus'tering**. — *adj* **clus'tery**. — **clus'ter-bean** the guar (qv); **cluster bomb** a bomb that opens on impact to throw out a number of small bombs; **clus'ter-cup** an aecidium; **clustered column** a pier which consists of several columns or shafts clustered together; **cluster fly** a large dark-brown fly related to the bluebottle, that gathers in large numbers in attics, etc during autumn; **cluster graft** (*surg*) an organ transplant in which the patient receives more than one organ; **cluster marketing** advertising, etc aimed at people with specific characteristics; **cluster physics** the physics of very small numbers of atoms; **cluster pine** the pinaster (*Pinus pinaster*), a pine with clustered cones. [OE *clyster*; LGer *kluster*; cf **clot**]

clutch[1] *kluch*, *vt* to close the hand upon; to hold firmly; to seize or grasp. — *vi* to make a snatching movement (with *at*). — *n* a claw (*archaic*); a grasping hand (often in *pl*); a device by which two shafts or rotating members may be connected or disconnected either while at rest or in relative motion; the pedal of a motor vehicle which controls such a device; grasp; a snatching movement; (in *pl*) power, control. — **clutch bag** a kind of handbag without strap or handle, carried in the hand or under the arm. [OE *clyccan* to clench]

clutch[2] *kluch*, *n* a brood of chickens; a sitting of eggs; (loosely) a number, group. — *vt* to hatch. [Cf **cleck**]

clutter *klut'ər*, *n* a clotted or confused mass; a disorderly accumulation; confusion; stir (*dialect*); noise (*dialect*); irregular interference on radar screen from echoes, rain, buildings, etc. — *vi* to crowd together; to go about in noisy confusion (*dialect*). — *vt* to litter, clog with superfluous objects, material, etc (often with *up*). [From **clot**; influenced in meaning by **cluster** and **clatter**]

cly *klī*, (*old slang*) *vt* to seize, steal. — **cly'-fāker** a pickpocket; **cly'-fāking** pocket-picking. [Prob related to **claw**; referred by some to Du *kleed* a garment, *to fake a cly* to take a garment]

Clydesdale *klīdz'dāl*, *adj* (of a breed of cart-horses) originating in *Clydesdale*, the area of Scotland through which the Clyde flows. — *n* a Clydesdale horse. — *adj* **Clyde'side** relating to *Clydeside*, the area along the Clyde estuary, or to shipbuilding, formerly its main industry. — *n* **Clyde'sider** an inhabitant of Clydeside or a worker in its shipbuilding industry.

clype or **clipe** *klīp*, (*Scot*) *vi* to tell tales. — Also *n*. [ME *clepien* to call]

clypeus *klip'i-əs*, *n* the shield-like plate on the heads of some insects. — *adj* **clyp'eal** of the clypeus. — *adj* **clyp'eate** or **clyp'ēiform** buckler-shaped. [L *clipeus* a round shield]

clyster *klis'tər*, (*archaic*) *n* a liquid injected into the rectum, an enema. — **clys'ter-pipe** a pipe or syringe for injecting a clyster. [Gr *klystēr* a clyster-pipe, from *klyzein* to wash out]

CM *abbrev*: *Chirurgiae Magister* (*L*), Master of Surgery; Corresponding Member.

Cm (*chem*) *symbol*: curium.

cm. *abbrev*: *carat métrique* (*Fr*), metric carat; *causa mortis* (*L*), by reason of death; centimetres.

CMEA *abbrev*: Council for Mutual Economic Assistance.

Cmdr. *abbrev*: Commander.

CMG *abbrev*: Companion of (the Order of) St Michael and St George.

CMH *abbrev*: Congressional Medal of Honor (*US*).

CMHR *abbrev*: combustion modified highly resilient.

CMI *abbrev*: computer-managed instruction.

CML *abbrev*: computer-managed learning.

CMOS (*comput technol*) *abbrev*: complementary metal oxide silicon.

CMS *abbrev*: Church Missionary Society.

CMV *abbrev*: cytomegalovirus.

c/n or **cn** *abbrev*: credit note.

CNAA *abbrev*: Council for National Academic Awards.

CNAG *abbrev*: Comunn na Gàidhlig, the national Scottish agency concerned with the development of Gaelic.
CNAR *abbrev*: compound net annual rate.
CND *abbrev*: Campaign for Nuclear Disarmament.
cnemial *k-nē'mi-əl*, (*anatom*) *adj* of or relating to the tibia or shin. [Gr *knēmē* tibia, leg, and **-ial**]
cnida (*k*)*nī'də*, *n* a nematocyst: — *n pl* **cnī'dae** (*-dē*). — *n* **cnidarian** a member of the *Cnidaria*, a division of the Coelenterata characterized by cnidae. — *n* **cnī'doblast** (*zool*; **-blast**) a stinging thread cell. — Also **nematoblast**. [New L, from Gr *knīdē* a nettle, a sea-anemone]
CNN *abbrev*: Cable News Network; certified nursery nurse.
CNR *abbrev*: Canadian National Railway.
CNRS *abbrev*: *Centre National de la Recherche Scientifique* (*Fr*), National Centre for Scientific Research.
CNS *abbrev*: central nervous system. — **CNS stimulant** (*med*) a drug (eg caffeine, amphetamine) that increases mental alertness.
CO *abbrev*: Colombia (IVR); Colorado (US state); combined operations; Commanding Officer; Commonwealth Office; conscientious objector; Crown Office.
Co. *abbrev*: Company; County.
Co (*chem*) *symbol*: cobalt.
c/o *abbrev*: care of.
co-. See **com-**.
coacervate *kō-as'ər-vāt* (or *-ûr'*), *vt* to heap; to cause to mass together. — Also *adj*. — *n* (also **coacervā'tion**) a reversible aggregation of particles of an emulsoid into liquid droplets before flocculation. [L *coacervāre*, *-ātum*, from *acervus* heap]
coach *kōch*, *n* a *usu* single-deck bus for tourists and sightseers; a railway carriage; a large, closed, four-wheeled carriage, *esp* one for state occasions or for conveyance of passengers; formerly, a private carriage; a ship's cabin near the stern; a private tutor; a professional trainer in athletics, football, etc. — *vt* to carry in a coach (*archaic*); to tutor, instruct, prepare for an examination, sporting event, etc. — *vi* to go by coach; to act as tutor; to study with a tutor. — *n* **coach'ee** or **coach'y** (*informal*) a coachman. — *n* **coach'er** a person who coaches; a coach-horse. — *n* **coach'ing** travelling by coach; tutoring; instruction. — *adj* **coach'y** pertaining to a coach. — *n* see under **coachee**. — **coach bolt** a large mushroom-headed bolt used for securing wood to masonry; **coach box** the driver's seat on a horse-drawn coach; **coach'builder** a craftsman who builds the bodies of cars, lorries, railway carriages, etc. — *n* **coach'building**. — *adj* **coach'built** (of a vehicle body) built to individual specifications and constructed by coachbuilders. — **coach'dog** a spotted dog, formerly kept as an attendant on carriages, a Dalmatian dog; **coach'-hire** money paid for the use of a hired coach; **coach'-horn** a post-horn; **coach'-horse** a horse used for pulling a coach; **coach house** a building in which a coach or carriage is kept; **coach'line** a decorative line along the body of a motor vehicle; **coach'load** the number of people a coach can carry; **coach'man** the driver of a coach; a servant employed to drive a private carriage; **coach party** a group of people travelling by coach; **coach road** formerly, a road for coaches, *esp* one kept in reasonable repair for mail coaches; **coach screw** a large square-headed screw; **coach tour** a holiday or outing on which people travel from place to place by coach; **coach'whip** a coachman's whip; a kind of whip-snake; **coach'whip-bird** either of two Australian birds of the genus *Psophodes*, that utter a sound like the crack of a whip; **coach'wood** an Australian tree (*Ceratopetalum apetalum*), yielding a light cross-grained wood used in furniture-making and (formerly) coachbuilding; this wood; **coach'work** vehicle bodywork. [Fr *coche*, from Hung *kocsi*, from *Kocs* in Hungary]
coact[1] *kō-akt'*, *vi* to act together. — *n* **coaction** (*kō-ak'shən*) joint action; mutual relations, *esp* between organisms in a community. — *adj* **cōac'tive** acting together. — *n* **cōactiv'ity**. [**co-** and **act**]
coact[2] *kō-akt'*, (*obs*) *vt* to compel. — *n* **coaction** (*kō-ak'shən*) compulsion. — *adj* **coac'tive** compulsory. [L *cōgere*, *cōāctum* to compel]
coad. *abbrev*: coadjutor.
coadapted *kō-ə-dap'tid*, *adj* mutually adapted. — *n* **coadaptātion**.
coadjacent *kō-ə-jās'ənt*, *adj* contiguous. — *n* **coadja'cency**.
coadjutant *kō-aj'ə-tənt*, *adj* mutually helping, co-operating. — *n* a person who helps or co-operates with another. — *n* **coadj'utor** a bishop appointed as assistant to a diocesan bishop; an associate: — *fem* **coadj'utress** or **coadj'utrix**. — *n* **coadj'utorship**. [L *adjūtor* a helper, from *ad* to, and *juvāre* to help]
coadunate *kō-ad'ū-nāt*, (*biol* and *phys*) *vt* to unite; to combine. — Also *adj*. — *n* **coadūnā'tion**. — *adj* **coad'ūnātive**. [L *adūnāre*, *-ātum* to unite, from *ad* to, and *unus* one]
co-agent *kō-ā'jənt*, *n* a joint agent. — *n* **co-ā'gency**.
coagulate *kō-ag'ū-lāt*, *vt* to cause to curdle, clot, or form into a semisolid mass by a chemical reaction. — *vi* to curdle, clot, or thicken into a semisolid mass. — *adj* clotted (*rare*); curdled. — *n* **cōagūlabil'ity**. — *adj* **cōag'ūlable**. — *n* **cōag'ūlant** a substance that causes or facilitates coagulation. — *n* **cōag'ūlāse** any enzyme that causes coagulation of the blood. — *n* **cōagūlā'tion**. — *adj* **cōag'ūlātive**. — *n* **cōag'ulator**. — *adj* **cōag'ūlatory**. — *n* **cōag'ūlum** a coagulated mass. — **coagulation factor** same as **clotting factor** at **clot**. [L *coāgulāre*, *-ātum*, from *agere* to drive]
coaita *kō-ī-tä'*, *n* the red-faced spider monkey (*Ateles paniscus*), of S America. [Tupí]
coal *kōl*, *n* a firm, brittle, generally black combustible carbonaceous rock derived from vegetable matter; a piece of this rock; charcoal (*obs*); a piece of charcoal, *esp* glowing; a cinder; an ember. — *vi* to take in coal. — *vt* to supply with coal; to char. — *n* **coal'er** a ship or train which transports coal. — *adj* **coal'y** of or like coal; covered with coal. — **coal'ball** a calcareous nodule found in coal; **coal'-bed** a stratum of coal. — *adj* **coal'-black** black as coal, very black. — **coal'-box** a box for holding coal; a shell that emits black smoke (*military slang*); **coal'-brass** iron pyrites found with coal; **coal bunker** a box, recess or compartment for storing coal; **coal cellar** a cellar or similar place for storing coal; **coal'-cutter** a machine for undercutting a coal-bed; **coal dust** coal in fine powder; **coal'face** the exposed surface of coal in a mine (see also **at the coalface** below); **coal'field** a district or area containing coal strata. — *adj* **coal'-fired** burning or fuelled by coal. — **coal'fish** a dusky fish of the cod family (*Pollachius virens*) — also called **coley, saithe** or (*US*) **pollack**; **coal gas** the mixture of gases produced by the distillation of coal, used for lighting and heating; **coal heaver** a person employed to carry or move coal; **coal hole** a small coal cellar; a hole in the pavement for filling a coal-cellar; **coalhouse** a covered-in place for keeping coal; **coaling station** a port at which ships take on coal; **coal'man** a man who sells and carries coal; **coal'master** the owner or lessee of a coalfield; **Coal Measures** (*geol*) the uppermost division of the Carboniferous; **coal merchant** a dealer in coal; **coal'mine** a pit or mine from which coal is dug; **coal'miner**; **coal mouse** see **coal-tit**; **coal oil** (*NAm*) rock-oil, shale-oil, paraffin; **coal'-porter** a person who carries coal; **Coal Sack** (*astron*) a dark patch in the Milky Way; **coal scuttle** a fireside container for holding coal; **coal'tar** a thick, black, opaque liquid formed when coal is distilled; **coal tit** a dark species of tit (*Parus ater*), with greyish plumage on its back and a black head marked with white patches at the nape (also **coal titmouse** or **coal mouse**). — **at the coalface** (*fig*) employed in physical or practical work or directly involved with production, as opposed to administrative or managerial work; working in an exposed, difficult and/or dangerous situation; **blow the coals** to excite passion, foment strife; **carry coals to Newcastle** to take

a thing where it is already most abundant; **haul** or **call over the coals** to reprimand, from the discipline applied to heretics; **heap coals of fire on someone's head** to excite someone's remorse and repentance by returning good for evil (from the Bible, Rom 12. 20). [OE *col*; cognate with ON *kol*, Ger *Kohle*]

coalesce *kō-ə-les'*, *vi* to grow together or unite into one whole; to fuse. — *n* **coalesc'ence** growing into each other; fusion. — *adj* **coalesc'ent**. [L *coalēscere*, from *alēscere* to grow up, increase]

Coalite® *kō'ə-līt*, *n* a smokeless fuel produced by low-temperature carbonization of coal.

coalition *kō-ə-lish'ən*, *n* the act of merging into one mass or body; a combination or alliance short of union, *esp* of states or political parties for some specific purpose. — *adj* **cōali'tional**. — *n* **cōali'tioner**. — *n* **cōali'tionism**. — *n* **cōali'tionist**. — **coalition government** government by a coalition of parties, sometimes called a national government. [L *coalitiō*; see **coalesce**]

coalize or **-ise** *kō'ə-līz*, *vt* and *vi* to bring or come into coalition. [Fr *coaliser*]

Coalport *kōl'pōrt* or *-pört*, *n* patterned porcelain ware made at *Coalport*, near Shrewsbury, during the 19c.

coaming *kōm'ing*, (*naut*) *n* (*usu* in *pl*) a raised framework around the edges of the hatches of a ship to keep water out. [Origin unknown]

Coanda effect *kō-an'də i-fekt'*, *n* the tendency of liquid, when it encounters a curved surface, to run along it. [Henri Marie *Coanda* (1885–1972) French engineer]

coapt *kō-apt'*, *vt* to adjust. — *n* **coaptā'tion**. [L *coaptāre*, from *aptāre*, to fit]

coarb *kō'ärb*, (*hist*) *n* the head of a family in an Irish sept; an ecclesiastical successor. — Also **comarb** (*kō'ärb*). [Ir *comharba* successor]

coarctate *kō-ärk'tāt*, *adj* compressed; constricted, narrowed. — *vi* to become constricted; to narrow. — *n* **cōarctā'tion**. [L *coar(c)tāre*, *-ātum*, from *ar(c)tāre* to draw together]

coarse *kōrs* or *körs*, *adj* common, base, inferior; rough; rude; uncivil; harsh; gross; large in grain, fibre or mesh, etc; without refinement; roughly approximate. — *adv* **coarse'ly**. — *vt* and *vi* **coars'en** to make or become coarse. — *n* **coarse'ness**. — *adj* **coars'ish** somewhat coarse. — **coarse fish** freshwater fish other than those of the salmon family (as opposed to *game fish*); **coarse fishing**. — *adj* **coarse'-grained** large in grain; coarse-natured; gross. — **coarse metal** impure cuprous sulphide obtained in the smelting process. [From phrase 'in course', hence *ordinary*]

coast *kōst* or (*obs*) **cost** or **coste** *kōst*, (also, eg *Spenser*) *kost*, *n* the border of land next to the sea; the seashore; (often with *cap*) the Pacific coast of the US (*NAm*); a side (*obs*); a limit or border (*obs*); a region (*obs*); direction (*obs*); footing, terms (*Spenser*); a hill suitable for tobogganing (*NAm*); an act or period of sliding down a slope. — *vi* to sail along or near a coast; to travel downhill on a sledge, on a cycle without pedalling or in a motor-car out of gear; to glide; to succeed or proceed with minimum effort; (also *obs* **cost**) to approach (*obs*). — *vt* to sail by or near to. — *adj* **coast'al**. — *n* **coast'er** a vessel engaged in coastal trade; a person or thing that coasts; a container or mat for a decanter or glasses on a table; in W Africa, a European resident; (*usu* with *cap*) in NZ, an inhabitant or native of the West Coast of South Island. — *adj* **coast'ing** keeping near the coast; trading between ports in the same country. — *n* the act of sailing, or of trading, along the coast; sliding downhill. — *adv* **coast'ward** or **coast'wards** toward(s) the coast. — *adv* **coast'wise** along or by the coast. — *adj* carried on along the coast. — **coast'guard** an organization with responsibility for watching coastal waters to prevent smuggling and illegal fishing, to assist shipping, and for life-saving; a member of this organization; **coast'guardsman** (chiefly *US*); **coast'line** the line or boundary of a coast; shoreline. — *adj* **coast-to-coast'** covering the whole country, nationwide. — **the coast is clear** there is no obstacle or danger in the way. [OFr *coste* (Fr *côte*), from L *costa* rib, side]

coat *kōt*, *n* an outer garment with sleeves; an overcoat; the hair or wool of an animal; any covering; a membrane or layer, as of paint, etc; a coat of arms (see below); a skirt or petticoat (*dialect*). — *vt* to clothe; to cover with a coat or layer. — *n* **coat'ee** a short close-fitting coat. — *n* **coat'er** a worker, machine, etc that applies a layer or covering. — *n* **coat'ing** a covering, layer; cloth for coats. — *adj* **coat'less** without a coat or a coat of arms. — **coat'-armour** a coat of arms, or heraldically embroidered garment worn over armour; armorial devices; **coat'-card** a card bearing the representation of a coated figure, the king, queen or knave (now called *court-card*); **coat'-dress** a tailored dress with fastening from neckline to hem, *usu* worn without a coat or jacket; **coated lens** a lens coated with a thin film of transparent material to reduce the reflection of light from its surface; **coat hanger** a curved piece of wood, etc, with a hook, by which clothes may be hung and kept in shape; **coat'rack** or **coat'stand** a rack or stand with pegs for hanging coats on; **coat tails** the long back-pieces of a tail-coat. — **coat of arms** the family insignia embroidered on the surcoat worn over the hauberk, or coat of mail; the heraldic bearings of a person, family or organization; **coat of mail** a piece of armour for the upper part of the body, made of metal scales or rings linked one with another; **on someone's coat tails** achieving one's position as a result of the promotion or advancement of a person to whom one has attached oneself, and not by one's own merit; **trail one's coat (tails)** (*orig Ir*) to be aggressive, pick a quarrel (*n* **coat'-trailing**); **turn one's coat** to change one's principles, or to turn from one party to another. [OFr *cote* (Fr *cotte*), from LL *cottus*, *cotta* a tunic; the further ety is uncertain]

coati *kō-ä'tē* or *-ti*, or *kə-wä'tē*, *n* a tropical American plantigrade carnivorous mammal of the genera *Nasna* and *Nasuella*, related to, but larger than, the raccoons. — Also **coati-mun'di** or **coati-mon'di**. [Tupí]

co-author *kō-ö'thər*, *n* a joint author.

coax[1] *kōks*, *vt* to persuade by fondling or flattery; to humour or soothe; to pet. — *n* **coax** or **coax'er**. — *adv* **coax'ingly**. [**cokes** a simpleton]

coax[2] or **co-ax** *kō'aks*, *n* short for coaxial cable.

coaxial *kō-ak'si-əl*, *adj* having the same axis. — *adv* **coax'ially**. — **coaxial cable** a cable consisting of one or more **coaxial pairs**, each a central conductor within an outer tubular conductor.

cob[1] *kob*, *n* a short-legged strong horse; a male swan (also **cob'-swan**); a lump (*esp* of coal, ore or clay); a rounded object; a cobloaf; the axis of a head of maize, a corncob; a cobnut; an irregularly-shaped Spanish-American dollar of the 17c to 19c (also **cob money**). — *adj* **cobb'y** like a cob; stout, brisk, lively, arrogant (*dialect*). — **cob'loaf** a rounded, round-headed or misshapen loaf; an archaic expression of contempt; **cob'nut** the nut of the European hazel; the European hazel; a children's game played with nuts; **cob'-pipe** a tobacco pipe made from a corncob. [Perh connected with **cop**[1]]

cob[2] *kob*, *n* (in parts of Britain and in New Zealand) a building material composed of clay and chopped straw; a building constructed of this material. — **cob cottage**; **cob wall**. [Origin unknown]

cob[3] *kob*, (*dialect*) *n* a wicker basket used by sowers. [Origin unknown]

cob[4] *kob*, *vt* to strike; to thump on the buttocks.

cob[5] or **cobb** *kob*, (*archaic*) *n* a gull, *esp* the greater black-backed gull. [Cf Du *kob* gull]

cobalamin *kō-bal'ə-min*, *n* a complex molecule containing cobalt that is a constituent of vitamin B_{12}. [*cobalt* and *vitamin*]

cobalt *kō'bölt*, *n* a metallic element (atomic no 27; symbol **Co**), having similarities to nickel; a blue pigment prepared from it (also **cō'balt-blue**). — *adj* of this deep-blue colour. — *adj* **cobalt'ic**. — *adj* **cobaltif'erous**. — *n*

cō'baltite a mineral containing cobalt, arsenic, and sulphur (also **cobalt glance**). — **cobalt bloom** erythrite; **cobalt bomb** a suggested bomb consisting of a hydrogen bomb encased in cobalt, with increased destructive qualities resulting from the cobalt-60 dust released; **cobalt-60** a radioactive isotope of cobalt used as a source of gamma rays, eg in radiotherapy. [Ger *Kobalt*, from *Kobold* a demon, a nickname given by the German miners, because they supposed it to be a mischievous and hurtful metal]

cobb. See **cob**[5].

cobber *kob'ər*, (*Austr* and NZ; *colloq*) *n* mate, chum, buddy. [Perh from dialect *cob* to take a liking to]

cobble[1] *kob'l* or **cobblestone** *-stōn*, *n* a rounded stone, *esp* formerly used in paving. — *vt* to pave with cobblestones. [Ety dubious]

cobble[2] *kob'l*, *vt* to mend shoes; to patch up, assemble, put together, or mend hastily or with parts or materials from various sources (often with *together* or *up*). — *n* see **coble**. — *n* **cobb'ler** a person who cobbles or mends shoes; an iced drink made up of wine or spirits, sugar, lemon, etc; a (*usu* fruit) pie with a thick crunchy topping; (in *pl*; *slang*) nonsense. — *n* **cobb'lery**. — *n* **cobb'ling**. — **cobbler's pegs** an Australian weed with peg-like bristles on the flowerheads; **cobbler's punch** a hot drink made of beer, with the addition of spirit, sugar and spice. [Origin unknown]

cobble[3]. See **coble**.

Cobdenism *kob'dən-izm*, *n* the policy of Richard *Cobden* (1804–65), the English 'Apostle of Free Trade'. — *n* **Cob'denite** a supporter of Cobdenism, *esp* a freetrader.

cobelligerent *kō-bi-lij'ə-rent*, *adj* cooperating in warfare. — Also *n*.

cobia *kō'bi-ə*, *n* the sergeant fish. [Perh of W Indian origin]

coble or **cobble** *kōb'l* or *kob'l*, *n* a small flat-bottomed boat for use on rivers and estuaries (*Scot*); a single-masted sea-fishing boat with a flat bottom and square stern (*NE Eng*). [Cf Welsh *ceubal* a hollow trunk, a boat]

COBOL or **Cobol** *kō'bōl*, *-bol*, *n* an internationally accepted computer programming language, for general commercial use, which uses statements in English. [*Co*mmon *b*usiness *o*riented *l*anguage]

cobra *kō'brə* or *kob'rə*, *n* any poisonous snake of the genus *Naja*, found in India and Africa, which dilates the skin of its neck so as to resemble a hood. — *adj* **cob'ric**. — *adj* **cob'riform** like or related to the cobra. [Port *cobra* (*de capello*) snake (of the hood)]

coburg *kō'bûrg*, *n* a thin fabric of worsted with cotton or silk, twilled on one side; the name of various pieces of bakery and confectionery, including a type of round loaf and a type of sponge cake (also *adj*). [*Coburg*, in Germany]

cobweb *kob'web*, *n* a spider's web or net; any snare or device intended to entrap; anything flimsy or easily broken; anything that obscures. — Also *vt*. — *n* **cobwebb'ery**. — *adj* **cob'webby**. [Prob *attercop-web*; see **attercop** and **web**]

cobza *kob'zə*, *n* a short-necked, ten-stringed, unfretted Romanian folk-instrument.

coca *kō'kə*, *n* either of two Andrean shrubs (*Erythroxylon coca* or *E. truxinense*) of a family related to flax, whose leaves contain cocaine. [Sp, from Quechua *coca*]

Coca-Cola® *kō-kə-kō'lə*, *n* a carbonated soft drink first made in the US (often shortened to **Coke**). — *adj* denoting the spread of American culture to other parts of the world. — **coca-colonizā'tion** or **-s-** (*facetious*) the invasion of other parts of the world by American culture and values as typified by the availability of the drink.

Cocagne, **Cocaigne**. Same as **Cockaigne**.

cocaine *ko-kān'*, *kō'kā-in* or *kō'kä-in*, *n* an alkaloid obtained from coca-leaves or produced synthetically; an addictive narcotic used medicinally as a local anaesthetic (often shortened to **coke**; *drug-taking slang*). — *n* **cocain'ism** a morbid condition induced by addiction to cocaine. — *n* **cocain'ist** — *n* **cocainizā'tion** or **-s-**. — *vt* **cocain'ize** or **-ise** to anaesthetize with cocaine. [**coca** and **-ine**]

coccid, etc. See under **coccus**.

coccineous *kok-sin'i-əs*, (*obs*) *adj* bright red. [L *coccineus*, from *coccum* cochineal]

cocco *kok'ō* or **coco** *kō'kō*, *n* the taro or other edible araceous tuber: — *pl* **cocc'os** or **co'cos**.

coccolite *kok'ō-līt*, *n* a variety of pyroxene; a small rounded body found in chalk formations, consisting of microscopic plates secreted by extinct algal plankton (also **cocc'olith**). [Gr *kokkos* a berry, and *lithos* a stone]

coccus *kok'əs*, *n* a one-seeded portion of a dry fruit that breaks up at maturity (*bot*); a spherical bacterium (*zool*): — *pl* **cocci** (*kok'sī*). — *adj* **coccal** (*kok'əl*). — *n* and *adj* **coccid** (*kok'sid*) (any insect) of the family **Coccidae** (*kok'si-dē*), which includes the scale insects, or of the superfamily *Coccoidea*. — *n* **coccidioidomycosis** (*-oi-dō-mī-kō-sis*) infection resulting from the inhalation of the spores of the fungus *Coccidioides immitis*, occurring either as an influenza-like respiratory illness, or as a severe, progressive disease affecting the skin, viscera, nervous system and lungs: — *pl* **coccid'ia**. — *n* **coccidiosis** (*kok-sid-i-ōs'is*) a contagious infection of birds and animals by coccidia. — *n* **coccidiostat** (*kok-sid'i-ō-stat*) an agent which builds up a resistance by the host to coccidia by retarding the latter's lifecycle, etc; any of various drugs used to prevent the development of coccidium-caused diseases, often added to feedstuffs or drinking-water. — *n* **coccidium** (*kok-sid'i-əm*) a parasitic protozoan of the order **Coccid'ia**. — *adj* **coccoid** (*kok'oid*). — *n* **Cocc'ūlus** a tropical genus of climbing plants (*Menispermaceae*). — **cocculus indicus** the dried fruit of *Anamirta cocculus* (same family), narcotic and poisonous. [New L, from Gr *kokkos* a berry]

coccyx *kok'siks*, (*anatom*) *n* the terminal triangular bone of the vertebral column in man and certain apes, consisting of four tiny bones fused together: — *pl* **coccyges** (*kok-sī'jēz*). — *adj* **coccygeal** (*kok-sij'i-əl*) or **coccyg'ian**. [Gr *kokkyx*, *-ȳgos* cuckoo, coccyx (its shape resembling a cuckoo's bill)]

co-chair *kō-chār*, *n* a joint chairperson, male or female.

Cochin *koch'in*, *n* a large feathery-legged domestic hen, *orig* from Cochin-China, now part of Vietnam. — Also **Cochin-China** (*-chī'nə*).

cochineal *koch'i-nēl* or *-nēl'*, *n* a scarlet dyestuff consisting of the dried bodies of the female **cochineal insect**, used as a colouring for foodstuffs, etc; the insect itself (*Dactylopius coccus*), that feeds on cacti in Mexico, the W Indies, etc. [Sp *cochinilla*, dimin of L *coccinus* scarlet, from *coccum* (Gr *kokkos*) a berry, as the similar coccid insect was formerly supposed to be the berry or seed of an oak]

cochlea *kok'li-ə*, *n* anything spiral-shaped, *esp* a snail-shell; the spiral cavity of the inner ear (*anatom*): — *pl* **coch'leae**. — *adj* **coch'lear** (*-li-ər*) pertaining to the cochlea of the ear; spoon-shaped. — *adj* **cochlear'iform** spoon-shaped. — *adj* **coch'leāte** or **coch'leated** twisted spirally. [L *coc(h)lea* a shell, screw, from Gr *kochlias* a snail]

cock[1] *kok*, *n* a male bird, *esp* of the domestic fowl (also often as *combining form*, eg **cock'bird**, **cock-rob'in**, **cock-sparr'ow**); a male crab, lobster or salmon; a weathercock; (sometimes as *old cock*) a familiar form of address to a man (*slang*); a strutting chief or leader (*slang*); anything set erect; a tap; part of the lock of a gun, held back by a spring, which, when released by the trigger, produces the discharge; a penis (*vulg*); nonsense (*colloq*). — *vt* to set erect or upright (often with *up*); to set up the brim of; to draw back (eg the cock of a gun); to turn up or to one side; to tilt up (one's head, ears, etc) knowingly, inquiringly or scornfully. — *vi* to strut; to swagger. — *adj* **cocked** set erect; turned up or to one side; (of a gun) with the cock drawn back, ready to fire. — *n* **cock'er** someone who follows cockfighting; a cocker spaniel (see below); a term of familiarity (*slang*). — *n* **cock'erel** a young cock. — *adv* **cock'ily**. — *n* **cock'iness**, **cocks'iness** or **cox'iness**. — *adj* **cock'y**, **cocks'y** or **cox'y** self-important, bumptious; pert. — **cock-a-doodle-doo'** (*imit*) the crow of a cock. — *vi* to crow. — *adj* **cock-a-hoop'** in exultant spirits. — **cockaleekie** see **cockieleekie** below; **cockalō'rum** a bumptious little person; a boys' jumping game. — *adj* **cock'-and-bull'** (of a story) fabricated and incredible. — **cock'-broth** the broth made from a boiled cock; **cockchafer** see separate entry; **cock'-crow** early morning, when cocks crow; **cocked hat** an old-fashioned three-cornered hat; a small triangle on a navigational chart formed by taking the third of three bearings (*naut*); **cocker spaniel** a small spaniel used to retrieve birds in game shooting; **cock'eye** a squinting eye. — *adj* **cock'eyed** having a cockeye; off the straight, awry (*colloq*); tipsy (*colloq*). — **cock'fight** or **cock'-fighting** a fight or contest between game-cocks; a fight; **cockhorse'** a child's imaginary or toy horse. — *adj* prancing, proud. — *adv* properly **a-cockhorse'** (ie on cockhorse) on horseback; exultingly. — **cockieleek'ie** or **cockyleek'y** or **cock(-)a(-)leek'ie** (*Scot*) soup made from a fowl and leeks; **cock'laird** (*Scot*) the owner of a small farm, who farms it in person; **cock'loft** a small room just under the roof; **cock'match** a cockfight; **cock-of-the-rock'** a S American bird of the cotinga family; **cock'pit** a sheltered depression in the deck of a yacht or small ship; (in aircraft) a compartment in the fuselage, *usu* for the pilot or rarely for the passenger(s); the driver's seat in a racing car; a pit or enclosed space where game-cocks fought; a frequent battleground; part of a ship-of-war's lower regions used for the wounded in action; **cock's'-comb** or **cocks'comb** the comb or crest on a cock's head; a jester's cap; a crest-like crystalline mineral aggregate (as in *cockscomb pyrites*); a name for various plants, *esp Celosia cristata*, (family Amarantaceae) with a fasciated inflorescence like a cock's comb, also yellow-rattle (*Rhinanthus*), and sainfoin; a coxcomb; **cocks'foot** a Eurasian grass (*Dactylis glomerata*) with inflorescences like a cock's foot; **cock'shot** a cockshy; **cock'shut** (*archaic* or *dialect*) twilight, *prob* referring to the time when poultry are shut up for the night; **cock'shy** a throw at a target, *orig* a cock, for amusement; an object set up for this purpose; an object of criticism or ridicule; **cock-sparr'ow** a male sparrow; a small, lively person; **cock'spur** a spur on the leg of a gamecock; a type of catch used on casement windows; **cockspur grass** (*Echinochloa crus-galli*) an invasive grass of warmer, *orig* only tropical, climates; **cock'sucker** (*vulg slang*) a contemptible person who attempts to ingratiate himself with his superiors; a toady; a male homosexual. — *adj* **cock'sure** irritatingly self-confident or self-assured. — **cock'teaser** (*vulg slang*) a woman who deliberately provokes a man's sexual arousal, then refuses sexual intercourse. — *adj* **cock'-up** turned up; rising above the tops of the other letters, superior (*printing*). — *n* (*colloq*) a muddle, mess, confusion. — **cockyleeky** see **cockieleekie**. — **cock a snook** see under **snook**[2]; **cock of the walk** a person who (thinks he) is the most important in a group; **go off at half cock** (*colloq*) to begin too soon, when not properly prepared; **knock into a cocked hat** to give a profound beating, to defeat; **live like fighting cocks** to have every luxury. [OE *coc*; ON *kokkr*]

cock[2] *kok*, *n* a small pile of hay, dung, etc. — *vt* to pile or heap into cocks. — *adj* **cocked** heaped up in cocks. [Cf ON *kökkr* a lump]

cock[3] *kok*, (*Shakesp*) *n* a cockboat. — **cock'boat** a ship's small boat; a small frail boat.

cock[4] *kok*, (*obs*) altered form of **god**. — **cock and pie** see under **pie**[2].

cock-a-bondy *kok-ə-bon'di* or (*colloq*) *kok-i-bun'di*, *n* a fly for angling. [Welsh *coch a bon ddu* red, with black stem]

cockabully *kok-ə-bo͝o'li*, *n* any of various small freshwater fish of New Zealand. [Maori *kokopu*]

cockade *kok-ād'*, *n* a rosette worn on the hat as a badge. [Fr *cocarde*, from *coq* cock]

Cockaigne or **Cockayne** *kok-ān'*, *n* (*orig* in medieval story) an imaginary country of luxury and delight. [Ety doubtful]

cock-a-leekie. See **cockieleekie** under **cock**[1].

cockalorum. See **cock**[1].

cockatoo *kok-ə-to͞o'*, *n* any of a number of large crested parrots (genus *Kakatoe*) of the Australian region; a small farmer (also **cock'y**) (*Austr* and *NZ*); a lookout (*Austr colloq*). — *n* **cockatiel** or **cockateel** (*-tēl'*) a small crested parrot of Australia. — **cocky's joy** (*Austr slang*) golden syrup; **cow cocky** (*Austr* and *NZ*) a dairy farmer. [Malay *kakatua*]

cockatrice *kok'ə-trīs* or *-tris*, *n* a fabulous monster, a serpent with the wings of a bird and the head of a cock; a cock-like monster with a dragon's tail (*heraldry*); a prostitute (*obs*); a mischievous or treacherous person (*fig*). [OFr *cocatris*]

Cockayne. See **Cockaigne**.

cockboat *kok'bōt*, *n* any small frail boat; a ship's small boat. — Also **cockle boat**. [Obs *cokke* a small boat, from OFr *coque*]

cockchafer *kok'chā-fər*, *n* a large European flying beetle (*Melolontha melolontha*), with reddish-brown wing-cases and fan-like antennae, the larvae of which are a serious pest of farm and garden crops. — Also called **May bug**. [**cock**[1] and **chafer**]

cocker[1] *kok'ər*, *vt* to pamper; to fondle; to indulge. [Ety doubtful; cf Du *kokelen*, OFr *conqueliner* to dandle]

cocker[2], **cockerel**. See **cock**[1].

Cocker *kok'ər*, *n* a standard of accuracy and orthodoxy (*esp* in the phrase *according to Cocker*). [From Edward *Cocker* (1631–75), author of a popular arithmetic book]

cockernony *kok-ər-non'i*, (*obs Scot*) *n* the gathering of hair in a fillet; a coiffure; a pad of false hair; a starched cap. [Origin obscure]

cocket *kok'it*, *n* the custom-house seal (*hist*); a custom-house certificate. [Origin doubtful]

cock-eye(d), **cockhorse**. See **cock**[1].

cockieleekie. See under **cock**[1].

cockle[1] *kok'l*, *n* a cornfield weed, *esp* now the corncockle. — **cock'lebur** a composite weed of the genus *Xanthium*; a spiny bur of this plant (also called **clotebur**). [OE *coccel*]

cockle[2] *kok'l*, *n* a large bivalve mollusc (*Cardium edule* or other species) with thick, ribbed, heart-shaped, equal-valved shell; its shell; a bivalve shell generally. — *adj* **cock'led** shelled like a cockle. — **cockle hat** a hat bearing a scallop shell, the badge of a pilgrim; **cockle'man** a cockle-fisherman; **cock'leshell** the shell of a cockle; a frail boat. — **cockles of the heart** one's inmost heart. [Fr *coquille*, from Gr *konchylion*, from *konchē* a cockle]

cockle[3] *kok'l*, *n* a pucker. — *vi* to pucker. — *vt* to cause to pucker. [Perh Fr *coquiller* to blister, from *coquille*; see **cockle**[2]]

cockle[4] *kok'l*, *n* a furnace or stove. [Perh Du *kachel*]

cockney *kok'ni*, *n* (often with *cap*) a person born in London, *strictly*, within hearing of Bow Bells; London dialect, *esp* of the East End; a young snapper fish (*Austr*). — *adj* (often with *cap*) characteristic of a Cockney. — *n* **cock'neydom** the domain of Cockneys. — *n* **cockneyficā'tion**. — *vt* **cock'neyfy** or **cock'nify** to make Cockney. — *adj* **cock'neyish**. — *n* **cock'neyism** a Cockney idiom or characteristic. [ME *coken-ey* cock's egg, hence, an oddity; or perh connected with Fr *coquin* a rogue, from L *coquus* a cook]

cockroach *kok'rōch*, *n* an orthopterous insect, the so-called black beetle. [Sp *cucaracha* woodlouse, cockroach]

cockscomb, **cocksfoot**, etc. See **cock**[1]

cockswain. See **coxswain**.

cocktail[1] *kok'tāl*, *n* a mixed drink containing spirits and other liquors; an appetizer consisting of eg seafood with a sauce; any mixture of substances or elements. —

adj (of food items) suitable to be served with cocktails. — **cocktail bar** or **lounge** a bar or room in a hotel or restaurant where cocktails and other spirits are served; **cocktail dress** a dress for semi-formal wear; **cocktail shaker** or **mixer** a container for mixing cocktails; **cocktail stick** a small wooden or plastic stick with pointed ends for holding a cherry, olive, small sausage, etc when eaten with drinks. — **fruit cocktail** a salad of finely-diced fruit. [**cock**[1] and **tail**[1]]

cocktail[2] *kok'tāl*, *n* an animal, *esp* a racehorse, of mixed breeding; a person of low breeding who pretends to be a gentleman; a horse with a docked tail. — *adj* **cock'tailed** having the tail cocked or tilted up.

cocky. See **cock**[1], **cockatoo**.

cockyleeky. See **cockieleekie** under **cock**[1].

coco[1] *kō'kō*, *n* a tropical seaside palm tree (*Cocos nucifera*) with curving stem (also **co'co-palm**, **co'conut-palm** or **co'co-tree**), which produces the coconut: — *pl* **cō'cos**. — **coco-de-mer** (*-də-mer'*; Fr) the double coconut (see below); **coco fibre** coir used as a growing medium in horticulture; **co'conut** less correctly **co'coanut** or **co'-kernut** a large edible nut, yielding **coconut-butt'er** (or **coconut-oil'**) and **coconut-milk'**; **coconut ice** a kind of sweet made of coconut and sugar; **co'conut-matting** matting made from the husk of the coconut; **co'conut-shy** a fairground throwing game with coconuts as targets or as prizes. — **double coconut** the large two-lobed nut of the Seychelles palm (*Lodoicea seychellarum*). [Port and Sp *coco* a grimace, grinning face; applied to the nut from the three marks at the end of it, which resemble a grotesque face]

coco[2]. See **cocco**.

cocoa *kō'kō*, *n* the seed of the cacao or chocolate tree; a powder made from the seeds; a drink made from the powder. — **co'coa-beans** the seeds, *esp* when dried and fermented; **co'coa-butter** or **co'coa-fat** a fat obtained from the seeds and used in confectionery, soaps, etc. [**cacao**]

cocoanut. See under **coco**[1].

cocoa-wood. See under **coco-wood**.

COCOM or **Cocom** *kōkom*, *abbrev*: Co-ordinating Committee for Multilateral Export Controls.

coconscious *kō-kon'shəs*, *adj* aware of the same things, or aware of various things within the same consciousness; pertaining to the co-conscious. — *n* mental processes in a subsidiary stream, apart from the main stream of consciousness. — *n* **cōcon'sciousness**.

cocoon *ko-kōōn'*, *n* the silken sheath spun by many insect larvae in passing into the pupa stage and by spiders for their eggs; the capsule in which earthworms and leeches lay their eggs; a preservative covering for military and other equipment; a cosy, secure place or situation. — *vt* to wrap or preserve carefully as in a cocoon. — *n* **cocoon'ery** a place for keeping silkworms when feeding and spinning cocoons. — *n* **cocoon'ing**. [Fr *cocon*, from *coque* a shell, from L *concha* a shell]

cocopan *kō'kə-pan*, *n* (in S Africa) a wagon on a narrow-gauge railway serving a mine. [Altered from Zulu *'ngkumbana*]

cocoplum *kō'kō-plum*, *n* a W Indian rosaceous tree (*Chrysobalanus icaco*); its edible fruit. [Sp *icaco*, and **plum**]

cocotte *ko-kot'*, *n* a small fireproof dish, *usu* for an individual portion, a casserole; a loose woman, prostitute. [Fr, child's word for hen, from *coq* cock]

coco-wood or **cocoa-wood** *kō'kō-wŏŏd*, *n* the wood of a W Indian mimosaceous tree, *Inga vera*; kokrawood.

coction *kok'shən*, *n* boiling; cooking. — *adj* **coc'tile** baked; hardened by fire, as a brick. [L *coquere*, *coctum* to boil, cook]

coculture *kō-kul'chər*, *vt* to grow (two or more organisms) in the same growing medium or culture; to grow (an organism) on or in more than one organic medium.

cocuswood *kō'kəs-wŏŏd*, *n* the so-called Jamaica ebony (*Brya ebenus*); a tradename for kokrawood.

cod[1] *kod* or **codfish** *kod'fish*, *n* a food-fish (*Gadus morrhua*) of northern seas; any fish of the genus *Gadus* or the family *Gadidae*. — *n* **codd'er** a cod fisherman or his boat. — *n* **cod'ling** a small cod. — **cod'-fisher**; **cod'-fishery**; **cod'-fishing**. — **cod-liver oil** a medicinal oil extracted from the fresh liver of the common cod or related fish. [Ety dubious]

cod[2] *kod*, (*obs*) *n* a bag; a pod; the scrotum. — *adj* **codd'ed** enclosed in a cod. — *adj* **codd'ing** (*Shakesp*) lecherous. — **cod'piece** a pouch once worn by men in the front of tight hose or breeches. [OE *codd* a small bag]

cod[3] *kod*, (*Scot*) *n* a pillow or cushion. [ON *koddi* a pillow]

cod[4] *kod*, (*slang*) *n* a jest; a hoax. — *adj* mock, sham; done, intended, etc as a joke or take-off. — *vt* to hoax; to poke fun at: — *pr p* **codd'ing**; *pa t* and *pa p* **codd'ed**. [Ety dubious]

cod[5] *kod*, (*dialect*) *n* a fellow, chap; a codger. [See **codger**]

Cod. *abbrev*: Codex.

c.o.d. *abbrev*: cash (or collect) on delivery.

coda *kō'də*, *n* a passage forming the completion of a piece, rounding it off to a satisfactory conclusion (*music*); any similar passage or piece in a story, dance sequence, etc. — *n* **codett'a** (*music*) a short coda. [Ital, from L *cauda* a tail]

codder. See **cod**[1].

coddle *kod'l*, *vt* to pamper, mollycoddle; to cook (*esp* eggs) gently over hot water. — *n* an effeminate person. [Ety dubious]

code *kōd*, *n* a collection or digest of laws; a system of rules and regulations (*specif* regarding education); established principles or standards (of art, moral conduct, etc); a volume; a system of signals; a system of words, letters or symbols which represent sentences or other words, to ensure economy or secrecy in transmission; a cipher; a set of rules and characters for converting one form of data to another (*comput*); the characters of the resulting representation of data (*comput*); the pattern of holes in a punched card or paper tape which represents a character or instructions. — *vt* to codify; to express in code. — *n* **codificā'tion** (*kod-* or *kōd-*). — *n* **codifier** (*kod'* or *kōd'*) or **cōd'ist** a person who codifies. — *vt* **codify** (*kod'* or *kōd'*) to put into the form of a code; to digest; to systematize: — *pr p* **cod'ifying**; *pa t* and *pa p* **cod'ified**. — *n* and *adj* **cod'ing**. — **code'book** a book containing the words, symbols, etc of a code or codes; **code'-breaker** a person who tries to interpret secret codes; **code'-breaking**; **code'-name** or **code'-number** a name or number used for convenience, economy, secrecy, etc. — *adj* **code'-named**. — **code of conduct** or **code of practice** an established method or set of rules for dealing with, behaving in, etc a particular situation. [Fr *code*; see **codex**]

codeclination *kō-dek-lin-ā'shən*, *n* polar distance.

codeine *kō'dēn* or *-di-in*, *n* an alkaloid, obtained from opium, used as an analgesic and sedative. [Gr *kōdeia* poppy-head]

co-dependant or (*esp US*) **co-dependent** *kō-di-pend'ənt*, (*psychol*) *n* a person who seeks to fulfil his or her own emotional needs by caring for or controlling a dependant. — *n* **co-depend'ency**. — *adj* **co-depend'ent**.

codex *kō'deks*, *n* a code; a manuscript volume: — *pl* **codices** (*kōd'i-sēz*). — *n* **cōdicol'ogy** the study of manuscript volumes. — *adj* **cōdicolog'ical**. [L *cōdex* or *caudex*, *-icis* the trunk of a tree, a set of tablets, a book]

codger *koj'ər*, *n* a man, a chap, *esp* if old and eccentric. [Prob a variant of **cadger**]

codicil *kod'i-sil*, *n* a supplement to a will. — *adj* **codicill'ary**. [L *cōdicillus*, dimin of *cōdex*]

codicology. See **codex**.

codification, etc. See **code**.

codilla *kō-dil'ə*, *n* the coarsest part of hemp or flax. [Dimin of Ital *coda*, from L *cauda* a tail]

codille *kō-dil'*, *n* a situation in ombre when the challenger loses. [Fr]

codling[1] *kod'ling* or **codlin** *kod'lin*, *n* a variety of elongated apple. — **codling moth** or **codlin moth** a brownish-gold moth (*Cydia pomonella*), whose larvae are a common pest of apples, quinces, pears, etc. [Ety uncertain]

codling[2]. See **cod**[1].
codon *kō'don*, (*biol*) *n* a triplet of bases in the messenger-RNA molecule, which determines a particular amino-acid in protein synthesis. [**code** and *-on*]
co-driver *kō'-drīvər*, *n* one of two alternating drivers, *esp* in a race or rally.
codswallop or **cod's-wallop** *kodz'wol-əp*, (*colloq*) *n* nonsense, rubbish. [Origin uncertain]
coeducation *kō-ed-ū-kā'shən*, *n* education of the sexes together. — *n* **co'ed** a girl or woman educated at a coeducational institution (*usu NAm*); a coeducational school. — *adj* **co'ed** or **coeducā'tional**.
coefficient *kō-if-ish'ənt*, *n* that which acts together with another thing; a numerical or literal expression for a factor of a quantity in an algebraic term (*math*); a numerical constant used as a multiplier to a variable quantity, in calculating the magnitude of a physical property (*phys*).
coehorn or **cohorn** *kō'hörn*, (*military hist*) *n* a small mortar for throwing grenades. [Baron van *Coehoorn* (1641–1704)]
coel- or **coelo-** (also *NAm* **cel-** or **celo**) *sēl(ō)*, *combining form* denoting a cavity, or hollow part. [Gr *koilos* hollow]
coelacanth *sē'lə-kanth*, *n* any of a group of primitive crossopterygian fishes all of which were thought to be extinct until 1938, when a living specimen of the genus *Latimeria* was discovered off the coast of E Africa. — *adj* **coelacan'thic** (*facetious*) ancient but worth preserving. [From Gr *koilos* hollow, and *akantha* spine]
coelanaglyphic *sēl-an-ə-glif'ik*, (*sculp*) *adj* in cavo-rilievo (hollow relief). [Gr *koilos* hollow, *ana* up, and *glyphein* to carve]
coelenterate *sə-len'tər-āt* or *sē-*, *n* any invertebrate of the phylum Coelenterata of many-celled animals, radially symmetrical, with a single body-cavity (the enteron) including the hydroids (Hydrozoa), jellyfish (Scyphozoa), sea anemones and corals (Actinozoa), and (in some classifications) the sea gooseberries (Ctenophora). — Also *adj*. [Gr *koilos* hollow, and *enteron* intestine]
coeliac or (*esp NAm*) **celiac** *sē'li-ak*, *adj* relating to the abdomen; pertaining to coeliacs, coeliac disease, etc. — *n* a person suffering from coeliac disease. — **coeliac disease** a condition of the intestines in which a sensitivity to gluten prevents the proper absorption of nutrients (also called **gluten enteropathy**). [Gr *koiliakos* from *koiliā* the belly]
coelom or (*esp NAm*) **celom** *sē'lōm* or *-lom*, *n* the body-cavity, or space between the intestines and the body-wall in animals above the coelenterates. — *n pl* **Coelō'mata** animals possessing a coelom. — *adj* **coe'lomate** having a coelom. — *n* a coelomate animal. — *adj* **coelomat'ic** or **coelom'ic**. [Gr *koilōma*, *-atos* a cavity]
coelostat *sē'lō-stat*, *n* an astronomical instrument consisting of a clock-driven mirror on an axis parallel to the earth's, so that light is reflected continuously from a celestial body such as the sun onto a telescope. [L *caelum* (misspelt *coelum*) sky, and Gr *statos* fixed]
coelurosaur *sēl'ū-rə-sör*, *n* a bipedal carnivorous dinosaur of the Triassic and Cretaceous periods, thought to be the ancestor of archaeopteryx.
coemption *kō-emp'shən*, *n* the buying up of the whole supply of a commodity; a form of marriage under the fiction of a mutual sale of the two parties (*Roman law*). [L *coemptiō*, *-ōnis*, from *emere* to buy]
coen- or **coeno-** (also chiefly *NAm* **cen-** or **ceno-**) *sēn-(ō)-*, *combining form* signifying common. [Gr *koinos* common]
coenaesthesis or **cenesthesis** *sē-nēs-thē'sis*, or *-nis-*, **coenesthesia** or **cenesthesia** *-thē'zi-ə* or *-zyə*, (*psychol*) *n* general consciousness or awareness of one's body. [Gr *koinos* common, and *aisthēsis* perception]
coenenchyma *sē-neng'ki-mə*, (*bot*) *n* gelatinous material uniting the polyps of an anthozoan colony. [Gr *koinos* common, and *enchyma* infusion]
coeno-. See **coen-**.
coenobite or **cenobite** *sēn'o-bīt*, *n* a monk who lives in a community. — *adj* **coenobitic** (*-bit'ik*) or **coenobit'ical**. — *n* **coen'obitism**. — *n* **coenō'bium** a religious community; a colony of unicellular organisms (*biol*): — *pl* **coenō'bia**. [Gr *koinobion*, from *koinos* common, and *bios* life]
coenocyte *sēn'ō-sīt*, (*biol*) *n* a multinucleate mass of protoplasm occurring when nuclei divide within a cell wall, as in fungi. [**coeno-** and **-cyte**]
coenosarc *sēn'ō-särk*, (*biol*) *n* the common tissue uniting the polyps of a coral or other colonial organisms. [Gr *koinos* common, and *sarx* flesh]
coenospecies *n* alternative spelling of **cenospecies**.
coenosteum *si-nos'ti-um*, (*biol*) *n* the calcareous skeleton of a coral colony. [Gr *koinos* common, and *osteon* bone]
coenourus *sē-nū'rəs*, *n* an encysted tapeworm larva consisting of a bladder from whose inner wall several heads develop. [New L, from Gr *koinos* common, and *oura* tail]
coenzyme *kō-en'zīm*, *n* a non-protein organic molecule (such as a vitamin) that bonds with a specific enzyme only while the biochemical reaction is being catalysed, being essential to, but unaffected by, the reaction. — **coenzyme A** see **acetylcoenzyme A**; **coenzyme Q** see **ubiquinone**.
coequal *kō-ē'kwəl*, *adj* equal with another of the same rank or dignity. — *n* one of the same rank. — *n* **cōequality** (*-i-kwol'*). — *adv* **coē'qually**.
coerce *kō-ûrs'*, *vt* to restrain by force; to compel. — *adj* **cōer'cible**. — *adv* **cōer'cibly**. — *n* **cōercim'eter** an instrument for measuring coercive force. — *n* **cōer'cion** restraint; government by force. — *n* **cōer'cionist**. — *adj* **cōer'cive** having power to coerce; compelling; tending to or intended to coerce. — *adv* **cōer'cively**. — *n* **cōer'civeness**. — *n* **coerciv'ity** the coercive force needed to demagnetize a material that is fully magnetized. — **coercive force** the reverse magnetizing force required to bring the magnetization of a ferromagnetic material to zero. [L *coercēre*, from *arcēre* to shut in]
coessential *kō-is-en'shəl* or *-es-*, *adj* being of the same essence or nature. — *n* **coessentiality** (*-shi-al'i-ti*).
coetaneous *kō-i-tā'ni-əs*, *adj* of the same age; coeval. [L *aetās*, *aetātis* age]
coeternal *kō-i-tûr'nəl* or *kō-ē-*, *adj* equally eternal; jointly eternal. — *adv* **coeter'nally**. — *n* **coeter'nity**.
coeval *kō-ē'vəl*, *adj* of the same age. — *n* a person or thing of the same age; a contemporary. [L *coaevus*, from *aevum* age]
coevolution *kō-ēv-ə-loo'shən*, *n* the process of adaptation in which the evolution of two (or more) organisms is dependent on, or is a response to, the interactions between them.
coexist *kō-igz-ist'* or *-egz-*, *vi* to exist at the same time or together. — *n* **coexist'ence**. — *adj* **coexist'ent**. — **peaceful coexistence** the condition of living side by side in mutual toleration.
coextend *kō-iks-tend'* or *-eks-*, *vi* to extend equally in space or time. — *n* **coexten'sion**. — *adj* **coexten'sive**.
C of A *abbrev*: Certificate of Airworthiness.
cofactor *kō-fak'tər*, *n* a factor which occurs along with other factors in multiplication; a nonprotein organic molecule or a metallic ion that binds with an enzyme and is essential to the enzyme's reaction (*biol*).
C of C *abbrev*: Chamber of Commerce.
C of E *abbrev*: Church of England; Council of Europe.
coff *kof*, (*Scot*) *vt* to buy: — *pa t* and *pa p* **coffed** or **coft**. [From pa p of **cope**[2]]
coffee *kof'i*, *n* a powder made by roasting and grinding the seeds of a tree (*Coffea arabica*, *robusta*, etc) of the madder family; a drink made from the powder. — **coffee bag** a small porous bag containing ground coffee beans, used to make coffee; **coffee bar** or **shop** a small restaurant where coffee, tea, cakes, etc are served; **coffee bean** the seed of the coffee tree; **coffee break** a short break for coffee during the working day; **coffee bug** an insect (*Lecania coffeae*) destructive to the coffee

tree; **coffee cup** a cup for coffee, *usu* smaller than a teacup; **coffee disease** a disease affecting the leaves of the coffee tree, caused by a rust fungus (*Hemileia vastatrix*); **coffee essence** concentrated liquid coffee extract; **coffee grounds** the sediment left after coffee has been infused; **coffee house** an establishment where coffee and other refreshments are sold; **coff'ee-housing** gossiping while a covert is drawn (*hunting*); talking during a game, *esp* in order to distract or mislead players (*cards*); **coffee klatsch** (*US*) a coffee party; **coff'ee-maker**; **coffee mill** a machine for grinding coffee beans; **coffee morning** a morning social gathering at which coffee is drunk; **coffee pot** a pot in which coffee is prepared and served; **coffee room** a room in a hotel where coffee and other refreshments are served; a public room; **coffee service** or **set** a set of utensils for serving and drinking coffee; **coffee shop** see **coffee bar**; **coffee stall** a movable street stall selling coffee and other refreshments; **coffee table** a small low table; **coffee tree**; **coffee whitener** whitener (qv) for coffee. — **coffee-table book** (*orig facetious*, sometimes *derog*) a large, expensive and profusely illustrated book of the kind one would set out on a coffee table for visitors to admire; **white** (or **black**) **coffee** coffee with (or without) **milk**. [Turk *kahveh*, from *Ar qahwah* orig meaning wine]

coffer *kof'ər*, *n* a chest for holding money or treasure; an ornamental deep panel in a ceiling; a cofferdam. — *vt* to hoard or store; to ornament with coffers. — *adj* **coff'ered**. — **coff'erdam** a watertight structure that is pumped dry, allowing underwater foundations, etc to be built; **coff'er-fish** any fish of the genus *Ostracion* that has a box-like bony covering enveloping its entire body. — Also called **box'-fish**, **trunkfish**. [OFr *cofre* a chest, from L *cophinus* a basket, from Gr *kophinos* a basket]

coffin *kof'in*, *n* a box for a dead body; a thick-walled container, *usu* of lead, for transporting radioactive materials, a flask; the horny part of a horse's hoof. — *vt* to place in a coffin. — **coffin bone** a bone enclosed in a horse's hoof; **coffin nail** (*slang*) a cigarette; **coffin ship** a dangerously unsound ship. — **drive a nail in one's coffin** to do something tending to hasten death or ruin. [OFr *cofin*, from L *cophinus*, from Gr *kophinos* a basket]

C of I *abbrev*: Church of Ireland.

coffinite *kof'in-īt*, *n* a uranium-yielding ore. [From R C *Coffin*, a worker of the ore in Colorado]

coffle *kof'l*, *n* a gang, *esp* of slaves tied together. [Ar *qāfilah* a caravan]

coffret *kof'rət*, *n* a small coffer; a small presentation box. [Fr, dimin of *coffre* coffer]

C of S *abbrev*: Chief of Staff; Church of Scotland.

coft *koft*, (*Scot*) *pa t* and *pa p* of **coff**.

cog[1] *kog*, *vt* to cheat or deceive; to wheedle; to manipulate (dice) so that they may fall in a given way. — *n* the act of cheating; deception. — *n* **cogg'er**. [Thieves' slang]

cog[2] *kog*, *n* a projection, eg on a toothed wheel; a cogwheel; an unimportant person in a large organization. — *vt* to furnish with cogs; to stop (a wheel) by putting a block before it: — *pr p* **cogg'ing**; *pa t* and *pa p* **cogged**. — **cog'wheel** a toothed wheel. [ME *cogge*; ety uncertain; cf Swed *kugge*]

cog[3] *kog*, (*building*) *n* a tenon used in cogging. — *vt* to join by means of cogs. — *n* **cogg'ing** a type of joint used to join two wooden beams, where the upper beam is bearing on the lower by cutting a tenon in the lower beam and a corresponding notch in the upper. [Poss **cog**[2]]

cog[4] *kog*, *n* formerly, a large merchant ship or warship; a small boat; a cockboat. [ME *cogge*, perh from OFr *cogue* a ship, or ON *kuggr* a merchant ship]

cog[5]. See **coggie**.

cog[6]. See **cogue**.

cog. *abbrev*: cognate.

COGB *abbrev*: Certified Official Government Business.

COGENE *kō'jēn*, *abbrev*: Committee on Genetic Experimentation (of the International Council of Scientific Unions).

cogener *kō'ji-nər*, *n* a variant of **congener**.

cogent *kō'jənt*, *adj* powerful; convincing. — *n* **cō'gence** or **cō'gency** convincing power. — *adv* **cō'gently**. [L *cōgēns*, *-entis*, pr p of *cōgere*, from *coagere* to drive]

coggie or **cogie** *kog'i* or *kōg'i*, (*Scot*) *n* a small wooden bowl. — Also **cog**. [Dimin of **cogue**]

coggle *kog'l*, *vi* to be unsteady, to wobble. — *n* a cobblestone. — *adv* **cogg'ly** (*Scot*) shaky. [Origin uncertain]

cogitate *koj'i-tāt*, *vi* to turn a thing over in one's mind; to meditate; to ponder. — *adj* **cog'itable** capable of being thought, conceivable. — *n* **cogitā'tion** deep thought; meditation. — *adj* **cog'itātive** having the power of thinking; given to cogitating. [L *cōgitāre*, *-ātum* to think deeply, from *co-*, and *agitāre* to put in motion]

cogito, ergo sum *cō'gi-tō er'gō sŏŏm*, (*L*) I think, therefore I am (the basic tenet of Descartes' philosophy).

Cognac *kon'yak*, *n* a French brandy made near *Cognac*, in Charente.

cognate *kog'nāt*, *adj* of the same family, kind or nature; derived from the same ancestor, root or other original; related or allied. — *n* someone related by blood (whether agnate or not) (*Roman law* and *generally*); often, any relative on either side other than an agnate; a relative on one's mother's side (*Scots law*). — *n* **cog'nateness**. — *n* **cognā'tion**. — **cognate object** a noun related in origin or meaning to a normally intransitive verb, and used as its object, as in *sing* a *song*. — **cognatic succession** succession to the throne by the eldest child, irrespective of sex. [L *cognātus*, from *co-*, and (*g*)*nāscī* to be born]

cognition *kog-nish'ən*, *n* the act or process of knowing, in the widest sense, including sensation, perception, etc, distinguished from emotion and conation; the knowledge resulting or acquired. — *adj* **cognit'ional**. — *adj* **cog'nitive** capable of, or pertaining to, cognition. — *adv* **cog'nitively**. — *n* **cognitiv'ity**. — *adj* **cognizable** or **-s-** (*kog'niz-ə-bl*; also *kon'iz-*) that may be known or understood; that may be judicially investigated. — *adv* **cog'nizably** or **-s-**. — *n* **cog'nizance** or **-s-** (or *kon'iz-*) knowledge or notice, judicial or private; observation; jurisdiction; that by which one is known, a badge. — *adj* **cog'nizant** or **-s-** (or *kon'iz-*) having cognizance or knowledge of. — *vt* **cognize'** or **-ise'** to become conscious of. — **cognitive dissonance** (*psychol*) the mental conflict resulting from incompatible cognitions; **cognitive enhancer** (*med*) another term for **smart drug**; **cognitive science** the study or science of cognition including aspects of psychology, philosophy, linguistics, semantics and artificial intelligence; **cognitive therapy** (*psychol*) a method of psythotherapy in which the patient is encouraged to replace negative attitudes with positive ones, most often applied in the treatment of depression (also **cognitive-behavioural therapy**). — **take cognizance of** to recognize, take into consideration. [L *cognitiō*, *-ōnis*, from *cognōscere*, *cognitum*, from *co-*, and (*g*)*nōscere* to know]

cognomen *kog-nō'mən*, *n orig* the last of the three names of an ancient Roman indicating the house or family to which he belonged; a surname; an epithet or nickname: — *pl* **cognō'mens** or **cognō'mina**. — *adj* **cognominal** (*-nom'*) like-named; relating to a cognomen. — *vt* **cognom'inate** to name. — *n* **cognominā'tion**. [L *cognōmen*, *-inis*, from *co-*, and (*g*)*nōmen* a name]

cognosce *kog-nos'*, (*Scots law*) *vt* to examine; to give judgement upon; to declare to be an idiot. — *adj* **cognosc'ible**. [L *cognōscere*, from *co-*, intens, and (*g*)*nōscere*, to know]

cognoscente *ko-nyō-shent'ā*, *n* a person professing an expert knowledge, *esp* of works of art, music, literature, etc; a connoisseur: — *pl* **cognoscent'i** (*-ē*). [Ital (modal *conoscente*), from L *cognōscere* to know]

cognovit *kog-nō'vit*, (*law*) *n* an acknowledgement by a defendant that the plaintiff's cause is just. [L *cognōvit actiōnem* (he) has acknowledged the action]

cogue or **cog** *kōg* or *kog*, (*esp Scot*) *n* a round wooden vessel, *usu* of staves and hoops. [Ety uncertain]

cohabit *kō-hab'it*, *vi* to dwell together as husband and wife, or as if husband and wife. — *n* **cohab'itant** someone living with another or others. — *n* **cohabitā'tion** living together; government by a head of state and a ruling party of opposing views. — *n* **cohabitee'** or **cohab'itor** (*colloq* short form **co'hab**). [L *cohabitāre*, from *co-*, and *habitāre* to dwell]

coheir *kō-ār'*, *n* a joint heir: — *fem* **coheir'ess**. — *n* **coheritor** (*kō-her'it-ər*) a coheir.

cohere *kō-hēr'*, *vi* to stick together; to be consistent. — *vt* to fit together in a consistent, orderly whole. — *n* **cohē'rence** or **cohē'rency** a tendency to cohere; a sticking together; consistency. — *adj* **cohēr'ent** sticking together; connected; consistent or orderly in thought or speech; (of a system of units) such that one unit multiplied or divided by another gives a third unit in the system exactly; (of a beam of radiation) showing definite, not random, relationships between points in a cross-section. — *adv* **cohēr'ently**. — *n* **cohēr'er** formerly, an apparatus for detection of electric waves by reduced resistance of imperfect contact, as if by cohesion. — *n* **cohēsibil'ity**. — *adj* **cohēsible** (*-hēz'*) capable of cohesion. — *n* **cohē'sion** (*-zhən*) the act of sticking together; a form of attraction by which particles of bodies stick together; concrescence of like parts (*bot*); logical connection. — *adj* **cohē'sive** (*-siv* or *-ziv*) having the power of cohering; tending to unite into a mass. — *adv* **cohe'sively**. — *n* **cohe'siveness**. [L *cohaerēre*, *-haesum*, from *co-*, and *haerēre* stick]

coheritor. See **coheir**.

cohibit *kō-hib'it*, (*rare*) *vt* to restrain. — *n* **cohibition** (*-ish'ən*). — *adj* **cohib'itive**. [L *cohibēre*, from *co-*, and *habēre* to have, hold]

coho or **cohoe** *kō'hō*, *n* a Pacific salmon, a species of *Oncorhynchus*: — *pl* **co'hos** or **co'hoes**. [Ety unknown]

cohobate *kō'hō-bāt*, (*chem*) *vt* to redistil (a liquid distillate), *esp* by pouring again and again over the matter from which it is distilled. [New L *cohobāre*]

cohog. Same as **quahog**.

cohorn. See **coehorn**.

cohort *kō'hört*, *n* a tenth part of a Roman legion; any band of warriors; formerly, a division of plants between a class and an order or, according to some, between a suborder and a family; in the classification of higher animals, one of the divisions between subclass and order; a group of individuals; a group with a shared characteristic, *esp* being the same age (*statistics*); (*popularly*) a companion or follower. [L *cohors*, *-tis* an enclosed place, a multitude enclosed, a company of soldiers]

cohortative *kō-hör'tə-tiv*, *adj* (*archaic*) encouraging. — *n* (*Heb gram*) lengthened form of the imperfect. [L *cohortārī*, *-ātus*, from *co-*, intensive, and *hortārī* to exhort]

co-host *kō'hōst*, *vt* to act as joint host to or of. — Also *n*.

COHSE *kō'zi*, *abbrev*: Confederation of Health Service Employees.

cohune *kō-hōōn'*, *n* a C and S American palm (*Attalea cohune*) yielding **cohune nuts** and **cohune oil**. [From Am Sp]

cohyponym *kō-hī'pō-nim*, *n* a word which is one of two or more hyponyms of another word.

COI *abbrev*: Central Office of Information.

coif *koif*, *n* a covering for the head, *esp* the close-fitting cap of white lawn or silk originally worn by serjeants-at-law; a covering for the head worn by women. — *vt* to provide with a coif; to dress (the hair). — *n* **coiffeur** (*kwä-fœr'*) a hairdresser: — *fem* **coiffeuse** (*-øz'*). — *n* **coiffure** (*kwä-fūr'*) a style of hairdressing; a headdress. — Also *vt*. [Fr *coiffe*, from LL *cofia* a cap]

coign or **coigne** *koin*, *n* variant spellings of **quoin** or **coin**. — **coign of vantage** an advantageous position.

coil[1] *koil*, *vt* to wind in rings; to enclose in twists. — *vi* to wind. — *n* a coiled object; one of the rings into which anything is coiled; a wire wound spirally to conduct electricity; a contraceptive device consisting of a metal or plastic coil fitted in the uterus. [OFr *coillir* (Fr *cueillir*), from L *colligere*, from *col-* together, and *legere* to gather; cf **cull and collect**]

coil[2] *koil*, (*archaic*) *n* tumult; hubbub; noise; fuss. — **mortal coil** (*Hamlet* III. 1. 68) the toil and trouble of human life. [Origin unknown]

coin *koin*, *n* a piece of metal legally stamped and current as money; money; a cornerstone or quoin (*archaic*). — *vt* to convert into money; to stamp; to invent, fabricate (*esp* a new word); to gain money by means of (*archaic*). — *n* **coin'age** the act of coining money; the currency; the pieces of metal coined; the invention, or fabrication, of something new, *esp* a word or phrase; what is invented. — *n* **coin'er** a person who coins money; a maker of counterfeit coins; an inventor (of words, etc). — *n* **coin'ing** minting; invention. — **coin box** a telephone or other machine which one operates by putting coins in a slot. — *adj* **coin'-operated**, **coin'op-** or **coin-in-the-slot'** (of a machine) operated by inserting a coin in a slot. — **coin a phrase** to use a new phrase or expression (*usu ironic*, ie to repeat a cliché); **coin money** or **coin it** to make a lot of money rapidly; **pay someone in his** or **her own coin** to give tit for tat; to give as good as one got. [Fr *coin* a wedge (see **quoin**), also the die to stamp money, from L *cuneus* a wedge]

coincide *kō-in-sīd'*, *vi* to occupy the same place or time; to agree; to correspond; to be identical. — *n* **coincidence** (*kō-in'si-dəns*) fact, event, or condition of coinciding; the occurrence of events simultaneously or consecutively in a striking manner but without any causal connection between them. — *n* **coin'cidency**. — *adj* **coin'cident**. — *adj* **coincidental** (*-dent'l*). — *adv* **coincident'ally**. — *adv* **coin'cidently**. [L *co-*, and *incidere*, from *in* in, and *cadere* to fall]

coinhere *kō-in-hēr'*, *vi* to inhere together. — *n* **coinhēr'ence**.

coinheritor *kō-in-her'it-ər*, *n* a joint heir. — *n* **coinher'itance**.

coinstantaneous *kō-in-stən-tā'ni-əs*, *adj* exactly simultaneous. — *n* **co-instantaneity** (*-stan-tə-nē'i-ti*) or **co-instantā'neousness**. — *adv* **coinstantā'neously**.

coinsurance *kō'in-shōō'rəns*, *n* insurance jointly with another, *esp* when the owner of the property to be insured bears part of the risk.

Cointreau® *kwɛ̃-trō* or *kwän'*, *n* an orange-flavoured liqueur.

coir *koir*, *n* the strong fibre of coconut husk, used in making rope and matting; a growing medium for garden and pot plants made from this fibre. [From Tamil or Malayalam]

coistrel or **coistril** *kois'tril*, *n* a groom (*obs*); a knave (*Shakesp*). [See **custrel**]

coit or **quoit** *koit*, (*Austr slang*) *n* the buttocks, the backside.

coitus *kō'it-əs* or **coition** *kō-ish'ən*, *n* sexual intercourse. — *adj* **cō'ital**. — **coitus interruptus** coitus intentionally interrupted by withdrawal of the penis from the vagina before semen is ejaculated; **coitus reservatus** coitus in which ejaculation is avoided. [L *coitiō*, *-ōnis*, from *co-* together, and *īre*, *itum* to go]

cojoin *kō-join'*, (*Shakesp*) *vt*. Same as **conjoin**.

cojones *kō-hō'nāz*, (*slang*, chiefly *US*) *n pl* testicles, balls; courage, spirit. [Sp]

coke[1] *kōk*, *n* a form of fuel obtained by the heating of coal in confined space whereby its more volatile constituents are driven off; the residue when any substance (eg petrol) is carbonized. — *vt* and *vi* to make into, or become, coke. — *adj* **cō'ky** like coke. — **coking coal** bituminous coal good for coking. [Ety uncertain]

coke[2] *kōk*, *n* cocaine (*slang*); (®; with *cap*) Coca-Cola.

cokernut. See under **coco**[1].

cokes *kōks*, (*obs*) *n* a simpleton. [Ety uncertain]

COL *abbrev*: computer-orientated language.

Col. *abbrev*: Colonel; Colorado (US state); (the Letter to the) Colossians (*Bible*).

col *kol, n* a depression or pass in a mountain range, a defile (*geog*); a region between two anticyclones giving a similar figure when represented in contour (*meteorol*). [Fr, from L *collum* a neck]

col. *abbrev*: column.

col-. See **com-**.

cola or **kola** *kō'lə, n* (with *cap*) a genus of W African trees (*Cola acuminata, C. nitida*) producing nuts used in drugs and for flavouring soft drinks; a soft drink so flavoured. [African name]

colander or **cullender** *kol'ən-dər, kul', n* a perforated vessel used as a strainer in cookery. [L *cōlāre* to strain]

colatitude *kō-lat'i-tūd, n* the complement of the latitude. [**co(mplement)** and **latitude**]

Colbertine *kol'bər-tin, n* a kind of lace, so called from Jean Baptiste *Colbert* (1619–83), Minister of Finance to Louis XIV, a great patron of the arts.

colcannon *kol-kan'ən, n* an Irish dish, consisting of boiled cabbage and potatoes mashed with butter. [**cole**, cabbage, and Ir *ceannan* white-headed]

colchicum *kol'ki-kəm, n* any Liliaceous plant of the genus *Colchicum*, meadow saffron or autumn crocus; its dried corm and seeds, used as a source of colchicine: — *pl* **col'chicums** or **col'chica**. — *n* **col'chicine** (*-chi-* or *-ki-sēn*) an alkaloid obtained from meadow saffron and used in the treatment of gout and to inhibit chromosome separation thus inducing polyploidy. [L, from Gr *kolchikon* meadow saffron, neuter of *Kolchikos*, relating to *Kolchis*, the sorceress Medea's country]

colcothar *kol'kō-thär, n* a dark-red iron peroxide powder formed by calcining iron sulphate, used as a pigment and for polishing glass, etc. [Ar *qolqotār*]

cold *kōld, adj* giving or feeling a sensation that is felt to be the opposite of hot; chilly; low in temperature; without passion or zeal; spiritless; unfriendly; indifferent; reserved; (of colours) suggesting cold rather than heat, as blue or grey; without application of heat; used of operations formerly requiring heat, eg **cold'-cast'ing**, **-forg'ing**, **-mould'ing** and **-weld'ing**; (in marketing, politics, etc) involving contacting people thought to be potential customers or supporters, without the contact having been prearranged or primed, and with no knowledge of the people's likely reactions or opinions, as in **cold call**, **cold calling** or **cold canvassing**. — *n* a relative absence of heat; the feeling or sensation caused by the absence of heat; coldness; a spell of cold weather; a catarrhal inflammation of the mucous membrane of the respiratory organs, caused by a virus, usually accompanied by hoarseness and coughing; catarrh; chillness. — *adj* **cold'ish** somewhat cold. — *adv* **cold'ly**. — *n* **cold'ness**. — *n* and *adj* **cold'blood** (of) a horse belonging to the heavy draught breeds (cf *hotblood* and *warmblood*). — *adj* **cold'-blooded** having a body temperature that varies with the temperature of the environment, as in fishes; (of persons) sensitive to cold (*informal*); (**cold-blood'ed**) lacking in feeling; (of persons or actions) hard-hearted. — *adv* **cold-blood'-edly**. — **cold-blood'edness**; **cold cathode** (*elec*) an electrode from which electron emission results from high-potential gradient at the surface at normal temperatures; **cold chisel** a strong and finely-tempered chisel for cutting cold metal; a tool used with a heavy hammer to cut or break stone, concrete, etc; **cold comfort** see under **comfort**; **cold cream** a creamy ointment used to remove make-up or as a cooling or moisturizing dressing for the skin. — *vt* (*colloq*) to apply cold cream to. — **cold cuts** slices of cold cooked meat. — *adj* **cold'-drawn** (of metal, wire, etc) drawn through a die without heating; (of vegetable oil) subjected to pressure without heat. — **cold duck** a drink made from equal parts of champagne and burgundy; **cold feet** loss of nerve; cooling off of courage or ardour; **cold fish** a person who shows no emotion; **cold frame** a structure, *usu* of wood and glass and without artificial heat, for protecting young plants; **cold front** the surface of an advancing mass of cold air where it meets a retreating mass of warmer air; **cold fusion** nuclear fusion without prior heating, ie effected at normal room temperature; **cold harbour** a wayside travellers' shelter. — *adj* **cold-heart'ed** lacking feeling; indifferent. — *adv* **cold-heart'edly**. — **cold-heart'-edness**; **cold moulding** the moulding of articles using resins that polymerize chemically; **cold pack** a wet pack prepared with cold water, to counteract fever, inflammation, etc. — *adj* **cold'-rolled** (of metal) rolled without heating. — **cold rubber** a hard-wearing synthetic rubber made at a temperature of 5°C (41°F). — *adj* **cold'-short** brittle when cold; (of feelings) brittle, sensitive. — *vt* **cold-should'er** to give the cold shoulder to (see below). — **cold slaw** cole-slaw; **cold snap** a sudden short spell of cold weather; **cold sore** a blister or group of blisters on or near the mouth, caused by a viral infection (*herpes simplex*); **cold start** (*comput*) the reloading of a computer program; **cold steel** cutting or stabbing weapons, as opposed to bullets; **cold storage** storage and preservation of goods in refrigerating chambers; abeyance; **cold turkey** the plain unvarnished truth; sudden withdrawal of narcotics; the symptoms experienced by a drug user on such withdrawal (also *fig*); **cold war** an intense, remorseless struggle for the upper hand by all means short of actual fighting, *orig* and *esp* as between the Communist and non-Communist powers after World War II; **cold water** water at its natural temperature in ordinary conditions; **cold wave** (*hairdressing*) an artificial wave produced by a chemical solution. — *vt* **cold'-weld** to force together (two like or unlike metals) so that normal oxide surface films are ruptured and adhesion occurs. — **cold welding**. — *vt* **cold'-work** to shape (metals) at or near atmospheric temperature by rolling, pressing, etc (*n* **cold work**). — **catch cold** to contract a cold; to make an unexpected loss; **cold as charity** a proverbial phrase expressing ironically great coldness or indifference; **cold dark matter** in cosmology, a material thought to be detectable in the microwave background of the universe whose existence may disprove the Big Bang theory; **come in from the cold** to gain acceptance or recognition after a period of isolation or neglect; **give** or **show the cold shoulder** to show studied indifference; to give a rebuff; **go cold (on)** to lose enthusiasm for or interest in; to peter out or disappear; to fail to respond to; **in a cold sweat** (as if) sweating with fear; **in cold blood** with deliberate intent, not under the influence of passion; **leave one cold** to fail to impress; **leave out in the cold** to neglect, ignore; **pour** or **throw cold water on** to discourage; **turn down cold** to refuse absolutely and immediately, allowing no discussion. [OE (Anglian) *cald* (WSax *ceald*); Scot *cauld*, Ger *kalt*; cf **cool**, ON *kala* to freeze, L *gelidus*, from *gelū* frost]

cole *kōl, n* a general name for plants of the cabbage family. — **cole'seed** the seed of rape; rape; **cole'slaw** (*-slö*; Du *koolsla* for *kool salade* cole salad) a salad consisting mainly of shredded cabbage with a dressing; **cole'wort** cabbage, *esp* varieties with no heart. [OE *cawel*; Ger *Kohl*, Scot **kail**; all from L *cōlis*, *caulis* a stem, esp of cabbage]

colemanite *kōl'mən-īt*, (*mineralogy*) *n* hydrated calcium borate, crystallized in the monoclinic system, occurring as nodules in clay. [From W T *Coleman* (1824–93), American mine owner]

coleopteran or **coleopteron** *kol-i-op'tər-ən, n* any insect of the order *Coleoptera*, having hard or horny forewings which serve as wing-cases for the functional wings, the beetles. — *adj* **coleop'teral** or **coleop'terous**. — *n* **coleop'terist** a student of beetles. [Gr *koleos* a sheath, and *pteron* a wing]

coleoptile *kol-i-op'tīl, n* (*bot*) a protective sheath around the first leaves of cereals. [Gr *koleos* a sheath, and *ptilon* a feather]

coleorhiza *kol-i-ō-rī'zə*, (*bot*) *n* a protective layer on the radicle of some plants, eg grasses. [Gr *koleos* sheath, and *rhiza* root]

coleslaw. See under **cole**.
coletit, **coletitmouse** alternative spellings of **coaltit**, **coaltitmouse**.
coleus *kō'li-əs*, *n* any plant of the genus *Coleus* with variegated coloured leaves often used for indoor decoration: — *pl* **cō'leuses**. [Gr *koleos* a sheath]
colewort. See **cole**.
coley *kō'li*, *n* an edible fish of the cod family.
colibri *kol'ib-rē* or *-lē'*, *n* a type of humming-bird. [Sp *colibrí*, Fr *colibri*, said to be the Carib name]
colic *kol'ik*, *n* severe spasmodic pain in the abdomen without diarrhoea, due to an obstruction of the intestine, intestinal infection or excessive intestinal gas. — *adj* **col'icky** like, suffering from or causing colic. [**colon**[2]]
coliform[1] *kol'-i-förm*, *adj* like a sieve. [L *cōlium* a strainer]
coliform[2]. See under **colon**[2].
colin *kol'in*, *n* the Virginian quail. [Ety uncertain; perh Sp]
coliseum or **colosseum** *kol-ə-sē'əm*, *n* a large building or stadium, used as a place of entertainment, named after the Flavian amphitheatre in Rome. [Med L, from L *colossus* (see **colossus**), from the huge statute of Nero near which the Flavian amphitheatre was built]
colitis. See **colon**[2].
coll *kol*, (*obs*) *vt* to embrace, hug. — *n* **coll'ing** embracing. [Fr *col*, from L *collum* the neck]
coll. *abbrev*: colleague; collective; collector; college; colloquial.
collaborate *kəl-ab'ər-āt*, *vi* to work in association (with); to assist or cooperate (with an enemy, *esp* one occupying one's country). — *n* **collaborā'tion**. — *n* **collaborā'tionism** collaboration wth an enemy. — *n* **collaborā'tionist** — *adj* **collab'orative**. — *n* **collab'orātor**. [L *collabōrāre*, *-ātum*, from *labōrāre* to work]
collage *kol-äzh'*, *n* a picture made from scraps of paper and other odds and ends pasted up; any work or construction put together from assembled fragments. — *n* **collag'ist**. [Fr, pasting]
collagen *kol'ə-jen*, *n* a protein in fibrous connective tissue, readily turned into gelatin. — *n* **coll'agenase** one of a group of enzymes that break down collagen. — *adj* **collagen'ic** or **collag'enous**. [Gr *kolla* glue, and *gen-*, the root of *gignesthai* to become]
collapse *kəl-aps'*, *n* a falling away or breaking down; any sudden or complete breakdown or prostration. — *vi* to cave in; to close or fold up; to break down; to go to ruin; to lose heart. — *vt* to fold up or close. — *n* **collap'sar** (*astron*) a black hole. — *n* **collapsibil'ity** or **collapsabil'ity**. — *adj* **collaps'ible** or **collaps'able** (*esp* of furniture) capable of being folded or dismantled. [L *collāpsus*, from *col-* together, and *lābī*, *lāpsus* to slide or fall]
collar *kol'ər*, *n* something worn round the neck by a person, horse, dog, etc; the neck or (sometimes detachable) neckband of a garment; the part of an animal's skin or coat, or a bird's feathers, round the neck; a marking around an animal or bird's neck; a surrounding band; the junction of root and stem in a plant; a piece of meat rolled up and tied; a joint of bacon from the neck; an arrest (*slang*). — *vt* to seize by the collar; to put a collar on; to seize or arrest (*slang*). — *adj* **coll'ared** having, or ornamented with, a collar; rolled up and bound with a string, as a piece of meat having the bones removed; captured. — *n* **collarette'** a small collar for a garment. — **collar beam** a horizontal piece of timber connecting or bracing two opposite rafters, to prevent sagging; **collar bone** the clavicle, a bone connecting the shoulder blade and breastbone; **collar cell** a choanocyte; **collared dove** a dove (*Streptopelia decaocto*) of Europe and Asia, with light grey plumage marked with a narrow black stripe around the back of the neck; **collar stud** a stud for fastening a shirt collar; **coll'ar-work** hard work by a draught-horse pulling against the horse-collar; drudgery. — **have one's collar felt** (*slang*) to be arrested or apprehended by the police; **hot under the collar** in a state of agitation or anger. [OFr *colier*, from L *collāre*, from *collum* the neck]
coll' arco *kol är'kō*, (*music*) with the bow. [Ital]
collard *kol'ərd*, *n* cole wort. [**cole wort**]
collat. *abbrev*: collateral; collaterally.
collate *kol-āt'*, *vt* to bring together for comparison; to examine and compare, eg books, and *esp* old manuscripts; to place (sheets of a book or document) in order for binding or stapling, and to examine with respect to completeness and sequence of sheets, etc; to merge (two or more files, sets of records, etc); to place in or confer a benefice upon. — *adj* **collā'table**. — *n* **collā'tion** the act of collating; a bringing together for examination and comparison; the presentation of a clergyman to a benefice; a description of a book as collated; a light meal taken on fast days in monasteries; any light meal. — *adj* **collā'tive** having the power of conferring; of livings where the bishop and patron are one and the same person. — *n* **collā'tor** a person who collates or compares; a person who bestows or presents; a machine which merges sets of punched cards or separates cards from a set; a machine which puts copied or printed sheets into sequential sets. [L *collātum*, used as supine of *conferre*, from pfx *col-*, and *lātum* (from *ferre* to bring)]
collateral *kol-at'ər-l*, *adj* side by side; running parallel or together; corresponding; descended from the same ancestor, through a different line. — *n* a collateral relation; a contemporary; a rival; collateral security. — *adv* **collat'erally**. — **collateral damage** (*military euphem*) civilian casualties or damage to property, etc that was not a military target; **collateral security** an additional and separate security for repayment of money borrowed. [L *col-*, and *latus*, *lateris* a side]
colleague[1] *kol'ēg*, *n* a person associated with another in some employment. — *n* **coll'eagueship**. [Fr *collègue*, from L *collēga*, from col and *legere* to choose]
colleague[2] *kol-ēg'*, (*obs*) *vi* to ally; to conspire: — *pr p* **colleaguing** (*kol-ēg'ing*); *pa t* and *pa p* **colleagued** (*kol-ēgd'*). [OFr *colliguer* to join in alliance, from L *colligāre* to bind together]
collect *kəl-* or *kol-ekt'*, *vt* to assemble or bring together; to put (one's thoughts) in order; to receive payment of; to call for and remove. — *vi* to come together; to accumulate. — *n* **collect** (*kol'*) a short prayer, specific to the liturgies of the Western Church, consisting of one sentence, conveying one main petition. — *adj* and *adv* (*-ekt'*; *NAm*; of a telephone call, telegram, etc) paid for by the recipient. — *adj* **collect'able** or **collect'ible** of interest to a collector. — *n* any item of interest to a collector; one of a set of toys or ornaments each purchasable separately but priced and marketed in such a way as to encourage the purchase of all or much of the range. — *n pl* **collectā'nea** a collection of passages from various sources; a miscellany. — *adj* **collect'ed** gathered together; (of a poet's or other writer's works) assembled in one volume, one set of volumes, etc; composed, cool. — *adv* **collect'edly**. — *n* **collect'edness** self-possession; coolness. — *n* and *adj* **collect'ing**. — *n* **collec'tion** the act of collecting; the gathering of contributions, *esp* of money; the money collected; money intended for collection in church; an accumulation; an assemblage; a book of selections; a regular removal of rubbish for disposal, or letters from a postbox for delivering; composure; (in *pl*) an examination at the end of the terms in certain colleges; the range of new fashion clothes shown by a couturier. — *adj* **collect'ive** considered as forming one mass or sum; congregated; common; denoting a number or group (of people, animals, etc) (*gram*). — *n* a gathering, assemblage; a unit of organization in a collectivist system; loosely, a group of people who run a business, etc, for their mutual benefit, often with no specifically designated jobs. — *adv* **collect'ively**. — *n* **collect'ivism** the economic theory that industry should be carried on with a collective capital, a form of socialism; a system embodying this. — *n* and *adj* **collect'ivist**. — *n*

collectiv'ity. — *vt* **collect'ivize** or **-ise** to give a collectivist organization to. — *n* **collect'or** something which or someone who collects; a person who seeks to acquire and set together examples or specimens, as of books, minerals, curiosities; any electrode that collects electrons that have already fulfilled their function, as in a screen grid; the outer section of a transistor which delivers a primary flow of charge carriers; in India, the chief official of a district, collecting revenue and acting as a magistrate. — *n* **collect'orate** or **collect'orship**. — **collect'ing-box** a box for specimens used by naturalists in the field; a box for receiving money contributions; **collective agreement** one reached by collective bargaining; **collective bargaining** negotiation on pay and conditions of service between one or more trade unions on one side and an employer or association of employers on the other; **collective farm** a state-controlled farm consisting of a number of small-holdings operated on a cooperative basis; **collective fruit** (*bot*) a multiple fruit, one derived from several flowers, eg fig, mulberry; **collective noun** a singular noun referring to a group of persons or things; **collective responsibility** the convention that all decisions of a cabinet, committee, etc are presented and treated as being unanimous; **collective security** general security among nations to be achieved through guarantee of each nation's security by all; **collective unconscious** (*psychol*) the part of the unconscious mind that originates in ancestral experience; **collector's item** or **piece** an object beautiful, valuable, interesting, etc enough to be sought for or included in a collection. — **collect on delivery** (*NAm*) cash on delivery. [L *colligere*, *collēctum*, from *legere* to gather]

colleen *kol'ēn* or *kol-ēn'*, *n* a girl, *specif* an Irish girl. [Irish *cailín*]

college *kol'ij*, *n* an incorporation, company or society of persons joined together generally for a specific function, often having exclusive privileges; a body or society that is a member of a university or is coextensive with a university; an institution for higher, professional or vocational education; a literary, political or religious institution; the premises housing a college; a prison (*slang*). — *n* **coll'eger** a member of a college; one of the foundationers at Eton College. — *adj* **collegial** (*kə-lē'ji-əl*) pertaining to a college or university, or to a collegium. — *n* **collē'gialism** the theory that the church is a self-governing body independent of the state. — *n* **collegial'ity** sharing by bishops in papal decision-making (*RC*); the process of making decisions, agreeing on actions, etc, shared by all the bishops of a church. — *n* **collē'gian** a member or inhabitant of a college; a student; an inmate of a prison (*obs slang*). — *n* **collē'gianer** a member of a college, a student. — *adj* **collē'giate** pertaining to or resembling a college; (of a town, etc) containing a college; instituted like a college; corporate. — *n* (*obs slang*) an inmate of a prison, etc. — **college pudding** a kind of steamed pudding containing dried fruit; **collegiate church** or **collegial church** a church having a college or chapter, consisting of a dean or provost and canons, attached to it; in Scotland, a church occupied by two or more pastors of equal rank (also **collegiate charge** (*hist*)). — **College of Arms** a collegiate body incorporated in 1483, presided over by the Earl Marshal, and including Garter, principal King-of-arms, Clarenceux and Norroy, besides six heralds and four pursuivants; **college of cardinals** (*RC*) the whole body of cardinals, electors of and advisors to the pope; **college of education** a college for training teachers; **College of Justice** in Scotland, the Court of Session, composed of judges, advocates, writers to the signet, and solicitors. [Fr *collège*, from L *collēgium*, from *col-*, and *legere* to gather]

collegium *ko-lēj'i-əm*, *n* college of cardinals; an administrative board, eg of a government department in the former USSR: — *pl* **collē'gia** or **collē'giums**. — **collegium musicum** (*ko-lēj'i-əm mū'si-kəm* or *ko-lāg'i-ŏŏm mōō'si-kŏŏm*) a group of amateur musicians, often connected with a university. [L *collēgium*; see **college**]

col legno *kol len'yō* or *kō lān'yō*, (*music*) an instruction to string players to use the wood of the bow. [Ital, with the wood]

collembolan *kol-em'bō-lən*, *n* a member of the order *Collembola* of wingless insects (the springtails) whose abdomen has no more than six segments and typically having a springing organ (a furcula). [Gr *kolla* glue, and *embolos* a peg]

collenchyma *kol-eng'ki-mə*, (*bot*) *n* a type of plant tissue having thickened cellulose walls (particularly at the angles of the cell walls) acting to strengthen and support, *esp* in leaves and young stems. — *adj* **collenchym'atous**. [Gr *kolla* glue, *en* in, and *chyma* that which is poured]

Colles' fracture *kol'is frak'chər*, *n* a fracture of the radius near the wrist, with backward displacement of the hand. [Abraham *Colles* (1773–1843) Irish surgeon]

collet *kol'it*, *n* a circular flange or collar; the collar of a plant; the part of a ring or other piece of jewellery which contains the stone. — **collet chuck** a device having a circular flange or collar for holding work or a tool on a lathe. [Fr, from L *collum*]

colliculus *ke-lik'ū-ləs*, (*zool*) *n* a small prominence, as on the surface of the optic lobe of the brain. [New L]

collide *kə-līd'*, *vi* to dash together; to clash. — *vt* to cause to collide. — *n* **collī'der** (in particle physics) a type of accelerator which causes subatomic particles to collide or be smashed together using electromagnets. — *n* **collision** (*-lizh'n*) the state of being struck together; a violent impact, a crash; conflict; opposition; clashing. — **collision course** a course which, if persisted in, will result in a collision (*lit* and *fig*). — **elastic collision** a collision in which both kinetic energy and momentum are conserved (*phys*); a collision in which the bombarding particle does not excite or break up the struck nucleus, and is simply scattered, the process being termed **elastic scattering** (*nuclear*); **inelastic collision** a collision in which momentum, but not kinetic energy, is conserved (*phys*); a collision in which there is a change in the total energies of the particles involved, the resultant scattering being termed **inelastic scattering** (*nuclear*). [L *collīdere*, *collīsum*, from *col-*, and *laedere* to strike]

collie or **colly** *kol'i*, *n* a long-haired, intelligent breed of sheepdog, originating in Scotland. [Origin uncertain]

collier *kol'yər*, *n* a coalminer; a ship that carries coal; a sailor in such a ship; a charcoal-burner or dealer in charcoal or coal (*obs*). — *n* **coll'iery** a coalmine. [**coal**]

collieshangie *kol-i-shang'i*, (*Scot*) *n* a noisy wrangling; an uproar; a disturbance. [Origin unknown]

colligate *kol'i-gāt*, *vt* to bind together. — *n* **colligā'tion** conjunction; bringing together under a general principle or conception. — *adj* **coll'igative** (*physical chem*) depending on the concentration, not the nature, of the atoms and molecules in a substance. [L *colligāre*, *-ātum*, from *col-*, and *ligāre* to bind]

collimate *kol'i-māt*, *vt* to make parallel; to adjust accurately the line of sight of (an optical instrument, such as a surveying telescope). — *n* **collimā'tion**. — *n* **coll'imātor** a device for obtaining a beam of parallel rays of light or other radiation, or one for obtaining a beam of particles moving in parallel paths; a subsidiary telescope for collimating other instruments. [*collīmāre*, a wrong reading for L *collīneāre* to bring into line with, from *col-* together, and *līnea* a line]

collinear *ko-lin'i-ər*, *adj* in the same straight line. — *n* **collinear'ity**.

Collins *kol'inz*, *n* a cocktail made with a spirit, lemon or lime juice, sugar and soda water (also without *cap*, eg **vodka collins**, **whiskey collins**). — **Tom Collins** or **John collins** this drink made with gin.

colliquate *kol'i-kwāt*, *vt* (*obs*) to melt; to fuse. — *adj* **colliq'uable** or **colliq'uant** (*obs*) melting, wasting. — *n* **colliquā'tion** the process of melting or wasting away. — *adj* **colliq'uative** profuse in flow; wasting. — *n*

colliquesc'ence readiness to liquefy. [L *col-* together, and *liquāre, -ātum* to cause to melt]
collision. See **collide**.
collocate *kol'ō-kāt, vt* to place together; to set; to arrange. — *n* **collocā'tion** the placing of something together with something else; the habitual placing together of one specific word with one or more other specific words (*linguistics*); the group of words so formed (*linguistics*). [L *collocāre, -ātum*, from *col-*, and *locāre* to place]
collocutor, collocutory. See under **colloquy**.
collodion *kol-ō'di-ən, n* a gluey solution of nitrated cotton (or cellulose nitrates) in alcohol and ether, used in surgery and photography. [Gr *kollōdēs*, from *kolla* glue, and *eidos* form, appearance]
collogue *kə-lōg', vi* to converse confidentially; to conspire or intrigue (*usu* with *with*). — *vt* to coax, flatter (*obs*). [Prob from L *colloquī* to speak together]
colloid *kol'oid, n* a substance in a state in which, though apparently dissolved, it cannot pass through a membrane; a substance that readily assumes this state; a colloidal system. — *adj* **colloid'al**. — **colloidal system** a dispersed substance plus the material in which it is dispersed. [Gr *kolla* glue, and *eidos* form]
collop *kol'əp*, (*dialect*) *n* a slice of meat; any small thing or piece of something. — **Collop Monday** the day before Shrove Tuesday, when collops-and-eggs were eaten. — **minced collops** (*Scot*) minced meat. [Origin obscure]
colloq. *abbrev*: colloquial; colloquially.
colloquy *kol'ə-kwi, n* a speaking together; mutual discourse; conversation. — *vi* (*rare*) to converse. — *n* **collocutor** (*kol-ok'ū-tər*). — *adj* **colloc'ūtory**. — *vi* **colloque** (*kol-ōk'*) to hold colloquy. — *adj* **colloquial** (*kə-lō'kwi-əl*) pertaining to or used in common conversation. — *n* **collō'quialism** a form of expression used in familiar talk. — *n* **collō'quialist**. — *adv* **collō'quially**. — *n* **coll'oquist** a speaker in a colloquy. — *n* **collō'quium** a conference; a meeting for discussion; a seminar: — *pl* **collō'quia** or **collō'quiums**. — *vi* **coll'oquize** or **-ise** to converse. [L *colloquium*, from *col-*, and *loquī* to speak]
collotype *kol'ō-tīp, n* a printing process using a hardened gelatine plate, used in book illustration and advertising; a print produced by this process. — *adj* **collotypic**. [Gr *kolla* glue, and **type**]
colluctation *kol-uk-tā'shən*, (*archaic*) *n* strife; opposition. [L *colluctārī*, from *col-*, and *luctāri* to wrestle]
collude *kol-ūd'* or *-ōōd', vi* to conspire, *esp* in a fraud. — *n* **collud'er**. — *n* **collu'sion** the act of colluding; a secret agreement to deceive, eg one made between the opposing parties in a lawsuit; conspiracy. — *adj* **collu'sive** pertaining to a collusion; conspiratorial. — *adv* **collu'sively**. [L *collūdere, collūsum*, from *col-*, and *lūdere* to play]
colluvies *ko-lū'* or *ko-lōō'vi-ēz, n* accumulated filth, a foul discharge; a rabble. [L *colluviēs* washings, from *colluere* to wash thoroughly]
colly[1] *kol'i, vt* (*archaic*) to begrime or darken, as with coal dust. — *n* soot, smut (*archaic* or *dialect*); (also **colly bird**) a blackbird (*dialect*). [See **coal**]
colly[2]. See **collie**.
collyrium *ko-lir'i-əm, n* eye lotion or ointment: — *pl* **collyr'ia** or **collyr'iums**. [Latinized from Gr *kollȳrion* eye-salve, dimin of *kollȳrā* a roll of bread]
collywobbles *kol'i-wob-lz*, (*facetious*) *n* abdominal pain or disorder; nervous stomach, or a state of apprehensiveness generally. [Prob **colic** and **wabble, wobble**]
Colmar *kol'mär, n* a kind of fan fashionable in Queen Anne's time; a kind of pear. [Perh *Colmar* in Alsace]
Colo. *abbrev*: Colorado (US state).
coloboma *kol-o-bō'mə*, (*med*) *n* a congenital defect of the eye affecting the development of the lens, iris or retina. [New L, from Gr *kolobos* cut short]
colobus *kol'ō-bəs, n* any arboreal African monkey of the genus *Colobus*, with black (or black and white) fur forming a crest down its back, a long tail and vestigial or absent thumbs: — *pl* **col'obi** (*-bī* or *-bē*) or **col'obuses**. — *adj* **col'obid**. [Gr *kolobos* maimed]
Colocasia *kol-ō-kā'zi-ə* or *-si-ə*, (*bot*) *n* a genus of plants of the arum family including the taro (*C. esculenta*) grown for its edible tubers, and several varieties grown for their decorative foliage. [Gr *kolokāsiā* waterlily root]
colocynth *kol'o-sinth, n* a cucurbitaceous plant of Europe and Asia, bearing bitter-tasting gourd-like fruits (*Citrullus colocynthis*); a purgative obtained from its dried fruit. [Gr *kolokynthis*]
cologarithm *kōlog'ə-ridhm* or *-rithm*, (math) *n* the logarithm of the reciprocal of a number (*abbrev* **colog**).
cologne *kə-lōn', n* a perfumed mixture of alcohol and essential oils, first made at Cologne in 1709 by Johann Farina. — Also called **Cologne water** or **eau de Cologne**.
colon[1] *kō'lən, n* the punctuation mark (:), used to indicate a distinct clause of a sentence, or to introduce a list, spoken or reported words, etc, or (in figures) to indicate ratio. [Gr *kōlon* a limb, member]
colon[2] *kō'lən, n* the large intestine from the caecum to the rectum; in insects, the wide posterior part of the hindgut. — *n* **colec'tomy** (*kə-*) surgical removal of all or part of the colon. — *n* **coliform** (*kol'i-förm*) the coliform bacillus. — *n* **colitis** (*kō-* or *ko-lī'tis*) or **colon'itis** inflammation of the colon. — *adj* **colon'ic** of the colon. — *n* a colonic irrigation. — *n* **colonos'copy** examination of the inside of the colon using a **colon'oscope**, a flexible viewing instrument passed into the colon through the anus. — *adj* **colorec'tal** pertaining to the colon and rectum. — *n* **colos'tomy** (*kə-*) a surgical procedure in which part of the colon is brought through an incision in the abdomen to form an artificial anus. — *n* **colot'omy** (*kə-*) cutting of or incision into the colon. — **coliform bacillus** or **colon bacillus** any of several bacilli living in the intestines of man and some animals; **colonic irrigation** (*med*) the injection of large amounts of water or other liquid into the colon in order to clean it out. [Gr *kolon* the large intestine]
colon[3] *kō-lōn', n* the monetary unit of El Salvador and Costa Rica: — *pl* **cō'lōns** or **colon'es**. [From Columbus (Sp *Colón*)]
colon[4] *kə-lon'* or Fr *ko-lɔ̃, n* a colonist, *esp* a colonial farmer, in Algeria. [Fr, see **colony**]
colonel *kûr'nəl, n* a senior army officer ranking between a lieutenant-colonel and a brigadier (US brigadier-general); in US, an officer of equivalent rank in the marines or the air force; in some regiments, an honorary rank given *usu* to a distinguished former member of the regiment; in US, an honorary title sometimes given to a person not connected with the armed forces; (loosely) a form of address to a lieutenant-colonel. — *n* **col'onelcy** (*-si*) the office or rank of colonel. — *n* **col'onelling** (*archaic*) (or *kor-ō-nel'ing*) playing the colonel. — *n* **col'onelship** colonelcy; the quality of being a colonel. — **Colonel Blimp** see **blimp**; **colonel-comm'andant** the commander of a brigade (sometimes given as an honorary rank); **colonel-in-chief'** an honorary colonel, in Britain generally a member of the Royal Family. [Older Fr and Sp *coronel*, from Ital *colonello*, the leader of a *colonna*, or column, from L *columna*; spelling assimilated to Mod Fr]
colonial, etc. See **colony**.
colonic. See **colon**[2].
colonnade *kol-ən-ād', n* a range of columns placed at regular intervals and *usu* supporting an entablature; a similar row, as of trees. — *adj* **colonnād'ed**. [Fr, from L *columna*]
colony *kol'ən-i, n* a name vaguely applied to a state's dependencies overseas or abroad (distinguished from a *dominion*); a military settlement planted in subject territory (*Roman hist*); a band of emigrants or their new home, connected with but without political ties to their city of origin (*ancient Gr hist*); a body of persons settled in a foreign country, or forming a separate ethnic, cultural or occupational group; the settlement so formed; the place they inhabit; a number of organisms, *esp* of one kind, living together as a community (*biol*); a coenobium; a group or company of Beaver Scouts. — *adj* **colonial** (*kə-lō'ni-əl*) pertaining

to, of the nature of, or dating from the time when a territory was, a colony. — *n* an inhabitant, citizen or member of a colony, a colonist. — *n* **colō'nialism** a trait of colonial life or speech; the colonial system (see below); the policy or practice of obtaining, or maintaining hold over, colonies, *esp* with the purpose of exploiting them. — *adj* and *n* **colō'nialist**. — *adv* **colō'nially**. — *n* **col'onist** an inhabitant of a colony; a voter set up for election purposes (*US hist*); a weed of cultivated ground (*bot*). — *n* **colonīzā'tion** or **-s-** the act or practice of colonizing; state of being colonized. — *vt* **col'onize** or **-ise** to plant or establish a colony in; to form into a colony; (of plants, animals, etc) to spread into a new habitat. — *vi* to settle as colonists. — **colonial animals** organisms consisting of numerous individuals in bodily union; **colonial goose** (*old Austr* and *NZ*) a joint of mutton, boned, stuffed and roasted; **Colonial Office** (*hist*) the government office dealing with the colonies; **colonial system** the theory that the settlements abroad should be treated as proprietary domains exploited for the benefit of the mother country. — **colonial experience man** (*old Austr*) a jackaroo; **colony stimulating factors** (*immunol*) substances which cause blood-forming stem cells to proliferate and differentiate into colonies of mature blood cells; **the Colonies** formerly, the subject territories of the British Empire; the thirteen states that formed the United States of America at the Declaration of Independence in 1776. [L *colōnia*, from *colōnus* a husbandman, from *colere* to till]

colophon *kol'ə-fon* or *-fən*, *n* a publisher's imprint or emblem; formerly, an inscription at the end of a book or literary composition, often naming the author and scribe or printer, with place and date of execution, etc, as on a modern title page. [L *colophōn*, from Gr *kolophōn* summit, finishing touch]

colophony *kol-of'ə-ni*, or *kol'*, *n* rosin. [Gr *kolophōniā* (*rhētinē* gum) from *Kolophōn* (Colophon), in Asia Minor]

coloquintida *kol-o-kwin'ti-də*, an alternative name for **colocynth**.

color. *NAm* spelling of **colour**.

Colorado beetle *kol-ər-ä'dō bē'tl*, *n* a yellow and black striped beetle (*Leptinotarsa decemlineata*), a serious pest of potatoes, originating in the US but now found in Europe and elsewhere. [*Colorado*, the US state]

coloration. See under **colour**.

coloratura *kol-or-ət-ōō'rə*, (*music*) *n* embellished vocal passages including runs, trills, etc. — *adj* florid, embellished. — **coloratura soprano** a high and flexible soprano voice, capable of singing coloratura passages; a singer with such a voice. [Ital, colouring]

colorectal. See under **colon**[2].

colorific, etc. See under **colour**.

Coloss. (*Bible*) *abbrev*: (the Letter to the) Colossians.

colossal *ko-* or *kə-los'əl*, *adj* like a colossus; gigantic.

colosseum. See **coliseum**.

colossus *kəl-os'əs*, *n* a person or organization of gigantic power and influence; *orig* a gigantic statue, *esp* that of Apollo at (but not astride) the entrance of the harbour of Rhodes: — *pl* **coloss'i** (*sī*) or **coloss'uses**. — **coloss'us-wise** (*Shakesp*) astride. [L, from Gr *kolossos*]

colostomy. See under **colon**[2].

colostrum *ko-los'trəm*, *n* a yellowish fluid produced from a mammal's nipples in the first few hours or days after giving birth, consisting mainly of lymphocytes and immunoglobins and preceding the production of milk. — *adj* **colos'tric** or **colos'trous**. [L]

colotomy. See under **colon**[2].

colour, also (*esp NAm*) **color**, etc *kul'ər*, *n* a sensation of light induced in the eye by electromagnetic waves of a certain frequency, the colour being determined by the frequency; a property whereby bodies have different appearances to the eye through surface reflection or absorption of rays; hue, one of the constituents into which white light can be decomposed; appearance of blood in the face; race or race-mixture other than Caucasian; appearance; plausibility; reason, pretext; tint; shade; paint; vividness; timbre (*music*); variety; (in *sing* or *pl*) a flag, ensign or standard; (in *pl*) a symbol of membership of a party, club, college, team, etc; (in particle physics) any of six varieties of a particular characteristic of quarks and antiquarks, used to define possible combinations of these particles in baryons and mesons. — *vt* to put colour on; to stain; to paint; to set in a favourable light; to exaggerate; to disguise; to misrepresent. — *vi* to take on colour; to blush. — *n* **col'orant** or **col'ourant** a substance used for colouring. — *n* **colorā'tion** or **colourā'tion** colouring; mode of colouring; disposition of colours. — *adj* **colorif'ic** (*kol-* or *kul-*) producing colours. — *n* **colorim'eter** (*kol-* or *kul-*) an instrument for comparison of colours. — *n* **colorim'etry**. — *adj* **colourable** (*kul'*) capable of being coloured; plausible; feigned. — *adv* **col'ourably**. — *adj* **col'oured** having colour; having a specious appearance, deceitful (*obs*); (of the complexion) other than white; (*loosely*; often *derog*) belonging to a dark-skinned race; (*usu* with *cap*) in S Africa, of mixed racial descent, partly Caucasian, partly of darker race; (also with *cap*) in S Africa, of one of the official racial groups, neither white nor African; not of Caucasian race. — *n* (*usu* with *cap*) in S Africa, a person of mixed racial descent; (also with *cap*) in S Africa, a member of one of the official racial groups, one who is neither white nor African; (in *pl*) coloured items of clothing for washing, as opposed to *whites*. — *n* **col'ourer**. — *adj* **col'ourful** full of or having colour; vivid. — *n* **col'ouring** any substance used to give colour; the actual colours of anything, and their arrangement; manner of applying colours; appearance, *esp* a person's hair and skin colour; tone. — *n* **col'ourist** a person who colours or paints; a person who excels in colouring or painting with colour. — *n* **colourīzā'tion** or **-s-**. — *vt* **col'ourize** or **-ise** to add colour to (a film made in black and white). — *adj* **col'ourless** without colour; transparent; pale; neutral; lacking distinctive character. — *adj* **col'oury** having much colour. — **colour bar** social discrimination *esp* by whites against other races. — *adj* **col'our-blind** unable to distinguish some colours from others. — **colour blindness**; **colour code** a system of identification, eg of electrical wires, by different colours. — *vt* **col'our-code** to mark with different colours for identification. — **colour contamination** (*image technology*) a fault in colour reproduction caused by incomplete separation of primary colours; **colour contrast** the perceived change in a colour when surrounded by another colour, used in psychology and tests for colour-blindness; **colour correction** in colour printing, compensation either by hand, by colour masking, or electronically, for inherent faults of the printing inks available; **coloured pencil** one containing a coloured lead as distinct from graphite or blacklead. — *adj* **col'ourfast** (of material, etc) with colours that are resistant to change when exposed to water, light or rubbing. — **colour fastness**; **colour film** a film for producing colour photographs; **colour filter** (*photog*) a transparent material, *usu* coloured glass or gelatin, used to modify the light transmitted through a camera's lens, by absorbing or transmitting selectively certain colours or wavelengths; **colour index** the difference between the photographic and visual magnitudes of a star used to calculate its temperature (*astron*); a number representing the dark-coloured heavy silicates in an igneous rock (*geol*); a systematic arrangement of colours according to their hue, saturation and brightness or an index giving chemical compositions of dyes and pigments; **colour line** a social and political separation between white and other races; **col'ourman** a person who prepares or sells paints; **colour masking** in photographic colour reproduction, the use of additional images to compensate for the deficiencies of the dyes forming the principal colour records; **colour music** the art of displaying colours on a screen with effect analogous to music; **colour organ** an instrument for doing this; **colour party** or **colour guard** a military guard carrying a flag or colours; **colour scheme** a planned combination of colours in a design or interior decoration; **colour screen** a colour filter; **col'our-sergeant** the sergeant who carries the colours of a regiment; **colour subcarrier** in colour television, a signal conveying the colour or chrominance information as a modulation, added to the monochrome video and synchronizing signals; **colour supplement** or **magazine** an illustrated magazine printed in colour and published *usu* as a part of a weekly newspaper. — Also **col'our-sup**, **-supp** or **-mag** (*colloq*). — *adj* of a style often pictured in such a magazine, ie expensive and rather exclusive. — **colour temperature** (*phys*) that temperature of a black body that radiates with the same dominant wavelengths as those apparent from a source being described or considered; **colour threshold** the luminance level below which colour differences are indiscernible; **col'ourwash** a cheap form of distemper coating. — *vt* to paint with this. — **col'ourway** one of several combinations of colours in which eg a patterned fabric is available. — **colour in** to fill in an area on a piece of paper, etc with colour; **colour up** to blush, flush; **false colours** a false pretence; **give colour** to give plausibility; **high colour** ruddiness of complexion; **in one's true colours** as one really is, one's real character; **join the colours** to enlist; **lose colour** to lose one's good looks; to become pale; to appear less probable (*fig*); **nail one's colours to the mast** to commit oneself to some party or plan of action; **off colour** faded; unwell; past one's best; slightly indecent; **primary colours** see **primary**; **see the colour of a person's money** to be sure that a person has sufficient money to pay before agreeing to a transaction; **with flying colours** with distinction or brilliance. [OFr *color*, from L *color*, *-ōris*; related to *cēlāre* to cover, to conceal]

colporteur *kol-pōr-tûr'*, *-pör-*, or *kol'pōrt-ər*, *n* a pedlar, *esp* one selling religious tracts and books. — *n* **col'portāge** (or *-täzh'*) the distribution of books by colporteurs. [Fr *colporteur*, from *col*, from L *collum* the neck, and *porter*, from L *portāre* to carry]

colposcope *kol'pō-skōp*, *n* an instrument for examining the neck of the uterus, *esp* for early signs of cancer. — *adj* **colposcop'ical**. — *adv* **colposcop'ically**. — *n* **colpos'copy** examination using a colposcope. [Gr *kolpos* the womb, and *skopeein* to see]

Colt® *kōlt* or *kolt*, *n* a single-action revolver invented by Samuel *Colt* (1814–62); any pistol, revolver, etc bearing this tradename.

colt *kōlt* or *kolt*, *n* a young horse; an awkward, somewhat clumsy, person; an inexperienced youth; *esp* in sports and games, a young, inexperienced player; a rope's end used as an instrument of punishment (*naut*). — *vi* (*archaic*) to frisk like a colt. — *vt* to cheat (*archaic*); to give the rope's end, to beat. — *adj* **colt'ish** like a colt; frisky. — **colts'foot** a composite plant (*Tussilago farfara*) with a shaggy stalk and large soft leaves. [OE *colt*; Swed *kult* a young boar, a stout boy]

colter. See **coulter**.

colubrid *kol'ū-brid*, *n* any snake of the family **Colū'bridae**, the largest family of snakes, of about 300 genera worldwide, being mostly non-venomous and including the grass snake, water snakes and whip snakes. — Also *adj*. — *adj* **colubriform** (*-ōō'* or *-ū'*) resembling the Colubridae. — *adj* **col'ūbrine** of, relating to or resembling the Colubridae; snakelike. [L *coluber* a snake]

colugo *ko-lōō'gō*, *n* the flying lemur (qv): — *pl* **colu'gos**. [Prob from Malaysian word]

Columba *kəl-um'bə*, *n* one of the southern constellations. — *adj* **Colum'ban** pertaining to St *Columba* (521–597), the Irish apostle who founded a monastery at Iona and converted the Northern Picts to Christianity. [L *columba* dove]

columbarium, columbary. See **columbine**.

Columbian *kəl-um'bi-ən*, *adj* of or relating to the United States, American (*poetic*). — *n* a size of type between English and Great Primer, *approx* 16-point (*printing*). — *n* **colum'bate** niobate. — *adj* **colum'bic** niobic. — *n* **columb'ite** a mineral, niobate and tantalate of iron and manganese. — *n* **colum'bium** the former name for niobium. [Christopher *Columbus*, discoverer of America]

columbine *kol'əm-bīn*, *adj* of or like a dove; dove-coloured. — *n* any plant of the ranunculaceous genus *Aquilegia*, with coloured sepals and spurred petals, giving the appearance of a bunch of pigeons; (with *cap*) in pantomime, the sweetheart of Harlequin. — *n* **columbā'rium** a dovecot; a niche for a sepulchral urn; a recess in a wall to receive the end of a rafter: — *pl* **columbāria**. — *n* **col'umbary** a dovecot. [L *columba* a dove]

Columbus *kə-lum'bəs*, *n* the European Space Agency's programme ensuring a European contribution to the International Space Station.

column *kol'əm*, *n* an upright cylinder, used as support or adornment; any upright body or mass like a column; a body of troops forming a long, narrow procession; a vertical row of figures, etc; a vertical section of a page or of a table of information; a particular section in a newspaper, often habitually written by the same person; a bundle of nerve-fibres; the central part of an orchid. — *n* **col'ūmel** a small column. — *n* **colūmell'a** (*biol*) the central axis of a spiral univalve; the auditory ossicle in lower vertebrates, homologous with the stapes in mammals (also **columella auris**); the central axis of the spore-case of mosses; the central axis of a fruit that remains after the carpels have split away: — *pl* **columell'ae** (*lē*). — *adj* **columnal** (*kə-lum'nl*) or **colum'nar** pertaining to columns; like a column; formed or arranged in columns. — *n* **columnar'ity**. — *adj* **columnated** (*kol'əm-nāt-id*, or *kə-lum'*), **columned** (*kol'əmd*) or **colum'niated** having columns. — *n* **columniation** (*kə-lum-ni-ā'shən*) the use or arrangement of columns. — *n* **columnist** (*kol'əm-ist* or *-nist*) a person who writes a regular column in a newspaper. — **column inch** the measure used in newspapers, etc, being an area one column wide by one inch deep. [L *columna*, related to *celsus* high; Gr *kolōnē* a hill; see **hill**]

colure *kō-lūr'*, *kōl'* or *kol'yər*, *n* a great circle of the celestial sphere passing through the poles of the equator and either the solstitial or the equinoctial points. [Gr *kolouros*, from *kolos* docked, and *ourā* tail]

colza *kol'zə*, *n* coleseed, yielding **col'za-oil**. [Du *koolzaad* cabbage-seed]

COM *kom*, *abbrev*: computer output on microfilm.

Com. *abbrev*: Commander; Commissioner; Committee; Commodore; Commonwealth; Communist.

com. *abbrev*: comedy; commerce; committee; common; commune.

com- *kom-*, **con-** *kon-* or **co-** *ko-* or *kō-*, also, by assimilation, **col-** *kol-*, or **cor-** *kor-*, *pfx* denoting: together, with; similar; used as intensive as in *consolidate*, *constant*. [L *com*, old form of *cum* with]

COMA *abbrev*: Committee on Medical Aspects of Food Policy.

coma[1] *kō'mə*, *n* a deeply unconscious state characterized by absence of response to external and internal stimuli, caused by an accumulation of poison in the brain tissue, head injury, cerebral haemorrhage, etc; stupor. — *adj* **com'atose** affected with coma; extremely drowsy or sleeping heavily (*facetious*). [Gr *kōma*, *-atos*]

coma[2] *kō'mə*, *n* a tuft of hairs attached to the testa of a seed (*bot*); a crown of leaves on certain trees; the nebulous envelope of the head of a comet (*astron*); (the manifestation of) a defect in an optical system (eg in a telescope) in which the image of a point appears as a blurred pear-shaped patch (*optics*): — *pl* **com'ae** (*mē*). — *adj* **cō'mal**, **cō'mate**, **cō'mose** or **cō'mous**. — *n* **comat'ulid** a feather-star. — **Coma Berenices** (*ber-ə-nī'sēz*) Berenice's Hair, a small northern constellation. [Gr *komē* the hair of the head]

comanchero *kō-man-che'rō*, *n* in the 19c, a person who traded with plains Indians of SW North America: — *pl* **comanche'ros**. [Mex Sp, from *Comanche* tribe]

comarb. See **coarb**.

comart *kō-märt'*, (*Shakesp*) *n* an agreement. [Perh pfx **co-** and **mart**; or a misprint for *cou'nant* ie **covenant**]

comate[1] *kō'māt'*, (*Shakesp*) *n* a mate or companion.

comate[2]. See **coma**[2].

comatose. See **coma**[1].

comb[1] *kōm*, *n* a toothed implement or part of a machine, for separating, arranging and cleaning hair, wool, flax, etc; anything of similar form; the fleshy crest on the head of some birds; the top or crest of a wave, of a roof, or of a hill; a regular structure made by bees for storing honey, a honeycomb. — *vt* to separate, arrange or clean by means of a comb or as if with a comb; to search methodically and thoroughly. — *vi* to break with a white foam, as the top of a wave does. — *adj* **combed**. — *n* **comb'er** someone or something that combs wool, etc; a long foaming wave. — *n pl* **comb'ings** hairs or wool fibres combed off. — *adj* **comb'less**. — *adj* **comb'y**. — *adv* **comb'wise**. — **comb out** to arrange (hair) by combing after rollers, etc have been removed; to remove (tangles, etc) from hair by combing; to search thoroughly for and remove (eg lice, men for military service; *n* **comb'-out**); **go over with a fine-tooth(ed) comb** to examine or search thoroughly. [OE *camb*]

comb[2], **combe**. See **coomb**[1,2].

combat *kom'bət* or *kum'bat* (*NAm usu kəm-bat'*; not standard in UK), *vi* to contend or struggle. — *vt* to fight against, to oppose; to contest; to debate: — *pr p* **com'bating**; *pa t* and *pa p* **com'bated**. — *n* (*kom'* or *kum'*) a struggle; a fight; fighting, military action. — *adj* (*esp US*) of or pertaining to fighting troops (as opposed to eg base units). — *adj* **com'batable**. — *adj* **com'batant** disposed to combat; taking part or liable to take part in military action. — *n* a person who takes part in (a) combat. — *adj* **com'bative** inclined to quarrel, aggressive. — *n* **com'bativeness**. — **combat fatigue** same as **battle fatigue**; **combat jacket** a jacket (in the style of those) worn by soldiers when fighting, *usu* khaki with camouflage markings. [Fr *combattre* to fight, from L pfx *com-* mutual, and *bātuere* to strike]

comber[1] *kom'bər*, *n* the gaper (a sea-perch); a species of wrasse.

comber[2]. See under **comb**[1].

combine *kəm-bīn'*, *vt* to join together; to unite chemically (with) to form a new compound; to bind, restrict (*Shakesp*). — *vi* to come into close union (with); to cooperate; to unite and form a new compound (*chem*). — *n* (*kom'bīn*) a syndicate, a trust, an association of trading companies; a combine harvester. — *n* **combinabil'ity**. — *adj* **combīn'able**. — *adj* **combinate** (*kom'bin-āt*) combined; betrothed (*Shakesp*). — *n* **combinā'tion** the act of combining; union, joining of individual things; chemical union, forming a new compound; a motorcycle with sidecar (also called **motorcycle combination**); a group of persons united for a purpose; in mathematics, a possible set of a given number of things selected from a given number, irrespective of arrangement within the set (distinguished from a *permutation*); the series of letters or numbers that must be dialled to open a combination lock. — *n pl* **combinā'tions** (*colloq* short form **coms** or **combs** (*komz*)) a warm undergarment covering the whole body with long sleeves and legs. — *adj* **com'binātive**. — *adj* **combinato'rial** (*math*) concerned with arrangements, combinations and permutations. — *n* **combinator'ics** (*math*) the branch of mathematics concerned with the theory and function of combinations and permutations. — *adj* **combin'atory**. — *adj* **combīned'**. — *adj* **combīn'ing**. — *n* **combo** (*kom'bō*) a small jazz or dance band; any combination (*colloq*); a white man who cohabits with an Aboriginal woman (*Austr*): — *pl* **com'bos**. — **combination lock** a lock used on safes, suitcases, etc, with numbered dials which must be turned in a special order a certain number of times, or to a certain number or numbers, to open it; **combination oven** an oven that functions both as a microwave and as a conventional oven; **combination room** at Cambridge University, a common room; **combined operations** (*military*) operations in which army, navy and air force work together; **combine harvester** (*agric*) a combined harvesting and threshing machine; **combining form** a linguistic element that is only used as part of a composite word. [L *combīnāre* to join, from *com-* and *bīnī*, two and two]

comble *kɔ̃-bl'*, (*Fr*) *n* the acme.

combo. See under **combine**.

combretum *kom-brē'təm*, *n* a member of the genus *Combretum* (family **Combretā'ceae**), tropical and subtropical trees and shrubs noted for the beauty of their flowers. [L *combrētum* an unknown plant]

combs. See under **combinations**.

comburgess *kom-bûr'jis*, *n* a fellow-burgess.

combust *kom-bust'*, *vt* to burn up. — *adj* in conjunction with the sun, or apparently very near it, so as to be obscured by its light, said of a planet when it is not more than $8\frac{1}{2}°$ from the sun. — *adj* **combust'ible** liable to catch fire and burn; excitable. — *n* something that will catch fire and burn. — *n* **combust'ibleness** the quality of being combustible. — *n* **combust'ion** (*-yən*) burning; the action of fire on combustible substances; oxidation or similar process with production of heat. — *adj* **combust'ious** (*Shakesp*) combustible, inflammable; turbulent. — *adj* **combust'ive** capable of catching fire. — *n* **combust'or** the system in a jet engine or gas turbine in which combustion takes place; a combustion chamber. — **combustion chamber** in a boiler furnace, the space in which combustion of gaseous products from the fuel takes place; in an internal-combustion engine, the space above the piston in which combustion occurs (*autos*). — **spontaneous combustion** burning caused by heat generated in the substance or body itself. [L *combūrere*, *combūstum* to consume, from *com-*, intens, and *ūrere* to burn]

Comdr. *abbrev*: Commander.

Comdt. *abbrev*: Commandant.

come *kum*, *vi* to move toward the place that is the point of view of the speaker or writer (the opposite of *go*); to draw near; to arrive at a certain state or condition; to issue, to happen, to turn out; to yield (*Shakesp*); to become; to amount (to); to reach; to begin to be in some condition; to achieve a sexual orgasm, to ejaculate (*slang*); to be had, got or gained; (only *3rd pers sing*; *esp* in *subjunctive*) when (a certain time) comes (as in *Come five o'clock, it will be dark outside*). — *vt* (*colloq*) to act the part of, assume the behaviour of, as in *Don't come the innocent with me*; (with *it*) to try to impress, assert one's authority over, etc: — *pr p* **com'ing**; *pa t* **came** (*kām*); *pa p* **come**. — *interj* (or *imperative*) expressive of encouragement, protest or reproof (often in phrases **come come** or **come now**). — *n* **com'er** (also *archaic* **comm'er**) someone who comes or has come; a person who shows promise (*colloq*). — *n* **com'ing** arrival or approach; (*esp* with *cap*) the Advent, or the hoped-for return (also **Second Coming**) of Christ. — *interj* or *pr p*, used as a response to a request or requirement for one's attention or presence. — *adj* future; of future importance; ready to make or meet advances (*archaic*). — **come-and-go'** passage to and fro. — *adj* **come-at'-able** (*colloq*) accessible. — **come'-back** a return, *esp* to a former activity or good, popular, successful, etc state; a revival; a retort, rejoinder; cause or ability to complain; recrimination; **come'down** a descent; a disappointment or deflation; a degradation; **come-hith'er** an invitation to approach; allure. — *adj* (of a look, manner, etc) inviting (*esp* sexually), alluring. — **come'-off** a conclusion; an evasion of duty; **come'-on** (*colloq*) encouragement, *esp* sexual; persuasion; **come'-o'-will** something that comes of its own accord; an illegitimate child (also **come'-by=chance**); **comeupp'ance** (*colloq*) deserved rebuke or punishment. — **all comers** everyone that arrives, volunteers, etc; **as it comes** however it is made, in any way whatsoever; **come about** to happen; to turn to face the opposite way (*naut*); **come across** to find (a specific thing) *esp* during a general search; to make an impression; to give or supply (often with *with*); **come again**? (*colloq*) what did you say?; pardon?; **come along** to progress; to arrive; (in *imperative*) make haste, hurry; **come and go** to fluctuate; to have freedom of movement or action; **come apart** to fall to pieces; **come at** to reach; to attack; to approach; **come away** to leave; to become detached; **come back** to return to popularity, office, etc after being in a losing position, a period of obscurity, etc; to return to life; to become fashionable again; to return to memory; to retort (*esp NAm*); **come between** to cause a rift between (two people, etc); to create a barrier or division between; **come by** to come near; to pass by; (as a command to sheepdogs) move to the left of the group of sheep being herded; to visit (*esp NAm*); to obtain or acquire; to come in; **come down** to descend; to be reduced, to decrease; to lose (*esp* financial) status; to emerge from the state induced by a hallucinogenic or addictive drug; (with *to*) to be a question of; to be an inheritance; **come down on** to be severe with, to punish; **come down with** to become ill with or contract (a disease); **come for** to arrive in order to collect; to attack; **come forward** to identify or present oneself (as a volunteer, as a witness, etc); **come home** to return to one's house; to touch one's interest or feelings closely, to affect (with *to*); (of an anchor) to drag or slip through the ground (*naut*); **come in** to enter; to arrive; to receive (money, income, etc); to have a role or function; to reply to a radio signal or call; to start an innings (*cricket*); to get within the opponent's guard (*fencing*); **come in for** to receive as, or as if as, one's share; to receive incidentally; **come in on** to become a partner, etc in (eg a business venture); **come into** to inherit; to be involved in; (of plants) to begin producing (flowers, leaves, etc); **come into one's own** to demonstrate or practise one's special skills, aptitudes, etc in a satisfactory way; **come of** to be a descendant of; to be the consequence of, arise or result from; to become of; **come of age** to reach full legal adult status; **come off** to come away; to become detached (from); to obtain a specified type of result (with *best*, worst, etc); to desist from; to prove successful; to have an orgasm (*vulg slang*); **come off it**! (*colloq*) don't be ridiculous!; **come on** to advance; to thrive, succeed; to proceed; to begin; to appear; to give the impression of being (*colloq*); often in *imperative* as a challenge or exhortation to attack, proceed, hurry, recover form low spirits, etc; **come on stream** (of oil-wells) to start regular production (also *fig*); **come on strong** (*colloq*) to speak or act forcefully or aggressively; **come out** to emerge; to appear; to result (well, etc); to be published; to become known or evident; to be solved; to enter society; to be released or leave (prison, hospital, etc); to declare openly one's homosexuality (*slang*); (of photographs) to develop successfully; (of stains, marks, etc) to be removed; to erupt (in spots, a rash, etc); to stop work, strike; to declare oneself (against or in favour of); **come out with** to utter, to say; to exclaim; **come over** to befall; to change sides or allegiance; to come into the mind of; to make an impression (with *as*); suddenly to experience a certain feeling or mood (as in *come over faint*; *colloq*); **come round** to come by a circuitous path; to visit; to happen in due course; to recur; to veer; to become favourable (in opinion, etc); to become amenable; to recover consciousness from a faint, etc; **come short of** to fail to attain; **come through** to survive; to succeed or complete successfully (an exam, test, etc); to arrive, having passed through a (*usu* administrative) process or system; to pass through; **come to** to obtain; to amount to; to be a question of; to proceed as far as; to recover consciousness; **come to grief** to meet with disaster or failure; **come to oneself** to return to one's normal state of mind; **come to pass** (*esp Bible*) to happen; **come to stay** to become permanent; **come true** to be fulfilled, to happen; **come under** to be included under; **come undone** or **unfastened**, etc to become detached, loose, etc; **come up** to present itself in discussion, etc; to appear; **come up against** to encounter (an obstacle, difficulty); **come up to** to reach (a specified point in space or time); to equal; **come upon** to attack; to affect; to hold answerable; to meet; to find; **come up with** to suggest; to overtake; **give someone the come-on** to invite or entice, *esp* sexually; **have it coming** (*colloq*) to have no chance of avoiding, or to get, one's just deserts; **how come**? how does it happen that?; **not know if one is coming or going** to be totally confused, perplexed or disorientated; **to come** future. [OE *cuman*; Ger *kommen*]

Comecon *kom'i-kon*, *n* a Communist organization, the *Co*uncil for *M*utual *Econ*omic Aid, or Assistance.

comeddle *kō-med'l*, *vt* to mix (*obs*); to temper (*Shakesp*).

Comédie Française *ko-mā-dē frā-sez*, (*Fr*) *n* the official name of Le Théâtre français, the French national theatre; **Comédie humaine** (*ü-men*) (*Fr*) the Human Comedy, the title of Balzac's series of novels, intended to form a complete picture of contemporary society.

comedo *kom'i-dō*, *n* a blackhead, a black-tipped white mass often found in the blocked skin pores: — *pl* **com'edos**. — *adj* **comedogen'ic** causing blackheads. [L *comedō*, *-ōnis* glutton, from *comedere* to eat up, from its wormlike appearance]

comedy *kom'i-di*, *n* a dramatic work or production having a pleasant or humorous character; the literary genre consisting of such works; a story with a happy ending; an incident of a comic or humorous nature. — *n* **comedian** (*kə-mē'di-ən*) a person who acts in or writes comedies; an entertainer who tells jokes, etc; an entertaining and amusing person (often *ironic*): — *fem* **comedienne** (*ko-me-* or *-mē- -di-en'*; *orig Fr*, and still often spelt **comédienne**). — *adj* **comē'dic** of or pertaining to comedy. — *n* **comēdiett'a** a short comic piece. — **comedy of manners** (a) satirical comedy dealing with the manners or fashions of a social class. [Fr *comédie*, from L *cōmoedia*, from Gr *kōmōidiā*, from *kōmos* revel, or *kōmē* village and *ōidē* song]

comely *kum'li*, *adj* pleasing; graceful; handsome or pretty. — *adv* in a pleasing or graceful manner. — *n* **come'liness**. [OE *cȳmlic* glorious, beautiful, from *cȳme* suitable, fine and *lic* like]

comestible *kom-est'ibl*, *adj* eatable. — *n* (*usu* in *pl*) food. [Fr, from L *comedere* to eat up]

comet *kom'it*, *n* a heavenly body with a (*usu*) elliptical orbit round the sun, having a main nucleus composed of rocky fragments held together with ice and surrounded by a cloud of dust and gas (the coma), which, when the comet nears the sun, may be driven away from the head of the comet to form a luminous tail. — *adj* **com'etary** or **cometic** (*-et'ik*). — *n* **cometog'raphy**. — *n* **cometol'ogy**. — **com'et-finder** a telescope of low power used to search for comets. [Gr *komētēs* long-haired, from *komē* hair]

comether *kəm-edh'ər*, (*dialect*) *n* wheedling; charm. [**come hither**, a call to cows, etc]

comfit *kum'fit*, *n* a sweet; a sugar-coated seed or almond. — *n* **com'fiture** (*obs*) conserve, preserved fruit. [A doublet of **confect**; Fr *confit*, *confiture*]

comfort *kum'fərt* (*Spenser kom-fort'*), *vt* to relieve from pain or distress; to soothe, cheer, console; to support or encourage. — *n* relief; something that gives ease, consolation, enjoyment, etc; freedom from annoyance; quiet enjoyment; ease, a degree of luxury; encouragement, support; a bed quilt (*US colloq*). — *adj* **com'fortable** imparting or enjoying comfort; easy (*fig*); confident in the (*esp* moral) correctness of a choice or decision; having enough money to live well. — *adv* **com'fortably**. — *n* **com'forter** a person who gives comfort; (with *cap*) the Holy Ghost (*Bible*); a long narrow woollen scarf; a dummy teat; a bed quilt (*US*). — *adj* **com'fortless**. — *n* **com'fortlessness**. — *adj* **com'fy**

(*colloq*) comfortable. — **cold comfort** little, if any, comfort; **comfort station** (*NAm*) a (public) lavatory. [OFr *conforter*, from L *con-* intensive, and *fortis* strong]

comfrey *kum'fri*, *n* a boraginaceous plant of the genus *Symphytum*, having hairy leaves often used in herbal medicine. [OFr *confirie*]

comic *kom'ik*, *adj* relating to comedy; raising mirth or laughter; funny, humorous. — *n* the quality or element that arouses mirth or laughter; an actor of humorous parts; a humorous entertainer on stage, in clubs, on TV, etc; an amusing person (*colloq*); a paper or magazine, *esp* for children, with illustrated stories, strip cartoons, etc (*orig* comic, later also serious, even horrific; also **comic book**). — *adj* **com'ical** funny, amusing. — *n* **comical'ity** or **com'icalness**. — *adv* **com'ically**. — **comic relief** relief from dramatic tension provided by humour or a comic episode; **comic strip** a strip cartoon. [See **comedy**]

comice *kom'is*, *n* a variety of pear (also **comice pear**).

Cominform *kom'in-förm*, *n* the *Com*munist *Inform*ation Bureau (1947–56), which succeeded the Comintern. — *n* **Com'informist**.

COMINT *kom'int*, *abbrev*: *Com*munications *Int*elligence, that branch of military intelligence concerned with monitoring and intercepting communications transmitted by the enemy. — Cf **ELINT**.

Comintern *kom'in-tûrn*, *n* the *Com*munist *Intern*ational (1919–43), or Third International (see under **international**).

comitadji. Same as **komitaji**.

comitatus *kom-i-tā'təs*, *n* a prince's escort or retinue; a county or shire. — *adj* **com'ital** relating to a count, earl, or county. — *adj* **com'itative** (of a grammatical case) expressing accompaniment. — *n* a comitative case. [L *comitātus*, *-ūs*, from *comes*, *-itis* companion, count]

comitia *ko-mish'i-ə* or *ko-mi'ti-a*, *n pl* the assemblies of the Romans for electing magistrates, passing laws, etc. — **comitia centuriata** (*sen-tū-ri-ā'tə* or *ken-to͞o-ri-ä'ta*) the assembly of Roman people, voting by centuries; **comitia curiata** (*kū-ri-ā'tə* or *ko͞o-ri-ä'ta*) that of the patricians, voting by curiae; **comitia tributa** (*tri-bū'tə* or *tri-bo͞o'ta*) that of the people, voting by tribes. [L, from *com* together, and *īre*, *itum* to go]

comity *kom'i-ti*, *n* courteousness; civility. — **comity of nations** (L *comitas gentium*) the international courtesy between nations in which recognition is accorded to the laws and customs of each state by others; a group of nations adhering to this code of behaviour. [L *cōmitās*, *-ātis*, from *cōmis* courteous]

comm. *abbrev*: commander; commentary; communication.

comma *kom'ə*, *n* a phrase (*rhetoric*); in punctuation, the sign (,) that marks the smallest division of a sentence; the smallest interval, break or discontinuity; a comma butterfly; a name for various minute intervals, *esp* the difference between twelve perfect fifths and seven octaves (*music*). — **comma bacillus** the microorganism (*Vibrio comma*) that causes cholera; **comma butterfly** a brown and orange nymphaline butterfly (*Polygoniac-album*), having wings with ragged outlines and with a white comma-shaped mark on the underside of the hind wing. — **inverted commas** a set of double or single superscript commas used to introduce and close a quotation, the introductory one(s) being inverted ("..'' or '..'). [L, from Gr *komma* a section of a sentence, from *koptein* to cut off]

command *kəm-änd'*, *vt* to order; to exercise supreme (*esp* military) authority over; to demand; to have within sight, range, influence or control. — *vi* to have chief authority; to govern. — *n* an order; authority; control; power to overlook, influence or use; the thing or people under one's authority; a military division under separate control; ability or understanding; a signal or message activating a mechanism or setting in motion a sequence of operations (*esp comput*); a command paper. — *n* **commandant** (*kom-ən-dant'* or *kom'*) an officer who has the command of a place or of a body of troops. — *n* **commandant'ship**. — *vt* **commandeer'** to seize for military use; to take over for one's own use, without asking. — *n* **command'er** a person who commands; an officer in the navy next in rank under a captain; a high-ranking police officer in charge of a district; a member of a higher class in an order of knighthood; a district administrator in religious military orders; the highest ranking officer in the Royal Society for the Prevention of Cruelty to Animals. — *n* **command'ership**. — *n* **command'ery** the district under a commander, *esp* in the religious military orders. — *adj* **command'ing** dominating, impressive, authoritative; strategic. — *adv* **command'ingly**. — *n* **command'ment** a command; a religious rule for living by, *esp* one of the Ten Commandments. — *n* **command'o** an armed force of Boers (*SAfr hist*); a unit of a special service brigade, *esp* the Royal Marine Corps (*military*); a person serving in such a unit: — *pl* **command'os**. — **command economy** an economy in which all means of creating wealth and business activities are controlled by government rather than market forces; **commander-in-chief'** the officer in supreme command of an army, or of the entire forces of the state; **command language** (*comput*) the language used to communicate with the operating system; **command module** the part of a spacecraft from which operations are directed; **command paper** a government document, *orig* one presented to parliament by command of the monarch; **command performance** a performance before royalty; **command post** a military unit's (temporary) headquarters. — **at one's command** available for use; **commander of the faithful** a title of the caliphs; **Ten Commandments** the ten commandments given by God to Moses on Mount Sinai, as described in the Old Testament Book of Exodus. [Fr *commander*, from LL *commandāre* (L *commendāre*), from L *mandāre* to entrust]

commeasure *kəm-ezh'ər*, *vt* to equal in measure; to coincide with. — *adj* **commeas'urable** same as **commensurable**.

commedia dell'arte *ko-mā'dē-a de-lär'te*, (*Ital*) *n* Italian Renaissance comedy, mainly improvised and with stock characters.

comme il faut *ko-mēl-fō*, (*Fr*) *adj* as it should be; proper; correct; approved by the fashionable world; genteel, well-bred.

Commelina *kom-ə-lī'nə*, *n* a tropical genus of monocotyledons, of the family **Commelinaceae** (*-li-nā'si-ē*). [After the Dutch botanists Johannes (1629–72) and Caspar (1667–1731) *Commelin*]

commemorate *kəm-em'ə-rāt*, *vt* to signify remembrance by a solemn or public act; to celebrate; to preserve the memory of. — *adj* **commem'orable**. — *n* **commemorā'tion** preserving the memory of some person or thing, *esp* by a solemn ceremony; the specification of individual saints in the prayers for the dead; the great festival of the Oxford academic year, *usu* taking place on the third Wednesday after Trinity Sunday. — *adj* **commem'orative** or **commem'oratory** tending or serving to commemorate. — *n* **commem'orātor**. [L *commemorāre*, *-ātum* to remember, from *com-* intensive and *memor* mindful]

commence *kəm-ens'*, *vi* and *vt* to begin; to originate. — *n* **commence'ment** the beginning; at certain universities, the act of taking a degree; the ceremony when degrees are conferred (*esp US*). [OFr *com(m)encier*, from L *com-* (intensive) and *initiāre* to begin, from *in* into, and *īre* to go]

commend *kəm-end'*, *vt* to commit as a charge or responsibility; to recommend as worthy; to praise; to adorn, set off (*obs*). — *adj* **commend'able** praiseworthy. — *n* **commend'ableness**. — *adv* **commend'ably**. — *n* **commend'am** an ecclesiastical benefice held, or the tenure or grant of a benefice held, *in commendam*, ie theoretically temporarily, until a pastor was provided for it, but often for life and without duties. — *n* **commendation** (*kom-ən-dā'shən*) the act of commending; praise; a public award for praiseworthy action. — *n* **comm'endator** a person who holds a benefice *in commendam*; a titular abbot, etc. — *adj* **commend'atory** commending; containing praise or commendation; presenting to favourable notice or reception; held or holding *in commendam*. — **commend me to** (*archaic*) remember me kindly to; give me by preference. [L *commendāre*, from *com-* (intensive) and *mandāre* to trust]

commensal *kə-men'səl*, *adj* eating at the same table; living together in close association, *esp* an association of less intimate kind than that called symbiosis (*biol*). — *n* a messmate; an organism living in partnership or association with another of a different species without affecting or benefiting it. — *n* **commen'salism**. — *n* **commensal'ity**. — *adv* **commen'sally**. [L *com-* together, and *mēnsa* a table]

commensurable *kəm-en'shə-rə-bl* or *-sū-*, *adj* having a common measure (*math*); capable of being measured exactly by the same unit (*math*); well-proportioned. — *n* **commensurabil'ity** or **commen'surableness**. — *adv* **commen'surably**. — *adj* **commen'surate** equal in measure or extent; in due proportion with (*with*). — *adv* **commen'surately**. — *n* **commen'surateness**. — *n* **commensurā'tion**. [L *com-*, and *mēnsūra* a measure, from *mētīrī*, *mēnsus* to measure]

comment *kom'ənt* or *-ent*, *n* a note conveying illustration or explanation; a remark, observation or criticism. — *vi* (or *kəm-ent'*) to make critical or explanatory notes (on); to make remarks, observations, etc; to annotate. — *vt* to say in comment. — *n* **comm'entary** a comment; a remark; a series or book of comments or critical notes; a continuous description of a sport, event, etc broadcast on television or radio (also **running commentary**). — *vi* **comm'entate** to give a running commentary. — *n* **commentā'tion** annotation. — *n* **comm'entātor** a person who comments; the writer of a critical commentary; a broadcaster of a running commentary. — *adj* **commentatō'rial** (or *-tö'*) pertaining to the making of commentaries. — *n* **comm'enter** or **comm'entor** (or *-ment'*). — **no comment** (*colloq*) I have nothing to say (*usu* to a newspaper or television reporter). [L *commentārī* to devise, contrive, from *com-* and *mēns*, *mentis* the mind]

commer (*archaic*). See under **come**.

commerce *kom'ûrs*, *n* interchange of merchandise on a large scale between nations or individuals; trade or traffic. — *vi* (*rare*) **commerce** (*kəm-ûrs'*) to trade; to have communication (with). — *adj* **commer'cial** (*-shl*) pertaining to commerce; mercantile; having profit as the main aim (sometimes implying disregard of quality); commercially viable. — *n* a commercial traveller; a commercially-sponsored advertisement on radio or TV; a commercial vehicle. — *n* **commercialese'** business jargon. — *n* **commer'cialism** commercial attitudes and aims; an expression characteristic of commercial language. — *n* **commer'cialist**. — *n* **commerciality** (*-shi-al'i-ti*). — *vt* **commer'cialize** or **-ise** to make profit the main aim of; to turn (something) into a source of profit (often *derog*). — *adv* **commer'cially**. — **commercial art** graphic art for commercial products or purposes, such as packaging, advertising, etc; **commercial break** a short break in a radio or TV programme to allow commercials to be broadcast; **commercial traveller** a travelling sales representative of a business concern; **commercial vehicle** generally, a goods-carrying vehicle; by some, understood to include passenger-carrying vehicles such as buses. [Fr, from L *commercium*, from *com-* mutual, and *merx*, *mercis* merchandise]

commère *kom-er'*, *n* fem of **compère**. [Fr, godmother; cf **cummer**]

commerge *kə-mûrj'*, *vi* to merge together.

commie or **commy** *kom'i*, (*colloq derog*) *n* and *adj* short form of **communist**.

comminate *kom'in-āt*, *vt* to threaten. — *n* **comminā'tion** (an instance of) threatening, denunciation; a recital of God's judgements against sinners, made on Ash Wednesday and at other times in the Ch of Eng. — *adj* **comm'inative** or **comm'inatory** threatening punishment. [L *comminārī*, *-ātum*, from *com-* (intensive) and *minārī* to threaten]

commingle *kəm-ing'gl*, *vt* and *vi* to mingle or mix together. — *adj* **comming'led**.

comminute *kom'in-ūt*, *vt* to reduce or break into minute particles or fragments; to pulverize. — *adj* **comm'inuted** pulverized; broken into tiny pieces. — *n* **comminū'tion**. — **comminuted fracture** see under **fracture**. [L *comminuere*, *-ūtum* to break into pieces, from *com-* (intensive) and *minuere* to make small, from root of *minus* less]

Commiphora *kom-if'ər-ə*, *n* a genus of plants of the family Burseraceae, natives of tropical Asia and Africa, yielding myrrh, bdellium and other resins. [Gr *kommi* gum, and *phoreein* to bear]

commis *ko'mē*, *n* an agent, deputy; an apprentice waiter, steward or chef. [Fr]

commiserate *kəm-iz'ər-āt*, *vt* and *vi* to feel or express sympathy or pity for (often with *with*). — *adj* **commis'erable** (*rare*) requiring commiseration; pitiable. — *n* **commiserā'tion** pity, sympathy. — *adj* **commis'erative** feeling or expressing sympathetic sorrow. — *n* **commis'erator**. [L *com-* with, and *miserāri* to deplore, from *miser* wretched]

commissar *kom'i-sär* or *-sär'*, *n* a commissary (officer); (also **People's Commissar**) formerly, in the Soviet Union, a head of a government department (after 1946 called **minister**); (also **political commissar**) in the Soviet Union, a Communist Party official responsible for political education, encouragement of party loyalty, etc, *esp* in military units. — *n* **commissā'riat** the department charged with the furnishing of provisions, eg for an army; the supply of provisions; the office of a commissary or of a commissar; a body of commissars. [LL *commissārius*, from *committere*, *commissum*]

commissary *kom'is-ər-i*, *n* a store supplying equipment and provisions (*US*); (the supply of) provisions, commissariat (*US*); a restaurant or canteen, *esp* in a film studio (*orig US*); an officer who supplies provisions, etc to an army; an officer representing a bishop, and performing his duties in distant parts of the diocese (*eccles*); a commissar; a person to whom any charge is committed; a deputy; the judge in a commissary court (*Scots law*). — *adj* **commissā'rial** pertaining to a commissary. — *n* **comm'issaryship**. — **commissary court** a Scottish court, abolished in 1836, with jurisdiction in matters that had formerly belonged to the bishops' courts; **commissary general** the head of the department for supplying provisions, etc to an army. [Ety as for **commissar**]

commission *kəm-ish'ən*, *n* the act of committing; the state of being commissioned or committed; that which is committed; a document, etc conferring authority, or the authority itself, *esp* that of a military, naval, or air officer, or a justice of the peace; a percentage paid to an agent; a body of persons appointed to perform certain duties; an order for a piece of work, *esp* of art; (of a warship, etc) the state of being manned, equipped, and ready for service; (of an office) temporary or permanent delegation to a number of persons who act jointly. — *vt* to give a commission to or for; to empower; to appoint; to put into service. — *vi* to be put into service. — *n* **commissionaire** (*-ār'*) a uniformed doorkeeper or messenger; a member of a corps of former soldiers and sailors employed as doorkeepers, etc. — *adj* **commiss'ioned**. — *n* **commiss'ioner** a person who holds a commission to perform some business; a member of a commission; the representative of high authority in a district, etc. — *n* **commiss'ionership**. — **commission agent** or **commission merchant** a person who transacts business for another for a commission; **commissioned officer** one appointed by commission. — **commissioner of oaths** a solicitor authorized to authenticate oaths on statements, etc; **High Commission** the embassy representing one country that is a member of the British Commonwealth in another such country; **High Commission Court** a court established in 1529 to investigate ecclesiastical cases, abolished as illegal in 1641; **High Commissioner** the chief representative in a High Commission; **in** (or **out of**) **commission** (of warships) prepared (or unprepared) for service; in (or not in) usable or working condition; **Lord High Commissioner** the representative of the Crown at the General Assembly of the Church of Scotland. [See **commit**]

Commissr *abbrev*: Commissioner.

commissure *kom'is-ūr*, *n* a joint; a joining surface; a bundle of nerve fibres connecting two nerve centres, eg those crossing the midline of the central nervous system. — *adj* **commissū'ral**. [L *commissūra* a joining; see **commit**]

commit *kə-mit'*, *vt* to give in charge or trust; to consign, send; to become guilty of, perpetrate; to involve (*esp* oneself) ; to pledge, promise: — *pr p* **committ'ing**; *pa t* and *pap* **committ'ed**. — *n* **commit'ment** the act of committing; an order for sending to prison; imprisonment; an obligation (to be) undertaken; declared attachment to a doctrine or cause. — *n* **committ'al** commitment; imprisonment; (the ceremony of) the placing of a coffin in a grave, crematorium furnace or the sea; a pledge, actual or implied. — *adj* **committ'ed** having entered into a commitment; (of literature or the work of a writer or other artist) advocating certain beliefs (*esp* religious or political ideology) or with some fixed purpose (eg to effect social reform) (also **engagé**). — **commit oneself** to make a definite decision or judgment (on); to make a definite agreement; **Committee of the whole House** the House of Commons or other legislative body, when it resolves itself into a committee with chairman, etc; **commit to memory** to learn by heart, memorize. [L *committere*, from *com-* with, and *mittere* to send]

committee *kə-mit'ē*, *n* a group selected from a more numerous body (or the whole body) to which some special business is committed; (*kom-i-tē'*) a person to whom something is committed; formerly, a person entrusted with the care of a lunatic or imbecile (*law*). — *n* **committ'eeman** a member of a committee. — *n* **committ'eeship**. — **committee stage** the stage in the passage of a bill through parliament, between the second and third readings, when it is discussed in detail in committee. — **in committee** participating in, during or subject to the deliberations of a committee. [ME, from *committen* to entrust]

commix *kə-miks'*, (*rare*) *vt* and *vi* to mix together. — *n* **commix'tion** (*-chən*) or **commix'ture** the act of mixing together; the state of being mixed; the compound formed by mixing; the rite of putting a piece of the host into the chalice, emblematic of the reunion of body and soul at the resurrection; sexual intercourse (*obs*).

commn *abbrev*: commission.

commo *kom'ō*, (*Austr colloq*) *n* a communist: — *pl* **comm'os**.

commode *kə-mōd*, *n* a small sideboard; an ornamental chest of drawers; a chair containing a chamberpot; a large high headdress formerly worn by ladies. [Fr]

commodious *kə-mō'dyəs*, *adj* roomy, spacious; comfortable; suitable or convenient (*archaic*); serviceable (*archaic*). — *adv* **commo'diously**. — *n* **commō'diousness**. [L *commodus*, from *com-* together, and *modus* measure]

commodity *kom-* or *kəm-od'i-ti*, *n* an article of trade; (in *pl*) goods, produce; profit, expediency, advantage, convenience or privilege (*archaic*). [MFr *commodité*, from L *commoditās*, *-ātis* fitness, convenience]

commodo or **comodo** *ko-mō'dō* or Ital *kom'o-do*, (*music*) *adj* and *adv* with ease; relaxed. [Ital, comfortable]

commodore *kom'ə-dōr* or *-dör*, *n* an officer of a rank between an admiral and a captain; the senior captain in a fleet of merchant ships; the president of a yacht club; a commodore's ship. [Perh from Du *kommandeur*]

common *kom'ən*, *adj* belonging equally to more than one; mutual; public; general; usual; frequent; ordinary; easily got or obtained; of little value; vulgar; of low degree. — *n* the commonalty (*Shakesp*); a tract of open land, used by all the inhabitants of a town, parish, etc; a right to take something from the land of another person (*law*). — *vi* to share (*Shakesp*); to board (*archaic*). — *adj* **comm'onable** held in common, mutually; (of animals) that may be pastured on common land. — *n* **comm'onage** the right of pasturing in common with others; the right of using anything in common; a common. — *n* **commonal'ity** the state of being common to all; standardization; frequency, prevalence; (*esp Scot*) the common people. — *n* **comm'onalty** the general body of ordinary people; the common people. — *n* **comm'oner** a person who is not a noble; a member of the House of Commons; at Oxford University, a student who pays for his or her commons him- or herself. — *n* **comm'oney** an ordinary playing marble. — *n* **common'oning** the conversion of land to common. — *adv* **comm'only** in a common manner; meanly, vulgarly; ordinarily; usually, frequently, often; generally; familiarly, intimately (*archaic*); publicly (*Bible*). — *n* **comm'onness**. — *n pl* **comm'ons** the common people, commonalty; (with *cap*) their representatives, ie the lower House of Parliament or **House of Commons**; common land, kept for the mutual benefit of ordinary people; food at a common table, *esp* at an Oxford college; the building or hall attached to a college serving as a dining room recreation area, etc; food in general, rations. — **common carrier** a person or company that deals with the transporting of goods, messages, etc for which he or it is legally responsible; **common chord** (*music*) a chord made up of three notes in a major or minor scale, ie the fundamental or generating note with its third and perfect fifth; **common cold** a viral infection causing inflammation of the mucous membranes lining the nose and throat, resulting in a runny nose, headache, etc; **common debtor** (*Scots law*) a debtor who is also owed money by a third party: the sum owed to him or her may be arrested (qv) and transferred directly to his or her creditor; **common denominator** see under **denominate**; **Common Era** the Christian Era; **common forms** the ordinary clauses which frequently occur in identical terms in writs and deeds; **common gender** the gender of a noun or pronoun having one form for male and female, such as L *bōs* bull or cow, Eng *student*; **common ground** a subject of mutual interest, argument, agreement, etc; **comm'onhold** a freehold held in common by a number of owners, who have joint responsibility for managing the property (eg a block of flats); **common law** the law of England based on custom and precedent, as opposed to **statute law** or **civil law**; **common-law marriage** in England, any of various informal types of marriage ceremony given legal recognition until 1753, some of which, if performed abroad, are still legally valid; loosely, the bond between a man (**common-law husband**) and woman (**common-law wife**) living together as husband and wife but not legally married; **common market** an association of countries as a single economic unit with internal free trade and common external tariffs; (with *caps*) see **European Economic Community**; **common measure** a quantity that is a measure of several quantities (*math*); common time (*music*); the usual form of a ballad stanza, a quatrain containing alternating four-stress and three-stress lines; **common metre** a four-line hymn stanza with eight syllables in the first and third lines, six in the second and fourth; **common-mode failure** (*nuc eng*) the failure of two or more supposedly independent parts of a system (eg a reactor) from a common external cause or from interaction between the parts; **common noun** (*gram*) a name that can be applied to all the members of a class (as opposed to *proper* noun). — *adj* **common-or-gar'den** ordinary. — **comm'onplace** a common topic or subject (*obs*); a platitude, pointless remark. — *adj* frequent, common, usual; lacking distinction; hackneyed, overused. — *vt* to make notes of; to put in a commonplace book. — *vi* to platitudinize. — **commonplace book** a book in which ideas, notes, memoranda, etc are jotted down; **comm'on-rid'ing** the equivalent of beating the bounds in the Scottish Borders; **common room** (in schools, colleges, etc) a sitting-room to which the students or teachers have common access; **common school** (*US*) a public elementary school; **common sense** average understanding; good sense or practical wisdom. — *adj* **commonsense'** or **commonsens'ical**. — **common-shore'** see under **shore**[4]; **common stair** an interior stair giving access to several independent flats or dwellings; **common stock** (*US*) ordinary shares; **common time** (*music*) rhythm with two, four, eight or sixteen beats to the bar. — **Book of Common Prayer** the liturgy of the Church of England; **common in the soil** (*law*) the ancient right to take stone, sand, gravel and minerals from common land; **common of pasture** (*law*) the ancient right to graze animals on common land; **Court of Common Bench** or **Common Pleas** one of the divisions of the High Court of Justice; **in common** together (*archaic*); together (with); shared or possessed equally; **make common cause with** to cast in one's lot with; to have the same interest and aims as; **philosophy of common sense** that school of philosophy which takes the universally admitted impressions of mankind as corresponding to the facts of things without any further scrutiny; **short commons** (*colloq*) meagre rations; **the common good** the interest of the community at large; the property of a former Scottish royal burgh which is not raised by tax nor held by special act of parliament; **the common people** the people in general. [Fr *commun*, from L *commūnis*, prob from *com-* together, and *mūnis* serving, obliging]

commonweal *kom'ən-wēl*, (*archaic*) *n* the common good, welfare of the community; commonwealth.

commonwealth *kom'ən-welth*, *n* the public or whole body of the people; a group of states united by a common interest or joint history, such as *the British Commonwealth*; a form of government in which the power rests with the people, *esp* that in England after the overthrow of Charles I; a state or dominion, *esp* applied to the Australian federation and certain states of America. — **Commonwealth Day** the second Monday in March, formerly kept as a day of celebration in the British Commonwealth; **comm'onwealth'sman** or **comm'onwealthsman** (*obs*) a (good) citizen; an adherent of Cromwell's Commonwealth. [See **wealth**]

commorant *kom'ər-ənt*, *n* and *adj* resident (*esp* at a university). [L *commorāns*, *-antis*, pr p of *commorārī* to abide]

commorientes *kom-mor-i-en'tēz*, (*law*) *n pl* persons who die together on the same occasion, where it cannot be determined which died first, and death is assumed to have taken place in order of seniority by age. [L]

commot or **commote** *kum'ət*, (*hist*) *n* a subdivision of a cantred. [Med L *commotum*, from Welsh *cymwd*]

commotion *kə-mō'shən*, *n* a violent motion or moving; excited or tumultuous action, physical or mental; agitation; tumult, noise, disturbance. — *adj* **commō'tional**. [See **commove**]

commove *kə-mōōv'*, (*archaic*) *vt* to put in motion; to agitate; to disturb, excite. [L *com-* (intensive) and *movēre*, *mōtum* to move]

comms *komz*, *abbrev*: communications.

communautaire *ko-mōō-nō-tār'*, *adj* of, pertaining to or in a spirit or attitude in keeping with or appropriate to the aims and principles of the European Community. — Also **commu'nitaire**. — Also *n*. [Fr]

commune[1] *kom'ūn*, *n* a corporation; in France, etc, a small administrative district with some self-government and a mayor; in some communist countries, an agricultural community; a group of people living together, sharing possessions, income, etc for the benefit of the group as a whole. — *adj* **communal** (*kom'ū-nl* or *kə-mū'*) pertaining to a commune or a community; owned in common, shared. — *n* **commū'nalism**. — *n* and *adj* **commū'nalist**. — *n* **commūnalīzā'tion** or **-s-**. — *vt* **commū'nalize** or *-ise* (or *kom'*) to make communal. — *adv* **comm'ūnally**. — *n* **Comm'ūnard** (or *-ärd'*) an adherent of the Paris *Commune* in 1871; (without *cap*) a communist; (without *cap*) a member of a commune. — **the Paris Commune** a revolt by Parisian workers, radicals and socialists in 1871 against the national government, with the aim that each city or district should be ruled independently by its own commune or local government. [Fr *commune*; see **common**]

commune[2] *kə-mūn'* or *kom'ūn*, *vi* to converse or talk together; to have intimate (*esp* spiritual) communication with (eg nature); to receive Holy Communion. — *n* and *adj* **commūn'ing**. [OFr *communer* to share]

commune bonum *ko-mū'nē bō'nəm* or *ko-mōō'ne bo'nōōm*, (*L*) the good of all, common good.

communibus annis *ko-mū'ni-bəs an'ēs* or *ko-mōō'ni-bōōs an'ēs*, (*L*) on the annual average.

communicate *kə-mū'ni-kāt*, *vt* to impart; to reveal, demonstrate; to bestow. — *vi* to succeed in conveying one's meaning to others; to have something in common (with another person); to have communication, correspondence, verbal or written contact (with *with*); to have a means of communication; to partake of Holy Communion. — *n* **commūnicability** (*-kə-bil'i-ti*) or **commū'nicableness**. — *adj* **commū'nicable** that may be communicated (*esp* of a disease). — *adv* **commū'nicably**. — *n* **commū'nicant** a person who partakes of Holy Communion. — *n* **commūnicā'tion** (an act of) communicating; that which is communicated; (a piece of) correspondence; a means of communicating, a connecting passage or channel; (in *pl*) means of giving and receiving information, such as speech, telecommunications, the press, and cinema; a means of transporting, *esp* troops and supplies. — *adj* **commū'nicative** inclined to communicate or give information; talkative; unreserved. — *adv* **commū'nicatively**. — *n* **commū'nicativeness**. — *n* **commū'nicātor**. — *adj* **commū'nicātory** imparting knowledge. — **communicable disease** any disease caused by a parasite or microorganism that may be transferred from one person (or animal) to another; **communicating door** a door which gives access from one room, office, etc to another; **communication cord** a cord in the wall or ceiling of a railway train which can be pulled in an emergency to stop the train; **communications satellite** an artificial satellite in orbit around the earth, used to relay radio, television and telephone signals; **communication** or **communications theory** the theory of the transmitting of information, *esp* to, from, or between machines. [L *commūnicāre*, *-ātum*, from *commūnis* common]

communi consensu *ko-mū'nī kon-sen'sū* or *ko-mōō'nē kon-sen'sōō*, (*L*) by common consent.

communion *kəm-ūn'yən*, *n* the act of communing; spiritual intercourse or contact; fellowship; the interchange of transactions; union of a number of people in a religious service; the body of people uniting in such a service; (**Holy Communion**) the Eucharist, the sacrament commemorating the Last Supper (*Christian relig*). — **communion card** a card used *esp* in the Presbyterian church to invite to, or register attendance at, Holy Communion; **commun'ion-cloth**, **commun'ion-cup**, and **commun'ion-table** those used at a service of Holy Communion; **communion rail** the rail in front of the altar in some churches, at which the communicants kneel. — **Communion of Saints** the spiritual fellowship of all true Christian believers, the blessed dead and the faithful living, in RC doctrine held to involve a mutual exchange of examples, prayers, merits and satisfactions; **take communion** to receive the bread and wine at a service of Holy Communion. [L *commūniō*, *-ōnis*, from *commūnis* common]

communiqué or **communique** *kom-ū'ni-kā*, *n* an official announcement or bulletin, *esp* one given to the press, radio or television. [Fr, related to **communicate**]

communism *kom'ūn-izm*, *n* a social theory according to which society should be classless, private property should be abolished, and land, factories, etc collectively owned and controlled; a system of government adhering to these principles; (often with *cap*) Marxian socialism as understood in Russia. — *n* **comm'ūnist** a supporter of or believer in communism; (often with *cap*) a member of a Communist party. — *adj* of or pertaining to communism; believing in or favouring communism. — *adj* **commūnistic** believing in or favouring communism; of or favouring communal living and ownership. — *vt* **comm'ūnize** or **-ise** to make common property; to make communist. [Fr *communisme*, from *commun* common]

community *kəm-ūn'i-ti*, *n* a body of people in the same locality; the public in general; people having common rights, etc; a body of persons leading a common life, or under socialistic or similar organization; a group of people who have common interests, characteristics or culture; a monastic body; any group of plants growing together under natural conditions and forming a recognizable sort of vegetation; a common possession or enjoyment; agreement; communion; commonness (*archaic*). — *adj* of, for or by a local community. — *n* **communitā'rian** a member of a community; an advocate of living in communities. — **community care** (responsibility for) the provision of social and welfare services to eg sick or old people in their own homes by local organizations rather than large institutions such as hospitals or old people's homes; **community centre** a place where members of a community may meet for social and other activities; **community charge** a tax replacing the rating system, itself replaced by the council tax, levied to pay for local government services and facilities, poll tax; **community chest** (*US*) a fund of voluntary contributions for local welfare; **community college** same as **village college**; a public junior college offering two year courses to students (*NAm*); **community council** a lay body elected to look after local interests; **community health** preventive health services, including the surveillance of special groups (children, the elderly, etc) in their homes, at special clinics, etc; **community home** the successor to the approved school (see under **approve**); **community medicine** a former name for **public health medicine**; **community nurse** a nurse (eg a health visitor, district nurse or midwife) employed by a local health authority to visit patients in their own homes, staff various clinics, etc; **community physician** a physician, appointed by the local health authority, with administrative responsibility for the medical and social welfare of an area (also **public health physician**); **community policing** the provision of police officers in an area who are either from the area or are well known to the residents; **community property** property owned equally by each partner in a marriage; **community radio** broadcasts made from stations independent of local radio, aimed at involving people in their own community, and serving specialist groups, eg ethnic minorities, jazz enthusiasts, etc; **community relations** the relationships, interactions and conflicts existing between different ethnic, social, political or religious groups in an area; the process or work of reconciling or mediating with these groups; **community school** a school that is open outside school hours for the use and recreation of the community; **community service** unpaid work for the community, eg that done by minor criminals as an alternative to imprisonment under a **community-service order**; **community singing** organized singing by a large gathering of people; **community spirit** the sense of belonging to, and participating in, a (local) community; **community work** a form of social work based on the needs of local communities; **community worker**. [OFr *communité*, from L *commūnitās*, *-ātis*, from *commūnis* common]

commute *kə-mūt'*, *vt* to substitute or exchange; to change or transform (into); to exchange (*esp* the death sentence) for a less severe punishment; to pay off (eg a debt being paid by instalments) early by a single payment, by a simpler or more convenient method, etc; to change (electric current) from alternating to direct or vice versa. — *vi* to travel some distance regularly, *esp* daily to work. — *n* **commūtabil'ity**. — *adj* **commūt'able** that may be commuted or exchanged. — *vt* **commūtate** (*kom'*; *elec*) to commute. — *n* **commūtā'tion** the act of commuting (a sentence, payment or current); change or exchange of one thing for another; the travelling done by a commuter (*NAm*). — *adj* **commū'tative** (or *kom'ū-tā-tiv*) relating to exchange; interchangeable; such that $x*y = y*x$, where * denotes a binary operation (*math*). — *adv* **commūtatively**. — *n* **comm'ūtātor** an apparatus for reversing electric currents. — *n* **commūt'er** a person who travels daily between home and work. — **commutation ticket** (*NAm*) a season ticket; **commuter belt** an area within travelling distance of a large city or town, from which people commute to work. [L *commūtāre*, from *com-* with, and *mūtāre* to change]

commutual *kə-mū'cho͞o-əl*, *adj* mutual, reciprocal.

comodo. See **commodo**.

comose, **comous**. See **coma**[2].

comp *komp*, (*informal*) *n* a compositor; an accompanist. — *vi* to work as a compositor; to play an accompaniment.

comp. *abbrev*: comparative (also **compar**.); compare; compiler; composer; compound; compounded; comprehensive; comprising.

compact[1] *kəm-pakt'*, *adj* closely placed or fitted together; tightly grouped, not spread out; (of a person) smallish; close; brief; of a car, medium-sized and economical (*NAm*). — *n* **compact** (*kom'*) a compacted body or structure, a combination (of elements); a small case containing face-powder for carrying in the handbag (also **powder compact**); a compact car (*NAm*); a compact camera. — *vt* (*-pakt'*) to press closely together; to consolidate. — *adj* **compact'ed**. — *adv* **compact'edly**. — *n* **compact'edness**. — *n* **compactificā'tion** the act or process of making or becoming compact or tightly grouped together. — *vt* **compact'ify**. — *n* **compac'tion** the act of compacting, or state of being compacted; sediments compacted by pressure from above (*geol*); an area formed by dumping rock waste, etc, pressing it together by means of heavy machines, and causing or allowing grass to grow over the whole. *adv* **compact'ly**. — *n* **compact'ness**. — *n* **compact'or** a machine which crushes and compacts eg solid waste into the ground. — **compact camera** a small 35mm camera, *usu* with automatic focusing and exposure and often with built-in interchangeable lens and automatic winding; **compact disc** (*usu abbrev* **CD**) a small audio disc from which digitally recorded sound can be read by laser, a laser disc; **compact disc player** a machine that plays compact discs by means of a laser beam; **compact video disc** (*abbrev* **CDV**) an audio-visual disc that records and plays both pictures and sound. [L *compāctus*, pa p of *compingere*, from *com-*, and *pangere* to fix]

compact[2] *kom'pakt*, *n* a mutual bargain or agreement; a league, treaty or union. — *adj* (*kom-pakt'*) united (eg in a league). [L *compactum*, from *compacīscī*, from *com-*, with *pacīscī* to bargain]

compadre *kom-pä'drā*, n a male friend or companion. [Sp, godfather]

compages *kəm-pā'jēz*, *n* a structure (also *obs* **compage'**): — *pl* **compa'ges**. — *vt* **compag'inate** to join, connect. — *n* **compagination** (*-paj-i-nā'shən*). [L *compāgēs*, *compāgināre*, *-ātum*, from *com-*, and root of *pangere* to fasten]

compagnie anonyme *kɔ̃-pa-nyē a-no-nēm*, (*Fr*). Same as **société anonyme**.

compagnon de voyage *kɔ̃-pa-nyɔ̃ də vwa-yäzh*, (*Fr*) *n* a travelling companion.

compander or **compandor** *kəm-pand'ər, n* a system of transmitting or reproducing sound by compressing and then re-expanding the volume-range so as to produce a clearer signal by reducing the contrast. [*com*press, ex*pand*, and *-er* or *-or*]

companing (*Spenser*). See under **company**.

companion[1] *kəm-pan'yən, n* a person who keeps company or frequently associates with another, either voluntarily or as a profession; a member of an order of knighthood, *esp* in a lower grade; one of a pair or set of things; an often pocket-sized book on a particular subject (as in *angler's companion*). — *vt* (*rare*) to accompany. — *adj* of the nature of a companion; accompanying. — *adj* **compan'ionable** fit to be a companion; agreeable. — *n* **compan'ionableness**. — *adv* **compan'ionably**. — *adj* **compan'ionate** acting as or resembling a companion; suited to be a companion. — *adj* **compan'ioned** having a companion. — *n* **compan'ionhood**. — *adj* **compan'ionless**. — *n* **compan'ionship** the state of being a companion; company, fellowship; a body of companions. — **companionate marriage** a form of marriage proposed in the 1920s with legalized birth control and divorce by mutual consent; **companion set** a set of fireside implements on a stand; **companion star** a star appearing to be close to another though not necessarily near it in space, eg the fainter component of a double star. — **Companion of Literature** (*abbrev* **CLitt**.) an honour (instituted 1961) conferred by the Royal Society of Literature. [Fr *compagnon*, from LL *compānium* a mess, from L *com-* with, and *pānis* bread]

companion[2] *kəm-pan'yən*, (*naut*) *n* the skylight or window frame through which light passes to a lower deck or cabin; a companion ladder. — **companion hatch** the covering of an opening in a deck; **companion ladder** the ladder or stair leading from the deck to a cabin or to the quarterdeck; **companionway** a staircase from the deck to a cabin. [Cf Du *kompanje*; OFr *compagne*; Ital *compagna* storeroom]

company *kum'pə-ni, n* a person or persons with whom one associates; any assembly of people, or of animals or birds; a group of people associated for trade, etc; a society; a subdivision of a regiment; the crew of a ship; a group of actors working together; a collective noun for a flock of widgeon; the state of being a companion; fellowship, companionship; social intercourse. — *adj* belonging to, relating to, or associated with, a commercial company. — *vt* (*archaic*) to accompany. — *vi* (*rare*) to associate; to cohabit: — *pr p* **com'panying**; *Spenser* **com'paning**; *pa t* and *pa p* **com'panied**. — **company doctor** an advisor, consultant or businessman who turns unprofitable or inefficient companies into profitable or efficient businesses (*colloq*); a medical practitioner who works for a company and oversees the health of the staff; **company man** an employee who puts loyalty to his company before his personal life, friends, etc; **company promoter** a person who promotes or superintends the formation of joint-stock companies; **company secretary** the chief administrative officer of a company, having certain duties and obligations, eg ensuring that company documentation is in order; **company sergeant major** the senior non-commissioned officer in a regiment or battalion responsible for discipline; **company union** (*NAm*) an association of workers within a single company, unaffiliated to any wider trade union body, a staff association. — **bad company** unsuitable, *esp* criminal, companions or associates; **be good** (or **bad**) **company** to have or lack companionable qualities; **in company** in the presence of other people outside one's immediate family or intimate acquaintance; **keep company** to associate (with *with*); to court; **know a man by his company** to assess a man's character by the quality of his friends; **part company** to separate, go different ways (*lit* or *fig*). [Fr *compagnie*; same root as **companion**[1]]

compar. *abbrev*: comparative; comparison.

compare[1] *kəm-pār'*, *vt* to put (as if) side by side so as to ascertain how far things agree or disagree (often with *with*); to liken or represent as similar (with *to*); to give the degrees of comparison of (*gram*). — *vi* to make comparison; to relate (well, badly, etc) in comparison; to vie or compete (*archaic*). — *n* (*obs*) compeer; comparison. — *n* **comparabil'ity**. — *adj* **comparable** (*kom'pər-ə-bl* or *kəm-par'ə-bl*). — *n* **com'parableness** or *kom-par'*). — *adv* **com'parably** (or *kəm-par'*). — *adj* **comparative** (*kəm-par'ə-tiv*) pertaining to or making comparison; estimated by comparing with something else; relative, not positive or absolute; (of adjectives and adverbs) expressing more or greater degree (*gram*; also *n*). — *adv* **compar'atively**. — *n* **compar'ator** any device for comparing accurately, so as eg to detect deviations from a standard or to confirm identity. — *n* **comparison** (*-par'i-sən*) the act of comparing; the capacity of being compared; a comparative estimate; a simile or figure by which two things are compared; the inflection of an adjective or adverb to express different relative degrees of its quality (*gram*). — **comparability study** a comparison of wages, conditions, etc in different jobs, or the same job in different areas, *usu* in order to determine future levels of wages; **comparison microscope** a microscope in which there are two objective lenses, so that images from each can be examined side by side. — **beyond compare** without any rival or equal; **compare notes** to share or exchange one's ideas (with someone else). [L *comparāre* to match, from *com-*, and *parāre* to make or esteem equal, from *par* equal]

compare[2] *kəm-pār'*, (*archaic*) *vt* to get or provide. [L *comparāre*, from *com-* (intensive) and *parāre* to prepare]

compartment *kəm-pärt'mənt, n* a partitioned-off or marked-off division of an enclosed space or area; a closed-off division of a railway carriage; a division of anything. — *vt* **compart'** (*rare*) to divide into parts. — *n* **compartmentalizā'tion** or **-s-**. — *vt* **compartment'alize** or **-ise** to divide into categories or into units, *esp* units with little intercommunication. — *adv* **compartment'ally**. — **compartment syndrome** (*med*) a painful muscle cramp due to obstruction of blood flow to a group of muscles compressed within a confined space after exercise or injury. [Fr *compartiment*, from L *com-* (intensive) and *partīrī* to divide, from *pars*, *partis* a part]

compass *kum'pəs, n* an instrument consisting of a magnetized needle, used to find directions; (in *pl*) a pair of jointed legs, for describing circles, etc (also **pair of compasses**); a circuit or circle; limit; range of pitch of a voice or instrument; circumference; girth. — *vt* to pass or go round; to surround or enclose; to grasp, comprehend; to bring about, accomplish, achieve or obtain; to contrive or plot (*obs*); to curve, bend (*Shakesp*). — *adj* **com'passable** capable of being compassed. — *n* **com'passing** (*obs*) contrivance, design. — *adj* **com'past** (*archaic*) rounded. — **compass card** the circular card of a compass marked with directional points and degrees; **compass plane** a plane, convex on the underside, for smoothing curved timber; **compass plant** any plant (such as *Silphium laciniatum* and certain species of lettuce) that alligns its leaves north and south to avoid the midday sun; **compass rose** the circular device showing the principal directions on a map or chart; **compass saw** a narrow-bladed saw for cutting in curves; **compass signal** a signal denoting a point in the compass; **compass tim'ber** curved timber, used for shipbuilding, etc; **compass window** a semicircular bay window. — **box the compass** see under **box**[2]. [Fr *compas* a circle, prob from LL *compassus*, from L *com-* (intensive) and *passus* a step]

compassion *kəm-pash'ən, n* a feeling of sorrow or pity for the suffering of another, *usu* with a desire to alleviate it. — *vt* (*archaic*) to pity. — *adj* **compass'ionable** pitiable. — *n* **compass'ionate** inclined to pity or mercy; merciful. — *adv* **compass'ionately**. — *n* **compass'ionateness**. — **compassionate leave, discharge**, etc leave, discharge, etc in exceptional circumstances for personal reasons; **compassion fatigue** progressive disinclination to show charity or compassion, *usu* due to the sheer volume of deserving cases. [Fr, from LL *compassiō, -ōnis*, from *com-* with, and *patī, passus* to suffer]

compast. See under **compass**.

compatible *kəm-pat'i-bl, adj* consistent (with), congruous; capable of coexistence; admissible in combination; able to be transplanted into another's body without rejection (*med* and *biol*); able to form grafts, or capable of self-fertilization (*bot*); (of drugs) able to be used simultaneously without undesirable side-effects or interaction (*chem*); (of a television system) enabling colour transmissions to be received in black and white by monochrome sets; enabling stereophonic signals to be treated as monophonic by mono equipment; (of computers, computer peripherals, machinery, etc) able to be used together without special modification). — *n* **compatibil'ity** or **compat'ibleness**. — *adv* **compat'ibly**. [Fr, from L *com-* with, and *patī* to suffer]

compatriot *kəm-pāt'ri-ət*, or *-pat'*, *n* a fellow-countryman. — Also *adj*. — *adj* **compatriotic** (*-ot'ik*). — *n* **compa'triotism**. [Fr *compatriote*, from L *compatriōta*; see **patriot**]

compear *kəm-pēr'*, (*Scots law*) *vi* to appear in court. — *n* **compear'ance**. — *n* **compear'ant**. [Fr *comparoir*, from L *compārēre*, from *com-* (intensive) and *pārēre* to appear]

compeer *kəm-pēr'* or *kom'pēr*, *n* a person who is the equal of another in rank, ability or status; a companion. — *vt* (*-pēr'*; *archaic*) to equal. [L *compār*, from *com-* (intensive) and *pār* equal]

compel *kəm-pel'*, *vt* to drive or urge on forcibly (to); to bring about or obtain by irresistible pressure; to force; to drive together (*archaic*): — *pr p* **compell'ing**; *pa t* and *pa p* **compelled'**. — *adj* **compell'able**. — *n* **compell'er**. — *adj* **compell'ing** forcing attention or interest, irresistible; powerfully persuasive. [L *com-* (intensive) and *pellere, pulsum* to drive]

compellation *kom-pə-lā'shən*, (*rare*) *n* an act or style of addressing someone; an appellation. — *adj* **compellative** (*kəm-pel'ə-tiv*). — *n* compellation. [L *compellāre, -ātum* to address, frequentative of *compellere*]

compendium *kəm-pen'di-əm*, *n* a shortening or abridgement; a summary of a larger work or subject, containing the most important or useful extracts or facts, an abstract; a collection of board-games or puzzles in one box: — *pl* **compen'diums** or **compen'dia**. — *adj* **compen'dious** short; concise but comprehensive. — *adv* **compen'diously**. — *n* **compen'diousness**. [L *compendium* what is weighed together, or saved (opposed to *dispendium* what is weighed out or spent), from *com-* together, and *pendere* to weigh]

compensate *kom'pən-sāt* or *kəm-pen'sāt*, *vt* to make (*esp* financial amends to, to recompense; to counterbalance. — *vi* to make amends (for). — *n* **compensā'tion** (*kom-*) the act of compensating; amends, *esp* financial, for loss, injury, etc sustained; the neutralization of opposing forces (*phys*); payment, remuneration (*NAm*); process of compensating for sense of failure or inadequacy by concentrating on achievement or superiority, real or fancied, in some other sphere; the defence mechanism involved in this (*psychol*). — *adj* **compensā'tional**, **com'pensātive** (or *kəm-pen'sə-tiv*) or **compen'satory** (also *sā'*) giving compensation. — *n* **com'pensātor**. — **compensation balance** or **pendulum** a balance wheel or pendulum so constructed as to counteract the effect of the expansion and contraction of the metal under variation of temperature; **compensation neurosis** (*psychol*) a set of physical and psychological symptoms affecting some victims of industrial, etc injury who have the prospect of receiving financial compensation for their injury, thought by some to be a genuine reaction to trauma and by others to be an attempt to profit from the initial injury; **compensation water** the water passed downstream from a reservoir to supply users who, before the construction of the reservoir dam, took their water directly from the stream. [L *com-* (intensive) and *pēnsāre*, frequentative of *pendere* to weigh]

compère *kɔ̃-per* or *kom'per*, *n* a person who introduces and provides the links between items of an entertainment: — *fem* **commère'**. — *vt* to act as compère to. [Fr, godfather, godmother]

compesce *kəm-pes'*, (*archaic Scot*) *vt* to restrain. [L *compēscere*]

compete *kəm-pēt'*, *vi* to seek or strive for something in rivalry with others; to contend for a prize. — *n* **competition** (*kom-pi-tish'ən*) the act of competing; rivalry in striving for the same goal; a match or trial of ability; those things or people with which or whom others are competing. — *adj* **competitive** (*kəm-pet'i-tiv*) pertaining to or characterized by competition; suitable to compete or relishing the challenge of competition; (of price) at a level likely to attract potential customers, being at least as cheap as or cheaper than competitors. — *n* **compet'itiveness**. — *n* **compet'itor** a person who competes; a rival or opponent. — **in competition** competing (with). [L *competere* to strive together, from *com-* together, and *petere* to seek, strive after]

competent *kom'pi-tənt, adj* suitable; sufficiently good or skilful; fit; efficient; belonging as a right; (of a witness) legally qualified; legitimate. — *n* **com'petence** or **com'petency** suitability; fitness; efficiency; capacity, ability; sufficiency; legal power or capacity. — *adv* **com'petently**. [L *competere* to come together, be convenient, from *com-*, and *petere* to seek]

comping *kom'ping*, (*informal*) *n* the hobby of entering competitions in newspapers, magazines, etc. — *n* **com'per** a person who regularly enters for such competitions. [Contraction of **competition**]

compile *kəm-pīl'*, *vt* to write or compose (a work, document, etc) by collecting the materials from other books or sources; to draw up or collect (a list, etc); (in golf, etc) to put together (a score of). — *n* **compilā'tion** (*-pil-* or *-pīl-*) the act of compiling; the thing compiled, eg a literary work made by gathering the material from various authors, sources, etc or a collection of audio recordings. — *n* **com'pilātor** a person who compiles. — *adj* **compī'latory**. — *n* **compile'ment** a compilation. — *n* **compīl'er** a person who compiles; a complex program which translates a whole program of computer instructions written in a program-language into machine code before the computer acts on any of the instructions in that program (*comput*; cf **interpreter**). [Fr *compiler*, prob from L *compīlāre*, from *com-* together, and *pīlāre* to plunder, or *pīlāre*, to pound down; influenced by **pile**]

compital *kom'pit-əl, adj* pertaining to crossroads, or to the intersection of leaf-veins; acutely intersecting. [L *compita* crossroads]

complacent *kəm-plā'sənt, adj* showing satisfaction, *esp* when self-satisfied, *usu* with insufficient regard to problems, dangers, etc; pleased; inclined to please, complaisant (*archaic*). — *n* **complā'cence** or **complā'cency** pleasure; (self-)satisfaction; complaisance (*archaic*). — *adv* **complā'cently**. [L *complacēre*, from *com-* (intensive) and *placēre* to please]

complain *kəm-plān'*, *vi* to express grief, pain, unfavourable opinion, grievance (at or about); to express a sense of injury or dissatisfaction; to make an accusation or charge; to make a mournful sound; to state that one has pain, an illness, etc (with *of*). — *vt* to utter as a complaint. — *n* (*obs* or *poetic*) complaint. — *n* **complain'ant** a person who complains; a person who raises a suit, a plaintiff (*law*). — *n* **complain'er** a complainant. — *n* and *adj* **complain'ing**. — *adv* **complain'ingly**. — *n* **complaint'** an instance or the act of complaining; an expression of grief and dissatisfaction; finding fault; the thing complained about; a grievance; a disease or illness, an ailment. [Fr *complaindre*, from LL *complangere*, from L *com-* (intensive) and *plangere* to bewail]

complaisant *kəm-plā'zənt* or *kom'ple-zant*, *esp* formerly *-zant'*, *adj* wishing to please or tending to comply with the wishes of others; obliging. — *n* **complais'ance** (or *kom'ple-zans* or *-zans'*) desire to please, *esp* in excess; an obliging manner or attitude. — *adv* **complai'santly**. [Fr, *complaire*, from L *complacēre*]

complanate *kom'plən-āt*, (*esp bot*) *adj* flattened. — *n* **complanā'tion**. [L *complānāre*, *-ātum* to make flat]

compleat. See **complete**.

complect *kəm-plekt'*, (*archaic*) *vt* to embrace; to interweave. — *adj* **complect'ed** interwoven. [L *complectī* to embrace, from *com-*, and *plectere* to twine]

complement *kom'pli-mənt*, *n* that which completes or fills up; a number or quantity required to make something complete; that amount by which an angle or arc falls short of a right angle or quadrant; one of the parallelograms not intersected by the diagonal of a given parallelogram when it is divided into four parallelograms by straight lines through a point in the diagonal; that by which a logarithm falls short of 10; all members of a set not included in a given subset (*math*); that which is added to certain verbs to make a complete predicate; that by which an interval falls short of an octave (*music*); either of a pair of colours which together give white; a group of proteins in blood plasma that combine with antibodies to destroy antigens (*immunol*); fullness (of the moon) (*heraldry*). — *vt* **complement** (*-ment'* or *kom'pli-mənt*) to be the complement of. — *adj* **complement'al** completing; — *adv* **complement'arily**. — *n* **complementar'ity** a concept, first adopted in microphysics, which accepts the existence of superficially inconsistent views of an object or phenomenon, eg which accepts a dual aspect of light (consisting of particles, as shown by certain experiments, and of waves, as shown by others). — *adj* **complement'ary** completing; together making up a whole, right angle, ten, an octave or white; (of medical treatment, therapies, etc) not mainstream, alternative. — *n* **complementā'tion** the full or partial restoration of normal function when two chromosomes each with a different recessive mutant gene combine in one cell (*genetics*); a method of representing negative numbers in the binary system (*comput*). [L *complēmentum*, from *com-* (intensive) and *plēre* to fill]

complete *kəm-plēt'*, *adj* free from deficiency; not lacking any part; perfect; finished; entire, whole; fully equipped; consummate, fully skilled. — Also **compleat** (*-plēt'*; *archaic*). — *vt* to finish; to make perfect or entire; to accomplish. — *vi* to finish. — *adj* **complēt'able**. — *adj* **complēt'ed**. — *adv* **complete'ly**. — *n* **complete'ness**. — *n* **complē'tion** the fact of completing; the state of being complete; fulfilment. — *adj* **complēt'ive**. — *adj* **complēt'ory** fulfilling; completing. [L *complēre*, *-ētum* to fill up, from *com-* (intensive) and *plēre* to fill]

complex *kom'pleks*, *adj* composed of more than one, or of many parts; not simple or straightforward; intricate; difficult. — *n* a complex whole; a group of (repressed and forgotten) ideas or impressions to which are ascribed abnormal mental conditions and abnormal bodily conditions due to mental causes (*psychol*); loosely applied to the mental condition itself; a complex chemical substance such as a coordination compound (qv); a collection of interrelated buildings, units, etc forming a whole, eg a *sports complex*. — *vt* to complicate; to combine into a complex. — *n* **complex'edness**, **com'plexness** or **complex'ity** the state of being complex; complication. — *n* **complexificā'tion**. — *vt* and *vi* **complex'ify** to make or become complex or complicated. — *adv* **com'plexly**. — *n* **complex'us** an aggregate of parts; a complicated system; a broad muscle of the back, passing from the spine to the head (*anatom*). — **complex number** the sum of a real and an imaginary number; **complex sentence** one consisting of a principal clause and one or more subordinate clauses. [L *complex*, from *com-* together, and root of *plicāre* to fold; see **complicate**]

complexion *kəm-plek'shən*, *n* colour or look of the skin, *esp* of the face; general character, aspect or nature (*fig*); general appearance, temperament or texture (*obs*). — *adj* **complex'ional** pertaining to the complexion. — *adj* **complex'ioned** having a certain specified complexion. — *adj* **complex'ionless** colourless; pale. [Fr, from L *complexiō*, *-ōnis* a combination, physical structure of body, from *com-* together and *plectere* to plait]

compliance *kəm-plī'əns*, *n* yielding; agreement, complaisance; assent; submission; under the deregulated stock market, self-policing by securities firms to ensure that the rules to prevent information passing between departments with potentially conflicting interests are being obeyed; the degree to which patients follow medical advice; the linear displacement produced by unit force in a vibrating system (*phys*). — *adj* **complī'able** disposed to comply. — *n* **complī'ancy** compliance. — *adj* **complī'ant** yielding; flexible, submissive; civil. — *adv* **complī'antly**. [See **comply**]

complicate *kom'pli-kāt*, *vt* to make complex; to entangle. — *adj* (*bot*) folded together. — *n* **com'plicacy** (*-kə-si*) the quality or state of being complicated, complexity. — *adj* **com'plicant** overlapping. — *adj* **com'plicated** intricate, complex; difficult, confused. — *n* **complicā'tion** an intricate blending or entanglement; a complexity; (*usu* in *pl*) further disease or illness starting during treatment of or recovery from an existing medical condition; something which causes or adds to difficulty or confusion. — *adj* **com'plicātive** tending to complicate. — **complicated fracture** a fracture where there is some other injury (eg a flesh wound not communicating with the fracture, a dislocation or a rupture of a large blood vessel). — **complication of diseases** a number of diseases present at the same time. [L *com-* together, and *plicāre*, *-ātum* to fold]

complice *kom'plis*, *n* (*obs*) an associate or accomplice. — *n* **complic'ity** the state or condition of being an accomplice; complexity.

complied, **complier**. See **comply**.

compliment *kom'pli-mənt*, *n* an expression of admiration or praise; (*usu* in *pl*) an expression of formal respect or civility. — *vt* **compliment** (*-ment'* or *kom'pli-mənt*) to pay a compliment to; to express respect for; to praise; to flatter; to congratulate. — *vi* to make compliments. — *adj* **compliment'al** expressing or implying compliment. — *adj* **compliment'ary** conveying or expressing civility or praise; using compliments; given free. — *n* **compliment'er**. — **back-handed** or **left-handed compliment** a remark intended to seem a compliment, but in reality an insult; **compliments of the season** compliments appropriate to special times, *esp* Christmas, New Year, etc; **pay** or **present one's compliments** to give one's respects or greeting. [Fr *compliment*, from L *complīmentum*; see **comply**]

complin or **compline** *kom'plin*, *n* (also *cap*) in the Christian liturgy, the seventh and last service of the day, at 9pm, completing the set hours for prayer. [OFr *complie* (Mod *complies*), from L *complēta* (*hōra*)]

complish *kom'plish*, (*archaic*) *vt* to accomplish.

complot *kom'plot*, (*archaic*) *n* a conspiracy. — *vi* (*kəm-plot'*) to plot together; to conspire. — *vt* to plan: — *pr p* **complott'ing**; *pa t* and *pa p* **complott'ed**. [Fr]

compluvium *kom-ploo͞'vi-əm*, *n* a quadrangular open space in the middle of a Roman house. [L, from *compluere* to flow together (being the space into which rain flowed from the surrounding roofs)]

comply *kəm-plī'*, *vi* to yield to the wishes of another; to agree or consent to (with *with*); to be ceremoniously complaisant or courteous (*obs*): — *pr p* **comply'ing**; *pa t* and *pa p* **complied'**. — *n* **complī'er**. — *adj* **comply'ing** compliant, yielding, flexible. [Ital *complire* to fulfil, to suit, to offer courtesies, from L *complēre* to fulfil; see **complete**]

compo[1] *kom'pō*, *n* a mortar of cement; a mixture of whiting, resin and glue for ornamenting walls and cornices; a bankrupt's composition: — *pl* **com'pos**. —

compo ration (*military*) a composite 'hard' ration for use in the field when no fresh food is available. [Abbrev of **composition**]

compo[2] *kom'pō*, *n* compensation for industrial injuries, paid out of a central fund (*colloq*); (unemployment) compensation, redundancy pay (*Austr slang*): — *pl* **com'pos**. [Abbrev of **compensation**]

component *kəm-pō'nənt*, *adj* making up; forming one of the elements or parts. — *n* one of the parts or elements of which anything is made up, or into which it may be broken down. — *n* **compō'nency**. — *adj* **componental** (*kom-pō-nent'l*) or **componential** (*-nen'shəl*). [L *compōnere* to compose]

compony or **componé** *kom-pō'ni*, (*heraldry*) *adj* consisting of a row of squares of alternate tinctures. [Origin doubtful]

comport[1] *kəm-pōrt'* or *-pört'*, *vi* to agree, suit (with *with*). — *vt* to bear (*obs*); (*reflexive*) to behave. — *n* **comport'ment** behaviour, bearing. [L *comportāre*, from *com-* with, and *portāre* to carry]

comport[2] *kom'pört*, **compote** *kom'pōt* or **compotier** *kɔ̃-po-tyā* or *kom-pō'*, *n* a dish, *usu* with a stemmed base, for serving desserts, fruit, etc. [See **compot**]

compose *kəm-pōz'*, *vt* to form by putting together or being together; to put in order or at rest; to settle or soothe; to design artistically; to set up for printing; to create (*esp* in literature and music). — *vi* to write (*esp*) music; to set type. — *adj* **composed'** settled; quiet; calm. — *adv* **compōs'edly**. — *n* **compōs'edness**. — *n* **compōs'er** a writer or author, *esp* of music. — *n* **composi'tion** the act or art of composing; the nature or proportion of the ingredients (of anything); a thing composed; a work of art, *esp* in music; an exercise in writing prose or verse; arrangement of parts; combination; an artificial mixture, *esp* one used as a substitute; mental or moral make-up; a compromise; a percentage accepted by a bankrupt's creditors in lieu of full payment; the compounding of vector quantities, such as velocities forces, into a single resultant; a picture or photograph formed from several images; the transition from a concept or assertion about individuals to one about the class to which they belong (*philos*). — *adj* **composi'tional**. — *n* **composure** (*kəm-pōzh'(y)ər*) calmness; self-possession; tranquillity; composition; temperament, character (*archaic*). — **composing room** a room in a printing works in which type is set; **composing-stick** (*printing*) a boxlike holder in which type is fitted before it is placed on the galley. [Fr *composer*, from L *com-* with, and *pausāre* to cease, rest; confused and blended in meaning with words from *pōnere*, *positum* to place]

composite *kom'pə-zit*, or formerly and *NAm -poz'*, *adj* made up of distinct parts or elements; (*esp* with *cap*) blending Ionic and Corinthian styles (*archit*); belonging to the **Compositae** (*kəm-poz'i-tē*), a large family of plants related to the campanulas but having small florets crowded together in heads on a common axis surrounded by bracts, the whole resembling and functioning as a single flower; (of a proposal, etc) combining points from several sources. — *n* a composite thing; something made up of distinct parts or diverse elements; a composite portrait (*esp NAm*); a plant of the Compositae; a material consisting of a matrix such as cement or plastic reinforced by fibres. — *vt* (*-zīt*) to pool and combine (proposals from various sources, eg local branches of a political party) so as to produce a list for discussion at a higher, *esp* national level. — *n* **com'positeness**. — *adj* **compositive** (*-poz'*). — *n* **compos'itor** a person who sets up type for printing. — *adj* **compos'itous** (*bot*) composite. — **composite carriage** a railway carriage with compartments of different class; **composite photograph** a photograph printed by superimposing several negatives; **composite portrait** a blend of several portraits; **composite resolution** a resolution or proposal made up from several similar resolutions and incorporating all their main points; **composite school** (*Can*) a school offering both academic and non academic courses. — **composition of felony** compounding of felony; **metal composite** a metal with steel wires or glass fibres incorporated in it. [L *compositus*, *compostus*, from *com-* together, and *pōnere* to place]

compos mentis *kom'pos men'tis*, (*L*) *adj* of sound mind, sane.

compossible *kəm-pos'i-bl*, *adj* possible in coexistence with something else. — *n* **compossibil'ity**.

compost *kom'post* or (*obs*) **composture** *kəm-pos'chər*, *n* a mixture; manure consisting of a mixture of decomposed organic substances. — *vt* to treat with compost; to convert into compost. — *n* **com'poster** an apparatus for converting garden waste into compost. — **compost heap** a pile of plant refuse, soil and often chemical fertilizer, which decomposes to form compost. [OFr *compost*, from L *compositum* (see **composite**.]

composure. See **compose**.

compot or **compote** *kom'pot* or *kom'pōt*, *n* fruit stewed in sugar or syrup; a dessert of stewed fruit; a savoury ragout, *usu* of game. [Fr *compote*; cf **composite**]

compotation *kom-pō-tā'shən*, *n* an act of carousing in company. — *n* **compotā'tionship**. — *n* **com'potātor** a drinking companion. — *adj* **compot'atory**. [L *compōtātiō*, *-ōnis*, from *com-* together, and *pōtāre* to drink]

compote, **compotier**. See **compot**, **comport**[2].

compound[1] *kəm-pownd'*, *vt* to make up; to combine (*chem*); to settle or adjust by agreement; to agree for a consideration not to prosecute (a felony); to intensify, make worse or greater. — *vi* to agree, or come to terms. — *adj* (*kom'*) mixed or composed of a number of parts; so united that the whole has properties of its own which are not necessarily those of its constituents, as in the case of a mixture (*chem*); not simple, dealing with numbers of various denominations of quantity, etc, as in *compound addition*, etc, or with processes more complex than the simple process, as in *compound proportion*. — *n* a mass made up of a number of parts; a word made up of two or more words; a compound substance (*chem*); a compounded drug. — *n* **compound'er**. — **compound animals** same as **colonial animals**; **compound engine** a condensing engine in which the mechanical action of the steam is begun in one cylinder, and ended in a larger cylinder; **compound eye** in insects, etc, an eye made up of many separate units; **compound fracture** see under **fracture**; **compound interest** interest added to the principal at the end of each period (*usu* a year) to form a new principal for the next period, thus giving further interest on the interest to date; **compound interval** (*music*) any interval plus an octave; **compound leaf** a leaf divided into leaflets by divisions reaching the midrib; **compound number** a quantity expressed in two or more different units, as in 3 *feet* 6 *inches*; **compound quantity** (*algebra*) a quantity consisting of more than one term, as $a+b$; **compound ratio** the product of ratios; **compound sentence** (*gram*) a sentence containing more than one principal clause; **compound time** (*music*) time in which each bar is made up of two or more simple measures. [OFr *compundre*, from L *compōnere*, from *com-* together, and *pōnere* to place]

compound[2] *kom'pownd*, *n* an enclosure round a house or factory (*esp* in India), or for housing labourers (S Africa), prisoners or detainees. [Malay *kampong*, *kampung* enclosure]

comprador or **compradore** *kom-prä-dōr'* or *-dör'*, *n* (*esp* in China and the Far East) a native agent or intermediary through whom a foreign firm trades; an agent of a foreign power. [Port, buyer, from L *com-* (intensive), and *parāre* to furnish]

comprehend *kom-prə-hend'*, *vt* to grasp with the mind, to understand; to comprise or include. — *n* **comprehensibil'ity** or **comprehen'sibleness**. — *adj* **comprehen'sible** capable of being understood. — *adv* **comprehen'sibly**. — *n* **comprehen'sion** understanding; power of the mind to understand; the intension of a term or the sum of the qualities implied in the term, connotation (*logic*); the inclusion of Nonconformists within the Church of England. — *adj* **comprehen'sive** having the quality or power of comprehending or containing much; including everything; complete. — *n* a comprehensive school; a detailed layout or proof. — *adv* **comprehen'sively**. — *n* **comprehen'siveness**. — *n* **comprehensivīzā'tion** or **-s-** the act of converting schools to comprehensives. — *vt* **comprehen'sivize** or **-ise**. — **comprehensive insurance** a form of motor insurance providing cover for most risks, including accidental damage; **comprehensive school** a secondary school, serving a particular area, that provides education for pupils of all levels of ability. [L *comprehendere*, *-hēnsum*, from *com-* and *prehendēre* to seize]

compress *kəm-pres'*, *vt* to press together; to force into a narrower space; to condense or concentrate; to embrace (*archaic*). — *n* (*kom'*; *surg*) a pad used to apply pressure to any part of the body, eg to reduce swelling; a folded cloth applied to the skin. — *adj* **compressed'** pressed together; compacted; laterally flattened or narrowed (*biol*). — *n* **compressibil'ity** the property of being reduced in volume by pressure; the ratio of the amount of compression per unit volume to the compressing force applied; a shock-wave phenomenon causing increased drag, which asserts itself when an aircraft in flight approaches the speed of sound, the hypothesis of the air as an incompressible fluid being no longer valid (*aerodynamics*). — *adj* **compress'ible** that may be compressed. — *n* **compress'ibleness**. — *n* **compression** (*kəm-presh'ən*) the act of compressing; the state of being compressed or condensed; flattening; deformation by pressure; the stroke that compresses the gases in an internal-combustion engine. — *adj* **compress'ional**. — *adj* **compress'ive** tending to compress. — *n* **compress'or** anything that compresses or raises pressure, such as a device that compresses air or gas; a muscle that compresses certain parts. — *n* **compressure** (*-presh'ər*). — **compressed air** air at more than atmospheric pressure; **compression-ignition engine** an internal-combustion engine in which ignition of the liquid fuel injected into the cylinder is performed by the heat of compression of the air charge. [L *compressāre*, from *com-* together, and *pressāre*, to press, from *premere*, *pressum* to press]

comprimario *kom-prē-mä'ri-ō*, *n* (in opera or ballet) a role of secondary importance; a singer or dancer playing such a role: — *pl* **comprimar'ios**. [Ital]

comprint *kəm-print'*, *vt* to share in printing of the former privilege shared with the Stationers' Company and the King's Printer by Oxford and Cambridge universities.

comprise *kəm-prīz'*, *vt* to contain, include; to comprehend; to consist of (often, incorrectly, with *of*). — *adj* **comprīs'able**. — *n* **comprīs'al** the act, condition or fact of comprising. [Fr *compris*, pa p of *comprendre*, from L *comprehendere*; see **comprehend**]

compromise *kom'prə-mīz*, *n* arbitration (*archaic*); a settlement of differences by concession on each side; partial waiving of theories or principles for the sake of settlement; anything of intermediate or mixed kind, neither one absolute nor another. — *vt* to settle by concession on each side; to involve or bring into question; to expose to risk of injury, suspicion, censure or scandal. — *vi* to make a compromise. [Fr *compromis*, from L *comprōmittere*, *-missum*, from *com-* together, and *prōmittere* to promise]

comprovincial *kom-prə-vin'shəl*, *adj* belonging to the same province.

Compsognathus *komp-sog'nə-thəs*, *n* one of the smallest known dinosaurs, lizard-hipped, bipedal and carnivorous. [Gr *kompsos* elegant, and *gnathos* jaw]

compt, **compter**, **comptible** *kownt*, *-ər*, *-ə-bl*. *Obs* forms of **count**², etc.

Comptometer® *komp-tom'ə-tər*, *n* a machine that adds, subtracts, multiplies and divides.

compte rendu *kɔ̃t rã-dü*, (*Fr*) *n* an account rendered; an official report.

comptroll, **comptroller**. See under **control**.

compulse *kəm-puls'*, *vt* (*obs*) to compel. — *adj* **compul'satory** or **compul'sative** (*Shakesp*) compulsory. [Ety as **compulsion**]

compulsion *kəm-pul'shən*, *n* the act of compelling; force; a strong irrational impulse. — *n* **compul'sionist** a believer in compulsion. — *n* **compul'sitor** (*Scots law*) a means of compelling. — *adj* **compul'sive** with power to compel; pertaining to compulsion; (of a person) driven by, (of an action) caused by, a specific, constant and irresistible impulse; (loosely) irresistible, fascinating. — *adv* **compul'sively**. — *adv* **compul'sorily**. — *adj* **compul'sory** obligatory; compelling. — *n* an exercise comprising specified compulsory figures, movements or dances, eg in ice-skating. — **compulsion neurosis** a disorder in which the patient suffers from compulsions and/or obsessions, depression, etc; **compulsory purchase** enforced purchase by a public authority of property needed for public purposes. [L *compulsāre*, frequentative of *compellere*; see **compel**]

compunction *kəm-pungk'shən*, *n* uneasiness of conscience (*obs*); remorse tinged with pity, regret. — *adj* **compunc'tious** of the nature of compunction; feeling compunction. — *adv* **compunc'tiously**. [OFr, from L *compunctiō*, *-ōnis*, from *com-* (intensive) and *pungere*, *punctum* to prick]

compurgation *kom-pûr-gā'shən*, *n* (in Old English and other Germanic law) the clearing of the accused by the evidence of a number of witnesses swearing to his or her innocence; evidence in favour of the accused; vindication. — *n* **com'purgator** a witness who testifies to the innocence or veracity of the accused. — *adj* **compurgatō'rial** (*kom-*). — *n* **compur'gatory**. [L *compūrgāre* to purify entirely, from *com-* (intensive) and *pūrgāre* to purify; see **purge**]

compursion *kəm-pûr'shən*, (*Sterne*) *n* a pursing together.

compute *kəm-pūt'*, *vt* to calculate, *esp* with a computer; to estimate. — *adj* **computable** (*kom'* or *-pūt'*) calculable. — *n* **com'putant**, **com'putātor** or **com'putist** a person who calculates. — *n* **computā'tion** the act of computing; (a) calculation; an estimate; arithmetic. — *adj* **computā'tional** involving calculation. — *adj* **com'putative** (or *-pūt'*) of or relating to computation. — *adj* **comput'erate** computer literate. — *n* **comput'er** a calculator; a person who computes; a machine or apparatus, mechanical, electric or electronic, for carrying out (*esp* complex) calculations, dealing with numerical data or with stored items of other information, also used for controlling manufacturing processes, or coordinating parts of a large organization. — *n* **computerese'** (*facetious*) computer language; the jargon used by people who deal with computers. — *n* **computerizā'tion** or **-s-**. — *vt* **comput'erize** or **-ise** to bring computer(s) into use to control (a process, an operation, or a system of operations formerly done by manual or mechanical means); to process (data) by computer. — **computer-aided design** the process of design using computer technology, eg the use of a computer terminal to manipulate, select and store data and as a draughting board (often *abbrev* **CAD**); **computer-aided diagnosis** (*med*) the use of computer technology to aid in the diagnosis of disease, such as imaging and scanning techniques, probability-based data systems and pattern recognition systems; **computer-aided learning** a tutorial method using a computer to teach, question and assess a student; **computer-aided manufacturing** a system of integrating various aspects of a manufacturing process using computers (often *abbrev* **CAM**); **computed** (or **computerized**) **axial tomography scanner** a machine which produces X-ray pictures of cross-sections of the body with the assistance of a computer (often *abbrev* **CAT** or **CT scanner**); **computer code** another name for **machine code**; **computer conferencing** a facility whereby individuals at widely scattered locations can communicate interactively using interconnected computer terminals; **computer crime** or **fraud** crime such as embezzlement committed through the manipulation of company finances, etc by computer; **computer dating**

the meetings arranged between men and women by an agency that matches seemingly compatible couples by using personal details held on computer; **computer game** a game on cassette or disk for playing on a home computer, the player(s) attempting to manipulate moving images on the screen by operating certain keys, a control pad or joystick; a video game; **computer graphics** diagrammatic or pictorial matter produced by computer, on a screen or in printed form; **computer language** a system of alphabetical or numerical signs used for feeding information into a computer, a programming language; **computer literacy**. — *adj* **computer literate** competent, or fully versed, in the use of computers. — *adj* **computer-read'able** able to be read and understood by computers. — **computer science** the sciences connected with computers, eg computer design, programming, data processing, etc; **computer scientist**; **computer typesetting** the use of electronic equipment to process keyed material, outputting justified, hyphenated, etc lines, the output being either a new tape to be used on a typesetting or filmsetting machine or, in many systems, the final product on paper or film; **computer virus** see **virus**. [L *computāre*, from *com-* (intensive) and *putāre* to reckon]

Comr. *abbrev*: Commissioner.

comrade *kom'rid* or *kum'rid* (*archaic -rād'*), *n* a close companion; an intimate associate or friend; a fellow-soldier; in some socialist and communist circles used as a term of address, or prefixed to a name; a communist (*derog slang*). — *adj* and *adv* **com'radely**. — *n* **com'radeship**. [Sp *camarada* a roomful, a room-mate, from L *camera* a room, from Gr *kamarā*]

coms *komz*. Short for **combinations**.

COMSAT or **comsat** *kom'sat*, *abbrev*: communications satellite.

Comsomol. Variant of **Komsomol**.

comstockery *kum'stok-ə-ri*, or *kom'*, (*esp US*) *n* vigorous censorship or suppression of literary and artistic material considered to be salacious. — *n* **com'stocker**. — *n* **com'stockism**. [From Anthony *Comstock* (1844–1915), an American denunciator of the salacious in literature and art]

Comtism *komt'izm* or *kɔ̃t-ēzm*, *n* the philosophical system of Auguste *Comte* (1798–1857), the founder of Positivism. — *n* and *adj* **Comt'ian** and **Comt'ist**.

Comus *kō'məs*, *n* a god of mirth and revelry, son of Bacchus and Circe (*Roman mythol*); (without *cap*) a revel. [L, from Gr *kōmos* a revel, carousal]

Con. *abbrev*: Conformist; Conservative; Consul.

con[1] *kon*, *adv* and *n* a contraction of L *contrā* against, as in **pro and con** for and against.

con[2] (*Spenser* **conne** or **kon**) *kon*, (*archaic*) *vt* to know; to learn; to study carefully, scan, pore over; to commit to memory; to acknowledge (as in *to con thanks*); to teach or show: — *pr p* **conn'ing**; *pa t* and *pa p* **conned**, *Spenser* **cond** (*kond*). — *n* **conn'er**. — *n* **conn'ing**. [Another form of **can**, OE *cunnan* to know; perh partly *cunnian* to seek to know, examine. (See **conner**[2])]

con[3] or **conn** *kun* or *kon*, (*naut*) *vt* to direct the steering of. — Also *vi*. — *n* the act or station of conning. — *n* **con'der** or **conner** (*kun'ər* or *kon'ər*) a person who directs steering; a lookout on land, who signals the movements of fish to fishermen. — *n* **conn'ing**. — **conn'ing-tower** the pilot house of a warship or the raised structure on the hull of a submarine, acting as a bridge when the submarine is on the surface. [Older forms *cond*, *condue*, etc, from Fr *conduire*, from L *condūcere*; see **conduct**]

con[4] *kon*, (*dialect*) *n* a knock. [Fr *cogner* to knock]

con[5] *kon*, (*slang*) *adj* short for **confidence**, as in **con game** or **con trick** a swindle, **con man** or **woman** a swindler, *esp* one with a persuasive way of talking. — *vt* **con** to swindle; to trick; to persuade by dishonest means. — *n* a trick, swindle.

con[6] *kon*, (*slang*) *n* a prisoner. [Abbrev of **convict**]

con. *abbrev*: conclusion; *contra* (*L*), against; conservation.

con-. See **com-**.

conacre *kon'ā-kər*, *n* the custom of letting farmland in Ireland in small portions for rent in money or labour; the farmland let in this way. — Also **corn'acre**. — *vt* to sublet in conacre. — *n* **con'acreism**. [**corn**[1] and **acre**]

con amore *kon am-ōr'e* or *-ö're*, *adj* and *adv* with love; heartily; with tenderness (*music*). [Ital]

conarium *kō-nā'ri-əm*, (*anatom*) *n* the pineal gland: — *pl* **conā'ria**. — *adj* **conā'rial**. [Gr *kōnarion* pineal gland, dimin of *kōnos* cone]

conation, **conative**. See **conatus**.

conatus *kō-nā'təs*, *n* an effort or striving; a natural impulse or tendency: — *pl* **conā'tus**. — *n* **conā'tion** the psychological processes, including desire, instinct and volition, that lead to purposeful action (cf *cognition*). — *adj* **conative** (*kon'* or *kōn'ə-tiv*). [L *cōnātus*, *-ūs* effort]

con brio *kon brē'ō*, (*music*) *adj* and *adv* with vivacity; forcefully. [Ital]

conc. *abbrev*: concentrated; concentration.

con calore *kon ka-lö're*, (*music*) *adj* and *adv* with warmth; passionately. [Ital]

concatenate *kən-kat'ə-nāt*, *vt* to link together as in a chain; to connect in a series. — *n* **concatenā'tion** a series of links united; a series of things depending on or resulting from each other. [L *con-*, and *catēna* a chain]

concause *kon'kōz*, *n* a cooperating cause.

concave *kon'kāv* or *kon-kāv'*, *adj* curved inwards (opposed to *convex*). — *n* a hollow; an arch or vault. — *vt* and *vi* to make or become hollow. — *adv* **con'cavely** (or *-kāv'*). — *n* **concavity** (*kən-kav'i-ti*) the quality of being concave; a hollow. — *adj* **concā'vō-con'cave** or **doub'le-con'cave** (both also *-kon-kāv'*) concave on both sides. — *adj* **concā'vō-con'vex** (or *-kon-veks'*) concave on one side, and convex on the other. [L *concavus*, from *con-* (intensive) and *cavus* hollow; see **cave**[1]]

conceal *kən-sēl'*, *vt* to hide completely or carefully; to keep secret; to disguise; to keep from telling. — *adj* **conceal'able**. — *n* **conceal'er**. — *n* **conceal'ment** hiding; keeping secret; secrecy; disguise; a hiding place; a mystery (*archaic*). [OFr *conceler*, from L *concēlāre*, from *con-* (intensive) and *cēlāre* to hide]

concede *kən-sēd'*, *vt* to yield or give up; to admit, allow. — *vi* to make a concession; to admit defeat. — *n* **conced'er**. [L *concēdere*, *-cēssum*, from *con-*, wholly and *cēdere* to yield]

concedo *kon-kā'dō*, (*logic*) *vt*, *1st pers sing* I admit; I grant. [L; see **concede**]

conceit *kən-sēt'*, *n* overbearing self-esteem, vanity; thought (*obs*); a witty thought, *esp* far-fetched, affected or (over-)ingenious; a fanciful idea; understanding (*archaic*); a small ornament (*obs*). — *vt* (*obs*) to conceive; to think or imagine. — *adj* **conceit'ed** clever, witty (*obs*); fantastical (*archaic*); having a high opinion of oneself; egotistical, vain. — *adv* **conceit'edly**. — *n* **conceit'edness**. — *adj* **conceit'ful** (*Spenser*) thoughtful. — *adj* **conceit'less** (*Shakesp*) without conceit, stupid. — *adj* **conceit'y** (*dialect*) characterized by conceit. — **out of conceit with** displeased with. [From **conceive** on the analogy of **deceive**, **deceit**]

conceive *kən-sēv'*, *vt* to receive into or form in the womb; to form in the mind; to imagine or think; to understand; to grasp as a concept; to express. — *vi* to become pregnant; to think. — *n* **conceivabil'ity** or **conceiv'ableness**. — *adj* **conceiv'able**. — *adv* **conceiv'ably**. [OFr *concever*, from L *concipere*, *conceptum*, from *con-* together, and *capere* to take]

concelebrate *kon-sel'ə-brāt*, *vt* (of two or more priests) to celebrate (mass) jointly. — *n* **concel'ebrant** a priest taking part in a concelebrated mass. — *n* **concelebrā'tion**. [L *con-* together, and **celebrate**]

concent *kən-sent'*, or **concentus** *-sent'əs*, (*archaic*) *n* a harmony or concord of sounds or voices. [L *concentus*, pa p of *concinere*, from *con-* together, and *canere* to sing]

concentrate *kon'sən-trāt*, sometimes *kən-sen'-*, *vt* to bring towards, or collect at, a common centre; to focus; to direct (attention, etc) exclusively upon the matter in hand; to condense, to increase the quantity of in a unit of space. — *vi* to move towards a common centre; to direct one's thoughts or efforts towards one object. — *n* a product of concentration; something in concentrated form. — *adj* **con'centrate** concentrated. — *n* **concentrā'tion** the act of concentrating; the condensing of anything; the number of molecules or ions to a unit of volume; the directing of the mind on something, *esp* for a sustained period. — *adj* **concen'trative** tending to concentrate. — *n* **concen'trativeness**. — *n* **con'centrator** an apparatus for concentrating solutions or for obtaining minerals from ores by physical means. — **concentration camp** a prison camp for people (*esp* civilians) whom the authorities wish to remove or segregate from society. [A lengthened form of **concentre**]

concentre or (*NAm*) **concenter** *kən-sent'ər*, *vi* to tend to or meet in a common centre; to be concentric. — *vt* to bring or direct to a common centre or point: — *pr p* **concent'ring** or **concent'ering**; *pa t* and *pa p* **concent'red** or **concent'ered**. — *adj* **concen'tric** or **concen'trical** having a common centre. — *adv* **concen'trically**. — *n* **concentricity** (*kon-sən-tris'i-ti*). [Fr *concentrer*, from L *con-*, and *centrum*, from Gr *kentron* point]

concept *kon'sept*, *n* a thing thought of, a general notion; an idea, invention. — *n* **conceptacle** (*kən-sep'tə-kl*; *obs*) a receptacle; a reproductive cavity. — *n* **concep'tion** the act of conceiving; the fertilization of an ovum; the formation, or power of forming in the mind, of a concept, plan, thought, etc; a concept; (often in negative expressions) a notion, thought, idea; a mere fancy (*Shakesp*); a plan. — *n* **Concep'tionist** a nun of an order founded in Portugal in 1489 in honour of the Immaculate Conception. — *adj* **concep'tious** (*Shakesp*) fruitful. — *adj* **concept'ive** capable of conceiving. — *adj* **concep'tual** pertaining to conception or concepts. — *n* **concep'tualism** the doctrine in philosophy that universals exist only in the mind. — *n* **concep'tualist**. — *adj* **conceptualis'tic**. — *n* **conceptualizā'tion** or **-s-**. — *vt* **concep'tualize** or **-ise** to form a concept, idea, notion or mental picture of. — *vi* to form concepts; to think abstractly. — *n* **concep'tus** (*-təs*) the products of conception; the developing foetus and surrounding tissue in the uterus: — *pl* **concep'tuses** or (incorrectly) **concep'tī** (the Classical *L pl* being *conceptūs*). — **concept car** a prototype car produced by a manufacturer to illustrate a general idea or genre of vehicle; **conceptual art** a revolutionary type of art of the 1960s and 1970s, concentrating not so much on a completed image as on the means of producing an image or concept. [L *concipere*, *-ceptum* to conceive]

concern *kən-sûrn'*, *vt* to relate or belong to; to have to do with, deal with, have as subject matter; to affect or interest; to involve by interest, occupation or duty; to trouble, make anxious; to bother (oneself) with. — *n* that which relates or belongs to one; affair; business; interest; regard; anxiety; a business establishment; in Quaker terminology, a spiritual directive to act in a given matter. — *n* **concern'ancy** (*Shakesp*) bearing, relevancy. — *adj* **concerned'** interested; involved; taking an active interest in current social, etc problems; troubled, anxious. — *adv* **concern'edly**. — *n* **concern'edness**. — *prep* **concern'ing** regarding; about. — *n* **concern'ment** concern; a matter of importance (*archaic*). — **as concerns** with regard to. [L *concernere* to distinguish, (later) to have respect to, from *con-* (intensive) and *cernere* to distinguish]

concert *kon'sərt*, *n* union or agreement in any undertaking; harmony, *esp* musical; a musical performance. — *vt* (*kən-sûrt'*) to construct or devise together; to arrange, adjust. — *n* **concertante** (*kon-sər-tan'tē*; Ital *kon-cher-tän'te*) a symphonic composition in which two or more solo instruments or voices take the principal parts alternately. — *adj* providing an opportunity for brilliant virtuosity by an instrumentalist or singer. — *adj* **concerted** (*-sûrt'*) mutually planned or orchestrated; arranged in parts (*music*). — *n* **concertino** (*kon-chər-tē'nō*) a short concerto: — *pl* **concerti'nos**. — *n* **concerto** (*kon-chûr'tō*) a composition for solo instrument(s) and orchestra in sonata form; applied by earlier composers to various combinations and forms: — *pl* **concer'tos** or **concer'ti**. — **con'cert-goer** a habitual attender of concerts; **concert grand** a grand piano suitable for concerts; **concert hall**; **con'certmaster** (*NAm* or as a translation of Ger *Konzertmeister*) the leader of an orchestra; **concerto grosso** a musical work in which solo parts are played by a small group of instruments, *usu* alternating with strings or an orchestra; **concert overture** a piece of music like an overture, but composed specially to be played at a concert; **concert party** a small group of performers, entertainers, etc, often at a private function; a group of people working together to buy shares separately, in order to use them later as one holding (*stock exchange slang*); **concert pitch** a standard of pitch that has varied considerably during musical history, but is now internationally standardized so that A above middle C has a frequency of 440 hertz (see **international concert pitch**, **French pitch**); a high state of readiness, tension, etc. — **in concert** working or conspiring together; performing at a concert venue. [Ital *concertare* to sing in concert, from L *con-* and *certāre* to strive]

concertina *kon-sər-tē'nə*, *n* a (*usu* hexagonal) musical instrument consisting of a pair of bellows, the sounds produced (when the bellows are squeezed and the buttons pressed) by free vibrating reeds of metal, as in the accordion; anything of similar folded-up shape. — *vi* and *vt* to collapse or fold up like a concertina: — *pr p* **concerti'naing**; *pa t* and *pa p* **concerti'naed**. [Ety as for **concert**, plus dimin suffix]

concession *kən-sesh'ən*, *n* the act of conceding; the thing conceded; a grant; in Canada, a piece of land granted by the government; the grant of such land; the right, granted under government licence, to drill for oil or gas in a particular area; (the right to conduct) a branch of one business within a branch or on the premises of a larger one; a reduced-price ticket (for the elderly, schoolchildren, the unwaged, etc). — *adj* **concessible** (*-ses'*). — *n* **concessionaire'** or **concessionnaire'** a holder of a concession, *esp* one granted by a business or government. — *adj* **concess'ionary**. — *n* **concess'ionist**. — *adj* **concess'ive** implying concession. — **concession road** in Canada, a road running between concessions. [See **concede**]

concetto *kon-chet'tō*, *n* an ingenious turn of expression; a flash of (*esp* affected or fanciful) wit; a conceit: — *pl* **concet'ti** (*-tē*). — *n* **concet'tism** the use of concetti. — *n* **concet'tist**. [Ital, from L *conceptum* conceit]

conch *kongk* or *konch*, *n* the name for various marine molluscs and their shells; such a shell used as a trumpet; a poor white inhabitant of the Florida Keys, *esp* if of Bahamian origin (from their feeding on conchs); a concha; a shell-like device for kneading and mixing chocolate during manufacture: — *pl* **conchs** (*kongks*) or **conches** (*kon'chiz*). — *n* **conch'a** (*kong'kə*) the semi-dome of an apse (*archit*); the apse itself; the outer ear, or its cavity; a small cigar tapered at each end: — *pl* **conchae** (*kong'kē* or *-chē*). — *adj* **conch'al**. — *adj* **conch'ate** or **conch'iform** shaped like a shell, *esp* one valve of a bivalve shell. — *vt* **conche** (*kongk* or *konch*) to knead and mix (chocolate) during manufacture. *adj* **conchif'erous** having a shell; shelly. — *n* **conchiolin** (*kon-kī'ə-lin*) a fibrous protein substance that forms the basic structure of the shell of molluscs. — *n* **conchī'tis** inflammation of the concha. — *n* **conch'oid** (*geom*) a plane curve, $(x^2\ \ y^2)(x - a)^2 = l^2x^2$, the locus of a point making with a fixed straight line a constant intercept on the ray of a pencil through a fixed point. — *adj* **conchoid'al** pertaining to a conchoid; shell-like, applied to a fracture like that seen in glass (*mineralogy*). — *adj* **concholog'ical**. — *n* **conchol'ogist**. — *n* **conchol'ogy** the study of molluscs and their shells. [L *concha*, from Gr *konchē* a cockle or mussel; connected with **chank**, and **cockle**[2]]

conchiglie *kon-kē'lē-e*, *n pl* shell-shaped pasta. [Ital]

conchy or **conchie** *kon'shi*, (*derog slang*) *n* a *consc*ientious objector; an overconscientious person (*Austr*).

concierge *kɔ̃-si-erzh'*, *n* a warden; a janitor; a hall porter (male or female). [Fr; ety unknown]

conciliar *kən-sil'i-ər*, *adj* of, from or pertaining to a council, *esp* an ecclesiastical council. — Also **concil'iary**. [L *concilium* council]

conciliate *kən-sil'i-āt*, *vt* to gain, or win over; to reconcile, bring together (*esp* opposing sides in an industrial dispute). — *vi* to make friends, having been hostile. — *adj* **concil'iable** (*obs*). — *n* **conciliā'tion** the act or process of conciliating. — *adj* **concil'iative** (or *-ā-tiv*). — *n* **concil'iātor**. — *adj* **concil'iatory**. [L *conciliāre*, *-ātum*, from *concilium* council]

concinnity *kən-sin'i-ti*, *n* harmony; congruity; elegance. — *adj* **concinn'ous** elegant; harmonious. [L *concinnus* well adjusted]

concipient *kən-sip'i-ənt*, *adj* conceiving. — *n* **concip'iency**. [L *concipiēns*, *-entis*, pr p of *concipere* to conceive]

concise *kən-sīs'*, *adj* cut short; brief but pertinent. — *vt* (*Milton*) to mutilate. — *adv* **concise'ly**. — *n* **concise'ness** the quality of being concise; terseness. [L *concīsus*, pa p of *concīdere*, from *con-* (intensive) and *caedere* to cut]

conclamation *kon-klə-mā'shən*, (*formal*) *n* a shout of many together. [L *conclāmātiō*, *-ōnis*]

conclave *kon'klāv*, *n* a private room (*obs*); the room in which cardinals meet to elect a pope; the body of cardinals; any secret assembly. — *n* **con'clāvist** an attendant on a cardinal in conclave. [L *conclāve*, from *con-* with, and *clāvis* a key]

conclude *kən-kloōd'*, *vt* to enclose (*archaic*); to restrain or debar (*obs*); to close; to end; to decide; to settle or arrange finally; to infer. — *vi* to end; to form a final judgement; to state the object sought (*Scots law*). — *adj* **conclud'ed** finished; settled. — *adj* **conclud'ing** final, closing. — *n* **conclu'sion** (*-zhən*) the act of concluding; the end, close, or last part; inference, result, assumption; judgement; an experiment (*obs*); a problem, a riddle (*Shakesp*). — *adj* **conclusive** (*-kloō'siv*) or **conclu'sory** final; convincing. — *adv* **conclus'ively**. — *n* **conclus'iveness**. — **in conclusion** finally; **jump to conclusions** see under **jump**; **try conclusions** to experiment; to engage in a contest (with). [L *conclūdere*, *conclūsum*, from *con-* (intensive) and *claudere* to shut]

concoct *kən-kokt'*, *vt* to fabricate; to plan, devise; to make up or put together; to prepare or mature. — *n* **concoct'er** or **concoct'or**. — *n* **concoc'tion** the action of concocting; something fabricated or made up from separate parts, eg a story, a lie, a food dish or drink; preparation of a medical prescription, etc. — *adj* **concoct'ive**. [L *concoquere*, *concoctum*, from *con-* together, and *coquere* to cook, to boil]

concolor *kon'kul-ər*, (*esp biol*) *adj* of uniform colour. — Also **concol'orate** or **concol'orous**. [L, from *con-* together, and *color* colour]

concomitant *kən-kom'i-tənt*, *adj* accompanying; conjoined; occurring along with, because of, or in proportion to (something else). — *n* someone who or or something that necessarily accompanies. — *n* **concom'itance** or **concom'itancy** the state of being concomitant. — *adv* **concom'itantly**. [L *con-* (intensive) and *comitāns*, *-antis*, pr p of *comitārī* to accompany, from *comes* a companion]

concord *kon'körd*, or *kong'*, *n* the state of being of the same opinion or feeling; harmony; agreement; a treaty or pact; a combination of sounds satisfying to the ear (as opposed to *discord*). — *vi* **concord'** (*kən-*) to agree; to harmonize. — *n* **concord'ance** agreement; an index of the words or passages of a book or author; any similar physical characteristic found in both of a pair of twins. — *adj* **concord'ant** harmonious, united. — *adv* **concord'antly**. — *n* **concord'at** a pact or agreement, eg between the pope and a secular government. — *adj* **concor'dial** harmonious. [Fr *concorde*, from L *concordia*, from *concors* of the same heart, from *con-*, and *cor*, *cordis* the heart]

concorporate *kən-kör'pər-āt*, (*archaic*) *vt* to unite in one body. — *adj* united in the body.

concours *kɔ̃-koōr*, (*Fr*) *n* a contest, competition; a competitive examination; a meeting. — **concours d'élégance** (*dā-lā-gãs*) a competition among cars in which marks are allotted for appearance, not speed.

concourse *kon'kōrs*, *kong'* or *-körs*, *n* a large hall; an open space, *esp* in a railway station, airport, etc for transit, meeting, etc; an assembly of people for some event; concurrence of an officer who has the legal right to grant it (*Scots law*). [Fr *concours*, from L *concursus*, from *con-*, and *currere* to run]

concreate *kon'krē-āt*, (*archaic*) *vt* to create with; to create at the same time.

concremation *kon-kri-mā'shən*, *n* complete burning; cremation; burning together; suttee. [L *concremāre*, *-ātum*, from *con-* (intensive) and *cremāre* to burn]

concrescence *kən-kres'əns*, (*biol* and *med*) *n* a coalescence or growing together of separate parts or organs. — *adj* **concresc'ent**. [L *concrēscentia*, from *con-*, and *crēscere* to grow]

concrete *kon'krēt* (or *kən-krēt'*), *adj* formed into one mass; real, actual, specific, not abstract, able to be experienced; (*kon'*) made of concrete. — *n* (*kon'*) a mixture of sand, gravel, etc and cement, used in building; a solid mass formed by parts growing or sticking together. — *vt* (*-krēt'*) to form into a solid mass; (*kon'*) to cover or fix with concrete. — *vi* (*-krēt'*) to harden. — *adv* **concrēte'ly** (or *kon'*). — *n* **concrēte'ness** (or *kon'*). — *n* **concrētion** (*-krē'shən*) a concreted mass; a nodule or lump formed within a rock by materials rearranging themselves about a centre (*geol*); a solid mass formed within an animal or plant body, whether by deposition or by accumulation of foreign matter (*biol* and *med*). — *adj* **concrē'tionary**. — *n* **con'cretism** regarding or representing abstract things as concrete. — *n* and *adj* **con'cretist**. — *adj* **concrēt'ive** having the power to concrete. — *n* **concretrizā'tion** or **-s-**. — *vt* **con'cretize** or **-ise** to render concrete, realize. — **concrete jungle** (*facetious*) an area of bleakly ugly (*esp* high-rise) buildings; **concrete mixer** a machine with a large revolving drum for mixing concrete; **concrete music** same as **musique concrète**; **concrete poetry** an art form which seeks to introduce a new element into poetry by means of visual effects such as special arrangements of the letters of the poem on the printed page; **concrete steel** reinforced concrete. [L *concrētus*, from *con-* together, and *crēscere*, *crētum* to grow]

concrew *kon-kroō'*, (*archaic*) *vi* to grow together. [Fr *concrû*, pa p of *concroître*, from L *concrēscere*]

concubine *kong'kū-bīn*, *n* a woman who cohabits with a man without being married; a kept mistress; (in certain polygamous societies) a secondary wife. — *n* **concubinage** (*kon-kū'bin-āj*) the state of living together as man and wife without being married; being or having a concubine. — *adj* **concū'binary**. — *n* **concū'bitancy** a custom by which marriage between certain persons is obligatory. — *n* **concū'bitant** a person subject to such an obligation. — Also *adj*. [Fr, from L *concubīna*, from *con-* together, and *cubāre* to lie down]

concupiscence *kən-kū'pis-əns*, *n* a strong desire; sexual appetite, lust. — *adj* **concū'piscent**. — *adj* **concū'piscible**. [L *concupīscentia*, from *concupīscere*, from *con-* (intensive) and *cupere* to desire]

concupy *kon*(*g*)'*kū-pi*, (*Shakesp*) *n* short form of **concupiscence** (or perhaps of **concubine**).

concur *kən-kûr'*, *vi* to agree; to assent; to coincide; to meet in one point; to run together: — *pr p* **concurr'ing**; *pa p* **concurred'**. — *n* **concurrence** (*-kur'*) agreement; assent; the meeting of lines in one point; coincidence. — *n* **concurr'ency**. — *adj* **concurr'ent** running, coming, acting or existing together or simultaneously; coinciding; accompanying; meeting in the same point. — *n* a person who or thing that concurs; formerly, a person who accompanied a sheriff's officer as witness (*obs*). —

adv **concurr'ently**. — *adj* **concurr'ing** agreeing. [L *concurrere*, from *con-* and *currere* to run]

concuss *kən-kus'*, *vt* to affect with concussion; to disturb; to shake; — *n* **concussion** (*-kush'*) the state of being shaken or jarred; (a state of brief or partial unconsciousness resulting from) a violent blow to the head or neck causing a (*usu* temporary) disturbance in brain function; a violent shock caused by the sudden contact of two bodies. — *adj* **concuss'ive** having the power or quality of concussion. [L *concussus*, pa p of *concutere*, from *con-* together, and *quatere* to shake]

concyclic *kon-sī'klik*, (*geom*) *adj* lying or situated on the circumference of the same circle. — *adv* **concy'clically**. [L *con-* together, and Gr *kyklos* wheel]

cond. See under **con**[2].

condemn *kən-dem'*, *vt* to declare (a person, action, etc) to be wrong, immoral, reprehensible, etc; to judge unfavourably or blame; to sentence (to imprisonment or death); to demonstrate the guilt of; to force into or doom to some fate or unhappy condition; to pronounce unfit for use or consumption. — *adj* **condemnable** (*-dem'nə-bl*) that may be condemned. — *n* **condemnātion** (*kon-dəm-nā'shən*) the state of being condemned; the act of condemning. — *adj* **condem'natory** expressing or implying condemnation. — *adj* **condemned'** pronounced to be wrong, guilty or worthless; belonging or relating to one who is sentenced to punishment by death (eg *condemned cell*); declared dangerous or unfit. [L *condemnāre*, from *con-* (intensive) and *damnāre* to hurt]

condense *kən-dens'*, *vt* to reduce to smaller extent or volume; to render more dense, intense or concentrated; to subject to condensation (*chem*). — *vi* to become condensed. — *n* **condensabil'ity**. — *adj* **condens'able**. — *vt* and *vi* **condens'āte** to condense. — *n* a product of condensation; a hydrocarbon liquid, a light form of oil. — *n* **condensā'tion** (*kon-*) the act of condensing; water which, having vaporized, returns to its liquid state, eg on a cold window; the union of two or more molecules of the same or different compounds with the elimination of water, alcohol, or other simple substances (*chem*); (loosely) applied to almost any reaction in which a product of higher molecular weight than the original substance is obtained. — *n* **condens'er** an apparatus for reducing vapours to a liquid form; a mirror or lens for focusing light, eg in a microscope; a capacitor. — *n* **condens'ery** a condensed-milk factory. — **condensation trail** a vapour trail; **condensed milk** milk reduced and thickened by evaporation, with added sugar; **condensed type** printing type of narrow face. [L *condēnsāre*, from *con-* (intensive) and *dēnsus* dense]

conder. See under **con**[3].

condescend *kon-di-send'*, *vi* to act graciously to inferiors; to deign (to do something) (now *usu facetious*); to stoop to what is unworthy of one; to comply (*obs*); to agree, consent (*obs*). — *vt* to concede or grant (*obs*); to specify (*esp Scots law*). — *n* **condescend'ence** condescension; an articulate statement annexed to a summons, setting forth the allegations in fact upon which an action is founded (*Scots law*). — *adj* **condescend'ing** gracious to inferiors; offensively patronizing. — *adv* **condescend'ingly**. — *n* **condescen'sion**. — **condescend upon** to specify; to mention. [L *con-* (intensive) and *dēscendere* to descend, from *dē* down from, and *scandere* to climb]

condiddle *kən-did'l*, (*Scott*) *vt* to steal. [L *con-* (intensive) and **diddle**]

condie. See **cundy**.

condign *kən-dīn'*, *adj* (*usu* of punishment) well deserved, fitting. — *adv* **condign'ly**. — *n* **condign'ness**. [L *condīgnus*, from *con-* (intensive) and *dīgnus* worthy]

condiment *kon'di-mənt*, *n* a seasoning, *esp* salt or pepper. — *vt* to season. [L *condīmentum*, from *condīre* to preserve, to pickle]

condisciple *kon-di-sī'pl*, *n* a fellow disciple; a schoolfellow, classmate; a fellow student. [L *condiscipulus*, from *con-* together, and *discipulus* (see **disciple**)]

condition *kən-dish'ən*, *n* the state in which things exist, eg *the human condition*; a good or fit state; a particular quality of existence, good, bad, etc; rank (as in *a person of condition*; *archaic*); prerequisite, prior requirement; temper (*obs*); a term of a contract; (in *pl*) circumstances; that which must be true for a further statement to be true (*logic*); a clause in a will, etc which requires something to happen before the will is enacted (*law*). — *vi* (*rare*) to make or impose terms. — *vt* to restrict, limit; to put into the required state; to prepare or train (a person or animal) for a certain activity or for certain conditions of living; to secure by training (a certain behavioural response to a stimulus which would not normally cause it; *psychol*). — *adj* **condi'tional** depending on conditions; expressing a condition or conditions. — *n* **conditional'ity**. — *adv* **condi'tionally**. — *vt* **condi'tionate** (*obs*) to act as a condition. — *adj* **condi'tioned** having a certain condition, state or quality; caused by psychological conditioning; subject to condition. — *n* **condi'tioner** a person, substance or apparatus that brings something into a good or required condition. — *n* **condi'tioning**. — **conditioned reflex** or **response** a reflex response to a stimulus which depends upon the former experience of the individual. — **in** or **out of condition** in good or bad condition; physically fit or unfit. [L *condiciō* (wrongly *conditiō*), *-ōnis* an agreement, from *condīcere*, from *con-* together, and *dīcere* to say]

condo *kon'dō*, (*NAm colloq*) *n* short for **condominium**.

condole *kən-dōl'*, *vi* to grieve (with another person); to express sympathy in sorrow. — *adj* **condol'atory** expressing condolence. — *n* **condole'ment**. — *n* **condol'ence** (*usu* in *pl*) an expression of sympathy with another's sorrow. — *adj* **condol'ent**. [L *con-* with, and *dolēre* to grieve]

con dolore *kon do-lō're* or *-lö're*, (*music*) *adj* and *adv* with grief, mournfully. [Ital]

condom *kon'dom* or *-dəm*, *n* a thin rubber sheath worn on the penis during sexual intercourse to prevent conception or infection. [Perh from the name of the inventor]

condominium *kon-do-min'i-əm*, *n* joint sovereignty; a country whose government is controlled by two or more other countries; a block of apartments in which each apartment is separately owned (*NAm*); such an apartment (*NAm*). [L *con-* together, and *dominium* lordship, ownership]

condone *kən-dōn'*, *vt* to forgive; to pass over without blame, overlook intentionally; to excuse. — *adj* **condōn'able**. — *n* **condonā'tion** (*kon-*) forgiveness; forgiveness granted by the injured party, often formerly a reason for refusing to grant a divorce on the grounds of adultery (*law*). [L *con-* (intensive) and *dōnāre* to give; see **donation**]

condor *kon'dör* or *-dər*, *n* either of two large American vultures, the Andean condor (*Vultur gryphus*) having black plumage and a wingspan up to 3.5m (11 1/2ft), and the nearly extinct Californian condor (*Gymnogyps californianus*), having grey-brown plumage and a slightly shorter wingspan. [Sp *cóndor*, from Quechua *cuntur*]

condottiere *kon-dot-tyā'rā*, *n* a leader of a mercenary band of military adventurers, *esp* in the 13c to 16c: — *pl* **condottie'ri** (*-rē*). [Ital, from *condotto* way, from L *condūcere* to assemble, from *con-* together, and *dūcere* to lead]

conduce *kən-dūs'*, *vi* to help to bring about, lead to, or contribute towards (a result). — *n* **conduce'ment** (*Milton*). — *adj* **conduc'ible**. — *adv* **conduc'ingly**. — *adj* **conduc'ive** leading, contributing or tending; favourable to or helping towards something. — **conducive to** helping towards, promoting or encouraging. [L *con-* together, and *dūcere* to lead]

conduct *kən-dukt'*, *vt* to lead or guide; to convey (water, blood, sap, etc); to direct; to manage (one's life, business affairs, etc); to behave (*esp* oneself); to carry, transmit, allow to pass (*elec*; also *n*); to beat time for and coordinate (an orchestra, piece of music, etc; also *vi*). — *n* (*kon'dukt*) the act or method of leading or managing; behaviour; guidance; management. — *n* **conduct'ance** a conductor's power of conducting electricity, the reciprocal of the resistance. — *n* **conductibil'ity**. — *adj* **conduct'ible** capable of conducting heat, etc; capable of being conducted or transmitted. — *n* **conduc'tion** the act or property of conducting or transmitting; transmission (of eg heat) by a conductor; the passage of a nerve impulse. — *adj* **conduct'ive** having the quality or power of conducting or transmitting. — *n* **conductiv'ity** the power of transmitting heat, electricity, etc; the power of a specific substance to conduct electricity. — *n* **conduct'or** the person or thing that conducts; a leader; a manager; a director of an orchestra or choir; a person sometimes in charge of taking fares on a bus, etc but not driving it (*fem* **conduc'tress**); a railway guard (*NAm*); anything that has the property of transmitting electricity, heat, etc. — *n* **conduct'orship** the office of conductor. — *n* **conduct'us** a style of metrical Latin song of the 12c and 13c (*usu* for no more than three voices), in which all the voice parts move together: — *pl* **conduc'tī**. — **conduct disorder** a persistent pattern of antisocial or aggressive behaviour, *usu* in children or adolescents, which may include vandalism, truancy, assault, substance abuse, etc; **conducted tour** a tour (of places of interest, a workplace, factory, etc) led by a guide; **conductive education** a system of teaching children (and sometimes adults) suffering from motor disorders (eg cerebral palsy) to achieve their maxium potential by guiding them to attain specific goals in their own way by providing a concentrated course of exercise and intellectual stimulation; **conductor rail** a rail which transmits electricity to an electric train; **safe-conduct** see under **safe**. [L *conductus*, from *condūcere*. See **conduce**]

conduit *kon'dit*, or *kun'*, also *kon'dū-it* or *-dwit*, *n* a channel, pipe, tube or duct conveying water or other fluid, or covering electric wires, etc; a means of transmission or communication; a fountain for supplying the public with water (*rare*). [Fr *conduit*, from L *conductus*, from *condūcere* to lead]

conduplicate *kən-dūp'li-kāt* or *-do͞op'*, *adj* folded together lengthwise. [L *conduplicāre*, *-ātus* to double, from *con-*, and *duplex* double]

condyle *kon'dil* or *-dīl*, (*anatom*) *n* a rounded protuberance at the end of a bone for articulation with another bone, such as the ball in a ball-and-socket joint. — *adj* **con'dylar** or **con'dyloid**. — *n* **condylō'ma** a raised warty growth on the skin, the mucous passages or around the genitals: — *pl* **condylō'mas** or **condylō'mata**. — *adj* **condylō'matous**. [Gr *kondylos* knuckle]

cone *kōn*, *n* a solid figure bounded by a plane base in the shape of a circle or ellipse tapering to a fixed point (the vertex) (*geom*); anything shaped like a cone; the typical flower (or fruit) or inflorescence of the Coniferae, woody and more or less conical, with a mass of scale-like sporophylls set closely about an axis; a similar structure in other plants, eg horsetails; an ice-cream cornet, often including the ice-cream; one of a series of plastic bollards, shaped like geometrical cones, placed round obstacles, etc in the road in order to divert traffic; one of the two types of light-sensitive cells in the retina of the eye; a volcanic hill; a fan of alluvium where a torrent is checked at the foot of a declivity or in a lake. — *vt* to shape like a geometrical cone. — *vi* to bear cones. — *adj* **conic** (*kon'ik*) or **con'ical** having the form of, or pertaining to, a cone. — *n* a conic section. — *adv* **con'ically**. — *n sing* **con'ics** the geometry of the cone and its sections. — *adj* **cō'niform** in the form or shape of a cone. — **cone shell** a mollusc of the family *Conidae* with large conical shells; **cone wheat** a bearded variety of wheat; **conic section** a curve made by the intersection of a cone by a plane. — **cone off** to close off (eg one carriage-way of a motorway) with cones. [Gr *kōnos*]

con espressione *kon es-pres-yō'ne*, (*music*) *adj* and *adv* with expression.

coney. See **cony**.

confabulate *kən-fab'ū-lāt*, *vi* to chat (*colloq* **confab'**); to invent past experiences, either consciously or unconsciously, to compensate for loss of memory (*psychiatry*). — *adj* **confab'ūlar**. — *adj* **confab'ūlatory**. — *n* **confabūlā'tion** a chat (*colloq* **confab** *kon'*); the act or process of confabulating (*psychiatry*). — *n* **confab'ūlātor**. [L *cōnfābulārī*, from *con-*, and *fābulārī* to talk]

confarreation *kən-far-i-ā'shən*, *n* a Roman patrician mode of marriage, in which a spelt cake was offered up. — *adj* **confarr'eāte**. [L *cōnfarreātiō*, from *con-* with, and *fār* spelt]

confect *kən-fekt'*, *vt* to prepare by combining ingredients; to preserve. — *n* (*kon'fekt*) fruit, etc, prepared with sugar; a sweet; a comfit. — *n* **confec'tion** composition, compounding, mixing; a sweet substance mixed with a medicinal preparation to make it more palatable; a sweet; a light, frothy entertainment; an elaborate article of clothing for women's wear. — *n* **confec'tionary** a place where confections are made or kept; a confection. — *adj* pertaining to or of the nature of confections. — *n* **confec'tioner** a person who makes or sells confectionery, sweet cakes or sweets; a sweet shop. — *n* **confec'tionery** confectioners' work or art; sweets in general. [L *cōnficere*, *cōnfectum* to make up together, from *con-*, and *facere* to make]

confederate *kən-fed'ər-ət*, *adj* leagued together; allied (*esp* with *cap*, of the seceding American states in the Civil War). — *n* a person, etc united in a league; (with *cap*) a supporter of the seceding states in the American Civil War; an ally; an accomplice. — *vi* and *vt* (*-āt*) to league together or join in a league. — *n* **confed'eracy** a league or alliance; people or states united by a league; a conspiracy; (with *cap*) the league of eleven seceding states in the American Civil War (*US hist*). — *adj* **confed'eral** belonging or pertaining to a confederation. — *n* **confederā'tion** a league; an alliance, *esp* of princes, states, etc; an association of more or less autonomous states united permanently by a treaty. — *adj* **confed'erative** of or belonging to a federation. [L *cōnfoederāre*, *-ātum*, from *con-*, and *foedus*, *foederis* a league]

confer *kən-fûr'*, *vt* to give or bestow (*esp* a privilege or honour); to compare (*obs*; now only in use as *abbrev* **cf**). — *vi* to talk or consult together: — *pr p* **conferr'ing**; *pa t* and *pa p* **conferred'**. — *n* **conferee'** (*kon-*) a person with whom one confers; a person on whom something is bestowed; a person taking part in a conference. — *n* **conference** (*kon'*) the act of conferring; an appointed meeting or series of meetings for instruction or discussion; (with *cap*) a kind of pear. — *n* **con'ferencing** the practice of holding a conference in which the participants are linked by telephone, by telephone and video equipment, or by computer. — *adj* **conferential** (*kon-fər-en'shl*). — *n* **confer'ment** bestowal; a thing bestowed. — *adj* **conferr'able**. — *n* **conferr'er**. — **in conference** attending a meeting; engaged, busy. [L *cōnferre*, from *con-* together, and *ferre* to bring]

conférence *kɔ̃-fā-rãs*, (*Fr*) *n* a lecture. — *n* **conférencier** (*-rã-syā*) a lecturer.

conferva *kon-fûr'və*, *n* any freshwater alga of the genus *Conferva* (class Heterocontae) forming slimy masses or tufts of unbranched filaments; loosely applied to any filamentous freshwater alga: — *pl* **confer'vae** (*-vē*) or **confer'vas**. — *adj* **confer'void** resembling conferva. [L *cōnferva* a kind of water plant]

confess *kən-fes'*, *vt* to acknowledge fully (*esp* something wrong); to own up to or admit; to make known (eg sins to a priest); (eg of a priest) to hear a confession from; to reveal, betray, or make manifest (*poetic*). — *vi* to make confession (*esp* to a priest). — *n* **confess'ant** a person who makes a confession of sins to a priest. — *adj* **confessed'** or **confest'** admitted; avowed; declared;

evident. — *adv* **confess'edly** or **confest'ly**. — *n* **confession** (*kən-fesh'ən*) acknowledgement or admission of a crime or fault; the act of confessing; the thing confessed; a statement of religious belief; acknowledgement of sin to a priest (*auricular confession*); a religious body of common belief (*obs*). — *n* **confess'ional** the seat or enclosed recess where a priest hears confessions; the institution of confession. — *adj* pertaining to confession. — *n* **confess'ionalism**. — *n* **confess'ionalist**. — *adj* **confess'ionary** of or belonging to confession. — *n* a confessional. — *n* **confess'or** (or *kon'*) a priest who hears confessions and grants absolution; a person who makes a declaration *esp* of religious faith; a person who endures persecution but not death: — *fem* **confess'oress**. — *n* **confess'orship**. — **confession of faith** a formal statement embodying the religious beliefs of a church or sect; a creed; **confess to** to admit, acknowledge; **stand confessed** (*formal* or *archaic*) to be revealed. [Fr *confesser*, from L *cōnfitērī*, *cōnfessus*, from *con-* (signifying completeness) and *fatērī* to confess, from *fārī* to speak]

confetti *kən-fet'i* or *kon-fet'tē*, *n pl* sweets or comfits (or plaster or paper imitations of them) flung in carnival in Italy; small pieces of coloured paper flung at brides and bridegrooms. — **confetti money** paper money which is virtually worthless, *esp* as a result of acute inflation. [Ital (sing *confetto*); see **comfit**, **confect**]

confide *kən-fīd'*, *vi* to trust wholly or have faith (with *in*); to impart secrets to someone as confidences (with *in*). — *vt* to entrust; to tell with reliance upon secrecy. — *n* **confidant** (*kon-fi-dant'*) a person confided in or entrusted with secrets, *esp* in love affairs; a close friend: — *fem* **confidante'**. — *n* **confidence** (*kon'fi-dəns*) firm trust or belief; faith; trust in secrecy; self-assurance, self-belief; assuredness, *esp* in the outcome of something; admission to knowledge of secrets or private affairs; a confidential communication. — *n* **con'fidency**. — *adj* **con'fident** trusting firmly; having full belief; (*esp* self-)assured; bold. — *n* a confidential friend. — *adj* **confidential** (*-den'shl*) given in confidence; admitted to a person's confidence; private. — *n* **confidential'ity**. — *adv* **confiden'tially**. — *adv* **con'fidently**. — *n* **confīd'er**. — *adj* **confīd'ing** trustful. — *adv* **confīd'ingly**. — *n* **confīd'ingness**. — **confidence interval** (*statistics*) an interval so constructed as to have a prescribed probability of containing the true value of an unknown parameter; **confidence trick** a swindler's trick, whereby (*usu*) a person is induced to hand over money to the swindler for something they will never receive (often *abbrev* **con trick** (see under **con**[5]); **confidence trickster**; **confident person** (*Scots law*) a confidential person, partner, agent, etc. — **in confidence** secretly, as a secret; **in someone's confidence** trusted by the person in question with confidential matters. [L *cōnfīdere*, from *con-* (signifying completeness), and *fīdere* to trust]

configuration *kən-fig-ū-rā'shən*, *n* external figure, shape or arrangement; outline; relative position or aspect, *esp* of planets; the spatial arrangement of atoms in a molecule (*chem*); Gestalt, the organized whole (*psychol*); a computer system, *esp* as a complex of physical components. — *adj* **configurā'tional**. — *vt* **config'urate** or **config'ure** to shape, arrange. [L *cōnfigūrāre* to form]

confine *kon'fīn*, *n* a border, boundary or limit (generally in *pl*); (*kən-fīn'*) confinement (*archaic*); a prison (*Shakesp*). — *vt* **confine'** to limit, enclose, bound; to imprison; to border (*obs*); to be adjacent to (*obs*). — *adj* **confin'able**. — *adj* **confined'** limited; imprisoned; narrow, small. — *adj* **confine'less** (*Shakesp*) without bound; unlimited. — *n* **confine'ment** the state of being shut up; restraint; imprisonment; the time during which a woman is confined to bed during labour and immediately after giving birth; (*nuc eng*) see **containment**. — *n* **confin'er**. — *adj* **confin'ing** bordering; limiting. — **be confined** to be limited; to be imprisoned; (of a woman) to go through the process of childbirth. [L *cōnfīnis* bordering, from *con-* together, and *fīnis* the end]

confirm *kən-fûrm'*, *vt* to strengthen; to fix or establish; to ratify; to repeat the assertion of (eg a statement, an order for goods) so as to make it more definite or certain; to verify, give proof of the truth or justification of; to assure; to put through a ceremony to admit to full religious communion. — *adj* **confirm'able**. — *n* **con'firmand** a candidate for religious confirmation. — *n* **confirmā'tion** a making firm or sure; convincing proof; the rite by which people are admitted to full communion in many Christian churches; ratification by a competent court of the appointment of an executor, constituting his right to act (*Scots law*). — *adj* **confirm'ative** tending to confirm. — *n* **con'firmator**. — *adj* **confirm'atory** giving additional strength to; confirming. — *adj* **confirmed'** settled; inveterate, habitual, addicted. — *n* **confirmee'** a person to whom a confirmation is made. — *n* **confirm'er**. — *n* **confirm'ing**. — *n* **confirm'or**. [OFr *confermer*, from L *cōnfirmāre*, from *con-* (intensive) and *firmāre*, from *firmus* firm]

confiscate *kon'fis-kāt* or (*obs*) *kən-fis'*, *vt* to appropriate to or seize for the state, as a penalty; to take possession of (property) by authority. — *adj* forfeited. — *adj* **con'fiscable** (or *-fis'*). — *adj* **confiscatory** (*kon'fis-kā-tər-i* or *kən-fis'kə-tər-i*) of the nature of confiscation. — *n* **confiscā'tion** the act of confiscating. — *n* **con'fiscātor** a person who confiscates. [L *cōnfiscāre*, *-ātum*, from *con-* together, and *fiscus* a basket, purse, treasury]

confiserie *kɔ̃-fēz-ə-rē*, (*Fr*) *n* a confectionery. — *n* **confiseur** (*kɔ̃-fēz-œr*) a confectioner.

confit *kon'fit*, *n* (*obs*). Same as **comfit**.

confiteor *kon-fit'i-ör*, (*RC*) *n* (often with *cap*) a form of prayer of public confession. [L *cōnfiteor* I confess]

confiture *kon'fit-ūr*, *n* (*obs*). Same as **comfiture**.

confix *kən-fiks'*, (*esp Shakesp*) *vt* to fix firmly. [L *cōnfīgere*, *-fīxum*, from *con-* (intensive) and *fīgere* to fix]

conflagrate *kon'flə-grāt*, *vt* and *vi* to burn up. — *adj* **conflāg'rant** (*archaic* or *formal*) burning. — *n* **conflagrā'tion** a great burning or fire; a war or other major destructive disturbance. [L *cōnflagrāre*, from *con-* (intensive) and *flagrāre* to burn; see **flagrant**]

conflate *kən-flāt'*, *vt* to fuse; to combine (eg two different versions of a text) into one. — *n* **conflā'tion**. [L *cōnflāre*, *-ātum* to blow together, from *con-*, and *flāre* to blow]

conflict *kon'flikt*, *n* unfortunate coincidence or opposition; violent collision; (a) struggle, contest, war, etc; a mental or emotional struggle. — *vi* (*kən-flikt'*) to fight; to contend; to be in opposition; to clash, be unfortunately simultaneous. — *adj* **conflict'ing** clashing; competing; contradictory. — *n* (*rare*) **conflic'tion**. — *adj* **conflict'ive** tending to conflict. — **in conflict** incompatible or irreconcilable (with). [L *cōnflīgere*, *-flīctum*, from *con-* together, and *flīgere* to strike]

confluence *kon'flōō-əns*, *n* a flowing together; a meeting place, *esp* of rivers; a concourse; the act of meeting together. — *adj* **con'fluent** flowing together; running into one; uniting. — *n* a stream uniting and flowing with another. — *adv* **con'fluently**. — *n* **con'flux** (*-fluks*) a flowing together. [L *cōnfluere*, from *con-* together, and *fluere*, *fluxum* to flow]

confocal *kon-fō'kl*, *adj* (of a microscope) in which an aperture in the illuminating system confines the illumination to a small spot on the specimen, and a corresponding aperture in the imaging system allows only light transmitted, reflected or emitted by that spot to contribute to the image. [**con-** (see **com-**)]

conform *kən-förm'*, *vt* to make like or of the same form or type; to adapt. — *vi* to be or become of the same form or type (often with *to*); to comply (with *to*); to obey (with *with*). — *adj* and *adv* (*Scot*) in conformity. — *n* **conformabil'ity** the state of being conformable. — *adj* **conform'able** corresponding in form or type; compliant, agreeable; (of rock layers, etc) as, or in the position in which, originally laid down (*geol*). — *adv*

conform'ably. — *adj* **conform'al** (of a map) representing small areas in their true shape. — *n* **conformā'tion** particular form, shape or structure; adaptation. — *n* **conform'er** or **conform'ist** a person who complies with social, etc norms; a person who complies with the practices of the Established Church. — *n* **conform'ity** similarity or adherence to the norm; compliance; consistency with a standard; conformability (*geol*). — **conformal transformation** see **transformation**; **conformational analysis** (*chem*) the study of the spatial arrangements of atoms in molecules, particularly in saturated organic molecules. — **in conformity with** in accordance with. [L *cōnfōrmāre*, from *con-* and *fōrmāre*, from *fōrma* form]

confound *kən-fownd'*, *vt* to overthrow, defeat; to confuse, fail to distinguish between; to throw into disorder; to defeat in argument (*obs*); to perplex; to astonish: — *pa p* (*Spenser*) **confound'**. — *adj* **confound'ed** confused; astonished; damned, blasted (a term of disapproval; *colloq*). — *adv* **confound'edly** (*colloq*) hatefully, shamefully; cursedly. — *adv* **confound'ingly** astonishingly. — **confound it, him, you**, etc (*interj*) a mild curse. [OFr *confondre*, from L *cōnfundere*, *-fūsum*, from *con-* together and *fundere* to pour]

confraternity *kon-frə-tûr'ni-ti*, *n* a brotherhood, *esp* a religious or charitable one; clan; brotherly friendship. [L *con-*, and *frāter* brother]

confrère *kɔ̃-frer*, *n* a colleague; a fellow member or associate. — *n* **confrérie** (*kɔ̃-frā-rē*) a brotherhood. [Fr, from L *con-* together, and *frāter* a brother]

confront *kən-frunt'*, *vt* to come or be face to face with; to face in opposition; to bring face to face; to compare. — *n* **confrontā'tion** (*kon-*) or (*archaic*) **confront'ment** the bringing of (*usu* opposing or hostile) people face to face; continued hostile attitude, with hostile acts or statements but without declaration of war. — *adj* **confrontā'tional** involving, causing, etc confrontation. — *n* **confrontā'tionism** the favouring of confrontation as a political means. — *n* and *adj* **confrontā'tionist**. — *adj* **confronté** (*kon-frunt'ā*) (*heraldry*) face to face. [Fr *confronter*, from L *con-* together, and *frōns*, *frontis* forehead; see **front**]

Confucian *kən-fū'shyən*, *adj* of or belonging to (the doctrines of) *Confucius*, the Chinese philosopher (551–479 BC). — *n* a follower of Confusianism. — *n* **Confū'cianism**. — *n* **Confū'cianist**.

con fuoco *kon fōō-ōk'ō* or *kon fwō'kō*, (*music*) *adj* and *adv* with fire. [Ital]

confuse *kən-fūz'*, *vt* to perplex; to throw into disorder; to fail to distinguish between; to cause to be embarrassed or flustered; to jumble or mix together so that things cannot be distinguished. — *vi* to be confused. — *adj* **confu'sable** or **confu'sible** liable to be confused. — Also *n*. — *adj* **confused'** perplexed; disordered. — *adv* **confu'sedly** in a confused manner; disorderly. — *n* **confu'sedness** the state of being confused; disorder. — *n* **confū'sion** (*-zhən*) the state of being confused; disorder; overthrow, perdition (*archaic*); perplexity; embarrassment, shame; turmoil. [See **confound**]

confute *kən-fūt'*, *vt* to prove to be false, disprove; to refute; to bring to naught or put an end to (*obs*). — *adj* **confūt'able**. — *n* **confūtā'tion** (*kon-*). — *adj* **confūt'ative** tending to confute. — *n* **confute'ment**. [L *cōnfūtāre* to silence]

Cong. *abbrev*: Congregation; Congregational; Congress; Congressional.

cong. (*pharm*) *abbrev*: *congius* (L), gallon.

conga *kong'gə*, *n* a Latin American dance in which dancers are linked in single file and move forward in a series of steps and side kicks; music for this dance; a conga drum. — Also *vi*. — **conga drum** a tall narrow drum beaten with the hands. [Am Sp, Congo]

congé or **congee** *kɔ̃-zhā* or *kon'ji*, *n* permission to depart; a dismissal; a discharge; leave, furlough (*military*); a type of concave moulding (*archit*). — *vi* to take leave. — **congé d'élire** (*dā-lēr*) permission to elect; the crown's formal permission to a dean and chapter to elect a certain person as bishop. [Fr *congé*, from L *commeātus* leave of absence, from *com-* together, and *meāre* to go]

congeal *kən-jēl'*, *vt* and *vi* to freeze; to change from fluid to solid, eg by cooling; to coagulate; to stiffen (also *fig*). — *adj* **congeal'able**. — *n* **congeal'ableness**. — *n* **congeal'ment** or **congelation** (*kon-ji-lā'shən*) the act or process of congealing; anything congealed. [L *congelāre*, from *con-* (intensive) and *gelū* frost]

congee. See **congé**, **conjee**.

congener *kon'ji-nər*, *n* something of the same kind or nature, *esp* a plant or animal of the same genus; a secondary product in an alcoholic beverage that helps to determine its flavour, colour and power to intoxicate. — *adj* akin, of the same kind or nature. — *adj* **congeneric** (*-ner'ik*) or **congener'ical** of the same genus, origin or nature; of the congeners of an alcoholic beverage. — *n* **congener'ic** a member of the same genus; in the manufacture of alcoholic beverages, a congener. — *adj* **congenerous** (*kən-jen'ər-əs*) of the same origin, nature or kind. — *adj* **congenetic** (*kon-ji-net'ik*) having a common origin. [L *con-* with, and *genus*, *generis* kind]

congenial *kən-jē'ni-əl*, *adj* pleasant, friendly or agreeable; of the same spirit or tastes; kindred, sympathetic; to one's taste; suitable. — *n* **congēniality** (*-al'i-ti*). — *adv* **congē'nially**. [L *con* with, and *geniālis* (see **genial**[1]).]

congenic *kən-jen'ik*, *adj* (of animal cells) bred so as to be genetically identical except for a single gene locus. [**con-** (see **com-**)]

congenital *kən-jen'i-təl*, *adj* (of diseases, defects or deformities) dating from birth, but not necessarily hereditary; complete or absolute, as if from birth (*esp* in the phase *congenital idiot*). — *adv* **congen'itally**. [L *congenitus*, from *con-* together, and *gignere*, *genitum* to beget]

conger[1] *kong'gər*, *n* a large sea fish of the eel family, *Congridae*. — Also **conger-eel'**. [L, from Gr *gongros* sea eel]

conger[2] *kong'gər*, (*hist*) *n* a society of cooperating booksellers. [Origin uncertain]

congeries *kon-jer'i-ēz* or *-jēr'*, *n* a collection, mass or heap: — *pl* **conger'ies**. [L *congeriēs*, from *con-* together, and *gerere*, *gestum* to bring]

congest *kən-jest'*, *vt* to bring together or heap up; to accumulate; to cause congestion in. — *vi* to become overcrowded. — *adj* **congest'ed** overcrowded; packed closely together; overcharged; clogged; affected with an accumulation of blood or mucous. — *adj* **congest'ible**. — *n* **congestion** (*-jes'chən*) an overcrowded condition; an accumulation of blood, lymph or mucous in any part of the body; fullness. — *adj* **congest'ive** indicating congestion or tending to become congested. [L *congerere*, *congestum*, from *con-* together, and *gerere*, *gestum* to bring]

congiary *kon'ji-ər-i*, *n* in ancient Rome, a gift distributed amongst the people or soldiery, *orig* in corn, oil, etc, later in money. [L *congiārium*, from *congius* the ancient Roman gallon]

congius *kon'ji-əs*, (*pharm*) *n* a unit of liquid measure equal to the imperial gallon. [L *congius* the ancient Roman gallon]

conglobe *kən-glōb'*, *vt* or *vi* to collect together into a globe or round mass. — *adj* **conglobate** (*kon'glō-bāt* or *kən-glō'bāt*) formed into a globe or ball. — *vt* or *vi* to form into a globe or ball. — *n* **conglobā'tion**. — *vi* **conglobūlate** (*-glob'*) to gather into a globule or small globe. — *n* **conglobūlā'tion**. [L *con-* together, and *globāre*, *-ātum*, from *globus* a ball, globe]

conglomerate *kən-glom'ər-it*, *adj* gathered into a mass; bunched; composed of pebbles cemented together (*geol*). — *vt* and *vi* (*-āt*) to gather into a ball. — *n* (*-it*) a conglomerate rock (*geol*); a miscellaneous mass or collection; an industrial group made up of companies which often have diverse and unrelated interests. — *adj* **conglomeratic** (*-at'ik*; *geol*) of the nature of conglomerate. — *n* **conglomerā'tion** the state of being conglomerated; a collection or jumble of things. [L *conglomerāre*, *-ātum*, from *con-* together, and *glomus*, *glomeris* a ball of thread]

conglutinate *kən-glōō'tin-āt*, *vt* to glue together; to heal by uniting or joining. — *vi* to unite or grow together. — *adj* **conglu'tinant**. — *n* **conglutinā'tion** a joining by means of some sticky substance; the process of healing by joining or growing together. — *adj* **conglu'tinātive** having power to conglutinate. — *n* **conglu'tinator**. [L *conglūtināre*, *-ātum*, from *con-* together, and *glūten* glue]

congo. See **congou**.

Congolese *kong-gōl-ēz'* or *kong'gō-lēz* or (now *rare*) **Congoese** *kong-gō-ēz'*, *n* a native of the Congo. — Also *adj*.

Congo red *kong'gō red*, *n* a scarlet dyestuff used as a chemical indicator for acid solutions in the pH range 3-5, and as a biological stain.

congou *kong'gōō*, *n* a kind of black tea from China. — Also **con'go**. [Chinese *kung hu* labour, referring to that expended in producing it]

congrats *kən-grats'*, (*colloq*) *n pl* and *interj* congratulations.

congratulate *kən-grat'ū-lāt*, *vt* to express pleasure in sympathy with; to felicitate; to consider clever (*esp reflexive*). — *adj* **congrat'ūlable**. — *adj* **congrat'ūlant** expressing congratulation. — *n* a congratulator. — *n* **congratūlā'tion**. — (In *pl*, as *interj*) an expression of joy or felicitation. — *n* **congrat'ūlator**. — *adj* **congrat'ūlative** or **congrat'ūlatory** (or *lā'*) expressing congratulation. [L *congrātulārī*, *-ātus*, from *con-* (intensive) and *grātulārī*, from *grātus* pleasing]

congree *kən-grē'*, (*archaic*) *vi* to agree; to accord. [L *con-* together, and Fr *gré* goodwill, from L *grātus* pleasing]

congreet *kən-grēt'*, (*archaic*) *vi* to greet one another. [L *con-* together, and **greet**]

congregate *kong'grə-gāt*, *vi* to flock together. — *vt* to gather together; to assemble. — *adj* (*Spenser*) congregated. — *n* **con'gregant** a member of a congregation (*esp* a Jewish one). — *adj* **con'gregated** assembled; gathered together. — *n* **congrega'tion** a body of people actually or habitually attending a particular church; an assemblage of people or things; the act of congregating; a board charged with some department of administration in the Roman Catholic Church; a name given to certain religious orders without solemn vows; the body of Protestant Reformers in Scotland in the time of Mary Stuart; a name given to the children of Israel (*Old Testament*); an academic assembly. — *adj* **congregā'tional** pertaining to a congregation; (with *cap*) pertaining to the Independent Church. — *n* **Congregā'tionalism** a form of church government in which each congregation is independent in the management of its own affairs (also called *Independency*). — *n* **Congregā'tionalist**. — **Congregation for the Doctrine of the Faith** see **Inquisition**. [L *congregāre*, *-ātum*, from *con-* together, and *grex*, *gregis* a flock]

congress *kong'gres*, *n* an assembly of delegates, specialists, ambassadors, etc for the discussion or settlement of problems, creating legislation, etc; (with *cap*) the federal legislature of the United States; the act of meeting together; sexual intercourse. — *vi* to meet in congress. — *adj* **congressional** (*-gresh'*). — *n* **Con'gressman**, *fem* **Con'gresswoman** a member of Congress, *esp* of the House of Representatives (also **Con'gressperson**). — **Congressional Record** (*US*) the official published record of the proceedings of Congress. [L *con-* together, and *gradi*, *gressus* to step, to go]

Congreve *kong'grēv*, *n* a rocket for use in war. — **Con'greve-match** a kind of friction match. [Both perh invented by Sir William *Congreve* (1772–1828)]

congrue *kong-grōō'*, *vi* (*Shakesp*) to agree. — *n* **con'gruence** or **con'gruency** suitability or appropriateness; agreement; the quality of being congruent (*geom*). — *adj* **con'gruent** suitable; agreeing or corresponding; congruous; identical in shape so that all parts correspond (*geom*); (of two numbers) having the same remainder when divided by a third number (*math*). — *n* **congru'ity** agreement between things; consistency; suitability. — *adj* **con'gruous** suitable or appropriate; consistent. — *adv* **con'gruously**. — *n* **con'gruousness**. [L *congruere* to run together]

conia. See under **coniine**.

conic, conical. See under **cone**.

conidium *kon-id'i-əm*, (*bot*) *n* an asexual fungal spore produced exogenously from a hyphal tip, not in a sporangium: — *pl* **conid'ia**. — *adj* **conid'ial**. — *n* **conid'iophore** (Gr *phoros* bearing) a hypha that produces conidia. — *n* **conid'iospore** a conidium. [Gr *konis* dust]

conifer *kon'* or *kōn'i-fər*, *n* any tree or shrub of the group *Coniferae*, including yews, pines, firs, etc, which typically bear cones. — *adj* **conif'erous** cone-bearing; of the conifer family. [L *cōnus* (Gr *kōnos*) a cone, and *ferre* to bear]

coniform. See **cone**.

coniine *kō'ni-ēn*, *n* a liquid, highly poisonous alkaloid ($C_8H_{17}N$) found in hemlock (*Conium*). — Also **cō'nia**, **cō'nine** or **cō'nin**. [Gr *kōneion* hemlock]

conima *kon'i-mə*, *n* the fragrant resin of a tropical American burseraceous tree (*Protium*). [Carib name]

conine. See **coniine**.

conirostral *kōn-i-ros'trəl*, (*zool*) *adj* (eg of most finches) having a strong conical beak. [L *cōnus* (Gr *kōnos*) cone, and *rōstrālis*, from *rōstrum* a beak]

conj. abbrev: conjunction; conjunctive.

conject *kən-jekt'*, *vi* (*Shakesp*; also as a modern back-formation) to conjecture. — *n* **conject'ure** an opinion formed without proof; an opinion formed on slight or defective evidence or none at all; a guess. — *vi* to guess. — *vt* to make conjectures regarding; to conclude by conjecture. — *adj* **conject'urable**. — *adj* **conject'ural** involving conjecture; given to conjecture. — *adv* **conject'urally**. — *n* **conject'urer**. [L *conjicere*, *conjectum* to throw together, from *con-*, and *jacere* to throw]

conjee or **congee** *kon'jē*, (*Anglo-Ind*) *n* water in which rice has been boiled; rice or millet gruel. — *vt* to starch with conjee. [Tamil *kañji*]

conjoin *kən-join'*, *vt* to join together; to combine. — *vi* to unite. — *adj* **conjoined'** united; in conjunction. — *adj* **conjoint'** joined together; united. — *adv* **conjoint'ly**. [Fr *conjoindre*, from L *con-*, and *jungere*, *junctum* to join; see **join**]

conjugal *kon'jōō-gəl* or *kən-jōō-gəl*, *adj* pertaining to marriage. — *n* **conjugality** (*-gal'i-ti*). — *adv* **con'jugally**. — **conjugal rights** the right of sexual relations with a spouse. [L *conjugālis*, from *conjux* a husband or wife, from *con-* together, and *jugum* a yoke]

conjugate *kon'jōō-gāt*, *vt* to give the various inflections or parts of (a verb) (*gram*); to unite (*biochem*). — *vi* to undergo inflection (*gram*); to unite (*biochem*). — *adj* (*gət* or *-gāt*) joined; connected or coupled; occurring in pairs (*bot*); reciprocally related, as of two complex numbers, having their real parts equal and their imaginary parts equal but of opposite sign (*math*); having the same root, cognate (*gram*). — *n* (*-gət*) a word with the same root as another word; anything joined or connected with, or related to, something else. — *n* **con'jugant** (*biol*) one of a pair of cells or individuals undergoing conjugation. — *n pl* **Conjuga'tae** (*-tē'*) a class of freshwater algae reproducing by conjugation of like gametes, including desmids, Spirogyra, etc. — *adj* **con'jugated** conjugate; (of atoms, groups, bonds, or the compounds in which they occur) showing a special type of mutual influence, *esp* characterized by an arrangement of alternate single and double bonds between carbon atoms (*chem*). — *adj* **conjugā'tional** or **con'jugative** conjugate. — *n* and *adj* **con'jugating**. — *n* **conjugā'tion** the set of all the inflectional forms of a verb, including tense, person, voice, aspect, etc (*gram*); inflection in verbs (*gram*); the act of joining; union; temporary or permanent union of two cells or individuals preparatory to the development of new individuals, *esp* the union of isogametes in some algae and fungi (*biol*); (in prokaryotes) the process by which genetic information is transferred from one bacterium to another (*biol*). — **conjugate diameters** two diameters in a conic section, such that each is parallel to the tangent at the extremity of the other; **conjugated protein** a biochemical compound in which a protein is combined with a non-protein; **conjugate foci** (*phys*) two points such that rays of light diverging from either of them are brought to a focus at the other; **conjugate mirrors** mirrors set so that rays from the focus of one are reflected to that of the other. [L *conjugāre*, *-ātum*, from *con-* together, and *jugāre*, from *jugum*, a yoke]

conjunct *kən-junkt'* or *kon'junkt*, *adj* conjoined; joint. — *n* **conjunc'tion** connection, union; combination; simultaneous occurrence in space and time; a word that connects sentences, clauses and words (*gram*); one of the aspects of the planets, when two bodies have the same celestial longitude or the same right ascension (formerly when they were in the same sign) (*astrol*). — *adj* **conjunc'tional**. — *adv* **conjunc'tionally**. — *n* **conjunctiva** (*kon-jungkt-ī'və*) the mucous membrane of the front of the eye, covering the external surface of the cornea and the inner side of the eyelid. — *adj* **conjunctī'val** of the conjunctiva. — *adj* **conjunc'tive** closely united; serving to join; connective (*anatom*); being a conjunction or related to (the use of) conjunctions (*gram*). — *adv* **conjunc'tively**. — *n* **conjunc'tiveness**. — *n* **conjunctivitis** (*-iv-ī'tis*; *med*) inflammation of the conjunctiva. — *adv* **conjunct'ly** conjointly; in union. — *n* **conjunc'ture** a combination of circumstances, *esp* one leading to a crisis. — **conjunctive mood** (*gram*) the subjunctive mood generally, or when used in a principal clause, or in the principal clause of a conditional sentence; **conjunct tetrachords** (*Gr music*) tetrachords in which the highest note of the lower is the lowest note of the higher. [L *conjunctiō*, *-ōnis*, from *conjungere*; see **conjoin**]

conjure *kun'jər*, *vi* to practise magical tricks, *esp* for public entertainment; to make an invocation; to conspire (*obs*). — *vt* (*usu kən-jo͞or'*) to call on or summon by a sacred name or in a solemn manner; to implore earnestly; to compel (a spirit) by incantations; to call before the imagination (often with *up*); to render, effect, cause to be or become, by magic (often with *out*, *away*, etc). — *n* **conjurā'tion** a magic trick or spell; the performing of magic tricks; a solemn appeal or entreaty, supplication (*archaic*). — *n* **con'jurātor**. — *n* **conjurer** or **conjuror** (*kun'* or *kon'*) a person who performs magic tricks by sleight-of-hand, etc. — *n* **con'juring** the performing of magic tricks; the production of apparently miraculous effects by natural means. — *n* **con'jury** magic. — **to conjure with** regarded as influential, powerful or important (*esp* in the phrase *a name to conjure with*). [Fr *conjurer*, from L *conjūrāre* to swear together, from *con-*, and *jūrāre* to swear]

conk[1] *kongk*, *n* the fructification of a fungal parasite on a tree (*NAm*); timber disease due to this parasite (*NAm*). — *n* **conk'er** a horse chestnut (or formerly a snail shell) threaded on a string and used in the game of **conkers**, in which each player seeks to break their opponent's by hitting it with their own; a horse chestnut. — *adj* **conk'y** affected by the disease conk. [Prob **conch**]

conk[2] *kongk*, (*slang*) *vi* to get out of order, fail, break down (*esp* with *out*); to fall asleep, collapse from exhaustion, die (with *out*). [Origin uncertain]

conk[3] *kongk*, (*slang*) *n* the nose; the head; a blow on the head. — *vt* to strike (a person) on the head.

con moto *kon mō'tō*, (*music*) *adj* and *adv* with movement; briskly. [Ital]

Conn. *abbrev*: Connecticut (US state).

conn. See **con**[3].

conn. *abbrev*: connected; connection.

connate *kon'āt*, *adj* inborn; innate; allied; congenital (*med*); united in growth (*biol*). — *n* **connā'tion** (*biol*) union, *esp* of similar parts or organs. — **connate water** water which has been trapped in sediments since their deposition. [L *con-*, and *nāscī*, *nātus* to be born]

connatural *kə-nach'ə-rəl*, *adj* of the same or similar nature; congenital (*med*). — *adv* **connat'urally**. [Ety as for **connate**]

conne. See under **con**[2].

connect *kən-ekt'*, *vt* to tie or fasten together; to establish a relation between; to associate. — *vi* to be or become joined; to be significant or meaningful (*colloq*); to hit a target with a blow, a kick, etc (*colloq*); to have or develop an understanding or rapport (*NAm*); to find a source of illicit drugs (*slang*). — *adj* **connect'able** or **connect'ible**. — *adj* **connect'ed** joined; linked; coherent; related. — *adv* **connect'edly**. — *n* **connect'er** or **connect'or**. — *n* **connection** or **connexion** (*-ek'shən*) the act of connecting; that which connects; a religious body or society held together by a set of shared beliefs; context; relation; intimacy; coherence; intercourse; the opportunity or time to change trains, buses, etc; a relative, *esp* a distant one, or one by marriage; (*usu* in *pl*) a friend or relative in a position of power or influence; (in *pl*) the owner and trainer of a racehorse and their associates; the supplying of narcotic drugs (*slang*); a supplier of such drugs, a dealer or pusher (*slang*). — *n* **connec'tionism** the theory that connections between neurons govern behaviour and thought (*psychol*); (in artificial intelligence) the modelling of systems on networks made up of electronic neurons connected in a simplified model of the network of neurons in the brain. — *adj* **connect'ive** binding together (*anatom*). — *n* a word that connects sentences and words. — *adv* **connect'ively**. — *n* **connectiv'ity**. — **connecting rod** a rod attached to two parts of a machine to allow motion in one part to cause motion in the other part, *esp* such a rod connecting a piston to a crankshaft; **connective tissue** any of several kinds of animal tissue fulfilling mechanical functions, consisting of an amorphous matrix embedded with specialized cells, and forming bone, cartilage, tendons, ligaments, and enswathing membranes. — *adj* **well-connect'ed** related to people of good social standing. — **in connection with** concerning. [L *con-* and *nectere*, *nexum* to tie]

conner[1] *kun'ər*, *n* an inspector or tester. [OE *cunnere*, from *cunnian* to learn, seek to know]

conner[2] or **cunner** *kun'ər*, *n* a kind of wrasse, the goldsinny or corkwing; a related American fish. [Origin obscure]

conner[3]. See under **con**[2,3].

connexion. See **connect**.

conning-tower. See **con**[3].

conniption *kə-nip'shən*, (*NAm slang*) *n* a fit of rage or hysteria (also **conniption fit**); a tantrum. [Perh Ger *knipsen* to snap, click]

connive *kən-īv'*, *vi* to plot or conspire (often with *with*); to agree to take no notice of, and thus tacitly encourage (a crime, wrongdoing, etc) (often with *at*); to have a private understanding (often with *with*). — *n* **conniv'ance**. — *n* **conniv'er**. [L *connīvēre*, *cōnīvēre* to wink]

connivent *kə-nī'vənt*, (*biol*) *adj* (of insect or plant parts) converging and touching, but not united or fused. — *n* **conniv'ence** or **conniv'ency**. [See **connive**]

connoisseur *kon-əs-ûr'* or *kon'*, *n* a person with a well-informed knowledge and appreciation, *esp* of fine food and wine or of the arts. — *n* **connoisseur'ship** the skill and knowledge of a connoisseur. [Fr (now *connaisseur*), from *connoître* (*connaître*), from L *cognōscere* to know]

connote *kon-ōt'*, *vt* to signify or suggest (ideas, associations, etc) in addition to the direct meaning; to imply as inherent attribute(s); to include as or involve a condition. — *vt* **connotate** (*kon'ō-tāt*) to connote. — *n* **connotā'tion** the act of connoting; an idea, association or implication additional to the idea, object, etc denoted. — *adj* **conn'otātive** (or *-nō'tə-tiv*) or **connō'tive**. [L *con-* with, and *notāre* to mark]

connubial *kən-ū'bi-əl*, *adj* pertaining to marriage. — *n* **connubiality** (*-al'i-ti*). — *adv* **connū'bially**. [L *con-* and *nūbere* to marry]

connumerate *kən-ū'mə-rāt*, *vt* to count together. — *n* **connumerā'tion**.

conodont *kon'ə-dont* or *kōn-*, *n* a microscopic phosphatic toothlike fossil, mainly from the Devonian period, derived from an unknown group of animals, but thought to be vertebrates. — Also *adj*. [Gr *kōnos* cone, and **odont**]

conoid *kōn'oid*, *n* anything like a cone in form; a solid generated by the revolution of a parabola, hyperbola or ellipse about its axis. — *adj* **cōn'oid**, **cōnoid'al**, **cōnoid'ic** or **cōnoid'ical**. [Gr *kōnos* a cone, and *eidos* form]

conquer *kong'kər*, *vt* to overcome or vanquish (also *fig*); to gain control of by force or with an effort (also *fig*). — *vi* to be the victor. — *adj* **con'querable**. — *n* **con'querableness**. — *adj* **con'quering**. — *adv* **con'queringly**. — *n* **con'queror** a person who conquers; a victor: — *fem* (*rare*) **con'queress**. — *n* **conquest** (*kong'kwest*) the act of conquering; that which is conquered or acquired by physical or moral force; the act of gaining the affections of another; the person whose affections have been gained; acquisition otherwise than by inheritance (*old Scots law*). — **the Conqueror** William I of England (L *conquestor*); **the Conquest** the acquisition of the throne of England by William, Duke of Normandy, in 1066. [OFr *conquerre*, from L *conquīrere*, *conquaerere*, from *con-* (intensive) and *quaerere* to seek]

conquistador *kong'kēs-ta-dōr'*, *-dör* or *-kwis'*, *n* a conqueror, *esp* applied to the Spanish conquerors of Mexico and parts of S America in the 16c: — *pl* **conquis'tadors** or **conquistadores** (*-dōr'es* or *-dör'es*). [Sp, from L *conquīrere*]

con-rod *kon'rod*, *n* short for **connecting-rod**.

cons. *abbrev*: consecrated; consigned; consignment; consolidated; consonant; constable; constitution; constitutional; construction; consulting.

consanguine *kon-sang'gwin*, *adj* related by blood; of the same family or descent (also **consanguin'eous**). — *n* **consanguin'ity** relationship by blood as opposed to affinity or relationship by marriage; a close relationship or connection. [L *cōnsanguineus*, from *con-* with, and *sanguis* or *sanguīs* blood]

conscience *kon'shəns*, *n* inmost thought, consciousness (*Shakesp*); the sense of moral correctness that governs or influences a person's actions or thoughts; scrupulousness, conscientiousness, diligence. — *interj* (*Scot*) an expression of surprise (also **my conscience**). — *adj* **con'scienceless**. — *adj* **con'scient** aware; conscious. — *adj* **conscientious** (*-shi-en'shəs*) regulated by a regard to conscience; scrupulous; tending to take great care, show diligence, etc. — *adv* **conscien'tiously**. — *n* **conscien'tiousness**. — *adj* **con'scionable** (*-shən-ə-bl*; *obs*) governed or regulated by conscience. — *n* (*obs*) **con'scionableness**. — *adv* (*obs*) **con'scionably**. — **conscience clause** a clause in a law, contract, etc which allows people with moral objections not to obey, be bound, etc; **conscience money** money given to relieve the conscience, as compensation for wrongdoing. — *adj* **con'science-stricken** stung by conscience, feeling guilty. — **conscientious objector** a person who objects on grounds of conscience, *esp* to military service. — **crisis of conscience** a state of acute unease over a difficult moral decision; **freedom of conscience** the right to hold religious or other beliefs without persecution; **good** (or **bad**) **conscience** an approving (or reproving) conscience; **in all conscience** certainly; by all that is right and fair (*colloq*); **make a matter of conscience** to have scruples about; **on one's conscience** causing feelings of guilt; **prisoner of conscience** a person imprisoned on account of his or her political beliefs; **speak one's conscience** (*Shakesp*) to speak frankly; to give one's opinion. [Fr, from L *cōnscientia* knowledge, from *cōnscīre* to know well, in one's own mind, from *con-* (intensive) and *scīre* to know]

conscious *kon'shəs*, *adj* having the feeling or knowledge of something; aware; having consciousness. — *n* the conscious mind. — **-conscious** *combining form* being very aware of and concerned about, as in *clothes-conscious*, *cost-conscious*. — *adv* **con'sciously**. — *n* **con'sciousness** the waking state of the mind; the knowledge which the mind has of anything that is acually being experienced; awareness; thought. — **con'sciousness-raising** development of awareness of one's identity and potential or of (*esp* public) awareness of social and political issues. — Also *adj*. [L *cōnscius*, from *cōnscīre* to know; see **conscience**]

conscribe *kən-skrīb'*, *vt* to enlist by conscription. — *adj* **conscript** (*kon'skript*) enrolled or registered, *esp* compulsorily. — *n* someone enrolled and liable to serve compulsorily, *esp* in the armed forces. — *vt* (*kən-skript'*) to enlist compulsorily. — *n* **conscrip'tion** a compulsory enrolment for service; the obtaining of recruits by compulsion. — *adj* **conscrip'tional**. — *n* and *adj* **conscrip'tionist**. — **conscript fathers** (L *patrēs cōnscrīptī*) the senators of ancient Rome; hence, any august legislators. [L *cōnscrībere* to enrol, from *con* together, and *scrībere*, *scrīptum* to write]

consecrate *kon'si-krāt*, *vt* to render holy or venerable; to set apart for a holy use; to hallow; to devote (time, energy, etc). — *adj* consecrated; sanctified; devoted. — *n* **consecrā'tion** the act or process of rendering holy. — *adj* **con'secrative**. — *n* **con'secrātor**. — *adj* **consecratory** (*-krā'tər-i*) making sacred or holy. [L *cōnsecrāre*, *-ātum* to make wholly sacred, from *con-* (intensive) and *sacrāre* to set apart as sacred, from *sacer* sacred]

consectary *kən-sek'tə-ri*, (*archaic*) *n* a deduction, conclusion or corollary. — *adj* consequent; following logically or naturally. [L *cōnsectārī*, frequentative of *cōnsequī*; see **consecutive**]

consecutive *kən-sek'ū-tiv*, *adj* following in regular order or one after another; expressing consequence (*gram*). — *n* **consecution** (*kon-si-kū'shən*) a train of consequences or logical deductions; a series of things that follow one another; succession of similar intervals in harmony (*music*). — *adv* **consec'utively**. — *n* **consec'utiveness**. [L *cōnsequī*, from *con-* (intensive) and *sequī*, *secūtus* to follow]

conseil *kɔ̃-sāy*, (*Fr*) *n* advice; council. — **conseil d'administration** a board of directors; **conseil de famille** (*də fa-mē-y'*) a family consultation; **conseil d'état** (*dā-ta*) a council of state.

consenescence *kon-sən-es'əns*, (*formal*) *n* general decay. — Also **consenesc'ency**. [L *con-* (intensive) and *senēscere* to grow old]

consensus *kən-sen'səs*, *n* agreement of various parts; agreement in opinion; unanimity; (loosely) trend of opinion. — *n* **consen'sion** mutual consent. — *adj* **consen'sual** relating to consent; existing by or based only on consent (*legal*); (of reflex actions) responding to stimulation in another part of the body (*med*). — *adv* **consen'sually**. — **consensual contract** a contract drawn up and requiring only the consent of all parties; **consensus sequence** a DNA sequence found with minor variations and similar function in widely divergent organisms. [L *cōnsēnsus*, from *cōnsentīre*; see **consent**]

consent *kən-sent'*, *vi* to agree; to give permission; to accede; to comply; to be of the same mind. — *vt* to agree. — *n* agreement; permission; accordance with or acceptance of the actions or opinions of another; concurrence; acquiescence. — *adj* **consentaneous** (*kon-sən-tā'ni-əs*) agreeable or accordant; consistent. — *adv* **consentā'neously**. — *n* **consentā'neousness** or **consentaneity** (*kon-sen-tə-nē'i-ti*). — *n* **consentience** (*kən-sen'shəns*) agreement. — *adj* **consen'tient** agreeing. — *adv* **consent'ingly**. — **consenting adult** a person over the age of 21, legally able to enter into a homosexual relationship in private (also *fig*). — **age of consent** the age at which a person is legally competent to give consent to certain acts, *esp* sexual intercourse; **with one consent** unanimously. [L *cōnsentīre*, from *con-* and *sentīre* to feel, to think]

consequence *kon'si-kwəns*, *n* that which follows or comes after as a result or inference; effect; importance; social standing; the relation of an effect to its cause (*logic*);

consequentiality; (in *pl*) a game describing the meeting of a man and a woman and its consequences, each player writing a part of the story, without knowing what previous writers have written. — *vi* (*archaic*) to draw inferences. — *adj* **con'sequent** following, *esp* as a natural effect or deduction; flowing in the direction of the original slope of the land (distinguished from *subsequent* and *obsequent*; *geol*). — *n* that which follows; the natural effect of a cause. — *adj* **consequential** (*-kwen'shl*) following as a result, *esp* an indirect result; significant, important; self-important. — *n* **consequen'tialism** (*ethics*) the principle stating that the morality of an action is judged according to how good or bad its consequences are. — *adv* **consequen'tially**. — *adv* **con'sequently**. — **in consequence (of)** as a result (of); **of no consequence** trivial, unimportant; **take the consequences** to accept the (often unpleasant) results of one's actions. [Fr, from L *cōnsequī*, from *con-* (intensive) and *sequī* to follow]

conservative *kən-sûr'və-tiv*, *adj* tending to support the preservation of established views, customs, institutions, etc; opposed or averse to change; traditional; moderate; cautious; (with *cap*) belonging, or pertaining, to the Conservative party. — *n* a person opposed or averse to change; a traditionalist; (with *cap*) a person belonging to or supporting the political party which favours the preservation of existing institutions and seeks to promote free enterprise. — *n* **conser'vatism** opposition to innovation; (with *cap*) the policies and principles of the Conservative party. — *adv* **conser'vatively** traditionally; in a traditional way; moderately or cautiously. — *n* **conser'vativeness** conventionality; moderation. — **Conservative Party** in the UK, Canada and Australia, the political party advocating support of established customs and institutions, opposition to socialism, and *usu* favouring free enterprise. [Ety as for **conserve**]

conserve *kən-sûrv'*, *vt* to keep in a whole, safe or undamaged state; to retain; to preserve; to preserve in sugar (*obs*). — *n* (also *kon'*) something preserved, eg fruits in sugar. — *adj* **conser'vable**. — *n* **conser'vancy** in the UK, a court or commission having authority to preserve a river, forest, port or area of countryside; the act of preserving; *esp* official care of a river, forest, etc. — *adj* **conser'vant**. — *n* **conservā'tion** (*kon-*) the act of conserving (*esp* old buildings, flora and fauna, the environment). — *adj* **conservā'tional**. — *n* **conservā'tionist** a person who is actively interested in conservation, *esp* of the environment or natural resources. — *n* **conservatoire** (*kɔ̃-ser-va-twär* or *kən-sûr-və-twär'*) or **conservatō'rium** a school of music. — *n* **con'servātor** (or *kən-sûr'və-tər*) a person who preserves from injury or violation; an official with (*usu* administrative) responsibility for a conservancy; a guardian, custodian: — *fem* **conservā'trix**. — *n* **conser'vatorship**. — *n* **conser'vatory** a storehouse; a greenhouse or place in which exotic plants are kept, *esp* one interconnecting with a house; a school of music. — *adj* (*rare*) preservative. — *n* **conser'ver**. — **conservation area** an area designated as being of special architectural or historic interest, and therefore protected from any alterations which would destroy its character; **conservation of mass and energy** (*phys*) the principle that the sum of the total amount of mass and energy in a given isolated system is constant. [L *cōnservāre*, from *con-* and *servāre* to keep]

consider *kən-sid'ər*, *vt* to look at attentively or carefully; to think or deliberate on; to take into account; to attend to; to regard as; to think, hold the opinion (that); to reward (*obs*). — *vi* to think seriously or carefully; to deliberate. — *adj* **consid'erable** large enough to be worthy of consideration, significant; worthy of respect or attention; of some importance; showing or having a high degree of (a quality, eg courage). — *n* **consid'erableness**. — *adv* **consid'erably**. — *n* **consid'erance** (*archaic*) consideration. — *adj* **consid'erate** (*-it*) thoughtful for the feelings and interests of others; considered, deliberate (*archaic*). — *adv* **consid'erately**. — *n* **consid'erateness** thoughtfulness for others. — *n* **considerā'tion** careful thought; something considered; motive or reason; considerateness; importance; recompense, payment; the reason or basis of an agreement or compact; the thing given or done or abstained from by agreement with another, dependent on or in consequence of that other giving, doing or abstaining from something (*law*). — *adj* **consid'erative** (*obs*) thoughtful; prudent; considerate. — *adv* **consid'eratively** (*obs*). — *adj* **consid'ered** carefully thought out, deliberate. — *prep* **consid'ering** in view of. — *conj* seeing that. — *adv* everything considered. — *adv* **consid'eringly** with consideration. — **in consideration of** because of; as payment for; **take into consideration** to allow for; **under consideration** being considered or dealt with. [L *cōnsīderāre*, perh orig a term of augury and from *con-*, and *sīdus*, *sīderis* star]

consign *kən-sīn'*, *vt* to entrust; to commit; to transmit; to transfer; to devote; to sign or seal (*obs*). — *adj* **consign'able**. — *n* **consignation** (*kon-sig-nā'shən*). — *n* **consignatory** (*kən-sig'nə-tər-i*) a co-signatory. — *adj* **consigned'** given in trust. — *n* **consignee** (*kon-sīn-ē'*) a person to whom anything is consigned or entrusted. — *n* **consign'er** or **consign'or**. — *n* **consign'ment** a thing consigned; a set of things consigned together; the act of consigning. [L *cōnsignāre* to attest]

consignify *kon-sig'ni-fī*, (*formal*) *vt* to mean when taken along with something else. — *n* **consignificā'tion**. — *adj* **consignif'icative**.

consilience *kən-sil'i-əns*, *n* concurrence; coincidence. — *adj* **consil'ient** agreeing. [L *con-* together, and *salīre* to leap]

consimilar *kən-sim'i-lər*, *adj* like each other. — *n* **consimilar'ity**. — *n* **consimil'itude**. — *n* **consimil'ity**. [L *cōnsimilis*]

consist *kən-sist'*, *vi* to be composed or formed (of); to exist, lie or have its being (in); to be expressed or shown (by); to be compatible or consistent. — *n* **consist'ence** consistency; substance. — *n* **consist'ency** consistence; degree of density or thickness; agreement with something previously stated or shown; harmony, compatibility. — *adj* **consist'ent** free from contradiction; fixed or steady; not fluid; agreeing together, harmonious, compatible; true to principles. — *adv* **consist'ently**. — *adj* **consistō'rial**. — *adj* **consistō'rian**. — *n* **con'sistory** (or *-sist'*) an assembly or council (*archaic*); a spiritual or ecclesiastical court or governing body; an assembly of cardinals and the pope (*RC*); the place where such a court or assembly meets. — Also *adj*. [L *cōnsistere*, from *con-* together, and *sistere* to set, stand]

consociate *kon-sō'shi-āt*, *vt* and *vi* to associate together or bring into association. — *adj* **consō'ciated**. — *n* **consociation** (*-si-* or *-shi-ā'shən*) companionship; association; alliance, *esp* of churches; a federal council of Congregational churches; a subdivision of an association dominated by one particular species (*bot*). — *adj* **consocia'tional**. — *n* **consocies** (*-sō'shi-ēz*) a community in nature with a single dominant species. [L *cōnsociāre*, *-ātum*, from *con-*, and *sociāre* to associate, from *socius* a companion]

console[1] *kən-sōl'*, *vt* to give solace or comfort to; to cheer in distress. — *adj* **consōl'able**. — *n* **consolā'tion** solace; alleviation of misery; a comforting action or circumstance. — *adj* **consolatory** (*kən-sol'ə-tər-i*, or *-sōl'*) comforting. — *n* **console'ment**. — *n* **consol'er**: — *fem* (*rare*) **consolā'trix**. — **consolā'tion-match**, **-prize**, **-race**, etc a match, prize, race, etc, for those participants who have been unsuccessful or have not won. [L *cōnsōlārī*, from *con-* (intensive) and *sōlārī* to comfort]

console[2] *kon'sōl*, *n* the key-desk of an organ; a panel or cabinet with dials, switches, etc, control unit of an electrical, electronic or mechanical system; an ornamental device resembling a bracket, frequently in the form of the letter S, used to support cornices, or for placing busts, vases or figures on; a large radio or television set or radiogram that stands, in a cabinet, on the floor; a cabinet for this or similar apparatus. — **console table** a table supported against a wall by consoles or brackets. [Fr; prob connected with **consolidate**]

consolidate *kən-sol'i-dāt*, *vt* to make solid; to form into a compact mass; to unite into one; to merge; to rearrange and strengthen (*military*). — *vi* to grow solid or firm; to unite. — *adj* made firm or solid; united. — *adj* **consol'idated**. — *n* **consolidā'tion** the act or process of consolidating; (in industry) a programme of compulsory redundancies (*euphem*). — *adj* **consol'idative** tending to consolidate; having the quality of healing. — *n* **consol'idator**. — **consolidated annuities** see **consols**; **consolidated fund** a fund made up by uniting the yield of various taxes, etc to meet standing charges, eg interest on national debt, grants to royal family, etc; **consolidation acts** acts of parliament which combine into one general statute several special enactments. [L *cōnsolidāre*, *-ātum*, from *con-* (intensive) and *solidus* solid]

consols *kon'solz* or *kon-solz'*, *n pl* government securities without a maturity date. [Short for **consolidated annuities**]

consolute *kon'sə-lo͞ot*, *adj* (of liquids) mutually or equally soluble. [L *consolūtus*, from *con-*, and *solvere* to dissolve]

consommé *kɔ̃-som-ā* or *kən-som'ā*, *n* a clear soup made from meat by slow boiling. [Fr, pa p, from L *cōnsummāre*, *-ātum* to consummate]

consonant *kon'sən-ənt*, *n* any speech sound other than a vowel; a letter of the alphabet representing such a sound. — *adj* consistent (with); suitable; harmonious. — *n* **con'sonance** a state of agreement or accord; agreement or unison of sounds, harmony; a combination of musical notes which can sound together without the harshness produced by beats; concord. — *n* **con'sonancy** harmony. — *adj* **consonantal** (*-ant'l*). — *adv* **con'sonantly**. — *adj* **con'sonous** harmonious. [L *cōnsonāns*, *-antis*, pr p of *cōnsonāre* to harmonize, from *con-* and *sonāre* to sound]

con sordino *kon sör-dē'nō*, (*music*) *adj* (of an instrument) played with a mute. [Ital]

consort *kon'sört* or *-sərt* (*archaic*, *-sört'*), *n* a partner; a companion; a wife or husband, *esp* of a reigning monarch; an accompanying ship; a partnership or association (*obs*); agreement, accord (*obs*); formerly, a small group of instruments played or musicians playing together. — *vt* **consort'** to accompany; to associate, combine or unite (with). — *vi* to associate or keep company (with); to agree. — *adj* **consort'ed** associated. — *n* **consort'er**. — *n* **con'sortism** symbiosis. — *n* **consortium** (*kon-sör'ti-əm*, *-shəm* or *-shi-əm*) a combination of several banks, business concerns, or other bodies; fellowship; association; the association of fungus and alga in a lichen; in marriage, the right of a spouse to the company, affection and assistance of the other (*law*): — *pl* **consor'tia** or (*esp NAm*) **consor'tiums**. — **in consort** in company; in harmony. [L *cōnsors*, *-sortis*, from *con-*, and *sors* a lot]

conspecific *kon-spə-sif'ik*, (*biol*) *adj* of the same species. — *n* a plant or animal of the same species. [L *con-* with, and **specific**; see **species**]

conspectus *kən-spek'təs*, *n* a comprehensive view or survey; a synopsis, summary. — *n* **conspectuity** (*kon-spek-tū'i-ti*; *Shakesp*) sight. [L *cōnspectus*, from *cōnspicere* to look at; see **conspicuous**]

conspicuous *kən-spik'ū-əs*, *adj* catching the eye; noticeable; prominent or attracting attention. — *n* **conspicū'ity** (*kon-*) or **conspic'uousness**. — *adv* **conspic'uously**. — **conspicuous consumption** extravagant, ostentatious spending on luxury goods in order to impress other people. [L *cōnspicuus*, from *cōnspicere*, from *con-* (intensive) and *specere* to look]

conspire *kən-spīr'*, *vi* to plot or scheme together; to devise; to act together to one end. — *vt* to plan, devise. — *n* **conspiracy** (*-spir'ə-si*) the act of conspiring; a banding together for a (often secret, *usu* unlawful) purpose; a plot; joint action, concurrence. — *adj* **conspīr'ant** conspiring. — *n* **conspir'ator** a person who conspires. — *adj* **conspiratōrial**. — *adv* **conspiratō'rially**. — *n* **conspīr'er** conspirator. — *adv* **conspīr'ingly**. — **conspiracy of silence** an agreement, *esp* between a group of people, not to talk about a particular matter in order to prevent others from obtaining information. [L *cōnspīrāre*, from *con-* together, and *spīrāre* to breathe]

con spirito *kon spir'i-tō* or *spēr'ē-tō*, (*esp music*) *adj* and *adv* with spirit. [Ital]

conspurcation *kon-spûr-kā'shən*, (*obs*) *n* defilement. [L *cōnspurcāre*, *-ātum* to defile]

const. *abbrev*: constant; constitution.

constable *kun'stə-bl*, or *kon'*, *n* a policeman or policewoman of the lowest rank; applied to various other peace officers; the warden or keeper of a royal castle or fort; a military or administrative officer in an area or district or high-ranking officer of the royal household (*Med hist*). — *n* **con'stableship**. — *n* **con'stablewick** (*hist*) the district of a constable. — *n* **constabulary** (*kən-stab'ū-lər-i*) an organized body of constables; a police force. — *adj* of or pertaining to constables, or peace-officers. — **Constable of France** chief of the household under the old French kings, then commander-in-chief of the army, judge in questions of chivalry, tournaments and martial displays; **High Constable** one of two constables formerly appointed in every hundred or franchise, to raise the military levy, and with responsibility for maintenance of the peace; **Lord High Constable of England** an officer of the crown, formerly a judge in the court of chivalry; **Lord High Constable of Scotland** a similar officer (now a mere hereditary title); **outrun the constable** to go too fast; to get into debt; **petty constable** a parish constable who was under the High Constable; **special constable** a person sworn in by the justices to preserve the peace, or to execute warrants in special circumstances. [OFr *conestable* (Fr *connétable*), from L *comes stabulī* count or companion of the stable]

constant *kon'stənt*, *adj* fixed; unchangeable; firm; continual; faithful. — *n* (*math*) a quantity (or parameter) which remains the same while the variables may change. — *n* **con'stancy** fixedness; unchangeableness; steadfastness; stability; faithfulness; perseverance (*Shakesp*); certainty (*Shakesp*). — *adv* **con'stantly**. [L *cōnstāns*, *-stantis*, from *cōnstāre* to stand firm, from *con-* (intensive) and *stāre* to stand]

constantan *kon'stən-tan*, *n* an alloy of about 40% nickel and 60% copper, having a high and constant resistance to flow of electricity or heat. [**constant**]

Constantia *kən-stan'shi-ə*, *n* a sweet wine produced around *Constantia*, near Cape Town.

constantia et virtute *kon-stan'shi-ə* (or-*ti-ä*) *et vûr-tū'tē* (also *vir-to͞o'te* or *wir-*), (*L*) by constancy and virtue.

Constantinian *kon-stən-tin'yən*, *adj* pertaining to Constantine I (AD *circa* 274–337), the first Christian Roman emperor (AD 306–337).

Constantinopolitan *kon-stan-ti-nō-pol'it-ən*, *adj* of or pertaining to *Constantinople* (now Istanbul).

constate *kən-stāt'*, *vt* to assert (*Gallicism*). — *n* **constatation** (*kon-stə-tā'shən*) a statement, assertion; ascertaining, verification. — *adj* **constative** (*kon'stə-tiv*, *-stā'tiv*; *philos*) (of a statement) that can be true or false; that implies assertion rather than performance. — *n* such a statement (opposed to *performative*). [Fr *constater*, from L *constat* it is certain]

constellate *kon'stəl-āt* or *kən-stel'āt*, *vt* to cluster; to compel or affect by stellar influence. — *vi* to cluster together. — *n* **constellā'tion** stars which form a group as seen from the earth; a group or gathering of famous or brilliant people; any group of people, ideas, factors in a situation, etc, related in some way; a particular disposition of the planets, supposed to influence the course of human life or character (*astrol*). — *adj* **constell'atory**. [L *cōnstellātus* studded with stars, from *con-*, and *stellāre*, from *stella* a star]

conster. See **construe**.

consternate *kon'stər-nāt, vt* to fill with dismay or confusion. — *n* **consternā'tion** dismay or amazement, often causing confusion or lack of understanding. [L *cōnsternāre, -ātum*, from *con-* wholly, and *sternere* to strew]

constipate *kon'stip-āt, vt* to cause an irregular and insufficient evacuation of the bowels of; to deprive of vigour or useful action (*fig*); to stop up or close (*obs*). — *adj* **con'stipated**. — *n* **constipā'tion**. [L *cōnstīpāre, -ātum* to press together, from *con-*, and *stīpāre* to pack]

constitute *kon'stit-ūt, vt* to form or make up; to establish or found; to set up; to appoint. — *n* **constituency** (*kən-stit'ū-ən-si*) the whole body of voters, or a district or population, represented by a member of parliament, etc; a set of people supporting, patronizing, or forming a power-base for, a business organization, pressure group, etc. — *adj* **constit'uent** constituting or forming; essential; component; electing; constitution or law-making. — *n* an essential part; one of those who elect a representative, *esp* to parliament; an inhabitant of the constituency of a member of parliament, etc. — *n* **constitū'tion** (*kon-*) a system of laws and customs established by the sovereign power of a state for its own guidance; an established form of government; the act of constituting; the natural condition of body or mind; disposition; a set of rules or guidelines by which an organization is governed; molecular structure, taking into account not only the kinds and numbers of atoms but the way in which they are linked (*chem*). — *adj* **constitū'tional** conforming to the constitution or frame of government; existing subject to fixed laws; inherent in the natural make-up or structure of a person or thing. — *n* a walk for the benefit of one's health. — *n* **constitū'tionalism** adherence to the principles of the constitution. — *n* **constitū'tionalist** or **constitū'tionist** a person who favours or studies a constitution or the constitution. — *n* **constitutional'ity**. — *vt* **constitū'tionalize** or **-ise** to make constitutional. — *adv* **constitū'tionally**. — *adj* **con'stitutive** that constitutes or establishes; having power to constitute; essential; component. — *n* **con'stitutor** someone or something that constitutes; a person who makes a constitution. — **constitutional monarchy** a monarchy in which the power of the sovereign is defined and limited by the constitution; **constitutive enzyme** an enzyme that is formed under all conditions of growth. [L *cōnstituere, cōnstitūtum*, from *con-* (intensive) and *statuere* to make to stand, to place]

constr. *abbrev*: construction.

constrain *kən-strān', vt* to force, compel; to confine, limit; to restrict by a condition; to cause constraint to. — *adj* **constrain'able**. — *adj* **constrained'** forced, compelled; lacking ease and spontaneity of manner, unnatural; embarrassed. — *adv* **constrain'edly**. — *n* **constraint'** compulsion; confinement; repression of one's feelings; embarrassment; a restricting condition. [OFr *constraindre*, from L *cōnstringere*, from *con-*, and *stringere* to press]

constrict *kən-strikt', vt* to press together; to contract; to cramp; to limit. — *adj* **constrict'ed** narrowed; cramped; narrowed in places (*bot*). — *n* **constric'tion** the process of narrowing or pressing together; contraction; tightness; something constricted; (in a chromosome) a narrow, localized region, normally found at the centromere and elsewhere including the nucleolar-organizing region. — *adj* **constrict'ive**. — *n* **constrict'or** something that constricts or draws together; a muscle that compresses an organ or hollow structure; a snake that crushes its prey in its coils. [L *cōnstringere, -strictum*]

constringe *kən-strinj', (rare) vt* to draw together; to cause to contract or shrink. — *vi* to contract or shrink. — *n* **constrin'gency**. — *adj* **constrin'gent** having the quality of contracting. [L *cōnstringere*]

construct *kən-strukt', vt* to build up; to make; to put together the parts of or from parts; to compose; to compile; to put in grammatical relation. — *adj* constructed. — *n* (*kon'strukt*) a thing constructed, *esp* in the mind; an image or object of thought constructed from a number of sense-impressions or images (*psychol*). — *adj* **construct'able** or **construct'ible**. — *n* **construct'er** or **construct'or**. — *n* **construc'tion** the act or process of constructing; anything constructed; a building; the syntactic relations of words in a sentence (*gram*); a word or group of words; interpretation; meaning. — *adj* **construc'tional** pertaining to construction; used for structures; making use of structures. — *n* **construc'tionist** (*US law*) a person, *esp* a judge, who interprets constitutional law in a particular way. — *adj* **construct'ive** capable of, tending towards, or concerned in, constructing; representing positive advice (as opposed to *destructive*). — *adv* **construct'ively**. — *n* **construct'iveness**. — *n* **construct'ivism** a non-representational style of art, *esp* sculpture and architecture, using man-made industrial materials and processes such as twisting and welding; a simplified, non-realistic style in stage sets, using steps, platforms, etc (also **construc'tionism**). — **constructive dismissal** action by an employer which leaves an employee no alternative but to resign; **construct state** in Semitic languages, the state of a noun depending on another noun, where in Indo-European languages the other would be in the genitive case, eg *House of God*, house being in the construct state. — **bear a construction** to allow of a particular interpretation. [L *cōnstruere, -structum*, from *con-*, and *struere* to build]

construe *kən-stro͞o'* or *kon'stro͞o*, (old form **conster** *kon'stər*), *vt* to interpret; to infer; to construct grammatically; to analyse the grammatical structure of (*esp* a classical Greek or Latin text), preparatory to translating. — *vi* to be capable of or permit grammatical analysis. — *n* (*kon'stro͞o*; *rare*) an act of construing; something construed, a piece of translation. — *n* **construabil'ity**. — *adj* **constru'able**. — *n* **construer** (*kon'* or *-stro͞o'*). [L *cōnstruere, constructum* to pile together]

constuprate *kon'stū-prāt, (obs) vt* to ravish. — *n* **constuprā'tion**. [L *cōnstuprāre*, from *con-* (intensive), and *stuprum* defilement, disgrace]

consubsist *kon-sub-sist', vi* to subsist together.

consubstantial *kon-sub-stan'shl, adj* of the same substance, nature or essence, *esp* (*Christian theol*) of the Trinity. — *n* **consubstan'tialism** the doctrine of consubstantiation. — *n* **consubstan'tialist** a believer in consubstantiation. — *n* **consubstantiality** (*-shi-al'i-ti*). — *adv* **consubstan'tially**. — *vt* and *vi* **consubstan'tiate** (*-shi-āt*) to unite in one common substance or nature, *esp* (*Christian theol*) bread and wine and the body of Christ. — Also *adj*. — *n* **consubstantiā'tion** the doctrine of the actual, substantial presence of the body and blood of Christ coexisting in and with the bread and wine used at the Lord's Supper (cf **transubstantiation**). — *n* **consubstantiā'tionist**. [L *consubstāntiālis*, from *con-* with, and *substantia* substance]

consuetude *kon'swi-tūd, n* (a) custom; familiarity. — *adj* **consuetū'dinary** customary. — *n* an unwritten law established by usage, derived by immemorial custom from antiquity; a ritual of customary devotions. [L *cōnsuētūdō, -inis* custom]

consul *kon'səl, n* an agent for a foreign government appointed to attend to the interests of its citizens and commerce; one of the two chief magistrates in the Roman republic; one of the three heads of the French republic, 1799–1804. — *n* **con'sulage** (*hist*) duty paid to a consul for protection of goods. — *adj* **con'sular** (*-sū-lər*) pertaining to a consul. — *n* a person of consular rank. — *n* **con'sulate** (*-sūl-* or *-səl-*) the office, residence, jurisdiction, government or time of a consul or consuls. — *n* **con'sulship** the office, or term of office, of a consul. — **consul general** a consul of the first rank: — *pl* **consuls general**. [L *cōnsul*]

consult *kən-sult', vt* to ask advice of; to look up for information or advice; to consider (wishes, feelings, etc of others); to discuss. — *vi* to consider jointly (with *with*); to take advice. — *n* (*kən-sult'* or *kon'sult*); *hist* consultation; council; a meeting for conspiracy or intrigue. — *n* **consult'ancy** an agency which provides professional advice; the post of consultant. — *n* **consultant** (*kən-sult'ənt*) a person who gives professional advice or takes part in consultation; the most senior grade of doctor in a given speciality in a hospital; a person who seeks advice or information. — Also *adj*. — *n* **consultā'tion** (*kon-səl-* or *-sul-*) deliberation, or a meeting for deliberation, *esp* of physicians or lawyers. — *adj* **consult'ative** of or pertaining to consultation, *esp* of bodies without vote on the final decision. — *adj* **consult'atory** of the nature of consultation. — *n* **consultee'** a person consulted. — *n* **consult'er** a person who consults. — *adj* **consult'ing** (of a physician, lawyer, etc) prepared to give professional advice to others in the same field. — *adj* **consult'ive**. — *n* **consult'or**. — *adj* **consult'ory**. — **consulting room** the room in which a doctor sees a patient. [L *cōnsultāre*, intensive of *cōnsulere* to consult]

consulta *kon-sōōl'tä*, (*Ital* and *Sp*) *n* a meeting of council.

consume *kən-sūm'* or *-sōōm'*, *vt* to use up; to devour; to waste or spend; to destroy by wasting, fire, evaporation, etc; to exhaust. — *vi* to waste away. — *adj* **consum'able**. — *n* something that can be consumed. — *adv* **consum'edly** (*archaic*) exceedingly. — *n* **consum'er** a person who consumes; a person who uses an article produced (opposite to *producer*). — *n* **consum'erism** (the promotion of) the protection of the interests of buyers of goods and services against defective or dangerous goods, etc; the theory that steady growth in the consumption of goods is necessary for a sound economy. — *n* **consum'erist**. — *n* and *adj* **consum'ing** wasting or destroying: engrossing. — **consumer durables** consumer goods designed to last a relatively long time, such as televisions, washing machines, cars, etc; **consumer goods** goods in a finished state for sale to and use of consumers; **consumer research** the study of the needs and preferences of consumers; **consumer terrorism** the deliberate contamination by harmful substances of certain food products, *usu* in order to blackmail the producers or retailers of the products; **consumer terrorist**. [L *cōnsūmere*, *-sūmptum* to destroy, from *con-* (signifying completeness), and *sūmere* to take]

consummate *kon'sum-āt*, *-səm-*, or *-sū-*, *vt* to raise to the highest point; to perfect or finish; to make (marriage) legally complete by sexual intercourse. — *adj* (*kən-sum'āt* or *-it* or *kon'sū-*), complete, supreme or perfect of its kind; skilled or competent. — *adv* **consumm'ately** perfectly; with accomplishment. — *n* **consummā'tion** the act of completing; perfection; the act of sexual intercourse which makes a marriage legally valid. — *adj* **consumm'ative**. — *n* **con'summātor**. — *adj* **consumm'atory**. [L *cōnsummāre*, *-ātum* to perfect, from *con-* (intensive) and *summus* highest, perfect, *summa* a sum]

consumption *kən-sum(p)'shən*, *n* the act or process of consuming or using up; the quantity consumed; wasting of the body; an earlier name for pulmonary tuberculosis. — *n* **consumpt** (*kon'sum(p)t* or *kən-sum(p)t'*; *Scot*) consumption. — *adj* **consump'tive** wasting away; pertaining to, inclined to or suffering from the disease consumption. — *n* a person affected by consumption. — *adv* **consump'tively**. — *n* **consump'tiveness** or **consumptiv'ity** (*kon-*). [See **consume**]

cont or **contd** *abbrev*: continued.

contabescent *kon-tab-es'ənt*, *adj* wasting away, atrophied; failing to produce pollen (*bot*). — *n* **contabesc'ence**. [L *contābēscēns*, *-entis*, from *contābēscere* to waste away]

contact *kon'takt*, *n* touch; meeting; association; means or occasion of communication; a person one can call upon for assistance, information, introductions, etc in a business or other organization; a person who has been exposed to contagion; meeting in a point without intersection (*math*); a coming close together such as to allow passage of electric current or communication of disease; a place or part where electric current may be allowed to pass; a contact lens. — *adj* involving contact; caused or made active by contact. — *vt* and *vi* (also *kon-takt'*) to bring or to come into contact; to get in touch with, or establish a connection with. — *adj* **contact'able** able to be contacted. — *n* **con'tactor** a device for repeatedly making and breaking an electric circuit. — *adj* **contact'ual** pertaining to contact. — **contact flight** navigation of an aircraft by ground observation alone; **contact lens** a lens, *usu* of thin plastic material, worn in direct contact with the eyeball, instead of spectacles, to correct defects of vision; **contact man** (*colloq*) an intermediary in transactions, *esp* shady ones; **contact-metamor'phism** (*geol*) alteration of rocks in the neighbourhood of igneous materials; **contact poison** a poison which can penetrate the skin, and which can act without being swallowed or inhaled; **contact print** (*photog*) a print made by putting a negative or positive transparency in direct contact with a sensitized paper or film and exposing to light; **contact tracing** a system used by health workers and certain clinics, to control the spread of a disease, eg sexually transmitted disease, by finding as many individuals who have had contact with a patient as possible. [L *contingere*, *contactum* to touch, from *con-* wholly, and *tangere* to touch]

contadino *kon-tä-dē'nō*, *n* an Italian peasant: — *pl* **contadi'ni** (*-nē*): — *fem* **contadi'na** (*-nä*): — *pl* **contadi'ne** (*-nā*) or **contadi'nas**. [Ital]

contagion *kən-tā'jən*, *n* transmission of a disease by direct contact with an infected person or object; a disease or poison transmitted in this way; the means of transmission; the transmission of an emotional state, eg excitement; a harmful influence. — *n* **contā'gionist** (*obs*) a person who believes in the contagiousness of certain diseases. — *adj* **contā'gious** (of disease) communicable by ordinary social contact (cf *infectious*); carrying disease or other contagion; noxious (*obs*); spreading easily (*fig*; *colloq*). — *adv* **contā'giously**. — *n* **contā'giousness**. — *n* **contā'gium** contagion; contagious matter. — **contagious abortion** see **brucellosis**. [L *contāgiō*, *-ōnis*, from *con-*, and *tangere* to touch]

contain *kən-tān'*, *vt* to have within, enclose; to comprise, include; to restrain; to keep fixed; to hold back; to keep in check; to retain (*archaic*). — *adj* **contain'able**. — *n* **contain'er** something that contains goods, etc for storage; a large box-like receptacle of standard shape and size in which goods are enclosed for transport on a lorry, train or ship; a vessel for holding gas. — *n* **containerizā'tion** or **-s-**. — *vt* **contain'erize** or **-ise** to put (freight) into standard sealed containers; to use such containers for (eg a transport operation). — *n* **contain'ment** the act of containing; the act or policy of preventing the spread beyond certain limits of a power or influence regarded as hostile, by means other than war; the successful result of this; in fusion, the use of shaped magnetic fields or of inertial confinement to contain a plasma (*nuc eng*; also **confinement**). — **container crane** a very large bridge-type quayside crane for handling large containers; **container ship** a ship designed for the most efficient stowing and transport of such containers; **container terminal** a port, railway station, etc, or part of one, set aside and equipped for handling containers. [OFr *contenir*, from L *continēre*, from *con-*, and *tenēre* to hold]

contaminate *kən-tam'i-nāt*, *vt* to pollute, eg by radioactivity; to infect; to defile by touching or mixing with; to corrupt. — *adj* contaminated. — *adj* **contam'inable**. — *n* **contam'inant**. — *n* **contaminā'tion** pollution; adulteration, corruption; defilement. — *adj* **contam'inative**. [L *contāmināre*, *-ātum*, from *contāmen* (for *contagmen*) pollution; see **contact**]

contango *kən-tang'gō*, (*stock exchange*) *n* a percentage paid by the buyer to the seller of stock for keeping back its delivery to the next settling-day, continuation (opposite to *backwardation*): — *pl* **contang'os**. — Also *vt*. — **contang'o-day** see **continuation-day**. [Arbitrarily from **continue**]

cont. bon. mor. *abbrev*: *contra bonos mores* (*L*), qv.

conte *kɔ̃t*, *n* a short story (as a literary genre). [Fr]

conté *kɔ̃-tā'* or *kon'tā*, *n* (sometimes with *cap*) a hard crayon, *usu* black, brown, or red, made of graphite and clay. [N J *Conté*, 18c Fr chemist]

conteck *kon'tek*, (*archaic*) *n* strife. [OFr *contek*, prob connected with *contekier* to touch]

contemn *kən-tem'*, *vt* to despise: — *pr p* **contemning** (-*tem'ing*); *pa t* and *pa p* **contemned'**, *Spenser pa p* **contempt'**. — *n* **contem'ner** or **contem'nor** (-*ər* or -*nər*) a person who contemns; a person who has been found guilty of contempt of court. — *adj* **contem'nible**. [L *contemnere*, *-temptum* to value little, from *con-* (intensive) and *temnere* to slight]

contemper *kən-temp'ər*, *vt* to blend together, to qualify by mixture; to adapt. — *n* **contemperā'tion** (*obs*). — *n* **contem'perature**. [L *contemperāre*]

contemplate *kon'tem-plāt*, older *kən-tem'plāt*, *vt* to consider or look at attentively; to meditate on or study; to intend. — *vi* to think seriously; to meditate (on or upon). — *adj* **contemp'lable**. — *n* **contem'plant**. — *n* **contemplā'tion** meditation; a meditative condition of mind; attentive viewing or consideration; matter for thought; purpose. — *n* **contemp'latist**. — *adj* **con'templātive** (or *kən-tem'plə-*) given to contemplation. — *n* a person leading a life of religous contemplation. — *adv* **con'templatively** (or -*tem'*). — *n* **con'templativeness** (or -*tem'*). — *n* **con'templātor** a person who contemplates; a student (*rare*). — **contemplative life** (*theol* and *philos*) life devoted to meditation (opposed to *active life*). — **in contemplation of** in the expectation of; bearing in mind as a possibility. [L *contemplārī*, *-ātus* to mark out carefully a *templum* or place for auguries, from *con-* (signifying completeness) and *templum*]

contemporaneous *kən-tem-pə-rā'nyəs*, *adj* living, happening or being at the same time; belonging approximately to the same relative place in the succession, not necessarily strictly synchronous (*geol*). — *n* and *adj* **contemporā'nean** contemporary. — *n* **contemporaneity** (-*ə-nē'i-ti*). — *adv* **contemporā'neously**. — *n* **contemporā'neousness**. — *n* **contem'porariness**. — *adj* **contem'porary** belonging to the same time (with); of the same age; (loosely) present-day, *esp* up-to-date, fashionable, etc; of a style of house decoration and furnishing popular in the 1950s. — *n* a person who lives at the same time as another; a newspaper or magazine of the same time. — *vt* **contem'porize** or **-ise** to make contemporary. [L *con-*, and *tempus*, *-oris* time]

contempt *kən-tempt'*, *n* scorn; disgrace; disregard of the rule of law, or an offence against the dignity of a court, etc, as in *contempt of court*, *contempt of Parliament*. — *n* **contemptibil'ity** or **contempt'ibleness**. — *adj* **contempt'ible** (*Spenser kon'*) despicable. — *adv* **contempt'ibly**. — *adj* **contempt'ūous** haughty, scornful. — *adv* **contempt'ūously**. — *n* **contempt'uousness**. [**contemn**]

contend *kən-tend'*, *vi* to strive; to struggle in emulation or in opposition; to dispute or debate (with *against*, *for*, *with* or *about*). — *vt* to maintain in dispute (that). — *n* **contend'ent** (*rare*) or **contend'er** a person who contends. — *n* and *adj* **contend'ing** striving. — *n* **conten'tion** strife; debate; a point argued. — *adj* **conten'tious** in, or relating to, dispute; controversial; quarrelsome; given to dispute. — *adv* **conten'tiously**. — *n* **conten'tiousness**. [L *contendere*, *-tentum*, from *con-*, and *tendere* to stretch]

contenement *kən-ten'i-mənt*, (*obs*) *n* property necessary to maintain one's station. [L *con-* (intensive) and **tenement**]

content[1] *kon'tent*, *n* that which is contained; capacity; the substance; (in *pl*) the things contained; (in *pl*) the list of chapters, sections, etc in a book; capacity. — **content word** a word which has a meaning independent of its context (as opposed to *function word*). [See **contain**]

content[2] *kən-tent'*, *adj* satisfied; quietly happy. — *n* peace of mind; satisfaction. — *interj* I am content or agreed, the formula of assent in the House of Lords. — *vt* to make content. — *n* **contentā'tion** (*obs*). — *adj* **content'ed** content. — *adv* **content'edly**. — *n* **content'edness** or **content'ment**. — *adj* **content'less** without content; discontented. [Fr, from L *contentus* contained, hence, satisfied, from *con-*, and *tenēre* to hold]

contention, **contentious**. See **contend**.

conterminous *kən-tûr'min-əs*, *adj* adjacent, meeting along a common boundary; meeting end to end; coincident; coextensive in range. — *adj* **conter'minal** adjacent; end to end. — *adj* **conter'minant** or **conter'minate** adjacent. [L *conterminus* neighbouring, from *con-*, and *terminus* a boundary]

contessa *kon-tes'ə*, *n* an Italian countess: — *pl* **contess'as**.

contesseration *kon-tes-ər-ā'shən*, (*rare*) *n* (the act of) forming friendship or union *orig*, in ancient Rome, by dividing a square tablet as token. [From L *contesserāre*, from *con-*, and *tessera* square stone, token (in full *tessera hospitalis* given by guest to host)]

contest *kən-test'*, *vt* to call in question or make the subject of dispute; to strive to gain. — *vi* to contend. — *n* (*kon'*) a struggle for victory; a competition; strife; a debate, dispute, argument. — *adj* **contest'able**. — *n* **contest'ant** a person who takes part in a contest. — *n* **contestā'tion** the act of contesting; contest, strife; emulation. — *adj* **contest'ed**. — *n* **contest'er**. — *adj* **contest'ing**. — *adv* **contest'ingly**. — **contested election** one in which there are more candidates than are to be elected; one whose validity is disputed (*US*). [Fr *contester*, from L *contestārī* to call to witness, from *con-* (intensive) and *testārī* to be a witness, from *testis* a witness]

context *kon'tekst*, *n* the parts of a piece of writing or speech which precede and follow a particular word or passage and may fix, or help to fix, its true meaning; associated surroundings, setting. — *adj* **context'ūal**. — *n* **contextūalizā'tion** or **-s-**. — *vt* **context'ūalize** or **-ise** to place in context; to study (words, etc) in their context. — *adv* **context'ūally**. — *n* **context'ure** the process or manner of weaving together; structure; fabric. [L *contextus*, *contexere*, from *con-*, and *texere*, *textum* to weave]

conticent *kon'tis-ənt*, (*Thackeray*) *adj* silent. [L *conticēns*, *-entis*, from *con-* (intensive) and *tacēre* to be silent]

contignation *kon-tig-nā'shən*, (*archaic*) *n* joining together of timber; framework boarding. [L *contignātiō*, *-ōnis*, from *contignāre*, from *con-*, and *tignum* beam]

contiguous *kən-tig'ū-əs*, *adj* touching, adjoining; near; next (to) in space or time. — *n* **contigū'ity**. — *n* **contig'uousness**. — *adv* **contig'uously**. [L *contiguus*, from *contingere* to touch on all sides, from *con-* wholly, and *tangere* to touch]

continent *kon'ti-nənt*, *n* a vast landmass not broken up by seas; one of the great divisions of the land surface of the globe; the mainland portion of one of these; (*usu* with *cap*) the mainland of Europe (as opposed to the British Isles); sum and substance (*archaic*); solid earth (*obs*); the main or whole body of anything (*obs*). — *adj* restraining within due bounds, or absolutely abstaining from, the indulgence of pleasure, *esp* sexual; able to control the movements of one's bladder and bowels; temperate; virtuous. — *n* **con'tinence** or **con'tinency** self-restraint or abstinence; chastity; ability to control one's bladder and bowels. — *adj* **continental** (-*ent'l*) of, characteristic of, or of the nature of, a continent, *esp* the mainland of Europe, the colonies of N America at the period of the War of Independence, or the main landmass of the United States. — *n* a native or inhabitant of a continent, *esp* the mainland of Europe; an American soldier of the War of Independence; a currency note of the Continental Congress. — *n* **continent'alism** anything peculiar to the usage of a continent, *esp* Europe. — *n* **continent'alist**. — *adv* **con'tinently** in a continent manner. — **continental breakfast** a light breakfast of rolls and coffee (cf **English breakfast**); **continental climate** the climate characteristic of the interior of a continent, with hot summers, cold winters, and little rainfall; **Continental Congress** an assembly of delegates of the American colonies, before the United States constitution was in force; **continental divide** a range of mountains forming the watershed of a continent; **continental drift** (*geol*) the theory of the slow drifting apart of land masses, as eg in A L Wegener's theory of the formation of world continents from one original land mass, now supported by the theory of **plate-tectonics**; **continental plate** a plate (qv) of the lithosphere; **continental quilt** a duvet; **continental shelf** a gently sloping zone, under relatively shallow seas, offshore from a continent or island; **Continental System** Napoleon's plan for excluding Britain from all commercial connection with Europe. [L *continēns*, *-entis*, from *continēre* to contain, from *con-*, and *tenēre* to hold]

contingent *kən-tin'jənt*, *adj* dependent on something else; liable but not certain to happen; accidental. — *n* an event liable but not certain to occur; a share, quota or group, *esp* of soldiers. — *n* **contin'gence** contact; contingency (*obs*). — *n* **contin'gency** the quality or state of being contingent; a possible future event; a chance happening or concurrence of events; something dependent on such an event (also *adj*); chance; uncertainty; an incidental; close connection; contact (*obs*). — *adv* **contin'gently**. — **contingency plans** plans or arrangements made in case a particular situation should arise. [L *contingēns*, *-entis*, from *con-* mutually, and *tangere* to touch]

continue *kən-tin'ū*, *vt* to draw out or prolong; to extend; to maintain; to go on with; to resume; to adjourn (*law*); to be a prolongation of. — *vi* to remain in the same place or state; to last or endure; to persevere. — *adj* **contin'uable**. — *adj* **contin'ual** without interruption; unceasing; persistent. — *adv* **contin'ually**. — *n* **contin'uance** duration; uninterrupted succession; stay; adjournment (*law*). — *adj* **contin'uant** continuing; capable of continuing. — *n* (*phonetics*) a consonant sound which is produced on an uninterrupted flow of breath. — Also *adj*. — *adj* **contin'uāte** closely united (*obs*); unbroken (*Shakesp*). — *n* **continuā'tion** going on; persistence; constant succession; extension; resumption; a further instalment. — *adj* **contin'uative** continuing. — *n* **contin'uator** a person who continues; a person who keeps up a series or succession. — *adj* **contin'ued** uninterrupted; unceasing; extended; resumed; in instalments. — *adv* **contin'uedly**. — *n* **contin'uedness**. — *n* **contin'uer** someone who or something that continues; a person who has the power of persevering. — *n* **continū'ity** the state of being continuous or consistent; uninterrupted connection; a complete scenario of a cinema film; the person who writes it (in full **continuity writer**); the ordering or arrangement of film or television shots and scenes, or of parts of a radio broadcast, in a correct or consistent way. — *n* **continuo** (*kon-tin'ū-ō*; Ital *-tēn'wō*) thorough-bass; the bass part as written for a keyboard instrument, with or without an accompaniment; the instruments playing this part: — *pl* **contin'uos**. — *adj* **contin'uous** joined together in space or time without interruption. — *adv* **contin'uously**. — *n* **contin'uousness**. — *n* **contin'ūum** that which is continuous; that which must be regarded as continuous and the same and which can be described only relatively: — *pl* **contin'uums** or **contin'ua**. — **continuā'tion-day** that on which contangos (qv) are fixed; **continuing education** part-time courses of study for adult students; **continuity announcer** (*radio*, *TV*) a person who supervises the continuity of a sequence of programmes, by linking programmes, filling gaps with interlude material, etc; **continuity girl** or **man** a person employed on the set of a cinema film to ensure continuity, *esp* in matters of costume, make-up, props, etc, between different shots; **continuous assessment** the assessment of the progress of a pupil or student by intermittent checks, eg class tests, essays, etc, throughout the year; **continuous creation** the notion of creation as going on always, not as a single act at one particular time (*philos*); the steady-state theory of cosmology (*astron*); **continuous stationery** (*comput*) stationery consisting of a long sheet of paper with regular perforations, *usu* folded fanwise and fed through a printer; **continuous wave** (*phys*) an electromagnetic wave of constant frequency and amplitude. — **space-time continuum** see under **space**. [L *continuāre*, from *continuus* joined, connected, from *continēre* to hold together]

contline *kont'līn*, *n* the space between stowed casks; a spiral interval between the strands of a rope. [Prob **cant**[2], and **line**[2]]

conto *kon'tō*, *n* a Portuguese and Brazilian monetary unit worth 1000 escudos or cruzeiros: — *pl* **con'tos**. [Port, million (reis), from L *computus* a sum]

contorno *kon-tör'nō*, *n* contour or outline: — *pl* **contor'nos**. — *n* **contor'niate** a coin or medal with a deep groove round the disc. — *adj* having this. [Ital *contorno* circuit, contour]

contort *kən-tört'*, *vt* to twist or turn violently; to writhe. — *adj* **contort'ed** twisted; twisted, as some flower-buds when each floral leaf overlaps its neighbour always on the same side round the circle; much and irregularly plicated (*geol*). — *n* **contor'tion** a violent twisting; deformation. — *adj* **contor'tional** or **contor'tionate**. — *n* **contor'tionism**. — *n* **contor'tionist** a gymnast who practises contorted postures; a person who twists words and phrases. — *adj* **contort'ive**. [L *con-* (intensive) and *torquēre*, *tortum* to twist]

contour *kon'to͞or*, *n* outline, shape or surface; general character or aspect; artistic quality of outline; a contour line; a point, line or surface at, along or on which some property or characteristic is constant, or its representation in a map or diagram. — *adj* having, showing or based on contours; contoured. — *vt* to mark with contour lines; to follow the contour lines of. — *adj* **con'toured** (of chairs, etc) shaped to fit the lines of the human body. — **contour feathers** feathers lying along a bird's body providing insulation and streamlining; **contour line** an imaginary line on the ground whose points are all at the same height above sea-level, or the intersection of the ground surface by a level surface of constant elevation; a representation of such a line on a map; **contour map** a map in which the configuration of land is shown by contour lines; **contour ploughing** the ploughing (and planting) of sloping land along the contour lines to limit erosion. [Fr *contour* (Ital *contorno*), from Ital *contornare*, to surround, outline, from L *con-*, and *tornāre* to turn in a lathe, from *tornus* (Gr *tornos*) a lathe]

contr. *abbrev*: contracted; contraction.

contra *kon'tra* or *-trə*, *adv* and *prep* against. — *n* an argument against; the opposing side.

contra- *kon'tra* or *-trə*, *pfx* denoting: against; contrary. [L *contrā*]

contraband *kon'trə-band*, *adj* forbidden by law to be imported or exported; illegally imported or exported, smuggled; prohibited. — *n* illegal trade; smuggled or prohibited goods; (in the American Civil War) a refugee slave. — *n* **con'trabandism** trading in contraband goods. — *n* **con'trabandist** a smuggler. — **contraband of war** commodities not to be supplied by neutral to belligerent powers. [Sp *contrabanda*, from Ital *contrabbando*, from L *contrā*, and LL *bandum* ban]

contrabass *kon'trə-bās*, *n* the double bass. — *adj* applied to other instruments taking a similar part. — Also **contrabasso**, **contrabbasso** (*-bäs'ō*) and (*rare*) **coun'terbase**. [Ital *contra(b)basso*, from pfx *contra-* (indicating an octave lower), and *basso* bass]

contrabassoon *kon'trə-bas-o͞on'*, *n* a metal or wooden instrument, like a bassoon but sounding an octave lower, the double bassoon. [*contra-* (see **contrabass** above) and **bassoon**]

contra bonos mores *kon'tra bō'nōs* (or *bo'*) *mō'rēz* (or *-rās*), (*L*) contrary to good manners or morals (*informal* short form **cont. bon. mor**).

contraception *kon-trə-sep'shən*, *n* the prevention of unwanted pregnancy. — *n* **contracep'tive** a drug, device or other means of contraception. — Also *adj*. [L *contrā* against, and **(con)ception**]

contract *kən-trakt'*, *vt* to draw together; to lessen; to shorten; to effect by agreement; to come into, become the subject of; to incur; to catch (a disease); to bargain for; to betroth. — *vi* to shrink; to become less; to become shorter; to make a contract (*with* or *for*). — *n* (*kon'trakt*), an agreement on fixed terms; a bond; a betrothal; the written statement representing an agreement; contract bridge; a final bid in contract bridge; an undertaking; an undertaking or agreement to kill a particular person, *esp* for an agreed sum of money (*underworld slang*). — *n* **contractabil'ity**. — *adj* **contract'able** (*kən-*) (*esp* of a disease or habit) able to be contracted. — *adj* **contract'ed** drawn together; shortened; narrow; mean; engaged to be married. — *adv* **contract'edly**. — *n* **contract'edness**. — *n* **contractibil'ity**. — *adj* **contract'ible** capable of being contracted or shortened. — *adj* **contract'ile** tending or having power to contract or to draw in. — *n* **contractil'ity** (*kon-*). — *n* **contrac'tion** (*kən-*) the act of contracting; a word shortened in speech or spelling; a symbol for shortening or a shortened form of (part of) a word (*palaeog*); a tightening of the muscles or muscle fibres, *esp* one of the regular spasms of the uterine muscles or fibres involved in the process of giving birth. — *adj* **contrac'tional** or **contrac'tionary** having the effect of contracting. — *adj* **contract'ive** tending to contract. — *n* **contract'or** a person who, or company that, engages to execute work or furnish supplies at a stated rate; one of the parties to a bargain or agreement. — *adj* **contract'ūal**. — *adj* **contrac'tural** pertaining to contracture (*med*); contractual (*nonstandard*). — *n* **contract'ure** persistent muscular contraction; a deformity or shortening of a part of the body due to shrinkage of the tissue in the muscles, skin, etc; tapering of a column (*archit*). — **contract bridge** a development of auction bridge, in which tricks beyond the number bid for count as honours; **contract in** to agree to participate on certain conditions; **contract out** to decide not to participate in a pension scheme, etc; to withdraw from an obligation, agreement, etc; to arrange that certain conditions shall not apply; to offer (work previously carried out by in-house staff, in a school, hospital, etc) to private contractors. [L *contractus*, from *con-* together, and *trahere*, *tractum* to draw]

contracyclical *kon'trə-sī'kli-kl*, *adj* (of an economic policy) offsetting fluctuation cycles in the economy by reducing taxes during a recession and raising them during a boom. [L *contrā* against, and **cyclical** (see **cycle**)]

contradance or **contredance** *kon'trə-däns*, *n* a country dance, *esp* a French version of the English country dance.

contradict *kon-trə-dikt'*, *vt* to deny what is affirmed by; to assert the contrary of; to deny; to be contrary to in character. — *adj* **contradict'able**. — *n* **contradic'tion** the act of contradicting; a statement asserting the contrary; denial; inconsistency. — *adj* **contradic'tious** prone to contradiction. — *adv* **contradic'tiously**. — *adj* **contradict'ive** contradicting or tending to contradict. — *adv* **contradict'ively**. — *n* **contradict'or**. — *adv* **contradict'orily**. — *n* **contradict'oriness** the quality of being contradictory. — *adj* **contradict'ory** affirming the contrary; inconsistent. — *n* a word, principle, etc that contradicts another; either of two propositions such that both cannot be true, or both cannot be false (*logic*). — **contradiction in terms** a group of words containing a contradiction. [L *contrādīcere*, *-dictum*, from *contrā-* against, and *dīcere* to say]

contradistinguish *kon'trə-dis-ting'gwish*, *vt* to distinguish by contrasting different qualities or conditions. — *n* **contradistinc'tion**. [**contra-**]

contrafagotto *kon-trə-fə-got'tō*, *n* the contrabassoon: — *pl* **contrafagot'tos**. [Ital *contra-* (indicating an octave lower), and *fagotto* bassoon]

contraflow *kon'trə-flō*, *n* a system of traffic regulation on motorways, when one carriageway is closed and the other is arranged for two-way traffic. [contra-]

contrahent *kon'trə-hənt*, (*hist*) *adj* entering into a contract. — *n* a contracting party. [L *contrahēns*, *-entis*, from *contrahere* to contract]

contrail *kon'trāl*, *n* short form of **condensation trail** (see under **condense**).

contraindicate *kon'trə-in'di-kāt*, *vt* to point to (a particular treatment or procedure) as unsuitable or unwise (*med*); to show or give as reason for not being, doing or having, etc; to forbid. — *n* **contrain'dicant**. — *n* **con'traindicā'tion** any factor in a patient's condition which indicates that surgery, drug therapy, inoculation, etc would involve a greater than normal degree of risk and is therefore unwise to pursue. — *adj* **contraindic'ative**.

contra ius gentium *kon'trə yōōs jen'shəm* or *kon'trä yōōs gen'ti-ōōm*, (*L*) against the law of nations.

contrair *kən-trār'*, an obsolete dialect form of **contrary**.

contralateral *kon-trə-lat'ə-rəl*, (esp *med*) *adj* on the opposite side, *esp* of the body; affecting the opposite side of the body. [**contra-**]

contralto *kən-tral'tō* or *-träl'*, *n* the lowest musical voice in women; a singer with such a voice; a part for such a voice: — *pl* **contral'ti** (*-tē*) or **contral'tos**. — Also *adj*. [Ital, from *contra-*, and **alto**]

contra mundum *kon'trə mun'dum* or *kon'trä mōōn'dōōm*, (*L*) against the world.

contranatant *kon-trə-nā'tənt*, *adj* swimming upstream. [L *contrā*, and *natāns*, *-antis*, pr p of *natāre* to swim]

contra pacem *kon'trə pā'sem* or *pä'chem*, or *kon'trä päkem*, (*L*) against the peace.

contraplex *kon'trə-pleks*, (*teleg*) *adj* having messages passing opposite ways at the same time. [L *contrā* against, and sfx *-plex*, as in **complex**]

contraposition *kon-trə-po-zish'ən*, *n* opposition, contrast; an immediate inference, which consists in denying the original subject of the contradictory of the original predicate (*logic*). — *adj* and *n* **contrapos'itive**.

contrapposto *kon-trə-po'stō*, (*art*) *n* a pose of the human body with hips, shoulders and head in different planes: — *pl* **contrappo'stos**. [Ital]

contraprop *kon'trə-prop*. Contraction of **contrarotating propeller**.

contraption *kən-trap'shən*, *n* a contrivance. [Perh *con-trivance adaption*]

contrapuntal, **contrapuntist**. See **counterpoint**[1].

contrarotating propeller *kon-trə-rō-tā'ting prə-pel'ər*, *n* one of a pair of propellers rotating in opposite directions. — Also **contrapropell'er**.

contrary *kon'trə-ri*, *adj* opposite; contradictory; (*usu kən-trā'ri*) perverse. — *n* an extreme opposite; a proposition so related to another that both cannot be true though both may be false (*logic*). — *vt* and *vi* to oppose; to contradict; to annoy. — *n* **contrariety** (*-rī'i-ti*) opposition; inconsistency; the relationship between two contraries (*logic*). — *adv* **contrarily** (*kon'* or *-trā'*). — *n* **contrariness** (*kon'* or *-trā'*). — *adj* **contrarious** (*kən-trā'ri-əs*; *archaic*) showing contrariety. — *adv* **contra'riously** (*archaic*) contrarily. — *n* **con'trariwise** (or *-trā'* or *-tra'*) in the contrary way; on the other side; on the other hand. — **contrary motion** (*music*) movement of parts in opposite directions, one up, another down. — **on the contrary** quite the opposite, not at all; **to the contrary** to the opposite effect. [L *contrārius*, from *contrā* against]

contrast *kən-träst'*, *vi* to stand in opposition. — *vt* to set in opposition to, in order to show difference. — *n* (*kon'träst*) opposition or unlikeness in things compared; a contrasting person or thing; the (degree of) difference in tone between the light and dark parts of a photograph or a television picture. — *adj* **contrast'ive**. — *adj* **contrast'y** (*photog*) (of prints or negatives) showing a high degree of contrast. — **contrast medium**

a suitable substance, eg barium sulphate, used in diagnostic radiology in order to give contrast. [Fr *contraster* from L *contrā* opposite to, and *stāre* to stand]

contrasuggestible *kon-trə-suj-est'i-bl*, (*psychol*) *adj* responding to suggestion by believing or doing the opposite. [**contra-**]

contrat *kɔ̃-tra*, (*Fr*) *n* a contract; an agreement. — **contrat aleatoire** (*ä-lāä-twär*) (*Fr law*) a conditional contract; **contrat de vente** (*də vɑ̃t*) a contract of sale; social contract.

contrate *kon'trāt*, *adj* (of wheels *esp* in watchmaking) having cogs parallel to the axis. [L *contrā* opposite]

contra-tenor *kon'trə-ten-ər*. Same as **counter-tenor**.

contraterrene *kon-trə-ter'ēn*, *adj* opposite in character to earthy or terrestrial. [**contra-**]

contravallation *kon-trə-val-ā'shən*, *n* a fortification built by besiegers about the place besieged. [L *contrā* against, and *vallāre*, *-atum* to fortify]

contravene *kon-trə-vēn'*, *vt* to oppose; to infringe. — *n* **contraven'tion**. [L *contrā*, against, and *venīre*, *ventum* to come]

contrayerva *kon-trə-yûr'və*, *n* a tropical American plant of the mulberry family, once believed to be an antidote to poisons; a Jamaican birthwort of similar reputation. [Sp (now *contrahierba*), from L *contrā* against, and *herba* a herb]

contrecoup *kɔ̃-tr'-ko͞o*, *n* an injury, *esp* to the brain within the skull, resulting from a blow on the side opposite to it (*med*); a kiss (*billiards*). [Fr, counterblow]

contre-jour *kɔ̃-tr'-zho͞or*, (*photog*) *n* the technique of taking photographs with the light source in front of the camera lens. [Fr *contre* against, and *jour* day, daylight]

contretemps *kɔ̃-tr'-tɑ̃*, *n* something happening inopportunely or at the wrong time, anything embarrassing or vexatious, a hitch. [Fr *contre* (L *contrā*) against, and *temps* (L *tempus*) time]

contrib. *abbrev*: contribution; contributor.

contribute *kən-trib'ūt* or *kon'*, *vt* to give along with others; to give for a common purpose; to add towards a common result, to a fund, etc; to write and send for publication with others. — *vi* to give or bear a part; to be a contributor. — *adj* **contrib'utable** payable; subject to contribution. — *n* **contribū'tion** (*kon-*) the act of contributing; something contributed; a levy or charge imposed upon a number of people; anything given for a common purpose or done towards a common end; a written composition supplied to a periodical, etc. — *adj* **contrib'utive** giving a share; helping. — *n* **contrib'utor** a person who contributes; a person who sends written articles for publication. — *adj* **contrib'utory** or (*obs*) **contrib'utary** given or giving to a common purpose or fund; having partial responsibility; (of a pension scheme) to which the employee makes a contribution as well as the employer. — *n* a person or thing that contributes; a director or member of a company who is liable to contribute to the assets if the company is wound up. — **contributory negligence** failure to take adequate precautions against an accident, etc, resulting in partial legal responsibility for injury, damage, etc. [L *con-*, and *tribere*, *-ūtum* to give]

contrist *kən-trist'*, (*obs*) *vt* to sadden. — *n* **contristā'tion**. [Fr *contrister*, from L *contristāre*, from *con-* (intensive) and *tristis* sad]

contrite *kon'trīt* or *kən-trīt'*, *adj* full of guilt and remorse for a wrongdoing or sin; wholly penitent; (of an action) showing a sense of guilt or sin. — *adv* **contritely**. — *n* **contriteness**. — *n* **contrition** (*kon-trish'ən*) remorse; deep sorrow for past sin and resolve to avoid future sin (*Christian relig*). [L *contrītus*, from *conterere*, from *con-* wholly, and *terere* to bruise]

contriturate *kən-trit'ū-rāt*, (*rare*) *vt* to pulverize. [*con-* (intensive) and **triturate**]

contrive[1] *kən-trīv'*, *vt* to plan; to invent; to bring about or effect; to manage or arrange; to plot; to conceive, understand (*archaic*). — *adj* **contriv'able** that may be contrived. — *n* **contriv'ance** an invention; the act of contriving; a deceitful plan. — *adj* **contrived'** laboured, artificially intricate. — *n* **contrive'ment** an act of contriving; the thing contrived; invention; design; artifice. — *n* **contriv'er** a schemer, a manager. [OFr *controver*, from *con-* (intensive) and *trover* to find]

contrive[2] *kən-trīv'*, (*Shakesp*) *vt* to spend, as time. [L *conterere*, *contrītum* (perf *contrīvī*) to wear out]

control *kən-trōl'*, *n* restraint; authority; command; regulation; a check; a means of operating, regulating, directing or testing; a station for doing so; a scientific experiment performed without variables to provide a standard of comparison for other experiments (also **control experiment**); a subject or group of subjects (**control group**) providing such a standard of comparison; a number or letter printed on a sheet of postage stamps as an indication of authenticity (also **control mark**); a disembodied spirit or other agency supposed to direct a spiritualistic medium; a lever ('joy-stick') or wheel to move ailerons and elevator, and so control the movements of aircraft (also **control column**, **lever** or **stick**); an aerofoil that controls the movements of an aircraft, such as rudder, elevator or stabilizer (also **control surface**); a secret service agent who supervises other agents. — *adj* pertaining to control. — *vt* to check; to restrain; to govern; to command or operate: — *pr p* **contrōll'ing**; *pa t* and *pa p* **contrōlled'**. — Formerly **comptroll'**, **control'**, **controul'**. — *n* **contrōllabil'ity**. — *adj* **controll'able** capable of or subject to control. — *n* **controll'er** a person who supervises financial affairs or examines financial accounts (also **comptroll'er**); an official authorized to control some activity or department; a person who controls or regulates; an apparatus for regulating, eg the speed of an electric car. — *n* **controll'ership**. — *n* **control'ment** the act or power of controlling; the state of being controlled; control. — **control character** (*comput*) a keyboard character which is not printed but which starts or controls an operation or device; **control key** (*comput*) a key on a computer keyboard which when used in conjunction with standard keys will perform a variety of functions, eg editing; **controlled air space** clearly defined areas in which an aircraft may fly only if it is under radio instructions from air-traffic control; **controlling interest** number of shares sufficient to ensure control over the running of a company; **control panel** or **board** a panel or board containing dials, switches and gauges for operating and monitoring electrical or other apparatus; **control register** (*comput*) one which stores the instructions controlling the operation of a computer for one cycle; **control rod** a rod moved in and out of a reactor core to vary reactivity (*nuc eng*); **control room** a room in which control instruments are placed, eg in a broadcasting station; **control total** (*comput*) a method of checking that data in a group of records has not been altered in error by comparing totals of certain items before and after processing; **control tower** a building at an airport from which take-off and landing instructions are given; **control unit** (*comput*) the part of a computer which interprets instructions and controls the execution of a program. [Fr *contrôle*, from *contre-rôle* a duplicate register, from L *contrā* against, and *rotulus* a roll]

contrôlé *kɔ̃-trō-lā*, (*Fr*) *adj* registered; hallmarked.

controvert *kon'trə-vûrt*, *vt* to oppose; to argue against; to dispute. — *n* **con'troverse** (*archaic*) dispute. — *adj* **controver'sial** (*-shəl*) relating to controversy; arousing controversy. — *n* **controver'sialist** a person given to controversy. — *adv* **controver'sially**. — *n* **con'troversy** (also *kən-trov'ər-si*) a debate; contention; dispute; a war of opinions, in books, pamphlets, etc. — *adj* **controvert'ible**. — *adv* **controvert'ibly**. — *n* **con'trovertist** (or *-vûrt'ist*). [L *contrā* against, and *vertere* to turn]

contubernal *kən-tūb'ər-nəl*, or (*archaic*) **contubernyal**, *adj* living together (in the same tent); pertaining to companionship. [L *contubernālis* (*n*), from *cum* with, together, and *taberna* hut, tavern]

contumacious *kon-tū-mā'shəs*, *adj* opposing lawful authority with contempt; obstinate; stubborn. — *adv* **contumā'ciously**. — *n* **contumā'ciousness**. — *n* **contumacity** (*-mas'i-ti*) or **con'tumacy** (*-məs-i*) obstinate disobedience or resistance; refusal to comply with the orders of a court of law. [L *contumāx*, *-ācis* insolent, from *con-* (intensive) and *tumere* to swell, or *temnere* to despise]

contumely *kon'tūm-li* (or *kon'tū-mi-li*), *n* scornful insolence; a scornful insult. — *adj* **contumē'lious** haughtily insolent. — *adv* **contumē'liously**. — *n* **contumē'liousness**. [L *contumēlia*, prob from the same source as *contumāx*]

contuse *kəntūz'*, *vt* to bruise (the body); to crush. — *vt* **contund** (*kən-tund'*; *archaic*); to bruise or pound. — *n* **contusion** (*-tū'zhən*) the act of bruising; the state of being bruised; a bruise. — *adj* **contū'sive** tending to bruise. [L *contundere*, *contūsum*, from *con-* (intensive) and *tundere* to bruise]

conundrum *kən-un'drəm*, *n* a riddle, *esp* one whose answer is a play on words; any puzzling question. [Origin unknown]

conurbation *kon-ûr-bā'shən*, *n* a dense cluster of neighbouring towns considered as a single unit in some respects, eg industrial, economic, administrative. — *adj* **conur'ban**. — *n* **conurbia** (*kən-ûr'bi-ə*) conurbations considered as a class. [L *con-* together, and *urbs* city]

conure *kon'ūr*, *n* one of several small S American parrots of the genus *Aratinga* and related genera. [Gr *kōnos* cone, and *ourā* tail]

convalesce *kon-vəl-es'*, *vi* to regain health, *esp* by resting. — *n* **convalesc'ence** or (*rare*) **convalesc'ency** (the period of) gradual recovery of health and strength. — *adj* **convalesc'ent** gradually recovering health; promoting or encouraging convalescence. — *n* a person recovering health. [L *con-* (intensive) and *valēscere*, from *valēre* to be strong]

Convallaria *kon-və-lā'ri-ə*, *n* the lily-of-the-valley, a genus of Liliaceae. [L *convallis* a sheltered valley]

convection *kən-vek'shən*, *n* a transmission, *esp* that of heat or electricity through liquids or gases by means of currents; vertical movement, *esp* upwards, of air or atmospheric conditions (*meteorol*). — *adj* **convec'tion**. — *adj* **convec'tional**. — *adj* **convec'tive**. — *n* **convec'tor** an apparatus for heating by convection. [L *convectiō*, *-ōnis* bringing together, from *con-*, and *vehere* to carry]

convenable. See **convenance**, **convene**, **convenient**.

convenance *kɔ̃-və-nãs* or *kon'vən-äns*, *n* what is suitable or proper; (in *pl*) the conventional usages or social proprieties, etiquette. — *adj* **convenab'le** (*-äbl'*, or *kon'*) conforming to the convenances. [Fr]

convene *kən-vēn'*, *vi* to come together; to assemble. — *vt* to call together; to summon before a court, etc. — *adj* **convēn'able**. — *n* **convēn'er** or **convēn'or** a person who convenes a meeting; a person who chairs a committee. [Fr *convenir*, *from* L *convenīre*, from *con-*, together, and *venīre* to come]

convenient *kən-vēn'yənt*, *adj* suitable; handy; commodious. — *adj* **convenable** (*kon'vən-ə-bəl*) (*obs*) fitting. — *n* **convēn'ience** suitability; an advantage; any means or device for promoting (*esp* domestic) ease or comfort; a lavatory or water-closet, *esp* (**public convenience**) a building containing several for use by the public. — *n* **convēn'iency** (*rare*) convenience. — *adv* **convēn'iently**. — **convenience food** food (partly) prepared before sale so as to be ready, or almost ready, for the table; **convenience store** (*NAm*) a small grocery shop, often part of a chain, that stays open after normal hours and is conveniently situated in a local area. — **at one's (earliest) convenience** (on the first occasion or at the earliest time) when it is suitable or opportune. [L *convenīre*]

convent[1] *kon'vənt*, *n* a closed community of people, *usu* women, devoted to a religious life; the house in which they live, a monastery or (now *usu*) nunnery. — *adj* **convent'ual** belonging to a convent. — *n* a monk or nun; (with *cap*) a member of one of the two divisions of the Franciscans, following a mitigated rule, the other division being the *Observants*. [Through Fr from L *convenīre*, *conventum* to come together]

convent[2] *kən-vent'*, (*Spenser*, *Shakesp*) *vt* to convene, summon, cite. — *vi* (*archaic*) to be suitable. [L *convenīre*, *conventum*, from *con-*, and *venīre* to come]

conventicle *kən-vent'i-kl* (earlier *kon'vənt-*), *n* a secret, illegal or forbidden religious meeting, applied *esp* to those of English dissenters and to the Scottish Presbyterians in the persecutions under Charles II and James II; any private, clandestine or irregular meeting or the place where it is held. — *vi* to hold such a meeting. — *n* **conven'ticler**. [L *conventiculum* a secret meeting of monks]

convention *kən-ven'shən*, *n* an assembly, *esp* of representatives or delegates for some common object; any extraordinary assembly called upon any special occasion; a parliament not summoned by the sovereign (*hist*); an assembly for framing or revising a constitution; the act of convening; fashion; established usage; any temporary treaty; an agreement; a meeting of political party delegates for nominating a candidate for the presidency or other purpose (*US*); in card games, a mode of play in accordance with a recognized code of signals, not determined by the principles of the game. — *adj* **conven'tional** customary; growing out of tacit agreement or custom; bound or influenced by convention; formed or adopted by convention; not spontaneous; stylized; arbitrary; (of weapons, warfare, energy sources) not nuclear. — *n* **conven'tionalism** adherence to, or advocacy of, that which is established conventionally, such as a mode of speech, etc; something conventional. — *n* **conven'tionalist** a person who adheres to a convention, or is influenced by conventionalism. — *n* **conventional'ity** the state of being conventional; something which is established by use or custom. — *vt* **conven'tionalize** or **-ise** to make conventional; to delineate according to a convention rather than nature. — *adv* **conven'tionally**. — *adj* **conven'tionary** acting under contract. — *n* **conventioneer'** (*NAm*) a person attending a convention. — *n* **conven'tioner** or **conven'tionist**. [L *conventiō*, *-ōnis*; see **convene**]

converge *kən-vûrj'*, *vi* to tend towards or meet in one point, value, quality, etc; (of animals) to undergo convergence. — *n* **conver'gence** the act or point of converging (also **conver'gency**); the moving inwards of the eyes in focusing on a near object (*physiol*); the property of having a limit, for infinite series, sequences, products, etc (*math*); the independent development, in animals not related evolutionarily, of similar features or characteristics; the movement towards a state of parity in the economies of the several countries of the EC; the accumulation of air over a particular region, giving rise to upward air currents (*meteorol*). — *adj* **conver'gent** converging; due to or characterized by convergence. — *n* **conver'ging** meeting or tending to meet in a point; coming nearer together (also *fig*). — **convergence zone** (*geol*) an area where tectonic plates collide causing earth tremors, volcanic eruptions, etc; **convergent thinking** (*psychol*) the examination of ideas by deductive thinking, *usu* following a set of rules or logical steps. [L *con-*, and *vergere* to bend, to incline]

conversazione *kon-vər-sat-si-ō'ni*, *n* a meeting for conversation, particularly on learned subjects; — *pl* **conversazio'nes** or **conversaziō'ni** (*-nē*). [Ital]

converse[1] *kən-vûrs'*, *vi* to talk (with or about); to commune spiritually (with); to associate familiarly (with; *obs*). — *n* (*kon'vûrs*) conversation; spiritual communing. — *adj* **convers'able** disposed to converse; sociable. — *adv* **convers'ably**. — *n* **convers'ance** or **convers'ancy** (also *kon'*) the state of being conversant; familiarity. — *adj* **convers'ant** (also *kon'*) acquainted by study; familiar. — *n* **conversā'tion** talk; an instance of communication by talking. — *adj* **conversā'tional**. —

n **conversā'tionalist** or **conversā'tionist** a person who enjoys or excels in conversation. — *n* **conversā'tionism** (*rare*) a colloquialism. — *adj* **conver'sative** (*obs*) ready to talk. — **conversation piece** an object that arouses comment by its novelty; a painting of a number of people in their usual environment, engaged in their usual pastimes, etc; a play, etc, in which the dialogue is as important as, or more important than, the action. [Fr *converser*, from L *conversārī* to turn about, go about, associate, dwell, from *con-* (intensive) and *versāre* to keep turning, from *vertere* to turn]

converse², **conversion**. See under **convert**.

convert *kən-vûrt'*, *vt* to turn about (*obs*); to change or turn from one thing, condition, opinion, party or religion to another; to cause to acquire faith in a particular religion; to change by a spiritual experience; to change into the converse; to alter into something else (eg iron into steel, a try into a goal, a large house into several flats, a merchant ship into a cruiser); to apply to a particular purpose; to exchange for an equivalent. — *vi* to undergo conversion; to be convertible (from one form into another); to switch (religious or political) allegiance. — *n* (*kon'vûrt*) a person who is converted, *esp* to a particular religious faith. — *adj* **con'verse** (or -*vûrs'*) reversed in order or relation. — *n* (only *kon'*) that which is the opposite of another; a proposition in which the subject and predicate have changed places (*logic*); a proposition in which that which is given and that which is to be proved in another proposition are interchanged (*math*). — *adv* **converse'ly**. — *n* **conver'sion** a change from one condition, use, opinion, party, religion or spiritual state to another; something (*esp* a building) adapted for a different purpose; the expression of repressed emotions as physical symptoms (*psychiatry*); the act of constructing a proposition in accordance with the rules of direct inference, in which the terms of another proposition are interchanged (*logic*). — *n* **con'vertend** the proposition to be converted (*logic*). — *n* **convert'er** someone or something that converts; a vessel in which materials are changed from one condition to another (*esp* iron into steel); apparatus for making a change in electric current (also **conver'tor**); a device which converts data from one form into another (*comput*); a reactor which converts fertile material into fissionable material. — *n* **convertibil'ity**. — *adj* **convert'ible** that may be converted; (of currency) that may be freely converted into other currencies, or into gold (or dollars) at a fixed price. — *n* anything convertible; a car with a folding top. — *adv* **convert'ibly**. — *n* **convertiplane** (*kən-vûr'tə-plān*) an earlier name for a vertical take-off and landing aircraft. — *n* **con'vertite** (*archaic*) a convert; a reformed prostitute. — **conversion course** a course of study designed to facilitate the change from one subject to another; **conversion disorder** (*psychol*) a form of neurosis in which a person represses painful emotions and unconsciously converts them into physical symptoms, particularly when the bodily site symbolizes the repressed idea. — **convertible-term insurance** a life insurance policy providing cover for a given period but which may be converted to eg a whole-life policy at some time during this period at favourable terms. [L *convertere*, *conversum*, from *con-*, and *vertere* to turn]

convex *kon'veks*, also *kon-veks'*, *adj* rising into a round form on the outside, the reverse of concave. — *n* a convex figure, surface, body or part. — *adj* **convexed'** made convex. — *adv* **convex'edly**. — *n* **convex'ity** roundness of form on the outside; a convex part or figure. — *adv* **con'vexly** (or -*veks'*). — *n* **con'vexness** (or -*veks'*). — *adj* **convexo-con'cave** (or -*kāv'*) convex on one side, and concave on the other. — *adj* **convexo-con'vex** (or -*veks'*) convex on both sides. [L *convexus* vaulted, from *convehere*, from *con-*, and *vehere* to carry]

convey *kən-vā'*, *vt* to carry; to transmit; to impart; to steal; to communicate (ideas, etc); to make over in law. — *adj* **convey'able**. — *n* **convey'al**. — *n* **convey'ance** the act or means of conveying; trickery; a vehicle of any kind; the act of transferring property (*law*); the document that transfers it. — *n* **convey'ancer** a person who prepares deeds for the transference of property. — *n* **convey'ancing**. — *n* **convey'er** or **convey'or** a person or thing that conveys in any sense; a mechanism for continuous transport of materials, packages, goods in process of manufacture, etc (also **convey'or-belt**). [OFr *conveier*, from L *con-*, and *via* a way]

convicinity *kon-vi-sin'i-ti*, (*rare*) *n* a neighbourhood.

convict *kən-vikt'*, *vt* to prove guilty; to pronounce guilty. — *n* (*kon'vikt*) a person convicted or found guilty of crime; a person who has been condemned to penal servitude. — *n* **convic'tion** the state of being convinced; strong belief; the act of convincing; an act or an instance of proving guilty; the condition of being consciously convicted of sin (*theol*). — *n* **con'victism** the convict system. — *adj* **convict'ive** able to convince or convict. — **carry conviction** to be convincing. [Ety as for **convince**]

convince *kən-vins'*, *vt* to persuade by evidence; to satisfy as to truth or error; to overcome, get the better of (*archaic*). — *n* **convince'ment** (*obs*). — *adj* **convinc'ible**. — *adj* **convinc'ing** producing conviction; certain, positive, beyond doubt; (of a victory, etc) by a large or significant margin. — *adv* **convinc'ingly**. [L *convincere*, from *con-* (signifying completeness) and *vincere*, *victum* to conquer]

convivial *kən-viv'i-əl*, *adj* social; jovial; feasting or drinking in company; relating to a feast. — *vi* **convive** (-*vīv'*; *archaic*) to feast together. — *n* (*kɔ̃-vēv*, *kon'vīv*; *archaic*) a companion at table. — *n* **conviv'ialist**. — *n* **convivial'ity**. — *adv* **conviv'ially**. [L *convīvium* a living together, a feast, from *con-* together, and *vīvere* to live]

convo *kon'vō*, (*Austr colloq*) *n* (a) conversation.

convoke *kən-vōk'*, *vt* to call together; to assemble (also **convocate** (*kon'vō-kāt*). — *n* **convocā'tion** the act of convoking; a synod of clergy, *esp* those of the provinces of Canterbury and York (*Ch of Eng*); a large (*esp* formal) assembly, eg of the members of a university court. — *adj* **convocā'tional**. — *n* **convocā'tionist**. [L *convocāre*, from *con-* together, and *vocāre*, -*ātum* to call]

convolve *kən-volv'*, *vt* to roll together, or one part on another. — *adj* **convolute** (*kon'və-lo͞ot*, -*lūt*) rolled together, or one part on another; coiled laterally with one edge inside, one outside (*bot*); of a flowerbud, contorted (*bot*); (of a gasteropod shell) having the inner whorls concealed or overlapped by the outer (*zool*). — *adj* **con'voluted** (of argument, style of speech or writing) intricate, tortuous, difficult to understand; unclear; convolute, rolled together. — *n* **convolution** (-*lo͞o'*, -*lū'*) a twist or coil; a fold or sinuosity, *esp* of the brain surface. [L *con-* together, and *volvere*, -*volūtum* to roll]

convolvulus *kən-vol'vū-ləs*, *n* any of a large number of twining or trailing plants of the genus *Convolvulus*, including bindweed. — *adj* **convol'vūlāceous** belonging or relating to the **Convolvulaceae** (*kən-vol-vū-lā'si-ē*), a family of plants with trumpet-shaped flowers and twirling or trailing stems. [L *convolvere*; see ety for **convolve**]

convoy *kon-voi'*, also *kon'voi*, *vt* to accompany (vehicles, *esp* ships) for protection; to escort. — *n* (*kon'*) the act of convoying; a ship or ships of war guarding a fleet of merchant-vessels; the ships protected in this way; an escort; any group of vehicles, *esp* lorries, travelling together; a supply of stores, etc under escort. [Fr *convoyer*; see **convey**]

convulse *kən-vuls'*, *vt* to agitate violently; to affect by spasms (also *fig*). — *n* **convuls'ant** an agent, *esp* a drug, that causes convulsions. — Also *adj*. — *adj* **convul'sible** subject to convulsion. — *n* **convul'sion** any violent involuntary contraction of the voluntary muscles of the body; any violent disturbance; (in *pl*) fits of uncontrollable laughter (*colloq*). — *adj* **convul'sional** or **convul'sionary** pertaining to convulsions. — *n* **con-**

vul'sionary a person who has convulsions, *esp* one of a fanatical sect of Jansenists in 18c France. — *n* **convul'sionist** a religious convulsionary; a believer in the importance of convulsions in geological history (opposed to *uniformitarian*). — *adj* **convuls'ive** causing or affected with convulsions; spasmodic. — *adv* **convuls'ively**. — *n* **convuls'iveness**. [L *con-* (intensive) and *vellere*, *vulsum* to pluck, to pull]

cony or **coney** *kō'ni* or (historically accurate) *kun'i*, *n* a rabbit; rabbit-skin; a hyrax (*Bible*); a term of endearment for a woman (*obs*); a dupe or fool (*obs*). — **co'ny-burrow** a rabbit-burrow. — *vt* **co'ny-catch** (*Shakesp*) to cheat. — **co'ny-catcher** (*obs*) a cheat; **co'ny-wool** rabbits' fur. [Prob through OFr *conil*, from L *cunīculus* a rabbit]

coo[1] *kōō*, *vi* to make a sound like a dove; (of lovers) to speak fondly. — *vt* to murmur softly or ingratiatingly; to effect as by cooing: — *pr p* **coo'ing**; *pa t* and *pa p* **cooed** (*kōōd*). — *n* the sound made by doves. — *n* and *adj* **coo'ing**. — *adv* **coo'ingly**. [Imit]

coo[2] *kōō*, (*slang*) *interj* expressive of surprise.

cooee or **cooey** *kōō'ē*, *n* a call to attract attention, *orig* a signal used in the Australian bush. — *vi* to utter the call. — *interj* attracting attention. — **within cooee** (*Austr* and *NZ colloq*) nearby, within calling distance. [Aboriginal]

coof *kōōf*, *kŏŏf* or *kif*, (*Scot*) *n* a lout; a fool. — Also **cuif**. [Origin obscure]

cook[1] *kŏŏk*, *vt* to prepare (food) by heating; to subject to great heat; to manipulate for any purpose, or falsify accounts, etc); to concoct (a story, excuse, etc) (often with *up*); to ruin, tire out (*slang*); to spoil or ruin; to prepare (*esp* an illegal drug) by heating (*slang*). — *vi* to practise cookery; to undergo cooking; (of, *esp* jazz, musicians) to play skilfully generating excitement (*slang*). — *n* a person who undertakes or is skilled in cooking. — *adj* **cook'able**. — *n* **cook'er** a stove, special vessel, or other apparatus for cooking; a variety (eg of apple) suitable for cooking. — *n* **cook'ery** the art or practice of cooking food; a place for cooking (*NAm*); a camp kitchen (*Can*). — *adj* **cook'-chill** (of foods and meals) cooked, then packaged and stored in a refrigerated state, requiring reheating before serving. — *n* the process of preparing food in this way. — **cooked breakfast** a breakfast which comprises or includes cooked food such as grilled or fried bacon, eggs, sausages, etc; **cooker hood** a canopy over a cooker, containing filters, for the extraction of steam and smells; **cook'ery-book** or **cook'book** a book of recipes for cooking dishes; **cook-gen'eral** or **cook-house'maid** a domestic servant combining the functions of cook and general servant or housemaid; **cook'house** a building or room for cooking in; **cook'ing-apple** an apple specially suitable for cooking; **cook'ing-range** a stove adapted for cooking several things at once; **cook'maid** a maid who cooks or assists a cook; **cook'out** (*NAm*) a barbecue party; **cook'room** a room in which food is cooked; **cook shop** a shop that sells cookery equipment; an eating-house (*US*); **cook'ware** pans, dishes, etc used for cooking. — **cook someone's goose** (*colloq*) to spoil someone's plans; **cook the books** (*colloq*) to falsify accounts, etc; **what's cooking?** (*slang*) what is being planned? [OE *cōc* a cook (cf Ger *Koch*), from L *coquus*]

cook[2] *kŏŏk*, *vi* to make the sound of the cuckoo.

cook[3] or **kook** *kŏŏk*, (*Scot*) *vi* to dart in and out of sight; to peep. [Origin obscure]

cookie *kŏŏk'i*, *n* a plain bun (*Scot*); a small sweet biscuit or cake (*US* also **cook'y**); a person (*esp* in the phrase *a smart cookie*). — **cook'ie-pusher** (*US slang*) an effeminate man or a sycophantic person, *esp* a man; **cook'ie-shine** (*old-fashioned joc*) a tea-party. — **that's how** (or **that's the way**) **the cookie crumbles** (*colloq*) that's what the situation is; that's the way things usually happen. [Du *koekje* a cake]

Cook's tour *kŏŏks tōōr*, (*colloq*) *n* a rapid but extensive tour; a wide-ranging superficial inspection. [Thomas *Cook*, English travel agent 1808–92)]

cool *kōōl*, *adj* slightly cold; free from excitement; calm, imperturbable; disinterested, unenthusiastic; indifferent; impudent; unemotional and relaxed; (of jazz music) restrained, economical and relaxed; excellent, admirable (*colloq*, *orig NAm*); acceptable (*colloq*); (of large amounts, *esp* of money) all of, not less than, as in *a cool million* (*colloq*). — *vt* to make cool; to allay or moderate (eg heat, excitement, passion, etc). — *vi* (often with *down*) to grow cool; to lose radioactivity. — *n* that which is cool; coolness, imperturbability, self-possession, sangfroid. — *n* **cool'ant** a cooling agent; a fluid used to cool the edge of a cutting tool (*eng*); a fluid used as the cooling medium in an engine (*eng*); the gas or liquid circulated through a reactor core to carry the heat generated in it to boilers or heat exchangers. — *n* **cool'er** anything that cools; a vessel in which something is cooled; a spritzer with additional fruit juice; jail, *esp* a military jail (*slang*). — *adj* **cool'ish** somewhat cool. — *adv* **cool'ly** in a cool manner; with composure; indifferently; impudently. — *n* **cool'ness** moderate cold; indifference; diminution of friendship; lack of zeal; lack of agitation; self-possession. — *n* **coolth** (*dialect*) coolness. — *adj* **cool'y** (*Spenser*) cool. — **cool box** or **bag** an insulated box or bag, used to keep food, etc cool; **cool change** (*Austr*) a change in wind direction resulting in cooler weather. — *adj* **cool'headed** not easily excited; capable of acting with composure. — **cool'house** a greenhouse kept at a cool temperature; **cooling-off** see **cool off**; **cooling tower** a large structure in which water heated in an industrial process is cooled for re-use; **cool'-tankard** an old name for a cooler with spices and borage; a local name of borage. — **cooling-off period** the time, *usu* a period of five to seven days, in which a consumer has the right to serve notice of cancellation of a credit, insurance, etc agreement; **cool it** (*slang*; often *imperative*) to calm down, act in a relaxed fashion; **cool off** to become less angry and more amenable to reason (*n* and *adj* **cooling-off'**); to grow less passionate (*n* and *adj* **cool'ing-off'**); **cool one's heels** to be kept waiting; **keep one's cool** (*colloq*) to remain calm, keep one's head; **lose one's cool** to become flustered. [OE *cōl*; cf Ger *kühl*]

coolabah, **coolibah** or **coolibar** *kōōl'ə-bä(r)*, *n* any of several species of Australian eucalyptus tree, *esp Eucalyptus microtheca*. [Aboriginal]

coolamon *kōō'lə-mon*, (*Austr*) *n* a shallow vessel made of wood or bark used by Australian aborigines to hold water, etc. [Aboriginal]

Cooley's anaemia *kōō'liz ən-ēm'i-ə*, *n* a former name for **thalassaemia**. [T B *Cooley* (1871–1945), US paediatrician]

Coolgardie safe *kōōl-gär'di sāf*, *n* a cupboard with fabric walls which are soaked with water, used, *esp* in the Australian outback, to keep food cool. [From *Coolgardie* in W Australia]

coolie or **cooly** *kōōl'i*, *n* an Indian or Chinese labourer who emigrated under contract to a foreign country; a hired native labourer in India and China (*offensive*); in S Africa, an Indian (*offensive*). — **coolie hat** a type of conical straw sunhat with a wide circular brim, as formerly worn by coolies. [Prob *Kolī*, a tribe of W India; or Tamil *kūli* hire]

coolly, **coolth**, etc. See **cool**.

coom[1] *kōōm*, *n* soot; coal-dust; dust or grime of various kinds. — *vt* to begrime. — *adj* **coom'y**. [Appar Northern form of **culm**[2]]

coom[2] *kōōm*, (*Scot*) *n* the wooden centering on which a bridge is built; anything arched or vaulted. — *adj* **coom'ceiled** said of an attic room with the inside ceiling sloping from the wall. [Origin obscure]

coomassie blue® *koo-mas'i blōō*, (*biochem*) *n* a dye used as stain to locate proteins separated by electrophoresis.

coomb[1], **coombe**, **comb** or **combe** *kōōm*, *n* a short deep valley; a hollow in a hillside. [OE *cumb* a hollow]

coomb[2] or **comb** *kōōm*, *n* an old measure of capacity = 4 bushels. [OE *cumb* a measure]
Coomb's test *kōōmz test*, *n* a test to detect rhesus antibodies on the surface of red blood cells, used in the diagnosis of haemolytic anaemia. [From R R A *Coombs* (born 1921), British immunologist]
coon *kōōn*, *n* the raccoon (*colloq*); a sly thief; a Black person (*offensive*). — **coon'hound** or **coon'dog** a hound (*usu* a crossbred bloodhound), or dog used to hunt raccoon; **coon'skin** the pelt of a raccoon. — **coon'-song** (*offensive*) a Black American song. **[raccoon]**
cooncan *kōōn'kan*, *n* a card game for two players in which they try to form sequences. [Sp *con quién* with whom]
coontie or **coonty** *kōōn'ti*, *n* an American plant (*Zamia floridana*) related to the cyclads, from whose roots a starch similar to arrowroot is obtained. [Seminole *kunti*]
coop *kōōp*, *n* a wicker basket; a box or cage for poultry or small animals; a confined, narrow place, *esp* a prison cell. — *vt* (often with *up*) to confine in a coop or elsewhere. [Perh from an unknown OE *cūpe*, related to *cȳpe* cask; cf L *cūpa* cask]
co-op *kō-op' or kō'op*, (*colloq*) *n* short for **co-operative society** or **co-operative store**.
cooper[1] *kōōp'ər*, *n* a person skilled in making barrels, casks, etc; a mixture of stout and porter. — *vt* to make or repair (tubs, etc); to prepare, patch up. — *vi* to work as a cooper. — *n* **coop'erage** the work or workshop of a cooper; the sum paid for a cooper's work. — *n* **coop'ering**. — *n* **coop'ery** the business of a cooper. [Also LGer, from LL *cūpārius*, from *cūpa* cask; cf **coop**]
cooper[2] *kōp'ər*. See **coper**[1].
co-operate or **cooperate**, etc *kō-op'ər-āt*, *vi* to work together. — *adj* **co-op'erant** working together. — *n* **co-operā'tion** joint operation; assistance; willingness to help; combination in co-operative societies; an interaction between two species which is of mutual benefit but on which neither is dependent (*ecol*). — *adj* **co-op'erative**. — *n* an organization in which there is collective owernship or control of the means of production and distribution such as *workers' cooperative*, *farming cooperative*, etc. — *n* **co-op'erātor**. — **co-operating grace** (*theol*) the RC, Arminian and Socinian doctrine that the human will co-operates with the divine in the matter of saving grace; **co-operative society** a commercial enterprise from which the profits are passed on to workers and customers; **co-operative store** the shop of a co-operative society. [Pfx **co-** together, and **operate**]
Cooper pairs *kōōp'ər pārz*, (*phys*) *n pl* pairs of weakly-bound electrons found in a superconducting material below its transition temperature. [L N *Cooper* (born 1930), US physicist]
Cooper's hawk *kōō'pərz hök*, *n* a small N American hawk (*Accipiter cooperii*). [W *Cooper* (died 1864), US ornithologist]
co-opt or **coopt**, etc *kō-opt'*, *vt* to elect into any body by the votes of its members. — *n* **co-optā'tion** or **co-op'tion**. — *adj* **co-op'tative** or **co-op'tive**. [L *cooptāre*, *-ātum*, from *co-* together, and *optāre* to choose]
co-ordinal or **coordinal** *kō-ör'di-nəl*, (*biol*) *adj* (of plants and animals) of or belonging to the same order.
co-ordinate (also **coor-** in all words) *kō-ör'di-nāt*, *vt* to place or classify in the same order or rank; to adjust the relations or movements of; to combine or integrate harmoniously (also *vi*); to harmonize (also *vi*); to match; to combine by means of a coordinate bond (*chem*). — *n* an element of the same order as another; each of a system of two or more magnitudes used to define the position of a point, line or surface by reference to a fixed system of lines, points, etc; (in *pl*) outer garments in harmonizing colour, material and pattern (cf **separates**). — *adj* of the same order or rank; pertaining to or involving co-ordination or co-ordinates. — *adv* **co-or'dinately**. — *n* **co-or'dinateness** the quality of being matched or harmonized. — *n* **co-ordinā'tion** ordered action together; balanced or skilful movement. — *adj* **co-or'dinative** co-ordinating; co-ordinated, indicating co-ordination. — *n* **co-ord'inator**. — **co-ordinate geometry** geometry by the use of co-ordinates, analytical geometry; **co-ordination compounds** (*chem*) compounds in which the atoms or groups are united by **co-ordinate bonds**, secondary valences supplementary to the principal valences (eg addition compounds), *esp* (**co-ordination complex compounds**) ones in which there is a central atom or ion.
cooser. See **cusser**.
coost *køst*, a Scottish form of **cast** (*pa t*).
coot[1] *kōōt*, *n* a short-tailed waterfowl, with black plumage, a white bill and an area of bare white skin (the frontal shield) on the forehead (hence the phrase, *bald as a coot*); a foolish or silly person (*colloq*). [ME *cote*; cf Du *koet*]
coot[2], **cootikin**. See **cuit**.
cootie *kōōt'i*, (*US* and *NZ slang*) *n* a head or body louse. [From Polynesian *kuty* parasite]
COP (*NZ*) *abbrev*: Certificate of Proficiency (a pass in a subject at university).
cop[1] *kop*, *n* a conical ball of thread on a spindle; a top or head of anything. — Also **copp'in**. — *adj* **copped** rising to a cop or head. [OE *cop*, *copp*]
cop[2] *kop*, (*slang*) *vt* to capture; to catch; to acquire, get, obtain. — *n* a policeman; a capture or arrest (as in the phrase *a fair cop*); a catch (as in the phrase *not much cop* of little value, not worth much). — *n* **copp'er** (*slang*) a policeman. — **cop'shop** (*slang*) a police station. — **cop a plea** (*underworld slang*) to plead guilty to a lesser charge in order to speed the judicial process and/or avoid a heavier sentence; **cop it** (*slang*) to suffer a punishment; **cop out** (*slang*) to avoid or evade responsibility for, to refuse to participate in (*n* **cop'-out**). [Perh Fr *caper* to seize, from L *capere*, *captum* to take; cf Du *kapen* to steal]
copacetic or **copesettic** *kō-pə-set'ik*, (*US colloq*) *adj* sound, satisfactory; excellent. — *interj* all clear. — Also **kopaset'ic**. [Origin obscure]
copaiba *kō-pī'bä* or *-pā'bä* or **copaiva** *-vä*, *n* a transparent resin obtained from S American caesalpiniaceous trees of the genus *Copaifera*, used in medicine and in varnishes; a tree of the genus *Copaifera*. [Sp and Port from Tupí]
copal *kō'pəl*, *n* a hard aromatic resin obtained from many tropical trees, and used to make varnishes and lacquers. [Sp, from Nahuatl *copalli* resin]
coparcener *kō-pär'sən-ər*, (*law*) *n* a joint heir to a property or an estate (also **parcener**). — *n* **copar'cenery** or **copar'cenary** joint ownership of property, *esp* by inheritance. — Also *adj*.
copartner *kō-pärt'nər*, *n* a joint partner. — *n* **copart'nership** or (*old-fashioned*) **copart'nery**.
copataine *kop'ə-tān*, (*rare*) *adj* high-crowned like a sugar-loaf. [Ety obscure]
copatriot. A form of **compatriot**.
COPD (*med*) *abbrev*: chronic obstructive pulmonary disease (emphysema).
cope[1] *kōp*, *n* a semicircular, sleeveless, hooded vestment worn over the alb or surplice by priests at certain Christian ceremonies; a covering shaped like a cope. — *vt* to cover as with a cope. — *n* **cop'ing** the covering course of masonry of a wall. — **cope'stone** or **cop'ing-stone** a stone that tops or forms part of the coping of a wall. [ME *cape*, from hypothetical OE *cāpe*, from LL *cāpa*; cf **cap**[1]]
cope[2] *kōp*, (*dialect*) *vt* and *vi* to barter or exchange. — *n* **cōp'er** a dealer, *esp* in horses. [Cf Du *koopen*]
cope[3] *kōp*, *vi* (*esp* with *with*) to contend; to deal (with) successfully. — *vt* to encounter, meet (*archaic*); to match (*Shakesp*). — **copes'-mate** or **cope'mate** (*obs*) a companion; an accomplice; a partner; an adversary; a paramour. [Fr *couper*, from L *colaphus* (Gr *kolaphos*) a blow with the fist]
cope[4] *kōp*, (*obs*) *vt* to tie or sew up the mouth of (a ferret). [Origin obscure; cf **uncape**, **uncope**]

cope[5] *kōp*, *vt* to cut (a piece of moulding) so that it fits over another piece. — **cop'ing-saw** a narrow saw blade held under tension in a wide, U-shaped metal frame, used for cutting curves. [Fr *couper* to cut]

copeck. Same as **kopeck**.

copepod *kō'pi-pod*, *n* any minute planktonic or parasitic crustacean of the subclass **Copepoda** (*kō-pep'əd-ə*), an important source of food for eg pelagic fish such as the herring. [Gr *kōpē* handle, oar, and *pous*, *podos* foot]

coper[1] or **cooper** *kōp'ər*, *n* a ship used clandestinely to supply alcohol to deep-sea fishermen. — *vi* to supply alcoholic liquor in such a way. [Du *kooper*, from *koopen* to trade (cf **cope**[2]); cf Ger *kaufen* to buy; OE *cēapan*]

coper[2]. See **cope**[2].

Copernican *ko-pûr'ni-kən*, *adj* relating to *Copernicus*, the famous Polish astronomer (1473–1543), or to his system, in which it was demonstrated that the earth revolves about the sun.

copesettic. See **copacetic**.

copia verborum *kō'pi-ə vûr-bō'rəm* or *kō'pi-a ver-bō'ro͝om*, also *wer-*, (*L*) plenty of words, fluency, prolixity.

copier. See **copy**.

coping. See **cope**[1].

co-pilot or **copilot** *kō'pī-lət*, *n* a second pilot in an aircraft.

copious *kō'pi-əs*, *adj* plentiful; overflowing; abounding. — *adv* **cō'piously**. — *n* **cō'piousness**. [L *cōpiōsus*, from *cōpia* plenty, from *co-* (intensive) and *ops*, *opis* wealth]

copita *ko-pēt'ə*, *n* a tulip-shaped sherry glass. [Sp]

coplanar *kō-plān'ər*, *adj* on the same plane. — *n* **coplanarity** (*kō-plān-ar'i-ti*).

co-polymer or **copolymer** *kō-pol'i-mər*, *n* a substance polymerized along with another, the result being a chemical compound, not a mixture. — *n* **co-polymerizā'tion** or **-s-**. — *vt* **co-pol'ymerize** or **-ise**.

co-portion *kō-pōr'shən* or *-pör'*, (*rare*) *n* a share.

copper[1] *kop'ər*, *n* a reddish moderately hard metallic element (atomic no 29; symbol **Cu** for L *cuprum*), perhaps the first metal used by man, and used as an electrical conductor and in alloys; a coin, made *orig* of copper or bronze; a copper vessel; a boiler (*orig* of copper) for laundry, etc; the reddish-brown colour of copper; any of several kinds of copper-coloured butterfly, eg the small copper, *Lycaena phlaeas*. — *adj* made of copper; of the colour of copper. — *vt* to cover with copper. — *n* **copp'ering** the act of sheathing with copper; a covering of copper. — *adj* **copp'erish** somewhat like copper. — *adj* **copp'ery** like copper. — **Copper Age** a stage in culture in some regions leading up to the Bronze Age, characterized by the use of copper unmixed with tin; **copper-beech'** a variety of the common beech with purplish, copper-coloured leaves. — *vt* **copper-bott'om** to cover the bottom of (a ship) with copper. — *adj* **copper-bott'omed** (of a ship) having the bottom covered with copper as protection; sound, safe, reliable, *esp* financially. — **copper-cap'tain** one who appropriates the title of captain without any right to it. — *adj* **copp'er-faced** faced with copper, as type. — *vt* **copp'er-fasten** to fasten with copper bolts; to make (an agreement) binding. — **copper glance** redruthite, cuprous sulphide, chalocite; **copp'erhead** a venomous reddish-brown snake of the eastern US, similar to the rattlesnake; a similar Australian snake; a northern sympathizer with the South in the Civil War (*US hist*); **copper nickel** niccolite, a copper-red mineral, arsenide of nickel; **copp'erplate** a plate of polished copper on which something has been engraved; an impression taken from such a plate; a fine handwriting based on the style used in copperplate engravings; **copper-pyrītēs** a yellow double sulphide of copper and iron, chalopyrite; **copp'ersmith** a smith who works in copper; **copper sulphate** a salt of copper ($CuSO_4$), used in solution as a fungicide; **copp'erwork** work in copper; (also *n sing* **copp'erworks**) a place where copper is worked or manufactured; **copp'erworm** the ship-worm. — **hot coppers** (*old slang*) a parched tongue and throat after a bout of drinking. [OE *copor*, from LL *cuper*, from L *cuprum* a form of *cyprium* (*aes*) Cyprian (brass), because found in *Cyprus*]

copper[2]. See **cop**[2].

copperas *kop'ər-əs*, *n* a name formerly applied to copper and other sulphates, now only to ferrous sulphate (see **melanterite**). [Fr *couperose* (Ital *coparosa*), perh from L *cuprī rosa* rose of copper, or *aqua cuprōsa* copper water]

coppice *kop'is* or **copse** *kops*, *n* a dense thicket of trees and bushes, *esp* one used for periodical cutting of twigs and branches; a thicket of sprouting branches growing from cut stumps. — *vt* to cut back (trees, bushes, etc) to form a coppice; to cover with coppice. — *vi* to form a coppice. — *n* **copp'icing**. — *adj* **cop'sy**. — **copse'wood**. [OFr *copeiz* wood, newly cut, from LL *colpare* to cut]

coppin. See **cop**[1].

copple *kop'l*, (*obs*) *n* a bird's crest. — **copp'le-crown**. — *adj* **copp'le-crowned**. [Appar from **cop**[1]]

copple-stone. An obsolete form of **cobblestone**.

coppy *kop'i*, (*dialect*) *n* a small stool. — Also **copp'y-stool**. [Origin uncertain]

copra *kop'rə*, *n* the dried kernel of the coconut, yielding coconut oil. [Port, from Malayalam]

co-presence or **copresence** *kō-prez'əns*, *n* presence together. — *adj* **copres'ent**.

copro- or **copr-** *kopr(ō)-*, *combining form* denoting dung, faeces, obscenity. — *n* **coprōlāl'ia** (Gr *lalia* talk; *psychiatry*) obsessive or repetitive use of obscene language, eg as a characteristic of Tourette's syndrome. — *adj* **coprōlāl'iac**. — *n* **coprolite** (*kop'rə-līt*; Gr *lithos* stone; *geol*) a phosphatic pellet thought to be the fossilized faeces of fish, reptiles and birds; any similar phosphatic concretion of indeterminate origin. — *n* **cop'rolith** (*med*) a mass of hard (sometimes calcified) faeces in the colon or rectum, due to chronic constipation. — *adj* **coprolitic** (*-lit'ik*) containing or made of coprolites; like, or pertaining to, coprolites. — *n* **coprol'ogy** the use of obscenity in speech, literature and art. — *n* **coproph'agan** (Gr *phagein* to eat) a dung-beetle. — *adj* **coprophag'ic** (*-aj'ik*). — *n* **coproph'agist** (*-jist*) a dung-eater. — *adj* **coproph'agous** (*-gəs*). — *n* **coproph'agy** (*-ji*). — *n* **coprophil'ia** (Gr *philiā* love) an abnormal interest in, or preoccupation with, faeces. — *adj* **coproph'ilous** abnormally interested in faeces or dung; (of plants, etc) growing on or in dung. — *n* **copros'terol** a compound formed from cholesterol in the intestine. — *adj* **coprozō'ic** (of animals) living in dung. [Gr *kopros* dung]

coprosma *kə-proz'mə*, *n* any Australian evergreen shrub or small tree of the genus *Coprosma* with glossy, leathery leaves and egg-shaped white or orange berries. [New L, from Gr *kopros* dung, and *osmē* smell]

copse, **copsewood**, **copsy**. See **coppice**.

Copt *kopt*, *n* a Christian descendant of the ancient Egyptians. — *adj* **Copt'ic**. — *n* the language of the Copts. [Gr *Aigyptios* Egyptian]

copter *kop'tər*, (*colloq*) *n* short for **helicopter**.

copula *kop'ū-lə*, *n* that which joins together; a bond or tie; the word joining the subject and predicate (*logic* or *linguistics*). — *adj* **cop'ular**. — *vi* **cop'ulāte** to have sexual intercourse (with). — *vt* (*obs*) to unite. — *n* **copulā'tion**. — *adj* **cop'ulātive** uniting; of or relating to copulation; indicating combination, not alternative or adversative relation. — *n* (*gram*) a conjunction that indicates combination. — *adj* **cop'ulatory**. [L *cōpula*, from *co-*, and *apere* to join]

copy *kop'i*, *n* an imitation; a transcript; a reproduction; that which is imitated or reproduced; a single specimen of a book, magazine, newspaper, etc; matter (eg a newspaper article) for printing; something newsworthy. — *vt* to write, paint, etc in the manner of; to imitate closely; to transcribe; to reproduce or duplicate; to provide a copy of (eg a letter) for (someone). — *vi* to make a copy of another's work and pass it off as one's own; to reproduce data from one part of a data storage device to another, or to another storage device without altering the data (*comput*): — *pr p* **cop'ying**; *pa t* and *pa p* **cop'ied**. — *n* **cop'ier** someone or something that copies; an imitator. — *n* **cop'yism** servile or plagiaristic copying. — *n* **cop'yist** a person whose job is to copy documents. — **cop'ybook** a writing or drawing book of models printed for imitation; a collection of copies of documents. — *adj* conventional, commonplace; (of an example, operation, etc) perfect, or carried out flawlessly. — **cop'ycat** (*colloq*) a term applied in resentful derision to an imitator. — *adj* imitated; done in imitation. — *vt* and *vi* to imitate. — *vt* **cop'y-edit** to prepare (newspaper copy, etc) for printing by correcting errors, etc. — **cop'y-editing**; **cop'yhold** (*Eng law*) formerly, a type of estate or right of holding land, according to the custom of a manor, by copy of the roll originally made by the steward of the lord's court; **cop'yholder** formerly, a holder of land by copyhold; an assistant who reads copy to a proofreader; a device that holds copy for a compositor; a piece of equipment which holds copy upright for a computer keyboard operator. — *vt* **cop'yread** (*US*) to subedit. — **cop'y-reading**; **cop'yright** the sole right to reproduce a literary, dramatic, musical or artistic work, or to perform, translate, film or record such a work (in the UK, since 1 July 1912, for books the term is the author's lifetime and fifty years after his or her death). — *adj* protected by copyright. — *vt* to secure the copyright of. — *adj* **cop'yrightable**. — **copyright library** one of six libraries in the UK entitled to receive a copy gratis of every book published in the UK; **copy taster** a person who selects items for publication or broadcast from the range of material submitted by reporters, etc; **cop'y-typing**; **copy typist** a typist who copies written, printed, etc matter, not working from shorthand or recorded sound; **cop'ywriter** a writer of copy (*esp* advertisements) for the press. [Fr *copie*, from L *cōpia* plenty; in LL a transcript]

coq au vin *kok-ō-vɛ̃*, (*Fr*) *n* a dish of chicken cooked in red wine, with onions, herbs and garlic. [Fr, cock in wine]

coquelicot *kok'li-kō*, *n* another name for the poppy (esp *literary*); a brilliant red, the colour of the red poppy. [Fr, poppy]

coquet or **coquette** *ko-* or *kō-ket'*, *vi* to flirt; to dally. — *vt* (*obs*) to flirt with: — *prp* **coquett'ing**; *pa p* and *pa t* **coquett'ed**. — *n* **cō'quetry** (*-kit-ri*) the act of coquetting; the attempt to attract admiration, without serious affection; deceit in love; any artful prettiness. — *n* **coquette'** a woman who flirts; a S American humming bird of the genus *Lophornis*. — Also *adj*. — *adj* **coquett'ish** practising coquetry; befitting a coquette. — *adv* **coquett'ishly**. — *n* **coquett'ishness**. [Fr *coqueter*, from *coquet*, dimin of *coq* a cock]

coquilla *kō-kil'yə*, *n* the nut of the piassava palm (*Attalea funifera*), whose mottled, dark-brown endosperm is used by button-makers and turners. [Sp; dimin of *coca* shell]

coquille *ko-kē'*, *n* (often in *pl*) a scallop or other seafood served in a scallop shell; a dish or pastry case in the shape of a scallop or shell; a pat, eg of butter; a basket-hilt of a sword in the shape of a shell (*fencing*). [Fr, from L *conchȳlium*, from Gr *konchylion* a cockle or mussel]

coquimbite *kō-kim'bīt*, *n* a yellowish hydrous sulphate of iron found in certain volcanic rocks. [From *Coquimbo* in Chile where it was originally found].

coquina *ko-kē'nə*, *n* a clastic limestone made up of cemented shell debris. [Sp, shell-fish]

coquito *kō-kē'tō*, *n* a Chilean palm (*Jubaea spectabilis*) having edible nuts: — *pl* **coqui'tos**. [Sp; dimin of *coco* coco-palm]

Cor. *abbrev*: (the Letters to the) Corinthians (*Bible*); Coroner.

cor. *abbrev*: corner; cornet.

cor[1] *kör*, (*colloq*) *interj* an expression of surprise. — **cor blimey** a form of **gorblim(e)y**. [Corruption of *God*]

cor[2] *kör*, *n* a Hebrew measure, the homer, 10 ephahs or baths (roughly 11 bushels). [Heb *kōr* round vessel]

cor-. See **com-**.

coraciiform *kor-ə-sī'i-förm*, (*zool*) *adj* of, belonging to or related to the *Coraciiformes*, an order of birds including the kingfishers, hornbills, bee-eaters and rollers.

coracle *kor'ə-kl*, *n* a small oval rowing-boat made by stretching hides over a wickerwork frame, now used in Wales and Ireland. [Connected with Welsh *corwg* anything round; cf Gaelic *curach* (see **currach**)]

coracoid *kor'ə-koid*, *adj* shaped like a crow's beak. — *n* (*anatom*) a paired ventral bone in the breast-girdle, forming, with the scapula, the articulation for the fore-limb; in mammals, except monotremes, reduced to a **coracoid process** fused to the scapula. [Gr *korax*, *korakos* a crow, and *eidos* form]

co-radicate or **coradicate** *kō-rad'i-kāt*, (*philol*) *adj* of the same root. [Pfx **co-** together, and **radicate** (see **radical**)]

coraggio *kor-ad'jō*, *interj* courage: — *pl* **corag'gios**. [Ital]

CORAL *kor'əl*, (*comput*) *n* a computer programming language used in a real-time system.

coral *kor'əl*, *n* a rocklike substance of various colours deposited on the bottom of the sea, formed from the skeletons, mostly calcareous, of certain invertebrates of the classes *Anthozoa* and *Hydrozoa*; the invertebrates themselves; a young child's toy of coral or other material for biting on while teething; (in *pl*) a necklace of coral; a deep orange-pink colour. — *adj* made of or like coral, *esp* red coral of a deep orange-pink. — *adj* **corallā'ceous** like, or having the qualities of, coral. — *n* **Corallian** (*-al'*; *geol*) a Jurassic stratum overlying the Oxfordian, including the Coral Rag and Coralline Oolite (also called *Lusitanian*). — *adj* **corallif'erous** containing coral. — *adj* **coralliform** (*-al'*) having the form of coral. — *adj* **corallig'enous** producing coral. — *adj* **cor'alline** of, like or containing coral. — *n* a common limy seaweed (Corallina) of a delicate pinkish or purplish colour; a coral-like substance or animal. — *n* **cor'allite** the cup of a simple coral or of one polyp; a fossil coral. — *adj* **cor'alloid** or **coralloid'al** in the form of coral; resembling coral. — *n* **corallum** (*-al'*) the skeleton of a coral colony: — *pl* **corall'a**. — **coral berry** an American shrub of the snowberry genus, or its red berry; **coral fern** a type of Australian fern with fronds shaped like branching coral; **cor'al-fish** any of several kinds of tropical, spiny-finned fish which inhabit coral reefs; **coral flower** any flowering plant of the N American genus *Heuchera*, of the family Saxifragaceae, typically having heart-shaped evergreen leaves and bell-shaped flowers on slender stems; **coral island** an island formed from coral; **Coralline Crag** (*geol*) a division of the English Pliocene, shelly sands and clays with fossil polyzoa; **Coralline Oolite** a massive limestone underlying the Coral Rag; **Coral Rag** a coarse limestone rock formed chiefly of coral in the Corallian formation; **cor'al-reef** a reef or bank formed by the growth and deposit of coral; **cor'al-rock** a limestone composed of coral; **cor'alroot** a species of *Cardamine* with knobbed root stock; an orchid of the genus *Corallorhiza* with branching coral-like roots; **coral snake** a venomous American elapid snake of the genus *Micrurus* and related genera; any of various brightly-coloured snakes of Africa and Asia; **coral spot** a fungus (*Nectria cinnabarina*) that *usu* lives on dead twigs but may become parasitic if it enters living shoots, killing branches and occasionally whole trees; **coral tree** a tree or shrub of the tropical genus *Erythrina*, with red coral-like flowers; **cor'alwort** coralroot, in either sense. [L *corallum*, from Gr *korallion*]

coram *kō'ram*, (*L*) *prep* before; in the presence of. — **coram domino rege** (*kō'ram dom'i-nō rē'jē* or *rā'ge*), before our lord the king; **coram nobis** (*nō'bis* or *-bēs*) before us (ie the monarch), in our presence; **coram paribus** (*par'i-bəs* or *pär'i-bo͝os*) before equals or one's peers; **coram populo** (*pop'ū-lō*, or *-o͞o-*,) in the presence of the people; publicly.

coramine *kor'a-mīn*. See **nikethamide**.

coranach. Same as **coronach**.

cor anglais *kör ã'glā* or *ong'-glā*, an oboe set a fifth lower than the ordinary oboe; an organ stop corresponding to this. — Also called (*Ital*) **corno inglese** (*kör'nō ing-glā'sā*): — *pl* **cors anglais** (*körz* or *kör*) or **cor'ni inglesi** (*kör'nē in-glā'sē*). [Fr, English horn, though it is probably not English]

coranto *ko-ran'tō*, *n* a rapid and lively dance; the music for it, in triple time: — *pl* **coran'tos** or **coran'toes**. — Also **courante'**. [Fr *courante* (literally) running, from L *currere* to run (Ital *coranta*, from Fr)]

corban *kör'bən*, (*Old Testament*) *n* anything devoted to God in fulfilment of a vow. [Heb *qorbān* an offering, sacrifice]

corbe *körb* (*Spenser*). See **corbel, courb**.

corbeau *kör-bō'*, *n* a blackish green colour. [Fr, crow, raven]

corbeil *kör'bel* or *-bāy'*, *n* a basket filled with earth, set up as a defensive missile (*fortif*); a carved representation of a basket (*archit*). — *n* **corbeille'** a basket of flowers. [Fr *corbeille*, from L *corbicula*, dimin of *corbis* a basket]

corbel *kör'bəl*, (*archit*) *n* a projection from the face of a wall, supporting a weight (*Spenser* **corbe**); a bracket. — *vt* to lay (stone, etc) so it forms a corbel. — *adj* **cor'belled** or (*NAm*) **cor'beled**. — *n* **cor'belling** or (*NAm*) **cor'beling**. — **corbel step** a corbie step; **corbel table** a row of corbels and the parapet or cornice they support. — **corbel out** or **corbel off** to (cause to) project on corbels. [OFr *corbel*, from LL *corvellus*, dimin of *corvus* a raven]

Corbett *kör'bət*, *n* a Scottish mountain of between 2 500 and 2 999 feet that has a re-ascent of 500 feet on all sides (cf **Munro**). [Orig list of these made by J R *Corbett*]

corbicula *kör-bik'ū-lə*, *n* the pollen basket of bees, consisting of the dilated posterior tibia with its fringe of long hairs: — *pl* **corbic'ulae** (*-lē*). — *adj* **corbic'ulate**. [L dimin of *corbis* a basket]

corbie *kör'bi*, (*Scot*) *n* a raven; a crow. — **corbie gable** a stepped gable; **corbie messenger** a messenger who returns too late, or not at all; **cor'bie-steps** the small stonework steps on the slops of a gable, crow-steps. [OFr *corbin*, from L *corvus* a crow]

corcass *kör'kəs*, *n* in Ireland, a salt-marsh, or land susceptible to flooding by a river. [Ir *corcach*]

Corchorus *kör'kə-rəs*, *n* the jute genus. [Gr *korchoros* the name of a plant]

cord *körd*, *n* a small rope or thick string; a part of the body resembling a cord (eg *spinal cord, umbilical cord*); a measure of cut wood (128cu feet), *orig* determined by use of a cord or string; a raised rib on cloth; ribbed cloth, *esp* corduroy (also *adj*); (in *pl*) corduroy trousers; a string crossing the back of a book in binding; a flex for an electrical apparatus. — *vt* to supply with a cord; to bind with a cord. — *n* **cord'age** a quantity of cords or ropes, such as the rigging of a ship, etc; a quantity of wood measured in cords. — *n* **cordec'tomy** surgical removal of a vocal cord. — *adj* **cord'ed** fastened with cords; wound about with cords (*heraldry*); ribbed; (of wood) piled in cords. — *n* **cord'ing** the act of binding; cordage. — *n* **cord'ite** a cordlike smokeless explosive. — *adj* **cord'less** (of an electrical device) operating without a flex; battery-powered. — *n* **cordocentē'sis** (*med*) the removal of a sample of foetal blood from the umbilical vein by inserting a hollow needle through the wall of the pregnant woman's abdomen. — *n* **cordot'omy** the surgical division of bundles of nerve fibres in the spinal cord to relieve severe or persistent pain (also **chordot'omy**). — **cord grass** a grass of the genus *Spartina* which is found in muddy salt-marshes and is used for making ropes; **cord'wood** wood cut up and stacked in cords. [Fr *corde*, from L *chorda*; see **chord**]

Cordaites *kör-dā-ī'tēz*, *n* a Palaeozoic genus of fossil plants of the family **Cordaitā'ceae**, gymnosperms nearer the conifers than the cycads. [Named after A K J *Corda* (1809–49), Bohemian botanist]

cordate *kör'dāt*, *adj* heart-shaped; having the base indented next to the petiole (*bot*). — *adj* **cord'iform** heart-shaped. [L *cordātus* (in modern sense), from L *cor*, *cordis* the heart]

Cordelier *kör-də-lēr'*, *n* a Franciscan friar, from the knotted cord worn as a girdle; (in *pl*) a club in the French Revolution which met in an old Cordelier convent. [OFr *cordele*, dimin of *corde* a rope]

cordial *kör'di-əl*, *adj* friendly; hearty; sincere; affectionate; reviving the heart or spirits. — *n* a soft drink with a fruit base, *usu* diluted before being drunk; a medicine or drink for refreshing the spirits; anything which revives or comforts the heart. — *n* **cordiality** (*-al'i-ti*). — *vi* **cor'dialize** or **-ise** to become cordial, to fraternize. — *adv* **cor'dially**. — *n* **cor'dialness**. [Fr, from L *cor*, *cordis* the heart]

cordierite *kör'di-ər-īt*, *n* the mineral iolite or dichroite. [After P L A *Cordier* (1777–1861), Fr mineralogist]

cordiform. See **cordate**.

cordillera *kör-dil-yā'rə*, *n* a chain of mountains, *esp* the chain including the Andes and the Rocky Mountains. [Sp, from Old Sp *cordilla*, from L *chorda* cord, from Gr *chordē*]

cordiner *kör'di-nər*. See **cordovan**.

cordite. See under **cord**.

córdoba *kor'dō-bə* or *-bä*, *n* the standard monetary unit of Nicaragua, divided into 100 centavos. [Named after Francisco Fernandez de *Córdoba* (died about 1518)]

cordon *kör'don* or *-dən*, *n* a cord or ribbon bestowed as a badge of honour; a line of police, soldiers, etc, or a system of road-blocks, encircling an area so as to prevent or control passage into or out of it; a row of stones along the line of a rampart (*fortif*); a single-stemmed fruit tree. — *vt* (often with *off*) to close (off) an area with a cordon of men, ring of barriers, etc. — **sanitary cordon** (*rare*) a cordon sanitaire. [Fr]

cordon bleu *kor-dɔ̃ blø*, (*Fr*) *n* formerly, the blue ribbon worn by the knights of the Holy Ghost; hence, a person of distinction, *esp* a cook of the highest excellence. — *adj* (of a cook or cookery) of a very high standard.

cordon sanitaire *kor-dɔ̃ sa-nē-ter*, (*Fr*) *n* a line of sentries posted to restrict passage into and out of an area and so keep contagious disease within that area; neutral states keeping hostile states apart; a barrier (*lit* or *fig*) isolating a state, etc considered dangerous.

cordotomy. See under **cord**.

cordovan *kör'də-vən* or (*archaic*) **cordwain** *körd'wān*, *n* goatskin leather, *orig* from *Cordova* (*Córdoba*) in Spain. — *n* **cord'wainer** or **cord'iner** (*archaic*) a worker in cordovan or cordwain; a shoemaker. — *n* **cord'wainery** (*archaic*).

corduroy *kör-də-roi'*, *kör'*, *n* a ribbed cotton pile fabric; (in *pl*) corduroy trousers (*colloq abbrev* **cords**). — *adj* made of corduroy. — **corduroy road** a track laid transversely with tree-trunks. [Perh Fr *corde du roi* king's cord, although the term is not used in French; perh **cord** and **duroy**]

cordwain, cordwainer. See **cordovan**.

cordyline *kör-di-lī'nē*, *n* any tropical or subtropical palmlike shrub or tree of the genus *Cordyline*, frequently cultivated for their handsome foliage, and including the New Zealand cabbage palm, and the good-luck plant or Ti tree. [Gr *kordylē* club]

CORE *kör*, *abbrev*: Congress of Racial Equality (*US*).

core[1] *kōr* or *kör*, *n* in an apple, pear, etc, the central casing containing the seeds; the innermost or most essential part of something (also *adj*); the central part of the earth (*geol*); a cylindrical sample of rock, soil, etc extracted by driving a hollow-core drill into strata; the lump of stone or flint remaining after flakes have been struck off it (*archaeol*); the part of a nuclear reactor containing the fissile material; (also **magnetic core**) a small ferromagnetic ring which, either charged or uncharged by electric current, can thus assume two states corresponding to the binary digits 0 and 1 (*comput*); a solid mass of specially prepared sand or loam placed in a mould to provide a hole or cavity in metal casting; a computer memory made up of a series of three rings (also **core store, core memory**). — *vt* to take out the core of (an apple, etc). — *adj* **cored** having the core removed; cast by means of a core; having a core. — *adj* **core'less** without a core; pithless; hollow. — *n* **cor'er** a device for removing the core of an apple, etc. — **core curriculum** see under **curriculum**; **core store** or **core memory** (*comput*) see **core** above; **core temperature** (*biol*) the mean temperature of the tissues of an organism located below the level of tissue that is affected by the ambient temperature; **core times** see **flexitime** under **flex**. [Poss L *cor* the heart, or Fr *cor* horn, corn (on the foot), or *corps* body]

core[2] *kōr* or *kör*, *n* a company, gang or shift. [**corps**]

coreferential *kō-ref-ər-en'shl*, *adj* (*philos*) (of more than one linguistic expression) designating the same individual or class.

coregent *kō-rē'jənt*, *n* a joint regent.

Coregonus *kor-i-gō'nəs* or *kör-*, *n* whitefish, a genus of herring-like fishes of the salmon family, pollan, vendace, etc. — *adj* **corego'nīne** (or *-nin*). [Gr *korē* pupil of the eye, and *gōniā* angle]

corelation, **corelative** *kō-*. Same as **correlation** and **correlative**.

coreligionist *kō-rə-lij'ən-ist*, *n* a follower of the same religion as another.

corella *kə-rel'ə*, *n* an Australian long-billed cockatoo. [Aboriginal]

coreopsis *kor-i-op'sis*, *n* any annual or perennial composite plant of the genus *Coreopsis*, mostly native to America, some species of which are cultivated for their showy flowers. [Gr *koris* a bug, and *opsis* appearance, from the shape of the seed]

corespondent *kō-rə-spond'ənt*, (*law*) *n* a man or woman cited in divorce cases as having committed adultery with the wife or husband who is the *respondent*. — **corespondent shoes** two-coloured shoes for men, generally black or brown and white.

corey. See **cory**.

corf *körf*, *n* a coalminer's basket, now *usu* a trolley or wagon; a cage for fish or lobsters: — *pl* **corves** (*körvz*). — Also *dialect* **cauf** (*köf*): — *pl* **cauves**. — **corf'house** (*Scot*) a salmon-curing house. [Du, from L *corbis* basket]

Corfam® *kör'fam*, *n* a synthethic, porous material used as a substitute for leather, *esp* in shoes.

Corfiot or **Corfiote** *kör'fi-ət*, *n* a native or citizen of Corfu. — Also *adj*.

CORGI *kör'gi*, *abbrev*: Confederation for Registration of Gas Installers (*UK*).

corgi *kör'gi*, *n* a Welsh breed of dog, having a foxlike head and short legs. [Welsh *corr* dwarf, and *ci* dog]

coriaceous. See **corium**.

coriander *kor-i-an'dər*, *n* a European umbelliferous plant (*Coriandrum sativum*), whose leaves and seeds are used as a flavouring in food. — **coriander seed**. [Fr *coriandre*, from L *coriandrum*, from Gr *koriannon*]

Corinthian *kor-inth'i-ən*, *adj* of *Corinth* (Gr *Korinthos*) in Greece; of an ornate style of Greek architecture, with acanthus capitals; (of literary style) over-embellished or over-brilliant; (of sport, sportsmen, etc) amateur; profligate, dissolute. — *n* a native or inhabitant of Corinth; an amateur sportsman; a dissolute man of fashion. — *n* **Cor'inth** (*obs*) a brothel. — *vi* **corinth'ianize** or **-ise** (*archaic*) to be licentious. — **Corinthian brass** or **bronze** an alloy made in Corinth, much valued in ancient times.

Coriolis effect *kor-i-ō'lis i-fekt'*, (*phys*) *n* the deflection (to the right in the Northern, left in the Southern, hemisphere) and acceleration of bodies, etc moving relative to the earth's surface, caused by the earth's rotation. [First studied by G B *Coriolis*, (1792–1843) Fr civil engineer)]

corium *kō'ri-əm* or *kö'*, *n* leather armour (*antiques*); the true skin, under the epidermis (*anatom*; also **dermis**.) — *adj* **coriā'ceous** or **co'rious** (*esp* of plant structures) having a leathery appearance. [L *corium*, from Gr *chorion* skin, leather]

corival, **corivalry**, **corivalship** *kō*. Same as **corrival**, etc.

cork *körk*, *n* the outer bark of the cork tree, a species of oak found in S Europe, N Africa, etc; a stopper, eg for a wine bottle, made of cork; any stopper; a tissue of close-fitting, thick-walled cells, almost airtight and watertight, forming bark or covering the surfaces of wounds (*bot*); a piece of cork; a fisherman's float made of cork. — *adj* made of cork. — *vt* to stop with a cork; to stop up; to bottle up or repress (with *up*; *fig*). — *n* **cork'age** a charge made in a restaurant, etc for serving wine not bought on the premises. — *adj* **corked** stopped as by a cork; (of wine) tainted as if by the cork, generally in fact by a fungus which develops on the cork; blackened by burnt cork; drunk (*old slang*). — *n* **cork'er** a person or thing that is an excellent example of its kind (*slang*); a person or device that inserts corks. — *n* **cork'iness**. — *adj* **cork'ing** (*slang*) surpassing; excellent; tremendous. — *adj* **cork'y** of or resembling cork; (of wine) corked (*NAm*). — **cork'board** a thin composite board made of cork and resin, used as flooring and as insulation; **cork'borer** an instrument for boring holes in corks to receive glass tubes in chemical apparatus; **cork cambium** phellogen; **cork'=cutter** a person employed in cutting corks for bottles, etc; an instrument used for this. — *adj* **cork'-heeled** (of shoes, etc) having cork heels; wanton (*obs*). — **cork oak** a S European species of oak (*Quercus suber*) from which cork is obtained for commercial use in Spain and Portugal; **cork'screw** a device, *usu* consisting of a piece of metal in the shape of a screw, for drawing corks from bottles. — *adj* like a corkscrew in shape. — *vi* to move in a spiral manner. — *vt* to pull out with difficulty (eg a cork); to obtain information from by force or cunning. — **cork-sole'** an inner shoe-sole made of cork. — *adj* **cork'-tipped** (of a cigarette) having a filter of cork. — **cork'tree** the cork oak; a name applied to various trees with corky bark or very light wood; **corkwing wrasse** a small reddish-brown or greenish wrasse (*Crenilabrus melops*), one of the species of wrasse found in N European waters; **cork'wood** very light wood; a name applied to many trees with light wood, eg balsa, alligator apple. [Perh from Sp *alcorque* cork slipper, which may be from L *quercus* oak, with the Arabic article *al*; Sp has also *corche*, *corcha*, *corcho*, perh from L *cortex* bark, rind]

corkir or **korkir** *kör'kər*, (*Scot*) *n* a lichen used for dyeing (red or purple). [Gaelic *corcur*, from L *purpura* purple]

corm *körm*, *n* a modified underground stem (without scale leaves, as in a bulb), the storage structure of the crocus, meadow saffron, etc. — *n* **corm'el** a small corm produced from the base of a larger one. — *n* **corm'ophyte** (*-fīt*) a plant differentiated into leaf, stem and root. — *adj* **cormophytic** (*-fit'*). — *adj* **corm'ous** producing corms. — *n* **corm'us** the differentiated body of a cormophyte; the whole body of a compound animal. [Gr *kormos* the lopped trunk of a tree]

cormidium *kör-mid'i-əm n* an aggregation of polyps in a colonial marine hydrozoan.

cormorant *kör'mə-rənt*, *n* a member of a genus (*Phalacrocorax*) of shiny black web-footed seabirds, related to the pelicans, that feeds on large quantities of fish and breeds in colonies on rocks and cliffs; a glutton. [Fr *cormoran*, from L *corvus marīnus* sea crow]

Corn. *abbrev*: Cornish; Cornwall.

corn[1] *körn*, *n* collectively, seeds of cereal plants, or the plants themselves, *esp* (in England) wheat, (in Scotland and Ireland) oats, (in N America) maize; a grain, a hard particle; a kernel or small hard seed; something old-fashioned or hackneyed. — *adj* of, for, pertaining to, made from, growing among, or feeding upon, corn; granular. — *vt* to make granular (*archaic*); to preserve with salt or brine; to give corn to (eg a horse) (*dialect*); to intoxicate (*old slang*). — *vi* to form seed. — *adj* **corned** salted. — *adj* **corn'y** (*colloq*) of, like or abounding in corn; old-fashioned; uninteresting from frequent use; dull; over-sentimental. — **cornacre** see **conacre**; **corn'ball** (*US*) a sweetened ball of popcorn; an unsophisticated person; something trite, banal or sentimental. — Also *adj*. — **corn'-beef** or **corned beef** preserved salted beef; **corn bin** a bin for storing corn; **corn'borer** a European moth (*Pyrausta nubilalis*) whose larvae have become a pest of maize in America; **corn'brake** a maize plantation; **cornbran'dy** spirits made from grain; whisky; **corn'brash** (*geol*) a clayey limestone whose presence in soil affords good growth for cereal crops; **corn'bread**, (or **corn'-cake**) (*US* and *W Indies*) bread (or cake) made of maize meal; **corn bunting** a common brown bunting (*Emberiza calandra*) of Europe and Asia; **corn'-chandler** a retailer of grain; **corn'-chandlery**; **corn circle** see **crop circle**; **corn cob** the woody core of a maize ear; **corn'cockle** a tall, beautiful cornfield weed (*Agrostemma githago*) with reddish-purple flowers, similar to the campion; **corn'-cracker** (*US*) a poor white; a Kentuckian; **corn'crake** a type of rail (*Crex crex*), of elusive habit and with a characteristic rasping cry, commonly nesting in hayfields; **corn'-dealer, corn'-factor** or **corn'-merchant** a merchant who buys and sells corn; **corn dodger** (*US*) a cake, small loaf or dumpling made of maize; **corn-dollie** see **kirn**[1]; **corn exchange** a building where trade in corn is (or was) carried on. — *adj* **corn'-fed** fed on corn; well fed. — **corn'field** a field in which corn is growing; **corn'flag** another name for a gladiolus; **corn'flake** a crazy or silly person (*US slang*); (in *pl*) toasted flakes of maize, eaten *esp* as a breakfast cereal; **corn'flour** finely ground maize, rice, or other grain, used *esp* for thickening sauces; **corn'flower** a beautiful blue-flowered cornfield weed of the Compositae (*Centaurea cyanus*); **corn'fly** the gout-fly; **corn'husk** (*NAm*) the outer covering of an ear of maize; **corn'husker** a person or machine that removes cornhusks; **corn'husking**; **corning house** formerly, a place where gunpowder was granulated; **corn'=kist** (*Scot*) a grain chest; **corn'land** ground suitable for growing grain; **corn law** a law regulating trade in grain, *esp* (in *pl* with *cap*) laws that restricted importation to Britain by a duty, repealed in 1846; **corn'loft** a granary; **corn'-maiden** see **kirn**[1]; **corn marigold** a yellow cornfield chrysanthemum (*Chrysanthemum segetum*); **corn'mill** a flour-mill; **corn'-miller**; **corn'moth** a moth of the clothes-moth genus (*Tinea granella*), whose larvae feed on grain; **corn oil** oil extracted from maize, used in cooking, etc; **corn'pipe** a musical instrument made of a stalk of an oat or other cereal; **corn pit** (*US*) part of an exchange where business is done in maize; **corn pone** (*US*) maize-bread, often baked or fried; a maize loaf; **corn popper** a pan or grating for popping corn; **corn poppy** the field poppy; **corn'rent** rent paid in corn, not money; **corn rig** (*Scot*) a ridge or strip on which oats are grown; **corn'row** a hairstyle, *esp* Afro-Caribbean, in which the hair is arranged in tightly braided flat rows; **corn'-salad** a plant of the genus *Valerianella*, of the valerian family (*esp V. locusta*) the common cornsalad, sometimes used as salads and formerly called lamb's lettuce; **corn shuck** (*NAm*) the husk enclosing a maize ear; **corn'-shucking** the removal of corn shucks; a machine for the purpose; **corn silk** (*NAm*) the silky tuft at the tip of an ear of maize, formerly used as a diuretic; **corn snake** a harmless snake (*Coluber guttatus*) of the southern US; **corn snow** (*NAm*) granular snow; **corn'-spirit** (*folklore*) a god or spirit concerned in the growth of corn; **corn spurrey** a common weed of cornfields (*Spergula arvensis*), with small white five-petalled flowers; **corn'stalk** a stalk of corn; a tall thin person, *esp* one born in New South Wales (*Austr*); **corn'starch** (*NAm*) corn flour; **corn'-stone** a silicious limestone, favourable for cereal growing; **corn thrips** a minute flying insect of the order Thysanoptera, that sucks the sap of grain; **corn weevil** a small weevil (*Calandra granaria*), destructive in granaries; **corn whisky** an American whisky made from maize; **corn'worm** a corn weevil; a corn moth larva. — **corn cob pipe** a tobacco-pipe with the bowl made of a maize cob; **corn on the cob** a cob of maize with grains still attached, cooked whole and eaten as a vegetable. [OE *corn*; Gothic *kaurn*; related to L *grānum*]

corn[2] *körn*, *n* a small hard growth chiefly on the toe or foot, resulting from thickening of the cuticle, caused by pressure or friction. — *adj* **corn'eous** horny. — *n* **corn'icle** or **cornic'ulum** a little horn; a hornlike process, *esp* one of the wax-secreting tubes of a greenfly. — *adj* **cornic'ulate** horned; horn-shaped. — *adj* **cornif'-erous** containing hornstone. — *adj* **cornif'ic** producing or forming horn or horns. — *n* **cornificā'tion**. — *adj* **corn'iform** shaped like a horn. — *adj* **cornigerous** (*kör-nij'ər-əs*) horned. — *n* **cor'nū** (*kör'nōō*; *anatom*) a horn, hornlike part or process: — *pl* **cor'nūa**. — *adj* **cor'nūal** hornlike. — *adj* **corn'y** of or pertaining to horns or corns; having corns; horny. — **corn'-cure** a remedy for corns; **corn'-cutter** a person who cuts corns; **corniferous limestone** a coral limestone with chert nodules in the Devonian of N America; **corn plaster** a remedial plaster for corns. — **tread on someone's corns** to hurt someone's feelings. [L *cornū* a horn]

cornaceous. See **cornel**.

cornage *körn'ij*, (*hist*) *n* a feudal service or rent fixed according to number of horned cattle, horngeld. [OFr, from L *cornū* horn]

cornea *kör'ni-ə*, *n* the transparent horny membrane that forms the front covering of the eye. — *adj* **cor'neal**. — **corneal graft** a surgical operation in which healthy corneal tissue is grafted on to a patient's eye to replace diseased or damaged tissue; **corneal lens** a contact lens covering the transparent part of the eye. [L *cornea* (*tēla*) horny (tissue)]

cornel *kör'nəl*, *n* any tree of the genus *Cornus*, particularly the cornelian-cherry or cornelian tree, a small tree (*Cornus mas*) of central and southern Europe. — *adj* **cornā'ceous** of or belonging to the **Cornāceae**, a family of trees and shrubs including the dogwood, cornel and spotted laurel. [LL *cornolium*, from L *cornus* cornel]

cornelian[1] *körnē'li-ən* or **carnelian** *kär-*, *n* a fine kind of quartz, generally translucent red. [Fr *cornaline*, from L *cornū* a horn, or *cornum* cornelian-cherry, from its appearance; confused with *carō*, *carnis* flesh]

cornelian[2] *kör-nē'li-ən*, *n* the fruit of the cornel tree; the tree itself. — **cornelian cherry**. [**cornel**]

cornemuse *kör'ni-mūz*, *n* a French bagpipe. [Fr]

corneous. See **corn**[2].

corner *kör'nər*, *n* the point where two lines or several planes meet; an angular projection or recess; a secret or confined place; an awkward or embarrassing position; a point in a rubber at whist (*obs*); a free shot, taken from the corner of the field, given to the opposite side when a player in eg football or hockey plays the ball over his own goal line; an operation by which the whole of a stock or commodity is bought up so that the buyers may resell at their own price. — *vt* to supply with corners; to put in a corner; to put in a fix or difficulty; to form a corner against; to get control of (a market for a particular commodity) by forming a corner. — *vi* to turn a corner. — *adj* **corn'ered** having corners; put in a difficult position. — *adv* **corn'erwise** or **corn'erways** with the corner in front; diagonally. — **corn'erback** (*Am football*) a defensive back; **corn'er=boy** (*Ir*) a loafer, a street-corner layabout; **corner'-man** the man at the end of the row in a negro-minstrel performance (*obs*); a street-corner layabout; **corn'er-stone** a stone that unites the two walls of a building at a corner; the principal stone, *esp* the corner of the foundation of a building; something of prime importance. — **cut corners** see under **cut**; **fight** or **stand one's (own) corner** to defend strongly, maintain, one's (own) position, stand, argument, etc; **(just) round the corner** close at hand; soon to be attained, reached, etc; **turn the corner** to go round the corner; to get past a difficulty or danger; to begin to pick up. [OFr *corniere*, from L *cornū* horn]

cornet[1] *kör'nit* (*NAm* also *-net'*), *n* a treble brass valve instrument, more tapering than the trumpet; an organ stop of various kinds; an old woodwind instrument (*usu* **cornett**); a cornet-player; any funnel-shaped object, eg a piece of gold for assaying, an ice-cream-filled wafer cone, or a cream-filled pastry. — *n* **cor'netist** or **cornett'ist** a cornet-player. — *n* **cornettino** (*-tē'nō*) an instrument of the cornet family with a compass a fourth above that of a cornet (also **small cornet**). — *n* **cornō'pean** a brass cornet. — **cornet-à-piston(s)** (*kor-nā-ä-pēs-tɔ̃*) (*Fr*) a brass cornet. [Fr *cornet*, dimin of *corne*, from L *cornū* horn]

cornet[2] *kör'nit*, *n* an old form of lady's headdress, with side lappets; a lappet of this; a cavalry standard (*obs*); up to 1871, a cavalry officer, later a sub-lieutenant; a standard-bearer at a common riding. — *n* **cor'netcy** the commission or rank of cornet. [Fr *cornette*, ult from L *cornū* horn]

cornet[3]. See **coronet**.

cornett, cornettino, cornettist. See **cornet**[1].

cornetto *kör-net'ō*, *n* an old woodwind instrument, now revived for performances of early music: — *pl* **cornett'i** (*-ē*). [Ital, ult from L *cornū* horn]

cornice *kor'nis*, *n* a projecting moulding along the top of a building, window, etc; a plaster moulding at the junction between a ceiling and walls; a picture moulding; an overhanging crest of snow on the edge of a mountain ridge, etc; the uppermost member of the entablature, surmounting the frieze (*classical archit*). — *vt* to provide with a cornice. — *adj* **cor'niced**. — **cor'nice-hook**, **cor'nice-pole** or **cor'nice-rail** a hook, pole or rail for hanging pictures, curtains, etc; **cornice ring** a ring or moulding on a cannon next below the muzzle-ring. [Fr, from Ital, poss from Gr *korōnis* a curved line, cf L *corōna*]

corniche *kor-nēsh*, (*Fr*) *n* a coast road built along a cliff-face; in Egypt, a boulevard along a bank of the Nile.

cornicle, corniculate, corniferous, cornigerous, etc. See under **corn**[2].

Cornish *kör'nish*, *adj* pertaining to Cornwall. — *n* the Celtic language of Cornwall, dead since the later 18c. — **Cornish clay** china-clay; **Cornish pasty** a pasty with meat and vegetables.

corno *kör'nō*, *n* the French horn: — *pl* **cor'ni** (*-nē*). — *n* **corn'ist** a horn-player. — **corno di bassetto** (*ba-set'ō*) the basset horn; an organ-stop; **corno inglese** see **cor anglais**. [Ital, from L *cornū* a horn]

cornopean. See under **cornet**[1].

cornu, cornual. See under **corn**[2].

cornucopia *kör-nū-kō'pi-ə*, *n* the horn of plenty, according to one fable, the horn of the goat that suckled Jupiter, placed among the stars as an emblem of plenty (*Gr mythol*); an ornamental vase in the shape of a horn overflowing with fruits; an abundant source of supply. — *adj* **cornucō'pian**. [L *cornū cōpiae*, from *cornū* horn, and *cōpia* plenty]

Cornus. See **cornel**.

cornute *kör-nūt'*, *vt* (*obs*) to cuckold. — *adj* **cornute'** or **cornut'ed** horned; hornlike; cuckolded (*obs*). — *n* **cornūt'o** (or *-nōō'*; *Ital*; *obs*) a cuckold: — *pl* **cornut'os**. [L *cornūtus* horned, from *cornū* horn]

corny. See **corn**[1,2].

corocore *kor'ō-kōr* or *-kör*, *n* a Malay form of boat. — Also **cor'ocorō** (*pl* **cor'ocoros**). [Malay *kurakura*]

corody. See **corrody**.

corol. *abbrev*: corollary.

corolla *kor-ol'ə* or *-ōl'ə*, (*bot*) *n* the inner circle or whorl of the floral envelopes. — *adj* **corollā'ceous**. — *n pl* **Corolliflorae** (*-i-flō'rē*; L *flōs*, *flōris* flower) in some classifications the Gamopetalae or Sympetalae. — *adj* **corolliflo'ral**. — *adj* **corolliflo'rous**. — *adj* **corolli'form**. — *adj* **coroll'ine** (or *kor'*). [L *corolla*, dimin of *corōna* a crown]

corollary *kər-ol'ə-ri* (rare *kor'əl-ā-ri*), *n* an easy inference; a natural consequence or result. [L *corollārium* a garland, money for a garland, a tip, from *corolla*]

coromandel *ko-rə-man'dəl* or *-rō-*, (sometimes with *cap*) *n* or *adj* (also **Coromandel wood**) calamander; (also **coromandel ebony**) a wood of the same genus (*Diospyros*) as calamander; the colour colcothar. — **Coromandel screen** a Chinese folding lacquered screen; **Coromandel work** lacquer work in which an incised design is filled with colour or with gold. [*Coromandel* Coast in SE India]

corona *ko-rō'nə* or *kə-*, *n* a crown or crownlike structure; the large, flat, projecting member of a cornice crowning the entablature (*archit*); the trumpet of a daffodil, etc, composed of ligules of the perianth leaves (*bot*); a coloured ring round the sun or moon, distinguished from a halo by having a red outerpart; one of the sun's envelopes, outside the chromosphere, observable during total eclipse (*astron*); a similar atmospheric envelope of a star (*astron*); a round pendent chandelier, as hung from the roof of a church (also **corona lucis** *lū'sis* or *lōō'kis*): — *pl* **corō'nas** or **corō'nae** (*-ē*). — *n* **coronagraph** or **coronograph** (*-ōn'ə-gräf*) a special telescope used to observe prominences and the corona around the edge of the sun. — *n* **cor'onal** (*-ə-nl*) a circlet, small crown or garland for the head. — *adj* **corō'nal** pertaining to a crown, a corona, or to the top of the head; like a crown. — *adj* **cor'onary** (*-ən-ə-ri*) coronal; surrounding a part, eg the heart. — *n* a coronary thrombosis. — *adj* **cor'onāte** or **cor'onāted** crowned; (of shells) having a row of projections round the apex. — *n* **coronā'tion** the ceremony of crowning. — *n* **corō'nium** the name given to a hypothetical element in the solar corona assumed to explain spectral lines now known to be due to iron and nickel atoms that have lost a large number of electrons. — **coronary artery** one of the branching arteries supplying blood to the heart-wall from the aorta; **coronary artery bypass** a surgical procedure to restore adequate oxygen supply to the heart muscle by attaching lengths of vein taken from eg the leg to the aorta and bypassing blocked coronary arteries (also **coronary bypass graft**); **coronary care unit** (*abbrev* **CCU**) a hospital ward in which patients are treated after a heart attack; **coronary thrombosis** a stoppage in a branch of a coronary artery by a clot of blood, which causes part of the heart muscle to die (see also **myocardial infarction**). [L *corōna* a crown]

coronach *kor'ə-nähh* or *-nəhh*, *n* a dirge. [Said to be a Gaelic word *corranach* (cf Ir *coránach*, from *comh-* with, together, and *rànach* a cry)]

coronal, coronary, etc. See **corona**.

coronation[1] (*Spenser*) an archaic variant of **carnation**.

coronation. See **corona**[2].

coroner *kor'ə-nər*, *n orig* the guardian of the pleas of the crown; now an official (*usu* a medical practitioner or lawyer) who presides at an inquest and enquires into the causes of accidental or suspicious deaths; in the Isle of Man, the principal officer of a sheading. [OFr *corouner*, from L *corōna* crown]

coronet *kor'ə-nit*, *n* a small crown worn by the nobility; an ornamental headdress; the part of a horse's pastern just above the coffin (also **cor'net**). — *adj* **cor'oneted**. [OFr *coronete*, dimin of *corone* crown, from L *corōna*]

coronis *ko-rō'nis*, *n* in Greek, a sign (') marking a crasis, as κἄν = καὶ ἄν. [Gr *korōnis* a curved line]

coronium, coronograph. See **corona**.

coronoid *kor'ə-noid* or *kor-ō'noid*, (*anatom*) *adj* like a crow's bill, as in the *coronoid process* of the lower jaw or the upper end of the ulna. [Gr *korōnē* a crow, and *eidos* form, shape]

co-routine *kō'rōō-tēn*, (*comput*) *n* a procedure in a computer program that can pass control to any other procedure, or suspend itself and continue later.

corozo *kor-ō'sō*, *n* a S American short-stemmed palm (*Phytelephas*) whose seed (**corozo nut**) gives vegetable ivory; the cohune palm: — *pl* **corō'zos**. [Sp, from an Indian language]

corp. *abbrev*: corporation; corporal.

corpora. See **corpus**.

corporal[1] *kör'pə-rəl*, *n* a non-commissioned officer next below a sergeant in rank; in the navy, a petty officer under a master-at-arms; the leader of a gang of miners, etc. — *n* **cor'poralship**. [Fr *caporal*, from Ital *caporale*, from *capo* the head, from L *caput* the head]

corporal[2] *kör'pə-rəl, adj* belonging or relating to the body; having a body; material; not spiritual. — *n* in Catholic and episcopal churches, the cloth on which the bread and wine of the Eucharist are laid out and with which the remains are covered (also **corporas** *-ras*; *obs*). — *n* **corporality** (*-al'i-ti*). — *adv* **cor'porally**. — **corporal punishment** punishment inflicted on the body, eg flogging. [L *corpus, corporis* the body]

corporate *kör'pə-rət, adj* legally united into a body so as to act as an individual; belonging or pertaining to a corporation; united. — *adv* **cor'porately**. — *n* **cor'porateness**. — *n* **corporā'tion** a succession or collection of people authorized by law to act as one individual and regarded as having a separate existence from the people who are its members; a town council; a company (*NAm*); a belly, *esp* a pot-belly (*colloq*). — *n* **cor'poratism** (the policy of) control of a country's economy through the combined power of the trade unions, large businesses, etc. — *n* and *adj* **cor'poratist**. — *adj* **cor'porative**. — *n* **cor'porātor** (*rare*) a member of a corporation. — **corporate hospitality** the entertainment by business companies of potential clients, *esp* by wining and dining them at prestigious sporting events; **corporate raider** a company or individual who seeks to gain control of a business by acquiring a large proportion of its stock; **corporate state** a system of government by corporations representing employers and employed, its purpose being to increase national production and obviate party politics; **corporate venturing** the provision of venture capital by a company to another with the intention of obtaining inside information relating to the borrower or in order to gain control of that company at some future date; **corporation aggregate** a corporation consisting of several persons; **corporation sole** a corporation which consists of one person and his or her successors; **corporation tax** a tax levied on the income of companies. [L *corpus, corporis* the body]

corporeal *kor-pō'ri-əl* or *-pö', adj* having a body or substance; material; not spiritual. — *n* **corpō'realism** materialism. — *n* **corpō'realist**. — *n* **corpōreality** (*-al'i-ti*). — *vi* and *vt* **corpō'realize** or **-ise**. — *adv* **corpō'really**. [L *corporeus* bodily, from *corpus* the body]

corporeity *kör-pə-rē'i-ti, n* the fact or quality of having a body; corporeality. — *n* **corporificā'tion** the act of corporifying. — *vt* **corpor'ify** to embody; to solidify. [L *corpus* the body]

corposant *kör'pə-zant, n* St Elmo's fire, an electrical discharge forming a glow about a masthead, etc. [Port *corpo santo*, from L *corpus sanctum* holy body]

corps *kōr* or *kör, n* a division of an army forming a tactical unit; a branch or department of an army; an organized body; a set of people working more or less together: — *pl* **corps** (*kōrz* or *körz*). — **corps diplomatique** (*dē-plō-ma-tēk*) the whole diplomatic staff at a particular capital. — **corps de ballet** (*kor də ba-le*) the company of ballet dancers at a theatre; **corps d'élite** (*kor dā-lēt*) a small number of people picked out as being the best in any group. [Fr, from L *corpus* body]

corpse *körps*, or *körs, n* a dead, *usu* human body. — *vi* (*theat slang*) (of an actor on stage) to forget one's lines, etc, to be incapable of speaking one's lines because of a sudden attack of hysterical laughter. — *vt* (*theat slang*) to cause (an actor) to corpse. — **corpse candle** a light seen hovering over a grave, an omen of death; **corpse'-gate** a lych-gate. [ME *corps*, earlier *cors*, from OFr *cors*, from L *corpus* the body]

corpus *kör'pəs, n* any mass of body tissue that may be distinguished from its surroundings; a body of literature, writings, etc; the main part of anything: — *pl* **cor'pora** (*-pə-rə*). — *n* **cor'pūlence** or **cor'pūlency** fleshiness of body; excessive fatness. — *adj* **cor'pūlent**. — *adv* **cor'pūlently**. — *n* **cor'puscle** (*-pus-l*; sometimes *-pus'l*) a cell or other minute body suspended in fluid, *esp* a red or white cell in the blood; a minute particle (also **corpus'cule**). — *adj* **corpus'cular**. — *adj* **corpuscūlā'rian**. — *n* a person who holds the corpuscular theory. — *n* **corpuscular'ity**. — **corpus callosum** (*kə-los'əm*; L *callosus*, callous, hard-skinned) (in humans and higher mammals) a broad band of nerve fibre between the two cerebral hemispheres: — *pl* **corpora callosa**; **corpus cavernosum** (*ka-vər-nō'səm*; L *cavernosus* cavernous, hollow) a section of erectile tissue in the penis or clitoris: — *pl* **corpora cavernosa**; **Corpus Christi** (*kris'tē* or *-tī*) the festival in honour of the Eucharist, held on the Thursday after the festival of the Trinity; **corpus delicti** (*di-lik'tī* or *de-lik'tē*; *law*) the substance or fundamental facts of the crime or offence, eg in a murder trial, that somebody is actually dead and has been murdered; **corpus iuris** a body of law, eg of a country or jurisdiction; **corpus luteum** (*lōō'ti-əm*; L *luteus* yellow) a mass of yellow glandular tissue that develops in a Graafian follicle after the eruption of an ovum and secretes progesterone to prepare the uterus for implantation: — *pl* **corpora lutea**; **corpus spongiosum** (*spun-ji'-ō'zəm*; New L *spongiosus* spongy) the blood sinus which together with the corpus cavernosum forms the erectile tissue in the penis; **corpus striatum** (*strī-ā'təm*; L *striātus* furrowed) the section of the basal ganglia in the cerebral hemispheres of the brain that consists of the claudate and lentiform nuclei; **corpus vile** (*vī'lē* or vē'le also *wē-*; L *vilis* worthless) a person or thing considered so expendable as to be a fit object for experimentation, regardless of the consequences: — *pl* **corpora vilia**. — **corpuscular theory of light** Newton's theory that light consists of a stream of material particles, applied in quantum theory; **Corpus Juris Canonici** (*jōō'ris* (or *ū'ris*) *ka-non'i-sī* (or *-i-kē*)) the body of the canon law; **Corpus Juris Civilis** (*si-vi'lis* (*kē-vē'* or *-wē'*)) the body of the civil law. [L *corpus* the body]

corr. *abbrev*: correspond; corrupted; corruption.

corrade *kə-rād'* or *kor-*, (*geol*) *vt* to wear away (land) through the action of loose solid material, eg pebbles in a stream or windborne sand. — *n* **corrasion** (*-rā'zhən*). [L *corrādere* to scrape together, from *con-* together, and *rādere, rāsum* to scratch]

corral *kə-* or *ko-ral', n* a pen for cattle; an enclosure to drive hunted animals into; a defensive ring of wagons. — *vt* to pen; to form into a corral: — *pr p* **corrall'ing**; *pa t* and *pa p* **corralled'**. [Sp]

correct *kə-* or *ko-rekt', vt* to make right or supposedly right; to remove or mark faults or supposed faults from or in; to do this and evaluate; to set (a person) right; to punish; to counterbalance; to bring into a normal state; to reduce to a standard. — *adj* right; according to standard; free from faults. — *adj* **correct'able** or **correct'ible**. — *n* **correc'tion** emendation or would-be emendation; amendment; reduction; compensation; quantity to be added to bring to a standard or balance an error; bodily punishment; a period of reversal or counteraction during a strong market trend (*US finance*). — *adj* **correc'tional**. — *n* **correc'tioner** (*Shakesp*) a person who administers correction. — *n* **correct'itude** correctness of conduct or behaviour. — *adj* **correct'ive** of the nature of or by way of correction; tending to correct; correcting. — *n* that which corrects; any agent or drug that modifies the action of another substance (also **corrigent**). — *adv* **correct'ly**. — *n* **correct'ness**. — *n* **correct'or** someone who or something that corrects; a director or governor; a proofreader. — *adj* **correct'ory** corrective. — **corrective training** reformative imprisonment for persistent offenders of 21 and over for periods from 2 to 4 years. — **under correction** subject to correction, often used as a formal expression of deference to a superior authority. [L *corrigere, corrēctum*, from *cor-* (intensive) and *regere* to rule]

corregidor *ko-rehh'i-dōr, n* the chief magistrate of a Spanish town. [Sp, corrector]

correlate *kor'i-lāt, vi* to be related to one another. — *vt* to bring into relation with each other; to establish relation or correspondence between. — *n* either of two things so related that the one implies the other or is complementary to it; an analogue (*rare*). — *adj* (*rare*) correlated. — *adj* **correlā'table**. — *n* **correlā'tion** the state or act of correlating; mutual relation, *esp* of phenomena regularly occurring together; interdependence, or the degree of it. — *adj* **correlative** (*-el'ə-tiv*). — *n* a person or thing correspondingly related to another person or thing. — *adv* **correl'atively**. — *n* **correl'ativeness** or **correlativ'ity**. [L *cor-* with, and **relate**]

correligionist *kor'ə-lij'ən-ist*. Same as **coreligionist**.

correption *kər-ep'shən*, (*obs*) *n* shortening in pronunciation; a reproof. [L *correptiō, -ōnis*, from *cor-* (intensive) and *rapere* to seize]

corres. *abbrev*: corresponding.

correspond *kor-i-spond'*, *vi* to answer, suit, agree (with *to* or *with*); to communicate, *esp* by letter. — *n* **correspond'ence** or (*archaic*) **correspond'ency** relation of agreement, part to part, or one to one; communication by letter; friendly communication (*archaic*); a body of letters; suitability; harmony. — *adj* **correspond'ent** answering; agreeing; suitable. — *n* a person with whom communication is kept up by letters; a person who contributes letters, or is employed to send special reports (eg *foreign correspondent, war correspondent*) to a periodical; a person or firm that regularly does business for another elsewhere. — *adv* **correspond'ently**. — *adj* **correspond'ing** similar, comparable, matching; suiting; carrying on correspondence by letters; correspondent; answering. — *adv* **correspond'ingly**. — *adj* **correspon'sive** corresponding; answering. — **correspondence course, school**, etc one conducted by postal correspondence; **correspondence principle** (*phys*) the principle stating that the predictions of quantum and classical mechanics must correspond in the limit of very large quantum numbers; **corresponding member** a member living at a distance who communicates with a society without taking part in its administration. — **doctrine of correspondences** the theory of Swedenborg that there is a spiritual antitype corresponding to every natural object and that Scripture contains the key to these correspondences. [L *cor-* with, and *respondēre* to answer]

corrida or **corrida de toros** *kō-rē'dhä* (*dā tō'rōs*), (*Sp*) *n* a bullfight.

corridor *kor'i-dör*, *n* a passageway or gallery communicating with separate rooms or dwellings in a building or compartments in a railway train; a strip of territory or airspace by which a country has access to a particular place, eg a port, or providing access through another's land for a particular purpose; (in *pl*) places outside the administrative centre where unofficial news circulates and gossip is carried on (*politics*). — **corr'idor-carriage** or **corr'idor-train** a railway carriage or train in which one can pass along from one compartment to another; **corridor work** (*informal*) discussion behind the scenes at a meeting. — **corridors of power** (*fig*) the higher reaches of government administration. [Fr, from Ital *corridore*, from Ital *correre* to run, from L *currere*]

corrie *kor'i*, *n* a semicircular hollow on a hillside (*Scot*); a bowl-shaped recess on a mountainside formed by a glacier (*geol*; also **cirque** or **cwm**). [Gaelic *coire* a cauldron]

corrie-fisted *ko'ri-fist'əd*, (*Scot*) *adj* left-handed. [From Gaelic *cearr* left(-handed)]

corrigendum *kor-i-jen'dəm* or *-gen'dŏŏm*, *n* something which requires correction: — *pl* **corrigen'da** (*esp*) corrections to be made in a book. [L, gerundive of *corrigere* to correct]

corrigent *kor'i-jənt*, *adj* corrective. — *n* something with corrective properties or function, *esp* a drug to reduce or counteract undesirable effects of others in a formula. — *n* **corrigibil'ity**. — *adj* **corr'igible** that may be corrected; open to correction. [L *corrigere* to correct; see **correct**]

corrival *kor-ī'vəl*, (*rare*) *n* a rival; a competitor; an equal. — *adj* contending; emulous. — *vt* to rival. — *vi* to vie. — *n* **corrī'valry**. — *n* **corrī'valship**. [L *con-* with, and **rival**]

corroborate *kər-ob'ə-rāt*, *vt* to confirm; to make more certain. — *adj* (*archaic*) confirmed. — *adj* **corrob'orable**. — *adj* **corrob'orant**. — *n* **corroborā'tion** confirmation. — *adj* **corrob'orative** tending to confirm. — *n* that which corroborates. — *n* **corrob'orātor**. — *adj* **corrob'oratory** corroborative. [L *cor-* (intensive) and *rōborāre, -ātum* to make strong; see **robust**]

corroboree *kə-rob'ə-rē*, *n* a ceremonial dance of Australian Aborigines; a song for such a dance; a festive gathering. — *vi* to hold a corroboree. [Aboriginal]

corrode *kər-ōd'*, *vt* to eat away by degrees, *esp* chemically; to rust. — *vi* to be eaten away. — *adj* **corrōd'ent** having the power of corroding. — *n* that which corrodes. — *n pl* **corrodentia** (*ko-rə-den'shyə*) the Psocoptera, or book-lice, etc. — *n* **corrōsibil'ity**. — *adj* **corrōs'ible** (also **corrōd'ible**). — *n* **corrosion** (*-rō'zhən*) the act or process of eating or wasting away. — *adj* **corrōs'ive** having the quality of eating away. — *n* that which has the power of corroding. — *adv* **corrōs'ively**. — *n* **corrōs'iveness**. — **corrosive sublimate** mercuric chloride. [L *cor-* (intensive) and *rōdere, rōsum* to gnaw]

corrody or **corody** *kor'ō-di*, *n* an allowance; a pension; *orig* the right of the lord to claim free lodging from the vassal. [OFr *conrei, conroi*]

corrugate *kor'ə-* or *kor'ŏŏ-gāt*, *vt* to wrinkle or draw into folds. — *n* **corrugā'tion** the act of wrinkling or state of being wrinkled; a wrinkle. — *n* **corr'ugator** (*anatom*) a muscle that creates wrinkles when contracted. — **corrugated iron** sheet iron bent by rollers into ridges for strength; **corrugated paper** a multi-layered paper with the top layer ridged, used as wrapping material. [L *cor-* (intensive) and *rūgāre, -ātum* to wrinkle, from *rūga* a wrinkle]

corrupt *kər-upt'*, *vt* to taint, destroy the purity of; to pervert; to debase; to spoil; to bribe. — *vi* to rot, go bad; to lose purity, spoil. — *adj* defiled; depraved; dishonest, venal; of the nature of, or involving, bribery; bribed; not genuine or pure; rotten, putrid; debased or made very faulty in transcription; (of a computer program or data in store) containing errors arising eg from a fault in the hardware or software. — *n* **corrupt'er**. — *n* **corruptibil'ity**. — *adj* **corrupt'ible** liable to be corrupted. — *n* **corrupt'ibleness**. — *adv* **corrupt'ibly**. — *n* **corrup'tion** the quality of being corrupt; a corrupt action; bribery; dishonesty; rottenness; impurity. — *n* **corrup'tionist** a person who defends or who practises corruption. — *adj* **corrupt'ive** having the quality of corrupting. — *adv* **corrupt'ly**. — *n* **corrupt'ness**. — **corruption of blood** the former inability of an attainted person to inherit or transmit lands, titles or dignities. [L *cor-* (intensive) and *rumpere, ruptum* to break]

corsac *kör'sak*, *n* an Asian fox, *Vulpes corsac*. [From Turk]

corsage *kör-säzh'*, *n* the bodice or waist of a woman's dress; a small bouquet to be worn there or elsewhere. [OFr, from *cors*, from L *corpus* the body]

corsair *kör'sār*, *n* a privateer (*esp* of Barbary); a privateering ship; a pirate. [Fr *corsaire* one who courses or ranges, from L *cursus* a running, from *currere* to run]

corse *körs*, *n* a poetic form of **corpse**.

corselet, corselette. See **corslet**.

corset *kör'sit*, *n* a close-fitting stiff inner bodice; stays; a stiff belt coming down over the hips; the controls imposed by the Bank of England to restrict banks' capacity to lend money, eg by limiting the amount of new interest-bearing deposits a bank can accept (*colloq*). — Also *adj*. — *vt* to supply with a corset: — *pr p* **cor'seting**; *pa t* and *pa p* **cor'seted**. — *n* **corsetier** (*kor-sə-tyā*, also *-tēr'*), *fem* **corsetière** (*kor-sə-tyer*, also *-tēr'*) a maker or seller of corsets. — *n* **cor'setry** corsets; the making or selling of corsets. [Dimin of OFr *cors*, from L *corpus* the body]

corsive *kör'siv*, (*obs*) *n* and *adj*. Same as **corrosive**.

corslet or **corselet** *körs'lit*, *n* a cuirass, a protective body-covering of leather, or steel, etc; a modified corset, or combined belt and brassière. — Also **corselette'**. — *adj* **cors'leted**. [Fr *corselet*, dimin of OFr *cors*, from L *corpus* the body]

corsned *körs'ned*, (*hist*) *n* a piece of bread or cheese, swallowed in trial by ordeal and believed to prove guilt if it stuck in the throat. [OE *corsnǣd*, from *gecor* (cf *coren*, pa p of *cēosan* to choose) and *snǣd*, a piece, from *snīdan* to cut]

corso *kör'sō*, *n* a race, run, course; a race of riderless horses; a procession of carriages; a street where these are held; an avenue, a wide street, a broad thoroughfare: — *pl* **cor'sos**. [Ital]

Cortaderia *kör-tə-dē'i-ə*, *n* a genus of tall-stemmed S American grasses with large thick panicles. [Am Sp *cortadera* a plant with sharp-edged leaves]

cortège *kör-tezh'*, *n* a train of attendants, a retinue; a procession, *esp* a funeral procession. [Fr, from Ital *corte* court]

Cortes *kor'tes*, *n* the parliament of Spain and of Portugal. [Sp and Port pl of *corte* a court]

cortex *kör'teks*, *n* the bark or skin of a plant between the epidermis and the vascular bundles (*bot*); the outer layer of certain organs, *esp* of the brain (*cerebral cortex*) (*zool*): — *pl* **cortices** (*kör'ti-sēz*) or sometimes **cor'texes**. — *adj* **cor'tical** pertaining to the cortex; external. — *adj* **cor'ticāte** or **corticāted** provided with bark. — *adj* **corti'colous** (*biol*) growing or living on the bark of trees, etc. — *n* **corticosteroid** (*kör-tik-ō-stē'roid* or *ster'*) or **cor'ticoid** any steroid hormone, eg cortisone, synthesized by the adrenal cortex; a group of drugs derived from or similar to naturally produced corticosteroid hormones. — *n* **corticotrophin** (*kör-tik-ō'trof-in*) adrenocorticotrophin (ACTH). [L *cortex*, *corticis* bark]

cortile *kör-tē'lā*, *n* an enclosed, *usu* roofless, courtyard within a building: — *pl* **cortili** (*-lē*). [Ital]

cortisol *kör'ti-sol*, *n* hydrocortisone. [*cortis*one]

cortisone *kör'ti-zōn* or *-sōn*, *n* 'compound E', a naturally-occurring cortico-steroid isolated from the adrenal cortex, or prepared from ox bile, etc, used as an anti-inflammatory agent and in the treatment of Addison's disease.

Corti's organ. Same as **organ of Corti**.

corundum *kə-run'dəm*, *n* a mineral consisting of alumina, second in hardness only to the diamond (varieties include sapphire, ruby, emery). [Tamil *kurundam*]

coruscate *kor'əs-kāt*, *vi* to sparkle; to throw off flashes of light. — *adj* **coruscant** (*-rus'*) flashing. — *adj* **cor'uscating** flashing; sparkling (*esp fig*, of wit). — *n* **coruscā'tion** a glittering; a sudden flash of light. [L *coruscāre*, *-ātum* to vibrate, glitter]

corvée *kör-vā'*, *n* the obligation to perform gratuitous labour (such as the maintenance of roads) for the sovereign or feudal lord (*hist*); a fatigue duty or party (*military*); extra duty (*fig*). [Fr, from LL *corrogāta*, from L *corrogāre*, from *cor-* together, and *rogāre* to ask]

corves. See **corf**.

corvet. Same as **curvet**.

corvette *kör-vet'*, *n* an escort vessel specially designed for protecting convoys against submarine attack; formerly, a flush-decked vessel, with one tier of guns. [Fr, from Sp *corbeta*, from L *corbīta* a slow-sailing ship, from *corbis* a basket]

corvus *kör'vəs*, *n* (with *cap*) a southern constellation; a grappling-hook in ancient Roman naval warfare; a hooked ram for destroying walls. — *n* **cor'vid** (*zool*) a member of the crow genus *Corvus*, of the family **Corvidae** (*-vi-dē*) and subfamily **Corvinae** (*-vī'-nē*). — *adj* **cor'vine** (*-vīn*). [L *corvus* a raven]

cory or **corey** *kör'i*, (*vulg slang*) *n* the penis. [Romany *kori* thorn]

corybant *kor'ə-bant*, *n* a priest of Cybele, whose rites were accompanied with noisy music and wild dances (*Gr antiq*); a reveller: — Eng *pl* **cor'ybants**; L (from Gr) *pl* **corybant'es** (*-tēz*). — *adj* **coryban'tic** wildly excited. — *n* **cor'ybantism**. [Gr *korybās*, *korybantos*]

corydalis *kor-id'ə-lis*, *n* any perennial plant of the genus *Corydalis* of the Papaveraceae, of Europe and Asia, having fern-like foliage and tubular flowers. — *n* **cor'ydaline** (or *-rid'*) an alkaloid ($C_{22}H_{27}O_4N$) obtained from the root of *Corydalis lutea*. [Gr *korydallis* crested lark, from a supposed resemblance of the flower]

Corydon *kor'i-don*, (*poetic*) *n* a generic proper name for a rustic. [L, from Gr *Korydōn*, a shepherd's name in Theocritus and Virgil]

corylopsis *kor-i-lop'sis*, *n* any deciduous flowering shrub or small tree of the genus *Corylopsis*, of China and Japan, typically having racemes of yellow flowers appearing before the leaves in spring. [New L, from **corylus** and Gr *opsis* appearance]

corylus *kor'i-ləs*, *n* a deciduous nut-bearing tree of the genus *Corylus* including *C. avellana*, the European hazel, and *C. maxima*, the filbert. [L]

corymb *kor'imb*, (*bot*) *n* a flattish-topped raceme. — *adj* **cor'ymbose** (or *-imb'*). [L *corymbus*, from Gr *korymbos* a cluster]

Corynebacterium *kor-ə-nē-bak-tē'-ri-əm*, *n* a genus of rodlike bacteria including *C. diptheriae* that occurs in three forms and is the causative organism of diptheria. [New L, from Gr *korynē* club, and **bacterium**]

Corypha *kor'i-fə*, *n* the talipot genus of gigantic tropical Asian palms. [Gr *koryphē* top]

coryphaeus *kor-i-fē'əs*, *n* the chief or leader, *esp* the leader or speaker of a Greek chorus: — *pl* **coryphaei** (*-fē'ī*). — Also (*archaic*) **coryphe** (*kor'if*). — *n* **coryphee** (*kor-ē-fā'*; Fr *coryphée*) *orig* a male dancer (*n* is *masc* in Fr); now, one of a group between soloists and corps de ballet, a leading ballet dancer (also **cor'yphe**). [L, from Gr *koryphaios*, from *koryphē* the head]

coryphene *kor'i-fēn*, *n* a fish of the genus *Coryphaena*, called the dolphin. [Gr *koryphaina*]

coryza *ko-rī'zə*, *n* a cold in the head; nasal catarrh as a result of a cold in the head or hay fever. [L, from Gr *koryza*]

CoS *abbrev*: Chief of Staff.

cos[1] *kos*, *n* a crisp, long-leaved lettuce. — Also **cos lettuce**. [Introduced from the Aegean island of Cos (Gr *Kōs*)]

cos[2]. See **cosine**.

'cos *koz* or *kəz*, (*colloq*) *adv* and *conj* because.

Cosa Nostra *kō'zə nos'trə*, *n* the Mafia organization, *esp* in US. [Ital, our thing]

coscinomancy *kos'i-nō-man-si*, *n* an ancient mode of divination by a sieve and pair of shears. [Gr *koskinon* a sieve, and *manteiā* divination]

cose *kōz*, (*rare*) *vi* to make oneself cosy. [See **cosy**]

cosecant *kō-sek'ənt* or *-sēk'*, *n* one of the six trigonometrical functions of an angle, the reciprocal of the sine, identical with the secant of the complementary angle (short form **cosec** *kō'sek*).

cosech *kōs-ek'*, *n* short for *h*yperbolic *cosec*ant.

coseismal *kō-sīz'məl*, *adj* experiencing an earthquake shock simultaneously. — Also **coseis'mic**. [L *co-* together, and Gr *seismos* earthquake]

cosentient *kō-sen'sh(y)ənt*, *adj* perceiving or aware at the same time.

coset *kō'set*, (*math*) *n* a set which when added to another set results in a larger set.

cosh[1] *kosh*, (*Scot*) *adj* cosy, snug. [Orig unknown]

cosh[2] *kosh*, (*slang*) *n* a bludgeon, truncheon, lead-pipe, piece of flexible tubing filled with metal, or the like, used as a weapon. — Also *vt*. — *n* **cosh boy** a thug, a mugger. [Prob Romany, from *koshter* a stick]

cosh[3] *kosh*, *n* short for *h*yperbolic *cos*ine.

cosher[1] *kosh'ər*, (*dialect*) *vt* to pamper, to coddle. — *vi* to chat in a friendly way.

cosher[2]. Same as **kosher**.

coshery *kosh'ər-i*, *n* the ancient right of an Irish chief to quarter himself and his retainers on his tenantry (also **cosh'ering**). — *vi* **cosh'er** to live on dependants. — *n* **cosh'erer**. [Ir *coisir* a feast]

COSHH *abbrev*: Control of Substances Hazardous to Health.

cosier. See **cozier**.

così fan tutte *kō-sē' fan too'tā*, (*Ital*) that is what all women do; all women are like that.

cosignatory *kō-sig'nə-tə-ri*, *adj* uniting with others in signing. — *n* a person who does so. — *adj* **cosignif'icative** (*rare*) having the same signification.

cosine *kō'sīn*, *n* one of the six trigonometrical functions of an angle, the ratio of the base to the hypotenuse, identical with the sine of the complementary angle (short form **cos** *kos*).

COSLA *koz'lə*, *abbrev*: Convention of Scottish Local Authorities.

cosmea *koz'mi-ə*, *n* a plant of the genus *Cosmos*.

cosmeceutical *koz-mə-sū'tik-əl*, *n* (in *pl*) products which overlap the cosmetics and drugs industries. [*cosme*tics and pharma*ceutical*]

cosmetic *koz-met'ik*, *adj* purporting to improve beauty, *esp* that of the complexion; correcting defects of the face, etc, or making good particular deficiencies (eg *cosmetic surgery*); involving or producing an apparent or superficial concession, improvement, etc without any real substance to it. — *n* (*usu* in *pl*) a preparation for the improvement of beauty, etc. — *n* **cosmē'sis** cosmetic surgery or treatment. — *adj* **cosmet'ical**. — *adv* **cosmet'ically**. — *n* **cosmetic'ian** a person who produces, sells, or is skilled in the use of, cosmetics (sometimes *fig*). — *n* **cosmet'icism**. — *vt* **cosmet'icize** or **-ise** to give cosmetic treatment to. — *n* **cosmetol'ogist**. — *n* **cosmetol'ogy** the art or profession of applying cosmetics or hairdressing, or of carrying out plastic surgery. — **cosmetic surgery** a surgical operation carried out to improve a patient's appearance rather than to cure disease or improve function. [Gr *kosmētikos*, from *kosmeein* to adorn, from *kosmos* order]

cosmism *koz'mizm*, *n* the notion of the cosmos as a self-existing whole. — *n* **cos'mist** a secularist. [Gr *kosmos* universe, world]

cosmochemistry *koz-mə-kem'is-tri*, *n* the study of the chemical composition of stars, planets etc. — *adj* **cosmochem'ical**.

cosmocrat *koz'mə-krat*, *n* (*rare*) a ruler of the world. — *adj* **cosmocrat'ic**. [**cosmos** and **-crat**]

cosmodrome *koz'mə-drōm*, *n* a launching-site for spacecraft, *esp* in the former Soviet Union. [Russ *kosmodrom*]

cosmogony *koz-mog'ə-ni*, *n* a theory or myth of the origin of the universe, *esp* of the stars, nebulae, etc. — Also **cosmogeny** (*-moj'*). — *adj* **cosmogon'ic** or **cosmogon'ical** relating to cosmogony. — *n* **cosmog'onist** a person who speculates on the origin of the universe. [Gr *kosmogonia*, from *kosmos* order, the universe, and root of *gignesthai* to be born]

cosmography *koz-mog'rə-fi*, *n* the science of the constitution of the universe; a description of the world or universe. — *n* **cosmog'rapher** — *adj* **cosmograph'ic** or **cosmograph'ical**. [Gr *kosmographia*, from *kosmos* the universe, and *graphein* to write]

cosmolatry *koz-mol'ə-tri*, (*rare*) *n* the worship of the world. [Gr *kosmos* world, and *latreiā worship*]

cosmology *koz-mol'ə-ji*, *n* the science of the universe as a whole; a treatise on the structure and parts of the system of creation. — *adj* **cosmological** (*-loj'*). — *n* **cosmol'ogist**. — **cosmological constant** a constant introduced by Einstein into his General Relativity equations to produce a solution in which the universe would be static, abandoned by him when the universe was later shown to be expanding, but still retained in various theoretical cosmological models with a value close to or equal to zero; **cosmological principle** according to the cosmology of general relativity, the principle that, at a given time, the universe would look the same to observers in other nebulae as it looks to us. [Gr *kosmos* order, the universe, and *logos* discourse]

cosmonaut *koz'mə-nöt*, *n* an astronaut, *specif* a Russian astronaut. — *n* **cosmonau'tics**. [Russ *kosmonaut*, from Gr *kosmos* the universe, and *nautes* a sailor]

cosmoplastic *koz-mə-plas'tik* or *-pläs-*, *adj* moulding or forming the universe; world-forming. [Gr *kosmos* the universe, world, and *plassein* to form]

cosmopolitan *koz-mə-pol'itən*, *n* a citizen of the world; someone free from local or national prejudices; a communist sympathetic towards or tolerant of non-communism in other countries. — *adj* belonging to, representative of, etc, all parts of the world; unprejudiced; sophisticated, worldly. — *n* **cosmopol'itanism**. — *n* and *adj* **cosmopolite** (*koz-mop'ə-līt*) (a) cosmopolitan. — *adj* **cosmopol'itic** or **cosmopolit'ical**. — *n sing* **cosmopol'itics** world politics. — *n* **cosmop'olitism** (or *-pol'*). [Gr *kosmopolitēs*, from *kosmos* the world, and *polītēs* a citizen, from *polis* a city]

cosmorama *koz-mə-rä'mə*, *n* a view, or a series of views, of different parts of the world, using mirrors, lenses, etc. — *adj* **cosmoramic** (*-ram'*). [Gr *kosmos* world, and *horāma* a spectacle]

cosmos[1] *koz'mos*, *n* any composite flowering plant of the American genus *Cosmos*, related to the dahlia. [Gr *kosmos* ornament]

cosmos[2] *koz'mos*, *n* the world or universe as an orderly or systematic whole (opposed to *chaos*); a complex or orderly system. — *adj* **cos'mic** relating to the cosmos; universal; orderly. — *adj* **cos'mical** cosmic; happening at sunrise (*astron*); rising with the sun (*astron*). — *adv* **cos'mically**. — *adj* **cosmogenic** (*-jen'ik*) of an isotope, capable of being produced by the interaction of cosmic rays with the atmosphere or the surface of the Earth. — *adj* **cosmothet'ic** or **cosmothet'ical** assuming an external world. — **cosmic abundance** the relative proportion of each atomic element found in the universe; **cosmic background radiation** see **microwave background**; **cosmic constant** same as **cosmological constant** (qv under **cosmology**); **cosmic dust** fine particles occurring in interstellar space; **cosmic rays** highly penetrating rays from interstellar space, consisting of protons, electrons, positrons, etc. [Gr *kosmos* order, world, universe]

cosmosphere *koz'mə-sfēr*, *n* an apparatus for showing the position of the earth at any given time with reference to the fixed stars.

cosmotheism *koz-mə-thē'izm*, *n* the belief that identifies God with the cosmos; pantheism. [Gr kosmos world and **theism**]

cosmotron. See **accelerator** under **accelerate**.

cosphered *kō-sfērd'*, (*archaic*) *adj* being in the same sphere.

cosponsor *kō-spon'sər*, *vt* to sponsor jointly. — Also *n*.

coss *kos*, *n* a measure of distance in India, averaging about $1\frac{3}{4}$ miles. [Hindi *kōs*, from Sans *krosà* a call]

Cossack *kos'ak*, *n* a member of a free peasant people in SE Russia, formerly holding by military tenure and serving as cavalry under the tsar. — *adj* of, or characteristic of, the Cossacks. — **Cossack boots** Russian boots; **Cossack hat** a brimless hat of fur or similar material. [Turk *quzzāq* freebooter]

cosset *kos'it*, *n* a hand-reared lamb; a pet. — *vt* to fondle; to pamper: — *pr p* **coss'eting**; *pa t* and *pa p* **coss'eted**. — *n* a hand-reared lamb or other pet. [Perh OE *cot-sǣta-*, *cot-setla* cot-dweller]

cossie *koz'i*, (*esp Austr colloq*) *n* a swimming costume.

cost[1] *kost*, *vt* or *vi* to be obtainable at a price of; to involve an expenditure of; to require to be outlaid or suffered or lost: — *pa t* and *pa p* **cost**. — *vt* to estimate the cost of production of: — *pa t* and *pa p* **cost'ed**. — *n* what is or would have to be outlaid, suffered or lost to obtain anything; (in *pl*) the expenses of a lawsuit. — *n* **cost'liness**. — *adj* **cost'ly** high-priced; valuable. — **cost'-accountant** a person who analyses and classifies elements of cost, eg material, labour, etc, or who devises systems of doing this; **cost'-accounting** (*vt* **cost'-account**). — **cost centre** a department, process or piece of equipment for whch costs can be worked out as part of the costing process in business. — *adj* **cost-effec'tive**

or **cost-effi'cient** giving adequate return for outlay. — **cost-effec'tiveness** or **cost efficiency**. — *adj* **cost-free'** free of charge. — Also *adv*. — **cost plus** a work contract where payment is based on the actual production cost plus an agreed percentage of that cost as profit. — *adj* **cost-plus'**. — **cost price** the price the dealer pays for goods bought; **cost push** (*econ*) inflation due to rising production costs. — Also **cost-push inflation**. — **at all costs** or **at any cost** no matter what the cost or consequences may be; **cost-benefit analysis** (or **assessment**) the comparison of the cost of a particular course of action with the benefits (to be) derived from it; **cost of living** the total cost of goods ordinarily required in order to live up to one's usual standard; **cost of living index** an official number showing the cost of living at a certain date compared with that at another date taken as a standard; **prime cost** the price of production, without regard to profit or overhead expenses. [OFr *couster* (Fr *coûter*), from L *cōnstāre* to stand at]

cost[2] or **coste** *kost*, (*Spenser*) *n*. See **coast**. — *vt* and *vi* (*Shakesp*, *Spenser*) to approach. [**coast**]

costa *kos'tə*, *n* a rib; a rib-like structure, vein, ridge; the fore-edge of an insect's wing; the nervure next to it: — *pl* **cos'tae** (*-ē*). — *adj* **cos'tal** of or near the ribs, the costa, or the side of the body. — *n* the costal nervure. — *n* **costalgia** (*-al'jə*), pain around the chest due to damage to a rib or a nerve running beneath the ribs. — *adj* **cos'tāte** or **costā'ted** having or resembling ribs. [L *costa* a rib]

co-star *kō'stär*, *n* a cinema, etc star appearing with other stars. — *vi* (with *with*) to appear with other stars: — *pr p* **co'-starring**; *pa t* and *pa p* **co'-starred**.

costard *kos'tərd*, *n* a large kind of apple; the human head (*archaic slang*). [Perh L *costa* a rib]

costate, **costated**. See **costa**.

coste. See **cost**[2].

costean *kos-tēn'*, *vi* to dig down to bedrock in prospecting. — *n* **costean'ing**. — **costean'-pit**. [Said to be from Cornish *cothas* dropped, and *stean* tin]

costermonger *kos'tər-mung-gər* or **coster** *kos'tər*, *n* a seller of fruit and other wares from a barrow. [Orig *costardmonger*, from **costard** and **monger**]

costive *kos'tiv*, *adj* constipated. — *adv* **cos'tively**. — *n* **cos'tiveness**. [Fr *constipé*; see **constipate**]

costmary *kost'mār-i*, *n* a composite plant of S Europe (*Chrysanthemum balsamita*), grown for its fragrant leaves and used as a seasoning and to flavour ale. [L *costum*, from Gr *kostos* costus, and *Maria* the Virgin Mary]

costrel *kos'trəl*, (*obs* or *dialect*) *n* an eared bottle or small flask, to be hung at the waist. [OFr *costerel*]

costume *kos'tūm* or (*NAm*) *-tōōm*, *n* a manner of dressing; dress, garb; a woman's outer dress as a unit; fancy dress; (a piece of) clothing for a particular purpose, as in *swimming-costume*. — *vt* (*kos-tūm'* or *NAm -tōōm'*) to dress. — *adj* **costumed'**. — *n* **costum'er** or **costum'ier** a person who makes or deals in costumes. — **costume drama**, **piece** or **play** one in which the actors wear the costumes of an earlier era; **costume jewellery** decorative jewellery made of paste and base metals rather than precious stones and gold or silver. [Fr, from Ital *costume*, from L *cōnsuētūdō*, *-inis* custom]

costus *kos'təs*, *n* an aromatic root wrongly assigned to the genus *Costus* of the ginger family, really a composite of Kashmir, *Saussurea hypoleuca* (also **cos'tus arab'icus** or **cos'tus-root**). [Latinized from Gr *kostos*]

cosy or (*NAm*) **cozy** *kō'zi*, (*orig Scot*) *adj* snug; comfortable. — *n* a covering used for a teapot, to keep the tea warm (also **tea'-cosy**); a similar covering for a boiled egg. — *adv* **cō'sily**. — *n* **cō'siness**. — **cosy along** (*colloq*) to reassure, often with falsehoods; **cosy up** (*colloq*, *esp US*; with *to* or *with*) to try to gain someone's favour or friendship; to snuggle up. [Ety unknown]

cot[1] *kot*, (*archaic* and *poetic*) *n* a small dwelling, a cottage. — *adj* **cott'ed** lined with cots. — **cot'-folk** (*Scot*) cottars; **cot'-house** (*Scot*) a house occupied by a cottar; **cot'land** land belonging to a cottage; **cot'quean** (*obs*) a scolding woman; a man who busies himself with women's affairs such as housework; **cot'town** (*Scot*) a group of cot-houses. [OE *cot*; cf ON and Du *kot*]

cot[2] *kot*, *n* a small bed, *esp* one with high sides for a young child; a swinging bed of canvas (for officers, the sick, etc) (*naut*); a camp-bed (*NAm*); a hospital bed. — Also **cott**. — **cot case** (*esp Austr*) a person who is drunk and incapable; **cot death** the sudden, unexplained death, often happening at night, of an apparently healthy baby. — Also called **sudden infant death syndrome**. [Anglo-Ind, from Hindi *khāṭ*]

cot[3] (*Spenser* **cott**) *kot*, *n* a small boat. [Ir]

cot[4]. See under **cotangent**.

cot[5]. See **cote**[1].

cotangent *kō-tan'jənt*, *n* one of the six trigonometrical functions of an angle, the reciprocal of the tangent — identical with the tangent of the complementary angle (short form **cot** *kot*).

cote[1] *kōt* or **cot** *kot*, *n* a place or shelter for animals (as in *dovecote* or *dovecot*, *sheep-cote*). [OE *cote*; cf **cot**[1]]

cote[2] *kōt*, (*archaic*) *vt* to pass by; to outstrip (as one dog another). [Poss connected with **coast**]

cote[3]. Shakespearian form of **quote**.

coteau *ko'tō*, (*NAm*) *n* a hilly upland area, rising ground; an upland or ridge between two valleys (esp *Can*): — *pl* **cot'eaux** (*-tō* or *-tōz*). [Fr, a sloping hillside, from OFr *costel*, dimin of *coste* slope]

cote-hardie *kōt'-här'di*, *n* a medieval close-fitting tight-sleeved body garment. [OFr]

côtelette *kōt-let*, (*Fr*) *n* a cutlet, a chop. — **côtelette de filet** a loin chop.

coteline *kōt-lēn'*, *n* a kind of muslin, corded or ribbed. [Fr *côte* a rib, from L *costa*]

cotemporaneous, etc (*kō-*). Same as **contemporaneous**, etc.

cotenant *kō-ten'ənt*, *n* a joint tenant. — *n* **co-ten'ancy**.

coterie *kō'tə-ri*, *n* a social, literary, or other exclusive circle. [Fr; orig a number of peasants holding land jointly from a lord, from LL *cota* a cot]

coterminous *kō-tûr'mi-nəs*. Same as **conterminous**.

coth *koth*, *n* short for *h*yperbolic *cot*angent.

cothurnus *kō-thûr'nəs* or **cothurn** *kō'thûrn* or *-thûrn'*, *n* the buskin worn in ancient Greek tragedy: — *pl* **cothur'nī** or **cothurns**. [Latinized from Gr *kothornos*]

coticular *kō-tik'ū-lər*, (*obs*) *adj* pertaining to whetstones. [L *cōticula*, dimin of *cos*, *cotis* whetstone]

cotidal *kō-tīd'l*, *adj* having high tide occurring at the same time.

cotillion *ko-til'yən* or **cotillon** *ko-tē'yɔ̃*, *n* a sort of lively dance with varied steps; a formal (*esp* a coming-out) ball (*NAm*). [Fr *cotillon* petticoat, from *cotte* a coat, from LL *cotta* a tunic; see **coat**]

cotinga *kō-ting'gə*, *n* any brightly plumaged passerine bird of the tropical American genus *Cotinga*, or the family **Cotingidae** (*-tin'ji-dē*). [Of Tupí origin]

cotise or **cottise** *kot'is*, (*heraldry*) *n* an ordinary, one quarter of a bend in breadth. — *vt* to border with cotises, barrulets, etc. [Fr *cotice*; origin obscure]

cotoneaster *ko-tō-ni-as'tər*, *n* any shrub or small tree of the genus *Cotoneaster*, related to hawthorn. [L *cotōnea* quince]

Cotswold *kots'wōld*, *n* a breed of sheep. — **Cotswold lion** (*jocular*) a sheep. [*Cotswold* Hills, SW England]

cott. See **cot**[2,3].

cotta *kot'ə*, *n* a short surplice. [LL *cotta*]

cottabus *kot'ə-bəs*, *n* in ancient Greece, an amusement among young men, consisting in throwing wine into a vessel, success at which supposedly indicated fortune in love. [L, from Gr *kottabos*]

cottage *kot'ij*, *n* a small dwelling-house; a country residence; a summer residence (*US*); a one-storey house, a bungalow (*Austr*); a public lavatory used by homosexuals for soliciting (*slang*). — *adj* **cott'aged** covered with cottages. — *n* **cott'ager** a person who lives in a cottage, *esp* a rural labourer. — *adj* **cott'agey** cottage-like. — *n* **cott'aging** (*slang*) soliciting by male homosexuals in public lavatories. — **cottage cheese** soft white loose cheese made from skim-milk curds; **cottage hospital** a small, rural hospital without resident doctors; **cottage industry** one in which the work is done wholly or largely by people in their own homes, *esp* one on a relatively small scale; **cottage loaf** a loaf shaped as a smaller lump on the top of a bigger one; **cottage orné** (Fr *ko-täzh or-nā*) an ornately-designed small country house built in rustic style; **cottage piano** a small upright piano; **cottage pie** shepherd's pie. [LL *cottagium*, from OE *cot*; see **cot**[1]]

cottar or **cotter** *kot'ər, n* one of a class of medieval villeins; a peasant occupying a cot or cottage for which he has to give labour (*Scot*). [**cot**[1]]

cotter *kot'ər, n* a pin or wedge for fastening and tightening. — *n* **cott'er-pin** a pin for keeping a cotter in place. [Origin obscure]

cottid, cottoid. See **cottus**.

cottier *kot'i-ər, n* a cottar; an Irish tenant holding land as the highest bidder. — *n* **cott'ierism** the cottier system of land tenure. [Fr *cotier*; see **cot**[1]]

cottise. See **cotise**.

cotton *kot'n, n* a soft substance like fine wool, the long hairs covering the seeds of the cotton-plant; the plant itself, individually or collectively; yarn or cloth made of cotton. — *adj* made of cotton. — *vi* to agree, to become friendly or attached. — *n* **cottonade'** an inferior cotton cloth. — *n* **cottonoc'racy** the cotton planting or cotton manufacturing interests. — *adj* **cott'ony** like cotton; soft; downy. — **cotton belt** (sometimes with *caps*) the region in the south-eastern US in which much cotton is produced; **cott'on-boll** the pod of the cotton-plant; **cotton bush** (*Austr*) any of various downy-leaved shrubs used to feed cattle, etc; **cotton cake** cakes or pellets of compressed cotton-seed, used as an animal feed; **cotton candy** (*NAm*) candy floss; **cott'on-gin** a machine for separating the seeds from the fibre of cotton; **cotton grass** a genus (*Eriophorum*) of sedges with long, silky or cottony hairs about the ripened ovary; **cott'on-mill** a factory where cotton is spun or woven; **cott'onmouth** the venomous water mocassin snake (from the white inside of its mouth). — *adj* **cott'on-picking** (*US slang*; sometimes *facetious*) used as a relatively mild pejorative. — **cotton plant** one of various species of *Gossypium* (family Malvaceae), yielding cotton; **cotton press** a press for compressing cotton into bales; **cotton sedge** (*Can*) cotton grass; **cott'onseed** the seed of the cotton-plant, yielding a valuable oil; **cotton spinner** a person who spins cotton, or employs those who do; **cott'ontail** any of several species of rabbits of the genus *Sylvilagus*, the ordinary rabbit of the US; **cotton thistle** a strong thistle (*Onopordon acanthium*) covered with a cottony down; **cotton tree** the American cotton wood; an Indian tree *Bombax malabaricum*; an Australian hibiscus; **cotton waste** refuse from cotton mills, used for cleaning machinery, etc; **cott'onweed** cudweed, a cottony seaside composite plant (*Diotis maritima*); **cott'onwood** any one of several American species of poplar; **cotton wool** cotton in its raw or woolly state; loose cotton pressed in a sheet as an absorbent or protective agent, for stuffing, etc; a protected, cushioned or cosseted state; padding, waffle; **cott'on-worm** the caterpillar of an owlet moth (*Aletia xylina*), destructive to American cotton crops; **cottony-cushion scale** a small insect (*Icerya purchasi*), a serious pest of citrus trees in western US. — **cotton on** (*slang*) (sometimes with *to*) to catch on, understand; **cotton on to** (*slang*) to take to. [Fr *coton*, from Ar *qutun*]

cottus *kot'əs*, or **cottid** *kot'id, n* any fish of the genus *Cottus* or family **Cottidae** (*-i-dē*) including the bullhead and father-lasher. — *adj* **cott'oid**. [Gr *kottos* a fish, perh the bullhead]

cotwal. See **kotwal**.

cotyle *kot'i-lē, n* an ancient Greek drinking-cup; a cup-like cavity (*zool*): — *pl* **cot'ylae** (*-lē*) or **cot'ylēs**. — *adj* **cotyl'iform** (*bot*) disc-shaped with raised rim. — *adj* **cot'yloid** cup-shaped. [Gr *kotylē*]

cotyledon *kot-i-lē'dən, n* a seed-leaf (*bot*); a convex subdivision of the mature placenta, each division containing a major blood vessel (*zool*); a plant of the S African genus *Cotyledon*. — *adj* **cotylē'donary**. — *adj* **cotylē'donous** pertaining to or having cotyledons. [Gr *kotylēdōn*, from *kotylē* a cup]

coubiliac. See **koubibiaca**.

coucal *kōō'käl, n* any member of a genus (*Centropus*) of common ground-dwelling birds in Africa, India and Australia, the lark-heeled cuckoos. [Imit]

couch[1] *kowch, vt* to lay down; to lower, place in a horizontal position; to arrange in language, to express; to depress or remove (a cataract in the eye) (*surg*). — *vi* to lie down for the purpose of sleep, concealment, etc. — *n* a kind of sofa with half back and one raised end; any sofa; any place for rest or sleep; a bed, *esp* for daytime use, eg one on which a doctor's or psychiatrist's patient lies for examination; the lair of a wild beast (*poetic*). — *adj* **couch'ant** lying down with head up (*heraldry*). — *n* **couch'ing** embroidery in which the surface is covered with threads and these are secured by stitches forming a pattern. — **couch potato** (*slang, orig US*) a person whose leisure time is spent sitting shiftlessly in front of the television or video. [Fr *coucher* to lay down, from L *collocāre* to place, from *col-* together, and *locus* a place]

couch[2] or **couch grass** *kowch'* or *kōōch'* (*gräs*), *n* a grass related to wheat, a troublesome weed owing to its creeping rootstocks. [A variant of **quitch**[1]]

couchee *kōō'shā, n* an evening reception. — Also (formerly) **couchée** or **couché**. [Fr *couché* a reception before going to bed; see **couch**[1]]

couchette *kōō-shet', n* a sleeping-berth on a continental train or a cross-channel boat, convertible from and into ordinary seating. [Fr]

cou-cou *kōō'-kōō, n* a W Indian dish of boiled corn meal with okra. [Origin uncertain]

coudé *kōō-dā'*, (*astron*) *adj* (of a reflecting telescope) in which one or more plane mirrors reflect the light down the polar axis. [Fr, bent like an elbow]

Couéism *kōō'ā-izm, n* psychotherapy by auto-suggestion. — *n* **Cou'éist**. [Emile *Coué* (1857–1926), its expounder]

cougar *kōō'gär, -gər* or **couguar** *-gwär, n* a puma. [Fr *couguar*, from Port *cucuarana*, adapted from a Tupí-Guaraní name]

cough *kof, vi* to expel air with a sudden opening of the glottis and a characteristic harsh sound; to confess to a crime or give information (*slang*). — *vt* to expel by coughing. — *n* the act or the sound of coughing; an ailment of which coughing is a symptom; (with *the*) equine flu. — *n* **cough'er**. — *n* **cough'ing**. — **cough drop** a cough lozenge; a person of spicy character; **cough lozenge** a medicated lozenge to relieve a cough; **cough mixture** a liquid medicine to relieve a cough. — **cough down** to silence (a speaker) by coughing; **cough up** (*slang*) to pay out, hand over, under compulsion. [ME *coughen*; cf Du *kuchen*, Ger *keuchen*, *keichen* to gasp]

could *kŏŏd, pa t* of **can**[1]. — **could be** (*colloq*) perhaps, maybe. [ME *coude*, *couth*, *from* OE *cūthe* for *cunthe* was able; *l* is inserted from the influence of *would* and *should*]

coulée *kōō-lā', n* a lava-flow; a rocky ravine (*NAm*). [Fr *couler* to flow]

couleur de rose *kōō-lœr də rōz*, (*Fr*) *adj* rose-coloured; seen or presented in a way that exaggerates attractiveness. — Also *n*.

coulis *kōō-lē*, (*Fr*) *n* a thin purée of fish, fowl, fruit or vegetables.

coulisse *kōō-lēs', n* a piece of grooved wood, eg the slides in which the side-scenes of a theatre run; hence (in *pl*) the wings (*theat*); (sometimes with *cap*) the part of the Paris Bourse where unofficial securities are traded. [Fr *couler* to glide, to flow, from L *cōlāre* to strain]

couloir *kōōl-wär', n* a gully, *esp* an Alpine gully. [Fr, passage]

coulomb *kōō-lom'*, *n* the MKSA and SI unit of electric charge (static or as a current), equal to the quantity of electricity transferred by one ampere in one second (symbol **C**). — *n* **coulom'eter** a voltameter. — Also **coulomb'meter**. — *adj* **coulomet'ric**. — *n* **coulom'etry** (chemical analysis by) the measuring of the number of coulombs used in electrolysis. [From C A de *Coulomb* (1736–1806), French physicist]

Coulommiers *kōō-lom-yā*, *n* a white, soft cheese, fresh or cured, made near *Coulommiers* in central France.

coulter or (*esp NAm*) **colter** *kōl'tər* (*Scot kōō'tər*), *n* the iron cutter in front of a ploughshare. [OE *culter*, from L *culter* knife]

coumarin or **cumarin** *kōō'mə-rin*, *n* a crystalline compound ($C_9H_6O_2$) obtained from Tonka beans, woodruff, melilot, etc, used medicinally to prevent coagulation of the blood. — *adj* **coumaric** (*-mar'*) or **coumaril'ic**. [Tupí *cumarú* Tonka bean]

council *kown'sl* or *-sil*, *n* an assembly called together for deliberation, advice, administration or legislation; the people making up such an assembly; the body directing the affairs of a town, county, parish, etc; an assembly of ecclesiastics met to regulate doctrine or discipline; a governing body in a university; a committee that arranges the business of a society. — Also *adj*. — *n* **coun'cillor** or (*NAm*) **coun'cilor** a member of a council. — *n* **coun'cilman** (esp *US*) a member of a municipal council. — **council cham'ber** the room where a council is held; **council estate** an area set apart for council houses; **council house** a building in which a council meets; a dwelling-house erected by a municipal council; **council school** a school governed by a town or county council; **council tax** a local government tax based on and banded according to property values, with each household deemed to have two residents (with discount for people living alone), a replacement for the poll tax or community charge. — **Council of Europe** a consultative body of European states, at first (1949) thought of as the parliament of a future European federation; **Council of Ministers** in the EC, the decision-making body comprising ministers of the member countries; **council of war** a conference of officers called to consult with the commander (also *fig*); **European Council** the body comprising the French head of state and the prime ministers of the other EC countries; **in council** in the council-chamber; in consultation; **legislative council** a council to assist a governor, with power to make laws. [Fr *concile*, from L *concilium*]

counsel *kown'sl*, *n* advice; consultation; deliberation; a person who gives counsel, a barrister or advocate. — *vt* to advise; to warn: — *pr p* **coun'selling**; *pat* and *pa p* **coun'selled**. — *adj* **couns'ellable** that may be counselled. — *n* **coun'selling** (a service consisting of) helping people to adjust to or deal with personal problems, etc by enabling them to discover for themselves the solution to the problems while receiving sympathetic attention from a counsellor; (sometimes) the giving of advice on miscellaneous problems. — Also *adj*. — *n* **coun'sellor** or (*US*) **coun'selor** a person who counsels; a person involved in counselling; a barrister. — *n* **coun'sellorship** or (*US*) **coun'selorship**. — **counsel of perfection** a commendation of something beyond the binding minimum, something not absolutely imperative, but commended as the means of reaching greater 'perfection'; an impractical ideal; **keep counsel** to keep a secret; **Queen's Counsel** (*abbrev* **QC**) or **King's Counsel** (*abbrev* **KC**) a barrister or advocate appointed by letters-patent (the office is honorary, but gives the right of precedence in all the courts). [Fr *conseil*, from L *consilium* advice, from *consulere* to consult]

count[1] *kownt*, *n* an imperial official (*Roman hist*); in continental Europe, a noble equal in rank to an earl. — *n* **count'ess** a lady of the same rank as a count or earl; the wife of a count or earl; a size of roofing slate, 508 × 254 mm (20 × 10in). — *n* **count'ship** a count's dignity or domain (also used as a title). [OFr *conte*, from L *comes*, *comitis* a companion, from *con-* with, and *īre* to go]

count[2] or **compt** (*obs*) *kownt*, *vt* to number, sum up; to name the numerals up to; to take into account, reckon as significant or to be recognized; to reckon, esteem, consider. — *vi* to number; to be numbered; to be of account; to be recognized in reckoning; to have a certain value; to reckon; to name the numerals in order. — *n* the act of numbering; reckoning; the number counted; a number indicating size of yarn; the counting (by a referee) of the seconds in which a boxer or wrestler may rise and resume fighting (also **count'-out**); esteem, consideration, account; a particular charge in an indictment (*law*). — *adj* denoting a noun which, since it denotes an entity of which there can be one or more than one, is able to form a plural. — *adj* **count'able** (*obs* **compt'able** or **compt'ible**) capable of being counted; to be counted; accountable; (of a noun) count. — *adj* **count'ed** accounted, reckoned. — *n* **count'er** a person or thing that counts; that which indicates a number; a disc or similar, used in reckoning or (*games*) as a substitute for a coin or a marker of one's position on a board; a table with a raised surface over which money is counted, goods are laid, food is served, etc; the name of certain prisons (officially **compt'er**; *obs*). — *adj* **count'less** that cannot be counted; innumerable. — **count'-down** a descending count or counted check to a moment of happening regarded as zero, as in the firing of a rocket; **count'er-caster** (*Shakesp*) an arithmetician, reckoner; **count'er-jumper** or **count'erskipper** contemptuous names for a shopkeeper or shop assistant; **counting frame** a frame having rows of movable beads, used for elementary counting, an abacus; **count'ing-house** or **count'ing-room** formerly, a room in which a merchant, etc kept his accounts and transacted business; **count'line** (of a confectionery bar) made as an individual line (eg a filled or chocolate-covered combination bar) as distinct from moulded chocolate; **count-out** see **count** above; **count wheel** a wheel with notched edge controlling the stroke of a clock in sounding the hours. — **count out** of a meeting (*esp* of the House of Commons), to bring to an end by pointing out that a quorum is not present; (in children's games) to eliminate (players) by counting while repeating a rhyme; to judge (a boxer, wrestler, etc) defeated by counting the maximum allowable seconds in which to resume; **keep count** to keep an accurate numerical record (of); **lose count** to fail to keep count (of); **out for the count** unable to rise and resume the fight during the count (*boxing*); in general, unconscious, or asleep; **over the counter** involving trading in shares not on the official Stock Exchange list; (*adj* **o'ver-the-count'er** of goods, *esp* drugs, legally sold directly to the customer); **under the counter** hidden from customers' sight (*adj* **un'der-the-count'er** reserved for the favoured customer; sold, or procured, illegally or secretly). [OFr *cunter* (Fr *compter*), from L *computāre*]

countenance *kown'tən-əns*, *n* the face; the expression of the face; favour, approbation; acquiescence, sanction; appearance (*obs*); demeanour shown towards a person (*obs*). — *vt* to favour, approve or sanction; to make a show of (*Spenser*). — *n* **coun'tenancer**. — **in countenance** unabashed; **out of countenance** abashed. [OFr *contenance*, from L *continentia* restraint, demeanour, from *continēre* to contain]

counter[1] *kown'tər*, *adv* the opposite way; in opposition. — *adj* contrary; opposing; opposite. — *n* that which is counter or opposite; the voice-part set in immediate contrast with the melody (*music*); a parry in which one foil follows the other in a small circle (*fencing*); the part of a horse's breast between the shoulders and under the neck; the part of a ship's stern from the lower moulding to the waterline (*naut*). — *vt* to contradict; to meet or answer by a stroke or move; to strike while receiving or parrying a blow (*boxing*). — **run counter to** to move in the opposite direction (to); to act or happen in a way contrary (to instructions, expectations, etc). [Partly aphetic for **encounter**, partly directly from AngloFr *countre*, OFr (Fr) *contre*, from L *contrā* against]

counter[2]. See **count**[2].

counter- *kown'tər-*, *combining form* signifying against. — *n* **coun'ter-agent** anything which counteracts. — *n* **coun'ter-attack** an attack in response to an attack. — Also *vt* and *vi*. — *n* **counter-attrac'tion** attraction in an opposite direction; a rival show. — *adj* **counter-attract'ive**. — *vt* **counterbal'ance** to balance by weight on the opposite side; to act against with equal weight, power or influence. — *n* **coun'terbalance** an equal weight, power or agency working in opposition. — *n* **counterbase** see **contrabass**. — *n* **coun'ter-batt'ery** (*military*) a battery erected to oppose another. — *n* **coun'terbid** a bid made in opposition to another bid. — *n* **coun'terbidder**. — *n* **coun'terblast** a defiant pronouncement or denunciation. — *n* **coun'terblow** a return blow. — *n* **coun'terbluff** actions or words intended as a bluff, made in opposition to someone else's bluff. — *n* **coun'terbond** a bond to protect from contingent loss a person who has given bond for another. — *n* **coun'terbore** a straight-sided widening of the end of a bored hole; a drill for making this. — *vt* to form a counterbore in. — *vt* **coun'terbrace** (*naut*) to brace or fasten (the head-yards and after-yards) in opposite ways. — *n* the lee-brace of the foretopsail-yard. — *n* **coun'terbuff** a stroke that stops motion or causes a recoil; a return blow; a rebuff. — *vt* to rebuff. — *n* **coun'terchange** a balanced contrast in a picture, etc between eg light on a dark background and dark on a light background; exchange (*Shakesp*); reciprocation (*Shakesp*). — *adj* **coun'terchanged** having the tinctures reversed or interchanged (*heraldry*). — *n* **coun'tercharge** a charge brought forward in opposition to another charge. — Also *vi*. — *vt* **coun'tercharm** to destroy or dissolve the effects of (another charm). — *n* that which destroys the effects of another charm. — *vt* **countercheck'** to check by opposing, separate or additional means; to rebuke. — *n* **coun'tercheck** a check in opposition or addition to another; a rebuke. — *n* **coun'ter-claim** (*esp law*) a claim brought forward as a partial or complete set-off against another claim. — *adv* **counter-clock'wise** in a direction contrary to that of the hands of a clock. — *n* **countercondi'tioning** (*psychol*) the conditioning of a response that is opposite to a response previously acquired or learned. — *n* **coun'ter-culture** a way of life deliberately different from that which is normal or expected. — *n* **coun'ter-current** a current flowing in an opposite direction. — *n* **coun'ter-drain** a drain alongside a canal, etc, to carry off water oozing out. — *vt* **coun'terdraw** to trace on oiled paper or other transparent material. — *n* **counter-esp'ionage** espionage directed against the enemy's spy system or action taken to counter it in one's own country. — *n* **counter-ev'idence** evidence brought forward in opposition to other evidence. — **counterexten'sion** *n* (in orthopaedics) the traction of part of a limb with the remainder held in a static position. — *adj* **coun'ter-fleury** (*heraldry*; *-flōō'ri* or *-flû'ri*) **-flō'ry** or **-flow'ered** with flowers placed the contrary way. — *n* **coun'terfoil** the part of a bank cheque, postal order, ticket, etc retained by the giver as a record of the transaction (see **foil**[2]). — *n* **coun'ter-force** an opposing force. — *n* **coun'terfort** a buttress or arch supporting a retaining wall. — *n* **coun'ter-gauge** an adjustable scribing gauge for marking the measurements of a mortise on a piece to be tenoned. — *n* **coun'ter-glow** gegenschein. — *n* **coun'terguard** (*fortif*) an outwork consisting of two lines of rampart running parallel to the faces of the bastion, to guard the bastion from being breached. — *n* **coun'ter-influence** an opposing influence. — *n* **counter-insur'gency** action taken against insurgents. — Also *adj*. — *n* **counter-intell'igence** activities, such as censorship, camouflage, use of codes, etc, aimed at preventing an enemy from obtaining information, or the organization that carries these out. — *adj* **counterintu'itive** not what would be intuitively expected; apparently improbable. — *n* **counterirr'itant** (*esp med*) an irritant used to relieve another irritation or discomfort. — *n* **counterirrita'tion**. — *n* **coun'terlight** (*painting*) a light opposite to any object, disturbing the effect of its light. — *vi* **coun'termarch** to march back or in a direction opposite to a former one. — *n* a marching back or in a direction opposite to a former one; a manoeuvre by which a body of men change front, and still retain the same men in the front rank (*military*). — *n* **coun'termark** an additional mark put on a bale of goods belonging to several merchants, so that it may not be opened except in the presence of all the owners; a mark put on standard metal by the London Goldsmiths' Company in addition to the artificer's; an artificial cavity made in the teeth of horses to disguise their age. — *n* **coun'termeasure** an action intended to counteract the effect of another action or happening. — *vt* **countermine'** to make a mine in opposition to; to oppose by means of a countermine; to frustrate by secret working (*fig*). — *n* a mine or chamber excavated by the besieged to counteract or destroy the mines made by the besiegers (*fortif*); any means of counteraction (*fig*). — **coun'termotion** an opposite motion. — *n* **coun'termove** or **coun'termovement** a contrary move or movement. — *n* **coun'termure** a wall-facing; a supplementary wall; a wall raised by besiegers against a wall (*fortif*). — *vt* (*-mūr'*) to defend with a countermure. — *n* **coun'ter-offensive** a counterattack; an attack by the defenders. — *n* **coun'teroffer** a response made by a seller to a buyer's bid, *usu* lowering the price *orig* asked for, in an attempt to clinch a bargain. — *n* **coun'ter-opening** an aperture or vent on the opposite side, or in a different place. — *n* **coun'terpace** a step in opposition to another; a contrary measure. — *adj* **coun'ter-paled** (*heraldry*) divided equally, as an escutcheon, first palewise, then by a line fesswise, with tinctures counterchanged. — *n* **coun'ter-parole** a word in addition to the password. — *adj* **counter-pass'ant** (*heraldry*) passing each other going in opposite directions. — *n* **coun'terplea** a replication to a plea or request. — *vt* **counterplead'** to plead the contrary of. — *vt* **coun'ter-plot** to plot against in order to frustrate another plot. — *n* a plot or stratagem opposed to another plot. — *vt* **coun'terpoise** (*obs* **coun'terpeise** *-pēz*) to poise, balance or weigh against or on the opposite side; to act in opposition to with equal effect. — *n* an equally heavy weight in the other scale (also *fig*). — *n* **coun'ter-poison** a poison used as the antidote of another. — *n* **coun'ter-pressure** opposing pressure. — *adj* **counterproduc'tive** acting against productivity, efficiency or usefulness. — *n* **counterproduc'tiveness**. — *n* **coun'terproof** an inverted impression obtained from a newly printed proof of an engraving, by laying it, while the ink is still wet, upon plain paper, and passing it through the press. — *n* **coun'ter-proposal** one which proposes an alternative to a proposal already made. — *n* **coun'ter-punch** to return a punch or blow (also *fig*). — *n* **Counter-Reforma'tion** (*hist*) a reform movement within the Roman Catholic Church, following and counteracting the Reformation. — *n* **counter-revolu'tion** a subsequent revolution counteracting the effect of a previous. — *n* and *adj* **counter-revolu'tionary** (a person) opposing a particular revolution or opposed to revolutions. — *n* **coun'ter-roll** (*law*) a copy of the rolls relating to appeals, inquests, etc, serving as a check on another's roll. — *adj* **counter-sa'lient** (*heraldry*) salient in opposite directions. — *n* **coun'terscarp** (*fortif*) the side of the ditch nearest to the besiegers and opposite to the scarp. — *vt* **counterseal'** (*Shakesp*) to seal with an extra seal for further security. — **counter-secur'ity** (*finance*) security given to someone who has become surety for another. — *n* **coun'ter-sense** an interpretation contrary to the real sense. — *n* **coun'tershading** (in animals) dark and light areas of colour on the body serving to camouflage or protect. — *n* **coun'tershaft** an intermediate shaft driven by the main shaft. — *vt* **countersign'** to sign on the opposite side of a document, etc; to sign in addition to the signature of a superior or principal signatory, to attest the authenticity of a document. — *n* **count'ersign** a military private sign or word, which must be given in order to pass a sentry; a counter-signature. — *n* **coun'ter-signal** a signal used in reply to another. — *n* **counter-sig'nature** a name countersigned to a document. — *vt* **coun'tersink** to enlarge the upper part of (a hole), eg for the head of a screw; to set the head or top of (eg a nail, screw, etc) on a level with, or below, the surface of the surrounding material: — *pa p* and *adj* **coun'tersunk**. — *n* **coun'terspy**. — *n* **coun'terspying** counter-espionage. — *n* **coun'ter-statement** a statement in opposition to another statement. — *n* **coun'terstroke** a stroke in return. — *vt* and *vi* **coun'tersue** to sue a person by whom one is being sued. — *n* **coun'tersubject** (*music*) a second theme by the first voice (*esp* in a fugue) when accompanying the second voice performing the main subject. — *n* **coun'ter-tenor** the highest alto male voice (so called because a contrast to tenor). — *n* **coun'ter-time** resistance, opposition; the resistance of a horse that interrupts his cadence and the measure of his manège. — *n* **coun'ter-trading** trading by barter. — *n* **coun'ter-turn** a turn in a play different from what was expected. — *n* **coun'ter-view** an opposing view; a posture in which two persons face each other; opposition; contrast. — *vt* **counter-vote'** to vote in opposition to. — *vt* **counter-weigh'** to weigh against, counterbalance. — *n* **coun'ter-weight** weight in an opposite scale; a counterbalancing influence or force. — *vi* **coun'ter-wheel** to wheel in an opposite direction. — *n* **coun'ter-work** a work intended to oppose another. — *vt* **counterwork'** to work in opposition to. [Anglo-Fr *countre*, OFr *contre*, from L *contrā* against]

counteract *kown-tər-akt'*, *vt* to act counter or in opposition to; to neutralize. — *n* **counterac'tion**. — *adj* **counterac'tive**. [**counter-**]

counterfeit *kown'tər-fit* or *-fēt*, *vt* to imitate; to copy without authority; to forge. — *n* something false or copied, or that pretends to be true and original. — *adj* (also *Spenser* **coun'terfect**) pretended; made in imitation; forged; false. — *n* **coun'terfeiter** a person who counterfeits. — *adv* **coun'terfeitly** in a counterfeit manner; falsely. — *n* **coun'terfeisance** (*-fēzəns*; or *archaic* **coun'terfēsaunce**) an act of counterfeiting; forgery. [OFr *contrefet*, from *contrefaire* to imitate, from L *contrā* against, and *facere* to do]

countermand *kown-tər-mänd'*, *vt* to give a command in opposition to one already given; to revoke. — *n* (*kownt'*) a revocation to a former order. — *adj* **countermand'able**. [OFr *contremander*, from L *contrā* against, and *mandāre* to order]

counterpane *kown'tər-pān* or (*obs*) **counterpoint** *-point*, *n* a coverlet for a bed. [OFr *contrepoint*, from *coulte-pointe*, from L *culcita puncta* a stitched pillow; see **quilt**]

counterpart *kown'ter-pärt*, *n* the part that answers to, fits into or completes another part, having the qualities which the other lacks; a corresponding or equivalent person or thing; a duplicate, a close or exact copy. [**counter-**]

counterpoint[1] *kown'tər-point*, *n* the art of combining melodies (*music*); a melody added to another (*music*); an opposite point. — *vt* to write in counterpoint; to set in contrast for effect. — *adj* **contrapuntal** (*kon-trə-punt'əl*). — *n* **contrapunt'ist** a composer skilled in counterpoint. [Fr *contrepoint* and Ital *contrappunto*, from L *contrā* against, and *punctum* a point, from the pricks, points or notes placed against those of the melody; also in some senses **counter-** and **point**]

counterpoint[2]. See **counterpane**.

countervail *kown'tər-vāl*, *vt* to be of avail against; to act against with equal effect; to be of equal value to; to compensate. — *adj* **countervail'able**. [OFr *contre-valoir*, from *contre* (from L *contrā* against), and *valoir* to be of avail (from L *valere* to be strong)]

countrol. See **control**.

country *kun'tri*, *n* a region; a state; a nation; rural districts as distinct from town; the land of one's birth or citizenship; the district hunted by a pack of foxhounds; the rock surrounding a mineral lode (also **coun'try-rock**); country music. — *adj* belonging to the country; rural; rustic. — *adj* **coun'trified** or **coun'tryfied** like or suitable for the country in style; like a person from the country in style, dress or manner. — **country-and-west'ern** a popularized form of music deriving from the rural folk-music of the United States. — Also *adj*. — **country club** a club in the country which has facilities for sport, leisure and social activities; **country code** a code of behaviour to be followed by people using the countryside, *esp* for recreational purposes; **country cousin** a relative from the country, unaccustomed to town sights or manners; **country dance** a dance as practised by country people; a type of dance in which either an indefinite number of couples in a circle or two lines, or groups of fixed numbers of couples in two lines, can take part, tracing a precise and sometimes complex pattern of movements; **country-dan'cing**; **coun'try-folk** fellow-countrymen; rural people; **country gentleman** a landed proprietor who resides on his estate in the country; **country-house'** or **country-seat'** the residence and estate of a country gentleman; **coun'tryman** a man who lives in the country; a man belonging to the same country, fellow-countryman; **country music** the folk music of the rural areas of the United States; country-and-western music; both of these taken together; **country party** (*hist*) the party opposed to the court; **country rock** electrically amplified music which combines the styles of rock-and-roll and country-and-western music; **country-rock** see under **country** above; **coun'tryside** a district or part of the country; rural districts in general; **country town** a small town in a rural district. — *adj* **countrywide'** all over the country. — **coun'trywoman** a woman who lives in the country; a woman of the same country. — **go to the country** (*politics*) to appeal to the voters of the country by calling a general election; **the country** (*cricket slang*) the outfield. [OFr *contrée*, from LL *contrāta*, *contrāda*, an extension of L *contrā* over against]

county[1] *kownt'i*, a portion of a country separated for administrative, parliamentary or other purposes, a shire; the territory or dominion of a count (*hist*). — *adj* of a, or the, county; of a county family. — **county borough** see **borough**; **county council** a council for managing the public affairs of a county; **county councillor**; **county court** the highest court of law within a county; **county cricket** cricket played in matches between clubs representing counties; **county family** a family of nobility or gentry (**coun'ty-people**) with estates and a seat in the county; **county hall** the administrative centre of a county; **county palatine** see under **palatine**; **County school** a school provided and maintained by a local education authority; **county seat** (*US*) the seat of county government; **county town** the town in which the public business of the county is transacted. [**count**[1]]

county[2] *kownt'i*, (*obs*) *n* a count. [Prob Anglo-Fr *counte*]

coup[1] *kōō*, *n* a blow, stroke; a sudden action or motion; a clever and successful stroke in a board or card game; a masterstroke, clever and successful stratagem; the act of putting a ball in a pocket without having hit another ball (*billiards*); a coup d'état. — **coup de bonheur** (*də bon-œr*) a stroke of luck; a lucky hit or shot; **coup d'éclat** (*dā-klä*) a bold stroke; **coup d'essai** (*de-sā*) an experimental work; a first attempt; **coup de foudre** (*də fōō-dr'*) a sudden and astonishing happening, a thunderclap; love at first sight; **coup de grâce** (*də gräs*) a finishing blow to put out of pain; a death blow; a finishing stroke generally; **coup de main** (*də mɛ̃*) a sudden vigorous attack; **coup de maître** (*də metr'*) a masterstroke; **coup de poing** (*də pwɛ̃*) a blow or punch with the fist; a typical Old Stone Age axe, a roughly pointed piece of stone held in the hand; **coup d'état** (*dā-tä*) a violent or subversive action resulting in a change of government or state policy; **coup de théâtre** (*də tä-ätr'*) a sudden and sensational turn eg in a play, a theatrical effect; **coup d'oeil** (*dœ-i*) a general view at a glance. [Fr, from LL *colpus*, from L *colaphus*, from Gr *kolaphos* a blow]

coup[2] *kowp*, (*Scot*) *vt* to exchange or barter. — *n* **coup'er** a dealer. [ON *kaupa* to buy]

coup[3] or **cowp** *kowp*, (*Scot*) *vt* and *vi* to overturn; to tip up. — *n* an upset; a tip for rubbish. [OFr *colp* blow]

coupe[1] *ko͞op*, (*Fr*) *n* a dessert, *usu* made with ice cream and often fruit, served in a glass bowl; a glass container for serving such a dessert, *usu* with a shallow bowl and a short stem.

coupe[2] *ko͞op*, (*NAm*) *n* a coupé (motor-car).

coupé *ko͞o-pā'*, *n* the front part of a French stagecoach; a four-wheeled carriage with interior seating for two and a separate seat for the driver; an end compartment of a railway carriage with a seat on one side only; a two-door motor car with a roof sloping towards the back; (in dancing) a salute to a partner, while swinging one foot (also **coupee** *ko͞o-pē'*). — *adj* (*heraldry*) (of the head or limb of an animal) cut off evenly. — Also **couped** (*ko͞opt*). [Fr pa p of *couper* to cut]

couple *kup'l*, *n* two of a kind joined together, or connected; two, a pair; two people considered as partners, *esp* a man and woman; that which joins two things together; a pair of equal forces acting on the same body in opposite and parallel directions (*statics*). — *vt* to join together. — *vi* to pair sexually. — *n* **coup'ledom**. — *n* **coup'lement** union; a couple. — *n* **coup'ler** someone who or something that couples or unites; an organ mechanism by which stops of one manual can be played from another or from the pedals. — *n* **coup'let** a pair, couple; a twin; two successive lines of verse (*esp*) that rhyme with each other. — *n* **coup'ling** that which connects; an appliance for transmitting motion in machinery, or for connecting vehicles, as in a railway train. — **coup'ling-box** the box or ring of metal connecting the contiguous ends of two lengths of shafts. — **a couple of** (loosely) two or three; a few. [OFr *cople*, from L *cōpula*]

coupon *ko͞o'pon*, *-pən*, *-pɔ̃* or *-pong*, *n* a billet, check, or other slip of paper cut off from its counterpart; a separate ticket or part of a ticket; a voucher certifying that payments will be made, services performed, goods sold, etc; a piece cut from an advertisement entitling one to some privilege; a party leader's recommendation of an electoral candidate; a printed betting form on which to enter forecasts of sports results. [Fr *couper* to cut off]

coupure *ko͞o-pūr'*, *n* a cutting, incision; an entrenchment made by the besieged behind a breach (*fortif*); the deletion of passages in a play, piece of music, etc. [Fr *couper* to cut]

cour and **coure**. Obsolete forms of **cover** and **cower**.

courage *kur'ij*, *n* the quality that enables people to meet danger without giving way to fear; bravery; spirit. — *interj* take courage. — *adj* **courageous** (*kə-rā'jəs*) full of courage; brave. — *adv* **courāgeously**. — *n* **courā'geousness**. — **Dutch courage** artificial courage induced by drinking alcohol; **pluck up courage** or **take one's courage in both hands** to nerve oneself; to gather boldness; **the courage of one's convictions** courage to act up to, or consistently with, one's opinions or principles. [OFr *corage* (Fr *courage*), from L *cor* the heart]

courant *ko͞o-rant'*, (*heraldry*) *adj* in a running position. — *n* **courante** or **courant** (*ko͞o-ränt'*) an old dance with a kind of gliding step, a coranto; music for it; (*ko͞o-rant'*) a newspaper (now in titles only). [Fr, pr p of *courir* to run; see **current**]

courb or **curb** *ko͞orb* or *kûrb*, (*archaic*) *vi* to bend or stoop in order to supplicate. — *adj* bent (also *obs* **corbe**). [Fr *courber*, from L *curvāre* to bend]

courbaril *ko͝or'bə-ril*, *n* the W Indian locust-tree, *Hymenaea courbaril*; its resin, gum anime. [Fr from Carib]

courbette *ko͝or-bet'*, *n* the French form of **curvet**.

courd. An obsolete form of **covered**.

coureur de bois *ko͞o-rœr də bwa*, (*Can hist*) *n* a French Canadian woodsman who traded furs with the Indian tribes. [Can Fr, literally, woods runner]

courgette *ko͝or-zhet'*, *n* a type of small marrow. — Also called **zucchini**. [Fr *courge* gourd, pumpkin]

courier *ko͞o'ri-ər*, *n* a messenger, *esp* one employed to deliver special or urgent messages or items; a state or diplomatic messenger; an official guide and organizer who travels with tourists; a title of certain newspapers. [Fr, from L *currere* to run]

courlan *ko͞or'lən*, *n* any bird of the American genus *Aramus*, related to the rails, the limpkin. [Fr, from a S American name]

course *kōrs* or *kōrs*, *n* the path in which anything moves; the ground over which a race is run, golf is played, etc; a channel for water; the direction pursued; a voyage; a race; regular progress from point to point; a habitual method of procedure; a prescribed series, sequence, process or treatment, eg of lectures, training, education, pills, etc; each of the successive divisions of a meal, ie soup, fish, etc; a range of bricks or stones on the same level in building; (in the lute, etc) one of two or more strings tuned in unison or in octaves (*music*); the series of positions of a bell in the changing order in which a set of bells is struck (*bell-ringing*); one of the sails bent to a ship's lower yards (*main course* mainsail, *fore course* foresail, and *mizzen course* crossjack; *naut*); (in *pl*) the menses. — *vt* to run, chase or hunt after; to use in coursing. — *vi* to run; to move with speed, as in a race or hunt. — *n* **cours'er** a runner; a swift horse; a person who courses or hunts; a swift running bird (*Cursorius*). — *n* **cours'ing** hunting of *esp* hares with greyhounds or lurchers, by sight rather than by scent. — **cours'ing-joint** a joint between two courses of masonry; **course'work** work that goes to make up an educational course. — **in course** in regular order; of course (*archaic*); **in due course** eventually; at a suitable later time; **in the course of** during; in the process of; undergoing (something); **in the course of time** eventually; with the passing of time; **of course** by natural consequence; indisputably; it must be remembered (often used to introduce a comment on a preceding statement); **run** (or **take**) **its** (or **their**) **course** to proceed or develop freely and naturally, *usu* to a point of completion or cessation; **stay the course** see under **stay**; **the course of nature**, or **the normal**, etc **course of events** the usual way in which things happen or proceed. [Fr *cours*, from L *cursus*, from *currere*, *cursum* to run]

court *kört* or *kōrt*, *n* an enclosed space, such as one surrounded by houses; a piece of ground or floor on which certain games are played; a division marked off by lines on such a place; the palace of a sovereign; the body of persons who form the sovereign's suite or council; an assembly of courtiers; a hall of justice (*law*); the judges and officials who preside there; any body of persons assembled to decide causes; a sitting of such a body; a court shoe. — *vt* to pay attentions to, to woo; to solicit; to seek. — *n* **court'ier** someone who frequents courts or palaces; someone who courts or flatters. — *n* **court'ierism** the behaviour or practices of a courtier. — *adj* and *adv* **court'ierlike**. — *adv* **court'ierly**. — *n* **court'ing** wooing. attendance at court (*Spenser*). — *n* **court'let** a petty court. — *adj* **court'like** courtly; polite. — *n* **court'liness**. — *n* **court'ling** a hanger-on at court. — *adj* **court'ly** having manners like those of, or befitting, a court; politely stately; fair and flattering. — *n* **court'ship** the act or process of wooing a woman in order to persuade her to become one's wife; the period of time over which this is carried out; courtly behaviour. — **court-bar'on** (*hist*) the assembly of freehold tenants of a manor under a lord; **court'-card** see **coat-card**; **court'craft** the courtier's art, intrigue; **court cupboard** (*hist*) a movable cupboard or sideboard on which plate was displayed; **court circular** a daily report in certain newspapers of the appointments, activities, etc of the sovereign and/or other members of a royal family; **court'-day** a day on which a judicial court sits; **court dress** the special formal costume worn on state or ceremonious occasions; **court fool** a fool or jester, formerly kept at court for amusement; **court hand** a modification of the Norman handwriting, as distinguished from the modern or Italian handwriting, in use in the English law-courts from the 16c to the reign of George II; **court'house** a building where the law-courts are held; **court'-leet** (*hist*) a court of record held in a manor before the lord or his steward; **courtly love** a conception and tradition of love, originating in late medieval European literature, in which the knight sublimates his love for his lady in submission, service and devotion; **court martial** a court held by officers of the army, navy or air force for the trial of offences against service laws (one improvised in time of war round an upturned drum for summary judgement was a **drumhead court martial**): — *pl* **courts martial** or (*colloq*) **court mar'tials**. — *vt* **court-mar'tial** to try before a court martial: — *pr p* **court-mar'tialling**; *pa t* and *pa p* **courtmar'tialled**. — **court order** a direction or command of a justiciary court; **court plaster** sticking-plaster made of silk, originally applied as patches on the face by ladies at court; **court'-roll** the record of a court of justice; **court'room** a room in a courthouse in which lawsuits and criminal cases are heard; **court shoe** a ladies' dress shoe without straps or laces; **court sword** a light sword worn as part of court dress; **court tennis** the game of real tennis (qv under **real**[2]), distinguished from lawn tennis; **court'yard** a court or enclosed ground attached to a house. — **court holy water** (*obs*) empty compliments; flattery; **court of first instance** a law-court in which proceedings are first heard; **go to court** to institute legal proceedings against someone; **hold court** to preside over admiring followers, etc; **laugh someone out of court** see under **laugh**; **out of court** without a trial in a law-court; without claim to be considered; **the ball's in your court** see under **ball**. [OFr *cort* (Fr *cour*), from LL *cortis* a courtyard, from L *cors, cohors, cohortis* an enclosure; related to Gr *chortos* an enclosed place, L *hortus* a garden (see **yard**[2])]

court-bouillon *ko͞or bo͞o-yɔ̃'*, *n* a seasoned stock made with water, vegetables and wine or vinegar, in which fish is boiled: — *pl* **courts-bouillons**. [Fr *court* short, from L *curtus*, and **bouillon**]

Courtelle® *ko͞or-tel'* or *kör-tel*, *n* a synthetic acrylic wool-like fibre.

courteous *kûrt'yəs* or *kört'yəs*, *adj* polite, considerate or respectful in manner and action; obliging. — *adv* **court'eously**. — *n* **court'eousness**. — *n* **courtesy** (*kûrt'ə-si*, or *kört'*) courteous behaviour; an act of civility or respect; a curtsy (*obs*); the life interest of the surviving husband in his wife's estate (*law*). — *vi* to make a curtsy: — *pr p* **court'esying**; *pa t* and *pa p* **court'esied**. — **courtesy light** a small light in a motor vehicle, *usu* operated by the opening and closing of the doors; **courtesy title** a title really invalid, but allowed by the usage of society, as for children of peers. [OFr *corteis, cortois*; see **court**]

courtesan or **courtezan** *kûrt'i-zan, kört'*, or *-zan'*, *n* a mistress or prostitute, *esp* of a man of status or wealth. [Fr *courtisane*, from Ital *cortigiana*, orig a woman of the court]

couscous or **kouskous** *ko͞os'ko͞os*, *n* hard wheat semolina; a N African dish of steamed couscous with meat, vegetables, etc. [Fr, from Ar *kuskus*, from *kaskasa* to pound; see **cuscus**[2]]

cousin *kuz'n*, *n* the son or daughter of an uncle or aunt; formerly, a kinsman generally; a term used by a sovereign in addressing another, or to one of his own nobles; a person belonging to a group related by common ancestry, interests, etc; something kindred or related to another. — *n* **cous'inage**. — *n* **cous'inhood**. — *adj* **cous'inly** like, or having the relation of, a cousin. — *n* **cous'inry** cousins collectively. — *n* **cous'inship**. — **cousin-ger'man** a first cousin; something closely related. — **cross cousin** the son or daughter of one's father's sister or mother's brother; **first cousin** the child of one's aunt or uncle, a full cousin; **first cousin once removed** the son or daughter of a cousin-german, sometimes loosely called *second cousin*; **forty-second cousin** *vaguely* a distant relative; **second cousin** the child of one's parent's first cousin; loosely, a first cousin once removed. [Fr, from L *consōbrīnus*, from *con-* (signifying connection), and *sobrīnus*, applied to the children of sisters, from the root of *soror* a sister]

couter *ko͞o'tər*, (*slang*) *n* a sovereign. [Said to be from Gypsy *cuta* a gold piece]

couth[1] *ko͞oth*, (*obs*) *pa t* and *pa p* of **can** could; knew; known; did. [OE *pa t cūthe*, pa p *cūth*]

couth[2] *ko͞oth*, *adj* good-mannered, refined, sophisticated. [Back-formation from **uncouth**]

couthie or **couthy** *ko͞oth'i*, (*Scot*) *adj* friendly, kindly; comfortable; snug. [Prob OE *cūth* known]

coutil or **coutille** *ko͞o-til'*, *n* a strong cotton fabric used in mattresses, etc. [Fr *coutil*]

couture *ko͞o-tür*, or (*US*) *-to͝or'*, *n* dressmaking or dress designing. — *n* **couturier** (*ko͞o-tür'yā*, or (*US*) *-to͝or-*), *fem* **couturière** (*-yer'*) a dressmaker or dress designer. [Fr]

couvade *ko͞o-väd'*, *n* a custom among certain peoples in many parts of the world for the father to take to his bed at the birth of a child, and submit to certain restrictions of food, etc; loosely, the symptoms occasionally experienced by an expectant father, eg stomach pains. [OFr *couvade*, from *couver* to hatch, from L *cubāre* to lie down]

couvert *ko͞o-ver*, (*Fr*) *n* a cover (at table).

COV *abbrev*: covariance (*statistics*); crossover value (*genetics*).

covalency *kō-vā'lən-si*, *n* the union of two atoms by the sharing of a pair of electrons, one from each atom (cf **electrovalency**). — *adj* **covā'lent**. [L *co-* together, and **valency**]

covariance *kō-vār'i-əns*, *n* the property of varying concomitantly (*math*); the mean value of the products of the deviations of two or more variates from the respective mean values of these variates (*statistics*). — *n* and *adj* **cōvār'iant**. — *vi* **cōvār'y**. [**co-** and **vary**]

cove[1] *kōv*, *n* a small inlet of the sea; a bay; a cavern or rocky recess; a curved junction of wall and ceiling (*archit*); the moulding covering the junction of wall and ceiling (also **cō'ving**). — *vt* to overarch. — *adj* **coved** formed with an arch. — *n* **cove'let** a small cove. [OE *cofa* a room; ON *kofi*, Ger *Koben*]

cove[2] *kōv*, (*Austr colloq* or *old Br slang*) *n* a fellow, a customer. [Origin obscure]

covellite *kō-vel'īt* or *kō'vəl-*, *n* a blue mineral, cupric sulphide. [N *Covelli*, (1790–1829), Ital mineralogist, its discoverer]

coven *kuv'in* or *-ən*, *n* a gathering of witches; a gang of thirteen witches. [See **covin**]

covenant *kuv'ə-nənt*, *n* a mutual agreement; the writing containing the agreement; an engagement entered into between God and a person or a people, a dispensation, testament. — *vi* to enter into an agreement. — *vt* to agree to; to stipulate. — *adj* **cov'enanted** agreed to by covenant; bound by covenant; holding a position under a covenant or contract. — *n* **covenantee'** the person to whom a covenant is made. — *n* **cov'enanter** (*usu* in Scotland *kuv-ə-nant'ər*) a person who signed or adhered to the *Scottish National Covenant* of 1638 (the *Solemn League and Covenant* of 1643 was in effect an international treaty between Scotland and England for securing civil and religious liberty). — *n* **cov'enantor** that party to a covenant who subjects himself or herself to the penalty of its breach. — **covenant of grace** or **redemption** (*Christian theology*) that by which life is freely offered to sinners on condition of faith in Christ; **covenant of works** that made with Adam as federal representative of the human race on condition of obedience. [OFr, from L *con-* together, and *venīre* to come]

covent *kov'ənt* or *kuv'ənt*, (*archaic*) *n* a variant of **convent**.

Coventry *kov'* or *kuv'ənt-ri*, *n* a city in the W Midlands of England. — **Coventry blue** a blue thread once made there. — **send to Coventry** to ostracize, *esp* to refuse to talk to.

cover *kuv'ər*, *vt* to put or spread something on, over or about; to come or be on, over or about; to hide; to clothe; to protect; to screen; to brood or sit on; to suffice for; to provide for or against; to comprise; to traverse; to take as field of operations; to play a higher card upon; to put down (a stake of equal value) in betting; (*esp* of a stallion) to copulate with; to protect with a weapon by being within range for returning fire against any attacker; (of a journalist) to report on (a news story). — *vi* to lay a table for a meal (*obs*); to put one's hat on. — *n* that which covers or is intended to cover; a bedcover; a lid; the binding of a book; the jacket of a book; an envelope, *esp* one with a stamp and postmark, as in *first-day cover*; undergrowth or thicket concealing game, etc; a pretext or disguise; an apparently genuine identity, job, etc used as a front, *esp* by spies; the protection provided by an insurance policy; the funds available to cover liabilities; a confederate; a table setting for one person (hence *cover charge* below); a cover version; a cover point. — *adj* intended to conceal the true nature or identity of a person, organization, etc. — Also as *combining form*. — *n* **cov'erage** the area or (*fig*) amount covered or included; the group or section of the community reached by an advertising medium; the (extent of) reporting of a topic, event, etc on television, in the press, etc; insurance cover. — *adj* **cov'ered** having a cover; sheltered, concealed; roofed over; with a hat on. — *n* **cov'ering**. — **cov'erall** a boiler suit (*US*; often in *pl*); a one-piece garment for babies, covering arms, legs and body. — *adj* covering or including everything. — **cover charge** a charge per person made by a restaurant, in addition to charge for food; **cover crop** a subsidiary crop grown partly to protect the soil; **cover drive** (*cricket*) a drive past cover point; **covered wagon** a large wagon with a bonnet-shaped canvas hood, *esp* that used by pioneers to the American West; used as a symbol of pioneering spirit; **covered way** or **covert way** (*fortif*) a path outside the ditch of a fort, sunk below the crest of the glacis to provide protection; **cover girl** a girl pictured on a magazine cover; **cover glass** (*microsc*) a coverslip; **covering letter** a letter to explain documents enclosed with it; **cover note** (*insurance*) a note certifying that the holder has a current insurance policy; a note issued to an insured person certifying that the latter has insurance coverage while their policy is being prepared; **cover point** (in cricket, etc) (the position of) the player who supports point and stands to his right; (in lacrosse) (the position of) one of the defending players; **cover price** (of magazines, etc) the price printed on the outside cover; **cov'erslip** a loose cover for a duvet; a thin slip of glass used for covering a specimen under a microscope (*microsc*); **cover-up** see **cover up**; **cover version** a recording of a song, etc which has been recorded by someone else, *usu* very similar to the original. — **cover for** to act in the place of (someone who is absent, etc); **cover in** to fill in; to complete the covering of, *esp* of a roof of a building; **cover into** to transfer into; **cover up** to cover completely; to conceal, withhold information (*colloq*; *n* **cov'er-up**); **from cover to cover** from beginning to end of a book. [Fr *couvrir* (Ital *coprire*), from L *cooperīre* from *co-*, and *operīre* to cover]

coverlet *kuv'ər-lit*, *n* a bedcover. — Also **cov'erlid**. [Fr *couvrir* to cover, and *lit* (from L *lectum*) a bed]

covers *kō'vûrs*, *abbrev*: coversed sine.

coversed sine *kō'vûrsd sīn*, *n* one of six trigonometrical functions of an angle equal to one minus the sine of a specified angle.

covert *kuv'ərt*, *adj* (also *kō'vûrt*) concealed; secret. — *n* a feather covering the quill-bases of wings and tail of a bird; a shelter; cover for game. — *adv* **cov'ertly** in a secret, stealthy or concealed manner. — *n* **cov'erture** covering, shelter; disguise. [ME, covered, from OFr pa p of *covrir* to cover]

covet *kuv'it*, *vt* to desire or wish for eagerly; to wish for (something belonging to another). — *vi* (*archaic*) to desire (with *for*): — *pr p* **cov'eting**; *pa t* and *pa p* **cov'eted**. — *adj* **cov'etable**. — *adj* **cov'eted**. — *adv* **cov'etingly**. — *n* **cov'etīse** (*obs*) covetousness; ardent desire. — *n* **cov'etiveness** (*obs*; *phrenol*) acquisitiveness. — *adj* **cov'etous** inordinately desirous; avaricious. — *adv* **cov'etously**. — *n* **cov'etousness**. [OFr *coveit(i)er* (Fr *convoiter*), from L *cupiditās*, *-ātis*, from *cupere* to desire]

covey[1] *kuv'i*, *n* a brood or hatch of partridges; a small flock of game birds; a party or set of people. [OFr *covée*, from L *cubāre* to lie down]

covey[2]. Dimin of **cove**[2].

covin or **covyne** *kōv'in*, *kuv'in*, *n* a compact (*archaic*); a conspiracy, *esp* (*law*) one between two or more people to act to the injury of another; a coven. — *adj* **covinous** (*kuv'*; *archaic*) fraudulent. — **cov'in-tree** a tree before a Scottish mansion at which guests were met and parted from. [OFr *covin*, from LL *convenium*, from *con-* together, and *venīre* to come]

coving *kō'ving*, (*archit*) *n* the projection of upper storeys over lower; the vertical sides connecting the jambs with the breast of a fireplace; a quadrant moulding covering the joint between wall and ceiling. [See **cove**[1]]

covyne. See **covin**.

cow[1] *kow*, *n* the female of the bovine animals; the female of certain other animals, such as the elk, elephant, whale, etc; an ugly, ungainly, slovenly or objectionable woman (*vulg*); an objectionable or rather despicable person or thing (*Austr slang*); a trying situation or occurrence (*usu a fair cow*) (*Austr slang*): — *pl* **cows**, (*older*) **kine** *kīn*, and (still in *Scots*) **kye** *kī*. — *adj* **cow'ish** like a cow; cowardly (*Shakesp*). — **cow'bane** the water hemlock (*Cicuta virosa* or other species), often fatal to cattle; **cow'bell** a bell for a cow's neck; **cow'berry** the red whortleberry (*Vaccinium vitis-idaea*); **cow'bird** or **cow blackbird** an American bird (*Molothrus*) of the troupial family, that accompanies cattle, and drops its eggs into other birds' nests; **cow'boy** a man who has the charge of cattle on a ranch (*NAm*); any rather rough male character in stories, etc of the old American West, such as a gunfighter or a man involved in fighting Indians; a rodeo performer (*NAm*); a young inexperienced lorry-driver, or anyone who drives an unsafe or overloaded lorry (*slang*); a person who behaves recklessly or irresponsibly (*slang*); a derogatory term for an often inadequately qualified or slapdash person providing inferior services or shoddy workmanship for a quick profit (*colloq*). — Also *adj*. — **cowboy boots** high-heeled boots, *usu* with ornamental stitching, etc, worn by, or reminiscent of styles worn by, cowboys and ranchers; **cow'-calf** a female calf; **cow'catcher** (*NAm*) an apparatus on the front of a railway engine to throw off obstacles; **cow cocky** see under **cockatoo**; **cow'-chervil**, **cow'-parsley** or **cow'-weed** wild chervil; **cow college** (*US slang*) a college in a remote rural area; **cow'-dung**; **cow'feeder** a dairyman; a device for dispensing feed to cattle; **cow'fish** a coffer-fish or trunk-fish (with cowlike head); a manatee; any small cetacean; **cow'girl** a young woman who dresses like and does the work of a cowboy; **cow'grass** perennial red clover; zigzag clover; **cow'hand** a cowboy (*NAm*); **cow'heel** the foot of an ox stewed to a jelly; **cow'herb** a European flowering plant (*Saponaria vaccaria*), related to the carnation; **cow'herd** a person who herds cows; cow-heard (see separate entry); **cow'hide** the hide of a cow; the hide of a cow made into leather; a coarse whip made of twisted strips of cowhide. — *vt* to whip with a cowhide. — **cow'house** a building in which cows are stalled, a byre; **cow'-leech** (*obs*) a cow-doctor; **cow'lick** a tuft of turned-up hair on the forehead (also **cow's lick**); **cow'man** a man who tends cows; a man who owns a cattle ranch (*US*); **cow-parsley** see **cow-chervil**; **cow parsnip** an umbelliferous plant, hogweed (*Heracleum sphondylium*) used as fodder; **cow'pat** a roundish lump of cow-dung; **cow'pea** a leguminous plant (*Vigna sinensis*) indigenous to Asia but cultivated in other parts of the world and used like French beans; **cow'-pilot** a W Indian demoiselle fish, said to accompany the cowfish; **cow'-plant** an asclepiadaceous plant of Ceylon (*Gymnema lactiferum*) with a milky juice; **cow'poke** (*US colloq*) a cowboy; **cow'pox** an infection similar to smallpox caused by the *Vaccinia* virus, and *usu* affecting cows (the cowpox virus was found to confer immunity to smallpox and was used in the vaccination programme to eradicate smallpox); **cow'-puncher** (*US colloq*) a cowboy; a herder of cows; **cow's arse** (*vulg*) a mess, botched job, etc; **cow'shed** a cowhouse; **cow's lick** see **cowlick**; **cow'tree** a S American tree (*Brosimum galactodendron*) of the mulberry family, that produces a nourishing fluid resembling milk; **cow-weed** see **cow-chervil**; **cow'-wheat** a yellow-flowered scrophulariaceous plant (*Melampyrum*), with seeds somewhat like grains of wheat. — **till the cows come home** for a long time of unforseeable duration. [OE *cū*, pl *cȳ*; Ger *Kuh*; Sans *go* a bull, cow]

cow[2] or **kow** *kow*, (*Scot*) *n* a branch, bunch of twigs, besom. [Poss OFr *coe*, from L *cauda* tail]

cow[3] *kow*, *vt* to subdue the spirit of; to keep under. — *adj* **cowed** abjectly depressed or intimidated. [Perh from ON *kūga*; Dan *kue* to subdue]

cow[4] *kow*, (*Dickens*) *n* a chimney cowl. [Variant of **cowl**[1]]

cowage. See **cowhage**.

cowal *kow'əl*, (*Austr*) *n* a shallow lake or swamp. [Aboriginal]

cowan *kow'ən*, (*Scot*) *n* a dry-stone-diker; a mason who never served an apprenticeship; someone who tries to enter a Freemasons' lodge, or the like, surreptitiously. [Origin doubtful]

coward *kow'ərd*, *n* a reprehensibly faint-hearted person; a person who lacks courage; someone who brutally takes advantage of the weak. — *vt* to make cowardly. — *adj* cowardly; with tail between legs (*heraldry*). — *n* **cow'ardice** (*-is*) lack of courage; timidity; brutal conduct towards the weak or undefended. — *n* **cow'ardliness**. — *adj* **cow'ardly** having the character of a coward; characteristic of or to be expected of a coward. — *adv* like a coward; with cowardice. — *n* (*obs*) **cow'ardry** (*Spenser* **cow'ardree**) or **cow'ardship** (*Shakesp*). [OFr *couard* (Ital *codardo*), from L *cauda* a tail]

cowdie-gum, cowdie-pine. Same as **kauri-gum, kauri-pine**.

cower *kow'ər*, *vi* to crouch or cringe in fear. — *adv* **cow'eringly**. — **cower away** to shrink back in fear. [Cf ON *kūra*, Dan *kure* to lie quiet]

Cow Gum® *kow gum*, *n* a rubber solution used as an easily removable quick-drying adhesive.

cowhage, cowage or **cowitch** *kow'ij* or *-ich*, *n* a tropical leguminous climbing plant (*Mucuna*); the stinging hairs on its pod, used as a vermifuge; its pods. [Hindi *kavāch*]

cowheard, cowherd. Spenserian spellings of **coward**.

cowitch. See **cowhage**.

cowl[1] *kowl*, *n* a large loose hood, *esp* of a kind worn by a monk; a cover, *usu* revolving, fitted over a chimney to improve ventilation; the part of a motor vehicle to which the windscreen and instrument panel are fixed; a cowling. — *vt* to cover like a cowl. — *adj* **cowled** wearing a cowl. — *n* **cowl'ing** the metal casing round an aeroplane engine. — *adj* **cowl'-necked** (of a dress, sweater, etc) having a collar which lies in loose folds over the neck and shoulders as a monk's cowl does. [OE *cugele*; ON *kofl*; related to L *cucullus* hood]

cowl[2] *kōl*, *kōōl* or *kowl*, (*dialect* or *archaic*) *n* a tub or large vessel for liquids. — **cowl'-staff** (*Shakesp*) a pole on which a basket or vessel is slung. [OE *cūfel* or OFr *cuvele*, both from L *cūpella* dimin of *cūpa a cask*]

co-worker *kō-wûr'kər*, *n* an associate; someone who works with one on a project, etc. [**co-**]

cowp. See **coup**[3].

Cowper's glands *kow'pərz glandz* or *kōō-*, *n* a pair of glands near the prostate in mammals which under sexual stimulation secrete mucus which forms part of the seminal fluid. — Also called **bulbourethral glands**. [Discovered by William *Cowper* (1666–1709), an English anatomist]

cowrie or **cowry** *kow'ri*, *n* a mollusc of a large genus (*Cypraea*) of gasteropods, the shells of which are used in certain primitive societies as money or invested with magical properties; a shell of the mollusc. [Hindi *kaurī*]

cowrie-pine. Same as **kauri-pine**.

co-write *kō-rīt*, *vt* to write with another or others.

cowslip *kow'slip*, *n* a species of primrose (*Primula veris*), with fragrent yellow flowers arranged in umbels, common in pastures; the marsh-marigold (*US*). — *adj* **cow'slip'd** (*poetic*) covered with cowslips. [OE *cūslyppe*, from *cū* cow, and *slyppe* slime, ie cow-dung]

cox *koks*. A short form of **coxswain**.

coxa *koks'ə*, *n* the hip bone; the proximal joint of an arthropod's leg: — *pl* **cox'ae** (*-ē*). — *adj* **cox'al**. — *n* **coxal'gia** (*ji-ə*) pain in the hip or disease of the hip joint. [L]

coxcomb *koks'kōm*, *n* a foolishly vain or conceited man; a strip of red cloth notched like a cock's comb, which professional fools used to wear; the head (*obs*). — *adj* **coxcombic** (*-kōm'* or *-kom'*), **coxcomb'ical** or **coxcom'-ical** foppish; vain. — *n* **coxcombical'ity**. — *adv* **coxcomb'ically**. — *n* **cox'combry** the behaviour of a coxcomb. [**cock's comb**]

coxiness. See **cock**[1].

Coxsackie virus *kōōk-sä'kē vīrəs*, *n* (sometimes without *cap*) any of a group of RNA-containing viruses that occur in the human intestinal tract and cause various diseases, including meningitis and inflammation of muscle, brain and heart tissue. [From *Coxsackie*, in New York state, where the virus was first discovered]

Cox's orange pippin *kok'səz o'rinj pip'in*, *n* a sweet-tasting variety of apple with a brownish-green skin tinged with orange when ripe (in *pl* often shortened to **Coxes** *kok'səz*). [From R *Cox*, English horticulturist]

coxswain or **cockswain** *kok'sn*, or *kok'swān*, *n* the helmsman of a lifeboat; (*usu* shortened to **cox**) the person who steers a racing eight or four (*rowing*); a petty officer in charge of a boat and crew. — *vt* and *vi* to act as coxswain (for). — Often shortened to **cox**. — *adj* **coxed** having a cox. [Obs *cock* a boat (cf **cockboat**) and **swain**]

coxy. See **cock**[1].

Coy (*military*) *abbrev*: Company.

coy *koi*, *adj* bashful, modest; affectedly shy; evasive. — *adv* **coy'ly**. — *n* **coy'ness**. [Fr *coi*, from L *quiētus* quiet]

coyote *koi'ōt*, *koi-ōt'(i)* or *kī-ōt'i*, *kī'ōt*, *n* a prairie-wolf, a small wolf of N America; a person who exploits illegal immigrants to the US, *esp* from Mexico (*US slang*): — *pl* **coyo'tes** or **coyo'te**. [Mex *coyotl*]

coyotillo *kō-yō-tēl'yō*, *n* a thorny shrub (*Karwinskia humboldtiana*) of Mexico and the US, related to the buckthorn, and bearing berries that can cause paralysis. [Mex Sp, literally, little coyote]

coypu *koi'pōō*, or *-pōō'*, or *-pū*, *n* a large S American aquatic rodent (*Myopotamus* or *Myocastor coypus*) now found wild in Europe, the source of nutria fur. [Native name]

coystrel, coystril. Same as **coistrel**.

coz *kuz*, (*archaic*) *n* a contraction of **cousin**.

coze *kōz*, *vi* to chat. — Also *n*. [Fr *causer*]

cozen *kuz'n*, *vt* to cheat. — *n* **coz'enage** deceit. — *n* **coz'ener**. [Perh Fr *cousiner* to claim kindred; see **cousin**]

cozier or **cosier** *kō'zi-ər*, (*Shakesp*) *n* a cobbler. [OFr *cousere* tailor, from L *cōnsuere* to sew together]

cozy. *NAm* spelling of **cosy**.

CP *abbrev*: Command Post; Common Prayer; Communist Party.

cp *abbrev*: candle power (qv); chemically pure.
cp. *abbrev*: compare.
CPAC *abbrev*: Consumer Protection Advisory Committee.
CPAG *abbrev*: Child Poverty Action Group.
Cpd *abbrev*: compound.
CPG *abbrev*: Coronary Prevention Group.
CPGB *abbrev*: Communist Party of Great Britain.
CPI *abbrev*: consumer price index, a method of demonstrating the inflation rate.
cpi (*comput*) *abbrev*: characters per inch.
Cpl *abbrev*: Corporal.
CP/M (*comput*) *abbrev*: Control Program for Microprocessors.
CPO *abbrev*: Chief Petty Officer; Crime Prevention Officer.
cpp *abbrev*: current purchasing power.
CPR *abbrev*: Canadian Pacific Railway.
CPRE *abbrev*: Campaign for the Protection of Rural England.
CPRS *abbrev*: Central Policy Review Staff, a former body (1971–83) reviewing and reporting on British Government strategy, also known as the **Government Think-Tank**.
CPS *abbrev*: Crown Prosecution Service.
cps *abbrev*: characters per second (*comput*); cycles per second (phys).
CPSA *abbrev*: Civil and Public Services Association.
CPU (*comput*) *abbrev*: central processing unit.
CQ (*radio*) *symbol*: transmitted by an amateur operator to establish communication with any other amateur operator.
Cr *abbrev*: Councillor.
Cr. (*chem*) *symbol*: chromium.
cr. *abbrev*: credit; creditor; crown.
crab[1] *krab*, *n* any of the marine decapod crustaceans, having a wide, flat carapace in which the abdomen is folded under the cephalothorax; its flesh as food; (with *cap*) the sign of the zodiac and constellation Cancer; a portable winch; a crab-louse. — *vi* to drift or move sideways; to fish for crabs. — *n* **crabb'er** a crab fisherman. — *adj* **crabb'y** crab-like. — *adj* **crab'like**. — *adj* and *adv* **crab'wise** with sideways motion like a crab's. — *adj* **crab'-faced** having a peevish expression. — **crab'-louse** a crab-shaped parasitic louse (*Pthirus pubis*) infesting the hair of the pubis, etc in humans; **Crab Nebula** the expanding cloud of gas in the constellation of Taurus, being the remains of a supernova observed in 1054 AD; **crab's'-eyes** or **crab'-stones** prayer-beads, the scarlet and black seeds of the Indian liquorice tree (*Abrus precatorius*); a limy concretion in the crayfish's stomach; **crab'-yaws** yaws on the soles and palms. — **catch a crab** (*rowing*) to sink the oar too deeply (or not enough) in the water and fall back in consequence. [OE *crabba*; Ger *Krebs*]
crab[2] *krab*, *n* a wild apple (tree or fruit); a sour-tempered person. — **crab'-apple**; **crab'stick** a walking-stick or cudgel made of crab-apple wood. [Ety uncertain]
crab[3] *krab*, *vt* (of hawks) to claw; to decry, criticize; to obstruct, wreck or frustrate. — *n* dejection; fault-finding. [**crab**[1]]
crabbed *krab'id*, *adj* ill-natured, perverse or irascible; (of handwriting) cramped or difficult to decipher. — *adv* **crabb'edly**. — *n* **crabb'edness**. — *adv* **crabb'ily**. — *n* **crabb'iness**. — *adj* **crabb'y** bad-tempered, ill-natured. [**crab**[1] conflated in meaning with **crab**[2]]
crabby. See **crab**[1], **crabbed**.
crab-nut, **-oil**, **-wood**. See **carap**.
crack *krak*, *vt* and *vi* to (cause eg a whip to) make a sharp sudden sound; to split; to break partially or suddenly; to fracture, the parts remaining in contact; to (cause to) give way under strain, torture, etc; (of petroleum, etc) to break into simpler molecules. — *vi* (of the voice) to change tone or register suddenly; to chat, gossip (*Scot* and *US*); to talk incessantly, to boast (with *on*; *colloq*). — *vt* to break open (a safe, etc); to solve the mystery of (a code, etc); to utter in jest; to hit with a resounding noise. — *n* a sudden sharp splitting sound; a partial fracture; a flaw; a sharp resounding blow; a friendly chat (*Scot* and *Ir*); (with *the*) the latest news, gossip (*Ir*); an expert; a quip, gibe; a try (*slang*); the vagina (*vulg slang*); a highly addictive form of cocaine mixed with other substances (*usu* baking powder) and sold and used in small pellet-like pieces. — *adj* (*colloq*) excellent, first-rate; expert. — *adj* **cracked** split; damaged; crazy (*informal*). — *n* **crack'er** a person or thing that cracks; a thin crisp biscuit; a colourful tubular package that comes apart with a bang, when the ends are pulled, to reveal a small gift, motto, etc; a small, noisy firework; the apparatus used in cracking petroleum; something exceptionally good or fine of its type (*colloq*). — *adj* **crack'ers** (*colloq*) crazy; unbalanced. — *adj* **crack'ing** (*colloq*) (of speed, etc) very fast; very good. — **crack baby** a baby born to a mother addicted to the drug crack that has suffered physical damage as a result of being exposed to the drug while in the womb, or is itself addicted; **crack'brain** a crazy person. — *adj* **crack'brained**. — **crackdown** see **crack down on**; **cracked wheat** wheat coarsely ground, boiled and then dried for use as a cereal food, bulgur; **crack'erjack** or **crack'ajack** a person or thing of highest excellence. — Also *adj*. — *adj* **crack'er-barrel** (*US*) rural, rustic, of homely philosophy. — **crack'head** a person who uses, or is addicted to, the drug crack; **crack house** a place where the drug crack is made and consumed. — *adj* **crack'jaw** hard to pronounce. — **crack'pot** a crazy person. — Also *adj*. — **cracks'man** a burglar. — **at the crack of dawn** at daybreak; very early in the morning; **crack a bottle, can**, etc to open or drink a bottle, can, etc; **crack a crib** (*thieves' slang*) to break into a building; **crack a joke** to utter a joke with some effect; **crack credit** to destroy one's credit; **crack down on** to take firm action against (*n* **crack'down**); **crack it** (*colloq*) to succeed, *esp* in the seduction of a woman; **crack on** (*colloq*) to proceed or go forward quickly; **crack the whip** to assert authority suddenly or forcibly; **crack up** to praise; to fail suddenly, to go to pieces; to suffer a mental breakdown; to distress considerably; **fair crack of the whip** a fair opportunity; **get cracking** to get moving quickly. [OE *cracian* to crack; cf Du *kraken*, Gaelic *crac*]
crackle *krak'l*, *vi* to make a slight but sustained cracking noise as a wood fire does; to rustle loudly. — *n* a slight crackling or loud rustling; a kind of porcelain with the glaze purposely cracked in the kiln as a form of decoration (also **crack'leware**); paper money, banknotes, money in general (*slang*). — *n* **crack'ling** the rind of roast pork; (in *pl*) the part of suet made up of skin without tallow. — *adj* **crack'ly** producing a crackling or rustling noise; brittle, crisp. [Frequentative of **crack**]
cracknel *krak'nəl*, *n* a light, brittle biscuit; (in *pl*) crisply fried pieces of fat pork (*NAm*). [ME *krakenelle*, perh from OFr *craquelin*]
-cracy *-krə-si*, *combining form* used to indicate rule, government (by a particular group, etc) as in *democracy*, *mobocracy*. — *combining form* **-crat** (*-krat*) a person supporting, or partaking in, government (by a particular group, etc). — *adj combining form* **-cratic** or **-cratical**. [Gr *-kratia*, from *kratos* power]
cradle *krā'dl*, *n* a small bed for a baby, *usu* suspended or on rockers; (with *the*) infancy; the place of origin or nurture of a particular person or thing; a stand, rest or holder for supporting something; a suspended platform or trolley which can be raised and lowered and from which work can be carried out on the side of a ship, building, etc; a framework, *esp* one for keeping bedclothes from pressing on a patient, or one under a ship for launching; a rocking box for gold-washing; an engraver's knife used with a rocking motion; a wooden pronged attachment for a scythe, for combining the operations of cutting and gathering. — *adj* having been so since infancy, as in *cradle Catholic*. — *vt* to lay or rock in a cradle; to hold and rock lovingly; to wash

(soil containing gold) into a rocking-box; to nurture. — *vt* and *vi* (in lacrosse) to keep (the ball) in the net of one's stick while running, by means of a rocking action. — *n* **crā'dling** (*archit*) a wooden or iron framework within a ceiling. — **cradle cap** a form of seborrhoeic dermatitis common in babies, in which patches of scaly skin form on the scalp; **cra'dle-scythe** a broad scythe used in a cradle framework for cutting grain; **cra'dle-snatcher** (*usu derog*) someone who chooses as a lover or marriage partner someone much younger than himself or herself (also **baby-snatcher**); **cra'dle-snatching**; **cra'dlesong** a lullaby. — **from the cradle to the grave** throughout one's life. [OE *cradol*; ety obscure]

craft *kräft*, *n* cunning; dexterity; art; creative artistic activity involving construction, carving, weaving, sewing, etc as opposed to drawing (also **craft'work**); a skilled trade; the members of a trade collectively; an occupation; a ship or ships of any kind (*orig* small); an air vehicle or a space vehicle. — *vt* to make or construct, *esp* with careful skill. — *adv* **craft'ily**. — *n* **craft'iness**. — *adj* **craft'less** free from craft; unskilled in any craft. — *adj* **craf'ty** having skill (*archaic*); cunning; wily. — **craft guild** an association of people engaged in the same trade; **craft shop** a shop in which materials and tools for creative activities such as embroidery, basketry, model-making, etc are sold; **crafts'man** a person engaged in a craft; **crafts'manship** or **craft'manship**; **crafts'person** (*pl* **crafts'people**); **crafts'woman**; **craft'-work** see **craft** above. — **arty-crafty** see under **art**[2]. [OE *cræft*; Ger *Kraft* power]

crag[1] *krag*, *n* a rough steep rock or point, a cliff; a shelly deposit mixed with sand, found in the Pliocene of E Anglia (*geol*). — *adj* **cragg'ed** craggy. — *n* **cragg'edness** or **cragg'iness**. — *adj* **cragg'y** full of crags or broken rocks; rough; rugged. — **crag-and-tail'** (*geol*) a hill-form with steep declivity at one end and a gentle slope at the other. — *adj* **crag'fast** (*mountaineering*) unable to move from a position on a crag. — **crags'man** a person skilled in rock-climbing. [Appar connected with Gaelic *creag*, *carraig*]

crag[2] *krag*, *n* the neck; the throat. [Cf Du *kraag*, Ger *Kragen* the neck]

craig *krāg*, *n* Scots form of **crag**[1] and **crag**[2]. — **craig'fluke** the witch (*Pleuronectes cynoglossus*), a flat fish.

crake[1] *krāk*, (*dialect*) *n* a crow, raven; a corncrake; a croak; the cry of the corncrake. — *vi* to utter a crake. — **crake'berry** crowberry. [Cf **corncrake**, **croak**]

crake[2] *krāk*, (*dialect* and *Spenser*) *n*, *vt* and *vi* (to) boast. [**crack**]

cram *kram*, *vt* to press closely together; to stuff; to fill to superfluity; to overfeed; to feed with a view to fattening; to make believe false or exaggerated tales (*old slang*); to teach, or learn, hastily for a certain occasion (such as an examination or a lawsuit). — *vi* to eat greedily; to prepare for an examination, etc by hasty and intensive learning: — *pr p* **cramm'ing**; *pa t* and *pa p* **crammed**. — *n* a crush; a lie (*old slang*); information that has been crammed (*obs*); the system of cramming. — *adj* **cramm'able**. — *adj* **crammed**. — *n* **cramm'er** a person or machine that crams poultry; someone who, or an establishment that, crams pupils or a subject. — *adj* **cram-full'**. [OE *crammian*; ON *kremja* to squeeze; Dan *kramme* to crumple]

crambo *kram'bō*, *n* a game in which one player gives a word to which another finds a rhyme; rhyme: — *pl* **cram'boes**. — **cram'boclink** or **crambo-jin'gle** (*Burns*) rhyming doggerel. [Prob from L *crambē repetīta* cabbage served up again]

crame *krām*, (*Scot*) *n* a booth for selling goods. [From Du or Low Ger]

cramoisy or **cramesy** *kram'əz-i*, (*archaic*) *adj* crimson. — *n* crimson cloth. [See **crimson**]

cramp *kramp*, *n* an involuntary and painful contraction of a voluntary muscle or group of muscles; (in *pl*) acute abdominal pain; restraint; a cramp-iron; a contrivance with a movable part that can be screwed tight so as to press things together. — *adj* (*old*) (used of handwriting) hard to make out; cramped; narrow. — *vt* to affect with spasms; to confine; to hamper; to fasten with a cramp-iron. — *adj* **cramped** (of handwriting) small and closely written; compressed; restricted, without enough room, confined. — *n* **cramp'et** or **cramp'it** a scabbard-chape; a cramp-iron; a crampon. — *adj* **cramp'ing** restricting, confining. — *n* **cramp'on** a grappling-iron; a spiked contrivance attached to the boots for climbing mountains or telegraph poles or walking on ice. — *adj* **cramp'y** affected or diseased with cramp; producing cramp. — **cramp'bark** (*US*) the guelder-rose, or its medicinal bark; **cramp'-bone** the patella of the sheep, an old charm for cramp; **cramp'-fish** the electric ray or torpedo; **cramp'-iron** a piece of metal bent at both ends for binding things together; **cramp'-ring** a ring formerly blessed by the sovereign on Good Friday against cramp and falling sickness. — **cramp someone's style** to restrict someone's movements or actions; **writer's cramp** a common disease affecting those in the habit of constant writing, the muscles refusing to respond only when an attempt to write is made (also called **scrivener's palsy**). [OFr *crampe*; cf Du *kramp*, Ger *Krampf*]

crampon. See **cramp**.

cran *kran*, *n* a measure of capacity for herrings just landed in port, equal to $37\frac{1}{2}$ gallons. — **coup the cran** (*Scot*) to upset, or be upset, (eg of plans). [Prob from Gaelic *crann* a measure]

cranberry *kran'bər-i*, *n* the red acid berry of a small evergreen shrub (*Vaccinium oxycoccos*) growing in peaty bogs and marshy grounds, or the larger berry of an American species (*V. macrocarpum*), both made into jellies, sauces, etc; extended loosely to other species of the genus; the shrub itself. — **cran'berry bush** or **cran'berry tree** (*US*) the guelder-rose. [For *crane-berry*; a late word; origin obscure; cf Ger *Kranbeere* or *Kranichbeere*]

cranch *kranch*, *n* and *vt*. Same as **crunch**.

crane[1] *krān*, *n* any bird of the *Gruidae*, large wading birds with long legs, neck and bill; a machine for raising heavy weights, *usu* having a rotating boom from the end of which the lifting gear is hung; a travelling platform for a film camera; a bent pipe for drawing liquor out of a cask. — *vt* to raise with a crane; to stretch one's neck as a crane does. — *vi* to stretch out the neck. — *n* **crān'age** the use of a crane; the price paid for the use of it. — **crane'fly** a fly (Tipula) with very long legs, the daddy-long-legs. — *adj* **crane'-necked**. — **cranes'bill** or **crane's'-bill** any wild species of the Geranium genus, from the beaked fruit. [OE *cran*; Ger *Kranich*, Welsh *garan*]

crane[2]. Same as **cranium**.

craniopharyngioma *krā-ni-ō-far-in-jō'mə*, *n* a tumour of the pituitary gland, which if untreated may cause permanent brain damage. [**cranium**, *pharyngi-* from Gr *pharunx*, *pharungos* pharynx, throat, and **-oma** tumour]

cranium *krā'ni-əm*, *n* the skull; the bones enclosing the brain: — *pl* **crā'niums** or **crā'nia**. — *adj* **crā'nial**. — *n pl* **Crāniā'ta** (*zool*) the main division of the Chordata, which has a cranium. — *n* **crāniec'tomy** (Gr *ektomē* cutting out) the surgical removal of a piece of the skull. — *n* **crāniog'nomy** (Gr *gnōmē* knowledge) cranial physiognomy. — *adj* **crāniolog'ical**. — *n* **crāniol'ogist**. — *n* **crāniol'ogy** the study of skulls; phrenology. — *n* **crāniom'eter** an instrument for measuring the skull. — *n* **crāniom'etry**. — *n* **crānios'copist** a phrenologist. — *n* **crānios'copy** phrenology. — *n* **crāniot'omy** (Gr *tomē* a cut) the act of compressing the skull of a foetus in obstructed deliveries (*obstetrics*); incision into or removal of part of the skull, *esp* for the purpose of neurosurgery. — **cranial index** the breadth of a skull as a percentage of the length. [LL *crānium*, from Gr *krānion* the skull]

crank[1] *krangk*, *n* an arm on a shaft for communicating motion to or from the shaft (*machinery*); a handle on this principle for starting a motor (also **crank'handle** or **starting handle**); a person of eccentric or faddy habits and tastes (*derog*); an irascible person (*NAm*); a whim. — *vi* to turn a crank (often with *up*). — *vt* to turn (a shaft) using a crank; to start (a motor) with a crank. — *adv* **crank'ily**. — *n* **crank'iness**. — *adj* **crank'y** eccentric, faddy and full of whims (*derog*); crabbed, ill-tempered (*NAm*); shaky, unsteady (*colloq*). — **crank'case** a box-like casing for the crankshaft and connecting-rods of some types of reciprocating-engine; **crank pin** the pin fitted into the arm of a crank and to which a connecting-rod is attached; **crank'shaft** the main shaft of an engine or other machine, which carries a crank or cranks for the attachment of connecting-rods. [OE *cranc*; cf Ger *krank* ill]

crank[2] *krangk*, (*drug-taking slang*) *n* any amphetamine drug. — **crank up** to inject narcotics. [From motoring image]

crank[3] *krangk*, or **crank-sided** *krangk-sī'did*, (*naut*) *adj* liable to capsize. — *n* **crank'ness** liability to capsize. [Ety uncertain]

crankle *krangk'l*, *n* a turn, winding, or wrinkle; an angular protuberance. — *vt* and *vi* to bend; to twist. [Frequentative of **crank**[1]]

crannog *kran'og*, (*archaeol*) *n* a lake-dwelling in Scotland and Ireland, typically a tiny island artifically enlarged and fortified. [Gaelic *crann* a tree]

cranny *kran'i*, *n* a fissure; a chink; a secret place. — *vi* to enter crannies. — *adj* **crann'ied** having crannies or fissures. [Fr *cran* a notch]

cranreuch *krän'ruhh*, (*Scot*) *n* hoar-frost. [Origin obscure; poss from Gaelic]

crants *krants*, (*Shakesp*) *n* the garland carried before the bier of a maiden and hung over her grave. [Ger *Kranz* a wreath, a garland]

crap[1] *krap*, *n* Scots form of **crop**. — *vt* to crop; to cram or stuff. — **crappit-head** or **crappit-heid** (*krap'it-hēd*,) a haddock's head stuffed with a mixture of oatmeal, suet, onions and pepper.

crap[2] *krap*, *n* excrement (*vulg*); rubbish, dirt (*slang*); worthless nonsense (*slang*); unpleasant or petty behaviour (*slang*). — *vi* to defecate (*vulg*). — *vt* to fear (something) (*vulg*; also **crap it**). — *adj* **crapp'y**. — **crap out** (*vulg*) to give up, opt out, chicken out. [ME *crappe* chaff, from MDu *krappe*, prob from *krappen* to tear off]

crap[3]. See under **craps**.

crape *krāp*, *n* a thin crinkled silk or other fabric formerly *usu* dyed black and used for mourning clothes; a band of this for putting round a mourner's hat or arm. — *adj* made of crape. — *adj* **crāp'y**. — **crape'hanger** or **crepe'hanger** (*colloq*) a pessimist; **crape'hanging** or **crepe'hanging**. [OFr *crespe* (Fr *crêpe*), from L *crispus* crisp; see also **crêpe**]

craple *krap'l*, (*Spenser*) *n*. Same as **grapple**.

craps *kraps*, *n sing* a gambling game in which a player rolls two dice (also **crap**). — *n* **crap** a losing throw in craps. — **crap out** to make a losing throw in craps (*US*); to fail (*US*); **shoot craps** to play craps. [**crab**[1], lowest throw at hazard]

crapulence *krap'ū-ləns*, *n* sickness caused by excessive drinking; intemperance. — *adj* **crap'ulent** or **crap'ulous**. — *n* **crapulos'ity**. [Fr *crapule*, from L *crāpula* intoxication]

craquelure *krak'ə-lūr* or *-lōōr*, *n* the fine cracking that occurs in the varnish or pigment of old paintings; this effect or pattern. [Fr]

crare or **crayer** *krār*, *n* a trading vessel. [OFr *craier*]

crases. See **crasis**.

crash[1] *krash*, *n* a noise as of things breaking or being crushed by falling; the shock of two bodies meeting; a collision between vehicles, etc; the failure of a commercial undertaking; economic collapse; a fall or rush to destruction; the complete breakdown of a computer system or program; the disagreeable after-effects of a high (*drug-taking slang*). — *adj* planned to meet an emergency quickly; involving suddenness, speed or short-term intensive effort. — *vt* and *vi* to dash or fall to pieces with a loud noise; to move with a harsh noise; to collide or cause to collide with another vehicle, etc; to fall or cause (an aircraft) to fall violently to earth or into the sea, *usu* with extensive damage; to gatecrash (*colloq*); to have or cause (a computer system or program) to break down completely. — *vi* to come to grief, fail disastrously; to suffer the unpleasant after-effects of a high (*drug-taking slang*). — *adj* **crash'ing** (*colloq*) extreme, overwhelming, *esp* in *a crashing bore*. — **crash barrier** a protective barrier, *usu* of steel, placed eg along the edge of a road or the central reservation of a motorway; **crash course** a short-lasting but intensive programme of instruction; **crash dive** a sudden dive of a submarine (also *vi* and *vt*); **crash'-helmet** a padded safety headdress for motorcyclists, racing motorists, etc. — *vi* and *vt* **crashland'** in an emergency, to land (an aircraft) abruptly, with resultant damage. — **crash'=land'ing**; **crash'-mat** a thick mattress used by athletes and gymnasts to absorb the impact of landing after a jump, etc; **crash'-matting**; **crash'pad** padding inside a motor vehicle to protect the occupants in case of accident; a place providing temporary accommodation (*slang*). — *adj* **crash'-proof** designed to withstand a crash. — **crash recorder** see **flight-recorder**. — *vt* **crash'=test** to test (a new product) to establish its breaking point by subjecting it to heat, pressure, impact, etc. — **crash out** (*slang*) to fall asleep; to become unconscious. [Imit]

crash[2] *krash*, *n* a coarse strong linen. [Perh from Russ *krashenina* coloured linen]

crasis *krā'sis*, (*gram*) *n* the mingling or contraction of two vowels into one long vowel, or into a diphthong: — *pl* **crā'sēs** (*-sēz*). [Gr *krāsis* mixture]

crass *kras*, *adj* coarse, boorish; grossly stupid, tactless or insensitive. — *n* **crassament'um** the thick part of coagulated blood; the clot. — *n* **crass'itude** coarseness; stupidity, tactlessness or insensitivity. — *adv* **crass'ly**. — *n* **crass'ness**. [L *crassus*]

crassulaceous *kras-ū-lā'shəs*, (*bot*) *adj* of, belonging to, or relating to the *Crassulaceae*, a family of succulent plants including the stonecrops and houseleeks. — **crassulacean acid metabolism** (*abbrev* **CAM**) a method of photosynthesis in plants of the *Crassulaceae*, in which carbon dioxide is taken in at night and stored to be used during the day. [From the genus name *Crassula* stonecrop, from L *crassus* thick]

-crat, **-cratic**, **-cratical**. See **-cracy**.

cratch *krach*, (*dialect* and *archaic*) *n* a crib to hold hay for cattle, a manger. — *n pl* **cratch'es** a swelling on a horse's pastern, under the fetlock. [Fr *crèche* manger; from a Gmc root, whence also **crib**]

crate *krāt*, *n* a strong metal, plastic, wooden or wickerwork case with partitions, for carrying breakable or perishable goods; a packing case; the contents of a crate; a decrepit aeroplane or car (*colloq*). — *vt* to pack in a crate. [L *crātis* a hurdle]

crater *krāt'ər*, *n* the bowl-like mouth of a volcano; a hole in the ground where a meteorite has fallen, or a shell, mine or bomb exploded; a circular rimmed depression in the surface of the moon; a cavity formed in the carbon of an electric arc; (*usu* **krat'er**) a large two-handled bowl for mixing wine in (*archaeol*). — *vt* to form craters in. — *adj* **crateriform** (*krat-er'i-förm* or *krāt'er-i-förm*) cup-shaped. — *adj* **crat'erous**. — **crater lake** a lake formed in the crater of an extinct volcano. [L, from Gr *krātēr* a mixing bowl]

craton *krāt'on*, (*geol*) *n* any of the comparatively rigid and immobile areas in the earth's crust. [Gr *kratos* strength]

cratur *krāt'ər*, (*Ir* and *Scot*) *n* a creature. — **the cratur** whisky.

craunch *krönch*. A dialect form of **crunch**.

cravat *krə-vat'*, *n* a formal neckerchief worn, *esp* by men, as an alternative to a tie. — *vt* to dress in a cravat. [Fr *cravate*, from *Cravates*, 17c Croatian mercenaries who wore a scarf in battle]

crave *krāv*, *vt* to ask for earnestly, to beg; to require; to long or yearn for. — *vi* to long (with *for* or *after*). — *n* a longing; a claim (*Scots law*). — *n* **crav'er** someone who craves; a beggar. — *n* **crav'ing** a longing or great desire. [OE *crafian* to crave; ON *krefja*]

craven *krāv'n*, *adj* cowardly; spiritless. — *n* a coward; a spiritless person. — *vt* (*Shakesp*) to render spiritless. — *adv* **crav'enly**. — *n* **crav'enness**. [ME *cravant*, perh from L *crepāre* crack]

craw *krö*, *n* the crop, throat or first stomach of fowls; the crop of insects; the stomach of animals generally. — **stick in one's craw** see **stick in one's throat** under **stick**. [ME *crawe*; not found in OE; cf Du *kraag* neck]

crawfish *krö'fish*, (*esp NAm*) *n* a crayfish. — *vi* to retreat or back out, *esp* from a position in which one is being challenged.

crawl[1] *kröl*, *vi* to move slowly with the body on or close to the ground; to move on hands and knees; to creep; to move slowly or stealthily; to behave abjectly or obsequiously; to be covered with crawling things (with *with*); to swim using the crawl stroke. — *n* the act of crawling; a slow pace; a swimming stroke in which the arms are held in front of the body and rotated from the shoulder alternately and the feet kicked up and down. — *n* **crawl'er** someone who or something which crawls; an abject, obsequious or sycophantic person; a sluggish or slow person; a creeping thing; a heavy slow-moving vehicle, *esp* one that moves on caterpillar tracks; a baby's overall, a romper suit. — *n* **crawl'ing**. — *adj* creeping; lousy, verminous. — *adj* **craw'ly** (*colloq*) with, or like the feeling of, something crawling over one; creepy. — **crawler lane** an extra lane for the use of slow-moving vehicles on an uphill stretch of a road; **crawling peg** (*econ*) a system of stabilizing prices or exchange rates by allowing a limited amount of rise or fall at predetermined intervals. [ME, perh from ON *krafla* creep]

crawl[2] *kröl*, *n* a pen for keeping fish or lobsters. [From Afrik *kraal* a pen]

crayer. See **crare**.

crayfish *krā'fish* or (*esp NAm*) **crawfish** *krö'fish*, *n* a large edible freshwater decapod crustacean; the Norway lobster; the spiny lobster. [ME *crevice*, from OFr *crevice* (Fr *écrevisse* a crayfish), from OHGer *krebiz* a crab]

crayon *krā'ən*, *n* a pencil made of chalk, wax or pipe-clay, variously coloured, used for drawing; a drawing done with crayons. — *vt* and *vi* to draw or colour with a crayon. [Fr *crayon*, from *craie* chalk, from L *crēta* chalk]

craze *krāz*, *vt* or *vi* to develop or cause (pottery, metal, etc) to develop a series of fine cracks; to shatter or break (*archaic*); to weaken; to impair; to become or to cause (the mind) to become deranged. — *n* a crack or flaw; a series of fine cracks; insanity; a fashion or fad; a small structural defect in plastic. — *adj* **crazed**. — *adv* **crāz'ily**. — *n* **crāz'iness**. — *adj* **crāz'y** demented, deranged; ridiculous, stupid; exuberantly wild in behaviour (*colloq*); extravagantly enthusiastic or passionate (about) (*colloq*); impractical; (of paving, etc) composed of flat, irregular pieces. — *n* a crazy person (*colloq*): — *pl* **cra'zies**. — **crazing mill** a mill for crushing tin-ore; **crazy bone** (*NAm*) the funny bone; **crazy golf** a form of putting in which balls have to be hit past, through, over, etc obstacles such as humps, tunnels, bends, etc to reach the hole; **crazy paving** paving composed of irregularly shaped slabs of stone or concrete, used for ornamental effect on terraces, garden paths, etc; **crazy quilt** a patchwork quilt made up haphazardly of irregular pieces of material sewn together. [Scand; cf Swed *krasa*, Dan *krase* to crackle; also Fr *écraser* to crush]

CRE *abbrev*: Commission for Racial Equality.

creagh or **creach** *krehh*, (*Scot*) *n* a foray; booty. [Gaelic *creach*]

creak *krēk*, *vi* to make a sharp grating or squeaking sound, as of an unoiled hinge or sagging floorboard. — *n* a grating noise. — *adv* **creak'ily**. — *adj* **creak'y** squeaky; tending to creak; badly made or performed (*fig*). [From the sound, like *crake* and *croak*]

cream *krēm*, *n* the oily substance that rises to the surface of milk, yielding butter when churned; the colour of this substance, yellowish-white; the best part of anything; the pick of a group of things or people; a food largely made of cream or like cream in consistency or appearance, as *ice cream*; any other substance having the appearance or consistency of cream, as *cold-cream* for skin. — *vt* to take off the cream from (milk), to skim; to select (the best) from a group, etc (with *off*); to beat or mix to the consistency of thick cream (eg a mixture of sugar and butter in cake-making); to treat with cream. — *vi* to form cream; to gather like cream. — *adj* of the colour of cream, yellowish-white; prepared with cream; (of sherry) sweet. — *n* **cream'er** a device for separating cream from milk; a small jug for cream (*esp NAm*); a substitute for milk, in powder form, for use in coffee, etc. — *n* **cream'ery** an establishment where butter and cheese are made from the milk supplied by a number of producers; a shop selling milk, butter, etc. — *n* **cream'iness**. — *adj* **cream'y** full of cream, or like cream in appearance, consistency, etc; forming or gathering like cream. — **cream'-bun** or **cream'-cake** a kind of bun or cake filled with cream or a substitute for cream; **cream-cheese'** soft white cheese. — *adj* **cream'-coloured** of the colour of cream, yellowish-white. — **cream cracker** a crisp, unsweetened type of biscuit, often eaten with cheese; **cream horn** a horn-shaped pastry filled with cream, etc; **cream jug** a small jug for serving milk or cream. — *adj* **cream'laid** (of paper) cream or white in colour with a laid watermark. — **cream'-nut** another name for the Brazil nut; **cream puff** a confection of puff pastry filled with cream; (*esp* used of men) an ineffectual person (*esp NAm*); **cream'-slice** a wooden blade for skimming cream from milk; **cream soda** (*esp NAm*) a vanilla-flavoured fizzy drink; **cream tea** a meal consisting of tea and scones filled with cream and jam; **cream'ware** a type of earthenware first produced in the 18c, having a cream-coloured glaze. — *adj* **cream'wove** (of wove paper) cream or white in colour. — **cream of chicken, mushroom**, etc **soup** chicken, mushroom, etc soup made with milk or cream; **cream of tartar** a white crystalline compound made by purifying argol, potassium hydrogen tartrate; **cream of tartar tree** another name for the baobab; an Australian tree of the same genus, *Adansonia gregorii*. [OFr *cresme*, *creme*, from LL *cramum* of Celtic origin, infl by eccelesiastical *chrīsma* unction]

creance *krē'əns*, (*falconry*) *n* the cord which secures the hawk in training. [Fr *créance*]

creant *krē'ənt*, *adj* creating; formative. [L *creāns*, *-antis*, pr p of *creāre*; see **create**]

crease[1] *krēs*, *n* a mark made by folding, pressing or crumpling; such a mark pressed centrally and longitudinally into a trouser-leg; a wrinkle or line on the face; any of three lines that regulate the positions of batsman and bowler at the wicket, ie *bowling crease*, from astride which the bowler must bowl, *popping-crease*, four feet in front of the bowling crease, at which the batsman or batswoman plays and behind which is his or her ground, and *return crease*, marking the sideward limits of the bowler (*cricket*); (in ice-hockey and lacrosse) a marked area round the goal. — *vt* to make a crease or creases in; to graze with a bullet, sometimes used as a method of temporarily disabling rather than killing (an animal). — *vi* to become creased. — *vt* and *vi* (*colloq*) to double up with laughter (often with *up*). — *n* **creas'er**. — *adj* **creas'y** full of creases; liable or tending to crease. — *adj* **crease'-resistant** or **crease'-resisting** (of a fabric) not becoming creased in normal wear. [Origin uncertain]

crease[2]. See **kris**.

creasote. See **creosote**.

create *krē-āt'*, *vt* to bring into being or form out of nothing; to bring into being by force of imagination; to make, produce or form; to design; to invest with a new form, office or character; to institute; to be the first actor to play (a certain role). — *vi* (*slang*) to make a fuss. — *n* **creation** (*krē-ā'-shən*) the act of creating; (with *cap* and *the*) God's act of creating the universe (*Christian relig*); that which is created; the world, the universe; a specially designed, elaborate, or particularly striking, garment, eg a hat. — *adj* **creā'tional**. — *n* **creā'tionism** the theory that everything that exists had its origin in special acts of creation by God (opposite to *evolutionism*); the theory that God immediately creates a soul for every human being born (opposite to *traducianism*; also **creā'tianism**). — *n* **creā'tionist**. — *adj* **creā'tive** having power to create; creating; showing or relating to imagination or originality; (*esp* of accounting or accountancy) characterized by an imaginative re-interpretation or dubious manipulation of established rules of procedure, for personal benefit or ease of operation (*euphem*). — *adv* **creā'tively**. — *n* **creā'tiveness**. — *n* **creativity** (*krē-ə-tiv'*) the state or quality of being creative; the ability to create. — *n* **creā'tor** someone who creates; a maker; (with *cap* and *the*) the Supreme being, God: — *fem* (*rare*) **creā'trix** or **creā'tress**. — *n* **creā'torship**. — *adj* **creatural** (*krē'chər-əl*) or **crea'turely** pertaining to a creature or thing created. — *n* **creature** (*krē'chər*) an animate being, *esp* an animal; a human being, in this sense often used in contempt or compassion; something created, whether animate or inanimate; a person completely under one's control, a dependent, instrument, or puppet; (*usu* with *the*) alcoholic liquor (*colloq*). — *n* **crea'tureship**. — **creation science** creationism treated as a scientific viewpoint or theory; **creative accounting** or **creative accountancy** see **creative** above; **creative therapy** the use of art, dance, music, etc to assist human development and social interaction, eg during recovery from illness; **creature comforts** material comforts such as food, drink, a place to sleep, etc; liquor, *esp* whisky; **the Creator** the Supreme being, God. [L *creāre*, *-ātum* to create, *creātūra* a thing created]

creatic *krē-at'ik*, adj relating to flesh. [See **creatine**]

creatine or **creatin** *krē'ə-tin* or *-tēn*, *n* a nitrogenous compound ($C_4H_9N_3O_2$), the product of protein metabolism, found in the striped (voluntary) muscle of vertebrates. — *n* **crē'atinine** (*-nin* or *-nēn*) dehydrated creatine ($C_4H_7N_3O$) found in urine and muscles. — **creatine phosphate** the phosphate of creatine forming a store of phosphate in the muscles and maintaining adequate levels of adenosine triphosphate (ATP). [Gr *kreas*, *kreatos* flesh]

creative, **creator**, **creature**. See under **create**.

crèche *kresh*, *n* a nursery for either brief or day-long care of young children; (sometimes with *cap*) a model representing the scene of Christ's nativity. [Fr *crèche* manger]

cred *kred*, (*slang*) *n* short for **credibility** (*esp* in the phrase **street cred**).

credal. See **creed**.

credence *krē'dəns*, *n* belief; trust; precautionary tasting of food before serving, eg to a king, etc (*obs*); a sideboard; the small table beside the altar on which the bread and wine are placed before being consecrated (also **credence table**); a shelf over a piscina (also **credence shelf**). — *n* **credendum** (*kri-den'dəm*) a thing to be believed, an act of faith: — *pl* **creden'da**. — *adj* **crē'dent** (*obs*) credible, believable; credulous, believing. — *adj* **credential** (*kri-den'shl*) recommending for credit or confidence. — *n pl* **creden'tials** evidence of competence, taken as one's entitlement to authority, etc; letters of introduction, certificates, etc entitling one to trust or confidence. — *n* **credenza** (*kri-den'zə*, *Ital krā-dent'sa*) a credence table or shelf; a sideboard; a bookcase, *esp* if without legs. [LL *crēdentia* trust, from L *crēdere* to believe]

credendum, **credential(s)**, **credenza**. See **credence**.

credible *kred'ible*, *adj* capable of being believed; seemingly worthy of belief or of confidence; reliable; (of a nuclear weapon) in whose use and effectiveness one can believe. — *n* **credibil'ity** (*kred-*) the quality of deserving belief or confidence; the amount of confidence placed in one on the basis of one's record, knowledge or proven abilities, eg in a particular social group or environment. — *n* **cred'ibleness**. — *adv* **cred'ibly**. — **credibility gap** (*politics*, etc) the discrepancy between what is claimed or stated and what actually is, or seems likely to be, the case. [L *crēdibilis* believable, from *crēdere* to believe]

credit *kred'it*, *n* belief; esteem; reputation or honour; distinction; good character; acknowledgement or recognition of something contributed or achieved; sale on trust; time allowed for payment; a balance in a person's favour in an account; an entry in an account making acknowledgement of a payment (*bookkeeping*); the side of an account on which such entries are made (*bookkeeping*); a sum placed at a person's disposal in a bank, up to which they may draw; certified completion of a course of study counting towards a final pass; (in *pl*) credit titles; (in *pl*) a list of acknowledgements in a book, etc. — *vt* to believe; to trust; to sell or lend to on condition that payment is made within a specified period; to enter on the credit side of an account; to ascribe to (with *to* or *with*); to mention in the credit titles. — *adj* **cred'itable** trustworthy; bringing credit or honour; praiseworthy. — *n* **cred'itableness**. — *adv* **cred'itably**. — *n* **cred'itor** a person (or business) to whom a debt is due. — **credit card** a card obtainable from a credit card company which, in places where the card is recognized, enables the holder to have purchases, services, etc debited to an account kept by the company; a similar card issued by other organizations, or by certain banks, some only to be used with a cheque book; **credit limit** the maximum amount of credit extended to an individual or business; **credit note** a document issued by a retailer, *esp* a shop or store, to a customer who has returned goods, which can be used to obtain other goods to the same value; **credit rating** (an assessment of) the level of a person's or business's creditworthiness; **credit scoring** the calculation of a person's credit rating by adding up points awarded according to the person's age, marital status, occupation, address, etc; **credit squeeze** a method of controlling the money supply in an economy by imposing restrictions on the amount of credit available to individuals and businesses, used by governments as a counter-inflationary instrument; **credit titles** (or, more usually, **cred'its**) acknowledgements of the work of participators shown at the beginning or end of a cinema film, television programme, etc; **credit transfer** a method of settling a debt by lodging cash at a post office or bank where it is transferred to the creditor's account; **credit union** a non-profit-making co-operative savings association which makes loans to its members at low interest; **cred'itworthiness** entitlement to credit as judged from earning capacity, promptness in debt-paying, etc. — *adj* **cred'itworthy**. — **be a credit to someone**, etc to achieve success, perform or act in praiseworthy manner as proof of time, trouble, etc well-invested in one by someone, etc; **give credit for** to acknowledge as having (a quality, certain level of competence, etc). [OFr *crédit*, from L *crēditum* loan, from *crēdere* to believe]

credo *krē'dō* or *krā-*, *n* a belief or set of beliefs; (with *cap*) the Apostles' Creed or the Nicene Creed, or a musical setting of either of these for church services; a belief or set of beliefs: — *pl* **crē'dōs**. [L, I believe]

credulity *kri-dū'li-ti*, *n* disposition to believe without sufficient evidence; credulousness. — *adj* **credūlous** (*kred'*) apt to believe without sufficient evidence; unsuspecting. — *adv* **cred'ūlously**. — *n* **cred'ūlousness**. [L *crēdulus* over-trustful, from *crēdere* to believe]

cree *krē*, *vt* and *vi* (of grain) to soften by boiling or soaking. [Fr *crever* to burst]

Cree *krē*, *n* a member of a N American Indian tribe living in Montana and parts of Canada; the Algonquian language of this people, or its syllabic writing system. [Short for Can Fr *Christianaux*, from Algonquian *kiristino*, *kinistino*]

Creed *krēd*, *n* a form of teleprinter. [From Frederick George *Creed* (1871–1957), its Canadian inventor]

creed *krēd*, *n* a summary of articles of religious belief; any system of belief or set of principles. — *adj* **creed'al** or **cred'al**. — **the Creed** the Apostles' Creed or the Nicene Creed. [OE *crēda*, from L *crēdō* I believe]

Creek *krēk*, *n* a member of any of the tribes of American Indians of Florida, Alabama and Georgia (now mainly in Oklahoma), who formed the **Creek Confederacy**; the Muskogean language of the Creek Indians. [Prob **creek** a river]

creek *krēk*, *n* a small inlet or bay, or the tidal estuary of a river; a small river or brook (*NAm*, *Austr* and *NZ*). — *adj* **creek'y** full of creeks; winding. — **up the creek (without a paddle)** (*slang*) in dire difficulties (without the means or ability to save oneself). [Prob Scand, ON *kriki* a nook; cf Du *kreek* a bay; Fr *crique*]

creel *krēl*, *n* a basket, *esp* a fish basket. [Origin obscure]

creep *krēp*, *vi* to move with the belly on or near the ground; to move or advance slowly or stealthily; to slip or encroach very gradually; to develop insidiously; to grow along the ground or on supports, as a vine does; to fawn or cringe; (of the skin or flesh) to have a shrinking sensation, as a concomitant of horror, etc; to shudder; to drag with a creeper (*naut*); to undergo creep (*metallurgy*). — *vt* (*Milton*, etc) to creep on: — *pa t* and *pa p* **crept**. — *n* the act or process or creeping; a slow slipping or yielding to stress; crystallization or rise of a precipitate on the side of a vessel above the surface of a liquid; gradual alteration of shape under stress (*metallurgy*); a narrow passage; an enclosure in which young farm animals may feed, with an approach too narrow to admit the mother; a cringing, unassertive or otherwise unpleasant person (*slang*). — *n* **creep'er** someone or something that creeps; a creeping plant, eg the Virginia creeper; a small bird that runs up trees, a tree-creeper (*NAm*); a kind of grapnel used for dragging the seabed, etc (*naut*); an endless chain or conveyor; a crêpe-soled, or other soft-soled, shoe (*colloq*); a wheeled board on which one may lie and move about while working under a vehicle eg as a mechanic; a ball bowled so as to stay low (*cricket*). — *adj* **creep'ered** covered with a creeper. — *n* **creep'ie** a low stool; a stool of repentance. — *adj* **creep'ing**. — *adv* **creep'ingly**. — *adj* **creep'y** mysterious, rather eerie or chilling. — **creep'-hole** a hiding hole; a subterfuge; **creeping bent grass** a common European pasture grass, *Agrostris palustris*; **creeping eruption** an irritating skin condition caused by the larvae of certain flies or nematodes which burrow through the skin tissue leaving thin red lines (also **larva migrans**); **creeping Jenny** moneywort, a creeping plant of the primrose family (*Lysimachia nummularia*); **creeping Jesus** (*derog slang*) a cringingly sanctimonious person. — *adj* **creep'mouse** (*archaic*) silent and shrinking; **creepy-crawl'y** (*informal*) a creeping insect (also *adj*). — **the creeps** (*colloq*) a feeling of horror or revulsion. [OE *crēopan*; Du *kruipen*]

creese. See **kris**.

creesh *krēsh*, (*Scot*) *vt* to grease. — *n* grease. — *adj* **creesh'y**. [OFr *craisse*, from L *crassus* fat]

crémaillère *krā-mī-yer'*, *n* a zigzag line of fortification; a rack railway. [Fr, pot-hook]

cremaster *kri-mas'tər*, *n* a muscle of the spermatic cord; a hook-like projection on the pupae of butterflies and moths from which the pupa is suspended. [Gr *kremastēr* suspender, from *kremannynai* to hang]

cremate *kri-māt'*, *vt* to burn (*esp* a dead body). — *n* **cremā'tion**. — *n* **cremā'tionist**. — *n* **cremāt'or** a person who undertakes cremations; a furnace for cremation; an incinerator. — *adj* **crematorial** (*krem-ə-tō'ri-əl* or *-tö'*). — *n* **crematō'rium** a place for cremating dead bodies. — *adj* **crem'atory** (*-ə-tər-i*). — *n* a crematorium. [L *cremāre*, *-ātum* to burn]

creme *krēm*, *n* a form of **cream**, used *specif* for skin creams, frequently used in proprietary names.

crème or **crême** *krem*, (*Fr*) *n* cream, applied to various creamy substances. — **crème brûlée** (*brü-lā'*) a dish of egg yolks, cream and vanilla topped with caramelized sugar; **crème caramel** (*kar-a-mel*) an egg custard baked in a dish lined with caramel; **creme de cacao** *kə-kä'ō* or *-kā'ō* a chocolate-flavoured liqueur; **crème de la crème** (*də la krem*) cream of the cream, the very best; **crème de menthe** (*də mãt*) a green peppermint-flavoured liqueur; **crème fraîche** (*fresh*) cream thickened with a culture of bacteria.

cremocarp *krem'ō-kärp*, (*bot*) *n* the characteristic fruit of the Umbelliferae, composed of two one-seeded halves which split apart and dangle from the top of the axis. [Gr *kremannynai* to hang, and *karpos* fruit]

Cremona *krim-ō-nə*, *n* the name applied to any of the superior violins or stringed instruments made at *Cremona* in Italy'(16c–18c), including those made by Stradivari.

cremona *kri-mō'nə*, and **cremorne** *kri-mör'nə*. Erroneous forms of **cromorna**.

cremor *krē'mör*, *n* thick juice. [L]

cremosin or **cremsin** *krem'zin*, *adj*. Obsolete forms of **crimson**.

crenate *krēn'āt*, *kren'āt* or *kren-āt'*, or **crenated** *-id*, (*bot*) *adj* (of plant leaves) having a notched or scalloped edge. — *n* **crē'na** a notch or tooth. — *n* **crēnā'tion** a crenated formation; the process of shrinkage and formation of scalloped edges on red blood cells in a hypertonic solution. — *n* **crenature** (*krē'* or *kren'*). — *adj* **cren'ulate** or **cren'ulated** finely or irregularly notched or serrated. [New L *crēnātus*, from an inferred L *crēna* a notch]

crenel or **crenelle** *kren'l*, (*archit*) *n* an indentation in a parapet, a crenellation. — *vt* to indent with crenels. — *vt* **cren'ellate** or (*US*) **cren'elate**. (*kren'i-lāt*) to provide with battlements. — *adj* **cren'ellate** or **cren'ellated** having or forming battlements; indented. — *n* **crenel-lā'tion**. — *adj* **cren'elled**. [OFr *crenel*, from inferred L *crēna* a notch]

crenulate. See **crenate**.

creodont *krē'ō-dont*, *n* any member of a group of primitive fossil carnivores, appearing in Eocene times. [Gr *kreas* flesh, and *odous*, *odontos*, tooth]

creole *krē'ōl* or *krē-ōl'*, *n* (*usu* with *cap*) strictly, applied in the former Spanish, French and Portuguese colonies of America, Africa and the W Indies to natives of pure European blood (as opposed to immigrants born in Europe or to coloured natives); (*usu* with *cap*) a native, but not aboriginal or indigenous; (*loosely*; *usu* with *cap*) a native of mixed blood, *esp* a W Indian of mixed Spanish or French and Negro blood; (*usu* with *cap*) applied to the native French or Spanish settlers in Louisiana (*US*); (*usu* with *cap*) a colonial patois (French, Spanish, etc); (also **creolized** or **creolised language**) a language formerly a pidgin which has developed and become the accepted language of a region, *esp* in the W Indies. — *adj* (sometimes with *cap*) pertaining to a Creole or creole; of a type of W Indian cookery, *usu* including rice, okra, peppers and spices or strong seasoning. — *n* and *adj* **creō'lian** an earlier form of **creole**. — *n* **crē'ōlist** a person who studies creole languages. — *n* **crēōlizā'tion** or **-s-** the development of a pidgin into a creole. [Fr *créole*, from Sp *criollo*, dimin of *criado* nursling, from *criar* literally to create, hence to bring up, nurse, from L *creāre*]

creophagous *krē-of'ə-gəs*, *adj* flesh-eating, carnivorous. [Gr *kreas* flesh, and *phagein* to eat]

creosol *krē'ə-sol*, *n* one of the active consituents of creosote, an oily insoluble liquid with a characteristic smoky aroma.

creosote or **creasote** *krē'ə-sōt*, *n* an oily liquid obtained by destructive distillation of wood-tar, used as an antiseptic; a somewhat similar liquid got from coal-tar, used to preserve wood (also **creosote oil** or **coal-tar creosote**). — *vt* to treat with creosote. — **creosote plant** an American bush (*Larrea mexicana*) that has an odour of creosote and forms dense scrub. [Gr *kreas* flesh, *sōtēr* saviour, from *sōzein* to save]

crepance *krē'pəns*, *n* a wound on a horse's hind ankle-joint, caused by the shoe of the other hind-foot. [L *crepāre* to break]

crêpe or **crepe** *krāp* or *krep*, *n* any of several finely wrinkled fabrics similar to crape (qv); rubber rolled in thin crinkly sheets (**crêpe rubber**); (*usu* **crêpe**) a thin pancake. — *n* **crep'erie** a restaurant or eating establishment that specializes in pancakes with various fillings. — *n* **cre'piness**. — *n* **crep'oline** a light crape-like dress material. — *n* **crep'on** a thick crape-like fabric made of silk or nylon. — *adj* **crêp'y**, **crep'y** or **crep'ey** (*esp* of skin) wrinkled, crêpe-like, crape-like. — **crêpe-de-chine** (*də shēn*; also **crepe-**) a crape-like fabric, *orig* of silk; **crepe'hanger** see under **crape**; **crêpe paper** thin crinkled paper; **crêpe sole**. — *adj* **crêpe'-soled** (of shoes) having a sole of crêpe rubber. — **crêpe suzette** (*sü-zet*) a thin pancake in a hot orange- or lemon-flavoured sauce, *usu* flambéed: — *pl* **crêpes suzettes**. [See **crape**]

crepitate *krep'i-tāt*, *vi* to crackle, snap; to rattle; (of beetles) to discharge an offensive fluid. — *adj* **crep'itant** crackling. — *n* **crepitā'tion** the act of crepitating; crackling; a soft crackling sound detected through a stethoscope, and *usu* resulting from inflammation due to pneumonia or other disease. — *adj* **crep'itātive**. [L *crepitāre*, *-ātum*, frequentative of *crepāre* to crack, rattle]

crepitus *krep'i-təs*, (*med*) *n* the grating sound produced when an arthritic joint is moved or when a fractured bone is disturbed. [L, a creaking or rattling]

crept *krept*, *pa t* and *pa p* of **creep**.

crepuscular *kri-pus'kū-lər*, *adj* of or pertaining to twilight; dim, dark; (of certain animals) active, or appearing, at twilight. — Also **crepus'culous**. — *n* **crepuscule** (*krep'əs-kūl*, or *-ūs'*) or **crepuscle** (*krep'əs-l*, or *-us'*) twilight. [L *crepusculum* twilight

Cres. *abbrev*: Crescent (in street names).

cresc. (*music*) *abbrev*: crescendo.

crescendo *kresh-en'dō*, (*music*) *adj* and *adv* gradually increasing in loudness. — *n* an increase of loudness; a passage of increasing loudness; a high point, a climax (*fig*): — *pl* **crescen'dos**. — Also *vi*. [Ital, increasing]

crescent *kres'ənt* or *krez'*, *n* (more *usu* **the crescent moon**) the waxing moon; a curved shape like the moon in its first or last quarter; the Turkish (*orig* Byzantine) standard or emblem; the Turkish power; (a symbol of) the Muslim faith; a curved street or terrace; a crescent-shaped roll or bun, a croissant. — *adj* shaped like the waxing moon; increasing, growing (*formal*). — *n* **cresc'entade** a religious war for Islam. — *adj* **cresc'ented** or **crescentic** (*-ent'ik*) formed like a crescent. — *adj* **cresc'ive** (*formal*) increasing. [L *crēscere* to grow, pr p *crēscēns*, *-entis*]

crescograph *kres'kə-grāf*, *n* a sensitive instrument capable of measuring and recording the rate of growth of plants. [L *crēscere* to grow, and **-graph**]

cresol *krēs'ol*, *n* a compound ($C_6H_4(CH_3)OH$) found in tar and creosote, resembling phenol and used as an antiseptic and disinfectant. — Also called **cresylic acid**.

cress *kres*, *n* a name for many pungent-leaved cruciferous plants of various genera often used as a culinary garnish and in salads, eg *Lepidium* (garden cress), *Rorippa* (watercress), *Arabis* (rock cress); extended to other plants of similar character, such as Indian cress (*Tropaeolum*). [OE *cresse*, *cerse*; cf Du *kers*, Ger *Kresse*]

cresset *kres'it*, (*hist*) *n* an iron basket in which oil or pitch could be burned to provide light, *usu* placed on the top of a pole; a torch generally. [OFr *cresset*, *crasset* (Fr *creuset*), from ODu *kruysel* a hanging lamp]

crest *krest*, *n* the comb or tuft on the head of a cock or other bird; a long narrow ridge forming the summit of anything, as a roof-ridge or the top of a hill or wave; the mane of a horse, etc; a ridge along the surface of a bone (*anatom*); a plume of feathers or other ornament on the top of a helmet; an accessory figure *orig* surmounting the helmet in a coat of arms, also used separately as a device on personal effects (*heraldry*). — *vi* to culminate, reach a high point. — *vt* to surmount (a hill or wave). — *adj* **crest'ed** having a crest; having an elevated appendage like a crest (*bot*). — *adj* **crest'less** without a crest; not of high birth. — **crested tit** a European tit (*Parus cristatus*) which has a speckled black and white crest. — *adj* **crest'fallen** dejected or cast-down. — **on** (or **riding**) **the crest of a wave** enjoying a run of success. [OFr *creste* (Fr *crête*), from L *crista*]

creston *kres-ton'*, (*geol*) an outcrop. [Sp]

cresylic *krə-sil'ik*, (*chem*) *adj* of cresol or creosote. — **cresylic acid** cresol. [From *cre*sol with sfx *-yl* and sfx *-ic*]

cretaceous *kri-tā'shəs*, *adj* composed of or like chalk; (with *cap*) belonging to the uppermost system of the Secondary or Mesozoic rocks, including in England the Wealden, the Gault and Greensand, and the Chalk. — Also *n*. [L *crētāceus*, from *crēta* chalk]

Cretan *krē'tən* or **Cretic** *krē'tik*, *adj* belonging to Crete. — *n* a native or inhabitant of Crete. — *n* **crē'tic** (*prosody*) a metrical foot consisting of one short syllable between two long. — *n* **crē'tism** a lie. [Gr *krētikos*, from *Krētē* Crete]

cretin *kret'in* or *krēt'in*, *n* a child suffering from a congenital deficiency of thryoxine (thyroid hormone) which, if untreated, can lead to mental retardation and incomplete physical development; a person affected by these conditions as a result of such a deficiency; an idiot (*colloq*). — *n* **cret'inism**. — *vt* **cretinize** or **-ise**. — *adj* and *n* **cret'inoid**. — *adj* **cret'inous**. [Fr *crétin*, from L *christiānus* human creature]

cretonne *kret-on'* or *kret'on*, *n* a strong printed cotton fabric used for curtains or for covering furniture. [Fr, prob from *Creton* in Normandy]

Creutzfeldt-Jakob disease *kroits'felt yak'-ob diz-ēz*, *n* a rare degenerative condition of the brain thought to be caused by infection with a slow-acting virus, and characterized by diminishing muscle coordination, deterioration of the intellect and often blindness and loss of speech. [From H G *Creutzfeldt* (1885–1964), and A M *Jakob* (1884–1931), German psychiatrists]

creutzer. Same as **kreutzer**.

crevasse *kriv-as'*, *n* a crack or split, *esp* applied to a cleft in a glacier; a fissure in a river embankment (*US*). — *vt* to make a fissure in (a dyke, etc) (*US*). [Fr; cf **crevice**]

crève-cœur *krev-kœr*, (*Fr*) *n* heartbreak.

crevette *krə-vet'*, (*Fr*) *n* a shrimp or prawn.

crevice *krev'is*, *n* a narrow crack or split, *esp* in a rock. [OFr *crevace*, from L *crepāre* to creak, break]

crew[1] *kroo͞*, *n* a gang; a ship's company; the oarsmen or oarswomen (and cox, where appropriate) of a racing boat; a group or team of people with individual duties in charge of a bus, train or aeroplane. — *vi* to act as a crew member on a ship, etc (*esp* with *for*). — **crew bus** a commercial vehicle with seating for several people, used *esp* for transporting workmen to and from their place of work; **crew cut** a style of haircut in which the hair is cut so close to the head that it stands upright; **crew neck** a round, close-fitting style of neck on a jersey (*adj* **crew'-necked**). [OFr *creue* increase, from *croistre* to grow]

crew[2] *kroo͞*, *pa t* of **crow**.

crewe *kroo͞*, (*archaic*) *n* a pot. [OFr *crue*]

crewel *kroo͞'əl*, *n* a fine worsted yarn used for embroidery and tapestry; embroidery or tapestry work in which crewels are used. — *vt* to work in crewel. — *n* **crew'elist**. — *n* **crew'ellery**. — *n* **crew'elwork**. [Orig a monosyllable, *crule*, *crewle*; ety uncertain]

crewels, **cruells** or **cruels** *kroo͞'əlz*, (*archaic Scot*) *n pl* the king's evil, scrofula. [Fr *écrouelles*]

criant *krī'ənt* or *krē-ã*, *adj* garish, discordantly coloured. [Fr]

crib *krib*, *n* a child's bed, *usu* with slatted sides, a cot (*esp US*); a manger or container for animal fodder; a representation, *esp* a model, of the scene around the manger that served as a bed for the newborn Christ; a stall for oxen; a rudimentary dwelling; a country cottage (*NZ*); a small confined space; a brothel (*slang*); a container for grain; a wickerwork basket; a timber framework for a dam, a pier foundation, a mine-shaft lining, etc (also **crib'work**); a pilfering, or the thing pilfered; an act of stealing, or something stolen, from another's work, a plagiarism; a key or baldly literal translation, used as an aid by students, etc; the discarded cards at cribbage, used by the dealer in scoring. — *vt* to put in a crib; to confine; to steal (another's work), to plagiarize: — *pr p* **cribb'ing**; *pa t* and *pa p* **cribbed**. — **crib'-biting** (in horses) a harmful habit of seizing the edge of the crib or manger in the teeth, often accompanied by the swallowing of air (wind-sucking); **crib death** (*NAm*) cot death; **crib'work** see **crib** above. [OE *crib*; Ger *Krippe*]

cribbage *krib'ij*, *n* a card game in which each player discards a certain number of cards for the *crib*, and scores by holding certain combinations and by bringing the sum of the values of cards played to certain numbers. — **cribb'age-board** a scoring-board for cribbage, with holes for pegs. [*crib* discarded cards; see under **crib**]

cribble *krib'l*, *n* a coarse screen or sieve used for sand, gravel or corn; coarse flour or meal (*obs*). — *vt* to sift or riddle (*obs*); (in engraving) to produce a dotted or punctured effect. — *adj* **cribb'led**. — *adj* **cribell'ar**. — *n* **cribell'um** a sieve-like spinning-organ of certain spiders: — *pl* **cribell'a**. — *adj* **criblé** (*Fr*; *krē-blā*; *engraving*) punctured like a sieve, dotted. — *adj* **crib'rāte** (or *krīb'*), **crib'rose** or **crib'rous** perforated like a sieve. — *n* **cribrā'tion** sifting. — *adj* **crib'riform** (*anatom* and *bot*) perforated, sieve-like. [L *crībrum*, dimin *crībellum* a sieve]

cribellar, **criblé**, **cribrate**, etc. See under **cribble**.

cricetid *krī-sē'tid*, *n* a member of the *Cricetidae*, a family of rodents including the hamsters. [New L, from Slav name for hamster]

crick[1] *krik*, *n* a spasm or cramp of the muscles, *esp* of the neck. — *vt* to produce or cause a crick in. [Prob imit]

crick[2] *krik*, (*NAm dialect*) *n* a creek.

cricket[1] *krik'it*, *n* a jumping insect of the family *Gryllidae*, related to the grasshopper and locust, the male of which makes a chirping sound by rubbing its forewings together. [OFr *criquet*; cf Du and LGer *krekel*]

cricket[2] *krik'it*, *n* an outdoor game played by two teams of eleven players on a large field with two wickets (22 yards apart) near the centre, in which batsmen from one team attempt to defend the wickets and score the maximum number of runs (by hitting a hard leather ball) without being bowled, caught or run out by members of the opposing team. — *vi* to play cricket. — *n* **crick'eter**. — *n* and *adj* **crick'eting**. — **not cricket** (*colloq*) not fair and sporting. [Fr *criquet* goalpost]

cricket[3] *krik'it*, (*now dialect*) *n* a low stool. — **cricket table** a small low table with a circular foldable top on a triangular base. [Ety unknown]

crickey, **cricky**. See **crikey**.

cricoid *krī'koid*, (*anatom*) *adj* ring-shaped. — *n* a ring-shaped cartilage forming the wall of the larynx. [Gr *krikoeides*, from *krikos* a ring, and *eidos* form]

cri de cœur *krē də kœr*, (*Fr*) *n* a cry from the heart, a heartfelt, passionate entreaty, complaint or reproach.

cri du chat (syndrome) *krē dü shä* (*sin'drōm*), *n* a rare, often fatal, congenital condition, so called because underdevelopment of the larynx results in a cat-like cry, and caused by the absence of a particular chromosome in all the body cells. [Fr]

cried, **crier**, **cries**. See **cry**.

crikey *krīk'i*, **cricky** or **crickey** *krik'i*, (*slang*) *interj* a mild oath or expression of surprise. [Euphemism for *Christ*]

crim *krim*, (*colloq*) *n* short for criminal.

crim. con. (*law*) *abbrev*: criminal conversation.

crime *krīm*, *n* a violation of law, *esp* if serious; an act punishable by law; such acts collectively or in the abstract; an act of serious moral wrongdoing; sin; something deplorable (*colloq*). — *vt* (*military*) to charge or convict of an infraction of regulations. — *adj* **crime'ful** criminal. — *adj* **crime'less** without crime, innocent. — *adj* **criminal** (*krim'*) relating to crime; guilty of crime; violating the law. — *n* a person who is guilty of crime. — *n* **criminalēse'** criminals' slang. — *n* **crim'inalist** a person versed in criminal law. — *n* **criminal'ity** the condition of being a criminal; guiltiness. — *n* **criminalīzā'tion** or **-s-**. — *vt* **crim'inalize** or **-ise** to declare someone or something criminal; to make illegal. — *adv* **crim'inally**. — *vt* **crim'inate** to accuse. — *n* **criminā'tion** the act of criminating; accusation. — *adj* **crim'inative** or **crim'inatory** involving crimination. — *adj* **criminogen'ic** causing crime. — *n* **criminol'ogist**. — *n* **criminol'ogy** the science and study of crime and criminals. — *adj* **crim'inous** criminal, chiefly in the ecclesiastical phrase *a criminous clerk*. — *n* **crim'inousness**. — **crime prevention** measures taken to deter or prevent criminal acts, *esp* those safeguards advocated by a police **crime prevention officer** to prevent theft, burglary, etc; **crime sheet** (*military*) a record of offences against regulations; **crime wave** a sharp rise in the level of criminal activity (see **wave**); **criminal conversation** (*law*; abbrev **crim. con.**) adultery; formerly, an action in which a husband could claim damages against the adulterer; **criminal court** a court in which those accused of criminal offences are tried (cf **civil court**); **criminal law** the body of law dealing with criminal offences, offenders and punishment; **criminal lawyer**. [Fr, from L *crīmen*, *-inis*]

crimen *krī'men* or *krē'men*, (*L*) *n* a crime: — *pl* **cri'mina**. — **crimen falsi** (*fal'sī*, *fal'sē*) the crime (or charge) of perjury; **crimen laesae majestatis** (*lē'sē maj-əs-tā'tis* or *lī'sī ma-yes-tä'tis*) high treason.

crime passionel *krēm pa-syo-nel*, (*Fr*) *n* a crime committed from (sexual) passion.

criminal, **criminologist**, etc. See under **crime**.

crimine or **crimini** *krim'i-ni*, (*archaic*) *interj* an ejaculation of surprise or impatience. [Perh from *Christ*; see **crikey**]

crimmer. See **krimmer**.

crimp *krimp*, *vt* to press into folds, flutes or ridges; to put tight waves or curls into (the hair) with curling tongs; to bend (eg metal) into shape; to thwart or hinder (*NAm*). — *n* a curl or wave; a bend or crease; a hindering factor (*NAm*). — *n* **crimp'er** a person who or device that crimps or corrugates; a hairdresser (*slang*). — *vt* **crimp'le** to curl, wrinkle or crumple. — *adj* **crimp'y**. — **crimp'ing-iron** an iron instrument used for crimping hair, fabric, etc; **crimp'ing-machine** a machine for forming crimps. [OE *gecrympan* to curl; cf **cramp**, and Du *krimpen* to shrink]

Crimplene® *krim'plēn*, *n* (a grease-resistant, synthetic fabric made from) a thick polyester yarn.

crimson *krim'zn*, *n* a deep red colour, tinged with blue; red in general. — *adj* deep red. — *vt* to dye crimson. — *vi* to become crimson; to blush. [ME *crimosin*, from OFr *cramoisin*; from Ar *qirmizī* scarlet, from *qirmiz* kermes, from which it is made]

crinal *krī'nəl*, *adj* of or belonging to the hair. — *adj* **crīn'ate** or **crīn'ated** having hair. — *adj* **crīnig'erous** hairy. — *adj* **crīnicul'tural** relating to the culture or growth of the hair. — *adj* **crī'nose** hairy. [L *crīnis* the hair]

crine *krīn*, (*Scot*) *vi* to shrink or shrivel. [Gaelic *crìon* dry]

cringe *krinj*, *vi* to stoop in a servile manner; to cower in fear; to behave timidly or obsequiously; to fawn or to flatter with mean servility; (loosely) to wince or flinch. — *n* a servile obeisance. — *n* **cringe'ling** or **crin'ger** a person who cringes. — *n* and *adj* **crin'ging**. — *adv* **crin'gingly** in an obsequious manner. — **cringe'-making** (*colloq*) embarrassing, sickening, excruciating. [Related to OE *crincan*, *cringan* to shrink; cf **crank**[1]]

cringle *kring'gl, n* a small piece of rope worked into the bolt-rope of a sail, and containing a metal ring or thimble. [LGer *Kringel* little ring]

crinicultural, crinigerous. See **crinal**.

crinite[1] *krī'nīt, adj* hairy; having or resembling a tuft of hair (*bot*). [See **crinal**]

crinite[2] *krī'nīt, n* an encrinite or fossil crinoid. [See **crinoid**]

crinkle *kringk'l, vt* to twist, wrinkle, crimp. — *vi* to wrinkle up, curl. — *n* a wrinkle; a virus disease of strawberry plants, transmitted by aphids; (also **crink'ly**) paper money, money in general (*slang*). — *adj* **crink'ly** wrinkly. — *n* (*slang*) an old person. — **crinkle-crank'le** (*dialect*) (something) winding or zigzag; **crinkum-crank'um** a whimsical term for something that is full of intricate twists and turns. [Related to OE *crincan*; see **cringe**]

crinoid *krin'oid* or *krī'noid, n* a primitive echinoderm of the class *Crinoidea*, with cup-shaped body and branching arms, including the feather-star, sea lily and numerous fossil forms. — Also adj. — *adj* **crinoid'al** shaped like a lily. [Gr *krinoeides* like a lily]

crinoline *krin'ə-lin, -lēn, n orig* a stiff fabric of horsehair and flax used to distend women's skirts; a hooped petticoat or skirt made to project all round by means of steel wire; a netting round ships as a guard against torpedoes. — *n* **crinolette'** a small crinoline causing the dress to project behind only. — *adj* **crin'olined**. [Fr, from *crin*, from L *crinis* hair, and *lin*, from L *linum* flax]

crinose. See **crinal**.

crinum *krī'nəm, n* any of various plants of the Amaryllis family, characterized by luxuriant clusters of lily-like flowers. [Gr *krinon* a lily]

criollo *krē-ōl'ō, n* a Latin American native of European, *esp* Spanish, blood; any of several S American breeds of animal; the name given to a fine variety of cocoa: — *pl* **crioll'os**. [Sp, native, indigenous; see **creole**]

crio-sphinx *krī'ō-sfingks, n* a ram-headed sphinx. [Gr *krīos* a ram, and *sphinx* a sphinx]

cripes *krīps*, (*slang*) *interj* an expression of surprise or worry. [Euphemism for *Christ*]

cripple *krip'l, n* a lame person; a person damaged, disabled or deficient in some way, as an *emotional cripple*; a bracket attached to a ladder on the ridge of a roof to support scaffold boards. — *adj* lame. — *vt* to make lame, to disable; to impair, undermine or curtail with disastrous effect. — *adj* **cripp'led**. — *n* **cripp'ling** a prop set up as a support against the side of a building. [OE *crypel*; connected with **creep**]

crise *krēz, n* a peak of emotional distress, an emotional crisis: — *pl* **crises** (*krēz*). — **crise de conscience** (*də-kɔ̃-syãs*) a crisis of conscience, a moral dilemma; **crise de foi** (*də-fwä*) an attack of doubt, distrust or disillusionment; **crise de nerfs** (*də-ner*) an attack of nerves, hysterics. [Fr]

crisis *krī'sis, n* a crucial or decisive moment; a turning-point, eg in a disease; a time of difficulty or distress; an emergency: — *pl* **crises** (*krī'sēz*). [Gr *krisis* a decision, judgement, from *krīnein* to decide]

crisp *krisp, adj* curling closely; so dry as to break or crumble easily, brittle; (of pastry) short; (of weather) fresh and bracing, *esp* when frosty; firm, the opposite of limp or flabby; (of wording) neat, terse, well-turned; (of manner) firm, decisive, authoritative. — *vt* and *vi* to make or become crisp. — *n* (*usu* in *pl*) a thin slice of potato fried until crisp, a potato-crisp; any piece of food fried or roasted until crisp. — *adj* **crisp'āte** (*bot* and *zool*) having a wavy edge. — *n* **crispā'tion** the state of being curled; a ripple or slight wave, as on the surface of water; a creeping or rippling sensation caused by a slight muscle contraction. — *n* **crisp'er** anything that crisps; a compartment in a refrigerator in which to keep lettuce, etc fresh. — *adv* **crisp'ly**. — *n* **crisp'ness**. — *adj* **crisp'y**. — **crisp'bread** a brittle, unsweetened type of biscuit of rye or wheat, *usu* eaten as a substitute for bread. [OE, from L *crispus* curled, wrinkled]

crispin *kris'pin, n* a poetic name for a shoemaker, from *Crispin* of Soissons, the patron saint of shoemakers, martyred 25 October 287.

criss-cross *kris'-kros, n* a network of crossing lines; the Latin cross at the beginning of the alphabet on a hornbook (see **criss-cross-row** under **Christ**); a mark formed by two lines in the form of a cross, as the signature of a person unable to write his or her name; a game of noughts and crosses (*esp NAm*). — *adj* and *adv* crosswise; consisting of a network of crossed lines. — *vt* and *vi* to cross repeatedly. [From **christ-cross**]

crissum *kris'əm, n* the area surrounding a bird's cloaca, including the under-tail feathers: — *pl* **criss'a**. [L *crissāre* to move the thighs sensuously]

crista *kris'tə, n* a crest; a ridge or fold resembling a crest, eg in the inner membrane of a mitochondrion (*biol*): — *pl* **cris'tae** (*-ē*). — *adj* **crist'ate** crested. — *adj* **crist'iform**. [L]

cristobalite *kris-tō'bəl-īt, n* one of the principal forms of silica, produced from quartz at high temperatures, occurring in volcanic rocks, slags, etc. [Cerro San *Cristóbal* in Mexico, where it was discovered]

crit *krit*, (*colloq*) *n* short for **criticism**.

crit. *abbrev*: critical.

criterion *krī-tē'ri-ən, n* a means or standard of judging; a test; a rule, standard or canon: — *pl* **critē'ria**. — *adj* **crite'rion-referenced** (of an examination or assessment) judging examinees on the basis of their demonstrated mastery of certain skills and abilities (rather than by comparison with the achievements of their peers; cf **norm-referenced**). — **crite'rion referencing**. [Gr *kritērion*, from *kritēs* a judge]

crith *krith*, (*phys*) *n* a unit of mass, that of 1 litre of hydrogen at standard temperature and pressure, ie 89.88mg. [Gr *krīthē* barleycorn, a small weight]

crithidial *krith-id'i-əl*, (*zool*) *adj* of, pertaining to or resembling the flagellate genus *Crithidia*, particularly applied to a stage in the life-cycle of certain trypanosomes.

crithomancy *krith'ō-man-si, n* divination by strewing meal over sacrificial animals. [Gr *krīthē* barley, and *manteiā* divination]

critic *krit'ik, n* someone who assesses the quality of something, a judge; a professional reviewer of literature, art, drama or music; a person skilled in textual studies and the ascertainment of the original words where readings differ; a fault-finder. — *adj* **crit'ical** at or relating to a turning-point, transition or crisis; decisive, crucial; (loosely) seriously ill; relating to criticism; rigorously discriminating; captious; of a condition in which a chain reaction is self-sustaining (*phys*). — *adv* **crit'ically**. — *n* **crit'icalness** or **critical'ity**. — *n* **crit'icaster** a petty critic (see **-aster**). — *n* **crit'icism** the art of judging, *esp* in literature or the fine arts; a critical judgment or observation. — *adj* **criticizable** or **-isable** (*-sīz'*). — *vt* **crit'icize** or **-ise** to analyse and pass judgment on; to find fault with, to censure. — **critical angle** the smallest possible angle of incidence at which a light ray is totally reflected; **critical apparatus** see **apparatus criticus**; **critical coupling** (*elec eng*) the coupling giving maximum energy transfer between two circuits or systems tuned to the same frequency; **critical damping** (*phys*) the minimum amount of damping that results in an oscillatory electric circuit or mechanical system sufficient to prevent free oscillation; **critical mass** (*nuc eng*) the minimum amount of fissile material needed to sustain a chain reaction; **critical philosophy** that of Kant which is based on a critical examination of the foundations of knowledge; **critical temperature** that temperature above which a gas cannot be liquefied by pressure alone. — **critical path analysis** the working out with the aid of a computer the sequence of operations that must be followed in order to complete a complex piece of work in the minimum time. [Gr *kritikos*, from *krīnein* to judge]

critique *kri-tēk, n* (the art of) criticism; a critical estimate of a work of literature, art, etc; a critical dissertation or review. — *vt* to discuss or analyse critically. [Fr, from Gr *kritikē* (*technē*) the art of criticism]

critter or **crittur** *krit'ər*, (*dialect* and *colloq*; now *esp US*) *n* a creature; an animal.

crivens or **crivvens** *kriv'ənz*, (*Scots slang*) *interj* an exclamation expressing amazement or dismay. [Perh from *Christ* combined with *heavens*]

croak *krōk*, *vi* (of eg a frog or raven) to utter a low hoarse sound; to speak similarly hoarsely; to grumble or talk dismally; to die (*slang*). — *vt* to utter (words) hoarsely; to kill (*esp NAm slang*). — *n* the sound or a sound similar to that of a frog or raven. — *n* **croak'er** an animal or bird that croaks; a grumbler; any of several types of tropical seafish of the Sciaenidae family that emit croaking noises. — *adv* **croak'ily**. — *n* **croak'ing**. — *adj* **croak'y**. [Imit]

Croat *krō'at*, *n* a native or inhabitant of Croatia, in the former Yugoslavia; the language of Croatia. — Also *adj*. — *adj* **Croatian** (*-ā'shən*) belonging to Croatia or its people. — *n* a Croat; the Croat language. [Serbo-Croatian *Hrvat*]

croc *krok*, (*colloq*) *n* short for **crocodile**.

croceate, **croceous**. See **crocus**[1].

crocein *krō'si-in*, *n* one of a group of red and yellow artificial dyes. [L *croceus* yellow]

croche *krōch*, *n* a knob at the top of a deer's horn. [Fr]

crochet *krō'shā*, *n* decorative work consisting of intertwined loops, executed in wool or thread with a small hook. — *vi* and *vt* to work in crochet: — *pr p* **crocheting** (*krō'shā-ing*); *pa t* and *pa p* **crocheted** (*krō'shād*). — *n* **cro'cheting** the action of crochet. — *n* crochetwork. [Fr *crochet*, from *croche*, *croc* a hook]

crocidolite *krō-sid'ə-līt*, *n* a fibrous mineral consisting mainly of silicate of iron and sodium, called *blue asbestos*; in S Africa also a golden alteration product or pseudomorph of this mineral, consisting largely of quartz. [From Gr *krokis*, *-idos* nap of cloth, and *lithos* stone]

crock[1] *krok*, *n* a pot or jar; a potsherd. — *adj* **crocked** (*NAm slang*) drunk. — *n* **crock'ery** earthenware; all types of domestic pottery. [OE *croc*; Ger *Krug*; perh of Celtic origin, as in Welsh *crochan* a pot, Gaelic *crogan* a pitcher]

crock[2] *krok*, (*dialect*) *n* dirt, smut. — *vt* to fill or cover with dirt or smut. [Origin doubtful]

crock[3] *krok*, (*colloq*) *n* a broken down or decrepit person or thing. — *vi* to break down (often with *up*). — *vt* to disable. [Cf Norw and Swed *krake* a poor beast]

crockery. See **crock**[1].

crocket *krok'it*, (*archit*) *n* an ornament on the sloping sides of a pediment, pinnacle, etc, *usu* like curled leaves or flowers. [See **croquet**]

crocodile *krok'ə-dīl*, *n* a large long-tailed tropical reptile of the genus *Crocodilus* (order *Crocodilia*), with powerful tapering jaws and a thick skin covered with bony plates; sometimes extended to the order *Loricata* including alligators and gavials; leather from crocodile skin; a double file of school pupils taking a walk. — *adj* and *n* **crocodilian** (*-dil'*). — **crocodile bird** an African bird (*Pluvianus aegyptius*) said to pick the crocodile's teeth or take leeches from its throat; **crocodile clip** a clip for making electrical connections, with serrated jaws that interlock; **crocodile tears** hypocritical grief, from the old story that crocodiles (which have large lachrymal glands) shed tears over the hard necessity of killing animals for food. [L *crocodīlus*, from Gr *krokodeilos* a lizard]

crocosmia *krə-koz'mi-ə*, *n* any tridaceous plant of the genus *Crocosmia*, including monbretia, typically bearing orange or yellow flowers in late summer. [Gr *krokos* crocus, and *osmē* smell]

crocus[1] *krō'kəs*, *n* a bulbous iridaceous plant with brilliant yellow, purple or white flowers: — *pl* **cro'cuses**. — *adj* **croceate** (*krō'si-āt*; *obs*) or **croceous** (*krō'shi-əs*) saffron-coloured. — *n* **crocoite** (*krō'kō-īt*) or **crocoisite** (*krō'*, or *-kō'*) a bright red mineral, lead chromate. [L *crocus*, from Gr *krokos*; prob of Eastern origin; cf Heb *karkom* and Ar *kurkum* saffron]

crocus[2] *krō'kəs*, (*slang*) *n* a quack doctor.

Croesus *krē'səs*, *n* a very rich man. [*Croesus*, king of Lydia, of fabulous wealth]

croft *kroft*, *n* a small piece of arable land, in Scotland *esp* adjoining a dwelling; a small farm. — *n* **croft'er** someone who runs or farms a croft. — *n* **croft'ing**. [OE *croft*; perh cognate with Du *kroft* hillock]

Crohn's disease *krōnz diz-ēz'*, *n* a chronic medical condition involving severe inflammation of the gastro-intestinal tract, particularly the ileum, and causing scarring and thickening of the bowel wall. [B *Crohn* (1884–1983), US physician]

croissant *krwä'sã*, *n* a crescent-shaped bread-roll made with a large quantity of butter and having a flaky consistency. [Fr]

croix de guerre *krwä də ger*, (*Fr*) *n* a military decoration for bravery in action.

cromack. Same as **crummock**, **crummack**.

Cro-Magnon *krō-mag'nən* or *krō-man'yɔ̃*, *adj* pertaining to an early type of *Homo sapiens*, long-skulled but short-faced, of late Palaeolithic times. [From *Cro-Magnon*, in Dordogne, where the first skulls of this type were found]

crombie *krom'bi*, *n* a woollen cloth manufactured in Aberdeen, used for overcoats, etc; a garment made from such cloth.

crome or **cromb** *krōm*, *kro͞om*, (*dialect*) *n* a hook or crook. — *vt* to draw with a crome. [Cf Du *kram*]

cromlech, *krom'lehh* or *-lek*, *n* a prehistoric stone circle; formerly applied to a dolmen. [Welsh *cromlech*, from *crom* curved, circular, and *llech* a stone]

cromorna or **cromorne** *krō-mörn'*(*ə*), *n* a krummhorn; a krummhorn stop. [Fr *cromorne*, from Ger *Krummhorn*]

Cromwellian *krom-wel'i-ən*, *adj* of or relating to Oliver *Cromwell*, Puritan and Lord Protector of the Commonwealth (1653–8). — *n* a supporter of Cromwell; a settler in Ireland in the settlement of 1652; a chair of plain design with leather seat and back, said to have been popularized by the Puritans.

crone *krōn*, *n* an old woman (*derog*); an old ewe. [Perh OFr *carogne* carrion, hag, directly or through Du]

cronet *krō'net*, (*obs*) *n* the hair growing over the top of a horse's hoof. **[coronet]**

cronk *krongk*, (*Austr colloq*) *adj* ill; of poor quality; fraudulent. [From **crank**[1]]

crony *krōn'i*, *n* an intimate companion. — *n* **crō'nyism** (*colloq*) the appointment of friends to well-paid posts regardless of their fitness for these posts. [Said to be orig university slang, from Gr *chronios* long-continued, perennial]

croodle[1] *kro͞od'l*, (*Scot*) *vi* to cower down, snuggle. [Origin unknown]

croodle[2] *kro͞od'l* or *kro͝od'l*, (*Scot*) *vi* to murmur like a dove. [Imit]

crook *kro͝ok*, *n* a bend, or something bent; a staff bent at the end, as a shepherd's or bishop's; a professional swindler, thief or criminal in general; a curved tube used to lower the pitch of a wind instrument; a curved tube carrying the mouthpiece of a bassoon; a gibbet (*obs*). — *adj* (*Austr* and *NZ colloq*) ill; unfair; wrong, dubious; inferior; nasty, unpleasant. — *vt* and *vi* to bend or form into a hook. — *adj* **crook'ed** bent like a crook; containing an angle or series of angles; twisted, contorted; not straight, tipped at an angle; dishonest or illegal (*colloq*); (often *kro͝okt*) angry with (with *on*) (*Austr* and *NZ*). — *adv* **crook'edly**. — *n* **crook'edness**. — **crook'back** (*Shakesp*) a hunchback. — *adj* **crook'-backed**. — **go crook** (*Austr colloq*) to lose one's temper; **go crook on** or **at** (*Austr* and *NZ colloq*) to upbraid, rebuke. [Prob ON *krōkr* hook; cf Swed *krok*, Dan *krog*]

Crookes glass *kro͝oks gläs*, *n* a type of glass that inhibits the passage of ultraviolet light, used in sunglasses, etc; **Crookes tube** (*phys*) a sealed, evacuated tube in which stratification in electric discharges can be observed. [Sir William *Crookes* (1832–1919), British scientist]

croon *kro͞on*, (*Scot krün*) *vi* to sing or hum in an undertone. — *vt* and *vi* to sing softly in a sentimentally contemplative manner. — Also *n*. — *n* **croon'er**. — *n* **croon'ing**. [Cf Du *kreunen* to groan]

crop *krop*, *n* a hunting whip with loop instead of lash; an end cut off; an act or mode of cutting; a style of cutting or wearing short hair; the total quantity produced, cut or harvested; the total growth or produce; a cultivated plant, collectively; a number, quantity (of products, ideas, etc) produced or appearing at a time, a supply; a season's yield; the craw, a dilatation of a bird's oesophagus; a similar structure in another animal; a finial (*archit*); an outcrop. — *vt* to cut off the top, ends, margins or loose parts of; to cut short; to mow, reap or gather; (*esp* of grazing animals) to bite off in eating; to raise crops on; to cut the hair of. — *vi* to yield a crop; to come to the surface (with *up* or *out*); hence, to come (up) casually, as in conversation: — *pr p* **cropp'ing**; *pa t* and *pa p* **cropped**. — *n* **crop'ful** as much as a bird's crop can hold: — *pl* **crop'fuls**. — *adj* **cropfull'** satiated, filled to repletion. — *n* **cropp'er** someone or something that crops; a plant that yields a crop; a person who raises a crop in exchange for a share of it (also **share cropper**); a kind of pigeon noted for its large crop; a small platen printing machine; a fall (*colloq*); a failure (*colloq*). — *n* **cropp'ing** the act of cutting off; the raising of crops; an outcrop (*geol*). — *n* **cropp'y** one of the Irish rebels of 1798 who cut their hair short, like the French Revolutionists. — *adj* **crop'bound** (of birds) suffering from impaction of the crop. — **crop circle** a swirled or flattened circle in a field of arable crop, *orig* thought to be a natural phenomenon caused by particular meteorological conditions on an undulating landscape but in most instances now proved to be man-made as a hoax (also called **corn circle**); **crop'duster** an aircraft that sprays crops from the air with fungicides or insecticides; the pilot of such an aircraft; **crop'-dusting**; **crop'-ear** (*obs*) a person, horse, dog, etc with cropped ears. — *adj* **crop'-eared** (of a person, horse, dog, etc) having the ears cropped; (of a Puritan) having hair cropped to show the ears (used by Cavaliers as jibe). — **crop'land** land used for growing crops; **crop'-marks** (*archaeol*) variations in the depth or colour of a crop growing in a field, which, viewed from the air, can show the presence of a structure beneath the soil. — **come a cropper** (*colloq*) to have a fall, perhaps from the phrase *neck and crop*. [OE *crop* the top shoot of a plant, the crop of a bird; Du *crop* a bird's crop]

croquante *krok-ãt*, (*cookery*) *n* a crisp pie or tart; a crisp cake containing almonds. [Fr]

croque-monsieur *krok mə-syø*, (*Fr*) *n* a type of toasted sandwich filled with ham and cheese.

croquet *krō'kā*, *n* a game in which wooden balls are driven by means of long-handled mallets, through a series of hoops. — *vt* to drive away by striking another ball in contact. [Northern Fr *croquet*, a dialect form of *crochet*, dimin of *croc*, *croche* a crook]

croquette *krō-ket'*, *n* a ball or cylindrical cake, *usu* of minced and seasoned meat, fish or potato, coated in breadcrumbs and fried. [Fr, from *croquer* to crunch]

croquis *kro-kē*, (*Fr*) *n* an outline or rough sketch.

crore *krōr* or *krör*, (*Anglo-Ind*) *n* (*esp* of rupees) ten million, or one hundred lakhs. [Hindi *karo*]

crosier or **crozier** *krō'z(h)yər*, *n* the pastoral staff or crook of a bishop or abbot; (*erroneously*) an archbishop's cross; the coiled growing tip of a young plant, *esp* a fern. — *adj* **cro'siered**. [ME *crose* or *croce*, from LL *crocia* a crook]

cross *kros*, *n* a gibbet on which the Romans exposed criminals, typically consisting of two pieces of timber, one placed transversely to the other; (with *cap*) the particular one on which Christ suffered; (with *cap*) the symbol of the Christian religion, or of the crusades; a representation of Christ's cross; any object, figure or mark formed by two parts or lines transverse to each other, with or without elaboration; such a mark used instead of a signature by an illiterate person; such a mark used to symbolize a kiss in a letter, etc, or as an indicator of location, intersection or error; a staff surmounted by a cross; a monument not always in the form of a cross, where proclamations are made, etc; a place in a town or village where such a monument stands or stood; a cross-shaped pendant or medal; the transverse part of an anchor, or the like; a surveyor's cross-staff; a crossing or crossway; anything that crosses or thwarts; adversity or affliction in general, or a burden or cause of suffering, as in *bear one's cross*; mixing of breeds, hybridization; a hybrid; something intermediate in character between two other things; unfairness or dishonest practices, *esp* in sport where a contestant corruptly allows himself or herself to be beaten; a game or race lost by collusion or which has been rigged; the obverse of a coin, formerly often stamped with a cross (*obs*); hence, a coin (*archaic*); a transverse pass, *esp* towards the opposing team's goal (*football*, etc). — *adj* lying across or crosswise; transverse; oblique; adverse; interchanged; peevish; angry, displeased (with); hybrid; dishonest; balancing, neutralizing. — *adv* and *prep* across. — *vt* to mark with a cross; to make the sign of the cross over; to set something, or draw a line, across; to set in position athwart the mast (*naut*); to place crosswise; to cancel by drawing cross lines; to pass from one side to the other of; to pass transversely, *esp* in the direction of the opposing team's goal (*football*); to extend across; to interbreed; to draw two lines across (a cheque), thereby restricting it to payment through a bank; to obstruct; to thwart; to annoy; to confront (*archaic*); to bestride. — *vi* to lie or pass across; to meet and pass; (of two reciprocal letters) to be in the postal system simultaneously, each having been posted before the other is received; (of telephone lines) to connect and interfere with each other causing callers on one line to hear conversations on another; to interbreed: — *pa t* and *pa p* **crossed**. — *adj* **crossed**. — *n* **cross'ing** the act of making the sign of the cross; the act of going across; a place where a roadway, etc, may be crossed; an intersection, *esp* of transepts and nave in a church; an act of thwarting; cross-breeding. — *adj* **cross'ing**. — *adj* **cross'ish**. — *n* **cross'let** a small cross. — *adv* **cross'ly**. — *n* **cross'ness**. — *adv* **cross'wise** across; in the form of a cross (*archaic*). — **cross action** (*law*) an action brought by the defender against the pursuer; **cross aisle** (*obs*) a transept; **cross-and-pile'** (or **-or-**) (*archaic*) heads or tails; a toss-up. — *adj* **cross'-armed** having the arms crossed. — **cross assembler** (*comput*) an assembler that runs on one computer, producing a machine code for a different computer. — *adj* **crossband'ed** (of a handrail) having the grain of the veneer run across that of the rail. — **cross'band**, **cross'banding**; **cross'bar** a horizontal bar, eg on a man's bicycle or across a pair of goal posts; a kind of lever. — *adj* **cross'barred**. — **crossbar switch** (*electronics*) a switch having two sets of paths, one vertical and one horizontal, with an electromagnetically operated means of connecting any path in the one set with any path in the other; **crossbar switching** using a crossbar switch system; **cross'beam** a large beam stretching across a building and serving to hold its sides together; **cross'bearer** a person who carries a cross in a procession; **cross bedding** (*geol*) another term for **false bedding**; **cross'bench** a bench laid crosswise; a bench on which independent or neutral members of the House of Commons or the House of Lords sit. — *adj* independent; impartial. — **cross'-bencher**; **cross bill** a bill brought by the defendant in a Chancery suit against the plaintiff; **cross'bill** a finch of the genus *Loxia* with mandibles crossing near the points. — *vt* **cross'bite** (*archaic*) to bite in return; to cheat in return; to outwit; to entrap. — **cross'bones** a figure of two thigh-bones laid across each other, forming with the skull a conventional emblem of death or piracy; **cross'bow** a weapon for shooting bolts, formed of a bow placed crosswise on a stock; **cross'-bower** or **cross'bowman**. — *adj* **cross'bred**. — **cross'-breed** a breed produced by crossing two distinct breeds; the offspring of such a cross; **cross'breeding**; **cross'buck** (*NAm*) a cross-shaped sign placed at a level crossing to warn motorists; **cross bun** see **hot cross bun**; **cross-butt'ock** a throw in which the hip is used to unbalance one's opponent in wrestling. — *vt* **cross'-check** to test the accuracy of eg a statement or piece of information by consulting various other sources of information; (in ice hockey) to check (one's opponent) illegally by hitting his upper body or stick. — Also *vi* and *n*. — **cross'claim** a claim made by the defendant against the plaintiff; **cross compiler** (*comput*) a compiler that runs on one computer, producing a machine code for a different computer; **cross correspondence** (*psychical research*) fitting together of communications separately unintelligible to give an intelligible whole. — *adj* and *adv* **cross'-coun'try** through fields, woods, over hills, etc, rather than by road, *esp* (of running, skiing, etc) over a long distance. — **cross-cross'let** a cross with a smaller cross at each of its ends. — *adj* **cross-cul'tural** pertaining to the differences between cultures; bridging the gap between cultures. — **cross'-current** (in the air, sea, or a river) a current flowing across the main current; **cross'cut** a transverse cut or course; a short way across from one point to another. — *adj* cutting transversely or across the grain. — *vt* (*-kut'*) to cut across. — **crosscut saw** a large saw worked by two men, one at each end, for cutting timber across the grain; **cross'cutting** (*cinema* and *TV*) cutting and fitting together film sequences so that in the finished picture the action moves from one scene to another and back again, thus increasing dramatic tension; **cross'-dāting** (*archaeol*) a method of dating one site, level, etc by comparison with others; **cross-divi'sion** division into groups or classes that overlap; **cross-dress'ing** transvestism, the wearing of clothes normally associated with the opposite sex; **crossed line** a telephone line connected in error to a different line or circuit; **cross-examinā'tion**. — *vt* **cross-exam'ine** to question minutely, or with a view to checking evidence already given; to subject to examination by the other side, *esp* by the prosecution or defence in a court of law. — **cross'-eye** a squint in which the eye turns inwards towards the nose. — *adj* **cross-eyed'** squinting. — *vt* **cross'-fade** (*TV* and *radio*) to cause (a sound source or picture) to fade away while gradually introducing another (also *vi*). — **cross'fall** the transverse inclination on a road; **cross'-fertilizā'tion** the fecundation of a plant by pollen from another; fruitful interaction of ideas from eg different cultures. — *adj* **cross'field** (*football*) (of a pass, etc) *usu* long and transverse in direction. — **cross'fire** (*military*) the crossing of lines of fire from two or more points (also *fig*); **cross'fish** another name for the common sea urchin (*Asterias rubens*); **cross-gar'net** a T-shaped hinge, used *esp* to attach a door to a door frame. — *adj* **cross-gar'tered** (*Shakesp*) wearing the garters crossed on the leg; **cross'-grained** having the grain or fibres crossed or intertwined; perverse; contrary; intractable. — *adv* across the grain; perversely. — **cross-grained'ness**; **cross guard** the bar, at right angles to the blade, forming the hilt-guard of a sword; **cross hairs** two fine lines crossing at right angles at the centre of the lens of an optical instrument, used for focusing; **cross'-hatching** (in drawing, etc) shading by intersecting sets of parallel lines; **cross'head** a beam across the head of something, *esp* the bar at the end of the piston-rod of an engine; **cross-infec'tion** infection of an already ill or injured person with another illness unrelated to his or her own complaint, liable to occur eg in hospitals where a variety of diseases are being treated; infection from one species to another. — *vt* **cross-infect'**. — **crossing over** (*biol*) the interchange of parts of paired chromosomes when they separate again after synapsis, producing variations in the inherited characteristics of offspring; **cross'ing-sweeper** (*obs*) a person who sweeps a street crossing; **cross'ing-warden** a lollipop man or woman; **cross'jack** (*naut*) a square sail set on the mizzenmast; **cross'-kick** a crossfield kick; **cross-lat'eral** a person affected with cross-laterality. — Also *adj*. — **cross-lateral'ity** a mixture of physical one-sidedness, eg the combination of a dominant left eye with a dominant right hand. — *adj* **cross'-leaved** having leaves in four rows, set crosswise. — *adj* **cross'-legged** having the legs crossed. — Also *adv*. — **cross'light** a light whose direction makes an angle with that of another light, and which illuminates additional parts or regions. — *adj* **cross'-lighted**. — **cross'-linking** (*chem*) the formation of side bonds between different chains in a polymer. — *adj* **cross-magnet'ic** diamagnetic. — **cross-marketing** see **cross-selling**. — *vt* **cross'-match** to test (blood samples from a donor and a recipient) for compatibility by checking that agglutination does not occur when red cells from each are put into the other's serum. — **cross'-matching**; **cross'over** a road passing over the top of another; another term for **crossing over** (*biol*); a place or point at which a crossing or transfer is made. — *adj* (of a musician, singer, etc) popular with or appealing to a wider audience beyond the category of music with which first associated; having, incorporating or combining two or more styles, functions, methods, etc. — **crossover network** (*acoustics*) a frequency selective network which divides an audio signal into two or more frequency ranges in a loudspeaker, etc; **crossover vote**; **crossover voter** (*US politics*) a person registered with one political party who votes for another in a primary. — *adj* **cross'-party** covering or drawn from all political parties. — **cross'patch** an ill-natured person (see **patch**[2]); **cross'piece** a piece of material of any kind crossing another; a timber over the windlass, with pins for belaying the running rigging (*naut*); **cross-ply tyre** a tyre in which the plies of fabric in the carcass are wrapped so as to cross each other diagonally; **cross-pollina'tion** transfer of pollen from the anther of one flower to the stigma of another (cf **self-pollination**); **cross-pur'pose** a contrary purpose; (in *pl*) a game in which answers to questions are transferred to other questions; (in *pl*) confusion in conversation or action by misunderstanding; **cross-quar'ters** an ornament of tracery like the four petals of a cruciform flower; a quatrefoil. — *vt* **cross-ques'tion** to cross-examine. — *vt* **cross-refer'** to refer or direct (a reader, etc) to another place, entry, passage, title, etc. — *vi* to make a cross-reference. — **cross-ref'erence** a reference in a book to another entry, passage or title; any similar reference, eg in a filing system, directing the user to another place or position for further information. — Also *vt*. — **cross'-rib** an arch supporting a vault; **cross'road** a road crossing the principal road, a bypath; a road joining main roads; (often in *pl*) a place where roads cross; (in *pl*) a stage at which an important decision has to be made. — *adj* **cross'roads**. — **cross'-row** same as **Christ-cross-row**; **cross-ruff'** (*cards*) (*esp* in whist and bridge) alternate trumping, by one of the partners, leading a suit that the other lacks; **cross'-section** a transverse section; a comprehensive representation; the effective target area of a nucleus for a particular reaction under specified conditions, measured in barns — when no reaction can take place, the cross-section is zero (*phys*). — *vt* to make a cross-section of. — *adj* **cross-sec'tional**. — **cross-sell'ing** or **cross-mark'eting** the selling of services in addition to the services normally associated with a particular business or organization, eg the selling of insurance by banks, building societies, etc to existing customers; **cross'-sill** a railway sleeper; **cross-spring'er** a rib following the line of the groin in a groined vault; **cross'-staff** a surveying instrument consisting of a staff surmounted with a frame carrying two pairs of sights at right angles; **cross'-stitch** a stitch in the form of a cross; needlework made up of such stitches; **cross'-stone** (*obs*) chiastolite; staurolite; harmotome; **cross'-talk** interference caused by the energy from one telephone conversation invading another by electrostatic or electromagnetic coupling; backchat; repartee; **cross'tie** a supporting tie placed transversely; a railway sleeper; **cross-tīn'ing** (*agric*) a method of harrowing crosswise. — *adj* **cross'town** (*NAm*) extending over, or crossing, a town, as in *crosstown bus*. — **cross'tree** a piece of timber or metal placed across the upper end of a ship's mast; **cross-vault'ing** vaulting formed by the intersection of simple vaults; **cross'walk** (*NAm*) a pedestrian crossing; **cross'way** a way that crosses another or links others; **cross'wind** a wind blowing across the path of eg an aeroplane; **cross'word** or **crossword puzzle** a type of puzzle invented in America in 1913, in which a square with blank spaces is to be filled with letters which, read across or down, will give words corresponding to clues given. — **cross a bridge when one comes to it** see under **bridge**[1]; **cross as two sticks** particularly perverse and disagreeable; **cross one's fingers** or **keep one's fingers crossed** to place one finger across another in the hope of ensuring good luck; **cross one's heart (and hope to die)** to emphasize that one is being truthful by making the sign of a cross over one's heart; **cross someone's lips** to be uttered by someone; **cross someone's mind** to flash across someone's mind; **cross someone's palm** to put a coin in someone's hand, as a payment; **cross someone's path** to come in someone's way, to meet someone; to thwart someone; **cross swords** to enter into a dispute (with); **on the cross** diagonally; dishonestly (*slang*). [OE *cros*, from ON *kross*, from L *crux*, *crucis*]

crossandra *kro-sän'drə*, *n* any evergreen shrub of the genus *Crossandra*, cultivated for their pink, yellow or red flowers. [New L, from Gr *krossos* fringed, and *andros* genitive of *anēr* male (signifying anther)]

crosse *kros*, *n* the stick with which the game of lacrosse is played, having at its top end a network of leather thongs enclosed in a triangular frame. [Fr]

crossette *kro-set'*, (*archit*) *n* a small projecting part of an impost-stone at the extremity of an arch; a shoulder in an arch-stone fitting into the stone next to it. [Fr]

crossopterygian *kros-op-tə-rij'ən*, *n* a member of a subclass (*Crossopterygii*) of mostly extinct bony fishes, thought to be the ancestors of amphibians, having paired fins with the axis fringed with rays, and including the coelocanthus. — Also *adj*. [New L *crossopterygii*, from Gr *krossoi* tassels, fringe, and *pteryx*, *-gos* fin]

crotal[1] *krō'təl*, *n* a crotalum; a small spherical bell. — *n* **crotalaria** (*krot-* or *krōt-ə-lā'ri-ə*) any plant of the sunn-hemp genus *Crotalaria*, family Papilionaceae, including the American rattleboxes (from their inflated pods). — *n pl* **Crotalidae** (*-tal'i-dē*) the rattlesnake family. — *adj* **crotaline** (*krot'ə-līn*) like a rattlesnake. — *n* **crot'alism** poisoning by crotalaria. — *n* **crotalum** (*krot'ə-ləm*) a clapper or castanet used in ancient religious rites: — *pl* **crot'ala**. — *n* **Crotalus** (*krot'*) the rattlesnake genus. [Gr *krotalon* a rattle, castanet]

crotal[2] or **crottle** *krot'l*, *n* a lichen (of various kinds) used for dyeing. [Gaelic *crotal*]

crotch *kroch*, *n* a fork, as of a tree; the bifurcation of the human body; the corresponding area in eg a pair of trousers; the human genital area. — *adj* **crotched**. [Ety obscure]

crotchet *kroch'it*, *n* a note in music, equal to half a minim, ♩; a crooked or perverse fancy; a whim, or conceit; a small hook (*obs*). — *adj* **crotch'ety** having crotchets or peculiarities; whimsical; short-tempered. — *n* **crotch'eteer** (*rare*) a crotchety person. [Fr *crochet* dimin of *croche* a hook; see **crochet**]

croton *krō'tən*, *n* any plant of the *Croton* genus of tropical plants of the spurge family or of the related genus *Codiaeum*. — **croton oil** a powerful purgative obtained from the seeds of *Croton tiglium*. [Gr *krotōn* a sheep-tick, which the seed resembles]

Croton bug *krō'tən bug n* the German cockroach. [From the *Croton* river, which supplies water to the city of New York]

crottle. See **crotal**[2].

crouch *krowch*, *vi* to squat or lie close to the ground; to bend low with legs doubled; to cringe; to fawn. — *vt* to bend. — *n* act or position of crouching. [Poss connected with **crook**]

crouch-ware *krowch'-wār*, *n* an old salt-glazed stoneware made at Burslem. [Origin unknown]

croup[1] *kro͞op*, *n* inflammation and consequent narrowing of the larynx and trachea in children, associated with difficulty in breathing and a peculiar ringing cough; a burr. — *vi* to croak or speak hoarsely. — *n* **croup'iness**. — *adj* **croup'ous**. — *adj* **croup'y**. [From the sound made]

croup[2] or **croupe** *kro͞op*, *n* the rump of a horse; the place behind the saddle. — *vi* (*dialect*) to squat on one's haunches. — *n* **croup'on** (*obs*) the croup; the human buttocks. [Fr *croupe* a protuberance; related to **crop**]

croupade *kro͞o-pād'*, (*dressage*) *n* a leap in which the horse draws up its hind-legs toward the belly. [Fr]

croupe. See **croup**[2].

crouper *kro͞op'ər*, *n*. An obsolete form of **crupper**.

croupier *kro͞o'pi-ər* or *-pi-ā*, *n* a person who officiates at a gaming-table, dealing the cards, collecting the stakes and paying the winners. [Fr, one who rides on the croup]

croupon. See **croup**[2].

croupous, croupy. See **croup**[1].

crouse *kro͞os*, (*Scot*) *adj* lively, cheerfully confident, brisk. — *adv* boldly, pertly. — *adv* **crouse'ly**. [ME *crūs*; cf LGer *krûs* gay, Ger *kraus*, Du *kroes* crisp, cross]

croustade *kro͞os-täd'*, *n* a case of fried bread or pastry for serving game, etc. [Fr]

crout *krowt*, *n*. Same as **sauerkraut**.

croûte *kro͞ot*, *n* a thick slice of fried bread for serving entrées. — *n* **croûton** (*-tɔ̃* or *-ton'*) a small cube of fried bread, as used in soups and salads. — **en croûte** (*cookery*) wrapped in pastry and baked. [Fr *croûte* crust]

crow *krō*, *n* any of several large black birds of the genus *Corvus*, *esp C. corone* (the so-called *carrion crow*); extended to other birds of this genus, *esp* the rook; the defiant or triumphant cry of a cock; an infant's inarticulate cry of joy; an ugly old woman (*slang*); short for crowbar. — *vi* to croak; to utter a crow; to boast, swagger, triumph (often with *over*): — *pa t* **crew** (*kro͞o*) or **crowed**; *pa p* **crowed** or **crown** (*krōn*). — **crow'bar** a heavy iron bar *usu* bent at one end, used as a lever; **crow'berry** a low creeping moorland shrub (*Empetrum*) producing small black berries; **crow boot** a boot made of leather and fur, as worn by Eskimos; **crow'-flower** applied to various plants, in *Shakesp* perhaps crowfoot; **crow'foot** a buttercup, sometimes extended to other plants (*pl* in this sense **crow'foots**); **crow'-quill** a pen made of the quill of a crow, etc, for fine writing or etching; **crow's'-bill** or **crow'-bill** (*surg*) a kind of forceps for extracting bullets, etc, from wounds; **crow's'-foot** one of the wrinkles spreading out from the corners of the eyes, formed as the skin ages (*pl* in this sense **crow's' feet**); a caltrop (*obs mil*); **crow's'-nest** (*naut*) an elevated platform near the top of a ship's mast for a man on lookout. — *n pl* **crow'-steps** step-like stonework on a gable. — **crow'-toe** applied to various plants, in Milton probably crowfoot. — **as the crow flies** in a straight line; **draw the crow** (*Austr*) to draw the short straw, come off worst in an allocation; **eat crow** or **eat (boiled) crow** to be forced to do something very disagreeable, humiliate oneself; **have a crow to pluck with** to have something to settle with someone; **stone the crows** (*esp Austr slang*) an expression of amazement, horror, etc. [OE *crāwe* a crow, *crāwan* to crow]

crowd[1] *krowd*, *n* a number of persons or things closely pressed together, without order; the rabble; multitude; a social set. — *vt* to gather into a lump or crowd; to fill by pressing or driving together; to compress; to thrust, put pressure on. — *vi* to press on; to press together in numbers; to swarm. — *adj* **crowd'ed**. — **crowd'-puller** a person, event, etc attracting a large audience. [OE *crūdan* to press]

crowd[2] *krowd*, (*obs* or *dialect*) *n* (*obs*) the crwth. — *n* **crowd'er** a fiddler. [See **crwth**]

crowdie *krowd'i*, (*Scot*) *n* a mixture of meal and water, brose; a soft curd cheese made from soured milk. [Ety unknown; perh in part from **crud**]

crown *krown*, *n* a circular head ornament, *esp* as a mark of honour; the diadem or state-cap of royalty; kingship; (*usu* with *cap*) the sovereign; governing power in a monarchy; honour; the top of anything, eg a head, hat, tree, arch; a type of spire or lantern, formed by converging flying buttresses (*archit*); a stag's surroyals; the visible part of a tooth; a substitute for this, made of gold or synthetic material, etc, fitted over a broken or decayed tooth; (in gem-cutting) the upper of the two conical surfaces of a brilliant; the junction of root and stem of a plant; a short rootstock; a clasping metal cap for a bottle; chief ornament; completion or consummation; a coin originally stamped with a crown, *esp* a 5-shilling piece; used to translate various coin names, such as krone; the old French écu; a British size of paper before metrication (or a US size of paper 15 × 19in), originally watermarked with a crown. — *vt* to cover or invest with a crown; to cap; to invest with royal dignity; to fill with foaming liquor; (in draughts) to convert into a king or crowned man by the placing of another draught on the top on reaching the crown-head; to adorn; to dignify; to complete happily; to hit on the head (*slang*). — *adj* **crowned**. — *n* **crown'er** a shaped paper label attached to a product, eg a bottle, printed with advertising or promotional material; a coroner (*obs*). — *n* **crown'et** a coronet. — *n* **crown'ing** coronation; the final stage of labour, when the top of the child's head passes through the vaginal opening (*obstetrics*). — *adj* **crown'less**. — *n* **crown'let** a small crown. — **crown agent** a solicitor in Scotland who prepares criminal prosecutions; (with *caps*) one of a British body of business agents operating internationally, appointed by the Overseas Development Administration; **crown antler** the uppermost tine of an antler; **Crown attorney** (*Can*) a lawyer who acts for the Crown in criminal cases; **crown'-bark** a kind of cinchona bark; **crown cap** a lined metal cap for a bottle; **crown colony** a colony administered directly by the home government; **crown courts** the system of courts in England and Wales that administer criminal jurisdiction; **Crown Derby** a late 18c porcelain made at Derby, marked with a crown; **crowned head** a monarch; **crown gall** a disease of plants caused by a bacterium (*Agrobacterium tumefaciens*), forming tumours along roots and shoots; **crown glass** alkali-lime glass; window glass formed in circular plates or discs; **crown graft** (*hortic*) insertion of scions between bark and wood; **crown green** a bowling-green with the centre higher than the edges; **crown'-head** (in draughts) the back row of squares, where a piece is crowned; **crown imperial** a garden plant, a species of fritillary having bell-shaped orange flowers; **crown jewels** the jewels, including the regalia, worn by the sovereign on state occasions; **crown land** land belonging to the crown or sovereign; **crown lawyer** a lawyer who acts for the crown in criminal cases; **crown living** a church living in the gift of the crown; **Crown Office** the administrative office of the Queen's Bench Division of the High Court; the office in which the great seal is affixed; **crown-of-thorns starfish** or **Crown of Thorns** a starfish that preys on living coral; **crown piece** a five-shilling piece; **crown'-post** a king-post in a roof; **crown prince** the heir-apparent to the crown; **crown princess** the female heir to a throne; the wife of a crown prince; **crown roast** roast ribs of lamb or pork arranged in a circle like a crown; **crown rot** a disease affecting rhubarb, caused by a soil-borne bacterium (*Erwinia rhapontici*); **crown saw** a saw consisting of a rotating cylinder with cutting teeth; **crown vetch** a trailing plant (*Coronilla varia*), of the pea family with pink or purple flowers; **crown'-wheel** (*horology*) a wheel with teeth set at right angles to its plane; **crown witness** a witness for the crown in a criminal prosecution instituted by it; **crown'work** the manufacture and fitting of artificial crowns for teeth; such an artificial crown or crowns; an outwork composed of a bastion between two curtains, with demi-bastions at the extremes (*fortif*). — **crown and anchor** a game played with dice marked with crowns and anchors; **crown of the causeway** the middle of the street; **Crown Prosecution Service** the independent prosecuting body in England and Wales which decides whether cases brought by the police should be tried in the courts. [OFr *corone*, from L *corōna*; cf Gr *koronos* curved]

crown[2]. See **crow**.

croze *krōz*, *n* the groove in the staves of a cask in which the edge of the head is set. [Perh OFr *croz* (Fr *creux*) groove]

crozier. See **crosier**.

CRT *abbrev*: cathode ray tube; composite rate tax.

cru *krü*, (*Fr*) *n* a vineyard or group of vineyards; a vintage.

crubeen *kroo-bēn'* or *kroo'bēn*, *n* a pig's trotter, as food. [Ir *crúibín*, dimin of *crúb* hoof]

cruces. See **crux**.

crucial *kroo'shəl*, *adj* testing or decisive; essential, very important; very good (*slang*); crosslike; of the nature of a crux; of or relating to Afro-Caribbean culture or street slang of Jamaican origin. [**crux**]

crucian or **crusian** *kroo'shən*, *n* a colourful carp, commonly kept as an aquarium fish. [LG *karusse* (Ger *Karausche*), from L *coracīnus*, from Gr *korakīnos*, a black perch-like fish, from *korax* raven]

cruciate *kroo'shi-āt*, *adj* cross-shaped; arranged like a cross. [L *crux*, *crucis* a cross]

crucible *kroo'si-bl*, *n* an earthen pot for melting ores, metals, etc. [LL *crucibulum*]

crucifer *kroo'si-fər*, *n* a cross-bearer in a procession; a member of the Cruciferae. — *n pl* **Crucif'erae** (*bot*) a family of archichlamydeous dicotyledons, with cross-shaped flowers, including cabbage, turnip, cress, wall-flower. — *adj* **crucif'erous** bearing or marked with a cross; with four petals placed crosswise; of the Cruciferae. [L *crux*, *crucis* a cross, and *ferre* to bear]

cruciform *kroo'si-förm* *adj* cross-shaped. [L *crux*, *crucis* a cross, and **-form**]

crucify *kroo'si-fī*, *vt* to expose or put to death on a cross; to fasten to a wheel or the like, as a military field punishment; to subdue completely; to mortify; to torment; to treat harshly or cruelly; to hold up to scorn or ridicule: — *pr p* **cru'cifying**: *pa t* and *pa p* **cru'cified**. — *n* **cru'cifier** someone who crucifies. — *n* **cru'cifix** a figure or picture of Christ fixed to the cross. — *n* **crucifixion** (*-fik'shən*). [OFr *crucifier*, from L *crucifīgere*, *crucifīxum*, from *crux* cross, and *fīgere* to fix]

cruciverbal *kroo-si-vûr'bəl*, (*usu facetious*) *adj* of or relating to (the compiling and solving of) crosswords. — *n* **cruciver'balism**. — *n* **cruciver'balist** a crossword addict. [L *crux* cross, and *verbum* a word]

cruck *kruk*, *n* one of a pair of curved timbers supporting a roof. [Cf **crook**]

crud *krud* or *krood*, (*slang*) *n* anything dirty, filthy, disgusting or worthless; excrement or anything similar to it; a gluey half-melted snow (*skiing slang*); radioactive waste; a contemptible person. — *vt* and *vt* to (cause to) be encrusted with or blocked with dirt, filth, etc (*usu* with *up*). — *vt* (*Spenser*) and *vi* **crudd'le** to curdle. — *adj* **crudd'y** (*slang*) dirty, unpleasant, worthless; contemptible. [**curd**]

crude *krood*, *adj* raw, unprepared; not reduced to order or form; unfinished; undigested; immature; unrefined; coarse, vulgar, rude; inartistic. — *n* crude oil. — *adv* **crude'ly**. — *n* **crude'ness**. — *n* **crud'ity** rawness; unripeness; that which is crude. — **crude oil** petroleum in its unrefined state. [L *crūdus* raw]

crudités *krü-dē-tā*, (*Fr*) *n pl* raw fruit and vegetables served as an hors d'oeuvre.

cruel *kroo'əl*, *adj* disposed to inflict pain, or deriving pleasure from the suffering of others; devoid of pity, merciless, savage; severe. — *adv* **cru'elly**. — *n* **cru'elness** (*obs*). — *n* **cru'elty**. [Fr *cruel*, from L *crūdēlis*]

cruels, **cruells**. Same as **crewels**.

cruet *kroo'it*, *n* a small jar or bottle for sauces and condiments for the table; a vessel for wine, oil, or water for religious ceremonies. — **cru'et-stand** a stand or frame for holding cruets. [Anglo-Fr, dimin of OFr *cruye* jar, from root of **crock**[1]]

cruise *krooz*, *vi* to sail to and fro; (of a vehicle, aircraft, etc) to progress smoothly at a speed economical in fuel, etc; to wander about seeking something (with *about*, etc; *colloq*); to go round public places looking for a sexual partner (*slang*; also *vt*). — *n* a sailing to and fro; a wandering voyage in search of an enemy or for the protection of vessels or for pleasure or health; a land journey of similar character. — *n* **cruis'er** someone who or that which cruises; a speedy warship, specially for cruising; a privateer; a cruising yacht; a cruiserweight boxer. — **cruise control** (in certain cars) an electronic device which controls cruising speed on motorways; **cruise missile** a subsonic guided missile using the air for support; **cruise'wear** clothing suitable for a leisure cruise; **cruis'er weight** a boxer between middle and heavy, a light heavyweight (see **heavyweight**); **cruise'-way** a canal for exclusively recreational use. [Du *kruisen* to cross]

cruisie. See **crusie**.

cruive, **cruve** or **croove** *kroov* (*Scot krøv* or *kriv*), *n* a pen or sty; a wattled fish-trap used in a river or estuary.

cruller *krul'ər*, (*NAm*) *n* a type of sweet cake fried in fat. — Also **krull'er**. [Cf Du *krullen* to curl]

crumb *krum*, *n* a small bit or morsel of bread; a small particle of anything; the soft part of bread; a worthless or contemptible person (*slang*). — *vt* to break into crumbs; to put crumbs in or on; to remove crumbs from. — *vi* to crumble. — *adj* **crumb'y** in crumbs; soft. — *adj* **crum'my** crumby; covered in lice (*slang*); not good, worthless, inferior, unpleasant, out of sorts, etc (*colloq*). — **crumb'-tray** a tray on to which crumbs are brushed from the table or one on which crumbs collect at the base of a toaster. [OE *cruma*; Du *kruim*; Ger *Krume*; **crimp**]

crumble *krum'bl*, *vt* to break into crumbs. — *vi* to fall into small pieces; to decay. — *n* a crumb; that which crumbles easily; a sweet dish consisting of a layer of stewed fruit covered with a crumbled mixture of flour, butter and sugar. — *n pl* **crum'blies** (*slang*) very old people. — *adj* **crum'bly**. [Orig dimin of **crumb**; Du *kruimelen*; Ger *krümeln*]

crumbs *krumz*, (*orig schoolchildren's slang*) *interj* expressing surprise, dismay, etc. [Euphem for *Christ*]

crumen *kroo'mən*, *n* a deer's tear-pit. — *n* **cru'menal** (*Spenser*) a purse. [L *crumēna* a purse]

crumhorn. See **krummhorn**.

crummock or **crummack** *krum'ək*, *n* a crook, a stick with a curved head. [Gaelic *cromag* hook, crook]

crummy[1] *krum'i*, (*Scot*) *n* a cow with a crumpled horn. [Scot *crum* to bend; cf MLGer *krummen*]

crummy[2]. See **crumb**.

crump[1] *krump*, (*military slang*) *n* (the sound of) an exploding bomb, etc. — *vi* to make such a sound. [Imit]

crump[2] *krump*, *adj* crisp, friable (*Scot*). — *adj* **crump'y** (*dialect*) crisp. [Imit; cf **crimp**]

crumpet *krum'pit*, *n* a pancake made of batter, variously small and thick or large and thin in different parts of the UK; a small thick yeast cake with holes on the top, *usu* eaten hot with butter, sometimes called a muffin; the head (*slang*); a woman, or women collectively, as sexual objects, now also used of a man or men (*slang*). [Ety uncertain]

crumple *krump'l*, *vt* to crush into irregular wrinkles; to wrinkle; to cause to collapse. — *vi* to wrinkle; to collapse. — *adj* **crump'led**. — *n* **crump'ling**. — **crumple zones** the front and rear portions of a motor car designed to crumple and absorb the impact in a collision while the passenger area remains intact. [**crump**[2]]

crunch *krunch*, *vt* to crush with harsh noise, with the teeth, under foot, or otherwise; to chew anything hard, and so make a noise; to process large quantities of (data, numbers, etc). — *vi* to make such a noise; to chew with, or bite into with, such a noise; to walk, or move, with such a noise. — *n* the act or sound or crunching; (with *the*) the real testing or critical moment, trial of strength, time or cause of difficulty, etc (*colloq*); a crisis, emergency (*colloq*). — *n* **crunch'iness**. — *adj* **crunch'y**. — **number-cruncher** and **number-crunching** see under **number**. [Altered form of *craunch*, prob influenced by *munch*]

crunkle *krunk'l*, *vi* to crumple. [Cf **crinkle**]

cruor *kroo'ör*, (*med*) *n* a mass of coagulated blood; a blood clot: — *pl* **cruores** (*kroo-ör-ēz*). [L]

crupper *krup'ər*, *n* a strap of leather fastened to the saddle and passing under the horse's tail to keep the saddle in its place; the hind part of a horse. [OFr *cropiere*, from *crope* the croup]

crural *kroo'rəl*, *adj* belonging to or like a leg. [L *crūrālis*, from *crūs*, *crūris* the leg]

crusade *kroo-sād'*, *n* any one of many medieval military expeditions under the banner of the cross to recover the Holy Land from the Muslims; any daring or romantic undertaking; concerted action to further a cause. — *vi* to go on a crusade. — *n* **crusād'er** someone engaged in a crusade. [Fr *croisade*, from Provençal *crozada*, from *croz*, from L *crux* a cross]

crusado *kroo-sā'dō*, *n* an old Portuguese coin, so called because the reverse side was marked with a cross: — *pl* **crusā'dos**. [Port *cruzado*]

cruse *krooz*, also *kroos*, *n* an earthenware pot; a small cup or bottle. [Cf ON *krūs*; Ger *Krause*]

cruset *kroo'sit*, *n* a goldsmith's crucible. [Cf Fr *creuset*, MDu *kruysel*, MLGer *krusel*]

crush *krush*, *vt* to press or squeeze so as to squash, deform or break; to break into tiny fragments; to beat down or overwhelm; to subdue; to ruin. — *vi* to become broken or crumpled under pressure; to have a crush or be infatuated with (with *on*). — *n* a violent squeezing; a close crowd of persons or things; a drink made from fruit pulp or fruit juice; a narrowing passage into which cattle, etc are driven; an infatuation (with *on*), or its object (*slang*). — *adj* **crush'able**. — *adj* **crushed**. — *n* **crush'er** someone who or something that crushes or subdues; a policeman (*slang*). — *adj* **crush'ing**. — *adv* **crush'ingly**. — **crush bar** a bar in a theatre for selling drinks in the intervals of a play, etc; **crush barrier** a barrier erected to restrain a crowd and prevent crushing; **crushed strawberry** the pinky colour of strawberries that have been crushed. — Also *adj*. — **crush hat** a collapsible opera hat; **crush room** a room where an audience may promenade during the intervals of the entertainment; **crush syndrome** a medical condition in which traumatic damage to a large amount of body muscle impairs the functioning of the kidneys and may lead to kidney failure. [OFr *croissir*; perh cognate with MHGer *krosen* to crunch]

crusian. See **crucian**.

crusie, **crusy** or **cruisie** *krooz'i*, (*Scot*) *n* an open iron lamp used with a rush wick. [From **cruset**]

crust *krust*, *n* the hard rind or outside coating of anything; the outer part of bread; a dried-up scrap of bread; a livelihood (*slang*); the covering of a pie, etc; ice on top of soft snow (*skiing*); the head (*usu* in the phrase *off one's crust*) (*slang*); the solid exterior of the earth, consisting mainly of sedimentary rocks resting on ancient igneous rocks; the dry scaly covering on a skin lesion; a layer of sediment on the side of the bottle in some wines and ports; impertinence (*old slang*). — *vt* to cover with a crust or hard case. — *vi* to gather into a hard crust. — *adj* **crust'al** pertaining to a crust, *esp* the earth's. — *adj* **crust'ate** or **crustāt'ed** covered with a crust. — *n* **crustā'tion** an adherent crust. — *adv*

crust'ily. — *n* **crust'iness**. — *adj* **crust'less**. — *adj* **crust'y** of the nature of or having a crust, as port or other wine; having a hard or harsh exterior; hard; snappy; surly. [L *crusta* rind]

crusta *krus'tə*, *n* a piece prepared for inlaying; a hard coating; a cocktail served in a glass, its rim encrusted in sugar: — *pl* **crus'tae** (*-tē*). [L]

crustacean *krus-tā'sh(y)ən* or *-shi-ən*, *n* a member of a large class (**Crustā'cea**) of arthropod animals with hard shells, almost all aquatic, including crabs, lobsters, shrimps, sand-hoppers, wood-lice, water-fleas, barnacles, etc. — Also *adj*. — *adj* **crustā'ceous** having a crust or a shell. [L *crusta* shell]

crusy. See **crusie**.

crutch *kruch*, *n* a staff with a crosspiece at the head to place under the arm of a lame person; any support of similar form; a bifurcation, crotch; a small figure inserted to show the number to be carried (*arith*). — *vt* to support; to prop; to clip wool from the hindquarters of (a sheep) (*Austr*). — *vi* to go on crutches. — *adj* **crutched** marked by the sign of, or wearing, a Cross. — **Crutch'ed-friars** or **Crouch'ed-friars** an order of mendicant friars so called from the cross which they wore. [OE *crycc*]

cruve. See **cruive**.

crux *kruks*, *n* a cross; something that occasions difficulty or perplexity, a puzzle; that on which a decision turns; the essential point, eg in a problem: — *pl* **crux'es** or **cruces** (*kroo'sēz*). — **crux ansata** (*an-sā'tə*, or *krooks an-sä'ta*) a T-shaped cross with a loop at the top, the ankh; **crux criticorum** (*krit-i-kō-rəm* or *-room*) a puzzle for the critics; **crux decussata** (*dē-kus-ā'tə* or *dā-koos-ä'ta*) an X-shaped cross, such as the cross of St Andrew or St Patrick; **crux medicorum** (*me-di-kö'rəm* or *-room*) a puzzle for the doctors. [L *crux*, *crucis* a cross]

cruzado *kroo-zā'dō*, *n* the former standard unit of currency of Brazil, replaced by the cruzeiro: — *pl* **cruzadōs** or **cruzadoes**.

cruzeiro *kroo-zā'rō*, *n* the standard unit of currency of Brazil, which replaced the cruzado: — *pl* **cruzei'ros**. [Port *cruz* cross]

crwth *krooth*, *n* the crowd, an old Welsh stringed instrument, four of its six strings played with a bow, two plucked by the thumb. [Welsh *crwth* a hollow protuberance, a fiddle; Gaelic, Ir *cruit*]

cry *krī*, *vi* to utter a shrill loud sound, *esp* one of pain or grief; to lament; to weep; to bawl; to call (*Scot*). — *vt* to utter loudly; to exclaim; to proclaim or make public; to offer for sale by crying out; to call (*Scot*); to proclaim the banns of marriage of (*Scot*): — *3rd pers sing* **cries**; *pr p* **cry'ing**; *pa t* and *pa p* **cried** (*krīd*). — *n* any loud sound, *esp* of grief or pain; a call or shout; a fit of weeping; a pack of hounds, hence of people; a particular sound uttered by an animal; bawling; lamentation; prayer; clamour; report or rumour; a general utterance; a watchword, battle-cry, or slogan; a street call of wares for sale or services offered: — *pl* **cries**. — *n* **crī'er** someone who cries, *esp* an official maker of proclamations. — *n* **cry'ing** the act of calling loudly; weeping. — *adj* calling loudly; claiming notice and immediate action or redress, as in *a crying need*; distressing, heartbreaking, lamentable, as in a *crying shame*. — **cry'baby** someone who cries too easily or frequently, like a baby. — **a far cry** a great distance; a very different matter; **cry down** to decry, disparage; **cry for the moon** to beg or sigh for something unattainable; **crying in the wilderness** voicing opinions or making suggestions that are not (likely to be) heeded; **cry off** to withdraw from an agreement; to back out; **cry on** (*Scot*) to call upon; **cry one's eyes** (or **heart**) **out** to weep copiously or bitterly; **cry out** to give a shout or shriek, eg of alarm, pain, etc; **cry out for** to be in urgent or obvious need of; **cry out to be** (**done**, **used**, etc) to be someone or something that very much ought to be (done, used, etc); **cry over spilt milk** to waste time in bemoaning what is irreparable; **cry quits** to declare a thing even; **cry stinking fish** to decry one's own goods; **cry up** to praise; **cry you mercy** (*obs*) I beg your pardon; **for crying out loud** (*slang*) an expression of frustration, impatience, etc; **great cry and little wool** much ado about nothing; **hue and cry** see under **hue**[2]; **in full cry** in full pursuit, *orig* used of dogs in hunt; **within cry of** within hearing distance. [Fr *crier*, from L *quirītāre* to scream]

crymotherapy. See **cryotherapy** (under **cryo-**).

cryo- *krī'ō-* or *krī-o'-*, *combining form* denoting frost, ice, ice-cold. — *adj* **cryobiolog'ical**. — *n* **cryobiol'ogist**. — *n* **cryobiol'ogy** the study of the effects of extreme cold on living organisms. — *n* **cryoc'onite** (Gr *konis* dust) dust found on the surface of polar ice. — *n* **cry'ogen** (*-jen*) (Gr root of *gignesthai* to become) a substance used for obtaining low temperatures, a freezing mixture. — *adj* **cryogen'ic** pertaining to the science of cryogenics, or to work done, apparatus used, or substances kept, at low temperatures. — *n sing* **cryogen'ics** the branch of physics concerned with phenomena at very low temperatures. — *n* **cryogeny** (*-oj'ə-ni*) refrigeration; cryogenics. — *n* **cryoglobulin** (*-glob'ū-lin*; *med*) an immunoglobulin formed in the blood in certain diseases which forms obstructions in small blood vessels when the extremities are subjected to low temperatures. — *n* **cry'olite** (Gr *lithos* a stone) an ice-stone or Greenland spar, sodium aluminium fluoride, earliest source of aluminium. — *n* **cryom'eter** (Gr *metron* measure) a thermometer for low temperatures. — *adj* **cryomet'ric**. — *adj* **cryon'ic**. — *n sing* **cryon'ics** the practice of preserving human corpses by freezing them, with the idea that advances in science may enable them to be revived at some future time. — *adj* **cryophil'ic** (Gr *phileein* to love; *biol*) able to thrive at low temperatures. — *n* **cryoph'orus** (Gr *pherein* to bear) an instrument for showing the decrease of temperature in water by evaporation. — *n sing* **cryophys'ics** low temperature physics. — *n* **cryoprecip'itate** a precipitate, eg from blood plasma, produced by freezing and thawing under controlled conditions. — *n* **cryopreservā'tion** the preservation of living cells (eg blood, human eggs and sperm) by freezing; cryonics. — *n* **cry'oprobe** a fine instrument with a cooled tip used in cryosurgery. — *n* **cry'oscope** an instrument for determining freezing-points. — *adj* **cryoscop'ic**. — *n* **cryos'copy** the study of the effect of dissolved substances on the freezing-points of solvents. — *n* **cry'ostat** apparatus for achieving or demonstrating cooling by evaporation; any apparatus for maintaining a low temperature. — *n* **cryosur'gery** surgery using instruments at very low temperatures to cut and destroy tissue. — *n* **cryother'apy** or **crymother'apy** (*krī-mō-*) medical treatment using extreme cold. — *n* **cry'otron** a tiny form of electronic switch operating in a bath of liquid helium a few degrees above absolute zero. — **cryonic suspension** cryonics. [Gr *kryos* frost]

crypt *kript*, *n* an underground cell or chapel; a small cavity, a tubular gland (*zool*). — *adj* **cryp'tal** pertaining to, or of the nature of, a crypt. [L *crypta*, from Gr *kryptē*, from *kryptein* to hide; cf **grot**]

crypt- *kript-*, or **crypto-** *-ō-* or *-o-*, *combining form* denoting hidden. — *n pl* **cryptadia** (*krip-tā'di-ə*; Gr) things to be kept secret. — *n* **cryptaesthesia** or (*NAm*) **cryptesthesia** (*kript-ēs-thē'zyə* or *-zhə*; Gr *aisthēsis* perception) supranormal perception, eg clairvoyance. — *adj* **cryptaesthet'ic**. — *ns* **cryptanal'ysis** the art of deciphering codes, etc. — *n* **cryptan'alyst**. — *n* **crypto-Chris'tian**. — *n* **crypto-comm'unist**. — *n* **cryptococcō'sis** a rare infection caused by the fungus *Cryptococcus neoformans*, which, if inhaled, may cause meningitis and growths in the lungs. — *adj* **cryptocryst'alline** with crystalline structure visible only under the microscope. — *n* **cryp'togam** any member of the **Cryptogamia** (*krip-tō-gā'mi-ə*), a former class of flowerless plants (including mosses, ferns, etc) that reproduce by means of spores rather than seeds. — *adj* **cryptogā'mian**. — *adj* **cryptogamic** (*-gam'ik*). — *n* **cryptog'amist**. — *adj* **cryptog'amous**. — *n* **cryptog'amy**. — *adj*

cryptogen'ic (of diseases) of unknown or obscure cause. — *n* **cryp'togram** or **cryp'tograph** anything written in cipher. — *n* **cryptog'rapher** or **cryptog'raph**. — *adj* **cryptograph'ic**. — *n* **cryptog'raphy**. — *adj* **crypto-log'ical**. — *n* **cryptol'ogist**. — *n* **cryptol'ogy** secret language; the scientific study of codes. — *n* **crypto-mē'ria** the Japanese cedar, *Cryptomeria japonica*. — *n* **cryptomnesia** (*-mnē'zi-ə* or *-zhə*) latent or subconscious memory. — *adj* **cryptomnēs'ic**. — *n* **crypton** see **krypton**. — *n* **cryp'tonym** (Gr *onyma* name) a secret name. — *adj* **crypton'ymous**. — *n* **cryptor'chid** a male human or animal in whom one or both testes fail to descend into the scrotum. — *n* **cryptor'chidism**. — *n* **crypto-sporidiō'sis** an infection affecting humans and domestic animals, caused by the protozoan **crypto-sporid'ium** (*pl* **-id'ia**), and characterized by diarrhoea, fever and stomach pains. [Gr *kryptos* hidden]

cryptic *krip'tik*, *adj* hidden; secret; unseen; mysteriously obscure. — *adj* **cryp'tical**. — *adv* **cryp'tically**. — **cryptic coloration** (*zool*) protective resemblance to some part of the environment by countershading or mimicry (eg of leaves or twigs). [LL *crypticus* from Gr *kryptikos*, from *kryptos* hidden]

crypto *krip'to*, *n* a person who is secretly a member of a party, sect, organization, etc, eg a crypto-communist. [**crypt-**]

crystal *kris'tl*, *n* rock-crystal, a clear quartz, like ice; a body, generally solid, whose atoms are arranged in a definite pattern, outwardly expressed by geometrical form with plane faces; a crystalline element, of piezo-electric or semiconductor material, functioning as eg a transducer, oscillator, etc in an electronic device; a globe of rock-crystal or the like in which one may see visions (also **crystal ball**); anything bright and clear; a superior glass of various kinds; cut glass; a watch-glass; cocaine or amphetamine (*drug-taking slang*). — *adj* composed of or like crystal. — *adj* **crys'talline** (*-īn*, *-in*, or in *poetry* also *-tal'*) like crystal or a crystal; composed of crystal, crystals, or parts of crystals; having the structure of a crystal. — *n* a crystalline substance. — *n* **crystallin'ity**. — *n* **crys'tallite** a small, imperfectly formed or incipient crystal; a minute body in glassy igneous rocks. — *n* **crystallī'tis** inflammation of the crystalline lens. — *adj* **crystallī'zable** or **-s-**. — *n* **crystallīzā'tion** or **-s-**. — *vt* and *vi* **crys'tallize** or **-ise** to form into crystals; to make or become definite or concrete; (*esp* of fruit) to coat with sugar crystals. — *n* **crystallogen'esis** origination of crystals. — *adj* **crystallo-genet'ic**. — *n* **crystallog'rapher**. — *adj* **crystallo-graph'ic**. — *n* **crystallog'raphy** the science of the structure, forms and properties of crystals. — *n* **crys'talloid** a substance in a state in which it dissolves to form a true solution which will pass through a membrane; a minute crystalline particle of protein (*bot*). — *adj* like a crystal; of the nature of a crystalloid. — *n* **crys'tallomancy** (Gr *manteiā* divination) divination by transparent bodies. — *adj* **crys'tal-clear** very or completely clear. — **crys'tal-gazer**; **crys'tal-gazing** gazing in a crystal or the like to obtain visual images, whether in divination or to objectify hidden contents of the mind; **crystalline heaven** or **sphere** in ancient astronomy, a sphere between the fixed stars and the *primum mobile*, assumed to explain precession of the equinoxes; **crystalline lens** the transparent refractive body of the eye; **crystal rectifier** a rectifier that depends on differential conduction in doped semiconductor crystals; **crystal set** a simple early type of wireless receiving apparatus having a crystal detector; **crystal violet** an antiseptic dye, hexamethylpararosaniline hydrochloride (also **gentian violet**). [OFr *cristal*, from L *crystallum*, from Gr *krystallos* ice, from *kryos* frost]

csárdás *chär'däsh*, *n* a Hungarian dance, or its music, in two movements, one slow and the other fast. — Also (wrongly) **czar'das**. [Hung]

CS *abbrev*: Chemical Society; Christian Science; Civil Service; Clerk to the Signet; Court of Session; Czechoslovakia (IVR). — See also **CS gas**.

Cs (*chem*) *symbol*: caesium.

c/s *abbrev*: cycles per second (hertz).

CSA *abbrev*: Confederate States of America.

CSCE *abbrev*: Conference on Security and Co-operation in Europe.

CSE *abbrev*: Certificate of Secondary Education.

CSEU *abbrev*: Confederation of Shipbuilding and Engineering Unions.

CSF *abbrev*: cerebrospinal fluid.

CS gas *sē'es gas*, *n* an irritant gas that affects vision and respiration, synthesized in 1928 by *C*arson and *S*taughton and used in riot control.

CSIRO *abbrev*: Commonwealth Scientific and Industrial Research Organization.

CSM *abbrev*: Committee on Safety of Medicines; Company Sergeant-Major.

CSO *abbrev*: community-service order.

CSP *abbrev*: Chartered Society of Physiotherapists; Council for Scientific Policy.

c-spring. See **cee-spring**.

CST *abbrev*: Central Standard Time (*NAm*); College of Speech Therapists.

CSU *abbrev*: Civil Service Union.

CSV *abbrev*: community service volunteer.

CSYS *abbrev*: Certificate of Sixth Year Studies.

CT *abbrev*: Connecticut (US state); same as **CAT** (see under **compute**).

Ct *abbrev*: Court (in addresses, etc).

ct *abbrev*: carat; cent; court.

CTC *abbrev*: city technical college; city technology college; Cyclists' Touring Club.

CTCC *abbrev*: Central Transport Consultative Committee.

ctene *tēn*, *n* a comb-like swimming organ in the Ctenophora. — *adj* **cteniform** (*tēn'* or *ten'*) or **cten'oid** comb-shaped. — *n* **ctenoph'oran** a member of the *Ctenophora*, a class of Coelenterates — transparent, free-swimming marine organisms resembling jellyfishes, moving by means of meridionally-placed comb-like plates. — Also *adj*. — *n* **cten'ophore** any member of the Ctenophora. [Gr *kteis*, *ktenos* comb]

Ctesiphon arch *tes'i-fon ärch*, (*archit*) *n* an arch of inverted catenary shape, such as the great ruined arch at Ctesiphon, on the Tigris south-east of Baghdad.

CTOL *abbrev*: conventional take-off and landing.

CTT *abbrev*: capital transfer tax.

CTV *abbrev*: continuous variable transmission.

Cu (*chem*) *symbol*: *cuprum* (L), copper.

Cu. or **cub.** *abbrev*: cubic.

cuadrilla *kwä-drēl'yə* or *-drēyə*, *n* the attendants of a matador. [Sp, gang, troop]

cub[1] *kub*, *n* the young of certain carnivorous animals, such as foxes, bears etc; a whelp; a rude or cheeky young boy or girl; (in full **Cub Scout**) a member of the junior section of the Scout Association; a beginner, novice, apprentice; a young or inexperienced person, *esp* a newspaper reporter. — *vt* and *vi* to bring forth (cubs); to hunt (fox-cubs): — *pr p* **cubb'ing**; *pa t* and *pa p* **cubbed**. — *n* **cubb'ing** cub-hunting. — *adj* **cubb'ish** like a cub; awkward or ill-mannered. — *n* **cub'hood**. — *adj* **cub'less**. — **cub'-hunting** hunting of young foxes. [Origin unknown]

cub[2] *kub*, *n* a cattle-pen; a chest. — *n* **cubb'y** or **cubb'y-hole** a snug enclosed place; a small compartment in a desk, cabinet, etc. [Prob from LGer]

Cuban *kū'bən*, *adj* pertaining to *Cuba* or its people. — *n* a native of Cuba. — **Cuban heel** (on footwear) a straight-sided heel of medium height.

cubby-hole. See **cub**[2].

cube *kūb*, *n* a solid body having six equal square faces, a solid square; anything with this shape; the third power of a quantity (*math*). — *vt* to raise to the third power (*math*); to cut into cubes; to calculate the amount or contents of in cubic units. — *n* **cūb'age** or **cū'bature** the act or process of finding the solid or cubic content of a body; the result thus found. — *adj* **cū'bic** or **cū'bical** pertaining to a cube; solid, three-dimensional; isometric (*crystallog*); (**cubic**) of or involving the third power or degree (*math*); (of volume) equal to that contained in a cube of specified dimensions. — *n* **cubic** (*math*) a cubic equation. — *adv* **cū'bically**. — *n* **cū'bicalness**. — *adj* **cū'biform**. — *n* **cū'bism** a modern movement in painting, which seeks to represent several aspects of an object seen from different viewpoints arbitrarily grouped in one composition, making use of cubes and other solid geometrical figures. — *n* and *adj* **cū'bist**. — *adj* **cūbist'ic**. — *adv* **cūbist'ically**. — *n* **cū'boid** (*math*) a solid with six rectangular faces, the opposite faces being of equal size. — *adj* **cū'boid** or **cū'boidal** resembling a cube in shape. — **cube root** (*math*) the quantity of which the given quantity is the cube; **cuboid bone** (*anatom*) (in the foot) the outer bone of the tarsus connected to the heel bone and the fourth and fifth metatarsal bones. [Fr, from L *cubus*, from Gr *kybos* a die]

cubeb *kū'beb*, *n* the dried berry of *Piper cubeba*, a Sumatran climbing pepper shrub, formerly used as a drug to treat infections of the urinary tract. [Fr *cubèbe*, from Ar *kabābah*]

cubic. See **cube**.

cubica *kū'bi-kə*, *n* a fine worsted fabric used for linings. [Sp *cubica*]

cubicle *kū'bi-kl*, *n* a bedroom; part of a dormitory or other large room which is partitioned off; a cell; a small compartment used for dressing and undressing as at a clinic, swimming pool, etc. [L *cubiculum*, from *cubāre* to lie down]

cubic zirconia. See under **zircon**.

cubism, etc. See **cube**.

cubit *kū'bit*, *n* an old measure, the length of the arm from the elbow to the tip of the middle finger, from 18 to 22 inches (*approx* 46 to 56cm). — Also **cū'bitus**. — *adj* **cū'bital** of the length of a cubit; relating to the elbow or forearm. [L *cubitum* the elbow; cf L *cubāre* to lie down]

cuboid, etc. See under **cube**.

cucking stool *kuk'ing stōōl*, (*hist*) *n* a stool in which scolds, dishonest traders and other miscreants were placed, *usu* before their own door, to be pelted and jeered at by the mob. [Mentioned in the Domesdsay Book as in use in Chester, and called *cathedra stercoris*; from an obs word *cuck*, to defecate; cf ON *kūka*]

cuckold *kuk'əld*, *n* a man whose wife has proved unfaithful. — *vt* to make a cuckold (of). — *vt* **cuck'oldize** or **-ise** to make a cuckold. — *n* **cuck'oldom** or **cuck'oldry** the state of a cuckold; the act of making a cuckold. [OFr *cucuault*, from *cucu* cuckoo]

cuckoo *kōō'kōō*, *n* a bird (*Cuculus canorus*) that cries *cuckoo*, noted for depositing its eggs in the nests of other birds who then rear the chicks as their own; any bird of this or related genera; the call of the cuckoo; a silly or slightly mad person. — *adj* (*colloq*) silly or slightly mad. — **cuckoo clock** a clock in which a mechanical bird pops out of a door, making the sound of a cuckoo to announce the hours; **cuckoo flower** a plant (*Cardamine pratensis*) commonly found in damp pastures in Europe and America, with divided leaves and small lilac or white flowers, lady's smock; another name for ragged robin; **cuckoo fly** a gold-wasp, so named from laying its eggs in the nests or larvae of other insects; **cuckoo pint** (*orig* **cuckoo pintle**) (*-pint* or *-pīnt*) a European plant, (*Arum maculatum*) with a cylindrical purple flowerhead (spadix) enclosed within a yellowish modified leaf (spathe), and poisonous red berries (also called **lords and ladies**); **cuckoo-spit** or **cuckoo-spittle** a froth secreted by froth-flies on plants, surrounding and protecting the larvae and pupae. [Imit; cf Fr *coucou*, Ger *Kuckuck*, L *cucūlus*, Gr *kokkyx*, *-ȳgos*]

cucullate *kū'kul-āt* or *-kul'*, or **cucullated** *-id*, *adj* hooded; shaped like a hood. [L *cucullatus*, from *cucullus* a hood]

cucumber *kū'kum-bər*, or *-kəm-*, *n* a climbing plant (*Cucumis sativus*) of the Cucurbitaceae, with bristly lobed leaves and tendrils; its long cylindrical fruit, used as a salad vegetable and pickle; a cucumber tree (*US*). — **cucumber tree** the bilimbi tree; a species of magnolia whose fruit resembles a cucumber (*US*). — *adj* **cūcūm'-iform**. — **cool as a cucumber** calm, imperturbable. [L *cucumis*, *-eris*]

cucurbit *kū-kûr'bit*, *n* a chemical vessel used in distillation, *orig* shaped like a gourd; a cucurbitaceous plant. — *adj* **cucur'bital** or **cucurbitā'ceous** pertaining to the **Cucurbitā'ceae**, a family of sympetalous dicotyledons, including gourd, marrow, melon, etc; gourd-like. [L *cucurbita* a gourd]

cud *kud*, *n* food brought back from the first stomach of a ruminating animal to be chewed again. — **cud'weed** a woolly composite plant of the genus *Gnaphalium*, or a related plant. — **chew the cud** (*colloq*) to meditate, to reflect. [OE *cwidu*]

cudbear *kud'bār*, *n* a purple or reddish dyestuff obtained from various lichens. [From Dr *Cuthbert* Gordon, an 18c Scottish chemist]

cuddeehih. See **cuddy**[2].

cudden, cuddie, cuddin. See **cuddy**[4].

cuddle *kud'l*, *vt* to hug; to embrace; to fondle. — *vi* to lie close and snug together. — *n* a close embrace. — *adj* **cudd'lesome** or **cudd'ly** pleasant to cuddle, being eg attractively plump, soft, etc; suggestive of, conducive to, cuddling. [Origin unknown]

cuddy[1] *kud'i*, *n* a small cabin or cookroom, in the forepart of a boat or lighter; in large vessels, the officers' cabin under the poop-deck. [Origin uncertain; cf Fr *cahute*; Du *kajuit*; Ger *Kajüte*]

cuddy[2] *kud'i*, (*hist*) *n* the right of a lord to entertainment from his tenant; rent. — Also (*obs*) **cudd'eehih**. [Irish *cuid oidhche*, from *cuid* a share, and *oidche* night]

cuddy[3] or **cuddie** *kud'i*, (*Scot* and *dialect*)) *n* a donkey; a horse; a stupid person. [Perh *Cuthbert*]

cuddy[4] or **cuddie** *kud'i*, (*Scot*) *n* a young coalfish. — Also **cudd'en** or **cudd'in**. [Gaelic *cudainn*, *cudaig*]

cudgel *kuj'l*, *n* a heavy staff; a club. — *vt* to beat with a cudgel: — *pr p* **cudg'elling**; *pa t* and *pa p* **cudg'elled**. — *n* **cudg'eller**. — *n* **cudg'elling**. — **cudgel one's brains** to think hard; **take up the cudgels** to join in defence or support, *esp* energetically or forcefully. [OE *cycgel*]

cue[1] *kū*, *n* the seventeenth letter of the alphabet (Q or q).

cue[2] *kū*, *n* the last words of an actor's speech serving as a signal to the next speaker to begin; any word or action that serves as a signal to begin a speech, action, operation, etc; a stimulus that produces a response (*psychol*); the part one has to play (*archaic*). — *vt* to give a cue to; to insert (eg a film sequence, sound effect, etc) into a script: — *pr p* **cue'ing** or **cū'ing**; *pa t* and *pa p* **cued**. — **cue someone in** (*orig US slang*) to inform (someone); **on cue** just at the right moment. [According to some from Fr *queue* tail (see next word); in 17c written Q, and derived from L *quando* when, ie when the actor was to begin]

cue[3] *kū*, *n* a twist of hair at the back of the head; a rod used in playing billiards, etc. — *vt* to form a cue in (hair); to hit (a ball) with a cue (also *vi*): — *pr p* **cue'ing** or **cū'ing**; *pa t* and *pa p* **cued**. — *n* **cue'ist** a billiard-player. — **cue ball** the ball struck by the cue in snooker, billiards, etc. [Fr *queue*, from L *cauda* a tail]

cuerpo. See **en cuerpo**.

cuesta *kwes'tə*, *n* (*esp* in SW US) a hill ridge having a steep scarp on one side and a gradual slope on the other, caused by denudation of gently dipping hard rock strata. [Sp]

cuff[1] *kuf*, *n* a light blow with the open hand. — *vt* to strike with the open hand; to beat. [Origin obscure; cf Swed *kuffa* to knock]

cuff[2] *kuf*, *n* the end of the sleeve near the wrist; a covering for the wrist; a handcuff; a turned-up fold at the bottom of a trouser leg (*NAm*). — *vt* (*police slang*) to put handcuffs on. — **cuff link** either of a pair of *usu* decorative fasteners, *orig* consisting of two buttons linked together, now *usu* one button-like object attached to a pivoting bar, used for fastening a shirt cuff.

— **off the cuff** unofficially and offhand; improvised; **on the cuff** (*US*) on tick; on the house. [Prob cognate with **coif**]

cuff[3] *kuf*, *n* a Scottish form of **scuff**[1], **scruff**[1].

cuffin *kuf'in*, *n* a man. — **queer cuffin** a justice of the peace; a churl. [Thieves' slang]

cuffle *kuf'l*, (*obs*) *vi* to scuffle.

cuffo *kuf'ō*, (*old US slang*) *adv* without any admission charge. [Prob derived from **on the cuff** see **cuff**[2]]

cuffuffle *kər-fuf'l*, (*informal*) *n*. Same as **carfuffle**.

Cufic. Same as **Kufic**.

cui bono? *kī* or *kwē bō'nō*, or *ko͞o'ē bo'nō*, (*L*) for whose benefit or advantage is it?; who is the gainer?

cui malo? *kī* or *kwē mä'lō*, or *ko͞o'ē mal'-ō*, (*L*) whom will it harm?

cuif. Same as **coof**.

cuique suum *kwē'kwə so͞o'əm*, (*L*) to each his own.

cuirass *kwi-ras'* (or *kū'*), *n* a defensive breastplate and backplate fastened together; a breastplate alone. — *vt* to equip or cover with a cuirass. — *n* **cuirassier** (-*ēr'*) a cavalry-soldier wearing a cuirass. [Fr *cuirasse*, from *cuir*, leather, from L *corium* skin, leather]

cuir-bouilli *kwēr-bo͞o'yē*, *n* leather boiled or soaked in hot water and moulded, *orig* used for armour. — Also **cuir-bou'illy**. [Fr, boiled leather]

Cuisenaire rods *kwē-zə-nār' rodz*, *n pl* a set of small wooden rods, of significant related sizes and colours, used in teaching arithmetic. [Georges *Cuisenaire*, a Belgian educationalist]

cuish. See **cuisse**.

cuisine *kwē-zēn'*, (*Fr*) *n* a kitchen or cooking department; the art or style of cooking; the dishes cooked. — *n* **cuisin'ier** (-*yā*) a cook. — **cuisine bourgeoise** plain cooking; **cuisine minceur** (*mɛ̃-sœr*) a style of cooking characterized by imaginative use of light, simple ingredients. — **nouvelle cuisine** (*no͞o-vel*) a style of simple French cooking excluding rich creamy sauces, etc in favour of fresh vegetables and light sauces. [From L *coquīna*, from *coquere* to cook]

cuisse *kwis* or **cuish** *kwish*, (*Shakesp* **cush** *kush*) *n* thigh armour. — **cuisse-madame** (-*däm'*) a jargonelle pear. [Fr *cuisse*, from L *coxa* hip]

cuisser. See **cusser**.

cuit, cute or **coot** *køt*, *küt* or *kit*, (*Scot*) *n* the ankle. — *n* **cuit'ikin, cut'ikin** or **coot'ikin** a gaiter. [Cf Du *koot*, lem *keute*]

cuit à point *kwēt ä pwɛ̃*, (*Fr*) done to a turn.

cuiter *küt'ər*, (*Scot*) *vt* to wheedle; to cocker, pamper.

cuittle *küt'l*, (*Scot*) *vt* to coax; to cajole; to curry (favour). [Origin obscure]

culch or **cultch** *kulch*, (*S Eng*) *n* rubbish; the flooring of an oyster-bed; oyster-spawn. [Origin doubtful]

culchie *kul'chi*, (*Irish*) *n* a rustic; a country labourer. [Origin unknown]

Culdee *kul'dē*, *n* one of a fraternity of monks living in Scotland from the 8c in groups of cells. [Old Irish *cēle de*, servant or companion of God, Latinized by Boece into *Culdei* (pl) as if *cultōrēs Deī*]

cul-de-four *kü(l)-də-fo͞or* (Fr *kü*), (*archit*) *n* a low vault shaped like a quarter sphere; a demicupola. [Fr *cul* bottom, *de* of, and *four* furnace]

cul-de-lampe *kül-də-lãp*, *n* an ornamental design used in filling up blank spaces in a book. [Fr *cul* bottom, *de* of, and *lampe* lamp]

cul-de-sac *ko͝ol'də-sak*, or *kul'*, *n* a street, etc closed at one end; a blind alley; a route that leads nowhere (*fig*). [Fr *cul* bottom, *de* of, and *sac* sack]

culet *kū'lit*, *n* the flat back or base of a brilliant-cut gemstone; armour protecting the hips and buttocks. [OFr *culet*, dimin of *cul* bottom]

culex *kū'leks*, *n* an insect of the genus *Culex*, of the gnat family **Culic'idae**, including the common European mosquito *C. pipiens*: — *pl* **culices** (*kū'li-sēz*). — *n* **cu'licid**. — *adj* **culiciform** (-*lis'*). — *n* and *adj* **cu'licine**. [L *culex*, *-icis*]

culinary *ku'lin-ər-i*, or *ū'*, *adj* pertaining to the kitchen or to cookery; used in the kitchen. [L *culīnārius*, from *culīna* a kitchen]

cull[1] *kul*, *vt* to gather; to select; to pick out and destroy (individuals, eg seal, deer), as inferior or superfluous members of a group. — *n* an act of culling; an unsuitable or superfluous animal eliminated from a flock or herd. — *n* **cull'er**. — *n* **cull'ing**. [Fr *cueillir* to gather, from L *colligere*, from *col-* together, and *legere* to gather]

cull[2]. See **cully**.

cullender. See **colander**.

cullet *kul'it*, *n* waste glass, melted up again with new material. [Fr *collet*, from L *collum* neck]

cullion *kul'yən*, (*archaic*) *n* a mean or base person; a wretch, rascal. — *adj* **cull'ionly** mean, base. [Fr *couillon* testicle, poltroon (Ital *coglione*), from L *cōleus* a leather bag, from Gr *koleos* sheath]

cullis[1] *kul'is*, (*now rare*) *n* a strong broth. [OFr *coleis*, from L *cōlāre* to strain]

cullis[2] *kul'is*, *n* a roof gutter or groove. [Fr *coulisse*]

cully *kul'i*, *n* a dupe (*archaic*); a pal, mate, a man generally (*slang*; *rare*). — *vt* (*archaic*) to deceive or cheat: — *pr p* **cull'ying**; *pa t* and *pa p* **cull'ied**. — *n* **cull** (*archaic*) a dupe. — *n* **cull'yism** (*archaic*) the state of being a cully. [Prob a contraction of **cullion**]

culm[1] *kulm*, *n* a stem of grass or sedge. — *vi* to form a culm. — *adj* **culmif'erous** having a culm. [L *culmus* a stalk]

culm[2] *kulm*, *n* coal-dust; anthracite dust; anthracite (*dialect*). — *adj* **culmif'erous** producing culm. — **Culm** or **Culm Measures** a Lower Carboniferous formation of Europe and SW England, with grits, sandstones, shales, etc. [Origin unknown; cf **coom**]

culmen *kul'men*, *n* the highest point; the top ridge of a bird's bill. [L; see **culminate**]

culmiferous. See **culm**[1,2].

culminate *kul'min-āt*, *vi* to reach the highest point (with *in*); to be on, or come to, the meridian, and thus the highest (or lowest) point of altitude (*astron*). — *vt* to bring to the highest point. — *adj* **cul'minant** at its highest point. — *n* **culminā'tion** the act of culminating; the top; the highest point; transit of a body across the meridian (*astron*). [LL *culmināre*, *-ātum*, from *culmen* or *columen*, *-inis* a summit]

culottes *kū-lot'*, or *ko͞o-*, *n pl* a divided skirt. — **sansculotte** see **sans**. [Fr *culotte* breeches]

culpable *kul'pə-bl*, *adj* meriting or deserving blame or condemnation; guilty, criminal (*archaic*). — *n* **culpabil'ity** or **cul'pableness** blameworthiness. — *adv* **cul'pably**. — *adj* **cul'patory** expressive of blame. [L *culpa* a fault]

culpa lata *kul'pə lāt'ə* or *ko͝ol'pa lä'ta*, (*L*) *n* gross negligence.

culpa levis *kul'pə lē'vis* or *ko͝ol'pa le'vis* or *-wis*, (*L*) *n* a fault of little importance; excusable neglect.

culprit *kul'prit*, *n* a person at fault; a criminal; a prisoner who has pled not guilty to a charge and is awaiting trial (*Eng law*). [From the fusion in legal phraseology of *cul.* (*culpable*, *culpābilis*), and *prit*, *prist* (OFr *prest*) ready]

cult *kult*, *n* a system of religious belief; a sect; an unorthodox or false religion; a great, often excessive, admiration for a person or idea; the person or idea giving rise to such admiration; (with *of*) a fad. — *adj* applied to objects associated with pagan worship; pertaining to, or giving rise to, a cult, extremely fashionable. — *adj* **cult'ic** or **cult'ish** pertaining to or characteristic of a cult. — *n* **cult'ism** adherence to a cult. — *n* **cult'ist**. [L *cultus*, from *colere* to worship]

cultch. Same as **culch**.

culter *kul'tər*, *n* an *obs* form of **couter**. — *adj* **cul'trate**, **cultrā'ted** or **cul'triform** knife-shaped. [L, knife]

cultigen *kul'ti-jən*, *n* a cultivated type of plant of uncertain origin. [See **cultivate**, and Gr root of *gignesthai* to become]

cultivar. See under **cultivate**.

cultivate *kul'ti-vāt*, *vt* to fill or produce by tillage; to prepare for crops; to devote attention to; to seek actively to gain or foster (an association, friendship, etc); to civilize or refine. — *adj* **cul'tivable** or **cultivāt'able** capable of being cultivated. — *n* **cultivar** (*kul'ti-vär*) a plant variety produced from a naturally occurring species, that has been developed and maintained by cultivation (*cultivated variety*). — *n* **cultivā'tion** the art or practice of cultivating; civilization; refinement. — *n* **cul'tivātor** a person who cultivates; an agricultural implement, a grubber. [LL *cultivāre*, *-ātum*, from L *colere* to till, to worship]

cultrate, **cultriform**. See **culter**.

culture *kul'chər*, *n* cultivation; the result of cultivation; the state of being cultivated; refinement in manners, thought, taste, etc; loosely, the arts; a type of civilization; the attitudes and values which inform a society; a crop of microorganisms, eg bacteria, grown in a solid or liquid medium in a laboratory. — *vt* to cultivate; to grow (living organisms or cells) in a culture medium. — *adj* **cul'turable**. — *adj* **cul'tural**. — *adv* **cul'turally**. — *adj* **cul'tured** cultivated; well educated, *esp* in the arts and humanities; refined. — *adj* **cul'tureless**. — *n* **cul'turist** a devotee of culture; a person who grows cultures in a laboratory. — **cultural anthropology** social anthropology; **cultural cringe** (esp *Austr*) a subservient attitude (*usu* of a nation) to what are regarded as the superior cultures of others; **cultural** or **culture shock** disorientation caused by a change from one environment, culture, ideology, etc to another that is radically different or alien; **cultured pearl** a pearl grown round a small foreign body deliberately introduced into an oyster's shell; **culture medium** a nutritive substance on which laboratory cultures can be grown, eg gelatin, agar, etc; **culture vulture** a derogatory term for someone who has an avid interest in the arts. [L *cultūra*, from *colere*]

cultus *kul'təs*, *n* a religious ritual; a cult. [L]

culver *kul'vər*, *n* a dove, a pigeon; a wood-pigeon. — **cul'ver-key** (often in *pl*) the cowslip; (in *pl*) ash-keys. — *adj* **cul'vertailed** dove-tailed. [OE *culfre*]

culverin *kul'vər-in*, *n* an early form of hand gun; later a type of cannon with a long barrel of relatively narrow bore, used in the 16c and 17c. — *n* **culverineer'**. [Fr *coulevrine*, from *couleuvre* snake, from L *colubrīnus* snake-like, from *coluber* snake]

Culver's physic *kul'vərz fiz'ik* or **root** *ro͞ot*, *n* the dried rhizome of a N American plant related to the speedwell (*Veronicastrum virginicum*), formerly used medicinally. [From Dr *Culver*, an 18th-century US physician]

culvert *kul'vərt*, *n* an arched construction or channel enclosing a drain or watercourse beneath a road, railway, etc. [Perh from Fr *couler* to flow, from L *colāre*]

culvertage *kul'vərt-tij*, (*hist*) *n* degradation of a vassal to the position of a serf. [OFr *culvert* a serf]

cum *kum*, *prep* combined with; with the addition of (as *cum-dividend*, of shares, including the right to the next dividend); used as a *combining form* to indicate dual function, nature, etc, as in *kitchen-cum-dining-room*. [L]

cumarin. See **coumarin**.

Cumb. *abbrev*: Cumbria.

cumbent *kum'bənt*, *adj* lying down; reclining. [L *cumbēns*, *-entis*, pr p of *cumbere* to lie down]

cumber *kum'bər*, *vt* to trouble or hinder with something useless; to get in the way of; to occupy obstructively. — *n* an encumbrance; cumbering. — *adj* **cum'bered** hampered; obstructed. — *n* **cum'berer**. — *adj* **cum'berless** unencumbered. — *n* **cum'berment**. — *adj* **cum'bersome** unwieldy, awkward, unmanageable. — *n* **cum'brance** an encumbrance; hindrance, burden. — *adj* **cum'brous** hindering; obstructing; unwieldy. — *adv* **cum'brously**. — *n* **cum'brousness**. [Appar OFr *combrer* to hinder, from LL *cumbrus* a heap, from L *cumulus* a heap]

cumec *kū'mek*, (*eng*) *n* short for *cu*bic *me*tre per se*c*ond, a unit for measuring volumetric rate of flow.

cum grano salis *kum grā'nō sā'lis* or *ko͞om grä'nō sa'lis*, (*L*) with a grain of salt.

cumin or **cummin** *kum'in* or *kū'min*, *n* an umbelliferous plant (*Cuminum cyminum*) of the Mediterranean region, with seeds like caraway, used for flavouring and valuable as carminatives. [OE *cymen*, from L *cumīnum*, from Gr *kymīnon*, cognate with Heb *kammon*]

cum laude *kum lö'dē* or *ko͞om lowd'de*, (*L*) with distinction (used on a diploma to denote special merit or the lowest grade of honours). — See also **magna cum laude**, **summa cum laude**.

cummer *kum'ər* or **kimmer** *kim'ər*, (*Scot*) *n* a godmother (*obs*); a gossip; a woman; a girl. [Fr *commère*, from L *con-*, with *māter* mother]

cummerbund *kum'ər-bund*, *n* a waistband, a sash. [Hindi *kamarband*, a loinband]

cummingtonite *kum'ing-tən-īt*, *n* a mineral of the amphibole group, hydrated magnesium iron silicate, occurring in metamorphic rocks. [From *Cummington*, a town in the US where it was first found]

cum multis aliis *kum mul'tis ā'lē-is* or *ko͞om mo͝ol'tēs a'lē-ēs*, (*L*) with many other things.

cum notis variorum *kum nō'tis vā-ri-ō'rəm* (or *-ö'*) or *ko͞om no'tēs va-ri-ō'ro͞om* (or *wa-*), (*L*) with notes of various (critics or commentators).

cum privilegio *kum priv-i-lē'ji-ō* or *ko͞om prē-vi-lā'gi-ō* (or *-wi-*), (*L*) with privilege.

cumquat. Same as **kumquat**.

cum-savvy *kum-sav'i*, (*slang*) *n* know-how.

cumshaw *kum'shö*, *n* a gift, a tip, gratuity. [Pidgin-Eng, from Chin *gam sia* grateful thanks]

cumulate *kūm'ū-lāt*, *vt* and *vi* to heap together; to accumulate. — *adj* **cum'ulate** or **cum'ulated** heaped up. — *n* **cumulā'tion** accumulation. — *adj* **cum'ulative** increasing by successive additions. — *adv* **cum'ulatively**. — **cumulative action** (*med*) (of a drug) toxic effects produced when repeated doses are taken and the body has had insufficient time to break down or excrete each dose; **cumulative dose** (*radiol*) the integrated radiation dose resulting from repeated exposure; **cumulative vote** a system by which a voter may distribute a number of votes at will among the candidates, giving more than one to a candidate if he or she chooses. [L *cumulāre*, *-ātum*, from *cumulus* a heap]

cumulus *kū'mū-ləs*, *n* a heap; a kind of cloud consisting of rounded heaps with a darker horizontal base: — *pl* **cū'mulī**. — *adj* **cū'muliform**. — *adj* **cū'mulose**. — **cū'mulocirr'us** a delicate cirrus-like cumulus cloud; **cū'mulonim'bus** a cumulus cloud of great height, often discharging showers or characteristic of thunderstorms; **cūmulostra'tus** (*-strā'* or *strä'*) a cumulus cloud with an extended base. [L *cumulus* a heap]

cunabula *kū-nab'ū-lə*, *n pl* a cradle; incunabula. [L *cūnābula*]

cunctator *kungk-tā'tər*, *n* someone who delays or procrastinates. — *n* **cunctā'tion** delay, procrastination. — *adj* **cunctā'tious**, **cunc'tative** or **cunc'tatory** inclined to delay or procrastinate. [L *cunctātor*, from *cunctārī* to delay, hesitate]

cundy *kun'di* or *kon'di*, (*Scot*) *n* a covered drain; a tunnel or passage. — Also **con'die**. [Altered form of **conduit**]

cuneal *kū'ni-əl* or **cuneate** *kū'ni-āt*, *adj* wedge-shaped. — *adj* **cuneat'ic** cuneiform. — *adj* **cuneiform** (*kū-nē'i-förm* or *kū'ni(i-)förm*) wedge-shaped — specially applied to the old Hittite, Babylonian, Assyrian and Persian writing, of which the characters were impressed by the wedge-shaped facets of a stylus. — *n* cuneiform writing. — **cuneiform bones** (*anatom*) (in the foot) three small bones of the tarsus. [L *cuneus* a wedge]

cunette *kū-net'*, (*fortif*) *n* a trench sunk along the middle of a dry ditch or moat, serving as a drain, a cuvette. [Fr, from Ital *cunetta*, aphetic from *lacunetta* a small lagoon or ditch]

cunjevoi *kun'ji-voi*, (*Austr*) *n* a sea squirt; a large-leaved araceous plant, (*Alocasia macrorrhiza*) with edible rhizomes. [Aboriginal]

cunner. See **conner**[2].

cunnilingus *kun-i-ling'gəs* or **cunnilinctus** *-lingk'təs*, *n* oral stimulation of the female genitalia. [L *cunnus* vulva, and *lingere* to lick]

cunning *kun'ing*, *adj* knowing, clever; skilful, ingenious; artful; crafty; dainty or quaintly pleasing (*NAm*). — *n* knowledge, cleverness; skill, ingenuity; the faculty of using stratagem to accomplish a purpose; craftiness; artifice. — *adv* **cunn'ingly**. — *n* **cunn'ingness** the quality of being cunning; artfulness, slyness. [OE *cunnan* to know]

cunt *kunt*, (*taboo slang*) *n* the female genitalia, *esp* the vagina; a woman regarded as a sexual object; an unpleasant, contemptible person of either sex. [ME *cunte*; ety dubious]

CUP *abbrev*: Cambridge University Press.

cup *kup*, *n* a drinking-vessel, roughly hemispherical, *usu* with one handle; a hollow; a cup-shaped structure (*biol*); either of the two cup-shaped supports for the breasts in a brassière; a cupful; a dry or liquid measure used in cooking, equal to *approx* half a pint (a little over one quarter of a litre); the liquid, etc contained in a cup; a mixed beverage made with wine (as *claret cup*); an ornamental vessel offered as a prize; a competition with such a vessel as a prize; the hole, or its metal lining, on the green (*golf*); the chalice, or the consecrated wine, at the Eucharist; that which one receives or undergoes in life, one's lot in life. — *vt* to form into the shape of a cup; to lodge in or as if in a cup; to draw blood to the surface of the skin by means of cupping-glasses in order to facilitate blood-letting or to relieve chest infection, etc (*med*); to make drunk (*obs*). — *vi* to become cup-shaped: — *pr p* **cupp'ing**; *pa t* and *pa p* **cupped**. — *n* **cup'ful** as much as fills a cup: — *pl* **cup'fuls**. — *n* **cup'pa** (*colloq*) a cup of tea. — *n* **cupp'er** a cupbearer; a person professionally engaged in cupping. — *n* **cupp'ing** (*med*) (*esp* formerly) the application of cups from which the air is removed in order to draw blood to the surface of the skin. — **cup'-and-ball** a ball and socket joint; the game of catching a tethered ball in a cup on the end of a stick; **cup'-and-ring (mark)** (*archaeol*) a cup-mark surrounded by one or more incised rings, carved on stones; **cup'bearer** a person who attends at a feast to fill and hand out wine cups; **cup'cake** a small round cake baked in a foil or paper case; an attractive woman (*NAm slang*); a mad or eccentric person (*NAm slang*); a term of endearment (*NAm*); **cup coral** a simple cup-shaped coral; **cup fungus** any fungus of the order Pezizales; **cup'gall** a cup-shaped gall in oak-leaves; **cup'head** a hemispherical (or nearly so) bolt-head or rivet-head; **cup lichen** or **cup moss** any lichen with cup-shaped structures; **cup'man** a boon companion; **cup mark** a cup-shaped hollow made by prehistoric man on rocks, standing-stones, etc; **cupp'ing-glass** a glass vessel used in cupping; **cup'-tie** (*sport*) one of a series of games to determine the winners of a cup. — *adj* **cup'-tied** (of a player) unable to play in a cup-tie because of injury or other disallowance; (of a team) involved in a cup-tie and therefore unable to play in other games. — **in one's cups** under the influence of liquor, drink; **one's cup of tea** see under **tea**; **there's many a slip 'twixt the cup and the lip** the success of a venture should not be assumed and the possibility of failure or disaster should be recognized. [OE *cuppe*, from L *cūpa*, *cuppa* a tub]

cupboard *kub'ərd*, *n* an item of furniture or a recess fitted with a door, used for storage. — *vt* to store. — **cup'board-love** hypocritical show of affection for material gain.

cupel *kū'pəl*, *n* a small vessel used by goldsmiths in assaying precious metals; the movable hearth of a reverberatory furnace for refining. — *vt* to assay in a cupel: — *pr p* **cū'pelling** or *NAm* **cūpeling**; *pa t* and *pa p* **cū'pelled** or *NAm* **cū'peled**. — *n* **cūpellā'tion** a method of refining precious metal in which impure metal is melted in a cupel and impurities are oxidized or run off. [L *cūpella*, dimin of *cūpa*; see **cup**]

Cupid *kū'pid*, *n* the Roman god of sexual love, identified with Greek Eros; (without *cap*) a winged figure of a young boy often carrying a bow and arrow representing love (*art*, etc); (without *cap*) a kind of jam-tart (*US*). — *adj* **cūpid'inous** full of desire, *esp* amorous. — *n* **cūpid'ity** covetousness. — **Cupid's bow** an archery bow in the shape of a double curve; the human lips shaped (either naturally or by lipstick) like this. [L *Cūpīdo*, *-inis*, from *cupere* to desire]

cupola *kū'pə-lə*, *n* a spherical vault, or concave ceiling, on the top of a building; the internal part of a dome; a dome; a lantern on the top of a dome; any dome-shaped structure, eg at the end of the cochlea (*anatom*); an armoured dome or turret to protect a gun; a furnace used in iron-foundries. — *vt* to furnish with a cupola. — *adj* **cū'pola'd** or **cū'polaed**. — *adj* **cū'polar**. — *adj* **cū'polated**. [Ital, from L *cūpula*, dimin of *cūpa* a cask]

cuppa. See **cup**.

cuprammonium *kū-prä-mō'ni-əm*, *n* a solution of cupric hydroxide in ammonia. — **cuprammonium rayon** artificial silk made by dissolving cellulose in cuprammonium. [L *cuprum* copper, and **ammonium**]

cupreous *kū'pri-əs*, *adj* of, containing, or like copper. — *adj* **cū'pric** of or containing bivalent copper. — *adj* **cūprif'erous** yielding copper. — *n* **cū'prite** red copper ore, ruby copper, cuprous oxide (Cu_2O). — *adj* **cū'prous** of or containing univalent copper. — **cū'pro-nick'el** an alloy of copper and nickel. [L *cupreus*, from *cuprum*; see **copper**]

Cupressus *kū-pres'əs*, *n* the cypress genus. [L]

cupric, etc, **cuprous**. See **cupreous**.

cupule *kū'pūl*, *n* a small cup in a liverwort containing gemmae (*bot*); a cup-shaped structure on the fruit of some trees, eg oak, beech, chestnut. — *adj* **cū'pūlar** or **cū'pūlate** cup-like; pertaining to a cupule. — *n pl* **Cūpūlif'erae** (*-ə-rē'*) in some classifications a family including beech, oak, chestnut, with or without birch, hazel, and hornbeam. — *adj* **cūpūlif'erous** of the Cupuliferae; bearing cupules. [L *cūpula*, dimin of *cūpa* tub]

cur *kûr*, *n* a worthless dog, of low breed; someone deserving contempt, a scoundrel. — *adj* **curr'ish**. — *adv* **curr'ishly**. — *n* **curr'ishness**. [ME *curre*; cf ON *kurra* to grumble]

cur. or **curt**. *abbrev*: current (ie this month).

curaçao *ko͞o-rä-sä'ō*, or **curaçoa** *kū'rə-sō* or *kū-ra-sō'*, *n* a liqueur flavoured with bitter orange peel. [*Curaçao*, island in the W Indies, where it was first made]

curacy. See **curate**.

curare or **curari** *kū-* or *ko͞o-rä'ri*, *n* a paralysing poison extracted from the bark of S American trees (eg *Strychnos* or *Chondodendron*), *orig* used by South American Indians to coat the tips of arrows, later used as a muscle relaxant, eg to control muscle spasm in tetanus, and in surgery. — Also **cura'ra**. — *n* **cura'rine** a highly poisonous alkaloid derivative, used in surgery in the form of tubocurarine, as a muscle relaxant. — *vt* **cu'rarize** or **-ise**. [Port from Carib *kurari*]

curassow *kū'rə-sō* or *kū-räs'ō*, *n* a large turkey-like S American bird. [From the island of *Curaçao*]

curat *kū'rət*, (*obs*) *n* a cuirass. [See **cuirass**]

curate[1] *kūr'it*, *n* someone who has the cure of souls (*archaic*); a clergyman in the Church of England, assisting a rector or vicar. — *n* **cur'acy** (*-ə-si'*) or **cur'ateship** the office, employment or benefice of a curate. — **curate's egg** anything of which some parts are excellent and some parts are bad. [LL *cūrātus*, L *cūra* care]

curate[2] *kū-rāt'*, *vt* to act as a curator for (eg an exhibition or museum). [Back-formation from **curator**]

curative. See **cure**[1].

curator *kūr-ā'tər* (in Scots law *kūr'ə-tər*), *n* a person who has the charge of anything; a superintendent, *esp* of a museum; a person appointed by law as guardian; a member of a board for electing university professors and the like: — *fem* **curā'trix**. — *adj* **curatorial** (*-ə-tö'ri-əl*). — *n* **curā'torship**. [L *cūrātor*]

curatory. See **cure**[1].

curb *kûrb*, *n* a chain or strap attached to the bit for restraining a horse; another spelling for **kerb** (chiefly *US*); a check or restraint; a disease of horses, marked by hard swellings on the leg; the swelling itself. — *vt* to furnish with or guide by a curb; to restrain or check. — *adj* **curb'able**. — *adj* **curb'less**. — **curb'stone** a *NAm* spelling of **kerbstone**. [Fr *courbe*, from L *curvus* bent]

curch *kûrch*, *n* a covering for the head, a kerchief. [See **kerchief**]

curculio *kûr-kū'li-ō*, *n* any member of the **Curcūlion'idae**, a family of weevils, many of which are serious pests of stored foodstuffs and fruit crops, *esp* the **plum curculio** of N America: — *pl* **curcu'lios**. [L, rice or grain weevil]

curcuma *kûr-kū'mə*, *n* any plant of the genus *Curcuma* (of the ginger family), especially *C. longa* yielding turmeric. — *n* **cur'cumine** or **cur'cumin** the saffron-yellow colouring matter of turmeric, used *esp* in food colouring. [Ar *kurkum* saffron]

curd *kûrd*, *n* milk thickened or coagulated by acid; the cheese part of milk, as distinguished from the whey; any substance of similar consistency; (in soap-making) the granular soap that rises in the lye upon salting; the fatty matter between the flakes of salmon flesh; the flowering head of cauliflower, broccoli, etc. — *vt* and *vi* to curdle. — *n* **curd'iness**. — *vt* and *vi* **curd'le** to turn into curd; to coagulate; to thicken. — *adj* **curd'y** like or full of curd. — **curd cheese** a mild white cheese made from skimmed milk curds. [Prob Celtic; Gaelic *gruth*, Irish *cruth*]

cure[1] *kūr*, *n* that which heals; a remedy, or course of remedial treatment; a means of improving a situation; a course or method of preserving or arresting decomposition; the total quantity cured; treatment by which a product is finished or made ready for use; care of the sick; an act of healing; care of souls or spiritual charge. — *vt* to heal or make better; to preserve by drying, salting, etc; to finish by means of chemical change, eg to vulcanize (a rubber), or to use heat or chemicals in the last stage of preparing (a thermosetting plastic). — *vi* to undergo a process or course of curing. — *n* **cūrabil'ity**. — *adj* **cūr'able**. — *n* **cūr'ableness**. — *adj* **cūr'ative** or **cūr'atory** tending to cure. — *adj* **cūre'less** that cannot be cured. — *n* **cūr'er**. — **cūre'-all** a panacea. [OFr *cure*, from L *cūra* care]

cure[2] *kūr*, (*slang*) *n* an odd or queer person. [Ety dubious]

curé *kū'rā*, *n* a parish priest in France. [Fr; see **curate**]

curettage *kū-ret'ij*, (*surg*) *n* the scraping of a body cavity or internal surface of an organ by means of a spoon-shaped instrument known as a **curette'**, *usu* to remove diseased tissue or a sample of tissue for diagnostic purposes. — *vt* **curette'** to scrape with a curette. — *n* **curette'ment** curettage. [Fr *curer* to clean, clear]

curfew *kûr'fū*, *n* a regulation obliging persons to be indoors within certain hours; the ringing of a bell at a certain hour as a traditional custom, or the bell itself; the time of curfew; in feudal times, the ringing of a bell as a signal to put out all fires and lights. — **cur'few-bell**. [OFr *covrefeu*; *couvrir* to cover, *feu* fire, from L *focus*]

curfuffle. See **carfuffle**.

curia *kū'ri-ə*, *n* the court of the papal see; one of the ten divisions of a Roman tribe; a building in which the senate met; a provincial senate. — *n* **cū'rialism**. — *n* **cū'rialist**. — *adj* **cūrialist'ic**. — **Curia Regis** see **aula**. — **curia advisari vult** (*law*) the court wishes to be advised, or consider (*abbrev* **cur**. **adv**. **vult** or **c.a.v**). [L *cūria* a division of a Roman tribe, a senate, a court]

curie *kū-rē'* or *kū'rē*, *n orig* the quantity of radon in radioactive equilibrium with a gram of radium; a unit of radioactivity, defined as 3.7×10^{10} disintegrations per second (becquerels), or the quantity of a radioactive substance which undergoes this number of disintegrations. — *n* **curium** (*kū'*) a chemical element (atomic no 96; symbol **Cm**). — **curiether'apy** a former name for the treatment of disease by radium. [After Marie and Pierre *Curie*, discoverers of radium]

curiet *kū'ri-et*, (*obs*) *n* a cuirass. [See **cuirass**]

curio *kū'ri-ō*, *n* any article of bric-à-brac, or anything considered rare and curious: — *pl* **cū'rios**. [For **curiosity**]

curiosa *kū-ri-ō'sə*, *n pl* strange or unusual objects, *specif* books, manuscripts, etc which are pornographic or erotic. [New L, from same root as **curious**]

curious *kū'ri-əs*, *adj* anxious to learn; inquisitive; skilfully made; singular; rare, unusual; odd, strange. — *n* **curiosity** (*-os'i-ti*) the state or quality of being curious; inquisitiveness; that which is curious; anything rare or unusual. — *adv* **cū'riously**. — *n* **cū'riousness**. [Fr *curieux*, from L *cūriōsus*, from *cūra*]

curium. See **curie**.

curl *kûrl*, *vt* to twist into ringlets; to coil; to cause to move in a curve; to ripple. — *vi* to shrink into ringlets; to move in curves; to writhe; to ripple; to eddy; to play at the game of curling. — *n* a ringlet of hair, or something resembling it; a wave, bending or twist; an eddy; a plant disease in which leaves curl; a curled condition. — *adj* **curled**. — *n* **curl'er** someone who, or that which, curls; a player at the game of curling. — *n* **curl'iness**. — *n* **curl'ing** a game played on ice, *esp* common in Scotland, in which two teams slide a series of heavy smooth stones with the aim of reaching a target circle and/or dislodging the opposing team's stone(s) already in the circle. — *adj* **curl'y** having curls; full of curls. — **curling īrons** another name for curling tongs; **curl'ing-pond** a pond on which curling is played; **curl'ing-stone** a heavy smooth stone with a handle, used in the game of curling; **curling tongs** an instrument consisting of a heated rod (round which hair is wound) and a hinged plastic or metal grip, used for curling the hair; **curlpaper** a strip of paper round which the hair is twisted to give it curl; **curl'y-greens** kale. — *adj* **curl'y-headed**. — **curl up** (*colloq*) to be embarrassed; **out of curl** lacking energy, limp. [ME *crull*; Du *krullen*, Dan *krolle* to curl]

curlew *kûr'lōō* or *-lū*, *n* a wading bird (*Numenius arquata*) of the woodcock family, inhabiting moorland, the shoreline and other damp areas, with a long curved bill and long legs, and a plaintive whistling cry; any related bird of the genus *Numenius*. — **cur'lew-berry** another name for crowberry; **stone curlew** see separate entry at **stone**. [OFr *corlieu*; prob from its cry]

curlicue *kûr'lə-kū*, *n* a fancy twist or curl, *esp* in handwriting. [**curly** and **cue**[2]]

curliewurlie *kûr'li-wûr'li*, (*Scot*) *n* and *adj* (of) a twisted or curled object or ornament.

curmudgeon *kər-muj'ən*, *n* an avaricious, ill-natured churlish fellow; a miser. — *adj* and *adv* **curmud'geonly**. [Origin unknown]

curmurring *kər-mûr'ing*, *n* a rumbling sound, *esp* that made in the bowels by flatulence. [Imit]

curn *kûrn*, (*Scot*) *n* a grain; a particle; a small quantity, a little. — *adj* **curn'y** or **curn'ey** granular, coarse-grained. [**corn**]

curnaptious. See **carnaptious**.

curpel *kûr'pl*, *n* a Scots form of **crupper**.

curr *kûr*, (*dialect*) *vi* to make a purring sound. [Imit]

currach or **curragh** *kur'əhh* or *kur'ə*, *n* a long-shaped boat of similar construction to a coracle. [Irish *curach*]

currajong. See **kurrajong**.

currant *kur'ənt*, *n* a small black raisin or dried seedless grape; extended to several species of Ribes (*black*, *red*, *white*, *flowering currant*), and to various other plants, and their fruits. — *adj* **curr'anty** full of currants. — **curr'ant-bread** a sweetened bread containing (grape) currants; **curr'ant-bun** or **curr'ant-loaf** a dark spiced cake full of currants; **curr'ant-cake** a cake with currants in it; **curr'ant-jelly** a jelly made from red or black currants; **curr'ant-wine**. [**Corinth** (currants orig known as *raisins of Corinth*)]

currawong *kur'ə-wong*, *n* any of several Australian crow-like birds of the genus *Strepera*, with a distinctive, resounding call. [Aboriginal]

current *kur'ənt*, *adj* belonging to the period of time now passing; up-to-date; present; generally or widely received; passing from person to person. — *n* a running or flowing; a stream; a portion of water or air moving in a certain direction; a flow of electricity; course. — *n* **curr'ency** that which circulates, *esp* the money of a country; circulation; general acceptance or prevalence; up-to-dateness; native-born Australians collectively, as opposed to immigrants (*old Austr slang*). — *adv* **curr'ently**. — *n* **curr'entness**. — **currency note** another name for **treasury note**; **current account** a bank account on which one is *usu* not paid interest and from which money may be withdrawn by cheque; **current bedding** (*geol*) false bedding. — *adj* **curr'ent-cost** (*accountancy*) of a system that values assets at the current cost of replacement (cf **historic cost**); **current coil** (*elec eng*) a coil connected in series with a circuit and therefore carrying the main current. — **pass current** to be received as genuine. [L *currēns*, *-entis*, from pr p of *currere* to run]

currente calamo *ku-ren'tē* (or *kŏŏ-ren'te*) *ka'la-mō*, (*L*) with a running pen, offhand.

curricle *kur'i-kl*, *n* a two-wheeled open chaise, drawn by two horses abreast. [L *curriculum* course, race, racing chariot, from *currere* to run]

curriculum *kə-rik'ū-ləm*, *n* a course, *esp* the course of study at a school, college, university, etc: — *pl* **curric'ula** or **curric'ulums**. — *adj* **curric'ular** of or relating to a curriculum or to courses of study. — **core curriculum** the subjects that a pupil or student is obliged to study while at school; **curriculum vitae** (*kə-rik'ūl-əm vī'tē* or *kŏŏr-ik'ŏŏ-lŏŏm vē'tī* or *wē'tī*) (a biographical summary of) the course of someone's life, *esp* details of education and achievements in chronological order requested by or supplied to potential employers (*abbrev* **cv** or **CV**). [L; see **curricle**]

currie. See **curry**[3].

curried, **currier**. See **curry**[2].

currish, **currishly**, etc. See **cur**.

curry[1] *kur'i*, *n* a dish of meat, eggs or vegetables cooked and seasoned with hot or aromatic spices, eg turmeric, chillies, cumin, coriander, etc. — *vt* to make a curry of by seasoning with mixed spices or adding curry sauce. — **curr'y-leaf** a rutaceous Indian tree (*Murraya koenigii*) whose leaves are an ingredient in curry powder; **curry powder** ground mixed spices, including turmeric, cumin, chillies, fenugreek, cloves, coriander, etc. [Tamil *kari* sauce]

curry[2] *kur'i*, *vt* to dress or treat (leather). — *n* to rub down and groom (eg a horse) with a currycomb; to beat; to scratch: — *pr p* **curr'ying**; *pa t* and *pa p* **curr'ied**. — *n* **curr'ier** a person who curries or dresses tanned leather; **curr'ying**. — **curr'ycomb** a metal instrument or comb with rows of teeth used for currying or grooming horses. — **curry favour** (*orig* **curry favell** to curry the chestnut horse) to seek to ingratiate oneself. [OFr *correier* (Fr *corroyer*), *conrei* outfit, from L *con-* with, and the root seen in **array**]

curry[3], **currie**. Obsolete forms of **quarry**[2].

cursal. See **cursus**.

curse *kûrs*, *vt* to invoke or wish evil upon; to blaspheme; to afflict with; to damn; to excommunicate. — *vi* to utter abuse; to swear. — *n* an invocation or wishing of evil or harm; evil invoked on another person; the excommunication sentence; an imprecation; any great evil; (with *the*) menstruation, a menstrual period (*colloq*). — *adj* **curs'ed** under or deserving a curse; hateful. — *adv* **curs'edly**. — *n* **curs'edness**. — *n* **curs'er**. — *n* **curs'ing**. — *adj* **curst** cursed; ill-tempered (*archaic*). — *n* **curst'ness** the state of being curst; peevishness; perverseness. — **curse of Scotland** (*cards*) the nine of diamonds (origin unknown). [OE *cursian*, from *curs* a curse; ety doubtful; not connected with **cross**]

curselarie, **cursenary**. See **cursorary** under **cursor**.

cursitor *kûr'si-tər*, *n* a clerk or officer in the Court of Chancery who made out original writs *de cursu*, ie of ordinary course; a vagrant (*obs*). [LL *cursitor*]

cursive *kûr'siv*, *adj* (of handwriting) written with a running hand; flowing; (of a typeface) designed to imitate handwriting. — *adv* **cur'sively**. [LL *cursīvus*, from L *currere* to run]

cursor *kûr'sər*, *n* a sliding part of a measuring instrument; one of several (*usu* flashing) devices appearing on a VDU screen used to indicate position, eg of the next input character, of a correction, etc. — *adj* (*obs*) **cur'sorary** (*Shakesp*; other readings **cur'senary**, **cur'-selarie**; *prob* intended for **cursitory**) cursory. — *adj* **curso'rial** (of an animal or bird or part of its anatomy) adapted for running. — *adv* **cur'sorily** (*-sər-*). — *n* **cur'soriness**. — *adj* **cur'sory** superficial; hasty; running quickly over. [L *cursor*, pl *cursōrēs* a runner, from *currere*, *cursum* to run]

curst. See **curse**.

cursus *kûr'səs*, *n* an elongated prehistoric earthwork found only in Britain, consisting of parallel banks with ditches outside: — *pl* **cur'si**. — *adj* **cur'sal**. [L, a course]

curt *kûrt*, *adj* short; concise; discourteously brief or summary. — *adv* **curt'ly**. — *n* **curt'ness**. [L *curtus* shortened]

curt. *abbrev*. See **cur**. (*abbrev*).

curtail *kər-tāl'*, *vt* to cut short; to cut off a part of; to abridge. — *n* **curtail'ment**. — **cur'tail-step** a round-ended step at the bottom of a flight. [Old spelling *curtal*, OFr *courtault*, from L *curtus* shortened]

curtain *kûr'tən*, *n* hanging drapery at a window, around a bed, etc; the part of a rampart between two bastions (*fortif*); a curtain wall; (in a theatre) a screen of cloth or metal concealing the stage, or restricting the spread of fire; the fall of the curtain, close of a scene or act (*theat*); a protective barrier in general, as the fire of many guns directed along a certain line to prevent the passage of an enemy (also called **cur'tain-fire**). — *vt* to enclose or furnish with curtains; (with *off*) to separate with, or as if with, a curtain. — **curtain call** a summons to a performer or performers from the audience to reappear after the curtain has been lowered at the end of a performance; **curtain lecture** a lecture or reproof given in bed by a wife to her husband; **curtain raiser** a short play preceding the main performance; an event which precedes a more important event; **curtain speech** a speech made before a theatre curtain; **curtain wall** a wall that is not load-bearing, eg does not support a roof; **curtain walling** prefabricated large framed sections of lightweight, *usu* predecorated, material used in building. — **bamboo curtain** see under **bamboo**; **be curtains (for)** to be the end or death (of) (*colloq*); **behind the curtain** away from public view; **draw the curtain** to draw it aside, so as to show what is behind, or to draw it in front of anything so as to hide it; **iron curtain** see under **iron**. [OFr *cortine*, from LL *cortīna*; prob L *cōrs*, *cōrtis* a court]

curtal *kûr'təl*, (*obs*) *n* a horse or other animal with a docked tail; anything docked or cut short, eg a kind of bassoon, cannon, etc. — *adj* docked or shortened. [See **curtail**]

curtalaxe *kûr'tə-laks*, (*archaic*) *n* a short, broad sword, a cutlass. [A corruption of the earlier forms *coutelas*, *curtelas*. See **cutlass**]

curtana *kûr-tä'nə* or *-tā'nə*, *n* a sword without a point, symbolic of mercy, carried at coronations. [L *curtus* short]

curtate *kûr'tāt*, *adj* shortened or reduced — applied to the distance of a planet from the sun or earth projected on the plane of the ecliptic. — *n* **curtā'tion**. [See **curt**]

curtesy *kûr'tə-si*, (*law*; now *rare*) *n* the right of a widower to a life estate in the land of his late wife.

curtilage *kûr'til-ij*, *n* a court, garden, field or area of land attached and belonging to a dwelling-house, etc. [OFr *courtillage*; see **court**]

curtsy or **curtsey** *kûrt'si*, *n* a formal indication of respect (by women) made by bending the knees. — *vi* to make or 'drop' a curtsy. [See **courtesy**]

curule *kū'rōōl*, *adj* of high authority, as a higher Roman magistrate who was entitled to a **curule chair**, one like a camp-stool with curved legs. [L *curūlis*, from *currus* a chariot]

curvaceous, **curvate**, etc. See **curve**.

curve *kûrv*, *n* a line that is not straight; a line (including a straight line) answering to an equation; a graph; the curved line on a graph representing the rise and fall of measurable data, eg birth-rate; a curved surface; anything bent; an arch; (in *pl*) the rounded contours of a woman's body (*colloq*). — *vt* to bend; to form into a curve. — *vi* to bend; to move in a curve. — *adj* **curvaceous** or **curvacious** (*kûr-vā'shəs*; *colloq*) (of a woman) having shapely curves. — *adj* **cur'vāte** or **curvā'ted** curved or bent in a regular form. — *n* **curvā'tion**. — *adj* **cur'vative** (*-və-tiv*). — *n* **cur'vature** (*-və-chər*) a curving or bending; the continual bending, or the amount of bending, from a straight line; the reciprocal of the radius at any point. — *adj* **curved**. — *adj* **curve'some** curvaceous. — *adj* **curvicau'date** having a crooked tail. — *adj* **curvicos'tate** having curved ribs. — *adj* **curvifō'liate** having curved leaves. — *adj* **cur'viform**. — *adj* **curvilin'eal** or **curvilin'ear** bounded by curved lines. — *n* **curvilinear'ity**. — *adj* **cur'ving**. — *adj* **curviros'tral** (of a bird) with the bill curved downward. — *adj* **cur'vital** of or pertaining to curvature. — *n* **cur'vity** the state of being curved. — *adj* **curv'y**. [L *curvus* crooked]

curvet *kûr'vet* or *kər-vet'*, *n* a light leap of a horse in which the forelegs are raised together, followed by the hindlegs with a spring before the forelegs touch the ground (*dressage*); a leap, frolic. — *vi* (*kər-vet'* or *kûr'vet*) to leap in curvets; to frisk: — *pr p* **curvett'ing** or **cur'veting**; *pa t* and *pa p* **curvett'ed** or **cur'veted**. [Ital *corvetta*, dimin of *corvo*, from L *curvus*]

curvicaudate, **curvifoliate**, **curvilineal**, etc. See **curve**.

cuscus[1] *kus'-kus*, or *kōōs'-kōōs*, *n* an arboreal phalanger of the Malay Archipelago, having thick fur, a long tail and large eyes. [Native name in the Moluccas]

cuscus[2] *kus'kus*, *n* the grain of the African millet. — See also **couscous**.

cuscus[3] *kus'kus*, *n* the fragrant fibrous root of an Indian grass (*Andropogon squarrosus*), used for making fans, etc. [Pers *khas khas*]

cusec *kū'sek*, (*eng*) *n* short for *cu*bic feet per *sec*ond, a unit for measuring volumetric rate of flow.

cush. See **cuisse**, **cushion**.

cushat *kush'ət*, (*Scot*) *n* the ringdove or wood-pigeon. [OE *cūscute*, perh from its note, and *scēotan* to shoot]

cushaw *kə-shö'*, *ku'* or *kōō'shö*. See **cashaw**.

Cushing's syndrome *kōōsh'ingz sin'drōm*, *n* a condition characterized by obesity, raised blood pressure, metabolic disorders, osteoporosis, etc, caused by excess amounts of corticosterid hormones in the body due to an adenoma of the pituitary gland (**Cushing's disease**), or a malignant tumour elsewhere. [Described by H W *Cushing* (1869–1939), American surgeon]

cushion *kōōsh'ən*, *n* a case of material, plastic, etc filled with some soft, elastic stuff, eg feathers or foam rubber, for resting on; a pillow; a pad; an engraver's pad; the pillow used in making bone-lace; the cap of a pier (*archit*); the padded lining of the inner side of a billiard-table (*colloq* **cush**); a body of steam remaining in the cylinder of a steam-engine, acting as a buffer to the piston; any body of air or steam acting as a protection against shock; anything that serves to deaden a blow, act as a protection against harm, unpleasant effects, etc. — *vt* to seat on, or provide with, a cushion; to serve as a cushion for or against; to suppress (complaints) by ignoring. — *adj* **cush'ioned** furnished with a cushion, padded; protected, shielded from anything unpleasant; having cushion-tyres. — *n* **cush'ionet** a little cushion. — *adj* **cush'iony** like a cushion, soft. — **cush'ion-plant** a plant of cushion-like form reducing transpiration; **cush'ion-tyre** or *NAm* **-tire** a cycle tyre of rubber tubing, with rubber stuffing. [OFr *coissin*, from L *coxīnum*, *coxa* hip, or perh L *culcita* mattress, cushion]

Cushite or **Kushite** *kōōsh'īt*, *n* a group of languages of eastern Africa, eg Ethiopia, Somalia, Sudan; a (member of a) race speaking any of these languages. — *adj* of or relating to the languages or the race. — Also **Cushitic** or **Kushitic** (*-it'ik*). [*Cush*, an ancient kingdom in the Nile valley, and **-ite**]

cushy *kōōsh'i*, (*slang*) *adj* easy and comfortable; not dangerous. [Perh Hindi *khush* pleasant, *khushī* happiness]

cusk *kusk*, (*NAm*) *n* the torsk.

cusp *kusp*, *n* a point; the point or horn of the moon, etc; a toothlike meeting of two branches of a curve, with sudden change of direction; a toothlike ornament common in Gothic tracery (*archit*); a cone-shaped prominence on a tooth, *esp* a molar or premolar; one of the folds of membrane forming a valve in the heart or in a vein; a division between signs of the zodiac (*astrol*). — *adj* **cus'pate**. — *adj* **cusped**. — *n* **cus'pid** a tooth with a single point, a canine tooth. — Also *adj*. — *adj* **cus'pidal**. — *adj* **cus'pidate** or **cus'pidated** (*biol*) having a rigid point or ending in a point. [L *cuspis*, *-idis* a point]

Cusparia bark *kə-spar'i-ə bärk*, *n* Angostura bark (qv).

cuspidor or **cuspidore** *kus'pi-dōr* or *-dör*, (*NAm*) *n* a spittoon. [Port, from L *conspuere* to spit upon]

cuss *kus*, (*slang*) *n* a curse; a fellow. — *vt* and *vi* to curse. — *adj* **cuss'ed** cursed; obstinate. — *n* **cuss'edness** contrariness. — **cuss'word** (*esp NAm*) a swearword. [**curse**; prob sometimes associated with **customer**]

cusser, **cuisser** or **cooser** *kus'ər*, *kōōs'ər* or *küs'ər*, (*Scot*) *n* a stallion. [**courser**]

custard *kus'tərd*, *n* a baked mixture of milk, eggs, etc, sweetened or seasoned (now *usu* **egg custard**); a cooked mixture of similar appearance, thickened with cornflour. — **custard apple** the fruit of a W Indian tree (*Anona reticulata*) with edible pulp of the appearance and consistency of custard; **custard pie (comedy)** slapstick, applied *esp* to early US films in which comedians threw **custard pies** (pies containing custard) at each other; **custard powder** a flavoured preparation containing cornflour, etc for using with milk and sugar to make custard; **custard tart** a pastry containing custard. [Earlier *custade*, a corruption of *crustade* a pie with a crust; see **crust**]

custock. See **castock**.

custody *kus'tə-di*, *n* guardianship of a minor, awarded by a court of law; care; security; a watching or guarding; the condition of being held by the police. — *adj* **custō'dial**. — *n* **custō'dian** or **custō'dier** a person who has care, *esp* of some public building. — *n* **custō'dianship**. [L *custōdia* guard, from *custōs*, *-ōdis* a keeper]

custom *kus'təm*, *n* what one is accustomed to doing; usage; frequent repetition of the same act; regular trade or business; any of the distinctive practices and conventions of a people or locality; an unwritten law dating back to time immemorial; a tax on goods; (in *pl*) duties on imports and exports; (in *pl*) the collecting authorities. — *adj* (*esp NAm*) made to order or individual specification. — *adj* **cus'tomable** (*archaic*) customary; common; dutiable. — *adv* **cus'tomarily**. — *n* **cus'tomariness**. — *adj* **cus'tomary** according to use and wont; usual; holding or held by custom; copyhold. — *n* (also **custumary** *kus'tūm-ər-i*) a body or book of the customs of a manor, etc or the ritual of a religious community. — *adj* **cus'tomed** accustomed; usual. — *n* **cus'tomer** a person who usually frequents a certain place of business; a buyer; a person (*slang*). — *n* **customīzā'tion** or **-s-**. — *vt* **cus'tomize** or **-ise** to make in such a way as to suit specified individual requirements. — *adj* **cus'tomized** or **-s-**. — *adj* **cus'tom-built** or **cus'tom-made** built or made to a customer's order or specification. — **cus'toms-house** or (*esp NAm*) **custom**

house the place, *esp* at a port, where customs or duties on exports and imports are collected; **customs union** a group of states having free trade between themselves, and a common tariff policy toward non-member states. [OFr *custume*, *costume*, from L *cōnsuētūdō*, *-inis*, from *cōnsuēscere* to accustom]

custos *kus'təs*, *n* a guardian, custodian or keeper; a superior in the Franciscan order: — *pl* **custō'des** (*-dēz*). — **custos rotulorum** (*ro-tū-lō'rəm* or *kōō'stōs ro-tōō-lō'rōōm*), (*L*) keeper of the rolls.

custrel *kus'trəl*, (*hist*) *n* an attendant on a knight; a knave. [OFr *coustillier*, from *coustille* dagger; cf **coistrel**]

custumary. See **custom**.

cut *kut*, *vt* to penetrate with a sharp edge, make an incision in; to cleave or pass through; to divide; to carve, hew, trim or make or fashion by cutting; to sever; to reap; to excise; to intersect, cross; to divide (a pack of cards) by lifting the upper portion at random; to expose (a card or suit) in this way; (in tennis, golf, etc) to strike obliquely, imparting spin to; to reduce, lessen or abridge; to wound, hurt or affect deeply; to shorten; to interrupt or break; to break off acquaintance with; to pass intentionally without greeting; to renounce, give up; to stay away from; to castrate; to perform or execute (eg a caper); to make (a sound recording, eg a disc); to grow (teeth) through the gums (see also **cut one's teeth (on)** below); to mix another substance with (an illegal drug) to increase weight and volume (*slang*); to dilute or adulterate. — *vi* to make an incision; to intersect; to strike obliquely; to be cut; to dash, go quickly; to run away, to be off (*slang*); (in film-making) to cease photographing; (of a film) to change rapidly to another scene: — *pr p* **cutt'ing**; *pa t* and *pa p* **cut**. — *n* a cleaving or dividing; an excavation for a road, railway, etc; a cross passage; a stroke or blow; (in various games) a particular stroke, generally implying obliquity and spin; (in cricket) a stroke to the off side with horizontal bat; the spin imparted to the ball; a reduction or diminution; an act of unkindness; the result of fashioning by cutting, carving, etc (eg clothes, hair, gemstones); the act, or outcome, of cutting a pack of cards; an incision or wound; an excision; a piece cut off; total quantity cut; a varying unit of length for cloth and yarn; an engraved block or the picture from it; manner of cutting, or fashion; an individual product obtained during the distillation of petroleum; a working horse (*archaic*); a rake-off or share (*slang*); a record, extract of a sound recording, etc (*slang*); (in films) the action of cutting or its result. — *adj* (*slang*) (of a drug) adulterated or diluted. — *n* **cutt'er** a person or thing that cuts; a cut-throat (*obs*); a tailor who measures and cuts out the cloth; a small vessel with one mast, a mainsail, a forestay-sail, and a jib set to bowsprit-end; any sloop of narrow beam and deep draught; a powerful motor-launch (as used by coastguard and navy) which may be armed; (in quarrying) a joint parallel to the dip of the rocks; a small whisky bottle holding half a mutchkin, shaped for carrying in the hip pocket (*Scot*); a medium-sized pig carcase, from which joints and fillets are taken. — *n* **cutt'ing** a dividing or lopping off; an incision; a piece cut from a newspaper; a piece of a plant cut off for propagation; an open excavation for road, railway, etc; editing of film or recording. — *adj* (of a remark, etc) intended to be cruel or hurtful; (of wind) cold and penetrating. — *adj* **cut-and-thrust** see **cut and thrust** below. — **cut'away** a coat with the skirt cut away in a curve in front; an angled edge on a door; a model or picture showing the interior workings of something, with the overlying parts removed; (in films or television) a shot of action that is related to, or happening simultaneously to, the central events. — *adj* having parts cut away. — **cut'back** a going back in a plot to earlier happenings; a reduction or decrease, *esp* in expenditure, workforce, production, etc; **cut flowers** flowers cut from their plants for display in vases, etc; **cut glass** flint glass shaped by cutting or grinding. — *adj* **cut'glass** made of cut glass; (of an accent) upper-class, refined. — **cut'-in** the act of cutting in. — *adj* **cut'-leaved** (*bot*) having leaves deeply cut. — **cut'line** (*US*) a caption; **cut'-off** that which cuts off or shortens, eg a straighter road, a shorter channel cut across a bend of a river; a bend thus cut off; a device for shutting off steam, water, light, electricity, supply of cartridges in a magazine rifle, etc; the point at which something ceases to operate or apply (also *adj*); **cut'-out** the act of cutting out; something which has been cut out; a safety device, eg for breaking an electric circuit. — *adj* **cut'-over** (*US*) (of land) having had its timber removed. — *adj* **cut-price'** at a reduced rate. — **cut'purse** (*hist*) a person who stole by slitting purses worn at the belt; a pickpocket. — *adj* **cut-rate'** (*esp NAm*) cut-price.— *n* **cut'-throat** an assassin; a ruffian; a modification of bridge, etc for three players, each playing alone; an open razor. — *adj* murderous; (of competition) extremely tough, relentless; (of card games) for three players. — **cutting edge** a part or area (of an organization, branch of study, etc) that breaks new ground, effects change and development, etc; **cutting list** (*building*) a list giving dimensions of timber required for any given work; **cut'-up** (*orig US*) a person who makes jokes or plays tricks; a literary collage, composed of cut-up and rearranged passages of prose or verse (also *adj*); **cut'-water** the forepart of a ship's prow; the angular edge of a bridge-pier; **cut'work** openwork embroidery or appliqué (also *adj*); **cut'worm** a caterpillar, *esp* of the moth genus *Agrotis*, that feeds on the stems of young plants near ground level. — **a cut above** something distinctly better (than); **cut across** to go or extend beyond the limits of; to take a shorter route across; **cut a dash** or **figure** to have a striking appearance; **cut along** (*colloq*) to leave, go away quickly; **cut and come again** abundant supply, from the notion of cutting a slice, and returning at will for another; **cut and cover** a method of constructing a tunnel by making an open cutting, arching it over, and covering in; **cut and dry** or **cut and dried** ready made; fixed beforehand, decided in advance; **cut and paste** (in the design of page layouts for newspapers, magazines, etc) a method of arranging areas of text, illustrations, etc by cutting and sticking down with paste; (in word processing, dtp, etc) a technique for moving blocks of text, etc; **cut and run** to be off or escape quickly; **cut and thrust** (in fencing) the use of the edges and the point of the weapon; swift, shrewd and cleverly-calculated action or reaction, argument, etc (*adj* **cut-and-thrust'**); **cut back** to prune close to the stem; to revert to a previous scene; to reduce (expenditure, etc); **cut both ways** (of a decision, action, situation, etc) to have or result in both advantages and disadvantages; **cut corners** to turn corners by the quickest way, not keeping close to the edge of the road; to do something (eg a piece of work) with the minimum of effort and expenditure and therefore often imperfectly; **cut dead** to refuse to recognize or acknowledge (another person); **cut down** to bring down by cutting; to reduce, curtail; **cut down to size** to cause (a person) to feel less important or to be less conceited; **cut in** to interpose; (of an electrical device) to begin working automatically; to deprive someone of a dancing partner; to intercept on the telephone; to manoeuvre into a line of traffic in front of an overtaken vehicle, etc, *esp* without adequate warning or indication; to come into a game by cutting a card; to give a share; **cut it** (*slang*) to succeed or manage; **cut it fine** to take risks by leaving insufficient margin for error; **cut it out** (*colloq*) to make an end of it, leave off; **cut it too fat** to overdo a thing; **cut loose** to break free from constraints; **cut no ice** see under **ice**; **cut off** to sever; to isolate; to put to an end prematurely; to intercept; to stop; (of an electrical device) to stop working, *usu* automatically, *esp* as a safety measure; to disinherit; **cut off with a shilling** to bequeath only a shilling; to disinherit; **cut one's coat according to one's cloth** to adapt oneself to (*esp* financial) circumstances; **cut one's losses** to have done with an unprofitable venture; **cut one's stick** to take one's departure; **cut one's teeth (on)** (*colloq*) to gain experience (by means of); to practise (on); **cut out** to shape; to contrive; to debar; to supplant; to separate from a herd; to pass out of a game on cutting a card; to pass out of a line of traffic in order to overtake; to capture and carry off (a ship) as from a harbour, etc, by getting between her and the shore; (of an engine) suddenly to stop functioning; **cut out for** naturally fitted for; **cut short** to abridge; to make short by cutting; to silence by interruption; **cut teeth** to have teeth grow through the gums, as an infant; **cut up** to cut into pieces; to criticize severely; to turn out (well or ill) when divided into parts; (in *passive*) to be deeply distressed; to make jokes, play tricks or behave in a boisterous manner (*NAm*); **cut up rough** to take something amiss, become difficult or angry; **miss the cut** (*golf*) to fail to qualify for the final round(s) of a tournament; **short cut** see under **short**. [Origin unknown]

cutaneous. See **cutis**.

cutch[1] *kuch*, *n* catechu. [Malay *kachu*]

cutch[2] or **kutch** *kuch*, *n* a set of tough paper or velum sheets used by gold-beaters. [Appar from Fr *caucher*, from L *calcāre* to tread]

cutcha *kuch'ə*, *adj* of dried mud; makeshift. [Hindi *kaccā* raw]

cutcherry, **cutchery**. Same as **kachahri**.

cute[1] *kūt*, *adj* daintily or quaintly pleasing; clever, astute. — *adv* **cute'ly**. — *adj* **cute'sy** (*esp US*) sentimentally or affectedly cute, twee. — *n* **cū'tie** or **cū'tey** a smart girl; something cute. — *n* **cute'ness**. — **cū'tie-pie** (*slang*) someone cute or sweet, a poppet. [**acute**]

cute[2]. See **cuit**.

Cuthbert *kuth'bərt*, *n* the apostle of Northumbria (c. 635–687); a derisive name given to someone suspected of evading military service, and hence to any shirker. — **(St) Cuthbert's beads** perforated joints of encrinites found on Holy Island; **(St) Cuthbert's duck** the eiderduck.

cuticle *kū'ti-kl*, *n* the outermost or thin skin; the dead skin at the edge of finger- and toenails; the waxy or corky layer on the epidermis of plants (*bot*); the protective outer layer of many invertebrates, eg insects (*zool*). — *adj* **cūtic'ūlar**. [L *cutīcula*, dimin of *cutis* skin]

cutikin. Same as **cuitikin**.

cutis *kū'tis*, *n* the dermis; the true skin, as distinguished from the cuticle (*anatom* and *zool*). — *adj* **cūtān'eous** belonging to or relating to the skin. — *n* **cū'tin** (*bot*) a waxy material forming plant cuticle. — *n* **cūtinizā'tion** or **-s-**. — *vt* and *vi* **cū'tinize** or **-ise**. [L]

cutlass *kut'ləs*, *n* a short, broad sword, with one cutting edge, formerly used in the navy. [Fr *coutelas*, augmentative from L *cultellus*, dimin of *culter* a ploughshare, a knife]

cutler *kut'lər*, *n* a person who makes or sells knives. — *n* **cut'lery** implements for eating food; edged or cutting instruments in general; the business of a cutler. [Fr *coutelier*, from OFr *coutel*, from L *culter* knife]

cutlet *kut'lit*, *n* a piece of rib and the meat belonging to it, *esp* of mutton, veal, etc; other food made up in the shape of a cutlet. [Fr *côtelette*, dimin of *côte*, from L *costa* a rib]

cuttle[1] *kut'l*, *n* a cephalopod mollusc (*Sepia*), able to eject a black, inky liquid (also **cutt'lefish**); extended to other cephalopods. — **cutt'le-bone** or **cuttlefish bone** the internal shell of the cuttlefish, used for making tooth-powder, for polishing the softer metals and for cage-birds to sharpen their beaks on. [OE *cudele*]

cuttle[2] *kut'l*, *n* a knife (*obs*); a bully (*archaic*). [Perh L *cultellum* knife; perh also for **cut-throat**, **cutpurse** or **cuttlefish**]

cutto or **cuttoe** *kut'ō*, *n* a large knife: — *pl* **cutt'oes**. [Fr *couteau*]

cutty *kut'i*, (*Scot*) *adj* short, curtailed. — *n* a short clay pipe; a short, dumpy girl; applied to a woman, a term of reprobation, serious or playful; a mischievous or teasing girl or woman. — **cutt'y-sark** a short shift, or its wearer; **cutt'y-stool** the stool of repentance in old Scottish church discipline. [**cut**]

cuvée *kü-vā* or *kōō-vā'*, *n* (the contents of) a vat of blended wine of uniform quality. [Fr]

cuvette *küv-et* or *kū-vet'*, *n* a shallow vessel or dish for holding liquids, eg in a laboratory; a cunette (*fortif*). [Fr, dimin of OFr *cuve* a cask, vat, from L *cupa*]

cuz *kuz*. An obsolete spelling of **coz**.

CV *abbrev*: *chevaux* (*Fr*), as in **2CV** *deux chevaux* two horsepower (car); Cross of Valour (*Austr* and *Can*); curriculum vitae.

cv *abbrev*: (or **CV**) curriculum vitae; *cursus vitae* (*L*), course or progress of life.

cva *abbrev*: cerebrovascular accident.

CVO *abbrev*: Commander of the (Royal) Victorian Order.

CVS *abbrev*: chorionic villus sampling.

CW *abbrev*: chemical warfare.

cwm *kōōm*, *n* the Welsh name for a valley or glen; a cirque or corrie (*geol*). [Welsh (cf **coomb**[1]), and Fr *combe*]

CWO or **cwo** *abbrev*: cash with order.

CWS *abbrev*: Co-operative Wholesale Society.

cwt *abbrev*: hundredweight(s). [*c* for L *centum* a hundred, and *wt* for *weight*]

CY *abbrev*: Cyprus (IVR).

cyan *sī'an*, *n* a greenish blue; blue ink used as a primary colour in printing. — *adj* of a greenish blue colour. — **cyan-** or **cyano-** *combining form* denoting blue or dark blue; relating to or indicating cyanide or cyanogen. — *n* **cyan'amide** the amide of cyanogen, a white crystalline substance ($NCNH_2$); loosely, applied to **calcium cyanamide** (NCNCa), a fertilizer. — *n* **cyanate** (*sī'ən-āt*) a salt of cyanic acid. — *adj* **cyan'ic** of or belonging to cyanogen. — *n* **cy'anide** a direct compound of cyanogen with a metal. — *vt* to treat with a cyanide. — *n* **cy'aniding** extraction of gold or silver from ore by means of potassium cyanide. — *n* **cy'anin** a plant pigment, blue in cornflower, but red in the rose because of its reaction with acids. — *n* **cy'anine** any of a group of dyes used as sensitizers in photography. — *n* **cyanite** see **kyanite**. — *vt* **cy'anize** or **-ise** to turn into cyanide. — *n* **cyanoacet'ylene** (*chem*) a large and complex organic molecule found in space. — *n* **cyanoac'rylate** any of several strong, fast-setting adhesives derived from acrylic acid. — *n* **cyanobactē'rium** a blue-green alga. — *n* **cyanocobal'amin** (*cobalt* and *vitamin*) vitamin B_{12}, which has a large and complicated molecule, in one form including a cyanide group, in all forms including a cobalt atom. — *n* **cyan'ogen** (*-jen*) a compound of carbon and nitrogen $(CN)_2$ forming a colourless poisonous gas with an almond-like odour, an essential ingredient of Prussian blue. — *n* **cyanogen'esis** (*bot*) the production of hydrogen cyanide by certain plants as a reaction to cell damage or invasion by disease. — *n* **cyanom'eter** an instrument for measuring the blueness of the sky or ocean. — *n* **cyan'ophyte** a blue-green alga. — *adj* **cy'anosed** (*colloq*). — *n* **cyanō'sis** bluish discoloration of the skin resulting from lack of oxygen in the blood. — *adj* **cyanot'ic**. — *n* **cyan'otype** blueprint. — *n* **cyan'ūret** (*obs*) a cyanide. — **cyanic acid** an acid composed of cyanogen, oxygen and hydrogen (HCNO). [Gr *kyanos* blue]

cyathus *sī'ə-thəs*, (*antiq*) *n* the ancient Greek or Roman filling or measuring cup; a measure equal to about $\frac{1}{2}$ pint. [L, from Gr *kyathos* a wine cup, a measure]

Cybele *sib'i-lē*, *n* a flora, treatise on the plants of a region. [L *Cybelē*, from Gr *Kybelē* the mother goddess]

cybernate *sī'bər-nāt*, *vt* to control (a manufacturing process, etc) by means of a computer. — *adj* **cy'bernated**. — *n* **cybernātion**. [*cyber*netics and *-ate*, suffix forming a verb]

cybernetics *sī-bər-net'iks*, *n sing* the comparative study of communication processes and automatic control systems in mechanical or electronic systems (such as in computers) and biological systems (such as the nervous system). — *adj* **cybernet'ic**. — *n* **cybernet'icist** (*-sist*). [Gr *kybernētēs* a steersman]

cyberphobia *sī-bər-fō'bi-ə, n* an intense or irrational fear of computers [*cyber*netics and **phobia**]

cyberpunk *sī'bər-pungk, n* a genre of science fiction featuring a bleak and wretched society controlled by computer networks in which the hero is *usu* a gifted young computer hacker who uses his or her skills to rebel against the system; a writer or devotee of this genre. [*cyber*netics and **punk**]

cyberspace *sī'bər-spās, n* virtual reality, an artificial environment created by computer, with which people can physically interact. [*cyber*netics and **space**]

cyborg *sī'börg, n* a robot made of biological and machine components. [*cyber*netics and *org*anism]

cybrid *sī'brid, (biol) n* a cell, plant, etc possessing the nuclear genome of one plant with at least some part of the chloroplastal or mitochondrial genome of the other, as opposed to a hybrid in which some parts of both parental nuclear genomes are present.

cycad *sī'kad, n* any member of an order of primitive gymnospermous plants, related to conifers but superficially resembling ferns and palms. — *adj* **cycadā'ceous**. [Formed from supposed Gr *kykas*, a misreading of *koïkas*, accusative pl of *koïx* doum-palm]

cycl-. See **cyclo-**.

cyclamate *sik'la-māt* or *sīk', n* any of a number of very sweet substances derived from petrochemicals, formerly used as sweetening agents in food, soft drinks, etc.

cyclamen *sik'lə-mən, n* a plant of the S European *Cyclamen* genus, related to the primulas, with nodding flowers and bent-back outer petals; a strong bright pink colour, characteristic of this plant (also *adj*). [Gr *kyklamīnos*]

cyclandelate *sī-klan'də-lāt, n* a drug whose effect is to dilate the veins, etc, used to improve circulation eg in cerebrovascular disease.

Cyclanthaceae *sī-klan-thā'si-ē, n pl* a tropical S American family of plants related to the screw-pines, with a spadix sometimes resembling a pile of discs. — *adj* **cyclanthā'ceous**. [Gr *kyklos* wheel, and *anthos* flower]

cycle *sī'kl, n* a period of time in which events happen in a certain order, and which constantly repeats itself; a recurring series of changes; an age; an imaginary circle or orbit in the heavens; a series of poems, romances, etc centring in a figure or event (also **cy'clus**); a group of songs with related subjects; a bicycle or tricycle; a complete series of changes in a periodically varying quantity, eg an alternating current, during one period; a sequence of computer operations which continues until a criterion for stoppage is reached, or the time of this. — *vt* to cause to pass through a cycle of operations or events; to transport or accompany on a cycle. — *vi* to move in cycles; to ride on a cycle. — *n* **cy'cler** (*NAm*) a cyclist. — *adj* **cy'clic** or **cy'clical** pertaining to or containing a cycle; recurring in cycles; arranged in a ring or rings. — *n* **cyclical'ity**. — *adv* **cy'clically**. — *n* **cy'clicism**. — *n* **cyclic'ity**. — *n* **cy'cling**. — *n* **cy'clist** a person who rides on a cycle. — *n* **cy'cloid** a figure like a circle; a curve traced by a point on the circumference of a circle which rolls along a straight line; a person of cyclothymic temperament, or one suffering from a cyclic type of manic-depressive psychosis (*psychol*). — *adj* nearly circular; (of fish) having scales with evenly curved border; cyclothymic; characterized by swings of mood (*psychol*). — *adj* **cycloid'al**. — *n* **cycloid'ian** a fish with cycloid scales. — *n* **cyclō'sis** circulation: — *pl* **cyclō'ses** (*-sēz*). — **cy'cleway** a track or path, often running alongside a road, constructed and reserved for cyclists; **cyclic AMP** (in full **cyclic adenosine monophosphate**) (*biol*) a compound which regulates processes within cells by its effects on enzymes; **cyclic compound** a closed-chain or ring compound in which the ring consists of carbon atoms only (*carbocyclic compound*) or of carbon atoms linked with one or more other atoms (*heterocyclic compound*); **cyclic group** (*math*) a group on which every element can be expressed as a power of a single element. — **cycle per second** see under **hertz**. [Gr *kyklos* circle]

cyclizine *sīkli-zēn, n* an antihistamine drug used to relieve travel and postoperative sickness, etc.

cyclo *sī'klō, (colloq) n* a trishaw: — *pl* **cy'clos**. [**cycle**]

cyclo- or **cycl-** *sīk-l(ō)-, combining form* denoting: cycle; ring; circle; cyclic compound; the ciliary body (*anatom*). — **cy'clo-cross** a pedal-cycle race over rough country in which bicycles have to be carried over natural obstacles. [Gr *kyklos* circle]

cyclobarbitone *sīklō-bärb'itōn, n* a barbiturate drug used as a hypnotic and sedative. [**cyclo-**]

cyclodialysis *sīklō-dīal'i-sis, (surg) n* an operation to reduce pressure in the eye in glaucoma patients, in which part of the ciliary body is separated from the sclera. [**cyclo-**]

cyclograph *sī'klō-gräf, n* an instrument for describing arcs of circles without compasses, an arcograph; a camera that can reproduce the whole surface of a cylindrical object as a single photograph. — *adj* **cyclograph'ic**. [**cyclo-**]

cyclohexane *sī-klō-heks'ān, n* a highly flammable chemical, C_6H_{12}, with a pungent odour, used in making synthetic fibres, as a paint solvent, etc. [**cyclo-**]

cycloid. See under **cycle**.

cyclolith *sī'klō-lith, n* a peristalith or stone circle. [**cyclo-** and Gr *lithos* a stone]

cyclone *sī'klōn, n* a system of winds blowing spirally inwards towards a centre of low barometric pressure; loosely a wind-storm; a separating apparatus, a kind of centrifuge. — *adj* **cyclon'ic**. [Gr *kyklōn*, contracted pr p of *kykloein* to whirl round]

cyclonite *sī'k'lə-nīt, n*. See **RDX**.

cyclopaedia or **cyclopedia** *sī-klō-pē'di-ə, n* a short form of **encyclopaedia**. — *adj* **cyclopae'dic**.

cyclopean, **cyclopian**, etc. See under **Cyclops**.

cyclopentolate *sīklə-pen'tə-lāt, n* a drug used in eye drops to dilate the pupil of the eye or to treat inflammation.

cycloplegia *sī-klə-plē'jə, (pathol) n* paralysis of the ciliary muscle in the eye, which impedes the adjustment of the lens. [**cyclo-**]

cyclopropane *sī-klō-prō'pān, n* a cyclic hydrocarbon, C_3H_6, a general anaesthetic. [**cyclo-**]

Cyclops *sī'klops, n* one of a fabled race of giants who lived chiefly in Sicily, with one eye in the middle of the forehead (*pl* **Cy'clops**, **Cyclō'pes**, or **Cy'clopses**); (without *cap*) a one-eyed monster (*pl* **cyclō'pes**); a genus of minute freshwater copepods with an eye in front; (without *cap*) a member of the genus (*pl* **cy'clops**). — *adj* **cyclopē'an**, **cyclō'pian** or **cyclop'ic** relating to or like the Cyclopes; giant-like; vast; pertaining to a prehistoric Greek style of masonry with immense stones of irregular form. [Gr *kyklōps*, pl *kyklōpes*, from *kyklos* a circle, and *ōps* an eye]

cyclorama *sī-klō-rä'mə, n* a circular panorama; a curved background in stage and cinematograph sets, used to give impression of sky distance, and for lighting effects. — *adj* **cycloram'ic**. [**cyclo-**, and Gr *horāma* view]

cycloserine *sī-klō-sēr'in, n* an antibiotic used against tuberculosis and other infections. [**cyclo-**, and *serine* an amino acid]

cyclospermous *sī-klō-spûr'məs, (bot) adj* with the embryo bent round the endosperm. [**cyclo-**, and Gr *sperma* seed]

cyclosporin A *sī-klō-spör'in ā, n* an immunosuppressant drug used following transplant surgery to reduce the risk of tissue rejection. [**cyclo-**, and Gr *spora* seed]

cyclostome *sī'klō-stōm, n* a member of the **Cyclostomata** (*-stō'mə-tə*), a class of animals with fixed open mouth, including the lampreys. — *adj* **cyclostomous** (*-klos'tə-məs*). [**cyclo-**, and Gr *stoma* mouth]

cyclostyle *sī'klō-stīl, n* a device for creating multiple copies of a written document by use of a pen with a small puncturing wheel. — Also *vt*. [**cyclo-**]

cyclothymia *sī-klō-thī'mi-ə, n* a temperament inclined to marked alternation of mood, from elation to misery, *usu* indicative of a personality disorder. — *n* **cy'clothyme** a person with such a temperament. — *adj* **cyclothy'mic**. [**cyclo-**, and Gr *thymos* spirit]

cyclotron *sī'klō-tron*, *n* a type of particle accelerator (see **accelerator** under **accelerate**) for accelerating the heavier atomic particles (such as protons), used in the treatment of cancer. [**cyclo-** and **-tron** (3)]

cyder. Same as **cider**.

cyesis *sī-ē'sis*, *n* pregnancy: — *pl* **cyē'ses** (*-sēz*). [Gr *kyēsis*]

cygnet *sig'nit*, *n* a young swan. [Dimin from L *cygnus*, directly or through Fr *cygne*, which seems to be a reshaping of *cisne*, from LL *cicinus*, L *cycnus*, from Gr *kyknos* a swan]

cylinder *sil'in-dər*, *n* a solid figure of uniform cross-section generated by a straight line remaining parallel to a fixed axis and moving round a closed curve, ordinarily in a circle perpendicular to the axis (giving a *right circular cylinder*); a roller-shaped object; a cylindrical part, solid or hollow, such as a rotating part of a printing press, the tubular chamber in which a piston works (*mech*). — *adj* **cylindrā'ceous** somewhat cylindrical. — *adj* **cylin'dric** or **cylin'drical**. — *adv* **cylin'drically**. — *n* **cylindricity** (*-dris'i-ti*). — *adj* **cylin'driform** in the form of a cylinder. — *n* **cylin'drite** a mineral of cylindrical habit, compound of tin, lead, antimony and sulphur. — *n* **cyl'indroid** a body like a cylinder. — Also *adj*. — **cylinder block** a casing in which the cylinders of an internal-combustion engine are contained; **cylinder head** the closed end of the cylinder of an internal-combustion engine; **cylinder lock** a type of lock comprising a movable cylinder which can be rotated inside a fixed cylinder only when the correct key is inserted; **cylinder seal** (*antiq*) a stone engraved in intaglio, used in the ancient East for rolling an impression on clay tablets; **cylindrical grinding** (*eng*) the operation of accurately finishing cylindrical work by a high-speed abrasive wheel. — (**firing** or **working**, etc) **on all cylinders** working at full strength or perfectly; in good working order. [Gr *kylindros* roller, from *kylindein* to roll]

cylix *sil'* or *sīl'iks*, (*Gr antiq*) *n* a shallow two-handled stemmed drinking cup: — *pl* **cyl'ices** (*-sēz*). — Also **kyl'ix**. [Gr *kylix*, *-ikos*]

Cym. *abbrev*: Cymric.

cyma *sī'mə*, (*archit*) *n* an ogee moulding of the cornice (**cyma recta** concave above, convex below; **cyma reversa** convex above, concave below). — *n* **cy'mograph** (*erron* **cy'magraph**) an instrument for tracing the outline of mouldings (see also **kymograph**). — *n* **cymā'tium** a cyma. [Gr *kyma* a billow]

cymar or **cimar** *si-mär'*, *n* a loose coat of various styles, formerly worn by women; an undergarment, a shift; a chimer. [Fr *simarre*, of comparable meanings, from Sp *zamarra* sheepskin; cf **chimer**]

cymbal *sim'bəl*, *n* a hollow brass plate-like musical instrument, beaten with a stick, etc or against another of a pair. — *n* **cym'balist** a cymbal-player. — *n* **cym'balo** the dulcimer: — *pl* **cym'baloes** or **cym'balos**. — *adj* **cym'biform** boat-shaped. [L *cymbalum*, from Gr *kymbalon*, from *kymbē* the hollow of a vessel]

cymbidium *sim-bid'i-əm*, *n* any orchid of the genus *Cymbidium*, with colourful, long-lasting flowers: — *pl* **cymbid'iums** or **cymbid'ia**. [New L *Cymbidium*, from L *cymba* a boat]

cyme *sīm*, (*bot*) *n* a young shoot; any sympodial inflorescence, the main shoot ending in a flower, the subsequent flowers growing on successive lateral branches. — *adj* **cym'oid**. — *adj* **cym'ose**. — *adj* **cym'ous**. [L *cyma*, *cīma*, from Gr *kȳma* a sprout]

cymograph. See under **cyma**.

cymoid. See **cyme**.

cymophane *sī'mō-fān*, (*mineralogy*) *n* cat's eye, a variety of chrysoberyl with wavy opalescence. — *adj* **cymophanous** (*-mof'ə-nəs*) opalescent. [Gr *kȳma* wave, and *phainein* to show]

cymose, cymous. See **cyme**.

cymotrichous *sī-mot'ri-kəs*, (*anthropol*) *adj* wavy-haired. — *n* **cymot'richy**. [Gr *kȳma* wave, and *thrix* (genitive *trichos*) hair]

Cymric *kim'rik*, *kum'*, or *sim'*, *adj* Welsh. — *n* **Cym'ry** the Welsh. [Welsh *Cymru* Wales]

cyn-. See **cyno-**.

cynanche *si-nang'kē*, *n* disease of the throat, *esp* quinsy. [Gr *kyōn*, *kynos* a dog, and *anchein* to throttle]

cynegetic *sin-ē-jet'ik*, *adj* relating to hunting. [Gr *kynēgetēs* huntsman, from *kyōn*, *kynos* dog, and *hēgetēs* leader]

cynghanedd *kəng-han'edh*, *n* a system of sound correspondences used in Welsh verse, *esp* alliteration and rhyme within a line. [Welsh, from *cym* with, and *canu* to sing]

cynic *sin'ik* or **cynical** *sin'ik-əl*, *adj* disinclined to recognize or believe in goodness or selflessness; literally doglike; surly, snarling. — *n* **Cyn'ic** one of a sect of philosophers founded by Antisthenes of Athens (born c. 444 BC), characterized by an ostentatious contempt for riches, arts, science and amusements (so called from their morose manners); (without *cap*) someone who takes a pessimistic view of human motives and actions. — *n* **cyn'icism** (*-i-sizm*) surliness; contempt for and suspicion of human nature; heartlessness, misanthropy; a cynical remark. — *adv* **cyn'ically**. — *n* **cyn'icalness**. [Gr *kynikos* doglike, from *kyōn*, *kynos* dog, or perh from *Kynosarges*, the gymnasium where Antisthenes taught]

cyno- or **cyn-** *sīn* or *sin(-ō)-*, *combining form* denoting dog or dogs. [Gr *kyon*, *kynos* dog]

cynophilia, **cynophilist**, **cynophobia**. See **canophilist**, **canophobia**.

cynosure *sin'* or *sīn'ō-shōōr* or *-zhōōr*, *n* the dog's tail, or Lesser Bear (*Ursa Minor*), the constellation containing the North Star; the North Star itself; hence, anything that strongly attracts attention or admiration. [Gr *kyōn*, *kynos* a dog, and *ourā* a tail]

cyperaceous *sip-* or *sīp-ə-rā'shəs*, *adj* of, belonging to, or resembling the *Cyperaceae*, a family of grasslike plants including the sedges, certain rushes and papyrus. [From Gr *kypeiros* sedge]

cypher. See **cipher**.

cy pres *sē prā*, (*law*) *n* the principle of applying the money donated to a charity, etc to some object as near as possible to the one specified by the donor or testator, when that itself is impracticable. [OFr, so near]

cypress[1] *sī'prəs* or *-pris*, *n* a coniferous tree (*Cupressus*), whose branches used to be carried at funerals; hence, a symbol of death; extended to various other trees, *esp* in America to the swamp-growing deciduous conifer *Taxodium distichum*. — **cypress knee** a hollow upgrowth from the root of the swamp-cypress, an organ of respiration; **cypress vine** a tropical American climbing plant (*Quamolit pennata*), frequently cultivated for its scarlet or orange tubular flowers. [OFr *ciprès* (Fr *cyprès*), from L *cupressus* from Gr *kyparissos*]

cypress[2] *sī'prəs* or *-pris*, (*obs*) *n* a thin transparent black fabric like crape. — *adj* made of cypress. — Also **cy'prus**. [Prob from the island of *Cyprus*]

Cyprian *sip'ri-ən*, *adj* of the island of Cyprus; lewd, licentious, Cyprus being the place where Aphrodite was worshipped. — *n* a Cypriot; (also without *cap*) a lewd woman. — *n* **Cyp'riot** or **Cyp'riote** a native of Cyprus. — **Cypro-Mino'an** an undeciphered Bronze Age script of Cyprus. — Also *adj*.

cyprid. See **cypris**.

cyprinid *si-prī'nid* or *si'pri-nid*, *n* a member of the carp family (**Cyprinidae** *si-prin'i-dē*) of freshwater fishes, including the common carp (*Cyprinus carpio*), goldfish, bream and many other related species, typically having pharyngeal teeth and a single dorsal fin. — Also *adj*. — *adj* **cyprine** (*sip'rīn*). — *n* **Cyprin'odont** (Gr *odous*, *odontous* tooth) any of several *esp* marine types of soft-finned tropical or subtropical fishes related to the carp, but with toothed jaws, including guppies and swordtails. — Also *adj*. — *adj* **cyp'rinoid** (*-rin-oid*) of, related to, or resembling the carp. [L, from Gr *kyprīnos* a kind of carp]

Cypriot, Cypriote. See **Cyprian**.

cypripedium *sip-ri-pē'di-əm*, *n* any orchid of the genera *Cypripedium* or *Paphiopedalum*, eg lady's slipper: — *pl* **cypripē'dia**. [Gr *Kypris* Aphrodite, and *podion* a little foot, modified by L *pēs* foot]

cypris *sip'ris*, *n* a bivalved barnacle of the genus *Cypris* of freshwater ostracod crustaceans: — *pl* **cyp'ridēs** (*-dēz*). — *n* **cyp'rid** any member of the genus; a cypris. [Gr *Kypris* Aphrodite]

cyproheptadine *sīprō-hept'ə-dēn*, *n* a powerful anti-histamine drug used to treat allergies and to stimulate the appetite.

Cypro-Minoan. See under **Cyprian**.

cyprus. See under **cypress**[2].

cypsela *sip'sə-lə*, (*bot*) *n* the fruit of members of the daisy family, consisting of two carpels fused together and surrounded by a calyx sheath. [New L, from Gr *kypselē* a hollow vessel]

Cyrenaic *sī-rin-ā'ik*, *adj* pertaining to *Cyrēnē*, or to the hedonism of its philosopher Aristippus.

Cyrillic *sir-il'ik*, *adj* pertaining to the alphabet attributed to St Cyril (9c), distinguished from the other Slavonic alphabet, the Glagolitic.

cyst *sist*, *n* a sac or bag-like structure, whether normal or containing morbid matter (*anatom* or *pathol*); a membrane enclosing an organism (such as a protozoon or parasitic worm) in a dormant stage of its life-cycle (*biol*). — *n* **cyste'ctomy** surgical removal of the bladder. — *adj* **cyst'ic** or **cyst'iform**. — *n* **cysticercō'sis** (*-ser-*) (disease caused by) infestation of the body tissues by cysticerci. — *n* **cysticer'cus** (*-ser'kəs*; Gr *kerkos* tail) the larval stage of certain tapeworms in which invagination of the neck and scolex forms a fluid-filled cyst, bladderworm: — *pl* **cysticerci** (*-ser'sī*). — *n* **cyst'id** or **cystid'ean** a cystoid. — *n* **cystī'tis** inflammation of the inner lining of the bladder. — *n* **cyst'ocarp** (Gr *karpos* fruit) the fructification in red seaweeds. — *n* **cys'tocele** (Gr *kēlē* tumour) hernia of the bladder. — *n* **cyst'oid** any echinoderm of the extinct class **Cystoid'ea**, globular or bladder-like animals enclosed in calcareous plates, stalked or sessile. — *n* **cyst'olith** (Gr *lithos* stone) a stalked limy concretion in some plant cells. — *n* **cystolithī'asis** the presence of calculi (stones) in the bladder. — *n* **cyst'oscope** (Gr *skopeein* to view) an instrument inserted up the urethra for examining the inside of the bladder. — *n* **cystos'copy**. — *n* **cystos'tomy** the surgical operation of creating an artificial opening from the bladder to the abdomen. — *n* **cystot'omy** (Gr *tomē* a cut) surgical incision into the bladder. — **cystic fibrosis** (*fī-brō'sis*) a hereditary disease of the exocrine glands, present from birth or appearing in infancy or childhood, characterized by secretion of sticky mucus, a tendency to chronic lung infections and an inability to absorb nutrients from food. [LL *cystis*, from Gr *kystis* a bladder]

cystine *sis'tēn* or *-tin*, *n* an amino acid, $C_6H_{12}0_4N_2S_2$, found in proteins, *esp* keratin. — *n* **cysteine** (*sis'ti-ēn* or *-in*) an amino acid, $C_3H_7O_2NS$, that oxidizes to form cystine. — *n* **cystinō'sis** a defect of the metabolism present from birth which leads to abnormal accumulations of cystine in the kidneys, blood, etc. — *n* **cystinū'ria** a condition in which excessive levels of the amino acid cystine are present in the urine, leading to formation of cystine stones in the kidney. [**cyst** and **-ine**]

cytase *sī'tās*, *n* an enzyme that breaks down cellulose.

-cyte *sīt*, (*biol*) *combining form* denoting cell. [Gr *kytos* vessel, hollow]

Cytherean *sith-ə-reē'ən*, *adj* pertaining to Aphrodite. [L *Cytherēa*, from Gr *Kythereia* Cytherean (goddess), Aphrodite, worshipped in the island of *Kythēra*]

cytisus *sit'i-səs*, *n* a plant of the broom genus *Cytisus* of the Papilionaceae: — *pl* **cyt'isī**. — *n* **cyt'isine** a poisonous alkaloid found in laburnum. [Gr *kytisos* a kind of medick, laburnum]

cyto- *sī'to-* or **cyt-** *sīt-*, *combining form* denoting cell. — *n* **cytochem'istry** the study of chemical compounds and their actions in living cells. — *n* **cyt'ochrome** any of a group of substances in living cells, of great importance in cell oxidation. — *n* **cyt'ode** a protoplasm body without nucleus. — *n* **cytodiagnos'is** medical diagnosis following the close examination of the cells of the body tissues or fluids, eg the smear test for cervical cancer. — *n* **cytodifferentiā'tion** the process of specialization, in cell development. — *n* **cytogen'esis** cell formation. — *adj* **cytogenet'ic**. — *adv* **cytogenet'ically**. — *n* **cytogenet'icist**. — *n sing* **cytogenet'ics** the science linking the study of genetics with cytology, *esp* the structure, function and origin of chromosomes. — *adj* **cyt'oid** cell-like. — *n* **cyt'okine** (*immunol*) a protein chemical messenger that assists the immune system in combating infection and has a role in cell-division; a drug based on this protein, used in the treatment of cancer, etc. — *n* **cytokīn'in** (Gr *kineein* to move) any of numerous substances which regulate plant growth by inducing cell division. — *adj* **cytolog'ical**. — *n* **cytol'ogist**. — *n* **cytol'ogy** (*biol*) the study of the structure and function of individual cells, *esp* used for the detection of abnormal cells. — *n* **cytol'ysis** (Gr *lysis* loosening) the dissolution of cells, *esp* by breakdown of their outer membrane. — *n* **cy'tomegalovī'rus** (*abbrev* **CMV**) any of a group of viruses containing DNA of the herpes family, which cause cells which they infect to enlarge and may cause an illness similar to glandular fever, or (if transmitted by a pregnant woman to her unborn child) brain damage or malformations in newborn babies. — *n* **cytom'eter** any of various devices for counting cells. — *adj* **cytomet'ric**. — *n* **cytom'etry**. — *n* **cyt'on** the body of a nerve-cell. — *n* **cytopathol'ogy** the study of cells in illness. — *n* **cytopē'nia** (Gr *penia* poverty) deficiency of one or more types of blood cell. — *n* **cyt'oplasm** (Gr *plasma* form, body) the protoplasm of a cell surrounding the nucleus. — *adj* **cytoplas'mic**. — *n* **cy'tosine** one of the nitrogen-containing bases forming nucleotides in deoxyribonucleic acids. — *adj* **cytoskel'etal**. — *n* **cytoskel'eton** the internal fibrous structure within cytoplasm, determining the shape of a cell, and influencing its movement. — *n* **cy'tosome** the part of a cell outside the nucleus. — *adj* **cytotox'ic**. — *n* **cytotoxic'ity**. — *n* **cytotox'in** a substance which damages or kills cells, *esp* a drug used to treat cancer. [Gr *kȳtos* vessel, hollow]

czapka. See **chapka**.

czar, czardom, czarevich, czarevna, czarina, etc. See **tsar**, etc.

czardas. An *erron* spelling of **csárdás**.

Czech *chek*, *n* a member of a westerly branch of the Slavs, the Bohemians, and sometimes also the Moravians; a Czechoslovak; an inhabitant of the Czech Republic; the language of the Czechs, Bohemian, closely related to Polish. — Also *adj*. — *adj* (*rare*) **Czech'ic**. — *n* **Czechoslō'vak** a native or citizen of *Czechoslovakia*; a member of the Slavic people including the Czechs and the Slovaks. — Also *adj*. — *adj* **Czechoslovak'ian**. [Polish]

D

D or **d** *dē*, *n* the fourth letter in the modern English alphabet, as well as in the Phoenician, Hebrew, Greek, and Latin alphabets (from the last of which it was immediately derived), having the sound of the voiced dental stop; the second note in the natural scale (*music*); anything shaped like the letter; the semicircular marking on a billiard table. — **D'-ring** a metal ring or clip in the shape of a capital D, used in various kinds of harness or as trimming on garments.

D or **D**. *abbrev*: Democrat or Democratic (*US*); Department; *Deus* (*L*), God; Deutsch (catalogue of Schubert's works); *Deutschland* (*Ger*), Germany (IVR); diamonds (*cards*); dimension; dinar; Director; *Dominus* (*L*), Lord; Dutch. — **D-day** (*dē'dā*; D for unnamed *day*) the opening day (6 June 1944) of the Allied invasion of Europe in World War II; any critical day of action; decimal day (15 February 1971), day of conversion from £.s.d. to decimal money; **D'-mark** Deutsche mark (see **mark**[2]); **D'-notice** (D for defence) a notice officially sent to newspapers, etc, asking them not to publish certain information. — **3-D** three-dimensional (see **dimension**).

D *symbol*: deuterium (*chem*); (Roman numeral) 500.

D *symbol*: electric flux (displacement).

d or **d**. *abbrev*: date; daughter; day; dead; deci-; degree; *dele* (L), delete; *denarius* or *denarii* (L), a penny or pence (before 1971); departs; depth; deserted; diameter; died; duke.

d (*phys*) *symbol*: density.

'd *d*, short form of **had** or **would**. See also **'dst**.

DA *abbrev*: dinar; Diploma in Anaesthetics; Diploma of Art; District Attorney (*US*); duck's arse (hairstyle).

D/A (*comput*) *abbrev*: digital-to-analogue.

da[1] or **dah** *dä*, *n* a heavy Burmese knife. [Burmese *da*]

da[2] *dä*, *n* dialect form of **dad**[1].

da[3] *abbrev*: deca-.

DAAG *abbrev*: Deputy Assistant Adjutant-General.

dab[1] *dab*, *vt* to touch or press gently with something soft or moist; to peck; to smear; to dress (the face of stone) using a steel point: — *pr p* **dabb'ing**; *pa t* and *pa p* **dabbed**. — *n* a gentle touch or wipe with something soft or moist; a small lump of anything soft or moist; (*usu* in *pl*) a fingerprint (*slang*); (with *cap*, in *pl*) Fingerprint Department of New Scotland Yard; a species (*Limanda limanda*) of fish of the Pleuronectidae; applied to other (*esp* small) flatfish. — *n* **dabb'er** a pad for dabbing ink on blocks or plates — *n* **dabb'ity** (*Scot*) a cheap pottery figure sold at fairgrounds, etc. — **dab'chick** the little grebe. [Cf MDu and early Mod Du *dabben* to pinch; Ger *Tappe* a pat; confused with **daub** and **tap**]

dab[2] *dab*, *n* an expert person. — Also *adj*. — *n* **dab'ster** (*colloq*). — **a dab hand at** an expert at. [Origin unknown]

dabble *dab'l*, *vt* to shake about in liquid; to spatter with moisture. — *vi* to play in liquid with hands or feet; to do anything in a trifling or small way. — *n* the act of dabbling. — *n* **dabb'ler**. — *n* and *adj* **dabb'ling**. — *adv* **dabb'lingly**. [Frequentative of **dab**[1]]

dabchick. See **dab**[1].

Daboecia. See **St Dabeoc's heath** under **saint**.

dabster. See **dab**[2].

da capo *dä kä'pō*, (*music*) an indication in music that the performer must return to the beginning of the piece and conclude at the double bar marked *Fine* (*abbrev* **DC**). [Ital, from the head or beginning]

d'accord *da-kör*, (*Fr*) *interj* and *adv* agreed; in tune.

dace *dās*, **dare** *dār* or **dart** *därt*, *n* a small river fish (*Leuciscus vulgaris*) of the carp family and chub genus. [ME *darce*, from OFr *dars*, from LL *dardus* a dart or javelin, of Gmc origin; from its quickness]

dacha *dä'chə*, *n* a country house or cottage in Russia. [Russ, orig gift (*esp* from a ruler)]

dachshund *däks'ho͝ont*, *daks'ho͝ond*, *-ho͝ont*, *n* a badger-dog or teckel, of German origin, with long body and very short legs. [Ger *Dachs* badger, and *Hund* dog]

dacite *dā'sīt*, *n* a fine-grained eruptive rock composed of quartz and plagioclase, with mica, etc. [From *Dacia*, a Roman province]

dacker *dak'ər*, **daker** or **daiker** *dā'kər*, (*Scot*) *vi* to lounge, saunter; to potter. [Origin unknown]

dacoit or **dakoit** *dä-koit'*, *n* one of a gang of robbers in India and Burma (now Myanma). — *n* **dacoit'y**, **dakoit'i** or **dacoit'age** robbery by gang-robbers, brigandage. [Hindi *dākait*, *dakait* a robber]

Dacron® *dak'ron* or *dāk'ron* *n* US name for **Terylene**®.

dactyl *dak'til*, *n* a digit (*zool*); a foot of three syllables, one long followed by two short, like the joints of a finger (*classical prosody*); in English, etc, a foot of three syllables, the first accented. — *adj* **dac'tylar** or **dactyl'ic**. — *adv* **dactyl'ically**. — *n* **dactyliog'raphy** or **dactyliol'ogy** the study or lore of finger-rings or engraved gems. — *n* **dactyl'iomancy** divination by means of a finger-ring. — *n* **Dac'tylis** the cocksfoot grass genus. — *n* **dac'tylist** a writer of dactylic verse. — *n* **dactyl'ogram** (or *dak'*) a fingerprint. — *n* **dactylog'raphy** the study of fingerprints; dactylology. — *n* **dactylol'ogy** the art of talking with the fingers using sign language. — *n* **dactylos'copy** identification by or classification of fingerprints. [Gr *daktylos* a finger, *daktylios* a finger-ring]

dad[1] *dad* or **daddy** *dad'i*, (*childish* and *colloq*) *n* father; used familiarly in addressing any older man. — **dadd'y-long'-legs** the crane-fly. — **the daddy of them all** (*colloq*) the biggest, best, etc. [History uncertain]

dad[2] *dad* or **daud** *död*, (*dialect*) *vt* to throw against something; to dash, thump. — *n* a lump; a blow, thump. [Derivation unknown]

Dada *dä'dä* or **Dadaism** *dä'dä-izm*, *n* a short-lived (from 1916 to c1920) movement in art and literature which sought to abandon all form and throw off all tradition. — *n* **Da'daist**. — *adj* **Dadais'tic**. [Fr, *dada* hobby-horse, a name said to have been arbitrarily chosen by the German writer Hugo Ball]

daddle[1] *dad'l*, (*dialect*) *vi* to walk in an unsteady manner, like a child or very old person; to totter. [Perh connected with **dawdle**]

daddle[2] *dad'l*, (*dialect*) *n* the hand. [Uncertain]

daddock *dad'ək*, (*dialect*) *n* the heart of a rotten tree. [Perh connected with **dodder**[2]]

daddy. See **dad**[1].

dado *dā'dō*, *n* the cubic block forming the body of a pedestal (*classical archit*); a deep border of wood along the lower part of the walls of a room, often merely represented by wallpaper or painting, etc: — *pl* **dā'dos** or **dā'does**. — *vt* to fit with a dado. [Ital; see **die**[2]]

dae *dā*, (*Scot*) *vt* and *vi*. A form of **do**.

daedal or **dedal** *dē'dəl*, *adj* formed with art; displaying artistic or inventive skill; intricate, varied. — *adj* **Daedalian** or **Dedalian** (*di-dā'li-ən*) of, pertaining to, or resembling the work of *Daedalus* (*Gr mythol*); (without *cap*) daedal. — *adj* **daedal'ic**. [From L *Daedalus*, Gr *Daidalos*, the mythical artist who constructed the Cretan labyrinth and made wings for his son Icarus and himself]

daemon *dē'mən* or **daimon** *dī-'mōn*, *n* a spirit holding a middle place between gods and men, such as the daemon or good genius of Socrates; an evil spirit, devil. — *adj* **daemonic** or **daimonic** (*-mon'ik*) supernatural; of power or intelligence more than human; inspired. [L *daemōn*, *-onis*, from Gr *daimōn*, *-onos* a spirit, a genius, and later a devil; see **demon**]

dae-nettle. See **day-nettle**.

daf *abbrev*: Doorn Automobielfabriek (Netherlands motor factory).

daff[1] *daf*, (*archaic*) *vi* to make sport, to play the fool. — *n* **daff'ing** foolery, gaiety. [Origin doubtful]

daff[2] *daf*, (*Shakesp*) *vt* to put off; to turn aside, dismiss, put by. [A variant of **doff**]

daff[3] *n* (*colloq*). Short for **daffodil**.

daffodil *daf'ə-dil*, often *colloq* **daff** or **daff'y**, *n* a yellow-flowered narcissus. — Also (*poetic*) **daffadowndilly** (*daf'ə-down-dil'i*) or **daffodill'y**. — *adj* pale yellow. [ME *affodille*, from OFr *asphodile*, from Gr *asphodelos* asphodel; the *d* is unexplained]

daffy[1] *daf'i*, *n* an 'elixir of health' invented by one Thomas *Daffy* (died 1680).

daffy[2] *daf'i*, (*colloq*) *adj* daft, crazy. [**daff**[1]]

daffy[3] *n* (*colloq*). Short for **daffodil**.

DAFS *abbrev*: Department of Agriculture and Fisheries for Scotland.

daft *däft*, (*colloq*) *adj* silly; weak-minded; insane; unreasonably merry; very fond (of) or enthusiastic (about) (*colloq*). — *n* **daft'ie**. — *adv* **daft'ly**. — *n* **daft'ness**. — **daft days** (*Scot*) the period of festivity and leisure at Christmas and New Year; the carefree days of one's youth. [ME *dafte* mild, meek. See **deft**]

daftar *daf'tär*, (*Ind*) *n* an office, *esp* a military orderly room; a bundle of documents. [Hindi]

DAG *abbrev*: Deputy Adjutant-General.

dag[1] *dag*, *n* a heavy pistol of the 15c and 16c. [Origin uncertain]

dag[2] *dag*, *n* a tag, scallop or laciniation (*obs*); a dirt-clotted tuft of wool on a sheep (also **dag'lock** or (in *pl*) **dagg'ings**); a scruffy, untidy, slovenly person (*Austr colloq*); a person, *esp* an adolescent, who is or feels socially awkward or graceless (*Austr colloq*). — *vt* to cut into dags; to bedraggle (*obs*); to cut off a sheep's dags. — *adj* **dagg'y** (*Austr* and *NZ colloq*) scruffy, dishevelled. [Origin uncertain]

dag[3] *dag*, (*Austr colloq*) *n* a person who is rather eccentric or comically entertaining (see also **dag**[2]). [UK dialect **dag** a dare]

dagaba. See **dagoba**.

dagga *dag'ə* or *duhh'ə*, *n* Indian hemp (called *true dagga*); an African labiate plant *Leonotis leonurus* or other species (*Cape* or *red dagga*) smoked as a narcotic, called the love-drug. [Hottentot *dachab*]

dagger *dag'ər*, *n* a knife or short sword for stabbing at close quarters; an obelus, a mark of reference † (*printing*). — **dagg'erboard** (*naut*) a light, narrow, completely removable centreboard. — **at daggers drawn** in a state of hostility; **double dagger** diesis ‡ (*printing*); **look daggers** to look in a hostile manner. [ME *dagger*; cf Fr *dague*]

daggings. See **dag**[2].

daggle *dag'l*, *vt* and *vi* to wet or grow wet by dragging or sprinkling. — **dagg'le-tail** a draggle-tail. [Frequentative of **dag**[2]]

daggy. See **dag**[1].

daglock. See **dag**[2].

dago *dā'gō*, (*offensive*) *n* a man of Spanish, Portuguese or Italian origin: — *pl* **dā'goes** or **dā'gos**. [Prob Sp *Diego*, from L *Jacōbus* James]

dagoba or **dagaba** *dä'gə-bä*, *n* in Sri Lanka, a dome-shaped memorial shrine (for Buddhist relics), a tope. [Sinh *dāgaba*]

Dagon *dā'gən* or *-gon*, (*Bible*) *n* the national god of the Philistines, half-man, half-fish. [Heb *dāgōn*, from *dāg* fish]

daguerreotype *də-ger'ō-tīp*, *n* a method of photography by mercury vapour development of silver iodide exposed on a copper plate; a photograph taken by this method; a faithful representation (*obs*). — *vt* to photograph by that process. — *adj* **daguerr'ean**. — *n* **daguerre'otyper** or **daguerre'otypist**. — *n* **daguerre'otypy** the art of daguerreotyping. [Fr, from Louis *Daguerre* (1789–1851)]

dagwood *dag'wŏŏd*. Same as **dogwood** (see under **dog**[1]).

dah[1] *dä*, *n* a word representing the dash in the spoken form of Morse code. See also **dit**[4].

dah[2]. See **da**[1].

dahabiyah, **dahabiyeh**, **dahabieh** or **dahabeeah** *dä-hä-bē'(y)ä*, *-ə*, *n* a Nile sailing boat. [Ar *dhahabīyah* golden]

dahl. See **dal**.

dahlia *dāl'yə*, in US *däl'yə*, *n* any plant of the Mexican genus *Dahlia* of perennial garden composites with large brightly-coloured flowers and tuberous roots. [From Anders *Dahl*, an 18c Swedish botanist]

daidle *dā'dl*, (*Scot*) *vi* to waddle; to stagger; to idle about; to trifle; to potter. — *adj* **daid'ling** feeble; dawdling. [**daddle**[1]]

daiker[1] *dā'kər*, (*obs Scot*) *vi* to decorate. [Perh Fr *décorer*]

daiker[2]. See **dacker**.

daikon *dī'kon*, *n* a long white Japanese root vegetable of the radish family, similar to a mooli. [Jap]

Dáil *doil* or **Dáil Eireann** (*ār'ən*), *n* the lower house of the legislature of the Republic of Ireland. [Ir, assembly (of Ireland)]

daily *dā'li*, *adj* coming, done or happening every day or every weekday; constant. — *adv* every day or every weekday; constantly, regularly. — *n* a daily paper; a non-resident servant, *esp* a cleaning woman; (in *pl*) film rushes (*US*). — **daily bread** one's living, livelihood; **daily double** (*horse-racing*) a single bet on the winners of two races on the same day; **daily dozen** (*colloq*) physical exercises done regularly, *usu* every morning. [**day**]

daimen *dem'ən*, *dām'ən*, (*Scot*) *adj* occasional. [Origin obscure]

daimio *dī'myō*, *n* a Japanese territorial noble under the old feudal system: — *pl* **dai'mios**. [Jap]

daimon. See **daemon**.

daine (*Shakesp*). Same as **deign**.

dainty *dān'ti*, *adj* pleasant to the taste, choice; delicate; tasteful; genteel; fastidious; choicely or fastidiously neat; elegant (*Spenser*). — *n* that which is dainty, a delicacy, *esp* a small cake. — *adj* (*Spenser*) **daint** or **daynt**. — *adv* **dain'tily**. — *n* **dain'tiness**. [ME *deintee* anything worthy or costly, from OFr *daintié* worthiness, from L *dignitās*, *-ātis*, from *dignus* worthy]

daiquiri *dī'kə-ri* or **daquiri** *dak'ə-ri*, *n* a cocktail containing rum and lime-juice. [*Daiquirí*, Cuban place name]

dairy *dā'ri*, *n* a place where milk is kept, and butter and cheese made; a shop where milk and other dairy produce is sold; a company which processes or supplies milk or milk products. — *n* **dai'rying**. — **dairy cattle** cattle reared mainly for the production of milk, as distinct from *beef cattle*, reared primarily for their meat products; **dairy cream** cream made from milk, not artificial substitutes; **dai'ry-farm**; **dai'rymaid**; **dai'ryman**; **dairy products** milk and its derivatives, butter, cheese, etc; **dayr''house** (*Spenser*) a dairy. [ME *deye*, from OE *dǣge* a dairymaid; orig a kneader of dough; see **dough**]

dais *dās*, *dā'is*, *n* a raised floor at the upper end of a dining-hall where the high table stands; a raised floor, *usu* with a seat or throne and perhaps a canopy; the canopy over an altar, etc; a platform for the use of speakers, etc. [OFr *deis*, from LL *discus* a table, from L *discus* a quoit, from Gr *diskos* a disc]

daisy *dā'zi*, *n* a composite wild or garden plant (*Bellis perennis*), with a yellow disc and white rays; extended to other plants such as the *ox-eye daisy*, which is a chrysanthemum; a general term of admiration, often ironical (*old US slang*). — *adj* **dai'sied** covered with daisies. — **dai'sy-chain** a string of daisies each threaded through the stem of the next; **dai'sy-cutter** a fast-going horse that does not lift its feet high (*archaic*); a cricket-ball (or the ball in other sports) skimmed along the ground; **dai'sy-wheel** a flat, horizontal, wheel-shaped device with printing characters at the end of the spokes. — **fresh as a daisy** bright and vigorous, with strength and spirits unimpaired; **New Zealand daisy bush** a half-hardy shrub of the genus *Olearia*, with daisy-like flowers; **pushing up the daisies** (*slang*) dead (and buried). [OE *dæges ēage* day's eye]

dak *däk* or **dawk** *dök*, *n* in India, the mail-post; hence mail, a letter, a parcel, etc; method of travelling like that of the mail (*orig* by relays of bearers or horses). — **dak bungalow** a house for travellers in India; **dak runner** a runner or horseman who carried mail. [Hindi *dāk* a relay of men]

daker. See **dacker**.

Dakin's solution *dā'kinz səl-, sol-ōō'shən* or *-ū'shən* (*chem*) *n* a dilute solution of sodium hypochlorite and boric acid, used as an antiseptic. [From Henry *Dakin* (1880–1952), British chemist]

dakoit. See **dacoit**.

dal, **dahl** or **dhal** *däl*, *n* the pigeon-pea, a pea-like plant (*Cajanus indicus*) cultivated in India and the tropics; pulse; a purée of pulse. — Also **dholl**. [Hindi *dal* to split]

dalai lama *dä'lī läm'ə*, *n* the head of the Tibetan Buddhist hierarchy. [Mongolian *dalai* ocean, and Tibetan *lama* high-priest]

dale *dāl*, *n* the low ground between hills; the valley through which a river flows. — **dales'man** *specif* a man of the dales of Yorkshire. [OE *dæl*, reinforced by ON *dalr*; cf Swed *dal*; Ger *Tal*]

Dalek *dä'lek*, *n* a mobile mechanical creature with a harsh staccato voice. [Created for the BBC television series *Dr Who*]

dali *dä'li*, *n* a tropical American tree related to nutmeg, yielding staves, etc, and wax seeds. [Native name]

Dalila, **Dalilah**. See **Delilah**.

dalle *däl*, *n* a slab or tile, *esp* decorative; (in *pl*) a rapid where a river runs in a gorge between steep rocks (*US*). [Fr]

dallop. See **dollop**.

dally *dal'i*, *vi* to waste time by idleness or trifling; to dawdle, delay; to play (with); to exchange caresses (*archaic*): — *pr p* **dall'ying**; *pa t* and *pa p* **dall'ied**. — *n* **dall'iance** dallying, toying or trifling; mutual exchange of embraces (*archaic*); delay. — *n* **dall'ier** a trifler. [OFr *dalier* to chat]

dalmahoy *dăl'mə-hoi, -hoi'*, (*hist*) *n* a bushy bob-wig worn in the 18c. [Said to be named from a wearer]

Dalmatian *dal-mā'shən*, *adj* belonging to *Dalmatia* (in Croatia, part of former Yugoslavia). — *n* a native or inhabitant of Dalmatia; a large, short-haired breed of dog, white with dark spots (also *adj*).

dalmatic *dal-mat'ik*, *n* a loose-fitting, wide-sleeved ecclesiastical vestment, worn *esp* by deacons in the RC Church, also sometimes by bishops. [LL *dalmatica* a robe worn by persons of rank, on the pattern of a dress worn in *Dalmatia*]

Dalradian *dal-rā'di-ən*, (*geol*) *adj* applied to a series of Pre-Cambrian rocks well represented in the Scottish Highlands. — Also *n*. [From the ancient kingdom of *Dalriada*]

dal segno *däl sān'yō*, (*music*) an indication that the performer must return to the sign :𝄋: (*abbrev* **DS**). [Ital, from the sign]

dalt or **dault** *dölt*, (*Scot*) *n* a foster-child. [Gaelic *dalta*]

dalton *döl'tən*, *n* another name for **atomic mass unit** (qv under **atom**). — *n* **Dal'tonism** (also without *cap*) colour-blindness; inability to distinguish red from green. — *adj* **Dalto'nian**. [From the English chemist and physicist, John *Dalton* (1766–1844), who described his own case of colour-blindness]

Daltonism[1] *döl'tən-izm*, *n* a school method (the **Dalton plan**) by which each pupil pursues separately in their own way a course divided into monthly instalments, and designed to suit each individual. [First tried in 1920 at *Dalton*, Massachusetts]

Daltonism[2], **daltonism**. See **dalton**.

dam[1] *dam*, *n* an embankment to restrain water; the water so confined; a millstream (*Scot*); a restraint (*fig*). — *vt* to keep back by a bank: — *pr p* **damm'ing**; *pa t* and *pa p* **dammed**. [Gmc; Du *dam*, Ger *Damm*, etc]

dam[2] *dam*, *n* a mother, *usu* of cattle, horses, etc, or *contemptuous*. [A form of **dame**[1]]

dam[3] *däm*, *n* an obsolete Indian copper coin, one fortieth of a rupee. [Hindi *dām*]

dam[4] *dam*, (*obs Scot*) *n* a draughtman. — *n sing* **dams** the game of draughts. — **dam'board** or **dam'brod** a draughtboard. [Fr *dame* lady]

dam[5] *dam*, (*colloq*) form of **damn** or **damned**. — *adj* **dam'fool'** stupid, ridiculous. — *interj* **damme** (*dam'(m)ē*) damn me. — *interj* **damm'it** damn it. — **as near as dammit** see under **near**.

damage *dam'ij*, *n* hurt, injury, loss; the value of what is lost; cost (*colloq*); (in *pl*) the financial reparation due for loss or injury sustained by one person through the fault or negligence of another (*law*). — *vt* to harm, cause injury to. — *vi* to be injured. — *n* **damageabil'ity**. — *adj* **dam'ageable**. — *adv* **dam'agingly**. — **damage feasant** (*fez'ənt*) doing damage (of beasts trespassing); **direct** or **general damages** damages awarded for the immediate consequences of a hurt as distinct from **indirect** or **special damages** turning on the remoter consequences; **what's the damage?** (*colloq*) how much do I owe? what is the cost? [OFr *damage* (Fr *dommage*), from L *damnum* loss]

daman *dam'an*, *n* the Syrian hyrax, the cony of the Bible. [Ar]

damar *dam'ər*. Same as **dammar**.

damascene *dam'ə-sēn, dam-ə-sēn'*, *n* a Damascus or damascened sword; inlay of metal (*esp* gold) or other materials on steel, etc; the structure or surface appearance of Damascus steel; a damson or damson plum; (with *cap*) a native or inhabitant of Damascus. — *vt* to decorate (*esp* steel) by inlaying or encrusting; to ornament with the watered or wavy appearance of Damascus steel, or in imitation of it. — Also **damasceene, damaskeen, damaskin** or **damasquin** (*-kēn*). — *n* **damascen'ing** inlaying upon steel; the production of watered appearance on steel. — **Damascus blade** a sword made from Damascus steel; **Damascus steel** a hard steel, repeatedly folded and hammered, giving a wavy surface pattern. [From *Damascus*, famous for its steel and (see **damask**) silk work]

damask *dam'əsk*, *n* material, originally of silk, now usually of linen, also of cotton or wool, woven with a pattern; Damascus steel or its surface appearance; the red colour of a damask rose. — *vt* to weave patterns into (cloth); to damascene. — *adj* red, like a damask rose. — *n* **dam'assin** damask with flowered patterns in gold or silver thread. — **damask plum** a damson; **damask rose** a fragrant pink or red variety of rose; **dam'ask-steel** Damascus steel. [From *Damascus* (see **damascene**)]

damboard, **dambrod**. See **dam**[4].

dame[1] *dām*, *n* the mistress of a house, a matron (now *usu jocular* or *patronizing*); a mother (*obs*); a woman (*slang*); the comic vulgar old woman of the pantomime, *usu* played by a male actor; a noble lady; (the title of) a lady of the same rank as a knight; a baronet's or knight's wife (as a formal title prefixed to the lady's name) (*obs*); a name given to members of certain orders of nuns, *esp* Benedictine. — **dame'-school** (*hist*) a school for young children, *usu* kept by a woman; **dame's'-vī'olet** a cruciferous plant (*Hesperis matronalis*) formerly cultivated in pots by ladies for its sweet scent at night. [Fr *dame*, from L *domina* a lady]

dame[2] *dam*, (*Fr*) *n* woman, lady. — **dame d'honneur** (*don-œr*) maid of honour; **dames de la halle** (*də la al*) market women.

damfool. See **dam**[5].

dammar or **dammer** *dam'ər*, *n* a hard resin used for making varnish, obtained from various conifers. [Malay *damar*]

damme, **dammit**. See **dam**[5].

damn *dam*, *vt* to censure; to sentence to eternal punishment; to doom; to curse or swear at. — *vi* to utter curses. — *n* an interjection expressing annoyance, disgust or impatience (*colloq*); something of little value (*colloq*); a curse. — *adj* **damnable** (*dam'nə-bl*) deserving or tending to damnation; hateful; pernicious. — *n* **dam'nableness** or **damnabil'ity**. — *adv* **dam'nably**. — *n* **damnation** (*-nā'shən*) condemnation; the punishment of the impenitent in the future state (*theol*); eternal punishment. — *adj* **dam'natory** (*-nə-tər-i*) consigning to damnation. — *adj* **damned** (*damd*; *poetic dam'nid*) sentenced to everlasting punishment (**the damned** *damd*, those so sentenced); hateful; thorough, complete; used to express surprise (as in *I'll be damned!*). — *adv* very, exceedingly. — *n* **damnification** (*dam-ni-fi-kā'shən*) infliction of injury or loss. — *vt* **dam'nify** to cause loss to. — *adj* **damning** (*dam'ing* or *-ning*) exposing to condemnation. — **damn all** (*colloq*) nothing at all; **damn with faint praise** to condemn in effect by expressing too cool approval; **do one's damnedest** (*damd'əst*; *colloq*) to do one's very best; **not give a damn** (*colloq*) to be completely unconcerned; **not worth a damn** (*colloq*) of no value; **the damned** see **damned** above. [Fr *damner*, from L *damnāre* to condemn, from *damnum* loss]

Damoclean *dam-ō-klē'ən*, *adj* like *Damoclēs*, flatterer of Dionysius of Syracuse, taught the insecurity of happiness by being made to sit through a feast with a sword suspended over his head by a single hair; hence, carrying the threat of imminent calamity.

damoisel, **damosel** or **damozel** *dam'ō-zel*, *n*. Same as **damsel**.

damp *damp*, *n* vapour, mist; moisture; moist air; (in mines, etc) any gas other than air; lowness of spirits (*archaic*); a gloom; discouragement. — *vt* to wet slightly; to discourage; to check; to make dull; to slow down the rate of burning (of a fire) (often with *down*; see also **damp down**); to diminish the amplitude of (*phys*). — *adj* moist; foggy; unenthusiastic (*colloq*). — *vt* and *vi* **damp'en** to make or become damp or moist; to stifle (*fig*). — *n* **damp'er** someone who or something which damps; a depressive influence; a door or shutter for shutting off or regulating a draught; a device for diminishing the amplitude of vibrations or cycles (*phys*); a mute (*music*); (in a piano or harpsichord, etc) the pad which silences a note after it has been played; a kind of unleavened bread (*orig Austr*); a cake of this. — *n* **damp'ing** reduction in vibration through dissipation of energy (*phys*); diminution in sharpness of resonance through the introduction of resistance (*electronics*). — *adj* **damp'ish**. — *n* **damp'ishness**. — *adv* **damp'ly**. — *n* **damp'ness**. — *adj* **damp'y** (*archaic* and *poetic*) damp. — **damp'-course** a layer of moisture-proof material in a masonry wall; **damp'ing-off'** a disease of seedlings caused by *Pythium* or other fungus in an excess of moisture. — *adj* **damp'-proof** impervious to moisture. — *vt* to make (eg a wall) damp-proof. — **damp-proof course** a damp course; **damp squib** something that fails to go off with the expected bang (*lit* and *fig*). — **damp down** to close down a furnace, etc (*n* **damp'ing-down'**). [ME *dampen*; related to Du *damp*, and Ger *Dampf* vapour]

damsel *dam'zəl*, *n* a young girl or unmarried woman (*archaic* or *poetic*). — **dam'selfish** a small brightly-coloured tropical fish of the family *Pomacentridae*; **dam'selfly** an insect of the order *Odonata*, resembling the dragonfly. [OFr *dameisele* (Fr *demoiselle*), from LL *domicella*, dimin of L *domina* lady]

damson *dam'zən*, *n* a rather small, oval, dark-purple plum. — **damson cheese** a thick damson jam. [Shortened from *Damascene*, from *Damascus*]

Dan *dan*, *n* a title of honour equivalent to Master or Sir formerly applied *esp* to monks, and now by the poets to great poets, etc. [OFr *dan* (Sp *don*; Port *dom*), from L *dominus* lord]

Dan. *abbrev*: (the Book of) Daniel (*Bible*); Danish.

dan[1] *dan*, (*dialect*) *n* a box for carrying coal; a tub.

dan[2] *dan*, *n* (in Japanese combative sports) a level of proficiency (*usu* 1st rising to 10th); a person who has gained such a level. [Jap]

dan[3] *dan*, *n* a small sea marker-buoy. — Also **dan buoy**. [Origin obscure]

dance *däns*, *vi* to move rhythmically, *esp* to music; to spring. — *vt* to cause to dance or jump; to perform or execute (as a dance). — *n* a sequence of steps or rhythmic movements, *usu* to music; the tune to which dancing is performed; the musical form of a dance-tune; a meeting for dancing; a series of dance-like movements performed by birds, etc, eg as a mating display. — *adj* **dance'able**. — *n* **danc'er**. — *n* **danc'ing**. — **dance'-band**; **dance'-hall** a public hall providing facilities for dancing; **dance'-music** music specially arranged for accompanying dancing; **dance'-tune**; **danc'ing-girl** a woman who entertains in a club, etc by dancing; **danc'ing-master**. — **dance a bear** (*obs*) to exhibit a performing bear; **dance attendance** to wait assiduously (on); **dance of death** a series of allegorical paintings symbolizing the universal power of death, which is represented as a skeleton; **dance to someone's tune** to conform to someone's wishes; **dance upon nothing** to be hanged; **lead someone a (merry) dance** to keep someone involved unnecessarily in a series of perplexities and vexations; **merry dancers** (*dialect*) the aurora borealis. [OFr *danser*, from Gmc; OHGer *dansôn* to draw along]

dancette *dän-set'*, *n* a zigzag or indented line or figure (*heraldry*); the chevron or zigzag moulding common in Romanesque architecture. — *adj* **dancetté**, **dancettee** or **dancetty** (*dän'set-i* or *-set'*) deeply indented. [OFr *dent*, *dant* tooth, notch, from L *dēns*, *dentis*]

D and C (*med*) *abbrev*: dilatation and curettage (a diagnostic and/or curative procedure frequently used in obstetrics and gynaecology, involving dilation of the cervix, and curettage, or cleaning out, of the uterus).

dandelion *dan'di-lī-ən*, *n* a common yellow-flowered composite (*Taraxacum officinale*) with jagged-toothed leaves. [Fr *dent de lion* lion-tooth]

dander[1] *dan'dər*, **dauner**, **daunder** or **dawner** *dön'(d)ər*, (*Scot* and *Northern dialect*) *vi* to stroll, saunter. — *n* a stroll, saunter. [Origin unknown]

dander[2] *dan'dər*, *n* a form of **dandruff**; anger; passion. — **get someone's** (or **one's**) **dander up** or **raise someone's** (or **one's**) **dander** to make or become angry.

dander[3] *dan'dər*, (*Scot*) *n* furnace cinders. [Origin unknown]

Dandie Dinmont *dan'di din'mənt*, *n* a short-legged rough-coated terrier of Scottish Border breed, of pepper or mustard colour. [From *Dandie Dinmont* in Scott's *Guy Mannering*, whose Peppers and Mustards are represented as the origin of the breed]

dandify, etc. See **dandy**[1].

dandiprat or **dandyprat** *dan'di-prat*, (*obs*) *n* a silver three-halfpenny piece; an insignificant person; a little boy. [Origin unknown]

dandle *dan'dl*, *vt* to play with; to fondle (a baby), toss it in the arms or dance it lightly on one's knee. — *n* **dand'ler**. [Origin unknown]

dandruff or (now *rarely*) **dandriff** *dand'rəf*, *n* a scaly scurf on the skin under the hair. [Origin unknown]

dandy[1] *dan'di*, *n* a foppish, silly fellow; a man who pays great attention to his dress; a dandy-cock; a dandy-roll. — *adj* (*colloq*) smart, fine, a word of general commendation. — *adj* **dandī'acal** or **dand'ified** inclined to be a dandy. — *vt* **dan'dify** to dress up. — *adv* **dan'dily**. — *adj* **dan'dyish**. — *n* **dan'dyism**. — **dan'dy-brush** a stiff-bristled brush for grooming a horse; **dan'dy-cart** (*hist*) a light spring-cart; **dan'dy-cock** and **-hen** (*dialect*) a bantam; **dan'dy-horse** an early bicycle without pedals, driven by kicking the ground; **dan'dy-roll** a wire-gauze cylinder that impresses the ribs and watermark on paper. [Origin unknown; orig Scots; poss a person spoiled by too much dandling]

dandy[2] *dan'di*, *n* a sloop-like vessel with jigger-mast abaft. — *adj* **dan'dy-rigged**.

dandy-fever. Same as **dengue**.

dandyfunk. See **dunderfunk**.

dandyprat. See **dandiprat**.

Dane *dān*, *n* a native or citizen of Denmark; a Scandinavian invader of Britain in the 9–10c; a very large dog (Great Dane); a Dalmatian dog (lesser Dane). — *adj* **Danish** (*dān'ish*) belonging to Denmark. — *n* the language of the Danes (also **Dan'isk** (*Spenser*)); a Danish pastry. — **Danish blue** a blue-veined, strongly-flavoured cheese; **Danish pastry** a flaky confection of sweetened dough, containing jam or other fillings and often iced. [Dan *Daner* (pl); OE *Dene*]

danegeld *dān'geld* or **danegelt** *-gelt*, *n* a tax imposed in the 10c to buy off the Danes or to defend the country against them (*hist*); payment or concessions made to avoid trouble. [OE *Dene* Danes, and *geld* payment]

dane-hole *dān'hōl*. Same as **dene-hole**.

Danelaw or **Danelagh** *dān'lö*, (*hist*) *n* that part of England, NE of Watling Street, occupied (9–11c) by the Danes; (without *cap*) the Danish law which prevailed there. [OE *Dena lagu* Danes' law]

dang[1] *dang*, (*euphem*) *vt* a form of **damn**.

dang[2]. See **ding**[1].

danger *dān'jər*, *n* peril, hazard or risk; insecurity; power (*obs*). — *vt* (*archaic*; *Shakesp*) to endanger. — *adj* **dan'gerous** full of danger; unsafe; insecure; arrogant, stand-offish (*obs*). — Also *adv* (*Shakesp*). — *adv* **dan'gerously**. — *n* **dan'gerousness**. — **danger line** the boundary between safety and danger; **danger money** extra money paid for doing a more than usually perilous job; **danger point** the place where safety gives way to danger; **dangerous drugs** certain specific drugs (*incl* morphine, cocaine, heroin, etc) to the dispensing of which stringent regulations apply (**Dangerous Drugs Act** the act under which these drugs are scheduled). — **in danger of** liable to; on the point of; **on the danger list** (in a hospital, etc) categorized as being dangerously ill (also *fig*). [OFr *dangier* absolute power (of a feudal lord), hence power to hurt, from LL *dominium* feudal authority, from L *dominus* a lord]

dangle *dang'gəl*, *vi* to hang loosely or with a swinging motion; to follow about. — *vt* to cause to dangle; to show as an encouragement or enticement. — *n* **dang'ler** (*archaic*) a person who dangles about after others, *esp* women. — *n* and *adj* **dang'ling**. — *adj* **dang'ly**. — **dangling participle** (*gram*) a misrelated participle. [Cf Dan *dangle*, from ON *dingla*]

Daniel *dan'yəl*, *n* a wise judge (in phrases such as *a second Daniel* and *a Daniel come to judgement* (both in Shakespeare's *Merchant of Venice*). [From Daniel in the Apocryphal *Book of Susannah*]

Daniell cell *dan'yəl sel* (*chem*; *hist*) *n* a type of primary cell with zinc and copper electrodes. [From John *Daniell* (1790–1845), British scientist]

danio *dā'ni-ō*, *n* any of several brightly-coloured tropical freshwater fish: — *pl* **da'nios**. [Origin obscure]

Danish. See **Dane**.

Danite *dan'īt*, *n* a member of a secret society amongst the early Mormons. [*Dan*; cf Gen 49. 16 and 17]

dank *dangk*, *adj* unpleasantly moist, wet. — *n* (*obs*; *Milton*) a wet place. — *adj* **dank'ish**. — *n* **dank'ness**. [Origin uncertain]

danke schön *dang'kə shœn*, (*Ger*) many thanks.

dannebrog *dan'e-brog*, *n* the Danish national flag; the second of the Danish orders instituted by King Valdemar in 1219. [Dan]

danse macabre *dās ma-käbr'*, (*Fr*) *n* dance of death (qv).

danseur *dā-sœr*, *n* a male ballet dancer. — *n* **danseuse** (*dā-sœz*) a female dancer; a female ballet dancer. — **danseur noble** (*nobl'*) a principal male ballet dancer: — *pl* **danseurs nobles** (*dā-sœr nobl'*). [Fr]

Dansker *dan'skər*, (*Shakesp*) *n* a Dane.

dant and **danton**. Earlier forms of **daunt** and **daunton**.

Dantean *dan'ti-ən* or **Dantesque** *dan-tesk'*, *adj* like (the work of) the Italian poet *Dante* Alighieri; sublime; austere. — *n* **Dan'tist** a Dante scholar. — *n* **Dantoph'ilist** a lover of Dante.

DAP (*comput*) *abbrev*: distributed array processor.

dap[1] *dap*, *vi* to bounce; to dip gently into water; to fish with a fly bounced gently on the surface. — *n* a bait so used; a bounce. — *n* **dapp'er**. [Origin obscure]

dap[2] *dap*, (*dialect*) *n* a gym shoe, plimsoll. [Prob **dap**[1]]

daphne *daf'ni*, *n* any plant of the *Daphne* genus (family *Thymelaeaceae*) of shrubs, *incl* mezereon and spurge-laurel. [Gr *daphnē* sweet bay]

Daphnia *daf'ni-ə*, *n* a genus of water flea. — *n* **daph'nid** (*-nid*) any member of the genus. [Gr *Daphne*]

dapper[1] *dap'ər*, *adj* quick; little and active; neat; spruce. — *n* **dapp'erling** (*archaic*) a dapper little fellow. — *adv* **dapp'erly**. — *n* **dapp'erness**. [Du *dapper* brave; cf Ger *tapfer* quick, brave]

dapper[2]. See **dap**[1].

dapple *dap'l*, *adj* marked with spots or splotches; mottled. — *vt* to variegate with splotches of colour or shade. — *adj* **dapp'led**. — *adj* and *n* **dapp'le-bay'** (an animal, *esp* a horse) of bay colour, variegated with dapples; **dapp'le-grey'** (an animal, *esp* a horse) of a pale grey colour with darker spots. [Origin unknown]

dapsone *dap'sōn*, *n* a drug widely used in the treatment of leprosy, dermatitis, etc. [*di*aminodi*p*henyl*s*ulph*one*]

daquiri. See **daiquiri**.

DAR *abbrev*: Daughters of the American Revolution, a patriotic women's organization dating from 1890.

daraf *dar'af*, (*elec*) *n* a unit of elastance, the reciprocal of capacitance in farads. [*Farad* backwards]

darbies *där'biz*, (*slang*) *n pl* handcuffs. [Appar from the personal name *Darby*]

Darby and Joan *där'bi-ənd-jōn'*, *n* a devoted elderly married couple. — **Darby and Joan Club** a social club for elderly people. [Poss from characters in an 18c song]

Darbyite *där'bi-īt*, *n* a member of the Plymouth Brethren, more particularly of the Exclusive branch of the sect. [From their principal founder, J N *Darby* (1800–82)]

darcy *där'si*, (*geol*) *n* a unit used to express the permeability coefficient of a rock, for example in calculating the flow of oil, gas or water: — *pl* **dar'cys** or **dar'cies**. [From H-P-G Darcy (1803–58), Fr engineer]

Dard *därd*, *n* a person belonging to any of the peoples who speak Dardic languages. — *adj* and *n* **Dard'ic** (of or relating to) a particular Indo-European language group spoken in parts of Northern India, Pakistan and Afghanistan.

Dardan *där'dən* or **Dardanian** *där-dā'ni-ən*. Same as **Trojan**.

dare[1] *dār*, *vi* and *vt* to be bold enough (to); to venture: — *3rd pers sing* **dare(s)**, before infinitive often **dare**; *pa t* **dared** or **durst** (now *rare*, used *esp* in subjunctive sense); *pa p* **dared**. — *vt* to challenge; to defy; to face: — *3rd pers sing* **dares**; *pa t* and *pa p* **dared**. — *n* an act of daring or a challenge to perform it; boldness (*obs*; *Shakesp*). — *adj* **dare'ful** (*obs*; *Shakesp*) full of daring, adventurous. — *adj* **dar'ing** bold; courageous; fearless. — *n* boldness. — *adv* **dar'ingly**. — **dare'-devil** a rash, daring person. — *adj* unreasonably rash and reckless. — **dare'-dev'ilry**; **dar'ing-do** same as **derring-do**. — *adj* **dar'ing-hard'y** (*Shakesp*) foolhardy. — **I dare say** or **I daresay** I suppose. [OE *durran* (preterite-present verb), pr t *dearr*, preterite *dorste*; Gothic *daursan*; related to Gr *tharseein*]

dare[2] *dār*, (*obs*) *vi* to lurk, crouch, shrink, be dismayed, doze, be fascinated, stare. — *vt* (*obs* or *dialect*; *Spenser* and *Shakesp*) to daze; to frighten. — *n* a contrivance with mirrors such as was once used to fascinate larks. [OE *darian* to lurk, be hidden]

dare[3] *dār*. Same as **dace**.

darg *därg*, (*Scot* and *Northern dialect*) *n* a day's work; a task. [Contraction from *dawerk*, *day-wark* day-work]

darga *dûr'gä*, *n* (a structure over) a place where a holy person was cremated or buried. [Hindi *dargāh*]

dargle *där'gl*, (*Scott*) *n* a dell. [Prob from the *Dargle* in County Wicklow, mistaken by Scott for a common noun]

dari. See **durra**.

daric *dar'ik*, *n* an old gold or silver Persian coin larger than an English sovereign named after *Darius* I of Persia.

dariole *da'rē-ōl* or *dar'yōl*, *n* a shell of pastry, etc, or small round mould; a dish comprising such a shell and its filling; one prepared in such a mould. [Fr]

dark *därk*, *adj* without light; black, or somewhat blackish; (of hair and skin colouring) not of a fair or light hue; gloomy; (of a theatre) closed; difficult to understand; unenlightened; secret; sinister. — *n* absence of light; nightfall; a state of ignorance. — *adv* (*Shakesp*) in a state of dark. — *vt* **dark'en** to make dark or darker; to sully. — *vi* to grow dark or darker. — *n* **dar'kie** see **darky** below. — *adj* **dark'ish**. — *vi* **dark'le** (*literary*) to grow dark (a back-formation from *darkling*). — *adv* and *adj* **dark'ling** dark; in the dark. — *adv* **dark'lings** (*poetic*) in the dark. — *adv* **dark'ly**. — *n* **dark'ness**. — *adj* **dark'some** dark; gloomy (*poetic*). — *n* **dark'y** a Black or coloured person (also **dark'ie** or **dark'ey**; *offensive*); a dark-lantern (also **dark'ey**; *slang*). — **Dark Ages** the period of European history from the 5c to the 9c or 12c (or 15c), once considered to be a time of intellectual darkness; **Dark Continent** Africa; **dark current** (*image technol* and *phys*) residual current in a photoelectric cell, video camera tube, etc, when there is no incident illumination; **darkfield microscope** an ultramicroscope (qv); **dark glasses** sunglasses; **dark-ground illumination** (*biol*) a method for the microscopic examination of living material by scattered light, specimens appearing luminous against a dark background (*opp* to **bright-field illumination**); **dark horse** (in racing) a horse whose capabilities are not known; a person whose abilities or motives are not known; a candidate not brought forward till the last moment (*esp US*); **dark'-house** (*Shakesp*) a mad-house; **dark'-lant'ern** a lantern whose light can be covered; **dark'mans** (*thieves' slang*) night; **dark matter** undetectable but influential matter, possibly in the form of neutrinos, making up a large proportion of the mass of the universe; **dark meat** the darker meat from the legs, etc of poultry (cf **white meat**); **dark'room** a room for developing and printing photographs free from such light as would affect photographic plates; **dark star** a star that emits no visible light, and can be detected only by its radiowaves, gravitational effect, etc. — **darken someone's door** (often with *neg*, often implying unwelcomeness) to appear as a visitor; **in the dark** ignorant, unaware; **keep dark** to be silent or secret; **keep it dark** to conceal it; **prince of darkness** Satan. [OE *deorc*]

darling *där'ling*, *n* a dearly-loved person (often as a form of address); a favourite. — *adj* (one) beloved; sweet; delightful (*colloq*). [OE *dēorling*; see **dear**[1]]

Darlingtonia *där-ling-tō'ni-ə*, *n* a Californian pitcherplant of the Sarracenia family. [Named after William *Darlington* (1782–1863), American botanist]

darn[1] *därn*, *vt* to mend by interwoven stitches; to embroider or sew with the stitches used in mending holes. — *n* a darned place. — *n* **darn'er** a person who darns; a darning needle. — *n* **darn'ing**. — **darning egg** or **darning mushroom** a smooth curved object, *usu* wooden, to support material being darned; **darn'ing-needle**. [Etymology uncertain]

darn[2] and **darned** *därnd*. Forms of **damn** and **damned**.

darnel *där'nəl*, *n* a species of rye-grass; *perh* the tares of the Bible. [Poss connected with OFr *darne* stupid, from its supposed narcotic properties]

darraign, **darraigne**, **darrain**, **darraine**, **darrayn** or **deraign** *də-rān'*, (*obs*) *vt* to vindicate; to justify; to prove; to claim; to challenge; to decide; to set in battle array, or to do (battle) (*Spenser* and *Shakesp*). [OFr *derainier*, *desraisnier* to plead, vindicate, from LL *dē-*, *dis-* *ratiōnāre*, from L *dē-* or *dis-*, and *ratiō* reason; cf **arraign**]

darre *där* (*Spenser*). Same as **dare**[1].

darred *därd*, *pa p* of **dare**[2].

darshan *där'shən*, (*Hinduism*) *n* a blessing conferred by seeing or touching a great or holy person. [Hindi]

dart[1] *därt*, *n* a pointed weapon or toy for throwing with the hand; anything that pierces; a tapering fold sewn on the reverse of material in order to shape it; (in *pl*) a game in which darts are thrown at a board; a sudden forward movement; a plan, scheme (*Austr colloq*); in some snails, a calcareous needle supposed to be used as a sexual stimulus; a cutworm moth (genus *Agrotis*) with a dart-like mark on the forewing (in full **dart'-moth**). — *vt* to hurl suddenly; to send or shoot out. — *vi* to move, start or shoot out rapidly (*frequentative* **dar'tle**). — *n* **dar'ter** a person who or thing which darts; a freshwater diving bird (genus *Plotus*) related to cormorants; an archerfish; applied also to various small American fishes of the perch family. — *adj* **dart'ing**. — *adv* **dart'ingly**. — **dart'board** the target used in the game of darts; **dart'-sac** the gland that secretes the dart in snails. — **Old Dart** (*Austr slang*) Great Britain. [OFr *dart*; cf OE *daroth*]

dart[2]. See **dace**.

dartle. See **dart**[1].

dartre *där'tər*, (*med*) *n* herpes, or some herpes-like skin disease. — *adj* **dar'trous**. [Fr]

Darwinism *där'win-izm*, *n* the theory of the origin of species propounded by Charles *Darwin* (1809–82). — *adj* and *n* **Darwin'ian** or **Dar'winist**.

darzi *där'zē*, *dûr'zē*, *n* a tailor. [Hindi *darzī*]

dash[1] *dash*, *vt* to throw, thrust or drive violently; to break by throwing together; to bespatter; to blotch; to frustrate; to confound; to modify by dilution or mixing. — *vi* to rush; to smash (against). — *n* a violent striking; a rush; a sprint (*athletics*; *esp NAm*); a violent onset; a blow; a splash; a splash of colour; a stroke of the pen or similar mark; a mark (—) at a break in a sentence or elsewhere; a euphemism for damn (sometimes represented by this sign); a mark (▼ or ▲) above or beneath a note indicating that it is to be played staccato (*music*); an acute accent used in algebra and in lettering of diagrams as a discriminating mark; a long element in the Morse code; verve; ostentation; a small quantity of added ingredient; a dashboard in a motor vehicle. — *n* **dash'er** someone who dashes; someone who makes a great show (*colloq*). — *adj* **dash'ing** spirited; showy; stylish. — *adv* **dash'ingly**. — **dash'board** a board, screen or partition in front of a driver on a horse-vehicle, to keep off splashes of mud; the instrument panel of a motor vehicle or small aircraft; **dash'-pot** a device for damping vibration by a piston moving in a cylinder containing liquid; **dash'-wheel** a washing-machine in the form of a partitioned drum. — **dash off** to throw off or produce hastily; to leave abruptly; **dash out** to knock out by striking against something. [ME *daschen*, *dassen* to rush, or strike with violence; cf Dan *daske* to slap]

dash[2] *dash*, *n* a gift accompanying a commercial transaction; a gratuity; a bribe. [Port *das* will you (*sing*) give?]

dasheen *da-shēn'*, *n* the taro. [Poss Fr *de Chine* of China]

das heisst *das hīst*, (*Ger*) that is. — *abbrev* **dh** equivalent to English *ie*.

dashiki or **dasheki** *da-shē'ki*, *n* a type of loose shirt worn in Africa, and also in the US. [West African]

dassie *das'i*, (*SAfr*) *n* the hyrax. [Du *dasje*, dimin of *das* badger; Afrik *dassie*]

dastard *däs'tərd*, *n* (*archaic*) a cowardly fellow; (loosely) someone who does a brutal act without giving their victim a chance. — *adj* (*archaic*) shrinking from danger; cowardly. — *adj* **das'tardly** despicable; cowardly (also *adv*). — *n* **das'tardness**, **das'tardliness** or **das'tardy**. [Prob connected with **dazed**]

dasyphyllous *das-i-fil'əs*, (*bot*) *adj* having crowded, thick, or woolly leaves. [Gr *dasys* thick, bushy, hairy, and *phyllon* leaf]

Dasypus *das'i-po͞os* or *-pəs*, *n* a genus of armadillos. — *n* **das'ypod** any member of the genus. — *n pl* **Dasipod'idae** the armadillo family. [Gr *dasypous* a hare, from *dasys* hairy, and *pous*, *podos* foot]

dasyure *das'i-ūr*, *n* any marsupial of the flesh-eating genus *Dasyurus* (called native cat) or the family *Dasyuridae* (Tasmanian devil, Tasmanian wolf, etc). [Gr *dasys* shaggy, and *ourā* tail]

DAT, **Dat** or **dat** *dat*. See **digital audio tape** under **digit**.

dat. *abbrev*: dative.

data *dā'tə*, (in US and technical Eng *dä'tə*), *n pl* (commonly treated as *sing*) facts given (quantities, values, names, etc) from which other information may be inferred; such facts, in the form of numbers or characters, which can be input to a computer: — *n sing* **da'tum** (qv). — *n* **datamā'tion** shortened term for **automatic data processing**. — **da'tabank** a body of information (a collection of databases or large files of data) stored in a computer, which can process it, and from which particular pieces of information can be retrieved when required; **da'tabase** an organized collection of files of information that has been systematically recorded, and may form the basis of a data-processing system; **da'tabus** or **data highway** (*comput*) a path for transferring data; **data communications** the sending of computer-encoded data by means of telecommunications (*abbrev* **da'tacomms**); **data flow** (*comput*) an approach to the organization of complex algorithms and machines, in which operations are triggered by the arrival of data; **data processing** see under **process**; **data protection** (*comput*) safeguards to protect the integrity, privacy and security of data; **data set** (*comput*) a file — **direct data capture** or **data capture** the putting of information, *esp* concerning (cash) sales, into a form that can be fed directly into a computer. [L *data* things given, pa p neuter pl of *dare* to give]

datacomms. See under **data**.

datal[1]. See **date**[1].

datal[2]. See **daytale** under **day**.

datamation. See **data**.

Datapost® *dā'tə-pōst*, *n* an express, door-to-door collection and delivery service for parcels and packages provided by the Royal Mail.

datary *dā'tə-ri*, *n* an officer of the papal court charged with registering and dating bulls, etc, and with duties relating to the granting of indults and graces; his office (also **datā'ria**). [LL *datārius*, from L *dare* to give]

date[1] *dāt*, *n* a statement of time, or time and place, of writing, sending or executing (on a letter, book, document, etc); a particular day of the month; the time of an event; duration, or end, of existence (*archaic*); term of life; death-day, doom (with pun on *debt*; *Spenser*); an appointment or engagement (*colloq*); the person dated (in the last sense of the *vt*). — *vt* to affix a date to; to ascertain the date of; to suggest the date of; to make an appointment with (*colloq*); to go out with (a member of the opposite sex), *esp* regularly (*colloq*). — *vi* to have begun (at a specified time); to be typical of a particular time; to become old-fashioned. — *adj* **dāt'able** or **dāt'eable**. — *adj* **dāt'al**. — *adj* **dat'ed** old-fashioned, out of date. — *adj* **date'less** without date or fixed limit; free from engagements. — *n* **dāt'er**. — *n* and *adj* **dāt'ing**. — **date'-coding** marking in code on the container a date after which food should not be used; **date line** short for International Date Line (qv); **date'= line** a line giving the date and location (as on a newspaper); **date rape** (chiefly *US*) the rape of a woman by a man with whom she has gone out on a date; **date'= stamp** a device for stamping the date on documents, etc; the impression made by this. — **out of date** see under **out**; **to date** until now; **up to date** aware of and following modern trends; having the latest knowledge and information, etc; adapted or corrected to the present time; modern. [OFr *date*, from L *datum* given]

date[2] *dāt*, *n* the fruit of the date-palm. — **date'-palm** or **-tree** a palm (*Phoenix dactylifera*) of N Africa; **date'-plum** a fruit of the ebony genus, persimmon; **date'-shell** the date-shaped shell of *Lithodomus*, or the animal itself, of the mussel family, a borer in limestone rocks; **date'-su'gar**. [Fr *datte*, from L *dactylus*, from Gr *daktylos* a finger, a date]

DATEC *abbrev*: data and telecommunications.

Datel® *dā'tel*, *n* a facility provided by British Telecom for the transfer of data between computers, via a central computer where it is processed and available for retrieval on demand. [*da*ta and *tel*ecommunications]

Datin. See **Datuk**.

dative *dāt'iv*, *adj* given or appointed (by a court) (*Scots law*); that may be disposed of or given (*Eng law*); expressing an indirect object (*gram*). — *n* the dative case; a word in the dative. — *adj* **dātī'val**. [L *datīvus*, from *dare* to give]

datolite *dat'ə-līt*, *n* a hydrated silicate of boron and calcium. [Gr *dateesthai* to divide, and *lithos* stone]

Datuk *da-to͝ok*, *n* a member of a senior chivalric order in Malaysia: — *fem* **Datin** (*da-tēn'*). [Malay *datu* chief]

datum *dā'təm*. *Sing* of **data** (qv). — **dā'tum-line**, **-level** or **-plane** the horizontal base-line from which heights and depths are measured; **datum point** a reference point against which measurements and comparisons can be made. [L *datum* given, from *dare* to give]

datura *də-tū'rə*, *n* any plant of the thorn-apple genus *Datura*, of the potato family, with strongly narcotic properties; the poison derived from these plants. — *n* **datū'rine** atropine, or a mixture of atropine with other alkaloids. [Hindi *dhatūrā*]

dau. *abbrev*: daughter.

daub *döb*, *vt* to smear; to paint crudely. — *n* a crude painting. — *n* **daub'er**. — *n* **daub'ery** (or *Shakesp* **dawb'ry**) a daubing, or crudely artful device, false pretence. — *n* **daub'ing**. — *adj* **daub'y** sticky. — **wattle and daub** see **wattle**[1]. [OFr *dauber* to plaster, from L *dealbāre* to whitewash; see **dealbate**]

daube *dōb*, (*Fr*) *n* a meat stew.

daud, **dawd** or **dod** *död*, (*Scot*) *vt* to knock, thump. — *n* a lump; large piece. [**dad**[2]]

daughter *dö'tər*, *n* a female in relation to her parent; a female descendant; woman (generally). — *adj* proceeding or formed, as from a parent; (of a cell) formed by division (*biol*); derived of a nuclide, formed by the radioactive decay of another (*phys*). — *n* **daugh'terliness**. — *n* **daugh'terling** a little daughter. — *adj* **daugh'terly** like or becoming a daughter. — **daughter board** (*comput*) a printed circuit board, or anything similar, which plugs into a motherboard; **daugh'ter-in-law** a son's wife; (formerly) a step-daughter: — *pl* **daugh'ters-in-law**. [OE *dohtor*; Scot *dochter*, Ger *Tochter*, Gr *thygatēr*]

dault. See **dalt**.

daunder, **dauner**. See **dander**[1].

daunt *dönt*, *vt* to frighten; to discourage; to subdue. — *n* **daunt'er**. — *adj* **daunt'less** not to be daunted, resolute, bold. — *adv* **daunt'lessly**. — *n* **daunt'lessness**. — *vt* **daun'ton** (*Scot*) to subdue; to dare (*obs*). [OFr *danter* (Fr *dompter*), from L *domitāre*, from *domāre* to tame]

dauphin *dö'fin*, (*hist*) *n* the eldest son of the king of France (1349–1830). — *n* **dauphine** (*dö-fēn'*) or **dau'phiness** his wife. [OFr *daulphin* (Fr *dauphin*), from *Delphinus*, family name of the lords of the Viennois; hence dolphins in their crest, and name Dauphiné for their province (ceded to the king, 1349)]

daur *dör*, (*Scot*). A form of **dare**[1].

daut or **dawt** *döt*, (*Scot*) *vt* to pet. — *n* **daut'ie** or **dawt'ie** a pet or darling. [Origin unknown]

daven *dä'vən*, (*Judaism*) *vi* to pray, to recite the prayers of the liturgies; to lead prayers. [Yiddish *davnen*]

davenport *dav'n-pōrt*, *-pört*, *n* a small ornamental writing-desk (also **dev'onport**); a large sofa. [Prob from the maker]

davenport-trick *dav'n-pōrt-trik*, *-pört-*, *n* an artifice by which someone can free themselves from ropes wound round them and tied. [From two impostors who practised it (fl. 1845–65)]

davidia *dav-id'iə*, *n* a shrub or small tree (*Davidia involucrata*), a native to China, with heart-shaped leaves and conspicuous white bracts.

Davis apparatus *dā'vis ap-ər-ā'təs*, *n* a device making possible escape from a crippled submarine, invented by Sir Robert *Davis* (1890–1965).

davit *dav'it*, *dā'vit*, *n* one of a pair of devices for hoisting and lowering, eg (on a ship) for lowering a boat. [Appar from the name *David*]

Davy *dā'vi* or **Davy-lamp** *-lamp*, *n* the safety-lamp used in coalmines, invented by Sir Humphry *Davy* (1778–1829).

Davy Jones *dā'vi jōnz*, *n* a sailor's familiar name for the (malignant) spirit of the sea, the devil. — **Davy Jones's locker** the sea, as the grave of men drowned at sea. [Origin unknown]

daw[1] *dö*, (*obs*) *vi* to dawn. [OE *dagian*, from *dæg* day]

daw[2] *dö*, *n* a bird of the crow family, *esp* a jackdaw; a simpleton (*archaic*). — *adj* **daw'ish**. — **daw'cock** (*archaic*) a cock jackdaw; a simpleton. [ME *dawe*]

dawbry (*Shakesp*). See **daub**.

dawd. See **daud**.

dawdle *dö'dl*, *vi* to waste time by trifling; to act or move slowly. — *n* **daw'dler**. — *adv* **daw'dlingly**. [Cf **daddle**]

dawk. See **dak**.

dawn *dön*, *vi* to become day; to begin to grow light; to begin to appear. — *n* **dawn** or **dawn'ing** daybreak; beginning. — **dawn chorus** the singing of birds at dawn; **dawn cypress** or **redwood** a conifer, abundant as a fossil, found growing in China in the 1940s and since planted widely; **dawn'-man** Eoanthropus (qv); **dawn raid** a stock market operation in which a large proportion of a company's shares are suddenly bought at a price much higher than their prevailing market rate. — **dawn on** to begin to become evident to or be understood by. [Appears first as **dawning**, prob from ON; cf Swed and Dan *dagning*]

dawner. See **dander**[1].

dawt, **dawtie**. See **daut**.

day *dā*, *n* the time of light, from sunrise to sunset, morning till night; twenty-four hours, from midnight to midnight (formerly by some reckoned from sunrise, or sunset, or (by astronomers) from noon); the time the earth takes to make a revolution on its axis (this being the *sidereal* day (between two transits of the first point of Aries, or approximately of the same star), distinguished from the *apparent solar* day (between two transits of the sun), and the *mean solar* day (between two transits of the mean, or imaginary uniformly moving, sun); morning and afternoon, as opposed to evening and night; the hours devoted to work (*working-day*); a day set apart for a purpose, such as for receiving visitors; lifetime; time of existence, vogue or influence; a time; daylight; the space between mullions of a window; ground surface over a mine. — *adv* (*colloq*) **days** during the day, each day. — **day'-bed** a kind of couch or sofa; a hospital-bed for a day-patient; a bed for resting on during the day; **day'-blind'ness** a defect of vision in which objects are best seen by a dim light, hemeralopia; **day'-board'er** a pupil who attends but does not sleep at a boarding-school; **day'-boat** a small pleasure-boat with no sleeping accommodation; **day'-book** (*bookkeeping*) a book for entering the transactions of each day; **day'-boy** or **-girl** see **day scholar** below; **day'break** dawn; **day care** daytime supervision and help given by trained nursing and other staff to a group of pre-school children, or elderly or handicapped people; **day care centre** or **day centre** a centre which provides social amenities and/or supervision for elderly or handicapped people, vagrants, alcoholics, petty offenders, etc; **day'-coal** the upper stratum of coal; **day'dream** a pleasant fantasy or reverie. — Also *vi*. — **day'dreamer**; **day'-fly** a mayfly; **day'-lā'bour** labour paid by the day; **day'-lā'bourer**; **day'-length** (*bot*) the number of hours of daylight in a day, a trigger for flowering in some plants; **day'-level** (*mining*) a level driven from the surface; **day'light** the light of day; a clear space; **daylight lamp** (*phys*) a lamp which emits light of wavelengths similar to those of ordinary daylight; **day'light-sav'ing** increasing the amount of daylight available for work or play, by advancing the clock, *usu* by one hour; **Daylight Saving Time** the time adopted for daylight-saving purposes; **day'-lil'y** a liliaceous plant (genus *Hemerocallis*) whose blossoms last only for a day. — *adj* **day'long** during the whole day. — **day'mark** an unlighted sea-mark; **day name** (*WAfr*) a personal name given to indicate the day of the week on which the person was born; **day-neutral plant** (*bot*) a plant in which flowering is not sensitive to day-length; **day'-nursery** a place where young children are cared for while their parents work. — *adj* **day'-old** one day old. — **day'-patient** a hospital patient who attends for treatment (eg minor sugery) and goes home the same day; **day'-peep** (*literary*; *Milton*) dawn; **day=release'** a system by which workers are freed from employment during the day so as to attend an educational course. — Also *adj*. — **day-return'** a *usu* reduced rail or bus fare for a journey to a place and back on the same day; a ticket for this type of journey; **day room** a room used as a communal living-room in a school, hospital or hostel, etc; **day'-sailor** a day-boat powered by sail; **day'-scholar** a pupil who attends a boarding-school during the school-hours, but lives at home (also **day'-boy** or **day'-girl**); **day'-school** a school held during the day, as opposed both to a night-school and to a boarding-school; **day'-shift** a group of workers that takes its turn during the day; the daytime period of work; **day'-sight** night-blindness; **days'man** (*archaic*) a person who appoints a day to hear a cause; an umpire; **day'spring** dawn; **day'star** the morning star; the sun; **day'tale** (*-tāl* or *-təl*) or **dā'tal** (*-təl*) (*old*) reckoning by the day, *esp* of work or wages; **day'taler** or **da'taller** (*-təl-ər*) a day-labourer; **day'time** the time of daylight; day as opposed to evening and night. — Also *adj*. — *adj* **day'-to-day'** daily, routine. — **day trip** a trip made to somewhere and back within one day; **day'-tripper**. — *adj* **day'-wea'ried** (*Shakesp*) wearied with the work of the day. — **day'-work**. — **all in a** (or **the**) **day's work** a normal or acceptable part of one's job or of what one is doing; **at the end of the day** (*fig*) when all is said and done; **call it a day** to announce a decision to leave off; **day about** on alternate days; **day by day** daily; **day in, day out** for an indefinite succession of days; **day of action** a day designated by an organization for industrial action, demonstrations, etc in support of a cause; **day off** a day's holiday; **day out** a day spent away from home for pleasure, as a holiday, etc; a servant's free day (*archaic*); **days of grace** three days allowed for payment of bills, etc beyond the day named; **from day to day** concerned only with the present; **have had its** (or **one's**) **day** to have become worn out or useless; **in this day and age** at the present time; **knock** or **beat the (living) daylights out of** (*colloq*) to beat severely; **make someone's day** to make the day memorable for someone; **one day** or **one of these days** at some indefinite time in the (near) future; **scare the (living) daylights out of** (*colloq*) to terrify; **see daylight** to arrive at some comprehension, illumination or prospect of a solution; **that will be the day** (*colloq*) that is very unlikely; **the day** the time spoken of or expected; today (*Scot*); **the day after the fair** too late; **the other day** not long ago; **the time of day** the hour of the clock; a greeting; **win the day** to gain the victory. [OE *dæg*; Ger *Tag*; not L *diēs*]

Dayak. See **Dyak**.

dayes-man; **daynt**; **dayr'house** (all *Spenser*). See **day (daysman)**; **dainty**; **dairy**.

dayglo or **Day-Glo**, *dā'glō*, *adj* of a luminously brilliant green, yellow, pink or orange. [*Day-glo*® a brand of paint]

day-nettle *dā'net'l*, *n* a dead-nettle; (in Scotland and N England) the hemp-nettle; a gathering on the finger. —

Also **dae'-nett'le**. [Perh for **dead-nettle**; but cf ON *(akr)dai* hemp-nettle]

day-woman (*Shakesp*). Same as **dey-woman**.

daze *dāz*, *vt* to stun, to stupefy. — *n* (a state of) bewilderment; mica (*archaic*). — *adj* **dazed** (*dāzd*). — *n* **da'zer**. — *adv* **dazedly** (*dāz'id-li*). — **in a daze** stunned. [ON *dasa-sk* (reflexive) to be breathless]

dazzle *daz'l*, *vt* to daze or overpower with strong light; to amaze by brilliancy, beauty or cleverness. — *vi* to be dazzled. — *n* **dazz'le** or **dazz'lement** the act of dazzling; that which dazzles. — *n* **dazz'ler**. — *n* and *adj* **dazz'ling**. — *adv* **dazz'lingly**. — **dazz'le-paint'ing** fantastic painting for camouflage. [Frequentative of **daze**]

dB *abbrev*: decibel(s).

dBA *symbol*: acoustic decibel.

DBE *abbrev*: Dame (Commander of the Order) of the British Empire.

dbl *abbrev*: double.

DBMS *abbrev*: database management system.

DBS *abbrev*: direct broadcast (or broadcasting) by satellite; direct broadcast (or broadcasting) satellite.

DC *abbrev*: *da capo* (*Ital*; *music*), return to the beginning; direct current (also **dc**; *elec*); District Commissioner; District of Columbia (US state); Doctor of Chiropractic.

DCC *abbrev*: digital compact cassette (qv under **digit**).

DCh *abbrev*: *Doctor Chirurgiae* (*L*), Doctor of Surgery.

DCF *abbrev*: discounted cash flow.

DCL *abbrev*: Distillers Company Limited; Doctor of Civil Law.

DCM *abbrev*: Distinguished Conduct Medal.

DCMG *abbrev*: Dame Commander of (the Order of) St Michael and St George.

DCS *abbrev*: Deputy Clerk of Session.

DCVO *abbrev*: Dame Commander of the (Royal) Victorian Order.

DD *abbrev*: *Deo dedit* (*L*), gave to God; direct debit (also **dd** or **d/d**); *Divinitatis Doctor* (*L*), Doctor of Divinity; *dono dedit* (*L*), gave as a gift (or **dd**).

D/D or **dd** *abbrev*: days after date; day's date.

dd or **d/d**. See **DD** and **D/D**.

D-day. See under **D** (*abbrev*).

DDD *abbrev*: *dat, dicat, dedicat* (*L*), gives, devotes and dedicates; *dono dedit dedicavit* (*L*), gave and dedicated as a gift.

DDR *abbrev*: (until October 1990) *Deutsche Demokratische Republik* (*Ger*), German Democratic Republic (East Germany; also IVR).

DDS *abbrev*: digital data storage; Doctor of Dental Surgery.

DDT. See under **dichlor(o)-**.

DE *abbrev*: Delaware (US state); Department of Employment.

de- *dē-*, *di-*, *pfx* (1) meaning down from, away; (2) indicating a reversal of process, or deprivation; (3) used intensively. [L, or Fr, from L]

DEA *abbrev*: Department of Economic Affairs; Drug Enforcement Administration (*US*).

deacon *dē'kən*, *n* in Episcopal churches, a member of the order of clergy under priests; (in some Presbyterian churches) an officer, man or woman, distinct from the elders, who attends to the secular affairs of the church; (in Congregational and some other churches) an officer who advises the pastor, distributes the bread and wine at communion, and dispenses charity; (in Scotland) the master of an incorporated company; an adept (*Scot*); the skin of a very young calf. — *n* **dea'coness** a female servant of the Christian society in the time of the apostles; (in a convent) a nun who has the care of the altar; a member of an order of women in some Protestant churches whose duties are pastoral, educational, social and evangelical. — *n* **dea'conhood**. — *n* **dea'conry**. — *n* **dea'conship**. — **permanent deacon** an officer in the Roman Catholic church, minimally below a priest. — See also **diaconate**. [L *diāconus*, from Gr *diākonos* a servant]

deactivate *dē-ak'tiv-āt*, *vt* to diminish or remove the activity of. — *n* **deactiva'tion**. [**de-** (2)]

dead *ded*, *adj* no longer alive; inanimate; deathlike; (of a ball) at rest, out of play; (of a golfball) within a certain putt, or into the hole; out of use; obsolete; inactive; cold and cheerless; dull; numb; insensitive; unproductive; as good as dead; inelastic; without vegetation; utter, complete, absolute (*slang*); unerring. — *vt* (*obs*) to deaden, dull; to benumb. — *vi* (*obs*) to lose vitality; to become numb. — *adv* in a dead manner; absolutely; utterly; directly; exactly (*colloq*); extremely, *esp* as *intensive* eg *dead easy*, *dead slow*. — *n* the time of greatest stillness, coldness, etc, eg *the dead of night*, *of winter*. — *vt* **dead'en** to make dead; to deprive partly of vigour, sensibility or sensation; to blunt; to lessen; to make soundproof. — *n* **dead'ener**. — *n* and *adj* **dead'ening**. — *n* **dead'er** (*colloq*) a corpse. — *n* **dead'liness**. — *adj* **dead'ly** causing death; fatal; implacable; very great (*colloq*). — *adv* in a manner resembling death; extremely (*colloq*). — *n* **dead'ness**. — *adj* **dead'-alive'** or **dead'-and-alive'** dull, inactive. — **dead'-beat** (*colloq*) a down-and-out. — *adj* **dead-beat'** (*colloq*) quite overcome, exhausted. — **dead'-bolt'** or **-lock** one moved by turning the key or knob without intervention of a spring. — *adj* **dead'-born** stillborn. — **dead'-cart** a cart for collecting the bodies of those who died of a pestilence. — **dead centre** in a reciprocating engine or pump, either of the positions, at top and bottom of a piston stroke, at which the crank and connecting-rod are in line and there is no actual turning effect (*usu* **top** or **bottom dead centre**); a non-rotating centre in the tail-stock of a lathe; **dead cert** (*slang*) something absolutely certain, eg a certain winner in a horse-race; **dead'-clothes** clothes to bury the dead in; **dead'-col'ouring** the first broad outlines of a picture; **dead'-deal** a board for measuring and lifting a corpse. — *adj* **dead'-do'ing** (*Spenser*) putting to death, destructive. — **dead duck** (*colloq*) a plan, idea or person, etc that has no chance of success or survival; **dead-end'** a pipe, passage, etc closed at one end; a blind alley (*lit* and *fig*). — *adj* leading nowhere (*lit* and *fig*). — **dead'-eye** (*naut*) a round, flattish wooden block with a rope or iron band passing around it, and pierced with three holes for a lanyard; **dead'-fall** a trap with a weight that falls when its support is removed; **dead'-fin'ish** (*Austr*) a thicket or a thicket-forming shrub of the mimosa family (genus *Albizzia* or *Acacia*); a complete standstill or vanquishment; **dead'-fire** an appearance of fire taken as a death-omen; **dead'-freight** money paid for the empty space in a ship by a person who engages to freight her, but fails to make out a full cargo; **dead'-ground** (*military*) ground that cannot be covered by fire; **dead'-hand** mortmain; **dead'-head** or **dead'head** a person who enjoys privileges without paying, eg a seat in a theatre, etc; an ineffective, unproductive person; a sprue (see **sprue**[1]). — *vt* to remove the withered heads of (flowers), in order to encourage further growth. — **dead-heat'** or **dead heat** a heat or race in which two or more competitors are equal; the result of this, a tie. — Also (**dead-heat'**) *vi*. — **dead'house** a mortuary; **dead language** one no longer spoken; **dead'-lett'er** a letter undelivered and unclaimed at the post-office; a law or ordinance made but not enforced; **dead'-lev'el** a stretch of land without any rising ground; sameness; **dead'-lift** or **-pull** a lift or pull made without help or leverage, etc; hence an effort under discouraging conditions; **dead'-lights** storm-shutters for a cabin window; **dead'line** closing date, last possible time; *orig* a line in a military prison, on going beyond which a prisoner was liable to be shot; **dead'lock** the case when matters have become so complicated that all is at a complete standstill; see also **dead-bolt**. — *vi* and *vt* to reach or bring to a standstill because of difficulties, etc. — **dead loss** a complete loss; a useless ally or endeavour (*fig*); **deadly-night'shade** belladonna; **deadly sin** a mortal sin (see under **seven**); **dead'-march** a piece of solemn music played at funeral processions, *esp* of soldiers; **dead'-**

meat the flesh of animals ready for the market; **dead'-men** (*colloq*) empty bottles after a party or drinking bout; the poisonous parts of a crab or other edible shellfish; **dead'-nettle** any species of *Lamium*, labiate plants superficially like nettles but stingless. — *adj* **dead-on'** (*colloq*) accurate, spot-on (see also **dead on** below). — **dead'pan** an expressionless face; a person having or assuming such a face. — *adj* expressionless; emotionless; completely serious or mock serious. — **dead'-pay** continued pay dishonestly drawn for men actually dead; **dead point** another (eg *eng*) name for **dead centre**; **dead'-reck'oning** an estimation of a ship's or aircraft's place simply by the log-book; **dead ringer** (*slang*) a person who, or a thing which, looks exactly like someone or something else; **dead'-rope** a rope not running in any block; **dead'-set'** a complete standstill, as of a gun dog pointing at game; a determined and prolonged onslaught, *esp* with a view to captivation. — *adj* absolutely determined. — **dead'-shot'** an unerring marksman; **dead's part** (*Scots law*) the part of a man's moveable property which he may bequeath by will, and which is not due to wife and children; **dead spit** exact image; **dead'stock** farm equipment. — *adj* **dead'stroke** without recoil. — **dead'-wall** a wall unbroken by windows or other openings; **dead'-wa'ter** still water; eddy water closing in behind a ship's stern; **dead'-weight'** unrelieved weight; heavy and oppressive burden; difference in a ship's displacement loaded and light; **dead'-wind** calm (in the vortex of a storm); head wind (*obs*); **dead wood** or **dead'-wood** pieces of timber laid on the upper side of the keel at either end; useless material or personnel; **dead'-work** work, itself unprofitable, but necessary as a preliminary. — **dead against** see **dead set against**; **dead as a dodo, as a door-nail, as a herring** or **mutton** absolutely dead; **dead-ball line** (*Rugby football*) a line marked out not less than 22 metres behind the goal line at each end of the pitch, beyond which the ball is out of play; **dead-beat escapement** a clock escapement in which there is no recoil to the escape wheel; **dead-cat bounce** (*stock exchange slang*) a temporary recovery of share prices following a sharp fall, not indicative of a true upturn but merely caused by some reinvestment by speculators who had already sold shares; **dead drunk** helplessly drunk; **dead-letter box** or **drop** a place where secret messages, etc may be left for later collection; **dead man's handle** a device, eg on an electric train, which allows current to pass only so long as there is pressure on it; **dead man's pedal** a foot-operated safety device on the same principle, used *esp* on diesel trains; **dead-men's bells** the foxglove; **dead men's fingers** a type of soft coral, a very common actinozoan coelenterate (*Alcyonium digitatum*); **dead men's shoes** succession to someone who dies; **dead on** (used of time, musical notes, etc) exact or exactly; **Dead Sea apple** or **fruit** apple of Sodom; **dead set** see under **set**; **dead set against** or **dead against** utterly opposed to; **dead to the world** very soundly asleep; unconscious; **leave for dead** to abandon, presuming dead; to surpass spectacularly (*colloq*); **over my dead body** when I am beyond caring, and not until then; **put the dead wood on** (*slang*) to gain a great advantage over; **the dead** those who are dead. [OE *dēad*; Gothic *dauths*, Ger *tot*, from root of **die**]

deaf *def*, *adj* with no, or with impaired, hearing; not willing to hear; inattentive; hollow, with no kernel (now *dialect*). — *vt* **deaf'en** to make deaf; to stun (with noise); to render impervious to sound. — *n* **deaf'ening** stuffing put into floors, partition-walls, etc to prevent sounds from passing through. — *adj* making deaf (with noise); very loud. — *adv* **deaf'ly**. — *n* **deaf'ness**. — **deaf'-aid** a hearing-aid; **deaf alphabet** digital and manual signs used to express letters (and words and phrases) visually (also **deaf-and-dumb alphabet**, a name now deprecated); **deaf language** sign language used by the deaf (also **deaf-and-dumb language**, a name now deprecated); **deaf'-mute'** a person who is both deaf and dumb (considered *offensive* by some deaf people). — *n* **deaf'-mut'ism**. — **turn a deaf ear** to pretend not to have heard; to ignore. [OE *dēaf*; Du *doof*, Ger *taub*]

deal[1] *dēl*, *n* a portion; an indefinite quantity; a large quantity; the act of distributing cards; a business transaction (*esp* a favourable one); treatment. — *vt* to divide, to distribute; to throw about; to deliver. — *vi* to transact business (in); to act; to distribute cards: — *pa t* and *pa p* **dealt** (*delt*). — *n* **deal'er** a person who deals (cards) or whose turn it is to deal, or who has dealt the hand in play; a trader. — *n* **deal'ership** the state of being a dealer; the authority to sell products or services as an appointed dealer; dealers as a group. — *n* **deal'ing** (often in *pl*) manner of acting towards others; business transactions. — **dealer brand** own-label. — **deal with** to have to do with, to treat of; to take action in regard to. [OE *dǣlan*, from *dǣl* a part; Ger *teilen*, from *Teil* a part or division; cf **dole**[1]]

deal[2] *dēl*, *n* a fir or pine board of a standard size, soft wood. — *adj* made of deal. — **deal'fish** a ribbonfish (genus *Trachypterus*). [MLGer *dele*; cf OE *thel*, *thille*, and mod **thill**[1]]

dealbate *dē-al'bāt*, *adj* whitened. — *n* **dealbā'tion**. [L *dealbāre*, *-ātum* to whitewash, from pfx *de-* in sense of over a surface, and *albus* white]

de-alcoholize or **-ise** *dē-al'ko-hol-īz*, *vt* to reduce the amount of alcohol in (wine, beer, etc).

dealt. See **deal**[1].

deambulatory *dē-am'bū-lə-tər-i*, *n* a place for walking about in; a passage or aisle round the choir and apse of a church. [L *deambulāre*, *-ātum* to walk about]

dean[1] or **dene** *dēn*, *n* a small valley. [OE *denu* a valley; cf **den**[1]]

dean[2] *dēn*, *n* a dignitary in cathedral and collegiate churches who presides over the canons; a rural dean; the chief cardinal-bishop of the College of Cardinals; the president of a faculty in a college or of the *Faculty of Advocates*; a resident fellow of a college who has administrative and disciplinary functions; the senior member of a corps or body; the chief chaplain of the Chapel Royal; the chief judge of the Court of Arches; the president of a trade-guild. — *n* **dean'ery** the office of a dean; a group of parishes presided over by a dean; a dean's house. — *n* **dean'ship** the office or dignity of a dean. — **Dean of Arches** dean of the Court of Arches (see under **arch**); **Dean of Faculty** president of the *Faculty of Advocates* in Scotland; **Dean of Guild** formerly a municipal functionary in Scotland who had authority over building and altering of houses; **rural dean** a clergyman who, under the bishop, has the special care and inspection of the clergy in certain parishes. [OFr *deien* (Fr *doyen*), from LL *decānus* or Gr *dekānos* a chief of ten, from L *decem* or Gr *deka* ten]

deaner *dēn'ər*, (*old slang*) *n* a shilling. [Prob L *denārius*]

dear[1] *dēr*, *adj* high in price; costly; characterized by high prices; scarce; highly valued; beloved; a conventional form of address used in letter-writing; earnest (*Shakesp*). — *n* a person who is dear or beloved; an affectionate term of address (also **dear'ie** or **dear'y**). — *adv* at a high price; dearly. — *interj* indicating surprise, pity, or other emotion. — *n* and *adj* **dear'ling** (*Spenser*) darling. — *adv* **dear'ly** affectionately; earnestly; at great cost. — *n* **dear'ness**. — *adj* **dear'bought** (*poetic*) precious. — **dear me** or **dearie** (or **deary**) **me** an expression of dismay, etc; **Dear John letter** (*colloq*; *orig US*) a letter from a girl to her husband or fiancé, etc ending their relationship; **dear knows** an expression of ignorance; **oh dear**! an expression of surprise, sorrow, pity or dismay. [OE *dēore*, *dȳre*; cognate with Ger *teuer*]

dear[2], **deare** or **deere** *dēr*, (*Spenser*; *Shakesp*; *Milton*) *adj* grievous. — Also *adv*. [OE *dēor*]

deare. See **dere**.

dearn, **dearnful**, **dearnly**. See **dern**[2], etc.

dearth *dûrth*, *n* scarcity; want; famine; barrenness; dearness, high price (*obs*). [**dear**[1]]

dearticulate *dē-är-tik'ū-lāt*, *vt* to disjoint. [**de-** (2)]

deasil *dēz'l, des'l, desh'l, dēsh'l*, (*Scot*) *n* sunwise motion (*opp* to *withershins*). — *adv* sunwise. — Also **dea'soil, dei'seal, dei'sheal** or **dea'siul**. [Gaelic *deiseil*]

deaspirate *dē-as'pir-āt*, *vt* to remove the aspirate from. — *n* **deaspirā'tion**. [**de-** (2)]

death *deth*, *n* the state of being dead; extinction or cessation of life; manner of dying; mortality; a deadly plague; the cause of death; the end or destruction of something; a thing considered as fearsome or painful, etc as death; spiritual lifelessness; the killing of the animal in hunting. — *adj* **death'ful** deadly, destructive; mortal; deathlike. — *adj* **death'less** never dying; everlasting. — *n* **death'lessness**. — *adj* **death'like** deadly; like death. — *n* **death'liness**. — *adj* **death'ly** deadly; deathlike. — *adv* **death'ward** or **death'wards**. — *adj* **death'y**. — **death'-add'er** a poisonous Australian snake (*Acanthophis antarcticus*); **death'-ag'ony** the struggle often preceding death; **death angel** death-cap; **death'-bed** the bed on which a person dies; the last illness; see also **on one's deathbed** below; **death'-bell** the passing bell; **death'-blow** a blow that causes death; **death'-cap** or **-cup** a very poisonous toadstool (*Amanita phalloides*) often mistaken for an edible mushroom; **death'-cell** a prison cell for condemned prisoners awaiting execution; **death certificate** a legal certificate on which a doctor states the fact and *usu* the cause of a person's death; **death'-damp** a cold sweat preceding death. — *adj* **death'-dealing**. — **death'-duty** (often in *pl*) duty paid on inheritance of property (now replaced by **inheritance tax** (qv)); **death'-fire** a light supposed to presage death; **death'-knell** the ringing of a bell to announce a death; something that announces the end of one's hopes, ambitions, etc (*fig*). — *adj* **death'=marked** marked for or by death, destined to die. — **death'-mask** a plaster cast taken from the face after death; **death penalty** the legal taking of a person's life as punishment for crime. — *adj* **death'-prac'tised** (*Shakesp*) threatened with death by malicious arts. — **death'-rate** the proportion of deaths to the population; **death'-ratt'le** a rattling in the throat that sometimes precedes death; **death'-ray** an imaginary ray that could destroy all life; **death'-roll** a list of the dead; **death row** (*US*) the part of a prison containing death-cells; **death's'-head** the skull of a human skeleton, or a figure of it; a memorial ring bearing such a figure; **deaths'man** (*Shakesp*) an executioner; **death'-song** a song sung before dying; **death squad** an unofficial terrorist group who murder those whose views or activities they disapprove of, often operating with the tacit or covert support of the government of the country; **death star** a small thin star-shaped metal plate with sharpened points, used as a missile; **death'-stroke** a death-blow; **death'-throe** the dying agony; **death'-token** (*Shakesp*) a sign or token of impending death, a plague-spot; **death'-trap** an unsafe structure or place that exposes one to great danger of death; **death'-warrant** an order from the authorities for the execution of a criminal; **death'watch** a vigil, a watch kept beside a dying person; deathwatch beetle; **death wish** (*psychol*) a wish, conscious or unconscious, for death for oneself or another; **death'-wound** a wound that causes death. — **at death's door** very near to death; **catch one's death (of cold)** (*colloq*) to catch a very bad cold; **death-bed repentance** repentance for one's faults, sins, etc when it is too late to reform one's life; **death's-head moth** a hawk-moth with pale markings on the back of the thorax somewhat like a skull; **death on** fatal to, fond of, good at; **deathwatch beetle** a beetle that produces a ticking noise, found *esp* in house timbers (genus *Anobium*); **do** or **put to death** to kill; to cause to be killed; **gates** or **jaws of death** the point of death; **in at the death** up on the animal before the dogs have killed it; present at the finish, crux, climax, etc of anything (*fig*); **like death warmed up** or **over** (*colloq*) very unwell; **like grim death** tenaciously; **on one's deathbed** about to die; **sign one's own death-warrant** to do something that makes one's downfall inevitable; **to death** (until) dead; to a state of exhaustion; **to the death** to the very end. [OE *dēath*; Ger *Tod*; see **dead** and **die**[1]]

deave or **deeve** *dēv*, (*Scot* and *dialect*) *vt* to deafen; to worry (*esp* with noise); to bother; to break. [See **deaf**]

deaw and **deawy** or **deawie** (*Spenser*). Same as **dew** and **dewy**.

deb. Colloquial form of **débutante**.

debacle or **débâcle** *di-bak'l* or *dā-bäk'l'*, *n* a complete break-up or collapse; a breaking up of ice on a river; a sudden flood of water leaving its path strewed with debris (*geol*); a stampede. [Fr *débâcle*; *dé-*, *des-*, and *bâcler* to bar, from L *baculus* a stick]

debag *di-bag'*, (*colloq*) *vt* to remove the trousers of, as a prank or punishment. — *n* **debagg'ing**. [**de-** (2) and **bags**]

debar *di-bär'*, *vt* to bar out; to exclude; to hinder: — *pr p* **debarr'ing**; *pa t* and *pa p* **debarred'**. — *n* **debar'ment**. [**de-** (3)]

debark *di-bärk'*, *vt* or *vi* to disembark. — *n* **dēbarka'tion** or **dēbarcā'tion**. [Fr *débarquer*, from *des* (from L *dis-*) away, and Fr *barque* a ship]

debarrass *di-bar'əs*, (*archaic*) *vt* to disembarrass, disentangle, free. [Fr *débarrasser*; *dé-*, *des-*, and *barre* a bar]

debase *di-bās'*, *vt* to lower; to make poor (of quality) or of less value; to adulterate. — *adj* **debased'** degraded; reversed (*heraldry*). — *n* **debās'edness**. — *n* **debase'ment** degradation. — *n* **debās'er**. — *adj* **debās'ing**. — *adv* **debās'ingly**. [**de-** (1)]

debate *di-bāt'*, *n* argument; a formal discussion, *esp* in parliament or some other forum; fight, strife (*obs*). — *vt* to contend for in argument; to argue about; to fight for (*archaic*). — *vi* to deliberate; to consider; to join in debate; to fight, contend (*obs*). — *adj* **debāt'able** or **debate'able** liable to be disputed; open to argument; contentious. — *adj* **debate'ful** (*obs*; *Spenser*) quarrelsome. — *n* **debate'ment** (*obs*; *Spenser* and *Shakesp*) controversy. — *n* **debāt'er**. — *adv* **debāt'ingly**. — **Debatable** (or **Debateable**) **Land** a tract of border land between Esk and Sark, formerly claimed by both England and Scotland. [OFr *debatre*, from L *dē*, and *batuere* to beat]

debauch *di-böch'*, *vt* to lead away from duty or allegiance; to corrupt with lewdness; to seduce; to vitiate. — *vi* to overindulge. — *n* a fit or period of intemperance or lewdness. — *adj* **debauched'** corrupt; profligate. — *adv* **debauch'edly**. — *n* **debauch'edness**. — *n* **debauchee** (*di-böch-ē'* or *-bösh-ē'*) a libertine. — *n* **debauch'er**. — *n* **debauch'ery** excessive intemperance; habitual lewdness. — *n* **debauch'ment**. [OFr *desbaucher* (Fr *débaucher*) to corrupt, from *des-* (L *dis-*) and *baucher* to hew]

debby. See **début**.

debel *di-bel'*, (*obs*; *Milton*) *vt* to conquer in war: — *pr p* **debell'ing**; *pa t* and *pa p* **debelled'**. [L *dēbellāre*, from *dē* down, and *bellāre* to war, from *bellum* war]

debenture *di-ben'chər*, *n* a written acknowledgment of a debt; a security issued by a company for money borrowed on the company's property, having a fixed rate of interest and *usu* fixed redemption rates; a certificate entitling an exporter of imported goods to a repayment of the duty paid on their importation. — *adj* **debent'ured** (of goods) entitled to drawback or debenture. [L *dēbentur* there are due (the first word of the receipt), 3rd pers pl passive of *dēbēre* to owe]

debilitate *di-bil'i-tāt*, *vt* to make weak; to impair the strength of. — *adj* **debile** (*deb'il* or *dē'bīl*; *archaic*) weak, feeble. — *n* **debilitā'tion**. — *adj* **debil'itating**. — *adj* **debil'itative**. — *n* **debil'ity** weakness and languor; a weak action of the bodily functions. [L *dēbilitāre*, *-ātum*, from *dēbilis* weak, from *dē*, and *habilis* able. See **ability**]

debit *deb'it*, *n* a debt or something due; an entry on the debtor side of an account, recording a sum owing (*bookkeeping*). — *vt* to charge with debt; to enter on the debtor side of an account. — *n* **deb'itor** (*obs*; *Shakesp*) a debtor. — **debit card** a card used by a purchaser by means of which money is directly transferred from his or her account to the retailers; **debit note** a document informing a buyer that their account has been debited with the amount shown. [L *dēbitum* what is due, from *dēbēre* to owe]

de-blur *dē-blûr'*, *vt* to make (blurred photographs) sharp, *esp* with the aid of computers: — *pr p* **de-blurr'ing**; *pa t* and *pa p* **de-blurred'**. [**de-** (2)]

debonair or **debonnaire** *deb-ə-nār'*, *adj* of good appearance and manners; elegant; courteous; carefree. — *adv* **debonair'ly**. — *n* **debonair'ness**. [Fr *de* of, *bon* good, and the old word *aire* (masc) manner, origin; mod Fr *débonnaire*]

debosh *di-bosh'*. An old form of **debauch**.

deboss *vt* to impress (a design, symbol, character, etc) into (*opp* of **emboss**[1]). [**de-** (2) and **boss**[1]]

debouch *di-bowch'*, *di-bōōsh'*, *vi* to issue or emerge, to march or flow out from a narrow pass or confined place. — *n* **débouché** (*dā-bōō-shā'*) an outlet. — *n* **debouch'ment** an act or place of debouching; **debouchure** (*di-bōōshür'*) the mouth of a river or strait. [Fr *déboucher*, from *de* from, and *bouche* mouth, from L *bucca* cheek]

Debrett *di-bret'* or **Debrett's Peerage** (*pēr'əj*), *n* a peerage edited and published from 1784 until his death by John Field *Debrett*, still in publication and the model for all exclusive lists.

débridement *dā-brēd-mã*, *dā-brēd'mənt* or *dī-*, (*med*) *n* the removal of foreign matter or dead or infected tissue from a wound. — *vt* **débride'** to clean or treat (a wound) by débridement; to remove (dead tissue, etc) by débridement. [Fr, literally unbridling]

debrief *dē-brēf'*, *vt* to gather information from a soldier or astronaut, etc, on return from a mission. — *n* **debrief'ing**. [**de-** (2)]

debris or **débris** *deb'rē*, *dəb-rē'*, *dāb'rē*, *n* wreckage; ruins; rubbish; a mass of rocky fragments. [Fr, from *briser*, related to **bruise**]

debruised *di-brōōzd'*, (*heraldry*) *adj* surmounted or partly covered by one of the ordinaries. [OFr *debruisier*, from *de-* apart, and *bruiser* to break]

debt *det*, *n* an amount owed by one person to another; what one becomes liable to do or suffer; a state of obligation or indebtedness; a duty; a sin (*Bible*). — *adj* **deb'ted** (*Shakesp*) indebted, obliged. — *n* **debtee'** a creditor. — *n* **debt'or** a person who or country, body, etc that owes a debt. — **debt bondage** a system (often amounting to virtual slavery) whereby a person is obliged to work for a moneylender in an attempt to pay off debt. — **bad debt** a debt of which there is no prospect of payment; **debt of honour** a debt not recognized by law, but binding in honour (*esp* a gambling or betting debt); **debt of nature** death; **floating debt** miscellaneous public debt, like exchequer and treasury bills, as opposed to **funded debt**, that which has been converted into perpetual annuities like consols in Britain; **in someone's debt** under an obligation (not necessarily pecuniary) to someone; **national debt** see under **nation**[1]. [OFr *dette*, from L *dēbitum*, *dēbēre* to owe]

debug *dē-bug'*, *vt* to remove concealed listening devices from; to find faults or errors in and remove them from (*esp* a machine or a computer program); to remove insects from (*colloq*). [L *dē* from, and **bug**]

debunk *dē-bungk'*, *vt* (*slang*) to clear of bunk or humbug; to remove the whitewash from (a reputation); to show up (eg a theory) as false. [**de-** (2)]

debus *dē-bus'*, *vt* and *vi* to unload from or get out of a bus or other vehicle: — *pr p* **debuss'ing**; *pa t* and *pa p* **debussed'**. [**de-** (1)]

debut or **début** *dā-bü'*, *n* a beginning or first attempt; a first appearance before the public, or in society. — *vi* to start, make a first appearance. — *n* **débutant** (*dā-bü-tã* or *deb'ū-tənt*) *n* a male performer who makes his first appearance. — *n* **débutante** (*-tãt* or *deb'ū-tənt*) a young woman making her first appearance in society (shortened to *colloq* **deb** or **debb'y**); a female performer making her first appearance. — *adj* **debb'y** (*colloq*) of or like a deb or debs. [Fr *début* a first stroke, from *débuter*, from *de* from, and *but* aim, mark]

Debye *də-bī'* or **Debye unit** (*ū'nit*), *n* a unit of electric dipole moment. [P J W *Debye* (1884–1966), Dutch physicist]

DEC *abbrev*: Disasters Emergency Committee.

Dec. *abbrev*: December.

dec. *abbrev*: deceased; declaration (also **dec**); declension (also **decl.**).

deca- *dek-ə-*, *pfx* signifying ten. [Gr *deka*]

decachord *dek'ə-körd*, *n* an old ten-stringed musical instrument. [Gr *dekachordos*, from *deka* ten, and *chordē* a string]

decade *dek'ād*, *dek-ād'* or (*obs*) **decad** *-ad*, *n* a series of ten years; any group or series of ten. — *adj* **dec'adal**. [Gr *dekas*, *-ados*, from *deka* ten]

decadence *dek'ə-dəns* or **decadency** *n* state of decay; a decline from a superior state, standard or time; applied to a school in late 19c French literature, the symbolists, and their like. — *adj* **dec'adent** decaying, declining; lacking in moral and physical vigour; symbolist (see *n* above). — *n* a degenerate person; a symbolist (see *n* above). — *adv* **dec'adently**. [Fr *décadence*, from LL *dēcadentia*, from L *dē* down, and *cadere* to fall]

decaffeinate *dē-kaf'i-nāt*, *vt* to extract (most of) the caffeine from (coffee, tea, cola, etc). — *n* **decaff'** (*colloq*) decaffeinated coffee. [**de-** (2)]

decagon *dek'ə-gon*, *n* a plane figure of ten angles and sides. — *adj* **decagonal** (*-ag'ən-əl*). [Gr *deka* ten, and *gōniā* an angle]

decagramme or **decagram** *dek'ə-gram*, *n* a weight of ten grammes. [Fr *décagramme*, from Gr *deka* ten, and **gramme**]

Decagynia *dek-ə-jin'i-ə*, (*bot*) *n pl* (in the Linnaean system) a class of plants with ten pistils. — *adj* **decagyn'ian** or **decagynous** (*-aj'*). [Gr *deka* ten, and *gynē* a woman]

decahedron *dek-ə-hē'drən*, *n* a solid figure having ten faces. — *adj* **decahē'dral**. [Gr *deka* ten, and *hedrā* a seat]

decal *dē'kal*, *dek'al*, *n* a transfer (picture or design). [Abbrev of **decalcomania**]

decalcify *dē-kal'si-fī*, *vt* to deprive of lime. — *n* **decalcificā'tion**. [**de-** (2)]

decalcomania *dē-kal'ko-mā-ni-a*, *n* the art or process of transferring a design from specially prepared paper on to another surface; a design transferred in this way. [Fr *décalcomanie*, from *décalquer* to trace, copy]

decalescence *dē-kəl-es'əns*, *n* the behaviour of iron or steel which in heating from red to white reaches a point where it seems to go back for a little (the *opp* of *recalescence*). [L *dē* down, and *calēscere* to grow hot]

decalitre *dek'ə-lēt-ər*, *n* ten litres, 2·20 imperial gallons, 2·64 US gallons. [Fr *décalitre*, from Gr *deka* ten, and *lītrā* a pound]

decalogue *dek'ə-log*, *n* the ten commandments (see under **command**). — *n* **decalogist** (*di-kal'ə-jist*) an exponent as of the decalogue. [Gr *deka* ten, and *logos* a discourse]

Decameron *di-kam'ə-ron*, *-rən*, *n* Boccaccio's book of a hundred tales, supposed to be told in ten days. — *adj* **decameron'ic**. [Gr *deka* ten, and *hēmerā* a day]

decamerous *di-kam'ər-əs*, *adj* having the parts in tens. [Gr *deka* ten, and *meros* part]

decametre *dek'ə-mēt-ər*, *n* ten metres. [Fr *décamètre*, from Gr *deka* ten, and *metron* a measure]

decamp *di-kamp'*, *vi* to make off, *esp* secretly; to break camp. — *n* **decamp'ment**. [Fr *décamper*]

decanal *dek-ān'əl*, *adj* pertaining to a dean or deanery; decani. — *adj* **decān'ī** dean's, ie south (of the side of a choir where the dean sits, opposed to **cantoris**); used (*music*) in antiphonal singing. [LL *decānus*, *-ī*]

Decandria *de-kan'dri-ə*, (*bot*) *n pl* (in Linnaean system) a class of plants with ten stamens. — *adj* **decan'drian**. — *adj* **decan'drous** with ten stamens. [Gr *deka* ten, and *anēr*, *andros* a man, male]

decane *dek'ān*, (*chem*) *n* a hydrocarbon ($C_{10}H_{22}$), tenth of the methane series. [Gr *deka* ten]

decani. See **decanal**.

decant *di-kant'*, *vt* to pour off, leaving sediment; to pour from one vessel into another; to move (people) to another area, etc. — *n* **decantā'tion** (*dē-*). — *n* **decant'er** an ornamental stoppered bottle for holding decanted liquor. [Fr *décanter* (Ital *decantare*), from L *dē* from, and *canthus* beak of a vessel, from Gr *kanthos* corner of the eye]

decantate *dē-kant'āt*, (*obs*) *vt* and *vi* to chant or say repeatedly. [L *dēcantāre*, from pfx *dē-*, and *cantāre*, intensive of *canere* to sing]

decapitalization or **-isation** *di-kap-it-əl-ī-zā'shən*, *n* loss or draining away of capital in industry. — *vt* **decap'italize** or **-ise**. [**de-** (2)]

decapitate *di-kap'i-tāt*, *vt* to behead. — *n* **decapitā'tion**. [LL *dēcapitāre*, from L *dē* from, and *caput*, *capitis* the head]

Decapoda *di-kap'ə-də*, *n pl* an order of higher crustaceans with ten feet (including pincers), ie crabs, lobsters, shrimps, prawns, etc; an order of cephalopods with ten arms. — *n* **dec'apod** a member of either of these orders. — Also *adj*. — *adj* **decap'odal**, **decap'odan** or **decap'odous**. [Gr *deka* ten, and *pous*, *podos* a foot]

decarbonize or **-ise** *dē-kär'bən-īz*, *vt* to remove carbon or carbon dioxide from (also **decar'būrize** and **-ise**; **decar'bonate**). — *n* **decarbonā'tion**. — *n* **decarbonīzā'tion** or **-s-**. — *n* **decarburīzā'tion** or **-s-**. — See also **decarb** under **decoke**. [**de-** (2)]

decarboxylase *dē-kär-bok'si-lāz*, (*bot*) an enzyme that catalyses the removal of CO_2 from its substrate. [**de-** (2), carboxyl, and *-ase* sfx denoting an enzyme]

decare *dek'är*, *dek-är'*, *n* 1000 square metres, 10 ares. [Gr *deka* ten, and **are**[1]]

decastere *dek'ə-stēr*, *n* ten steres. [Gr *deka* ten, and **stere**]

decastich *dek'ə-stik*, *n* a poem of ten lines. [Gr *deka* ten, and *stichos* a row, a verse]

decastyle *dek'ə-stīl*, (*archit*) *n* a portico with ten columns in front. — Also *adj*. [Gr *deka* ten, and *stȳlos* a column]

decasyllable *dek-ə-sil'ə-bl*, *n* a verse-line or a word of ten syllables. — *adj* **decasyllabic** (*-ab'ik*). [Gr *deka* ten, and *syllabē* a syllable; see **syllable**]

decathlon *dek-ath'lon*, *n* a two-day contest of ten events held at the modern Olympic Games since 1912. — *n* **decath'lete**. [Gr *deka* ten, and *athlon* a contest]

decaudate *dē-kö'dāt*, *vt* to cut off the tail of. [L *dē* from, and *cauda* tail]

decay *di-kā'*, *vi* to fall away from a state of health or excellence; to waste away; to decompose, rot; (of eg magnetism, radioactivity) to decrease in strength as the source of energy is removed. — *vt* to cause to waste away; to impair. — *n* a falling into a worse or less perfect state; a wearing away; rotting; bad or rotten matter (eg in a tooth); loss of fortune; ruin, downfall (*obs*); disintegration of a radioactive substance. — *adj* **decayed'** rotten; reduced in circumstances, impoverished. — **decay heat** (*nuc eng*) the heat produced by the radioactive decay of fission products in a nuclear reactor. [OFr *decair*, from L *dē* from, and *cadere* to fall]

Decca® *dek'ə*, *n* the **Decca Navigator System**, consisting of a series of chains of long-wave radio transmitting stations, each chain formed of a master station and three slaves, providing a navigator or pilot with meter readings that have to be interpreted by special charts, or, alternatively, with a direct picture of the aircraft's track on a **Decca Flight Log**.

deccie *dek'i*, (*slang*) *n* short for interior decoration or (also with *cap*) an interior decoration enthusiast or interior designer.

decease *di-sēs'*, *n* death. — *vi* to die. — *adj* **deceased'** dead; lately dead. — *n sing* or *n pl* the dead person or people in question. [OFr *deces* (Fr *décès*), from L *dēcessus* departure, death, from *dē* away, and *cēdere*, *cēssum* to go]

decedent *di-sē'dənt*, *n* (*US law*) a deceased person. [L *dēcēdēns*, *-entis*, pr p of *dēcēdere* to depart, from *dē* away, and *cēdere* to go]

deceit *di-sēt'*, *n* the act of deceiving; anything intended to mislead another; fraud; falseness. — *adj* **deceit'ful** full of deceit; disposed or tending to deceive; insincere. — *adj* **deceit'fully**. — *n* **deceit'fulness**. [OFr *deceite*, from L *dēcipere*, *dēceptum* to deceive]

deceive *di-sēv'*, *vt* to mislead or cause to err; to cheat; to disappoint (*archaic*). — *adj* **deceiv'able** that may be deceived; exposed to imposture. — *n* **deceivabil'ity** or **deceiv'ableness**. — *adj* **deceiv'ably**. — *n* **deceiv'er**. [Fr *décevoir*, from L *dēcipere*, *dēceptum* to deceive]

decelerate *dē-sel'ər-āt*, *vt* and *vi* to retard, slow down. — *n* **decelerā'tion**. — *n* **decel'erator**. — *n* **decelerom'eter** an instrument for measuring deceleration. [L *dē* down, and *celer* swift]

December *di-sem'bər*, *n* in Roman times the tenth, now the twelfth, month of the year. — *adj* **Decem'berish** or (*obs*) **Decem'berly** wintry, cold. — *n* **Decem'brist** one of those who took part in the Russian conspiracy of December 1825. [L *December*, from *decem* ten]

decemvir *di-sem'vər*, *n* a member of a body of ten men; *esp* of those who drew up the Laws of the Twelve Tables at Rome (451–450 BC): — *pl* **decem'virs** or **decem'virī** (L; *dek'em-wi-rē* or *-vi-rī*). — *adj* **decem'viral**. — *n* **decem'virāte** a body of ten men in office; the term of office of decemvirs. [L *decem* ten, and *vir* a man]

decency. See **decent**.

decennary *di-sen'ər-i*, *n* a period of ten years — also **decenn'ium**. — *adj* **decenn'ial** consisting of, or happening every, ten years. [L *decem* ten, and *annus* a year]

decennoval *di-sen'ō-vəl*, (*obs*) *adj* pertaining to the number 19. [L *decemnovalis*, from *decem* ten, and *novem* nine]

decent *dē'sənt*, *adj* becoming; seemly; proper; modest; moderate; fairly good; passable; showing tolerant or kindly moderation (*colloq*); nice, pleasant (*colloq*). — *n* **dē'cency** conformity to accepted moral and ethical standards; fairness; (in *pl*) the conventions of respectable behaviour. — *adv* **dē'cently**. [L *decēns*, *-entis*, pr p of *decēre* to be becoming]

decentralize or **-ise** *dē-sen'trəl-īz*, *vt* to withdraw from the centre; to transform by transferring functions from a central government, organization, authority or head to smaller local centres. — *n* **decentralizā'tion** or **-s-**. [**de-** (2)]

deception *di-sep'shən*, *n* act of deceiving; state of being deceived; means of deceiving or misleading; trick; illusion. — *n* **deceptibil'ity**. — *adj* **decept'ible** capable of being deceived. — *adj* **decep'tious** (*Shakesp*) deceitful. — *adj* **decep'tive** tending to deceive; misleading. — *adv* **decep'tively**. — *n* **decep'tiveness**. — *adj* **decep'tory** tending to deceive. — **deceptive cadence** (*music*) same as **interrupted cadence**. [OFr, from LL *dēceptiō*, *-ōnis*, from *dēcipere* to deceive]

decerebrate *dē-ser'ə-brāt*, *vt* to deprive of the cerebrum. — Also **decer'ebrize** or **-ise**. — *n* **decerebrā'tion**. [**de-** (2)]

decern *di-sûrn'*, (*Scots law*) *vt* and *vi* to judge; to decree; to pass judgement. [OFr *decerner*, from L *dēcernere*, from *dē*, and *cernere* to distinguish]

decession *di-sesh'ən*, (*rare*) *n* departure. [See **decease**]

déchéance *dā-shā-ãs*, (*Fr*) *n* forfeiture.

dechristianize or **-ise** *dē-krist'yən-īz*, *vt* to turn from Christianity. — *n* **dechristianiza'tion** or **-s-**. [**de-** (2)]

deci- *des'i-*, *pfx* signifying one-tenth. [L *decimus* tenth]

deciare *des'i-är*, *n* the tenth part of an are. [Fr, from L *deci-* (in *decimus*), and **are**]

decibel *des'i-bel*, *n* a term used to express a relationship between two currents, power levels or voltages, or to express a level of sound (the tenth part of a bel; this unit more commonly used than **bel** (qv)). [L *deci-*, and **bel**]

decide *di-sīd'*, *vt* to determine; to end; to settle; to resolve. — *vi* to make up one's mind. — *adj* **decid'able** capable of being decided. — *adj* **decid'ed** determined; clear, unmistakable; resolute. — *adv* **decid'edly**. — *n* **decid'er**

someone who, or that which, decides; an action, etc that proves decisive, such as the winning goal in a match (*colloq*). [OFr *decider*, from L *dēcīdere*, from *dē* away, and *caedere* to cut]

deciduous *di-sid'ū-əs, adj* liable to be shed at a certain period; transitory, not permanent; shedding all the leaves together (*opp* to *evergreen*; *bot*); shedding wings (as some insects do). — *n* **decid'ua** (*med* and *zool*) a membrane of the uterus discharged after parturition: — *pl* **decid'uas** or **deciduae** (*di-sid'ū-ē*). — *adj* **decid'ual**. — *adj* **decid'uāte**. — *n* **decid'uousness**. [L *dēciduus*, from *dēcidere*, from *dē* from, and *cadere* to fall]

decigram or **decigramme** *des'i-gram, n* the tenth part of a gram(me).

decilitre or (*NAm*) **deciliter** *des'i-lē-tər, n* a tenth part of a litre.

decillion *di-sil'yən, n* a million raised to the tenth power; in American notation, a thousand raised to the eleventh power. — *adj* and *n* **decill'ionth**. [L *decem* ten, and **million**]

decimal *des'i-məl, adj* numbered or proceeding by tens. — *n* a decimal fraction. — *n* **dec'imalism** use or advocacy of a decimal system. — *n* **dec'imalist**. — *vt* **dec'imalize** or **-ise** to convert to a decimal system, *esp* the metric system. — *n* **decimalizā'tion** or **-s-**. — *adv* **dec'imally**. — **decimal classification** see **Dewey decimal system**; **decimal currency** one in which the basic unit is divided into ten (or a multiple of ten) parts; **decimal fraction** a fraction expressed by continuing ordinary decimal notation into negative powers of ten, a point being placed after the unit figure; **decimal notation** a system of writing numbers based on ten and powers of ten, our ordinary system; **decimal places** the number of figures written after the point (**decimal point**) which separates the unit and the decimal fraction; **decimal system** a system in which each unit is ten times the next below it, *esp* the metric system of weights and measures; **decimal tab** a facility of most word processors and some computers which arranges a column of numbers so that the decimal points are aligned. [L *decima* (*pars*) a tenth (part)]

decimate *des'i-māt, vt* to take or destroy the tenth part of; to punish by killing every tenth man; (loosely) to reduce very heavily. — *n* **decimā'tion**. — *n* **dec'imātor**. [L *decimāre*, *-ātum*, from *decimus* tenth, from *decem* ten]

décime *dā-sēm*, (*hist*) *n* a French coin equal to $\frac{1}{10}$ franc. [Fr, from L *decima* (*pars*) tenth (part)]

decimetre or (*NAm*) **decimeter** *des'i-mē-tər, n* a tenth of a metre.

decinormal *des-i-nör'məl*, (*chem*) *adj* of one-tenth of normal concentration. [L *decimus* tenth, and **normal**]

decipher *di-sī'fər, vt* to uncipher; to read or transliterate or interpret from secret, unknown, or difficult writing; to make out; to detect (*obs*; *Shakesp*); to reveal (*obs*; *Shakesp*); to show forth (*obs*). — *n* **decīpherabil'ity**. — *adj* **decī'pherable**. — *n* **decī'pherer**. — *n* **decī'pherment**. [**de-** (2)]

decision *di-sizh'ən, n* the act or product of deciding; settlement; judgement; the quality of being decided in character. — *adj* **decisive** (*-sīs'iv*) having the power of deciding; showing decision; final; positive. — *adv* **decī'sively**. — *n* **decī'siveness**. — *adj* **decī'sory** decisive. — **decision support system** (*comput*) a system which assists in decision-making by using one or more computers and programs to provide and organize data; **decision table** (*logic* and *comput*) a table comprising four sections showing a number of conditions and actions to be taken if these are or are not met, indicating the action to be taken under any condition or set of conditions. [See **decide**]

decistere *des'i-stēr, n* one-tenth of a stere.

decitizenize or **-ise** *dē-sit'i-zən-īz, vt* to deprive of citizenship. [**de-** (2)]

decivilize or **-ise** *dē-siv'i-līz, vt* to reduce from a civilized to a more savage state. [**de-** (2)]

deck *dek, vt* to cover; to clothe; to adorn; to provide with a deck (see also **deck over**); to pile up on a platform. — *n* a covering (*obs*); a horizontal platform extending from one side of a vessel to the other, thereby joining the sides together, and forming both a floor and a covering (*naut*); a floor, platform, or tier as in a bus, bridge, etc; the ground (*slang*); the platform of a skateboard; a pile of things laid flat; a pack of cards; the part of a pack used in a particular game, or the undealt part; the platform supporting the turntable of a record-player; that part of a tape-recorder or computer in which the magnetic tapes are placed, and the mechanism for running them; a set of punched cards (*comput*); a packet of heroin or other narcotic drug (*slang*). — *adj* **decked** (*dekt*) adorned, decorated. — *n* **deck'er** the person or thing that decks; a vessel, vehicle or other structure that has a deck or decks (used only as *combining form*, as in *three-decker*); a person who adorns. — *n* **deck'ing** adornment; a platform. — **deck'-bridge** a bridge whose upper stringer carries the roadway; **deck'-cargo** cargo stowed on the deck of a vessel; **deck'chair** a chair, *usu* folding and made of canvas and wood, such as passengers sit or lie on deck in; **deck'-game** a game played on a ship's deck; **deck'-hand** a person employed on deck; an ordinary sailor; **deck'house** a house, room, or box on deck; **deck'-load** a deck-cargo; **deck officer** a ship's officer dealing with navigation, cargo, etc, rather than engineering; **deck'-passage** a passage securing only the right of being on deck, without cabin accommodation; **deck'-pass'enger**; **deck'-quoits** quoits as played on a ship's deck, with rope rings; **deck'-tenn'is** lawn-tennis modified for playing on board ship. — **clear the decks** to tidy up, remove encumbrances, *esp* in preparation for action (*orig* naval action, now often *fig*); **deck out** to adorn, decorate; **deck over** to complete building the upper deck of (a vessel); to construct a roof over (eg a railway station) and build up upon that surface; **hit the deck** (*slang*) to lie, fall or be pushed down quickly (*esp* for safety); to get out of bed; **pedestrian deck** a safe-way for pedestrians. [Verbal meanings from Du *dekken* to cover: cf **thatch**; Ger *decken*; L *tegere*; noun meanings from MDu *dec* roof, covering]

deckle *dek'l, n* (in paper-making) a contrivance for fixing width of sheet; a deckle-edge. — *adj* **deckled** (*dek'ld*) deckle-edged. — **deck'le-edge** the raw or ragged edge of handmade paper or an imitation of it. — *adj* **deck'le-edged** having a rough uncut edge. [Ger *Deckel* lid]

decko. See **dekko**.

decl. See **dec**.

declaim *di-klām', vi* to make a set or rhetorical speech; to harangue; to recite. — *vt* to utter, repeat or recite declamatorily. — *n* **declaim'ant**. — *n* **declaim'er**. — *n* and *adj* **declaim'ing**. — *n* **declamation** (*dek-lə-mā'shən*) act of declaiming; a set speech in public; display in speaking. — *adv* **declamatorily** (*di-klam'ə-tə-ri-li*). — *adj* **declam'atory** of the nature of declamation; appealing to the passions; noisy and rhetorical. [L *dēclāmāre*, from *de-* (intensive) and *clāmāre* to cry out]

declare *di-klār', vt* to make known; to announce; to assert; to make a full statement of (eg goods at customs); to expose and claim a score for (*bezique*, etc); to announce one's choice of trump-suit or no trumps (*bridge*). — *vi* to make a statement; to announce one's decision or sympathies; to show cards in order to score; to end an innings voluntarily before ten wickets have fallen (*cricket*). — *adj* **declār'able** capable of being declared, exhibited, or proved. — *n* **declār'ant** a person who makes a declaration. — *n* **declaration** (*dek-lə-rā'shən*) the act of declaring; that which is declared; a written affirmation; a formal announcement (eg of war); an official announcement of entry for a race, etc;. in the criminal law of Scotland, the statement made by the prisoner before the magistrate; in common law, the pleading in which the plaintiff in an action at law sets forth his or her case against the defendant. — *adj* **declarative** (*di-klar'ə-tiv*) making a statement or declaration; declaratory. — *adj* **declar'atory** explanatory; declarative. — *adv* **declar'atively** or **declar'atorily**. — *n* **declar'ator** a form of action in the Court of Session, with the view of having a fact judicially ascertained and declared. — *adj* **declāred'** avowed, stated. — *adv* **declā'redly** avowedly. — *n* **declār'er** a person who declares. — **declaratory act** an act intended to explain an obscure or disputed law. — **declare an interest** (of a member of parliament, etc) formally to make known that they have (financial) connections with an organization with which (parliamentary) discussions are concerned; **declare off** to renounce; to withdraw; to cancel; **(well) I declare!** *interj* expressing surprise. [L *dēclārāre*, *-ātum*, from pfx *dē-* wholly, and *clārus* clear (partly through Fr *déclarer*)]

declass *dē-kläs'*, *vt* to remove or degrade from one's class. — *adj* **déclassé**, *fem* **déclassée** (*dā-klä-sā*; *Fr*) having lost caste or social standing. [Fr *déclasser*]

declassify *dē-klas'i-fī*, *vt* to take off the security list; to remove from a classification. [**de-** (2)]

declension *di-klen'shən*, *n* a falling off; decay; descent; a system of cases and case-endings (*gram*); a class of words similarly declined; a statement in order of the cases of a word. — *adj* **declen'sional**. [See **decline**]

decline *di-klīn'*, *vi* to bend or turn away; to deviate; to refuse; to bend or slope down; to fail or decay, eg in health or fortune; to stoop or condescend; to draw to an end. — *vt* to bend down; to turn away from; to refuse; to avoid; to give the various cases of (*gram*). — *n* a falling off; deviation; decay; a period of gradual deterioration; a gradual sinking of the bodily faculties, consumption (*archaic*); a down-slope. — *adj* **declīn'able** having inflection for case. — *adj* **declī'nal** bending downward. — *adj* **declinant** (*dek'lin-ənt*; *heraldry*) having the tail hanging down. — *adj* **dec'linate** (*bot*) curving downwards. — *n* **declinā'tion** act of declining (*US*); a sloping or bending downwards; deviation; the angular distance of a heavenly body from the celestial equator (*astron*). — *n* **dec'linātor** an instrument determining declination. — *adj* **declīn'atory** containing a declination or refusal. — *n* **declīn'ature** act of declining or refusing; a plea declining the jurisdiction of a judge (*law*). — *n* **declinom'eter** an instrument for measuring declination in various senses, *esp* the **declination of the compass** or **magnetic declination** (ie the deviation of the magnetic needle from the true north), or the declination or dip of a compass needle (see **dip of the needle**). — **on the decline** in the process of becoming less, deteriorating. [L *dēclīnāre*, from *dē* down, away from, and *clīnāre* to bend (partly through Fr *décliner*)]

declivity *di-kliv'i-ti*, *n* a place that slopes downward, (*opp* of *acclivity*); inclination downwards. — *adj* **decliv'itous**. — *adj* **declī'vous** (*rare*). [Fr *déclivité*, from L *dēclīvitās*, *-ātis*, from *dē* downward, and *clīvus* sloping, related to *clīnāre*]

declutch *dē-kluch'*, *vi* to release the clutch (of a motor vehicle). [**de-** (2)]

Deco or **deco** *dek'ō*, *adj* pertaining to art deco (qv).

decoct *di-kokt'*, *vt* to prepare by boiling; to extract the substance of by boiling; to boil; to devise. — *adj* **decoc'tible**. — *adj* **decoc'tive**. — *n* **decoc'tion** an extract of anything got by boiling. — *n* **decoc'ture** a substance prepared by decoction. [L *dēcoquere*, *dēcoctum*, from *dē* down, and *coquere* to cook]

decode *dē-kōd'*, *vt* to translate from a code. — *vt* and *vi* to convert from sound or writing to meaning, or from a foreign language to one's own language (*linguistics*); to convert computer data into human-readable form; to convert coded information into analogue information (*electronics*). — *n* (*dē'kōd*) a decoded message. — *n* **decō'der**. [**de-** (2)]

decoherer *dē-kō-hē'rər*, (*old elec*) *n* a device for bringing a coherer back to its former condition after it has been affected by an electric wave. [**de-** (2)]

decoke *dē-kōk'* and earlier **decarb** *dē-kärb'*, (*colloq*) *vt* to decarbonize (an internal combustion engine). [**de-** (2)]

decollate[1] *dē-kol'āt*, *vt* (*archaic*) to behead. — *adj* **decoll'ated** rounded off, as the apex of a shell. — *n* **decollā'tion** the act of beheading; a picture of a decapitation, *esp* of the head of St John the Baptist on a platter; the festival of the Baptist, 29 August. — *n* **decoll'ator**. [L *dēcollāre*, from *dē* from, and *collum* the neck]

decollate[2] *vt* and *vi* to separate continuous stationery into separate sheets or forms. — *n* **decolla'tion**. — *n* **decolla'tor**.

décolleté *dā-kol-tā*, *adj* wearing a low-cut dress; (of clothes) low-cut. — *n* **décolletage** (*dā-kol-täzh'*) a low-cut neckline; a dress with this; the exposure of the neck and shoulders in such a dress. [Fr, pa p of *décolleter* to bare the neck and shoulders, from *collet* collar. Cf **decollate**]

decolonize or **-ise** *dē-kol'ə-nīz*, *vt* to release from being a colony, grant independence to. — *n* **decolonizā'tion** or **-s-**. [**de-** (2)]

decolour or **decolor** *dē-kul'ər*, *vt* to deprive of colour. — Also **decol'o(u)rize** or **-ise**. — *n* and *adj* **decol'orant** (a substance) that bleaches or removes colour. — *vt* **decol'orate** to deprive of colour. — *adj* without colour. — *n* **decolorā'tion** removal or absence of colour. — *n* **decolo(u)rīzā'tion** or **-s-**. [L *dēcolōrāre*, from *dē* from, and *color* colour]

decommission *dē-kəm-ish'ən*, *vt* to take out of commission or operation (eg a warship or atomic reactor). — *n* **decommiss'ioner**. — *n* **decommiss'ioning**. [**de-** (2)]

decomplex *dē'kom-pleks*, *adj* repeatedly compound. [**de-** (3)]

decompose *dē-kom-pōz'*, *vt* to separate the component parts of; to resolve into elements; to break down, rot. — *vi* to decay, rot; to break down into elements or components. — *n* **decompōsabil'ity**. — *adj* **decompōs'able**. — *n* **decompōs'er**. [Fr *décomposer*, from pfx *dé-* (L *dis-*) apart, and *composer*; see **compose**]

decomposition[1] *di-kom-pə-zish'ən*, *n* act or state of decomposing; decay. — *vt* **decompound** (*dē-kəm-pownd'*) to decompose. — *adj* **decompound'able**. [Fr pfx *dé-* (L *dis-*) apart, and **composition**; accidentally associated in meaning with **decompose**]

decomposition[2] *dē-komp-ə-zish'ən*, *n* the compounding of things already compound. — *adj* **decomp'osite** (or *-oz'-*) doubly or further compounded. — *vt* **decompound** (*-kəm-pownd'*) to compound again, or further. — *adj* (*dē'*) compounded more than once; having leaflets themselves composed of separate parts (*bot*). [**de-** (3)]

decompound. See **decomposition**[1,2].

decompress *dē-kəm-pres'*, *vt* to release from pressure. — *n* **decompression** (*-presh'ən*) the act or process of releasing from pressure; the gradual release of air pressure on persons (such as divers, construction workers, etc) on returning to normal atmospheric conditions; any operation to relieve excessive pressure (*surg*). — *adj* **decompress'ive**. — *n* **decompress'or**. — **decompression chamber** a chamber in which excessive pressure can be reduced gradually to atmospheric pressure, or in which a person can be subjected gradually to decreased atmospheric pressure; **decompression sickness** bends, a painful and sometimes fatal disorder affecting divers, etc who are too suddenly subjected to decreased air pressure, caused by the formation of nitrogen bubbles in the body as nitrogen comes rapidly out of solution from the blood and other body fluids [**de-** (2)]

decongest *dē-kən-jest'*, *vt* to relieve or end the congestion of. — *n* **deconges'tant** (*med*) an agent that relieves congestion. — *n* **decongest'ion** (*-yən*). — *adj* **deconges'tive**. [**de-** (2)]

deconsecrate *dē-kon'si-krāt*, *vt* to deprive of the character given by consecration; to secularize. — *n* **deconsecrā'tion**. [**de-** (2)]

deconstruction *dē-kən-struk'shən*, *n* a method of critical analysis applied *esp* to literary texts, which, questioning the ability of language to represent reality adequately, asserts that no text can have a fixed and stable meaning, and that readers must eradicate all philosophical or other assumptions when approaching a text. — *vt* **deconstruct'**. — *n* and *adj* **deconstruc'tionist**. [**de-** (2) and **construct**]

decontaminate *dē-kən-tam'in-āt*, *vt* to free from contamination. — *n* **decontam'inant**. — *n* **decontaminā'tion**. — *adj* **decontam'inative**. — *n* **decontam'inātor**. [**de-** (2)]

decontrol *dē-kən-trōl'*, *vt* to remove (*esp* official) control from. — *n* removal of control. [**de-** (2)]

décor or **decor** *dā'kör*, *n* scenery and stage embellishments; ornament; the general decorative effect (colour-scheme, furnishings, etc) of a room. [Fr, decoration]

decorate *dek'ə-rāt*, *vt* to ornament, to beautify; to paint, put wallpaper on (a house, etc); to honour with a badge or medal. — *adj* **dec'orated**. — *n* **decorā'tion** ornament; the applied paint and wallpaper in eg a house; the badge of an order; a medal; (in *pl*) flags, bunting, paper chains, etc put out or hung at a time of celebration. — *adj* **dec'orative** (*-rə-tiv*) ornamental. — *adv* **dec'oratively**. — *n* **dec'orativeness**. — *n* **dec'orātor** a person who decorates, *esp* houses. — **Decorated style** (*archit*) a style of Gothic architecture, elaborate and richly decorated, which prevailed till near the end of the 14c; **Decoration Day** see **Memorial Day**. [L *decorāre*, *-ātum*, from *decus* what is becoming, from *decēre* to be becoming]

decorous *de'kə-rəs*, or (*old-fashioned*) *-kō'*, *-kö'*, *adj* becoming; suitable; proper; decent. — *adv* **dec'orously**. — *n* **dec'orousness**. — *n* **decō'rum** that which is in keeping, congruous; that which is becoming in outward appearance; propriety of conduct; decency. [L *decōrus* becoming; L *decēre* to be becoming]

decorticate *dē-kör'ti-kāt*, *vt* to remove the bark, husk or peel of; to remove the cortex of (*med*). — *n* **decorticā'tion**. [L *dēcorticāre*, *-ātum*, from *dē* from, and *cortex* bark]

decoupage or **découpage** *dā-koo-päzh'*, *n* the craft (originating in the 18c) of applying decorative paper cut-outs to eg wood surfaces; a picture produced in this way. [Fr *découper* to cut out]

decouple *dē-kup'l*, *vt* to reduce or prevent unwanted distortion or oscillation within (a circuit or circuits) (*electronics*); to separate from, end the connection with. — *n* **decoup'ling**. [**de-** (2)]

decoy *di-koi'*, *vt* to allure; to entrap; to lure into a trap. — *n* (*dē'koi*) anything intended to lure into a snare (*lit* and *fig*); a person, etc employed to lure others into a snare; an apparatus of hoops and network for trapping wild ducks (sometimes **duck'-coy**). — **de'coy-duck** a wild duck tamed and trained to entice others into a trap; a person employed to lure others into a snare (*fig*). [Perh Du *de* the, or L pfx *dē* down, and Du *kooi*, from L *cavea* a cage; or poss Du *eendekooi* a duck-trap]

decrassify *dē-kras'i-fī*, (*rare*) *vt* to make less crass. [**de-** (2), and **crass**]

decrease *di-krēs'*, *vi* to become less. — *vt* to make less. — *n* (*dē'krēs*) a growing less; loss. — *adv* **decreas'ingly**. [OFr *decrois* a decrease, from L *dēcrēscere*, from *dē* from, and *crēscere* to grow]

decree *di-krē'*, *n* an order by someone in authority; an edict or law; a judicial decision; a predetermined purpose (*theol*). — *vt* to decide or determine by sentence in law; to appoint. — *vi* to make a decree: — *pr p* **decree'ing**; *pa t* and *pa p* **decreed'**. — *adj* **decree'able** capable of being decreed. — *n* **decreet'** (*Scots law*; *archaic*) a court judgement. — *adj* **decrē'tal** (*Spenser dec'*) pertaining to a decree or decretal. — *n* a decree, *esp* a papal edict; a book containing decrees; (*specif* in *pl*; often with *cap*) the second part of the canon law, the decrees of various popes determining points of ecclesiastical law. — *n* **decrē'tist** in medieval universities, a student of the decretals, a student of law. — *adj* **decrē'tive**. — *adj* **decrē'tory** pertaining to a decree, judicial; having the force of a decree. — **decree absolute** a final decree; (in a divorce) that which makes the former partners free to marry again; **decree nisi** (*nī'sī*; L *nisi* unless) a provisional decree which will be made absolute in due time unless cause is shown to the contrary (granted *esp* in divorce cases). [OFr *decret* and L *dēcrētālis*, from L *dēcrētum*, from *dēcernere* to decide]

decrement *dek'ri-mənt*, *n* the act or state of decreasing; the quantity lost by decrease; the decrease in value of a variable (*math*); the ratio of each amplitude to the previous one in an oscillator (*phys*). — *vt* to decrease the value of by a given amount; (in computer programming) to substract 1 from (the value in a storage location). [L *dēcrēmentum*]

decrepit *di-krep'it*, *adj* worn out by the infirmities of old age; in the last stage of decay. — *n* **decrep'itness** or **decrep'itude** the state of being decrepit or worn out with age. [L *dēcrepitus* noiseless, very old, from *dē* from, and *crepitus* a noise]

decrepitate *di-krep'i-tāt*, (*phys*) *vi* to crackle (like salts when heated). — *vt* to roast so as to cause a continual crackling, to calcine. — *n* **decrepitā'tion**. [L *dē-* (intensive) and *crēpitāre* to rattle much, frequentative of *crepāre*]

decrescent *di-kres'ənt*, *adj* becoming gradually less. — *n*, *adj* and *adv* **decrescendo** (*dā-kre-shen'dō*; *Ital*; *music*) (a) becoming quieter; diminuendo: — *pl* **decrescend'os**. [L *dē* and *crēscere*]

decretal, etc. See **decree**.

decrew *di-kroo'*, (*Spenser*) *vi* to decrease. [OFr *decru*, pa p of *decroistre*. See **decrease**]

decriminalize or **-ise** *dē-krim'in-əl-īz*, *vt* to make (a practice, etc) no longer a criminal offence in law. — *n* **decriminalizā'tion** or **-s-**. [**de-** (2)]

decrown *dē-krown'*, *vt* to discrown. [**de-** (2)]

decrustation *dē-krus-tā'shən*, *n* removal of a crust. [**de-** (2)]

decry *di-krī'*, *vt* to cry down; to condemn; to criticize as worthless; to blame: — *pr p* **decry'ing**; *pa t* and *pa p* **decried'**. — *n* **decrī'al**. — *n* **decrī'er**. [Fr *dé-*, *des-* (L *dis-*), and *crier* to cry; see **cry**]

decrypt *dē-kript'*, *vt* to decode. — *n* **decryp'tion**. [**de-** (2) and **crypt-**]

dectet *dek-tet'*, *n* a group of ten (musicians, lines of verse, etc); a composition for ten musicians. [L *decem* ten, and **quartet**, **quintet**, etc]

Dectra® *dek'trə*, *n* a long-range modification of **Decca**.

decubitus. See under **decumbent**.

decuman *dek'ū-mən*, *adj* principal, large (of waves, etc); connected with the principal gate of a Roman camp (near which the 10th cohort of the legion was stationed). — *n* a great wave, as every tenth wave was supposed to be. [L *decumānus*, from *decem* ten]

decumbent *di-kum'bənt*, *adj* lying down; reclining on the ground; lying flat but having a rising tip (*bot*). — *n* **decubitus** (*-kūb'i-təs*; *med*) posture in bed. — *n* **decum'bence** or **decum'bency** the act or posture of lying down. — *adv* **decum'bently**. — *n* **decum'biture** the time when a sick person takes to bed. — **decubitus ulcer** (*med*) a bedsore. [L *dēcumbēns*, *-entis*, from *dē* down, and *-cumbere* (in compounds only) to lie]

decuple *dek'ū-pl*, *adj* tenfold. — *n* a number repeated ten times. — *vt* to make tenfold, multiply by ten. [Fr *décuple*, from L *decuplus*]

decurion *di-kū'ri-ən*, (*hist*) *n* in a Roman army, an officer over ten soldiers; any overseer of ten; a councillor. — *n* **decū'ria** or **decury** (*dek'ū-ri*) a company of ten (or more) — *n* **decū'rionate**. [L]

decurrent *di-kur'ənt*, *adj* running or extending downward (*obs*); continued down the stem (*bot*). — *n* **decurr'ency**. — *adv* **decurr'ently**. — *n* **decursion** (*-kûr'*) a running down (*obs*); a military manoeuvre or parade (*hist*). — *adj* **decur'sive**. — *adv* **decur'sively**. [L *dēcurrēns*, *-entis*, from *dē* down, and *currere*, *cursum* to run]

decurve *di-kurv'*, (*biol*) *vi* to curve downwards. — *n* **decurvā'tion**. — *adj* **decurved'**. [**de-** (1)]

decury. See **decurion**.

decussate *di-kus'āt*, *vt* to divide in the form of an X. — *vi* to cross in such a form; to cross, intersect, as lines, etc.

— *adj* **decuss'ate** or **decuss'ated** crossed; arranged in pairs which cross each other, like some leaves. — *adv* **decuss'ately**. — *n* **decussā'tion** (*dek-*). [L *decussāre*, *-ātum*, from *decussis* a coin of ten *asses* (*decem asses*) marked with X, symbol of ten]

DEd. *dē-ed'*, *abbrev*: Doctor of Education.

dedal, Dedalian. See **daedal**.

dedans *də-dã*, *n* an open gallery at the end of the service side of a court in real tennis; spectators (collectively) at a court tennis match. [Fr]

dedicate *ded'i-kāt*, *vt* to set apart and consecrate to some sacred purpose; to devote wholly or chiefly; to inscribe or give orally in tribute (to anyone); to inaugurate or open (*US*). — *adj* devoted; dedicated (*obs*; *Shakesp*). — *n* **ded'icant** a person who dedicates. — *adj* **ded'icated** consecrated; giving one's whole interest and work to a particular cause or belief; single-minded, determined; manufactured or set aside for a specific purpose (eg *a dedicated calculator*), or made to work in conjunction with another specific piece of equipment (eg a *dedicated flash gun*). — *n* **dedicatee** (*ded-i-kə-tē'*) a person to whom a thing is dedicated. — *n* **dedicā'tion** the act of dedicating; the state of being dedicated; an address or tribute to a patron, mentor, etc prefixed to a book. — *adj* **dedicā'tional**, **dedicatorial** (*-kə-tō'ri-əl* or *-tö'*), **ded'icatory** (*-kə-* or *-kā-*) or **ded'icative**. — *n* **ded'icātor**. — **Feast of Dedication** a name for **Hanukkah**. [L *dēdicāre*, *-ātum*, from *dē* down, and *dicāre* to declare]

dedifferentiation *dē-dif-ər-en-shi-ā'shən*, (*biol* and *med*) *n* a change by which specialized or heterogeneous tissue reverts to a generalized or homogeneous form. [**de-** (2)]

dedimus *ded'i-məs*, (*law*) *n* a writ commissioning a person who is not a judge to act as a judge. [From the opening, L *dedimus* (*potestātem*) we have given (power), from *dare* to give]

dedramatize or **-ise** *dē-drä'mə-tīz*, *vt* to play down the importance of, lessen or keep low the tension or friction caused by. [**de-** (2)]

deduce *di-dūs'*, *vt* to derive, work out logically (that); to infer from what precedes or from premises, clues, remarks, etc. — *n* **deduce'ment** what is deduced. — *adj* **dedūc'ible** that may be deduced or inferred. — *n* **dedūcibil'ity** or **dedūc'ibleness** the quality of being deducible. — *vt* **deduct** (*-dukt'*) to take away; to separate (*obs*); to subtract; to reduce, weaken (*obs*; *Spenser*); to deduce (*obs*). — *n* **deductibil'ity**. — *adj* **deduct'ible**. — *n* **deduc'tion** the act of deducing; that which is deduced; the inference of a particular truth from a general truth previously known, as distinguished from *induction*, leading from particular truths to a general truth; the act of deducting; the thing or amount deducted; abatement. — *adj* **deduct'ive** (of thought or reasoning) concerned with deduction from premises or accepted principles. — *adv* **deduct'ively**. — **deducted spaces** see **tonnage**. [L *dēdūcere*, *dēductum*, from *dē* from, and *dūcere* to lead]

dee[1] *dē*, *vi*. Scottish form of **die**.

dee[2] *dē*, *n* the fourth letter of the alphabet (D, d); anything shaped like it. — *n*, *vt* and *interj* (*euphem*) a substitute for **damn**.

deed[1] *dēd*, *n* something done; an act; an exploit, *esp* heroic; a legal transaction, *esp* involving the transfer of property; the documentary evidence of it, signed, sealed and delivered. — *vt* (*NAm*) to transfer (property). — *adj* **deed'ful** (*Tennyson*) marked by deeds or exploits. — *adv* **deed'ily**. — *adj* **deed'less** (*Shakesp*, etc) not having performed deeds. — *adj* **deed'y** (*dialect*) industrious, active. — **deed poll** a deed executed by one party, *esp* one by which a person changes his/her name, originally having the edge *polled* or cut even, not indented. — **deed of covenant** a legal agreement in which a person promises to pay a fixed sum (to another person or organization) for an agreed period of time, enabling the payer to deduct tax from the total payment; **deed of saying** (*Shakesp*) performance of what has been said or promised; **in deed** in reality. [OE *dǣd*, from *dōn* to do; Ger *Tat*]

deed[2] *dēd*, a Scottish form of **indeed**; also of **died** and **dead**.

dee-jay or **deejay** *dē'jā* or *-jā'*, (*colloq*) *n* a phonetic representation of the initials **DJ**, *abbrev* of **disc jockey**. — *vi* to act as a dee-jay.

deek *dēk*, *vt imperative* look at, see. [Gipsy *dik* to look, see]

deem *dēm*, *vt* or *vi* to judge; to think; to believe: — *pa t* and *pa p* **deemed** (*Spenser* **dempt**). — *n* (*obs*; *Shakesp*) opinion. — *n* **deem'ster** a judge (now only in the Isle of Man). — *n* **dempster** (*dem'stər*) a judge (*obs*); formerly in Scotland an officer who repeated the sentence after the judge (also **doom'ster**). [OE *dēman* to form a judgement, from *dōm* judgement; see **doom**]

de-emphasize or **-ise** *dē-em'fə-sīz*, *vt* to take the emphasis away from, treat or consider as of little or less importance. [**de-** (2)]

deen *dēn*, (*Spenser*) for **din**.

deep *dēp*, *adj* extending or placed far down or far from the outside; great in extent from top to bottom; penetrating a (relatively) long way; greatly recessed; very distant; greatly involved; engrossed (in); difficult to understand; very secret; wise and perceptive; profoundly versed; cunning; very still; profound; intense; excessive; heartfelt; sunk low; low in pitch; (of a road) encumbered with mud, sand or ruts; in the outfield, not close to the wickets (*cricket*). — *adv* in a deep manner; at or to a great depth; far (in time); intensely, profoundly. — *n* that which is deep; the sea (*poetic*); a deep place; the middle, deepest, or most intense part; anything profound or incomprehensible. — *vt* **deep'en** to make deeper in any sense; to increase. — *vi* to become deeper. — *n* **deep'ie** (*colloq*) a three-dimensional cinematograph film. — *adv* **deep'ly**. — *adj* **deep'most** deepest. — *n* **deep'ness**. (see also **depth**). — *adj* **deep'-browed** of high intellectual powers. — **deep drawing** a process of shaping metal that involves considerable plastic distortion (*eng*). — *adj* **deep'=draw'ing** (of ships) requiring considerable depth to float in. — *adj* **deep'-drawn**. — *adj* **deep'-dyed** thoroughgoing, extreme (in a bad sense). — *adj* **deep'felt**. — *adj* **deep'-fet** (*Shakesp*) fetched from a depth. — **deep field** (*cricket*) fielding position deep behind the bowler; **deep'-freeze'** storage of foodstuffs, or other perishable substances, at very low temperature; the appliance in which such goods are stored. — Also *vt*. — *vt* **deep'-fry'** to fry (food) completely submerged in fat or oil. — **deep kiss** a French kiss, a kiss using the tongue; **deep kissing**. — *adj* **deep'-laid** secretly plotted or devised. — **deep litter** a method of keeping hens in a henhouse with a deep layer of peat material on the floor. — *adj* **deep'-mouthed** (*archaic*) with deep voice. — *adj* **deep'-read** profoundly versed. — *adj* **deep-root'ed** (*lit* and *fig*). — *adj* **deep'-sea** pertaining to the deeper parts of the sea. — *adj* **deep'=seat'ed** not superficial, ingrained. — *adj* **deep'-set** (*esp* of eyes) set deeply (into the face). — **deep'-sink'er** (*Austr*) a drinking vessel of the largest size; **Deep South** a region of the US, roughly Georgia, Alabama, Mississippi and Louisiana; **deep space** the area of space beyond the moon's orbit; **deep structure** (*linguistics*) the underlying grammatical concepts and relationships of words in a sentence from which its **surface structure** (qv) derives; **deep therapy** the treatment of disease by deep X-rays or gamma rays; **deep throat** (*colloq*) a highly confidential informant. — *adj* **deep'-toned'** having a deep tone or timbre. — **deepwa'terman** a seagoing ship: — *pl* **deepwa'termen**. — **go in, dive in** or **be thrown in at the deep end** to plunge, or be plunged, straight into an activity, job, etc with little or no experience or preparation; **go off the deep end** to express strong feelings without restraint; to lose one's temper completely; **in deep water** in difficulties; **two deep, three deep**, etc, in two, three, etc layers or rows. [OE *dēop*; Ger *tief*; cf **dip, dive**]

deer *dēr*, *n* any kind of animal (as in *small deer*; *obs*); any animal of the *Cervidae*, a family of even-toed hoofed animals characterized by the possession of antlers by the males at least, *incl* red deer, reindeer, etc: — *pl* **deer**. — *n* **deer'let** a chevrotain. — **deer'berry** the huckleberry (genus *Gaylussacia*); the fruit of a gaultheria; that of *Vaccinium stamineum*, an inedible American whortleberry; **deer'-fence** a very high fence that deer should not be able to jump over; **deer'-forest** a wild tract of land (not necessarily woodland) reserved for deer; **deer'-hair** a small species of club-rush; **deer'horn** or **deer'-horn** a deer's antler or its material; a freshwater mussel (*US*); **deer'-hound** a large rough-coated greyhound; **deer'-lick** a spot of salt ground to which deer come to lick the earth; **deer'-mouse** the American deer-footed mouse (so called from its agility); **deer'-neck** a thin ill-shaped neck (of horses); **deer'-park**; **deer'skin** skin of the deer, or the leather made from it; **deer'stalker** a person who stalks deer; a sportsman's helmet-shaped cap; **deer'stalking**. [OE *dēor*; Ger *Tier*, Du *dier*; ON *dyr*]

deere. See **dear**[2].

deev *dēv*. Same as **div**[2].

deeve. See **deave**.

def *def*, (*slang*) *adj* excellent, brilliant (*orig* in hip-hop culture). [Appar from *def*initive or *def*initely]

def. *abbrev*: defendant; definition.

deface *di-fās'*, *vt* to destroy or mar the face or external appearance of, to disfigure; to obliterate; to put out of countenance (*obs*); to defame (*obs*). — *n* **deface'ment** the act of defacing; injury to form or appearance; that which defaces. — *n* **defā'cer**. — *adv* **defā'cingly**. [OFr *desfacer*, from L *dis-* away, and *faciēs* face]

de facto *dē* or *dā fak'tō*, (*L*) actual, if not rightful or legally recognized (eg *the de facto ruler*); in fact, actually. — *n* (*Austr*) a de facto husband or wife.

defaecate. Same as **defecate**.

defalcate *dē'* or *de'fal-kāt*, or *di-fal'kāt* or (*rare*) *-föl'*, *vt* (*obs*) to deduct a part of. — *vi* to embezzle money held on trust. — *n* **defalcā'tion** a diminution; a defection; a misappropriation of funds entrusted to someone; the amount misappropriated. — *n* **de'falcator** someone guilty of defalcation. [LL *dēfalcāre*, *-ātum* to cut away, from L *dē* from, and *falcāre* to cut, from *falx*, *falcis* a sickle]

defame *di-fām'*, *vt* to take away or destroy the good fame or reputation of; to say malicious things about; to speak evil of; to charge falsely (*archaic*). — *n* (*obs*; *Spenser*) infamy. — *n* **defamation** (*def-ə-mā'shən*) the act of defaming; calumny; slander or libel. — *adv* **defamatorily** (*di-fam'ə-tər-i-li*). — *adj* **defam'atory** containing defamation; injurious to reputation; calumnious. — *n* and *adj* **defā'ming**. [OFr *diffamer*, from L *diffāmāre*, from *dis-* away, and *fāma* report]

defast or **defaste**. Spenserian spellings of **defaced** (*pa p*).

defat *dē-fat'*, *vt* to remove fat or fats from: — *pr p* **defatt'ing**; *pa t* and *pa p* **defatt'ed**. [de- (2)]

default *di-fölt'*, *n* a fault, failing or failure; defect; neglect to do what duty or law requires; failure to fulfil a financial obligation; the value of a variable used, or pre-set course of action taken, by a computer system when no specific instruction is given by the user or keyer to override it (also *adj*); fault or offence (*archaic*). — *vi* to fail through neglect of duty; to fail to appear in court when called upon; to fail to fulfil a financial obligation (with *on* or *in*). — *n* **default'er** a person who fails to appear in court, or to account for money entrusted to his or her care, or to settle an ordinary debt or debt of honour; a military offender. — **by default** because of a failure to do something; **in default of** in the absence of; for lack of; **judgement by default** judgement given against a person because he or she fails to plead or make an appearance in court. [OFr *defaute* (noun) and *default* (3rd sing of *defaillir*), from L pfx *dē-* and *fallere*; see **fault**]

defeasance *di-fēz'əns*, *n* undoing, defeat (*obs*); a rendering null or void (*law*); a condition whose fulfilment renders a deed void (*law*). — *adj* **defeas'anced** liable to be forfeited. — *adj* **defeas'ible** that may be annulled. — *n* **defeasibil'ity**. — *n* **defeas'ibleness**. — **deed of defeasance** (*Eng law*) an instrument which defeats the operation of some other deed or estate. [OFr *defesance*, from *desfaire*; see **defeat**]

defeat *di-fēt'*, *vt* to win a victory over; to get the better of; to frustrate; to ruin, undo (*obs*; *Shakesp*); to annul (*law*); to disfigure (*obs*; *Shakesp*). — *n* a frustration of plans; ruin; overthrow, eg of an army in battle; loss of a game, race, etc; annulment (*law*). — *n* **defeat'ism** readiness or inclination to accept, welcome or help to bring on, defeat. — *n* **defeat'ist**. — Also *adj*. — *n* **defeat'ure** (*obs*) undoing (*Spenser*); defeat; disfigurement (*Shakesp*; from **feature**). — *vt* (*archaic*) to disfigure. [OFr *defait*, from *desfaire* to undo, from L *dis-* (negative) and *facere* to do]

defecate *def'i-kāt*, *vt* to clear of dregs or impurities; to purify from extraneous matter. — *vi* to void excrement. — *n* **defecā'tion**. — *n* **def'ecātor**. [L *dēfaecāre*, *-ātum* to cleanse, from *dē* from, and *faex*, *faecis* dregs]

defect *di-fekt'*, *dē'fekt*, *n* a deficiency; a lack; an imperfection; a blemish; a fault; an imperfection in a crystal lattice which may be caused by the presence of a minute amount of a different element in a perfect lattice (*crystallog*). — *vi* (*di-fekt'*) to desert one's country or a cause, transferring one's allegiance (to another). — *n* **defectibil'ity**. — *adj* **defect'ible** liable to imperfection; deficient. — *n* **defec'tion** (an act of) desertion; a failure to carry out a duty; (an act of) revolt. — *n* **defec'tionist**. — *adj* **defect'ive** having defects; lacking in some necessary quality; imperfect; faulty; insufficient; incomplete in inflexions or forms (*gram*). — *n* a person who is subnormal in physical or mental powers. — *adv* **defect'ively**. — *n* **defect'iveness**. — *n* **defect'or** a person who deserts or betrays their country, etc. — **defective equation** (*math*) an equation derived from another, but with fewer roots than the original; **defective virus** (*biol*) a virus that is unable to replicate without a *helper*, eg a plasmid which provides a replicative function. — **the defects of one's qualities** virtues carried to excess, the faults apt to accompany or flow from good qualities. [L *dēficere*, *dēfectum* to fail, from *dē* down, and *facere* to do]

defence *di-fens'* or *NAm* **defense** *dē'fens*, *n* (an act of) defending; capability or means of resisting an attack; protection; a protective piece of armour; vindication, justification (for an action, etc); a defendant's plea or argument (*law*); the defending party in legal proceedings; the members of a (football, hockey, etc) team who are in defending positions, eg halves, backs, goalkeeper. — *adj* **defenced'** fortified. — *adj* **defence'-less**. — *adv* **defence'lessly**. — *n* **defence'lessness**. — *vt* **defend** (*di-fend'*) to keep off anything hurtful from; to guard or protect; to maintain against attack; to prohibit, forbid (*obs*); to ward off; to resist (eg a claim) (*law*); to act as a lawyer for (a defending party); to contest. — *vi* to have, and act on, the responsibility for preventing scoring (*sport*). — *adj* **defend'able** that may be defended. — *n* **defend'ant** a defender; a person accused or sued (*law*). — *adj* **defend'ed** guarded; protected; maintained against attack; forbidden (*obs*; *Milton*). — *n* **defend'er** a person who defends; a player who defends the goal, etc; the holder of a championship, etc who seeks to maintain his or her title; a person who accepts a challenge (*obs*); a person sued or accused (*Scots law*); (in *pl* with *cap*; *hist*) an Irish Roman Catholic society formed at the end of the 18c in opposition to the Peep-o'-day Boys and the Orangemen. — *n* **Defend'erism** (*esp hist*) the policies of the Defenders. — *n* **defen'sative** (*obs*) a protection. — *n* **defensibil'ity**. — *adj* **defens'ible** capable of being defended. — *adv* **defens'ibly**. — *adj* **defens'ive** defending; cautious, attempting to justify one's actions; in a state or posture of defence. — *n* that which defends; posture of defence. — *adv* **defens'ively**. — **defence'man** or (*esp NAm*) **defense'man** (in ice-hockey and lacrosse) a player (other than the goalkeeper) who defends the goal; **defence mechanism** an unconscious mental process by which an individual excludes ideas or experiences painful or unacceptable to him or her (*psychiatry*); a response by the body in reaction to harmful organisms (*med*). — **defender of the faith** a title held by the sovereigns of England since Henry VIII, on whom it was conferred in 1521 for his book against Luther; **stand** or **be on the defensive** to be in the position of defending oneself, not attacking. [L *dēfendere dēfēnsum* to ward off]

defenestration *dē-fen-is-trā'shən*, *n* (an act of) flinging someone out of a window. [L *dē* from, and *fenestra* window]

defense, etc. See **defence**.

defer[1] *di-fûr'*, *vt* to put off to another time; to delay: — *pr p* **deferr'ing**; *pa t* and *pa p* **deferred'**. — *adj* **defer'able** or **deferr'able**. — *n* **defer'ment**. — *n* **deferr'al**. — *n* **deferr'er** a procrastinator. — **deferred annuity** see under **annuity**; **deferred pay** an allowance paid to soldiers on their discharge, or to their relations on their death; a government servant's pension; **deferred payment** payment by instalments; **deferred sentence** a legal sentence which is delayed until such time as the criminal's conduct can be examined; **deferred shares** shares not entitling the holder to a full share of profits, and sometimes to none at all, until the expiration of a specified time or the occurrence of some event. [L *differre*, from *dis-* asunder, and *ferre* to bear, carry; cf **differ**]

defer[2] *di-fûr'*, *vi* to yield (to the wishes or opinions of another person, or to authority). — *vt* to submit to or lay before somebody: — *pr p* **deferr'ing**; *pa t* and *pa p* **deferred'**. — *n* **deference** (*def'ər-əns*) a deferring or yielding in judgement or opinion; respectful compliance or acknowledgement; submission. — *adj* **def'erent** bearing away, carrying off; deferential. — *n* a deferent duct (as opposed to an *afferent* one) in the body; in the Ptolemaic system of astronomy, any of the large eccentric circles which with the smaller epicycles were used to account for the apparent movements of the moon and the planets round the earth. — *adj* **deferential** (*-en'shl*) showing deference. — *adv* **deferen'tially**. [L *dēferre*, from *dē* down and *ferre* to bear]

defervescence *dē-fər-ves'əns*, *n* abatement of heat; coolness; decrease of feverish symptoms (*med*). — Also **defervesc'ency**. [L *dēfervēscere* to cease boiling, from *dē* down, and *fervēscere*, from *fervēre* to boil]

defeudalize or **-ise** *dē-fū'dəl-īz*, *vt* to deprive of feudal character. [**de-** (2)]

deffly (*Spenser*) for **deftly**.

defiance *di-fī'əns*, *n* the act of defying; a challenge to combat; aggressiveness; brave or bold contempt of opposition. — *adj* **defī'ant** full of defiance, insolently bold. — *adv* **defī'antly**. — *n* **defī'antness** (*rare*). — **bid defiance to** to defy. [**defy**]

defibrillation *de-fib-ril-ā'shən* or *-fīb-*, (*med*) *n* the application of an electric current to the heart to restore the normal rhythm after fibrillation has occurred. — *n* **defib'rillator** (or *-fīb'*) (*med*) *n* a machine which applies an electric current to the chest or heart to stop irregular contractions, or fibrillation, of the heart. [Pfx **de-** (2)]

defibrinate *dē-fī'bri-nāt*, *vt* to deprive of fibrin. — Also **defī'brinize** or **-ise**. — *n* **defībrinā'tion**. [**de-** (2), and **fibrin**]

deficient *di-fish'ənt*, *adj* lacking (in); less than complete; defective. — *n* a defective. — *n* **defic'iency** (sometimes **defic'ience**) defect; shortage; the amount which is lacking for completeness; the amount by which a non-profit-making organization's annual income falls short of the annual expenditure (*bookkeeping*). — *adv* **defic'iently**. — *n* **defic'ientness**. — **deficiency disease** a disease due to lack of necessary substances (*esp* vitamins) in the diet, such as rickets, scurvy, beri-beri, pellagra. [L *dēficere*; see **defect**]

deficit *def'i-sit* or *-fis'*, *n* shortfall, *esp* of revenue, as compared with expenditure; the amount of a shortfall. [Fr *déficit*, from L *dēficit*, 3rd pers sing present indicative of *dēficere* to lack]

de fide *dē fī'dē* or *dā fē'de*, (*L*) (of a teaching) in which belief is obligatory.

defied, **defier**, etc. See **defy**.

defilade. See **defile**[1].

defile[1] *di-fīl'*, *vi* to march off in single file, or file by file. — *n* (*dē'fīl* or *di-fīl'*) a long narrow pass or way, in which troops can march only in file, or with a narrow front; a gorge. — *vt* **defilade** (*def-i-lād'*) to plan a fortification so as to protect it or those in it from raking crossfire. — Also *n*. — *n* **defile'ment** act of defilading. [Fr *défiler*, from L *dis-*, and *fīlum* a thread]

defile[2] *di-fīl'*, *vt* to befoul; to pollute or corrupt; to violate. — *n* **defile'ment** (an act of) defiling; foulness. — *n* **defīl'er**. [L *dē*, and OE *fȳlan*, from *fūl* foul; confused with OFr *defouler* to trample, violate]

defilement. See **defile**[1,2].

defiliation *dē-fil-i-ā'shən*, (*Lamb*) *n* depriving a parent of their child. [L *dē* from, and *filius* a son]

define *di-fīn'*, *vt* to bring to an end (*obs*); to decide; to fix the bounds or limits of; to determine with precision; to describe accurately; to fix or describe the meaning of. — *n* **defīnabil'ity**. — *adj* **defīn'able**. — *adv* **defīn'ably**. — *n* **define'ment** (*rare*; *Shakesp*) description. — *n* **defin'er**. — *adj* **definite** (*def'i-nit*) defined; having distinct limits; fixed; certain, sure; exact; clear; sympodial or cymose (*bot*); referring to a particular person or thing (*gram*; see also **article**). — *adv* **def'initely** in a definite manner; determinately; yes indeed (*colloq*). — *n* **def'initeness**. — *n* **defini'tion** a defining; a description of a thing according to its properties; an explanation of the exact meaning (of a word, term or phrase); sharpness of outline, visual clarity. — *adj* **defini'tional**. — *adj* **definitive** (*di-fin'i-tiv*) defining or limiting; positive; final; most authoritative, expert or complete. — *n* (*gram*) an adjective used to limit the extent of meaning of a noun, eg *this*, *that*. — *adv* **defin'itively**. — *n* **defin'itiveness**. — *n* **defin'itude**. [L *dēfīnīre*, *-ītum* to set bounds to, from *dē*, and *fīnis* a limit]

definiendum *di-fin-ē-en'dəm*, *n* a word or phrase that is, or that is to be, defined, as in a dictionary: — *pl* **definien'da**. — Cf **definiens**. [L, neuter gerundive of *dēfīnīre*; see **define**]

definiens *di-fin'ē-ənz*, *n* the word or words used as a definition, as in a dictionary: — *pl* **definien'tia**. — Cf **definiendum**. [L, pr p of *dēdīnīre*; see **define**]

deflagrate *def'lə-grāt*, *vi* and *vt* to burn suddenly, generally with flame and crackling noise. — *n* **deflagrabil'ity**. — *adj* **deflag'rable** which deflagrates; deflagrating readily. — *n* **deflagrā'tion**. — *n* **def'lagrātor** apparatus for deflagration. — **def'lagrating-spoon** a cup with long vertical shank for handling chemicals that deflagrate. [L *dēflagrāre*, from *dē* down, and *flagrāre* to burn]

deflate *dē-flāt'*, *vt* and *vi* to collapse or cause to collapse due to emptying of gas; (of one's hopes, ego, etc) to reduce in extent due to disappointment, criticism, etc; (of an economy) to cause deflation in or suffer from deflation. — *n* **deflā'ter** or **deflātor**. — *n* **deflā'tion** the act or process of deflating; the state of being deflated; a financial condition in which there is a decrease in the amount of money available relative to its buying power (*opp* to *inflation*; *econ*); removal of loose soil material by the wind. — *adj* **deflā'tionary**. — *n* **deflā'tionist** someone who favours deflation of currency. — Also *adj*. [L *dē* from, and *flāre* to blow]

deflect *di-flekt'*, *vi* and *vt* to turn aside; to swerve or deviate from a correct line or proper course. — *adj* **deflect'ed** (*bot*) bent abruptly downward. — *n* **deflec'tion** or **deflex'ion** (*L dēflexiō*) (an act of) bending or turning away; deviation. — *adj* **deflec'tional** or **deflex'ional**. — *adj* **deflec'tive** causing deflection. — *n* **deflec'tor** a device for deflecting a flame, electric arc, etc. — *vt* **deflex'** (*zool* and *bot*) to bend down. — *adj* **deflexed'**. — *n* **deflex'ure** deviation. [L *dē* from, down, and *flectere*, *flexum* to bend, turn]

deflorate *dē-flō'rāt* or *-flō'*, *adj* (*bot*) past flowering; (of an anther) having shed its pollen. — *vt* (*rare*) to deflower.

— *n* **deflorā'tion** the act of deflowering. [L *dēflōrāre*; see **deflower**]

deflower *di-flowr'*, *vt* to strip of flowers; to deprive of grace and beauty, or of virginity; to rape (*euphem*). — *n* **deflower'er**. [OFr *desflorer*, from LL *dēflōrāre* to strip flowers off, from L *dē* from, and *flōs*, *flōris* a flower]

defluent *def'lōō-ənt*, *adj* running down, decurrent. — *n* **defluxion** (*di-fluk'shən*; *obs*) a downflow; a disease supposedly due to a flow of humour; a discharge of fluid in the body. [L *dēfluere*, from *dē* down, and *fluere*, *fluxum* to flow]

defoaming agent *dē-fō'ming āj'ənt*, (*chem*) *n* a substance added to a boiling liquid to prevent or diminish foaming.

defoliate *di-fō'li-āt*, *vt* to strip of leaves. — *adj* **defōl'iate** or **defōl'iated** — *n* **defō'liant** a chemical preparation used to remove leaves. — *n* **defōliā'tion** the falling off of leaves; the time of shedding leaves. — *n* **defō'liātor**. [LL *dēfoliāre*, *-ātum*, from *dē* off, and *folium* a leaf]

deforce *di-fōrs'* or *-förs'*, *vt* to keep out of possession by force (*law*); to resist (an officer of the law in the execution of his or her duty) (*Scots law*). — *n* **deforce'ment**. — *n* **deforc'īant** someone who deforces. — **deforciā'tion** (*obs*) a legal distress. [Anglo-Fr *deforcer*, from *de-* (L *dis-*); see **force**[1]].

deforest *dē-for'ist*, *vt* to disforest, to strip of forests. — *n* **deforestā'tion**. [**de-** (2)]

deform *di-förm'*, *vt* to alter or injure the form of; to disfigure; to change the shape of without breaking into pieces. — *vi* to become altered in shape without breaking into pieces. — *adj* (*archaic*; *Milton*, etc) hideous, unshapely. — *n* **deformabil'ity**. — *adj* **deform'able**. — *n* **dēformā'tion**. — *adj* **deformed'** misshapen, disfigured, etc. — *adv* **deform'edly**. — *n* **deformed'ness**. — *n* **deform'er**. — *n* **deform'ity** the state of being deformed; lack of proper shape; ugliness; disfigurement; anything that destroys beauty; an ugly feature or characteristic. [L *dēfōrmis* ugly, from *dē* from, and *fōrma* beauty]

defoul *di-fowl'*, (*obs*) *vt* to befoul, defile. [OE *fūl* foul, with *de-* from confusion with OFr *defouler* to trample; cf **defile**[2]]

defraud *di-fröd'*, *vt* to deprive by fraud (of); to cheat or deceive. — *n* **defraudā'tion**. — *n* **defraud'ment**. — *n* **defraud'er**. [L *dēfraudāre*, from *dē* from, and *fraus*, *fraudis* fraud]

defray *di-frā'*, *vt* to pay, settle; to satisfy, appease (*Spenser*): — *pr p* **defray'ing**; *pa t* and *pa p* **defrayed'**. — *adj* **defray'able**. — *n* **defray'al** or **defray'ment**. — *n* **defray'er**. [OFr *desfrayer*, from *des-* (*L dis-*) and *frais* expenses]

defreeze *dē-frēz'*, *vt* to thaw out, defrost (*esp* frozen foods). [**de-** (2)]

defrock. Same as **unfrock**.

defrost *dē'frost'*, *vt* to remove frost or ice from; to thaw out. — Also *vi*. — *n* **defrost'er** a device for defrosting *esp* a windscreen. [**de-** (2)]

deft *deft*, *adj* handy, clever, dexterous, *esp* in movement. — *adv* **deft'ly**. — *n* **deft'ness**. [ME *defte*, *dafte* simple, meek; OE *gedæfte* meek, from *dæftan*, *gedæftan* to prepare, make fit; the stem appears in *gedafen* fit]

defunct *di-fungkt'*, *adj* having finished the course of life, dead; finished, no longer working or in use (*fig*). — *n* a dead person. — *n* **defunc'tion** (*Shakesp*) death. — *adj* **defunc'tive** pertaining to the dead. [L *dēfungī*, *dēfunctus* to finish, from *dē* (intensive) and *fungī* to perform]

defuse[1] *di-fūz'*, (*Shakesp*) *vt* to disorder. — *adj* **defūs'd'**. [For **diffuse**[1]]

defuse[2] or (*esp US*) **defuze** *dē-fūz'*, *vt* to remove the fuse of (a bomb, etc), so making it harmless. — Also *fig*.

defy *di-fī'*, *vt* to challenge (*archaic*); to brave, dare; to flout, or to resist (eg authority, convention, an order, a person); to discard, dislike (*obs*): — *pr p* **defy'ing**; *pa t* and *pa p* **defied'**; *3rd pers sing present indicative* **defies'**. — *n* (*Dryden*) a defiance. — *n* **defī'er**. [OFr *defier*, from LL *diffīdāre* to renounce faith or allegiance, from L *dis-* asunder, and *fīdere* to trust, from *fidēs* faith]

deg. *abbrev*: degree or degrees.

dégagé *dā-gä-zhā*, (*Fr*) *adj* unembarrassed, unconstrained, easy; uninvolved. [Pa p of Fr *dégager* to disentangle]

degarnish. Same as **disgarnish**.

degas *dē-gas'*, *vt* to remove gas from; to eject or emit in the form of a gas. [**de-** (2)]

degauss *dē-gows'*, *vt* to protect against magnetic mines by equipment for neutralizing a ship's magnetic field; to remove the magnetic field from (*esp* a television tube). [**de-** (2) and **gauss**]

degender *di-jen'dər*, (*obs*; *Spenser*) *vi* to degenerate. [Fr *dégénerer*, influenced by **gender**[2]]

degenerate *di-jen'ər-it*, *adj* having neglected the high qualities of mankind, become base, immoral, etc; of two or more quantum states, having the same energy (*phys*). — *n* a person who is degenerate. — *vi* (*-āt*) to decline from a more moral, desirable, etc state; to grow worse in quality or standard. — *vt* (*Milton*) to cause to degenerate. — *n* **degen'eracy** the act or process of becoming degenerate; the state of being degenerate. — *adv* **degen'erately**. — *n* **degen'erateness**. — *adj* **degen'erāting**. — *n* **degenerā'tion** the act or process of degenerating. — *n* **degenerā'tionist** someone who believes that the tendency of man is not to improve, but to degenerate. — *adj* **degen'erative** tending or causing to degenerate. — *adj* **degen'erous** (*obs*). — **degenerative joint disease** same as **osteo-arthritis**. [L *dēgenerāre*, *-ātum* to depart from its kind, from *dē* from, down, and *genus*, *generis* kind]

deglutinate *di-glōō'tin-āt*, *vt* to separate (things glued together); to remove gluten from. — *n* **deglutinā'tion**. [L *dēglūtināre*, *-ātum*, from *dē* from, and *glūtināre*, from *glūten* glue]

deglutition *dē-glōō-tish'ən*, (*physiol*) *n* the act or power of swallowing. — *adj* **deglu'titive**. — *adj* **deglu'titory**. [L *dē* down, and *glūtīre* to swallow; see **glut**]

dégoût *dā-gōō*, (*Fr*) *n* distaste.

degrade *di-grād'*, *vt* to lower in grade or rank; to deprive of office or dignity; to lower in character, value or position, or in complexity; to disgrace; to wear down, erode (*geol*); to decompose (*chem*). — *vi* to decompose (*chem*). — *adj* **degrād'able** able to decompose chemically or biologically. — *n* **degradation** (*deg-rə-dā'shən*) becoming degraded; disgrace; degeneration; abortive structural development; a lowering in dignity; decomposition (*chem*); wearing down, erosion. — *adj* **degrād'ed** reduced in rank; base, degenerate, declined in quality or standard; low; placed on steps (*heraldry*). — *adj* **degrād'ing** morally debasing; disgraceful. [OFr *degrader*, from L *dē* down, and *gradus* a step. See **grade**]

degras *deg'räs*, *n* a fat obtained from sheepskins. [Fr *dégras*, from *dégraisser* to degrease]

degrease *dē-grēs'*, *vt* to strip, or cleanse of, grease. — *n* **degreas'ant** a substance which removes grease. [**de-** (2)]

degree *di-grē'*, *n* a grade or step (*archaic*); a gradation on a scale, or that which it measures; a unit of temperature; one of a series of advances or steps; relative position; rank; extent, amount; a mark of distinction conferred by universities and some colleges, either earned by examination or research or granted as a mark of honour; the 360th part of a revolution or circle; 60 geographical miles; nearness (of relationship); comparative amount (of criminality, severity, etc); one of the three stages (*positive*, *comparative* and *superlative*) in the comparison of an adjective or adverb; the highest sum of exponents in any term (*algebra*); the number of points in which a curve may be met by a straight line. — **degree'-day** a unit used in measuring the heating requirements in a building, ie a fall of one degree of heat in one day. — **by degrees** by small amounts, gradually; **degree of dissociation** (*chem*) the fraction of the total number of molecules which are dissociated; **degree of freedom** (*phys*) any one of the independent variables defining the state of a system (eg temperature, pressure, concentration); a capability of variation (eg a system having two variables one of which is dependent on the other has one degree of freedom); **first**, **second** and **third degree burn** (*med*) the three categories of seriousness of a burn, third degree being most serious; **first**, **second** and **third degree murder** (*NAm*) the three categories of criminality of (and therefore severity of punishment for) a murder, first degree being most serious; **forbidden degrees** the degrees of blood relationship within which marriage is not allowed; **Songs of degrees** or **Songs of ascents** Psalms 120-134, either because sung by the Jews returning from captivity, or by the Jews coming up annually to attend the feasts at Jerusalem; **third degree** a method of extracting a confession by bullying and/or torture; any ruthless interrogation; **to a degree** to a certain extent; to a great extent, to extremes. [Fr *degré*, from L *dē* down, and *gradus* a step]

degression *di-gresh'ən, n* a gradual decrease, *esp* on tax rates. — *adj* **degressive** (*di-gres'iv*). [L *dēgredī*, *dēgressus* to descend]

dégringoler *dā-grɛ̃-go-lā*, (*Fr*) *vi* to descend rapidly or steeply; to decline, fail. — *n* **dégringolade** (*-go-läd*) a sudden descent; a quick deterioration. — Also *vi*.

degum *dē-gum', vt* to free from gum. [**de-** (2)]

degust *dē-gust'*, (*rare*) *vt* to taste, to relish. — *vi* to have a relishing taste. — *vt* **degust'āte** to degust. — *n* **degustā'tion** the act of tasting. — *adj* **degust'atory**. [L *dē* down, and *gustāre* to taste]

dehisce *di-his', vi* to gape, burst open (*bot*, etc). — *n* **dehisc'ence**. — *adj* **dehisc'ent**. [L *dehīscere*, from *dē*, (intensive) and *hīscere*, inceptive of *hiāre* to gape]

dehorn *dē-hörn', vt* to remove the horns from; to prune (a tree). — *n* **dehorn'er**. [**de-** (2)]

dehort *di-hört', vt* to dissuade. — *n* **dehortā'tion** (*dē-*) dissuasion. — *adj* **dehor'tative** or **dehor'tatory** dissuasive. — *n* **dehort'er**. [L *dehortārī*, from *dē* off, and *hortārī* to exhort]

dehumanize or **-ise** *dē-hū'mən-īz, vt* to deprive of specifically human qualities, render inhuman. [L *dē* from, down, and **humanize**]

dehumidify *dē-hū-mid'i-fī, vt* to rid of moisture, dry. — *n* **dehumidificā'tion**. — *n* **dehumid'ifier**. [**de-** (2)]

dehydrate *dē-hī'drāt, dē', vt* to remove water from chemically; to remove moisture from, dry; to deprive of strength, interest, etc (*fig*). — *vi* to lose water. — *n* **dēhydrā'tion** loss or withdrawal of moisture; excessive loss of water from the tissues of the body (*med*); the removal of water from oil or gas. — *n* **dēhy'drātor** or **dēhy'drater**. [L *dē* from, and Gr *hydōr* water]

dehypnotize or **-ise** *dē-hip'nə-tīz, vt* to bring out of a hypnotic trance. — *n* **dehypnotizā'tion** or **-s-**. [**de-** (2)]

de-ice *dē-īs', vt* to dislodge ice from (aircraft surfaces, windscreens, etc), or to treat them so as to prevent its formation. — *n* **dē-īc'er** any means of doing this, whether a fluid, a paste, or a mechanical or pneumatic device. [**de-** (2)]

deicide *dē'i-sīd, n* the killing or killer of a god. — *adj* **deicī'dal**. [L *deus* a god, and *caedere* to kill]

deictic. See **deixis**.

deid *dēd*, Scots form of **dead** or **death**. — **deid'-thraw** death-throe.

deify *dē'i-fī, dā'i-fī, vt* to exalt to the rank of a god; to worship as a deity; to make godlike: — *pr p* **dē'ifying**; *pa t* and *pa p* **dē'ified**. — *adj* **dēif'ic** or **deif'ical** making, or treating as if, godlike or divine. — *n* **dēificā'tion** the act of deifying; a deified embodiment. — *n* **dē'ifier**. — *adj* **dē'iform** formed or appearing like a god. [Fr *déifier*, from L *deificāre*, from *deus* a god, and *facere* to make]

deign *dān, vi* to condescend, stoop (to doing something). — *vt* to condescend to give or (*obs*; *Shakesp*) take. [Fr *daigner*, from L *dīgnārī* to think worthy, from *dīgnus* worthy]

dei gratia *dē'i grā'shi-ə* or *dā'ē grä'ti-a*, (*L*) by the grace of God.

deil *dēl, n* Scots form of **devil**.

deindustrialize or **-ise** *dē-in-dus'tri-əl-īz, vt* to disperse or reduce the industrial organization and potential of a nation, area, etc. — *n* **deindustrializā'tion** or **-s-**. [**de-** (2)]

deino-, **Deinoceras**, **Deinornis**, **deinosaur**, **Deinotherium**. See **dino-**.

de integro *dē in'ti-grō* or *dā in-teg'rō*, (*L*) anew.

deiparous *dē-ip'ə-rəs, adj* bearing a god (used of the Virgin Mary). [L *deus* a god, and *parere* to bring forth]

deipnosophist *dīp-nos'ə-fist, n* a person who converses learnedly at dinner, a table-philosopher (from Athenaeus's work, *Deipnosophistai* (end of 2c). [Gr *deipnon* dinner, and *sophos* wise]

deiseal or **deisheal**. Same as **deasil**.

deist *dē'ist, dā'ist, n* a person who believes in the existence of God, but not in a divinely revealed religion. — *n* **de'ism**. — *adj* **deist'ic** or **deist'ical**. — *adv* **deist'ically**. [L *deus* a god]

deity *dē'i-ti, dā'i-ty, n* godhood; divinity; godhead; a god or goddess; (with *cap* and with **the**) the Supreme Being. [Fr *déité*, from LL *deitās*, from L *deus* a god; Sans *deva*]

deixis *dīk'sis*, (*gram*) *n* the use of words relating to the time and place of utterance, eg personal pronouns, demonstrative adverbs, adjectives and pronouns. — *adj* **deictic** (*dīk'tik*) designating words relating to the time and place of utterance (also *n*); proving directly (*logic*). — *adv* **deic'tically**. [Gr *deiknynai* to show]

déjà vu *dā-zhä vü, n* in any of the arts, unoriginal material, old stuff; an illusion of having experienced before something that is really being experienced for the first time, a form of the memory disorder paramnesia (*psychology*). [Fr, already seen]

deject *di-jekt', vt* to depress the spirits of. — *adj* (*archaic*; *Shakesp*) cast down. — *adj* **deject'ed** cast down; dispirited. — *adv* **deject'edly**. — *n* **deject'edness**. — *n* **dejec'tion** lowness of spirits; (often in *pl*) faecal discharge (*med*; also **dejec'ta**); defecation. — *adj* **dejec'tory** promoting evacuations of the bowel. [L *dējicere*, *-jectum*, from *dē* down, and *jacere* to cast]

dejeune *di-jōōn'*, (*archaic*) *n* breakfast or lunch.—See **disjune**, **déjeuner**.

déjeuner *dā-zhø-nā*, (*Fr*) *n* breakfast or lunch. — **petit déjeuner** (*pə-tē*) (little breakfast) coffee and rolls on rising; **déjeuner à la fourchette** (*a la fōōr-shet*) meat (literally fork) breakfast, early lunch.

de jure *dē jōō'rē, dā zhōō're*, (*L*) by right; rightful.

Dekabrist *dek'ə-brist, n* a Decembrist. [Russ *Dekabr'* December]

dekalogy *di-kal'ə-ji, n* a group of ten novels. [Gr *deka* ten, and *logos* discourse, by analogy with **trilogy**]

dekko or **decko** *dek'ō*, (*slang*) *n* a look: — *pl* **dekk'os** or **deck'os**. — *vi* to look. — **have** or **take a dekko** to have a (quick) look. [Hindi *dekho*, imperative of *dekhnā* to see]

Del. *abbrev*: Delaware (US state).

del *del, n* another name for **nabla**.

del. *abbrev*: delegate; *delineavit* (*L*), (he or she) drew it.

delaine *di-lān', n* an untwilled light dress material, originally of wool. [Fr *mousseline de laine* wool muslin]

delaminate *di-lam'i-nāt, vi* to split into layers. — *n* **delaminā'tion**. [L *dēlamināre*, from *dē*, and *lāmina* a layer]

delapse *di-laps'*, (*obs*) *vi* to sink down. — *n* **delap'sion**. [L *dē* down, and *lābī*, *lapsus* to slip]

délassement *dā-las-mã*, (*Fr*) *n* relaxation.

delate[1] *di-lāt', vt* to pass on (*archaic*); to publish (*obs*); to charge with a crime (*archaic*). — *n* **delā'tion**. — *n* **delā'tor**. [L *dēlātum*, used as supine of *dēferre* to bring a report against, to inform on, from *dē-* (intensive) and *ferre*, *lātum* to bear]

delate[2] (*Shakesp*) for **dilate**.

delay[1] *di-lā', vt* to put off to another time; to defer; to hinder or retard (eg an engine's timing). — *vi* to pause, linger, or put off time: — *pr p* **delay'ing**; *pa t* and *pa p*

delay'ed. — *n* a putting off or deferring; the (amount of) time during which something is put off; a pause; a hindrance; a device by which the operation of a mechanism can be timed to take place after an interval. — *n* **delay'er**. — *adv* **delay'ingly**. — **delayed action** the operation of a switch, detonation of explosives, etc some time after the mechanism has been set; **delayed drop** (*aeronautics*) a parachute descent in which the parachutist deliberately delays pulling the ripcord; **delayed neutrons** (*phys*) those neutrons resulting from fission which are emitted with a measurable time delay. [OFr *delaier*]

delay[2] *di-lā'*, (*Spenser*, etc) *vt* to temper, dilute, weaken. [Fr *délayer* to dilute, from L *dēliquāre* to clarify or *dis-*, and *ligāre* to bind]

del credere *del krād'ər-i*, *adj* applied to an agent who becomes surety for the solvency of persons to whom he or she sells. [Ital *del* of the, and *credere* to believe, trust]

dele *dē'li*, *vt imperative* delete, efface, a direction in proofreading to remove a letter or word, indicated by *δ* or other sign. — *adj* **deleble** or **delible** (*del'*) that can be deleted. — *n pl* **delen'da** things to be deleted. [L *dēlē* imperative of *dēlēre* to delete; or for *dēleātur* subjunctive passive; *dēlenda*, neuter pl of gerundive]

delectable *di-lekt'ə-bl* (or *Spenser* and *Shakesp*, *del'*), *adj* delightful; very pleasing. — *n* **delect'ableness** or **delectabil'ity**. — *adv* **delect'ably**. — *n* **delectā'tion** (*dē-*) delight, enjoyment. [Fr, from L *dēlectābilis*, from *dēlectāre* to delight]

delegate *del'i-gāt*, *vt* to send as a legate or representative; to entrust or commit (to a subordinate). — *n* (*-gət*) a person who is delegated; a deputy or representative; a person elected to Congress to represent a territory (eg Guam or American Samoa) as distinguished from the representatives of the States (*US*). — *adj* delegated, deputed. — *adj* **del'egable**. — *n* **del'egacy** the act or system of delegating; a delegate's appointment or authority; a body of delegates; (in some universities) an elected standing committee; a department of a university. — *n* **delegā'tion** a delegating; the act or process of giving tasks to staff with authority to carry them out, whilst retaining the overall responsibilty (*business*); a deputation; a body of delegates (*US*); a body of delegates that was appointed every ten years by each of the two portions of the Dual Monarchy to negotiate a treaty between the Austrian Empire and the Kingdom of Hungary (*hist*). — **delegated legislation** rules and orders with the force of law made by the executive under statutory authority. [L *dē* away, and *lēgāre*, *-ātum* to send as ambassador]

delenda. See **dele**.

delete *di-lēt'*, *vt* to blot out; to erase, take out (something written or printed), cancel; to destroy. — *n* **delē'tion**. — *adj* **delē'tive**. — *adj* **delē'tory**. — **deletion mutation** (*biol*) a mutation in which a base or bases are lost from the DNA. [L *dēlēre*, *dēlētum* to blot out]

deleterious *del-i-tē'ri-əs*, *adj* harmful or destructive; poisonous. — *adv* **deletē'riously**. — *n* **deletē'riousness**. [Gr *dēlētērios* hurtful, from *dēleesthai* to hurt]

delf[1] or **delph** *delf* or **delft** *delft*, *n* (in full **Delft'ware**) a kind of earthenware originally made at *Delft*, Holland.

delf[2] or **delph** *delf*, *n* a drain, ditch, excavation; a charge representing a square sod (*heraldry*): — *pl* **delfs**, **delphs** or **delves**. [OE *delf*; *delfan* to dig]

deli. Short form of **delicatessen**.

Delian *dē'li-ən*, *adj* pertaining to *Dēlos*, in the Aegean Sea, by tradition birthplace of Apollo and Artemis.

delibate *del'i-bāt*, (*obs*) *vt* to sip. — *n* **delibā'tion**. [L *dēlībāre*, from *dē* from, and *lībāre* to take, taste]

deliberate *di-lib'ər-āt*, *vt* to consider, think about carefully. — *vi* to consider the reasons for and against anything; to reflect; to consider; to take counsel; to debate. — *adj* (*-it*) well considered; not impulsive; intentional; (of movement) slow and careful; considering carefully; slow in determining; cautious. — *adv* **delib'erately** in a deliberate manner; (loosely) quietly, without fuss or haste. — *n* **delib'erateness**. — *n* **deliberā'tion** the act of deliberating; mature reflection; calmness; coolness. — *adj* **delib'erative** proceeding or acting by deliberation. — *adv* **delib'eratively**. — *n* **delib'erativeness**. — *n* **delib'erātor**. [L *dēlīberāre*, *-ātum*, from *dē-* (intensive) and *lībrāre* to weigh, from *lībra* a balance]

delible. See **dele**.

delicate *del'i-kit*, *adj* gently pleasing to the senses, *esp* the taste; not strong; dainty; discriminating or perceptive; fastidious; of a fine, slight texture or constitution; tender; not robust (*esp* in health); (of a colour) pale; requiring careful handling (*lit* and *fig*); refined in manners; not immodest; gentle, polite; luxurious. — *n* a luxurious or fastidious person (*obs*); a luxury (*obs*); a delicacy (*archaic*). — *n* **del'icacy** (*-kə-si*) the state or quality of being delicate; refinement; nicety; tenderness, weakness (*esp* of health); luxuriousness; anything delicate or dainty, *esp* to eat; a special culinary luxury. — *adv* **del'icately**. — *n* **del'icateness**. [L *dēlicātus*, prob connected with *dēliciae* allurements, luxury, from *dēlicere*, from *dē* (intensive) and *lacere* to entice]

delicatessen *del-i-kə-tes'n*, *n pl* or *sing* prepared foods, *esp* cooked meats, pâtés, and unusual or foreign foods; (as *n sing*; also *colloq* short form **del'i**) a shop selling these. [Ger pl of Fr *délicatesse* delicacy]

delicious *di-lish'əs*, *adj* pleasing to the senses, *esp* taste; giving exquisite pleasure. — *n* **delice** (*obs*; *di-lēs'*; in *Spenser del'is*) delight; a delight; a delicacy. — *adv* **deli'ciously** in a delicious manner; luxuriously (*Bible*). — *n* **deli'ciousness**. — **flower delice** (*Spenser*, also *del'is*) see **fleur-de-lis**. [L *dēliciōsus*, from *dēliciae* or *dēlicium* delight]

delict *di-likt'*, (*legal*, *esp Scots law*) *n* a transgression, a misdemeanour. [L *dēlictum* an offence; see **delinquent**]

deligation *del-i-gā'shən*, (*surg*) *n* a binding up, ligature. [L *dēligāre*, to bind up, from *dē* (intensive) and *ligāre* to bind]

delight *di-līt'*, *vt* to please highly. — *vi* to have or take great pleasure (with *in*); to please greatly. — *n* a high degree of pleasure; extreme satisfaction; that which gives great pleasure. — *adj* **delight'ed** greatly pleased; delightful (*Shakesp*); capable of delight (*Shakesp*). — *adv* **delight'edly**. — *n* **delight'edness**. — *adj* **delight'ful** causing or full of delight. — *adv* **delight'fully**. — *n* **delight'fulness**. — *adj* **delight'less** giving no delight. — *n* (*archaic*) **delight'some** delightful. [OFr *deliter*, from L *dēlectāre*, intensive of *dēlicere*; cf **delicate** and **delicious**; spelling influenced by confusion with **light**]

Delilah *di-lī'lə*, *n* the Philistine woman who tricked Samson; a courtesan; a temptress; an alluring object. — Also **Dali'lah** or **Dalila** (*Milton dal'i-lə*).

delimit *di-lim'it* or **delimitate** *di-lim'i-tāt*, *vt* to determine or mark the limit or limits of. — *n* **delimitā'tion**. — *adj* **delim'itative**. [L *dēlīmitāre*, from *dē* (intensive) and *līmitāre*; see **limit**]

delineate *di-lin'i-āt*, *vt* to mark out with, or as if with, lines; to represent by a sketch or picture; to draw; to describe. — *adj* **delin'eable**. — *n* **delineā'tion** the act of delineating; a sketch, representation or description. — *adj* **delin'eative**. — *n* **delin'eātor**. [L *dēlīneāre*, *-ātum*, from *dē* down, and *līnea* a line]

delineavit *di-lin-i-ā'vit* or *-ä'wit*, (*L*) (he or she) drew (this), sometimes added to the signature of the artist or draughtsman on a drawing.

delinquent *di-ling'kwənt*, *adj* failing in duty; of or concerning a bad debt or debtor. — *n* a person who fails in his or her duty, *esp* to pay a debt; an offender, *esp* a young criminal; a person lacking in moral and social sense, without showing impairment of intellect. — *n* **delin'quency** failure in or omission of duty, *esp* financial; a fault; crime, the state of being delinquent. — *adv* **delin'quently**. [L *dēlinquēns*, *-entis*, pr p of *dēlinquere*, from *dē-* (intensive) and *linquere*, *lictum* to leave]

deliquesce *del-i-kwes'*, *vi* to melt and become liquid by absorbing moisture, as certain salts, etc do. — *n*

deliquesc'ence. — *adj* **deliquesc'ent** liquefying in the air; (of the veins of a leaf) breaking up into branches (*bot*). [L *dēliquēscere*, from *dē-* (intensive) and *liquēscere* to become fluid, from *liquēre* to be fluid]

deliquium *di-lik'wi-əm*, *n* a swoon (*obs*); eclipse (*archaic*); melting away (*Carlyle*). [Really two different words, partly confused: (1) L *dēliquium*, from *dēlinquere* to leave, fail; (2) L *dēliquium*, from *dēliquāre* to melt]

delirious *di-lir'i-əs*, *adj* wandering in the mind, *esp* through fever or other illness; lightheaded; insane; tremendously pleased, happy or excited (*colloq*). — *n* **delirā'tion** (*del-*) madness, aberration. — *adj* **delir'iant**. — *adj* **delirifacient** (*di-lir-ifā'shənt*) producing delirium. — *n* that which produces delirium. — *adv* **delir'iously**. — *n* **delir'iousness**. — *n* **delir'ium** the state of being delirious, *esp* through fever; wild excitement, happiness or wild enthusiasm: — *pl* **delir'iums** or **delir'ia**. — **delirium tremens** (*trē'menz* or *tre'*; *colloq abbrev* **DTs**) a delirious disorder of the brain produced by over-absorption of alcohol, often marked by convulsive or trembling symptoms and hallucination. [L *dēlīrus* crazy, from *dēlīrāre* literally to turn aside, from *dē* from, and *līra* a furrow; *tremēns* the pr p of *tremere* to tremble]

delitescent *del-i-tes'ənt*, (*med*) *adj* latent. — *n* **delitesc'ence**. [L *dēlitēscēns*, *-entis*, pr p of *dēlitēscere*, from *dē* from, and *latēscere*, from *latēre* to lie hid]

deliver *di-liv'ər*, *vt* to liberate or set free (from restraint or danger); to rescue (from evil or fear); to give up; to hand over, distribute or convey to the addressee; to communicate, pronounce (a speech, message, etc); to unleash, throw (a blow, a ball, etc); to discharge (eg water); to assist (a mother) at the birth (of). — *adj* (*obs*) nimble. — *n* **deliverabil'ity**. — *adj* **deliv'erable**. — *n* **deliv'erance** liberation; release; parturition, giving birth (*obs*); the utterance of a judgement or authoritative opinion. — *n* **deliv'erer**. — *adv* **deliv'erly** (*obs*). — *n* **deliv'ery** the act of delivering; a giving up; the act or manner of speaking in public, of discharging a shot, or water, of throwing a cricket-ball, etc; the voluntary transfer of possessions from one person to another in a contract for the sale of goods (*law*); withdrawal of a pattern from a mould; a distribution; the route or a round of distribution; (the manner of) an act of giving birth. — **deliv'ery-man** a man who goes round delivering goods; **delivery note** a document sent with goods to the customer, detailing the goods and signed on receipt as evidence of their delivery; **deliv'ery-pipe** or **-tube** one that delivers water, etc at the place where it is required; **deliv'ery-van** a tradesman's van for delivering goods at customers' premises. — **be delivered of** (*archaic*) to give birth to; **deliver the goods** (*slang*) to carry out what is required or promised; **general delivery** the delivery of letters at a post-office to the persons to whom they are addressed (as opposed to *house-to-house delivery*); **jail** or **gaol delivery** see **jail**. [Fr *délivrer*, from L *dē* from, and *līberāre* to set free, from *līber* free]

dell[1] *del*, *n* a deep hollow or small valley, *usu* covered with trees; a hole (*obs*; *Spenser*). [OE *dell*; cf **dale**]

dell[2] *del*, (*archaic slang*) *n* a young girl; a trull, a prostitute.

Della-Cruscan *del-ə-krus'kən*, *del-la-krōō s'kən*, (*hist*) *n* a member of the old Florentine Accademia *della Crusca* (Ital, literally academy of the bran, as sifters of the language 1582), or of a group of sentimental poetasters crushed by Gifford's *Baviad* and *Maeviad* (1794 and 1796). — Also *adj*.

Della-Robbia *del-la-rob'bya*, *n* a term applied to enamelled terracotta, after a 15c Florentine sculptor, Luca *della Robbia*, who is said to have perfected the art of producing it.

delope *di-lōp*, (*hist*) *vi* in a duel, to fire one's gun into the air. [Orig uncertain].

delouse *dē-lows'*, *vt* to free from lice, or (*fig*) from landmines, etc. [**de-** (2)]

delph. See **delf**[1,2].

Delphic *del'fik*, *adj* relating to *Delphi*, a town of ancient Greece, or to its famous oracle; (also without *cap*) like an oracle, *esp* if ambiguous or difficult to interpret. — Also **Del'phian**. — *adv* **del'phically**. [Gr *Delphikos* from *Delphi*]

delphin *del'fin*, *adj* pertaining to the *dauphin* (qv) of France, or to an edition of the Latin classics prepared for his use, 64 volumes, 1674–1730.

Delphinidae *del-fin'i-dē*, *n pl* a family of cetaceans, *incl* dolphins, grampuses, etc. — *adj* **del'phinoid**. [L *delphīnus*, from Gr *delphīs*, *-īnos* a dolphin]

delphinium *del-fin'i-əm*, *n* any plant of the *Delphinium* genus of Ranunculaceae, comprising the larkspurs and stavesacre: — *pl* **delphin'iums** or **delphin'ia**. [Latinized from Gr *delphīnion* larkspur, dimin of *delphīs* dolphin (from the appearance of the flowers)]

Delphinus *del-fī'nəs*, (*astron*) *n* the Dolphin, a northern constellation between Pegasus and Aquila. [L]

delt (*colloq*) *n* short for **deltoid muscle**.

delta *del'tə*, *n* the fourth letter (Δ or δ) of the Greek alphabet, equivalent to *d*; an alluvial deposit at the mouth of a stream or river, Δ-shaped in the case of the Nile, where the flow splits into several channels; as an ancient Greek numeral δ' = 4, ͵δ = 4000; in classification, the fourth or one of the fourth grade, the grade below gamma. — *adj* **deltā'ic** pertaining to a delta. — *adj* **del'toid** of the form of the Greek Δ; triangular. — *n* a deltoid muscle. — *adj* and *n* **del'ta-wing** (a jet aeroplane) with triangular wings. — **deltoid muscle** the large triangular muscle of the shoulder. [Gr, from Heb *daleth* a tent-door]

deltiology *del-ti-ol'ə-ji*, *n* the study and collection of picture postcards. — *n* **deltiol'ogist**. [Gr *deltion* small writing-tablet]

delubrum *di-lū'brəm*, *-lōō'*, *n* a temple, shrine, sanctuary; a church having a font; a font. [L *dēlūbrum*]

deluce. See **fleur-de-lis**.

delude *di-lōōd'*, *di-lūd'*, *vt* to play with (someone) so as to frustrate them or their hopes (*obs*); to elude (*obs*); to deceive or cause to accept what is false as true. — *adj* **delud'able**. — *adj* **delud'ed** holding or acting under false beliefs. — *n* **delud'er**. [L *dēlūdere* to play false, from *dē* down, and *lūdere*, *lūsum* to play]

deluge *del'ūj*, *n* a great overflow of water; a flood, *esp* the original biblical flood of Noah; an overwhelming flow or quantity (*fig*). — *vt* to inundate; to overwhelm with, or as if with, water. [Fr *déluge*, from L *dīluvium*, from *dīluere*, from *dis-* away, and *luere* to wash]

delundung *del'ən-dung*, *n* the weasel-cat of Java and Malacca, a small carnivore related to the civet. [Javanese]

delusion *di-lōō'zhən*, *di-lū'zhən*, *n* the act of deluding; the state of being deluded; a hallucination; a false belief (*esp psychol*); error. — *adj* **delu'sional** pertaining to or afflicted with delusions. — *n* **delu'sionist**. — *adj* **delu'sive** (*-siv*) or **delu'sory** apt or tending to delude; deceptive. — *adv* **delu'sively**. — *n* **delu'siveness**. [See **delude**]

delustrant *dē-lus'trənt*, (*textiles*) *n* dense inorganic material added to a man-made fibre that allows a range of fibres with different lustres and opacities to be obtained. [**de-** (2) and *lustrant*, from **lustre**[1]]

de luxe *də lüks'*, *di lōōks'*, *luks'*, *adj* sumptuous, luxurious; having refinements or superior qualities. [Fr, of luxury]

delve *delv*, *vt* and chiefly *vi* (with *in* or *into*) to dig (*esp* with a spade or the hands); to search or rummage deep (with *in*); to make deep research (*fig*); (of a path, road, etc) to dip, slope suddenly. — *n* (*archaic*; *Spenser*) a hollow, hole, depression, a cave. — *n* **delv'er**. [OE *delfan* to dig; connected with **dale**, **delf**[2], **dell**[1]]

delves. See **delf**[2].

demagnetize or **-ise** *dē-mag'nit-īz*, *vt* to deprive of magnetic properties. — *n* **demagnetīzā'tion** or **-s-**. — *n* **demag'netizer** or **-s-**. [**de-** (2)]

demagogue *dem'ə-gog*, *n* a leader of the people; a popular orator who appeals to the baser emotions of his or her audience. — *adj* **demagogic** or **demagogical** (*-gog'*, *-goj'*). — *n* **demagogism** or **demagoguism** (*dem'ə-gog-ism*). — *n* **dem'agoguery** (*-gog-*). — *n* **dem'agogy** (*-goj-*). [Gr *dēmagōgos*, from *dēmos* people, and *agōgos* leading, from *agein* to lead]

demain. See **demesne**.

demaine. See **demean**[1].

demand *di-mänd'*, *vt* to claim; to ask for peremptorily or authoritatively; to require, insist upon; to ask (a question) (*obs*). — *n* the asking for what is due; peremptory asking for something, insistence upon something; a claim; desire shown by consumers; the amount of any article, commodity, etc that consumers will buy; inquiry. — *adj* **demand'able** that may be demanded. — *n* **demand'ant** someone who demands; a plaintiff (*law*). — *n* **demand'er**. — *adj* **demand'ing** requiring much attention, effort, etc. — **demand feeding** the practice of feeding a baby when it wants food, rather than at set times; **demand forecasting** (in marketing) finding out what the demand for a product, etc will be at various selling prices so as to discover at which price the greatest profit will be made. — **in (great) demand** much sought after, desired; **on demand** whenever required. [Fr *demander*, from LL *dēmandāre* to demand, from L *dē-* (intensive) and *mandāre* to put into one's charge]

demanning *dē-man'ing*, *n* the deliberate reduction of the number of employees in a particular industry, etc. — *vt* **deman'**: — *pr p* **demann'ing**; *pa t* and *pa p* **demanned'**. [**de-** (2)]

demarcation or **demarkation** *dē-märk-ā'shən*, *n* the act of marking off or setting boundaries; separation; a fixed limit; in trade unionism, the strict separation of the area of work of one craft or trade from that of another. — *vt* **dē'marcate** (or *di-märk'*) to mark off or limit; to separate. — Also **demark'**. — **demarcation dispute** a disagreement between trade unions in a particular factory or industry about which union's members are responsible for performing a particular task. [Sp *demarcación*, from *de* from, and *marcar* to mark. See **mark**[1]]

démarche *dā-märsh*, (*Fr*) *n* a step, measure or initiative (*esp* diplomatic).

dematerialize or **-ise** *dē-mə-tē'ri-əl-īz*, *vt* and *vi* to become, or cause to become, invisible, to vanish, cease to exist. — *vt* to deprive of material qualities or character. — *vi* to become immaterial, lose material form or character. — *n* **dematerializā'tion** or **-s-**. [**de-** (2)]

demayne. See **demean**[1].

deme *dēm*, *n* a subdivision of ancient Attica and of modern Greece, a township; a group of plants or animals that are closely related and live in a single distinct locality (*biol*). [Gr *dēmos* people]

demean[1] *di-mēn'*, *vt* to bear, behave or conduct (*reflexive*); to treat (*Spenser*, etc); to ill-treat (*Spenser*, etc; *obs Scot*). — *n* (*Spenser* **demaine'**, **demayne'** or **demeane'**) air, bearing; treatment. — *n* **demeanour** or *NAm* **demean'or** (*di-mēn'ər*; *Spenser* **demeasnure**) behaviour; manner towards another. [OFr *demener*, from *de-* (intensive) and *mener* to lead, from L *mināre* to drive, orig from *minārī* to threaten]

demean[2] *di-mēn'*, *vt* to lower in status, reputation, or (often *reflexive*) dignity. [Prob on the analogy of *debase*, from pfx **de-** (1) and **mean**]

demeasnure. See **demean**[1].

dement *di-ment'*, (*rare*) *vt* to drive crazy, cause to become insane. — *vi* to deteriorate mentally, *esp* in old age. — *adj* (*archaic*) insane, demented. — *n* (*archaic*) a demented person. — *vt* **dement'āte** (*archaic*) to dement. — *adj* **dement'ed** out of one's mind; insane; crazy (*colloq*); suffering from dementia. — *adv* **dement'edly**. — *n* **dement'edness**. — *n* **dementia** (*di-men'shi-ə*; *psychol*) any form of insanity characterized by the failure or loss of mental powers; the organic deterioration of intelligence, memory, and orientation, often in advancing age. — **dementia praecox** or **precox** (*prē'koks*) an older name for schizophrenia. [L *dēmēns*, *dēmentis* out of one's mind, from *dē* from, and *mēns* the mind]

démenti *dā-mã-tē*, *n* a contradiction, denial. [Fr *démentir* to give the lie to]

dementia. See **dement**.

demerara *dem-ə-rā'rə*, *-rä'*, *n* a type of brown sugar in large crystals; a type of rum. [*Demerara* in Guyana]

demerge[1] *dē-mûrj'*, (*obs*) *vt* to immerse, plunge. [L *dē* down, and *mergere* to plunge]

demerge[2] *dē-mûrj'*, *vi* (of companies, etc) to undergo a reversal of a merger, to become separate again. — *n* **demer'ger**. [**de-** (2)]

demerit *dē-* or *di-mer'it*, *n* a fault or defect *esp* in a person; a mark given for a fault or offence, *esp* in schools or the army, etc (*NAm*); lack of merit; desert, merit (*obs*). [L *dēmerērī*, *dēmeritum* to deserve fully, later understood as to deserve ill, from *dē-* fully, and *merēri* to deserve]

demerse *də-mûrs'*, *vt* (*obs*) to immerse. — *adj* **demer'sal** subaqueous, living underwater; found on or near the bottom. — *adj* **demersed'** (*bot*) growing under water. — *n* **demer'sion**. [L *dē* down, and *mergere*, *mersum* to plunge]

demesne *di-mān'*, *-mēn'*, or **demain** *di-mān'*, *n* a manor-house with lands adjacent to it not let out to tenants; any estate in land. [Forms of **domain**]

demi- *dem'i*, *combining form* denoting half or half-sized. — *n* **dem'i-bast'ion** (*fortif*) a kind of half-bastion, consisting of one face and one flank. — *n* **dem'i-cann'on** (*Shakesp*; *hist*) an old kind of gun which threw a ball weighing from 30 to 36 lb. — *n* **demi-caractère** (*də-mē-kar-ək-tār*; Fr, half-character) in ballet, a character dance that uses the classical technique. — Also *adj*. — *n* **dem'i-cul'verin** (*hist*) an old kind of cannon which threw a shot of 9 or 10 lb. — *vt* **demi-de'ify** to treat as a demigod; to go halfway towards deifying. — *n* **dem'i-dev'il** a half-devil. — *n* **dem'i-dis'tance** (*fortif*) the distance between the outward polygons and the flank. — *n* **dem'i-dī'tone** (*music*) a minor third. — *n* **dem'igod** a half-god; a person whose nature is partly divine, *esp* a hero fabled to be, or idolized as, the offspring of a god and a mortal: — *fem* **dem'igoddess**. — *n* **dem'i-gorge** (*fortif*) the part of the polygon remaining after the flank is raised, going from the curtain to the angle of the polygon. — *n* **dem'i-lance** (*hist*) a short, light spear of the 16c; a soldier armed with such a weapon. — *n* **dem'i-lune** (*-lōōn*; *fortif*) a half-moon; an old name for **ravelin**. — *n* **demi-monde** (*dem'i-mond*, *də-mē-mɔ̃d'*) a class of women in an unrespectable social position, the kept mistresses of society men; the shady section of a profession or group. — *n* **demi-mondaine** (*-en'*) a woman member of the demi-monde. — Also *adj*. — *n* **demi-pension** (*də-mē-pã-syɔ̃*; Fr, boarding-house) the provision of bed, breakfast and one other meal, in hotels, etc, half board. — *adj* **demipique** (*dem'i-pēk*) (of an 18c war-saddle) having a lower peak than usual. — Also *n*. — *n* **dem'irep** (*old*; for *demi-reputable*) a person, *esp* a woman, of dubious reputation. — *n* **demirep'dom**. — *n* **demi-semiquaver** (*dem-i-sem'i-kwā-vər*; *music*) a note equal in time to half of a semiquaver. — *n* **dem'i-volt** or **-volte** a half-turn of a horse, the forelegs being raised in the air. — *n* **dem'i-wolf** (*Shakesp*) a half-wolf, the offspring of a dog and a wolf. [Fr *demi*, from L *dīmidium*, from *di-* apart, and *medius* the middle]

demic. See **demos**.

demicannon . . . to . . . **demigorge**. See under **demi-**.

demies. See **demy**.

demigration *dem-i-grā'shən*, *n* change of abode. [L *dēmigrāre*, *-ātum* depart, from *dē*, and *migrāre*]

demijohn *dem'i-jon*, *n* a glass bottle with a full body and narrow neck often with handles and enclosed in wickerwork. [Fr *dame-jeanne* Dame Jane, analogous to **bellarmine**, **greybeard**; not from the town *Damaghan*]

demi-jour *də-mē-zhōōr*, (*Fr*) *n* half-light, twilight, subdued light.

demi-lance. See under **demi-**.

demilitarize or **-ise** *dē-mil'i-tər-īz*, *vt* to release from military control, remove forces from. — *n* **demilitarīzā'tion** or **-s-**. [**de-** (2)]

demi-lune. See under **demi-**.

demineralize or **-ise** *dē-min'ə-rə-līz*, *vt* to remove salts from (water or the body). — *n* **demineralizā'tion** or **-s-**. [**de-** (2)]

demi-mondaine ... to ... **demirepdom**. See under **demi-**.

demise *di-mīz'*, *n* a transferring by lease; death (*euphem* or *formal*), as of a sovereign or a distinguished person; a transfer of the crown or of an estate to a successor. — *vt* to give to a successor; to bequeath by will; to transfer by lease. — *adj* **demī'sable**. [OFr *demise*, pa p of *desmettre* to lay down, from L *dis-* aside, and *mittere*, *missum* to send]

demi-semiquaver. See under **demi-**.

demiss *di-mis'*, (*rare*) *adj* humble. — *n* **demission** (*di-mish'ən*) lowering; degradation; depression; relinquishment; resignation. — *adj* **demiss'ive** (*obs*) humble. — *adv* **demiss'ly** (*obs*). [L *dēmittere*, *-missum*, from *dē* down, and *mittere* to send]

demist *dē-mist'*, *vt* to clear (eg a car windscreen) of condensation. — Also *vi*. — *n* **demist'er** a mechanical device which does this, *usu* by blowing hot air. [**de-** (2)]

demit[1] *di-mit'*, *vt* to send down; to lower. [See **demiss**]

demit[2] *di-mit'*, (*esp Scot*) *vt* to dismiss (*archaic*); to relinquish; to resign. [Fr *démettre*, from L *dimittere*, from *dis-* apart, and *mittere* to send]

demitasse *dem'i-tas*, *n* (the quantity contained by) a small cup of, or for, (*esp* black) coffee. [Fr, half-cup]

demiurge *dem'i-ûrj*, *n* the maker of the world; among the Gnostics, the creator of the world and man, subordinate to God the supreme. — Also **demiur'gus** (*-gəs*). — *adj* **demiur'geous** (*-jəs*) or **demiur'gic** (*-jik*) or **demiur'gical**. — *adv* **demiur'gically**. [Gr *dēmiourgos*, from *dēmos* the people, and *ergon* a work]

demi-volt(e), **demi-wolf**. See under **demi-**.

demo *dem'ō*, (*colloq*) *n* short for **demonstration**, *esp* in the sense of a public expression of feeling: — *pl* **dem'os**.

demobilize or **-ise** *di-mōb'il-īz*, *vt* to take out of action; to disband; to discharge from the army (*colloq*). — *n* **demobilizā'tion** or **-s-**. — *n* and *vt* **demob** (*dē-mob'*; *pr p* **demobb'ing**; *pa p* **demobbed'**) *colloq* shortening of **demobilization** and **demobilize**. — Also *adj*. [**de-** (2)]

democracy *di-mok'rə-si*, *n* a form of government in which the supreme power is vested in the people collectively, and is administered by them or by officers appointed by them; the common people; a state of society characterized by recognition of equality of rights and privileges for all people; political, social or legal equality; (*usu* with *cap*) the Democratic party (*archaic*; *US*). — Also (formerly) **democraty** (*-ok'*; *Milton*). — *n* **democrat** (*dem'ō-krat*) a person who adheres to or promotes democracy as a principle; (sometimes with *cap*) a member of the Democratic party in the United States, the party generally inclining to look to marginally left of centre; a member of any British, Irish, German, etc political party with *Democratic* in its title (*colloq*); a light four-wheeled cart with several seats (*US hist*; also **democrat wagon**). — *adj* **democrat'ic** or **democrat'ical** relating to democracy; insisting on, advocating or upholding equal rights and privileges for all. — *adv* **democrat'ically**. — *adj* **democratifī'able** capable of being made democratic. — *vt* **democratize** or **-ise** (*di-mok'*) to render democratic. — *n* **democratīzā'tion** or **-s-**. — *n* **democ'ratist** a democrat. [Fr *démocratie*, from Gr *dēmokratiā*, from *dēmos* the people, and *kratos* strength]

démodé *dā-mö-dā*, (*Fr*) *adj* out of fashion.

demoded *dē'mōd'id*, *adj* (*disparagingly*) no longer in fashion. [**de-** (2)]

demodulate *dē-mod'ū-lāt*, (*radio*) *vt* to perform demodulation on (a wave). — *n* **demodulā'tion** the inverse of modulation, a process by which an output wave is obtained that has the characteristics of the original modulating wave. — *n* **demod'ulator**. [**de-** (2)]

Demogorgon *dē-mō-gör'gən*, *n* a mysterious infernal deity first mentioned about AD450. [Appar Gr *daimōn* deity, and *gorgō* Gorgon, from *gorgos* terrible]

demography *dē-mog'rə-fi*, *n* the study of population, *esp* with reference to size, density and distribution. — *n* **demog'rapher**. — *adj* **demographic** (*-ō-graf'ik*). [Gr *dēmos* the people, and *graphein* to write]

demoiselle *dəm-wä-zel'*, *n* a young lady (*archaic* or *facetious*); a graceful variety of crane (*Anthropoides virgo*; *ornithol*); a dragonfly; a fish of the genus *Pomacentrus* or its family (related to the wrasses); a tiger-shark. [Fr; see **damsel**]

demolish *di-mol'ish*, *vt* to ruin, lay waste; to destroy, put an end to, cause to collapse. — *n* **demol'isher**. — *n pl* **demol'ishments**. — *n* **demoli'tion** (*dem-ō-*) the act of pulling down; ruin. — *n* **demoli'tionist**. [Fr *démolir*, from L *dēmōliri* to throw down, from *dē* down, and *mōlīrī* to build, from *mōlēs* a heap]

demology *dē-mol'ə-ji* *n* demography; the theory of the origin and nature of communities. [Gr *dēmos* people, and *logos* a discourse]

demon *dē'mən*, *n* an evil spirit, a devil; sometimes (like **daemon**) a friendly spirit or good genius; a person of great energy or enthusiasm or skill (*fig*): — *fem* **dē'moness**. — Also *adj*. — *adj* **demoniac** (*di-mōn'i-ak*). — *n* a person possessed by a demon or evil spirit. — *adj* **demoniacal** (*dē-mə-nī'ə-kl*) pertaining to or like demons or evil spirits; influenced by demons. — *adv* **demonī'acally**. — *n* **dēmonī'acism** (*-ə-sizm*) the state of being a demoniac. — *adj* **demō'nian** (*Milton*). — *n* **demō'nianism** possession by a demon. — *adj* **demonic** (*dē-mon'ik*) demoniac. — *n* **dē'monism** a belief in or worship of demons. — *n* **dē'monist**. — *vt* **dē'monize** or **-ise** to convert into a demon; to control or possess by a demon. — *n* **dēmonoc'racy** the power of demons. — *n* **dēmonol'ater**. — *n* **dēmonol'atry** the worship of demons. — *adj* **dēmonolog'ic** or **dēmonolog'ical**. — *n* **dēmonol'ogist**. — *n* **dēmonol'ogy** an account of, or the study of, demons and their ways. — *n* **dēmonomā'nia** a form of mania in which the subject believes himself or herself to be possessed by devils. — *n* **dē'monry** demoniacal influence. [L *daemōn*, from Gr *daimōn* a spirit, genius; in New Testament and Late Greek, a devil; see **daemon**]

demon. See **demonstr**.

demonetize or **-ise** *dē-mun'i-tīz*, *-mon'*, *vt* to remove from currency as money. — *n* **demonetīzā'tion** or **-s-**. [**de-** (2)]

demonstr. *abbrev*: demonstrative (also **demon**. or **demons**.).

demonstrate *dem'ən-strāt* *vt* to make apparent; to give proof of; to prove with certainty; to teach, expound, explain or exhibit by practical means. — *vi* to exhibit one's feelings; to act as demonstrator. — *n* **demonstrabil'ity**. — *adj* **demon'strable** (or *dem'ən-*) that may be demonstrated. — *n* **demon'strableness**. — *adv* **dem'onstrably** (or *di-mon'*). — *n* **demonstrā'tion** a pointing out, indication; proof beyond doubt; expression of the feelings by outward signs; a public expression of feelings (*esp* of protest), as by a mass-meeting, a procession, etc; show; a movement to exhibit military intention, or to deceive an enemy; a practical lesson, explanation or exhibition. — Also *adj*. — *adj* **demon'strative** pointing out (eg a *demonstrative adjective*); making evident; proving with certainty; of the nature of proof; given to showing one's feelings openly. — *adv* **demon'stratively**. — *n* **demon'strativeness**. — *n* **dem'onstrātor** a person who proves beyond doubt; a teacher or assistant who helps students with practical work; a person who goes about exhibiting the uses and merits of a product; a person who takes part in a public protest demonstration; a vehicle or other piece of merchandise used for demonstration to customers. — *adj* **demon'stratory** demonstrative. [L *dēmōnstrāre*, *-ātum*, from *dē-* (intensive) and *mōnstrāre* to show]

demoralize or **-ise** *dē-mor'əl-īz*, *vt* to corrupt morally; to lower the morale of, to deprive of spirit and confidence;

to throw into confusion. — *n* **demoralīzā'tion** or **-s-** the act of demoralizing; corruption or subversion of morals. — *adj* **demoralīz'ing** or **-s-**. [**de-** (2)]

demos *dē'mos*, *n* the people (*esp contemptuously*). — *adj* **dem'ic** (*rare*) of the people. — *adj* **demot'ic** pertaining to the people; popular; of a simplified kind of writing distinguished from the hieratic, or priestly, and from hieroglyphics (*Egyp antiq*). — *n* **demot'icist** or **demot'ist** a student of demotic script. [Gr *dēmos*]

Demosthenic *de-mos-then'ik*, *adj* of or like *Dēmosthenēs* the Athenian orator; oratorical; eloquent.

demote *dē-mōt'*, *vt* to reduce in rank. — *n* **demō'tion**. [On the analogy of **promote**; **de-** (2)]

demotic. See **demos**.

demotivate *dē-mōt'i-vāt*, *vt* to cause a loss of motivation in (someone, etc). [**de-** (2)]

demount *dē-mownt'*, *vt* to take down from a support, place of display, etc; to take (eg a building) to pieces in such a way that it can be reassembled. — *adj* **demount'-able**. [**de-** (2) and **mount** to set in position]

dempster. Same as **deemster**. [See under **deem**]

dempt *demt*, (*Spenser*), *pa p* and *pa t* of **deem**.

demulcent *di-mul'sənt*, *adj* soothing. — *n* a medicine that soothes irritation. [L *dēmulcēns*, *-entis*, from *dē* down, and *mulcēre* to stroke, to soothe]

demulsify *dē-mul'si-fī*, *vt* to separate from an emulsion; to make resistant to emulsification. — *n* **demulsificā'tion**. — *n* **demul'sifier**. [**de-** (2) and **emulsify**]

demur *di-mûr'*, *vi* to object, balk, dissent; to hesitate from uncertainty or before difficulty (*archaic*). — *vt* (*obs*; *Milton*) to hesitate about: — *pr p* **demurr'ing**; *pa t* and *pa p* **demurred'**. — *n* an act of demurring, objection; a pause, hesitation (*archaic*); a stop (*obs*). — *adj* **demurr'-able**. — *n* **demurr'age** undue delay or detention of a vessel, railway wagon, etc, and thus in the completion of a contract; compensation for such detention; a charge made by the Bank of England for exchanging notes or gold for bullion. — *n* **demurr'al** (*rare*) demur. — *n* **demurr'er** a person who demurs; an objection (*law*); a plea in law that, even if the opponent's facts are as they say, they still do not support his or her case (*law*). [Fr *demeurer*, from L *dēmorārī* to loiter, linger, from *de-* (intensive) and *morārī* to delay, from *mora* delay]

demure *di-mūr'*, *adj* sober; staid (in dress or manners); modest, chaste; affectedly modest; making a show of gravity. — *vi* (*obs*; *Shakesp*) *appar*, to look demurely. — *adv* **demure'ly**. — *n* **demure'ness**. [OFr *meur* (Fr *mûr*), from L *matūrus* ripe; pfx unexplained]

demy *dem'i* or *di-mī'*, *n* before metrication, a size of printing and writing paper approximating to **A2**; a writing paper, 52.5 by 40cm (21 by 16in; *US*); a holder of certain scholarships in Magdalen College, Oxford, *orig* allowed half the commons (the allowance of food and drink) assigned to a fellow: — *pl* **demies'**. — *n* **demy'ship**. [Fr *demi*, from L *dīmidium* half, from *dis-* apart, and *medius* the middle]

demyelinate *dē-mȳ'ə-lin-āt*, (*med*) *vt* to destroy the myelin of (nerve fibres). — *n* **demyelinā'tion**. [**de-** (2)]

demystify *dē-mis'ti-fī*, *vt* to clear of mystification, to make no longer mysterious or obscure. — *n* **demystificā'tion**. [**de-** (2)]

demythologize or **-ise** *dē-mith-ol'ə-jīz*, *vt* to remove mythology from (*esp* the Bible) in order to arrive at the basic meaning. — *n* **demythologīzā'tion** or **-s-**. [**de-** (2)]

den[1] *den*, *n* the hollow lair of a wild animal; a pit or cave; a haunt of vice or misery; a private domestic room or office for work or pleasure (*colloq*); a narrow valley, a dean (*Scot*). — *vi* to retire to a den. — **den mother** (*US*) an adult female leader of a Cub Scout group; any adult female protective figure in general. [OE *denn* a cave, lair; related to *denu* a valley]

den[2] *den*, (*obs*) *n* used for **good-e'en** or **good-even**.

denary *dēn'ər-i*, *adj* containing or having as a basis the number ten; ten. — *n* the number ten; a group of ten. — *n* **denarius** (*di-nā'ri-əs*) the chief Roman silver coin under the Republic, divided into ten asses (about 8d); translated *penny* in the New Testament, hence the use of d for penny (before the introduction of decimal coinage): — *pl* **dena'rii** (*ri-ī*). [L *dēnārius*, from *dēnī* ten by ten, from *decem* ten]

denationalize or **-ise** *dē-nash'ən-əl-īz*, *vt* to deprive of national rights or character; to return from state to private ownership, to privatize. — *n* **denationalizā'tion** or **-s-**. [**de-** (2)]

denaturalize or **-ise** *dē-nach'ər-əl-īz*, *vt* to make unnatural; to deprive of naturalization as a citizen. — *n* **dēnaturalīzā'tion** or **-s-**. [**de-** (2)]

denature *dē-nā'chər*, also **denaturize** or **-ise** *dē-nā'chər-īz*, *vt* to change the nature or properties of (eg a protein by heat or other treatment); to render (alcohol, etc) unfit for human consumption; to add (non-radioactive material) to radioactive material, in order to prevent its being used in an atomic bomb (*nuclear*). — *n* **denā'turant** a substance used to denature another. [**de-**(2)]

denay *di-nā'*, *obs* form of **deny** and **denial**.

denazify *dē-nät-si-fī*, *vt* to free from Nazi influence and ideology. — *n* **denazificā'tion**. [**de-** (2)]

dendron *den'dron*, *n* a branching projection of a nerve-cell. — *n* **dendrachate** (*den'drə-kāt*; Gr *achātēs* agate) arborescent agate. — *adj* **den'driform** treelike. — *n* **den'drite** (Gr *dendrītēs* of a tree) a treelike crystalline aggregate or skeleton crystal; a dendron. — *adj* **dendrit'ic** or **dendrit'ical** treelike, arborescent; marked with branching figures like plants. — *n* **dendrō'bium** (Gr *bios* life) any plant of the *Dendrobium* genus of epiphytic orchids, chiefly of tropical Asia. — *n* **Dendrocal'amus** (Gr *kalamos* cane) a genus of bamboos. — *adj* **dendrochronolog'ical**. — *n* **dendro-chronol'ogist**. — *n* **dendrochronology** (*den-drō-kron-ol'ə-ji'*) the fixing of dates in the past by comparative study of the annual growth rings in timber and in ancient trees. — *n* **dendroclimatol'ogy** the study of growth rings in trees as evidence of climatic change. — *n* **den'droglyph** (*-glif*; Gr *glyphē* carving) an ancient carving on a tree. — *n* **den'drogram** a diagram with branches indicating the relationships of items in a classification. — *adj* **den'droid** or **den'droidal** treelike. — *n* **dendrol'atry** (Gr *latreiā* worship) the worship of trees. — *adj* **dendrolog'ical** or **dendrol'ogous**. — *n* **dendrol'ogist**. — *n* **dendrol'ogy** a treatise on trees; the natural history of trees. — *n* **dendrom'eter** an instrument for measuring trees. — *n* **den'drophis** (Gr *ophis* snake) a snake of the genus *Dendrophis*, tree snakes found in India and Australia. [Gr *dendron* tree]

dene[1] *dēn*, *n* a small valley. [See **dean**[1]]

dene[2] *dēn*, *n* a sandy tract, a dune. [Ety doubtful]

Deneb *den'eb*, *n* the brightest star in the constellation Cygnus. — *n* **Deneb'ola** a star at the tail of the constellation Leo. [Ar *dhanab* tail, and *al-asad* of the lion]

denegation *den-i-gā'shən*, *n* a denial. [L *dēnegāre*, *-ātum* to deny, from *dē-* (intensive) and *negāre* to deny]

dene-hole *dēn'hōl*, *n* a prehistoric artificial chamber in the chalk, in Kent, Essex, etc, perhaps a flint-mine or a storehouse. [Perh from **dene**[1], or OE *Dene* Danes, from popular association; and **hole**[1]]

denervated *den'ər-vāt-id*, (*med*) *adj* deprived of nerve supply. [**de-** (2) and **nervate**]

DEng. *dē-eng'*, *abbrev*: Doctor of Engineering.

dengue *deng'gā*, *n* an acute tropical epidemic fever, seldom fatal — also called **breakbone fever** or **dan'dy-fever**. [Appar Swahili *dinga*]

deniable, **denial**, **denier**, etc. See **deny**.

denier *də-nēr'*, *n* an old small French silver coin (*obs*; *Shakesp*); also later, a copper coin of the value of $\frac{1}{2}$ sou, hence a very trifling sum; a unit of silk, rayon and nylon yarn weight (*usu den'i-ər*). [Fr, from L *dēnārius*]

denigrate *den'i-grāt*, *vt* to blacken (*esp* a reputation). — *adj* blackened. — *n* **denigrā'tion**. — *n* **den'igrātor**. [L *dē-* (intensive) and *nigrāre* to blacken, from *niger* black]

denim *den'im*, *n* coloured twilled cotton fabric for jeans, overalls, etc; (in *pl*) a garment (*esp* a pair of jeans) made of denim. [Fr *de* of, and *Nîmes*, town in S France]

denitrate *dē-nī'trāt*, *vt* to free from nitric acid or other nitrogen compounds. — *n* **dēnītrā'tion** or **dēnītrificā'tion** removal of nitrogen or its compounds. — *n* **dēnī'trificātor**. — *vt* **dēnī'trify**. [**de-** (2)]

denizen *den'i-zn*, *n* an inhabitant (human, animal or plant); a person admitted to the rights of a citizen (of a given place); a wild plant, probably foreign, that keeps its footing when it has been introduced; a naturalized foreign word or expression. — Also *adj*. — *vt* to make a denizen; to provide with occupants. — *vi* to inhabit. — *n* **denizā'tion** act of making a person a citizen. — *n* **den'izenship**. [OFr *deinzein*, from *deinz*, *dens* (Fr *dans*) within, from L *dē intus* from within]

dennet *den'it*, *n* a light type of gig popular during the early 19c. [Prob a surname]

denominate *di-nom'in-āt*, *vt* to give a name to; to call. — *adj* **denom'inable**. — *n* **denominā'tion** the act of naming; a name or title; a class or group, *esp* of units in weights, money, etc; (of coins, etc) an allotted value; a collection (of individual plants, etc) called by the same name; a religious sect. — *adj* **denominā'tional** belonging to a denomination or sect. — *adv* **denominā'tionally**. — *n* **denominā'tionalism** a denominational or class spirit or policy; devotion to the interests of a sect. — *n* **denominā'tionalist**. — *adj* **denom'inative** giving or having a title. — *adv* **denom'inatively**. — *n* **denom'inātor** the person who, or that which, gives a name (*archaic*); the lower number in a vulgar fraction, which names the parts into which the whole number is divided (*arith*). — **common denominator** a number that is a multiple of each of the denominators of a set of fractions, *esp* the least; something that makes comparison, communication, agreement, etc between things or people possible. [L *dē-* (intensive) and *nōmināre* to name, from *nōmen* name]

denote *di-nōt'*, *vt* to note or mark off (a limit, border, etc); to indicate by a sign; to signify or mean; to indicate the objects comprehended in a class (*logic*). — *adj* **denō'table**. — *vt* **dē'nōtate** (*obs*) to denote. — *n* **dēnotā'tion** (*logic*) that which a word denotes, in contradistinction to that which it connotes. — *adj* **denō'tative** (or *dē'*). — *adv* **denō'tatively** (or *dē'*). — *n* **denōte'ment** (*Shakesp*) a sign or indication. [Fr *dénoter*, from L *dēnotāre*, *-ātum*, from *dē* (intensive) and *notāre* to mark]

dénouement or **denouement** *dā-nōō-mã*, *n* the unravelling of a plot or story; the issue, event or outcome. [Fr *dénouement* or *dénoûment*, from *dénouer*, OFr *desnoer* to untie, from L *dis-*, and *nodāre* to tie, from *nodus* a knot]

denounce *di-nowns'*, *vt* to inform against or accuse publicly; to condemn (*esp* an argument or theory); to inveigh against; to proclaim as imminent (*obs*); to notify formally termination of (treaties, etc); to announce (*obs*); to give formal notice of a claim for mining rights covering (*US*; through *Sp*). — *n* **denounce'ment** denunciation. — *n* **denounc'er**. [Fr *dénoncer*, from L *dēnuntiāre*, from *dē-* (intensive) and *nuntiāre* to announce]

de novo *dē nō'vō* or *dā nō'wō*, (*L*) *adv* anew, again from the beginning.

dense *dens*, *adj* thick, closely-spaced, compact; extremely stupid (*colloq*). — *adv* **dense'ly**. — *n* **dense'ness**. — *n* **dens'ifier**. — *vt* **dens'ify** to increase the density of (wood, etc) by compression. — *n* **densim'eter** an instrument for measuring the relative density or the closeness of grain of a substance. — *adj* **densimet'ric**. — *n* **densim'etry**. — *n* **densitom'eter** an instrument for measuring the optical transmission or reflecting properties of a material or the strength of colour of a photographic image. — *adj* **densitomet'ric**. — *n* **densitom'etry**. — *n* **dens'ity** the quality or degree of being thick, closely spaced or compact; the proportion of a mass to its bulk or volume; the quantity of matter per unit of bulk; the extent to which data can be packed on to a magnetic disk (*comput*). — **dense-media process** (*mineral ext*) a method of separation in which dispersion of a heavy mineral in water separates lighter (floating) ore from heavier (sinking) ore; **density gradient centrifugation** (*biol*) the separation of cells, cell components or complex molecules on the basis of their density differences by centrifuging them in a prepared solution. [L *dēnsus* thick, dense]

dent[1] *dent*, *n* a hollow in a surface, caused by a blow. — *vt* to make such a hollow in; to do injury to (someone's pride, etc). — See also **dint**, **dunt**[1]. [Confused with **dent**[2]]

dent[2] *dent*, (*obs*) *n* a notch. — *vt* to notch. [Fr, tooth; see ety for **dental**; also infl by **indent**]

dent. *abbrev*: dental; dentist; dentistry.

dental *dent'əl*, *adj* pertaining to or concerned with the teeth or dentistry; produced by the aid of the teeth. — *n* (*phonetics*) a sound pronounced by applying the tongue to the teeth or (loosely) the gums. — *adj* **dent'ary** (*zool*) belonging to dentition; bearing teeth. — *n* a bone of the lower jaw of some vertebrates *usu* bearing teeth. — *adj* **dent'ate** or **dent'ated** toothed; notched; having a tooth-shaped pattern. — *n* **dentā'tion** condition of being dentate; a toothlike projection. — *n* **dent'ex** a strongly toothed voracious fish related to perch, found in the Mediterranean. — *n* **dent'icle** a small toothlike structure; a dentil. — *adj* **dentic'ulāte** or **dentic'ulāted** notched; having dentils. — *n* **denticulā'tion**. — *adj* **dent'iform** having the shape of a tooth or of teeth. — *n* **dent'ifrice** (*-fris*; L *fricāre* to rub) a substance used in rubbing or cleaning the teeth, toothpaste or toothpowder. — *adj* **dentigerous** (*-ij'*) bearing teeth. — *adj* **dentilin'gual** (L *lingua* tongue) formed between the teeth and the tongue, as *th* in *thin* and *this*. — *n* a consonant sound so formed. — *n* **dent'ine** (*-ēn*) or **den'tin** the hard, calcareous substance of which teeth are mainly composed. — *adj* **dentiros'tral** (L *rōstrum* a beak) with notched bill. — *n* **dent'ist** a person qualified to treat diseases and malformations of, and injuries to, teeth. — *n* **dent'istry** the art or work of a dentist. — *n* **dent'ition** the cutting or growing of teeth; the shape, number, and typical arrangement of the teeth in a given species. — *adj* **dent'oid** (Gr *eidos* form) formed or shaped like a tooth. — *n* **dent'ure** a set of (*esp* artificial) teeth. — **dental floss** see **floss**; **dental formula** a formula showing the number and distribution of the different kinds of teeth in an animal's jaws; **dental hygiene** the (study, practice of, advice on, etc) maintenance of healthy teeth and gums, as by careful cleaning, scaling, etc; **dental hygienist** a person trained and qualified in dental hygiene. [L *dēns*, *dentis* a tooth; dimin *denticulus*]

dentalium *den-tā'li-əm*, *n* any mollusc or shell of the genus *Dentalium*, of scaphopod molluscs whose shells resemble an elephant's tusk: — *pl* **dentā'liums** or **dentā'lia**. [New L, from LL *dentālis* dental, from L *dens*, *dentis* a tooth]

dentaria *den-tā'ri-ə*, *n* any plant of the genus *Dentaria*, *incl* the cruciferous toothwort. [New L, from L *dens*, *dentis* a tooth]

dentary, **dentate**, etc. See **dental**.

dentel. See **dentil**.

dentelle *den-tel'*, *dã-tel*, *n* lace, lacework; an ornamental pattern or border resembling lace and featuring toothed outlines, used in decorating book covers. [Fr, literally little tooth, from OFr *dentele*, dimin of *dent* tooth]

dentex, **denticle**, **denticulate**, **dentifrice**, etc. See under **dental**.

dentil *den'til*, (*archit*) *n* one of a series of square blocks or projections as in the bed-moulding of a cornice of columns, a denticle. — Also **dent'el**. [*dentille*, obs fem dimin of *dent* tooth]

dentine, **dentist**, etc, **dentoid**, **denture**. See under **dental**.

denuclearize or **-ise-** *dē-nū'klē-ə-rīz*, *vt* to remove nuclear weapons from (a country, state, etc). — *n* **denuclearīzā'tion** or **-s-**. [**de-** (2)]

denude *di-nūd'*, *vt* to make nude or naked; to strip (*esp* an area of land; also rarely **denūd'ate**). — *vi* to divest oneself of a title, etc. — *n* **denudation** (*den-ū-dā'shən*) a making nude or bare; the wearing away of rocks whereby the underlying rocks are laid bare (*geol*). [L *dēnūdāre*, from *dē-* (intensive) and *nūdāre*, *-ātum* to make naked]

denumerable *di-nū'mər-əbl*, (*math*) *adj* able to be put in a one-to-one correspondence with the positive integers. — *adv* **denū'merably**. [**de-** (3)]

denunciate *di-nun'si-āt* or *shi-āt*, *vt* to denounce. — *n* **denunciā'tion** any formal declaration; the act of denouncing; a threat. — *n* **denun'ciātor** a person who denounces. — *adj* **denun'ciatory** containing a denunciation; threatening. [L *dēnunciāre* or *dēnuntiāre*; see **denounce**]

Denver boot *den'vər bōōt*, (*slang*) *n* a wheel-clamp. [From *Denver*, US, its original place of use]

deny *di-nī'*, *vt* to gainsay or declare not to be true; to reject; to refuse; to refuse to admit; to refuse a visitor (access to); to disown: — *pr p* **deny'ing**; *pa t* and *pa p* **denied'**. — *n* **denīabil'ity**. — *adj* **denī'able**. — *adv* **denī'ably**. — *n* **denī'al** the act of denying; refusal; rejection. — *n* **denī'er**. — *adv* **deny'ingly**. — **deny oneself** to refuse to allow oneself pleasure (in); to exercise self-denial. [Fr *dénier*, from L *dēnegāre*, from *dē-* (intensive) and *negāre* to say no]

Deo *dē'ō*, *dā'ō*, (*L*) to, for or with God. — **Deo favente** (*fə-ven'tē* or *-wen'tā*) with God's favour; **Deo gratias** (*grā'ti-äs* or *grā'shi-əs*) thanks to God; **Deo Optimo Maximo** (*op'ti-mō mak'si-mō*; *abbrev* **DOM**) to God, the best, the greatest (the motto of the Benedictines); **Deo volente** (*vo-len'tē* or *wo-len'tā*; *abbrev* **DV**) God willing.

deobstruent *dē-ob'strōō-ənt*, (*med*) *adj* removing obstructions. — Also *n*. [L *dē* away; see **obstruct**]

deoch-an-doruis *dohh-ən-do'ris*, *n* a stirrup cup, a parting drink. — Also **doch-an-doris**, **doch-an-dorach** (*-əhh*) or **deuch-an-doris**. [Gaelic *deoch* drink, *an* the, and *doruis*, genitive of *dorus* door]

deodand *dē'ō-dand*, *n* (in old English law) a personal chattel which had been the immediate accidental cause of the death of a human being, forfeited to the crown for pious uses. [L *deō* to God, and *dandum* that must be given, from *dare* to give]

deodar *dē'ō-där*, *n* a cedar tree (*Cedrus deodara*) of the Himalayas, much praised by Indian poets; its hard, sweet-smelling wood. [Sans *deva-dāru* divine tree]

deodate *dē'ō-dāt*, (*obs*) *n* a gift to God; extended to mean a gift from God. [L *deō* to God (*ā Deō* by God), and *datum* given, pa p of *dare* to give]

deodorize or **-ise** *dē-ō'dər-īz*, *vt* to take the (*usu* unpleasant) odour or smell from; to make inoffensive by euphemism, evasion, etc (*fig*). — *n* **deō'dorant**, also **deō'dorizer** or **-s-** a substance that destroys or conceals unpleasant smells. — *n* **deōdorīzā'tion** or **-s-**. [**de-** (2)]

deontology *dē-on-tol'ə-ji*, *n* the science of duty, ethics. — Also *n sing* **deon'tics**. — *adj* **deon'tic**. — *adj* **deontological** (*-tə-loj'*). — *n* **deontol'ogist**. [Gr *deon*, *-ontos* neuter pr p of *deein* to be necessary, to behove, and *logos* discourse]

deoppilate *dē-op'i-lāt*, (*obs*; *med*) *vt* to free from obstruction. — *n* **deoppilā'tion**. — *adj* **deopp'ilative**. [**de-** (2)]

deoxidate *dē-oks'i-dāt*, *vt* to remove oxygen from, or reduce (*chem*). — Also **deox'idize** or **-ise**. — *n* **deoxidā'tion**. — Also **deoxidīzā'tion** or **-s-**. — *n* **deox'idīzer** or **-s-** a substance that deoxidizes. — *vt* **deoxygenate** (*dē-oks'ij-ən-āt*) to remove oxygen from. — Also **deox'ygenize** or **-ise**. — *pfx* **deoxy-** or **desoxy-** containing less oxygen. — **deoxyribonucleic acid** (*dē-oks-i-rī'bō-nū-klē'ik*) nucleic acid containing **deoxyrī'bōse** (sugar), consisting of complex molecules, present in chromosomes of all plant and animal cells, and carrying in coded form instructions for passing on of hereditary characteristics (*abbrev* **DNA**). [**de-** (2)]

Dep. or **dep.** *abbrev*: department; deputy.

dep. *abbrev*: depart or departs; departure; deposed.

depaint *di-pānt'*, (*Spenser*) *vt* to paint; to depict. [Fr *dépeindre*, from L *dēpingere*; see **depict**]

depart *di-pärt'*, *vi* to go away; to quit or leave; to die (*euphem*); to separate from one another (*obs*). — *vt* (*obs*) to separate, divide. — *n* (*obs*; *Shakesp* and *Spenser*) departure, parting. — *n* **depart'er**. — *n* **depart'ing**. — *n* **depart'ure** act of departing; a going away from a place; deviation (from a normal course of action, etc); the distance in nautical miles travelled by a ship due east or west; a death (*euphem*). — **a new departure** a change of purpose, method or activity, a new course procedure; **the departed** (*euphem*) a person (or people) who has (or have) died. [Fr *départir*, from L *dis-* apart, and *partīre* (*partīrī*) to part, to divide]

department *di-pärt'mənt*, *n* a part; a special or allotted function, sphere of activity, duty or expertise; a section of an administration, university, office or other organization, headed by a manager responsible for a specific area of work; a section of a large shop or store, selling a particular type of goods; a division of a country, *esp* a département of France. — *adj* **departmental** (*dē-pärt-ment'l*). — *vt* **department'alize** or **-ise** to form into separate departments; to deal with (a large amount of work, etc) by allotting a specific share to different departments. — *n* **departmentalizā'tion** or **-s-**. — *n* **department'alism** too strict division of work among departments with little intercommunication. — *adv* **department'ally**. — **department store** (*orig US*) a large shop selling a great variety of goods in different departments. [Fr *département*, from *départir* (see **depart**)]

département *dā-pär-təm-ã*, *n* any of the regional government divisions into which France is split. [Fr]

depasture *di-päs'chər*, *vt* to eat bare; to put to pasture; to afford pasture for. — *vi* to graze. [**de-** (2)]

depauperize or **-ise** *di-pö'pər-īz*, *vt* to remove from the state of pauper. — *vt* **depau'perate** to impoverish. — *adj* impoverished. [**de-** (2) and (3)]

dépêche *dā-pesh*, (*Fr*) *n* dispatch, message.

depeinct *di-pānt'*, (*Spenser*) *vt* to paint. [**depaint**]

depend *di-pend'*, *vi* to hang down (*rare*); to be sustained by or connected with anything; to be pending; to rely (on); to rest (on). — *adj* **depend'able** that may be relied on; reliable. — *adv* **depend'ably**. — *n* **depend'ant** (also **depend'ent**) a person who depends on another for support (*esp* financial); a hanger-on. — *n* **depend'ence** (rarely **depend'ance**) state of being dependent; reliance, trust; that on which one depends; a quarrel or duel pending (*archaic*). — *n* **depend'ency** that which depends; connected consistency (*Shakesp*); a foreign territory dependent on a country, a kind of subordinate colony without self-government; dependence (*rarely*; *Shakesp* **depend'acie** submissiveness). — *adj* **depend'ent** (also **depend'ant**) depending, relying, contingent, relative. — *adj* **depend'ing** still undetermined; awaiting settlement (*obs*). — *adv* **depend'ingly**. — **dependency culture** a type of society which relies upon, and (in a *derog* sense) expects, state benefits and support to maintain it. — **depending on** or **dependent on** according as. [Fr *dépendre*, from L *dēpendēre*, from *dē* from, and *pendēre* to hang]

depersonalize or **-ise** *dē-pûr'sən-əl-īz*, *vt* to take away the characteristics or personality of; to make impersonal, dehumanize. — *n* **dēpersonalizā'tion** or **-s-**. [**de-** (2)]

dephlegmate *di-fleg'māt*, (*old chem*) *vt* to free from water; to concentrate, rectify. — *n* **dephlegmā'tion** (*dē-*). — *n* **dephlegmā'tor**. [**de-** (2)]

dephlogisticate *dē-flo-jis'ti-kāt*, (*old chem*) *vt* to deprive of phlogiston. — **dephlogisticated air** Priestley's name for oxygen. [**de-** (2)]

depict *di-pikt'*, *vt* to paint or draw; to make a likeness of; to describe, *esp* minutely. — *n* **depict'er** or **depict'or**. — *n* **depic'tion**. — *adj* **depict'ive**. [L *dēpingere*, *dēpictum*, from *dē-* (intensive) and *pingere* to paint]

depicture *di-pik'chər*, (*archaic*) *vt* to picture; to paint; to represent. — *n* depicting, representation. [**de-** (3) and **picture** (verb)]

depilate *dep'i-lāt*, *vt* to remove the hair from. — *n* **depilā'tion** the removal or loss of hair. — *n* **dep'ilātor**. — *n* **depilatory** (*di-pil'ə-tər-i*) an application for removing superfluous hairs. — *adj* possessing this ability. [L *dēpilāre*, *-ātum*, from *dē* out, and *pilus* hair]

deplane *dē-plān'*, (*NAm*) *vi* to disembark from an aeroplane. [**de-** (2) and **plane**[2]]

deplete *di-plēt'*, *vt* to empty, reduce, exhaust, use up. — *n* **deplē'tion** the act of emptying or exhausting; the reduction in total value of a natural resource (eg oil, coal) as more of it is extracted and used or sold; the act of relieving congestion or plethora (*med*). — *adj* **deplē'table**. — *adj* **deplē'tive**. — *adj* **deplē'tory**. — **depleted uranium** (*chem*) a sample of uranium having less than its natural content of ^{235}U; **depletion layer** (*electronics*) in semiconductor materials, the area where mobile electrons do not neutralize the combined charge of the donors and acceptors, barrier layer. [L *dēplēre*, *dēplētum* to empty, from *dē-* (negative) and *plēre* to fill]

deplore *di-plōr'*, *-plör'*, *vt* to feel or express deep grief for; to express strong disapproval or disgust at; to give up as hopeless (*obs*). — *adj* **deplor'able** lamentable, causing great regret; sad; hopelessly bad. — *n* **deplor'ableness** or **deplorabil'ity**. — *adv* **deplor'ably**. — *n* **deplorā'tion** (*dep-* or *dēp-*) lamentation. — *adv* **deplor'ingly**. [L *dēplōrāre*, from *dē-* (intensive) and *plōrāre* to weep]

deploy *di-ploi'*, *vt* to unfold; to open out or extend; to spread out and place strategically (any forces). — *vi* to open; (of a body of troops) to extend from column into line, to take up strategic positions. — *n* **deploy'** or **deploy'ment**. [Fr *déployer*, from L *dis-* apart, and *plicāre* to fold]

deplume *di-plōōm'*, *vt* to strip of plumes or feathers. — *n* **deplumā'tion** (*dē-*). [**de-** (2)]

depolarize or **-ise** *dē-pō'lər-īz*, (*phys*) *vt* to deprive of polarity. — *n* **depolarīzā'tion** or **-s-**. [**de-** (2)]

depoliticize or **-ise** *dē-po-lit'i-sīz*, *vt* to remove the political nature or awareness from. [**de-** (2)]

depolymerize or **-ise** *dē-pol'i-mər-iz*, *vt* to break a large molecule into simpler ones that have the same basic formula. — *vi* to decompose in this way. — *n* **depolymerizā'tion** or **-s-**. [**de-** (2)]

depone *di-pōn'*, *vt* (mainly *Scots law*) to lay down; to deposit; to testify upon oath. — *adj* **depō'nent** (*gram*) having a passive form but active meaning, as if having laid aside the passive (really middle or reflexive) meaning. — *n* a deponent verb; a person who makes a deposition, *esp* under oath, or whose written testimony is used as evidence in a court of justice. [L *dēpōnere*; pr p *dēpōnēns*, *-entis*, from *dē* down, and *pōnere* to place, lay]

Depo-Provera® *de-pō-prō-vä'rə*, *n* an injectable contraceptive for women, used *esp* in developing countries.

depopulate *dē-pop'ū-lāt*, *vt* to overrun and lay waste (*obs*); to rid of people, remove the population from. — *vi* to become devoid of people. — *adj* depopulated. — *n* **depopulā'tion** act of depopulating; havoc; destruction. — *n* **depop'ulātor**. [L *dēpopulārī*, *-ātus*, from *dē-* (intensive) and *populārī* to swarm over, to spread over a country, said of hostile people (L *populus*), hence to ravage, to destroy; later understood as to deprive of people]

deport[1] *di-*, *dē-pōrt'*, *-pört'*, *vt* to transport, to exile; to expel (eg as an undesirable alien or foreigner). — *n* **deportā'tion** (*dē-*). — *n* **deportee'** (*dē-*). [Fr *déporter*, from L *dēportāre*, from *dē-* away, and *portāre*, *-ātum* to carry]

deport[2] *di-pōrt'*, *-pört'*, *vt* to behave (*reflexive*). — *n* **deport'ment** behaviour; physical bearing, stance, gait; manners. [OFr *deporter*, from L *dē-* (intensive) and *portāre* to carry]

depose *di-pōz'*, *vt* to remove from a high office or post; to degrade; to set down; to remove; to attest; to examine or put upon oath (*Shakesp*). — *vi* to give testimony; to swear (*obs*; *Shakesp*) — *adj* **depōs'able**. — *n* **depōs'al**. — *n* **depōs'er**. [Fr *déposer*, from L *dē* from, and *pausāre* to pause, (later) to place]

deposit *di-poz'it*, *vt* to put or set down; to place; to lay; to lay up, set aside for later use; to entrust (*esp* money); to lodge as a pledge, give (*esp* money) as security; to lay down as a coating, bed, vein, etc (*geol*). — *n* that which is deposited or put down; a sum of money paid to secure an article, service, etc, the remainder of the cost being paid later; an accumulation by sedimentation, precipitation, sublimation, or other natural means (*geol*); something entrusted to another's care, *esp* a sum of money put in a bank; a pledge; a bailment where one entrusts goods to another to be kept without recompense (in *Scots law*, **depositā'tion**); the state of being deposited. — *n* **depos'itary** a person with whom anything is left for safe keeping; a guardian (also **depos'itory**). — *adj* **depos'itive**. — *n* **depos'itor**. — *n* **depos'itory** a place where anything is deposited for safekeeping (also **depos'itary**). — **deposit account** a bank account *usu* used for savings, in which money is lodged to gain interest, and for which cheques are not used; **deposit money** (*econ*) deposits in bank current accounts, the largest part of the money supply; **depos'it-receipt'** a receipt for money deposited in a bank, etc. [L *dēpositum* placed, from *dēpōnere*, from *dē* down, and *pōnere* to place]

deposition *dēp-ə-zish'ən*, *n* the act of deposing; the act of deponing; declaration, written sworn testimony, to be used as a substitute for the production of the witness in open court; removal; the act or process of depositing; what is deposited, sediment. — *adj* **deposi'tional**. [**deposit**; blended with root of **depose**]

depot *dep'ō*, *di-pō'*, *dā'pō* or *dē'pō*, *n* a place of deposit; a storehouse; a military station where stores are kept and recruits trained; the headquarters of a regiment; the portion of a regiment left at home; a bus or railway station (*NAm*); a place where buses or tram-cars are kept. [Fr *dépôt*, from L *dēpōnere*, *-positum* to put down, to place]

deprave *di-prāv'*, *vt* to represent as bad (*obs*); to make morally bad or worse; to corrupt. — *n* **depravation** (*dep-rə-vā'shən*) act of depraving; state of being depraved; depravity. — *adj* **deprāved'** corrupt. — *adv* **deprāv'edly**. — *n* **deprāv'edness**. — *n* **deprāve'ment** (*archaic*) vitiation. — *adv* **deprāv'ingly**. — *n* **depravity** (*di-prav'i-ti*) a vitiated or corrupt state of moral character; extreme wickedness; corruption; the hereditary tendency of man toward sin (*theol*); original sin (*theol*). [L *dēprāvāre*, from *dē-* (intensive) and *prāvus* bad]

deprecate *dep'ri-kāt*, *vt* to regret deeply; to argue or protest against; to express disapproval of; to disparage, belittle; to try to ward off by prayer (*archaic*); to desire earnestly the prevention or removal of; to invoke or beseech with a view to the averting or withholding of evil (*archaic*). — *adj* **dep'recable** to be deprecated. — *adj* **dep'recating** expressing contempt, disapproval, disparagement. — *n* **deprecā'tion** act of deprecating, earnest prayer, *esp* a special petition against some evil, in litanies. — *adv* **dep'recātingly**. — *adj* **dep'recātive**. — *adj* **dep'recātory**. — *n* **dep'recātor**. — *adv* **dep'recātorily**. [L *dēprecārī*, *-ātus* to pray away or against, from *dē* away, and *precārī* to pray]

depreciate *di-prē'shi-āt*, *vt* to lower the worth of; to undervalue, to be contemptuous of the value of; to disparage. — *vi* to fall in value. — *adv* **deprē'ciātingly**. — *n* **depreciātion** (*-s(h)i-ā'shən*) the falling of value; the loss in value of assets due to wear and tear, obsolescence or passage of time (*accountancy*); the rate at which a fixed asset loses value; disparagement, ridicule. — *adj* **deprē'ciative** or **deprē'ciatory** tending to depreciate or lower. — *n* **deprē'ciātor**. [L *dēpretiāre*, *-ātum*, from *dē* down, and *pretium* price]

depredate *dep'ri-dāt*, *vt* to plunder or prey upon; to rob; to lay waste; to devour. — *n* **depredā'tion** the act of plundering; state of being depredated; (*usu* in *pl*) hardship, damage. — *n* **dep'redātor**. — *adj* **depredatory** (*di-pred'ət-ə-ri*). [L *dēpraedārī*, *-ātus*, from *dē-* (intensive) and *praedārī*, from *praeda* plunder]

deprehend *dep-ri-hend'*, (*obs*) *vt* to catch, seize; to apprehend; to detect. [L *dēpraehendere*, from *dē-* aside, and *praehendere* to take]

depress *di-pres'*, *vt* to press down; to let down; to lower; to cause to sink; to humble; to make subject; to dispirit, deject or cast a gloom over. — *n* **depress'ant** anything which lowers activity or spirits; a sedative; a chemical that causes a mineral to sink in flotation (*mining*). — Also *adj*. — *adj* **depressed'** pressed down; lowered; flattened or slightly hollowed; humbled; dejected; dispirited; (of a market, trade, etc) reduced, not flourishing. — *adj* **depress'ible**. — *adj* **depress'ing** able or tending to depress, *esp* in spirits. — *adv* **depress'ingly**. — *n* **depression** (*di-presh'ən*) a falling in or sinking; a lowering (eg of vital functions, or of vitality); a region of low barometric pressure, a cyclone; a hollow; a state of deep dejection and a pervasive feeling of helplessness, together with apathy and loss of self-esteem, causing retardation of thought and body functions (*med*); a condition of reduced trade activity and prosperity. — *adj* **depress'ive** tending to depress; (of a person) suffering from periods of depression. — *n* a person suffering from periods of depression. — *n* **depress'or** an oppressor; something which lowers activity; a muscle that draws down; a surgical instrument for pressing down. — **depressed area** a region suffering from reduced trade, and often consequently one of specially heavy unemployment, poor housing, etc. [L *dēprimere -pressum*, from *dē* down, and *premere* to press]

depressurize or **-ise** *dē-presh'ər-īz*, *vt* to reduce the air pressure in (eg an aircraft cabin) *esp* suddenly. — *n* **depressurizā'tion** or **-s-**. [**de-** (2)]

deprive *di-prīv'*, *vt* to dispossess; to keep from enjoyment (of); to degrade (*esp* a clergyman) from office; to bereave. — *adj* **deprīv'able**. — *n* **deprīv'al** or **deprivā'tion** (*dep-ri-* or *dē-prī-*) the act of depriving; the state of being deprived; degradation from office; loss; bereavement. — *adj* **deprived'** having been dispossessed (of); suffering from hardship, *esp* the lack of good educational, social, medical, etc facilities. — *adj* **depriv'ātive**. — *n* **deprīve'ment**. [LL *dēprīvāre* to degrade, from L *dē* from, and *prīvāre* to deprive]

de profundis *dē prə-fun'dis*, *dā pro-fŏŏn'dēs*, (*L*) out of the depths (from Psalm 130).

deprogram *dē-prō'gram*, *vt* to remove a program from (a computer); (*usu* **deprō'gramme**) to prevail upon (a person) to reject obsessive beliefs, fears, etc. [**de-** (2)]

depside *dep'sīd*, (*chem*) *n* a product formed from hydroxy-aromatic acids by the condensation of the carboxyl group of one molecule with the phenol group of a second, functioning in plant cells. [Gr *depsein* to knead]

Dept. or **dept**. *abbrev*: department (also **Dept** or **dept**); deputy.

depth *depth*, *n* deepness; the measure of deepness down or inwards; a deep place; intensity (of eg feeling); the innermost or most intense part, as in *depth of winter*; difficulty of understanding, obscurity; extent of wisdom and penetration of mental powers. — *adj* **depth'less** having no depth; bottomless. — **depth'-bomb** or **-charge** a powerful bomb that explodes under water (dropped over or near submarines); **depth psychology** the psychology of the unconscious mind; **depth psychologist**. — **depth of field** the distance between the nearer and farther planes in an area photographed, seen through a microscope, etc, over which the image is in reasonably sharp focus; **depth of focus** the distance between a camera lens and the film at which the image will be clear; **in depth** extending far inwards; (of defence) consisting of several successive lines; extensive(ly) and thorough(ly) (*adj* **in'-depth'** see under **in**); **out of one's depth** in water where one cannot touch bottom with one's head above the surface, or too deep for one's safety; in a situation, etc beyond one's understanding; **the depths** the lowest pitch of humiliation and misery. [Not in OE; possibly ON *dȳpth*; or formed from **deep** on analogy of **length**, etc]

depurate *dep'ū-rāt*, *di-pū'rāt*, *vi* to purify. — *adj* and *n* **dep'ūrant**. — *n* **depūrā'tion**. — *n* **dep'ūrātor**. — *n* and *adj* **depurative** (*dep'ū-rā-tiv* or *di-pūr'ə-tiv*). — *adj* **depū'ratory**. [LL *dēpūrāre*, *-ātum* to purify, from L *dē-* (intensive) and *pūrāre* to purify, from *pūrus* pure]

depute *di-pūt'*, *vt* to appoint or send as a substitute or agent; to send with a special commission; to give (one's authority) to someone else. — *combining form* (*dep'ūt*) in Scotland, appointed deputy (as in *sheriff-depute*, often simply *the depute*). — *n* **deputation** (*dep-ū-tā'shən*) the act of deputing; the person or persons deputed or appointed to transact business for another; a representative body of people sent to state a case in a dispute; the privilege of shooting game, or a document granting it, formerly given by the lord of a manor, nominally as to a gamekeeper. — *vt* **dep'ūtize** or **-ise** to appoint as deputy. — *vi* to act as deputy. — *n* **dep'ūty** a person deputed or appointed to act for another, *esp* (*London*) for an alderman or (*US*) for a sheriff; a delegate or representative, or substitute; a legislator, member of a chamber of deputies; a person who attends to safety arrangements in a coal-mine. [L *dēputāre* to prune, (later) to select]

der. *abbrev*: derivation; derivative; derived.

deracialize or **-ise** *dē'rāsh'əl-īz*, *-yə-līz*, *vt* to divest of racial character. [**de-** (2) and **racial**]

deracinate *dē-ras'i-nāt*, *vt* to root up (*lit* and *fig*). — *n* **deracinā'tion**. — *adj* **déraciné** (*dā-ras-ē-nā*; *Fr*) uprooted (*lit* and *fig*). [Fr *déraciner*, from L *dē* from, and LL *rādicīna*, dimin of L *rādix* a root]

deraign. See **darraigne**.

derail *di-rāl'*, (*lit* and *fig*) *vt* to cause to leave the rails. — *vi* to go off the rails. — *n* **derail'er**. — *n* **derail'ment**. [**de-** (2)]

dérailleur *dā-ra-yœr* or **dérailleur gear** (*gēr*), *n* a variable bicycle-gear depending on a mechanism by means of which the chain can be transferred from one sprocket wheel to another of different size. [Fr *dérailler* to derail]

derange *di-rānj'*, *vt* to put out of place or order; to disorder, put into confusion; to make insane. — *adj* **deranged'** disordered; insane. — *n* **derange'ment** disorder, disarray; insanity; obsolete psychiatric term for psychosis. [Fr *déranger*, from *dé-* (L *dis-*) asunder, and *ranger* to rank]

derate *dē-rāt'*, *vt* to relieve (wholly or partially) from paying local rates; to reduce the maximum capacity ratings of electrical equipment to allow for deterioration, etc. — *n* **derat'ing**. [**de-** (2)]

deration *dē-ra'shən*, *vt* to free from rationing. [**de-** (2)]

deray *di-rā'*, (*obs*) *vt* to derange. — *vi* to go wild. — *n* tumult, disorder. [OFr *desreer*, from *des-* (negative) and *rei*, *roi* order; see **array**]

Derby *där'bi*, *n* a kind of porcelain made at *Derby*; a horse-race held annually on Epsom Downs (from Derby stakes, instituted by Earl of *Derby*, 1780); (*dûr'bi*) a horse-race run at Churchill Downs, Kentucky; (often without *cap*) any race attracting much interest, or a keen sporting contest, *esp* one between neighbouring teams; (*dûr'bi*; *US*; often without *cap*) a bowler hat; (sometimes without *cap*) a strong type of boot. — **Derby dog** a dog straying on a race-course; an intruder or an interruption (*fig*); **Derbyshire neck** a form of goitre; **Derbyshire spar** fluorite.

der-doing *dûr'-dŏŏ'ing*, (*Spenser*) *adj* doing daring deeds. [See **derring-do**]

dere or **deare**, *dēr*, (*obs*) *vt* to injure. — *n* (*Spenser*) injury. [OE *derian*]

derecognize or **-ise** *dē-rek'əg-nīz*, *vt* to withdraw recognition from (*esp* a trade union). — *n* **derecogni'tion**. [**de-** (2)]

deregister *dē-rej'is-tər*, *vt* to remove from a register. — *n* **deregistrā'tion**. [**de-** (2)]

de règle *də regl'*, (*Fr*) according to rule.

deregulate *dē-reg'ū-lāt*, *vt* to free from regulations or controls. — *n* **deregulā'tion**. [**de-** (2)]

derelict *der'i-likt*, *adj* forsaken; abandoned, falling in ruins; neglectful of duty (chiefly *NAm*). — *n* anything (*esp* a ship) forsaken or abandoned; a person abandoned by society, a down-and-out. — *n* **derelic'tion** act of forsaking (*esp* duty), unfaithfulness or remissness; state of being abandoned; land gained from the water by a change of waterline. [L *dērelinquere*, *-lictum*, from *dē* (intensive), *re-* behind, and *linquere* to leave]

dereligionize or **-ise** *dē-ri-lij'ən-īz*, *vt* to make irreligious. [**de-** (2)]

derequisition *dē-rek-wi-zi'shən*, *vt* to return (something that has been used for a military purpose) to civilian use. [**de-** (2)]

derestrict *dē-ri-strikt'*, *vt* to free from restriction (*esp* a road from a speed limit). — *n* **derestric'tion**. [**de-** (2)]

derham. See **dirhem**.

deride *di-rīd'*, *vt* to laugh at; to mock. — *n* **derid'er**. — *adv* **derid'ingly**. — *adj* **derisible** (*-riz'*). — *n* **derision** (*di-rizh'-ən*) act of deriding; mockery; a laughing-stock. — *adj* **derisive** (*di-rīs'iv* or *riz'*) scoffing, mocking. — *adv* **derīs'ively** (or *-riz'*). — *n* **derīs'iveness** (or *-riz'*). — *adj* **derīs'ory** scoffing; ridiculous. [L *dērīdēre*, *-rīsum*, from *dē* (intensive) and *rīdēre* to laugh]

derig *dē-rig'*, *vt* to dismantle and remove (equipment, *esp* sound and lighting gear; *theat*, etc). — Also *n*. [**de-** (2)]

de rigueur *də rē-gœr*, (*Fr*) required by strict etiquette, or by fashion, etc.

derision, **derisive**, **derisory**, etc. See **deride**.

deriv. *abbrev*: derivation; derivative; derived.

derive *di-rīv'*, *vt* to conduct, draw, take, obtain, proceed or receive (from a source or origin); to infer; to trace to or from an origin; to bring down (upon oneself; *obs*; *Shakesp*). — *vi* to descend, issue or originate. — *adj* **derīv'able**. — *adv* **derīv'ably**. — *adj* **derivate** (*der'i-vāt*) derived. — *n* a derivative. — *n* **derivā'tion** act of deriving; a drawing off; the tracing of a word to its root; source, origin; that which is derived; descent or evolution; a sequence of statements showing how a certain result must follow from other statements already accepted, as in a mathematical formula, logical progression, etc. — *adj* **derivā'tional**. — *n* **derivā'tionist**. — *adj* **derivative** (*di-riv'ə-tiv*) derived or taken from something else; (sometimes *derog*) not radical or original, unoriginal. — *n* that which is derived; a word formed from another word, *esp* by prefixation or suffixation; a product derived from one already produced; a differential coefficient (*math*); (in *pl*) futures and options (*stock exchange*). — *adv* **deriv'atively**. — **derived demand** (*econ*, *marketing*, etc) a demand that exists only as a result of another demand; **derived unit** a unit of measurement derived from the fundamental units of a system. [Fr *dériver*, from L *dērivāre*, from *dē* down, from, and *rīvus* a river]

derm *dûrm*, *n* the true skin, below the outer layer — also **der'ma** or **der'mis**. — *n* **dermabrā'sion** a cosmetic operation in which the facial skin is scrubbed, peeled away and allowed to heal. — *adj* **der'mal**, **dermat'ic** or **der'mic** pertaining to the skin; consisting of skin. — *npl* **Dermap'tera** an order of insects with forewings, when present, in the form of firm elytra, the earwigs. — *n* **dermatī'tis** (*med*) inflammation of the skin. — *n* **dermat'ogen** (*bot*) the layer from which epidermis is formed at the growing-point. — *n* **dermatoglyph'ics** (Gr *glyphein* to carve) (*n pl*) skin patterns, *esp* of the skin on the under-surfaces of the hands and feet; (*n sing*) the science of the study of skin patterns. — *n* **dermatograph'ia** (*med*) a type of urticaria in which the physical allergy causes stroking or scratching, etc to raise a red weal on the skin. — *adj* **dermatograph'ic**. — *n* **dermatog'raphy** anatomical description of the skin (also **dermog'raphy**). — *adj* **der'matoid** of the form of skin; skin-like. — *adj* **dermatolog'ical**. — *n* **dermatol'ogist**. — *n* **dermatol'ogy** the branch of science that concerns itself with the skin. — *n* **derm'atome** (Gr *tomos* a slice, section, from *temnein* to cut) a surgical instrument for cutting layers of skin, *esp* for grafting; the part of an embryonic somite, or skin segment, that produces the dermis; the area of skin supplied with nerves from a single spinal root. — *n* **dermatomyosī'tis** a disease characterized by inflammation of the skin and muscles, and wasting of the muscles. — *n* **der'matōphyte** a parasitic fungus of the skin. — *adj* **dermatoplas'tic**. — *n* **dermatoplas'ty** (Gr *plassein* to mould) a plastic operation on the skin, *esp* grafting. — *n* **dermatō'sis** any skin disease: — *pl* **dermatō'ses** (*-sēz*). — *n* **der'moid** a cyst of similar cell structure to that of skin, *usu* congenital or occurring in the ovary. — *n pl* **Dermop'tera** an order of mammals, the flying lemurs, sometimes included in Insectivora. [Gr *derma*, *-atos* the skin]

dern[1]. See **durn**.

dern[2] or **dearn** *dûrn*, (*archaic* and *dialect*) *adj* secret; hidden; dreadful (*Shakesp*). — *n* secrecy; hiding. — *adj* **dern'ful** or **dearn'ful** solitary; mournful. — *adv* **dern'ly** or **dearn'ly** secretly; sorrowfully; grievously. [OE *dyrne*, *derne* secret]

dernier *der-nyā*, (*Fr*) *adj* last. — **dernier cri** (*krē*) the last word (literally cry), the latest fashion; **dernier ressort** (*res-sör*) a last resort.

derogate *der'ō-gāt*, *vi* and *vt* to lessen by taking away; to detract. — *adj* (*Shakesp*) degenerate. — *adv* **der'ogately** (*Shakesp*) in a derogatory manner. — *n* **derogā'tion** a taking from; detraction; depreciation; the allowed breaking of a rule. — *adj* **derog'ative**. — *adv* **derog'atively**. — *adv* **derogatorily** (*di-rog'ə-tər-i-li*). — *n* **derog'atoriness**. — *adj* **derog'atory** detracting; injurious; insulting, adversely critical. [L *dērogāre*, *-ātum* to repeal part of a law, from *dē* down, from, and *rogāre* to propose a law]

derrick *der'ik*, *n* an arrangement for hoisting materials, by a boom hung from a central post; a framework or tower over a borehole or the like. — *vt* to luff (the jib of a crane). [From *Derrick*, a 17c hangman]

derrière *der-yer*, *der'i-er*, (*Fr*) *n* the behind, buttocks.

derring-do or **derring do** or **doe** *der'ing-doo͞*, (*false archaic*) *n* daring action. — *adj* **der-do'ing**. — **derr'ing doo'er**. [Spenser mistook Lydgate's *dorryng do*, ie daring (to) do (misprinted *derrynge do*) for a noun]

derringer *der'in-jər*, *n* a short American pistol. [Inventor's name]

derris *der'is*, *n* any plant of the tropical genus (*Derris*) of papilionaceous plants (related to peas and beans) whose roots yield an insecticide powder. [Gr *derris* a leather coat]

derry *der'i*, (*slang*, *esp Austr*) *n* a feeling of dislike or resentment, *esp* in the phrase **have a derry on (someone)**. [Prob from old refrain **derry down**]

der Tag *dār tähh*, *täg*, (*Ger*) the day when the struggle begins (*orig*, in Germany, the day when a career of conquest by Germany was to begin).

derth *dûrth*, (*Spenser*) *n*. Same as **dearth**.

derv *dûrv*, *n* diesel engine fuel oil. [From *d*iesel *e*ngined *r*oad *v*ehicle]

dervish *dûr'vish*, *n* (sometimes with *cap*) a member of one of numerous Muslim fraternities, professing poverty and leading an austere life. [Turkish *dervīsh*, from Pers *darvish* a dervish, literally a poor man]

DES *abbrev*: Department of Education and Science.

desacralization or **-isation** *dē-sak-rə-lī-zā'shən* or *-sā'krə-*, *n* the removal of sacred character, operation, tradition, etc; secularization. — *vt* **desa'cralize** or **-ise**. [**de-** (2), **sacral**, **-ize** and *-ation*]

désagrément *dāz-ag-rā-mã*, (*Fr*) *n* something disagreeable.

desalinate *dē-sal'in-āt*, *vt* to remove salt from (*esp* sea water). — Also **desal'inize** or **-ise**. — *n* **desalinā'tion**. — *n* **desal'inātor**. — *n* **desalinizā'tion** or **-s-**. [**de-** (2)]

desalt *dē-sölt'*, *vt* to remove salt from. — *n* **desalt'īng**. [**de-** (2)]

desaturation *dē-sat-ū-rā'shən*, (*phys*). See **saturation**.

descale *dē-skāl*, *vt* to remove scales from (*esp* fish); to scrape away an encrustation from. [**de-** (2)]

descant *des'kant*, *n* an accompaniment above and harmonizing with the main melody (*music*); counterpoint (*obs*; *music*); a discourse or disquisition under several heads. — *adj* (of a musical instrument) having a higher register and pitch than most others of the same family. — *vi* **descant'** (*Shakesp des'*) to sing a descant; to discourse at length (*obs*); to comment (*obs*). [ONFr *descant*, from L *dis-* apart, and *cantus* a song]

descend *di-send'*, *vi* to climb down; to pass from a higher to a lower place or condition; to move from general to particular topics, details, etc; to make an invasion; to be derived (from); (of the testes) to move from the abdominal cavity into the scrotum. — *vt* to move down upon, to traverse downwards. — *n* **descend'ant** a person who descends, ie offspring from an ancestor; the point on the ecliptic opposite the ascendant (*astrol*). — *adj* **descend'ed** derived by descent. — *adj* **descend'ent** going down; proceeding from an ancestor. — *n* **descend'er** the part of a letter such as *j* or *p* that comes below the line on which *x* sits (*printing*). — *adj* **descend'ible** (also **descend'able**) that may descend or be descended; capable of transmission by inheritance, heritable. — *adj* **descend'ing**. — *n* (*Shakesp*) lineage. — *n* **descen'sion**. — *adj* **descen'sional**. — *n* **descent'** an act of descending; transmission by succession, inheritance; motion or progress downward; slope; a raid or invasion; derivation from an ancestor; a generation, a degree in genealogy; descendants collectively. — **descent from the cross** a picture representing Christ being taken down from the cross. [Fr *descendre*, from L *dēscendere*, from *dē* down, and *scandere* to climb]

deschool *dē-skōōl'* *vt* and *vi* to free children from the restrictions of traditional classroom learning and a set curriculum, and educate them in a less formal way, *esp* at home. — *n* **deschool'er**. — *n* **deschool'ing**. [**de-** (2)]

descramble *dē-skram'bəl*, *vt* to unscramble, decipher. [**de-** (2)]

describe *di-skrīb'*, *vt* to trace out or delineate; to give an account of, recount the physical appearance or details of. — *adj* **descrīb'able**. — *n* **describ'er**. — *n* **description** (*di-skrip'shən*) the act of describing; an account of anything in words; loosely sort, class, or kind. — *adj* **descrip'tive** containing description. — *adv* **descrip'tively**. — *n* **descrip'tiveness**. — *n* **descrip'tivism** the use of, or belief in, descriptive linguistics (see below); a theory of ethics by which only empirical statements are acceptable. — *n* **descrip'tor** (*comput*) a symbol or form of words that identifies a particular subject in a storage system, or gives information on how particular material is stored; a key word or a heading. — **descriptive geometry** the study of three-dimensional figures when projected on to a two-dimensional surface; **descriptive linguistics** the study of the description of a language structure as it occurred individually at a particular time, ie with no reference to its history, any other language, etc. [L *dēscrībere*, from *dē* down, and *scrībere*, *scrīptum* to write]

descrive *di-skrīv'*, (*obs*) *vt* to describe. [OFr *descrivre*, from L *dēscrībere*]

descry *di-skrī'*, *vt* to reveal (*obs*; *Spenser*); to discover by looking; to espy: — *pr p* **descry'ing**; *pa t* and *pa p* **descried'**. — *n* (*obs*) discovery; a thing discovered (*Shakesp*). [Appar two words: OFr *descrire* for *descrivre*, from L *dēscrībere*, and OFr *descrier*, *decryer* to proclaim, announce, from *des-*, *de-*, and *crier* to cry; cf **describe**, **decry**]

desecrate *des'i-krāt*, *vt* to make no longer consecrated; to profane, damage (something sacred). — *n* **des'ecrater** or **des'ecrator**. — *n* **desecrā'tion** act of desecrating; profanation, damage (of anything sacred). [Coined on the analogy of **consecrate**, with L *dē* from (L *dēsecrāre* meant to consecrate)]

desegregate *dē-seg'ri-gāt*, *vt* to abolish racial segregation in (eg a university). — *n* **desegregā'tion**. — *n* and *adj* **desegregā'tionist**. [**de-** (2)]

deselect *dē-sə-lekt'*, *vt* (of a political party at constituency or ward level) not to select (the candidate who is already an MP or councillor) as a candidate for re-election; (of a selection panel or other body) not to reselect (eg an athlete) for a place on a team, to represent a country, county or the like. — *n* **deselec'tion**. [**de-** (2)]

desensitize or **-ise** *dē-sen'sit-īz*, *vt* and *vi* to make or become less sensitive. — *n* **desensitīzā'tion** or **-s-**. — *n* **desen'sitizer** or **-s-**. [**de-** (2)]

deserpidine *di-zûrp'i-din*, *-dēn*, *n* a synthetic sedative drug of which the natural base is *Rauwolfia serpentina*.

desert[1] *di-zûrt'*, *n* anything which is deserved; claim to reward; merit. — *adj* **desert'less** (*rare*) without merit. [OFr, pa p of *deservir*; see **deserve**]

desert[2] *di-zûrt'*, *vt* to leave; to forsake. — *vi* to run away; to leave a service, eg the army, without permission. — *n* **desert'er** someone who deserts from or quits any of the armed forces without permission. — *n* **deser'tion** an act of deserting; the state of being deserted; wilful abandonment of a legal or moral obligation. — **desert the diet** (*Scots law*) to give up a charge. [L *dēserere*, *dēsertum*, from *dē-* (negative) and *serere* to bind]

desert[3] *dez'ərt*, *adj* deserted; desolate; uninhabited; uncultivated. — *n* a desolate or barren tract, *usu* with little or no water; a waste; a place of solitude. — *n* **desertificā'tion**, **desertīzā'tion** or **-s-** the deterioration or reversion of land to desert conditions, owing to over-grazing, erosion, etc. — **desert boots** laced suede ankle boots with rubber soles; **desert pea** (*usu* **Sturt's desert pea**) an Australian glory-pea (*Clianthus*) with a predominantly scarlet flower; **desert rat** a jerboa, hence (from the divisional sign of a jerboa) a soldier of the British 7th Armoured Division with service in North Africa in 1941–42. [OFr *desert*, from L *dēsertum*, from *dēserere* to desert, unbind]

deserve *di-zûrv'*, *vt* to be entitled to by merit; to warrant, be worthy of. — *vi* to be worthy of reward. — *adj* **deserved'**. — *adv* **deserv'edly**. — *n* **deserv'edness**. — *n* **deserv'er**. — *adj* **deserv'ing** worthy. — *adv* **deserv'ingly** according to what is deserved; justly. [OFr *deservir*, from L *dēservīre*, from *dē* (intensive) and *servīre* to serve]

desex *dē-sex'*, *vt* to desexualize. [**de-** (2)]

desexualize or **-ise** *dē-seks'ū-əl-īz*, *vt* to deprive of sexual character or quality. — *n* **desexualīzā'tion** or **-s-**. [**de-** (2)]

déshabillé. See **dishabille**.

desiccate *des'i-kāt*, *vt* to dry (up); to preserve by drying. — *vi* to grow dry. — *adj* **des'iccant** or **desiccative** (*di-sik'ə-tiv*) drying; having the power of drying. — *n* a drying agent. — *n* **desiccā'tion** the act or process of drying up; the state of being dried up. — *n* **des'iccātor** apparatus for drying. [L *dēsiccāre*, *-ātum* to dry up, from *dē-* (intensive) and *siccus* dry]

desiderate *di-zid'ər-āt*, *vt* to long for or earnestly desire; to want or miss. — *n* **desiderā'tion** the act of desiderating; the thing desiderated. — *adj* **desid'erative** implying desire (as in *desiderative verb*). — *n* **desiderā'tum** (or *-ä'*) something desired or much wanted: — *pl* **desidera'ta**. — *n* **desiderium** (*des-i-dē'ri-əm*) longing; grief for what is lost. [L *dēsīderāre*, *-ātum* to long for; *dēsīderium* longing. A doublet of **desire**]

design *di-zīn'*, *vt* to indicate (*Shakesp*, *Spenser*, etc; *obs*); to draw; to plan and execute artistically; to form a plan of; to contrive, invent; to intend; to set apart or destine. — *n* a drawing or sketch; a plan in outline; a plan or scheme formed in the mind; arrangement of form and appearance; a plot; intention. — *adj* **design'able**. — *adv* **designedly** (*di-zīn'id-li*) by design; intentionally. — *n* **design'er** a person who provides designs or patterns; a draughtsman; a plotter; someone who designs sets for plays, operas, films, etc. — *adj* of or pertaining to a designer; designed by (and bearing the name of) a known fashion designer; designed, created to follow the fashionable trend or image (loosely; slightly *derog*); custom-made, for a specific purpose or effect. — *adj* **design'ful** full of design. — *adj* **design'ing** artful; scheming; working secretly for self-interest. — *n* the art of making designs or patterns. — *adv* **design'ingly**. — *adj* **design'less**. — *n* **design'ment** (*obs*) the design or sketch of a work; intention, purpose, enterprise (*Shakesp*), etc. — **design engineer** a designer in engineering; **designer drug** a drug manufactured so as to produce the same (*esp* hallucinogenic or narcotic) effects as one already existing (*esp* one restricted or illegal), by modifying the contents; a drug designed for a specific purpose. — **argument from design** the argument for the existence of God from evidence of design in creation; **by design** intentionally. [Fr *désigner*, from L *dēsignāre*, *-ātum*, from *dē-* off, and *signum* a mark]

designate *dez'ig-nāt*, *vt* to mark out so as to make known; to show, indicate; to name; to be a name or label for; to appoint or nominate. — *adj* nominated to but not yet in possession of an office (used after the noun, as in *chairman designate*). — *n* **designā'tion** a showing or pointing out; a name; a title; a style of address descriptive of occupation, standing, etc; the line typed after the signature in the complimentary close of a formal or business letter; nomination to office. — *adj* **des'ignative**. — *adj* **designā'tory**. — *n* **des'ignātor**. [L *designātus*, pa p of *designare* to designate; see **design**]

desilver *dē-sil'vər*, *vt* to remove silver from. — Also **desil'verize** or **-ise**. — *n* **desilverizā'tion** or **-s-**. [**de-** (2)]

desine (*Spenser*). Same as **design**.

desinent *des'in-ənt*, or **desinential** *des-i-nen'shəl*, (*obs* or *archaic*) *adj* terminal. — *n* **des'inence** ending. [L *dēsinēns*, *-entis*, pr p of *dēsinere* to leave off, from *dē* from, and *sinere* to allow]

desipient *di-sip'i-ənt*, *adj* playing the fool; trifling. — *n* **desip'ience**. [L *dēsipiēns*, *-entis*, pr p of *dēsipere*, from *dē-* (negative) and *sapere* to be wise]

desire *di-zīr'*, *vt* to long for; to wish for; to ask; to regret the loss of (*archaic*; *Bible*). — *vi* to be in a state of desire. — *n* an earnest longing or wish; a prayer or request; the object desired; lust. — *n* **desīrabil'ity**. — *adj* **desīr'able** worthy of desire or approval; to be approved of; pleasing; agreeable. — *n* a desirable person or thing. — *n* **desīr'ableness**. — *adv* **desīr'ably**. — *adj* **desire'less**. — *n* **desīr'er**. — *adj* **desīr'ous** (*usu* with *of*) full of desire; wishful, wanting; eager; desirable (*obs*). — *adv* **desīr'ously**. — *n* **desīr'ousness**. [Fr *désirer*, from L *dēsīderāre*]

desist *di-zist'*, *-sist'*, *vi* to leave off, stop (doing something). — *n* **desist'ance** or **desist'ence**. [L *dēsistere*, from *dē-* away from, and *sistere* to cause to stand]

desk *desk*, *n* a sloping or flat table for writing or reading, often fitted with drawers, etc; a shut-up writing-box; a pulpit or lectern; a counter in a public place for information, registration, etc; a department of a newspaper office, eg *the news desk*; a music-stand; in an orchestra, *esp* among strings, (players in) a seating position determined by rank (eg *the first desk*). — *adj* **desk'bound** or **desk'-bound** confined to a desk (eg of someone doing paperwork and administration rather than active or practical work); (of equipment, eg a computer) not portable. — *adj* **desk'top** (of a computer, etc) designed for use on a desk. — *n* such a computer. — **desktop publishing** (a system for) the production on a desktop computer of all the pre-press stages of publication, ie typesetting, design, layout, illustration, etc; **desk'-work** work done at a desk, eg by a clerk or author. [ME *deske*, from L *discus*, from Gr *diskos*; see **dish**[1] and **disc**]

deskill *dē-skil'*, *vt* to remove the element of human skill from (a job, process, operation, etc) through automation, computerization, etc. [**de-** (2)]

desman *des'mən*, *n* a Russian aquatic insectivore with long snout and musk-glands; a related Pyrenean species. [Swed *desman* musk]

desmid *dez'mid*, *n* (*bot*) one of a group of microscopic algae, unicellular or strung in chains. — *n* **desmine** (*dez'mēn* or *-min*) the mineral stilbite occurring in bundles. — *n* **desmōd'ium** a plant of the telegraph-plant genus *Desmodium*: — *pl* **desmo'diums**. — *adj* **desmodrom'ic** (*mech*; Gr *dromos* running) denoting a system, used in some motorcycle and racing car engines, that employs eg cams, rockers, etc to ensure that the opening and closing of valves, when the vehicle is at high speed, is fully controlled. — *adj* **des'moid** arranged in bundles. — *adj* **desmosō'mal**. — *n* **des'mosome** (*biol*) a small thickened patch on the membrane of a cell, such patches serving as points of adhesion between cell and cell, eg in the skin. [Gr *desmos* a chain, fetter, *desmē* a bundle, and *eidos* form]

desmoid *dez'moid*, (*zool*) *adj* resembling a fascia or a ligament. — *n* a firm swelling composed of scar tissue. [Ety as for **desmid**, and **-oid**]

désobligeante *dāz-ob-lēzh-ãt*, *n* a carriage for one. [Fr, unaccommodating]

désœuvré *dāz-œv-rā*, (*Fr*) *adj* unoccupied; at a loose end.

desolate *des'ō-lāt*, *vt* to make lonely or forlorn; to make extremely sad; to deprive of inhabitants; to lay waste. — *adj* (*-lit*) comfortless; dreary; forlorn; lonely; totally lacking in inhabitants; laid waste. — *adv* **des'olately**. — *n* **des'olateness**. — *n* **des'olāter** or **des'olātor**. — *n* **desolā'tion** waste; destruction; a place desolated; misery, wretchedness. — *adj* **des'olatory**. [L *dēsōlāre*, *-ātum*, from *dē-* (intensive) and *sōlāre* to make alone, from *sōlus* alone]

desorb. See **desorption**.

désorienté *dāz-or-ē-ã-tā*, (*Fr*) *adj* having lost one's bearings, confused.

desorption *dē-sörp'shən*, (*chem*) *n* release from an adsorbed state. — *vt* **desorb'**. [**de-** (2)]

desoxy-. See **deoxy-** under **deoxidate**.

despair *di-spār'*, *vi* to be without hope (of). — *n* hopelessness; anything which causes despair. — *adj* **despair'ful** (*archaic*; *Spenser*). — *adj* **despair'ing** apt to despair; full of despair. — *adv* **despair'ingly**. [OFr *desperer*, from L *dēspērāre*, *-ātum*, from *dē-* (negative) and *spērāre* to hope]

despatch. See **dispatch**.

desperado *des-pər-ä'dō*, *-ā'dō*, *n* a desperate person, reckless of danger; a wild ruffian: — *pl* **despera'dos** or **despera'does**. [Old Sp (mod *desesperado*), from L *dēspērātus*]

desperate *des'pər-it*, *adj* in a state of despair; hopeless; beyond hope; despairingly reckless; (loosely) furious; extremely bad; extremely anxious or eager (for, to do, etc) (*colloq*). — *adv* **des'perately**. — *n* **des'perateness**. — *n* **desperā'tion** a state of despair; despairing; disregard of danger; fury; recklessness. [See **despair**]

despicable *dis-pik'ə-bl*, *des'pik-*, *adj* deserving to be despised; contemptible; worthless. — *n* **despicabil'ity** or **despic'ableness** (or *des'pik-*). — *adv* **despic'ably** (or *des'*). [See **despise**]

despight *di-spīt'*. An old spelling of **despite**.

despise *di-spīz'*, *vt* to look down upon with contempt, scorn, hate. — *adj* **despīs'able**. — *n* **despīs'al** contempt. — *n* **despīs'edness** (*Milton*). — *n* **despīs'er**. [OFr *despire* (*despis-*), from L *dēspicere*, from *dē* down, and *specere* to look]

despite *di-spīt'*, *n* (*obs*) a looking down with contempt; violent malice or hatred. — *prep* in spite of; notwithstanding. — *adj* **despite'ful** (*archaic*). — *adv* **despite'fully** (*archaic*). — *n* **despite'fulness** (*archaic*). — *adj* **despiteous** (*dis-pit'i-əs*; *archaic*; *Spenser*, etc). [OFr *despit* (mod *dépit*), from L *dēspectus*, from *dēspicere*; see **despise**]

despoil *di-spoil'*, *vt* to plunder completely; to strip; to bereave; to rob. — *n* **despoil'er**. — *n* **despoil'ment**. [OFr *despoiller* (mod *dépouiller*; see **despoliation**)]

despoliation *di-spōl-i-ā'shən*, *n* despoiling. [L *dēspoliāre*, from *dē-* (intensive) and *spolium* spoil]

despond *di-spond'*, *vi* to be lacking in hope, to be dejected. — *n* (*Bunyan*) despondency. — *n* **despond'ence** or **despond'ency** lack of hope, dejection. — *adj* **despond'**-

ent. — *adv* **despond'ently**. — *n* and *adj* **despond'ing**. — *adv* **despond'ingly**. [L *dēspondēre* to promise, to devote, to resign, to despond, from *dē* away, and *spondēre* to promise]

despot *des'pot, -pət, n* someone invested with absolute power; a tyrant. — *n* **des'potat** or **des'potate** a territory governed by a despot. — *adj* **despotic** (*dis-pot'ik*) or **despot'ical** pertaining to or like a despot; having absolute power; tyrannical. — *adv* **despot'ically**. — *n* **despot'icalness**. — *n* **des'potism** absolute power; a state governed by a despot. — *n* **despotoc'racy** government by a despot. [OFr *despot*, from Gr *despotēs* a master]

despumate *di-spū'māt* or *des'pū-māt, vi* to throw off impurities in foam or scum. — *vt* to skim. — *n* **despumā'tion**. [L *dēspūmāre, -ātum*, from *dē-* off, and *spūma* foam]

desquamate *des'kwə-māt, vi* (*esp* of the skin affected by disease) to scale off. — *n* **desquamā'tion** a scaling off; the separation of the cuticle or skin in scales. — *adj* **desquamative** (*di-skwam'ə-tiv*). — *adj* **desquam'atory**. [L *dēsquāmāre, -ātum*, from *dē-* off, and *squāma* a scale]

des res *dez rez*, (*colloq; facetious*, or *property jargon*) *n* a desirable residence. [From abbrev used in small ads, brochures, etc]

desse *des*, (*Spenser*) *n* a desk. [**dais**]

dessert *diz-ûrt', n* a final course of a meal, pudding or other sweet item; fruit, sweetmeats, etc served at the end of a meal. — **dessert'-serv'ice** the dishes used for dessert; **dessert'spoon** a spoon used for eating desserts, smaller than a tablespoon and larger than a teaspoon; **dessert'spoon'ful**: — *pl* **dessert'spoonfuls**. [OFr *dessert*, from *desservir* to clear the table, from *des-* (L *dis-*) away, and *servir* to serve, from L *servīre*]

dessiatine, **dessyatine** or **desyatin** *des'yə-tēn, n* a Russian measure of land, 2·7 English acres (about 1·1 hectares). [Russ *desyatīna* a measure of land, a tenth; *desyat'* ten]

destabilize or **-ise** *dē-stā'bil-īz, vt* to make unstable or less stable (*lit* and *fig*). — *n* **destā'bilizer** or **-s-**. [**de-** (2)]

de-Stalinize or **-ise** *dē-stä'li-nīz, vt* to remove the influence of Joseph Stalin from (Russian politics, etc). — *n* **de-Stalinīzā'tion** or **-s-**.

destemper. See **distemper**[1].

De Stijl *də stīl*, an (*orig* Dutch) artistic movement of the 1920s, embracing neoplasticism and Dada, and having an influence on contemporary architecture and design. [Du, the style (the title of the movement's magazine)]

destine *des'tin, vt* (often by fate) to ordain or appoint to a certain use or state; to intend; to fix; to doom. — Also **des'tinate** (*obs*). — *n* **destinā'tion** the purpose or end to which anything is destined or appointed; end; purpose; design; fate; the place to which one is going; (the nomination of) the series of heirs to whom property, etc is to pass (*Scots law*). — *n* **des'tiny** the purpose or end to which any person or thing is appointed; unavoidable fate; necessity. [Fr *destiner*, from L *dēstināre*, from *dē-* (intensive) and root of *stāre* to stand]

destitute *des'ti-tūt, adj* left alone, forsaken (*obs*); in utter poverty; entirely lacking in (with *of*). — *vt* (*obs*) to forsake; to deprive. — *n* **destitu'tion** the state of being destitute; poverty; deprivation of office. [L *dēstituere, -ūtum*, from *dē-* away, and *statuere* to place]

destrier *des'tri-ər, des-trēr'*, (*archaic*) *n* a warhorse. [Fr, from L *dextrārius* led by the (squire's) right hand]

destroy *di-stroi', vt* to demolish, pull down; to overturn; to defeat or kill; to ruin; to put an end to: — *prp* **destroy'ing**; *pa t* and *pa p* **destroyed'**. — *adj* **destroy'-able**. — *n* **destroy'er** a person or thing that destroys; a small, fast-moving warship. — **destroying angel** *Amanita phalloides* or *Amanita virosa*, two poisonous toadstools, whitish in colour, with a volva at the base of the stalk. [OFr *destruire* (Fr *détruire*), from L *dēstruere, dēstructum*, from *dē-* down, and *struere* to build]

destruction *di-struk'shən, n* the act or process of destroying; overthrow; physical or moral ruin; death; a cause of destruction. — *vt* **destruct'** to destroy a rocket or missile in flight. — Also *vi*. — *adj* **destruc'tible** capable of being or liable to be destroyed. — *n* **destructibil'ity** or **destruc'tibleness**. — *adj* **destruc'tional**. — *n* **destruc'-tionist** a person engaged in destruction; a person who believes in the final annihilation of the damned. — *adj* **destruc'tive** causing or concerned with destruction; (of eg criticism) unhelpfully negative (*opp* of *constructive*); mischievous. — *n* a destroying agent. — *adv* **destruc'-tively**. — *n* **destruc'tiveness**. — *n* **destruc'tivist** a representative of destructive principles. — *n* **destruct-iv'ity** (*dē-*). — *n* **destruc'tor** (*di-*) a destroyer; a furnace for burning up refuse. — **destructive distillation** the decomposition of solid substances by heating, and the subsequent collection of the volatile substances produced. [L *dēstruere, -structum*; see **destroy**]

desuetude *di-sū'i-tūd, des'wi-tūd, n* disuse; discontinuance. [L *dēsuētūdō*, from *dēsuētum, dēsuēscere*, from *dē* (negative) and *suēscere* to become used]

desulphur *dē-sul'fər, vt* to remove sulphur from. — Also **desul'phūrāte** or **desul'phūrize** or **-ise**. — *n* **desulphūrā'-tion**. — *n* **desulphūrizā'tion** or **-s-**. — *n* **desul'phūrizer** or **-s-**. [**de-** (2)]

desultory *des'əl-tər-i, adj* jumping from one thing to another; without rational or logical connection; rambling; hasty; loose. — *adv* **des'ultorily**. — *n* **des'ultoriness**. [L *dēsultōrius*, from *dēsultor* a vaulter, *dēsilīre, -sultum* to leap, from *dē* from, and *salīre* to jump]

desyatin. See **dessiatine**.

desyne (*Spenser*). Same as **design**.

detach *di-tach', vt* to unfasten; to take away or separate; to withdraw; to send off on special service (*military*). — *vi* to separate. — *adj* **detach'able**. — *adj* **detached'** unconnected; separate; impartial; aloof; free from care, passion, ambition and worldly bonds. — *adv* **detach'edly**. — *n* **detach'edness**. — *n* **detach'ment** the state of being detached; the act of detaching; that which is detached, eg a unit of troops from the main body. [Fr *détacher*, from OFr pfx *des-* (L *dis-*) apart, and root of **attach**]

detail *di-tāl'* or *dē'tāl vt* to relate minutely; to enumerate; to set apart for a particular service. — *vi* to give details about anything. — *n* (*dē'tāl*, or *esp NAm di-tāl'*) a small or unimportant part; an item; a particular account; too much attention to relatively unimportant particulars; (chiefly *military*) a small body set apart for special duty. — *adj* **detailed'** giving full particulars; exhaustive. — **detail drawing** (*building*) large-scale working drawing (*usu* of a part only) giving information which does not appear on small-scale drawings of the whole construction. — **go into detail** to study, discuss, etc a matter deeply, considering the particulars; **in detail** circumstantially, point by point; piecemeal. [Fr *détailler*, from *de-* (intensive) and *tailler* to cut]

detain *di-tān', vt* to hold back; to withhold; to delay; to stop; to keep; to keep in custody. — *n* (*Spenser*) detention. — *adj* **detain'able**. — *n* **detain'ee** a person kept in custody. — *n* **detain'er** a person who detains; the holding of what belongs to another (*law*); a warrant to a sheriff to keep in custody a person already in confinement. — *n* **detain'ment** detention. [OFr *detenir*, from L *dētinēre*; see **detent**]

detect *di-tekt', vt* to discover; to discern; to find out (*esp* something elusive or secret); to uncover, expose (*obs*); to accuse (*obs; Shakesp*). — *adj* **detect'able** or **detect'-ible**. — *n* **detec'tion** the discovery of something hidden or not easily observed; the state of being found out. — *adj* **detect'ive** employed in or concerned with detection. — *n* a policeman, *usu* not in uniform, or other person (*private detective*) who investigates cases of crime or watches the behaviour of suspected persons. — *n* **detect'ivist** a writer of detective fiction. — *n* **detect'ōphone** a secret telephone for eavesdropping. — *n* **detec'tor** someone who detects; an apparatus for detecting something, eg smoke, tampering with a lock, pressure of electric currents, electric waves, etc. — **detective story** one in which clues to the detection of a criminal are set forth and unravelled. [L *dētegere*, *-tēctum*, from *dē-* (negative) and *tegere*, to cover]

detent *di-tent'*, *n* anything that checks motion; a catch, *esp* for regulating the striking of a clock. — *n* **deten'tion** the act of detaining; the state of being detained; confinement, or restriction of liberty, *esp* of a political prisoner or any offender; delay. — **detention centre** a place of confinement for young offenders from 14 to 20 years old for periods of up to 6 months. [L *dētinēre*, *dētentum*, from *dē* from, and *tenēre* to hold]

détente *dā-tāt*, (*Fr*) *n* relaxation of strained relations (*esp* between countries).

détenu *dā-tə-nü*, (*Fr*) *n* a prisoner, *esp* a political prisoner in India: — *fem* **détenue**.

deter *di-tûr'*, *vt* to frighten (from); to hinder or prevent: — *pr p* **deterr'ing**; *pa t* and *pa p* **deterred'**. — *n* **deter'ment**. — *n* **deterrence** (*di-ter'əns*). — *adj* **deterrent** (*di-ter'ənt*) serving to deter. — *n* anything that deters; *specif* a nuclear weapon. [L *dēterrēre*, from *dē* from, and *terrēre* to frighten]

deterge *di-tûrj'*, *vt* to wipe off; to cleanse (eg a wound). — *n* **deterg'ence** or **deterg'ency**. — *n* **deterg'ent** (also *rarely* **deters'ive**) that which cleanses; a cleansing agent, such as an abrasive, a solvent or mixture of solvents, and certain water-soluble oils, *esp* (commonly) a soapless cleanser. — *adj* (also **deters'ive**) cleansing; purging. [L *dētergēre*, *dētersum*, from *dē* off, and *tergēre* to wipe]

deteriorate *di-tē'ri-ə-rāt*, *vt* to make worse. — *vi* to grow worse. — *n* **dete̅riorā'tion** the act of making worse; the process of growing worse. — *n* **dete̅riorā'tionist** a believer in deteriorism. — *adj* **dete̅'riorātive**. — *n* **dete̅'riorism** the doctrine that the world grows worse. — *n* **dete̅riority** (*-or'i-ti*; *obs*) worseness. [L *dēteriōrāre*, *-ātum* to make worse, from *dēterior* worse, from *dē* down]

determine *dē-tûr'min*, *vt* to put terms or bounds to; to limit; to fix or settle; to define; to decide; to resolve; to cause to resolve; to put an end to (*law*). — *vi* to come to a decision; to come to an end (*law*); to cease to exist (*Shakesp*); to take part in a dispute, *esp* in completing the degree of bachelor of arts (*obs*). — *n* **determin-abil'ity**. — *adj* **deter'minable** capable of being determined, decided or finished. — *n* **deter'minableness**. — *adv* **deter'minably**. — *n* **deter'minacy** (*-ə-si*). — *adj* **deter'minant** serving to determine. — *n* that which serves to determine; the sum of all the products obtained by taking one from each row and column of a square block of quantities, each product being reckoned positive or negative according as an even or an odd number of transpositions reduces it to the order of the rows (or of the columns), used for the solution of equations and other purposes (*math*); a hypothetical unit in the germ-plasm determining the course of development of a cell (*bot*); a determining candidate for the BA degree (*obs*). — *adj* **deter'mināte** determined or limited; fixed; decisive; cymose, having the main stem and branches ending in flowers (*bot*). — *vt* (*obs*; *Shakesp*) to determine. — *adv* **deter'minately**. — *n* **determinā'tion** the act of determining; the condition of being determined; that which is determined or resolved on; end (*law*); direction to a certain end; resolution; fixedness of purpose; decision of character. — *adj* **deter'minātive** that determines, limits or defines. — *n* (in hieroglyphics) an additional sign attached to a word as a guide to its meaning. — *adj* **deter'mined** ascertained; fixed; firm in purpose; resolute. — *adv* **deter'minedly**. — *n* **deter'miner** someone who, or that which, determines; a determinant (*bot*); a limiting adjective or modifying word such as *any*, *each*, *that*, *my*, etc (*gram*). — *n* **deter'minism** the doctrine that all things, including the will, are determined by causes (the converse of free-will); necessitarianism. — *n* **deter'-minist**. — *adj* **determinis'tic**. [L *dēterminăre*, *-ātum*, from *dē* (intensive) and *terminus* a boundary]

deterrent. See **deter**.

detersion *di-tûr'shən*, *n* the act of cleansing. — *adj* and *n* **deter'sive** detergent. [See **deterge**]

detest *di-test'*, *vt* to hate intensely. — *adj* **detest'able** (*Spenser* and *Shakesp dē'*) worthy of being detested; extremely hateful; abominable. — *n* **detestabil'ity** or **detest'ableness**. — *adv* **detest'ably**. — *n* **detestation** (*dē-tes-tā'shən*) (an object of) extreme hatred. [Fr, from L *dētestāri*, from *dē* (intensive) and *testāri* to call to witness, execrate, from *testis* a witness]

dethrone *di-thrōn'*, *vt* to remove from a throne. — *n* **dethrone'ment**. — *n* **dethrōn'er**. — *n* **dethrōn'ing**. [**de-** (2)]

detinue *det'in-ū*, (*law*) *n* wrongful detention of property. [OFr *detenue*, fem pa p of *detenir*; see **detain**]

detonate *det'ə-nāt* or *dēt'ō-nāt*, *vt* and *vi* to explode or cause to explode rapidly and loudly; in an internal-combustion engine, to explode by spontaneous combustion with a hammering sound (pinking or knock). — *n* **detonā'tion** an explosion with report; in an internal-combustion engine, premature combustion of part of the mixture, causing knocking or pinking. — *n* **det'onātor** a substance that detonates; a substance or contrivance whose explosion initiates that of another explosive. [L *dētonāre*, *-ātum*, from *dē* down, and *tonāre* to thunder]

detort *di-tört'*, *vt* (*obs*) to distort; to untwist; to twist the other way. — *n* (*biol*) **detor'sion** or (*obs*) **detor'tion**. [L *dētorquēre*, *dētortum*; *dē* away (also negative) and *torquēre* to twist]

detour *dē'*, *dā'to͞or* *n* a deviation; a circuitous way. — Also *vt* and *vi*. [Fr *dé-* (L *dis-*) asunder, and *tour* turning]

detox *dē-toks*, (*orig US*; *colloq*) *vt* short form of **detoxify**. — *n* (*dē'toks*) short form of **detoxification**; a detoxification centre (also **detox tank**).

detoxicate *dē-toks'i-kāt*, or **detox'ify** *-i-fī*, *vt* to rid of poison or the effects of it. — *n* **detox'icant** a substance that detoxicates. — Also *adj*. — *n* **detoxicā'tion** or **detoxificā'tion**. — **detoxification centre** a centre for the treatment of alcoholism or drug addiction. [**de-** (2)]

detract *di-trakt'* *vt* to take away, abate; to distract; to defame (*obs*). — *vi* (with *from*) to take away from; to reduce in degree; to diminish. — *n* **detract'or** a belittler or disparager: — *fem* **detract'ress**. — *n* and *adj* **detract'ing**. — *adv* **detract'ingly**. — *n* **detrac'tion** depreciation; slander. — *adj* **detract'ive** or **detract'ory** tending to detract; derogatory. — *adv* **detract'ively**. [L *dētrahere*, from *dē* from, and *trahere*, *tractum* to draw]

detrain *dē-trān'*, *vt* to set down out of a railway train. — *vi* to alight from a train. — *n* **detrain'ment**. [**de-** (2)]

détraqué *dā-trä-kā*, *fem* **détraquée**, *n* a person who is deranged. [Fr, upset, out of order]

detribalize or **-ise** *dē-trī'bə-līz*, *vt* to cause to lose tribal characteristics, customs, etc, *usu* in favour of an urban way of life. — *n* **detribalīzā'tion** or **-s-**. [**de-** (2)]

detriment *det'ri-mənt*, *n* diminution; damage; loss; a thing that causes diminution, damage or loss. — *adj* **detrimental** (*-ment'l*). — *n* (*archaic slang*) a suitor undesirable owing to lack of means or other defect; someone whose presence lessens the chances of a good match. — *adv* **detriment'ally**. [L *dētrīmentum*, from *dē* off, and *terere*, *trītum* to rub]

detritus *di-trī'təs*, *n* a mass of substance gradually worn off solid bodies; an aggregate of loosened fragments, *esp* of rock; accumulated debris. — *adj* **detrī'tal**. — *n* **detrition** (*di-trish'ən*) wearing away. [L *dētrītus* worn, from *dē* off, and *terere*, *trītum* to rub]

de trop *də trō*, (*Fr*) *adj* (used after the noun) superfluous; in the way.

detrude *di-tro͞od'*, *vt* to thrust down. — *n* **detru'sion**. [L *dētrūdere*, from *dē* down, and *trūdere* to thrust]

detruncate *di-trung'kāt*, *vt* to cut short; to lop; to mutilate. — *n* **detrunca'tion** (*dē-*). [L *dētruncāre*, *-ātum*, from *dē* off, and *truncāre*, to lop]

detumescence *dē-tū-mes'əns*, *n* diminution of swelling (*opp* to *intumescence*). [**de-** (2)]

detune *dē-tūn'*, *vt* to alter the oscillations of (violin strings, an electronic circuit, etc); to reduce the performance and efficiency of (a motor-car engine). [**de-** (2)]

deuce[1] *dūs* or *NAm dōōs*, *n* a card or die with two spots; a situation ('forty all') in which one side must gain two successive points to win the game, or ('five all', 'games all') two successive games to win the set (*tennis*); a throw of two at dice; two dollars (*US slang*). — **deuce'-ace** a throw of two dice turning up deuce and ace; bad luck. [Fr *deux* two, from L *duōs* accusative of *duo* two]

deuce[2] *dūs*, *n* (in exclamatory phrases) the devil. — *adj* **deuced** (*dū'sid* or *dūst*) (as an intensifier) damned, absolute, etc. — *adv* confoundedly; extremely. — Also **deuc'edly**. [Prob from the **deuce** (see **deuce**[1]), the lowest throw at dice]

deuch-an-doris. See **deoch-an-doruis**.

deuddarn *dī'dhärn*, *n* a Welsh dresser or sideboard in two stages. [Welsh]

deus *dē'əs*, *dā'ōōs*, (*L*) *n* god: — *pl* **di** (*dī* or *dē*). — **Deus avertat** (*a-vûr'tat*, *ä-wer'tat*) God forbid; **Deus det** (*det*) God grant; **deus ex machina** (*eks mak'in-a*, sometimes *mə-shē'nə*) *orig*, a god brought on the stage by a mechanical device; a contrived and inartistic solution of a difficulty in a plot; **Deus vobiscum** (*vō-bis'kəm*, *wō-bēs'kōōm*) God be with you; **Deus vult** (*vult* or *wōōlt*) God wills it (the Crusaders' cry).

Deut. (*Bible*) *abbrev*: (the Book of) Deuteronomy.

deuter- *dū-tər-*, or **deutero-** *dū-tər-ō-*, *combining form* denoting second or secondary. — *n* **deuterag'onist** the second actor in a Greek drama. — *n* **deu'teranope** a person suffering from deuteranopia. — *n* **deuteranō'pia** (Gr *ops* eye) a type of colour-blindness in which red and green are confused, blue and yellow only being distinguished. — *adj* **deuteranop'ic**. — *vt* **deu'terate** to add deuterium to, or to replace hydrogen by deuterium in (molecules). — *n* **deuterā'tion**. — *n* **deu'teride** a hydrogen compound containing another element. — *n* **deuterium** (*-tē'ri-əm*) heavy hydrogen, an isotope of hydrogen of double mass. — *adj* **deuterocanon'ical** (Gr *kanōn* rule) pertaining to a second canon of inferior authority, ie the Old Testament Apocrypha and the New Testament Antilegomena. — *n* **deuterog'amist** a person who allows or practises deuterogamy. — **deuterog'amy** (Gr *gamos* marriage) second marriage, *esp* of the clergy, after the death of the first wife. — *n* **deu'teron** the nucleus of heavy hydrogen, of mass 2, carrying unit positive charge. — *n* **Deuteronomy** (*-on'ə-mi* or *dū'*; Gr *nomos* law) the fifth book of the Pentateuch, containing a repetition of the decalogue and laws given in Exodus. — *adj* **Deuteronom'ic** or **Deuteronom'ic**. — *n* **Deuteron'omist** the author of the book of Deuteronomy or part of it. — *n* **deu'teroplasm** same as **deutoplasm**. — *n* **deuteros'copy** (Gr *skopiā* a look-out) a second view or meaning (*obs*); second sight. — *adj* **deuteroscop'ic**. — **deuterium oxide** heavy water. [Gr *deuteros* second]

deuton *dū'ton*, (*obs*) older form of **deuteron**.

deutoplasm *dū'tō-plazm*, (*biol*) *n* the food material, such as yolk or fat, within an egg or cell. — *adj* **deuto-plas'mic**. [Fr *deutoplasme*]

Deutschmark *doich'märk* or **Deutsche Mark** *doich'ə märk* *n* the standard monetary unit (100 pfennig) of Germany (and of West Germany prior to unification). [Ger]

Deutzia *dūt'si-ə* or *doit'si-ə*, *n* a genus of saxifragaceous plants with panicles of white flowers, introduced from China and Japan. [After Jan *Deutz*, 18c Dutch naturalist]

Deuxième Bureau *dø-zyem bü-rō*, (*Fr*) *n* the French Department of Military Intelligence.

deva *dā'vä*, (*Hinduism* and *Buddhism*) *n* a god; a good spirit. [Sans *deva* a shining one, a god]

devall *di-völ'*, *vi* to sink, decline (*obs*); to cease (*Scot*). — *n* (*Scot*) a stop. [Fr *dévaler*, from L *dē-* down, and *vallis* a valley]

devalue *dē-val'ū*, *vt* to reduce the value of. — Also *vi* (*esp* of currency). — *n* **devalorizā'tion** or **-s-** devaluation. — *n* **devaluā'tion** (*econ*) reducing the value internationally of a country's money, by lowering the exchange rate. — *vt* **deval'orize** or **-ise**. — *vt* **deval'uate**. [**de-** (2)]

devanagari *dā-və-nä'gə-ri*, *n* the script in which Sanskrit and Hindi are *usu* written and printed (the official script for Hindi); used also for other Indian languages. — Also with *cap*. [Sans *devanāgari* town-script of the gods; see **nagari**]

devastate *dev'əs-tāt*, *vt* to lay waste; to plunder; to shock or greatly disappoint (*colloq*). — *adj* **dev'astating** ravaging; overpoweringly effective (*colloq*). — *adv* **dev'astatingly**. — *n* **devastā'tion** the act of devastating; the state of being devastated; havoc; waste of property by an executor. — *adj* **dev'astātive**. — *n* **dev'astātor**. — *n* **dēvastā'vit** (L, has wasted) a writ lying against an executor for devastation; the offence of devastation. [L *dēvastāre*, *-ātum*, from *dē-* (intensive) and *vastāre* to lay waste]

devel. See **devvel**.

develop (earlier also **develope**) *di-vel'əp*, *vt* to unroll (*obs*); to lay open by degrees (*obs*); to free from integuments or that which envelops; to bring out what is latent or potential in; to bring to a more advanced or more highly organized state; to work out the potentialities of; to elaborate; to cause to grow or advance; to evolve; to contract (a disease); to make more available; to exploit the natural resources of (a region); to build on or prepare (land) for building on; to bring into a position useful in attack (*chess*); to disclose; to express in expanded form (*math*); to unroll into a plane surface (*geom*); to render visible the image on a negative by the use of chemicals (*photog*). — *vi* to open out; to evolve; to advance through successive stages to a higher, more complex, or more fully grown state: — *pr p* **devel'oping**; *pa t* and *pa p* **devel'oped**. — *adj* **devel'opable**. — *adj* **devel'oped**. — *n* **devel'oper** a person who develops, *esp* property; a reagent for developing photographs; an apparatus for developing muscles. — *n* **develop'ment** the act or process of developing; the state of being developed; a gradual unfolding or growth; evolution; the expression of a function in the form of a series (*math*); elaboration of a theme, or that part of a movement in which this occurs (*music*); new situations that emerge. — *adj* **development'al** pertaining to development. — *adv* **development'ally**. — **development area** a region of heavy unemployment where new industry is given official encouragement. [Fr *développer*, opposed to *envelopper*, of obscure origin]

devest *di-vest'*, *vt* to undress (*Shakesp*); to alienate (*law*); to take off; to strip. [A form of **divest**]

Devi *dā'vē*, *n* in India, used as a title for a married woman (following her name). [Sans, goddess]

deviate *dē'vi-āt*, *vi* to go from the way; to turn aside from a certain course; to diverge or differ, from a standard, mean value, etc; to err; to step outside one's fundamental contractual duty (*law*). — *vt* to cause to diverge. — *n* (*dē'vi-ət*; *psychol*) a person who deviates much from the norm, *esp* sexually; a deviant. — *n* **dē'viance** or **dē'viancy**. — *n* **dē'viant** someone who deviates from the norm, *esp* sexually. — Also *adj*. — *n* **dēviā'tion**. — *n* **dēviā'tionism**. — *n* **dēviā'tionist** a communist whose doctrine deviates from the strictly orthodox. — *n* **dē'viātor**. — *adj* **dēviā'tory**. — **deviation of the compass** departure of the mariner's compass from the magnetic meridian, owing to the ship's magnetism or other local causes; **standard deviation** the square root of the variance of a number of observations (*math*). [L *dēviāre*, *-ātum*, from *dē* from, and *via* a way]

device *di-vīs'*, *n* that which is devised or designed; a contrivance; a plan or scheme; one of a number of physical parts of a system, eg a computer system (as *input device*, *storage device*); power of devising; an emblem (*heraldry*); a motto; a conceit (*obs*); a masque (*obs*). — *adj* **device'ful** (*Spenser*; now *rare*) full of devices. — **leave someone to their own devices** to leave someone alone, not distracting or interfering with them. [OFr *devise*; see **devise**]

devil *dev'l* or *-il*, *n* an evil spirit; (with *cap*) the supreme spirit of evil; a wicked person; reckless, lively person; (*usu* pitying) a fellow; an animal, thing, problem, difficult, etc to deal with; someone who excels or exceeds in anything; a printer's devil; a drudge (*esp legal* or *literary*); a firework; a grilled or highly seasoned dish; a dust-storm; fighting spirit; a plumber's portable furnace; a machine of various kinds, *esp* for tearing; used as a mild oath, an expression of impatience, irritation, etc, or a strong negative. — *vt* to season highly and broil. — *vi* to perform another person's drudgery; to do very menial work: — *pr p* **dev'illing** or (*NAm*) **dev'iling**; *pa t* and *pa p* **dev'illed** or (*NAm*) **dev'iled**. — *n* **dev'ildom**. — *n* **dev'iless**. — *n* **dev'ilet**, **dev'iling** or **dev'ling** a young devil; a swift (*dialect*). — *adj* **dev'ilish** fiendish, malignant; very bad. — *adv* (often *dev'lish*; *colloq*) very, exceedingly. — *adv* **dev'ilishly**. — *n* **dev'ilism**. — *n* **dev'ilkin**. — *adj* **dev'illed**. — *n* **dev'ilment** frolicsome mischief. — *n* **dev'ilry**. — *n* **dev'ilship**. — *n* **dev'iltry** (*US*). — **dev'il-crab** the velvet crab; **dev'il-dodger** (*slang*) a preacher, *esp* of the ranting kind; someone who attends churches of various kinds, to be on the safe side; **dev'il-fish** the fishing-frog or angler; the giant ray of the United States; the octopus; **dev'il-in-a-bush** a garden flower, love-in-a-mist. — *adj* **dev'il-may-care'** reckless, audacious. — **dev'il-on-the-neck** an old instrument of torture; **dev'il-on-two-sticks** older name for diabolo; **devil's advocate** advocatus diaboli, the Promoter of the Faith, an advocate at the papal court whose duty it is to propose objections against a canonization (*RC*); a person who states the case against a proposal, course of action, etc, *usu* for the sake of argument; **dev'il's-bit** a species of scabious (*Succisa pratensis*) with rootstock as if bitten off; **devil's bones** dice; **devil's books** playing-cards; **devil's coach-horse** a large dark-coloured beetle (*Ocypus olens*); **devil's darning-needle** (*colloq*) a dragonfly or damselfly; **devil's dozen** thirteen; **devil's dung** asafoetida; **devil's dust** shoddy made by a machine called the **devil**; **devil's food cake** (chiefly *US*) a kind of chocolate cake; **dev'ils-on-horse'back** prunes wrapped in bacon, grilled, and served on toast; **devil's own** a name given to the 88th Regiment in the Peninsular War, also to the Inns of Court Volunteers; **devil's picture-books** (also in *sing*) same as **devil's books**; **devil's snuff-box** a puff-ball; **devil's tattoo** see under **tattoo**[1]; **dev'il-worship** the worship of the Devil, or of devils; Satanism; the Yezidi religion; **dev'il-worshipper**. — **between the devil and the deep (blue) sea** in a desperate dilemma; faced with alternatives which are equally undesirable; **devil a bit, a one** or **a thing** etc, not at all, not one, etc; **devil of a mess** a very bad mess; **devil take the hindmost** take care of yourself and never mind about others; **go to the devil** to become ruined; (*interj*) go away!; **play the devil** to make havoc (with); **printer's devil** the youngest apprentice in a printing-office; a printer's errand-boy; **raise hell** or **raise the devil** see under **raise**; **talk of the devil** here comes the person we were talking of; **the devil and all** much fuss; turmoil; **the devil to pay** serious trouble (as a consequence of an action, etc). [OE *dēofol*, *dēoful*, from L *diabolus*, from Gr *diabolos*, from *diaballein* to throw across, to slander, from *dia* across, and *ballein* to throw; cf Ger *Teufel*, Fr *diable*, Ital *diavolo*, Sp *diablo*]

devious *dē'vi-əs*, *adj orig*, remote, out of the way (*archaic*); roundabout, winding; erring; insincere; tortuous of mind; scheming; deceitful. — *adv* **dē'viously**. — *n* **dē'viousness**. [L *dēvius*; see **deviate**]

devise *di-vīz'*, *vt* to imagine; to compose; to scheme, think out; to contrive; to bequeath (*law*); to suppose, guess (*Spenser*); to purpose (*Spenser*); to meditate (*obs*); to describe (*obs*); to depict (*obs*). — *vi* (*obs*) to consider; to talk; to scheme. — *n* the act of bequeathing; a will; property bequeathed by will. — *adj* **devīs'able**. — *n* **devīs'al**. — *n* **devīsee** (*dev-ī-zē'*) a person to whom property is bequeathed. — *n* **devī'ser** a person who contrives. — *n* **devīs'or** a person who bequeaths. — **devisal of arms** formerly synonymous with grant of arms, now used by the English College of Arms where the petitioner is an American corporate body and therefore ineligible for a grant of arms. [OFr *deviser*, *devise*, from LL *dīvīsa* a division of goods, a mark, a device, from L *dīvidere*, *dīvīsum* to divide]

devitalize or **-ise** *dē-vī'tə-līz*, *vt* to deprive of vitality or life-giving qualities. — *n* **devitalīzā'tion** or **-s-**. [**de-** (2)]

devitrify *dē-vit'ri-fī*, *vt* to change from glassy to minutely crystalline. — *n* **devitrification** (*-fi-kā'*). [**de-** (2)]

devling. See **devilet** under **devil**.

devocalize or **-ise** *dē-vō'kə-līz* or **devoice** *dē-vois'*, *vt* to make voiceless. [**de-** (2)]

devoid *di-void'*, *adj* (with *of*) destitute, free; empty. [OFr *desvoidier*, from *des-* (L *dis-* away), and *voider*, from L *viduāre*, from *viduus* deprived]

devoir *dev'wär* (historically *dev'ər*), *n* (often in *pl*) what is due, duty (*archaic*); service (*obs*); a courtesy; an act of civility. [Fr, from L *dēbēre* to owe]

devolution *dēv-* or *dev-ə-lo͞o'shən*, *-lū'*, *n* a passing from one person to another; a handing over of powers; a modified home rule, the delegation of certain powers to regional governments by a central government. — *adj* **devolu'tionary**. — *n* **devolu'tionist**. [See **devolve**]

devolve *di-volv'*, *vt* to roll down (*archaic*); to pass on; to hand down; to deliver over, *esp* powers to regional governments by a central government. — *vi* to roll down (*archaic*); to fall or pass over in succession (with *on*). — *n* **devolve'ment**. [L *dēvolvere*, *-volūtum*, from *dē* down, and *volvere* to roll]

Devonian *di-vō'ni-ən*, *adj* belonging to *Devonshire*; (of rock) belonging to a period between the Silurian and the Carboniferous, and *esp* to the marine type, well seen in Devon (the continental type being the Old Red Sandstone; *geol*). — *n* a native of Devonshire; the Devonian rock system. — **Devon** or **Devon minnow** an angler's lure that imitates a swimming minnow.

devonport *dev'n-pōrt*, *-pört*. Same as **davenport**.

Devonshire cream *dev'n-shər krēm*, *n* clotted cream.

dévot *dā-vō*, *fem* **dévote** *dā-vōt*, (*Fr*) *n* a devotee.

devote *di-vōt'*, *vt* to set apart or dedicate by a vow or solemn act; to give up (oneself or something) wholly (to); to doom (*obs*). — *adj* (*Shakesp* and *archaic*) devoted. — *adj* **devōt'ed** given up (to), as by a vow; strongly attached (to); zealous; doomed (*obs*). — *adv* **devōt'edly**. — *n* **devōt'edness**. — *n* **devotee** (*dev-ə-tē'* or *dev'*) a person wholly or superstitiously devoted, *esp* to religion; a votary; someone strongly and consistently interested in something (with *of*). — *n* **devōte'ment** (*Shakesp* and *archaic*). — *n* **devō'tion** the act of devoting; the state of being devoted; consecration; giving up of the mind to the worship of God; piety; prayer; strong affection or attachment; ardour; faithful service; (in *pl*) prayers; religious offerings (*obs*); alms (*obs*). — *adj* **devō'tional**. — *n* **devō'tionalist**. — *n* **devōtional'ity**. — *n* **devō'tionalness**. — *n* **devō'tionist**. — *adv* **devō'tionally**. [L *dēvovēre*, *dēvōtum*, from *dē* away, and *vovēre* to vow]

devour *di-vowr'*, *vt* to swallow greedily; to eat up; to consume or waste with violence or wantonness; to take in eagerly by the senses or mind. — *n* **devour'er**. — *adj* **devour'ing**. — *adv* **devour'ingly**. — *n* **devour'ment**. [OFr *devorer*, from L *dēvorāre*, from *dē* (intensive) and *vorāre* to swallow]

devout *di-vowt'*, *adj* given up to religious thoughts and exercises; pious; solemn; earnest. — *adv* **devout'ly**. — *n* **devout'ness**. [OFr *devot*, from L *dēvōtus*; see **devote**]

devvel or **devel** *dev'l*, (*Scot*) *n* a hard blow. — *vt* to hit hard; to stun with a blow. [Ety dubious]

dew[1] *dū*, *n* moisture deposited from the air on cooling, *esp* at night, in minute specks upon the surface of objects; a similar deposit or exudation of other kinds; early freshness. — *vt* to moisten (as) with dew (*poetic*). — *adv* **dew'ily**. — *n* **dew'iness**. — *adj* **dew'y**. — **dew'-berry** a kind of bramble or blackberry (*Rubus caesius*; in

America, other species) having a bluish, dew-like bloom on the fruit; **dew'-bow** a rainbow-like appearance seen on a dewy surface; **dew'-claw** a rudimentary inner toe, *esp* on a dog's leg; **dew'-drop** a drop of dew; a drip, a drop of mucous on the end of the nose (*colloq*); **dew'-fall** the deposition, or time of deposition, of dew; **dew'point** the temperature at which a given sample of moist air becomes saturated and forms dew; **dew'-pond** a hollow thought to be supplied with water by mist; **dew'-retting** the process of rotting away the gummy part of hemp or flax by exposure on the grass to dew and rain; **dew'-worm** the common earthworm. — *adj* **dew'y-eyed** fresh, innocent (often *ironic*). — **mountain dew** (*colloq*) whisky. [OE *dēaw*; cf ON *dögg*, Ger *Tau* dew]

dew² *dū*, *n* an obsolete spelling of **due**. — *adj* **dew'full** (*Spenser*) due.

Dewali. Same as **Diwali**.

dewan or **diwan** *dē-wän'*, *n* in India, a financial minister; a state prime minister; the native steward of a business house. — *n* **dewani** or **dewanny** (*dē-wä'nē*) the office of dewan. [Pers *dīwān*; see **divan**]

Dewar-flask *dū'ər-fläsk*, *n* (sometimes without *cap*; also **dew'ar**) a type of vacuum flask. [From Sir James *Dewar* (1842–1923), its inventor]

dewater *dē-wö'tər*, *vt* to drain or pump water from (eg coal). — *n* **dewat'ering** partial or complete drainage by eg thickening, sedimentation or filtering to facilitate shipment or drying of a product. [**de-** (2)]

Dewey decimal system *dū'i des'i-məl sis'tim* or **Dewey decimal classification** *klas'i-fi-kā'shən*, *n* a system of library classification, based on the division of books into numbered classes, with further subdivision shown by numbers following a decimal point. — Also **decimal classification**. [Invented by Melvil *Dewey* (1851–1931), US librarian]

dewitt *di-wit'*, *vt* to lynch. [From the fate of Jan and Cornelius *De Witt* in Holland in 1672]

dewlap *dū'lap*, *n* the pendulous skin under the throat of oxen, dogs, etc; the fleshy wattle of the turkey. — *adj* **dew'lapped** or **dew'lapt**. [Prob **dew** and OE *læppa* a loose hanging piece]

dexamphetamine. See **dextroamphetamine** under **dextro-**.

Dexedrine® *dek'sə-drēn*, *n* dextroamphetamine.

dexiotropic *deks-i-ō-trop'ik*, *adj* turning to the right. [Gr *dexios* right, and *tropos* turning]

dexter¹ *deks'tər*, *adj* on the right-hand side; right; of that side of the shield on the right-hand side of the bearer, the spectator's left (*heraldry*); so sometimes in description of a picture, to avoid ambiguity. — *adv* **dex'terwise**. [L, right]

dexter² *deks'tər*, *n* a small breed of Kerry cattle. — Also *adj*. [Prob breeder's name]

dexterity *deks-ter'i-ti*, *n* skill of manipulation, or generally; adroitness; right-handedness (*rare*). — *adj* **dex'terous** or **dex'trous** *orig* right-handed; adroit; subtle; skilful. — *adv* **dex'terously** or **dex'trously**. — *n* **dex'terousness** or **dex'trousness**. [L *dexter* right]

dextral *deks'trəl*, *adj* right; turning to the right; of the right-hand side of the body; of flatfish, lying right-side-up; of a spiral shell, turning in the normal manner, ie anticlockwise from the top. — *n* **dextral'ity** right-handedness. — *adv* **dex'trally**. [Med L *dextrālis*, from *dextra* right hand]

dextran *deks'tran*, *n* a carbohydrate formed in sugar solutions by a bacterium (*Leuconostoc mesenteroides*), a substitute for blood plasma in transfusion. [**dextro-**]

dextrin *deks'trin* or **dextrine** *-trēn*, *n* British gum, a gummy mixture obtained from starch by heating or otherwise, used as a thickener in foods and in adhesives.

dextro- *deks-trō-*, *combining form* denoting to, or towards, the right. — *n* **dextroamphet'amine** or **dexamphet'amine** the dextrorotatory isomer of amphetamine, used as a stimulant. — *n* **dextrocar'dia** (Gr *kardiā* heart) a condition in which the heart lies in the right side of the chest, not the left. — *n* **dextrocar'diac** a person who has this condition. — *adj* **dextrogyrate** (*-jīr*) or **dex'trogyre** (*-jīr*) causing to turn to the right hand. — *n* **dextrophos'phate** an anticoagulant and cholesterol-lowering drug whose usefulness in AIDS research is currently being tested. — *adj* **dextrorō'tatory** rotating to the right (clockwise), *esp* rotating thus the plane of polarization of light. — *n* **dextrorōtā'tion**. [L *dexter*; Gr *dexios*, Sans *dakṣiṇa* on the right, on the south]

dextrorse *deks-trörs'* or *deks'*, (*biol*) *adj* rising spirally and turning to the left, ie crossing an outside observer's field of view from left to right upwards (like a screw-nail); formerly used in the contrary sense (sinistrorse). [L *dextrōrsus* towards the right, from *dexter*, and *vertere* to turn]

dextrose *deks'trōs*, *-trōz*, *n* glucose.

dextro tempore *deks'trō tem'pər-ē*, *-por-e*, (*L*) at a lucky moment.

dextrous. See **dexterity**.

dey¹ *dā*, (*obs* or *dialect*) *n* a dairy-maid. — Also **dey'-woman**. [See **dairy**]

dey² *dā*, *n* the pasha or governor of Algiers before the French conquest. [Turk *dāi*, orig a maternal uncle, a familiar title of the chief of the janizaries]

DF *abbrev*: Defender of the Faith.

DFC *abbrev*: Distinguished Flying Cross.

DFM *abbrev*: Distinguished Flying Medal.

dft *abbrev*: defendant; draft.

DG *abbrev*: *Dei gratia* (L), by the grace of God; Director-General.

dg *abbrev*: decigram(s).

DGFT *abbrev*: Director General of Fair Trading.

d.h. *abbrev*. See **das heisst**.

dhak *däk*, *n* an Indian *Butea*. [Hindi *dhāk*]

dhal. Same as **dal**.

dharma *där'mə*, *dûr'*, *n* virtue or righteousness arising from observance of social and moral law (*Hinduism*); truth as laid down in the Buddhist scriptures; the law. [Sans]

dharmsala *dûrm-sä'lä*, *n* a building having a religious or charitable purpose, as a free or cheap lodging for travellers. — Also **dharmshala**. [Hindi *dharmsālā*, from Sans *dharma*, and *śālā* hall]

dharna *dûr'nä*, *n* calling attention, *esp* to injustice, by sitting or standing in a place (where one will be noticed, *esp* sitting and fasting at the door of an offender). [Hindi]

dhobi *dō'bi*, *n* an Indian washerman. — **dhobi itch** a tropical allergic dermatitis. [Hindi *dhobī*]

dhole *dōl*, *n* the Indian wild dog. [Supposed to be from an Indian language]

dholl. Same as **dal**.

dhooly. Same as **doolie**.

dhoti *dō'ti* or **dhooti** *dōō'ti*, *n* the Hindu loincloth; a cotton fabric used for this. [Hindi *dhotī*]

dhow, also **dow** *dow*, *n* an Arab lateen-sailed vessel of the Indian Ocean. [Origin unknown; cf Ar *dāw*, Marathi *dāw*]

DHSS *abbrev*: (until 1989) Department of Health and Social Security (now **DSS** — Department of Social Services).

dhurra. See **durra**.

dhurrie. Same as **durrie**.

DI *abbrev*: Detective Inspector; donor insemination (qv under **donation**).

di. Plural of **deus**.

di- *dī*, *pfx* denoting two, twice or double. — See also **dis-**. [Gr *dis* twice]

dia. *abbrev*: diameter.

dia- *dī'a-* or *-ə-*, *pfx* denoting: through; across; during; composed of. [Gr]

diabase *dī'əbās*, *n* (formerly) diorite; an altered dolerite or basalt. — *adj* **diabā'sic**. [Appar orig a faulty derivative of Gr *di-* double, and *basis* base; associated with *diabasis*, transition]

diabetes *dī-ə-bē'tēz*, *n* any of several diseases, marked by an excessive discharge of urine, notably **diabetes insipidus** a disease caused by a disorder of the pituitary gland leading to malfunction of the kidney, and

diabetes mellitus (*L*, honied) caused by insulin deficiency or, rarely, an excess of insulin, with excess of sugar in the blood and urine. — *adj* **diabetic** (*-bēt'* or *-bet'*) or less commonly **diabet'ical** relating to, or suffering from, diabetes; for the use of diabetics. — *n* **diabet'ic** a person suffering from diabetes. — *n* **diabetol'ogist** a doctor specializing in the study and treatment of diabetes and the care of diabetics. [Gr *diabētēs* a siphon, from *dia* through, and *bainein* to go]

diable *dē-äbl'* or *dē-abl'*, *n* an unglazed earthenware casserole with a handle and a wide base tapering up to a narrow neck. [Fr]

diablerie or **diablery** *dē-äb'lə-rē*, *n* magic; the black art; sorcery; mischief. [Fr *diable*; see **devil**]

diabolic *dī-ə-bol'ik*, *adj* of the devil; satanic; like a devil; extremely cruel. — *adj* **diabol'ical** (*colloq*) very shocking, annoying or difficult; outrageous; (as an intensifier) complete or absolute. — *adv* **diabol'ically**. — *n* **diab'olism** devil worship; devilry. — *n* **diab'olist** a person knowledgeable on diabolism. — *vt* **diabolize** or **-ise** (*-ab'ə-līz*) to make devilish. — *n* **diabol'ogy** or **diabolol'ogy** the doctrine of devils; devil-lore. [Gr *diabolikos*, from *diabolos*; see **devil**]

diabolo *di-a'bol-ō* or *dī-*, *n* a game in which a two-headed top is spun, tossed, and caught on a string attached to two sticks, held one in each hand. [Gr *diaballō* I throw over, toss, or from *diabolos* devil; see also **devil**]

diacatholicon *dī-ə-kə-thol'i-kon*, (*obs*) *n* a purgative electuary, the drug being mixed with honey or syrup; a panacea. [Gr *dia katholikōn* of universal (ingredients)]

diacaustic *dī-ə-kös'tik*, (*math* and *phys*) *adj* pertaining to or denoting a caustic curve or caustic surface formed by refraction. — *n* a curve so formed. [**dia-** and **caustic** (*math*)]

diacetylmorphine. See **diamorphine**.

diachronic *dī-ə-kron'ik*, *adj* of the study of a subject (*esp* a language) through its historical development (*opp* of *synchronic*). — *adv* **diachron'ically**. — *n* **diachronism** (*dī-ak'*). — *adj* **diachronist'ic** or **diach'ronous**. [**dia-** and Gr *chronos* time]

diachylon *dī-ak'i-lon* or **diachylum** *dī-ak'i-ləm*, *n* formerly a plaster of plant juices; now lead-plaster. [Gr *dia chȳlōn* through (ie composed of) juices, or *diachȳlon* (neuter) juicy]

diacid *dī-as'id*, (*chem*) *adj* having two replaceable hydrogen atoms; capable of replacing two hydrogen atoms of an acid. [**di-**]

diacodion *dī-ə-kō'di-on* or **diacodium** *dī-ə-kō'di-əm*, (*obs*) *n* a syrup of poppies. [L, from Gr *dia kōdeiōn* composed of poppy-heads, from *kōdeia* a poppy-head]

diaconate *dī-ak'ə-nāt*, *n* the office or period of service of a deacon. — *adj* **dīac'onal** pertaining to a deacon. [See **deacon**]

diaconicon *dī-ə-kon'i-kən*, *n* a sacristy for sacred vessels, in a Greek church, on the south side of the bema or sanctuary. [Gr *diākonikon*]

diacoustic *dī-ə-kōō'stik*, old-fashioned *-kow'*, *adj* pertaining to the refraction of sound. — *n* **diacoust'ics** the branch of physics that deals with refracted sounds. [**dia-**, and **acoustic**]

diacritic *dī-ə-krit'ik* or **diacritical** *-əl*, *adj* distinguishing, a term used of marks (eg accents, cedillas, etc) attached to letters to indicate modified sound, value, etc. — *n* **diacrit'ic** such a mark. [Gr *diakritikos*, from *dia* between, and *kritikos*; see **critic**]

diact *dī'akt*, (*zool*) *adj* two-rayed. — *adj* **diactinal** (*-ak'* or *-tī'*) or **diact'ine**. [**di-** and Gr *aktīs*, *aktīnos* ray]

diactinic *dī-ak-tin'ik*, (*phys*, *optics*, etc) *adj* capable of transmitting actinic rays. [**dia-**, and Gr *aktīs*, *aktīnos* ray]

diadelphous *dī-ə-del'fəs*, (*bot*) *adj* (of stamens) united by the filaments in two bundles; having stamens so joined. — *n pl* **Diadel'phia** (in the Linnaean classification) a class with stamens so joined. [**di-**, and Gr *adelphos* brother]

diadem *dī'ə-dem*, *n* a crown, a jewelled headband, or the like; an arch of a crown; regal power; a crowning glory. — *adj* **dī'ademed** wearing a diadem. — **diadem spider** the common garden spider (from its markings). [OFr *diademe*, from L *diadēma*, from Gr *diadēma*, from *dia* round, and *deein* to bind]

diadochi *dī-ad'o-kī*, *n pl* the generals who became monarchs of the various kingdoms (Syria, Egypt, etc) into which the empire of Alexander the Great split after his death (323BC). [Gr *diadochos* succeeding, a successor; *diadechesthai* to succeed]

diadrom *dī'ə-drom*, *n* a course or passing; a vibration. — *adj* (of leaf nerves) radiating fanwise. [Gr *dia* across, and *dromos* a run]

diaeresis or **dieresis** *dī-ēr'i-sis* or *-er'*, *n* a mark (¨) placed over a vowel-letter, *esp* the second of two adjacent ones to show that it is to be pronounced separately, as in *naïf*; a pause or break where the end of the word coincides with the end of a foot (*prosody*): — *pl* **diaer'eses** or **dier'eses** (*-ēz*). [Gr *diairesis* separation, from *dia* apart, and *haireein* to take]

diagenesis *dī-ə-jen'i-sis*, *n* the conversion of sediment into rock; reconstitution of crystals to form a new product (*chem*). — *adj* **diagenetic** (*-ji-net'ik*). [**dia-** and **genesis**]

diageotropic *dī-ə-jē-ō-trop'ik*, (*bot*) *adj* taking a position perpendicular to the direction of gravity. — *adv* **diageotrop'ically**. — *n* **diageotropism** (*-ot'*). [**dia-**]

diaglyph *dī'ə-glif*, *n* an intaglio. [Gr *dia* through, and *glyphein* to carve]

diagnosis *dī-əg-nō'sis*, *n* the identification of a disease by means of its symptoms; a formal determining description, *esp* of a plant: — *pl* **diagnō'ses** (*-ēz*). — *n* **diagnosabil'ity**. — *adj* **dī'agnosable** (or *-nō'*). — *vt* **dī'agnose** (or *-nōz'*, or (*esp US*) *-nōs* or *-nōs'*) to identify (eg a disease) from symptoms. — *adj* **diagnos'tic** of, or useful in, diagnosis; distinguishing; differentiating. — *n* that by which anything is known; a symptom. — *n* **diagnosti'cian** (*-nos-tish'ən*) a person skilled in diagnosis. — *n sing* **diagnos'tics** diagnosis as a branch of medicine. — **diagnostic characters** (*zool*) characteristics by which one genus, species, family or group can be differentiated from another; **diagnostic program** or **routine** a program or routine used in most computers as an aid in the debugging of programs and systems. [Gr, from *dia* between, and *gnōsis* knowing]

diagometer *dī-ə-gom'i-tər*, *n* a form of electroscope for ascertaining electric conductivity. [Gr *diagein* to conduct, and *metron* a measure]

diagonal *dī-ag'ə-nəl*, *adj* through the corners, or joining two vertices that are not adjacent, of a polygon; (of a plane) passing through two edges (not adjacent) of a polyhedron; slantwise. — *n* a straight line or plane so drawn. — *adv* **diag'onally**. — **diagonal scale** a scale for laying down small fractions of the unit of measurement, by lengthwise parallel lines intersected by two sets of parallel lines, crosswise and oblique. [L *diagōnālis*, from Gr *diagōnios*, from *dia* through, and *gōniā* a corner]

diagram *dī'ə-gram*, *n* a figure or plan intended to explain rather than represent actual appearance; an outline figure or scheme; a curve symbolizing a set of facts; a record traced by an automatic indicator. — *adj* **diagrammatic** (*-grə-mat'ik*). — *adv* **diagrammat'ically**. [Gr *diagramma*, from *dia* round, and *graphein* to write]

diagraph *dī'ə-gräf*, *n* an instrument for copying, enlarging or projecting drawings. — *adj* **diagraphic** (*-graf'ik*). [Gr *dia* round, and *graphein* to write]

diagrid *dī'ə-grid*, (*eng*) *n* a structure of diagonally intersecting beams, used for support. [*dia*gonal *grid*]

diaheliotropic *dī-ə-hē-li-ō-trop'ik*, (*bot*) *adj* turning transversely to the light. — *n* **diaheliotropism** (*-ot'rə-pizm*). [**dia-**]

dial *dī'əl*, *n* an instrument for showing the time of day by the sun's shadow (as in *sundial*); a timepiece (*obs*); the face of a watch or clock; a graduated plate on which a movable index shows the value of some quantity measured, or can be set to make an adjustment (such as the temperature control of an oven, etc or the tuning device on a radio); the numbered plate on a telephone, and the moveable disc fitted on top; a miner's compass with sights for surveying; a face (*slang*). — *vt* to measure or indicate or get into communication with by dial; to use a telephone dial or keypad to select (a telephone number). — *vi* to use a telephone dial or keypad: — *pr p* **di'alling** or (*NAm*) **di'aling**; *pa t* and *pa p* **di'alled** or (*NAm*) **di'aled**. — *n* **di'alist** a maker of dials; someone skilled in dialling. — *n* **di'aller** a person who surveys by dial. — *n* **di'alling** the art of constructing sundials; the science which explains the measuring of time by the sundial; surveying by dial. — **dialling code** a group of numbers dialled to obtain the desired exchange in an automatic dialling system; **dialling tone** or (*NAm*) **dial tone** the continuous sound heard on picking up a telephone receiver which indicates that the equipment is functioning and ready to accept an input telephone number; **di'al-plate** the plate to which the pillars of a watch are fixed. [LL *diālis* daily, from L *diēs* a day]

dial. *abbrev*: dialect.

dialect *dī'ə-lekt*, *n* a variety or form of a language peculiar to a district or class, *esp* but not necessarily other than a literary or standard form; a peculiar manner of speaking; any of two or more variant forms of a particular computer language. — *adj* **dialect'al**. — *adv* **dialect'ally**. — *n* **dialect'icism**. — *n* **dialectol'ogist**. — *n* **dialectol'ogy** the study of dialect(s). [Through Fr and L from Gr *dialektos* speech, manner of speech, peculiarity of speech, from *dia* between, and *legein* to speak]

dialectic *dī-ə-lek'tik* or **dialec'tical** *-əl*, *adj* pertaining to discourse or to dialectics; logical. — *n* **dialec'tic**, or *n sing* **dialec'tics** the art of discussing, *esp* a debate which seeks to resolve the conflict between two opposing theories, rather than disprove any one of them; that branch of logic which teaches the rules and modes of reasoning. — *adv* **dialec'tically**. — *n* **dialecti'cian** a person skilled in dialectics, a logician. — **dialectical materialism** see under **materialism**. [Gr *dialektikos*]

diallage[1] *dī-al'ə-jē*, (*rhetoric*) *n* a figure of speech by which arguments, after having been considered from various points of view, are all brought to bear upon one point. [Gr *diallagē*; see **diallage**[2]]

diallage[2] *dī'əl-āj*, *n* a mineral, a brown, grey or green form of augite with play of colour. — *adj* **diallagic** (*-aj'ik*) or **diallagoid** (*-al'ə-goid*). [Gr *diallagē* change, from *dia* between, and *allassein* to change, from *allos* other]

dialogite *dī-al'ə-jīt*, *n* a rose-red manganese carbonate. [Gr *dialogē* selection, doubt]

dialogue or (*NAm* sometimes) **dialog**, *dī'ə-log*, *n* conversation between two or more people, *esp* of a formal or imaginary nature; the lines spoken by characters in plays, films, novels, etc; an exchange of views in the hope of ultimately reaching agreement. — *vi* (*esp NAm*) to take part in a dialogue, converse (often with *with*). — *vt* (*obs*; *Shakesp*) to put into dialogue form. — *adj* **dialog'ic** (*-loj'*). — *n* **dial'ogist** a writer or speaker of dialogues. — *adj* **dialogist'ic** or **dialogist'ical**. — *vi* **dialogize** or **-s-** (*dī-al'ə-jīz*) to discourse in dialogue. [Fr, from L *dialogus*, from Gr *dialogos* a conversation, from *dialegesthai* to discourse]

dialypetalous *dī-ə-li-pet'ə-ləs*, (*bot*) *adj* having the petals separate, polypetalous. [Gr *dialyein* to separate, from *dia* asunder, *lyein* to loose, and *petalon* a leaf]

dialysis *dī-al'i-sis*, (*chem*) *n* the separation of substances by diffusion through a membranous septum or partition; diaeresis; dissolution; separation; removal of impurities from the blood by a kidney machine (qv) (*med*): — *pl* **dial'yses** (*-sēz*). — *adj* **dialysable** or (*NAm*) **-z-** (*dī-ə-līz'ə-bl*). — *vt* **dialyse** or (*NAm*) **dialyze** (*dī'ə-līz*) to separate by dialysis. — *vi* to use a kidney machine. — *n* **di'alyser** or (*NAm*) **-z-**. — *adj* **dialytic** (*-lit'ik*). [Gr *dialysis*, from *dia* asunder, and *lyein* to loose]

diam. *abbrev*: diameter.

diamagnetic *dī-ə-mag-net'ik*, *adj* applied to any substance of which a rod suspended between the poles of a magnet arranges itself across the lines of force (*opp* to *paramagnetic*). — *n* **diamag'net** a diamagnetic substance. — *adv* **diamagnet'ically**. — *n* **diamag'netism** the form of magnetic action possessed by diamagnetic bodies; the branch of magnetism which deals with diamagnetic phenomena. [**dia-**]

diamanté *dē-a-mã-tā*, *dī-ə-man'ti*, *n* a decoration, eg on a dress, consisting of glittering particles; a fabric so decorated. — Also *adj*. — *adj* **diamantine** (*dī-ə-man'tīn*) of, or resembling, diamonds. [Fr *diamant* diamond]

diamantiferous *dī-ə-man-tif'ər-əs*, *adj* yielding diamonds. [Fr *diamantifère*]

diameter *dī-am'i-tər*, *n* the measure through or across; a straight line passing through the centre of a circle or other figure, terminated at both ends by the circumference; in the parabola, a straight line parallel to the axis extending from the curve to infinity. — *adj* **diam'ētral** or **diametric** (*dī-ə-met'rik*), also **diamet'rical**, in the direction of a diameter; pertaining to the diameter; as of opposite ends of a diameter (as in *diametrical opposition*). — *adv* **diam'etrally** in a diametral manner. — *adv* **diamet'rically** along a diameter; as at the ends of a diameter. — **tactical diameter** the perpendicular distance between a ship's courses before and after turning 180°. [Through Fr and L from Gr *diametros*, from *dia* through, across, and *metron* a measure]

diamond *dī'ə-mənd*, *n* a highly prized gemstone, and the hardest of all minerals, consisting of carbon crystallized in the cubic system; a rhombus; a card of a suit distinguished by pips of that form; a baseball field, or the part between bases (*US*); one of the smallest kinds of English printing type (about 4½-point). — *adj* resembling, made of or marked with diamonds; lozenge-shaped, rhombic. — *adj* **dī'amonded** furnished with diamonds. — *adj* **dīamondif'erous** yielding diamonds. — **di'amond-back** a N American terrapin with diamond-shaped markings on its shell; a N American rattlesnake (*Crotalus adamanteus*), with diamond-shaped markings; **di'amond-bee'tle** a beautiful sparkling S American weevil; **diamond bird** any of several small insectivorous Australian songbirds; a pardalote; **diamond dove** a small Australian dove (*Geopelia cuneata*) with white markings on the wings, often kept in cage or aviary; **di'amond-drill** a borer whose bit is set with bort; **di'amond-dust** or **-pow'der** the powder made by the friction of diamonds on one another in the course of polishing; **di'amond-field** a region that yields diamonds; **di'amond-hitch** a mode of fastening a rope for heavy burdens; **diamond jubilee** a sixtieth anniversary (of marriage, **diamond wedding**); **diamond snake** a carpet snake with diamond-shaped markings; **di'amond-wheel** a wheel covered with diamond-dust and oil for polishing diamonds, etc. — **black diamonds** (*fig*) coal; **diamond cut diamond** an encounter between two very sharp people; **rough diamond** an uncut diamond; a person possibly of great worth, but of rough appearance and unpolished manners. [ME *diamaunt*, from OFr *diamant*, from LL *diamas*, *-antis*, from Gr *adamas*, *-antos*; see **adamant**]

diamorphine *dī-ə-mör'fēn*, *n* a short form of **diacetylmor'phine** (*dī-as'ə-til-*) an acetyl derivative of morphine, commonly known as heroin.

diamyl *dī-am'il*, (*chem*) *adj* having two amyl groups. [**di-**]

Diana *dī-an'ə*, *n* the Roman goddess of light, the moon-goddess, representative of chastity and hunting, identified with the Greek Artemis (*mythol*); a huntress. — Also **Dī'an**. — **Diana monkey** a large long-tailed W African monkey (*Cercopithecus diana*) with a white crescent on the forehead; **Diana's tree** tree of silver (see under **tree**). — **Diana of the Ephesians** a goddess of fertility worshipped at Ephesus. [L *Diāna*]

diandrous *dī-an'drəs*, *adj* having, or allowing, two husbands or male mates (at a time); (of a flower or flowering plant) having two stamens or antheridia. —

n pl **Dian'dria** (in Linnaeus's classification) a class of plants with two stamens. — *n* **dian'dry** the practice or condition of being diandrous. [Gr *dis* twice, and *anēr, andros* a man, male]

DIANE *abbrev*: Direct Information Access Network for Europe.

dianetics® *dī-ə-net'iks, n sing* the former name for Scientology. [Gr *dia* through, and *nous* mind]

dianodal *dī-ə-nō'dəl,* (*math*) *adj* passing through a node. [**dia-**]

dianoetic *dī-ə-nō-et'ik, adj* capable of or relating to thought. [Gr *dianoētikos*, from *dia* through, and *noeein* to think]

dianthus *dī-an'thəs, n* any plant or flower of the *Dianthus* genus of herbaceous flowers to which carnations and pinks belong. [Poss Gr *Dios anthos* Zeus's flower; or *dianthēs* flowering in succession]

diapason *dī-ə-pā'zən, -sən,* (*music*) *n* a whole octave (*obs*); a bass part (*obs*); harmony (*obs*); a full volume of various sounds in concord; the whole range or compass of tones; a standard of pitch; a foundation-stop of an organ (*open* or *stopped diapason*) extending through its whole compass. — Also (*Spenser*; *poetic*) **dī'apase**. [Gr *dia pasōn chordōn symphōniā* concord through all the notes]

diapause *dī'ə-pöz, n* (in insects and the embryos of some animals) a period of suspended animation and growth. [Gr *diapausis* pause, from *diapauein* to pause, from *dia* between, and *pauein* to stop]

diapedesis *dī-ə-pi-dē'sis,* (*physiol*) *n* the migration of white blood-corpuscles through the walls of the blood vessels without apparent rupture. — *adj* **diapedetic** (*-det'ik*). [Gr *dia* through, and *pēdēsis* leaping]

diapente *dī-ə-pen'ti, n* the interval of a fifth (*music*); a medicine of five ingredients. [Gr *dia* through, and *pente* five]

diaper *dī'ə-pər, n* (*esp NAm*) a baby's nappy; linen or cotton cloth with a square or diamond pattern, used chiefly for table linen and towels; the pattern itself; a pattern for ornamentation, woven, not coloured, in textiles; a floral or geometric pattern in low relief in architecture, often repeated over a considerable surface; paving in a chequered pattern. — *vt* to variegate with figures, as in diaper. — *n* **dī'apering**. [OFr *diaspre, diapre*, from LL *diasprus*, from Byzantine Gr *diaspros* from *dia* through, and *aspros* white]

diaphanous *dī-af'ə-nəs, adj* transparent; translucent; pellucid; clear; light, delicate. — *n* **diaphaneity** (*dī-ə-fə-nē'i-ti*). — *n* **dīaphanom'eter** an instrument for measuring the transparency of the air. — *adv* **dīaph'anously**. — *n* **dīaph'anousness**. [Gr *diaphanēs*, from *dia* through, and *phainein* to show, shine]

diaphone *dī'ə-fōn, n* a siren-like fog-signal; an organ stop made louder by vibrating material; all the variants of a phoneme. [Gr *dia* across, and *phōnē* voice]

diaphoresis *dī-ə-for-ē'sis,* (*med*) *n* sweat, *esp* artificially induced. — *adj* **diaphoretic** (*-et'ik*) promoting sweating. — *n* a sudorific, a diaphoretic substance. [Gr *diaphorēsis* sweating, from *dia* through, and *pherein* to carry]

diaphototropic *dī-ə-fō-tō-trop'ik,* (*bot*) *adj* diaheliotropic, turning transversely to the light. — *n* **diaphototrōp'ism**. — *n* **diaphototropy** (*-tot'rə-pi*). [**dia-**]

diaphragm *dī'ə-fram, -frəm, n* a thin partition or dividing membrane; the midriff, the muscular structure separating the chest from the abdomen (*anatom*); a metal plate with a central hole, for cutting off side-rays in optical instruments; a strengthening or stiffening plate (*eng*); (in a telephone, etc) a thin vibrating disc that converts electrical signals into sound waves and vice versa; a contraceptive device, a thin rubber or plastic cap placed over the neck of the uterus. — *adj* **diaphragmal** (*-frag'*). — *adj* **diaphragmatic** (*-frag-mat'*). — *n* **diaphragmatī'tis** (*-frag-*) inflammation of the diaphragm. — **diaphragm pump** a pump which has a flexible membrane instead of a piston. [Gr *diaphragma* partition, midriff, from *dia* across, and *phragma* a fence]

diaphysis *dī-af'i-sis, n* an abnormal elongation of the axis (*bot*); the shaft of a long bone (*anatom*). [Gr *diaphysis* a separation, from *dia* through, and *phyesthai* to grow]

diapir *dī'ə-pēr,* (*geol*) *n* an anticlinal fold in which the overlying rock has been pierced by material from beneath. — *adj* **diapi'ric**. — *n* **diapi'rism** the upward movement of material through denser rocks to form diapirs. [Gr *diapeirainein* to pierce]

diapophysis *dī-ə-pof'i-sis,* (*anatom*) *n* a dorsal transverse process of a vertebra: — *pl* **dīapoph'ysēs** (*-sēz*). — *adj* **diapophysial** (*dī-ap-ō-fiz'i-əl*). [Gr *dia* apart, and *apophysis* offshoot]

diapositive *dī-ə-poz'i-tiv, n* a transparent photographic positive; a slide. [**dia-**]

diapyesis *dī-ə-pī-ē'sis,* (*pathol*) *n* suppuration. — *adj* **diapyetic** (*-et'ik*) producing suppuration. — *n* a medicine of this property. [Gr *diapyēsis*, from *dia* through, and *pyon* pus]

diarch *dī'ärk,* (*bot*) *adj* having two xylem strands. [Gr *di-* twice, and *archē* origin]

diarchy *dī'är-ki, n* a form of government in which two people, states, or bodies are jointly vested with supreme power (also less correctly **dī'narchy** or **dy'archy**). — *adj* **diarch'al** or **diarch'ic**. [Gr *di-* twice, and *archein* to rule]

diarise, diarize. See **diary**.

diarrhoea or (*NAm*) **diarrhea** *dī-ə-rē'ə, n* a persistent purging or looseness of the bowels, evacuation of liquid faeces; an excessive flow of anything (*fig*; *colloq*). — *adj* **diarrhoe'al** or **diarrhoe'ic** or (*NAm*) **diarrhē'al** or **diarrhē'ic**. [Gr *diarroia*, from *dia* through, and *rhoiā* a flow]

diarthrosis *dī-är-thrō'sis,* (*anatom*) *n* articulation admitting free movement, as eg the shoulder joint. [Gr *diarthrōsis* jointing, from *dia* through, and *arthron* joint]

diary *dī'ə-ri, n* a daily record; a book for making daily records, noting engagements, etc. — *adj* **diarial** (*dī-ā'ri-əl*) or **dīā'rian**. — *n* **dī'arist** a person who keeps a diary. — *vt* **diarize** or **-ise** (*dī'e-riz*) to enter in a diary. — *vi* to keep a diary. [L *diārium*, from *diēs* day]

diascope *dī'ə-skōp, n* an optical projector used for showing transparencies on a screen; a slide projector. [**dia-**, and Gr *skopeein* to view]

diascordium *dī-ə-skör'di-əm,* (*obs*) *n* a medicine made from water-germander, etc. [Medical L, from Gr *dia skordiōn* composed of *skordion* (perhaps water-germander)]

diaskeuast *dī-ə-skū'ast, n* a reviser; an interpolator. [Gr *diaskeuazein* to make ready, from *dia* through, and *skeuos* a tool]

Diasone® *dī'ə-sōn, n* a proprietary name for a sulphonamide (a derivative of *diaminodiphenylsulphone*) used against leprosy.

diaspora *dī-as'por-ə, n* (with *cap*) dispersion, used collectively for the dispersed Jews after the Babylonian captivity, and also in the apostolic age for the Jews living outside of Palestine, now, for Jews outside Israel; a similar dispersion or migration of other peoples or communities. — Also *adj*. [Gr *diasporā*, from *dia* through, and *speirein* to scatter]

diaspore *dī'ə-spōr, -spör, n* a mineral, aluminium hydroxide, AlO(OH). [Gr *diasporā* scattering, from its decrepitation]

diastaltic *dī-ə-stal'tik,* (*Gr music*) *adj* (of intervals) extended; (of style) bold. [Gr *diastaltikos* expanding]

diastase *dī'ə-stās,* (*biol*) *n* an enzyme that converts starch into sugar, produced in germinating seeds and in pancreatic juice. — *adj* **diastā'sic** or **diastatic** (*-stat'ik*). [Gr *diastasis* division, from *dia* apart, and *stasis* setting]

diastasis *dī-as'tə-sis,* (*surg*) *n* separation of bones without fracture. [See **diastase**]

diastema *dī-ə-stē'mə,* (*zool* and *anatom*) *n* a natural space between two consecutive teeth, or series of teeth: — *pl*

diastē'mata. — *adj* **diastemat'ic**. [Gr *diastēma*, *-atos* interval]

diaster *dī-as'tər*, (*biol*) *n* in cell-division, a stage in which the daughter chromosomes are situated in two groups near the poles of the spindle, ready to form the daughter nuclei. [Gr *di-* twice, and *astēr* a star]

diastereoisomer *dī-ə-stē-ri-ō-ī'sō-mər*, (*chem*) *n* a stereo-isomer which is not an enantiomorph. — *adj* **diastereo-isomeric** (*-me'rik*). — *n* **diastereoisom'erism**. [**dia-**]

diastole *dī-as'tə-lē*, *n* dilatation of the heart, auricles and arteries (*opp* to *systole*, or contraction; *physiol*); the lengthening of a short syllable, as before a pause. — *adj* **diastolic** (*dī-ə-stol'ik*). [Gr *diastolē*, from *dia* asunder, and *stellein* to place]

diastrophism *dī-as'trō-fizm*, (*geol*) *n* processes of deformation of the earth's crust. — *adj* **diastrophic** (*dī-ə-strof'ik*). [Gr *diastrophē* distortion, from *dia* aside, and *strophē* a turning]

diastyle *dī'ə-stīl*, (*archit*) *adj* with columns about three diameters apart. — *n* a building or colonnade so proportioned. [Gr *diastȳlos*, from *dia* apart, and *stȳlos* column]

diatessaron *dī-ə-tes'ə-ron*, *-rən*, *n* an arrangement of the four Gospels as a single narrative, *esp* the earliest, that of Tatian (*prob* AD110–180); the interval of a fourth (*music*); a medicine of four ingredients. [Gr *dia tessarōn* through, or composed of, four]

diathermic *dī-ə-thûr'mik*, *adj* permeable by or able to conduct radiant heat. — Also **diather'mal**, **diather'-manous** and **diather'mous**. — *n* **diather'macy**, **dia-ther'mancy** or **diathermanē'ity** permeability by or conductibility of radiant heat. — *n* **di'athermy** heating of internal parts of the body by electric currents. [Gr *dia* through, and *thermē* heat]

diathesis *dī-ath'i-sis*, *n* a particular condition or habit of body, *esp* one predisposing to certain diseases (*med*); a habit of mind. — *adj* **diathetic** (*dī-ə-thet'ik*). [Gr *diathesis*, from *dia* asunder, and *tithenai* to place]

diatom *dī'ə-təm*, *n* one of a class of microscopic unicellular algae with flinty shells in two halves, fitting like box and lid. — *adj* **diatomā'ceous**. — *n* **dī'atomist** a person who studies diatoms. — *n* **diatomite** (*dī-at'əm-īt* or *dī'ət-*) diatomaceous earth or kieselguhr, a powdery siliceous deposit of diatom frustules. — **diatom ooze** a deep-sea deposit of diatom frustules. [Gr *diatomos* cut through, from *dia* through, and *temnein* to cut]

diatomic *dī-ə-tom'ik*, *adj* consisting of two atoms; having two replaceable atoms or groups; bivalent. [**di-** and **atom**]

diatonic *dī-ə-ton'ik*, *adj* proceeding by the tones and intervals of the natural scale in Western music. — *adv* **diaton'ically**. [Gr *diatonikos*, from *dia* through, and *tonos* tone]

diatretum. See **cage-cup**.

diatribe *dī'ə-trīb*, *n* a continued discourse or disputation (*archaic*); an abusive or bitter harangue. — *n* **dī'atribist** a writer or utterer of such. [Gr *diatribē* a spending of time, from *dia* through, and *tribein* to rub, wear away]

diatropism *dī-at'rō-pizm*, *n* (of plants or parts of plants) orientation at right angles to the direction of a stimulus. — *adj* **diatropic** (*dī-ə-trop'ik*). [Gr *dia* across, and *tropos* turning]

diaxon *dī-aks'on*, (*zool*) *adj* having two axes or two axis-cylinder processes. — *n* a bipolar nerve-cell (*anatom*). [Gr *di-* twice, and *axōn* an axis]

diazepam *dī-az'i-pam*, *n* a tranquillizing drug which relieves tension and acts as a muscle relaxant. [**di-**, *azo-* and *epoxide*]

diazeuxis *dī-ə-zūk'sis*, (*Gr music*) *n* the separation of two tetrachords by a whole tone. — *adj* **diazeuc'tic**. [Gr *diazeuxis* disjunction, from *dia* apart, and *zeuxis* yoking]

diazo *dī-az'ō*, *adj* (of compounds) containing two nitrogen atoms and a hydrocarbon radical; (of a photocopying process) using a diazo compound decomposed by exposure to light (also **dyeline**). — *n* a copy made by the diazo method: — *pl* **diaz'os** or **diaz'oes**. — Also **dyeline**. — **diazonium** (*dī-ə-zō'ni-əm*) **salts** a group of diazo compounds used in the manufacture of certain dyes. [**di-** and **azo-**]

dib[1] *dib*, *vi* to dip; to fish by letting the bait bob up and down on the surface of the water: — *pr p* **dibb'ing**; *pa t* and *pa p* **dibbed**. [Prob a form of **dab**[1]]

dib[2] *dib*, *n* one of the small bones of a sheep's leg; (in *pl*) a children's game, played by throwing up such small bones or stones (**dib'-stones**) etc from the palm and catching them on the back of the hand (also *jacks*, or in Scots *chuckie-stanes* or *chucks*); (in *pl*) money (*slang*; also **dibbs**). [Ety uncertain]

dibasic *dī-bā'sik*, *adj* capable of reacting with two equivalents of an acid; (of acids) having two replaceable hydrogen atoms. [**di-**]

dibber. See **dibble**.

dibble *dib'l* or **dibber** *dib'ər*, *n* a pointed tool used for making holes for seeds or plants. — *vt* **dibb'le** to plant with a dibble. — *vi* to make holes; to dip the bait lightly in and out of the water (*angling*). — *n* **dibb'ler** someone who, or that which, dibbles; a dibble; a small carnivorous Australian marsupial (*Antechinus apicalis*) with long snout and short hairy tail. [Prob connected with **dab**[1]]

dibranchiate *dī-brang'ki-āt*, (*zool*) *adj* having two gills. — *n pl* **Dibran'chia** or **Dibranchiā'ta** the two-gilled sub-class of cephalopods. [Gr *di-* twice, and *branchia* gills]

dibromo- *dī-brō'mō-*, *combining form* signifying having two atoms of bromine, *esp* replacing hydrogen.

dibutyl *dī-bū'til*, (*chem*) *adj* having two butyl groups. — **dibutyl phthalate** (*thal'āt*) the dibutyl ester of phthalic acid, used to keep off insects.

dicacity *di-kas'i-ti*, (*archaic*) *n* raillery, banter. — *adj* **dicacious** (*di-kā'shəs*). [L *dicāx* sarcastic]

DIC *abbrev*: Diploma of the Imperial College.

dicarpellary *dī-kär'pəl-ər-i* or *-pel'*, (*bot*) *adj* of or with two carpels. [**di-**]

dicast or **dikast** *dik'ast*, (*Gr hist*) *n* one of the 6000 Athenians annually chosen to act as judges. — *n* **dicas'tery** their court. — *adj* **dicas'tic**. [Gr *dikastēs*, from *dikē* justice]

dice[1], **dicey**, **dicing**. See **die**[2].

dice[2] *dīs*, *vt* (*Austr colloq*) to reject.

dicentra *dī-sen'trə*, *n* any plant of the *Dicentra* genus of the fumitory family, *incl* bleeding-heart (*D. spectabilis*), with the two outer petals broadly pouched. — Also **dielytra** (*dī-el'i-trə*; *orig* a misprint). [Gr *di-* double, and *kentron* a point, spur]

dicephalous *dī-sef'ə-ləs*, *adj* two-headed. [Gr *dikephalos*, from *di-* double, and *kephalē* a head]

dich *dich*, (*Shakesp*) supposed to be for **do it**, may it do.

dichasium *dī-kā'zi-əm*, (*bot*) *n* a cymose inflorescence in which each axis in turn produces a pair of nearly equal branches: — *pl* **dichā'sia**. — *adj* **dichā'sial**. [Gr *dichāsis* division, halving]

dichlamydeous *dī-klə-mid'i-əs*, (*bot*) *adj* having both a calyx and a corolla. [Gr *di-* double, and *chlamys*, *-ydos* mantle]

dichlor- or **dichloro-** *dī-klōr(-ō)-*, *-klör-*, *combining form* signifying having two atoms of chlorine, *esp* replacing hydrogen. — *n* **dīchlō'rōdīphēn'yltrichlō'roēth'ane** known as **DDT**, a white powder *orig* used to kill lice and thus prevent the spread of typhus, effective also against other insects, but having long-term disadvantages. — *n* **dichlor'vos** a pesticide used in fish-farming to reduce sea lice.

dichloralphenazone *dī-klōr-əl-phen'ə-zōn*, *-klör-*, *n* a drug, $C_{15}H_{18}Cl_6N_2O_5$, used as a hypnotic and sedative. [**di-**, **chloral (hydrate)**, and *phenazone*, an antipyretic drug]

dichogamy *dik-* or *dīk-og'ə-mi*, (*bot*) *n* an arrangement for preventing the self-fertilization of hermaphrodite flowers, the stamens and stigmas ripening at different times. — *adj* **dichog'amous**. [Gr *dicha* in two, and *gamos* marriage]

dichord *dī'körd*, *n* an ancient two-stringed lute. [Gr *dichordos*]

dichotomy *dik-* or *dīk-ot'ə-mi, n* a division into two strongly contrasted groups, classes, opinions, etc; (loosely) a problem, situation, etc in which there is a clear split or difference of opinion, a variance, discrepancy or divergence; repeated branching (*bot*). — *adj* **dichot'omic**. — *n* **dichot'omist**. — *vt* and *vi* **dichot'omize** or **-ise**. — *adj* **dichot'omous**. — *adv* **dichot'omously**. — **dichotomous question** a question in a questionnaire that requires a simple answer of 'Yes' or 'No'. [Gr *dichotomiā*, from *dicha* in two, and *tomē* a cut, from *temnein* to cut]

dichroism *dī'krō-izm, n* the property of showing different colours exhibited by doubly refracting crystals when viewed in different directions by transmitted light. — *adj* **dichrō'ic** or **dichrōit'ic**. — *n* **dī'chrōīte** a strongly dichroic mineral, iolite or cordierite. — *n* **dī'chrōoscope** or **dī'chrōscope** an instrument for testing the dichroism of crystals. — *adj* **dichrōoscop'ic** or **dichrōscop'ic**. [Gr *dichroos* two-coloured, from *di-* twice, and *chroā* colour]

dichromate *dī-krō'māt, n* a salt of **dichro'mic acid** ($H_2Cr_2O_7$) containing two chromium atoms. — Also called **bichromate**. [**di-** and **chromate**]

dichromatic *dī-krō-mat'ik, adj* having two colours, *esp* in different individuals of the same species; able to see two colours and two only, as in red-green colour-blind persons who see only blue and yellow. — *n* a person of dichromatic vision, a dichromat. — *n* **dī'chrōmat** or **dī'chrōmate** a person who can distinguish two colours only. — *n* **dichrō'matism**. — *adj* **dichrō'mic** dichroic; dichromatic. — *n* **dichrō'mism**. [Gr *di-* twice, and *chrōma, -atos* colour]

dichromic. See **dichromate** and **dichromatic**.

dicht or **dight** *dihht*, (*Scot*) *vt* to wipe. — *n* a wipe. [**dight**]

dick [1] *dik*, (*slang*) *n* a man, a fellow (sometimes with *cap*; now *usu derog*); a detective; a penis (*vulg*). — **dick'head** (*vulg*) an idiot; a fool; someone despised. — **clever Dick** a know-all. [*Dick* for Richard]

dick[2] *dik*, (*old slang*) *n* fine words (used for **dictionary**); also used for **declaration**, as in *to take one's dick*, and probably in *up to dick*, meaning excellent (up to declared value).

dickcissel *dik-sis'l, n* the black-throated bunting, an American migratory bird. [Imit of call]

dickens *dik'ənz, n* the deuce, the devil, as in *what the dickens* or *play the dickens*. [Appar *Dickon* Richard, as a substitute for **devil**]

Dickensian *dik-en'zi-ən, adj* pertaining to Charles *Dickens* (1812–70), the novelist; pertaining to conditions, *esp* squalid social or working conditions, like those described in his novels. — *n* an admirer or student of Dickens.

dicker[1] *dik'ər*, (*NAm*) *n* haggling or bargaining; petty trade by barter, etc. — *vi* to haggle; to hesitate or dither. [Prob the obs *dicker* used for the number ten, *esp* for counting hides or skins, from L *decuria*]

dicker[2] *dik'ər*, (*slang*) *n* (in Ireland) someone who spies on army patrols, and reports back to the IRA. [*dick* (slang) to look, peer]

dickey[1], **dicky** or **dickie** *dik'i, n* a leather apron for a gig, etc; the driver's seat in a carriage; a seat for servants at the back of a carriage; a folding seat at the back of a motor car; a false shirt-front; (or **dickey bow**) a bow tie. [Perh from *dick*, a dialect Eng word for a leathern apron; perh Du *dek* a cover]

dickey[2,3]. See **dicky**[1,2].

dickie. See **dickey**[1].

Dickin medal *dik'in med'əl, n* a British award for animal heroism in wartime, instituted in 1943. [Maria Elisabeth *Dickin*, founder of the People's Dispensary for Sick Animals, which makes the awards]

Dicksonia *dik-sōn'i-ə, n* a tropical and southern genus of ferns, mainly tree-ferns. [After James *Dickson* (died 1822), botanist]

dickty. See **dicty**.

dicky[1] or **dickey** *dik'i, n* (*E Anglian*) an ass. — **dick'y-bird** a small bird (*childish*); a word (*rhyming slang*). [*Dick*, for Richard]

dicky[2] or **dickey** *dik'i*, (*colloq*) *adj* shaky; not in good condition. [Poss from *Tom and Dick*, Cockney rhyming slang for *sick*.]

dicky[3]. See **dickey**[1].

diclinous *dī'kli-nəs* or *-klī'*, (*bot*) *adj* having the stamens and pistils in separate flowers, whether on the same or on different plants. — *n* **dī'clinism**. [Gr *di-* twice, double, and *klīnē* a bed]

dicotyledon *dī-kot-i-lē'dən*, (*bot*) *n* (often shortened to **dī'cot**) a plant of the **Dīcotylē'donēs** (*-ēz*) or **Dīcot'ylae** (*-i-lē*), one of the two great divisions of Angiosperms, having embryos with two seed-leaves or cotyledons, leaves commonly net-veined, the parts of the flowers in twos, fives, or multiples of these, and the vascular bundles in the axes usually containing cambium. — *adj* **dicotylē'donous**. [Gr *di-* twice, and **cotyledon**]

dicrotic *dī-krot'ik, adj* (of the pulse) having two beats to one beat of the heart. — Also **dī'crotous**. — *n* **dī'crotism**. [Gr *di-* twice, double, and *krotos* beat]

dict. See **dictate**.

dict. *abbrev*: dictation; dictator; dictionary.

dicta. See **dictum**.

Dictaphone® *dik'tə-fōn, n* a recording apparatus for dictating letters, etc. [L *dictāre* to dictate, and Gr *phōnē* sound]

dicta probantia *dik'tə prō-ban'shi-ə* or *dik'ta prō-ban'ti-a*, (*L*) *n pl* proof texts.

dictate *dik-tāt'*, or formerly *dik'tāt, vt* to say or read for another to write; to lay down with authority; to command. — *vi* to give orders; to behave dictatorially. — *n* (*dik'tāt*) an order, rule, direction. — *n* **dict** (*obs*) a saying. — *vt* (*obs*) to dictate. — *n* **dictā'tion** the act, art or practice of dictating; speaking or reading of words for a pupil, secretary, etc to write; the words dictated; overbearing command. — *n* **dictā'tor** a person invested with absolute authority, *orig* an extraordinary Roman magistrate; someone who, or that which, dictates: — *fem* **dictā'tress** or **dictā'trix**. — *adj* **dictatorial** (*dik-tə-tō'ri-əl* or *-tö'*) like a dictator; absolute; overbearing. — *adv* **dictatō'rially**. — *n* **dictā'torship**. — *n* **dictā'ture**. — *adj* **dic'tatory**. [L *dictāre, -ātum*, frequentative of *dīcere* to say]

diction *dik'shən, n* a saying or speaking (*obs*); manner of speaking or expressing; choice of words; style; enunciation. [L *dictio*, *-ōnis*, from *dicere, dictum* to say]

dictionary *dik'shən-ə-ri, n* a book containing the words of a language alphabetically arranged, with their meanings, etymology, etc; a lexicon; an additional program available in some word-processing packages which will check text for spelling errors against a dictionary contained on the disk (*comput*); a work containing information on any area of knowledge, alphabetically arranged. [LL *dictiōnārium*; see **diction**]

Dictograph® *dik'tō-grāf, n* an instrument for transmitting speech from room to room, with or without the speaker's knowledge, *usu* by means of a small concealed microphone. [L *dictum* thing said, and Gr *graphein* to write]

dictum *dik'təm, n* something said; a saying; a popular maxim; an authoritative saying: — *pl* **dic'ta**. [L]

dicty or **dickty** *dik'ti*, (*US slang*) *adj* proud, snobbish; high-class; excellent. [Origin unknown]

dictyogen *dik'ti-ō-jen*, (*obs*; *bot*) *n* a monocotyledon with net-veined leaves. [Gr *diktyon* a net, and *gennaein* to produce]

dicyclic *dī-sīk'lik, adj* having two whorls or rings. [Gr *di-* twice, double, and *kyklos* wheel]

dicynodont *dī-sin'ō-dont, n* an extinct tusked reptile, showing affinities with mammals. [Gr *di-* twice, *kyōn, kynos* dog, and *odous, odontos* tooth]

did *did, pa t* of **do**.

didactic *di-dak'tik, dī-*, or **didac'tical** *adj* fitted or intended to teach; instructive (sometimes pedantically or dictatorially so); preceptive. — *adv* **didac'tically**. — *n* **didac'ticism** (*-sizm*). — *n sing* **didac'tics** the art or science of teaching. [Gr *didaktikos*, from *didaskein* to teach; related to L *docēre*, *discere*]

didactyl *dī-dak'til*, *adj* two-fingered, two-toed, or two-clawed. — Also *n*. — *adj* **didac'tylous**. [Gr *di-* twice, and *daktylos* finger, toe]

didakai, didakei. See **diddicoy**.

didapper *dī'dap-ər*, *n* the dabchick or little grebe; someone who disappears and bobs up again. [**dive** and **dapper**, a variant of **dipper**; cf OE *dūfedoppa* pelican]

didascalic *did-as-kal'ik*, *adj* didactic. [Gr *didaskalikos*, from *didaskalos* teacher]

didder *did'ər*, (*dialect*) *vi* to shake. [See **dither**.]

diddicoy, didicoy or **didicoi** *did'i-koi*, **didakai** or **didakei** *did'ə-kī*, *n* an itinerant tinker or scrap-dealer, not a true gypsy. [Romany]

diddle[1] *did'l*, *vt* to cajole, swindle; to waste time, to dawdle (*NAm*). — *n* **didd'ler**. [Origin uncertain]

diddle[2] *did'l*, (*Scot*) *vt* and *vi* to make mouth music, sing without words (often dance tunes). — *n* **didd'ler**. [Onomatopoeic]

diddy[1] *did'i*, (*colloq*) *adj* small; tiny.

diddy[2] *did'i*, (*dialect*) *n* a female breast, a nipple or teat. [Perh from **tit**[2] or from Ir *dide* a teat]

didelphic *dī-del'fik*, (*zool*) *adj* having or pertaining to a double womb. — *n pl* **Didel'phia** the marsupials. — *adj* **didel'phian, didel'phine** or **didel'phous**. — *n* **didel'phid** an animal of the **Didel'phidae** (*-ē*) or, less commonly, **Didelphyidae** (*-fī'i-dē*), the opossum family. — *n* **Didel'phis** (*-fis*; less commonly **Didel'phys**) an American genus of opossums. [Gr *di-* double, and *delphys* womb]

didgeridoo *did'jər-i-doō'*, *n* an Australian Aboriginal musical instrument, consisting of a very long tube producing a low-pitched resonant sound. [Aboriginal word]

didicoi, didicoy. See **diddicoy**.

dido *dī'dō*, (*US colloq*) *n* an antic, caper; a frivolous or mischievous act: — *pl* **dī'does** or **dī'dos**. — **act dido** to play the fool; **cut up didoes** to behave in an extravagant way. [Origin unknown]

didrachma *dī-drak'mə* or **didrachm** *dī'dram*, *n* a double drachma. [Gr *di-* double, and **drachma**]

didst *didst*, (*archaic*) *2nd sing pa t* of **did**.

Didunculus *di-dung'kū-lus*, *n* a genus of birds, the tooth-billed pigeon of Samoa. [Dimin of *Didus*, zoological name of the dodo, from its similar bill]

didymium *di-* or *dī-dim'i-əm*, *n* a supposed element discovered in 1841, later resolved into neodymium and praseodymium. [Gr *didymos* twin, from its constant association with *lanthanum*]

didymous *did'i-məs*, (*biol*) *adj* twin; twinned; growing in pairs; composed of two parts slightly connected. [Gr *didymos* twin]

Didynamia *did-i-nā'mi-ə*, *n pl* a class of plants in the Linnaean system with two long stamens and two short. — *adj* **didynā'mian** or **didyn'amous**. [Gr *di-* double, and *dynamis* strength]

die[1] *dī*, *vi* (or *vt* with object *death*) to lose life; to perish; to wither; (of an engine) to stop working; (*esp* **be dying**; *hyperbolically*) to languish, suffer, long, or be very eager (for); to be overcome by the effects (of); to merge: — *pr p* **dy'ing**; *pa t* and *pa p* **died** (*dīd*). — *adj* **die'-away** languishing. — **die'-hard** an irreconcilable conservative; a resolute, obstinate or dauntless person. — Also *adj*. — **die away** to disappear by degrees, become gradually inaudible; **die back** (*bot*) to die by degrees from the tip backwards (*n* **die'back**); **die down** to subside; (of plants) to die above ground, leaving only roots or rootstocks; **die game** to keep up one's spirit to the last; **die hard** to struggle hard against death, to be long in dying; to be difficult to suppress, eradicate, or persuade (*n* and *adj* **die'-hard**); **die off** to die quickly or in large numbers; **die out** to become extinct, to disappear; **die the death** (*theat slang*) to arouse no response from one's audience; **never say die** never give up. — See also **dying**. [Prob from a lost OE (Anglian) *dēgan*; but commonly referred to a Scand root seen in ON *deyja*, *döyja*; related to MHGer *touwen*, whence Ger *Tod*. The OE word in use was *steorfan* (see **starve**)]

die[2] *dī*, *n* (also **dice** *dīs*) a small cube with faces numbered or otherwise distinguished, thrown in games of chance, etc; (also **dice**) a small cubical piece; (also **dice**) hazard; a stamp for impressing coin, etc; applied to various tools for shaping things by stamping or cutting: — *pl* (gaming, cookery, etc) **dice** or (stamping and shaping) **dies** (*dīz*). — *vi* **dice** to play with dice; to take great risks. — *vt* to cut into dice; to chequer: — *pr p* **dīc'ing**; *pa t* and *pa p* **diced**. — *adj* **diced** ornamented with a chequered pattern; cut into dice. — *n* **dīc'er**. — *adj* **dīc'ey** (*colloq*) risky; tricky; uncertain in result. — *n* **dīc'ing** a chequered pattern; dice-playing. — **dice'-box** an hour-glass-shaped box from which dice are thrown; **dice'-coal** a coal that breaks into cubical blocks; **dice'-play**; **dice'-player**. — *vt* **die'-cast** to shape (metal or plastic) by casting in a metal mould. — **die'-casting**; **die'-sink'er**; **die'-sink'ing** the engraving of dies for embossing, etc; **die'-stock** a contrivance for holding the dies used in screw-cutting; **die'-work** ornamentation of a metal surface by impressions with a die. — **dice with death** to take great risks; **no dice** no answer, or a negative answer; no success; **straight as a die** (ie a gaming die; *fig*) completely honest; **the die is cast** an irrevocable step has been taken; there is no turning back now. [OFr *de*, pl *dez* (Provençal *dat*, Ital *dado*), from LL *dadus* = L *datus* given or cast]

dieb *dēb*, *n* a jackal of northern Africa. [Ar *dhīb*]

died. See **die**[1].

diedral. See **dihedral**.

dièdre *dē-edr'*, *n* a rock angle, or re-entrant corner, *usu* with a crack in it. [Fr]

diegesis *dī-ē-jē'sis*, (*rhetoric*) *n* (in an oration) the narration of the facts. [Gr *diēgēsis*]

dieldrin *dēl'drin*, *n* a crystalline organochlorine compound used as a contact insecticide. [O *Diels* (1876–1954), German chemist, and **aldrin**]

dielectric *dī-i-lek'trik*, *adj* non-conducting; transmitting electric effects without conducting. — *n* a substance, solid, liquid or gas, capable of supporting an electric stress, and hence an insulator. — **dielectric constant** relative permittivity (see **permit**); **dielectric heating** the heating of a non-conducting substance as a result of loss of power in dielectric. [Gr *dia* through, and **electric**]

dielytra *dī-el'i-trə*, (also with *cap*) *n* an erroneous name for **dicentra** (qv). [As if Gr *di-* double, and *elytron* cover]

diencephalon *dī-en-sef'ə-lon*, *-kef'*, (*zool* and *anatom*) *n* the posterior part of the forebrain in vertebrates, connecting the cerebral hemispheres with the midbrain. [**dia-**]

diene *dī'ēn*, (*chem*) *n* an organic compound containing two double bonds between carbon atoms. [**di-**, and *-ene* as in **alkene, benzene**, etc]

dieresis. See **diaeresis**.

dies[1] *dī'ēz*, *dē'ās*, (*L*) *n* day: — *pl* **dies**. — **dies fasti** (*fas'tī* or *fäs'tē*) and **dies profesti** (*pro-fes'tī* or *-tē*) days on which judgement could be pronounced, on which courts could be held in ancient Rome, lawful days; **dies faustus** (*fös'təs* or *fows'toōs*) lucky day; **dies festi** (*fes'tī* or *-tē*) or **dies feriae** (*fer'i-ē* or *-ī*) days of actual festival; **dies infaustus** (*in-fös'təs* or *in-fows'toōs*) unlucky day; **dies irae** (*īr'ē* or *ēr'ī*) the day of wrath; the day of judgement (from a Latin hymn); the hymn itself, used in the Mass for the dead; **dies nefasti** (*ni-fas'tī* or *ne-fäs'tē*) days on which a judgement could not be pronounced or assemblies of the people be held, in ancient Rome; **dies non** (*non* or *nōn*) a day on which judges do not sit, or one on which normal business is not transacted.

dies[2]. See **die**[2].

diesel *dēz'l*, *n* a diesel engine; a locomotive, train, etc driven by a diesel engine; diesel oil. — *n* **dieselizā'tion** or **-s-**. — *vt* and *vi* **dies'elize** or **-ise** to equip, or be equipped with, a diesel engine, locomotive or train. — *adj* **dies'el-elec'tric** using power obtained from a diesel-operated electric generator. — **diesel engine** a compression-ignition engine in which the oil fuel is introduced into the heated compressed-air charge as a jet of liquid under high pressure. — *adj* **dies'el-hydraul'ic** using power transmitted by means of one or more mechanisms (torque convertors) filled with oil. — **diesel oil** heavy fuel oil used in diesel engines. [Rudolph *Diesel* (1858–1913), German engineer]

diesis *dī'i-sis*, *n* the difference between a major and a minor semitone (*music*); the double-dagger (‡) (*printing*): — *pl* **dī'eses** (*-sēz*). [Gr *diesis* a quarter-tone]

diestrus. See **dioestrus**.

diet[1] *dī'ət*, *n* mode of living, *usu* now only with especial reference to food; a planned or prescribed selection of food, *esp* one designed for weight-loss or the control of some disorder; the food habitually consumed by a person or animal; allowance of provisions (*obs*). — *adj* and *combining form* (*esp* of drinks, often with brand name) having less sugar than the regular version. — *vt* to supply with food (*archaic*); to prescribe a diet for or put on a diet; to keep fasting. — *vi* to feed (*archaic*); to take food according to rule, *esp* in order to lose weight. — *n* **dīetā'rian** (*rare*) a person who observes prescribed rules for diet. — *adj* **dī'etary** pertaining to diet or the rules of diet. — *n* a course of diet; allowance of food, *esp* in large institutions. — *n* **dī'eter** someone who is on a diet; someone who regulates diet (*Shakesp*). — *adj* **dīetet'ic** or **dietet'ical** pertaining to diet. — *adv* **dīetet'ically**. — *n sing* **dīetet'ics** the study of, or rules for regulating, diet. — *n* **dī'etist**, **dīetitian** or **dīetician** (*-ish'ən*) an authority on diet. — **dietary fibre** fibrous substances in fruits, vegetables and cereals which keep bowel movements regular and are thus thought to help prevent certain diseases (also called **roughage**); **di'et-bread** bread designed for people on a diet; **di'et-drink** (*obs*) a medically prescribed drink; **diet sheet** a list of permitted foods (and the quantities recommended) for a person on a diet. [Fr *diète*, from LL *diaeta*, from Gr *diaita* mode of living, diet]

diet[2] *dī'ət*, *n* a national, federal, or provincial assembly, council, or parliament, *esp* (*usu* with *cap*) the national legislature of Japan; a conference; the proceedings under a criminal libel (*Scots law*); a clerical or ecclesiastical function in Scotland, such as a *diet of worship*. — *n* **dī'etine** a minor or local diet. — **desert the diet** to abandon criminal proceedings under a particular libel (*Scots law*). [OFr *diete*, from LL *diēta*, from Gr *diaita*; or according to Littré, from L *diēs* a (set) day, with which usage cf Ger *Tag* day, *Reichstag*]

diethyl *dī-eth'il*, (*chem*) *adj* having two ethyl groups. — *n* **diethylamine** (*-mēn'*) a liquid resembling ethylamine, answering to ammonia, with ethyl groups replacing two hydrogen atoms. **[di-]**

Dieu *dyø*, (*Fr*) *n* God. — **Dieu avec nous** (*a-vek nōō*) God with us; **Dieu défend le droit** God defends the right; **Dieu et mon droit** (*ā mɔ̃ drwä*) God and my right; **Dieu vous garde** (*vōō gärd*) God keep you.

diff. *abbrev*: difference; different.

diffarreation *di-far-i-ā'shən*, (*hist*) *n* a divorce from an ancient Roman marriage by *confarreation*. [L *dif-* (*dis-*) asunder]

differ *dif'ər*, *vi* to be unlike, distinct or various (used by itself, or followed by *from*); to disagree (with *with* or sometimes *from*); to fall out, dispute (*with*). — *n* (*Scot*) a difference of opinion. — *n* **diff'erence** or (*archaic*) **diff'erency** dissimilarity; the quality distinguishing one thing from another; a contention or quarrel; the point in dispute; the excess of one quantity or number over another; differentia; a distinguishing mark; a modification to distinguish the arms of a branch from those of the main line (*heraldry*); discrimination. — *vt* (*rare*) to make or perceive a difference between or in. — *adj* **diff'erent** distinct; separate; unlike; not the same (with *from*, also with *to* and (*esp US*) *than*); out of the ordinary (*colloq*); novel. — *n* **differentia** (*-en'shi-ə*; *L*; *logic*) that property which distinguishes a species from others: — *pl* **differen'tiae** (*-ē*). — *adj* **differen'tial** (*-shəl*) constituting or pertaining to a difference or differentia; discriminating; pertaining to infinitesimal differences (*math*). — *n* an infinitesimal difference; a differential gear; a price difference; the difference between rates of pay set for each category of employees within an industry; the difference in rates of pay between different industries. — *adv* **differen'tially**. — *vt* **differentiate** (*-en'shi-āt*) to make different, cause to develop difference(s); to classify as different; to constitute a difference between; to obtain the differential coefficient of (*math*). — *vi* to become different by specialization; to distinguish (*from* or *between*). — *n* **differentiā'tion** the act of distinguishing; description of a thing by giving its differentia; exact definition; a change by which what was generalized or homogeneous became specialized or heterogeneous; the act or process of differentiating, or determining the ratio of the rates of change of two quantities one of which is a function of the other (*math*). — *n* **differen'tiātor** someone who or that which differentiates. — *adv* **diff'erently**. — **difference tone** or **differential tone** a tone heard when two tones are sounded together, its frequency the difference of their frequencies; **differential calculus** see under **calculus**; **differential coefficient** the ratio of the rate of change of a function to that of its independent variable; **differential equation** one involving total or partial differential coefficients; **differential gear** a gear enabling one driving wheel of a vehicle to move faster than another, eg when cornering; **differential motion** a mechanical movement in which the velocity of a driven part is equal to the difference of the velocities of two parts connected to it; **differential thermometer** a thermometer for measuring difference of temperature. — **agree to differ** to agree to accept amicably a difference of opinion without further argument; **difference of opinion** a matter about which two or more people or groups disagree; **with a difference** with something special; in a special way. [L *differe*, from *dif-* (for *dis-*) apart, and *ferre* to bear]

difficile *di-fis'il*, *dif'i-sil*, (*archaic* or reintroduced) *adj* difficult. [OFr and Fr *difficile*; see **difficult**]

difficult *dif'i-kəlt*, *adj* not easy; hard to do; requiring labour and pains; hard to please; not easily persuaded; unmanageable; hard to resolve or extricate oneself from; potentially embarrassing, etc. — *adv* **diff'icultly** (mainly *chem*; eg *difficultly soluble*). — *n* **diff'iculty** the quality or fact of being difficult; a difficult situation; laboriousness; an obstacle; an objection; that which cannot be easily understood or believed; (*usu* in *pl*) embarrassment of affairs, *esp* financial trouble; a quarrel. — **make difficulties** to be hard to please; to make objections. [The adj was formed from *difficulty*, from Fr *difficulté*, from L *difficultās*, *-ātis*, from *difficilis*, from *dif-* (*dis-*) (negative) and *facilis* easy]

diffident *dif'i-dənt*, *adj* distrusting (*obs*); lacking in self-confidence; overly shy or modest. — *n* **diff'idence**. — *adv* **diff'idently**. [L *diffīdēns*, *-entis*, pr p of *diffīdere* to distrust, from *dif-* (*dis-*) (negative) and *fīdere* to trust, from *fidēs* faith]

diffluent *dif'lōō-ənt*, *adj* readily flowing away; fluid; deliquescent. [L *dis-* apart, and *fluēns*, *-entis*, pr p of *fluere* to flow]

difform *di-förm'*, (*obs*) *adj* unlike; irregular in form. — *n* **difform'ity**. [L *dis-* apart, and *fōrma* form]

diffract *di-frakt'*, *vt* to break up; to subject to diffraction. — *n* **diffrac'tion** the spreading of light or other rays passing through a narrow opening or by the edge of an opaque body or reflected by a grating, etc, with interference phenomena, coloured and other. — *adj* **diffrac'tive**. — *n* **diffractom'eter** an instrument used in the examination of the crystal structure of matter by means of diffraction of X-rays, or of the atomic structure of matter by means of diffraction of electrons or neutrons. — *n* **diffrangibil'ity** (*-franj-*). — *adj*

diffrang'ible capable of being diffracted. [L *diffringere*, *diffrāctum*, from *dis-* asunder, and *frangere* to break]

diffuse[1] *di-fūz'*, *vt* to pour out all round; to send out in all directions; to scatter; to circulate; to publish. — *vi* to spread. — *adj* **diffūsed'** spread widely; loose. — *adv* **diffūs'edly**. — *n* **diffūs'edness**. — *n* **diffūs'er** someone or something that diffuses; an attachment for a light fitting that prevents glare; a duct that, as it widens out, reduces the speed of an airflow or fluid. — *n* **diffūsibil'ity**. — *adj* **diffūs'ible**. — *n* **diffū'sion** a spreading or scattering abroad; extension; distribution; the movement of molecules and ions in a fluid from areas of high to areas of low concentration; spread of cultural elements from one region or community to another (*anthropol*). — *n* **diffū'sionism** (*anthropol*) the theory that diffusion is mainly responsible for cultural similarities. — *n* **diffū'sionist**. — *adj* **diffū'sive** (*-siv*) extending; spreading widely. — *adv* **diffū'sively**. — *n* **diffū'siveness** or **diffūsiv'ity**. — **diffused lighting** lighting that is transmitted or reflected in all directions and, being evenly distributed, produces no glare; **diffusion plant** (*nuc eng*) a plant used for isotope separation by gaseous or thermal diffusion; **diffu'sion-tube** an instrument for determining the rate of diffusion for different gases. [L *diffundere*, *diffūsum*, from *dif-* (*dis-*) asunder, and *fundere* to pour out]

diffuse[2] *di-fūs'*, *adj* diffused; widely spread; wordy; not concise. — *adv* **diffuse'ly**. — *n* **diffuse'ness**. [Root as for **diffuse**[1]]

DIG *dig*, *abbrev*: Disablement Income Group.

dig *dig*, *vt* to excavate; to turn up with a spade or otherwise; to get or put by digging; to poke or thrust; to taunt; to understand or approve (*old slang*); to take note of (*old slang*). — *vi* to use a spade; to seek (for) by digging (*lit* and *fig*); to burrow; to mine; to lodge (*colloq*); to study hard (*NAm slang*): — *pr p* **digg'ing**; *pa t* and *pa p* **dug** or (*archaic*; *Bible*) **digged**. — *n* an act or course of digging; an archaeological excavating expedition; an excavation made by archaeologists; a poke; a taunt; a hard-working student (*NAm slang*). — *adj* **digg'able**. — *n* **digg'er** a person or animal that digs; a miner, *esp* a gold-miner; an Australian or New Zealand soldier; an Australian *colloq* form of address; a machine for digging. — *n pl* **digg'ings** places where mining is carried on, *esp* for gold; digs. — *n pl* **digs** (*colloq*) accommodation; lodgings. — **digg'er-wasp** a burrowing wasp of various kinds; **digging stick** a primitive tool, a pointed stick, sometimes weighted, for digging the ground. — **dig a pit for** (*fig*) to set a trap for; **dig in** to cover over by digging; to work hard; to take up a defensive position (*lit* or *fig*); to begin eating (*colloq*); **dig oneself in** to entrench oneself; to establish oneself in a position; **dig one's heels in** to refuse to be moved or persuaded; **dig out** to decamp (*US slang*); to unearth (*lit* or *fig*); **dig up** to remove from the ground by digging; to excavate; to obtain by seeking (*colloq*); to produce, *esp* reluctantly (*colloq*). [Prob OFr *diguer* to dig; of Gmc origin]

digamma *dī-gam'ə*, *n* vau, the obsolete sixth letter (Ϝ, Ͱ, later ς) of the Greek alphabet with the sound of our *w*; as a numeral ς′ = 6, ͵ς = 6000. — See **episemon**. [Gr *di-* twice, and *gamma*, from its form like one capital *Γ* over another]

digamy *dig'ə-mi*, *n* a second marriage (after death of partner or divorce). — *n* **dig'amist**. — *adj* **dig'amous**. [Gr *di-* twice, and *gamos* marriage]

digastric *dī-gas'trik*, (*anatom*) *adj* double-bellied, or fleshy at each end, as is one of the muscles of the lower jaw. [Gr *di-* double, and *gastēr* the belly]

digest[1] *di-jest'* (also *dī-*), *vt* to dissolve in the stomach; to soften by heat and moisture (*chem*); to distribute and arrange; to prepare or classify in the mind; to think over, to take in gradually, the meaning and implications of; to endure (eg an insult) without protest (*old-fashioned*). — *vi* to be dissolved in the stomach; to be softened by heat and moisture. — *adv* **digest'edly**. — *n* **digest'er** someone who digests; a closed vessel in which by heat and pressure strong extracts are made from animal and vegetable substances. — *n* **digestibil'ity**. — *adj* **digest'ible** that may be digested. — *n* **digestion** (*di-jest'yən*) the dissolving of the food in the stomach; orderly arrangement; mental assimilation; exposing to slow heat, etc (*chem*). — *adj* **digest'ive** pertaining to digestion; promoting digestion. — *n* something which promotes digestion; (also **digestive biscuit**) a round, semi-sweet biscuit, the basic ingredient of which is meal. — *adv* **digest'ively**. — **digestive tract** the alimentary canal. [L *dīgerere*, *dīgestum* to carry asunder or dissolve, from *dī-* (*dis-*) asunder, and *gerere* to bear]

digest[2] *dī'jest*, *n* a body of laws collected and arranged, *esp* the Justinian code of civil laws; a synopsis; an abstract; a periodical abstract of news or current literature. [L *dīgesta*, neuter pl of *dīgestus*, pa p of *dīgerere* to carry apart, to arrange]

dight *dīt*, *vt* to adorn (*archaic*); to equip (*archaic*); (*dihht*) another spelling of **dicht**. — *adj* disposed; adorned. [OE *dihtan* to arrange, prescribe, from L *dictāre* to dictate (whence Ger *dichten* to write poetry)]

digit *dij'it*, *n* a finger or toe; a finger's breadth as a unit of measurement (1·9 cm or $\frac{3}{4}$ inch); a figure, *esp* one used in arithmetic to represent a number; any one of the Arabic numerals from 0 to 9; the twelfth part of the diameter of the sun or moon (*astron*). — *adj* **dig'ital** pertaining to the fingers, or to arithmetical digits; showing numerical information by a set of digits to be read off, instead of by a pointer on a dial, etc (as in *digital clock*, *digital thermometer*); (of electronic circuits) responding to and producing signals which at any given time are at any one of a number of possible discrete levels, generally either one of two levels; (of continuous data, eg sound signals) separated into discrete units to facilitate transmission, processing, etc, or of the transmission, etc of sound, etc, in this form (**digital transmission** (*comput*) the sending of computer data from one location to another by using a modem to convert the data into electronic impulses which can be sent along telecommunications lines to a distant point, where a modem converts the impulses back to the original form of the data). — *n* a finger (*joc*); a key of a piano, etc. — *n* **digitalin** (*dij-i-tā'lin* or *dij'it-ə-lin*) a glucoside or mixture of glucosides obtained from digitalis leaves, used as a heart-stimulant. — *n* **digitā'lis** any plant of the foxglove genus *Digitalis*; dried foxglove leaves used as a drug. — *n* **dig'italization** or **-s-**. — *vt* and *vi* **dig'italize** or **-s-** to give digitalis to (a patient) for the treatment of certain heart conditions. — *adj* **dig'itate** or **dig'itated** (of leaves) consisting of several fingerlike sections. — *adv* **dig'itately**. — *n* **digitā'tion** fingerlike arrangement; a fingerlike division. — *adj* **digit'iform** formed like fingers. — *adj* **dig'itigrade** walking on the toes. — *n* an animal that walks on its toes. — *n* **digitīzā'tion** or **-s-**. — *vt* **dig'itize** or **-ise** to put (data) into digital form, eg for use in a digital computer. — *n* **dig'itizer** or **-s-** (*comput*) a device which converts analogue signals to digital codes (also **analogue-to-digital** or **A/D converter**); a device which converts pictures captured by a video camera into digital form for computer input (also **video digitizer**). — *n* **digitō'rium** a pianist's dumb keyboard for finger exercises. — **digital audio tape** (*abbrev* **DAT**, **Dat** or **dat**) a magnetic audio tape on which sound has been recorded digitally; this form of recorded sound, affording greater clarity and compactness, and less distortion than conventional recording; **digital clock** or **watch** a clock or watch, without a conventional face, on which the time is indicated directly by numbers; **digital compact cassette** (*abbrev* **DCC**) a digital audio tape, in standard cassette format, that is played via a fixed-head tape recorder; this form of recorded sound; **digital compact disc** a compact disc (qv); **digital computer** an electronic calculating machine using arithmetical digits, generally binary or decimal notation; **digital recording** a digital means of storing and transmitting information electronically, eg in sound recording where frequency and amplitude features of the sound wave are measured, expressed and stored in digital form (as on compact disc or digital audio tape); **digital socks** socks with individual toe-coverings similar to the fingers of gloves; **digitizing board**, **pad**, **table** or **tablet** a device consisting of a flat surface on which diagrams may be drawn with a special stylus, the co-ordinates of the position of the stylus at any given point on the diagram being digitized for storage, etc. [L *digitus* finger, toe]

digladiate *dī-glad'i-āt, vi* (*obs*) to fight with swords; to fence; to wrangle. — *n* **digladiā'tion**. — *n* **diglad'iātor**. [L *dīgladiārī* to contend fiercely, from *dis-* this way and that, and *gladius* sword]

diglot *dī'glot, adj* bilingual. — *n* a bilingual person or book. [Gr *diglōttos*, from *di-* double, and *glōtta*, tongue]

diglyph *dī'glif*, (*archit*) *n* an ornament consisting of a double groove. [Gr *di-* double, and *glyphē* carving]

dignify *dig'ni-fī, vt* to invest with honour; to exalt; to lend an air of dignity to (as in *dignify with the name of*): — *pr p* **dig'nifying**; *pa t* and *pa p* **dig'nified**. — *n* **dignificā'tion**. — *adj* **dig'nified** marked or consistent with dignity; exalted; noble; grave; ranking as a dignitary. [LL *dīgnificāre*, from *dīgnus* worthy, and *facere* to make]

dignity *dig'ni-ti, n* the state of being dignified; elevation of mind or character; grandeur of bearing or appearance; elevation in rank, place, etc; degree of excellence; preferment; high office; a dignitary. — *n* **dig'nitary** someone in a high position or rank, *esp* in the church. — **beneath one's dignity** degrading, at least in one's own estimation; **stand on one's dignity** to assume a manner that asserts a claim to be treated with respect. [Fr *dignité*, from L *dīgnitās, -ātis*, from *dīgnus* worthy]

digonal *dig'ə-nl*, (*math*, etc) *adj* (of symmetry about an axis) such that a half-turn (180°) gives the same figure. [Gr *di-* twice, and *gōniā* angle]

digoneutic *dig-ə-nūt'ik*, (*zool*) *adj* breeding twice a year. [Gr *di-* twice, and *goneus* a parent]

digraph *dī'gräf, n* two letters expressing a single sound, such as *ph* in *digraph*. [Gr *di-* twice, and *graphē* a mark, a character, from *graphein* to write]

digress *dī-gres', di-gres', vi* to depart from the main subject; to introduce irrelevant matter. — *n* **digression** (*-gresh'ən*) a departure from the main point; a part of a discourse not about the main subject. — *adj* **digress'ional** or **digress'ive** of the nature of a digression; departing from the main subject. — *adv* **digress'ively**. [L *dīgredī, digressus*, from *dī-* (*dis-*) aside, and *gradī* to step]

digs. See **dig**.

Digynia *dī-jin'i-ə, n pl* in various Linnaean classes of plants, an order with two styles or a deeply cleft style. — *adj* **digyn'ian**. — *adj* **digynous** (*dij'* or *dī'i-nəs*) digynian; with two styles or two carpels. [Gr *di-* twice, and *gynē* a woman]

DIH *abbrev*: Diploma in Industrial Health.

dihedral *dī-hē'drəl*, sometimes **diedral** *dī-ē'drəl*, (*math*, etc) *adj* bounded by two planes, or two plane faces. — *n* a dihedral angle. — *n* **dihē'dron** the limiting case of a double pyramid when the vertices coincide. — **dihedral angle** the angle made by the wing of an aeroplane with the horizontal axis. [Gr *di-* twice, and *hedrā* a seat]

dihybrid *dī-hī'brid*, (*biol*) *n* a cross between parents that differ in two independently heritable characters. — Also *adj*. [Gr *di-* double, twice, and **hybrid**]

dihydric *dī-hī'drik*, (*chem*) *adj* having two hydroxyl groups. [**di-**]

dijudicate *dī-jōō'di-kāt, vt* and *vi* to judge; to decide. — *n* **dijudicā'tion**. [L *dī-* (*dis-*) asunder, and *jūdicāre* to judge]

dika *dī'kə, dē'kə, n* a West Indian tree of the Simarubaceae (*Irvingia gabonensis*), the so-called wild mango. — **di'ka-bread** a compressed mass of dika and other seeds, smelling like chocolate; **di'ka-butter** or **-oil** a fat expressed from its seeds. [From a W Afr name]

dikast. See **dicast**.

dik-dik *dik'dik, n* a name for several very small E African antelopes, of the genus *Madoqua*. [Said to be a name in Ethiopia]

dike[1] or **dyke** *dīk, n* a trench, or the earth dug out and thrown up; a ditch; a mound raised to prevent flooding; in Scotland, a wall (**dry-stane dike** a wall without mortar; **fail'-dike** a wall of turf), sometimes even a thorn-hedge; an igneous mass injected into a fissure in rocks, sometimes weathered out into wall-like forms (*geol*); a lavatory (*old slang*). — *vt* to provide with a dike. — *vi* to make a dike. — *n* **dīk'er** a person who makes dikes. — **dike'-louper** (*Scot*) an animal which jumps the fence, etc around its pasture; an immoral person (*fig*); **dike swarm** (*geol*) a series of dikes of the same age, *usu* trending in a constant direction over a wide area. [OE *dīc*, whence also **ditch**, this and related words in the Germanic languages denoting both a trench dug out and the mound of earth so formed; cf Ger *Teich* a pond, *Deich* (orig LGer) an embankment, Du *dijk* a bank, dam, Dan *dige* a bank, dam, Swed *dike* a ditch, trench]

dike[2] or **dyke** *dīk*, (*slang*) *n* a lesbian. — *adj* **dīk'ey** or **dyk'ey**. [Origin unknown]

dikkop (*SAfr*) *n* the stone-curlew. [Afrik *dik* thick, and *kop* head]

diktat *dik-tät', n* a harsh settlement forced on the defeated or powerless; an order or statement allowing no opposition. [Ger, something dictated]

dil. *abbrev*: dilute.

dilacerate *di-las'ər-āt, vt* to rend or tear asunder. — *n* **dilacerā'tion**. [L *dī-* asunder, and **lacerate**]

dilapidate *di-lap'i-dāt, vt* to pull down stone by stone; to waste; to allow to go to ruin. — *adj* **dilap'idated** in ruin; in a state of disrepair. — *n* **dilapidā'tion** the state of ruin; (in *pl*) damage done to a building during tenancy (*law*); impairing of church property during an incumbency (*eccles*); (in *pl*) money paid at the end of an incumbency by the incumbent or his heirs for the purpose of putting the parsonage, etc in good repair (*eccles*). — *n* **dilap'idātor**. [L *dīlapidāre*, from *dī-* asunder, and *lapis, lapidis* a stone]

dilate *dī-lāt', di-lāt', vt* to spread out in all directions; to expand; to enlarge; to set forth at full length (*Shakesp*, etc). — *vi* to widen; to swell out; to expand; to speak at length. — *n* **dilātabil'ity**. — *adj* **dilāt'able** that may be dilated or expanded. — *n* **dilāt'ancy** (*chem*) the property shown by some colloidal systems of thickening or solidifying under pressure or impact. — *adj* **dilāt'ant** tending to dilate; showing dilatancy. — *n* **dilatation** (*-lə-tā'shən*) or (irregularly formed) **dilā'tion** expansion; a transformation which produces a figure similar to, but not congruent with, the original (*math*). — *n* **dil'atātor** an instrument or a muscle that expands. — *adj* **dilāt'ed** expanded and flattened. — *n* **dilā'tor** a dilatator; someone who dilates (also **dilāt'er**). — *adj* **dilāt'ive**. [L *dīlātāre* to spread out, from *dī-* (*dis-*) apart, and *lātus* wide]

dilatory *dil'ə-tə-ri, adj* slow; given to procrastination; loitering; tending to delay. — *adv* **dil'atorily**. — *n* **dil'atoriness**. [L *dīlātōrius*, from *differre, dīlātum* to postpone]

dildo *dil'dō, n* an object serving as an erect penis substitute (also **dil'doe**; *slang*); word used in refrains of songs (*obs*); a weak or effeminate man (*obs*); a cylindrical curl; a W Indian spiny cactus (*Lemaireocereus hystrix*): — *pl* **dil'dos** or **dil'does**. — **dil'do-glass** a cylindrical glass. [Origin uncertain]

dilemma *di-, dī-lem'ə, n* a position where each of two alternative courses (or of all the feasible courses) is eminently undesirable; (loosely) a predicament, problem; a form of argument in which the maintainer of a certain proposition is committed to accept one of two propositions each of which contradicts his or her original contention (the argument was called a 'horned syllogism', and the victim compared to a man certain to be impaled on one or other of the horns of an infuriated bull, hence the **horns of a dilemma**; *logic*). — *adj* **dilemmat'ic**. — **on the horns of a dilemma** in a dilemma (see comments above). [L, from Gr *dilēmma*, from *di-* twice, double and *lēmma* an assumption, from *lambanein* to take]

dilettante *dil-et-an'ti*, *n* a person who loves the fine arts but in a superficial way and without serious purpose (the *amateur* usually practises them); a dabbler in art, science or literature: — *pl* **dilettan'ti** (*-tē*). — Also *adj*. — *adj* **dilettan'tish**. — *n* **dilettan'tism** or **dilettan'teism**. [Ital, pr p of *dilettare*, from L *dēlectāre* to delight]

diligent *dil'i-jənt*, *adj* steady and earnest in application; industrious. — *n* **dil'igence** steady application; industry; a warrant to produce witnesses, books, etc, or a process by which persons or goods are attached (*Scots law*); (also pronounced *dē-lē-zhās*) a French or continental stagecoach (also **dill'y**; *hist*). — *adv* **dil'-igently**. [Fr, from *dīligēns*, *-entis*, pr p of L *dīligere* to choose]

dill[1] *dil*, *n* an umbelliferous annual Eurasian herb related to parsnip, the fruits or 'seeds' of which are used in condiments and as a carminative. — **dill pickle** pickled cucumber flavoured with dill; **dill'-wat'er** a medicinal drink prepared from the seeds. [OE *dile*; Ger *Dill*, Swed *dill*]

dill[2] *dil*, (*Austr colloq*) *n* a fool. [Prob **dilly**[3]]

dilli. See **dilly-bag**.

dilling *dil'ing*, *n* a darling (*obs*); the youngest child (*obs*); the weakling of a litter (*dialect*). [Origin doubtful]

dilly[1]. See **diligence** and **dilly-bag**.

dilly[2] *dil'i*, (*colloq*) *n* an excellent or very pleasing person or thing. — Also *adj*. [Perh contraction of **delightful**]

dilly[3] *dil'i*, (*Austr colloq*) *adj* foolish, silly. [Prob **daft** and **silly**]

dilly-bag *dil'i-bag*, *n* an Australian Aboriginal bag, made of woven grass or fibre; a small bag. — Also **dill'i** or **dill'y**. [Aboriginal *dilli*, and **bag**]

dilly-dally *dil'i-dal'i*, (*colloq*) *vi* to loiter or trifle. [Reduplication of **dally**; cf **shilly-shally**]

dilucidate *di-lū'si-dāt*, *di-lōō'*, (*obs*) *vt* to elucidate. — *n* **dilucidā'tion**. [L *dīlūcidāre*, *-ātum*]

dilute *di-lūt'*, *di-lōōt'*, or *dī*, *vt* to make thinner or more liquid; to diminish the concentration of, by mixing, *esp* with water; to make less strong, powerful or forceful; (of labour) to increase the proportion of unskilled to skilled in. — *vi* to become mixed. — *adj* (*di-* or *dī-lūt'*, *-lōōt'*, or *dī'*) diminished in concentration by mixing. — *adj* **diluent** (*dil'ū-ənt*) diluting. — *n* that which dilutes. — *adj* **dilut'able**. — *n* a drink such as a fruit squash which is diluted before being drunk. — *n* **dilut'ee** an unskilled worker introduced into a skilled occupation. — *n* **dilute'ness**. — *n* **dilut'er** or **dilut'or** someone who or that which dilutes. — *n* **dilu'tion**. — *adj* **dilu'tionary** tending to dilute. [L *dīluere*, *dīlūtum*, from *dī-* away, and *luere* to wash]

diluvium *dil-ū'vi-əm*, *dil-ōō'*, *n* an inundation or flood; a loose glacial deposit of sand, gravel, etc; a deposit of sand, gravel, etc made by extraordinary currents of water (*geol*; *obs*). — Also **dilu'vion**. — *adj* **dilu'vial** pertaining to a flood, *esp* that told of in the Bible, in the time of Noah; caused by a deluge; composed of diluvium. — *n* **dilu'vialism**. — *n* **dilu'vialist** someone who explains geological phenomena by Noah's flood, told of in the Bible. — *adj* **dilu'vian** diluvial. [L *dīluvium* a deluge, from *dīluere* to wash away]

dim *dim*, *adj* not bright or distinct; obscure; not seeing clearly; mentally dull, stupid (*colloq*). — *vt* to make dark; to dip (headlights) (*NAm*); to obscure. — *vi* to become dim: — *pr p* **dimm'ing**; *pa t* and *pa p* **dimmed**. — *adv* **dim'ly**. — *n* **dimm'er** a device for regulating the supply of light. — *adj* **dimm'ish** somewhat dim. — *n* **dim'ness**. — **dim'wit** (*colloq*) a stupid person. — **a dim view** (*colloq*) an unfavourable view; **dim out** to reduce the lighting (of) gradually (*n* **dim'-out'**). [OE *dimm*; related to ON *dimmr* dark, and Ger *Dämmerung* twilight]

dim. *abbrev*: dimension; diminuendo (also **dimin.**; *music*); diminutive (also **dimin.**).

di majorum gentium *dī mə-jō'rəm*, or *-jö' jen'sh(y)əm* or *dē ma-yō'rōōm gen'ti-ōōm*, (*L*) the divinities of superior rank, ie the twelve greater gods of classical mythology.

dimble *dim'bl*, (*dialect*) *n* a dell, a dingle.

dime *dīm*, *n* the tenth part of an American and Canadian dollar, 10 cents; a coin of this value; a small sum of money. — **dime museum** a cheap show; **dime novel** a cheap novel, *usu* sensational; **dime store** (*US*) a shop selling cheap goods (*orig* costing not more than a dime). — **a dime a dozen** cheap, commonplace. [Fr, orig *disme*, from L *decima* (*pars*) a tenth (part)]

dimension *dī-* or *di-men'shən*, *n* measure in length, breadth or thickness (the three dimensions of space); scope, extent (also *fig*); size; the sum of the indices in a term (*algebra*); a factor or aspect; a concept, development in range or quality, etc. — *vt* to give the dimensions of; to make to specified dimensions. — *adj* **dimen'sional** concerning dimension. — *combining form* of so many dimensions, as in *three-dimensional*. — *adj* **dimen'-sioned**. — *adj* **dimen'sionless**. — **dimension work** masonry in stones of specified size. — **fourth dimension** an additional dimension attributed to space; (in relativity theory, etc) time; **new dimension** a fresh aspect; **third dimension** depth, thickness; a rounding out, completeness, given by added information, detail, etc (*fig*). [Fr, from L *dīmēnsiō*, *-ōnis*, from *dīmētīrī*, *dīmēnsus*, from *dī* (*dis-*) apart, and *mētīrī* to measure]

dimer *dī'mər*, (*chem*) *n* a compound whose molecule has twice as many atoms as another compound of the same empirical formula (the *monomer*). — *adj* **dīmeric** (*-mer'ik*). — *n* **dīmerizā'tion** or **-s-**. — *vt* **dī'merize** or **-ise**. [**di-**, and mono*mer*]

dimerous *dim'ə-rəs*, *adj* consisting of two parts; with two members in each whorl (*bot*); having two-jointed tarsi (*entomol*). — *adj* **dimeric** (*dī-mer'ik*) bilaterally symmetrical; dimerous. — *n* **dimerism** (*dim'ər-izm*). [Gr *di-* double, twice, and *meros* a part]

dimeter *dim'i-tər*, (*prosody*) *adj* containing two measures. — *n* a verse of two measures. [L, from Gr *dimetros*, from *di-* twice, and *metron* a measure]

dimethyl *dī-meth'il*, *n* ethane. — *adj* containing two methyl radicals in combination. — *n* **dimeth'ylamine** (*-ə-mēn*) a compound answering to ammonia with methyl replacing two hydrogen atoms. — *n* **dimethylan'iline** an oily liquid, aniline heated with methyl alcohol and hydrochloric acid, from which dyes are obtained. [**di-**]

dimetric *dī-met'rik*, (*crystallog*) *adj* tetragonal. [**di-** and **metric** pertaining to distance]

dimidiate *di-mid'i-āt*, *adj* divided into halves; having a shape that appears as if halved; having only one side developed (*biol*); split on one side (*bot*). — *vt* (*heraldry*) to represent the half of. — *n* **dimidiā'tion**. [L *dīmidiāre*, *-ātum* to halve, from *dīmidius* half, from *dis-* apart, and *medius* the middle]

dimin. See **dim**. (*abbrev*).

diminish *di-min'ish*, *vt* to make less; to take a part from; to degrade or belittle. — *vi* to grow or appear less; to subside. — *adj* **dimin'ishable**. — *adj* **dimin'ished** made smaller; lessened; humbled; of a semitone less than perfect or minor (*music*). — *n* and *adj* **dimin'ishing**. — *adv* **dimin'ishingly**. — *n* **dimin'ishment**. — **diminished responsibility** limitation in law of criminal responsibility on the grounds of mental weakness or abnormality, not merely of actual insanity; **diminishing glass** a lens or combination of lenses that makes objects appear smaller. — **law of diminishing returns** the fact that there is a point beyond which any additional amount of work, expenditure, taxation, etc results in progressively smaller output, profits, yields, etc. [Coined from (archaic) **minish**, in imitation of L *dīminuere* to break in pieces, from *dī-* (from *dis-*) apart, and *minuere* to make less, which in LL replaced the earlier *dēminuere* to lessen, from *dē* from, and *minuere*]

diminuendo *di-min-ū-en'dō*, (*music*) *adj* and *adv* letting the sound die away. — Also *n*: — *pl* **diminuen'does** or **diminuen'dos**. [Ital, from LL *dīminuendus*, for L *dēminuendus*, gerundive of *dēminuere* to lessen (see **diminish**)]

diminution *dim-in-ū'shən*, *n* a lessening; decrease. — *adj* **dimin'utive** of a diminished size; very small; contracted. — *n* a word formed from another to express a little one of the kind (*gram*); one of the smaller ordinaries, of the same shape as one of the larger ones (*heraldry*). — *adv* **dimin'utively**. — *n* **dimin'utiveness**. [**diminish**]

dimissory *dim'is-ə-ri*, *di-*, *dī-mis'ə-ri*, *adj* sending away or giving leave to depart to another jurisdiction. [L *dīmissōrius*, from *dīmittere*, *dīmissum*, from *dis-* apart, and *mittere* to send]

dimity *dim'i-ti*, *n* a stout white cotton, striped or figured in the loom by weaving with two threads. [Gr *dimitos*, from *di-* twice, and *mitos* a thread]

dimmer, **dimming**. See **dim**.

dimorphism *dī-mör'fizm*, *n* the occurrence of two forms in the same species (*biol*); the property of crystallizing in two forms (*chem*). — *n* **dī'morph** either of the two forms of a dimorphous species or substance. — *adj* **dimor'phic** or **dimor'phous**. [Gr *di-* twice, and *morphē* form]

dimple *dim'pl*, *n* a small hollow, *esp* on a person's cheek or chin; a shallow depression in a surface; a depression or bubble in glass. — *vi* to form dimples. — *adj* **dim'pled**. — *n* **dim'plement** (*rare*). — *adj* **dim'ply**. [Appar cognate with Ger *Tümpel* pool]

dim sum *dim sum*, *n* a selection of Chinese foods, often eaten as an appetiser, *usu* including steamed dumplings with various fillings. [Chin]

dimwit. See **dim**.

dimyarian *dim-i-* or *dī-mī-ā'ri-ən*, (*zool*) *adj* having two adductor muscles. [Gr *di-* twice, and *mȳs*, *myos* muscle]

DIN *din*, *n* a unit of measurement of the speed of photographic film; a standard system of plugs and sockets used to connect domestic audio and video equipment. [Abbrev Ger *D*eutsche *I*ndustrie *N*orm, German Industry Standard]

din *din*, *n* a loud continued jarring noise. — *vt* to assail (the ears) with noise; to annoy with clamour; to obtrude noisily and persistently: — *pr p* **dinn'ing**; *pa t* and *pa p* **dinned**. — *adj* **din'ful**. — **din into** (*colloq*) to instil (knowledge) into (a person) by forceful repetition. [OE *dynn*, *dyne*; cf ON *dynr*, Dan *dön* noise]

dinanderie *dē-nã-də-rē*, *n* (also with *cap*) domestic decorative brassware, originally that made at *Dinant* in Belgium; extended to Indian and Levantine brassware. [Fr]

Dinantian *din-an'shi-ən*, (*geol*) *adj* Lower Carboniferous. [*Dinant* in Belgium]

dinar *dē-när'*, *n* the monetary unit of Yugoslavia, and of Algeria, Tunisia, Iraq, and other Arab countries; an ancient Arab gold coin of 65 grains' weight. [L *dēnārius*]

dinarchy. See **diarchy**.

dindle. See **dinnle**.

dine *dīn*, *vi* to take dinner. — *vt* to provide with a dinner. — *n* (*obs*) dinner, dinner-time. — *n* **din'er** a person who dines; a dining-car on a train; a small, inexpensive restaurant (*esp NAm*). — *n* **dinette'** an alcove or other part of a room or kitchen set apart for meals. — **din'er-out** a person who goes much to dinner parties; **din'ing-car** a railway carriage in which meals are served; **din'ing-hall**; **din'ing-room**; **din'ing-table**. — **dine off** or **on** to have as one's dinner; **dine out** to dine somewhere other than at home; **dine out on** to be invited to dinner, or (loosely) to enjoy social success, on the strength of (one's possession of eg interesting information); **dine with Duke Humphrey** (*hist*) to go without a meal, loiter about Duke Humphrey's Walk in Old St Paul's. [OFr *disner* (Fr *dîner*) prob from L *dis-* expressing undoing, and *jējūnus* fasting (cf **disjune**); according to others, from L *dē-* (intensive) and *cēna* a meal]

DIng *abbrev*: *Doctor Ingeniariae* (*L*), Doctor of Engineering.

ding[1] *ding*, *vt* (all senses *archaic* or *dialect*) to dash; to beat; to thump; to knock; to surpass (*Scot*). — *vi* to beat (*Scot*); to dash (*obs*): — *pa t* **dinged**, **dang** or **dung**; *pa p* **dinged** or **dung**. — *n* **ding'er** (*slang*) anything superlative in its kind. — **ding doun** (*do͞on*; *Scot*) to knock or throw down. [ME *dingen*, *dyngen*; cf ON *dengja*, Swed *dänga* to bang]

ding[2] *ding*, *vi* to ring; to sound; to keep sounding. — *vt* to reiterate to a wearisome degree. — **ding'-dong'** the sound of bells ringing; monotony; sameness; an argument or fight. — *adj* and *adv* like a bell ringing; hammer-and-tongs; keenly contested with rapid alternations of success. — *vt* and *vi* to ring; to nag. [Imit, but partly confused with **ding**[1]]

Ding an sich *ding an zihh*, (*Ger*; *philos*) *n* the thing-in-itself, the noumenon.

dingbat *ding'bat*, (*US slang*) *n* something whose name one has forgotten, or does not want to use; a foolish or eccentric person; a tramp; money. — *adj* **ding'bats** (*Austr* and *NZ colloq*) daft, crazy. — **the dingbats** (*Austr* and *NZ colloq*) delirium tremens. [Perh **ding**[1] and **bat**[1]]

dinge[1] *dinj*, (*US derog slang*) *n* a Negro. — *adj* of or relating to Negroes.

dinge[2]. See **dingy**.

dinges *ding'əs*, (*SAfr colloq*) *n* an indefinite name for any person or thing whose name one cannot or will not remember. — Also **ding'us**. [Du, from Afrik *ding* thing; cf Eng **thingummy** and **thingumbob**]

dinghy or (*esp* formerly) **dingy** or **dingey** *ding'gi*, *n* a small open boat, propelled by oars, sails or an outboard motor; an inflatable boat, *esp* one kept for use in emergencies. [Hindi *dingī* a small boat]

dingle *ding'gl*, *n* a wooded hollow; a dell. [Origin uncertain]

dingle-dangle *ding'gl-dang'gl*, *adv* swinging to and fro. [Reduplication of **dangle**]

dingo *ding'gō*, *n* the tawny-coloured wild dog of Australia; a cheat or coward (*Austr slang*): — *pl* **ding'oes**. [Name in obs Aboriginal dialect]

dingus. See **dinges**.

dingy[1] *din'ji*, *adj* dim or dark; shabby and dirty-looking; dull; soiled. — *n* **dinge** dinginess. — *vt* to make dingy. — *n* **din'giness**. [Origin obscure]

dingy[2]. See **dinghy**.

dinic *din'ik*, (*rare*) *adj* relating to vertigo or dizziness. — *n* a remedy for dizziness. [Gr *dīnos* whirling]

dinitro- *dī-nī'trō-*, *combining form* denoting (a chemical) having two nitro-groups (NO_2), *esp* replacing hydrogen. — *n* **dinitroben'zene** $C_6H_4(NO_2)_2$, corresponding to *benzene*, C_6H_6.

dink[1] *dingk*, *adj* (*Scot*) neat, trim. — *vt* and *vi* (*Scot*) to dress neatly; to adorn. — *adj* **dink'y** (*colloq*) neat; dainty; trivial, insignificant (*NAm*).

dink[2] *dingk*, (*tennis*; *US*) *n* a drop-shot, *esp* one that drops just past the net. — *vt* and *vi* to play such a shot. [Imit]

dinkum *ding'kəm*, (*Austr* and *NZ colloq*) *adj* real, genuine; square, honest. — Also *adv*. — Emphatically **fair dinkum**. — Also **dink'y-di** or **-die**. [Eng dialect *dinkum* a fair share of work]

dinky[1] *ding'ki*, (*colloq*) *n* *d*ouble- (or *d*ual-) *i*ncome *n*o *k*ids, an acronym applied to a member of a young, childless (*usu* married) couple both earning a good salary, who thus enjoy an affluent lifestyle: — *pl* **dink'ies**. — Also *adj*.

dinky[2]. See **dink**[1].

dinmont *din'mənt*, *n* a Border name for a male sheep between the first and second shearing. [Origin obscure]

dinner *din'ər*, *n* the chief meal of the day, at midday or (*usu*) in the evening; a formal meal or public banquet, often in celebration of a person or event. — *vi* to dine. — *vt* to provide with dinner. — *adj* **dinn'erless**. — **dinn'er-dance** a dance following a formal dinner; **dinn'er-gown** a less formal evening dress; **dinner hour**;

dinner jacket a man's tailless dress-jacket, *usu* black; **dinner lady** a woman who cooks and/or serves meals in a school canteen; **dinn'er-pail** a vessel in which a workman carries his dinner (*US*); **dinner party** a party at which dinner is served; **dinner plate**; **dinner service** or **dinner set** a complete set of plates and dishes for a company at dinner; **dinner table**; **dinn'er-time**; **dinn'er-wagon** *orig* a shelved trolley for a dining-room; a sideboard in two tiers, for holding dishes, etc. [OFr *disner* (properly) breakfast; see **dine**]

dinnle *din'l*, (*Scot*) *vi* to tingle; to shake, vibrate. — *vt* to cause to tingle, shake or vibrate. — *n* a thrill, vibration, tremor, tingling. — Also **din'dle**. [Prob imitative]

dino- or (*archaic*) **deino-** *dī-nō-*, *combining form* denoting huge, terrible. — *n* **Dinoceras** or **Deinoceras** (*-nos'ə-rəs*; Gr *keras* horn) a large Eocene fossil stump-footed ungulate of Wyoming, also known as Uintatherium, named from three pairs of protuberances on the skull; **Dinornis** or **Deinornis** (*dī-nör'nis*; Gr *ornis* a bird) a genus of moas, including the biggest. — *n* **dinosaur** or **deinosaur** (*dī'nə-sör*; Gr *sauros* a lizard) any extinct (Mesozoic) reptile of the order **Dinosaur'ia** from two to eighty feet in length; a chance survivor of a type characteristic of a bygone era (*fig*). — *adj* (*fig*) **dinosaur'ic**. — *n* **dinothere** or **deinothere** (*dīn'ə-thēr*), **dinotherium** or **deinotherium** (*-thē'ri-əm*; Gr *thērion* a beast) any extinct elephantine mammal of the genus *Deinotherium* with downward-curving tusks. [Gr *deinos* terrible]

dinoflagellate *dī-nō-flaj'ə-lāt*, *n* a unicellular organism, a plant-like flagellate with two flagella. [Gr *dīnos* whirl, and **flagellate**]

Dinornis, **dinosaur**, etc. See under **dino-**.

dint *dint*, *n* a blow or stroke (*archaic*); the mark of a blow (*archaic*, now *usu* **dent**); force (as in *by dint of*). — *vt* (*archaic*) to make a dint in. [OE *dynt* a blow; cf **dunt**[1]; ON *dyntr*]

diocese *dī'ə-sis* or *-sēs*, *n* the circuit or extent of a bishop's jurisdiction. — *adj* **diocesan** (*dī-os'i-sn* or *-zn*) pertaining to a diocese. — *n* a bishop in relation to his diocese; one of the clergy in the diocese. [Through Fr and L from Gr *dioikēsis*, from *dioikeein* to keep house, from *di-*, for *dia-* (signifying completeness) and *oikeein* to keep house, from *oikos* a house]

diode *dī'ōd*, (*electronics*) *n* a semiconductor device which allows current to flow in only one direction around a circuit (also **semiconductor diode**); the earliest and simplest type of valve, an electron tube with heated cathode and anode. [Gr *di-* twice, and *hodos* way]

Diodon *dī'ə-don*, *n* a genus of globe fishes with all the teeth in each jaw consolidated. [Gr *dis-* twice, double, and *odous*, *odontos* a tooth]

dioecious *dī-ē'shəs*, (*biol*) *adj* having the sexes in separate individuals or creatures; not hermaphrodite; having male and female flowers on different plants. — *n pl* **Dioe'cia** (*dī-ē'shə*) a class in the Linnaean system, dioecious plants. — *n* **dioe'cism** (*dī-ē'sizm*). [Gr *di-* twice, and *oikos* a house]

dioestrus or (*NAm*) **diestrus** *dī-ēs'trəs*, *n* a sexually quiescent period following ovulation, in the oestrous cycle in mammals.

Diogenic *dī-ə-jen'ik*, *adj* pertaining to the Cynic philosopher *Diogenēs* (c.412–323 BC); cynical.

Dionaea *dī-ə-nē'ə*, *n* Venus's fly-trap, Venus Fly Trap (*Dionaea muscipula*), an American droseraceous insectivorous plant. [L, from Gr *Diōnaiā* Aphrodite, from her mother *Diōnē*]

Dionysia *dī-ə-niz'i-ə* or *-nis'*, (*Gr hist*) *n pl* dramatic and orgiastic festivals in honour of *Dionȳsos* (Bacchus), Greek god of wine. — *adj* **Dionys'iac** Bacchic. — *adj* **Dionys'ian** relating to *Dionȳsos* or to *Dionȳsios* (Dionysius of Syracuse, the Areopagite, Exiguus, or any other of the name).

Diophantine *dī-ə-fan'tīn*, *adj* pertaining to the Alexandrian mathematician *Diophantos* (c.AD275). — **Diophantine analysis** (*math*) the part of algebra concerned with finding particular rational values for general expressions under a surd form; **Diophantine equations** (*math*) indeterminate equations for which integral or rational solutions are required.

Diophysite. See **Diphysite**.

diopside *dī-op'sīd*, (*mineralogy*) *n* a strongly birefringent monoclinic calcium-magnesium pyroxene. [Gr *di-* double, and *opsis* a view]

dioptase *dī-op'tās*, (*mineralogy*) *n* an emerald-green acid copper silicate. [Gr *dia* through, and *optazein* to see; from its internal glitter]

dioptric *dī-op'trik* or **dioptrical** *-əl*, *adj* pertaining to dioptrics or a diopter; transparent (as in *dioptric beehive*). — *n* **diop'ter** an ancient form of theodolite; the index-arm of a graduated circle; a dioptre (*esp US*). — *n* **diop'tre** a unit of measurement of the power of a lens, the reciprocal of the focal distances in metres, negative for a divergent lens. — *adj* **diop'trate** (*entomol*) having the compound eye divided transversely. — *n sing* **diop'trics** the part of optics that deals with refraction. [Gr *dioptrā* a levelling instrument, *dioptron* a spyglass, from *dia* through, and the root of *opsesthai*, used as future of *horaein* to see]

diorama *dī-ə-rä'mə*, *n* an exhibition of translucent pictures seen through an opening with lighting effects; a miniature three-dimensional scene with figures; a display of eg a stuffed animal in a naturalistic setting in a museum, etc; a miniature film or television set. — *adj* **dioram'ic**. [Gr *dia* through, and *horāma* a sight]

diorism *dī'ə-rizm*, *n* distinction, definition. — *adj* **dioris'tic** or **dioris'tical**. — *adv* **dioris'tically**. [Gr *diorizein* to divide, from *dia* through, and *horos* a boundary]

diorite *dī'ə-rīt*, *n* a crystalline granular igneous rock composed of plagioclase and hornblende. — *adj* **diorit'ic**. [Gr *diorizein* to distinguish, from *dia* through, and *horos* a boundary]

diorthosis *dī-ör-thō'sis*, *n* the reduction of a dislocation (*surg*); the correction of a deformity; a critical revision of a text. — *adj* **diorthot'ic**. [Gr *dia* through, and *orthos* straight]

Dioscorea *dī-os-kōr'i-ə*, *-kör'i-ə*, *n* the yam genus, of the monocotyledonous family **Dioscoreā'ceae**. — *adj* **dioscoreā'ceous**. [From the 1c (AD) Greek physician *Dioskoridēs*]

Dioscuri *dī-os-kū'rī*, (*Gr mythol*) *n pl* Castor and Pollux together, as sons of Zeus. [Gr *Dios*, genitive of *Zeus*, and *koros* (Ionian *kouros*) a son, a lad]

diosgenin *dī-os'jən-in*, *n* a crystalline substance obtained from the Mexican yam (genus *Dioscorea*), used in the preparation of steroid hormones.

diota *dī-ō'tə*, *n* a two-handled ancient vase. [Gr *diōtos* two-handled, from *di-* twice, and *ous*, *ōtos* ear]

Diothelism, **Diothelite**. See **ditheletism**.

dioxan *dī-oks'ən*, or **dioxane** *-ān*, (*chem*) *n* a colourless, flammable, toxic liquid, $C_4H_8O_2$ used as a solvent for waxes, resins, etc.

dioxide *dī-ok'sīd*, *n* an oxide with two atoms of oxygen in the molecule. [**di-** and **oxide**]

dioxin *dī-ok'sin*, *n* an extremely toxic poison found in certain weedkillers and bleaching agents, known to cause cancer, skin, liver, and kidney disease, and birth defects.

Dip. *abbrev*: Diploma, as in eg **Dip. Ed.** Diploma in Education, **Dip. Tech.** Diploma in Technology, **Dip. SW** Diploma in Social Work.

dip *dip*, *vt* to immerse for a time; to lower; to lower and raise again (eg a flag); to cause (headlights) to shine below the eye-level of oncoming motorists; to baptize by immersion; to lift by dipping (*usu* with *up*); to dye, clean or coat by dipping; to immerse (fruit, wood, etc) in a preservative solution; to immerse (*esp* sheep) in a chemical solution to prevent or clear infestation by insects, etc; to moisten, suffuse (*Milton*); to involve in money difficulties (*colloq*); to mortgage; to pawn. — *vi* to plunge and emerge; to sink; to reach down into something; to enter slightly; to fish by lowering the bait slightly into the water, then bobbing it gently on the surface; to look cursorily; to incline downwards; to dip snuff (see below): — *prp* **dipp'ing**; *pa t* and *pa p* **dipped**. — *n* the act of dipping; a hollow; a sag; that which is taken by dipping; an inclination downwards; a sloping; (of the headlights of a car, etc) the state of being dipped; the angle a stratum of rock makes with a horizontal plane (*geol*); the angle between the horizontal and the earth's magnetic field; magnetic dip; a bath; a short swim; a liquid (such as a chemical solution or a dye) in which anything is dipped (such as sheep, garments, etc); a creamy mixture into which bread, biscuits, etc are dipped before being eaten; a candle made by dipping a wick in tallow; a pickpocket (*slang*). — *n* **dipp'er** someone who or that which dips; a ladle; a bucket or scoop of a dredge or excavator; a device for directing motor car headlights upwards or downwards (also **dip'-switch**); a dipping bird (*Cinclus*), the water-ouzel; the dabchick (*US*); (with *cap*) the Plough (*astron*); a nickname for a Baptist, *esp* a Dunker. — *n* **dipp'ing** the action of the verb; snuff-dipping. — **dip'-circle** or **dipp'ing-needle** an instrument for determining magnetic dip; **dip'-net** a long-handled net for dipping up fish; **dip'-pipe** a pipe with submerged outlet, *esp* in gasworks; **dip'-sec'tor** an instrument for determining the dip of the visible horizon; **dip'-slope** (*geol*) a slope of ground coinciding with the dip of the rocks; **dip'stick** a rod for measuring depth of liquid in a sump, etc; a stupid or foolish person (*colloq*; *derog*); **dip'-switch** see **dipper** above; **dip'-trap** a bend in a pipe containing liquid to cut off gases. — **dip in** to take a share; **dip into** to put one's hand into to remove something; to take or use (eg money from a fund); to read cursorily in; **dip of the horizon** the angle of the visible horizon below the level of the eye; **dip of the needle** the angle a balanced magnetic needle makes with the horizontal plane; **dip snuff** *orig*, in the southern US, to rub the gums and teeth with a wet stick dipped in snuff; to suck a pinch or small bag of snuff held between one's cheek and gum (*n* **snuff'-dipper** and **snuff'-dipping**). [OE *dyppan*, causal of *dȳpan* to plunge in, from *dēop* deep; cf Dan *dyppe*; Ger *taufen* to immerse]

dipchick *dip'chik*. Same as **dabchick**.

di penates *dī pə-nā'tēz* or *dē pe-nä'tās*, (*L*) *n pl* household gods.

dipeptide *dī-pep'tīd*, (*chem*) *n* a peptide formed by the combination of two amino acids. [**di-** and **peptide** (see **pepsin**)]

dipetalous *dī-pet'ə-ləs*, *adj* having two petals. [Gr *di-* twice, and *petalon* a leaf]

diphenyl *dī-fē'nil*, *n* a hydrocarbon, $C_{12}H_{10}$, consisting of two phenyl groups, used as a fungicide and in dye-manufacture, etc (also **bīphē'nyl**). — *adj* having two phenyl groups, *esp* replacing hydrogen. [**di-**]

diphone *dī'fōn*, *n* a shorthand sign representing a diphthongal sound. [Gr *di-* twice, and *phōnē* sound]

diphtheria *dif-thē'ri-ə*, *n* an infectious throat disease in which the air-passages become covered with a leathery membrane. — *adj* **diphtheric** (*-ther'ik*) or **diphtheritic** (*-thər-it'ik*). — *n* **diphtherī'tis** diphtheria. — *adj* **diph'theroid**. [Fr *diphthérie*, *diphthérite* (now *diphtérie*), from Gr *diphtherā* leather]

diphthong *dif'thong* or *dip'thong* *n* two vowel-sounds pronounced as one syllable (as in *out* or *mind*); (loosely) a digraph; the ligature *æ* or *œ*. — *adj* **diphthongal** (*-thong'gəl*) or **diphthongic** (*-thong'gik*). — *adv* **diphthong'ally**. — *vt* **diph'thongize** or **-ise** (*-gīz*). [OFr *di(p)tongue* (Fr *diphtongue*), from L *dip(h)thongus*, from Gr *diphthongos*, from *di-* twice, and *phthongos* sound, vowel, reconstructed to more closely resemble the Greek]

diphycercal *dif-i-sûr'kəl*, (*zool*) *adj* having the tail symmetrical about the vertebral column, which runs horizontally (of fishes, etc). [Gr *diphyēs* of double nature, twofold, and *kerkos* a tail]

diphyletic *dī-* or *dī-fil-et'ik*, (*biol*) *adj* of dual origin; descended from two distinct ancestral groups. [Gr *di-* double, and *phȳletikos* pertaining to a tribesman, from *phȳlē* a tribe]

diphyodont *dif'i-ō-dont*, (*zool*) *adj* having two sets of teeth (milk and permanent). — *n* a mammal with these. [Gr *diphyēs* of double nature, and *odous*, *odontos* a tooth]

Diphysite *dif'i-zīt* or *-sīt*, *n* a believer in the existence of two natures in Christ, a divine and a human (*opp* to *Monophysite*). — Also **Dyoph'ysite**, or less correctly **Dioph'ysite**. — *n* **Diph'ysitism** (*-it-izm*). — All words also without *cap*. [Gr *di-* double, and *physis* nature]

dipl- *dip-l-* or **diplo-** *dip-lō-*, *combining form* signifying double. — *n* **diplococcus** (*dip-lə-kok'əs*) (*bacteriol*) a coccus which divides by fission, the two resulting individuals remaining paired. — *n* **diplodocus** (Gr *dokos* beam, bar, from its appearance) any gigantic, quadrupedal, herbivorous dinosaur of the genus *Diplodocus*, belonging to the sauropod group, remains of which have been found in the Jurassic rocks of the Rocky Mountains. — *n* **dip'logen** (from **hydrogen**) an alternative name for deuterium or heavy hydrogen. — *n* **diplogen'esis** (Gr *genesis* generation) doubling of parts normally single. — *adj* **dip'loid** (Gr *eidos* form; *biol*) having the full or unreduced number of chromosomes characteristic of the species, as in body cells (*opp* to *haploid*). — *n* **diploid'y**. — *n* **dip'lon** an alternative name for deuteron, the nucleus of heavy hydrogen. — *n* **dip'lont** (Gr *on*, *ontos*, pr p of *einai* to be; *biol*) an animal or plant body containing diploid nuclei. — *n* **diplō'pia** (Gr *ōps* eye) double vision. — *adj* **diplostē'monous** (Gr *stēmōn* a thread; *bot*) having two whorls of stamens, the outer alternating with the petals, the inner with the outer. — *n* **diplozō'on** (Gr *zōion* an animal) a flatworm of the genus *Diplozoon* that lives fused together in pairs parasitically upon the gills of minnows, etc: — *pl* **diplozo'a**. [Gr *diploos* double]

diplegia (*med*) *n* bilateral paralysis of similar parts of the body. [**bi-** and Gr *plege* a blow]

dipleidoscope *di-plī'də-skōp*, *n* an instrument for ascertaining the moment of meridian passage by observing the coincidence of two images. [Gr *diploos* double, *eidos* appearance, and *skopeein* to view]

diplex *dī'pleks*, (*telecomm*) *adj* pertaining to the transmission of two simultaneous messages over one wire in the same direction. [**duplex**, with substitution of Gr *di-* double]

diplo-. see **dipl-**.

Diplock court *dip'lok kört*, *n* in Northern Ireland, a court of law which sits without a jury.

diplodocus. See under **dipl-**.

diploe *dip'lō-ē*, (*anatom*) *n* the spongy tissue between the hard inner and outer tables of the skull. [Gr *diploē* doubling, fold]

diplogen, **diplogenesis**, **diploid**. See under **dipl-**.

diploma *di-plō'mə*, *n* a document conferring some honour or privilege, such as a university degree, etc. — *vt* to confer a diploma upon. — *n* **diplomate** (*dip'lə-māt*) someone who holds a diploma. — *vt* (*obs*) to confer a diploma on. [L, from Gr *diplōma* a letter folded double, from *diploos* double]

diplomacy *di-plō'mə-si* or *-plo'*, *n* the art of negotiation, *esp* in relations between states; tact in management of people concerned in any affair. — *n* **diplomat** (*dip'lə-mat*) a person employed or skilled in diplomacy. — *n* **diplomatese** (*-ēz'*; *colloq*) the jargon or obscure language used by diplomats. — *adj* **diplomat'ic** or **diplomat'ical** pertaining to diplomacy; tactful and skilful in negotiation or in dealing with people. — *n* **diplomatic** (*-mat'ik*) a minister at a foreign court; diplomatics. — *adv* **diplomat'ically**. — *n sing* **diplomat'ics** the science of deciphering ancient writings, such as charters, etc; palaeography. — *n* **diplo'matist** a diplomat. — *vi* and *vt* **diplo'matize** or **-ise** to practise, or bring about by, diplomacy. — *n* **diplomatol'ogy** the study or science of diplomatics, charters, decrees, etc. — **diplomatic bag** a bag used for sending documents, etc to and from embassies, free of customs control; the contents of such a bag; **diplomatic corps** the whole body of foreign diplomats resident in any capital; **diplomatic immunity** immunity from local laws and taxation enjoyed by diplomats abroad; **diplomatic relations** formal relations between states marked by the presence of diplomats in each other's country. [Fr *diplomatie* (pronounced *-sie*), from *diplomate*, *diplomatique*, ultimately from L (see **diploma**)]

diplon, **diplont**, **diplopia**, **diplostemonous**, **Diplozoon**. See under **dipl-**.

Dipnoi *dip'nō-ī*, *n pl* an order of fishes, the lung-fishes. — *adj* and *n* **dip'nōan**. — *adj* **dip'nōous** having both lungs and gills. [Gr *di-* double, and *pnoē* breath]

Dipodidae *dī-pod'i-dē*, *n pl* the jerboa family of rodents. [Gr *dipous* two-footed, from *di-* twice and *pous*, *podos* a foot]

dipody *dip'ə-di*, (*prosody*) *n* a double foot. [Gr *di-* double, and *pous*, *podos* a foot]

dipolar *dī-pō'lər*, *adj* having two poles. — *n* **di'pole** two equal and opposite electric charges or magnetic poles of opposite sign set a small distance apart; a body or system containing either of these; a type of radio or television aerial. [**di-**]

dippy *dip'i*, (*colloq*) *adj* crazy; insane. [Origin obscure]

diprionidian *dī-prī-ə-nid'i-ən*, (*palaeontol*) *adj* serrated on both sides (of graptolites). [Gr *di-* twice, and *priōn* a saw]

diprotodont *dī-prō'tō-dont*, (*palaeontol*) *n* any marsupial of the **Diprotodont'ia**, the suborder (in some classifications) including kangaroos, wombats, etc, with one pair of incisors in the lower jaw. — *n* **dīprō'tōdon** any animal of the extinct genus *Diprotodon*, the largest known marsupials. — *n* **diprotodon'tid** an animal of the **Diprotodon'tidae** (*-ē*), an extinct family of marsupials including the genus *Diprotodon*. [Gr *di-* twice, *prōtos*, first, and *odous*, *odontos* tooth]

Dipsacus *dip'sə-kəs*, *n* the teasel genus, giving name to the **Dipsacā'ceae** related to the valerian and madder families. [Gr *dipsakos* teasel, from *dipsa* thirst, because the leaf-axils hold water]

dipsas *dip'sas*, *n* a snake whose bite was believed to cause intense thirst (*pl* **dip'sades**; *-dēz*); (with *cap*) a genus of non-venomous snakes. [Gr *dipsas*, from *dipsa* thirst]

dipsomania *dip-sō-mā'ni-ə*, *n* an intermittent pathological craving for alcoholic stimulants. — *n* **dipsomā'niac** a person who suffers from dipsomania (*colloq* **dip'sō**: — *pl* **dip'sōs**). [Gr *dipsa* thirst, and *maniā* madness]

Diptera *dip'tər-ə*, *n* the genus of two-winged insects or flies; (without *cap*) any insect of the genus. — *adj* **dip'teral** two-winged; with double peristyle (*archit*). — *n* **dip'teran** a dipterous insect. — *n* **dip'terist** a person who studies flies. — *n* **dip'teros** (*archit*) a building with double peristyle or colonnade. — *adj* **dip'terous** with two wings or winglike expansions. [Gr *dipteros* two-winged, from *di-* twice, and *pteron* a wing]

dipterocarp *dip'tər-ō-kärp*, *n* any tree of the genus *Dipterocarpus* or its family **Dipterocarpā'ceae** (chiefly Indian), in which some of the sepals enlarge as wings for the fruit. — *adj* **dipterocarpā'ceous** or **dipterocarp'-ous**. [Gr *di-* double, *pteron* wing, and *karpos*, fruit]

diptych *dip'tik*, *n* a double-folding wooden writing-tablet; a register of bishops, saints, etc read aloud during the eucharist; a pair of pictures, *esp* with a religious theme, painted on hinged wooden panels. [Gr *diptychos*, from *di-* twice, and *ptychē* a tablet, a fold]

Dir. *abbrev*: Director.

dirdum or **dirdam** *dir'dəm*, (*Scot*) *n* uproar; a scolding, punishment; blame. [Origin obscure]

dire *dīr*, *adj* dreadful; calamitous in a high degree; urgent; portentous. — *adj* (*poetic*) **dire'ful**. — *adv* **dire'fully**. — *n* **dire'fulness**. [L *dīrus*]

direct *di-rekt'*, *dī'rekt*, *adj* straight; straightforward; by the shortest way; forward, not backward or oblique; at right angles; immediate; without intervening agency or interposed stages; (of a dye) fixing itself without a mordant; in the line of descent; outspoken; sincere; unambiguous; unsophisticated in manner. — *n* (*music*) an indication of the first note or chord of next page or line. — *adv* straight; by the shortest way; without deviation, intervening agency or interposed stages. — *vt* to keep or lay straight; to point or aim; to point out the proper course to; to guide; to order; to address, mark with the name and residence of a person; to plan and superintend (the production of a film or play). — *vi* to act as director of a film, play, etc; to direct letters, etc. — *n* **direc'tion** aim at a certain point; the line or course in which anything moves or on which any point lies; guidance; command; the body of persons who guide or manage a matter; the address, or written name and residence of a person; the work of the director of a film, play, etc. — *adj* **direc'tional** relating to direction in space. — *adj* **direc'tionless** not moving, looking, etc in any particular direction; aimless. — *adj* **direct'ive** having the power or a tendency to direct. — *n* a general instruction; a law passed by the European Economic Community, addressed to member states, requiring the national Parliament to make changes to their law so as to effect the directive. — *n* **directiv'ity** the property of being directional. — *adv* **direct'ly** in a direct manner; without intermediary; immediately (in time and otherwise). — *conj* (often with *that*; *colloq*) as soon as. — *n* **direct'ness**. — *n* **direct'or** a person who directs; a person who directs the shooting of a cinema film, etc; a manager or governor; a member of a board conducting the affairs of a company; a counsellor; a father confessor or spiritual guide; part of a machine or instrument which guides the motion; in automatic trunk dialling, the apparatus which obtains a channel through exchange junctions to the required exchange; a device that continuously calculates the position of a moving target and supplies firing data: — *fem* **direct'ress** or **direct'rix**. — *n* **direct'orate** the office of director; a body of directors; (with *cap*) the French Directory or Directoire. — *adj* **directorial** (*-tō'* or *-tö'*). — *n* **direc'torship**. — *adj* **direct'ory** containing directions; guiding. — *n* a body of directions; a guide; a book with the names, telephone numbers and residences of the inhabitants of a place; a similar reference book compiled for a specific purpose, eg Fax users, members of one profession or trade; a body of directors; (with *cap*) the *Directoire*, or French Republican government of 1795–99. — *n* **direct'rix** see **director** above; a line serving to describe a conic section, which is the locus of a point whose distances from focus and directrix have a constant ratio (*geom*): — *pl* **directrices** (*-tri'sēz*). — **direct access** (*comput*) the ability to access data in a storage and retrieval system directly without having to scan any part of the storage file first (also **random access**); **direct action** coercive methods of attaining industrial or political ends as opposed to pacific, parliamentary or political action; **direct broadcast satellite** (*telecomm*) a high power geostationary communications satellite from which television programmes are beamed directly to the viewer, rather than being redistributed by cable or other means; **direct cost** (*accountancy*) one that can be measured and identified as being incurred on a specific job, contract or process; **direct current** an electric current flowing in one direction only; **direct debit** an arrangement by which a creditor can claim payment direct from the payer's bank account, and the payee can vary the amount paid; **direct drilling** the ploughing and sowing of a field in one operation; **direct injection** a system of fuel injection in an internal-combustion engine where a carburettor is not used but fuel is injected directly into the cylinder; **directional aerial** one that can receive or transmit radio waves in one direction only; **directional drilling** (*oil industry*) a method of drilling in which the well is not drilled vertically, a technique used *esp* in offshore drilling where a number of wells may be drilled from a single platform; **direc'tion-finder** a radio receiver that determines the direction of arrival of incoming waves, used *esp* in navigation; **direc'tion-indicator** an aerial navigation device in which needles of actual and desired course overlap when the aircraft is on its true course; **direct labour** labour employed directly, not through a contractor; **direct mail** (*marketing*) the sending of promotional material to named potential customers by means of the postal service; **direct mail advertising** (*marketing*); **direct mailshot** (*marketing*) a single mailing in a campaign for a particular product or service etc; **direct marketing** selling of products or services by manufacturers or producers directly to consumers without using a retail outlet; **direct method** a method of teaching a foreign language through speaking it, without translation, and without formal instruction in grammar; **direct motion** (*music*) progression of parts in the same direction; **direct object** a word or group of words denoting that upon which the action of a transitive verb is directed; **director circle** the locus of the intersection of a pair of tangents to a conic at right angles to each other; **direct'or-gen'eral** a chief administrator of a *usu* non-commercial organization; **director's chair** a light folding chair with seat and back of canvas or similar material and arm-rests; **directory enquiries** a telephone service in which a customer will be told the relevant telephone number from the directory for any name and address specified to the operator; **direct speech** speech reported as spoken, in the very words of the speaker (L *ōrātiō rēcta*); **direct tax** one levied directly from individuals or organizations, rather than on goods or services. — **directed-energy weapon** a weapon whose destructive force consists of beams of light, electromagnetic pulses, subatomic particles, or the like; **direct-grant school** (until 1979) a fee-paying school which received a state grant on condition that it took a specified number of non-fee-paying pupils. [L *dīrigere*, *dīrēctum*, from *dī-*, apart, and *regere*, to rule]

Directoire *dē-rek-twär*, (*hist*) *n* the French Directorate of 1795–99. — *adj* after the fashion in dress or furniture prevailing at that time; (of knickers) knee-length, with elastic at waist and knee. [Fr; see **direct**]

directress, **directrices**, **directrix**. See under **direct**.

diremption *dī-remp'shən*, *n* separation into two, disjunction. — *vt* **dīrempt'**. [L *diremptiō*, *-ōnis*, from *dirimere*, *diremptus* to separate; cf **diriment**]

dirge *dûrj*, *n* a funeral song or hymn; a slow and mournful piece of music. [Contracted from *dīrige* (imperative of L *dīrigere* to direct), the first word of an antiphon sung in the office for the dead, from the words from the Vulgate, Psalm 5, 8]

dirham *dûr-ham'*, *də-ram'*, *dē'ram* or **dirhem** *dûr-hem'*, *n* an oriental unit of weight, *orig* two-thirds of an Attic drachma (*usu* **dirhem**); (the following *usu* **dirham**) the monetary unit of Morocco (100 centimes); a coin equal to this in value; a coin used in several N African and Middle Eastern countries, with varying value. — Also **derham'**. [Ar, Pers, and Turk forms of the Greek *drachmē* a drachma or dram]

dirige *dir'i-ji*, (*obs*) *n* a dirge.

dirigible *dir'i-ji-bl*, *-rij'*, *adj* that can be directed. — *n* a navigable balloon or airship. — *adj* **dir'igent** directing. [See **direct**]

dirigisme *dē-rēzh-ēzm'*, *n* control by the State in economic and social spheres. — Also **dirigism'**. — *adj* **dirigiste** (*-ēst'*). [Fr, from Ital *dirigismo*]

diriment *dir'i-mənt*, *adj* nullifying. [L *dirimere*]

dirk[1] *dûrk*, *n* a Highland dagger; a sidearm worn by midshipmen and naval cadets (*hist*). — *vt* to stab with a dirk. [Orig Scots, in form *durk*; ety uncertain, but cf Du, Dan, Swed *dolk* dagger; Ir *duirc* is probably from the English word]

dirk[2] or **dirke** *dûrk*, *adj*, *adv* and *vt* (*Spenser* etc) for **dark**, **darkly** or **darken**.

dirl *dirl*, (*Scot*) *vi* and *vt* to (cause to) thrill, vibrate. — *n* vibration; a tingling as after a blow. [**drill**[1] and **thrill**]

dirndl *dûrn'dl*, *n* an Alpine peasant woman's dress with close-fitting bodice and full skirt; an imitation of this, *esp* a full skirt with a tight, often elasticated, waistband. [Ger dialect, dimin of *dirne* girl]

dirt *dûrt*, *n* any filthy substance, such as dung, mud, etc; foreign matter adhering to anything; loose earth; a mixture of earth, gravel and cinders, used as a surface for race-tracks, etc; rubbish; obscenity; a worthless or despised person or thing; spiteful gossip. — *vt* to make dirty. — *adv* **dirt'ily**. — *n* **dirt'iness**. — *adj* **dirt'y** marked with dirt; soiled; foul, filthy; (of a colour) not bright or clear; stormy; obscene; unclean in thought or conversation; despicable; showing anger or reproof; mean; sordid; dishonest, treacherous. — *vt* to soil with dirt; to sully: — *pr p* **dirt'ying**; *pa t* and *pa p* **dirt'ied**. — **dirt'-bed** a quarryman's term for a layer representing an old soil, *esp* in the Purbeck group. — *adj* **dirt'-cheap'** cheap as dirt, very cheap. — **dirt'-eating** a practice of eating clay as among various primitive peoples; a morbid impulse to eat dirt; **dirt farmer** (*US*) a person who farms their own land, *esp* without hired help; **dirt'-pie** mud moulded by children in play. — *adj* **dirt'-poor** utterly poor, destitute. — **dirt'-road** (*Austr*, *US*, *NZ*) a soft road, unpaved and unmacadamized. — *adj* **dirt'-rott'en** (*Shakesp*) wholly decayed. — **dirt'-track** a rough unsurfaced track; a motor cycle racing-track, with earthy or cinder surface; **dirty bomb** one that produces a large amount of radioactive contamination; **dirty dog** (*slang*) a dishonest or contemptible person; **dirty linen** (*colloq*) personal problems or grievances (*esp* in the phrase *wash one's dirty linen in public*); **dirty look** (*colloq*) a look of anger, disapproval or reproof; **dirty money** money earned by base means; (in dock labour) extra pay for unloading offensive cargo; extra pay for any unpleasant, dirty, etc task; **dirty trick** a dishonest or despicable act; a political intrigue (*esp* in the phrase *dirty-tricks campaign* or *operation*); **dirty word** an obscene word; a word for something (such as a feeling, principle, or belief) that is regarded with disfavour at the present time; **dirty work** work that dirties the hands or clothes; dishonourable practices, *esp* undertaken on behalf of another person; foul play. — **dirty old man** (*colloq*) a man whose sexual aspirations and actions are considered appropriate only to a younger man; **dish the dirt** (*colloq*) to distribute spiteful gossip, deal out malicious stories (about a person); **do the dirty on** to play a low trick on, cheat; **eat dirt** to acquiesce submissively in a humiliation; **throw dirt** to besmirch a reputation. [ME *drit*, prob ON *drit* excrement; cf OE *gedrītan* to defecate]

Dis *dis* or *dēs*, *n* a name for Pluto, hence, the infernal world. [L *Dīs*, cognate with *deus*, *dīvus*]

dis. *abbrev*: discontinued.

dis- *dis* or **di-** *di-*, *pfx* (1) meaning in two, asunder, apart; (2) meaning 'not' or a reversal; (3) indicating a removal or deprivation; (4) used intensively. [L *dis-*, *dī-*]

Disa *dī'sə*, *dīzə*, *n* an orchid of the *Disa* genus of African orchids with dark green leaves, or of certain other genera. [Origin unknown]

disable *dis-ā'bl*, *vt* to deprive of power; to weaken; to cripple or incapacitate; to disqualify legally; to depreciate, disparage, undervalue (*Shakesp*). — *adj* **disā'bled** having physical disabilties; designed or intended for people with physical disabilities. — *n* **disā'blement**. — *n* **disabil'ity** lack of power; lack of legal power or qualification; a disqualification; a difficulty, *esp* physical. [**dis-** (2)]

disabuse *dis-ə-būz'*, *vt* to undeceive or set right. [**dis-** (2)]

disaccharide *dī-sak'ə-rīd*, *n* a sugar that hydrolyses into two molecules of simple sugars. [**di-**]

disaccommodate *dis-ə-kom'ə-dāt*, *vt* to put to inconvenience. — *n* **disaccommodā'tion**. [**dis-** (2)]

disaccord *dis-ə-körd'*, *vi* to refuse to accord; to be at discord; not to agree. — Also *n*. — *adj* **disaccord'ant**. [**dis-** (2)]

disaccustom *dis-ə-kus'təm*, *vt* to make to be lost through disuse. [**dis-** (2)]

disacknowledge *dis-ək-nol'ij*, *vt* to refuse to acknowledge, disown. [**dis-** (2)]

disadorn *dis-ə-dörn'*, (*obs* and *rare*) *vt* to deprive of ornaments. [**dis-** (3)]

disadvance *dis-əd-väns'*, (*obs*) *vt* to cause to retreat; to draw back, cease to put forward (*Spenser*). [**dis-** (2)]

disadvantage *dis-əd-vänt'ij*, *n* unfavourable circumstance or condition; loss; damage. — *adj* **disadvan'tageable** (*obs*). — *adj* **disadvan'taged** deprived of the resources and privileges (*usu* social) enjoyed by the majority of people; in unfavourable conditions relative to other (specified) people. — *adj* **disadvantageous** (*dis-ad-vənt-ā'jəs*) involving or bringing disadvantage; unfavourable. — *adv* **disadvantā'geously**. — *n* **disadvantā'geousness**. [**dis-** (2)]

disadventurous *dis-əd-ven'chə-rəs*, (*obs*) *adj* unfortunate. — *n* **disadven'ture** or **disaven'ture** (*Spenser*, etc) a mishap. — *adj* **disaven'trous** (*Spenser*) unfortunate. [**dis-** (2)]

disaffect *dis-ə-fekt'*, *vt* to take away the affection of; to make discontented or unfriendly: — *pa p* and *adj* **disaffect'ed** ill-disposed or alienated; tending to break away. — *adv* **disaffect'edly**. — *n* **disaffect'edness**. — *n* **disaffec'tion** the state of being disaffected; lack of affection or friendliness; alienation; ill-will; political discontent or disloyalty. — *adj* **disaffec'tionate**. [**dis-** (3)]

disaffiliate *dis-ə-fil'i-āt*, *vt* and *vi* to end an affiliation (to); to separate oneself (from). — *n* **disaffiliā'tion**. [**dis-** (2)]

disaffirm *dis-ə-f urm'*, *vt* to contradict; to repudiate or reverse (*law*). — *n* **disaffirm'ance** or **disaffirmā'tion** (*dis-a-*). [**dis-** (2)]

disafforest *dis-ə-for'ist*, *vt* to bring out of the operation of forest laws; to take away the legal status of a forest from; to clear of forest, disforest. — *n* **disafforestā'tion**. — *n* **disaffor'estment**. [L *dis-* reversal, and LL *afforestāre* to make into a forest. See **forest**]

disaggregate *dis-ag'ri-gāt*, *vt* to separate (something) into its component parts. — *n* **disaggregā'tion**. [**dis-** (1)]

disagree *dis-ə-grē'*, *vi* to differ or be at variance; to disaccord; to dissent; to quarrel; to be opposed; to prove unsuitable or a source of annoyance (eg of food upsetting the stomach). — *adj* **disagree'able** not amicable; unpleasant; offensive. — *n* **disagreeabil'ity**. — *n* **disagree'ableness**. — *n pl* **disagree'ables** annoyances. — *adv* **disagree'ably**. — *n* **disagree'ment** lack of agreement; difference; unsuitableness; dispute. [**dis-** (2)]

disallow *dis-ə-low'*, *vt* not to allow; to refuse to sanction; to deny the authority, validity or truth of; to reject, to forbid; to dispraise (*obs*). — *vi* (*obs*) to disapprove. — *adj* **disallow'able**. — *n* **disallow'ance**. [**dis-** (2)]

disally *dis-ə-lī'*, *vt* to break the alliance of; to separate or sunder (*Milton*). [**dis-** (2) and (1)]

di salto *dē säl'tō*, (*Ital*) at a leap.

disambiguate *dis-am-big'ū-āt*, *vt* to take away the ambiguity from; to make unambiguous. — *n* **disambigua'tion**. [**dis-** (3)]

disamenity *dis-ə-mē'ni-ti*, *-men'-*, *n* a lack of amenity; a disadvantage or drawback (eg of a property or district). [**dis-** (3)]

disanalogy *dis-an-a'lə-ji*, *n* a non-correspondence; an aspect or feature in which something is not analagous to something else. — *adj* **disanal'ogous** (*-gəs*). [**dis-** (2)]

disanchor *dis-angk'ər*, *vt* to free from the anchor. — *vi* to weigh anchor. [**dis-** (3)]

disanimate *dis-an'i-māt*, *vt* to deprive of spirit or animation; to deject (*Shakesp*, etc). [**dis-** (3)]

disannex *dis-ə-neks'*, *vt* to disjoin. [**dis-** (1)]

disannul *dis-ə-nul'*, *vt* to annul completely. — *n* **disannull'er**. — *n* **disannul'ment** or **disannull'ing**. [**dis-** (4)]

disanoint *dis-ə-noint'*, *vt* to undo the anointing or consecration of. [**dis-** (2)]

disapparel *dis-ə-par'əl*, *vt* to disrobe. [**dis-** (2)]

disappear *dis-ə-pēr'*, *vi* to vanish from sight; to become lost; to leave or take flight without explanation or warning; to cease to exist, be felt or be known. — *vt* to cause (someone) to vanish, be no longer around, *esp* by imprisoning or killing them *usu* for political reasons. — *n* **disappear'ance**. [**dis-** (3)]

disapply *dis-ə-plī'*, *vt* to render (a law) inapplicable. — *n* **disapplicā'tion**. [**dis-** (2)]

disappoint *dis-ə-point'*, *vt* to deprive of what is appointed (*obs*); to frustrate the hopes or expectations of; to prevent the fulfilment of. — *vi* to cause disappointment. — *adj* **disappoint'ed** saddened by the frustration of hopes, etc; balked; frustrated; unequipped or ill-equipped (*obs*; *Shakesp*). — *adj* **disappoint'ing** causing disappointment; unsatisfactory, of a less than adequate or expected standard. — *n* **disappoint'ment** the defeat of one's hopes or expectations; frustration; the vexation accompanying failure. [OFr *desapointer*, from *des-* (L *dis-*) away, and *apointer* to appoint. See **appoint**]

disapprobation *dis-ap-rō-bā'shən*, *n* disapproval. — *adj* **disapp'robātive** or **disapp'robātory**. [**dis-** (2)]

disappropriate *dis-ə-prō'pri-āt*, *vt* to take away from the condition of being appropriated. — *adj* (*-it*) deprived of appropriation. [**dis-** (3)]

disapprove *dis-ə-proo̅v'*, *vt* and *vi* to give or have an unfavourable opinion (of); to reject. — *n* **disapprov'al**. — *adv* **disapprov'ingly**. [**dis-** (2)]

disarm *dis-ärm'*, *vt* to deprive of arms; to strip of armour; to render defenceless; to deprive of the power to hurt; to conciliate or placate (*fig*); to deprive of suspicion or hostility; to reduce to a peace footing. — *vi* to disband troops, reduce national armaments. — *n* **disarm'ament** the reduction of national armaments; the act of disarming or the state of being disarmed. — **disarm'er** someone who or that which disarms; a person in favour of reducing national armaments. — *adj* **disarm'ing** charming; tending to placate. [**dis-** (3)]

disarrange *dis-ə-rānj'*, *vt* to undo the arrangement of; to disorder; to derange. — *n* **disarrange'ment**. [**dis-** (2)]

disarray *dis-ə-rā'*, *vt* to break the array of; to throw into disorder; to strip of array or dress. — *n* lack of array or order; untidiness; undress (*archaic*). [**dis-** (2) and (3)]

disarticulate *dis-är-tik'ūl-āt*, *vt* to separate the joints of. — *vi* to separate at a joint. — *n* **disarticulā'tion**. [**dis-** (1)]

disassemble *dis-ə-sem'bl*, *vt* to take apart. — **disassem'bler** (*comput*) a program which translates from machine code to an assembly language. — *n* **disassem'bly**. [**dis-** (1)]

disassimilate *dis-ə-sim'i-lāt*, *vt* to subject to katabolism. — *n* **disassimilā'tion**. — *adj* **disassim'ilative**. [**dis-** (2)]

disassociate *dis-ə-sō'shi-āt*, *vt* (with *from*) to disconnect; to dissociate. — *n* **disassociā'tion**. [**dis-** (2)]

disaster *diz-äs'tər*, *n* an adverse or unfortunate event; a great and sudden misfortune; a calamity. — *adj* **disas'trous** calamitous, ruinous; gloomy, foreboding disaster. — *adv* **disas'trously**. — **disaster area** an area in which there has been a disaster (eg flood or explosion), requiring special official aid; (loosely) any place where a misfortune has happened; anything which is untidy, ugly, disadvantageous, etc (*colloq*); **disaster movie** a film which has as its main theme or focus of action a disaster or catastrophe. [OFr *desastre*, from *des-* (L *dis-*) with evil sense, and *astre* a star, destiny, from L *astrum*, Gr *astron* star]

disattire *dis-ə-tīr'*, (*Spenser*) *vt* to undress. [**dis-** (2)]

disattribution *dis-at-ri-bū'shən*, *n* the act of adjudging a work of art, etc to be no longer the product of a particular artist, etc; an instance of this. [**dis-** (2)]

disattune *dis-ə-tūn'*, *vt* to put out of harmony. [**dis-** (2)]

disauthorize or **-ise** *dis-ö'thər-īz*, *vt* to deprive of authority. [**dis-** (3)]

disavaunce (*Spenser*). Same as **disadvance**.

disaventrous, disaventure. See **disadventure**.

disavouch *dis-ə-vowch'*, (*obs*) *vt* to disavow. [**dis-** (2)]

disavow *dis-ə-vow'*, *vt* to disclaim knowledge of, or connection with; to disown; to deny. — *n* **disavow'al**. [OFr *desavouer*, from *des-* (L *dis-*) away, and *avouer* to avow. See **avow**]

disband *dis-band'*, *vt* to disperse, break up (a group, unit, etc). — *vi* to break up. — *n* **disband'ment**. [OFr *desbander* to unbind, from *des-* (L *dis-*) reversal, and *bander* to tie]

disbar *dis-bär'*, (*law*) *vt* to expel from the bar. — *n* **disbar'ment**. [**dis-** (3)]

disbark[1] *dis-bärk'*, (*obs*) *vt* to land from a ship; to disembark. [OFr *desbarquer*, from *des-* (L *dis-*) reversal, and *barque* bark]

disbark[2] *dis-bärk'*, *vt* to strip of bark, to bark. [**dis-** (3)]

disbelieve *dis-bə-lēv'*, *vt* to believe to be false; to refuse to believe. — *vi* to have no faith (*in*). — *n* **disbelief'**. — *n* **disbeliev'er**. [**dis-** (2)]

disbench *dis-bench'*, *-bensh'*, *vt* to drive from a bench or seat (*Shakesp*); to deprive of the status of a member of a governing body in the Inns of Court. [**dis-** (3)]

disbenefit *dis-ben'i-fit*, *n* a drawback, disadvantage, loss, inconvenience, etc; absence or loss of a benefit. [**dis-** (2) and (3)]

disbodied *dis-bod'id*, *adj* disembodied. [**dis-** (3)]

disbosom *dis-bŏŏz'əm*, *vt* to make known, reveal. [**dis-** (1)]

disbowel *dis-bow'əl*, (*fig*) *vt* to disembowel: — *pr p* **disbow'elling**; *pa t* and *pa p* **disbow'elled**. [**dis-** (3)]

disbranch *dis-bränch'*, *-bränsh'*, *vt* to remove branches from; to sever. [**dis-** (3)]

disbud *dis-bud'*, *vt* to remove buds from. [**dis-** (3)]

disburden *dis-bûr'dn* or **disburthen** *dis-bûr'dhn*, *vt* to rid of a burden; to free; to unload, discharge. [**dis-** (3)]

disburse *dis-bûrs'*, *vt* to pay out. — *n* **disburs'al** or **disburse'ment** a paying out; that which is paid. [OFr *desbourser*, from *des-* (L *dis-*) apart, and *bourse* a purse]

disc or (*esp NAm*) **disk** *disk*, *n* any flat thin circular body or structure; a quoit thrown by ancient Greek athletes; a circular figure, such as that presented by the sun, moon and planets; the enlarged torus of a flower; the inner part of a capitulum in composite plants; a layer of fibrocartilage between vertebrae, the slipping of which (*slipped disc*) causes pressure on spinal nerves and hence pain; a gramophone record; (usu as **disk**) a magnetic disc or a disk file (see entry at **disk**; *comput*); a compact disc; a video disc. — *vt* and *vi* to work with a disc harrow. — *adj* **disc'al** pertaining to, or of the nature of a disc. — *adj* **disc'oid** or **discoid'al** in the form of a disc; (of a capitulum) without ray-flowers (*bot*). — *n* **discog'raphy** collection or description, etc, of gramophone records; the history or description of musical recording; a list of recordings by one composer or performer. — *n* **discog'rapher**. — *n* **disc'ophile** (*-ō-fīl*) someone who makes a study of and collects gramophone records. — **disc brake** one in which the friction is obtained by pads hydraulically forced against a disc on the wheel; **disc'-flower** or **-flor'et** one of the tubular inner flowers of a capitulum (*opp* to *ray-flower*); **disc harrow** or **disc plough** a harrow or plough in which the soil is cut by inclined discs; **disc jockey** a person who introduces and plays recordings (*esp* of popular music) on a radio or television programme, in a club etc; **disc parking** a system according to which the motorist is responsible for affixing to his or her car special disc(s) showing the time of arrival and the time when permitted parking ends, there being no charge during the permitted period; **disc player** a machine for playing videodiscs; **disc wheel** a wheel on a motor vehicle, etc in which the hub and rim are connected by a solid piece of metal rather than by spokes. [Gr *diskos*]

disc. *abbrev*: discount; discoverer.

discage *dis-kāj'*, *vt* to free from a cage. [**dis-** (2)]

discalced *dis-kalst'*, *adj* without shoes, bare-footed or wearing only sandals, as a branch of the Carmelite order of friars and nuns noted for their austerity. — *n* and *adj* **discal'ceate**. [L *discalceātus*, from *dis-* (negative) and *calceāre*, *-ātum* to shoe, from *calceus* a shoe, from *calx* the heel]

discandy or **discandie** *dis-kan'di*, (*Shakesp*) *vi* to dissolve or melt from a state of being candied. — *n* **discan'dering** (*Shakesp*) supposed to be for **discandying**. [**dis-** (2)]

discant *dis'kant*. Same as **descant**.

discapacitate *dis-kə-pas'i-tāt*, *vt* to incapacitate. [**dis-** (2)]

discard *dis-kärd'*, *vt* and *vi* to reject; to get rid of as unwanted; to cast off; (of cards) to throw away, as not needed or not allowed by the game; (in whist, etc) to throw down a (useless) card of another suit when one cannot follow suit and cannot or will not trump; to discharge. — *n* (also *dis'*) the act of discarding; the card or cards thrown out of the hand; discharge, dismissal, abandonment; a cast-off, anything discarded. — *n* **discard'ment**. — **throw into the discard** (*US*) to throw on the scrap-heap. [**dis-** (3)]

discarnate *dis-kär'nit*, *-nāt*, *adj* disembodied; separated from its or the body. [**dis-** (1), and L *carō*, *carnis* flesh]

discase *dis-kās'*, (*Shakesp*, etc) *vt* to remove a case or covering from, to undress. [**dis-** (3)]

discept *di-sept'*, *vi* to dispute, debate. — *n* **disceptā'tion** (*archaic*). — *adj* **disceptā'tious** (*obs*). — *n* **disceptā'tor** (*obs*). — *adj* **disceptatō'rial** (*obs*). [L *disceptāre*, *-ātum* to contend, from *dis-*, and *captāre*]

discern *di-sûrn'*, *-zûrn'*, *vt* to make out; to distinguish by the eye or understanding; to judge (*obs*; a blunder for **decern**). — *n* **discern'er**. — *adj* **discern'ible**. — *adv* **discern'ibly**. — *adj* **discern'ing** discriminating; showing acute judgement. — *n* **discern'ment** the power or faculty of discriminating; judgement; acuteness. [L *discernere*, from *dis-* thoroughly, and *cernere* to sift, perceive]

discerp *di-sûrp'*, *vt* (*rare*) to separate. — *n* **discerpibil'ity** capability of being disunited. — *adj* **discerp'ible** (*obs*) or **discerp'tible**. — *n* (*rare*) **discerp'tion**. — *adj* (*rare*) **discerp'tive**. [L *discerpere* to tear in pieces, from *dis-* apart, and *carpere* to pluck]

discharge *dis-chärj'*, *vt* to free from or relieve of a charge of any kind (burden, explosive, electricity, liability, accusation, etc); to set free; to acquit; to dismiss from employment; to fire (eg a gun); to take the superincumbent weight from; to set down or send forth; to eject; to pour out; to emit or let out; to perform (eg a task or duty); to pay; to give account for; to distribute (as weight); to forbid (*obs*). — *vi* to unload; to become released from a charged state; to allow escape of contents; to flow away or out. — *n* (*usu dis'chärj*) the act of discharging; release from a charge of any kind; unloading; liberation; acquittal; dismissal; outflow; rate of flow; emission; release of tension; payment; performance; that which is discharged. — *n* **discharg'er** someone who discharges; an apparatus for discharging (*esp* electricity, eg a spark-gap or discharging tongs); an apparatus for firing an explosive. — **discharge tube** a tube in which an electric discharge takes place in a vacuum or in a gas at low pressure; **discharging arch** an arch built in a wall to protect a space beneath from the weight above; **discharging tongs** metal tongs used for discharging condensers. [OFr *descharger*, from *des-* apart, and *charger*; see **charge**]

dischuffed *dis-chuft'*, (*colloq*) *adj* displeased; disappointed. [**dis-** (2)]

dischurch *dis-chûrch'*, (*obs*) *vt* to deprive of church rank or privileges. [**dis-** (3)]

discide *di-sīd'*, (*obs*; *Spenser*, etc) *vt* to cut asunder, to divide. [L *dis-* asunder, and *caedere* to cut]

discinct *di-singkt'*, *adj* ungirded. [L *discingere*, *-cinctum* to ungird]

disciple *dis-ī'pl*, *n* a person who professes to receive instruction from another; a person who follows or believes in the doctrine of another; a follower, *esp* one of the twelve apostles of Christ. — *vt* (*Spenser*, etc) to teach. — *n* **discī'pleship**. — **Disciples of Christ** a sect that seeks a restoration of New Testament Christianity, by some called Campbellites. [Fr, from L *discipulus*, from *discere* to learn; related to *docēre* to teach]

discipline *dis'i-plin*, *n* training designed to engender self-control and an ordered way of life: the state of self-control achieved by such training; instruction; a branch of learning, or field of study; a branch of sport; an event in a sports meeting; subjection to control; order; severe training; mortification; punishment; an instrument of penance or punishment. — *vt* to subject to discipline; to train; to educate; to bring under control; to chastise. — *adj* **disc'iplinable**. — *adj*

disc'iplinal (or *-plī'*). — *n* **disc'iplinant** a person who subjects themselves to a discipline, *esp* one of an order of Spanish flagellants. — *n* **disciplinā'rian** a person who enforces strict discipline. — *adj* disciplinary; advocating or practising strict discipline. — *n* **disciplinā'rium** a scourge for penitential flogging. — *adj* **disc'iplinary** pertaining to or of the nature of discipline. — *n* **disc'ipliner** a person who disciplines. — **First** and **Second Book of Discipline** two documents (1560 and 1578) embodying the constitution and order of procedure of the Church of Scotland from the period of the Reformation. [L *disciplīna*, from *discipulus*]

discission *di-sish'ən*, *n* an incision into a tumour or cataract. [L *dīscissiō*, *-ōnis*, from *dīscindere*, *-scissum*, from *dī-* apart, and *scindere* to cut]

disclaim *dis-klām'*, *vt* to renounce all claim to; to refuse to acknowledge or be responsible for; to repudiate; to reject; to cry out against the claim of. — *vi* to make a disclaimer; to declaim, cry out (*obs*). — *n* **disclaim'er** a denial, disavowal or renunciation. — *n* **disclamā'tion** (*-kləm-*) a disavowal. [OFr *disclaimer*, from L *dis-* apart, and *clāmāre* to cry out]

disclose *dis-klōz'*, *vt* to unclose; to open; to lay open; to bring to light; to reveal; to hatch (*Shakesp*); to transform and give vent to (*Spenser*): — *pa p* (*Spenser*) **disclōst'**. — *n* a disclosure; emergence from the egg (*Shakesp*). — *n* **disclō'sure** (*-zhər*) the act of disclosing; a bringing to light or revealing; that which is disclosed or revealed. — **disclosing tablet** a tablet which, when chewed, reveals by means of a coloured dye any areas of plaque to be removed from the teeth. [OFr *desclos*, from L *dis-* apart, and *claudere*, *clausum* to shut]

disco *dis'kō*, (*colloq*) *n* short for **discothèque**: — *pl* **dis'cos**. — *adj* suitable or specially produced for discothèques, such as *disco dancing*, *disco dress*, *disco music*. — *vi* (*colloq*) to go to a disco; to dance to disco music: — *pr p* **dis'coing**; *pa t* and *pa p* **dis'coed**. — *n* **dis'coer** someone who frequents discos.

discobolus *dis-kob'ə-ləs*, *n* a disc-thrower (*classical Gr hist*); the name of a famous lost statue ascribed to Myron, of which copies exist. [L, from Gr *diskobolos*, from *diskos* a quoit and *ballein* to throw]

discographer, **discography**, **discoid**, **discoidal**, etc. See **disc**.

discolour or (*NAm*) **discolor**, *dis-kul'ər*, *vt* to take away colour from; to change or to spoil the natural colour of; to alter the appearance of; to mark with other colours, to stain; to dirty, disfigure. — *vi* to become discoloured. — *n* **discolourā'tion** the act of discolouring; the state of being discoloured; stain. — *adj* **discol'oured** stained, etc; many-coloured (*Spenser*). [OFr *descolorer*, from L *dis-* apart, and *colōrāre*, from *color* colour]

discombobulate *dis-kəm-bob'ōō-lāt*, *-ū-lāt* or **discomboberate** *-bob'ər-āt*, (*esp NAm slang*) *vt* to disconcert, upset. [Origin obscure]

Discomedusae *dis-kō-me-dū'sē*, *n pl* an order of jellyfishes with flattened umbrella. — *n* and *adj* **discomedū'san**. [Gr *diskos* disc, and **medusa**]

discomfit *dis-kum'fit*, *vt* to disconcert or balk; to defeat or rout: — *pr p* **discom'fiting**; *pa t* and *pa p* **discom'fited**. — *n* (*Milton*) defeat. — *n* **discom'fiture**. [OFr *desconfit*, pa p of *desconfire*, from L *dis-* (negative), and *conficere* to prepare, from *con-* (intensive), and *facere* to make]

discomfort *dis-kum'fərt*, *n* lack of comfort; uneasiness; slight pain. — *vt* to deprive of comfort; to make uneasy. — *adj* **discom'fortable** causing discomfort (*obs*); uncomfortable. [OFr *desconforter*, from *des-* (privative) and *conforter* to comfort; see **comfort**]

discommend *dis-kəm-end'*, *vt* to blame; to dispraise. — *adj* **discommend'able**. — *n* **discommend'ableness**. — *n* **discommendation** (*dis-ko-mən-dā'shən*). [**dis-** (2)]

discommission *dis-kə-mish'ən*, (*Milton*) *vt* to deprive of a commission. [**dis-** (3)]

discommode *dis-kə-mōd'*, *vt* to inconvenience. — *adj* **discommō'dious**. — *adv* **discommō'diously**. — *n* **discommodity** (*-mod'-*) inconvenience. [**dis-** (2), and obsolete verb *commode* to suit]

discommon *dis-kom'ən*, *vt* to deprive of the right of common, or (at Oxford and Cambridge) of dealing with undergraduates. [**dis-** (3), and **common** (noun)]

discommunity *dis-kə-mūn'i-ti*, (*rare*) *n* lack of community. [**dis-** (2)]

discompose *dis-kəm-pōz'*, *vt* to deprive of composure; to disturb or agitate; to disarrange or disorder. — *n* **discompō'sure** (*-zhər* or *-zhyər*). [**dis-** (2)]

Discomycetes *dis-kō-mī-sē'tēz*, (*bot*) *n pl* a group of fungi (*Ascomycetes*) with open apothecia. — *n* **dis'comycete**. — *adj* **discomycē'tous**. [Gr *diskos* disc, and *mykētes*, pl of *mykēs* a fungus]

disconcert *dis-kən-sûrt'*, *vt* to throw into confusion; to disturb; to frustrate; to defeat; to put out of countenance, to embarrass. — *n* **disconcert** (*dis-kon'sərt*) disunion. — *n* **disconcer'tion** confusion. — *n* **disconcert'ment**. [Obs Fr *disconcerter*, from *des-* (L *dis-*) apart, and *concerter* to concert]

disconformable *dis-kən-förm'ə-bl*, *adj* not similar or consistent; (of strata) with their original relative positions disturbed (*geol*); not conformable. — *n* **disconform'ity** lack of conformity; unconformity (*geol*). [**dis-** (2)]

disconnect *dis-kən-ekt'*, *vt* and *vi* to separate or disjoin (from); to break the connection, *esp* electrical (between). — *adj* **disconnect'ed** separated; (eg of a discourse) loosely united. — *adv* **disconnect'edly**. — *n* **disconnec'tion** or **disconnex'ion**. [**dis-** (1)]

disconsent *dis-kən-sent'*, (*obs*) *vi* to differ or dissent. [**dis-** (2)]

disconsolate *dis-kon'sə-lit*, *adj* beyond consolation or comfort; very sad or disappointed. — *adv* **discon'solately**. — *n* **discon'solateness**. — *n* **disconsolā'tion**. [L *dis-* (negative) and *consōlārī*, *consōlātus* to console]

discontent *dis-kən-tent'*, *adj* not content; dissatisfied. — *n* lack of contentment; dissatisfaction; a discontented person (*Shakesp*). — *vt* to deprive of contentment; to stir up to ill-will. — *adj* **discontent'ed** dissatisfied. — *adv* **discontent'edly**. — *n* **discontent'edness**. — *adj* **discontent'ful**. — *adj* **discontent'ing** not contenting or satisfying; discontented (*Shakesp*). — *n* **discontent'ment**. [**dis-** (2), (3)]

discontiguous *dis-kon-tig'ū-əs*, *adj* not contiguous, not in contact. — *n* **discontigū'ity**. [**dis-** (2)]

discontinue *dis-kən-tin'ū*, *vt* to cease to continue; to put an end to; to leave off; to stop. — *vi* to cease; to be separated (*obs*). — *n* **discontin'uance** or **discontinuā'tion** a breaking off or ceasing. — *n* **discontinu'ity** (*-kon-*). — *adj* **discontin'uous** not continuous; broken off; separated; interrupted by intervening spaces. — *adv* **discontin'uously**. [OFr *discontinuer*, from L *dis-* reversal, and *continuāre* to continue]

discophile. See **disc**.

Discophora *dis-kof'ə-rə*, *n pl* the order of jellyfishes known as *Discomedusae*. — *n* and *adj* **discoph'oran**. — *adj* **discoph'orous**. [Gr *diskos* disc, and *phoros* carrying]

discord *dis'körd*, *n* disagreement, strife (*opp* of *concord*); difference or contrariety of qualities; a combination of inharmonious sounds; uproarious noise; a dissonance, *esp* unprepared. — *vi* **discord'** to disagree. — *n* **discord'ance** or **discord'ancy**. — *adj* **discord'ant** without concord or agreement; inconsistent; contradictory; harsh; jarring. — *adv* **discord'antly**. — *adj* **discord'ful** (*Spenser*). — **apple of discord** see under **apple**. [OFr *descord*, from L *discordia*, from *dis-* apart, and *cor*, *cordis* the heart]

discorporate *dis-kör'pər-it*, *adj* disembodied. [**dis-** (2)]

discothèque or **discotheque** *dis'kə-tek*, *n* a club or party where music for dancing is provided by records, *usu* played by a disc jockey, and often accompanied by special lighting effects; the equipment and records used to provide such music and effects. — Now *usu* (*colloq*) **dis'co** (qv). [Fr, a record-library, from Gr *diskos* disc, and *thēkē* case, library]

discounsel *dis-kown'səl*, (*Spenser*, *etc*) *vt* to dissuade. [OFr *desconseillier*, from *des-* apart, and *conseillier* to counsel]

discount *dis'kownt*, *n* a deduction made for prompt payment of an account, or according to some other negotiated agreement; the rate or percentage of the deduction granted; a deduction made for interest in advancing money on a bill; the amount by which the price of a share or stock unit is below the par value. — *vt* **discount'** to disregard, or reject as unimportant; to reduce the effect of (eg an extravagant statement, a fabulous story or an event foreseen); to sell at a reduced price; to allow as discount; to allow discount on; to pay (rarely to receive) beforehand the present worth of a bill of exchange; to ignore. — *vi* to practise discounting. — *adj* **discount'able**. — *n* **discount'er**. — **dis'count-broker** a person who cashes notes or bills of exchange at a discount; **discount house** a company trading in bills of exchange, etc; (also **discount store**) a shop where goods are sold at less than the usual retail price; **discount rate** the rate at which a discount is granted; the rate at which banks can borrow funds using bills as security; (*NAm*) bank rate. — **at a discount** below par; not sought after; superfluous; depreciated in value; **discounted cash flow** (*accountancy*) the present value of future estimated cash flows. [OFr *descompter*, from *des-* (L *dis-*) away, and *compter* to count]

discountenance *dis-kown'tən-əns*, *vt* to put out of countenance; to abash; to refuse approval of or support to; to discourage. — *n* cold treatment; disapprobation. [OFr *descontenancer*, from *des-* reversal, and *contenance* countenance]

discourage *dis-kur'ij*, *vt* to take away the courage of; to dishearten; to oppose by showing disfavour. — *n* **discour'agement** act of discouraging; that which discourages; dejection. — *n* and *adj* **discour'aging** disheartening, depressing. — *adv* **discour'agingly**. [OFr *descourager*. See **courage**]

discoure *dis-kowr'*, (*Spenser*) *vt* to discover.

discourse *dis-kōrs'*, *-körs'*, or *dis'*, *n* speech or language generally; conversation; the reasoning faculty (*obs* or *archaic*); a treatise; a speech; a sermon; (apparently) process of combat (*Spenser*) — *vi* to talk or converse; to reason; to treat formally (with *on*). — *vt* to utter or give forth. — *n* **discours'er** (*Shakesp*). — *adj* **discours'al**. — *adj* (*obs*) **discours'ive**. [Fr *discours*, from L *discursus*, from *dis-* away, and *currere* to run]

discourteous *dis-kûrt'yəs*, *-kōrt'* or *-kört'*, *adj* lacking in courtesy; uncivil. — Also (*Spenser*) **discour'teise**. — *adv* **discourt'eously**. — *n* **discourt'eousness**. — *n* **discourt'esy** discourteousness; a discourteous remark or act. [**dis-** (2)]

discover *dis-kuv'ər*, *vt* to find or find out, *esp* for the first time; to uncover (*obs*); to lay open or expose (*archaic*); to exhibit (*rare*); to reveal (*rare*); to make known (*archaic*); to espy. — Also (*Spenser*, etc) **discoure'** and **discure'**. — *adj* **discov'erable**. — *n* **discov'erer** a person who makes a discovery, *esp* of something never before known; an informer (*obs*); a scout (*Shakesp*). — *n* **discov'ery** the act of finding out; the thing discovered; gaining knowledge of the unknown; the unravelling of a plot; exploration or reconnaissance (as in **voyage of discovery** voyage of exploration). — **discovery well** an exploratory oil well which proves to yield a commercially viable amount of oil. [OFr *descouvrir*, from *des-* (L *dis-*) away, and *couvrir* to cover; see **cover**]

discovert *dis-kuv'ərt*, (*law*) *adj* (of a spinster or widow) not under the bonds of matrimony. — *n* **discov'erture**. [Literally, uncovered, unprotected; OFr *descovert*; see **discover** and **cover**]

discredit *dis-kred'it*, *n* lack of credit; bad credit; ill-repute; disgrace; a person or thing bringing ill-repute or disgrace. — *vt* to refuse to believe in; to deprive of credibility; to deprive of credit; to disgrace. — *adj* **discred'itable** bringing discredit; disgraceful. — *adv* **discred'itably**. [**dis-** (2) and (3)]

discreet *dis-krēt'*, *adj* careful in one's actions and choice of words, *esp* able to keep secrets; tactful; prudent; modest; unpretentious; discrete, separate, detached (*archaic*). — *adv* **discreet'ly**. — *n* **discreet'ness**. [OFr *discret*, from L *discrētus*, from *discernere* to separate, to perceive; see **discern** and **discrete**]

discrepancy *dis-krep'ən-si*, *n* disagreement, variance of facts or sentiments. — *n* **discrep'ance** (or *dis'*). — *adj* **discrep'ant** (or *dis'*) contrary, disagreeing. [L *discrepāns*, *-antis* different, from *dis-* apart, and *crepāns*, pr p of *crepāre* to sound]

discrete *dis-krēt'*, *adj* separate; discontinuous; consisting of distinct parts; referring to distinct objects; abstract (*opp* to *concrete*). — *adv* **discrete'ly**. — *n* **discrete'ness**. — *adj* **discret'ive** separating; disjunctive. — *adv* **discret'ively**. [L *discrētus*; cf **discreet**]

discretion *dis-kresh'ən*, *n* quality of being discreet; prudence; liberty to act at pleasure. — *adj* **discre'tional** or **discre'tionary** left to discretion; unrestricted. — *adv* **discre'tionally** or **discre'tionarily**. — **discretionary income** the amount of income remaining from a person's salary or wages after all regular fixed expenditure on necessary items has been met. — **age** or **years of discretion** mature years; **at discretion** according to one's own judgement or pleasure; **be at someone's discretion** to be completely under someone's power or control; **surrender at discretion** to surrender unconditionally, ie to another's discretion. [OFr *discrecion*, from L *discrētiō*, *-ōnis*, from *discernere*, *-crētum*]

discriminate *dis-krim'i-nāt*, *vt* to note the difference of or between; to distinguish; to select from others. — *vi* to make or note differences or distinctions; to distinguish (with *between*); (with *in favour of* or *against*) to treat differently, *esp* because of one's feelings or prejudices about a person's sex, race, religion, etc. — *n* (*math*) a special function of the roots of an equation, expressible in terms of the coefficients, zero value of the function showing that at least two of the roots are equal. — *adj* (*-nit*) discriminated; discriminating. — *adj* **discrim'inant** discriminating. — *adv* **discrim'inately**. — *adj* **discrim'ināting** noting distinctions; gifted with judgement and penetration. — *adv* **discrim'inātingly**. — *n* **discriminā'tion** the act or process of discriminating; judgement; good taste; the selection of a signal having a particular characteristic (frequency, amplitude, etc) by the elimination of all the other input signals (*telecomm*). — *adj* **discrim'inative** that marks a difference; characteristic; observing distinctions. — *adv* **discrim'inatively**. — *n* **discrim'inātor** a person who or thing which discriminates; a device which affects the routing and/or determines the fee units for a call originating at a satellite exchange (*telecomm*); a circuit which converts a frequency or phase modulation into amplitude modulation for subsequent demodulation (*telecomm*); a circuit which rejects pulses below a certain amplitude level and shapes the remainder to standard amplitude and profile (*telecomm*). — *adj* **discrim'inatory** biased, unfair, revealing prejudice; discriminative; making fine distinctions. — **positive discrimination** discrimination in favour of those who were formerly discriminated against, *esp* in the provision of social and educational facilities and employment opportunities. [L *discrīmināre*, *-ātum*, from *discrīmen* that which separates; cf *discernere* to discern]

discrown *dis-krown'*, *vt* to deprive of a crown. [**dis-** (3)]

disculpate *dis-kul'pāt*, *vt* to free from blame. [**dis-** (3)]

discumber *dis-kum'bər*, (*archaic*) *vt* to disencumber. [**dis-** (2)]

discure. See **discover**.

discursive *dis-kûr'siv*, *adj* running from one thing to another; (of writing or speaking style) proceeding from one subject to another with no formal plan, given to digression, roving, desultory; proceeding regularly from premises to conclusion, intellectual or rational, rather than intuitive (*philos*). — *n* **discur'sion** (*rare*) desultory talk; act of reasoning. — *n* **discur'sist** (*obs*) a disputer. — *adv* **discur'sively**. — *n* **discur'siveness**. —

adj **discur'sory** discursive. — *n* **discur'sus** (*LL*) discourse, reasoned treatment. [See **discourse**]

discus *dis'kəs*, *n* a disc, a flat circular image or object; a heavy wooden disc, thickening towards the centre, thrown for distance in athletic contests, *orig* in ancient Greece; (*usu* with *cap*) a popular freshwater aquarium fish, a brightly-coloured, disc-shaped S American cichlid. [L, from Gr *diskos*]

discuss *dis-kus'*, *vt* to examine in detail in speech or writing; to talk or argue about in conversation; to debate; to sift; to consume (eg a bottle of wine; *facetious*); to throw off (*obs*; *Spenser*); to dispel; to settle, decide (*obs*); to declare, make known (*obs*; *Shakesp*). — *adj* **discuss'able** or **discuss'ible**. — *n* **discussion** (*dis-kush'ən*) debate, argument or conversation; a detailed treatment in speech or writing; the dispersion of a tumour (*surg*). — *adj* **discuss'ive** or **discutient** (*-kū'shi-ənt*) (*med*) able or tending to discuss or disperse tumours. — *n* **discū'tient** a medicine with this property. [L *discutere*, *discussum*, from *dis-* apart, and *quatere* to shake]

disdain *dis-dān'*, *vt* to think unworthy; to scorn. — *n* a feeling of contempt, generally tinged with superiority; haughtiness. — *adj* **disdained'** (*Shakesp*) disdainful. — *adj* **disdain'ful** feeling or showing disdain. — *adv* **disdain'fully**. — *n* **disdain'fulness**. [OFr *desdaigner* with substitution of *des-* (L *dis-*) for L *dē* in L *dēdīgnārī*, from *dīgnus* worthy]

disease *diz-ēz'*, *n* an unhealthy state of body or mind; a disorder, illness or ailment with distinctive symptoms, caused eg by infection; unhealthiness, or a specific ailment, in plants; a social evil (*fig*); uneasiness (in this sense often written **dis-ease** and pronounced *dis'ēz'*; *archaic*). — *vt* (*Spenser*, etc) to make uneasy. — *adj* **diseased'** affected with disease. — *n* **diseas'edness**. — *adj* **disease'ful** (*obs*). [OFr *desaise*, from *des-* (L *dis-* not), and *aise* ease; see **ease**]

diseconomy *dis-ə-kon'ə-mi*, *n* (an instance of) something which is economically wasteful or unprofitable. [**dis-** (2)]

disedge *dis-ej'*, (*Shakesp*, etc) *vt* to deprive of the edge; to blunt; to dull. [**dis-** (3)]

disembark *dis-im-bärk'*, *vi* to leave a ship; to land. — *vt* to set ashore; to take out of a ship. — *n* **disembarkā'tion** (*dis-em-* or *dis-im-*) or **disembark'ment**. [OFr *desembarquer*, from *des-* (L *dis-* removal), and *embarquer*. See **embark**]

disembarrass *dis-im-bar'əs*, *vt* to free from an embarrassment, burden or complication (with *of*). — *n* **disembarr'assment**. [**dis-** (2)]

disembellish *dis-im-bel'ish*, *vt* to deprive of embellishment. [**dis-** (2)]

disembitter *dis-im-bit'ər*, *vt* to free from bitterness. [**dis-** (2)]

disembody *dis-im-bod'i*, *vt* to remove or free (a spirit) from the body; to discharge from military embodiment. — *adj* **disembod'ied**. — *n* **disembod'iment**. [**dis-** (3)]

disembogue *dis-im-bōg'*, *vt* (*usu reflexive*) and *vi* to discharge at the mouth, as a stream (with *into*). — *n* **disembogue'ment**. [Sp *desembocar*, from *des-* (L *dis-*) apart, and *embocar* to enter the mouth, from *en* (L *in*) into, and *boca* (L *bucca*) cheek, mouth]

disembosom *dis-im-bo͝oz'əm*, *vt* to separate from the bosom; to disburden. [**dis-** (1)]

disembowel *dis-im-bow'əl*, *vt* to take out the bowels of; to tear out the inside of. — *n* **disembow'elment**. [**dis-** (3)]

disembrangle *dis-im-brang'gl*, (*obs*) *vt* to free from dispute. [**dis-** (2)]

disembroil *dis-im-broil'*, *vt* to free from broil or confusion. [**dis-** (2)]

disemburden *dis-im-bûr'dn*, *vt* to disburden. [**dis-** (3)]

disemploy *dis-im-ploi'*, (*rare*) *vt* to remove from employment. — *adj* **disemployed'**. — *n* **disemploy'ment**. [**dis-** (2)]

disenable *dis-in-ā'bl*, *vt* to make unable; to disable; to deprive of power (*obs*). [**dis-** (2)]

disenchain *dis-in-chān'*, *vt* to free from restraint. [**dis-** (2)]

disenchant *dis-in-chänt'*, *vt* to free from enchantment, to disillusion. — *n* **disenchant'er**, *fem* **disenchant'ress**. — *n* **disenchant'ment**. [**dis-** (2)]

disenclose *dis-in-klōz'*, *vt* to free from the condition of being enclosed; to dispark. — Also **disinclose'**. [**dis-** (2)]

disencumber *dis-in-kum'bər*, *vt* to free from an encumbrance; to disburden. — *n* **disencum'brance**. [**dis-** (2)]

disendow *dis-in-dow'*, *vt* to take away the endowments of (*esp* of an established church). — *adj* **disendowed'**. — *n* **disendow'ment**. [**dis-** (3)]

disenfranchise *dis-in-fran'chīz*, *-shīz*, (*rare*) *vt* to disfranchise; to deprive of suffrage. — *n* **disenfran'chisement** (*-chiz-*, *-shis-*). [**dis-** (2)]

disengage *dis-in-gāj'*, *vt* to separate or free from being engaged; to separate; to set free; to release. — *vi* to come loose; to break off from a fight. — *adj* **disengaged'** at leisure, without engagement. — *n* **disengag'edness**. — *n* **disengage'ment** a separating, releasing; a mutual withdrawal from a position. [OFr *desengager*, from *des-* (L *dis-* negative) and *engager* to engage]

disennoble *dis-i-nō'bl*, *vt* to deprive of title, or of what ennobles; to degrade. [**dis-** (2)]

disenrol *dis-in-rōl'*, *vt* to remove from a roll. [**dis-** (2)]

disenshroud *dis-in-shrowd'*, *vt* to divest of a shroud, to unveil. [**dis-** (3)]

disenslave *dis-in-slāv'*, *vt* to free from bondage. [**dis-** (2)]

disentail *dis-in-tāl'*, *vt* to break the entail of (an estate) (*law*); to divest (*obs*). — *n* the act of disentailing. [**dis-** (2)]

disentangle *dis-in-tang'gl*, *vt* to free from entanglement or disorder; to unravel; to disengage or set free. — *n* **disentang'lement**. [**dis-** (2)]

disenthral or **disenthrall** *dis-in-thröl'*, *vt* to free from enthralment. — *n* **disenthrall'ment** or **disenthral'ment**. [**dis-** (2)]

disenthrone *dis-in-thrōn'*, (*Milton*, etc) *vt* to dethrone. [**dis-** (2)]

disentitle *dis-in-tī'tl*, *vt* to deprive of title or right. [**dis-** (2)]

disentomb *dis-in-to͞om'*, *vt* to take out from a tomb. [**dis-** (2)]

disentrail or **disentrayle** *dis-in-trāl*, (*Spenser*) *vt* to let forth as if from the entrails. [**dis-** (3)]

disentrain *dis-in-trān'*, *vt* to set down from a train. — *vi* to alight from a train. — *n* **disentrain'ment**. [**dis-** (3)]

disentrance *dis-in-träns'*, *vt* to awaken from a trance or entrancement; to arouse from a reverie. — *n* **disentrance'ment**. [**dis-** (2)]

disentrayle. See **disentrail**.

disentwine *dis-in-twīn'*, *vt* to untwine. [**dis-** (2)]

disenvelop *dis-in-vel'əp*, *vt* to free from that in which a thing is enveloped; to unfold. [**dis-** (2)]

disenviron *dis-in-vī'rən*, *vt* to deprive of environment. [**dis-** (3)]

disepalous *dī-sep'ə-ləs*, (*bot*) *adj* having two sepals. [**di-** and **sepal**]

disequilibrium *dis-ek-wi-lib'ri-əm*, *n* lack of balance, *esp* in economic affairs: — *pl* **disequilib'ria**. — *vt* **disequil'ibrate** to cause a disequilibrium in. [**dis-** (2)]

disespouse *dis-is-powz'*, (*Milton*) *vt* to separate after espousal or betrothal. [**dis-** (1)]

disestablish *dis-is-tab'lish*, *vt* to undo the establishment of; to deprive (a church) of established status. — *n* **disestab'lishment**. [**dis-** (2)]

disesteem *dis-is-tēm'*, *n* lack of esteem; disregard. — *vt* to disapprove; to dislike. — *n* **disestimā'tion** (*-es-tim-*). [**dis-** (2)]

diseur *dē-zœr* or *fem* **diseuse** *dē-zœz*, (*Fr*) *n* a reciter or entertainer.

disfame *dis-fām'*, (*rare*) *n* evil reputation. [**dis-** (2)]

disfavour or (*NAm*) **disfavor** *dis-fā'vər*, *n* the state of being out of favour or disapproved of; hostility, disapproval or dislike; a disobliging act. — *vt* to be hostile to; to disapprove; to oppose. — *n* **disfā'vourer**. [**dis-** (2)]

disfeature *dis-fē'chər*, *vt* to deprive of a feature; to deface. [**dis-** (3)]

disfellowship *dis-fel'ō-ship*, *n* lack of or exclusion from fellowship. — *vt* to excommunicate. [**dis-** (2)]

disfigure *dis-fig'ər*, *vt* to spoil the appearance of, to blemish or mar; to deface; to deform or distort. — *n* **disfigūrā'tion** or **disfig'urement**. [OFr *desfigurer*, from L *dis-* (negative) and *figūrāre* to figure]

disflesh *dis-flesh'*, (*archaic* and *poetic*) *vt* to deprive of flesh, to disembody. [**dis-** (3)]

disfluency *dis-floo'ən-si*, *n* a lack of fluency in speech, with hesitations, repetitions, stammering, etc. — *adj* **disflu'ent**. [**dis-** (2)]

disforest *dis-for'ist*, *vt* to strip of trees, to deforest; to disafforest (*law*). [**dis-** (2)]

disform *dis-förm'*, *vt* to alter the form of. [**dis-** (2)]

disfranchise *dis-fran'chīz*, *-shīz*, *vt* to deprive of a franchise, or of rights and privileges, *esp* that of voting for a member of parliament. — *n* **disfran'chisement**. [**dis-** (2)]

disfrock *dis-frok'*, *vt* to unfrock, deprive of clerical garb or character. [**dis-** (3)]

disfurnish *dis-fûr'nish*, (*Shakesp* and *literary*) *vt* to strip, render destitute. — *n* **disfur'nishment**. [**dis-** (2)]

disgarnish *dis-gär'nish*, *vt* to despoil. [**dis-** (3)]

disgarrison *dis-gar'i-sn*, *vt* to deprive of a garrison. [**dis-** (3)]

disgavel *dis-gav'l*, (*law*) *vt* to relieve from the tenure of gavelkind. [**dis-** (3)]

disgest *dis-jest'* or *-jēst'*, and **disgest'ion** *-yən*, *obs* or *dialect* forms of **digest**[1] and **digestion**.

disglorify *dis-glō'ri-fī*, *-glö'*, (*Milton*) *vt* to deprive of glory. [**dis-** (3)]

disgodded *dis-god'id*, *adj* deprived of divinity. [**dis-** (2)]

disgorge *dis-görj'*, *vt* to discharge from the throat; to vomit; to discharge in great volume or with violence; to give up, *esp* reluctantly; to remove sediment from (champagne) after fermentation in the bottle. — *n* **disgorge'ment**. [OFr *desgorger*, from *des* away, and *gorge* throat. See **gorge**]

disgospelling *dis-gos'pəl-ing*, (*Milton*) *adj* withholding the gospel, stopping the channel of the gospel. [**dis-** (3)]

disgown *dis-gown'*, *vt* or *vi* to strip of a gown; to deprive of or to renounce orders or a degree. [**dis-** (3)]

disgrace *dis-grās'*, *n* the state of being out of favour or of being dishonoured; a cause of shame, someone or something shameful; disrepute or dishonour; disfigurement; ugliness; defect of grace. — *vt* to put out of favour; to bring disgrace or shame upon. — *adj* **disgrace'ful** bringing disgrace; causing shame; dishonourable. — *adv* **disgrace'fully**. — *n* **disgrace'-fulness**. — *n* **disgra'cer**. — *adj* **disgracious** (*-grā'shəs*; *obs*; *Shakesp*, etc) ungracious, unpleasing. — **in disgrace** out of favour; shamed. [Fr *disgrâce*, from L *dis-* not, and *grātia* favour, grace]

disgrade *dis-grād'*, (*archaic*) *vt* to deprive of rank or status. — *n* **disgradation** (*-grə-dā'shən*). [OFr *desgrader*, with substitution of *des-* (L *dis-*) for L *dē* in LL *dēgradāre*, from *gradus* a step]

disgregation *dis-gri-gā'shən*, *n* separation; scattering. [L *disgregātiō*, *-ōnis*, from *dis-* apart, and *grex*, *gregis* flock]

disgruntle *dis-grun'tl*, (*colloq*) *vt* to disappoint or displease. — *adj* **disgrun'tled** out of humour, discontented, sulky. — *n* **disgrun'tlement**. [**dis-** (4) and **gruntle**, frequentative of **grunt**]

disguise *dis-gīz'*, *vt* to change the appearance or character of; to conceal the identity of, eg by dress intended to deceive, or by a counterfeit manner and appearance; to mask or hide (facts or feelings); to misrepresent; to intoxicate (*usu* in the phrase *disguised in liquor*; *archaic* and *slang*). — *n* dress intended to disguise the wearer; a false appearance; a misleading representation; change of behaviour in intoxication (*archaic* and *slang*). — *adj* **disguis'able**. — *adj* **disguised'**. — *adv* **disguis'edly**. — *n* **disguis'edness**. — *adj* **disguise'less**. — *n* **disguise'ment**. — *n* **disguis'er**. — *n* **disguis'ing**. [OFr *desguiser*, from *des-* (L *dis-* reversal), and *guise* manner; see **guise**]

disgust *dis-gust'*, *n* loathing, distaste, extreme disapproval, or annoyance; (formerly, eg in Milton, Johnson, Jane Austen) distaste, disfavour, displeasure. — *vt* to cause disgust in. — *adj* **disgust'ed**. — *adv* **disgust'edly**. — *n* **disgust'edness**. — *adj* **disgust'ful**. — *adv* **disgust'fully**. — *n* **disgust'fulness**. — *adj* **disgust'ing**. — *adv* **disgust'ingly**. — *n* **disgust'ingness**. — **in disgust** with or because of a feeling of disgust. [OFr *desgouster*, from *des-* (L *dis-*) and *gouster*, from L *gustāre* to taste]

dish[1] *dish*, *n* a vessel, *esp* one that is flat, or shallow, or not circular, for holding or serving food at table; a dishful; the food in a dish; a cup (of tea, coffee, etc) (*archaic*); food prepared in a particular way for the table; a hollow; concavity of form, as in a wheel or a chair-back; (also **dish aerial**) a microwave aerial in the form of a parabolic reflector used for radar or radio telescopes and for satellite broadcast reception; a good-looking person, *esp* of the opposite sex (*colloq*). — *vt* to put in a dish, for serving at table; to make concave; to outwit, circumvent (*colloq*); to ruin (*colloq*). — *adj* **dished** having a concavity; (of a pair of wheels on a car, etc) sloping in towards each other at the top; completely frustrated (*colloq*). — *n* **dish'ful**. — *n* **dish'ing** putting in a dish; a hollow, a concavity. — *adj* hollow like a dish. — *adj* **dish'y** (*colloq*) good-looking, attractive. — **dish aerial** see **dish** (*n*) above; **dish'-cloth** or (*archaic* or *dialect*) **dish'-clout** a cloth for washing, drying or wiping dishes; **dish'-cover** a cover for a dish to keep it hot. — *adj* **dish'-faced** having a round, flat face, or (in animals) a concavity in the face. — **dish'-rag** a dish-cloth; **dish'towel** a cloth for drying dishes, a tea-towel (*esp NAm*); **dish'washer** a machine which washes dishes, cutlery, etc; a person employed to wash dishes; **dish'water** water in which dishes have been washed; a liquid deficient in strength or cleanliness. — **dish out** to serve out; to share (food) among several people; to give, give out (*colloq*; *usu disparagingly*; *esp* with *it*, of rough treatment, punishment, etc); **dish the dirt** see under **dirt**; **dish up** to serve up, (*esp fig* of old materials presented again). [OE *disc* a plate, a dish, a table, from L *discus*, from Gr *diskos*; cf **disc**, **desk** and Ger *Tisch* table]

dish[2] *dish*, (*printing*) *vt* to distribute (type).

dishabilitate *dis-(h)ə-bil'i-tāt*, *vt* to disqualify; to attaint. — *n* **dishabilitā'tion**. [**dis-** (2)]

dishabille *dis-ə-bēl'*, *n* careless attention to one's dress, appearance, etc; a state of undress; an undress garment. — Also **déshabillé** (*dā-zä-bē-yā*). [Fr *déshabillé*, pa p of *déshabiller* to undress, from *des-* (L *dis-*) apart, and *habiller* to dress]

dishabit *dis-hab'it*, (*Shakesp*) *vt* to drive from a habitation. [OFr *deshabiter*, from L *dis-* (privative) and *habitāre* to inhabit]

dishable *dis-hā'bl*, an obsolete form (*Spenser*, etc) of **disable**.

dishallow *dis-hal'ō*, *vt* to desecrate. [**dis-** (2)]

disharmony *dis-här'mə-ni*, *n* lack of harmony; discord; disagreement, dissent; incongruity. — *adj* **disharmonic** (*-mon'*) out of harmony; discordant; incongruous; dysharmonic. — *adj* **disharmonious** (*-mō'*). — *adv* **disharmō'niously**. — *vt* and *vi* **dishar'monize** or **-ise** to put out of, or be out of, harmony. [**dis-** (2)]

dishearten *dis-härt'n*, *vt* to deprive of courage or spirits; to discourage or demoralize; to depress. — *adj* **disheart'ened**. — *adj* **disheart'ening**. — *adv* **disheart'-eningly**. [**dis-** (2)]

dishelm *dis-helm'*, *vt* to divest of a helmet. [**dis-** (3)]

disherit *dis-her'it*, (*Spenser*, etc) *vt* to disinherit. — *n* **disher'ison** (*-zən*). — *n* **disher'itor**. [OFr *desheriter*, from L *dis-* (negative) and LL *hērēditāre* to inherit, from L *hērēs* heir]

dishevel *di-shev'l*, *vt* to ruffle (hair) or disarrange (clothing); to cause to hang loose. — *vi* to spread in disorder: — *pr p* **dishev'elling**; *pa t* and *pa p* **dishev'elled**.

— *adj* **dishev'elled** (of a person) untidy or bedraggled in appearance; (of hair) hanging loose, or merely untidy. — *n* **dishev'elment**. [OFr *discheveler*, from LL *discapillāre* to tear out or disorder the hair, from L *dis-* in different directions, and *capillus* the hair]

dishome *dis-hōm'*, *vt* to deprive of a home. [**dis-** (3)]

dishonest *dis-on'ist*, *adj* not honest; lacking integrity; disposed to cheat; insincere; unchaste (*obs*; *Shakesp*). — *adv* **dishon'estly**. — *n* **dishon'esty**. [OFr *deshoneste*, from *des-* (L *dis-*; negative) and *honeste* (L *honestus*) honest]

dishonour or (*NAm*) **dishonor** *dis-on'ər*, *n* lack of respect or honour: disgrace; shame; something that brings discredit; an affront; reproach; failure of a debtor to make good a promise to pay. — *vt* to deprive of honour; to disgrace; to cause shame to; to seduce; to degrade; to refuse the payment of (eg a cheque). — *adj* **dishon'orary** causing dishonour. — **dishon'ourable** or (*NAm*) **dishon'orable** not in accordance with a sense of honour; disgraceful. — *n* **dishon'ourableness** or (*NAm*) **dishon'orableness**. — *adv* **dishon'ourably** or (*NAm*) **dishon'orably**. — *n* **dishon'ourer** or (*NAm*) **dishon'orer**. — **dishonorable discharge** dismissal from the US armed forces for serious misconduct (such as theft or desertion). — **dishonorably discharged**. [OFr *deshonneur*, from *des-* (L *dis-*) (negative) and *honneur*, (from L *honor*) honour]

dishorn *dis-hörn'*, *vt* to deprive of horns. [**dis-** (3)]

dishorse *dis-hörs'*, *vt* to unhorse. [**dis-** (3)]

dishouse *dis-howz'*, *vt* to deprive of house or housing; to turn out of doors; to clear of houses. [**dis-** (3)]

dishumour *dis-(h)ū'mər*, (*obs*) *n* ill-humour. — *vt* to put out of humour. [**dis-** (2)]

dishy. See **dish**[1].

disillude *dis-i-lo͞od'*, *-lūd'*, *vt* to free from illusion. [**dis-** (3)]

disilluminate *dis-i-lo͞o'mi-nāt*, *-lū'*, (*Swinburne*) *vt* to destroy the light of, to darken. [**dis-** (2)]

disillusion *dis-i-lo͞o'zhən*, *-lū'*, *n* a freeing from illusion; state of being disillusioned. — *vt* to destroy the illusions of, to disenchant; to disabuse. — *adj* **disillu'sionary**. — *adj* **disillu'sioned** disenchanted, disabused of an illusion; often, bereft of comfortable beliefs whether they were false or true. — *vt* **disillu'sionize** or **-ise**. — *n* **disillu'sionment**. — *adj* **disillu'sive** (*-siv*). [**dis-** (3)]

disimagine *dis-i-maj'in*, *vt* to banish from the imagination; to imagine not to be. [**dis-** (3) and (2)]

disimmure *dis-i-mūr'*, *vt* to release from walls; to liberate. [**dis-** (2)]

disimpassioned *dis-im-pash'ənd*, *adj* free from the influence of passion, tranquil. [**dis-** (2)]

disimprison *dis-im-priz'n*, *vt* to free from prison or restraint. — *n* **disimpris'onment**. [**dis-** (2)]

disimprove *dis-im-pro͞ov'*, *vt* to render worse. — *vi* to grow worse. [**dis-** (2)]

disincarcerate *dis-in-kär'sər-āt*, *vt* to free from prison. — *n* **disincarcerā'tion**. [**dis-** (2)]

disincentive *dis-in-sen'tiv*, *n* a discouragement to effort; a deterrent. — Also *adj*. [**dis-** (2)]

disinclination *dis-in-kli-nā'shən*, *n* lack of inclination; unwillingness. — *vt* **disincline** (*-klīn'*) to render unwilling, reluctant or averse. — *adj* **disinclined'** not inclined; averse. [**dis-** (2)]

disinclose. See **disenclose**.

disincorporate *dis-in-kör'pə-rāt*, *vt* to deprive of corporate rights. — *n* **disincorporā'tion**. [**dis-** (2)]

disindividualize or **-ise** *dis-in-di-vid'ū-əl-īz*, *vt* to deprive of individuality. [**dis-** (2)]

disindustrialize or **-ise** *dis-in-dus'tri-əl-īz*, *vt* to deprive of industry, reduce the amount of industry in. — *n* **disindustrializā'tion** or **-s-**. [**dis-** (2)]

disinfect *dis-in-fekt'*, *vt* to rid of disease-causing bacteria, etc by cleaning, *esp* with a chemical. — *n* **disinfect'ant** a chemical, etc that destroys bacteria. — Also *adj*. — *n* **disinfec'tion**. — *n* **disinfect'or**. [**dis-** (2)]

disinfest *dis-in-fest'*, *vt* to rid (a place or animal, etc) of vermin. — *n* **disinfestā'tion**. [**dis-** (2)]

disinflation *dis'in-flā-shən*, (*econ*) *n* return to the normal condition after inflation; deflation which reduces or stops inflation. — *adj* **disinflā'tionary**. [**dis-** (2)]

disinformation *dis-in-fər-mā'shən*, *n* deliberate leakage of misleading information. [**dis-** (2)]

disingenuous *dis-in-jen'ū-əs*, *adj* not ingenuous; not frank or open; crafty, devious. — *n* **disingenu'ity** (*rare*). — *adv* **disingen'uously**. — *n* **disingen'uousness**. [**dis-** (2)]

disinherit *dis-in-her'it*, *vt* to cut off from hereditary rights; to deprive of an inheritance. — *n* **disinher'ison** (*-zən*) act of disinheriting. — *n* **disinher'itance**. [**dis-** (3)]

disinhibit *dis-in-hib'it*, *vt* to remove restraints on (used *esp* of drugs affecting behaviour). — *n* **disinhibition** (*-hi-bish'ən*). — *adj* **disinhib'itory**. [**dis-** (2)]

disinhume *dis-in-hūm'*, *vt* to take out of the earth, to disinter. [**dis-** (2)]

disintegrate *dis-in'ti-grāt*, *vt* and *vi* to separate into parts; to break up; to crumble. — *adj* **disin'tegrable**. — *n* **disintegrā'tion** the act or state of disintegrating; a process in which a nucleus ejects one or more particles, *esp* in spontaneous radioactive decay (*nucleonics*). — *adj* **disin'tegrative**. — *n* **disin'tegrātor** a machine for crushing or pulverizing. [**dis-** (1)]

disinter *dis-in-tûr'*, *vt* to remove from a grave or from the earth; to dig up or bring to light; to bring out of obscurity: — *pr p* **disinterr'ing**; *pa t* and *pa p* **disinterred'**. — *n* **disinter'ment**. [**dis-** (2)]

disinterest *dis-in'tər-ist*, *n* disadvantage (*rare*); impartiality, freedom from prejudice; lack of interest, unconcern. — *vt* to free from interest. — *adj* **disin'terested** not influenced by private feelings or considerations; not deriving personal advantage; impartial; unselfish, generous; (revived from obsolescence) uninterested. — *adv* **disin'terestedly**. — *n* **disin'terestedness**. — *adj* **disin'teresting** (*obs*) uninteresting. [**dis-** (2)]

disinthral. Same as **disenthral**.

disintricate *dis-in'tri-kāt*, *vt* to free from intricacy. [**dis-** (2)]

disinure *dis-in-ūr'*, (*obs*; *Milton*) *vt* to render unfamiliar. [**dis-** (2)]

disinvest[1] *dis-in-vest'*, *vt* to divest. — *n* **disinvest'iture** the action of disinvesting. [**dis-** (2)]

disinvest[2] *dis-in-vest'*, *vi* and *vt* to remove investment (from) or cease investment (in; with *in*). — *n* **disinvest'ment**. [**dis-** (2)]

disinvigorate *dis-in-vig'ər-āt*, (*rare*) *vt* to weaken. [**dis-** (2)]

disinvolve *dis-in-volv'*, *vt* to unfold; to disentangle. [**dis-** (2)]

disjaskit *dis-jas'kit*, (*Scot*) *adj* jaded; worn out. [Prob **dejected**]

disject *dis-jekt'*, *vt* to dismember; to scatter. — *n* **disjec'tion**. [L *disjicere*, *-jectum*, from *dis-* apart, and *jacere* to throw]

disjoin *dis-join'*, *vt* to separate after having been joined; to form a disjunction of. — *vi* to separate, disconnect. — *adj* **disjoin'ing** disjunctive. [OFr *desjoindre*, from L *disjungere*, from *dis-* apart, and *jungere* to join]

disjoint *dis-joint*, *vt* and *vi* to disconnect or come apart at the joints; to dislocate or disunite; to break the natural order or relations of; to make incoherent. — *adj* **disjoint'ed** (of discourse, narrative, etc) incoherent; lacking connection or continuity; separated at the joints; badly assorted. — *adv* **disjoint'edly**. — *n* **disjoint'edness**. [OFr *desjoinct*, from *desjoindre* to disjoin.]

disjunct *dis-jungkt'*, also *dis'jungkt*, *adj* disjoined; having deep constrictions between the different sections of the body (*zool*); (of tetrachords) having the highest note of the lower and the lowest of the upper a tone or semitone apart (*ancient Gr music*). — *n* (*logic*) one of the propositions in a disjunction; a disjunctive proposition. — *n* **disjunc'tion** the act of disjoining; disunion; separation; the separation during meiosis of the two members of each pair of homologous chromosomes (*biol*); a compound statement comprising propositions connected by an element denoting 'or', an *inclusive disjunction* being true when at least one proposition is true, an *exclusive disjunction* being true when at least one but no more than one of the propositions is true (*logic*). — *adj* **disjunct'ive** disjoining; tending to separate; (of conjunctions) indicating an alternative or opposition (*gram*); relating to, containing, forming or being part of a disjunction (*logic*). — *n* a disjunctive word or element. — *adv* **disjunct'ively**. — *n* **disjunct'or** a device for breaking an electric circuit; a weak place where separation between conidia occurs (*bot*). — *n* **disjunct'ure** disjunction. [OFr *desjoinct*, *desjoindre* to disjoin]

disjune *dis-jōōn'*, (*Scot*; *archaic*) *n* breakfast. [OFr *desjun*, from L *dis-* expressing undoing, and *jējūnus* fasting]

disk *disk*, *n* a disc (**disc**[1] qv; *esp US*); a magnetic disc used for backing up and storing information and programs (*comput*). — *n* **diskette'** (*comput*) a small magnetic floppy disk. — *adj* **disk'less**. — **disk capacity** (*comput*) the amount of storage space on a disk; **disk drive** a computer peripheral with a head that records data on, and retrieves data from disks; **disk file** or **store** (*comput*) a random access device consisting of disks coated with magnetizable material, on which data is stored in tracks; **disk pack** (*comput*) a set of magnetic disks fitted on a common spindle. — **disk operating system** (*abbrev* **DOS**) software that manages the storage and retrieval of information on disk on personal computers. [Variant of **disc**]

disleaf *dis-lēf'*, *vt* to deprive of leaves. — Also **disleave'**. [**dis-** (2)]

disleal *dis-lē'l*, (*Spenser*) *adj* disloyal, dishonourable. [See **disloyal**]

disleave. See **disleaf**.

dislike *dis-līk'*, *vt* to have an aversion to, to find unpleasant or disagreeable; to disapprove of; to be displeased with; to displease (*obs*). — *n* (*dis-līk'*, sometimes *dis'*) disinclination; aversion; distaste; disapproval. — *adj* **dislike'able** or **dislīk'able**. — *adj* **dislike'ful**. — *vt* **dislik'en** (*Shakesp*) to make unlike. — *n* **dislike'ness** (*obs*) unlikeness. [**dis-** (2) and **like**[2]; the genuine Eng word is *mislike*]

dislimb *dis-lim'*, *vt* to tear the limbs from; to dismember. [**dis-** (1)]

dislimn *dis-lim'*, (*Shakesp*) *vt* to efface. [**dis-** (3)]

dislink *dis-lingk'*, *vt* to unlink, to separate. [**dis-** (2)]

disload *dis-lōd'*, *vt* to unload, to disburden. [**dis-** (3)]

dislocate *dis'lō-kāt*, *vt* to displace (a bone) from its joint, to put out of joint; to disrupt, disorganize or disturb. — *adv* **dis'locatedly**. — *n* **dislocā'tion** a dislocated joint; displacement; disorganization; derangement (of traffic, plans, etc); a fault (*geol*). [LL *dislocāre*, *-ātum*, from L *dis-* apart, and *locāre* to place]

dislodge *dis-loj'*, *vt* to prise, knock or force out of position; to drive from a lodgement or place of rest; to drive from a place of hiding or of defence. — *vi* to go away. — *n* **dislodge'ment** or **dislodg'ment**. [OFr *desloger*, from *des-* (L *dis-*) apart, and *loger* to lodge]

disloign *dis-loin'*, (*Spenser*) *vt* to put far apart or at a distance, to remove. [OFr *desloignier*, from *des-* (L *dis-*) apart, and *loignier* to remove]

disloyal *dis-loi'əl*, *adj* not loyal; unfaithful. — *adv* **disloy'ally**. — *n* **disloy'alty**. [OFr *desloyal*, from *des-* (L *dis-* negative), and *loyal*, *leial*, from L *lēgālis* legal]

dislustre *dis-lus'tər*, (*archaic* or *poetic*) *vt* to deprive of lustre. — *vi* to lose lustre. [**dis-** (3)]

dismal *diz'məl*, *adj* gloomy; dreary; sorrowful; lugubrious; depressing. — *n* unlucky days (*obs*); (with *cap*, *usu* in *pl*) a swamp (*old US dialect*); a dismal person; (in *pl*) the dumps; (in *pl*) mournings (*obs*). — *adv* **dis'mally**. — *n* **dis'malness**. — *n* **dismality** (*-mal'i-ti*). — **dismal day** (*Spenser*) a day of ill omen; **dismal Jimmy** (*colloq*) a confirmed pessimist. — **the dismal science** political economy. [OFr *dismal*, from L *diēs malī* evil or unlucky days]

disman *dis-man'*, *vt* to deprive (a country or ship) of men; to unman; to deprive of human character (of the body by death) (*obs*). [**dis-** (3)]

dismantle *dis-man'tl*, *vt* to take to bits, pull down; to demolish; to undo the structure of (an organization, etc) in consequence of a decison to terminate it; to strip; to deprive of furniture, fittings, etc, so as to render useless; to raze the fortifications of. — *n* **disman'tlement**. — *n* **disman'tler**. [OFr *desmanteller*, from *des-* (L *dis-*) away, and *mantele*, from *mantel* a mantle]

dismask *dis-mäsk'*, *vt* to strip a mask from; to remove a disguise from; to uncover. [OFr *desmasquer*, from *des-* (L *dis-*; negative) and *masquer* to mask]

dismast *dis-mäst'*, *vt* to topple or remove a mast or masts. — *n* **dismast'ment**. [**dis-** (3)]

dismay *dis-*, *diz-mā'*, *vt* to appal or alarm; to discourage; to distress (*Spenser*). — *vi* (*Shakesp*, etc) to be daunted. — *n* alarm or consternation; the loss of strength and courage through fear; a discouraging onslaught (*Spenser*). — *n* **dismay'edness**. — *adj* **dismay'ful**. — *adv* **dismay'fully** (*Spenser*). — *adj* **dismay'ing**. [Appar through OFr, from L *dis-* (negative) and OHGer *magan* (Ger *mögen*; OE *magan*) to have might or power; see **may**[1]]

dismayd *dis-mād'*, (*Spenser*) *adj* apparently, misshapen, deformed, mismade. [**dis-** (2)]

dismayl *dis-māl'*, (*obs*) *vt* to deprive of mail (armour); to break mail from (*Spenser*). [OFr *desmailler*, from *des-* (L *dis-*; privative), and *maille* mail]

disme *dīm*, (*Shakesp*, etc) *n* a tenth or tithe. [OFr; see **dime**]

dismember *dis-mem'bər*, *vt* to cut up or tear (a body) limb from limb; to separate a limb from; to disjoint; to tear to pieces; to divide up, break up; to carve (certain birds, eg herons, cranes) for the table (*obs*). — *adj* **dismem'bered** (*heraldry*) without limbs or with limbs detached. — *n* **dismem'berment**. [OFr *desmembrer*, from *des-* (L *dis-*) apart, and *membre* a member (L *membrum*)]

dismiss *dis-mis'*, *vt* to send away or allow to go; to dispatch; to discard, dispose of (a suggestion, etc); to remove from office or discharge from employment, to sack, to terminate a contract of employment; to reject, to put out of court (a case or claim), to discharge (*law*); to put out (a batsman or a team) for a stated number of runs (*cricket*). — *vi imperative* (as a military command) fall out. — *n* **dismiss'al** or (*esp* formerly) **dismission** (*-mish'ən*). — *adj* **dismiss'ible**. — *adj* **dismiss'ive**. — *adj* **dismiss'ory**. — **dismissal with disgrace** dismissal from the British armed forces for serious misconduct — a court-martial ruling. [**dis-** (3), and L *mittere*, *missum* to send; L *dimissus*]

dismoded *dis-mōd'id*, *adj* out of fashion. [**dis-** (2) and **mode**]

dismount *dis-mownt'*, *vi* to come down; to get down from a horse or a bicycle, etc. — *vt* to throw or bring down from any elevated place; to remove from a stand, framework, setting, carriage or the like. [OFr *desmonter*, from *des-* (L *dis-*; negative) and *monter* to mount]

dismutation *dis-mū-tā'shən*, (*biochem*) *n* simultaneous oxidation and reduction. [**dis-** (2)]

disnatured *dis-nā'chərd*, *adj* unnatural, devoid of natural affection. — *vt* **disnaturalize** or **-ise** (*-nat'* or *-nach'*) to make alien or unnatural. [**dis-** (2)]

disnest *dis-nest'*, *vt* to dislodge from a nest; to clear (of nestlings). [**dis-** (3)]

Disneyesque *diz-ni-esk'*, *adj* in the style of the characters, etc appearing in the cartoon films of Walt *Disney* (1901–66), American cartoonist and film producer; fantastical, whimsical, unreal. — *vt* **Dis'neyfy** to present or process the history of, or facts concerning (a site, etc) by means of video films or other visual aids, *esp* simplistically for the convenience of the tourist, instead of encouraging exposure to the actual environment: — *pr p* **Dis'neyfying**; *pa t* and *pa p* **Dis'neyfied**. — *n* **Dis'neyficātion**.

disobedient *dis-ō-bēd'yənt*, *adj* neglecting or refusing to obey. — *n* **disobed'ience**. — *adv* **disobed'iently**. [**dis-** (2)]

disobey *dis-ō-bā'*, *dis-ə-bā'*, or *dis'*, *vt* and *vi* to neglect or refuse to obey. [OFr *desobeir*, from *des-* (L *dis-*; negative) and *obeir* to obey]

disoblige *dis-ō-blīj'*, *-ə-blīj'*, *vt* to relieve from an obligation (*obs*); to refuse or fail to oblige or grant a favour to; to disregard the wishes of; to offend or injure thereby; to inconvenience (*colloq*). — *n* **disobligation** (*dis-ob-li-gā'shən*) freedom from obligation; act of disobliging. — *adj* **disobligatory** (*-gə-tə-ri*) releasing from obligation. — *n* **disobligement** (*-blīj'*). — *adj* **disoblīg'ing** not obliging; not careful to attend to the wishes of others; unaccommodating; unkind. — *adv* **disoblīg'ingly**. — *n* **disoblīg'ingness**. [**dis-** (2)]

disoperation *dis-op-ər-ā'shən*, (*ecology*) *n* a mutually harmful relationship between two organisms in a community. [**dis-** (2)]

disorbed *dis-örbd'*, (*archaic* and *poetic*) *adj* (of a star) thrown from its sphere (*Shakesp*); (of a ruler) deprived of the orb of sovereignty. [**dis-** (3)]

disorder *dis-ör'dər*, *n* lack of order; confusion; disturbance among the public, breach of the peace, crowd violence, rioting, etc; a malfunction of the body, an ailment or illness. — *vt* to throw out of order; to disarrange, to reduce to confusion; to disturb the balance of (the mind, etc); to disturb the health of, to produce disease in. — *adj* **disor'dered** confused, deranged. — *n* **disor'derliness**. — *adj* **disor'derly** out of order; untidy in a state of confusion; irregular; lawless, unruly; causing a disturbance of the peace (*law*); defying the restraints of decency. — *adv* confusedly; in a lawless manner. — *n* a disorderly person. — **disorderly conduct** (*law*) any of several minor infringements of the law likely to cause a breach of the peace; **disorderly house** a brothel or gambling establishment, in either of which disorderly behaviour might be expected. [OFr *desordre*, from *des-* (L *dis-*; negative) and *ordre* order]

disordinate *dis-ör'di-nit*, *adj* not in order (*rare*); disorderly (*rare*); inordinate (*Milton*). — *adv* **disor'dinately**. [**dis-** (2)]

disorganize or **-ise** *dis-ör'gən-īz*, *vt* to disarrange or disrupt; to disturb the system or structure of; to destroy the organic structure of. — *adj* **disorganic** (*-gan'*). — *adj* **disor'ganized** or **-s-** disordered; unsystematic, muddled. — *n* **disorganizā'tion** or **-s-**. [**dis-** (2)]

disorient *dis-ō'ri-ənt*, *-ö'*, *vt* (literally) to turn from the east; to confuse as to direction, cause (someone) to lose their bearings; to throw out of one's reckoning. — Also **diso'rientate**. — *n* **disorientā'tion**. [**dis-** (2)]

disown *dīs-ōn'*, *vt* to refuse to own or acknowledge as belonging to oneself; to deny any connection with; to repudiate, cast off. — *n* **disown'er**. — *n* **disown'ment**. [**dis-** (2)]

dispace *dis-pās'*, (*Spenser*) *vi* to range about. — Also *vt* (*reflexive*). [Perh L *di-* apart, and *spatiāri* to walk about or from **dis-** (1) and **pace**[1]]

disparage *dis-par'ij*, *vt* to dishonour by comparison with what is inferior (*obs*); to talk slightingly of, to belittle; to match in marriage with an inferior; to lower in rank or estimation (*obs*); to dishearten (*Spenser*). — *n* **dis'parage** (*obs*; *Spenser*) an unequal match. — *n* **dispar'agement**. — *n* **dispar'ager**. — *adv* **dispar'agingly**. [OFr *desparager*, from *des-* (*L dis-*; negative) and *parage*; see **parage**]

disparate *dis'pər-it*, *-āt*, *adj* unequal; essentially unalike, and therefore incapable of being compared. — *n* (in *pl*) things too unalike to be compared. — *adv* **dis'parately**. — *n* **dis'parateness**. [L *disparātus*, from *dis-* not, and *parāre* make ready; influenced by *dispar* unequal]

disparity *dis-par'i-ti*, *n* inequality; unlikeness so great as to render comparison difficult and union unsuitable. [L *dispar* unequal, from *dis-* (negative) and *par* equal]

dispark *dis-pärk'*, *vt* to throw open, deprive of the character of a park; to remove from a park. [**dis-** (2) and (3)]

dispart *dis-pärt'*, *vt* to part asunder (*obs*); to divide, to separate (*archaic*). — *vi* (*archaic*) to separate. — *n* the difference between the thickness of metal at the breech and the mouth of a gun. [**dis-** (1)]

dispassion *dis-pash'ən*, *n* freedom from passion; a calm state of mind. — *adj* **dispass'ionate** (*dis-pash'ə-nət*) free from passion; not affected by personal feelings; calm, cool; unprejudiced, fair, impartial. — *adv* **dispass'ionately**. [**dis-** (2)]

dispatch or **despatch** *dis-pach'*, *vt* to send off (mail, or a person to do a task, etc); to send away hastily; to send out of the world; to kill or put to death; to dispose of; to perform or deal with speedily. — *vi* (*Shakesp*, etc) to make haste. — *n* a sending away in haste; dismissal; rapid performance of a task, etc; haste, promptitude; death, eg by execution or murder; the sending away of mail, a messenger, etc; that which is dispatched, such as a message, *esp* telegraphic; (in *pl*) state-papers or other official papers (diplomatic or military, etc). — *n* **dispatch'er**. — *adj* **dispatch'ful** (*Milton*, etc) swift. — **dispatch'-boat** a vessel for carrying dispatches; **dispatch box** or **case** a box or case for holding dispatches or valuable papers; **dispatch rider** a carrier of dispatches, on horseback or now *esp* motorcycle. — **mentioned in dispatches** as a distinction, commended in official military dispatches for bravery, etc; **with dispatch** (*archaic*) quickly; without delay. [Ital *dispacciare* or Sp *despachar*, from L *dis-* apart, and some LL word from the root of *pangere*, *pactum* to fasten; not connected with Fr *dépêcher*]

dispathy. An *obs* misspelling of **dyspathy**.

dispauperize or **-ise** *dis-pö'pər-īz*, *vt* to free from pauperism or from paupers. — *vt* **dispau'per** to declare no longer a pauper. [**dis-** (2)]

dispeace *dis-pēs'*, *n* lack of peace; dissension. [**dis-** (2)]

dispel *dis-pel'*, *vt* to drive away and scatter; to cause to disappear. — *vi* to scatter or melt away: — *pr p* **dispell'ing**; *pa t* and *pa p* **dispelled'**. [L *dispellere*, from *dis-* away, and *pellere* to drive]

dispence *dis-pens'* (*Spenser*, etc). Same as **dispense**.

dispend *dis-pend'*, (*obs*) *vt* to expend, pay out. [OFr *despendre*, from L *dis-* out, and *pendere* to weigh]

dispensary. See **dispense**.

dispense *dis-pens'*, *vt* to deal out or distribute; to administer (justice, etc); to make up (medicine, etc) for distributing or administering. — *vi* (*Spenser*) to make amends; to compound. — *n* expense; expenditure; supplies; dispensation (*Milton*). — *n* **dispensabil'ity**. — *adj* **dispens'able** able to be dispensed with, expendable, inessential; able to be dispensed; pardonable (*archaic*). — *n* **dispens'ableness**. — *adv* **dispens'ably**. — *n* **dispens'ary** a place where medicines, etc are dispensed and medical care given (*esp* formerly, gratis; now eg in a hospital or school). — *n* **dispensation** (*dis-pən-sā'shən*) the act of dispensing or dealing out; administration (of justice, etc); the regulation or ordering of events by God, Providence or nature; a divinely-ordained religious system specific to a community or period; licence or permission to neglect a rule, *esp* of church law in the RC church; ground of exemption. — *adj* **dispensā'tional**. — *adj* **dispens'ative** granting dispensation. — *adv* **dispens'atively**. — *n* **dis'pensātor** a dispenser; a distributor; an administrator. — *adv* **dispens'atorily**. — *adj* **dispens'atory** granting dispensation. — *n* a book containing medical prescriptions. — *adj* **dispensed'**. — *n* **dispens'er** a person who dispenses, *esp* a pharmacist who dispenses medicines; a container, or machine that gives out (a commodity) in prearranged quantities. — **dispense with** to permit the lack of; to disregard, forgo or waive; to do without. [Fr *dispenser*, from L *dis-*, and *pēnsāre* to weigh]

dispeople *dis-pē'pl*, *vt* to empty of inhabitants. [**dis-** (2)]

dispermous *dī-spûr'məs*, (*bot*) *adj* having or yielding two seeds. [**di-** and Gr *sperma* seed]

disperse *dis-pûrs'*, *vt* to scatter in all directions; to spread; to diffuse; to drive asunder; to cause to vanish, to dissipate; to suspend (particles) in a medium so as to form a colloid (*phys*). — *vi* to separate; to spread widely; to vanish. — *n* **dispers'al** dispersion; distribution; the spread of a species to new areas. — *n* **dispers'ant** a substance causing dispersion. — *adv* **dispers'edly**. — *n* **dispers'edness**. — *n* **dispers'er**. — *n* **dispersion** (*dis-pûr'shən*) a scattering, or state or process of being scattered; the removal of inflammation (*med*); the spreading out of rays owing to different refrangibility (*phys*); the range of deviation of values of a variable from the average (*statistics*); the state of a finely divided colloid; a substance in that state; the diaspora. — *adj* **dispers'ive** tending or serving to disperse. — *n* **dispers'oid** a substance in a state of dispersion (also **disperse phase**). — **dispersal prison** a prison designed to accommodate a certain number of particularly dangerous or high-risk prisoners in addition to other categories of detainees. [L *dīspergere*, *dīspersum*, from *dī-* asunder, apart, and *spargere* to scatter]

dispirit *dis-pir'it*, *vt* to dishearten; to discourage. — *adj* **dispir'ited** dejected, discouraged; feeble, spiritless. — *adv* **dispir'itedly**. — *n* **dispir'itedness**. — *adj* **dispir'iting** disheartening. — *adv* **dispir'itingly**. — *n* **dispir'itment**. [**dis-** (2)]

dispiteous *dis-pit'i-əs*, (*obs*) *adj* despiteous, contemptuous, malicious; pitiless. — *adv* **dispit'eously**. — *n* **dispit'eousness**. [See **despite**; influenced by **piteous**]

displace *dis-plās'*, *vt* to put out of place; to disarrange; to remove from a state, office or post; to supplant, replace or supersede; to substitute something for. — *adj* **displace'able**. — *n* **displace'ment** a putting or being out of place; a supplanting or superseding; the difference between the position of a body at a given time and that occupied at first; the quantity of water displaced by a ship afloat or an immersed body; the disguising of emotional feelings by unconscious transference from one object to another (*psychol*). — **displaced person** a person forced from his or her country by war, revolution, persecution or oppression, a refugee or stateless person. [OFr *desplacer*, from *des-* (L *dis-*; negative) and *place* place]

displant *dis-plänt'*, *vt* to remove from a fixed position; to drive from an abode. — *n* **displantā'tion**. [OFr *desplanter*, from L *dis-* (negative) and *plantāre* to plant]

display *dis-plā'*, *vt* to unfold or spread out; to exhibit; to set out ostentatiously; to present (advertising copy, etc) in an eye-catching way (*printing*). — *n* a displaying or unfolding; an exhibition or demonstration; presentation of advertising copy, etc so as to attract attention, through appropriate deployment of typefaces, use of space, illustrations, etc; ostentatious show; an animal's or bird's behaviour when courting, threatening intruders, etc, in which the crest is raised, feathers spread, etc; the 'picture' on a cathode-ray tube screen making the information visible (*electronics*). — *adj* **displayed'** unfolded; spread; printed in prominent letters; erect, with wings expanded, as a bird (*heraldry*). — *n* **display'er**. [OFr *despleier*, from *des-* (L *dis-*; negative) and *plier*, *ploier*, from L *plicāre* to fold; doublet **deploy**; see **ply**[1].]

disple *dis'pl*, (*Spenser*, etc) *vt* to discipline, chastise. [Apparently from **discipline**]

displease *dis-plēz'*, *vt* to offend; to annoy, irritate; to be disagreeable to. — *vi* to raise aversion or be displeasing. — *n* **displeasance** (*dis-plez'əns*; *Spenser*, etc) displeasure. — *adj* **displeas'ant** (*obs*). — *adj* **displeased'** vexed, annoyed. — *adv* **displeas'edly**. — *n* **displeas'edness**. — *adj* **displeas'ing** causing displeasure; disagreeable; giving offence. — *adv* **displeas'ingly**. — *n* **displeas'ingness**. — *n* **displeasure** (*dis-plezh'ər*) the condition of being displeased; anger, annoyance; a cause of irritation. — *vt* (*archaic*) to displease, offend. [OFr *desplaisir*, from *des-* (L *dis-*) reversal, and *plaisir* to please]

displenish *dis-plen'ish*, (*Scot*) *vt* to deprive (eg a farm) of plenishing or furniture, implements, etc; to sell the plenishing of. — *n* **displen'ishment**. [**dis-** (3)]

displode *dis-plōd'*, (*Milton*) *vt* to discharge, to explode. — *vi* to explode. — *n* **displōsion** (*-plō'zhən*). [L *displōdere*, from *dis-* apart, and *plaudere* to beat]

displume *dis-ploōm'*, *vt* to deprive of plumes or feathers. [**dis-** (3)]

dispondee *dī-spon'dē*, (*prosody*) *n* a double spondee. — *adj* **dispondā'ic**. [Gr *dispondeios*, from *di-* twice, and *spondeios* spondee]

dispone *dis-pōn'*, *vt* to set in order, dispose (*archaic*); to make over to another (*Scots law*); to convey legally. — *n* **disponee'** the person to whom anything is disponed. — *n* **dispon'er**. [L *dispōnere* to arrange]

disponge. See **dispunge**.

disport *dis-pōrt'* or *-pört'*, (*literary*) *vt* (*usu reflexive*) to divert or amuse (oneself). — *vi* to play about, frolic or gambol. — *n* **disport'ment**. [OFr (*se*) *desporter* to carry (oneself) away from one's work, to amuse (oneself), from *des-* (L *dis-*), and *porter*, from L *portāre* to carry; see **sport**]

disposable, **disposal**. See **dispose**.

dispose *dis-pōz'*, *vt* to arrange or settle; to distribute; to place in order, or arrange in position; to apply to a particular purpose; to make over by sale, gift, etc; to bestow; to incline (with *to* or *towards*). — *vi* to settle things; to ordain what is to be; to make a disposition. — See also **dispose of** below. — *n* disposal, management; behaviour, disposition. — *n* **dispōsabil'ity**. — *adj* **dispōs'able** able to be disposed of; intended to be thrown away or destroyed after use; (of assets, etc) available for one's use. — *n* a product intended for disposal after use. — *n* **dispōs'ableness**. — *n* **dispōs'al** the act of disposing or of dealing with something; the act or process of getting rid of something; the act of bestowing, transferring or assigning property, etc; arrangement, disposition, deployment; management; right of bestowing; availability for use, control, service, etc. — *adj* **disposed'** inclined; liable, having a tendency (with *to*); (used after *well*, *ill* or *kindly*, etc) having friendly or unfriendly, etc feelings (with *to* or *towards*). — *adv* (*rare*) **dispōs'edly** in good order; with measured steps. — *n* **dispōs'er**. — *n* and *adj* **dispōs'ing**. — *adv* **dispōs'ingly**. — *n* **disposure** (*-pō'zhər*) disposal, arrangement; disposition. — **disposable income** a person's gross income less any compulsory deductions, the income available for spending, saving, investing, etc. — **at one's disposal** at one's service, available for one's use; under one's management or control, to deploy as one wishes; **dispose of** to deal with, *esp* finally and decisively; to sell, transfer, part with or give away; to get rid of or throw away; to prove (an adversary, argument or claim) wrong; to consume (food, etc), *esp* in haste; to kill. [Fr *disposer*, from *dis-* (L *dis-*) apart, and *poser* to place, from L *pausāre* to pause, (late) to place]

disposition *dis-pə-zish'ən*, *n* an arrangement, deployment or distribution; the act of or a plan for dealing with affairs etc, bestowing or assigning property, etc; a natural tendency or inclination; temperament or personality; ministration (*New Testament*); a giving over to another, conveyance or assignment (often *disposition and settlement*), a deed for the disposal of a person's heritable property at their death (*Scots law*). — *adj* **disposi'tional**. — *adj* **disposi'tioned**. — *adj* **dispositive** (*-poz'i-tiv*). — *adv* **dispos'itively**. — *n* **dispos'itor** (*astrol*) a planet that disposes or controls another. [Fr, from L, from *dis-* apart, and *pōnere*, *positum* to place]

dispossess *dis-pə-zes'*, *vt* to deprive of property, land, etc. — *adj* **dispossessed'** deprived of possessions, property, etc; deprived of one's home, country or rights; deprived of hopes, expectations, etc. — *n* **dispossession** (*dis-pə-zesh'ən*). — *n* **dispossess'or**. [**dis-** (2)]

dispost[1] *dis-pōst'*, *vt* to displace from a post. [**dis-** (2)]

dispost[2] *dis-pōst'*, (*Spenser*) for **disposed**.

disposure. See **dispose**.
disprad (*Spenser*). See **dispread**.
dispraise *dis-prāz'*, *n* the expression of an unfavourable opinion; blame; reproach. — *vt* to blame; to censure. — *n* **disprais'er**. — *adv* **disprais'ingly**. [OFr *despreisier*, from *des-* (L *dis-*) reversal, and *preisier* to praise]
dispread *dis-pred'*, *vt* to spread in different ways. — *vi* to spread out; to expand. — Spenser has the forms **dispred**; *pl* **dispredden**; *pa p* **disprad**. [**dis-** (1)]
disprinced *dis-prinst'*, (*Tennyson*) *adj* deprived of the appearance of a prince. [**dis-** (3)]
disprison *dis-priz'n*, (*poetic*) *vt* to set free. [**dis-** (2)]
disprivacied *dis-priv'ə-sid*, (*poetic*) *adj* deprived of privacy. [**dis-** (3)]
disprivilege *dis-priv'i-lij*, *vt* to deprive of a privilege. [**dis-** (3)]
disprize *dis-prīz'*, (*archaic*) *vt* to set a low price upon; to undervalue. [**dis-** (2)]
disprofess *dis-prə-fes'*, *vt* to cease to profess, renounce. [**dis-** (3)]
disprofit *dis-prof'it*, (*archaic*) *n* loss, damage. [**dis-** (2)]
disproof *dis-pro͞of'*, *n* the disproving of something; evidence or argumentation that disproves something, refutation. [**dis-** (2)]
disproove *dis-pro͞ov'*, (*Spenser*) *vt* to disapprove of. [**dis-** (2)]
disproperty *dis-prop'ər-ti*, (*Shakesp*) *vt* to deprive one of possession of. [**dis-** (3)]
disproportion *dis-prə-pōr'shən*, *-pör'*, *n* lack of appropriate proportion; lack of balance, symmetry or equality. — *vt* to make unsuitable in form or size, etc. — *adj* **dispropor'tionable** (*archaic*). — *n* **dispropor'tionableness**. — *adv* **dispropor'tionably**. — *adj* **dispropor'tional**. — *adv* **dispropor'tionally**. — *adj* **dispropor'tionate** out of proportion; not of the appropriate size or amount (*usu* too large or too much) in relation to something. — *adv* **dispropor'tionately**. — *n* **dispropor'tionateness**. [**dis-** (2)]
dispropriate *dis-prō'pri-āt*, (*obs*) *vt* to disappropriate. [**dis-** (3)]
disprove *dis-pro͞ov'*, *vt* to prove to be false or wrong; to disapprove (*archaic*): — *pa p* **disproved'** or **disproven** (*-prōv'* or *-pro͞ov'*). — *adj* **disprov'able**. — *n* **disprov'al**. [OFr *desprover*; see **prove**]
disprovide *dis-prō-vīd'*, (*archaic*) *vt* to leave or render unprovided. [**dis-** (2)]
dispunge (*Shakesp*) or **disponge** *dis-punj'*, *vt* to sprinkle or discharge as if from a sponge. [**dis-** (1)]
dispurse *dis-pûrs'*, (*Shakesp*) *vt* to disburse. [**dis-** (1)]
dispurvey *dis-pər-vā'*, (*archaic*) *vt* to deprive of provisions. — *n* **dispurvey'ance** (*Spenser*). [**dis-** (3)]
dispute *dis-pūt'*, *vt* to argue about; to contend for; to oppose by argument; to call in question. — *vi* to argue or debate (with *about* or *over*). — *n* a contest with words; an argument; a debate; a quarrel. — *adj* **dis'putable** (also *-pūt'*) that may be called in question; of doubtful certainty. — *n* **disputabil'ity** or **dis'putableness**. — *adv* **dis'putably**. — *n* **dis'putant** a contestant in a debate, or party in an argument. — *adj* engaged in debate or argument. — *n* **disput'er**. — *n* **disputā'tion** a contest in argument; an exercise in debate. — *adj* **disputā'tious** or **disput'ative** inclined to dispute, cavil, or controvert. — *adv* **disputā'tiously** or **disput'atively**. — *n* **disputā'tiousness** or **disput'ativeness**. — **beyond, past** or **without dispute** indubitably, certainly; **in dispute** being debated or contested. [OFr *desputer*, from L *disputār*, from *dis-* apart, and *putāre* to think]
disqualify *dis-kwol'i-fī*, *vt* to render or declare unsuitable, unfit or unable to do a particular thing; to debar: — *pr p* **disqual'ifying**; *pa p* and *pa t* **disqual'ified**. — *adj* **disqualifī'able**. — *n* **disqualificā'tion** state of being disqualified; anything that disqualifies or incapacitates. — *n* **disqual'ifier**. [**dis-** (3)]
disquiet *dis-kwī'ət*, *adj* (*archaic*) unquiet, uneasy, restless. — *n* lack of quiet; uneasiness, restlessness; anxiety. — *vt* to render unquiet; to make uneasy or anxious; to disturb or upset. — Also **disquī'eten**. — *adj* **disquī'etful**. — *adj* **disquī'eting**. — *adv* **disquī'etingly**. — *adj* **disquī'etive**. — *adv* **disquī'etly** (*Shakesp*). — *n* **disquī'etness**. — *adj* **disquī'etous**. — *n* **disquī'etude** a feeling of anxiety or unease. [**dis-** (2)]
disquisition *dis-kwi-zish'ən*, *n* a carefully or minutely argued examination of a topic; an essay. — *adj* **disquisi'tional**, **disquisi'tionary**, **disquis'itory**, or **disquis'itive** pertaining to or of the nature of a disquisition. [L *disquīsītiō*, *-ōnis*, from *disquīrere*, from *dis-* (intensive) and *quaerere*, *quaesītum* to seek]
disrank *dis-rangk'*, *vt* to reduce to a lower rank; to throw into confusion (*obs*). [**dis-** (3)]
disrate *dis-rāt'*, (*naut*) *vt* to reduce (eg a petty officer) to a lower rating or rank. [**dis-** (3)]
disregard *dis-ri-gärd'*, *vt* to pay no attention to; to ignore; to dismiss as unworthy of attention. — *n* lack of attention; neglect; lack of respect. — *adj* **disregard'ful**. — *adv* **disregard'fully**. [**dis-** (2)]
disrelish *dis-rel'ish*, *vt* not to relish; to dislike the taste of; to dislike. — *n* distaste; dislike; disgust. — *adj* **disrel'ishing** offensive. [**dis-** (2)]
disremember *dis-ri-mem'bər*, (*dialect* or *US colloq*) *vt* not to remember, to forget. [**dis-** (2)]
disrepair *dis-ri-pār'*, *n* a worn-out or dilapidated condition; an unsatisfactory working condition; the state of needing to be repaired. [**dis-** (2)]
disrepute *dis-ri-pūt'*, *n* bad repute; discredit. — Also **disreputation** (*dis-rep-ū-tā'shən*). — *adj* **disrep'utable** unreliable or untrustworthy; disgraceful; not respectable; disordered and shabby, dingy, not presentable. — *n* **disrep'utableness** or (*rare*) **disreputabil'ity**. — *adv* **disrep'utably**. [**dis-** (2)]
disrespect *dis-ri-spekt'*, *n* lack of respect; discourtesy; incivility. — *vt* (*archaic*) not to respect. — *adj* **disrespect'able** (*rare*) not respectable. — *adj* **disrespect'ful** showing disrespect; irreverent; uncivil. — *adv* **disrespect'fully**. — *n* **disrespect'fulness**. [**dis-** (2)]
disrobe *dis-rōb'*, (*esp literary*) *vt* and *vi* to undress; to take off robes. — *vt* to remove the covering or concealment from. [**dis-** (2) and (3)]
disroot *dis-ro͞ot'*, *vt* to uproot. [**dis-** (3)]
disrupt *dis-rupt'*, *vt* and *vi* to interrupt (growth, progress, etc); to upset or throw into disorder or confusion; to split or burst. — *n* **disrupt'er** or **disrupt'or**. — *n* **disrup'tion** interruption, disturbance or upheaval; (with *cap*) in Scottish ecclesiastical history, the separation of the Free Church from the Established Church for the sake of spiritual independence (1843). — *adj* **disrup'tive** having an upsetting or unsettling effect; obstreperous, unruly. — *adv* **disrupt'ively**. [L *disruptus*, *dīruptus*, from *dīrumpere*, from *dis-* apart, asunder, and *rumpere* to break]
diss[1] *dis*, *n* an Algerian reedy grass (*Ampelodesma tenax*), used for cordage, etc. [Ar *dīs*]
diss[2] *dis*, (*rapper slang*) *vt* to reject or dismiss with contempt. [Appar abbrev of **disrespect**]
diss. *abbrev*: dissertation.
dissatisfactory *dis-sat-is-fak'tər-i*, *adj* causing dissatisfaction. — *n* **dissatisfac'tion** the state of being dissatisfied; discontent; uneasiness. — *n* **dissatisfac'toriness**. [**dis-** (2)]
dissatisfy *dis-sat'is-fī*, *vt* to fail to satisfy; to disappoint; to make discontented; to displease. — *n* **dissatisfac'tion**. — *adj* **dissat'isfied** discontented; not pleased. [**dis-** (2)]
dissaving *dis-sā'ving*, (*econ*) *n* the spending of savings made in the past to finance an excess of spending over disposable income, thus diminishing accumulated assets. [**dis-** (2)]
disseat *dis-sēt'*, *vt* to unseat. [**dis-** (2) and (3)]
dissect *di-sekt'*, *vt* to cut apart, to cut into small pieces; to cut (a dead animal or a plant, etc) into parts for the purpose of minute examination; to divide and examine; to analyse or criticize minutely. — *adj* **dissect'ed** deeply cut into narrow segments (*bot*); cut up by valleys (*geol*). — *adj* **dissect'ible**. — *n* **dissect'ing**. — *n* **dissec'tion** the act or the art of cutting in pieces a plant

or animal in order to ascertain the structure of its parts; anatomy. — *adj* **dissect'ive** tending to dissect. — *n* **dissect'or**. — **dissected map** or **picture** a map or picture on a board cut up so as to form a puzzle; **dissecting microscope** a form of microscope that allows dissection of the object under examination; **dissecting room** and **table** a room in which, and a table on which, anatomical dissection is practised. [L *dissecāre*, *dissectum*, from *dis-* apart, and *secāre* to cut]

disseise or **disseize** *dis-sēz'*, (*law*) *vt* to deprive of seisen or possession of an estate of freehold; to dispossess wrongfully. — *n* **disseis'in** or **disseiz'in** wrongful dispossession. — *n* **disseis'or** or **disseiz'or**. [**dis-** (3)]

disselboom *dis'əl-bōōm*, (*SAfr*) *n* the single shaft of an ox-wagon or other cart or wagon. [Du *dissel* shaft, and *boom* beam]

dissemble *di-sem'bl*, *vt* to disguise or mask (one's true feelings or character); to feign (*obs*). — *vi* to pretend; to assume a false appearance; to play the hypocrite; to dissimulate. — *n* **dissem'blance** (*rare*) lack of resemblance; the act of dissembling. — *n* **dissem'bler**. — *n* **dissem'bling**. — *adj* deceiving, hypocritical. — *adv* **dissem'blingly**. [L *dissimulāre*, from *dissimilis* unlike, from *dis-* (negative) and *similis* like; perh remodelled on *resemble*]

dissembly *dis-em'bli*, *n* the breaking up of an assembly; a Dogberryism for assembly (*Shakesp*). [**dis-** (1)]

disseminate *di-sem'i-nāt*, *vt* to sow or scatter abroad; to propagate; to diffuse. — *adj* scattered. — *n* **dissemi-nā'tion**. — *adj* **dissem'inative**. — *n* **dissem'inātor**. — *n* **dissem'inule** (*bot*) any part or organ of a plant that serves for dissemination. — **disseminated sclerosis** an older name for **multiple sclerosis**. [L *dissēminare*, *-ātum*, from *dis-* apart, and *sēminare* to sow, from *sēmen*, *sēminis* a seed]

dissent *di-sent'*, *vi* not to assent; to think differently; to disagree in opinion; to differ (with *from*); to break away from an established church and adopt new religious beliefs or practices. — *n* the act of dissenting; difference of opinion; a protest by a minority; a differing or separation from an established church. — *n* **dissen'sion** disagreement in opinion; discord; strife. — *n* **dissent'er** someone who disagrees; (with *cap*) someone, *esp* a Protestant, who refuses to conform to the established church, a nonconformist. — *adj* **dissent'erish**. — *n* **dissent'erism**. — *adj* **dissen'tient** (*-shənt*) declaring dissent; disagreeing. — *n* a person who disagrees; a person who declares his or her dissent. — *adj* **dissent'ing**. — *adv* **dissent'ingly**. — *adj* **dissen'tious** (*-shəs*; *Shakesp*, etc, now *rare*) disposed to discord, contentious [L *dissentīre*, *dissēnsum*, from *dis-* apart, and *sentīre* to think]

dissepiment *di-sep'i-mənt*, *n* a partition in an ovary (*bot*); a partition partly cutting off the bottom of a coral cup (*zool*). — *adj* **dissepimental** (*-ment'l*). [L *dissaepīmentum* a partition, from L *dissaepīre*, from *dis-* apart, and *saepīre* to hedge in, to fence]

dissertate *dis'ər-tāt*, *vi* (*rare*) to discourse. — Also (*archaic*) **dissert'**. — *n* **disserta'tion** a formal discourse; a treatise, a written thesis, *usu* based on the author's research, often a requirement for an academic qualification. — *adj* **disserta'tional**. — *adj* **diss'ertātive**. — *n* **diss'ertātor**. [L *dissertāre*, intensive of *disserere* to discuss, from *dis-*, and *serere* to put together]

disserve *dis-sûrv'*, *vt* (*archaic*) to do a bad turn to; to clear (a table). — *n* **disserv'ice** injury, sometimes done in an attempt to help; mischief; a bad turn. — *adj* **disserv'-iceable**. [OFr *desservir*, from L *dis-* (negative) and *servīre* to serve]

dissever *di-sev'ər*, *vt* and *vi* to sever; to part in two; to separate; to disunite. — *n* **dissev'erance**, **disseverā'tion** or **dissev'erment** a dissevering or parting. — *adj* **dissev'ered** disunited. [OFr *dessevrer*, from L *dis-* apart, and *sēparāre* to separate]

dissheathe *dis-shēdh'*, (*rare*) *vt* to unsheathe. [**dis-** (2)]

disshiver *dis-shiv'ər*, *vt* (*Spenser*) and *vi* to shiver in pieces. [**dis-** (1)]

dissident *dis'i-dənt*, *adj* dissenting. — *n* a dissenter, *esp* one who disagrees with the aims and procedures of the government. — *n* **diss'idence** disagreement. [L *dissidēns*, *-entis*, pr p of *dissidēre*, from *dis-* apart, and *sedēre* to sit]

dissight *di(s)-sīt'*, (*archaic*) *n* an unsightly object. [**dis-** (2)]

dissilient *di(s)-sil'yənt*, *adj* springing apart; bursting open with force (*bot*). — *n* **dissil'ience**. [L *dissiliēns*, *-entis*, from *dis-* apart, and *salīre* to leap]

dissimilar *di-sim'ilər*, *adj* not similar; unalike, different. — *n* **dissimilarity** (*-ar'*) unlikeness. — *adv* **dissim'ilarly**. [**dis-** (2)]

dissimilate *di-sim'i-lāt*, *vi* and *vt* (*esp* of sounds, *philol*) to become or make dissimilar. — *n* **dissimilā'tion** the process of becoming or of rendering dissimilar; katabolism. [**dis-** (2)]

dissimile *di-sim'i-li*, *n* the opposite of a simile, a comparison by contrast. [**dis-** (2)]

dissimilitude *dis-i-mil'-i-tūd*, *n* the quality of being unalike, dissimilarity. [**dis-** 2]

dissimulate *di-sim'ū-lāt*, *vt* to pretend the contrary of; to conceal or disguise (one's real feelings, etc), to dissemble. — *vi* to practise dissimulation, play the hypocrite. — *n* **dissimulā'tion** the act of dissembling; a hiding under a false appearance; false pretension; hypocrisy. — *adj* **dissim'ulative**. — *n* **dissim'ulātor**. [L *dissimulāre*, *-ātum* to dissimulate, from *dis-* (negative) and *similis* like]

dissipate *dis'i-pāt*, *vt* to scatter or disperse; to squander; to waste; to dispel. — *vi* to separate or disperse and disappear; to waste away; to be dissolute in conduct; to indulge in trivial amusements. — *adj* **diss'ipable** that may be dissipated. — *adj* **diss'ipated** dissolute, *esp* addicted to drinking. — *adv* **diss'ipatedly**. — *n* **dissipā'tion** intemperate, extravagant or dissolute living; the process of dissipating or being dissipated; the wasteful spending of something. — *adj* **diss'ipātive** tending to dissipate or disperse; connected with the dissipation of energy. — **dissipation trail** (*meteorol*) a lane of clear atmosphere formed by the passage of an aircraft through a cloud. — **dissipation of energy** degradation of energy, or progressive loss of availability of a portion for doing work at each transformation. [L *dissipāre*, *-ātum*, from *dis-* apart, and (archaic) *supāre* to throw]

dissociate *di-sō'shi-āt*, *di-sō'si-āt*, *vt* to separate; to treat or regard as separate and distinct; (*reflexive*) to distance (oneself), declare (oneself) to be unconnected with something (with *from*). — *vi* and *vt* to subject to or undergo dissociation. — *adj* separated. — *n* **dissōciabil'ity** (*-shə-*). — *adj* **dissō'ciable** not sociable; ill associated; incongruous; capable of being dissociated. — *n* **dissō'ciableness**. — *adv* **dissō'ciably**. — *adj* **dissō'cial** (*archaic*) not social. — *n* **dissociality** (*-sō-shi-al'*). — *vt* **dissō'cialize** or **-ise** to make unsocial. — *n* **dissociā'tion** (*-sō-shi-* or *-sō-si-*) the act of dissociating; the process or state of being dissociated; separation into simpler constituents, *esp* a reversible separation caused by heat, or separation into ions (*chem*); the splitting off from consciousness of certain ideas and their accompanying emotions leading to fragmentation of the personality into independent identities, as in cases of split or multiple personality (*psychol*); breaking of associations. — *adj* **dissō'ciative** (*chem*) tending to dissociate. [L *dissociāre*, *-ātum*, from *dis-* apart, and *sociāre* to associate]

dissoluble *dis-ol'ū-bl* *adj* capable of being dissolved, soluble. — *n* **dissolūbil'ity** — *n* **dissol'ūbleness**. [L *dissolūbilis*, from *dissolvere* to dissolve]

dissolute *dis'ə-lōōt* or *-lūt*, *adj* loose, *esp* in morals, debauched. — *n* a dissolute person. — *adv* **diss'olutely**. — *n* **diss'oluteness**. — *adj* **diss'olutive**. [L *dissolūtus* lax, from *dissolvere* to loosen]

dissolution *dis-ə-lō'shən* or *-lū'shən* *n* break-up, disintegration into parts; decay and death; the annulment or ending of a partnership or relationship; the dispersal of an assembly, as of Parliament before an election; loosening; melting; dissoluteness or dissolute behaviour (*archaic*). — *n* **dissolu'tionism**. — *n* **dissolu'tionist**. [L *dissolūtiō*, *-ōnis* a breaking up, from *dissolvere*]

dissolve *di-zolv'* *vt* and *vi* to (cause to) go into solution; to (cause to) become liquid, to melt; to separate or break up and disperse; to terminate or dismiss (an assembly, such as Parliament) or be terminated or dismissed. — *vt* to annul or terminate (eg a partnership or marriage); to resolve (eg doubts or riddles; *archaic*). — *vi* to collapse or subside emotionally, eg into tears; to break up; to waste away; to fade away; to fade out one scene gradually while replacing it with another (also *n*; *cinema* and *TV*). — *n* **dissolvabil'ity**. — *adj* **dissolv'able** capable of being dissolved. — *n* **dissolv'ableness**. — *n* **dissolv'ent** (*rare*) a solvent. — *adj* having power to dissolve or disperse. — *n* and *adj* **dissolv'ing**. [L *dissolvere*, *dissolūtum*, from *dis-* , and *solvere*, *-ūtum* to loose]

dissonant *dis'ə-nənt*, *adj* (of sounds, *esp* musical) discordant, inharmonious; jarring, clashing, incompatible, conflicting, contradictory or incongruous. — *n* **diss'onance** disagreement of sound; lack of harmony; discord; disagreement; *specif* (a chord or interval containing) a combination of musical sounds that calls for resolution or produces beats (also **diss'onancy**). — *adv* **diss'onantly**. [L *dissonāns*, *-antis*, from *dis-* apart, and *sonāre* to sound]

dissuade *di-swād'*, *vt* to deter, *esp* through advice or argument, to persuade not to do something (with *from*); to give advice against (*obs*); to seek to divert by advice (*obs*). — *n* **dissuā'der**. — *n* **dissuā'sion** (*-zhən*). — *adj* **dissuā'sive** (*-siv*) tending to dissuade. — *n* that which tends to dissuade. — *adv* **dissuā'sively**. — *n* and *adj* **dissuā'sory** (*rare*). [L *dissuādēre*, from *dis-* apart, and *suādēre*, *suāsum* to advise]

dissunder *dis-sun'dər*, (*archaic*) *vt* to sunder. [**dis-** (4)]

dissyllable. A variant of **disyllable**.

dissymmetry *dis-sim'i-tri*, *n* lack of symmetry; enantiomorphy (the symmetry of right and left hand, or of object and mirror-image). — *adj* **dissymmetric** or **dissymmetrical** (*-et'*). — *adv* **dissymmet'rically**. [**dis-** (2)]

dist. *abbrev*: distance; distilled; distinguish; district.

distaff *dis'täf*, *n* the stick that holds the bunch of flax, tow or wool in spinning; women's work (*literary*). — **distaff side** the female part, line, side, or branch of a family or descent, the male equivalent being the *spear side*. [OE *distæf*, from the root found in LGer *diesse* the bunch of flax on the staff; and *stæf* staff; see **dizen**]

distain *dis-tān'*, (*archaic*) *vt* to stain; to sully. [OFr *desteindre* to take away the colour of, from L *dis-* (negative) and *tingere* to colour]

distal *dis'təl*, (*biol*) *adj* farthest from the point of attachment (*opp* to *proximal*; *anatom* and *zool*); farthest from the centre (*opp* to *mesial*; *dentistry*). — *adv* **dis'tally**. [Formed from **distance** on the analogy of *central*]

Distalgesic® *dis-tal-jē'zik*, *n* a pain-killing drug in tablet form, containing paracetamol. [*Dist*iller's Co Ltd and an*algesic*]

distance *dis'təns*, *n* the gap or interval between two points in space or time; the extent of such a gap or interval; remoteness or separation in space or time; a remote place, region or time; the remotest part of one's field of vision, or the equivalent part in a picture; progress, headway; degree of remoteness; opposition; stand-offishness or aloofness of manner; the scheduled duration of a boxing match, etc; in horse-racing, a point 240 yards back from the winning post (*UK*), or a final stretch of the course (*US*), which a horse, in heat-races, must reach by the time the winner has covered the whole course, in order to run in the final heat. — *adj* (*athletics*; of races) over a long distance. — *vt* to place at a distance; to hold (oneself) aloof (with *from*); to leave at a distance behind. — *adj* **dis'tanceless** not allowing a distant view (of hazy weather); having no indications of distance (of pictures). — **distance education** or **teaching** the provision of educational courses, eg by television or correspondence course, for students unable to attend in person the educational institution concerned; **distance learning** the following of such educational courses; **middle distance** the part of a scene between the foreground and the furthest part. — **go the distance** to complete what one has started (*colloq*); to endure to the end of a (boxing, etc) bout; **keep someone at a distance** to treat someone with aloofness; **keep one's distance** to abstain from familiarity (with); to keep aloof (from). [See **distant**]

distant *dis'tənt*, *adj* at a certain distance; at a great distance; remote, in time, place, resemblance or connection; indistinct; reserved or aloof in manner. — *adv* **dis'tantly**. — *n* **dis'tantness**. — **dis'tant-signal** on a railway, a signal farther from the destination than the home-signal. [Fr, from L *distāns*, *-antis*, from *dī-* apart, and *stāns*, *stantis*, pr p of *stāre* to stand]

distaste *dis-tāst'*, *n* disrelish (for); repugnance or dislike (for); an unpleasant experience (*obs*); an offence (*obs*). — *vt* to dislike (*archaic*); to offend (*obs*); to spoil the taste of (*obs*; *Shakesp*). — *vi* (*obs*; *Shakesp*) to be distasteful. — *adj* **distaste'ful** unpalatable; unpleasant; disagreeable; full of or indicating distaste (*obs*; *Shakesp*). — *adv* **distaste'fully**. — *n* **distaste'fulness**. [**dis-** (2)]

distemper[1] *dis-temp'ər*, *n* a mode of painting in size, water-glass, or other watery medium giving body to the pigment; paint of this kind for indoor walls, stage scenery, etc. — *vt* to paint in distemper. — Also **destemp'er**. [L *dis-* (reversal) and *temperāre* to regulate, mix in proportion; cf **distemper**[2]]

distemper[2] *dis-temp'ər*, *n* a morbid or disorderly state of body or mind (*archaic*); any of several infectious diseases affecting animals, *esp* a viral illness (**canine distemper**) of dogs, foxes, ferrets and mink; ill-humour (*archaic*). — *vt* (*archaic*) to derange the temper; to disorder or disease. — *adj* **distemp'erate** not temperate, immoderate; diseased. — *n* **distemp'erature** (*archaic*) lack of proper temperature; intemperateness, disturbance; uneasiness of mind; indisposition. — *adj* **distem'pered** disordered; intemperate, ill-humoured, put out of sorts. [OFr *destemprer* to derange, from L *dis-* apart, and *temperāre* to govern, regulate]

distend *dis-tend'*, *vt* to stretch forth or apart; to stretch in three dimensions; to swell; to exaggerate. — *vi* to swell up, expand, inflate, (as though as a result of increasing internal pressure). — *n* **distensibil'ity** capacity for distension. — *adj* **disten'sible** that may be stretched. — *adj* **disten'sile** (*-sīl*) distensible; able to cause distension. — *n* **disten'sion** an act of distending or stretching; the state of being stretched; breadth (*rare*; sometimes **disten'tion**). — *adj* **disten'sive** capable of stretching or of being stretched. — *adj* **distent'** (*Spenser*) extended; distended, swollen. [L *distendere*, from *dis-* apart, and *tendere*, *tēnsum* or *tentum* to stretch]

disthene *dis'thēn*, *n* kyanite, so called from its difference in hardness when scratched in different directions. [Gr *di-* twice, and *sthenos* strength]

disthrone *dis-thrōn'*, *vt* to dethrone. — Also (*Spenser*) **disthrōn'ize**. [**dis-** (2) and (3)]

distich *dis'tik*, *n* (*prosody*) two lines or verses, complete in themselves; a couplet: — *pl* **distichs** (*-tiks*). — *adj* having two rows. — *adj* **dis'tichal**. — *adj* **dis'tichous** in or having two rows; (*esp bot*) arranged in or having two opposite vertical rows. [Gr *distichos*, from *di-* twice, and *stichos* a line]

distil or (*NAm*) **distill** *dis-til'*, *vi* to fall in drops; to flow gently; to evaporate and condense again; to use a still. — *vt* to let fall or cause to fall in drops; to convert from liquid into vapour by heat, and then to condense again; to extract as an essence or concentrate by evaporation and condensation; to accumulate or amass little by little in pure form (*fig*); to reduce to essentials by sorting and sifting (*fig*): — *pr p* **distill'ing**; *pa t* and *pa p* **distilled'**. — *adj* **distill'able**. — *n* **dis'tilland** that which is to be, or is being, distilled. — *n* **dis'tillāte** the product of distillation. — *n* **distillā'tion** the process of distilling. — *adj* **distill'atory** of or for distilling. — *n* **distill'er**. — *n* **distill'ery** a place where distilling, *esp* of alcoholic spirits, is carried on. — *n* **distill'ing**. — *n* **distil'ment** (*Shakesp*) that which is distilled. — **destructive distillation** the collection of volatile matters released when a substance is destroyed by heat in a closed vessel (as coal is when making gas); **fractional distillation** the separation by distilling of liquids having different boiling-points, the heat being gradually increased and the receiver changed; **vacuum distillation** distillation under reduced pressure (effecting a lowering of the boiling-point). [OFr *distiller*, with substitution of prefix, from L *dēstillāre*, *-ātum*, from *dē* down, and *stillāre* to drop, from *stilla* a drop]

distinct *dis-tingkt'*, *adj* separate; different; well-defined; clear; definite, unmistakable; distinguished, differentiated (*obs*; *Milton*, etc); marked, variegated (*poetic*; *Spenser*, *Milton*). — *adv* **distinct'ly** clearly; definitely, unmistakably. — *n* **distinct'ness**. — *n* **distincture** (*-tingk'chər* or *-tyər*) distinctness. [L *dīstinctus* separate]

distinction *dis-tingk'shən*, *n* separation or division; discrimination; a distinguishing mark or character; distinctness (*obs*); difference; a mark or honorific recognition of excellence; an honour; discriminating favour; noticeable eminence; outstanding merit; impressive and meritorious individuality. [L *dīstinctio*, *-ōnis* separation, distinction]

distinctive *dis-tingk'tiv*, *adj* marking out as different, distinguishing; characteristic, readily recognizable, serving to identify. — *n* a distinctive feature. — *adv* **distinct'ively**. — *n* **distinct'iveness**. [*dīstinct*, stem of pa p of L *dīstinguere*, and sfx *-ive*]

distincture. See **distinct**.

distingué, *fem* **distinguée** *dē-stɛ̃-gā*, (*Fr*) *adj* distinguished; striking.

distinguish *dis-ting'gwish*, *vt* to mark off, set apart, differentiate (often with *from*); to recognize by characteristic qualities; to make out, identify; to make distinctions in or concerning (*obs*); to bring by drawing distinctions; to separate by a mark of honour; to make eminent or known; to conduct (oneself) noticeably well; to hold to be not directly comparable (*Scots law*). — *vi* to make or show distinctions or differences, to recognize a difference (often with *between*). — *adj* **disting'uishable** capable of being distinguished. — *adv* **disting'uishably**. — *adj* **disting'uished** illustrious, eminent; dignified in appearance or manner; remarkable (with *for*). — *n* **disting'uisher**. — *adj* **disting'uishing** peculiar, serving to identify. — *n* **disting'uishment** (*Shakesp*, etc) distinction. — **Distinguished Conduct Medal** (*abbrev* **DCM**), **Distinguished Flying Cross** (*abbrev* **DFC**), and **Distinguished Service Medal** (*abbrev* **DSM**; also *US*), **Distinguished Service Order** (*abbrev* **DSO**) military decorations awarded for distinguished conduct in action. [L *dīstinguere*, *dīstinctum*, from *dī-* apart, and *stinguere* originally to prick, and *-ish*, in imitation of Fr verbs in *-ir*]

distort *dis-tört'*, *vt* to twist or pull awry, spoil the natural shape of, deform; to misrepresent (statements or facts, etc); to pervert, warp; to alter or make indistinct (a signal or sound) in transmission or reproduction (*radio* and *telecomm*). — *adj* **distort'ed**. — *n* **distortion** (*-tör'shən*) the process of distorting or being distorted; deformation; misrepresentation; change of waveform in course of transmission resulting in loss of clarity (*radio* and *telecomm*); crookedness; warping, perversion. — *adj* **distort'ive** causing distortion. [L *dis-* apart, and *torquēre*, *tortum* to twist]

distract *dis-trakt'*, *vt* to draw the attention of (someone) away from something; to divert someone or someone's attention in another or several other directions; to confuse; to harass; to render crazy; to madden; to divert, amuse, entertain. — *adj* separate (*Shakesp*, *dis'-*); distracted (*Milton*, *-trakt'*). — *adj* **distract'ed** confused, bewildered; harassed; crazy, mad, maddened. — *adv* **distract'edly**. — *n* **distract'edness**. — *n* **distractibil'ity**. — *adj* **distract'ible**. — *adj* **distract'ing**. — *adv* **distract'ingly**. — *n* **distrac'tion** the state of being distracted; that which distracts; perplexity; agitation; madness; a diversion, amusement; recreation, relaxation. — *adj* **distract'ive** causing perplexity. — *adv* **distract'ively**. [L *distrahere*, *-tractum*, from *dis-* apart, and *trahere* to draw]

distrail. Same as **dissipation trail**.

distrain *dis-trān'*, (*law*) *vt* to seize (*esp* goods for debt, *esp* for non-payment of rent or rates); to pull apart, burst (*Spenser*). — *vi* to seize the goods of a debtor. — *adj* **distrain'able**. — *n* **distrainee'** a person whose property has been distrained. — *n* **distrain'er** or **distrain'or**. — *n* **distrain'ment**. — *n* **distraint'** seizure of goods. [OFr *destraindre*, from L *dī-* apart, and *stringere* to draw tight]

distrait *dēs-tre*, *fem* **distraite** *dēs-tret*, (*Fr*) *adj* absent-minded.

distraught *dis-tröt'*, *adj* distracted; frantic, eg with grief or worry; mad; perplexed; drawn aside or apart (*Spenser*). [Modified form of **distract** (adj), modified by association with words like **caught** and **taught**]

distress *dis-tres'*, *n* extreme pain or suffering, *esp* mental or emotional; that which causes suffering; calamity; misfortune; acute poverty; exhaustion; peril; difficulty; compulsion (*archaic*); act of distraining goods (*law*); the goods seized; (in a structure) a sign of weakness arising from stress. — *vt* to afflict with (*esp* mental or emotional) pain or suffering; to harass; to grieve; to reduce financially, impoverish; to impart an antique appearance to (furniture), age artificially, by knocking, scraping, etc; to distrain (*law*). — *adj* **distressed'** suffering mentally or physically; impoverished; (of furniture) deliberately battered so as to appear antique. — *n* **distress'er**. — *adj* **distress'ful**. — *adv* **distress'fully**. — *n* **distress'fulness**. — *adj* **distress'ing**. — *adv* **distress'ingly**. — **distressed area** a region of unusually severe unemployment; **distress signal** a radio signal or flare put out by a ship, etc in distress. — **in distress** (of a ship or aircraft) in danger, needing help. [OFr *destresse*, from L *dīstringere*; see **distrain**]

distribute *dis-trib'ūt* or *dis'*, *vt* to divide amongst several; to deal out or allot; to classify; to disperse about a space; to spread out; to separate (type) and put back in compartments (*printing*); to use (a term) with full extension, including every individual to which it is applicable (*logic*). — *n* **distrib'uend** that which is to be distributed. — *adj* **distrib'utable** that may be divided. — *adj* **distrib'utary** distributing. — *n* a branch of a distributing system; an off-flow from a river that does not return to it (eg in a delta). — *n* **distributee'** (*US law*) a person who shares in the estate of a deceased person. — *n* **distributer** see **distributor** below. — *n* **distribu'tion** the act or process of distributing; dispersal; the business activity of transferring goods from the producer to the consumer, *incl* packaging, transport and warehousing; division; range; allotment; classification; the application of a general term to all the objects denoted by it (*logic*); the manner in which the products of industry are shared among the people (*econ*); the range of values of a variable presented in terms of frequency (*statistics*). — *adj* **distribu'tional**. — *adj* **distrib'utive** that distributes, separates or divides; giving to each his own; referring individually to all members of a group, as the words *each*, *every*, *either*, *neither* (*gram*); (of a general term) applying to all objects denoted by it (*logic*); such that $a.(x+y+z+\ldots) = a.x+a.y+a.z+\ldots$ (*math*). — *n* a distributive word, like *each* or *every*, that indicates the several individuals of a number taken separately (*gram*). — *adv* **distrib'utively**. — *n* **distrib'utiveness**. — *n* **distrib'utor** or **distrib'uter** someone who, or that which, distributes; an agent, or middleman, between the manufacturer and the retailer or customer, a wholesaler, a retailer; a device in a petrol engine whereby a high tension current is transmitted in correct sequence to the sparking plugs. — **distributed logic** computer systems where central processing unit operations are distributed among a number of terminals rather than located centrally; **distributed processing** (*comput*) the distribution of processing power away from the centre to other terminals; **distribution coefficient** (*chem*) same as **partition coefficient**. — **geographical distribution** see under **geography**. [L *distribuere*, from *dis-* apart, and *tribuere*, *tribūtum* to allot]

district *dis'trikt*, *n* a portion of territory defined for political, judicial, educational, or other purposes (such as a registration district, a militia district, the District of Columbia); generally, an area, locality or region; (in local government) an administrative subdivision of a Scottish region or of an English or Welsh county; a constituency (*US*); a subdivision of a division (*India*). — *vt* to divide into districts. — **district attorney** (*US*) a public prosecutor for a district; **district council** in British local government, the council elected to govern a district; **district court** (*US*) the federal court for a district; **district heating** the distribution of heat from a central source to buildings in the surrounding area; **district judge** (in England and Wales) judicial officer for each county court and district court empowered to try certain cases, and to supervise certain stages of others (before 1991 called *registrar* and *district registrar*); **district nurse** a nurse appointed to attend to patients in their own homes; **district visitor** a church worker who visits parishioners in a district. [Fr, from LL *dīstrictus* jurisdiction, from *dīstringere*; see **distrain**]

distringas *dis-tring'gas*, *n* formerly, a writ directing a sheriff or other officer to distrain. [Second pers sing present subjunctive of L *dīstringere*; see **distrain**]

distrouble *dis-trub'l*, (*obs*) *vt* to trouble greatly, to perplex, to disturb. [L *dis-* (intensive) and **trouble**]

distrust *dis-trust'*, *n* lack of trust; lack of faith or confidence; doubt. — *vt* to have no trust in; to disbelieve; to doubt. — *n* **distrust'er**. — *adj* **distrust'ful** full of distrust; apt to distrust; suspicious; to be distrusted (*rare*). — *adv* **distrust'fully**. — *n* **distrust'fulness**. — *adj* **distrust'less**. [**dis-** (2) and (3)]

distune *dis-tūn'*, (*archaic*) *vt* to put out of tune. [**dis-** (3)]

disturb *dis-tûrb'*, *vt* to interrupt; to inconvenience; to throw into confusion; to agitate; to upset. — *n* disturbance. — *n* **disturb'ance** interruption; a commotion or fracas; derangement; agitation; interference, molestation (*law*); perplexity. — *adj* and *n* **disturb'ant** disturbing. — *adj* **disturb'ative**. — *n* **disturbed'** worried; confused, *esp* emotionally; maladjusted. — *n* **disturb'er**. — *adj* **disturb'ing**. [OFr *destourber*, from L *disturbāre*, from *dis-* apart, and *turbāre* to agitate, from *turba* a crowd]

distyle *dis'tīl*, *dī'stīl*, (*archit*) *n* a portico with two columns. [Gr *di-* twice, and *stȳlos* column]

disulfiram *dī-sul-fē'rəm*, *n* a drug used to treat chronic alcoholism, acting by inducing nausea, etc if alcohol is taken.

disulphate *dī-sul'fāt*, *n* a pyrosulphate; formerly, an acid sulphate. — *n* **disul'phide** a sulphide containing two atoms of sulphur to the molecule. — Also (*obs*) **disul'phūret**. — *adj* **disulphū'ric** pyrosulphuric. [**di-**]

disunion *dis-ūn'yən*, *n* lack of union, dissension, disagreement; breaking up of union or concord; separation, estrangement. — *n* **disun'ionist** someone who favours dissolution of a union. — *vt* **disunite'** to separate from union, detach, divide; to sever or sunder; to estrange, drive apart. — *vi* to fall apart; to part, separate. — *n* **disu'nity** lack of unity, dissension. [**dis-** (2) and (1)]

disuse *dis-ūs'* or *dis'ūs*, *n* the state of being out of use, no longer used, observed or practised; neglect, desuetude. — *vt* (*dis-ūz'*) to cease to use or practise; to leave out of use. — *n* **disusage** (*dis-ūz'ij*) gradual cessation of use or custom. — *adj* **disused** no longer observed or practised. — **disuse atrophy** (*med*) the wasting away of a part as a result of diminution or cessation of functional activity. [**dis-** (2) and (3)]

disutility *dis-ū-til'i-ti*, *n* an inconvenience, drawback, disadvantage. [**dis-** (2)]

disvalue *dis-val'ū*, (*rare*) *vt* to disparage. [**dis-** (3)]

disvouch *dis-vowch'*, (*Shakesp*) *vt* to disavow. [**dis-** (3)]

disworship *dis-wûr'ship*, (*Milton*) *n* dishonour, disgrace. [**dis-** (2)]

disyllable or **dissyllable** *dīs-il'ə-bl*, *n* a word of two syllables. — *adj* **disyllabic** (*-ab'ik*). — *n* **disyllabificā'tion**. — *vt* **disyllab'ify** to make into two syllables. — *n* **disyll'abism** the character of having two syllables. [Through Fr *dissyllabe*, *dissilabe*, and L from Gr *di-* twice, and *syllabē* a syllable; with *l* as in **syllable**]

disyoke *dis-yōk'*, (*Tennyson*) *vt* to free from the yoke. [**dis-** (3)]

dit[1] or **ditt** *dit*, (*archaic*) *n* a poem; the words of a song. [Appar formed by Spenser from **dite**[1] influenced by **ditty**]

dit[2] *dit*, (now *Scot*) *vt* to stop, block: — *pa t* and *pa p* **ditt'ed** or **ditt'it**; *pa p* also **dit**. [OE *dyttan* to shut]

dit[3] *dē*, (*Fr*) *adj* named; reputed.

dit[4] *dit*, *n* a word representing the dot in the spoken form of Morse code. See also **dah**[1].

dita *dē'tə*, *n* an apocynaceous tree (*Alstonia scholaris*), of India and the Philippines, with tonic bark. [Tagálog or Visayan]

dital *dī'təl*, *n* a thumb key for sharpening a lute or guitar string by a semitone. [Ital *dito* finger, with *-al* after **pedal**, **manual**]

ditch *dich*, *n* a trench dug in the ground for drainage or irrigation, or to serve to mark a boundary; any long narrow depression carrying water; the border of a bowling-green; the sea (*slang*). — *vi* to make, repair or clean a ditch or ditches; (of an aircraft or pilot) to come down in the sea (*colloq*). — *vt* to dig a ditch in or around; to drain by ditches; to throw, or drive, into a ditch; to crash (a vehicle) deliberately; to abandon, or get rid of (*slang*); to escape from or leave (a person) in the lurch (*slang*); to derail (*US*); to bring (an aircraft) down in the sea (*colloq*). — *n* **ditch'er** a man or machine that makes, cleans or repairs ditches. — **ditch'-dog** (*Shakesp*) a dead dog rotting in a ditch; **ditch'-water** stagnant foul water such as is found in ditches, proverbially dull. [OE *dīc*, whence also **dike**; see notes at **dike**[1]]

dite[1] *dīt*, (*obs*) *n* writing; a composition. — *vt* to compose, indite; to dictate; to indict. [OFr *dit* a saying, from *ditier*, *diter* to write, from L *dictum* an utterance, from *dictāre*, frequentative of *dīcere* to say]

dite[2] (*Spenser*) *vt*. Same as **dight** (*archaic*).

dithecal *dī-thē'kl*, (*bot*) *adj* having two thecae. — Also **dīthē'cous**. [**di-**]

ditheism *dī'thē-izm*, *n* the doctrine of the existence of two supreme gods. — *n* **dī'theist**. — *adj* **ditheist'ic** or **ditheist'ical**. [Gr *di-* twice, and *theos* a god]

Ditheletism *dī-thel'ət-izm*, *n* the doctrine that Christ on earth had two wills, human and divine (*opp* to *Monotheletism*). — Also **Dī'thelism**, **Dīoth'elism**, **Dȳoth'elism**, **Dȳothel'etism** or **Dīthel'itism**. — *n* **Dī'thelēte** a believer in the doctrine. — Also **Dīoth'elēte**, **Dȳoth'elēte** or **Dȳoth'elite**. — *adj* **Dīthelet'ic** or **Dīthelet'ical**. — Also **Dīothelet'ic(al)**, **Dȳothelet'ic(al)**, **Dȳothelit'ic(al)**. — All words also without *cap*. [Gr *di-* twice (or *dyo* two), and *thelētēs* a willer, from *thelein* to will]

dither *didh'ər*, *vi* to waver, vacillate; to agitate (chiefly *US*); to tremble, shiver, quake. — *vt* to perturb, confuse. — *n* a state of irresolution; a trembling condition; a quaking fit; tremulous excitement; perturbation. — Also **didd'er**. — *n* **dith'erer**. — *adj* **dith'ery**. — **all of a dither** nervous, agitated. [Probably imit]

dithionate *dī-thī'ən-āt*, *n* a salt of **dithionic** (*-on'ik*) **acid**, otherwise hyposulphuric acid ($H_2S_2O_6$) [Gr *di-* twice, and *theion* sulphur]

dithyramb *dith'i-ram(b)*, *n* in ancient Greece, a wild impassioned choral hymn sung in honour of Bacchus; a poem or piece of writing in wildly rapturous or bombastic vein. — *adj* **dithyram'bic** of or like a dithyramb; rapturous; wild and boisterous. — *adv* **dithyram'bically**. — *n* **dithyram'bist**. [Gr *dīthyrambos*]
ditokous *dit'o-kəs*, (*zool*) *adj* producing two at a birth or in a clutch. [Gr *di-* twice, and *tokos* birth]
ditone *dī'tōn*, *n* in ancient Greek music, an interval of two major tones. [**di-**]
ditriglyph *dī-trī'glif*, (*archit*) *n* a space for two triglyphs in the entablature between columns. — *adj* **ditriglyph'ic**. [**di-**]
ditrochee *dī-trō'kē*, (*prosody*) *n* a trochaic dipody. — *adj* **dītrochē'an**. [**di-**]
ditsy or **ditzy** *dit'si*, (*US colloq*) *adj* amiably eccentric, scatterbrained; precious, affected.
ditt. See **dit**[1].
dittander *di-tan'dər*, *n* a pepperwort (*Lepidium latifolium*), a pungent cruciferous plant; dittany. [A form of **dittany**]
dittany *dit'ə-ni*, *n* an aromatic rutaceous plant (*Dictamnus albus*), secreting much volatile oil. [OFr *dictame*, from L *dictamnus*, from Gr *diktamnos*; prob from Mt *Diktē* in Crete]
dittay *dit'ā*, (*obs Scots law*) *n* an indictment, charge. [OFr *ditté*, from L *dictātum*; cf **ditty** and **dictate**]
dittit. See **dit**[2].
ditto *dit'ō*, (in writing abbreviated to **do**, or replaced by ditto marks (qv below)) *n* that which has been said; the same thing: — *pl* **ditt'os**. — *adv* as before, or aforesaid; in the same manner, likewise; (as assenting rejoinder) same here. — *vt* to duplicate, echo: — *pr p* **ditt'oing**; *pa t* and *pa p* **ditt'oed**. — *n pl* **ditt'os** a suit of clothes of the same colour throughout. — **ditto marks** a sign " written immediately below a word, etc to show that it is to be understood as repeated. [Ital *ditto*, from L *dictum* said, pa p of *dīcere* to say]
dittography *di-tog'rə-fi*, *n* unintentional repetition of letters or words by a scribe or printer in copying a manuscript. [Gr *dittos* double, and *graphein* to write]
dittology *di-tol'ə-ji*, *n* a double reading or interpretation. [Gr *dittologiā*, from *dittos* double, and *legein* to speak]
ditty *dit'i*, *n* a simple song; a little poem to be sung. — *vt* to set to music. [OFr *ditie*, from L *dictātum*, neuter perfect participle (passive) of *dictāre* to dictate]
ditty-bag *dit'i-bag*, *n* a sailor's bag for personal belongings. — Also **ditt'y-box**. [Origin unknown]
ditzy. See **ditsy**.
diuretic *dī-ū-ret'ik*, *adj* increasing the flow of urine. — *n* a medicine that increases the flow of urine. — *n* **diurē'sis** increased or excessive excretion of urine. [Gr *diourētikos*, from *dia* through, and *ouron* urine]
diurnal *dī-ûr'nəl*, *adj* daily; relating to or performed in or lasting a day; (of animals) at rest during the night and active during the day (*biol*); (of flowers) open during the day; belonging to the daytime. — *n* a service-book containing the day hours, except matins (a night-office; *eccles*); a diary, journal (*archaic*). — *n* **diur'nalist** (*archaic*) a journalist. — *adv* **diur'nally**. [L *diurnālis*, from *diēs* a day; see **journal**]
diuturnal *dī-ū-tûr'nəl*, *adj* lasting long. — *n* **diutur'nity**. [L *diūturnus*, from *diū* long]
Div. *abbrev*: Division.
div[1] *div*, (*Scot*; in *present indicative* only) *vt* a form of **do** (auxiliary).
div[2] *dēv*, *n* an evil spirit of Persian mythology. [Pers *dīv*]
div[3] *div*, *n* short for **dividend**.
div. *abbrev*: divide; divine; division; divorce or divorced.
diva *dē'vä*, *n* a great female singer, *esp* an operatic prima donna. [Ital, from L *dīva*, fem of *dīvus* divine]
divagate *dī'və-gāt*, *vi* to wander about; to digress. — *n* **divagā'tion**. [L *dīvagārī* to wander]
divalent *dī-vā'lənt* or *div'əl-ənt*, *n* a chemical element or atom capable of uniting with two atoms of hydrogen or their equivalent. — *adj* having two combining equivalents. — Also **bivalent**. — *n* **diva'lency**. [Gr *di-* twice, and L *valēre* to be worth]
Divali. See **Diwali**.
divan *di-van'*, *n* a couch without back or sides; a bed of similar design (also **divan'-bed'**); (*esp* formerly) a smoking-room; (in some Muslim countries) a council chamber, court of justice or council of state, or a counting house; any council or assembly (*poetic*); an (*orig Pers*) name for a collection of poems; a dewan. [Ar and Pers *dīwān* a long seat]
divaricate *dī-var'i-kāt*, (*biol*) *vi* to part into two branches, to fork; to diverge. — *vt* to divide into two branches. — *adj* widely divergent, spreading apart. — *n* **divari-cā'tion**. [L *dīvaricāre*, *-ātum*, from *dis-* apart, and *varicāre* to spread the legs, from *varus* bent apart]
dive *dīv*, *vi* to plunge headfirst into or down through water or down through the air; (of a submarine) to submerge; (of an aircraft) to descend steeply, nose-first; to go headlong into a recess, forest, etc, or suddenly investigate the interior of a container, etc (with *into*); to plunge or go deeply into any matter; to involve oneself wholeheartedly (with *into*). — *vt* to plunge, dip: — *pa t* **dived** or (*NAm*) **dove** (*dōv*). — *n* a plunge; a swoop; a headlong descent; a refuge; a resort, generally disreputable, often underground, eg a bar (*slang*); a subway; a faked knockout (*boxing*). — *n* **div'er** a person who dives or can dive; a person who dives for pearls; a person who works from a diving-bell or in a diving-suit beneath water; any member of a genus (*Gavia*) of ducklike diving birds; (loosely; *esp* formerly) any of various diving birds such as the auk, grebe, penguin, etc; a pickpocket (*slang*). — *n* and *adj* **div'ing**. — *vt* and *vi* **dive'-bomb** to attack with, or as if with, a dive-bomber; to discharge bombs while diving. — **dive'-bomber** an aeroplane that discharges a bomb while in a steep dive; **dive'-bombing**; **dive-dapp'er** (*Shakesp*) a didapper, dabchick, little grebe; **div'ing-bell** a hollow vessel or chamber, originally bell-shaped, open at the bottom and supplied with air by a tube from above, in which one may descend into and work under water; **div'ing-board** a board for diving from; **div'ing-suit** or (formerly) **-dress** a watertight costume for a diver, with special provision for receiving air, etc. [OE *dȳfan*, *dūfan*, from ON *dȳfa*]
divellent *dī-vel'ənt*, *adj* drawing apart. — *vt* **divell'icate** to pull in pieces; to pluck apart. [L *dī-* apart, and *vellere*, *vellicāre* to pluck]
diver. See **dive**.
diverge *di-* or *dī-vûrj'*, *vi* to incline or turn apart; to tend from a common point in different directions; to vary from the standard; to deviate, differ; (of a mathematical series) to increase indefinitely. — *vt* to deflect, cause to diverge. — *n* **diverge'ment**. — *n* **diverg'ence** or **diverg'ency** the act or amount of diverging; the condition of being divergent; the flow of air away from a particular region, *usu* associated with fine weather (*meteorol*); (of an infinite series, etc) the property of having no limit (*math*); the turning outward of the eyes in focusing on a distant object (*physiol*); initiation of a chain reaction in which more neutrons are released than are absorbed and lost (*nucleonics*). — *adj* **diverg'ent** diverging; (of thought or thinking) following unconventional routes, so as to produce a variety of solutions in problem-solving (*psychol*). — *adv* **diverg'ently**. — *adj* **diverg'ing**. — *adv* **diverg'ingly**. — **divergent thinking** (*behav*) thinking that is productive and original, involving the creation of a variety of ideas or solutions that tend to go beyond conventional categories (*opp* to **convergent thinking**). [L *dī-* apart, and *vergere* to incline]
divers *dī'vərz*, (*archaic* and *literary*) *adj* sundry; several; more than one; same as **diverse** (*Bible*). — *adv* (*Milton*) in different directions. [L *dīversus* turned different ways, contrary, different]
diverse *dī'vərs* or *dī'vûrs'*, *adj* various, assorted; multiform; different; distinct; distracting (*Spenser*). — *vi* (*Spenser*) to turn aside. — *adv* **di'versely** or **diverse'ly**.

— *adj* **diversifī'able**. — *n* **diversificā'tion**. — *adj* **diver'sified**. — *vt* **divers'ify** to differentiate (*obs*); to give variety to, to vary, variegate or modify; to make (investments) in securities of different types so as to lessen risk of loss; to engage in production of a variety of (manufactures, crops), or in a variety of operations, so as to expand or lessen risk of failure or loss. — Also *vi*: — *pr p* **diver'sifying**; *pa t* and *pa p* **diver'sified**. — *n* **diver'sion** the act of diverting or turning aside; something which diverts; amusement, recreation; something done to turn the attention of an opponent; an official detour to avoid (part of) a road which is temporarily closed. — *adj* **diver'sionary** of the nature of a diversion, designed to distract the attention of an opponent. — *n* **diver'sionist** a deviationist. — *n* **diver'sity** state of being diverse; difference; dissimilarity; variety. — *adv* **dī'versly** in divers ways. [L *dīversus* different, various]

divert *di-vûrt'*, *dī-*, *vt* to turn aside (also *archaic*, *vi*); to change the direction of; to distract from business or study; to amuse. — *n* (*Scot*) an amusing person or thing. — *adj* **divert'ible**. — *n* **divertibil'ity**. — *adj* **divert'ing** tending to divert; amusing, entertaining. — *adv* **divert'ingly**. — *n* **divertisement** (*di-vûrt'iz-mənt*) a diversion; a divertimento. — *adj* **divert'ive** tending to divert. [Fr, from L *dīvertere*, *dīversum* from *dī-* aside, and *vertere* to turn]

diverticulum *dī-vər-tik'ū-ləm*, (*anatom*) *n* a sac or pouch formed eg by herniation in the wall of a tubular organ, *esp* the intestines: — *pl* **divertic'ula**. — *adj* **dīvertic'ular**, **dīvertic'ulate**, or **divertic'ulated**. — *n* **dīverticūlī'tis** inflammation of one or more diverticula. — *n* **dīverticūlō'sis** the presence of several diverticula in the intestines. [L *dīverticulum* a byway, retreat]

divertimento *di-vûr-ti-men'tō*, (*music*) *n* an entertaining piece of music, *esp* a suite for orchestra or chamber ensemble: — *pl* **divertimen'ti** (*-t-ē*). [Ital]

divertissement *dē-ver-tēs'mã*, (*Fr*) *n* a short entertainment, eg a ballet interlude, between the acts of a play, or between plays; generally, a diversion or entertainment.

Dives *dī'vēz*, *n* the rich man at whose gate Lazarus lay (*Bible*: Luke 16. 19); a rich and luxurious person. [L *dīves* rich (man), understood as a proper name]

divest *dī-vest'*, *vt* to remove clothes from, strip (with *of*); to strip or deprive (with *of*); to disencumber or free (oneself) (with *of*). — *adj* **divest'ible**. — *n* **divest'iture**, **divest'ment** or **divest'ure**. [OFr *desvestir*, with change of prefix (*dis-* for *dē-*) from L *dēvestīre*, from *dē* away from, and *vestīre* to clothe, from *vestis* a garment]

divi. See **divvy**.

divide *di-vīd'*, *vt* to split up, or mark off, into parts, actually or in imagination; to separate, part; to distinguish, set apart; to classify; to share, distribute; to allot; to deal out; to ascertain how many times a quantity is contained in (*math*); to perform with division or floridly (*music*); to be a boundary or a subject of difference between; to keep apart; to set at variance, cause disagreement between; to cause to vote for and against a motion; to sever. — *vi* to separate; to fall apart; to branch; to vote for and against a motion; to be capable of or be susceptible of division; to be contained a specified number of times in another number (with *into*). — *n* the act of dividing (*colloq*); an area of high land between two water systems, a watershed (*esp NAm*); something that divides or separates, a gap or split. — *adj* **divīd'able** (or *div'id-*) divisible; divided (*Shakesp*). — *adj* **divīd'ant** (*Shakesp*) distinguishable, separable. — *adv* **divīd'edly**. — *n* **divīd'er** someone who, or that which, divides; a screen or partition (also **room'-divider**); a soup-ladle (*Scot*); (in *pl*) a kind of compasses for measuring. — *adj* **divīd'ing** separating. — *n* separation. — *adj* **divid'ual** divisible; separable (*Milton*); shared in common with others (*Milton*). — *adj* **divid'uous** divided, special, accidental. — **divided highway** (*NAm*) a dual carriageway; **divided skirt** wide-legged knee-length trousers for women, having the appearance of a skirt, culottes; **divīd'ing-en'gine** an instrument for marking accurate subdivisions or graduating scales. [L *dīvidere*, *dīvīsum*, from *dis-* apart, and the root *vid* to separate]

dividend *div'i-dend*, *n* a number that is to be divided by another; the share of a sum divided that falls to each individual, by way of interest or otherwise; the sum payable to creditors of an insolvent estate (*law*). — **dividend stripping** a method of evading tax on dividends by a contrived arrangement between a company liable to tax and another in a position to claim repayment of tax; **div'idend-warr'ant** a certificate entitling to payment of dividend. — **declare a dividend** to announce the sum per cent a trading concern is prepared to pay its shareholders. [L *dīvidendum* to be divided, from *dīvidere*]

divider. See **divide**.

dividivi *div'i-div-i*, *n* the curved pods of a small tropical American tree (*Caesalpinia coriaria*), used for tanning and dyeing; the tree itself. [Carib name]

dividual, **dividuous**. See **divide**.

divine *di-vīn'*, *adj* belonging to or proceeding from a god; holy; excellent in the highest degree; wonderful, splendid (*colloq*); prescient, having forebodings (*Milton*). — *n* a person skilled in divine things; a minister of the gospel; a theologian. — *vt* to foresee or foretell as if divinely inspired; to guess or make out; to prognosticate; to make divine (*Spenser*); to search for (underground water, etc), *esp* with a divining rod. — *vi* to profess or practise divination; to have forebodings. — *n* **divinā'tion** the art or practice of divining; seeking to know the future or hidden things by supernatural means; instinctive prevision; prediction; conjecture. — *n* **div'inātor** (*archaic*) or **divīn'er** a person who divines or professes divination; a conjecturer: — *fem* **divīn'eress**. — *adj* **divinatō'rial** or **divin'atory** relating to divination, conjectural. — *adv* **divīne'ly**. — *n* **divīne'ness**. — **diviner**, **divineress** see **divinator** above. — *vt* **divin'ify**, or **div'inize** or **-ise** to treat as divine. — **divine right** the concept that monarchs rule by the authority of God rather than by consent of the people; any authority supposed to be unquestionable (*colloq*); **divīn'ing rod** a rod, *usu* of hazel, used by those professing to discover water or metals under ground. [OFr *devin* soothsayer, and L *dīvīnus*, from *dīvus*, *deus* a god]

diving. See **dive**.

divinify. See under **divine**.

divinity *di-vin'i-ti*, *n* godhead; the nature or essence of a god; a celestial being; a god; the science of divine things; theology. — **divinity hall** (*Scot*) a theological college or department. [OFr *devinite*, from L *dīvīnitās*, *-tātis*; see **divine**]

divinise, **divinize**. See under **divine**.

divisible *di-viz'i-bl*, *adj* capable of being divided or separated; capable of being divided without remainder (*math*). — *n* **divisibil'ity** or **divis'ibleness**. — *adv* **divis'ibly**. [L *dīvīsibilis*, from *dīvīdere* to divide]

divisim *di-vī'zim*, *dē-wē'sim*, (*L*) *adv* separately.

division *di-vizh'ən*, *n* the act of dividing; the state of being divided; that which divides; a partition; a barrier; a portion or section; one of a set of graded classes or groups; one of the parts of a territorial or business, etc unit, divided for administrative, etc purposes; in India, a part of a province under a commissioner, divided into districts; an army unit (*usu* half an army corps) containing almost all branches of the service; separation; the taking of a vote; difference in opinion, etc; disunion; the process of finding how many times one quantity is contained in another (*math*); a taxonomic grouping, the equivalent of a phylum (*bot*); a florid passage or performance in which many short notes may be regarded as taking the place of a long note (*music*; *archaic*). — *adj* **divisional** (*-vizh'*) relating to or marking a division or separation (also **divis'ionary**); relating to or belonging to a part of a larger unit. — *n* **divisionaliza'tion** or **-s-**. — *n* **divis'ionism** (often with *cap*; *painting*) pointillism. — *n* **divis'ionist**. — **division-lobby** see **lobby**. — **division of labour** the assigning of different functions to different agents; **fallacy of division** (*logic*) the fallacy of assuming that the part or individual partakes of the characteristic of the whole or group. [L *dīvīsiō*, *-ōnis*, *dīvīsor*, *-ōris*, from *dīvīdere* to divide]

divisive *di-vī'siv*, *adj* forming division or separation; tending to divide or separate; tending to create dissension. — *adv* **divī'sively**. — *n* **divī'siveness**. [LL *dīvīsīvus*, from *dīvīdere* to divide]

divisor *di-vī'zer*, (*math*) *n* the number which divides the dividend; a number that divides another without remainder, a factor. [L *dīvīsor*, from *dīvīdere* to divide]

divorce *di-vōrs'*, *-vörs'*, *n* the legal dissolution of a marriage or the decree that dissolves it; complete separation or severance (*fig*). — *vt* to dissolve the marriage of; to give or obtain a divorce (to a couple or one's spouse, or from one's spouse); to separate, sever. — *vi* to obtain a divorce; to separate by divorce. — *adj* **divorce'able**. — *n* **divorcee'** a divorced person. — Also **divorcé** *masc* and **divorcée** *fem* (*di-vör'sā*; *Fr*). — *n* **divorce'ment** (*Bible*) divorce. — *n* **divor'cer**. — *adj* **divor'cive** having power to divorce. [Fr, from L *dīvortium*, from *dīvortere*, another form of *dīvertere* (of a woman) to leave one's husband)]

divot *div'ət*, *n* a thin sod, cut for roofing, etc (*Scot*); a small piece of turf gouged out by a golfer's club-head, or by a horse's hoof. — **feal and divot** (*Scots law*) a right of cutting sods. [Origin unknown]

divulge *di-* or *dī-vulj'*, *vt orig* to spread abroad among the vulgar or the people; to make public; to reveal, disclose. — *vt* **divul'gate** (*-gāt*; *archaic*) to publish. — *n* **dīvulgā'tion**, **divul'gence** or **divulge'ment**. [L *dīvulgāre*, from *dī-* abroad, and *vulgāre* to publish, from *vulgus* the common people]

divulsion *di-* or *dī-vul'shən*, *n* act of pulling or rending apart or away. — *adj* **divul'sive** tending to pull apart. [L *dīvulsiō*, *-ōnis*, from *dī-*, and *vellere*, *vulsum* to pull]

divvy or **divi** *div'i*, (*slang*) *n* a dividend; a share. — **divvy up** to divide (spoils, etc); to go shares: — *pr p* **divv'ying**; *pa t* and *pa p* **divv'ied**. [Abbrev of **divide** and **dividend**]

Diwali *di-wä'lē*, *n* the Hindu or Sikh festival of lamps held in October or November. — Also **Dewali** or **Divali**. [Hindi *divālī*]

diwan. Same as **dewan**.

dixi *dēk'sē*, (*L*) I have spoken.

dixie or **dixy** *diks'i*, *n* a military cooking-pail or camp-kettle. [Perh Hindi *degcī*, from Pers *degcha*, dimin of *dīg* large metallic cooking utensil]

Dixieland *dik'si-land*, *n* an early style of jazz in New Orleans, played by small combinations of instruments. [*Dixie* name given to southern states of the US]

DIY *dee'ī-wī'*, *abbrev*: do-it-yourself (qv under **do**[1]).

dizain *di-zān'*, (*prosody*) *n* a ten-line stanza or poem. [Fr *dix* ten, from L *decem* ten]

dizen *dī'zn* or *diz'n*, (*obs*) *vt* to dress or charge (a distaff) with flax; to dress up, dress gaudily. [From the root seen in **distaff**]

dizygotic *dī-zī-got'ik*, (*biol*) *adj* developed from two zygotes or fertilized eggs. — **dizygotic twins** fraternal twins, ie twins which have developed from two zygotes. [Gr *di-* twice, and **zygote**]

dizzard *diz'ərd*, (*obs*) *n* a blockhead. [Perh ME and OFr *disour* story-teller]

dizzy *diz'i*, *adj* giddy; confused, bewildered; (of a height) so elevated as to cause giddiness in anyone looking down (often *fig*); (generally) giddy-making, confusing, bewildering; silly (*colloq*); extreme (*colloq*). — *vt* to make dizzy; to confuse: — *pr p* **dizz'ying**; *pa t* and *pa p* **dizz'ied**. — *adv* **dizz'ily**. — *n* **dizz'iness**. — *adj* **dizz'ying** making one dizzy. — *adv* **dizz'yingly**. [OE *dysig* foolish; cf Dan *dösig* drowsy; cf also **doze**]

DJ *dē-jā'*, *n* a dee-jay, disc jockey; a dinner jacket (*colloq*). [Abbrev]

djebel. See **jebel**.

djellaba or **djellabah** *jə-lä'bə* or *jel'ə-bə*, *n* a cloak with a hood and wide sleeves. — Also **jellab'a** or **jelab'**. — See also **gal(l)abi(y)a(h)**. [Ar *jallabah*, *jallāb*]

djibbah *jib'ä*. Same as **jubbah**.

djinn, **djinni**. See **jinn**.

DK *abbrev*: Denmark (IVR).

dk *abbrev*: dark; deck; dock.

DL *abbrev*: Deputy Lieutenant.

D/L *abbrev*: demand loan.

dl *abbrev*: decilitre(s).

DLit or **DLitt** *dē-lit'*, *abbrev*: *Doctor litterarum* or *litteraturae* (*L*), Doctor of Letters or Doctor of Literature.

dlr *abbrev*: dealer.

dlvy *abbrev*: delivery.

DM *abbrev*: Deutschmark or Deutsche Mark.

dm *abbrev*: decimetre(s).

DMA (*comput*) *abbrev*: direct memory access.

D-mark or **D-mark**. Same as **DM** (*abbrev*).

DMD (*med*) *abbrev*: Duchenne muscular dystrophy.

DM's or **DMs** (*colloq*) *abbrev*: Doc Martens®.

DMS *abbrev*: database management system.

DMus *dē-muz'*, *abbrev*: Doctor of Music.

DMZ *abbrev*: demilitarized zone.

DNA *dē-en-ā*, *n* deoxyribonucleic acid (qv at **deoxidate**). — **DNA library** (*biol*) a mixture of cloned DNA sequences derived from a single source and containing all or most of the sequences from that source; **DNA profiling** genetic fingerprinting (see under **genetic**).

DNB *abbrev*: Dictionary of National Biography (a reference work containing the biographies of famous British people.)

D-notice. See **D** (*abbrev*).

Dnr *abbrev*: dinar (standard unit of currency of former Yugoslavia).

Do. *abbrev*: dominee.

do[1] *dōō* or *də*, *vt* to put in some condition, eg to clean, to tidy; to render; to confer; to bestow; to perform; (of a vehicle) to (have the power to) travel at a (maximum) speed of; to accomplish, complete; to finish; to exhaust; to work at; to perform work upon; to beat up, thrash, assault (*slang*); to prepare, set in order, arrange; to cook; to cheat, or overreach (*slang*); to raid, rob (*slang*); to treat; to make the round of, see the sights of (*colloq*); to spend (a period of time) in prison; to take or use (a drug; *US slang*); to put, place (*obs*); to cause (*obs*). — *vi* to act, be active; to behave; to fare; to thrive; to suffice; to be just good enough; to serve (with *for*); to arrange, devise or effect in respect of something or someone (with *with*): — *2nd sing* (*archaic*) **do'est** or **dost** (*dust*), *3rd* **does** (*duz*), also (*archaic*) **do'eth** or **doth** (*duth*); *pa t* **did**; *pr p* **do'ing**; *pa p* **done** (*dun*) in *Spenser*, *infinitive* **doen**, **done**, and **donne**, *3rd pl pa t* **doen**. — *Do* serves as a substitute for a verb that has just been used. It is used as an auxiliary verb (where there is no other auxiliary) with an infinitive in negative, interrogative, emphatic, and rhetorically inverted sentences, in some dialects merely periphrastically, and in verse sometimes to gain a syllable or postpone the accent; but these uses are limited with the verbs *have* and *do*. — *n* activity (*obs*); a feast, celebration; a swindle, hoax (*slang*); what one has to do (*obs*); fuss (*archaic*): — *pl* **do's** or **dos**. — *adj* **do'able** able to be done. — *n* **do'er** a person who does, or habitually does, anything; an agent; a busy, active or energetic person; a person who prefers taking action, or practical steps, to contemplation and discussion; a healthy farm animal (*NZ*); a horse in respect of its appetite, as in *a good doer* (*horse racing*). — *adj* **do'ing** active (as in *up and doing*). — *n* (*colloq*) a scolding; thrashing; severe treatment; the agency or handiwork of someone seen as instrumental in something; (in *pl*) activities, behaviour; (in *pl*) fancy dishes or adjuncts; (in *pl*) what's-its-name (*slang*). — **done** *pa p* of **do**; *infinitive* of **do** (*Spenser*). — *adj* utterly exhausted (now *usu* **done in**); finished, completed; cooked to a degree suitable for eating; (of behaviour, etc) socially acceptable. — *interj* (used in clinching a bargain, etc) agreed. — *n* (*cookery*) **done'ness** the state of being, or degree to which something is, cooked. — **do'-all** a factotum;

do'-good'er a slighting name for someone who tries to benefit others by social reforms, etc, implying that his or her efforts are unwelcome, self-righteous or ineffectual; **do'-good'ery** (*derog*); **do'-good'ing**. — Also *adj*. — **do'-good'ism** (*derog*). — *adj* **do-it-yourself'** designed to be built or constructed, etc by an amateur rather than by someone specially trained. — Also *n*. — **do-it-yourself'er**; **do'-naught**, **do'-nought** or **do'-noth'-ing** a lazy or idle person; a fainéant (see **donnot**); **do'-noth'ingism**; **do'-noth'ingness**. — **all done** completely finished, used up; **be done** to be at an end; to have done or finished (*Scot*); **be** or **have done with** to finish with, end contact or dealings with; **do away with** to abolish, destroy; **do brown** to cook or roast to brownness; to hoax, swindle (*slang*); **do by** to act towards; **do down** to put down, subdue (*obs*); to cheat, get the better of (*colloq*); **do for** to suit; to provide for; to ruin; to kill (*colloq*); to do domestic work for (*colloq*); **do in** (*colloq*) to deceive, to get the better of; to exhaust; to ruin; to murder; **do or die** to make a final desperate attempt to do or achieve something, no matter what the cost or consequences (*adj* **do'-or-die'**); **do out** (*colloq*) to clean (a room, etc) thoroughly; **do out of** to deprive of by cheating; **do over** to do again, repeat (*US*); to cover over, eg with paint; to beat up (*slang*); **do's and don'ts** advice or rules for action, *esp* in particular circumstances; **do someone proud** (*colloq*) to make someone feel flattered; to treat lavishly; **do something**, etc **for** to improve, enhance; **do to death** to murder; to repeat too often; **do up** to fasten up; to put up, make tidy, arrange, tie up; to redecorate; to apply cosmetics to; to dress, array oneself becomingly; to fatigue utterly; **do well** to be justified; to be wise or sensible to take a particular step; to prosper; **do with** to make use of; to meddle with; to get on with; **do without** not to be dependent on, to dispense with; **have done** to desist; to stop it; to have no more dealings; **have to do with** to have any sort of connection with; **have you done**? (*colloq*) are you finished?; **how do you do**? a conventional phrase used as a greeting; **I**, etc **can't be doing with** I, etc can't abide, have no patience with; **make do** see under **make**; **nothing doing** no; **that's done it** it is completed; (*interj* indicating dismay) it is spoiled, ruined; **what are you**, etc **doing with (something)**? why have you, etc got (something)?; **what's to do**? what is the matter? [OE *dōn*, *dyde*, *gedōn*; Du *doen*, Ger *tun*; connected with Gr *tithenai* to put, place]

do². See **doh**.

do (*abbrev*). See **ditto**.

DOA *abbrev*: dead on arrival.

doab *dō'äb*, *n* a tongue of land between two rivers (*esp* the Ganges and Jumna). [Pers *dōāb* two waters]

doable. See do¹.

doat, etc. See **dote**.

dob *dob*, (*Austr colloq*) *vt* (*usu* with *in*) to inform on or betray: — *prp* **dobb'ing**; *pa t* and *pa p* **dobbed**. — *n* **dobb'er**. — *n* **dobb'er-in**. [Br dialect *dob* to put down]

dob *abbrev*: date of birth.

dobbin *dob'in*, *n* a workhorse. [An altered dimin of *Robert*, traditionally used as a name for a horse]

dobby or **dobbie** *dob'i*, *n* a dotard; a brownie; an attachment to a loom for weaving small figures. [Perh from *Robert*]

dobchick *dob'chik*. Same as **dabchick** (see under **dab**¹).

Doberman *dō'bər-mən* or **Doberman pinscher** (*pin'shər*), *n* a breed of terrier, large and muscular with a smooth black and tan coat, and long forelegs. — Also **Dobermann (pinscher)**. [*Dobermann*, the first breeder, and Ger *Pinscher* a type of terrier]

dobhash *dō'bash*, *n* an interpreter. [Hindi *dōbāshī*, *dūbhāshiya*, from *dō*, *dū* two, and *bhāshā* language]

Dobro® *dō'brō*, *n* an acoustic steel guitar with metallic resonator, of a type *usu* laid flat on the knee to play, particularly associated with country music and producing a wavering sound.

Dobson unit *dob'sən ū-nit*, *n* a unit of measurement of the ozone layer, expressed in terms of its hypothetical thickness at sea-level pressure, 100 Dobson units representing a thickness of one millimetre. [G M B *Dobson* (1889–1976), English meteorologist]

DOC *abbrev*: *Denominazione di Origine Controllata* (*Ital*), the Italian equivalent of appellation contrôlée (qv); District Officer Commanding.

doc *dok*, *n* a familiar contraction of **doctor**.

docent *dō'sənt*, *dō-sent'*, (*US*) *n* a teacher or lecturer at a college or university. [From Ger, see **privat-dozent**]

Docetism *dō-sē'tizm*, *n* a 2c heresy, that Christ's body was only a semblance, or else of ethereal substance. — *n* **Do'cēte** or **Docē'tist** a holder of this belief: — *pl* **Docē'tae** (*-tē*) or **Docētists**. — *adj* **Docetic** (*-sēt'* or *-set'*) or **Docetist'ic**. [Gr *dokēsis* a phantom, semblance, from *dokeein* to seem]

DOCG *abbrev*: *Denominazione di Origine Controllata Garantita* (*Ital*), a designation of wines, guaranteeing quality, strength, etc.

doch-an-doris, **doch-an-dorach**. See **deoch-an-doruis**.

dochmius *dok'mi-əs*, *n* (*prosody*) a foot of five syllables, typically with first and fourth short, the rest long. — *adj* **doch'miac** or **dochmī'acal**. [L, from Gr *dochmios*]

docht. See **dow**².

docile *dō'sīl* or (*US*) *dos'il*, *adj* easy to teach or train; willing to learn; easily managed, obedient, compliant. — *n* **docibil'ity**. — *adj* (*obs*) **do'cible**. — *n* **doc'ibleness** or **docil'ity** (*-sil'*). [Fr, from L *docilis*, from *docēre* to teach]

docimasy *dos'i-mə-si*, *n* scrutiny; application of tests; assaying; examination of drugs. — *adj* **docimastic** (*-mas'tik*). — *n* **docimol'ogy** the art of assaying. [Gr *dokimasiā* examination, from *dokimazein* to test]

dock¹ *dok*, *n* a polygonaceous weed (genus *Rumex*) with large leaves and a long root. — *n* **dock'en** (*Scot*, perh *orig pl*) a dock. — **dock'-cress** the nipplewort. [OE *docce*]

dock² *dok*, *vt* to cut short; to curtail; to cut off the whole or part of (an animal's tail); to cut the tail off (an animal); to clip; to reduce (someone's pay), or deduct (a certain amount) from it. — *n* the part of a tail left after clipping; the rump (*Scot*). [ME *dok*, prob from ON *dokkr* stumpy tail]

dock³ *dok*, *n* (often used in *pl*) an artificial basin for the reception of vessels and cargo; the waterway between two wharves or two piers; a wharf or pier; in a railway station, the place of arrival and departure of a train; in the theatre, a space for storing scenery. — *vt* to embed in sand or ooze (*obs*; *Shakesp*); to place in a dock; to bring into dock; to equip with docks; to join (spacecraft) together in space. — *vi* to enter a dock: to join together in space. — *n* **dock'age** accommodation in docks for ships; dock-dues. — *n* **dock'er** a dockside labourer whose job is to load and unload ships. — *n* **dock'ing**. — *n* **dockizā'tion** or **-s-**. — *vt* **dock'ize** or **-ise** to convert into docks. — **dock'-dues** payments for use of a dock; **dock'-la'bourer** a docker; **dock'land** a district round about docks; **dock'-master** the person superintending a dock; **dock'side** the area alongside a dock; **dock'-warrant** a warehouse receipt; **dock'yard** a naval establishment with docks, building-slips, stores, etc. — **dry dock** a dock from which the water can be pumped, in order to effect repairs to the underside of a ship (*vt* **dry'-dock** to put in dry dock). — **in the dock** (*facetious*; of a vehicle) undergoing repairs and so unavailable for use. [Origin obscure; cf ODu *dokke*]

dock⁴ *dok*, *n* the enclosure for the accused in a court of law. — **in the dock** on trial in a court of law; under attack, facing criticism (with *for*). [Flem *dok* cage, hatch, sty]

docken. See **dock**¹.

docket *dok'it*, *n* a summary of the contents of a document, etc; a bill or ticket affixed to anything indicating its contents; a label; a list or register of cases in court, or of legal judgements, or (*US*) business to be transacted; an official permit to buy; a customhouse certificate of payment. — *vt* to make a summary of the contents of a document, etc; to enter in a book; to mark the contents of papers on the back; to fix a label to: — *pr p* **dock'eting**; *pa t* and *pa p* **dock'eted**. — Also **docquet** (as if French). [Perh a dimin of **dock** to curtail]

Doc Martens® *dok mär'tənz, n pl* a make of lace-up, *esp* black leather, boots with light thick resilient soles.

doctor *dok'tər, n* a licensed medical practitioner; a dentist (*NAm*); a veterinary surgeon (*NAm*); a mender or repairer of something; a name for various contrivances for removing defects or superfluities in manufacture; a person who has received a doctorate from a university (or the Archbishop of Canterbury), the most senior academic degree in any subject (*orig* implying competency to teach); a learned man, *esp* a teacher (*archaic*); one of a small number of *esp* revered early ecclesiastical writers (also **Doctor of the Church**); a cleric especially skilled in theology or ecclesiastical law; a ship's cook or camp-cook (*slang*); in some warm countries, a cool sea-breeze conducive to health; material used to sophisticate, refine, adjust, etc something; brown sherry (*old slang*); counterfeit coin (*old slang*); (in *pl*) loaded dice (*old slang*); a fish, the sea-surgeon; a type of angler's fly. — *vt* to treat, as a doctor does; to patch up, repair; to sophisticate, tamper with, falsify; to address as doctor; to confer a doctor's degree upon; to spay, castrate (*colloq*). — *vi* to practise medicine. — *adj* **doc'toral** relating to the academic degree of doctor. — *n* **doc'torand** a candidate for the doctorate. — *vt* **doc'torate** to confer the degree of doctor upon. — *n* the academic degree of doctor. — *n* **doc'toress** or **doc'tress** (*facetious*) a female doctor; a doctor's wife. — *adj* **doctorial** (*-tō'ri-əl* or *-tö'ri-əl*). — *adj* appropriate to a doctor, showing a doctor's skill or concern. — *adj* **doc'torly** — *n* **doc'torship**. — **doc'tor-fish** a sea-surgeon; **Doctors' Commons** before the establishment of the Divorce Court and Probate Court in 1857, the college of the doctors of civil law in London, incorporated by royal charter in 1768; **doctor's stuff** medicine. — **go for the doctor** (*Austr colloq*) to make an all-out effort, give one's all; **what the doctor ordered** (*colloq*) the very thing that's needed. [L, a teacher, from *docēre* to teach]

doctrinaire *dok-tri-nār', n* an unpractical theorist, disposed to carry principles to logical but unworkable extremes; in France, in 1815–30, one of a school who desired constitutional government. — *adj* theoretical; preoccupied with theory, inclined to carry principles to logical but unworkable extremes; impractical; dogmatic. — *n* and *adj* **doctrinā'rian** doctrinaire. — *n* **doctrinair'ism** or **doctrinā'rianism** blind adhesion to one-sided principles. [Fr, from LL *doctrīnārius*]

doctrine *dok'trin, n* teaching (*archaic*); a body of religious, political, etc teaching; a guiding principle, belief or precept. — *adj* **doctrinal** (*dok-trī'nl* or *dok'tri-nl*). — *adv* **doctri'nally** (or *dok'*). [L *doctrīna*, from *docēre* to teach]

docudrama *dok'ū-drä-mə, n* a play or film reproducing real events and characters. [*docu*mentary *drama*]

document *dok'ū-mənt, n* a paper, *esp* of an official character, affording information, proof or evidence of anything; evidence, proof (*archaic*); instruction (*Spenser*, etc); warning (*obs*). — *vt* (also *-ment'*) to furnish (eg a ship) with documents; to support or prove by documents or evidence. — *adj* **documental** (*-ment'*) documentary. — *n* **document'alist** a specialist in documentation; a person who collects and classifies documents. — *adv* **documentar'ily**. — *n* **documen'tarist** a person who makes documentaries. — *n* **documentarizā'tion** or **-s-**. — *vt* and *vi* **document'arize** or **-ise** to present in, or make documentaries. — *adj* **document'ary** relating to or found in documents; (of films, TV programmes, etc) aiming at presenting reality, presenting facts not fiction. — *n* a film or radio or TV programme about real people or events, without fictional colouring or professional actors. — *n* **documentā'tion** instruction (*archaic*); preparation, setting forth, or use of documentary evidence and authorities; documents or other material provided in support, amplification or authentication; (in fiction) realistic reproduction of records, real or supposed; the written information on the structure and operation of hardware or software (*comput*). — **document reader** (*comput*) a form of optical character reader which converts the characters into code and feeds them automatically into the computer. [Fr, from L *documentum*, from *docēre* to teach]

DOD (*US*) *abbrev*: Department of Defense.

dod[1] *dod*, (*obs* or *dialect*) *vt* to cut the hair of; to poll; to pollard; to clip. — *n* (*Scot*) a rounded hilltop, *esp* a shoulder of a greater hill. — *adj* **dodd'ed** polled; hornless; pollard. — *n* **dodd'y** (*Scot*) a hornless cow. [ME *dodden*]

dod[2] *dod*, (*Scot*) *n* a slight fit of ill-humour; (in *pl*; often with *the*) the sulks. — *adj* **dodd'y**. [Gaelic *dod* peevishness]

dod[3] *dod, n* an old or archaic minced form of **God**, used in oaths.

dod[4]. See **daud**.

doddard. See **doddered**.

dodder[1] *dod'ər, n* a leafless, twining, pale parasitic plant (genus *Cuscuta*) of or related to the convolvulus family. [ME *doder*; cf Ger *Dotter*]

dodder[2] *dod'ər, vi* to shake, to tremble, to totter or progress unsteadily, as a result of age; to potter; to ramble in talk; to be decrepit in mind or body. — *n* **dodd'erer** (*derog*) a feeble, senile person. — *adj* **dodd'ering** (*derog*) decrepit in body and feeble in mind, senile. — *adj* **dodd'ery** unsteady with age. [Perh connected with **doddered**]

doddered or (*obs*) **doddard** *dod'ərd, adj* perhaps *orig* pollard; decayed with loss of branches. [Cf **dod**[1]]

doddipoll. See **doddypoll**.

doddle *dod'l*, (*colloq*) *n* something very easily accomplished. [Poss from **dodder**[2]]

doddy. See **dod**[1,2].

doddypoll or **doddipoll** *dod'i-pōl*, (*obs*) *n* a blockhead. — Also **dottipoll**. [Appar **dote** and **poll**]

dodeca- *dō-dek-ə-, combining form* denoting twelve. — *n* **dodec'agon** (Gr *gōniā* an angle) a plane figure with twelve angles and sides. — *n pl* **Dodecagyn'ia** (*-jin'i-ə*; Gr *gynē* a woman, a female) in some classes of the Linnaean classification, an order of plants with twelve styles. — *adj* **dodecagyn'ian** or **dodecag'ynous** (*-aj'i-nəs*). — *n* **dodecahedron** (-hē'dron; Gr *hedrā* a seat) a solid figure, having twelve faces (equal pentagons in a *regular* dodecahedron, rhombs in a *rhombic* dodecahedron). — *adj* **dodecahē'dral**. — *n pl* **Dodecan'dria** (Gr *anēr*, *andros* a man, male) a Linnaean class of plants, having twelve stamens. — *adj* **dodecan'drous**. — *adj* **dodecaphon'ic** (*music*; Gr *phōnē* voice) twelve-tone. — *n* **dodecaph'onism** twelve-tone music. — *n* **dodecaph'onist** a composer or admirer of twelve-tone music. — *n* **dodecaph'ony**. — *adj* **dodecastyle** (*dō'dek-ə-stīl* or *dō-dek'ə-stīl*; *archit*; Gr *stȳlos* a pillar) having twelve columns in front. — *n* a portico so built. — *n* **dodecasyll'able** (*prosody*) a line of twelve syllables. — *adj* **dodecasyllab'ic**. [Gr *dōdeka* twelve]

dodge *doj, vi* to start aside or shift about, to move out of the way of a blow, etc; to evade or use mean tricks; to shuffle or quibble; (in change-ringing) to make two bells change order in the sequence (*bell-ringing*). — *vt* to evade (a blow, etc) by a sudden shift of place or position; to evade by astuteness or deceit. — *n* an evasion; a trick, ruse, stratagem; a quibble; an instance of dodging (*bell-ringing*). — *n* **dodg'er** a person who dodges, a shirker; a clever trickster; a screen on a ship's bridge for shelter in rough weather; food, *esp* bread (*dialect* and *Austr colloq*); an advertising leaflet (*US*). — *n* **dodg'ery** trickery. — *n* **dodg'ing** (*image technol*) manipulation of the light projected through a negative by an enlarger to lighten or darken selected parts of the resultant print. — *adj* **dodg'y** artful, tricky; difficult to do or carry out; risky, tricky; uncertain, unstable, unreliable. — **dodge the column** (*slang*) to evade one's duties. [Origin obscure]

Dodgems® *doj'əmz, n* (also without *cap*) a fairground amusement in which drivers of small electric cars within an enclosure try to bump others without being bumped. — *n* **Dodgem**® one of these cars.

dodkin *dod'kin, n* a doit. — Also **doit'kin**. [**doit**]

dodman *dod'mən*, (*dialect*) *n* a snail. [Origin unknown]

dodo *dō'dō, n* a clumsy flightless bird, about the size of a turkey (native of Mauritius) which became extinct about the end of the 17c; an old-fashioned or stupid person (*colloq*): — *pl* **do'does** or **do'dos**. [Port *doudo* silly]

Dodonaean *dō-dō-nē'ən, adj* pertaining to *Dodona* in Epirus, or its oracle sacred to Zeus, situated in a grove of oaks. — Also **Dodō'nian**.

DOE *abbrev*: Department of Energy (*US*); Department of the Environment.

Doe *dō, n* **John Doe** and **Jane Doe** names for unidentified male and female characters, *esp* in US detective stories, films. — *n* **John Doe** and **Richard Roe**, imaginary plaintiff and opponent in the old legal action for ejectment, proverbial as a legal fiction.

doe *dō, n* the female of the smaller deer such as the fallow deer or roe-deer; extended to the female of antelope, kangaroo, rabbit, hare, and some other animals. — *adj* **doe'-eyed** having large, dark eyes like those of a deer. — **doe'-skin** the skin of a female fallow deer; a smooth, close-woven, woollen cloth. [OE *dā*; Dan *daa*, deer]

doek *do͝ok*, (*SAfr*) *n* a square cloth for tying round the head, worn by African women. [Afrik, cloth]

doen, doer, does, doest, doeth. See **do**[1].

doff *dof, vt* to take off, remove (a piece of one's clothing); to put off; to lift (one's hat) in greeting someone. — *n* **doff'er** part of a carding machine that strips the cotton from the cylinder when carded; a person who removes full bobbins from a machine. [**do**[1] and **off**]

DOG *abbrev*: Directory of Opportunities for Graduates.

dog[1] *dog, n* a wild or domestic animal of the genus (*Canis*) which includes the wolf and fox; the domestic species, diversified into a large number of breeds; a male of this and other species; a mean scoundrel; a term of contempt for a man or boy; generally, a fellow (eg *a jolly dog*); either of the two constellations, the Greater and the Lesser Dog (Canis Major and Minor); an andiron; a hook for holding logs; a gripping appliance of various kinds; a cock, eg of a gun; a dogfish; a prairie dog; heavy ostentation (*slang*); (in *pl*) greyhound races (*colloq*); a failure, something less than satisfactory (*NAm colloq*); a boring or unattractive woman (*slang*). — *adj* and as *combining form* of dogs; male (*opp* to *bitch*); spurious, base, inferior (as in *dog Latin*). — *adv esp* as *combining form* utterly. — *vt* to follow like a dog; to track and watch constantly; to worry, plague, infest; to hunt with dogs; to fasten with a dog: — *pr p* **dogg'ing**; *pa t* and *pa p* **dogged'**. — *adj* **dogg'ed** doglike; stubbornly persevering or determined; sullen; pertinacious. — *adv* (*slang*) very. — *adv* **dogg'edly**. — *n* **dogg'edness**. — *n* **dogg'er** someone who dogs. — *n* **dogg'ery** doggish ways or doings; dogs collectively; rabble; a drinking resort (*US*). — *n* **dogg'ess** (*facetious*) a bitch. — *n* **dogg'iness**. — *n* **dogg'ing** shooting with dogs; following like a dog. — *adj* **dogg'ish** doglike; characteristic of dogs; churlish; brutal. — *adv* **dogg'ishly**. — *n* **dogg'ishness**. — *adj* **dogg'y** fond of dogs; of, for or characteristic of, a dog or dogs; dashing, beauish. — Also *n* (also **dogg'ie**) *dimin* of **dog**. — *n* **dog'ship** the quality or personality of a dog. — **dog'-ape** a baboon (from the shape of its head); **dog'bane** or **dog's' bane** a plant (*Apocynum*) said to be poisonous to dogs; **dog'-bee** (*obs*) a drone; **dog'-belt** a broad belt put round the waist for hauling; **dog'berry** the fruit of the wild cornel or dogwood; extended to many other plants and their fruits; (with *cap*) a pompous, muddle-headed fellow (from the character in Shakespeare's play *Much Ado About Nothing*); **Dog'berrydom**; **Dog'berryism** an utterance worthy of Dogberry, ie wordy consequential blundering and malapropism; **dog'-bis'cuit** a hard kind of biscuit for feeding dogs; **dog'bolt** *orig* a kind of arrow; a contemptible fellow (*obs*); **dog'cart** a two-wheeled horse-vehicle with seats back to back, *orig* used to carry sporting dogs. — *adj* **dog'-cheap** extremely cheap. — **dog'-collar** a collar for a dog; a clerical collar fastened behind; a woman's stiff collar or neck ornament; **dog'-crab** a very small crab; **dog'-dai'sy** the common daisy; the ox-eye daisy; **dog'days** the period when the Dogstar rises and sets with the sun (*usu* reckoned 3 July to 11 August) — erroneously supposed to be the time when dogs are specially liable to hydrophobia; **dog'-ear** a dog's-ear; a fold at the corner of a page in a book. — *adj* **dog'-eared** (of pages of a book) turned down like the ears of a dog; hence, shabby and scruffy. — **dog'-eat-dog'** a ruthless pursuit of one's own interests, savage self-concern. — Also *adj*. — **dog'-end** (*slang*) a cigarette-end. — *adj* **dog'-faced**. — **dog'-fancier** a breeder or seller of dogs; **dog fennel** see **dog's fennel** below; **dog'fight** a fight between dogs; any confused fight or mêlée; a fight between fighter aircraft, *esp* at close quarters; **dog'fish** a small shark of various kinds; **dog'fox** a male fox; **dog'-grass** or **dog'-wheat** couch-grass or a related species; **dog'gy-bag** a bag used by diners to carry home leftover food from a restaurant (for their pets); **dog'gy-paddle** or **dog'-paddle** a simple swimming stroke with alternate arm movements, similar to the swimming action of a dog; **dog'-hand'ler** a policeman, etc in charge of a specially trained dog; **dog'-head** the hammer of a gunlock; **dog'-hip** or **-hep** (*dialect*) hip or fruit of the dog rose; **dog'hole** a hole fit only for a dog; a wretched dwelling; **dog'-house** a dog-kennel (*esp US*); a place of disgrace (*fig*); **dog'-kennel**; **dog'-Lat'in** spurious or sham Latin; **dog'-leech** (*obs*) a person who treated diseases of dogs; **dog'-leg** a sharp bend, like that in a dog's hindleg; something bent in that way, eg (*golf*) a hole with a bent fairway. — *adj* (also **dog'-legged**) bent like a dog's hind leg; (of stairs) having successive flights running opposite ways without a well-hole; (of a fence) made of poles laid on cross-shaped supports. — *vi* to become, or be bent like a dog's leg. — *vt* to make such a bend in. — **dog'-lett'er** *r* (from its growling sound); **dog'-louse**; **dog-paddle** see **doggy-paddle**; **dog'-pars'ley** fool's parsley; **dog'-per'iwinkle** a species of *Purpura* (also **dog'-whelk**); **dog' rose** a species of wild rose (*Rosa canina*); **dog's age** (*colloq*) a long time; **dog'-salmon** keta and humpback, Pacific species of salmon; **dog's'-body** (*orig naut slang*) pease-pudding; a dish of biscuit, water and sugar; a junior naval (or other) officer; (*usu* **dogs'body**) a general drudge; someone who does menial, monotonous work for others; **dog's breakfast** or **dog's dinner** anything very untidy; **dog's chance** a bare chance; no chance; **dog's disease** (*Austr colloq*) any minor ailment, eg influenza; **dog's'-ear** a fold at the corner of a page in a book. — *vt* to fold at the corner. — **dog's'-fenn'el** mayweed; **dog'shores** pieces of timber used to shore up a vessel before launching. — *adj* **dog'-sick'** thoroughly sick, sick as a dog. — **dog'skin** leather made of or in imitation of dog's skin. — Also *adj*. — **dog'sled** (*esp NAm*) or **dog sledge** a sledge pulled by a team of dogs; **dog'sleep** a light sleep, very easily broken; **dog sleigh** a dogsled; **dog's life** a wretched, miserable life; **dog's'-meat** scraps and refuse sold as food for dogs; **dog's'-mer'cury** a euphorbiaceous plant (*Mercurialis perennis*); **dog's'-nose** gin and beer, or similar mixture; **dog'-soldier** a soldier going on all-fours (*military slang*); **dog's'-tail-grass'** a common British pasture grass (*Cynosurus*); **Dog'star** Sirius, in the constellation of the Great Dog, the brightest star in the heavens, giving name to the dogdays; **dog's'-tongue** hound's-tongue, a plant of the borage family; **dog's'-tooth** a broken-check pattern used extensively in the weaving of tweeds; **dog's-tooth-grass'** a seaside sand-binding grass (*Cynodon*); **dog's-tooth violet** see **dog-tooth violet** below; **dog tag** a metal identity disc for a dog or (*colloq*) for a soldier; **dog'-tick**. — *adj* **dog'-tired'** or (*Shakesp*) **dog'-wea'ry** completely worn out. — **dog'tooth** a moulding in later Norman architecture, consisting of a series of ornamental square pyramids; a canine tooth; **dog'tooth-spar'** calcite crystals like canine teeth; **dog'tooth-vi'olet** or **dog's-tooth violet** any plant of the liliaceous genus *Erythronium*; **dog'town** a prairie-dog community; **dog'-trick** a low trick; **dog'trot** a gentle trot like a dog's; a jogtrot; **dog'vane** (*naut*) a small vane to show direction of wind; **dog'-vi'olet** a scentless wild violet, *esp Viola canina*; **dog'-watch** (*naut*) on shipboard, a watch 4–6 pm or 6–8 pm, consisting of two hours only, instead of four; **dog-weary** see **dog-tired** above; **dog-wheat** see **dog-grass**; **dog'-whelk'** a gasteropod of the genus *Nassa*, like a small whelk; a dog-periwinkle; **dog'wood'** the wild cornel (*Cornus* (or *Swida*) *sanguinea*), a small tree with white flowers and purple berries, the shoots and leaves turning red in autumn; extended to many other shrubs and trees. — **dog in the manger** a person who will not let others enjoy what they themselves have no use for; **dogs of war** (*fig*) troops, aggressors, mercenaries, warlike people (from *Shakesp*); **go to the dogs** to be ruined; **hot dog** a roll containing a hot sausage; **like a dog's dinner** (*slang*) very smart, dressed up flamboyantly, overdressed; **not to lead the life of a dog** to lead a life so wretched that even a dog would not be content with it; **put on the dog** (*US*) to put on airs, behave showily; **throw, give** or **send to the dogs** to throw away or abandon. [Late OE *docga* ; cf Du *dog* a mastiff, and Ger *Dogge*]

dog[2] *dog*, (*obs*) *n* used in oaths for **God**. — *interj* **doggone** (*dog-gon'*) (*US*) expressing vexation (*adj* and *adv* **doggone'** or **doggoned'**), from **dog on (it)**, God damn (it).

doge *dōj*, or *dō'jā*, *n* formerly the title of the chief magistrate in republican Venice and Genoa. — *n* **dogaressa** (*dō-gä-res'a*) a doge's wife. — *n* **dogate** (*dō'gāt*). — *n* **dogeate** (*dō'jāt*). — **doge'ship**. [Ital (Venetian dialect) for *duce* duke, from L *dux* a leader]

dogged, etc. See **dog**[1].

dogger[1] *dog'ər*, *n* a two-masted Dutch fishing-vessel. — **dogg'erman**. [Du]

dogger[2] *dog'ər*, (*geol*) *n* a concretion, *esp* of ironstone; a sandy ironstone or ferruginous sandstone; (with *cap*) part of the Middle Jurassic. [Origin uncertain; a northern word]

dogger[3]. See **dog**[1].

doggerel *dog'ər-əl*, *n* irregular measures in burlesque poetry, so named in contempt; poor quality comic or trivial verse; nonsense. — *adj* irregular in rhythm, mean. — Also **dogg'rel**. [Origin unknown]

doggery ... to ... **doggishness**. See **dog**[1].

doggo *dog'ō*, (*colloq*) *adv* quiet and hidden, as *esp* in the phrase *to lie doggo* until it is safe, appropriate, etc to emerge. [Poss from **dog**[1]]

doggy. See **dog**[1].

dogie or **dogy** *dō'gi*, (*US*) *n* a motherless calf. [Origin obscure]

dogma *dog'mə*, *n* a settled opinion; a principle or belief, or code of belief, principles or doctrines; a doctrine laid down with authority. — *adj* **dogmatic** (*-mat'ik*) or **dogmat'ical** pertaining to a dogma; asserting a thing as if it were a dogma; asserting positively; overbearing. — *adv* **dogmat'ically**. — *n sing* **dogmat'ics** (*theol*) the statement of Christian doctrines, systematic theology. — **dog'matism** dogmatic or positive assertion of opinion. — *n* **dog'matist** a person who makes positive assertions. — *vi* **dog'matize** or **-ise** (*-mə-tīz*) to state one's opinion dogmatically or arrogantly. — *n* **dog'-matizer** or **-s-**. — *n* **dogmatol'ogy** the science of dogma. — *adj* **dog'matory**. [Gr *dogma, -atos* an opinion, from *dokeein* to think, seem]

dogy. See **dogie**.

DoH *abbrev*: Department of Health.

doh or **do** *dō*, (*music*) *n* in sol-fa notation, a syllable representing the first note of the scale: — *pl* **dohs, dos** or **do's**. — **up to high doh** (*colloq*) in a state of great excitement or agitation. [Perh L *Do*minus (Lord), *do* replacing the syllable *ut* used by the Italian originator]

dohyo *dō'yō*, (in sumo wrestling) the ring or marked area in which the wrestlers compete. [Jap]

DoI *abbrev*: Department of Industry.

doilt *doilt*, (*Scot*) *adj* crazy, foolish. — Also **doiled**. [Origin obscure]

doily *doi'li*, *n orig* an old kind of woollen fabric (*obs*); a small lace or lacy paper, etc ornamented napkin, often laid on or under dishes. — Also **doy'ley** or **doy'ly**. [From *Doily* or *Doyley*, a famous haberdasher]

doing. See **do**[1].

doit *doit*, *n* a small obsolete Dutch coin; a thing of little or no value. — Also **doit'kin**. [Du *duit*]

doited or **doitit** *doit'id, -it*, (*Scot*) *adj* in dotage, senile. [Origin obscure]

dojo *dō'jō n* a place where judo or karate, etc are taught or practised: — *pl* **do'jos**. [Jap]

dol. *abbrev*: dolce (*music*); dollar.

dolabriform *dō-lab'ri-form*, *adj* like a hatchet or cleaver. [L *dolābra* a cleaver, and *fōrma* form]

Dolby® *dol'bi*, *n* an electronic device which reduces the amount of extraneous noise on recorded or broadcast sound. [R *Dolby* (born 1933), its inventor]

dolce *dol'chā*, *adj* and *adv* sweet or sweetly (*esp* of music). — *n* a soft-toned organ-stop. — *adv* **dolcemente** (*-men'tā*; *music*) softly and sweetly. — **dolce far niente** (*fär nē-en'tā*; *Ital*) literally, sweet doing-nothing, pleasant idleness; **dolce vita** (*vē'ta*; *Ital*, sweet life) a life of wealth, pleasure and self-indulgence. [Ital, from L *dulcis*]

doldrums *dol'drəmz*, *n pl* those parts of the ocean near the equator where calms and baffling winds prevail (*naut*); a state of inactivity or stagnation; low spirits. [Prob connected with obsolete *dold* stupid, or *dol*, dull]

dole[1] *dōl*, *n* a share (*archaic*); a dealing out; something given in charity (*old*); state pay to unemployed (*colloq*); a small portion. — *vt* (*usu* with *out*) to deal out in small portions. — **on the dole** (*colloq*) living on unemployment or other benefit. [OE *dāl*; related to **deal**[1]]

dole[2] *dōl*, *n* pain or grief (*archaic* and *dialect*); heaviness at heart (*archaic* and *poetic*). — Also **dool** (*dōōl*) and (*obs*) **doole**. — *adj* **dole'ful** full of dole or grief; melancholy. — *adv* **dole'fully**. — *n* **dole'fulness**. — *adj* **do'lent** (*obs*). — *adj* **dole'some** dismal. — *adv* **dole'somely**. [OFr *doel* (Fr *deuil*) grief, from L *dolēre* to feel pain]

dole[3] *dōl*, *n* guile (*obs*); criminal intention (*Scots law*). [L *dolus*, from Gr *dolos* guile]

dolerite *dol'ər-it*, (*geol*) *n* a basic igneous rock like basalt in composition but coarser grained. — *adj* **dolerit'ic**. [Fr *dolérite*, from Gr *doleros* deceptive]

dolia. See **dolium**.

dolicho- *dol-i-kō-*, *combining form* denoting long. — *n* **dolichocephal** (*-sef'əl*) a long-headed person. — *adj* **dolichocephalic** (*-sif-al'ik*; Gr *kephalē* the head) long-headed, ie having a breadth of skull (from side to side) less than 75 (or 78) per cent of the length (front to back) (*opp* to *brachycephalic*). — Also **dolichoceph'alous**. — *n* **dolichoceph'aly** or **dolichoceph'alism**. — *n* **Dolichos** (*dol'i-kos*; Gr, long, also a podded plant) a genus of long-podded leguminous plants allied to the haricot; (without *cap*) any plant of the genus. — *n* **Dolichosaurus** (*-sö'rəs*; Gr *sauros* lizard) the typical genus of **Dolichosau'ria**, a group of Cretaceous fossil reptiles. — *n* **Dolichotis** (*-kō'tis*; Gr *ous, ōtos* the ear) a genus of long-eared S American rodents — the mara or Patagonian hare. [Gr *dolichos* long]

dolichurus *dol-i-kū'rəs*, (*prosody*) *n* a dactylic hexameter with a redundant syllable at the end. [Gr *dolichouros* long-tailed]

dolina *dō-lēn'ə*, or **doline** *dō-lēn'*, (*geol*) *n* a swallow-hole. [Russ *dolina* valley, plain]

dolium *dō'li-əm*, (*antiq*) *n* a Roman earthenware jar for wine, oil or grain, etc: — *pl* **dō'lia**. [L *dōlium*]

doll[1] *dol*, *n* a puppet; a toy in the form of a human being, *esp* a baby; an over-dressed and rather silly woman; a young woman, *esp* (*NAm*) an attractive one (*slang*); the smallest or pet pig in a litter. — *vi* and *vt* to dress (often with *up*) in a showy way. — *n* **doll'dom**. — *n* **doll'hood**. — *n* **doll'iness**. — *adj* **doll'ish**. — *n* **doll'ishness**. — *n* **doll'y** (dimin of **doll**) an attractive but rather silly young girl (also **dolly girl** or **dolly bird**); formerly, a dolly-mop (qv); a slow, easy catch (*cricket*) or shot. — Also *adj*. — **doll's'-house** or (*US*) **doll'-house**; **doll'y-mixture** a mixture of small brightly-coloured sweets; one of these sweets; **doll'y-mop** (*old slang*) a slut; a prostitute; **doll'y-shop** (*hist*) a marine store (a low pawn-shop) often having a black doll as sign. [Prob from *Dolly*, familiar dimin of *Dorothy*]

doll² *dol*, (*horse-racing*) *n* a hurdle used as a barrier on a race-course to exclude certain areas from use by riders. — **doll off** or **doll out** to mark off by means of dolls.

dollar *dol'ər*, *n* a silver coin (= 100 cents), the standard unit of money of many countries, *incl* the US, Canada, Australia, New Zealand, Mexico, Hong-Kong, etc; a thaler; five shillings (*old slang*). — *adj* **doll'ared**. — *n* **dollariza'tion** or **-s-**. — *adj* **doll'arless**. — *n* **dollaroc'racy**. — *n* **doll'arship**. — **dollar area** those countries as a whole whose currencies are linked to the US dollar; **dollar diplomacy** diplomacy dictated by financial interests; diplomacy that employs financial weapons to increase political power; **dollar gap** the excess of imports from a dollar country over exports to it, necessitating settlement by dollar exchange or in gold. [Ger *T(h)aler* (LGer *daler*), short for *Joachimsthaler* because first coined at the silver-mines in Joachimsthal (Joachim's dale) in Bohemia]

dollop *dol'əp*, *n* a lump; a tuft of grass or weeds (*obs*); a rank patch in a field (*obs*). — Also **dall'op**. [Prob connected with Norw dialect *dolp* a lump]

dolly¹. See **doll¹**.

dolly² *dol'i*, *n* a complimentary offering of flowers, sweetmeats, etc on a tray. [Anglo-Ind, from Hindi *dālī*]

dolly³ *dol'i*, *n* an implement used to wash ore (*mining*); a wooden shaft attached to a disc with projecting arms, used for beating and stirring clothes in a washing-tub (*old*); a trolley, truck or platform on wheels or rollers; a tool for holding the head of a rivet. — *vt* to operate upon, yield or obtain with a dolly; to wheel or roll with a dolly; to beat with a hammer. — *adj* **doll'ied**. — *n* **doll'ier**. — **dolly camera** a camera moving on a dolly; **doll'y-shop** see under **doll¹**; **dolly shot** a shot taken with a dolly camera; **dolly switch** a switch (for an electric light, etc) consisting of a pivotal lever pushed up and down vertically; **doll'y-tub** a tub for washing clothes or ores with a dolly. [Prob from *Dolly*, the familiar form of *Dorothy*]

Dolly Varden *dol'i var'dən*, *n* a flowered muslin dress for women, with pointed bodice and tucked-up skirt; a large hat, one side bent downwards, abundantly trimmed with flowers; a large American fish of the char genus. [Named from a character in Dickens's novel *Barnaby Rudge*]

dolma *dol'mə*, *n* a vine or cabbage leaf with a savoury stuffing: — *pl* **dol'mas** or **dolmades** (Gr, *-mä'des*). [Turk]

dolman *dol'mən*, *n* a Turkish robe with slight sleeves and open in front; a hussar's jacket, worn like a cloak, with one or both sleeves hanging loose; a woman's mantle. — **dolman sleeve** a kind of sleeve which tapers from a very wide armhole to a tight wrist. [Turk *dōlāmān*]

dolmen *dol'mən*, *n* a stone table; a prehistoric structure, possibly a tomb, of erect unhewn stones, supporting a flattish stone. [Fr *dolmen*; usually explained as derived from Breton *dol*, *taol* table, and *men* stone; but *tolmēn* in Cornish meant hole of stone]

dolomite *dol'ə-mīt*, *n* a mineral, double carbonate of calcium and magnesium; a rock composed of that mineral, magnesian limestone. — *adj* **dolomitic** (*-mit'ik*). — *n* **dol'omitīzātion** or **-s-**. — *vt* **dol'omitize** or **-ise** to convert into dolomite. [After the French geologist D Guy de *Dolomieu* (1750–1801)]

dolour or (*NAm*) **dolor** *dol'ər*, *dōl'ər*, or (*hist*) *dul'ər*, (*poetic*) *n* pain; grief; anguish. — *adj* **dolorif'erous** or **dolori'fic** causing or conveying dolour, pain or grief. — *adv* **dolorō'sō** (Ital; *music*) in a soft and pathetic manner. — *adj* **dol'orous** full of pain or grief; doleful. — *adv* **dol'orously**. — *n* **dol'orousness**. [OFr, from L *dolēre* to grieve]

dolphin *dol'fin*, *n* any of a group of animals of the whale kind belonging to the family *Delphinidae*, about 2.5–3m (8 to 10 ft) long, with a beak-like snout; sometimes used loosely in the US to include the porpoise; either of two fish of the genus *Coryphaena* about 1.5m (5 ft) in length, *esp C. hippurus*, noted for the brilliancy of its colours when dying (also **dol'phin-fish**); (with *cap*) a northern constellation (see **Delphinus**); a buoy or pile for mooring; a structure of piles used to protect a harbour entrance, etc. — *n* **dolphinarium** (*-ā'ri-əm*) an aquarium for dolphins: — *pl* **dolphinā'riums** or **dolphinā'ria** (*-ə*). — *n* **dol'phinet** (*Spenser*) a female dolphin. — **dol'phin-fish** see **dolphin** above; **dol'phin-fly** a black aphis or plant-louse, destructive to beanplants. [OFr *daulphin*, from L *delphinus*, from Gr *delphīs*, *-phīnos*]

dols *abbrev*: dollars.

dolt *dōlt*, *n* a dull or stupid fellow. — *adj* **dolt'ish** dull; stupid. — *adv* **dolt'ishly**. — *n* **dolt'ishness**. [For **dulled**; see **dull**]

DOM *abbrev*: *Deo optimo maximo* (*L*), see **Deo**; Dominican Republic (IVR); *Dominus omnium magister* (*L*), God the master of all; dirty old man.

Dom¹ *dom*, *n* the Portuguese form of *Don* (see **don¹**); also a title given to certain Catholic dignitaries and members of some monastic orders, *esp* the Benedictine. [L *dominus* lord]

Dom² *abbrev*: Dominical; Dominican; Dominion; *Dominus* (*L*), Lord.

-dom *-dom* or *-dəm*, *sfx* forming nouns, denoting: dominion, power, state or condition; a group of people (with a specified characteristic, eg *officialdom*). [OE *dōm* judgement; Ger *-tum*]

domain *dō-mān'*, *n* what one is master of or has dominion over; an estate or territory that is owned or governed by a person, a family or a ruler; ownership; a public park or recreation area (*Austr* and *NZ*); the scope or range of any subject or sphere of knowledge; an aggregate to which a variable belongs (*math*). — *adj* **domain'al** or **domā'nial**. [Fr *domaine*, from L *dominicum*, from *dominus* a master]

domal *dōm'əl*, *adj* of or relating to a house, or dome. [L *domus* a house]

domatium *do-mā'sh(y)əm*, (*bot*) *n* a plant structure that harbours mites or other symbiotic organisms: — *pl* **domā'tia**. [Latinized form of Gr *dōmation*, dimin of *dōma* house]

Domdaniel *dom-dan'yəl*, (*literary*) *n* a hall under the sea inhabited by a sorcerer and his disciples (*Southey*); an infernal cave, den of iniquity generally (*Carlyle*). [Fr, from Gr *dōma Daniēl* house of Daniel; from Chavis and Cazotte's French continuation of the *Arabian Nights*]

dome¹ *dōm*, *n* a structure, *usu* hemispherical, raised above a large building; a large cupola; a cathedral (*obs*); a building, *esp* a great or stately building (*poetic*); anything approaching the form of a hemispherical vault, eg a head, the cover of a reverberatory furnace, the steam-chamber on a locomotive boiler or a clip-fastener that fits into a hold; a pair of crystal-faces parallel to a lateral axis, meeting in a rooflike edge (*crystallog*). — *vt* to cover with a dome; to make into the shape of a dome. — *vi* to become dome-shaped. — *adj* **domed** or **domical** (*dōm'* or *dom'*) having a dome. — *adj* **dōm'y**. [L *domus* a house; Fr *dôme*, Ital *duoma*, Ger *Dom*]

dome² (*Spenser*). Same as **doom**.

Domesday-book or **Doomsday-book** *dōōmz'dā-bŏŏk*, *n* a book compiled by order of William the Conqueror, containing a survey of all the lands in England, their value, owners, etc, so called from its authority in judgement (OE *dōm*) on the matters contained in it.

domestic *dō-*, *də-mes'tik*, *adj* belonging or relating to the home or family; remaining much at home, enjoying or accustomed to being at home; private; tame; not foreign. — *n* a servant in the house; (in *pl*) articles of home manufacture, *esp* homemade cotton cloths. — *adj* **domes'ticable** capable of being domesticated. — *adj* **domes'tical** (*archaic*). — *adv* **domes'tically**. — *vt* **domes'ticate** to make domestic or familiar; to tame. — *adj* **domes'ticated** adapted to or content with home life and activities; tamed. — *n* **domesticā'tion**. — *n* **domes'ticātor**. — *n* **domesticity** (*dō-* or *do-mis-tis'i-ti*) domestic or domesticated state; home life; (in *pl*) home conditions and arrangements. — *vt* **domesticize** or **-ise** domesticate. — **domestic architecture** the architecture of mansions, dwelling-houses, cottages, etc; **domestic economy** the principles of running a household efficiently; **domestic science** the household skills of cooking, sewing, etc; the older term for home economics (qv). [L *domesticus*, from *domus* a house]

domett *dom'ət* or *-it*, *n* a plain cloth with cotton warp and woollen weft. [Perh a proper name]

domical. See **dome**[1].

domicile *dom'i-sīl*, *-sil*, or **dom'icil** *dom'i-sil n* a dwelling-place, abode; a person's legally recognized place of residence. — *vt* **dom'icile** (*-sīl*) to establish in a fixed residence. — *adj* **dom'iciled**. — *adj* **domiciliary** (*-sil'*) of or relating to the domicile; dealing with or available to people in their own homes. — *vt* **domiciliāte** (*-sil'*) to establish in a permanent residence. — *n* **domiciliā'tion**. — **domiciliary visit** an authorized visit to a private house for the purpose of searching it; a visit made by a doctor, etc to a patient's or client's home. [Fr, from L *domicilium*, from *domus* a house]

dominant *dom'in-ənt*, *adj* prevailing; predominant; having a commanding position; of an ancestral character, appearing in the first generation of crossbred offspring to the exclusion of the alternative character in the other parent, which may yet be transmitted to later generations (*genetics*). — *n* the fifth above the tonic (*music*); a dominant gene or the character determined by it (*genetics*); one of the prevailing species in a plant or animal community. — *n* **dom'inance** or **dom'inancy** ascendancy; the state of being dominant. — *adv* **dom'inantly**. [L *dominans*, *-antis*, pr p of *dominārī* to be master]

dominate *dom'in-āt*, *vt* to be lord over; to have command or influence over, to govern; to prevail over; to tower over; to command a view of; to be the controlling position of; to be predominant in; to project one's personality, influence, etc strongly over. — Also *vi*. — *n* the Roman Empire in its later more avowedly absolute form. — *n* **dominā'tion** government; absolute authority; tyranny; (in *pl*) the angelic dominions (qv). — *adj* **dom'inative** governing; arbitrary (*rare*). — *n* **dom'inātor** a ruler or governor (*Shakesp*); a ruling influence. [L *dominārī*, *-ātus* to be master, from *dominus* a master, from *domāre* to tame]

dominee *dōō'mi-ni*, (*SAfr*) *n* a minister of the Dutch Reformed Church or any other Afrikaner church. [See **dominie**]

domineer *dom-in-ēr'*, *vi* (often with *over*) to rule imperiously; to command arrogantly; to be overbearing. — *adj* **domineer'ing** overbearing, authoritarian. [Prob through Du from OFr *dominer*, from L *dominārī*]

dominical *do-min'i-kl*, *adj* belonging to the Lord (as the Lord's Prayer or the Lord's Day). — **dominical letter** one of the first seven letters of the alphabet, used in calendars to mark the Sundays throughout the year. [LL *dominicālis*, from L *dominicus*, from *dominus* lord, master]

Dominican *do-min'i-kən*, *adj* belonging to St *Dominic* or to the Dominicans. — *n* a friar or monk of the order of St Dominic (founded in 1215), the *Fratres Predicatores*, or *Black Friars* (from their black mantle).

dominie *dom'i-ni*, *n* a schoolmaster, a tutor (*esp Scot*); a clergyman (*US dialect*). [L *domine*, vocative of *dominus* master]

dominion *də-min'yən*, *n* lordship; sovereignty; rule, power or authority; a domain or territory with one ruler, owner or government; a completely self-governing colony, not subordinate to but freely associated with the mother country; control; (in *pl*) a class of angelic spirits (Col 1. 16). — **Dominion Day** until 1983, the name of Canada Day (qv). [LL *dominiō*, *-ōnis*, from *dominus* master]

domino *dom'i-nō*, *n* a cape with a hood worn by a master or by a priest; a long cloak of black silk with a hood, used at masked balls, or its wearer; a mask covering the upper half of the face; one of the oblong pieces with which the game of **dom'inoes** (*-nōz*) is played, *usu* twenty-eight in number, divided into two compartments, each of which is a blank or marked with from one to six spots; a card game played in a similar way; the end; a mistake in performance (*music*; *colloq*): — *pl* **dom'inoes** or **dom'inos**. — *adj* (*surg*) involving a series of multiple transplant operations on different patients; (*obstetrics*) denoting antenetal and postnatal care, together with a hospital delivery supervised by one's own midwife. — **domino theory** the theory that one event sets off a series of similar events, thus exhibiting the **domino effect**, the fall of one domino standing on end causing the whole row to fall in turn. [Appar Sp *dominó*, *dómino*, in some way connected with L *dominus* master]

DOMS *abbrev*: Diploma in Ophthalmic Medicine and Surgery.

domy. See **dome**[1].

don[1] *don*, *n* (with *cap*) a Spanish title, corresponding to English Sir and Mr, formerly applied only to noblemen, now to all classes (*fem* **Doña** (*dōn'ya*), Italian form **Don'na**); a Spanish nobleman, a Spaniard; a fellow of a college or university; any member of the teaching staff of a college or university; an expert (*Austr* and *NZ*); a swell, adept (*colloq*). — *n* **dona** or **donah** (*dō'nə*) a sweetheart (corruption of **Doña** or **Donna**). — *adj* **donn'ish** pertaining to or acting like a college don. — *n* **donn'ism** self-importance. — *n* **don'ship** the rank or dignity of a don. — **Don Juan** (*hwän* or *jōō'ən*) a legendary Spanish licentious nobleman, subject of plays, poems, and operas in several European languages; an attractive libertine and profligate. [Sp, from L *dominus*]

don[2] *don*, *vt* to do or put on; to assume: — *pr p* **donn'ing**; *pa t* and *pa p* **donned**. [**do** and **on**]

Doña. See **don**[1].

dona, donah. See **don**[1].

Donat or **Donet** *dō'nət*, (*obs*) *n* a grammar, a primer. [OFr *donat*, from Aelius *Dōnātus*, author about AD358 of a long-famous Latin grammar]

donation *dō-nā'shən*, *n* an act of giving; that which is given, a gift of money or goods; the act by which a person freely transfers their title to anything to another (*law*). — *n* **dō'nary** a thing given to a sacred use. — *n* **dō'natary** (*Scots law*) a person to whom lands escheated to the crown are made over. — *vt* **dōnate'** (a back-formation from **donation**) to give as gift; to contribute, *esp* to charity. — *n* **dōnative** (or *don'*) a gift; a gratuity; a benefice presented by the founder or patron without reference to the bishop. — *adj* vested or vesting by donation. — *n* **dōnā'tor** a person who makes a gift, a donor. — *n* **dōn'atory** (or *don'*) a recipient. — *n* **dōnee'** the person to whom a gift is made. — *n* **dō'ning** (*colloq*; back-formation from **donor**) the act of donating (eg blood). — *n* **dō'nor** a giver; a benefactor; a person who (or animal which) provides blood, semen, or tissue or organs for use in transplant surgery; an impurity in semiconductor material which increases the conductivity by contributing electrons (*electronics*). — **donor card** a card carried by a person willing to have (sometimes specified) parts of his or her body used in transplant surgery in the event of his or her death;

donor insemination artificial insemination using semen from a donor. — **dona nobis** the last section of the mass, beginning *Dona nobis pacem* Give us peace. [Fr, from L *dōnāre*, *-ātum*, from *dōnum* a gift, from *dare* to give]

Donatist *dōn'*, *don'ə-tist*, *n* a member of an African Christian sect of the 4c and 5c, who protested against any diminution of the extreme reverence paid to martyrs, treated the lapsed severely, and rebaptized converts from the Catholic Church. — *n* **dōn'atism**. — *adj* **dōnatis'tic** or **donatis'tical**. [From *Dōnātus*, one of their leaders]

donder *don'ə*, (*SAfr slang*) *vt* to beat up, thrash. — *n* a scoundrel, rogue. [Afrik, to thrash, from Du *donderen* to swear, bully]

done. See **do**[1].

donee. See under **donation**.

doner kebab. See **kebab**.

Donet. See **Donat**.

dong[1] *dong*, *n* a deep ringing sound, such as that of a large bell. — Also *vi*. [Imit]

dong[2] *dong*, (*vulg*; *orig* and *chiefly US*) *n* the penis.

dong[3] *dong*, *n* the standard monetary unit of Vietnam.

donga *dong'gə*, (*orig SAfr*) *n* a gully made by soil erosion. [Zulu, a bank, side of a gully]

dongle *dong'gl*, *n* a device plugged into a computer which prevents the unauthorized use of software on a different machine.

doning. See **donation**.

donjon *dun'jən*, *n* a strong central tower in ancient castles, to which the garrison retreated when hard pressed. [A doublet of **dungeon**]

donkey *dong'ki*, *n* an ass; a stupid person; a person used by drug dealers to carry drugs being smuggled through customs (*slang*): — *pl* **don'keys**. — **donkey derby** one or more races by contestants on donkeys, eg at a fête; **don'key-en'gine** a small auxiliary engine; **donkey jacket** a strong jacket, with shoulders of leather or (*usu*) a substitute, and patch pockets; **don'key-man** (*-man*) a man in charge of a donkey; (*-mən*) in the merchant navy, (formerly) a man in charge of a donkey-engine, (*now*) a petty officer or senior rating in a ship's engine-room; **don'key-pump** an extra steam-pump; **donkey vote** (*Austr*) in a preferential system of voting, a vote accepting the order of candidates on the ballot paper; such votes collectively; **don'key-work** drudgery. — **argue** or **talk the hindlegs** (or **-leg**) **off a donkey** to argue or talk persistently and therefore *usu* persuasively; **donkey's years** a long time (a pun on *ears*). [Still regarded as slang in 1823; perh a double dimin of *dun*, from its colour; or from *Duncan*]

Donna. See under **don**[1].

donnard, **donnart**. See **donnered**.

donnat. See **donnot**.

donne. See under **do**[1].

donné or **donnée** *do'nā*, *n* a datum; basic assumption(s), as eg a given situation, on which a work of literature is founded; the main fact or condition determining the character and timing of an action: — *pl* **donn'és** or **donn'ées** (*-ā(z)*). [Fr]

donnered, **donnered**, **donnert**, **donnard** or **donnart** *don'ərd*, *-ərt*, (*Scot*) *adj* stupid; dull-witted.

Donnerwetter *don'ər-vet-ər*, (*Ger*) *n* thunderstorm (used as an interjection of annoyance, etc).

donned, **donning**. See **don**[2].

donnish, **donnism**. See **don**[1].

donnot or **donnat** *don'ət*, (*Yorkshire*) *n* a good-for-nothing; an idler. [Appar partly **do-naught** (**do**[1]), and partly *dow-nought* (**dow**[2])]

Donnybrook or **donnybrook** *don'i-brŏŏk*, *n* a riotous assembly, a rowdy brawl. [From the fair at *Donnybrook*, Dublin]

donor. See **donation**.

donship. See **don**[1].

donsie *don'si*, (*Scot*) *adj* unlucky, perverse (*obs*); neat, trim (*obs*); sickly; stupid. [Origin unknown]

don't *dōnt*, contraction of **do not**. — *n* something one must not do. — **don't'-know** (the answer given by) someone whose mind is not made up with regard to some, *esp* political, issue.

donut. See **doughnut** under **dough**.

donzel *don'zəl*, (*obs*) *n* a squire, aspirant to knighthood. [Ital *donzello*, from LL *domnicellus*, dimin of L *dominus* lord]

doo *dōō*, (*Scot*) *n* a dove. — **doocot** or **dooket** (*dŏŏk'ət*) a dovecote.

doob *dōōb*, *n* dog's-tooth grass. [Hindi *dūb*]

doodah *dōō'dä* or (*esp US*) **doodad** *dōō'dad*, *n* a small ornament or trinket; a piece of decoration; a gadget; thingamy. — **all of a doodah** very agitated. [Both coined from **do**[1]]

doodle[1] *dōōd'l*, *vi* to scrawl or scribble meaninglessly or aimlessly. — *n* something doodled. — *n* **dood'ler**.

doodle[2] *dōōd'l*, (*Scot*) *vt* to dandle.

doodle[3] *dōōd'l*, (*Scot*) *vt* to drone or play, as a bagpipe. [Ger *dudeln*]

doodlebug *dōōd'l-bug*, *n* the larva of an ant-lion or other insect (used in divination in America; *US*); any instrument, scientific or unscientific, used by prospectors to indicate the presence of minerals; the V-1, a flying bomb (*World War II slang*).

dook[1] *dŏŏk*, (*Scot*) *n* a plug of wood driven into a wall to hold a nail, etc; a bung. [Unknown]

dook[2] *dŏŏk*, (*Scot*) *vt* and *vi* to duck; to bathe. — *n* an act of plunging, dipping or bobbing; a bathe; an inclined adit at a mine. [**duck**[2]]

dook[3]. See **duke**.

dooket. See **doocot** under **doo**.

dool[1], **doole**. See **dole**[2] and **dule**.

dool[2] *dōōl*, or **dule** (*Scot*) *dül*, *n* a boundary mark; a goal. — **hail the dules** to score a goal. [Cf Du *doel*, LGer *dole*, Fris *dôl*, *dôle*]

doolally *dōō-la'li*, (*slang*) *adj* mentally unbalanced; crazy. [Deolali, a town near Bombay]

doolie *dōō'li*, *n* a litter or palanquin. [Hindi *dolī*]

doom *dōōm*, *n* destiny, fate; ruin; catastrophe; death; judgement or condemnation; final judgement; a picture of the Last Judgement. — *vt* to condemn to destiny or catastrophe; to pronounce judgement on; to sentence: — *pr p* **doom'ing**; *pa t* and *pa p* **doomed**. — *adj* **doomed** under sentence; fated; destined to inevitable death, failure or ruin. — *adj* **doom'ful** (*Spenser*, etc) dispensing judgement. — *adv* **dooms** (*Scot*) very, exceedingly. — *n* **doom'ster** a judge (*archaic*); a dempster; a pessimist (*colloq*); a doomwatcher (*colloq*). — *adj* **doom'y** (*colloq*) pessimistic; depressed; depressing. — **doom'-merchant** (*colloq*) a pessimist; someone continually expecting, and forecasting, disaster; **doom'-sayer**; **doom'saying**; **dooms'day** the day of doom, the last judgement; a day of reckoning; **dooms'man** (*archaic*) someone who pronounces doom or sentence, a judge; a pessimist (*colloq*); **doom'watch** pessimism about the contemporary situation and about the future, *esp* of the environment; observation of the environment to prevent its destruction by pollution, overpopulation, etc; a generally pessimistic view of the future. — Also *adj* and *vi*. — **doom'watcher**; **doom'-watching**. — **Doomsday-book** see **Domesday-book**. — **crack of doom** the last trump; **till doomsday** forever. [OE *dōm* judgement]

doom-palm. See **doum-palm**.

doona *dōō'nə*, (*Austr*) *n* a continental quilt. [Orig a trademark.]

door *dōr* or *dör*, *n* the usual entrance into a house, room or passage; a solid sheet (of wood, metal, glass, etc) hung so that it permits access through or closes up an entrance; a house, etc (as in *three doors away*); a means of approach or access. — **door'bell**; **door'-case** the frame which encloses a door; **door'-cheek** (*Scot*) a side-post of a door; **door'-keeper**; **door'knob**; **door'knock** (*Austr*) a fundraising appeal in which agents go from door to door soliciting donations. — Also *adj* and *vi*. — **door'knocker** a knocker on a door; a person who doorknocks (*Austr*); **door'mat** a mat for wiping shoes on, or for some other purpose at a door; an uncomplaining person whom others treat inconsiderately (*colloq*); **door'nail** a stud for a door, proverbially dead; **door'-plate** a plate on or at a door with the householder's name on it; **door'post** the jamb or side-piece of a door; **door'-sill** the threshold of a doorway; **doors'-man** or **doors'man** a porter, doorkeeper; **door'stead** a doorway; **door'step** a step at a door; a thick slice of bread (*colloq*). — *vt* to go from door to door round (an area), eg canvassing in an election; (*esp* of journalists) to pester someone, by waiting on their doorstep: — *pr p* **door'stepping**; *pa t* and *pa p* **door'-stepped**. — **door'stepper**; **door'stepping**; **door'stone**; **door'stop** a wedge to prevent a door swinging shut; a knob fixed to floor or wall to prevent a door opening too far. — *adj* **door'-to-door'** calling at each house in an area in order to sell, canvass, etc. — Also *adv*. — **door'way** an opening where there is or might be a door; **door'-yard** (*US*) a yard about the door of a house. — **close** (or **open**) **the door to** to make impossible (or possible); **doorstep selling** going from house to house to (try to) sell goods or services; **lay at someone's door** to blame someone (for); **leave the door open** to preserve a situation in which something remains possible; **next door (to)** in the next house; near or bordering upon; very nearly (*fig*); **on one's doorstep** close to one's house, etc; **out of doors** see under **out**; **show someone the door** to turn someone out of the house. [OE *duru* (fem) and *dor* (neuter); cf Ger *Tür*, *Tor*, Gr *thyrā*, L *forīs*, Sans *dvār* a door]

doorn *dōōrn*, (*SAfr*) *n* thorn. — **doorn-boom** (*dōōrn'bōōm*) a S African acacia. [Du *doorn* thorn, and *boom* tree]

doo-wop *dōō'wop*, (*music*) *n* vocalizing in harmony in the style of rhythm-and-blues, *orig* developed in the US during the 1950s.

dop[1] *dop*, *n* a copper cup in which a gem is fastened for cutting or polishing; Cape brandy made from grape-skins (*SAfr*); a tot (eg of wine; *SAfr*); a drink container (having the capacity of about one third of a bottle); an empty shell (of a nut); a cartridge-case (*usu* **dopp'ie**). [Du *dop* shell, husk]

dop[2] *dop*, (*obs*) *vt* and *vi* to dip; to dap. — *n* a curtsy; a bob. — *n* **dopp'er** a didapper; a rod for dapping. — *n* **dopp'ing** a flock of sheldrake. [OE *dop-* (in compounds); connected with **dip**]

dopa *dō'pə*, *n* a naturally-occurring amino-acid, a form of which, **L-dopa**, is used in the treatment of Parkinson's disease. [From *d*i*o*xy*p*henyl*a*lanine, a former name for the compound]

dopamine *dō'pə-mēn*, *n* a chemical found in brain tissue that acts as a neurotransmitter, necessary for the normal functioning of the brain. [**dopa** and **amine**]

dopatta or **dupatta** *dō-put'ə*, *n* a silk or muslin shawl or headscarf. [Hindi]

dope *dōp*, *n* a thick liquid, semi-liquid, or pasty material (*US*); an absorbent; lubricating grease; aeroplane varnish; a substance added to improve the efficiency or modify the properties of anything; opium; a drug, *esp* one illegally administered to an athlete, a racehorse, or taken by an addict; drug-taking; confidential or fraudulent information in advance (*colloq*); information in general (*colloq*); anything supplied to dull, blind or blunt the conscience or insight; a fool (*colloq*). — *vt* to give or apply dope to; to drug; to add impurities to (a semiconductor) to modify or improve its properties (*electronics*). — *vi* to take dope. — *n* **dōp'ant** (*electronics*) a substance used in doping. — *n* **dōp'er** someone who applies, administers, deals in, or takes dope. — *adj* **dope'y** or **dōp'y** narcotic; stupefied; stupid. — *n* **dōp'iness**. — *n* **dōp'ing** drugging; the addition of known impurities to a semiconductor, to achieve the desired properties in diodes and transistors (*electronics*). — **dope'-fiend** a drug addict. [Du *doop* a dipping, sauce; *doopen* to dip]

doppelgänger *dop'l-geng'ər*, *n* a ghostly double of a human person, an apparition; a wraith. — Also **doppelgang'er** (*-gang'*). [Ger, literally double-goer]

Dopper *dop'ər*, *n* a Baptist or Anabaptist; a member of a strict and conservative denomination, an offshoot of the Dutch Reformed Church in S Africa. [Du *dooper*, from *doopen* to dip]

doppie. See **dop**[1].

doppio movimento *dop'pi-ō mo-vē-men'tō*, (*Ital*; *music*) double speed.

dopplerite *dop'lər-it*, *n* a black elastic substance (calcium salts of humus acids) found in peat beds. [Named after Christian *Doppler*; see ety for **Doppler principle**]

Doppler (or **Doppler's**) **principle** *n* the law of change of wavelength when a source of vibrations is moving towards or from the observer, explaining the fall of pitch of a railway whistle when the engine passes, and enabling astronomers to measure the radial velocity of stars by the displacement of known lines of the spectrum; **Doppler effect** or **shift** this observed change, used in eg Doppler radar to determine velocities of observed objects. [From Christian *Doppler* (1803–53), an Austrian physicist, who announced the principle in 1842]

dopy. See **dope**.

Dor. *abbrev*: Doric.

dor[1] *dör*, (*obs*) *n* a scoff, mockery, as in *to give* (any one) *the dor*. — *vt* to mock, put out of countenance. [Prob ON *dār* scoff]

dor[2] or **dorr** *dör*, *n* a kind of dung-beetle, also called **dor'beetle** and **dor'-fly**; a cockchafer (in US called **dor'bug**); a drone (*obs*). — **dor'hawk** the nightjar. [OE *dora* a humble-bee]

Dora *dō'rä* or *dö'*, (*colloq*; *hist*) *n* the *D*efence *o*f the *R*ealm *A*ct (1914) which imposed wartime restrictions.

dorado *də-rä'dō*, *n* the coryphene, a large edible marine fish, so called from its iridescent gold/blue colour when dying; the so-called golden salmon, a S American river fish (*Salminus*) of the Characinidae; (with *cap*) a small southern constellation, the Swordfish: — *pl* **dora'dos**. [Sp, from *dorar* to gild, from L *deaurāre*, *-ātum*; see **dory**[1], and **el Dorado**]

Doras *dō'rəs* or *dö'*, *n* a S American genus of Siluridae, bony-plated river fish with spines, with the habit of walking overland when drought threatens. — *n* **do'rad** any member of the genus, or of the group to which it belongs. [Gr *dory* spear]

Dorcas *dör'kəs*, *n* in the Bible, Acts 9. 36, the Greek translation (*Dorkas*) of *Tabitha* (Aramaic, denoting gazelle), the name of a woman famous for good works, hence **Dorcas society** (*hist*) a ladies' society for making and providing clothes for the poor. [Gr *dorkas* gazelle]

doree. See **dory**[1].

Dorian *dō'ri-ən* or *dö'*, *adj* belonging to *Doris* in Greece or to the Dorians; Doric. — *n* a native of Doris; a member of one of the main divisions of the ancient Greeks who arrived about 1100BC and made their home in Doris, SE Peloponnese, Crete, Rhodes, etc. — **Dorian mode** a mode of ancient Greek music consisting of two tetrachords with a semitone between the two lowest notes in each, the tetrachords separated by a whole tone (as efga or bcde — but reckoned downwards by the Greeks), traditionally of a stirring, solemn, simple and martial quality; an authentic mode of old church music, extending from d to d with d as its final. [L *Dōrius*, from Gr *Dōrios*, from *Dōris*]

Doric *dor'ik*, *adj* belonging to *Doris* in Greece, or the Dorians, or their dialect; denoting one of the Greek orders of architecture, distinguished by its simplicity and massive strength. — *n* an Ancient Greek dialect; any dialect thought to resemble it, *esp* Scottish. — *n* **Doricism** (*dor'i-sizm*) a peculiarity of the Doric dialect. — *n* **Dō'rism** Doricism; a Dorian characteristic. — *vt* and *vi* **dōr'ize** or **-ise** to render or become like the Dorians, in language, manners, etc. [L *Dōricus*, from Gr *Dōrikos*, from *Dōris*]

Doris *dō'ris* or *dö'*, *n* a genus of nudibranchiate gasteropods, shell-less molluscs with a plumy tuft of gills on the back, giving name to the family **Dorid'idae**. — *n* and *adj* **do'ridoid**. [Gr *Dōris* a sea-goddess]

dork *dörk*, (*slang*) *n* an idiot, an object of contempt; a penis (*US*). — *adj* **dork'y**.

Dorking *dörk'ing*, *n* a square-bodied breed of poultry, variously coloured, and with five claws on each foot (so named from *Dorking* in Surrey).

dorlach *dör'lahh*, (*Scot*) *n* a bundle, a truss; a sheaf; a valise. [Gaelic]

dorm *dörm*, (*colloq*) *n* short for **dormitory**.

dormant *dör'mənt*, *adj* sleeping; hibernating; (of seeds, etc) alive but not active or growing; (of volcanoes) inactive but not extinct; torpid, lethargic; resting; not used, in abeyance (as a title); in a sleeping posture (*heraldry*). — *n* a crossbeam; a joist. — *n* **dor'mancy**. [OFr *dormant*, pr p of *dormir*, from L *dormīre* to sleep]

dormer *dör'mər*, *n* a dormitory or bedroom (*obs*); a dormer-window. — **dor'mer-win'dow** a small window with a gable, projecting from a sloping roof (*orig* a dormitory window). [OFr *dormeor*, from L *dormītōrium*, from *dormīre* to sleep]

dormie. See **dormy**.

dormient *dör'mi-ənt*, (*archaic*) *adj* sleeping; dormant. [L *dormiēns*, *-entis*, pr p of *dormīre* to sleep]

dormition *dör-mish'ən*, *n* falling asleep; death. — *n* and *adj* **dor'mitive** soporific. [Fr, from L *dormīre* to sleep]

dormitory *dör'mi-tər-i*, *n* a large sleeping-room with many beds, whether in separate cubicles or not; a resting-place; a college hostel (*US*); a small town or a suburb (also **dormitory town** or **suburb**), the majority of whose residents work elsewhere. — **dor'mitory-car** (*US*) a railway sleeping-carriage. [L *dormītōrium*, from *dormīre* to sleep]

Dormobile® *dör'mə-bēl*, *n* a type of van equipped for living and sleeping in.

dormouse *dör'mows*, *n* any member of the *Myoxidae*, a family of rodents related to mice but somewhat squirrel-like in form and habit: — *pl* **dor'mice**. [Perh connected with L *dōrmīre* to sleep (from their hibernation) and prob **mouse**]

dormy or **dormie** *dör'mi*, *adj* (in golf) as many holes up or ahead as there are yet to play. [Perh connected with L *dormīre* to sleep; the player who is *dormy* cannot lose even by going to sleep]

dornick *dör'nik*, *n* a kind of stout figured linen, originally made at *Doornik* or Tournai in Belgium.

doronicum *dər-on'ik-əm*, *n* a composite plant of the genus *Doronicum*, having yellow, daisy-like flower heads. [L, from Ar *dorunaj*]

Dorothy bag *dor'ə-thi bag*, *n* a type of ladies' handbag closed by draw-strings at the top and hung from the wrist.

dorp *dörp*, *n* a Dutch or S African village or small town; a town considered as provincial and backward (*colloq*; *derog*) [Du and Afrik *dorp*; OE *thorp*]

dorr. See **dor**[2].

dorsal *dör'sl*, *adj* relating or belonging to the back. — *n* a dorsal fin; a dorsal vertebra; a dossal. — *adv* **dor'sally**. — *n* **dorse** the back of a book or writing; a dossal; the back. — *n* **dor'sel** a dossal. — *n* **dor'ser** a dosser. — *adj* **dorsibranchiate** (*-brangk'*) having gills on the back. — *adj* **dorsif'erous** having sori on the back (*bot*); carrying young on the back (*zool*). — *adj* **dor'sifixed** (*bot*; of an anther) attached by the whole length of the back to the filament. — *adj* **dor'siflex** bent towards the back. — *n* **dorsiflex'ion** a bending backwards; a bending of the back, a bow. — *adj* **dor'sigrade** walking on the back of the toes. — *adj* **dorsiven'tral** possessing two sides distinguishable as upper or ventral and lower or dorsal (eg as a leaf). — *n* **dorsiventral'ity**. — *adj* **dorsolum'bar** of or relating to the dorsal and lumbar vertebrae, or the area of the body which they occupy. — *n* **dor'sum** the back: — *pl* **dor'sa**. — **dorsal suture** the seam at the midrib of a carpel. — **send to dorse** (*obs slang*) to throw on the back. [L *dorsum* the back]

dorse[1] *dörs*, *n* a small cod. [Low Ger *dorsch*]

dorse[2], **dorsel**, **dorser**. See under **dorsal**.

dort *dört*, (*Scot*) *vi* to sulk. — *n pl* **dorts** sulks. — *adj* **dor'ty** pettish; delicate. [Origin unknown]

dorter or **dortour** *dör'tər*, (*archaic*) *n* a dormitory, *esp* monastic. [OFr *dortour*, from L *dormītōrium*; see **dormer** and **dormitory**]

dory[1] *dō'ri*, *dö'*, *n* a golden-yellow fish (*Zeus faber*) of the mackerel family, officially called sea wolf. — Also called **John Dory** and **doree**. [Fr *dorée*, from *dorer* to gild, from L *deaurāre* to gild, from *dē-*, in the sense of over, and *aurum* gold]

dory[2] *dō'ri* or *dö'*, (*esp US*) *n* a small boat, with flat bottom, sharp bow and stern, especially suited for surf-riding. [Perh from a Central American language]

DOS *dos*, (*comput*) *abbrev*: disk operating system (see **disk**).

dos or **do's**. See **do**[1].

dos-à-dos *dō-za-dō'*, *adv* (*archaic*) back to back. — *n* a sofa constructed for sitting so; a square-dance figure in which dancers pass each other back to back (*dō-sē-dō'*; also **dosi-do'**: — *pl* **dosi-dos'**). [Fr]

dose *dōs*, in Scotland commonly *dōz*, *n* the quantity of medicine, electric current, X-rays, etc, administered at one time; a portion, *esp* a measured portion, of something given or added; anything disagreeable or medicinal to be taken; a bout, *esp* of an illness or something unpleasant. — *vt* to order or give in doses; to give doses to. — *n* **dōs'age** the practice, act or method of dosing; the regulation of dose; the addition of an ingredient; the proper size of dose. — *n* **dōsim'eter** an instrument for measuring radiation, a small ionization chamber with a scale on which can be read the dose which has caused it partially to discharge (also **dose'-meter**). — *n* **dōsim'etry**. — *n* **dōsiol'ogy** or **dosol'ogy** the science of doses. — **dose equivalent** a quantity of absorbed radiation dosage, measured in sieverts or (*esp* formerly) in rems, being the value of the absorbed dose (qv below) adjusted to take account of the different effects different types of radiation have on the human body, etc. — **absorbed dose** the amount of radiation absorbed by a body, etc, measured in grays or (*esp* formerly) rads. [Fr, from Gr *dosis* a giving, from *didonai* to give]

doseh *dō'se*, *n* a religious ceremony at Cairo (abolished 1884), during the festival of the Prophet's birth, when the sheikh of the Sa'di dervishes rode on horseback over the prostrate bodies of his followers. [Ar *dawsah* treading]

dosh *dosh*, (*slang*) *n* money. [Poss *do*llars and ca*sh*]

dosi-do. See **dos-à-dos**.

doss *dos*, (*slang*) *n* a bed, sleeping-place (*esp* in a dosshouse); a sleep. — *vi* to sleep; to go to bed. — *n* **doss'er** a person who lodges in a dosshouse, or wherever they can, a vagrant. — **doss'house** a very cheap lodging-house. — **doss down** to go to bed in a dosshouse, or in a makeshift bed elsewhere. [Perh from *doss*, a dialectal Eng name for a hassock; or perh **dorse** (see under **dorsal**)]

dossal or **dossel** *dos'əl*, *n* a cloth hanging for the back of an altar, sides of a church chancel, etc. [LL *dossāle*, *dorsāle*, from L *dorsum* back]

dosser[1] *dos'ər*, (*hist*) *n* a rich hanging or tapestry for the walls of a hall or of a chancel; a pannier. [OFr *dossier*, from *dos*, from L *dorsum* back]

dosser[2], **dosshouse**. See under **doss**.

dossier *do'si-ā*, *do-syā'*, *dos'i-ər*, (orig *law*) *n* a set of documents relating to a person, event or case; a brief. [Fr, from *dos*, from L *dorsum* back]

dossil *dos'il*, *n* a plug, spigot; a cloth roll for wiping ink from an engraved plate in printing; a pledget or wad of lint for dressing a wound (*surg*). [OFr *dosil*, from LL *ducillus* a spigot]

dost. see **do**[1].

dot[1] *dot*, *n* a very small spot, a speck or mark; (in writing and printing) such a mark used as a full stop or point, one of a series used to indicate an omission, used to form the letters *i* and *j* or used as a diacritic; the symbol representing the short element in the written representation of Morse code; the symbol for the decimal point (*math*); the symbol indicating multiplication or logical conjunction (*logic*, *math*); the symbol used after a note or rest to indicate that its length is increased by half its value (*music*); the symbol used above or below a note to indicate that it should be played staccato (*music*); anything like a dot, a very small object; a very small amount. — *vt* to mark with a dot or dots; to scatter with objects; to jot; to hit (*slang*); to place or stand, etc at irregular and relatively widely spaced intervals. — *vi* to form dots; to limp: — *prp* **dott'ing**; *pat* and *pap* **dott'ed**. — *adj* **dott'ed** composed of dots; marked with a dot or dots. — *n* **dott'iness**. — *adj* **dott'y** composed of or covered with dots; unsteady (*colloq*); feeble-minded, eccentric (*colloq*); (with *about*) crazy about, extremely fond of (*colloq*). — **dotted line** a line composed of dots or dashes that (on printed forms, etc) one is instructed to sign on or tear along, etc; **dotted note** or **rest** (*music*) one whose length is increased by one half by a dot placed after it; **dotted rhythm** one characterized by the use of dotted notes; **dot matrix** (*comput*) a method of printing using a rectangular matrix consisting of lines of pins, a selection of which is used to make each letter shape (hence **dot-matrix printer** or **dot matrix printer**). — **dot and carry** (*arith*) to set down the units and carry over the tens to the next column; **dot one's i's and cross one's t's** to pay great attention to detail; **dotted around** or **over**, etc, here and there; **on the dot** (**of**) exactly (at) (a given time); **the year dot** (*colloq*) the very beginning of time. [OE has *dott* head of a boil; Du *dot* tuft, knot]

dot[2] *dot*, *n* a marriage portion. — *adj* **dōt'al** pertaining to dowry or to dower. — *n* **dōtā'tion** the bestowing of a dowry; an endowment. [Fr, from L *dōs*, *dōtis*]

dote or **doat** *dōt*, *vi* to be stupid or foolish (*archaic*); to be weakly affectionate; to show excessive love (with *upon* or *on*); (of timber) to decay. — *n* **dōt'age** a doting; the childishness of old age; excessive fondness. — *n* **dōt'ant** (*Shakesp*) a dotard. — *n* **dōt'ard** someone who dotes; someone showing the weakness of old age, or excessive fondness. — *adj* **dōt'ed** (*obs*) stupid. — *n* **dōt'er** or **doat'er** someone who dotes. — *adj* and *n* **dōt'ing** or **doat'ing**. — *adv* **dot'ingly**. — *adj* **dōt'ish** silly. — *adj* **dōt'y** (*dialect*) decaying (of timber). — **dot'ing-piece** or **doat'ing-piece** someone who is doted on. [Cf Old Du *doten* to be silly; Fr *radoter* to rave, is from the same root]

doth. See under **do**[1].

dot-matrix, **dotted**. See under **dot**[1].

dotterel or **dottrel** *dot'*(*ə*)*rəl*, *n* a kind of plover, named from its apparent stupidity in allowing itself to be approached and caught; a stupid fellow, a dupe. [**dote**]

dottiness, **dotting**. See **dot**[1].

dottipoll. See **doddypoll**.

dottle[1] *dot'l*, *n* a plug, *esp* of tobacco left at the bottom of a pipe. [**dot**[1]]

dottle[2] *dot'l*, (*Scot*) *n* a fool, a silly person, a dotard. — *adj* foolish, crazy; in dotage. — Also *adj* **dott'led**. [**dote**]

dottrel. See **dotterel**.

dotty. See **dot**[1].

doty. See **dote**.

douane *dōō-än'* or *dwän*, *n* a custom-house. — *n* **douanier** (*dwä-nyā'*), a custom-house officer. [Fr, from Ar *dīwān*; cf **divan** and **diwan** (see under **dewan**)]

douar *dōō'är*. See **duar**.

Douay *dōō'ā*, among Catholics often *dow'i*, *n* the town of *Douai* in France (Nord), historically famous for its English and other Catholic colleges. — **Douay Bible** an English Roman Catholic translation of the Bible, the New Testament in the Rhemish version, the Old done at Douai in 1609–10.

double *dub'l*, *adj* twofold; twice as much; of about twice the weight, size, quality or strength; two of a sort together; in pairs; paired; for two people; having two interpretations, ambiguous; acting two parts, insincere, hypocritical, deceitful; folded once; duple, having two beats in a bar (*music*); sounding an octave lower (*music*); having stamens in the form of petals, or having ligulate in place of tubular florets (*bot*). — *adv* to twice the extent; twice over; two together; deceitfully. — *vt* to multiply by two; to make twofold; to make twice as much or as many; to be the double of; (in acting) to play (two parts) in the one production; to be a substitute for or counterpart of; (in bridge) to raise the scores at stake in (a hand); to duplicate in unison or in another octave above or below (*music*); to line (*heraldry*); to fold; to clench (one's fist(s)); to pass (*esp* sail) round or by; (*billiards*, etc) to cause (a ball) to rebound. — *vi* to increase to twice the quantity; to turn sharply back on one's course; to go or move at twice the usual speed; to act as substitute; to perform two functions, to serve in two capacities; to understudy (*usu* with *for*; *theat*); (in acting) to play two different parts in the same piece; to (be able to) play one or more musical instruments in addition to one's usual one (*music*); (in bridge) to make a double (bid); (*billiards*, etc; of a ball) to rebound from a cushion. — *n* a quantity twice as much; a double measure of spirits (*colloq*); the score of twice the amount shown in the narrow outer ring of a dartboard; a hit on this (*darts*); a stroke causing the ball one hits to rebound against a cushion and into the opposite pocket (*billiards*); a combination of two things of the same kind (such as a binary star); (in *pl*) a game with two players on each side (*tennis*, etc); a double fault, two faults in succession (*tennis*); a bid which, if successful, increases one's score for the hand and, if unsuccessful, increases one's penalty (*bridge*); a win or a defeat in two events on the same programme, in the same championship or series, or against the same opponent; a combined bet on two races, stake and winnings from the first being bet on the second; to place two pawns or two rooks of the same colour on the same file, one behind the other (*chess*); a Guernsey copper coin, $\frac{1}{8}$th of a penny; a duplicate; an actor's substitute; a quick pace, at twice the speed of a normal march; one's wraith or apparition; an exact counterpart; a turning upon one's course; a trick; a feast on which the antiphon is said both before and after the psalms (*eccles*); a size of roofing slate, 330 x 152 mm (13 x 6 inches). — *n* **doub'leness** the state of being double; duplicity. — *n* **doub'ler** someone who or that which doubles. — *n* **doub'leton** (the possession of) two cards of a suit in a hand. — *n* **doub'ling** the act of making double; a turning back in running; a trick; a plait or fold; mantling (*heraldry*). — *adj* shifting, manoeuvring. — *adv* **doub'ly**. — **double act** (*theat*) a variety act for two people to perform; the two entertainers. — *adj* **doub'le-act'ing** applying power in two directions; producing a double result. — **double-a'gent** an agent secretly acting simultaneously for two opposing powers; **double-axe'** a religious symbol of Minoan Crete and the Aegean, a double-headed axe, associated with the mother-goddess and her son (Zeus). — **double axel** (*ice-skating*) an axel incorporating two and a half turns. — *vt* and *vi* **double-bank** to double-park; to ride two at a time on a bicycle or horse, etc (*Austr* and *NZ*). — *adj* **doub'le-banked'** having two men at each oar, or having two tiers of oars one above the other, as in ancient galleys; double-parked. — **dou'ble-banking** double-parking. — **double-bar'** a double vertical line or a single heavy vertical one marking the end of a movement or piece of music or one of its important divisions. — *adj* **doub'le-barr'elled** or (*NAm*) **doub'le-barr'eled** having two barrels; (of a surname) hyphenated; (of a compliment) ambiguous. — **doub'le-bass'** the largest and lowest-pitched instrument of the violin family, playing an octave below the cello; **double bed** a bed wide enough for two people; **double bill** see under **bill**[3]; **double bind** (*psychiatry*) a situation in which conflicting cues are given so that any choice of behaviour will be considered wrong; a dilemma. — *adj* **doub'le-bit'ing** cutting on either side. — *adj* **doub'le-blind'** denoting a comparative experiment or trial, etc in which the identities of the control group are known neither to the subjects nor to the experimenters; **double bluff** an action or statement meant to seem to be a bluff, but in fact genuine; **double boiler** (*NAm*) a double saucepan; **double bond** (*chem*) a covalent bond involving the sharing of two pairs of electrons. — *vt* to accept two reservations for (the same room, seat or time, etc); **doub'le-bott'om** or **double-bottom lorry** an articulated lorry pulling a second trailer. — Also **drawbar outfit**. — *adj* **doub'le-breast'ed** (of a coat, etc) having two fronts, one overlapping the other. — **doub'le-bubb'le** (*prison slang*) one hundred per cent interest. — *vt* **doub'le-charge'** to load with double measure; to charge twice for (an item, service, etc). — *vt* and *vi* **doub'le-check'** to check a second time. — Also *n*. — **double chin** a chin with a fold of flesh beneath it. — *adj* **doub'le-chinn'ed**. — **doub'le-co'conut** the coco-de-mer; **double concerto** a concerto for two solo instruments; **double cream** a cream with a higher fat content than single cream; **doub'le-cross** a betrayal or deceiving of someone for whom one was supposed to be betraying or deceiving someone else. — *vt* to betray by double-cross. — **doub'le-cross'er**; **doub'le-dagg'er** a diesis (‡); **doub'le-deal'er** a deceitful person; **doub'le-deal'ing** duplicity, deceit. — *adj* **doubl'le-decked** having two decks or layers. — **doub'le-deck'er** a double-decked ship; a bus, tram-car, etc in two stories or tiers; a sandwich having three pieces of bread and two layers of filling; a novel or film, etc in two separate parts; anything consisting of two layers (*colloq*). — Also *adj*. — *vi* **doub'le-declutch'** (*autos*) to change into a different gear by first changing to neutral, increasing the engine speed, then engaging the chosen gear, disengaging the clutch at both stages. — **doub'le-decomposi'tion** a chemical action in which two compounds exchange some of their constituents. — *adj* **doub'le-dens'ity** (*comput*) (of a disk) capable of recording double the normal number of bytes. — *adj* **doub'le-dig'it** double-figure. — **double disapproval** an arrangement by which airlines are free to set the level of fares for a route unless the governments at both ends of the route raise objections to the rate set; **double door** or **doors** a door consisting of two parts hung on opposite posts; **double-dotted note** or **rest** (*music*) one whose length is increased by three-quarters, marked by two dots placed after it; **double-dotted rhythm** one characterized by double-dotted notes; **doub'le-Dutch** incomprehensible talk. — *adj* **doub'le-dyed** twice-dyed; deeply imbued; inveterate, confirmed. — **doub'le-eagle** (*US*) a gold coin worth $20; a heraldic representation of an eagle with two heads, as in the old arms of Russia and Austria. — *adj* **doub'le-edged'** having two edges; cutting or working both ways. — **doub'le-end'er** anything having two ends alike; a cross-cut sawing machine with two adjustable circular saws for sawing both ends of timber; **double entendre** see separate entry; **doub'le-en'try** (*bookkeeping*) a method by which two entries are made of each transaction in order to reflect its credit and debit aspects; **double exposure** (*photog*) accidental or deliberate superimposition of one image on another. — *adj* **doub'le-eyed** doubly keen of sight. — *adj* **doub'le-faced** hypocritical, false; (of fabric, etc) finished so that either side may be used as the right side. — **doub'le-fa'cedness** (*-sid-*); **double fault** (*tennis*, etc) two faults served in succession, causing the loss of a point. — *vi* **doub'le-fault'**. — **double feature** a cinema programme involving two full-length films. — *adj* **doub'le-fig'ure**. — **double figures** a score or total, etc of any number equal to or greater than 10 but less than 100; **double first** a university degree with first-class honours in two different subjects; a person who has such a degree; **doub'le-flat'** (*music*) a note already flat flattened again by a semitone; a sign indicating this. — *adj* **doub'le-flower'ed** (of a plant) having double flowers. — *adj* **doub'le-formed'** having, or combining, two forms. — *adj* **doub'le-fount'ed** having two sources. — *adj* **doub'le-front'ed** (of a house) having main-room windows on both sides of the front door. — *vt* **doub'le-gild** to gild with double coatings of gold; to gloss over. — **doub'le-glaz'ing** a double layer of glass in a window with an air-space between the layers to act as insulation; the provision of this. — *adj* **doub'le-glazed'**. — **double Gloucester** or **double Gloster** (*glos'tər*) a Gloucestershire cheese of extra richness. — *adj* **doub'le-hand'ed** having two hands; two-handled. — *adj* **doub'le-head'ed** having two heads. — **double-head'er** a coin with a head on each side (*colloq*; *esp Austr*); two games played on the same day (*sport*; *NAm*); a train pulled by two locomotives coupled together. — *adj* **doub'le-heart'ed** treacherous. — **double helix** the DNA molecule, two spirals coiled round an axis. — *adj* **doub'le-hung'** (of a window) having top and bottom sashes each balanced by sash-cord and weights, so as to be capable of vertical movement in its own groove. — **double jeopardy** second trial for the same offence. — *adj* **doub'le-joint'ed** having loose joints admitting some degree of movement backward. — **double knit** a fabric knitted on two sets of needles, producing a double thickness joined by interlocking stitches. — *adj* **double-knit**. — *adj* **doub'le-līved'** having two lives. — *adj* **doub'le-locked'** locked with two locks or bolts; locked by two turns of the key, as in some locks and many novels. — *adj* **doub'le-manned'** supplied with twice the complement of men. — *adj* **doub'le-mean'ing** ambiguous. — Also *n*. — *adj* **doub'le-mind'ed** undetermined, wavering. — **doub'le-mind'edness**. — *adj* **doub'le-mouthed'** speaking with contradictory voices. — **doub'le-na'tured** having a twofold nature. — **double negative** a construction consisting of two negatives, *esp* when only one is logically required. — **double obelisk** (*printing*) a double dagger (see above); **double-page spread** or **double spread** the two facing pages of a publication, as used for an advertisement or illustration, etc across both pages. — *vt* and *vi* **doub'le-park'** to park (a car, etc) alongside vehicles already parked at the kerb. — **double play** (*baseball*) a play putting out two runners; **double pneumonia** pneumonia of both lungs. — *adj* and *adv* **doub'le-quick'** at a pace approaching a run; very fast. — *n* the double-quick pace. — **double salt** a salt whose crystals dissolve to give two different salts in solution; **double saucepan** a pair of saucepans, the top one fitting closely into the lower one, and heated by boiling water in the lower one. — *vt* **doub'le-shade'** (*Milton*) to double the darkness of. — **doub'le-sharp'** (*music*) a note already sharp sharpened again by a semitone; a sign indicating this. — *adj* **doub'le-shott'ed** (of cannon) with double charge. — **doub'le-shuff'le** a scraping movement made twice with each foot; a dance of such steps; a trick. — *vt* and *vi* **doub'le-space'** to type with a space of one line between each typed line. — **doub'le-speak** double-talk; **double spread** see **double-page spread** above; **double standard** a principle, etc applied in such a way as to allow different standards of behaviour to different people, groups, etc; (in *pl*) the practice of advocating (for others) certain moral, etc standards not followed by oneself; bimetallism; **double star** (*astron*) a binary star; two unrelated stars appearing close together when seen through a telescope; **doub'le-stopp'ing** (*music*) simultaneous playing on two (stopped) strings of an instrument at once. — *adj* **doub'le-sto'rey** (of a building) having two floors or tiers. — **doub'le-stout'** extra strong stout or porter; **doub'le-take'** a second look impelled by surprise or admiration; delayed reaction; **doub'le-talk** talk that sounds relevant but means nothing; ambiguous, deceptive talk; **doub'lethink** the faculty of simultaneously harbouring two conflicting beliefs, coined by George Orwell in his novel *Nineteen Eighty-Four* (1949); **double-threaded screw** (*eng*) a screw having two threads, whose pitch is half the lead. — Also **two-start thread**; **double time** payment to a worker at twice the usual rate; a time twice as fast as the previous time (*music*); a slow running pace, a regulation running pace keeping in step as a troop; a fast marching pace (*US*). — *vi* **double-tongue'** (*music*) to produce a staccato sound by rapid articulation when playing a wind instrument (*n* **double-tongu'ing**). — *adj* **doub'le-tongued'** having two tongues or a cleft tongue; self-contradictory; deceitful. — **double top** (*darts*) a score of double twenty; **double vision** seeing two images of the same object, because of lack of co-ordination between the two eyes; **double-u** or **double-you** (*dub'l-ū*) the twenty-third letter of the alphabet (W, w); **double wedding** a wedding involving two couples; **double whammy** see **whammy** under **wham**; **double zero option** see **zero-zero option**; **doubling time** (*nuc eng*) the time required for the neutron flux in a reactor to double; in a breeder reactor, the time required for the amount of fissile material to double — **at the double** very quickly; — **bent double** folded; doubled up, bending forward; stooping; **double back** to go back in the direction one has just come, but *usu* not by the same route; **double or quits** (in gambling) the alternative, left to chance, of doubling or cancelling payment (*adj* **double'-or-quits'**); **double up** to fold double; to clench (one's fists); to bend over (as with laughter or pain); to come at the double; to share with another; to join together, couple. [OFr *doble*, from L *duplus* double, from *duo* two, and the root seen in Eng **fold**, Gr *haploos*]

double entendre *dōō-blã-tã'dr'*, *n* (the use of) a word or phrase with two meanings, one usually more or less indecent. [Fr of 17c, superseded now by (*mot*) *à double entente*]

doublet *dub'lit*, *n* a close-fitting garment for the upper part of the body with *hose*, the typical masculine dress during the 14–17c; a thing that is repeated or duplicated; one of a pair, *esp* one of two words *orig* the same but varying in spelling and meaning, eg *balm*, *balsam*. [OFr, dimin of *double*]

doubletree *dub'l-trē*, *n* the horizontal bar on a vehicle to which the whippletree (with harnessed animals) is attached.

doubloon *dub-lōōn'*, *n* an obsolete Spanish gold coin, originally = 2 pistoles. [Sp *doblón*, augmentative of *doble* double; see **double**]

doubly. See **double**.

doubt *dowt*, *vi* to be undecided in opinion; to be apprehensive (*obs*). — *vt* to be uncertain about; to question; to hesitate or scruple; to incline to believe only with fear or hesitation; to distrust; to incline to think (*esp Scot*); to suspect (*archaic*; also *reflexive*); to cause to doubt or fear (*obs*). — *n* uncertainty of opinion; a suspicion; fear (*obs*); a thing doubtful or questioned (*obs*); danger (*obs*; *Spenser*) — *adj* **doubt'able**. — *adj* **doubt'ed** questioned; feared, redoubted (*Spenser*). — *n* **doubt'er**. — *adj* **doubt'ful** feeling or full of doubt; undetermined; subject to doubt; not clear; insecure; suspicious; not confident; not likely or not certain to participate, co-operate, etc. — *n* a doubtful person or thing. — *adv* **doubt'fully**. — *n* **doubt'fulness**. — *n* and *adj* **doubt'ing**. — *adv* **doubt'ingly**. — *adj* **doubt'less** free from doubt or (*obs*; *Shakesp*, etc) fear. — *adv* without doubt; certainly; no doubt (often only allowing for the possibility). — *adv* **doubt'lessly**. — **doubting Thomas** a doubter or sceptic; someone who needs proof before believing something (from the doubting of *Thomas*, in the Bible: John 20. 25). — **beyond doubt** or **beyond a shadow of doubt** certain or certainly; **in doubt** not certain, undecided; **no doubt** surely. [OFr *douter*, from L *dubitāre*, related to *dubius* doubtful, moving in two (*duo*) directions]

douc *dōōk*, *n* a variegated monkey of SE Asia. [Fr, from Cochin name]

douce *dōōs*, *adj* sweet (*obs*); sober, peaceable, sedate (*Scot*). — *adv* **douce'ly**. — *n* **douce'ness**. — *n* **doucet** or **dowset** (*dōō'* or *dow'sit*; *obs*) a sweet dish; (in *pl*) a deer's testicles. — *n* **douceur** (*dōō-sûr'*) sweetness of manner (*obs*); a compliment (*archaic*); a conciliatory present, bribe or tip. [Fr *doux*, *douce* mild, from L *dulcis* sweet]

doucepere. See **douzepers**.

douche *dōōsh*, *n* a jet of water directed upon or into the body from a pipe, etc; an apparatus for producing such a jet. — *vt* and *vi* to use a douche (on). [Fr, from Ital *doccia* a water-pipe, from L *dūcere* to lead]

doucine *dōō-sēn'*, (*archit*) *n* a cyma recta. [Fr]

dough *dō*, *n* a mass of flour or meal moistened and kneaded, but not baked; money (*slang*). — *n* **dough'iness**. — *adj* **dough'y** like dough; soft; (of complexion) pallid, pasty. — *adj* **dough'-baked** half-baked, defective in intelligence. — **dough'-boy** a boiled flour dumpling (also **dough'-ball**); an American infantryman (*military slang*). — *adj* **dough'faced** over-persuadable, *specif* of N American politicians too inclined to favour the South at the time of the Civil War. — *adj* **dough'-kneaded** (*Milton*) soft. — **dough'nut** or (*esp US*) **donut** sweetened dough fried in fat; an accelerating tube in the form of a toroid (*nucleonics*); a toroidal assembly of enriched fissile material for increasing locally the neutron intensity in a reactor for experimental purposes, a tokamak (*nucleonics*; also **toroid**); a pile of annular laminations in toroidal shape for magnetic testing or a loading coil in toroidal shape on transmission lines, permitting exact balance in addition to inductance (*elec eng*). — *vi* to practise doughnutting. — **dough'nutting** the surrounding of a speaker in parliament by other members to give an impression, *esp* to television viewers, of a packed house. [OE *dāh* dough; Ger *Teig*, ON *deig* dough; cf **duff**[1]]

dought. See **dow**[2].

doughty *dow'ti*, *adj* able, strong; brave. — *adv* **dough'tily**. — *n* **dough'tiness**. [OE *dyhtig* (later *dohtig*) valiant, from *dugan* to be strong; Ger *tüchtig* able]

Douglas fir *dug'ləs fûr*, *n* a tall western American coniferous timber tree (*Pseudotsuga douglasii*). [David *Douglas* (1798–1834), who introduced it to Britain]

Doukhobor. See **Dukhobor**.

douleia, **doulocracy**. See **dulia**.

douma. See **duma**.

doum-palm *dowm'-päm*, *dōōm'-päm*, *n* an African palm (*Hyphaene*), with a branched stem, and a fruit with the taste of gingerbread. — Also **doom'-** or **dum'-palm**. [Ar *daum*, *dūm*]

doup *dowp*, (*Scot*) *n* the bottom section of an eggshell; the buttocks; the bottom or end of anything. — **can'dle-doup** a candle-end. [Cf ON *daup* a hollow]

dour *dōōr*, *adj* obstinate, determined; sullen; grim. — *n* **dour'ness**. [Appar L *dūrus* hard]

doura. See **durra**.

dourine *dōō-rēn'*, *dōō'rēn*, *n* a contagious disease of horses due to a trypanosome. [Fr *dourin*]

douroucouli or **durukuli** *dōō-rōō-kōō'lē*, *n* a night-ape, any monkey of the S American genus *Nyctipithecus*. [SAm name]

douse[1] or **dowse** *dows*, *vt* to plunge into water. — *vi* to fall suddenly into water. [Cf Swed *dunsa* fall heavily; prob from sound; cf *souse*]

douse[2] or **dowse** *dows*, *vt* to strike (*obs*); to strike or lower (a sail). — *n* a heavy blow. [Prob related to Old Du *dossen* to beat]

douse[3] or **dowse** *dows*, *vt* to put out, extinguish (*esp* in the *slang* **douse the glim** to put out the light). — *n* **dous'er** a shutter for cutting off light in a cinema projector. [Perh connected with **dout**[1] or with **douse**[2]]

dout[1] *dowt*, *vt* to put out, extinguish. — *n* **dout'er**. [**do** and **out**]

dout[2]. See **dowt**.

douzepers *dōō'zə-pār*, (*archaic*) *n pl* the twelve peers of Charlemagne, or a similar group: — *sing* **dou'zeper** or **dou'cepere** (*Spenser*) a champion, great knight or noble. [OFr *douze pers* twelve peers]

dove[1] *duv*, *n* a pigeon (often in combination, as eg *ring-dove*, *turtle-dove*) and used *esp* of the smaller species; an old word of endearment; an emblem of innocence and gentleness, also of the Holy Spirit (*Bible*: Matt 3. 16); in politics and industrial relations, etc, a person who seeks peace and conciliation rather than confrontation or war (*opp* to *hawk*). — *vt* to treat as a dove. — *n* **dove'let** a small dove. — *adj* **dove'like** like a dove; innocent. — *adj* **dov'ish** or **dove'ish** dovelike; seeking peace and conciliation rather than confrontation or war. — *n* **dove'ishness**. — **dove'-colour** a greyish, bluish, pinkish colour; **dove'cot** or **dove-cote** a small building or structure in which pigeons breed; a pigeon-house. — *adj* **dove'-drawn** (*Shakesp*) drawn by doves. — *adj* **dove'-eyed** meek-eyed. — **dove'-house** a dovecot; **dove's'-foot** a name for some species of cranesbill (*Geranium dissectum*, *Geranium molle*, etc); **dove'tail** a tenon shaped like a dove's spread tail, for fastening boards; a joint of alternate tenons and mortises of that shape. — *vt* and *vi* to fit by one or more dovetails; to fit or join together neatly (often with *into* or *with*). — **dove'tailing**. — **flutter the dovecots** to disturb commonplace, conventional people, as the eagle would a dovecot (see Shakespeare's play *Coriolanus* V. 6. 115). [OE *dūfe*, found only in the compound *dūfe-doppa* a diving bird; Ger *Taube*]

dove[2] *dōv*, (*Scot*) *vi* to be half asleep or stupefied. — *vi* **dō'ver** (*Scot*) to snooze, doze. — *vt* to stun. — *n* a snooze; a swoon; half-consciousness. — *adj* **dō'vie** (*Scot*) stupid. [OE *dofian* to be stupid]

dove[3] *dōv*, *NAm pa t* of **dive**.

dovecot, doveish. See under **dove**[1].

dovekie *duv'ki*, *n* the little auk or rotch; the black guillemot. [Dimin of **dove**[1]]

Dover's powder *dō'vərz pow'dər*, *n* a sudorific compounded of ipecacuanha root, opium and potassium sulphate (or, in the US, lactose). [First prescribed by Dr Thomas *Dover* (1660–1742)]

dover. See under **dove**[2].

dovetail, dovish. See under **dove**[1].

dow[1]. See **dhow**.

dow[2] *dow*, (*obs* and *Scots*) *vi* to be good for a purpose; to avail; to be able: — *3rd pers sing* **dow** or **dows**; *pa t* **docht, dought** (*dohht*) or **dowed**. — **dow'na** (*neg*) cannot; cannot be bothered. — **dow'na-do** powerlessness. [OE *dugan*]

dowable. See **dower**.

dowager *dow'ə-jər*, *n* a widow with a dower or jointure; a title given to a widow to distinguish her from the wife of her husband's heir (also *adj*); an elderly woman of imposing appearance. — **Dowager's hump** a prominent curvature of the spine below the base of the neck that can develop due to osteoporosis (*colloq*). [OFr *douagere*, from LL *dōtārium* dower, from L *dōtāre* to endow]

dowar. See **duar**.

dowd *dowd*, or **dowdy** *dowd'i*, *n* a woman who wears dull-looking, clumsy, ill-shaped clothes. — *adv* **dowd'ily**. — *n* **dowd'iness**. — *adj* **dowd'y**. — *adj* **dowd'yish**. — *n* **dowd'yism**. [Origin unknown]

dowed. See **dow**[2].

dowel *dow'əl*, *n* a pin for fastening things together by fitting into a hole in each. — *vt* to fasten by means of dowels. — *n* **dow'elling** long, thin, *usu* wooden rod of circular section. — **dow'el-joint**; **dow'el-pin**; **dow'el-rod**. [Prob related to Ger *Döbel*, *Dübel* a plug]

dower *dow'ər*, *n* a jointure; a dowry; an endowment. — *vt* to give a dowry to; to endow. — *adj* **dow'able** that may be endowed. — *adj* **dow'erless**. — **dow'er-house** the house set apart for the widow, *usu* on her late husband's estate. [OFr *douaire*, from LL *dōtārium*, from L *dōtāre* to endow]

dowf *dowf*, (*Scot*) *adj* dull, heavy, spiritless. — *n* **dowf'ness**. [Prob ON *daufr* deaf]

dowie *dow'i*, (*Scot*) *adj* dull, low-spirited, sad; dismal. [Prob OE *dol* dull]

dowitcher *dow'ich-ər* *n* a name given to two species of sand piper (*Limnodromus griseus* and *Limnodromus scolopaceus*; family *Scolopacidae*), found in arctic and subarctic N America. [From Iroquoian]

Dow-Jones average or **index** *dow'jōnz' av'ər-ij* or *in'deks*, (*US*) *n* an indicator of the relative prices of stocks and shares on the New York Stock exchange, based on the average price of a certain agreed list of securities. [Charles H *Dow* (1851–1902), and Edward D *Jones* (1856–1920), American economists]

dowl or **dowle** *dowl*, (*obs* or *dialect*; *Shakesp*) *n* a portion of down in a feather; a piece of fluff. [Origin obscure]

dowlas *dow'ləs*, *n* a course linen cloth. [From *Daoulas* or *Doulas*, near Brest, in Brittany]

down[1] *down*, *n* soft feathers; a soft covering of fluffy hair. — *adj* **downed** filled or covered with down. — *n* **Down'ie**® a duvet. — *n* **down'iness**. — *adj* **down'y** covered with or made of down; like down; knowing (*slang*). — **down'-bed**; **down'-quilt**. — **the downy** (*old slang*) bed. — The spellings **dowlne** and **dowlney** (*Shakesp*) show confusion with **dowl**. [ON *dūnn*; Ger *Daune*, LGer *dune*]

down[2] *down*, *n* a bank of sand thrown up by the sea (same as **dune**); a treeless upland; (in *pl*) an undulating upland tract of pasture-land, *esp* in SE England (**the Downs**); the roadstead off E Kent. — *n* **down'land**. [OE *dūn* a hill, from Celtic *dun*]

down[3] *down*, *adv* (passing into *adj* in predicative use) to a lower position, level or state; away from a centre (capital, city, university, etc); southward; to leeward; in a low or lowered position or state; below; on or to the ground; downstairs; under the surface; from earlier to later times; to a further stage in a series; from greater to less (in size, grain, activity, intensity, etc); to a standstill, exhaustion or conclusion; to a final state of defeat, subjection, silence, etc; in a fallen state; in adversity; at a disadvantage; ill; behindhand; in writing or record, in black and white; in flood; on the spot, immediately in cash; in readiness to pounce; in a state of alert awareness and understanding; in watchful opposition or hostility (with *on*, *upon*); broken, not operational (*comput*). — Also elliptically, passing into an interjection or verb by omission of *go*, *come* or *put*, etc, often followed by *with*. — *adj* going, reaching, directed towards or having a lower position or level; depressed; low; broken, not operational (*comput*). — *prep* in a descent along, through or by; to or in a lower position on or in; along in the direction of the current; along. — *n* a descent; a low place; a reverse of fortune, a time of comparative bad luck; an act of throwing or putting down; a tendency to treat one harshly; a feeling of dislike; one of four consecutive periods of play, during which a team must score or advance the ball 9 m (10 yd) in order to retain possession (*Am football*). — *vt* to knock, throw, shoot or put down; to put down, overthrow; to depress. — *interj* ordering (*esp* a dog) to go or stay down; (with *with*) expressing a wish for the downfall of someone or something. — *n* **down'er** (*slang*) a depressant drug; any depressing experience, etc. — *adv* **down'ward** (*-wərd*) or **down'wards** (*-wərdz*) from higher to lower; from source to outlet; from more ancient to modern; in the lower part. — *adj* **down'ward**. — *adv* **down'wardly**. — *n* **down'wardness** a sinking tendency; a state of being low. — *adj* **down'-and-out'** at the end of one's resources; destitute and rejected by, or rejecting, society. — *n* **down'-and-out'**. — *n* **down'-and-out'er**. — *adj* **down'-at-heel'** having the back of the shoe trodden down; generally shabby. — **down'beat** a downward movement of the conductor's baton; an accented beat. — *adj* (*colloq*) relaxed, unworried; unemphatic; depressed; gloomy; depressing. — **down'bow** (*music*) a movement of the bow over the strings beginning at the nut end; **down'burst** same as **microburst**. — *adj* **down'cast** dejected. — *n* a current of air into a mine; a shaft carrying it (**down'cast-shaft'**); a downward throw; a down-throw. — **down'-come** a fall, ruin; a heavy pour of rain; **down'-draught** a current of air downwards; **down'-east'er** (*US*) someone living *down east* from the speaker, a New Englander, and *esp* an inhabitant of Maine; **down'fall** fall, failure, humiliation, ruin; a heavy fall of rain. — *adj* **down'fallen** ruined. — **down'flow** a running or flowing down; something which runs or flows down; **down'force** aerodynamically-caused downward force in a car, etc which eg improves its road holding. — *adj* **down'-going**. — **down-go'ing** (or *down'*); **down'grade** a downward slope or course. — *adj* and *adv* downhill. — *vt* to reduce in status, etc; to belittle, underrate. — *adj* **down'-gyved** (*Shakesp*) hanging down like fetters. — **down'-haul** a rope by which a jib, etc is hauled down when set. — *adj* **down'-heart'ed** dejected. — *adj* **down'hill** descending, sloping. — Also *n*. — *adv* **downhill'**. — *adj* **down'hole** of the drills, measuring instruments, and equipment used down a borehole (*mineral ext*); applied to equipment that is used within the well (*oil industry*). — *adj* **down'-home** (*US colloq*) characteristic of the southern states of the US; characteristic of the country or country-dwellers; homemade; friendly. — **down'-line** the line of a railway leading from the capital, or other important centre, to the provinces; **down'lighter** a downward directed light-fitting, attached to or recessed in the ceiling. — **download'** (*comput*) to transfer (data or programs) from one computer to another; to broadcast programmes of material for specialist groups (eg doctors) outside normal broadcasting hours (often to be recorded on videotape for viewing later). — *adj* **down'looked** (*Dryden*) downcast, gloomy. — **down'-ly'ing** (*dialect*) time of retiring to rest; a woman's confinement during childbirth. — *adj* **down'-mar'ket** of (buying, selling or using) commodities relatively low in price, quality or prestige. — Also *adv*. — *adv* and *adj* **down'most** superlative of *down*. — **down payment** a deposit on an article, service, etc; **down'pipe** a drainpipe which takes rainwater from the gutter of a roof. — *vt* **down'play** to play down. — **down'pour** a heavy fall of rain, etc. — *adv* **down'right** perpendicular (*obs*); in plain terms; utterly. — *adj* plain-spoken; brusque; utter, out-and-out (as in *downright madness*); thorough. — **down'rightness**; **down'rush** a rushing down (as of gas, hot air, etc); **down'-sett'ing** a setting down, a snub; **down'side** the adverse or disadvantageous aspect of a situation (also *adj*). — **down'-sitt'ing** sitting down, time of rest (*Bible*: Psalms 139. 2); a sitting, session (*Scot*); a settlement, establishment (*esp* by marriage; *Scot*). — *vt* **down'size** to reduce in size (*esp* a workforce by redundancy); to design or make a smaller model of (a car, etc). — **down'spout** (*NAm*) a downpipe, drainpipe. — *adv* **down'stage'** towards the footlights (also *adj*). — *adv* **downstairs'** in or towards a lower storey; belowstairs, in the servants' quarters. — *n* a lower storey, *usu* the ground floor. — *adj* **down'stair** or **down'stairs**. — *adv* **downstream'** with the current. — *adj* **down'stream** further down the stream; going with the current; in the hydrocarbons industry, denoting any stage subsequent to oil production, eg refining, the production of oil derivatives, etc (sometimes with *of*). — **down'stroke** a downward line made by the pen in writing; **down'swing** a downward trend in volume of trade, etc; the part of the swing where the club is moving down towards the ball (*golf*). — *adj* **down'-the-line** (of a ballet-dancer) inconspicuously placed, unimportant. — **down'-throw** act of throwing down, or state of being thrown down; the amount of vertical displacement of the relatively lowered strata at a fault (*geol*); **down'time** a period when work is halted, due to equipment failure, lack of materials, bad weather, etc. — *adj* **down'-to-earth'** sensible; practical; realistic. — *adj* and *adv* **down'-town'** in or towards the lower part or (*esp US*) the business and shopping centre of the town. — *n* this part of a town. — **down'-train** a railway train which leaves from the chief terminus; **down'trend** a downward trend. — *adj* **down'-trod** or **down'-trodden** trampled on; tyrannized over. — **down'turn** a downward trend, decline. — *adj* **down'turned** folded or turned down. — *adj* and *adv* **down'wind'** in the direction in which the wind is blowing; in or to a position (relative to someone or something) in this direction (often with *of*). — **down east** (*US*) in or into Maine and adjoining parts of New England; **down in the mouth** in low spirits; **down on one's luck** in unfortunate circumstances; **down south** (*US*) in the southern states; **down to** (*slang*) the fault or responsibility of; **down tools** to stop work, strike; **down to the ground** (*colloq*) completely; **down town** in or towards the centre of a town; **down under** in or to Australia and New Zealand; **down with** put down; swallow; (as *interj*) depose, get rid of, abolish; **go down** (often with *with*) to be received (well or badly) (by); (often with *with*) to be acceptable (to); (with *with*) to contract (illness); **go downhill** to deteriorate (in health, prosperity or morality); **go downstream** to begin operating the downstream stages of oil exploitation; **up and down** alternately well and ill; to and fro. [ME *a-down, adun*, from OE *of dūne* from the hill (dative case of *dūn* hill; see **down**[2] and **adown**)]

downa, downa-do. See **dow**[2].

Downie®. See **down**[1].

Downing Street *down'ing strēt, n* the street in London where the Prime Minister's official residence is, as well as the Foreign and Commonwealth Office; the British government (*colloq*).

Down's syndrome *downz' sin'drōm, n* a congenital disease caused by chromosomal abnormality, in which there is mental deficiency and a broadening and flattening of the features. — Formerly known as **Mongolism**. [John L H *Down* (1828–96), English physician]

Downs. See **down**[2].

downy. See **down**[1].

dowp. Same as **doup**.

dowry *dow'ri, n* the property which a woman brings to her husband at marriage, sometimes used for dower; sometimes a gift given to or for a wife at marriage; a natural endowment. [See **dower**]

dows. See under **dow**[2].

dowse[1] *dows, vt* and *vi*. See **douse**[1,2,3].

dowse[2] *dowz, vi* to look for water with a divining-rod. — *n* **dows'er** a person who divines water [Origin unknown]

dowset. See **douce**.

dowt or **dout** *dowt*, (*Scot*) *n* a cigarette-end. [From **dout**[1]]

doxographer *doks-og'rə-fər, n* a compiler of opinions of philosophers. — *n* **doxog'raphy**. [Gr *doxa* opinion, reputation, glory, and *graphein* to write]

doxology *doks-ol'əji*, (*Christian relig*) *n* a hymn or liturgical formula ascribing glory to God. [Gr *doxa* opinion, reputation, glory, and *logos* discourse]

doxy[1] *dok'si, n* (*slang*; *archaic*) a mistress (*Shakesp*, etc); a woman of loose character. [Origin unknown]

doxy[2] *dok'si*, (*colloq, esp facetious*) *n* an opinion ('Orthodoxy', said Warburton, 'is my doxy — heterodoxy is another man's doxy'). [Gr *doxa* opinion]

doyen *doi'ən, dwä-yã, n* a dean or senior member (of an academy, diplomatic corps, class, profession, etc): — *fem* **doyenne** (*doi-en'* or *dwä-yen*). [Fr, from L *decānus*]

doyley, doyly. See **doily**.

doz. (sometimes *duz*) *abbrev*: dozen.

doze *dōz, vi* to sleep lightly, or to be half-asleep; to be in a dull or stupefied state. — *vt* to spend in drowsiness (with *away*). — *n* a short light sleep. — *adj* **dozed** drowsy. — *vt* **dō'zen** (*Scot*) to stupefy. — *vi* to become stupefied. — *n* **dō'zer**. — *n* **dō'ziness**. — *n* **dō'zing**. — *adj* **dō'zy** drowsy; not alert, stupid (*colloq*); beginning to decay. [Cf ON *dūsa*, Dan *döse*]

dozen[1] *duz'n, n* a set of twelve; also used, *esp* in *pl*, for a less exact number: — *pl* **doz'en** when preceded by a numeral, otherwise **doz'ens**. — *adj* and *n* **doz'enth**. — **baker's, devil's** or **long dozen** thirteen; **daily dozen** see under **daily**; **half'-a-doz'en** six; approximately six; **round dozen** a full dozen. [OFr *dozeine*, from L *duodecim* (*duo* two, and *decem* ten), and neuter pl ending *-ēna* (cf Sp *docena*)]

dozen[2]. See **doze**.

dozer *dō'zər*. *Colloq* for **bulldozer** or **calfdozer**.

DP *abbrev*: data processing; displaced person.

DPA *abbrev*: Data Protection Authority; Discharged Prisoners' Aid.

DPH *abbrev*: Diploma in Public Health.

DPh. or **DPhil**. *abbrev*: Doctor of Philosophy.

dpi (*comput*) *abbrev*: dots per inch.

DPM *abbrev*: Diploma in Psychological Medicine.

DPP *abbrev*: Director of Public Prosecutions.

dpt *abbrev*: department.

DR *abbrev*: dry riser.

Dr *abbrev*: debtor; Doctor; Driver; Drummer.

Dr. *abbrev*: drachma; Drive (in street names).

dr. *abbrev*: dram; drawer.

DRV *abbrev*: dietary reference values.

drab[1] *drab*, *n* a low, sluttish woman; a whore. — *vi* to associate with drabs. — *n* **drabb'er** someone who associates with drabs. — *n* **drabb'iness**. — *adj* **drabb'ish** or **drabb'y** sluttish. [Poss Gaelic *drabag*; Ir *drabog* slut; or LGer *drabbe* dirt]

drab[2] *drab*, *n* thick, strong, grey cloth; a grey or dull-brown colour, *perh* from the muddy colour of undyed wool; uninteresting unvaried dullness. — *adj* of the colour of drab; dull and monotonous. — *n* **drabb'et** a coarse linen fabric used for smock-frocks. — Also **drabette'**. — *adv* **drab'ly**. — *n* **drab'ness**. [Perh Fr *drap* cloth, from LL *drappus*, prob Gmc; see **drape**]

drabble *drab'l*, *vt* to besmear, bedraggle. — *n* **drabb'ling** a manner of fishing for barbels with a rod and long line passed through a piece of lead. — *n* **drabb'ler** or **drab'ler** an additional piece of canvas, laced to the bottom of the bonnet of a sail, to give it greater depth. [LGer *drabbeln* to wade about]

Dracaena *drə-sē'nə*, *n* the dragon-tree genus. [LL *dracaena* a she-dragon, from Gr *drakaina*, feminine of *drakōn* dragon]

drachm *dram*, *n* a drachma; a dram.

drachma *drak'mə*, *n* in ancient Greece, a weight and a silver coin of different values; the standard unit of modern Greek currency (100 *lepta*): — *pl* **drach'mas**, **drach'mae** (*-mē*) or **drach'mai** (*-mī*). [Gr *drachmē*, from *drassesthai* to grasp with the hand]

Draco *drā'kō*, *n* the Dragon, a northern constellation; a dragon-lizard. — *n* **dracone** (*dra'kōn*, sometimes *dra-kō'ni*; also with *cap*; ® in US) a large sausage-shaped, bag-like container for transporting liquids, towed on the surface of the sea, etc. — *adj* **draconian** (*drək-*, *drak-ō-ni-ən*) or **draconic** (*-on'ik*) of or of the nature of a dragon. — *n* **draconites** (*drak-ə-nī'tēz*) a precious stone fabled to come from a dragon's brain. — *n* **dracontiasis** (*drak-ən-tī'ə-sis*) guinea-worm disease. — *n* **Dracontium** (*drə-kon'shi-əm*) a S American araceous genus formerly of medical repute. — *n* **dracunculus** (*drə-kungk'ū-ləs*) (with *cap*) the green dragon genus of Araceae; the dragonet; the guinea-worm. [L *dracō*, *-ōnis*, and Gr *drakōn*, *-ontos* a dragon or snake, dimins L *dracunculus*, Gr *drakontion*, prob from the root of Gr *derkesthai* to look]

Draconian *drə-* or *drā-kō'ni-ən*, **Draconic** *-kon'ik* or **Dracontic** *-kont'ik*, *adj* extremely severe, like the laws of *Draco* (Gr *Drakōn*), archon at Athens 621 BC. — *n* **Draconism** (*drak'ən-izm*). — All words also without *cap*.

drad *drad*, (*Spenser*) *pa t* and *pa p* of **dread**. — *adj* (*Spenser*) dread.

draff *drăf*, *n* dregs; the refuse of malt after brewing. — *adj* **draff'ish** or **draff'y** worthless. [Prob related to Du *draf*, Ger *Treber*, *Träber*]

draft *dräft*, *n* anything drawn; the selecting of a smaller body (of people, animals or things) from a larger; the body so selected (*esp military*); a member of it; conscription (*US*); an order eg to a bank for the payment of money; a demand (upon resources, credulity, patience, etc); a plan; a preliminary sketch, or version of a piece of writing; (occasional and *US*) a draught (in various senses). — *vt* to draw an outline of; to draw up in preliminary form; to draw off; to detach. — *n* **draftee'** a conscript. — *n* **draft'er** or **draught'er** a person who drafts; a draught-horse. — **draftiness**, **drafty** see **draught**. — **draft'-bar** a draw-bar; **draft'-dodger** (*US colloq*) a person who avoids conscription; **draft'-dodging**. — **draft'-horse**, **draft'-ox**, **drafts**, **drafts'man**, **drafts'manship** see under **draught**. [**draught**]

drag *drag*, *vt* to draw by force; to draw slowly; to pull roughly and violently; to trail; to explore with a dragnet or hook; to apply a drag to. — *vi* to hang so as to trail on the ground; to be forcibly drawn along; to move slowly and heavily; to lag; to give the feeling of being unduly slow or tedious: — *pr p* **dragg'ing**; *pa t* and *pa p* **dragged**. — *n* anything dragged; an act of dragging; a dragging effect; the component of the aerodynamic force on a body travelling through a fluid (*esp* a vehicle travelling through air) that lies along the longitudinal axis; a net or hook for dragging along to catch things under water; a heavy harrow; a device for guiding wood to the saw; a car, lorry or wagon (*slang*); a mail-coach; a long open carriage, with transverse or side seats; a brake, *esp* an iron shoe that drags on the ground; any obstacle to progress; a tedious, dreary occupation or experience (*slang*); influence, pull (*US slang*); a trail of scent left by an animal, or a trail of broken undergrowth caused by an animal dragging off its prey; an artificial scent dragged on the ground for foxhounds to follow; a short 'draw' on a cigarette (*slang*); a retarded motion of the cue-ball imparted by striking somewhat under the centre (*billiards*, etc); (the wearing of) transvestite clothing, now *usu* women's dress worn by a man, or a form of entertainment involving this (*slang*; also *adj*); a homosexuals' party (*slang*). — *adj* (*slang*) **dragg'y** boring, tedious. — *n* **drag'ster** a car for drag-racing. — **drag'-bar** a draw-bar; **drag'-chain** a chain used as drag to a wheel; a chain for coupling railway vehicles; **drag'hound** a foxhound trained to follow a drag; **drag'-hunt**; **drag'line** an excavating machine, crane-like in appearance, moving on articulated tracks (or **walking dragline**, on 'legs' having steel plates as 'feet'), and drawing towards itself a bucket suspended from a long jib; **drag'-man** a fisherman who uses a dragnet; **drag'net** a net to be dragged along the bottom of water or the ground; a systematic police search for a wanted person; **drag'-parachute** a small parachute attached to the rear of an aircraft, which opens on landing to assist deceleration; **drag'-queen** a professional female impersonator; **drag race** a motor car or motorcycle contest in acceleration, with standing start and over a quarter-mile course; **drag'-racing**; **drag'-shot** a shot that imparts drag to a billiard-ball; **drags'man** the driver of a drag or coach. — **drag by** to pass slowly; **drag on** to continue slowly and tediously; **drag one's feet** or **heels** to hang back deliberately in doing something (*n* **foot'-dragging**); **drag out** to prolong unnecessarily or tediously; **drag out of** to get (information, etc) from (someone) with difficulty, sometimes by force; **drag up** (*colloq*) to mention or quote (a story, etc, *esp* defamatory) inappropriately or unnecessarily; to bring up (a child) badly. [Northern from OE *dragan* or ON *draga*]

dragée *drä'zhā*, *n* a sweet enclosing a drug, or a nut or fruit, etc; a medicated sweet; a chocolate drop; a small silvered ball for decorating a cake. [Fr]

draggle *drag'l*, *vt* or *vi* to make or become wet and dirty, as if by dragging along the ground; to trail. — **dragg'le-tail** a slut. — *adj* **dragg'le-tailed**. [Frequentative of **drag**, and a doublet of **drawl**]

draggy. See **drag**.

dragoman *drag'ō-mən*, *n* an interpreter or guide in Eastern countries: — *pl* **drag'ōmans**. [Fr, from Ar *tarjumān*, from *tarjama* to interpret]

dragon *drag'ən*, *n* a fabulous winged scaly-armoured fire-breathing monster, often a guardian of treasure, ravaging a country when its hoard is rifled; a fierce, intimidating or watchful person; a paper kite; a dragon lizard; applied to various plants, *esp* Dracunculus (green dragon), and Dracontium; (with *cap*) a northern constellation (Draco); (also with *cap*) a racing yacht of the International Dragon class, 8.88m (29.2 feet) long. — *n* **drag'oness** a she-dragon. — *n* **drag'onet** a little dragon; a fish of the genus *Callionymus*. — *adj*

drag'onish. — *n* **drag'onism** unremitting watchfulness. — *vt* **drag'onize** or **-ise** to turn into a dragon; to watch like a dragon. — *adj* **drag'onlike**. — *adj* **dragonné** (*drag-o-nā'*; *heraldry*) like a dragon in the rear part. — **drag'on-fish** a dragonet; a fish of the genus *Pegasus*; **drag'onfly** a predaceous long-bodied often brilliantly-coloured insect of the *Odonata*; **drag'onhead** or **drag'-on's-head** a labiate garden plant (genus *Dracocephalum*; from the shape of the corolla); **dragon lizard** a small tree-dwelling E Indian lizard (genus *Draco*) with parachute of ribs and skin; a S American lizard (*Thorictis*); a monitor, *esp* a species (*Varanus komodoensis*) found in Komodo (in Indonesia), reaching 3 metres (10 feet) in length; **drag'on-root** (*US*) an araceous plant (*Arisaema*) or its tuberous root, used in medicine; **drag'on's-blood** a red resinous exudation from the dragon-tree and many other trees, used for colouring varnishes, etc; **drag'on-stand'ard** a standard in, or bearing, the form of a dragon; **drag'on-tree** a great tree of the Canary Islands (*Dracaena draco*), of the Liliaceae, remarkable for its resin (a variety of dragon's blood), its growth in thickness like a dicotyledon, and the great age it attains. — **chase the dragon** (*slang*) to smoke heroin by heating it and inhaling the fumes; **to sow dragon's teeth** to stir up trouble, cause contention. [Fr, from L *dracō*, *-ōnis*, from Gr *drakōn*, *-ontos*, perh from root *drak*, as in *edrakon*, aorist of *derkesthai* to see clearly]

dragonnade *drag-ən-ād'*, *n* the persecution of French Protestants under Louis XIV by means of dragoons (*hist*); any persecution by military means (*usu* in *pl*). [Fr, from *dragon* dragoon]

dragoon *drə-gōōn'*, *n* an old fire-spitting musket; a mounted infantryman armed with it (*obs*); a heavy cavalryman, as opposed to hussars and lancers, a term surviving in the names of certain regiments. — *vt* to compel by military bullying; to compel by force. — **dragoon'-bird** the umbrella-bird. [Fr *dragon* dragon, dragoon]

dragsman, **dragster**. See under **drag**.

drail *drāl*, *n* the iron bow of a plough from which the traces draw; a piece of lead round the shank of the hook in fishing. — *vi* to draggle. [Prob a combination of **draggle** and **trail**]

drain *drān*, *vt* to draw off by degrees; to filter; to draw off water, sewage or other liquid from; to provide a means of drainage, to instal a drain; to make dry; to drink dry; to exhaust. — *vi* to flow off gradually; to lose liquid gradually (eg by trickling or dripping); to discharge. — *n* a watercourse; a channel allowing liquid to drain; a ditch; a sewer; a drink (*slang*); expenditure that exhausts or diminishes. — *adj* **drain'-able**. — *n* **drain'age** act, process, method or means of draining; means of discharging water; the system of drains in a town. — *n* **drain'er** a device on which articles are placed to drain. — **drain'age-basin** the area of land that drains into one river; **drain'age-tube** a tube for discharge of pus, etc; **drain'ing-board** a sloping surface beside a sink, where dishes, etc are placed to drain when washed; **drain'pipe** a pipe to carry away waste water or rainwater; (in *pl*; *colloq*; also **drainpipe trousers**) very narrow trousers; **drain'-tile**; **drain'-trap** a contrivance for preventing the escape of foul air from drains, while admitting water to them. — **down the drain** (*slang*) gone for good; wasted. [OE *drēahnian*]

draisine or **draisene** *drā-zēn*, (*hist*) *n* dandy-horse. [Invented in early 19c by Baron *Drais*, of Mannheim]

drake[1] *drāk*, *n* the male of the duck; a flat stone thrown so as to skip along the surface of water in playing *ducks and drakes* (also **drake'stone**). [Ety obscure; cf provincial Ger *draak*; OHGer *antrahho*, Ger *Enterich*, the first element usually explained as *eend*, *end*, *anut* duck]

drake[2] *drāk*, *n* a dragon (*archaic*); a fiery meteor (*obs*); a beaked galley, or Viking ship of war (*hist*); an angler's name for species of Ephemera. [OE *draca* dragon, from L *dracō*]

Dralon® *drā'lon*, *n* a type of acrylic fibre.

DRAM *dram*, (*comput*) *abbrev*: dynamic random access memory: — *pl* **DRAMs**.

dram *dram*, *n* a contraction of **drachm**; $\frac{1}{16}$th of an ounce avoirdupois; formerly (still *US*) apothecaries' measure of $\frac{1}{8}$th of an ounce; a small drink of alcohol, *esp* whisky; a tipple. — *vi* to drink a dram. — *vt* to give a dram to. — **dram'-drink'er**; **dram'-shop** a bar. [Through Fr and L, from Gr *drachmē*; see **drachma**]

drama *drä'mə*, *n* a story showing life and action, intended for representation by actors; a composition intended to be represented on the stage, radio or film, etc; the total range of dramatic literature; theatrical entertainment; a dramatic situation, or series of absorbing, exciting, tense or tragic, etc events. — *adj* **dramat'ic** (*drə-mat'ik*) belonging to or of drama: appropriate to or in the form of drama; with the force and vividness of a drama; impressive or important because of speed, size, suddenness, etc. — *adj* **dramat'ical** (*old*) dramatic. — *adv* **dramat'ically**. — *n* **dramat'icism**. — *n* (*usu sing*) **dramat'ics** the acting, production and study of plays; a show of excessive, exaggerated emotion (*colloq*). — *n* **dram'atist** a writer of plays. — *adj* **dramatīz'able** or **-s-** (*dram-*). — *n* **dramatīzā'tion** or **-s-** the act of dramatizing; the dramatized version of a novel or story. — *vt* **dram'atize** or **-ise** to compose in or turn into the form of a drama or play; to exaggerate the importance of or emotional nature of. — **drama documentary** see **faction**; **dramatic irony** a situation, etc in a play, the irony of which is clear to the audience but not to the characters; **dram'atis persō'nae** (*-e* or *-ī*) the characters of a drama or play. [L, from Gr *drama*, *drāmatos*, from *drāein* to do]

Dramamine® *dram'ə-mēn*, *n* a drug used *esp* to treat travel sickness.

dramaturgy *dram'ə-t ur-ji*, *n* the principles of dramatic composition; theatrical art. — *n* **dram'aturg'** (from Ger) a member of a theatrical company who selects the repertoire and may assist in the arranging and production of the plays, compiling notes for the programme, etc. — *n* **dram'aturge** or **dram'aturgist** a playwright. — *adj* **dramatur'gic** or **dramatur'gical**. [Through Fr from Gr *drāmatourgiā*, *drāmatourgos* playwright, from *drāma*, and *ergon* a work]

Drambuie® *dram-bōō'i*, *-bū'i*, *n* a Scotch whisky liqueur. [**dram**, and Gaelic *buidhe* yellow, golden, or agreeable, pleasant]

dramma giocoso *dram'ma jō-kō'sō*, *n* (Ital, comic drama) comic opera. — **dramma per musica** (*per mōō'zē-ka*; Ital, drama through music) an *esp* 17 and 18c term for opera, or for the musical drama that was its forerunner.

drammock *dram'ək*, *n* meal and water mixed raw. — Also **dramm'ach**. [Cf Gaelic *drama*(*i*)*g* a foul mixture]

Drang nach Osten *drang nahh ō'stən*, *n* (*Ger*, *hist*) eastward thrust, the policy of German expansionists.

drank *drangk*, *pa t* of **drink**.

drant or **draunt** *dränt*, *drönt*, (*dialect*) *vi* and *vt* to drawl, to drone. — *n* a droning tone.

drap *drap*, *n* and *v*. Scots form of **drop**. — *n* **drapp'ie** or **drapp'y** (*Scot*) a little drop, *esp* of spirits.

drap-de-Berry *drä-də-ber-ē'*, (*obs*) *n* a woollen cloth made in Berry, in France. — Also *adj*. [Fr, Berry cloth]

drape *drāp*, *vt* to cover as with cloth; to hang cloth in folds about; (also *reflexive*) to put (oneself or a limb) in a casual and graceful pose. — *n* a hanging or curtain (*NAm* and *theat*); (in *pl*) a drape suit. — *adj* **draped**. — *n* **drāp'er** a dealer in cloth, textiles and clothing. — *adj* **drāp'eried** draped. — *n* **drāp'ery** cloth, textiles, etc; hangings; the draper's business; the representation of clothes and hanging folds of cloth (*art*): — *pl* **drāp'eries**. — *vt* to drape. — *n* **drapet** (*drap'it*; *Spenser*) a cloth covering. — *n* **drapier** (*drāp'i-ər*; *obs*) a draper. — **drape suit** a man's suit with narrow trousers and a **drape coat** or **jacket**, a very long jacket (*esp* with velvet collar and cuffs), particularly popular during the 1950s.

[OFr *draper* to weave, drape, *drapier* draper, from *drap* cloth, prob Gmc; see **drab**]

drappie, **drappy**. See **drap**.

drastic *dras'tik*, *adj* forcible, powerful in action; violent; unsparing; great and quick or sudden; dramatic; bad, unpleasant; extreme. — *n* (*med*) a severe purgative. — *adv* **dras'tically**. [Gr *drastikos*, from *drāein*, to act, to do]

drat *drat*, *interj* used to express vexation, (sometimes with an object). — *adj* **dratt'ed**. [Aphetic from **God rot**]

dratchell *drach'l*, (*dialect*) *n* a slut.

draught *dräft*, *n* the act of drawing or pulling; a pull; attraction; the thing or quantity drawn; readiness for drawing from the cask; the act of drinking; the quantity drunk in one breath; a dose of liquor or medicine; the outline of a picture, or a preliminary sketch or plan (*usu* **draft**); that which is taken in a net by drawing; a chosen detachment of men (*usu* **draft**); a current of air; the depth to which a ship sinks in the water; a move in a game (*obs*); a thick disc used in the game of draughts (also **draughts'man**); (in *pl*) a game played by two persons moving draughtmen alternately on a chequered board; a cesspool or privy (*Shakesp*, etc). — *adj* on draught. — *vt* to sketch out or make a preliminary plan of or attempt at (also **draft**); occasionally for **draft** in sense of draw off or set apart from a larger body. — *n* **draughter** see **draft**. — *n* **draught'iness** or (*NAm*) **draf'tiness**. — *adj* **draught'y** or (*NAm*) **draf'ty** full of draughts or currents of air. — **draught'-animal**, **-horse**, **-ox**, etc, one used for drawing heavy loads; **draught-bar** see **draw-bar**; **draught'board** a chessboard used for playing draughts; **draught'en'gine** the engine over the shaft of a coal-pit. — *n pl* **draught'-hooks** large iron hooks fixed on the cheeks of a cannon-carriage. — **draught'-house** (*Bible*, etc) a sink or privy; **draught'man** a piece used for playing draughts; **draught'-net** a dragnet. — *adj* **draught'-proof** sealed, filled, etc to prevent draughts. — Also *vt*. — **draught'-proofing**; **draught'-screen** a screen for warding off a current of air; **draughts'man** a piece used in playing draughts; someone skilled or employed in drawing; someone who draughts or draws up documents (in this sense usually **draftsman**); **draughts'manship**. — **feel the draught** (*fig*) to be unpleasantly conscious of difficult conditions, *esp* being short of money; **on draught** (of liquor) sold from the cask. [OE *draht*, from *dragan* to draw; see **drag** and **draw**]

draunt. See **drant**.

drave *drāv*. Old *pa t* of **drive**.

Dravidian *drə-vid'i-ən*, *adj* belonging to a dark, long-headed, wavy-haired race of S India; belonging to a group of languages in S India, *incl* Tamil, Malayalam, Kannada, Telugu, etc. — Also *n*. [Sans *Drāviḍa* an ancient province of S India]

draw *drö*, *vt* to pull; to drag; to pull along; to bring forcibly towards or after one; to pull into position; to pull back; to pull back the string of; to pull together or away; to take (eg a raffle ticket) at random from a number; to entice, attract; to coax into giving information; to encourage to talk freely (*usu* **draw out**); to inhale; to take out; to unsheathe; to withdraw; to cause to flow out; to evoke or bring out by some artifice; to extract by pulling; to extract the essence of; to eviscerate; to pull through a small hole, as in making wire; to deduce; to lengthen; to extend to the full length; to force to appear (eg to force a badger from its hole); to receive or take from a source or store; to demand by a draft; to get by lot; to trace; to construct in linear form; to make a picture of by drawing lines; to describe; to put into shape, to frame; to write out (eg a cheque); to require as depth of water for floating; to finish without winning or losing; to glance (*cricket*); to hit (the ball) too much to the left (if right-handed) or to the right (if left-handed) (*golf*); to deliver (a bowl) so that it moves in a curve to the point aimed for (*bowls*); to deliver gently (*curling*); to force one's opponents to play (all their cards of a suit, *esp* trumps) by continually leading cards of that suit (*bridge*, etc); to hit (the cue ball) so that it recoils after striking another ball (*billiards*, etc); in a foundry, etc, to remove a pattern from a mould. — *vi* to pull; to practise drawing; to move; to make one's way, go; to resort; to approach; to make a draught; (of a flue, etc) to have a good current of air; to act as drawer; to draw a card, a sword or lots; to infuse; to end a game without winning or losing; to move in a curve to the point aimed for (*bowls*): — *pa t* **drew** (*drōō*); *pa p* **drawn**. — *n* the act of drawing; assignment by lot of prizes, opponents in a game, etc; anything drawn; a drawn or undecided game; an attraction; a drawer (of a chest of drawers; *US*). — *adj* **draw'able**. — *n* **drawee'** the business or person on whom a bill of exchange is drawn; the bank on which a cheque is drawn. — *n* **draw'er** a person or thing that draws; the person that signs a cheque or bill of exchange; someone who draws beer or fetches liquor in a tavern; (*drör*) a thing drawn out, such as the sliding box in a **chest of drawers**; (in *pl*) a close-fitting undergarment for the lower part of the body and the legs. — *n* **draw'ing** the art of representing objects or forms by lines drawn, shading, etc; a picture in lines; the act of assigning by lot; the act of pulling, etc. — *n pl* **drawings** any monies or other assets taken by the owner of a business, or paid by the business on the owner's behalf. — *adj* **drawn** pulled together; closed; neither won nor lost; unsheathed; eviscerated; strained, tense; etiolated (*bot*). — **draw'back** a disadvantage; a receiving back of some part of the duty on goods on their exportation; **draw'bar** a sliding bar; a bar used in coupling railway vehicles (also **drag'-bar** and **draught'-bar**); **drawbar outfit** a lorry, whether or not articulated, with a trailer; **draw'-boy** *orig* the boy who pulled the cords of the harness in figure-weaving; a mechanical device for this purpose; **draw'bridge** a bridge that can be drawn up or let down as required; bridge played by two people, with two dummy hands, not exposed; **draw'-down** a reduction, diminution; **draw'-gear** the apparatus by which railway-cars are coupled; **draw hoe** a hoe designed for pulling soil towards one, having a flat blade at about right angles to the handle; **draw'ing board** a slab on which paper can be pinned for drawing on; the planning stage of a project, etc (*fig*); **draw'ing-frame** a machine in which carded wool, cotton or the like is drawn out fine; **draw'ing-knife** a knife with a handle at each end, used by a cooper for shaving hoops by drawing it towards him; **draw'ing-master**; **draw'ing-paper**; **draw'ing-pen**; **draw'ing-pencil**; **draw'ing-pin** or **drawing pin** a short broad-headed pin for fastening paper to a drawing board, etc; **draw'ing-room** in engineering, a room where plans and patterns are drawn (see also separate article); **draw'ing-table** (also **draw-leaf table**, **draw-table** and **draw-top table**) a table which can be extended in length by drawing out sliding leaves; **draw'-net** same as **dragnet**; **drawn'-thread' work** or **drawn work** ornamental needlework done by pulling out some of the threads of a fabric; **draw'-plate** a plate supporting dies for drawing wire or tubing; **draw'-sheet** (in nursing) a sheet that can be drawn out from under a patient; **draw'-string** or **draw'string** a string or cord, etc, in a casing in or threaded through material, by which the material may be drawn or gathered up. — *adj* having or closed by such a string. — **draw-table**, **draw-top table** see **drawing-table**; **draw'-tube** a tube sliding within another, as in a form of telescope; **draw'-well** a well from which water is drawn up by a bucket and apparatus. — **at daggers drawn** openly hostile; **draw attention to** see under **attention**; **draw a bead on** see under **bead**; **draw a blank** literally, to get a lottery ticket that wins no prize; to get no result; **draw a cover** (or **covert**) to send the hounds into a cover to frighten out a fox; **draw back** to recoil; to withdraw; **draw blank** to draw a cover, but find no fox; **draw, hang and quarter** see under **hang**; **draw in** to reduce, contract; to become shorter; **draw it fine** to be too precise; **draw it mild**

(*colloq*) to refrain from exaggeration; **draw near** to approach; **draw off** to cause to flow from a barrel, etc; to withdraw; **draw on** to approach; to pull on; **draw on** or **upon** to make a draught upon; to make a demand upon (eg one's credulity, patience or resources); to draw one's weapon against; **draw on one's imagination** to make imaginative or lying statements; **draw on one's memory** to try to remember; to make use of what one remembers; **draw out** to leave the place (of an army, etc); to lengthen; to entice into talk and self-expression; **draw rein** to slacken speed, to stop; **draw someone's attention to** see under **attention**; **draw stumps** to end play in cricket by removing the wickets; **draw the cloth, board** or **table** (*archaic*) to clear up after a meal; **draw the line** to fix a limit; to find finally and positively unacceptable; **draw the long bow** see under **bow**[2]; **draw the teeth of** to make harmless; **draw to a head** to mature; **draw up** to form in regular order; to compose, put into shape; to stop; **in drawing** correctly drawn; **out of drawing** inaccurately drawn, or drawn in violation of the principles of drawing; **out of the top drawer** of top grade, *esp* socially. [OE *dragan*; cf **drag**]

Drawcansir *drö-kan'sər*, (*literary*) *n* a blustering bully. [*Drawcansir* (parodying Dryden's *Almanzor*), who 'kills 'em all on both sides' in Buckingham's play *The Rehearsal* (performed 1671)]

drawing-room[1] or **drawing room** *drö'ing-ro͝om*, *n* a room to which the company withdraws after dinner, a formal sitting-room; (formerly) a reception of company at court; a private compartment of a railway parlor-car (*US*). — *adj* suitable for the drawing-room. [Orig **withdrawing-room**]

drawing-room[2]. See under **draw**.

drawl *dröl*, *vi* to speak in a slow lengthened tone; to dawdle (*obs*). — *vt* to say in a slow and sleepy manner. — *n* a slow, lengthened utterance. — *n* **drawl'er**. — *adv* **drawl'ingly**. — *n* **drawl'ingness**. [Connected with **draw**]

drawn *drön*, *pa p* of **draw**, and *adj*.

dray[1] *drā*, *n* a low strong cart for heavy goods; a timber sledge; that which is dragged or drawn. — *n* **dray'age**. — **dray'-horse**; **dray'man**; **dray'-plough**. [Cf OE *dræge* dragnet, from *dragan* to draw; see **drag** and **draw**]

dray[2]. See **drey**.

drazel *dräz'l*, (*dialect*) *n* a slut. [Origin unknown]

dread *dred*, *n* great fear; awe; an object of fear or awe; fury (*Spenser*). — *adj* dreaded; inspiring great fear or awe. — *vt* to fear greatly; to reverence; to feel great apprehension towards or dismay about (*colloq*); to cause to fear, to frighten (*obs*). — *adj* **dread'ed** (now *usu facetiously*; with **the**) fearsome, terrifying. — *n* **dread'er**. — *adj* **dread'ful** *orig*, full of dread; producing great fear or awe; terrible; very bad, unpleasant (*colloq*). — *adv* **dread'fully** in a dreadful way; very (much) (*colloq*). — *n* **dread'fulness**. — *adj* **dread'less**. — *adv* (*Spenser*, etc) doubtless. — *adv* **dread'lessly**. — *n* **dread'lessness**. — *adv* **dread'ly**. — **dread locks** or **dread'locks** the long tightly curled or plaited hairstyle adopted by Rastafarians; **dread'nought** or **dread'-naught** someone who dreads nothing; a thick woollen cloth or garment made of it for wear in inclement weather; a powerful type of battleship or battle-cruiser (dating from 1905–6). — **penny dreadful** a cheap sensational serial or book, etc. [ME *dreden*, from OE *ondrǣdan* to fear; ON *ondrēda*, OHGer *intratan* to be afraid]

dream[1] *drēm*, *n* a train of thoughts and images experienced during sleep, a vision; something only imaginary; a distant hope or ideal, probably unattainable. — *vi* to experience dreams during sleep; to think idly (with *of*); to think (of) as possible, contemplate as imaginably possible. — *vt* to see or imagine in, or as in, a dream: — *pa t* and *pa p* **dreamed** or **dreamt** (*dremt*). — *n* **dream'er**. — *n* **dream'ery** a place favourable to dreams; dream-like fancies. — *adj* **dream'ful** (*Tennyson*) dreamy. — *adv* **dream'ily**. — *n* **dream'iness**. — *n* and *adj* **dream'ing**. — *adv* **dream'ingly**. — *adj* **dream'less**. — *adv* **dream'lessly**. — *n* **dream'lessness**. — *adj* **dream'y** full of dreams; given to dreaming; appropriate to dreams; dream-like; lovely (*colloq*). — **dream'boat** (*slang*) someone wonderful and desirable, *usu* of the opposite sex; **dream'-land** the land of dreams, reverie, or imagination; **dream ticket** (*orig US*; *esp* a pair of candidates considered) the ideal or optimum electoral ticket; **dream'time** in the mythology of Australian Aboriginals, the time when the earth and patterns of life on earth took shape; **dream'while** the duration of a dream; **dream'-world** a world of illusions. — **dream up** to plan in the mind, often unrealistically; **go like a dream** to work or progress, etc very well. [ME *dream*, *drēm*; perh the same word as **dream**[2]]

dream[2] *drēm*, (*obs*) *n* joy; mirth; minstrelsy; music; sound. — **dream'hole** a hole in the wall of a steeple, tower, etc for admitting light. [OE *drēam* joy, mirth]

dreary *drēr'i*, *adj* gloomy; cheerless; dull and tedious. — *adj* **drear** dreary. — *n* (*Spenser* **dreare** or **drere**) dreariness; gloom; mishap. — *n* **drear'ihead**, **drear'iment**, **drear'iness**, **drear'ing** (all *Spenser*) or **drear'ihood**. — *adv* **drear'ily**. — *adj* **drear'isome** desolate, forlorn. [OE *drēorig* mournful, bloody, from *drēor* gore]

dreck *drek*, (*slang*) *n* rubbish, trash. — *adj* **dreck'y**. [Yiddish *drek*, Ger *Dreck* dirt, filth, dung]

dredge[1] *drej*, *n* a bag-net for dragging along the bottom to collect oysters, biological specimens, mud, etc; a machine for deepening a harbour, canal, river, etc, for excavating under water or on land, or for raising alluvial deposits and washing them for minerals, by means of buckets on an endless chain, pumps, grabs, or other devices. — *vt* and *vi* to gather, explore or deepen with a dredge. — *n* **dredg'er** someone who dredges; a machine for dredging; a boat, ship or raft equipped for dredging. [Connected with **drag** and **draw**]

dredge[2] *drej*, *vt* to sprinkle. — *n* **dredg'er**, **dredge'-box** or **dredg'ing-box** a container with a perforated lid for dredging. [OFr *dragie* sugar-plum, from Gr *tragēmata* dessert]

dree *drē*, (*Scot*) *vt* to endure, bear. — **dree one's weird** to undergo one's destiny. [OE *drēogan* to suffer, accomplish]

dreg *dreg*, *n* a trace, a small quantity. [ON *dregg*]

dregs *dregz*, *n pl* impurities in liquid that fall to the bottom, the grounds; dross; the most worthless part of anything. — *n* **dregg'iness**. — *adj* **dregg'y** containing dregs; muddy; foul. [ON *dregg*]

dreich *drēhh*, (*Scot*) *adj* long drawn out; tedious; dreary. [See **dree**]

dreikanter *drī'kān-tər*, *n* a pebble faceted by wind-blown sand, properly having three faces: — *pl* **drei'kanter** or **drei'kanters**. [Ger *Dreikant* solid angle, from *drei* three, and *Kante* edge]

drek. Same as **dreck**.

drench *drench*, *drensh*, *vt* to fill with drink or liquid; to wet thoroughly; to soak; to force a drench upon (an animal); to drown (*obs*). — *vi* (*obs*) to drown. — *n* a draught; a dose of liquid medicine forced down the throat (of an animal). — *n* **drench'er**. [OE *drencan* to cause to drink (*drincan* to drink), *drenc* drink, drowning; Ger *tränken* to soak; see **drink**]

drent *drent* (*Spenser*), *obs pa p* of **drench** to drown.

drepanium *dri-pā'ni-əm*, (*bot*) *n* a cymose inflorescence in which each daughter axis is on the same side of its parent axis, and all in one plane. [Latinized from Gr *drepanion*, dimin of *drepanon* a reaping-hook]

drere, drerihead, etc. Spenserian forms of **drear**, etc.

Dresden china, or **Dresden porcelain** or **ware** *drez'dən* (*chī'nə*, *pōrs'lin* or *wār*), *n* fine decorated china made in Saxony (Royal Saxon porcelain factory established at Meissen, 1710).

dress *dres*, *vt* to clothe; to apply suitable materials to; to straighten; to flatten; to smooth; to erect; to set in order; to prepare, arrange; to adorn; to finish or trim; to draw (a fowl), to gut and trim (a fish, etc); to add seasoning to (food); to manure; to treat; to tend; to tie (a fly) (*angling*); to treat with severity; to chide; to thrash. — *vi* to put on clothes; to put on finer, more elaborate, or more formal clothes; to come into line: — *pa t* and *pa p* **dressed**, sometimes (now *obs*) **drest**. — *n* the covering or ornament of the body; a woman's one-piece skirted garment; style of clothing; ceremonial or formal clothing. — *adj* pertaining to (formal) evening dress. — *n* **dress'er** a person who dresses; a medical student who dresses wounds; a lady's maid; a person who assists an actor to dress (*theat*); a tool or machine for dressing; a table on which meat is dressed or prepared for use; a kitchen sideboard, *esp* with a high back and shelves; a chest of drawers or dressing-table (*US*). — *n* **dress'ing** dress or clothes; the action of someone who dresses; material applied to a wound; material applied to goods, eg a coat of preservative; matter used to give stiffness and gloss to cloth; sauce or (*US*) stuffing, etc, used in preparing a dish for the table, etc; manure or the like applied to land; an ornamental moulding; a thrashing. — *adj* **dress'y** fond of dress; showy; indicating care in dressing. — **dress'-cir'cle** part of a theatre (*usu* the first gallery), *orig* intended for people in evening dress; **dress'-coat** a man's fine black coat with narrow or cut-away skirts, worn in full dress (see below); **dressed day** (formerly) the second day of a three days' visit; **dress form** a dressmaker's (*usu* adjustable) model. — *n pl* **dress'-goods** fabrics for making women's and children's gowns, frocks, etc. — **dress'guard** (*archaic*) an arrangement of strings to protect the rider's dress from contact with a bicycle wheel; **dress'-improver** (*obs*) a bustle; **dress'ing-case** a case for toiletry requisites; **dress'ing-down** a severe scolding; a thrashing; **dress'ing-gown** a loose garment worn before or whilst dressing, or in dishabille, etc; **dress'ing-jacket** or (*obs*) **dress'ing-sack** a jacket worn by women in dressing; **dress'ing-room**; **dress'ing-station** a place where wounded are collected and tended by members of a field-ambulance; **dress'ing-table**; **dress'-length** enough (fabric) to make a dress; **dress'-maker** a person who makes clothes; a person who makes clothes for women and children as a living (*vi* **dress'make** *colloq* back-formation); **dress'making** the art or process of making clothes; **dress'-reform** a late 19c movement seeking to make dress more practical; **dress'-rehears'al** a full rehearsal in costume with everything as for the performance. — Also *fig*. — **dress sense** sense of style in dress, knowledge of what suits one; **dress'-shield** a device to protect the armpit of a dress, etc against sweat; **dress'-shirt'**, **dress'-suit'** and **dress'-tie'** those for formal evening dress; **dress uniform** a formal, ceremonial uniform. — **dress down** to handle with severity; to reprimand severely; to thrash; to dress deliberately informally; **dress up** to dress elaborately; to dress for a part; to masquerade; to treat so as to make appear better or more interesting, etc than it really is; **evening dress** or **full dress** the costume prescribed by fashion for evening receptions, dinners, balls, etc; **get dressed** to put one's clothes on. [OFr *dresser* to prepare, from an inferred LL *dīrectiāre* to straighten; see **direct**]

dressage *dres'äzh*, *n* training of a horse in deportment and response to controls; this equestrian discipline practised in competition; the manoeuvres practised. [Fr]

drest *drest*, (*obs*) *pa t* and *pa p* of **dress**.

drevill *drev'il*, (*Spenser*) *n* a foul person. [Cf MDu *drevel* scullion]

drew *dro͞o*, *pa t* of **draw**.

drey or **dray** *drā*, *n* a squirrel's nest. [Ety dubious]

drib *drib*, *vi* (*obs*) to trickle; to go little by little. — *vt* (*obs*) to let trickle; to take a little, filch; to lead gradually; to shoot (an arrow) short or wide. — *n* a drop; a trickle; a small quantity — *n* **dribb'er**. (*obs*). — *n* **dribb'let** or **drib'let** a drop; a trickle; a small quantity. — **dribs and drabs** small quantities at a time. [Related to **drip**]

dribble *drib'l*, *vi* to fall in small drops; to drop quickly; to trickle; to slaver, like a child or an idiot. — *vt* to let fall in drops; to give out in small portions; to drib (*archery*; *Shakesp*). — *vt* and *vi* to move the ball forward little by little, tricking opponents (*football*, *hockey*, etc). — Also *n*. — *n* **dribb'ler**. — *adj* **dribb'ly**. [Frequentative of **drib**]

dricksie. See **druxy**.

dried, **drier**, **dries**, **driest**. See **dry**.

drift *drift*, *n* a driving; a drove (*archaic*); a heap of matter (eg snow) driven together; floating materials driven by water; a driving shower; a streaming movement; the direction in which a thing is driven; a slow current caused by the wind; leeway; passive travel with the current, wind, etc; abandonment to external influences; tendency; a cattle-track, drove-road; a group of animals driven or herded; a pin or bar driven into a hole, eg to enlarge it (also **drift'pin**); a drift-net; a set of nets; the object aimed at; the meaning or implication of words used; loose superficial deposits, *esp* glacial or fluvio-glacial (*geol*); a horizontal or oblique excavation or passage (*mining*); a ford (*SAfr*; from *Du*). — *vt* to drive; to carry by drift; to cause or allow to drift; to pierce or tunnel. — *vi* to be floated along; to be driven into heaps; to leave things to circumstances; to wander around, or live, without any definite aim. — *n* **drift'age** that which is drifted; the amount of deviation from a ship's course due to leeway. — *n* **drift'er** someone who or something which drifts; an aimless shiftless person; a fisherman or a fishing-boat that uses a drift-net. — *adj* **drift'less** without drift. — *adj* **drift'y** full of or forming drifts. — **drift'-anchor** an anchor for keeping the ship's head to the wind; **drift'-bolt** a steel bolt used to drive out other bolts; **drift'-ice** floating masses of ice drifting before the wind; **drift'-land** an old tribute paid for the privilege of driving cattle through a manor; **drift'-mining** gold-mining by means of drifts in the gravel and detritus of old river-beds; coal-mining by means of drifts; **drift'-net** a net which is allowed to drift with the tide; **drift'pin** see **drift** *n* above; **drift'-sail** a sail immersed in the water, used for lessening the drift of a vessel during a storm; **drift transistor** (*radio*) one in which resistivity increases continuously between emitter and collector junctions, improving high-frequency performance; **drift tube** (*electronics*) tube-shaped electrode in which electrons pass without significant change in velocity, while the accelerating radio frequency voltage changes; **drift'-way** a road over which cattle are driven; drift (*mining*); **drift'-weed** gulf-weed; tangle; seaweed thrown up on the beach; **drift'wood** wood drifted by water. [ME; ON *drift* snowdrift; root as **drive**]

drill[1] *dril*, *vt* to bore, pierce; to make with a drill; to pierce with a bullet or bullets (*slang*); to exercise (soldiers, pupils, etc) by repeated practice; to sow in rows. — *n* an instrument for boring stone, metal, teeth, or other hard substances; a large boring instrument used in mining, etc; a type of shellfish which bores into the shells of oysters; a training exercise, or a session of it; a drill-master; a ridge with seed or growing plants on it (*esp* vegetables such as turnips, potatoes, etc); the plants in such a row; the machine for sowing the seed; correct procedure or routine (*colloq*). — *n* **drill'er**. — **drill'-barrow** a grain-drill driven by hand; **drill bit** a removeable cutting and boring head in a drill; **drill'-harrow** a harrow for working between drills; **drill'-hole** a hole bored in the ground eg for rock samples; **drill'-husbandry** the method of sowing seed in drills or rows; **drill'ing-machine**, **drill'ing-lathe** or **drill'-press** a machine for boring with a drill or drills; **drilling mud** a mixture of clays, water, density-increasing agents and sometimes thixotropic agents pumped down through the drilling pipe and used to cool, lubricate and flush debris from the drilling assembly, providing the hydrostatic pressure to contain the oil and gas when this is reached; **drilling pipe** the tube which connects the drilling platform to the drill bit and imparts rotary motion to the latter; **drilling platform** a floating or fixed offshore structure supporting a drilling rig; **drilling rig** or **drill rig** the complete apparatus and structure required for drilling an oil well; **drill'-master** a person who teaches drill, or who trains in anything, *esp* in a mechanical manner; **drill'-plough** a plough for sowing grain in drills; **drill-press** see **drilling-machine**; **drill rig** see **drilling rig**; **drill'-sergeant** a sergeant who drills soldiers; **drill'ship** a free-floating ship-shaped drilling platform. [Prob borrowed from Du *drillen* to bore; *dril, drille* a borer; cf **thrill**]

drill[2] *dril, n* a W African baboon, smaller than the mandrill. [Perh a W Afr word]

drill[3] *dril, n* a stout twilled linen or cotton cloth. — Also **drill'ing**. [Ger *Drillich* ticking, from L *trilīx* three-threaded; *trēs, tria* three, and *līcium* thread]

drilling. See **drill**[1, 3].

drily. See under **dry**.

D-ring. See under **D** (noun).

drink *dringk, vt* to swallow (a liquid); to empty (a glass, bowl, etc) by swallowing the contents; to absorb; to take in through the senses; to smoke (tobacco; *obs*). — *vi* to swallow a liquid; to drink alcohol; to drink alcohol to excess: — *pr p* **drink'ing**; *pa t* **drank**, *archaic* **drunk**; *pa p* **drunk**. — *n* an act of drinking; a quantity drunk; something to be drunk; a beverage; intoxicating liquor, alcohol. — *adj* **drink'able**. — *n* **drink'ableness**. — *n* **drink'er** a person who drinks; a tippler. — *n* **drink'ing**. — *adj* fit to drink; for drinking. — *adj* **drink-drive'** pertaining to drink-driving. — *vi* to drive under the influence of alcohol. — **drink-dri'ver** someone who drives a vehicle after having drunk alcohol, *esp* more than the legally permitted amount. — *n* and *adj* **drink-dri'ving**. — *interj* **drink'-hail** an Early Middle English reply to a pledge in drinking (*waes hail* (later **wassail**), be healthy, or lucky, was answered with *drinc hail* drink healthy or lucky, *hail* being ON adj *heill*, not OE *hāl*). — **drink'ing-bout**; **drink'ing-fountain**; **drink'ing-horn**; **drinking-up time** in a public house, the few minutes allowed after official closing time for customers to finish their last drinks before leaving; **drink'-money** a gratuity, ostensibly given to buy liquor for drinking to the health of the giver; **drink'-offering** an offering of wine, oil, blood, etc to a god. — **drink oneself drunk** to drink until one is drunk; **drink in** to absorb (rain, etc), as dry land does; to take in eagerly (something seen, said, etc); **drink off** to quaff wholly and at a gulp; **drink (someone** or **the others**, etc) **under the table** to continue drinking and remain (comparatively) sober after others have completely collapsed; **drink to, drink to the health of** or **drink the health of** to drink wine, etc, with good wishes for the health, prosperity, etc of, to toast; **drink up** to empty by drinking; to finish drinking; **in drink** (while) intoxicated; **strong drink** alcoholic liquor; **the drink** (*slang*) the sea; a bribe. — See also **drunk**. [OE *drincan*; Ger *trinken*]

drip *drip, vi* to fall in drops; to let fall drops. — *vt* to let fall in drops: — *pr p* **dripp'ing**; *pa t* and *pa p* **dripped**. — *n* a falling in drops; that which falls in drops; the projecting edge of a roof or sill, etc; a device for passing a fluid slowly and continuously, *esp* into a vein of the body (also **drip'-feed**); the material so passed; a weak, pathetic person (*colloq*); drivel, *esp* sentimental (*slang*). — *n* **dripp'ing** that which falls in drops, *esp* fat from meat during roasting. — *adj* **dripp'y** (*colloq*) silly, inane. — *adj* **drip'-dry'** (of a material or garment) which, when allowed to dry by dripping, requires no, or little, ironing. — Also *vi* and *vt*. — **drip'-feed** a drip (see above). — *vt* to treat (a patient, etc) with a drip. — **drip irrigation** a system of irrigation in which water is supplied through pipes to the roots of a crop; **dripp'ing-pan** a pan for receiving the dripping from roasting meat; **dripping roast** a source of easy and continuous profits; **drip'-stone** a projecting moulding over a doorway, etc, serving to throw off the rain; **drip'-tip** (*bot*) a prolonged leaf-tip, serving to shed rain. — **right of drip** a right in law to let the drip from one's roof fall on another's land. [OE *dryppan*, from *drēopan*]

drisheen *dri-shēn', n* a type of Irish sausage made with sheep's blood. [Ir *drisín*]

drive *drīv, vt* to urge along; to hurry on; to control or guide the movements or operations of; to convey or carry in a vehicle; to urge or force in or through; to push briskly; to provide motive power to; to urge (a point of argument); to carry through (eg a bargain); to impel; to compel; to send away with force, eg a ball, *esp* (*golf*) to play from the tee or with a driver, (*cricket*) to hit strongly down the pitch, and (*tennis*) to return forcibly underarm; to chase; to excavate (eg a tunnel); to sort out (feathers) in a current of air. — *vi* to control an engine, vehicle or draught-animal, etc; to press forward with violence; to be forced along (like a ship before the wind); to be driven; to go in a motor vehicle or carriage; to aim or tend towards a point (with *at*); to strike with a sword or the fist, etc (with *at*): — *pr p* **drīv'ing**; *pa t* **drōve** or *archaic* **drāve**, and *Spenser* **drive** (*driv*); *pa p* **driv'en**. — *n* an excursion in a vehicle; a road for driving on, *esp* the approach to a house within its own grounds; a driving stroke (*sport*); impulse; impulsive force; power of getting things done; a motivational concept used to describe changes in responsiveness to a consistent external stimulus (*behav*); the chasing of game towards the shooters, or the sport so obtained, or the ground over which the game is driven; pushing sales by reducing prices; an organized campaign to attain any end; a meeting in order to play certain games, eg whist; apparatus for driving. — *n* **drivabil'ity** or **driveabil'ity**. — *adj* **driv'able** or **drive'able**. — *n* **driv'er** a person who or thing which drives, in all senses; a club used in golf to propel the ball from the tee. — *adj* **driv'erless** running or able to run, without a driver. — **drive'-in** a refreshment stop, store, cinema, etc where patrons are catered for while still remaining in their motor cars. — Also *adj*. — **drive'way** a carriage drive; a drive, *esp* connecting a house or other premises with the public road; **driv'ing-band** the band or strap that communicates motion from one machine, or part of a machine, to another; **driv'ing-box** a box on which a driver sits; **driv'ing-gear** apparatus by which power is transmitted from shaft to shaft; **driving licence** an official licence to drive a motor vehicle; **driv'ing-mirror** a small mirror in which a driver can see what is behind his or her vehicle; **driving seat** the seat in a vehicle in which the driver sits; a position of control; **driv'ing-shaft** a shaft from a driving-wheel communicating motion to machinery; **driving test** a test of ability to drive safely, *esp* an official and obligatory test; **driv'ing-wheel** a main wheel that communicates motion to other wheels; one of the main wheels in a locomotive. — **drive a coach and horses through** (*colloq*) to demolish (an argument, etc) by demonstrating the obvious faults in it; to brush aside, ignore completely; **drive home** to force (eg a nail) completely in; to make completely understood or accepted; **let drive** to aim a blow. [OE *drīfan* to drive; Ger *treiben* to push]

drivel *driv'l, vi* to dribble, slaver like an infant; to speak like an idiot; to be foolish: — *pr p* **driv'elling**; *pa t* and *pa p* **driv'elled**. — *n* slaver; nonsense. — *n* **driv'eller**. [ME *drevelen, dravelen*; OE *dreflian*]

driven. See **drive**.

drizzle *driz'l, vi* to rain in fine drops. — *vt* to shed in fine drops; to pour (a liquid) in drops (*over*) (*cookery*); to cover in fine drops or in mist. — *n* a small, light rain. — *adj* **drizz'ly**. [Frequentative of ME *dresen*, from OE *drēosan* to fall; Gothic *driusan*]

droger or **drogher** *drō'gər, n* a W Indian coasting vessel, with long masts and lateen sails. [Du, orig a vessel on which fish were dried, from *droogen* to dry]

drogue *drōg, n* the drag of boards, attached to the end of a harpoon-line, checking the progress of a running whale; a conical canvas sleeve open at both ends, used as one form of sea-anchor, or to check the way of an aircraft, etc; (or **drogue parachute**) a parachute used to reduce speed of a falling object, eg one fired from a descending space capsule; a funnel device on the end of the hose of a tanker aircraft; a wind-sock; an air target of similar shape. — **drogue bomb** an improvised terrorist bomb, made with a grenade or plastic explosive, using a plastic bag or similar as a drogue to stabilize it when thrown. [Origin obscure]

droguet *dro-gā'*, *n* a ribbed woollen dress fabric, a variety of rep. [Fr; cf **drugget**]

droich *drōhh*, (*Scot*) *n* a dwarf. — *adj* **droich'y** dwarfish. [Gaelic *troich* or *droich*; orig from OE (see **dwarf**)]

droil *droil*, (*obs*) *vi* to drudge. [Perh Du *druilen* to loiter]

droit *drwä* (before a vowel *drwät*; *Eng droit*), *n* right, legal claim. — **droit administratif** (*ad-mēn-ē-stra-tēf*) in France, administrative law; **droit au travail** (*ō-tra-vä-y'*) right to work; **droit des gens** (*dā zhā*) international law; **droit du seigneur** (*dü se-nyœr*) same as **jus primae noctis** (qv under **jus**[1]). [Fr]

drôle *drōl*, *n* a rogue or knave. — *adj* amusing; odd. [Fr]

droll *drōl*, *adj* odd; amusing; laughable. — *n* someone who excites mirth; a jester. — *vi* to practise drollery; to jest. — *n* **droll'ery** drollness; waggery; a comic show, picture or story; a jest; a puppet-show. — *n* **droll'ing**. — *adj* **droll'ish** rather droll. — *n* **droll'ness**. — *adv* **drolly** (*drōl'li*). [Fr *drôle*, prob from Du *drollig* odd, from *trold* a hobgoblin; cf Ger *Droll* a short thick person]

drome *drōm*, (*colloq*) *n* an aerodrome.

dromedary *drum'i-dər-i*, *drom'*, *n* a thoroughbred camel; a one-humped Arabian camel. — (*Spenser*) **drom'edare**. [OFr *dromedaire*, from LL *dromedārius*, from Gr *dromas*, *dromados* running, from *dromos* a course, run]

dromond *drom'* or *drum'ənd*, *n* a swift medieval ship of war. — Also **drom'on**. [OFr, from LL *dromō*, *-ōnis*, from Byzantine Gr *dromōn*, from *dromos* a running, and *dramein* (aorist) to run]

dromophobia *drom-ō-fō'bi-ə*, *n* a morbid fear of crossing streets. [Gr *dromos* public walk, and *phobos* fear]

dromos *drom'os*, *n* a Greek race-course; an entrance-passage or avenue, as to a subterranean tomb, etc (*archaeol*): — *pl* **drom'oi**. — *adj* **drom'ic** or **drom'ical** pertaining to a race-course; basilican. [Gr]

drone *drōn*, *n* the male of the honey-bee; someone who lives on the labour of others, like the drone-bee; a lazy, idle fellow; a deep humming sound; a bass-pipe of a bagpipe; its note; a pedal bass; the burden of a song; a monotonous speaker or speech; an aircraft piloted by remote control. — *vi* to emit a monotonous humming sound; (with *on*) to talk at length in a monotonous or expressionless way. — *vt* to say in such a tone. — *adv* **drōn'ingly**. — *adj* **drōn'ish** like a drone; lazy, idle. — *adv* **dron'ishly**. — *n* **drōn'ishness**. — *adj* **drōn'y**. — **drone'-pipe** a pipe producing a droning sound. [OE *drān* bee, but the quantity of the *a* is doubtful, and relations obscure: perh from Old Saxon]

drongo *drong'gō*, *n* any member of the family *Dicruridae*, glossy-black fork-tailed insect-catching birds of the Old World tropics (also **drong'o-shrike**); a nitwit, a no-hoper (*Austr slang*): — *pl* **drong'oes** or **drong'os**. — **drong'o-cuck'oo** a cuckoo that resembles a drongo. [From Malagasy]

droog *drōōg*, *n* a gang-member, *specif* a violent hooligan of the type portrayed by Anthony Burgess in his novel *A Clockwork Orange* (1962). — *adj* **droog'ish** (of dress, behaviour, etc) reminiscent of a droog. [Coined by Burgess after Russ *drug* a friend]

drook, **drookit**. See **drouk**.

drool *drōōl*, *vi* to slaver; to drivel; to show effusive or lascivious pleasure (with *over*). — *n* drivel. **[drivel]**

droome *drōōm*, (*Spenser*) *n*. Another form of **drum**[1].

droop *drōōp*, *vi* to hang down; to grow weak or faint; to decline. — *vt* to let hang down. — *n* a drooping position. — *adv* **droop'ily**. — *n* **droop'iness**. — *adv* **droop'ingly**. — *adj* **droop'y**. — **droop nose** (*colloq* **droop snoot**; *aeronautics*) a cockpit section hinged on to the main fuselage to provide downward visibility at low speeds. [ON *drūpa* to droop; see **drop**]

drop *drop*, *n* a small rounded blob of liquid that hangs or falls at one time; a very small quantity of liquid; anything hanging like a drop; a pendant; a small round sweet; a curtain dropped between acts (also **drop'-cur'tain**; *theat*); (in *pl*) a medicine taken or applied in drops; a fall; a vertical descent or difference of level; the distance by which something falls or may fall; a lowering; a landing by parachute; an instance of dropping anything; an unpleasant surprise; a trap in the gallows scaffold, the fall of which allows the person being executed to drop; a device for lowering goods into a ship's hold. — *combining form* **drop-** used of something that drops or that causes something to drop or that is used in or for dropping. — *vi* to fall in drops; to let drops fall; to fall suddenly, steeply or sheer; to let oneself fall gently; to sink; to lapse; to diminish; to subside into a condition, come gradually to be; to come casually or accidentally; to move slowly with the tide. — *vt* to let fall in drops; to let fall; to let go, relinquish, abandon, part with; to omit; to lower; to lay; (of an animal) to give birth to; to spot, bespatter, sprinkle; to say casually; to write and send (a note) in an offhand or informal manner; to set down, part with; to cause to fall; to hole, etc (a ball); to score (a goal) with a drop-kick; to set down from a vehicle or a ship; to cease to associate with; to lose (a sum of money or a game as part of a contest); to take one more (shot, stroke) than par (*golf*); to cause to fall; to bring down by a shot: — *pr p* **dropp'ing**; *pa t* and *pa p* **dropped**. — *n* **drop'let** a little drop. — *n* **dropp'er** someone who or something which drops; a tube or contrivance for making liquid come out in drops; a shoot that grows downward from a bulb and develops a new bulb (*hortic*); a dog, eg a setter, that drops to earth on sighting game; an artificial fly attached to the leader (also **drop'fly**; *angling*). — *n* **dropp'ing** that which is dropped; (*usu* in *pl*) dung, excrement. — *n* **dropp'le** (*rare*) a trickle. — *adv* **drop'wise** by drops. — *adj* **drop'-dead** (*slang*, *esp US*) stunning, sensational, breathtaking. — **drop'-drill'** an apparatus for dropping seed and manure into the soil simultaneously; **drop'-forging** the process of shaping metal parts by forging between two dies, one fixed to the hammer and the other to the anvil of a steam or mechanical hammer (*n* and *vt* **drop'-forge**); **drop'-goal'** (*Rugby football*) a goal secured by a drop-kick; **drop'-hamm'er** or **drop'-press** a swaging, stamping or forging machine; **drophead coupé** a car whose top can be opened. — *adj* **drop-in** see **drop in** below. — **drop'-kick** a kick made when the ball rebounds from the ground after dropping from the hand (*Rugby football*; also *vt*); a kick made by both feet while jumping in the air (*wrestling*). — *adj* **drop'-leaf** (of a desk or table) with a hinged leaf (or leaves) which can be raised or dropped to horizontal position, but lies vertical when not in use. — **drop'-lett'er** (*US old*) a letter left at a post-office merely for local delivery; **drop lock** or **drop'lock loan** (*finance*) a bank loan for which interest rates vary with the market, but if the long-term interest rates fall to a specified level it is converted to a fixed-rate long-term bond; **drop'-net** a net suspended from a boom, to be suddenly dropped on a passing shoal of fish; **drop-out** a drop-kick taken following the defender's touchdown (*Rugby football*); a person who has withdrawn from an academic course or from conventional society; a patch which fails to record data on a magnetic tape (*comput*); **dropp'ing-well** (*fig* in Tennyson) a well supplied by water falling in drops from above. — *adj* **drop'-ripe** so ripe as to be ready to drop from the tree. — **drop'-scene** a drop-curtain (see under **drop** *n*); **drop'-scone** or **dropped'-scone** a small thick pancake, a Scotch pancake; **drop serene** (*Milton*) an old medical name for (a type of blindness) amaurosis, literally translated from L *gutta serēna*; **drop'-shot** (*tennis*, etc) a ball made to drop close to the net immediately after clearing it; **drop'stone** a stalactitic calcite; **drop tank** (*aeronautics*) a tank, *esp* for fuel, that can be dropped during flight; **drop'-wort** a species of spiraea (*S. filipendula*) with bead-like root tubercles. — **a drop in the bucket** or **ocean** an infinitesimally small quantity; **at the drop of a hat** immediately; on the smallest provocation; **drop a brick** see under **brick**; **drop a curtsy** to curtsy; **drop astern** (*naut*) to get left more and more behind; **drop away** to depart, disappear; **drop down** to sail, move or row down a coast, or down a river to the sea; **drop in** to come, fall or set, etc in, or to arrive or visit casually, informally unintentionally, or one by one (*n* and *adj* **drop'-in**); **drop off** to fall asleep; to become less, to diminish; to depart, disappear; **drop on** or **drop down on** to single out for reproof or an unpleasant task; **drop out** to disappear from one's place; (of sound) to disappear (during a transmission, etc); to make a drop-kick (*Rugby football*); to withdraw, *esp* from an academic course or from conventional life in society (*n* and *adj* **drop'-out**); **dropping fire** unremitting irregular discharge of small-arms; **drop someone a line** (*colloq*) to write someone a letter; **get the drop on one** (*US*) to be ready to shoot first; hence to have at a disadvantage; **let drop** to disclose inadvertently, or seemingly so; **Prince Rupert's drops** or **Rupert's drops** drops of glass that have fallen in a melted state into cold water, and have assumed a tadpole-like shape, the whole falling to dust with a loud report if the point of the tail be nipped off. [OE *dropa* a drop, *dropian*, *droppian* to drop; Du *drop*, Ger *Tropfe*]

dropsy *drop'si*, *n* a condition characterized by unnatural accumulation of watery fluid in any part of the body (now *usu* called **oedema**). — *adj* **drop'sical** or **drop'sied** (*Shakesp*, etc) affected with dropsy. [Aphetic for **hydropsy**]

drosera *dros'ə-rə*, *n* any plant of the sundew genus of **Droserā'ceae**, a family of insectivorous plants. — *adj* **droserā'ceous**. [Feminine of Gr *droseros* dewy, from *drosos* dew]

droshky *drosh'ki*, or **drosky** *dros'ki*, *n* a low four-wheeled open carriage used in Russia; a German four-wheeled cab. [Russ *drozhki*]

drosometer *dros-om'i-tər*, (*meteorol*) *n* an instrument for measuring dew. [Gr *drosos* dew, and *metron* measure]

drosophila *dros-of'i-lə*, *n* any fly of the *Drosophila* genus of small yellow flies, fruit-flies, which breed in fermenting fruit juices and are used in genetic experiments. [Gr *drosos* dew, moisture, and *phileein* to love]

dross *dros*, *n* the scum of melting metals; waste matter; small or waste coal; refuse; rust; lucre. — *n* **dross'iness**. — *adj* **dross'y** like dross; impure; worthless. [OE *drōs*]

drostdy *dros'dā*, (*SAfr*) *n* (formerly) the house and office of a landdrost. [Afrik, from Du *drost* bailiff, sheriff; cf Ger *Drost*, *Drostei*]

drought *drowt* or **drouth** *drowth* (*Scot drōōth*), *n* dryness; a shortage of rain or of water; a condition of atmosphere favourable to drying; thirst. — *n* **drought'iness** or **drouth'iness**. — *adj* **drought'y** or **drouth'y** very dry; lacking rain; thirsty. [OE *drūgath* dryness, from *drūgian* to dry]

drouk or **drook** *drōōk*, (*Scot*) *vt* to drench. — *n* **drouk'ing** or **drook'ing**. — *adj* **drouk'it** or **drook'it**. [Origin obscure; cf ON *drukna* to be drowned; Dan *drukne*]

drouth, etc. See **drought**.

drove *drōv*, *pa t* of **drive**. — *n* a number of cattle, or other animals, driven or herded together; a crowd or horde, eg of people, moving along together; a broad-edged chisel for dressing stone; a drove road (*esp E Anglia*). — *n* **drov'er** a person whose occupation is to drive cattle; a fishing boat, drifter (*Spenser*, etc). — *n* **drov'ing** the occupation of a drover; the action of herding cattle, etc. — **drove'-road** an old generally grassy track used or once used by droves of cattle. [OE *drāf*, *drīfan* to drive]

drow[1] *drow*, (*Shetland* and *Orkney*) a form of **troll**[1].

drow[2] *drow*, (*Scot*) *n* a drizzling mist; a squall. [Origin obscure]

drown *drown*, *vi* to die of suffocation in liquid. — *vt* to kill by suffocation in liquid; to submerge; to flood; to extinguish; to make indistinguishable or imperceptible. — *adj* **drownd'ed** (*Spenser*; now *illiterate*) drowned. — *n* **drown'er**. — *n* and *adj* **drown'ing**. — **drowned valley** a river valley which has been drowned by a rise of sea level relative to the land, due either to actual depression of the land or to a rise in sea level. — **drown someone out** (*colloq*) to make someone inaudible by making a louder noise. [ME *drounen*; origin obscure; the word used in OE was *druncnian*]

drowse *drowz*, *vi* to doze, sleep lightly. — *vt* to make heavy with sleep, cause to doze; to stupefy; to pass in a half-sleeping state. — *n* a half-sleeping state. — *n* **drows'ihead** or **drows'ihed** (*Spenser*) drowsiness, sleepiness. — *adv* **drows'ily**. — *n* **drows'iness**. — *adj* **drows'y** sleepy; heavy; dull; inducing sleep. [Appar OE *drūsian* to be sluggish; but not known between OE times and the 16c]

drub *drub*, *vt* to beat or thrash: — *pr p* **drubb'ing**; *pa t* and *pa p* **drubbed**. — *n* **drubb'ing** a cudgelling; (in games) a thorough defeat. [Ar *daraba* to beat, bastinado, from *darb* a beating, has been suggested]

drucken *druk'ən*, (*Scot*) *adj* drunken. — Used also as *pa p* of **drink**. — *n* **druck'enness**. [ON *drukkinn*, pa p of *drekka* to drink]

drudge *druj*, *vi* to do dull, laborious or lowly work. — *n* someone who does heavy monotonous work; a slave; a menial servant; dull task-work. — *n* **drudg'er**. — *n* **drudg'ery** or **drudg'ism** the work of a drudge; uninteresting toil; hard or humble labour. — *adv* **drudg'ingly**. [Ety unknown; perh from root of OE *drēogan* to perform, undergo]

drug[1] *drug*, *n* any substance used in the composition of medicine to cure, diagnose or prevent disease; a narcotic substance, *esp* an addictive one; a poisonous or stupefying substance; something one is intoxicated by or craves for (*fig*); an article that cannot be sold, generally owing to overproduction. — *vt* to mix or season with drugs; to administer a drug to; to dose to excess; to poison or stupefy with drugs. — *vi* to administer drugs or medicines; to take drugs, *esp* narcotics, habitually: — *pr p* **drugg'ing**; *pa t* and *pa p* **drugged**. — *n* **drugg'er** a druggist (*obs*); someone who drugs. — *n* **drugg'ie** (*colloq*) a drug addict. — *n* **drugg'ist** a person who deals in drugs; a pharmacist (*NAm*). — *adj* **drugg'y**. — **drug'-addict** or **drug'-fiend** a habitual, addicted taker of (*esp* non-medicinal) drugs; **drug'-pusher** a pusher, someone who peddles narcotics illegally; **drug resistance** the medical condition in which tissues become resistant after treatment with drugs, commonly found with many anti-tumour treatments; **drug'-runner** someone who smuggles drugs; **drug'-running**; **drug'-store** (mainly *NAm*) a chemist's shop (usually selling a variety of goods, including refreshments). [OFr *drogue*, of uncertain origin]

drug[2] *drug*, (*obs*; *Shakesp*) *n* a form of **drudge**.

drugget *drug'it*, *n* a woven and felted coarse woollen fabric; a protective covering, made of such fabric, for a floor or carpet. [OFr *droguet*]

druid *drōō'id*, *n* (also with *cap*) a priest among the ancient Celts of Britain, Gaul and Germany; an Eisteddfod official; a member of a benefit society (founded 1781), its lodges called *groves*: — *fem* **dru'idess** (also with *cap*). — *adj* **druid'ic** or **druid'ical**. — *n* **dru'idism** the doctrines which the druids taught; the ceremonies they practised. — **druidical circle** a fanciful 18c name for a stone circle (not made by the druids). [L pl *druidae*, from a Celtic stem *druid-*, whence OIr *drai*, Ir and Gaelic *draoi* magician]

drum[1] *drum*, *n* a percussion instrument, a skin stretched on a frame; anything shaped like a drum; the tympanum of the ear; the upright part of a cupola (*archit*); a cylinder, *esp* a revolving cylinder; a magnetic drum (*comput*; see under **magnet**); a cylindrical barrel; a bundle or swag (*Austr*); a house (*slang*); a large and tumultuous evening party (said to be so called because rival hostesses vied with each other in drumming up crowds of guests; *obs*); a drumfish. — *vi* to beat a drum; to beat rhythmically; to solicit orders (*US*). — *vt* to expel to the sound of a drum or drums (with *out*;

esp military; also *fig*); to summon, call together (with *up*); to impress or stress by repetition: — *pr p* **drumm'ing**; *pa t* and *pa p* **drummed**. — *n* **drumm'er** a person who drums; a commercial traveller (*esp US*); a swagman (*Austr*). — **drum'beat**; **drum'-belly** see **hoove**[1]; **drum brake** a type of brake in which two shoes grip the inside of the brake drum; **drum'fish** any fish of the Sciaenidae; **drum'fire** massed artillery-fire with a rolling sound; **drum'head** the head or skin of a drum; the top part of a capstan; (also **drumhead cabbage**) a type of flat-headed cabbage. — *adj* (*military*) improvised in the field (see **court-martial**). — **drum'-ma'jor** the marching leader of a military band; **drum majorette** a girl who heads a marching band, *usu* twirling a baton, in a parade, etc; a majorette; **drum'stick** the stick with which a drum is beaten; the tibia of a dressed fowl; **drum table** a round, deep-topped table on a central leg, *usu* with drawers. — **beat** or **bang the drum** to indulge in publicity. [From a Gmc root found in Du *trom*, Ger *Trommel* a drum; prob imit]

drum[2] *drum, n* a ridge, drumlin (in many place names). — *n* **drum'lin** (*geol*) a usually oval ridge formed under the ice-sheet of the Glacial Period (also **drum**). [Scot and Ir Gaelic *druim* back]

drumble *drum'bl*, (*Shakesp*; now *dialect*) *vi* to be sluggish. — *n* **drum'bledor** a dumbledore.

drumlin. See **drum**[2].

drumly *drum'li*, (*Scot*) *adj* turbid, muddy; gloomy.

drummer. See **drum**[1].

drummock *drum'ək*. Same as **drammock**.

Drummond light *drum'ənd līt, n* the limelight or oxy-hydrogen light invented by Captain T *Drummond* (1797–1840).

drunk *drungk*, *pa p* and old-fashioned *pa t* of **drink**. — *adj* intoxicated (also *fig*); saturated. — *n* a drunk person; drunken bout. — *n* **drunk'ard** a person who frequently drinks to excess; a habitual drinker. — *adj* **drunk'en** given to excessive drinking; worthless, besotted; resulting from intoxication; (sometimes) drunk. — *adv* **drunk'enly**. — *n* **drunk'enness** intoxication; habitual intoxication.

drupe *drōōp, n* any fleshy fruit with a stone. — *adj* **drupā'ceous** producing or pertaining to drupes or stone-fruits. — *n* **drup'el** or **drupe'let** a little drupe, forming part of a fruit, as in the raspberry. [L *drūpa*, from Gr *dryppā* an olive]

Druse, Druze or **Druz** *drōōz, n* (one of) a people inhabiting chiefly a mountainous district in the south of Syria, whose religion contains elements found in the Koran, the Bible, Gnosticism, etc. — Also *adj*. — *adj* **Drus'ian**. [Perh from *Darazi* an early exponent of the religion]

druse *drōōz, n* a rock cavity lined with crystals (by geologists *usu* called a **drusy cavity**), a geode. — *adj* **dru'sy** rough with or composed of minute crystals; miarolitic. [Ger *Druse*, from Czech *druza* a piece of crystallized ore]

druthers *dru'dhərz*, (*US colloq*) *n* choice, preference. [Contraction of I'*d rather* do]

druxy *druk'si, adj* (of timber) having decayed spots concealed by healthy wood. — Also **drick'sie**. [Origin unknown]

Druz, Druze. See **Druse**.

dry *drī, adj* (*compar* **drī'er**, *superl* **drī'est**) without water or liquid, contained or adhering; free from or deficient in moisture, sap or rain; thirsty; out of water; failing to yield water, or milk, or other liquid; (of a fruit) not fleshy; not green; (of eg toast) unbuttered; not drawing blood; (of wines, etc) free from sweetness and fruity flavour; (of beer) brewed by a method that removes the bitter taste, aftertaste and smell of traditional beer; legally forbidding the liquor trade (*colloq*); enforcing or subjected to prohibition; uninteresting; frigid, precise, formal; (of humour) quiet, restrained, uttered in a matter-of-fact way, as if not intended to be humorous; (of manner) distantly unsympathetic; (of a cough) not producing catarrh; (of natural gas) containing only small amounts of liquid constituents. — *vt* to free from or empty of water or moisture (often with *off*). — *vi* to become dry (often with *off*); to evaporate entirely: — *pr p* **dry'ing**; *pa t* and *pa p* **dried**; *3rd pers sing pr t* **dries**. — *n* a prohibitionist; a person who favours strict adherence to hardline right-wing Conservative policies (*UK politics*). — *n* **drī'er** or **dry'er** someone or something that dries; a machine for extracting moisture from cloth, grain, etc; a drying agent for oils, paint, etc. — *adv* **drī'ly** or **dry'ly** in a dry manner. — *n* and *adj* **dry'ing**. — *adj* **dry'ish**. — *n* **dry'ness**. — **Dry'asdust** a character in the prefatory matter of some of Scott's novels; a dull, pedantic, learned person. — Also *adj*. — **dry battery** (*elec*) a battery composed of dry-cells. — *vt* **dry'beat** (*obs*; *Shakesp*, etc) to drub, but without shedding blood. — **dry'-bi'ble** a disease of horned cattle in which the third stomach, or bible, is very dry; **dry blowing** the use of a current of air to separate particles of mineral (*esp* gold) from the material in which it is found; **dry bob** at Eton, a boy who plays cricket during the summer term (*opp* to the *wet bob*, who rows). — **dry'-cell** (*elec*) an electric cell in which the electrolyte is not a liquid but a paste. — *vt* **dry'-clean** to clean (clothes, etc) using eg a petroleum-based solvent rather than water. — **dry construction** (*building*) the use of timber or plasterboard for partitions, lining of walls and ceilings, to eliminate the traditional use of plaster and the consequent drying out period. — Also **dry lining**; **dry'-cupping** (*old med*) application of cups without previous scarification. — *vt* **dry'-cure** to cure by drying. — **dry'-dock** see **dry dock** at **dock**[3]. — *adj* **dry'-eyed** tearless. — **dry farming** a system of tillage in dry countries, surface soil being kept constantly loose, so as to retain scanty rains and reduce evaporation; **dry-'fist** (*obs*) a niggard. — *adj* and *adv* **dry-fist'ed** (*obs*) taking payment for gains and owing for losses. — *adj* **dry'-fly** (of fishing) without sinking the fly in the water. — *adv* **dry'-foot** (*Shakesp*) by scent of the foot alone. — *n pl* **dry'-goods** drapery and the like distinguished from groceries, etc. — **dry hole** a well which does not yield commercially viable quantities of oil or gas; an unsuccessful project (*fig*); **dry ice** and **dry-iced** see under **ice**; **dry lining** see **dry construction**. — *n pl* **drying oils** vegetable or animal oils which harden by oxidation when exposed to air. — **drying-up cloth** a cloth or towel for drying dishes, a dishtowel; **dry land** land as opposed to sea; **dry light** (*archaic*) an undeceptive light; an unprejudiced view; **dry Mass** or **dry service** *Missa sica*, a rite in which there is neither consecration nor communion; **dry measure** a system of measure by bulk, used for grain, etc (see eg **bushel**[1], **peck**[1], **pint**); **dry'mouth** xerostomia; **dry'-nurse** a nurse who does not suckle. — Also *vt*. — **dry'-plate** a sensitized photographic plate, with which a picture may be made without the preliminary use of a bath; **dry'-point'** a sharp needle by which fine lines are drawn in copper-plate engraving; a plate or impression produced with it; **dry riser** a vertical pipe with an outside access through which water can be pumped from the street to the individual floors of a building in the event of a fire; **dry'-rot** a decay of timber caused by *Merulius lacrymans* and other fungi which reduce it ultimately to a dry brittle mass; a concealed decay or degeneration (*fig*); **dry run** a practice exercise (*military*); a rehearsal, test. — *vt* **dry'-salt'** to cure (meat) by salting and drying. — *n* **dry'salter** a dealer in gums, dyes, etc, or (*obs*) in salted or dry meats, pickles, etc; **dry'saltery**; **dry service** see **dry Mass** above. — *adj* and *adv* **dry'-shod** without wetting the shoes or feet. — **dry ski** an adaptation of a ski with which one can practise skiing on a dry surface; **dry skiing**; **dry steam** steam unmixed with liquid drops. — *adj* **dry'-stone** built of stone without mortar, as some walls. — **dry'-stove** a kind of hot-house with dry heat; **dry suit** a close-fitting air- and watertight synthetic suit for wearing in *esp* cold water, that retains warmth by a layer of air, and allows clothing to be worn underneath it; **dry'-transfer lettering** lettering on the back of a plastic sheet that can be rubbed down onto paper, etc; **dry'-wall'er** a person who builds walls without mortar; **dry'-wash'** the bed of an intermittent stream. — **cut and dried** or **cut and dry** see under **cut**; **dry out** (*colloq*) to take or give a course of treatment to cure oneself or another person of alcoholism; **dry up** to dry thoroughly or completely; to cease to produce liquid (water, milk, etc); (of an actor, etc) to forget one's lines or part (*colloq*); to stop talking (*slang*); **go dry** to adopt liquor prohibition; **high and dry** see under **high**; **the dry** (sometimes with *cap*; *Austr colloq*) the dry season in central and northern Australia. [OE *drȳge*; cf Du *droog*, Ger *trocken*]

dryad *drī'ad, -əd*, (*Gr mythol*) *n* a wood nymph; a forest-tree: — *pl* **dry'ads** or **dry'adēs**. [Gr *dryas, -ados*, from *drȳs* oak tree]

DS *abbrev*: dal segno (*music*); disseminated sclerosis; Doctor of Surgery.

DSC *abbrev*: Distinguished Service Cross.

DSc. *abbrev*: *Doctor Scientiae* (*L*), Doctor of Science.

DSM *abbrev*: Distinguished Service Medal.

DSO *abbrev*: (Companion of the) Distinguished Service Order.

dso, dsobo, dsomo. See under **zho**.

dsp *abbrev*: *decessit sine prole* (*L*), died without issue.

DSS *abbrev*: Department of Social Services.

DST *abbrev*: Daylight Saving Time.

'dst *dst*, a shortened form of **hadst, wouldst**, etc.

DT *abbrev*: data transmission.

DTh. or **DTheol.** *abbrev*: *Doctor Theologiae* (*L*), Doctor of Theology.

DTI *abbrev*: Department of Trade and Industry.

DTP *abbrev*: desktop publishing.

DT's or **dt's** (*colloq*) *abbrev*: delirium tremens (see under **delirious**).

Du. *abbrev*: Dutch.

duad. See **dual**.

dual *dū'əl*, *adj* twofold; consisting of two; expressing or representing two things (*gram*). — *n* a grammatical form indicating duality; a word in the dual number. — *vt* to make (a road) into dual carriageway. — *n* **dū'ad** a dyad; a pair (*rare*). — *n* **dū'alin** an explosive mixture of sawdust, saltpetre and nitroglycerine. — *n* **dū'alism** (*philos*) that view which seeks to explain the world by the assumption of two radically independent and absolute elements, eg (1) the doctrine of the entire separation of spirit and matter, thus being opposed both to *idealism* and to *materialism*, and (2) the doctrine of two distinct principles of good and evil, or of two divine beings of these characters. — *n* **dū'alist** a believer in dualism. — *adj* **dūalis'tic** consisting of two; relating to dualism. — *adv* **dūalis'tically**. — *n* **duality** (*dū-al'i-ti*) doubleness; state of being double. — *adv* **dū'ally**. — *n* **dū'archy** a faulty form of **diarchy**. — **dual carriageway** a road consisting of two separated parts, each for use of traffic in one direction only; **dual control** joint control or jurisdiction. — *adj* **du'al-control** able to be operated by either or both of two persons. — *adj* **du'al-density** (*comput*) same as **double density**. — **dual monarchy** two (more or less) independent states with one and the same monarch; (*specif*) Austria-Hungary (before 1918); **dual personality** a condition in which the same individual shows at different times two very different characters; **dual pricing** differential pricing. — *adj* **du'al-pur'pose** serving or intended to serve two purposes; (of cattle) bred to produce meat and milk. — **dual school** one for both boys and girls. [L *duālis*, from *duo* two]

duan *dōō'än* or *dōō'-an*, *n* a division of a poem, a canto. [Gaelic]

duar *dōō'är*, *n* a circular Arab encampment or tent village. — Also **douar** or **dowar**. [Ar *dūār*]

duarchy. See under **dual**.

dub[1] *dub*, *vt* to confer knighthood upon (from the ceremony of striking the shoulders with the flat of a sword); to confer any name or dignity upon; to smooth with an adze; to trim; to cut the comb and wattles from; to rub a softening and waterproof mixture into (leather); to dress (a fly) for fishing: — *pr p* **dubb'ing**; *pa p* **dubbed**. — *n* **dubb'ing** the accolade; (also **dubb'in**) a preparation of grease for softening leather. [OE *dubbian* to dub knight]

dub[2] *dub*, (*dialect*; *esp Scot*) *n* a pool of foul water; a puddle; (in *pl*) mud. [Cf LGer *dobbe*]

dub[3] *dub*, *vt* to give (a film) a new soundtrack, eg one in a different language; to add sound effects or music; to transfer (recorded music, etc) to a new disc or tape; to combine so as to make one record (music, etc from more than one source, eg a live performance and a recording). — **dub poet**; **dub poetry** a style of poetry, of W Indian origin, performed spontaneously in reggae rhythm to dubbed or recorded music. [Abbrev of **double**]

dubbin, dubbing. See **dub**[1].

dubious *dū'bi-əs*, *adj* doubtful, causing or having doubt; uncertain; of uncertain result or outcome; arousing suspicion or disapproval; hesitating (about). — *n* **dūbiety** (*-bī'i-ti*) doubt. — *adv* **dū'biously**. — *n* **dūbios'ity** or **dū'biousness**. [L *dubius*]

dubitate *dū'bi-tāt*, *vi* to doubt, hesitate. — *adj* **dū'bitable**. — *adv* **dū'bitably**. — *n* (*obs*) **dū'bitancy**. — *n* **dūbitā'tion**. — *adj* **dū'bitative**. — *adv* **dū'bitatively**. [L *dubitāre, -ātum*]

ducal *dū'kəl*, *adj* pertaining to a duke. — *adv* **dū'cally**. [Fr, from LL *ducālis*, from L *dux* leader]

ducat *duk'ət*, (*hist*) *n* a gold or silver coin of varying values, formerly much used on the Continent. — *n* **ducatoon'** an old silver coin in Venice and elsewhere. [OFr *ducat*, from Ital *ducato*, from LL *ducātus* a duchy]

ducdame *dōōk'də-mi, dōōk-dä'mi*, (Shakesp play *As You Like It*), *interj* perhaps a meaningless refrain; explained as L *duc ad mē* bring to me, as Welsh *dewch 'da mi* come with me, and as Romany *dukrā'mē* I tell fortunes, etc.

duce *dōō'chā*, *n* the title assumed by the Italian dictator Mussolini. [Ital, leader, from L *dux*]

Duchenne muscular dystrophy *dü-shen' mus'kū-lər dis'trə-fi*, *n* (short form **Duchenne**) a common and severe form of muscular dystrophy, which strikes children (*esp* boys) under 10 years old. [Guillaume *Duchenne* (1806–75), French physician]

duchess, duchesse. See **duchy**.

duchy *duch'i*, *n* the territory of a duke, a dukedom. — *n* **duch'ess** the wife or widow of a duke; a woman of the same rank as a duke in her own right; a size of roofing slate 610 × 305 mm (24 x 12 inches). — *n* **duchesse** (*duch'es* or *dü-shes'*; Fr, duchess) a table-cover or centrepiece. — Also **duchesse cover**. — **duchesse lace** Flemish pillow lace with designs in cord outline; **duchesse potatoes** piped shapes of mashed potato, butter, milk and egg-yolk baked until light brown; **duchesse set** a set of covers for a dressing-table; **duchy court** the court of a duchy. [OFr *duché*, from LL *ducātus*; Fr *duchesse*, from LL *ducissa*]

duck[1] *duk*, *n* a kind of coarse cotton or linen, etc cloth for small sails, sacking, etc; (in *pl*) garments made of duck. [Du *doek* linen cloth; Ger *Tuch*]

duck[2] *duk*, *vt* to dip for a moment in water; to avoid (*colloq*). — *vi* to dip or dive; to lower the head suddenly; to cringe, yield. — *n* a quick plunge, dip; a quick lowering of the head or body, a jerky bow. — *n* **duck'er** someone who ducks; a diving-bird. — *n* **duck'ing**. — **duck'ing-pond**; **duck'ing-stool** (*hist*) a stool or chair in which adjudged offenders were tied and ducked in the water. — **duck out of** to shirk, avoid (responsibilities, etc). [ME *douken* from an assumed OE *dūcan* to duck, dive; Ger *tauchen*, Du *duiken*]

duck[3] *duk*, *n* any bird of the family *Anatidae*, the prominent features of which are short webbed feet, with a small hind-toe not reaching the ground, netted scales in front of the lower leg, and a long bill; the female duck as distinguished from the male *drake*; (originally *duck's egg* for zero (0), in a scoring-sheet) no runs (*cricket*); a darling, sweetheart (used loosely as a term of address; *colloq*); (*usu* **lame duck**) a defaulter, bankrupt; an oscillating shape used in wave-power technology (also **nodding duck**). — *n* **duck'ing** duck-hunting. — *n* **duck'ling** a young duck. — *n* **ducks** or **duck'y** (*colloq*) a term of endearment. — *adj* **duck'y**. — **duck'-ant** a Jamaican termite nesting in trees; **duck'bill** a platypus. — *adj* **duck'-billed** having a bill like a duck. — **duck'-board** a board with slats nailed across it, used for walking in excavations, etc, on swampy ground, or as steps in repair work on roofs; **duck-coy** see **decoy**. — *adj* **duck'-footed**. — **duck'-hawk** a moor-buzzard or marsh-harrier; a peregrine falcon (*US*). — *adj* **duck'-legged** short-legged. — **duck'mole** the duckbill; **duck'-pond**; **duck's arse** (or *US* **ass**; *slang*; *abbrev* **DA**) a man's hairstyle in which the hair is swept back to a point on the neck resembling a duck's tail, worn *esp* by Teddy boys; **duck's'-foot** lady's-mantle; **duck'-shot** shot for shooting wild-duck. — *vi* **duck'shove** (*Austr* and *NZ*; *colloq*) to jump a queue (*orig* of taxi-drivers); to cheat; to steal; to avoid responsibilities. — **duck'-shover** (*Austr* and *NZ*, *colloq*); **duck's'-meat** duckweed; **duck soup** (*US slang*) something very easy, a cinch; someone easy to handle, a pushover; **duck'-tail** a white Teddy boy of S Africa; **duck'weed** any plant of the family *Lemnaceae*, monocotyledons most of which consist of a small flat green floating plate, from which one or more roots dangle. — **Bombay duck** a small Indian fish, the bummalo, dried and eaten as a relish; **break one's duck** (*cricket*) to make one's first run (see **duck** above); **lame duck** a defaulter; a bankrupt; anything disabled; an inefficient or helpless person or organization; **like a dying duck** languishing; **make** or **play ducks and drakes** to make flat stones skip on the surface of water; to use recklessly; to squander, waste (with *of* or *with*); **sitting duck** an easy target, helpless victim; **wild'-duck** the mallard, *esp* the hen-bird. [OE *dūce* (or perh *duce*) a duck; cf **duck**[2]]

duck[4] *duk*, *n* a kind of amphibious military transport vehicle or landing craft. [From manufacturers' code initials, DUKW]

ducking. See **duck**[2,3].

duct *dukt*, *n* a tube conveying fluids in animal bodies or plants; a pipe for an electric cable; a hole, pipe or channel for carrying a fluid; an air-passage. — *vt* to carry along, or as if along, a duct. — *adj* **duct'less**. — **ducted fan** see **turbofan**; **ductless glands** (*anatom*) masses of glandular tissue that lack ducts and discharge their products directly into the blood. [L *ductus*, from *dūcere* to lead]

ductile *duk'tīl*, *-til*, *adj* yielding; capable of being drawn out into threads; easily led. — *n* **ductility** (*-til'-iti*) or **duc'tileness** capacity of being drawn out without breaking. [Fr, from L *ductilis*, from *dūcere* to lead]

dud[1] *dud*, (*colloq*) *n* (in *pl*) poor or ragged clothes, tatters; (in *pl*) clothes. — *n* **dudd'ery** (*dialect*) a shop where old clothes are sold; rags collectively. — *adj* **dudd'ie** or **dudd'y** (*Scot*) ragged. — **duddie weans** (*wānz*; *Burns*) ragged children; (with *caps*) a Scottish literary society. [There is a ME *dudde* birrus, a cloak; cf ON *duthi* swaddling-clothes]

dud[2] *dud*, (*colloq*) *n* a bomb or projectile that fails to go off; a dishonoured cheque; a counterfeit; any useless or ineffective person or thing; a failure. — Also *adj*. [Origin unknown]

dudder *dud'ər*, (*dialect*) *n* confusion. [Cf **dither**]

duddery, duddie, duddy. See **dud**[1].

dude *dūd*, *dōōd*, (orig *US slang*) *n* a fop or dandy; a man from the city holidaying out West; a fellow. — *adj* **du'dish**. — *n* **du'dism**. — **dude ranch** a ranch run as a holiday resort or for training in ranching. — **dude up** to dress up flashily. [Origin unknown]

dudeen *dōō-dēn'*, *-dhēn'*, *n* a short clay tobacco-pipe. — Also **dudheen'**. [Ir *dúidín*, dimin of *dúd* pipe]

dudgeon[1] *duj'ən*, *n* resentment; offended indignation, *esp* as in *in high dudgeon*. [Origin unknown]

dudgeon[2] *duj'ən*, *n* the haft of a dagger; a small dagger (*archaic*). [Anglo-Fr *digeon* knife-handle]

dudheen. See **dudeen**.

dudish, dudism. see **dude**.

duds. See **dud**[1].

due[1] *dū*, *adj* owed; that ought to be paid or done to another; proper; appointed, under engagement (to be ready, arrive, etc). — *adv* exactly, directly. — *n* something which is owed; what one has a right to or has earned; fee, toll, charge or tribute; (in *pl*) subscription to a club or society. — *adj* **due'ful** or **dewfull** (*Spenser*) proper, fit. — **due date** the date by which a payment must be paid; the date on which a payment falls due. — **due to** caused by; owing to, because of (a use still deprecated by some, but now almost standard); (of horses) pregnant by; **give someone his** (or **her**) **due** to be fair to someone; **give the devil his due** to acknowledge some commendable quality, etc in someone otherwise disapproved of; **in due course** in the ordinary way when the time comes. [OFr *deü*, pa p of *devoir*, from L *debēre* to owe]

due[2] *dū*, (*Shakesp*) *vt* to endue.

duel *dū'əl*, *n* a prearranged fight between two people under fixed conditions and generally on an affair of honour; single combat to decide a quarrel; any fight or struggle between two parties. — *vi* to fight in a duel: — *pr p* **dū'elling**; *pa t* and *pa p* **dū'elled**. — *n* **dū'eller**. — *n* **dū'elling**. — *n* **dū'ellist**. — *n* **duello** (*dōō-el'ō*) a duel (*obs*); duelling; the laws which regulate duelling: — *pl* **duell'os**. — *adj* **dū'elsome** given to duelling. [Ital *duello*, from L *duellum*, the original form of *bellum*, from *duo* two]

duende *dwen'de*, (*Sp*) *n* literally a ghost, goblin, demon; inspiration, magnetism, ardour: — *pl* **duen'des**.

duenna *dū-en'ə*, *n* a lady who acts the part of governess in Spain; a lady who watches over or chaperons a younger. [Sp *dueña*, a form of *doña* mistress, from L *domina*, feminine of *dominus* lord]

duet, **duett** *dū-et'* or **duetto** *dōō-et'tō*, *n* a composition in music for two performers; the performance of this; the performers of this; any action involving two parties: — *pl* **duets'**, **duetts'**, **duett'os** or **duett'i** (*-ē*). — *vi* to perform a duet: — *pr p* **duett'ing**; *pa t* and *pa p* **duett'ed**. — *n* **duettino** (*-tē'nō*) a simple duet: — *pl* **duettin'os**. — *n* **duett'ist** (*dū-*). [Ital *duetto*, dimin of *duo*, from *due* two, from L *duo*]

duff[1] *duf*, *n* dough; a stiff flour pudding boiled in a bag; decaying vegetable matter, fallen leaves; coal-dust. — **up the duff** (*Austr* and *UK slang*) pregnant. [A form of **dough**]

duff[2] *duf*, (*slang*) *vt* to make to look new; to alter brands on (stolen cattle); to steal cattle. — *n* **duff'ing**, **duff'ing-up** or **duff'ing-over**. — **duff up** or **duff over** to beat up. [Perh a back-formation from **duffer**[2]]

duff[3] *duf*, *vt* to misplay by hitting the ground behind the ball (*golf*); to bungle. [Back-formation from **duffer**[1]]

duff[4] *duf*, (*colloq*) *adj* no good; broken, not working. [Prob **duff**[3]]

duff[5] *duf*, (*slang*) *n* the buttocks, rump. [Perh **duff**[1]]

duffel or **duffle** *duf'l*, *n* a thick, coarse woollen cloth, with a thick nap; sporting or camping kit (*US*). — **duffel bag** a canvas bag, cylindrical in shape, *orig* used for a sailor's kit; **duffel coat** a jacket or coat, *usu* hooded, made of duffel. [Du, from *Duffel* a town near Antwerp]

duffer[1] *duf'ər*, *n* an unskilful or worthless person; a fogey, a useless old fellow; a counterfeit coin; an unproductive mine. — *n* **duff'erdom** or **duff'erism**. [Origin unknown]

duffer[2] *duf'ər*, *n* a peddler of sham jewellery, etc; someone who fakes up sham articles or duffs cattle. [Origin unknown: thieves' slang]

duffle. See **duffel**.

dug[1] *dug*, *n* a nipple or udder of a cow or similar animal. [Cf Swed *dægga*, Dan *dægge* to suckle]

dug[2] *dug*, *pa t* and *pa p* of **dig**. — **dug'out** a boat made by hollowing out the trunk of a tree; a rough dwelling or shelter dug out of a slope or bank or in a trench; a (*usu* sunken) shelter or covered bench area beside a sports pitch in which players, etc wait when not in the game; a superannuated person brought back to employment (*slang*).

dugong *dōō'gong*, *n* a herbivorous marine mammal of the order *Sirenia*, up to 3m long, with flipperlike forelimbs (the supposed original of the mermaid). [Malayan *dūyong*]

duike or **duyker** *dī'kər*, *dā'kər*, *n* a small S African antelope; (*dī'kər*) a cormorant (*SAfr*). [Du, diver (from plunging into the bush, or into the sea)]

duke *dūk*, *n* a sovereign prince of a small state; a nobleman of the highest order; a chief (*obs*; *Bible*); (as *dōōk*; *slang*) the fist (also **dook**). — *vt* (with *it*) to play the duke; to fight or hit with the fists (often *duke it out*; *US slang*). — *n* **duke'dom** the title, rank or lands of a duke. — *n* **duke'ling** a petty duke. — *n* **dūk'ery** a duke's territory or seat. — *n* **duke'ship**. — **the Dukeries** a group of ducal seats in Nottinghamshire. [OFr *duc*, from L *dux*, *ducis* a leader, from *dūcere* to lead]

Dukhobor or **Doukhobor** *dōō'hhō-bör*, *dōō'kō-bör*, *n* a member of a Russian sect who trust to an inner light, reject the doctrine of the Trinity, and refuse military service, many of them settled in Canada since 1899: — *pl* **D(o)u'khobors** or **Dukhobort'sy**. [Russ *Dukhoborets*, from *dukh* spirit, and *borets* fighter, from *borotŷ* to fight]

dukkeripen *dōōk-ə-rip'ən*, *n* fortune-telling. [Romany *drukeriben*]

DUKW. See **duck**[4].

dulcamara *dul-kə-mā'rə*, *-mä'rə*, *n* the plant bittersweet. [L *dulcis* sweet, and *amāra* (feminine) bitter]

dulce et decorum est pro patria mori *dōōl'chā et dā-kö'rōōm est prō pat'ri-a mö'ri*, (*L*) it is sweet and glorious to die for one's country. [Horace, *Odes* III 2. 13]

dulcet *duls'it*, *adj* sweet; melodious, harmonious. — *n* **dul'cian** (*dul'si-ən*; *obs* or *hist*) a small bassoon. — *n* **dulciana** (*dul-si-ä'nə*) an open diapason organ stop of pleasing tone and small scale. — *n* **dulcificā'tion**. — *adj* **dulcif'luous** flowing sweetly. — *vt* **dul'cify** (*rare*) to make sweet. — *n* **dulcil'oquy** a soft manner of speaking. — *n* **dul'cite**, **dul'citol** or **dul'cose** (*-kōs*) a saccharine substance derived from various plants (in its crude form, *Madagascar manna*). — *n* **Dul'citone**® a keyboard instrument in which graduated tuning-forks are struck by hammers. — *n* **dul'citude** sweetness. — **dulcified spirit** a compound of alcohol with mineral acid. [L *dulcis* sweet]

dulcimer *dul'si-mər*, *n* a musical instrument like a flat box, with sounding-board and wires stretched across bridges; a Jewish musical instrument, probably a bagpipe. [Sp *dulcemele*, from L *dulce melos* a sweet song, from *dulcis* sweet, and Gr *melos* a song]

Dulcinea *dul-sin-ē'ə*, *dul-sin'i-ə*, (*literary*) *n* a sweetheart. [From *Dulcinea* del Toboso, the name given by Don Quixote to the mistress of his imagination]

dulcite, **Dulcitone**, **dulcose**, etc. See under **dulcet**.

dule[1] *dül*, (*Scot*) *n* woe. — Also **dool** or (*obs*) **doole**. — **dule'-tree** the gallows. [See **dole**[2]]

dule[2]. See **dool**[2].

dulia or **douleia** *dū-* or *dōō-lī'ə*, (*RC*) *n* the inferior veneration accorded to saints and angels (as opposed to **hyperdulia**, that accorded to the Virgin Mary, and **latria**, that accorded to God alone). — *n* **douloc'racy** or **dulo'cracy** government by slaves. — *n* **dulō'sis** enslavement, practised by certain ants upon other kinds. — *adj* **dulot'ic**. [Gr *douleiā* servitude, *doulōsis* enslavement, from *doulos* a slave]

dull *dul*, *adj* slow to learn or to understand; lacking sharpness in hearing (or other sense); insensible; without life or spirit; uninteresting; slow-moving; drowsy; sleepy; sad; downcast; cheerless; lacking brightness or clearness; cloudy; dim; muffled; obtuse; blunt. — *vt* to make dull or stupid; to blunt; to damp; to cloud. — *vi* to become dull. — *n* **dull'ard** a dull and stupid person; a dunce. — *adj* **dull'ish**. — *n* **dull'ness** or **dul'ness** the state or quality of being dull. — *adj* (*poetic*) **dull'y** somewhat dull. — *adv* **dully** (*dul'li*). — *adj* **dull'-brained** (*Shakesp*). — *adj* **dull'-browed**. — *adj* **dull'-eyed** (*Shakesp*). — *adj* **dull'-sighted**. — *adj* **dull'-witted**. [Related to OE *dol* foolish, and *dwellan* to err; Du *dol*, Ger *toll* mad]

dulocracy, **dulosis**, **dulotic**. See under **dulia**.

dulse *duls*, *n* an edible red seaweed, *esp Rhodymenia palmata*. [Gaelic *duileasg*, possibly from *duille* a leaf, and *uisge* water]

duly *dū'li*, *adv* properly; fitly; at the proper time. [See **due**[1]]

duma or **douma** *dōō'mə*, *n* an elected council, *esp* (*hist*) the Russian parliament of 1906–17. — *n* **dum'aist** a duma member. [Russ *duma*, of Gmc origin; cf **doom**]

dumb *dum*, *adj* without the power of speech; silent; soundless; stupid (orig *US* after Ger or Du). — *vt* (*Shakesp*) to render dumb. — *adv* **dumb'ly** in silence; mutely. — *n* **dumb'ness**. — *n* **dumm'erer** (*old slang*) a dumb person, *esp* a rogue who feigns dumbness. — **dumb'-bell** a double-headed weight swung in the hands to develop the muscles; any object or figure of the same shape; a stupid person (*US*); **dumb blonde** (in films, etc) the stock character of a blonde-haired beauty of limited intelligence; **dumb'-cane** a tropical American araceous plant (*Dieffenbachia seguine*) whose acrid juice swells the tongue; **dumb'-cluck** a fool (orig *US*; same as **cluck**). — *vt* **dumbfound'** or **dumfound'** to strike dumb; to confuse greatly; to astonish. — *vt* **dumbfound'er** or **dumfound'er** to dumbfound. — **dumb'-pia'no** a soundless keyboard for piano practice; **dumb'-show'** gesture without words; pantomine. — *adj* **dumb'struck** silent with astonishment. — **dumb terminal** (*comput*) an input or output terminal which has no independent processing capability; **dumb'-wait'er** a movable platform used for conveying food, dishes, etc at meals; a stand with revolving top for holding dessert, etc; a small lift for food and dishes. — **strike dumb** to silence with astonishment. [OE *dumb*; Ger *dumm* stupid, Du *dom*]

dumbledore *dum'bl-dōr*, *-dör*, (*dialect*) *n* the bumblebee; the brown cockchafer.

dumbo *dum'bō*, (*colloq*) *n* a dimwit. [**dumb**]

dumdum *dum'dum*, *n* a soft-nosed expanding bullet, first made at *Dum Dum* near Calcutta. — **dumdum fever** kala-azar.

dumfound, **dumfounder**. See **dumb**.

dumka *dōōm'kə*, (*music*) *n* a lament; a slow movement or piece: — *pl* **dumky** (*-kē*). [Czech]

dummerer. See **dumb**.

dummy *dum'i*, *n* a sham or counterfeit article taking the place of a real one; a block, lay-figure or mannequin; a dumb person; a sample, eg an unprinted model of a book; a rubber teat for pacifying an infant; an exposed hand of cards; the imaginary player of such a game or hand; a feint of passing or playing the ball (*Rugby football*, etc). — *vt* and *vi* to sell the dummy (to; see below). — *adj* silent; sham, feigned. — *n* **dumm'iness**. — **dummy run** an experimental run; a try-out or testing. — **sell the dummy (to)** (*Rugby football*, etc) to deceive an opponent by a feint of passing or playing the ball (also *fig*). [**dumb**]

dumortierite *dū-mör'ti-ər-īt*, *n* a blue, greenish-blue, pink or violet semi-precious gemstone, aluminium borosilicate. [From the 19c French palaeontologist Eugène *Dumortier*, who discovered it]

dumose *dū'mōs*, (*bot*; *rare*) *adj* bushy (also **dū'mous**). — *n* **dumos'ity**. [L *dūmus* a thorn-bush]

dump[1] *dump*, *vt* to set down heavily or with a thump; to unload; to land and sell at prices below cost of production in the exporting country, or (according to some) in the importing country (*econ*); to tip (*esp* rubbish); to get rid of; to transfer data held in computer memory to a printer or disk (*comput*). — *n* a thud; a place for the discharge of loads, or for rubbish; a deposit; store (*military*); a dirty, dilapidated place; a printout or other copy of data held in computer memory. — *n* **dump'er** someone who, or something which dumps; a dumper truck; (in surfing) a wave that crashes suddenly downwards with great force, causing surfers to fall. — **dump'bin** (in a shop) a display stand or container, eg for bargain items; **dumper truck** or **dump truck** a lorry which can be emptied by raising the front of the carrier to allow the contents to slide out the back (also **dump'er**). — **dump on** (*US slang*) to do down, belittle; to take advantage of. [Cf Dan *dumpe*, Norw *dumpa* to fall plump]

dump[2] *dump*, *n* dullness or gloominess of mind, ill-humour, low spirits (now only used in the *pl* **dumps**); an obsolete slow dance or dance-tune in 4-4 time; a melancholy strain (*obs*; *Shakesp*, etc); any tune (*obs*). — *adj* **dump'ish** depressed in spirits. — *adv* **dump'ishly**. — *n* **dump'ishness**. — **(down) in the dumps** (*colloq*) in bad spirits; depressed. [Prob related to ODu *domp* mist; or Ger *dumpf* gloomy]

dump[3] *dump*, *n* a deep hole in a river-bed, a pool. [Prob Norw *dump* pit]

dump[4] *dump*, *n* a short thick person or thing; a marble; a counter; a small coin; (in *pl*) money (*slang*). [Perh a back-formation from **dumpy**]

dum-palm. See **doum-palm**.

dumper. See **dump**[1].

dumpish. See **dump**[1].

dumple. See **dumpy**.

dumpling *dump'ling*, *n* a kind of thick pudding or mass of paste; a dumpling-shaped person or animal; a silly person. [Origin obscure]

dumps. See **dump**[2].

dumpy *dump'i*, *adj* short and thick. — *n* a dumpy person or animal, *esp* one of a breed of very short-legged fowls; a short umbrella. — *n* **dump'iness**. — *vt* **dump'le** (*rare*) to make or cook, as a dumpling; to round into a dumpy shape. — **dump'y-lev'el** a surveyor's level with rigid connection of the telescope to the vertical spindle. [18c; perh from **dumpling**]

dum spiro, spero *dŏŏm spēr'ō, spär'ō*, (*L*) while I breathe, I hope.

dum vivimus, vivamus *dŏŏm vēv'i-mŏŏs, vē-vä'mŏŏs*, (*L*) let us live while we are alive.

dun[1] *dun*, *adj* greyish brown; mouse-coloured; dingy; dusky. — *n* a dun colour; a horse of dun colour. — *vt* (*New Eng*) to cure and brown (eg cod). — *vi* to become dun-coloured. — *n* **dunn'ing**. — *adj* **dunn'ish** somewhat dun. — **dun'-bird** the pochard, *esp* the female; **dun'-cow** a ray with a skin of shagreen; **dun'-div'er** the goosander, *esp* the female or young male; **dun'-fish** codfish cured by dunning. [OE *dun*, prob not Celtic]

dun[2] *dun*, *vt* to importune for payment; to plague, pester, harass: — *prp* **dunn'ing**; *pa t* and *pa p* **dunned**. — *n* someone who duns; a demand for payment. [Perh related to **din**]

dun[3] *dun*, *n* a hill; a fortified mound. [Celtic; in many place names; adopted in OE as *dūn*; see **down**[2]]

dunce *duns*, *n* a slow learner; a stupid person. — *n* **dunce'dom** the class of dunces. — *n* **dun'cery** stupidity. — *n* **Dun'ciad** Pope's epic of dunces. — **dunce's cap** a tall conical hat, formerly worn at school to indicate stupidity. [*Duns* Scotus (died 1308), the Subtle Doctor, leader of the schoolmen, from him called *Dunses*, who opposed classical studies on the revival of learning, hence any opposer of learning, a blockhead]

dunch or **dunsh** *dunsh*, (*Scot*) *vt* to jog, nudge, bump; to butt. — Also *n*. [Ety doubtful]

dunder *dun'dər*, *n* lees, dregs of sugar-cane juice. [Sp *redundar* to overflow]

dunderfunk *dun'dər-fungk*, (*naut*) *n* ship-biscuit, soaked in water, mixed with fat and molasses, and baked in a pan. — Also **dan'dyfunk**.

dunderhead *dun'dər-hed*, *n* a stupid person (also **dun'-derpate**.) — *adj* **dun'derheaded**. — *n* **dun'derheadism**. — *n* **dun'derheadededness**. [Origin uncertain]

Dundonian *dun-dō'ni-ən*, *n* and *adj* (a person) belonging to, coming from or born in Dundee, Scotland.

Dundreary *dun-drēr'i*, *adj* like Lord *Dundreary*, in Tom Taylor's *Our American Cousin* (in Sothern's creation of the part, a lisping and brainless dandy, wearing long side-whiskers).

dune *dūn*, *n* a low hill of sand, *esp* on the seashore. — **dune'-buggy** (*orig US*) a beach buggy, a *usu* small car with large tyres, used for driving on beaches. [Fr, from ODu *duna*; cf **down**[2]]

dung[1] *dung*, *n* excrement; manure; a tailor or other worker submitting to low rates of pay (*opp* to *flint*; *obs slang*) — *vt* to manure with dung. — *vi* to void excrement. — *adj* **dung'y**. — **dung'-bee'tle** the dor-beetle; a scarabaeid beetle generally; **dung'-cart**; **dung'-fly** any of a number of small two-winged flies (*Scatophagidae*) that breed on dung or decaying vegetable matter; **dung'-fork** a fork used for moving stable manure; **dung'-heap** or **dung'-hill** a heap of dung; any squalid situation or place; **dung'-hunt'er** a skua; **dung'mere** a manure-pit. [OE *dung*; cf Dan *dynge* a heap; Ger *Dung*]

dung[2]. See **ding**[1].

dungaree *dung-gə-rē'* or *dung'gə-rē*, *n* a coarse Indian calico; (in *pl*) work overalls made of it, *esp* loose trousers with a bib front and shoulder straps; (in *pl*) a similar garment for casual wear. [Hindi *dūgrī*]

dungeon *dun'jən*, *n orig* the principal tower of a castle; a close, dark prison; a cell under ground. — *vt* to confine in a dungeon. — *n* **dun'geoner** a gaoler. [OFr *donjon*, from LL *domniō*, *-ōnis*, from L *dominus* a lord]

duniewassal, dunniewassal or **duniwassal** *dŏŏn-i-wos'l*, *n* a Highland gentleman of inferior rank. [Gaelic *duine* man, and *uasal* of gentle birth]

dunite *dun'īt*, *n* crystalline rock composed almost entirely of olivine. [*Dun* Mountain, near Nelson, in New Zealand]

duniwassal. See **duniewassal**.

dunk *dungk*, *vt* and *vi* to dip (cake, etc that one is eating) in one's coffee or other beverage. — *n* **dunk'er**. [Ger *tunken* to dip; cf **Dunker**]

Dunker *dungk'ər*, *n* a member of a sect of German-American Baptists who practise triple immersion. — Also **Tunk'er**. [Ger, dipper]

Dunkirk *dun-kûrk'* or *dun'*, *n* a successful military evacuation by sea against odds, as by the British in 1940 at *Dunkirk*; a complete abandonment of one's position; a rapid or desperate withdrawal.

dunlin *dun'lin*, *n* the red-backed sandpiper (*Calidris alpina*) a gregarious shore-bird, also known as the **ox-bird**: — *pl* **dunlins** or (*collectively*) **dunlin**. [Dimin of **dun**[1]]

Dunlop *dun-lop'*, *n* a cheese made of unskimmed milk. [From *Dunlop* in Ayrshire]

dunnage *dun'ij*, *n* loose wood of any kind laid in the bottom of the hold to keep the cargo out of the bilge-water, or wedged between parts of the cargo to keep them steady; sailor's baggage. [Ety unknown]

dunnakin *dun'ə-kin*, *n*. Same as **dunny**[2].

dunnart *dun'ärt*, *n* a marsupial mouse of Australia and Papua New Guinea (genus *Sminthopsis*). [Aboriginal]

dunniewassal. See **duniewassal**.

dunnite *dun'īt*, *n* a kind of explosive based on ammonium picrate. [From its inventor, the US army officer, Col B W *Dunn* (1860–1936)]

dunno *də-nō'*. *Colloq* contraction of **(I) don't know**.

dunnock *dun'ək*, *n* the hedge-sparrow. [Dimin of **dun**[1]]

dunny[1] *dun'i*, (*dialect*) *adj* deaf; stupid. [Origin obscure]

dunny[2] *dun'i*, (*colloq* or *dialect*) *n* a lavatory, often an outside lavatory (*esp Austr* and *NZ*); a basement or cellar (of a tenement building, etc; *Scot*).

dunsh. See **dunch**.

Dunstable *dun'stə-bl*, *n* a kind of straw-plait, first made at *Dunstable* in Bedfordshire; a straw hat, etc. — **Dunstable road** or **highway** anything plain and direct.

dunt[1] *dunt*, (*Scot*) *n* a thump; the wound or mark made by a thump. — *vt* to thump, beat. [See **dint**]

dunt[2] *dunt*, (*dialect*) *n* the disease gid or sturdy in sheep, etc. [Origin obscure]

dunt[3] *dunt*, *vt* (of ceramics) to crack in the oven because of too rapid cooling. [Origin obscure]

duo *dōō'ō*, *dū'ō*, *n* a duet; two persons, etc, associated in some way (eg a pair of musicians or variety artists): — *pl* **dū'os**. [Ital, from L *duo* two]

duodecennial *dū-ō-di-sen'yəl*, *adj* occurring every twelve years. [L *duodecim* twelve, and *annus* year]

duodecimal *dū-ō-des'i-ml*, *adj* computed by twelves; twelfth; (in *pl*) a method of calculating the area of a rectangle when the length and breadth are stated in feet and inches. — Also *n*. — **duodecimal system** a system of numbers in which each denomination is twelve times the next, instead of ten times, as in ordinary (decimal) arithmetic; the name given to the division of unity into twelve equal parts. [L *duodecim* twelve, from *duo* two, and *decem* ten]

duodecimo *dū-ō-des'i-mō*, *adj* (*printing* and *publishing*) formed of sheets folded so as to make twelve leaves. — *n* a book of such sheets, *usu* written **12mo**; an interval of a twelfth (*music*): — *pl* **duodecimos**. [L *in duodecimō*, in twelfth (ablative of *duodecimus* twelfth) from *duo* two, and *decem* ten]

duodenary *dū-ō-dē'nə-ri*, *adj* relating to twelve, twelvefold. [L *duodēnārius*]

duodenum *dū-ō-dē'nəm*, (*anatom* and *zool*) *n* the first portion of the small intestine (so called because it is about twelve fingers'-breadth in length): — *pl* **duodē'na**. — *adj* **duodē'nal**. — *n* **duodēnec'tomy** excision of the duodenum. — *n* **duodēnī'tis** inflammation of the duodenum. [Formed from L *duodēnī* twelve each]

duologue *dū'ō-log*, *n* a dialogue between two actors. [Irregularly formed from L *duo* (or Gr *dyo*) two, and Gr *logos* discourse]

duomo *dwō'mō*, *n* (an Italian) cathedral: — *pl* **duō'mos** or **duō'mi** (*-ē*). [Ital. See **dome**[1]]

duopoly *dū-op'ə-li*, *n* a situation in which two companies, etc monopolize trading in a commodity. [L *duo* (or Gr *dyo*) two, and mono*poly*]

duotone *dū'ō-tōn*, *n* and *adj* (a drawing, print, etc) done in two tones or colours. [L *duo* two, and **tone**]

DUP *abbrev*: Democratic Unionist Party (the Protestant nationalist party of Northern Ireland).

dup *dup*, (*Shakesp*) *vt* to undo, open. [**do up**; cf **don**[2] and **doff**]

dup. *abbrev*: duplicate.

dupatta. See **dopatta**.

dupe *dūp*, *n* someone who is cheated. — *vt* to deceive; to trick. — *n* **dūpabil'ity**. — *adj* **dū'pable**. — *n* **dū'per**. — *n* **dū'pery** the art of deceiving others. [Fr *dupe*; of uncertain origin]

dupion *dū'pi-ən*, *-on*, *n* a double cocoon, made by two silkworms spinning together; a kind of coarse silk made from these cocoons. [Fr *doupion*, from Ital *doppione* double]

duple *dū'pl*, *adj* double, twofold; having two beats in the bar (*music*). — *n* **dū'plet** a like throw of two dice; a pair of electrons forming a single bond between two atoms; a group of two notes occupying the time of three (*music*). [L *duplus* double; cf **double**]

duplex *dū'pleks*, *adj* twofold, double; having some part doubled; allowing communication and transmission in both directions simultaneously (*comput*, *teleg*, etc). — *n* a duplex apartment or house. — *n* **du'plexer** (*telecomm* and *radar*) a system allowing the use of the same aerial for transmission and reception. — **duplex apartment** a flat on two floors; a building on two floors, consisting of a flat on each (*Can*); **duplex house** (*NAm*) a house, divided either horizontally or vertically, providing accommodation for two families. [L *duplex*, *-icis*]

duplicate *dū'pli-kit*, *adj* double; twofold; like, equivalent or alternative. — *n* another (*esp* subsidiary or spare) thing of the same kind; a copy or transcript; the condition of being in two copies. — *vt* (*-kāt*) to double; to copy; to repeat; to fold. — *n* **dūplicand'** (*Scots law*) double feu-duty, due on certain occasions. — *n* **dūplicā'tion**. — *adj* **dū'plicative**. — *n* **dū'plicātor** a copying machine. — *n* **dū'plicāture** a doubling; anything doubled; the fold of a membrane. — *n* **dūply'** a second reply in Scots law. — *vt* to say in duply. — **duplicate bridge** a form of competition bridge in which each pair or four plays the same set of hands as all other pairs or fours; **duplicate ratio** ratio of the squares of the quantities. — **in duplicate** in two copies, or original accompanied by a copy; **duplication of the cube** the problem eagerly discussed by the early Greek geometers, of constructing a cube equal to twice a given cube, impossible by use of straight line and circle only, but soluble by means of other curves. [L *duplicāre*, *-ātum*, from *duo* two, and *plicāre* to fold]

duplicity *dū-plis'i-ti*, *n* doubleness, *esp* in conduct or intention; insincerity; double-dealing. — *adj* **duplic'itous**. [L *duplex*, *-icis* double]

duply. See under **duplicate**.

dupondius *dū-pon'di-əs*, (*hist*) *n* an ancient Roman coin: — *pl* **dupon'diī**. [L]

duppy *dup'i*, *n* a ghost. [W Indian word]

Dupuytren's contracture *dū-pwē'trenz kən-trak'chər*, (*pathol*) *n* a condition in which one or more fingers (or, more rarely, toes) are caused to be bent towards the palm of the hand (or sole of the foot) by the contraction of a fibrous chord in the palmar (or plantar) tissue. — Also **Dupuytren's contraction**. [Baron Guillaume *Dupuytren* (1777–1835), French surgeon]

dura[1]. See **durra**.

dura[2] *dū'rə*, *n* short for **dura mater**.

durable *dūr'ə-bl*, *adj* able to last or endure; hardy; permanent. — *n* something that will endure, *esp* (*pl*) goods that do not need replacing frequently. — *n* **durabil'ity** or **dur'ableness**. — *adv* **dur'ably**. — *n* **dur'ance** continuance (*obs*); durability (*obs*); a durable cloth (*obs*); imprisonment (*archaic*). — *n* **dur'ant** a strong cloth in imitation of buff-leather. — *n* **durā'tion** continuance in time; time indefinitely; power of continuance; length of time. — *adj* **durā'tional**. — **for the duration** (*colloq*) as long as the war (or the situation under discussion) continues. [L *dūrāre* to harden, endure, last]

Duralumin® *dūr-al'ū-min*, *n* (also without *cap*; also **dūr'al** or **dūralūmin'ium**) a strong, light, aluminium alloy containing copper. [L *dūrus* hard, and *alumin*ium]

dura mater *dū'rə mā'tər*, *dōō'ra mä'ter*, (*anatom* and *zool*) *n* the exterior membrane of the brain and spinal column distinguished from the other two, the arachnoid and the pia mater. [L *dūra māter* hard mother, a translation of the Arabic name]

duramen *dū-rā'mən*, (*bot*) *n* heartwood. [L *dūrāmen* hardness, from *dūrus* hard]

durance, **duration**, etc. See under **durable**.

durante bene placito *dū-ran'tē ben'ē plas'i-tō*, *dōō-ran'te ben'e plak'i-tō*, (*LL*) during good pleasure; **durante vita** (*vī'tə*, *vē'tə* or *wē'tä*) during life.

durbar *dur'bär*, *n* an audience-chamber; a reception or levee; an Indian court (*hist*); the body of officials at an Indian court. [Pers *darbār* a prince's court, literally a door of admittance]

durchkomponiert or **durchkomponirt** *dōōrhh-kom-pon-ērt'*, (*Ger*) *adj* having the music specially adapted to each stanza.

Durchlaucht *dōōrhh'lowhht*, (*Ger*) *n* Serene Highness.

Durchmusterung *dōōrhh-mōōs'tər-ōōng*, (*Ger*, examination, scrutiny) *n* a star-catalogue.

durdum. Same as **dirdum**.

dure *dūr*, (*obs*) *vi* to endure, last or continue. — *adj* **dure'ful** (*Spenser*) enduring, lasting. [Fr *durer*, from L *dūrāre*, from *dūrus* hard]

duress or **duresse** *dūr-es'*, *dūr'es*, *n* constraint, force; imprisonment; coercion illegally exercised to force a person to perform some act; compulsion, pressure. [OFr *duresse*, from L *dūritia*, from *dūrus* hard]

durgan *dûr'gən*, (*dialect*) *n* a dwarf, any undersized creature. — *adj* **dur'gy** (*-gi* or *-ji*). [Related to **dwarf**]

Durham *dur'əm*, *n* one of a particular breed of shorthorned cattle. — Also *adj*. [From the English county]

durian *dōō'ri-ən* or *dū'*, *n* a tall Indian and Malayan bombacaceous fruit-tree (*Durio zibethinus*), with leaves like a cherry's; its large fruit, with hard rind and foul-smelling but pleasant-tasting pulp. — Also **du'rion**. [Malay *dūrī* thorn]

during *dū'ring*, *prep* throughout the time of; in the course of. [Orig *pr p* of **dure**]

durmast *dûr'mäst*, *n* a European oak bearing sessile acorns, with leaves downy below, noted for its tough wood (*Quercus petraea* or *sessiliflora*). [Origin unknown: perh a blunder for *dun mast*]

durn *dûrn*, (*dialect*) *n* a doorpost. — Also **dern**. [Prob Norse]

duro *dōō'rō*, *n* a Spanish peso: — *pl* **dur'os**. [Sp (*peso*) *duro* hard (peso)]

duroy *dōō-roi'*, (*obs*) *n* a type of coarse woollen fabric. [Orig uncertain]

durra *dōō'rə*, *n* Indian millet, a grass (*Sorghum vulgare*) related to sugar-cane, much cultivated for grain in Asia and Africa, or other species of the genus. — Also **dou'ra**, **dhu'rra**, **du'ra** and **dari** (*dur'i*). [Ar *dhurah*]

durrie *dur'i*, *n* an Indian cotton carpet fabric with fringes, used for curtains, covers, etc. [Hindi *darī*]

durst *dûrst*, *pa t* of **dare**[1], to venture. [OE *dorste*, pa t of *durran* to dare]

durukuli. See **douroucouli**.

durum *dū'rəm* or **durum wheat** (*hwēt* or *wēt*), *n* a kind of spring wheat (*Triticum durum*), grown *esp* in Russia, N Africa and N America, whose flour is used in making spaghetti, etc. [L *trīticum dūrum* hard wheat]

dush *dush*, (*Scot*) *vt* to strike heavily against; to throw down. — *n* a heavy impact.

dusk *dusk*, *adj* darkish; of a dark colour. — *n* twilight; partial darkness; darkness of colour. — *vt* and *vi* to make or become dusky; to dim. — *vt* and *vi* **dusk'en** to make or grow dark. — *adv* **dusk'ily**. — *n* **dusk'iness**. — *adj* **dusk'ish**. — *adv* **dusk'ishly**. — *n* **dusk'ishness**. — *adv* **dusk'ly**. — *n* **dusk'ness**. — *adj* **dusk'y** partially dark or obscure; dark-coloured; sad; gloomy. [Appar connected with OE *dox* dark]

dust *dust*, *n* fine particles of solid matter, *esp* earth, powdery matter or dirt; a cloud of this; the earth; the grave; a debased or shabby condition; (with **the**) pneumoconiosis (*miners' slang*); gold-dust, hence money; turmoil (*slang*); a disturbance, a brawl (*colloq*). — *vt* to free from dust (also *vi*); to trash, beat (*colloq*); to pass or leave in a trail of dust (*US colloq*); to sprinkle. — *n* **dust'er** someone who or something which dusts; a cloth or brush for removing dust; a sprinkler; a dustcoat (*US*). — *adv* **dust'ily**. — *n* **dust'iness**. — *adj* **dust'less**. — *adj* **dust'y** covered or sprinkled with dust; like dust; contemptible, bad (as in the phrases *not so dusty* and *a dusty answer*; *slang*). — **dust bag** a cloth or paper sack intended to hold the material sucked up by a vacuum cleaner; **dust'-ball**, a ball of grain-dust, etc, in a horse's intestine; **dust'-bath** the action of birds in rubbing dust into their feathers, probably to get rid of parasites; **dust'bin** a receptacle for household rubbish; a repository for anything unwanted, unimportant, etc (*fig*); **dust'-bowl** a drought area subject to dust-storms (**Dust Bowl** the region of the US along the western edge of the Great Plains); **dust'-brand** smut; **dust'-brush** a light brush for removing dust; **dust'cart** a cart for taking away household rubbish; **dust'-coat** an overall; a light overcoat; **dust cover** the jacket of a book; a dustsheet; **dust'-devil** or **-storm'** a small storm in which a whirling column of dust or sand travels across a dry country; **dust explosion** an explosion resulting from the ignition of small concentrations of flammable dust (eg coal dust or flour) in the air; **dust'-hole** (*obs*) dustbin; **dusting powder** fine powder, *esp* talcum powder; **dust jacket** the jacket or dust cover of a book; **dust'man** a person employed to remove household rubbish; **dust'-pan** a pan or shovel for removing dust swept from the floor. — *adj* **dust'proof** impervious or inaccessible to dust. — **dust'sheet** a cloth for protecting furniture from dust; **dust'-shot** the smallest size of shot; **dust-storm** see **dust-devil**; **dust'-up** (*colloq*) a quarrel, a brawl; **dusty answer** an unsatisfying, unfruitful, or sordid response (*fig*); **dust'y-foot** see **piepowder**; **dust'y-mill'er** the auricula, from the white dust on its leaves and flowers. — **bite the dust** see under **bite**; **dust someone's jacket** to give someone a beating; **kick up** or **raise a dust** see under **kick**; **throw dust in someone's eyes** (*fig*) to deceive someone. [OE *dūst*; cf Ger *Dunst* vapour]

Dutch *duch*, *adj* pertaining to the Netherlands, its people or language; German, Teutonic (*obs*, except *rare* or *archaic US*); heavy, clumsy, as in *Dutch-built*. — *n* the language of the Netherlands; German (*High* and *Low Dutch*, *Hoch* and *Nieder* or *Platt Deutsch*, High and Low German; *obs* and *US*); (as *pl*) the people of the Netherlands; Germans (*obs* and *US*). — **Dutch'man** a native or citizen of the Netherlands; an Afrikaner (*SAfr*; *derog*); a German or Teuton (*US*): — *pl* **Dutch'men**; *fem* **Dutch'woman**: — *pl* **Dutch'women**. — **Dutch auction** see under **auction**; **Dutch bargain** a one-sided bargain; **Dutch barn** a storage barn consisting of a roof on a steel framework; **Dutch cap** see under **cap**[1]; **Dutch carpet** a mixed material of cotton and wool for floor coverings; **Dutch cheese** a small round cheese made on the Continent from skimmed milk; **Dutch clinker** a hard yellow brick for paving, etc; **Dutch clock** a clock of wood and wire with brass wheels, made in the Black Forest; **Dutch clover** white clover; **Dutch comfort** 'Thank God it's no worse'; **Dutch concert** a concert in which singers sing their various songs simultaneously, or each person sings a verse of any song of their choosing between bursts of some familiar chorus; **Dutch courage** see under **courage**; **Dutch doll** a wooden doll with jointed legs; **Dutch drops** a once popular medicine, composed of oil of turpentine, tincture of guaiacum, etc; **Dutch gold**, **leaf** or **metal** a copper-zinc alloy, a substitute for gold leaf; **Dutch hoe** a hoe with blade attached as in a spade; **Dutch liquid** ethylene dichloride ($C_2H_4C_{12}$), an anaesthetic discovered by Dutch chemists; **Dutch lunch** or **Dutch supper** one at which each person brings or pays for their own share; **Dutchman's breeches** Dicentra; **Dutchman's pipe** a species of Aristolochia; **Dutch oven** a heavy covered cooking-pot used by burying in coals; a heavy stewpot or casserole; a tin for roasting before an open fire; **Dutch pink** see **pink**[4]; **Dutch rush** a horse-tail (*Equisetum hyemale*) with much silica in its stem, used for polishing; **Dutch tiles** see under **tile**; **Dutch treat** an occasion (eg a meal or an entertainment) when each person pays for himself or herself; **Dutch uncle** someone who criticizes or reprimands one unsparingly; **Dutch wife** an open frame of rattan or cane used in the East Indies, to rest the limbs upon in bed; a bolster used for the same purpose. — **double Dutch** any unknown or unintelligible language; **Dutch elm disease** a fungal, *usu* fatal, disease of elm trees, spread by bark beetles, causing a gradual withering; **go Dutch** (*colloq*) to pay each for himself or herself; **High Dutch** see **Dutch** (*n*) above; formerly, Dutch as spoken in the Netherlands as opposed to S African Dutch; double Dutch (*obs*); **I'm a Dutchman** an expression used ironically to show disbelief and rejection of an earlier statement; **Pennsylvania Dutch** the mixed German dialect of the descendants of German settlers in Pennsylvania; **talk like a Dutch uncle** to utter a rebuke. [Ger *deutsch*, (literally) belonging to the people, from OHGer *diutisc*; cf OE *thēod*, Gothic *thiuda* nation; see **Teutonic**]

dutch *duch*, (*cockney slang*) *n* a wife. [Probably **duchess**]

duty *dū'ti*, *n* that which is due; what one is bound by any (*esp* moral) obligation to do; one's proper business; service; attendance; supervision of pupils out of school hours; performance of function or service; the work done by a machine under given conditions, or for a specified amount of energy supplied; the amount of water needed to irrigate an area for a particular crop; respect, deference; tax on goods, etc. — *adj* **dū'teous** devoted to duty; obedient. — *adv* **dū'teously**. — *n* **dū'teousness**. — *adj* **dū'tiable** subject to custom duty.

— *adj* **dū'tied** subjected to duties and customs. — *adj* **dū'tiful** attentive to duty; respectful; expressive of a sense of duty. — *adv* **dū'tifully**. — *n* **dū'tifulness**. — *adj* **du'ty-bound'** obliged by one's feeling of duty; honour-bound. — *adj* **du'ty-free'** free from tax or duty. — *n* (*colloq*) a shop, *usu* at an airport or on board a ship, where duty-free articles are on sale; an article on sale at such a shop; **duty officer** the officer on duty at any particular time. — *adj* **du'ty-paid'** on which duty has been paid. — **do duty for** to serve as, to act as substitute for; **on duty** performing one's duties, or liable to be called upon to do so, during a specified period of time (*opp* to **off duty**). [Anglo-Fr *dueté*; see **due**[1]]

duumvir *dōō-, dū-um'vir, -vər, n* one of two men associated in the same office or post: — *pl* **duum'virs** or **duum'viri** (-*ī*; (*L*) *dōō-ōōm-wir'ē*). — *adj* **duum'viral**. — *n* **duum'virate** an association of two men in one office or post; a government by duumvirs. [L *duumvirī*, for *duovirī*, from *duo* two, and *vir* a man]

duvet *dōō'vā*, (*Fr dü-vā*), *n* a quilt stuffed with eiderdown, swan's-down or man-made fibres, used on a bed in place of blankets, etc; a quilted coat or jacket: — *pl* **du'vets**. [Fr]

duvetyn *dū'və-tēn, duv'tin, n* a soft fabric with a nap, made of cotton, wool, silk or rayon, and often used for women's clothes. — Also **duvetyne** or **duvetine**. [Fr *duvetine*, from *duvet* down]

dux *duks, n* a leader; the top academic prize-winner in a school or class (*esp Scot*). [L, a leader]

duxelles *duk-sel', dōōk-, -z, n* a seasoning made from chopped mushrooms, onions or shallots, and parsley. [The Marquis *d'Uxelles*, 17c French nobleman]

duyker. See **duiker**.

DV *abbrev*: *Deo volente* (*L*), God willing.

Dv. *abbrev*: Drive (in street names).

dvandva *dvän'dvä*, (*gram*) *n* a compound word, each element being equal in status (eg *tragicomedy*, *bittersweet*). [Sans *dvaṁdva* a pair]

DVLA *abbrev*: Driver and Vehicle Licensing Agency (formerly Centre).

DVORAK keyboard *dvör'zhak kē'bōrd, -börd*, (*comput*) *n* a typewriter, etc keyboard laid out so as to minimize finger movement.

dvornik *dvor'nēk, dvör', n* a Russian concierge or porter. [Russ, caretaker, from *dvor* yard, court]

dwale *dwāl, n* deadly nightshade (*bot*); a stupefying drink (*obs*); a black colour (*heraldry*). [ON *dvöl, dvali* delay, sleep]

dwam or **dwalm** *dwäm*, or **dwaum** *dwöm*, (*Scot*) *n* a swoon (*obs*); a sudden sickness; a dream, state of inattention. — *vi* to swoon (*obs*); to fail in health. [OE *dwolma* confusion]

dwang *dwang*, (*Scot* and *NZ*) *n* a piece of timber used to reinforce joists, etc, a strut. [Du, force, a constraint, from *dwingen* to force]

dwarf *dwörf, n* an abnormally small person, *esp* (in general but non-technical usage) a person with abnormally short limbs but normal body and head; a small manlike being, *esp* a metal-worker (*folklore*); an animal or plant much below the ordinary height; anything very small of its kind; a small star of high density and low luminosity (**white dwarf**, **red dwarf**, **brown dwarf**, etc according to strength of light emitted): — *pl* **dwarfs** or (*rare*) **dwarves**. — *adj* dwarfed; dwarfish; very small. — *vt* to hinder from growing; to make to appear small. — *vi* to become dwarfed. — *adj* **dwarfed**. — *adj* **dwarf'ish** like a dwarf; very small; despicable. — *adv* **dwarf'ishly**. — *n* **dwarf'ishness**. — *n* **dwarf'ism** condition of being a dwarf. — **dwarfed tree** bonsai. [OE *dweorg*; Du *dwerg*, ON *dverg*, Ger *Zwerg*]

dweeb *dwēb*, (*US slang*) *n* a fool, nerd.

dwell *dwel, vi* to abide or reside (*formal* or *archaic*); to remain; to rest attention (on); to continue long (in; *obs*). — *vt* (*Milton*) to inhabit; to cause to dwell: — *pr p* **dwell'ing**; *pa t* and *pa p* **dwelt** or **dwelled**. — *n* a pause or hesitation in the working of a machine (*eng*); a part of a cam shaped so as to allow a pause in operation at the point of maximum lift (*eng*). — *n* **dwell'er**. — *n* **dwell'ing** (*formal* or *archaic*) the place where one dwells; a house; habitation; continuance. — **dwell'ing-house** a house used as a dwelling, in distinction from a place of business or other building; **dwell'ing-place** a place of residence. [OE *dwellan* to go astray, delay, tarry]

dwile *dwīl, n* a floorcloth or mop. [Cf Du *dweil* a mop]

dwindle *dwind'l, vi* to grow less; to waste away; to grow feeble; to become degenerate. — *vt* to lessen. — *n* decline. — *n* **dwin'dlement**. [Dimin of **dwine**]

dwine *dwīn, vi* to pine; to waste away (*Scot*). [OE *dwīnan* to fade; cf ON *dvīna*, Dan *tvine* to pine away]

DY *abbrev*: Benin (formerly Dahomey) (IVR).

Dy (*chem*) *symbol*: dysprosium.

dyad *dī'ad, n* a pair of units treated as one; a bivalent atom, radical, or element (*chem*). — *adj* **dyad'ic**. [Gr *dyas, -ados*, from *dyo* two]

Dyak or **Dayak** *dī'ak, n* a member of any of the indigenous, generally non-Muslim tribes of the interior of Borneo; their languages and dialects. [Malay *dayak* up-country]

dyarchy *dī'ärk-i, n* a common but undesirable spelling of **diarchy**.

dybbuk *dib'ək*, (*Jewish folklore*) *n* an evil spirit, or the soul of a dead person, that enters the body of a living person and controls his or her actions. [Heb *dibbūq*]

dye[1] *dī*, (*Spenser*) *n*. Same as **die**[2].

dye[2] *dī, vt* to stain; to give a new colour to: — *pr p* **dye'ing**; *pa t* and *pa p* **dyed**. — *n* colour produced by dyeing; tinge; stain; a colouring liquid. — *adj* **dy'able** or **dye'able**. — *adj* **dyed**. — *n* **dye'ing**. — *n* **dy'er** a person whose trade is to dye cloth, etc. — *n* **dyester** (*dī'stər*; *Scot*) a dyer. — **dye'-house** a building in which dyeing is done; **dyeline** (*dī'līn*) see **diazo**; **dy'er's-green'weed** or **dy'er's-broom** a papilionaceous shrub (*Genista tinctoria*), a source of yellow colouring matter; **dy'er's-rock'et**, **-weld** or **-yell'owweed** a plant (*Reseda luteola*), related to mignonette, yielding a yellow dye; **dy'er's-weed** a name for various plants that yield dyes (woad, weld, dyer's-greenweed, etc); **dye'stuff** a substance used in dyeing; **dye'-wood** any wood from which material is obtained for dyeing; **dye'-work** or **-works** an establishment for dyeing. — **dye in the wool** to dye (the wool) before spinning, to give a more permanent result (*adj* **dyed-in-the-wool** (*fig*) (too) fixed in one's opinions or attitudes). [OE *dēagian* to dye, from *dēag, dēah* colour]

dying *dī'ing, pr p* of **die**[1]. — *adj* destined for death; mortal; declining; occurring immediately before death, eg *dying words*; pertaining to death; last, final. — *n* death. — *adv* **dy'ingly**. — *n* **dy'ingness**. — **dying declaration** (*law*) declaration made by a dying person who does not survive through the trial of the accused; **dying shift** (*mining*) the night shift. [See **die**[1]]

dyke, **dykey**. See **dike**[1,2].

dyn *abbrev*: dynamo; dynamometer; dyne.

dynamic *dīn-am'ik*, or *din-*, *adj* relating to force; relating to dynamics; relating to the effects of forces in nature; relating to activity or things in movement; relating to dynamism; causal; forceful, very energetic. — *n* a moving force; any driving force instrumental in growth or change (*esp* social); pattern of growth or change. — *adj* **dynam'ical**. — *adv* **dynam'ically**. — *n* **dynam'icist** a person who studies dynamics. — *n sing* **dynam'ics** the science of matter and motion, mechanics, sometimes restricted to kinetics; (often as *n pl*) (signs indicating) varying levels of loudness (*music*). — *n* **dyn'amism** a theory which explains the phenomena of the universe by some immanent energy; operation of force; dynamic quality; quality of restless energy; quality of suggesting forceful movement (*art*, etc). — **dyn'amist**. — *adj* **dynamis'tic**. — *vt* **dyn'amize** or **-ise** to make dynamic. [Gr *dynamikos*, from *dynamis* power, from *dynasthai* to be able]

dynamite *dīn'ə-mīt* (formerly also *din'*), *n* an explosive consisting of absorbent matter, such as porous silica, saturated with nitroglycerine; something highly dangerous to deal with; someone or something excellent or thrilling (*slang*). — *vt* to blow up with dynamite (also *fig*). — *n* **dyn'amiter** or **dyn'amitard** (*-mit-ärd*) (*archaic*) a user of dynamite, *esp* for political purposes. [Gr *dynamis* power]

dynamo *dīn'ə-mō*, *n* contraction for **dynamo-electric machine**, a machine for generating electric currents by means of the relative movement of conductors and magnets: — *pl* **dyn'amos**. — *adj* **dyn'amo-elec'tric** or **dyn'amo-elec'trical**. — *n* **dynamogen'esis** or **dynamog'eny** production of increased nervous activity. — *n* **dynamograph** (*-am'*) a recording dynamometer. — *n* **dynamom'eter** an instrument for measuring force, or (brake horse-) power. — *adj* **dynamomet'ric** or **dynamomet'rical**. — *n* **dynamom'etry**. — *n* **dyn'amotor** an electrical machine with two armature windings, one acting as a motor and the other as a generator, and a single magnetic field, for converting direct current into alternating current. — *n* **dyn'atron** (*electronics*) a four-electrode thermionic valve used to generate continuous oscillation. — **human dynamo** a person of exceptional energy. [Gr *dynamis* power]

dynast *din'ast*, *-əst*, also (*US*) *dīn'*, *n* a ruler. — *adj* **dynas'tic** or **dynas'tical** relating to a dynasty. — *adv* **dynast'ically**. — *n* **dyn'asty** (*-əs-ti*) a succession of monarchs of the same family, or of members of any powerful family or connected group. [Fr *dynastie*, or LL *dynastīa*, from Gr *dynasteia* power, dominion, from *dynasthai* to be able]

dynatron. See under **dynamo**.

dyne *dīn*, *n* the force which (in the centimetre-gram-second system) acting on a mass of one gramme, produces an acceleration of one centimetre per second per second, equal to 10^{-5} of a newton. — *n* **dyn'ode** (*electronics*) an intermediate electrode (between the cathode and final anode) which causes amplification by secondary emission of electrons. [Gr *dynamis* force]

Dyophysite. Same as **Diphysite**.

Dyothelete, **Dyotheletism**, **Dyothelism**. See **Ditheletism**.

dys- *dis-*, *pfx* signifying ill, bad or abnormal. [Gr]

dysaesthesia *dis-əs-thē'si-ə*, *-zhi-ə*, *-zhə*, or *-ēs-*, (*med*) *n* impaired sensation, partial insensibility. — *adj* **dysaesthetic** (*-thet'ik*). [**dys-** and Gr *aisthēsis* sensation, from *aisthanesthai* to feel]

dysarthria *dis-är'thri-ə*, (*med*) *n* impaired ability to articulate speech resulting from damage to the central or peripheral nervous system. [**dys-**, and Gr *arthron* a joint]

dyschroa *dis'krō-ə*, (*med*) *n* discoloration of the skin from disease. — Also **dyschroia** (*-kroi'ə*). [**dys-** and Gr *chroā*, *chroiā* complexion]

dyscrasia *dis-krā'si-ə*, *-zhi-ə*, *-zhə*, (*obs pathol*) *n* a disordered condition of the body attributed originally to unsuitable mixing of the body fluids or humours. [**dys-** and Gr *krāsis* a mixing]

dyscrasite *dis'kras-īt*, *n* a mineral composed of silver and antimony. [**dys-** and Gr *krāsis* mixture]

dysentery *dis'ən-tər-i*, *-tri*, (*med*) *n* a term formerly applied to any condition in which inflammation of the colon was associated with the frequent passage of bloody stools; now confined to *amoebic dysentery*, the result of infection with the *Entamoeba histolytica*, and to *bacillary dysentery*, due to infection with *Bacterium dysenteriae*. — *adj* **dysenteric** (*-ter'ik*). [Gr *dysenteria*, from *dys-* amiss, and *enteron* intestine]

dysfunction *dis-fungk'shən* or *dis-fung'shən*, *n* impairment or abnormality of the functioning of an organ. — *adj* **dysfunc'tional**. [**dys-**]

dysgenic *dis-jen'ik*, (*zool*) *adj* unfavourable to racial improvement. — *n sing* **dysgen'ics** the study of race degeneration; cacogenics. [**dys-**, and the root of *gennaein* to beget]

dysgraphia *dis-graf'i-ə*, *n* inability to write, due to brain damage or other cause. — *adj* **dysgraph'ic**. [**dys-** and Gr *graphein* to write]

dysharmonic *dis-här-mon'ik*, *adj* unbalanced, lacking in harmony of proportion. [**dys-**]

dyskinesia *dis-kin-ē'zi-ə*, (*pathol*) *n* lack of control over bodily movements; impaired performance of voluntary movements. [**dys-** and Gr *kīnēsis* movement]

dyslexia *dis-leks'i-ə*, *n* word-blindness, great difficulty in learning to read or spell, unrelated to intellectual competence and of unknown cause. — *adj* and *n* **dyslec'tic** or **dyslex'ic**. [**dys-** and Gr *lexis* word]

dyslogistic *dis-lə-jis'tik*, *adj* conveying censure, opprobrious. — *adv* **dyslogis'tically**. — *n* **dys'logy** dispraise. [**dys-** and Gr *logos* discourse]

dysmelia *dis-mēl'i-ə*, *-mel'*, *-yə*, *n* the condition in which one or more limbs are misshapen or incomplete. — *adj* **dysmel'ic**. [**dys-** and Gr *melos* limb]

dysmenorrhoea or (*esp US*) **dysmenorrhea** *dis-men-ō-rē'ə*, (*med*) *n* difficult or painful menstruation. — *adj* **dysmenorrhoe'al** or **dysmenorrhe'al**. — *adj* **dysmenorrhoe'ic** or **dysmenorrhe'ic**. [**dys-** and Gr *mēn* month, and *rhoiā* flow]

dysmorphophobia *dis-mör-fō-fō 'bi-ə*, *n* abnormal fear of any personal physical deformity. [**dys-**, **morpho-** and **phobia**]

dysodyle, **dysodile** or **dysodil** *dis'ō-dīl*, *-dil*, *n* a yellow or greyish laminated bituminous mineral (often found with lignite) that burns vividly, with an odour of asafoetida. [Gr *dysōdēs* stinking, from *dys-* ill, *ozein* to smell, and *hȳlē* matter]

dyspareunia *dis-pä-rōō'ni-ə*, *n* painful or difficult coitus. [**dys-** and Gr *para* beside, and *eunē* a bed]

dyspathy *dis'pə-thi*, *n* antipathy, dislike. — *adj* **dyspathet'ic**. [**dys-** and Gr *pathos* feeling]

dyspepsia *dis-pep'si-ə*, (*med*) *n* indigestion. — Also **dyspep'sy**. — *n* **dyspep'tic** a person afflicted with dyspepsia. — *adj* **dyspep'tic** or **dyspep'tical** afflicted with, pertaining to, or arising from indigestion; gloomy, bad-tempered. — *adv* **dyspep'tically**. [Gr *dyspepsiā*, from *dys-* ill, and *pepsis* digestion, from *peptein* to digest]

dysphagia *dis-fā'ji-ə*, (*pathol*) *n* difficulty in swallowing. — Also **dys'phagy** (*-fə-ji*). — *adj* **dysphagic** (*-faj'ik*). [**dys-** and Gr *phagein* (aorist) to eat]

dysphasia *dis-fāz'i-ə*, *-fā'zhə*, *n* difficulty in expressing or understanding thought in spoken or written words, caused by brain damage. [**dys-** and Gr *phasis* speech]

dysphemism *dis'fə-mizm*, *n* the replacing of a mild or inoffensive word or phrase by an offensive one; the offensive word or phrase substituted. — *adj* **dysphemis'tic**. [From **dys-** and **euphemism**]

dysphonia *dis-fō'ni-ə*, *n* difficulty in producing sounds. — *adj* **dysphon'ic**. [**dys-** and Gr *phōnē* sound]

dysphoria *dis-fō'ri-ə*, *-fö'*, *n* impatience under affliction; morbid restlessness; uneasiness; absence of feeling of wellbeing. — *adj* **dysphor'ic**. [Gr *dysphoriā* affliction, pain, from *dys-* ill, and the root of *pherein* to bear]

dysplasia *dis-plā'zi-ə*, (*pathol*) *n* abnormal development or growth of a cell, tissue, organ, etc. — *adj* **dysplas'tic**. [**dys-** and Gr *plāsis* moulding]

dyspnoea or (*esp US*) **dyspnea** *disp-nē'ə*, *n* difficult or laboured breathing. — *adj* **dyspnoe'al** or **dyspne'al**. — *adj* **dyspnoe'ic** or **dyspne'ic**. [Gr *dyspnoia*, from *dys-* ill, and *pnoē* breathing]

dyspraxia *dis-prak'si-ə*, (*pathol*) *n* an impaired ability to perform deliberate actions. [**dys-** and Gr *prāxis* doing]

dysprosium *dis-prōz'i-əm*, *n* a metallic element of the rare earths (atomic no 66; symbol **Dy**). [Gr *dysprositos* difficult to reach, from *dys-* ill, difficult, *pros* to, and *ienai* to go]

dysrhythmia *dis-ridh'mi-ə*, *n* abnormal or defective rhythm. [**dys-** and Gr *rhythmos* rhythm]

dystectic *dis-tek'tik*, *adj* not easily fused. [Gr *dystēktos*, from *dys-* ill, and *tēkein* to melt]

dysteleology *dis-tel-i-ol'ə-ji*, *n* the doctrine of purposelessness, or denial of final causes; the study of functionless rudimentary organs in animals and plants. — *adj* **dysteleological** (*-i-ə-loj'i-kl*). — *n* **dysteleol'ogist**. [**dys-** (in a negative sense)]

dysthesia *dis-thē'si-ə*, *n* a morbid habit of body, resulting in general discomfort and impatience. — *adj* **dysthetic**

(*-thet'ik*). [Gr *dysthesiā*, from *dys-* ill, and *thesis* position]

dysthymia *dis-thī'mi-ə*, (*psychiatry*) *n* abnormal anxiety and despondency. — *n* **dysthȳm'iac** a person who suffers from dysthymia. — *adj* **dysthȳm'ic**. [**dys-** and Gr *thymiā* despair]

dystocia *dis-tō'shi-ə*, (*med*) *n* abnormal or difficult labour or childbirth. [**dys-** and Gr *tokos* birth]

dystonia *dis-tō'ni-ə*, (*med*) *n* a disorder of muscle tone, causing muscle spasm. — *adj* **dystonic** (*-ton'ik*). [**dys-** and Gr *tonos* tension]

dystopia *dis-tō'pi-ə*, *n* a place thought of as the opposite to Utopia, ie where everything is as bad as possible. — *adj* **dysto'pian**. [From **dys-** and **utopia**]

dystrophy *dis'trə-fi*, (*biol*) *n* impaired or imperfect nutrition; any of several disorders in which there is wasting of muscle tissue, etc. — Also **dystrō'phia**. — *adj* **dystrophic** (*-tro'fik*; of a lake) over-acidic and lacking sufficient nutrients. — *n* **dys'trophin** a protein essential to normal muscle function, found to be lacking in muscular dystrophy sufferers. — **muscular dystrophy** see under **muscle**. [**dys-** and Gr *trophē* nourishment]

dysuria *dis-ū'ri-ə*, (*med*) *n* difficulty or pain in passing urine. — Also **dys'ury**. — *adj* **dysū'ric**. [Gr *dysouriā*, from *dys-* ill, and *ouron* urine]

Dytiscus *di-* or *dī-tis'kəs*, *n* a genus of carnivorous water-beetles, *incl* a common large British species, *D. marginalis*. — Also **Dyticus** (*dit'*). — *adj* and *n* **dytiscid** (*di-* or *dī-tis'id*). [Gr *dytikos* diving, from *dyein* to dive]

dyvour *dī'vər*, (*obs Scot*) *n* a bankrupt. — *n* **dyv'oury** bankruptcy. [Perh from Fr *devoir* to owe]

DZ *abbrev*: Algeria (IVR, from the Arabic name *al-Djazā'ir*).

dz. *abbrev*: dozen.

dzeren *dzē'rən*, *n* a Central Asian antelope. [Mongolian]

dzho, **dzo**. See **zho**.

dziggetai *dzig'ə-tī*, *n* a Central Asian wild ass (*Equus hemionus*), rather like a mule. [Mongolian *tchikhitei*]

E

E or **e** *ē*, *n* the fifth letter in the modern English alphabet, with various sounds, as in m*e*, g*e*t, *E*ngland, h*e*r, pr*e*y, and often mute, commonly indicating a preceding long vowel or diphthong: cf not, not*e*; bit, bit*e*; in music, the third note or sound of the natural diatonic scale, the major third above the tonic C.

E *abbrev*: East; Ecstasy, the drug (*colloq*); electromotive force (*phys*); (also *E*) energy (*phys*); English; Spain (ie España; IVR); European (as in *E number*); exa-. — **E'-boat** (enemy *boat* or Ger *Eilboot*, from *Eile* speed) a fast German motor torpedo-boat; **E. coli** see **Escherichia coli**; **E'-fit**® a form of identikit, the image being composed on screen and adjustable by fine degrees; **E-layer** or **E-region** see **Kennelly-Heaviside layer**; **e'-mail** or **E'-mail** electronic mail (qv); **E number** an identification code required by EEC law for food additives such as colourings and preservatives, consisting of the letter E followed by a number.

E *symbol*: as medieval Roman numeral, 250; **Ē** = 250 000.

e (*math*) *symbol*: the base of the natural system of logarithms (see **Napierian**); the eccentricity of a conic section.

ea *ē'ə* or *ē*, (*dialect*) *n* a river; running water; a drainage channel in the Fens, sometimes **eau**, as if taken from French. [OE *ēa*; related to L *aqua* water]

each *ēch*, *adj* and *pronoun* every one separately considered. — *adv* **each'where** (*obs*) everywhere. — **each other** a compound reciprocal pronoun, one another, sometimes restricted in application to two; **each way** in betting, for a win and for a place (*adj* **each'-way**). [OE *ǣlc*, from *ā* ever, and *gelīc* alike]

eadish. Obsolete form of **eddish**.

eager[1] *ē'gər*, *adj* excited by desire; longing to do or (with *for*) obtain; earnest (*obs*); keen, severe; (*Shakesp* **aygre**) sour, acid, bitter (*obs*). — *adv* **ea'gerly**. — *n* **ea'gerness**. — **eager beaver** an enthusiast; a zealous person; a person who is too eager for work. [OFr *aigre*, from L *ācer*, *ācris* sharp]

eager[2]. Same as **eagre**.

eagle *ē'gl*, *n* a name given to many large birds of prey of the family Falconidae; a military standard carrying the figure of an eagle; a lectern in the form of an eagle; the badge of certain orders, such as the Prussian **black** (1701) and **red** (1705) **eagle**, the Polish, afterwards Russian, **white eagle** (1705); a gold coin of the United States, formerly worth ten dollars and now available in denominations of 5, 10, 25 and 50 dollars; a colonel's shoulder insignia (*US*); a hole at golf played in two strokes less than par. — *n* **ea'glet** a young or small eagle. — *adj* **ea'gle-eyed** or **ea'gle-sighted** sharp-eyed; discerning. — *adj* **ea'gle-flighted** flying high. — **ea'gle-hawk** a name applied to several eagles of comparatively small size; **ea'gle-owl** any of a number of large horned owls of the genus Bubo; **ea'gle-ray** a large sting-ray; **ea'gle-stone** a hard-encrusted nodule of argillaceous oxide of iron. — *adj* **ea'gle-winged** having an eagle's wings. [OFr *aigle*, from L *aquila*]

eaglewood *ē'gl-wŏŏd*, *n* a genus (Aquilaria) of the daphne family, large spreading trees of E India, whose heartwood contains a resinous substance fragrant when burnt. [From the accidental resemblance of its name in some Eastern languages to **eagle**, L *aquila*; cf **agalloch** and **agila**]

eagre *ā'gər* or *ē'gər*, *n* a bore or sudden rise of the tide in a river. [Origin doubtful; hardly from OE *ēgor* flood]

EAK *abbrev*: Kenya (ie East Africa Kenya; IVR).

ealdorman. Obsolete form of **alderman**.

eale prob *ēl*, (Shakesp, *Hamlet* 1. 4. 36) *n* various conjectures, generally supposed to be for **evil** but perh a misprint.

ean *ēn*, (*Shakesp*) *vt* and *vi* to give birth (to). — *n* **ean'ling** a young lamb. [OE *ēanian*]

eaon *abbrev*: except as otherwise noted.

EAP *abbrev*: English for academic purposes.

ear[1] *ēr*, *n* the part of a cereal plant containing the seeds, *esp* of corn. — *vi* to produce ears. — *adj* **eared** (of corn) having ears. — **ear'-cockle** a disease of wheat caused by a threadworm (*Tylenchus*). [OE *ēar*; Ger *Ähre*]

ear[2] *ēr*, (*obs*) *vt* to plough or till. — *n* **ear'ing** (*obs*) ploughing. [OE *erian*; cf L *arāre* and Gr *aroein*]

ear[3] *ēr*, *n* the organ of hearing, or just the external part; the sense or power of hearing; the faculty of distinguishing sounds *esp* of a different pitch; attention; anything projecting or shaped like an ear, such as the auricle of a leaf, the lug of a vessel or a projecting part for support, attachment, etc. — *adj* **eared** having ears or external ears. — *n* **ear'ful** (*colloq*) rough or scolding words, a reprimand; as much talk or gossip as one's ears can stand. — *n* **ear'ing** (*naut*) one of a number of small ropes for fastening the upper corner of a sail to the yard. — *adj* **ear'less** without ears, or external ears. — **ear'ache** an ache or pain in the ear. — *vi* **ear'bash** (*Austr colloq*) to talk incessantly. — **ear'bob** an earring; **ear'-bone**. — *adj* **ear'-bussing** (*Shakesp*; another reading **ear'-kissing**) whispered. — **ear'-cap** (*archaic*) an earflap; **ear defenders** plugs or muffs for insertion into, or fitting over, the ear to reduce noise reception; **ear'drop** a pendant earring; (in *pl*) a medicine taken in the form of drops put into the outer ear; **ear'drum** the tympanic membrane, a thin partition between the outer ear and the organs of the middle ear, which vibrates as sound waves strike it; the cavity of the middle ear, tympanum; **ear'flap** one of two coverings for the ears, attached to a cap, to protect them from cold or injury; **ear'-hole** the opening in the ear; **ear'lap** the tip of the ear; an earflap; **ear'lobe** the soft lower part of the outer ear; **ear'lock** a curl near the ear worn by Elizabethan dandies; **ear'mark** a distinctive mark; an owner's mark on an animal's ear. — *vt* to set aside or intend for a particular purpose; to put an earmark on. — **ear'muffs** a pair of ear coverings joined by a band across the head; **ear'phone** a headphone; **ear'pick** an instrument for clearing the ear; **ear'piece** the part of a telephone, etc that is placed next to the ear; a square box for advertisement, etc printed at the top of a newspaper page. — *adj* **ear'-piercing** shrill, screaming. — *n* the piercing of the lobe of the ear in order to insert earrings. — **ear'plug** a plug of soft material inserted into the outer ear to keep out sound, water, etc; **earring** (*ēr'ing*) a piece of jewellery hung from or fixed on or in the ear; **ear'-shell** any shell of the family Haliotidae; **ear'shot** the distance within which a sound can be heard. — *adj* **ear'-splitting** ear-piercing. — **ear'-trumpet** a trumpet-shaped tube formerly used as a hearing-aid; **ear'wax** a waxy substance secreted by the glands of the ear; **ear'wig** (OE *ēarwicga*, from *ēare* ear, and *wicga* insect or beetle) any dermapterous insect of the family Forficulidae, once supposed to creep into the ear; a flatterer. — *vt* to gain the ear of (*archaic*); to bias (*archaic*); to pester with continual demands (*archaic*); to eavesdrop (*slang*). — *adj* **ear'wiggy**. — **ear'-witness** a witness that can testify from his or her own hearing. — **about one's ears** said of something falling around one (eg a building or missiles) (also *fig*); **a thick ear** (*colloq*) a blow on the ear, by way of chastisement; **a word in**

someone's ear a private word with someone; **be all ears** to give every attention; **fall on deaf ears** (of a remark, request, etc) to be ignored; **give ear** to attend (to); **go in (at) one ear and out (at) the other** to make no permanent impression; **have itching ears** to want to hear novelties (2 Tim 4.3); **have** or **keep one's ear to the ground** to keep oneself well informed about what is going on around one; **have someone's ear** to be sure of someone's favourable attention; **lend an ear** to listen (to); **make a pig's ear of** see **pig**[1]; **make someone's ears burn** to discuss someone in his or her absence; **out on one's ear** (*colloq*) turned out, dismissed; **pin back one's ears** to listen attentively; **pin back someone's ears** to reprimand, rebuke; **play by ear** to play on a musical instrument without the help of written music; **play it by ear** to deal with a situation as it develops without advance planning; **set by the ears** to set violently against each other; **tickle the ear of** to gratify, pander to the taste of or flatter; **turn a deaf ear** to refuse to listen (to); **up to one's ears in** deeply involved in; **walls have ears** someone may be listening; **wet behind the ears** (*colloq*) naïve, immature. [OE *ēare*; cf Ger *Ohr* and L *auris*]

earcon *ēr'kon*, (*comput*) *n* an audio signal given by a computer, eg indicating what task it is performing, as distinct from an *icon*, or visual signal. [Artificial coinage, from *ear* and *icon*]

eard, eard-hunger. See **yird**.

earl *ûrl*, *n* a British nobleman ranking between a marquis and a viscount (*fem* **countess**). — *n* **earl'dom** the lands or rank and title of an earl. — **Earl Marshal** an English officer of state, president of the Heralds' College: Scottish form **Earl Marischal**. [OE *eorl* a warrior or hero, a Danish under-king, later a nobleman equivalent to a count; cf ON *jarl*]

early *ûr'li*, *adv* near the beginning (of a time, period or series); soon; in good time; beforehand; before the appointed time: — *compar* **ear'lier**; *superl* **ear'liest**. — *adj* belonging to or happening in the first part of a time, period or series; belonging to or happening in the first stages of development; beforehand; ready, advanced, awake or on the spot in good time; happening in the remote past or near future; (of temperatures, figures, etc) low. — *n* (*hortic*; *usu* in *pl*) early potatoes. — *vt* **ear'lierize** or **-ise** to do at a date earlier than that arranged. — *n* **ear'liness**. — **early bird** the proverbial catcher of the (early) worm; an early riser; (with *caps*) a name given to a type of communications satellite; **early closing** the keeping of a weekly half-holiday by the shopkeepers of town; closing of public houses early in the night. — *adj* **early-clos'ing**. — **early door** an entrance to a theatre or hall open before the ordinary door at a higher price; **Early English** the form of Gothic architecture in which the pointed arch was first employed in Britain, succeeding the *Norman* towards the end of the 12c and merging into the *Decorated* at the end of the 13c. — Also *adj*. — *adj* (*philol*) see under **English**. — *adj* **early-Victor'ian** belonging to or characteristic of the early part of Queen Victoria's reign 1837–1901. — *adj* **early-warn'ing** (also as two words) belonging to or part of an early warning system (see below). — **early wood** (*bot*) the wood formed in the first part of a growth layer during the spring, typically with larger cells and thinner cell walls than the *late wood*. — **earlier on** previously; **early and late** at all times; **early day motion** a parliamentary motion for consideration on a day when business finishes early, ie (as such days rarely exist) merely to draw attention to a matter; **early on** before much time has elapsed; **early warning system** a system of advance warning or notice, *esp* of nuclear attack; **(it's) early days** (*colloq*) (it's) too soon to know, have a result, etc; **keep early hours** to rise and go to bed early. [OE *ǣrlīce* (adv), from *ǣr* before]

earn[1] *ûrn*, *vt* to gain by labour; to acquire; to deserve; to bring to someone. — *n* **earn'er** a person who earns; something (*esp* illegal or slightly shady) that brings a good income or profit (*slang*). — *n pl* **earn'ings** what one has earned; money saved; the profits from a venture; income from investments. — **earn out** to make enough money from sales to recover costs or make a profit. [OE *earnian* to earn; cf OHGer *aran* harvest; Ger *Ernte*]

earn[2] *ûrn*, (*dialect*) *vt* and *vi* (of milk) to curdle. — *n* **earn'ing** rennet. — Also **yearn, yearning**. [OE *iernan* = *rinnan*, to run, and *ærnan* = *rennan* to cause to run; *gerinnan*, and causative *gerennan* to curdle]

earn[3] *ûrn*, (*Spenser*, *Shakesp*) *vi*. See **yearn**[1].

earnest[1] *ûr'nist*, *adj* intent; sincere in intention; serious, *esp* over-serious, in disposition; determined or whole-hearted; fervent or impassioned. — *n* used in the expression **in earnest** (see below). — *adv* **ear'nestly**. — *n* **ear'nestness**. — **in all earnestness** most sincerely; urgently; **in earnest** serious, not joking; in a determined or unequivocal way; in reality. [OE *eornost* seriousness; Ger *Ernst*]

earnest[2] *ûr'nist*, *n* payment given in token of a bargain made (also **ear'nest-money** or **ear'nest-penny**); a pledge; first-fruits. [ME *ernes*, from OF *erres* pledges, from Gr *arrabon* pledge, from Heb '*ērābōn*]

earst. Obsolete form of **erst**.

earth *ûrth*, *n* the third planet in order from the sun (often with *cap*); the material on the surface of the globe; soil, a mixture of disintegrated rock and organic material, in which plants are rooted; dry land as opposed to sea; the world; the inhabitants of the world; dirt; dead matter; the human body; a burrow; an electrical connection with the earth, *usu* by a wire soldered to a metal plate sunk in moist earth; an old name for certain oxides of metals (see **alkaline earth, rare earth**). — *vt* to connect to earth electrically; to bury, inter (*obs*); to hide or make hide in the earth or in a hole; to clog, cover, smear or partially cover with earth (often with *up*). — *vi* (*poetic* or *rhetoric*) to burrow; to hide. — *adj* **earth'en** made of earth or clay; earthly. — *n* **earth'iness**. — *n* **earth'liness**. — *n* **earth'ling** a person living on the earth; a worldly-minded person. — *adj* **earth'ly** belonging to the earth; vile; worldly; conceivably possible on earth. — *n* (*colloq*) chance (for *earthly chance*). — *adv* **earth'ward** (also **earth'wards**) towards the earth. — *adj* **earth'y** consisting of, relating to or resembling earth; inhabiting the earth; gross; unrefined. — **earth'-bag** a sack of earth used in fortifications; **earth'-bath** a bath of earth or mud; **earth'-board** the board of a plough or other implement that turns over the earth. — *adj* **earth'born** born from or on the earth. — *adj* **earth'bound** confined to the earth; heading towards the earth. — *adj* **earth'-bred** bred from earth; mean, grovelling. — **earth-chest'nut** same as **earth'-nut**; **earth'-closet** a lavatory in which the excreta are covered with earth. — *adj* **earth'-created** made of earth. — **earth'enware** crockery; coarse pottery; **earth'fall** a landslide. — *adj* **earth'fast** fixed in the earth. — *adj* **earth'-fed** contented with earthly things. — **earth'flax** asbestos; **earth'-hog** the aardvark; **earth'-house** an underground stone-lined gallery associated with the Iron Age, which may have functioned as a storehouse or dwelling, a souterrain, also called **Picts' house**; **earth'-hunger** passion for acquiring land; **earthing tyres** aircraft tyres that discharge static electricity on grounding; **earth-light** see **earth-shine**. — *adj* **earth'ly-mind'ed** having the mind intent on earthly things. — **earth'ly-mind'edness**; **earth'man** or **earth'woman** *esp* in science fiction, a person who lives on the planet earth; **earth mother** the earth personified as a goddess; a woman, typically fertile and of generous proportions, who seems to symbolize motherhood. — *adj* **earth'-motherly**. — **earth'-movement** (*geol*) elevation, subsidence or folding of the earth's crust; **earth'mover** any piece of machinery designed to move earth, eg a bulldozer. — *adj* **earth'-moving**. — **earth'-nut** the edible root-tuber of *Conopodium flexuosum*, a woodland umbelliferous plant; the plant itself (also *arnut*, *pig-nut*, *earth-chestnut*); the peanut (Arachis); **Earth observation** (*space*) observation of the Earth from satellites by remote sensing techniques; **earth'-pea** the peanut; **earth'-pillar** (*geol*) a column of soft material protected from erosion by an overlying stone; **earth'-plate** a buried plate of metal forming the earth connection of a telegraph-wire, lightning-conductor, etc; **earth'quake** a quaking or shaking of the earth; a heaving of the ground; a disruptive event, upheaval (*fig*). — *adj* **earth'quaked** shaken, destroyed or visited by an earthquake. — *adj* **earth'quaking**. — **earth science** any of the sciences dealing with the earth, eg geography or geology. — *adj* **earth'shaking** or **earth'shattering** of great importance or consequence. — **earth'-shine** or **earth'-light** the faint light visible on the part of the moon not illuminated by the sun; **earth'-smoke** (*bot*) fumitory; **earth'-star** a fungus (*Geaster*) related to the puffballs that opens out into a starlike form; **earth'-table** (*building*) a course of stone or brick just above the ground; **earth-tone** a colour like that of the earth, eg a brown or green; **earth'-tremor** a slight earthquake; **earth'wax** ozokerite; **earth'wolf** the aardwolf; **earthwoman** see **earthman**; **earth'work** a fortification of earth; an embankment; the act or process of excavation and embanking; **earth'worm** the common worm; a mean person, a poor creature. — **cost the earth** (*colloq*) to be very expensive; **down** or **back to earth** back to reality (*adj* **down-to-earth** see under **down**[3]); **go to earth** to search for or take refuge in a hole or hiding-place (also *fig*); **green earth** see **green**[1]; **on earth** used for emphasis in phrases such as *how on earth, why on earth*, etc; absolutely, without exception, as in *best on earth*; **run to earth** to search out or find; to go to earth (*lit* and *fig*); **the Earthshaker** (*mythol*) Poseidon (qv), the god responsible for causing earthquakes. [OE *eorthe*; cf Du *aarde* and Ger *Erde*]

ease *ēz*, *n* freedom from pain or disturbance; rest from work; quiet, peace; freedom from difficulty; naturalness; unconstrained manner. — *vt* to free from pain, trouble or anxiety; to make comfortable; to relieve; to loosen or relax; to calm; to move gently; to manoeuvre little by little. — *vi* to become less acute or severe (often with *off* or *up*); to move very gradually; (of the price of shares, etc) to fall slightly. — *adj* **ease'ful** ease-giving; quiet, fit for rest. — *adj* **ease'less**. — *n* **ease'ment** relief, easing (*rare*); assistance (*obs*); support (*obs*); gratification (*obs*); the right to use something (*esp* land) not one's own or to prevent its owner from making an inconvenient use of it (*legal*). — *adv* **eas'ily**. — *n* **eas'iness**. — *adj* **eas'y** not difficult; at ease; free from pain; tranquil; unconstrained; giving ease; convenient; yielding; not straitened (in circumstances); not tight; not strict; in plentiful supply; (of the stock market) not showing unusually great activity (*finance*). — Also *adv* (*esp colloq*). — *interj* a command to lower, to go gently, to stop rowing, etc. — *adj* **ease'-giving**. — *adj* **eas'y-care** (*esp* of materials) easy to look after, clean, etc. — **eas'y-chair** a comfortable arm-chair. — *adj* **easy-go'ing** (*colloq*) placid; indolent. — **eas'y-goer**; **easy listening** a category of modern popular music comprising pleasant but undemanding songs and tunes. — Also *adj*. — **easy meat**, **game** or **mark** a person or thing that is easy to beat, fool, persuade, hit, destroy, etc; **easy money** money made without much exertion or difficulty. — *adj* **eas'y-ō'sy** (*colloq*) easy-going; without strong feelings, indifferent. — **easy street** (*colloq*) a situation of comfort or affluence; **easy terms** a phrase used in describing a hire-purchase agreement to imply or emphasize that the payments will not be a burden to the customer; **easy touch** see under **touch**. — **at ease** free from anxiety; in a comfortably relaxed frame of mind or physical attitude; (of soldiers) standing with feet apart, not at attention; **be easy** to be quite willing to fall in with any arrangement; **chapel of ease** see under **chapel**; **ease off** to slacken gradually; to make or become less intense; **ease oneself** (*archaic*; *euphem*) to urinate or defecate; **easy does it** take your time, do (it) slowly or carefully; **easy on the eye** (*colloq*) good to look at; **easy over** (*colloq*, *esp US*) (of an egg) fried on both sides; **go easy on** to be lenient with; to use sparingly; **honours easy** honours evenly divided (at cards, etc); **ill at ease** anxious; embarrassed or uneasy; uncomfortable; **stand at ease** (*military*) a command to soldiers, etc to stop standing at attention, to stand with feet apart; **stand easy** (*military*) a command to stand in a still more relaxed position; **take it easy** to avoid exertion; to be in no hurry; **take one's ease** to make oneself comfortable. [OFr *aise*; cognate with Ital *agio*, Provençal *ais* and Port *azo*; ult from L *adjacēns*, see **adjacent**]

easel *ēz'l*, *n* a frame for supporting a blackboard, a picture during painting, etc. [Du *ezel* or Ger *Esel* an ass]

easily, **easiness**. See **ease**.

easle or **aizle** *āz'l*, (*Burns*) *n* hot ashes. [OE *ysle*]

eassel or **eassil** *ēs'l*, (*Scot*) *adv* eastward; easterly. — *adv* **eass'elgate** or **eass'elward**. [**east**]

east *ēst*, *n* the part of the heavens where the sun rises at the equinox; one of the four cardinal points of the compass; the east part of a region; the east wind. — *adj* and *adv* towards the compass point of the east; (blowing) from the east. — *vi* (*archaic*) to move or turn east. — *adj* **east'bound** travelling in an eastward direction. — *adj* **east'er** (*obs*) or **east'ern** towards the east; connected with the east; living in the east. — *n* **east'erling** a native of the east; a trader from the shores of the Baltic (*hist*). — *adj* **east'erly** situated in the east; coming from the east; looking toward the east. — *adv* on the east; towards the east. — *n* an east wind. — *n* **east'erner** a native or inhabitant of the east, *esp* of the United States. — *adj* **east'ernmost** or **east'most** situated furthest east. — Also **east'ermost** (*obs*). — *n* **east'ing** the course taken to the eastward; the distance eastward from a given meridian. — *adj* **east'ling** or **east'lin** (*Scot*) easterly. — *adv* **east'lings** or **east'lins** (*Scot*) eastward. — *adv* **east'ward** or **east'wards** toward the east. — *adj* **east'ward**. — *adj* **east'bound** bound for the east; travelling east. — **east-by-north'** (or **east-by-south'**) $11\frac{1}{4}$ degrees north (or south) from due east; **East End** the eastern part of London or another town, often an area inhabited by poorer people; **East-end'er**; **Eastern Church** or **Eastern Orthodox Church** the churches which follow the ancient rite of the East and accept the first seven councils, rejecting papal supremacy (also **Orthodox Church**, **Greek Church**, **Greek Orthodox Church**, **Orthodox Eastern Church**); **Eastern Time** or **Eastern Standard Time** the time used on the east coast of N America, being 5 hours behind GMT (abbrev **ET** or **EST**); **East-Ind'iaman** (*hist*) a ship used in the East Indian trade; **East Indian** and **Indies** see under **Indian**. — *adj* **east'land** belonging to or coming from an eastern district or country. — **east'-north-east'** (or **east'-south-east'**) $22\frac{1}{2}$ degrees north (or south) from the east; **East Side** the eastern part of the city of New York. — **about east** (*old US slang*) correctly; **East Coast fever** also called **African coast fever**, a protozoan cattle disease resembling redwater, transmitted by ticks; **the East** the countries between the Balkans and China (see also **Near East**, **Middle East** and **Far East**); in mid-to-late 20c politics, the countries, chiefly of the eastern hemisphere, under communist rule; the eastern part of the United States, used relatively and vaguely, but *usu* the part to the east of the Allegheny Mountains, or to the east of the Mississippi River and to the north of Maryland. [OE *ēast*; Ger *Ost*; related to Gr *ēōs* the dawn]

Easter *ēst'ər*, *n* a Christian festival commemorating the resurrection of Christ, held on the Sunday after the first full moon following the spring equinox (21 March). — **Easter cactus** a S American cactus having coral-coloured flowers; **Easter Day** the day of the Easter festival, also **Easter Sunday**; **Easter dues** or **offerings** customary sums of money paid to the priest by his congregation at Easter; **Easter egg** a painted, decorated, stained or artificial egg, now *esp* made of chocolate, given as a present at Easter; **Easter lily** any of several white-flowered lilies; **East'ertide** or **East'-**

ertime the days around Easter; the fifty days from Easter to Whitsuntide (*eccles*). [OE *ēastre*; Ger *Ostern*; Bede derives the word from *Eostre* (variant of *Eastre*), a goddess whose festival was held at the spring equinox]

easy. See **ease**.

EAT *abbrev*: Tanzania (ie East Africa Tanzania; IVR).

eat *ēt*, *vt* to take into the body by the mouth as food; to bite, chew or swallow; to include or tolerate in one's diet; to consume (often with *up*); to corrode or destroy (often with *away*); to upset, irritate or worry (*colloq*). — *vi* to take food; to take a meal, eg at a stated time; to make inroads, make a hole or gnaw (with *into* or *through*); to be eatable, to taste: — *pr p* **eat'ing**; *pa t* **ate** (*et* or *āt*); *pa p* **eaten** (*ē'tən*) or *obs* **eat** (*et*). — *n* (*archaic* in *sing*, *colloq* in *pl*) food. — *adj* **eat'able** edible or fit to be eaten. — *n* anything used as food (chiefly in *pl*; *colloq*). — *n* **eat'age** grass or fodder for horses, etc; the right to eat. — *n* **eat'er** someone who or something which eats or corrodes; a variety of fruit, vegetable, etc suitable for eating uncooked. — *n* **eat'ery** (*slang*) a restaurant. — *n* and *adj* **eat'ing**. — **eat'ing-apple**, etc one suitable for eating uncooked; **eat'ing-house** a restaurant; **eat'ing irons** (*slang*) knife, fork and spoon. — **eat away** to destroy gradually; to gnaw; **eat crow**, **dirt** or **humble pie** see under **crow**, **dirt**, **humbles**; **eat in** of acid, to corrode, etch, etc (a metal); to eat at home; **eat into** of acid, to corrode, etc; to consume, use up or make inroads into; **eat off** to clear (a crop) by setting cattle to eat it; **eat one's hat** to be very surprised (if something turns out contrary to one's expectations); **eat one's head off** to cost more for food than one is worth; **eat one's heart out** to pine away, brooding over misfortune; **eat one's terms** (*legal*) to study for the bar, with allusion to the number of times in a term that a student must dine in the hall of an Inn of Court; **eat one's words** to take back what one has said; **eat out** to have a meal away from home, *usu* in a restaurant; to eat everything edible in (a place); to encroach upon; **eat the air** (*Shakesp*) to be deluded with hopes; **eat up** to devour entirely; to consume or absorb; (*esp* in *passive*) to obsess or preoccupy wholly; **what's eating you?** (*colloq*) what is worrying or irritating you? [OE *etan*; cf Ger *essen*, ON *eta*, L *edere* and Gr *edein*]

Eatanswill *ēt'ən-swil*, *n* a corrupt election or selection, from the name of the pocket borough in Charles Dickens' novel *Pickwick Papers* at which an election takes place.

eatche *ēch*, (*Scott*) *n* a Scots form of **adze**.

eath, **eathe** or **ethe** *ēth* or *eth*, (*Spenser*, etc) *adj* easy. — *adv* easily. — *adv* **eath'ly**. [OE *ēathe* easy or easily]

EAU *abbrev*: Uganda (ie East Africa Uganda; IVR).

eau[1] *ō*, *n* the French word for water, used in English in various combinations. — **eau des creoles** (*dā krā-ol'*) a fine Martinique liqueur, made by distilling the flowers of the mammee-apple with alcohol; **eau de Cologne** (*də kə-lōn*) a perfume, first make at Cologne in 1709; **eau de Javelle** see **Javel water**; **eau de Nil** (*də nēl*) a pale-green colour, Nile green; **eau de vie** (*də vē*) brandy.

eau[2]. See **ea**.

eaves *ēvz*, *n pl* (*orig sing*) the projecting edge of the roof; anything projecting. — **eaves'drip** or **eaves'drop** the water that falls from the eaves of a house; the place where the drops fall; (**eavesdrop**) an act of eavesdropping. — *vi* **eaves'drop** to stand under the eaves or near the windows of a house to listen; to try to overhear other people's private conversations. — Also *vt*: — *pr p* **eaves'dropping**; *pa p* and *pa p* **eaves'dropped**. — **eaves'dropper** someone who listens in this way; someone who tries to overhear private conversation; **eaves'dropping**. [OE *efes* the clipped edge of thatch; cf Icel *ups*]

EAZ *abbrev*: Tanzania (ie East Africa Zanzibar; IVR).

EB *abbrev*: epidermolysis bullosa (qv under **epidermis**); Epstein-Barr (virus).

ébauche *ā-bōsh*, (*Fr*) *n* rough draft or sketch.

ebb *eb*, *n* the going back or lowering of the tide; a decline. — *vi* to flow back; to sink; to decline. — *adj* (*obs* or *dialect*; *Scott*) shallow. — *adj* **ebb'less**. — **ebb'tide** the ebbing tide. — **at a low ebb** (*fig*) in a low or weak state. [OE *ebba*]

EBCDIC *eb'si-dik*, (*comput*) *abbrev*: extended binary coded decimal interchange code, the other main code used in addition to ASCII.

ebenezer *eb-ən-ēz'ər*, *n* a memorial stone set up by Samuel after the victory of Mizpeh (1 Samuel 7.12); a name sometimes applied to a chapel or religious meeting-house. [Heb *eben-hā-'ezer* stone of help]

ébéniste *ā-bā-nēst*, (*Fr*) *n* a cabinetmaker.

Ebionite *ē'bi-ən-īt*, *n* a member of a group of early Christians who believed they were bound by the Mosaic law and denied the apostolate of Paul and the miraculous birth of Jesus. — *adj* **ebionitic** (*-it'ik*). — *n* **e'bionītism** or **e'bionism**. — *vt* **e'bionize** or **-ise**. [Heb *ebyōn* poor]

Eblis *eb'lis* or **Iblis** *ib'lis*, *n* the chief of the fallen angels in Muslim mythology. [Ar *Iblīs*]

Ebola disease *ē-bō'lə diz-ēz'*, *n* a virus disease occurring in Africa, similar to, but with a much higher mortality rate than, green monkey disease (qv under **green**).

ebony *eb'ən-i*, (*rare*, *esp poetic*, **ebon** *eb'ən*), *n* a kind of wood produced by various species of the *Diospyros* tree (family **Ebenā'ceae**) almost as heavy and hard as stone, usually black and capable of being finely polished; a tree producing it; a black person (*US archaic* and *derog*), *now* black people in general, their concerns and sensibilities. — *adj* made of ebony; black as ebony. — *n* **eb'onist** a worker in ebony. — *n* **eb'onite** black vulcanized rubber, vulcanite. — *vt* and *vi* **eb'onize** or **-ise** to make or become like ebony. [L (*h*)*ebenus*, from Gr *ebenos*; cf Heb *hobnīm*, pl of *hobni* or *obni*, from *eben* a stone]

Ebor. *ē'bör* or *e'bör*, *abbrev*: *Eboracum* (*L*) York; *Eboracensis* (*L*), of York.

éboulement *ā-bōōl'mā*, *n* the falling in of the wall of a fortification; a landslide or landslip. [Fr]

ebracteate *ē-brak'ti-āt*, (*bot*) *adj* without bracts. — *adj* **ebract'eolate** without bracteoles. [L *ē-* without or from, and *bractea* a thin plate]

EBRD *abbrev*: European Bank for Reconstruction and Development.

ebriate *ē'bri-āt*, or **ebriated** *-id*, *adj* intoxicated. — *n* **ebriety** (*ē-brī'i-ti*) drunkenness. — *adj* **e'briōse** drunk. — *n* **ebrios'ity**. [L *ēbriāre*, *-ātum* to make drunk]

ébrillade *ā-brē-(l)yäd'*, *n* the sudden jerking of a horse's rein when he refuses to turn. [Fr]

EBU *abbrev*: European Broadcasting Union.

ebullient *i-bul'yənt*, *adj* boiling up or over; agitated; enthusiastic or exuberant. — *n* **ebull'ience** or **ebull'iency** cheerful enthusiasm; a boiling over. — *adv* **ebull'iently**. — *n* **ebull'ioscope** an apparatus for determining the boiling-points of liquids. — *adj* **ebullioscop'ic** or **ebullioscop'ical**. — *adv* **ebullioscop'ically**. — *n* **ebullios'copy**. — *n* **ebullition** (*eb-ə-lish'ən*) the act of boiling; agitation; an outbreak. [L *ēbulliēns*, *-entis*, pr p of *ēbullīre*, from *ē* out, and *bullīre* to boil]

eburnean *eb-ûr'ni-ən*, *adj* of or like ivory. — Also **ebur'neous**. — *n* **eburnā'tion** (*ēb-* or *eb-*; *med*) an abnormal change of bone by which it becomes very hard and dense. — *n* **eburnificā'tion** the art of making like ivory. [L *eburneus*, from *ebur* ivory]

EC *abbrev*: East Caribbean; East Central; Ecuador (IVR); Established Church; European Community.

ECA *abbrev*: Economic Commission for Africa.

ecad *ek'ad*, (*bot*) *n* a plant form which is assumed to have adapted to its environment. [Gr *oikos* home, and **ad**[1]]

ecardinate *ē-kärd'in-āt*, *adj* hingeless. — *n pl* **Ecard'inēs** (*zool*) a class of brachiopods without hinge or arm skeleton. [L *ē-* without, and *cardō*, *-inis* hinge]

écarté[1] *ā-kär'tā*, *n* a game in which cards may be discarded for others. [Fr, discarded, from *é-* (from L *ēx* out of or from), and *carte* a card]

écarté[2] *ā-kär'tā*, *n* in ballet, a position in which the arm and leg are extended to the side. [Fr, spread or separated]

ecaudate *ē-kö'dāt*, *adj* tailless. [L *ē-* without, and *cauda* tail]

ecblastesis *ek-blas-tē'sis*, (*bot*) *n* proliferation of a floral axis. [Gr *ekblastēsis* budding forth, from *ek* out of, and *blastos* a sprout]

ecbole *ek'bo-lē*, *n* a digression (*rhetoric*); the raising or sharpening of a tone (*music*). — *adj* **ecbol'ic** (*med*) inducing contractions of the uterus leading to childbirth or abortion. — *n* a drug having this effect. [Gr *ekbolē* throwing out, from *ek* out of, and *ballein* to throw]

eccaleobion *e-kal-i-ō-bī'on*, (*hist*) *n* a kind of incubator. [Gr *ekkaleō bīon* I call forth life]

ecce *ek'si*, *ek'ā*, *ek'e* or *ech'ā*, (*L*) *interj* behold. — **ecce homo** (*hō'mō* or *hom'ō*; L, man) behold the man (John 9.5); a portrayal of Christ crowned with thorns (*art*); **ecce signum** (*sig'nəm* or *-nŏŏm*) behold the sign or proof.

eccentric *ek-sen'trik*, *adj* (of behaviour, etc) odd or unconventional; unusual, departing from the norm; not positioned centrally; with the axis to one side, not at the centre; (of superimposed circles) not concentric, not having the same centre. — *n* a circle not having the same centre as another; a device for taking an alternating rectilinear motion from a revolving shaft (*mech*); an eccentric person. — *adj* (*archaic*) **eccen'trical**. — *adv* **eccen'trically**. — *n* **eccentricity** (*-sən-tris'*) the condition of being eccentric; in a conic section, the constant ratio of the distance of a point on the curve from the focus to its distance from the directrix (*usu* represented by *e*; *geom*); peculiarity of behaviour; oddness. [Gr *ek* out of, and *kentron* centre]

ecchymosis *ek-i-mō'sis*, (*med*) *n* discoloration caused by bleeding under the skin. — *adj* **ecch'ymosed**. — *adj* **ecchymot'ic**. [Gr *ekchȳmōsis*, from *ek* out of, and *chȳmos* juice]

Eccl. or **Eccles.** *abbrev*: in the Bible, the book of Ecclesiastes. — **eccl.** or **eccles.** ecclesiastical.

Eccles cake *ek'lz kāk*, *n* a small cake or bun filled with raisins, currants, etc. [*Eccles* in Lancashire]

ecclesia *i-klē'zi-ə*, *n* a popular assembly, *esp* of Athens, where the people exercised full sovereignty and every male citizen above twenty years could vote; applied by the Septuagint commentators to the Jewish commonwealth, and from them to the Christian Church. — *adj* **ecclē'sial**. — *n* **ecclē'siarch** (*-ärk*) a ruler of the church. — *n* **ecclē'siast** 'the preacher', the name given to the author of Ecclesiastes; an ecclesiastic. — *n* **Ecclesias'tes** one of the books of the Old Testament, traditionally supposed to have been written by Solomon. — *n* **ecclesias'tic** a person consecrated to the church, such as a priest or a clergyman. — *adj* **ecclesias'tic** or **ecclesias'tical** relating to the church or to the clergy. — *adv* **ecclesias'tically**. — *n* **ecclesias'ticism** (*-sizm*) excessive regard for ecclesiastical rules and observances; the churchman's temperament or spirit. — *n* **Ecclesias'ticus** one of the books of the Apocrypha. — *n* **ecclesiol'atry** (Gr *latreiā* worship) excessive reverence for church forms and traditions. — *n* **ecclesiol'ater**. — *adj* **ecclesiolog'ical**. — *n* **ecclesiol'ogist**. — *n* **ecclesiol'ogy** the study of church forms and traditions and of church architecture and decoration; the study or knowledge of the church. — **ecclesiastical year** see under **year**. [LL, from Gr *ekklēsia* an assembly called out of the world, the church, from *ek* out of, and *kaleein* to call]

Ecclus. *abbrev*: in the Bible, the apocryphal book of Ecclesiasticus.

ecco *ek'kō*, (*Ital*) *imperative* here is; there; look there.

eccoprotic *ek-ō-prot'ik*, *adj* laxative, mildly cathartic. — *n* a laxative. [Gr *ekkoprōtikos*, from *ek* out of, and *kopros* dung]

eccrinology *ek-ri-nol'ə-ji*, *n* the branch of physiology relating to the secretions of the eccrine glands. — *adj* **eccrine** (*ek'rīn*) of a gland, *esp* the sweat glands, secreting externally. [Gr *ek* out of, and *krīnein* to separate, secrete]

eccrisis *ek'ri-sis*, *n* expulsion of waste or abnormal matter. — *n* **eccrit'ic** a medicine having this effect. [Gr *ekkrisis* secretion, from *ek* out, and *krisis* separation]

ecdysis *ek'di-sis*, *n* the act of casting off skin or outer covering, sloughing. — *n* **ecdysiast** (*-diz'*; *facetious*) a striptease performer. [Gr *ekdysis*, from *ek* out of, and *dyein* to put on]

ECE *abbrev*: Economic Commission for Europe.

ECG *abbrev*: electrocardiogram or electrocardiograph.

ECGD *abbrev*: Export Credit Guarantee Department.

ech. See **eche**.

échappé *ā-sha'pā*, (*ballet*) *n* a double leap from two feet, starting in fifth position, landing in second or fourth, and finishing in fifth. [Fr, pa p of *échapper*, to escape]

eche *ēch*, (*Shakesp*) *vt* to eke out; to augment. — Also **ech**, **eech**, **ich**. [OE *ēcan*; related to L *augēre* to increase; see **eke**]

echelon *esh'ə-lon* or *āsh-lɔ̃*, *n* an arrangement of troops, ships, planes, etc as if in steps; a particular level in the hierarchy of an organization; the group of people at any one of these levels. [Fr *échelon*, from *échelle* ladder, stair; see **scale**[2]]

echeveria *ek-* or *ech-ə-vē'ri-ə*, *n* a plant of the genus *Echeveria* of succulent plants of the Crassulaceae family. [Named after the 19c Mexican botanical artist *Echeveri*]

echidna *ek-id'nə*, (*zool*) *n* a member of the genus *Echidna* (family *Tachyglossidae*) of Australian toothless, spiny, egg-laying, burrowing monotremes, also called **spiny ant-eater**. — *n* **echid'nine** snake-poison. [Gr *echidna* viper]

echinus *e-kī'nəs*, *n* a sea-urchin; the convex projecting moulding (an eccentric curve in Greek examples) supporting the abacus of the Doric capital (*archit*). — *adj* **echinate** (*ek'in-āt*) or **echinated** (*-id*) prickly like a hedgehog; bristly. — *n* **Echīnocac'tus** a large genus of ribbed, generally very spiny, cactuses. — *n* **echīnococc'us** the bladder-worm stage (parasitic in cow, sheep, pig and man) of the dog tapeworm. — *n* **echī'noderm** (*zool*) any one of the **Echīnoder'ma** or **Echīnoder'mata**, a phylum of radially symmetrical marine animals, with a body-wall strengthened by calcareous plates, and usually moving by tube-feet, distensible finger-like protrusions of a part of the coelom known as the water-vascular system, including starfishes, sea-urchins, brittle-stars, sea-cucumbers and sea-lilies. — *adj* **echinoder'mal**. — *adj* **echinoder'matous**. — *adj* **echī'noid** like a sea-urchin. — *n* a sea-urchin. — *n pl* **Echīnoid'ea** the sea-urchins, a class of Echinoderma. — *n* **Echīn'ops** (*bot*) a genus of Compositae found in southern Europe, the globe thistle, with flowers in globular clusters. [Gr *echīnos* a hedgehog]

echo *ek'ō*, *n* the sending back or reflection of sound or other waves; the repetition of sound by reflection; a reflected sound; a soft-toned organ-stop forming a part of some large organs; a device in verse in which a line ends with a word which recalls the sound of the last word of the preceding line; response; (in *pl*) reverberations or repercussions; repetition; imitation; an imitator; something that reminds one of something else; a memory evoked; the signal emitted by an object being scanned by radar; the visual signal from such an object, appearing on screen; in card games, conventional play to indicate what cards one holds; in musical recording, an electronic reverberating effect: — *pl* **echoes** (*ek'ōz*). — *vi* to reflect sound; to be sounded back; to resound; to play a card as echo. — *vt* to send back (sound or other waves); to send back the sound of; to repeat; to imitate; to follow slavishly: — *pr p* **ech'ōing**; *pa t* and *pa p* **ech'oed** (*-ōd*). — *n* **ech'ōer**. — *adj* **echō'ic** of the nature of an echo; onomatopoeic (*philol*). — *n* **ech'ōism** the formation of imitative words. — *n* **ech'ōist** a person who repeats like an echo. — *vi* **ech'ōize** or **-ise**. — *adj* **ech'oless** giving no echo;

unresponsive. — *n* **echocar'diogram** the record produced by **echocardiog'raphy**, the investigation by means of ultrasound of certain internal parts of the heart and the ways in which they move in order to detect disease *esp* of the heart valves. — *n* **echoenceph'alogram** the record produced by **echoencephalog'raphy**, the investigation of brain tissues by means of ultrasound waves beamed through the head. — *n* **ech'ogram** the record produced in echo-sounding. — *n* **echolalia** (*ek-ō-lā'li-ə*; Gr *laliā* talk) senseless or compulsive repetition of words heard; occurring in forms of mental illness. — *n* **echoprax'ia** or **echoprax'is** (Gr *praxis* doing) in mental illness, the imitation of postures or movements of those around. — **echo chamber** a room in which sound can be echoed for recording or radio effects or when measuring acoustics; **echo location** determining the position of objects by means of supersonic vibrations echoed from them, as a bat does; **ech'o-sounder** the apparatus used in echo-sounding; **ech'o-sounding** a method of measuring the depth of water, locating shoals of fish, etc, by noting the time taken for an echo to return from the bottom, the shoal, etc; **echo virus** any of a group of viruses which can cause respiratory and intestinal diseases and meningitis (*e*nteric *c*ytopathogenic *h*uman *o*rphan virus). — **cheer to the echo** to applaud heartily. [L, from Gr *ēchō* a sound]

echt *ehht*, (*Ger*) *adj* genuine, authentic.

ECLAC *abbrev*: Economic Commission for Latin America and the Caribbean.

éclair *ā-kler'* or *-klār'*, or *i-*, *n* a cake, long in shape but short in duration, with cream filling and *usu* chocolate icing. [Fr *éclair* lightning]

éclaircissement *ā-kler-sēs'mã*, *n* the act of clearing up a misunderstanding; explanation. — **come to an éclaircissement** to come to an understanding; to explain conduct that seemed equivocal. [Fr *éclaircir*, from L *ex* out, and *clārus* clear]

eclampsia *i-klamp'si-ə*, (*pathol*) *n* a condition resembling epilepsy; now only applied to acute toxaemia with convulsive fits in the last three months of pregnancy. — Also **eclamp'sy**. — *adj* **eclamp'tic**. [Gr *eklampsis*, from *eklampein* to flash forth, to burst forth violently (eg of a fever), from *ek* out of, and *lampein* to shine]

éclat *ā-klä*, *n* a striking effect; showy splendour; distinction; applause. [Fr *éclat*, from OFr *esclater* to break, to shine]

eclectic *ek-lek'tik* or *i-*, *adj* selecting or borrowing from a variety of styles, systems, theories, etc; characterized by such selection or borrowing; choosing the best out of everything; broad, as opposed to exclusive. — *n* someone who selects opinions from different systems *esp* in philosophy. — *adv* **eclec'tically**. — *n* **eclec'ticism** (*-sizm*) the practice of an eclectic; the doctrine of the **eclec'tics**, a name applied to certain Greek thinkers in the 2c and 1c BC, and later to Leibniz and Cousin. [Gr *eklektikos*, from *ek* from, and *legein* to choose]

eclipse *i-klips'*, *n* the total or partial disappearance of a heavenly body by the interposition of another between it and the spectator, or by passing into its shadow (it can be *total*, *partial* or *annular* (qv)); an overshadowing; loss of brilliancy; darkness. — *vt* to hide completely or partially; to darken; to overshadow, cut out or surpass. — *n* **eclip'tic** (*astron*) the great circle in which the plane containing the centres of the earth and sun cuts the celestial sphere; the apparent path of the sun's annual motion among the fixed stars; a great circle in which that plane cuts the earth's surface at any moment. — *adj* characteristic of or belonging to an eclipse or the ecliptic. — **eclipse plumage** dull plumage apparent in certain usually brilliant-coloured birds out of the mating season. [OFr, from L *eclīpsis*, from Gr *ekleipsis* failure, from *ek* out of, and *leipein* to leave]

eclogite or **eklogite** *ek'lə-jīt*, *n* a crystalline rock composed of red garnet and green omphacite or smaragdite. [Gr *eklogē* selection (from the unusual minerals that compose it), from *ek* out of, and *legein* to choose]

eclogue *ek'log*, *n* a short pastoral poem like Virgil's *Bucolics*. [L *ecloga*, from Gr *eklogē* a selection, esp of poems, from *ek* out of, and *legein* to choose]

eclosion *i-klō'zhən*, *n* emergence, *esp* of an insect from a pupal case or a larva from an egg. — *vi* **eclose'**. [Fr *éclosion*, from L *ex-*, and *claudere* to shut]

ECO *abbrev*: English Chamber Orchestra.

eco- *ēk'*, *ek'ō-* or *ek'ə-*, *combining form* denoting concerned with habitat and environment in relation to living organisms. — The form is currently very productive, and is found also as an *adj* form **ē'co** ; only a selection of the commoner derivatives is given. — *n* **ec'ocīde** the destruction of the aspects of the environment which enable it to support life. — *n* **ec'ofreak** or **ec'onut** (*derog slang*) a person concerned with the state and protection of the environment, an environmentalist. — *adj* **ecofriend'ly** ecologically acceptable, in harmony with, or not threatening to, the environment. — *n* **e'co-label** a label used by manufacturers of products claiming to be environmentally acceptable, specifying to the consumer the exact nature of their ecological soundness; a label certifying that certain standards of ecological soundness have been reached. — *n* **e'co-labelling**. — *n* **ecophō'bia** fear of one's home surroundings. — *n* **ec'ospecies** a group of ecotypes. — *n* **ec'osphere** the parts of the universe or *esp* the earth in which life is possible. — *n* **ec'osystem** a unit consisting of a community of organisms and their environment. — *n* **eco-tour'ism** small-scale, carefully managed development of the natural environment for the holiday market. — *adj* **ecotox'ic** poisonous to plants or animals, deleterious to the environment. — *n* **ecotoxicol'ogist**. — *n* **ecotoxicol'ogy** the study of the destructive effect of waste materials, etc on the environment. — *n* **ec'otype** a group of organisms which have adapted to a particular environment and so have become different from other groups within the species.

ecod *i-kod'*, (*archaic*) *interj*. Same as **egad**.

E. coli *abbrev*: Escherichia coli.

ecology *ē-kol'ə-ji*, *ek-ol'*, or *ik-*, *n* the scientific study of plants, animals, or peoples and institutions, in relation to environment. — *adj* **ecologic** (*-ko-loj'ik*) or **ecolog'ical** relating to or concerned with ecology; using, concerned with or relating to methods, processes, etc beneficial to the natural environment. — *adv* **ecolog'ically**. — *n* **ecol'ogist**. — Also **oecology**, etc. — **ecological efficiency** the ratios between the amount of energy flow at different points along a food chain; **ecological niche** the position or status of an organism within its community or ecosystem; **ecological succession** see **succession** under **succeed**. [Gr *oikos* house, and *logos* discourse]

economy *ē-kon'ə-mi*, *i-kon'*, or *e-*, *n* the administration of the material resources of an individual, community or country; the state of these resources; a frugal and judicious expenditure of money; thrift; the management of a household (*archaic*); a dispensation, as *the Christian economy*; the efficient use of something, eg speech, effort, etc; making one's presentation of doctrine, etc suit the needs or not offend the prejudices of one's hearers (*theol*); an organized system; regular operations, eg of nature. — *adj* of or pertaining to a cheaper class of air or sea travel; (of goods) of a larger size so costing less than several small sizes (of packets, etc). — *adj* **economet'ric** or **economet'rical**. — *n* **econometrician** (*-mə-trish'ən*). — *n sing* **economet'rics** statistical analysis of economic data and their interrelations. — *n* **economet'rist**. — *adj* **economic** (*ē-kə-nom'ik* or *ek-ə-*) relating or referring to economy or to economics; relating to industry or business, eg *economic geography*, *history*, etc, from the utilitarian viewpoint; operated at or capable of yielding a profit; economical. — *adj* **econom'ical** conducive to thrift; frugal; careful; economic. — *adv* **econom'ically**. — *n sing* or *n pl* **econom'ics** financial position and management; financial or economic aspects; the science of household management (*obs*; but see **home economics**

under **home**). — *n sing* political economy. — *n* **econ'omism** a belief, sometimes too great, that economic causes and theories are of primary importance. — *n* **econ'omist** a person who studies or is an expert on political economy; an economizer. — *n* **economizā'tion** or **-s-** the act of economizing. — *vi* **econ'omize** or **-ise** to manage with economy; to spend money carefully; to save. — *vt* to use prudently; to spend frugally. — *n* **econ'omīzer** or **-s-** a person who is economical; a device for saving heat, fuel, etc. — **economic determinism** the belief that all cultural, political, social, etc activity stems from economic considerations; **economic refugee** someone who flees from his or her country because of poverty rather than religious or political considerations; **economic zone** the coastal sea-area which a country claims as its own territory (for fishing, mining, etc). [L *oeconomia*, from Gr *oikonomiā*, from *oikos* a house, and *nomos* a law]

e contra *ē* (or *ā*) *kon'tra*, (*LL*) contrariwise, conversely.

e contrario *ē kon-trār'i-ō* or *ā kon-trä'ri-ō*, (*LL*) on the contrary.

e converso *ē kon-vûr'sō* or *ā kon-ver'*, (or *-wer'*), (*LL*) conversely, by logical conversion.

écorché *ā-kör-shā'*, *n* a figure in which the muscles are represented stripped of the skin, for the purposes of artistic study. [Pa p of Fr *écorcher* to flay]

ECOSOC *abbrev*: United Nations Economic and Social Council.

écossaise *ā-ko-sez'*, *n orig* a dance or dance-tune of Scottish origin in 3-4 or 2-4 time; later, a lively country-dance or its music in 2-4 time. — **douche écossaise** the alternation of hot and cold douches. [Fr, fem of *écossais* Scottish]

ecostate *ē-kos'tāt*, *adj* ribless. [L *ē* from, and *costa* rib]

ECOWAS *abbrev*: Economic Community of West African States.

ecphonesis *ek-fō-nē'sis*, *n* exclamation (*rhetoric*); in the Greek Church, the part of the service spoken in an audible tone: — *pl* **ecphonē'ses**. [Gr *ekphōnēsis*, from *ek* out, and *phōnē* voice]

ecphractic *ek-frak'tik*, (*obs med*) *adj* serving to remove obstructions. — *n* a drug with such properties. [Gr *ekphraktikos*, from *ek* from, and *phrassein* to enclose]

écraseur *ā-kra-zœr'*, *n* a surgical instrument in the form of a wire or chain loop which cuts as it tightens. [Fr *écraser* to crush]

écritoire *ā-krē-twär*, (*Fr*) *n* the modern form of **escritoire**.

ecru *e-* or *ā-kroo'*, or *-krü'*, *n* unbleached linen; its off-white or light greyish-brown colour. — Also *adj*. [Fr *écru*, from L *ex* (intens), and *crūdus* raw]

ECS *abbrev*: European Communications Satellite.

ECSC *abbrev*: European Coal and Steel Community.

ecstasy *ek'stə-si*, *n* a state of exalted pleasure or happiness, rapture; a state of temporary mental alienation and altered or diminished consciousness; excessive joy; enthusiasm or any exalted feeling; (often with *cap*) a drug taken for its stimulant and hallucinogenic properties, *methylene-dioxymethamphetamine* (*slang*; often *abbrev* **E**). — *vt* to fill with joy. — *adj* **ec'stasied** enraptured. — *n* **ec'stasis** ecstasy. — *vt* and *vi* **ec'stasize** or **-ise**. — *adj* **ecstat'ic** causing ecstasy; amounting to ecstasy; rapturous. — *n* a person (often) in a state of ecstasy; a user of the drug Ecstasy; something spoken in a state of ecstasy. — *adv* **ecstat'ically**. [Gr *ekstasis*, from *ek* from, and the root of *histanai* to make stand]

ECT *abbrev*: electroconvulsive therapy.

ectasis *ek'tə-sis*, *n* the lengthening of a short syllable; abnormal stretching (*med*): — *pl* **ectases** (*-tā'sēz*). [Gr *ektasis* stretching]

ecthlipsis *ek-thlip'sis*, *n* the suppression of a sound, *esp* of a syllable ending in *m* in verse before a vowel: — *pl* **ecthlipses** (*-sēz*). [Gr *ekthlīpsis*, from *ek* from, and *thlībein* to rub or squeeze]

ecthyma *ek-thī'mə*, *n* an eruption of the skin forming large pustules. [Gr *ekthȳma* a pustule]

ecto- *ek-tō-* or *ek-tə-*, *combining form* denoting outside (often opposed to **endo-**, **ento-**; see also **exo-**). — *n* **ec'toblast** (Gr *blastos* a shoot or bud; *biol*) the outer cell-layer of a gastrula, the epiblast. — *adj* **ectoblas'tic**. — *n* **ec'tocrine** an organic substance released in minute amounts by an organism into the environment, which exerts an effect on its own and other species' form, development or behaviour. — *n* **ec'toderm** (Gr *derma* skin; *biol*) the external germinal layer of epiblast of the embryo, or any part of the mature animal derived from it. — Also **ex'oderm**. — *adj* **ectoderm'al** or **ectoderm'ic**. — *n* **ectoen'zyme** an exoenzyme. — *n* **ec'tomorph** (Gr *morphē* form) a person of light and delicate build, thought to accompany a type of personality characterized by alertness, inhibition and intellectual activity; cf **endomorph** and **mesomorph**. — *adj* **ectomorph'ic**. — *n* **ec'tomorphy**. — *n* **ectopar'asite** an external parasite. — *n* **ec'toplasm** (Gr *plasma* something moulded) the outer layer of cytoplasm of a cell (*biol*); a substance believed by some spiritualists to emanate from the body of a medium. — *adj* **ectoplas'mic**. — *adj* **ectoplas'tic**. — *n* **ec'tosarc** (Gr *sarx*, *sarkos* flesh; *zool*) ectoplasm. — *n* **ec'totherm** a cold-blooded animal. — *adj* **ectotherm'ic**. — *adj* **ectotroph'ic** (Gr *trophē* food; *bot*) of a mycorrhiza, having its hyphae mainly on the outside of the root that it feeds. — *n* and *adj* **ectozō'an**. — *adj* **ectozō'ic**. — *n* **ectozō'on** (Gr *zōion* animal) an animal ectoparasite: — *pl* **ectozō'a**. [Gr *ektos* outside]

ectogenesis *ek-tō-jen'i-sis*, (*biol*) *n* development outside the body; variation in response to outside conditions. — *adj* **ectogenetic** (*-jən-et'ik*) produced by or characteristic of ectogenesis. — *adj* **ectogen'ic** of external origin; ectogenous. — *adj* **ectogenous** (*ek-toj'ə-nəs*) capable of living independently, or outside the body of the host (as some parasites). — *n* **ectog'eny** the effect of pollen on the tissues of a plant. [Gr *ektos* outside, and *genesis* generation]

ectomorph, etc, **ectoparasite**. See **ecto-**.

ectophyte *ek'tō-fīt*, (*bot*) *n* a vegetable ectoparasite. — *adj* **ectophytic** (*-fit'ik*). [Gr *ektos* outside, and *phyton* a plant]

ectopia *ek-tō'pi-ə* or **ectopy** *ek'to-pi*, (*pathol*) *n* abnormal displacement of parts; a condition in which the foetus is outside the womb. — *adj* **ectop'ic** in an abnormal position. — **ectopic pregnancy** the development of a foetus outside the uterus, *esp* in a Fallopian tube. [Gr *ek* from, and *topos* place]

ectoplasm ... to ... **ectozoon**. See **ecto-**.

ectropion *ek-trōp'i-on* or **ectropium** *-əm*, *n* the turning out of the margin of the eyelid, so that the red inner surface is exposed. — *adj* **ectrop'ic**. [Gr *ek* out of, and *trepein* to turn]

ectype *ek'tīp*, *n* a reproduction or copy. — *adj* **ectypal** (*ek'ti-pəl*). — *n* **ectypog'raphy**. [Gr *ek* from, and *typos* a stamp]

ECU, **Ecu** or **ecu** *ā'kū* or *ek'ū*, *n* short for **European currency unit**, a unit of currency whose rate is based on a range of European currencies within the EMS, used eg as a reserve currency and seen as the notional single European currency. — **hard ECU**, **Ecu** or **ecu** an ECU based on the narrow band of the exchange rate mechanism, designed not to devalue against any other European currency and to bring about stability and low inflation.

écu *ā-kü* or *ā-kū'*, *n* a French silver coin, *usu* considered as equivalent to the English crown; a French gold coin weighing about 60 grains, etc (both *hist*); more recently, a common name for the five-franc piece. [Fr, from L *scutum* a shield]

écuelle *ā-kwel'* or *ā-kü-el'*, *n* a two-handled soup bowl. [Fr, from L *scutella* drinking-bowl]

ecumenic *ē-kū-* or *ek-ū-men'ik*, or **ecumenical** *-əl*, *adj* general, universal or belonging to the entire Christian Church; of or relating to the ecumenical movement. — *adv* **ecumen'ically**. — *n* **ecumen'icalism**, **ecumen'icism** (*-is-izm*) or **ecumen'ism** (or *i-kū'mə-nizm*) doctrines and practice of the Christian ecumenical movement (also *fig*). — *n sing* **ecumen'ics** the study of ecumenical awareness and the ecumenical movement in the

Christian church. — Also **oecumenic**, etc. — **ecumenical movement** a movement within the Christian church towards unity on all fundamental issues of belief, worship, etc. [L *oecumenicus*, from Gr *oikoumenikos*, from *oikoumenē* (*gē*) inhabited (world)]

écurie *ā-kü-rē'*, *n* a team of cars under individual or joint ownership which take part in motor racing. [Fr, a stable]

ECUSA or **Ecusa** *i-ko͞o'sə*, *abbrev*: Episcopal Church of the United States of America.

ECWA *abbrev*: Economic Commission for Western Africa.

eczema *ek'si-mə* or *ig-zē'mə*, *n* a skin disease in which part of the skin is red, with numerous small papules that turn into vesicles. — *adj* **eczematous** (*-sem'*, *-zem'ət-əs* or *-zēm'*). [Gr *ekzeein*, from *ek* out of, and *zeein* to boil]

Ed. *abbrev*: editor.

ed. or **edit**. *abbrev*: edited; edition.

edacious *i-*, *ē-* or *e-dā'shəs*, (*literary* or *facetious*) *adj* given to eating; gluttonous. — *adv* **edā'ciously**. — *n* **edā'ciousness**. — *n* **edacity** (*i-das'i-ti*). [L *edāx*, *edācis*, from *edere* to eat]

Edam *ē'dam*, *n* a type of mild Dutch cheese shaped into globes with a red outer skin. [After *Edam* near Amsterdam]

edaphic *i-daf'ik*, (*bot* or *ecol*) *adj* pertaining to the soil. — *n* **edaphology** (*ed-ə-fol'ə-ji*). — **edaphic factor** any property of the soil, physical or chemical, that influences plants growing on that soil. [Gr *edaphos* ground]

EdB *abbrev*: Bachelor of Education.

EDC *abbrev*: ethylene dichloride; European Defence Community.

Edda *ed'ə*, *n* the name of two Scandinavian books, the *Elder Edda*, a collection of ancient mythological and heroic songs (9c–11c or earlier), and the *Younger* or *Prose Edda*, by Snorri Sturluson (c. 1230), mythological stories, poetics and prosody. — *adj* **Eddā'ic** or **Edd'ic**. [ON, appar related to *ōdr* mad, and *ōthr* spirit, mind or poetry; cf **wood**[2], Ger *Wut* fury, and L *vātēs* poet or seer]

eddish *ed'ish*, (*dialect*) *n* pasturage, or the eatable growth of grass after mowing. [Dubiously referred to OE *edisc* a park]

eddoes *ed'ōz*, *n pl* the tubers of various plants *esp* taro (*Colocasia*): — *sing* **edd'o**. [From a W African word]

eddy *ed'i*, *n* a current running back against the main stream, so causing a circular motion in the water; a similarly whirling motion of smoke, mist or wind; a whirlpool; a whirlwind. — *vi* to move round and round: — *pr p* **edd'ying**; *pa t* and *pa p* **edd'ied**. — **eddy current** an electric current caused by varying electromotive forces which are due to varying magnetic fields, and causing heating in motors, transformers, etc. — Also **Foucault current**; **eddy vortex** a column of air spinning inward and upward, sometimes forming in conditions of atmospheric temperature contrast. [Cf ON *itha*; prob connected with OE pfx *ed-* back]

edelweiss *ā'dəl-vīs*, *n* a small white composite plant (*Leontopodium alpinum*) with woolly heads, found in damp places on the Alps. [Ger *edel* noble, and *weiss* white]

edema, **edematose**, **edematous**. See **oedema**.

Eden *ē'dən*, *n* the garden in which Adam and Eve lived before the Fall (*Bible*); a paradise. — *adj* **Edenic** (*-den'*). [Heb *ēden* delight or pleasure]

Edenburgen. *abbrev*: *Edenburgensis* (*L*), of Edinburgh.

edentate *ē-den'tāt*, *adj* without teeth; lacking front teeth. — *n* a member of the **Edentā'ta**, a New World order of mammals having no front teeth or no teeth at all, such as sloths, ant-eaters, armadillos, and formerly certain Old World edentate animals such as the pangolins. — *adj* **eden'tal** of the edentates. — *adj* **eden'tulous** toothless. [L *ēdentātus* toothless, from *ē* out of, and *dēns*, *dentis* a tooth]

EDF *abbrev*: European Development Fund.

edge *ej*, *n* the border of anything; a rim; the brink; the intersection of the faces of a solid figure; a ridge or crest; the cutting edge of an instrument; something that wounds or cuts; keenness; incisiveness or trenchancy; sharpness of mind or appetite; irritability; advantage (*colloq*). — *vt* to put an edge or border on or round; to border, form or be a border for; to egg or urge on (*archaic*); to move or push gradually, *esp* sideways or edgeways; to trim the edge of; to strike with the edge of the bat (*cricket*). — *vi* to move sideways; to move gradually. — *combining form* **-edged** denoting having an edge or edges of the stated kind or number, as in *sharp-edged*, *two-edged*. — *adj* **edged**. — *adj* **edge'less** without an edge; blunt. — *n* **edg'er** someone or something that edges; a garden tool for trimming the edge of a lawn. — *adv* **edge'ways** or **edge'wise** with edge foremost or uppermost; in the direction of the edge; sideways. — *n* **edg'iness** angularity or over-sharpness of outline; the state of being on edge. — *n* **edg'ing** any border eg round a garment, flower-bed, etc; (a strip of) material, eg lace, for using as a trimming around the edge. — *adj* **edg'y** with edges; sharp or hard in outline; irritable, on edge. — **edge coal** a steeply dipping coal-seam; **edge effect** (*image technol*) see **border effect**; **edge rail** a rail of a form in which the carriage-wheels roll on its edges, being held there by flanges; **edge tool** or **edged tool** a tool with a sharp edge. — **edge in a word** or **get a word in edgeways** to get a word in with difficulty; **edge out** to remove or get rid of gradually; to defeat by a small margin (*US*); **go** or **be over the edge** (*colloq*) to go or have gone beyond what can be endured; to have or have had a nervous breakdown; **have the** or **an edge on** or **against** to have the advantage, or an advantage, over; **inside** or **outside edge** a skating movement on the inner or outer edge of the skate; **on edge** in a state of expectant irritability; nervous or tense with anticipation; all agog; **play with edge tools** to deal carelessly with dangerous matters; **set on edge** to excite; **set someone's teeth on edge** to set up a disagreeable sensation in the teeth and mouth, as sour fruit does; to cause to wince, irritate acutely; formerly, to make eager or stimulate desire. [OE *ecg*; cf Ger *Ecke*, and L *aciēs*]

edgebone. Same as **aitchbone**.

edh. See **eth**.

edible *ed'i-bl*, *adj* able to be eaten. — *n* something for food. — *n* **edibil'ity** or **ed'ibleness** fitness for being eaten. [L *edibilis*, from *edere* to eat]

edict *ē'dikt*, *n* something proclaimed by authority; an order issued by a king or lawgiver. — *adj* **edict'al**. — *adv* **edict'ally**. [L *ēdictum*, from *ē* out of, and *dīcere*, *dictum* to say]

edifice *ed'i-fis*, *n* a building; a large building or house. — *adj* **edificial** (*-fish'l*) structural. [Fr *édifice*, from L *aedificium*, from *aedificāre*; see **edify**]

edify *ed'i-fī*, *vt* to improve the mind of; to strengthen spiritually towards faith and holiness; to build up the faith of; to build (*archaic*); to establish (*obs*); to furnish with buildings (*Spenser*): — *pr p* **ed'ifying**; *pa t* and *pa p* **ed'ified**. — *n* **edificā'tion** instruction; progress in knowledge or in goodness. — *adj* **edif'icatory** (or *ed'*) giving edification. — *n* **ed'ifier** a person who edifies. — *adj* **ed'ifying** instructive; improving. — *adv* **ed'ifyingly**. [L *aedificāre*, from *aedēs* a temple or house, and *facere* to make]

edile. Same as **aedile**.

Edin. *abbrev*: Edinburgh.

Edinburgh rock *ed'in-bə-rə rok'*, *n* a sweet in the form of brittle pastel-coloured sticks. [First manufactured by an Edinburgh confectioner in 1822]

edit *ed'it*, *vt* to prepare (a writer's work or works) for publication; to correct and improve (a piece of text, etc) ready for publication; to reword; to supervise the publication of; to be the editor of (a newspaper or periodical); to compile (a reference work); to garble or cook up; to revise; to censor or bowdlerize; to make up the final version of a film, video, etc by selection, rearrangement, etc of material filmed previously; to prepare for broadcasting. — *n* an act or instance of editing. — *n* **edi'tion** one of the different forms in which a book is published; the form given to a text by its editor; the number of copies of a book printed at a time, or at different times without alteration; the publication of a book (*obs*); a number of identical articles, eg copies of a work of art, issued at one time; reproduction. — *n* **ed'itor** a person who edits books, etc; a person in charge of a newspaper, periodical, etc or a section of it: — *fem* (*archaic*) **ed'itress**. — *adj* **edito'rial** of or belonging to an editor. — *n* an article in a newspaper written by an editor or leader writer. — *n* **editorializā'tion** or **-s-**. — *vi* **edito'rialize** or **-ise** to introduce personal opinions or bias into reporting; to expound one's views in an editorial or in the style of one. — *adv* **edito'rially**. — *n* **ed'itorship**. — **edit out** to remove (a piece of film, tape, etc) during editing. [L *ēdere*, *ēditum*, from *ē* from, and *dare* to give]

edite, bibite *e'di-tē, bi'bi-tē* or *e'di-te, bi'bi-te*, (*L*) eat, drink.

edition. See **edit**.

édition de luxe *ā-dē-syɔ̃ də lüks*, (*Fr*) *n* a splendid and expensive edition of a book.

editio princeps *i-dish'i-ō prin'seps* or *ā-dit'i-ō prin'keps*, (*L*) *n* the original edition, *esp* of a work till then known only in MS.

editor, etc. See **edit**.

EDP *abbrev*: electronic data processing.

edriophthalmic *ed-ri-of-thal'mik*, *adj* (of crustaceans) with stalkless eyes. — Also **edriophthal'mian** or **edriophthal'mous**. [Gr *hedrion*, dimin of *hedrā* seat, and *ophthalmos* eye]

EDS *abbrev*: English Dialect Society.

EDT (*NAm*) *abbrev*: Eastern Daylight Time.

educate *ed'ū-kāt*, *vt* to bring up and instruct; to teach; to train. — *n* **educabil'ity**. — *n* **educātabil'ity**. — *adj* **ed'ucable**. — *adj* **ed'ucated** having had a (good) education; cultivated, knowledgeable, refined in judge ment or taste; (of a guess) authoritative, backed by experience, to be accorded credence. — *n* **educā'tion** bringing up or training, eg of a child; instruction; strengthening of the powers of body or mind; culture. — *adj* **educā'tional**. — *n* **educā'tionalist** or **educā'tionist** a person skilled in methods of educating or teaching; a person who promotes education. — *adv* **educā'tionally**. — *adj* **ed'ucātive** of or pertaining to education; producing education. — *n* **ed'ucātor**. — *adj* **educatory** (*ed'* or *-kā'tə-ri*). [L *ēducāre*, *-ātum* to rear, from *ēdūcere*, from *ē* from, and *dūcere* to lead]

educe *i-* or *ē-dūs'*, *vt* to draw out; to extract; to make appear, to elicit; to develop; to infer. — *n* **educe'ment**. — *adj* **educ'ible**. — *n* **educt** (*ē'dukt*) what is educed. — *n* **eduction** (*ē-duk'shən*) the act of educing; the exhaust of an engine. — *n* **educ'tor** someone who or something which educes. [L *ēdūcere*, *ēductum*, from *ē* from, and *dūcere* to lead]

edulcorate *i-dul'kə-rāt*, *vt* to sweeten (*obs*); to free from soluble particles by washing. — *adj* **edul'corant**. — *n* **edulcorā'tion**. — *adj* **edul'corātive**. — *n* **edul'corātor**. [L *ē-* (intens), and *dulcōrāre* to sweeten, from *dulcis* sweet]

eduskunta *ā-do͞os-ko͞on'tä*, *n* the single-chamber Finnish parliament, elected every four years. [Finn]

Edwardian *ed-wörd'i-ən* (*archaic* and *US* also *-wärd'*), *adj* belonging to or characteristic of the reign of (any) King *Edward*, *esp* Edward VII; (of a motor-car) built in the period 1905 to 1918 — between veteran and vintage cars. — Also *n*. — *n* **Edwardian'a** (*-ä'nə*) furniture, ornamentation, artefacts, etc of the Edwardian period. — *n* **Edward'ianism**.

EE *abbrev*: early English; (also **ee**) errors excepted.

ee *ē*. Scots form of **eye**[2]: — *pl* **een**.

-ee *-ē*, *combining form* signifying the person affected by some action, eg *evacuee*, *interviewee*; a person in a particular situation, eg *absentee*; a person performing some action, eg *attendee*, *standee* (esp *US*). [Fr pa p sfx *-é* or *-ée*, from L *-ātus*, *-āta*]

EEC *abbrev*: European Economic Community.

eech. See **eche**.

EED *abbrev*: electro-explosive device.

EEF *abbrev*: Engineering Employers' Federation.

EEG *abbrev*: electroencephalogram or encephalograph.

eek *ēk*, *interj* of fright, used conventionally in children's comics, etc. [Representative of a shriek or squeal]

eel *ēl*, *n* any fish of the *Anguillidae*, *Muraenidae* or other family of *Apodes*, fishes with long smooth cylindrical or ribbon-shaped bodies, without pelvic fins and almost or totally scaleless; extended to various other fishes of similar form, such as the **sand eel** (or launce), and the **electric eel**; extended also to some eel-like threadworms (also **eel'worm**); a devious or evasive person, a slippery character. — *adj* **eel'y**. — **eel'-basket** a basket for catching eels; **eel'fare** (OE *faran* to travel) a migratory passage of young eels; a brood of young eels; a young eel; **eel'grass** or **eel'wrack** grasswrack (*Zostera*), a grasslike flowering plant of the pondweed family, growing in sea-water; **eel'pout** (*-powt*; OE *ǣlepūte*) the burbot; the viviparous blenny; **eel'-set** a net placed across a river to catch eels; **eel'-spear** an instrument with broad prongs for catching eels; **eel'worm** a nematode. — **salt eel** (*obs*) a rope's end. [OE *ǣl*; Ger *Aal*, and Du *aal*]

een. See **ee**.

e'en *ēn*. A poetic contraction of **even**[1,2].

EEO *abbrev*: Energy Efficiency Office.

EEPROM (*comput*) *abbrev*: electronically erasable programmable read-only memory.

e'er *ār*. A contraction of **ever**.

eerie or **eery** *ē'ri*, *adj* strangely frightening; weird; affected with fear, timorous (*dialect*). — *adv* **ee'rily**. — *n* **ee'riness**. [Scot; ME *arh*, *eri*, from OE *ærg* (*earg*) timid]

EET *abbrev*: Eastern European Time.

EETPU *abbrev*: Electrical, Electronic, Telecommunications and Plumbing Union.

EETS *abbrev*: Early English Text Society.

eeven, eevn, eev'n or **eevning**. Old spellings (*Milton*) of **even** (*n*, *adj* and *adv*) and **evening**.

EEZ *abbrev*: exclusive economic zone.

ef *ef*, *n* the sixth letter of the alphabet (F, f).

EFA *abbrev*: European fighter aircraft.

eff *ef*, *euphem* for **fuck** *esp* in *adj* **eff'ing** and *vi* **eff off**. — **effing and blinding** swearing.

effable *ef'ə-bl*, (*archaic*) *adj* capable of being expressed. [Fr, from L *effārī*, from *ex* out, and *fārī* to speak]

efface *i-* or *e-fās'*, *vt* to destroy the surface of; to rub out or erase; to obliterate, wear away. — *adj* **efface'able**. — *n* **efface'ment**. — **efface oneself** to avoid notice. [Fr *effacer*, from L *ex* out, and *faciēs* face]

effect *i-fekt'*, *n* the result of an action; the impression produced; the meaning conveyed; reality; (in *pl*) goods or property; (in *pl*) sound and lighting devices contributing to the illusion of the place and circumstance in which the action is happening (*theatre*, *cinema*, etc). — *vt* to produce; to accomplish or bring about. — *n* **effec'ter**. — *adj* **effec'tible** that may be effected. — *adj* **effec'tive** having power to effect; causing something; successful in producing a result or effect; powerful; serviceable; actual; in force. — *n* a soldier or body of soldiers ready for service. — Also *adj*. — *adv* **effec'tively**. — *n* **effec'tiveness**. — *adj* **effect'less** without effect, useless. — *n* and *adj* **effec'tor** (*biol*) (an organ or substance) that produces a response to stimulus. — *adj* **effec'tual** successful in producing the desired effect; decisive (*Shakesp*). — *n* **effectual'ity**. — *adv* **effec'tually**. — *n* **effec'tualness**. — *vt* **effec'tuate** to accomplish. — *n* **effectuā'tion**. — **effective rate** (also **sterling effective rate**) the percentage deviation of sterling from its Smithsonian parity (qv) against an average of selected foreign currencies, weighted according to their UK trade importance; **effectual calling** (*theol*) the invitation to come to Christ received by the elect. — **come**, etc or **put**, etc **into effect** to become or make operative; **for effect** so as to make a telling impression; **general effect**

the effect produced by a picture, etc as a whole; **give effect to** to carry out, perform; **in effect** in truth, really; substantially; in operation or operative; **leave no effects** to die without property to bequeath; **take effect** to begin to operate; to come into force; **to that effect** with the previously indicated purport. [OFr, from L *effectus*, from *ex* out, and *facere* to make]

effeir[1] or **effere** *e-fēr'*, (*Scot*) *n* affair; appearance, show, array. [**affair**]

effeir[2] or **effere** *e-fēr'*, (*obs*) *vi* to appertain; to suit. [OFr *afferir*, from L *ad* to, and *ferrīre* to strike]

effeminate *i-fem'in-ət*, *adj* womanish; unmanly; weak; soft; voluptuous; feminine (*Shakesp*). — *n* an effeminate person. — *vt* (*-āt*; *archaic*) to make womanish; to weaken or unman. — Also *vi* (*archaic*). — Also **effem'inize** or **-ise**. — *n* **effem'inacy** (*-ə-si*) unmanly softness or weakness; indulgence in unmanly pleasures. — *adv* **effem'inately**. — *n* **effem'inateness**. [L *effēmināre*, *-ātum* to make womanish, from *ex* out, and *fēmina* a woman]

effendi *e-fen'di*, *n* in Turkey, a former title for civil officials, abolished in 1934 and now used orally with the force of *Mr*; generally, in the Eastern Mediterranean, a title of respect for educated or high-ranking people. [Turk; from Gr *authentēs* an absolute master]

effere. See **effeir**[1,2].

efferent *ef'ə-rənt*, *adj* conveying outward or away, as in (*zool*) **efferent nerve**, a nerve carrying impulses away from the central nervous system. — *n* **eff'erence**. [L *ē* from, and *ferēns*, *-entis*, pr p of *ferre* to carry]

effervesce *ef-ər-ves'*, *vi* to boil up; to bubble and hiss; to fizz or froth up; to behave or talk vivaciously. — *n* **effervesc'ence** or **effervesc'ency**. — *adj* **effervesc'ent** boiling or bubbling from the release of gas; lively, vivacious or exuberant. — *adj* **effervesc'ible**. — *adv* **effervesc'ingly**. [L *effervēscere*, from *ex* (intens), and *fervēre* to boil]

effete *e-fēt'*, *adj* exhausted; degenerate, decadent; having become barren (*obs*). — *adv* **effete'ly**. — *n* **effete'ness**. [L *effētus* weakened by having given birth, from *ex* out, and *fētus* the act of giving birth]

efficacious *ef-i-kā'shəs*, *adj* able to produce the result intended. — *adv* **efficā'ciously**. — *n* **efficā'ciousness**, **efficacity** (*-kas'i-ti*) or **eff'icacy** (*-kə-si*) the power of producing an effect; effectiveness. [L *efficāx*, *-ācis*, from *efficere*; see **efficient**]

efficient *i-fish'ənt*, *adj* capable of doing what may be required; effective; competent or proficient; working with speed and economy. — *combining form* **-effi'cient** economical in the use or consumption of a particular resource, as in *energy-efficient*. — *n* (*archaic*) the person or thing that effects. — *n* **effi'cience** (*archaic*) efficient action or power. — *n* **effi'ciency** the power to produce the result intended; the quality of being efficient; the ratio of a machine's output of energy to its input; a small flat (*US*; also **efficiency apartment**). — *adv* **effi'ciently**. [Fr, from L *efficiēns*, *-entis*, pr p of *efficere*, from *ex* out, and *facere* to make]

effierce *e-fērs'*, (*Spenser*) *vt* to make fierce.

effigurate *e-fig'u-rāt*, *adj* having a definite shape. — *n* **effigurā'tion** an axial outgrowth in a flower. [L *ef-*, from *ex-* (intens), and **figurate**]

effigy *ef'i-ji*, *n* a likeness or figure of a person; the head or impression on a coin — (*archaic*) **effigies** (*ef-ij'i-ēz*): — *pl* **effigies** (*ef'i-jiz*; *archaic ef-ij'i-ēz*). — **burn** or **hang in effigy** to burn or hang a figure of a person, as an expression of hatred or disapproval. [L *effigiēs*, from *effingere*, from *ex* (intens) and *fingere* to form]

effing. See **eff**.

effleurage *ef-lə-räzh'*, *n* a stroking movement in massage. — Also *vi* and *vt*. [Fr, glancing or grazing]

effloresce *ef-lo-res'*, *vi* to blossom forth; to become covered with a powdery crust (*chem*); to form a powdery crust. — *n* **effloresc'ence** the production of flowers; the time of flowering; a redness of the skin; a powdery surface crust; the formation of such a crust; the giving up of the water of crystallization to the atmosphere. — *adj* **effloresc'ent**. [L *efflōrēscere*, from *ex* out, and *flōrēscere* to blossom, from *flōs*, *flōris* a flower]

effluent *ef'lŏŏ-ənt*, *adj* flowing out. — *n* liquid industrial waste; outflow from sewage during purification; a stream that flows out of another stream or lake. — *n* **eff'luence** a flowing out; emanation. [L *effluēns*, *-entis* pr p of *effluere*, from *ex* out, and *fluere* to flow]

effluvium *e-flōō'vi-əm*, *n* disagreeable vapours rising from decaying matter; minute particles that flow out from bodies; a generally unpleasant exhalation: — *pl* **efflu'via**. — *adj* **efflu'vial**. [LL, from L *effluere*]

efflux *ef'luks*, *n* the act of flowing out; something that flows out. — Also **effluxion** (*e-fluk'shən*). [L *effluere*, from *ex* out, and *fluere*, *fluxum* to flow]

efforce *e-fōrs'*, (*obs*) *vt* to compel; to force; to force open; to do violence to; to put forward with force. [Fr *efforcer*, from LL *exfortiāre*, from *ex* out, and *fortis* strong]

effort *ef'ərt*, *n* exertion of body or mind; an attempt; (a) struggle; a piece of work produced by way of attempt; anything done or produced (*colloq*). — *adj* **eff'ortful** done with effort, laboured. — *adj* **eff'ortless** making no effort, passive; easy, showing no sign of effort. [Fr, from L *ex* out, and *fortis* strong]

effray, **effraide**. Obsolete forms of **affray** or **afraid**.

effrontery *i-* or *e-frunt'ər-i*, *n* shamelessness; impudence or impudent audacity; insolence. [Fr *effronterie*, from L *effrōns*, *effrontis*, from *ex* out, without, and *frōns*, *frontis* forehead]

effulge *i-* or *e-fulj'*, *vi* to shine out; to beam: — *pr p* **effulg'ing**; *pa t* and *pa p* **effulged'**. — *n* **efful'gence** great brilliance or brightness; a flood of light. — *adj* **efful'gent** giving off a brilliant light; shining; radiant; splendid. — *adv* **efful'gently**. [L *effulgēre* to shine out, pr p *effulgēns*, *-entis*, from *ex* out, and *fulgēre* to shine]

effuse *e-fūz'*, *vt* to pour out; to spread out; to pour forth (eg words); to shed (eg blood); to spread; to let loose (*Thomson*). — *vi* to flow out. — *n* (*e-fūs'*; *Shakesp*) effusion or shedding. — *adj* (*e-fūs'*) poured out; loosely spreading (*bot*); (of shells) with the lips separated by a groove. — *n* **effusiometer** (*e-fūz-i-om'i-tər*) an apparatus for comparing molecular weights of gases by observing the relative time taken to stream out through a small hole. — *n* **effusion** (*e-fū'zhən*) pouring or streaming out; emission; shedding (eg of blood); an abnormal outpouring of fluid into the tissues or cavities of the body (*med*); an unrestrained outpouring of words, *esp* expressing warmth or enthusiasm; a literary outpouring, *esp* in poetic form (often *derog*); effusiveness; the act of pouring, or process of being poured, out; something poured over or shed. — *adj* **effusive** (*e-fū'ziv*) poured out abundantly; poured out at the surface in a state of fusion, volcanic (*geol*); expressing emotion in an over-demonstrative manner; gushing. — *adv* **effus'ively**. — *n* **effus'iveness**. [L *effundere*, *effūsum*, from *ex* out, and *fundere* to pour]

Efik *ef'ik*, *n* (a member of) a people of SE Nigeria; the language of this people.

EFL *abbrev*: English as a foreign language.

eft[1] *eft*, *n* a lizard (*obs*); a newt. [OE *efeta*; see **newt**]

eft[2] *eft*, (*obs*) *adv* afterwards; again; forthwith; moreover. — *adv* **eftsoons** (*eft-sōōnz'*; *obs*) soon afterwards or forthwith. [OE *æft* or *eft* after or again; see **aft**]

EFTA or sometimes **Efta** *ef'tə*, *abbrev*: European Free Trade Association.

eftest *eft'ist*, (*Warwickshire* and *Worcestershire*; *Shakesp*) *adj superl* readiest; most convenient.

EFTPOS or **Eftpos** *eft'pos*, (*comput*) *abbrev*: electronic funds transfer at point of sale.

EFTS (*comput*) *abbrev*: electronic funds transfer system.

eftsoons. See **eft**[2].

EG *abbrev*: equivalent grade.

eg or **ex gr** *abbrev*: *exempli gratia* (*L*), for example.

egad *i-gad'*, (*archaic*) *interj* a mild oath. [Perh orig **ah God**]

egal *ē'gəl*, *adj* (*Shakesp*) equal. — *adj* and *n* **egalitā'rian** (*i-gal-*) equalitarian; (a person) believing in and upholding the principle of equality among people. — *n* **egalitā'rianism**. — *n* **egality** (*ē-* or *i-gal'*) equality. — *adv* **ē'gally** (*Shakesp*). [OFr *egal*, from L *aequālis*, from *aequus* equal]

égarement *ā-gar-mã*, (*Fr*) *n* confusion, bewilderment.

egence *ē'jəns* or **egency** *-si*, *n* need. [L *ēgēre* to be in need]

eger *ē'gər*, *n*. Same as **eagre**.

Egeria *ē-jē'ri-ə* or *e-*, *n* a female adviser. [L *Ēgeria* or *Aegeria*, the nymph who instructed Numa Pompilius]

egest *ə-jest'* or *ē-jest'*, *vt* to discharge; to expel from the body in any way. — *n pl* **egest'a** things thrown out; excreta; waste materials removed from the body. — *n* **egestion** (*e-jest'yən*). — *adj* **egest'ive**. [L *ēgerere*, *ēgestum*, from *ē* out, and *gerere* to carry]

egg[1] *eg*, *n* an oval, round, etc body laid by the female of birds, reptiles, fish, insects and certain other animals from which the young is hatched, *esp* that laid by a hen and eaten as food; an ovum or female gamete (also **egg'-cell**); a zygote, the fertilized ovum, or the organism growing within it; anything shaped like a hen's egg; a bomb or mine (*slang*). — *vt* to add egg to, *usu* in cooking. — *n* **egg'er** a person who collects wildfowl's eggs; any moth of the family *Lasiocampidae*, whose cocoons are egg-shaped (also **egg'ar**). — *n* **egg'ery** (*archaic*) a place where eggs are laid. — *n* **egg'ler** (*archaic*) a dealer in eggs. — *adj* **egg'y** abounding in eggs; having just laid or about to lay an egg; tasting or smelling of or marked or covered with eggs. — **egg'-and-anch'or**, **egg'-and-dart'**, **egg'-and-tongue'** (*archit*) ornaments *esp* found on cornice mouldings, in the form of eggs alternating with anchors, darts or tongues; **egg'-apparatus** (*bot*) the egg and the synergidae in the embryo-sac of an angiosperm; **egg'-apple** the egg-fruit; **egg'-beater** an egg-whisk; a helicopter (esp *NAm colloq*); **egg'-binding** inability to expel an egg; **egg'-bird** the sooty tern. — *adj* **egg'-bound** in the state of being unable to expel eggs. — **egg'-box** a protective partitioned container for holding *usu* six eggs. — *adj* used of a type of building which looks like a simple square box or a number of these put together. — **egg'-capsule**, **egg'-case** or **egg'-purse** a protective covering in which the eggs of some animals are enclosed; **egg'-cōsy** a cover for keeping a boiled egg hot; **egg'cup** a small cup for holding a boiled egg (still in its shell) at table; **egg custard** see under **custard**; **egg'-dance** a dance performed blindfold among eggs; **egg'-flip** a drink made of ale, wine, spirits or milk, with eggs, sugar, spice, etc; **egg'-fruit** the fruit of the egg-plant; **egg'-glass** an egg-timer; **egg'head** (*colloq*) an intellectual; **egg'mass** (*colloq*) intellectuals as a group. — Also *adj*. — **egg'nog** a drink of eggs and hot beer, spirits, etc; **egg'-plant** the aubergine, *orig* an East Indian annual plant (*Solanum melongena*) with edible egg-shaped fruit; **egg'-plum** a yellowish egg-shaped plum; **egg'-powder** a powder of dried eggs, or a substitute; **egg'-purse** egg-capsule; **egg'shell** the hard calcareous covering of a bird's egg; a smooth gastropod shell; a very thin kind of porcelain. — *adj* thin and delicate; (of paint, etc) having only a slight gloss. — **egg'-slice** a utensil for lifting fried eggs out of a pan; **egg'-spoon** a small spoon used for eating boiled eggs from the shell; **egg'-timer** a small sand-glass for timing the boiling of eggs; **egg'-tooth** a hard point on the beak by which an unhatched bird or reptile breaks the eggshell; **egg'wash** a thin mixture of egg and milk (or water) used as a glaze for pastry; **egg'-whisk** an instrument for beating raw eggs. — **a bad egg** (*colloq*) a worthless person; **egg-and-spoon race** a race in which each competitor carries an egg in a spoon; **eggs Benedict** (*ben'i-dikt*) a slice of ham and a poached egg placed on a slice of toast and covered with hollandaise sauce; **good egg** (*colloq*) an exclamation of approval; **have** or **put all one's eggs into one basket** to risk all on one enterprise; **have**, **get** or **be left with egg on one's face** (*slang*) to be left looking foolish; **lay an egg** (*slang*, chiefly *US*) (of a joke, comedian, theatrical performance, etc) to fail, flop; **take eggs for money** to be put off with mere promises of payment; **teach your grandmother to suck eggs** to presume to teach someone older and wiser than oneself; to teach someone something that he or she knows already; **tread upon eggs** to walk warily, to steer one's way carefully in a delicate situation. [ON *egg*; cf OE *ǣg*, Ger *Ei*, perh L *ōvum*, Gr *ōon*]

egg[2] *eg*, *vt* (with *on*) to incite, urge on. [ON *eggja*, from *egg* an edge; cognate with OE *ecg*; see **edge**]

eggar, **egger**, **eggery**, **eggler**, **eggy**. See **egg**[1].

egis. Same as **aegis**.

eglandular *ē-glan'dū-lər*, *adj* having no glands. — *adj* **eglan'dulose**. [L *ē-* without, and *glandula* gland]

eglantine *eg'lən-tīn* or *eg'lən-tin*, *n* a fragrant species of wild rose, the sweet-brier; perhaps the honeysuckle (*Milton*). [Fr, from OFr *aiglent*, as if from a L *aculentus* prickly, from *acus* a needle, and sfx *-lentus*]

eglatere *eg-lə-tēr'*, (*archaic*) *n* eglantine.

egma *eg'mə*, *n* Costard's attempt at *enigma* in Shakespeare's *Love's Labour's Lost*.

ego *e'gō* or *ē'gō*, *n* the 'I' or self, that which is conscious and thinks; an image of oneself; self-confidence; egotism. — *adj* **egocen'tric** self-centred; regarding or regarded from the point of view of the ego. — Also *n*. — *n* **egocentri'city**. — *n* **e'gōism** the doctrine that we have proof of nothing but our own existence (*philos*); the theory of self-interest as the principle of morality (*ethics*); over-concern for one's own well-being; selfishness; self-centredness; egotism. — *n* **e'gōist** a person who holds the doctrine of egoism; a person who thinks and speaks too much of himself or of things as they affect himself; an egotist. — *adj* **egōist'ic** or **egōist'ical** pertaining to or displaying egoism. — *adv* **egōis'tically**. — *n* **egō'ity** the essential element of the ego. — *n* **egomā'nia** abnormal egotism. — *n* **egomā'niac**. — *adj* **egomanī'acal**. — *n* **e'gotheism** (or *-thē'*) the deification of self; identification of oneself with God. — *n* **e'gotism** a frequent use of the pronoun I; thinking or speaking too much of oneself; self-exaltation. — *n* **e'gotist** an egotistic person. — *adj* **egotis'tic** or **egotis'tical** showing egotism; self-important; conceited. — *adv* **egotist'ically**. — *vi* **e'gotize** or **-ise** to talk a lot about oneself. — **ego ideal** (*psychol*) one's personal standards, ideals, ambitions, etc acquired as one recognizes parental and other social standards, formed into a composite of characteristics to which one would like to conform; one's idealized picture of oneself; **e'go-trip** (*slang*) an action or experience which inflates one's good opinion of oneself; **e'go-tripper**. — **massage someone's ego** (*facetious*) to flatter someone, rub someone up the right way. [L *ego*, *egō*, and Gr *egō* I]

egregious *i-grē'jəs*, *adj* prominent, distinguished (*archaic*); outrageous; notorious. — *adv* **egrē'giously**. — *n* **egrē'giousness**. [L *ēgregius* chosen out of the flock, from *ē* out of, and *grex*, *gregis* a flock]

egress *ē'gres*, *n* the act of going out; departure; the way out; the power or right to depart. — *n* **egression** (*i-* or *ē-gresh'ən*) the act of going out; departure. [L *ēgredī*, *ēgressus*, from *ē* out of, and *gradī* to go]

egret *ē'gret*, *n* a white heron of several species; an aigrette. [See **aigrette**]

EGU *abbrev*: English Golf Union.

egurgitate *ē-gûr'ji-tāt*, (*rare*) *vt* to vomit; to cast forth. [L *ēgurgitāre*, *-ātum*, from *ē* out of, and *gurges*, *-itis* a whirlpool]

Egypt, or *archaic* **Aegypt**, *ē'jipt*, *n* a country of NE Africa. — *adj* **Egyptian** (*ē-jip'shən*) belonging to Egypt; (of type) antique (*printing*). — *n* a native or citizen of Egypt; a gypsy (*archaic*). — *adj* **Egyptolog'ical**. — *n* **Egyptol'ogist**. — *n* **Egyptol'ogy** the science of Egyptian antiquities. — **Egyptian darkness** darkness like that of Exod 10.22 in the Bible.

eh *ā*, *interj* expressing inquiry, failure to hear or slight surprise. — *vi* to say 'Eh'.

EHF *abbrev*: extremely high frequency.

EHO *abbrev*: Environmental Health Officer.
EI *abbrev*: East Indian; East Indies.
EIA *abbrev*: environmental impact assessment.
EIB *abbrev*: European Investment Bank.
Eid al-Adha, **Eid al-Fitr**. See **Id-al-Adha** and **Id-al-Fitr**.
eident *ī'dənt*, (*Scot*) *adj* busy, diligent. [ME *ithen*, from ON *ithinn* diligent]
eider *ī'dər*, *n* the **ei'der-duck**, a northern sea-duck, sought after for its fine down. — **ei'derdown** the soft down of the eider-duck, used for stuffing bedcovers; a bedcover, *usu* quilted. [Prob through Swed from ON *æthar*, genitive of *æthr* an eider-duck]
eidetic *ī-det'ik*, (*psychol*) *adj* (of a mental image) extraordinarily clear and vivid, as though actually visible; (of a person or memory) reproducing, or able to reproduce, a vividly clear visual image of what has been previously seen. — *n* a person with this ability. — *adv* **eidet'ically**. [Gr *eidētikos* belonging to an image, from *eidos* form]
eidograph *ī'dō-gräf*, *n* an instrument used for copying drawings. [Gr *eidos* form, and *graphein* to write]
eidolon *ī-dō'lon*, *n* an image; a phantom or apparition; a confusing reflection or reflected image: — *pl* **eidō'la**. [Gr; see **idol**]
eigen- *ī-gən-*, *combining form* denoting proper, own. — *n* **ei'gen-frequency** (*physics*) one of the frequencies with which a particular system may vibrate. — *n* **ei'genfunction** a solution of a wave function that satisfies a set of boundary conditions. — *n* **ei'gentone** (*physics*) a tone characteristic of a particular vibrating system. — *n* **ei'genvalue** (*math* and *physics*) any of the possible values for a parameter of an equation for which the solutions will be compatible with the boundary conditions. [Ger]
eight *āt*, *n* the cardinal number one above seven; a symbol (8, viii, etc) representing that number; a set of eight things or persons (syllables, leaves, rowers, etc); an eight-oar boat; an eight-cylinder engine or car; a card with eight pips; a shoe or other article of a size denoted by 8; the eighth hour after midday or midnight; a score of eight points, tricks, etc; the age of eight years. — *adj* of the number eight; eight years old. — *adj* and *adv* **eight'fold** in eight divisions; eight times as much. — *adv* by eight times as much. — *adj* **eighth** (*ätth*) last of eight; next after the seventh; equal to one of eight equal parts. — *n* an eighth part; a person or thing in eighth position; an octave (*music*). — *adv* **eighthly** (*ätth'li*) in the eighth place. — *n* **eight'some** a group of eight; eight together; a Scottish reel for eight dancers (also **eightsome reel**). — *n* and *adj* **eight'vo** same as **octavo**: — *pl* **eight'vos**. — *adj* **eight'-day** lasting or running for eight days. — **eight'foil** (*heraldry*) an eight-leaved flower. — *adj* **eight'foot** eight feet in measure (also *adv*); for musical sense see under **foot**. — *adj* **eight'-hour** consisting of eight hours or eight working hours. — *adj* **eight'-oar** manned by eight rowers. — *n* an eight-oar boat. — **eight'pence** the value of eight pennies. — *adj* **eight'penny** costing eightpence. — *n* and *adj* **eight'score** eight times twenty. — **eights'man** one of a crew or team of eight. — *adj* **eight'-square** regularly octagonal. — **an eight days** a week; **figure of eight** a figure shaped like an 8 made in skating, etc; **one over the eight** (*colloq*) one (alcoholic) drink too many; **piece of eight** an old Spanish coin worth eight reals; **the eights** annual bumping boat-races between the various Oxford colleges in the summer term. [OE (Anglian) *æhta* (W Sax *eahta*); Ger *acht*, L *octō*, Gr *oktō*]
eighteen *ā-tēn'* or *ā'tēn*, *n* and *adj* eight and ten; (**18**) a certificate designating a film suitable only for people of eighteen and over. — *adj* and *n* **eighteen'mo** octodecimo: — *pl* **eighteen'mos**. — *adj* **eigh'teenth** (or *-tēnth'*) last of eighteen; next after the seventeenth; equal to one of eighteen equal parts. — *n* an eighteenth part; a person or thing in eighteenth position. — *adv* **eighteenth'ly**. — *adj* **eigh'teen-hole** having eighteen golf-holes. — **eigh'teen-pence**. — *adj* **eigh'teen-penny**. — **eighteen-penny piece** an obsolete English coin. [OE (Mercian) *æhtatēne* (W. Sax *eahtatīene*)]
eighty *ā'ti*, *n* and *adj* eight times ten. — *n pl* **eight'ies** the numbers eighty to eighty-nine; the years so numbered in life or any century; a range of temperatures from eighty to just less than ninety degrees. — *adj* **eigh'tieth** last of eighty; next after the seventy-ninth; equal to one of eighty equal parts. — *n* an eightieth part; a person or thing in eightieth position. [OE *æhtatig* (W Sax *eahtatig* or *hundeahtatig*)]
eigne *ān*, (*archaic*) *adj* first born. [Fr *aîné*]
EIIR. See **ER**.
eik *ēk*. Scots form of **eke**[1].
eikon. Same as **icon**.
eild[1]. Same as **eld**.
eild[2] *ēld*, (*Scot*) *adj* not bearing young; not yielding milk. [See **yeld**]
eilding. See **eldin**.
eine *īn* or *ēn*, (*obs*) *n pl* eyes. [See **een** under **ee**]
Einsteinian *īn-stī'ni-ən*, *adj* of or relating to Albert *Einstein*, physicist and mathematician (1879–1955) or his theories, *esp* that of relativity. — *n* **einstein'ium** the radioactive metallic element (symbol **Es**; atomic number 99) artificially produced from plutonium and named after Einstein.
eirack *ē'rək*, (*Scot*) *n* a young hen. [Gaelic *eireag*]
eirenicon or **irenicon** *ī-rē'ni-kon*, *n* a proposition or scheme for peace; a peace-making message; the deacon's litany at the beginning of the Greek liturgy, from its opening petitions for peace. — *adj* **eirē'nic** same as **irenic**. [A partly Latinized spelling of Gr *eirēnikon*, neuter of *eirēnikos* peaceful or peaceable, from *eirēnē* peace]
EIS *abbrev*: Educational Institute of Scotland.
eisel or **eisell** *ā'səl* or *ī'səl*, (*obs*) *n* vinegar. [OFr *aisil*, *aissil*, from LL dimin of L *acētum* vinegar]
Eisen und Blut. See **Blut und Eisen**.
eisteddfod *ī-sted'fəd* or *īs-tedh'vod*, *US* *ās-*, *n orig* a competitive congress of Welsh bards and musicians, now any of several gatherings in Wales for competitions in music, poetry, drama, etc, *esp* (with *cap*) the Royal National Eisteddfod: — *pl* **eistedd'fods** or **eisteddfodau** (*-vo-dī*). — *adj* **eisteddfod'ic**. [W, (literally) session, from *eistedd* to sit]
either *ī'dhər* or *ē'dhər*, *adj* the one or the other; one of two; each of two, the one and the other. — *pronoun* the one or the other. — *conj* correlative to *or*; or (*Bible*). — *adv* (used in conjunction with a negative) also, likewise (not), as in *He isn't hungry and she isn't either*; (after a negative) moreover, besides, as in *She's a golfer, and not a bad one, either*. [OE *ǣgther*, contraction of *ǣghwæther*, from *ā* aye, pfx *ge-*, and *hwæther* whether; see also **each**]
ejaculate *i-jak'ū-lāt*, *vt* to utter with suddenness, to exclaim; to eject. — *vi* to utter or make an ejaculation; to emit semen. — *n* (*-lət*) semen. — *n* **ejacūlā'tion** ejection or emission; a sudden utterance in prayer, etc; an unpremeditated emotional prayer or remark; emission of semen. — *adj* **ejac'ūlative** (or *-lā-*). — *adj* **ejac'ūlatory** (or *-lā-*). [L *ē* from, and *jaculārī*, *-ātus*, from *jacere* to throw]
eject *i-* or *ē-jekt'*, *vt* to throw out; to dismiss; to turn out; to expel. — *vi* to make oneself be ejected as from an aircraft or spacecraft. — *n* **eject** (*ē'jekt*) a mental state other than one's own, a thing thrown out of one's own consciousness, as distinguished from *object*, a thing presented in one's consciousness. — *n pl* **eject'a** or **ejectament'a** matter thrown out, *esp* by volcanoes. — *n* **ejec'tion** discharge; expulsion; the state of being ejected; vomiting; something that is ejected. — *adj* **ejec'tive**. — *n* **eject'ment** expulsion; dispossession; an action for the recovery of the possession of land (*law*). — *n* **eject'or** a person who ejects or dispossesses another of his or her land; any mechanical apparatus for ejecting or discharging. — **eject'or-seat** or (*US*) **ejection seat** a seat that can be shot clear with its occupant in an emergency. [L *ējectāre*, frequentative of *ējicere*, *ējectum*, from *ē* from, and *jacere* to throw]

ejusd. *abbrev*: *ejusdem* (*L*), of the same. — **ejusdem generis** *ē-jus'dəm jen'ə-ris* or *ā-ūs'dem ge'ne-ris*, (*L*) of the same kind.
eka- *ā'kə-* or *ē'kə-*, *pfx* formerly prefixed to the name of an element to give a provisional name for the hypothetical undiscovered element that should follow in the periodic table. [Sans *eka* one]
EKCO *ek'ō*, *abbrev*: E K Cole (manufacturer of electrical goods).
ek dum *ek dum*, at once. [Hindi *ek dam*]
eke[1] (*Scot* **eik**) *ēk*, *vt* (now only with *out*) to add to or increase; to lengthen; to supplement or make up to the required measure. — *n* (*Scot*) an addition or supplement. [OE *ēcan* (W Sax *īecan*); cf **eche**; L *augēre*; Gr *auxanein*]
eke[2] *ēk*, (*archaic*) *adv* in addition; likewise. [OE *ēac*; Ger *auch*, perh from root of **eke**[1]]
ekistics *ek-is'tiks*, *n sing* a word coined by a Greek, C A Doxiadis, for the science or study of human settlements. — *adj* **ekis'tic**. — *n* **ekistician** (*-tish'ən*). [From Mod Gr coinage *oikistikē*, from Gr *oikistikos* of or relating to settlement, from *oikizein* to settle or colonize, from *oikos* a house]
ekka *ek'ə*, *n* a small one-horse carriage. [Hindi, from *ekkā* one, from Sans *eka*]
eklogite. See **eclogite**.
ekphrasis *ek'frə-sis*, (*art*) *n* a description of a work of art, possibly imaginary, produced as a rhetorical exercise, those of antiquity having provided inspiration for artists of the Renaissance. [Gr, description]
ekuele *ā-kwā'lā* or **ekpwele** *ek-pwā'lā*, *n* between 1973 and 1985, the name of the standard monetary unit of Equatorial Guinea (100 céntimos): — *pl* **ekue'le** or **ekpwe'les**. [Native name]
el[1] *el*, *n* the twelfth letter of the modern English alphabet (L, l); anything of that shape; a wing giving a building the shape of the letter L (*US*).
el[2] *el*, (*US colloq*) *n* an *el*evated railroad.
e-la *ē'-lä'*, *n* the highest note in old church music, E, the fourth space in the treble, sung to the syllable *la* in the highest hexachord; the highest pitch of anything. — *n* **e-la-mi** (*ē'-lä'-mē'*) E, the third space in the bass ('in bass') or the first line in the treble ('in alt'), sung to *la* in the first and fourth hexachords respectively, and *mi* in the second and fifth.
elaborate *i-lab'ər-āt*, *vt* to produce by labour; to work out in detail; to build up from raw or comparatively simple materials; to add detail to; to convert (eg food) into complex substances (*physiol*). — *vi* (with *on* or *upon*) to add detail, more information, etc to a bare account; to become elaborate. — *adj* (*i-lab'ər-ət*) done with fullness and exactness; highly detailed; complicated; wrought with labour. — *adv* **elab'orately**. — *n* **elab'orateness**. — *n* **elaborā'tion** the act or process of elaborating; a refinement, detail or complication added; the process by which substances are built up in the bodies of animals or plants. — *adj* **elab'orative** (or *-rā-*). — *n* **elab'orātor** someone who elaborates. — *n* **elab'oratory** (*obs*) a laboratory. [L *ēlabōrāre*, *-ātum*, from *ē* from, and *labōrāre*, from *labor* labour]
Elaeagnus *el-i-ag'nəs*, *n* the oleaster genus, giving name to the family **Elaeagnā'ceae**. [Gr *elaiagnos* goat willow]
Elaeis *el-ē'is*, *n* the oil-palm genus. [Gr *elaion* olive oil]
elaeolite *el-ē'ō-līt*, *n* a greasy-looking nepheline. [Gr *elaion* olive oil, and *lithos* stone]
El Al *el al* the Israeli airline, (literally) towards the sky.
élan *ā-län'* or *ā-lã*, *n* impetuosity; dash or style. — **élan vital** (*ā-lã vē-tal*; *Bergson*) the creative force responsible for the growth and evolution of organisms. [Fr]
elance *i-läns'*, *vt* to throw as a lance. [Fr *élancer*]
eland *ē'lənd*, *n* a S African antelope, resembling the elk in having a protuberance on the larynx. [Du, from Ger *Elend* (now *Elen*), from Lith *élnis* elk]
elanet *el'ə-net*, *n* a kite of the genus **Elanus**. [Gr *elanos* a kite]
elaphine *el'ə-fīn*, *adj* like or belonging to a red deer. [Gr *elaphos* stag]
Elaps *ē'laps*, *n* an American genus of snakes, also called **Micrurus**, the coral-snake; sometimes applied to a S African genus, also called **Homorelaps**, the garter-snake. [A form of **ellops**]
elapse *i-laps'*, *vi* to slip or glide away; (of time, or units of time) to pass silently. — *n* passing. [L *ēlāpsus*, *ēlābī*, from *ē* from, and *lābī*, *lāpsus* to slide]
elasmobranch *i-laz'mō-brangk*, or *-las'*, *n* any member of the **Elasmobranch'iī**, a class of fishes including sharks and skates which have a cartilaginous skeleton and plate-like gills. [Gr *elasmos* a beaten-metal plate, and *branchia* gills]
elastic *i-las'tik*, or *-läs'*, *adj* having a tendency or the ability to recover the original form or size after stretching, compression or deformation; springy or resilient; able to recover quickly a former state or condition, eg after a shock (*fig*); stretchy; flexible; capable of stretching to include a large number or amount (*lit* and *fig*); made of elastic. — *n* a string or ribbon woven with rubber strands. — *n* **elas'tance** (*phys*) the reciprocal of the capacity of a condenser, from its electromechanical analogy with a spring. — *n* **elas'tase** an enzyme found in the pancreatic juice that decomposes elastin. — *adv* **elas'tically**. — *vt* **elas'ticate** to make elastic. — *adj* **elas'ticated**. — *n* **elasticity** (*el-* or *ēl-əs-tis'i-ti*) power of returning to its original form or size after stretching, compression or deformation; springiness, flexibility, resilience or stretchiness; power to recover from shock, depression, etc, or financial restraint. — *vt* **elas'ticize** or **-ise** (*-ti-sīz*) to make elastic. — *n* **elas'ticness**. — *n* **elas'tin** a protein, the chief constituent of elastic tissue. — *n* **elastomer** any rubber-like substance. — *adj* **elastomeric** (*-mer'*). — **elastic band** a narrow strip of rubber formed into a loop for holding objects together, etc (also called **rubber band**); **elastic collision** or **scattering** see under **collide**; **elastic limit** the greatest stress a material can be subjected to without permanent deformation; **elastic tissue** tissue having fibres with elastic quality, occurring *esp* in ligaments and tendons. [Late Gr *elastikos*, from *elaunein* to drive]
Elastoplast® *i-last'ō-pläst* or *-plast*, *n* a dressing for a wound, consisting of gauze on a backing of adhesive tape.
elate *i-lāt'*, *adj* (*rare*) lifted up; puffed up with success; exalted. — *vt* to raise or exalt (*obs*); to raise the spirits of, cheer or exhilerate; to make exultant, proud or euphoric. — *adv* **elāt'edly**. — *n* **elāt'edness**. — *n* **elā'tion** pride resulting from success; exaltation, high spirits or euphoria. — *adj* **ē'lative** (*gram*) (of a noun case), expressing place 'from which', as eg in Finnish. — *n* the elative case. [L *ēlātus*, used as pa p of *efferre*, from *ē* from, and *lātus* carried]
elater *el'ə-tər*, *n* an elastic filament aiding spore-dispersal in certain fungi, in liverworts and in horse-tails (*bot*); a skipjack beetle. — *n* **elatē'rium** a substance contained in the juice of the fruit of the squirting cucumber, producing the purgative **elat'erin**. — **elaterite** (*i-lat'ər-īt*) elastic bitumen, a rubber-like mineral resin. [Gr *elatēr* driver, from *elaunein* to drive]
elbow *el'bō*, *n* the joint where the arm bends; the corresponding joint in vertebrates; the part of a sleeve which covers the elbow; any sharp turn or bend, eg in a road. — *vt* to push with the elbow, to jostle. — **el'bow-chair** an armchair; **el'bow-grease** (*facetious*) vigorous rubbing; hard work; **elbow macaroni** macaroni cut longer than usual, and with a pronounced bend; **el'bow-room** room to extend the elbows; space enough for moving or acting; freedom and scope. — **at one's elbow** close at hand, ready for use; **bend**, **crook** or **lift the elbow** to drink alcohol, *esp* too much; **out at elbow** wearing a ragged coat or threadbare, *orig* worn at the elbows; **up to the elbows** completely engrossed or involved. [OE *elnboga*; see **ell**[1] and **bow**[1] *n* and *vt*]
elchi, **eltchi** or **elchee** *el'chē* or *-chi*, *n* an ambassador. [Turk *īlchī*]

eld *eld*, (*archaic*) *n* age; old age or senility; former times or antiquity. [OE *eldo*]

elder[1] *eld'ər*, *n* a shrub or tree (*Sambucus*) of the Caprifoliaceae, related to honeysuckle, with pinnate leaves, small flowers (with a wheel-shaped corolla) and three-seeded fruits. — **eld'erberry** the acidulous purple-black drupaceous fruit of the elder; **eld'er-gun** a popgun made from a length of elder by removing the pith; **eld'erberry wine** a wine made from elderberries; **elder-flower water** a distilled water made from the flowers. [OE *ellærn*]

elder[2] *eld'ər*, *adj* older; having lived a longer time; prior in origin. — *n* an older person; an ancestor; *esp* in primitive communities, a person advanced to the office of adviser or administrator on account of age; one of a class of office-bearers in the Presbyterian Church (*presbyter* of the New Testament). — *n* **eld'erliness**. — *adj* **eld'erly** rather old; bordering on old age. — *n* (with *the*) elderly people. — *n* **eld'ership** the state of being older; the office of an elder. — *adj* **eld'est** oldest. — **Elder Brethren** the governing members of Trinity House; **elder** or **eldest hand** in card-playing, the player on the dealer's left, who leads; **elders' hours** respectable hours, usually meaning not after 10pm; **elder statesman** a retired statesman consulted by the government; any administrator of age and experience; (in *pl*, with *caps*) a reactionary group of retired statesmen who exercised a power behind the throne in Japan. [OE *eldra* (W Sax *ieldra*, *yldra*) compar, and *eldesta* (W Sax *ieldesta*) superl of *ald* (W Sax *eald*) old]

eldin *el'din* or **elding** *el'ding* (*Northern*), also (*Scot*) **eilding** *ēl'ding*, *n* fuel. [ON *elding*, from *eldr* fire]

ELDO *abbrev*: European Launcher Development Organization (now **ESA**).

El Dorado or **Eldorado** *el-də-rä'dō*, the golden land or city imagined by the Spanish conquerors of America; any place where wealth is easily to be acquired. [Sp *el* the, and *dorado*, pa p of *dorar* to gild, from 'the gilded man', the king of the legendary city of Manoa who smeared himself with gold-dust; afterwards transferred to the city itself]

eldritch *el'(d)rich*, (*Scot*) *adj* weird; uncanny. [Perh connected with **elf**]

Eleatic *el-i-at'ik*, *adj* belonging to *Elea*, a Greek city of Lower Italy, or to the school of philosophers connected with it, including Xenophanes, Parmenides and Zeno. — *n* a philosopher belonging to this school.

elec. or **elect.** *abbrev*: electric; electricity.

elecampane *el-i-kam-pān'*, *n* a composite plant (*Inula helenium*) formerly much cultivated for its medicinal root; a sweet flavoured with an extract from the root. [L *enula* or *inula campāna*, field or Campanian]

elect *i-lekt'*, *vt* to choose in preference to other options; to select for any office or purpose; to select by vote. — *adj* chosen; taken by preference from among others; chosen for an office but not yet in it (almost always after the noun); in Christian doctrine, chosen by God for salvation (*theol*). — *n* (with *the*) those chosen or set apart, *esp* by God for salvation. — *n* **electabil'ity**. — *adj* **elect'able**. — *n* **elec'tion** (*-shən*) the act of electing or choosing; the public choice of a person for office, *usu* by the votes of a constituent body; free will; the exercise of God's sovereign will in the predetermination of certain persons to salvation (*theol*); those elected in this way (*Bible*). — *vi* **electioneer'** to labour to secure the election of a candidate. — *n* **electioneer'er**. — *n* and *adj* **electioneer'ing**. — *adj* **elect'ive** relating to, concerning, dependent on, or exerting the power of choice; optional. — *n* an optional subject of study (*US*); an elective placement with a hospital, or to study abroad, etc (*med*). — *adv* **elect'ively**. — *n* **electiv'ity** (*ē-* or *e-*). — *n* **elect'or** a person who elects; a person who has a vote at an election; in US a member of the **electoral college**; (*usu* with *cap*) the title formerly belonging to those princes and archbishops of the German empire who had the right to elect the Emperor: — *fem* **elect'ress** or **elect'oress**. — *adj* **elect'oral** or **electō'rial** (*ē-* or *e-*) relating to elections or to electors; consisting of electors. — *n* **elect'orate** the dignity or the territory of an elector; the body of electors. — *n* **elect'orship**. — **electoral college** in US, the body of people who elect the President and Vice-President, themselves elected by popular vote; any body of electors with a similar function; **electoral vote** (*US*) the vote of the members of the electoral college. [L *ēligere*, *ēlectum*, from *ē* from, and *legere* to choose]

Electra complex *i-lek'trə kom'pleks*, (*psychol*) *n* the attachment of a daughter to her father, with hostility to her mother. [From the Greek story of *Electra*, who helped to avenge her mother's murder of her father]

electret *i-lek'trit*, (*elec*) *n* a permanently polarized (piece of) dielectric material. [*Electr*icity and magn*et*]

electric *i-lek'trik*, *adj* relating to electricity; charged with or capable of being charged with electricity; producing or produced by, conveying, operated by or making use of electricity; thrilling (*fig*); full of tension and expectation, as though charged with electricity; producing a sudden startling effect. — *n* a non-conductor of electricity, such as amber, glass, etc, capable of being electrified by friction. — *adj* **elec'trical**. — *n pl* (*finance*) shares in electricity companies. — *adv* **elec'trically**. — *n* **electrician** (*el-ik-trish'ən*) someone who studies or is trained in the science of electricity; someone who makes, instals or repairs electrical apparatus. — *n* **electricity** (*el-ik-tris'i-ti*) the magnetic power of amber and other substances when rubbed; an imaginary fluid supposed to explain this and related phenomena; the manifestation of a form of energy associated with separation or movement of charged particles, such as electrons and protons; the science that deals with this; an electric charge or current; a feeling of excitement. — *n* **electrīzā'tion** or **-s-**. — *vt* **elec'trize** or **-ise** to electrify. — **electrical engineer** a specialist in the practical applications of electricity as a branch of engineering; **electrical engineering**; **electric arc** a luminous space between electrodes when a current passes across; **electric battery** a group of cells connected in series or in parallel for generating an electric current by chemical action; **electric blanket** a blanket incorporating an electric element, used for warming a bed; **electric blue** a vividly bright blue colour; **electric calamine** the mineral hemimorphite, which becomes positively electrified at one end and negatively at the other when its temperature rises, and *vice versa* as it cools; **electric chair** in the US, the seat on which a condemned criminal is put to death by electrocution; (with *the*) execution by electrocution in this manner; **electric eel** a cyprinoid fish, *Electrophorus electricus*, of S America, shaped like an eel and able to give powerful electric shocks by means of an electric organ in its long tail; **electric eye** a photo-electric cell; a miniature cathode ray tube; **electric fence** an electrically charged wire fence; **electric field** a region in which attracting or repelling forces are exerted on any electric charge present; **electric fire**, **heater** or **radiator** an apparatus using an electric current, for heating a room; **electric furnace** an apparatus for getting very high temperatures by means of an electric current; **electric guitar** a guitar with an electrical amplifying device; **electric hare** a dummy animal worked by electricity for racing greyhounds to chase; **electric motor** any device for converting electrical energy into mechanical energy; **electric organ** an organ in which the sound is produced by electrical devices instead of wind (*music*); in certain fishes, a structure that generates, stores and discharges electricity (*zool*); **electric piano** one in which the sounds are produced electrically; **electric ray** the fish Torpedo; **electric seal** dyed rabbit or hare skin; **electric storm** a violent disturbance in the electric condition of the atmosphere; **electric torch** a portable electric light. [L *ēlectrum*, from Gr *ēlektron* amber, in which electricity was first observed]

electrify *i-lek'tri-fī*, *vt* to introduce electricity into, to charge with electricity; to adapt to electricity as the motive power; to excite suddenly; to astonish: — *pr p* **elec'trifying**; *pa t* and *pa p* **elec'trified**. — *adj* **elec'trifiable**. — *n* **electrificā'tion**. [L *electrum* and *facere* to make]

electro- *i-lek'trō-* or *el-ik-tro'*, *combining form* denoting electric or electrolytic. — *n* **elec'tro** (*colloq*) short for **electroplate** and **electrotype**: — *pl* **elec'tros**. — *n sing* **electroacous'tics** the technology of converting acoustic energy into electrical energy and vice versa. — *adj* **electroacous'tic**. — *n* **electroanal'ysis** separation by electrolysis. — *adj* **electroanalyt'ical**. — *n* **electrobiol'ogist**. — *n* **electrobiol'ogy** the science of the electrical phenomena in living organisms; an old name for hypnotism. — *n* **electrocar'diogram** a photographic record of the electrical variations that occur during contraction of the muscle of the heart. — *n* **electrocar'diograph** a galvanometer used for making such records. — *n* **electrocardiog'raphy** the study of electric currents produced during muscular activity of the heart. — *n* **electrocement'** cement made in an electric furnace by adding lime to molten slag. — *adj* **electrochem'ic** or **electrochem'ical**. — *n* **electrochem'ist**. — *n* **electrochem'istry** the study of the relation between electricity and chemical change. — *adj* **electroconvuls'ive**. — **electroconvulsive therapy** shock therapy (*abbrev* **ECT**). — *n* **elec'troculture** the cultivation of plants under the stimulus of electricity. — *vt* **elec'trocute** to inflict a death penalty by means of electrocution; to kill by electricity. — *n* **electrocū'tion**. — *n* **elec'trōde** (Gr *hodos* way) a conductor by which a current of electricity enters or leaves an electrolytic cell, gas discharge tube or thermionic valve. — *n* **electrodeposi'tion** deposition of a layer of metal by electrolysis. — *n sing* **electrodynam'ics** the study of electricity in motion, or of the interaction of currents and currents, or currents and magnets. — *n* **electrodynamom'eter** an instrument for measuring electric currents by the attraction or repulsion between current-bearing coils. — *n* **electroenceph'alogram** (*-sef'* or *-kef'*) a record made by an **electroenceph'alograph**, an instrument recording small electrical impulses produced by the brain. — *n* **electroencephalog'raphy**. — *n* **electroextrac'tion** or **electrowinn'ing** the recovery of a metal from its salts by passing an electric current through a solution. — *n* **elec'troforming** (*electronics*) electrodeposition of copper on stainless steel formers to obtain waveguide components. — *n* **elec'trogen** a molecule which emits electrons when it is illuminated. — *n* **electrogen'esis** the production of electricity, *esp* in living cells, etc. — *adj* **electrogen'ic** producing electricity; of or capable of electrogenesis. — *n* **electrogild'ing** electroplating with gold. — *n* **elec'trograph** a recording electrometer. — *n* **electrog'raphy**. — **electrohydraulic forming** shaping a piece of metal with a die by means of a shock wave in water set up by discharge of energy between immersed electrodes. — *n sing* **electrokinet'ics** the branch of science that deals with the distribution of electric currents. — *n* **electrolier** (*-lēr'*) an electric-light fixture resembling a chandelier. — *n* **electrol'ogy** the science of electricity; electrotherapy. — *n* **electroluminesc'ence** luminescence produced by the application of an electric field to a dielectric phosphor. — **electrolyse**, etc see separate entry. — *n* **electromag'net** a piece of soft iron, etc, made magnetic by a current of electricity passing through a coil of wire wound round it. — *adj* **electromagnet'ic** of or relating to an electromagnet or electromagnetism. — **electromagnetic interaction** (*phys*) an interaction between charged elementary particles intermediate in strength between *strong* and *weak interactions*, completed in about 10^{-18}s. — **electromagnetic theory** Clerk Maxwell's theory explaining light in terms of electromagnetic waves. — **electromagnetic unit** any unit, such as the abampere or abvolt, in a centimetre-gram-second system of units based on the magnetic forces exerted by electric currents. — **electromagnetic wave** a travelling disturbance in space produced by the acceleration of an electric charge, comprising an electric field and a magnetic field at right angles to each other, both moving at the same velocity in a direction normal to the plane of the two fields. — *n* **electromag'netism** a branch of science dealing with the relation between, and properties of, electric and magnetic force. — *adj* **electromechan'ical** of or relating to any mechanical process or device involving the use of electricity; of or relating to electromechanics. — *adv* **electromechan'ically**. — *n sing* **electromechan'ics** the mechanics of the electric circuit. — *n* **elec'tromer** a substance showing electromerism. — *adj* **electromer'ic**. — *n* **electrom'erism** (*chem*) a form of tautomerism caused by a redistribution of electrons among the atoms of a molecule or group. — *adj* **electrometallur'gical**. — *n* **electromet'allurgist** (or *-al'*). — *n* **electromet'allurgy** (or *-al'*) the industrial working of metals by means of electricity. — *n* **electrom'eter** an instrument for measuring difference of electric potential. — *adj* **electromet'ric** or **electromet'rical**. — *adv* **electromet'rically**. — *n* **electrom'etry** the science of electrical measurements. — *adj* **electromō'tive** of or relating to the motion of electricity or the laws governing it. — **electromotive force** difference of potential or the force generated by this, being the force of an electric current (also called **electromō'tance**). — *n* **electromō'tor** an apparatus for applying electricity as a motive power. — *n* **electromy'ograph** an instrument for recording voltages produced by muscular contraction. — *n* **electromyog'raphy** the study of electric currents set up in muscles by their functioning. — *adj* **electroneg'ative** carrying a negative charge; tending to form negative ions. — *n* **electronegativ'ity** an electronegative state; the power of eg an atom to attract electrons. — *adj* **electro-op'tic** or **electro-op'tical**. — **electro-optical effect** see **Kerr effects**. — *n sing* **electro-op'tics** the study of the effects that an electric field has on light crossing it. — *n* **electro-osmo'sis** movement of liquid under an applied electric field through a fine tube or membrane. — *n* **elec'trophile** an electrophilic substance. — *adj* **electrophil'ic** having or involving an affinity for electrons (ie for negative charge), electron-seeking. — *n* **electrophorē'sis** (Gr *phoreein* to bear) migration of suspended particles such as protein macromolecules under the influence of an electric field. — *adj* **electrophoretic** (*-et'ik*) of or relating to electrophoresis. — *n* **electroph'orus** an instrument for obtaining static electricity by means of induction. — *n* **electrophotog'raphy** photography by means of electric rather than chemical processes, as in xerography. — *adj* **electrophotograph'ic**. — *adj* **electrophysiolog'ical**. — *n* **electrophysiol'ogist**. — *n* **electrophysiol'ogy** the study of electric phenomena of living organisms. — *vt* **elec'troplate** to plate or cover, *esp* with silver, by electrolysis. — *n* electroplated ware. — *n* **elec'troplater**. — *n* **elec'troplating**. — *adj* **electropō'lar** having, as an electrical conductor, one end or surface positive and the other negative. — *adj* **electropos'itive** carrying a positive charge; tending to form positive ions. — *n* **elec'troscope** an instrument for detecting the presence of electricity in a body and the nature of it. — *adj* **electroscop'ic**. — *n* **elec'troshock** an electric shock. — *n* **elec'trosonde** a sonde for measuring atmospheric electricity. — *adj* **electrostat'ic** of or relating to electricity at rest. — **electrostatic unit** any unit, such as the statampere and statvolt, in a centimetre-gram-second system of units based on the forces of repulsion existing between static electric charges. — *adv* **electrostat'ically**. — *n sing* **electrostat'ics** the branch of science concerned with electricity at rest. — *n sing* **electrotech'nics** (also **electrotechnol'ogy**) electric technology. — *n sing* **electrotherapeu'tics** (also **electrother'apy**) treatment of disease by electricity. — *adj* **electrotherm'al** or **electrotherm'ic** of or relating to electricity and heat, or heat obtained electrically. — *n sing* **electrotherm'ics**. — *n* **electrotherm'y**. — *n* **elec'trotint** a printing block produced by drawing with varnish on a metal plate, and depositing metal electrically on the parts not covered. — *adj* **electroton'ic**. — *n* **electrot'onus** the state of a nerve subjected to a steady discharge of electricity. — *n* **elec'trotype** a printing plate made by electrolytically coating a mould with copper; a facsimile of a coin made by this process. — Also *adj*. — *n* **elec'trotyper** a person who makes electrotypes. — *adj* **electrotȳp'ic**. — *n* **elec'trotypist**. — *n* **elec'trotȳpy**. — *n* **elec'trovalency** union within a chemical compound achieved by transfer of electrons, the resulting ions being held together by electrostatic attraction (cf *covalency*). — *adj* **elec'trovalent**. — *n* **electrowinning** see **electroextraction**. [Gr *ēlektro*, combining form of *ēlektron* (see **electron**)]

electrolyse or **electrolyze** *il-ek'trə-līz*, *vt* to break down by electrolysis; to subject to electrolysis. — *n* **electrolysis** (*-trol'i-sis*) decomposition by electric current, with migration of ions shown by changes at the electrodes; the removal of hair by applying an electrically charged needle to the follicle. — *n* **elec'trolyte** (*-līt*) a substance able to be broken down by electrolysis. — *adj* **electrolytic** (*-lit'ik*). — *adv* **electrolyt'ically**. [**electro-** and Gr *lysis* loosing]

electron *i-lek'tron*, *n* a natural alloy of gold and silver used in ancient times (also Latinized as **elec'trum**); a minute particle charged with electricity, or a unit charge having inertia, normally forming part of an atom but capable of isolation as in cathode rays. — **electron camera** any device that converts an optical image into a corresponding electric current directly by electronic means; **electron capture** the capture of an electron by the nucleus of its own atom, the change of a proton into a neutron decreasing by one the atomic number of the atom; **electron gun** the assembly of electrodes in a cathode ray tube which produces the electron beam; **electron micrograph** a photograph obtained by substituting a photographic plate for the fluorescent viewing screen of an electron microscope; **electron microscope** a microscope that makes use of a beam of electrons instead of light; **electron optics** the study of the effects of electric and magnetic fields on the direction of beams of electrons; **electron pair** a duplet; an electron and a positron; **electron probe** an X-ray device that bombards the specimen under examination with a very narrow beam of electrons, allowing non-destructive analysis; **electron ring accelerator** an accelerator in which an intense ring of circulating electrons, being accelerated, can carry along and accelerate protons or stripped ions; **electron shell** a group of electrons surrounding a nucleus of an atom and having adjacent energy levels; **electron telescope** an optical instrument with electronic image converter used with a normal telescope; **electron tube** an electronic device in which the electron conduction is in a vacuum or gas inside a gas-tight enclosure, eg a thermionic valve; **elec'tron-volt** a unit of energy equal to that acquired by an electron when accelerated by a potential of one volt. [Gr *ēlektron* amber]

electronegative, **electronegativity**. See **electro-**.

electronic *el-*, *il-* or *ēl-ik-tron'ik*, *adj* of or relating to electronics or electrons; worked or produced by devices made according to the principles of electronics; concerned with or working with such devices. — *adv* **electron'ically**. — *n sing* **electron'ics** the science and technology of the conduction of electricity in a vacuum, a gas or a semiconductor; the devices, etc based on this. — **electronic brain** any electronic computer; **electronic countermeasures** (*military*) the use of electronic systems and reflectors to impair the effectiveness of enemy guidance, surveillance or navigational equipment; **electronic flash** an extremely intense and brief flash for high-speed photography produced by passing an electric charge through a gas-filled tube; the apparatus for producing it; **electronic mail** the sending and receiving of messages by any electronic means; **electronic mailbox** a section of a central computer's memory reserved for a particular individual, into which messages can be directed; **electronic music** music made by arranging electronically produced sounds either directly from a keyboard, etc, or previously generated in the laboratory and recorded on tape (cf **musique concrète**); **electronic organ** (*music*) an organ in which the sound is produced electronically; **electronic piano** a kind of synthesizer; **electronic tagging** a monitoring system allowing the supervision of an offender outside prison by means of an electronic tag (eg a bracelet or anklet fitted with a transmitter) which maintains regular signals to a central computer. — **electronic funds transfer** (**system**) a method whereby financial credits and debits are transferred electronically (between banks and shops, etc) by computer network (**at point of sale** signifying such a system in operation at a shop checkout, etc, enabling payment by debit or credit card rather than by cash or cheque); **electronic point of sale** (at shop checkouts) a computerized till system in which a cash till with a bar-code reader is directly linked to a stock control system. [Ety as for **electron**]

electrophoresis ... to ... **electrowinning**. See **electro-**.

electrum. See **electron**.

electuary *i-lek'tū-ər-i*, *n* a medicine mixed with honey or syrup. [LL *ēlectuārium*, perh from Gr *ekleikton* from *ekleichein* to lick up]

eleemosynary *el-ē-moz'*, *el-i-ē-moz'i-nər-i*, or *-mos'*, *adj* relating to charity or almsgiving; dependent on charity; of the nature of alms. [Gr *eleēmosynē* alms, from *eleos* pity; see **alms**]

elegant *el'i-gənt*, *adj* pleasing to good or fastidious taste; very careful or ornate in dress; graceful in form and movement; refined and luxurious; (of style) polished; (of apparatus or work in science or mathematics) simple and effective; excellent (*slang*). — *n* **el'egance** or **el'egancy** the state or quality of being elegant; the finest propriety of manners (*archaic*); refinement; an exemplification of elegance. — *adv* **el'egantly**. [Fr, from L *ēlegāns*, *-antis*, from *ē* from, and root of *legere* to choose]

elegit *i-lē'jit* or *ā-lā'git*, (*law*) *n* a writ of execution, abolished in England in 1956, whereby a debtor's property and lands could be delivered to the plaintiff until the debt was satisfied by profits, rents, etc. [L, he has chosen, from *eligere* to chose]

elegy *el'i-ji*, *n* a song of mourning; a funeral-song (*archaic*); a poem of serious, pensive, or reflective mood; a poem written in elegiac metre. — *adj* **elegī'ac** belonging to elegy; mournful; used in elegies, *esp* applied to classical verse in couplets of hexameter and pentameter lines (**elegiac couplets**), or two stanzas of four iambic pentameters rhyming *abab* (**elegiac stanzas**). — *n* elegiac verse. — *adj* **elegī'acal**. — *adv* **elegi'acally**. — *n* **elegiast** (*e-lē'ji-ast*; *Goldsmith*) or **el'egist** a writer of elegies. — *vi* **el'egize** or **-ise** to write elegiacally. — *vt* to write an elegy on. [L *elegīa*, from Gr *elegeiā* from *elegos* a lament]

element *el'ə-mənt*, *n* a first principle; one of the essential parts of anything; an ingredient; the proper medium, habitat or sphere of any thing or being; any one of the four substances, fire, air, earth and water, supposed by the ancients to be the foundation of everything (in China a fifth, wood, was included); (in *pl*) the rudiments of learning; (*usu* in *pl*) the bread and wine used in the Eucharist; a substance that cannot be resolved by chemical means into simpler substances (*chem*); a member or unit of a structure; a resistance wire in an electric heater; an electrode; a determining fact or condition in a problem; the sky (*archaic*); a celestial sphere; (in *pl*) the weather or the powers of nature. — *adj* **elemental** (*-ment'l*) of or concerned with the elements; belonging to, produced by or inhabiting the elements. — *n* an elemental spirit; a nature spirit; a disembodied spirit. — *n* **element'alism** the worship of elemental spirits; the theory which resolves the divinities of antiquity into the elemental powers. — *adv* **element'ally**. — *adj* **element'ary** of a single element; primary or fundamental; rudimentary; simple; uncompounded; of or relating to the elements; treating of first principles. — **elemental spirits** beings in medieval belief who presided over the four elements, living in and ruling them; **elementary particle** any of a number of particles, eg electron, proton, neutron, neutrino, kaon or pion, so-called because supposed indivisible; **elementary school** a school in which the first years of formal education are given, in UK *obs* since 1944, but still current in NAm. — **elements of an orbit** (*math*) the data mathematically necessary to determine it; **in one's element** in the surroundings most natural or pleasing to one. [L *elementum*, pl *elementa*, first principle(s)]

elemi *el'im-i*, *n* a fragrant resinous substance obtained from various tropical trees, *esp* a species of Canarium, used *esp* in varnishes and inks. [Perh Ar]

elenchus *i-lengk'əs*, (*logic*) *n* refutation; a sophism: — *pl* **elench'ī**. — *n* (*obs*) **elench** (*i-lengk'*). — *adj* **elenc'tic** relating to argument, cross-examining or refuting. [L, from Gr *elenchos*, from *elenchein* to refute]

elephant *el'i-fənt*, *n* a Proboscidean (*Elephas*), the largest living land mammal, having a very thick skin, a trunk, and ivory tusks, found in two surviving species, the **African elephant** having larger ears and a flatter head than the **Indian** or **Asian elephant**, and in several extinct species; a size of paper before metrication. — *n* **elephantī'asis** (Gr *elephantiāsis*) a disease chiefly of tropical climates, consisting of an overgrowth of the skin and connective tissue usually of the legs and scrotum. — *adj* **elephant'ine** of or relating to an elephant; like an elephant; very large or ungainly; (of a memory) capacious and reliable. — *adj* **elephant'oid** elephant-like. — **elephant cord** thick, wide-ribbed corduroy; **elephant folio** a folio of the largest size; **elephant grass** a kind of reed-mace, *Typha elephantum*; **elephant gun** a large-calibre rifle designed for killing elephants or other large animals; **elephant seal** the largest of the seals, the male measuring about 6m (20 feet) in length; **el'ephant's-ears** or **-ear** any of various begonias or varieties of ornamental arum with heart-shaped leaves; applied also to other large-leaved plants such as bergenias and species of Colocasia; **el'ephant's-foot** Hottentot bread, a plant (*Testudinaria elephantipes*) of the yam family, whose root-stock resembles an elephant's foot, eaten by the Hottentots; a tropical composite plant, Elephantopus, from the shape of its radical leaves; **elephant shrew** any member of the African family Macroscelidae, long-nosed, long-legged Insectivora, agile jumpers over loose sand. — **pink elephants** hallucinations caused by over-indulgence in alcoholic drink; **white elephant** anything that gives more trouble than it is worth (a (so-called) white elephant being an honourable but onerous gift from the kings of Siam to a courtier they wished to ruin); an unwanted possession, often given away to a jumble sale; something which proves to be useless. [Remodelled after L from ME *olifaunt*, from OFr *olifant*, or poss OE *olfend* camel, from L *elephantus*, *elephās*, from Gr *elephās*, *-antos*]

Eleusinian *el-ū-sin'i-ən*, *adj* relating to the town of *Eleusis* in Attica in ancient Greece. — **eleusinian mysteries** the religious festivities of Demeter celebrated there.

eleutherian *el-ū-thē'ri-ən*, *adj* freedom-giving. — *n* **eleu'therarch** (*-thər-ärk*; Gr *archos* chief; *Shelley*) the chief of an invented secret society of **eleu'therī**. — *n* **eleutherococ'cus** a creeping shrub found in Siberia, from which a drug is prepared that apparently increases stamina and concentration. — *adj* **eleutherodac'tyl** (Gr *daktylos* toe) (of birds) having the hind-toe free. — *n* **eleutheroma'nia** a manic desire for freedom. — *n* **eleutheropho'bia** fear of freedom. — *n* and *adj* **eleutheropho'bic**. [Gr *eleutheros* free]

elevate *el'i-vāt*, *vt* to raise to a higher position; to raise in mind and feelings; to exhilarate. — *adj* **el'evated** or (*archaic* or *poetic*) **el'evate** raised; lofty; exhilarated. — *n* **elevā'tion** the act of elevating or raising, or the state of being elevated or raised; exaltation; an elevated place; a rising ground; height; the external flat side or face of a building, or a mathematically accurate drawing of it (*archit*); angular height above the horizon; an angle made by a line with the plane of the horizon; a leap with apparent suspension in the air (*ballet*); in the Eucharist, the lifting up (of the Host) in view of the people. — *n* **el'evātor** a person or thing that lifts up; a lift or machine for raising grain, etc, to a higher floor or level; a lift (*US*); a storehouse for grain; a muscle raising a part of the body; a movable control surface or surfaces at the tail of an aeroplane by which it is made to climb or dive. — *adj* **el'evātory** able or tending to raise. — *n* **elevon** (*el'ə-vən*) a wing flap on delta-wing or tailless aircraft acting both as an *elev*ator and as an ailer*on*. — **elevated railroad** (*US*) a raised railway over a roadway, *colloq* **el** or **L**). [L *ēlevāre*, *-ātum*, from *ē* from, and *levāre* to raise, from *levis* light; see **light**[2]]

eleven *i-lev'n*, *n* the cardinal number next above ten; a team of eleven (in cricket, association football, etc); the eleventh hour after noon or midnight. — *adj* of the number eleven. — *n* (*usu n pl*, sometimes *n sing*) **elev'enses** or **elev'ens** (*colloq*) an eleven o'clock snack; morning coffee or other refreshment. — *adj* **elev'enth** next after the tenth; equal to one of eleven equal parts. — *n* an eleventh part; an octave and a fourth (*music*). — *adv* **elev'enthly**. — **eleven and twenty long** (*Shakesp*) exactly right (the score aimed at in the game of one-and-thirty); **eleventh hour** the very last moment, referring to Matt 20.6, 9 (*adj* **elev'enth-hour**); **eleven-plus** or **eleven-plus examination** formerly in England and Wales, a school examination taken by pupils about the age of eleven to decide to which type of secondary education (academic, non-academic or technical) they were to proceed; this or any similar system of selection, still operated by a few local education authorities in the UK. [OE *en(d)le(o)fan*; cf Gothic *ainlif*; perh (ten and) *one left*, from the root of L *linquere*, Gr *leipein* to leave]

elevon. See **elevate**.

ELF *abbrev*: extremely (or extra) low frequency.

elf *elf*, *n* in European folklore, a supernatural being, generally of human form but diminutive size, sometimes more malignant than a fairy; a fairy; a dwarf; a mischievous or fairylike being, *esp* a child: — *pl* **elves** (*elvz*). — *vt* (*Shakesp*) to entangle (hair). — *n* **elf'hood**. — *adj* **elf'in** small, with delicate frame; small, mischievous and charming; pertaining to a good-natured elf. — *n* a little elf; a child. — *adj* **elf'ish**, **elv'an** or **elv'ish** elf-like or mischievous; tricky; distraught; self-willed. — **elf'-arrow** or **elf'-bolt** an elf-shot; **elf'-child** a changeling, or a child supposed to have been left by elves in the place of one stolen by them; **elf'land** the land of the elves or fairies; **elf'locks** (*Shakesp*) locks of hair tangled together, supposedly by elves. — *vt* **elf'-shoot** to shoot with an elf-arrow, bewitch. — **elf'-shot** a prehistoric flint or stone arrow-head, supposed to be used by elves; sickness attributed to it. — *adj* shot with an elf-arrow; bewitched. [OE *ælf*; cf ON *ālfr* and Swed *elf*]

eliad. See **œillade**.

Elian *ē'li-ən*, *adj* of or like the work of Charles Lamb, who wrote under the name of *Elia*. — *n* a devotee or imitator of Lamb.

elicit *i-*, *ē-* or *e-lis'it*, *vt* to draw forth; to evoke. — *n* **elicitā'tion**. — *n* **elic'itor**. [L *ēlicere*, *ēlicitum*]

elide *ē-* or *i-līd'*, *vt* to rebut (*archaic*); to cut off (*esp* a syllable in verse); to suppress or abridge. — *n* **elision** (*i-lizh'ən*) the suppression of a vowel or syllable; an omission. [L *ēlīdere*, *ēlīsum*, from *ē* from, and *laedere* to strike]

Elien. *abbrev*: *Eliensis* (*L*) of (the diocese of) Ely.

eligible *el'i-ji-bl*, *adj* fit or worthy to be chosen; legally qualified for election or appointment; desirable. — *n* (*colloq*) an eligible person or thing. — *n* **eligibil'ity**. — *adv* **el'igibly**. [Fr, from L *ēligere*; see **elect**]

eliminate *i-*, *ē-* or *e-lim'in-āt*, *vt* to remove, cancel or get rid of; to expel (waste matter); to thrust out (*archaic*). — *adj* **elim'inable**. — *adj* **elim'inant** (*med*) causing elimination of waste or abnormal matter. — *n* an eliminating agent. — *n* **eliminā'tion**. — *adj* **elim'inative**. — *n* **elim'inātor** one who or that which eliminates; *esp* a device for substituting an electric main for a battery in a wireless receiving set. — *adj* **elim'inatory**. [L *ēlimināre*, *-ātum*, from *ē* from, and *līmen*, *-inis* a threshold]

ELINT *el'int*, *abbrev*: *El*ectronic *Int*elligence, the branch of military intelligence concerned with monitoring and recording electronic output (as opposed to intercepting communications; cf **COMINT**).

elision. See **elide**.

élite or **elite** *i-*, *e-* or *ā-lēt'*, *n* a chosen or select part or group, the pick or flower of anything (in this sense, sometimes used as *pl*); a size of typewriter type allowing twelve letters to the inch. — Also *adj*. — *n* **élit'ism** or **elit'ism** (belief in) government by an élite; consciousness of belonging to an élite; the favouring or creation of an élite. — *adj* **élit'ist** or **elit'ist** favouring, creating, etc an élite. — Also *n*. [Fr *élite*, from L *ēlecta* (*pars* a part, understood); see **elect**]

elixir *i-*, *ē-* or *e-liks'ər*, *n* a liquor once supposed to have the power of indefinitely prolonging life (**elixir of life**) or of transmuting metals; the quintessence of anything; a substance which invigorates; a clear, syrupy, alcoholic or flavoured solution masking the taste of an unpalatable medicine; a panacea; a nostrum; a strong tincture; a compound tincture. [LL, from Ar *al-iksīr* the philosopher's stone, from *al-* the, and *iksīr*, prob from Late Gr *xērion* a desiccative powder for wounds, from Gr *xēros* dry]

Elizabethan *i-* or *e-liz-ə-bē'thən*, *adj* pertaining to a Queen *Elizabeth* or her reign, *esp* to the first Queen Elizabeth (1533–1603) or her reign (1558–1603), applied to dress, manners, literature, etc. — *n* a person, *esp* poet or dramatist, of that age. — *n* **Elizabēth'anism**. — **Elizabethan architecture** the mixed style that sprang up on the decline of Gothic, marked by Tudor bow-windows and turrets decorated with classic cornices and pilasters, long galleries, enormous square windows, large apartments, plaster ceilings divided into compartments, etc.

elk *elk*, *n* a deer of N Europe and Asia, identical or closely related to the moose of N America, the largest of all living deer; the wapiti (*NAm*). — **elkhorn fern** a fern of the genus *Platycerium*, tropical epiphytic ferns with a large leaf like an elk's horn; **elk'hound** a large strong Norwegian spitz breed of dog with a thick coat and curled tail. — **Irish elk** a giant deer now extinct, known from the remains found in the Pleistocene, *esp* in Ireland. [Poss OE *elh* (W Sax *eolh*)]

ell[1] *el*, *n* a varying measure of length originally taken from the arm; a cloth measure equal to $1\frac{1}{4}$yd (*obs*). — **ell'wand** a measuring rod. — **give him an inch and he'll take an ell** a concession will encourage the taking of liberties. [OE *eln*; Du *el*, Ger *Elle*, L *ulna*, Gr *ōlenē* elbow]

ell[2] *el*. Same as **el**[2].

ellagic *e-laj'ik*, *adj* pertaining to gall-nuts, applied to an acid, $C_{14}H_6O_8$. [Fr *galle* gall, spelt backwards]

ellipse *i-* or *e-lips'*, (*geom*) *n* a figure produced by the section of one branch of a right circular cone by a plane passing obliquely and failing to meet the other branch. — *n* **ellip'sis** a figure of syntax by which a word or words are left out and merely implied (*gram*); mark(s) indicating ellipsis (*printing*): — *pl* **ellip'sēs**. — *n* **ellip'sograph** an instrument for describing ellipses. — *n* **ellip'soid** (*geom*) a surface of which every plane section is an ellipse or a circle; a solid object of this shape. — *adj* **ellipsoi'dal**. — *adj* **ellip'tic** or **ellip'tical** of or relating to an ellipse; oval; having a part understood; concise or comprehensive; obscure or dubious; (loosely) circumlocutory; rather narrow, slightly acute at each end and broadest in the middle (*bot*); of or relating to ellipsis. — *adv* **ellip'tically**. — *n* **ellipticity** (*el-ip-tis'i-ti*) deviation from the form of a circle or sphere; the difference between the equatorial and polar diameters of the earth. — **elliptic geometry** or **space** Riemannian geometry or space. [L *ellipsis*, from Gr *elleipsis* from *elleipein* to fall short, from *en* in, and *leipein* to leave]

ellops *el'ops*, (*obs*) *n* a kind of snake (*Milton*); a kind of sturgeon (also **el'ops**); a sea-serpent (*Goldsmith*). [Gr *ellops*, also *elops*, *elaps* perh mute, perh scaly, also an unknown fish and an unknown snake; cf **Elaps**, **elops**]

elm *elm*, *n* a tree (genus *Ulmus*) with serrated leaves unequal at the base and small flowers in clusters appearing before the leaves; its timber (also called **elm'wood**). — *adj* of elm. — *adj* **elm'en** (*obs*) made of elm. — *adj* **elm'y** full of or covered with elms. [OE *elm*; Ger *Ulme*, L *ulmus*]

El Niño *el nē'nyō*, *n* a warm current affecting the Peruvian coast every ten or so years. [Sp, the child, short for *El Niño de Navidad* the Christ Child, from the arrival of the current at Christmas]

Elo *el'o*, *adj* denoting a scale on which the ability of chess-players is assessed, devised by Arpad *Elo*, 20c US professor of physics. — **Elo ratings**; **Elo scale**.

elocution *el-ə-kū'shən*, *n* the art of effective speaking, *esp* public speaking, in terms of enunciation and delivery; eloquence (*obs*). — *vi* **el'ocute** (often *facetious*) to declaim. — *adj* **elocū'tionary**. — *adj* **eloc'ūtory** (*rare*). — *n* **elocū'tionist** a person trained or expert in or practising elocution; a teacher of elocution; a reciter. [L *ēlocūtiō*, *-ōnis*, from *ēloquī*, *-cūtus*, from *ē* from, and *loquī* to speak]

Elodea *e-lō'di-ə*, (*bot*) *n* an American genus of Hydrocharitaceae, to which the Canadian waterweed belongs. — Also called **Helodea**, **Anacharis** and **Phyllotria**. [Gr *helōdēs* marshy or marsh-dwelling, from *helos* marsh, and *eidos* form]

éloge *ā-lōzh'*, **elogium** *ē-lō'ji-əm*, (*obs*) or **elogy** *el'ə-ji*, (*obs*) *n* a funeral oration; a panegyric. — *n* **el'ogist** someone who delivers an éloge. [Fr *éloge* and its source L *ēlogium* a short statement or an inscription on a tomb, perh confused with **eulogy**]

Elohim *e-lō'him*, *n* a Hebrew name for God. — *n* **Elō'hist** the writer or writers of the passages of the Old Testament in which the Hebrew name Elohim (for God) is used instead of Yahweh (Jehovah). — *adj* **Elōhist'ic** relating to these passages. [Heb pl of *Eloah*, explained by Delitzsch as a plural of intensity]

eloin or **eloign** *e-loin'*, (*archaic*) *vt* to convey to a distance; to separate and remove. — *n* **eloin'er** or **eloign'er**. — *n* **eloin'ment** or **eloign'ment**. [OFr *esloignier* (Fr *éloigner*), from LL *ēlongāre*; see **elongate**]

elongate *ē'long-gāt* or *i-long'gāt*, *vt* to make longer; to extend. — *vi* to grow longer. — *adj* **elongate** or **elongated**. — *n* **elongā'tion** the act of lengthening out; distance (*obs*); the angular distance of a moon or planet from the sun. [LL *ēlongāre*, *-ātum*, from *ē* from, and *longus* long]

elope *e-* or *i-lōp'*, *vi* to escape privately, *esp* with a lover (*usu* to get married); to run away or bolt. — *n* **elope'ment**. — *n* **elō'per**. [Cf ODu *ontlōpen*, Ger *entlaufen* to run away]

elops *el'ops*, *n* see **ellops**; (with *cap*) a genus of fish (family *Elopidae*) related to the tarpon. [See ety of **ellops**]

eloquent *el'ə-kwənt*, *adj* having eloquence; persuasive; strongly expressive. — *n* **el'oquence** the power, art or practice of uttering strong emotion in correct, appropriate, expressive and fluent language; the art of such language; persuasive speech. — *adv* **el'oquently**. [L *ēloquēns*, *-entis*, pr p of *ēloquī* to utter]

elpee *el-pē'*, (*colloq*) *n* a long-playing record, a phonetic representation of the abbrev **LP**.

Elsan® *el'san*, *n* a type of portable lavatory in which chemicals are used to kill bacteria and destroy smell. [*E L* Jackson, the manufacturer, and *san*itation]

else *els*, *adj* (or *adv*) other (in addition or instead). — *adv* otherwise; besides; except that mentioned. — *adv* **elsewhere'** in or to another place. — *adv* **elsewhith'er**. — *adv* **else'wise** in a different manner; otherwise. [OE *elles* otherwise, orig genitive of *el* other; cf OHGer *alles* or *elles*, L *alius*, Gr *allos* other]

elsin *el'sin*, or **elshin** *el'shin*, (*Scot*) *n* an awl. [From ODu *elssene* (Mod *els*); cf **awl**]
ELT *abbrev*: English language teaching (to non-English speakers).
elt *elt*, (*dialect*) *n* a young sow. [Cf **yelt** and **gilt**[2]]
eltchi. See **elchi**.
eluant, **eluate**. See **elution**.
elucidate *ē-* or *i-lū'si-dāt*, or *-lōō'*, *vt* to make lucid or clear; to throw light upon; to illustrate. — *n* **elucidā'tion**. — *adj* **elu'cidative** or **elu'cidatory** making clear; explanatory. — *n* **elu'cidator**. [LL *ēlūcidāre*, *-ātum*, from *ē-* (intens) and *lūcidus* clear]
elucubration. Obs form of **lucubration**. [L *ē-* (intens)]
elude *ē-* or *i-lūd'*, or *-lōōd'*, *vt* to escape by design or craftiness; to baffle; (of a fact, etc) to fail to be discovered, remembered, etc. — *n* **elu'der**. — *adj* **elu'dible**. — *n* **elu'sion** (*-zhən*) the act of eluding; evasion. — *adj* **elu'sive** (*-ziv* or *-siv*) practising elusion; deceptive. — *adv* **elu'sively**. — *n* **elu'soriness**. — *adj* **elu'sory** tending to elude or cheat; evasive; deceitful. [L *ēlūdere*, *ēlūsum*, from *ē* from, and *lūdere* to play]
Elul *e'ləl* or *-lōōl*, *n* the 12th month of the Jewish civil year, and 6th of the ecclesiastical. [Heb, from *âlal* to reap]
elution *ē-* or *i-lōō'shən*, or *-lū'*, (*chem*) *n* purification or separation by washing. — *n* **el'uant** or **el'uent** a liquid used for elution. — *n* **el'uate** liquid obtained by eluting. — *vt* **elute'**. — *n* **elu'tor** a vessel for elution. [L *ēlūtiō*, *-ōnis* washing, from *ēluere*, *ēlūtum*, from *ē* from, and *luere* to wash]
elutriate *ē-* or *i-lōō'tri-āt*, or *-lū'*, *vt* to separate by washing into coarser and finer portions. — *n* **elutriā'tion**. — *n* **elu'triātor** an apparatus for elutriating. [L *ēlutriāre*, *-ātum* to wash out, from *ēluere*, from *ē* from, and *luere* to wash]
eluvium *i-*, *ē-lōō'vi-əm* or *-lū'*, *n* an accumulation of rock debris formed on the spot or moved by wind only, such as loess. — *adj* **elu'vial**. [Formed on the analogy of **alluvium** and **diluvium**; L *ē* from, and *luere* to wash]
ELV *abbrev*: expendable launch vehicle (see under **expend**).
elvan[1] *elv'ən*, *n* a granular crystalline dyke rock, composed of quartz and orthoclase. — Also **elv'anite**. [Cornish miners' name; prob Cornish *elven* spark]
elvan[2], **elves**, **elvish**. See under **elf**.
elver *el'vər*, *n* a young eel. [**eelfare** (see **eel**)]
Elysium *ē-*, *i-* or *e-liz(h)'i-əm*, *n* the abode of the blessed dead (*Gr mythol*); any delightful place. — *adj* **Elys'ian**. — **elysian fields** Elysium. [L, from Gr *elysion* (*pedion*), the Elysian (plain)]
elytrum *el'it-rəm* or **elytron** *el'it-ron*, *n* a beetle's forewing modified to form a case for the hindwing; a dorsal plate in certain worms: — *pl* **el'ytra**. — *adj* **el'ytral**. — *adj* **elyt'riform**. — *adj* **elytrigerous** (*-trij'ər-əs*). [Latinized from Gr *elȳtron* a sheath]
Elzevir *el'zi-vēr* or *-vər*, *adj* published by the *Elzevirs*, a celebrated family of printers at Amsterdam, Leyden and other places in Holland, whose small neat editions were chiefly published between 1592 and 1681; of or relating to the type used in their 12mo and 16mo editions of the Latin classics. — *n* a special form of printing type.
em *em*, *n* the thirteenth letter of the alphabet (M or m); the unit of measurement (12-point lower-case 'm') used in spacing material and in estimating dimensions of pages (*printing*); see also **quadrat**).
em- *em-*, *pfx* a form of **en-** used before *b*, *m* or *p*.
'em *əm*, (*colloq*) *pronoun* them; to them. [Orig the unstressed form of *hem*, dative and accusative pl of **he** (OE *him*, *heom* dative pl); but now used colloq as if an abbreviation of **them**]
EMA *abbrev*: European Monetary Agreement.
emaciate *i-mā'shi-āt*, or *-si-*, *vt* to make meagre or lean; to deprive of flesh; to waste. — *vi* to become lean; to waste away. — *adj* **emā'ciate** or **ema'ciated**. — *n* **emāciā'tion** the condition of becoming emaciated or lean; leanness. [L *ēmaciāre*, *-ātum*, from *ē-* (intens) and *maciāre* to make lean, from *maciēs* leanness]
e-mail or **E-mail** *ē'-māl*, *n* short for electronic mail.
emalangeni. See **lilangeni**.
emanate *em'ə-nāt*, *vi* to flow out of or from anything; to proceed from some source; to arise. — *adj* **em'anant** flowing out. — *n* **emanā'tion** a flowing out from a source, such as the universe considered as issuing from the essence of God; the *generation* of the Son and the *procession* of the Spirit, as distinct from the origination of created beings (*theol*); that which issues or proceeds from a source; a radioactive gas given off by radium, thorium and actinium, also called radon. — *n* **em'anatist** someone who believes in emanation (*theol*). — *adj* **em'anative**, **em'anatory** or **emanā'tional**. [L *ēmānāre*, *-ātum*, from *ē* out from, and *mānāre* to flow]
emancipate *e-* or *i-man'si-pāt*, *vt* to set free from restraint or bondage or disability of any kind. — *n* **emancipā'tion** the act of setting free from bondage or disability of any kind; the state of being set free. — *n* **emancipā'tionist** an advocate of the emancipation of slaves. — *n* **eman'cipātor**. — *adj* **emancipa'tory**. — *n* **eman'cipist** (*hist*) convict who has served his time of punishment in a penal colony. [L *ēmancipāre*, *-ātum*, from *ē* away from, and *mancipāre* to transfer property, from *manceps*, *-cipis* someone who gets property, from *manus* the hand, and *capere* to take]
emarginate *ē-mär'jin-āt*, *vt* to take away the margin of. — *adj* depressed and notched instead of pointed at the tip, such as a leaf (*bot*); having all the edges of the primitive form crossed by a face (*mineralogy*); having the margin broken by a notch or segment of a circle (*zool*). — *n* **emarginā'tion**. [L *ēmargināre*, *-ātum*, from *ē* out, and *margināre* to provide with a margin, from *margō* a margin]
emasculate *i-* or *ē-mas'kū-lāt*, *vt* to deprive of male characteristics; to castrate; to deprive of masculine vigour; to make effeminate; to lessen or take away the power, force or effectiveness of (*fig*). — *adj* emasculated. — *n* **emasculā'tion**. — *n* **emas'culātor**. — *adj* **emas'culatory** (*-lə-tər-i*). [LL *ēmasculāre*, *-ātum*, from *ē* from, and *masculus*, dimin of *mās* a male]
embace. See **embase**.
embail *im-* or *em-bāl'*, (*obs*) *vt* to encircle; to hoop in: — *pa p* (*Spenser*) **embayld'**. [**em-** (from **en-** (1a))]
embale *im-* or *em-bāl'*, *vt* to make up, eg into a bale; to bind up; to enclose. [Fr *emballer*, from *em-* (L *in*) in, and *balle* a bale]
emball *em-böl'*, *vt* to ensphere. — *n* **emball'ing** (*Shakesp*) the receiving of the ball (of sovereignty). [**em-** (from **en-** (1a))]
embalm *im-* or *em-bäm'*, *vt* to preserve (*esp* a dead body) from decay by aromatic drugs; to preserve with fragrance; to preserve unchanged but lifeless; to impregnate with balm or perfume. — *n* **embalm'er**. — *n* **embalm'ing** or **embalm'ment**. [Fr *embaumer*, from *em-* in, and *baume*; see **balm**]
embank *im-* or *em-bangk'*, *vt* to enclose or defend with a bank or dike. — *n* **embank'er**. — *n* **embank'ment** the act of embanking; a bank or mound made to keep water within certain limits; a mound constructed so as to carry a level road or railway over a low-lying place. [**em-** (from **en-** (1a))]
embar *im-* or *em-bär'* or (*obs*) **imbar**, *vt* to shut in (*archaic*); to hinder or stop (*archaic*); to put under embargo (*archaic*): — *pr p* **embarr'ing**; *pa t* and *pa p* **embarred'**. — *n* **embarr'ing**. [**em-** (from **en-** (1a))]
embarcation. Same as **embarkation**.
embargo *em-bär'gō*, *n* a temporary order from the Admiralty to prevent the arrival or departure of ships; a stoppage of trade for a short time by authority; a prohibition or ban: — *pl* **embar'goes**. — *vt* to lay an embargo on; to seize: — *pr p* **embar'gōing**; *pa t* and *pa p* **embar'goed** (*-gōd*). — *n* **embarque'ment** (*Shakesp*) a placing under embargo. [Sp, from *embargar* to impede or restrain, from Sp pfx *em-* in, and LL (and Sp) *barra* a bar]

embark *im-* or *em-bärk'*, *vt* to put on board ship; to engage or invest in any affair. — *vi* to go on board ship; to engage in or commerce (with (*up*)*on* or *in*). — *n* **embarkā'tion** (*em-*) a putting or going on board; anything which is embarked; a vessel (*obs*). — *adj* **embarked'**. — *adj* **embark'ing**. — *n* **embark'ment**. [Fr *embarquer*, from *em-* in, and *barque* bark]

embarquement. See **embargo**.

embarras de or **du choix** *ā-ba-ra də* (*dü*) *shwa*, (*Fr*) a perplexing number of things to choose from, (literally) embarrassment in choice; **embarras de** or **des richesses** (*də* (*dā*) *rē-shes*) a perplexing or disconcerting profusion of wealth or abundance of any kind.

embarrass *im-* or *em-bar'əs*, *vt* to put out of countenance or disconcert; to perplex; to involve in difficulty, *esp* in money matters; to encumber. — *vi* to become disconcerted or discomposed. — *adj* **embarr'assed** perplexed; constrained; disconcerted; out of countenance. — *n* **embarr'assment** the state of feeling embarrassed; something which makes one feel embarrassed; difficulties in money matters; a perplexing amount (see **embarras de choix**, etc). [Fr *embarrasser*, from *em-* in, and *barre*, LL *barra* bar]

embase or **imbase** (*Spenser* **embace**) *im-bās'*, *vt* to lower; to bring down; to degrade; to debase: — *pa p* and *pa t* **embased'**, (*Spenser*) **embaste'**. — *adj* **embased'**. — *n* **embase'ment**. [**em-** (from **en-** (1b)) and **base**, or Fr *bas* low]

embassy *em'bə-si*, *n* an ambassador's residence; the charge or function of an ambassador; the person or body of persons sent on an undertaking. — *n* **em'bassade** (*Shakesp*) an embassy. — *adv* (*Spenser -bas'*) on an embassy. — *n* **embassador** (*-bas'*; *obs*) an ambassador. — *n* **em'bassage** embassy; the sending or business of an embassy. [See **ambassador**]

embaste. See **embase**.

embathe or **imbathe** *im-bādh'*, (*archaic*) *vt* to bathe; to immerse; to bedew. [**em-** (from **en-** (1c))]

embattle[1] *im-bat'l*, *vt* to equip with battlements. — *adj* **embatt'led** having battlements; having an outline like a battlement (*heraldry*). — *n* **embatt'lement** battlement. [**em-** (from **en-** (1c)) and OFr *bataillier* to embattle; see **battlement**]

embattle[2] *im-bat'l*, *vt* to range in order of battle; to arm (*Spenser*). — *adj* **embatt'led** arranged for battle; involved in battle (*esp fig*). [OFr *embataillier*, from *em-* in, and *bataille* battle]

embay[1] *im-bā'*, *vt* to enclose in a bay; to land-lock. — *n* **embay'ment** a bay. [**em-** (from **en-** (1a))]

embay[2] *em-bā'*, (*Spenser*) *vt* to bathe, steep or imbue. [Fr *em-* in, and apparently *baigner*; see **bagnio**]

embayld. See **embail**.

embed or sometimes **imbed** *im-bed'*, *vt* to place, set or plant firmly in a mass of matter (also *fig*); to lay, as in a bed; to enclose deeply or snugly. — *n* **embedd'ing** (*biol*) the technique in which specimens are embedded in a supporting medium, such as paraffin wax or epoxy resin, in preparation for sectioning with a microtome. — *n* **embed'ment** the act of embedding; the state of being embedded. [**em-** (from **en-** (1a))]

embellish *im-bel'ish*, *vt* to make beautiful with ornaments; to decorate; to make graceful; to illustrate pictorially (eg a book); to add interesting and possibly untruthful details to (an account, narrative, etc). — *n* **embell'isher**. — *adv* **embell'ishingly**. — *n* **embell'ishment** the act of embellishing or adorning; a decoration; ornament. [Fr *embellir*, *embellissant*, from *em-* in, and *bel* (*beau*) beautiful]

ember *em'bər*, *n* a piece of live coal or wood; (the following definitions chiefly in *pl*) red-hot ashes; the smouldering remains of a fire, or (*fig*) of love, passion, etc. [OE *æmerge*; ON *eimyrja*]

Ember-days *em'bər-dāz*, *n pl* the three Fast-days (Wednesday, Friday and Saturday) in each quarter, following the first Sunday in Lent, Whitsunday, Holy Cross Day (14 Sep), and St Lucia's Day (13 Dec). — **Em'ber-week** the week in which they occur. [OE *ymbryne* a circuit, from *ymb* round (cf Ger *um*, L *ambi-*), and *ryne* a running, from *rinnan* to run]

ember-goose *em'bər-gōōs*, *n* the great northern diver. [Norw *emmer*; Ger *Imber*]

embezzle *im-bez'l*, *vt* to appropriate (money or property that has been entrusted to one) fraudulently; to impair (*obs*). — *n* **embezz'lement** fraudulent appropriation of money or property entrusted to one. — *n* **embezz'ler**. [Anglo-Fr *embesiler* to make away with; perh influenced by **imbecile** (qv)]

embitter *im-bit'ər*, *vt* to make bitter or more bitter; to make more bitterly hostile. — Also **imbitt'er** (*archaic*). — *adj* **embitt'ered** soured; having been made misanthropical, cynical or disappointed. — *n* **embitt'erer**. — *n* and *adj* **embitt'ering**. — *n* **embitt'erment**. [**em-** (from **en-** (1b))]

emblaze[1] *im-blāz'*, *vt* to light up; to set on fire. [**em-** (from **en-** (1b))]

emblaze[2] *im-blāz'*, *vt* to describe or depict heraldically; to celebrate; to adorn heraldically. [**em-** (from **en-** (1c))]

emblazon *im-blā'zn*, *vt* to adorn with figures (*heraldry*); to depict heraldically; to celebrate, glorify or praise. — *n* **emblā'zoner**. — *n* **emblā'zonment** an emblazoning. — *n* **emblā'zonry** the art of emblazoning or adorning; devices on shields. [**em-** (from **en-** (1c))]

emblem *em'bləm*, *n* a symbolic device or badge; a picture representing to the mind something different from itself; a type or symbol; an inlaid ornament (*Milton*). — *vt* (*archaic*) to symbolize. — *n* **emblema** (*em-blē'mə*) an inlaid ornament: — *pl* **emblē'mata**. — *adj* **emblemat'ic** or **emblemat'ical** pertaining to or containing emblems; symbolical; representing (with *of*). — *adv* **emblemat'ically**. — *n* **emblem'atist** a writer or inventor of emblems. — *vt* **emblematize** or **-ise** (*-blem'ə-tīz*), **em'blemize** or **-ise** to represent by an emblem. [L, from Gr *emblēma*, *-atos* a thing inserted, from *en* in, and the root of *ballein* to throw]

emblements *em'bli-mənts*, (*law*) *n pl* crops raised by the labour of the cultivator of land (but not tree-fruits or grass) or the profits arising from these. [OFr *emblaer* to sow with corn, from LL *imbladāre*, from *in* in, and *bladum* wheat]

emblic *em'blik*, *n* an E Indian tree (*Phyllanthus emblica*) of the spurge family; its fruit, used for tanning. — Also **emblic myrobalan**. [Ar *amlaj*, from Pers *amleh*]

embloom *im-blōōm'*, *vt* to cover with bloom. [**em-** (from **en-** (1a))]

emblossom *im-blos'əm*, *vt* to cover with blossom. [**em-** (from **en-** (1a))]

embody *im-bod'i*, *vt* to form into a body; to make tangible or material; to express (in words, in tangible form, etc); to typify or personify; to make part of a body, to incorporate; to organize. — Also **imbody** (*archaic*). — *vi* to unite in a body or mass; to become corporeal, carnal or sensual: — *pr p* **embod'ying**; *pa t* and *pa p* **embod'ied**. — *adj* **embod'ied**. — *n* **embod'iment** the act of embodying; the state of being embodied; that in which something is embodied. [**em-** (from **en-** (1a))]

embog *im-bog'*, *vt* to bog. [**em-** (from **en-** (1c))]

embogue *im-bōg'*, *vi* to disembogue.

emboil *em-* or *im-boil'*, (*obs*) *vi* (*Spenser*) to burn with anger. — *vt* to make burn with anger; to irritate. [**em-** (from **en-** (1c))]

emboîtement *ā-bwät-mā'*, *n* encasement. — **emboîtement theory** the abandoned theory of earlier embryologists that the egg contained the germs of all future descendants, box within box. [Fr]

embolden *im-bōld'n*, *vt* to make bold or courageous; to give the necessary courage for some action; to set in bold type (*typography*). — *n* **embold'ener**. [**em-** (from **en-** (1b))]

embolism *em'bol-izm* or *-bəl-*, *n* the presence of one or more obstructing clots, etc in the blood vessels (*med*); an intercalation of days in the calendar to correct error; an intercalated prayer for deliverance from evil coming after the Lord's Prayer. — *adj* **embolic** (*-bol'*) relating to an embolus or to an emboly. — *adj*

embolis'mal. — *adj* **embolis'mic**. — *n* **em'bolus** a clot obstructing a blood-vessel. — *n* **em'boly** an invagination. — **embolismic year** see **year**. [Late Gr *embolismos* intercalation, from Gr *embolos* a stopper, *embolē* insertion, ramming, from *emballein* to throw in]

embonpoint *ã-bɔ̃-pwɛ̃'*, *adj* stout, plump or full in figure; well-fed. — *n* stoutness, plumpness or well-fed condition. [Fr, from *en bon point* in good form]

emborder *em-börd'ər* or *im-*, or **imborder**, (*Milton*) *vt* to set as a border; to border. [**em-** (from **en-** (1c))]

emboscata *em-bos-kä'tə* or *-kā'tə*, *n* an erroneous form of Ital *imboscata* or Sp *emboscada* an ambuscade.

embosom or **imbosom** *im-bŏŏz'əm*, *vt* to take into or clasp to the bosom; to receive into the affections; to implant in the bosom or mind; to enclose or surround protectively. [**em-** (from **en-** (1a))]

emboss[1] *im-bos'*, *vt* to raise in relief; to ornament with raised work; to cover with bosses; to raise bosses on. — *adj* **embossed'** raised or standing out in relief; formed or covered with bosses; having a protuberance in the centre (*bot*). — *n* **emboss'er**. — *n* **emboss'ment** a prominence like a boss; raised work. [**em-** (from **en-** (1a))]

emboss[2], **imboss** *im-bos'* or **imbosk** *-bosk'*, (*obs*) *vi* to go into the depths of a wood. — *vt* to drive to extremity; to make foam at the mouth: — *pa p* **embossed'**, *Milton* **embost'**. [OFr *embosquer*, from *em-* (L *in* in), and *bosc* a wood; see **ambush**]

emboss[3] *em-bos'*, (*Spenser*) *vt* to clothe; to wrap; to enclose. [Origin obscure]

embouchure *ã-bŏŏ-shür'*, *n* the mouth of a river; the mouthpiece of a wind instrument; the disposition of the mouth in playing a wind instrument. [Fr, from *emboucher* to put to the mouth or discharge, from *en* in, and *bouche* a mouth]

embound *em-bownd'*, (*Shakesp*) *vt* to enclose. [**em-** (from **en-** (1a))]

embourgeoise *im-bŏŏr'zhwäz* or *ã-bŏŏr-zhwaz'*, *vt* to cause to become bourgeois or middle-class: — *pr p* **embourgeoising**; *pa t* **embourgeoised**. — *n* **embourgeoisement** (*im-bŏŏr'zhwäz-mənt* or *ã-bŏŏr-zhwaz-mã*). [Fr *embourgeoiser*; see **bourgeois**]

embow *em-bow'* or *em-bō'*, (*archaic*) *vt* to bend; to arch or vault; to ensphere. — *adj* **embowed'** bent. [**em-** (from **en-** (1a))]

embowel *im-bow'əl*, *vt* to enclose (*obs*); to disembowel or remove the entrails from; to enclose in, or (*Spenser*) to thrust into, the bowels (*obs*): — *pr p* **embow'elling**; *pa t* and *pa p* **embow'elled**. — *n* **embow'elment**. [**em-** (from **en-** (1a))]

embower or **imbower** *im-bow'ər*, *vt* to place in a bower; to shelter, eg with trees. — *vi* to take or give shelter. — *n* **embow'erment**. [**em-** (from **en-** (la))]

embox *im-boks'*, *vt* to set in a box. [**em-** (from **en-** (1a))]

embrace[1] *im-brās'*, *vt* to take in the arms; to clasp affectionately to the bosom; to take eagerly or willingly; to comprise; to admit, adopt or receive. — *vi* to join in an embrace: — *pr p* **embrac'ing**; *pa t* and *pa p* **embraced'**. — *n* an act of embracing; a loving hug; (in *pl*) sexual intercourse (*archaic*). — *n* **embrace'ment**. — *n* **embrac'er**. — *adj* **embrac'ing**. — *adj* **embrac'ive**. — *adv* **embrac'ingly**. — *n* **embrac'ingness**. [OFr *embracer* (Fr *embrasser*), from L *in* in or into, and *brā(c)chium* an arm; see **brace**]

embrace[2] *em-brās'*, (*Spenser*) *vt* to brace, fasten or bind. [**em-** (from **en-** (1a))]

embracer, **embraceor** or **embrasor** *em-brā'sər*, (*law*) *n* a person who seeks to influence jurors by corrupt means to deliver a partial verdict. — *n* **embrac'ery** the offence of an embracer. [OFr *embraceor*, from *embraser* to set on fire]

embraid *em-brād'*, (*Spenser*) *vt* to braid. [**em-** (from **en-** (1c))]

embranchment *im-bränch'mənt* or *-sh-*, *n* a branching off, such as an arm of a river, a spur of a mountain, etc. [Fr *embranchement*]

embrangle or **imbrangle** *im-brang'gl*, (*archaic*) *vt* to confuse or perplex. — *n* **embran'glement**. [**em-** (from **en-** (1a))]

embrasor. See **embracer**.

embrasure[1] *em-brās'yər*, (*Shakesp*) *n* embrace. [**em-** (from **en-** (1a))]

embrasure[2] *im-brā'zhər*, (*archit*) *n* an internally splayed recess of a door or window; the slant of such a recess; an opening in a wall for cannon to fire through. — Also **embrā'zure**. [Fr, from OFr *embraser* to slope the sides of a window, from *em-* (from L *in*), and *braser* to skew]

embrave *em-brāv'*, *vt* to make showy, to decorate (*Spenser*); to inspire with bravery. [**em-** (from **en-** (1b))]

embread *em-brēd'*, (*Spenser*) *vt* to embraid. [**em-** (from **en-** (1c))]

embreathe *em-brēdh*, (*archaic*) *vt* to breathe into; to breathe in. [**em-** (from **en-** (1a))]

embrewe (*Spenser*). See **imbrue**.

embrittle *im-brit'əl*, (*archaic*) *vt* and *vi* to make or become brittle. — *n* **embrit'tlement**. [**em-** (from **en-** (1b))]

embrocate *em'brō-kāt*, *vt* to moisten and rub eg with a lotion. — *n* **embrōcā'tion** the act of embrocating; the lotion used. [LL *embrocāre*, *-ātum*, from Gr *embrochē* a lotion, from *embrechein* to soak or embrocate, from *en-* in or into, and *brechein* to wet]

embroglio. See **imbroglio**.

embroider *im-broid'ər*, *vt* to ornament with designs in needlework; to add ornament or fictitious detail to. — *n* **embroid'erer**. — *n* **embroid'ery** the art of producing ornamental designs in needlework on textile fabrics, etc; ornamental needlework; variegation or diversity; artificial or elaborate ornamentation; embellishment; exaggeration or invented detail. [ME *embrouderie*, from OFr *embroder*; confused with or influenced by OE *bregdan* to weave or braid]

embroil *im-broil'*, *vt* to involve in a broil or in perplexity (with); to entangle; to distract; to throw into confusion. — *n* **embroil'ment** a state of perplexity or confusion; disturbance. [Fr *embrouiller*, from pfx *em-*, and *brouiller* to break out]

embrown or **imbrown** *im-brown'*, *vt* to make brown; to darken or obscure. — *adj* **embrown'ing**. [**em-** (from **en-** (1b))]

embrue. See **imbrue**.

embrute. See **imbrute**.

embryo *em'bri-ō*, also (*archaic*) **embryon** *em'bri-on*, *n* a young animal or plant in its earliest stages of development; the beginning of anything: — *pl* **em'bryos** or **em'bryons**. — Also *adj*. — *n* **embryogen'esis** or **embryogeny** (*-oj'i-ni*) the formation and development of the embryo. — *n* **em'bryoid** (*bot*) an embryo-like structure produced in tissue culture. — *adj* **embryolog'ic** or **embryolog'ical**. — *n* **embryol'ogist**. — *n* **embryol'ogy** the science of the formation and development of the embryo. — *adj* **em'bryonal** embryonic. — *adj* **em'bryonate** or **em'bryonated** (*obs*) (of minerals, etc) embedded in other material. — *adj* **embryon'ic** or **embryot'ic** of or relating to anything in an imperfect or incomplete state; rudimentary. — *n* **embryot'omy** (Gr *tomē* a cut) the division of a foetus to effect removal. — *n* **embryulcia** (*-ul'shi-ə*; Gr *holkē* dragging) forcible extraction of a foetus. — **em'bryo-sac** the megaspore of a flowering plant, one of the cells of the nucellus; **embryo transfer** (abbrev **ET**) surgical transfer of the young embryo into the uterus, a technique used in the treatment of infertility. [LL, from Gr *embryon*, from *en* in, and *bryein* to swell]

embus *im-bus'*, *vt* to put (*esp* troops) into a bus. — *vi* to board a bus: — *pr p* **embuss'ing**; *pa t* and *pa p* **embussed'**. [**em-** (from **en-** (1a))]

embusqué *ã-bü-skā*, (*Fr*) *adj* in ambush. — *n* a slacker or shirker; a person who evades military service.

embusy *em-biz'i*, (*Spenser*) *vt* to occupy or make busy. [**em-** (from **en-** (1b))]

emcee *em-sē'*, (*colloq*) *n* a master of ceremonies, a phonetic representation of the abbrev **MC**. — *vi* and *vt* to act as a master of ceremonies (for).

eme *ēm*, (*obs*) *n* an uncle. [OE *ēam*; Du *oom*]

emeer. See **emir**.

emend *ē-mend'*, *vt* to make alterations in with a view to improving (a text); to remove faults or blemishes from (now *rare*). — *adj* **ēmend'able** that may be emended. — *n pl* **ēmend'als** (*law*) funds set apart for repairs, in the accounts of the Inner Temple. — *vt* **ē'mendate** to correct errors. — *n* **ēmendā'tion** the removal of an error or fault; correction. — *n* **ē'mendātor** a corrector of errors in writings; a person who corrects or improves. — *adj* **ēmen'datory** mending or contributing to correction. [L *ēmendāre*, *-ātum*, from *ē* from, and *mendum* a fault]

emerald *em'ər-əld*, (*Spenser* **emeraude**) *n* a gemstone, a beautiful velvety green variety of beryl; (also **emerald green**) its colour. — **em'erald-copper** dioptase; **em'erald-cut** in gemstones, a multifaceted flat-topped rectangular cut; **Emerald Isle** Ireland, from its greenness; **emerald type** (*printing*) a small size of type. [OFr *esmeralde*, from L *smaragdus*, from Gr *smaragdos*]

emerge *i-* or *ē-mûrj'*, *vi* to rise out of anything; to issue or come out; to reappear after being concealed; to come into view; to come into being in the course of evolution; to crop up. — *n* **emer'gence** the act of emerging; a sudden appearance; an emergency (*obs*); an outgrowth of subepidermic tissue along with epidermic, an appendage more complex in structure than a hair (*bot*); in insects, the appearance of the imago from the cocoon, pupa-case or pupal integument. — *n* **emer'gency** an unexpected occurrence, requiring immediate action; pressing necessity; emergence (*obs*); a substitute in reserve. — Also *adj*. — *adj* **emer'gent** emerging; suddenly appearing; arising unexpectedly; urgent; coming into being in the course of evolution; (of a state) having recently become independent. — *adv* **emer'gently**. — *adj* **emer'ging** developing; becoming important. — *adj* **emersed** (*ē-mûrst'*; *bot*) (eg of leaves) rising above the surface of water. — *n* **emer'sion** (*-shən*) the act of emerging; the reappearance of a heavenly body after eclipse or occultation (*astron*). — **emergency exit** an exit to be used only in an emergency, eg fire. — **state of emergency** a situation in which a government suspends the normal constitution in order to deal with an emergency such as a natural disaster or civil disorder. [L *ēmergere*, *ēmersum*, from *ē* out of, and *mergere* to plunge]

emeritus *i-* or *ē-mer'i-təs*, *adj* (often following a noun) honourably discharged from the performance of public duty, *esp* denoting a retired professor. — *n* a person who has been honourably discharged from public duties: — *pl* **emer'itī**. [L *ēmeritus* having served one's time, from *ēmerērī* to earn, from *ē-* (signifying completeness) and *merērī* to deserve]

emerods *em'ə-rodz*, (*Bible*) *n pl* haemorrhoids; representations of them in gold, used as charms.

emersed, **emersion**. See under **emerge**.

emery *em'ər-i*, *n* a very hard mineral, a variety of corundum, used as powder for polishing, etc. — *vt* to rub or coat with emery. — **em'ery-bag** a bag of emery-powder for cleaning and sharpening needles; **em'ery-board** a small flat strip of wood or card coated with emery-powder, used in manicure; **em'ery-cloth** or **em'ery-paper** cloth or paper covered with emery-powder for polishing; **em'ery-powder** ground emery; **em'ery-wheel** a wheel coated with emery for polishing. [OFr *esmeril*, *emeril*, from LL *smericulum*, from Gr *smēris*, *smȳris*]

emetic *i-met'ik*, (*med*) *adj* causing vomiting. — *n* a medicine that causes vomiting. — *n* **emesis** (*em'i-sis*) vomiting. — *adj* **emet'ical**. — *adv* **emet'ically**. — *n* **em'etin** or **em'etine** the alkaloid forming the active principle of ipecacuanha root, violently emetic. — *n* **emetophō'bia** a pathological fear of vomiting. [Gr *emetikos*, from *emeein* to vomit]

emeu. See **emu**.

émeute *ā-møt'*, sometimes *i-mūt'*, *n* a popular rising or uproar. [Fr]

EMF *abbrev*: electromotive force (also **emf**); European Monetary Fund.

EMI *abbrev*: electromagnetic interference (also **emi**); EMI Limited (*orig* Electrical and Musical Industries Limited).

emicate *em'i-kāt*, *vi* to sparkle. — *adj* **em'icant** sparkling; flashing. — *n* **emicā'tion**. [L *ēmicāre*, *-ātum*]

emiction *i-mik'shən*, *n* the discharging of urine. — *adj* **emic'tory** promoting the flow of urine. [L *ēmingere*, *ēmictum*, from *ē* from, and *mingere* to urinate]

emigrate *em'i-grāt*, *vi* and *vt* to move from one country or state to another as a place of abode. — *adj* **em'igrant** emigrating or having emigrated. — *n* someone who emigrates or has emigrated. — *n* **emigrā'tion**. — *adj* **emigrā'tional**. — *n* **emigrā'tionist** an advocate or promoter of emigration. — *adj* **em'igrātory**. — *n* **émigré** (*ā-mē-grā'*) a royalist who fled from France during the Revolution; an (*esp* political) emigrant. [L *ēmīgrāre*, *ēmigrāre*, *-ātum*, from *ē* from, and *migrāre* to remove]

éminence grise *ā-mē-nās grēz*, (*Fr*) *n* someone exercising power in the background, as did Cardinal Richelieu's private secretary and *alter ego* Père Joseph, nicknamed *l'Éminence Grise* ('the Grey Eminence').

eminent *em'i-nənt*, *adj* distinguished; exalted in rank or office; rising above others; conspicuous. — *n* **em'inence** a part eminent or rising above the rest; a rising ground; a ridge or knob; height; distinction; a title given in 1631 to cardinals, previously styled Most Illustrious; advantage or upper hand (*Shakesp*). — *n* **em'inency**. — *adj* **eminen'tial** (*-shəl*; *obs*). — *adv* **em'inently**. — **eminent domain** the right by which the supreme authority in a state may appropriate an individual's property for public use. [L *ēminēns*, *-entis*, pr p of *ēminēre*, from *ē* from, and *minēre* to project]

emir *ā-mēr'*, sometimes *ē'mər*, *n* a title given in the East and in N Africa to all independent chieftains, and also (*perh* improperly) to all the supposed descendants of Mohammed through his daughter Fatima. — *n* **emir'ate** the office, jurisdiction, or state of an emir. — Also **ameer**, **amir** (*a-mēr'*, *ə-*) or **emeer**. [Ar *amīr* ruler]

Emi-Scanner® *em'i-skan-ər*, *n* a machine which produces computer-assisted X-ray pictures of the head or body. [**EMI**]

emit *i-* or *ē-mit'*, *vt* to send out; to throw or give out; to issue; to utter (a declaration): — *pr p* **emitt'ing**; *pa t* and *pa p* **emitt'ed**. — *n* **emissary** (*em'is-ər-i*) someone sent out on a mission, *esp* on behalf of a government or state; an agent sent out on a secret mission; a spy; an underground outlet, *esp* of a lake. — *adj* sent forth; outgoing. — *adj* **emiss'ile** able to be pushed out or forward. — *n* **emission** (*-mish'ən*) the act of emitting; that which is issued at one time; the discharge of semen or other fluid from the body; the release of electrons from parent atoms on absorption of energy exceeding the average (*phys*). — *adj* **emiss'ive** emitting or sending out. — *n* **emissiv'ity** (*ē-*) the property or power of emitting or radiating. — *n* **emitt'er** in a transistor, the region from which charge carriers are injected into the base. — **emission current** (*electronics*) the total electron flow from an emitting source; **emission theory** the corpuscular theory of light. [L *ēmittere*, *ēmissum*, from *ē* out of, and *mittere* to send]

emma *em'ə*, *n* formerly, a signallers' name for the letter *m*.

Emmanuel or **Immanuel** *i-man'ū-əl* or *-el*, (*Bible*) *n* the symbolic name of the child announced by Isaiah (Isaiah 7.14) and applied to Jesus as the Messiah in Matt 1.23. [Gr *Emmanouēl*, from Heb *'Immānūēl*, from *'im* with, *ānū* us, and *ēl* God]

emmarble *i-mär'bl*, *vt* to turn to marble; to represent in marble; to adorn with marble. [**em-** (from **en-** (1b))]

emmenagogue *em-ēn'ə-gog*, or *-en'*, *n* medicine intended to restore or to bring on menstruation. — Also *adj*. — *adj* **emmenagogic** (*-goj'ik*). — *n* **emmenol'ogy** the study of menstruation. [Gr *emmēna* menstruation, (from *mēn* a month) and *agōgos* drawing forth]

Emmental or **Emmenthal** *em'ən-täl*, *n* a hard Swiss cheese, similar to Gruyère, made in the Emmental or

Emme valley. — Also **Emmentaler** or **Emmenthaler** (*em'ən-täl-ər*). — Also *adj*.

emmer *em'ər*, *n* a species of wheat, *Triticum dicoccum*. [Ger dialect]

emmesh. See **enmesh**.

emmet *em'it*, (*archaic* and *dialect*) *n* the ant; in Cornwall, a tourist. [OE *ǣmete*]

emmetropia *em-e-trō'pi-ə*, *n* the normal condition of the refractive media of the eye. — *n* **emm'etrope** an emmetropic person. — *adj* **emmetropic** (*-trop'ik*). [Gr *en* in, *metron* measure, and *ops* the eye]

emmew, **immew** *i-mū'* or **enmew** *in-mū'*, *vt* to confine or mew up; in Shakespeare, appar for **enew**. [**em-** (from **en-** (1a))]

emmove *e-mōōv'*, (*Spenser*) *vt* to move or excite. — Also **enmove**.

Emmy *em'i*, *n* a television trophy, corresponding to the cinema Oscar, awarded annually by the American Academy of Television Arts and Sciences: — *pl* **Emm'ys** or **Emm'ies**. [Origin uncertain]

emollient *i-mol'yənt*, *adj* softening; making supple. — *n* (*med*) a softening application such as a poultice, fomentation, etc. — *n* **emollesc'ence** incipient fusion. — *vt* **emoll'iate** to soften; to make effeminate. — *n* **emolli'tion** the act of softening or relaxing. [L *ēmollīre*, *ēmollītum*, from *ē* (intens), and *mollīre* to soften, from *mollis* soft]

emolument *i-mol'ū-mənt*, *n* (often in *pl*) profit arising from employment, such as salary or fees; advantage (*obs*). — *adj* **emolumen'tal**. — *adj* **emolumen'tary**. [L *ēmolimentum*, prob from *ēmolere* to grind out, from *ē-* and *molere* to grind, rather than from *ēmōlīrī* to work out, from *mōlīrī* to toil]

emong, **emonges**, **emongest**, **emongst**. Obs forms of **among**, **amongst**.

emotion *i-mō'shən*, *n* a moving of the feelings; agitation of mind; any of various phenomena of the mind, such as anger, joy, fear or sorrow, associated also with physical symptoms; feeling as distinguished from cognition and will (*philos*). — *vi* **emote** (*i-mōt'*) to show or express exaggerated emotion. — *adj* **emō'tionable**. — *adj* **emō'tional**. — *n* **emō'tionalism** a tendency to emotional excitement (also **emōtional'ity**); the habit of working on the emotions; the indulgence of superficial emotion. — *adv* **emō'tionally**. — *adj* **emō'tionless**. — *adj* **emō'tive** (*-tiv*) of or relating to the emotions; emotional; tending to arouse emotion. — *n* **emō'tivism** (*ethics*) the theory that moral statements express the emotions of the speaker rather than an objective accepted truth. — *vt* **emove** (*i-mōōv'*; *archaic*) to affect with emotion. [L *ēmōtiō*, *-ōnis*, from *ēmovēre*, *-mōtum* to stir up]

EMP *abbrev*: European Member of Parliament.

Emp. *abbrev*: Emperor; Empire; Empress.

empacket *im-pak'it*, (*Scott*) *vt* to pack up. [**em-** (from **en-** (1c))]

empaestic *em-pē'stik*, *adj* pertaining to the art of embossing; stamped or inlaid. [Gr *empaiein* to emboss]

empaire (*Spenser*). See **impair**[1].

empale *em-pāl'*. See **impale**.

empanel *im-pan'əl*, *vt* to enter (the names of a prospective jury) on a list; to select (a jury) from such a list: — *pr p* **empan'elling**; *pa t* and *pa p* **empan'elled**. — *n* **empan'elment**. — Also **impanel** or **impannel**. [**em-** (from **en-** (1a))]

empanoply *im-pan'o-pli*, *vt* to clothe in full armour. [**em-** (from **en-** (1a))]

emparadise (*Milton*). See **imparadise**.

empare (*Spenser*). See **impair**[1].

emparlaunce (*Spenser*). See under **imparl**.

empart (*Spenser*). See **impart**.

empassionate, **empassioned** (*Spenser*). See **impassion**.

empathy *em'pə-thi*, *n* the power of entering into another's personality and imaginatively experiencing his or her experiences; the power of entering into the feeling or spirit of something (*esp* a work of art) and so appreciating it fully. — *adj* **empathet'ic**. — *adj* **em-path'ic**. — *vi* **em'pathize** or **-ise**. [Gr *en* in, and *pathos* feeling]

empatron *em-pā'trən*, (*Shakesp*) *vt* to patronize. [**em-** (from **en-** (1c))]

empayre *Spenser*. See **impair**[1].

empeach (*Spenser*). See **impeach**.

empennage *em-pen'ij* or *ā-pen-äzh'*, *n* an aeroplane's tail unit, including elevator, rudder and fin. [Fr, the feathering of an arrow, from L *penna* feather or wing]

empeople *im-pē'pl*, (*obs*) *vt* to fill with people; to form into a people or community. [**em-** from (**en-** (1a))]

emperce. See **empierce**.

emperish *im-per'ish*, (*Spenser*, etc) *vt* to impair. [Perh (irregularly) from Fr *empirer*; cf **impair**[1]]

emperor *em'pər-ər*, *n* the head of an empire; a high title of sovereignty; before metrication, a paper size (48 × 72in): — *fem* **em'press**. — *vt* **em'perize** or **-ise** (*obs*) to play the emperor. — *n* **em'perorship**. — *n* **em'pery** (esp *poetic*) empire or power. — **emperor moth** the second largest British moth, with a wingspan of about three inches; **emperor penguin** the largest of the penguins. [OFr *emperere*, from L *imperātor* a commander (fem *imperātrix*), from *imperāre* to command]

Empfindung *emp-fin'dōōng*, (*Ger*) *n* sensation or feeling.

emphasis *em'fə-sis*, *n* forcible or impressive expression; an insistent or vigorous way of attributing importance or enforcing attention; stress; accent; prominence; the use of language to imply more than is said (*obs*): — *pl* **em'phases** (*-sēz*). — *vt* **em'phasize** or **-ise** to make emphatic; to lay stress on. — *adj* **emphat'ic** (*im-* or *em-fat'ik*) or **emphat'ical** (*rare*) expressed or expressing with emphasis; stressed forcibly; impressive; strongly marked. — *adv* **emphat'ically**. — *n* **emphat'icalness**. [Gr *emphasis* image, outward appearance, significance or implied meaning, from *en* in, and *phainein* to show]

emphlysis *em'fli-sis*, *n* a vesicular eruption: — *pl* **em'-phlyses**. [Gr *en* in, and *phlysis* eruption, from *phlȳein* to bubble or break out]

emphractic *em-frak'tik*, *adj* stopping the pores of the skin. — *n* a substance with this property. [Gr *emphraktikos* obstructive, from *en* in, and *phrassein* to stop]

emphysema *em-fis-ē'mə*, (*med*) *n* an unnatural distension of a part of the body with air; distension of the lung, with breathing difficulties, etc. — *adj* **emphysē'matous**. — *n* **emphysē'mic** a sufferer from emphysema. [Gr *emphȳsēma*, from *emphȳsaein* to inflate]

emphyteusis *em-fit-ū'sis*, *n* in Roman law, a perpetual right in a piece of land, for which a yearly sum was paid to the proprietor. — *adj* **emphyteu'tic**. [Gr, from *emphyteuein* to implant]

empiecement *em-pēs'mənt*, *n* an insertion in a garment. [Fr *empiècement*]

empierce or **emperce** *em-pērs'*, (*Spenser*) *vt* to pierce. [**em-** (from **en-** (1c))]

empight *em-pīt'*, (*Spenser*) *adj* fixed. [**pitch**[2]]

empire *em'pīr*, *n* a dominion or group of states, peoples, nations, etc under the same sovereign power (*esp* an emperor) and spread over an extended area; supreme control or dominion; the government or office of an emperor; the time of the duration of an empire; a large industrial organization embracing many firms; a country whose sovereign owes no allêgiance to another (*hist*). — *adj* (*usu* with *cap*, *esp* of dress or furniture) relating to or in the style of the first French Empire (1804–14). — **em'pire-building** the practice or policy of increasing one's power or authority. — Also *adj*. — **em'pire-builder**; **Empire Day** *formerly* a public holiday celebrated on or near 24 May (Queen Victoria's birthday); **Empire gown** a gown with low neckline and high waist such as was worn during the first French Empire. [Fr, from L *imperium*]

empiric *em-pir'ik*, formerly *em'*, *adj* empirical. — *n* a person who makes trials or experiments; someone whose knowledge is obtained from experience only; a quack. — *adj* **empir'ical** depending on trial or experiment; known or knowing only by experience. — *adv* **empir'ically**. — *n* **empir'icism** (*-sizm*) the system which accepts only knowledge based on direct experience (*philos*); the practice of empirical methods; the dependence of a physician on his experience alone without a regular medical education; the practice of medicine without a regular education; quackery. — *n* **empir'icist** (*-sist*) someone who practises empiricism. — *adj* **empiricūt'ic** (*Shakesp* **emperick qutique**; modelled on *therapeutic*; *obs*) empirical. — **empirical formula** (*chem*) a formula showing in simplest form the ratio of atoms in a molecule, not the absolute number. [Fr, from L *empīricus*, from Gr *empeirikos*, from *en* in, and *peira* a trial]

emplacement *im-plās'mənt*, *n* the act of placing; a gun-platform (*military*). — *vt* **emplace'** (back-formation) to put in or provide with an emplacement. [Fr *emplacement*]

emplane *im-plān'*, *vt* to put or take on an aeroplane. — *vi* to board an aeroplane. — Also **enplane'**. [**em-** (from **en-** (1a)) and **plane**[2]]

emplaster *em-pläs'tər*, (*obs*) *n* and *v* plaster. — *adj* **emplastic** (*-plas'*) glutinous; adhesive. — *n* a medicine that stops the pores. — *n* **emplas'tron** (*Gr*) or **emplas'trum** (*L*) a medicated plaster. [OFr *emplastre(r)*, from L *emplastrum*]

emplecton *em-plek'ton*, (*archaic*) *n* ashlar masonry filled up with rubble. — Also **emplec'tum** (*L*). [Gr *emplekton*, from *en* in, and *plekein* to weave]

emplonge (*Spenser*). See **implunge**.

employ *im-ploi'*, *vt* to occupy the time or attention of; to use as a means or agent; to give work to. — *n* employment. — *adj* **employ'able** fit or able to be employed. — *adj* **employed'** having employment, in a job. — *n* **employ'ee** (or *em-ploi-ē'*) a person employed. — *n* **employ'er**. — *n* **employ'ment** the act of employing; something which engages or occupies; occupation. — **employment agency** an agency which finds work for the unemployed and employees for vacant positions; **employment office** a job centre; **Employment Service** a government agency run by the Department of Employment, which finds work for the unemployed, pays out unemployment benefit, etc (formerly called *employment exchange* or *Labour Exchange*); **Employment Training** a government scheme intended to train or retrain unemployed people to enable them to find work (abbrev **ET**). [Fr *employer*, from L *implicāre* to enfold, from *in* in, and *plicāre* to fold; cf **imply** and **implicate**]

emplume *im-ploōm'*, (*archaic* or *poetic*) *vt* to provide with a plume. [**em-** (from **en-** (1a))]

empoison *im-poi'zn*, (*archaic*) *vt* to put poison into; to poison (*obs*); to embitter or corrupt. — *adj* **empoi'soned**. — *n* **empoi'sonment**. [**em-** (from **en-** (1a))]

empolder. See **impolder**.

emporium *em-pö'ri-əm*, *n* a commercial or trading centre or mart; a big shop: — *pl* **empō'ria** or **empō'riums**. [L, from Gr *emporion* a trading station, from *emporos* a wayfarer or trader, from *en* in, and *poros* a way]

empoverish. *Obs* form of **impoverish**.

empower *im-pow'ər*, *vt* to authorize. — *n* **empow'erment** the giving to individuals of power to take decisions in matters relating to themselves, *esp* (in an organization) in relation to self-development. [**em-** (from **en-** (1a))]

empress. See **emperor**.

empressement *ā-pres-mā*, (*Fr*) *n* demonstrative warmth of manner. — *adj* **empressé** (*-pres-ā*; *Fr*) eager or enthusiastic.

emprise *em-prīz'*, (*archaic*) *n* an enterprise; a dangerous undertaking. [OFr *emprise*, from pa p fem of *emprendre*, from L *in* in, and *praehendere* to take]

emption *emp'shən*, *n* the act of buying, purchase. — *adj* **emp'tional**. [L *emptiō*, *-ōnis*, from *emere* to buy]

empty *emp'ti*, *adj* having nothing inside; unoccupied; unfurnished; without effect; unsatisfactory; lacking substance; meaningless; empty-headed; hungry (*colloq*); devoid (of; *Shakesp* with *in*). — *vt* to make empty; to deprive of contents; to remove from a receptacle. — *vi* to become empty; to discharge: — *pr p* **emp'tying**; *pa t* and *pa p* **emp'tied**. — *n* an empty bottle, box, sack, etc: — *pl* **emp'ties**. — *n* **emp'tier**. — *adv* **emp'tily**. — *n* **emp'tiness** the state of being empty; lack of substance; unsatisfactoriness; inanity. — *n* **emp'tying**. — *adj* **empty-hand'ed** bringing or taking away nothing or no gift. — *adj* **empty-head'ed** frivolous. — **empty-nest'er** a parent whose children have left the parental home. [OE *ǣmetig*, from *ǣmetta* leisure or rest; the *p* is excrescent]

emptysis *emp'ti-sis*, *n* spitting, *esp* of blood. [Gr *emptysis* spitting, from *en* in, and *ptyein* to spit]

empurple *im-pûr'pl*, *vt* to dye or tinge purple. [**em-** (from **en-** (1b))]

Empusa *em-pū'zə*, *n* a goblin or spectre sent by Hecate (*Gr mythol*; also without *cap*; also **empuse'**); a genus of fungi parasitic upon houseflies and other insects. [Gr *Empousa*]

empyema *em-pī-ē'mə*, or *-pi-*, *n* a collection of pus in any cavity, *esp* the pleura. — *adj* **empye'mic**. — *n* **empyesis** (*-ē'sis*) an eruption on the skin containing pus. [Gr *empyēma*, *empyēsis*, from *en* in, and *pyon* pus]

empyreal *em-pir-ē'əl*, (*Milton*, *Pope em-pir'i-əl*) *adj* formed of pure fire or light; of or relating to the highest and purest region of heaven; sublime. — *adj* **empyre'an** empyreal. — *n* the highest heaven, where the pure element of fire was supposed to subsist; the heavens. [Gr *empyros* fiery, from *en* in, and *pȳr* fire]

empyreuma *em-pir-ū'mə*, *n* the burned smell and acrid taste that occur when vegetable or animal substances are burned: — *pl* **empyreu'mata**. — *adj* **empyreumat'ic** or **empyreumat'ical**. — *vt* **empyreu'matize** or **-ise**. [Gr *empȳreuma*, *-atos* embers, from *en* in, and *pȳr* fire]

EMS *abbrev*: Emergency Medical Service; European Monetary System, a system of monetary co-operation between EEC member countries, limiting fluctuations in currency rates between them.

EMU *abbrev*: Economic and Monetary Union or European Monetary Union; electromagnetic unit (also **emu**).

emu or **emeu** *ē'mū*, *n* a flightless, fast-running Australian bird, *Dromaius novaehollandiae*, the largest living bird after the ostrich. — **emu wren** a small Australian bird (*Stipiturus*) with tail-feathers structurally similar to those of the emu. [Port *ema* an ostrich]

emulate *em'ū-lāt*, *vt* to try to equal or surpass (*esp* a person or thing that one admires); to rival successfully; (loosely) to imitate. — *adj* (*Shakesp*) ambitious, eager to rival. — *n* **emulā'tion** the act of emulating or attempting to equal or excel; rivalry; competition; contest; jealous rivalry (*obs*). — *adj* **em'ulātive** inclined to emulation, rivalry or competition. — *n* **em'ulātor**: — *fem* **em'ulātress** (*obs*). — *vt* **em'ule** (*Southey*) to emulate. — *adj* **em'ulous** eager to emulate; keen to achieve or obtain the same success or excellence as someone else; engaged in competition or rivalry. — *adv* **em'ulously**. — *n* **em'ulousness**. [L *aemulārī*, *-ātus*, from *aemulus* emulous]

emulge *i-mulj'*, (*archaic*) *vt* to milk or drain out. — *n* **emul'gence**. — *adj* **emul'gent** (*med*) acting as a drain for. [See **emulsion**]

emulsion *i-mul'shən*, *n* a colloidal suspension of one liquid in another; a light-sensitive coating on photographic plates; a liquid mixture containing globules of fat (such as milk), or of resinous or bituminous material; emulsion paint. — *n* **emulsificā'tion**. — *n* **emul'sifier** a chemical which forms or preserves an emulsion, *esp* one used as a food-additive to prevent the constituents of processed foods separating out; apparatus for preparing emulsions. — *vt* **emul'sify**. — *n* **emul'sin** an enzyme obtained from bitter almonds. — *vt* **emul'sionize** or **-ise**. — *adj* **emul'sive**. — *n* **emul'soid** an easily dispersed colloid, giving a suspension readily formed again after coagulation. — *n* **emul'sor** an emulsifying apparatus. — **emulsifying agent** a substance whose presence in small quantities stabilizes an emulsion; **emulsion paint** a water-thinnable paint made from a pigmented emulsion of a resin in water. [L *ēmulgēre*, *ēmulsum* to milk out, from *ē* from, and *mulgēre* to milk]

emunctory *i-* or *ē-mungk'tər-i*, (*rare*) *adj* conveying waste; pertaining to nose-blowing. — *n* any organ or passage of the body that discharges waste; an excretory duct. — *n* (*rare*) **emunc'tion**. — *vt* **emunge** (*i-munj'*; *obs*) to clean. [L *ēmunctōrium* a pair of snuffers, a means of cleansing, from *ēmungere*, *ēmunctum* to blow the nose, to cleanse]

emure *i-mūr'*, (*Shakesp*) *vt* and *n* a variant of **immure**. [**em-** (from **en-** (1a))]

emys *em'is*, *n* any member of a genus (*Emys*) of freshwater and marsh terrapins: — *pl* **em'ydēs**. [Gr *emys*, *-ydos*]

EN *abbrev*: Enrolled Nurse.

en *en*, *n* the fourteenth letter of the modern English alphabet (N or n); half of an em (*printing*; see also **quadrat**). — *n* **enn'age** (*printing*) the length of a piece of type measured in ens.

en- *en-* or *in-*, *pfx* (1) in words derived from L through Fr (a) used to form verbs with the sense of *in, into, upon*; (b) used to form verbs with the sense *cause to be*; (c) used intensively or almost meaninglessly; (2) in words derived from Gr used to form verbs with the sense of *in*.

enable *in-ā'bl*, *vt* to make able; to give power, strength or authority to; to make possible. — *n* **enab'ler**. — *adj* **enab'ling**. — **enabling act**, **bill** or **resolution** one giving or proposing to give power to act. [**en-** (1b)]

enact *in-akt'*, *vt* to perform; to act the part of; to establish by law. — *n* (*Shakesp*) an enactment. — *adj* **enact'ing**. — *adj* **enact'ive**. — *n* **enac'tion** (*-shən*) or **enact'ment** the passing of a bill into law; that which is enacted; a law. — *n* **enact'or** a person who practises or performs anything; a person who forms decrees or establishes laws. — *n* **enac'ture** (*Shakesp*) fulfilment. [**en-** (1b) and **act**]

enallage *en-al'ə-jē*, (*gram*) *n* the exchange of one case, mood, tense, etc, for another. [Gr *enallagē*, from *en* in, and *allassein* to change]

enamel *in-am'əl*, *n* vitrified coating fired on to a metal or other surface; any glossy enamel-like surface or coating, *esp* that of the teeth; a work of art in enamel; a paint giving an enamel-like finish. — *vt* to coat with or paint in enamel; to form a glossy surface on, like enamel: — *pr p* **enam'elling**; *pa t* and *pa p* **enam'elled**. — *n* **enam'eller** or **enam'ellist**. — *n* **enam'elling**. [OFr *enameler*, from *en* in, and *esmail* enamel; see **smelt**[2] and **melt**]

en ami *ã-na-mē*, (*Fr*) as a friend.

enamour or (*US*) **enamor** *in-am'ər*, *vt* to inspire with love; to charm. — *n* **enamorado** (*en-äm-ō-rä'dō*; *obs*; *Sp*) a lover: — *pl* **enamorad'os**. — *adj* **enam'oured**. — *adj* **enam'ouring**. — **enamoured of** in love with; keen on. [OFr *enamourer*, from pfx *en-*, and *amour*, from L *amor*, *-ōris* love]

enantiodromia *en-an-ti-ō-drō'mi-ə*, *n* the process by which something becomes or is superseded by its opposite, *esp* the adopting of values, beliefs, etc opposite to those previously held; the interaction of such opposing values, beliefs, etc. — *adj* **enantiōdrom'iacal** (or *-drō-mī'ə-kl*). — *adj* **enantiōdrō'mic**. [Gr, from *enantios* opposite, and *dromos* running]

enantiomer *en-an'ti-ō-mər*, *n* an enantiomorph. — *adj* **enantiomer'ic**. [Gr *enantios* opposite, and *meros* part]

enantiomorph *en-an'ti-ō-mörf*, (*chem*) *n* a shape or object (such as a crystal or molecule) exactly similar to another except that right and left are interchanged, each being a mirror-image of the other. — *adj* **enantiomorph'ic**. — *adj* **enantiomorph'ous**. — *n* **enantiomorph'ism**. — *n* **enantiomorph'y**. [Gr *enantios* opposite, and *morphē* shape]

enantiopathy *en-an-ti-op'ə-thi*, *n* allopathy. [Gr *enantios* opposite, and *pathos* suffering]

enantiosis *en-an-ti-ō'sis*, (*rhetoric*) *n* the expression of an idea by negation of its contrary (litotes), or by substitution of the contrary (antiphrasis, irony). [Gr *enantiōsis* contradiction]

enantiostyly *en-an-ti-ō-stī'li*, (*bot*) *n* a dimorphous condition in which the style projects at one side or the other in different flowers. — *adj* **enantiostȳ'lous**. [Gr *enantios* opposite, and *stȳlos* a column]

enantiotropy *en-an-ti-o'trə-pi*, (*physical chemistry*) *n* the existence in a substance of two crystal forms, one stable above, the other below, a transition temperature. — *adj* **enantiōtrop'ic**. [Gr *enantios* opposite, and *tropos* turn, habit]

enarch. See **inarch**.

enarched *en-ärcht'*, (*heraldry*) *adj* arched; like an arch. [**en-** (1b)]

enarm *en-ärm'*, *vt* to arm (*obs*); to lard (*obs*). — *adj* **enarmed** (*heraldry*) having horns, hoofs, etc of a different colour from the body. [**en-** (1b)]

enarration *ē-nə-rā'shən*, (*archaic*) *n* exposition; detailed narration. [L *ēnarrātiō*, *-ōnis*, from *ē-* out, and *narrāre* to relate]

en arrière *ã-na-ryer*, (*Fr*) behind or in the rear.

enarthrosis *en-är-thrō'sis*, (*anatom*) *n* a ball-and-socket joint. — *adj* **enarthrō'dial**. [Gr *enarthrōsis*, from *en* in, and *arthron* a joint]

enate *ē'nāt*, (*biol*) *adj* growing out. — *n* **enā'tion** an outgrowth. [L *ē-* from, and *nātus* born]

en attendant *ã-na-tã-dã*, (*Fr*) in the meantime or while waiting.

enaunter *en-ön'tər* or *en-än'tər*, (*obs*) *conj* lest by chance. [Contraction of *in a(d)venture*]

en avant *ã-na-vã*, (*Fr*) forward.

en badinant *ã ba-dē-nã*, (*Fr*) roguishly or humorously.

en beau *ã bō*, (*Fr*) in a flattering style, eg of a person shown in a portrait.

en bloc *ã blok*, (*Fr*) as one unit or wholesale.

en brochette *ã bro-shet*, (*Fr*) (of food) on a skewer.

en brosse *ã bros*, (of hair) cut short and standing up stiffly. [Fr, like a brush]

en caballo *ān kä-bä'lyō*, (*Sp*) on horseback.

en cabochon. See **cabochon**.

encaenia *en-sē'ni-ə*, *n* the annual commemoration of founders and benefactors at Oxford, held in June. [L, from Gr *enkainia* (pl) a feast of dedication, from *en* in, and *kainos* new]

encage, (*obs*) **incage** *in-kāj'*, *vt* to shut up in a cage. [**en-** (1a)]

encalm *in-käm'*, (*obs*) *vt* to becalm. [**en-** (1b)]

encamp *in-kamp'*, *vt* to form into a camp; to lodge in a camp. — *vi* to pitch tents; to make or stay in a camp. — *n* **encamp'ment** the act of encamping; the place where a camper or company is encamped; a camp. [**en-** (1b)]

encanthis *en-kan'this*, (*med*) *n* a small tumour of the inner angle of the eye. [Gr *enkanthis*, from *en* in, and *kanthos* a canthus]

encapsulate *in-kap'sūl-āt*, *vt* to enclose in or as if in a capsule; to capture the essence of, to describe succinctly but sufficiently. — *n* **encapsulā'tion**. [**en-** (1a)]

encarnalize or **-ise** *in-kär'nəl-īz*, *vt* to embody; to make carnal or sensual. [**en-** (1b)]

encarpus *en-kär'pəs*, *n* a festoon of fruit ornamenting a frieze. [Gr *enkarpa* (neut pl), from *en* in, and *karpos* fruit]

encase or **incase** *in-kās'*, *vt* to enclose in a case; to surround or cover; to line. — *n* **encase'ment** or **incase'ment** the act of encasing; an enclosing substance; a covering; a lining. [**en-** (1a)]

encash *in-kash'*, *vt* to convert into cash. — *n* **encash'ment**. [**en-** (1b)]

encaustic *en-kös'tik*, *adj* having the colours burned in; of or pertaining to encaustic. — *n* an ancient method of painting in melted wax. — **encaustic tile** a decorative glazed and fired tile, having patterns of different coloured clays inlaid in it and burnt with it. [Gr *enkaustikos*, from *enkaiein* to burn in, from *en* in, and *kaiein* to burn]

en cavalier *ã ka-va-lyā*, (*Fr*) in a cavalier manner; astride (a horse) as opposed to side-saddle.

encave *en-kāv'*, (*Shakesp*) *vt* to hide. [Fr *encaver* to put in a cellar, from *en* in, and *cave* cellar]

enceinte[1] *ã-sẽt'*, (*fortif*) *n* an enclosure, generally the whole area of a fortified place. [Fr, from *enceindre* to surround, from L *in* in, and *cingere*, *cinctum* to gird]

enceinte[2] *ã-sẽt'*, *adj* pregnant, expecting a child. [Fr, from L *incincta* girt about or ungirt]

Encephalartos *en-sef-əl-är'tos*, *n* the Kaffir-bread genus of cycads. [Gr *enkephalos* within the head, or palm-cabbage, and *artos* bread]

encephalon *en-sef'əl-on*, or *-kef'*, (*anatom* and *zool*) *n* the brain. — *adj* **encephalic** (*-al'ik*) belonging to the head or brain. — *n* **encephalin** or **encephaline** (*-sef'ə-lin*) a rarer spelling of **enkephalin** (qv). — *adj* **encephalit'ic** pertaining to encephalitis. — *n* **encephalī'tis** inflammation of the brain. — *n* **enceph'alocele** (*-əl-ō-sēl*; Gr *kēlē* tumour) a protrusion of a portion of the brain through the skull, where the bones are incomplete in infancy. — *n* **enceph'alogram** or **enceph'alograph** an X-ray photograph of the brain. — *n* **encephalog'raphy** radiography of the brain, its cavities having been filled with air or dye injected into the space around the spinal cord. — *adj* **enceph'aloid** resembling the matter of the brain. — *n* **encephalop'athy** a degenerative brain disease. — *n* **encephalot'omy** (Gr *tomē* a cut) dissection of the brain. — *adj* **enceph'alous** cephalous. — **encephalitis lethargica** (*-ji-kə*) an acute disease marked by profound physical and mental lethargy and popularly called *sleeping-sickness* or *sleepy-sickness*. [Gr *enkephalos*, from *en* in, and *kephalē* head]

enchafe *en-chāf'*, (*obs*) *vt* to make warm; to irritate. [Earlier *enchaufe* or *eschaufe*, from OFr *eschauffer*, from *es-* (L *ex*), and *chauffer*; see **chafe**]

enchain *in-chān'*, *vt* to put in chains; to hold fast (*fig*); to link together (*obs*). — *n* **enchain'ment** the act of enchaining; the state of being enchained. [Fr *enchaîner*, from *en* in, and *chaîne* chain, from L *catēna*]

enchant *in-chänt'*, *vt* to cast a spell upon; to compel by enchantment; to act on by songs or rhymed formulas of sorcery; to charm; to delight utterly. — *adj* **enchant'ed** under the power of enchantment; beguiled or captivated; delighted; possessed by witches or spirits. — *n* **enchant'er** a person who enchants; a sorcerer or magician; a person who charms or delights: — *fem* **enchant'ress**. — *adj* **enchant'ing**. — *adv* **enchant'ingly** with the force of enchantment; in a charming or delightful manner. — *n* **enchant'ment** the act of enchanting; the use of magic arts; an enchanted state; something that enchants. — **enchanter's nightshade** a plant (*Circaea lutetiana*) of the evening primrose family, growing in shady places, the name transferred apparently from another plant (perhaps mandrake or swallow-wort) for no obvious reason. [Fr *enchanter*, from L *incantāre* to sing a magic formula over, from *in* on, and *cantāre* to sing]

encharge *in-chärj'*, *vt* to enjoin (*obs*); to entrust (*archaic*). [OFr *encharger*; see **charge**]

encharm *in-chärm'*, (*obs*) *vt* to cast a spell on; to charm. [**en-** (1c)]

enchase *in-chās'*, *vt* to fix in a border or setting; to enshrine (*obs*); to enclose (*obs*); to enshrine in verse (*obs*); to insert or let in; to set with jewels; to engrave or chase; to adorn with raised or embossed work; *prob* to fewter or sheathe (*Spenser*). — *n* (*Spenser*) enchasing. — *adj* **enchased'**. [Fr *enchâsser*, from *en* in, and *châsse* shrine, setting, from L *capsa* a case; see **case**[1] and **chase**[3]; **chase**[2] is a contraction]

encheason *en-chē'zn*, (*Spenser*) *n* a reason, cause or occasion. [OFr *encheson*, from *encheoir* to fall in; influenced by L *occāsiō*, *-ōnis* occasion]

encheer *in-chēr'*, (*archaic*) *vt* to cheer or comfort. [**en-** (1c)]

enchilada *en-chi-läd'ə*, *n* a Mexican dish consisting of a rolled stuffed tortilla cooked with a chilli-flavoured sauce. [Am Sp, from Sp *enchilar* to season with chilli]

enchiridion or **encheiridion** *en(g)-kī-rid'i-on*, *n* a book to be carried in the hand for reference; a manual. [Gr *encheiridion*, from *en* in, and *cheir* hand]

enchondroma *en-kon-drō'mə*, (*pathol*) *n* an abnormal cartilaginous growth: — *pl* **enchondro'mas** or **enchondro'mata** (*-tə*). [Gr *en* in, and *chondros* cartilage]

enchorial *en-kö'ri-əl*, *adj* belonging to or used in a country (*rare*); used by the people, *esp* (in ancient Egypt, of a writing system) demotic. — Also **enchoric** (*-kor'*). [Gr *enchōrios*, from *en* in, and *chōrā* a place or country]

encierro *en-thye'rō*, (*Sp*) *n* in Spanish towns, an event in which bulls are driven through the streets to the bull-ring: — *pl* **encier'ros**. [Literally, enclosure]

encincture *in-singk'chər*, *vt* to girdle. — *n* a girdling; an enclosure. [**en-** (1b)]

encipher *in-sī'fər*, *vt* to put into cipher. [**en-** (1a)]

encircle *in-sûrk'l*, *vt* to enclose in a circle; to go round (something). — *n* **encirc'ling**. — *n* **encir'clement**. [**en-** (1a)]

en clair *ã kler*, (*Fr*) not in cipher, uncoded.

enclasp *in-kläsp'*, *vt* to clasp. [**en-** (1c)]

enclave *en'klāv*, also *en-klāv'*, or *ã-kläv'*, *n* a piece of territory entirely enclosed within foreign territory; an enclosure. — *vt* to surround. [Fr, from LL *inclāvāre*, from L *in* in, and *clāvis* a key]

enclitic *en-klit'ik*, *adj* (of a word, *esp* a particle) without accent or stress, behaving as if not a separate word or, in ancient Greek, transferring its accent to the preceding word (*gram*); inclined. — *n* (*gram*) a word or particle which always follows another word and which is enclitic to it. — *n* **enclisis** (*eng'klis-is*). — *adv* **enclit'ically**. [Gr *enklitikos*, from *en* in, and *klīnein* to lean]

encloister *in-klois'tər*, (*obs*) *vt* to immure. [**en-** (1a)]

enclose or **inclose** *in-klōz'*, *vt* to close or shut in; to confine; to surround; to put within, *esp* of something sent within a letter or within its envelope; to seclude; to fence (*esp* waste land). — *n* **enclos'er** or **inclos'er**. — *n* **enclosure** or **inclosure** (*-klō'zhər*) the act of enclosing; the state of being enclosed; that which is enclosed, *esp* in a letter; a space fenced off; that which encloses; a barrier; the framing of a window. — **enclosed order** a Christian religious order leading an entirely contemplative life, not going out into the world to work. [**en-** (1a) and **close**[2]]

enclothe *in-klōdh'*, *vt* to clothe. [**en-** (1a)]

encloud *in-klowd'*, *vt* to cover with clouds. [**en-** (1a)]

encode *in-kōd'*, *vt* to encipher; to record in a form other than plain written or printed text; to convert an idea or message into words, or translate (something) into a foreign language (*linguistics*). [**en-** (1a)]

encoignure *ã-kwa-nür'* or *-nūr'*, *n* a piece of furniture, *esp* ornamental, eg a cupboard or cabinet, made to fit into a corner. [Fr, from *encoigner* to fit into a corner, from *en* in, and *coin* a corner]

encolour *in-kul'ər*, *vt* to colour or tinge. [**en-** (1b)]

encolpion *en-kol'pi-on*, *n* a reliquary, cross, etc worn on the breast. — Also (Latinized) **encol'pium**. [Gr, from *en* in or on, and *kolpos* bosom]

encolure *en(g)-kol-ūr'*, (*Browning*) *n* a horse's mane. [Fr, horse's neck]

encomienda *ān-kō-mē-ān'da*, (*Sp*) *n* a commandery or commander's district. — *n* **encomendero** (Sp; *ān-kō-mān-dā'rō*) its commander: — *pl* **encomender'os**.

encomium *en-kō'mi-əm*, also **encō'mion** (*-on*), *n* high commendation; a eulogy: — *pl* **encō'miums** or **encō'mia**. — *n* **encō'miast** a person who utters or writes encomiums; a praiser. — *adj* **encomias'tic** or **encomias'tical** bestowing praise. — *adv* **encomias'tically**. [L, from Gr *enkōmion* a song of praise, from *en* in, and *kōmos* festivity]

encompass *in-kum'pəs*, *vt* to surround or enclose; to include or embrace; to go round (*obs*); to bring about. — *n* **encom'passment**. [**en-** (1a)]

encore *ã-* or *ong-kör'*, *interj* calling for repetition of a performance or an additional item. — *n* a call of encore; an item given in response to such a call. — *vt* to call encore to. — *vi* to perform an encore. [Fr, again or still]

encounter *in-kown'tər, vt* to meet face to face, *esp* unexpectedly; to meet in a contest; to oppose or confront. — *n* an unexpected or chance meeting; an interview; a fight or battle; a contentious meeting; a manner of meeting or accosting (*Shakesp*); an encounter group meeting; — **encounter group** a group which meets with a view to establishing greater self-awareness and greater understanding of others by indulging in unrestrained verbal and physical confrontation and contact. [OFr *encontrer*, from L *in* in, and *contrā* against]

encourage *en-kur'ij, vt* to put courage in; to inspire with spirit or hope; to incite or spur on; to give patronage to; to cherish or sustain. — *n* **encour'agement** the act of encouraging; something that encourages. — *n* **encour'ager**. — *n* and *adj* **encour'aging**. — *adv* **encour'agingly**. [OFr *encoragier* (Fr *encourager*), from pfx *en-*, and *corage* courage]

encradle *en-krā'dl*, (*Spenser*) *vt* to lay in a cradle. [**en-** (1a)]

encraty *en'krə-ti, n* self-control. — *n* **En'cratism** the doctrine of the Encratites. — *n* **En'cratite** one of a heretical sect in the early church who abstained from marriage, and from meat and wine. [Gr *enkrateia* self-control, from *en* in, and *kratos* strength]

encrease. *Obs* form of **increase**.

encrimson *en-krim'zn, vt* to tinge with a crimson colour. — *adj* **encrim'soned**. [**en-** (1b)]

encrinite *en(g)'kri-nīt, n* a fossil crinoid; a crinoid. — *adj* **en'crinal**. — *adj* **encrin'ic**. — *adj* **encrinī'tal**. — *adj* **encrinitic** (*-it'ik*). [Gr *en* in, and *krinon* a lily]

encroach *in-krōch', vi* to seize on the rights of others; to intrude beyond boundaries; to extend into the territory, sphere, etc, of others. — *n* **encroach'er**. — *adv* **encroach'ingly**. — *n* **encroach'ment** an act of encroaching; something that is taken by encroaching. [OFr *encrochier* to seize, from *en-* and *croc* a hook]

en croupe *ã kro͞op*, (*Fr*) on the crupper, on a pillion.

en croûte. See **croûte**.

encrust or **incrust** *in-krust', vt* to cover with a crust or hard coating; to form a crust on the surface of. — *vi* to form a crust. — *n* **encrust'ment**. — *n* **encrustā'tion** (*en-*; or **incrustā'tion** *in-*) the act of encrusting; a crust or layer of anything; an inlaying of marble, mosaic, etc. [L *incrustāre*, *-ātum*, from *in* on, and *crusta* crust]

encryption *in-krip'shən, n* the putting of messages or information into code. — *vt* **encrypt'**. — *adj* **encrypt'ed**. [See **crypt-**]

en cuerpo *ān kwār'pō*, (*Sp*) in close-fitting dress; without a cloak or coat; in undress, eg in one's shirt-sleeves; sometimes erroneously for stark naked, the Spanish for which is *en cueros* (*kwār'ōs*). — Also **in cuerpo** and **in querpo**.

encumber *in-kum'bər, vt* to impede the motion of; to hamper; to embarrass; to burden; to load, eg with debts, etc. — *n* **encum'berment** the act of encumbering; the state of being encumbered. — *n* **encum'brance** something which encumbers or hinders; a legal claim on an estate; someone dependent on another, *esp* a child. — *n* **encum'brancer**. [OFr *encombrer*, from *en-*, and *combrer* (see **cumber**)]

encurtain *in-kûr'tin, vt* to curtain or veil. [**en-** (1a)]

ency., **encyc.** or **encycl.** *abbrev*: encyclopedia; encyclopedic.

encyclical *en-sīk'lik-l*, or *-sik'*, *adj* (also **encyc'lic**) sent round to many persons or places. — *n* a letter addressed by the Pope to all his bishops. [Gr *enkyklios*, from *en* in, and *kyklos* a circle]

encyclopedia or **encyclopaedia** *en-sī-klō-pē'di-ə, n* the circle of human knowledge; a work containing information on every department, or on a particular department, of knowledge, generally alphabetically arranged; *esp* (with *cap*) that by Diderot, D'Alembert and others. — *adj* **encyclope'dian** embracing the whole circle of learning. — *adj* **encyclope'dic** or **encyclope'dical** of or relating to an encyclopedia; all-comprehensive; full of information. — *n* **encyclope'dism** comprehensive knowledge; the rationalistic attitude of the French Encyclopedists. — *n* **encyclope'dist** the compiler or someone who assists in the compilation of an encyclopedia; *esp* (*Encyclopédiste*) a writer for the French *Encyclopédie* (1751–65). [False Gr *enkyklopaideiā*, a wrong reading for *enkyklios paideiā* general education (opposed to professional or special) *enkyklios* circular, recurring, everyday, from *en* in, and *kyklos* circle, and *paideiā* education, from *pais*, *paidos* a child]

encyst *en-sist'*, (*biol*) *vt* or *vi* to enclose or become enclosed in a cyst or vesicle. — *n* **encystā'tion**. — *n* **encyst'ment**. — *adj* **encyst'ed**. [**en-** (1a)]

end *end, n* the last point or portion; termination or close; death; consequence; an object aimed at; a fragment or odd piece; half a unit length of cloth; a warp thread; a waxed thread ending in a bristle (*shoemaker's end*); one of the two sides of a field, court, pitch, etc defended by a team, player, etc (*sport*); part of a game played from one end (of the bowling-green, archery-ground, etc); an outer district; a region; a cottage room (*Scot*). — *vt* to bring to an end; to destroy. — *vi* to come to an end; to cease; to be at the end. — *adj* **end'ed** brought to an end; having ends. — *n* **end'ing** a termination; a conclusion; death; extremity; something that is at the end; the final syllable or portion of a word, *esp* an inflection (*gram*). — *adj* concluding; finishing; completing; dying. — *adj* **end'less** without end; returning upon itself; everlasting; incessant; objectless. — *adv* **end'lessly**. — *n* **end'lessness**. — *adv* **end'long** (*Scot* **end'lang**) lengthwise on end (*archaic*); continuously (*archaic*); straight on (*archaic*). — *prep* (*obs*) along. — *adj* (*rare*) set on end. — *adj* **end'most** farthest. — *adv* **end'ways** or **end'wise** on end; with the end forward. — **end'-all** something that ends everthing (see also **be-all and end-all** under **be**); **end'game** the final stage of a game of chess or certain other games; a person's manner of playing the endgame; **endless chain** a chain whose ends are joined; **endless gearing**, **screw** or **worm** an arrangement for producing slow motion in machinery, consisting of a screw whose thread gears into a wheel with skew teeth; **end man** the man at the end of a row of performers, etc. — *adv* and *adj* **end'-on'** in the direction in which the end points. — **end organ** a specialized sensory or motor structure at a nerve-end; **end'-paper** a paper at the beginning or end of a book, pasted to the binding and leaving an additional fly-leaf; **end'-product** the final product of a series of operations; **end'-reader** one who peeps at the end of a novel to see the outcome; **end result** the final result or outcome; **end'ship** (*obs*) a village. — *adj* **end'-stopped** (*poetry*) having a pause at the end of each line (of verse). — **end use** the final use to which anything, *esp* a manufactured article, is put; **end'-user** the person, company, etc who will be the recipient of a product being sold; (*usu* **end-user certificate**) in international trade, documentation naming the end-user of a product being sold, required eg in the exporting of arms. — **all ends up** completely; convincingly; **at a loose end** or **at loose ends** with nothing to do; in a state of uncertainty or confusion as to one's course of action; **at an end** terminated; discontinued; exhausted; **at one's wit's end** see under **wit**[2]; **at the end of one's tether** utterly exasperated; without further resource; **be the end of** to cause the death of (often a *colloq* exaggeration); **end for end** with the position of the ends reversed; **end of story** (*colloq*) that's that; **end up** to arrive or find oneself eventually or finally; to finish (with *with* or *by*); to become in the end; **get hold of the wrong end of the stick** to misunderstand blunderingly; **get** or **have one's end away** (*slang*) to have sexual intercourse; **in the end** after all; at last; **keep one's end up** to maintain one's part position, appearance, etc; to be content to keep one's wicket standing without trying to score (*cricket*); **loose end** (often in *pl*) an unsettled matter; **make (both) ends meet** to live within one's income (both ends meaning both ends of the year); **no end** (*colloq*) very much; **on**

end erect; at a stretch; **the end** the last straw; the limit; **the end of the road** the point beyond which one can no longer continue or survive. [OE *ende*; cf Ger *Ende*, Dan *ende*, Gothic *andeis*; Sans *anta*]

endamage *in-dam'ij*, *vt* to damage. — *n* **endam'agement** damage, injury or loss. [**en-** (1b)]

endamoeba. See **entamoeba**.

endanger *in-dān'jər*, *vt* to put in danger; to expose to loss or injury. — *n* **endan'gerer**. — *n* **endan'germent** hazard, peril. [**en-** (1b)]

endarch *end'ärk*, (*bot*) *adj* having the protoxylem on the inner edge. [Gr *endō* within, and *archē* origin]

endart or **indart** *in-därt'*, (*Shakesp*) *vt* to dart in. [**en-** (1a)]

endear *in-dēr'*, *vt* to make dear or more dear; to bind in gratitude (*Shakesp*). — *adj* **endeared'** beloved. — *adj* **endear'ing** making dear; arousing affection; expressing love (*archaic*). — *adv* **endear'ingly**. — *n* **endear'ingness**. — *n* **endear'ment** the act of endearing; the state of being endeared; something that excites or increases affection; a caress or a spoken or written expression of love. [**en-** (1b)]

endeavour or (*US*) **endeavor** *in-dev'ər*, *vi* to strive; to attempt. — *n* an exertion of power towards some object; an attempt or trial. — *n* **endeav'ourment** (*Spenser*) endeavour. — **do one's endeavour** (*archaic*) to do one's utmost. [From such phrases as to *put oneself in devoir* (Fr *se mettre en devoir*) to do what one can or make it one's duty, from Fr *en* in, and *devoir* duty]

endecagon. A faulty form of **hendecagon**.

endeictic *en-dīk'tik*, *adj* showing, exhibiting or demonstrating. — *n* **endeix'is** an indication. [Gr *endeiktikos*]

endemic *en-dem'ik*, *adj* prevalent or regularly found among a people or in a district; confined to a particular area (*biol*). — *n* an endemic disease or plant. — *adj* **endemial** (*-dē'mi-əl*) or **endem'ical**. — *adv* **endem'ically**. — *n* **endemicity** (*-is'i-ti*) or **en'demism** the state of being endemic. — *n* **endemiol'ogy** (*-dem-* or *-dēm-*) the scientific study of endemic diseases. [Gr *endēmios*, from *en* in, and *dēmos* a people or a district]

endenizen *en-den'i-zn*, *vt* to naturalize, to make a denizen. [**en-** (1b)]

endermic *en-dûrm'ik* or **endermical** *-ik-l*, *adj* through or applied directly to the skin. — Also **endermat'ic**. — *n* **en'deron** the corium, derma or true skin. [Gr *en* in, *derma* and *deros* skin]

endew *en-dū'*, (*obs*) *vt* (see **endue**) to endow (*Spenser*).

endiron. Same as **andiron**.

endite. *Obs* form of **indict** or **indite**.

endive *en'div* or *-dīv*, *n* a salad plant (*Cichorium endivia*) of the chicory genus, with crisp, succulent, curly or broad leaves; (*esp US*; loosely) chicory. [Fr, from L *intubus*]

endlang, **endlong**. See **end**.

endo- *en'dō-* or *en-do'-*, *combining form* often interchanging with **ento-**(and *opp* to **ecto-** and **exo-**) inside or within. — *n* **en'doblast** (Gr *blastos* a shoot or bud) the inner cell-layer of a gastrula, the hypoblast. — *adj* **endocar'diac** or **endocar'dial** (Gr *kardiā* heart) within the heart. — *n* **endocardī'tis** inflammation of the endocardium, *esp* over the valves. — *n* **endocar'dium** the lining membrane of the heart. — *n* **en'docarp** (Gr *karpos* fruit; *bot*) a differentiated innermost layer of the pericarp, *usu* hard, such as a plum stone. — *adj* **endochylous** (*en-dok'i-ləs*; Gr *chȳlos* juice; *bot*) having internal water-storing cells. — *adj* **endocrī'nal**. — *adj* **en'docrine** (or *-krin*; Gr *krīnein* to separate; *physiol*) secreting internally; applied *esp* to certain glands that pour secretions into the blood (also *n*). — *adj* **endocrinic** (*-krin'ik*). — *n* **endocrinol'ogy** the science of the discharge of ductless glands. — *adj* **endocritic** (*-krit'ik*) endocrine. — *n* **en'doderm** (Gr *derma* skin) the inner layer of cells in a gastrula; the tissues derived from that layer. — *adj* **endoderm'al** or **endoderm'ic**. — *n* **endoderm'is** a close-set sheath, one cell thick, enclosing the central cylinder in plants. — *n* **en'dodyne** same as **autodyne**. — *adj* **endogamic** (*-gam'ik*) or **endogamous** (*-dog'ə-məs*). — *n* **endogamy** (*en-dog'əm-i*; Gr *gamos* marriage) the custom forbidding marriage outside one's own group; inbreeding; pollination between two flowers on the same plant; the union of female gametes. — *n* **en'dogen** (*-jen*; Gr *genēs* born; *obs*) any plant, including the monocotyledons, regarded as growing from within. — *adj* **endogen'ic** pertaining to the processes of change within the earth. — *adj* **endogenous** (*en-doj'i-nəs*) increasing by internal growth; formed within; (of depression) with no external cause. — *n* **endog'eny**. — *n* **en'dolymph** the fluid within the membranous labyrinth of the ear. — *adj* **endomēt'rial**. — *n* **endometrī'tis** (Gr *mētra* womb) inflammation of the endometrium. — *n* **endomētriō'sis** (a condition caused by) the presence of active endometrial tissue where it should not be, *esp* when affecting other organs of the pelvic cavity. — *n* **endomēt'rium** the mucous membrane lining the cavity of the uterus. — *n* **endomitos'is** (*bot*) the process in which the chromosomes divide without cell division, giving double the original number of chromosomes in the cell. — *n* **endomix'is** (Gr *mixis* mingling) in Protozoa, a nuclear reorganization without conjugation. — *n* **en'domorph** (Gr *morphē* form) a mineral enclosed within another mineral, the latter being termed a perimorph; a person of generally heavy or rounded body build, thought to accompany a type of personality characterized by placidity, lack of anxiety or tension, and the pursuit of pleasure (cf **ectomorph** and **mesomorph**). — *adj* **endomorph'ic**. — *n* **endomorph'y**. — *n* **endopar'asite** a parasite living inside the body of its host. — *n* **endonuc'lease** an enzyme that cuts a polynucleotide chain internally. — *adj* **endophagous** (*en-dof'ə-gəs*). — *n* **endoph'agy** (*-ə-ji*; Gr *phagein* aorist, to eat) cannibalism within the family or tribe; eating away from within. — *adj* **endophyllous** (*-fil'əs*; Gr *phyllon* a leaf; *bot*) being or formed within a sheathing leaf; living inside a leaf. — *n* **endophyte** (*en'dō-fīt*; Gr *phyton* a plant; *bot*) a plant living within another, whether parasitically or not. — *adj* **endophytic** (*-fit'ik*). — *n* **en'doplasm** (*biol*) the inner portion of the cytoplasm of a cell. — *adj* **endoplas'mic** or **endoplas'tic**. — *n* **endopleura** (*-ploo'rə*; Gr *pleurā* a side; *bot*) the inner seed coat. — *n* **endopodite** (*en-dop'ə-dīt*; Gr *pous*, *podos* a foot) the inner branch of a crustacean's leg. — *n* **endoradiosonde** (*med*) a miniature battery-powered transmitter designed to be swallowed by the patient to send out information about a bodily function such as digestion (see **radiosonde** under **radio-**). — *adj* **endorhizal** (*-rī'zl*; Gr *rhiza* root; *bot*) having the radicle of the embryo enclosed within a sheath, as in monocotyledons; monocotyledonous. — *n* **en'dosarc** (Gr *sarx*, *sarkos* flesh) endoplasm. — *n* **en'doscope** (Gr *skopeein* to look) an instrument for viewing the cavities of internal organs. — *adj* **endoscopic** (*-skop'ik*). — *n* **endoscopy** (*en-dos'kə-pi*) any technique for viewing internal organs, such as by fibre optic apparatus. — *adj* **endoskel'etal**. — *n* **endoskel'eton** the internal skeleton or framework of the body. — *n* **endosmō'sis** osmosis inwards, ie towards the solution. — Also **en'dosmose** (*-mōs*). — *n* **endosmom'eter** an instrument for measuring endosmotic action. — *adj* **endosmomet'ric**. — *adj* **endosmot'ic** pertaining to or of the nature of endosmosis. — *adv* **endosmot'ically**. — *n* **en'dosperm** (Gr *sperma* seed) (in a seed) nutritive tissue formed from the embryo-sac. — *adj* **endosper'mic**. — *n* **en'dospore** (Gr *sporos* seed; *bot*) the innermost layer of a spore-wall; a spore formed within a mother-cell. — *adj* **endos'teal** (Gr *osteon* bone) within a bone. — *n* **endos'teum** (*anatom*) the internal periosteum. — *n* **endosym'biont** an organism living within the body of its symbiotic host. — *adj* **endosymbiot'ic**. — *adj* **endothē'lial**. — *n* **endothē'lium** (*biol*) the layer of cell tissue on the internal surfaces of blood-vessels, lymphatics, etc: — *pl* **endothē'lia**. — *adj* **endotherm'ic** (Gr *thermē* heat) accompanied by, characterized by, or formed with absorption of heat. — *adj* **endotroph'ic** (Gr *trophē* food) of a mycorrhiza, occurring mainly within the root of the plant it feeds. — *n*

endozō'on (Gr *zōion* animal) an entozoon: — *pl* **endozō'a**. — *adj* **endozō'ic** (*bot*) entozoic, having seeds dispersed by animals that swallow them. [Gr *endon* or *endō* within]

endorphin *en-dör'fin*, *n* any of a group of opiate-like substances produced by the brain and the pituitary gland with pain-killing and other properties similar to morphine. [**endo-** and **morphine**]

endorse[1] or **indorse** *in-dörs'*, *vt* to write (*esp* one's signature, a note of contents, a record of an offence) on the back of; to assign by writing on the back of; to give one's sanction to; to express approbation of; to do so as a form of advertising, *usu* in return for money; to lay on the back to load (*archaic*). — *adj* **endors'able**. — *n* **endorsee'** (*en-*) the person to whom a bill, etc is assigned by endorsement. — *n* **endorse'ment** the act of endorsing; that which is written on the back; a sanction; a record of a motoring offence on a driving licence; an additional clause on a policy altering the coverage in some way (*insurance*). — *n* **endors'er**. — **endorse out** (*SAfr*) to order (a person) to leave a place because he or she lacks official permission to be there. [**endoss** changed under the influence of LL *indorsāre*, from *in* on, and *dorsum* the back]

endorse[2] *en-dörs'*, (*heraldry*) *n* a vertical band or stripe on a shield, one-fourth or one-eighth of the width of a pale. — *adj* **endorsed'** (of a pale) with an endorse on each side of it; (of wings) thrown back. [Origin obscure]

endosarc ... to ... **endospore**. See **endo-**.

endoss *en-dos'*, (*obs*) *vt* to endorse; to inscribe (*Spenser*). [ME *endosse*, from OFr *endosser*]

endosteal ... to ... **endotrophic**. See **endo-**.

endow *in-dow'*, *vt* to give a dowry or marriage portion to; to settle a permanent provision on; to provide permanent means of support for; to enrich with any gift or faculty; to present. — *adj* **endowed'** having (a gift, ability, etc) (with *with*). — *n* **endow'er**. — *n* **endow'ment** the act of endowing; something that is settled on any person or institution; a quality, aptitude or skill bestowed on anyone. — **endowment assurance** or **insurance** a form of insurance providing for the payment of a certain sum at a certain date or at death if earlier. [Fr *en* (from L *in*), and *douer* to endow, from L *dōtāre*, from *dōs*, *dōtis* a dowry]

endozoon, etc. See **endo-**.

endue or **indue** (*Spenser*, etc **endow** or **indew**), *in-dū'*, *vt* to take into the stomach, like a hawk (*obs*); to digest (*obs*); to take in or digest mentally (*Spenser*); to bring to (*Shakesp*); to put on (eg clothes); to invest with; to clothe; to supply or provide with. [OFr *enduire*, from L *indūcere*, from *in* into, and *dūcere* to lead, influenced by *induere* to put on]

endungeon *in-dun'jən*, *vt* to shut up in a dungeon or similar confinement. [**en-** (1a)]

endure *in-dūr'*, *vt* to tolerate, bear or put up with without giving in or up; to harden (*Spenser*); to remain firm under. — *vi* to continue to exist; to remain firm; to last. — *adj* **endur'able** that can be endured or borne; lasting. — *n* **endur'ableness**. — *adv* **endur'ably**. — *n* **endur'ance** the state or power of or capacity for enduring, bearing or surviving; patient suffering; patience; continuance; duration (*obs*); lasting quality; maximum performance under given conditions; captivity (*obs*). — *n* **endur'er**. — *adj* **endur'ing** lasting. — *adv* **endur'ingly**. [OFr *endurer*, from L *indūrāre*, from *in* in, and *dūrus* hard]

endways or **endwise**. See **end**.

ENE *abbrev*: east-north-east.

ene. Same as **e'en** (see under **even**[2]).

en effet *ã-ne-fe*, (*Fr*) in effect; in fact.

enema *en'i-mə*, *n* a fluid injected into the rectum; the process of injecting such a fluid: — *pl* **en'emas** or **ene'mata**. [Gr *enema*, *-atos*, from *enienai* to send in, from *en* in, and *hienai* to send]

enemy[1] *en'i-mi*, *n* a person who hates or dislikes, or who is hated or disliked; a foe; a hostile nation or force; something which is harmful to or which acts against (*fig*). — *adj* hostile. — **enemy at the door** (*usu fig*) a person, force, event, etc that is a present or increasing threat; **how goes the enemy**? (*colloq*) what time is it?; **the enemy** or **the old enemy** the Devil; **the last enemy** death. [OFr *enemi* (Fr *ennemi*), from L *inimīcus*, from *in-* (neg), and *amīcus* a friend]

enemy[2]. A dialect form of **anemone**.

energid. See **energy**.

energumen *en-ər-gū'mən*, (*obs*) *n* a person who is possessed; a demoniac. [LL *energūmenus*, from Gr *energoumenos*, from *energeein*, from *en* in, and *ergon* work]

energy *en'ər-ji*, *n* the power required for doing work, for action, etc; the power exerted in working etc; intensity; vigorous activity; vigour; forcefulness; the capacity of a material body or of radiation to do work (*phys*). — *adj* **energet'ic** having, requiring or showing energy; active; forcible; effective. — Also **energet'ical**. — *adv* **energet'ically**. — *n sing* **energet'ics** the science of the general laws of energy; the production and use of energy, eg in animals. — *adj* **ener'gic** (*in-ûr'jik*) exhibiting energy. — *n* **ener'gid** a protoplasmic unit; the nucleus and active cytoplasm of a cell. — *vt* **en'ergize** or **-ise** to give strength or active force to; to stimulate to activity. — *vi* to release energy, *esp* by acting vigorously; to act with force. — **energy gap** the amount by which energy requirements exceed the energy supply; **energy-mass equation** see **mass-energy equation**. — **conservation of energy** see **conservation**. [Gr *energeia*, from *en* in, and *ergon* work]

enervate *en'ər-vāt*, still sometimes *i-nûr'*, *vt* to weaken by depriving of nerve, strength, courage or vitality. — *adj* weakened; spiritless. — *adj* **en'ervating** or **en'ervative**. — *n* **enervā'tion**. — *vt* **enerve'** (*obs*) to enervate. [L *ēnervāre*, *-ātum*, from *ē* out of, and *nervus* a nerve]

enew *e-nū'*, (*falconry*) *vt* to drive or (*reflexive*) plunge into water. [OFr *enewer*, from *en* in, and OFr *ewe* (Fr *eau*) water]

enface *in-fās'*, *vt* to stamp or print on the face of a document, bill, etc. — *n* **enface'ment**. [**en-** (1a)]

en face *ã fas*, (*Fr*) in front; opposite; straight in the face; facing forward.

en famille *ã fa-mē-y'*, (*Fr*) (literally) amongst the family; as at a family gathering; at home; without ceremony.

enfant *ã-fã*, (*Fr*) *n* a child. — **enfant de la maison** (*də la me-zɔ̃*) a child of the house, quite at home; **enfant de son siècle** (*də sɔ̃ sye-kl'*) a person who reflects the spirit of his or her time, (literally) a child of his or her century; **enfant gâté** (*gä-tā*) a spoilt child (*fem* **gâtée**); **enfants perdus** (*ã-fã per-dü*) forlorn hope or shock troops, (literally) lost children; **enfant terrible** (*te-rē-bl'*) a precocious child whose sayings and actions cause embarrassment to other (*esp* older) people; a person whose behaviour, etc is indiscreet, embarrassing or (loosely) unconventional; **enfant trouvé** (*trōō-vā*) a foundling.

enfeeble *in-fē'bl*, *vt* to make feeble; to weaken. — *n* **enfee'blement** weakening; weakness. [**en-** (1b)]

enfelon *en-fel'ən*, (*Spenser*) *vt* to make fierce. [**en-** (1b)]

enfeoff *in-fef'* or *en-fēf'*, *vt* to give a fief to; to invest with a possession in fee; to give up as a fief; to surrender. — *n* **enfeoff'ment** the act of enfeoffing; the deed which invests someone with the fee of an estate. [OFr *enfeffer*, from *en-*, and *fief* (see **fief** and **feoff**)]

enfested *en-fest'id*, (*Spenser*) *adj* embittered. [Perh for **infest** hostile or **enfestered**]

enfestered *en-fest'ərd*, *adj* festered. [**en-** (1b)]

en fête *ã fet*, (*Fr*) in festivity or in festive mood; keeping, dressed for, etc a holiday.

enfetter *en-fet'ər*, (*Shakesp*) *vt* to bind in fetters. [**en-** (1c)]

enfierce *en-fērs'*, (*Spenser*) *vt* to make fierce. [**en-** (1b)]

enfilade *en-fi-lād'*, *n* a number of things arranged as if threaded on a string; a series of rooms with the doors in line affording a continuous passage; a vista; a discharge of firearms that sweeps a line or position from end to end (*military*); a situation or a body open from end to end. — *vt* to discharge or be in position to discharge firearms along the whole length of a line. — Also *adj*. — *adj* **enfiled** (*en-fīld'*; *heraldry*) thrust through like a sword. [Fr *enfiler*, from *en* (L *in*), and *fil*, from L *fīlum* a thread; see **file** a line or wire]

enfire *en-fīr'*, (*Spenser*) *vt* to set on fire or inflame.

enfix. See **infix**.

enflame. *Obs* form of **inflame**.

enflesh *in-flesh'*, *vt* to turn into flesh. [**en-** (1b)]

enflower *in-flow'ər*, *vt* to cover with flowers. [**en-** (1a)]

enfold or **infold** *in-fōld'*, *vt* to wrap up; to embrace or enclose; to encompass. — *n* **enfold'ment** the act of enfolding; something that enfolds. [**en-** (1a)]

enforce *in-förs'*, *vt* to gain by force; to impose by force; to give force to; to emphasize or reinforce; to put in force; to give effect to; to urge; to impress; to drive; to compel; to apply force to. — *vi* (*Spenser*) to strive. — *adj* **enforce'able**. — *adv* **enfor'cedly** by violence, not by choice. — *n* **enforce'ment** the act of enforcing; compulsion; a giving effect to; something that enforces. — *n* **enforc'er** someone who or something which enforces; a member of a gang, etc who uses strong-arm tactics to enforce the power of the gang or its leaders (*slang*, *orig US*). — **enforcement notice** (*law*) an order served on someone who has breached town-planning regulations; **enforcement officer**; **enforcement work**. [OFr *enforcer*, from *en* (L *in*), and *force*]

enforest *in-for'əst*, *vt* to turn into forest. [**en-** (1b)]

enform (*Spenser*). *Obs* form of **inform**[1].

enfouldered *en-fōl'dərd*, (*Spenser*) *adj* charged with or like lightning. [**en-** (1c) and OFr *fouldre* (Fr *foudre*), from L *fulgur* lightning]

enframe *in-frām'*, *vt* to put in a frame. [**en-** (1a)]

enfranchise *in-fran'chīz* or *-shīz*, *vt* to set free; to give a franchise or political privileges to. — *n* **enfran'chisement** (*-chiz-* or *-shiz-*) the act of enfranchising; liberation; admission to civil or political privileges. [OFr *enfranchir*, from *en*, and *franc* free; see **franchise**]

enfree *en-frē'* or **enfreedom** *en-frē'dəm*, (*Shakesp*) *vt* to set free; to give freedom to. [**en-** (1b)]

enfreeze *en-frēz'*, *vt* to freeze; to turn to ice: — *pa p* (*Spenser*) **enfrōs'en**. [**en-** (1c)]

EN(G) *abbrev*: Enrolled Nurse (General), formerly a State Enrolled Nurse.

ENG *abbrev*: Electronic News Gathering.

eng *eng*, (*phonetics*) *n* the symbol ŋ, representing the sound of English *ng*. — Also called **agma**. [From the sound]

Eng. *abbrev*: England; English.

eng. *abbrev*: engineer; engineering; engraver; engraving.

engage *in-gāj'*, *vt* to pledge (*obs*); to bind by a promise; to render liable (*obs*); to secure for service, ensure the services of; to enlist; to win over or attract; to betroth; to bespeak or reserve; to hold or occupy; to begin an action against (*military*); to fasten (*archit*); to interlock; to entangle (*archaic*). — *vi* to promise; to become bound; to take part; to become occupied or involved; to begin an action (*military*). — *adj* **engaged'** pledged; promised, *esp* in marriage; greatly interested; taken or booked; occupied; partly built or sunk into, or so appearing (*archit*); geared together or interlocked; (of literature or a writer) committed (cf **engagé**). — *n* **engage'ment** the act of engaging; the state of being engaged; something that engages or binds; betrothal; promise; appointment; employment; a fight or battle; commitment (cf **engagé**). — *n* **engāg'er** someone who engages in any sense; (with *cap*; *hist*) an adherent of the *Engagement* of 1647, a secret treaty between Charles I and the Scottish Commissioners. — *adj* **engāg'ing** charming, winning or attractive. — *adv* **engāg'ingly**. — *n* **engāg'ingness**. — **engagement ring** a ring given *esp* by the man to the woman as a token of their engagement to marry. — **engage for** (*archaic*) to answer for. [Fr *engager*, from *en gage* in pledge; see **gage**[1]]

engagé *ã-ga-zhā'*, *adj* committed to a point of view or to social or political action. — *n* **engagement** (*ã-gazh-mã*; sometimes *in-gāj'mənt*) commitment. [Fr]

engaol *en-jāl'*, (*Shakesp*) *vt* to put in gaol. [**en-** (1a)]

en garçon *ã gar-sɔ̃*, (*Fr*) like a bachelor; in bachelor style.

en garde *ã gärd*, (*Fr*; *fencing*) a warning to assume a defensive position in readiness for an attack.

engarland *in-gär'lənd*, *vt* to put a garland round. [**en-** (1a)]

engarrison *in-gar'i-sn*, *vt* to establish as a garrison. [**en-** (1b)]

engender *in-jen'dər*, *vt* to beget, generate or start the development of; to bear; to breed; to sow the seeds of; to cause to exist; to produce. — *vi* to be caused or produced. — *n* **engen'derer**. — *n* **engen'derment**. — *n* **engen'drure** or **engen'dure** (*archaic*) the act of engendering; generation. [Fr *engendrer*, from L *ingenerāre*, from *in*, and *generāre* to generate]

Enghalskrug *eng'hals-kroŏk*, (*Ger*) *n* a type of beer jug. [Ger *eng* narrow, *Hals* neck, and *Krug* jug]

engild *en-gild'*, (*Shakesp*) *vt* to gild. [**en-** (1c)]

engine *en'jin*, *n* a mechanical contrivance, *esp* a complex piece of machinery in which power is applied to do work; a locomotive; a military machine; anything used to effect a purpose; a source of power (*fig*); a device, contrivance or trick (*obs*); a snare (*obs*); an instrument of torture (*obs*); a person used as a tool (*archaic*); (see also **ingine**) ability, ingenuity, genius or turn of mind (*obs*). — *vt* to equip with an engine or engines; to contrive (*obs*). — *n* **engineer'** someone who designs or makes, or puts to practical use, engines or machinery of any type, including electrical; someone who designs or constructs public works, such as roads, railways, sewers, bridges, harbours, canals, etc; someone who constructs or manages military fortifications, etc (*hist*), or engines (*obs*); a soldier trained for construction work, such as digging trenches, road-making, etc; an officer who is responsible for a ship's engines; an engine-driver (*esp US*); someone who does public work requiring little skill (*US*; *facetious*); someone who plots (*obs*) or who contrives to bring about (with *of*). — *vi* to act as engineer. — *vt* to arrange or contrive; to manoeuvre or guide; to produce by engineering. — *n* **engineer'ing** the art or profession of an engineer; extended to apply to certain techniques or processes not connected with the work of engineers, such as *protein engineering*. — *n* **en'giner** (*Shakesp*) engineer. — *n* **enginery** (*en'jin-ri*) the art of managing engines; engines collectively; machinery. — **en'gine-driver** a person who controls an engine, *esp* a railway locomotive; **engineer's chain** a chain 50 or 100 feet long, made up of one-foot (0.3m) links; a unit of length of 100 feet (30.48m); **en'gine-fitter** a person who fits together the parts of an engine; **en'gine-man** a person who drives an engine; **en'gine-room** the room in a ship, industrial plant, etc in which the engines are; the source of strength or power (*fig*). — *adj* **en'gine-turned**. — **en'gine-turning** a kind of ornament made by a rose-engine, such as on the backs of watches, etc. [OFr *engin*, from L *ingenium* skill; see **ingenious**]

engird *in-gûrd'*, *vt* to gird round; to encircle: — *pa p* and *pa t* **engirt'**. — *vt* **engir'dle**. [**en-** (1a)]

engiscope. See **engyscope**.

English *ing'glish*, *adj* belonging to *England* or its inhabitants; (loosely, and deprecated by the Scots, Welsh and Northern Irish) British; of or relating to the English language. — *n* the English people (as *pl*); a Germanic language spoken in the British Isles, USA, most parts of the British Commonwealth, etc; 14-point type (*printing*); side (*NAm*; *billiards*). — *vt* to translate into English (*archaic* or *rare*); to make English or anglicise; to influence with English characteristics, customs, etc; to impart side to (*NAm*; *billiards*). — *n* **Eng'lander** (*facetious*, as though a mistaken translation of eg German *Engländer*) an Englishman. — *adj* **Eng'lified** like the English of England in speech or ways; Southroun in speech, *esp* affectedly so (*Scot*). — *n* **Eng'lisher** a translator into English; an Englishman

(*Scot*). — *n* **Eng'lishism** (*US rare*) an expression or idiom originating in or found only in the English of England or Britain; a custom or practice peculiar to England; great admiration or enthusiasm for England and its customs, etc. — *n* **Eng'lishman** or **Eng'lishwoman** a native or naturalized inhabitant of England. — *n* **Eng'lishry** the fact of being English; in Ireland, the population of English descent. — **Basic English** see under **base**[1]; **Early English** often used vaguely, eg for early Middle English or for Middle and early Modern English; for *archit* use see **early**; **English breakfast** a cooked breakfast, *usu* consisting of several dishes or courses (cf **continental breakfast**); **English disease** the British disease; **English flute** the recorder; **English horn** the cor anglais; **English sickness** same as **English disease**; **English sweat** (*hist*) the sweating sickness (see **sweat**). — **in plain English** in clear, simple language; **little Englander** a 19c British opponent of British imperalism and empire-building; a late-20c British supporter of the view that Britain should retain its individual national identity rather than become part of a more integrated Europe; **little Englanderism** or **Englandism**; **Middle English** the English used in Britain from about 1100 or 1150 AD till about 1500; **Modern English** the English used in Britain from about 1500 onwards; **Old English** a kind of black-letter type-face (*printing*); the English language down to about 1100 or 1150 AD (formerly, and still popularly, called *Anglo-Saxon*); **presentment of Englishry** (*hist*) the offering of proof that a person murdered belonged to the English race, to escape the fine levied on the hundred or township for the murder of a Norman; **Young England** see under **young**. [OE *Englisc*, from *Engle* Angles]

englobe *in-glōb'*, *vt* to enclose in or as if in a globe; to form into a globe. [**en-** (1a,b)]

engloom *in-glo͞om'*, *vt* to make gloomy. [**en-** (1b)]

englut *in-glut'*, *vt* to glut or fill; to swallow: — *pr p* **englutt'ing**; *pa t* and *pa p* **englutt'ed**. [**en-** (1c)]

engobe *en-gōb'*, *n* a slip applied to ceramics before the glaze, eg to mask their natural colour. [Fr]

engore *in-gör'*, *vt* to gore (*Spenser*); to pierce (*obs*); to wound (*obs*); to make gory. [**en-** (1c)]

engorge *in-görj'*, *vt* to glut; to devour (*Spenser*). — *vi* (*Milton*) to feed voraciously. — *adj* **engorged'** congested or excessively full of blood, etc. — *n* **engorge'ment** the act of swallowing greedily; congestion eg with blood (*med*). [**en-** (1c)]

engouement or **engoûment** *ã-go͞o-mã'*, *n* excessive fondness; infatuation. [Fr]

engouled *en-go͞old'*, (*heraldry*) *adj* of bends, crosses, etc, having ends that enter the mouths of animals. [Fr *engoulée*, from *en* in, and OFr *goule* (Fr *gueule*) a beast's mouth]

engrace *in-grās'*, *vt* to put grace into. [**en-** (1a)]

engraff. An obsolete form of **engraft**.

engraft *in-gräft'*, *vt* to graft; to insert; to join on (to something already existing); to fix deeply; to cuckold (*obs*). — *n* **engraftā'tion** (*en-*) the act of engrafting. — *n* **engraft'ment** engrafting; the thing engrafted; a scion. — Also (*obs*) **ingraft'**, etc. [**en-** (1a)]

engrail *in-grāl'*, *vt* to border with little semicircular indents (*heraldry*); to make rough (*archaic*). — *vi* to form an edging or border; to run in indented lines. — *n* **engrail'ment** the ring of dots round the edge of a medal; indentation in curved lines (*heraldry*). [OFr *engresler* (Fr *engrêler*), from *gresle* slender, from L *gracilis*]

engrain or **ingrain** *in-grān'*, *vt* to dye in a fast or lasting colour; to fix a dye firmly in; to instil (a habit or attitude) deeply in. — *adj* **engrained'** or **ingrained'** (or *in'*) dyed in grain; deeply coloured or permeated; deep-rooted and established, eg *engrained laziness*; thorough-going (*fig*). — *n* **engrain'er**. [Orig to dye in grain, ie with grain, the dye]

engram *en'gram*, sometimes **engramma** *en-gram'ə*, (*psychol*) *n* a permanent impression made by a stimulus or experience; a stimulus impression supposed to be inheritable; a memory trace. — *adj* **engrammat'ic**. [Ger *Engramm*, from Gr *en* in, and *gramma* that which is written]

en grande tenue *ã grãd tə-nü*, (*Fr*) in full dress.

en grand seigneur *ã grã sen-yœr*, (*Fr*) like a great lord.

engrasp *en-gräsp'*, (*Spenser*) *vt* to grasp. [**en-** (1c)]

engrave[1] *in-grāv'*, *vt* to cut with a special tool on wood, steel, etc; to cut into; to impress deeply; to form or represent by engraving: — *pa p* **engraved'** or **engrāv'en**. — *n* **engrāv'er**. — *n* **engrāv'ery** (*obs*) the art of the engraver. — *n* **engrāv'ing** the act or art of cutting or incising designs on metal, wood, etc in order to print impressions from them (in metal, the lines to be printed are sunk or incised, in wood, they appear in relief, the wood between them being cut away); an impression taken from an engraved plate; a print. [**en-** (1a) and **grave**[1]]

engrave[2] *in-grāv'*, (*obs*) *vt* to deposit in the grave. [**en-** (1a)]

engrenage *ã-grə-näzh*, (*Fr*) *n* gearing (also *fig*); a series of events, decisions, etc, each of which leads inevitably to further ones; the taking of such decisions as moves towards some goal, thus avoiding the necessity of discussing the desirability of the goal itself.

engrieve *en-grēv'*, (*Spenser*) *vt* to grieve. [**en-** (1c)]

engroove or **ingroove** *in-gro͞ov'*, *vt* to cut a groove or furrow in; to fit into a groove. [**en-** (1a)]

engross *in-grōs'*, *vt* to buy up wholesale or completely; to monopolize; to take wholly to oneself; to absorb the attention, interest or powers of completely; to copy in large writing or in distinct characters; to write in legal form; to prepare a legal or official document; to name in a list or document (*obs*); to make thick (*Spenser*); to fatten (*Shakesp*). — *adj* **engrossed'**. — *n* **engross'er**. — *adj* **engross'ing** absorbing; monopolizing. — *n* **engross'ment** buying up wholesale; something (eg a document) which has been engrossed; a fair copy. — **engrossing a deed** writing it out in full and regular form for signature. [Fr *en gros*, from L *in* in, and *grossus* large; see **gross**]

enguard *en-gärd'*, (*Shakesp*) *vt* to guard or defend. [**en-** (1c)]

engulf or **ingulf** *in-gulf'*, *vt* to swallow up completely; to cause to be swallowed up; to overwhelm. — Also (*obs*) **engulph'** or **ingulph'**. — *n* **engulf'ment**. [**en-** (1a)]

engyscope *en'ji-skōp*, (*obs*) *n* a microscope, *esp* a kind of reflecting microscope. — Erroneously **en'giscope**. [Gr *engys* near, and *skopeein* to view]

enhalo *in-hā'lō*, *vt* to surround with a halo. [**en-** (1a)]

enhance *in-häns'*, *vt* to lift (*obs*); to raise in value or quality; to heighten; to intensify; to add to or increase; to make more important; to improve. — *vi* to increase; to rise in value. — *n* **enhance'ment**. — *n* **enhanc'er** something that enhances; a DNA sequence that can stimulate transcription of gene while being at a distance from it (*biol*). — *adj* **enhanc'ive**. — **enhanced radiation weapon** a neutron bomb. [Anglo-Fr *enhauncer*, prob from OFr *enhaucer*, from L *in*, and *altus* high; cf **hance**]

enharmonic *en-här-mon'ik* or **enharmonical** *-ik-l*, *adj* pertaining to music constructed on a scale containing intervals of less than a semitone; of a scale of music current among the Greeks in which an interval of $2\frac{1}{2}$ tones was divided into two quarter tones and a major third; of a minute pitch difference eg between F sharp and G flat, not identifiable in a scale of equal temperament. — *adv* **enharmon'ically**. — **enharmonic modulation** for instruments of equal temperament, change of notation without change of tone. [Gr *enharmonikos*, from *en* in, and *harmoniā* harmony]

enhearse. See **inhearse**.

enhearten *in-härt'n*, *vt* to encourage; to cheer. [**en-** (1b)]

enhunger *en-hung'gər*, *vt* to make hungry. [**en-** (1b)]

enhydros *en-hī'dros*, (*mineralogy*) *n* a chalcedony nodule with water or other liquid in a cavity. — *n* **enhy'drite** a mineral with fluid inclusions. — *adj* **enhydrit'ic** or **enhy'drous**. [Gr *enydros* containing water, from *en* in, and *hydōr* water]

enhypostasia *en-hī-pō-stā'zi-ə*, (*theol*) *n* substantial or personal existence; personality not existing independently but by union with another, as the human nature of Christ was said to be dependent on his divine nature. — *adj* **enhypostatic** (*-stat'ik*). — *vt* **enhypostatize** or **-ise** (*-pos'tə-tīz*). [Gr *en*, in, and *hypostasis* (see **hypostasis**)]

eniac *en'i-ak*, *n* an American pioneer electronic computer, in full, *e*lectronic *n*umerical *i*ntegrator *a*nd *c*alculator.

enigma *in-ig'mə*, *n* a statement with a hidden meaning to be guessed; anything very obscure; a mysterious person or situation; a riddle; (with *cap*) a cipher used by Germany during World War II. — *adj* **enigmat'ic** or **enigmat'ical** (*en-*) relating to, containing or resembling an enigma; obscure; puzzling; open to more than one interpretation. — *adv* **enigmat'ically**. — *n* **enig'matist** a person who makes up or deals in riddles; a person who expresses himself or herself in riddles. — *vt* **enig'matize** or **-ise** to express enigmatically or symbolically. — *n* **enigmatog'raphy** the composition of enigmas. [L *aenigma*, from Gr *ainigma*, from *ainissesthai* to speak darkly, from *ainos* a fable]

enisle or **inisle** *in-īl'*, *vt* to put on or make into an island; to isolate. [**en-** (1a, b)]

enjambment or **enjambement** *in-jam(b)'mənt* or *ã-zhãb-mã'*, *n* in verse, the continuation of the sense without a pause beyond the end of the line. — *vt* and *vi* **enjamb** (*in-jam'*). [Fr *enjambement*, from *enjamber* to stride, encroach, from *en* in, and *jambe* leg]

enjoin *in-join'*, *vt* to impose (a command, etc) on; to order or direct, *esp* with authority or urgency; (*law*) to forbid or prohibit by injunction. — *n* **enjoin'er**. — *n* **enjoin'ment**. [Fr *enjoindre*, from L *injungere*, from *in* in, and *jungere* to join]

enjoy *in-joi'*, *vt* to take pleasure or delight in; to feel or perceive with pleasure; to possess or use with satisfaction or delight; to have the use or benefit of; (*usu* of a man) to have sexual intercourse with (*archaic*). — *adj* **enjoy'able** capable of being enjoyed; giving pleasure, delightful. — *n* **enjoy'ableness**. — *adv* **enjoy'ably**. — *n* **enjoy'er**. — *n* **enjoy'ment** the state, act or condition of enjoying; the satisfactory possession or use of anything; pleasure; happiness. — **enjoy oneself** to have a pleasant time. [OFr *enjoier* to give joy to, from *en* (L *in*), and *joie* joy; or OFr *enjoir* to enjoy, from *en*, and *joir*, from L *gaudēre* to rejoice]

enkephalin or **enkephaline** *en-kef'ə-lin*, *n* a chemical found in small quantities in the brain, which relieves pain and can now be produced synthetically. [Gr *en* in, and *kephalē* head]

enkernel *in-kûr'nl*, *vt* to enclose in a kernel. [**en-** (1a)]

enkindle *in-kin'dl*, *vt* to kindle or set on fire; to inflame; to excite or rouse. — *adj* **enkin'dled**. [**en-** (1c)]

enlace *in-lās'*, *vt* to encircle as though with laces; to embrace; to entwine; to entangle; to cover with a network or with lace; to interlace. — *n* **enlace'ment**. — Also **inlace'**. [**en-** (1c)]

en l'air *ã ler*, (*Fr*) in the air; being discussed or expected; without reality.

enlard *in-lärd'*, (*Shakesp*) *vt* to grease or baste. [**en-** (1a)]

enlarge *in-lärj'* (*Spenser* **enlarg'en**), *vt* to increase in size or quantity; to expand; to amplify; to make wider; to reproduce on a larger scale, *esp* of a photograph; to set free. — *vi* to grow large or larger; to speak or write expansively; to expatiate. — *adj* **enlarged'**. — *adv* **enlar'gedly**. — *n* **enlar'gedness**. — *n* **enlarge'ment** the act of enlarging; the state of being enlarged; increase; extension; diffuseness of speech or writing; a photograph reproduced on a larger scale; the act of setting free; release. — *n* **enlarg'er** an apparatus with a lens for enlarging photographs. [OFr *enlarger*, from *en* (L *in*), and *large* large]

enlevement *in-lēv'mənt*, *n* (*esp Scots law*) the abduction of a woman or child. — Also (as Fr) **enlèvement** (*ã-lev-mã*). — *adj* **enlevé** (*Fr*; *ã-lə-vā*) carried away or kidnapped.

enlight *in-līt'*, (*archaic*) *vt* to shed light on; to light up or kindle. — *vt* **enlight'en** to impart knowledge or information to; to make aware or uplift by knowledge or religion; to free from prejudice and superstition; to lighten or shed light on (*archaic*); to give light to (*archaic*); to make clear to the mind (*obs*). — *n* **enlight'enment** the act of enlightening; the state of being enlightened; (*usu* with *cap*) the spirit of the French philosophers of the 18c, with a belief in reason and human progress and a questioning of tradition and authority. [OE *inlīhtan*, from *in* in, and *līhtan* to light; or independently formed later]

enlink *in-lingk'*, *vt* to connect closely. [**en-** (1c)]

enlist *in-list'*, *vt* to enrol; to engage as a soldier, etc; to obtain the support and help of, for a cause or undertaking. — *vi* to engage in public service, *esp* as a soldier; to support a cause with enthusiasm. — *n* **enlist'ment** the act of enlisting; the state of being enlisted. — **enlisted man** (*US*) a member of the armed forces below the rank of warrant officer, other than a cadet or midshipman. [**en-** (1a)]

enliven *in-līv'n*, *vt* to put life into; to excite or make active; to make cheerful or bright; to animate. — *n* **enlīv'ener**. — *n* **enlīv'enment**. [**en-** (1b)]

enlock *in-lok'*, *vt* to lock up; to enclose. [**en-** (1a)]

enlumine *en-lōō'min*, (*Spenser*) *vt*. Same as **illumine**.

en masse *ã mas*, (*Fr*) in a body; all together.

enmesh or **inmesh** *in-mesh'*, **emmesh** or **immesh** *em-(m)esh'*, *im-(m)esh'*, *vt* to catch in a mesh or net; to entangle. [**en-** (1a)]

enmew. See **emmew**.

en militaire *ã mē-lē-ter*, (*Fr*) as a military man.

enmity *en'mi-ti*, *n* the quality of being an enemy; unfriendliness; ill-will; hostility. [OFr *enemistié*, from L *inimīcus*; see **enemy**]

enmossed *in-most'*, *adj* covered with moss. [**en-** (1a)]

enmove *en-mōōv'*, (*Spenser*) *vt*. Same as **emmove**.

ennage. See **en**.

ennea- *en'i-ə-*, *combining form* denoting nine. — *n* **ennead** (*en'i-ad*; Gr *enneas*, *-ados*) the number nine; a set of nine things. — *adj* **ennead'ic**. — *n* **enn'eagon** (*-ə-gon*; Gr *gōniā* angle) a polygon with nine angles, a nonagon. — *adj* **enneagonal** (*-ag'ən-l*). — *n* **enneahē'dron** a solid figure with nine faces. — *adj* **enneahē'dral**. — *n pl* **Ennean'dria** (Gr *anēr*, *andros* man or male) the ninth Linnaean class of plants, with nine stamens. — *adj* **ennean'drian**. — *adj* **ennean'drous**. — *adj* **enn'eastyle**. (Gr *stȳlos* column) having nine columns. [Gr *ennea* nine]

ennoble *i-nō'bl*, *vt* to make noble; to elevate or distinguish; to raise to the ranks of the nobility. — *n* **ennō'blement** the act of making noble; conferment of the rank of noble. — *adj* **enno'bling**. [Fr *ennoblir*, from Fr *en* (L *in*), and *noble*]

ennui *ã-nwē'*, *on'wē* or *on-wē'*, *n* a feeling of weariness or languor; boredom; the occasion of these feelings. — *vt* (found mostly as *pap*) to weary; to bore: — *prp* **ennuying**; *pa t* and *pa p* **ennuied'** or **ennuyed'**. — *adj* **ennuyé** (*Fr*; *-yā*) bored. [Fr, distress, from OFr *anoi*, from L *in odiō*, as *in odiō habeō* I hold in hatred, ie I am tired of; see **annoy**]

ENO *abbrev*: English National Opera.

enodal *ē-nō'dl*, *adj* without nodes.

enoki *ə-nok'ē*, *n* a thin white edible mushroom with a very small cap, native to Japan. [Jap]

enomoty *e-nom'o-ti*, (*ancient Greece*) *n* a band of sworn soldiers, *esp* the smallest subdivision of the Spartan army. [Gr *enōmotiā*, from *en* in, and *omnynai* to swear]

enormous *i-nör'məs*, or (*obs*) **enorm'**, *adj* immense; huge; abounding, exceeding the normal *esp* in a bad sense (*archaic*); outrageous (*archaic*); atrocious (*archaic*); considerable, very much, large extent of (*colloq*); exceedingly good (*colloq*). — *n* **enor'mity** a great crime; great wickedness; outrage; immenseness or vastness; iniquity; abnormality (*obs*). — *adv* **enor'mously**. — *n* **enor'mousness**. [L *ēnormis*, from *ē* out of, and *norma* rule]

enosis *en'ō-sis* or *en-ō'sis*, *n* union, the aim and rallying-cry of the Greek Cypriot movement for union with Greece: — *pl* **enoses**. [Gr (ancient and mod) *henosis*, from *heis*, *henos* one]

enough *i-nuf'*, *adj* as much as needed to satisfy a requirement, lack, demand, etc; sufficient; giving content; satisfying. — *adv* sufficiently; quite; fairly; tolerably; used in phrases which stress or admit the state of something, eg *oddly enough*, *fair enough*. — *n* sufficience; as much as satisfies a desire or want; a sufficient degree or extent. [OE *genōh* (nominative, neuter accusative and adv for earlier *genōg*); Gothic *ganōhs*; Ger *genug*; ON *gnōgr*]

enounce *i-* or *ē-nowns'*, *vt* to enunciate; to proclaim; to utter or articulate. [Fr *énoncer*, from L *ēnuntiāre*]

enow[1] *i-now'*, (*archaic*) *adj* and *adv* enough; formerly used as plural of *enough*. [OE *genōge*, with *-g* preserved in inflected forms; cf **enough**]

enow[2] *ē-nōō'*, *adv* (*Scot* and *dialect*) a moment ago; presently. [Prob **even now**]

ENP *abbrev*: electronic number plate.

en pantoufles *ā pā-tōō-fl'*, unconstrained, at one's ease. [Fr, in slippers]

en papillote *ā pa-pē-yot*, (of food) cooked and served in an envelope of oiled paper or foil. [Fr *papillote* buttered or oiled paper for cooking in]

en passant *ā-pa-sā*, (*Fr*) in passing; by the way; applied in chess to the taking of a pawn that has just moved two squares as if it had moved only one.

en pension *ā-pā-syɔ̃*, (*Fr*) at a fixed rate for board and lodging.

enplane. See **emplane**.

en plein air *ā ple-ner*, (*Fr*) in the open air.

en plein jour *ā plɛ̃ zhōōr*, (*Fr*) in broad daylight.

en poste *ā post*, (*Fr*) of a diplomat, resident at a place in an official capacity.

en primeur *ā prē-mœr*, (of tasting, buying or investing in wine) when the wine is new. [Fr *en* in, and *primeur* (of wine) youth or newness]

en prince *ā prɛ̃s*, (*Fr*) in princely style.

en principe *ā prɛ̃-sēp*, (*Fr*) in principle.

enprint *en'print*, *n* an enlarged photographic print, *esp* 5 × 3½in (approx 12.7cm × 9cm). ['*En*velope-size print' and '*en*larged print' have both been suggested as origins]

en prise *ā prēz*, (*Fr*) (of a piece in chess) exposed to capture.

en pure perte *ā pür pert*, (*Fr*) to mere loss or to no purpose.

en queue *ā ko*, (*Fr*) like a tail; in a string or line; (of hair) tied at the nape of the neck, in a queue or ponytail.

enquire. See **inquire**.

enrace *en-rās'*, (*Spenser*) *vt* to implant. [**en-** (1a)]

enrage *in-rāj'*, *vt* to make furiously angry. — *adj* **enraged'** very angry; furious. — *n* **enrage'ment** the act of enraging; the state of being enraged; rapture (*Spenser*). [OFr *enrager*, from *en* (L *in*), and *rage* rage]

enragé *ā-rä-zhā*, (*Fr*; *hist*) *n* any of a group of revolutionaries during the French Revolution in favour of proto-socialist economic reform rather than political reform as a means of alleviating the distress of the populace. [Fr, violently angry or crazy]

enranckle *in-rang'kl*, (*Spenser*) *vt* to enrage. [**en-** (1b)]

enrange *en-rānj'* or **enraunge** *en-rönj'*, (*Spenser*) *vt* to arrange; to rove over. [**en-** (1c)]

enrank *en-rangk'*, (*Shakesp*) *vt* to place in order. [**en-** (1a)]

en rappel *ā ra-pel*, (*Fr*; *mountaineering*) using a rope which is easily pulled free after descent. [Fr, from *rappel* recall]

en rapport *ā ra-pör*, (*Fr*) in direct relation; in close touch or sympathy.

enrapture *in-rap'chər*, *vt* to put in rapture or ecstasy; to transport with pleasure or delight. — *adj* **enrap'tured** or **enrapt'** in ecstasy. [**en-** (1a)]

enraunge. See **enrange**.

enravish *en-rav'ish*, *vt* to enrapture. [**en-** (1c)]

enregiment *in-rej'(i)-mənt*, *vt* to form into a regiment. [**en-** (1b)]

enregister *in-rej'is-tər*, *vt* to register; to enrol; to record; to put on record as ratified. [**en-** (1c)]

en règle *ā re-gl'*, (*Fr*) in due order; according to regulations.

en retraite *ā rə-tret*, (*Fr*) in retirement; on half-pay.

en revanche *ā rə-vāsh*, (*Fr*) in return or requital.

enrheum *en-rōōm'*, (*obs*) *vt* to give a cold to or cause to catch a cold. — *adj* (*archaic*) **enrheumed'**. [OFr *enrheumer*, from *en* (see **en-** (1b), and Gr *rheuma* (see **rheum**)]

enrich *in-rich'*, *vt* to make rich; to fertilize; to decorate; to enhance or improve; to increase the proportion of some valuable substance in; to increase the proportion of one or more particular isotopes in a mixture of the isotopes of an element, eg to raise the proportion of fissile nuclei above that for natural uranium in reactor fuel (*phys*). — Also *vi* (*rare*). — *n* **enrich'ment** the act of enriching; something that enriches; ornamentation. [**en-** (1b)]

enridged *en-rij'id*, (*Shakesp*) *adj* formed into ridges. [**en-** (1b)]

enring *in-ring'*, *vt* to encircle; to put a ring on. [**en-** (1a)]

enriven *en-riv'n*, (*Spenser*) *adj* torn. [**en-** (1c)]

enrobe *in-rōb'*, (*formal*) *vt* to dress, clothe, or invest. [**en-** (1c)]

enrol or (*archaic* or *US*) **enroll** *in-rōl'*, *vt* to insert in a roll, list or register; to enter in a list as pupil, member, etc; to enlist; to record; to put in writing; to form into a roll (*Spenser*); to enwrap (*Spenser*). — *vi* to enrol oneself: — *pr p* **enroll'ing**; *pa t* and *pa p* **enrōlled'**. — *n* **enroll'er**. — *n* **enrol'ment** or **enroll'ment** the act of enrolling; that in which anything is enrolled; a register. [OFr *enroller* (Fr *enrôler*), from *en*, and *rolle* roll]

enroot *in-rōōt'*, *vt* to fix by the root; to implant firmly; to entangle (*Shakesp*). [**en-** (1c)]

enrough *in-ruf'*, (*archaic*) *vt* to make rough. [**en-** (1b)]

enround *en-rownd'*, (*Shakesp*) *vt* to surround. [**en-** (1a)]

en route *ā rōōt*, on the road, on the way. — *interj* let us go, march. — **en route for** on the way towards. [Fr]

ens *enz*, (*metaphys*) *n* being or existence; an entity, as opposed to an attribute: — *pl* **entia** (*en'shi-ə*). — **ens per accidens** (*enz pər ak'si-dənz* or *per a-ki-dāns'*; *Aristotelian metaphys*) that which exists only as an accident of a substance (an **ens per se** (*sē* or *sā*)); **ens rationis** (*rā-shi-ō'nis* or *ra-ti-ō'*) an entity of reason, existing purely in the mind opposed to **ens reale** (*rē-ā'lē* or *re-ä'le*) which exists actually or potentially outside the mind. [LL *ēns*, pr p of L *esse* to be]

ENS *abbrev*: European Nuclear Society.

Ens. *abbrev*: Ensign.

ENSA *en'sə*, *abbrev*: Entertainments National Services Association, which provided entertainment for the armed forces during World War II.

ensample *en-säm'pl*, (*archaic*) *n* example. — *vt* to give an example of. [OFr *essample*; see **example**]

ensanguine *in-sang'gwin*, *vt* to stain or cover with blood. — *adj* **ensan'guinated** or (*esp facetious*) **ensan'guined** bloody. [Fr pfx *en-* in, and L *sanguis*, *-inis* blood]

ensate *en'sāt*, (*bot*) *adj* sword-shaped. [L *ēnsis* sword]

enschedule *en-shed'ūl*, (*Shakesp*) *vt* to insert in a schedule. [**en-** (1a)]

ensconce *in-skons'*, *vt* to settle comfortably; to hide safely; to cover or protect with a sconce or earthwork (*obs*). [**en-** (1a)]

enseal *en-sēl'*, (*archaic*) *vt* to put one's seal to; to seal up. [**en-** (1c)]

enseam[1] *en-sēm'*, *vt* to mark as if with a seam. [**en-** (1c), and **seam**[2]]

enseam[2] *en-sēm'*, *vt* to grease (*obs*); to defile (*Shakesp*); to free from superfluous fat (*obs*). [**en-** (1c), and **seam**[1]]

enseam[3] *en-sēm'*, (*obs*) *vt* to contain; to introduce to company. [Origin obscure; cf ME *in same* or *in seme*, OE *ætsomne* or *tosomne* together, ON *semja* to put together]

ensear *en-sēr'*, (*Shakesp*) *vt* to dry up. [**en-** (1b), and **sear**[2]]

ensemble *ã-sã-bl'*, *n* all parts of a thing taken together; a group of musicians playing together (*music*); the performance of such a group; the combined effect of the performance; a costume consisting of several (matching) garments; a group of supporting dancers, a corps de ballet; a set of a very large number of systems, all dynamically identical to a system under statistical consideration, but differing in the initial condition (*phys*). — Also *adj*. — **tout ensemble** (*tōō-tã-*) general appearance or effect. [Fr *ensemble* together, from L *in* in, and *simul* at the same time]

ensepulchre *en-sep'əl-kər*, *vt* to put in a sepulchre. [**en-** (1a)]

ensew (*Spenser*). Same as **ensue**.

ensheathe, **ensheath** or **insheathe** *in-shēdh'*, *vt* to enclose as a sheath. [**en-** (1a)]

enshell. Same as **inshell**. — *adj* **enshield'** (*Shakesp*), *prob* **enshelled** or **inshelled**.

enshelter *en-shel'tər*, (*Shakesp*) *vt* to put in shelter. [**en-** (1a)]

enshield[1] *en-shēld'*, *vt* to shield or protect. [**en-** (1c)]

enshield[2]. See **enshell**.

enshrine *en-shrīn'*, *vt* to enclose in or as if in a shrine; to consider sacred, to cherish. — *n* **enshrine'ment**. [**en-** (1a)]

enshroud *en-shrowd'*, *vt* to cover up; to cover with a shroud; to cover, hide or envelop as if with a shroud. [Pfx **en-** (1a)]

ensiform *en'si-förm*, (*bot* and *med*) *adj* sword-shaped. [L *ēnsis* a sword, and *fōrma* form]

ensign *en'sin* or *-sīn*, *n* a badge, sign or mark; a sign or flag distinguishing a nation or a regiment (see also under **blue**, **red** and **white**); a soldier who carries the colours; until 1871, the officer of lowest commissioned rank in the British infantry; an officer of lowest commissioned rank (*US navy*). — *vt* (*-sīn'*; *heraldry*) to mark with a badge or sign placed above. — *n* **en'signcy** or **en'signship** (*hist*) the rank or commission of an ensign in the army. [OFr *enseigne*, from L *īnsignia* pl of *īnsigne* a distinctive mark, from *in* on, and *signum* a mark]

ensilage *en'sil-ij* or *in-sī'lij*, *n* the storing of green fodder in pits or silos. — *vt* **ensile** (*en-sīl'* or *en'sīl*) or **en'silage** to store by ensilage. [Fr, from Sp *en* in, and *silo*, from L *sīrus*, from Gr *siros*, *sīros* or *seiros* pit for corn]

ensky *en-skī'*, (*Shakesp*) *vt* to place in the sky. [**en-** (1a)]

enslave *in-slāv'*, *vt* to make a slave or slaves of; to subject to a dominating influence. — *adj* **enslaved'**. — *n* **enslave'ment** the act of enslaving; the state of being enslaved; slavery; captivity. — *n* **enslav'er**. [**en-** (1b)]

ensnare *in-snār'*, *vt* to catch in a snare; to entrap; to entangle. [**en-** (1a)]

ensnarl *en-snärl'*, (*Spenser*) *vt* to entangle. [**en-** (1a)]

ensorcell *in-sör'səl* or *-sör'*, (*archaic* and *poetic*) *vt* to bewitch. [OFr *ensorceler*, from *en*, and *sorcier* a sorcerer]

ensoul or **insoul** *in-sōl'*, *vt* to join with the soul; to animate as a soul; to bestow a soul on. — *n* **ensoul'ment** or **insoul'ment**. [**en-** (1b)]

en spectacle *ã spek-ta-kl'*, (*Fr*) as a spectacle.

ensphere or **insphere** *in-sfēr'*, *vt* to enclose or place in or as if in a sphere; to give a spherical form to: — *pap* (*Milton*) **insphear'd**. [**en-** (1a)]

enstamp *in-stamp'*, *vt* to mark as with a stamp. [**en-** (1c)]

enstatite *en'stət-īt*, *n* a rock-forming mineral, an orthorhombic pyroxene, magnesium silicate. [Gr *enstatēs* adversary, from its refractory character]

ensteep *en-stēp'*, (*Shakesp*) *vt* to steep; to place under water. [**en-** (1c)]

enstructured *en-struk'chərd*, *adj* incorporated into or made part of the structure of something. [**en-** (1a) and **structure**]

enstyle *in-stīl'*, (*archaic*) *vt* to style or call. [**en-** (1c)]

ensue *in-sū'*, *vi* to follow or come after; to result (with *from*). — *vt* (*Bible*; *archaic*) to follow after: — *pr p* **ensū'ing**; *pa t* and *pa p* **ensūed'**. [OFr *ensuir* (Fr *ensuivre*), from L *in* after, and LL *sequere*, from L *sequī* to follow]

en suite *ã swēt*, *adv* forming a unit or a set; in succession or a connected series; with an en suite bathroom. — *adj* (of a bathroom) connecting directly with a bedroom. — *n* an en suite bathroom. [Fr, in sequence or in succession]

ensure *in-shōōr'*, *vt* to make sure; to make safe; to betroth (*obs*); to insure (*obs*). — *n* **ensur'er**. [See **insure**]

enswathe *in-swādh'*, *vt* to wrap round. — Also **inswathe'**. — *n* **enswathe'ment**. [**en-** (1c)]

ensweep *in-swēp'*, (*archaic*) *vt* to sweep over. [**en-** (1c)]

ENT (*med*) *abbrev*: ear, nose and throat, a specialized field of medicine.

ent. or **entom.** *abbrev*: entomology.

ent-. See **ento-**.

entablature *en-tab'lə-chər*, *n* in classical architecture, the part which surmounts the columns and rests upon the capitals; any similar structure, such as an engine framework upon columns. [Ital *intavolatura*, from *in* in, and *tavola*, from L *tabula*, a table]

entablement *in-tā'bl-mənt*, *n* a platform above the dado on a pedestal, on which a statue rests; an entablature. [Fr]

entail[1] or **entayle** *en-tāl'*, (*obs*) *vt* and *vi* to carve. — *n* cut or fashion. [OFr *entailler*, from LL *intaleāre*, from *in* into, and *taleāre* to cut]

entail[2] *in-tāl'*, *vt* to bring on or result in as an inevitable consequence; to settle on a series of heirs for (an estate), so that the immediate possessor may not dispose of it (*law*). — *n* the settlement of an entailed estate; an estate entailed; the transmission or rule of descent of an estate. — *n* **entail'er**. — *n* **entail'ment** the act of entailing; the state of being entailed. [**en-** (1a) and **tail**[2]]

entame *en-tām'*, (*Shakesp*) *vt* to tame. [**en-** (1c)]

entamoeba *en-tə-mē'bə*, *n* any amoeba of the genus *Entamoeba*, one species of which causes amoebic dysentery in humans. — Also **endamoe'ba**. [**ento-** or **endo-** and **amoeba**]

entangle *in-tang'gl*, *vt* to twist into a tangle, or so as not to be easily separated; to involve in complications or in an embarrassing or compromising situation; to perplex or confuse; to ensnare. — *n* **entang'lement** a confused state; perplexity or confusion; a tangled obstacle; a tangle; the condition of being entangled; an entangling situation or involvement. [**en-** (1c)]

entasis *en'tə-sis*, (*archit*) *n* the slightly swelling outline of the shaft of a column or similar structure, used to counteract the illusion of concavity that an absolutely straight column would produce. [Gr *entasis*, from *en* in, and *tasis* a stretch]

entayle. See **entail**[1].

entelechy *en-tel'ə-ki*, (*philos*) *n* actuality; distinctness of realized existence; a vital principle supposed by vitalists to direct processes in an organism towards realization of a certain end. [Gr *entelecheia*, from *en* in, *telos*, perfection or end, and *echein* to have]

entellus *en-tel'əs*, *n* the hanuman monkey of India. [Appar from *Entellus*, the old Sicilian in Virgil's *Aeneid*, from its old-mannish appearance]

entender or **intender** *in-tend'ər*, (*obs*) *vt* to make tender; to weaken. [**en-** (1b)]

entente *ã-tãt*, *n* an understanding; a friendly agreement or relationship between states, eg the **entente cordiale** (*kör-dē-äl'*) between Britain and France (1904). [Fr]

enter *en'tər*, *vi* to go or come in; to penetrate; to come on to the stage; to take possession; to become a member; to put down one's name (as competitor, candidate, etc); to join in or become a party or participator. — *vt* to come or go into; to penetrate; to join or engage in; to begin; to put into; to enrol or record; to admit; to inscribe or have inscribed; to register (a vessel leaving a port, a horse for a race, a pupil for a school, etc); to insert a record of; to initiate; to become a member of; to take possession of; to obtain right of pre-emption to by recording one's name in a land office, etc (*US*). — *n*

(*Shakesp*) ingoing. — *adj* **en'terable**. — *n* **en'terer**. — *n* and *adj* **en'tering**. — **enter a protest** to write it in an official document; thence simply, to protest; **enter into** to become concerned or involved in; to be interested in; to participate actively or heartily in; to understand sympathetically; to take up the discussion of; to be part of; **enter on** or **upon** to begin; to engage in. [Fr *entrer*, from L *intrāre* to go into, related to *inter* between]

enter-[1]. Form of **inter-**, *orig* through Fr *entre* between, etc.

enter-[2] *en'tər-* or **entero** *en'tərō-*, *combining form* denoting intestine. — *adj* **en'teral** pertaining to, within, or by way of the intestine. — *adj* **en'terate** having an alimentary canal. — *n* **enterec'tomy** (Gr *ektomē* a cutting out) surgical removal of part of the bowel. — *adj* **enteric** (*en-ter'ik*) pertaining to the intestines; possessing an alimentary canal. — *n* short form of **enteric fever**, typhoid fever, an infectious disease due to a bacillus, characterized by fever, rose-red rash, enlargement of the spleen and ulceration of the intestines. — *n* **enterī'tis** inflammation of the intestines, *esp* the small intestine. — *n* **en'terocele** (*-sēl*; Gr *kēlē* tumour) a hernia containing intestine. — *n* **enterocentesis** (*-sen-tē'sis*; Gr *kentēsis* pricking) operative puncturing of the intestine. — *n* **en'terolith** (Gr *lithos* stone) a concretion of organic matter with lime, bismuth or magnesium salts formed in the intestine. — *n* **Enteromor'pha** (Gr *morphē* form) a genus of green seaweeds of tubular form. — *n* **en'teron** in coelenterates (animals with only one body-cavity) the body-cavity itself; in higher animals, the gut or alimentary canal: — *pl* **en'tera**. — *n* **enteropneust** (*en'tər-op-nūst*; Gr *pneein* to breathe) any animal of the **Enteropneus'ta** (literally gut-breathers) the Hemichordata or a division of them including Balanaglossus. — *adj* **enteropneust'al**. — *n* **enteroptos'is** downward displacement of the intestines. — *n* **enteros'tomy** (Gr *stoma* mouth) surgical formation of an opening in the intestine. — *n* **enterot'omy** incision of the intestinal wall. — *n* **enterotox'in** an intestinal toxin which causes food poisoning. — *n* **enterovī'rus** any of several viruses occurring in and infecting the intestine. [Gr *enteron* gut]

enterchaunge *en-tər-chönj'*. An *obs* form of **interchange**.

enterdeale (*Spenser*). See **interdeal**.

entero-. See **enter-**[2].

enterprise *en'tər-prīz*, *n* an undertaking or new project, *esp* when bold or dangerous; readiness, initiative and daring in undertaking; a business concern. — *vt* (*archaic*) to undertake. — *n* **en'terpriser** an adventurer (*archaic*); an entrepreneur. — *adj* **en'terprising** bold and imaginative in undertaking; adventurous; full of initiative. — *adv* **en'terprisingly**. — **enterprise culture** a culture based on an economic policy that encourages commercial initiative and audacious, imaginative planning; **enterprise zone** any of a number of sites in depressed areas in which industrial and commercial renewal is encouraged by the government by means of financial and other incentives. [OFr *entreprise*, pa p of *entreprendre*, from *entre* between (L *inter*), and *prendre*, from L *praehendere* to seize]

entertain *en-tər-tān'*, *vt* to provide food or drink as refreshment for; to give lodging or hospitality to; to treat hospitably; to hold the attention or thoughts of; to hold the attention of in a pleasant or diverting manner; to amuse; to give pleasure or amusement to by means of a performance, show, etc; to receive and take into consideration; to keep or hold in the mind; to maintain or keep up (*obs*); to take on (as a servant, etc) (*obs*); to treat (*obs*); to receive (*obs*); to meet or experience (*Spenser*). — *n* (*Spenser*; *Shakesp*) entertainment. — *n* **entertain'er** a person who entertains in any sense; a person who gives performances professionally, eg a singer or comedian. — *adj* **entertain'ing** giving entertainment; amusing. — Also *n*. — *adv* **entertain'ingly**. — *n* **entertain'ment** the act of entertaining; the reception of and provision for guests; hospitality at table; something that entertains or amuses; amusement; a performance or show intended to give pleasure; the provisions of the table (*archaic*); a banquet (*archaic*). [Fr *entretenir*, from L *inter* among, and *tenēre* to hold]

entertake *en-tər-tāk'*, (*Spenser*) *vt* to receive.

entertissued. See **intertissued**.

entêté *ã-te-tā*, (*Fr*) *adj* infatuated; opinionated: — *fem* **entêtée**.

enthalpy *en-thal'pi* or *en'thəl-pi*, (*phys*) *n* the heat content of a substance per unit mass, defined as $h = u + pv$ (u = internal energy, p = pressure, and v = volume). [Gr *enthalpein* to warm in]

enthetic *en-thet'ik*, *adj* (of diseases, etc) introduced from outside the body. [Gr *enthetikos*, from *entithenai* to put in]

enthral or (*esp US*) **enthrall** *in-thröl'*, *vt* to bring into bondage or slavery; to hold in bondage or slavery; to hold spellbound: — *pr p* **enthrall'ing**; *pa t* and *pa p* **enthralled'**. — *n* **enthral'dom** (*archaic*) the condition of being enthralled. — *adj* **enthrall'ing**. — *n* **enthral'ment** or (*esp US*) **enthrall'ment** the act of enthralling; slavery. — Also (*obs*) **inthrall'** or **inthral'**. [**en-** (1a)]

enthrone *in-thrōn'*, *vt* to place on a throne; to exalt to the seat of royalty; to install as bishop; to exalt. — *n* **enthrōne'ment** the act of enthroning or of being enthroned. — Also **enthroniza'tion** or **-s-**. — *vt* **enthrō'nize** or **-ise** (or *en'*) to enthrone (eg a bishop); to exalt. [**en-** (1a)]

enthusiasm *in-* or *en-thū'zi-azm*, or *-thōō'*, *n* intense and lively interest; passionate zeal; possession by a god, inspiration or religious exaltation (*obs*); religious extravagance (*obs*). — *vt* and *vi* **enthuse'** (back-formation) to make, be, become, or appear enthusiastic. — *n* **enthu'siast** a person filled with enthusiasm; a person deeply interested in a particular subject. — *adj* **enthusias'tic** or **enthusias'tical** filled with enthusiasm; zealous; ardent. — *adv* **enthusias'tically**. [Gr *enthousiasmos* a god-inspired zeal, from *enthousiazein* to be inspired by a god, from *en* in, and *theos* a god]

enthymeme *en'thi-mēm*, *n* an argument of probability only (*rhetoric*); a syllogism in which one premise is suppressed (*logic*). — *adj* **enthymemat'ical**. [Gr *enthȳmēma* a consideration, from *enthȳmeesthai* to consider, from *en* in, and *thȳmos* the mind]

entia. See **ens**.

entice *in-tīs'*, *vt* to attract by exciting hope or desire; to tempt; to lead astray. — *adj* **entice'able**. — *n* **entice'ment** the act of enticing; something which entices or tempts; allurement. — *n* **entīc'er**. — *n* and *adj* **entīc'ing**. — *adv* **entīc'ingly**. [OFr *enticier* to provoke; prob related to L *titiō* a firebrand]

entire *in-tīr'*, *adj* whole; complete; unmingled; intact; unimpaired; untired (*Spenser*); not castrated (*esp* of a horse); with untoothed and unlobed margin (*bot*); inner or inward (*Spenser*); genuine (*archaic*). — *adv* (*archaic*) within; sincerely. — *n* the whole (*rare*); completeness (*rare*); a stallion; a stamped, used or unused, envelope (*philat*); porter or stout as delivered from the brewery. — *adv* **entire'ly**. — *n* **entire'ness** or **entī'rety** completeness; the whole. — **in its entirety** in its completeness; (considered, taken, etc) as a whole. [OFr *entier*, from L *integer* whole, from *in-* not, and root of *tangere* to touch; in some senses showing confusion with **interior**]

entitle *en-tī'tl*, *vt* to give a title to; to style; to give a right or claim to. — *n* **entī'tlement** something to which one has a right or claim. [OFr *entiteler*, from LL *intitulāre*, from *in* in, and *titulus* title]

entity *en'ti-ti*, *n* being or existence; something that exists independently; the basic essential nature of something; an abstraction or archetypal conception. — *adj* **en'titative**. [LL *entitās*, *-ātis*, from *ēns* (see **ens**)]

ento- *en'tō-* or *en-to'*, or **ent-** *ent-*, *combining form* denoting inside, often interchanging with **endo-** and *opp* to **ecto-** and **exo-**. — *n* **en'toblast** (Gr *blastos* shoot or bud) endoderm; a cell nucleolus. — *n* **en'toderm**

endoderm. — *adj* **entophytal** (*-fī'tl*). — *n* **en'tophyte** (*-fīt*; Gr *phyton* plant) an endophyte. — *adj* **entophytic** (*-fit'ik*) or **entophytous** (*en-tof'i-təs* or *en-tō-fī'təs*). — *adj* **entop'ic** developed, etc, in the usual place. — *adj* **entoplas'tral**. — *n* **entoplas'tron** the unpaired plate behind the epiplastra in a turtle's plastron. — *adj* **entopt'ic** (Gr *ōps*, *ōpos* eye) within the eyeball; pertaining to the visibility to the eye of objects within itself. — *n sing* **entop'tics** the study of such appearances. — *adj* **ento'tic** (Gr *ous*, *ōtos* ear) of the interior of the ear. — *adj* **entozō'al**. — *adj* **entozō'ic**. — *n* **entozō'on** (Gr *zōion* an animal) an animal living parasitically within the body of its host: — *pl* **entozō'a**. [Gr *entos* within]

entoil *in-toil'*, *vt* to entangle or ensnare. — *n* **entoil'ment**. [**en-** (1a)]

entomb *in-tōōm'*, *vt* to place in a tomb; to bury. — *n* **entomb'ment** burial. [OFr *entoumber*, from *en* in, and *tombe* a tomb]

entomic *en-tom'ik*, *adj* pertaining to insects. — *adj* **entomolog'ical** (*-loj'*). — *adv* **entomolog'ically**. — *n* **entomol'ogist** a scientist who specializes in entomology. — *vi* **entomol'ogize** or **-ise**. — *n* **entomol'ogy** (*-ə-ji*) the science of insects. — *adj* **entomoph'agous** (*-fə-gəs*; Gr *phagein* to eat (aorist)) insectivorous, insect-eating. — *n* **entomoph'agy** (*-fə-ji*) the practice of eating insects. — *adj* **entomoph'ilous** (Gr *phileein* to love) specially adapted for pollination by insects. — *n* **entomoph'ily** pollination by insects; adaptation to pollination by insects. [Gr *entoma* insects, from *entomos* cut up, from *en* in, and *tomē* a cut]

Entomostraca *en-tō-mos'trə-kə*, *n pl* a general name for the lower orders of Crustacea, ie *Phyllopods*, *Ostracods*, *Copepods* and *Cirripedes*. — *n* and *adj* **entomos'tracan**. — *adj* **entomos'tracous**. [Gr *entomos* cut up, from *en* in, *tomē* a cut, and *ostrakon* a shell]

entophytal ... to ... **entotic**. See **ento-**.

entourage *ā-tōō-räzh'*, *n* surroundings, followers, attendants. [Fr, from *entourer* to surround, from *en* in, and *tour* a circuit]

en tout cas *ā-tōō-kä'*, *n* a parasol that can be used as an umbrella. — **En-Tout-Cas**® a hard tennis court that can be used in all weathers. [Fr, in any case]

entozoon, etc. See **ento-**.

entr'acte *ā-trakt'*, *n* the interval between acts in a play; a piece of music or other performance between acts. [Fr, from *entre* between, and *acte* act]

entrail *en-trāl'*, (*Spenser*) *vt* to interlace or entwine. — *n* twisting or entanglement. [OFr *entreillier*, from *en* in, and *treille* trelliswork]

entrails *en'trālz*, (*Spenser* **entralles** *en'trōlz*), *n pl* the internal parts of an animal's body, the bowels; the inside of anything; the seat of the emotions (*obs*): — *sing* (*rare*) **entrail** (*Spenser* **entrall** *en-trōl'*). [OFr *entraille*, from LL *intrālia*, from *inter* within]

entrain[1] *in-trān'*, *vt* to put (*esp* troops) into a railway train. — *vi* to get into a train; to take a train. — *n* **entrain'ment**. [**en-** (1a)]

entrain[2] *in-trān'*, *vt* to transport one substance, eg small liquid particles, in another, eg a vapour (*phys*); to suspend bubbles or particles in a moving fluid (*phys*); to draw after (*archaic*). — *n* **entrain'ment**. [Fr *entraîner*]

entrain[3] *ā-trɛ̃*, (*Fr*) *n* liveliness or spirit. — *n* **entraînement** (*ā-tren-mā*) enthusiasm.

en train *ā trɛ̃*, (*Fr*) in progress.

entrall(es). See **entrails**.

entrammel *in-tram'l*, *vt* to trammel or fetter. [**en-** (1c)]

entrance[1] *en'trəns*, *n* a place of entering; a door; an act of entering; a coming on to the stage; the power or right to enter; the beginning (*archaic*). — *n* **en'trant** someone who or something which enters. — **entrance fee** the money paid on entering a society, club, etc. [Fr *entrer*, from L *intrāre* to enter]

entrance[2] *in-* or *en-träns'*, *vt* to fill with enthusiastic or rapturous delight; to put into a trance. — *n* **entrance'ment** a state of trance or of great or excessive joy. — *adj* **entranc'ing** charming, delightful. [**en-** (1a)]

entrant. See **entrance**[1].

entrap *in-trap'*, *vt* to catch in or as if in a trap; to ensnare; to entangle. — *n* **entrap'ment** the act of entrapping; the state of being entrapped; the act of luring a person into the commission of a crime so that he or she may be arrested and prosecuted (*law*). — *n* **entrapp'er**. [OFr *entraper*, from *en* in, and *trappe* a trap]

en travesti *ā tra-ves-tē*, (*Fr*) (*esp* of a female dancer, singer or actress) wearing the clothes of the opposite sex.

entreasure *in-trezh'ər*, (*archaic*) *vt* to store in or as if in a treasury. [**en-** (1a)]

entreat *in-trēt'*, *vt* to ask earnestly; to beseech; to beg for; to induce (*obs*); to treat, deal with or behave towards (*obs*); to occupy oneself with (*Spenser*); to pass or spend (time) (*Shakesp*). — *vi* to beseech or ask. — *adj* **entreat'able** (*obs*). — *adj* **intreat'full** (*Spenser*). — *adj* **entreat'ing**. — *adv* **entreating'ly**. — *adj* **entreat'ive** (*obs*). — *n* **entreat'ment** the act of entreating; treatment (*obs*); perhaps discourse, verbal intercourse, or favours as objects of entreaty (*Shakesp*). — *n* **entreat'y** the act of entreating; earnest prayer. — Also (*Spenser*) **intreat'**, etc. [OFr *entraiter*, from *en*, and *traiter* to treat]

entrechat *ā-tr-shä'*, (*ballet*) *n* a leap during which a dancer beats his or her heels together. [Fr, from Ital *intrecciata* plaited or complicated (caper)]

entrecôte *ā'tr'kōt*, *n* a steak cut from between two ribs. — Also *adj*. [Fr]

entrée *ā'* or *on'trā*, *n* entry, freedom of access, admittance; introduction or means of access; a dish served at dinner between the chief courses ie between fish and roast, also (*esp US*) a main course, and (*esp Austr*) a starter; an introduction or prelude (*music*); the act of entering, a formal entrance, or music for it. — **entrée dish** a dish, usually silver, with a cover, suitable for an entrée. [Fr]

entremets *ā'trə-mā* or *-me*, *n* a light dish served at table between the chief courses, formerly **entremes** or **entremesse**. [OFr *entremes*, from *entre* between, and *mes* (Fr *mets*) dish]

entrench or **intrench** *in-trench'* or *-trensh'*, *vt* to dig a trench around; to fortify with a ditch and parapet; to establish in a strong position (*esp military*); to establish or fix firmly because of an unwillingness to change or in such a way that change is difficult or impossible; to cut into or wound (*Spenser*). — *vi* to encroach. — *n* **entrench'ment** or **intrench'ment** a defensive earthwork of trenches and parapets; any protection; an encroachment (*obs*). — **entrenched provisions** in the constitution of S Africa, provisions specially safeguarded by being made subject to amendment or repeal only by exceptional procedure. [**en-** (1c)]

entre nous *ā-tr' nōō*, (*Fr*) between ourselves.

entrepot or **entrepôt** *ā'trə-pō*, *n* a storehouse; a bonded warehouse; a port through which exports and imports pass, *esp* one from which imports are re-exported without duty being charged on them. [Fr]

entrepreneur *ā-trə-prə-nœr'*, *n* a person who undertakes an enterprise *esp* a commercial one, often at personal financial risk; the managing proprietor of a firm who supplies the capital, bears the risks of production and is the controller of day-to-day management and marketing; a contractor or employer; an organizer of musical or other entertainments: — *fem* **entrepreneuse** (*-nœz'*). — *adj* **entrepreneur'ial** (*-nœr'i-əl*, *-nū'* or *-nōō'*). — *n* **entrepreneur'ialism**. — *n* **entrepreneur'ship**. [Fr]

entresol *en'tər-sol* or *ā'tr'-sol*, *n* a low storey between two main storeys of a building, generally between the ground floor and the first floor. [Fr, from *entre* between, and *sol* the ground]

entrez *ā-trā*, (*Fr*) *imperative* come in.

entrism, etc. See **entryism** under **entry**.

entrold, another reading **introld** *in-trōld'*, (*Spenser*; *appar* a past participle of unknown meaning) enrolled, in the sense of encircled, has been conjectured.

entropion *en-trō'pi-on* or **entropium** *en-trō'pi-əm*, *n* inversion of the edge of the eyelid. [Gr *en* in, and *tropē* turning]

entropy *en'trə-pi*, (*phys*) *n* a measure of unavailable energy, energy still existing but lost for purpose of doing work because it exists as the internal motion of molecules; a measure of the disorder of a system; a measure of heat content, regarded as increased in a reversible change by the ratio of heat taken in to absolute temperature. [Gr *en* in, and *tropē* turning, intended to represent 'transformation content']

entrust or **intrust** *in-trust'*, *vt* to give in trust; to commit as a trust; to give responsibility to trustingly. — *n* **entrust'ment**. [**en-** (1c)]

entry *en'tri*, *n* the act of entering in any sense; a coming on to the stage; the coming in of an instrument or performer; entrance; a narrow lane between houses (*dialect*); a lobby or vestibule; a hostel (*obs*); the act of recording in writing; the thing so written; a list of competitors; a young hound, or hounds collectively old enough to begin training; a taking possession (*law*). — *n* **en'tryism** or **en'trism** the practice of joining *esp* a political body in sufficient numbers to swing its policy, *specif* of Trotskyists, etc in branches of the Labour Party. — *n* and *adj* **en'tryist** or **en'trist**. — **entry corridor** (*space flight*) same as **re-entry corridor**; **entry fee** entrance fee; **entry portal** (*radiol*) an area through which a beam of radiation enters the body. — **card of entry** (*bridge*, etc) a card with which to win a trick in order to take the lead; **port of entry** see **port**[4]. [Fr *entrée*, from *entrer*, from L *intrāre* to go into]

Entryphone® *en'tri-fōn*, *n* a telephonic device at the entrance to eg a block of flats, allowing communication between individual occupiers and visitors and usually incorporating a means of opening the main door.

Ent. Sta. Hall *abbrev*: Entered at Stationers' Hall, until 1924 a book registration requirement for copyright purposes.

entwine *in-twīn'*, *vt* to interlace; to weave together. — Also **intwine'**. [**en-** (1c)]

entwist *in-twist'*, *vt* to twist round. — Also **intwist'**. [**en-** (1c)]

enucleate *in-ū'kli-āt*, *vt* to extract (eg a tumour, eyeball or swelling) (*surg*); to deprive of a kernel or nucleus; to explain. — *adj* without a nucleus. — *n* **enucleā'tion**. [L *ēnucleāre*, from *ē* from, and *nucleus* a kernel]

enumerate *i-nū'mər-āt*, *vt* to count the number of; to give a list of, one by one. — *n* **enūmerā'tion** the act of numbering; a detailed account; a summing-up (*rhetoric*). — *adj* **enū'merative**. — *n* **enū'merātor** someone who or something that enumerates; a person who collects and deals with population census figures, voters' lists, etc. [L *ē* from, and *numerāre*, *-ātum* to number]

enunciate *i-nun'si-āt* or *i-nun'shi-āt*, *vt* to state formally; to pronounce distinctly; to utter. — *adj* **enun'ciable** (*-si-* or *-shi-*) capable of being enunciated. — *n* **enunciation** (*i-nun-si-ā'shən*) the act of enunciating; the manner of speaking or pronouncing; a distinct statement or declaration; the words in which a proposition is expressed. — *adj* **enun'ciative** (*-si-ā-*, *-syā-*, *-sh(y)ā-* or *-shə-*) or **enun'ciatory** containing enunciation or utterance; declarative. — *n* **enun'ciātor** someone who or something that enunciates. [L *ēnuntiāre*, *-ātum*, from *ē* from, and *nuntiāre* to tell, from *nuntius* a messenger]

enure. See **inure**[1].

enuresis *en-ū-rē'sis*, (*med*) *n* incontinence of urine. — *adj* and *n* **enūret'ic**. [Gr *en* in, and *ourēsis* urination]

envassal *en-vas'əl*, (*obs*) *vt* to make a vassal. [**en-** (1c)]

envault *en-vǒlt'*, (*obs*) *vt* to enclose in a vault. [**en-** (1a)]

enveigle. See **inveigle**.

envelop *en-* or *in-vel'əp*, *vt* to cover by wrapping; to surround entirely; to hide. — *n* **envelope** (*en'vəl-ōp*) something which envelops, wraps or covers; a cover for a letter (in this sense sometimes pronounced *on'* or *ā'* in imitation of French); one of the coverings of a flower, the calyx or corolla (*bot*); the gas-bag of a balloon or airship; the locus of ultimate intersections of a series of curves (*math*); the outer containing vessel of a discharge tube (*electronics*); the curve connecting the peaks of successive cycles of a modulated carrier wave (*telecomm*). — *adj* **envel'oped** (*heraldry*) entwined, eg with serpents or laurels. — *n* **envel'opment** a complete wrapping or covering. — **envelope stuffer** (*marketing*) an item of promotional material enclosed with a letter, invoice, statement, etc. [OFr *enveloper*; origin obscure]

envenom *in-ven'əm*, *vt* to put venom into; to poison; to taint with bitterness or malice. — *adj* **enven'omed**. [OFr *envenimer*, from *en* in, and *venim* venom]

en ventre sa mère *ā vā-tr' sa mer*, (*law*; *Fr*) in his or her mother's womb.

en vérité *ā vā-rē-tā*, (*Fr*) in truth.

envermeil *en-vûr'mil*, (*Milton*) *vt* to dye red or give a red colour to. [OFr *envermeiller*, from *en* in, and *vermeil* red or vermilion]

Env. Ext. *abbrev*: Envoy Extraordinary.

en ville *ā vēl*, (*Fr*) in town; not at home.

environ *in-vī'rən*, *vt* to surround; to encircle. — *n pl* **environs** (*in-vī'rənz* or *en'vi-*) the places that environ; the outskirts of a city; neighbourhood. [Fr *environner*, from *environ* around, from *virer* to turn round; cf **veer**]

environment *in-* or *en-vī'rən-mənt*, *n* surroundings; external conditions influencing development or growth of people, animals or plants; living or working conditions. — *adj* **envīronment'al**. — *n* **environment'alism** concern about the environment and its preservation from the effects of pollution, etc; the belief that environment rather than heredity is the main influence on a person's behaviour and development (*psychol*). — *n* **environment'alist** a person who is concerned with the protection of the environment, *esp* from pollution; a person who advocates environmentalism (*psychol*). — *n sing* **environics** (*en-vī-ron'iks*) the study of methods of influencing behaviour by controlling environmental factors. — *adj* **environment'ally-friend'ly** having or designed to have a beneficial relationship with the environment; not harmful to the environment. — **environmental health officer** an official whose duty is to enforce regulations regarding matters which might affect the health of the general public eg hygiene in food-handling shops, maintenance of a clean water supply, waste disposal, etc (*abbrev* **EHO**) — formerly **public health inspector** and **sanitary inspector**; **environmental pathway** a route by which a radionuclide in the environment can reach man; **Environmental Protection Agency** a federal agency responsible for the protection of the environment and pollution control (*US*; *abbrev* **EPA**). [Ety as for **environ**]

envisage *in-viz'ij*, *vt* to face (*archaic*); to consider or contemplate; to picture in one's mind; to visualize; to see, suggest or expect as a possible or likely future target, result, etc. — *n* **envis'agement**. [Fr *envisager*, from *en* in, and *visage* the face]

envision *in-vizh'ən*, *vt* to see as if in a vision; to visualize; to envisage. [**en-** (1c)]

envoy[1] *en'voi*, *n* a messenger, *esp* one sent to transact business with a foreign government; a diplomatic minister of the second class. — *n* **en'voyship**. [Fr *envoyé*, from pa p of *envoyer* to send]

envoy[2] or **envoi** *en'voi*, *n* the concluding part of a poem or a book; the author's final words, *esp* the short stanza concluding a poem written in certain archaic metrical forms. [OFr *envoye*, from *envoiier* to send, from *en voie* on the way, from L *in* on, and *via* a way]

envy *en'vi*, *n* ill-will or hostility (*obs*); a feeling of discontent at the good looks, qualities, fortune, etc, of another; an object or person contemplated with grudging or envious feelings. — *vt* (formerly *in-vī'*) to feel vexation at (*obs*); to feel envy towards or on account of; to wish to have or to covet someone's property, good fortune, skills, etc; to grudge (*obs*); to desire with emulation or rivalry: — *pr p* **en'vying**; *pa t* and *pa p* **en'vied**. — *adj* **en'viable** that is to be envied; causing envy. — *n* **en'viableness**. — *adv* **en'viably**. — *n* **en'vier** someone who envies. — *adj* **en'vious** feeling envy; directed by envy; enviable (*Spenser*). — *adv* **en'viously**. — *n* **en'viousness**. — *n* **en'vying** (*Bible*) jealousy or ill-will. [Fr *envie*, from L *invidia*, from *invidēre* to look askance at, to envy, from *in* on, and *vidēre* to look]

enwall or **inwall** *in-wöl'*, *vt* to enclose within a wall. [**en-** (1a)]

enwallow *en-wol'ō*, (*Spenser*) *vt* to roll about wallowingly. [**en-** (1c)]

enwheel *en-(h)wēl'*, (*Shakesp*) *vt* to encircle. [**en-** (1a)]

enwind or **inwind** *in-wīnd'*, *vt* to wind about or enwrap. [**en-** (1a)]

enwomb *en-wōōm'*, *vt* to make pregnant (*Spenser*); to conceive or have in the womb (*Shakesp*); to contain. [**en-** (1a)]

enwrap or **inwrap** *in-rap'*, *vt* to cover by wrapping; to enfold; to engross. — *n* **enwrap'ment**. — *adj* and *n* **enwrapp'ing**. [**en-** (1a)]

enwreathe or **inwreathe** *in-rēdh'*, *vt* to wreathe; to envelop; to encircle with or as if with a wreath. [Pfx **en-** (1a)]

Enzed *en-zed'*, (*Austr* and *NZ colloq*) *n* New Zealand; (also **Enzedd'er**) a New Zealander. [The abbrev **NZ** phonetically represented]

enzian *ent'si-ən*, *n* a type of schnapps flavoured with gentian roots, drunk in the Tyrol. [Ger *Enzian* gentian]

enzone *in-zōn'*, *vt* to engirdle; to enclose with or as if with a zone or belt. [**en-** (1a)]

enzootic *en-zō-ot'ik*, *adj* of animal diseases, prevalent in a particular district or at a particular season. — *n* a disease of this kind. [Gr *en* in, and *zōion* animal, in imitation of *endemic*]

enzyme *en'zīm*, *n* any one of a large class of protein substances produced by living cells which, *usu* in the presence of other substances eg coenzymes, act as catalysts in biochemical reactions. — *adj* **enzymat'ic** or **enzym'ic**. — *n* **enzymol'ogist**. — *n* **enzymol'ogy** the scientific study of enzymes. [Gr *en* in, and *zȳmē* leaven]

E O *ē'ō'*, *n* a mid-18c gambling game, depending on a ball falling into slots marked either *E* or *O*.

e o *abbrev*: ex officio.

eoan *ē-ō'ən*, *adj* of or pertaining to dawn. [L, from Gr *ēōs* dawn]

Eoanthropus *ē-ō-an-thrō'pəs*, *n* what was thought to be an early form of man, represented by parts of a skull found at Piltdown, Sussex in 1912, but in 1953 exposed as a hoax when the jawbone was shown to be an ape's. [Gr *ēōs* dawn, and *anthrōpos* man]

EOC *abbrev*: Equal Opportunities Commission.

Eocene *ē'ō-sēn*, (*geol*) *adj* belonging to the oldest division of the Tertiary formation. — *n* the Eocene system, period or strata. [Gr *ēōs* daybreak, and *kainos* new, from the very small proportion of living species of molluscs among its fossils; cf **Miocene** and **Pliocene**]

eod *abbrev*: every other day.

Eohippus *ē-ō-hip'-əs*, *n* the oldest known horselike animal, an Eocene fossil. [Gr *ēōs* dawn, and *hippos* horse]

EOKA *ā-ō'kə*, *abbrev*: *Ethnikē Organōsis Kypriākou Agōnos* (*Gr*), the National Organization of the Cypriot Struggle, a secret Greek Cypriot organization which fought for the union of Cyprus with Greece.

Eolian, **Eolic**. Same as **Aeolian**, **Aeolic**.

éolienne *ā-ol-yen'*, *n* dress material of fine silk and wool. [Fr]

eolipile. Same as **aeolipile**.

eolith *ē'ō-lith*, *n* a very early roughly-broken stone implement, or one naturally formed but assumed to have been used by man. — *adj* **eolith'ic**. [Gr *ēōs* dawn, and *lithos* stone]

eon. See **aeon**.

eonism *ē'ə-nizm*, (*psychiatry*) *n* adoption by a male of female dress and manner. [Chevalier d'*Éon*, Fr diplomat (died 1810) who chose female dress as a disguise]

eo nomine *ē'ō nom'i-nē* or *e'ō nom'i-ne*, (*L*) by that name, on that claim.

eorl. Obs form of **earl**.

eosin *ē'ō-sin*, *n* a red dyestuff, $C_{20}H_8Br_4O_5$. — *adj* **eosin'ophil** (Gr *philos* loving) readily staining with eosin. — *n* a type of white blood cell, so called because it is easily stained by eosin. — *n* **eosinophil'ia** the condition of staining readily with eosin; the condition in which there is an abnormally large number of eosinophils in the blood. — *adj* **eosinophil'ic** or **eosinoph'ilous** eosinophil; pertaining to eosinophils or eosinophilia. [Gr *ēōs* dawn]

eothen *ē-ō'then*, (*archaic*) *adv* from the east, the name given by Kinglake to his book of travel in the East (1844). [Gr *ēōthen* (literally) from morn, at earliest dawn]

Eozoon *ē-ō-zō'on*, *n* what was thought to be a fossil organism in the Archaean system of Canada, which would have been the oldest known living thing, or the banded arrangement of calcite and serpentine at that time supposed to be its remains. — *adj* **Eozō'ic**. [Gr *ēōs* dawn, and *zōion* an animal]

EP *abbrev*: electroplated; European Parliament; extended play (of records).

Ep. See **Epis**.

ep-. See **epi-**.

EPA *abbrev*: Environmental Protection Agency (*US*); European Productivity Agency.

epacris *ep-ak'ris* or *ep'ə-kris*, *n* a plant of the chiefly Australian genus *Epacris* of heath-like plants, giving name to the family **Epacridā'ceae**, closely related to the heaths. — *n* **epac'rid** (or *ep'*) any member of the genus, or the family. [Gr *epi* upon, and *akris* a summit]

epact *ē'pakt*, *n* the moon's age at the beginning of the year; the excess of the calendar month or solar year over the lunar. [Fr *épacte*, from Gr *epaktos* brought on, from *epi* on, and *agein* to bring]

epaenetic *ep-ə-net'ik* or **epainetic** *ep-ī-net'ik*, (*archaic*) *adj* eulogistic. [Gr *epainetikos*, from *epainein* to praise]

epagoge *ep-ə-gō'gē* or *-jē*, (*logic*) *n* induction. — *adj* **epagog'ic**. [Gr *epagōgē*, from *epi* on, and *agōgē* leading]

epagomenal *ep-ə-gom'ə-nəl*, *adj* (*esp* of days) intercalary, or inserted between others. [Gr *epagomenos*, from *epi* upon or in, and *agein* to bring]

epainetic. See **epaenetic**.

epanadiplosis *ep-a-nə-di-plō'sis*, (*rhetoric*) *n* a figure by which a sentence begins and ends with the same word, eg 'Rejoice in the Lord alway, and again I say, rejoice'. — *pl* **epanadiplō'sēs**. [Gr]

epanalepsis *ep-a-nə-lep'sis*, (*rhetoric*) *n* repetition or resumption with the same words. — *pl* **epanalep'sēs**. [Gr]

epanaphora *ep-ə-naf'o-rə*. Same as **anaphora**.

epanodos *ep-an'o-dos*, (*rhetoric*) *n* recapitulation of the chief points in a discourse. [Gr *epanodos*]

epanorthosis *ep-an-ör-thō'sis*, (*rhetoric*) *n* the retracting of a statement in order to correct or intensify it, as *For Britain's guid! for her destruction!*: — *pl* **epanorthō'sēs**. [Gr]

eparch *ep'ärk*, *n* the governor of a modern Greek province; a metropolitan (*eccles*). — *n* **ep'archate** or **ep'archy** the province, territory or diocese of an eparch. [Gr *eparchos*, from *epi* upon, and *archē* dominion]

épatant *ā-pa-tã*, (*Fr*) *adj* wonderful or marvellous.

epaule *e-pöl'*, *n* the shoulder of a bastion (*military*). — *n* **epaule'ment** a side-work of a battery or earthwork to protect it from flanking fire (*military*); a particular position of a dancer's shoulders, one forward, one back (*ballet*). [Fr *épaule* shoulder, from L *spatula*]

epaulette or (*esp US*) **epaulet** *ep'əl-et*, *n* an ornament on the shoulder of military or naval officers' uniform (now disused in the British Army) or of civilian clothing; a shoulder-piece. [Fr *épaulette*, from *épaule* the shoulder]

epaxial *ep-aks'i-əl*, (*zool*) *adj* above the axis. [Gr *epi* on or over, and **axis**]

epedaphic *ep-ə-daf'ik*, *adj* pertaining to atmospheric conditions. [Gr *epi* above, and *edaphos* ground]

épée *ā-pā'*, *n* a sharp-pointed, narrow-bladed sword without a cutting edge, used for duelling and, with a button on the point, for fencing. [Fr]

epeira *ep-īr'ə*, *n* a spider of the genus *Epeira*, the type of the **Epeir'idae**, including the common garden spider. — *n* **epeir'id** a member of the family. [Perh Gr *epi* on, and *eirein* to string]

epeirogenesis *ep-ī-rō-jen'i-sis*, (*geol*) *n* the building of continents by movement of the earth's crust. — Also **epeirogeny** (*-roj'i-ni*). — *adj* **epeirogen'ic** or **epeirogenetic** (*-jin-et'ik*). — **epeirogenic earth movements** continent-building movements, such as gentle uplift or depression, involving the coastal plain and the recently submerged continental shelf of the great land areas. [Gr *ēpeiros* mainland, and *genesis* formation]

epencephalon *ep-en-sef'ə-lon*, or *-kef'*, *n* the cerebellum. — *adj* **epencephalic** (*-si-fal'ik*, or *-ki-*). [Gr *epi* on, and *enkephalon* brain]

epenthesis *e-pen'thə-sis*, *n* the insertion of a sound within a word: — *pl* **epenthesēs**. — *adj* **epenthetic** (*-thet'ik*). [Gr]

epeolatry *ep-i-ol'ə-tri*, *n* worship of words. [Gr *epos* word, and *latreiā* worship]

éperdu (*fem* **éperdue**) *ā-per-dü*, (*Fr*) *adj* distracted. — **éperdument amoureux** (*fem* **amoureuse**) (*ā-per-dü-mā a-mōō-rø* (*-røz*)) desperately in love.

epergne *i-pûrn'*, *n* a branched ornamental centrepiece for the table. [Fr *épargne* (literally) saving, as used in phrases *taille* or *gravure d'épargne* metal or etching with parts left in relief]

epexegesis *ep-eks-i-jē'sis*, *n* the addition of words to make the sense more clear: — *pl* **epexegēsēs**. — *adj* **epexeget'ic** (*-jet'ik*) or **epexeget'ical**. — *adv* **epexeget'ically**. [Gr *epexēgēsis*, from *epi* in addition, and *exēgeesthai* to explain]

EPG *abbrev*: Eminent Persons' Group.

Eph. (*Bible*) *abbrev*: (the Letter to the) Ephesians.

epha or **ephah** *ē'fə*, *n* a Hebrew measure for dry goods. [Heb; prob of Egyptian origin]

ephebe *ef-ēb'*, **ephebus** or **ephebos** *-əs*, *n* in ancient Greece, a young male citizen from 18 to 20 years of age: — *pl* **ephebes'** or **ephē'bī**. — *adj* **ephēb'ic** of or belonging to an ephebe; pertaining to the adult period in the life-history of an individual (*biol*). — *n* **ephēbophilia** (*-fil'*) sexual desire for youths or adolescents. [L *ephēbus*, from Gr *ephēbos*, from *epi* upon, and *hēbē* early manhood]

ephedra *ef'ed-rə*, *ef-ēd'rə* or *ef-ed'rə*, *n* a plant of the sea-grape genus (*Ephedra*) of jointed, nearly leafless desert plants of the Gnetaceae. — *n* **eph'edrine** (or *ef-ed'rin*) an alkaloid obtained from Ephedra or produced synthetically, used in treating hay fever, asthma, etc. [Gr *ephedrā* horsetail]

ephelis *e-fē'lis*, (*med*) *n* a freckle; a coloured patch on the skin: — pl **ephelides** (*e-fel'i-dēz* or *-fēl'*). [L, from Gr]

ephemera *ef-em'ər-ə*, or *-ēm'*, *n* an insect of the mayfly genus *Ephemera*, whose adult life is very short; something which lasts a short time (but see also **ephemeron** below): — *pl* **ephem'eras** or **ephem'erae**. — *adj* **ephem'eral** existing only for a day; short-lived; fleeting. — *n* anything very short-lived. — *n* **ephemeral'ity**. — *n* **ephem'erid** an insect of the mayfly family **Ephemer'idae** (*-mer'i-dē*; order Plectoptera or **Ephemerop'tera**). — *adj* **ephemerid'ian**. — *n* **ephem'eris** an astronomical almanac tabulating the daily positions of the sun, moon, planets and certain stars, etc; an account of daily transactions (*archaic*); a journal (*archaic*): — *pl* **ephemerides** (*ef-e-mer'i-dēz*). — *n* **ephem'erist** someone who studies the daily motions of the planets; a student or collector of ephemera. — *n* **ephem'eron** an insect that lives only for a day; (*usu* in *pl*) an object of limited worth or usefulness, having no lasting value; anything ephemeral: — *pl* **ephem'era**. — *adj* **ephem'erous**. — **ephemeris time** time measured by orbital movement of earth, moon and planets, differing from mean solar time in that it allows for irregularities due to variations in rate of rotation of the earth, an **ephemeris second** being a fixed fraction of the solar year 1900. [Gr *ephēmeros* living a day, from *epi* for, and *hēmerā* a day]

Ephesian *ef-ē'zi-ən* or *-ē'zhən*, *adj* of or pertaining to *Ephesus*, an ancient Greek city in modern Turkey. — *n* an inhabitant of Ephesus; a jolly companion (*Shakesp*).

ephialtes *ef-i-al'tēz*, (*archaic*) *n* an incubus; a nightmare: — *pl* **ephial'tes**. [Gr *ephialtēs*]

ephod *ef'od*, *n* a kind of linen surplice worn by the Jewish priests (*Old Testament*); a surplice, generally. [Heb *ēphōd*, from *āphad* to put on]

ephor *ef'ör* or *ef'ər*, *n* in ancient Doric Greece, *esp* Sparta, a class of powerful senior magistrates elected annually. — *n* **eph'oralty**. [Gr *epi* upon, and root of *horaein* to see]

epi- *ep-i-* or **ep-** *ep-* before a vowel or *h*, *pfx* above, over, upon or on, as in *epidermis*; in addition or after, as in *epiphenomenon* and *epirrhema*. [Gr *epi* on or over]

epiblast *ep'i-bläst*, *n* the outer germinal layer of an embryo. — *adj* **epiblast'ic**. [Gr *epi* upon, and *blastos* a germ or shoot]

epic *ep'ik*, *adj* applied to a long narrative poem that relates heroic events in an elevated style; characteristic of an epic poem; impressive; large-scale. — *n* an epic poem; epic poetry as a genre; a story comparable to that of an epic poem, *esp* a long adventure novel or film; an epic poet (*obs*). — *adj* **ep'ical**. — *adv* **ep'ically**. — *n* **ep'icism** (*-sizm*). — *n* **ep'icist**. — **epic dialect** Homer's Greek; **epic theatre** the theatre of **epic drama**, episodic drama with alienation (qv), narrative passages, etc. [Gr *epikos*, from *epos* a word]

epicalyx *ep-i-kāl'iks*, or *-kal'*, (*bot*) *n* an apparent accessory calyx outside the true calyx, composed of bracts or of fused stipules of sepals. [Gr *epi* on, and **calyx**]

epicanthus *ep-i-kan'thəs*, *n* a fold of skin over the inner canthus of the eye, characteristic of the Mongolian race. — *adj* **epican'thic**. [Gr *epi* on, and **canthus**]

epicarp *ep'i-kärp*, (*bot*) *n* the outermost layer of the pericarp or fruit. [Gr *epi* upon, and *karpos* fruit]

epicede *ep'i-sēd*, or **epicedium** *ep-i-sē'di-əm* or *-dī'*, *n* a funeral ode: — *pl* **ep'icedes** or **epicē'dia** (or *-dī'*). — *adj* **epicē'dial** or **epicē'dian** elegiac. [L *epicēdīum*, from Gr *epikēdeion*, from *epi* upon, and *kēdos* care]

epicene *ep'i-sēn*, *adj* common to both sexes; having characteristics of both sexes or neither; effeminate; of common gender (*gram*); sometimes restricted to those words that have one grammatical gender though used for both sexes. — Also *n*. [Gr *epi* upon, and *koinos* common]

epicentre or (*US*) **epicenter** *ep'i-sen-tər*, *n* that point on the earth's surface directly over the point of origin of an earthquake. — Also *fig*. — *adj* **epicen'tral**. [Gr *epi* upon or over, and *kentron* a point]

epicheirema *ep-i-kī-rē'mə*, (*logic*) *n* a syllogism confirmed in its major or minor premise, or both, by an incidental proposition. [Gr *epicheirēma* an attempt or an attempted proof short of demonstrating, from *epi* upon, and *cheir* hand]

épicier *ā-pē-syā*, (*Fr*) *n* a grocer.

epicism, epicist. See **epic**.

epiclesis *ep-i-klē'sis*, *n* in the Eastern church, an invocation of the Holy Spirit at the consecration of the elements: — *pl* **epiclēsēs**. [Gr *epiklēsis* invocation, from *epikalein* to summon]

epicondyle *ep-i-kon'dīl* or *-dil*, (*anat*) *n* the upper or proximal part of the condyle of the humerus or femur. — *n* **epicondylitis** (*-dil-ī'tis*) inflammation of an epicondyle; inflammation of the tissues beside the epicondyle of the humerus. [**epi-**]

epicotyl *ep-i-kot'il*, (*bot*) *n* the stem of an embryo plant or seedling between the cotyledons and the next leaf. [Gr *epi* over, and **cotyledon**]

epicritic *ep-i-krit'ik*, *adj* (of certain sensory nerve fibres in the skin) able to discriminate accurately between small degrees of sensation. [Gr *epikritikos* determining, from *epi* on, and *krīnein* to judge]

epicure *ep'i-kūr*, *n* a person of refined and fastidious taste, *esp* in food, wine, etc; an Epicurean (*obs*); a person devoted to sensual enjoyment (*obs*). — *adj* **Epicurē'an** of or relating to *Epicurus* (341–270 BC), the Greek philosopher, who taught that the real world is a chance composition of atoms or particles and that pleasure controlled by social convention (misrepresented by opponents as brutish sensuality) is the greatest good; (without *cap*) devoted to luxury, *esp* refined luxury. — *n* a follower of Epicurus; (without *cap*) a hedonist or epicure. — *n* **Epicurē'anism** the doctrines of Epicurus; devotion to these doctrines; epicurism. — *vi* **ep'icurize** or **-ise** (*archaic*) to act as an epicure; to profess the philosophy of Epicurus. — *n* **ep'icurism** pursuit of pleasure; fastidiousness in luxury; (also *ep-i-kūr'izm*; *archaic*) Epicureanism. [L *Epicūrus*, from Gr *Epikouros*]

epicuticle *ep-i-kū'ti-kəl*, (*biol*) *n* the waxy outermost layer of an insect's cuticle. — *adj* **epicūtic'ular**. [**epi-**]

epicycle *ep'i-sī-kl*, *n esp* in Ptolemaic astronomy, a circle whose centre is carried round the circumference of another circle; the circle on whose circumference is the point which describes an epicycloid. — *adj* **epicy'clic**. — *n* **epicy'cloid** the curve described by a point on the circumference of a circle rolling round the outside of the circumference of another circle. — *adj* **epicycloi'dal**. — **epicyclic gear** a system of gears consisting of one or more wheels travelling round the outside or inside of another wheel whose axis is fixed. [Gr *epi* upon, and *kyklos* a circle]

epideictic *ep-i-dīk'tik* or **epideictical** *-əl*, *adj* done for show or display. [Gr *epi* upon, and *deiknynai* to show]

epidemic *ep-i-dem'ik*, *adj* affecting a community at a certain time; prevalent. — *n* a disease that attacks great numbers in one place at one time, and itself travels from place to place; a widespread outbreak. — *adj* **epidem'ical**. — *adv* **epidem'ically**. — *n* **epidemic'ity**. — *adj* **epidēmiolog'ical** pertaining to epidemiology. — *n* **epidēmiol'ogy** the science of epidemics and their occurrence, severity, distribution, etc. — *n* **epidēmiol'ogist**. [Gr *epidēmos* general, from *epi* among, and *dēmos* the people]

epidendrum *ep-i-den'drəm*, *n* an orchid of the genus *Epidendrum* of orchids mainly growing on other plants. — Also **epiden'drone**. [Gr *epi* upon, and *dendron* tree]

epidermis *ep-i-dûr'mis*, *n* cuticle or scarf-skin, forming an external protective covering for the true skin or corium (*zool*); an outer sheath of close-set cells, *usu* one deep (*bot*). — *adj* **epider'mal**. — *adj* **epider'mic**. — *adj* **epiderm'oid**. — *n* **Epidermophyton** (*-mof'i-tən*; Gr *phyton* a plant) a genus of parasitic funguses or dermatophytes, a cause of athlete's foot. — **epidermolysis bullosa** (*-mol'i-sis bōō-lō'sə*; Gr *lysis* loosening, New L *bulla* blister) a mutilating and incapacitating hereditary skin disease in which the skin on slight contact readily becomes covered with blisters (*abbrev* **EB**). [Gr *epidermis*, from *epi* upon, and *derma* the skin]

epidiascope *ep-i-dī'ə-skōp*, *n* an optical device for projecting images of objects whether opaque or transparent. [Gr *epi* upon, *dia* through, and *skopeein* to look at]

epididymis *ep-i-did'i-mis*, (*anatom*) *n* a mass of sperm-carrying tubes at the back of the testis: — *pl* **epidid'ymides** (*-mi-dēz* or *-dī-dim'-*). [Gr, from *epi* on, and *didymos* a testicle or a twin]

epidiorite *ep-i-dī'ə-rīt*, (*geol*) *n* a dioritic or gabbroitic rock more or less metamorphosed, the pyroxene being changed to amphibole. [Gr *epi* after, and **diorite**]

epidote *ep'i-dōt*, (*geol*) *n* a greenish mineral, silicate of calcium, aluminium, and iron. — *n* **epidosite** (*ep-id'ə-sīt*) a rock composed of epidote and quartz. — *adj* **epidotic** (*-dot'*). — *n* **epidotizā'tion** or **-s-**. — *adj* **epid'otized** or **-ised** changed into epidote. [Gr *epididonai* to give in addition or superadd, from the great length of the base of the crystal]

epidural *ep-i-dūr'əl*, *adj* situated on, or administered outside, the lowest portion of the spinal canal. — *n* short for **epidural anaesthetic**, the epidural injection of an anaesthetic, *esp* in childbirth. — **epidural anaesthesia** loss of painful sensation in the lower part of the body produced by injecting an anaesthetic into the lowest portion of the spinal canal. [Gr *epi* upon, and **dura** (**mater**)]

epifocal *ep-i-fō'kl*, *adj* epicentral.

epigaeal or **epigeal** *ep-i-jē'əl*, **epigaeous** or **epigeous** *-əs*, **epigaean** or **epigean** *-ən*, *adj* growing or living close to the ground; with cotyledons above ground. [Gr *epigaios* or *epigeios*, from *epi* on, and *gaia* or *gē* earth]

epigamic *ep-i-gam'ik*, *adj* attractive to the opposite sex. [Gr *epigamos* marriageable, from *epi* upon, and *gamos* marriage]

epigastrium *ep-i-gas'tri-əm*, (*anatom*) *n* the part of the abdomen extending from the sternum towards the navel, the pit of the stomach. — *adj* **epigas'tric**. [Gr *epi* upon, and *gastēr* the stomach]

epigeal, etc. See **epigaeal**.

epigene *ep'i-jēn*, (*geol*) *adj* acting or taking place at the earth's surface. [Fr *épigène*, from Gr *epigenēs* born after]

epigenesis *ep-i-jen'i-sis*, *n* the theory, now universally accepted, that the development of an embryo consists of the gradual production and organization of parts (as opposed to the theory of preformation, which supposed that the future animal or plant was already present complete, although in miniature, in the germ). — *n* **epigen'esist**. — *n* **epigenet'icist**. — *adj* **epigenet'ic** pertaining to epigenesis; (of minerals) formed subsequently to the enclosing rock. — *n sing* **epigenet'ics** the science which studies the causes at work in development. [Gr *epi* upon or after, and *genesis* formation]

epiglottis *ep-i-glot'is*, *n* a cartilaginous flap over the glottis. — *adj* **epiglott'ic**. [Gr *epiglōttis*, from *epi* over, and *glōttis* glottis]

epigon *ep'i-gon* or **epigone** *ep'i-gōn*, *n* one of a later generation; (*usu* in *pl*) a son or successor; an inferior follower or imitator: — *pl* **ep'igons**, **ep'igones** (*-gōnz*) or (often with *cap*) **epig'onī** descendants (*esp* of the Seven against Thebes), or successors (*esp* of Alexander); undistinguished descendants, followers or imitators of the great. [Gr *epi* after, and *gonē* birth]

epigram *ep'i-gram*, *n* any concise and pointed or sarcastic saying; a short poem expressing an ingenious thought with point, usually satirical. — *adj* **epigrammatic** (*-grəm-at'ik*), or **epigrammati'ical** relating to or dealing in epigrams; like an epigram; concise and pointed. — *adv* **epigrammat'ically**. — *n* **epigramm'atist** someone who writes epigrams. — *vt* **epigramm'atize** or **-ise** to make an epigram on. [Through Fr and L, from Gr *epigramma*, from *epi* upon, and *gramma* a writing, from *graphein* to write]

epigraph *ep'i-gräf*, *n* an inscription, *esp* on a building; a citation or motto at the beginning of a book or section of a book. — *vt* to provide with an epigraph. — *n* **epigrapher** (*ep-ig'rə-fər*) or **epig'raphist** someone who studies inscriptions. — *adj* **epigraphic** (*-graf'ik*). — *n* **epig'raphy**. [Gr *epigraphē*, from *epi* upon, and *graphein* to write]

epigynous *e-pij'i-nəs*, (*bot*) *adj* growing upon the top of the ovary; having calyx, corolla and stamens inserted on the top of an inferior ovary. — *n* **epig'yny**. [Gr *epi* upon, and *gynē* woman or female]

epilate *ep'i-lāt*, *vt* to remove (hair) by any method. — *n* **epilā'tion**. — *n* **ep'ilator**. [Fr *épiler*, from L *ex* from, and *pilus* hair]

epilepsy *ep'i-lep-si*, *n* a chronic functional disease of the nervous system, shown by recurring attacks of sudden unconsciousness or impairment of consciousness, commonly accompanied by convulsive seizures. — *n*

epilep'tic a sufferer from epilepsy. — *adj* **epilep'tic** or **epileptical**. [Gr *epilēpsiā*, from *epi* upon, and root of *lambanein* to seize]

epilimnion *ep-i-lim'ni-ən*, *n* the upper, warm layer of water in a lake. [Gr *epi* upon, and *limnion*, dimin of *limnē* a lake]

epilobium *ep-i-lōb'i-əm*, *n* a willow-herb, a plant of the genus *Epilobium*. [Gr *epi* upon, and *lobos* a pod, from the position of the petals]

epilogue or (*US*) also **epilog** *ep'i-log*, *n* the concluding section of a book, etc; a short poem or speech at the end of a play; the actor giving the epilogue; the conclusion (*usu* religious) of a day's radio or TV programmes. — *adj* **epilogic** (*-loj'ik*) or **epilogistic** (*-jis'*). — *n* **epil'ogist**. — *vi* **epilogize** or **-ise** (*ep-il'ə-jīz*, or *ep'*), **epiloguize** or **-ise** (*-gīz*) to speak or write an epilogue. [Fr, from L *epilogus*, from Gr. *epilogos* conclusion, from *epi* upon, and *legein* to speak]

epimeletic *ep-i-mel-et'ik*, (*animal behaviour*) *adj* of a type of social behaviour in which the young are cared for by the parents or other individuals of the same species, eg worker bees.

epimer *ep'i-mər*, *n* an isomeric compound, differing from its corresponding isomer only in the relative positions of an attached hydrogen and hydroxyl. — *adj* **epimeric** (*-mer'ik*) having the characteristics or relationship of epimers. [*epi-* and iso*mer*]

epinasty *ep'i-nas-ti*, (*bot*) *n* the down-curving of an organ, caused by a more active growth on its upper side (opposed to *hyponasty*). — *adj* **epinas'tic**. — *adv* **epinas'tically**. [Gr *epi* upon, and *nastos* pressed close]

epinephrine *ep-i-nef'rin* or *-rēn*, *n* (*esp US*) adrenaline. [Gr *epi* upon, and *nephros* kidney]

epineural (*zool*) *adj* in Echinodermata, lying above the radial nerve; in vertebrates, lying above or arising from the neural arch of a vertebra. [Gr *epi* upon, and **neural**]

epinikion *ep-i-nik'i-ən* or **epinicion** *ep-i-nis(h)'i-ən*, *n* in ancient Greece, a song of victory; an ode in honour of a victor or winner. — *adj* **epinik'ian** or **epinic'ian**. [Gr *epinīkion*, from *epi* on or after, and *nīkē* victory]

epinosic *ep-i-nos'ik*, *adj* unhealthy; unwholesome. [Gr *epi-*, and *nosos* disease]

epipetalous *ep-i-pet'ə-ləs*, (*bot*) *adj* inserted or growing on a petal or petals.

Epiphany *e-pif'ə-ni*, *n* a church festival celebrated on 6 Jan in commemoration of the manifestation of Christ to the wise men of the East (or in the Eastern church in commemoration of Christ's baptism and first miracle at Cana); the manifestation of a god; a *usu* sudden revelation or insight into the nature, essence or meaning of something: — *abbrev* **Epiph**. — *adj* **epiphanic** (*-fan'*). [Gr *epiphaneia* appearance, from *epi* to, and *phainein* to show]

epiphenomenon *ep-i-fin-om'ən-ən*, *n* an accompanying phenomenon, a fortuitous, less important or irrelevant by-product; something appearing after, a secondary symptom of a disease (*pathol*): — *pl* **epiphenom'ena**. — *n* **epiphenom'enalism** interpretation of mind as an epiphenomenon upon the physical. — *n* and *adj* **epiphenom'enalist**. [Gr *epi* after, and *phainomenon* neuter pr p passive of *phainein* to show]

epiphonema *ep-i-fō-nē'mə*, (*rhetoric*) *n* an exclamation; a phrase or reflection added as a finishing touch. [Gr *epiphōnēma*]

epiphragm *ep'i-fram*, *n* the disc with which certain molluscs close the aperture of their shell. [Gr *epiphragma* covering, from *epiphrassein* to obstruct]

epiphyllous *ep-i-fil'əs*, (*bot*) *adj* growing upon a leaf, *esp* on its upper surface. [Gr *epi* upon, and *phyllon* a leaf]

epiphysis *ep-if'i-sis*, *n* any portion of a bone having its own centre of ossification; the pineal gland (*epiphysis cerebri*); an ossicle of Aristotle's lantern in a sea-urchin; an upgrowth around the hilum of a seed: — *pl* **epiph'ysēs**. [Gr, excrescence]

epiphyte *ep'i-fīt*, *n* a plant growing on another plant without being parasitic; a vegetable parasite on the surface of an animal (*pathol*). — *adj* **epiphyt'al**, **epiphytic** (*-fit'ik*) or **epiphyt'ical**. — *n* **ep'iphytism** (or *-fīt'*) the condition of being epiphytic; a similar relation among animals. [Gr *epi* upon, and *phyton* a plant]

epiplastron *ep-i-pläs'tron*, *n* the anterior lateral piece of the nine forming the plastron of a turtle: — *pl* **epiplas'tra**. — *adj* **epiplas'tral**.

epiploon *e-pip'lō-on*, (*anatom*) *n* the great omentum. — *adj* **epiplō'ic**. [Gr *epiploon*, from *epipleein* to float on]

epipolism *e-pip'o-lizm*, *n* fluorescence. — *adj* **epipol'ic**. [Gr *epipolē* surface]

epirrhema *ep-i-rē'mə*, *n* in Greek comedy the address of the Coryphaeus to the audience after the parabasis. — *adj* **epirrhēmat'ic**. [Gr, from *epi* on or after, and *rhēma* word]

Epis. *abbrev*: Episcopal (also **Episc**.); Epistle (also **Ep**.; *Bible*).

episcopacy *e-pis'kə-pəs-i*, *n* church government by bishops; the office of a bishop; a bishop's period of office; the bishops, as a class. — *adj* **epis'copal** governed by bishops; belonging to or vested in bishops. — *adj* **episcopā'lian** pertaining to bishops or to an episcopal church; pertaining to government by bishops. — *n* a person who belongs to an episcopal (*esp* Anglican) church. — *n* **episcopā'lianism** or **epis'copalism** episcopalian government and doctrine. — *adv* **epis'copally**. — *n* **epis'copant** (*Milton*) a holder of a bishopric. — *n* **epis'copate** a bishopric; the office of a bishop; a bishop's period of office; the order of bishops. — *vi* (*Milton*) to act as a bishop. — *vt* **epis'copize** or **-ise** to make a bishop of; to make episcopalian. — *vi* to play the bishop (also *vt* with *it*). — *n* **epis'copy** (*Milton*) survey or superintendence. [Gr *episkopos* an overseer]

episcope *ep'i-skōp*, *n* an optical device for projecting images of opaque objects. [Gr *epi* on or over, and *skopeein* to look]

episemon *ep-i-sē'mon*, *n* a badge or characteristic device; one of three obsolete Greek letters used as numerals: ϛ or Ϝ, vau or digamma (6); Ϙ, koppa (90); and ϡ, san, sampi (900). — *adj* **episēmat'ic** (*zool*) serving for recognition, distinguishing. [Gr *episēmon* a badge, from *epi* on, and *sēma* a sign]

episepalous *ep-i-sep'əl-əs*, (*bot*) *adj* growing or inserted upon a sepal or sepals. [**epi-**]

episiotomy *ep-iz-i-ot'ə-mi*, (*med*) *n* an incision made in the perineum to facilitate the delivery of a foetus. [Gr *epision* pubic region, and **-tomy**]

episode *ep'i-sōd*, *n* a story introduced into a narrative or poem to give variety; an interesting or distinctive incident or occurence; an occurrence, *esp* when one of a series of similar occurrences; a passage giving relief from the principal subject (*music*); an incident or period detachable from a novel, play, etc; a part of a radio or television serial which is broadcast at one time. — *adj* **ep'isōdal**, **episō'dial**, **episodic** (*-sod'*) or **episod'ical** pertaining to or contained in an episode; brought in as a digression; having many episodes; (only **episodic** or **episodical**) sporadic, occurring at intervals. — *adv* **episod'ically** by way of episode; incidentally. [Gr *epeisodion*, from *epi* upon, and *eisodos* a coming in]

episome *ep'i-sōm*, *n* a genetically active particle found *esp* in bacteria, able to exist and multiply either independently or integrated in a chromosome. [**epi-** and *-some*, from Gr *sōma* body]

epispastic *ep-i-spas'tik*, (*med*) *adj* blistering. — *n* a blistering agent. [Gr *epispastikos*, from *epi* upon, and *spaein* to draw]

episperm *ep'i-spûrm*, (*bot*) *n* the outer seed-coat. [Gr *epi* upon, and *sperma* seed]

epispore *ep'i-spör*, (*bot*) *n* the outermost layer of a spore-wall. [**epi-**]

epistasis *i-pis'tə-sis*, *n* the suppression by a gene of another non-allelomorphic gene; the arrest of a discharge or secretion; a scum which forms on the surface of a liquid, *esp* urine: — *pl* **-stasēs**. — *adj* **epistatic** (*ep-i-*

stat'ik). [Gr, stopping, from *epi* on, and *stasis* stoppage]

epistaxis *ep-i-stak'sis*, (*med*) *n* bleeding from the nose. [Gr *epistazein* to shed in drops]

epistemology *ep-is-tə-mol'ə-ji*, *n* the theory of knowledge. — *adj* **epistē'mic** relating to knowledge, epistemology or epistemics. — *n sing* **epistē'mics** the scientific study of knowledge, its acquisition and its communication. — *adj* **epistemological** (*-ə-loj'*). — *n* **epistemol'ogist**. [Gr *epistēmē* knowledge, and *logos* discourse]

episternum *ep-i-stûr'nəm*, (*anatom*) *n* the interclavicle; the epiplastron; the presternum of mammals. — *adj* **epister'nal**.

epistilbite *ep-i-stil'bīt*, (*mineralogy*) *n* a zeolite closely related to stilbite. [Gr *epi* on, after or in addition to, and **stilbite**]

epistle *i-pis'l*, *n* something written and sent to someone, a letter; (often with *cap*) *esp* a letter to an individual or church from an apostle, such as the Epistles of Paul in the Bible; (often with *cap*) the extract from one of the apostolical epistles read as part of the communion service; a verse composition in letter form. — *vt* (*Milton*) to preface. — *n* **epistler** see **epistoler** below. — *n* **epistolā'rian** a letter-writer. — *n* **epis'tolary** a book containing the Epistles, used for readings in church. — *adj* **epistolā'rian, epis'tolary, epis'tolatory, epistolic** (*ep-is-tol'ik*) or **epistol'ical** pertaining to or consisting of epistles or letters; suitable in or for an epistle; contained in letters. — *n* **epistoler** (*i-pist'ə-lər*) or **epistler** (*-pis'* or *-pist'*) the reader of the Epistle in church; a letter-writer. — *n* **epis'tolet** a short letter. — *n* **epis'tolist** a writer of letters. —vi **epis'tolize** or **-ise** to write a letter. — *n* **epistolog'raphy** letter-writing. — **epistle side** of a church, the south side (*opp* to *gospel side*). [OFr, from L *epistola*, from Gr *epistolē*, from *epi* on the occasion of, and *stellein* to send]

epistrophe *e-pis'trə-fē*, *n* the ending of successive clauses with the same word (*rhetoric*); a refrain in music. [Gr *epistrophē* a return, from *epi* upon, and *strephein* to turn]

epistyle *ep'i-stīl*, (*archit*) *n* an architrave. [Gr *epi* upon, and *stȳlos* a pillar]

epitaph *ep'i-täf*, *n* a tombstone inscription; a composition in the form of a tombstone inscription. — *vt* to compose an epitaph upon. — *n* **epitapher** (*ep'i-täf-ər*) or **ep'itaphist** a composer of epitaphs. — *adj* **epitaph'ian** or **epitaph'ic**. [Gr *epitaphion*, from *epi* upon, and *taphos* a tomb]

epitasis *e-pit'ə-sis*, *n* the main action of a Greek drama leading to the catastrophe (*opp* to *protasis*): — *pl* **epit'asēs**.

epitaxy *ep'i-tak-si*, (*crystallog*) *n* the growth of a thin layer of crystals on another crystal so that they have the same structure. — *adj* **epitax'ial**. — *adv* **epitax'ially**. [Gr *epi* on, and *taxis* arrangement]

epithalamium *ep-i-thə-lā'mi-əm*, or **epithalamion** *-on*, *n* a song or poem in celebration of a marriage: — *pl* **epithalā'mia**. — *adj* **epithalam'ic**. (*ep-i-thə-la'mik*). [L *epithalamium*, Gr *epithalamion*, from *epi* upon, and *thalamos* a bride-chamber]

epithelium *ep-i-thē'li-əm*, (*anatom*) *n* the cell-tissue that covers the outer surface of the body and the mucous membranes connected with it, and also the closed cavities of the body. — *adj* **epithē'lial**. — *n* **epithēliō'ma** carcinoma of the skin: — *pl* **epithelio'mas** or **epithelio'mata** (*-mə-tə*). — *adj* **epithēliō'matous**. [New L, from Gr *epi* upon, and *thēlē* nipple]

epithem *ep'i-them*, *n* a soft external application (*med*); a group of cells exuding water in some leaves (*bot*). — Also **epithema** (*ep-i-thē'mə* or *ep-ith'i-mə*): — *pl* **ep'ithems** or **epithe'mata**. [Gr *epithema*, *epithēma*, *-atos*, from *epi* on, and *tithenai* to place]

epithermal *ep-i-thûr'məl*, *adj* having energy just above the energy of thermal agitation. [**epi-**]

epithesis *ep-ith'i-sis*, *n* the addition of one or more letters to a word, a paragoge. [Gr, setting on]

epithet *ep'i-thet*, *n* an adjective or adjectival phrase expressing some quality of the person or thing to which it is applied; a descriptive term; a term, expression (*Shakesp*). — *vt* to term. — *adj* **epithet'ic** pertaining to an epithet; having or using many epithets. — *n* **epith'eton** (*Shakesp* **apath'aton**) an epithet. [Gr *epitheton*, neuter of *epithetos* added, from *epi* on, and *tithenai* to place]

epithymetic *ep-i-thim-et'ik*, *adj* pertaining to desire. [Gr *epi* upon, and *thȳmos* the soul]

epitome *i-pit'ə-mē*, *n* an abridgement or short summary of anything, eg a book; a short or concentrated expression of something; a typical example; a personification. — *adj* **epitomic** (*ep-i-tom'ik*) or **epitom'ical**. — *n* **epit'omist** an epitomizer. — *vt* **epit'omize** or **-ise** to make an epitome of; to shorten; to condense; to typify; to personify. — *n* **epit'omizer** or **-s-** someone who abridges. — **in epitome** on a small scale. [Gr *epi* upon, and *tomē* a cut]

epitonic *ep-i-ton'ik*, *adj* overstrained. [Gr *epitonos*, from *epi* upon, and *teinein* to stretch]

epitope. See **antigenic determinant**.

epitrachelion *ep-i-tra-kē'li-ən*, *n* an Orthodox priest's or bishop's stole. [Gr, on the neck, from *epi* upon, and *trachēlos* neck]

epitrite *ep'i-trīt*, (*prosody*) *n* a foot made up of three long syllables and one short. [Gr *epitritos*, from *epi* in addition to, and *tritos* third]

epitrochoid *ep-i-trō'koid*, *n* a curve like an epicycloid but generated by any point on a radius. [Gr *epi* on, and *trochos* wheel]

epizeuxis *ep-i-zūk'sis*, (*rhetoric*) *n* the immediate repetition of a word for emphasis. [Gr, joining on]

epizoon *ep-i-zō'on*, *n* an animal that lives on the surface of another animal, whether parasitically or commensally: — *pl* **epizō'a**. — *adj* and *n* **epizō'an**. — *adj* **epizō'ic** dwelling upon an animal; having seeds dispersed by animals. — *adj* **epizootic** (*ep-i-zō-ot'ik*) pertaining to epizoa; affecting animals as an epidemic affects humans; containing fossil remains, as subsequent to the appearance of life (*geol*; *obs*). — *n* an epizootic disease. — *n sing* **epizōot'ics** the science or study of epidemic animal diseases. [Gr *epi* upon, and *zōion* an animal]

EPNS *abbrev*: electroplated nickel silver; English Place-Name Society.

EPOCH *abbrev*: End Physical Punishment of Children.

epoch *ēp'ok*, *ēp'ohh* or *ep'ok*, *n* a point of time fixed or made remarkable by some great event from which dates are reckoned; the particular time, used as a point of reference, at which the data had the values in question (*astron*); a planet's heliocentric longitude at the epoch (*astron*); a precise date; a time from which a new state of things dates; an age (geological, historical, etc). — Also (*archaic*) **ep'ocha**. — *adj* **epochal** (*ep'ok-l*). — *adj* **ep'och-māking** important enough to be considered as beginning a new age. — *adj* **ep'och-marking**. — **epoch of osculation** (*astron*) see **osculating orbit** [Gr *epochē*, from *epechein* to stop, take up a position, from *epi* upon, and *echein* to hold]

epode *ep'ōd*, *n* a kind of lyric poem invented by Archilochus, in which a longer verse is followed by a shorter one; the last part of a lyric ode, sung after the strophe and antistrophe. — *adj* **epodic** (*-od'ik*). [Gr *epōidos*, from *epi* on, and *ōidē* an ode]

eponychium *ep-o-nik'i-əm*, (*anatom*) *n* a narrow band of cuticle over the base of a nail. [Gr *epi* on, and *onyx*, *onychos* nail]

eponym *ep'ə-nim*, *n* a person, real or mythical, from whose name another name, *esp* a place name, is derived; the name so derived; a hero invented to account for the name of a place or people; a character who gives a play, etc its title; a distinguishing title. — *adj* **eponym'ic** or **eponymous** (*i-pon'i-məs*). [Gr *epōnymos* eponymous, from *epi* upon, to, and *onyma*, *onoma* a name]

epopee *ep'o-pē*, or **epopoeia** *ep-o-pē'yə*, *n* epic poetry; an epic poem. [Gr *epopoiiā*, from *epos* a word, an epic poem, and *poieein* to make]
epopt *ep'opt*, *(Gr hist) n* someone initiated into the Eleusinian mysteries. [Gr *epoptēs*, from *epi* upon, and root *op-* to see]
EPOS *abbrev*: electronic point of sale.
epos *ep'os*, *n* the elementary stage of epic poetry; an epic poem; a series of events of the kind that form the subject of epic poetry: — *pl* **ep'oses**. [Gr *epos* a word]
epoxy *e-pok'si*, *adj* containing oxygen bound to two other atoms, often carbon, which are already attached in some way. — *n* an epoxy resin. — *n* **epox'ide** an epoxy compound. — **epoxy** (or **epoxide**) **resins** synthetic polymers used as structural plastics, surface coatings, adhesives and for encapsulating and embedding electronic components.
EPP *abbrev*: European People's Party.
épris *ā-prē*, or *fem* **éprise** *-prēz*, *(Fr) adj* captivated or smitten.
EPROM *ē'prom (comput) abbrev*: electrically programmable read only memory; erasable programmable read only memory (qv under **erase**). — *n (comput)* a chip with EPROM. — Also **eprom**.
éprouvette *ā-proo-vet'*, *n* an apparatus for testing the strength of gunpowder. [Fr *éprouver* to try]
epsilon *ep-sī'lən* or *ep'si-lon*, *n* the fifth letter (E or ε) of the Greek alphabet, short e; as a numeral ε' = 5 and ͵ε = 5000. [Gr *e psīlon* bare or mere e]
epsomite *ep'səm-īt*, *n* a mineral, hydrated magnesium sulphate ($MgSO_4{\cdot}7H_2O$). — **Epsom salt** or **salts** a purgative medicine of similar composition to that originally obtained from the springs at Epsom in Surrey, used also in dyeing, etc.
Epstein-Barr virus *ep-stīn-bär' vī'rəs*, *n* a virus which causes glandular fever and which is thought to be associated with various human cancers. [M A *Epstein* and Y M *Barr*, British virologists, who first isolated it in 1964]
EPT *abbrev*: Environmental Protection Technology.
EPU *abbrev*: European Payments Union.
épuisé or *fem* **épuisée** *ā-pwē-zā*, *(Fr) adj* worn out.
epulation *ep-ū-lā'shən*, *(rare) n* feasting. — *adj* **ep'ulary**. [L noun *epulātiō*, adj *epulāris*, from *epulāri*, *-ātus* to feast]
epulis *e-pū'lis*, *(pathol) n* a tumour of the gums, either benign or malignant, and growing from the periosteum of the jaw. [Gr *epi* upon, and *oulon* gum]
epulotic *ep-ū-lot'ik*, *(med) adj* forming a scar over a wound. — *n* a substance which encourages the forming of scar-tissue. [Gr *epoulōtikos*, from *epi* upon, and *oulē* a scar]
epurate *ep'ū-rāt*, *vt* to purify. — *n* **epurā'tion** or **épura'tion** purification or purging, *esp* in reference to the denazification process in France after World War II. [Fr *épurer*]
epyllion *e-pil'i-ən*, *n* a poem with some resemblance to an epic but shorter. [Gr, dimin of *epos* word]
Epyornis. A spelling of **Aepyornis**.
equable *ek'wə-bl*, *adj* even or uniform; smooth; without wide variations or extremes; even-tempered. — *n* **equabil'ity** or **e'quableness**. — *adv* **e'quably**. [L *aequābilis*, from *aequāre*, from *aequus* equal]
eq *abbrev*: equal; equation; equivalent.
equal *ē'kwəl*, *adj* identical in quantity; of the same value; adequate; in correct proportion; fit; equable; uniform; equitable; evenly balanced; just; equally developed on each side (*bot*). — *n* one of the same age, rank, etc; equality (*Spenser*). — *vt* to be or make equal to; to reach the same level as (*bot*): — *pr p* **e'qualling**; *pa t* and *pa p* **e'qualled**. — *adj* **equalitār'ian** (*-kwol-*) of or pertaining to the equality of mankind. — *n* a person who believes in or supports the political and social equality of mankind. — *n* **equalitā'rianism**. — *n* **equality** (*ē-kwol'i-ti*) the condition of being equal; sameness; evenness. — *n* **equalizā'tion** or **-s-** the act of making equal; the state of being equalized. — *vt* **e'qualize** or **-ise** to make equal or uniform; to equal (*obs*). — *vi* to become equal; to make one's score equal to one's opponent's. — *n* **equalī'zer** or **-s-** a person or thing that equalizes; a goal, etc that levels the score; see also **graphic equalizer**. — *adv* **equally** (*ē'kwə-li*). — *n* **e'qualness** equality, equability. — *n* **ē'quant** in Ptolemy's astronomical system, a point on the line on which the earth and the centre of a given planet's deferent stand, or a circle centred on such a point, used to reconcile observed planetary motions with the hypothesis of uniform planetary velocity. — *adj* (*crystallog*) of the geometric form taken by a crystal in which its diameter is equal or nearly equal in all directions. — *vt* **equāte'** to reduce to an average or to a common standard of comparison; to state as equal; to regard as equal. — *vi* to be or be regarded, treated, etc as equal. — *n* **equā'tion** (*i-kwā'zhən* or *i-kwā'shən*) the act of making equal; a statement of the equality of two quantities; reduction to a common standard; correction to compensate for an error, irregularity or discrepancy; the quantity added for this purpose; a formula expressing a chemical action and the proportions of the substances involved. — **equal opportunities** in employment, etc, the avoidance of any discrimination between applicants, etc on the grounds of sex, race, etc, monitored by the government-appointed **Equal Opportunities Commission**; **equal** or **equals sign** the symbol =, which indicates that two (numerical) values are equal; **equal temperament** see under **temperament**. — **equal to the occasion** fit or able to cope with an emergency; **equation of time** (*astron*) mean solar time minus apparent solar time, or the right ascension of the true sun minus that of the mean sun; **personal equation** a correction to be applied to the reading of an instrument on account of the observer's tendency to read too high, too low, etc; any tendency to error or prejudice due to personal characteristics for which allowance must be made. [L *aequālis* equal, and *aequāre*, *-ātum* to make equal, from *aequus* equal]
equanimity *e-kwə-nim'i-ti* or *ē-*, *n* evenness of mind or temper. — *adj* **equanimous** (*i-kwan'i-məs*). — *adv* **equan'imously**. [L *aequanimitās*, from *aequus* equal, and *animus* the mind]
equant, equate, equation. See **equal**.
equator *i-kwā'tər*, *n* an imaginary great circle passing round the middle of the Earth and equidistant from the N and S poles; the imaginary great circle in which the plane of the earth's equator intersects the celestial sphere (so called because day and night are equal when the sun reaches it); the middle belt or line of any globular or nearly globular body that has some sort of polarity. — *adj* **equatorial** (*ek-wə-tö'ri-əl* or *ēk-*) of, pertaining to, of the nature of, or in the neighbourhood of an equator. — *n* a telescope mounted on an axis, capable of moving parallel to the equator and so following a star in any part of its diurnal course. — *adv* **equato'rially** so as to have motion or direction parallel to the equator. [See **equal**]
equerry *ek'wə-ri* or *ik-wer'i*, *n* an official who attends upon a member of the royal family; royal stables (*obs*); an officer responsible for the royal stables (*archaic*). [Fr *écurie*, from LL *scūria* a stable]
equestrian *i-kwes'tri-ən*, *adj* of or relating to horsemanship, or to the Roman order of *equitēs* or knights; on horseback. — *n* a horse-rider; a performer on horseback: — *fem* (sham *Fr*) **equestrienne'**. — *n* **eques'trianism** horsemanship. [L *equester*, *equestris*, from *eques* a horseman, from *equus* a horse]
equi- *ē-kwi-* or *ek'wi-*, *pfx* denoting equal. — *adj* **equian'gular** having equal angles (**equiangular spiral** a curve whose radius vector makes a constant angle with the tangent or *logarithmic spiral*). — *n* **equiangular'ity**. — *n* and *vt* **equibal'ance** equipoise. — *adj* **equidiff'erent** having equal differences. — *n* **equidis'tance**. — *adj* **equidis'tant** equally distant. — *adv* **equidis'tantly**. — *adj* **equilat'eral** (L *latus*, *-eris* side) having all sides equal. — *n* **equimul'tiple** a number multiplied by the

same number as another. — *adj* **equipō'tent** of equal power. — *adj* **equipoten'tial** of equal power, capability, potential or potentiality. — *adj* **equiprob'able** equal in degree of probability. — *n* **equiprobabil'ity**. — *adj* **e'quivalve** having valves of similar size and form. [L *aequus* equal]

Equidae *ek'wi-dē*, *n pl* a family of hoofed mammals consisting of the genus **Eq'uus** (horse, ass and zebra) and various fossil forms. — *n* **equid** a member of the family Equidae. [L *equus* horse]

equidifferent ... to ... **equilateral**. See **equi-**.

equilibrium *ēk-*, *ek-wi-lib'ri-əm*, *n* balance; the state of even balance; a state in which opposing forces or tendencies neutralize each other. — *vt* and *vi* **equilibrate** (*ēk-wi-līb'rāt*, *-lib'rāt* or *-kwil'*) to balance; to counterpoise. — *n* **equilibrā'tion**. — *n* **equil'ibrator** (or *-līb'*) a balancing or stability device, *esp* an aeroplane fin. — *n* **equil'ibrist** (or *lib'*, or *-līb'*) someone who does balancing tricks. — *n* **equilib'rity**. [L *aequilībrium*, from *aequus* equal, and *lībra* balance]

equimultiple. See **equi-**.

equine *e'* or *ē'kwīn* or **equinal** *e-* or *ē-kwīn'əl*, *adj* pertaining to or of the nature of a horse or horses. — *n* **equinia** (*i-* or *ē-kwin'i-ə*) glanders. — *n* **equin'ity** equine nature. — **equine infectious anaemia** another name for **swamp fever**. [L *equīnus*, from *equus* a horse]

equinox *ek'* or *ēk'wi-noks*, *n* either of the two annual occasions when the sun crosses the equator, making the night equal in length to the day, about 21 Mar and 23 Sep; an equinoctial point. — *adj* **equinoc'tial** pertaining to the equinoxes, the time of the equinoxes, or to the regions about the equator. — *n* the celestial equator or **equinoctial line**. — *adv* **equinoc'tially** in the direction of the equinox. — **equinoctial gales** high gales popularly supposed to prevail about the times of the equinoxes (the belief is unsupported by observation); **equinoctial point** either of the two points in the heavens where the equinoctial line cuts the ecliptic; **equinoctial year** see under **year**. [L *aequus* equal, and *nox*, *noctis* night]

equip *i-kwip'*, *vt* to fit out; to furnish with everything needed: — *pr p* **equipp'ing**; *pa t* and *pa p* **equipped'**. — *n* **equipage** (*ek'wi-pāj*) something with which one is equipped (*archaic*); the apparatus required for any operation, eg making tea (*archaic*); a carriage and attendants; retinue. — *vt* (*obs*) to equip. — *n* **equip'ment** the act of equipping; the state of being equipped; things used in equipping or furnishing; outfit; a set of tools, etc. [Fr *équiper*, prob from ON *skipa* to set in order, and *skip* a ship; partly influenced by confusion with L *equus* horse]

equiparate *i-kwi'pər-āt*, (*obs*) *vt* to regard or treat as equal or the same; to put on an equal footing. — *adj* equal or the same. — *n* **equipara'tion**. [L *aequiparāre*]

équipe *ā-kēp*, (*Fr*) *n* (in motor-racing and other sport) a team.

equipoise *ek'wi-poiz*, *n* a state of balance; a counterpoise. — *vt* to balance; to counterpoise. [L *aequus* equal, and **poise**]

equipollent *ē-* or *e-kwi-pol'ənt*, *adj* having equal power or force; equivalent. — *n* an equivalent. — *n* **equipoll'ence** or **equipoll'ency**. [L *aequus* equal, and *pollēns*, *pollentis*, pr p of *pollēre* to be strong, able]

equiponderate *ē-* or *e-kwi-pon'dər-āt*, *vi* to be equal in weight; to balance. — *adj* (*-ət*) equal in weight. — *n* **equipon'derance**. — *adj* **equipon'derant**. [L *aequus* equal, and *pondus*, *ponderis* weight]

equipotent ... to ... **equiprobability**. See **equi-**.

equisetum *ek-wi-sē'təm*, *n* a plant of the *Equisetum* genus, the only surviving genus of the family **Equisetā'ceae**, constituting the **Equisetī'nae** or **Equisetā'les**, a class of pteridophytes, stiff herbaceous plants with almost leafless articulated and whorled stems and branches. — Also *horsetail*, *scouring-rush* or *Dutch rush*. — *adj* **equisetā'ceous**. — *adj* **equisēt'ic**. — *adj* **equisēt'iform**. [L *equus* a horse, and *sēta* a bristle]

equitation *ek-wi-tā'shən*, *n* the art of riding on horseback. — *adj* **eq'uitant** riding; straddling or overlapping; of leaves, folded lengthwise over succeeding leaves (*bot*). [L *equitāre* to ride, from *equus* a horse]

equity *ek'wi-ti*, *n* right as founded on the laws of nature; moral justice, of which laws are the imperfect expression; the spirit of justice which enables us to interpret laws rightly; a system of law which along with the common law is the main historical source of English law, a body of legal principles designed to ensure natural justice or 'fair play' (no longer administered by separate courts); fairness; an equitable right; the value of property in excess of any charges upon it; the total assets of a company after liabilities are taken into account; (in *pl*) ordinary shares; (with *cap*) the trade union for the British acting profession. — *adj* **eq'uitable** possessing or showing or in accordance with equity; held or exercised in equity; pertaining to a concept or rule of law which has its origin in the law of equity; fair or just. — *n* **eq'uitableness**. — *adv* **eq'uitably**. — **equity finance** or **equity share capital** capital subscribed by ordinary shareholders. [OFr *equité*, from L *aequitās*, *-ātis*, from *aequus* equal]

equivalent *i-kwiv'ə-lənt*, *adj* equal in value, power, meaning, etc; interchangeable; of similar combining value (*chem*). — *n* a thing equivalent; an equivalent weight (*chem*). — *n* **equiv'alence** or **equiv'alency**. — *adv* **equiv'alently**. — **equivalent weight** (*chem*) that weight which displaces or combines with or otherwise represents a standard unit, atomic weight, or atomic weight divided by valence. [Fr, from L *aequus* equal, and *valēns*, *valentis* pr p of *valēre* to be worth]

equivalve. See **equi-**.

equivocal *i-kwiv'ə-kl*, *adj* capable of meaning two or more things; of doubtful meaning; capable of a double explanation; suspicious; questionable. — *adv* **equiv'ocally**. — *n* **equivocal'ity**. — *n* **equiv'ocalness**. — *vi* **equiv'ocāte** to use equivocal or doubtful words in order to mislead. — *n* **equivocā'tion** the misleading use of equivocal or doubtful words; an instance of this; a fallacy caused by ambiguity (*logic*). — *n* **equiv'ocātor**. — *adj* **equiv'ocatory** containing or characterized by equivocation. — *n* **equivoke** or **equivoque** (*ek'wi-vōk*) an equivocal expression; equivocation; a quibble; a pun. [L *aequus* equal, and *vōx*, *vōcis* the voice or a word]

Equus. See **Equidae**.

ER *abbrev*: *Edwardus Rex* (*New L*) King Edward; *Elizabeth Regina* (*New L*) Queen Elizabeth (**EIIR** Queen Elizabeth II).

Er (*chem*) *symbol*: erbium.

er *ûr*, *interj* expressing hesitation.

-er[1] *-ər*, *sfx* marks the agent (person or thing); designates people according to occupation (eg writ*er*), or place of abode (eg London*er*). [OE *-ere*; some similar-looking words, eg groc*er* and offic*er*, are from Fr *-ier* (L *-arius*]

-er[2] *-ər*, *sfx* marks the comparative degree of adjectives (long*er*) and some adverbs (fast*er*). [OE *-ra* (adj), and *-or* (adv)]

ERA *abbrev*: earned run average (*baseball*); Equal Rights Amendment.

era *ē'rə*, *n* a series of years reckoned from a particular point, or that point itself; an important date; an age; a main division of geological time. — *n* **ē'rathem** (*geol*) the stratigraphical unit of rock strata corresponding to a geological era. [LL *aera* a number, orig counters or pieces of copper used in counting, pl of *aes* copper]

eradiate *i-* or *ē-rā'di-āt*, *vt* and *vi* to shoot out like a ray of light. — *n* **eradiā'tion**. [L *ē-* from, and *radius* a ray]

eradicate *i-rad'i-kāt*, *vt* to destroy or get rid of; to root out; to pull up by the roots. — *adj* **erad'icable**. — *adj* **erad'icāted** rooted up; of a tree, or part of a tree, torn up by the roots (*heraldry*). — *n* **eradicā'tion** the act of eradicating; the state of being eradicated. — *adj* **erad'icātive** serving to eradicate or drive thoroughly away. — *n* **erad'icātor**. [L *ērādīcāre*, *-ātum* to root out, from *ē* from, and *rādīx*, *-īcis* a root]

erase *i-rāz'*, *vt* to rub or scrape out; to efface; to destroy; to destroy a recording on audio or video tape; to replace the data of a storage area with characters representing zero (*comput*). — *adj* **erā'sable**. — *adj* **erased'** rubbed out; effaced; torn off, so as to leave jagged edges (*heraldry*). — *n* **erā'ser** someone who or something which erases eg *ink-eraser*. — *n* **erā'sion** (*-zhən*), **erase'ment** or **era'sure** (*-zhər*) the act of erasing; a rubbing out; scraping away; the place where something written has been rubbed out. — **erasable programmable read only memory** (*abbrev* **EPROM**; *comput*) a chip containing a program which it will hold until it is erased by exposure to ultraviolet light and which can then be reprogrammed; **erasable read only memory** (*abbrev* **EROM**; *comput*) a chip similar to the above, but which cannot be reprogrammed. [L *ērādere*, from *ē* from, and *rādere*, *rāsum* to scrape]

ERASMUS *i-raz'məs*, *abbrev*: European Community Action Scheme for the Mobility of University Students.

Erastian *e-ras'ti-ən* or *-tyən*, *n* a follower of Thomas *Erastus* (1524–83), a Swiss physician, who denied the church the right to inflict excommunication and disciplinary penalties; a person who would subordinate the church jurisdiction to the state (a position not held by Erastus at all). — *adj* relating to the Erastians or their doctrines. — *n* **Eras'tianism** control of the church by the state.

erathem. See **era**.

Erato *er'ə-tō*, (*Gr mythol*) *n* the Muse of lyric love poetry. [Gr *Eratō*]

erbium *ûr'bi-əm*, *n* a rare metal (atomic no 68; symbol **Er**) found in gadolinite at Ytt*erby*, near Stockholm. — *n* **er'bia** erbium oxide.

Erdgeist *ārt'gīst*, (*Ger*) *n* earth-spirit.

ere[1] *ār*, (*usu literary*) *adv*, *prep* and *conj* before. — *adv* **ere long** or **erelong'** before long; soon. — *adv* **ere now** or **erenow'** before this time. — *adv* **erewhile'** (*archaic*) formerly; some time before. [OE *ǣr*; cf Du *eer*]

ere[2]. Same as **ear**[2].

Erebus *er'i-bəs*, (*mythol*) *n* the dark and gloomy cavern between earth and Hades; the lower world or hell. [L, from Gr *Erebos*]

erect *i-rekt'*, *adj* upright; directed upward; right end up, not inverted; not decumbent (*bot*); turgid and raised (*zool*). — *vt* to set upright; to set erect; to set at right angles; to raise; to build; to exalt; to establish. — *adj* **erect'ed**. — *n* **erect'er** or **erect'or** someone who or something which erects or raises; a muscle which assists in erecting a part or an organ; an attachment to a compound microscope for making the image erect instead of inverted. — *adj* **erect'ile** (*-īl*) that may be erected. — *n* **erectility** (*e-* or *ē-rek-til'i-ti*). — *n* **erec'tion** the act of erecting; the state of being erected; exaltation; anything erected; a building of any kind; an enlarging and hardening of the penis *usu* in response to sexual stimulation. — *adj* **erect'ive** tending to erect. — *adv* **erect'ly**. — *n* **erect'ness**. [L *ērigere*, *ērēctum* to set upright, from *ē* from, and *regere* to direct]

eremacausis *er-i-mə-kö'sis*, (*chem*) *n* very slow oxidation. [Gr *ērema* quietly or slowly, and *kausis* burning, from *kaiein* to burn]

eremic *e-rē'mik*, *adj* of or belonging to deserts. [Gr *erēmikos*, from *erēmiā* desert or solitude]

eremite *er'i-mīt*, *n* a recluse who lives alone, *esp* from religious motives; a hermit. — *adj* **eremī'tal**. — *adj* **eremitic** (*-mit'ik*) or **eremit'ical**. — *n* **er'emītism**. [LL *erēmīta*, from Gr *erēmītēs*, from *erēmos* desert]

e re nata *ē rē nā'tə* or *ā rā nä'ta*, (*LL*; *legal*) according to the exigencies of the case.

erepsin *e-rep'sin*, *n* an enzyme of the small intestine, acting upon casein, gelatine, etc. [L *ēripere*, *ēreptum*, from *ē* from, and *rapere* to snatch]

erethism *er'e-thizm*, *n* excitement or stimulation of an organ; abnormal irritability. — *adj* **erethis'mic**. — *adj* **erethis'tic**. — *adj* **erethit'ic**. [Gr *erethismos*]

Erewhon *er'e-(h)won*, *n* the imaginary country of Samuel Butler's satirical Utopian romances *Erewhon* (1872) and *Erewhon Revisited* (1901). — *n* and *adj* **Erewhō'nian**. [Formed from *nowhere* spelt backwards]

erf *ûrf*, (*SAfr*) *n* a garden plot or small piece of ground: — *pl* **er'ven**. [Du; cf OE *erfe* inheritance]

erg[1] *ûrg*, *n* the unit of work in the centimetre-gramme-second system ie the quantity of work done when the point of operation of a force of one dyne is allowed to move one centimetre in the direction of the force. — *n* **er'gogram** a record by ergograph. — *n* **er'gograph** an instrument for measuring and recording muscular work. — *n* **ergomā'nia** abnormal desire to work, addiction to work. — *n* **ergomā'niac**. — *n* **ergom'eter** an instrument for measuring work done, a dynamometer. — *adj* **ergonom'ic**. — *adv* **ergonom'ically**. — *n sing* **ergonom'ics** (Gr *nomos*, from *nemein* to manage) the scientific study of man in relation to his physical working environment; the adaptation of machines and general conditions to fit the individual so that he or she may work at maximum efficiency. — *n* **ergon'omist**. — *n* **ergopho'bia** abnormal dislike of work. — **erg'-nine'**, **erg'-ten'**, etc an erg multiplied by ten to the power of nine, ten, etc. [Gr *ergon* work]

erg[2] *ûrg*, *n* a Saharan area of shifting sand dunes: — *pl* **ar'eg** or **ergs**. [Fr, from Ar *'irj*]

ergates *ûr'gə-tēz* or **ergate** *ûr'gāt*, *n* a worker ant, an undeveloped female. — *n* **ergatan'dromorph** (Gr *andromorphos* of male form) an ant combining characters of males and workers. — *n* **ergataner** (*ûr-gə-tā'nər* or *-tä'nər*; Gr *anēr* man) a worker-like wingless male ant. — *adj* **er'gative** (*gram*) of a grammatical case which, in certain languages, eg Eskimo and Basque, indicates the subject of a transitive verb (also **ergative case**). — *n* **ergativ'ity**. — *n* **ergatoc'racy** (Gr *kratos* power) rule by the workers. — *n* **ergatogyne** (*-jī'nē*; Gr *gynē* woman) a worker-like wingless female ant. — *adj* **er'gatoid** worker-like, wingless but sexually perfect. — *n* **er'gatomorph** an ergatoid ant. — *adj* **ergatomorph'ic**. [Gr *ergatēs* workman, from *ergon* work]

ergo *ûr'gō*, (*logic*) *adv* therefore (used to introduce the conclusion of a syllogism). — *vi* **er'gotize** or **-ise** to wrangle (see also **ergot**). [L *ergō* therefore]

ergodic *ər-god'ik*, (*math*) *adj* of or relating to the probability that in a system any state will occur again. — *n* **ergodic'ity** (*-dis'*). [Gr *ergon* work, and *hodos* way]

ergogram, etc. See **erg**.

ergon *ûr'gən* or *er'gon*, (*Gr*) *n* work or business.

ergonomic, etc. See **erg**.

ergosterol. See **ergot**.

ergot *ûr'got*, *n* a disease of grasses (*esp* rye) and sedges due to *Claviceps purpurea*; a seed so diseased. — *n* **ergos'terol** an unsaturated sterol obtained from ergot. — *vt* **er'gotize** or **-ise** to affect with ergot or with ergotism (see also **ergo**). — *n* **er'gotism** poisoning caused by eating bread made of rye diseased with ergot. [Fr]

ERI *abbrev*: *Edwardus Rex Imperator* (*New L*) Edward, King (and) Emperor.

eric *er'ik*, *n* the blood-fine paid by a murderer to his victim's family in old Irish law. — Also **er'iach** or **er'ick**. [Ir *eiric*]

erica *er'i-kə*, *n* a plant of the heath genus *Erica*. — *adj* **ericaceous** (*er-i-kā'shəs*) belonging to plants of the genus Erica, or its family **Ericā'ceae**; heathlike. — *adj* **er'icoid** with heatherlike leaves. [L, from Gr *ereikē* heath]

erigeron *e-rij'ə-ron*, *n* a plant of the flea-bane genus *Erigeron* of composite plants. [Gr *ērigeron* groundsel, from *ēri* early, and *gerōn* old]

eringo. Same as **eryngo**.

erinite *er'i-nīt*, *n* a basic arsenate of copper found in Cornwall and Ireland. [*Erin* Ireland]

Erinys *e-ri'nis*, *n* a Fury: — *pl* **Erinyes** (*e-rin'i-ēz*). [Gr *Erīnȳs*, pl *Erīnyes*]

erio- *er-i-ō-* or *-o-*, *combining form* denoting wool or fibre. — *n* **Eriocaulon** (*-ō-kö'lon*; Gr *kaulos* stalk) the pipewort genus, giving name to the **Eriocaul(on)ā'ceae**, a family of monocotyledons, related to the Bromelias. — *n* **Eriōden'dron** (Gr *dendron* tree) the silk-cotton genus of trees. — *n* **eriometer** (*-om'ət-ər*; Gr *metron* measure) an optical instrument for measuring small diameters, eg of fibres. — *n* **er'ionite** a mineral which occurs in white wool-like crystals. — *n* **eriophorum** (*-of'ər-əm*; Gr *phoros* carrying) a plant of the cotton-grass or cotton-sedge genus *Eriphorum*. — *adj* **eriophorous** (*-of'ər-əs*) very cottony. [Gr *erion* wool]

eristic *er-is'tik* or **eristical** *-is'tik-l*, *adj* of or pertaining to controversy or argument. [Gr *eristikos*, from *eris* strife]

erk *ûrk*, (*airmen's slang*) *n* an aircraftsman. [From *airk*, for aircraftsman]

erl-king *ûrl'-king*, *n* for German *Erlkönig*, a mistranslation (alder-king) of the Danish *ellerkonge* (from *elverkonge* king of the elves).

ERM *abbrev*: exchange rate mechanism.

ermelin *ûr'mə-lin*, (*archaic*) *n* ermine.

ermine *ûr'min*, *n* the stoat; a white fur, the stoat's winter coat in northern lands, used with the black tail-tip (or an imitation) attached for the ceremonial robes of royalty, the nobility, judges and magistrates. — *adj* **er'mined** trimmed or decorated with ermine. [OFr *ermine* (Fr *hermine*), perh from L (*mūs*) *Armēnius*, literally (mouse) of Armenia, whence it was brought to Rome; but according to some from OHGer *harmin* (Ger *Hermelin*) ermine-fur]

ern. An old spelling (*Milton*) of **earn**.

erne[1] *ûrn*, *n* an eagle, *esp* the sea-eagle. [OE *earn*; cf ON *örn*, Du *arend*]

erne[2] *ûrn*, (*Spenser*). Same as **yearn**[1].

Ernie *ûr'ni*, *n* the computer which picks random numbers to be used as winning numbers on premium bonds. [Abbreviation of *e*lectronic *r*andom *n*umber *i*ndicator *e*quipment]

erode *i-* or *e-rōd'*, *vt* to eat away or wear away; to form or shape by wearing away. — Also *vi*. — *adj* **erō'ded** or **erose** (*-rōs'*) irregularly notched as if bitten. — *adj* and *n* **erō'dent** caustic. — *adj* **erod'ible** able to be eroded. [L *ē* from, and *rōdere*, *rōsum* to gnaw]

erodium *e-rō'di-əm*, *n* a plant of the stork's-bill genus *Erodium* of the geranium family. [Gr *erōdios* a heron]

erogenic *e-rō-jen'ik* or **erogenous** *e-roj'ən-əs*, *adj* producing erotic desire or gratification. [**Eros**]

EROM *ē'rom* (*comput*) *abbrev*: erasable read only memory (qv under **erase**).

Eros *ēr'os* or *er'os*, *n* the Greek love-god, identified by the Romans with Cupid; an asteroid discovered in 1898, notable for its near approach to the earth. — *adj* **erotic** (*e-rot'ik*) or (*rare*) **erot'ical** pertaining to or arousing sexual desire; amatory; amorous. — *n* **erot'ic** a person who is particularly susceptible to sexual arousal; an amatory poem or composition. — *n pl* **erot'ica** erotic literature. — *n* **erot'icism** (*-sizm*) amorous temperament or habit; erotism. — *n* **erot'icist**. — *vt* **erot'icize** or **-ise** to make erotic; to arouse sexually. — *n* **er'otism** sexual desire; the manifestations of sex in its widest application. — *adj* **erotogenic** (*er-ət-ō-jen'ik*) or **erotogenous** (*-oj'*) producing erotic desire or gratification. — *n* **erōtomā'nia** unhealthily strong sexual passion. — *n* **erōtomā'niac**. — *n* **erōtophō'bia** fear of or aversion to any form of sexual involvement. [Gr *Erōs*, *-ōtos*, the Greek love-god]

erosion *i-* or *ē-rō'zhən*, (*geol*) *n* eating away or wearing down; the denuding action of weathering, water, ice, wind, etc. — *adj* **erosive** (*-rō'ziv*). [Ety as for **erode**]

erostrate *ē-ros'trāt*, (*bot*) *adj* beakless. [L *ē* from, and *rōstrum* a beak]

erotema *er-ō-tē'mə*, **eroteme** *er'ō-tēm* or **erotesis** *er-ō-tē'sis*, *n* a rhetorical question. — *adj* **erotetic** (*-tet'ik*) interrogatory. [Gr *erōtēma*, *erōtēsis*, from *erōtaein* to question]

erotic, **erotism**, **erotogenic**, etc. See **Eros**.

err *ûr*, *vi* to miss the mark; to be inaccurate; to make a mistake; to sin; to wander (*archaic*); to wander from the right way (*archaic*); to go astray (*archaic*): — *pr p* **erring** (*ûr'ing*, *er'ing*); *pa t* and *pa p* **erred** (*ûrd*). — *adj* **err'able** (*er'*; *obs*) capable of erring. — *adj* **err'ing** wandering (*archaic*); straying from the truth or right conduct. — *n* wandering (*archaic*); straying (*archaic*); making mistakes. — *adv* **err'ingly**. — *adj* **erroneous** (*i-rō'ni-əs*) erring; full of errors; wrong; mistaken; wandering or straying (*archaic*). — *adv* **errō'neously**. — *n* **errō'neousness**. — *n* **error** (*er'ər*) a blunder or mistake; wrong-doing; the difference between a quantity obtained by observation and the true value; a fault or mistake causing the failure of a computer program or system to produce expected results; mistaken opinion; deviation from the right way (*archaic*); a wandering, a winding course (*archaic*). — *n* **err'orist** (*archaic*). — **error message** (*comput*) a message on a computer screen to help the user correct a fault such as a missing file or incorrect keyboard input. [L *errāre* to stray; cognate with Ger *irren* and *irre* astray]

errand *er'ənd*, *n* a verbal message (*archaic*); a mission (*archaic*); a commission to say or do something usually involving a short journey; (in *pl*) shopping (*dialect*). — **err'and-boy** or **err'and-girl**. — **a fool's errand** or **a sleeveless errand** a futile journey; **make an errand** to invent a reason for going; **once'-errand**, **yince'-errand** or **ance'-errand** (*Scot*) for the express purpose and nothing else; **run errands** to be sent to convey messages or perform small pieces of business. [OE *ǣrende*; ON *eyrindi*; prob connected with Gothic *āirus*, ON *ārr* a messenger]

errant *er'ənt*, *adj* wandering; roving; quixotic; thorough (*obs*; cf **arrant**); erring. — *n* a knight-errant. — *adv* **err'antly**. — *n* **err'antry** an errant or wandering state; a rambling about like a knight-errant. [ME *errant*, from OFr pr p of *errer* to travel, from LL *iterāre*, confused with pr p of *errer* to err, from L *errāre*]

erratic *e-ra'tic*, *adj* wandering; having no certain course; not stationary; irregular, capricious, irregular or unpredictable in behaviour. — *n* a wanderer; an erratic block or boulder. — *adj* (*archaic*) **errat'ical**. — *adv* **errat'ically**. — *n* **erratum** (*e-rä'tum*) an error in writing or printing, *esp* one noted in a list in a book (*pl* **errata** *e-rä'tə*). — **erratic block** a mass of rock transported by ice and deposited at a distance. [L *errāticus*, from *errāre* to stray]

errhine *er'īn*, *adj* and *n* (something) causing sneezing or running of mucus from the nose. [Gr *errīnon*, from *en* in, and *rhīs*, *rhīnos* the nose]

erroneous, **error**, etc. See under **err**.

ers *ûrs*, *n* the bitter vetch. [Fr, from L *ervum*]

ersatz *er'zats*, *ûr'-* or *er-zats'*, *n* a substitute; a supplementary reserve from which waste can be made good (*military*). — *adj* substitute; fake. [Ger]

Erse *ers* or *ûrs*, *n* formerly, and still occasionally, the name given by Lowland Scots to the language of the people of the West Highlands, as being of Irish origin; sometimes used for Irish Gaelic, as opposed to Scottish Gaelic. [Variant of **Irish**]

erst *ûrst*, *adv* at first; formerly. — *adv* **erst'while** or **erstwhile'** formerly. — *adj* former. [OE *ǣrest*, superl of *ær*; see **ere**]

erubescent *er-ōō-bes'ənt*, *adj* growing red; blushing. — *n* **erubesc'ence** or **erubesc'ency**. — *n* **erubesc'īte** the mineral bornite. [L *ērubēscere* to grow red; see **rubescent** and **ruby**]

Eruca *i-rōō'kə*, *n* a genus of herbs of the family Cruciferae. — **erucic acid** (*i-rōō'sik*) a crystalline fatty acid found in rape-seed, wallflower seed and mustard seed, used in some edible oils. [L *ērūca* rocket (see **rocket**[2]); see also **eruciform**]

eruciform *e-rōō'si-förm*, *adj* like a caterpillar. [L *ērūca* caterpillar, and *fōrma* form]

eruct *i-rukt'*, or **eructate** *-āt*, *vt* to belch out, (eg wind from the stomach; also *vi*; also *fig*); of a volcano, to emit (fumes and ash or lava). — *n* **eructā'tion** (*ē-*). [L *ēructāre*, *-ātum*, from *ē* from, and *ructāre* to belch forth]

erudite *er'ōō-dīt*, or *-ū-*, *adj* learned. — *n* a learned person. — *adv* **er'uditely**. — *n* **erudi'tion** the state of being learned; knowledge gained by study; learning, *esp* in literature. [L *ērudītus*, from *ērudīre*, *ērudītum* to free from rudeness, from *ē* from, and *rudis* rude]

erumpent *i-rum'pənt*, (*bot*) *adj esp* of fungal hyphae, breaking through suddenly. [Ety as for **erupt**]

erupt *i-rupt'*, *vi* to break out or through, eg of a volcano, a tooth from the gum or a rash on the skin. — Also *vt*. — *n* **erup'tion** a breaking or bursting out; something which bursts out; a breaking out of spots on the skin; the action of a volcano. — *adj* **erup'tional**. — *adj* **erupt'ive** breaking out; attended by or producing eruption; produced by eruption. — *n* **erupt'iveness** or **eruptiv'ity**. [L *ērumpere*, *ēruptum*, from *ē* from, and *rumpere* to break]

ervalenta. See **revalenta**.

erven. See **erf**.

eryngo *e-ring'gō*, *n* the candied root of sea-holly; the plant itself, a superficially thistle-like umbellifer: — *pl* **eryn'gos** or **eryn'goes**. — *n* **eryn'gium** (*-ji-əm*) a plant of the genus *Erygium* of bristly plants including the sea-holly (family Umbelliferae). [Gr *ēryngos*]

Erysimum *er-is'i-məm*, *n* the treacle-mustard genus of Cruciferae. [Latinized from Gr *erysimon* hedge-mustard]

erysipelas *er-i-sip'i-ləs*, *n* an inflammatory disease, generally in the face, marked by a bright redness of the skin. — *adj* **erysipelatous** (*-el'ə-təs*). [Gr; prob from root of *erythros* red, and *pella* skin]

erythema *er-i-thē'mə*, *n* redness of the skin. — *adj* **erythemal** (*er-ith'*). — *adj* **erythemat'ic**. — *adj* **erythem'atous**. [Gr *erythēma*, from *erythainein* to redden, from *erythros* red]

erythro- or **erythr-** *er-ith-r(ō)-*, *combining form* denoting red. — *n* **erythrī'na** a plant of the kaffir-boom genus *Erythrina* of Papilionaceae, tropical and subtropical trees with brilliant red flowers. — *n* **eryth'rism** red colouring, *esp* exceptional or abnormal. — *n* **eryth'rīte** a reddish hydrous arsenate of cobalt. — *adj* **erythrit'ic**. — *n* **eryth'roblast** (*-bläst*; Gr *blastos* a sprout) a cell in bone marrow that develops into an erythrocyte. — *n* **eryth'rocyte** (Gr *kytos* case) a red blood corpuscle. — *n* **erythroleukae'mia** a malignant disorder of the blood characterized by an abnormal presence of erythroblasts and myeloblasts in the blood. — *n* **erythromycin** (*-mī'sin*; Gr *mykēs* fungus) an antibiotic similar to penicillin. — *n* **erythropē'nia** diminution below normal of the number of red cells in the blood. — *n* **erythrophō'bia** a fear of blushing; a neurotic tendency to blush; an aversion to red. — *n* **erythropoiesis** (*-poi-ēs'is*; Gr *poiēsis* making) the formation of red blood cells. — *n* **erythropoi'etin** a hormone which increases the rate of formation of red blood cells; a drug with the same effect. [Gr *erythros* red]

Erziehungsroman *er-tsē'ōōngs-rō-män'*, (*Ger*). Same as *Bildungsroman*.

ES *abbrev*: El Salvador (IVR).

Es (*chem*) *symbol*: einsteinium.

es *es*, *n* the nineteenth letter of the alphabet (S or s); anything of that shape. — Also **ess**.

ESA *abbrev*: Environmentally Sensitive Area; European Space Agency.

ESB *abbrev*: electrical stimulation of the brain.

Esc *abbrev*: escudo, the Portuguese unit of currency.

esc *esk*, (*comput*) *abbrev*: escape (key).

ESCA *abbrev*: electron spectroscopy for chemical analysis.

escadrille *es-kə-dril'*, *n* a French squadron of aircraft; a flotilla. [Fr, flotilla]

escalade *es-kə-lād'*, *n* the scaling of the walls of a fortress by means of ladders. — Also **escalā'dō** (for Sp *escalada*): — *pl* **escalā'does**. — *vt* to scale; to mount and enter by means of ladders. [Fr, from Sp *escalada*, from *escala* a ladder, from L *scāla*]

escalate *es'kə-lāt*, *vi* to ascend or descend on an escalator; to increase rapidly in scale or intensity. — Also *vt*. — *n* **escalā'tion**. — *n* **es'calātor** a moving staircase; short form of escalator clause (see below). — *adj* **es'calātory**. — **escalator clause** or **escalation clause** a clause in an agreement allowing for adjustment up or down according to change in circumstances, as in cost of material in a work contract or in cost of living in a wage agreement. [*escalate* is a back-formation from *escalator*, orig a trademark, prob from **escalade** and elev*ator*]

escalier *es-ka-lyā*, (*Fr*) *n* a staircase. — **escalier dérobé** (*dā-ro-bā*) a private staircase.

escallonia *es-kal-ōn'i-ə*, *n* a plant of the S American genus *Escallonia* of shrubs of the saxifrage family. [Discovered by *Escallon*, an 18c Spanish traveller]

escallop *is-kal'əp*, *n* a variant of **scallop**. — *adj* **escall'oped** (*heraldry*) covered with scallop-shells.

escalop. A variant of **scallop** except in heraldry.

escalope *es'ka-lop*, *n* a boneless slice of meat, cut thin and often beaten out still thinner. [Fr]

escamotage *es-ka-mo-täzh*, (*Fr*) *n* juggling.

escape *is-kāp'*, *vt* to free oneself from; to pass out of danger from; to evade or elude. — *vi* to come off or come through in safety; to emerge into or gain freedom; to flee; to slip out; to issue; to leak. — *n* the act of escaping; a means of escaping; flight; flight from reality; an outlet; an escape valve; a leakage; an accidental or inadvertent emission; an outburst; a person or thing that has escaped, *esp* a garden plant maintaining itself wild; a function key on some computer keyboards, used to cancel commands, to leave a program, etc (*abbrev* **esc**, *comput*); a sally; a prank (*obs*); a venial offence (*obs*); a transgression (*obs*). — *adj* of literature, providing escape from reality; (of a clause in an agreement) defining the conditions under which a party is relieved of obligation. — *adj* **escap'able**. — *n* **escapade** (*es-kə-pād'*) an escape (*archaic*); an exciting, *esp* mischievous, adventure. — *n* **escapado** (*-ā'dō*) an escaped evil-doer; an escapade (*Sp escapada*): — *pl* **escapā'does**. — *n* **escapee'** a person who has escaped from prison. — *adj* **escape'less**. — *n* **escape'ment** part of a timepiece connecting the wheel-work with the pendulum or balance, and allowing a tooth to escape at each vibration; the clearance in a pianoforte between the string and the hammer after it has struck the string, while the key is held down; an escape (*archaic*). — *n* **escāp'er**. — *n* **escāp'ism** escape from (*esp* unpleasant) reality. — *n* **escāp'ist** someone who seeks escape, *esp* from reality. — Also *adj*. — *n* **escapol'ogist**. — *n* **escapol'ogy** the study or use of methods of escape from any sort of constraint or confinement; (loosely) escapism. — **escape clause** a clause in a contract, etc that releases one from that contract under certain circumstances; **escape hatch** an emergency means of escape from a ship, submarine, etc; **escape mechanism** (*psychol*) a mental process by which a person avoids something unpleasant; **escape road** a short track leading off a road on a steep hill, sharp bend, etc, for vehicles going out of control; **escape valve** a valve to let steam, etc escape when wanted; **escape velocity** (*phys*) the minimum velocity needed to escape from the gravitation field of a body; **escape wheel** the wheel that the pallets act upon in a clock. [OFr *escaper* (Fr *échapper*), from LL *ex cappā* (literally) out of one's cape or cloak]

escargot *es-kar-gō*, (*Fr*) *n* an edible snail.

escarmouche *e-skär'mōōsh*, (*obs*) *n* a skirmish. [Fr]

escarole *es-ka-rōl* or *-röl*, *n* a broad-leaved, non-curly endive. [Fr]

escarp *is-kärp'*, *vt* to make into a scarp or sudden slope. — *n* a scarp or steep slope; the side of the ditch beside the rampart (*fortif*). — *n* **escarp'ment** the precipitous side of a hill or rock; escarp. [Fr *escarper* to cut steeply, from the root of **scarp**]

ESCB *abbrev*: European System of Central Banks.

eschalot. See **shallot**.

eschar *es'kär*, (*pathol*) *n* a slough or portion of dead or disorganized tissue, *esp* an artificial slough produced by caustics. — *adj* **escharot'ic** tending to form an eschar; caustic. — *n* a caustic substance. [L, from Gr *escharā* a hearth, or the mark of a burn]

eschatology *es-kə-tol'ə-ji*, (*theol*) *n* the doctrine of the last or final matters, such as death, judgement and the state after death. — *adj* **eschatolog'ic** or **eschatolog'ical**. — *n* **eschatol'ogist**. [Gr *eschatos* last, and *logos* a discourse]

escheat *is-chēt'*, *n* property that falls to the feudal lord or to the state for lack of an heir or by forfeiture; plunder or gain (*obs*; *Spenser* **excheat'**). — *vt* to confiscate. — *vi* to fall to the lord of the manor or the state. — *adj* **escheat'able**. — *n* **escheat'age**. — *n* **escheat'ment**. — *n* **escheat'or** (*hist*) an official who watched over escheats. [OFr *eschete*, from *escheoir* (Fr *échoir*), from L *ex* from, and *cadere* to fall]

Escherichia *esh-ə-rik'i-ə*, *n* a genus of rod-shaped, gram-negative bacteria of the family *Enterobacteriaceae*. — **Escherichia coli** the type species of this genus, occurring naturally in the intestines of vertebrates and sometimes pathogenic (abbrev **E. coli**). [T *Escherich*, Ger physician (died 1911)]

eschew *is-cho͞o'*, *vt* to shun; to flee from (*obs*); to abstain from. — *n* **eschew'al**. — *n* **eschew'er**. [OFr *eschever*; cognate with Ger *scheuen* to shun]

eschscholtzia or **eschscholzia** *e-sholt'si-ə*, *n* a plant of the genus *Echshol(t)zia* of the poppy family Papaveraceae, including the Californian poppy, a showy garden annual. [J F von *Eschscholtz*, a member of the expedition that discovered the poppy in 1821]

esclandre *es-klã-dr'*, *n* notoriety; any unpleasantness. [Fr, from L *scandalum*]

escolar *es-kō-lär'*, *n* an Atlantic and Southern fish of spectacled appearance. [Sp, scholar]

escopette *es-kō-pet'*, (*US*) *n* a carbine. [Sp *escopeta*]

escort *es'kört*, *n* anyone or anything accompanying another or others for protection, guidance, courtesy, etc; an armed guard; a police officer accompanying a person under arrest, in order to prevent escape; a man who accompanies a woman on an evening out; a person, usually of the opposite sex, hired to accompany someone to entertainments, etc; a member of an aircraft, etc crew whose duty is to look after children travelling alone; attendance. — Also used as *adj*. — *vt* **escort'** to accompany or attend as escort. — *n* (*US*) **escort'age**. — **escort agency** one which provides people to act as hired escorts; **escort carrier** a small aircraft-carrier used for escorting naval convoys or in support of military landings. [Fr *escorte*, from Ital *scorta*, from *scorgere* to guide, from L *ex* out, and *corrigere* to set right]

escot *es-kot'*, (*Shakesp*) *vt* to pay for or maintain. [OFr *escoter*, *escot* a tax; of Gmc origin; cf **scot**[1] and **shot**[2]]

escribano *ā-skrē-bä'nō*, (*Sp*) *n* a notary: — *pl* **escriba'nos**.

escribe *ē-skrīb'*, (*geom*) *vt* to draw (a circle) so as to touch one side of a triangle externally, the others (produced) internally. [L *ē* out, and *scrībere* write]

escritoire *es-krē-twär'*, *n* a writing-desk. — *adj* **escritō'rial** (or *-ör'*). [Fr *escritoire*, from LL *scrīptōrium*, from L *scrībere*, *scrīptum* to write]

escroc *es-krō*, (*Fr*) *n* a swindler.

escroll or **escrol** *es-krōl'*, *n* an escrow; a scroll (*heraldry*). — *n* **escrow** (*es-krō'*; *law*) a deed in the hands of a third party, to take effect when a condition is fulfilled. [Anglo-Fr *escroele*, *escroe*; see **scroll** and **scrow**]

escuage *es'kū-ij*, *n* scutage. [Anglo-Fr; see **scutage**]

escudo *es-ko͞o'dō*, *n* the Portuguese unit of currency; a coin representing this; formerly, a coin or currency unit of various values in other countries: — *pl* **escu'dos**. [Port and Sp, shield]

Esculapian. See **Aesculapian**.

esculent *es'kū-lənt*, *adj* eatable; fit to be used for human food. — *n* something that is eatable. [L *esculentus* eatable, from *esca* food, from *edere* to eat]

escutcheon *es-kuch'ən*, *n* a shield on which a coat of arms is represented; a family shield; the part of a vessel's stern bearing her name; a shield-shaped object or ornament, etc as a shield over a keyhole. — *adj* **escutch'eoned** having an escutcheon. — **a blot on the escutcheon** a stain on one's good name; **escutcheon of pretence** (*heraldry*) an escutcheon placed with the arms of an heiress in the centre of her husband's coat. [OFr *escuchon*, from L *scūtum* a shield]

Esd. (*Bible*) *abbrev*: (the Apocryphal Books of) Esdras.

ESE *abbrev*: east-south-east.

-ese *-ēz*, *sfx* denoting country or region of origin, as in *Japanese*, *Maltese*; the literary style, jargon, etc of a specified group, as in *journalese*, *officialese*.

esemplastic *es-əm-plas'tik*, *adj* unifying. — *n* **esemplasy** (*es-em'plə-si*) the unifying power of imagination. [Gr *es* into, *hen* (neuter) one, and *plastikos* moulding]

esile *ā'sil*, (*obs*). Same as **eisel**.

esker or **eskar** *esk'ər*, (*geol*) *n* a ridge of gravel and sand laid down by a subglacial stream or one which issues from a retreating glacier, a kame. [Ir *eiscir* a ridge]

Eskimo *es'ki-mō*, *n* one of a people inhabiting arctic America with its islands, Greenland, and the nearest Asiatic coast (the Eskimos themselves prefer to be called *Inuit* or *Yupik*); their language: — *pl* **Es'kimo** or **Es'kimos**. — Also *adj*. — **Eskimo dog** one of a breed of powerful dogs with a double coat of hair, widely distributed in the Arctic regions and indispensable for drawing sledges (also called **malamute**); **Eskimo roll** (*canoeing*) a complete roll-over under water. [Prob from an Indian word meaning eaters of raw flesh]

Esky® *es'ki*, (*Austr*) *n* (also without *cap*) a portable insulated container for keeping drinks, etc cool. [Prob from **Eskimo**]

ESL *abbrev*: English as a second language.

esloin or **esloyne** *es-loin'*, (*obs*). Same as **eloin**.

ESN *abbrev*: educationally subnormal, formerly used to describe people with special educational needs.

esne *ez'ni*, (*hist*) *n* a domestic slave in OE times. [OE]

esnecy *es'nə-si*, (*obs*) *n* the eldest daughter's right of first choice in dividing an inheritance. [OFr *ainsneece* (Fr *aînesse*)]

ESOP *abbrev*: employee share ownership plan.

esophagus. A chiefly *US* spelling of **oesophagus**.

esoteric *es-ō-ter'ik*, *adj* inner; secret; mysterious; taught to a select few (*opp* to *exoteric*; *philos*): — *n pl* **esoter'ica** esoteric objects, etc. — *adv* **esoter'ically**. — *n* **esoter'icism** (*-i-sizm*) or **esoterism** (*es-ot'ər-izm*) the holding of esoteric opinions. — *n* **esoter'icist**. — *n* **es'otery** (*rare*) secret doctrine. — **esoteric Buddhism** theosophy. [Gr *esōterikos*, from *esōterō*, compar of *esō*, *eisō* within]

ESP *abbrev*: English for special (or specific) purposes; extrasensory perception.

esp. or **espec.** *abbrev*: especially.

espada *es-pä'dha*, (*Sp*) *n* a sword; a swordfish; a matador.

espadrille *es-pə-dril'*, *n* a rope-soled shoe. [Fr, from Provençal *espardillo*, from *espart* esparto]

espagnole *es-pan-yol'* or **espagnole sauce** (*sōs*), *n* a brown sauce flavoured with tomatoes and sherry. — Also (*Fr*) **sauce espagnole** (*sōs es-pan-yol*). [Fr, Spanish (sauce)]

espagnolette *es-pan-yō-let'*, *n* the fastening of a French window. [Fr, dimin of *espagnol* Spanish]

espalier *es-pal'yər*, *n* a lattice-work of wood to train trees across; a fruit-tree trained on stakes; a row of trees so trained (*obs*). — *vt* to train as an espalier. [Fr, from Ital *spalliera* a support for the shoulders, from *spalla* a shoulder; cf **epaulette**]

esparto *es-pär'tō*, *n* a strong grass (*Stipatenacissima* and others) grown in Spain, N Africa, etc, and used for making paper, baskets, cordage, etc: — *pl* **espar'tos**. [Sp, from L *spartum*, from Gr *sparton* a kind of rope]

espec. See **esp**.

especial *is-pesh'l*, *adj* special; particular; principal; distinguished. — *adv* **espec'ially**. — **in especial** (*archaic*) in particular. [OFr, from L *speciālis*, from *speciēs* species]

esperance *es'pər-əns*, (*Shakesp*) *n* hope. [Fr *espérance*, from L *spērāre* to hope]

Esperanto *es-pər-an'tō*, *n* an international language devised by Dr Zamenhof, published 1887. — Also *adj*. — *n* **Esperan'tist** a speaker of Esperanto. [Inventor's pseudonym, (literally) the hoping one]

espial. See **espy**.

espiègle *es-pē-eg'l'*, *adj* roguish or frolicsome; arch. — *n* **espièg'lerie** roguishness; frolicsomeness. [Fr, from Ger *Eulenspiegel*; see **owl**]

espionage *es-pyon-äzh'*, *es'pi-ə-nij* or *es-pī'ə-nij*, *n* spying; use of spies. [Fr *espionner*, from *espion* spy]

esplanade *es-plə-nād'*, *n* a level space between a citadel and the first houses of the town; any level space for walking or driving in, *esp* by the sea. [Fr, from Sp *esplanada*, from L *explānāre*, from *ex* out, and *plānus* flat]

espouse *is-powz'*, *vt* to give or take in marriage or betrothal; to take upon oneself or embrace (eg a cause). — *n* **espous'al** the act of espousing or betrothing; the taking upon oneself of eg a cause; (in *pl*) a contract or mutual promise of marriage; a wedding; a formal betrothal. — *n* **espous'er**. [OFr *espouser* (Fr *épouser*), from L *spōnsāre* to betroth, from *spondēre*, *spōnsum* to vow]

espresso *es-pres'ō*, *n* a form of coffee-making machine giving high extraction under pressure; coffee made in this way: — *pl* **espress'os**. — Also *adj*, *esp* of a type of coffee bar or the coffee. [Ital, pressed]

ESPRIT *abbrev*: European Strategic Programme of Research into Information Technology, a European Community initiative to develop fifth generation computer techniques.

esprit *es-prē*, (*Fr*) *n* wit or liveliness. — **esprit de corps** (*es-prē də kor*) regard for the honour of the body to which one belongs; loyalty of a member to the whole; **esprit de l'escalier** (*də-les-kal-yā*; or sometimes incorrectly **d'escalier**) thinking of an apt or witty retort after the opportunity of making it is past; the retort itself; **esprit fort** (*for*) a free-thinker. [Fr *esprit* spirit, *de* of, *corps* body, *escalier* staircase, and *fort* strong]

esprit follet *es-prē fo-le*, (*Fr*) *n* mischievous goblin.

espumoso *es-pōō-mō'sō* (*Sp*) *n* a sparkling wine: — *pl* **espumo'sos**.

espy *es-pī'*, (*archaic* or *literary*) *vt* to watch; to see at a distance; to catch sight of; to observe; to discover unexpectedly: — *pr p* **espy'ing**; *pa t* and *pa p* **espied'**; *3rd pers sing* **espies'**. — *n* **espi'al** the act of espying; observation. [OFr *espier*; see **spy**]

Esq. or **Esqr**. *abbrev*: esquire.

-esque *-esk*, *sfx* forming adjectives from nouns, *esp* proper names, and denoting in the style or manner of or similar to, eg *Kiplingesque*, *statuesque*.

Esquimau *es'ki-mō*, a French spelling of **Eskimo**: — *pl* **Esquimaux** (*es'ki-mōz*).

esquire *es-kwīr'*, sometimes *es'*, *n orig* a squire or shield-bearer; an attendant on a knight (*archaic*); a landed proprietor; a title of dignity next below a knight; a gentleman acting as escort; a general title of respect in addressing letters (*usu abbrev* **Esq.**): — *fem* (*hist*; *rare*) **esquiress**. [OFr *esquier* (Fr *écuyer*), from L *scūtārius*, from *scūtum* a shield]

esquisse *es-kēs*, (*Fr*) *n* a sketch or outline.

ESRC *abbrev*: Economic and Social Research Council.

ESRO *ez'rō*, *abbrev*: European Space Research Organization, which became part of ESA in 1975.

ESS *abbrev*: evolutionarily stable strategy.

ess *es*, see **es**. — **collar of esses** a chain of links (also written SS) in the form of the letter S, worn by various dignitaries.

-ess *sfx* denoting the female of a specified species, occupation, etc, eg *lioness*, *princess*, *poetess*. [OFr *-esse*, from LL *-issa*, from Gr *-issa*]

essay *es'ā*, *n* an attempt; a tentative effort; a written composition less elaborate than a treatise; a first draft (*archaic*); a trial (*archaic*); an experiment (*archaic*). — *vt* **essay'** to try; to attempt; to make experiment of (*archaic*): — *pr p* **essay'ing**; *pa t* and *pa p* **essayed'**. — *n* **essay'er**. — *n* **essayette'** a little essay. — *adj* **ess'ayish**. — *n* **ess'ayist** a person who essays (*archaic*); a writer of essays. — *adj* **essayis'tic**. [OFr *essai*, from L *exagium* weighing, from *exagere* to try or examine]

esse *es'i*, (*philos*) *n* actual existence; essence. — **in esse** in existence (*opp* to *in posse*, in potentiality). [L *esse* to be]

essence *es'əns*, *n* the inner distinctive nature of anything; the qualities which make any object what it is; a being; an alcoholic solution of a volatile or essential oil; a perfume of such composition; the extracted virtues of any drug; a liquid having the properties of the substance from which it is obtained; (also **Essen'cia**) a particularly fine variety of Tokay wine. — *adj* **essential** (*is-* or *es-en'shl*) relating to, constituting or containing the essence; necessary to the existence of a thing; indispensable or important in the highest degree; highly rectified; pure; (of eg a disease) having no known cause. — *n* something necessary; a leading principle. — *n* **essen'tialism** an educational theory that concentrates on teaching basic skills; a philosophical doctrine that distinguishes between the essence of material objects and their existence or appearance. — *n* **essen'tialist**. — *n* **essentiality** (*is-en-shi-al'i-ti*) the quality of being essential; an essential quality or element. — *adv* **essen'tially**. — *n* **essen'tialness**. — **essential minerals** those whose presence is considered necessary to entitle a rock to the name it bears (*opp* to *accessory* minerals); **essential oils** oils forming the odorous principles of plants, also called *ethereal oils* or *volatile oils*; **essential organs** (*bot*) stamens and carpels. — **in essence** basically, fundamentally; **of the essence** of the utmost importance. [Fr, from L *essentia*, from *essēns*, *essentis*, assumed pr p of *esse* to be]

Essene *es-ēn'* or *es'ēn*, *n* one of a small religious fraternity among the ancient Jews leading retired ascetic lives and holding property in common. — *n* **Ess'enism**. [Gr *essēnos*; origin doubtful]

essential, etc. See **essence**.

Essex Man *es'iks man*, *n* an archetypal, southern English working-class male without cultural interests or good taste but with a large disposable income which he spends freely, mainly on consumer goods and entertainment. — *n* **Essex Girl** the archetypal daughter of such a man, with similar tastes and limited intelligence. [The county in SE England]

essive *es'iv*, (*gram*) *adj* denoting a state of being. — *n* the essive case. [Finn *essivi*, from L *esse* to be]

ESSO *es'ō*, *abbrev*: Standard Oil.

essoin or **essoyne** *es-oin'*, *n* an excuse for not appearing in court (*law*); an excuse (*Spenser*). — *n* **essoin'er**. [OFr *essoine* (Fr *exoine*), from *es*, from L *ex* out of, and *soin* care]

essonite *es'ən-īt*, or **hessonite** *hes'ən-īt*, *n* cinnamon-stone. [Gr *hēssōn* inferior (ie in hardness, to hyacinth which it resembles)]

EST *abbrev*: Eastern Standard Time (*NAm*); electric shock treatment.

Est. *abbrev*: Estate (in addresses, etc); estuary.

est *est*, *n* a philosophical and psychological programme designed to raise awareness and develop human potential, originated in California by Werner Erhard and used by some business organizations. [*E*rhard *S*eminars *T*raining]

est. *abbrev*: established; estimated.

-est *-əst*, *sfx* marks the superlative degree of adjectives (eg long*est*) and some adverbs (eg fast*est*). [OE *-est* or *-ost*]

establish *is-* or *es-tab'lish*, *vt* to settle or fix; to set up; to place in fixed position, possession, or power; to make good; to confirm (*archaic*); to prove; to ordain; to found; to set up in business; to institute by law as the recognized state church, and to recognize officially. — *adj* **estab'lished** fixed; ratified; instituted by law and backed by the state. — *n* **estab'lisher**. — *n* **estab'lishment** the act of establishing; a fixed state; something which is established; a permanent civil or military force; permanent staff; a person's residence, household and style of living; a business; a settlement; the church established by law; (with **the** and *cap*; often *derog*) the class in a community or in a field of activity who hold power, *usu* because they are linked socially, and who are *usu* considered to have conservative opinions and conventional values. — *adj* pertaining to an establishment or the Establishment. — *adj* **establishmentār'ian** maintaining the principle of church establishment; favouring or upholding the Establishment. — Also *n*. — *n* **establishmentar'ianism**. [OFr *establir*, pr p *establissant*, from L *stabilīre*, from *stabilis* firm, from *stāre* to stand]

estacade *es-tə-kād'*, *n* a dike of piles in a morass, river, etc against an enemy. [Fr, from Sp *estacada*]

estafette *es-tə-fet'*, *n* a military courier or express. [Fr, from Ital *staffetta*, from *staffa* stirrup; cf OHGer *stapho* a step]

estaminet *es-tam'ē-nā*, *n* a small bar or café. [Fr]

estancia *es-tän'syə*, *n* a Spanish-American cattle-estate. — *n* **estanciero** (*-syā'rō*) a farmer on such an estate: — *pl* **estancie'ros**. [Sp, station, from L *stāre* to stand]

estate *is-* or *es-tāt'*, *n* state (*archaic*); rank; worldly condition; total possessions; property, *esp* landed property of some size; a piece of land built over either privately or by a local authority, with houses (**housing estate**) or factories (**trading** or **industrial estate**); a piece of land given over to the cultivation of a particular crop; an order or class of people in the body politic; a chair or canopy of state, or a dais (*obs*); an estate car (see below). — *vt* to give an estate to (*archaic*); to bestow upon (*archaic*). — **estate agent** someone who values, buys and sells, and leases and manages property for clients; the manager of landed property. — *adj* **estate'-bottled** of wine, bottled on the estate where it has been made. — **estate car** a car designed to carry passengers and goods, *usu* with a large area behind the seats for luggage, etc, and a rear door; **estate duty** death duty; **estates'man** (*NEng*) a statesman. — **man's estate** the state of manhood; **personal estate** see **person**; **real estate** see **real**[1]; **the estates of the realm** the three divisions of the body politic, Lords Spiritual, Lords Temporal and Commons; often misused for the legislature, ie king, lords and commons: the ancient parliament of Scotland consisted of the king and the **three estates**, ie (1) archbishops, bishops, abbots and mitred priors (2) the barons and the commissioners of shires and stewartries (3) the commissioners from the royal burghs; in France, the nobles, clergy and **third estate** (*tiers état*) remained separate down to 1780; **the fourth estate** (*colloq*) the press. [OFr *estat* (Fr *état*), from L *status* a state]

ESTEC *abbrev*: European Space Research and Technology Centre.

esteem *is-* or *es-tēm'*, *vt* to set a high estimate or value on; to regard with respect or friendship; to consider or think. — *n* high estimation or value; favourable regard; estimation of worth. — *adj* **esteemed'** respected; in commercial correspondence, a colourless complimentary word. [Fr *estimer*, from L *aestimāre*]

ester *es'tər*, *n* a compound formed by the condensation of an alcohol and an acid, with elimination of water. — *n* **esterificā'tion** (*-ter-*). — *vt* **ester'ify** (or *es'*). [Named by Leopold Gmelin (1788–1853), prob from *Es*sig vinegar, and Ä*ther* ether]

Esth. (*Bible*) *abbrev*: (the Book of) Esther.

Esth, **Esthonian**. See **Estonian**.

esthesia, **esthesiogen**, etc. US spellings of **aesthesia**, **aesthesiogen**, etc.

estimable *es'ti-mə-bl*, *adj* that can be estimated or valued; worthy of esteem; deserving our good opinion. — *adv* **es'timably**. — *vt* **estimate** (*es'ti-māt*) to judge the worth of; to ascertain how much is present of; to calculate. — *n* (*-mət*) reputation (*Shakesp*); a valuing in the mind; judgement or opinion of the worth or size of anything; a rough calculation; a preliminary statement of the probable cost of a proposed undertaking; estimation. — *n* **estimā'tion** an act of estimating; a reckoning of value; esteem or honour; importance (*archaic*); conjecture. — *adj* **es'timātive**. — *n* **es'timātor**. — **hold in estimation** to esteem highly; **the estimates** accounts laid before parliament, etc, showing the probable expenditure for the year. [Ety as for **esteem**]

estipulate. See **exstipulate**.

estival, etc. US spelling of **aestival**, etc.

estoc *es-tok'*, *n* a short sword. [Fr]

estoile *es-twäl'*, (*heraldry*) *n* a star with wavy points. [OFr *estoile* (Fr *étoile*) a star]

Estonian or **Esthonian** *es-t(h)ō'ni-ən*, *adj* of or belonging to *Estonia*, a Baltic republic, till 1918 a province of Russia, incorporated in 1940 as a republic of the USSR and declaring itself fully independent in 1991. — *n* a native or citizen thereof; its language. — *n* **Esth** an Estonian of the original Finnish stock.

estop *es-top'*, *vt* to stop or bar (*archaic*); to hinder or preclude (*law*): — *pr p* **estopp'ing**; *pa t* and *pa p* **estopped'**. — *n* **estopp'age** (*law*) the state of being estopped. — *n* **estopp'el** (*law*) a conclusive admission which cannot be denied by the party whom it affects. [OFr *estoper*, from *estoupe*, from L *stuppa* flax; see **stop** and **stuff**]

estover *es-tō'vər*, (*law*) *n* a right to necessaries allowed by law, such as wood to a tenant for necessary repairs, etc. — **common of estovers** the right of taking necessary wood from another's estate for household use and the making of implements of industry. [OFr *estover* to be necessary, necessaries]

estrade *es-träd'*, *n* a low platform. [Fr, from Sp *estrado*]

estramazone. Same as **stramazon**.

estrange *is-trānj'*, *vt* to cut off or remove; to alienate, *esp* from friendship; to divert from its original use or possessor. — *adj* **estranged'** alienated; disaffected. — *n* **estrang'edness**. — *n* **estrange'ment**. — *n* **estrang'er**. [OFr *estranger* (Fr *étranger*), from L *extrāneāre*, from *extrāneus*; see **strange**]

estrangelo or **estranghelo** *es-trang'gə-lō*, *n* a cursive form of the old Syriac alphabet. — Also *adj*. [Syriac, perh from Gr *strongylos* round]

estrapade *es-tra-pād'*, *n* a horse's attempt to throw its rider. [Fr]

estray *e-strā'*, *n* a beast found within a manor or lordship, wandering from its owner. — *vi* to stray. [See **astray**]

estreat *es-trēt'*, (*law*) *n* a true extract, copy or note of some original writing or record, *esp* of fines and amercements to be levied by bailiffs or other officers. — *vt* to extract from the records of a court, eg a forfeited recognizance; to levy or exact. [OFr *estraite*, from L *extrahere*, from *ex* from, and *trahere* to draw; see **extract**]

estrepe *es'trēp*, (*law*) *vt* to commit waste (as a tenant) on lands, eg cutting down trees, etc. — *n* **estrepe'ment**. [MFr *estreper*, from L *exstirpāre* to root out]

estrich *es'trich* or **estridge** *es'trij*, (*obs*) *n* the ostrich.

Estrildidae *e-stril'di-dē*, *n pl* a family of oscinine birds, the weaver-finches. — *adj* and *n* **estril'did**. [From *astrilda*, the name of a particular species in Linnaeus's classification]

estro *es'trō*, (*Ital*) *n* enthusiasm or height of poetic inspiration.

estrogen, **estrum**, etc. US spellings of **oestrogen**, **oestrum**, etc.

estuary *es'tū-ər-i*, *n* the wide lower tidal part of a river. — *adj* **estūarial** (*-ā'ri-əl*). — *adj* **estūā'rian**. — *adj* **es'tūarine** (*-ə-rīn*). [L *aestuārium*, from *aestus* burning, boiling, commotion or tide]

ESU *abbrev*: English-Speaking Union; (also without *cap*) electrostatic unit.

esurient *es-ū'ri-ənt*, *adj* hungry; rapacious. — *n* **esū'rience** or **esū'riency** greedy hunger; needy rapacity. — *adv* **esu'riently**. [L *ēsuriēns*, *-entis*, pr p of *ēsurīre* to be hungry, from the desiderative of *edere* to eat]

ET *abbrev*: Arab Republic of Egypt (IVR); Eastern Time; embryo transfer; Employment Training (scheme) or Employment Trainee; ephemeris time; extraterrestrial.

Et (*chem*) *symbol*: ethyl.

ETA *abbrev*: Entertainment Trades' Alliance; estimated time of arrival; *(et'ə) Euzkadi ta Askatasuna*, a militant Basque separatist organization.

eta[1] *ē'tə* or *ā'tə*, *n* the seventh letter of the Greek alphabet, long e (H or *η*); as a numeral *η'* = 8, *ˌη* = 8000. — *n* **etacism** (*ā'tə-sizm*) the pronunciation of eta as close e (in this dictionary represented in the respelling as *ā*) (*opp* to *itacism*). [Gr *ēta*]

eta[2] *ā'tə*, *n* (also with *cap*) *esp* formerly, a member of the lowest Japanese class, which did work considered menial or degrading. [Jap]

etaerio *et-ē'ri-ō*, (*bot*) *n* an aggregated fruit, a group of achenes or drupels: — *pl* **etae'rios**. [Fr *étairion*, from Gr *hetaireiā* association]

étage *ā-täzh*, (*Fr*) *n* a floor storey.

étagère *ā-ta-zher*, (*Fr*) *n* a display stand with shelves for small objects or ornaments, etc

et al *abbrev*: *et alibi* (*L*), and elsewhere; *et alii*, *aliae* or *alia* (*L*), and other (people or things).

étalage *ā-ta-läzh*, (*Fr*) *n* a display, *esp* of goods in a shop window.

etalon *āt'əl-on*, (*phys*) *n* an interferometer used to measure wavelengths, consisting of an air film enclosed between half-silvered plane-parallel glass or quartz plates. [Fr, from MFr *estalon* standard of weights and measures, from OFr *estal* place]

étape *ā-tap*, (*Fr*) *n* a storehouse; a halting-place; a day's march; rations; forage.

état *ā-ta*, (*Fr*) *n* state or rank. — *n* **étatisme** (*ā-ta-tēzm'*) extreme state control over the individual citizen. — *adj* and *n* **étatiste** (*-tēst*). — **état-major** (*ma-zhor*) the staff of an army, regiment, etc.

États-Généraux *ā-ta zhā-nā-rō*, (*Fr*) *npl* the States-General.

ETB *abbrev*: English Tourist Board.

etc *abbrev*: et cetera or et ceteri.

et cetera *et set'ər-ə* or **etcetera** *usu abbrev* **etc** or **&c**, and the rest, and so on. — *n* something in addition, which can easily be understood from the context. — *npl* **et cet'eras** additional people or things. — **et ceteri** (*et set'ər-ē*) and the other people, and the rest (*abbrev* **etc**). [L *et* and, and *cetera* or *ceteri*, neuter pl or masc pl, the rest of the things or people]

etch *ech*, *vt* and *vi* to design on metal, glass, etc by eating out the lines with an acid; to eat away or corrode. — *n* **etch'ant** an acid or corrosive used in etching. — *n* **etch'er** a person who etches. — *n* **etch'ing** the act or art of etching or engraving; the impression from an etched plate. — **etching ground** the coating of wax or varnish on a plate prepared for etching; **etching needle** a fine-pointed steel instrument used in etching. [Ger *ätzen* to corrode by acid; from same root as Ger *essen*; see **eat**]

ETD *abbrev*: estimated time of departure.

eten or **ettin** *et'ən*, (*archaic*) *n* a giant. [OE *eten*, *eoten*; ON *jötunn*]

etepimeletic *et-ep-i-mel-et'ik*, (*animal behaviour*) *adj* of a type of social behaviour shown by young animals to elicit epimeletic behaviour.

eternal *i-* or *ē-tûr'nl*, *adj* without beginning or end of existence; everlasting; ceaseless; unchangeable; seemingly endless, occurring again and again (*colloq*). — (*archaic*) **eterne'**. — *n* **eter'nalist** someone who thinks that matter has existed eternally. — *n* **eternaliza'tion** or **-s-**, **eterniza'tion** or **-s-**. — *vt* **eter'nalize** or **-ise**, **eter'nize** or **-ise** (or *ē'tər-nīz*) to make eternal; to immortalize with fame. — *adv* **eter'nally**. — *n* **eter'nity** eternal duration; the state or time after death. — **eternal triangle** a sexual relationship, full of tension and conflict, between two men and a woman or two women and a man; **eternity ring** a ring set all round with stones, symbolizing continuity and everlasting love. — **The Eternal** God; **the Eternal City** Rome; **the eternal feminine** the spiritualizing and purifying influence of women in social and literary matters (see **das Ewig-Weibliche** in Quotations from Foreign Languages); **the eternities** the eternal reality or truth. [Fr *éternel*, from L *aeternus*, from *aevum* an age]

etesian *e-tē'zh(y)ən* or *-zyən*, *adj* periodical; blowing at stated seasons, such as certain winds, *esp* the NW winds of summer in the Aegean. [L *etēsius*, from Gr *etēsios* annual, from *etos* a year]

ETH *abbrev*: Ethiopia (IVR).

eth or **edh** *edh*, *n* a letter (Ð or ð), a barred D, used in Old English without distinction from thorn for voiced or voiceless th, in Icelandic and by phoneticians used for the voiced sound, thorn standing for the voiceless.

ethal *ē'thal*. Same as **cetyl alcohol**.

ethambutol *eth-am'bū-tol*, *n* a drug used in the treatment of tuberculosis. [*eth*ylene, *am*ine and *but*an*ol*]

ethane *eth'ān* or *ēth'*, *n* a colourless, odourless hydrocarbon ($H_3C{\cdot}CH_3$) of the methane series. — *n* **eth'anol** ethyl alcohol. — *npl* **ethanol'amines** derivatives of ethanol used in detergents and cosmetics. [**ether**]

ethe. See **eath**.

ethene. See under **ethyl**.

Etheostoma *e-thi-os'to-mə*, *n* a genus of small American freshwater fishes related to perch. — *adj* **etheos'tomine**. [Gr *ētheein* to sift, and *stoma* mouth]

ether *ē'thər*, *n* the clear, upper air; a medium, not matter, assumed in the 19c to fill all space and transmit electromagnetic waves (in these senses also **aether**); (*specif* **ethyl ether** or **diethyl ether**) a colourless, transparent, volatile liquid ($C_2H_5{\cdot}O{\cdot}C_2H_5$) of great mobility and high refractive power, used as a solvent, an anaesthetic, and in the preparation of explosives; extended to the class of compounds in which two alkyl groups are united with an oxygen atom. — *adj* **ethē'real** or **ethē'rial** consisting of ether; heavenly; airy; spirit-like. — *n* **ethēreal'ity**. — *n* **ethērealizā'tion** or **-s-**. — *vt* **ethē'realize** or **-ise** to convert into ether, or the fluid ether; to render spirit-like. — *adv* **ethē'really**. — *adj* **ethē'reous** (*Milton*), **etheric** (*ē-ther'ik*) or **ether'ical** ethereal. — *n* **etherificā'tion** (*-ther-*). — *vt* **etherify** to convert into ether. — *n* **ethē'rion** a very light gas once supposed to exist in air. — *n* **e'therism** the condition induced by using ether; addiction to the taking of ether. — *n* **e'therist** someone who takes or who administers ether. — *n* **etherizā'tion** or **-s-**. — *vt* **e'therize** or **-ise** to convert into ether; to stupefy with ether. — *n* **etheromā'nia** addiction to the taking of ether. — *n* **etheromā'niac**. — **ethereal oils** essential oils. [L *aethēr*, from Gr *aithēr* the heavens, from *aithein* to light up]

ethercap. See **ettercap**.

ethic *eth'ik*, (now *rare*) *adj* ethical. — *n* (more commonly *n sing* **eth'ics**) the science of morals, that branch of philosophy which is concerned with human character and conduct; a system of morals or rules of behaviour; a treatise on morals. — *adj* **eth'ical** relating to morals, the science of ethics or professional standards of conduct; relating to, or in accord with, approved moral behaviour; (of advertising) decent, honest and informative, not misleading, dishonest or unscrupulous; denoting a proprietary pharmaceutical not advertised to the general public and only available to the general public on doctor's prescription (also *n*). — *n* **ethical'ity** or **eth'icalness**. — *adv* **eth'ically**. — *n* **eth'icism** the tendency to moralize or ethicize; great interest in ethics or passion for ethical ideals. — *n* **eth'icist** an expert on or student in ethics; a person who detaches ethics from religion. — *vt* **eth'icize** or **-ise** (*-sīz*) to make ethical; to treat as ethical. — **eth'ico-** *combining form* denoting something ethical or of ethics. — **ethical dative** or **ethic dative** a dative implying an indirect interest in the matter, used to give a livelier tone to the sentence (eg *He could swear me as fluently as any bargee*); **ethical genitive** a genitive implying interest (eg *talking as usual about his Roman heating system*; see **your**); **situation ethics** ethics based on the proposition that no conduct is good or bad in itself and that one must determine what is right or wrong in each situation as it arises. [Gr *ēthikos*, from *ēthos* custom or character]

Ethiopian *ē-thi-ō'pi-ən*, *adj* of or belonging to Ethiopia or its people or their languages; of or belonging to the countries south of Egypt; (of people) black (*archaic*). — *n* a native of Ethiopia; an Ethiopian language; a black person (*archaic*). — *n* (*archaic*) **Ē'thiop** (*-op*). — *adj* **Ēthiop'ic** belonging to Ethiopia, to the Ethiopian church, or to a group of Semitic languages including Ge'ez, Amharic and Tigre. — *n* the Ge'ez language. — *n* **ē'thiops** in old chemistry, a name given to various, dull, dingy or black compounds. — Also (*archaic*) **Aethiopian**, etc. — **Ethiopian pepper** see **Negro pepper** under **pepper**; **Ethiopian region** a biological region consisting of Africa and Arabia south of the Tropic of Cancer. [Gr *Aithiops*, from *aithein* to burn, and *ops*, *ōps* face]

ethmoid *eth'moid*, *adj* like a sieve. — *adj* **ethmoid'al**. — **ethmoid bone** one of the bones forming the front part of the brain-case. [Gr *ēthmos* a sieve, and *eidos* form]

ethnic *eth'nik*, or **ethnical** *-nik-əl*, *adj* concerning nations or races; pertaining to gentiles or the heathen; pertaining to the customs, dress, food, etc of a particular racial group or cult; belonging or pertaining to a particular racial group; foreign; exotic; between or involving different racial groups. — *n* **eth'narch** (*-närk*; Gr *archos* leader) a ruler or governor of a people. — *n* **eth'narchy**. — *n* **eth'nic** a gentile or heathen (*obs*); a member of a racial or cultural minority group. — *adv* **eth'nically**. — *n* **eth'nicism** (*-sizm*; *obs*) heathenism; gentile religion. — *n* **ethni'city** (*-si-ti*). — *adj* **ethnobotan'ical**. — *adv* **ethnobotan'ically**. — *n* **ethnobot'anist**. — *n* **ethnobot'any** (the study of) traditional plant-lore, plant classification, plant use, etc. — *adj* **ethnocen'tric**. — *adv* **ethnocen'trically**. — *n* **ethnocen'trism** belief in the superiority of one's own cultural group or society and corresponding dislike or misunderstanding of other such groups. — *n* **eth'nocide** (*-sīd*; L *caedere* to kill) the extermination of a racial or cultural group. — *n* **ethnog'rapher**. — *adj* **ethnograph'ic** or **ethnograph'ical** pertaining to ethnography; of objects useful in the study of ethnography. — *n pl* **ethnograph'ica** (a collection of) ethnographic objects; (loosely) exotica. — *n* **ethnog'raphy** the scientific description of the races of the earth. — *n* **eth'nolinguist**. — *adj* **ethnolinguist'ic**. — *n sing* **ethnolinguist'ics** the study of the relationship between language and cultural behaviour. — *adj* **ethnolog'ical**. — *adv* **ethnolog'ically**. — *n* **ethnol'ogist**. — *n* **ethnol'ogy** cultural anthropology; the science concerned with the varieties of the human race (*obs*). — *n* **ethnomethodol'ogist**. — *n* **ethnomethodol'ogy** the study of communication in the language of everyday conversation. — *n* **ethnomusicol'ogist** a person who makes a study of music and/or musical instruments in relation to the cultures in which they are found. — *n* **ethnomusicol'ogy**. — *n* **ethnosci'ence** ethnography — **ethnic cleansing** the removal from an area by the militarily superior ethnic group, either by extermination or forced migration, of members of the other ethnic groups, *esp* and *orig* in the former Yugoslavia. [Gr *ethnos* a nation]

et hoc (or **id**) **genus omne** *et hok* (or *id*) *jē'nəs om'nē* or *gen'ōōs om'ne*, (*L*) and all that sort of thing.

ethos *ē'thos*, *n* the distinctive habitual character and disposition of an individual, group, race, etc; moral significance. — *adj* **etholog'ic** or **etholog'ical**. — *adv* **etholog'ically**. — *n* **ethol'ogist**. — *n* **ethol'ogy** the science of character; bionomics (see under **bio-**); the scientific study of the function and evolution of animal behaviour patterns. [Gr *ēthos* custom or character]

ethyl *eth'il* or *ēth'īl*, *n* the base (C_2H_5) of common alcohol, ether, etc; (with *cap* (US®)) an anti-knock compound containing lead tetraethyl $Pb(C_2H_5)_4$; petrol using this compound. — *n* **eth'ylamine** (*-ə-mīn*) a substance ($NH_2 \cdot C_2H_5$) resembling ammonia, with one atom of hydrogen replaced by ethyl. — *vt* **eth'ylate** to introduce an ethyl group into (a molecule). — *n* **eth'ylene** (also **eth'ene**) an oil-forming gas, hydrogen combined with carbon (C_2H_4). — **ethyl alcohol** ordinary alcohol; **ethylene glycol** a thick liquid alcohol used as an antifreeze; **ethyl ether** see **ether**. [**ether** and Gr *hȳlē* matter]

ethyne *eth'īn* or *ēth'*, *n* acetylene.

etiolate *ē'ti-o-lāt*, *vt* to cause to grow pale with small yellow leaves for lack of light, to blanch (*bot*); to make pale. — *vi* to become pale. — *adj* **e'tiolated**. — *n* **etiolā'tion**. — *n* **e'tiolin** a yellow pigment found in etiolated plants. [Fr *étioler* to become pale, to grow into stubble, from *éteule* stubble, from L *stipula* a stalk, straw]

etiology. An alternative (*esp US*) spelling of **aetiology**.

etiquette *et'i-ket* or *-ket'*, *n* forms of civilized manners or decorum; ceremony; the conventional laws of courtesy observed between members of the same profession, sport, etc. [Fr *étiquette*; see **ticket**]

etna *et'nə*, *n* a vessel for heating liquids in a saucer of burning alcohol. — *adj* **Etnē'an** or **Aetnē'an** of, pertaining to, resembling or characteristic of the volcano Etna. [L *Aetna*, from Gr *Aitnē*]

étoile *ā-twal*, (*Fr*) *n* a star; a star-shaped object.

Eton *ē'tn*, *n* a town opposite Windsor in England with an old-established public school; (in *pl*) an Eton suit. — *n* **Etonian** (*ē-tōn'i-ən*) a person educated at *Eton* College. — Also *adj*. — **Eton collar** a boy's broad starched turned-down collar; a similar-shaped collar on a woman's jumper, etc; **Eton crop** a ladies' hairstyle, short and sleeked flat; **Eton jacket** a boy's black dress-coat, without tails; **Eton suit** an Eton jacket with waistcoat and trousers in keeping.

étourdi, *fem* **étourdie** *ā-tōōr-dē*, (*Fr*) *adj* thoughtless, foolish or light-minded. — *n* **étourderie** (*ā-tōōr-drē*) heedlessness or stupid blundering.

étranger *ā-trã-zhā*, *fem* **étrangère** *-zher*, (*Fr*) *adj* foreign. — *n* a foreigner.

étrenne (*usu* in *pl* **étrennes**) *ā-tren*, (*Fr*) *n* a New Year's gift.

étrier *ā-trē-yā'*, *n* a small rope ladder of 1–4 rungs used as a climbing aid by mountaineers. [Fr, stirrup]

Etruria *i-trōō'ri-ə*, *n* an ancient state in Italy N of the Tiber; part of Hanley, Stoke-on-Trent in England where Josiah Wedgwood made the china known as *Etruria ware*. — *n* and *adj* **Etru'rian** Etruscan. — *adj* **Etruscan** (*i-trus'kən*) pertaining to Etruria, or to the language, culture, etc of the Etruscans. — *n* a person inhabiting or from Etruria; the non-Indo-European language of the Etruscans. — *n* **Etruscol'ogist**. — *n* **Etruscol'ogy**. [L *Etrūria* and *Etrūscus*]

et sequens *et sē'kwənz* or *se-kwāns'*, (*L*) and what follows (*abbrev* **et seq.** or **et sq.**); **et sequentes** (*si-kwen'tēz* or *se-kwen'tās*), *neuter* **et sequentia** (*si-kwen'shi-ə* or *se-kwen'ti-a*), and those that follow (*abbrev* **et sqq.**).

et sic de ceteris *et sik dē set'ə-ris* or *et sēk dā kā'te-rēs*, (*LL*) and so about the rest.

et sic de similibus *et sik dē si-mil'i-bəs* or *et sēk dā si-mil'i-bōōs*, (*L*) and so of the like.

et sq. or **et sqq.** See **et sequens**.

ETSU *abbrev*: Energy Technology Support Unit, a UK government department which evaluates research on renewable energy.

-ette noun-forming *sfx* (1) female, as *usherette*; (2) small, as *kitchenette*; (3) *esp* in tradenames, imitation or substitute, as *leatherette*.

ettercap *et'ər-kap*, or **ethercap** *edh'ər-kap*, *n* Scots forms of **attercop**.

ettin. See **eten**.

ettle *et'l*, (*Scot*) *vt* to purpose or intend; to aim; to aspire. — *n* purpose or intent. [ON *ætla* to think]

ETU *abbrev*: Electrical Trades Union (now **EETPU**).

ETUC *abbrev*: European Trade Union Confederation.

étude *ā-tüd'*, (*music*) *n* a composition intended either to train or to test the player's technical skill. [Fr, study]

étui or **etwee** *ā-twē'* or *et-wē'*, *n* a small case for holding small sewing articles. [Fr *étui* a case or sheath]

ety *abbrev*: etymology.

etym. or **etymol.** *abbrev*: etymological.

etymon *et'i-mon*, *n* the true origin of a word; an original root; the genuine or literal sense of a word (*rare*): — *pl* **et'yma** or **et'ymons**. — *adj* **etym'ic**. — *adj* **etymo-**

log'ical. — *adv* **etymolog'ically**. — *n* **etymolog'icon** or **etymolog'icum** an etymological dictionary. — *n* **etymol'ogist**. — *vi* **etymol'ogize** or **-ise** to inquire into or discuss etymology. — *vt* to trace or suggest an etymology for. — *n* **etymol'ogy** the science or investigation of the derivation and original signification of words; an etymon. [Neuter of Gr *etymos* true]

etypic *ē-tip'ik* or **etypical** *-ik-əl, adj* unconformable to type. [L *ē* from, and Gr *typos* type]

EU *abbrev*: Evangelical Union.

Eu (*chem*) *symbol*: europium.

Eubacteriales *ū-bak-tē-ri-ā'lēz, n pl* an order of Schizomycetes, nonfilamentous, unbranched bacteria. — *n* **eubactē'rium** a member of the Eubacteriales; any typical bacterium: — *pl* **eubactē'ria**. [Gr *eu* well, and **bacteria**]

eucaine or **eucain** *ū-kā'in, -kā'īn* or *-kān'*, (*med*) *n* a safer substitute for cocaine as a local anaesthetic. [Gr *eu* well, and **cocaine**]

eucalyptus *ū-kə-lip'təs, n* a tree or shrub of the large characteristically Australian genus *Eucalyptus* of the myrtle family, forest trees, some gigantic, and mallee scrub, with leathery often glaucous leaves turned edgewise to the sun, many yielding timber, and some giving oils and gum; eucalyptus oil: — *pl* **eucalyp'tuses** or **eucalyp'tī**. — *n* **eu'calypt** a eucalyptus. — *n* **eucalyp'tol** or **eucalyp'tole** cineol, a constituent of the various oils obtained from eucalyptus leaves. [Latinized from Gr *eu* well, and *kalyptos* covered]

eucaryon, **eucaryot**, **eucaryote**, **eucaryotic**. Same as **eukaryon**, etc.

eucharis *ū'kər-is* or *ū-kar'is, n* a plant of the *Eucharis* genus of S American bulbous plants with fragrant white flowers. [Gr, charming, from *eu* well, and *charis* grace]

Eucharist *ū'kə-rist*, (*Christian relig*) *n* the sacrament of the Lord's Supper; the elements of the sacrament, bread and wine. — *adj* **Eucharist'ic** or **eucharist'ical**. [Gr *eucharistiā* thanksgiving, from *eu* well, and *charizesthai* to show favour, from *charis* grace or thanks]

euchlorine *ū-klō'rēn, n* a very explosive green-coloured gas, a mixture of chlorine with chlorine peroxide. — *adj* **euchlo'ric**. [Gr *eu* well, and *chlōros* green]

euchologion *ū-ko-lō'ji-on, n* a formulary of prayers, primarily that of the Greek Church. — Also **euchology** (*-kol'ə-ji*). [Gr *euchologion*, from *euchē* a prayer, and *logos*, from *legein* to speak]

euchre *ū'kər, n* a N American card game for two, three, or four players, with the 32, 28 or 24 highest cards of the pack. If a player fails to make three tricks they are *euchred* and their adversary scores against them. — *vt* to score over, as above; to outwit. — *adj* **eu'chred** (*Austr* and *NZ slang*; *usu* with *out*) exhausted, at the end of one's tether. [Ety unknown]

euclase *ū'klās*, (*mineralogy*) *n* a hydrated beryllium aluminium silicate occurring in pale-green transparent crystals. [Fr, from Gr *eu* well, and *klasis* breaking]

Euclidean *ū-klid'i-ən* or *ū-kli-dē'ən, adj* pertaining to Euclid, a geometrician of Alexandria *c*300 BC, or to space according to his theories and assumptions. — **Euclidean geometry** a geometry based on the theories and assumptions of Euclid.

eucrite *ū'krīt*, (*mineralogy*) *n* a gabbroitic rock composed of lime-feldspar, pyroxenes and olivine. — *adj* **eucritic** (*-krit'ik*). [Gr *eu* well, and *kritos* distinguished]

eucyclic *ū-sī'klik*, (*bot*) *adj* having the same number of floral leaves in each whorl. [Gr *eu* well, and *kyklos* wheel]

eudaemonism or **eudemonism**, *ū-dē'mən-izm, n* a system of ethics that makes happiness the test of rectitude (whether *egoistic* as Hobbes's or *altruistic* as Mill's). — *adj* **eudaemon'ic** conducive to happiness. — *n sing* **eudaemon'ics**. — *n* **eudae'monist**. — *n* **eudae'mony** or **eudaemō'nia** happiness or wellbeing; in Aristotelian philosophy, a full, active life governed by reason. [Gr *eudaimoniā* happiness, from *eu* well, and *daimōn* a spirit]

eudialyte *ū-dī'ə-līt*, (*mineralogy*) *n* a silicate of zirconium, sodium, calcium and iron, occurring in Greenland, easily dissolved by acids. [Gr *eu* well, and *dialyein* to dissolve]

eudiometer *ū-di-om'i-tər, n* an apparatus for gas analysis, a graduated tube holding the gas over mercury, *usu* with wires for sparking. [Gr *eudios* clear or fine (as weather), and *metron* measure]

euge *ū'jē, interj* well! well done! [Gr *euge*]

eugenia *ū-jē'ni-ə, n* any plant of the clove genus *Eugenia* of the myrtle family. — *n* **eugenol** (*ū'jin-ol*) the chief constituent of oil of cloves ($C_{10}H_{12}O_2$). — Also **eugenic** (*-jen'ik*) **acid**. [Named after Prince *Eugene* of Savoy (1663–1736)]

eugenic[1] *ū-jen'ik, adj* pertaining to genetic improvement of a race (*esp* human) by judicious mating and helping the better stock to prevail. — *adv* **eugen'ically**. — *n sing* **eugen'ics** the science of genetic improvement of *esp* the human race. — *n* **eu'genism** (*-jin-*). — *n* **eu'genist**, **eugen'ecist** or **eugen'icist**. [Gr *eugenēs* of good stock]

eugenic[2]. See **eugenol** under **Eugenia**.

eugh, **eughen** and **ewghen**. *Obs* spellings (*Spenser* and *Shakesp*) of **yew** and **yewen**.

Euglena *ū-glē'nə, n* a genus of aquatic unicellular organisms of the order **Euglenoidī'na** or (*bot*) **Euglenā'les**, with a single flagellum and reddish eyespots. [Gr *eu* well, and *glēnē* eyeball]

Eugubine *ū'gū-bin* or *-bīn, adj* pertaining to the ancient town of *Eugubium* or *Iguvium* (now *Gubbio*) or to its famous seven tablets of bronze, the chief monument of the ancient Umbrian language.

euharmonic *ū-här-mon'ik*, (*music*) *adj* resulting in perfect harmony. [Gr *eu* well, and *harmoniā* harmony]

Euhemerism *ū-hē'mə-rizm, n* the theory which explains mythology as growing out of real history, its deities as merely larger-than-life people. — *n* and *adj* **euhē'merist**. — *adj* **euhemeris'tic**. — *adv* **euhemeris'tically**. — *vt* and *vi* **euhē'merize** or **-ise**. [From *Euhēmerus*, Gr *Euēmeros*, a 4c (BC) Sicilian philosopher]

euk, **ewk** *ūk*. See **yuke**.

eukaryon *ū-kar'i-ən*, (*biol*) *n* the highly organized cell nucleus, surrounded by a membrane, characteristic of higher organisms (cf *prokaryon*). — *n* **eukar'yote** or **eukaryot** (*-ōt* or *-ət*) an organism whose cells have such nuclei. — Also *adj*. — *adj* **eukaryot'ic**. — Also **eucaryon**, etc. [Gr *eu* well, and *karyon* kernel]

eulachon *ū'lə-kən, n* the N Pacific candle-fish, so oily that it is dried for use as a candle. — Also **eulachan**, **oolakan**, **oulakan**, **oulachon**, **ulicon**, **ulichon** and **ulikon**. [Chinook jargon *ulâkân*]

eulogium *ū-lō'ji-əm* or **eulogy** *ū'lə-ji, n* praise; a speech or writing in praise; a funeral oration: — *pl* **eulō'gia**, **eulō'giums** or **eu'logies**. — *n* **eu'logist** a person who extols another, *esp* a dead friend, etc. — *adj* **eulogist'ic** or **eulogist'ical** full of praise. — *adv* **eulogist'ically**. — *vt* **eu'logize** or **-ise** to extol. [LL *eulogium*, from Gr *eulogion* (classical *eulogiā*), from *eu* well, and *logos* a speaking]

eumelanin *ū-mel'ə-nin, n* any melanin pigment of darker type. [*eu-* good or most typical, from Gr *eu* well]

Eumenides *ū-men'i-dēz*, (*Gr mythol*) *n pl* a euphemistic name for the Erinyes or Furies (see under **fury**). [Gr *Eumenides* the gracious ones, from *eu* well, and *menos* disposition]

eumerism *ū'mər-izm*, (*biol*) *n* aggregation of similar parts. [Gr *eu* well, and *meros* part]

Eumycetes *ū-mī-sē'tēz*, (*bot*) *n pl* the higher fungi, Ascomycetes and Basidiomycetes. [Gr *eu* well, and **mycetes**]

eunuch *ū'nək, n* a castrated man, *esp* one in charge of a harem, or a high-voiced singer; an ineffectual person, lacking in some way in force or power (*fig*). — *n* **eu'nuchism** the condition of being a eunuch. — *vt* **eun'uchize** or **-ise** (*lit* and *fig*). — *n* **eu'nuchoidism** a condition in which there is some deficiency of sexual development and in which certain female sex characteristics, eg high voice, are often present. — *n* and *adj*

eu'nuchoid. [Gr *eunouchos*, from *eunē* bed, and *echein* to have (charge of)]

euoi. See **evoe**.

euonymus *ū-on'i-məs*, *n* a plant of the spindle-tree and burning bush genus *Euonymus* of Celastraceae. — *n* **euon'ymin** an extract of bark of burning bush. [Gr *euōnymos* spindle-tree]

euouae. See **evovae**.

eupad *ū'pad*, *n* an antiseptic powder containing hypochlorous acid. [*E*dinburgh *U*niversity *Pa*thology *D*epartment, where it originated]

eupatrid *ū-pat'rid*, *n* a member of the aristocracy in ancient Greek states. [Gr *eupatridēs*, from *eu* well, and *patēr* father]

eupepsy *ū-pep'si* or **eupepsia** *-pep'si-ə*, *n* good digestion (*opp* of *dyspepsia*). — *adj* **eupep'tic** pertaining to good digestion; cheerful (*fig*). — *n* **eupepticity** (*-tis'i-ti*). [Gr *eupepsiā* digestibility, from *eu* well, and *pepsis* digestion, from *peptein* to digest]

euph. *abbrev*: euphemism; euphemistic; euphemistically.

Euphausia *ū-fö'zi-ə*, *n* a genus of shrimplike malacostracan crustaceans of the family **Euphausiidae** (*-ī'i-dē*) order **Euphausiacea** (*-ā'si-ə*) common in plankton. — *n* **euphausia'cean**. — *adj* and *n* **euphaus'iid** or **euphaus'id** (a creature) belonging to the Euphausiidae or to the Euphausiacea. [Gr *eu* well, *phainein* to show, and *ousiā* substance]

euphemism *ū'fim-izm*, *n* a figure of rhetoric by which an unpleasant or offensive thing is described or referred to by a milder term; such a term. — *adj* **euphemist'ic**. — *adv* **euphemist'ically**. — *vt* **eu'phemize** or **-ise** to express by a euphemism. — *vi* to use euphemistic terms. [Gr *euphēmismos*, from *euphēmizein* to speak words of good omen, from *eu* well, and *phanai* to speak.

euphenics *ū-fen'iks*, *n sing* the science concerned with the physical improvement of human beings by modifying their development after birth (cf *eugenics*). [By analogy, from **eugenics** and **phenotype** (Gr *eu* well, and *phainein* to show)]

euphobia *ū-fō'bi-ə*, *n* a fear of good news. [Gr *eu* well, and *phobos* fear]

euphony *ū'fə-ni*, *n* an agreeable sound; a pleasing, easy pronunciation, often created by modification of the original sounds. — Also (*obs*) **euphonia** (*-fō'*). — *n* **eu'phon** a form of glass harmonica invented by Chladni in 1790. — *adj* **euphonic** (*-fon'ik*), **euphon'ical** or **euphō'nious** agreeable in sound. — *adv* **euphō'niously**. — *n* **eu'phonism** the use or custom of using euphonious words or phrases. — *n* **euphō'nium** a member of the saxhorn family, the bass tuba; the euphon. — *vt* **eu'phonize** or **-ise** to make euphonious. [Gr *euphōniā*, from *eu* well, and *phōnē* sound]

euphorbia *ū-för'bi-ə*, *n* a plant of the spurge genus *Euphorbia*, giving name to the **Euphorbiā'ceae**, an isolated family of archichlamydeous dicotyledons. — *adj* **euphorbiā'ceous**. — *n* **euphor'bium** a gum resin obtained from some spurges. [*Euphorbos*, Greek physician to Juba, king of Mauritania]

euphoria *ū-fō'ri-ə* or *-fö'*, or (*rare*) **euphory** *ū'fə-ri*, *n* an exaggerated feeling of wellbeing, *esp* irrational or groundless. — *adj* **euphor'iant** inducing euphoria. — *n* a drug which does this. — *adj* **euphoric** (*-for'ik*). [Gr *euphoriā*]

euphrasy *ū'frə-si* or *-zi*, (*bot*) *n* eyebright (*Euphrasia*) once thought good for disorders of the eyes. [Gr *euphrasiā* delight, from *euphrainein* to cheer, from *eu* well, and *phrēn* the mind]

euphroe *ū'frō*, (*naut*) *n* the wooden block through which the lines of a crowfoot are rove. — Also **ū'phroe**. [Du *juffrouw*, from *jong* young, and *vrouw* woman]

Euphrosyne *ū-froz'i-nē*, or *-fros'*, (*Gr mythol*) *n* one of the three Charites or Graces. [Gr *Euphrosynē*, from *euphrōn* cheerful]

Euphuism *ū'fū-izm*, *n* the affected and bombastic literary style brought into vogue by John Lyly's romance *Euphues* (1579–80); (without *cap*) a high-flown expression in this style. — *n* **eu'phuist**. — *adj* **euphuist'ic**. — *adv* **euphuist'ically**. — *vi* **eu'phuize** or **-ise**. [Gr *euphyēs* graceful or goodly]

Eur- or **Euro-** *ū'r(ō)-*, *combining form* denoting European; of or pertaining to the European Community; of or pertaining to Europe. — *adj* **Euraf'rican** pertaining to Europe and Africa, or Europe and N Africa, jointly; of a human race common to Europe and N Africa, the Mediterranean race; of mixed European and African parentage or descent. — *n* a person of Eurafrican race in either sense. — *adj* **Eurā'sian** of mixed European and Asian parentage or descent; of, or pertaining to, Europe and Asia (*Eurasia*) considered as one continent. — *n* a person of mixed European and Asian parentage. — *n* **Eurat'om** (*ū-rat'əm*) the European Atomic Energy Community (set up in 1958), an association for joint peaceful development of nuclear energy. — *n* **Eu'ro-Amer'ican** (also *adj*). — *n* **Eu'robond** a borrowing in Eurocurrency by a company from subscribers, which may or may not be sellable and for which the rate and life may be either fixed or variable; a security on which the named currency is not the currency of the country in which it has been issued. — *adj* **Eurocent'ric** of history, culture, etc, concentrating on Europe, sometimes to the exclusion of other influences. — *n* **Eurocentri'city** or **Eurocent'rism**. — *n* **Eur'ocheque** a special type of cheque drawn on the user's own bank which may be cashed in banks and used for making purchases in any of a number of European and non-European countries. — *n* **Eurocomm'unism** the theory of communism professed by Communist parties in Western Europe, more pragmatic than the traditional Soviet theory and asserting independence from it. — *n* **Eurocomm'unist**. — *n* **Eurocracy** (*ū-rok'rə-si*). — *n* **Eu'rocrat** an official concerned with the administration of any organization within the European Community, a European bureaucrat. — *adj* **Eurocrat'ic**. — *n* **Eu'rocurrency** the currency of any of the countries of the European Community. — *n pl* **Eu'ro-dollars** US dollars deposited in European banks to facilitate financing of trade between the US and Europe. — *n* **Eu'romarket** or **Eu'romart** the European Common Market; one of the West European stock exchanges. — *n* **Eu'ro-MP** a member of the European Parliament, an MEP. — *n* **Eu'ronet** an information network linking various European databanks. — *n* **Eur'o-Parliament** the European Parliament. — *n* **Eur'o-passport** a standard form of passport issued to all eligible citizens of the European Community. — *n* **Eu'rophile** (*ū'rō-fīl*; Gr *philos* friend) a lover of Europe, *esp* the European Community. — Also *adj*. — *n* **Eu'ro-sceptic** a person, *esp* a politician, who is sceptical about the desirability of closer links between the UK and the European Community. — *n* **Eu'roseat** a constituency in the European Parliament. — *n* **Eu'rospeak** (*facetious*) the jargon used by European Community officialdom. — *n* **Eu'rosterling** sterling as part of Eurocurrency. — *n* **eu'roterminal** the end station of a railway line, coach-route, etc that operates a direct service from the UK into Europe. — *n* **Eu'rotunnel** the Channel tunnel. — *n* **Eu'rovision** the European television network.

Euraquilo *ū-rak'wi-lō*, *n*. See **Euroclydon**.

Eurasian, **Euratom**. See under **Eur-**.

eureka, rarely **heureka** (*h*)*ū-rē'kə*, *interj* announcing a discovery. — *n* a brilliant discovery. [Gr *heurēka* I have found, perfect tense of *heuriskein* to find, the cry of Archimedes when he thought of a method of detecting the adulteration of the gold in Hiero's crown]

eurhythmy or **eurythmy**, *ū-rith'mi*, or *-ridh'*, *n* rhythmical movement or order; harmony of proportion; (*usu* with *cap*) an artistic, therapeutic and educational system based on rhythmic body movement correlated to poetry, music, etc, created by Rudolf Steiner (1861–1925). — *adj* **eurhyth'mic** or **eurhyth'mical**. — *n sing* **eurhyth'mics** the art or system of rhythmic movement expounded by E Jaques-Dalcroze (1865–1950). — *n* **eurhyth'mist**. [Gr *eurythmiā*, from *eu* well, and *rhythmos* rhythm]

euripus *ū-rī'pəs*, *n* an arm of the sea with strong currents, *specif* that between Euboea and Boeotia in classical Greece; a ditch round the arena in a Roman amphitheatre. [L, from Gr *eurīpos*]

Euro-. See **Eur-**.

euro *ū'rō*, (*Austr*) *n* a wallaroo, any of several types of large kangaroo: — *pl* **eu'ros**. [Aboriginal]

Euroclydon *ū-rok'li-don*, *n* the tempestuous wind by which St Paul's ship was wrecked (Acts 27.14). [Gr *Euroklydōn*, as if from *Euros* east wind, and *klydōn* a wave; supposed to be a wrong reading for *Eurakylōn*, L *Euraquilō*, from *Eurus* (Gr *Euros*) and *Aquilō* north wind]

Eurocommunism ... to ... **Europassport**. See under **Eur-**.

European *ū-rō-pē'ən*, *adj* belonging or relating to Europe; belonging or relating to the European Community. — *n* an inhabitant or native of Europe; a member of the pale-skinned race of man characteristic of Europe; a Europeanist. — *n* **Europē'anism**. — *n* **Europē'anist** a person who favours the European Community and seeks to uphold or develop it. — *n* **Europeaniza'tion** or **-s-**. — *vt* **europē'anize** or **-ise** to assimilate or convert to European character or ways; to integrate into the European Community. — **European Commission** an executive body composed of members of the European Community countries, which is responsible for the formulation of community policy and which initiates and drafts most community legislation; **European Community** (*abbrev* **EC**) the 12 member states of the European Economic Community, but often used loosely for the EEC itself; **European Court of Justice** the court of the European Community whose jurisdiction covers the hearing of disputes on issues of European Community law; **European Currency Unit** (*abbrev* **ECU**) the unit of currency used in the European Monetary Sustem (see below), made up of proportions of the currencies of a number of member countries; **European Economic Community** (*abbrev* **EEC**) the common market formed in 1957 by the Treaty of Rome by France, W Germany, Italy, Belgium, the Netherlands and Luxembourg; joined in 1973 by the United Kingdom, Denmark and the Republic of Ireland, in 1981 by Greece and in 1986 by Spain and Portugal; **European Free Trade Association** (*abbrev* **EFTA**) a free trade area created in 1960 by Norway, Sweden, Denmark, Austria, Portugal, Switzerland and the UK; **European Monetary Fund** (*abbrev* **EMF**) the managing body of the European Monetary System, which issues the European Currency Unit; **European Monetary System** (*abbrev* **EMS**) a system linking the values of member countries' currencies in order to limit fluctuations and support weaker currencies; **European Parliament** the legislative assembly of the European Community; **European plan** (*US*) in hotels, the system of charging for lodgings and service without including meals (cf **American plan**); **European Space Agency** (*abbrev* **ESA**) a European organization promoting international co-operation in space research and technology. [Gr *Eurōpē*]

Europhile. See under **Eur-**.

europium *ū-rō'pi-əm*, *n* a rare-earth metal (atomic no 63; symbol **Eu**) discovered spectroscopically by Demarçay in 1896. [**Europe**]

Europocentric *ū-rōp-ō-sent'rik* or **Eurocentric** *ū-rō-sent'-rik*, *adj* centred or concentrating on Europe or its civilization. [**Europe** and **centric** (see **centre**)]

Euroseat ... to ... **Eurovision**. See under **Eur-**.

Eurus *ū'rəs*, (*Gr mythol*) *n* the SE or, less exactly, E wind. [L, from Gr *Euros*]

Eurypharynx *ū-ri-far'ingks*, *n* the pelican-fish genus. [Gr *eurys* wide, and *pharynx* pharynx]

Eurypterus *ū-rip'tər-əs*, *n* a genus of Eurypterida. — *n* **euryp'terid** any member of the Eurypterida. — *n pl* **Eurypterida** (*-ter'i-də*) a Palaeozoic fossil order of Arachnida, scorpion-like aquatic animals, sometimes over six feet long, with the last (sixth) pair of appendages expanded. — *adj* **euryp'teroid** like or of the Eurypterida. — *n* a eurypterid. [Gr *eurys* wide, and *pteron* wing]

eurytherm *ū'ri-thûrm*, (*biol*) *n* an organism which tolerates a wide variation in temperature. — *adj* **eurytherm'al**, **eurytherm'ic** or **eurytherm'ous**. [Gr *eurys* wide, and *therme* heat]

eurythmy, etc. Alternative, *esp* American, spelling of **eurhythmy**.

Eusebian *ū-sē'bi-ən*, *adj* pertaining to *Eusebius* of Caesarea, father of ecclesiastical history (died 340), or to the Arian *Eusebius* of Nicomedia (died 342).

Euskarian *ūs-kā'ri-ən*, *adj* Basque. [Basque *Euskara* the Basque language]

eusol *ū'sol*, *n* an antiseptic solution obtained by treating eupad with water. [*E*dinburgh *U*niversity *s*olution *o*f *l*ime]

eusporangiate *ū-spor-an'ji-āt*, (*bot*) *adj* of a group of ferns, having each sporangium derived from a group of cells (*opp* of *leptosporangiate*). [Gr *eu* well, and **sporangium**]

Eustachian *ū-stā'shən* or *ū-stā'ki-ən*, *adj* pertaining to the Italian physician Bartolommeo *Eustachio* (died 1574). — **Eustachian tube** the tube leading from the middle ear to the pharynx; **Eustachian valve** the rudimentary valve at the entrance of the inferior vena cava in the heart.

eustacy or **eustasy** *ū'stə-si*, *n* changes in world shoreline level, probably caused by rise or fall of the sea-level and not by subsidence or elevation of the land. — *adj* **eustat'ic**. [Gr *eu* well, and *stasis* standing or *statikos* causing to stand]

eustyle *ū'stīl*, *adj* with columns spaced at about two diameters and a quarter. — *n* a colonnade or building so proportioned. [Gr *eustȳlos*, well intercolumniated, from *eu* well, and *stȳlos* column]

eutaxy *ū'tak-si*, *n* good order. — *n* **eutax'ite** a volcanic rock with banded structure. — *adj* **eutaxit'ic** having such a structure. [Gr *eu* well, and *taxis* arrangement]

eutectic, **eutectoid**. See **eutexia**.

Euterpe *ū-tûr'pē*, (*Gr mythol*) *n* the Muse of music and lyric poetry; a genus of palms. — *adj* **Euter'pean** pertaining to Euterpe or to music. [Gr *Euterpē*, from *eu* well, and *terpein* to delight]

eutexia *ū-tek'si-ə*, (*phys*) *n* the property of being easily melted. — *n* **eutec'tic** a mixture in such proportions that the melting-point (or freezing-point) is as low as possible, the constituents melting (or freezing) simultaneously. — *adj* of maximum ease of fusibility; pertaining to a eutectic. — *n* **eutec'toid** an alloy similar to a eutectic but involving formation of two or three constituents from another solid (not melted) constituent. — Also *adj*. — **eutectic point** the temperature at which a eutectic melts or freezes. [Gr *eutēktos* easily melted, from *eu* well, and *tēkein* to melt]

euthanasia *ū-thən-ā'zi-ə*, *n* an easy mode of death (*archaic*); the act or practice of putting painlessly to death, *esp* in cases of incurable suffering. — Also **euthanasy** (*-than'ə-si*). — *n* **euthanā'siast** a supporter of or believer in euthanasia. [Gr *euthanasiā*, from *eu* well, and *thanatos* death]

euthenics *ū-then'iks*, *n sing* the science concerned with the improvement of living conditions. — *n* **euthen'ist**. [Gr *euthēneein* to flourish]

Eutheria *ū-thē'ri-ə*, *n pl* the placental mammals. — *n* and *adj* **euthē'rian**. [Gr *eu* well, and *thēr* a beast]

Euthyneura *ū-thi-nū'rə*, *n pl* a subclass of gasteropods in which the visceral nerve-loop is not twisted. [Gr *euthys* straight, and *neuron* nerve]

eutrapelia *ū-trə-pē'li-ə* (*obs*) and **eutrapely** *ū-trap'ə-li*, *n* wit, ease and urbanity of conversation. [Gr *eutrapelia*, from *eutrapelos* pleasant in conversation]

eutrophy *ū'trə-fi*, *n* healthy nutrition; the state (of a body of water) of being eutrophic. — *adj* **eutrophic** (*ū-trof'ik*) pertaining to healthy nutrition; (of a body of water) over-rich in nutrients either naturally or as a result of artificial pollutants, and hence having a too-abundant growth of water-plants and animals. — *n* **eutrophicā'tion** the process of becoming or making (a body of water) eutrophic. [Gr *eutrophiā*]

eutropy *ū'trə-pi*, *n* regular variation of the crystalline form of a series of compounds with the atomic number of the element. — *adj* **eutropic** (*-trop'ik*) according to eutropy; turning sun-wise (*bot*). — *adj* **eu'tropous**. [Gr *eu* well, and *tropos* a turn]

Eutychian *ū-tik'i-ən*, *adj* of or pertaining to the doctrine of *Eutyches*, a 5c archimandrite of Constantinople, who held that Christ's human nature was merged in the divine. — *n* a follower of Eutyches.

EUW *abbrev*: European Union of Women.

euxenite *ūks'ə-nīt*, *n* a mineral, niobate and titanate of yttrium, erbium, cerium and uranium. [Gr *euxenos* hospitable, as containing many rare elements]

EV (*Bible*) *abbrev*: English version.

eV *abbrev*: electron-volt.

EVA (*astronautics*) *abbrev*: extravehicular activity.

evacuate *i-* or *ē-vak'ū-āt*, *vt* to throw out the contents of; to discharge, empty or void; to withdraw; to move or remove eg from a place of danger; to clear out troops, inhabitants, etc from; to create a vacuum in (*phys*); to nullify (*law*). — *vi* to move away (from a place of danger, *usu* temporarily); to void excrement, empty the bowels. — *adj* and *n* **evac'uant** a purgative or laxative. — *n* **evacuā'tion** an act of evacuating; withdrawal or removal; the material discharged, excreted, etc. — *adj* **evac'uātive**. — *n* **evac'uātor**. — *n* **evacūee'** a person moved or removed in an evacuation. [L *ē* from, and *vacuāre*, *-ātum* to empty, from *vacuus* empty]

evade *i-* or *ē-vād'*, *vi* to escape or slip away (*rare*). — *vt* to escape or avoid by cunning; to shirk; to baffle or elude (*fig*). — *adj* **evā'dable**. — *n* **evad'er**. [L *ēvādere*, from *ē* from, and *vādere* to go]

evagation *ē-* or *e-vag-ā'shən*, *n* wandering; a digression. [L *ēvagārī*, from *ē* from, and *vagārī* to wander]

evaginate *i-* or *ē-vaj'i-nāt*, *vt* to turn outside in (*med*); to evert; to remove from a sheath. — *adj* without a sheath. — *n* **evaginā'tion**. [L *ēvāgīnāre*, *-ātum* to unsheathe, from *ē* from, and *vāgīna* a sheath]

evaluate *i-* or *ē-val'ū-āt*, *vt* to determine or estimate the value of. — *n* **evaluā'tion**. — *adj* **eval'uative** tending or serving to evaluate, or functioning as an evaluation. [Fr *évaluer*]

Evan. or **evan.** *abbrev*: evangelical.

evanescent *ev-ən-es'ənt*, *adj* fleeting or passing; vanishing. — *vi* **evanesce'** to fade away or vanish. — *n* **evanesc'ence**. — *adv* **evanesc'ently**. [L *ēvānēscēns*, *-entis*, from *ē* from, and *vānēscere* to vanish, from *vānus* empty]

Evang. or **evang.** *abbrev*: evangelical.

evangel *i-van'jəl*, *n* good news (*poetic*); the Christian gospel; a doctrine set up as a saving principle, *esp* in morals or politics. — *n* **evangeliar** (*ev-ən-jel'*), **evangeliā'rion, evangeliā'rium** or **evangel'iary** a book of passages from the Gospels to be used at mass or in other services. — *adj* **evangelical** (*ev-* or *ēv-an-jel'ik-əl*) or (*archaic*) **evangel'ic** of or pertaining to the Christian Gospel; relating to the four Gospels; according to the doctrine of the Gospel; maintaining or promoting the teaching of the Gospel; Protestant; of the school of religious belief that insists especially on the total depravity of unregenerate human nature, the justification of the sinner by faith alone, the free offer of the Gospel to all, and the plenary inspiration and exclusive authority of the Bible; believing in and inspired by the necessity of carrying the Christian faith to those not already within the community of the Christian church; active and ardent in one's advocacy of some principle or cause. — *n* **evangel'ical** a person inspired by evangelical beliefs of any kind; a person who belongs to the evangelical school of religious belief. — *n* **evangel'icalism**. — *adv* **evangel'ically**. — *n* **evangel'icalness**. — *n* **evangel'icism** (*-sizm*) evangelical principles. — *n* **evan'gelism** evangelizing; evangelicalism. — *n* **evan'gelist** a person who evangelizes, religiously or otherwise; (with *cap*) an author of a Gospel, *esp* Matthew, Mark, Luke or John; an assistant of the apostles; a person who is authorized to preach but who is without responsibility for a fixed area; an itinerant preacher; a lay missionary in the Catholic Apostolic Church, a minister of the third grade; an active and keen advocate of some principle or cause. — *n* **evangelis'tary** a book of the Gospels or of passages from them to be read at divine service; a table of such passages. — Also **evangelistā'rion**. — *adj* **evangelis'tic** tending or intended to evangelize, religiously or otherwise. — *n* **evangelīzā'tion** or **-s-** (*i-van-jəl-*) the act of proclaiming the Gospel; Christianization; the attempt to persuade others of the rightness of some principle or cause. — *vt* **evan'gelize** or **-ise** to make acquainted with the Gospel; to convert to Christianity. — *vi* to preach the Gospel from place to place; to try to persuade others to support some principle or cause. — *n* **evan'gely** (*obs*) the Gospel. — **Evangelical Union** see **Morisonian**. [L *evangelicus*, from Gr *euangelikos*, from *eu* well, and *angellein* to bring news]

evanish *i-van'ish*, (chiefly *poetic*) *vi* to vanish; to die away. — *n* **evan'ishment**. — *n* **evanition** (*ev-ə-nish'ən*). [OFr *evanir*, *evaniss-*, from L *ex* from, and *vānus* empty; cf **evanesce**]

evaporate *i-vap'ər-āt*, *vi* to change into vapour; to pass into an invisible state; to depart, vanish or disappear (*fig*). — *vt* to convert into vapour; to dry by evaporation; to draw moisture off (a metal) in vapour form. — *adj* **evap'orable** able to be evaporated or converted into vapour. — *n* **evaporabil'ity**. — *n* **evaporā'tion** the act of evaporating or drawing off moisture in the form of steam or gas; the process by which a substance changes into vapour. — *adj* **evap'orātive**. — *n* **evap'orātor**. — *n* **evaporim'eter** or **evaporom'eter** an instrument for measuring the rate of evaporation. — *n* **evap'orite** a sedimentary rock formed by the evaporation of salt water. — *n* **evap'orograph** a device giving direct or photographic images of objects in darkness by focusing infrared radiations from them on to an oil-film, which evaporates in proportion to the amount of radiation and leaves an image. — **evaporated milk** milk thickened by evaporation of some of its water content, unsweetened. [L *ē* from, and *vapōrāre*, *-ātum*, from *vapor* vapour]

evapotranspiration *i-vap-ō-tran-spə-rā'shən*, *n* the return of water into the atmosphere as vapour, by evaporation (from soil, water bodies, etc) and emissions or *transpiration* (from plants); the total amount converted by this process. [**evaporate** and **transpiration**]

evasion *i-vā'zhən*, *n* the act of evading or eluding; an attempt to escape the point of an argument or accusation; an excuse. — *adj* **evasible** (*i-vā'zi-bl*) capable of being evaded. — *adj* **evā'sive** (*-siv*) evading or attempting to evade; elusive; devious, not straightforward; shuffling (*archaic*). — *adv* **evā'sively**. — *n* **evā'siveness**. — **take evasive action** to move or act in such a way as to avoid an object or consequence. [L *ēvādere*, *ēvāsum*; see **evade**]

eve. See **even**[2].

evection *i-* or *ē-vek'shən*, (*astron*) *n* a lunar inequality, the combined effect of the irregularity of the point of the moon's orbit at which it is nearest to Earth and the alternate increase and decrease of the eccentricity of the moon's orbit. [L *ēvectiō*, *-ōnis*, from *ē* from, and *vehere*, *vectum* to carry]

evejar. See under **even**[2].

even[1] *ēv'n*, *adj* flat; level; smooth; calm or unexcited; uniform; in a straight line or plane; straightforward (*Shakesp*); balanced equally; equal; fair or just; exact; (of people) not owing each other anything; divisible by two without a remainder; denoted by such a number. — *vt* to make even or smooth; to put on an equal basis; to compare; to make (scores, etc) equal; to act up to (*Shakesp*). — *vi* (often with *up*) to become even. — *adv* (also *archaic* **e'en**) exactly (*colloq*); nearly; indeed, in fact; so much as; still, yet, emphasizing a comparative, as in *even better*; used when speaking or writing of something extreme or completely unexpected, as in *even an idiot would know*. — *n* **ev'ener**. — *adv* **ev'enly**.

— *n* **ev'enness**. — *n pl* **ev'ens** even money. — *adj* and *adv* quits. — **even chance** an equal probability (of success or failure, etc); **ev'en-Chris'tian** (*obs*) fellow-Christian; **even date** the same date. — *adj* **ev'en-down** (*dialect* or *archaic*) straight-down (of rain); downright or honest. — *adv* thoroughly. — *adj* **even-hand'ed** impartial; just or fair. — *n* **even-hand'edness**. — *adj* **even-mind'ed** having an even or calm mind; equable. — *n* **even money** in betting odds, considered extremely likely to win or happen, and paying out only the equal of the stake. — *adj* **even-tem'pered** of placid temperament, calm. — **be even with** to be revenged on (also **get even with**); to be quits with; **even as** at that or this very moment when; **even-even nuclei** nuclei in which there are an even number of protons and also of neutrons; **even-odd nuclei** nuclei in which there are an even number of protons and an odd number of neutrons; **even now** a very little while ago (*archaic*); after all that has happened; **even on** (*Scot*) without intermission; **even out** to become even or equal; **even so** nevertheless; **even up on** to requite or come square with; **on an even keel** balanced, not tilting to one side or the other (often *fig*); (of eg business affairs) running smoothly, settled or well-organized. [OE *efen*; Du *even*, Ger *eben*]

even[2] *ēv'n* or **e'en** *ēn*, (*obs*, *poetic* or *dialect*) *n* evening; eve. — *n* **eve** (*ēv*) evening (*poetic*); the night or the whole day before a festival; the time just preceding an event. — *n* **evening** (*ēv'ning*) the close of the day; the decline or end (of life); an evening party, gathering or entertainment; an evening newspaper. — *adv* **eve'nings** (*esp NAm*) in the evening (on a number of occasions). — **eve'jar** (*dialect*) the nightjar; **ev'enfall** early evening, twilight; **evening class** a class held in the evenings, *usu* for people who work during the day; **eve'ning-dress** the (men's or women's) dress conventionally appropriate to formal social functions in the evening; **evening primrose** a N American plant (Oenothera) with pale yellow flowers that open in the evening; **evening-star'** a planet, *usu* Venus or Mercury, seen in the western sky and setting soon after the sun; **ev'ensong** evening prayers, the Anglican form appointed to be said or sung at evening; the time appropriate for these prayers; **ev'entide** (*poetic*) evening or the time of evening; **eventide home** a residential home for old people. [OE *ǣfen*, *ǣfnung*]

événement *ā-ven-mã*, (*Fr*) *n* an event or happening; *specif* a political strike or demonstration.

event *i-vent'*, *n* anything which happens; result; any incident or occurrence, *esp* a memorable one; contingency or possibility of occurrence; an item in a programme (of sports, etc); a type of horse-riding competition, often held over three days (**three-day event**), consisting of three sections, ie dressage, cross-country riding and show-jumping; fortune or fate (*obs*); an organized activity at a particular venue, eg for sales promotion, fund-raising, etc. — *vi* to ride in a horse-riding event. — *n* **event'er** a horse trained to take part in events; the rider of such a horse, eg *three-day eventer*. — *adj* **event'ful** full of events; memorable, momentous. — *n* **event'ing** taking part in riding events; the sport of horse-riding in three-day events. — *adj* **event'ūal** happening as a consequence; final, after a time. — *n* **eventūal'ity** an occurrence or happening; a contingency; the faculty of observing the order or chronology of events (*phrenology*). — *vi* **event'ūalize** or **-ise** to happen; to come into being. — *adv* **event'ūally** finally; at length, after some time. — *vi* **event'ūate** to turn out. — **event horizon** (*astron*) the boundary of a black hole. — **at all events** or **in any event** no matter what happens, anyway; **in the event** as things turn or turned out; if it should turn out (that); **in the event of** in the case of (a specified thing happening). [L *ēventus*, from *ēvenīre* to come out or happen, from *ē* from, and *venīre* to come]

eventration *ē-ven-trā'shən*, *n* the act of opening the belly; the protrusion of an organ from the abdomen. — *vt* **even'trate**. [Fr *éventration*, from L *ē* from, and *venter* belly]

ever *ev'ər*, *adv* always; eternally; at all times; continually; at any time; on record, in history or in the world (eg *the biggest ever* the biggest that has at any time been or happened); in any degree; at all or possibly; very or extremely (*slang*, *orig NAm*; used as part of an interjection or statement, eg *was I ever hungry* I was very hungry). — *sfx* giving complete generality to relative adverbs and pronouns, eg *whatever*, etc. — *adj* **ev'ergreen** in leaf throughout the year; always fresh and green; unfading; never failing, retaining one's (or its) vigour, freshness, popularity, interest, etc for ever. — *n* a tree or shrub that is green throughout the year; a person, piece of music, etc which retains freshness, popularity, etc through the years. — *adj* **everlast'ing** endless; perpetual; unceasing; eternal; wearisomely long (*colloq*). — *n* (with *the*) eternity; (with *cap* and *the*) God; a flower (of *Helichrysum*, *Antennaria* or other genus) that may be kept for years without much change of appearance; a very durable type or cloth. — *adv* **everlast'ingly**. — *n* **everlast'ingness**. — *adj* **ev'er-living** (*Shakesp*) immortal; deathless. — *adv* **evermore'** (or *ev'*) for all time to come (also **for evermore**); ever; unceasingly. — **ever and anon** (*archaic* and *poetic*) from time to time; **ever so** to a very great extent; to any extent (*archaic*); **ever such a** (*colloq*) a very; **for ever** for all eternity, always; for a long time (*colloq*). [OE *ǣfre*]

Everest *ev'ə-rəst*, *n* the name of the highest mountain in the world, in the Himalayas; anything extremely difficult to accomplish or conquer, the height of ambition. — **Everest pack** a light aluminium frame, carried on the back, with camping equipment strapped to it.

everglade *ev'ər-glād*, *n* a large shallow lake or marsh; (with *cap*; chiefly in *pl*) such a marsh in southern Florida, enclosing thousands of islets covered with dense thickets. [Perh **ever** and **glade**]

evert *ē-* or *i-vûrt'*, *vt* to turn inside out; to turn outwards. — *adj* **ever'sible**. — *n* **ever'sion**. — *n* **evert'or** a muscle that turns outwards. [L *ēvertere*, from *ē* from, and *vertere*, *versum* to turn]

every *ev'ri*, *adj* each of a number or collection; all taken separately. — *pronoun* **ev'erybody** or **ev'eryone** every person. — *adj* **ev'eryday** of or happening every day, daily; common or usual; (*esp* of clothes) pertaining to or appropriate for weekdays, not Sunday. — Also *n*. — *n* **ev'erydayness**. — *n* **Ev'eryman** (also without *cap*) the hero of an old morality play, representing mankind, everybody or anybody. — *adv* **ev'eryplace** (*US*) everywhere. — *pronoun* **ev'erything** all things taken singly; all. — *adv* **ev'eryway** in every way or respect. — *adv* **ev'erywhen**, **ev'erywhence** or **ev'erywhither** (*all rare*). — *adv* **ev'erywhere** in every place. — **every bit** or **whit** the whole, all of it; quite or entirely; **every here and there** all over in various places; **every last** (emphatically) every; **every man Jack** or **every mother's son** everyone without exception; **every now and then** or **every now and again** at intervals, periodically; **every other** every second or alternate; **every so often** at intervals or periodically; **every which way** (*US*) every direction or method; in disorder; **have everything** (*colloq*) to be well endowed with possessions, attractiveness, etc. [OE *ǣfre* ever, and *ǣlc* each]

evet *ev'it*, *n*. Same as **eft**[1].

evgs *abbrev*: evenings.

evhoe. See **evoe**.

evict *i-* or *ē-vikt'*, *vt* to dispossess by law; to expel (*usu* from a dwelling). — *n* **evic'tion** the act of evicting from house or lands; the dispossession of one person by another having a better title to property or land. — *n* **evic'tor**. — **eviction order** a court order by which a person may be evicted. [L *ēvictus*, pa p of *ēvincere* to overcome]

evident *ev'i-dənt*, *adj* that can be seen; clear to the mind; obvious. — *n* that which serves as evidence. — *n* **ev'idence** that which makes anything evident; means of proving an unknown or disputed fact; support (eg for a belief); indication; information in a law case; testimony; a witness or witnesses collectively. — *vt* to make evident, apparent or visible; to attest or prove; to indicate. — *adj* **evidential** (*-den'shəl*) or **eviden'tiary** providing evidence; tending to prove. — *adv* **eviden'tially**. — *adv* **ev'idently** visibly (*Bible*); obviously; manifestly. — **in evidence** received by the court as competent testimony; plainly visible, conspicuous or present (adopted from the Fr *en évidence*); **turn Queen's** or **King's evidence** or (*US*) **turn State's evidence** to give evidence for the prosecution against an accomplice in a crime. [L *ēvidēns, -entis*, from *ē* from, and *vidēre* to see]

evil *ē'v(i)l, adj* wicked or bad; mischievous; very disagreeable or angry; unfortunate (*rare* or *archaic*). — *adv* (*usu* in compounds) in an evil manner; badly or terribly. — *n* something which produces unhappiness or misfortune; harm; wickedness or depravity; sin; illness, disease or curse (eg **king's-evil**). — *adv* **evilly** (*ē'vil-i*) in an evil manner; badly or terribly. — *n* **e'vilness** the state of being evil; wickedness. — **e'vil-doer** a person who does evil; **evil eye** a supposed power to cause harm by a look. — *adj* **e'vil-eyed**. — *adj* **evil-fā'voured** having a repulsive appearance; ugly. — **evil-fā'vouredness** (*Bible*) ugliness; deformity. — *adj* **evil-mind'ed** inclined to evil; malicious; wicked. — *adv* **evil-mind'edly**. — **evil-mind'edness**; **evil-speak'ing** the speaking of evil; slander. — Also *adj*. — *adj* **evil-starred'** (*Tennyson*) born under the influence of an unpropitious star, unfortunate. — *adj* **evil-tem'pered** bad-tempered, unpleasant or spiteful. — **e'vil-worker** someone who does evil. — **speak evil of** to slander; **the evil one** the devil. [OE *yfel*; Du *euvel*; Ger *übel*; cf **ill**]

evince *i-vins', vt* to overcome or overpower (*archaic*); to prove beyond doubt; to show clearly; to make evident; to give indication of. — *n* **evince'ment**. — *adj* **evinc'ible**. — *adv* **evinc'ibly**. — *adj* **evinc'ive** tending to evince, prove or demonstrate. [L *ēvincere* to vanquish, from *ē-* (intens), and *vincere* to overcome]

Evipan® *ev'i-pan, n* the proprietary name of a drug, hexobarbitone sodium, used intravenously and intramuscularly as a basic anaesthetic.

evirate *ē'* or *e'vir-āt, vt* to castrate; to make weak or unmanly. [L *ēvirāre*, from *ē* from, and *vir* a man]

eviscerate *ē-* or *i-vis'ər-āt, vt* to tear out the viscera or bowels of; to gut (*lit* and *fig*). — *n* **evisceră'tion**. — *n* **evisc'erator**. [L *ē* from, and *viscera* the bowels]

evitable *ev'it-ə-bl, adj* avoidable. — *vt* **evite** (*i-vīt'*; *archaic*) and **ev'itate** (*Shakesp*) to avoid. — *n* **evitā'tion** the act of shunning or avoiding. [L *ēvitāre, -ātum*, from *ē* from, and *vītāre* to shun]

eviternal *ēv-i-tûr'nl, adj* eternal. — *adv* **eviter'nally**. — *n* **eviter'nity**. [L *aeviternus*; see **eternal**]

evocation, etc. See **evoke**.

evoe, evhoe, evohe *ē-vē'* or *ē-vō'i*, or **euoi** *ū-oi', interj* expressing Bacchic frenzy. [L *eu(h)oe*, from Gr *euoi, eu hoi*]

evoke *i-vōk', vt* to call out; to draw out or bring forth; to call up or awaken (*esp* memories) in the mind. — *adj* **evocable** (*i-vok'ə-bl*). — *vt* **evocate** (*ev'ō-kāt*) to evoke; to call up from the dead. — *n* **evocā'tion**. — *adj* **evocative** (*i-vok'ə-tiv*) or **evoc'atory**. — *adv* **evoc'atively**. — *n* **evoc'ativeness**. — *n* **evocator** (*e'vō-kā-tər*).— *n* **evok'er**. [L *ēvocāre*, from *ē* from, and *vocāre* to call]

évolué *ā-vol-ü-ā', n* a member of a primitive group of people who has been educated to the standards of a more advanced civilization. — Also *adj*. [Fr, developed]

evolution *ēv-* or *ev-ə-lōō'shən, n* the cumulative change in the characteristics of populations of organisms over succeeding generations, resulting in species totally different from remote ancestors; the act of unrolling or unfolding (*archaic*); the giving off (of heat, etc); gradual working out or development; a series of things following in sequence; the calculation of roots (*math*); (*usu* in *pl*) orderly movements eg of a body of troops, flock of birds, etc. — *n* **ev'olute** (*math*) an original curve from which another curve (the *involute*) is described by the end of a thread gradually unwound from the former. — *adj* rolled back. — *vt* and *vi* to develop by evolution. — *adj* **evolu'tional** or **evolu'tionary** of or pertaining to evolution. — *n* **evolu'tionism** the doctrine of evolution. — *n* **evolu'tionist** a person skilled in evolutions or military movements; a person who believes in evolution as a principle in science. — *adj* **evolutionis'tic**. — *adj* **ev'olutive**. — **evolutionarily stable strategy** (*biol*) a strategy such that, if most members of a population adopt it, there is no mutant strategy that would give higher reproductive fitness (*abbrev* **ESS**). [L *ēvolūtiō, -ōnis*, from *ēvolvere*; see **evolve**]

evolve *i-* or *ē-volv', vt* to unroll; to disclose; to develop; to give off (heat, etc); to unravel. — *vi* to change gradually, *esp* according to the theory of evolution; to become apparent gradually; to result (with *into*). — *adj* **evolv'able** that can be drawn out. — *n* **evolve'ment**. — *adj* **evolv'ent** evolving. — *n* **evol'ver**. [L *ēvolvere*, from *ē-* from, and *volvere, volūtum* to roll]

evovae *i-vō'vē* or **euouae** *ū-ōō'ē*, (*music*) *n* names for a Gregorian cadence, obtained from '*seculorum* (formerly written SECVLORVM) *Amen*' in the doxology 'Gloria Patri'.

EVR *abbrev*: electronic video recording and reproduction.

evulgate *ē-* or *e-vul'gāt, vt* to divulge; to publish. [L *ēvulgāre, -ātum*, from *ē* out, and *vulgus* the people]

evulse *i-* or *ē-vuls', vt* to pluck out. — *n* **evul'sion**. [L *ēvellere, ēvulsum*, from *ē* from, and *vellere, vulsum* to pluck]

evzone *ev'zōn, n* a soldier in an élite Greek infantry regiment. [Mod Gr *euzōnos*, from Gr, girt for action, from *eu* well, and *zōnē* girdle]

ewe *ū, n* a female sheep. — **ewe'-cheese** cheese made from the milk of ewes; **ewe'-lamb** a female lamb; a poor man's only possession, one's dearest possession (in reference to 2 Sam 12); **ewe'-milk**; **ewe'-neck** of horses, a thin hollow neck. — *adj* **ewe'-necked**. [OE *ēowu*; cf L *ovis*, Gr *oïs*, Sans *avi* a sheep]

ewer *ū'ər, n* a large water jug with a wide spout. [Through Fr from L *aquārium* (neuter of *aquārius* of water), from *aqua* water]

ewest *ū'ist*, (*Scot*) *adj* or *adv* near. [Appar from OE *on nēaweste* in the neighbourhood, wrongly divided as *on ewest*]

ewftes *ūfts*, (*Spenser*) *n pl* efts. [See **eft**[1]]

ewghen. An old spelling of **yewen**.

ewhow *ā'(h)wow'*, (*Scot*) *interj* expressing regret.

Ewigkeit *ā'vihh-kīt, n* eternity. [Ger]

ewk. See **yuke**.

ewt. See **newt**.

Ex. (*Bible*) *abbrev*: (the book of) Exodus.

ex[1] *eks, n* the twenty-fourth letter of the modern English alphabet (X or x).

ex[2] *eks, prep* direct from (as *ex works* or *ex warehouse*; *commerce*); without (as *ex dividend*, without the next dividend); used when stating the former name of a ship. [L, out of or from]

ex. *eks, abbrev*: examination or examined; example; except, excepted or exception; exchange; excursion or excursus; executed; executive; export; express; extra.

ex- *eks-, pfx* former but still living (as **ex-emperor**); formerly employed, etc by. — *n* **ex** (*colloq*) someone who is no longer what he or she was, *esp* a person's former husband or wife: — *pl* **ex's** or **ex'es**.

exa- *ek'sə-* or *ek-sa'*, (*math*) *abbrev*: 10^{18}.

ex abundantia *a-bən-dan'shi-ə* or *a-bōōn-dan'ti-ä* (*L*) out of abundance. — **ex abundanti cautela** (*-dan'tī kō-tē'lə* or *-dan'tē kow-tā'lä*) from excessive caution.

ex accidenti *eks ak-si-den'tī* or *a-ki-den'tē*, (*LL*) accidentally (as opposed to essentially).

exacerbate *iks-* or *igz-as'ər-bāt, vt* to make (eg an awkward situation or a disease) worse, more violent or more severe; to embitter; to provoke. — *n* **exacerbā'tion** or (*archaic*) **exacerbesc'ence** increase of irritation or violence, *esp* the increase of a fever or disease; embitterment. [L *exacerbāre*, *-ātum*, from *ex* and *acerbāre*, from *acerbus* bitter]

exact *igz-akt'*, *vt* to force out; to compel payment of; to demand and obtain; to extort; to require as indispensable or prerequisite. — *vi* to practise extortion. — *adj* precise; rigorous; accurate; absolutely correct; finished; consummate; strict in correctness of detail. — *adj* **exact'able** — *adj* **exact'ing** compelling full payment; unreasonable in making demands; demanding much, challenging or difficult. — *adv* **exact'ingly**. — *n* **exac'tion** the act of exacting or demanding strictly; an oppressive demand; something which is exacted, as (excessive) work or tribute. — *n* **exact'itude** exactness; correctness. — *adv* **exact'ly**. — *n* **exact'ment**. — *n* **exact'ness** the quality of being exact or precise; accuracy. — *n* **exact'or** or **exact'er** a person who exacts; an extortioner; someone who claims rights, often too strictly: — *fem* **exact'ress**. — **exact sciences** the mathematical sciences, whose results are precisely measurable. — **not exactly** not altogether; not at all (*colloq* or *ironic*). [L *exigere*, *exāctum* to demand or to weigh strictly, from *ex* from, and *agere* to drive]

ex aequo *eks ē'kwō*, or *ī'*, (*LL*) equally or equitably.

exaggerate *igz-aj'ər-āt*, *vt* to magnify unduly; to overstate; to represent too strongly; to intensify. — *vi* to speak hyperbolically, to overstate the case. — *adj* **exagg'erated**. — *adv* **exagg'eratedly**. — *n* **exaggerā'tion** extravagant overstatement; a statement displaying this. — *adj* **exagg'erative** or **exagg'eratory** containing exaggeration or tending to exaggerate. — *n* **exagg'erātor**. [L *exaggerāre*, *-ātum*, from *ex-*, and *aggerāre* to heap up, from *agger* a heap]

exalbuminous *eks-al-bū'min-əs*, (*bot*) *adj* without albumen.

exalt *igz-ölt'*, *vt* to place in a high position (of respect, etc); to elate or fill with the joy of success; to extol or praise; to refine or subtilize (*old chem*). — *n* **exaltā'tion** (*egz-öl-*) elevation in rank or dignity; high estate; elation or rejoicing; a planet's position of greatest influence (*astrol*); a collective noun for larks, a flight. — *adj* **exalt'ed** elevated or high; lofty; dignified. — *adv* **exalt'edly**. — *n* **exalt'edness**. [L *exaltāre*, from *ex-*, and *altus* high]

exam. Short for **examination**.

examine *igz-am'in*, *vt* to test; to inquire into; to question; to look closely at or into; to inspect. — *n* **exā'men** examination, *esp* of one's conscience, as a RC religious exercise. — *n* **examinabil'ity**. — *adj* **exam'inable**. — *n* **exam'inant** an examiner; someone who is being examined. — *n* **exam'inate** someone who is examined. — *n* **examinā'tion** careful search or inquiry; close inspection; trial; a test of capacity and knowledge (*colloq* contracted to **exam'**); formal interrogation in court of a witness or accused person (*law*). — *adj* **examina'tional**. — *n* **examinee'** a person under examination. — *n* **exam'iner** or **exam'inātor** a person who examines. — *n* **exam'inership**. — *adj* **exam'ining**. — **examinā'tion-in-chief** (*law*) questioning of one's own witness (cf **cross-examination**). — *vt* **exam'ine-in-chief**. — **need one's head examined** (*slang*) to be crazy, stupid, etc. [Fr *examiner*, from L *exāmināre*, from *exāmen* the tongue of a balance]

example *igz-äm'pl*, *n* a specimen or sample; an illustration; a copy of a book; a person or thing to be imitated or not to be imitated; a pattern; a warning; an instance. — *vt* (*rare*) to exemplify; to instance. — *n* **exam'plar** (*archaic*) an exemplar. — **for example** for instance; as an illustration; **make an example of** to punish severely as a warning to others. [OFr, from L *exemplum*, from *eximere* to take out, from *ex* out of, and *emere*, *emptum* to take]

exanimate *egz-* or *igz-an'i-māt*, *adj* lifeless; spiritless; depressed. — *n* **exanimā'tion**. [L *exanimātu* from *ex* from, and *anima* breath]

ex animo *eks an'i-mō*, (*L*) from the mind or earnestly.

ex ante *eks an'ti*, based on prediction and extrapolation. [L, from before]

exanthem *eks-an'thəm* or **exanthema** *eks-an-thē'mə*, (*med*) *n* a skin eruption, *esp* accompanied by fever; a disease characterized by these symptoms: — *pl* **exan'thems** or **exanthē'mata**. — *adj* **exanthemat'ic** or **exanthē'matous**. [Gr *exanthēma*, *-atos*, from *ex-* out, and *antheein* to blossom]

exarate *eks'ər-āt*, *adj* containing grooves or furrows; used of pupae in which the wings and legs are free. — *n* **exara'tion** (*rare*) the act of writing; composition. [L *exarātus*, from *exarāre* to plough up or to trace letters on a tablet]

exarch[1] *eks'ärk*, *n* a Byzantine provincial governor, *esp* of Italy (*hist*); a metropolitan bishop (*Orthodox Ch*); a bishop ranking between a patriarch and a metropolitan bishop (*Orthodox Ch*); the head of the Bulgarian church; a bishop's representative; an ecclesiastical inspector; a legate. — *adj* **exarch'al**. — *n* **exarch'ate** (or *eks'*) or **ex'archy** the office, jurisdiction or province of an exarch. — *n* **exarch'ist** (or *eks'*) a supporter of the Bulgarian exarch. [Gr *exarchos* leader]

exarch[2] *eks'ärk*, (*bot*) *adj* having the protoxylem on the outer edge. [Gr *ex-* out, and *archē* beginning, origin]

exasperate *igz-äs'pər-āt*, *vt* to make rough or harsh (*obs*); to make more grievous or more painful; to make very angry; to irritate to a high degree. — *adj* irritated; rough with hard points (*bot*). — *adj* **exas'perāting**. — *adj* **exas'perātive**. — *n* **exasperā'tion**. — *n* **exas'perātor**. [L *ex-* (intens), and *asperāre* to make rough, from *asper* rough]

ex auctoritate mihi commissa *eks ök-to-ri-tā'tē mī'hī kə-mis'ə*, or *owk-tō-ri-tä'te mi'hi ko-mi'sa*, (*L*) by the authority entrusted to me.

Exc. *abbrev*: Excellency.

exc. *abbrev*: excellent; except; exception; excursion.

Excalibur *eks-kal'ib-ər*, *n* the name of King Arthur's sword. [OFr *Escalibor*, for *Caliburn*; cf *Caladbolg*, a famous sword in Irish legend]

excambion *eks-kam'bi-on*, (*Scots law*) *n* exchange of lands. — Also **excam'bium**. — *vt* **excamb'** to exchange. [LL *excambiāre*; cf **cambist**, **cambium**, **exchange**]

excarnate *eks-kär'nāt*, *vt* to remove the flesh from. — *n* **excarna'tion**. [LL *excarnāre*, *-ātum*, from L *ex* from, and *carō*, *carnis* flesh]

ex cathedra *eks kə-thē'drə* or *eks kath'ə-dra*, (*LL*) from the chair of office, *esp* the Pope's throne in the Consistory or a professor's chair; hence authoritatively or judicially. — *adj* **ex-cathe'dra** spoken with or as if with authority; implying authoritativeness; to be obeyed completely, *esp* by Roman Catholics of papal decree.

excaudate *eks-kö'dāt*, (*zool*) *adj* having no tail. [L *ex-* without, and *cauda* tail]

excavate *eks'kə-vāt*, *vt* to dig out; to lay open by digging; to hollow or scoop out. — *n* **excavā'tion** the act of excavating; a hollow or cavity made by excavating; an archaeological site, a dig. — *n* **ex'cavātor** a person who excavates; a machine used for excavating. [L *excavāre*, from *ex-* out, and *cavus* hollow]

exceed *ik-sēd'*, *vt* to go beyond the limit or measure of; to surpass or excel. — *vi* to go beyond a given or proper limit (*archaic*); to be intemperate (*archaic*); to be outstanding. — *adj* **exceed'ing** surpassing; excessive; projecting beyond a neighbouring member (*bot*). — *adv* (*Bible*) exceedingly. — *adv* **exceed'ingly** very much; greatly. [L *ex-* beyond, and *cēdere*, *cēssum* to go]

excel *ik-sel'*, *vt* to be superior to or better than; to surpass; to exceed (*Milton*). — *vi* to have good qualities in large measure; to perform exceptional actions; to be superior or better: — *pr p* **excell'ing**; *pa t* and *pa p* **excelled'**. — *n* **excellence** (*eks'ə-ləns*) or **exc'ellency** great merit; any excellent quality; worth; greatness. — *n* **Exc'ellency** a title of honour given to persons high in rank or office. — *adj* **exc'ellent** surpassing others in some good quality; of great virtue, worth, etc; extremely good. — *adv* **exc'ellently**. — *interj* **excel'sior** (L *compar adj*, taller, loftier) higher still (after Longfellow). — *n* (sometimes with *cap*; *orig US*) a trade name for wood shavings for packing. [L *excellere*, from *ex-* out or up, and *celsus* high]

excellence *ek-se-lãs*, (*Fr*) *n* excellence. — **par excellence** as an example of excellence; superior to all others of the same sort.

excentric. Same as **eccentric** in mechanical senses.

except *ik-sept'*, *vt* to take out or leave out; to exclude. — *vi* to object (*usu* with *to* or *against*). — *prep* leaving out; not including; but. — *conj* (*archaic*) unless. — *adj* and *n* **except'ant**. — *prep* **except'ing** with the exception of, except. — *n* **excep'tion** the act of excepting; something which is excepted; exclusion; objection; offence. — *adj* **excep'tionable** objectionable. — *adv* **excep'tionably**. — *adj* **excep'tional** unusual (*esp* in a good sense). — *n* **excep'tionalism**. — *adv* **excep'tionally**. — *adj* **excep'tious** (*archaic*) disposed to take exception. — *adj* **excep'tive** including, making or being an exception. — *adj* **except'less** (*Shakesp*) making no exception, usual. — *n* **excep'tor**. — **take exception** to object (to); **the exception proves the rule** the existence of an exception to a supposed rule proves the general truth of the rule (often used in argument when no such conclusion is justified); a distorted translation of a part of a legal Latin phrase meaning 'the making of an exception proves that the rule holds in cases not excepted'. [L *excipere*, *exceptum*, from *ex* from, and *capere* to take]

exceptis excipiendis *ik-sep'tis ik-sip-i-en'dis* or *eks-kep'tēs eks-ki-pi-en'dēs*, (*LL*) excepting what is to be excepted; with proper exceptions.

excerpt *ek'sûrpt* or *ek-sûrpt'*, *n* a passage selected from a book, opera, etc, an extract. — *vt* **excerpt'** to select extracts from; to extract. — *adj* **excerpt'ible**. — *n* **excerpt'ing**. — *n* **excerp'tion**. — *n* **excerp'tor**. [L *excerptum*, pa p of *excerpere*, from *ex* from, and *carpere* to pick]

excerpta *ik-sûrp'tə* or *eks-kerp'ta*, (*L*; *pl* of **excerp'tum** *-təm* or *-to͝om*), *n pl* extracts, selections.

excess *ik-ses'* or *ek'ses*, *n* a going beyond what is usual or proper; intemperance; something which exceeds; the degree or amount by which one thing exceeds another; usury (*Shakesp*). — *adj* more than usual, proper, allowed, etc. — *adj* **excess'ive** beyond what is usual or right; immoderate; extreme. — *adv* excessively. — *adv* **excess'ively**. — *n* **excess'iveness**. — **excess capacity** the operating situation of a firm or industry when output is below the level at which all its productive resources are fully employed; **excess demand** a situation in which the quantity of a product or service which buyers wish to buy at the prevailing price exceeds that which sellers are prepared or able to sell; **excess fare** payment for distance travelled beyond, or in a higher class than, that allowed by the ticket; **excess luggage** or **baggage** luggage above the weight allowed free; **excess postage** payment due from the addressee when insufficient stamps have been put on a letter or packet; **excess supply** the operating situation of a firm or industry in which the quantity of a product or service which sellers wish to sell at the prevailing price exceeds the quantity which buyers wish to buy. — **carry to excess** to do (something) too much; **excess profits tax** a tax on profits in excess of those for a specified base period or over a rate adopted as a reasonable return on capital; **in excess of** more than. [L *excēssus*, from *excēdere*, *excēssum* to go beyond]

exch. *abbrev*: exchange; exchequer.

exchange *iks-chānj'*, *vt* to give or give up in return for something else; to receive in return for something else (*obs*); to give and take mutually; to barter; to change (*obs*). — *vi* to transfer in mutual ownership, position, etc. — *n* the giving and taking of one thing for another; barter; the thing exchanged; a process by which accounts between distant parties are settled by bills instead of money; money-changing business, trade; exchanging currency of one country for that of another (also **foreign exchange**); the difference between the value of money in different places; a stock exchange, etc; the building or other place where merchants, etc meet for business; a central office where telephone lines are connected; a bar-room (*archaic US slang*); in chess, the taking by both players of an opposing piece in consecutive moves; see **Employment Service**. — *n* **exchangeabil'ity**. — *adj* **exchange'able** that may be exchanged. — *adv* **exchange'ably**. — *n* **exchan'ger** a person who exchanges money, goods, etc, *esp* professionally; a money-changer or banker (*Bible*). — **exchangeable disk pack** (*comput*) a disk pack that can be removed for storage and later use on the same or a compatible machine; **exchange control** the official control of the level of a country's foreign exchange transactions so as to conserve its holding of foreign currency and to protect the stability of the national currency; **exchange rate** (or **rate of exchange**) the ratio at which one currency can be exchanged for another; **exchange rate mechanism** an arrangement set up to regulate exchange rate fluctuations between participating currencies in the EMS by fixing their rates, and limiting fluctuation, against the ECU; **exchange student** or **teacher** a student or teacher spending some time at a school, college or university in a foreign country while one from that country attends his or her school, etc, or a school, etc in his or her country. — **exchange words** or **blows** to quarrel verbally or physically; **force the exchange** in chess, to play so as to force one's opponent to take one piece for another; **win** (or **lose**) **the exchange** in chess, to gain (or lose) a superior piece in exchange for an inferior. [OFr *eschangier* (Fr *échanger*), from LL *excambiāre*, from L *ex* from, and LL *cambiāre* to barter]

excheat *eks-chēt'*, (*Spenser*) *n*. Same as **escheat**.

exchequer *iks-chek'ər*, *n* (also with *cap*) a department of state having charge of revenue, so named from the chequered cloth which *orig* covered the table, on which the accounts were reckoned; the Court of Exchequer (see below); a national treasury; one's funds, finances or purse (*joc*). — *vt* to proceed against in the Court of Exchequer (*rare*). — **exchequer bill** a bill issued by the Exchequer, as security for money advanced to the government. — **Chancellor of the Exchequer** see under **chancellor**; **Court of Exchequer** in England *orig* a revenue court developed out of the judicial branch of the Exchequer, which acquired a general common-law jurisdiction by a legal fiction, became a division of the High Court of Justice in 1875, and is now merged in the Queen's (or King's) Bench Division; in Scotland a revenue court abolished in 1886, when its jurisdiction transferred to the Court of Session. [See **chequer**, **check** and **chess**]

excide *ek-sīd'*, (*archaic*) *vt* to cut off. [L *excīdere*, from *ex* from, and *caedere* to cut]

excipient *ek-sip'i-ənt*, *n* a substance mixed with a medicine to give it consistence, or used as a means of its administration. [L *excipiēns*, *-entis*, pr p of *excipere* to take out or receive, from *ex* from, and *capere* to take]

excise[1] *ek'sīz* or *-sīz'*, *n* a tax on certain home commodities, and on licences for certain trades (also **excise tax** or **excise duty**); the department in the civil service concerned with this tax. — Also *adj*. — *vt* to subject to excise duty. — *adj* **excīs'able** liable to excise duty. — **excise law** (*US*) a liquor law or licensing law; **ex'ciseman** (or *-sīz'*) an officer charged with collecting excise duty. [MDu *excijs*, from OFr *acceis* tax, from LL *accensāre* to tax, from *ad* to, and *cēnsus* a tax]

excise[2] *ek-sīz'*, *vt* to cut off or out. — *n* **excision** (*ek-sizh'ən*) a cutting out or off of any kind; a complete removal, purging. — **excision repair** an enzymatic DNA repair process in which a mismatching DNA sequence is removed, the gap being filled by synthesis of a new sequence complementary to the remaining strand. [L *excīdere* to cut out, from *ex* from, and *caedere* to cut]

excite *ik-sīt'*, *vt* to cause to become active; to stir up (people, feelings of any kind, etc); to rouse, *esp* sexually; to energize; to produce electric or magnetic activity in (*phys*); to sensitize; to stir emotionally; to raise (a nucleus, atom, molecule, etc) to an excited state. — *n* **excitabil'ity**. — *adj* **excit'able** capable of being excited; responsive to stimulus (*phys*); easily excited. — *n* **excit'ableness**. — *n* **excitancy** (*ek'si-tən-si*) excitant property. — *n* **excitant** (*ek'si-* or *ek-sī'*) something which excites or rouses the vital activity of the body; a stimulant (*med*); the electrolyte in an electric cell. — *adj* exciting; stimulating. — *n* **excitā'tion** (*ek-si-* or *sī-*) the act of exciting; a means of or reason for excitement; a state of excitement. — *adj* **excīt'ative** or **excit'atory** tending to excite. — *adj* **excit'ed** agitated; roused emotionally or sexually; in a state of great activity; having energy higher than that of the ground, or normal, state (*phys*). — *adv* **excit'edly**. — *n* **excit'edness**. — *n* **excite'ment** agitation; something which excites emotionally. — *n* **excit'er** someone who or something which excites; an auxiliary machine supplying current for another machine; a sparking apparatus for producing electric waves. — *adj* **excit'ing** tending to excite; stirring or thrilling. — *adv* **excit'ingly**. — *n* **excīt'on** (or *ek'si-ton*; *phys*) a bound pair comprising an electron and a hole. — *n* **excī'tor** exciter; a nerve bringing impulses to the brain, stimulating a part of the body. [Fr *exciter*, from L *excitāre*, *-ātum*, from *exciēre*, from *ex-* out, and *ciēre* to set in motion]

excl. *abbrev*: exclamation; excluding; exclusive.

exclaim *iks-klām'*, *vt* and *vi* to cry out (in shock, surprise, indignation or other strong emotion); to utter or speak boldly or sharply. — *n* (*rare*) an exclamation or outcry. — *n* **exclamation** (*eks-klə-mā'shən*) a sharp cry or other utterance; outcry; an uttered expression of surprise, etc; the mark expressing this (!) (also **exclamation mark** or (*US*) **point**); an interjection. — *adj* **exclama'tional**. — *adj* **exclamative** (*eks-klam'ə-tiv*) or **exclam'atory** containing or expressing exclamation. [Fr *exclamer*, from L *exclāmāre*, *-ātum*, from *ex-* out, and *clāmāre* to shout]

exclaustration *eks-klös-trā'shən*, *n* the return of a religious to the outside world on release from his or her vows. [L *ex* out, and *claustrum* an enclosed place]

exclave *eks'klāv*, *n* a part of a country, province, etc, disjoined from the main part, being enclosed in foreign territory. [See **enclave**]

exclosure *eks-klō'zhər*, *n* an area shut off from intrusion (*opp* to *enclosure*). [L *ex-* from, and **close**[1]]

exclude *iks-klōōd'*, *vt* to shut out; to push out, eject; to prevent from entering; to omit; to prevent from taking part; to except or leave out; to exempt (from a law, regulation, etc); to hatch. — *adj* **exclud'able**. — *adj* **exclud'ed** (*bot*) exserted. — *n* **excludee'** someone who is excluded. — *n* **exclud'er**. — *n* **exclu'sion** (*-zhən*) a shutting or putting out; ejection; exception; prevention from inclusion or entry. — *adj* **exclu'sionary**. — *n* **exclu'sionism**. — *n* **exclu'sionist** someone who excludes, or wishes to exclude, another from a privilege. — *adj* **exclu'sive** (*-siv*) able or tending to exclude; (mutually) incompatible; preventing from participation; of the nature of monopoly; socially inaccessible or aloof; sole or only; not to be had elsewhere or from another source; select, fashionable, few; without taking into account (*esp* with *of*); not included. — *n* an exclusive product; a news story published by one newspaper, TV channel, etc only; one of a number who exclude others from their society. — *adv* **exclu'sively**. — *n* **exclu'siveness** or **exclusiv'ity**. — *n* **exclu'sivism** the practice of being exclusive. — *n* **exclu'sivist**. — *adj* **exclu'sory** acting or tending to exclude. — **excluded employee** one who is not qualified to make a claim under certain employment legislation, eg one who has reached retirement age; **exclusion clause** a contractual term or other notice which attempts to exclude a person from liability which would otherwise arise, eg certain risks being excluded from an insurance policy; **exclusion order** an order prohibiting the presence in, or entry to, Britain of any person known to be concerned in acts of terrorism; **exclusion principle** or **Pauli** (*pow'li*) **exclusion principle** (*phys*) a fundamental law of quantum mechanics that no two particles of a group called fermions can exist in identical quantum states ie have the same set of quantum numbers (this constraint explains the electronic structure of atoms and also the general nature of the periodic table); **Exclusive Brethren** see **Close Brethren**; **exclusive dealing** the act of abstaining deliberately from any business or other transactions with people of opposite political or other convictions to one's own; a euphemism for *boycotting*; **exclusive zone** or **exclusive economic zone** territorial waters within a certain limit in which foreign exploitation is totally banned. — **law of excluded middle** (*logic*) the principle that everything is either true or false; **to the exclusion of** so as to exclude. [L *exclūdere*, *-clūsum*, from *ex-* out, and *claudere* to shut]

excogitate *eks-koj'i-tāt*, *vt* to discover by thinking; to think out earnestly or laboriously. — *n* **excog'itator**. — *n* **excogitā'tion** laborious thinking; invention by thinking out; contrivance. — *adj* **excog'itātive**. [L *excōgitāre*, *-ātum*, from *ex-* out, and *cōgitāre* to think]

excommunicate *eks-kəm-ūn'i-kāt*, *vt* to forbid or expel from the communion of (any branch of) the church; to deprive of church privileges. — *adj* **excommun'icable**. — *adj* **excommun'icate** (*-kit* or *-kāt*) excommunicated. — Also *n*. — *n* **excommunicā'tion** or (*Milton*) **excommun'ion** the act of expelling from the communion of (a branch of) the church. — *n* **excommun'icator**. — *adj* **excommun'icatory** or **excommun'icative** of or pertaining to excommunication. [From LL *excommūnicāre*, from L *ex* out, and *commūnis* common]

ex concessis (or **concesso**) *eks kən-se'sis* (or *kən-se'sō*), also *kon-kā'sēs* (or *kon-kā'sō*), (*LL*) from what has been conceded.

ex consequenti *eks kon-si-kwen'tī* or *-se-kwen'tē*, (*LL*) by way of consequence.

ex converso. Same as **e converso**.

excoriate *eks-kō'ri-āt*, or *-kö'ri-*, *vt* to strip the skin from; to criticize severely. — *n* **excoriā'tion** the act of excoriating; the state of being excoriated. [L *excoriāre*, *-ātum*, from *ex* from, and *corium* the skin]

excorticate *eks-kör'ti-kāt*, *vt* to strip the bark off. — *n* **excorticā'tion**. [L *ex* from, and *cortex*, *-icis* bark]

excrement[1] *eks'kri-mənt*, *n* waste matter discharged from the digestive system, faeces; dregs. — *adj* **excremental** (*-ment'l*), **excrementitial** (*-tish'l*) or **excrementi'tious** pertaining to or containing excrement. [L *excrēmentum*, from *excernere*, from *ex-* out, and *cernere* to sift]

excrement[2] *eks'kri-mənt*, (*Shakesp*) *n* an outgrowth, a moustache. — *adj* **excremental** (*-ment'l*). [L *excrēmentum*, from *ex-* out, and *crēscere* to grow]

excrementa *eks-kri-men'tə* or *-kre-men'ta* (*L*; *pl* of **excrementum** *-təm* or *-tōōm*), *n pl* waste matter or rubbish.

excrescence *iks-kres'əns*, *n* an outgrowth or projection, *esp* abnormal, grotesque or offensive; a wart or tumour; a superfluous or unattractive part; outbreak. — *n* **excresc'ency** the state of being excrescent; an excrescence. — *adj* **excresc'ent** growing out; superfluous; of a sound or letter, added to a word for euphony, etc without etymological justification. — *adj* **excrescential** (*eks-kri-sen'shl*). [L *excrēscere*, from *ex-* out, and *crēscere* to grow]

excrete *eks-krēt'*, *vt* to discharge, *esp* from the bowels, bladder, sweat glands, etc; to eject in a similar or analagous manner. — *n pl* **excrē'ta** (*esp* waste) products discharged from the body. — *adj* **excre'tal**. — *n* **excre'ter**. — *n* **excrē'tion** the excreting of matter from an organism; that which is excreted. — *adj* **excrē'tive** able to excrete; concerned with excretion. — *adj* **excrē'tory** (or *eks'kri-tər-i*) having the quality or power of excreting. — *n* a duct that helps to receive and excrete matter. [L *ex* from, and *cernere*, *crētum* to separate]

excruciate *iks-kroo'shi-āt*, *vt* to torture; to rack; to inflict severe pain; to irritate greatly. — *adj* **excru'ciāting** extremely painful; racking; torturing; agonizing; intensely irritating (*fig*). — *adv* **excru'ciatingly**. — *n* **excruciā'tion** torture; irritation or annoyance. [L *excruciāre* to torture, from *ex-* out, and *cruciāre*, *-ātum* to crucify, from *crux*, *crucis* a cross]

excubant *eks'kū-bənt*, *adj* on guard. [L *excubāns*, *-antis*, pr p of *excubāre* to sleep out or lie on guard, from *ex* out, and *cubāre* to lie]

excudit *eks-kū'dit* or *-koo'*, (*L*) (he or she) struck, hammered, forged or printed (this).

exculpate *eks'kul-pāt*, also *-kul'*, *vt* to clear from the charge of a fault or crime; to absolve; to vindicate. — *adj* **excul'pable**. — *n* **exculpā'tion**. — *adj* **excul'patory** freeing from the charge of fault or crime. [L *ex* from, and *culpa* a fault]

ex curia *eks kū'ri-ə* or *koo'ri-ä*, (*L*) out of court.

excurrent *eks-kur'ənt*, *adj* having the main stem reaching to the top (*bot*); having the midrib reaching beyond the lamina (*bot*); flowing outwards (*zool*); carrying an outgoing current. [L *ex* from, and *currēns*, *-entis*, pr p of *currere* to run]

excursion *iks-kûr'shən* or *iks-kûr'zhən*, *n* a going out or forth; a deviation from the normal course; a pleasure trip; a group of people on a pleasure outing; a wandering from the main subject; rapid increase of reactor power above set operation level (*nuc eng*); a digression; an escapade; a raid; a sally. — Also *vi*. — *vi* **excurse'** (*archaic*) to digress. — *n* **excur'sionist** soemone who goes on a pleasure trip. — *vi* **excur'sionize** or **-ise** (*rare*) to go on an excursion. — *adj* **excur'sive** rambling; deviating from the main point or topic. — *adv* **excur'sively**. — *n* **excur'siveness**. — *n* **excur'sus** a dissertation or discussion on some particular matter appended to the main body of a book or chapter: — *pl* **excur'suses**. — **excursion fare** a special cheap fare allowed on certain journeys by public transport; **excursion ticket**; **excursion train** a special train, *usu* with reduced fares, for people making an excursion *esp* for pleasure. [L *ex-* out, and *currere*, *cursum* to run]

excuse *iks-kūz'*, *vt* to free from blame or guilt; to exonerate; to overlook or forgive; to pardon or condone (in small matters); to free (from an obligation); to release or dispense with temporarily; to allow to go out of one's presence; to seek to explain or justify a person or their actions; to make an apology or ask pardon for. — *vi* (*archaic*) to make excuse. — *n* (*iks-kūs'*) a plea offered in extenuation or explanation, in order to avoid punishment; pardon or forgiveness; indulgence. — *adj* **excūsable** (*iks-kūz'ə-bl*). — *n* **excūs'ableness**. — *adv* **excūs'ably**. — *n* **excūs'al**. — *adj* **excūs'atory** making or containing excuse; apologetic. — *n* **excus'er**. — *adj* **excusive** (*eks-kūs'iv*). — **be excused** to leave a room, etc; to go to the lavatory to relieve oneself (*euphem*); **excuse for** (*iks-kūs'*) a very poor example of; **excuse me** an expression used as an apology for any slight or apparent impropriety, *esp* as a request to pass, leave, interupt or catch someone's attention or for contradicting a statement that has been made; **excuse-me** or **excuse-me dance** a dance during which one may change partners; **excuse oneself** to ask permission and then leave; to explain and seek pardon (*for* a misdeed). [L *excūsāre*, from *ex* from, and *causa* a cause or accusation]

ex debito justitiae *eks deb'i-tō jəs-tish'i-ē* or *dā'bi-tō ūs-ti'ti-ī*, (*LL*) from what is due to justice.

ex delicto *eks di-lik'tō* or *dā-lik'tō*, (*LL*) owing to a crime.

ex-directory *eks-dī-rek'tə-ri*, or *-di-*, *adj* (of a telephone number) not listed in a directory; (of a person) having such a number. [**ex**[2] and **directory** (see **direct**)]

ex div or **ex-div** *eks('-)div'*. Short form of **ex dividend**, denoting a purchase of stocks and shares in which the seller and not the purchaser is entitled to the next payment of interest or dividends. [L *extra dividendum* without dividend]

ex dono *eks dō'nō*, (*L*) by gift, as a present from.

exeat *eks'i-at*, *n* formal leave of absence, *esp* for a student to be out of college for more than one night. [L, let him or her go out, 3rd pers sing pr subjunctive of *exīre*]

exec. *eg-zek'*, *abbrev*: executive; executor.

execrate *eks'i-krāt*, *vt* to curse; to utter evil against; to denounce; to detest. — *adj* **ex'ecrable** deserving execration; detestable; accursed; very bad or of low quality. — *n* **ex'ecrableness**. — *adv* **ex'ecrably**. — *n* **execrā'tion** the act of execrating; a curse pronounced; something which is execrated. — *adj* **ex'ecrātive** of or belonging to execration. — *adv* **ex'ecrātively**. — *adj* **ex'ecrātory**. [L *exsecrārī*, *-ātus* to curse, from *ex* from, and *sacer* sacred]

execute *eks'i-kūt*, *vt* to perform; to give effect to; to carry into effect; to put to use or bring into action; to put to death by law; to carry out the instructions in (a compiled version of a program), to run (a program) (*comput*). — *adj* **executable** (*eks'i-kūt-ə-bl* or *ek-sek'ūt-ə-bl*) that can be executed. — *n* **execūtancy** (*eg-zek'*) technique in music. — *n* **execūtant** (*eg-zek'*) someone who executes or performs; a technically accomplished performer of music. — *n* **execūter** (*eks'*). — *n* **execū'tion** the act of, or skill in, executing or performing; accomplishment; completion; the infliction of capital punishment; the carrying into effect of the sentence of a court of law; the warrant for so doing. — *n* **execū'tioner** a person who executes, *esp* one who carries out a sentence of death. — *adj* **executive** (*eg-zek'ū-tiv*) concerned with performance, administration or management; qualifying for or pertaining to the execution of the law; administrative; for the use of business executives; hence (loosely) expensive or sophisticated; active; designed or fitted to execute or perform. — *n* the power or authority in government that carries the laws into effect; the persons who administer the government or an organization; a person in an executive position in government or business; the head of an executive, eg a president, governor, mayor, etc (*US*; also **chief executive**). — *adv* **exec'ūtively**. — *n* **execūtor** (*eg-zek'*) a person who executes or performs; a person appointed by a testator to see a will carried into effect (*law*): — *fem* **exec'ūtrix** (*pl* **exec'ūtrixes** or **execūtrī'cēs**). — Also **exec'utress**. — *adj* **execūtō'rial**. — *n* **exec'ūtorship**. — *adj* **exec'ūtory** executing official duties; designed to be carried into effect. — *n* **exec'ūtry** executorship; moveable or heritable estate and effects (*Scots law*). — **execution error** (*comput*) a programming error which comes to light when the program is run (also called **run-time error**); **Executive Council** a ministerial council headed by the Governor (-General) (*Austr* and *NZ*); **executive officer** (in certain countries, eg US) a naval officer responsible for the general adminstration of a ship; **executive program** (*comput*) a program which controls the use of a computer and controls the running of compiled program; **executive session** (*US*) a meeting of the Senate for executive business, *usu* held in private; any meeting in private. [L *exsequī*, *exsecūtus*, from *ex* out, and *sequī* to follow]

exedra *eks'i-drə* or *eks-ed'rə*, *n* a portico, hall or vestibule; a seated room; a columned recess in classical Greek and Roman architecture, containing a continuous semicircular bench, used for holding discussions in; any outdoor bench in a recess; an apse, recess or niche. — Also **exhedra**: — *pl* **exedrae** or **exhedrae**. [L, from Gr *exedrā*, from *ex-* out, and *hedrā* seat]

exeem or **exeme** *eks-ēm'*, (*obs Scot*) *vt* to release or exempt. [L *eximere*, from *ex* from, and *emere* to take]

exegesis *eks-i-jē'sis*, *n* a critical interpretation of a text, *esp* Biblical. — *n* **ex'egēte** or **exegēt'ist** a person who interprets or expounds. — *adj* **exegetic** (*-jet'ik*) or **exeget'ical** pertaining to exegesis; explanatory. — *adv* **exeget'ically**. — *n sing* **exeget'ics** the science of exegesis. [Gr *exēgēsis*, from *exēgeesthai* to explain, from *ex-* out, and *hēgeesthai* to guide]

exeme. See **exeem**.

exempla. See **exemplum**.

exemplar *egz-em'plər* or *-plär*, *n* a person or thing to be imitated; the ideal model; a type; an example; a copy of a book or other text. — *adv* **exem'plarily**. — *n* **exem'plariness**. — *n* **exemplarity** (*-plar'*) exemplariness; exemplary conduct. — *adj* **exem'plary** worthy of imitation or notice; serving as model, specimen, illustration or warning. — **exemplary damages** (*law*) damages in excess of the value needed to compensate the plaintiff, awarded as a punishment to the offender (also called **punitive damages**). [L *exemplar*, from *exemplum* example]

exemple *eg-zãpl'*, (*Fr*) *n* example or model. — **par exemple** for example.

exemplify *igz-em'pli-fī*, *vt* to illustrate by example; to make an attested copy of; to prove by an attested copy: — *pr p* **exem'plifying**; *pa t* and *pa p* **exem'plified**. — *adj* **exem'plifiable**. — *n* **exemplificā'tion** the act of exemplifying; something which exemplifies; an attested copy or transcript. — *adj* **exemp'lificative**. — *n* **exemp'lifier**. [L *exemplum* example, and *facere* to make]

exempli gratia *ig-zem'plī grä'shi-ə* or *eks-em'plē grä'ti-ä*, (*L*) by way of example, for instance (*usu abbrev* **eg**).

exemplum *ig-zem'pləm*, *n* an example; a short story or anecdote illustrating a moral: — *pl* **exem'pla** (*-plə*). [L, example]

exempt *igz-empt'* or *-emt'*, *vt* to free, or grant immunity (from); to set apart (*Milton*). — *adj* taken out; (often with *from*) not liable (for) or subject (to); of goods and services, carrying no value-added tax, but on which tax charged by suppliers, etc cannot be reclaimed. — *n* an exempt person or organization; an officer who commanded in absence of his superiors, exempted on this account from ordinary duties (*hist*). — *n* **exemp'tion** the act of exempting; the state of being exempt; freedom from any service, duty, burden, etc; immunity. — **exemption clause** a contractual term or notice which attempts to exclude or restrict a person's liability; **exempt rating** a rating by which a business is exempted from charging or reclaiming VAT on the goods it supplies (the goods concerned being themselves exempted from VAT). — See also **zero-rating**; **exempt supplies** goods or services supplied by a business which do not require the business to charge VAT. [Fr, from L *eximere*, *exemptum*, from *ex* from, and *emere* to buy]

exenterate *eks-en'tər-āt*, (*obs*) *vt* to disembowel. — *adj* (*-it*) disembowelled. — *n* **exenterā'tion**. [L *exenterāre*, from Gr *exenterizein*, from *ex* from, and *enteron* intestine]

exequatur *eks-i-kwā'tər*, *n* an official recognition of a consul or commercial agent given by the government of the country in which he or she is to be based. [L *exequātur* let him execute, from the opening word]

exequy *eks'i-kwi* (*usu* in *pl* **exequies** *-kwiz*), *n* a funeral procession; funeral rites. — *adj* **exequial** (*eks-ē'kwi-əl*). [L *exequiae*, from *ex* from, and *sequī* to follow]

exercise *eks'ər-sīz*, *n* exertion of the body for health or amusement or the acquisition of a skill; a similar exertion of the mind; a task designed or prescribed for these purposes; a putting in practice; a written school task; a study in music; a set of problems, passages for translation, etc in a text-book; an academic disputation; accomplishment (*Shakesp*); (in *pl*) military drill or manoeuvres; a ceremony or formal proceeding (*NAm*); an act of worship or devotion; a discourse, *esp* the discussion of a passage of Scripture, giving the coherence of text and context, etc (the *addition* giving the doctrinal propositions, etc); a meeting of a presbytery for this purpose; hence, formerly, the presbytery itself. — *vt* to put in practice; to use; to train by use; to improve by practice; to give exercise to; to trouble; to wield. — *vi* to take exercise; to drill. — *adj* **ex'ercisable**. — *n* **ex'erciser** someone who or something which exercises; a device, *usu* with elasticated cords, to help in exercising the muscles. — **ex'ercise-book** a book for writing school exercises in. — **the object of the exercise** the purpose of a particular operation or activity. [OFr *exercice*, from L *exercitium*, from L *exercēre*, *-citum*, from *ex-* and *arcēre* to shut up or restrain]

exercitation *egz-ûr-sit-ā'shən*, *n* putting into practice; employment; exercise; a discourse. [L *exercitātiō*, *-ōnis*, from *exercēre* to exercise]

exergonic *eks-ûr-gon'ik*, *adj* of a biochemical reaction, accompanied by the release of energy and therefore capable of proceeding spontaneously. [Ety as for **exergue**]

exergue *eks'* or *eks-ûrg'*, *n* a part on the reverse of a coin, below the main device, often filled up by the date, etc. — *adj* **exer'gual**. [Fr, from Gr *ex* out of, and *ergon* work]

exert *igz-ûrt'*, *vt* to cause (oneself) to make a strenuous (*esp* physical) effort; to bring into active operation; to put forth (*obs*); to do or perform (*obs*). — *n* **exer'tion** a bringing into active operation; striving; strenuous activity. — *adj* **exert'ive** having the power or tendency to exert; using exertion. [L *exserere*, *exsertum*, from *ex* from, and *serere* to put together]

exes *eks'əz*, *n pl* a slang abbreviation of **expenses**; see also **ex** under **ex-**.

exeunt *eks'i-unt* or *-ŏŏnt*, (*stage direction*) (they) go out or leave the stage. — **exeunt omnes** (*om'nēz* or *-nās*) all go out. [L; see **exit**]

exfoliate *eks-fō'li-āt*, *vt* (of skin, bark, rocks, etc) to shed in flakes or layers; to remove in flakes, etc. — *vi* to come off in flakes; to separate into layers. — *n* **exfoliā'tion**. — *adj* **exfō'liative**. — *n* **exfō'liātor** an exfoliating agent. — **exfoliative cytology** (*biol*) the study for diagnostic purposes of cells shed from internal body surfaces. [L *exfoliāre*, *-ātum* to strip of leaves, from *ex* from, and *folium* a leaf]

ex gratia *eks grā'shi-ə* or *grä'ti-ä*, (*L*) as an act of grace; given or made as a favour, not out of obligation, and with no acceptance of liability (as *ex gratia payment*). — *abbrev* **ex gr**.

exhale[1] *eks-hāl'* or *egz-āl'*, *vt* to breathe forth; to emit or send out (as) a vapour, smell, etc; to cause or allow to evaporate; to emit through a membrane (*pathol*). — *vi* to breathe out; to rise or come off as a vapour, smell or emanation; to evaporate; to ooze out. — *adj* **exhāl'able**. — *adj* **exhāl'ant** exhaling; emitting vapour or liquid. — *n* an organ or vessel that emits vapour or liquid. — *n* **exhalation** (*eks-* or *egz-ə-lā'shən*) the act or process of exhaling; evaporation; anything exhaled, vapour, effluvium or emanation; a mist; a meteoric phenomenon, a meteor (*archaic*). [L *exhālāre*, from *ex* from, and *hālāre*, *-ātum* to breathe]

exhale[2] *eks-hāl'*, (*Shakesp*) *vt* to hale or draw out. [**ex-** and **hale**[2]]

exhaust *igz-öst'*, *vt* to draw off; to draw out the whole of; to use the whole strength of; to use up; to empty; to wear or tire out; to treat of or develop completely (an idea, theme, etc). — *vi* of exhaust gases in an engine, to be emitted. — *n* an outward current, or means of producing it; the exit of gases or fluids as waste products from the cylinder of an engine, a turbine, etc; the period of discharge of the gases or fluids; the gases or fluids so escaping (**exhaust gas** or **exhaust steam**). — *adj* **exhaust'ed** drawn out; emptied; consumed; tired out. — *n* **exhaust'er** someone or something that exhausts. — *adj* **exhaust'ible** that can be exhausted. — *n* **exhaustibil'ity**. — *n* **exhaustion** (*-öst'yən*) the act of exhausting or consuming; the state of being exhausted; extreme fatigue. — *adj* **exhaust'ive** tending to exhaust; investigating all parts or possibilities; thorough. — *adv* **exhaust'ively**. — *n* **exhaust'iveness**. — *adj* **exhaust'less** that cannot be exhausted. — **exhaust pipe** or **exhaust valve** the pipe or valve through which exhaust gases pass out. [L *exhaurīre*, *exhaustum*, from *ex* from, and *haurīre* to draw]

exhedra. See **exedra**.

exheredate *eks-her'i-dāt*, (*rare*) *vt* to disinherit. — *n* **exheredā'tion**. [L *exhērēdāre*, from *ex* out, and *hērēs*, *-ēdis* heir]

exhibit *igz-ib'it*, *vt* to hold forth or display; to present formally or publicly; to show or manifest (a quality, etc); to give as a remedy (*med*; *archaic*). — *n* a document or object produced in court to be used as evidence (*law*); something exhibited; an article at an exhibition. — *n* **exhib'iter**. — *n* **exhibition** (*eks-i-bish'ən*) presentation to view; display; showing off; a public show, *esp* of works of art, manufactures, etc; that which is exhibited; a public performance at the end of a school year; a grant or gift; an allowance towards support, *esp* to students at a university; the administration of a remedy (*archaic*). — *n* **exhibi'tioner** a university student who has been awarded an exhibition at a university. — *n* **exhibi'tionism** extravagant behaviour aimed at drawing attention to oneself; perversion involving public exposure of one's sexual organs (*psychiatry*). — *n* **exhibi'tionist**. — *adj* **exhibitionist'ic**. — *adv* **exhibitionist'ically**. — *adj* **exhib'itive** (*igz-*) serving for exhibition; representative. — *adv* **exhib'itively**. — *n* **exhibitor** (*igz-ib'i-tər*). — *adj* **exhib'itory** exhibiting. — **make an exhibition of oneself** to behave foolishly, making oneself ridiculous. [L *exhibēre*, *-itum*, from *ex-* out, and *habēre*, *-itum* to have]

exhilarate *igz-il'ə-rāt*, *vt* to make hilarious or merry; to raise the spirits of; to refresh the body and mind of; to enliven; to cheer. — *adj* **exhil'arant** exhilarating; exciting joy, mirth or pleasure. — *n* an exhilarating medicine. — *adj* **exhil'arāting** cheering; gladdening. — *adv* **exhil'arātingly**. — *n* **exhilarā'tion** the state of being exhilarated; joyousness. — *adj* **exhil'arātive** or **exhil'aratory**. — *n* **exhil'arātor**. [L *exhilarāre*, *-ātum*, from *ex-* (intens), and *hilaris* cheerful]

exhort *ig-zört'*, *vt* to urge strongly and earnestly; to counsel. — *n* **exhortā'tion** (*eks-* or *egz-*) the act of exhorting; language, speech or writing intended to exhort; counsel; a religious discourse. — *adj* **exhort'ative** or **exhort'atory** (*igz-*) tending to exhort or advise. — *n* **exhort'er** someone who exhorts; in some churches a layman appointed to give religious exhortation. [L *exhortārī*, *-ātus*, from *ex-* (intens), and *hortārī* to urge]

exhume *eks-hūm'* or *ig-zūm'*, *vt* to take out of the ground or place of burial; to disinter; to bring back into use; to bring to light; to bring up or mention again. — Also **exhumate** (*eks'hūm-āt*). — *n* **exhumā'tion** (*eks-*). — *n* **exhum'er**. [L *ex* out of, and *humus* the ground]

ex hypothesi *eks hī-poth'ə-sī*, (*LL*) from the hypothesis.

exies *ek'sāz*, (*Scot*) *n pl* a fit, eg of hysterics or ague. [**access**]

exigent *eks'i-jənt*, *adj* pressing; urgent; exacting; demanding immediate attention or action. — *n* extremity (*obs*); the last strait, the end of all (*Shakesp*); a needed amount (*Browning*). — *adj* **exigeant** (*egz-ē-zhã*; *Fr*) exacting: — *fem* **exigeante** (*-zhãt*). — *n* **ex'igence** or **ex'igency** (or *-ij'*) pressing necessity; emergency; distress. — *adv* **ex'igently**. [L *exigēns*, *-entis*, from pr p of *exigere*, from *ex-*, and *agere* to drive]

exigible *eks'i-jib-l*, *adj* liable to be exacted. [See ety for **exact**]

exiguous *egz-*, *eks-ig'ū-əs*, *adj* scanty; slender. — *adv* **exig'uously**. — *n* **exigū'ity** (*eks-*). — *n* **exig'ūousness**. [L *exiguus*, from *exigere* to weigh strictly; see **exact**]

exile *eks'* or *egz'īl*, *n* enforced or regretted absence from one's country or home; banishment; (with *cap*) the captivity of the Jews in Babylon (in these senses formerly *egz-īl'*); someone who is in exile; a banished person. — *vt* (formerly *egz-īl'*) to expel from one's country, to banish. — *n* **ex'ilement** (*rare*) banishment. — *adj* **exilic** (*egz-il'ik* or *eks-*) or **exil'ian** pertaining to exile, *esp* that of the Jews in Babylon. [OFr *exil*, from L *exsilium* banishment, from *ex* out of, and root of *salīre* to leap; affected by L *exsul* an exile]

exility *egz-* or *eks-il'i-ti*, (*obs*) *n* slenderness or smallness; refinement. [L *exīlitās*, *-ātis*, from *exīlis* slender]

eximious *eg-zim'i-əs*, (*archaic*) *adj* excellent or distinguished. — *adv* **exim'iously**. [L *eximius*, from *eximere*, from *ex* from, and *emere* to take]

ex improviso *eks im-prə-vī'zō* or *im-prō-vē'sō*, also *-wē'*, (*L*) unexpectedly.

exine *eks'in* or *-īn*. See **extine**. [L *ex* out of]

ex int. (*banking*) *abbrev*: *ex interest*, without interest. [L *ex* without]

exist *igz-ist'*, *vi* to have actual being; to live; to occur; to continue to live, *esp* in unfavourable circumstances. — *n* **exist'ence** the state of existing or being; livelihood; life; anything and everything that exists; being. — *adj* **exist'ent** having being; now existing. — *adj* **existential** (*eks-is-ten'shəl*) of or relating to (*esp* human) existence; of or relating to existentialism. — *n* **existen'tialism** a term covering a number of related philosophical doctrines denying objective universal values and holding that people, as moral free agents, must create values for themselves through actions and must accept the ultimate responsibility for those actions in the seemingly meaningless universe. — *n* and *adj* **existen'tialist**. — *adv* **existen'tially**. [L *existere*, *exsistere* to stand forth, from *ex-* out, and *sistere* to stand]

Exit *ek'sit* or *eg'zit*, *n* a British organization encouraging voluntary euthanasia, and campaigning for its legislation.

exit *ek'sit* or *eg'zit*, *n* the departure of a player from the stage; any departure; a passage out; a way of departure; death (*literary*); a place on a motorway where vehicles can leave by a slip road; the last instruction of a subroutine (*comput*): — *pl* **ex'its**. — *vi* to make an exit; to leave or depart; to die (*literary*); to lose the lead deliberately (*cards*): — *pa p* and *pa t* **ex'ited**. — *n* **ex'itance** (*phys*) the amount per unit area of light or other radiation emitted from a surface. — **exit poll** a poll of a sample of voters, taken as they leave the polling-station, used to give an early indication of voting trends in a particular election. [Partly from the L stage direction *exit* goes out (in pl *exeunt* go out), from *exīre* to go out, from *ex-* out, and *īre*, *itum* to go; partly from L *exitus* a way out]

ex lib *eks lib*, *abbrev*: *ex libris* (*L*), from the books (of X) (eg on bookplates). — *n* **ex-libris** (*eks-lī'bris* or *-li'*) a name-label pasted into the front of a book, a bookplate. — *n* **ex-li'brism**. — *n* **ex-li'brist** a collector or student of bookplates. [L *ex librīs* from the books (of so-and-so)]

ex mero motu *eks mē'rō mō'tū* or *me'rō mō'to͞o*, (*L*) from his or her own impulse; of his, her or its own accord.

ex natura rei *eks na-tū'rə rē'ī* or *na-to͞o'ra re'ē*, (*LL*) from the nature of the case; **ex natura rerum** (*rē'rəm* or *rā'ro͞om*) from the nature of things.

ex nihilo *eks nī'hi-lō* or *ni'*, (*L*) out of nothing, eg in *creation ex nihilo*.

exo- *eks'ō-* or *eks-o'-*, *combining form* outside (often *opp* to **endo-** or **ento-**; see also **ecto-**). — *adj* **exobiolog'ical**. — *n* **exobiol'ogy** the study of (possible) extraterrestrial life. — *n* **exobiol'ogist**. — *n* **ex'ocarp** (Gr *karpos* fruit; *bot*) the outer layer of the part of a fruit which contains the seeds; the epicarp. — *adj* **ex'ocrine** (Gr *krīnein* to separate; *physiol*) of glands, secreting through a duct. — *n* an exocrine gland. — *n* **exocytō'sis** (*biol*) the discharge from a cell of particles too large to diffuse throught the wall. — *n* **ex'oderm** exodermis; ectoderm. — *adj* **exoderm'al**. — *n* **exoder'mis** (Gr *dermis* skin) the outer cortex layer of a root. — *n* **exoen'zyme** an enzyme that functions outside the cell producing it, an ectoenzyme. — *adj* **exoergic** (*-ûr'jik*; Gr *ergon* work; *nuc eng*) of a process in which energy is released. — *n* **exog'amy** (Gr *gamos* marriage) the practice of marrying only outside of one's own group; the union of gametes not closely related (*biol*). — *adj* **exogam'ic** or **exog'amous**. — *n* **ex'ogen** (*obs*) a dicotyledon, so called because its stem thickens by layers growing on the outside of the wood. — *adj* **exogenet'ic** (*med*) not genetic, not caused by genetic factors. — *adj* **exog'enous** growing by successive additions to the outside; developing externally; having an external origin. — *n* **ex'onym** (Gr *onoma* a name) a name for a town, country, etc in a foreign language. —

n **exoph'agy** (Gr *phagein* to eat) the custom among cannibals of eating only the flesh of persons not of their own kin. — *adj* **exoph'agous**. — *n* **ex'oplasm** ectoplasm. — *n* **exop'odite** or **ex'opod** (Gr *pous*, *podos* foot) the outer branch of a crustacean limb. — *adj* **exopod'itic**. — *n* **exoskel'eton** a hard supporting or protective structure secreted externally by the ectoderm. — *adj* **exoskel'etal**. — *n* **ex'osphere** (Gr *sphaira* sphere) the outermost layer of the earth's atmosphere; the boundary of the earth's atmosphere and interplanetary space. — *adj* **exospher'ic** or **exospher'ical**. — *n* **ex'ospore** (Gr *sporos* a seed) the outer layer of a spore wall; a spore formed by abstriction, not within a mother-cell. — *adj* **exospor'al**. — *adj* **exospor'ous**. — *adj* **exother'mal** or **exother'mic** (Gr *thermē* heat; *chem*) involving evolution of heat. — *adv* **exother'mally** or **exother'mically**. — *n* **exothermi'city**. — *adj* **exotox'ic**. — *n* **exotox'in** (*biol*) a toxin produced by a micro-organism and secreted into the surrounding medium. [Gr *exō* outside]

Exocet® *eks'ə-set*, *n* a subsonic tactical missile, launched from ship, plane or submarine and travelling at low altitude. [Fr, from New L *Exocoetus volitans* the flying fish]

Exod. (*Bible*) *abbrev*: (the Book of) Exodus.

exode *ek'sōd*, *n* the concluding part of a Greek drama; a farce or afterpiece. [Gr *exodion*]

exodus *eks'ə-dəs*, *n* a going out, *esp* that of the Israelites from Egypt; (with *cap*) the second book of the Old Testament. — *adj* **exodic** (*-od'*). — *n* **ex'odist** a person who goes out; an emigrant. [L, from Gr *exodos*, from *ex-* out, and *hodos* a way]

ex officio *eks o-fish'i-ō* or *-fik'*, (*L*) by virtue of office or position. — *abbrev* **ex off.**

exomis *eks-ō'mis*, *n* a one-sleeved or (in Rome) sleeveless garment (also *Browning* **exo'mion**). [Gr *exōmis*, from *ex-* out, and *ōmos* shoulder]

Exon. *abbrev*: *Exonia* (*L*), Exeter; *Exoniensis* (*L*), of Exeter.

exon[1] *eks'on*, *n* one of the four commanding officers of the Yeomen of the Guard. [Appar intended to express the pronunciation of Fr *exempt* (see **exempt**)]

exon[2] *eks'on*, (*biol*) *n* any segment of a gene which consists of codons (*opp* of *intron*). — *adj* **exon'ic**. [L *ex* out of, and Gr neuter sfx *-on*]

exonerate *igz-on'ər-āt*, *vt* to free from the burden of blame or obligation; to acquit. — *n* **exonerā'tion** the act of exonerating. — *adj* **exon'erative** freeing from a burden or obligation. — *n* **exon'erator**. [L *exonerāre*, *-ātum*, from *ex* from, and *onus*, *oneris* burden]

ex opere operato, **ex opere operantis**. See under **opus**.

exophthalmia *eks-of-thal'mi-ə*, **exophthalmos** or **exophthalmus** *eks-of-thal'məs*, (*pathol*) *n* a protrusion of the eyeballs. — *adj* **exophthal'mic**. — **exophthalmic goitre** a form of hyperthyroidism marked by exophthalmia and swelling of the thyroid gland. [Gr *ex* out, and *ophthalmos* eye]

exor *abbrev*: executor.

exorable *eks'ər-ə-bl*, *adj* capable of being moved by entreaty. — *n* **exorabil'ity**. — *n* **exorā'tion** (*obs*) entreaty. [L *exōrāre*, from *ex-* thoroughly, and *ōrāre* to entreat]

exorbitant *igz-ör'bi-tənt*, *adj* going beyond the usual limits; excessive. — *n* **exor'bitance** or **exor'bitancy** great excess. — *adv* **exor'bitantly**. — *vi* **exor'bitate** (*obs*) to stray. [L *exorbitāns*, *-antis*, pr p of *exorbitāre*, from *ex* out of, and *orbita* a track, from *orbis* a circle]

exorcize or **-ise** *eks'ör-sīz*, *vt* to call forth or drive away (a spirit); to deliver from the influence of an evil spirit; to command by some holy name. — *n* **ex'orcism** (*-sizm*) the act of exorcizing or expelling evil spirits by certain ceremonies; a formula for exorcizing. — *n* **ex'orcist** a person who exorcizes or pretends to expel evil spirits by command (also **ex'orcīzer** or **-s-**); the third of the minor orders (*RC*). [LL from Gr *exorkizein*, from *ex-* out, and *horkos* an oath]

exordium *egz-ör'di-əm*, *n* an introductory part, *esp* of a discourse or composition: — *pl* **exor'diums** or **exor'dia**. — *adj* **exor'dial** pertaining to the exordium; introductory. [L, from *exordīrī*, from *ex* out of, and *ordīrī* to begin]

exosmosis *eks-os-mō'sis* or *eks-oz-*, *n* osmosis outwards, ie away from the solution (also **ex'osmose** *-mōs*). — *adj* **exosmotic** (*-mot'ik*). [Gr *ex-* out, and **osmosis**]

exostosis *eks-os-tō'sis*, (*anatom*) *n* abnormal enlargement of a bone: — *pl* **exostō'ses** (*-sēz*). [Gr *exostōsis*, from *ex-* out, and *osteon* a bone]

exoteric *eks-ō-ter'ik*, *adj* external (*obs*); intelligible to the uninitiated; popular or commonplace (*opp* to *esoteric*). — *adj* **exoter'ical**. — *adv* **exoter'ically**. — *n* **exoter'icism** (*-sizm*). [Gr *exōterikos*, from *exōterō* compar of *exō* outside]

exotic *igz-ot'ik*, *adj* introduced from a foreign country; alien (also *fig*); applied to various high-energy fuels used eg to propel rockets; foreign-looking; outlandish; romantically strange, rich and showy, or glamorous; pertaining to striptease or belly-dancing. — *n* anything of foreign origin; something not native to a country, such as a plant, a word or a custom; an exotic dancer. — *n pl* **exot'ica** exotic objects; theatrical or musical items with an unusual theme or with a foreign flavour. — *adv* **exot'ically**. — *n* **exot'icism** (*-sizm*). — *n* **exot'icness**. — **exotic dancer** a striptease artist or belly-dancer. [Gr *exōtikos*, from *exō* outside]

exp. *abbrev*: expired; exponential; export; exporter; express.

expand *iks-pand'*, *vt* to spread out; to lay open; to enlarge in bulk or surface area; to develop or bring out in fuller detail; to express at length, as in terms of a series or without contractions. — *vi* to become opened; to increase in volume; to enlarge; to spread; to become communicative (*fig*); to speak or write more fully (on). — *n* **expandabil'ity**. — *adj* **expand'able**. — *n* **expand'er** or **expand'or** an electronic device which increases the range of amplitude variations in a transmission system. — *n* **expanse** (*-pans'*) a wide extent; a stretch; the amount of spread or stretch; the firmament. — *n* **expansibil'ity**. — *adj* **expans'ible** capable of being expanded. — *adv* **expans'ibly**. — *adj* **expans'ile** (*-īl*) capable of expansion. — *n* **expan'sion** the act of expanding; the state of being expanded; enlargement; something which is expanded; amount of expanding; territorial extension; immensity; extension. — *adj* **expan'sional**. — *adj* **expan'sionary** tending to expand. — *n* **expan'sionism** the principle or practice of expanding the territory or the economy of a country. — *n* **expan'sionist** someone who favours territorial or currency expansion. — Also *adj*. — *adj* **expansionist'ic**. — *adj* **expans'ive** widely extended; diffusive; causing expansion; worked by expansion; effusive; talkative or communicative; marked by excessive feeling of well-being and delusions of self-importance (*psychiatry*). — *adv* **expans'ively**. — *n* **expans'iveness**. — *n* **expansiv'ity** (*eks-*). — **expanded metal** steel, etc stretched to form a mesh, used for reinforcing concrete, etc; **expanded plastic** (*esp* **expanded polystyrene**) foam plastic (or polystyrene); **expanding metal** a metal or alloy that expands in the final stage of cooling from liquid; **expanding universe (theory)** (*astron*) the theory that the whole universe is constantly expanding and the galaxies moving away from each other; **expansion board** or **card** (*comput*) a printed circuit board which can be inserted into an **expansion slot**, a connector in a computer which allows extra facilities to be added temporarily or permanently; **expansion bolt** a bolt that expands within a hole, crack, etc, thus providing a firm support, eg in mountaineering; **expansion joint** (*eng*) a gap left at a joint between eg lengths of rail or sections of concrete, to allow for heat expansion. [L *expandere*, from *ex-* out, and *pandere*, *pānsum* to spread]

ex parte *eks pär'tē* or *pär'tè*, (*law*) *adj* on one side only, or in the interests of one party only; partial; prejudiced. [L *ex* from, and *parte*, ablative of *pars*, *partis* party or side]

expat *eks'pat*, *n* short for **expatriate**.

expatiate *eks-pā'shi-āt*, *vi* to walk about (*archaic*); to wander at large (*usu fig*); to enlarge in discourse, argument or writing. — *n* **expatiā'tion**. — *adj* **expā'tiative** or **expā'tiatory** expansive. — *n* **expā'tiātor**. [L *exspatiārī*, *-ātus*, from *ex* out of, and *spatiārī* to roam, from *spatium* space]

expatriate *eks-pā'tri-āt* or *-pa'*, *vt* to send out of one's country; to banish or exile (oneself or another); to deprive of citizenship. — Also *adj* (*-tri-ət*). — *n* an exile, voluntary or compulsory; a person who lives abroad permanently, for financial or other reasons; a person working abroad for a period. — *n* **expatriā'tion** the act of expatriating; exile, voluntary or compulsory. [LL *expatriāre*, *-ātum*, from *ex* out of, and *patria* fatherland]

expect *iks-pekt'*, *vt* to await (*obs*); to look forward to as likely to come or happen, or as due; to suppose. — *vi* (*obs*) to wait. — *n* (*Shakesp*) expectation. — *adj* **expect'able**. — *adv* **expect'ably**. — *n* **expect'ance** or **expect'ancy** the act or state of expecting; something which is expected; hope. — *adj* **expect'ant** looking or waiting for something; in expectation; not yet but expecting to be; pregnant. — *n* a person who expects; a person who is looking or waiting for some benefit or office. — *adv* **expect'antly**. — *n* **expectā'tion** (*eks-*) the act or state of expecting; the prospect of future good; that which is or may fairly be expected; that which should happen, according to general norms of custom or behaviour; the degree of probability; the value of something expected; (in *pl*) prospect of fortune or profit by a will. — *adj* **expect'ative** giving rise to expectation; reversionary. — *n* an expectancy; an anticipatory grant of a benefice not yet vacant. — *adj* **expect'ed**. — *adv* **expect'edly**. — *n* **expect'er**. — *n* and *adj* **expect'ing**. — *adv* **expect'ingly** in a state of expectation. — **Expectation Week** (*Christian relig*, *esp Ch of Eng*) the period between Ascension Day and Whit Sunday, commemorating the Apostles' expectation of the Holy Spirit. — **be expecting** (*colloq*) to be pregnant; **life expectancy** or **expectation of life** the average length of time that one may expect to live. [L *expectāre*, *-ātum*, from *ex* out, and *spectāre* to look, frequentative of *specere* to see]

expectorate *eks-pek'tə-rāt*, *vt* to expel from the chest, air-passages or lungs by coughing, etc; to spit out. — *vi* to discharge or eject phlegm from the throat; to spit. — *adj* **expec'torant** tending to promote expectoration. — *n* a medicine that promotes expectoration. — *n* **expectorā'tion** the act of expectorating; something which is expectorated; spittle or phlegm. — *adj* **expec'torātive** having the quality of promoting expectoration. — *n* **expec'torātor**. [L *expectorāre*, *-ātum*, from *ex* from, and *pectus*, *pectoris* breast]

expedient *iks-pē'di-ənt*, *adj* suitable or appropriate; profitable or convenient rather than fair or just; advisable; expeditious (*Shakesp*). — *n* a means suitable to an end; something which serves to promote; contrivance or shift. — *n* **expē'dience** haste or despatch (*Shakesp*); enterprise (*Shakesp*); expediency. — *n* **expē'diency** appropriateness; desirableness; conduciveness to the need of the moment; something which is opportune; self-interest. — *adj* **expēdien'tial** (*-en'shl*). — *adv* **expedien'tially**. — *adv* **expē'diently**. [L *expediēns*, *-entis*, pr p of *expedīre* (see **expedite**)]

expeditate *eks-ped'it-āt*, *vt* to deprive of three claws or of the ball of the foot. — *n* **expeditā'tion**. [LL *expeditāre*, *-ātum*, from *ex* from, and *pēs*, *pedis* foot]

expedite *eks'pi-dīt*, *vt* to free from impediments; to hasten; to send forth; to despatch with speed and efficiency. — *adj* (*obs*) free from impediment; unencumbered; quick; prompt. — *adv* **ex'peditely**. — *n* **ex'pediter** or **ex'peditor**. — *n* **expedition** (*-di'shən*) speed; promptness; an organized journey to attain some object, such as hunting, warfare, exploration, etc; the party undertaking such a journey. — *adj* **expedi'tionary** belonging to an expedition; of the nature of an expedition. — *adj* **expedi'tious** characterized by expedition or rapidity; speedy; prompt. — *adv* **expedi'tiously**. — *n* **expedi'tiousness**. — *adj* **exped'itive**. [L *expedīre*, *-ītum*, from *ex* from, and *pēs*, *pedis* a foot]

expel *iks-pel'*, *vt* to drive out; to eject; to discharge in disgrace (from school, etc); to banish; to keep off (*Shakesp*): — *pr p* **expell'ing**; *pa t* and *pa p* **expelled'**. — *adj* and *n* **expell'ant** or **expell'ent**. — *n* **expellee'** a person who is expelled. [L *expellere*, *expulsum*, from *ex* from, and *pellere* to drive]

expend *iks-pend'*, *vt* to lay out (money); to employ or consume in any way; to spend. — *adj* **expend'able** that may be expended, *esp* that may be sacrificed to achieve some end. — Also *n*. — *n* **expendabil'ity**. — *n* **expen'der**. — *n* **expend'iture** the act of expending; something which is expended; the process of using up; money spent. — *n* **expense** (*-pens'*) expenditure; outlay; cost; a payment, debt or amount of an asset used up in the course of business activity during a particular accounting period; (in *pl*) money from one's own pocket spent in the performance of one's job, etc; such money reimbursed by one's company, etc or an allowance made to cover the amount usually spent; (in *pl*; *Scots law*) costs in a lawsuit. — *adj* **expens'ive** causing or requiring much expense; costly; lavish. — *adv* **expens'ively**. — *n* **expens'iveness**. — **expendable launch vehicle** (*space flight*) a launch system that is made up of expendable stages and has no recoverable parts (*abbrev* **ELV**); **expense** (or **expenses**) **account** an arrangement by which expenses incurred during the performance of an employee's duties are reimbursed by the employer (sometimes with the implication that the employee claims far more than is justified); a statement of such incurred expenses. — **at the expense of** to the cost or detriment of (often **at someone's expense**); with the loss or sacrifice of; **be at the expense of** to pay the cost (of). [L *expendere*, from *ex-* out, and *pendere*, *pēnsum* to weigh]

experience *iks-pē'ri-əns*, *n* test, trial or experiment (*obs*); practical acquaintance with any matter gained by trial; long and varied observation, personal or general; wisdom derived from the changes and trials of life; the passing through any event or course of events by which one is affected; such an event; anything received by the mind, such as sensation, perception or knowledge. — *vt* to have practical acquaintance with; to prove or know by use; to have experience of; to feel, suffer or undergo. — *adj* **expē'rienced** taught by experience; having much experience; practised and knowledgeable in sexual matters (*facetious*); skilful; wise. — *adj* **expē'rienceless** having little or no experience. — *adj* **expērien'tial** (*-en'shl*) pertaining to or derived from experience. — *n* **expērien'tialism** the philosophical doctrine that all knowledge comes from experience. — *n* **expērien'tialist**. — *adv* **expērien'tially**. — **experience meeting** a meeting for the relating of religious experiences. [Fr *expérience* and L *experientia*, from *experīrī*, from *ex-* (intens), and old verb *perīrī* to try]

experiment *iks-per'i-mənt*, *n* something done to test a theory or to discover something unknown; a trial; experience (*obs*). — *vi* (also *-ment'*) to make an experiment or trial; to search by trial. — *vt* (*obs*) to make trial of. — *adj* **experiment'al** pertaining to experiment; based on or proceeding by experiment; trying out new styles or techniques; tentative; experienced, having experience (*obs*). — *n* **experiment'alism** use of or reliance on experiment. — *n* **experiment'alist**. — *vi* **experiment'alize** or **-ise**. — *adv* **experiment'ally**. — *n* **experimentā'tion**. — *adj* **experiment'ative**. — *adj* **exper'imented** (*obs*) experienced; practised. — *n* **exper'imenter** (or *-ment'*) or **exper'imentist** a person who makes experiments. [L *experīmentum*, from *experīrī* to try thoroughly; see **experience**]

experimentum crucis *iks-per-i-men'təm kroo͞'sis* or *eks-pe-ri-men'to͞om kroo͞'kis*, (*L*) *n* a crucial test.

expert *eks'pûrt*, *adj* taught by practice; having a thorough knowledge; having a facility of performance (with *at* or *in*); skilful or adroit (with *at* or *in*). — *vt* (*Spenser*) to experience. — *n* someone who is skilled in any art or science; a specialist; a scientific or professional witness. — *n* **expertise** (*-ēz'*) expert knowledge; expertness; expert appraisal or valuation. — *vi* and *vt* **ex'pertize** or **-ise** (*-īz*) to give an expert opinion (on). — *adv* **ex'pertly**. — *n* **ex'pertness**. — **expert system** (*comput*) a program which enables a specific field of human knowledge to be stored in the form of facts and rules and uses artificial intelligence techniques to make decisions or solve problems. [Fr, from L *expertus*, from *experīrī* to try thoroughly; see **experience**]

expiate *eks'pi-āt*, *vt* to make complete atonement for; to make satisfaction or reparation for. — *adj* (*Shakesp*) expired or at an end. — *adj* **ex'piable** capable of being expiated, atoned for or done away with. — *n* **expiā'tion** the act of expiating; the means by which atonement is made; atonement. — *n* **ex'piātor**. — *adj* **ex'piatory** (*-ə-* or *-ā-tər-i*). [L *expiāre*, *-ātum*, from *ex-* (intens), and *piāre* to appease or atone for]

expire *iks-* or *eks-pīr'*, *vt* to breathe out; to emit; to bring to an end (*Spenser*). — *vi* to breathe out; to die; to come to an end; to lapse; to become invalid by lapse of time; to fulfil a term (*Spenser*). — *adj* **expī'rable** that may expire or come to an end. — *n* **expī'rant** someone expiring. — *n* **expirā'tion** (*eks-pi-* or *-pī-*) the act of breathing out; death (*obs*); end; something which is expired. — *adj* **expī'ratory** pertaining to expiration or the emission of the breath. — *adj* **expīred'** dead; extinct; lapsed; obsolete. — *adj* **expī'ring** dying; pertaining to or uttered at the time of dying. — *n* **expī'ry** the end or termination, *esp* by lapse of time; expiration. [Fr *expirer*, from L *ex* from, and *spīrāre*, *-ātum* to breathe]

expiscate *eks-pis'kāt*, (*Scot*) *vt* to find out by skilful means or by strict examination. — *n* **expiscā'tion**. — *adj* **expis'catory**. [L *expiscārī*, *expiscātus*, from *ex* from, and *piscārī* to fish, from *piscis* a fish.

explain *iks-plān'*, *vt* to make plain or intelligible; to unfold and illustrate the meaning of; to expound; to account for. — *vi* to give an explanation. — *adj* **explain'able**. — *n* **explain'er**. — *n* **explana'tion** (*eks-plə-nā'shən*) the act of explaining or clearing from obscurity; that which explains or clears up; the meaning or sense given to anything; a mutual clearing up of matters, reconciliation. — *adv* **explan'atorily** (*iks-plan'ə-tər-i-li*). — *adj* **explan'atory** or **explan'ative** serving to explain or clear up; containing explanations. — **explain away** to modify the force of by explanation, generally in a bad sense. [L *explānāre*, from *ex-* out, and *plānāre* to level, from *plānus* flat or plain]

explantation *eks-plän-tā'shən*, *n* the culture in an artificial medium of a part or organ removed from a living individual. — *n* and *vt* **explant'**. [L *explantāre*, from *ex-* out, and *plantāre* to plant]

expletive *eks-* or *iks-plē'tiv*, or *eks'pli-tiv*, *adj* filling out; added merely to fill up (a line of verse). — *n* a swear-word of any kind; a meaningless oath; a word or anything present merely to fill a gap; a word inserted to fill up a sentence or line of verse; a meaningless word serving a grammatical purpose only. — *adj* **explē'tory** (also *eks'pli-*) serving to fill up; expletive; supplementary. [L *explētivus*, from *ex* out, and *plēre* to fill]

explicate *eks'pli-kāt*, *vt* to unfold or develop (a theory, etc); to lay open or explain the meaning of. — *adj* **explic'able** (or *eks'*) capable of being explicated or explained. — *n* **explicā'tion** the act of explicating or explaining; explanation. — *adj* **explic'ative** or **explic'atory** (or *eks'*) serving to explicate or explain. — *n* **ex'plicātor**. [L *explicāre*, *explicātum* or *explicitum*, from *ex* out, and *plicāre* to fold]

explication de texte *eks-plē-ka-syɔ̃ də tekst*, *n* a method of literary criticism based on a detailed analysis of the text of the work. [Fr, (literally) explication of (the) text]

explicit[1] *iks-plis'it*, *adj* not merely implied but distinctly stated; plain in language; outspoken; clear; unreserved. — *adv* **explic'itly**. — *n* **explic'itness**. [See ety for **explicate**]

explicit[2] *eks'pli-sit*, (*obs*) *n* a conclusion. [From the medieval custom of writing *explicit* at the end of a book or section: orig appar for L *explicitum est* it is completed, later taken to be 3rd sing pr indicative, and supplied with a plural *expliciunt*; see **explicate**]

explode *iks-plōd'*, *vt* to cause to blow up; to bring into disrepute and reject; to cry down or hoot off (eg an actor) (*archaic*). — *vi* to burst with violence and *usu* a loud noise; to burst out or break forth suddenly; of population, to increase suddenly and rapidly. — *adj* **explō'ded** blown up; (of a theory, etc) rejected because proved false; (of a drawing or diagram of a machine, building, organism, etc) showing the internal structure and separate parts and their relationship. — *n* **explō'der**. — *adj* **explō'sible** liable to explode. — *n* **explō'sion** (*-zhən*) the act of exploding; a sudden violent burst with a loud noise; an outburst; breaking out of feelings, etc; a great and rapid increase or expansion, as in *population explosion*; release of breath after stoppage in articulating a stop consonant in certain positions. — *adj* **explō'sive** (*-siv* or *-ziv*) causing or liable to cause an explosion; worked, set in place, etc by an explosion; bursting out with violence and noise. — *n* something that will explode, *esp* a substance *specif* created to do so; a stop consonant pronounced with explosion. — *adv* **explō'sively**. — *n* **explō'siveness**. — **exploding star** a star that flares up, such as a nova or supernova; **explosion shot** a golf stroke to send a ball forcibly out of a bunker; **explosion welding** welding metals with very different melting points by means of pressure produced by an explosion; **explosive bolt** a bolt that can be blown out of position because it contains a small explosive charge; **explosive rivet** a rivet fixed in inaccessible places by detonation of a small charge in its end. [L *explōdere*, *explōsum*, from *ex* from, and *plaudere* to clap the hands]

exploit *eks'ploit*, *n* a deed or achievement, *esp* a heroic one; a feat. — *vt* (*iks-ploit'*) to work or make available; to turn or adapt to use; to make gain out of or at the expense of. — *adj* **exploit'able**. — *n* **exploit'age**. — *n* **exploitā'tion** (*eks-*) the act of successfully applying industry to any object, such as the working of mines, etc; the setting-up and getting into production of an oilfield, mine, etc; the act of using for selfish purposes. — *adj* **exploit'ative** or **exploit'ive**. — *n* **exploit'er**. — **exploitable girth** the minimum girth at breast height at or above which trees are considered suitable for felling or for other specified purpose. [OFr *exploit*, from L *explicitum* unfolded; see **explicate**]

explore *iks-plōr'*, *vt* and *vi* to search or travel through for the purpose of discovery; to examine thoroughly. — *n* **explorā'tion** (*eks-*) the act of searching or searching for (something) thoroughly; travel for the sake of discovery; examination of a region's geology, etc in a search for mineral resources. — *n* **explorā'tionist** a scientist engaged in mineral exploration. — *adj* **explor'ative** or **explor'atory** (*-or'-*) serving to explore or investigate; searching out. — *n* **explor'er** a person who explores, *esp* a member of a geological, etc exploration; (with *cap*) any of the first series of US satellites. — *adj* **explor'ing**. [Fr, from L *explōrāre*, *-ātum* to search out]

explosion. See **explode**.

expo *eks'pō*, *n* an exhibition or public showing: — *pl* **ex'pos**. [*expo*sition]

exponent *eks-pō'nənt*, *adj* setting forth; expounding. — *n* an interpreter of an art by performance; an example, illustration or type (of); an expounder (of); a symbol showing what power a quantity is raised to, an index (*math*). — *adj* **exponential** (*eks-pō-nen'shl*) pertaining to or involving exponents; (loosely) of a rate of increase, increasingly steep. — *n* an exponential function. — *adv* **exponen'tially**. — **exponential curve** a curve expressed by an exponential equation; **exponential equation** one in which the variable occurs in the exponent of one or more terms; **exponential function** a quantity with a variable exponent, *esp* e^x, where *e* is the base of natural logarithms; **exponential growth** a stage of growth occurring in populations of unicellular micro-organisms when the logarithm of the cell member increases linearly with time; **exponential series** a series in which exponential quantities are developed; **exponential theorem** gives a value of any number in terms of its natural logarithm, and from it can at once be derived a series determining the logarithm. [L *expōnēns*, *-entis* setting forth, from *ex-* out, and *pōnere* to place]

exponible *eks-pō'ni-bl*, *adj* able to be, or requiring to be, explained. [L *expōnere* (see **exponent**)]

export *eks-pört'*, *vt* to carry or send out of a country (eg goods in commerce); to save (a file) in a format that allows it to be loaded into other programs (*comput*). — *n* **ex'port** the act of exporting; something which is exported; a commodity which is or may be sent from one country to another as a business transaction; a type of strong brown beer. — *adj* **export'able**. — *n* **exportabil'ity**. — *n* **exportā'tion**. — *n* **export'er**. — **Export Credit Guarantee Department** a government department which insures UK exporters against losses arising from exporting goods (*abbrev* **ECGD**); **export multiplier** (*commerce*) the ongoing or multiplying effect on a country's national income of a rise or fall in its exports; **export reject** a manufactured article that is flawed in some way and so not passed for export, often sold at a reduced price on the home market. — **invisible exports** such items in a national trade balance as money spent by tourists from abroad, etc (as opposed to **visible exports**, goods sold abroad by traders). [L *exportāre*, *-ātum*, from *ex-* out of, and *portāre* to carry]

expose *iks-pōz'*, *vt* to lay out to view; to deprive of cover, protection or shelter; to make bare; to abandon (a child or animal); to submit (to an influence, such as light or weather); to put up (for sale); to explain (*archaic*); to disclose; to show up. — *n* (*US*) an exposé. — *adj* **expos'able**. — *n* **expōs'al** exposure; exposition. — *n* **exposé** (*eks-pō'zā*) an article or programme exposing crime, scandal, etc to public notice; a formal statement or exposition; an exposing; a shameful showing up. — *adj* **exposed'** unprotected; shelterless. — *n* **expōs'edness** the state of being exposed. — *n* **expōs'er**. — *n* **exposure** (*-pō'zhər* or *-zhyər*) the act of laying open or bare; subjection to an influence; the act of allowing access of light, or a section of film, etc which has been exposed to light (*photog*); the combination of duration of such access (shutter speed) with lens aperture chosen for the taking of a photograph; the act of showing up an evil; a state of being laid bare; openness to danger; in finance, a vulnerable, over-extended commitment or position; a shelterless state; position with regard to the sun, influence of climate, etc; appearance in public, *esp* on television; the total number of potential viewers, listeners, readers, etc of a particular advertising medium. — **exposure meter** (*photog*) an instrument, now often incorporated in the camera, for measuring the light falling on or reflected from a subject. — **expose oneself** to expose one's sexual organs in public. [Fr *exposer*, from L *ex-* out, and *pausāre* to rest, confused with *expōnere* to expose; see **exponent** and **exposition**, and cf **pose**[1], **compose**, **repose**, etc]

exposition *eks-pō-zish'ən*, *n* the act of exposing; a setting out to public view; the abandonment of a child; a public exhibition; a large international public exhibition or display, *esp* of industrial products (*commerce*; also **expo**); the act of expounding; explanation; commentary; an expository discourse; the enunciation of themes in a composition; that part of a sonata, fugue, etc in which themes are presented (*music*). — *adj* **exposit'ional**. — *adj* **expositive** (*-poz'*) serving to expose or explain; explanatory; exegetical. — *adv* **expos'itively**. — *n* **expos'itor** someone who or something which expounds; an interpreter: — *fem* **expos'itress**. — *adj* **expos'itory** serving to explain; explanatory. — *n* **exposture** (*-pos'chər*; *Shakesp*) exposure. [L *expositiō*, *-ōnis*, and *expositor*, *-ōris*, from *expōnere*, *expositum* to expose or set forth; see **expound**]

ex post facto *eks pōst fak'tō*, retrospective; retrospectively. [L, *literally* from what is done or enacted after]

expostulate *iks-post'ū-lāt*, *vi* to remonstrate; to discuss or reason (with); to discuss (*Shakesp*); to claim (*Milton*). — *n* **expostūlā'tion**. — *adj* **expost'ūlātive** (or *-ə-tiv*) or **expost'ūlatory** (*-ā-* or *-ə-tər-i*) containing expostulation. — *n* **expost'ūlator**. [L *expostulāre*, *-ātum*, from *ex* (intens), and *postulāre* to demand]

exposture. See **exposition**.

exposure. See **expose**.

expound *iks-pownd'*, *vt* to expose or lay open the meaning of; to explain; to interpret; to explain in a certain way. — *vi* to speak, talk informatively or pass comment (on), often at length. — *n* **expound'er**. [OFr *espondre*, from L *expōnere*, from *ex-* out, and *pōnere* to place]

express *iks-pres'*, *vt* to put into words; to symbolize; to state explicitly; to press or force out; to emit; to represent or make known by a likeness, words, signs, symbols, etc; to reveal; to designate; to dispatch rapidly. — *adj* clearly brought out; exactly representing; directly stated; explicit; clear; intended or sent for a particular purpose; expeditious, *esp* of or sent by special messenger service, etc. — *adv* with haste; specially; by express train or messenger; by express. — *n* a regular and quick conveyance; a system for the speedy transmission of messages or goods; an express train; an express messenger; a messenger or vehicle sent on a special errand; a special message. — *n* **express'age** the system of carrying by express; the charge for doing so. — *adj* **express'ible**. — *n* **expression** (*-presh'ən*) the act, mode or power of representing or giving utterance; representation or revelation by language, art, the features, etc; the manner in which anything is expressed; a word or phrase; a symbol; intonation; due indication of feeling in performance of music, etc; the act of forcing out by pressure; the effect which a gene produces (*biol*). — *adj* **express'ional** of or pertaining to expression. — *n* **express'ionism** (often with *cap*) in literature and painting, a revolt against impressionism, turning away from the representation of external reality to the expression of the artist's emotions and reactions to experience. — *n* and *adj* **express'ionist**. — *adj* **expressionis'tic**. — *adj* **express'ionless**. — *adv* **express'ionlessly**. — *adj* **express'ive** serving to express or indicate; full of expression; vividly representing (with *of*); emphatic; significant. — *adv* **express'ively**. — *n* **express'iveness**. — *n* **expressiv'ity** the quality of being able to express; the extent to which a gene produces an effect (*biol*). — *adv* **express'ly** explicitly; for the express purpose; definitely. — *n* **express'ness**. — *n* **expressure** (*eks-presh'ər*) pressing out; expression (*Shakesp*); representation (*Shakesp*). — **express agency** or **company** one that undertakes speedy transmission of goods; **express delivery** immediate delivery by special messenger; delivery by express agency; **express fee** a fee for express delivery; **expression mark** a direction written on a piece of music (*usu* in Italian); **expression stop** a stop in a harmonium by which the performer can regulate the air to produce expression; **expression vector** in genetic engineering, a vector that is specially constructed so that a large amount of the protein product, coded by an inserted sequence, can be made; **express letter**, **packet**, **parcel**, etc one sent by special messenger; **express'man** someone working in express delivery (*esp archaic US*); **express messenger** a special messenger delivering goods faster than the standard service; **express rifle** a rifle for big game at short range, with a heavy charge of powder and a light bullet; **express term** (*law*) an oral or written undertaking in a contract which has been expressly agreed by the parties; **express train** a railway-train which travels at high speed and with few stops; **express'way** (*NAm*) a motorway. — **express oneself** to give expression to one's thoughts, ideas and opinions. [L *exprimere*, *expressum*, from *ex* from, and *premere*, *pressum* to press; partly through Fr *exprès*, etc]

expressis verbis *eks-pre'sis vûr'bis* or *eks-pre'sēs ver'bēs* or *wer'*, (*L*) in express terms.

expresso *eks-pres'ō*, *n* and *adj*. Same as **espresso**.

exprobrate *eks'prō-brāt*, (*archaic*) *vt* to reproach with; to upbraid. — *n* **exprobrā'tion**. — *adj* **exprō'brative**. — *adj* **exprō'bratory**. [L *exprobrāre*, *-ātum*, from pfx *ex-* indicating source, and *probrum* disgrace]

ex professo *eks prə-fe'sō*, or *pro-*, (*L*) avowedly.

expromission *eks-pro-mish'ən*, (*law*) *n* the intervention of a new debtor, substituted for the former one, who is consequently discharged by the creditor. — *n* **expromissor** (*-mis'ər*). [L *exprōmittere*, *-missum* to promise to pay, from *ex-* (intens), and *prōmittere* to promise]

expropriate *iks-prō'pri-āt*, *vt* to dispossess (of property), *esp* for use by the state. — *adj* **exprō'priable**. — *n* **expropriā'tion**. — *n* **exprō'priator**. [L *expropriāre*, *-ātum*, from *ex* from, and *proprium* property]

ex propriis *eks prō'pri-is*, *prō'prē-ēs* or *pro'*, (*L*) from one's own resources.

ex proprio motu *eks prō'pri-ō mō'tū* or *pro'pri-ō mō'tōō*, (*LL*) of his or her own accord.

expugn *iks-pūn'*, *vt* to take by storm; to storm; to overcome. — *adj* **expugnable** (*-pug'* or *-pū'nəbl*) capable of being taken or vanquished. — *n* **expugnā'tion** (*-pug-*). [L *expugnāre*]

expulse *iks-puls'*, (*obs*) *vt* to expel forcibly or eject. — *n* **expul'sion** the act of expelling or state of being expelled; banishment. — *adj* **expul'sive** able or serving to expel. [L *expulsāre*, frequentative of *expellere* (see **expel**)]

expunge *iks-punj'*, *vt* to wipe out; to efface; to mark for deletion. — Also **expunct** (*iks-pungkt'*; *archaic*). — *n* **expunc'tion** (*-pungk'shən*). — *n* **expun'ger**. [L *expungere*, *-punctum* to mark for deletion by a row of dots, from *ex-* out, and *pungere* to prick]

expurgate *eks'pûr-gāt*, also *-pûr'*, *vt* to purge out or make pure; to revise (a book, etc) by removing anything supposed to be offensive, noxious or erroneous. — *n* **expurgā'tion** the act of expurgating or purifying; the removal of anything hurtful or evil; bowdlerizing; exculpation. — *n* **expurgator** (*eks'pûr-gā-tər* or *eks-pûr'gə-tər*) someone who expurgates or purifies. — *adj* **expurgato'rial** (*-gə-tö'ri-əl*) or **expur'gatory** pertaining to expurgation; tending to expurgate or purify. — *vt* **expurge** (*-pûrj'*) to purify or expurgate. [L *expurgāre*, *-ātum*, from *ex-* out, and *purgāre* to purge]

exquisite *eks'kwiz-it*, also *-kwiz'it*, *adj* of the most delicate and intricate workmanship; of the highest excellence; attracting the highest admiration; of delicate perception or close discrimination; not easily satisfied; fastidious; exceeding or extreme, as of pain or pleasure; delicious; far-fetched (*Shakesp*); abstruse (*obs*). — *n* a person who is obsessively or fashionably exact or fastidious in dress; a fop. — *adv* **exquisitely**. — *n* **exquisiteness**. [L *exquīsītus*, from *ex* out, and *quaerere* to seek]

ex quocunque capite *eks kwō-kun'kwi* (or *-kōōn'kwe*) *kap'it-ē* (or *-e*), (*L*) from whatever source.

exr *abbrev*: executor.

ex re nata (*L*). Same as **e re nata**.

exrx *abbrev*: executrix.

exsanguinous *iks-sang'gwin-əs*, *adj* without blood; anaemic. — Also **exsang'uine**, **exsang'uined**, **exsang'uinous** and **exsanguin'eous**. — *vt* **exsang'uinate** (*med*) to drain of blood. — *n* **exsanguinā'tion**. — *n* **exsanguin'ity**. [L *ex-* without, and *sanguis*, *-inis* blood]

exscind *ik-sind'*, *vt* to cut off. [L *ex* from, and *scindere* to cut]

exsect *ik-sekt'*, *vt* to cut out. — *n* **exsec'tion**. [L *ex* from, and *secāre*, *sectum* to cut]

exsert *ik-sûrt'*, *vt* to protrude. — *adj* **exsert'ed** projecting. — *adj* **exser'tile** (*-tīl*, or *US -til*). — *n* **exser'tion**. [L *exserere*, *-sertum*; see **exert**]

ex-service *eks-sûr'vis*, *adj* having formerly served in one of the armed services. — *n* **ex-ser'viceman** or **ex-ser'vicewoman**.

exsiccate *ek'si-kāt*, *vt* to dry up. — *adj* **exsicc'ant**. — *n* **exsiccā'tion**. — *adj* **exsicc'ative** (or *ek'si-kāt-*). — *n* **ex'siccātor** a drying agent or apparatus. [L *exsiccare*, from *ex-* out, and *siccus* dry]

exstipulate *iks-tip'ū-lāt*, (*bot*) *adj* without stipules. — Also **estip'ulate**.

exsuccous *ik-suk'əs*, *adj* sapless. [L *exsuccus*, from *ex-* out, and *succus* juice]

exsufflicate *ik-suf'li-kāt*, *adj* puffed out (*Shakesp*). — *vt* **exsuff'late** to blow away; to exorcize by blowing away. — *n* **exsufflā'tion** expiration; forced expiration; exorcism by blowing. [L *ex-* out, and *sufflāre* to blow out, from *sub* under, and *flāre* to blow]

ext. *abbrev*: extension; external or externally; extinct; extra; extract.

ex tacito *eks ta'si-tō* or *ta'ki-tō*, (*L*) silently.

extant *iks-tant'* or *eks'tənt*, *adj* standing out, or above the rest (*archaic*); still standing or existing; surviving. [L *extāns*, *-antis*, from *ex-* out, and *stāre* to stand]

extasy and **extatic**. *Obs* forms of **ecstasy** and **ecstatic**.

extempore *iks-tem'pə-ri*, *adv* on the spur of the moment; without preparation; suddenly. — *adj* composed and delivered or performed impromptu; without help of written notes; rising at the moment; sudden. — *n* (*obs*) an impromptu speech, etc. — *adj* **extem'poral**. — *n* **extemporaneity** (*-ə-nē'i-ti*). — *adj* **extemporā'neous** impromptu; temporary or improvised. — *adv* **extemporā'neously**. — *n* **extemporā'neousness**. — *adv* **extem'porarily**. — *n* **extem'porariness**. — *adj* **extem'porary** done on the spur of the moment; hastily prepared; speaking extempore; done without preparation; off-hand. — *n* **extemporizā'tion** or **-s-**. — *vt* **extem'porize** or **-ise** to speak, or compose and play, extempore or without previous preparation; to make a speech without notes; to improvise (a solution, etc). [L *ex* out of, and *tempore*, ablative of *tempus* time]

extend *iks-tend'*, *vt* to stretch out; to prolong in any direction; to enlarge; to expand; to widen; to unfold; to straighten out; to hold out; to offer or accord; to exert to the full; to seize (*law*; *Shakesp*); to value or assess. — *vi* to stretch or reach; to be continued in space or time. — *n* **extendabil'ity**. — *adj* **extend'able**. — *adj* **extend'ant** (*heraldry*) displayed. — *adj* **extend'ed** occupying space; having extension; stretched out; extensive. — *adv* **extend'edly**. — *n* **extend'er** someone or something that extends; a university extension lecture; a substance added to paint to give body, or to food to give extra bulk. — *n* **extendibil'ity**. — *adj* **extend'ible**. — *adj* **extense** (*-tens'*; *obs*) extensive. — *n* **extensibil'ity**. — *adj* **extens'ible** or **extensile** (*eks-ten'sīl* or *-sil*) that may be extended. — *n* **extensificā'tion** an agricultural policy within the European Community by which land is farmed less intensively and savings made in expenditure on feed, fertilizers and pesticides to balance lower production. — *n* **extension** (*iks-* or *eks-ten'shən*) an act of extending; the condition of being extended; an added piece; a wing or annex of a house; the property of occupying space; the extent of the application of a term or the number of objects included under it (*opp* of *intension*; *logic*); a word or words added to subject, predicate or object (*gram*); an additional telephone using the same line as the main one. — *adj* **exten'sional**. — *adv* **exten'sionally**. — *n* **exten'sionalism** or **extensional'ity**. — *n* **exten'sionist** an advocate of extension; a university extension lecturer or student. — *n* **exten'sity** massiveness or spatial quality in sensation from which perception of extension is derived. — *adj* **extens'ive** large; widespread; comprehensive; (*eks-*) pertaining to extension; seeking or deriving a comparatively small crop cheaply from a wide area (*opp* of *intensive*; *agric*). — *adv* **extens'ively**. — *n* **extens'iveness**. — *n* **extensivīzā'tion** the extensive method of agriculture (see also **extensification** above). — *n* **extensom'eter** or **extensim'eter** (*eks-*) an instrument for measuring small changes in length, etc in metal to which tension has been applied. — *n* **exten'sor** a muscle that extends or straightens any part of the body. — *n* **extent'** the space or degree to which a thing is extended; bulk; compass; scope; degree or amount (as in *to some extent*); a stretch or extended space; a valuation of property; a writ directing the sheriff to seize the property of a debtor, for the recovery of debts of record due to the Crown (*law*); seizure (*Shakesp*); attack (*Shakesp*); an act of extending (justice, courtesy, etc) (*Shakesp*). — *adj* stretched out. — **extended credit** a form of purchase where the goods become the property of the buyer immediately, as opposed to hire purchase where ownership is not transferred until the last payment is made; **extended family** a social unit comprising not only a couple and their children but other relatives, eg aunts, uncles and grandparents; **extended play** (of a gramophone record) giving longer reproduction because of a closer groove and the use of a larger part of its surface area. — **university extension** the enlargement of the aim of a university, in providing extramural instruction for those unable to become regular students. [L *extendere*, *extentum* or *extēnsum*, from *ex-* out, and *tendere* to stretch]

extenuate *iks-ten'ū-āt*, *vt* to lessen; to weaken the force of; to palliate; to underrate. — *n* and *adj* **exten'ūāting** palliating. — *adv* **exten'ūātingly**. — *n* **extenūā'tion** the act of representing anything as less wrong or criminal than it seems; palliation; mitigation. — *adj* **exten'ūātive** or **exten'ūatory** tending to extenuate; palliative. — *n* **exten'ūātor**. [L *extenuāre*, *-ātum*, from *ex-* (intens), and *tenuis* thin]

exterior *eks-tē'ri-ər*, *adj* outer; outward or external; on or from the outside; foreign, involving or dealing with foreign nations. — *n* the outside or outer surface; outward form or deportment; appearance; an outdoor scene in a cinema film, television drama, etc; an outer part (*esp* in *pl*). — *n* **extēriority** (*-or'i-ti*). — *n* **exterioriza'tion** or **-s-**. — *vt* **extēr'iorize** or **-ise** to externalise; to bring an internal part temporarily outside the body (*surg*). — *adv* **extē'riorly** outwardly. — **exterior angle** (*math*) the angle between any extended side and the adjacent side of a polygon. [L *exterior*, compar of *exter*, *exterus* outward, from *ex* from]

exterminate *iks-tûr'mi-nāt*, *vt* to drive out (*obs*); to destroy utterly; to put an end to; to root out. — *adj* **exter'minable** that can be exterminated; illimitable (*Shelley*). — *n* **extermina'tion** complete destruction or eradication. — *adj* **exter'minātive** or **exter'minatory** serving or tending to exterminate. — *n* **exter'minātor**. — *vt* **exter'mine** (*Shakesp*) to exterminate. [L *extermināre*, *-ātum* to drive beyond the boundary, from *ex* out of, and *terminus* boundary]

external *eks-tûr'nəl*, *adj* exterior; lying outside; outward; belonging to the world of outward things; that may be seen; not innate or intrinsic; accidental; foreign or involving foreign nations. — *n* exterior; (in *pl*) the outward parts; (in *pl*) outward or non-essential forms and ceremonies; (in *pl*) outward circumstances or appearances. — *adj* (*obs*) **extern'** or **externe'** external or outward. — *n* a non-resident, such as a day-scholar, an out-patient, or a non-resident physician or surgeon. — *n* **exter'nalism** undue regard to mere externals or non-essential outward forms, *esp* of religion. — *n* **exter'nalist**. — *n* **externality** (*-nal'i-ti*) external character; superficiality; undue regard to externals. — *n* **externalīzā'tion** or **-s-**. — *vt* **exter'nalize** or **-ise** to give form or apparent reality to; to give external expression to; to assign (one's feelings) to things outside oneself (*psychol*); to ascribe to causes outside oneself; to regard as consisting of externals only. — *adv* **exter'nally**. — *n* **externat** (*eks-ter-nä*; *Fr*) a day-school. — **external-combustion engine** one in which the fuel is burned outside the working cylinder; **external examiner** an examiner from another institution who has had no part in teaching the examinees; **external liabilities** (*commerce*) amounts owing to person or businesses other than shareholders; **external store** or **storage** (*comput*) any portable storage medium, eg magnetic disks; **external student** one examined (for an **external degree**) by a university in which he or she has not studied. [L *externus* outward, from *exter* outside]

exteroceptor *eks'tər-ō-sep-tər*, (*zool*) *n* a sensory organ, eg the eye, which receives impressions from outside the body. — *adj* **exterocep'tive**. [L *exterus* exterior, and *receptor*]

exterritorial, etc *eks-ter-i-tō'ri-əl*. Same as **extraterritorial**, etc.

extinct *iks-tingkt'*, *adj* put out; extinguished, quenched or squashed; no longer existing; (of a volcano) no longer erupting; obsolete; dead. — *adj* **extinct'ed** (*Shakesp*) extinguished. — *n* **extinc'tion** the state of being extinct; extinguishing, quenching or wiping out; destruction; suppression; the cutting off of polarized light at certain angles when a section of doubly refracting mineral is rotated between crossed nicols; the absorbing by the earth's atmosphere of a planet's or star's light (*astron*); the inhibition of a conditioned reflex (*psychol*). — *adj* **extinct'ive** tending to extinguish. — *n* **extinct'ure** (*Shakesp*) extinction. [L *ex(s)tinctum* (see **extinguish**)]

extine *eks'tin*, *-tēn* or *-tīn*, (*bot*) *n* the outer membrane of a pollen-grain or spore. — Also **ex'ine**. [From the root of L *exter*, *extimus* outer or outermost]

extinguish *iks-ting'gwish*, *vt* to quench or put out; to make extinct; to put an end to; to destroy or annihilate; to obscure by superior splendour; to pay off (a debt) (*law*). — *vi* to die out. — *adj* **exting'uishable**. — *n* **exting'uishant** a substance used to extinguish fires. — *n* **exting'uisher** someone or something that extinguishes; a small hollow conical instrument for putting out a candle, etc; a device for putting out fire; a conical structure resembling a candle extinguisher. — *n* **exting'uishment** the act of extinguishing; putting an end to a right by consolidation or union (*law*). [L *ex(s)tinguere*, *ex(s)tinctum*, from *ex-* out, and *stinguere* to quench]

extirpate *eks'tər-pāt*, *vt* to root out; to destroy totally; to remove surgically; to exterminate (*Spenser*, *Shakesp* **extirp** (*eks-tûrp'*)). — *adj* **extirpable** (*eks-tûrp'ə-bl*). — *n* **extirpā'tion** extermination; total destruction. — *n* **ex'tirpātor** someone who extirpates; an implement for weeding. — *adj* **ex'tirpative**. — *n* **extirpatory** (*eks-tûrp'ə-tər-i*). [L *exstirpāre*, *-ātum*, from *ex-* out, and *stirps* a stock or root]

extol *iks-tōl'* or *-tol'*, *vt* to lift up (*Spenser*); to praise highly: — *pr p* **extoll'ing**; *pa t* and *pa p* **extolled'** (*Spenser* **extold'**). — *n* **extoll'er**. — *n* **extol'ment** the act of extolling; the state of being extolled. [L *extollere*, from *ex-* up, and *tollere* to lift or raise]

extort *iks-tört'*, *vt* to wring out; to gain or draw out (money, a promise, etc) by compulsion or violence. — *adj* extorted; wrongfully obtained. — *adj* **extors'ive** serving or tending to extort. — *adv* **extors'ively**. — *n* **extortion** (*-tör'shən*) illegal securing of money by compulsion or violence; something which is extorted. — *adj* **extor'tionary** pertaining to or implying extortion. — *adj* **extor'tionate** (of a price) extremely high; (of a person) using extortion; oppressive; exacting, demanding too much. — *adv* **extor'tionately**. — *n* **extor'tioner** or **extor'tionist** someone who practises extortion. — *adj* **extort'ive**. [L *extorquēre*, *extortum*, from *ex-* out, and *torquēre* to twist]

extra[1] *eks'trə*, *adj* beyond or more than the usual or the necessary; extraordinary; additional. — *adv* unusually or exceptionally. — *n* what is extra or additional, such as an item above and beyond the ordinary school curriculum, something over and above the usual course or charge in a bill, etc; a special edition of a newspaper containing later news; a run scored at cricket from a bye, leg-bye, wide or no-ball (not hit); a person temporarily engaged for a minor part in a film, etc, eg to be one of a crowd. — *adj* **extra-condensed'** (*printing*) extremely narrow in proportion to the height. — **extra cover** in cricket, a fielding position between cover point and mid-off, or the player in this position; **extra jam** or

marmalade under EC regulations, jam or marmalade containing a considerably higher percentage (by weight) of fruit than that in ordinary jam or marmalade. — *adj* **extra-spec'ial** very special. — *n* a special late edition of an evening newspaper called for by some news of great importance. — **extra time** additional time allowed at the end of a match because of time lost through injury, etc; **extra virgin** or **extra-virgin** (of olive oil) of the best quality, extracted by pressing, not by chemical processes. [Probably contracted from **extraordinary**]

extra² *eks'trə* or *eks'trä*, (*L*) *prep* outside. — **extra modum** (*mō'dəm* or *mo'dŏŏm*) beyond measure, extravagant; **extra muros** (*mū'rōs* or *mōō'rōs*) beyond the walls.

extra- *eks'tra-* or *-trə-*, *pfx* outside. — *adj* **extra-ax'illary** (*bot*) not in the axil of a leaf. — *adj* **extracanon'ical** not part of the canon of the Bible. — *adj* **extracell'ular** (*biol*) outside the cell-walls. — *adj* **extracorpor'eal** outside the body. — *adj* **extra-curric'ular** of a subject or activity, outside and additional to the regular academic course. — *adj* **extradō'tal** not forming part of the dowry. — *adj* **extraflo'ral** not in a flower. — *adj* **extraforā'neous** outdoor. — *adj* **extragalac'tic** (*astron*) outside our galaxy. — *vt* **extra-ill'ustrate** (or *-lus'*) to illustrate from other printed books, to grangerize. — *n* **extra-illustrā'tion**. — *adj* **extrajudi'cial** not made in court, beyond the usual course of legal proceeding. — *adv* **extrajudi'cially**. — *adj* **extralim'ital** (*zool*) not found within a given faunal area; lying outside a prescribed area. — Also **extralim'itary**. — *adj* **extramar'ital** (of sexual relations, etc) outside marriage. — *adj* **extramet'rical** (*prosody*) in excess of the recognized number of syllables in the line. — *adj* **extramun'dane** beyond the material world. — *adj* **extramū'ral** without or beyond the walls; connected with a university but not under its direct control. — *adj* **extranū'clear** (*biol*) outside the nucleus (of a cell or an atom). — *adj* **extra=parō'chial** beyond the limits of a parish. — *adj* **extra=phys'ical** not subject to physical laws. — *adj* **extra=profess'ional** not belonging to a particular profession; outside the usual limits of professional duty or practice. — *adj* **extra-provin'cial** outside the limits of a particular province. — *adj* **extra-reg'ular** unlimited by rules. — *adj* **extrasen'sory** outside the ordinary senses as in clairvoyant and telepathic perception. — **extrasensory perception** the ability to perceive without the normal senses (cf **sixth sense**). — *adj* **extra-sō'lar** beyond the solar system. — *adj* **extraterres'trial** outside, or from outside, the earth. — Also *n*. — *adj* **extraterrito'rial** outside a territory or territorial jurisdiction (also **exterritor'ial**). — *n* **extraterritorial'ity** the privilege of being outside the jurisdiction of the country one is in (also **exterritorial'ity**). — *adj* **extratrop'ical** outside the tropics. — *adj* **extra-ū'terine** outside the uterus. — *adj* **extravas'cular** (*biol*) outside the vascular system or a vessel; not vascular. — *adj* **extravehic'ūlar** situated, used or happening outside a spacecraft. [L *extrā* outside]

extract *iks-* or *eks-trakt'*, *vt* to draw out by force or otherwise; to choose or select; to find out; to derive (pleasure, etc); to extort; to take a copy of (*Scots law*); to copy passages from; to publish passages from; to obtain by chemical or physical means from containing or combined matter; to exhaust or treat by extraction. — *adj* (*obs* except *Scots law*) extracted; derived. — *n* **extract** (*eks'*) anything drawn from a substance by heat, distillation, solvents, etc as an essence; a passage taken from a book or writing; wool obtained from rags from which cotton has been chemically removed. — *adj* **extract'able** or **extract'ible**. — *n* **extractabil'ity**. — *n* **extract'ant** (*chem*) a solvent used for extraction. — *n* **extrac'tion** the act of extracting; derivation from a stock or family; birth; lineage; something which is extracted. — *adj* **extract'ive** tending or serving to extract; of the nature of an extract. — *n* an extract. — *n* **extract'or** someone or something that extracts; (also **extractor fan**) an electric fan which extracts air, gas, etc from a room or building. — **extractive industries** those such as mining, forestry, agriculture, etc which draw out natural resources and process them into marketable form for the manufacturing sector of industry; **extractive matter** the soluble portions of any drug. — **extract the root of a quantity** to find its root by a mathematical process. [L *extrahere*, *extractum*, from *ex* from, and *trahere* to draw]

extradition *eks-trə-dish'ən*, *n* a delivering up of accused people by one government to another. — *adj* **extraditable** (*-dīt'ə-bl*). — *vt* **ex'tradite** to hand over for trial or punishment to a foreign government. [L *ex* from, and *trāditiō*, *-ōnis*, from *trādere*, *trāditum* to deliver up]

extrados *eks-trā'dos*, (*archit*) *n* the convex surface of an arch; the external curve of the keystone of an arch. [Fr, from L *extrā* outside, and Fr *dos* back]

extrait *eks-tre*, (*Fr*) *n* extract.

extraneous *eks-trān'yəs*, *adj* external; foreign; not belonging to or dependent on; not essential; irrelevant. — *n* **extraneity** (*-trə-nē'i-ti*) or **extrān'eousness**. — *adv* **extrān'eously**. [L *extrāneus* external, *extrā* outside]

extraordinary *eks-trörd'i-nə-ri* or *-in-ri*, also *eks-trə-örd'* or *iks-trörd'*, *adj* not usual or regular; remarkable or wonderful; special or additional (eg *physician extraordinary* in a royal household, and *extraordinary professor* in a German university, both being subordinate to the ordinary official); for a particular purpose (eg *extraordinary general meeting*). — *n pl* **extraord'inaries** things that exceed the usual order, kind or method. — *adv* **extraord'inarily**. — *n* **extraord'inariness**. — **extraordinary ray** in double refraction, the ray that does not obey the ordinary law of refraction. [L *extraordinārius*, from *extrā* outside, and *ordō*, *-inis* order]

extrapolate *iks-trap'ō-lāt* or *-ə-lāt*, also *eks'*, *vt* to estimate from observed tendencies the value of (any variable) outside the limits between which values are known; to infer or conjecture from what is known; to forecast future trends on the basis of past facts and events; to project into a new area of experience or activity. — Also *vi*. — *n* **extrapolā'tion**. — *adj* **extrap'olātive** or **extrap'olatory**. — *n* **extrap'olātor**. [L *extrā* and **interpolate**]

extrapose *eks-trə-pōz'*, (*gram*) *vt* to move an item normally positioned within a phrase or sentence to the end, to focus attention on it. — *n* **extraposition** (*-zish'ən*). [L *extrā* outside]

extraught *iks-tröt'*, (*Shakesp*) *pa p* of **extract**.

extravagant *iks-trav'ə-gənt*, *adj* spending a lot of money; wasteful; excessive; unrestrained; irregular; wandering beyond bounds (*archaic*). — *n* **extrav'agance** excess; lavish expenditure; digression (*Milton*). — *n* **extrav'agancy** extravagance; vagrancy (*Shakesp*). — *adv* **extrav'agantly**. — *vi* (*archaic*) **extrav'agate** to wander; to exceed proper bounds. — *n* **extravagā'tion**. [L *extrā* beyond, and *vagāns*, *-antis* pr p of *vagārī* to wander]

extravaganza *iks-trav-ə-gan'zə*, *n* an extravagant or eccentric musical, dramatic or literary production; extravagant conduct or speech. [Ital *(e)stravaganza*]

extravasate *iks-trav'ə-sāt*, *vt* to let or force (blood or other fluid) out of the proper vessels; to pour out (lava). — *adj* extravasated. — *n* **extravasā'tion** the act of extravasating; the escape of any of the fluids of the living body from their proper vessels. [L *extrā* out of, and *vās* a vessel]

extravert, **extraversion** and **extraversive**. Same as **extrovert**, etc.

extreat *eks-trēt'*, (*Spenser*) *n* extraction. [**estreat**]

extreme *iks-trēm'* (*archaic eks'*), *adj* outermost; most remote; last; highest in degree; greatest; most violent; (of opinions, etc) not moderate, going to great lengths; stringent: — *superl* (*rare*) **extrēm'est**; *compar* (*rare*) **extrēm'er**. — *n* the utmost point or verge; end; the utmost or the highest limit or degree; (in *pl*; *obs*) great necessity. — *adv* **extrēme'ly**. — *n* **extreme'ness**. — *n* **extrē'mism**. — *n* **extrē'mist** someone ready to go to extremes; a holder of extreme opinions; an advocate of extreme action. — *n* **extremity** (*-trem'i-ti*) the utmost limit; the highest degree; greatest necessity or distress; extreme condition; an end; a hand or foot. — **extreme unction** see under **unction**. — **extremely high frequency** see under **frequent**; **go to extremes** to go too far; to use extreme measures; **in the extreme** in the last, highest degree; extremely; **the last extremity** the utmost pitch of misfortune; death. [OFr *extreme*, from L *extrēmus*, superl of *exter*, *exterus* on the outside]

extricate *eks'tri-kāt*, *vt* to free from entanglements or perplexities; to disentangle; to set free. — *adj* **ex'tricable**. — *n* **extricā'tion** disentanglement; the act of setting free. [L *extricāre*, *-ātum*, from *ex* from, and *trīcae* hindrances]

extrinsic *iks-trin'sik*, *adj* external; not contained in or belonging to a body; foreign; not essential; of a muscle, running from the trunk to limb or girdle (opposed to *intrinsic*). — *adj* **extrin'sical**. — *n* **extrinsical'ity**. — *adv* **extrin'sically**. [Fr *extrinsèque*, from L *extrīnsecus*, from *exter* outside, sfx *-in* and *secus* beside]

extrorse *iks-trörs'* or **extrorsal** *iks-trörs'əl*, *adj* turned outward; (of an anther) opening towards the outside of the flower. [Fr, from L *extrorsus*, from *extrā* outside, and *versus* turned]

extrovert *eks'trə-* or *-trō-vûrt*, *vt* to turn outward or outside in; to make manifest. — *n* (*eks'*; *psychol*) a person interested mainly in the world external to himself or herself (opposed to *introvert*); hence (loosely) a sociable, outgoing, lively person. — Also *adj*. — *n* **extrover'sion**. — *adj* **extrover'sive**. [L *extrā* outside, and *vertere* to turn; the *extro-* forms by analogy with **introvert**]

extrude *iks-trōōd'*, *vt* to force or urge out; to expel; to protrude; to make rods, tubes, etc by extrusion. — *vi* to protrude. — *n* **extrud'er**. — *adj* **extru'sible**. — *n* **extrusion** (*-trōō'zhən*) the act of extruding, thrusting or throwing out; expulsion; a rock formed by the cooling of magma or lava; the operation of producing rods, tubes, etc of metal or plastic by forcing suitable material through a die by means of a ram. — *adj* **extrusive** (*-trōō'siv*). — *adj* **extru'sory** (*-sər-i*). [L *extrūdere*, *extrūsum*, from *ex-* out, and *trūdere* to thrust]

exuberant *eg-* or *ig-zū'bər-ənt*, also *-zōō'*, *adj* luxuriant; overflowing; abounding; in high spirits; lavish. — *n* **exu'berance** or **exu'berancy** the quality of being exuberant; luxuriance or an overflowing quantity; redundancy; outburst. — *adv* **exu'berantly**. — *vi* **exu'berate** (*rare*) to be exuberant; to grow profusely. [L *exūberāns*, *-antis*, pr p of *exūberāre*, from *ex-* (intens), and *ūber* rich]

exude *igz-* or *iks-ūd'*, *vt* to discharge by sweating; to discharge through pores or incisions; to exhibit or show (a feeling, etc). — *vi* to flow out of a body through the pores; to ooze out. — *n* **exudate** (*eks'*) exuded matter. — *n* **exudā'tion** (*eks-*) the act of exuding or discharging through pores; that which is exuded. — *adj* **exūd'ative**. [L *exūdāre*, from *ex* from, and *sūdāre* to sweat]

exul *ek'sul*, (*Spenser*) *n* an exile. [L *ex(s)ul*]

exulcerate *igz-ul'sər-āt*, *vt* to exasperate or afflict as if with an ulcer. — *n* **exulcerā'tion** ulceration; exasperation. [L *exulcerāre*, *-ātum*, from *ex-* (intens), and *ulcerāre* to ulcerate]

exult *igz-ult'*, *vi* to rejoice exceedingly; to triumph over. — *n* **exult'ance** or **exult'ancy** exultation; triumph. — *adj* **exult'ant** exulting; triumphant. — *adv* **exult'antly**. — *n* **exultā'tion** (*egz-*) triumphant delight; joyousness, *esp* spiritual. — *adv* **exult'ingly**. [L *ex(s)ultāre*, *-ātum*, from *ex(s)ilīre*, from *ex* out, and *salīre* to leap]

exurb *eks'ûrb*, (*orig US*) *n* a residential area, *esp* a prosperous one, outside the suburbs of a town. — *adj* **exur'ban**. — *n* and *adj* **exur'banite**. — *n* **exur'bia** exurbs collectively. [L *ex-* outside, and sub*urbia*]

ex utraque parte *eks ū-trā'kwi pär'tē* or *ōō-trä'kwe pär'te* (*L*) on either side.

exuviae *igz-* or *iks-ū'vi-ē*, *n pl* cast-off skins, shells or other coverings of animals; fossil remains of animals (*geol*). — *adj* **exū'vial**. — *vi* **exū'viate** to shed or cast off (a skin). — *n* **exuviā'tion** the act of exuviating. [L, from *exuere* to draw off]

ex voto *eks vō'tō*, or *wō'*, (*L*) according to one's prayer, by reason of a vow; votive. — *n* a votive offering.

EXW *abbrev*: ex works.

eyalet *ā-yä'let*, *n* a division of Turkey, a vilayet. [Turk, from Ar *iyālah*]

eyas *ī'əs*, *n* an unfledged hawk. — *adj* (*Spenser*) unfledged. — **ey'as-musket** an unfledged male hawk; a child (*Shakesp*). [*An eyas* for *a nyas*, from Fr *niais*, from L *nīdus* nest]

eye[1] *ī*, (*obs*) *n* a brood, *esp* of pheasants. [*An eye* for *a nye*, from OFr *ni*, from L *nīdus* nest]

eye[2] *ī*, *n* the organ of sight or vision; the power of seeing; sight; a tinge or suffusion (*Shakesp*); regard; aim; keenness of perception; anything resembling an eye; a central spot; the hole of a needle; the aperture for inserting the bias in a bowl; a round aperture; a mine entrance; a spring of water; a wire loop or ring for a hook; a round hole or window; the seed-bud of a potato; a spot on an egg; a spectacle lens; the central calm area of a cyclone; (in *pl*) the foremost part of a ship's bows, the hawse-holes: — *pl* **eyes**; *archaic* **eyne** (*īn*); *Scot* **een** (*ēn*). — *vt* to look on; to observe narrowly. — *vi* (*Shakesp*) to appear: — *pr p* **eye'ing** or **ey'ing**; *pa t* and *pa p* **eyed** (*īd*). — *adj* **eyed** having eyes; spotted as if with eyes. — *n* **eye'ful** as much as the eye can take in; something worth looking at, eg a fascinating sight or an attractive person (*slang*). — *adj* (*dialect*) sightly; careful, having an eye to. — *adj* **eye'less** without eyes or sight; deprived of eyes; blind. — *n* **eyelet** see separate entry. — **eye'ball** the ball or globe of the eye. — *vt* (*colloq*) to face someone eyeball to eyeball, to confront; to examine closely; to glance over (a page, etc). — *adj* (of a measurement) by eye only, not exact. — **eye bank** see **bank**[3]; **eye'-bath** a small cup that can be filled with a cleansing or medicinal solution, etc and held over the eye to bathe it; **eye'=beam** a glance of the eye; **eye'-black** mascara; **eye'bolt** a bolt with an eye instead of the normal head, used for lifting on heavy machines, fastening, etc; **eye'bright** a little plant of the genus Euphrasia (family Scrophulariaceae) formerly used as a remedy for eye diseases; **eye'brow** the hairy arch above the eye. — *vt* to provide with artificial eyebrows. — *adj* **eye'browless** without eyebrows. — **eye'-catcher** a part of a building designed specially to catch a person's eye (*archit*); a striking person, *esp* an attractive woman. — *adj* **eye'-catching** striking. — **eye contact** a direct look between two people; **eye'-cup** (*esp NAm*) an eye-bath; an eye-piece; **eye'-drop** (*Shakesp*) a tear; (in *pl* without hyphen) a medicine for the eye administered in the form of drops; **eye'-flap** a blinker on a horse's bridle; **eye'-glance** a quick look; **eye'glass** a glass to assist the sight, *esp* a monocle; (in *pl*; *usu NAm*) spectacles; an eye-piece; the lens of the eye (*Shakesp*); **eye'-hole** an eyelet; an eye-socket; a peep-hole; **eye'hook** a hook on a ring at the end of a rope or chain; **eye'lash** the row, or one, of the hairs that edge the eyelid. — *adj* **eye-leg'ible** (of headings, etc on microfilm or microprint) able to be read by the naked eye. — *adj* and *n* **eye'-level** (at) the same height above ground as the average person's eyes. — **eye'lid** the lid or cover of the eye; the portion of movable skin by means of which the eye is opened or closed; **eye'liner** a kind of cosmetic used for drawing a line along the edge of the eyelid in order to emphasize the eye; **eye lotion**; **eye muscle** a muscle controlling the eye or a part of it; a long muscle running down the back beside the spine; **eye'-opener** something that opens the eyes literally or figuratively, *esp* a startling enlightenment; a drink, *esp* in the morning (*colloq*); **eye'-piece** the lens or combination of lenses at the eye end of an optical instrument; **eye'-pit** the socket of the eye; **eye'-rhyme** similarity of words in spelling but not in pronunciation; **eye'-salve** salve or ointment for the eyes; **eye'-servant** someone who does his or her duty only when under the eye of his or her master; **eye'-service** service so performed; formal worship; **eye'-shade** a piece of stiff, *usu* tinted, transparent material, worn like the peak of a cap to protect the eyes from the sun or other bright light; **eye'shadow** a coloured cosmetic for the eyelids; **eye'-shot** the reach or range of sight of the eye; a glance; **eye'sight** power of seeing; view; observation; **eye socket** either of the two recesses in the skull in which the eyeballs are situated, the orbit; **eye'sore** anything that is offensive to look at; **eye'-splice** a kind of eye or loop formed by splicing the end of a rope into itself; **eye'-spot** a spot like an eye; any of several diseases of plants causing eye-shaped spots to appear on the growth; a rudimentary organ of vision. — *adj* **eye'-spotted** (*Spenser*) marked with spots like eyes. — **eye'stalk** a stalk on the dorsal surface of the head of many Crustacea, bearing an eye; **eye'strain** tiredness or irritation of the eyes; **eye'-string** the muscle that raises the eyelid; **eye'-tooth** a canine tooth, *esp* in the upper jaw, below the eye; **eye'-wash** a lotion for the eye; nonsense (*colloq*); deception (*colloq*); **eye'-water** water flowing from the eye; a lotion for the eyes; **eye'-wink** (*Shakesp*) a rapid lowering and raising of the eyelid; a glance; the time of a wink; **eye'-witness** someone who sees a thing happening or being done. — **all my eye** (*slang*) nonsense; **be all eyes** to give all attention; **be a sheet in the wind's eye** to be intoxicated; **clap, lay** or **set eyes on** (*colloq*) to see; **cry one's eyes out** see under **cry**; **cut one's eye-teeth** to cease to be a child; to become shrewd; **electric eye** see **electric**; **eyeball to eyeball** (of a discussion, confrontation, diplomacy, etc) at close quarters, dealing with matters very frankly and firmly (also **eye to eye**); **eye for an eye** retaliation, *lex talionis* (Exod 21.24); justice enacted in the same way or to the same degree as the crime; **eye of day** the sun; **eyes down** the start of a bingo game, or of any non-physical contest; **eye up** (*colloq*) to consider the sexual attractiveness of; **get** or **keep one's eye in** to become or remain proficient; **give an eye to** to attend to; **glad eye, green-eyed** see **glad** and **green**[1]; **have an eye to** to contemplate; to have regard to; to incline towards; **have one's eye on** to keep in mind; to consider acquisitively; **hit one in the eye** to be obvious; **in eye** in sight; **in one's mind's eye** in imagination; **in the eyes of** in the estimation or opinion of; **in the wind's eye** against the wind; **keep one's** (or **an**) **eye on** to observe closely; to watch; **keep one's eye** or **eyes skinned** or **peeled** (**for**) to be keenly watchful (for); **make a person open his** or **her eyes** to cause him or her astonishment; **make eyes at** to look at in an amorous way, to ogle; **mind your eye** (*slang*) take care; **my eye** used to express mild disagreement; **naked eye** see under **naked**; **one in the eye** a rebuff; **open a person's eyes** to make someone see; to show someone something of which he or she is ignorant; **pick the eyes out of** (*Austr colloq*) to choose and take the best parts of; **pipe one's eye** or **put a finger in the eye** to weep; **private eye** see under **private**; **put a person's eye out** to blind someone; to supplant someone in favour; **raise an eyebrow** to be mildly surprised, shocked or doubtful; **see eye to eye** from Isaiah 52.8 (*AV*) meaning see with one's own eyes, but used in the sense of to think alike; **see with half an eye** to see without difficulty; **shut one's eyes to** to ignore; **throw** or **make sheep's eyes at** to ogle; **turn a blind eye to** to pretend not to see, to wink at; **under the eye of** under the observation of; **up to the eyes** or **eyebrows** deeply involved (in); extremely busy; **with** or **having an eye to** considering. [OE *ēage*; cf Gothic *augo*, Ger *Auge*, Du *oog*, ON *auga*]

eyelet *ī'lit*, *n* a small eye or hole to receive a lace or cord, as in garments, sails, etc; a small hole for seeing through (also **eye'let-hole**); a little eye. — *vt* to make eyelets in. — *n* **eyeleteer'** an instrument for making eyelet-holes. [OFr *oillet*, from L *oculus*, influenced by **eye**]

eyeliad, eyliad. See **oeillade**.

Eyeti, Eyetie or **Eytie** *ī'tī*, (*slang*) *n* an Italian.

eyne *īn*, (*archaic*) *n pl* eyes. [OE *ēagan*]

eyot *āt*. See **ait**[1].

eyra *ī'rə*, *n* a South American wild cat. [Guaraní]

eyre *ār*, (*hist*) *n* a journey or circuit; a court of itinerant justices in the late 12c and 13c. [OFr *eire* journey, from L *iter* a way, a journey, from *īre*, *itum* to go]

eyrie or **eyry** (also **aerie**, **aery** or **ayrie**) *ā'ri*, *ē'ri* or *ī'ri*, *n* the nest of a bird of prey, *esp* an eagle; a house or stronghold perched on some high or steep place; any high or inaccessible place; the brood in the nest, or a stock of children (*Shakesp*). [OFr *aire*; origin unknown]

Ez. (*Bible*) *abbrev*: (the Book of) Ezra.

Ezek. (*Bible*) *abbrev*: (the Book of) Ezekiel.

F

F or **f** *ef*, *n* the sixth letter in the modern English and Latin alphabets, derived from the Greek digamma, its sound a labiodental fricative formed by bringing the lower lip into contact with the upper teeth; the fourth note of the natural diatonic scale of C (*music*); ff in medieval script was used instead of a capital F. — **F'-clef** a clef marking F, the fourth line in the bass, the bass-clef; **f'-hole** either of a pair of holes in the belly of a violin, etc, shaped like an italic *f*; **f'-number** (*photog*) the ratio of the focal length to the true diameter of a lens; **f'-stop** a setting on a camera to show the f-number currently in use. — **the three F's** free sale, fixity of tenure, fair rent.

F *abbrev*: Fahrenheit; Fellow (of a society, etc); fighter plane (as in *F*-15, *F*-16, *F*-111, etc) (*US*); fine (on lead pencils); franc or francs; France (IVR). — **the F-word** (*euphem*) fuck.

F *symbol*: medieval Roman numeral 40 ($\bar{F}$ = 40 000); farad (*phys*); filial generation, thus F_1 first or F_2 second filial generation (*genetics*); fluorine (*chem*).

F *symbol*: force.

f or **f.** *abbrev*: farthing; fathom or fathoms; female; feminine; femto-; folio; following; foot; forte (*music*).

f *symbol*: frequency.

FA *abbrev*: Faculty of Actuaries; Football Association. — see also **Fanny Adams**.

Fa. *abbrev*: Florida (US state).

fa *fä*, *n* the fourth note in the sol-fa notation — also anglicized in spelling as **fah**. [See **Aretinian**]

fa' *fö*. Scots for **fall**.

FAA *abbrev*: Federal Aviation Administration (of the US).

fa'ard or **faurd** *färd*, *förd*. Scots for **favoured**.

fab *fab*, (*slang*) *adj* excellent, marvellous. [Contraction of **fabulous**]

fabaceous *fə-bāsh'əs*, *adj* bean-like. [L *faba* a bean]

Fabergé *fa-ber-zhā* or *fab-ər-jā'*, *n* delicate gold and enamel ware made in Russia in the 19c and early 20c. [Peter Carl *Fabergé* (1846–1920)]

Fabian *fā'bi-ən*, *adj* delaying, avoiding battle, cautious, practising the policy of delay; favouring the gradual introduction and spread of Socialism. — *n* a member or supporter of the *Fabian Society* founded (1884) for this purpose. — *n* **Fā'bianism**. — *n* **Fā'bianist**. [From Q *Fabius* Maximus, surnamed Cunctator (delayer), from the masterly tactics with which he wore out the strength of Hannibal, whom he dared not meet in battle]

fable *fā'bl*, *n* a narrative in which things irrational and sometimes inanimate are, for the purpose of moral instruction, made to act and speak with human interests and passions; any tale in literary form, not necessarily probable in its incidents, intended to instruct or amuse; the plot or series of events in an epic or dramatic poem (*archaic*); a fiction or myth; a ridiculous story, an old wives' tale; a falsehood; subject of common talk. — *vi* to tell fictitious tales; to tell lies (*obs*). — *vt* to feign; to invent; to relate as if true. — *adj* **fā'bled** mythical; renowned in story; feigned. — *n* **fā'bler**. — *n* and *adj* **fā'bling**. — *adj* **fabular** (*fab'ū-lər*). — *n* **fab'ulist** a person who invents fables. — *vi* **fab'ulize** or **-ise** to write fables or to speak in fables. [Fr *fable*, from L *fārī* to speak]

fabliau *fab'li-ō*, *n* a metrical tale similar to those, *usu* coarsely humorous in quality, produced in France in the 12c and 13c: — *pl* **fabliaux** (*fab'li-ōz*). [Fr, from dimin of *fable*]

fabric *fab'rik*, *n* manufactured cloth; any system of connected parts; framework (also *fig*); a building; buildings, stonework, etc; texture; anything created as the result of skill and hard work; the act of constructing. — *vt* (*Milton*) to construct. — *n* **fab'ricant** (*archaic*) a manufacturer. — *vt* **fab'ricate** to create with skill and hard work; to manufacture; to produce; to devise falsely. — *n* **fabricā'tion** construction; manufacture; that which is fabricated or invented; a story; a falsehood. — *adj* **fab'ricātive**. — *n* **fab'ricātor**. [L *fābrica* fabric, from *fāber* a worker in hard materials; partly through Fr *fabrique*]

fabular, etc. See **fable**.

fabulous *fab'ū-ləs*, *adj* feigned or false; spoken or written about in fable; celebrated in story; immense, amazing; excellent (*colloq*). — *n* **fabulos'ity** legendary nature. — *adv* **fab'ulously**. — *n* **fab'ulousness**. [L *fābula*, from *fārī* to speak; see also **fable**]

faburden *fa'bər-dən*, (*music hist*) *n* harmony in thirds and sixths; an early kind of counterpoint; an undersong; a refrain; in 4-part harmonization of a hymn, having the tune in the tenor; a descant. [Fr *faux-bourdon*, from *faux* false, and *bourdon* bourdon]

façade or **facade** *fa-säd'*, *n* the exterior front or face of a building; the appearance presented to the world, *esp* if showy and with little behind it (*fig*). [Fr, from *face*, after Ital *facciata* the front of a building, from *faccia* the face]

face *fās*, *n* the front part of the head, including forehead, eyes, nose, mouth, cheeks, and chin; the outside form or appearance; the front or surface of anything; a flat surface of a solid geometrical figure, crystal, etc; the striking surface of a golf club, etc; the edge of a cutting-tool, etc; the front or upper surface, or that usually on view; the exposed surface in a cliff, mine or quarry; a principal cleavage-plane (*geol*); the dial of a watch, etc; the printed surface of a playing-card; a style of letter or type (*printing*); special appearance or facial expression; aspect, look, configuration; command of facial expression and bearing; boldness, effrontery; a grimace; presence; anger or favour (*Bible*). — *vt* to meet in the face or in front; to stand opposite to or looking towards; to confront; to stand up to; to brave; to resist; to put an additional face or surface on; to cover in front; to trim. — *vi* (often with *on*, *to* or *towards*) to direct or turn the face; to take or have a direction; to show a face, *esp* bold or false (*obs*). — *adj* **faced** having a face; having the outer surface dressed; with the front covered with another material. — *adj* **face'less** having no face; (of a person or people concerned in some action) with identity unknown or concealed; robot-like, *esp* of bureaucratic officials who allow no degree of personality to intrude on their decision-making processes. — *n* **fac'er** a person who faces something; a person who puts on a false show (*obs*); a bold-faced person (*obs*); a tool for smoothing or facing a surface; a severe blow on the face (*slang*); an affront (*colloq*); anything that staggers one, a sudden problem or difficulty (*colloq*). — *adj* **facial** (*fā'shl*) of or relating to the face; for the face. — *n* a beauty treatment to the face (*colloq*). — *adv* **fa'cially**. — *n* **fac'ing** a covering in front for decoration or protection. — **face'-ache** neuralgia in the nerves of the face; an ugly person (*slang*; *usu* used as a mild or facetious insult); **face'-card** a playing-card bearing a face (king, queen or knave); **face'-cloth** or **face-flann'el** a cloth used in washing the face; (**face-cloth**) a cloth laid over the face of a corpse or living person; **face'-cream** a cosmetic cream for the face; **face'-fung'us** (*colloq*) a moustache or beard; **face'-guard** or **face'-mask** a kind of mask to guard or protect the face. — *vt* **face'-hard'en** to harden on the surface, to case-harden (*lit* and *fig*). — **face'-lift** a renovating process, *esp* one applied to the outside of a building; a surgical operation to smooth and firm the tissues of the face; **face'man** or **face'worker** a miner who works at the coal-face, as opposed to elsewhere in or at the mine; **face'-mask** a face-guard; a face pack; **face'-off** (in ice-hockey, etc) the dropping of the puck between two players to start the game; a confrontation (*fig*); **face pack** a creamy cosmetic mixture put on to the face to cleanse and tone the complexion, and removed when dry; **face'-plate** a disc on which a piece of wood, etc can be fixed for turning on a lathe; a protective plate in front of a piece of machinery; a flat transparent panel on the front of a protective helmet; **face'-powder** a cosmetic powder for the face; **face'-saver** a course of action that saves one's face (see below); **face'-saving** saving one's face (see below). — Also *adj*. — **face value** the value as stated on the face of a coin, share certificate, etc; the apparent value of anything, which may not be the same as its real value; **facial angle** (in skull measurement) the angle formed by lines drawn from the middle of the forehead to the upper jaw above the incisor teeth and from the opening of the ear to the opening of the nose; **facial mapping** a forensic technique for reconstructing the original face beneath a disguise. — **face down** to abash by stern looks; to confront and make concede; **face out** to carry off by confident appearance; to face down; **face the music** (*colloq*) to accept unpleasant consequences at their worst; to brave a trying situation, hostile reception, etc; **face to face** opposite; in actual presence, in person; in confrontation (*adj* **face'-to-face'**); **face up to** to face or stand up to; to recognize (a fact or facts) and prepare to endure or act bravely; **fly in the face of** to set oneself directly against; **have two faces** to be two-faced (see under **two**); **in the face of** in defiance of, despite; **look (someone) in the face** to look at (someone) without shame or embarrassment; **lose face** to lose prestige; **loss of face** humiliation, loss of dignity; **make** or **pull faces at** to distort one's face into exaggerated expressions in order to amuse, annoy, etc; **on the face of it** on its own showing; as is palpably plain; at first glance; **pull a long face** to look dismal; **put a good** or **brave face on (it)** to adopt a good-natured or stoical attitude in a troublesome situation; **put one's face on** (*colloq*) to apply cosmetics to the face; **right face**!, **left face**! or **right about face**! words of command, on which soldiers turn to the side specified; **run one's face** (*obs slang*) to obtain things on credit by sheer impudence; **save one's face** to avoid humiliation or appearance of climbing down; **set one's face against** to oppose strenuously; **show one's face** to appear; **to one's face** in one's presence, openly. [Fr *face*, from L *faciēs* form or face; perh from *facere* to make]

facet *fas'it*, *n* a small surface, eg of a crystal or gem; an aspect or view; a small flat area on eg a bone (*anatom*). — *vt* to cut a facet on, or cover with facets. — *adj* **fac'eted** having or formed into facets. [Fr *facette*, dimin of *face* face]

facetious *fə-sē'shəs*, *adj* humorous in a flippant or inappropriate way, often mildly cutting or deprecating; given to joking, waggish; pertaining to facetiae. — Also **facete** (*-sēt'*; *archaic*). — *n pl* **face'tiae** (*-shi-ē*) witty or humorous sayings or writings; a bookseller's term for improper books, of all degrees of indecency. — *adv* **facē'tiously**. — *n* **facē'tiousness**. [L *facētia*, from *facētus* merry or witty]

facia *fash'i-ə*, *fas'i-ə*. Same as **fascia**.

facies *fā'shi-ēz*, *n* general aspect, *esp* of plant, animal or geological species or formations; facial appearance or expression, *esp* when characteristic of a disease or condition: — *pl* **fā'cies**. [L *faciēs* face]

facile *fas'īl*, *-il*, *adj* affable (*obs*); easily persuaded; yielding; mentally weak, short of idiocy, but weak enough to be easily persuaded to actions prejudicial to oneself (*Scots law*); easy to accomplish; easy; working with ease; fluent (*usu* disparagingly); easily said, etc, but unthinkingly stupid. — *adv* **fac'ilely**. — *n* **fac'ileness**. — *vt* **facilitāte** (*fə-sil'*) to make easy or easier. — *n* **facilitā'tion**. — *adj* **facil'itātive**. — *n* **facil'itātor**. — *n* **facil'ity** ease in performance or action; fluency; easiness to be persuaded; pliancy; affability (*obs*); a condition of being facile (*Scots law*); (*esp* in *pl* **facil'ities**) means or opportunities that render anything readily possible; anything specially arranged or constructed to provide a service, recreation, etc; an agreed amount of money made available for borrowing (*econ*); (in *pl*) a lavatory (*colloq*). [Fr, from L *facilis* easy, from *facere* to do]

facile princeps *fas'i-lē prin'seps* or *fa'ki-le prin'keps*, (*L*) obviously pre-eminent. — *n* an easy first.

facilitate, facility, etc. See under **facile**.

facinorous *fa-* or *fə-sin'ə-rəs*, (*archaic*) *adj* atrociously wicked. — Also **facinē'rious** (*Shakesp*). — *n* **facin'orousness**. [L *facinorōsus*, from *facinus* a crime, from *facere* to do]

façon de parler *fa-sɔ̃ də par-lā*, (*Fr*) way of speaking, a mere form of words.

façonné *fa-so-nā*, *fas-ə-nā'* or *fas'*, *n* fabric with a self-coloured pattern of small figures woven into it; the pattern on such a fabric. — Also *adj*. [Fr, pa p of *façonner* to work or fashion]

facsimile *fak-sim'i-li*, *n* an exact copy, eg of handwriting, a coin, a document, etc; accurate reproduction; facsimile telegraph; (also **facsimile transmission**) fax (qv), a system for transmitting exact copies of documents: — *pl* **facsim'iles**. — *adj* exactly corresponding. — *vt* to make a facsimile of, to reproduce: — *pr p* **facsim'ileing**; *pa t* and *pa p* **facsim'iled**. — *n* **facsim'ilist**. — **facsimile edition** an edition of a book, etc that is an exact reproduction of an earlier edition; **facsimile telegraph** the transmission of a still picture over a telegraph circuit and its reproduction. [L *fac*, imperative of *facere* to make, and *simile* neuter of *similis* like]

fact *fakt*, *n* anything that happens; a truth; truth; reality, or a real state of things, as distinguished from a mere statement or belief; a deed, act, or anything done (*archaic*); an assertion of the truth; a crime committed (*obs* except in **after** and **before the fact**). — *n* **facticity** (*-is'i-ti*) the quality of being a fact, factualness. — *adj* **fact'ūal** pertaining to facts; actual. — *n* **factūal'ity**. — *n* **fact'ūalness**. — *n* **fact'um** (*law*) a thing done, a deed. — *adj* **fact'-finding** appointed to ascertain, or directed towards ascertaining, all the facts of a situation. — **fact sheet** a paper setting out briefly information relevant to a particular subject. — **as a matter of fact** in reality; **facts of life** the details of reproduction, *esp* human reproduction; the realities of a situation; **in fact** or **in point of fact** indeed; **the fact of the matter** the plain truth about the subject in question. [L *factum*, neuter pa p of *facere* to do]

factice *fakt'is*, *n* (formerly also **fact'is**) a rubber-like material made from vegetable oils, used as a rubber substitute. [L *factīcius*, *factitīvus*, from *facere* to make]

facticity. See under **fact**.

faction[1] *fak'shən*, *n* a small group of people formed of dissenting members of a larger group, *esp* in politics, *usu* used in a negative sense; any rebellious group; dissension. — *adj* **fac'tional**. — *n* **fac'tionalism**. — *n* **fac'tionalist**. — *n* **fac'tionary** a member of a faction. — *n* **fac'tionist**. — *adj* **fac'tious** turbulent; given to faction; proceeding from party spirit; seditious. — *adv* **fac'tiously**. — *n* **fac'tiousness**. [L *factiō*, *-ōnis*, from *facere* to do]

faction[2] *fak'shən*, *n* a play, programme, piece of writing, etc that is a mixture of fact and fiction; this type of writing, etc. — Also called **drama documentary** or **news fiction**. [**fact** and *ion* from **fiction**]

factitious *fak-tish'əs*, *adj* artificial; made; produced by artificial conditions. — *adv* **facti'tiously**. — *n* **facti'tiousness**. — *adj* **fac'titive** causative; (of a verb) which can take both a direct object and a complement. — *adj*

fac'tive (*linguistics*) making. [L *factīcius*, *factitīvus*, from *facere* to make]

factoid *fak'toid*, *n* an unprovable statement which has achieved unquestioning acceptance by frequent repetition. [**fact** and **-oid**]

factor *fak'tər*, *n* a doer or transactor of business for another person; a person or organization that buys and sells goods for others, on commission; an agent managing heritable estates for another person (*Scot*); one of two or more quantities which, when multiplied together, result in the given quantity — eg 6 and 4 are factors of 24 (*math*); an element in the composition of anything, or in bringing about a certain result; a fact, etc which has to be taken into account or which affects the course of events; (in heredity) a gene; a blood product given eg to haemophiliacs to aid coagulation. — *vi* to work, act, etc as a factor. — *n* **factorabil'ity**. — *adj* **fac'torable**. — *n* **fac'torage** the fees or commission of a factor. — *adj* **factō'rial** of or pertaining to a factor. — *n* the product of all whole numbers from a given number down to one. — *n* **fac'toring** the work of a factor; the business of buying up trade debts, or lending money on the security of these. — *n* **factorizā'tion** or **-s-**. — *vt* **fac'torize** or **-ise** to resolve into factors; to warn not to pay or give up goods (*US*); to attach (the effects of a debtor in the hands of another person, eg of the heir). — *n* **fac'torship**. — *n* **fac'tory** a place where goods are manufactured; a trading settlement in another country. — **factor 8** or **factor VIII** one of the proteins which form the clotting agent in blood, absent in haemophiliacs; **Factory Acts** laws dealing with working conditions, safety, etc in places of work, enforced by the **factory inspectorate**; **factory farm** one carrying out **factory farming**, farming by methods of feeding and housing animals in which everything is subordinated to achieving maximum production, rapid growth, and qualities in demand on the market; **factory-gate price** or **charge** the price of goods calculated by the seller exclusive of freight charges to the buyer; **fac'tory-ship** a whaling-ship on which whales are processed; a ship which freezes or otherwise processes the catch of a fishing fleet. — **factors of production** (*econ*) everything which may contribute to the production of goods, thought of generally as land, capital and labour (and also sometimes the entrepreneur); **judicial factor** a person appointed by the Court to manage the estate of a person under some incapacity; **safety factor** see under **safe**. [L *facere* to do]

factotum *fak-tō'təm*, *n* a person employed to do all kinds of work for another: — *pl* **facto'tums**. [LL, from L *fac* imperative of *facere* to do, and *tōtum* all]

factual, **factuality**, **factualness** and **factum**. See under **fact**.

facture *fak'chər*, *n* the act or process of making (*rare*); the result of making, workmanship. [L *factūra*, from *facere* to make]

facula *fak'ū-lə*, *n* a spot brighter than the rest of the surface, *esp* as seen on the sun: — *pl* **fac'ulae** (*-lē*). — *adj* **fac'ular**. [L *facula* dimin of *fax* torch]

faculty *fak'əl-ti*, *n* facility or power to act; any particular ability or aptitude; an original power of the mind; any physical or mental capability or function; personal quality or endowment; right, authority or privilege to act; licence; a department of learning at a university, or the professors and lecturers constituting it; the members of a profession; executive ability. — *adj* **fac'ultātive** optional; incidental; of or relating to a faculty; conferring privilege, permission or authority; able to live under different conditions (*zool*). — *adv* **fac'ultatively**. — **facultative parasite** (*bot*) a parasite able to live on dead or decaying organic matter as well as on its living host (cf **obligate parasite**). — **Court of Faculties** a court established by Henry VIII, whereby authority is given to the Archbishop of Canterbury to grant dispensations and faculties; **Faculty of Advocates** the Scottish college of advocates. [Fr *faculté*, from L *facultās*, *-ātis*, from *facilis* easy]

facundity *fə-kun'di-ti*, *n* eloquence. [L *fācunditās*, *-ātis*]

fad *fad*, *n* a hobby or interest intensely pursued at first, but soon passed over for another; an overriding personal preference or taste, *esp* trifling. — *n* **fadd'iness**. — *adj* **fadd'ish**. — *n* **fadd'ishness** or **fadd'ism**. — *n* **fadd'ist** a person who is a slave to some fad. — *adj* **fadd'y**. [Ety unknown]

fadaise. See under **fade²**.

faddle *fad'l*, (*dialect*) *vi* to trifle. — *n* nonsense, trifling, *usu* in **fiddle-faddle**.

fade¹ *fād*, *vi* to lose strength, freshness, loudness, brightness or colour gradually; to grow pale, dull or faint; to die away; to disappear. — *vt* to cause to fade: to cause to change gradually in distinctness (as in *fade out*, *fade in*); to impart a fade to (*golf*). — *n* a fading; a slight, delayed (often deliberate) slice (*golf*). — *adj* (*archaic*) faded, weak. — *adj* **fā'dable**. — *adv* **fā'dedly**. — *n* **fā'dedness**. — *adj* **fāde'less** unfading; not liable to fade. — *adv* **fāde'lessly**. — *n* **fā'der** a sliding control as used eg on audio and lighting equipment to set levels of sound and light. — *n* and *adj* **fād'ing**. — *adj* **fā'dy** wearing away. — **fade'-away** a gradual disappearance. — **fade down** (of sound or light) to fade out (*n* **fade'-down**); **fade in** in films, radio, television, etc, to introduce (sound or a picture) gradually, bringing it up to full volume or clarity (*n* **fade'-in**); **fade out** in films, radio, television, etc, to cause (sound or a picture) to disappear gradually (*n* **fade'-out**); **fade up** (of sound or light) to fade in (*n* **fade'-up**). [OFr *fader*, from *fade*, perh from L *vapidum* dull, insipid]

fade² *fad*, (*Fr*) *adj* insipid, colourless. — *n* **fadaise** (*fa-dez*) a silly saying; twaddle. — *n* **fadeur** (*fa-dœr*) dullness.

fadge *faj*, (*archaic*) *vi* to agree, hit it off; to succeed, turn out. [Ety doubtful; not connected with OE *fēgan* to join]

fading *fā'ding*, *n* an old dance, probably Irish; the burden or refrain of a song (*Shakesp*). [Origin unknown]

fado *fä'dōō*, *n* a type of Portuguese folk-song or dance: — *pl* **fad'os**. [Port, fate, from L *fātum*]

faeces or (*US*) **feces** *fē'sēz*, *n pl* excrement; sediment after infusion or distillation; dregs. — *adj* **faecal** or (*US*) **fecal** (*fē'kl*). [L, pl of *faex*, *faecis* dregs or grounds]

faerie or **faery** fā'(ə)ri, (*archaic*) *n* the world of fairies, fairyland; a fairy. — Also *adj*. [A variant of **fairy**]

faex populi *fēks pop'ū-lī* or *fīks po'pōō-lē*, (*L*) *n* dregs of the people, the mob.

faff *faf*, (*colloq*) *vi* to dither, fumble (*usu* with *about* or *around*). [Origin obscure]

fag¹ *fag*, *n* a schoolboy forced to do menial work for another, *usu* older, boy; a tiresome piece of work; drudgery; *orig* an inferior cigarette (for *fag-end*; *slang*); hence any cigarette (*colloq*). — *vi* to become weary or tired out (*colloq*); to work hard; to be a fag for someone. — *vt* to weary; to use as a fag: — *pr p* **fagg'ing**; *pa t* and *pa p* **fagged**. — *n* **fagg'ery** drudgery; fagging. — *n* and *adj* **fagg'ing**. — **fag'-end** the end of a web of cloth that hangs loose; the untwisted end of a rope; the end, remaining or worthless part of a thing; the stump of a cigar or cigarette (*colloq*). — **fagged out** (*colloq*) very tired, exhausted; **fag out** to field, as a fag, in cricket. [Ety doubtful; perh a corruption of **flag¹**, to droop (qv)]

fag². See under **faggot**.

faggot or **fagot** *fag'ət*, *n* a bundle of sticks for fuel, etc; a stick; anything like a faggot; a bundle of pieces of iron or steel cut off into suitable lengths for welding; a soldier numbered on the muster-roll, but not really existing (*hist*); a voter who has obtained his or her vote expressly for party purposes, on a spurious or sham qualification (*hist*); a roll or ball of minced meat, *esp* pig's liver, mixed with bread and savoury herbs for cooking as food; an old woman (*derog*); a male homosexual (also **fag**; *slang*, *orig US*). — *adj* got up for a purpose, as in *faggot vote* (*hist*). — *vt* to tie together; to practise faggoting. — *n* **fagg'oting** or **fag'oting** a kind of embroidery in which some of the cross-threads are drawn together in the middle. — **burn one's faggot** to recant a heresy. [Fr *fagot* a bundle of sticks]

Fagin *fā'gin*, *n* a person who trains young thieves, receives stolen goods, etc. [Character in Dickens' novel *Oliver Twist*]

fagotto *fəg-ot'ō*, *n* a bassoon: — *pl* **fagott'i** (-*ē*). — *n* **fagott'ist** a person who plays the bassoon. [Ital]

Fagus *fā'gəs*, *n* the beech genus of trees, giving name to the family **Fagā'ceae**. — *adj* **fagā'ceous**. [L *fāgus* beech; cf Gr *phēgos* oak, and OE *bōc* beech]

fah. See **fa**.

fahlband *fäl'bänt*, *n* in crystalline rocks, a pale band rich in metals. — *n* **fahl'erz** (-*erts*) tetrahedrite; also tennantite. — *n* **fahl'ore** (-*ōr* or -*ör*) tetrahedrite or tennantite. [Ger *fahl* dun-coloured, *Band* band, *Erz* ore, and Eng **ore**]

Fahrenheit *fa'* or *fä'rən-hīt*, *adj* (of a thermometer or thermometer scale) having the freezing-point of water marked at 32, and the boiling-point at 212 degrees (to convert °F into °C, subtract 32 and take 5/9 of the remainder). [Named from the inventor, Gabriel D *Fahrenheit* (1686–1736)]

faible *feb'l*, *n* a foible; the part of a foil blade between the middle and the point, the weak part. [Fr, weak]

faience or **faïence** *fä-yãs*, *n* glazed coloured earthenware. [Fr; prob from *Faenza* in Italy]

faik *fāk*, (*Scot*) *vi* and *vt* to abate; to excuse.

faikes. See **fakes**.

fail[1] *fāl*, (*Scot*) *n* a turf, sod. — **fail'-dike** a turf wall. [Perh Gaelic *fàl* a sod]

fail[2] *fāl*, *vi* to fall short or be lacking (with *in*); to fall away, to dwindle; to decay; to die; to prove deficient under trial, examination, pressure, etc; not to achieve; to be disappointed or baffled; to become insolvent or bankrupt. — *vt* not to be sufficient for; to leave undone, omit; to disappoint or desert; to deceive (*Spenser*); to declare unsuccessful or lacking in knowledge after examination. — *n* a failure, *esp* in an examination. — *adj* **failed** that has failed; decayed, worn out; bankrupt. — *n* **fail'ing** a fault, weakness; a foible; failure. — *adj* that fails. — *prep* in default of, in the absence of. — *n* **fail'ure** a falling short or cessation; lack of success; omission; decay; bankruptcy; an unsuccessful person. — *adj* **fail'-safe** (of a mechanism) incorporated in a system to ensure that there will be no accident if the system does not operate properly; (of a system) designed to revert to a safe condition in the event of failure. — Also *fig*. — **fail of** to fall short of accomplishing (a purpose); **fail safe** to revert to a safe condition in the event of failure; **without fail** for certain. [OFr *faillir*, from L *fallere* to deceive; cf Du *feilen*, Ger *fehlen* and ON *feila*]

faille *fāl*, *fīl* or *fä-y'*, *n* a soft, closely-woven silk or rayon fabric with transverse ribs. [Fr]

failure. See under **fail**.

fain[1] *fān*, (*archaic* and *poetic*) *adj* glad or joyful; eager (with *to*); content for lack of anything better; compelled; wont (*Spenser*). — *vt* (*Spenser*) to delight in; to desire. — *adv* gladly. — *adv* **fain'ly** gladly. — *n* **fain'ness** eagerness. [OE *fægen* joyful; cf ON *feginn* glad]

fain[2] or **faine** *fān*, (*Spenser*) *vt*. Same as **feign**.

fainéant *fen'ā-ã*, *adj* and *n* do-nothing, applied *esp* to the later Merovingian kings of France, mere puppets, whose mayors of the palace governed the country. — *n* **fai'néance** (-*ãs*), **fai'neancy** (-*ən-si*) or **fainéantise** (-*tēz'*). [Fr, as if from *faire* to do, and *néant* nothing; really, from OFr *faignant* pr p of *faindre* to skulk]

fains *fānz*, (*schoolchildren's slang*) *interj* a plea for exemption or a truce. — Also **fain'ites** and **fains I**. [Form of **fen**[2]]

faint *fānt*, *adj* lacking in strength (*archaic*); dim; lacking distinctness; not bright or having any force; weak in spirit (*archaic*); lacking courage (*archaic*); done in a feeble way; inclined to lose consciousness momentarily; sickly-smelling, oppressive (*archaic*). — *vi* to become feeble or weak (*archaic*); to lose strength, colour, etc (*archaic*); to lose consciousness momentarily, to swoon; to fade or decay (*archaic*); to vanish (*archaic*); to lose courage or spirit (*archaic*). — *vt* (*rare*) to render faint. — *n* a swoon. — *adj* **faint'ed** (*Milton*) exhausted. — *n* and *adj* **faint'ing**. — *adj* **faint'ish** slightly faint. — *n* **faint'ishness**. — *adv* **faint'ly**. — *n* **faint'ness** lack of strength; feebleness of colour, light, etc; dejection. — *n pl* **faints** impure spirit produced at the beginning and end of distillation (also **feints**). — *adj* **faint'y** faintish. — *adj* **faint'-heart** (also *n*) or **faint-heart'ed** spiritless, lacking courage; timorous. — *adv* **faint-heart'edly**. — **faint-heart'edness**. [OFr *feint* feigned, from L *fingere* to feign]

fair[1] *fār*, *adj* bright; clear; clean; free from blemish; pure; pleasing to the eye; beautiful; of a light hue; free from rain, fine, dry; unobstructed; open; smoothly curving; prosperous; impartial; just; equitable; good, pleasing; plausible; civil; specious; reasonable; likely; favourable; pretty good; passable; out-and-out, veritable (*dialect*); a general expression of commendation or courtesy (as in *fair sir*; *archaic*). — *n* that which is fair; a woman (*archaic*); beauty (*Shakesp*). — *vt* to make fair. — *vi* to clear up, as the weather from rain. — *adv* in a fair manner (in all senses); full, square, directly (eg *hit fair in the centre*); quite (*dialect*) — *n* **fair'ing** adjustment or testing of curves in ship-building; streamlined external fittings on an aeroplane, car, motorcycle, etc, to reduce drag. — See also **fair**[2]. — *adj* **fair'ish** somewhat fair; pretty well; pretty drunk (*dialect*). — *adv* **fair'ly** tolerably; fully, quite; justly; reasonably; plainly; beautifully (*archaic*); neatly (*archaic*); gently (*obs*). — *n* **fair'ness**. — *adj* **fair'-and-square'** honest (also *adv*); **fair'-bod'ing** (*Shakesp*) auspicious. — **fair catch** (*Am football*) an unopposed catch by a receiving team member; **fair comment** honest expression of one's views in criticism, not motiviated by malice, and therefore not punishable as libel or slander; **fair copy** a clean copy after correction, *esp* of a legal document; **fair-deal'ing**. — *adj* **fair'-faced** with a light complexion; beautiful; specious (*archaic*). — **fair field** just conditions; **fair game** a legitimate object for attack or ridicule. — *adj* **fair'-haired** or **fair'-headed** having light-coloured hair. — **Fair Isle** a type of design used in knitwear, named from a Shetland island; **fair'lead** or **fair-leader** a ring, hole or set of holes, etc, or more elaborate device, for guiding a rope, etc so as to reduce friction. — *adj* **fair'-minded** judging fairly. — **fair play** honest dealing; justice. — *adj* **fair'-seeming** appearing fair. — *adj* **fair-spok'en** bland or civil in language and address. — **fair trade** smuggling (*euphem*); a mild form of the protective system, in which the basis of economic policy is supposed to be reciprocity or free trade only with such nations as grant similar privileges — also used adverbially; **fair'way** the navigable channel or usual course of vessels in a river, etc; the smooth turf between tee and putting-green, distinguished from the uncut rough and from hazards (*golf*). — *adj* **fair'-weath'er** suitable only for, or found only in, fair weather or (*esp* of friends or supporters) favourable circumstances. — **bid fair** see under **bid**; **fair befall** or **fall** (*archaic*) good luck to; **fair dinkum** (*Austr*) honest or honestly; **fair do's** (*dōōz* — *pl* of **do**; *colloq*) an expression appealing for, or agreeing to, fair play, strict honesty, etc; **fair enough** expressing acceptance, though not necessarily full agreement; **in a fair way to** see under **way**; **in all fairness** being scrupulously fair; **keep fair with** to keep on amicable terms with; **speak fair** see under **speak**; **stand fair with** to be in the good graces of; **the fair** or **the fair sex** (often *patronizing*) the female sex. [OE *fæger*]

fair[2] *fār*, *n* a large market held periodically for one kind of merchandise, or for the general sales and purchases of a district, with or without amusements; often reduced to a collection of shows, swing-boats, etc; a charity bazaar; a trade show. — *n* **fair'ing** a present given at or from a fair; any complimentary gift. — See also **fair**[1]. — **fair'-day**; **fair'ground**. — **a day after the fair** or

behind the fair too late; **get one's fairing** (*Scot*) to get one's deserts. [OFr *feire*, from L *fēria* holiday]

fairnitickle, **fairniticle**, **fairnytickle** or **fairnyticle**. See under **fern**.

fairy *fār'i*, *n* a creature of folklore, an imaginary being, generally of diminutive and graceful human form, capable of kindly or unkindly acts towards man; fairyland (see also **faerie**); an enchantress; a creature of overpowering charm; a male homosexual (*disparagingly*). — *adj* like a fairy, fanciful, whimsical, delicate. — *adv* **fair'ily**. — *n* **fair'ydom**. — *n* **fair'yhood**. — *n* **fair'yism**. — *adj* and *adv* **fair'ylike** like fairies or like something in fairyland; very delicate and charming. — **fair'y-beads** joints of the stems of fossil sea-lilies, or crinoids; **fairy-butt'er** a name applied in northern England to certain gelatinous fungi; **fai'ry-cycle** a small child's bicycle; **fairy-god'mother** a benefactress (or, loosely, a benefactor), *esp* an unexpected one; **fair'yland** the country of the fairies; **fairy light** (*usu* in *pl*) a small coloured light used as decoration, *esp* on Christmas trees; **fair'y-money** or **fairy gold** money reputedly given by fairies, which changes into withered leaves, slate, stones, etc; money that comes unsought, hence, illusory riches; **fairy moss** a small floating fern, *Azolla caroliniana*; **fair'y-ring** a ring of darker-coloured grass due to outward spread of a fungus (as the fairy-ring mushroom or champignon, *Marasmius oreades*), attributed to the dancing of fairies; **fair'y-stone** a fossil sea-urchin; a concretion; **fairy story** or **fair'ytale** a story about fairies or other supernatural beings; a folk-tale; a romantic tale; an incredible tale; a lie (*euphem*); a marvel. — *n* **fair'ytale** see **fairy story**. — *adj* beautiful, fortunate, etc, as in a fairytale. [OFr *faerie* enchantment, from *fae* (mod Fr *fée*); see **faerie** and **fay**[1]]

fait accompli *fe-ta-kɔ̃-plē*, (*Fr*) *n* an accomplished fact, a thing already done or done in advance, eg of obtaining permission.

faites vos jeux *fet vō zhø*, (*Fr*) place your stakes (eg in roulette).

faith *fāth*, *n* trust or confidence; belief in the statement of another person; belief in the truth of revealed religion; confidence and trust in God; the living reception of religious belief; that which is believed; any system of religious belief, *esp* the religion one considers true; fidelity to promises; honesty; word or honour pledged; faithfulness. — *interj* (*archaic*) by my faith; indeed. — *vt* (*fādh*; *Shakesp*) to believe. — *adj* **faith'ful** full of faith, believing; firm in adherence to promises, duty, friendship, love, etc; loyal; constant; corresponding to truth; worthy of belief; true; exact. — *adv* **faith'fully** with confidence; with fidelity; with sincerity; with scrupulous exactitude; solemnly (*colloq*); a word customarily used in concluding a letter. — *n* **faith'fulness**. — *adj* **faith'less** without faith or belief; not believing, *esp* in God or Christianity; not adhering to promises, duty, etc; inconstant, fickle; adulterous; untrustworthy; deceptive. — *adv* **faith'lessly**. — *n* **faith'lessness**. — *n* **faith'worthiness** trustworthiness. — *adj* **faith'worthy** worthy of faith or belief. — **faith'-healer**; **faith'-healing** or **faith'cure** a system of belief, based on James 5.15, that sickness may be cured without medical advice or appliances, if the prayer of Christians is accompanied in the sufferer by true faith; cure by suggestion. — **bad faith** treachery; insincerity or disingenuousness; the breaking of a promise; **Father of the faithful** Abraham; the spiritual leader of Islam, the caliph; **in good faith** with honesty and sincerity; acting honestly; **keep faith** to act honestly, according to one's promise (with); **the Faithful** believers, *esp* Muslims; (without *cap*) adherents, supporters, etc (*colloq*). [ME *feith* or *feyth*, from OFr *feid*, from L *fidēs*, from *fīdere* to trust]

faitor *fā'tər*, (*obs*) *n* an impostor. — Often **fai'tour**. [OFr *faitor*, from L *factor*, *-ōris* a doer]

faix *fāks*, (*dialect*) *interj* faith. [Prob short for *faykins*; see **fay**[2]]

fajitas *fa-hhē'təs*, *n pl* a Mexican dish of chicken, beef, etc, served sizzling hot, wrapped in flour tortillas.

fake[1] *fāk*, *vt* to fold, coil. — *n* a coil of rope, etc. [ME *faken*; cf Scot *faik* fold]

fake[2] *fāk*, *vt* to doctor, cook, pretend or counterfeit; to rob or attack; to filch. — *n* a swindle, dodge or sham; a faked object — also **fake'ment**. — *adj* false or counterfeit. — *n* **fak'er**. — *n* **fak'ery**. [Prob the earlier *feak* or *feague*, Ger *fegen* to furbish up]

fakes or **faikes** *fāks*, *n pl* thin-bedded shaly or micaceous sandstone or sandy shale.

fakir *fä-kēr'* or *fā'kər*, *n* a religious (*esp* Muslim) mendicant, ascetic or wonder-worker in India, etc. — *n* **fakir'ism** (or *fā'*). [Ar *faqīr* a poor man]

fa-la *fä-lä'*, *n* an old kind of madrigal. — **fa la** (**la**, etc) syllables used as a refrain.

falafel. See **felafel**.

falaj *fal'aj*, *n* a water channel, *specif* one forming part of the ancient irrigation system of Oman: — *pl* **aflaj'**. [Ar, stream]

Falange *fä-läng'hhā* (*Sp*), also *fə-lanj'* or *fā'*, *n* the Spanish fascist movement, established in 1933, and the only legal political party under Franco. — *n* **Falangism** (*fə-lan'jizm*) (also without *cap*). — *n* **Falan'gist** (also without *cap*). [Sp, from Gr *phalanx* phalanx (qv)]

Falasha *fə-lä'shə*, *n* one of a community of black Ethiopian Jews. [Amharic, immigrant]

falbala *fal'bə-lə*, *n* a trimming or flounce. [Ety doubtful; cf **furbelow**]

falcade *fal-kād'*, *n* the motion of a horse when it throws itself on its haunches in a very quick leap or curvet. [Fr, from L *falcāta* (fem) bent]

falcate *fal'kāt* or **falcated** *fal-kā'tid*, *adj* bent like a sickle. — *n* **falcā'tion**. — *adj* **falciform** (*fal'si-förm*) sickle-shaped. — *n* **fal'cūla** a falcate claw. — *adj* **fal'cūlate**. [L *falx*, *falcis* a sickle]

falces. See **falx**.

falchion *föl'shən* or *-chən*, *n* a short, broad sword, bent rather like a sickle. [OFr *fauchon*, through LL from L *falx* a sickle]

falciform. See under **falcate**.

falcon *föl'kən*, *fol'kən*, *fö'kən*, or (rarely) *fal'kən*, *n* any of the long-winged birds of prey of the genus *Falco* or related genera; a bird of prey of a kind trained to hunt small game; by falconers confined to the female (*esp* peregrine) falcon (cf **tercel**); a kind of cannon. — *n* **fal'coner** a person who hunts with, or who breeds and trains, falcons or hawks. — *n* **fal'conet** a small field-gun in use till the 16c. — *adj* **fal'conine**. — *n* **fal'conry** the art or practice of training, or hunting with, falcons. — *adj* **fal'con-eyed** keen-eyed. — **falcon-gen'til** or **falcon-gen'tle** the female of the peregrine falcon. [OFr *faucon*, from LL *falcō*, *-ōnis*]

falcula, etc. See under **falcate**.

faldage *föld'ij* or *fald'ij*, (*hist*) *n* the right of the lord of a manor of folding his tenant's sheep in his own fields for the sake of the manure; a fee paid by the tenant in lieu of this. [Law L *faldāgium*, from OE *fald* fold]

falderal *fal'dər-al'*, *n* a meaningless refrain in songs; any kind of flimsy trifle — also **folderol** (*fol'dər-ol'*) or **fal de rol**. — **falderal it** to sing meaningless sounds.

faldetta *fäl-det'ə*, *n* a Maltese woman's combined hood and cape. [Ital]

faldstool *föld'stōōl*, *n* a folding or camp stool; a coronation stool; a bishop's armless seat; a small desk in churches in England, at which the litany is sung or said. — *n* **fald'istory** (*obs*) a bishop's seat within the chancel. [LL *faldistolium* or *faldistorium*, from OHGer *faldstuol*, from *faldan* (Ger *falten*) to fold, and *stuol* (Ger *Stuhl*) stool]

Falernian *fa-lûr'ni-ən*, *adj* pertaining to a district (*Falernus ager*) in Campania (area around Rome), once famous for its wine.

fall[1] *föl*, *vi* to descend, *esp* freely and involuntarily by force of gravity; to drop; to drop prostrate; to throw oneself down; to collapse; to become lower literally or figuratively (in position, degree, intensity, value, pitch, etc); to die away; to subside; to abate; to ebb; to decline; to sink; (of the face) to relax into an expression of disappointment or dismay; to flow downwards; to slope or incline down; to hang, dangle or trail down; to be cast or shed; to drop dead or as if dead, *esp* in a fight; to be overthrown; to come to ruin; to lose power, station, virtue or repute; to be degraded; to be taken or captured; to become a victim; to yield to temptation; to pass into any state or action, to become, to begin to be (as in *fall asleep*, *fall in love*, *fall a-weeping*); to become pregnant (*dialect*); to rush; to become involved; to take oneself (to); to come to be; to come about; to come by chance or as if by chance; to come in due course; to happen or occur; to chance or light (on); to issue or come forth; to appertain (to); to be apportioned or assigned (to); to come as one's share, lot, duty, etc; to take up a set position; to be found at a specific place; to be disposed; to impinge; to lapse; to terminate; to revert. — *vt* to cause to fall (*archaic* or *US*); to let fall (*archaic*); to get (as what happens to one) (*obs*; *Burns*): — *pr p* **fall'ing**; *pa t* **fell**; *pa p* **fallen** (*fö'lən*). — *n* the act, manner, occasion or time of falling or of felling; descent by gravity, a dropping down; that which falls; as much as comes down at one time; onset; overthrow; descent from a better to a worse position; slope or declivity; descent of water; a cascade; length of drop or amount of descent; decrease in value; a sinking of the voice; a cadence; the time when the leaves fall, autumn (chiefly *US*); a bout of wrestling; the passing of a city or stronghold to the enemy; a lapse into sin, *esp* that of Adam and Eve, 'the Fall (of Man)'; a falling band, a hanging fringe, flap or ornament; a lot, chance or fortune (*archaic*); a lowering or hoisting rope. — *adj* **fall'en** having fallen; killed, *esp* in battle; overthrown; seduced; in a degraded state, ruined. — *n pl* (*esp literary*; *usu* with *the*) those killed in battle. — *n* **fall'er**. — *n* **fall'ing**. — *adj* **fall'-back** used as a retreat, or second alternative. — Also *n*. — **fallen star** a gelatinous mass of a blue-green alga (Nostoc, etc) once popularly thought to be of meteoric origin; **fall-in** see **fall in** below; **falling band** a 17c man's collar of fine material turned down on the shoulders; **falling-off'** a decline; **falling sickness** (*archaic*) epilepsy; **falling star** a meteor; **falling stone** a portion of an exploded meteor; **fall'out** by-product, side benefit (*colloq*); a deposit of radioactive dust from a nuclear explosion or plant; the aftermath of any explosive occurrence or situation (*fig*); see also **fall out** below; **fall'-trap** a trap that operates by causing the victim to fall. — **fall about** to laugh hysterically, to collapse (with laughter); **fall across** (*archaic*) to meet by chance; **fall among** to find oneself in the midst of; **fall apart** to disintegrate; to fail; to collapse or go to pieces; **fall away** to slope down; to decline gradually; to dwindle or waste away; to lose enthusiasm and so leave (a club, etc); to languish; to grow lean; to revolt or abandon one's beliefs, principles, etc; **fall back** to retreat, give way; **fall back** or **fall edge** (*obs*) no matter what may happen; **fall back upon** to have recourse to as an expedient or resource in reserve; **fall behind** to lag; to be outstripped; to get in arrears; **fall between two stools** to be neither one thing nor the other; to succeed in neither of two alternatives; **fall down on** (*colloq*) to fail in; **fall flat** to fail completely, have no effect; **fall flat on one's face** to come to grief or fail dismally; **fall for** (*colloq*) to develop a liking or love for (*usu* a person); to be taken in by (a trick, etc); **fall foul of** see under **foul**; **fall in** to (cause to) take places in ranks (*military*; *n* **fall'-in'**); to become hollowed; to revert; to cave in or collapse; **fall in with** to concur or agree with; to comply with; to meet by chance; to begin to associate with; **fall off** to become detached and drop; to deteriorate; to die away, to perish; to revolt or abandon one's beliefs, principles, etc; to draw back; **fall on** to begin eagerly; to make an attack; to meet (*archaic*); **fall on one's feet** to come well out of a difficulty; to gain any unexpected good fortune; **fall out** to quarrel; to happen (that); to turn out; to (cause to) break ranks (*military*; *n* **fall'-out'**); **fall over** to tumble or trip up (on); to go over to the enemy (*Shakesp*); to go to sleep (*Scot*); **fall over backwards** see **backwards** under **back**; **fall over oneself** (*colloq*) to take a lot of trouble, to be in great haste or eagerness (to do something); **fall short** to turn out to be short or insufficient; to become used up; to fail to attain or reach what is aimed at (with *of*); **fall through** to fail or come to nothing; **fall to** to begin hastily and eagerly; to apply oneself to; to begin to eat; **fall upon** to attack; to rush against; to devolve upon or be the duty of; to chance or come upon; **try a fall** to take a bout at wrestling. [OE *fallan* (WS *feallan*); Ger *fallen*; prob connected with L *fallere* to deceive]

fall[2] *föl*, *n* a trap. — **fall'-guy** or **fall guy** (*colloq*; *esp NAm*) a dupe or easy victim; a scapegoat. [OE *fealle*, from *feallan* to fall]

fall[3] *föl*, *n* the cry given when a whale is sighted or harpooned; the chase of a whale. — **loose fall** the losing of a whale. [Perh from the north-eastern Scottish pronunciation of **whale**]

fallacy *fal'ə-si*, *n* deceptive appearance; an apparently genuine but really illogical argument; deception or deceitfulness (*obs*); a wrong but prevalent notion. — *adj* **fallacious** (*fə-lā'shəs*) of the nature of (a) fallacy; deceptive; misleading; not well founded; causing disappointment. — *adv* **fallā'ciously**. — *n* **fallā'ciousness**. [L *fallācia*, from *fallāx* deceptive, from *fallere* to deceive]

fallal *fal-al'*, *n* a streamer of ribbon; any trifling ornament. — *adj* (*obs*) foppish, trifling. — *n* **fallal'ery**. — *adv* **fallal'ishly**.

fallible *fal'i-bl*, *adj* capable of making mistakes, liable to error. — *n* **fall'ibilism** (*philos*) the doctrine that knowledge gained empirically can never be certain. — *n* **fall'ibilist**. — Also *adj*. — *n* **fallibil'ity** capacity or tendency to make mistakes. — *adv* **fall'ibly**. [LL *fallibilis*, from *fallere* to deceive]

Fallopian *fə-lō'pi-ən*, *adj* relating to the Italian anatomist Gabriele *Fallopio* (1523–62). — **Fallopian tubes** two tubes or ducts through which the ova pass from the ovary to the uterus, perhaps discovered by him.

fallow[1] *fal'ō*, *adj* left unploughed or unsown for a time. — *n* land that has lain a year or more unploughed or unsown after having been ploughed. — *vt* to plough without seeding. — *n* **fall'owness**. — **fall'ow-chat** or **fall'ow-finch** the wheatear, a small songbird of the genus *Oenanthe*, a summer visitor to Britain. — **green fallow** land re-fertilized between crops by sowing a green crop, eg comfrey. [OE *fealgian* to fallow; *fealh* fallow land]

fallow[2] *fal'ō*, *adj* brownish-yellow. — **fallow deer** a yellowish-brownish deer smaller than the red deer, with broad flat antlers. [OE *falu* (*fealu*); cf Ger *fahl*, and ON *fölr*]

false *föls*, *adj* wrong; erroneous; deceptive or deceiving; untruthful; unfaithful (*old*); untrue; not genuine or real, counterfeit; improperly so called; (of teeth, etc) artificial, as opposed to natural; out of tune. — *adv* incorrectly; untruly; dishonestly; faithlessly. — *n* (*obs*) falsehood; untruth. — *vt* (*obs*) to deceive, be false to; to feign; to falsify. — *n* **false'hood** the state or quality of being false; lack of truth; deceitfulness (*obs*); false appearance (*obs*); an untrue statement; the act of lying; a lie. — *adv* **false'ly**. — *n* **false'ness**. — *n* **fals'er** a falsifier, counterfeiter (*obs*); a deceiver, a liar (*Spenser*). — *n* **fal'sie** (*colloq*; *usu* in *pl*) a pad of rubber or other material inserted into a brassière to enlarge or improve the shape of the breast. — *adj* **fals'ish** somewhat false. — *n* **fals'ism** a self-evident falsity. — *n* **fals'ity** the quality of being false; a false assertion. — **false acacia** one of the robinia, shrubs and trees of the N American genus *Robinia*, to which the locust tree also belongs; **false alarm** a warning of danger which turns out to have been unnecessary. — *adj* **false-bedd'ed**. — **false bedding** (*geol*) irregular lamination running obliquely to the general stratification, due to deposition in banks by varying currents; **false bottom** (eg in a suitcase) a partition cutting off and hiding a space between it and the true bottom; **false card** a card played to deceive. — *vi* **false-card'**. — **false conception** a uterine growth consisting of non-foetal material; **false dawn** deceptive appearance simulating dawn. — Also *fig*. — **false face** a mask. — *adj* **false'-faced** (*Shakesp*) hypocritical. — **false gallop** (*archaic*) a canter. — *adj* **false'-heart'ed** treacherous or deceitful. — **false hem** a strip of fabric added to the bottom of a garment, etc in order to deepen the hem; **false imprisonment** illegal detention by force or influence; **false leg** the abdominal leg of an insect larva, a proleg; **false pregnancy** a psychological disorder in which many of the symptoms of pregnancy are simulated, pseudocyesis (see under **pseud-**); **false pretences** deception; **false quantity** pronunciation or use of a long vowel as short or short as long; **false relation** (*music*) occurrence in different parts together or in succession of a tone and a chromatic derivative; **false rib** one that does not reach the breastbone; **false shame** shame felt for something which is not shameful; **false start** in a race, a start that is declared invalid (*sport*); an unsuccessful attempt to begin an activity; **false teeth** artificial teeth, dentures; **false'work** a temporary framework used to support a building, etc during construction. — **play someone false** to act falsely or treacherously towards a person; **put in a false position** to bring anyone into a position in which he or she will be misunderstood. [OFr *fals* (mod *faux*), from L *falsus*, pa p of *fallere* to deceive]

falsetto *föl-set'ō*, *n* (*usu* in a man) a forced (*esp* singing) voice of a range or register above its natural one; a person who uses such a voice; false or strained sentiment: — *pl* **falsett'os**. — *adj* and *adv* in falsetto. [Ital *falsetto*, dimin of *falso* false]

falsi crimen *fal-sī krī'mən* or *fal'sē krē'men*, (*LL*) *n* the crime of falsification, *esp* forgery.

falsidical *föl-sid'i-kəl*, (*rare*) *adj* conveying a meaning that is false. [L *falsus*, and *dīcere* to say]

falsify *föls'i-fī*, *vt* to forge or counterfeit; to tamper with; to misrepresent; to prove or declare to be false; to be false to (*obs*); to feign (*obs*). — *vi* (*obs*) to lie: — *pr p* **fals'ifying**; *pa t* and *pa p* **fals'ified**. — *n* **falsifīabil'ity**. — *adj* **fals'ifīable**. — *n* **falsificā'tion**. — *n* **fals'ifīer**. [Fr *falsifier*, from LL *falsificāre*, from L *falsus* false, and *facere* to make]

falsish, **falsism** and **falsity**. See under **false**.

Falstaffian *föl-stäf'i-ən* or *-staf'*, *adj* like or pertaining to Shakespeare's *Falstaff*, ie corpulent, jovial, humorous, dissolute and irrepressibly impudent.

faltboat *fölt'bōt*, also *folt'* or **foldboat** *fōld'bōt*, *n* a small collapsible boat of rubberized sailcloth. [Ger *Faltboot* folding boat]

falter *föl'tər*, *vi* to stumble; to go unsteadily; to hesitate in speech as if taken aback; to flinch; to waver; to flag; to fail. — *vt* to utter falteringly. — *n* unsteadiness. — *n* and *adj* **fal'tering**. — *adv* **fal'teringly**. [Prob a frequentative of ME *falden* to fold; connection with *fault* (in which the *l* is late) is not possible]

falx *falks*, (*med*) *n* a sickle-shaped or projecting part, as of the dura mater, the outside membrane of the brain and spinal columns: — *pl* **falces** (*fal'sēz*). [L, a sickle]

fam. *abbrev*: familiar; family.

fame *fām*, *n* public report or rumour (*archaic*); renown or celebrity, chiefly in a good sense. — *vt* (*rare*) to report; to make famous. — *adj* **famed** renowned. — *adj* **fame'less** lacking renown. — **fama clamosa** (*Scot*) any notorious rumour ascribing immoral conduct to a minister or office-bearer in a church; **house of ill fame** (*euphem*) a brothel. [Fr, from L *fāma* report, rumour or fame, from *fārī* to speak; cf Gr *phēmē*, from *phanai* to say]

familial. See under **family**.

familiar *fə-mil'yər*, *adj* well acquainted or intimate; in the manner of a close friend; intimate to an unwelcome degree, impertinently informal or friendly; free from constraint; unceremonious; having a thorough knowledge; well known or understood; private or domestic; common or everyday. — *n* a person with whom one is well or long acquainted; a spirit or demon supposed to come to a person, *esp* a witch, etc, at his or her call; a member of a pope's or bishop's household; the officer of the Inquisition who arrested those who were suspected. — *n* **familiarity** (*-i-ar'i-ti*) intimate acquaintanceship; any unusual or unwarrantable freedom in act or speech toward another person, an act of licence (*usu* in *pl*); freedom from constraint. — *vt* **famil'iarize** or **-ise** to make thoroughly acquainted with; to make easy by practice or study. — *adv* **famil'iarly**. [OFr *familier*, from L *familiāris*, from *familia* a family]

famille jaune *fam-ē zhōn* or **famille noire** *nwär*, *n* Chinese porcelain in which the background of the design is respectively yellow or black; **famille rose** (*rōz*) or **famille verte** (*vert*) Chinese porcelain with designs in which respectively pink or green is prominent. [Fr, family, yellow, black, pink and green]

family *fam'i-li*, *n* the household, or all those who live in one house (eg parents, children and servants); parents and their children; the children alone; the descendants of one common ancestor; race; honourable or noble descent; a group of people related to one another, or otherwise connected; a group of animals, plants, languages, etc, often including more than one genus; a collection of curves in the equations of which different values are given to the parameter or parameters (*math*). — *adj* of or concerning the family; belonging to or specially for a family; suitable for the whole family, or for children as well as parents. — *adj* **famil'ial** (*fəm-*) characteristic of a family. — *adj* **famil'iar** see separate entry above. — *n* **familism** (*fam'-*) the tendency of a family to cohere as a group; (with *cap*) the principles of the Familists. — *n* **Fam'ilist** a member of the 16c mystical sect known as the Family of Love, which based religion upon love independently of faith. — *adj* **familis'tic**. — **family allowance** an allowance formerly paid by the state for the support of children, now replaced by child benefit; **family baker**, **butcher**, etc a small retailer who supplies individual families, not merely institutions; **family Bible** a large Bible for family worship, with a page for recording family events; **family circle** the members of the family taken collectively; one of the galleries in a theatre; **family coach** formerly, a large carriage able to carry a whole family; a parlour game; **family credit** a payment by the state to a family whose income from employment is below a certain level; **family doctor** a general practitioner; **family fruit tree** or **family tree** a fruit tree bearing different varieties of the same fruit grafted on to it; **family grouping** same as **vertical grouping**; **family income supplement** a payment by the state to a family whose income from employment is below a certain level; **family jewels** everything of value in a household (*usu joc*); **family man** a man with a wife and children; a domesticated man; a man dedicated to, and who enjoys sharing activities with, his wife and children; **family name** surname; **family planning** regulating the number and spacing of children, eg by using contraceptives; **family tree** a diagram showing the branching of a family. — **in a family way** in a familiar or informal manner; **in the family way** (*euphem*) pregnant; **official family** (*US*) the cabinet. [L *familia*, from *famulus* a servant]

famine *fam'in*, *n* extreme general scarcity of food; scarcity of anything; extreme hunger, starvation. [Fr, from L *famēs* hunger]

famish *fam'ish*, *vt* to starve. — *vi* (*archaic*) to die of or suffer extreme hunger or thirst. — *n* **fam'ishment** starvation. — **be famished** or **famishing** to feel very hungry. [Obs *fame* to starve, from L *famēs* hunger]

famous *fā'məs*, *adj* renowned; noted; well known; excellent (*colloq*). — *vt* (*archaic*) to make famous. — *adv* **fā'mously**. — *n* **fā'mousness**. [OFr, from L *fāmōsus*, from *fāma* fame]

famulus *fam'ū-ləs*, *n* a private secretary or factotum; an attendant, *esp* on a magician or scholar. [L, a servant]

fan[1] *fan*, *n* a broad, flat instrument, *esp* used by women to cool themselves, typically in or spreading into the shape of a sector of a circle; a rotating ventilating or blowing apparatus; any fan-shaped structure, eg a deposit of alluvium; anything spreading in a fan shape, eg a bird's wing or tail; a propeller screw or propeller blade; a small sail to keep a windmill to the wind; a whale's tail-fluke; a basket formerly used for winnowing corn by throwing it in the wind; any instrument for winnowing. — *vt* to move by a fan or the like; to direct a current of air upon; to cool or to kindle with, or as if with, a fan; to fire (a non-automatic gun) by pulling back and releasing the hammer with the other hand; to winnow. — *vi* to move like a fan; to flutter; to spread out like a fan: — *pr p* **fann'ing**; *pa t* and *pa p* **fanned**. — *n* **fann'er** a fanning apparatus for winnowing, ventilation, etc. — *n pl* **fann'ings** the material strained from tea. — *adv* **fan'-wise** in the manner of a fan. — **fan belt** (in motor vehicles) a continuous belt that drives the alternator and the cooling fan for the radiator; **fan dance** a solo dance in the nude (or nearly so) in which the performer attempts concealment (or nearly so) by tantalizing manipulation of a fan or fans or a bunch of ostrich, etc feathers. — *adj* **fan'fold** (of paper) in a continuous strip, scored or perforated so as to fall flat in sections, used for computer print-out. — **fan'-jet** (an aeroplane with) an engine in which air is taken in through a fan and some of it, bypassing compressors, combustion chamber and turbines, mixes with the jet formed by the rest; **fan'light** a window sometimes resembling an open fan in shape; **fan palm** any palm with palmate or hand-shaped leaves, *esp* palmetto. — *adj* **fan'-shaped** forming a sector of a circle. — **fan'tail** a tail shaped like a fan; a variety of domestic pigeon with tail feathers spread out like a fan; a member of various other classes of fantailed birds such as the Australian genus of flycatchers *Rhipidura*; an artificially bred goldfish with double anal and caudal fins; a feature having parts radiating from a centre (*archit*). — Also *adj* (also **fan'tailed**). — **fan tracery** or **fan vaulting** (*archit*) tracery rising from a capital or a corbel, and diverging like the folds of a fan over the surface of a vault; **fan wheel** a wheel with fans on its rim for producing a current of air. — **fan out** to fan or spread like a fan from a centre. [OE *fann*, from L *vannus* a basket for winnowing; cf Fr *van*]

fan[2] *fan*, *n* a devotee or enthusiastic follower of some sport or hobby or public figure. — *n* **fan'dom**. — *n* **fan'zine** (*-zēn*) a magazine by and for amateur enthusiasts, *esp* of science fiction, pop music, or football. — **fan club** a group united by devotion to a celebrity; **fan mail** letters from devotees to a celebrity. [From **fanatic**]

Fanagalo *fan'ə-gə-lō*, *n* a South African pidgin language, a mixture of Zulu, Afrikaans and English.

fanal *fā'nəl*, (*archaic*) *n* a lighthouse or beacon. [Fr, from Gr *phanos* a lantern, and *phainein* to show]

Fanariot. See **Phanariot**.

fanatic *fə-nat'ik* (by some *fan'ə-tik*), *n* a person frantically or excessively enthusiastic, *orig* on religious subjects. — *adj* fanatical. — *adj* **fanat'ical** extravagantly or unreasonably zealous, *orig* in religious matters; excessively enthusiastic; extravagant (*Shakesp*). — *adv* **fanat'ically**. — *n* **fanat'icism** (*i-sizm*) wild and excessive religious or other enthusiasm. — *vt* **fanat'icize** or **-ise** (*-i-sīz*) to make fanatical. — *vi* to act like a fanatic. [L *fānāticus* belonging to a temple inspired by a god, from *fānum* a temple]

fan-cricket. Same as **fen-cricket** under **fen**[1].

fancy *fan'si*, *n* that faculty of the mind by which it recalls, represents, or conjures up past images or impressions, ie imagination, *esp* of a lower, passive, or more trivial kind; an image or representation thus formed in the mind; an unreasonable, lightly-formed or capricious opinion; a whim; a fantasia (*music*); capricious inclination or liking; taste; an individual fancy cake (*Scot*); love (*Shakesp*). — *adj* pleasing to, guided by, or originating in fancy or caprice; fantastic; capriciously departing from the ordinary, the simple, or the plain; ornate; (of flowers) parti-coloured; (of gems, *esp* diamonds) of a colour other than the normal one. — *vt* to picture in the mind; to imagine; to be inclined to believe; to have a liking for or be sexually attracted to (*colloq*); to be pleased with; to breed or cultivate (eg pigeons), with a view to development of conventionally accepted points: — *pr p* **fan'cying**; *pa t* and *pa p* **fan'cied**. — *interj* (also **fancy that**) an exclamation of surprise. — *adj* **fanciable** (*colloq*) (of a person) sexually attractive. — *adj* **fan'cied** formed or conceived by whim, etc; imagined; favoured, *esp* in betting. — *n* **fan'cier** a person who fancies; a person who has a liking for anything and is supposed to be a judge of it; a breeder of distinctive varieties. — *adj* **fan'ciful** guided or created by fancy; imaginative; whimsical; wild; unreal. — *adv* **fan'cifully**. — *n* **fan'cifulness**. — *adj* **fan'ciless** completely lacking in imagination, etc. — **fancy bread** bread other than plain bread; **fancy cake** a cake decorated with icing, filled with cream, etc; **Fancy Dan** (*colloq*) a stylish rather than effective performer; **fancy dress** a costume chosen for fun, *esp* for a party, and *usu* representing a famous type or character; dress arranged according to the wearer's fancy, to represent some character; **fancy dress ball** or **fancy ball** a ball at which fancy dress is worn; **fancy fair** a special sale of fancy articles for some charitable purpose. — *adj* **fancy-free'** carefree; free of responsibilities; not currently in love. — **fancy goods** fabrics of variegated rather than simple pattern, applied generally to ornaments and other articles of show; **fancy man** a woman's lover (*colloq derog*); a pimp; **fancy monger** (*Shakesp*) a person who makes love, *esp* the love affairs of others, his or her business. — *adj* **fan'cy-sick** (*Shakesp*) lovesick. — **fancy stitch** a more intricate and decorative stitch than *plain stitch*; **fancy woman** (*colloq derog*) a mistress; a prostitute; **fan'cywork** ornamental needlework. — **fancy oneself** to think too highly of oneself; **the fancy** (*old*) sporting characters generally, *esp* boxers; boxing; enthusiasts for a particular sport or pastime; **tickle** or **take someone's fancy** to attract someone mildly in some way. [Contracted from **fantasy**]

fand[1] *fand*, (*Scot*) *pa t* of **find**.

fand[2] *fand* or **fond** *fond*, (*obs*) *vi* to try or attempt; to proceed: — *pa t* and *pa p* **fand'ed**, **fond'ed** or (*Spenser*) **fond**. [OE *fandian*]

fandangle *fan-dang'gl*, *n* elaborate ornament; nonsense. [Perh from **fandango**]

fandango *fan-dang'gō*, *n* an old Spanish dance for two, or its music in 3-4 time, with castanets; a gathering for dancing, a ball (*US dialect*): — *pl* **fandang'os**. [Sp]

fane[1] *fān*, (*obs*) *n* a flag; a weathercock. [OE *fana* flag; cf Ger *Fahne*; cf **vane** and L *pannus* a cloth]

fane[2] *fān*, *n* a temple. [L *fānum*]

fanfare *fan'fār*, *n* a flourish of trumpets or bugles; a display of enthusiasm; an elaborate style of bookbinding. — *vt* to herald or acclaim with a fanfare. — *n* **fanfarade** (*fan-fər-ād'*) a fanfare. — *n* **fan'faron** a person who uses bravado; a blusterer or braggart. — *n* **fanfarō'na** (*Scott*; Sp *fanfarrona* trumpery) a gold chain. — *n* **fanfaronade'** vain boasting; bluster; ostentation. — *vi* to bluster. [Fr, perh from the sound]

fang *fang*, *n* the tooth of a wolf, dog, etc; a claw or talon (*obs*); the venom-tooth of a snake; the embedded part of a tooth, etc; a point (of a tool); a prong; a grip or catch (*Shakesp*); grip or power of suction in a pump (*Scot*). — *vt* to seize upon or catch; (*obs*; *Shakesp* **phang**); to prime a pump. — *adj* **fanged** having fangs or anything resembling them. — *adj* **fang'less**. [OE *fang*, from the same root as *fōn* to seize]

fangle *fang'gl*, *n* (*Milton* and *Bunyan*) fancy. — *vt* (*Milton*) to fabricate or decorate in a fancy way. — *adj* **fang'led**

(*Shakesp*) foppish. [Mistaken back-formation from **newfangle** or **newfangled**]

fango *fang'gō*, *n* a clay or mud from thermal springs in Italy, *esp* at Battaglio, used in the treatment of gout, rheumatism, etc: — *pl* **fang'os**. [Ital, mud, from Gmc]

fanion *fan'yən*, *n* a small flag, *esp* one used in surveying. — *n* **fan'on** a cloth for handling holy vessels or offertory bread; a narrow strip of material worn on the left arm by a priest, a maniple (see also **fannel**); a short cape worn by the Pope when celebrating High Mass. [OFr *fanion* or *fanon*, from LL *fanō*, *-ōnis* banner, napkin, from OHGer *fano*; cf **fane**[1] and **vane**]

fank[1] *fangk*, (*Scot*) *n* a coil; a noose; a tangle. [Connected with **fang**]

fank[2] *fangk*, (*Scot*) *n* an enclosure for sheep. [Gaelic *fang*]

fankle *fang'kl*, (*Scot*) *vt* to entangle. — *n* a tangle, muddle. [Connected with **fang**]

fannel or **fannell** *fan'əl*, *n* a narrow strip of material worn on the left arm by a priest, a maniple (see also **fanion**). [LL *fanonellus* and *fanula*, dimins of *fanō*; see **fanion**]

fanny *fan'i*, (*slang*) *n* the buttocks (chiefly *US*); the female genitals (*vulg*).

Fanny Adams *fan'i ad'əmz*, (*slang*) *n* tinned mutton. — **sweet Fanny Adams** or **sweet FA** (*slang*, in the Services a euphemism) nothing at all. [The name of a girl murdered and cut up c. 1812]

fanon. See **fanion**.

fantad. See **fantod**.

fan-tan *fan'tan*, *n* a Chinese gambling game where players try to guess the number of objects remaining after some have been removed from the total. [Chin]

fantasia *fan-tā'zi-ə*, *-tä'*, *-zhə* or *-tə-zē'ə*, *n* a musical or other composition not governed by the ordinary rules of form. [Ital, from Gr *phantasiā*; see **fantasy**]

fantasy or **phantasy** *fan'tə-si* or *-zi*, *n* fancy; imagination; mental image; love (*obs*); caprice; fantasia; a story, film, etc not based on realistic characters or setting; preoccupation with thoughts about unobtainable desires. — *vt* (*archaic*) to fancy or conceive mentally. — *adj* **fan'tasied** filled with fancies. — *n* **fan'tasist** a person who creates or indulges in fantasies. — *vt* and *vi* **fan'tasize** or **-ise** to indulge in gratifying fantasies; to have whimsical notions. — *n* **fan'tasm** same as **phantasm**. — *adj* **fantasque** (*-task'*; *obs*) fantastic. — *n* (*obs*) fantasy. — *n* **fan'tast** (*obs*) a person of fantastic ideas. — *n* **fantas'tic** (*obs*) a person who is fantastical; a dandy or fop. — *adj* **fantas'tic** or **fantas'tical** fanciful; not real; capricious; whimsical; wild; foppish (*obs*); (not **fantastical**) incredible; (not **fantastical**) excellent (*slang*). — *n* **fantastical'ity** or **fantas'ticalness**. — *adv* **fantas'tically**. — *vt* and *vi* **fantas'ticate** to fantasize over something; to give fantastic or whimsical treatment to. — *n* **fantastica'tion**. — *n* **fantas'ticism** (*-sizm*). — *n* **fantas'tico** (*Shakesp*; *Ital*) a dandy: — *pl* **fantas'ticoes**. — *n* **fan'tastry**. [OFr *fantasie*, through L from Gr *phantasiā*, from *phantazein* to make visible; cf **fancy** and **fantasia**]

fanteeg. See under **fantod**.

Fanti or **Fantee** *fan'tē*, *n* a Ghanaian people; their language. — **go Fanti** (*Kipling* and *G K Chesterton*) to adopt the ways of the natives.

fantigue. See under **fantod**.

fantoccini *fan-to-chē'nē*, *n pl* marionettes; a marionette show. [Ital, pl of *fantoccino*, dimin of *fantoccio* a puppet, from *fante* a boy, from L *īnfāns*, *-antis*]

fantod *fan'tod* or **fantad** *-täd*, (*slang*) *n* a fidgety, fussy person, *esp* a ship's officer; (*usu* in *pl*) fidgets. — *n* **fantigue** or **fanteeg** (*fan-tēg'*) anxiety or agitation.

fantom. Same as **phantom**.

fantoosh *fan-tōōsh'*, (*Scot*) *adj* fashionable; pretentious or showy. [Poss connected with Eng dialect *fanty-sheeny* fussy or showy, from Ital *fantoccino* marionette]

fanzine. See under **fan**[2].

FAO *abbrev*: Food and Agriculture Organization (of the United Nations).

fap *fap*, (*Shakesp*) *adj* fuddled or drunk.

faquir *fäk-ēr'*, *n*. Same as **fakir**.

far *fär*, *adj* remote, distant; more distant of two (in *Shakesp* as *compar*); (of an animal) off, right-hand (ie the side furthest from a person leading it); advanced (*obs*). — *adv* to, at, or over a great distance or advanced stage; remotely; in a great degree; very much; long (*obs*). — *vt* (*dialect*) to remove to a distance. — *adv* **far'most** most distant or remote. — *n* **far'ness** the state of being far; remoteness or distance. — *adj* **far'away** distant; abstracted or absent-minded. — *n* (*rare*) the distance. — **faraway'ness**; **far cry** a long distance; **Far East** China, Korea, Japan, etc; often also the countries from Myanma (Burma) to Indonesia and the Philippines and, as used by some, the countries of the Indian subcontinent. — *adj* **far'-fetched'** (*obs* **far'fet**) fetched or brought from a remote place (*archaic*); forced or unnatural; improbable, unlikely, unconvincing. — *adj* **far'-flung** placed or situated far and wide; extensive. — *adv* **far'-forth** (*Spenser*) far. — **Far North** the Arctic regions. — *adj* and *adv* **far'-off** in the distance. — *adj* **far'-out'** wonderful or amazing (*rather old*); avant-garde; (of jazz or its addicts) more up to date than 'cool'; intellectual; satisfying. — *adj* **far-reach'ing** having wide validity, scope, or influence. — *adj* **far-see'ing** able to foresee future events. — *adj* **far-sight'ed** seeing far; having or exhibiting foresight or shrewdness of judgement; having defective eyesight for near objects. — **far-sight'edness**. — *adj* **far'-sought** sought at a distance. — **Far South** the Antarctic regions. — *adj* **far'-spent** far advanced. — **Far West** (*esp* formerly) the Great Plains, Rocky Mountains and Pacific side of North America; (now *usu*) the area between the Rockies and the Pacific. — **as far as** to the extent that; up to (a particular place); **by far** in a very great degree; **far and away** by a great deal; **far and near** or **far and wide** everywhere, all about; **far between** at wide intervals; rare; **far be it** God forbid; **far from it** on the contrary; **go too far** to go beyond reasonable limits, *esp* of tact or behaviour; **I'll see you far** (or **farther**) **first** I will not do it by any means; **in so far as** to the extent that. — See also **farther**. [OE *feor*); Du *ver*; ON *fiarre* or *feorr*]

farad *far'əd*, *n* a unit of electrical capacitance, the capacitance of a capacitor between the plates of which appears a difference of potential of one volt when it is charged by one coulomb of electricity. — *n* **far'aday** a unit used in electrolysis, equal to 96 500 coulombs. — *adj* **faradic** (*-ad'ik*) pertaining to Faraday, *esp* in connection with induced currents. — *n* **far'adism** treatment by induced currents. — *n* **faradizā'tion** or **-s-**. — *vt* **far'adize** or **-ise** (*med*) to stimulate by induced currents. [From Michael *Faraday* (1791–1867), Eng chemist and physicist]

farand, **farrand** *far'ənd*, *fär'* or **farrant** *-ənt*, (*Scot*) *adj* having a certain appearance or manner, *esp* in such compound forms as *auld-farand* old-fashioned, quaint, precocious, sagacious; *fair-farand* goodly, specious. [ME *farand* comely. Origin obscure; prob pr p of **fare**]

farandine or **farrandine** *far'ən-dēn*, or **ferrandine** *fer'*, (*obs*) *n* a cloth or a dress of silk with wool or hair. [Fr *ferrandine*]

farandole *far-ən-dōl'*, *n* a Provençal dance performed in a long string; music for it, in 6-8 time. [Provençal *farandoula*]

farborough *fär'bər-ə*, *n* Goodman Dull's pronunciation of **thirdborough** (*Love's Labour's Lost*, I.1. 182). — Another reading, **tharborough**.

farce *färs*, *vt* to cram; to stuff, fill with stuffing; to swell out (*Shakesp*). — *n* stuffing or force-meat; comedy of extravagant humour, buffoonery, and improbability; a ridiculous or meaningless display; a hollow formality. — *n* **farceur** (*fär-sœr'*; *Fr*) a joker or buffoon; a person who writes or acts in farces: — *fem* **farceuse** (*-sœz'*). — *adj* **farci** (*fär-sē*; *Fr*; *cookery*) stuffed. — *adj* **far'cical**. — *n* **farcical'ity** farcical quality. — *adv* **far'cically**. — *vt* **far'cify** to turn into a farce. — *n* **farc'ing** (*cookery*) stuffing. [Fr *farce* stuffing, from L *farcīre* to stuff; the connecting links of meaning seem to be interpolation, theatrical gag, buffoonery; cf **farse**]

farcy *fär'si*, *n* chronic glanders, a disease *esp* of horses. — Also (*obs*) **far'cin**. — *adj* **far'cied**. — **far'cy-bud** a swollen lymphatic gland, as occurs in farcy. [Fr *farcin*, from LL *farcīminum*]

fard *färd*, *n* white paint for the face. — *vt* to paint with fard; to gloss over; to trick out. [Fr, of Gmc origin]

fardage *fär'dij*, (*naut*; *obs*) *n* wood placed in the bottom of a ship's hold to keep cargo out of the bilge-water, dunnage. [Fr]

fardel[1] *fär'dl*, (*obs*) *n* a fourth part. [OE *fēortha dæl*, fourth deal]

fardel[2] *fär'dl*, *n* a pack; anything cumbersome or irksome; the third stomach of a ruminant, the manyplies or omasum. — **far'del-bag** the omasum. — *adj* **far'del-bound** constipated, *esp* of cattle and sheep, by the retention of food in the omasum. [OFr *fardel* (Fr *fardeau*), dimin of *farde* a burden, poss from Ar *fardah* a package]

farden or **farding** *fär'dən* (*obs* or *dialect*). Same as **farthing**.

fare *fār*, *vi* to travel; to get on or succeed; to happen well or badly to; to be in any particular state, to be, to go on; to be fed. — *n* (*orig Spenser*) a course or passage; the price of passage; a passenger (or passengers); food or provisions for the table. — *interj* **farewell'** may you fare well, a parting wish for safety or success; goodbye. — *n* good wishes at parting; the act of departure. — *adj* (*fār'wel*) parting; said when bidding farewell; final. [OE *faran*; Ger *fahren*]

farfet. See **far-fetched** under **far**.

farina *fə-rī'nə* or *fə-rē'nə*, *n* ground corn; meal; starch; pollen; a mealy powder. — *adj* **farinaceous** (*far-i-nā'shəs*) mealy; consisting of cereals. — *adj* **far'inose** (*-i-nōs*) yielding farina. [L *farīna*, from *fār* corn]

Faringee. See **Feringhi**.

farl or **farle** *färl*, (*Scot*) *n* the quarter of a round cake of flour or oatmeal; a cake. [**fardel**[1]]

farm *färm*, *n* a tract of land (*orig* one leased or rented) used for cultivation and pasturage, along with a house and other necessary buildings; a farmhouse; a farmstead; a piece of land or water used for breeding animals (eg *fox-farm* or *oyster-farm*); a place for treatment and disposal (*sewage-farm*); a place where eg children are handed over to be taken care of; a fixed payment (*obs*); a lease (*Spenser*); a fixed payment by way of taxes, etc (*hist*); the letting out of the right to collect rents, taxes, etc in exchange for a fixed sum (*hist*). — *adj* of, belonging to, appropriate to, a farm. — *vt* to cultivate; to use as a farm; to arrange for maintenance of at fixed price; to grant or receive the rents, taxes, etc from for a fixed sum; to rent to or from another person. — *vi* to practise the business of a farmer. — *n* **farm'er** a person who farms land; the tenant of a farm; a person who receives taxes, etc in return for fixed payment: — *fem* (*rare*) **far'meress**. — *n* **farm'ery** the buildings of a farm. — *n* **farm'ing** the business of cultivating land. — **farmer general** a member of a group who, in pre-Revolutionary France, had bought the right to receive certain taxes; **Farmer Giles** (*UK* and *Austr rhyming slang*) piles, haemorrhoids; **farmer's lung** a lung disease caused by the spores of the fungus actinomycetes which develop in hay baled while it is still damp; **farm'-hand** or **farm-labourer** a person who works on a farm for wages; **farm'house** the farmer's house attached to a farm. — *adj* **farm'-in** (*econ*) acquired by farming into (qv below) a company. — *npl* **farm'-offices** outbuildings on a farm. — **farm'-place**, **farm'stead** or **farm steading** a farmhouse with buildings belonging to it — **farm'-toun** (*-tōōn*; *Scot*); **farm'yard** a yard or enclosure surrounded by farm buildings. — **farm into** to take shares in a company or concern (*usu* of a company obtaining an interest in another); **farm out** to board out for fixed payment; to give (eg work for which one has made oneself responsible) to others to carry out. [LL *firma* a fixed payment, from L *firmus* firm]

farmost. See under **far**.

farnesol *fär'ni-sol*, *n* an alcohol, $C_{15}H_{25}OH$, found in various essential oils and used in perfumes. [From *Acacia farnesiana*, after Odoardo *Farnese*, 16c Italian cardinal]

faro *fār'ō*, *n* a game of chance played by betting on the order of appearance of certain cards. [Perh from *Pharaoh*; reason unknown]

farouche *fə-rōōsh'* or *fa-*, *adj* shy or ill at ease; sullen and unsociable; socially inexperienced and lacking polish. [Fr, wild, shy, savage]

farrago *fə-rā'gō* or *fä-rä'gō*, *n* a confused mass of objects or people (*obs*); any disordered mixture: — *pl* **farrag'oes**. — *adj* **farraginous** (*fə-rāj'in-əs* or *-raj'*) miscellaneous, jumbled. [L *farrāgō*, *-inis* mixed fodder, from *fār* grain]

farrand or **farrant**. See **farand**.

farrandine. See **farandine**.

farren *far'ən*, (*dialect*) *n* a division of land; a right of common (qv under **right**). [Origin uncertain]

farrier *far'i-ər*, *n* a person who shoes horses; a person who cures horses' diseases; a person in charge of cavalry horses. — *n* **farr'iery** the farrier's art; veterinary surgery. [OFr *ferrier*, from L *ferrum* iron]

farrow[1] *far'ō*, *n* a litter of pigs. — *vi* or vt to give birth to (pigs). [OE *fearh*, a pig; Ger (dimin) *Ferkel*; L *porcus*]

farrow[2] *far'ō*, *adj* (of a cow) not pregnant for the time being. [Ety doubtful; cf Flem *verwekoe*, *varwekoe* with *farrow cow*]

farruca *fa-rōō'ka*, (*Sp*) *n* a Spanish gypsy dance with abrupt variations of tempo and mood.

farse *färs*, *n* an explanation of the Latin epistle in the vernacular. — *vt* to extend by interpolation. [**farce**]

Farsi *fär'sē*, *n* Modern Persian, an Indo-European language and the official spoken language of Iran. [*Fars* ('Persia'), province of SW Iran]

fart *färt*, (*vulg*) *vi* to break wind from the anus. — *n* an act of breaking wind; a worthless person (*slang*). — **fart about** or **around** to fool about; to waste time. [OE (assumed) *feortan*; cf Gr *perdesthai*]

farthel *fär'dhəl*, (*Scot*) *n*. Same as **farl**.

farther *fär'dhər*, **far'thermore**, **far'thermost** and **far'thest**. Same as **further**, etc, and sometimes preferred where the notion of distance is more prominent. [A variant (ME *ferther*) of **further**[1] that came to be thought a compar of **far**]

farthing *fär'dhing*, *n* a fourth part (*obs*); the fourth of a pre-1971 penny (from January 1961, not legal tender); anything very small; the Gr *assarion* (L *as*) and also *kodrantēs* (L *quadrāns*), one fourth of an *as* (*Bible*). — *adj* **far'thingless**. — **far'thingland** a varying area of land; **far'thingsworth** as much as a farthing will buy. [OE *fēorthing* a fourth part, from *fēortha* fourth, and sfx *-ing*]

farthingale *fär'dhing-gāl*, *n* a kind of crinoline of whalebone for extending a woman's dress outward from the waist. [OFr *verdugale*, from Sp *verdugado* hooped, from *verdugo* rod]

fartlek *färt'lek*, *n* alternate fast and slow running in one session, done as training work for marathons and other long-distance races. [Swed *fart* speed, and *lek* play]

FAS *abbrev*: Fellow of the Antiquarian Society; Fellow of the Society of Arts; foetal alcohol syndrome; (also **fas**) free alongside ship.

fasces *fas'ēz*, *n pl* the bundle of rods, with or without an axe, borne before an ancient Roman magistrate of high grade. [L *fascēs*, pl of *fascis* bundle]

Fasching *fa'shing*, (*Ger*) *n* (Shrovetide) carnival.

fascia *fā'shi-ə*, *n* a board over a shop-front, commonly bearing the shopkeeper's name; (also **fasc'ia-board**) the instrument-board of a motor car; a band or fillet (*obs*); a broad flat band, as in an architrave, or over a shop-front (*archit*); any bandlike structure; (*fash'i-ə*) connective tissue ensheathing a muscle (*zool*). — *adj* **fasc'ial**. — *adj* **fasc'iate** or **fasc'iated**. — *n* **fasciā'tion** (*bot*) union of a number of parts side by side in a flat plate. — *n* **fasciola** (*fə-sī'ō-lə*) or **fasciole** (*fas'i-ōl*) a band of colour. [L *fascia* band, bandage]

fascicle *fas'i-kl*, *n* a bundle or bunch, *esp* a bunched tuft of branches, roots, fibres, etc; a part of a book issued in parts. — Also **fasc'icūle** or **fascic'ūlus**: — *pl* **fascic'ūlī**. — *adj* **fasc'icled**, **fascic'ūlar**, **fascic'ūlate** or **fascic'ūlated**. — *n* **fascicūla'tion** [L *fasciculus*, dimin of *fascis* bundle]

fascinate *fas'i-nāt*, *vt* to bewitch, enchant or cast the evil eye upon (*obs*); to interest exceedingly, intrigue; to control by the eye like a snake; to hold spellbound; to charm; to captivate. — *adj* **fasc'inating** charming, delightful; intriguing, deeply interesting; compelling, irresistible. — *n* **fascinā'tion** the act of fascinating; power to harm, control, allure, or render helpless by looks or spells; the state of being fascinated. — *n* **fasc'inātor** a person who fascinates; a woman's light, soft, head-covering. [L *fascināre*, *-ātum*; perh allied to Gr *baskainein* to bewitch]

fascine *fas-ēn'*, *n* a brushwood bundle, used to fill ditches, protect a shore, etc from attack. [Fr, from L *fascīna*, from *fascis* a bundle]

fascio *fä'shō*, *n* an organized political group or club: — *pl* **fasci** (*fä'shē*). [Ital *fascio* bundle or group, with a hint of **fasces** (qv)]

Fascism *fash'izm* (*Ital* **Fascismo** *fä-shēz'mō*) the authoritarian form of government in Italy from 1922–43, characterized by extreme nationalism, militarism, anti-communism and restrictions on individual freedom; (also without *cap*) the methods, doctrines, etc of fascists or the Fascists. — *n* **Fasc'ist** (*Ital* **Fascista** *fä-shēs'tə*) a member of the ruling party in Italy from 1922–43, or a similar party elsewhere; (also without *cap*) an exponent or supporter of Fascism or (loosely) anyone with extreme right-wing, nationalistic, etc views or methods: — *pl* **Fasc'ists** (*Ital* **Fascis'ti**; *-tē*). — Also *adj*. — *adj* **fascis'tic**. [Ety as for **fascio**]

fasciola and **fasciole**. See under **fascia**.

fash *fash*, (*Scot*) *vt* to trouble or bother. — *vi* to be vexed; to take trouble or pains; to annoy. — *n* pains or trouble; annoyance. — *n* **fash'ery**. — *adj* **fashious** (*fash'əs*) troublesome or vexatious. — *n* **fash'iousness**. — **never fash your thumb** take no trouble in the matter. [OFr *fascher* (Fr *fâcher*), from L *fastīdium* disgust]

fashion *fash'n*, *n* the make or cut of a thing; form or pattern; vogue or trend; the prevailing mode or shape of dress or that imposed or favoured by those whose lead is accepted; a prevailing custom; manner; sort, type or kind; awareness of, and attention to, the latest trends in dress, behaviour, activities, enthusiasms, etc; high society; appearance. — *vt* to make; to mould according to a pattern; to suit or adapt. — *adj* **fash'ionable** according to prevailing fashion; prevailing or in use at any period; observant of the fashion in dress or living; moving in high society; frequented by people of fashion. — *n* a fashionable person. — *n* **fash'ionableness**. — *adv* **fash'ionably**. — *n* **fash'ioner**. — *n* **fash'ionist** a follower or setter of fashion. — **fashion house** an establishment in which fashionable clothes are designed, made and sold; **fashion jewellery** costume jewellery. — *adj* **fash'ionmongering** or **fash'ionmonging** (*Shakesp*) behaving like a fop. — **fashion plate** a picture showing the latest style of (*esp* formal) dress; a well-groomed, fashionably dressed person. — **after** or **in a fashion** in a way; to a certain extent; **do something**, etc **as though it were going out of fashion** (*slang*) to do something with extra vigour or enthusiasm, fast and furiously, as though for the last time; **in fashion** currently favoured; fashionable; **in the fashion** in accordance with the prevailing style of dress, etc; **out of fashion** old-fashioned; unfashionable. [OFr *fachon*, from L *factiō*, *-ōnis*, from *facere* to make]

fashions *fash'ənz*, (*Shakesp*) *n pl* for **farcin**, farcy.

fashious, etc. See under **fash**.

fast[1] *fäst*, *adj* quick; rapid; (of a clock) showing a time in advance of the correct time; promoting rapid play; for quick-moving traffic, as in *fast lane*; seeking excitement; rash; dissolute; sexually promiscuous. — *adv* swiftly; in rapid succession; in advance of the correct time; extravagantly or dissipatedly. — *adj* **fast'ish** somewhat fast. — *n* **fast'ness**. — **fast'back** a car whose roof slopes smoothly down towards the rear, giving a streamlined effect; a particular breed of pig; **fastball** (*baseball*) a high-speed, rising delivery from the pitcher; **fast bowling** (*cricket*) bowling in which the ball is delivered fast, pace bowling; **fast bowler**; **fast-breeder reactor** a nuclear reactor using fast neutrons which produces at least as much fissionable material as it uses; **Fastext** a facility on some television sets for scrolling through teletext pages faster than normal; **fast food** or **foods** kinds of food, eg hamburgers, chips, etc, which can be prepared and served quickly; **fast forward** the facility provided in a sound or video cassette player for winding a tape quickly forward without playing it. — *vt* **fast-for'ward** to advance (a tape) quickly by this means. — *vi* (*colloq*) to pass or move on without delay. — **fast neutron** a neutron of very high energy, *usu* over 10 000 electron volts; **fast reactor** a nuclear reactor using fast neutrons, and little or no moderator; **fast stream** (in eg the civil service) a category of personnel who have been selected for rapid promotion to senior posts. — *vt* **fast'-talk** to persuade with rapid, plausible talk. — *adj* **fast'-talking**. — **fast track** (*colloq*) the routine for accelerating the progress of a proposal, etc through its formalities; the quick but competitive route to advancement. — *adj* **fast'-track**. — *vt* to process or promote speedily. — **fast worker** a person who gains his or her ends quickly and easily, *esp* by unscrupulous means. — **a fast buck** (*slang*) money quickly and easily obtained; **fast and furious** (or **furiously**) rapidly and vigorously; **(life) in the fast lane** (a way of life) full of pressure, excitement and glamour; **pull a fast one** or **put a fast one over** (*colloq*) to gain an advantage by trickery. [A special use of **fast**[2] derived from Scand sense of urgent]

fast[2] *fäst*, *adj* firm; fixed; steadfast; fortified; (of sleep) sound; (of colours) not liable to fade or run. — Also used in combination (*esp archaic*) to denote firmly fixed, as in *handfast*, an agreement confirmed by handshaking, *lockfast*, firmly locked, and *colourfast*. — *adv* firmly, unflinchingly; soundly or sound (asleep); close or near (*archaic* or *literary*). — *adv* **fast'ly** (*Shakesp*) firmly. — *n* **fast'ness** fixedness; a stronghold, fortress, castle. — **fast'-and-loose'** a cheating game practised at fairs, the dupe being invited to put a stick in the loop of a coiled belt so that it cannot be pulled away — called also **prick-the-garter**. — *adj* **fast'-hand'ed** tight-fisted, mean. — **fast by** close to, close by; **hard and fast** (of a rule, etc) unalterable, inflexible, strict; **play fast and loose** (from the cheating game) to be unreliable or shifty; to behave without sense of moral obligation; to trifle (with *with*). [OE *fæst*; Ger *fest*]

fast[3] *fäst*, *vi* to abstain from food completely or restrict one's diet, eg as a religious duty; to go hungry. — *n* abstinence from food; special abstinence ordered by the church; the day or time of fasting. — *n* **fast'er** a person who fasts. — *n* **fast'ing** religious abstinence from food. — **fast'-day** a day of religious fasting; a day for humiliation and prayer, *esp* before communion; **Fast'ens** short for **Fastens-eve** (*Scot* **Fasten-e'en** and **Fastern's-e'en**) or **Fastens Tuesday** Shrove Tuesday (OE *fæstenes* genitive of *fæsten* fast). [OE *fæstan* to fast; Ger *fasten*]

fast[4] *fäst*, (*Spenser*) a spelling of **faced**.

fasten *fäs'n*, *vt* to make fast or firm; to fix securely; to attach. — *vi* to be capable of being fastened; to become fastened; to remain stationary. — *n* **fastener** (*fäs'nər*) a clip, catch, or other means of fastening. — *n* **fas'tening** (*fäs'ning*) a device which fastens. — **fasten on** to direct (one's eyes) on; to seize on, eg a fact; to fix the blame, responsibility for, on (a person) (*slang*). [**fast**[2]]

fasti *fas'tī* or L *fäs'tē*, *n pl* those days among the ancient Romans on which it was lawful to transact legal or public business (opposite of *nefasti*); an enumeration of the days of the year, a calendar; annals. [L]

fastidious *fas-tid'i-əs*, *adj* easily repelled or disgusted; meticulous or over-meticulous; difficult to please; exacting in taste, highly discriminating; (of bacteria) having complex requirements for growth. — *adv* **fastid'iously**. — *n* **fastid'iousness**. [L *fastīdiōsus*, from *fastīdium* loathing]

fastigiate *fas-tij'i-āt*, *adj* (of a roof) pointed, sloping to a point or edge; with branches more or less erect and parallel (*bot*); conical. — *adj* **fastig'iated**. — *n* **fastig'ium** the apex of a building; a gable-end; a pediment. [L *fastīgium* a gable-end or roof]

fastuous *fas'tū-əs*, (*archaic*) *adj* haughty; ostentatious. [L *fastuōsus*, from *fastus* arrogance]

fat[1] *fat*, *adj* plump, fleshy; well filled out; thick, full-bodied (as of printing types); corpulent; obese; having much, or of the nature of, adipose tissue or the substance it contains; oily; fruitful or profitable; (of a theatrical role) yielding rich oportunities for displaying one's talent; rich in some important constituent; gross; fulsome: — *compar* **fatt'er**; *superl* **fatt'est**. — *n* a substance found in adipose tissue; solid animal or vegetable oil; any member of a group of naturally occurring substances consisting of the glycerides of higher fatty acids, eg palmitic acid, stearic acid, oleic acid (*chem*); the richest part of anything; a piece of work offering more than usual profit for effort; a role or passage that enables an actor or musician to show his or her talent; inclination to corpulence; a fat animal; money (*slang*). — *adv* (in golf) striking the ground before the ball. — *vt* to make fat. — *vi* to grow fat: — *pr p* **fatt'ing**; *pa t* and *pa p* **fatt'ed**. — *n* **fat'ling** a young animal fattened for slaughter. — *adj* small and fat. — *adv* **fat'ly** grossly; lumberingly. — *n* **fat'ness** quality or state of being fat; fullness of flesh; richness; fertility; that which makes something fertile. — *adj* **fatt'ed**. See **kill the fatted calf** below. — *vt* **fatt'en** to make fat or fleshy; to enrich; to make fertile. — *vi* to grow fat. — *n* **fatt'ener**. — *n* **fatt'ening** (also *adj*). — *adj* **fatt'iness**. — *adj* **fatt'ish** somewhat fat. — *adj* **fatt'y** containing fat; having (some of) the qualities of fat. — *n* (*derog*) a fat person. — *adj* **fat'brained** (*Shakesp*) stupid. — **fat camp** (*US*) a residential slimming camp for overweight children; **fat cat** (*US slang*) a wealthy, prosperous person. — *adj* **fat'-cat**. — **fat city** (also with *caps*; *US slang*) easy circumstances, prosperous conditions. — *adj* **fat'-face** or **fat-faced'** having a fat or broad face. — **fat'-head** a stupid, dim-witted person. — *adj* **fat-head'ed**. — **fat'-hen** any one of various thick-leaved plants, *esp* of the goosefoot family. — *adj* **fat'-kidney'd** (*Shakesp*). — **fat'-lute** a mixture of pipe-clay and linseed oil, for filling joints in wood, *esp* in shipbuilding; **fat mouse** any of several kinds of mouse of the genus *Steatomys*, found in dry regions of Africa, that store fat and are eaten as a delicacy; **fat stock** or **fat'stock** livestock fattened for market. — *adj* **fat'-tailed** having much fat in the tail, as do certain Asiatic and African sheep. — **fatty acids** acids which with glycerine form fats; **fatty degeneration** morbid deposition of fat; **fatty heart**, etc, fatty degeneration of the heart, etc. — *adj* **fat'-witted** dull-witted, stupid. — (**a**) **fat chance** (*slang*) little or no opportunity or prospect; **a fat lot** (*slang*) not much; **kill the fatted calf** to have an extravagant celebration for someone returning after a long absence; **the fat is in the fire** a critical act has precipitated the trouble. [OE *fætt* fatted]

fat[2] *fat*, *n* a vessel for holding liquids; a vat; a dry measure of nine bushels. [See **vat**]

fatal *fā'tl*, *adj* belonging to or appointed by fate; announcing fate; causing death; mortal; bringing ruin; calamitous; decisive, critical, fateful; destined, unavoidable. — *n* **fāt'alism** the doctrine that all events are subject to fate, and happen by unavoidable necessity; acceptance of this doctrine; lack of effort in the face of threatened difficulty or disaster. — *n* **fāt'alist** a person who believes in fatalism. — *adj* **fātalist'ic**. — *n* **fatality** (*fə-tal'i-ti*) the state of being fatal or unavoidable; the decree of fate; fixed tendency to disaster or death; mortality; a fatal occurrence; a person who has been killed, *esp* in an accident, etc. — *adv* **fāt'ally**. — **the fatal sisters** see under **fate**. [L *fatalis*, from *fatum*; see **fate**]

fata Morgana *fä'tə mör-gä'nə*, *n* a striking kind of mirage seen most often in the Strait of Messina. [Supposed to be caused by the fairy (Ital *fata*) *Morgana* of Arthurian romance]

fate *fāt*, *n* inevitable destiny or necessity; appointed lot; destined term of life; ill-fortune; doom; final issue; (in *pl*; with *cap*; *Gr mythol*) the three goddesses of fate, Clotho, Lachesis, and Atropos, who determine the birth, life, and death of men and women, **the fatal sisters**. — *adj* **fāt'ed** doomed; destined; invested with the power of destiny (*Shakesp*); enchanted (*Dryden*). — *adj* **fate'ful** critical, decisive, having significant consequence; bringing calamity or death; prophetic, portentous; controlled by, or revealing the power of fate. — *adv* **fate'fully**. — *n* **fate'fulness**. [L *fātum* a prediction, from *fātus* spoken, from *fārī* to speak]

father *fä'dhər*, *n* a male parent; a protector who shows the love, concern, etc of a male parent; an ancestor or forefather; a contriver or originator; a title of respect applied to a venerable man, to confessors, monks, priests, etc; a member of certain fraternities; (*usu* in *pl*) a member of a ruling body, such as *conscript fathers*, *city fathers*; the oldest member, or member of longest standing, of a profession or body; any of a group of ecclesiastical writers of the early centuries, *usu* ending with Ambrose, Jerome, and Augustine; (with *cap*) the first person of the Christian Trinity. — *vt* to be the father of, procreate or beget; to adopt; to acknowledge that one is the father or author of; to ascribe to someone as his offspring or production. — *n* **fa'therhood** the state or fact of being a father; fatherly authority (*archaic*). — *adj* **fa'therless** having no living father; without a known author. — *n* **fa'therlessness**. — *adj* **fath'erlike**. — *n* **fa'therliness**. — *adj* **fa'therly** like a father; paternal. — *n* **fa'thership**. — **Father Christmas** same as **Santa Claus**; **fa'ther-figure** a senior person of experience and authority looked on as a trusted leader or protector; **fa'ther-in-law** the father of one's husband or wife; a stepfather (*archaic*): — *pl* **fa'thers-in-law**; **fa'therland** native land, *esp* Germany (*Vaterland*); the country of one's ancestors; **fa'ther-lash'er** a name applied to two bullhead fish found round the British coasts; **Father's Day** a day on which fathers are honoured, the third Sunday in June, the tradition being of US origin, dating from the early 20c. — **be gathered to one's fathers** (*Bible*) to die and be buried; **Holy Father** the Pope; **like father, like son** said when remarking inherited tendencies; **the father and mother of** see under **mother**. [OE *fæder*; Ger *Vater*, L *pater*, Gr *patēr*]

fathom *fadh'əm*, *n orig*, the reach of the outstretched arms; now, a unit of measurement for the depth of water, equal to 6 feet or 1·8 metres; penetration of mind; a timber measure equal to 216 cubic feet: — *pl* **fath'om** or **fath'oms**. — *vt* to measure or encompass with outstretched arms (*archaic*); to discover the depth of; to comprehend or get to the bottom of. — *adj* **fath'omable**. — *adj* **fath'omless** unfathomable. — *n* **fathom'eter** a sonic depth measurer. — **fath'om-line** a sailor's line and lead for taking soundings. [OE *fæthm*; Du *vadem*, Ger *Faden*]

fatidical *fā-* or *fə-tid'i-kl*, *adj* having the power to foretell future events; prophetical. — *adv* **fatid'ically**. [L *fātidicus*, from *fātum* fate, and *dīcere* to tell]

fatigue *fə-tēg'*, *n* weariness from physical or mental work; toil; lessened power of response to stimulus, resulting from activity (*physiol*); failure under repeated stress, as in metal; fatigue-duty (sometimes allotted as a punishment; *military*); (in *pl*) military overalls. — *vt* to reduce to weariness; to exhaust the strength or power of recovery of: — *pr p* **fatigu'ing**; *pa t* and *pa p* **fatigued'**. — *adj* **fatigable** or **fatiguable** (*fat'ig-ə-bl*) capable of being fatigued; easily fatigued. — *n* **fat'igableness** or **fat'iguableness**. — *adj* **fatigate** (*fat'i-gāt*; *Shakesp*) fatigued. — *vt* (*obs*) to fatigue. — *adv* **fatigu'ingly**. — **fatigue'-dress** soldiers' working dress; **fatigue'-duty** the part of a soldier's work distinct from the use of arms; **fatigue'-party** a group of soldiers on fatigue-duty. [Fr *fatigue*, from L *fatīgāre* to weary]

Fatimid *fat'i-mid*, *n* a descendant of Mohammed's daughter *Fatima* and his cousin Ali, *esp* one of a dynasty ruling parts of northern Africa from 909 to 1171. — Also *adj*.

fatiscent *fă-* or *fə-tis'ənt*, (*geol*) *adj* gaping with cracks. — *n* **fatis'cence**. [L *fatīscēns*, *-entis* pr p of *fatīscere* to gape]

fatsia *fat'si-ə*, *n* an evergreen spreading shrub of the ivy family, with leathery leaves and clusters of white flowers in the form of umbels. [Perh Jap *yatsude*, the name of this plant]

fatso *fat'sō*, (*derog slang*) *n* a fat person: — *pl* **fat'sos** or **fat'soes**. [**fat**[1]]

fatten, **fatter**, **fatty**, etc. See under **fat**.

fattrels *fat'rəlz* or *fät'*, (*Scot*) *n pl* ends of ribbon. [OFr *fatraille* trumpery]

fatuous *fat'ū-əs*, *adj* foolish, inane, asinine, *esp* in a cheerfully complacent way. — *adj* **fatū'itous**. — *n* **fatū'ity** or **fat'ūousness** complacent stupidity. — **fatuous fire** ignis fatuus, will-o'-the-wisp. [L *fatuus*]

fatwa or **fatwah** *fat'wə*, *n* a formal legal opinion or decision issued by a Muslim judicial authority, eg that someone should die or be killed; (non-Muslim) ultimate sanctions, sentence of death (*fig*, *esp humorous*). — *vt* (in a non-Muslim context) to put under threat of terrible revenge: — *pa t* and *pa p* **fat'wa'd**. [Ar]

faubourg *fō-bŏŏr*, (*Fr*) *n* a suburb just beyond the walls or a district recently included within a city.

fauces *fö'sēz*, *n pl* the upper part of the throat, from the root of the tongue to the pharynx; the throat of a flower. — *adj* **fau'cal** (*-kl*) of or produced in the fauces, as are certain Semitic guttural sounds. — *adj* **faucial** (*fö'shl*) of the fauces. [L *faucēs*]

faucet *fö'sit*, *n* a pipe inserted in a barrel to draw off liquid; a tap (*US*). [Fr *fausset*]

fauchion and **fauchon** *fö'shən* or *-chən*, *n*. Obsolete forms of **falchion**.

faucial. See under **fauces**.

faugh *fö*, *interj* expressing disgust.

faulchion and **faulchin**. Obsolete forms of **falchion**.

fault *fölt*, formerly *föt*, *n* a failing or weakness of character; an error; a blemish or flaw; imperfection; a misdeed or slight offence; a dislocation of strata or veins where a fracture has occurred in the earth's crust (*geol*); a defect in an electronic circuit; a stroke in which the player fails to serve the ball properly or into the proper place (*tennis*); a penalty point for failing to hit the correct ball or other error (*snooker* or *billiards*); a penalty point for refusing or failing to clear a fence (*showjumping*); culpability for something which has gone wrong. — *vi* to fall short (*obs*); to be faulty; to develop or show a fault (*geol*); to commit a fault. — *vt* to censure, find fault with; to find a flaw or flaws in; to cause a fault in (*geol*). — *adj* **fault'ful** (*Shakesp*) full of faults or crimes. — *adv* **fault'ily**. — *n* **fault'iness**. — *adj* **fault'less** without fault or defect. — *adv* **fault'lessly**. — *n* **fault'lessness**. — *adj* **fault'y** imperfect, defective; guilty of a fault; culpable. — **fault'-finder**; **fault'-finding** criticism, captiousness; the detection and investigation of faults and malfunctions in electronic equipment (**find'-fault** see under **find**); **fault plane** (*geol*) a *usu* uncurved surface of rock strata where a fault has occurred; **fault tolerance** (*comput*) the ability of a system to execute specific tasks correctly regardless of failures and errors. — **at fault** (of dogs) unable to find the scent; at a loss; to blame, culpable; guilty; **find fault** to carp, be critical; (with *with*) to censure for some mistake or defect; **in fault** (*archaic*) to blame; **to a fault** excessively. [OFr *faute*, *falte*, from L *fallere* to deceive]

faun *fön*, (*Roman mythol*) *n* the protector of shepherds, a rural deity similar to a satyr, having a man's body, with a goat's horns, ears, tail and hind legs. [L *Faunus*, a deity of woods and pastures]

fauna *fö'nə*, *n* the assemblage of all forms of animal life of a region or period, *esp* as distinct from plant life (*flora*); a list or account of this: — *pl* **faun'as** or **faun'ae** (*-ē*). — *adj* **faun'al**. — *n* **faun'ist** a person who studies faunas. — *adj* **faunist'ic**. [L *Fauna* and *Faunus* tutelary deities of shepherds, from *favēre*, *fautum* to favour]

faurd. See **fa'ard**.

Faustian *fow'sti-ən*, *adj* in the manner of *Faust* who, in German legend, made a bargain with the devil to gain limitless knowledge in exchange for his soul. — Also without *cap*.

faute de mieux *fōt də myø*, (*Fr*) for want of anything better.

fauteuil *fō-tœ-y'*, also *fō'til*, *n* an armchair, *esp* a president's chair; the seat of one of the forty members of the French Academy; a theatre stall. [Fr]

fautor *fö'tər*, *n* a favourer; a patron; an abettor. [L *fautor*, from *favēre* to favour]

Fauve *fōv* or **Fauvist** *fōv'ist*, *n* a member of a group of expressionist painters at the beginning of the 20c, including Matisse, who viewed a painting as essentially a two-dimensional decoration in colour, not necessarily imitative of nature. — *n* **Fauv'ism** this style of painting. [Fr *fauve* wild beast]

fauvette *fō-vet'*, *n* a warbler. [Fr]

faux *fō*, (*Fr*) *adj* false. — **faux ami** (*fōz a-mē*) literally, a false friend, hence a word in a foreign language that does not mean what it appears to, eg in Italian, *pretendere* does not mean 'to pretend'. — *n* and *adj* **faux-naïf** (*fō-na-ēf'*) (a person) seeming or pretending to be simple and unsophisticated. — **faux pas** (*fō pä*) literally, a false step, hence a mistake or blunder, *esp* an offence against accepted standards of politeness, decorum, etc.

fauxbourdon *fō-bŏŏr-dɔ̃*. Same as **faburden**.

fave *fāv*, *adj* (*teenage slang*) favourite.

favel or **favell** *fā'vəl*, (*obs*) *adj* light-brown; chestnut. — *n* (with *cap*) a name for a chestnut horse, *esp* used proverbially to mean craftiness or cunning, from the deceitful but much-courted horse *Fauvel* in the OFr *Roman de Fauvel*; hence **curry favell** (see **curry**[2]), from OFr *estriller* or *toucher Fauvel*.

favela *fä-vä'lə*, *n* (*esp* in Brazil) a shanty town. [Port]

faveolate *fə-vē'ō-lāt*, *adj* honeycombed. [L *favus* honeycomb]

favism *fā'vizm*, *n* an acute type of anaemia in which haemolysis is precipitated by contact with broad beans (by ingestion or pollen-inhalation), the original lesion being an enzyme deficiency in the red blood cells. [L *fava* broad bean, and *-ism*]

Favonian *fə-vō'ni-ən*, *adj* pertaining to the west wind, favourable. [L *Favōnius* the west wind]

favour or (*esp US*) **favor** *fā'vər*, *n* approval; esteem; goodwill; a kind deed; an act of grace or clemency; indulgence; partiality; advantage; (*usu* in *pl*) sexual intimacy regarded as a pleasure granted by one person to another, *esp* by a woman to a man (*literary* or *facetious*); a knot of ribbons worn at a football match, election, etc to show one's allegiance; a thing given or worn as a token of favour or love (*esp hist*); appearance, face (*archaic*); a letter or written communication (*commercial jargon*); an attraction or grace (*Shakesp*); an object of favour (*Milton*). — *vt* to regard with goodwill; to be on the side of; to show partiality to; to treat indulgently; to give support to; to afford advantage to; to resemble (*colloq*); to choose to wear, etc. — *adj* **fā'vourable** or (*esp US*) **favorable** friendly; propitious; conducive (with *to*); advantageous; satisfactory, promising. — *n* **fā'vourableness** or (*esp US*) **favorableness** — *adv* **fā'vourably** or (*esp US*) **favorably**. — *adj* **fā'voured** or (*esp US*) **favored** enjoying favour or preference; (of an area, etc) well liked, convenient; wearing favours; having a certain appearance, featured, as in *ill-favoured, well-favoured.* — *n* **fā'vouredness** or (*esp US*) **favoredness**. — *n* **fā'vourer** or (*esp US*) **favorer**. — *n* **fā'vourite** or (*esp US*) **favorite** (*-it*) a person or thing regarded with special preference; a person unduly loved and indulged, *esp* by a king; a person, horse, etc expected to win; a kind of curl of the hair, affected by ladies of the 18c. — *adj* esteemed, preferred, best loved. — *n* **fā'vouritism** or (*esp US*) **favoritism** inclination to partiality; preference shown to favourites. — *adj* **fā'vourless** or (*esp US*) **favorless** without favour; not favouring (*Spenser*). — **curry favour** see **curry**[2] and **favel**; **favours to come** favours still expected; **in favour** approved of; **in favour of** for; on the side of; for the advantage or benefit of; **out of favour** not approved of. [OFr, from L *favor*, from *favēre* to favour or befriend]

favrile *fəv-rēl'* or *fav'rəl*, *n* a type of iridescent glassware developed in America at the turn of the 20c by L C Tiffany. [Orig trademark, from obs *fabrile*, pertaining to a craftsman]

favus *fāv'əs*, *n* a fungal skin disease, chiefly of the scalp, giving a honeycombed appearance. — *adj* **favose** (*fə-vōs'* or *fā'vōs*) honeycombed. — *adj* **fā'vous** like a honeycomb; relating to favus. [L *favus* a honeycomb]

faw *fö*, *n* a gypsy. [From the surname *Faa*]

fawn[1] *fön*, *n* a young deer, *esp* a fallow deer; its colour, light greyish or yellowish brown. — *adj* of this colour. — *vt* and *vi* (of a deer) to give birth to young. [OFr *faon*, through LL from L *fētus* offspring]

fawn[2] *fön*, *vi* to try to please, or flatter, in a servile way (with *on* or *upon*); (of an animal, *esp* a dog) to lick, rub against, jump on, etc, in a show of affection. — *n* (*rare*) a servile action or gesture; cringing flattery. — *n* **fawn'er** a person who flatters to gain favour. — *n* and *adj* **fawn'ing**. — *adv* **fawn'ingly**. — *n* **fawn'ingness**. [A variant of **fain**[1], from OE *fægen* glad]

fax *faks*, *n* a shortening of **facsimile** as in **fax machine**, a machine that scans a document, etc electronically and transfers the information by a telephone or radio link to a receiving machine which reproduces the document; the system for such transfer of information; a fax machine; a copy produced in this way. — *vt* to transmit the contents of (a document, etc) using a fax machine.

fay[1] *fā*, (*poetic*) *n* a fairy. [OFr *fae*, from LL *fāta*; see **fate**]

fay[2] *fā*, (*Shakesp*) *n* faith. [OFr *fei*]

fay[3]. See **fey**[1].

fay[4] *fā*, (*obs* or *dialect*) *vt* and *vi* to fit or unite closely. — **fay'ing-face** a prepared surface of contact. [OE *fēgan*; Ger *fügen*]

fay[5] or **fey** *fā*, (*dialect*) *vt* to clean out, eg a ditch. [ON *fægja* to cleanse]

fayalite *fā'ə-līt* or *fä-yäl'īt*, *n* iron-olivine, a silicate of iron found in slag and occurring naturally. [*Fayal* in the Azores, where it was found, prob in ballast]

fayence. Same as **faience**.

fayne *fān*, (*Spenser*) *vt*. See **feign**.

fayre. An archaic or archaizing spelling of **fair**[2].

faze *fāz*, *vt* to drive or drive off (*obs*); to settle the business of (*Shakesp*); to beat (*obs*); to worry, perturb, unsettle. — Also **feese, feeze, pheese, pheeze** or **phese**. — *n* a rush (*dialect*); a rub (*obs*); perturbation, disquiet. — *adj* **fazed**, etc unsettled, mystified, thrown off balance. [OE *fēsian* to drive away]

fazenda *fə-zen'də*, *n* (*esp* in Brazil) a large estate, plantation or cattle ranch. — *n* **fazendeiro** (*fa-zen-dā'rō*) a person who owns or runs such a property: — *pl* **fazendei'ros**. [Port; see **hacienda**.]

FBA *abbrev*: Fellow of the British Academy.

FBI *abbrev*: Federal Bureau of Investigation (of the USA).

FBR *abbrev*: fast-breeder reactor.

FC *abbrev*: football club.

FCA *abbrev*: Fellow of the Institute of Chartered Accountants in England and Wales, or in Ireland.

FCCA *abbrev*: Fellow of the Chartered Association of Certified Accountants.

FCII *abbrev*: Fellow of the Chartered Insurance Institute.

FCMA *abbrev*: Fellow of the Institute of Cost and Management Accountants.

FCO *abbrev*: Foreign and Commonwealth Office.

fcp or **fcap** *abbrev*: foolscap.

FD *abbrev*: *Fidei Defensor* (*L*), Defender of the Faith, appearing on coins since decimalization.

FDA *abbrev*: Food and Drug Administration (of the USA); First Division Association, a trade union for high-ranking civil servants.

FDR *abbrev*: *Freie Demokratische Republik* (*Ger*), Free Democratic Republic (the former West Germany).

Fe *symbol*: *ferrum* (*L*), iron.

feague *fēg*, (*obs*) *vt* to whip; to perplex. [Cf Du *vegen*, Ger *fegen*]

feal[1] *fēl*, (*obs*) *adj* loyal, faithful. [OFr *feal*, from L *fidēlis*]

feal[2] *fēl*, (*dialect*) *vt* to conceal. [ON *fela*]

feal[3] *fēl*. Same as **fail**[1].

fealty *fē'əl-ti* or *fēl'ti*, *n* the vassal's obligation of fidelity to his feudal lord (*hist*); loyalty. [OFr *fealte*, from L *fidēlitās, -tātis*, from *fidēlis* faithful, from *fīdere* to trust]

fear *fēr*, *n* a painful emotion excited by danger; apprehension of danger or pain; alarm; solicitude, anxiety; that which causes alarm; risk or possibility; reverence or awe (*relig*); piety towards God (*old relig*). — *vt* to regard with fear, be afraid of; to expect with alarm; to be regretfully inclined to think; to revere (*relig*); to be anxious or in fear about (*obs*); to stand in awe of (*relig*); to venerate (*relig*); to terrify (*obs*); to make afraid (*obs*). — *vi* to be afraid; to suspect some danger to (with *for*); (*esp* in *neg*) to be in doubt. — *adj* **feared** (*fērd*; *archaic* and *Scot*) afraid. — *adj* **fear'ful** timorous; producing intense fear; terrible; (loosely) very great, very bad. — *adv* **fear'fully**. — *n* **fear'fulness**. — *adj* **fear'less** without fear; daring; brave. — *adv* **fear'lessly**. — *n* **fear'lessness**. — *adj* **fear'some** causing fear, frightful. — *adv* **fear'somely**. — **fear'nought** dreadnought cloth, a thick cloth for overcoats, etc. — **for fear** in case, lest; **for fear of** in order to avoid; **no fear** (*interj*; *slang*) definitely not. [OE *fǣr*, fear and *fǣran* to terrify]

feare. See **fere**[1].

feasible *fē'zi-bl*, *adj* practicable, possible; (loosely) probable, likely. — *n* **feas'ibleness** or **feasibil'ity**. — *adv* **feas'ibly**. — **feasibility study** an investigation to determine whether a particular project, system, etc is desirable, practicable, etc. [Fr *faisable* that can be done, from *faire, faisant*, from L *facere* to do]

feast *fēst*, *n* a rich and abundant meal; a regularly occurring religious celebration commemorating a person or event, honouring a deity, etc; (something that supplies) rich gratification of the senses (eg a *feast for the eyes*) or stimulation for the mind. — *vi* to hold a feast; to eat abundantly and well (with *on*); to receive intense delight. — *vt* to provide a feast for; to delight, gratify (one's senses; with *on*). — *n* **feast'er**. — *adj* **feast'ful** (*archaic*) festive, joyful, luxurious. — *n* **feast'ing**. — **feast'-day** a day on which a religious festival occurs; **feast'-rite** a rite or custom observed at religious feasts. — *adj* **feast'-won** (*Shakesp*) won or bribed by feasting. — **Feast of Dedication** see under **dedicate**; **Feast of Fools** and **Feast of Asses** medieval festivals held between Christmas and Epiphany, in which a mock bishop was enthroned in church, a burlesque mass was said, and an ass driven round in triumph; **Feast of Lots** the Jewish festival of purim; **Feast of Tabernacles** see under **tabernacle**; **Feast of Weeks** see under **week**; **movable feast** a feast of variable date, such as Easter. [OFr *feste* (Fr *fête*), from L *fēstum* a holiday, *fēstus* solemn, festal]

feat *fēt*, *n* an act or deed (*obs*); a deed manifesting extraordinary strength, skill or courage, an exploit, achievement; art, skill (*Spenser*). — *vt* (*Shakesp*) *perh* to fashion, to make feat or neat. — *adj* (*Shakesp*) neat, deft. — *adv* (*Shakesp*) **feat'ly** neatly; dexterously. [Fr *fait*, from L *factum*, from *facere* to do; cf **fact**]

feateous and **feateously**. See under **featous**.

feather *fedh'ər*, *n* one of the light growths that form the soft covering of a bird; anything resembling this, eg an ornament; a set of these, or synthetic substitutes, on the end of an arrow, to aid flight; plumage; condition; birds collectively; anything light or trifling; a projecting longitudinal rib or strip; feather-edge; a wedge; a formation of hair, eg on the legs of certain breeds of dog or horse; the act of moving an oar edgewise through the air, to lessen resistance; a foamy wave or wave-crest, *esp* that caused by a submarine's periscope. — *vt* to provide, cover or adorn with a feather or feathers; to turn (an oar) parallel to the water, to lessen air-resistance, or to make (a propeller-blade, etc) rotate in such a way as to lessen resistance; to shape (hair) by trimming and thinning. — *vi* to take on the appearance of a feather; to quiver the tail. — *adj* **feath'ered** covered or fitted with feathers, or anything featherlike; like the flight of a feathered animal, swift. — *n* **feath'eriness**. — *n* **feath'ering** plumage; the addition of a feather or feathers; a featherlike appearance; an arrangement of small arcs separated by cusps, within an arch (*archit*). — *adj* **feath'ery** pertaining to, resembling, or covered with feathers or an appearance of feathers. — **feather bed** a mattress filled with feathers or down. — *vt* **feath'erbed** to pamper; to protect (an industry, workers, etc) by such practices as overmanning in order to save jobs. — **featherbed'ding**; **feath'er-boarding** same as **weather-boarding**; **feather-bonn'et** a Highland soldier's feather-covered headdress; **feath'er-brain** (also **feath'er-head** or **feath'er-pate** (*archaic*)) a frivolous, silly person; **feather-dust'er** a light brush of feathers, used for dusting; **feath'er-edge** an edge of a board or plank thinner than the other edge; **feath'er-grass** a perennial grass (*Stipa*) with a feathery beard; **feather palm** any palm with feather-shaped leaves; **feath'er-star** see **crinoid**; **feath'er-stitch** one of a series of stitches making a zigzag line; **feath'erweight** the lightest weight that may be carried by a racehorse; a weight category applied variously in boxing, wrestling and weightlifting; a sportsman or sportswoman of the specified weight for the category (eg in professional boxing above bantamweight, **junior-featherweight** (maximum 55 kg/122lb), **featherweight** (maxiumum 57 kg/126 lb) and **super-featherweight** (maximum 59 kg/130lb); anyone of little consequence. — **a feather in one's cap** an achievement of which one can be proud; **birds of a feather** people of similar character; **feather one's nest** to accumulate wealth for oneself while working for others in a position of trust; **in full** or **high feather** greatly elated or in high spirits; **make the feathers fly** to create a turmoil or uproar; **ruffle someone's feathers** to upset or offend someone; **show the white feather** to show signs of cowardice, a white feather in a gamecock's tail being considered as a sign of degeneracy; **tar and feather** see under **tar**; **you could have knocked me down with a feather** I was astounded. [OE *fether*; Ger *Feder*; L *penna*, Gr *pteron*]

featous *fēt'əs*, **feat'eous** *-i-əs* or **feat'uous** *-ū-əs*, (*archaic*) *adj* shapely; well-made; handsome; dexterous; neat. — *adv* **feat'eously** (*Spenser*) dexterously, neatly. [OFr *fetis*, from L *factīcius* ,from *facere* to make; cf **factitious**]

feature *fē'chər*, *n* beauty (*obs*); shape, phantom (*archaic*); form, outward appearance; shape of face; any part of the face, such as the eyes, mouth, etc; an element or prominent trait of anything; a characteristic; (in *pl*) the face; a non-news article in a newspaper; a feature film; anything offered as a special attraction or distinctive characteristic. — Also *adj*. — *vt* to have as a feature; to make a feature of; to present prominently; to have features resembling (*colloq*). — *vi* to play an important part or role (with *in*), be a feature (of). — *combining form* **-feat'ured** having features of a specified type, as in *sharp-featured*. — *adj* **feat'ureless** completely lacking in distinct features. — *adj* **feat'urely** (*archaic*) handsome. — **feature film** a long film forming the basis of a cinema programme. — *adj* **feat'ure-length** (of films) of similar length to a feature film. — **feature programme** a radio or TV programme that reconstructs dramatically the life of a prominent person, or an important event, or gives a dramatic picture of a profession or activity. [OFr *faiture*, from L *factura*, from *facere* to make]

Feb. *abbrev*: February.

feblesse. See under **feeble**.

febrifuge *feb'rə-fūj*, (*med*) *n* a medicine, etc that reduces fever. — *adj* **febrifugal** (*fib-rif'ū-gəl* or *feb-rə-fū'gəl*) [MedL *febrifugia* feverfew]

febrile *fēb'*, *feb'rīl* or *-ril*, *adj* relating to fever; feverish. — *n* **febricity** (*fi-bris'i-ti*) feverishness. — *n* **febricula** (*fi-brik'ū-lə*) or **febricule** (*feb'*) a slight short fever. — *adj* **febrifacient** (*fē-bri-fā'shənt*; L *faciēns*, *-entis* making) producing fever. — *adj* **febrif'ic** (*fi-*) febrifacient; feverish. — *n* **febril'ity**. [Med L *febrīlis*, from *febris* fever]

Febronianism *feb-rō'ni-ən-izm*, *n* a system of doctrine antagonistic to the claims of the Pope and asserting the independence of national churches, propounded in 1763 by Johann Nikolaus von Hontheim under the pseudonym Justinus *Febronius*.

February *feb'rōō-ər-i*, *n* the second month of the year. [L *Februārius* (*mēnsis*) the month of expiation, and *februa* the feast of expiation]

fec. *abbrev*: fecit.

feces and **fecal**. See **faeces**.

fecht *fehht* and **fechter** *-ər*. Scots forms of **fight** and **fighter**.

fecial. See **fetial**.

fecit *fē'sit* or *fā'kit*, (*L*) (he or she) made or did (this).

feck *fek*, *n* (*Scot*) meaning, tenor (*obs*); substance (*obs*); efficacy; quantity, number; the bulk. — *adj* **feck'less** feeble, ineffectual; helpless; futile. — *adv* **feck'lessly**. — *n* **feck'lessness**. — *adv* (*archaic*) **feck'ly** mostly; nearly. [Aphetic for **effect**]

fecula *fek'ū-lə*, *n* starch obained as a sediment; sediment, dregs. — *n* **fec'ulence** or **fec'ulency**. — *adj* **fec'ulent** containing or consisting of faeces or sediment; foul; turbid. [L *faecula* dimin of *faex* dregs]

fecund *fēk'und* or *fek'und*, also *-ənd*, *adj* fruitful; fertile; prolific. — *vt* **fec'undāte** to make fruitful or fertile; to make pregnant, to fertilize or impregnate. — *n* **fecundā'tion**. — *n* **fecundity** (*fi-kund'i-ti*) fruitfulness, fertility; productiveness; the number of young produced by a species or individual (cf **fertility**; *ecol*). [L *fēcundus* fruitful]

Fed[1] *fed*, (*US slang*) *n* a Federal (agent), ie an agent of the Federal Bureau of Investigation. — Also without *cap*. [Contraction of **Federal**]

Fed[2] *abbrev*: Federal Reserve Board (of the US).

fed *fed*, *pa t* and *pa p* of **feed**[1].

fedarie, **foedarie** *fē'dər-i*, **federarie** or **federary** *fed'ər-ər-i*, *n*. Shakespearian words for a confederate accomplice. [L *foedus*, *-eris* treaty; moulded on **feudary**]

fedayee *fə-dä'yē*, *n* an Arab commando, *esp* one involved in the conflict against Israel: — *pl* **feda'yeen**. [Ar *fidā'ī*]

fedelini *fed-e-lē'nē*, *n* vermicelli. [Ital]

federal *fed'ər-əl*, *adj* pertaining to or consisting of a treaty or covenant; confederated, founded upon mutual agreement; (of a union or government) in which several states, while independent in home affairs, combine for national or general purposes, as in the United States (in the American Civil War, *Federal* was the name applied to the states of the North which defended the Union against the *Confederate* separatists of the South); of or relating to the national or central government in such a union, as opposed to any regional or state government. — *n* a supporter of federation; a Unionist soldier in the American Civil War. — *n* **fed'eracy**. — *n* **fed'eralism** the principles or cause maintained by federalists. — *n* **fed'eralist** a supporter of a federal constitution or union. — *n* **federalizā'tion** or **-s-**. — *vt*

fed'eralize or **-ise**. — *n* **fed'erary** (*Shakesp*) see **fedarie**. — **federal** (or **covenant**) **theology** that first worked out by Cocceius (1603–69), based on the idea of two covenants between God and man, of Works and of Grace (see also **covenant**). — **Federal Bureau of Investigation** (in the US) a bureau or subdivision of the Department of Justice that investigates crimes, such as smuggling and espionage, that are the concern of the federal government; **Federal Reserve Board** (in the US) the board of governors in charge of the **Federal Reserve System**, which, comprising twelve **Federal Reserve Banks**, controls banking activities and supply of money and credit. [L *foedus, foederis* a treaty, related to *fīdere* to trust]

federarie and **federary**. See **fedarie**.

federate *fed'ə-rāt*, *vt* and *vi* to join together in a league or federation. — *adj* united in a league; confederated. — *n* **federā'tion** the act of uniting in a league; a federal union. — *adj* **fed'erātive** united in a league. [L *foederāre*, from *foedus, foederis* a treaty]

fedora *fi-dō'rə* or *-dö'*, *n* a brimmed felt hat dented lengthways. [Said to be from *Fédora*, a play by Sardou]

fee *fē*, *n* the price paid for services, such as to a lawyer or physician; recompense, wages; the sum exacted for any special privilege; a grant of land for feudal service (*hist*); feudal tenure; service (*obs*); fee simple; inheritance (*obs*); possession (*obs*); ownership (*obs*); cattle, livestock (*obs*); property (*obs*); money (*obs*). — *vt* to pay a fee to; to hire (*Scot*): — *pr p* **fee'ing**; *pa t* and *pa p* **feed** or **fee'd**. — **fee'-farm** (*Shakesp*) tenure by fee simple at a fixed rent without services; **fee'-grief** (*Shakesp*) a private grief; **fee'ing-market** (*Scot*) a fair or market at which farm-servants are hired for the year or half-year following; **fee simple** unconditional inheritance; **fee tail** an entailed estate, which may descend only to a certain class of heirs. — **base fee** qualified fee, a freehold estate of inheritance to which a qualification is annexed; **conditional fee** a fee granted on condition, or limited to particular heirs; the estate of a mortgagee of land, possession of which is conditional on payment; **great fee** the land-holding of a tenant of the Crown. [Partly OE *feoh* cattle or property; Ger *Vieh*, ON *fē*; allied to L *pecus* cattle, and *pecūnia* money; partly AFr *fee*, prob ultimately Gmc and of the same origin]

fée *fā*, (*Fr*) *n* a fairy. — *n* **féerie** (*fā-rē*) fairyland; an extravaganza (*theat*).

feeble *fē'bl*, *adj* very weak, frail; (of a joke, excuse, etc) tame, lame, unconvincing or thin; vacillating, lacking resolve; faint. — *vt* (*Spenser*) to make feeble. — *n* **fe'blesse** (*Spenser*). — *n* **fee'bleness**. — *adj* **fee'blish**. — *adv* **fee'bly**. — *adj* **feeble-mind'ed** mentally impaired to the extent of being unable to compete with others or to manage one's affairs with ordinary prudence; lacking resolve. — *adv* **feeble-mind'edly**. — **feeble-mind'edness**. [OFr *foible*, for *floible* , from L *flēbilis* lamentable, from *flēre* to weep]

feed[1] *fēd*, *vt* to give, supply, or administer food to; to give as food (with *to*); to nourish; to provide with necessary material; to foster; to give as food or as material to be used progressively; to furnish (an actor) with cues or opportunities of achieving an effect; in football, to pass the ball to. — *vi* to take food; to nourish oneself by eating (with *on*): — *pr p* **feed'ing**; *pa t* and *pa p* **fed**. — *n* an amount or allowance of food given eg to babies or to cattle; food for livestock feeding; pasture; a plentiful meal (*colloq*); material supplied progressively for any operation; the means, channel, motion or rate of such supply; rate of progress of a tool; an actor who feeds another, a stooge. — *n* **feed'er** a person who consumes food (*esp* in a specified way, eg *a big feeder*) or provides or administers it to another; an actor who feeds another; something which supplies (water, electricity, ore, paper, etc); any channel of supply to a main system; a transport route linking outlying areas to the trunk line; a tributary; an overhead or underground cable, of large current-carrying capacity, used to transmit electric power between generating stations, substations and feeding points; a container for food for small animals, birds, etc; a feeding-bottle; a bib; a person who fattens cattle; a shepherd (*obs*); a dependant, a servant (*archaic*). — *adj* secondary, subsidiary, tributary. — *n* **feed'ing** the act of eating; that which is eaten; pasture; the placing of the sheets of paper in position for a printing or ruling machine. — **feed'back** return of part of the output of a system to the input as a means towards improved quality or self-correction of error (*negative feedback*) or, when in phase with the input signal, resulting in oscillation and instability (*positive feedback*); used also in speaking of biological, etc self-adjusting systems; response or reaction providing useful information or guidelines for further action or development; (in a public address system, etc) the unintentional returning of some of the sound output back to the microphone, producing a whistle or howl; **feed'-head** a cistern that supplies water to a boiler; **feed'-heater** an apparatus for heating water for a boiler; **feed'ing-bottle** a bottle for supplying liquid food to an infant; **feeding point** (*elec*) the junction point between a feeder and distribution system; **feed'-line** a line fed to an actor; a cue; **feed'lot** a unit in which cattle are kept indoors and made to put on weight rapidly by means of processed and blended feed supplied to them automatically; **feed'-pipe** a pipe for supplying liquid, such as water to a boiler or cistern; **feed'-pump** a force-pump for supplying a boiler with water; **feed'stock** raw material used in an industrial process; **feed'stuff** any type of food for animals, *esp* cattle, pigs, sheep, etc; **feed'-water** water supplied to a boiler, etc. — **fed to the (back) teeth** (*slang*) fed up; **fed up** (*slang*) sated (*obs*); jaded; disgruntled; bored; (with *with*) tired of, annoyed by; **feed one's face** (*slang*) to eat heartily; **off one's feed** without appetite, disinclined to eat. [OE *fēdan* to feed]

feed[2] *fēd*, *pa t* and *pa p* of **fee**.

fee-faw-fum *fē'-fö'-fum'* or **fee-fi-faw-fum** *fee'-fī'-fö'-fum'*, *interj* expressive of bloodthirstiness, in fairy tales, etc. — *n* words, etc intended to terrify. [From *Jack the Giantkiller*]

feel *fēl*, *vt* to perceive by the touch; to investigate by touching or handling; to find (one's way) by groping; to be conscious of; to be keenly sensible of; to have an inward persuasion of, to believe, consider or think; to caress the genitals of (with *up*; *vulg*). — *vi* to be aware that one is (well, ill, happy, etc); to explore or investigate with one's hand (with *in*, etc); to impart a particular impression when touched, as in *to feel smooth, sharp*, etc; to be emotionally affected; to have sympathy or compassion (with *for*): — *pr p* **feel'ing**; *pa t* and *pa p* **felt**. — *n* the sensation of touch; an instinct, touch, knack; an act of feeling something; an impression imparted by something being felt; a general impression or atmosphere associated with something. — *n* **feel'er** a person, etc that feels; a remark cautiously dropped, or any indirect stratagem, to sound out the opinions of others; a tentacle; a jointed organ in the head of insects, etc capable of a delicate sense, an antenna. — *n* **feel'ing** the sense of touch; perception of objects by touch; consciousness of pleasure or pain; an impression received physically or mentally; tenderness; (an) emotion; sensibility, susceptibility, sentimentality; an opinion, sentiment; an instinctive grasp or appreciation (with *for*); mutual or interactive emotion, such as *bad feeling* (resentment or animosity), *good feeling* (friendliness), *ill-feeling*, *fellow-feeling*; (in *pl*) the affections or passions; (in *pl*) one's sensibilities,or amour-propre, as in *hurt someone's feelings*. — *adj* expressive of great sensibility or tenderness; easily or strongly affected by emotion; sympathetic; compassionate; pitying; deeply felt. — *adj* **feel'ingless**. — *adv* **feel'ingly**. — **feeler gauge** (*eng*) a thin strip of metal of known thickness, used to measure or set the distance between surfaces or parts; **feel'-good** or **feel'good** (*colloq*) a feeling of personal well-being, optimism or (smug) self-satisfaction, often as *adj*, *esp* in the phrase *feel-good factor*, often apparent in research into voting, buying, etc intentions. — **bad feeling** resentment or animosity; ill-feeling; **feel after** (*Bible*) to search for; **feelings (are) running high** (there is) a general feeling of anger, emotion, etc; **feel like** to want, have a desire for; **feel oneself** to feel as fit as normal; **feel one's feet** or **way** to accustom oneself to a new situation, job, etc; **feel up to** (with *neg*) to feel fit enough to; **good feeling** friendly feeling; amicable relations; **no hard feelings** no offence taken. [OE *fēlan* to feel; Ger *fühlen*; prob akin to L *palpāri* to stroke]

feer[1]. See **fere**[1].

feer[2] *fēr*, (*Scot*) *vi* to draw the first furrow in ploughing, to mark out the rigs. — *n* **feer'in** or **feer'ing** a first guiding furrow. [Perh OE *fȳrian* to make a furrow, from *furh* furrow]

féerie. See under **fée**.

feese. See **faze**.

feet *fēt*, *pl* of **foot**. — *adj* **feet'less** footless. — See also **foot**.

feeze, **feese**, **pheese**, **pheeze** or **phese**. See **faze**.

fegary *fi-gā'ri*, *n* a variant of **vagary**.

fegs *fegz*, (*dialect*) *interj* in faith, truly. [See **fay**[2], **faith** and **faix**]

Fehm or **Fehmgericht**. Same as **Vehm** or **Vehmgericht**.

FEI *abbrev*: *Fédération Équestre Internationale* (*Fr*), International Equestrian Federation.

feign (*Spenser* **fain**, **faine** or **fayne**) *fān*, *vt* to fashion, shape (*obs*); to invent; to imagine falsely (*obs*); to assume fictitiously; to imagine (*archaic*); to make a show or pretence of, to counterfeit, simulate; to dissemble (*Spenser*). — *adj* **feigned** pretended; simulated; imagined (*archaic*); fictitious. — *adv* **feign'edly**. — *n* **feign'edness**. — *n* **feign'ing**. [Fr *feindre*, pr p *feignant* to feign, from L *fingere*, *fictum* to form]

feijoa *fā-jō'ə* or *fī-*, *n* any of various evergreen shrubs or trees of the genus *Feijoa*; the aromatic quince-like fruit they bear. [J da Silva *Feijo*, 19c Sp naturalist]

feint[1] *fānt*, *n* a mock assault; a deceptive movement in fencing, boxing, etc; a false show; a pretence. — *vi* to make a feint. [Fr *feinte*, from *feindre* to feign]

feint[2] *fānt*, *adj* a printers' or stationers' word for the faint horizontal rules sometimes printed on stationery. — *n pl* **feints** same as **faints**.

feis *fesh*, *n* an ancient Irish assembly for the proclamation of laws and the holding of artistic, intellectual and sports competitions; an Irish festival on the ancient model, including sports events, folk music and dancing: — *pl* **feiseanna** (*fesh'ə-nə*). [Ir, festival or assembly]

feisty *fī'sti*, (*colloq*, *orig US*) *adj* excitable, irritable, touchy; spirited. — *n* **fei'stiness**. [From old US dialect *fist* a small aggressive dog, from ME *fisten* to break wind]

felafel or **falafel** *fə-lä'fəl*, *n* a deep-fried ball of ground chick-peas, with onions, peppers, etc and spices. [Ar *falāfil*]

feldgrau *felt'grow*, *n* and *adj* field-grey, the colour of German military uniforms. [Ger *Feld* field, and *grau* grey]

feldsher *feld'shər* or *fel'shər*, *n* in Russia and parts of Eastern Europe), a partly trained person who practises medicine; a person who assists a doctor, *esp* on the battlefield. [Russ *fel'dsher*, from Ger *Feldscher* army surgeon]

feldspar *feld'spär* or *fel'spär* or **felspar** *fel'spär*, *n* any member of the most important group of rock-forming minerals, anhydrous silicates of aluminium along with potassium (such as *orthoclase*, *microcline*), sodium, calcium, or both (the *plagioclases*), or sodium and barium (*hyalo-phane*). — Also (*obs*) **feld'spathol**. — *adj* **feldspathic** or **felspathic** (*-spath'ik*). — *n* **feld'spathoid** or **fel'spathoid** any mineral of a group chemically related to feldspar, including nepheline, leucite, sodalite, etc. [Swed *feldtspat* a name given in 1740 by D Tilas, from Swed *feldt* or *fält*, field, and *spat* spar, apparently because of the abundance of feldspar in tilled fields of SW Finland; confused with Ger *Fels* rock]

Félibre *fā-lē'br'*, *n* a member of the **Félibrige** (*-brēzh'*), a Provençal literary brotherhood, founded in 1854 by Joseph Roumanille (1818–91) and six others. [Provençal, perh doctors of the law]

felicia *fə-li'shi-ə*, *n* any member of a South African genus of herbs and subshrubs of the daisy family, with blue or lilac flowers. [L *fēlix*, *-icis* happy]

feliciter *fi-lis'i-tər* or *fā-lē'ki-ter*, (*L*) *adv* happily; successfully.

felicity *fi-lis'i-ti*, *n* happiness; delight; a blessing; a happy event; elegance or aptness of wording or expression. — *adj* **felicif'ic** producing happiness. — *vt* **felic'itate** to express joy or pleasure to; to congratulate. — *n* **felicitā'tion** the act of congratulating; (in *pl*) congratulations. — *adj* **felic'itous** happy; prosperous; delightful; appropriate. — *adv* **felic'itously**. [OFr *felicité*, from L *fēlīcitās*, *-ātis*, from *fēlix*, *-icis* happy]

felid *fē'lid*, *n* a member of the *Felidae*, the cat family. [NL *fēlidae*, from L *fēlēs* a cat]

feline *fē'līn*, *adj* pertaining to cats or the cat family; like a cat. — *n* any animal of the cat family. — *n* **felinity** (*fi-lin'i-ti*). — *n* **Fē'lis** the cat genus, typical of the family **Fē'lidae** and sub-family **Fēlī'nae**. [L *fēlīnus*, from *fēlēs* a cat]

fell[1] *fel*, *n* a hill; an upland tract of wasteland, pasture or moorland. — **fell'-walking** and **fell'-running** the pastime of walking, or sport of running, over fells; **fell'-runner**; **fell'walker**. [ON *fjall*; Dan *fjeld*]

fell[2] *fel*, *pa t* of **fall**.

fell[3] *fel*, *vt* to cause to fall; to knock down; to bring to the ground; to cut down; to prostrate (eg by illness; *dialect*); to turn under and stitch down the edges of (a seam; *needlework*). — *n* a quantity felled at a time; a number of lambs born at one time; a felled seam. — *adj* **fell'able**. — *n* **fell'er**. [OE *fælla(n)*, *fella(n)* (WSax *fiellan*), causative of *fallan* (*feallan*) to fall]

fell[4] *fel*, *n* a skin; a membrane; a covering of rough hair. — **fell'monger** a person who prepares skins for the tanner. [OE *fell*; cf Ger *Fell*, L *pellis*, Gr *pella*]

fell[5] *fell*, (*Spenser*) *n* gall or bitterness. [L *fel*]

fell[6] *fel*, *adj* cruel; dire; ruthless; fierce; deadly; keen; doughty; pungent (*Scot*); great, mighty (*Scot*). — *adv* in a fell manner; very (*Scot*); very much (*Scot*). — *n* **fell'ness**. — *adv* **felly** (*fel'li*). — *adj* **fell-lurk'ing** (*Shakesp*) lurking with treacherous purpose. — **at one fell swoop** with a single deadly blow; in one quick operation. [OFr *fel* cruel, from LL *fellō*, *-ōnis*; see **felon**]

fella or **fellah**. See **fellow**.

fellah *fel'ə*, *n* a peasant, *esp* in Egypt: — *pl* **fell'ahs**, **fellaheen** or **fellahin** (*-hēn'*). [Ar *fellāh* tiller]

fellatio *fe-lā'shi-ō*, *n* oral stimulation of the penis: — *pl* **fellā'tios**. — Also **fellā'tion**. — *vt* **fellāte'** (back-formation) to perform fellatio on. [L, from *fellātus*, pa p of *fellāre* to suck]

feller. See **fell**[3] and **fellow**.

felloe *fel'ō* or **felly** *fel'i*, *n* a curved piece in the circumference of a wheel; the circular rim of a wheel. [OE *felg*; Ger *Felge*]

fellow *fel'ō*, *n* a man or boy, sometimes used dismissively; a boyfriend (*colloq*); an associate or companion; someone with something in common with one, one's peer or equal in a specified way (often *combining form*, as in *fellow-worker*); one of a pair, a mate; a counterpart; a senior member of a college; a member of the governing body of a university; a postgraduate student receiving a stipend for a stated period of research; (often with *cap*) a member of an academic, scientific or professional society; a worthless or contemptible person. — Also (*colloq*) **fell'a**, **fell'ah** or **fell'er**. — *adj* **fell'owly** (*Shakesp*) companionable. — *n* **fell'owship** the state of being a fellow or partner; friendship; communion; an association; an endowment in a college for the support of postgraduate fellows; the position and income of a university fellow; the reckoning of proportional division of profit and loss among partners. — **fellow-cit'izen** a person belonging to the same city as oneself or another; **fellow-comm'oner** at Cambridge and elsewhere, one of a privileged class of undergraduates, dining at the fellows' table; **fellow-coun'try-man** a person from the same country as oneself or another; **fellow-crea'ture** a creature like oneself or another; **fellow-feel'ing** a feeling of common interest; sympathy; **fellow-heir'** a joint heir; **fellow-man'** a human being like oneself or another; **fellow-mem'ber** a member of the same organization, etc; **fellow-serv'ant** a servant who has the same master or mistress as oneself or another; **fellow-towns'man** a dweller in the same town; **fellow-trav'eller** a person who travels in the same railway carriage, bus, etc, or along the same route as oneself or another; a person who, though not a party member, holds the same political (*esp* communist) views, a sympathizer (*transl* of *Russ* word; *derog*). — **good fellowship** companionableness; **the right hand of fellowship** the right hand given in welcome, *esp* by one minister or elder to another at an ordination in some churches. [ME *felawe*, from ON *fēlagi*, a partner in goods, from *fē* (OE *feoh*; Ger *Vieh*) cattle or property, and root *lag-* a laying together, a law. Cf **fee**, **law**, **lay**]

felly[1]. See **felloe**.

felly[2]. See under **fell**[6].

felo de se *fē'lō dē sē* or *fe'lō də sē*, (*Anglo-L*) literally, felon of himself, a suicide.

felon[1] *fel'ən*, *n* a person guilty of a felony; a wicked person (*obs*). — *adj* (*archaic*) wicked or cruel; fell; fierce; mighty. — *adj* **felonious** (*fi-lō'ni-əs*) wicked (*archaic*); depraved (*archaic*); pertaining to a felony. — *adv* **felō'niously**. — *n* **felō'niousness**. — *adj* **fel'onous** (*Spenser*) cruel, ruthless, fell. — *n* **fel'onry** a body of felons. — *n* **fel'ony** *orig* a crime punished by total forfeiture of lands, etc; a grave crime, formerly classed legally as one more serious than a misdemeanour (still classed as such in the USA because of the harsher punishments imposed). [OFr, from LL *fellō*, *-ōnis* a traitor]

felon[2] *fel'ən*, *n* an inflamed sore. [Perh **felon**[1]]

felsite *fel'sīt*, *n* a fine-grained mixture of quartz and orthoclase; a devitrified acid igneous rock, characterized by felsitic structure. — *adj* **felsitic** (*-sit'ik*) consisting of a fine patchy mosaic of quartz and feldspar (also **fel'sic**). [**feldspar**]

felspar. See **feldspar**.

felstone *fel'stōn*, *n* (*old-fashioned*) felsite. [Ger *Felsstein*, partly anglicized]

felt[1] *felt*, *pa t* and *pa p* of **feel**.

felt[2] *felt*, *n* a soft fabric formed without weaving, filaments pressed together using the natural tendency of the fibres of wool and certain kinds of hair to interlace and cling together; any material made in a similar way, eg the bituminous matting used to line roofs. — *vt* to make into felt; to cover with felt. — *vi* to become felted or matted. — *vt* **felt'er** to mat together like felt. — *n* **felt'ing** the art or process of making felt or of matting fibres together; the felt itself. — *adj* **felt'y**. — **felt-tip pen**, **felt-tipped pen** or **felt pen** a pen with a nib of felt or similar fibrous substance. [OE *felt*; cf Du *vilt*, Ger *Filz*]

felucca *fe-luk'ə*, *n* a small merchant vessel used in the Mediterranean, with two masts, triangular (lateen) sails, and often a rudder at each end. [Ital *feluca*; cf Ar *falūkah*]

felwort *fel'wûrt*, *n* a gentian. [OE *feldwyrt*, from *feld* field, and *wyrt* wort]

fem or **fem**. *abbrev*: feminine.

female *fē'māl*, *n* a woman or girl (sometimes *derog*); any animal or plant of the same sex as a woman. — *adj* of the sex that produces young or eggs, or (structures containing) spores or seeds; for, belonging to, characteristic of, or fancifully attributed to that sex; womanish (*Shakesp*); of the sex characterized by relatively large gametes (*biol*); (of parts of a mechanism) hollow and adapted to receive a counterpart (*machinery*). — Also (*Milton*) **fe'mal**. — *n* **fē'maleness**. — *n* **femality** (*fē-mal'i-ti*). — **female circumcision** surgical removal of part or all of the clitoris, clitoridectomy; **female screw** a cylindrical hole with a thread or groove cut on the innner surface. [Fr *femelle*, from *L fēmella* a girl, dimin of *fēmina* woman; the second syllable influenced by association with **male**]

feme *fem* or *fēm*, (*law*) *n* a woman. — **feme covert** (*kuv'ərt*) a married woman; **feme sole** a spinster, widow, or married woman legally in the position of an unmarried woman. [OFr *feme*]

femerall *fem'ər-əl*, *n* an outlet for smoke in a roof. [OFr *fumeraille*, from L *fūmus* smoke]

femetary. See **fumitory**.

feminal *fem'in-əl*, *adj* (of a man) thinking and acting in a way traditionally thought of as characteristic of women. — *n* **feminality** (*-al'i-ti*), **feminē'ity**, **feminil'ity**, **fem'inineness**, or **femin'ity** femaleness; the quality of being female, feminine, womanly or womanish. [L *fēmina* woman]

feminine *fem'in-in*, *adj* female; characteristic of, peculiar or appropriate to, women or the female sex; womanish; of that gender to which words denoting females, and in some languages various associated classes of words, belong (*gram*). — *n* the female sex or nature; a word of feminine gender. — *adv* **fem'ininely**. — *n* **fem'ininism** an idiom or expression supposedly characteristic of women; an addiction to feminine ways. — *n* **feminin'ity** the quality of being feminine. — **feminine caesura** one which does not immediately follow the rhythmical or metrical stress; **feminine ending** (*prosody*) in French verse, the ending of a line in a mute *e* (the French feminine suffix); the ending of a verse or musical phrase on an unstressed syllable or note; **feminine rhyme** a two-syllable rhyme, the second syllable being unstressed. [L *fēminīna*, dimin of *fēmina* woman]

feminism *fem'in-izm*, *n* advocacy of women's rights, or of the movement for the advancement and emancipation of women. — *n* **fem'inist** an advocate or favourer of feminism; a student of women. — Also *adj*. — *adj* **feminist'ic**. [L *fēmina* woman]

feminize or **-ise** *fem'in-īz*, *vt* and *vi* to (cause a male animal to) develop female characteristics. — *n* **feminīzā'tion** or **-s-**. [L *fēmina* woman]

femiter *fem'i-tər*. See **fumitory**.

femme *fam*, (*Fr*) *n* a woman, wife. — **femme de chambre** (*də shã-br'*) a lady's-maid; a chambermaid; **femme du monde** (*dü mɔ̃d*) a woman of the world; a society woman; **femme fatale** (*fa-tal*) an irresistibly attractive woman who brings difficulties or disaster on men; a siren; **femme incomprise** (*ɛ̃-kɔ̃-prēz*) a woman who is misunderstood or unappreciated; **femme savante** (*sa-vãt*) a learned woman, a blue-stocking. — See also **feme**.

femto- *fem'tō-*, *pfx* a thousand million millionth (10^{-15}). [Dan or Norw *femten* fifteen, from ON *fimmtān*]

femur *fē'mər*, *n* the thigh-bone; the third segment of an insect's leg: — *pl* **fē'murs** or **femora** (*fem'ər-ə*). — *adj* **femoral** (*fem'*) belonging to the thigh. — **femoral artery** the main artery of the thigh. [L *femur*, *-oris* thigh]

fen[1] *fen*, *n* low marshy land often, or partially, covered with water; a morass or bog. — *adj* **fenn'ish** or **fenn'y**. — **fen'-berry** the cranberry; **fen'-crick'et** the mole-cricket (see under **mole**[3]); **fen'-fire** the will-o'-the-wisp; **fen'land**; **fen'man** a person who lives in fen country. — *adj* **fen'-sucked** (*Shakesp*) drawn out of bogs. [OE *fenn*; ON *fen*]

fen[2] *fen*, (*obs*) *vt* used only as a prohibitory exclamation in boys' games, to bar an action, right or privilege. [Cf **fend**[1]; or perhaps from **feign**]

fen[3] *fen*, *n* a Chinese monetary unit, $\frac{1}{100}$ of a yuan; a coin of this value. [Chin]

fence *fens*, *n* a barrier, *esp* of wood or wood and wire, for enclosing, bounding or protecting land; a barrier of varying design for a horse to jump (*showjumping* and *steeplechasing*); the art of fencing; defence (*archaic*); a receiver of stolen goods (*thieves' slang*); a place where stolen goods are received (*thieves' slang*). — *vt* to enclose with a fence; to fortify; to shield; to keep off. — *vi* to build fences; to guard; to practise or take part in fencing; to be a receiver or purchaser of stolen goods (*thieves' slang*); to answer or dispute evasively; to leap fences. — *adj* **fenced** enclosed with a fence. — *adj* **fence'less** without a fence or enclosure, open. — *n* **fenc'er** a person who makes or repairs fences; a person who fences with a foil, etc; a horse trained to jump fences in steeplechasing. — *adj* **fenc'ible** capable of being fenced or defended. — *n* (*hist*) a militiaman or volunteer soldier enlisted in a crisis, *esp* to fight in a local or regional conflict. — *adj* **fenc'ing** defending or guarding. — *n* the act of erecting a fence; material for fences; fences collectively; the leaping of fences; receiving stolen goods (*thieves' slang*); the act, art or sport of attack and defence with a foil, sword, or similar weapon. — **fence'-lizard** a small American lizard (*Sceloporus*); **fence-mending** see **mend one's fences** below; **fence month** close season; **fenc'ing-master** or (*fem*) **fencing mistress** a man or woman who teaches fencing. — **fence the tables** in early, now limited, Scottish usage, to debar the unworthy from taking communion; **mend one's fences** to improve or restore one's relations, reputation, or popularity, *esp* in politics (*n* and *adj* **fence'-mending**); **sit on the fence** to avoid committing oneself; to remain neutral; **sunk fence** a ditch or water-course. [Aphetic from **defence**]

fend[1] *fend*, *vt* to ward (off); to shut out; to defend (*archaic*). — *vi* to offer resistance; to provide (for). — *n* (*Scot*) self-support, the effort one makes for oneself. — *adj* **fend'y** (*Scot*) resourceful; thrifty. [Aphetic for **defend**]

fend[2] *fend*, (*Milton*). Same as **fiend**.

fender *fend'ər*, *n* a guard in front of a hearth to confine the ashes; a protection for a ship's side against piers, etc, consisting of a bundle of rope, etc; a mudguard (*US*); a wing of a car (*NAm*); any structure serving as a guard against contact or impact. — **fend'er-stool** a long stool placed beside a fireside fender. [**fend**[1]]

fenestella *fen-is-tel'ə*, *n* a small window or window-like opening; in a church, a niche containing the piscina, the drain into which the washing water from the sacred vessels was poured; (with *cap*; *biol*) a Palaeozoic genus of lace-like Polyzoa. [L, dimin of *fenestra* a window]

fenestra *fi-nes'trə*, *n* a window or other wall-opening; a perforation; a translucent spot, eg that on a moth's wing (*zool*). — *n* **fenes'tral** a window with some other translucent material instead of glass. — *adj* of or like a window; perforated; with translucent spots. — *adj* **fenestrate** (*fen'is-trit*, *fi-nes'trit* or *-trāt*) or **fenestrated** having windows or the appearance of windows (*archit*); pierced; perforated; having translucent spots. — *n* **fenestrā'tion** the arrangement of windows in a building (*archit*); the fact of being fenestrate; perforation; the operation of making an artificial fenestra when the fenestra ovalis has been clogged by growth of bone (*surg*). — **fenestra ovalis** or **rotunda** (*biol*) the oval or round windows, two membrane-covered openings between the middle and the internal ear. [L]

feni or **fenny** *fen'i*, *n* an alcoholic spirit produced in Goa from coconuts or cashew nuts.

Fenian *fē'nyən*, *n* a member of an association of Irish people founded in New York in 1857 for the overthrow of the British government in Ireland; a (*esp* Irish) Catholic (*offensive*). — *adj* belonging to the legendary *fiann*, or to the modern Fenians; Catholic (*offensive*). — *n* **Fē'nianism**. [Old Ir *Féne*, one of the names of the ancient population of Ireland, confused in modern times with *fiann*, the militia of Finn and other ancient Irish kings]

fenitar *fen'i-tər*. See **fumitory**.

fenks *fengks* or **finks** *fingks*, *n* the refuse of whale-blubber. [Origin unknown]

fennec *fen'ək*, *n* a little African fox with large ears. [Ar *fenek*]

fennel *fen'əl*, *n* a yellow-flowered umbelliferous plant of the genus *Foeniculum*, related to dill, but distinguished by the cylindrical, strongly-ribbed fruit, the seeds and leaves being used for seasoning. — **fenn'el-flower** a plant of the genus *Nigella*. — **dwarf**, **Florence**, **French** or **sweet fennel** see **finocchio**; **giant fennel** an umbelliferous plant, *Ferula communis*. [OE *finul*, from L *fēniculum*, *fēnuc(u)lum* fennel, from *fēnum* hay]

fennish and **fenny**[1]. See under **fen**[1].

fenny[2]. See **feni**.

fent *fent*, *n* a slit or crack; a remnant or odd, short, or damaged piece of cloth (*NEng*). — **fent'-merchant**. [OFr *fente*, from L *findere* to cleave or split]

fenugreek *fen'ū-grēk*, *n* a plant (*Trigonella foenum-graecum*), related to melilot, the aromatic seeds of which are used as a food flavouring. [L *fēnum graecum* Greek hay]

feod, **feodal** and **feodary**. Same as **feud**[2], **feudal** and **feudary**.

feoff *fef* or *fēf*, *n* a fief. — *vt* to grant possession of a fief or property in land. — *n* **feoffee'** the person invested with the fief. — *n* **feoff'er** or **feoff'or** the person who grants a fief. — *n* **feoff'ment** the gift of a fief. [OFr *feoffer* or *fiefer*, from OFr *fief*. See **fee**]

feracious *fi-rā'shəs*, *adj* fruitful. — *n* **feracity** (*fi-ras'i-ti*; *rare*). [L *ferāx*, *-ācis*, from *ferre* to bear]

ferae naturae *fē'rē nə-tū'rē* or *fe'rī na-tōō'rī*, (*L*) (of animals) wild, undomesticated.

feral[1] *fē'rəl* or *fer'əl*, *adj* wild; untamed; uncultivated (*bot*); run wild; animal (*derog*). — *adj* **fer'alized** or **-s-** run wild following domestication. — *adj* **ferine** (*-rīn* or *-rin*) pertaining to or like a wild beast; wild; animal (*derog*). — *n* **ferity** (*fer'i-ti*; *rare*) wildness; uncultivated state; savagery. [L *fera* a wild beast]

feral[2] *fē'rəl*, *adj* deadly; funereal. [L *fērālis*]

fer-de-lance *fer'də-lās*, *n* the lance-headed or yellow viper of tropical America. [Fr, lance-head (literally, iron)]

fere[1], **feare**, **feer**, **fiere** or **pheere** *fēr*, (*archaic*) *n* a companion; a mate; a spouse; an equal. — **in fere** or (*adv*) **yfere'** together, in company. [OE *gefēra* companion, and *gefēre* company]

fere[2] *fēr*, (*Scot*) *adj* able, sound. [OE *fēre*]

feretory *fer'i-tər-i*, *n* a shrine for relics, carried in processions. [L *feretrum*, from Gr *pheretron* bier or litter, from *pherein* to bear]

ferial *fē'ri-əl*, *adj* pertaining to holidays; belonging to any day of the week which is neither a fast nor a festival (*RC*). [L *fēria* a holiday]

ferine and **ferity**. See under **feral**[1].

Feringhi or **Feringhee** *fer-ing'gē*, *n* an Indian name for a European. — Also **Farin'gee**. [**Frank**]

ferly *fûr'li*, (*Scot*) *adj* fearful; sudden; peculiar. — *n* (*fār'li*) a wonder. — *vi* to wonder. [OE *fǣrlic* sudden; cf Ger *gefährlich* dangerous]

ferm *fûrm*, *n* a farm; lodging (*Spenser*). [Variant of **farm**]

fermata *fûr-mä'tə*, (*music*) *n* a pause: — *pl* **ferma'tas** or **fermate** (*-tē*). [Ital]

Fermat's principle of least time (*phys*). See **principle of least time** under **principle**.

ferment *fûr'mənt*, *n* a substance that produces fermentation; internal motion amongst the parts of a fluid; agitation; tumult. — *vt* **ferment** (*-ment'*) to produce fermentation in; to work up or excite. — *vi* to rise and swell by the action of fermentation; (of wine) to undergo alcoholic fermentation; to be in excited action; (of emotions, etc) to agitate in the mind. — *n* **fermentabil'ity**. — *adj* **ferment'able** capable of fermentation. — *n* **fermentā'tion** a slow decomposition process of organic substances induced by micro-organisms, or by complex nitrogenous organic substances (*enzymes*) of vegetable or animal origin, *usu* accompanied by evolution of heat and gas, eg alcoholic fermentation of sugar and starch, and lactic fermentation; the act or process of fermenting; restless action of the mind or feelings. — *adj* **ferment'ative** causing or consisting of fermentation. — *n* **ferment'ativeness**. — *adj* **ferment'ed**. — *adj* **fermentesc'ible** capable of being fermented. — *adj* **fermentitious** (*-ish'əs*). — *adj* **fer-**

ment'ive. [Fr, from L *fermentum*, for *fervimentum*, from *fervēre* to boil]

fermi *fûr'mi*, (*phys*) *n* a unit equal to 10^{-5} angstrom or 10^{-15} metres. — *n* **fer'mion** one of a group of subatomic particles, such as protons, electrons and neutrons, having half-integral spin and obeying the exclusion principle. — *n* **fer'mium** an element (symbol **Fm**; atomic no 100), a radioactive metal artifically created out of the neutron bombarment of plutonium. [Italian physicist Enrico *Fermi* (1901–54)]

fern *fûrn*, *n* one of the class of higher or vascular flowerless plants, Filices, many species of which have feather-like leaves. — *n* **fern'ery** a place for rearing ferns. — *n* **fern'ing** (*med*) (of cervical mucus, etc) a tendency to develop a feathery or fern-like appearance. — *adj* **fern'y**. — **fern'-ally'** (*-al'*) a vascular flowerless plant, a pteridophyte, other than a fern; **fern'bird** a small brown-and-white New Zealand bird, *Bowdleria punctata*, related to the warblers, which is found in swamps and marshy scrub and which has somewhat fern-like tail feathers; **fern land** (in New Zealand) land covered or formerly covered by bracken; **fern'-owl** the nightjar; the short-eared owl; **fern'-seed** the spores of ferns, once believed to confer invisibility; **fern'shaw** a thicket of ferns; **fern'tickle** or **fern'ticle** (*obs* or *dialect*), also **fair'nitickle**, **fair'niticle**, **fair'nytickle**, **fair'nyticle**, **fer'nitickle**, **fer'niticle**, **fer'nytickle** or **fer'nyticle** (*Scot*) a freckle. — *adj* **fern'tickled** or **fern'ticled**. [OE *fearn*; Ger *Farn*]

ferocious *fə-rō'shəs*, *adj* savage, fierce; cruel. — *adv* **ferō'ciously**. — *n* **ferō'ciousness** or **ferocity** (*-ros'i-ti*) savage cruelty of temperament; untamed fierceness. [L *ferōx*, *ferōcis* wild, from *ferus* wild]

ferrandine. See **farandine**.

ferrate *fer'āt*, *n* a salt of ferric acid. — *adj* **ferr'eous** pertaining to, containing, or like iron. [L *ferrum* iron]

ferrel. See **ferrule**.

ferret[1] *fer'it*, *n* narrow silk or cotton ribbon. — Also *adj*. [Ital *fioretto*, dimin, from L *flōs*, *flōris* flower]

ferret[2] *fer'it*, *n* a half-tamed albino variety of the polecat, employed in unearthing rabbits; a diligent searcher or investigator. — *vt* to drive out of a hiding-place; to search out persistently and indefatigably. — *vt* or *vi* to hunt with a ferret: — *pr p* **ferr'eting**; *pa p* and *pa t* **ferr'eted**. — *n* **ferr'eter** a person who ferrets. — *adj* **ferr'ety** like a ferret in appearance. [OFr *furet* a ferret, dimin, from LL *fūrō*, *-ōnis* ferret, robber, from L *fūr* a thief]

ferri- *fer-i*, *combining form* signifying the presence of iron, *usu* in its trivalent form. — *n* **ferricy'anide** a salt of hydroferricyanic acid. — *n* **ferricyan'ogen** the trivalent radical, $Fe(CN)_6$, of the ferricyanides. — *adj* **ferrimagnetic**. — *n* **ferrimagnetism** iron magnetism in which the magnetic moments of neighbouring ions are non-parallel.

ferriage. See under **ferry**.

ferric *fer'ik*, *adj* of iron; containing iron in its trivalent form (**ferric acid** a hypothetical acid H_2FeO_4) (*chem*). — *adj* **ferrif'erous** bearing or yielding iron. — **ferric oxide** a red crystalline oxide of iron used as a coating on magnetic tape and as a metal polish (also called *jeweller's rouge*). [L *ferrum* iron]

Ferris wheel *fer'is wēl*, *hwēl*, (*orig US*) *n* a fairground attraction, a large upright wheel having seats suspended on the circumference which remain horizontal while the wheel rotates. [G W G *Ferris*, American engineer]

ferrite *fer'īt*, *n* a form of pure iron; any of a number of new magnetic materials (generally mixtures of iron oxide with *usu* cobalt, nickel or zinc) which are also electric insulators. — *adj* **ferrit'ic** consisting mainly of ferrite. — *n* **ferr'itin** a protein in which iron is stored in the liver and spleen. [L *ferrum* iron]

ferro- *fer-ō*, *combining form* signifying the presence of iron, *usu* in its divalent form; relating to iron. — *n* **ferro-all'oy** (*-oi'*) an alloy of iron and some other metal. — *n* **ferro-chro'mium** (or **ferro-chrome'**), **ferro-mang'anese**, **ferro-molyb'denum** and **ferro-nick'el** an alloy of iron with much chromium, manganese, etc. — *n* **ferrocon'crete** reinforced concrete. — *n* **ferrocy'anide** a salt of hydroferrocyanic acid. — *n* **ferrocyan'ogen** the quadrivalent radical, $Fe(CN)_6$, of the ferrocyanides. — *adj* **ferroelec'tric** exhibiting electric polarization. — *n* **ferroelectric'ity**. — *n* **ferrog'raphy** the technique of studying wear in machinery by measuring magnetically the ferous content of lubricants, the results being shown by **ferr'ograms**. — *adj* **ferromagnēs'ian** containing iron and magnesium. — *adj* **ferromagnet'ic** strongly magnetic; formerly, paramagnetic. — *n* **ferromag'netism** the typical form of iron magnetism, with high permeability and hysteresis. — *n* **ferr'o-print** a photograph made by means of iron salts. — *n* **ferropruss'iate** ferrocyanide. — *adj* **ferrosoferr'ic** combining ferrous and ferric. — *n* **ferr'otype** an old form of photograph taken using a film on an iron plate. [L *ferrum* iron]

ferronière or **ferronnière** *fer-on-yer'*, *n* a jewel held on the forehead by a chain, as in Leonardo da Vinci's 'La Belle Ferronnière'. [Fr *ferronnière*, fem of *ferronnier* ironmonger]

ferrous *fer'əs*, *adj* containing iron; containing iron in its divalent form. — **ferrous sulphate** a salt of iron, *usu* used in tanning, etc. [L *ferrum* iron]

ferruginous *fe-rōō'jin-əs* or *fə-rōō'jin-əs*, *adj* of the colour of iron-rust; impregnated with iron. — Also **ferrugin'eous** (*fer-*). — *n* **ferru'go** (*-gō*) rust disease of plants. [L *ferrūgō*, *-inis* iron-rust, from *ferrum* iron]

ferrule *fer'ōōl*, *-əl*, *n* a metal band, ring or cap on the tip of a stick, etc for reinforcing it; a threaded cylindrical fitting for joining two pipes or rods. — Also **ferr'el** (*Scot* **virl**). [OFr *virole*, from L *viriola* a bracelet]

ferry *fer'i*, *vt* to carry or convey (*esp* over water in a boat or ship, or sometimes an aircraft); to deliver (an aircraft coming from a factory) under its own power. — *vi* to cross by ferry: — *pr p* **ferr'ying**; *pa t* and *pa p* **ferr'ied**. — *n* a boat for the conveyance of passengers and *usu* vehicles across a stretch of water (also **ferr'y-boat**); the service thus provided; a place or route of carriage over water; the right of conveying passengers. — *n* **ferr'iage** provision for ferrying; the fare paid for it. — **ferr'y-boat** see **ferry** above; **ferr'y-house** a ferryman's house; a place of shelter or refreshment at a ferry; **ferr'yman**. [OE *ferian* to convey, *faran* to go; Ger *Fähre* a ferry, from *fahren* to go, to carry]

fertile *fûr'tīl*, (*US*) *-təl*, *adj* able to bear or produce young, fruit, etc abundantly; giving such ability; rich in resources; inventive; capable of breeding, hatching, or germinating; able to become fissile or fissionable (*phys*). — *adv* **fer'tilely**. — *n* **fertility** (*-til'i-ti*) fruitfulness, richness, abundance; the state of being fertile; the ability to produce young; the number or percentage of eggs produced by a species or individual that develop into living young (cf **fecundity**; *ecol*). — *n* **fertilization** or **-s-** (*-ti-lī-zā'shən*) the act or process of fertilizing. — *vt* **fer'tilize** or **-ise** to make fertile or fruitful; to enrich; to impregnate; to pollinate. — *n* **fer'tilizer** or **-s-** a person who or thing which fertilizes. — **Fertile Crescent** a crescent-shaped region stretching from Armenia to Arabia, formerly fertile but now mainly desert, considered to be the cradle of civilization; **fertile material** an isotope (eg uranium-238) that can be readily transformed into fissionable material; **fertility drug** a drug given to apparently infertile women to induce ovulation. [Fr, from L *fertilis*, from *ferre* to bear]

ferule *fer'ōōl*, *n* a cane or rod used for punishment. — *n* **fer'ula** a ferule; a staff of command; (with *cap*) the giant fennel genus. — *adj* **ferulā'ceous** like a cane, reed, or Ferula. [L *ferula* a giant fennel, from *ferīre* to strike]

fervent *fûr'vənt*, *adj* hot (*archaic*); warm in feeling, friendly or affectionate (*archaic*); passionate, ardent; zealous. — *n* **fer'vency** heat; eagerness; emotional warmth. — *adv* **fer'vently**. — *adj* **fervescent** (*-ves'ənt*) growing hot. — *adj* **fer'vid** very hot; having burning desire or emotion; glowing; zealous. — *n* **fervid'ity**. — *adv* **fer'vidly**. — *n* **fer'vidness**. — *n* **Fervidor'** the eleventh month of the French Revolutionary calendar, Thermidor. — *adj* **fer'vorous**. — *n* **fer'vour** heat; vehemence, ardour; zeal. [L *fervēre* to boil, *fervēscere*, *fervidus* fiery, glowing, *fervor* violent heat]

Fescennine *fes'ə-nīn* or *-nin*, *adj* scurrilous. — **Fescennine verses** rude extempore verses, generally in Saturnian measure, in which the parties bantered and ridiculed one another. [The Etruscan town of *Fescennium*]

fescue *fes'kū*, *n* any one of the grasses, closely related to the brome-grasses, of the genus *Festuca*, which includes many pasture and fodder grasses; a pointer used in teaching. [OFr *festu*, from L *festūca* a straw]

fesse or **fess** *fes*, (*heraldry*) *n* one of the simple heraldic forms, a horizontal band over the middle of an escutcheon, *usu* one-third of the whole. — *adv* **fesse'wise** or **fess'-wise**. — **fesse'-point** the centre of an escutcheon. [Fr *fasce*, from L *fascia* a band]

fest *fest*, *n* (*usu* in composition) a party or gathering, or (in writing) a collection, *esp* for a particular activity, as in *songfest*. [Ger *Fest* festival]

festa *fes'ta*, (*Ital*) *n* a holiday, festival or saint's day.

festal *fes'tl*, *adj* relating to a feast or holiday; joyous; festive. — *n* a festivity. — *adv* **fes'tally**. — *n* **festil'ogy** or **festol'ogy** a treatise on ecclesiastical festivals. [See **feast**]

fester *fes'tər*, *vi* to rot or putrefy; to suppurate; to rankle; to be idle (*colloq*). — *vt* to cause to fester or rankle. — *n* a sore discharging pus. [OFr *festre*, from L *fistula* an ulcer]

festilogy. See under **festal**.

festina lente *fes-tē'na len'ti*, (*L*) make haste slowly.

festinate *fes'ti-nāt*, *vt* (*esp med*) to accelerate. — *adj* (*Shakesp*) hurried, hasty. — *adv* **fes'tinately** (*Shakesp*). — *n* **festinā'tion** quickening, *esp* of physical movements. [L *festīnāre*, *-ātum* to hurry]

festival *fes'tiv-əl*, *n* a joyful or honorific celebration; a religious feast; a season or series of performances of music, plays, etc. — Also *adj*. [Med L *festīvālis* relating to a feast, from *festīvus* festive]

festive *fes'tiv*, *adj* relating to a feast or holiday; celebratory, joyful. — *adv* **fes'tively**. — *n* **festiv'ity** conviviality; joyfulness; gaiety; (in *pl*) joyful celebrations. — *adj* **fes'tivous** (or *-tī'*) festive. [L *fēstīvus*, from *fēstus*]

festology. See under **festal**.

festoon *fes-tōōn'*, *n* a garland suspended between two points; an ornament like a garland (*archit*). — *vt* to adorn, hang or connect with festoons. — *vi* to hang in festoons. — *n* **festoon'ery** festoons collectively. — **festoon blind** a window blind ruched to fall in festoon-like folds. [Fr *feston*, appar connected with L *fēstum* a festival]

festschrift *fest'shrift*, *n* a celebratory publication, commonly a collection of learned papers, presented by their authors and published in honour of some person. [Ger, festival writing]

FET *abbrev*: field-effect transistor.

fet *fet*, *vt*. Obsolete form of **fetch**[1].

feta *fet'ə*, *n* a crumbly white low-fat cheese originating in Greece and the Middle East, traditionally made from goat's or ewe's milk but now sometimes with cow's milk. — Also **fett'a**. [Mod Gr *pheta* a slice (ie of cheese), from Ital *fetta*]

fetal. See under **foetus**.

fetch[1] *fech*, *vt* to bring; to go and get; to be sold for (a certain price); to cause to come; to call forth; to draw (eg blood, breath); to achieve control over, to take; to derive; to reach or attain; to utter (a sigh or groan); to administer (a blow, etc, *usu* with *indirect object*). — *vi* to make one's way; to arrive; to be effective. — *n* an act of bringing; the distance travelled by a wind or wave without obstruction; a stratagem. — *adj* **fetch'ing** fascinating, charming; attractive. — **fetch a compass** or **circuit** to go round in a wide curve; **fetch and carry** to perform humble services for another person; **fetch a pump** to pour water in so as to make it draw; **fetch off** to bring out of danger or difficulty; to make away with (*Shakesp*); to fleece (*Shakesp*); **fetch out** to draw forth or develop; **fetch up** to recover; to come to a stop; to bring up, rear (eg children) (*US*); to vomit (*slang*). [OE *feccan*, appar an altered form of *fetian* to fetch; cf Ger *fassen* to seize]

fetch[2] *fech*, *n* the apparition, double, or ghost of a living person. — **fetch'-candle** a nocturnal light, supposed to portend a death. [Ety unknown]

fête *fet* or *fāt*, *n* an outdoor function with entertainments, stalls, refreshments, etc, often in aid of a charity; a festival; a holiday; the festival of the saint whose name one bears. — *vt* to entertain at a feast; to honour with festivities. — **fête champêtre** (*shã-pe-tr'*) a rural festival or garden party; an early 18c genre of French painting, typically showing courtly figures in a rural setting (also called **fête galante**), associated mainly with Jean Antoine Watteau (1684–1721); **Fête-Dieu** (*dyø*) the festival in honour of the Eucharist, Corpus Christi. [Fr]

fetial *fē'shəl*, *adj* pertaining to the Roman *fētiālēs*, a priestly college of heralds; heraldic, ambassadorial. — Also **fē'cial**.

fetich, **fetiche**, etc. See **fetish**.

feticide. See under **foetus**.

fetid or **foetid** *fē'tid* or *fet'id*, *adj* stinking; having a strong offensive smell. — *n* **fē'tidness**, **foe'tidness**, **fē'tor** or **foe'tor**. [L *fētidus*, *fētor*, from *fētēre* to stink]

fetish, **fetich** or **fetiche** *fe'tish* or *fē'tish*, *n* an object believed to procure for its owner the services of a spirit lodged within it; an inanimate object to which a pathological sexual attachment is formed; such an attachment; a person who is the object of an obsessive fixation; a fixation; something regarded with irrational reverence. — *n* **fet'ishism** or **fet'ichism** the worship of a fetish; a belief in charms; pathological attachment of sexual interest to an inanimate object. — *n* **fet'ishist** or **fet'ichist**. — *adj* **fetishist'ic** or **fetichis'tic**. — *vt* **fet'ishize** or **-ise** or **fet'ichize** or **-ise** to make a fetish of (a person). [Fr *fétiche*, from Port *feitiço* magic; a name given by the Portuguese to the gods of W Africa, from Port *feitiço* artificial, from L *factīcius*, from *facere* to make]

fetlock *fet'lok*, *n* a tuft of hair that grows above a horse's hoof; the part where this hair grows. — *adj* **fet'locked** having a fetlock; tied by the fetlock. [History obscure; long felt as a compound of **foot** and **lock**[2] (of hair); cf Ger *Fissloch*]

fetoscopy. See **foetoscopy** under **foetus**.

fett, *fet*, *vt*. Obsolete form of **fetch**[1].

fetta. See **feta**.

fetter *fet'ər*, *n* (*usu* in *pl*) a chain or shackle for the feet; (*usu* in *pl*) anything that restrains. — *vt* to put fetters on; to restrain. — *adj* **fett'erless**. — **fett'erlock** (*heraldry*) a shackle for a horse, as a design on a shield. [OE *feter*; connected with *fōt* foot]

fettle *fet'l*, *vt* to make ready, set in order or arrange; to tidy up (*dialect*); to knock or rub excess material off the edges of (a casting or piece of pottery); to line (a furnace). — *vi* to potter fussily about. — *n* condition, trim or form, *esp* in *in fine fettle*; lining for a furnace. — *n* **fett'ler** a person who fettles, *esp* (*Austr*) a maintenance worker on the railway. — *n* **fett'ling**. [Prob OE *fetel* a belt]

fettuccine, **fettucine** or **fettucini** *fet-ōō-chē'nā* or *-nē*, *n* pasta made in long ribbons, tagliatelle. [Ital]

fetus. See **foetus**.

fetwa *fet'wä*, *n*. A variant spelling of **fatwa**.

feu *fū*, (*Scot*) *n* a tenure where the vassal, in place of military services, makes a return in grain or in money; a right to the use of land, houses, etc in perpetuity, for a stipulated annual payment (**feu'-dū'ty**); a piece of land held in feu. — *vt* to grant land to a person who undertakes to pay the feu-duty. — *n* **feu'ar** a person who holds real estate in return for payment of feu-duty. — *adj* **feud'al** pertaining to a feu. [OFr *feu*; see **fee**]

feu d'artifice *fø dar-tē-fēs*, (*Fr*) *n* a firework: — *pl* **feux d'artifice**. — *n* **feu de joie** (*də zhwä*) a bonfire; (in English, *not* in French) a firing of guns as a symbol of joy: — *pl* **feux de joie**.

feud[1] *fūd*, *n* a war waged by private individuals, families or clans against one another on their own account; a bloody strife; a persistent state of private enmity. — Also *vi*. — *n* and *adj* **feud'ing**. — **right of feud** the right to protect oneself and one's family, and to deal out punishment to those who do one wrong. [OFr *faide*, *feide*, from LL *faida*, from OHGer *fēhida*; vowel change unexplained; see **foe**]

feud[2] or **feod** *fūd*, *n* a fief or land held on condition of service. — *adj* **feud'al** or **feod'al** pertaining to feuds or fiefs; pertaining to or typical of feudalism. — *n* **feud'alism** the feudal system, a system of social organization prevalent in W Europe in the Middle Ages, in which powerful land-owning lords granted degrees of privilege and protection to lesser subjects holding a range of positions within a rigid social hierarchy; a class-conscious social or political system resembling the medieval feudal system. — *adj* **feud'alist**. — *adj* **feudalis'tic**. — *n* **feudal'ity** the state of being feudal; the feudal system. — *n* **feudalīzā'tion** or **-s-**. — *vt* **feud'alize** or **-ise**. — *adv* **feud'ally**. — *adj* **feud'ary**, **feod'ary** or **feud'atory** holding lands or power by a feudal tenure. — Also *n*. — *n* **feud'ist** a writer on feuds; a person versed in the laws of feudal tenure. — **feudal system** feudalism. [LL *feudum*; see **fee**]

feudal. See **feud**[2] and under **feu**.

feuilleté *fœy-tā*, (Fr) *n* puff-pastry.

feuilleton *fœy-tɔ̃*, *n* in French and other newspapers, a part ruled off the bottom of a page for a serial story, critical article, etc; a contribution of this kind. — *n* **feu'illetonism** (*-tən-izm*). — *n* **feu'illetonist**. [Fr, dimin of *feuillet* a leaf, from L *folium*]

feutre. Same as **fewter**.

fever *fē'vər*, *n* an abnormally high body temperature, asociated with a raised pulse rate and hot, dry skin; any of many, *usu* infectious, diseases in which this is a marked symptom, such as *scarlet fever* or *yellow fever*; an extreme state of excitement or nervousness; a painful degree of anxiety. — *vt* to put into a fever. — *vi* (*obs*) to become fevered. — *adj* **fē'vered** affected with fever; excited. — *adj* **fē'verish** slightly fevered; indicating fever; restlessly excited; morbidly eager, frenzied. — *adv* **fē'verishly**. — *n* **fē'verishness**. — *adj* **fē'verous** feverish; marked by sudden changes; apt to cause fever. — **fē'ver-heat** the heat of fever; an excessive degree of excitement; **fever pitch** a state of great excitement or agitation; **fever therapy** cure by inducement of fever; **fe'ver-tree** a southern African tree of the genus *Acacia*, *usu* found in swampy, mosquito-infested places, and hence regarded (*esp* formerly) as an indicator of malarious spots to be avoided and by some even thought to be itself a cause of malaria; any of various species of trees, such as the Australian *Eucalyptus globulus* or the American *Pinckneya pubens*, which yield substances useful in the treatment of fevers. [OE *fēfor*, from L *febris*]

feverfew *n* (OE *fēferfūge*) a perennial plant of the daisy family, closely related to camomile, formerly believed efficacious in reducing fever. [MedL *febrifugia*, this plant, from *febris* fever and *fugare* to put to flight]

few *fū*, *adj* small in number; not many, hardly any. — *n* **few'ness** smallness of number; few words, brevity (*Shakesp*). — **a few** a small number (of), used as a noun, or virtually a compound adjective; also facetiously as an *adv*, a little; **a good few** or **quite a few** (*colloq*) a considerable number; **every few hours** or **days**, etc at intervals of a few hours, days, etc; **few and far between** very rare; **have had a few** (*facetious*) to have consumed a large number of alcoholic drinks, be drunk; **in few** (*formal*) in a few words, briefly; **no fewer than** as many as (a stated number); **not a few** a good number (of); **some few** an inconsiderable number; **the few** the minority. [OE *fēa*, pl *fēawe*; cf L *paucus* small]

fewmet. Same as **fumet**[1].

fewter or **feutre** *fū'tər*, *n* (*obs*) a spear-rest. — *vt* (*Spenser*) to set in a rest. [OFr *feutre* felt or a felt-lined socket]

fewtrils *fū'trilz*, (*dialect*) *n pl* little things, trifles. [**fattrels**]

fey[1], **fay** or **fie** *fā*, *adj* doomed, fated soon to die, under the shadow of a sudden or violent death, imagined to be marked by extravagantly high spirits (chiefly *Scot*); foreseeing the future, *esp* calamity (chiefly *Scot*); eccentric, slightly mad; whimsical; supernatural; fairy-like; elfin. [ME *fay* or *fey*, from OE *fæge* doomed; cf Du *veeg* about to die]

fey[2]. See **fay**[5].

fez *fez*, *n* a red brimless truncated conical cap of wool or felt, with black tassel, worn in Egypt, formerly in Turkey (also called the *tarboosh*): — *pl* **fezz'es** or **fez'es**. — *adj* **fezzed** (*fezd*). [From *Fez* in Morocco]

FF *abbrev*: French franc or francs.

ff or **ff.** *symbol*: *fecerunt* (*L*), (they) did it or made it; folios (*printing*); following pages, lines, etc; fortissimo (*music*).

fiacre *fē-ak'r'*, *n* a hackney coach; a cab. [Fr, from the Hôtel de St *Fiacre* in Paris, where first used]

fiancé, *fem* **fiancée** *fē-â'sā*, *n* the person one is betrothed to, one's betrothed. — *n pl* **fiançailles** (*fē-ã-sī-y'*) betrothal. [Fr]

fianchetto *fyäng-ket'to*, (*chess*) *n* the development of a bishop on a diagonal following the movement of the adjacent knight's pawn: — *pl* **fianchet'ti** (*-tē*). — Also *vt*. [Ital, dimin of *fianco* flank]

Fianna Fáil *fē'an-ä foil*, *n* the Irish republican party. [Ir, militia of Fál (a stone monument at Tara, hence Ireland); cf **Fenian**]

fiar *fē'ər*, (*Scots law*) *n* the owner of the fee simple of a property (in contrast to a *life-renter* of the property). [**fee**]

fiars *fē'ərz*, (*Scot*) *n pl* the prices of grain legally *struck* or fixed for the year at the *Fiars* Court, so as to regulate the payment of stipend, rent, and prices not expressly agreed upon (*usu* **fiars prices**). [OFr *feor* or *fuer* fixed price or standard, from L *forum* market]

fiasco *fē-as'kō*, *n* a flask or bottle; a failure in a musical performance; a complete failure of any kind: — *pl* **fias'cos** or **fias'coes**. [Ital *fiasco* bottle, perh from L *vasculum* a little vessel, from *vas* a vessel]

fiat *fī'at*, or (*L*) *fē'ät*, *n* a formal or solemn command; a short order or warrant of a judge for making out or allowing processes, letters-patent, etc (*Spenser* **fiaunt'**). — *vt* to sanction. — **fiat money** or **currency** (*esp US*) money (paper or coin) made legal tender and assigned a value by government decree, with a commodity value lower than its face value, not convertible into other specie of equivalent value, and generally with a lower purchasing power than nominally equivalent specie. [L *fiat* (or *fiant*), let it (or them) be done, 3rd *pers sing* (*pl*) present subjunctive of *fierī*, serving as passive of *facere* to do]

fib[1] *fib*, *n* a not very serious lie. — *vi* to tell a fib or lie; to speak falsely: — *pr p* **fibb'ing**; *pa p* **fibbed**. — *n* **fibb'er** a person who fibs. — *n* **fibb'ery** (*rare*) the habit of fibbing. — *n* **fib'ster** a fibber. [Perh **fable**]

fib[2] *fib*, *vt* to punch; to pummel: — *pa t* and *pa p* **fibbed**; *pr p* **fibb'ing**. [Ety unknown]

fiber. See **fibre**.

Fibonacci numbers, **sequence** or **series** *fē-bō-nä'chē num'-bərz*, *sē'kwəns* or *sē'rēz*, *n* a series of numbers in which each term is the sum of the preceding two terms. [Leonardo (*Fibonacci*) of Pisa (1170–1230)]

fibre or (*US*) **fiber** *fī'bər*, *n* a filament or thread-like cell of animal, vegetable or mineral origin, natural or synthetic; a structure or material composed of such filaments; texture; stamina; dietary fibre, roughage. — *adj* **fī'bred** or (*US*) **fi'bered** having fibre. — *adj* **fī'breless** or (*US*) **fib'erless** without fibre, strength or nerve. — *adj* **fī'briform** fibre-like. — *n* **fī'brin** an insoluble protein precipitated as a network of fibres when blood coagulates. — *n* **fībrin'ogen** (*-jən*) a protein that forms fibrin. — *n* **fībrinol'ysin** an enzyme in the blood which causes the breakdown of fibrin in blood clots; a drug having the same effect. — *adj* **fī'brinous** of or like fibrin. — *n* **fī'brō** (*Austr*) a wall-board of a compressed asbestos and cement mixture (also **fī'brocement'**®); a house constructed of such material: — *pl* **fi'bros**. — Also *adj* (also **fī'brocement'**®). — *n* **fī'broblast** a cell in connective tissue from which fibrous tissue is formed. — *adj* **fibroblast'ic**. — *n* **fibrocar'tilage** cartilage with embedded fibres. — *n* **fibrocement** see **fibro** above. — *n* **fī'brocyte** a normally inactive fibroblast which proliferates following tissue damage. — *adj* **fī'broid** of a fibrous nature. — *n* a fibrous tumour. — *n* **fibroin** (*fī'brō-in*) the chief chemical constituent of silk. — *n* **fī'broline** (*-lēn*) a yarn of flax, hemp and jute waste, used with linen or cotton for the backs of carpets, etc. — *n* **fī'brolite** a fibrous variety of the mineral sillimanite. — *n* **fibrō'ma** a tumour composed of fibrous tissue: — *pl* **fibrō'mata** or **fibrō'mas**. — *vi* **fibrose** (*fī-brōs'*) to form fibrous tissue. — *adj* (*fī'brōs*) fibrous. — *n* **fibrō'sis** a morbid growth of fibrous tissue. — *n* **fibrosī'tis** inflammation (*esp* rheumatic) of fibrous tissue. — *adj* **fibrot'ic** pertaining to fibrosis. — *adj* **fī'brous** composed of or like fibres. — *adj* **fibrovas'cūlar** composed of fibres and conducting elements. — **fī'breboard** or (*US*) **fi'berboard** a material formed made from compressed wood fibres; **fī'breglass** or (*US*) **fi'berglass** a synthetic fibre made of extremely fine filaments of molten glass, used in textile manufacture, in heat and sound insulation, and in reinforced plastics; **fibre optics** (as *adj usu* **fibre optic**) a technique using **fibre optic** (or **optics**) **bundles** or **cables**, bundles of extremely thin flexible glass fibres suitably coated, used in optical instruments to transmit maximum light by total internal reflection, and giving images of maximum clarity, and designed, because of their flexibility, for seeing into otherwise inaccessible places; **fi'brescope** or (*US*) **fi'berscope** a medical instrument using fibre optic bundles that allows examination of internal structures, eg the alimentary canal. — **to the very fibre of one's being** deeply or fundamentally. [Fr, from L *fibra* thread or fibre]

fibril *fī'bril*, *n* a small fibre; a root-hair; a minute thread-like structure such as the longitudinal contractile elements of a muscle-fibre. — *n* **fibrill'a** (*fī-* or *fi-*) a fibril filament: — *pl* **fibrill'ae** (*-ē*). — *adj* **fi'brillar**, **fi'brillary**, **fi'brillate** or **fi'brillated** pertaining to, of the nature of, or having fibrils or a fibrous structure. — *vi* **fi'brillate** to undergo fibrillation. — *n* **fibrillā'tion** the production or formation of fibrils or fibres; a mass of fibrils; a twitching of muscle fibres; uncoordinated contraction of muscle-fibres in the heart (*med*). — *n* **fi'brillin** a protein found in connective tissue. — *adj* **fi'brillose** having, or covered with, small fibres or the appearance of small fibres. — *adj* **fi'brillous** pertaining to or having small fibres. [New L *fibrilla* a little fibre]

fibrin, **fibro**, etc. See under **fibre**.

fibster. See under **fib**[1].

fibula *fib'ū-lə*, *n* a brooch in the shape of a safety pin; the outer and thinner of the two bones from the knee to the ankle in the human skeleton, or a corresponding bone in other animals. — *adj* **fib'ūlar**. [L *fībula* brooch]

fiche *fēsh*, *n* a card or strip of film containing miniaturized data. — Also short for **microfiche**. [Fr, a slip of paper, etc]

fichu *fi'shōō* or *fē'-shü*, *n* a three-cornered cape worn over the shoulders in the 18c and 19c, the ends crossed on the chest; a triangular piece of muslin, etc for the neck. [Fr]

fickle *fik'l*, *adj* inconstant in affections, loyalties or intentions; changeable. — *vt* (*Scot*) to perplex or puzzle. — *n* **fick'leness**. [OE *ficol*; *gefic* fraud]

fico *fē'kō*, (*Shakesp*) *n* a fig, as a measure of how little one cares, a whit; a sign of contempt made by placing the thumb between the next two fingers: — *pl* **fic'os**. [Ital, fig]

fictile *fik'tīl*, *-til*, *adj* used or made by a potter; capable of being moulded, *esp* in clay; relating to pottery. [L *fictilis*, from *fingere* to form or fashion]

fiction *fik'shən*, *n* an invented or false story; a falsehood; romance; the novel or story-telling as a branch of literature; a supposition, for the sake of argument, that a possibility, however unlikely, is a fact (*law*). — *adj* **fic'tional**. — *vt* **fic'tionalize** or **-ise** to give a fictional character to (a narrative dealing with real facts). — *adj* **fic'tionalized** or **-s-**. — *n* **fic'tionist** (*rare*) a writer of fiction. — *adj* **fic'tive** fictitious or imaginary. [Fr, from L *fictiō*, *-ōnis*, from *fictus*, pa p of *fingere* to form or fashion]

fictitious *fik-tish'əs*, *adj* of the nature of fiction; imaginary; not real or authentic; invented. — *adv* **ficti'tiously**. [L *ficticius* counterfeit or feigned]

fictor *fik'tər*, *n* (*obs*) a person who makes images from clay, etc. [L *fictor*; see **fiction**]

ficus *fī'kəs*, *n* any plant of the genus *Ficus*, which includes the fig-tree and others. [L]

fid *fid*, *n* a conical pin of hard wood, used by sailors to open the strands of rope in splicing; a square bar, with a shoulder, used to support the weight of the topmast or top-gallant mast. [Origin unknown]

Fid Def *abbrev*: *Fidei Defensor* (*L*), Defender of the Faith, used on coins before decimalization.

fiddious *fid'i-əs*, (*Shakesp*) *vt appar*, to treat as Coriolanus treated *Aufidius*.

fiddle *fid'l*, *n* a violin, *esp* when used to play folk music; extended (*colloq*) to any violin; extended to similar instruments such as *bass fiddle*; a violin-player; a raised rim round a table to keep dishes from sliding off it (*naut*); a swindle, *esp* petty (*slang*). — *vt* and *vi* to play on a fiddle. — *vt* to swindle; to falsify (records, accounts, etc). — *vi* to trifle or idle (with *about* or *around*); to handle things aimlessly (with *with*). — *n* **fidd'ler** a violinist (*colloq*); a trifler; a swindler; (also **fiddler crab**) a small crab of the genus *Uca* or *Gelasimus*, from the movements of its enlarged claw. — *adj* **fidd'ling** trifling; fiddly. — *adj* **fidd'ly** time-consuming; difficult to handle or do because requiring delicate movements of the fingers. — **fidd'le-back** the fiddle-shaped front of a chasuble; a chair with a fiddle-shaped back; **fidd'leback** a wavy grain found in some woods commonly used for the manufacture of violins, and also in woods used for other purposes. — Also *adj*. — **fiddle block** (*naut*) a block having two sheaves of different diameters one above the other; **fidd'le-bow** a bow strung with horsehair, with which the strings of the fiddle are played. — *interj* **fidd'le-de-dee** (*archaic*) nonsense. — *vi* **fidd'le-faddle** to trifle or idle. — *n* trifling talk or behaviour. — *adj* fussy, trifling. — *interj* nonsense. — **fidd'le-faddler**. — *adj* **fidd'le-faddling**. — **fidd'lehead** an ornament at a ship's bow, over the prow or cutwater, consisting of a scroll turning aft or inward; **fiddle pattern** a design of spoon or fork in which the handle is violin-shaped (*adj* **fidd'le-pattern**); **fiddler's green** the sailors' heaven, full of wine, women and song; **fiddler's money** small coins, such as sixpences; **fidd'lestick** a violin bow; a mere nothing, a trifle (*derisive*). — *interj* **fidd'lesticks** or **fidd'lestick** nonsense. — **fidd'le-string** a string for a fiddle; **fidd'lewood** (the valuable hard wood of) a tropical American tree (*Citharexylum*; family Verbenaceae). — **a face like a fiddle** a long or dismal face; **as fit as a fiddle** in the best of condition; **play first** or **second fiddle** to act as a first violin or a second violin player in an orchestra; to take a leading, or (*esp* unwillingly) a subordinate, part in anything; **Scotch fiddle** scabies (from the motion of the fingers against the palm). [OE *fithele*; Ger *Fiedel*; see **viol**]

fiddley *fid'li*, *n* iron framework round a hatchway opening. [Origin obscure]

FIDE *abbrev*: *Fédération Internationale des Echecs* (Fr), the International Chess Federation.

fide et amore *fī'dē et a-mö'rē* or *fi'dā et a-mō're*, (*L*) by faith and love; **fide et fiducia** (*fi-dū'shi-ə* or *fi-dōō'ki-ä*) by faith and confidence; **fide et fortitudine** (*for-ti-tū'di-*

nē or *for-ti-tōō'di-ne*) by faith and fortitude; **fidei defensor** (*fi'dē-ī di-fen'sör*, *fi-dā'ē dā-fen'sör*) defender of the faith (see under **defence**, and see also **Fid Def**); **fide non armis** (*non är'mis* or *ar'mēs*) by faith, not arms; **fides et justitia** (*fī'dēz et jus-tish'i-ə* or *fi'dāz et ūs-ti'ti-a*) fidelity and justice; **fides implicita** (*im-plis'i-tə* or *im-plik'i-tä*) implicit unquestioning faith; **fides Punica** (*pū'-ni-kə* or *pōō'ni-ka*) Punic faith; treachery.

fideism *fē'dā-izm*, *n* the doctrine that knowledge depends on faith rather than reason. — *n* **fi'deist**. — *adj* **fideist'ic**. [L *fīdere* to trust]

fidelity *fi-del'i-ti*, *n* faithfulness; sexual faithfulness to a husband or wife; honesty; firm adherence; accuracy in reproduction. [L *fidēlitās*, *-ātis*, from *fidēlis* faithful, from *fīdere* to trust]

fidget *fij'it*, *vi* to move about restlessly; to touch and handle things aimlessly (with *with*). — *vt* to cause to feel restless and uneasy: — *pr p* **fidg'eting**; *pa t* and *pa p* **fidg'eted**. — *n* a person who fidgets; restlessness; (in *pl*) general nervous restlessness, an inability to keep still. — *vi* **fidge** (*dialect*) to move about restlessly; to be eager. — *n* **fidg'etiness**. — *adj* **fidg'ety** restless; uneasy. [Perh related to **fike**]

fidibus *fid'i-bəs*, (*obs*) *n* a paper spill for lighting a pipe, etc. [Ger]

Fido *fī'dō*, *n* a method of dispersing airfield fog by burning petrol. [*Fog Investigation Dispersal Operation*]

fi donc! *fē dɔ̃*, (*Fr*) for shame!

fiducial *fi-dū'shyəl* or *-shəl*, *adj* (of a point or line) serving as a basis of reckoning (*phys* and *surveying*); showing confidence or reliance; of the nature of trust. — *adv* **fidū'cially**. — *adj* **fidū'ciary** of the nature of a trust; depending upon public confidence; held in trust. — *n* a person who holds anything in trust; a person who depends for salvation on faith alone, without adherence to the moral law, an antinomian (*obs theol*). [L *fīdūcia* confidence, from *fīdere* to trust]

fidus Achates. See **Achates**.

fidus et audax *fī'dəs et ö'daks* or *fi'dōōs et ow'däks*, (*L*) faithful and bold.

fie[1] *fī*, (*old* or *facetious*) *interj* denoting disapprobation or disgust, real or feigned. — **fie upon** an expression of disapprobation of the thing or person named. [Cf Fr *fi*; L *fī*; ON *fȳ* or *fei*; Ger *pfui*]

fie[2]. See **fey**[1].

fief *fēf*, *n* (*hist*) land held in return for feudal service or on condition of military service. — *n* **fief'dom** a piece of land held as a fief (*hist*); any area of influence autocratically controlled by an individual or organization. [Fr, from LL *feudum*; see **fee** and **feoff**]

field *fēld*, *n* country or open country in general; a piece of ground enclosed for cultivation or pasture; the range of any series of actions or energies; speciality; an area of knowledge, interest, etc; a region of space in which forces are at work (*phys*); the locality of a battle; the battle itself; an area of ground reserved and marked out for playing games, etc; a place removed from the classroom, office, etc where practical experience is gained; a wide expanse; the area visible to an observer at one time (eg in a microscope); one of the two interlaced sets of scanning lines making up the picture (*TV*); one scanning of a field from top to bottom and back (*TV*); an area of land in which a mineral, etc is mined; the surface of a shield (*heraldry*); the background of a coin, flag, etc; those taking part in a hunt; the entries collectively against which a contestant has to compete; all parties collectively, the entire set of competitors, runners, etc (as in *to bet on the field* in a horse-race); disposition of fielders (*cricket* or *baseball*); a system or collection of elements upon which binary operations of addition, subtraction, multiplication and division can be performed except that division by 0 is excluded (*math*); a set of characters comprising a unit of information (*comput*). — *vt* to catch (the ball) or stop and return it to the principal playing area (*cricket* or *baseball*); to handle skilfully (*esp* questions); to put into the field for play, military action or (*fig*) other form of contest. — *vi* to stand in position for catching or stopping the ball (*cricket* or *baseball*). — *adj* **field'ed** (*Shakesp*) encamped. — *n* **field'er** a person who fields. — *n* **field'ing** playing in the field at cricket as distinguished from batting. — *adv* **field'ward** or **field'wards** towards the fields. — **field allowance** a small extra payment to officers on active service; **field ambulance** a medical unit on the field of battle; **field artillery** mobile ordnance for active operations in the field; **field battery** a battery of field artillery; **field bed** a camp or trestle bed; a bed for use in the open air; **field book** the notebook used by a surveyor in the field; **field'boots** knee-length boots; **field botany**, **field geology**, etc, botany, geology, etc pursued in the open air; **field capacity** (*geol*) the water-retaining capacity of soil; **field club** a club of field naturalists. — *n pl* **field colours** small flags used for marking the position for companies and regiments in the field; hence, any regimental headquarters' flags. — **field'-cornet** the magistrate of a township (*SAfr hist*); a rank equivalent to lieutenant, *assistant field-cornet* equal to second lieutenant (*SAfr military*); **field day** a day when troops are taken out for instruction in field exercises; any period of great activity, success or enjoyment; **field'-dew** (*Shakesp*) dew of the fields; **fielded panel** a panel, sometimes subdivided into smaller panels, raised above or recessed into surrounding woodwork; **field emission** (*electronics*) emission from a metallic surface as a result of an intense electric field at the surface caused by a high-voltage gradient; **field-emission microscope** a microscope in which a very strong electric field is applied to a metal point and movement of atoms at the point is seen on a fluorescent screen; **field event** an athletic event other than a race; **field'fare** (*ety* doubtful) a species of thrush, having a reddish-yellow throat and breast spotted with black; **field glass** or **glasses** a binocular telescope for use in the field or open air; **field goal** (*Am football* or *basketball*) a goal scored from normal play; **field gray** or **grey** a grey (*Feldgrau*) adopted for uniforms in the German army in World War I; a German soldier dressed thus; **field gun** a light cannon mounted on a carriage; **field hand** an outdoor farm labourer; **field hockey** (*NAm*) hockey played on grass (as opposed to *ice hockey*); **field hospital** a temporary hospital near the scene of battle; **field ice** ice formed in the polar seas in large surfaces, as distinguished from icebergs; **field-ion microscope** a modification, with greater resolving power, of the field-emission microscope, in which ions of a gas (*usu* helium) which is adsorbing on the metal point are repelled and produce the image on the screen; used in conjunction with an instrument such as a mass spectrometer to identify the atoms, it is known as an **atom-probe-field-ion microscope**; **field kitchen** portable cooking equipment for troops, or the place where it is set up; **field lark** an American bird (*Sturnella*) of the Icteridae (see under **icterus**), not a lark; **field marshal** an army officer of highest rank; **field meeting** a secret religious meeting, a conventicle; **field'mouse** or **field'-vole** a name for various species of mouse and vole that live in the fields; **field naturalist** a person who studies natural history out of doors; **field night** a night marked by some important gathering, discussion, etc. — *n pl* **field notes** data noted in the field, to be worked up later. — **field officer** a military officer above the rank of captain, and below that of general; **field of view** or **vision** what is visible to one at any given moment; **field'piece** a cannon or piece of artillery used in the field of battle; **field preacher** an open-air preacher; **field preaching**. — *adj* **field'-sequential** (*TV*) relating to the association of individual primary colours with successive fields. — **fields'man** a fielder (*cricket* or *baseball*). — *n pl* **field sports** sports of the field, such as hunting, racing, etc. — **field'stone** (chiefly *US*) stone used for building, taken from a field; **field strength** the intensity of an electric or magnetic field; **field train** a department of the Royal Artillery responsible for the safety and supply of ammunition during war; **field trial** a test in practice, as distinct from one under laboratory conditions; **field trip** an expedition (*esp* by students) to observe and study something at its location; **field'vole** see **fieldmouse** above; **field'work** farm work in fields; work (scientific surveying, etc) in the field, as opposed to in a laboratory, office, etc; (often in *pl*) a temporary fortification erected by troops in the field, either for protection or to cover an attack on a stronghold; **field'worker** a practical research worker. — **keep the field** to keep the campaign going; to maintain one's ground; **play the field** see under **play**; **take the field** to assemble on a playing-field; to begin warlike operations. [OE *feld*; cf Du *veld* the open country, Ger *Feld*]

fiend *fēnd*, *n* a devil; a person driven by the most intense wickedness or hate; an addict; a devotee. — *adj* **fiend'ish** like a fiend; devilishly cruel. — *adv* **fiend'ishly**. — *n* **fiend'ishness**. — *adj* **fiend'-like** like a fiend; fiendish. [OE *fēond* enemy, orig pr p of *fēon* to hate; Ger *Feind*, Du *vijand*]

fient *fēnt*, *fint*, (*Scot*) *n* a fiend or devil; often used, like *devil* in English, as an emphatic negative (eg *fient ane*, devil a one, not one). [Ety as for **fiend**]

fierce *fērs*, *adj* savage; ferocious; (of competition or opposition) strong or intense; violent. — *adv* **fierce'ly**. — *n* **fierce'ness**. [OFr *fers* (Fr *fier*), from L *ferus* wild, savage]

fiere. See **fere**[1].

fieri facias *fī'ə-rī fā'shi-as* or *fē'e-rē fak'i-äs*, (*LL*) literally, cause to be done, the name of a writ commanding the sheriff to distrain the defendant's goods.

fiery *fīr'i*, *adj* like or consisting of fire; ardent; impetuous; irritable; (of ground in games) dry, hard, fast. — *adv* **fier'ily**. — *n* **fier'iness**. — **fiery cross** a charred cross dipped in blood, formerly carried round in the Scottish Highlands as a call to arms; a burning cross, symbol of the Ku-Klux Klan; **fiery mine** (*min ext*) a mine in which there is a possiblity of explosion from gas or coal-dust. [**fire**]

fiesta *fē-es'tə*, *n* a saint's day; a holiday; a carnival or festivity. [Sp]

FIFA *fē'fə*, *abbrev*: *Fédération Internationale de Football Association* (*Fr*), International Football Federation.

fife *fīf*, *n* a smaller variety of the flute. — *vi* to play on the fife. — *n* **fif'er** a fife-player. — **fife'-ma'jor** (*obs*) the chief fifer in a regiment; **fife rail** the rail round the mainmast, where a fifer sat at heaving of the anchor. [Ger *Pfeife* pipe, or Fr *fifre* fifer, both from L *pīpāre* to cheep]

Fifish *fīf'ish*, *adj* cranky or queer (supposed qualities of **Fif'ers**, inhabitant of *Fife*, Scotland).

FIFO *fī'fō*, *abbrev*: first in, first out (of redundancies).

fifteen *fif'tēn* or *fif-tēn'*, *adj* and *n* five and ten. — *n* a set, group or team of fifteen (such as, formerly, the Court of Session); **15** a certificate designating a film passed as suitable to be seen only by people of fifteen and over. — *n* **fifteen'er** (*rare*) a verse of fifteen syllables. — *adj* **fifteenth'** (or *fif'*) last of fifteen; next after the fourteenth; equal to one of fifteen equal parts. — *n* a fifteenth part; a person or thing in fifteenth position; a double octave (*music*); an organ stop sounding two octaves above the diapason. — *adv* **fifteenth'ly**. — **the Fifteen** the Jacobite rebellion of 1715. [OE *fīftēne*; see **five** and **ten**]

fifth *fifth*, *adj* last of five; next after the fourth; equal to one of five equal parts. — *n* one of five equal parts; a person or thing in fifth position; an interval of four (conventionally called five) diatonic degrees (*music*); a tone at that interval from another; a combination of two tones separated by that interval; (with *cap*) the Fifth Amendment (*US*). — *adv* **fifth'ly** in the fifth place. — **Fifth Amendment** an amendment to the US constitution which allows a person on trial not to testify against himself or herself and forbids a second trial if a person has been acquitted in a first; **fifth column** people within a country, etc who sympathize, and will act, with its enemies (expression used by a Spanish insurgent general when four columns were advancing upon Madrid); **fifth columnist** (*kol'əm-ist*); **fifth generation** (*comput*) the type of computer which incorporates aspects of artificial intelligence (*adj* **fifth'-generation**); **Fifth'-monarchism**; **Fifth'-monarchist**; **Fifth-monarchy men** an extreme sect at the time of the Puritan revolution, who looked for a new reign of Christ on earth in succession to Daniel's four great monarchies of Antichrist; **fifth wheel** the spare wheel of a four-wheeled vehicle; a superfluous or useless person or thing. — **take the Fifth** (*US colloq*) to refuse to testify, in accordance with the Fifth Amendment. [OE *fīfta*, assimilated to other ordinals in *-th*]

fifty *fif'ti*, *adj* and *n* five tens or five times ten. — *n pl* **fif'ties** the numbers fifty to fifty-nine; the years so numbered (of a life or century); a range of temperatures from fifty to just less than sixty degrees. — *adj* **fif'tieth** last of fifty; next after the forty-ninth; equal to one of fifty equal parts. — *n* a fiftieth part; a person or thing in fiftieth position. — *adj* **fif'tyish** apparently about fifty years old. — *n*, *adj* and *adv* **fif'ty-fif'ty** half-and-half; fifty per cent of each of two things; share and share alike. — **fifty-pence** or **fifty-penny piece** (in Britain) a coin worth 50 pence. [OE *fīftig*, from *fīf* five and *-tig*, the sfx *-ty*]

FIG *abbrev*: *Fédération Internationale de Gymnastique* (Fr), International Gymnastics Federation.

fig[1] *fig*, *n* any of a genus (*Ficus*) of tropical and subtropical trees and shrubs of the mulberry family which produce a soft pear-shaped fruit packed with seeds; the fruit itself, often eaten dried; a thing of little or no consequence, a negligible amount, a jot; piles (*obs*). — *vt* (*Shakesp*) to subject to an insulting gesture made by putting the thumb between the next two fingers. — **fig'-bird** any Australian oriole (genus *Sphecotheres*) feeding on figs, etc; **fig'-leaf** the leaf of the fig-tree; a representation of such a leaf for veiling the genitals of a statue or picture; any scanty clothing (from the Bible: Gen 3.7); any prudish evasion; a substitute or makeshift; something intended to conceal the reality of actions or motives, *esp* political or international; **fig'-pecker** the beccafico, a garden warbler; **fig'-tree** any tree which produces figs; **fig'wort** (*bot*) any species of Scrophularia; pilewort. [Fr *figue*, from L *fīcus* a fig or fig-tree]

fig[2] *fig*, (*colloq*) *n* figure; dress; form. — *vt* to dress or get up (with *out*); (of a horse) to display in an artificially lively condition (with *out* or *up*): — *pr p* **figg'ing**; *pa t* and *pa p* **figged**. — *n* **figg'ery** dressy ornament. — **in full fig** in full dress or array. [Perh **figure**]

fig. *abbrev*: figurative; figuratively; figure.

fight *fīt*, *vi* to strive or struggle; to contend in war or in single combat. — *vt* to engage in conflict with; to contend against; to maintain or contend for, or oppose, by combat, legal action, etc; to achieve by struggle; to cause to contend or enter into conflict: — *pr p* **fight'ing**; *pa t* and *pa p* **fought** (*föt*). — *n* a struggle; a combat; a strong disagreement; a battle or engagement; fighting spirit; inclination to fight; a screen to cover the men in a naval fight (*Shakesp*). — *adj* **fight'able** able to be fought. — *n* **fight'er** a person, etc who fights; a boxer; a relatively small military aircraft equipped to attack targets which are both in the air and on the ground. — *adj* **fight'ing** engaged in, eager for, or fit for war or strife. — *n* the act of fighting or contending. — **fighting chance** a chance of success given supreme effort; **fighting cock** a gamecock; a pugnacious person; **fighting fish** a small freshwater fish of Thailand (*Betta pugnax*), kept for its extraordinary readiness for fighting, bets being laid on the outcome. — **fight back** to retaliate; to counter-attack (*n* **fight'back**); **fighting drunk** drunk and very aggressive; **fighting fit** in good physical condition; **fight it out** to struggle on until the end; **fight off** to resist or repel; **fight shy of** to avoid owing to mistrust; **fight to the finish**, **to the ropes** or **to the last ditch** to fight until completely exhausted; **live**

like **fighting cocks** to habitually get the best available food and drink. [OE *fehtan* (WS *feohtan*); Ger *fechten*]

figment *fig'mənt*, *n* a fabrication or invention. [L *figmentum*, from *fingere* to form]

figo *fē'gō*, (*Shakesp*) *n* a sign of contempt, a fico: — *pl* **fig'os**. [OSp]

figuline *fig'ū-līn* or *-lin*, *adj* of earthenware; fictile. — *n* an earthenware vessel. [L *figulīnus*, from *figulus* potter]

figure *fig'ər*, (*US* and *dialect*) *-yər*, (*old-fashioned*) *fig'ūr*, *n* the form of anything in outline; appearance; a shape; a geometrical form; a diagram; a horoscope (*Shakesp*); a design; an illustration; bodily shape; a human form or representation of it; a personality, personage or character; an impressive, noticeable, important, ludicrous or grotesque person; a written character denoting a number; amount; value or price; a deviation from the ordinary mode of expression (*rhetoric*); the form of a syllogism with respect to the position of the middle term (*logic*); a group of notes felt as a unit (*music*); a series of steps or movements in a dance or in skating; an emblem. — *vt* to form or shape (*obs*); to symbolize (*archaic*); to foreshow (*obs*); to make an image of; to represent; to mark with figures or designs; to imagine; to reckon, to work out (often with *out*); to note by figures. — *vi* to make figures; to appear as a figure, make an appearance or show; to follow as a logical consequence, be expected (*colloq*). — *n* **figūrabil'ity** the quality of being figurable. — *adj* **fig'ūrable**. — *adj* **fig'ūral** represented by a figure or figures. — *n* **figurant** (*fig'ū-rənt*) or **figurante** (*fēg-ōō-rän'tā*; *Ital*) a ballet dancer, one of those who form a background for the solo dancers. — *adj* **fig'ūrate** of a certain definite form; florid (*music*). — *n* **figūrā'tion** the act of giving figure or form; representation by or in figures or shapes, *esp* significant, typical or emblematic figures; a figure of this kind; ornamentation with a design; florid treatment (*music*). — *adj* **fig'ūrative** representing by, containing or filled with figures of speech (*rhetoric*); metaphorical; representing a figure; emblematic or symbolic; of a style of painting, sculpture, etc characterized by the realistic depiction of people, objects, etc (as opposed to *abstract* art). — *adv* **fig'ūratively**. — *n* **fig'ūrativeness**. — *adj* **fig'ured** (*-ərd*) having a figure; marked or adorned with figures; delineated in a figure; in the form of figures. — *n* **fig'ūrine** (*-ēn* or *-ēn'*) a small carved or moulded figure. — *n* **fig'urist** a person who uses, or interprets, by figures. — **figurate numbers** a series of numbers such that if each be subtracted from the next, and the series so formed be treated in the same way, by a continuation of the process equal differences will ultimately be obtained; **fig'ure-caster** an astrologer (*obs*); a person who prepares casts of figures; **fig'ure-casting** astrology (*obs*); the art of preparing casts of animal or other forms; **fig'ure-dance** a dance consisting of elaborate formalized movements; **figured bass** a bass with numerals added to indicate chords; **fig'urehead** the figure or bust under the bowsprit of a ship; a merely nominal head, eg of an organization or a government. — *adj* nominal, but lacking real power. — **figure of merit** (*elec eng*) a general parameter which describes the quality of performance of eg an instrument or a circuit; **figure of speech** any of various devices (such as simile or metaphor) for using words in such a way as to make a striking effect; **figure skater**; **figure skating** skating in prescribed patterns on ice; **fig'ure-weaving** the weaving of figured fancy fabrics; **fig'urework** counting or calculation using numbers. — **cut a figure** to make a bold impression through one's appearance; **figure on** to count upon or expect; to plan (*US*). [Fr, from L *figūra*, from *fingere* to form]

fike *fīk*, (*Scot*) *vi* to fidget restlessly. — *n* restlessness; any annoying requirement or detail in work; a pernickety exacting person. — *n* **fīk'ery** fuss. — *adj* **fīk'ish** or **fīk'y**. [Prob ON *fīkja*]

fil. See **fill**[2].

filabeg. See **filibeg**.

filaceous *fil-ā'shəs*, *adj* composed of threads. [L *fīlum* a thread]

filacer *fil'ə-sər*, *n* formerly, an officer who filed writs. — Also **fil'azer**. [OFr *filacier*, from *filace* a file for papers, from apparently L *fīlum* a thread]

filagree. See **filigree**.

filament *fil'ə-mənt*, *n* a slender or threadlike object; a fibre; the stalk of a stamen (*bot*); a chain of cells; a thread of high resistance in an incandescent lamp or thermionic valve (*elec*). — *adj* **filamentary** (*-ment'ə-ri*) like a filament. — *adj* **filament'ous** threadlike. [L *fīlum* a thread]

filander *fil-and'ər*, *n* a threadlike intestinal worm in hawks; (in *pl*) the disease it causes. [OFr *filandre*, from L *fīlum* thread]

filar *fī'lər* (*optics*) *adj* having threads or wires. [L *fīlum* a thread]

Filaria *fi-lā'ri-ə*, *n* a genus of nematode worms of the family *Filarioidea*, introduced into the blood by mosquitoes; (without *cap*) any worm of the genus. — *adj* **filā'rial**. — *n* **filariasis** (*-lə-rī'ə-sis*) a disease caused by the presence of filaria in the blood, inflammation of the lymphatic vessels. [L *fīlum* thread]

filasse *fil-as'*, *n* vegetable fibre prepared for manufacture. [Fr, from L *fīlum* thread]

filature *fil'ə-chər*, *n* the putting of silk on to reels, or the place where it is done. — *n* **fil'atory** a machine for forming or spinning threads. [Fr, from L *fīlum* a thread]

filazer. Same as **filacer**.

filbert *fil'bərt*, *n* the nut of the cultivated hazel. Also (*obs*) **fil'berd**. [Prob from St *Philibert*, whose day (22 Aug) fell in the nutting season (OSax)]

filch *filch*, *vt* to steal; to pilfer. — *n* **filch'er** a thief. — *n* and *adj* **filch'ing**. — *adv* (*rare*) **filch'ingly**. [Ety unknown]

file[1] *fīl*, *n* a thread (*obs*); any contrivance for keeping papers in order, *orig* a line or wire on which papers were strung; a collection of papers arranged for reference; a collection of data in any form, *esp* on computer; a roll or list (*Shakesp*); a line of soldiers, chessboard squares, etc ranged one behind another; a small body of soldiers. — *vt* to put upon a file; to arrange in an orderly way; to put on record; to bring before a court; to deposit or lodge (a complaint, etc). — *vi* to march in file. — *adj* **fil'ed**. — *n* **fil'er** a person or thing that files; a filing cabinet (*colloq*). — **file copy** a copy filed for reference; an editor's copy of a book in which errors, possible changes, etc are noted; **file'-leader** the person at the head of a file; **file'name** (*comput*) a name used to refer to a given collection of data; **file server** (*comput*) a filing store available to all the terminals in a linked system; **filing cabinet** a cabinet for storing files. — **file off** to wheel off at right angles to the original or previous direction; **file with** (*archaic*) to rank with or be equal to; **on file** on record, catalogued; **single file** or **Indian file** one behind another. [L *fīlum* a thread]

file[2] *fīl*, *n* an instrument with sharp-edged furrows for smoothing or rasping metals, etc; a small metal or emery-paper instrument for shaping or smoothing finger- or toenails, a nailfile; a shrewd or cunning person (*obs*); a pickpocket (*obs*). — *vt* to cut or smooth with, or as if with, a file; to polish or improve, *esp* of a literary style. — *adj* **filed** polished or smooth. — *n* **fil'er** a person or thing that files. — *n* (*usu* in *pl*) **fil'ing** a particle rubbed off with a file. — **file'-cutter** a maker of metal files; **file'-fish** a fish of the Balistes or a related genus, with skin granulated like a file. [OE *fȳl* (WSax *fēol*); Ger *Feile*; Du *vijl*]

file[3] *fīl*, (*Shakesp* or *Scot*) *vt* to defile or pollute. [OE *gefȳlan*; cf **foul**]

filemot *fil'i-mot*, *adj* of a dead-leaf colour, dull brown. — *n* the colour itself. — Also **phil'amot** or **phil'omot**. [Fr *feuillemorte* dead leaf]

filet *fē-le*, (*Fr*) *n* undercut of beef, tenderloin; a kind of lace consisting of embroidery on a square-mesh net.

filet mignon *fē-le mē-nyɔ̃*, (*Fr*) *n* a small boneless cut of beef from the underside of a sirloin.

filfot. See **fylfot**.

filial *fil'i-əl*, *adj* pertaining or appropriate to a son or daughter; in the relation of a child. — *adv* **fil'ially**. [Fr, from LL *fīliālis*, from L *fīlius* a son]

filiate and **filiation**. Same as **affiliate** and **affiliation**.

filibeg, **filabeg**, **fillibeg**, **philabeg**, **phillabeg**, **philibeg** or **phillibeg** *fil'i-beg*, *n* the kilt. [Gaelic *feileadhbeag*, from *feileadh* pleat or fold, and *beag* little]

filibuster *fil'i-bus-tər*, *n* a pirate or buccaneer; a military adventurer or revolutionary; a person who obstructs legislation by making lengthy speeches, introducing motions, etc; obstruction by such means in a legislative body. — *vi* to act as a filibuster. — *n* **filibus'terer**. — *n* **filibus'tering**. — *n* **filibus'terism**. — *adj* **filibus'terous**. [Sp *filibustero*, through Fr *flibustier* or *fribustier*, from Du *vrijbuiter* (cf Eng **freebooter** (under **free**), Ger *Freibeuter*), from *vrij* free, and *buit* booty]

Filices *fil'i-sēz*, *n pl* the ferns, *esp* the true (homosporous leptosporangiate) ferns. — *n pl* **Filicales** (*-kā'lēz*) or **Filicineae** (*-sin'i-ē*) the ferns, leptosporangiate and eusporangiate, with or without water-ferns. — *adj* **filicin'ean**. [L *filix*, *-icis* fern]

filicide *fil'i-sīd*, *n* the murder of one's own child; a person who murders his or her child. [L *fīlius*, *fīlia* son or daughter, and *caedere* to kill]

filiform *fil'i-form*, *adj* threadlike. — *adj* **filipen'dulous** (*fil-*) hanging by or strung on a thread. [L *fīlum* a thread]

filigree *fil'i-grē*, *n* a kind of ornamental metallic lacework of gold and silver, twisted into convoluted forms, joined and partly consolidated by soldering; a delicate structure resembling this. — Also **fil'agree**; earlier forms **fil'igrain** and **fil'igrane**. — *adj* **fil'igreed** ornamented with filigree. [Fr *filigrane*, from Ital *filigrana*, from L *fīlum* thread, and *grānum* a grain]

filing. See under **file**[2].

filiopietistic *fi-li-ō-pī-ə-tis'tik*, *adj* marked by an excess of filial piety, or excessive veneration of one's ancestors. [See **filial** and **piety**]

filioque *fil-i-ō'kwi*, *n* the clause inserted into the Nicene Creed at Toledo in 589, which asserts that the Holy Ghost proceeds from the Son, as well as from the Father – not accepted by the Eastern Church. [L, and from the son]

filipendulous. See under **filiform**.

Filipino *fil-i-pē'nō*, *n* a native of the *Philippine* Islands: — *pl* **Filipi'nos**: — *fem* **Filipi'na**. — Also *adj*. [Sp]

filius nullius *fil'i-əs nul'i-əs* or *fē'li-o͞os no͞o'li-o͞os*, (*L*) a son of nobody, a bastard; **filius populi** (*po'pū-lī* or *po'po͞o-lē*) a son of the people; **filius terrae** (*te'rē* or *te'rī*) son of the soil, a person of low birth.

fill[1] *fil*, *vt* to make full; to put into until all the space is occupied; to supply abundantly; to satisfy; to glut; to perform the duties of; to take up (a vacant post); to increase the bulk of (soap, cotton fabrics, etc) by mixing in a lower-grade substance; to put amalgam, gold, etc into (a cavity in a tooth); to fulfil or carry out (*esp US*); to make up (a prescription) (*US*). — *vi* to become full; to become satiated. — *n* as much as fills or satisfies; a full supply; the fullest extent; a single charge of anything; anything used to fill. — *n* **fill'er** a person or thing that fills, eg any of various paste-like substances used to fill cracks in wood, plaster, etc; a vessel from which liquid is poured into a bottle; any item used to fill a gap in eg a page of newsprint or a broadcasting schedule; a substance added to various materials to impart desired qualities. — *n* **fill'ing** anything used to fill up, stop a hole, to complete, etc, such as amalgam, etc in a tooth, or the woof in weaving; (in *pl*) the quantity of new whisky spirit that a blender puts into store for maturation in eg a year, or the output of a distillery supplied for such purposes. — **filler cap** a device for closing the filling pipe of a petrol tank in a motor vehicle; **filler metal** (*eng*) the metal required to be added at the weld in welding processes; **filler rod** (*eng*) same as **welding rod**; **fill'-in** something used to fill in (time or space); fill-in flash; **fill-in flash** *usu* weak flash lighting used to compensate for strong back-lighting or heavy shadow in outdoor photography; **filling station** a roadside installation where petrol and oil are sold to motorists, etc. — **fill in** to occupy (time); to add what is necessary to complete (eg a form); to act as a temporary substitute (for; *colloq*); **fill out** to make or become more substantial, larger or fuller; to complete (a form, etc) (*esp US*); **fill someone in** (*colloq*) to give someone detailed information about a situation; to thrash or beat up someone (*slang*); to murder someone (*slang*); **fill the bill** to be adequate; **fill up** to fill, or be filled, by addition of more; **fill up with** to stuff with (*lit* and *fig*); **have one's fill of** to have enough of, *esp* something unpleasant or tiresome. [OE *fyllan*, from *full* full]

fill[2] or **fil** *fil*, (*Shakesp*) *n* a thill or shaft of a vehicle. — **fill'-horse**, **phil'horse** or **pil'horse** (*Shakesp*) a thill-horse, the horse nearest the carriage in a team. [See **thill**[1]]

fille *fē-y'*, (*Fr*) *n* a girl; a daughter. — **fille de chambre** (*də shã-br'*) a chambermaid; **fille de joie** (*zhwä*) a prostitute; **fille d'honneur** (*do-nœr*) a maid of honour.

fillet *fil'ət*, *n* meat or fish boned and rolled; a piece of meat without bone, *esp* the fleshy part of the thigh or the undercut of the sirloin; a boned whole, or thick boneless slice of, fish; a narrow piece of wood, metal, etc; a band for the hair; a small space or band used along with mouldings (*archit*). — *vt* to bone; to make into fillets; to bind or adorn with a fillet: — *pr p* **fill'eting**; *pa t* and *pa p* **fill'eted**. — **fillet weld** a weld at the junction of two parts at right angles to each other, a fillet of welding material being laid down in the angle created by the intersection of the surfaces of the parts. [Fr *filet*, dimin of *fil*, from L *fīlum* a thread]

fillibeg. See **filibeg**.

fillip *fil'ip*, *vt* to strike with the fingernail released from the ball of the thumb with a sudden jerk, to flick; to incite or stimulate: — *pr p* **fill'iping**; *pa t* and *pa p* **fill'iped**. — *n* a jerk of the finger from the thumb; a stimulus, *esp* of encouragement, a boost. [A form of **flip**]

fillipeen. US form of **philop(o)ena**.

fillister *fil'is-tər*, (*woodworking*) *n* a kind of rabbeting plane. [Origin unknown]

filly *fil'i*, *n* a young mare; a lively girl or young woman (*old colloq*). [Dimin of **foal**; prob from ON]

film *film*, *n* a thin skin or membrane; a thin layer or coating; a pellicle or scum on liquids; a gauze of very slender threads; a mistiness; a thin sheet of *usu* plastic-based material used for wrapping; a coating of a sensitive substance for taking a photograph; a sheet or strip of celluloid or a similar plastic prepared with such a coating for use in still or cinema photography; a motion picture, a series of images photographed (and *usu* sounds recorded) on such a strip which, when projected in succession and at speed, or broadcast, on to a screen, tell a story, present a subject, etc; (often in *pl*) this technique of storytelling, etc as an art form, a medium of communication, or an industry, the cinema. — *vt* to cover with a film; to photograph or record on film; to make a motion picture of; to adapt and enact for the cinema. — *vi* to become covered with a film; to make a motion picture. — *adj* **film'able** suitable for making a film of. — *n* **film'dom** or **film'land** the cinema industry. — *adj* **film'ic** pertaining to the cinema. — *n* **filmi'ness**. — *adj* **film'ish** having a flavour of the cinema. — *n* **filmog'raphy** a list of the films of a particular actor or director. — *adj* **film'y** composed of or like a film; covered with a film; gauzy or semi-transparent; clouded. — **film badge** a badge containing sensitive film worn by those risking exposure to radioactivity to detect and *usu* indicate the amount of exposure; **film colour** a vague textureless area of colour, such as the sky or that seen with closed eyes, as opposed to colour seen on the surface of an object; **film fan** a devotee of the cinema; **film'goer**; **film noir** (*nwär*) a style of cinema film, popular in American cinema in the 1940s and 50s, in which the darker side of human nature is presented, in a bleak, often starkly urban setting; **film set** the scenery, furniture, etc arranged for the scene of a cinema film. — *vt* (*printing*) **film'set** to set by a process of typesetting. — **film'setting** typesetting by exposing type on to film which is then transferred to printing plates; **film star** a favourite cinema performer; **film'-strip** a film consisting of a series of stills to be shown separately and consecutively; **filmy ferns** a family of ferns with very thin leaves, the Hymenophyllaceae. — **sheet film** film in the same sizes as photographic plates and superseding plates, used in printing and in large-format cameras. [OE *filmen*, connected with *fell* skin]

FILO *fī'lō*, *abbrev*: first in, last out (of redundancies).

filo or **phyllo** *fē'lō*, *n* a type of Greek, etc pastry made in thin sheets. [Gr *phyllon* a leaf]

Filofax® *fī'lə-faks*, *n* a small, loose-leaf filing system containing a diary and a selection of information, eg addresses, maps, indexes, to assist the user to organize his or her time, business, etc.

filoplume *fil'ō-ploom*, *n* a slender hairlike feather. — *n* **filopō'dium** (*fil-*; *biol*) a threadlike pseudopodium consisting of ectoplasm: — *pl* **filopō'dia**. [L *fīlum* a thread]

filose *fī'lōs adj* threadlike; having a threadlike end. [L *filum* a thread]

filoselle *fil-ō-sel'*, *n* coarse floss silk. [Ital *filosello*, from LL *folexellus* cocoon; infl by Ital *filo* thread]

fils *fēs*, (*Fr*) *n* son; (following a name) junior.

filter *fil'tər*, *n* an apparatus for purifying a fluid of solid matter by pouring it through porous material; a device for wholly or partly eliminating undesirable frequencies from light, radio or electric currents; (at a road junction) an auxiliary traffic light in the form of a green arrow which allows one lane of traffic to move while the main stream is held up. — *vt* to pass through a filter; to separate by a filter (*esp* with *out*). — *vi* to pass through a filter; to percolate; to pass gradually and dispersedly through obstacles; to join gradually a stream of traffic; (of a lane of traffic) to move in the direction specified by the filter; to become known gradually (*fig*). — *n* **filterabil'ity** or **filtrabil'ity**. — *adj* **fil'terable** or **fil'trable** able to pass through a filter (see **filter-passer** below); capable of being filtered. — *vt* and *vi* **fil'trate** to filter or percolate. — *n* a filtered liquid. — *n* **filtrā'tion** (an) act or process of filtering. — **fil'ter-bed** a bed of sand, gravel, clinker, etc used for filtering water or sewage; **fil'ter-paper** porous paper for use in filtering; **fil'ter-passer** and **filterable virus** terms used formerly for a virus in the sense of submicroscopic disease agent; **fil'ter-tip** a cigarette with a filter at the mouth end, to reduce the smoker's ingestion of impurities. [OFr *filtre*, from LL *fīltrum* felt]

filth *filth*, *n* repellent dirtiness, or any foul matter; anything that defiles, physically or morally; obscenity; (with *the*) the police (*derog slang*). — *adv* **filth'ily**. — *n* **filth'iness**. — *adj* **filth'y** foul; unclean; impure. [OE *fȳlth*, from *fūl* foul]

filtre (*Fr*). See **café filtre** under **cafe**.

fimble *fim'bl*, *n* the male plant of hemp, weaker and shorter in fibre than **carl-hemp**. [Du *femel* female]

Fimbra *fim'brə*, *abbrev*: Financial Intermediaries, Managers and Brokers Regulatory Association.

fimbria *fim'bri-ə*, *n* (*anatom*) a fringing filament. — *adj* **fim'briate** fringed (*anatom*); having a narrow border (*heraldry*). — *vt* (*anatom*) to fringe; to hem. — *adj* **fim'briated**. — *n* **fimbria'tion**. [L *fimbriae* fibres or fringe]

fimicolous *fim-ik'ə-ləs*, (*bot*) *adj* growing on dung. [L *fimus* dung, and *colere* to inhabit]

fin[1] *fin*, *n* an organ by which an aquatic animal steers, balances or swims; a fixed vertical surface on the tail of an aeroplane; a portion of a mechanism like a fish's fin in shape or purpose; a thin projecting edge or plate; a hand or arm (*slang*). — *adj* **fin'less**. — *adj* **finned** having fins. — *n* **finn'er** a finback. — *adj* **finn'y** finned. — **fin'back** or **fin'-whale** a rorqual. — *adj* **fin'-foot'ed** web-footed; having fringed toes. — **fin'-ray** a horny rod supporting a fin. — *adj* **fin'-toed'** having lobate or fringed toes. [OE *finn*; L *pinna* a feather or a fin]

fin[2] *fin*, (*US slang*) *n* a five-dollar bill. [Yiddish *finf* five]

FINA *fē'nə*, *abbrev*: Fédération Internationale de Natation Amateur (*Fr*), International Amateur Swimming Association.

finable. See under **fine**[2].

finagle *fi-nā'gəl*, *vt* to obtain by guile or swindling, to wangle; to cheat (a person; *usu* with *out of*). — Also *vi* and *n*. [Eng dialect *fainaigue* cheat or shirk]

final *fī'nl*, *adj* last; decisive or conclusive; relating to or constituting an end or motive; (of a judgement) ready for execution. — *n* the last of a series (eg of letters in a word, games in a contest, examinations in a curriculum, etc); in the old church modes, the keynote or tonic, the lowest note in the authentic modes, a fourth above it in the plagal; (in *pl*) final approach (*colloq*; *aeronautics*). — *n* **fī'nalism** (*philos*) teleology, interpretation in terms of purpose; belief that an end has been reached. — *n* **fī'nalist** a teleologist (*philos*); a person who reaches the final stage in a competition; a student taking his or her final examinations; a person who believes that finality has been reached (*philos*). — *n* **fīnality** (*-al'i-ti*) the state of being final; completeness or conclusiveness; the principle of final cause (*philos*); that which is final. — *vt* **fī'nalize** or **-ise** to put the finishing touches to; to put an end to completely. — *adv* **fī'nally**. — **final approach** (*aeronautics*) the part of the landing procedure from when the aircraft turns into line with the runway until the flare-out is started (*colloq* **fī'nals**); **final cause** (*philos*) the end or objective for which a thing is done, *esp* the design of the universe; **final demand** or **final notice** a last bill rendered before legal action is taken to recover a debt; **final solution** (*hist*) the English version of the name (Ger *Endlösung*) for the German Nazi policy and process, from 1941, of exterminating European Jews. [Fr, from L *fīnālis*, from *fīnis* an end]

finale *fi-nä'lā* or *-li*, *n* the end or climax; the last movement in a musical composition; the concluding part of any performance, eg the last song in a stage musical, *usu* impressively energetic or lavish. [Ital *finale* final, from L *fīnālis*]

finance *fī-*, *fi-nans'* or *fī'*, *n* money affairs or revenue, *esp* of a ruler or state; money, *esp* public money; the art of managing or administering public money; (in *pl*) money resources. — *vt* to manage financially; to provide or support with money. — *vi* to engage in money business. — *adj* **finan'cial** (*-shəl*) pertaining to finance. — *n* **finan'cialist** a financier. — *adv* **finan'cially**. — *n* **finan'cier** (*-si-ər*; *US fin-an-sēr'*) a person skilled in finance; a person who administers the public revenue. — *vi* and *vt* (*-sēr'*) to finance; to swindle. — **finance company** or **house** a company specializing in lending money against collateral, *esp* to finance hire-purchase agreements; **financial year** any annual period for which accounts are made up; the annual period ending 5 April, functioning as the income-tax year, over which the Government's financial policies and estimates are made; the annual period ending, for many public bodies, on 31 March. [Fr, from OFr *finer* to settle, from L *fīnis* an end]

finback. See under **fin**[1].

finch *finch*, *-sh*, *n* a name applied to many passerine or perching birds, *esp* to those of the genus *Fringilla* or family Fringillidae, including the bullfinch, chaffinch, goldfinch, etc. — *adj* **finched** finch-backed. — *adj* **finch'-backed** striped or spotted on the back. [OE *finc*; Ger *Fink*]

find *fīnd*, *vt* to come upon or meet with; to discover or arrive at; to come to perceive; to experience; to regain (a former position, state, etc); to determine after judicial inquiry; to supply or succeed in getting; to manage to reach, hit, land on, etc. — *vi* to come upon game: — *pr p* **find'ing**; *pa t* and *pa p* **found**. — *n* an act of finding; something found, *esp* something of value or interest. — *n* **find'er** a person who finds; a small telescope attached to a larger one, or a lens attached to a camera, to facilitate the directing of it at the object viewed. — *n* **find'ing** the act of any person who finds; that which is found; a judicial verdict; (in *pl*; *esp US*) the tools which some workmen have to supply themselves, *esp* (of shoemakers) everything except leather; (in *pl*) accessories such as buttons and zips (*US*). — **find'-fault** (*Shakesp*) a person who finds fault with another. — **finders keepers** (*colloq*) those who find something are entitled to keep it; **find one's account in** to find satisfactory profit or advantage in; **find oneself** to feel, as regards health, happiness, etc (*formal*); to come to terms with oneself; to discover one's true personality, vocation or interests; **find one's feet** to become able to stand or able to cope readily with new conditions; **find out** to discover or detect; **find someone in** (*obs*) to supply someone with. [OE *findan*; Ger *finden*]

fin de siècle *fɛ̃ də sye-kl'*, (*Fr*) the end of the 19c, or of an era; characteristic of the ideas, etc of the late 19c, *esp* modernistic; decadent.

findon-haddock and **findram**. See **finnan**.

fine[1] *fīn*, *adj* excellent (often *ironic*); beautiful; not coarse or heavy; consisting of small particles; subtle; slender; sharp; keen; exquisite; nice; delicate; sensitive; over-refined; over-elaborate (*obs*); pretentious (*obs*); showy; splendid; striking or remarkable; egregious, distinguished (*archaic*); pure; refined; containing so many parts of pure metal out of twenty-four (as 22 carats, or ounces, fine, 22/24 gold or silver), or out of a thousand. — *vt* to make fine; to refine; to purify; to change by imperceptible degrees (*esp* with *away* or *down*). — *adj* and *adv* at a more acute angle with the line of flight of the ball (eg *fine leg*); (of a billiards, etc stroke) making very slight contact. — *adv* well or well enough (*colloq*); narrowly; with little to spare. — *adj* **fine'ish** (also **fīn'ish**) somewhat fine. — *adv* **fine'ly**. — *n* **fine'ness** state, fact or degree of being fine; state of subdivision; (of gold or silver) number of parts in a thousand. — *n* **fin'er** a refiner. — *n* **fin'ery** splendour; showy adornments; a place where anything is fined or refined; a furnace for making iron malleable. — *n pl* **fines** material (ore, coal, etc) in a fine state of division, separated out by screening. — *n* **fīn'ing** the process of refining or purifying; a clarifying agent (often in *pl*; *winemaking*). — **fine art** or **arts** see under **art**; **fine chemicals** chemicals produced in small quantities *usu* of high purity, as opposed to **heavy chemicals**. — *vt* **fine'-draw** to draw or sew up so finely that no seam can be seen; to draw out finely or too finely. — *adj* **fine'-drawn**. — **fine gentleman** or **lady** an idle person, *usu* ostentatiously fashionable, sometimes refined; **fine metal** comparatively pure cuprous sulphide obtained from *coarse metal*. — *adj* **fine'-spoken** using fine phrases. — *adj* **fine'-spun** finely spun out; over-subtle. — **fine-tooth** (or **fine-toothed**) **comb** or **fine comb** a comb with slender teeth set close together. — *vt* **fine-tune'** to make delicate adjustments to. — **fine-tun'ing**; **fine writing** literary matter or style which is pretentiously ornate; **fīn'ing-pot** a vessel used in refining. — **cut it fine** to do something with little time or space to spare; **go over** or **through with a fine-tooth** (or **fine-toothed**) **comb** to investigate very thoroughly. [Fr *fin*, prob a back-formation from L *fīnītus* finished, pa p of *fīnīre* to finish, from *fīnis* an end]

fine[2] *fīn*, *n* an end or conclusion (*obs* except in the phrase *in fine*); a final settlement; a fictitious suit as a means of conveying property or barring an entail (*law*); a composition, or percentage accepted by a bankrupt's creditors, given by money payment; a fee paid on some particular occasion; a money penalty. — *vt* to bring to an end (*Shakesp*); to pledge or pawn (*Shakesp*); to impose a fine on; to punish by fine. — *adj* **fīn'able** liable to a fine. — *adj* **fine'less** (*Shakesp*) endless. — **foot of fine** see under **foot**. [L *fīnis* an end]

fine[3] *fēn*, *n* ordinary French brandy. — **fine Champagne** (*shã-pany'*) brandy distilled from wine made from grapes grown in the Charente area of France. [Fr]

fineer[1] *fi-nēr'*, an old form of **veneer** (*n* and *vt*).

fineer[2] *fi-nēr'*, (*obs*) *vi* to get goods on credit by fraud or deception. [Prob Du; cf **finance**]

Fine Gael *fē'nə gāl*, *n* (literally, Family of Gaels) a moderate political party of the Republic of Ireland.

fines herbes *fēn-zerb*, (*Fr*; *cookery*) *n pl* a mixture of herbs used as a garnish or, chopped, as a seasoning.

finesse *fi-nes'*, *n* subtlety of invention or design; sophisticated accomplishment; skill or expertise; an attempt by a player holding a higher card to take the trick with a lower card, risking loss (*bridge*). — *vt* and *vi* to play a finesse. — *vi* to use subtle intention of design. — *vt* to manage or administer with finesse, to manipulate subtly to a desired conclusion. — *n* **finess'er**. — *n* **finess'ing**. [Fr]

fingan *fin-gän'*, *n* a small coffee-cup without a handle, used with an ornamental holder called a zarf. — Also **finjan** (*-jän'*). [Egyptian *fingān*, Ar *finjān*.]

finger *fing'gər*, *n* one of the five terminal parts of the hand, or *usu* of the four other than the thumb; anything shaped like this; the part of a glove that covers such a part; the breadth of a person's finger, *esp* as a rough measure of alcoholic spirit poured into a glass; touch; agency (*esp* of God); share or interest; (in *pl*) grip or control. — *vt* to handle or perform with the fingers; to pilfer; to toy or meddle with; to make or indicate choice of fingers in performing (*music*); to indicate or identify a guilty person (*slang*). — *vi* to use or move the fingers. — *adj* **fing'ered** having fingers, or anything like fingers, or indication of fingering. — *n* **fing'ering** act or manner of touching with the fingers; the choice of fingers in playing a musical instrument; the written or printed indication of this. — *adj* **fing'erless** having no, or only rudimentary or short, fingers. — *n* **fing'erling** a very diminutive being or thing (*archaic*); a fish no bigger than a finger, *esp* a salmon parr or young trout less than a year old. — **fing'er-alphabet** an alphabet for the deaf or hard of hearing; **fing'er-and-toe'** a disease of turnips in which the taproot branches; another turnip disease, anbury; **fing'erboard** the part of a violin, etc against which the strings are stopped by the fingers; **fing'erbowl** or **fing'erglass** a bowl for water to clean the fingers at table; **fing'er-breadth** or **fing'ers-breadth** the breadth of a finger, a digit, as a unit of measurement (1·4 cm or $\frac{3}{4}$ of an inch); **finger buffet** a buffet consisting of **finger foods**, food (such as sandwiches) which may be eaten with the fingers as opposed to a knife and fork; **fing'er-end** or **fing'er's-end**; **fing'er-grass** a grass of the genus *Digitaria*, with fingerlike spikes; **fing'erguard** the crosspiece of a sword-handle; **fing'erhold** a grasp by the fingers; something by which the fingers can hold on (also *fig*); **fing'erhole** a hole in a wind instrument closed by the finger to modify the pitch. — *adv* or *adj* **fing'erlickin'** (*slang*) extremely (good). — **fing'ermark** a mark, *esp* a dirty one, made by a finger; **fing'ernail**; **fing'er-paint** a somewhat thick gelatinous paint used *esp* by children and applied with the hands and fingers rather than with a brush. — Also *vt*. — **fing'er-painting**; **fing'erplate** a plate to protect a door from dirty fingers; **fing'er-pointer** an accuser; **fing'er-pointing**; **fing'erpost** a post with a finger pointing the way to a destination; **fing'erprint** an impression of the ridges of the finger-tip, unique to each human being and used as a means of identification, *esp* of criminals; an accurate and unique identification feature or profile produced by chemical analysis, genetic analysis, etc (*fig*); the basic features (*fig*). — *vt* to take the fingerprints of (also *fig*). — **fing'erprinting** (also *fig*); **fing'erstall** a covering for protecting the finger; **fing'ertip**. — **a finger in the pie** a share in the doing of anything (often said of annoying meddling); **be all fingers and thumbs, have one's fingers all thumbs**, etc see under **thumb**; **burn one's fingers** or **get one's fingers burnt** see under **burn**; **cross one's fingers** see under **cross**; **get** or **pull the** (or **one's**) **finger out** (*colloq*) to start working hard or doing one's job properly or efficiently; **give someone** (or **get**) **the finger**

(*slang*) to make, or be the target of, an obscene gesture of contempt made by extending the middle finger vertically; **have at one's finger-ends**, **finger's-ends** or **fingertips** to be master of (a subject); **keep one's fingers crossed** see under **cross**; **lay** or **put a finger on** to touch; **not lift a finger** to take no action; **point the finger at** to call attention to in accusation; **put** or **lay one's finger on** to indicate, comprehend and express, or recall, precisely; **to one's fingertips** completely; in all respects; **twist**, **wind** or **wrap someone round one's little finger** to control someone completely, or influence someone to a great extent. [OE *finger*]

fingering[1] *fing'gər-ing*, *n* a woollen yarn of two or more strands, used in hand-knitting, *orig* and *esp* for stockings. [Perh Fr *fin grain* fine grain]

fingering[2]. See under **finger**.

fini *fē-nē*, (*Fr*) *adj* finished or completed; ruined or broken.

finial *fin'i-əl*, *n* a decoration on the top of a gable, spire, etc, often in the form of a spike or a bunch of leaves. [L *finis* end]

finical *fin'i-kl*, *adj* affectedly or excessively precise in unimportant matters; foppish. — *n* **finicality** (*-kal'i-ti*) the state of being finical; something finical. — *adv* **fin'ically**. — *n* **fin'icalness** or **fin'icking** fussiness and fastidiousness. — *adj* **finick'ety**, **fin'icking**, **fin'icky** or **fin'ikin** particular about unimportant matters; (**finicky**) (of a job) intricate, tricky, fiddly, requiring attention to small details, delicate manipulations, etc. [Prob connected with **fine**[1]]

fining. See under **fine**[1].

finis *fi'nis* or *fī'*, (*L*) *n* the end; the conclusion: — *pl* **finēs**.

finish *fin'ish*, *vt* to end; to complete the making of; to perfect; to give the last touches to; to complete the education of, *esp* for life in polite society; to complete the course of (a race); to put an end to or destroy. — Also *vi*. — *n* something which finishes or completes; the end of a race, hunt, etc; the last touch, elaboration or polish; the last coat of plaster or paint; (applied to cattle and sheep) the amount of flesh and fat on an animal. — *adj* **fin'ished** brought to an end or to completion; complete; consummate; perfect. — *n* **fin'isher** a person who finishes; a person who completes or perfects, *esp* in crafts. — *n* and *adj* **fin'ishing**. — **finishing post** the post marking the end of a race (*esp* for horses); **finishing school** an expensive establishment where some girls complete their education, with emphasis on social refinements, etc rather than academic achievement; **finishing touches** or **strokes** the last minor improvements needed to achieve perfection. — **finish up** to finish; to end up, be or become in the end. [Fr *finir*, *finissant*, from L *fīnīre* to end]

finite *fī'nīt*, *adj* having an end or limit; subject to limitations or conditions (opposed to *infinite*). — *adv* **fī'nītely**. — *n* **fī'nīteness** or **finitude** (*fin'i-tūd* or *fīn'*). — **finite verb** a verb limited by person, number, tense or mood, as opposed to an infinitive, gerund or participle. [L *fīnītus*, pa p of *fīnīre* to limit]

finjan. See **fingan**.

fink *fingk*, (*slang*) *n* a strike-breaker; an informer; loosely, an unpleasant person. — Also *vi* (often with *on*). [Origin uncertain]

finks. Same as **fenks**.

Finn *fin*, *n* a member of a people living in Finland and adjacent regions; more generally, a member of the group of peoples speaking Finnic languages. — *n* **Fin'lander** a native or citizen of Finland. — *n* **Finlandīzā'tion** or **-s-** in relations with the former Soviet Union, a policy of accommodation rather than confrontation. — *adj* **Finn'ic** of or relating to one of the two branches of the Finno-Ugrian family of languages, which includes Finnish, Estonian and Lapp, or to the peoples who speak these languages. — *adj* **Finn'ish** pertaining to the Finns, or to Finland, or its language. — *n* the Finno-Ugrian language of Finland. — *adj* **Finno-Ugrian** (*fin'ō-ū'gri-ən* or *-ōō'gri-ən*) or **Finno-Ugric** (*-grik*) belonging to the NW group of Ural-Altaic languages and peoples — Finnish, Estonian, Lapp, Cheremiss, Mordvin, Zyrian, Votyak, etc. — Also **U'gro-Finn'ic**. [OE *finnas* Finns]

Finn. *abbrev*: Finnish.

finnac or **finnack**. See **finnock**.

finnan *fin'ən* or (*obs*) **findram** *fin'rəm*, *n* a kind of smoked haddock, *prob* named from Findon, Kincardineshire, not from the Findhorn river. — Also **finnan** or **findon haddock** or **haddie**.

finnesko *fin'e-skō*, **finnsko** or **finsko** *fin'skō*, *n* a reindeer-skin boot with the hair on: — *pl* **finn'eskō**, etc. [Norw *finnsko*, from *Finn* Lapp, and *sko* shoe]

finnock, **finnack** or **finnac** *fin'ək*, *n* a young sea trout. [Gaelic *fionnag*, from *fionn* white]

fino *fē'nō*, *n* a dry sherry: — *pl* **fi'nos**. [Sp, fine or excellent]

finocchio, **finnochio** or **finochio** *fin-ok'i-ō*, *n* a dwarf variety of fennel, *Foeniculum* (*vulgare*) *dulce*, the leaf stalks of which are used in stews, salads, etc. — Also called **dwarf**, **Florence**, **French** or **sweet fennel**. [Ital, fennel]

finsko. See **finnesko**.

fiord or **fjord** *fyōrd* or *fyörd*, *n* a long, narrow, rock-bound inlet. [Norw *fjord*]

fiorin *fī'ə-rin*, *n* a variety of creeping bent-grass (*Agrostis stolonifera*). [Ir *fiorthán*]

fioritura *fyor-i-tōō'rə*, (*music*) *n* a florid embellishment: — *pl* **fioriture** (*-rā*). [Ital, flowering, from L *flōs*, *flōris*]

fippence *fip'əns*, (*colloq*) *n*. A shortened form of **fivepence**.

fipple *fip'l*, *n* the under-lip (*dialect*); (in wind instruments) the plug in the mouthpiece, often together with the sharp edge against which it directs the wind. — **fipp'le-flute** a flute with a fipple, a recorder or flageolet. [Cf ON *flipi* a horse's lip]

fir *fûr*, *n* the name of several conifers, *esp* of the genera *Abies* and *Picea*, resinous trees valuable for their timber. — *adj* **firr'y** having many firs; of fir. — **fir'-cone**; **fir'-tree**; **fir'-wood**. [OE *fyrh*; cf Ger *Föhre*]

fire *fīr*, *n* a substance formerly reckoned to be one of the four principal elements out of which all living things were made; the heat and light of burning; a mass of burning matter, such as fuel in a grate; flame or incandescence; a conflagration; the discharging of a firearm; fuel; a heating apparatus; heat or light from sources other than burning; lightning (*poetic*); volcanic or subterranean heat; great heat; the heat of fever or inflammation; glowing appearance; a sparkle of light; discharge of firearms (also *fig*); enthusiasm; ardour; passion; spirited vigour or animation; refraction of light in a gemstone. — *vt* to ignite; to cause to explode; to expose to heat; to bake (*pottery*); to cauterize (*farriery*); to fuel; to affect as if by fire; to discharge (a firearm); to send or direct (eg questions) forcefully or rapidly, as if from a firearm; to drive out; to dismiss (from employment, etc); to inflame; to animate; to rouse to passion of any kind. — *vi* to catch fire; to shoot with firearms; to become inflamed; to break out in anger; to make a fast, direct shot aimed merely at displacing an opponent's bowls (*bowls*); (of a car, engine, etc) to start. — *adj* **fired** affected, or having the appearance of having been affected, with fire; baked (*pottery*); ignited; kindled; discharged. — *adj* **fire'less**. — *n* **fir'er** a person who fires, in any sense. — *n* **fir'ing** ignition; discharge of guns, etc; simultaneous ringing of a peal of bells; fuelling; firewood; fuel; cautery; injury by overheating; subjection to heat. — **fire'-alarm** an apparatus for giving warning of fire; a warning of fire; **fire'arm** a weapon discharged by explosion (*usu* in *pl*); **fire'-arrow** a dart or arrow with an ignitable head; **fire'-back** a red-backed Sumatran pheasant; the back wall of a fireplace; an ornamental plate of iron placed there; **fire'ball** a burning meteor, a bolide; ball lightning; an incendiary or illuminating projectile; a flaming ball of burning gases; the luminous sphere of hot gases at the centre of a nuclear explosion; **fire'-balloon** a balloon carrying fire and raised by the heating and rarefaction of air; a balloon discharging fireworks in the air; **fire'-bar** a bar of a fire-grate; a heating element in an electric radiator; **fire'-basket** a portable firegrate, a brazier; **fire'-bird** the Baltimore oriole, or other bird of orange and red plumage; **fire blanket** a blanket of non-flammable material for extinguishing small fires; **fire'-blast** a blight of hops, due to a mite, giving a scorched appearance; **fire'-blight** a bacterial disease of fruit-trees, giving a scorched appearance; **fire'-bomb** an incendiary bomb. — Also *vt*. — **fire'-bombing**; **fire'-bote** (*hist*) a tenant's right to cut wood for fuel; **fire'box** a chamber for the fire in a steam engine, etc; **fire'brand** a burning piece of wood; an energetic person; a person who stirs up trouble; **fire'brat** a small insect found in bakehouses; **fire'-break** a strip of land kept clear to stop the spread of a fire (also *fig*); **fire'brick** a brick resistant to fire, used for furnace linings, grates, etc; **fire brigade** a body of fire-fighters; **fire bucket** a bucket containing sand or water for putting out fires; **fire'bug** (*colloq*) an arsonist; **fire'-clay** a clay poor in lime and iron, suitable for making fire-resistant pottery and firebricks; **fire'-control** a system of controlling the whole gunfire of a ship from one centre; **fire'cracker** a device for making a noise, a cylinder of paper or cardboard containing an explosive and a fuse; **fire'crest** or **fire-crested wren** a bird closely related to the goldcrest, a kinglet; **fire'damp** a combustible gas given off by coal, etc, chiefly methane; **fire'dog** an andiron; **fire door** a fire-resistant door to prevent the spread of fire within a building; an emergency exit; **fire'-drake** (*archaic*) a fire-breathing dragon; a luminous phenomenon; a kind of firework; **fire drill** a primitive instrument for making fire by twirling a stick; a practice in putting out or escaping from a fire; **fire'-eater** a juggler who seems to eat fire; a person who looks for quarrels; **fire'-edge** (*dialect*) a cutting edge hardened by fire; crispness in a newly baked cake; first eagerness; **fire engine** a vehicle which carries fire-fighters and equipment to put out fires; **fire escape** a fixed or movable way of escape from a burning building; **fire extinguisher** a portable device for spraying water, chemicals, foam, etc on to a fire to put it out. — *adj* **fire'-eyed** (*Shakesp*) having fiery eyes. — **fire'-fighter** a person whose job is the putting out of fires and the rescuing of people in danger; **fire'-fighting** the job of a fire-fighter; dealing with events as they arise, without long-term planning (*fig*); **fire'-flag** (*Coleridge*) and **fire'-flaught** (*Swinburne*) a flash of fire, lightning, etc; **fire'float** a boat or raft used in harbours for extinguishing fires; **fire'fly** any of various nocturnal insects which emit phosphorescent light; **fire'-grate** a grating to hold a fire; **fire'guard** a protective wire frame or railing in front of a fireplace; **fire'-hook** a hook formerly used to tear down burning buildings; **fire hose** a hose for extinguishing fires; **fire'house** (*obs*) a house with a fireplace, a dwelling-house; a fire station (*US*); **fire insurance** insurance against loss by fire; **fire'-irons** fireside implements, ie poker, tongs, shovel, not necessarily of iron; **fire'light** the light of a (*usu* domestic) fire; **fire'lighter** a piece of readily flammable material or other means of lighting a fire; **fire'lock** a gun discharged by a lock with flint and steel; **fire'man** a male fire-fighter; a stoker; a train driver's assistant (stoker on a steam railway engine); a person who looks after safety conditions in a mine; a person who explodes charges; a reporter sent out (*esp* abroad) to cover a specific event; **fireman's lift** a method of carrying someone by putting them face down over one's shoulder, *esp* used by fire-fighters in rescuing unconscious or injured people; **fire'mark** a metal plate formerly placed by insurance companies to mark an insured building; **fire'-marshal** (*US*) or **fire'-master** the head of a fire brigade. — *adj* **fire'-new** fresh from the fire; brand-new. — **fire'-office** a fire insurance office; **fire'-opal** a flame-coloured variety of opal; **fire'pan** a metal vessel for holding fire; **fire'place** the place for a domestic fire, the chimney-opening and surrounding area; **fire'-plough** (*US* **fire-plow**; *archaeol*) a stick rubbed in a wooden groove to make fire; **fire'-plug** a hydrant for use against fires; **fire'-policy** a written document of insurance against fire; **fire'pot** (*hist*) an earthen pot full of combustible material, used as a missile; **fire'-power** the amount of ammunition that can be fired with effect in a given time (*military*); the total offensive power or materials of a fighting force or any one of its machines or units (*military*); the total weight of influence, argument, etc of an individual, organization, etc (*fig*). — *adj* **fire'proof** rendered completely immune to the effects of fire; incombustible. — *vt* to make fireproof. — **fire'proofing**; **fire'-raiser** an arsonist; **fire'-raising** arson. — *adj* **fire'-resistant** or **fire'-resisting** immune to the effects of fire up to a required degree. — **fire'-risk** something which is likely to cause a fire, or to be consumed if there is one. — *adj* **fire'-robed** (*Shakesp*) robed in fire. — **fire sale** a sale of goods damaged by fire; any quick sale of goods at cheap bargain prices (*US*; *usu fig*); **fire'screen** a screen for intercepting the heat of a fire; **fire'ship** (*hist*) a ship carrying combustible materials sent among the enemy's ships; **fire'-shovel**; **fire'side** the side of the fireplace; the hearth; home. — *adj* domestic; familiar. — **fire station** a place where fire engines, fire-fighters, etc are kept in readiness to attend fires; **fire'-step** or **fir'ing-step** (*hist*) a ledge on which soldiers stand to fire over a parapet, a banquette; **fire'-stick** a primitive implement for making fire by friction; **fire'stone** a rock, *esp* sandstone, that can withstand great heat; **fire'-storm** a huge blaze (*esp* a result of heavy bombing) which fans its own flames by creating its own draught (also *fig*); **fire'thorn** (*bot*) pyracantha; **fire'-trap** a building, etc inadequately provided with fire exits and fire escapes; **fire'-tube** a tube through which fire passes, eg in a steam railway engine; **fire'-walk** or **fire'-walking** the (religious) ceremony of walking barefoot over hot stones, ashes, etc; **fire'-walker**; **fire'-warden** (*NAm*) an official responsible for the prevention and extinction of fires; **fire'-watcher** a person who watches out for fires resulting from bombing or in eg forested areas; **fire'-watching**; **fire'-water** (*humorous*) strong alcoholic spirits; **fire'weed** the rose-bay willow-herb, which springs up after forest, etc fires; **fire'woman** a female fire-fighter; **fire'wood** wood for fuel; **fire'work** a combustible or explosive mixture used in warfare, or a projectile carrying it (*obs*); a device containing combustible chemicals, for producing coloured sparks, flares, etc, often with loud noises; (*now* only in *pl*) a display of these; (in *pl*) an impressive technical display in music, talk, etc; (in *pl*) a display of temper; **fire'worm** a glow-worm; a firefly; **fire'-worship** worship of fire; loosely, homage to fire (as among Parsees) as a symbol of deity but not itself a god; **fire'-worshipper**; **firing line** an area, or the troops, within range of the enemy for practical purposes; a position of exposure to fierce criticism, etc, *esp* in the phrase *in the firing line*; **firing order** (*autos*) the sequence in which the cylinders of a multi-cylinder combustion engine fire; **firing party** a detachment detailed to fire over a grave or shoot a condemned prisoner; **firing pin** a pin that strikes the detonator and explodes the cartridge in a rifle; **firing point** the temperature at which a flammable oil catches fire spontaneously; **firing squad** a firing party, a detachment detailed to shoot a condemned prisoner. — **catch** or **take fire** to become ignited; to become aroused about something; **fire and brimstone** hell, formerly an exclamation of wrath or extreme irritation; a priest's evocation of eternal damnation (*adj* **fire'-and-brim'stone**); **fire and sword** military devastation; **fire away** (*usu imperative*; *colloq*) to go ahead; to begin; **fire in one's belly** ardour or passion in speaking, etc; drive or ambition; **fire off** to discharge; to ask or utter in rapid succession; **fire out** (*Shakesp*) to expel; **fire up** to start a fire; to fly into a passion; **go on fire** (*Scot* or *Ir*) to catch fire; **go through fire and water** see under **go**; **hang fire** see under **hang**; **on fire** in a state of fiery combustion; **play with fire** to expose oneself to unnecessary risk; to treat lightly a situation which could prove dangerous; **St Anthony's fire** see under **Anthony**; **St Elmo's fire** see under **Saint**; **set on fire** or **set fire to** to ignite; **under fire** exposed to the enemy's fire; exposed to criticism. [OE *fȳr*; Ger *Feuer*; Gr *pȳr*]

firk *fûrk*, (*obs*) *vt* to drive; to rouse; to whip or beat (*Shakesp*). [OE *fercian* to conduct]

firkin *fûr'kin*, *n* a measure equal to one-quarter of a barrel (*brewing*); 9 gallons (*brewing*); 56 lb of butter. [With dimin sfx *-kin*, from ODu *vierde* fourth]

firlot *fûr'lət*, *n* an old Scottish dry measure, one-quarter of a boll. [Earlier *ferthelot*; cf ON *fiōrthe hlotr* fourth lot]

firm[1] *fûrm*, *adj* fixed; compact; strong; not easily moved or disturbed; unshaken; resolute; decided; (of prices, commodities, markets, etc) steady or stable (*commerce*). — Also *adv*. — *vt* to make firm. — *vi* to become firm; to become stable or rise slightly (*commerce*). — *adj* (*obs*) **firm'less** wavering. — *adv* **firm'ly**. — *n* **firm'ness**. — **firm'ware** (*comput*) a set of software or similar instructions forming a more or less permanent and unerasable part of a computer's memory. — **firm down** to make (ground, etc) firm or firmer; **firm up** (of prices, etc) to firm (*commerce*); to make (a promise, etc) firm or firmer. [OFr *ferme*, from L *firmus*]

firm[2] *fûrm*, *n* a business house or partnership, a company. [Ital *firma*, from L *firmus*; see **farm**]

firmament *fûr'mə-mənt*, *n* the solid sphere in which the stars were formerly thought to be fixed; the sky. — *adj* **firmamental** (*-ment'l*). [L *firmāmentum*, from *firmus* firm]

firman *fûrm'man*, *fer-män'*, *n* a decree or judicial decison. [Pers *fermān*]

firmer *fûr'mər* or **firmer chisel** *chiz'l*, *n* a carpenter's or woodworker's wood-cutting chisel. [Fr *fermoir*, an alteration of *formoir*, from *former* to form]

firn *firn* or *fûrn*, *n* snow on high glaciers while still granular. [Ger *firn* of last year; cf obs Eng *fern* former]

firring. Same as **furring** under **fur**[1].

first *fûrst*, *adj* foremost; in front of or before all others; most eminent; chief; referring to the speaker or writer (*gram*). — *n* a person or thing that is first or of the first class; a place in the first class; an academic degree of the first class; first gear. — *adv* before anything or anyone else; for the first time. — *n* **first'ling** (*rare*) the first produce or offspring, *esp* of animals. — *adv* **first'ly** in the first place. — **first-aid'** treatment of a wounded or sick person before the doctor's arrival; **first-aid'er**. — *adj* **first-attack'** same as **first-strike**. — *adj* **first'-begotten** born first; eldest. — *adj* **first'-born** born first. — *n* the first in order of birth; the eldest child. — *adj* **first'-class'** of the first class, rank or quality. — **first-class mail** or **post** mail sent at a dearer rate to obtain quicker delivery; **first'-day** (*obs*) Sunday; **first-day cover** an envelope with stamps postmarked on their first day of issue; **first degree burn** and **first degree murder** see under **degree**; **first floor** (*adj* **first'-floor**) see under **floor**; **first'-foot'** (*Scot*) the first person to enter a house after the beginning of the new year. — *vt* to visit as first-foot. — *vi* to go around making visits as first-foot. — **first'-foot'er**; **first'-fruit'** or **first-fruits'** the fruits first gathered in a season; first products or effects of anything; payment in the form of first crops of a season, or annates, to a superior; **first gear** see under **gear**. — *adj* **first-genera'tion** (*comput*) of the early type of calculating and computing machine, using thermionic valves. — *adj* **first'-hand** obtained directly, or in order to obtain (information, etc) directly, without an intermediary. — *adv* **first-hand'**. — **first lady** the wife of the chief executive of a city, state or country, *esp* of the president of the USA, or any woman chosen by him to carry out official duties as hostess, etc (*US*; often with *caps*); a prominent or leading woman in any field, profession, etc; **first lieutenant** (in the Royal Navy) the executive officer, not necessarily a lieutenant, of a ship or naval establishment; **first light** the time when daylight first appears in the morning; **first name** a Christian name, or the name that comes first in a full name; **first night** the first public performance of a theatrical production; **first-night'er** a person who habitually goes to the theatre on first nights; **first offend'er** a person convicted for the first time. — *adj* **first'-past'-the-post'** denoting or relating to a system of voting in which each voter casts only one non-transferable vote, the candidate receiving the most votes being declared the winner. — **first person** (*gram*) the writer or speaker (*adj* **first'-person**). — *adj* **first'-rate** of highest rank or excellence; pre-eminent in quality, size or estimation. — *n* a warship so rated. — *adv* **first-rate'** excellently. — **first refusal** the chance to buy (*esp* property) before it is offered to others; **first school** a school for children aged five to eight, nine or ten; **first strike** a pre-emptive attack on an enemy, intended to destroy their nuclear weapons before they can be brought into use (*adj* **first'-strike**). — *adj* **first'-time** immediate; carrying out an action, eg the purchase of a house, for the first time. — **first water** the first or highest quality, or purest lustre, of diamonds and pearls (also *fig*); **First World** the richest and most technologically developed countries of the world; **first year allowance** an amount of capital expenditure which can be set against tax in the accounts pertaining to the actual year of spending. — **at first** at the beginning, in the early stages, etc; **first thing** before doing anything else; **not know the first thing about** to know nothing about. [OE *fyrst*, superl; cf *fore* before]

firth[1] *fûrth*, *n* an arm of the sea, *esp* a river-mouth. — Also **frith** (*frith*). [ON *fiörthr*; Norw *fjord*]

firth[2]. See **frith**[3].

FIS *abbrev*: Family Income Supplement; *Fédération Internationale de Ski* (Fr), International Ski Federation.

FISA *fē'sə*, *abbrev*: *Fédération Internationale de Sport Automobile* (Fr), International Automobile Sports Federation; Finance Industry Standards Association.

fisc or **fisk** *fisk*, (*obs*) *n* the state treasury; the public revenue; one's purse. [Ety as for **fiscal**]

fiscal *fis'kəl*, *adj* pertaining to the public treasury or revenue. — *n* a treasurer (*obs*); a public prosecutor, chief law officer of the crown under the Holy Roman Empire (*hist*); (in Scotland) an officer who prosecutes in criminal cases in local and inferior courts (in full, **procurator-fiscal**). — *adv* **fis'cally**. — **fiscal drag** the means by which the inland revenue automatically benefits from any increase in earned income without any actual increase in taxation rates; **fiscal year** (*esp US*) a financial year. — **the fiscal question** free trade or protection. [L *fiscus* a basket or purse]

fisgig. See **fizgig**.

fish[1] *fish*, *n* a vertebrate that lives in water and breathes through gills; loosely, any exclusively aquatic animal; the flesh of fish as food; a person, as in *a queer fish*; a fish-dive: — *pl* **fish** or **fish'es**. — *vi* to catch or try to catch or obtain fish, or anything that may be likened to a fish (such as seals, sponges, coral, compliments, information or husbands; often with *for*); to serve the purpose of fishing. — *vt* to catch and bring out of water; to bring up or out from a deep or hidden place, obscurity, etc; to elicit (with *out*); to practise the fisherman's craft in; to ransack; to hoist the flukes of (*naut*). — *adj* **fish'able**. — *n* **fish'er** a fisherman (now *rare*); an inappropriate name for the pekan or wood-shock, a type of marten. — *n* **fish'ery** the business of catching fish; a place for catching fish; a place where fish are reared for sale; a right of fishing. — *adj* **fish'ful** (*obs*) containing many fish. — *vt* **fish'ify** (*Shakesp*) to turn into fish, or make fish-like. — *n* **fish'iness**. — *adj* **fish'ing** used in fishing. — *n* the art or practice of catching fish; a fishing-ground or stretch of water where one fishes. — *adj* **fish'y** consisting of fish; like a fish; containing many fish; dubious, as of a story; equivocal, unsafe. — **fish'ball** see **fish cake**. — *adj* **fish'-bell'ied** swelled out downwards like the belly of a fish.

— **fish'-bone**; **fish'burger** a flat cake, similar to a hamburger, made of minced fish; **fish cake** or **fish'ball** a ball or cake of chopped fish and mashed potatoes, fried; **fish'-carv'er** or **fish'-trowel** a large flat implement for carving fish at table; **fish'-creel** an angler's basket; a fishwife's basket; **fish'-day** a day on which fish is eaten rather than meat; **fish'-dive** (*slang*) a ballerina's leap on to a partner's outstretched arms; **fish eagle** any of various fish-eating eagles, *Haliaetus vocifer*, of central and southern Africa; **fish eaters** (*rare*) a knife and fork for eating fish with; **fish'erman** a person who fishes for sport or as a business; **fisherman's luck** getting wet and catching no fish; **fisherman's ring** a signet ring, with the device of St Peter fishing, used in signing papal briefs; **fish'eye** (*slang*) an unfriendly, suspicious stare; **fish'eye lens** (*photog*) an ultra-wide-angle lens covering up to 180°; **fish'-fag** (*archaic*) a woman who sells fish; **fish'-farm**; **fish'-farmer**; **fish'-farming** rearing fish in ponds or tanks, for sale; **fish'-fing'er** a fairly small oblong cake of fish coated in batter or breadcrumbs; **fish'-garth** an enclosure on a river for the preserving or taking of fish (also **fish'-weir**); **fish'-glue** isinglass, or any other glue made from the skins, air-bladders, etc of fish; **fish'-god** a deity wholly or partly like a fish in form, like the Philistine Dagon; **fish'-guano** fish-manure; **fish'-guts**; **fish'-gutter**; **fish'-gutting**; **fish'-hatchery** a place for the artificial rearing of fish; **fish'-hawk** an osprey; **fish'-hook** a barbed hook for catching fish; **fish'ing-frog** the devil-fish; **fish'ing-ground** an area of water, *esp* of the sea, where fish are caught; **fish'ing-line** (a) fine strong *usu* nylon filament used (eg with a rod, hooks, etc) to catch fish; **fish'ing-rod** a long slender rod to which a line is fastened for angling; **fish'ing-tack'le** tackle — nets, lines, etc — used in fishing; **fish'-kett'le** a long oval dish for boiling or poaching fish; **fish'-knife** a knife with a broad, blunt-edged, *usu* decorated blade for eating fish with; a broad-bladed knife for cutting and serving fish with; **fish'-ladd'er** or (*NAm*) **fish'-way** an arrangement of steps and shelters for enabling fish to ascend a waterfall, etc; **fish'-louse** a copepod or other crustacean which is a parasite on fishes; **fish'-manure'** fish used as a fertilizer; **fish'-meal** dried fish, ground to meal; a meal of fish (*Shakesp*); an abstemious, sparing diet; **fish'monger** a dealer in fish. — *adj* **fish'-net** woven as a fine net. — **fish'-oil** oil obtained from fish and other marine animals; **fish'-packing**; **fish'-pond** a pond in which fish are kept (formerly also **fish'-stew**); **fish'-salesman** a person who receives consignments of fish for sale by auction to retail dealers; **fish'-scrap** fish or fishskins from which oil or glue has been extracted; **fish'skin** the skin of a fish; (also **fishskin disease**) ichthyosis; **fish'-slice** a flat implement for carving fish at table; a broad, flat implement for turning fish, etc in the frying-pan; **fish'-spear** a spear or dart for catching fish; **fish'-stew** (*obs*) a fish-pond; **fish stick** (*US*) a fish-finger; **fish'-strainer** a metal colander for taking fish from a boiler. — *adj* **fish'-tail** shaped like the tail of a fish. — *vi* to swing the tail of an aircraft from side to side to reduce speed while gliding downward; (of the back of a vehicle) to swing or skid from side to side; **fish-torpē'do** a self-propelling torpedo; **fish'-way** (*NAm*) a fish-ladder; **fish'-weir** a fish-garth; **fish'wife** or **fish'-woman** a woman who carries fish about for sale; a coarse, loud-mouthed woman; **fish'yback** (*US*) transportation of freight containers and trailers by ship or barge. — **a fish out of water** a person in an unaccustomed, unsuitable situation which makes him or her ill at ease; **big fish** (*slang*) an important or leading person; **drink like a fish** to drink (*usu* alcohol) to excess; **fish in troubled waters** to take advantage of disturbed times to further one's own interests; **have other fish to fry** to have something else to do or attend to; **make fish of one and flesh (or fowl) of another** to make offensive distinctions; **neither fish nor flesh (nor good red herring)** or **neither fish, flesh, nor fowl** neither one thing nor another; **odd fish** or **queer fish** a person of odd habits, or of a nature with which one is not in sympathy; **pretty kettle of fish** see under **kettle**. [OE *fisc*; Ger *Fisch*; ON *fiskr*; L *piscis*; Gaelic *iasg*]

fish[2] *fish, n* a piece of wood placed alongside another to strengthen it (*naut*); a counter in various games. — *vt* to strengthen with a fish or fish-plate. — **fish'-joint** a place where things are joined by fish-plates; **fish'-plate** an iron plate used in pairs to join railway rails. [Prob Fr *fiche* peg or mark]

fishgig. See **fizgig**.

fisk[1] *fisk*, (*obs*) *vi* to frisk; to gad about. [Prob a frequentative of OE *fȳsan* to hurry, or of *fȳsian* to feeze]

fisk[2]. See **fisc**.

fisnomie *fiz'no-mi*, (*Shakesp*) *n* physiognomy.

fissicostate *fi-si-kos'tāt, adj* having divided ribs. [L *fissus*, from *findere* to cleave, and *costa* rib]

fissile *fis'īl* or *-il, adj* readily split; capable of nuclear fission. — *n* **fissility** (*-il'*) ability to be split. [**fissure**]

fissilingual *fi-si-ling'gwəl, adj* with cloven tongue. [L *fissus*, from *findere* to cleave, and *lingua* tongue]

fission *fish'ən, n* a cleaving; reproduction by dividing; the splitting of the nucleus of an atom into two roughly equal parts accompanied by enormous release of energy. — *adj* **fiss'ionable** capable of nuclear fission. — *adj* **fiss'ive**. — **fission bomb** a bomb deriving its energy from nuclear fission; **fission fungus** a bacterium; **fission reactor** a reactor in which nuclear fission takes place; **fission spectrum** the wide range of elements and isotopes formed in fission. [**fissure**]

fissiparous *fi-sip'ə-rəs, adj* reproducing by fission. — *n* **fissip'arism**, **fissipar'ity** or **fissip'arousness**. — *adv* **fissip'arously**. [L *fissus*, from *findere* to cleave, and *parere* to bring forth]

fissiped *fi-si-ped'* or **fissipede** *-pēd', adj* with digits separate. — *n* an animal with digits separate. [L *fissus*, from *findere* to cleave, and *pēs*, *pedis* foot]

fissirostral *fi-si-ros'trəl, adj* with deep-cleft or gaping beak. [L *fissus*, from *findere* to cleave, and *rōstrum* beak]

fissle *fis'l*, (*Scot*) *vi* to rustle. [Imit]

fissure *fish'ər, n* an act of cleaving; a narrow opening, a chasm, cleft or groove; a sulcus, *esp* one of the furrows on the surface of the brain, such as the longitudinal fissure separating the hemispheres; a small abnormal crack in the mucous membrane. — *vt* to crack, cleave or divide. — *adj* **fiss'ured** cleft or divided. [L *findere*, *fissum* to cleave]

fist *fist, n* the closed or clenched hand; handwriting (*colloq*); an index (*printing*). — *vt* to strike or grip with the fist. — *n* **fist'ful** a handful. — *n pl* **fistiana** (*-ä'nə, -ā'nə; facetious*) anecdotes about boxing and boxers. — *adj* **fist'ic** or **fist'ical** (*facetious*) pugilistic. — *adj* **fist'y**. — **fist'icuff** a blow with the fist; (in *pl*; often *facetious*) boxing; (in *pl*; often *facetious*) a fight with fists; **fist'-law** the law of brute force; **fist'mele** (*-mēl*; **meal**[1] in sense of *measure*; *hist*) the breadth of a fist with the thumb extended, *esp* as used as the measure of the correct distance between the string and the handle of a braced bow. — **make a good, a reasonable, not a bad** etc, **fist of** to do (something) fairly well, not badly, etc. [OE *fȳst*; Ger *Faust*]

fistula *fist'ū-lə, n* a narrow passage or duct; an artificially made opening (*med*); a long narrow pipe-like ulcer (*pathol*); a tube through which the wine of the eucharist was once sucked from the chalice (also **calamus**): — *pl* **fist'ulae** (*-lē*) or **fist'ulas**. — *adj* **fist'ūlar**, **fist'ūlose** or **fist'ūlous**. [L *fistula* a pipe]

fit[1] *fit, adj* suitable; in suitable condition; meeting required standards; of suitable ability; convenient; befitting, appropriate; well trained and ready; in good condition; in good health; having a high level, or the required level, of stamina, suppleness or other athletic strength. — *n* success in fitting; adjustment and correspondence in shape and size; a thing (*esp* a garment) that fits. — *vt* to make suitable or able; to alter or make so as to be in adjustment; to adjust; to piece together; to be suitable or becoming for; to be of such size and shape as to adjust closely to; to be in agreement or correspondence with; to furnish or supply; to drive by fits (*Shakesp*). — *vi* to be suitable or becoming; to go into place with accurate adjustment to space; to be of such size and shape as to be able to do so: — *pr p* **fitt'ing**; *pa t* and *pa p* **fitt'ed**. — *adv* **fit'ly** (*compar* **fit'lier**; *superl* **fit'liest**). — *n* **fit'ment** a due (*Shakesp*); something fitted to an end (*Shakesp*); an article of furniture or equipment; a fitting. — *n* **fit'ness** the state of being suitable or (*esp* referring to health) fit; the average contribution of one allele or genohype to the next generation, compared with that of other alleles or genohypes (cf **Darwinian** and **inclusive fitness** below). — *adj* **fitt'ed** (of a cover, clothing, etc) made, cut, sewn, etc to fit exactly; (of a cupboard, etc) constructed to fit a particular space and attached to, or built into, the wall of a room; (of a room) fully furnished with (matching) fitted cupboards, etc. — *n* **fitt'er** a person or thing that fits or makes fit; a person who fits on clothes; a person who assembles or repairs the parts of a machine, etc. — *adj* **fitt'ing** fit; appropriate. — *n* anything used in fitting up, *esp* (in *pl*) equipment accessories; a fixture; a device used for supporting or containing a lamp, together with its holder and its shade or reflector (*elec eng*); the work of a fitter; the act or time of trying on an article of clothing so that it can be adjusted to fit the wearer. — *adv* **fitt'ingly**. — **fit'-out** (*obs*) outfit; **fitt'ing-out** a supply of things fit and necessary; **fitting-out basin** or **dock** a dock where a ship is completed after launching: **fitt'ing-shop** a shop in which pieces of machinery are fitted together; **fit'-up** temporary, improvised stage and properties (*theat*); a frame-up or false criminal charge, *esp* by the police (*slang*). — **Darwinian fitness** the number of offspring of an individual that live to reproduce in the next generation; **fit in** to find enough room or time for (someone or something); to be, or cause to be, in harmony (with); **fit on** to try on; to try on a garment on (a person); **fit out** to provide or equip; **fit up** to provide with fittings; to frame (*slang*); **inclusive fitness** Darwinian fitness, with the addition of those genes that the individual shares with its relatives and are passed on by them. [Origin obscure]

fit[2] *fit*, *n* a crisis (*obs*); the approach of death (*Spenser*); a painful experience (*Spenser*); an attack of illness, *esp* epilepsy; a convulsion or paroxysm; a temporary attack or outburst of anything, eg laughter; a sudden effort or motion; a mood or passing humour. — *vt* (*Shakesp*) to wrench or cause to start with a sudden movement. — *adj* **fit'ful** marked by sudden impulses; unpredictably intermittent; spasmodic. — *adv* **fit'fully**. — *n* **fit'fulness**. — **fit of the face** (*obs*) a grimace; **fits and starts** spasmodic and irregular bursts of activity; **throw a fit** see under **throw**[1]. [OE *fitt* a struggle]

fit[3] *fit*, (*archaic*) *n* a song; a division of a poem, a canto; a strain of music. — Also **fitt**, **fitte** or **fytte**. [OE *fitt* a song]

FITA *fē'tə*, *abbrev*: *Fédération Internationale de Tir à l'Arc* (*Fr*), International Archery Federation.

fitch[1] *fich*, *n* vetch; in Isaiah 28.25, black cumin (*Nigella sativa*); in Ezekiel 4.9, a species of wheat, spelt. [**vetch**]

fitch[2] *fich*, *n* a polecat; polecat fur; a paint-brush of polecat hair; a small hog's-hair brush. — *n* **fitch'et** or **fitchew** (*fich'ōō*) the polecat or its fur. [MDu *visse* and OFr *fissle*, *fissau*, from the root of Du *visse* nasty]

fitché or **fitchée** *fich'ā*, (*heraldry*) *adj* cut to a point. — Also **fitch'y**. [Fr *fiché*, pa p of *ficher* to fix]

fitt and **fitte**. See **fit**[3].

fitz- *fits-*, *pfx* son of; used in England, *esp* of the illegitimate sons of kings and princes, as in *Fitzclarence*, etc. [Anglo-Fr *fiz* (Fr *fils*), from L *filius*]

five *fīv*, *n* four and one; a symbol (5, v, etc) representing that number; a group of five; a score of five points, strokes, etc; a card with five pips; an article of the size so numbered; the fifth hour after midnight or midday; the age of five years. — *adj* of the number five; five years old. — *adj* and *adv* **five'fold** in five divisions: five times as much; folded in five thicknesses. — *n* **fiv'er** (*colloq*) a five-pound note; a five-dollar note (*US*). — **Five Articles** or **Five Points** statements of the distinctive doctrines of the Arminians and Calvinists respectively, the former promulgated in 1610, the latter sustained by the Synod of Dort in 1619 (see **Calvinism**); **five'-a-side'** a form of association football with five players on each side, instead of eleven. — Also *adj*. — *adj* **five'-bar** (of a gate) having five bars. — **five-day week** a week, five days of which are working days; **five-eighth'** (*Rugby football*) a stand-off; **second five-eighth** an inside centre, a player positioned on the outside of the five-eighth (*Austr* and *NZ*); **five'finger** or **five'fingers** a name for various plants (cinquefoil, oxlip, etc); a starfish. — *adj* **five'-finger** (of eg a piano exercise) for five fingers. — **Five Nations** (*hist*) a confederacy of five northern Iroquoian peoples; **five-o'clock shadow** (*colloq*) the new growth of hair that becomes noticeable on a man's shaven face in the late afternoon. — *adj* **five'-parted** in five parts; divided into five nearly to the base (*bot*). — **five'pence**, **fivepence piece** or **fivepenny piece** in Britain, a coin worth 5 pence (also **five'penny-piece'**). — *adj* **five'penny**. — **five'pins** a game with five 'pins', resembling ninepins and tenpins (*adj* **five'pin** as in *fivepin bowling alley*); **fives'-and-threes'** a variety of the game of dominoes. — *adj* **five'-square** (*Bible*) regularly pentagonal. — **five'-stones** the game of dibs or jacks played with five stones. — **bunch of fives** (*slang*) the fist; **give someone five** (*slang*) to shake hands, or slap hands above one's head (**high five**) with someone in congratulation or greeting; **Rugby fives** see under **Rugby**. [OE *fīf*; Ger *fünf*; Gothic *fimf*; Welsh *pump*; L *quinque*; Gr *pente*, *pempe*; Sans *pañca*]

fives[1] *fīvz*, (*Shakesp*) *n*. Same as **vives**.

fives[2] *fīvz*, *n pl* a ball game played with the (gloved) hand (or a bat) in a walled court. [Origin obscure]

fix *fiks*, *vt* to make firm or fast; to establish; to drive in; to settle; to make or keep permanent, solid, rigid, steady or motionless; to fasten or attach; to put to rights or mend; to arrange or attend to (a matter, sometimes by means of trickery); to prepare; to prevent from causing further trouble (*slang*); to get even with (*slang*); to chastise (*slang*). — *vi* to settle or remain permanently; to become firm, stable or permanent. — *n* a difficulty (*colloq*); a dilemma (*colloq*); the position of an aircraft, a ship, etc as calculated from instrument readings; the establishment of a position by any means; a shot of heroin or other drug (*slang*); a dose or experience of anything seen as or felt to be addictive (*colloq*); something fraudulently or covertly arranged (*colloq*). — *adj* **fix'able** capable of being fixed. — *vt* **fix'āte** to fix or make stable; to direct (the eyes) on an object; to arrest the emotional development of (*psychol*); to preoccupy. — *n* **fixā'tion** the act of fixing or state of being fixed; steadiness, firmness; a state in which a body does not evaporate; conversion of atmospheric nitrogen into a combined form; emotional arrest of personality, instinctive forces maintaining their earlier channels of gratification; loosely, an abnormal attachment or an obsession. — *n* **fix'ative** (*esp photog*) a fixing agent. — *n* **fix'ature** a gummy preparation for fixing the hair. — *adj* **fixed** settled; not apt to evaporate; steadily directed; fast, lasting, permanent; not varying or subject to alteration; used substantively for fixed stars (*Milton*). — *adv* **fix'edly**. — *n* **fix'edness**. — *n* **fix'er**. — *n* **fix'ing** the act or process of making fixed; arrangement; the process of removing unreduced silver halides after development of an emulsion (*image technol*); (in *pl*) adjuncts or trimmings; (in *pl*) equipment. — *n* **fix'ity** fixedness. — *adj* **fix'ive**. — *n* **fix'ture** fixing; a movable thing that has become fastened to land or to a house; a fixed article of furniture; a thing or person permanently established in a place; a fixed or appointed time or event, such as a horse-race. — *n* **fix'ure** (*Shakesp*) stability, position or firmness. — **fixed air** the name given by Dr Joseph Black in 1756 to what in 1784 was named by Lavoisier carbonic acid; **fixed assets** (*commerce*) buildings and plant, as opposed to consumables; **fixed capital** see under **capital**[1]; **fixed charges** overheads such as interest payments, allowance for depreciation, and fixed costs, which do not vary with the volume of business done; **fixed costs** overheads such as rent and rates which do not vary with the volume of business done; **fixed idea** a monomania; **fixed income** one which does not increase or decrease, such as income from a fixed-interest investment. — *adj* **fixed-in'terest** having an invariable rate of interest. — **fixed odds** a betting method whereby a stated amount per unit stake is offered for a certain result or combination of results; **fixed oils** those which, on the application of heat, do not volatilize without decomposition. — *adj* **fixed-pen'alty** of or relating to an offence, such as illegal parking, the penalty for which is invariable and obligatory, eg a fine which may be imposed and paid without the offender appearing in court. — *adj* **fixed'-price** (of a menu, contract, etc) having a price that cannot be varied. — **fixed satellite** a geostationary satellite; **fixed stars** stars which appear always to occupy the same position in the heavens, as opposed to *planets*; **fixed-wheel bicycle** a bicycle in which the pedals are so connected to the back wheel that free-wheeling is impossible, and on which only the front wheel has a conventional brake; **fixed-wing aircraft** an aircraft in which the wings are attached to the fuselage, as opposed to eg a helicopter with rotating 'wings' or propellers. — **fix on** to single out or decide upon; **fix up** to arrange or make arrangements for; to settle; to put to rights or attend to. [L *fīgere*, *fīxus* to fix, prob through LL *fīxāre*]

fizgig or **fisgig** *fiz'gig*, *n* a giddy or flirtatious girl; a firework of damp powder; a gimcrack, whimsy or trifle; a harpoon (also **fish'gig**); (**fiz'gig**; also **fizz'gig**) a police informer (*Austr slang*). [**gig**]

fizz or **fiz** *fiz*, *vi* to make a hissing or sputtering sound; to produce bubbles; (also **be fizzing**) to be very angry (*colloq*): — *pr p* **fizz'ing**; *pa t* and *pa p* **fizzed**. — *n* a sputtering sound; bubbly quality; a frothy drink, *esp* champagne. — *n* **fizz'er** something which fizzes; anything excellent (*colloq*); a very fast ball in cricket. — *n* and *adj* **fizz'ing**. — *vi* **fizz'le** to hiss or sputter; to go out with a sputtering sound (often with *out*); to come to nothing, be a fiasco or fail (often with *out*). — *n* an abortive effort. — *adj* **fizz'y**. [Formed from the sound]

fizzen and **fizzenless**. See **foison**.

FJI *abbrev*: Fellow of the Institute of Journalists; Fiji (IVR).

fjord. Same as **fiord**.

FL *abbrev*: Florida (US state); Liechtenstein (IVR).

fl. *abbrev*: florin; *floruit* (*L*), flourished.

Fla. *abbrev*: Florida (US state).

flabbergast *flab'ər-gäst*, (*colloq*) *vt* to stun or confound. [Prob connected with **flabby** and **gast**, to astonish]

flabby *flab'i*, *adj* soft or yielding, eg of muscles; (of people) having flabby muscles or flesh; overweight; hanging loose. — *n* **flab** (*colloq*) excess body fat. — *adv* **flabb'ily**. — *n* **flabb'iness**. [**flap**]

flabellum *flə-bel'əm*, *n* a fan, traditionally used to drive away flies from the chalice during the celebration of the eucharist; a fan-like structure (*biol*). — *adj* **flabell'ate** fan-shaped. — *n* **flabellation** (*flab-ə-lā'shən*) the action of fanning. — *adj* **flabell'iform**. [L, a fan]

flaccid *fla'sid* or *flak'sid*, *adj* limp; flabby; lax; easily yielding to pressure; soft and weak. — *adv* **flac'cidly**. — *n* **flac'cidness** or **flaccid'ity**. [L *flaccidus*, from *flaccus* flabby]

flack *flak*, (*NAm slang*) *n* a person who handles publicity and public relations; a press agent. [Origin uncertain; poss from **flak**]

flacker *flak'ər*, (*dialect*) *vi* to flap or flutter. [Cf OE *flacor* fluttering]

flacket *flak'it*, (*dialect*) *n* a flask or bottle. [OFr *flasquet*]

flacon *flak-ɔ̃'*, *n* a scent-bottle, etc. [Fr]

flaff *flaf*, (*Scot*) *vi* to flap; to pant. — *n* a flutter of the wings; a puff. — *vi* **flaff'er** to flutter. [Imit]

flag[1] *flag*, *vi* to droop; to flap feebly; to grow languid or spiritless: — *pr p* **flagg'ing**; *pa t* and *pa p* **flagged**. — *n* **flagg'iness**. — *adj* **flagg'y** limp or drooping; flabby. [Perh OFr *flac*, from L *flaccus*; prob influenced by imit forms, such as **flap**]

flag[2] *flag*, *n* an iris; reed-grass (*Bible*). — *n* **flagg'iness**. — *adj* **flagg'y** having many flags. — **flag'-basket** a reed basket for tools; **flag iris**; **flag'-worm** a worm or grub bred among flags or reeds. [Ety obscure; cf Du *flag*]

flag[3] *flag*, *n* a piece *usu* of bunting or other cloth with a design, used as an emblem for military or naval purposes, signalling, decoration, display, propaganda, etc; a conspicuous sign to mark a position, eg of a golf-hole, or to convey information, such as that a taxi is available for hire; a flagship (*hist*); a bushy tail. — *vi* to indicate or inform by flag-signals. — *vt* to decorate with flags; to inform by flag-signals; to mark (eg a passage or item in a book) for attention, by means of a bookmark, pen or pencil mark, etc; to indicate or code (material on computer tape, etc) so that particular items or classes of data may be found or extracted. — *adj* **flagg'y** like a banner; spreading, flabby. — **flag'-captain** the captain of a flagship; **flag'-day** a day on which collectors solicit contributions to a charity in exchange for small flags as badges to secure immunity for the rest of the day; 14 June, anniversary of the adoption of the Stars and Stripes (*US*); **flag'-lieutenant** an officer in a flagship, corresponding to an aide-de-camp in the army; **flag of convenience** a foreign flag under which a shipping company registers its tonnage to avoid taxation or other burdens at home; **flag of distress** a flag displayed as a signal of distress, *usu* upside down or at half-mast; **flag'-officer** a naval officer privileged to carry a flag denoting his rank — admiral, vice-admiral, rear-admiral or commodore; **flag of truce** a white flag displayed during a battle when some peaceful communication is desired; **flag'pole**, **flag'staff** or **flag'stick** a pole, etc for displaying a flag; **flag'ship** the ship carrying an admiral and flying his flag; anything of great importance or pre-eminence (*fig*; also *adj*); **flag'-wagging** signalling by flag; aggressive patriotism or imperialism (also **flag'-waving**); **flag'-waver**. — *adj* **flag'-waving** serving merely to show (superficial) support for or allegiance to eg a nation or a political party. — **black**, **red**, **white** and **yellow flag** see under **black**, **red**, **white** and **yellow** respectively; **dip the flag** to lower the flag and then hoist it as a token of respect; **flag down** to signal (eg a taxi) to stop; **show**, **carry** or **fly the flag** or **keep the flag flying** to (continue to) show support for or allegiance to one's own country, organization, etc; to put in an appearance or otherwise ensure that one, or the nation, firm, etc one represents, is not overlooked; **strike** or **lower the flag** to pull down the flag as a token of relinquishment of command, or in respect, submission, or surrender. [Origin unknown; cf Dan *flag*; Du *vlag*, Ger *Flagge*]

flag[4] *flag*, *n* a stone that separates in slabs; a flat paving-stone (also **flag'stone**). — *vt* to pave with flagstones. — *n* **flagg'ing** flagstones; a pavement constructed from them. — *adj* **flagg'y**. [ON *flaga* a slab]

flagellum *flə-jel'əm*, *n* a whip or scourge; a long runner (*bot*); a long cilium or whiplike appendage (*biol*): — *pl* **flagell'a**. — *adj* **flag'ellant** scourging. — *n* a person who whips, *esp* himself or herself in religious discipline or sexual gratification. — *n* **flag'ellantism**. — *n pl* **Flagellata** (*flaj-ə-lā'tə*) unicellular organisms with flagella. — *vt* **flag'ellate** to whip. — *n* any member of the Flagellata. — *adj* having a flagellum or flagella. — *adj* **flag'ellated**. — *n* **flagellā'tion**. — *n* **flag'ellātor**. — *adj* **flag'ellatory**. — *adj* **flagellif'erous**. — *adj* **flagell'iform**. — *n* **flagellōmā'nia** excessive enthusiasm for beating and flogging. — *n* and *adj* **flagellōmā'niac**. [L *flagellum*, dimin of *flagrum* a whip]

flageolet[1] *flaj-ō-let'* or *flaj'*, *n* a small high-pitched flute with two thumb-holes. [Fr, dimin of OFr *flageol, flajol* a pipe; not L *flauta* flute]

flageolet[2] *flaj-ō-let'*, *n* a variety of kidney bean. [Corruption of Fr *fageolet*; L *faseolus*]

flagitate *flaj'i-tāt*, *vt* to entreat or importune. — *n* **flagitā'tion**. [L *flagitāre, -ātum*]

flagitious *flə-jish'əs*, *adj* grossly wicked; guilty of heinous crimes. — *adv* **flagi'tiously**. — *n* **flagi'tiousness**. [L *flāgitiōsus*, from *flāgitium* a disgraceful act, from *flagrāre* to burn]

flagon *flag'ən*, *n* a large lidded jug for wine; a large bottle in which alcohol, *esp* wine or cider, is sold, *specif* one containing two pints or 1·13 litres. [Fr *flacon*, from *flascon*, from LL *flascō, -ōnis*; see **flask**]

flagrant *flā'grənt*, *adj* burning or raging (*archaic*); notorious; outrageous or conspicuous. — *n* **flā'grance** or **flā'grancy**. — *adv* **flā'grantly**. [L *flagrāns, -antis*, pr p of *flagrāre* to burn]

flagrante bello *flə-gran'tē be'lō* or *fla-gran'te*, (*L*) while war is raging; **flagrante delicto** (*di-lik'tō* or *dā-lik'tō*) in the very act (literally 'while the crime is blazing').

flagship. See under **flag**[3].

flail *flāl*, *n* an implement for threshing corn, consisting of a wooden bar (the *swingle*) hinged or tied to a handle; a medieval weapon with a spiked iron swingle. — *vt* to strike with, or as if with, a flail. — *vi* to move like a flail (often with *about*). [OE *fligel*, influenced by OFr *flaiel*, prob from L *flagellum* a scourge]

flair *flār*, *n* intuitive discernment; a faculty for nosing out; popularly and loosely, a natural aptitude. [Fr, sense of smell, from *flairer* to smell, from LL *flagrāre*, from L *fragrāre* to emit a smell]

flak *flak*, *n* anti-aircraft fire (*military slang*); adverse criticism (*colloq*); heated disagreement or dissension. — **flak jacket** a heavy protective jacket reinforced with metal. [Initials of Ger *Flieger-* (or *Flug-*) *abwehrkanone* anti-aircraft cannon]

flake[1] *flāk*, *n* a small flat scale or layer; a very small loose mass, eg of snow; a spark or detached flame; a flash (*Spenser*); an eccentric, a crazy person (*US colloq*). — *vt* to form into flakes; to sprinkle with, or as if with, flakes. — *vi* to come off in flakes. — *n* **flak'iness**. — *adj* **flak'y** formed of, or tending to form, flakes; (of pastry) formed of thin, crumbly layers; stupid, inept, incompetent (*colloq*); crazy, eccentric (*US colloq*). — *n* (*slang*) an angry outburst, a fit of temper. — **flake'-white** the purest white lead for painting, made in the form of scales or plates. — **flake out** to collapse from weariness or illness. [Perh connected with ON *flōke* flock of wool; OHGer *floccho*]

flake[2] *flāk*, *n* a movable hurdle for fencing; a stage hung over a ship's side for caulking, etc (*naut*); a frame or rack for storing or drying food. [Cf ON *flake*; Du *vlaak*]

flake[3]. Same as **fake**[1].

flam[1] *flam*, *n* a whim (*archaic*); an idle fancy (*archaic*); a falsehood; a trick. — *vt* to deceive; to get, manage, etc by deception. [Perh **flim-flam** or **flamfew**]

flam[2]. See **flawn**.

flambé *fläm'bā* or *flã-bā*, *adj* (of a Chinese ceramic glaze) dense and iridescent with streaky colour effect (*usu* red and blue) produced by irregular application or uneven firing; decorated with such a glaze; (also **flambéed** *fläm'bād*) in cookery, prepared or served with a dressing of flaming liquor, *usu* brandy. [Fr, pa p of *flamber* to flame or singe]

flambeau *flam'bō*, *n* a flaming torch: — *pl* **flam'beaux** or **flam'beaus** (*-bōz*). [Fr, from OFr *flambe*, from L *flamma*]

flamboyant *flam-boi'ənt*, *adj* late French Gothic (15c–16c) with flame-like tracery (*archit*); wavy in form; gorgeously coloured or decorated; (of a person, style, action, etc) ostentatious, colourful or extravagant. — *n* (also **flamboy'ante**) a tropical tree of the Caesalpinia family (*Poinciana regia*) with flame-coloured flowers. — *n* **flamboy'ance** or **flamboy'ancy**. — *adv* **flamboy'antly**. — **flamboy'ant-tree** or **flamboy'ante-tree**. [Fr, pr p of *flamboyer* to blaze]

flame *flām*, *n* the visible flickering luminous streams produced by a gaseous matter undergoing combustion; the gleam or blaze of a fire; rage; ardour of temper; vigour of thought; warmth of affection; love or its object, *esp* in the phrase '*an old flame*'. — *vi* to burn as flame; to break out in passion. — *vt* to set aflame. — *adj* **flamed** (*Spenser*) inflamed. — *adj* **flame'less**. — *n* **flame'let** a small flame. — *adj* **flam'ing** brilliantly red; gaudy; violent; furious; often used intensively or to express irritation, etc (*colloq*). — *adv* **flam'ingly**. — *n* **flammabil'ity**. — *adj* **flamm'able** capable of being set on fire. — *adj* **flammif'erous** producing flame. — *adj* **flam'y** pertaining to, or like, flame. — *adj* **flame'-coloured** of the colour of flame, bright reddish-yellow. — **flame-grill'**. — *adj* **flame-grilled'** cooked on a grill over a direct flame, *esp* produced by solid fuel rather than gas. — **flame'-leaf** (*bot*) a Poinciana tree; **flame'-thrower** a weapon of war that releases a powerful jet of burning liquid; **flame'-tree** a thick-stemmed Australian tree, *Brachychiton acerifolium*, with glossy leaves and scarlet bell-shaped flowers; applied to various other trees, *specif* the flamboyant-tree (see under **flamboyant**), the yellow-flowered *Acacia farnesiana* of SW USA, the scarlet-flowered *Butea frondosa* of India and Myanma, and the *Nuytsia floribunda* of W Australia, which has orange flowers. [OFr *flambe*, from L *flamma*]

flamen *flā'mən*, *n* (in ancient Rome) a priest serving one particular god. — *adj* **flamin'ical**. [L *flāmen, -inis*]

flamenco *flä-meng'kō*, *n* a type of emotionally intense gypsy song, or the dance performed to it, *orig* from the S Spanish region of Andalusia: — *pl* **flamen'cos**. [Sp, Flem, gypsy]

flamfew *flam'fū*, (*obs*) *n* a fantastic trifle or gewgaw. [Fr *fanfelue*]

Flamingant *flä-mɛ̃-gã'*, *n* a person who favours the Flemish language or Flemish nationalism. [Fr]

flamingo *flə-ming'gō*, *n* a large tropical or subtropical wading bird of a pink or bright-red colour, with long legs and neck and a downward-curving bill: — *pl* **flaming'os** or **flaming'oes**. [Sp *flamengo* (now *flamenco*)]

flamm. See **flawn**.

flammability and **flammable**. See under **flame**.

Flammenwerfer *fläm'ən-ver-fər*, (*Ger*) *n* a flame-thrower.

flammiferous. See under **flame**.

flammule *flam'ūl*, *n* a little flame, such as in a picture of a Japanese god. — *adj* **flamm'ūlāted** ruddy. — *n* **flammūlā'tion** flamelike marking. [L *flammula*, dimin of *flamma* flame]

flan *flan*, *n* a flat open tart filled with a sweet or savoury mixture; the blank metal disc on which a design is stamped to produce a coin. [**flawn**]

flanch[1] *flanch, flänch, flansh* or *flänsh*, *n* a flange; a design formed on each side of a shield by the segment of a circle (*heraldry*). — *adj* **flanched** having a pair of flanches. [Prob related to **flank**]

flanch[2] *flanch, flänch, flansh* or *flänsh* or **flaunch** *flönch* or *flönsh*, *vi* to widen, *esp* outwards or upwards, to flare (often with *out*). — *vt* to cause to slope in towards the top (often with *up*). — *n* **flanch'ing** or **flaunch'ing** the action or state of the verb; (**flaunching**) a sloping piece of cement, eg round the base of a chimney-pot. [Ety obscure]

flanconade *flang-kə-nād'*, (*fencing*) *n* a thrust in the flank or side. [Fr, from *flanc* the side]

flâneur *flä-nœr'*, *n* a person who saunters about, a stroller. — *n* **flânerie** (*flän-rē*) idling. [Fr *flâner* to lounge]

flange *flanj*, *n* a projecting or raised edge or flank, such as of a wheel or rail, used to give strength or to make a connection or attachment secure. — *vi* to widen out. — *vt* to put a flange on. — *adj* **flanged**. [Perh connected with **flank**]

flank *flangk*, *n* the side of an animal from the ribs to the thigh; a cut of beef from this part of the animal;

loosely, the corresponding part of the human body; the side or wing of anything, *esp* of an army or fleet; a body of soldiers on the right or left extremity. — *vt* to be on, pass round, attack, threaten or protect the flank of. — *n* **flank'er** a fortification that commands the flank of an attacking force; either one of the two outside men of the second row of the scrum (also **flank forward** or **wing forward**; *Rugby football*). — *vt* (*obs*) to defend by flankers; to attack sideways. — **do**, **pull** or **work a flanker** (*slang*, *orig military*) to trick, deceive, cheat, etc someone. [Fr *flanc*]

flannel *flan'əl*, *n* a light woollen textile used for clothing; a piece of this or other cloth used for washing or rubbing, now *esp* a piece of towelling for washing the face, a face-cloth; flattery, soft soap, words intended to hide one's ignorance, true opinions, etc (*colloq*); (in *pl*) trousers, *esp* of flannel or a similar cloth. — *vt* to wrap in flannel; to rub with a flannel; to flatter, to soft-soap, to utter flannel to (*colloq*; also *vi*). — *n* **flannelette'** a cotton imitation of flannel, widely used to make bed-linen, nightwear, etc. — *adj* **flann'elled**. — *adj* **flann'elly**. — *n* **flann'en** (*obs* or *dialect*) flannel. — **flann'elboard** or **flann'elgraph** a display board covered with flannel or felt, on which letters, pictures, etc backed with material will stick when pressed against it; **flann'el-flower** an Australian perennial plant with daisy-like flowers. [Poss OFr *flaine* blanket, or Welsh *gwlanen*, from *gwlan* wool]

flap *flap*, *n* the movement of a broad object hanging loose, or the action or sound of it striking a surface; anything broad and flexible hanging loose, such as material covering an opening; skin or flesh detached from the underlying part for covering and growing over the end of an amputated limb; a fluster, a panic (*colloq*); any surface attached to the wing of an aircraft which can be adjusted in flight to alter the lift as a whole; an 'r' sound produced by a single light tap of the tongue against the alveolar ridge or uvula (*phonetics*). — *vt* to beat or move with a flap; to fluster. — *vi* to move, as of wings; to hang like a flap; to get into a panic or fluster: — *pr p* **flapp'ing**; *pa t* and *pa p* **flapped**. — *adj* **flapp'able** not unflappable, easily perturbed, agitated, irritated, flustered, etc. — *n* **flapp'er** a person or thing that flaps; a flipper (*biol*); a young wild duck or partridge; a girl nearing womanhood (*obs slang*); in the 1920s, a flighty young woman, *esp* one ostentatiously unconventional in dress or behaviour (*slang*). — *n* **flapp'erhood**. — *adj* **flapp'erish**. — *adj* **flapp'ing** moving with or like a flap; (of or pertaining to races, animals, etc) not subject to Jockey Club or National Hunt Committee regulations (*horse-racing*) or not registered under the National Greyhound Racing Club (*greyhound racing*). — *n* the action of the verb; racing at flapping meetings (*horse-racing* or *greyhound racing*). — *adj* **flapp'y** (*colloq*) in a state of nervousness or panic; in a fluster. — **flap'doodle** the food of fools; gross flattery, etc; nonsense; **flap'-dragon** a game in which small edible items such as raisins are snatched from burning brandy, and swallowed. — *adj* **flap'-eared** (*Shakesp*). — **flap'jack** a kind of broad, flat pancake (*Shakesp* and *US*); a biscuit or cake made with rolled oats and syrup; a flat face-powder compact; an apple-puff (*dialect*). — *adj* **flap'-mouthed**. — **flap'track** or **flapping track** a racetrack for flapping. [Prob imit]

flare *flār*, *vi* to spread; to widen out like a bell; to burn with a glaring, unsteady light; to glitter or flash; to blaze up, literally or in anger (with *up*). — *vt* to display glaringly; to dispose of (superfluous gas or oil) by burning (with *off*; *chem eng*). — *n* a widening out, as in the bell of a horn, a bowl, or a skirt; an unsteady glare; an unshaded flame; a sudden blaze; a torch; a signalling light; (the flame or light produced by) a device composed of combustible material, activated to give warning, illumination, etc or to signal for help, eg at sea; a device for the safe disposal of superfluous gas, oil, etc by burning in the open (*chem eng*). — *n pl* **flares** trousers that widen (greatly) below the knee, popular in the late 1960s and early 1970s. — *adj* **flār'ing**. — *adv* **flā'ringly**. — *adj* **flā'ry**. — **flare'-out** (*aeronautics*) the controlled approach path of aircraft immediately prior to landing; **flare'-path** a path lit up to enable an aircraft to land or take off when natural visibility is insufficient; **flare stack** (*chem eng*) a tall chimney with an automatic igniter at the top, for the safe disposal of superfluous gas, etc by burning; **flare star** a star, *usu* a red dwarf, which has a periodical sudden and unpredictable increase in brightness; **flare'-up** a sudden bursting into flame; a sudden outbreak of violence, anger, etc. [Poss connected with Norw *flara* to blaze]

flaser *flä'zər*, (*geol*) *n* irregular streaky lenticular structure developed in metamorphic rocks. [Ger, streak]

flash[1] *flash*, *n* a momentary gleam of light; a sudden, short-lived flare or flame; (the momentary illumination from) a flashbulb or flashgun (*photog*); a sudden burst, eg of merriment; a moment or instant; a sudden rush of water; a board for directing or modifying a stream of water; a bright garter or ribbon worn on the hose with knickerbockers or kilt, a small portion showing below the part folded over; a distinctive mark on a uniform; a sticker or overprinted label on a piece of merchandise advertising a reduction in price, etc; a brief news announcement; in a film, a scene inserted by way of explanation or comment, *esp* a scene of the past, a flashback; vulgar ostentation (*colloq*); a thin surplus piece of metal at the sides of a forging or casting, or a similar extrusion in other materials; excess material forced out of a mould. — *adj* showy; vulgar; of, like, or pertaining to criminals (*slang*); fashionable (*archaic*). — *vi* to burst out, as a sudden light (*lit* and *fig*); to emit flashes of light; to sparkle brilliantly; to blaze out; to break out into intellectual brilliance; to burst out into violence; to move like a flash; to expose oneself indecently in public (*slang*). — *vt* to cause to flash; to expand (eg blown glass) into a disc; to send by some startling or sudden means; to show briefly; to display ostentatiously (often with *about* or *around*). — *n* **flash'er** a person or thing that flashes; a device for turning off and on lights eg in advertising, warning, etc signs; the signs themselves; (on a vehicle) a direction indicator; a person in the habit of indecently exposing himself or herself in public (*slang*). — *adv* **flash'ily**. — *n* **flash'iness**. — *n* **flash'ing** the act of blazing; a sudden burst, eg of water; (a method of producing) irregular colouring of bricks (by periodically stopping air supply in burning them, or other means); a thin metal strip put over a junction between roof tiles, slates, etc to make it watertight; the practice of indecently exposing oneself in public (*slang*). — *adj* emitting flashes; sparkling. — *adj* **flash'y** dazzling for a moment; showy but empty; vapid (*Milton*); gaudy; tawdry. — **flash'back** or **flashfor'ward** (in a film, novel, etc) a scene of the past or future, inserted as comment or explanation; an echo of the past or vision of the future. — Also *vi*. — **flash blindness** blindness caused by the flash of the explosion of a powerful bomb, etc; **flash'-board** one of a set of boards set up at the sides of a water-channel to deepen it; **flash'bulb** an oxygen-filled electric bulb in which aluminium or other foil or filament may be fired to provide a brilliant flash, *esp* for illuminating a photographic subject; **flash burn** one sustained as the result of exposure to a flash of intense heat, eg from a nuclear explosion; **flash card** a card on which a picture or word is printed or written, to be shown briefly to a child as an aid to learning; one of a set of large brightly-coloured cards each held up by an individual eg in a sports stadium and together forming a picture or message; **flash chip** see **flash memory**; **flash'cube** (*photog*) a plastic cube containing four flashbulbs, rotated as the film is wound on; **flash fire** a sudden extensive (increase in) fire caused eg by flash-over; **flash flood** a sudden, severe, brief flood caused by a heavy rainstorm; **flash flooding**; **flash'gun** a device holding and firing a flashbulb; **flash'-house** (*obs*) a brothel; **flash'light** a light that flashes periodically; light produced by flashbulbs, used to take photographs; an electric torch (*esp NAm*); **flash memory** or **flash chip** a form of non-volatile computer memory which can be erased electrically; **flash'-over** an electric discharge over the surface of an insulator (*elec engin*); instant combustion of material that has reached a high temperature (in a burning building, etc) as soon as oxygen reaches it; **flash'-point** the temperature at which a liquid gives off enough flammable vapour to ignite when a light is applied to it; a point in the development of a tense situation when violent action takes place; a place in the world where an outbreak of hostilities may occur at any time as a result of tension. — **flash in the pan** see under **pan**[1]; **news'flash** a brief preliminary dispatch about news just becoming known. [Prob imit; cf Swed dialect *flasa* to blaze]

flash[2] *flash*, (*obs* or *dialect*) *n* a pool, pond or marshy place. [Onomatopoeic; perh infl by Fr *flache* a hollow or pool]

flask *fläsk*, *n* a narrow-necked container for liquids; a bottle; a *usu* flat pocket-bottle; a moulding box of wood, cast-iron or pressed steel for holding the mould in which a casting is made; a lead case for storing or transporting radioactive sources (also **cask** or **coffin**); a container for the transport of irradiated nuclear fuel (also **cask** or **coffin**); a horn or metal vessel for carrying powder. — *n* **flask'et** (*hist*) a dish in which food is served; a basket (*Spenser*). [OE *flasce*; Ger *Flasche*; prob from LL *flascō*, from L *vasculum* a flask]

flat *flat*, *adj* smooth; level; lacking points of prominence or interest; shallow; spread out; monotonous; uniform; fixed, unvarying; exact; vapid, no longer brisk or sparkling; defeated; failing in effect; dejected; downright, out-and-out, sheer; (of drink) having lost all effervescence; (of feet) having little or no arch; (of shoes) not having a raised heel; low relative to the semitone above (*music*); below the right pitch (*music*); having flats in the key-signature (*music*); voiced (*phonetics*); (of a battery) dead, unable to generate. — *n* a level part; a plain; (often in *pl*) an area of land covered by shallow water; something broad; a storey or floor of a house, *esp* one, or part of one, used as a separate residence; the floor of a particular compartment (*naut*); a flat piece of scenery slid or lowered on to the stage (*theat*); an insipid passage (*music*); a simpleton or dupe (*colloq*); a character (♭) that lowers a note a semitone (*music*); a note so lowered (*music*); a punctured tyre. — *adv* in or to a flat position; evenly; too low in pitch; without qualification; exactly (used in giving time taken for eg a race). — *n* **flat'let** a small flat of two or three rooms. — *adv* **flat'ling**, **flat'lings** or **flat'long** (*Spenser* or *Shakesp*) with the flat side; flat side on; not edgewise; prostrate. — *adv* **flat'ly**. — *n* **flat'ness**. — *adj* **flatt'ed** made flat (*obs*); divided into flats. — *vt* **flatt'en** to make flat; to knock to the ground (*colloq*); to knock out (*colloq*); to amaze. — *vi* to become flat. — *n* **flatt'ing** painting leaving a non-glossy finish. — *adj* **flatt'ish** somewhat flat. — *adj* or *adv* **flat'ways** or **flat'wise** with or on the flat side. — **flat'back** a pottery figure with a flat back, designed to stand on a mantelpiece, etc and so be viewed only from the front; **flat'bed** or **flatbed truck** (*esp NAm*) a lorry with a flat sideless platform for its body; **flat'boat** a large flat-bottomed boat for transporting goods on a river, canal, etc; **flat'-cap** a low-crowned hat worn by London citizens in the 16c and 17c; hence, a London citizen or apprentice; a cloth cap, an unstiffened cap of wool or other soft cloth, with a peak, widely regarded as a symbol of the working-class man; **flat-earth'er** a person who maintains that the earth is flat; **flat'fish** a marine fish that habitually lies on one side, and has an unsymmetrical flat body, eg flounder, turbot, etc; **flat'foot** a condition in which the arch of the instep is flattened; a policeman (*derog slang*). — *adj* **flat'-footed** having flat feet; resolute (*US*); ponderous; unimaginative; uninspired; unprepared (*NAm*). — **flat-foot'edness**. — *adj* **flat'head** having an artifically flattened head; (with *cap*) of or designating a N American Indian people of Montana (once mistakenly believed to practise flattening children's skulls, as did the neighbouring Chinook; also *n*).— *n* (*US slang*) a simpleton, idiot; any of various species of edible flat-skulled fish of the Pacific and Indian Oceans; **flat'iron** an old-fashioned iron for pressing clothes, heated on a stove, etc; **flat'mate** a person with whom one shares a flat; **flat race** a race over open or clear ground, without jumps; **flat racing**; **flat rate** a fixed uniform rate (eg of charge or payment); **flat spin** rotation in a horizontal plane about a vertical axis; confused excitement (*colloq*); **flatter squarer tube** a television screen which is flat and perfectly square, eliminating the distortion produced by convex screens; **flat tyre** a punctured tyre; **flat'ware** domestic cutlery; plates and saucers; **flat'worm** a tapeworm or other member of the Platyhelminthes. — **flat broke** (*colloq*) having no money whatsoever; **flat out** at full speed; using every effort; **flatten out** to bring (an aeroplane) into a horizontal position; **that's flat** I tell you plainly; **the flat** flat racing. [ON *flatr* flat]

flatter *flat'ər*, *vt* to treat with insincere praise and servile attentions, *esp* in order to gain some advantage; to please with false hopes or undue praise; to overpraise; to represent over-favourably; to coax; to gratify. — *n* **flatt'erer**. — *adj* **flatt'ering**. — *adv* **flatt'eringly**. — *adj* **flatt'erous** (*archaic*) flattering. — *adv* **flatt'erously** (*archaic*). — *n* **flatt'ery** exaggerated or insincere praise. [Connected with OFr *flater* (Fr *flatter*); Gmc; cf ON *flathra*]

flatus *flā'təs*, *n* a puff of wind or blast; a breath; gas generated in the stomach or intestines: — *pl* **fla'tuses**. — *n* **flatulence** (*flat'ū-ləns*) or **flat'ūlency** distension of the stomach or bowels by gases formed during digestion; windiness; emptiness of utterance; pretentiousness. — *adj* **flat'ūlent**. — *adv* **flat'ūlently**. — *adj* **flat'ūous**. [L *flātus*, *-ūs* a blowing, from *flāre* to blow]

flaught[1] *flöt* (*Scot flöhht*), *n* a flight or a flapping. — *n* **flaugh'ter** a fluttering motion. — *vi* to flutter or flicker. [Related to **flight**]

flaught[2] *flöt* (*Scot flöhht*), *n* a flake (of snow); a skin or hide; a tuft (of hair, wool, etc); a gust; a flash (of lightning); a spark; a turf. — *vt* to strip or skin; to card (wool). — *vi* **flaugh'ter** to cut turfs, etc. — *n* a paring of turf; a spade (**flaugh'ter-spade**) for cutting turfs. [Cf **flake**[1], **flaw**[1], **flay**[1]]

flaunch. A variant of **flanch**[2].

flaune. See **flawn**.

flaunt *flönt*, *vt* to display ostentatiously; to show off. — *vi* to wave in the wind; to move or wave ostentatiously; to have a gaudy or saucy appearance. — *n* (*Shakesp*) anything displayed for show. — *n* **flaunt'er**. — *adj* **flaunt'ing** or **flaunt'y**. — *adv* **flaunt'ingly**. [Prob Scand]

flautist *flöt'ist* or (*esp US*) **flutist** *flōō'tist*, *n* a flute player. [Ital *flautista*]

flavescent *flə-* or *flā-ves'ənt*, *adj* yellowish or turning yellow. [L *flāvēscēns*, *-entis*, pr p of *flāvēscere* to become yellow, from *flāvus* yellow]

Flavian *flāv'i-ən*, *adj* of or pertaining to *Flavius* Vespasian and his sons Titus and Domitian, known collectively as the Flavian emperors of Rome (AD 69–96).

flavin *flā'vin* or **flavine** *flā'vēn*, *n* a yellow dye made from the bark of quercitron, a N American oak; any of various antiseptic substances, of which acriflavine is one. — *n* **flavone** (*flā'vōn*) a crystalline compound occurring in certain plants, eg primroses; any of a class of yellow pigments derived from this. [L *flāvus* yellow]

flavour or (*US*) **flavor** *flā'vər*, *n* that quality in food and drink perceived by the mouth, the joint response of the senses of taste and smell; the pleasantness or degree of this quality; a smack or relish; characteristic quality or atmosphere (*fig*); (in particle physics) any of the five, or probably six, types of quark. — *vt* to impart flavour to. — *adj* **flā'vorous**. — *n* **flā'vouring** or (*US*) **flā'voring** any substance used to give a flavour to food. — *adj* **flā'vourless** or (*US*) **flā'vorless**. — *adj* **flā'voursome** or

(*US*) **flā'vorsome**. — **flavour** or (*US*) **flavor of the week, month**, etc the favourite person or thing at a given time. [OFr *flaur*; prob influenced by **savour**]

flaw[1] *flö*, *n* a gust of wind; a sudden rush; an outburst of passion; uproar. [Cf Du *vlaag*, Swed *flaga*]

flaw[2] *flö*, *n* a flake, fragment or splinter (*Shakesp*); a break or crack; a defect. — *vt* to crack or break; to make defective. — *adj* **flawed**. — *adj* **flaw'less**. — *adj* **flaw'y**. [ON *flaga* a slab]

flawn or **flaune** *flön*, **flam** or **flamm** *flam*, (*archaic*) *n* a custard; a pancake. [OFr *flaon*, from LL *fladō*, *-ōnis*, from OHGer *flado*]

flax *flaks*, *n* the fibres of the plant *Linum*, which are woven to make linen cloth; the plant itself. — *adj* **flax'en** made of or resembling flax; (*esp* of hair) light yellow. — *adj* **flax'y** like flax; of a light colour. — **flax'-bush** or **flax-lil'y** a New Zealand plant (*Phormium*) of the lily family, yielding a valuable fibre, **New Zealand flax**; **flax'-comb** a toothed instrument or hackle for cleaning the fibres of flax; **flax'-dresser** a person who prepares flax for the spinner by the successive processes of rippling, retting, grassing, breaking, and scutching; **flax'-mill** a mill for making flax into linen; **flax'-seed** linseed; **flax'-wench** (*hist*) a woman or girl who spins flax. — **purging flax** a small wild species of flax (*Linum catharticum*). [OE *flæx* (WSax *fleax*); Ger *Flachs*]

flay[1] *flā*, *vt* to strip off the skin from; to flog; to subject to savage criticism: — *pr p* **flay'ing**; *pa t* and *pa p* **flayed**. — *n* **flay'er**. — **flay'-flint** (*archaic*) a skinflint. [OE *flēan*; ON *flā* to skin]

flay[2]. See **fley**.

flea *flē*, *n* any of an order of wingless, very agile, parasitic, blood-sucking insects. — *adj* **flea'some**. — **flea'-bag** (*slang*) a sleeping-bag; a distasteful place, *esp* used of lodgings; a scruffy, apparently flea-bitten, old woman or animal (*colloq*); **flea'-bane** a name for various composite plants (*Erigeron*, *Pulicaria*, etc) whose strong smell is said to drive away fleas; **flea'-beetle** a jumping beetle that infests various vegetables, eg turnips and cabbages; **flea'-bite** the bite of a flea; a small mark caused by the bite; a trifle, an only slight inconvenience (*fig*). — *adj* **flea'-bitten** bitten by fleas; shabby, badly looked after; mean (*fig*); having small reddish spots on a lighter background, *esp* of horses. — **flea circus** a show of performing fleas; **flea market** (*colloq*) a shop, collection of stalls, etc selling second-hand goods, *orig esp* clothes; **flea'pit** a shabby public building, *esp* a cinema, supposedly infested with vermin; **flea'wort** any of several European and Eurasian plants, some of which were formerly used to drive away fleas; see **ploughman's spikenard** under **spikenard**. — **a flea in one's ear** a stinging rebuff or rejoinder. [OE *flēah*; cf Ger *Floh*, Du *vloo*]

fleam *flēm*, *n* an instrument for bleeding diseased cattle. [OFr *flieme* (Fr *flamme*), from Gr *phlebotomon* a lancet, from *phleps*, *phlebos* a vein, and *tomē* a cut]

flèche *flesh*, *n* a spire; a slender spire rising from the intersection of the nave and transepts in some large churches (*archit*); a parapet with two faces forming a salient angle at the foot of a glacis or slope (*fortif*); a point on a backgammon board. [Fr, arrow]

fléchette or **flechette** *flā-shet'*, *n* a steel dart dropped or thrown from an aeroplane, *esp* in World War I; a dart fired from a gun. [Fr, dart, dimin of *flèche* arrow]

fleck *flek*, *n* a spot or speckle; a little bit of a thing. — *vt* **fleck** or **fleck'er** to spot, streak or speckle. — *adj* **flecked** spotted or dappled. — *adj* **fleck'less** without a spot or spots. [ON *flekkr* a spot; Ger *Fleck*, Du *vlek*]

flection. A less common spelling of **flexion**.

fled *fled*, *pa t* and *pa p* of **flee**.

fledge *flej*, *vt* to provide with feathers or wings; to bring up (a young bird) until it is ready to fly. — *vi* to acquire feathers for flying. — *adj* (*Milton*) fledged. — *adj* **fledged**. — *n* **fledg'ling** or **fledge'ling** a bird just fledged; a very immature or inexperienced person, a recently formed organization, etc (also *fig*). — Also *adj*. — *adj* **fledg'y** (*Keats*) feathery. [ME *fligge*, *flegge*, from an assumed OE (Kentish) *flecge*; cf OE *unflycge* unfledged; see **fly**]

flee[1] *flē*, *vi* to run away, eg from danger; to disappear. — *vt* to keep at a distance from; to run away from or leave hurriedly: — *pr p* **flee'ing**; *pa t* and *pa p* **fled**. — *n* **flē'er**. [OE *flēon*; Ger *fliehen*; not related to *fly*, but influenced by it, the *f* representing an earlier *th*]

flee[2] *flē*, *n* and *vi*. Scots form of **fly**.

fleece *flēs*, *n* a sheep's coat of wool; the wool shorn from a sheep at one time; anything like a fleece in appearance or texture. — *vt* to shear; to plunder; to charge (a person) exorbitantly; to cover with or as if with wool. — *adj* **fleeced** having a fleece. — *adj* **fleece'less**. — *n* **fleec'er** a person who strips, plunders or charges exorbitantly. — *adj* **fleec'y** woolly; like a fleece in appearance or texture. — **fleece'-wool** the wool cut from a sheep at any of its clippings subsequent to its first, or yearling, clipping. [OE *flēos*; Du *vlies*, Ger *Fliess*, now *Vlies*]

fleech *flēch*, (*Scot*) *vt* and *vi* to flatter, coax or beg. — *n* **fleech'ing** or **fleech'ment**. [Origin obscure]

fleer *flēr*, *vi* to make wry faces in contempt; to jeer. — *vt* to mock. — *n* mockery; a jibe. — *n* **fleer'er**. — *n* and *adj* **fleer'ing**. — *adv* **fleer'ingly**. [Cf Norw *flira*, Swed *flissa* to titter]

fleer[2]. See under **flee**[1].

fleet[1] *flēt*, *n* a number of ships, aircraft, motor cars, etc owned by the same company or otherwise associated; a navy; a division of a navy under an admiral. — **Fleet Air Arm** the airborne forces of the Royal Navy. [OE *flēot* a ship, from *flēotan* to float; connected with Du *vloot* and Ger *Flotte*]

fleet[2] *flēt*, *adj* swift; nimble; transient (*obs*). — *adv* **fleet'ly**. — *n* **fleet'ness**. — *adj* **fleet'-foot** (*Shakesp*) nimble or swift of foot. [Prob ON *fliōtr* swift; but ult cognate with **fleet**[3]]

fleet[3] *flēt*, *vi* to float (*obs*); to flow (*Spenser*); to flit or pass swiftly. — *vt* (*Shakesp*) to cause to pass quickly. — *adj* (*dialect*) shallow. — *adj* **fleet'ing** passing quickly; transient; temporary. — *adv* **fleet'ingly**. [OE *flēotan* to float]

fleet[4] *flēt*, *n* a shallow creek, bay, brook or drain, as in North*fleet*, *Fleet*-ditch, etc. — **Fleet Prison** or **the Fleet** a London gaol until 1842, near the Fleet river, long a place of confinement for debtors, and in which clandestine marriages were solemnized until 1754 by **Fleet parsons**, broken-down clergymen confined for debt; **Fleet Street** journalism or its ways and traditions, from the street in London in which many newspaper offices were formerly situated. [OE *flēot* an inlet]

fleg *fleg*, (*Scot*) *n* a fright. — *vt* to frighten. [OE *flecgan* to put to flight].

fleme *flēm*, (*Scot*) *vt* to put to flight: — *pa t* and *pa p* **flēm'it**. [OE *flieman*]

Flemish *flem'ish*, *adj* of or belonging to the Flemings, or to Flanders. — *n* the Flemings as a people; one of the two languages of Belgium, virtually identical with Dutch. — *vt* (without *cap*; *naut*) to flemish down. — *n* **Flem'ing** a native of Flanders; a Flemish-speaking Belgian. — **Flemish bond** a bricklayer's bond of alternate headers and stretchers in every course; **Flemish coil** (*naut*) a flat coil of rope with the end in the centre; **Flemish school** a school of painting formed by the brothers Van Eyck, reaching its height in Rubens, Vandyck and Teniers; **Flemish stitch** a stitch used in making certain kinds of point-lace. — **flemish down** (*naut*) to stow (a rope) in a Flemish coil. [Du *Vlaamsch*]

flench *flench*, **flense** *flens* or **flinch** *flinch*, *vt* to cut up the blubber of (eg a whale); to flay. [Dan *flense*]

flesh *flesh*, *n* muscular tissue; all the living substance of the body of similar composition to muscle; the soft substance that covers the bones of animals; the bodies of animals and (sometimes) birds, but not fish, used as food; the body, not the soul; animals, or animal nature; human bodily nature; mankind; kindred; one's own family; bodily appetites; excess weight; the soft substance of fruit, *esp* the part fit to be eaten. — *vt* to reward with flesh; to train to have an appetite for flesh (*esp* dogs for hunting); to inure or harden (eg to warfare or killing); to use on flesh (eg a sword); to use for the first time; to gratify with fleshly indulgence; to put flesh upon or fatten; to scrape flesh from. — *adj* **fleshed** (*flesht*) having flesh; fat. — *n* **flesh'er** an instrument for scraping hides; a butcher (*esp Scot*). — *n* **flesh'hood** (*Elizabeth Barrett Browning*) the state of being in the flesh. — *n* **flesh'iness**. — *n pl* **flesh'ings** actors' flesh-coloured tights. — *adj* **flesh'less** without flesh; lean. — *n* **flesh'liness**. — *adj* **flesh'ling** a sensualist. — *adj* **flesh'ly** corporeal; carnal; not spiritual. — Also *adv*. — *n* **flesh'ment** (*Shakesp*) the act of fleshing or initiating; excitement arising from success. — *adj* **flesh'y** fat; pulpy; plump. — **flesh'-broth** broth made by boiling meat; **flesh'-brush** a brush used for rubbing the skin to excite circulation; **flesh'-colour** the normal colour of the skin of a member of a white-skinned race; **flesh'-eater**; **flesh'-fly** a fly (*esp* Sarcophaga) whose larvae feed on flesh; **flesh'-hook** a hook for lifting meat from a pot; **flesh'-market**; **flesh'-meat** flesh of animals used for food; **flesh'monger** a person who deals in flesh; a whoremonger (*Shakesp*); a procurer, pimp or slave-dealer; **flesh pot** a pot or vessel in which meat is cooked (*hist*); abundance of flesh (*obs*); (*usu* in *pl*) high living; a place where entertainment of a sexual nature is on offer, eg a striptease club; a city known to provide an abundance of this kind of entertainment; **flesh'-pottery** sumptuous living; **flesh'-pressing** see **press flesh** under **press**[1]; **flesh'-tint** a tint or colour that represents the human body; **flesh'worm** (*archaic*) a worm or maggot that feeds on flesh; **flesh wound** a wound not reaching beyond the flesh. — **an arm of flesh** human strength or help; **flesh and blood** bodily or human nature; **flesh out** to give substance to or elaborate on (an idea, etc); **in flesh** in good condition; fat; **in the flesh** in bodily life, alive; incarnate; in person, actually present; **make someone's flesh creep** to arouse a feeling of horror in someone; **one flesh** (*relig*) united in marriage; **one's own flesh and blood** one's own relations; **press flesh** see under **press**[1]; **proud-flesh** see under **proud**. [OE *flǣsc*; cognate forms in all Gmc languages; Ger *Fleisch*, etc]

fletch *flech*, *vt* to feather (an arrow). — *n* **fletch'er** a person who makes arrows. [Fr *flèche* an arrow, OFr *flecher* a fletcher]

fletton *fle'tən*, *n* a type of brick made near *Fletton* in Cambridgeshire, of a mottled yellow and pink colour, with sharp arrises or edges.

fleur-de-lis or **fleur-de-lys** *flœr-də-lē'* or *-lēs'*, *n* the iris; an ornament and heraldic design of disputed origin (an iris, three lilies, etc), borne by the kings of France: — *pl* **fleurs-de-lis** or **fleurs-de-lys** (*flœr-*). — Also **flower delice**, **flower-delice**, **flower-de-luce**, **flower deluce** or **flower-deluce** — *n* **fleuret** (*flo͞or'ət*) an ornament like a small flower (also **fleurette** *flœ-ret'*); (*-et'*) a fencing foil. — *n* **fleuron** (*flœ-rɔ̃*) a flowerlike ornament, in architecture, printing, etc. — *adj* **fleury** (*flo͞o'ri*) (*heraldry*) having fleurs-de-lis (also **flo'ry** *flö'ri*). — **fleur de coin** (*kwɛ̃*) mint condition of a coin. [Fr; *lis* being OFr *liz*, from L *lilium* lily]

flew[1] *flo͞o*, *pa t* of **fly**; *colloq* used for **fled** (*pa t*).

flew[2] *flo͞o*, *n* the pendulous upper lip of a bloodhound or similar dog (*usu* in *pl*). — *adj* **flewed** (*Shakesp*). [Ety unknown]

flew[3]. See **flue**[3].

flex *fleks*, *vt* and *vi* to bend; to contract (a muscle). — *n* a bending; a flexible cord or line, *esp* of insulated electrical cable. — *combining form* **flex'i-** flexible. — *n* **flexibil'ity**. — *adj* **flex'ible** easily bent; pliant; adaptable; docile. — *n* **flex'ibleness** (*rare*). — *adv* **flex'ibly**. — *n* **flex'i-cover** (a book with) a flexible, plasticized cover offering greater durability than paper covers (also *adj*). — *n pl* **flex'ihours** hours of working under flexitime. — *adj* **flex'ile** (*-īl* or (*esp NAm*) *-əl*) flexible. — *n* **flexion** (*flek'shən*) a bend; a fold; the action of a flexor muscle; inflexion (*gram*). — *n* **flex'itime** or **Flex'time**® a system of flexible working hours in which an agreed total of hours may be worked at times to suit the worker, often with the proviso that on each day certain hours (**core times**) are included. — *n* **flexog'raphy** (Gr *graphein* to write) (printed matter, *esp* on plastic, produced by) a method of rotary printing using flexible rubber plates and spirit-based inks. — *n* **flex'or** a muscle that bends a joint, as opposed to an *extensor*. — *adj* **flex'ūose** or **flex'ūous** full of windings and turnings; undulating. — *adj* **flexural** (*flek'shər-əl*). — *n* **flex'ure** a bend or turning; the curving of a line or surface (*math*); the bending of loaded beams; obsequious bowing (*Shakesp*). — **flexible disk** (*comput*) a floppy disk; **flexible drive** a means of conveying rotational motion along a flexible cable, or the cable itself. — **flex one's muscles** to cause the muscles of one's arms, shoulders, etc to contract, in order to display them, test them as a preliminary to a trial of strength, etc (often *fig*). [L *flectere*, *flexum* to bend]

fley or **flay** *flā*, *vt* (*Scot*) to cause to flee; to frighten. — *vi* to be frightened. [ME *flayen*, from OE *flēgan* (as in compound *āflēgan*, *āflīegan* to put to flight); cf ON *fleyja*, Gothic *flaugjan*]

flibbertigibbet *flib'ər-ti-jib'it*, *n* a flighty, gossipy or mischievous person; an imp. [Poss imit of meaningless chatter]

flic *flēk*, (*Fr*; *slang*) *n* a policeman.

flichter *flihh'tər*, (*Scot*) *n* a flutter. — *vt* and *vi* to flutter or quiver.

flick[1] *flik*, *vt* to strike lightly, eg with a lash or a fingernail. — *n* a stroke of this kind. — **flick'-knife** a knife the blade of which springs out when a button in the handle is pressed. — **flick through** to turn the pages of (a book, etc) idly, or in order to get a rough impression of it. [Echoic]

flick[2] *flik*, (*slang*) *n* a cinema film; (in *pl*) the cinema. [**flicker**[1]]

flicker[1] *flik'ər*, *vi* to flutter and move the wings like a bird; to burn unsteadily, as of a flame. — *n* an act of flickering, a flickering movement or light. — *adv* **flick'eringly**. — **flick'ertail** (*NAm*) a ground-squirrel. [OE *flicorian*; imit]

flicker[2] *flik'ər*, *n* an American woodpecker. [Echoic]

flier and **flies**. See under **fly**.

flight[1] *flīt*, *n* a passing through the air; a soaring; distance flown; (of a ball in sports) pace or trajectory; a wandering or digression, eg of imagination or fancy; a series (of steps); a flock of birds flying together; a group of birds born in the same season; a volley; a long-distance arrow (*Shakesp*); a device attached to the blunt end of an arrow or dart, made of plastic or feathers, to stabilize its trajectory; the power of flying; the art or the act of flying with wings or in an aeroplane or other machine; a unit of the air force equivalent to a platoon in the army; a regular air journey, numbered and at a fixed time; an aircraft making such a journey; a journey of a spacecraft; a line of hurdles across a race track. — *vt* to cause (birds) to fly up; to shoot (wildfowl) in flight; to put a feather or feathers in (an arrow); to impart a deceptive trajectory or a deceptively slow speed to (a cricket ball). — *vi* (of birds) to rise or migrate in a flock. — *adj* **flight'ed** (*Milton*) flying. — *adv* **flight'ily**. — *n* **flight'iness**. — *adj* **flight'less** unable to fly. — *adj* **flight'y** swift (*Shakesp*); fanciful; changeable; giddy-minded, irresponsible; flirtatious. — **flight attendant** (*orig NAm*) a member of the cabin crew on an aeroplane, a steward or stewardess; **flight crew** the members of an aircraft crew whose responsibility is operation and navigation; **flight'-deck** the deck of an aircraft-carrier where the planes take off or land; the compartment for the crew in an aircraft; **flight'-feather** a quill of a bird's wing; **flight lieutenant** a Royal Air Force officer of rank corresponding to naval lieutenant or army captain; **flight path** the course (to be) taken by an aircraft, spacecraft, etc; **flight plan** a statement of the proposed schedule of an aircraft flight; **flight'-recorder** a device which records on tape or other electronic medium information about the functioning of an aircraft and its systems, used in determining the cause of an air crash (also **crash recorder**). — **flight of fancy** an instance of rather free speculation or indulgence in imagination; **in the first** or **top flight** in the highest class. [OE *flyht*, from *flēogan* to fly]

flight[2] *flīt*, *n* an act of fleeing. — **take (to) flight** to flee; to disappear quickly (*fig*). [Assumed OE *flyht*; cf *flēon* to flee]

flim-flam *flim'flam*, *n* a trick or deception; idle, meaningless talk; nonsense. [Cf **flam**]

flimp *flimp*, (*slang*) *vt* to rob (someone) while a partner hustles. [Cf WFlem *flimpe* to knock or rob]

flimsy *flim'zi*, *adj* thin; lightweight; without solidity, strength or reason; weak. — *n* transfer-paper or tracing-paper; a banknote (*slang*); reporters' copy written on thin paper; a carbon copy on thin paper. — *adv* **flim'sily**. — *n* **flim'siness**. [First in 18c; prob suggested by **film**]

flinch[1] *flinch* or *flinsh*, *vi* to shrink back, out of pain, fear, etc; to fail (in a duty, etc; often with *from*). — *n* **flinch'er**. — *n* and *adj* **flinch'ing**. — *adv* **flinch'ingly**. [Prob connected with ME *fleechen*, OFr *flechir*, L *flectere* to bend]

flinch[2]. Same as **flench**.

flinder *flin'dər*, (*rare*) *n* (*usu* in *pl*) a splinter or small fragment. [Norw *flindra* a splinter]

flindersia *flin-dûr'si-ə*, *n* any tree of the Australian genus *Flindersia*, valuable trees of the *Rutaceae* family. — **Flinders grass** a native pasture grass of Australia. [From the explorer Matthew *Flinders* (1774–1814)]

fling *fling*, *vt* to throw, cast or toss; to send forth; to dart, to send suddenly; to cause to fall; to throw out (*colloq*). — *vi* to throw the body about; to kick or throw (out); to dash or rush, throw oneself impetuously; to throw missiles: — *pr p* **fling'ing**; *pa t* and *pa p* **flung**. — *n* a cast or throw; a try; a passing attack; a jibe or taunt; a brief period of complete freedom, full enjoyment of pleasure; a lively Scottish country-dance. — *n* **fling'er**. — **fling mud at** see under **mud**; **fling out** to break out in impetuous plain-speaking; **fling to the winds** see under **wind**[1]; **full fling** at the utmost speed, recklessly. [Cf ON *flengja*; Swed *flänga*]

flint *flint*, *n* a hard mineral, a variety of quartz, which sparks easily when struck with steel; a concretion of silica; a piece of flint, *esp* one from which sparks are struck, or one manufactured into an implement before (or after) the use of metals; a small piece of an iron alloy, used to produce a spark in cigarette lighters; anything proverbially hard; a tailor or other worker demanding full union rates of pay (opposed to *dung*, one submitting to low rates; *obs slang*). — *adj* made of flint; hard. — *vt* **flint'ify** to turn to flint. — *adv* **flint'ily**. — *n* **flint'iness**. — *adj* **flint'y** consisting of, containing a lot of, or like flint; hard; cruel; obdurate. — **flint glass** a very fine and pure lead glass, *orig* made of calcined flints. — *adj* **flint'-heart** or **flint-heart'ed** (*Shakesp*) having a hard heart. — **flint'-knapper** a person who flakes or chips flints; **flint'-knapping**; **flint'lock** a gunlock or gun with a flint from which a spark is struck to ignite the powder. [OE *flint*; Dan *flint*; Gr *plinthos* a brick]

flip *flip*, *vt* and *vi* to fillip, to flick with the fingernail suddenly released from the ball of the thumb; to spin in the air; to flap. — *vi* to become very excited or enthusiastic (*slang*; often with *out*); to go mad (*slang*; often with *out*). — *n* a fillip or flick; a hot drink of beer and spirits sweetened, or any similar concoction; a somersault; a trip in an aeroplane, a pleasure-flight (*colloq*). — *adj* flippant; pert, over-smart. — *n* **flipp'er** an animal's limb adapted for swimming; a hand (*colloq*); a rubber foot-covering imitating an animal's flipper, worn by swimmers, divers, etc. — *adj* and *adv* **flipp'ing** (*colloq*) nasty or unpleasant; often used intensively or meaninglessly. — **flip'-chart** a large blank pad, bound at the top, on which information can be displayed in sequence during a presentation, etc; **flip'-dog** an iron for heating flip (the drink). — *adv* **flip'-flop'** with repeated flapping (also **flip'-flap'**). — *n* a fruit-seller's dance (*hist*); a form of somersault; a firework; the sound of regular footfalls; a flighty woman; a revolving apparatus for public amusement; (*orig*, and still *US* and *comput*) a bistable pair of valves, transistors or circuit elements, two stable states being switched by pulses; in Britain, a similar circuit with one stable state temporarily achieved by pulse; a type of flimsy sandal, *esp* one held on the foot by a thong between the toes. — *adj* **flipp'erty-flopp'erty** (*rare*) loose or dangling. — **flip'-side** the side of a gramophone record carrying the song, etc of lesser importance, the reverse of the side on whose merits the record is expected to sell; a less familiar aspect of anything. — *adj* **flip'-top** having a hinged lid which can be flipped up. — *n* a flip-top pack (*esp* of cigarettes). — **flip one's lid** (*slang*) to go mad. [Cf **fillip** and **flap**]

flippant *flip'ənt*, *adj* pert and frivolous in speech; showing disrespectful levity; nimble (*obs*); playful (*obs*). — *n* **flipp'ancy** or **flipp'antness** pert fluency of speech; impertinence; levity. — *adv* **flipp'antly**. [Cf **flip** and ON *fleipa* to prattle]

flirt *flûrt*, *vt* to jerk; to cause to move about quickly; to flick or rap. — *vi* to play at courtship, to indulge in light-hearted amorous or sexual banter (with); to trifle, toy or dally (with); to move briskly about. — *n* a pert, giddy girl; a person who behaves flirtatiously. — *n* **flirtā'tion** the act of flirting; a light-hearted and short-lived amorous attachment. — *adj* **flirtā'tious** (*colloq*) given to flirting; representing a light-hearted sexual invitation. — *adv* **flirta'tiously**. — *n* **flirt'ing**. — *adv* **flirt'ingly**. — *adj* **flirt'ish** indicative of a flirt (*obs*). — *adj* **flirt'y** flirting, flirtatious. — **flirt'-gill** (*-jil*; *Shakesp*) a pert or wanton woman. — **flirt with** to treat (death, danger, etc) lightly, by indulging in dare-devil behaviour, etc; to entertain thoughts of adopting (an idea, etc) or joining (a movement, etc). [Origin obscure; perh connected with Fr *fleureter* to talk sweet nothings]

flisk *flisk*, (*Scot*) *vi* to skip or caper about; to be restive. — *n* a whim. — *adj* **flisk'y**. [Onomatopoeic]

flit[1] *flit*, *vi* to move about lightly; to fly silently or quickly; to be unsteady or easily moved; to move house (*colloq*, esp *Scot*); to do this stealthily in order to avoid creditors, etc. — *vt* to remove or transfer: — *pr p* **flitt'ing**; *pa t* and *pa p* **flitt'ed** or (*Spenser*) **flitt**. — *n* **flitt'ing**. [ON *flytja*; Swed *flytta*]

flit[2] or **flitt** *flit*, (*obs*) *adj* fleet; fleeting; light. [**fleet**]

flitch *flich*, *n* a side of pork salted and cured. [OE *flicce*; ON *flikki*]

flite. Same as **flyte**.

flitt. See **flit**[1,2].

flitter[1] *flit'ər*, *vi* to flutter. — **flitt'er-mouse** (*archaic*) a bat. [**flit**[1]]

flitter[2] *flit'ər*, *n* (*usu* in *pl*, sometimes collectively in *sing*) a fragment, tatter or strip. [Connected with **flitter**[1]]

flittern *flit'ərn*, (*dialect*) *n* an oak sapling.

flivver *fliv'ər*, (*slang*) *n* a failure; a small cheap motor car or aeroplane; a small destroyer. [Origin uncertain]

flix[1] *fliks*, *n* fur or beaver-down. [Origin uncertain]

flix[2] *fliks*. An old form of **flux**. — **flix'-weed** a species of hedge-mustard, possibly so called from its use in treating the bloody flux or dysentery.

float *flōt*, *vi* to be supported on or suspended in a fluid; to be buoyed up; to move lightly, supported by a fluid; to seem to move in such a way; to be free from the usual attachment; to drift about aimlessly; to flow (*Milton*); to be flooded (*Spenser* and *Pope*); (in weaving) to pass threads without interweaving with them; to use a float; (of a currency) to be free to fluctuate in value in international exchange (*econ*). — *vt* to cause to float; to cover with liquid (*obs*); to convey on floats; to levitate; to separate by flotation; to smooth; to pare off (eg turf); to launch (eg a scheme); to circulate (eg a rumour); to offer (stocks, etc) for sale to raise capital;

to launch (a company) by drawing up various documents and raising cash by selling shares; to negotiate (a loan). — *n* state of floating (*Keats*, etc); a wave (*lit* and *fig*; *obs*); a contrivance for floating or for keeping something afloat, eg a raft, the cork or quill of a fishing-line, the ball of a ballcock, etc; a blade in a paddle-wheel or water-wheel; a floating indicator attached to a fishing-line, that moves when a fish takes the bait; a tool for smoothing; a plasterer's trowel; a low cart for carrying cattle, milk, etc or decorated as an exhibit in a street parade, etc; a footlight or the footlights collectively; money in hand for a purpose such as to give change to customers, to provide for expenses, etc; a soft fizzy drink with ice-cream floating on the top (*NAm*). — *adj* **float'able**. — *n* **float'age** or **flō'tage** buoyancy; anything which floats; flotsam; the part of a ship above the waterline. — *n* **float'ant** an agent that causes something to float. — *n* **floatā'tion** same as **flotation**. — *n* **floatel** see **flotel**. — *n* **float'er** a person or thing that floats; a vagrant, or a person who drifts from job to job or allegiance to allegiance; a blunder (*slang*); a floating policy (*US*); a meat pie floating in pea soup (*Austr*); a dark speck that appears to float before one's eyes, caused by dead cells and fragments of cells in the lens and vitreous humour. — *adj* **float'ing** that floats, in any sense; not fixed; fluctuating; circulating; not clearly committed to one side or the other (*politics*). — *n* the action of the verb; the spreading of plaster on the surface of walls; flotation therapy (see under **flotation**). — *adv* **float'ingly**. — *adj* **float'y**. — **float'-board** a board of an undershot water-wheel or a paddle-wheel; **float glass** glass hardened while floating on the surface of a liquid; **float grass** or **floating grass** floating meadow-grass (*Glyceria fluitans*); **floating battery** a vessel or hulk which is heavily armed, used in the defence of harbours or in attacks on marine fortresses; **floating bridge** a bridge supported on pontoons; **floating capital** goods, money, etc; capital not permanently invested; **floating charge** (*law* and *econ*) a fluctuating borrowing facility secured on the total assets of a company; **floating crane** a large crane carried on a pontoon, used in docks; **floating currency** a national (unit of) currency whose value is allowed to fluctuate freely in the international trading market; **floating debt** (an) unfunded debt or short-term government loan; **floating dock** a floating structure that can be sunk by admitting water to its air chambers, and raised again carrying a vessel to be repaired; **floating island** a floating mass of driftwood, or of vegetation buoyed up from the bottom by marsh gas, or anything similar; a dessert consisting of meringues floating in custard; **floating kidney** an abnormally mobile kidney; **floating light** a lightship; **floating-point notation** (*comput*) the expressing of numbers in the general form $\pm\ a \times b^n$ (eg $2{\cdot}3 \times 10^5$); **floating-point number** (*comput*) a number so expressed; **floating-point operation** (*comput*) the addition, subtraction, multiplication or division of two floating-point numbers; **floating policy** an insurance policy covering movable property irrespective of its location; **floating rib** see under **rib**[1]; **floating vote** the votes of electors who are not permanently attached to any one political party; **floating voter**; **float plane** a seaplane; **float'-stone** a porous spongelike variety of silica, so light as to float for a while on water; a bricklayer's smoothing tool; **float tank** see **flotation tank** under **flotation**. [OE *flotian* to float; ON *flota*]

floccus *flok'əs*, *n* a tuft of woolly hair; a tuft, *esp* at the end of a tail; the covering of unfledged birds: — *pl* **flocci** (*flok'sī*). — *n* **floccillā'tion** (*flok-si-*) fitful plucking at the bedclothes by a delirious patient. — *n* **floc'cinau'cini'hilipil'ificā'tion** (*facetious*) setting at little or no value (from the Latin genitives *floccī* and *naucī* at a trifle, *nihilī* at nothing, *pilī* at a hair, and *facere* to make). — *adj* **flocc'ose** (or *-ōs'*) woolly. — *adj* **flocc'ūlar**. — *adj* **flocc'ūlate**. — *vt* and *vi* to collect or mass together in tufts, flakes or cloudy masses. — *n* **floccūlā'tion**. — *n* **flocc'ule** a flocculus. — *n* **flocc'ūlence** flocculated condition. — *adj* **flocc'ūlent** woolly; flaky; flocculated. — *n* **flocc'ūlus** a small flock, tuft or flake; a small outgrowth of the cerebellum (*med*); a light or dark patch on the sun's surface, *usu* near sunspots, caused by calcium or hydrogen vapour: — *pl* **flocculi** (*flok'ū-lī*). [L *floccus* a lock or trifle; dimin *flocculus*]

flock[1] *flok*, *n* a company of animals, eg sheep, birds, etc; a company generally; a church congregation, considered as the charge of a minister. — *vi* to gather or go in flocks or in crowds. — **flock'-master** an owner or overseer of a flock; a sheep-farmer or shepherd. [OE *flocc* a flock or company; ON *flokkr*]

flock[2] *flok*, *n* a lock of wool; a tuft; cloth refuse, waste wool (also in *pl*); a woolly-looking precipitate (also in *pl*); fine particles of wool or other fibre applied to cloth to give a raised velvety surface or pattern. — **flock'-bed** a bed stuffed with wool; **flock'-paper** or **flock wallpaper** a wallpaper dusted over with flock. [OFr *floc*, from L *floccus* a lock of wool]

floe *flō*, *n* a field of floating ice. [Prob Norw *flo* layer, from ON *flō*]

flog *flog*, *vt* to beat or strike; to lash; to chastise with blows; to sell, sometimes illicitly (*slang*). — *vi* and *vt* to move or progress toilingly: — *pr p* **flogg'ing**; *pa t* and *pa p* **flogged**. — *n* **flogg'ing**. — **flog a dead horse** (*colloq*) to waste time and energy on a lost or impossible cause; **flog to death** (*colloq*) to talk about, advertise, persuade, etc too much, often producing the opposite to the desired effect. [17c cant; prob an abbrev of **flagellate**]

flokati *flə-kä'tē*, *n* a hand-woven Greek rug with a very thick shaggy wool pile. [Gr *phlokatē* a peasant's blanket]

flong *flong*, (*printing*) *n* papier-mâché for making moulds in stereotyping. [Fr *flan*]

flood *flud*, *n* a great flow of water; an inundation; a deluge; a condition of abnormally great flow in a river; a river or other water (*poetic*); the rise of the tide; any great inflow or outflow, eg of light, tears or visitors; a floodlight (*colloq*). — *vt* to submerge (land) in water; to overflow; to inundate; to supply in excessive quantity. — *vi* (of land) to be submerged in water; to overflow; of a woman, to bleed profusely, as after childbirth or in exceptionally heavy menstruation. — *adj* **flood'ed**. — *n* **flood'ing**. — **flood'gate** a gate for allowing or stopping the flow of water, a sluice or lock-gate; **flood lamp** a floodlight; **flood'light** lighting of a large area or surface by illumination from lamps situated at some distance (also **floodlighting**); one of the lamps providing such lighting. — Also *vt*: — *pa t* and *pa p* **flood'lighted** or **flood'lit**. — **floodlight projector** housing and support for a floodlight lamp with a reflector for directing the light into a suitable beam; **flood'mark** the mark or line to which the tide or a flood has risen; **flood'-plain** an extensive level area beside a river, formed of deposits of sediment brought downstream and spread by the river in flood; **flood'tide** the rising tide; **flood'wall** a wall built as protection against floods; **flood'water**; **flood'way** an artificial passage for floodwater. — **the Flood** the deluge, described in the Old Testament, that covered the whole Earth, and from which Noah and his family and livestock escaped in the ark. [OE *flōd*; Du *vloed*, Ger *Flut*; cf **flow**[2]]

floor *flōr*, *flör*, *n* the lower supporting surface of a room, etc; a platform; all the rooms in a building on the same level; a bottom surface; that on which anything rests or any operation is performed; a levelled area; the ground (*colloq*); the part of a legislative assembly where members sit and speak; the (part of a hall, etc accommodating) members of the public at a meeting, etc; the right to speak at a meeting (*esp* in the phrases *have* and *be given the floor*); the part of a stock, etc exchange on which dealers operate; a lower limit of prices, etc; a quantity of grain spread out to germinate. — *vt* to furnish with a floor; to throw or place on, or knock to, the floor; to defeat or stump (*colloq*). — *adj* **floored**. — *n* (*colloq*) **floor'er** a knock-down blow; a decisive retort, etc; an examination question one cannot answer. — *n* **floor'ing** material for floors; a platform. — **floor'board** one of the narrow boards making up a floor; **floor'cloth** a covering for floors, *esp* of linoleum or the like (*rare*); a cloth for washing floors; **floor'head** the upper end of a ship's floor timber; **flooring saw** a saw curved towards the toe with extra teeth on the back above the toe, used for cutting along the cracks between floorboards, etc; **floor limit** an amount above which a credit card sale must be authorized by the card company, varying from one shop, etc to another; **floor pan** the underside of a car, on which the body shell, doors, etc are built up; **floor plan** a diagram showing the layout of rooms, etc on one storey of a building; **floor price** a fixed lowest limit to the possible price of something; **floor show** a performance on the floor of a ballroom, nightclub, etc, not on a platform; **floor timber** a timber placed immediately across a ship's keel, on which her bottom is framed; **floor'walker** a supervisor of a section of a large store, who attends to customers' complaints, etc. — **cross the floor** (of a member of parliament, etc) to change one's allegiance from one party to another; **first floor** the floor in a house above the ground floor, the second storey; the ground floor (*NAm*) (*adj* **first'-floor**); **hold the floor** to dominate a meeting by speaking at great length; to speak too much, boringly; **take the floor** to rise to address a meeting; to take part in a dance. [OE *flōr*; Du *vloer* a flat surface, Ger *Flur* flat land; Welsh *llawr*]

floozie or **floosie** *floo͞o'zi*, (*slang*) *n* a young woman of doubtful sexual morals; a prostitute, *esp* a slovenly one. — Also **floo'zy** or **floo'sy**. [Origin uncertain]

flop[1] *flop*, *n* a limp, heavy, flapping movement, fall or sound; a collapse; a fiasco or failure; a place to sleep (*NAm slang*). — *adv* with a flop. — *vt* and *vi* to move with a flop; to drop heavily; to change over in nature or politics (*US*). — *vi* to collapse; to fail dismally; to go to bed or sleep (often with *at*; *NAm*). — *adv* **flopp'ily**. — *n* **flopp'iness**. — *adj* **flopp'y**. — *n* (*comput*) a floppy disk. — **flop'house** (*orig US*) a cheap hotel; a doss-house; **floppy disk** or **disc** (*comput*) a storage device in the form of a thin, flexible disc, sometimes encased in a stiff plastic cover. [A form of **flap**]

flop[2] *flop*, (*comput*) *n* a *fl*oating-point *op*eration (see under **float**).

flor *flŏr*, *n* a yeasty growth which is allowed to form on the surface of sherry wines after fermentation and which gives them a nutty taste. [Sp, flower or mould, from L *flōs*, *flōris* a flower]

Flor. *abbrev*: Florida (US state).

flor. *abbrev*: florin; *floruit* (L), flourished.

flora *flō'rə* or *flö'*, *n* the assemblage of all forms of vegetable life of a region or age, *esp* as distinct from animal life (*fauna*); a list or descriptive enumeration of these: — *pl* **flo'ras** or **flo'rae**. — *adj* **flo'ral** pertaining to the goddess Flora, to floras, or to flowers. — *adv* **flo'rally**. — *n* **Floréal** (*flō-rā-äl*; *Fr*) the 8th month of the French revolutionary calendar, the month of flowers, about 20 April–20 May. — *n* **florescence** (*flor-es'əns*) a bursting into flower; a time of flowering (*bot*). — *adj* **floresc'ent** bursting into flower. — *n* **floret** (*flor'it*) a small flower; one of the single flowers in the head of a composite flower; one of the branches in the head of a cauliflower. — *adj* **flo'riated** or **flo'reated** (*archit*) decorated with a floral ornament. — *n* **floribunda** (*flor-*, *flōr-* or *flör-i-bun'də*) a plant, *esp* a rose, whose flowers grow in clusters. — *adj* **floricul'tural** (*flōr-* or *flör-*). — *n* **flor'iculture** the growing of flowers or plants. — *n* **floricul'turist**. — *adj* **florif'erous** bearing or producing flowers. — *adj* **flo'riform** flower-shaped. — *n* **flor'igen** (*-i-jən*; Gr *gennaein* to produce) a postulated flower-forming hormone. — *n* **florilegium** (*-lē'ji-əm*; L *legere* to gather) an anthology or collection of choice extracts: — *pl* **florilē'gia**. — *n* **flor'ist** a seller, or grower, of flowers; (*flō'* or *flö'rist*) a student of flowers or of floras. — *adj* **florist'ic**. — *adv* **florist'ically**. — *n sing* **florist'ics** the study of floras. — *n* **flor'istry** the art of cultivating or selling flowers. — *adj* **flo'ry** having fleur-de-lys (*heraldry*); showy or conceited (*Scott*). — **floral diagram** a figure showing the arrangement of the parts of a flower in ground-plan. [L *Flōra*, goddess of flowers; *flōs*, *flōris* a flower]

floreat *flō'rē-at* or *flö'rā-at*, (*L*) may (it) flourish.

Florentine *flor'ən-tīn*, *adj* of or relating to *Florence* in Tuscany; (sometimes without *cap*; *cookery*) containing spinach. — *n* a native or inhabitant of Florence; (without *cap*) a durable silk textile fabric (also **flor'ence**); a pie with no crust beneath the meat; (also without *cap*) a biscuit covered on one side with fruit and nuts on a chocolate base. — **Florence flask** a long-necked round flask; **Florentine iris** see **orris**[1]. [L *Flōrentīnus*, from *Flōrentia*]

florescent, **floret**, **floribunda**, etc. See under **flora**.

florid *flo'rid*, *adj* having many flowers (*obs*); flowery; bright in colour; flushed with red; (of a complexion) ruddy, often unhealthily so; characterized by flowery rhetoric, melodic figures, or other ornament; over-adorned; richly ornamental. — *n* **florid'ity**. — *adv* **flor'idly**. — *n* **flor'idness**. [**flora**]

Florideae *flor-id'i-ē*, (*bot*) *n pl* a large subclass of the Rhodophyceae or red seaweeds. — *n* and *adj* **florid'ean**. — *adj* **florid'eous**. [L *flōridus* florid]

florin *flor'in*, *n orig* a Florentine gold coin with a lily stamped on one side, first struck in the 13c; a former British silver or cupro-nickel coin worth one-tenth of a pound, first minted in 1849 (a **double florin** was coined in 1887); in the Netherlands, the guilder. [Fr, from Ital *fiorino*, from *fiore* a lily, from L *flōs*, *flōris*]

florist, etc. See under **flora**.

floruit *flō'rū-it*, *flö'roo͞-*, *flor'ū-* or *-o͞o-*, *n* a period during which a person flourished, was most active, produced most works, etc. — Also *vi*. [L, 3rd pers sing perf indicative of *flōrēre* to flourish]

flory. See under **flora** and at **fleury** under **fleur-de-lis**.

floscule *flos'kūl*, *n* a floret (see under **flora**). — *adj* **flos'cūlar** or **flos'cūlous**. [L *flōsculus*, dimin of *flōs* a flower]

floss *flos*, *n* the rough outside of the silkworm's cocoon, and other waste from silk manufacture; fine silk in spun strands not twisted together, used in embroidery and (**dental floss**) tooth-cleaning; any loose downy or silky plant substance; fluff (also **flosh**). — *vi* and *vt* to use dental floss (on). — *n* **floss'ing**. — *adj* **floss'y** made of, like, or relating to floss; showy or overdressed (*slang*). — **floss silk** or **flox silk**. [Prob OFr *flosche* down, or from some Gmc word cognate with **fleece**; cf ON *flos* nap]

flota *flō'tə*, *n* a commercial fleet; formerly, the fleet which annually conveyed the produce of America to Spain. [Sp]

flote *flōt*, *n* (*obs*) a wave. — *n* **flō'tage** see **floatage** under **float**. — *adj* **flō'tant** (*heraldry*) floating in air or in water. — *n* **flotā'tion** the act of floating; the science of floating bodies; the act of starting a business, *esp* a limited liability company, by drawing up various documents and raising capital by selling shares; (also **froth flotation**) a method of separating ore from the rock in which it is embedded by forming a froth, the ore particles clinging to the bubbles. — **flotation therapy** (*med*) an alternative therapy for stress in which the patient floats for about an hour in a sealed salt-water-filled capsule (a **flotation tank** or **float tank**), with music sometimes piped in. — **plane** or **line of flotation** the plane or line in which the horizontal surface of a fluid cuts a body floating in it. [See **float**]

flotel or **floatel** *flō-tel'*, *n* a platform or boat containing the sleeping accommodation and eating, leisure, etc facilities for workers on oil rigs. [**float** and **hotel**]

flotilla *flo-til'ə*, *n* a fleet (of small ships). [Sp, dimin of *flota* a fleet]

flotsam *flot'səm*, *n* goods lost by shipwreck and found floating on the sea (see also **jetsam**). [Anglo-Fr *floteson* (Fr *flottaison*), from OFr *floter* to float]

flounce[1] *flowns*, *vi* to move abruptly, impatiently or disgustedly. — *n* an impatient or disgusted fling, flop or movement. — *adv* with a flounce. [Prob cognate with Norw *flunsa* to hurry, and Swed dialect *flunsa* to plunge]

flounce[2] *flowns*, *n* a hanging strip gathered and sewn to the skirt of a dress by its upper edge. — *vt* to provide with flounces. — *n* **floun'cing** material for flounces. — *adj* **floun'cy** decorated with flounces. [See **frounce**[1]]

flounder[1] *flown'dər*, *vi* to struggle with violent and awkward movements; to stumble helplessly in thinking or speaking. — *n* an act of floundering. [Prob an onomatopoeic blending of the sound and sense of earlier words like **founder** and **blunder**]

flounder[2] *flown'dər*, *n* a name given to a number of species of flatfish of the family Pleuronectidae, in Europe *Platichthys flesus*, in the US certain species of *Pseudopleuronectes*, *Limanda*, etc. [Anglo-Fr *floundre*, OFr *flondre*, most prob of Scand origin; cf ON *flythra*; Swed *flundra*]

flour *flowr*, *n* the finely-ground meal of wheat, or of any other grain; the fine soft powder of any substance. — *vt* to reduce into or sprinkle with flour. — *vi* (of mercury) to break up into fine globules in the amalgamation process. — *adj* **flour'y** covered with flour; like flour. — **flour bolt** a machine for separating flour from bran; **flour mill** a mill for making flour. [Same word as **flower**]

flourish *flur'ish*, *vi* to bloom (*obs* and *Scot*); to grow luxuriantly; to thrive; to be in full vigour; to be prosperous; to use copious and flowery language; to move in fantastic patterns; to display ostentatiously; to play or sing ostentatious passages, or ostentatiously (*music*); to play a fanfare; to make ornamental strokes with the pen; to show off. — *vt* to adorn with fantastic patterns or ornaments; to make attractive (*Shakesp*); to brandish in show, triumph or exuberance of spirits. — *n* decoration (*obs*); showy splendour; a figure made by a bold stroke of the pen; the waving of a weapon or other object; a flowery passage of words; a showy, fantastic or highly ornamental passage of music; a mass of blossom on a fruit-tree (*dialect*). — *adj* **flour'ished** decorated with flourishes. — *adj* **flour'ishing** thriving; prosperous; making a flourish. — *adv* **flour'ishingly**. — *adj* **flour'ishy** full of flourishes. — **flourishing thread** thread used in ornamental needlework. — **flourish of trumpets** a fanfare heralding an important person or people; any ostentatious introduction. [OFr *florir*, *floriss-*, from L *flōs*, *flōris* flower]

flouse *flows*, (*dialect*) *vt* and *vi* to splash. — Also **floush** (*flowsh*). [Cf **flush**[1]]

flout *flowt*, *vt* to jeer at, to mock; to treat with contempt; to reject or defy (orders, etc). — *vi* to jeer (with *at*). — *n* a jeer; a contemptuous act or speech. — *adv* **flout'ingly**. — **flout'ingstock** (*Shakesp*) a person or thing that is flouted. [Prob a specialized use of *floute*, ME form of **flute**, to play on the flute; cf Du *fluiten*]

flow[1] *flō*, *vi* (of water, etc) to run; to move or change form like a fluid; (of the tide) to rise or come in; to move in a stream; to glide smoothly; to abound or run over; to run in smooth lines; to issue or proceed smoothly and effortlessly; to stream or hang, loose and waving; to melt (*obs*). — *vt* to cover with water: — *pa t* and *pa p* **flowed**; *pa p* (*Shakesp* and *Milton*) **flown** (*flōn*). — *n* a stream or current; movement of, or like that of, a fluid; anything which flows or has flowed; mode of flowing; the setting in of the tide; copious fluency; menstruation (*colloq*). — *n* **flow'age** (an) act of flowing; the state of being flooded. — *adj* **flow'ing** moving, as a fluid; fluent; smooth and continuous; falling or hanging in folds or waves. — *adv* **flow'ingly**. — *n* **flow'ingness**. — **flow chart**, **diagram** or **sheet** a chart pictorially representing the nature and sequence of operations to be carried out, eg in a computer program or an industrial process; **flow cytometry** (*biol*) a technique for sorting cells or cell components, *usu* involving staining of specific cells, etc with a fluorescent molecule; **flow'meter** a device for measuring, or giving an output signal proportional to, the rate of flow of a fluid in a pipe; **flow'-on** (*Austr*) the process by which a wage or salary increase awarded to one group of workers results in a similar increase for other workers; such an increase; **flow-sorted chromosomes** those sorted on the basis of size by flow cytometry. [OE *flōwan*]

flow[2] *flōw*, *flow*, (*Scot*) *n* a morass; a flat, moist tract of land; a quicksand; a moorland pool; a sea basin or sound. [Cf Icel *flói* a marshy moor; Norw dialect *floe* pool in a swamp; ON *flóa* to flood]

flower *flow'ər* or *flowr*, *n* a growth comprising the reproductive organs of seed plants; the blossom of a plant, or the state of being in blossom; any plant that produces blossoms, *esp* one grown for its blossom; the prime of life; the best of anything; the person or thing most distinguished; the embodiment of perfection; a figure of speech; ornament of style; (in *pl*) menstrual discharge (*obs*); (in *pl*) a sublimate (eg **flowers of sulphur**; *chem*); (in *pl*) applied to some fungous growths, eg **flowers of tan**, a slime fungus on tan-bark. — *vi* to blossom; to flourish. — *vt* to adorn with flowers or a floral design. — *n* **flower'age** flowers collectively; the flowering state of a plant. — *adj* **flower'ed** decorated with flower designs; decorated with fleurs-de-lis (*heraldry*). — *n* **flower'er** a plant that flowers; an embroiderer of floral designs. — *n* **flower'et** a little flower; a floret (see under **flora**). — *n* **flower'iness**. — *n* and *adj* **flower'ing**. — *adj* **flower'less**. — *adj* **flower'y** full of or adorned with flowers; highly embellished or florid. — **flower'-bed** a garden bed for flowers; **flower'-bell** a blossom shaped like a bell; **flower'-bud** a bud with the unopened flower; **flower child** one of the Flower People; **flower'-clock** a collection of flowers so arranged that the time of day is indicated by their times of opening and closing; **flower-de-leuce**, **flower-deluce**, **flower deluce** (*-di-lōōs'*), **flower-delice** and **flower delice** (*-di-lēs'*, *-līs'* or *-del'is*) old names for the iris, or for the fleur-de-lis; **flower'-garden**; **flower'-girl** a girl or woman who sells flowers in the street; **flower'-head** a close inflorescence in which all the florets grow together at the tip of the stem, rather than on separated stalks; **flowering rush** a monocotyledonous plant (*Butomus*), with large linear three-edged leaves and an umbel of rose-coloured flowers; **flower of Jove** a campion with heads of purple or scarlet flowers, and leaves with silky-white hairs; **Flower People** (also without *cap*) colourfully dressed adherents of a cult (**Flower Power**; also without *caps*) arising in the mid-1960s which rejected materialism and advocated peace and universal love; **flower'pot** a pot in which a plant is grown; **flower'-service** a church service where offerings of flowers are made; **flower'-show** an exhibition of flowers; **flower'-stalk** the stem that supports the flower. — *adj* **flowery-kir'tled** (*Milton*) with a flowery petticoat. — **the flowery land** (*archaic*) China. [OFr *flour* (Fr *fleur*), from L *flōs*, *flōris* a flower]

flown *flōn*, *pa p* of **fly**; old *pa p* of **flow**[1]. — **flown cover** (*philat*) an envelope which has been carried by air over at least part of its delivery route.

flox silk. Same as **floss silk** (see under **floss**).

fl. oz. *abbrev*: fluid ounce or ounces.

flu or (*rare*) **flue** *flōō*, *n* a shortened form of **influenza**. — *adj* (*colloq*) **flu'ey**.

fluate *flōō'āt*, (*obs*) *n* a fluoride.

flub *flub*, (*NAm colloq*) *vt* to botch, make a mess of. — Also *vi*. — *pr p* **flubb'ing**; *pa t* and *pa p* **flubbed**. — *n* a gaffe; a mistake; a person given to making mistakes. [Ety unknown]

fluctuate *fluk'tū-āt*, *vi* to vary this way and that; to go up and down or to and fro; to move like a wave. — *vt* to throw into fluctuation. — *adj* **fluc'tūant**. — *adj* **fluc'tūāting**. — *n* **fluctūā'tion** rise and fall; motion to and fro; wavelike motion; alternate variation, vacillation. [L *fluctuāre*, *-ātum*, from *fluctus* a wave, from *fluere* to flow]

flue[1] *flōō*, *n* a pipe for conveying hot air, smoke, flame, etc; a small chimney; a flue pipe (*music*); the opening by which the air escapes from the foot of a flue pipe. — *vt* **flue'-cure** to cure (tobacco) by heat introduced through flues. — *adj* **flue'-cured**. — **flue pipe** a pipe, *esp* in an organ, in which the sound is produced by air impinging upon an edge; **flue'work** (in an organ) the flue pipes collectively. [Origin uncertain]

flue[2] *flōō*, *n* light fluff, such as collects in unswept places; soft down or fur. — *adj* **flu'ey**. [Origin doubtful]

flue[3] or **flew** *flōō*, (*dialect*) *adj* shallow or flat; flared; splayed. [Origin uncertain]

flue[4]. Same as **flu**.

fluellin *flōō-el'in*, *n* a name given to various speedwells (*esp Veronica serpyllifolia* and *Veronica officinalis*) and toadflaxes (*esp Linaria elatine* and *Linaria spuria*). [Welsh *llysiau Llewelyn* Llewelyn's herbs]

fluent *flōō'ənt*, *adj* able to speak and write a particular language competently and with ease (*usu* with *in*); spoken or written competently and with facility; voluble; marked by copiousness; (of a movement) smooth, easy or graceful. — *n* (*math*) the variable quantity in fluxions. — *n* **flu'ence** (*Milton*), **flu'ency** or **flu'entness**. — *adv* **flu'ently**. [L *fluēns*, *fluentis*, pr p of *fluere* to flow]

fluey. See **flu** and **flue**[2].

fluff *fluf*, *n* a soft down from cotton, etc; anything downy; a fault in performing (a play, piece of music, etc) (*colloq*); a duffed stroke at golf, etc (*colloq*). — *vt* to make fluffy (often with *up*). — *vt* and *vi* to bungle, in sport, musical or dramatic performance, etc. — *n* **fluff'iness**. — *adj* **fluff'y**. — **a bit of fluff** (*slang*, often *offensive*) a sexually attractive woman. [Perh connected with **flue**[2]]

flügel or **flugel** *flü'hhəl* or *flōō'gl*, *n* a grand piano. — **flü'gelhorn** or **flu'gelhorn** a hunting-horn, a kind of bugle with keys; **flü'gelhornist** or **flu'gelhornist**; **flugelman** (*flōō'gl-man*) same as **fugleman**. [Ger, wing]

fluid *flōō'id*, *n* a substance whose particles can move about with freedom; a liquid or gas. — *adj* that flows; unsolidified; of, using or pertaining to fluids; likely or tending to change; easily changed; (of a movement) smooth and graceful. — *adj* **flu'idal**. — *adj* **fluid'ic**. — *n sing* **fluid'ics** the science and technology of using a flow of liquid or gas for certain operations in place of a flow of electrons. — *vt* **fluid'ify**. — *n* **fluid'ity** or **flu'idness**. — *n* **fluidizā'tion** or **-s-**. — *vt* **flu'idize** or **-ise** to make fluid; to cause (fine particles) to move as a fluid, eg by suspending them in a current of air or gas; to fill with a specified fluid. — **fluid drive** a system of transmitting power smoothly, through the medium of the change in momentum of a fluid, *usu* oil; **fluidized bed** (*chem eng*) a bed of fluids which has been fluidized by an upward flow of liquid or gas. [L *fluidus* fluid, from *fluere* to flow]

fluke[1] *flōōk*, *n* a flounder; a trematode, parasitic worm, *esp* that which causes liver-rot in sheep, so called because of its resemblance to a miniature flounder (also **fluke'-worm**); a variety of kidney potato. [OE *flōc* a plaice; cf ON *flōke*]

fluke[2] *flōōk*, *n* the barb of an anchor; a barb; a lobe of a whale's tail. — *adj* **fluk'y**. [Prob a transferred use of **fluke**[1]]

fluke[3] *flōōk*, *n* an accidental success. — *vt* to make, score, etc by a fluke. — *adj* **fluk'ey** or **fluk'y**. [Origin unknown]

flume *flōōm*, *n* an artificial channel for water, for use in industry or as an amusement on which rides, *usu* in special boats, can be taken; a ravine with a stream flowing through it. — **be** or **go up the flume** (*rare*) to come to grief, to be done for. [OFr *flum*, from L *flūmen* a river, from *fluere* to flow]

flummery *flum'ər-i*, *n* a pudding made from the husks of oats, the Scots sowens; blancmange; anything insipid; empty compliment, humbug or pretentiousness. [Welsh *llymru*, from *llymrig* harsh, raw, from *llym* sharp or severe]

flummox *flum'əks*, (*colloq*) *vt* to perplex or puzzle. [Ety unknown]

flump *flump*, (*colloq*) *vt* to throw down heavily. — *vi* to move or fall with a flop or thud. — *n* the dull sound so produced. [Imit]

flung *flung*, *pa t* and *pa p* of **fling**.

flunk *flungk*, (*slang*, *esp NAm* and *NZ*) *vi* to fail in an examination; to be dismissed from college, etc for such a failure (with *out*). — Also *vt* and *n*. [Perh combined **flinch**[1] and **funk**[1]]

flunkey or **flunky** *flung'ki*, *n* a uniformed servant or footman; any servant; a servile person. — *n* **flun'keydom**. — *adj* **flun'keyish**. — *n* **flun'keyism**. [Perh originally *flanker* a person who runs alongside]

Fluon® *flōō'on*, *n* a proprietary name for **polytetrafluoroethylene**.

fluor *flōō'ər* or *-ör*, *n* fluorite. — *vi* **fluoresce** (*-ər-es'*) to demonstrate fluorescence. — *n* **fluorescein** (*-es'ē-in*) a fluorescent dyestuff, $C_{20}H_{12}O_5$. — *n* **fluoresc'ence** the property of some substances (eg fluor) of emitting, when exposed to radiation, rays of greater wavelength than those received. — *adj* **fluoresc'ent**. — *adj* **fluoric** (*-or'ik*). — *vt* **flu'oridate**, **flu'oridize** or **-ise** to add a fluoride to (a water or milk supply). — *n* **fluoridā'tion**. — *n* **flu'oride** a compound of fluorine with another element or radical; loosely, sodium fluoride or sodium monofluorophosphate as the active ingredient in toothpaste. — *vt* **flu'orinate** to introduce fluorine into a chemical compound. — *n* **fluorinā'tion**. — *n* **flu'orine** (*-ēn*) an element (symbol **F**; atomic no 9), a pale greenish-yellow gas. — *n* **fluorite** (*flōō'ər-īt*) a mineral, calcium fluoride, commonly purple, also green, colourless, etc, crystallizing in cubes and octahedra, found abundantly in Derbyshire. Its coloured varieties may fluoresce strongly in ultraviolet light. — **fluorescence microscopy** (*biol*) light microscopy in which the specimen is irradiated at wavelengths which will excite the natural or artificially introduced fluorochromes; **fluorescent lighting** brighter lighting obtained for the same consumption of electricity, by using fluorescent material to convert ultraviolet radiation in the electric lamp into visible light; **fluorimeter** see **fluorometer** below; **flu'orocarbon** an alkane in which hydrogen atoms are replaced by fluorine atoms, any of a series of compounds of fluorine and carbon (corresponding to the hydrocarbons) highly resistant to heat and chemical action; **flu'orochrome** (*chem*) a molecule or chemical group which fluoresces on irradiation; **fluorom'eter** or **fluorim'eter** an instrument for measuring intensity of fluorescence. — *adj* **fluoromet'ric** or **fluorimet'ric**. — **flu'oroscope** an instrument for X-ray examination by means of a fluorescent screen. — *adj* **fluoroscop'ic**. — **fluoros'copy**; **fluorō'sis** chronic poisoning by fluorine; **flu'orotype** (*obs*) photography by means of fluorides; **flu'orspar** fluorite. [L *fluor* flow, from its use as a flux]

Fluothane® *flōō'ō-thān*, *n* a proprietary name for **halothane** (see under **haloid**).

flurry *flur'i*, *n* a sudden blast or gust; agitation; a sudden commotion; bustle; the death-agony of the whale; a fluttering collection or mass of things, eg snowflakes. — *vt* to agitate or confuse: — *pr p* **flurr'ying**; *pa t* and *pa p* **flurr'ied**. — *vt* **flurr** (*flûr*; *rare*) to scatter. — *vi* to fly up. [Prob onomatopoeic, suggested by **flaw**[1], **hurry**, etc]

flush[1] *flush*, *n* a sudden flow; a flow of blood to the skin, causing redness; a suffusion of colour, *esp* red; the device on a lavatory which is operated to release a flow of water to clean the pan; a sudden growth; a renewal of growth; a rush of feeling; a puddle (*obs*); a watery place near a spring, etc (*obs*); bloom, freshness or vigour; abundance. — *vi* to glow; to become red in the face; to flow swiftly, suddenly or copiously. — *vt* to cleanse by a copious flow of water (as in a lavatory); to clear by a blast of air; to cause to glow; to elate or excite the spirits of. — *adj* overflowing; abounding; well supplied, *esp* with money (*colloq*); in full bloom (*Shakesp*); flushed. — *adj* **flushed** suffused with ruddy colour; excited. — *n* **flush'er** a person who flushes sewers. — *n* **flush'ing**. — *n* **flush'ness**. — *adj* **flush'y** reddish. — **flush'-box** a tank for flushing a lavatory, a cistern. — **in the** (or **one's**) **first flush** young or youthful; **in the first flush of** in the early stages of (*esp* youth), when one is at a peak of vigour, enthusiasm, etc. [Prob **flush**[2] influenced by **flash** and **blush**]

flush[2] *flush*, *vi* to start like an alarmed bird. — *vt* to rouse and cause (*esp* birds) to move off; to force out of concealment (with *out*). — *n* the act of starting (*esp* birds); a bird or a flock of birds so started (*Spenser*). [Prob onomatopoeic; suggested by **fly**, **flutter** and **rush**[1]]

flush[3] *flush*, *vt* to make even; to fill up to the level of a surface (often with *up*). — *adj* having the surface in the same plane as the adjacent surface (with *with*); (of a deck) having the same level throughout the ship's length. — Also *adv*. [Prob related to **flush**[1]]

flush[4] *flush*, *n* a hand in which all the cards or a specified number are of the same suit. — *adj* (*poker*) consisting of cards all of the same suit. — **busted flush** a flush that is never completed (*poker*); something that has to be abandoned as a failure (*fig*); **straight flush** (*poker*) a sequence of five cards of the same suit (**royal flush**, if headed by the ace). [Prob Fr *flux*, from L *fluxus* flow; influenced by **flush**[1]]

fluster *flus'tər*, *n* hurrying; flurry; heat (*obs*); confused agitation. — *vt* to confuse; to make hot and flurried; to fuddle with drink. — *vi* to bustle; to be agitated or fuddled. — *n* **flus'terment**. — *adj* **flus'tery** confused. — *vt* **flus'trate** (*obs*) to fluster. — *n* **flustrā'tion** (*obs*). [ON *flaustr* hurry]

Flustra *flus'trə*, *n* one of the commonest genera of Polyzoa, a division of aquatic animals. [Ety unknown]

flute *flōōt*, *n* a wind instrument, *esp* either of two types consisting of a wooden or metal tube with holes stopped by the fingertips or by keys, one type blown from the end through a fipple, the other (also called **transverse flute**) held horizontally and played by directing the breath across a mouth-hole; (in organ-building) a stop with stopped wooden pipes, having a flute-like tone; a longitudinal groove, such as on a pillar (*archit*); a tall, narrow wine-glass; a shuttle in tapestry-weaving, etc. — *vi* to play the flute; to make fluty sounds. — *vt* to play or sing in soft flute-like tones; to form flutes or grooves in (*archit*). — *adj* **flut'ed** ornamented with flutes, channels or grooves. — *n* **flut'er**. — *n* **flutina** (*-tē'*) a kind of accordion. — *n* **flut'ing** flute-playing or similar sounds; longitudinal grooving. — *n* **flut'ist** same as **flautist**. — *adj* **flut'y** like a flute in tone. — **flûte-à-bec** (*flüt-ä-bek*; *Fr*) a fipple-flute, a recorder or flageolet; **flute'-bird** a piping crow, an Australian bird of the shrike family; **flute'mouth** a fish (*Fistularia*) similar to the sticklebacks. [OFr *fleüte*; ety dubious]

flutter *flut'ər*, *vi* to move about nervously, aimlessly or bustlingly; (of a bird) to flap wings; (of a flag, etc) to flap in the air; to vibrate or, eg of a pulse, to beat irregularly; to be agitated or uncertain; to be frivolous (*obs*); to toss a coin (*archaic*). — *vt* to throw into disorder; to move in quick motions. — *n* quick, irregular motion; agitation; confusion; a bet or wager (*colloq*); a small speculation (*colloq*); (in wind-instrument playing) rapid movement of the tongue as for a rolled 'r' (also **flutt'er-tonguing**); (in sound reproduction) undesirable variation in pitch or loudness; abnormal oscillation of a part of an aircraft. [OE *flotorian* to float about, from the root of *flēotan* to float]

fluvial *flōō'vi-əl*, *adj* of, belonging to, found or occurring in rivers. — *n* **flu'vialist** a person stressing the role of rivers in the explanation of phenomena. — *adj* **fluviat'ic** or **flu'viatile** (*-tīl* or *-til*) belonging to or formed by rivers. — *adj* **fluvio-glā'cial** pertaining to glacial rivers. [L *fluviālis*, from *fluvius* a river, and *fluere* to flow]

flux *fluks*, *n* (an) act of flowing; a flow of matter; a state of flow or continuous change; a discharge generally from a mucous membrane (*med*); matter discharged; excrement (*euphem*); an easily fused substance, *esp* one added to another to make it more easily soldered; the rate of flow of mass, volume or energy (*phys*). — *vt* to melt; to apply flux to when soldering. — *vi* to flow; to fuse. — *n* **fluxion** (*fluk'shən*) a flowing or discharge; excessive flow of blood or fluid to any organ (*med*); a difference or variation; the rate of change of a continuously varying quantity (*math*); (in *pl*) the name given by Newton to that branch of mathematics which with a different notation (developed by Leibniz) is known as differential and integral calculus. — *adj* **flux'ional** or **flux'ionary** (*archaic*) variable; inconstant. — *n* **flux'ionist** a person skilled in fluxions. — *adj* **flux'ive** (*Shakesp*) flowing with tears. — **flux density** (*phys*) the number of photons (or particles) passing through unit area normal to a beam, or the energy of the radiation passing through this area. — **in a state of flux** in an unsettled, undetermined state. [OFr, from L *fluxus*, from *fluere* to flow]

fly *flī*, *vi* to move through the air, *esp* on wings or in aircraft; to operate an aircraft; to move swiftly; to hurry; to pass quickly; to flee; to burst quickly or suddenly; to flutter. — *vt* to avoid or flee from; to cause (eg a kite, aircraft, etc) to fly; to conduct or transport by air; to cross or pass by flying: — *pr p* **fly'ing**; *pa t* **flew** (*flōō*); *pa p* **flown** (*flōn*); 3rd *sing present indicative* **flies**. — *n* any insect of the order *Diptera*; often so widely used, *esp* in composition (eg *butterfly*, *dragonfly*, *mayfly*) as to be virtually equivalent to *insect*; a fish-hook dressed so as to imitate a fly; collectively, an insect pest; a familiar spirit (*archaic*); an attendant parasite (*obs*); a flight; a flap, *esp* a tent-door; a flap of material covering eg a trouser opening; a trouser fastener, eg a zip; the free end of a flag, or anything similar; a fast stagecoach (*hist*); a light vehicle on hire, at first drawn by a man, later by a horse (*hist*); a flywheel; (in *pl*) the large space above the proscenium in a theatre, from which the scenes, etc are controlled: — *pl* **flies**. — *adj* (*slang*) knowing; surreptitious or sly. — *n* **flier** or **flyer** (*flī'ər*) a person who flies or flees; an aircraft pilot; an object, eg a train, moving at top speed; an ambitious person, *esp* one for whom fast promotion in the workplace is assured (also **high-fli'er** or **high-fly'er**); a *usu* risky financial speculation (*slang*); a part of a machine which moves rapidly; a rectangular step in stairs; a flying leap (*colloq*); a (*usu* single-sheet) promotional leaflet used (*esp* as an insert to other printed material) for advertising purposes. — *adj* **fly'able** (of weather) in which it is safe to fly; (of an aircraft) able, or fit, to be flown. — *n* **fly'ing**. — *adj* that flies or can fly; moving or passing very rapidly; organized for speedy action or transfer to any location as the need arises; (of a visit) very brief. — **fly agaric** a poisonous type of toadstool, *Amanita muscaria*, used in the production of flypaper and having hallucinogenic properties; **fly ash** fine particles of ash released into the air during eg the burning of fossil fuels in power stations, also used in brick-making and as a partial substitute for cement in concrete. — *adj* **fly'away** streaming; flighty; (of hair) too fine to hold a style for long. — **fly'bane** poison for flies; a name for various plants used for this; **fly'belt** a belt of country infested by tsetse fly. — *adj* **fly'-bitten** marked by, or as if by, the bites of flies. — **fly'blow** the egg of a fly, *esp* when found in meat — *adj* **fly'-blown** tainted with flies' eggs or maggots (also *fig*). — **fly'boat** a long, narrow, swift boat used on canals; **fly'book** a case like a book for holding fishing-flies; **fly'-by** a flight, at low altitude or close range, past a place, or a body in space, for observation; **fly'-by-night** a person who gads about at night; an absconding debtor; an irresponsible person. — *adj* irresponsible, *esp* in business matters; unreliable; transitory. — *adj* **fly-by-wire'** (of the control systems of an aircraft) controlled by computer and operated electronically, not mechanically. — **fly'catcher** a name for various birds that catch flies on the wing; **fly cemetery** (*humorous*) an Eccles cake or Garibaldi biscuit; **fly'-dressing** fly-tying; **fly'-drive** a package holiday in which the rental of a car, etc is included and the vehicle collected at the destination. — Also *adj.* — **fly'-dumping** fly-tipping. — *vi* **fly'-fish** to fish using artificial flies as lure. — **fly'-fisher**; **fly'-fishing**; **fly'-flap** a fly swat (see below); **fly'-flapper**; **fly front** a concealed fastening on a jacket, shirt, etc. — *adj* **fly-front'ed**. — **fly-half'** (*Rugby football*) a stand-off half; **flying bedstead** a testing framework resembling a bedstead in shape, that can be raised vertically from the ground by a jet engine; **flying boat** a seaplane with a boat's body; **flying bomb** a bomb in the form of an unpiloted jet-propelled aeroplane; **flying bridge** a ferry-boat moving under the combined forces of a river or stream and the resistance of a long cable; a pontoon bridge; the highest bridge of a ship; **flying buttress** an arch-shaped prop (*archit*); **flying camp** or **flying column** a body of troops for rapid deployment from one place to another. — *n pl* **flying colours** unfurled flags; triumphant success. — **Flying Corps** the precursor (1912–18) of the Royal Air Force; **flying doctor** a doctor, *esp orig* in the remote parts of Australia, who can be called by radio, etc and who flies to visit patients; **Flying Dutchman** a black ghostly Dutch ship, or its captain, condemned to sweep the seas around the Cape of Good Hope for ever; **flying fish** a fish that can leap out of the water and sustain itself in the air for a short time by its long pectoral fins, as if flying; **flying fox** a large fruit-eating bat; **flying jib** in a ship with more than one jib, the one set furthest forward; **flying leap** a leap made from a running start; **flying lemur** an animal (not in fact a lemur) of the genera *Cynocephalus* or *Galeopithecus* of the islands of SE Asia, whose fore and hind limbs are connected by a fold of skin, included in the Insectivora or made a separate order, Dermoptera; **flying lizard** a dragon or Komodo lizard; **flying machine** a power-driven aircraft; **flying officer** an officer in the Royal Air Force of rank equivalent to sub-lieutenant in the navy and lieutenant in the army (formerly called **observer**); **flying party** a small body of soldiers, equipped for rapid movements, used to harass an enemy; **flying phalanger** a general name for animals similar to the phalangers with a parachute of skin between fore and hind legs; **flying pickets** mobile pickets available for reinforcing the body of local pickets during a strike; **flying saucer** any of several disc-like flying objects reported to have been seen by various people and alleged to be craft from outer space; **flying shore** a horizontal baulk or shore; **flying shot** a shot at something in motion; **flying squad** a body of police, etc with special training, available for duty where the need arises, or one organized for fast action or movement; **flying squid** a squid with broad lateral fins by which it can spring high out of the water; **flying squirrel** a name for several kinds of squirrels with a parachute of skin between the fore and hind legs; also applied to the flying phalanger; **flying start** (in a race) a start given with the competitors already in motion; an initial advantage; a promising start; **flying suit** a pilot's one-piece suit; a similar fashion garment, worn *esp* by women; **flying wing** an arrowhead-shaped aircraft designed to minimize drag at very high speeds; **fly'-kick** a kick made while running; **fly'leaf** a blank leaf at the beginning or end of a book; **fly line** a line for angling with an artificial fly; **fly'maker** a person who ties artificial flies for angling; **fly'-man** a person who works the ropes in theatre flies; a person who drives a fly; **fly orchis** an orchid (*Ophrys muscifera* or *insectifera*) with a fly-like flower; **fly'over** a road or railway line carried over the top of another one at an intersection; a processional flight of aircraft, a fly-past (*US*); **fly'paper** a sticky or poisonous paper for attracting and killing flies; **fly'-past** a ceremonial flight analogous to a march past; a fly-by in space; **fly'pitch** (*colloq*) a market stall for which the operator has no licence; **fly'pitcher**; **flypost'ing** the practice of sticking political, advertising, etc bills illegally, on walls, etc; **fly powder** a powder used for killing flies; **fly rail** a leg that turns out to support the leaf of a table; **fly rod** a light flexible rod used in fly-fishing, *usu* in three pieces, butt, second-joint, and tip; **fly'-sheet** a piece of canvas that can be fitted to the roof of a tent to give additional protection from rain; a handbill. — *adj* **fly'-slow** (*Shakesp*; doubtful reading and sense) slow-flying. — **fly'-speck** a small spot of flies' excrement; **fly'-spray** (an aerosol containing) an insecticide; **fly swat** or **swatter** a device with which to hit or drive away flies; **fly'-tipping** unauthorized disposal of waste materials; **fly'-tower** a central tower in a modern theatre from which the flies can be hung over the stage; **fly'trap** a trap to catch flies; a plant that traps flies, *esp* the American dogbane and Venus's flytrap; **fly'-tying** making artificial flies for angling; **fly'-under** a road or railway line carried under another one at an intersection; **fly'way** a migration route used by birds; **fly'weight** a weight category applied variously in boxing, wrestling and weightlifting; a sportsperson of the specified weight for the category (eg in professional boxing the lowest weight — **mini-flyweight** (under 48 kg/105 lb), **light-flyweight** or **junior-flyweight** (maximum 49 kg/108lb), **flyweight** (maximum 51 kg/112 lb) and **super-flyweight** (maximum 52 kg/115 lb)); **fly'-wheel** a large wheel with a heavy rim, applied to machinery to equalize the effect of the driving effort. — **a fly in the ointment** some slight flaw which corrupts a thing of value (Eccles 10.1); a minor disadvantage in otherwise favourable circumstances; **a fly on the wall** the invisible observer that one would like to be on certain occasions (*adj* **fly'-on-the-wall**); **fly a kite** see **kite-flying** under **kite**[1]; **fly at** or **upon** to attack suddenly; **fly high** to aim high or be ambitious; **fly in the face of** to insult (*obs*); to oppose or defy; to be at variance with; **fly off the handle** (*colloq*) to lose one's temper; **fly open** to open suddenly or violently; **fly out** to break out in a rage; **let fly** to attack (also *fig*); to throw or send off; **like flies** (dying, etc) in vast numbers, with as little resistance as insects; **make the feathers fly** see under **feather**; **no flies on** no lack of alertness or astuteness in. [OE *flēogan* to fly, pa t *flēah*; *flēoge* fly or insect; Ger *fliegen*, *Fliege*]

Flymo® *flī'mō*, *n* a proprietary name for a type of lawnmower which hovers on a cushion of air.

flype *flīp*, *vt* to strip back; to turn partly outside in. [Prob Scand; cf Dan *flip* a flap]

Flysch or **flysch** *flish*, *n* a great Alpine mass of Cretaceous and Lower Tertiary sandstone with shales. [Swiss Ger]

flyte or **flite** *flīt*, (*Scot*) *vi* to quarrel; to brawl. — *vt* to scold; to rail at. — *n* **flyte** or **flyt'ing** an open debate; a contest in the exchange of (poetic) abuse (*hist*). [OE *flītan* to strive; Ger *befleissen*]

Fm (*chem*) *symbol*: fermium.

fm *abbrev*: fathom.

FMCGs *abbrev*: fast-moving consumer goods.

Fmk *abbrev*: Finnish markka (unit of currency).

FMS *abbrev*: flexible manufacturing system.

FO *abbrev*: Field Officer; Flying Officer; Foreign Office; Full Organ.

fo. or **fol.** *abbrev*: folio.

foal *fōl*, *n* the young of any animal of the horse family. — *vi* and *vt* to five birth to (a foal). — **foal'foot** (*bot*) coltsfoot. — **in foal** or **with foal** (of a mare) pregnant. [OE *fola*; Ger *Fohlen*, Gr *pōlos*; L *pullus*]

foam *fōm*, *n* bubbles on the surface of liquid; a suspension of gas in a liquid; frothy saliva or perspiration; any of many light, cellular materials, rigid or flexible, produced by aerating a liquid, then solidifying it; the sea (*poetic*). — *vi* to gather, produce or be full of foam; to be furious (*colloq*). — *vt* to pour out in foam; to fill or cover with foam. — *adv* **foam'ily**. — *n* **foam'iness**. — *n* and *adj* **foam'ing**. — *adv* **foam'ingly**. — *adj* **foam'less**. — *adj* **foam'y** frothy. — **foam glass** a very lightweight material made by firing crushed glass with carbon, used as a heat insulator, a construction material, and a filling in lifebelts, etc; **foam** or **foamed plastics** cellular plastics, soft and flexible like sponges, or rigid, with excellent heat-insulation properties; **foam rubber** rubber in cellular form, used chiefly in upholstery. — **foam at the mouth** to produce frothy saliva; to be extremely angry (*colloq*). [OE *fām*; Ger *Feim*, prob related to L *spūma*]

fob[1] *fob*, *n* (*archaic*) a trick. — *vt* (*archaic* except with *off*) to cheat; to give as genuine; to put off; to foist or palm. [Cf Ger *foppen* to jeer]

fob[2] *fob*, *n* a small watch pocket in a waistcoat or the waistband of trousers; a chain attaching a watch to a waistcoat, etc; a decoration hanging from such a chain; a decorative tab on a key-ring. — **fob'-watch**. — *vt* (*obs*) to pocket. [Perh connected with L Ger *fobke* little pocket, HGer dialect *fuppe* pocket]

f o b *abbrev*: free on board.

FOC *abbrev*: father of the chapel (in a trade union).

f o c *abbrev*: free of charge.

focal, **foci** and **focimeter**. See under **focus**.

fo'c'sle *fōk'sl*, contracted form of **forecastle**.

focus *fō'kəs*, *n* a fixed point such that the distances of a point on a conic section from it and from the directrix have a constant ratio (*geom*); a point in which rays converge after reflection or refraction, or from which (*virtual focus*) they seem to diverge (*optics*); any central point; the point or region of greatest activity; the point of origin (eg of an earthquake); the position, or condition, of sharp definition of an image; — *pl* **foci** (*fō'sī*) or **fo'cuses**. — *vt* to bring or adjust to a focus; to adjust so as to get a sharp image of; to concentrate: — *pr p* **fo'cusing** or **focussing**; *pa t* and *pa p* **fo'cused** or **foc'ussed**. — *adj* **fō'cal** of, belonging or pertaining to a focus. — *n* **focalizā'tion** or **-s-**. — *vt* **fō'calize** or **-ise** to focus. — *adv* **fō'cally**. — *n* **focimeter** (*fō-sim'i-tər*) an instrument for measuring the focal length of a lens. — **focal infection** a localized bacterial infection, eg of a gland, etc; **focal length** the distance between the centre of a lens and its focus; **focal-plane shutter** a camera shutter in the form of a blind with a slot, which is pulled rapidly across, and as close as is practicable to, the film or plate, speed being varied by adjusting the width of the slot; **focal point** (*optics*) focus; **focusing cloth** a cloth thrown over a photographic camera and the operator's head and shoulders to exclude extraneous light when focusing. — **conjugate foci** two points such that each is the focus for rays proceeding from the other; **in focus** placed or adjusted so as to secure distinct vision, or a sharp, definite image; **principal focus** the focus for rays parallel to the axis. [L *focus* a hearth]

fodder *fod'ər*, *n* food supplied to cattle; food (*slang*); people seen, callously, as a plentiful and expendable commodity (as in *cannon fodder*). — *vt* to supply with fodder. — *n* **fodd'erer**. — *n* **fodd'ering**. [OE *fōdor*; Ger *Futter*; cf **food**[1] and **feed**[1]]

FOE or **FoE** *abbrev*: Friends of the Earth.

foe *fō*, (*literary* or *archaic*) *n* an enemy: — *pl* **foes**; (*Spenser*) **fone** or **foen** (*fōn*). — **foe'man** an enemy in war (*pl* **foe'men**). [ME *foo*, from OE *fāh*, *fā* (adj) and *gefā* (noun)]

foedarie. See **fedarie**.

foederatus *fed-ə-rā'təs* or *foi-de-rä'tōōs* (*pl* **foederati** *-rā'tī* or *-rä'tē*; *L*) *n* a (conquered) ally of Rome; an auxiliary soldier fighting for the Romans.

foehn. See **föhn**.

foetid and **foetor**. See **fetid**.

foetus (the usual but etymologically unsatisfactory form of **fetus**) *fē'təs*, *n* the young animal in the egg or in the womb, after its parts are distinctly formed. — *adj* **foe'tal** or **fē'tal**. — *adj* **foeticī'dal** or **fetici'dal**. — *n* **foe'ticide** or **fē'ticide** destruction of a foetus. — *n* **foetos'copy** or **fetos'copy** a procedure for viewing the foetus directly, within the uterus, or for taking a sample of foetal blood from the placenta, by inserting a hollow needle through the abdomen into the uterus, for ascertaining any disorder. — **foetal** or **fetal alcohol syndrome** the congenital defects characteristic of babies born to mothers whose intake of alcohol is excessive, including short stature, retardation, and pixie-like features. [L *fētus* offspring]

fog[1] *fog*, *n* (a) thick cloudlike mist near the ground; cloudy obscurity; confusion or bewilderment; blurring on a negative, print or transparency (*photog*). — *vt* to shroud in fog; to obscure; to confuse; to produce fog on (*photog*). — *vi* to become coated, clouded, blurred or confused (*esp* with *up* or *over*); to be affected by fog (*photog*). — *adj* **fogged** (*fogd*) clouded, obscured; bewildered. — *n* **fogg'er** or **fog'man** a person who sets railway fog-signals. — *adv* **fogg'ily**. — *n* **fogg'iness**. — *adj* **fogg'y** misty; damp; fogged; clouded in mind; stupid. — *adj* **fog'less** without fog, clear. — **fog'-bank** a dense mass of fog like a bank of land; **fog'-bell** a bell rung by waves or wind to warn sailors in fog. — *adj* **fog'bound** impeded or brought to a standstill by fog. — **fog'-bow** a whitish arch like a rainbow, seen in fogs; **fog'-dog** a whitish spot seen near the horizon in fog; **fog'horn** a horn used as a warning signal by or to ships in foggy weather; a siren; a big bellowing voice; **fog index** a formula for calculating the readability of a text, used *esp* for children's books; **fog'-lamp** a lamp, *esp* on a vehicle, used to improve visibility in fog; **fog'-signal** a detonating cap or other audible warning used in fog; **fog'-smoke** fog. — **not have the foggiest** (*colloq*) not to have the least idea. [Origin obscure; perh connected with **fog**[2]; perh with Dan *fog*, as in *snee-fog* thick falling snow]

fog[2] *fog* or **foggage** *fog'ij*, *n* grass that grows after the hay is cut; moss (*Scot*). — *vi* to become covered with fog. — *adj* **fogg'y**. [Origin unknown; Welsh *ffwg* dry grass, is borrowed from English]

fogash *fog'osh*, *n* the pike-perch. [Hung *fogas*]

fogey. See **fogy**.

foggage. See **fog**[2].

fogle *fō'gəl*, (*slang*) *n* a silk handkerchief. [Origin obscure]

fogy or **fogey** *fō'gi*, (*derog*) *n* an old person, *esp* one with old-fashioned views: — *pl* **fo'gies** or **fo'geys**. — Also **old fogy** or **old fogey**. — *adj* **fō'gram** antiquated. — *n* a fogy. — *n* **fō'gramite** or **fogram'ity**. — *n* **fō'gydom** or **fo'geydom**. — *adj* **fō'gyish** or **fo'geyish**. — *n* **fō'gyism** or **fo'geyism**. — **young fogy** or **young fogey** (*derog*) a young person who adopts old-fashioned opinions, appearance, etc. [Prob from **foggy** moss-grown]

foh, **pho** (*pl* **phos**) or **phoh** *fō*, (*archaic*) *interj* expressing disgust or contempt.

föhn or **foehn** *fœn*, *n* a hot dry wind blowing down a mountain valley, *esp* in the Alps. [Ger, from Romansch *favugn*, from L *Favōnius* the west wind]

foible *foi'bl*, *n* a weakness; a penchant; a failing; a faible (*fencing*). [OFr *foible* weak; cf **faible** and **feeble**]

foid *foid*, *n* an internationally agreed term for **feldspathoid**. [*f*eldspath*oid*]

foie gras *fwä-grä*, (*Fr*) *n* fattened liver (of goose) made into **pâté de foie gras** (or **foies gras**) (*pä-tā də*).

foil[1] *foil*, *vt* to defeat; to baffle; to frustrate; to beat down or trample with the feet (*obs*); to destroy a trail by crossing (*hunting*). — *n* a check, repulse or frustration (*obs*); an incomplete fall in wrestling; a blunt fencing sword with a button on the point. — **put on the foil** to overcome or bring to nothing. [OFr *fuler* to stamp or crush, from L *fullō* a fuller of cloth]

foil[2] *foil*, *n* a leaf or thin plate of metal, eg tinfoil; a mercury coating on a mirror; metal-coated paper; a thin leaf of metal put under a precious stone to show it to advantage; anything that serves to set off something else; a small arc in tracery; an aerofoil or hydrofoil. — *adj* **foiled**. — *n* **foil'ing**. — *adj* **foil'borne** (of a craft) lifted up from, or travelling along, the water on hydrofoils. [OFr *foil* (Fr *feuille*), from L *folium* a leaf]

foin *foin*, (*archaic*) *vi* to thrust with a sword or spear. — *n* a thrust with a sword or spear. — *adj* **foin'ingly**. [OFr *foine*, from L *fuscina* a trident]

foison *foi'zn*, *n* plenty (*archaic*); plentiful yield (*archaic*); strength, vitality or essential virtue (*Scot*; also **fushion**, **fusion** *fōōzh'ən*, *fizh'ən* or **fizz'en**). — *adj* **foi'sonless**

weak or feeble (*Scot*; also **fush'ionless, fu'sionless** or **fizz'enless**). [OFr, from L *fūsiō, -ōnis*, from *fundere, fūsum* to pour forth]

foist *foist*, *vt* to pass off (*on* or *upon*) the person affected; to insert wrongfully (*in* or *into* the thing affected); to bring in by stealth. — *n* **foist'er**. [Prob Du dialect *vuisten* to take in hand; *vuist* fist]

fol. *abbrev*: followed; following.

folacin *fō'lə-sin*, *n* folic acid.

folate. See under **folic acid**.

fold[1] *fōld*, *n* a doubling of anything upon itself; a crease; the concave side of anything folded; a part laid over on another. — *vt* to lay in folds or double over; to enclose in a fold or folds or wrap up; to embrace. — *vi* to become folded; to be capable of being folded; to yield (*obs*); (of a business, etc) to collapse or cease functioning (also with *up*; *colloq*). — *adj* **fold'able**. — *n* **fold'er** a person or thing that folds; a flat knife-like instrument used in folding paper; a folding case for loose papers; a folded circular. — *adj* **fold'ing** that folds or that can be folded. — *n* a fold or pleat; the bending of strata, *usu* as the result of compression (*geol*). — *adj* **fold'away** which can be folded and put away. — **foldboat** see **faltboat**; **folded mountains** (*geol*) mountains produced by folding processes; **folding door** a door consisting of two parts hung on opposite jambs; **fold'ing-machine** a mechanism that automatically folds printed sheets; **folding money** (*colloq*) paper money. — *adj* and *n* **fold'-out** (a large page, eg containing a diagram) folded to fit into a book, and to be unfolded for reading (also **gate'fold**). — **fold in** (*cookery*) to mix in carefully and gradually, without stirring. [OE *faldan* (WSaxon *fealdan*) to fold; Ger *falten*]

fold[2] *fōld*, *n* an enclosure for protecting domestic animals, *esp* sheep; a flock of sheep; a church or its congregation (*fig*); the Christian Church (*fig*). — *vt* to confine in a fold. — *n* **fold'ing**. [OE *falod, fald* a fold or stall]

-fold *fōld sfx* (with numbers) times, as in *tenfold*. [Ety as for **fold**[1]]

folderol. See **falderal**.

foliage *fō'li-ij*, *n* leaves collectively; a mass of leaves; plant forms in art. — *adj* **fōliāceous** (*-ā'shəs*) leaflike; like a foliage leaf; leaf-bearing; laminated. — *adj* **fō'liaged** having foliage; worked like foliage. — *adj* **fō'liar** pertaining to leaves; resembling leaves. — *vt* **fō'liate** *orig* to beat into a leaf; to cover with leaf metal; to number the leaves (not pages) of. — *vi* to split into laminae (*med*); (of a plant) to grow leaves. — *adj* **fō'liated** beaten into a thin leaf; decorated with leaf ornaments or foils; consisting of layers or laminae. — *n* **fōliā'tion** the production of leaves, *esp* in plants; the act of beating a metal into a thin plate, or of spreading foil over a piece of glass to form a mirror; the numbering of leaves (not pages) in a book (see **folio**); the alternation of more or less parallel layers or folia of different mineralogical nature, of which the crystalline schists are composed (*geol*); decoration with cusps, lobes or foliated tracery (*archit*). — *n* **fō'liature** foliation. — *adj* **fō'liolate** or **fō'liolose** composed of or pertaining to leaflets. — *n* **fō'liole** a leaflet of a compound leaf (*bot*); a small leaflike structure. — *adj* **fō'liose** leafy; leaflike. — *n* **folium** a leaf; a lamina or lamella (*med*): — *pl* **fō'lia**. — **foliage leaf** an ordinary leaf, not a petal, bract, etc; **foliage plant** one grown for the beauty of its foliage; **foliar feed** a plant food applied in solution to the leaves. [L *folium* a leaf; cf **blade**; Gr *phyllon*]

folic acid *fō'lik, fo'lik as'id*, *n* an acid in the vitamin B complex (*tetrahydrofolate*), found in leaves, liver, etc, or a similar acid, deficiency of which causes some of the symptoms of pernicious anaemia (see also **pterin**). — *adj* **fo'late** of or pertaining to folic acid. — *n* (a salt of) folic acid. [L *folius* a leaf (because occurring in green leaves)]

folie *fo-lē*, (*Fr*) *n* madness, insanity; folly. — **folie à deux** (*a dø*) a form of mental illness in which two people, generally close to one another, share the same delusion; **folie de doute** (*də doōt*) mental illness characterized by inability to make decisions, however trifling; **folie de grandeur** (*grã-dœr*) delusions of grandeur.

folio *fō'li-ō*, *n* a leaf (two back-to-back pages) of a book; a leaf of paper in a manuscript, numbered only on the front and blank on the verso; a sheet of paper folded once; a large-format book of such sheets; the size of such a book; one of several sizes of paper adapted for folding once into well-proportioned leaves; a page in an account-book, or two opposite pages numbered as one (*bookkeeping*); a certain number of words taken as a basis for computing the length of a document (*law*); a page number in a book (*printing*); a wrapper for loose papers: — *pl* **fō'lios**. — *adj* consisting of paper folded only once; of the size of a folio. — *vt* to number the leaves or pages of; to mark off the end of every folio of, in law copying: — *pr p* **fō'lioing**; *pa t* and *pa p* **fō'lioed**. — **in folio** in sheets folded once; in the form of a folio. [L *in foliō* on leaf (so-and-so), used in references; L *folium* a leaf or a sheet of paper]

folk *fōk*, *n* people, collectively or distributively; a nation or people; the people or commons (*archaic*); those of one's own family, relations (*colloq*); now generally used as a *pl* (either **folk** or **folks**) to mean people in general; folk music. — *adj* as practised, etc by ordinary people, and handed down by tradition (found also in *folk-art*, *folk-craft folk-medicine*, etc). — *n* **folk'ie** (*colloq*) a lover of folk music; a folk musician. — *n* **folk'siness**. — *adj* **folk'sy** (chiefly *US*) everyday; friendly; sociable; of ordinary people; (artificially) traditional in style. — **folk'-dance** a dance handed down by tradition of the people; **folk'-etymol'ogy** popular unscientific attempts at etymology. — *adj* **folk'-free** (*archaic*) having the rights of a freeman. — **folk hero** a hero in the eyes of the ordinary people, or in the traditions of a people; **folk'land** (OE *folcland*) in Old English times, probably land held by folk-right, opposed to *bōcland* (bookland); **folk'lore** the ancient observances and customs, the notions, beliefs, traditions, superstitions and prejudices of the common people; the study of these observances, etc, the science of the survival of archaic belief and custom in modern ages (a name suggested by W J Thoms in 1846). — *adj* **folk'lōric**. — **folk'lōrist** a person who studies folklore; **folk-mem'ory** a memory of an event that survives in a community through many generations; the power of remembering as attributed to a community; **folk'moot** an assembly of the people among the Old English; **folk music** the music (*esp* song) handed down in the popular tradition of the people, or contemporary music of a similar style; **folk'-right** the common law or right of the people; **folk rock** a form of popular music which adapts folk melodies to the rhythm of rock music; **folk'-singer**; **folk'-song** any song or ballad (frequently anonymous) originating among the people and traditionally handed down by them; a modern song composed and performed in the same idiom (*esp* by a singer-songwriter); **folk'-speech** the dialect of the common people of a country, in which ancient idioms are embedded; **folk'-tale** a popular story handed down by oral tradition from a more or less remote antiquity; **folk'-tune** a tune handed down among the people; **folk'way** a traditional way of thinking, feeling or acting, followed unreflectingly by a social group; **folk'-weave** a loosely woven fabric. [OE *folc*; ON *folk*; Ger *Volk*]

Folketing *fōl'kə-ting*, *n* the lower house of the Danish parliament or Rigsdag. [Dan, from *folk* the people, and ON *thing* assembly]

follicle *fol'i-kl*, *n* a fruit formed from a single carpel containing several seeds, splitting along the ventral suture only (*bot*); a Graafian follicle (*zool*); any small sac-like structure, eg the pit surrounding a hair-root (*zool*). — *adj* **follic'ūlated, follic'ūlar, follic'ūlose** or **follic'ūlous**. — **follicle-stimulating hormone** (*abbrev* **FSH**) a hormone secreted in the pituitary gland, which stimulates growth of the Graafian follicles of the ovary, and sperm production. [L *folliculus*, dimin of *follis* a wind-bag]

follow *fol'ō*, *vt* to go after or behind; to keep along the line of; to come after or succeed; to pursue; to attend; to support (eg a team or sportsperson); to believe in (eg a religious leader or teaching); to imitate; to obey (eg orders); to adopt (eg an opinion); to keep the eye or mind fixed on; to grasp or understand the whole course or sequence of; to result from, as an effect from a cause; to strive to obtain (*Bible*). — *vi* to come after; to result; to be the logical conclusion. — *n* a stroke that causes the ball to follow the one it has struck (*billiards*; commonly **follow-through'**); a second helping. — *n* **foll'ower** a person who comes after; a person who copies; a disciple, supporter or devotee; a retainer or attendant; a servant-girl's sweetheart (*old*); a part of a machine driven by another part. — *n* **foll'owing** a body of supporters. — *adj* coming next after; to be next mentioned; (of a wind) blowing in the same direction as a boat, aircraft, etc is travelling. — *prep* after. — **foll'ow-board** (in moulding) the board on which a pattern is laid; **follow-my-lead'er** a game in which all other players have to mimic whatever the leader does; **follow-on'** or **follow-through'** an act of following on or through. — **follow home** to follow to the point aimed at, to the heart of the matter; **follow on** to continue endeavours (*Bible*); optionally to take a second innings immediately after the first, as the result of being short in number of runs (*cricket*); to follow immediately (*colloq*); to start where another (person, etc) left off (*colloq*); **follow out** to carry out (eg instructions); to follow to the end or conclusion; **follow suit** to play a card of the same suit as the one which was led (*cards*); to do what another person has done; **follow through** to complete the swing of a stroke after hitting the ball (*sport*); to carry any course of action to its conclusion; **follow up** to pursue an advantage closely; to pursue a question that has been started (*n* **foll'ow-up**). [OE *folgian*, *fylgan*; Ger *folgen*]

folly *fol'i*, *n* silliness or weakness of mind; a foolish thing; sin (*obs*); a monument of folly, such as a great useless structure, or one left unfinished, because it was begun without establishing the cost. — *vi* (*archaic*) to act with folly. [OFr *folie*, from *fol* foolish]

Fomalhaut *fō'məl-howt*, *-hŏt*, *-ə-lōt*, *n* a first-magnitude star in the constellation of the Southern Fish. [Ar *fam-al-hūt* the whale's mouth]

foment *fō-ment'*, *vt* to foster (*usu* evil); to apply a warm lotion to; to treat or relieve by applying heat or moisture (*obs*). — *n* **fomentā'tion** instigation; the application of a warm lotion or a warm, moist preparation such as a poultice, to reduce inflammation and pain (extended sometimes to a dry or cold application); the lotion, etc so applied. — *n* **fomen'ter**. [L *fōmentum* for *fovimentum*, from *fovēre* to warm]

fomes *fō'mēz*, (*med*) *n* a substance capable of carrying infection: — *pl* **fomites** (*fō'mi-tēz*). [L *fōmes*, *-tis* touchwood]

fon *fon*, (*obs*) *n* a fool. — *vi* to be foolish or play the fool. — *vt* to fool (someone); to toy with. — *adv* **fon'ly** foolishly. [**fond**[1]]

fonctionnaire *fɔ̃k-syo-ner*, (*Fr*) *n* an official; a civil servant.

fond[1] *fond*, *adj* foolish, *esp* foolishly tender and loving (*archaic*); credulous or foolishly hopeful (*archaic*); weakly indulgent; prizing highly (with *of*); very affectionate; kindly disposed. — *vi* (*obs*) to dote. — *adv* **fond'ly**. — *n* **fond'ness**. [Pa p of **fon**, from ME *fonnen* to act foolishly, and *fon* a fool]

fond[2] *fond*, (*Spenser*), *pa t* of **fand**[2] and *pa t* and *pa p* of **find**.

fond[3] *fɔ̃*, (*Fr*) *n* basis, foundation or background.

fonda *fon'dä*, (*Sp*) *n* a tavern.

fondant *fon'dənt*, *n* a soft sweet made with flavoured sugar and water, that melts in the mouth. [Fr, from *fondre* to melt, from L *fundere*]

fondle *fon'dl*, *vt* to handle with fondness; to caress. — *n* **fond'ler**. — *n* **fond'ling** a pet (*obs*); a fool (*obs*); the action of the verb. [Ety as for **fond**[1]]

fonds *fɔ̃*, (*Fr*) *n* landed property; capital; money; fund (*lit* and *fig*).

fondue *fon'do͞o* or *fɔ̃-dü*, *n* a sauce made by heating a mixture of cheese and wine, etc, eaten by dipping pieces of bread, etc in the mixture (also **Swiss fondue**); a dish consisting of small cubes of meat cooked at the table on forks in hot oil and served with piquant sauces (also **fondue bourguignonne** *bo͞or-gē-nyon*); a soufflé with bread or biscuit crumbs. [Fr, from fem pa p of *fondre* to melt]

fone. See **foe**.

fons et origo *fons et o-rī'gō*, *-rē'*, (*L*) the source and origin.

font[1] *font*, *n* a vessel for baptismal water (*eccles*); a fount, origin or fountain (*poetic*). — *adj* **font'al** pertaining to a font or origin. — *n* **font'let** a little font. — **font name** (*eccles*) baptismal name; **font'-stone** (*eccles*) a baptismal font made of stone. [OE *font*, from L *fōns*, *fontis* a fountain]

font[2] *font*. See **fount**[1].

fontanelle or **fontanel** *fon-tə-nel'*, *n* a membrane-covered gap between the immature parietal bones in the skull of a foetus or infant; an opening for discharge (*med*). [Fr dimin, from L *fōns*, *fontis* a fountain]

fontange *fɔ̃-tãzh'*, (*hist*) *n* a tall head-dress worn in the 17th and 18th centuries. [Fr, from *Fontanges* the territorial title of one of Louis XIV's mistresses]

Fontarabian *fon-tə-rā'bi-ən*, *adj* of or relating to *Fontarabia* or Fuenterrabia at the west end of the Pyrenees (confused by Milton with Roncesvalles).

fonticulus *fon-tik'ū-ləs*, *n* the depression just over the top of the breastbone. [L *fonticulus*, dimin of *fōns* fountain]

fontinalis *fon-tin-ā'lis*, *n* a moss of the *Fontinalis* genus of aquatic mosses allied to *Hypnum*. [L *fontinālis* of a spring, from *fōns*]

food[1] *fo͞od*, *n* a substance, or substances, that a living thing feeds on; a substance which, when digested, nourishes the body; anything that nourishes or promotes growth or activity; substances produced by plants from raw materials taken in (*bot*). — *adj* **food'ful** (*rare*) able to supply food abundantly. — *n* **food'ie** or **food'y** (*colloq*) a person who is greatly (even excessively) interested in the preparation and consumption of good food. — *n* **food'ism** great interest in or concern over food. — *adj* **food'less** without food. — **food canal** the alimentary canal; **food'-card** a card entitling its holder to obtain his or her quota of rationed foodstuffs; **food chain** a series of organisms connected by the fact that each forms food for the next higher organism in the series; **food'-controller** an official who controls the storing, sale and distribution of food in time of emergency; **food conversion ratio** the ratio of the weight of foodstuffs which a cow, pig, chicken, etc consumes, to its own bodyweight; **food court** an area in a shopping precinct containing a variety of (fast-)food booths and a section of communal seating and tables for the customers; **food'-fish** an edible fish; **food poisoning** a gastrointestinal disorder caused by the ingestion of foods naturally toxic to the system or of foods made toxic by contamination with bacteria or chemicals; **food processor** an electrical appliance for cutting, blending, mincing, etc food, *esp* in the home; **food'stuff** a substance used as food; **food values** the relative nourishing power of foods. [OE *fōda*; Gothic *fōdeins*, Swed *föda*]

food[2] *fo͞od*, *n* (*Spenser*) Same as **feud**[1].

fool[1] *fo͞ol*, *n* a person lacking in wisdom, judgement or sense; a weak-minded person; a jester; a dupe or victim; a vague term of endearment (*obs*); a person with a weakness (with *for*). — *vt* to deceive; to cause to appear foolish; to obtain by fooling. — *vi* to play the fool; to trifle. — *adj* (*Scot* and *US*) foolish. — *n* **fool'ery** an act of folly; habitual folly; fooling. — *n* **fool'ing** playing the fool; acting the jester; a characteristic streak of jesting; trifling. — *adj* **fool'ish** lacking intellect; lacking discretion; unwise, ill considered; ridiculous, idiotic, silly; marked by folly; paltry. — *adv* **fool'ishly**. — *n* **fool'ishness**. — *adj* **fool'begged** (*Shakesp*) *perh*, foolish enough to be begged for a fool (qv under **beg**; in allusion to the custom of seeking the administration of a lunatic's estate for one's own advantage). — *adj* **fool'-born** (*Shakesp*) born of a fool or of folly. — *adj* **fool'-happy** happy or lucky without contrivance or judgement. — **foolhard'iness** (*Spenser* **foolhardize** or **-ise**; *-īz'* or *-härd'*). — *adj* **fool'hardy** foolishly bold; rash or incautious. — *adj* **fool'ish-witt'y** (*Shakesp*) wise in folly and foolish in wisdom. — *adj* **fool'proof** infallible; guaranteed not to cause damage or injury if misused. — **fool's cap** a jester's head-dress, *usu* having a coxcomb hood with bells; **fool's errand** a silly or fruitless enterprise; a search for what cannot be found; **fool's gold** iron pyrites; **fool's mate** (*chess*) the simplest of the checkmates (in two moves by each player); **fool's paradise** a state of happiness based on fictitious hopes or expectations; **fool's parsley** a poisonous umbelliferous plant (*Aethusa cynapium*) that a great enough fool might take for parsley. — **All Fools' Day** see under **all**; **fool around** to waste time; to mess about; to trifle with someone's affections, or to be unfaithful to them with a reckless attitude; to have sex, or indulge in sexual frolicking; **fool away** to squander to no purpose or profit; **fool with** to meddle with officiously, irresponsibly or thoughtlessly; **make a fool of** to cause (someone) to look ridiculous or stupid; to humiliate or dupe; to disappoint; **nobody's fool** a sensible, shrewd person; **play** or **act the fool** to behave like a fool; to be reckless or foolish; to be exuberantly comical or high-spirited. [OFr *fol* (Fr *fou*), from L *follis* a windbag]

fool[2] *fōōl*, *n* a purée of fruit scalded or stewed, mixed with cream or custard and sugar, such as *gooseberry fool*. [Prob a use of **fool**[1] suggested by *trifle*]

foolscap *fōōl'skap*, *n* a (now little-used) size of long folio writing- or printing-paper, generally 13½ by 17 inches (or by 8½ as a single sheet), *orig* bearing the watermark of a *fool's cap* and bells.

foot *fŏŏt*, *n* the part of its body on which a human or animal stands or walks; the part on which anything stands; the base; the lower or less dignified end; a measure (= 12 inches/0.3048 metres), *orig* the length of a man's foot; the corresponding square or cubic unit (sq foot = 144 sq inches/0.0929 sq metres; cu foot = 1728 cu inches/0.0086 cu metres); foot-soldiers; a division of a line of poetry; a manner of walking; a part of a sewing machine that holds the fabric in place under the needle; a muscular development of the ventral surface in molluscs; the absorbent and attaching organ of a young sporophyte (*bot*): — *pl* **feet**; also, as a measure, **foot**; in some compounds and in sense of dregs, or footlights, **foots**. — *vt* and *vi* (*esp* with *it*) to dance: to walk; to sum up. — *vt* to kick; to pay (the bill); to add a foot to; to grasp with the foot: — *pr p* **foot'ing**; *pa t* and *pa p* **foot'ed**. — *n* **foot'age** measurement or payment by the foot; the length of organ pipe giving the lowest note; an amount (ie length) of cinema or TV film. — *adj* **foot'ed** provided with a foot or feet; having gained a football (*Shakesp*). — *combining form* **-foot'ed** having a specified number of feet; having a specified manner of walking. — *n* **foot'er** a line of type printed at the foot of each page (*printing*); football (*colloq*). — *combining form* **-foot'er** something of a specified length in feet, *usu* a boat (eg *he sails a twenty-four-footer*). — *n* **foot'ie** or **foot'y** football (*colloq*, *esp Austr* and *NZ*); footsie (see **play footsie**) below. — *n* **foot'ing** a place for the foot to rest on, *esp* a secure and stable one; standing; terms; a place of installation; a fee charged on the installation of a person to a new position (*archaic*); a foundation or basis; the lower part of a column or wall, immediately above the foundation; position or rank; a track or surface; a tread; a dance; plain cotton lace. — *adj* **foot'less** having no feet; very drunk (*colloq*). — **foot-and-mouth disease** a contagious disease of cloven-footed animals, characterized by vesicular eruption, *esp* in the mouth and in the clefts of the feet; **foot'ball** a large ball for kicking about in sport; a game played with this ball, *esp* soccer (see under **association football**); a bargaining-point, point of controversy, etc that is tossed around (*esp* a *political football*; *fig*); **foot'baller** or (*rare*) **foot'ballist** a football player. — *adj* **foot'balling** of or relating to football. — **foot'bar** the bar, controlled by the pilot's feet, for operating the rudder in aircraft; **foot'-bath** an act of bathing the feet; a bowl, etc for this purpose; **foot'board** a support for the feet in a carriage or elsewhere; the footplate of a locomotive engine; an upright board at the foot of a bed; **foot'boy** a young boy attendant in livery; **foot brake** a brake operated by the foot; **foot'breadth** the breadth of a foot; **foot'bridge** a bridge for pedestrians; **foot'-candle** a former unit of incident light, equivalent to one lumen per sq foot (= 10·764 lux); **foot'cloth** a pack-horse cloth reaching to the feet of the horse; **foot'-dragging** see **drag one's feet** under **drag**; **foot'fall** the sound of a footstep; **foot fault** (*lawn tennis*) a fault made by stepping over the baseline when serving. — *vt* and *vi* **foot'fault**. — **foot'gear** shoes and stockings. — *n pl* **foot'guards** (*military*) guards that serve on foot. — **foot'hill** a minor elevation below a higher mountain or range (*usu* in *pl*); **foot'hold** a place to fix the foot in, eg when climbing; a grip; a firm starting position. — *adj* **foot-in-the mouth'** of or pertaining to a verbal faux pas. — **foot'-jaw** a maxilliped variety of crustacean (*zool*); **foot-lam'bert** a former unit of emitted or reflected light, equivalent to one lumen per sq foot (= 10·764 lux); **foot-land'-raker** (*Shakesp*) a footpad; **foot'-licker** a fawning, slavish flatterer; **foot'light** one of a row of lights along the front of a theatre stage; (in *pl*) the theatre as a profession. — *adj* **foot'loose** free or unhampered by (eg family) ties. — **foot'man** a person who goes on foot; a servant or attendant in livery; a foot-soldier; a servant running before a coach or rider; a low stand for fireside utensils: — *pl* **foot'men**; **foot'mark** see **foot'print** below; **foot'muff** a muff for keeping the feet warm; **foot'note** a note of reference or comment at the foot of a page; **foot'pace** (*obs*) a walking pace; a dais; **foot'pad** (*archaic*) a highwayman on foot; **foot'page** a boy attendant; **foot'-passenger** one who travels on foot; **foot'path** a way for walkers only; a side pavement; **foot'-patrol** a patrol on foot **foot'plate** a platform for **foot'platemen** or **foot'platewomen** (*n sing* **foot'plateman** or **foot'platewoman**), train driver and assistant (on a steam locomotive, the stoker); **foot'post** a post or other messenger that travels on foot; **foot'-pound** or **foot-pound force** the energy needed to raise a mass of one pound through the height of one foot in normal gravity; **foot'print** the mark left on the ground or floor by a person's or animal's foot (also **foot'mark**); the area surrounding an airport, or the part of an aircraft's flight path, in which the noise is liable to be above a certain level; the area covered by the down-driven blast of air which supports a hovercraft; the area on a floor, desk, etc occupied by a computer or part of one; the area covered by the beam of a direct broadcast satellite; **foot'-pump** a pump held or operated by the foot; **foot'-race** a race on foot; **foot'-racing**; **foot'rest** a support for the foot; **foot'-rope** a rope stretching along under a ship's yard for the crew to stand on when furling the sails; the rope to which the lower edge of a sail is attached; **foot'rot** ulceration of the coronary band, or any other infection of the feet in sheep or cattle; **foot'rule** a rule or measure a foot in length or measured off in feet. — *vi* **foot'slog** to march or tramp. — **foot'slogger**; **foot'slogging**; **foot'-soldier** a soldier serving on foot. — *adj* **foot'sore** having sore or tender feet, *usu* from much walking. — **foot'stalk** (*bot*) the stalk or petiole of a leaf; **foot'-stall** a side-saddle stirrup; **foot'step** a tread; a footfall; a footprint; a raised step for ascending or descending; (in *pl*; *fig*) a path or example; **foot'stool** a stool for placing one's feet on when sitting. — *adj* **foot'stooled**. — *adj* **foot'tapping** (of music) that makes one tap, or want to tap, one's feet in time with it. — **foot'-ton** or **foot-ton force** a unit of work or energy equal to the work done in raising one ton one foot against normal gravity, 2240 foot-pounds; **foot'-warmer** a device for keeping the feet warm; **foot'way** a path for people on foot; a mineshaft with ladders; **foot'wear** a collective term for boots, shoes, socks, etc; **foot'well** either of the recessed hollows for the feet in front of the front seats of a vehicle; **foot'work** the use or management of the feet, as in sport. — *adj* **foot'worn** footsore; showing signs of much wear by feet. — **a foot in the door** a first step towards a *usu* difficult desired end; **at the feet of** in submission, homage, supplication or devotion to or under the spell of; **catch on the wrong foot** to catch (someone) unprepared; **cover the feet** (*Bible*) to defecate; **drag one's feet** see under **drag**. — *adj* **eight'-foot** (*music*) having the pitch of an open organ-pipe eight feet long, or having that pitch for the lowest note. — **foot it** to walk; to dance; **foot of fine** (*law*) the bottom part (preserved in the records) of a tripartite indenture in case of a fine of land; **foot the bill** to pay up; **get off on the wrong foot** to make a bad beginning; **have one foot in the grave** to be not far from death; **have one's feet on the ground** to act habitually with practical good sense; **have the ball at one's feet** to have nothing to do except seize one's opportunity; **my foot**! *interj* expressing disbelief, *usu* contemptuous; **on foot** walking or running; in progress; **play footsie (with)** (*colloq*) to rub one's foot or leg against (another person's), *usu* with amorous intentions; to make furtively flirtatious advances towards (*fig*); **put a** or **one's foot wrong** (*usu* in *neg*) to make a mistake or blunder; **put one's best foot forward** to make one's best effort; **put one's foot down** to take a firm decision, *usu* against something; **put one's foot in it** to spoil anything by some tactless blunder or remark; **set foot in** to enter; **set on foot** to originate, start; **shoot oneself in the foot** see under **shoot**. [OE *fōt*, pl *fēt*; Ger *Fuss*, L *pēs*, *pedis*, Gr *pous*, *podos*, Sans *pad*]

footle *fōōt'l*, *vi* to trifle, waste time or potter (with *about* or *around*). — *n* silly nonsense. — *n* and *adj* **foot'ling**. [Origin obscure]

footra. See **fouter**.

Footsie *fōōt'si*. See **FTSE**.

footsie. See **play footsie** under **foot**.

footy[1] *fōōt'i*, (*dialect*) *adj* mean. [Origin obscure]

footy[2]. See **footie** under **foot**.

foo yung or **yong**. See **fu yung**.

foozle *fōōz'l*, (*colloq*) *n* a tedious person; a bungled stroke at golf, etc. — *vi* to fool away one's time. — *vi* and *vt* to bungle. — *n* **fooz'ler**. — *n* and *adj* **fooz'ling**. [Cf Ger dialect *fuseln* to work badly or potter]

fop *fop*, *n* an affected dandy. — *n* **fop'ling** a vain affected person. — *n* **fopp'ery** vanity in dress or manners; affectation; folly. — *adj* **fopp'ish** vain and showy in dress; affectedly refined in manners. — *adv* **fopp'ishly**. — *n* **fopp'ishness**. [Cf Ger *foppen* to hoax]

for *fōr* or *fər*, *prep* in the place of; in favour of; wanting or wishing to have; on account of; in the direction of; having as goal or intention, in quest of; with respect to; in respect of; by reason of; appropriate or adapted to, or in reference to; beneficial to; notwithstanding, in spite of; in recompense of; during; in the character of; to the extent of. — *conj* because. — **as for** as far as concerns; **be for it** or **be in for it** to have something unpleasant about to happen, *esp* a scolding; **for all (that)** notwithstanding; **for that** (*obs*) because; **for to** (*archaic* or *dialect*) in order to; to; **for why** (*obs*) why; because; **there is nothing for it but (to)** there is no other possible course of action but (to); **what is he for a man**? (*obs*) what kind of man is he? [OE *for*]

f o r *abbrev*: free on rail.

for- *fōr-* or *fər-*, *pfx* (1) in words derived from OE, used to form verbs with the senses: (a) away or off; (b) against; (c) thoroughly or utterly (intensive); (d) exhaustion; (e) destruction. (2) used in words derived from OE to form *adjs* with superlative force. (3) a contraction of *fore-*. (4) in words derived from L *forīs* outside, *forās* forth or out. No longer a living prefix.

fora. See **forum**.

forage *for'ij*, *n* fodder, or food for horses and cattle; provisions; the act of foraging. — *vi* to go about and forcibly carry off food for horses and cattle; to rummage about (for what one wants). — *vt* to plunder. — *n* **for'ager**. — **for'age-cap** the undress cap worn by infantry soldiers. [Fr *fourrage*, OFr *feurre* fodder, of Gmc origin; cf **fodder**]

foramen *fō-rā'mən* or *fō-*, *n* (*zool* or *anatom*) a small opening: — *pl* **foramina** (*-ram'i-nə*). — *adj* **foram'inal**. — *adj* **foram'inated** or **foram'inous** pierced with small holes; porous. — *n* **foraminifer** (*for-ə-min'i-fər*) any member of the **Foraminif'era** (*-am-* or *-ām-*) an order of rhizopod protozoa with a shell *usu* perforated by pores (*foramina*; L *ferre* to bear). — *adj* **foraminif'eral** or **foraminif'erous**. — **forāmen magnum** the great hole in the occipital bone through which the spinal cord joins the medulla oblongata. [L *forāmen*, from *forāre* to pierce]

forane *for-ān'*, *adj* a form of **foreign**, outlying or rural, as in **vicar-forane** (see under **vicar**).

forasmuch *fōr-* or *fər-əz-much'*, (*archaic* or *formal*) *conj* because or since (with *as*).

foray *for'ā*, *n* a raid; a venture or attempt; a journey. — *vt* and *vi* to raid; to forage. — *n* **for'ayer**. [Ety obscure, but ult identical with **forage**]

forb *fōrb*, *n* any herb which is not, or does not resemble, a grass. [Gr *phorbē* food]

forbad and **forbade**. See **forbid**.

forbear[1] *fōr-* or *fər-bār'*, *vi* to keep oneself in check; to abstain or refrain. — *vt* to abstain or refrain from; to avoid voluntarily; to spare or withhold; to give up (*obs*): — *pa t* **forbore'**; *pa p* **forborne'**. — *n* **forbear'ance** the exercising of patience or restraint; command of temper; clemency. — *adj* **forbear'ant** (*obs*) or **forbear'ing** long-suffering; patient. — *adv* **forbear'ingly**. [OE *forberan*, pa t *forbær*, pa p *forboren*; see pfx **for-** (1a), and **bear**[1]]

forbear[2] *fōr'bār*. Same as **forebear** (see under **fore-**).

forbid *fər-* or *fōr-bid'*, *vt* to prohibit; to command not to: — *pa t* **forbade** (*-bad'* or sometimes *-bād'*) or **forbad'**; *pa p* **forbidd'en**. — *n* **forbidd'al** or **forbidd'ance** (*obs*) prohibition; command or edict against a thing. — *adj* **forbidd'en** prohibited; unlawful; not permitted, *esp* in certain scientific rules; (of a combination of symbols) not in an operating code, ie revealing a fault (*comput*). — *adv* **forbidd'enly** (*Shakesp*) in a forbidden or unlawful manner. — *n* **forbidd'er**. — *n* **forbidd'ing**. — *adj* uninviting; sinister; unprepossessing; threatening or formidable in appearance. — *adv* **forbidd'ingly**. — *n* **forbidd'ingness**. — *n* **forbode** (*fōr-bōd'*; *archaic*) prohibition. — **forbidden degrees** see under **degree**; **forbidden fruit** (*Bible*) that forbidden to Adam (Gen 2.17); anything tempting and prohibited; (or **Adam's apple**) a name fancifully given to the fruit of various species of Citrus, *esp* to one having tooth-marks on its rind. — **over God's forbode** (*archaic*) God forbid. [OE *forbēodan*, pa t *forbēad*, pa p *forboden*; see pfx **for-** (1a) and **bid**; cf Ger *verbieten*]

forbore and **forborne**. See **forbear**[1].

forby, **forbye** or (*Spenser*) **foreby** *fər-bī'*, *adv* and *prep* near (*obs*); past (*obs*); by (*obs*); besides (*Scot*). [**for**, adv, and **by**]

forçat *fōr-sä*, (*Fr*) *n* a convict condemned to hard labour.

force[1] *fōrs* or *fōrs*, *n* strength, power or energy; efficacy; validity; influence; vehemence; violence; coercion; a group of people assembled for collective action (eg *police force*); (in *pl*; sometimes with *cap*) a navy, army or air force; an armament; any cause which changes the direction or speed of the motion of a portion of matter (*phys*). — *vt* to draw or push by strength; to thrust; to compel; to constrain; to overcome the resistance of by force; to achieve or bring about by force; to break or break open by force; to ravish; to take by violence; to cause to grow or ripen rapidly (*hortic*); to strain or work up to a high pitch; to induce or cause (someone) to play in a particular way (*cards*); to cause the playing of (*cards*); to strengthen (*Shakesp*); to attribute importance to (*obs*). — *vi* to strive (*obs*); to make way by force; to care (*obs*). — *adj* **forced** accomplished by great effort, eg a *forced march*; strained, excessive or unnatural; artificially produced. — *adv* **forc'edly**. — *n* **forc'edness** the state of being forced; constraint; unnatural or undue distortion. — *adj* **force'ful** full of force or strength; energetic; driven or acting with power. — *adv* **force'fully**. — *n* **force'fulness**. — *adj* **force'less** weak. — *n* **forc'er** a person or thing that forces, *esp* the piston of a force-pump. — *adj* **forc'ible** having force; done by force. — *n* **forc'ibleness** or **forcibil'ity**. — *adv* **forc'ibly**. — **forced labour** compulsory hard labour, as a punishment for a crime. — *vt* **force'-feed** to feed (a person or animal) forcibly, *usu* by the mouth: — *pa t* and *pa p* **force'-fed**. — **force'-feeding**. — *vi* **force'-land** to make a forced landing. — **forced landing** (*aeronautics*) a landing at a place where no landing was *orig* planned, necessary because of some mishap or emergency; **force'-pump** or **forc'ing-pump** a pump that delivers liquid under pressure greater than its suction pressure; a pump for cleaning out pipes by blowing air through; **forcible detainer** or **entry** taking property into custody or forcing an entry into it by violence or intimidation; **forcible feeble** (*Shakesp*) a weak man with a pretence of valour; **forc'ing-house** a hothouse for forcing plants, or a place for hastening the growth of animals; **forc'ing-pit** a frame sunk in the ground over a hotbed for forcing plants. — **force and fear** (*Scot*) that amount of constraint or compulsion which is enough to annul an engagement or obligation entered into under its influence; **force the pace** to bring and keep the speed up to a high pitch by competition; **in force** operative or legally binding; in great numbers. [Fr, from LL *fortia*, from L *fortis* strong]

force[2] *fōrs* or *förs* or **foss** *fos*, *n* a waterfall. [ON *fors*]

force[3] *fōrs* or *förs*, (*cookery*) *vt* to stuff (eg fowl). — **force'meat** meat chopped fine and highly seasoned, used as a stuffing or alone. [For **farce**]

force de frappe *fors də frap*, (*Fr*) *n* a strike force, *esp* a nuclear one. — **force majeure** (*mä-zhœr*) superior power; an unforeseeable or uncontrollable course of events, excusing one from fulfilling a contract (*legal*).

forceps *för'seps*, *n* a pincer-like instrument with two blades, for holding, lifting or removing (eg in surgery): — *pl* **for'ceps** (also **for'cepses** or **for'cipēs** *-si-pēz*). — *adj* **for'cipāte** or **for'cipated** formed and opening like a forceps. — *n* **forcipā'tion** torture by pinching with forceps. [L, from *formus* hot, and *capere* to hold]

forcible, etc. See under **force**[1].

ford *fōrd* or *förd*, *n* a place where water may be crossed by wading. — *vt* to wade across. — *adj* **ford'able**. [OE *ford-faran* to go; cf Ger *furt-fahren*, Gr *poros*, L *portus*, and **fare**, **ferry** and **far**]

fordo *för-* or *fər-dōō'*, (*archaic*) *vt* to destroy; to ruin; to overcome; to exhaust: — *pr p* **fordo'ing**; *pa t* **fordid'**; *pa p* **fordone** *-dun'*. — *adj* **fordone'** exhausted. — **from fordonne** (*Spenser*) from being fordone. [OE *fordōn*; Ger *vertun* to consume]

fore *fōr* or *för*, *adj* in front; former or previous (*obs*). — *adv* at or towards the front; previously. — *n* the front; the foremast. — *interj* (*golf*) a warning cry to anybody in the way of the ball. — *adj* **foremost** (*fōr'mōst* or *för'*; double *superl*, from OE *forma* first, *superl* of *fore*, and *superl* suffix *-st*) first in place; most advanced; first in rank and dignity. — *adj* and *adv* **fore'-and-aft'** lengthwise (*orig* of a ship); without square sails. — **fore-and-aft'er** a schooner, etc with a fore-and-aft rig; a hat peaked at the front and the back; **fore-and-aft sail** any sail not set on yards and lying fore-and-aft when untrimmed; **fore'bitt** one of the bitts, posts for fastening cables, at the foremast; **fore'bitter** a ballad sung at the forebitts. — **at the fore** displayed on the foremast (of a flag); **to the fore** at hand; in being or alive (*Scot*); loosely, prominent, towards the front. [OE *fore*, radically the same as **for**, prep]

fore- *fōr*, *för-*, *pfx* before or beforehand; in front. — *vt* **fore-admon'ish** to admonish beforehand. — *vt* **fore-advise'** to advise beforehand. — *n* **fore'arm** the part of the arm between the elbow and the wrist. — *vt* **forearm'** to arm or prepare beforehand. — *n* **forebear** or **forbear** (*fōr'bār* or *för'*; *orig Scot*) an ancestor (from **be** and *sfx* **-er**[1]). — *vt* **forebode'** to prognosticate or foretell; to have a premonition of (*esp* of evil). — *n* **forebode'ment** a feeling of coming evil. — *n* **forebod'er**. — *n* **forebod'ing** a perception beforehand; apprehension of coming evil. — *adv* **forebod'ingly**. — *n* **fore'-body** (*naut*) the part in front of the mainmast. — *n* **fore'-brace** (*naut*) a rope attached to the fore yard-arm, for changing the position of the foresail. — *n* **fore'brain** the front part of the brain, the prosencephalon. — *prep* **foreby'** (*Spenser*) same as **forby**. — *n* **fore'cabin** a cabin in a ship's forepart. — *n* **fore'-caddy** (*golf*) a caddy posted up ahead so as to see where the balls go. — *n* **fore'car** a small car carrying a passenger in front of a motorcycle. — *n* **fore'carriage** the front part of a carriage, with an arrangement for independent movement of the fore-wheels. — *vt* **fore'cast** to assess or calculate beforehand; to foresee; to predict. — *vi* to devise beforehand: — *pa t* and *pa p* **fore'cast** (sometimes **fore'casted**). — *n* a previous calculation; foresight; a prediction; a weather forecast (see under **weather**). — *n* **fore'caster**. — *n* **forecastle** or **fo'c'sle** (*fōk'sl* or sometimes *fōr'käs-l* or *för'*) a short raised deck at the fore-end of a ship; the forepart of a ship under the maindeck, the quarters of the crew. — *adj* **forechos'en** chosen beforehand. — *adj* **fore-ci'ted** quoted before or above. — *n* **fore'cloth** a cloth that hangs over the front of an altar, an antependium. — *n* **fore'course** a foresail. — *n* **fore'court** a court in front of a building; an outer court; the front area of a garage or filling-station, where the petrol pumps are situated; the part of a tennis court between the net and the service line. — *vt* **foredate'** to date (eg a cheque) before the true time. — *n* **fore'-day** (*Scot*) forenoon. — *n* **fore'deck** the forepart of a deck or ship. — *vt* **foredoom'** to doom beforehand. — *n* **fore'-edge** the outer edge of a book, furthest from the spine, placed outward in a medieval library. — *n* **fore'-end** the early or fore part of anything. — *n* **fore'father** an ancestor. — *vt* **forefeel'** to feel beforehand. — *adv* **forefeel'ingly**. — *adj* **forefelt'**. — *n* **fore'finger** the finger next to the thumb. — *n* **fore'foot** either of the front feet of a quadruped (*zool*); the foremost end of the keel, where the stem is found (*naut*): — *pl* **fore'feet**. — *n* **fore'front** the front or foremost part. — *n* **fore'gleam** a glimpse into the future. — *vt* and *vi* **forego'** to go before or precede; chiefly in its *pr p* **forego'ing** (or *fōr'* or *för'*) and *pa p* **foregone'** (or *fōr'* or *för'*); *pa t* **forewent'** (*rare*); formerly also *pa p*. — See also **forgo**. — *n* **foregō'er** (*fōr'* or *för'*). — *n* **forego'ing**. — *adj* **fore'gone** (**foregone conclusion** a conclusion come to before examination of the evidence; an obvious or inevitable conclusion or result). — *n* **foregone'ness**. — *n* **fore'ground** the part of a picture or field of view nearest the observer's eye, as opposed to the *background* (also *fig*). — *vt* (*orig US*; *fig*) to spotlight or emphasize. — *n* **fore'gut** the front section of the digestive tract of an embryo or of an invertebrate animal, from which the forepart of the alimentary canal develops. — *n* **fore'-hammer** a sledge-hammer. — *n* **fore'hand** the upper hand, advantage or preference; the part of a horse that is in front of its rider; the front position or its occupant (*tennis*); the part of the court to the right of a right-handed player or to the left of a left-handed player (*tennis*); a stroke played forehand (*tennis*). — *adj* done beforehand; anticipating or of anticipation (*Shakesp*); with the palm in front, opposed to *backhand* (*sport*); (of an arrow) for shooting point-blank (*Shakesp*). — *adv* with the hand in the forehand position. — *adj* **fore'handed** done beforehand, as payment for goods before delivery, or for services before rendered; seasonable; planning ahead, with thought or provision for the future (*US*); well-off (*US*); forehand (*US*; *tennis*); (of a horse, etc) shapely in the foreparts. — *n* **forehead** (*for'id, -ed, fōr'hed* or *fŏr'hed*) the front of the head above the eyes, the brow; confidence or audacity (*obs*). — *n* **fore'-horse** the foremost horse of a team. — *vt* **forejudge'** to judge before hearing the facts and proof; see also **forjudge**. — *n* **forejudg'ement** or **forejudg'ment**. — *n* **fore'king** (*Tennyson*) a preceding king. — *vt* **foreknow'** (*fōr-* or *för-*) to know beforehand; to foresee. — *adj* **fore-know'able**. — *adj* **foreknow'ing**. — *adv* **foreknow-'ingly**. — *n* **foreknowledge** (*-nol'ij*). — *adj* **foreknown'**. — *n* **fore'land** a point of land running forward into the sea, a headland; a front region. — *vt* **forelay'** to devise or plan beforehand; to wait for in ambush; to hinder; *pa t* of **forelie**. — *n* **fore'leg** a front leg. — *vt* **forelend'** or **forlend'** (*archaic*) to grant or resign beforehand: — *pa p* and *pa t* (*Spenser*) **forelent'** or **forlent'**. — *vt* **forelie'** to lie in front of: — *pa t* (*Spenser*) **forelay'**. — *vt* **forelift'** (*Spenser*) to raise in front. — *n* **fore'limb**. — *n* **fore'lock** the lock of hair on the forehead (**pull**, **touch** or **tug the forelock** to raise one's hand to the forehead in sign of respect, subservience, etc; **take time by the forelock** to seize an opportunity quickly); a cotter-pin. — *n* **fore'man** the first or chief man, one appointed to supervise, or act as spokesman for, others; an overseer: — *pl* **fore'men**. — *n* **fore'mast** the mast that is forward, or nearest to the bow of a ship. — *n* **fore'mastman** any sailor below the rank of petty officer. — *vt* **foremean'** (*archaic*) to intend beforehand. — *adj* **fore'men'tioned** mentioned before in writing or speech. — *n* **fore'name** the first or Christian name. — *adj* **fore'named** mentioned before. — *n* **fore'night** (*Scot*) the early part of the night before bedtime, the evening. — *n* **forenoon** (*fōr-nōōn', för-, fōr'nōōn* or *för'*; *chiefly Scot* and *Ir*) the morning; the part of the day before midday, as opposed to early morning. — *adj* (*fōr'* or *för'*) pertaining to this time. — *n* **fore'-notice** notice of anything in advance of the time. — *vt* **foreordain'** to arrange or determine beforehand; to predestine. — *n* **foreordinā'tion**. — *n* **fore'part** the front; the early part. — *adj* **fore'past** (*obs*) bygone. — *n* **fore'paw** a front paw. — *n* **fore'payment** payment beforehand. — *n* **fore'peak** the narrow part of a ship's hold, close to the bow. — *vt* **foreplan'** to plan beforehand. — *n* **fore'play** sexual stimulation before intercourse. — *vt* **forepoint'** to foreshadow. — *n* **fore'quarter** the front portion of a side of meat, *incl* the leg; (in *pl*; of an animal, *esp* a horse) the forelegs and shoulders, and the body areas adjoining them. — *adj* **fore-quo'ted** quoted or cited before. — *vt* **foreran'** *pa t* of **forerun**. — *n* **fore'-rank** the front rank. — *vi* **forereach'** (*naut*) to glide ahead, *esp* when going in stays (with *on*). — *vt* to sail beyond. — *vt* **foreread'** to foretell: — *pa t* **foreread** (*-red'*). — *n* **fore'reading**. — *adj* **fore-reci'ted** (*Shakesp*) recited or named before. — *vt* **forerun'** to run or come before; to precede. — *n* **fore'runner** a runner or messenger sent before; a person or thing coming before another, a precursor; a forewarning or omen. — *adj* **fore'said** already mentioned (see also **foresay**). — *n* **foresail** (*fōr'sl, för'* or *-sāl*) the chief and lowest square sail on the foremast; a triangular sail on the forestay. — *vt* **foresay'** to predict or foretell; to ordain (*Shakesp*); see also **forsay**. — *vt* and *vi* **foresee'** to see or know beforehand: — *pa t* **foresaw'**; *pa p* **foreseen'**. — *n* **foreseeabil'ity**. — *adj* **foresee'able**. — *adj* **foresee'ing**. — *adv* **foresee'ingly**. — *vt* **foreshad'ow** to give, or have, some indication of in advance; to shadow or typify beforehand. — *n* **foreshad'owing**. — *vt* **foreshew** see **foreshow**. — *n* **fore'ship** the forepart of a ship. — *n* **fore'shock** an earth tremor preceding an earthquake. — *n* **fore'shore** the space between high and low water marks. — *vt* **foreshort'en** to draw or cause to appear as if shortened, by perspective. — *n* **foreshort'ening**. — *vt* **foreshow** or **foreshew** (*fōr-shō'* or *för-*; *archaic*) to show or represent beforehand; to predict: — *pa t* **foreshowed** or **foreshewed** (*-shōd'*); *pa p* **foreshown** or **foreshewn** (*-shōn'*), also (*Spenser*) **foreshewed'**. — *n* **fore'side** the front side; outward appearance (*Spenser*). — *n* **fore'-sight** the act or power of foreseeing; wise forethought or prudence; the sight on the muzzle of a gun; a forward reading on a graduated levelling staff (*surveying*). — *adj* **fore'sighted**. — *adj* **fore'sightful**. — *adj* **fore'sightless**. — *vt* **foresig'nify** (*archaic*) to give a sign of beforehand; to foreshow; to typify. — *n* **fore'skin** the retractable skin that covers the glans penis, the prepuce. — *n* **fore'skirt** (*Shakesp*) the loose front part of a coat. — *vt* **forespeak'** to predict; to engage beforehand (*Scot*); see also **forspeak**. — *vt* **forespend'** to spend beforehand: — *pa p* **forespent'**. — See also **forspend**. — *n* **fore-spurr'er** (*Shakesp*) a person who rides in advance. — *n* **fore'stair** (*Scot*) an outside stair at the front of a house. — *vt* **forestall** (*fōr-stöl'* or *för-*; OE *foresteall* ambush, literally, a place taken beforehand, from *steall* a stand or station) to buy up before reaching the market, so as to sell again at higher prices; to anticipate; to hinder by anticipating; to bar. — *n* **forestall'er**. — *n* **forestall'ing** or **forestal'ment**. — *n* **fore'stay** a rope reaching from the foremast-head to the bowsprit end to support the mast. — *n* **fore'taste** a taste before buying, etc; a brief encounter with or exposure to something to be experienced, presented, etc in full at a later time; anticipation. — *vt* **foretaste'** to taste before possession; to anticipate; to taste before another. — *vt* **foreteach'** (*archaic*) to teach beforehand: — *pa t* and *pa p* **foretaught.'** — *vt* **foretell'** to tell before; to prophesy. — *vi* to utter prophecy: — *pa t* and *pa p* **foretold'**. — *n* **foretell'er**. — *vt* **forethink'** to anticipate in the mind; to have foreknowledge of: — *pa t* and *pa p* **forethought'**. — *n* **forethink'er**. — *n* **fore'thought** thought or care for the future; anticipation; thinking beforehand. — *adj* **forethought'ful**. — *n* **fore'time** past time. — *n* **fore'token** a token or sign beforehand. — *vt* **foretō'ken** to signify beforehand. — *n* and *adj* **fore-tō'kening**. — *n* **fore'tooth** a tooth in the forepart of the mouth: — *pl* **fore'teeth**. — *n* **fore'top** the platform at the head of the foremast (*naut*); the forepart of the crown of the head (*obs*); a lock of hair (*usu* upright) over the forehead; an appendage to a shoe (*obs*). — *n* **foretop'-mast** the mast erected at the head of the foremast, at the top of which is the **fore'top-gallant-mast**. — *adj* **fore-vouched'** (*Shakesp*) affirmed or told before. — *n* **fore'-ward** (*archaic*) an advance guard; the front (*Shakesp*). — *vt* **forewarn'** to warn beforehand; to give previous notice; see also **forwarn**. — *n* **forewarn'ing**. — *vt* **foreweigh'** (*archaic*) to estimate beforehand. — **fore-went'** *pa t* (*Spenser* also *pa p*) of **forego** (see also **forgo**). — *n* **fore'-wheel** either of the pair of front wheels of a wheeled vehicle. — *n* **fore'wind** a favourable wind. — *n* **fore'wing** either of an insect's front pair of wings. — *n* **fore'woman** a woman overseer, a headwoman or a spokeswoman for a group (eg for a jury): — *pl* **fore'-women**. — *n* **fore'word** a preface. [OE *fore*; Ger *vor*]

foreanent. See **fornent**.

forearm... to ... **forecited**. See under **fore-**.

foreclose *fōr-klōz', för-, vt* to close beforehand; to preclude; to prevent; to stop; to bar the right of redeeming (a mortgage, etc). — *adj* **foreclos'able**. — *n* **foreclosure** (*-klō'zhər*) the act, or an instance, of foreclosing; the process by which a mortgagor, failing to repay the money lent on the security of a property, is compelled to forfeit his or her right to redeem it (*law*). [OFr *forclos*, pa p of *forclore* to exclude, from L *forīs* outside, and *claudere*, *clausum* to shut]

forecloth... to ... **forecourt**. See under **fore-**.

fore-damned *fōr-dam'ned*, (*obs*) *adj* utterly damned (or *poss* damned beforehand). [Pfx **for-** (1c), (or possibly **fore-**)]

foredate... to ... **forefront**. See under **fore-**.

foregather. See **forgather**.

foregleam and **forego**[1], etc. See under **fore-**.

forego[2]. See **forgo**.

foreground... to ... **forehead**. See under **fore-**.
forehent. See **forhent**.
fore-horse. See under **fore-**.
foreign *for'in*, *adj* belonging to another country; from abroad; pertaining to, characteristic of or situated in another country; alien; extraneous; not belonging; unconnected; not appropriate. — *n* **for'eigner** a person belonging to, or from, another country; a stranger or outsider. — *n* **for'eignism** a mannerism, turn of phrase, etc, typical of a foreigner. — *n* **for'eignness** the quality of being foreign; lack of relation to something; remoteness. — **foreign aid** financial or other aid given by richer to poorer countries; **foreign bill** or **draft** a bill or draft payable in a different country, state, etc from that in which it was drawn. — *adj* **foreign-built'** built in a foreign country. — **foreign correspondent** a newspaper correspondent working in a foreign country in order to report its news, etc; **foreign exchange** the exchange, conversion, etc of foreign currencies; **foreign legion** an army unit consisting of foreigners; (with *caps*) a former French army unit, consisting of soldiers of all nationalities, serving outside France; **Foreign Office** the British government department dealing with foreign affairs. [OFr *forain*, from LL *forāneus*, from L *forās* out of doors]
forejudge[1]. See under **fore-**.
forejudge[2]. See **forjudge**.
foreknow, etc. See under **fore-**.
forel *for'əl*, (*archaic*) *n* a kind of parchment for covering books. [OFr *forrel*, dimin of *forre*, *fuerre* sheath]
foreland... to ... **fore-notice**. See under **fore-**.
forensic *fə-ren'sik*, *adj* belonging to courts of law, *orig* held by the Romans in the forum; used in law pleading; appropriate or adapted to argument; of or relating to sciences or scientists connected with legal investigations. — *n* **forensical'ity**. — *adv* **foren'sically**. — *n sing* **foren'sics** the art or study of public debate. — **forensic medicine** medical jurisprudence, the application of medical knowledge to the elucidation of doubtful questions in a court of justice. [L *forēnsis*, from *forum* market-place or forum]
forensis strepitus *for-en'sis strep'it-əs* or *-o͝os*, (*L*) the clamour of the forum.
foreordain... to ... **foresay**[1]. See under **fore-**.
foresay[2]. See **forsay**.
foreshadow... to ... **forskirt**. See under **fore-**.
foreslack and **foreslow**. See **forslack** and **forslow**.
forespeak[1] and **forespend**[1]. See under **fore-**.
forespeak[2] and **forespend**[2]. See **forspeak** and **forspend**.
fore-spurrer. See under **fore-**.
FOREST *for'ist*, *abbrev*: Freedom Organization for the Right to Enjoy Smoking Tobacco.
forest *for'ist*, *n* a large uncultivated tract of land covered with trees and undergrowth; woody ground and rough pasture; a royal preserve for hunting, governed by a special code called the **forest law**; any area resembling a forest because thickly covered with tall, upright objects. — *adj* of, pertaining to, or consisting of (a) forest; sylvan; rustic. — *vt* to cover with trees; to cover thickly with tall, upright objects. — *n* **for'estage** an ancient duty paid by foresters to the king; the rights of foresters. — *adj* **for'estal** or **foresteal** (*fər-est'i-əl*). — *n* **forestā'tion** tree-planting on a large scale, afforestation. — *adj* **for'ested**. — *n* **for'ester** a person who has charge of a forest; a person who has care of growing trees; (with *cap*) a member of the Ancient Order of Foresters or a similar friendly society; an inhabitant of a forest; a large kangaroo (*Austr*). — *adj* **for'estine**. — *n* **for'estry** the science and art of planting, tending and managing forests; forest country; an expanse of trees. — *adj* **for'est-born** (*Shakesp*) born in a forest. — *adj* **for'est-bred**. — **for'est-fly** a two-winged insect (*Hippobosca equina*) that annoys horses; **Forest Marble** (*geol*) a Middle Jurassic fissile limestone of which typical beds are found in Wychwood Forest, Oxfordshire; **for'est-oak** a species of Casuarina, a mainly Australian tree; **for'est-tree** a large tree, *esp* a timber-tree, that grows in forests. [OFr *forest* (Fr *forêt*), from LL *forestis* (*silva*) the outside wood, as opposed to the *parcus* (park) or walled-in wood, from L *forīs* out of doors]
forestair... to ... **foretopmast**. See under **fore-**.
forever *fər-ev'ər*, *adv* for ever, for all time to come; eternally; everlastingly; continually. — *n* an endless or indefinite length of time, or one that seems so. — *adv* **forev'ermore'** for ever hereafter.
forevouched... to ... **foreward**. See under **fore-**.
forewarn[1]. See under **fore-**.
forewarn[2]. See **forwarn**.
foreweigh... to ... **foreword**. See under **fore-**.
forex *fo'reks*, *abbrev*: foreign exchange.
forfair *fər-fār'*, *vi* to perish or decay (*obs*). — *adj* (*Scot*) **forfairn'** worn out; exhausted. [OE *forfaran*]
forfaiting *för'fā-ting*, *n* a method of export finance whereby debts on exported goods are bought and then sold on to banks, etc. — *n* **for'faiter** a person who, or company which, buys and sells such debts. [Fr *forfait* forfeit or contract]
forfeit *för'fit*, *n* something to which a right is lost; a penalty for a crime, or breach of some condition; a fine; (*esp* in *pl*) a game in which a player surrenders some item (a **forfeit**) which can be redeemed only by performing a task, or fulfilling a challenge, set by the others; a penalty incurred in such a game. — *adj* forfeited. — *vt* to lose the right to (something) by some fault or crime; to confiscate (*archaic*); to penalize by forfeiting; loosely, to give up voluntarily. — *adj* **for'feitable**. — *n* **for'feiter** (*Shakesp*) a person who incurs punishment by forfeiting his or her bond. — *n* **for'feiture** act of forfeiting; the state of being forfeited; the thing forfeited. — Also (*obs*) **forfault**, etc, by association with **fault**. [OFr *forfait*, from LL *forisfactum*, from L *forīs* outside, and *facere* to make]
forfend *fər-fend'*, (*archaic*) *vt* to ward off or avert. [Pfx **for-** (1a) and **fend**[1]]
forfex *för'feks*, *n* a pair of scissors or pincers; the pincers of an earwig, etc (*entomol*). — *adj* **for'ficate** (*ornithol*) deeply forked, *esp* of certain birds' tails. — *n* **Forfic'ūla** the common genus of earwigs. — *adj* **forfic'ūlate** like scissors. [L *forfex*, *-icis* shears or pincers]
forfoughten *fər-fö'tən* (*Scot* **forfoughen** *fər-fohh'ən*, **forfeuchen** *-fūhh'*), (*dialect*) *adj* exhausted. [Pfx **for-** (1c)]
forgat. See **forget**.
forgather or **foregather** *fər-gadh'ər*, *vi* to meet, *esp* by chance; to fraternize (with *with*). [Pfx **for-** (1c)]
forgave. See **forgive**.
forge[1] *fōrj* or *förj*, *n* the workshop of a person who works in iron, etc; a furnace, *esp* one in which iron is heated; a smithy; a place where anything is shaped or made. — *vt* to form by heating and hammering, by heating and pressure, or by pressure alone (in the last case, often **cold forge**); to form or fashion (an object or, *fig*, a link or connection); to fabricate; to counterfeit for purposes of fraud; to form by great pressure, electricity or explosion. — *vi* to commit forgery. — *adj* **forge'able**. — *n* **forg'er** a person who forges, *esp* illegally. — *n* **forg'ery** fraudulently making or altering anything, *esp* anything printed; anything which is forged or counterfeited; deceit (*obs*). — *adj* **forg'etive** (*Shakesp*) creative. — *n* **forg'ing** a piece of metal shaped by hammering; the act of a criminal forger. — **forge'man** a worker in an iron workshop, etc. [OFr *forge*, from L *fabrica*, from *faber* a workman]
forge[2] *fōrj* or *förj*, *vi* to move steadily on (*usu* with *ahead*). [Origin obscure]
forge[3] *fōrj* or *förj*, *vi* (of a horse) to click the hind shoe against the fore. [Origin obscure]
forget *fər-get'*, *vt* to lose or drop from the memory; to fail to remember or think of; to leave behind accidentally; to neglect: — *pr p* **forgett'ing**; *pa t* **forgot'** (*archaic* **forgat'**); *pa p* **forgott'en** (also, now *rare* or *US*, but otherwise *archaic*, **forgot'**). — *adj* **forget'ful** apt to forget; inattentive. — *adv* **forget'fully**. — *n* **forget'fulness**. — *adj* **forgett'able**. — *n* **forgett'er**. — *n* **forgett'ery** (*colloq facetious*) a capacity for forgetting;

a bad memory. — *n* and *adj* **forgett'ing**. — *adv* **forgett'ingly**. — *adj* **forgott'en**. — *n* **forgott'enness**. — **forget'-me-not** a plant with clusters of small blue flowers (genus *Myosotis*), regarded as an emblem of loving remembrance. — **forget it** (*colloq*; *esp* in *imperative*) used to state that there is no need to offer apologies, thanks, etc, or to say or do anything further about a particular matter; used to deny a request, or dismiss a suggestion, out of hand; **forget oneself** to lose one's self-control or dignity, to descend to words and deeds unworthy of oneself. [OE *forgetan* (*forgietan*), from pfx *for-* away, and *getan* (*gietan*) to get]

forgive *fər-giv'*, *vt* to pardon; to overlook; to pardon a debt or offence (*Shakesp*); to give up (*Spenser*). — *vi* to show mercy or compassion, or give a pardon: — *pa t* **forgave'**; *pa p* **forgiv'en**. — *adj* **forgiv'able** capable of being forgiven. — *n* **forgive'ness** pardon; remission; a readiness to forgive. — *adj* **forgiv'ing** ready to pardon; merciful; compassionate. [OE *forgiefan*, from pfx *for-* away, and *giefan* to give; cf Ger *vergeben*]

forgo or **forego** *fōr-*, *fȯr-* or *fər-gō'*, *vt* to leave (*obs*); to give up or relinquish; to do without; to refrain from using or benefiting from; to forfeit (*archaic*). — *vi* to go or pass away: — *pr p* **forgo'ing** or **forego'ing**; *pa p* **forgone'** or **foregone'**; *pa t* **forwent'** or **forewent'**. — See also **forego**. [OE *forgān* to pass by or abstain from, from pfx *for-* away, and *gān* to go]

forgot and **forgotten**. See **forget**.

forhaile *fȯr-hāl'*, (*Spenser*) *vt* to distract. [Pfx **for-** (1a)]

forhent or **forehent** *fȯr-hent'*, *vt* to overtake; to seize: — *pa p* (*Spenser*) **forhent'**. [Pfx **for-** (1c)]

forhow *fȯr-how'*, *vt* to despise (*obs*); (also **forhoo** *fər-hōō'* or **forhooie** *fər-hōō'ē*) to desert or abandon (*Scot*). [OE *forhogian*, from pfx *for-* away, and *hogian* to care]

forinsec *fər-in'sek*, *adj* (of feudal service) due to the lord's superior. — *adj* **forin'secal** (*obs*) foreign; alien; extrinsic. [L *forīnsecus* from without, from *forīs* out of doors, and *secus* following]

forint *for'int*, *n* the monetary unit of Hungary since 1946 (100 *fillér*). [Hung, from Ital *fiorino* florin]

forisfamiliate *fōr* or *for-is-fə-mil'i-āt*, (*law*) *vt* to emancipate from paternal authority; (of a father) to put (a son) in possession of land which is accepted as the whole portion of the father's property. — *vi* (of a son) to renounce one's title to a further share. — *n* **forisfamiliā'tion**. [LL *forīsfamiliāre*, *-ātum*, from L *forīs* out of doors, and *familia* a family]

forjeskit *fər-jes'kit* or **forjaskit** *-jas'*, (*Scot*) *adj* tired out. [Pfx **for-** (1c); cf **disjaskit**]

forjudge or **forejudge** *fōr-juj'* or *fȯr-*, (*law*) *vt* to deprive of a right, object, etc by a judgement. [OFr *forjugier*, from *fors*, from L *foris* out, and *jugier* (Fr *juger*) to judge]

fork *fȯrk*, *n* any pronged instrument (such as an eating implement or garden tool) for spiking and lifting, etc; anything that divides into prongs or branches; a branch or prong; the space or angle between branches, *esp* on a tree or between the legs; a confluent, tributary or branch of a river; one of the branches into which a road divides; a dividing into two branches, a bifurcation; a place of bifurcation; a barbed arrowhead; the part of a bicycle to which a wheel is attached; the appearance of a flash of lightning; the bottom of a sump in a mine; a simultaneous attack on two pieces by one piece (*chess*). — *vi* to branch; to follow a branch road. — *vt* to form as a fork; to move or lift with a fork; to stab or dig with a fork; to attack (two pieces) simultaneously (*chess*); to pump dry. — *adj* **forked** shaped like a fork; insincere or deceitful (as in *forked tongue*). — *adv* **fork'edly**. — *n* **fork'edness**. — *n* **fork'er**. — *n* **fork'ful** as much as a fork will hold: — *pl* **fork'fuls**. — *n* **fork'iness**. — *adj* **fork'y**. — **fork'-chuck** a forked lathe-centre in wood-turning; **forked lightning** lightning in the form of zigzag flashes; **fork'head** an arrowhead (*Spenser*); the forked end of a rod, holding a connecting pin; **fork'it-tail** or **fork'y-tail** (*dialect*) an earwig; **fork-lift truck** (or in short **fork'-lift**) a power-driven truck with an arrangement of steel prongs which can lift, raise up high and carry heavy packages and stack them where required (often used with a pallet); **fork lunch** or **luncheon**, **fork supper**, etc, a buffet-type meal suitable for eating with a fork only; **fork'tail** a name for various fish and birds, eg the kite. — *adj* **fork'-tailed**. — **fork out**, **over** or **up** (*slang*) to hand or pay over, *esp* unwillingly. [OE *forca*, from L *furca*]

forlana *fȯr-lä'nə* or **furlana** *fōōr-*, *n* a Venetian dance in 6-8 time. [Ital *Furlana* Friulian]

forlend. See **forelend**.

forlorn *fər-lȯrn'*, *adj* quite lost; forsaken; neglected; wretched. — *n* (*Shakesp*) a forsaken person; a forlorn hope. — *orig pa p* of the *obs* **forlese** (*for-lēz'*) *vt* to lose; to forsake (*pa t* and *pa p*, *Spenser*, **forlore** *-lōr'* or *-lȯr*). — *adv* **forlorn'ly**. — *n* **forlorn'ness**. [OE *forloren*, pa p of *forlēosan* to lose, from pfx *for-* away, and *lēosan* to lose; Ger *verloren*, pa p of *verlieren* to lose]

forlorn hope *fər-lȯrn' hōp*, *n orig*, a body of soldiers selected for some service of especial danger; a desperate enterprise of last resort; a vain or faint hope (from association with hope, in the sense of expectation). [Du *verloren hoop* lost troop]

form *fȯrm*, *n* shape; a mould; something that holds or shapes, eg a piece of formwork (see below); a species or kind; a pattern or type; a way of being; a manner of arrangement; order; regularity; system, eg of government; beauty (*obs*); style and arrangement; structural unity in music, literature, painting, etc; a prescribed set of words or course of action; ceremony; behaviour; condition of fitness or efficiency; a schedule to be filled in with details; a specimen document for imitation; the inherent nature of an object (*philos*); that in which the essence of a thing consists (*philos*); a complete set of crystal faces similar with respect to the symmetry of the crystal (*crystallog*); forme (*printing*); a long seat or bench; a school class; the bed of a hare, shaped by the animal's body; a criminal record (*slang*); the condition of fitness of eg a horse or athlete; a record of past performance of an athlete, horse, etc; (*colloq*; with *the*) the correct procedure; (*colloq*; with *the*) the situation or position. — *vt* to give form or shape to; to bring into being; to make; to contrive; to conceive in the mind; to go to make up; to constitute; to establish. — *vi* to assume a form. — *adj* **form'able**. — *adj* **form'ative** giving form, determining, moulding; capable of development; growing; serving to form words by derivation or inflection, not radical (*gram*). — *n* (*gram*) a derivative (*old*); a formative element; any grammatical element from which words and sentences are constructed. — *adj* **formed**. — *n* **form'er** someone or something that forms, shapes or moulds; a tool for giving a coil or winding the correct shape (*elec eng*). — *n* **form'ing**. — *adj* **form'less**. — *adv* **form'lessly**. — *n* **form'lessness**. — **form class** (*linguistics*) a class of forms (words and phrases) that will fit into the same position in a construction; **form critic**; **form criticism** biblical criticism that classifies parts of scripture according to literary form and relates literary forms to historical background; **form genus** a group of species with similar morphological characters, but which are not certainly known to be related in descent; **form horse** the favourite, the expected winner (*horse-racing*; also *fig*); **form letter** a letter with a fixed form and contents, used *esp* when writing to a number of people about the same or essentially similar matters; **form master**, **mistress** or **teacher** (*esp* in a secondary school) the teacher who is responsible for the administration, welfare, etc of a particular form or class; **form'work** shuttering to contain concrete. — **good** or **bad form** good or recognized, or bad or unaccepted, social usage. [L *fōrma* shape]

-form *fȯrm* or **-iform** *-i-fȯrm*, *combining form* (used to mean) having a specified form or number of forms. [L *fōrma* form]

formal *fȯrməl*, *adj* according to form or established style; relating to form; ceremonious, punctilious or methodical; having the outward form only; sane (*Shakesp*); having the power of making a thing what it is; essential. — *n* **form'alism** excessive observance of form or conventional usage, *esp* in religion; stiffness of manner; concentration on form or technique at the expense of social or moral content (*art*). — *n* **form'alist** a person having exaggerated regard to rules or established usages; a person who practises formalism (*art*). — Also *adj*. — *adj* **formalist'ic**. — *n* **formal'ity** the precise observance of forms or ceremonies; a matter of form; a ceremonious observance; stiffness or conventionality; mere convention at the expense of substance. — *n* **formalīzā'tion** or **-s-**. — *vt* **form'alize** or **-ise** to make formal; to make official or valid; to make precise or give a clear statement of. — *vi* to be formal. — *adv* **form'ally**. — **formal logic** see under **logic**; **formal verdict** (*law*) one in which the jury follows the judge's directions; in a fatal accident inquiry, a finding of death by misadventure with no apportioning of blame (*Scot*). [**form**]

formaldehyde *för-mal'di-hīd*, *n* a formic aldehyde, formalin.

formalin *för'mə-lin* or **formol** *för'mol*, *n* a formic aldehyde used as an antiseptic, germicide or preservative. [**formil**]

formaliter *för-mal'i-tər* or *-ter*, (*LL*) *adv* formally or in respect of the formal element.

formant *för'mənt*, *n* a component of a speech sound determining its particular quality (*acoustics*); anything that determines, limits or defines. [Ger *Formant*, from L *formāns*, *-antis*, pr p of *formare* to form]

format *för'mat* or (*rare*) *för'mä*, *n* (of books, etc) the size, form or shape in which they are issued; the style, arrangement and contents of eg a radio or television programme; (the description of) the way data is, or is to be, arranged in a file, on a card, disk, tape, etc (*comput*). — *vt* to arrange (a book, etc) into a specific format; to arrange (data) for use on a disk, tape, etc (*comput*); to prepare (a disk, etc) for use by dividing it into sectors (*comput*): — *pr p* **form'atting**; *pa t* and *pa p* **form'atted**. — *n* **form'atter** (*comput*) a program for formatting a disk, tape, etc. [Fr]

formate[1] *för-māt'*, *vi* (of aircraft) to join, or fly, in formation; to form (*obs*); to state precisely or formulate (*obs*). — *n* **formā'tion** a making or producing; something formed or made, a structure; an arrangement (of eg troops, aircraft or players); a group of strata used as a basis for rock mapping (*geol*); a plant community (*bot*). — *adj* **formā'tional**. [**form**]

formate[2]. See under **formic**.

forme *förm*, (*printing*) *n* metal type and blocks from which an impression is to be made, assembled and secured in a chase or frame ready for printing. — Also **form**. [**form**]

former *förm'ər*, *adj* (*compar* of **fore**) before in time; past; first mentioned (of two); beforehand or first (of two) (*Shakesp*). — *adv* **form'erly** in former times; before this time. [Formed late on analogy of ME *formest* foremost, by adding compar sfx *-er* to base of OE *forma* first, itself superlative]

formic *för'mik*, *adj* pertaining to ants. — *n* **for'mate** a salt of formic acid. — Also **for'miate**. — *adj* **for'micant** crawling like an ant; (of a pulse) very small and unequal. — *n* **formicā'rium** (*pl* **formicā'ria**) or **for'micary** an ant-hill, ants' nest, or colony. — *adj* **for'micate** resembling an ant. — *n* **formicā'tion** a sensation like that of ants creeping on the skin. — **formic acid** a fatty acid, H·CO·OH, found in ants and nettles. [L *formīca* an ant]

Formica® *för-mī'kə*, *n* a brand of plastic laminates used to provide hard, heat-resistant, easily-cleaned surfaces.

formidable *för'mid-ə-bl* or *-mid'*, *adj* causing fear; inspiring awe; redoubtable. — *n* **formidabil'ity** or **for'midableness**. — *adv* **for'midably**. [Fr, from L *formīdābilis*, from *formīdō* fear]

formol. See **formalin**.

formula *förm'ū-lə*, *n* a prescribed form, *esp* a fixed phrase or set of phrases traditionally used on a ceremonial, etc occasion; a formal statement of doctrines; a recipe; a milk substitute (prepared from dried ingredients) for bottle-feeding babies; a statement of joint aims or principles worked out for practical purposes by diplomats of divergent interests; a solution or answer worked out by different sides in a dispute, etc; a technical specification governing *orig* cars entered for certain motor-racing events, now also applied to other racing vehicles or craft; a general expression for solving problems (*math*); a set of symbols expressing the composition of a body (*chem*); a list of ingredients of a patent medicine: — *pl* **formulae** (*förm'ū-lē*) or **form'ūlas**. — *adj* **formulaic** (*-lā'ik*). — *adj* **form'ūlar** or **formūlaris'tic**. — *n* **formūlarīzā'tion** or **-s-** or **formūlā'tion**. — *vt* **form'ūlarize** or **-ise**. — *n* **form'ūlary** a formula; a book of formulae or precedents. — *adj* prescribed; ritual. — *vt* **form'ūlate** or **form'ūlize** or **-ise** to reduce to or express in a formula; to state or express in a clear or definite form. — *n* **form'ūlism** excessive use of, or dependence on, formulae. — *n* **form'ūlist**. [L *fōrmula*, dimin of *fōrma*]

fornent *fər-nent'*, (*Scot*) *adv* and *prep* right opposite to (in location). — Also **foreanent'** or **fornenst'**. [**fore** and **anent**]

fornicate[1] *för'ni-kāt*, *adj* arched (*archit*); arching over (*bot*). — *n* **fornicā'tion**. [L *fornicātus*, from *fornix* a vault or arch]

fornicate[2] *för'ni-kāt*, *vi* to commit fornication. — *n* **fornicā'tion** voluntary sexual intercourse between unmarried people, sometimes extended to cases where only one of the pair concerned is unmarried (*legal*); adultery (*Bible*); idolatry (*fig*). — *n* **for'nicātor**: — *fem* **for'nicātress**. [L *fornīcārī*, *-ātus*, from *fornix* a vault or brothel]

fornix *för'niks*, *n* something resembling an arch (*archit*); an arched formation of the brain (*med*). — *adj* **forn'ical**. [L]

forpine *för-pīn'*, *vi* (*Spenser*) to waste away. [Pfx **for-** (1c)]

forpit or **forpet** *fōr-pət*, (*Scot*) *n* a fourth part (now of a peck measure). [**fourth part**]

forrad *for'əd* or (*dialect*) **forrit** *for'ət* or *för'it*, (*Scot*) *adv* forms of **forward**: — *compar* **forr'ader**.

forray *for-ā'*, *n* and *vt* (*Spenser*) foray.

forren *for'in*, (*Milton*) *adj* foreign.

forsake *fər-sāk'* or *för-*, *vt* to desert; to abandon: — *pr p* **forsāk'ing**; *pa t* **forsook'**; *pa p* **forsāk'en**. — *adj* **forsāk'en**. — *adv* **forsāk'enly**. — *n* **forsāk'enness**. — *n* **forsāk'ing** abandonment. [OE *forsacan*, from *for-* away, and *sacan* to strive]

forsay or **foresay** *för-sā'*, *vt* to forbid (*obs*); to renounce (*Spenser*); to banish (*Spenser*). [OE *forsecgan*, from *for-* against, and *secgan* to say]

forset-seller. See **fosset-seller**.

forslack or **foreslack** *för-slak'*, *vi* (*obs*) to be or become slack or neglectful. — *vt* (*Spenser*) to harm by slackness. [Pfx **for-** (1c)]

forslow, **forsloe** or **foreslow** *för-slō'*, *vt* (*Spenser*) to delay. — *vi* (*Shakesp*) to delay. [OE *forslāwian*, from *for*, intensive, and *slāwian* to be slow]

forsooth *fər-sōōth'* or *för-*, *adv* in truth; certainly (now only *ironic*). [**for sooth**]

forspeak or **forespeak** *fər-spēk'* or *för-*, *vt* to forbid (*obs*); to speak against (*Shakesp*); to bewitch (*Scot*). [Pfx **for-** (1b)]

forspend or **forespend** *fər-spend'*, *vt* to wear out physically; to exhaust (resources): — *pa t* and *pa p* **forspent'**. [Pfx **for-** (1c)]

forswatt *för-swöt'*, (*Spenser*) *adj* covered with sweat. [Pfx **for-** (1c) and *swat*, old pa p of **sweat**]

forswear *fər-swār'* or *för-*, *vt* to deny or renounce upon oath. — *vi* to swear falsely: — *pa t* **forswore'**; *pa p* **forsworn'**. — *adj* **forsworn'** perjured, having forsworn oneself. — *n* **forsworn'ness**. — **forswear oneself** to swear falsely. [Pfx **for-** (1b)]

forswink *fər-swingk'* or *fȫr-*, (*obs*) *vt* to exhaust by labour. — *adj* **forswunk'** or (*Spenser*) **forswonck'** overworked. [Pfx **for-** (1b) and OE *swincan* to labour]

forsythia *för-sī'thi-ə* or *-si'*, *n* any shrub of the genus *Forsythia*, a popular garden plant producing clusters of yellow jasmine-like flowers in the spring. [After William *Forsyth* (1737–1804), botanist]

fort *fört* or *fört*, *n* a small fortress; an outlying trading-station (*NAm*). — *vt* to fortify. — **hold the fort** to take temporary charge. [Fr, from L *fortis* strong]

fortalice *fört'ə-lis*, (*hist*) *n* a fortress; a small outwork of a fortification. [LL *fortalitia*, from L *fortis*]

forte[1] *fört*, now *usu* for the first meaning *fört'i*, *n* the thing in which one excels; the upper half of a sword or foil blade, the strong part. [Fr *fort* strong]

forte[2] *för'ti*, (*music*) *adj* and *adv* loud: — *superl* **fortis'-simo**, *double superl* **fortissis'simo** as loud as possible. — *n* a loud passage in music. — *n* **fortepi'anist**. — *n* **fortepia'no** the 18c name for an early type of piano. — *adj* and *adv* loud with immediate relapse into softness. [Ital]

forth *förth* or *förth*, *adv* (*archaic*) forward; onward; out; into the open; in continuation; abroad. — *prep* (*Shakesp*) out of or forth from. — *vi* (*obs*) **forthcome'** to come forth. — *adj* **forthcom'ing** about to appear or happen; (of a person) friendly, communicative; just coming forth (*archaic*); approaching (*archaic*); at hand, ready to be produced (*archaic*). — *n* (*obs*) **forth'going** a going forth. — *n* **forth'-putting** the action of putting forth (*obs*); undue forwardness (*US*; *archaic*). — *adj* (*US*) forward. — *adv* **forth'right** (or *-rīt'*; *obs*) straightforward; at once. — *n* (*Shakesp*) a straight path. — *adj* straightforward; downright. — *adv* **forth'rightly**. — *n* **forth'rightness**. — *adv* **forthwith** (*-with'*, *-widh'* or *förth'*) immediately. — **and so forth** and so on, et cetera. [OE *forth*, from *fore* before; Du *voort*, Ger *fort*]

forthink *fər-thingk'*, *vt* (*Spenser*) to be sorry for or regret; to rethink. — *vi* (*dialect*) to change one's mind. [From OE *forthencan*, from OE *for-* and *thencan* to think or *thyncan* to seem]

forthy *för-dhī'*, (*Spenser*) *adv* therefore; for that. [OE *forthȳ*, from *for* and *thȳ*, instrumental case of *thæt* that]

forties and **fortieth**. See under **forty**.

fortify *för'ti-fī*, *vt* to strengthen with forts, etc against attack; to invigorate; to confirm; to strengthen (*esp* certain wines) by adding alcohol; to enrich (a food) by adding eg vitamins. — *vi* to put up fortifications: — *pr p* **for'tifying**; *pa t* and *pa p* **for'tified**. — *adj* **for'tifīable**. — *n* **fortificā'tion** the art of strengthening a military position by means of defensive works; (often in *pl*) the work so constructed; something which fortifies. — *n* **for'tifīer**. [Fr *fortifier*, from LL *fortificāre*, from *fortis* strong, and *facere* to make]

fortilage *för'ti-lāj* or *för'*, (*Spenser*) *n* a variant of **fortalice**.

fortis *för'tis*, (*phonetics*) *adj* (of a consonant) articulated with relatively great muscular effort and pressure of breath (opposed to *lenis*). — Also *n*: — *pl* **fortēs**. [L, strong]

fortissimo. See under **forte**[2].

fortiter et recte *för'ti-tər et rek'tē* or *for'ti-ter et rek'te*, (*L*) bravely and uprightly.

fortitude *för'ti-tūd*, (*US*) *-tōōd*, *n* courage in endurance; strength (*obs*). — *adj* **fortitū'dinous**. [L *fortitūdō*, *-inis*, from *fortis* strong]

fortlet *fört'lət* or *fört'*, *n* a little fort.

fortnight *fört'nīt*, *n* two weeks or fourteen days. — *adj* and *adv* **fort'nightly** once a fortnight. — *n* a magazine, etc appearing fortnightly. [OE *fēowertȳne niht* fourteen nights]

Fortran *för'tran*, *n* a problem-orientated computer language widely used in scientific work. [*For*mula *tran*slation]

fortress *för'trəs* or *för'*, *n* a fortified place; a defence. — *vt* (*Shakesp*) to guard. [OFr *forteresse*, another form of *fortelesce* (see **fortalice**)]

fortuitous *för-tū'i-təs*, (*US*) *-tōō'*, *adj* happening by chance; fortunate. — *n* **fortū'itism** belief in evolution by chance variation. — *n* **fortū'itist**. — *adv* **fortū'-itously**. — *n* **fortū'itousness** or **fortū'ity**. [L *fortuītus*]

fortune *för'chən*, *n* whatever comes by lot or chance; luck; the arbitrary ordering of events; the lot that falls to one in life; a prediction of one's future; success; a great accumulation of wealth; a large amount of money; an heiress (*obs*). — *vi* (*obs*) to befall. — *vt* (*obs*) to determine the fortune of. — *adj* **for'tunate** happening by good fortune; lucky; auspicious; felicitous. — *adv* **for'tunately** in a fortunate way, by good luck; I'm glad to say or happy to report. — *n* **for'tunateness**. — *adj* **for'tuned** (*archaic*) supplied by fortune. — *adj* **for'-tuneless** without a fortune; luckless. — *vt* (*Spenser*) **for'tunize** to make fortunate or happy. — **for'tune book** a book for use in fortune-telling; **fortune cookie** (*US*) a piece of dough wrapped and cooked around a piece of paper which has a (supposed) horoscope or a maxim on it, served *esp* in Chinese homes and restaurants; **for'tune-hunter** (*derog*) a person who hunts for a wealthy marriage. — *vi* **for'tune-tell** (back-formation). — **for'tune-teller** a person who professes to foretell one's fortune. — *n* **for'tune-telling**. — **a small fortune** quite a large amount of money. [Fr, from L *fortūna*]

forty *för'ti*, *adj* and *n* four times ten. — *n* (with *cap* and *the*) the French Academy. — *n pl* **for'ties** the numbers forty to forty-nine; the years so numbered (of a life or century); a range of temperature from forty to just less than fifty degrees; (with *cap* and *the*) the sea area lying between NE Scotland and SW Norway, with a minimum depth of 40 fathoms. — *adj* **for'tieth** the last of forty; next after the thirty-ninth; equal to one of forty equal parts. — *n* one of forty equal parts; a person or thing in fortieth position. — *adj* **for'tyish** apparently about forty years old. — **for'ty-five'** a record played at a speed of 45 revolutions per minute; (with *cap* and *the*) the Jacobite rebellion of 1745; **for'ty-nin'er** a gold-seeker in the 1849 rush in California; **forty winks** a short nap, *esp* after dinner. — **roaring forties** the tract of stormy W winds S of 40°S latitude (occasionally also in the Atlantic N of 40°N). [OE *fēowertig*, from *fēower* four, and *-tig* ten (as sfx)]

forum *fō'rəm* or *fö'*, *n orig* a market-place, *esp* that in Rome where public business was transacted and justice dispensed; the courts of law as opposed to Parliament (*rare*); a meeting to discuss topics of public concern; a publication, regular meeting, etc serving as a medium for debate: — *pl* **fo'rums** or **fo'ra**. [L *forum*, related to *forās* out of doors]

forwander *fər-won'dər*, *vi* to wander till wearied (*archaic*); to stray far (*Spenser*). — *adj* (*archaic*) **forwan'dered** strayed. [Pfx **for-** (1d)]

forward *för'wərd*, *adj* near or at the front; in advance; well advanced; ready; too ready; lacking due modesty or respect, presumptuous; officious; earnest (*archaic*); early ripe. — *vt* to help on; to send on. — *adv* **for'ward** or **for'wards** towards what is in front; onward; progressively. — *adv* **forward** (*for'əd*) towards or in the front part of a ship. — *n* **for'ward** a player in the front line (*football*, etc). — *n* **for'warder** a person or company engaged in forwarding. — *n* **for'warding** the act or business of despatching merchandise, etc. — *adv* **for'wardly**. — *n* **for'wardness**. — **forward delivery** delivery of goods at a future date. — *adj* **for'ward-looking** having regard to the future; progressive. — **forward market** a market in which commodities, etc are contracted to be bought and sold at a future date at an agreed price (**forward price**); **forward pass** (*Rugby football*) an illegal pass in which the ball is thrown forward towards the opponents' goal-line. [OE *fore-ward* (WSax *foreweard*), from *fore*, and *-ward* (*-weard*) signifying direction; the *s* of *forwards* is a genitive ending (cf Ger *vorwärts*)]

forwarn or **forewarn** *fər-* or *för-wörn'*, *vt* to forbid. [Pfx **for-** (1b), against, and **warn**]

forwaste *för-wāst'*, (*Spenser*) *vt* to waste utterly. [Pfx **for-** (1c)]

forweary *fər* or *för-wē'ri*, (*Spenser*) *vt* to weary out. [Pfx **for-** (1c)]

forwent *fər-* or *för-went'*. See **forgo**.

forwhy *för-(h)wī'*, (*archaic*) *conj* because. — *adv* why. [**for** and **why**]

forworn *fər-wōrn'* or *-wörn'*, (*Spenser*) *adj* much worn. [Pfx **for-** (1c)]

forzando and **forzato**. See **sforzando**.

Fosbury flop *foz'bə-ri flop*, *n* a method of high-jumping in which the athlete goes over the bar horizontally on his or her back. [R *Fosbury* (born 1947), US athlete]

foss[1] or **fosse** *fos*, *n* a ditch, moat, trench or canal. — *adj* **fossed**. — *n* **fossette'** a small hollow. — **Foss Way** or **Fosse Way** the Roman road that runs between Exeter and Lincoln; (without *cap*) any of the British Roman roads having a fosse on either side. [Fr *fosse*, from L *fossa*, from *fodere*, *fossum* to dig]

foss[2]. See **force**[2].

fossa[1] *fos'ə*, (*anatom*) *n* a pit or depression: — *pl* **foss'ae** (*-ē*). — *n* **foss'ūla** a small depression or groove. — *adj* **foss'ūlate**. [L, a ditch]

fossa[2] *fos'ə* or **foussa** *fo͞os'ə*, *n* a Madagascan animal (*Cryptoprocta ferox*) more or less similar to the civets; (**Fossa**) a genus of Madagascan civets. [Malagasy]

fosse. See **foss**[1].

fosset-seller *fos'it-sel'ər*, (*Shakesp*) *n* apparently, a person who sells faucets (another reading is **for'set-seller**). [*fosset* and *forset*, obs forms of **faucet**]

fossette. See under **foss**[1].

fossick *fos'ik*, (*Austr*) *vi* to search for gold, on the surface or in abandoned workings; to rummage. — *vt* to dig out. — *n* **foss'icker**. — *n* **foss'icking**. [Perh connected with Eng dialect *fossick* a troublesome person]

fossil *fos'l* or *-il*, *n* a rock or mineral substance dug from the earth (*obs*); a relic or trace of a former living thing preserved in rock (*geol*); an antiquated, out-of-date, or unchanging person or thing (*fig*; *derog*). — *adj* dug out of the earth; in the condition of a fossil; antiquated. — *adj* **fossilif'erous** bearing or containing fossils. — *n* **fossilizā'tion** or **-s-**. — *vt* **foss'ilize** or **-ise** to convert into a fossil (also *fig*). — *vi* to become a fossil; to look for fossils (*colloq*). — *adj* **foss'il-fired** (of a power station, etc) burning fossil fuel. — **fossil fuel** coal, oil, etc produced in the earth by a process of fossilization; **fossil water** water which has been trapped in an underground reservoir since a previous geological age. [Fr *fossile*, from L *fossilis*, from *fodere* to dig]

fossor *fos'or*, (*archaic*) *n* a grave-digger. — *adj* **fossorial** (*-ō'ri-əl* or *-ö'*; *zool*) adapted for digging. [L *fossor*, from *fodere* to dig]

fossula and **fossulate**. See under **fossa**[1].

foster[1] *fos'tər*, *vt* to bring up or nurse (*esp* a child not one's own); to put (a child) into the care of someone not its parent; to treat (eg the elderly) in a similar fashion; to encourage; to promote; to cherish. — *vi* to care for a child or elderly person in a foster-home. — *adj* of or concerned with fostering. — *n* **fos'terage** the act or custom of fostering or nursing; the condition or relation of foster-child; the care of a foster-child; the act of encouraging or cultivating. — *n* **fos'terer**: — *fem* **fos'tress**. — *n* **fos'tering**. — *n* **fos'terling** a foster-child. — **fos'ter-brother** a male child nursed or brought up with a child or children of different parents; **fos'ter-child** a child nursed or brought up by someone who is not its parent; **fos'ter-daughter**; **fos'ter-father** a man who brings up a child in place of its father; **fos'ter-home**; **fos'ter-mother** a woman who brings up a child in place of its mother; an apparatus for rearing chickens; **fos'ter-nurse**; **fos'ter-parent**; **fos'ter-sister**; **fos'ter-son**. [OE *fōstrian* to nourish, from *fōster* food]

foster[2] *fos'tər*, (*Spenser*) *n* a forester.

fother[1] *fodh'ər*, *vt* to cover (a sail, etc) with yarn and oakum, as stopping for a leak. [Perh Du *voederen* (modern *voeren*), or LGer *fodern* to line]

fother[2] *fodh'ər*, *n* a load or quantity (*dialect*); a cartload (*dialect*); a definite weight, *specif* of lead, 19½ hundredweight (*obs*). [OE *fōther*; Ger *Fuder*]

fother[3] *fodh'ər*, *n* a dialect variant of **fodder**.

fothergilla *fo-dhər-gil'ə*, *n* any plant of the *Fothergilla* genus of N American deciduous shrubs of the witch-hazel family (*Hamamelis*), also called witch-alder. [Dr John *Fothergill*, 18c British physician and botanist]

fou[1] *fo͞o*, (*Scot*) *adj* full; drunk.

fou[2] *fo͞o*, (*obs Scot*) *n* a bushel. [Perh **full**]

fouat or **fouet** *fo͞o'ət*, (*Scot*) *n* the house-leek.

Foucault *fo͞o'kō*. — **Foucault current** same as **eddy current** (see under **eddy**); **Foucault's pendulum** (*astron*) an instrument, consisting of a heavy metal ball suspended by a very long fine wire, devised by Foucault in 1851 to demonstrate the rotation of the Earth. [J B L *Foucault* (1819–68), Fr physicist]

foud *fowd*, *n* a bailiff or magistrate in Orkney and Shetland. — *n* **foud'rie** his or her jurisdiction. [ON *fōgeti*; Ger *Vogt*; from L *vocātus*, from *vocāre* to call]

foudroyant *fo͞o-droi'ənt* or *-drwä'yã*, *adj* thundering (*archaic*); dazzling (*archaic*); sudden and overwhelming (*pathol*). [Fr, pr p of *foudroyer*, from *foudre* lightning]

fouet. See **fouat**.

fouetté *fwe'tā*, *n* a ballet-step in which the foot makes a whip-like movement. [Fr]

fougade *fo͞o-gäd'* or **fougasse** *fo͞o-gäs'*, (*military*) *n* a piece of improvised artillery, a small pit charged with powder or shells and loaded with stones. [Fr]

fought *föt*, *pa t* and *pa p* or **foughten** *föt'n*, *old pa p* of **fight**.

foughty *fow'ti* or *fo͞o'ti*, (*dialect*) *adj* musty; mouldy; tainted. [OE *fūht* moist]

foul *fowl*, *adj* filthy; dirty; disfigured; untidy; loathsome; obscene; impure; shameful; gross; in bad condition; stormy; unfavourable; unfair; of little worth; choked up; entangled; full of errors (*printing*); ugly (*Shakesp*); bad (*colloq*). — *vt* to make foul; to tackle in a way that constitutes a breach of the rules; to collide with or come into accidental contact with; to obstruct. — *vi* to collide. — *n* the act of fouling; any breach of the rules in games or contests. — *adv* in a foul manner; unfairly. — *adv* **foul'ly**. — *n* **foul'ness**. — **foul'-brood** a bacterial disease of bee larvae; **foul'-fish** fish during the spawning season; **foul'mart** see **foumart**. — *adj* **foul'-mouthed** or **foul'-spok'en** addicted to the use of foul or profane language. — **foul'-mouth'edness**; **foul play** unfair action in any game or contest; dishonest dealing generally; violence or murder; **foul'-up** see **foul up** below. — **claim a foul** to assert that a rule has been broken, and claim the penalty; **fall foul of** to come into accidental contact with; to clash with; to assail; **foul befall** or **foul fall** (*obs*) bad luck to; **foul up** to make dirty; to (cause to) be or become blocked or entangled; to spoil (*colloq*); to cause to fail or break down (*colloq*); to bungle or make a mistake in (*colloq*); *n* **foul'-up**); **make foul water** (*naut*) to come into such shallow water that the keel throws up mud. [OE *fūl*; Ger *faul*, Gothic *fūls*]

foulard *fo͞o-lärd'* or *-lär'*, *n* a soft untwilled silk fabric; a silk handkerchief. [Fr]

foulder *fowl'dər*, (*Spenser*) *vi* to thunder. [OFr *fouldre*, from L *fulgur* lightning]

foulé *fo͞o-lā*, (*Fr*) *n* fulled cloth, *esp* a light woollen smooth-surfaced dress material.

foumart *fo͞o'märt* or *-mərt*, *n* a polecat. — Also **foul'mart**. [ME *fulmard*, from OE *fūl* foul, and *mearth* a marten]

found[1] *fownd*, *pa t* and *pa p* of **find**. — *n* **found'ling** a little child found deserted. — **all found** see under **all**; **found money** financial gain obtained for nothing; **found object** a natural or man-made object displayed as a work of art, either exactly as found or touched up ('composed').

found[2] *fownd*, *vt* to lay the bottom or foundation of; to establish on a basis; to originate; to endow. — *vi* to rely (with *on*). — *n* **foundā'tion** the act of founding; (often in *pl*) the base of a building; the groundwork or basis of anything; a permanent fund for a benevolent purpose or for some special objective; a cosmetic preparation used as a base for facial make-up; a priming substance applied to a canvas or board as a base for oil-painting. — *adj* **foundā'tional**. — *n* **foundā'tioner** a person supported from the funds or foundation of an institution. — *n* **found'er** a person who founds, establishes or originates; an endower: — *fem* **found'ress**. — **foundation course** an introductory course of study; **foundation garment** a woman's undergarment for supporting or controlling the figure; **foundā'tion-muslin** and **foundā'tion-net** gummed fabrics used for stiffening dresses, etc; **foundā'tion-stone** one of the stones forming the foundation of a building, *esp* a stone laid with public ceremony; **foundā'tion-stop** any organ stop whose sounds are those belonging to the keys, or differing by whole octaves only; a fundamental flue stop; **found'er-member** one of those members of a society who were instrumental in its foundation; **founders' shares** same as **deferred shares** (see under **defer**[1]); **founding father** a person who forms or establishes an institution, organization, etc. [Fr *fonder*, from L *fundāre*, *-ātum* to found, from *fundus* the bottom]

found[3] *fownd*, *vt* to merit (*obs*); to make (*esp* metals) by melting and allowing to harden in a mould; to cast. — *n* **found'er**. — *n* **found'ing**. — *n* **found'ry** the art of founding or casting; a place where founding is carried on; articles produced by founding. [Fr *fondre*, from L *fundere*, *fūsum* to pour]

founder *fownd'ər*, *vi* (of a building) to subside; to collapse in ruins (also *fig*); to go to the bottom (of the sea); (of a ship) to fill with water and sink; (of a horse) to stumble or go lame; to stick in mud. — *vt* to cause to founder. — *n* a collapse; inflammation of a horse's hoof, laminitis. — *adj* **found'erous** causing to founder. [OFr *fondrer* to fall in, from *fond*, from L *fundus* bottom]

foundling. See under **found**[1].

fount[1] *font* or *fownt*, (*printing*) *n* a complete assortment of types of one sort, with all that is necessary for printing in that kind of letter. — Also **font**. [Fr *fonte*, from *fondre*, from L *fundere* to cast]

fount[2] *fownt*, *n* a spring of water; a source. — *adj* **fount'ful** (*poetic*) full of springs. [L *fōns*, *fontis*]

fountain *fownt'in*, *n* a spring of water, a jet; a structure for supplying drinking water or other liquid; an ornamental structure with jets, spouts and basins of water; a reservoir from which oil, ink, etc flows, as in a lamp or pen; the source of anything. — *vi* to spring up or gush, eg from a fountain. — *adj* **fount'ainless**. — **fount'ain-head** the head or source; the beginning; **fountain-pen'** a pen with a reservoir for ink. [Fr *fontaine*, from LL *fontāna*, from L *fōns*, *fontis* a spring]

four *fōr* or *för*, *n* the cardinal number next above three; a symbol representing that number; a set of four things or people (leaves, rowers, etc); a four-oar boat; a four-cylinder engine or car; a shoe or other article of a size denoted by 4; a card with four pips; a score of four points, tricks, strokes, etc; the fourth hour after midday or midnight; (in *pl*) a snack taken at 4 o'clock (also **fours'es**; *dialect*); the age of four years. — *adj* of the number four; four years old. — *adj* and *adv* **four'fold** in four divisions; folded in four thicknesses; four times as much. — *n* **four'foldness**. — *n* **four'some** a group of four; anything in which four act people act together, *esp* a game of golf (two against two, partners playing the same ball) or a reel — also *adj*. — **four'-ale** ale sold at fourpence a quart (*obs*); cheap ale. — *adj* **four'-ball** (*golf*) played two against two with four balls, best ball counting. — Also *n*. — **four'-by-four'** or **4 x 4** a vehicle with four-wheel drive. — **four'-by-two'** the piece of cloth in a rifle pull-through; an army biscuit; a piece of wood, etc four (inches, etc) by two (inches, etc). — *adj* **four-col'our** (*photog* or *printing*) involving or using four colours (magenta, cyan, yellow and black) as primary. — *adj* **four-dimen'sional** having four dimensions, *esp* length, breadth and depth with the addition of time. — *n sing* **four'-eyes** the fish *Anableps* (also **four-eyed fish**); a person wearing spectacles (*derog slang*). — *adj* **four'-figure** running into four figures; expressed to four decimal places. — **four'-flush** four cards of the same suit in a five-card poker hand. — *vi* to bluff with a four-flush; to bluff generally. — *adj* bluffing; not genuine. — **four-flush'er**. — *adj* **four'-foot** measuring four feet (**four-foot way** in British and some other railways, the space of 4 ft 8½ inches (1·435 metres) between rails); having the pitch of an open organ pipe four feet long, or having that pitch for its lowest note. — *adj* **four'-footed** having four feet. — **four-function calculator** an electronic calculator which can add, subtract, multiply and divide. — *adj* **four'-handed** having four hands; played by four players (*cards*). — *adj* **four'-horse** drawn by four horses. — **four'-hours** (*Scot* *fowr'o͞orz*) a refreshment taken about four o'clock. — *adj* **four'-inched** (*Shakesp*) four inches wide. — **four'-in-hand** a coach drawn by four horses, two by two, driven by one person; the team drawing it; a necktie tied with a flat slip-knot, with dangling ends. — Also *adj* and *adv*. — *adj* **four'-leaved**, **four'-leafed** and **four'-leaf**. — *adj* **four'-legged** (also *leg'id*). — **four-letter word** any of a number of vulgar short words, *esp* of four letters, referring to sex or excrement; **four'-oar** a boat rowed with four oars; **four'-o'clock** a brightly coloured flowering plant (*Mirabilis jalapa*), also known as the marvel of Peru; a similar red-flowered plant (*Mirabilis laevis*) found in California; the friar-bird, an Australian honey-eater; **four'-pack** (*colloq*) four cans of drink packaged together and sold as a single item. — *adj* **four'-part** or **four-part'ed** in four parts; divided into four nearly to the base. — **four'pence** the value of four pennies; **four'penny** an old silver coin worth fourpence. — *adj* sold or offered for fourpence. — **fourpenny one** (*old slang*) a blow or punch; **four-post'er** a large bed with four curtain posts; **four-pound'er** a gun that fires a four-pound shot; a four-pound object, eg a loaf. — *adj* **four'score** (*archaic*) eighty. — *adj* **four'scorth** (*obs*) eightieth. — **four'-seater** a vehicle with seats for four. — *adj* **four'-square'** (also *adv*) square; presenting a firm bold front; frank, honest and forthright. — **four-stroke cycle** (in an internal-combustion engine) a recurring series of four strokes of the piston, comprising an out-stroke drawing the mixed gases into the cylinder, an in-stroke compressing them, an out-stroke impelled by their explosion and working the engine, and an in-stroke driving out the burnt gas. — *adj* **four'-wheel** acting on or by means of four wheels. — **four-wheel drive** (of a vehicle) having drive transmitted to all four wheels. — Also *n*. — *adj* **four'-wheeled**. — **four'-wheel'er** a cab or other vehicle with four wheels. — **on all fours** on four feet, or hands and feet, or hands and knees; analogous or strictly comparable (with *with*; *colloq*); **the Four Freedoms** the four essential human freedoms as proclaimed by US President Franklin D Roosevelt in 1941, ie freedom of speech, freedom of worship, freedom from want and freedom from fear; **the four hundred** (*US*) the exclusive social set; **the four seas** see under **sea**. [OE *fēower*; Ger *vier*]

fourchette *fo͞or-shet'*, *n* anything forked; a forked piece between glove fingers, uniting the front and back parts; a combination of the card next above and that next below the one just played; the furcula or wishbone of a bird; an animal's web foot; part of the external female genitals, a membrane at the posterior junction of the labia minora. [Fr, dimin of *fourche*, from L *furca* fork]

Fourcroya *fo͞or-kroi'ə*. Same as **Furcraea**.

fourgon *fo͞or-gɔ̃'*, *n* a baggage-wagon. [Fr]

Fourier *fo͞o'ri-ā*. — **Fourier analysis** the determination of the harmonic components (the terms of which form the *Fourier series* that represents the waveform) of a complex waveform; **Fourier principle** the principle showing that all repeating waveforms can be resolved into sine wave components consisting of a fundamental frequency and a series of harmonics at multiples of this frequency. [J B J *Fourier* (1768–1830), Fr mathematician]

Fourierism *fo͞o'ri-ər-izm*, *n* the socialistic system of F M Charles *Fourier* (1772–1837), in which society is reorganized into small co-operative communities, or *phalanges*, allowing free development to human talent and emotions. — *adj* **Fourieris'tic**.

fou rire *fōō rēr*, (*Fr*) *n* wild laughter, helpless giggling.

fourteen *fōr-*, *fôr-tēn'*, or *fōr'* or *fôr'tēn*, *n* and *adj* four and ten. — *n* **fourteen'er** a verse line of fourteen syllables. — *adj* **four'teenth** (or *-tēnth'*) last of fourteen; next after the thirteenth; equal to one of fourteen equal parts. — *n* a fourteenth part; a person or thing in fourteenth position. — *adv* **fourteenth'ly**. [OE *fēowertēne* (*-tīene*); see **four** and **ten**]

fourth *fōrth* or *fôrth*, *adj* last of four; next after the third; equal to one of four equal parts. — *n* one of four equal parts, a quarter; a person or thing in fourth position; an interval of three (conventionally called four) diatonic degrees (*music*); a tone at that interval from another (*music*); a combination of two tones separated by that interval (*music*). — *adv* **fourth'ly**. — **fourth dimension** that of time, as opposed to the three spatial dimensions; anything which is beyond ordinary experience. — *adj* **fourth-dimen'sional**. — **fourth estate** a group of people other than the lords, commons and clergy, who influence a country's politics; the press. — *adj* **fourth'-rate** of the fourth order; inferior. — **fourth wall** an idea of the naturalistic theatre, that the open front of the stage-set represents as solid a wall as the other three sides; **Fourth World** the poorest and least developed of the poor countries of the world; the poorest people in the developed countries. [OE *fēowertha*, *fēortha*]

foussa. See **fossa**[2].

fousty *fōōst'i*, (*Scot*) *adj* mouldy or damp; having a musty smell; fusty.

fouter or **foutre** *fōō'tər*, or **footra** (*Shakesp*) or **foutra** (*Shakesp*) *-trə*, *n* a fig (as a type of worthlessness); a worthless despicable fellow (*Scot*). — *vi* to mess around aimlessly. [OE *foutre*, from L *futuere* to copulate with]

fouth or **fowth** *fōōth*, (*Scot*) *n* abundance. [**full** and sfx *-th*]

fovea *fō'vi-ə*, (*anatom*) *n* a depression or pit: — *pl* **fō'veae** (*-vi-ē*). — *adj* **fō'veal** of or like a fovea; of the fovea centralis. — *adj* **fō'veate** pitted. — *n* **fovē'ola** a small depression — also **fō'veole**. — **fovea centralis** (*sen-trä'lis* or *-rā'*) a fovea in the centre of the back of the retina, the place where vision is sharpest. [L *fovea*]

fowl *fowl*, *n* a bird; a bird of the poultry kind, a cock or hen; its flesh as food: — *pl* **fowls** or **fowl**. — *vi* to kill or try to kill wildfowl. — *n* **fowl'er** a person who fowls. — *n* **fowl'ing**. — **fowl'ing-net** a net for catching birds; **fowl'ing-piece** a light gun for small shot, used in fowling; **fowl'-pest** an acute contagious virus disease of birds (also **fowl'-plague**); another similar disease, Newcastle disease. [OE *fugol*; Ger *Vogel*]

fowth. See **fouth**.

fox *foks*, *n* a wild animal related to the dog, having upright ears, a pointed snout, red or grey fur, and a long bushy tail: — *fem* **vix'en**; extended to other animals, eg black-fox (pekan) and flying fox; anyone notorious for cunning; an attractive young woman (*US colloq*); a kind of sword (*obs*). — *vt* (*colloq*) to baffle, deceive or cheat. — *vi* (*colloq*) to act cunningly; to cheat. — *vi* and *vt* (of paper) to discolour, showing brownish marks. — *adj* **foxed** (of books) discoloured; drunk; baffled. — *n* **fox'iness** craftiness; decay; a harsh, sour taste; discoloration as in books. — *n* **fox'ing** the act of a person who foxes; discoloration (as of paper). — *n* **fox'ship** (*Shakesp*) the character of a fox, craftiness. — *adj* **fox'y** of foxes; fox-like; cunning; reddish brown; sexually attractive (*colloq*, *esp US*). — **fox'-bat** a flying fox, a fruit-bat; **fox'berry** the bearberry, a type of heather (*bot*); the cowberry or red whortleberry; **fox'-brush** the tail of a fox; **fox'-earth** a fox's burrow; **fox'-evil** alopecia, baldness; **fox'glove** a tall plant (*Digitalis*) with spikes of drooping (typically purple) bell-shaped flowers and leaves from which the drug digitalis is produced; **fox'-grape** an American grape (*Vitis labrusca*; also *Vitis rotundifolia*); **fox'hole** a fox's earth; a small entrenchment (*military*); **fox'-hound** a hound used for chasing foxes; **fox'-hunt**; **fox'-hunter**; **fox'-hunting**; **fox'-mark** a brownish mark on paper that has foxed; **fox'shark** a large long-tailed shark, the thresher; **fox'-tail** a fox's brush; a genus (*Alopecurus*) of grasses, with a head like a fox's tail; **fox-terr'ier** a terrier of a breed *orig* trained to unearth foxes; **fox'-trap**; **fox'-trot** a horse's pace with short steps, as in changing from trotting to walking; (**fox'-trot**) a ballroom dance to syncopated music; a tune to which this is danced. — *vi* to dance the foxtrot: — *pr p* **fox'trotting**; *pa t* and *pa p* **fox'trotted**. — **fox and geese** a game played with pieces on a board, where the object is for certain pieces called the geese to surround or corner one called the fox or prevent him from passing. [OE *fox*; Ger *Fuchs*]

foy[1] *foi*, (*Spenser*) *n* allegiance. [Fr *foi* faith]

foy[2] *foi*, (*dialect*) *n* a parting entertainment or gift. [Du *fooi*]

foyer *foi'ā* or *foi'ər* (Fr *fwä-yā*), *n* in theatres, a public room, an anteroom; the entrance hallway of a hotel, etc. [Fr, from L *focus* hearth]

foyle and **foyne**. Spenserian spellings of **foil**[1,2] and **foin**.

fozy *fōz'i*, (*Scot*) *adj* spongy; lacking in freshness; fat; slow-witted. — *n* **fō̃z'iness** softness; lack of spirit. [Cf Du *voos* spongy]

FP *abbrev*: fireplug; former pupil; Free Presbyterian.

fp *abbrev*: fortepiano; freezing-point.

FPA *abbrev*: Family Planning Association.

FPS or **fps** *abbrev*: foot-pound-second.

Fr *abbrev*: Father (*relig*); franc; France; French; Friar; Friday.

Fr *chem symbol*: francium.

fr *abbrev*: fragment; franc; frequently.

fra *frä*, (*Ital*) *n* brother or friar.

frab *frab*, (*dialect*) *vt* to worry. — *adj* **frabb'it** peevish.

frabjous *frab'jəs*, *adj perh* joyous; surpassing. — *adv* **frab'jously**. [Invented by Lewis Carroll]

fracas *frak'ä* or *frä-kä'*, *n* uproar; a noisy quarrel: — *pl* **fracas** (*-käz*). [Fr, from Ital *fracasso*, from *fracassare* to make an uproar]

frack *frak* or *fräk*, (*Scot*) *adj* prompt; eager; lusty. [OE *fræc*, *frec*]

fracking *frak'ing*, (*min ext*) *n* the process of forcing liquid containing sand or other material into the strata round a well bottom to split them and prevent them closing.

fract *frakt*, *vt* to break; to violate (*Shakesp*). — *adj* **fract'ed** broken; violated; having a part displaced, as if broken (*heraldry*). [L *frangere*, *fractum* to break (partly through Fr)]

fractal *frak'təl*, *n* an apparently irregular or chaotic geometric entity generated by repeating, according to a mathematical formula, ever-diminishing subdivisions of a basic geometric shape, much used in computer graphics. — *adj* of, relating to or produced by such a generative process. — *n* **fractal'ity**. [Fr, from L *fractus*, pa p of *frangere* to break]

fraction *frak'shən*, *n* a fragment or small piece; any part of a unit (*arith*; see **decimal** and **vulgar**, **proper** and **improper**); a breach of friendly relations (*Shakesp*); a portion separated by fractionation, eg a mixture of hydrocarbons with similar boiling-points obtained by fractional distillation in a refinery; the breaking of the bread in the Eucharist (*Christian relig*); a group of Communists acting as a unit within a larger non-Communist body; a faction or schismatic group within the Communist party. — *adj* **frac'tional** belonging to a fraction or fractions; of the nature of a fraction; tiny, insignificant. — *n* **frac'tionalism** the state of consisting of discrete units; the action of forming a fraction within the Communist party. — *n* **frac'tionalist** a breaker-up of political unity. — *n* **fractionalīzā'tion** or **-s-**. — *vt* **frac'tionalize** or **-ise** to break up into parts. — *adv* **frac'tionally**. — *adj* **frac'tionary** fractional; fragmentary. — *vt* **frac'tionate** to break up into smaller units; to separate the components of by distillation or otherwise. — *n* **fractionā'tion**. — *n* **frac'tionātor** a plant for carrying out fractional distillation. — *n* **fractionīzā'-**

tion or **-s-**. — *vt* **frac'tionize** or **-ise** to break up into fractions. — *n* **frac'tionlet** a small fraction. — **fractional distillation** a distillation process for the separation of the various constituents of liquid mixtures by means of their different boiling-points. [Ety as for **fract**]

fractious *frak'shəs*, *adj* ready to quarrel; cross. — *adv* **frac'tiously**. — *n* **frac'tiousness** [L *frangere* to break]

fractography *frak-tog'rə-fi*, *n* the microscopic study of fractures in metal surfaces. [Ety as for **fract**, and **-graphy**]

fracture *frak'chər*, *n* (a) breaking; the breach or part broken; the surface of breaking, other than cleavage; the breaking of a bone. — *vt* and *vi* to break through; to crack. — **Colles' fracture** see **Colles'**; **comminuted fracture** a fracture in which the bone is splintered; **compound fracture** the breaking of a bone, communicating with a co-existing skin wound; **greenstick fracture** a fracture where the bone is partly broken, partly bent, occurring *esp* in limbs of children; **impacted fracture** a fracture in which the ends of bone are driven into each other; **simple fracture** a fracture of a bone without a wound in the skin. [Ety as for **fract**]

frae. See **fro**.

fraenum. Same as **frenum**.

frag *frag*, *vt* to kill with a fragmentation grenade (*esp* as in the Vietnam War): — *pr p* **fragg'ing**; *pa t* and *pa p* **fragged** (*fragd*). [**fragment**]

Fragaria *frə-gā'ri-ə*, *n* the strawberry genus. [L *frāgum* the strawberry]

fragile *fraj'īl*, (*US*) *-əl*, *adj* easily broken; frail; delicate. — *adv* **fra'gilely**. — *n* **fragility** (*frə-jil'*) or **fra'gileness** the state of being fragile. [Fr, from L *fragilis*, from *frangere*, *frāctum* to break]

fragment *frag'mənt*, *n* a piece broken off; a *usu* small piece of something broken or smashed; an unfinished portion (eg of a writing). — *vt* and *vi* (*frag-ment'*) to break into fragments. — *adj* **fragmental** (*-ment'*; also *frag'mən-təl*) composed of fragments of older rocks; in fragments. — *adv* **frag'mentarily**. — *n* **frag'mentariness**. — *adj* **frag'mentary** or **fragment'ed** consisting of fragments; broken; in fragments; existing or operating in separate parts, not forming a harmonious unity. — *n* **fragmentā'tion** division into fragments; cell division without mitosis (*biol*). — **fragmentation bomb** or **grenade** one which shatters into small destructive fragments on explosion. [L *fragmentum*, from *frangere*, *frāctum* to break]

fragor *frā'gör*, (*obs*) *n* a crash. [L]

fragrant *frā'grənt*, *adj* sweet-scented. — *n* **fra'grance** or **fra'grancy** pleasantness of smell; sweet or pleasant influence (*fig*). — *vt* to perfume or give a fragrance to. — *adv* **fra'grantly**. — *n* **fra'grantness**. [L *frāgrāns*, *-antis*, pr p of *frāgrāre* to smell]

fraîcheur *fre-shœr*, (*Fr*) *n* freshness or coolness.

frail[1] *frāl*, *adj* very easily shattered; feeble and infirm (*esp Scot*); decrepit; morally weak; unchaste (*euphem*); tender (*Spenser*). — *n* (*slang*) a woman. — *adj* **frail'ish** somewhat frail. — *adv* **frail'ly**. — *n* **frail'ness** or **frail'ty** (*Spenser* **fra'iltee**) weakness; infirmity. [OFr *fraile*, from L *fragilis* fragile]

frail[2] *frāl*, *n* a rush (*bot*); a basket made of rushes. [OFr *frayel*]

fraim. See **fremd**.

fraise[1] *frāz*, *n* a horizontal or nearly horizontal palisade (*fortif*); a tool for enlarging a drillhole; a 16c ruff. — *vt* to fence with a fraise. [Fr]

fraise[2] *frāz*, (*dialect*) *n* commotion.

fraise[3] *frāz*. See **froise**.

Fraktur *fräk-tōōr'*, *n* a German black-letter typeface. [Ger, from L *frāctūra* breaking]

framboesia *fram-bē'zi-ə*, *n* a tropical skin disease, yaws. [Fr *framboise* raspberry]

frame *frām*, *vt* to form; to shape; to put together; to plan, adjust or adapt; to contrive, devise or concoct; to bring about; to articulate; to direct (one's steps); to set about; to enclose in a frame or border; to make (someone) the victim of a frame-up. — *vi* (*rare*) to make one's way; to resort; to pretend (*dialect*); to make a move; to give promise of progress or success; to contrive (*Bible*). — *n* the body; a putting together of parts; a structure; a case made to enclose, border or support anything; the skeleton of anything; the rigid part of a bicycle; a structure on which embroidery is worked; a stocking-making machine; a loom (*obs*); a structure on which bees build a honeycomb; a structure for the cultivation or sheltering of plants; state (of mind) or mood; act of devising (*Shakesp*); the individual unit picture in cinema film or in a (still or movie) photographic film, cartoon strip, etc; formerly, the British term for field (*TV*); the total TV picture; a triangular support in which the balls are grouped for the break (*snooker*, etc); the balls so grouped (*snooker*, etc); in the jargon of certain games, a definite part of a game, a game, or a definite number of games. — *n* **fram'er** a person who forms or constructs; a person who makes frames for pictures, etc; a person who devises; a person who formulates (eg law). — *n* **fram'ing** the act of constructing; a frame or setting. — **frame'-breaker** (*hist*) a person who broke stocking-frames on their introduction; **frame'-house** a house consisting of a skeleton of timber, with boards or shingles laid on; **frame'-maker** a maker of picture-frames; **frame'-saw** a thin saw stretched in a frame; **frame'-up** a trumped-up affair, *esp* a false criminal charge against an innocent person; a staged or preconcerted event; **frame'work** the work that forms the frame; the skeleton or outline of anything. — **frame of reference** a set of axes with reference to which the position of a point, etc is described; any set of limits or standards as a context within which to place a specific action, event, behaviour type, etc. [OE *framian* to be helpful, related to *fram* forward]

frampold *fram'pōld* or *-pəld*, (*obs*) *adj* peevish or intractable; fiery. — Also **fram'pal** (*Scott*). — *n* **fram'pler** (*Scott*) a brawler. [Ety obscure]

franc *frangk*, *n* a coin forming since 1795 the unit of the French monetary system (**new** or **heavy franc** introduced 1960 — 'new' dropped 1963); the unit of currency in Belgium, Switzerland, etc. [OFr *franc*, from the inscription *Francorum rex* on the first coins]

franchise[1] *fran'chīz* or *-shīz*, *n* liberty; a privilege or exemption by prescription or grant; the right to vote, *esp* for a representative in a national government; voting qualification; a commercial concession by which a retailer is granted by a company the generally exclusive right of retailing its goods or providing its services in a specified area, with use of the company's expertise, marketing, trademark, etc; a similar concession granted by a public authority to a broadcasting company; a percentage below which the underwriter incurs no responsibility (*insurance*). — *vt* (*obs*) to enfranchise. — *n* **franchisee'** a person to whom a franchise is granted. — *n* **fran'chisement** (*-chiz-* or *-shiz-*; *obs*) liberation. — *n* **fran'chīser** a voter; a firm, etc which grants a commercial concession. [OFr, from *franc* free]

franchise[2] *frā-shēz*, (*Fr*) *n* candour or frankness.

Franciscan *fran-sis'kən*, *adj* belonging to the order of mendicant friars in the RC Church, founded by St *Francis* of Assisi (1182–1226). — *n* a friar of this order. [L *Franciscus* Francis]

francium *fran'si-əm*, *n* an element (symbol **Fr**; atomic no 87), an unstable radioactive metal present in uranium ore, discovered by a Frenchwoman. [**France**]

franco *fräng'kō*, (*Ital*) *adj* and *adv* post-free; franked.

Franco- *frangk'ō-*, *combining form* French; French and, as in eg **Fran'co-German**, **Fran'co-Russian**, etc. — *n* **Francomā'nia**, **Franc'ophil**, **Franc'ophile**, **Franc'ophobe** and **Francopho'bia** (also without *cap*) same as **Gallomania**, etc (see under **Gallic**). — *adj* **Franc'ophone** (also without *cap*) French-speaking (used eg of Africans for whom French is a second mother-tongue, or of French-speaking Canadians).

francolin *frang'kō-lin*, *n* a bird of the *Francolinus* genus of partridges. [Fr]

franc-tireur *frã tē-rœr*, (Fr) *n* a sniper; a guerrilla.

frangible *fran'ji-bl*, *adj* easily broken. — *n* **frangibil'ity**. [L *frangere* to break; see **fract**]

frangipani *fran-ji-pä'nē*, *n* the red jasmine or other species of *Plumeria*, tropical American shrubs of the dogbane genus with scented flowers; a perfume made from or imitating red jasmine; (also **frangipane** *fran'ji-pān*) a pastry-cake filled with cream, almonds and sugar. [From the name of the inventor of the perfume *Frangipani*]

Franglais *frã-gle*, (*usu humorous*) *n* French with many English words and forms; a jocular cross between English and French. [Fr *Français* and Ang*lais*]

franion *fran'yən*, *n* a paramour (*obs*); a boon companion (*obs*); a loose woman (*Spenser*). [Ety dubious]

Frank *frangk*, *n* a German from a confederation in Franconia of which a branch conquered Gaul in the 5c, and founded France; (in the East) a Western European. — *adj* **Frank'ish**. [See **frank**[1]]

frank[1] *frangk*, *adj* free or open; liberal (*obs*); open or candid in expression; unrestrained (*obs*); unmistakable or true (*med*; as in *frank pus* or *asthma*). — *vt* to sign or mark so as to ensure free carriage, eg at a post-office; to send thus signed or marked; to mark by means of a **frank'ing-machine** to show that postage has been paid. — *n* the signature of a person who had the right to frank a letter; the mark left by a franking-machine; a franked envelope. — *adv* **frank'ly** to be frank; in a frank manner. — *n* **frank'ness**. — **frank'-fee** tenure in fee-simple (*feudal law*); **frank'-pledge** a mutual suretyship by which the members of a tithing were made responsible for one another (*feudal law*); **frank'=tenement** freehold (*feudal law*). [OFr *franc*, from LL *francus*; OHGer *Franko* Frank, hence a free man]

frank[2] *frangk*, (*Shakesp*) *n* a pigsty. — *vt* to shut up in a sty; to cram or fatten. [OFr *franc*]

frankalmoign *frangk'al-moin*, (*Eng law*) *n* a form of land tenure in which no obligations were enforced except religious ones, eg praying. [OFr *franc* free, and *almoigne* alms]

Frankenia *frang-kē'ni-ə*, *n* the sea-heath genus, constituting a family **Frankeniā'ceae**, related to the tamarisk family. [Named after John *Frankenius* (1590–1661), Swedish physician and botanist]

Frankenstein *frangk'ən-stīn*, *n* the hero of Mary Shelley's novel of that name, who by his skill creates an animate being like a man, only to his own torment; hence, by confusion, any creation that brings disaster to its maker, *esp* a monstrous-looking humanoid creature.

frankfurter *frangk'fûr-tər* or *-fo͝or-tər*, *n* a small smoked sausage. [Short for Ger *Frankfurter Wurst* Frankfurt sausage]

frankincense *frangk'in-sens*, *n* olibanum, a sweet-smelling resin from Arabia, used as incense; spruce resin. — **herb frankincense** laserwort, one of a genus of perennial herbs. [OFr *franc encens* pure incense]

franklin *frangk'lin*, (*hist*) *n* an English freeholder, free from feudal servitude to a subject-superior. [LL *francus*; see **frank**[1]]

franklinite *frangk'lin-īt*, *n* a zinc-manganese mineral, mined at *Franklin Forge*, New Jersey, USA.

frantic *fran'tik*, *adj* mad or furious; wild, *esp* with anxiety; marked by hurried activity or frenzy. — *adv* **fran'tically** or (*Shakesp*) **fran'ticly**. — *n* **fran'ticness** the state of being frantic. — *adj* **fran'tic-mad** (*obs*) raving mad. [OFr *frenetique*, from L *phrenēticus*, from Gr *phrenētikos* mad, from *phrēn* the mind; see **frenetic** and **frenzy**]

franzy *fran'zi*, (*dialect*) *adj* cross; peevish. [Variant of **frenzy**]

frap *frap*, *vt* to strike (*now dialect*); to secure by many turns of a lashing (*naut*): — *pr p* **frapp'ing**; *pa t* and *pa p* **frapped**. [Fr *frapper* to strike]

frappant *fra-pã*, (*Fr*) *adj* striking; affecting.

frappé *fra'pā*, *adj* (of coffee or other drinks) iced; artificially cooled: — *fem* **frapp'ée**. — *n* an iced drink. [Fr, pa p of *frapper* to strike]

frass *fras*, *n* excrement or other refuse of wood-boring larvae. [Ger, from *fressen* to eat; cf **fret**[1]]

frat *frat*, *abbrev*: fraternize; fraternity.

fratch *frach*, (*dialect*) *n* a quarrel or brawl. — *adj* **fratch'ety** or **fratch'y**. — *adj* **fratch'ing**. [Perh imit]

frate *frä'tā*, (*Ital*) *n* a friar, a mendicant Franciscan: — *pl* **fra'ti** (*-tē*).

frater[1] *frā'tər*, *n* a refectory; sometimes applied in error to a monastic common-room or to a chapter-house (by confusion with *frater*[2]). — Also **fra'ter-house** or **frā'try**. [OFr *fraitur* for *refreitor*, from LL *refectōrium*]

frater[2] *frā'tər*, *n* a friar; a comrade. [L, a brother]

Fratercula *fra-tûr'kū-lə*, *n* the puffin genus. [Ety as for **fraternize**]

fraternal *frə-tûr'nl*, *adj* belonging to a brother or brethren; brotherly; (of twins) dizygotic, not identical. — *adv* **frater'nally**. [Ety as for **fraternize**]

fraternize or **-ise** *frat'ər-nīz*, *vi* to associate as brothers; to seek brotherly fellowship; to come into friendly association (with). — *n* **frater'nity** the state of being brothers; a brotherhood; a society formed on a principle of brotherhood; an all-male N American college association; any set of people with something in common. — *n* **fraternīzā'tion** or **-s-** associating as brothers. — *n* **frat'ernizer** or **-s-**. — *n* **fratry** (*frāt'ri*) or **frāt'ery** a fraternity; a convent of friars (see also **frater**[1]). — **fraternity house** or (*colloq*) **frat house** (*US*) a college fraternity lodging-house. [L *frāter* a brother; cf **brother**, Gr *phrātēr* a clansman, Sans *bhrātr*]

fratricide *frat'ri-sīd* or *frāt'*, *n* a person who kills his or her brother; the murder of a brother. — *adj* **fratricī'dal**. [Fr, from L *frāter*, *frātris*, and *caedere* to kill]

frau or **Frau** *frow*, *n* a (*usu* married) woman (often *derog*); a wife; (used of or to a German or German-speaking woman) Mrs. — *n* **fräulein** or **Fräulein** (*froi'līn*) an unmarried woman; often applied to a German governess; (used of or to a German or German-speaking woman) Miss. [Ger]

fraud *fröd*, *n* deceit; impersonation with intent to deceive; criminal deception done with the intention of gaining an advantage; a snare (*Milton*); a deceptive trick; a cheat or swindler (*colloq*); a fraudulent item. — *adj* (*rare*) **fraud'ful** deceptive. — *adv* (*rare*) **fraud'fully**. — *n* **frauds'man** a person involved in criminal fraud. — *n* **fraud'ster** a swindler. — *n* **fraud'ūlence** or **fraud'ūlency**. — *adj* **fraud'ūlent** using fraud. — *adv* **fraud'ūlently**. — **fraudulent bankruptcy** bankruptcy in which the insolvent is implicated in the misappropriation of the funds owing to his or her creditors. [OFr *fraude*, from L *fraus* fraud]

Frauendienst *frow'ən-dēnst*, (*Ger*) *n* courtly love.

fraught *fröt*, (*obs*) *n* a load or cargo; the freight of a ship. — *vt* (*obs*) to load. — *vi* (*Shakesp*) to form the freight of a vessel. — *adj* freighted or laden (*obs*); filled (with); having or causing (*esp* something bad or undesirable, eg danger; with *with*); feeling or making anxious or distressed; tension-filled. — *n* **fraught'age** or **fraut'age** (*Shakesp*) loading or cargo. [Prob ODu *vracht*; cf **freight**]

fräulein. See under **frau**.

Fraunhofer's lines *frown'hō-fərz līnz*. See under **line**[2].

fraus pia *frös pī'ə* or *frows pē'a*, (*L*) a pious fraud.

Fraxinus *frak'si-nəs*, *n* the ash genus of trees. — *n* **fraxinell'a** an aromatic plant, dittany (from its ash-like leaves). [L]

fray[1] *frā*, *n* an affray; a brawl. — *vt* to frighten. [Aphetic from **affray**]

fray[2] *frā*, *vt* to wear off by rubbing; to unravel the end or edge of; to cause a strain on (eg nerves, temper, etc). — *vi* to become frayed; (of deer, etc) to rub off the velvet from the new antlers. — *n* **fray'ing** the action of the verb; frayed-off material. — **fray at the edges** to wear, (*fig*) become problematic or unmanageable, or (of someone's patience or temper) begin to run out. [Fr *frayer*, from L *fricāre* to rub]

frazil *fraz'il* or *frä'zil*, *n* ground-ice; ice in small spikes and plates in rapid streams. [Can Fr *frasil*; prob Fr *fraisil* cinders]

frazzle *fraz'l*, *vt* to fray or wear out. — *n* the state of being worn out; a shred. — **burnt**, etc **to a frazzle** completely burnt, etc. [Origin unknown]

FRCP *abbrev*: Fellow of the Royal College of Physicians (**-Edin**, of Edinburgh; **-Lond**, of London; **-Irel**, of Ireland).

FRCPS Glasg *abbrev*: Fellow of the Royal College of Physicians and Surgeons of Glasgow.

FRCS *abbrev*: Fellow of the Royal College of Surgeons (**-Ed**, of Edinburgh; **-Eng**, of England; **-Irel**, of Ireland).

freak[1] *frēk*, *n* a caprice; an abnormal production of nature, a monstrosity; an eccentric; a weirdly unconventional person; a person who is wildly enthusiastic about something (*esp* as a combining form, as in *film-freak*, *football-freak* or *Jesus freak*). — *adj* capricious; wildly unusual. — *vi* to freak out. — *n* **freak'iness** or **freak'ishness**. — *adj* **freak'ish**, **freak'ful** or **freak'y** apt to change the mind suddenly; very unusual, odd. — *adv* **freak'ishly**. — **freak'-out** (*slang*) a (drug-induced) hallucinatory or (loosely) wildly exciting or unconventional experience or occurrence. — *vi* **freak out** to have such an experience, etc, or have a strong fit of anger, anxiety, etc. — *vt* to cause to freak out. — **phone freak(ing)** see under **phone**. [A late word; cf OE *frīcian* to dance]

freak[2] *frēk*, *vt* to spot or streak (*Milton*); to variegate (*Milton*). — *n* (*obs*) a streak of colour. [Perh the same as **freak**[1]]

freckle *frek'l*, *vt* to spot; to colour with spots. — *n* a yellowish or brownish-yellow spot on the skin *esp* of fair-haired people; any small spot. — *n* **freck'ling** a little spot. — *adj* **freck'ly** or **freck'led** covered in freckles. [ON *freknur* (pl), Dan *fregne*]

fredaine *frə-den*, (*Fr*) *n* an escapade or prank.

free *frē*, *adj* not bound; at liberty; not under arbitrary government; not strict, or bound by rules; not literal; unimpeded; unconstrained; readily cut, separated or wrought; ready (*esp* in the phrase *free to confess*); guiltless; frank; lavish; uncombined; (of a morpheme) able to stand alone as a word (opposite of *bound*; *linguistics*); unattached; exempt (with *from*); not suffering from or encumbered with (with *of* or *from*); having a franchise (with *of*); without, or not necessitating, payment; bold; indecent: — *compar* **freer** (*frē'ər*); *superl* **freest** (*frē'ist*). — *adv* freely; without payment; without obstruction. — *vt* to give liberty to; to deliver from whatever confines (something); to rid (with *from* or *of*): — *pr p* **free'ing**; *pa t* and *pa p* **freed**. — *combining form* free from, as in *trouble-free*. — *n* **free'bie** (*orig US*; *slang*; also **free'bee**) something supplied free of charge. — Also *adj*. — *n* **free'dom** liberty; frankness; outspokenness; unhampered boldness; separation; privileges connected with a city (often granted as a merely symbolic honour); improper familiarity; licence. — *adv* **free'ly**. — *n* **free'ness**. — *n* **freer** (*frē'ər*) a liberator. — **free agency** the state or power of acting freely, or without necessity or constraint upon the will; **free agent**; **free-and-eas'y** an informal public-house club. — *adj* informal in manners, lacking in ceremony. — *adj* **free'-arm** with the arm unsupported. — **free association** a technique in psychoanalysis based either on the first association called forth by each of a series of words or on a train of thought suggested by a single word; **free atom** an unattached atom assumed to exist briefly during certain chemical reactions; **free'base** (*slang*) cocaine refined for smoking by being heated with ether, often also inhaled during the process. — *vt* to refine (cocaine) in this way. — *vi* to smoke freebase. — **free'-bench** (*hist*) a widow's right to an endowment out of her husband's lands; **free'-board** the distance between waterline and the deck or the upper edge of the side of a vessel (*naut*); a strip of land outside a fence, or a right to this; **free'booter** a person who roves about freely in search of booty (Du *vrijbuiter*); **free'bootery**. — *adj* and *n* **free'booting**. — **free'booty**. — *adj* **free'born** born free. — **Free Church** that branch of the Presbyterians in Scotland which left the Established Church in the Disruption of 1843; the small minority of that group who refused to combine with the United Presbyterians in the **United Free Church** (see **United Presbyterian Church** under **presbyter**); in England, a Nonconformist church generally; **free'-city** a city constituting a state in itself; **free collective bargaining** collective bargaining (see under **collect**) without government-imposed or other restrictions; **free companion** (*hist*) a member of a **free company**, a medieval band of mercenaries ready for any service; **free'-cost** freedom from charges; **free'-diver** a skin-diver; **free'-diving** skin-diving; **freed'man** and **freed'woman** a man or woman who has been a slave and has been freed: — *pl* **freed'men** and **freed'women**; **freedom fighter** a person who fights in an armed movement for the liberation of a nation, etc from a government considered unjust, tyrannical, etc; **free drop** a ruling allowing one to lift a golf ball from its resting place and drop it elsewhere without penalty; **free energy** (*chem*) the capacity of a system to perform work; **free enterprise** the conduct of business without interference from the state; **free fall** the motion of an unpropelled body in a gravitational field, eg that of a spacecraft in orbit; **free'-fall** the part of a parachute jump before the parachute opens; any fast, uncontrolled descent (*fig*). — *adj* of or pertaining to free fall or to a parachute jump which is partly a free-fall. — *vi* to fall with one's parachute kept closed. — **free-fall'ing**; **free fight** a confused, haphazard or indiscriminate fight; **free'-fisher** a person who has a right to take fish in certain waters; **free flight** the flight of a rocket, etc when its motor is no longer producing thrust; **Free'-fone**® a British Telecom service allowing callers eg to a business or organization to make their calls free of charge, the charges being paid by the business or organization concerned (also, loosely, **free'phone**); **free'-food'er** an opponent of taxes on food. — *adj* **free'-footed** (*Shakesp*) not restrained in movement. — **free'-for-all** a contest open to anybody; a public brawl. — Also *adj*. — **free gift** something given free with a product as an incentive to buy. — *adj* **free'hand** executed by the unguided hand. — **free hand** complete freedom of action. — *adj* **free'-hand'ed** open-handed; liberal. — **free'-hand'edness**. — *adj* **free'-heart'ed** open-hearted; liberal. — **free'-heart'edness**; **free'hold** a property held by fee simple, fee tail, or for life; the holding of property in any of these ways. — Also *adj*. — **free'holder** a person who possesses a freehold; **free house** a public house that is not tied to a particular supplier; **free kick** (*football*) a kick allowed without interference, as a penalty against the opposing side for infringing the rules; **free'-labour** voluntary, not slave, labour; **free'lance** one of the mercenary knights and men-at-arms who after the Crusades wandered about Europe; an unattached politician, etc; anyone who works for himself or herself, employed or paid by others only for particular, *usu* short-term, assignments (also **free'lancer**). — Also *adj*, *adv* and *vi*. — **free list** the list of people admitted without payment to a theatre, etc, or of those to whom a book, etc is sent; **free-liv'er** a person who freely indulges his or her appetite for eating and drinking; a glutton. — *vi* **free'load** (*esp US*; *colloq*) to eat at someone else's expense; to sponge; to gain from others' efforts. — *n* a free meal. — **free'loader**. — *n* and *adj* **free'loading**. — **free love** (the claim to) freedom in sexual relations, unshackled by marriage; **free-lov'er** a person who advocates, or is thought to advocate, free love, eg (with *cap*) a Perfectionist (see under **perfect**); **free lunch** something given with apparently no strings attached, but *usu* received with suspicion; **free'man** and **free'woman** a person who is free or enjoys liberty; a person who holds a particular franchise or privilege: — *pl* **free'men**

and **free'women**; **free market** a capitalist economic system where prices are allowed to fluctuate solely according to supply and demand. — *adj* **free'-market**. — **free-marketeer'**; **free'māson** in the Middle Ages, a stone-mason of a superior grade; (often with *cap*) a member of a secret male fraternity, united in lodges for social enjoyment and mutual assistance. — *adj* **free-mason'ic**. — **freemā'sonry** (also with *cap*) the institutions, practices, etc of freemasons; instinctive understanding and sympathy. — *adj* **free-mind'ed** with a mind free or unperplexed; without a load of care. — **freephone** see **Freefone**®; **free'-port** a port open on equal terms to all traders; a free-trade zone adjacent to a port, allowing duty-free import and re-export of goods; **Free'post**® a Royal Mail service which allows inquirers or potential customers to write to a business or organization free of charge, the postage costs being paid by the business or organization concerned; **free radical** a group of atoms containing at least one unpaired electron existing briefly during certain chemical reactions. — *adj* **free'-range** (of poultry) allowed some freedom to move about, not kept in a barn or battery; (of eggs) laid by free-range hens. — *adj* **free'-reed** (*music*) having a reed that does not touch the side of the aperture. — **free ride** the ability to benefit from a situation, etc without having to bear any of its costs and responsibilities; **free-rid'er** (*colloq*) a person who enjoys benefits obtained for workers by a trade union without being a member of that trade union; **free'-school** a school where no tuition fees are exacted. — *vi* **free'-select** (*Austr*) to take up crown land under a scheme making land available for small farms. — **free'-selection** the process of doing so; the land so taken; **free'-selector** (also **selec'tion** and **selec'tor**); **free'sheet** a newspaper distributed free; **free'-shot** (Ger *Freischütz*) a legendary hunter and marksman who gets a number of bullets (*Freikugeln*) from the devil, six of which always hit the mark, while the seventh remains at the devil's disposal; **free skating** competitive figure skating in which the skater selects movements from an officially approved list of jumps, spins, etc. — *adj* **free'-soil** in favour of free territory and opposed to slavery. — **free-soil'er**. — *adj* **free'-space** (of a radio, etc) able to operate only where there is **free space**, ie where the radio waves are not affected by surrounding objects such as buildings, hills, etc. — **free speech** the right to express one's opinions freely in public; **free spirit** a person of an independent and individualistic turn of mind. — *adj* **free-spōk'en** accustomed to speaking without reserve. — **free-spōk'enness**. — *adj* **free'-standing** not supported by or attached to anything else. — **Free States** in America, before the Civil War of 1861–65, those of the United States in which slavery did not exist, as opposed to *Slave States*; **free'stone** any easily wrought building stone without a tendency to split into layers; a freestone fruit. — *adj* (of a type of peach, etc) having a stone from which the pulp easily separates (opposite of *clingstone*). — *adj* **free'style** (of a (eg swimming or skiing) race or competition) in which a competitor is free to choose which style or method to use or which movements to perform; (of wrestling) all-in; (of a competitor) taking part in freestyle competitions, etc. — *n* freestyle competitions; (in swimming now *usu*) the front crawl (see under **front**). — **free'styler** a competitor in such competitions. — *adj* **free'-swimming** swimming about, not attached. — **free'-thinker** a person who rejects authority in religion; a rationalist. — *n* and *adj* **free'-thinking**. — **free'-thought**. — *adj* **free'-tongued** free-spoken. — **free trade** free or unrestricted trade; free interchange of commodities without protective duties; **free-trad'er** a person who practises or advocates this; a smuggler; a smuggling vessel; **free verse** verse defying the usual conventions as to regularity of metre, rhyme, length of lines, etc; rhythmic prose arranged as irregular verses; **free'-verser** a writer of free verse, a verslibrist; **free vote** a vote left to individual choice, free from party discipline; **free'way** a toll-free road for high-speed traffic (*US*); a motorway (*SAfr*); **free'wheel** the mechanism of a bicycle by which the rear-wheel may be temporarily disconnected and set free from the driving-gear. — *vi* **freewheel'** to cycle with the rear wheel so disconnected; (of a motor vehicle or its driver) to coast; to move, act or live without restraint or concern (*fig*). — *n* and *adj* **freewheel'ing**; **free will** freedom of the will from restraint; freedom of choice; the power of self-determination. — *adj* **free'-will** spontaneous; voluntary. — **freewoman** see **freeman** above; **Free World** the collective name used of themselves by non-communist countries. — **for free** (*colloq*) given without desire for payment or other return; **free alongside ship** delivered to the quayside free of charge, but exclusive of the cost of loading on to the ship (*abbrev* **fas**); **free on board** delivered on a vessel or other conveyance at no charge at all (*abbrev* **fob**); **free on rail** delivered to a railway station and loaded on to a train free of charge (*abbrev* **for**); **it's a free country** (*colloq*) there is no objection to or law against the carrying-out of whatever action has been proposed; **make free with** to be familiar with or take liberties with; to help oneself liberally to; **make so free as to** to venture to. [OE *frēo*; Ger *frei*; ON *frī*]

freebie, **Freefone**®, etc. See under **free**.

freemartin *frē'mär-tin*, *n* the female of a pair of twin calves which has internal male organs and external and rudimentary internal female organs; a similar animal of another species. [Ety unknown; perh connected with Ir *mart* a heifer]

freesia *frē'zi-ə*, a plant of the S African genus *Freesia* of scented greenhouse plants of the iris family. [After F H T *Freese* or H Th *Frees*, German physicians, or according to some, E M *Fries*, Swedish botanist]

freet and **freety**. See **freit**.

freeze *frēz*, *vi* to become ice; to become solid owing to fall of temperature; to be at a temperature at which water would freeze; to be very cold; to become motionless, stiff, attached or stopped by, or as if by, cold. — *vt* to cause to freeze; to fix; to stabilize; to prevent the use of or dealings in; to stop at or not develop beyond a particular state or stage; to put a temporary stop to; to stop (a moving film) at a particular frame; to preserve (*esp* food) by freezing and storing below freezing-point; to anaesthetize (a part of the body): — *pr p* **freez'ing**; *pa t* **frōze** or (*Milton*) **freez'd**; *pa p* **frōz'en**; *obs* or *dialect* **frōze**, **frōre** or **frōrn**. — *n* a frost; a stoppage. — *adj* **freez'able**. — *n* **freez'er** a freezing apparatus; anything that freezes; a compartment in a refrigerator designed to freeze fresh foods; an apparatus or room for storing food, etc below freezing-point, a deep-freeze. — *n* **freez'ing**. — *adj* very cold. — *vt* **freeze'-dry**. — **freeze-dry'ing** rapid freezing and evaporation to dryness in a vacuum for preservation or storage of a substance; **freeze'-frame** a frame of a cinema film repeated, or a frame of a video film held, to give a still picture; **freeze'-out** see **freeze out** below; **freeze'-up** (*NAm*) the period when ice forms on lakes, etc, at onset of winter; **freez'ing-down** lowering of the body temperature; **freez'ing-mixture** a mixture, eg of pounded ice and salt, cold enough to freeze a liquid by the rapid absorption of heat; **freez'ing-point** the temperature at which a liquid solidifies, that of water being 32° Fahrenheit, 0° Celsius (centigrade). — **freeze down** to lower the body temperature in preparation for heart and other operations; **freeze out** (*colloq*) to oblige to leave; to exclude (*n* **freeze'-out**). [OE *frēosan*, pa p *froren*; Du *vreizen*, Ger *frieren*]

freight *frāt*, *n* the lading or cargo, *esp* of a ship; the charge for transporting goods. — *vt* to load (*esp* a ship); to hire or let out. — *adj* (*obs*) freighted; fraught. — *n* **freight'age** money paid for freight. — *n* **freight'er** a person who freights a vessel; a cargo-carrying boat, etc; a transporting agent (*US*). — **freight'-car** (*US*) a luggage van; a goods van or wagon; **freight'liner** a train having specially designed containers and rolling-stock and used for rapid transport of goods; (with *cap*

®) a British Rail system for transporting goods in containers suitable for carriage by rail, road and ship. — Also *adj*. — **freight shed** a goods shed or warehouse; **freight'-train** a goods train. [Prob ODu *vrecht*, a form of *vracht*]

freit or **freet** *frēt*, (*Scot*) *n* an omen. — *adj* **freit'y** or **freet'y** superstitious. [ON *frētt* news]

fremd *fremd* or *frāmd*, **fremit** *frem'it* or *frām'it* or **fraim** *frām*, (*Scot*) *adj* foreign; strange; not related or similar; estranged, cold or unfriendly. — *n* a stranger; people to whom one is not related, strangers. — Also (*Spenser*) **frenne** (*fren*). [OE *fremde*; cf Ger *fremd*]

fremescent *frəm-es'ənt*, (*rare*) *adj* growling or muttering. — *n* **fremesc'ence**. [L *fremere* to growl]

fremit. See **fremd**.

fremitus *frem'i-təs*, (*pathol*) *n* a palpable vibration, eg of the walls of the chest. [L, a murmur]

frena. See **frenum**.

French *french* or *-sh*, *adj* belonging to *France* or its people; originating in France (sometimes without *cap*). — *n* the people of France; the language of France, also an official language in Belgium, Switzerland, Canada and other countries; oral sex, fellatio (*vulg slang*). — *n* **Frenchificā'tion**. — *vt* **French'ify** to make French or Frenchlike; to infect with the manner of the French. — *n* **French'iness**. — *adj* **French'y** with an exaggerated French manner. — *n* a contemptuous name for a French person. — **French bean** the common kidney bean (*Phaseolus vulgaris*) eaten, pods and all, as a table vegetable; **French berry** the berry of a species of buckthorn, used as a yellow dye. — *adj* **French-Canā'dian** of or from the French-speaking part of Canada. — *n* a French-Canadian person; the French language of Canada; **French chalk** soapstone, *esp* as used to mark out patterns in dressmaking; **French cricket** a game (*esp* of children) resembling cricket, in which the batsman's legs serve as the wicket; **French cuff** a cuff of double thickness, *usu* fastened by a cuff-link, formed by folding back the band at the end of a shirt-sleeve, etc; **French curve** a thin plate, *usu* of plastic, with the outlines of various curves on it, used for drawing curves; **French dressing** a salad dressing consisting of oil and vinegar or lemon juice, and *usu* seasoning; **French fry** (*pl* **French fries**) or **French fried potato** a potato-chip; **French heel** a way of turning the heel in knitting; a high curved heel for women's shoes; **French horn** the orchestral brass horn; **French kiss** a kiss in which the tongue is inserted into one's partner's mouth; **French knickers** a type of wide-legged knickers; **French leave** see **take French leave** below; **French letter** (*slang*) a condom; **French loaf** a loaf of crusty bread baked in a long narrow shape with tapered ends; **French'man** and **French'woman**: — *pl* **French'men** and **French'women**; **French pitch** (*music*) a standard pitch established by the French government in 1859, and later widely adopted, being 435 cycles per second at 15°C for A (see **international (concert) pitch** under **international**); **French pleat** see **French roll** below; **French plum** a prune or dried plum; **French polish** a varnish for furniture, consisting chiefly of shellac dissolved in spirit. — *vt* **French-pol'ish** to treat with French polish. — **French-pol'isher**; **French-pol'ishing**; **French pox** (*obs*) syphilis; **French roll** or **pleat** a hairstyle in which the hair is formed into a vertical roll at the back of the head; **French roof** a modified mansard roof, really N American; **French sash** a French window (see below); **French seam** a seam stitched on the right side then on the wrong side to enclose raw edges; **French stick** a very narrow French loaf; **French toast** bread dipped in egg (and milk) and fried; **French White** see **China White**; **French window** a window of floor-to-ceiling height, acting as a door; **Frenchwoman** see **Frenchman** above. — **Free French** (from 1942 **Fighting French**) continuers under General de Gaulle of resistance to Germany in World War II after the French capitulation of 1940; **pardon** or **excuse my French** (*colloq*) pardon my bad language; **take French leave** to depart without notice or permission; to disappear suspiciously. [OE *Frencisc*, from L *Francus*, from OHGer *Franko*]

frenetic or (*rare*) **phrenetic** *fri-net'ik*, formerly *fren'*, *adj* delirious; frantic; frenzied; mad; distracted. — *n* (*archaic*) a madman. — *adj* **frenet'ical** or **phrenet'ical**. — *adv* **frenet'ically** or **phrenet'ically**. [OFr *frénétique*, from L *phrenēticus*, from late Gr *phrenētikos*, from Gr *phrenītis* delirium, from *phrēn* heart or mind; see **phrenesiac**]

frenne *fren*, (*Spenser*). See **fremd**.

frenum or **fraenum** *frē'nəm*, *n* a ligament restraining the motion of a part of the body: — *pl* **fre'na** or **frae'na**. — *n* **fren'ulum** a small stiff hair on the hind wing of some insects, serving to bond hind and front wings during flight: — *pl* **fren'ula**. [L *frēnum* a bridle]

frenzy *fren'zi*, *n* a state of violent excitement, agitation, hurry, etc; a paroxysm of madness. — *vt* to drive to frenzy. — *adj* **fren'zical** or **fren'zied**. [OFr *frenesie*, from L and late Gr *phrenēsis* , from Gr *phrenītis*; see **frenetic**]

Freon® *frē'on*, *n* any of the family of chemicals containing fluorine, used as refrigerants, etc (also without *cap*). — **Freon-12**' dichlorodifluoromethane (CF_2Cl_2), widely used in household refrigerators.

frequent *frē'kwənt*, *adj* coming or occurring often; crowded (*obs*); addicted (*Shakesp*). — *vt* (*fri-kwent'*) to visit (a place) often; to associate with; to resort to (*obs*); to crowd (*obs*). — *n* **frē'quence** a crowd or assembly (*Milton*); frequency. — *n* **frē'quency** resort (*obs*); commonness of recurrence; the number of vibrations, cycles or other recurrences in unit time (in ascending order, *high*, *very high*, *ultra-high*, *extremely high*, *super-high frequency*). — *n* **frēquentā'tion** the act of visiting often. — *adj* **frequentative** (*fri-kwent'ə-tiv*; *gram*) denoting the frequent repetition of an action. — *n* (*gram*) a verb expressing this repetition. — *n* **frequent'er**. — *adv* **frē'quently**. — *n* **frē'quentness**. — **frequency modulation** modulation in radio transmission by varying the frequency of the carrier wave, giving greater fidelity than amplitude modulation and (almost) freedom from atmospherics. — **high frequency** a radio frequency of between 3 and 30 megahertz; **low frequency** a radio frequency of between 30 and 300 kilohertz. [L *frequēns*, *frequentis*; connected with *farcīre* to stuff]

frère *frer*, (*Fr*) *n* a brother.

frescade *fres-kād'*, *n* a cool walk. [Fr, from Ital *frescata*]

fresco *fres'kō*, *n* a mode of painting on walls covered with damp freshly-laid plaster (*true fresco*), or partly-dried plaster (*dry fresco* or *fresco secco*); a picture painted in this way: — *pl* **fres'coes** or **fres'cos**. — *vt* to paint in fresco. — *adj* **fres'coed** (*-kōd*). — *n* **frescoer** (*fres'kō-ər*). — *n* **fres'coing**. — *n* **fres'coist**. [Ital *fresco* fresh]

fresh *fresh*, *adj* in a state of activity and health; in new condition; not stale, faded or soiled; new or recently added; raw or inexperienced; in youthful bloom; cool and invigorating; brisk; amorously over-free or cheeky (*slang*); without salt; not preserved by pickling, drying, salting, etc; not frosty, thawing (*Scot*); cheeky or pert. — *adv* freshly; afresh; newly. — *n* time of freshness; a small stream of fresh water (*Shakesp*); a thaw or open weather (*Scot*). — *vt* (*obs*) to freshen. — *vt* **fresh'en** to make fresh; to take the saltness from; to refill (a glass or drink) (*US*). — *vi* to grow fresh or (of wind) stronger. — *vt* and *vi* to make (oneself) fresh by washing, etc (often with *up*). — *n* **fresh'ener**. — *n* **fresh'er** a university or college student in his or her first year, a freshman. — *n* **fresh'erdom**. — *n* **fresh'et** a stream of fresh water; a flood. — *adj* **fresh'ish**. — *adv* **fresh'ly** with freshness; newly; anew. — *n* **fresh'ness**. — *adj* **fresh'-blown** newly blossomed, as a flower. — *n* **fresh'man** a newcomer; a fresher. — *n* **fresh'manship**. — *adj* **fresh'-new** (*Shakesp*) quite new. — *adj* **fresh'-run** (of eg a salmon) newly come up from the sea. — *adj* **fresh'water** of or pertaining to, or living in, fresh water, not salt water; accustomed to sailing only on fresh water. — **freshwater college** (*US*) a provincial, *esp* unsophisticated, college. [OE *fersc*; cf Ger *frisch*]

fresnel *frā'nəl*, *n* a unit of optical frequency, equal to 10^{12}Hz (= 1 *terahertz*). — **Fresnel ellipsoid** a method, used in crystal optics, of representing the doubly refracting properties of a crystal; **Fresnel lens** (*image technol*) a lens having a surface of stepped concentric circles, thinner and flatter than a conventional lens of equivalent focal length; **Fresnel zones** (*phys*) zones into which a wave-front is divided according to the phase of the radiation reaching any point from it. [A J *Fresnel* (1788–1827), Fr physicist]

fret[1] *fret*, *vt* to eat into; to corrode; to wear away by rubbing; to rub or chafe; to ripple or disturb; to vex or irritate. — *vi* to wear away; to vex oneself; to worry; to chafe; (of a liquid) to work or ferment (*dialect*): — *pr p* **frett'ing**; *pa t* and *pa p* **frett'ed**. — *n* agitation of the surface of a liquid; irritation; worry; a worn or eroded spot; sea fret. — *adj* **fret'ful** peevish. — *adv* **fret'fully**. — *n* **fret'fulness**. — *adj* **frett'ing** vexing. — *n* peevishness. [OE *fretan* to gnaw, from pfx *for-* intens, and *etan* to eat; Ger *fressen*]

fret[2] *fret*, *vt* to ornament with interlaced work; to variegate: — *pr p* **frett'ing**; *pa t* and *pa p* **frett'ed**. — *n* ornamental network; a type of decoration originating in ancient Greece, for a cornice, border, etc, consisting of lines meeting *usu* at right angles, the pattern being repeated to form a continuous band (also called **grecque key** or **grecque meander**); bendlets, dexter and sinister, interlaced with a mascle (*heraldry*). — *adj* **frett'ed** or **frett'y** ornamented with frets. — **fret'saw** a saw with a narrow blade and fine teeth, used for fretwork, scrollwork, etc; **fret'work** ornamental work consisting of a combination of frets; perforated woodwork. [OFr *freter* to adorn with interlaced work and *frete* trelliswork; prob influenced by or confused with OE *frætwa* ornament]

fret[3] *fret*, *n* any of the wooden or metal ridges on the fingerboard of a guitar or other instrument on to which the strings are pressed in producing the various notes. — *vt* to provide with frets: — *pr p* **frett'ing**; *pa t* and *pa p* **frett'ed**. [Prob same as **fret**[2]]

Freudian *froid'i-ən*, *adj* pertaining to Sigmund *Freud* (1856–1939), his theory of the libido, or his method of psychoanalysis. — *n* a follower of Freud. — **Freudian slip** an error or unintentional action, *esp* a slip of the tongue, supposed to reveal an unconscious thought.

FRG *abbrev*: Federal Republic of Germany, the former W Germany.

Fri *abbrev*: Friday.

friable *frī'ə-bl*, *adj* apt to crumble; easily reduced to powder. — *n* **frī'ableness** or **frīabil'ity**. [Fr, from L *friābilis*, from *friāre*, *friātum* to crumble]

friand *frē-ã*, (*Fr*) *adj* dainty or delicate: — *fem* **friande** (*frē-ãd*). — *n* an epicure.

friar *frī'ər*, *n* a member of one of the mendicant religious orders of men in the RC Church, ie the Franciscans (*Friars Minor* or *Grey Friars*), Dominicans (*Friars Preachers* or *Black Friars*), Carmelites (*White Friars*), Augustinians (*Austin Friars*), and others; a pale patch on a printed page. — *adj* **fri'arly** like a friar. — *n* **fri'ary** a convent of friars. — **fri'arbird** an Australian honey-eater with featherless head; **friar's balsam** a tincture of benzoin, storax, tolu and aloes used as an inhalant; **friar's cap** a type of aconite, wolf's-bane (*bot*); **friar's cowl** wake-robin (*bot*); **friar's lantern** the will-o'-the-wisp. [OFr *frere*, from L *frāter* a brother]

fribble *frib'l*, (*obs*) *vi* to trifle. — *n* a trifler. — *n* **fribb'ler**. — *adj* **fribb'ling** or **fribb'lish** trifling. [Onomatopoeic; prob influenced by **frivol**]

fricadel. See **frikkadel**.

fricandeau *frik-ən-dō'* or *frik'*, *n* a thick slice of veal, etc, larded: — *pl* **fricandeaux** (*-dōz*). [Fr]

fricassee *frik-ə-sē'*, *n* a dish of fowl, rabbit, etc cut into pieces and served in sauce. — *vt* to prepare as a fricassee: — *pr p* **fricassee'ing**; *pa t* and *pa p* **fricasseed'**. [Fr *fricassée*; origin unknown]

fricative *frik'ə-tiv*, *adj* produced by friction; pertaining to, or being, a fricative. — *n* (*phonetics*) a consonant produced by the breath being forced through a narrow opening. [L *fricāre*, *frictum* to rub]

fricht. See **fright**.

friction *frik'shən*, *n* rubbing; a resisting force met by one body moving against the surface of another; disagreement or jarring. — *adj* **fric'tional**. — *adj* **fric'tionless**. — **friction tape** (*NAm*) insulating tape (*usu* the cloth variety); **friction welding** welding in which the necessary heat is produced by means of friction, eg by rotating one part and forcing the parts together. [L *fricāre*, *frictum* to rub]

Friday *frī'di*, *n* the sixth day of the week. — **Friday (afternoon) car** (*colloq*) a new car with many faults in it, supposedly built on a Friday (afternoon) when workers' concentration is poor. — **Black Friday** Good Friday, from the black vestments of the clergy and altar in the Western Church; any Friday marked by a great calamity; **Good Friday** the Friday before Easter, kept in commemoration of Christ's Crucifixion; **Holy Friday** one of the three fast-days in each church quarter (also **Golden Friday**), sometimes used for Good Friday itself; **Man Friday**, **Girl Friday**, and **Person Friday** see under **man**, **girl** and **person**. [OE *Frīgedæg* day of (the goddess) Frīg]

fridge[1] *frij*, (*colloq*) *n* short for **refrigerator**. — **fridge-freez'er** a refrigerator and a deep-freeze constructed as a single unit.

fridge[2] *frij*, (*Sterne*) *vt* to rub or fray. [Prob imit]

fried. See **fry**[1].

friend *frend*, *n* a person loving or attached to another; a close or intimate acquaintance; a favourer, wellwisher or supporter; a member of a society so named; a relative (*Scot*); a lover (*obs* or *euphem*). — *vt* (*archaic*) to befriend. — *adj* **friend'ed** (*archaic*) supplied with friends. — *n* **friend'ing** (*Shakesp*) friendliness. — *adj* **friend'less** without friends; destitute. — *n* **friend'lessness**. — *adv* **friend'lily**. — *n* **friend'liness**. — *adj* **friend'ly** like a friend; having the disposition of a friend; favourable; amicable; (of a sports match, etc) played for amusement or practice rather than competitively (also *n*: — *pl* **friend'lies**); pertaining to the Society of Friends or Quakers; able to handle small variations in the input format and/or enabling the easy correction of input errors (*comput*). — **-friendly** *combining form* compatible with, helpful to or in sympathy with. — *n* **friend'ship** attachment from mutual esteem; friendly assistance. — **friendly fire** (*military*) accidental firing upon one's allies rather than one's enemies; **friendly lead** (*archaic*) an entertainment for the benefit of a person in need; **friendly numbers** (*math*) pairs of numbers each of which is the sum of the factors of the other, including unity (also called **amicable numbers**; cf **perfect number**); **friendly society** a benefit society, an association for relief in sickness, old age or widowhood, by provident insurance; **Friends of the Earth** an organization of conservationists and environmentalists. — **be friends with** to be on good terms with or well disposed towards; **have a friend at court** to have a friend in a position where his or her influence is likely to prove useful; **(Religious) Society of Friends** the proper designation of a sect of Christians better known as Quakers. [OE *frēond* (orig a pr p; cf *frēon* to love); Ger *Freund*]

frier[1] *frī'ər*, (*Milton*) *n* a friar.

frier[2] and **fries**. See under **fry**[1].

Friesian. See **Frisian**.

frieze[1] *frēz*, *n* a rough, heavy woollen cloth. — *adj* **friezed** having a nap. [Fr *frise*]

frieze[2] *frēz*, *n* the part of the entablature between the architrave and cornice, often ornamented with figures (*classical archit*); a decorated band along the top of the wall of a room (*archit*). — *vt* to put a frieze on. [OFr *frise*; Ital *fregio*; perh L *Phrygium* (*opus*) Phrygian (work)]

frig[1] *frig*, (*vulg*) *vi* and *vt* to masturbate; loosely, to have sexual intercourse with; (often with *about*) to potter about: — *pr p* **frigg'ing**; *pa t* and *pa p* **frigged**. — *n* masturbation. — *n* **frigg'ing** masturbation; pottering about. — *adj* and *adv* as an intensive, to a great extent or very; often used as a colourless descriptive. — **frig off** (*usu* in imperative) to go away. [Late ME *friggen*, from L *fricāre* to rub]

frig[2] *frij*, (*colloq*) *n* short for **refrigerator**.

frigate *frig'it*, (*naval*) *n* formerly, a vessel in the class next to ships of the line; now denoting an escort vessel. — *n* **frigatoon'** a small Venetian vessel with a square stern and two masts. — **frigate bird** a large tropical sea-bird (*Fregata*) with very long wings. [OFr *fregate*, from Ital *fregata*; ety dubious]

frigger *frig'ər*, *n* a glass ornament.

fright *frīt*, *n* sudden fear; terror; a figure of grotesque or ridiculous appearance (*colloq*). — *vt* **fright** (now *rare*, except as Scot **fricht** *frihht*) or **fright'en** to make afraid; to alarm; to drive by fear: — *pa p* **fright'ened** or (*dialect*) **frit**. — *adj* **fright'ened**. — *n pl* **fright'eners** (*slang*; also in *sing*) something intended to frighten, *esp* for criminal purposes. — *adj* **fright'ening**. — *adv* **fright'eningly**. — *adj* **fright'ful** terrible; horrible; unpleasant (*colloq*); great or huge (*colloq*). — *adv* **fright'fully** dreadfully; very (*colloq*). — *n* **fright'fulness** the quality of being frightful; terrorism. — *adj* **fright'some** frightful; feeling fright. — *adj* (*dialect*) **frit** frightened. — **put the frighteners on someone** (*slang*) to frighten someone into (not) doing something, *esp* for criminal purposes; **take fright** to become afraid. [OE *fyrhto*; cf Ger *Furcht* fear]

frigid *frij'id*, *adj* frozen or stiffened with cold; cold; chillingly stiff; without spirit or feeling; unanimated; leaving the imagination untouched; (*usu* of a woman) sexually unresponsive. — *n* **frigid'ity** coldness; coldness of affection; lack of animation; sexual unresponsiveness. — *adv* **frig'idly**. — *n* **frig'idness**. — **frigid zones** the parts of the earth's surface within the polar circles. [L *frīgidus*, from *frīgēre* to be cold, from *frīgus* cold]

frigidarium *frij-i-dār'i-əm* or *frig-i-där'i-o͝om*, (*L*) *n* the cooling room of a Roman public baths, often with a swimming-bath.

frigorific *frig-ər-if'ik*, *adj* causing cold; freezing. — *n* **frigorif'ico** (*Sp*) a slaughtering and meat-freezing establishment: — *pl* **frigorif'icos**. [L *frīgus*, *-oris* cold, and *facere* to make]

frigot *frig'ət*, (*Spenser*) *n*. Same as **frigate**.

frijol or **frijole** *frē'hhōl* or *frē-hhōl'*, *n* the kidney bean, or any species of Phaseolus: — *pl* **frijoles** (*-les*). [Sp *fríjol*, *frijol* or *fréjol*]

frikkadel or **fricadel** *frik'ə-del*, (*SAfr*) *n* a fried ball of minced meat. [Afrik, from Fr; cf **fricandeau**]

frill *fril*, *vi* (*archaic*) to ruffle, as a hawk ruffles its feathers, when shivering. — *vt* to provide with a frill. — *n* a ruffle; a ruffled or crimped edging; superfluous ornament; (in *pl*) affected airs and graces. — *n pl* **frill'ies** (*colloq*) light and pretty underwear for women. — *n* **frill'ing**. — *adj* **frill'y**. — **frilled lizard** a large Australian lizard (Chlamydosaurus) with an erectile frill around its neck. — **no frills** or **without frills** (in a manner, form, etc which is) straightforward, clear, without posturing, with no superfluous additions, etc. [Origin unknown]

Frimaire *frē-mār'*, *n* the third month of the French revolutionary calendar, about 21 November–20 December, the frosty month. [Fr *frimas* hoar-frost]

fringe *frinj*, *n* a border of loose threads; hair falling over the brow; a border; anything bordering on or additional to an activity. — *vt* to adorn with a fringe; to border. — *adj* bordering, or just outside, the recognized or orthodox form, group, etc as in *fringe medicine*, *fringe theatre*; unofficial or not part of the main event, as in *fringe meeting*; less important or popular, as in *fringe sports*. — *adj* **fringed**. — *adj* **fringe'less**. — *adj* **fring'y** decorated with fringes. — **fringe benefit** something in addition to wages or salary that forms part of the regular remuneration from one's employment; **fringe'-dweller** (*Austr*) a person, *esp* an Aborigine, who lives, *usu* in poverty and squalor, on the edge of a town or community; **fringe effect** (*image technol*) see **border effect**; **fringe tree** a large American shrub (*Chionanthus virginica*) of the olive family, whose very numerous snow-white flowers have long narrow corolla-segments. — **lunatic fringe** any (*usu* small) group of fanatics or extremists within a political party, pressure group, etc. [OFr *frenge*, from L *fimbriae* threads, related to *fibra* a fibre]

fringillaceous *frin-ji-lā'shəs*, *adj* pertaining to the finches or **Fringill'idae**. — *adj* **fringill'id**, **fringill'iform** or **fringill'ine**. [L *fringilla* a finch]

fripon *frē-pɔ̃*, (*Fr*) *n* a knave or scamp. — *n* **friponnerie** (*frē-pon-ə-rē*) knavery.

frippery *frip'ər-i*, *n* cast-off clothes (*obs*); an old-clothes shop, or the old-clothes trade (*obs*); tawdry finery; foppish triviality; useless trifles. — *adj* useless; trifling. — *n* **fripp'er** or **fripp'erer** (*archaic*) an old-clothes dealer. [OFr *freperie*, from *frepe* a rag]

fris *frish* or **friska** *frish'kö*, *n* the quick dance movement of a Hungarian csárdás. [Hung]

Frisbee® *friz'bi*, *n* a plastic saucer-shaped disc which can be made to skim through the air, used in various catching-games, etc.

frisée *frē-zā*, (*Fr*) *n* a variety of curly endive.

frisette *frē-zet*, (*Fr*) *n* a fringe of curls on the forehead. — *n* **friseur** (*frē-zœr*) a hairdresser. — *n* **frisure** (*frē-zür*) a mode of curling.

Frisian *friz'i-ən*, *n* a native of the Dutch province of *Friesland*; the Low German language of Friesland. — *adj* of or from Friesland, its people, or their language. — *adj* **Friesian** (*frēz'*) Frisian, *esp* of a heavy breed of dairy-cattle. — *n* a Frisian; a Friesian bull or cow. — *adj* **Fries'ic** or **Fries'ish**.

frisk *frisk*, *vi* to gambol; to leap playfully. — *vt* to search (a person or his or her pockets) (*slang*); to search for radioactive radiation by contamination meter. — *n* a frolicsome movement. — *n* **frisk'er**. — *adj* **frisk'ful** brisk or lively. — *adv* **frisk'ily**. — *n* **frisk'iness**. — *n* and *adj* **frisk'ing**. — *adv* **frisk'ingly**. — *adj* **frisk'y** lively; jumping with gaiety; frolicsome. [OFr *frisque*]

friska. See **fris**.

frisket *frisk'it*, (*printing*) *n* the light frame between the tympan and the forme, to hold in place the sheet to be printed. [Fr *frisquette*]

frisson *frē-sɔ̃*, *n* a shiver; a shudder; a thrill. [Fr]

frist *frist*, (*obs*) *n* delay or respite. — *vt* to postpone; to grant time, eg for payment. [OE *first* time or respite]

frisure. See under **frisette**.

frit[1] *frit*, *n* the mixed materials for making glass, pottery glazes, etc. — *vt* to fuse partially: — *pr p* **fritt'ing**; *pa t* and *pa p* **fritt'ed**. — **frit porcelain** an artificial soft-paste English porcelain (from its vitreous nature). [Fr *fritte*, from Ital *fritta*, from L *frīgere*, *frīctum* to roast]

frit[2] *frit*, *n* a small fly destructive to wheat and other cereal crops. — Also **frit'fly**. [Ety unknown]

frit[3]. See under **fright**.

frith[1]. See **firth**[1].

frith[2] *frith*, (*obs* or *hist*) *n* peace; sanctuary. — **frith'borh** (*-borhh*) a surety for keeping the peace, frankpledge; **frith'gild** a union of neighbours pledged to one another for the preservation of peace; **frith'soken** sanctuary or asylum (OE *frithsōcn*); **frith'stool** a chair of sanctuary, placed near the altar in a church, as at eg Hexham and Beverley (OE *frithstōl*). [OE *frith* peace; Ger *Friede*]

frith[3] *frith* or **firth** *fûrth*, *n* wooded country; brushwood; underwood. [OE (*ge*)*fyrhthe*]

fritillary *frit'il-ər-i* or *-il'*, *n* a member of the genus (*Fritillaria*) of the lily family, the best-known species having chequered purple flowers; a name for several butterflies of similar pattern. [L *fritillus* a dice-box]

fritter[1] *frit'ər*, *n* a piece of fruit, etc fried in batter. [OFr *friture*, from L *frīgere*, *frīctum* to fry]

fritter[2] *frit'ər*, *n* (*obs*) a fragment. — *vt* to break into fragments (*obs*); to squander piecemeal (often with *away*). — *n* **fritt'erer** a person who wastes time. [Perh

OFr *freture*, from L *frāctūra*, from *frangere*, *frāctum* to break]

fritto misto *frē'tō mēs'tō*, (*Ital*) *n* a mixed dish of fried food.

friture *frē-tür*, (*Fr*) *n* a dish of fried food; a fritter.

fritz *frits*: **on the fritz** (*US colloq*) out of order. [Origin unknown]

frivolous *friv'ə-ləs*, *adj* trifling; lacking (due) seriousness, silly. — *vt* and *vi* **friv'ol** (*rare*; back-formation) to trifle. — *n* **frivolity** (*-ol'*) a trifling habit or nature; levity. — *adv* **friv'olously**. — *n* **friv'olousness**. [L *frīvolus*]

frize. *Obs* form of **freeze** or **frieze**.

frizz or **friz** *friz*, *vt* to curl tightly. — *n* a curl; frizzed hair. — *adj* **frizzed** having the hair crisped into frizzes. — *adj* **frizz'y**. [OFr *friser* to curl; perh connected with **frieze**[1]]

frizzante *frē-dzan'tā*, (*Ital*) *adj* (of wine) sparkling.

frizzle[1] *friz'l*, *vt* to form in small short curls. — *vi* to go into curls. — *n* a curl; frizzled hair. — *adj* **frizz'ly**. [Related to **frizz** and **frieze**[1]]

frizzle[2] *friz'l*, *vt* and *vi* to fry; to scorch. [Perh onomatopoeic adaptation of **fry**[1], from sputtering noise]

fro *frō*, *prep* (*obs* except in Scots form **frae** *frā*) from. — *adv* away, only used in **to and fro** (see under **to**). [ON *frā*]

frock *frok*, *n* a monk's wide-sleeved garment; a frock-coat; a smock-frock; a sailor's jersey (*archaic*); a woman's or child's dress; an undress regimental coat; a wearer of a frock (*obs*). — *vt* (*rare*) to provide with a frock; to invest with priestly office. — *adj* **frocked** clothed in a frock. — *n* **frock'ing** cloth suitable for frocks, coarse cotton twill. — *adj* **frock'less**. — **frock'-coat** a double-breasted full-skirted coat for men. [OFr *froc* a monk's frock, from LL *frocus*, from L *floccus* a flock of wool; or from LL *hrocus*, from OHGer *hroch* (Ger *Rock*) a coat]

Froebelian *frœ-bēl'i-ən*, *adj* pertaining to Friedrich *Froebel*, German educationist (1782–1852) or to his system (the **Froebel system**) of kindergarten schools. — *n* **Froe'belism**.

frog[1] *frog*, *n* a tailless web-footed amphibian, *esp* one of the genus *Rana*, more agile than a toad; a swelling (in the throat); (with *cap*) a contemptuous name for a French person; (on a railway) a structure in the rails allowing passage across or to another track; a depression made in the face(s) of a brick; the block by which the hair is attached to the heel of a violin, etc bow. — *n* **frogg'ery** frogs collectively; a place where frogs abound or are kept. — *adj* **frogg'y** froglike; having or abounding in frogs. — *n* (with *cap*) a contemptuous name for a French person. — *n* **frog'let** or **frog'ling** a little frog. — **frog'bit** a small aquatic plant (*Hydrocharis morsus-ranae*), related to the water-soldier, but with floating leaves; **frog'-eater** a person who eats frogs; a contemptuous name for a French person; **frog'-fish** a name for various fishes, *esp* the angler-fish; **frog'-hopper** a froth-fly (see under **froth**); **frog'man** an underwater swimmer fitted with webbed froglike feet. — *vt* **frog'march** (sometimes **frog's'-march**) to carry an unco-operative or drunken prisoner, etc face downwards between four people, each holding a limb; now *usu* to seize from behind and force forwards while holding firmly by the arms or clothing; *sometimes* to propel backwards between two people, each holding an arm. — *n* the act or process of frogmarching. — **frog'mouth** any bird of the mopoke family or subfamily (Australian and S Asian) related to or included in the goatsuckers; **frog's'-mouth** antirrhinum or snapdragon; **frog'-spit** cuckoo-spit; **frog test** (*med*) a pregnancy test in which the woman's urine is injected into the dorsal lymph sac of the platanna frog, deemed to be positive if spermatozoa are present in the frog's urine within three hours. — **a frog in the** (or **one's**) **throat** hoarseness. [OE *frogga*; also *frox*; cognate with ON *froskr*; Ger *Frosch*]

frog[2] *frog*, *n* a V-shaped band of horn on the underside of a horse's hoof. [Perh same as **frog**[1]. Gr *batrachos* means frog in both senses; also influenced by Ital *forchetta* dimin of fork]

frog[3] *frog*, *n* an ornamental fastening or tasselled or braided button; an attachment to a belt for carrying a weapon. — *adj* **frogged** having ornamental stripes or workings of braid or lace, mostly on the breast of a coat. — *n* **frogg'ing**. [Perh Port *froco*, from L *floccus* a flock or lock]

froise *froiz* or **fraise** *frāz*, *n* a thick pancake, often with slices of bacon. [Origin unknown]

frolic *frol'ik*, *adj* (*archaic*) merry; pranky. — *n* gaiety; a prank; a gambol; a merrymaking. — *vi* to play wild pranks or light-hearted tricks; to gambol: — *pr p* **frol'icking**; *pa t* and *pa p* **frol'icked**. — *adj* **frol'icsome** merry; sportive. — *adv* **frol'icsomely**. — *n* **frol'icsomeness**. [Du *vrolijk* merry; cf Ger *fröhlich* joyful or merry]

from *from* or *frəm*, *prep* out of; away, to or at a greater distance relatively to; springing out of; beginning at; apart relatively to; by reason of. [OE *fram*, *from*; related to Gothic *fram* and ON *frā*]

fromage frais *from'äzh frā* or *frōm'äzh fre*, (*Fr*) *n* a light creamy cheese with a consistency similar to thick yoghourt, sold in tubs. [Fr, literally, fresh cheese]

fromenty. See **frumenty**.

frond *frond*, *n* a leaf, *esp* of a palm or fern; a leaflike thallus or plant body, or a leaflike organ of obscure morphological nature. — *n* **frond'age** fronds collectively. — *adj* **frond'ed** having fronds. — *adj* **frond'ent** leafy. — *n* **frondesc'ence** the development of leaves. — *adj* **frondesc'ent** leaflike; leafy; springing into leaf. — *adj* **frondif'erous** bearing or producing fronds. — *adj* **frond'ose** leaflike; leafy. [L *frōns*, *frondis* a leaf]

Fronde *frönd* or *frɔ̃d*, *n* a rebellious movement established in opposition to Mazarin and the court in France during Louis XIV's minority. — *n* **frondeur** (*frön-dûr'* or *frɔ̃-dœr*) a member of the Fronde; an irreconcilable or a dissident. [Fr, sling, from L *funda* sling]

front *frunt*, *n* the forehead (*poetic*); the face or appearance; the forepart of anything; the side open to view; the face of a building, *esp* the principal face; the part facing the sea or other water; a seaside promenade; the foremost line (of soldiers or battle); the scene of hostilities; the direction in which troops are facing when lined up (*military*); a combined face presented against opponents; a group of people, organizations or parties having the same or broadly similar (*esp* political or revolutionary) outlook and aims, who act together against opponents, as in *popular front* (see under **popular**); a set of false curls for the forehead; the breast of a man's shirt, a dickey; the middle part of the tongue; the auditorium of a theatre; the bounding surface between two masses of air of different density and temperature (*meteorol*); the apparent or nominal leader behind whom the really powerful person works anonymously (also **front man**); (something acting as) a cover or disguise for secret or disreputable activities; boldness; impudence. — *adj* of, relating to, or in, the front; articulated with the front of the tongue (*phonetics*). — *vt* to stand in front of or opposite; to face towards; to meet or oppose face to face; to add a front to; to serve as a front to; to change into or towards a front sound (*phonetics*); to act as the front man of; to act as the compère or frontman of; to stand, perform, etc in front of or at the front of, as eg the singer with a band. — *vi* to be foremost (*Shakesp*); to face; to act as a front for someone else or as a cover for something secret or illicit. — *n* **front'age** the front part of a building; extent of front; ground in front. — *n* **front'ager** (*law*) a person who owns or occupies property along a road, river or shore. — *adj* **front'al** (*frunt'l*; also *front'l*) of or belonging to the front, or the forehead; pertaining to a front (*meteorol*). — *n* the façade of a building; something worn on the forehead or face; a pediment over a door or window (*obs*); a hanging of silk, satin, etc embroidered for an altar, now *usu* covering only the top, the *superfrontal*, formerly covering the whole of the front, corresponding to the *antependium*. — *adj* **front'ed** formed with a front; changed into or towards a front sound (*phonetics*). — *adj* **front'less** lacking a front; devoid of shame or modesty (*archaic*). — *adv* **front'lessly**. — *n* **front'let** a band worn on the forehead. — *n* **frontogen'esis** (*meteorol*; Gr *genesis* generation) the formation or intensification of a front. — *n* **frontol'ysis** (*-is-is*; *meteorol*; Gr *lysis* dissolution) the weakening or disappearance of a front. — *adv* **front'ward** or **front'wards** towards the front. — *adv* **front'ways** or **front'wise** with face or front forward. — *adj* **front'-bench** sitting on a front bench in parliament, as a minister, or an opposition member of similar standing. — **front-bench'er**; **front crawl** (*swimming*) the crawl stroke performed face down; **front door**; **front-end computer** or **processor** a subsidiary computer which receives and processes data before passing it to a more powerful computer for further processing; **front-end load** an initial charge made to a person taking on a long-term savings or investment plan. — *adj* **front-end loaded** or **front'-loaded**. — **front-end loading** or **front'-loading** the taking of a large part of the total costs and commission of an investment or insurance policy out of the early payments or profits made; any similar weighting of borrowing, deduction, etc towards the early stages of a financial transaction or accounting period; **front-end system** that part of a computerized printing system which receives the matter to be printed and provides the input to the typesetter; **front line** the battle positions closest to the enemy; the most active, exposed or dangerous position or role in any activity or situation, *esp* a conflict (*fig*). — *adj* **front'-line** of or relating to the front line; of or relating to a state bordering on another state in which there is an armed conflict, and often involved in that conflict. — *adj* **front-loaded** see **front-end-loaded** above. — **front'-loader** a washing-machine which is loaded through a door at the front. — *adj* **front'-loading** (see also **front-end loading** above). — **front'man** the person who appears on television as presenter of a programme, *esp* a documentary programme; **front man** see **front** *n* above. — *adj* **front'-of-house**. — **front of the house** (in a theatre) the collective activities such as box-office and programme selling carried on in direct contact with the public. — *adj* **front'-page** suitable for the front page of a newspaper; important. — *vt* to print a (story) on the front page of a newspaper. — *adj* **front'-rank** of foremost importance. — **front'-ranker**; **front row** (*Rugby football*) the players in the front row of the scrum (also **front-row fowards**); **front'-runner** (in a race) a person who runs best while leading the field or one who sets the pace for the rest of the runners; a person or thing that is most popular, most likely to succeed, etc, *esp* in some kind of competition; **front-wheel drive** a system in which the driving power is transmitted to the front wheels of a vehicle as opposed to the rear wheels. — **come to the front** to become noticeable; to attain an important position; **in front** or **in front of** before. [L *frōns*, *frontis* the forehead]

frontier *frunt'* or *front'ēr*, *-yər* or *-ēr'*, *n* the border of a country; the border of settled country, *esp* in the USA, the advancing limit of the West pioneered in the 19c; an outwork (*fortif*; *Shakesp*); (in *pl*) the extreme limit (of knowledge and attainment) in a particular discipline or line of inquiry. — *adj* belonging to a frontier; bordering. — *vt* (*Spenser*) to border. — **front'iersman** or **front'ierswoman** (or *-tērz'*) a dweller on a frontier. [OFr *frontier*, from L *frōns*, *frontis*]

frontispiece *frunt'is-pēs* or *front'*, *n* the principal face of a building (*archit*); an illustration at the front of a book facing the title-page. — *vt* to put as a frontispiece; to provide with one. [Fr *frontispice*, from LL *frontispicium*, from *frōns*, *frontis* forehead, and *specere*, *spicere* to see; not connected with **piece**]

fronton[1] *frun'tən*, (*archit*) *n* a pediment. — Also **frontoon** (*-tōō n'*). [Fr, from Ital *frontone*]

fronton[2] *fron'tən* or *fron-ton'*, *n* the wall against which the game of pelota is played. [Sp *frontón*, from L *frōns*, *frontis* forehead]

frore *frōr* or *frör*, (*obs*, *dialect* or *poetic*), also (*obs* or *dialect*) **froren** *frōr'ən*, **frorne** or **frorn** *frörn*, *adj* frozen or frosty. — *adj* **frō'ry** (*Spenser*) frozen. [OE *froren*, pa p of *frēosan* to freeze]

frost *frost*, *n* a state of freezing; temperature at or below the freezing-point of water; frozen dew, or *hoar-frost*; a disappointment or failure (*slang*); coldness of manner or relations. — *vt* to affect with frost; to cover with hoar-frost; to make like hoar-frost; to sharpen (the points of a horse's shoe) so that it does not slip on ice. — *vi* to assume a frostlike appearance. — *adj* **frost'ed** covered by frost; having a frostlike appearance (eg a cake or Christmas card by sprinkling, or glass by roughening); damaged by frost. — *adv* **frost'ily**. — *n* **frost'iness**. — *n* **frost'ing** a coating of hoar-frost; material or treatment to give the appearance of hoar-frost; icing (*esp US*). — *adj* **frost'less** free from frost. — *adj* **frost'like**. — *adj* **frost'y** producing, characterized by, or covered with, frost; chill (*lit* and *fig*); frostlike. — **frost'bite** inflammation, sometimes leading to gangrene, in a part of the body, caused by exposure to cold. — *vt* to affect with frost. — *adj* **frost'bitten** bitten or affected by frost (*lit* and *fig*); suffering from frostbite. — *adj* **frost'bound** bound or confined by frost. — **frost'-nail** a projecting nail in a horse-shoe serving to prevent slipping on ice, an ice-calk. — *vt* to provide with frost-nails. — **frost'-smoke** a vapour frozen in the atmosphere, and having a smoke-like appearance; **frost'-work** tracery made by frost, eg on windows; work resembling frost tracery, etc. [OE *frost*, *forst*, from *frēosan*; cf Ger *Frost*]

froth *froth*, *n* foam; chatter (*fig*); something frivolous or trivial. — *vt* to cause froth on. — *vi* to make froth. — *n* **froth'ery** mere froth. — *adv* **froth'ily**. — *n* **froth'iness**. — *adj* **froth'less**. — *adj* **froth'y** full of or like froth or foam; empty; insubstantial. — **froth'-blower** (*slang*) a beer-drinker; **froth flotation** see **flotation** under **flote**; **froth'-fly** or **froth'-hopper** a frog-hopper, any insect of the family *Cercopidae*, whose larvae live surrounded by froth (cuckoo-spit) on plants. — *adj* **froth-fo'my** (*Spenser*) foaming. [ON *frotha*; Dan *fraade*]

frottage *fro-täzh'*, *n* rubbing; the use of rubbing or rubbings to obtain texture effects in a work of art; a work of art made by this means; a type of sexual activity in which sexual pleasure, and often orgasm, is obtained by rubbing against someone or something (*psychol*). — *n* **frotteur** (*fro-tœr'*; *psychol*) a person who practises sexual frottage. [Fr]

frou-frou *frōō'frōō*, *n* the rustling of silk; elaborate trimmings, eg frills; fussy decoration. [Fr]

froughy. Same as **frowy**.

frounce[1] *frowns*, (*obs*) *vt* to plait; to curl; to wrinkle up. — *vi* to wrinkle; to frown. — *n* a wrinkle, plait or curl; affected ornament. [OFr *froncier*; see **flounce**[2]]

frounce[2] *frowns*, (*obs*) *n* a disease of the mouth in hawks. [Origin unknown]

frow *frow*, *n* a Dutchwoman. [Du *vrouw*]

froward *frō'ərd*, (*archaic*) *adj* turned away; self-willed; perverse; unreasonable (opposed to *toward*). — *adv* (*Spenser*) in an averse direction. — *prep* (also **fro'wards**) in a direction away from. — *adv* **fro'wardly**. — *n* **fro'wardness**. [**fro** and sfx *-ward*]

frown *frown*, *vi* to wrinkle the brow, eg in anger; to look angry, gloomy or threatening; to show disapproval. — *vt* to express, send or force by a frown. — *n* a wrinkling or contraction of the brow in displeasure, etc; a stern look. — *adj* **frown'ing** gloomy; disapproving; threatening. — *adv* **frown'ingly**. — **frown on** or **upon** to disapprove of. [From OFr *froignier* (Fr *refrogner*) to knit the brow; origin unknown]

frowst *frowst*, *vi* (*obs*) to luxuriate in hot stuffiness and stupefaction. — *n* hot stuffy fustiness; a spell of frowsting (*obs*). — *n* **frowst'er**. — *n* **frowst'iness**. — *adj*

frowst'y fusty; close-smelling; foul-smelling. [Origin unknown]

frowy or **froughy** (*Spenser* **frowie**) *frō'i* or *frow'i*, *adj* musty or rancid (*Spenser*); (of timber) soft and brittle (*dialect*). [Prob OE *thrōh* rancidity]

frowzy or **frowsy** *frow'zi*, (*dialect*) *adj* fusty; stuffy or offensive; unkempt. [Origin unknown]

frozen *frōz'n*, *pa p* of **freeze**. — *adj* preserved by keeping at a low temperature; very cold; stiff and unfriendly; (of assets, bank accounts, etc) prevented from being accessed by the owner or account holder. — **frozen shoulder** (*med*) a shoulder joint which has become stiff owing to enforced immobilization, or to injury to the joint or its surrounding tissue.

FRPS *abbrev*: Fellow of the Royal Photographic Society.

FRS *abbrev*: Fellow of the Royal Society.

FRSE *abbrev*: Fellow of the Royal Society of Edinburgh.

fructans *fruc'tənz*, *n* a polymer of fructose, found in grasses and some vegetables. [L *frūctus* fruit]

fructed *fruk'tid*, *adj* (*heraldry*) bearing fruit. — *adj* **fructif'erous** bearing fruit. — *n* **fructificā'tion** fruit-production; a fruiting body (*bot*). — *vt* **fruc'tify** to make fruitful; to fertilize. — *vi* to bear fruit. — *adj* **fruc'tive** productive or fruitful. — *adj* **fructiv'orous** (L *vorāre* to devour) fruit-eating. — *n* **fruc'tose** a water-soluble simple sugar found in honey and fruit. — *n* **fruc'tūary** a person enjoying the fruits of anything. — *vi* **fruc'tūate** to come to fruit; to fructify. — *n* **fructūā'tion** coming to fruit or bearing of fruit. — *adj* **fruc'tūous** fruitful. [L *frūctus* fruit]

Fructidor *frük-tē-dör*, *n* the twelfth month in the French revolutionary calendar, the month of fruit, about 18 August–16 September. [Fr, from L *frūctus* fruit, and Gr *dōron* a gift]

frugal *frōō'gl*, *adj* economical in the use of anything; sparing; meagre; thrifty. — *n* **fru'galist** a person who is frugal. — *n* **frugality** (-*gal'*) economy; thrift. — *adv* **fru'gally**. [L *frūgālis*, from *frūx*, *frūgis* fruit]

frugiferous *frōō-jif'ə-rəs*, *adj* (L *ferre* to bear) fruit-bearing. — *adj* **frugiv'orous** (L *vorāre* to eat) feeding on fruits or seeds. [L *frūx*, *frūgis* fruit]

fruit (*obs* **fruict**) *frōōt*, *n* the produce of the earth, which supplies the needs of humans and animals; an edible part of a plant, generally sweet, acid and juicy, *esp* a part that contains the seed, but sometimes extended to include other parts (eg the leaf-stalk in rhubarb), and popularly distinguished from the vegetable, its savoury, firm-fleshed counterpart; a fructification, *esp* the structure that develops from the ovary and its contents after fertilization, sometimes including also structures formed from other parts of the flower or axis (*bot*); the offspring of animals (*archaic*); (often in *pl*) product, effect or advantage; a male homosexual (*derog slang*, *esp US*). — *vi* to produce fruit. — *n* **fruit'age** fruit collectively; fruits. — *n* **fruitā'rian** a person who lives on fruit. — Also *adj*. — *adj* **fruit'ed** having produced fruit. — *n* **fruit'er** a fruiterer (now *dialect*); a tree, etc as a producer of fruit, as in *good fruiter*; a fruit-grower. — *n* **fruit'erer** a person who deals in fruit: — *fem* **fruit'eress**. — *n* **fruit'ery** a place for storing fruit; fruitage. — *adj* **fruit'ful** productive. — *adv* **fruit'fully**. — *n* **fruit'fulness**. — *n* **fruit'ing** the process of bearing, or coming into, fruit. — *adj* **fruit'less** barren, sterile; without profit; useless; in vain. — *adv* **fruit'lessly**. — *n* **fruit'lessness**. — *n* **fruit'let** a small fruit; one of the small fruit-like parts that forms an aggregate or multiple fruit. — *adj* **fruit'y** like, or tasting like, fruit; rich; (of a voice) mellow or resonant; salacious, saucy or smutty; crazy (*US slang*); male homosexual (*slang*, *esp US*). — **fruit'-bat** any bat of the suborder Megacheiroptera, large fruit-eating bats of the Old World; **fruit body** see **fruiting body**; **fruit'-bud** a bud that produces fruit; **fruit-cage** an enclosure with mesh sides and a roof to protect growing fruit and vegetables from birds, etc; **fruit'cake** a cake containing dried fruit; a slightly mad person (*colloq*); **fruit cocktail** a fruit salad, *esp* one of small, *usu* diced, pieces of fruit; **fruit'-fly** an insect of genus *Drosophila*; **fruiting body** (*bot*) a seed or spore-bearing structure, eg the large spore-bearing structures of many fungi (also **fruit body**); **fruit'-knife** a small knife with a blade of silver, etc for cutting fruit; **fruit'-machine** a coin-operated gaming machine in which chance must match with any of a variety of stated winning combinations the pictures, traditionally of different fruits, on a set of revolving wheels; **fruit salad** a mixture of pieces of fruit, fresh or preserved; **fruit'-tree** a tree yielding edible fruit; **fruit'wood** the wood of a fruit-tree (also *adj*). — **bush fruits** small fruits growing on woody bushes; **first-fruits** see under **first** and see **annat**; **small** or **soft fruit** or **fruits** strawberries, currants, etc. [OFr *fruit*, *fruict*, from L *frūctus*, from *fruī*, *frūctus* to enjoy]

fruition *frōō-ish'ən*, *n* enjoyment; maturation, fulfilment or completion; use or possession, *esp* accompanied with pleasure; bearing fruit, fruiting. — *adj* **fru'itive**. [OFr *fruition*, from L *fruī* to enjoy]

frumentation *frōō-mən-tā'shən*, *n* a gift of grain bestowed on starving or rebellious people in ancient Rome. — *adj* **frumentā'ceous** made of or resembling wheat or other grain. — *adj* **frumentā'rious** pertaining to corn. [L *frūmentātiō*, *-ōnis*, from *frūmentārī* to provide with corn, from *frūmentum* corn]

frumenty *frōō'mən-ti*, *n* hulled wheat boiled in milk, sometimes flavoured with spices, eggs, rum, etc. — Also **frō'menty**, **fur'menty**, **fur'mety** or **fur'mity** (*fûr'*). [OFr *frumentee*, from *frument*, from L *frūmentum*]

frump *frump*, *n* a dowdy woman; a jeer or snub (*obs*). — *vt* (*obs*) to snub. — *adj* **frump'ish** or **frump'y** ill-dressed or dowdy.

frumple *frum'pl*, (*dialect*) *vt* to wrinkle.

frush[1] *frush*, *vt* (*Shakesp*) to break or bruise. — *adj* (*Scot*) brittle; crumbly. — *n* (*Scot*) a crash; splinters. [OFr *froissier* to bruise, from L *frustum* fragment]

frush[2] *frush*, *n* (*dialect*) the frog of a horse's foot; a disease in that part of a horse's foot. [Origin uncertain; cf OE *forsc* frog (animal); see **frog**[2]]

frust *frust*, *n* (*Sterne*) a fragment. — *n* **frust'ule** (*bot*) the siliceous two-valved shell of a diatom alga, with its contents. — *n* **frust'um** a slice of a solid body; the part of a cone or pyramid between the base and a parallel plane, or between two planes: — *pl* **frust'ums** or **frust'a**. [L *frustum* a bit]

frustrate *frus-trāt'* or *frus'trāt*, *vt* to make useless or of no effect; to bring to nothing; to balk; to thwart. — *adj* (*frus'*; *archaic*) useless or ineffectual; balked. — *adj* **frustra'ted** thwarted; having a sense of discouragement and dissatisfaction; sexually unfulfilled. — *adj* **frustra'ting**. — *adv* **frustra'tingly**. — *n* **frustrā'tion**. — **frustrated export** an article *orig* intended for export which for some reason has to be offered for sale on the home market. [L *frustrārī*]

frutex *frōō'teks*, (*bot*) *n* a shrub: — *pl* **fru'tices** (-*ti-sēz*). — *adj* **fru'ticose** shrubby. [L *frutex*, *-icis* a shrub]

frutify *frōō'ti-fī*, (*Shakesp*) *vt* Launcelot Gobbo's blunder for **notify** or **specify**.

fry[1] *frī*, *vt* to cook in oil or fat in a pan; to burn or scorch (often *fig*); to torture with heat (*obs*). — *vi* to undergo frying; to foam (*Spenser*): — *pr p* **fry'ing**; *pa t* and *pa p* **fried**; *3rd pers present indicative* **fries**. — *n* a dish of anything fried, *esp* the offal of a pig, lamb, etc; (in *pl*) fried potato-chips. — *n* **fri'er** or **fry'er** a person who fries (*esp* fish); a pan or container for frying; a fish suitable for frying. — *n* and *adj* **fry'ing**. — **fried'cake** (*US*) a cake fried in deep fat; a doughnut; **fry'ing-pan** a broad, shallow pan for frying food in; **fry'-up** (*colloq*) mixed fried foods, or the frying of these. — **fry in one's fat** suffer the consequences of one's behaviour; **out of the frying-pan into the fire** out of one difficult situation into a worse. [Fr *frire*, from L *frīgere*; cf Gr *phrȳgein*]

fry[2] *frī*, *n* young, collectively; a swarm of young, *esp* of fishes just spawned; young salmon in their second year; a number of small things. — **small fry** small things collectively, people or things of little importance; children. [ON *friō* seed; Dan and Swed *frø*]

FSA *abbrev*: Fellow of the Society of Antiquaries. — **FSAScot** *abbrev*: Fellow of the Society of Antiquaries of Scotland.

FSH *abbrev*: follicle-stimulating hormone; (of a car; often without *caps*) full service history.

FST *abbrev*: flatter, squarer tube (see under **flat**).

FT *abbrev*: Financial Times (newspaper).

ft *abbrev*: feet; foot.

FTA *abbrev*: Freight Transport Association.

fth or **fthm** *abbrev*: fathom.

FT Index *abbrev*: Financial Times (Industrial Ordinary Share) Index.

FTSE, **FT-SE 100** or **FT-SE** (often *foot'si*) *abbrev*: Financial Times Stock Exchange 100-Share Index, which records the share prices of the top 100 UK public companies. Also (*colloq*) **Foot'sie**.

fub *fub*, *vt* (*archaic*) to put off; to fob. — *n* **fubb'ery** (*obs*) a deception. — **fub off** (*Shakesp*) to put off or evade by a trick or a lie. [See **fob**[1]]

fubby *fub'i* or **fubsy** *fub'zi*, (*dialect*) *adj* chubby; squat. [Ety dubious]

fuchsia *fū'shə*, *n* any plant of a S American genus (*Fuchsia*) of the evening primrose family, with long pendulous flowers typically red or purple; a reddish-purple colour. — Also *adj*. — *n* **fuchsine** (*fŏŏks'ēn*) the dyestuff magenta, a green solid, purplish-red in solution (from its colour, similar to that of the flower). [Named after Leonard *Fuchs* (1501–66), German botanist]

fuchsite *fŏŏks'īt*, *n* a brilliant green chromium mica. [J N von *Fuchs* (1774–1856), German mineralogist]

fuci. See **fucus**.

fuck *fuk*, (old word, long *taboo*; all words and meanings still *vulg*) *vi* to have sexual intercourse; (with *about* or *around*) to play around or act foolishly; (with *off*) to go away. — *vt* to have sexual intercourse with (*usu* of a male); (with *about* or *around*) to deal inconsiderately with; (with *up*) to botch, damage or break (*n* **fuck'-up**). — *n* an act of sexual intercourse; a person, *esp* female, considered as a (good, poor, etc) partner in sexual intercourse; something of very little value; used in various phrases expressing displeasure, emphasis, etc; a term of abuse, a fucker. — *interj* an expression of displeasure, etc (often with an object, as in *fuck him!*). — *adj* **fucked** exhausted; useless. — *n* **fuck'er** a person who fucks; a term of abuse; a fellow; a person. — *n* **fuck'ing** sexual intercourse. — *adj* expressing scorn or disapprobation; often used as an intensifier or meaningless qualification. — *adv* very or to a great extent. — **sweet fuck all** or **fuck all** nothing at all. [Ety doubtful; perh Ger *ficken* to strike or copulate with]

fucus *fū'kəs*, *n* paint for the face, cosmetics (*obs*); any plant of the *Fucus* or bladder-wrack genus of seaweeds, the type genus of the family *Fucaceae*: — *pl* **fū'ci** (*-sī*) or **fū'cuses**. — *adj* **fū'coid** like, pertaining to or containing bladder-wrack, or seaweed, or seaweed-like markings. — *n* a marking like a fossil seaweed; a seaweed of the genus *Fucus*. — *adj* **fūcoid'al**. — *adj* **fū'cused** painted. [L *fūcus* the red dye orchil or rouge; Gr *phȳkos*]

fud *fud*, (*Scot*) *n* a rabbit's or hare's tail; the buttocks.

fuddle *fud'l*, *vt* to stupefy, eg with drink; to confuse. — *vi* to drink to excess or habitually: — *pr p* **fudd'ling**; *pa t* and *pa p* **fudd'led**. — *n* intoxicating drink (*obs*); intoxication; a drinking bout; confusion. — *n* **fudd'ler** a drunkard. — *n* and *adj* **fudd'ling** tippling. — **fudd'le-cap** (*obs*) a hard drinker. [Origin obscure]

fuddy-duddy *fud'i-dud-i*, *n* an old fogy or stick-in-the-mud; a fault-finder. — *adj* old-fogyish; old-fashioned; stuffy; prim; censorious. [Origin unknown]

fudge[1] *fuj*, *n* stuff, nonsense, humbug (*archaic*); a soft sweet made from butter, cream and sugar, often flavoured with vanilla, rum, etc. — *interj* (*archaic*) bosh. [Origin obscure]

fudge[2] *fuj*, *n* an inserted patch in a newspaper, or space reserved for it; the act of fudging; distortion; evasion. — *vi* to fadge (*archaic*); to cheat; to fail; to dodge. — *vt* to patch up; to fake; to distort; to dodge; to obscure or cover up. [Variant of **fadge**]

Fuehrer. Same as **Führer**.

fuel *fū'əl*, *n* material for burning as a source of heat or power; something that maintains or intensifies emotion, etc (*fig*); food, as maintaining bodily processes; fissile material for a nuclear reactor. — *vt* to provide with fuel; to incite, encourage or stimulate (*esp* anger, hate, violence, etc). — *vi* to take or get fuel: — *pr p* **fū'elling**; *pa t* and *pa p* **fū'elled**. — *n* **fū'eller**. — **fuel assembly** a group of nuclear fuel elements forming a single unit for purposes of charging or discharging a reactor; **fu'el-cell** a cell generating electricity for an external circuit as part of a chemical reaction between an electrolyte and a combustible gas or vapour supplied from outside the cell (the reaction taking place at more or less ordinary temperatures). — *adj* **fuel'-injected** having **fuel'-injection**, a system of operating an internal-combustion engine in which vaporized liquid fuel is introduced under pressure directly into the combustion chamber, so dispensing with a carburettor. — **fuelling machine** see **charge (-discharge) machine**; **fuel oil** heavy oil distillates used as fuel; **fuel reprocessing** the processing of nuclear fuel after use to remove fission products, etc and to recover fissile and fertile materials for further use (also **reprocessing**); **fuel rod** a unit of nuclear fuel in rod form for use in a reactor. — **add fuel to the fire** or **fires** to make an angry person angrier, a heated discussion more heated, etc. [OFr *fowaille*, from LL *focāle*, from L *focus* a fireplace]

fuero *fwā'rō*, *n* a code or body of law or privileges, *esp* in the Basque provinces, a constitution: — *pl* **fue'ros**. [Sp, from L *forum*]

fuff *fuf*, (*Scot*) *n* a puff; the spitting of a cat; a burst of anger. — *vt* and *vi* to puff; to spit like a cat. — *adj* **fuff'y** light and soft. [Imit]

fug *fug*, *n* a very hot, close, often smoky state of atmosphere; a person who fugs; dusty fluff. — *vi* to sit or revel in a fug. — *vt* to cause a fug in. — *adj* **fugg'y**. [Origin unknown]

fugacious *fū-gā'shəs*, *adj* inclined to run away or flee; fleeting; (of petals, etc) readily shed. — *n* **fugā'ciousness** or **fugacity** (*-gas'*). [L *fugāx*, *-ācis*, from *fugere* to flee]

fugal, **fugato** and **fughetta**. See under **fugue**.

fugitive *fū'ji-tiv*, *adj* inclined to run away, fleeing; fleeting; occasional, written for some passing occasion. — *n* a person who flees or has fled; a person difficult to catch; an exile. — *n* **fū'gie** (*Scot*) a cock that will not fight; a runaway. — *n* **fūgitā'tion** (*Scots law*) absconding from justice; sentence of outlawry. — *adv* **fū'gitively**. — *n* **fū'gitiveness**. — **fū'gie-warr'ant** (*Scot*) a warrant to apprehend a debtor supposed to be about to abscond, *prob* from the phrase *in meditatione fugae*. [L *fugitīvus*, from *fugere* to flee]

fugleman *fū'gl-mən*, *n* a soldier who stands before a company at drill as an example; a ringleader or mouthpiece of others. — *vi* **fū'gle** (*Carlyle*) to act like a fugleman. [Ger *Flügelmann* the leader of a file, from *Flügel* a wing, and *Mann* man]

fugue *fūg*, *n* a form of composition in which the subject is given out by one part and immediately taken up by a second (in *answer*), during which the first part supplies an accompaniment or counter-subject, and so on (*music*); a form of amnesia which is a flight from reality. — *adj* **fū'gal**. — *adv* **fū'gally**. — *adj* and *adv* **fugato** (*fū-gä'tō* or (*Ital*) *fŏŏ-gä'tō*) in the manner of a fugue without being strictly a fugue. — Also *n*: — *pl* **fuga'tos**. — *n* **fughetta** (*fū-get'ə* or (*Ital*) *fŏŏ-get'ta*) a short fugue. — *n* **fuguist** (*fūg'ist*) a person who writes or plays fugues. [Fr, from Ital *fuga*, from L *fuga* flight]

Führer *fū'rər* or (*Ger*) *fü'rər*, *n* the title taken by Hitler as dictator of Nazi Germany. [Ger, leader or guide]

fulcrum *ful'krəm* or *fŏŏl'*, *n* the prop or fixed point on which a lever moves or pivots (*mech*); a support; a means to an end (*fig*): — *pl* **ful'crums** or **ful'cra**. — *adj* **ful'crate** supported with fulcrums. [L *fulcrum* a prop, from *fulcīre* to prop]

fulfil or (*US*) **fulfill** *fŏŏl-fil'*, *vt* to fill full (*archaic*); to complete; to accomplish; to carry into effect; to bring to consummation; to develop and realize the potential of: — *prp* **fulfill'ing**; *pa t* and *pa p* **fulfilled'**. — *n* **fulfill'er**. — *n* **fulfill'ing** or **fulfil'ment** full performance; completion; accomplishment. [OE *fullfylla*, from *full* full, and *fyllan* to fill]

fulgent *ful'jənt*, *adj* shining; bright. — *n* **ful'gency**. — *adv* **ful'gently**. — *adj* **ful'gid** flashing. — *n* **ful'gor** or **ful'gour** (*-gör* or *-gər*) splendour. — *adj* **ful'gorous** flashing. [L *fulgēns*, *-entis*, pr p of *fulgēre* to shine, *fulgidus* shining, *fulgor* brightness]

fulgurate *ful'gū-rāt*, *vi* to flash like lightning. — *adj* **ful'gūral** pertaining to lightning. — *adj* **ful'gūrant** flashing like lightning. — *n* **fulgūrā'tion** flashing; (in assaying) the sudden and final brightening of the fused globule; the destruction of tissue, *esp* tumours, by electric sparks (*med*). — *n* **ful'gūrite** a tube of vitrified sand formed by lightning. — *adj* **ful'gūrous** resembling lightning. [L *fulgur* lightning]

fulham *fōōl'əm*, (*gambling*) *n* a die loaded at the corner to ensure that certain numbers are thrown. — Also **full'am** or **full'an**. [Prob the place-name *Fulham* in London]

fuliginous *fū-lij'i-nəs*, *adj* sooty; dusky. — *n* **fūliginos'ity**. — *adv* **fūlig'inously**. [L *fūlīgō*, *-nis* soot]

full[1] *fōōl*, *adj* holding all that can be contained; having no empty space; replete; abundantly supplied or furnished; abounding; copious; filling; containing the whole matter; complete; perfect; maximum; strong; clear; intense; swelled or rounded; protuberant; having an excess of material; at the height of development or end of course; (with *of*) unable to think or talk of anything but; drunk (*colloq*): — *compar* **full'er**; *superl* **full'est**. — *n* the completest extent, eg of the moon; the highest degree; the whole; the time of full moon. — *vt* to make with gathers or puckers. — *vi* to become full. — *adv* quite; thoroughly or veritably; directly. — *adj* **full'ish** inclined to fullness. — *n* **full'ness** or **ful'ness** the state of being full; the moment of fulfilment; plenty or wealth (*Shakesp*). — *adv* **full'y** completely; entirely; quite. — *adj* **full'-a'corned** (*Shakesp*) full-fed with acorns. — *adj* **full'-aged** having reached majority. — **fullback** a player in the defence, placed nearest his own goal-line (*Am football*); see also **back**[1]; **full blast** full operation. — *adv* **full'-blast'** with maximum energy and fluency. — **full'-blood** an individual of pure blood. — *adj* **full'-blood'ed** having a full supply of blood; vigorous, using maximum force or energy; thoroughbred or of unmixed descent; related through both parents. — *adj* **full'-blown** fully expanded, as a flower; beyond the first freshness of youth; fully qualified, developed or admitted; puffed out to fullness. — *adj* **full'-bod'ied** with much body, flavour or substance. — *adj* **full'-bore** (of a firearm) of larger calibre than small-bore. — **full'-bottom** a full-bottomed wig. — *adj* **full'-bott'omed** having a full or large bottom, eg of a wig. — *adj* **full'-bound** (*bookbinding*) with the boards covered as well as the back. — **full brother** or **sister** a son or daughter of the same parents as another. — *adj* **full'-charged** fully loaded (*lit* and *fig*). — *adv* **full'-cir'cle** round in a complete revolution; so as to return to an original position, state, etc. — **full'-cock'** the position of a gun cock drawn fully back, or of a tap fully open. — *adv* in that position. — *adj* **full'-cocked'**. — **full cousin** the son or daughter of an uncle or aunt, a first cousin. — *adj* **full'-cream'** (of milk) not skimmed; made with unskimmed milk. — *adj* **full'-dress** in or requiring the dress (**full dress**) worn on occasions of state or ceremony. — **full-dress debate** a set debate of some importance in which the leaders take part. — *adj* **full'-eyed** with large prominent eyes. — *adj* **full'-face** or **full'-faced** facing straight towards the viewer; having a full or broad face; (of type) bold-faced. — *adj* **full-fashioned** see **fully-fashioned** below. — *adj* **full'-fed** fed to plumpness or satiety. — *adj* **full-fledged** see **fully-fledged** below. — *adj* **full'-fraught** (*Shakesp*) fully charged, equipped or endowed, all-round. — *adj* **full'-front'al** of the front view of a completely naked man or woman (also **full'-front'**); with no detail left unrevealed (*fig*). — *n* such a view or picture. — *adj* **full'-grown** grown to full size. — **full hand** see **full house** below. — *adj* **full'-hand'ed** bearing something valuable, eg a gift. — *adj* **full'-heart'ed** full of heart or courage; fraught with emotion. — *adj* **full'-hot** (*Shakesp*) heated to the utmost. — **full house** a performance at which every seat is taken (*theat*); three cards of a kind and a pair (*poker*; also **full hand**); (in bingo) all the numbers needed to win; a complete set (of anything). — *adj* **full'-length'** extending the whole length. — *n* a portrait showing the whole length of a person. — *adv* stretched to the full extent. — *adj* **full'-manned** (*Shakesp*) having a full crew. — **full marks** the maximum marks possible in an examination (also used as an expression of approval); **full moon** the moon with its whole disc illuminated, when opposite the sun; the time when the moon is full. — *adj* **full'-mouthed** (*archaic*) having a full set of teeth; having food in plenty; loud; sonorous. — **full nelson** a type of wrestling hold, a nelson. — *adj* **full'-orbed** (*archaic*) having the orb or disc fully illuminated, as the full moon; round. — **full organ** the organ, or great organ, with all or most of the stops in use. — *adj* **full'-out** at full power; total. — *adj* **full'-page** occupying a whole page. — *adv* **full'-pelt'**, **full'-speed'**, **full'-split'** or **full-tilt'** with highest speed and impetus. — **full pitch** or **full toss** a ball which does not or would not bounce before passing or hitting the batsman's wicket. — *adj* **full'-rigged'** having three or more masts square-rigged. — *adv* **full'-sail'**. — *adj* **full'-sailed** having all sails set; having sails filled with wind; advancing with speed and momentum. — *adj* **full'-scale** of the same size as the original; involving full power or maximum effort. — **full score** a complete musical score with a staff or line for every part; **full service history** (*abbrev* **FSH** or **fsh**) the complete details of repairs and servicing done to a vehicle from new; **full sister** see **full brother** above. — *adv* **full-speed** and **full-split** see **full-pelt** above. — **full stop** a point marking the end of a sentence; an end or halt. — *adj* **full'-summed** (*archaic*) complete in all its parts. — *adj* **full'-throat'ed** or **full'-voiced** singing, etc with the whole power of the voice. — *adv* **full-tilt** see **full-pelt** above. — **full time** the end of a football, rugby, etc match. — *adj* **full'-time** occupied during or extending over the whole working day, week, etc. — **full'-tim'er**; **full toss** see **full pitch** above. — *adj* **full-voiced** see **full-throated** above. — *adj* **full'-winged** (*Shakesp*) having wide, strong wings. — *adj* **full'y-fashioned** or **full'-fashioned** (of garments, *esp* stockings) shaped to fit the body closely. — *adj* **full'y-fledged** or **full'-fledged** completely fledged; having attained full rank or membership. — **at the full** at the height, eg of one's good fortune, etc; **full and by** (*naut*) closehauled to the wind; **full-line forcing** the supplying of a particular product by a company to a customer only on condition that the customer takes the whole range of the company's product; **full of oneself** having a high or exaggerated opinion of one's own importance, etc (also **full of one's own importance**), too much the subject of one's own conversation; **full of years** old or aged; at a good old age; **full steam ahead** see under **steam**; **full up** full to the limit; sated or wearied (*colloq*); **in full** without reduction; **in full cry** (*esp* of hounds) in hot pursuit; **in full rig** (*naut*) with maximum number of masts and sails; **in full swing** at the height of activity; **in the fullness of time** at the due or destined time; **to the full** in full measure or completely. [OE *full*; Gothic *fulls*, ON *fullr*, Ger *voll*]

full[2] *fōōl*, *vt* to scour and beat, as a means of finishing or cleansing woollens; to scour and thicken in a mill. — *n* **full'age** the charge for fulling cloth. — *n* **full'er** a person who fulls cloth. — **fuller's earth** an earthy hydrous aluminium silicate, capable of absorbing grease; a division of the English Jurassic (*geol*); **full'er's-herb** a tall herb, soapwort; **full'ing-mill** a mill in which woollen cloth is fulled. [OFr *fuler* (see **foil**[1]) and OE *fullere* fuller, both from L *fullō* a cloth-fuller]

fullam and **fullan**. See **fulham**.

fullerene *fo͝ol'ər-ēn*, *n* a ball-shaped molecule consisting of carbon atoms. [**buckminster fullerene**]

fulmar *fo͝ol'mär* or *-mər*, *n* a gull-like bird of the petrel family. [Perh ON *fūll* foul, and *mār* gull]

fulminate *ful'min-āt*, *vi* to thunder or make a loud noise; to detonate; to issue decrees with violence or threats; to inveigh; to flash. — *vt* to cause to explode; to utter or publish (eg a denunciation); to denounce. — *n* a salt of fulminic acid (often dangerously detonating). — *adj* **ful'minant** fulminating; developing suddenly or rapidly (*pathol*). — *n* a thunderbolt; an explosive. — *adj* **ful'minâting** detonating. — *n* **fulminā'tion** an act of thundering, denouncing or detonating; a denunciation. — *adj* **ful'minatory**. — *vt* and *vi* **fulmine** (*ful'min*; *Spenser* and *Milton*) to fulminate. — *adj* **fulmin'eous** or **ful'minous** pertaining to thunder and lightning. — **fulminating gold** a green powder made from auric (gold) oxide and ammonium hydroxide; **fulminating mercury** fulminate containing bivalent mercury; **fulminating silver** a black solid made from silver oxide and ammonium hydroxide; **fulmin'ic acid** an acid isomeric with cyanic acid. [L *fulmināre*, *-ātum*, from *fulmen*, *-inis* lightning, from *fulgēre* to shine]

fulness. See under **full**[1].

fulsome *fo͝ol'səm*, *adj* sickeningly obsequious; nauseatingly affectionate, admiring or praiseful; loosely, copious or lavish; excessive; (eg of a voice or a woman's figure) well-developed, well-rounded. — *adv* **ful'somely**. — *n* **ful'someness**. [**full**[1] and affix *-some*]

fulvous *ful'vəs*, *adj* dull yellow; tawny. — *adj* **ful'vid**. [L *fulvus* tawny]

fum. See **fung**.

fumado *fū-mā'dō*, *n* a smoked fish, *esp* a pilchard: — *pl* **fumā'does** or **fuma'dos**. [Sp, smoked, from L *fūmāre* to smoke]

Fumaria *fū-mā'ri-ə*, *n* the fumitory genus, giving name to the **Fumariā'ceae**, a family related to the poppies. — **fumaric acid** (*fū-mar'ik*) an acid isomeric with maleic acid, found in Fumaria and other plants. [L *fūmus*; see **fumitory**]

fumarole *fūm'ə-rōl*, *n* a hole emitting gases in a volcano or volcanic region. — Also **fum'erole**. — *adj* **fumarol'ic**. [Fr *fumerolle* or Ital *fumaruola*, from L *fūmus* smoke]

fumatorium and **fumatory**. See under **fume**.

fumble *fum'bl*, *vi* to grope about awkwardly; to make bungling or unsuccessful attempts; to drop or mishandle the ball, eg in American football; to mumble (*obs*). — *vt* to handle, manage or effect awkwardly or bunglingly; to drop or mishandle (the ball), eg in American football; to huddle (*archaic*); to mumble (*obs*). — *n* an act of fumbling; a dropped or fumbled ball, eg in American football. — *n* **fum'bler**. — *adv* **fum'blingly**. [Cf Du *fommelen* to fumble; Dan *famle*; ON *fālma* to grope about]

fume *fūm*, *n* smoke or vapour, often odorous (often in *pl*); any volatile matter; rage or fretful excitement; a passionate person (*archaic*); anything unsubstantial, a pointless conceit. — *vi* to smoke; to give off vapour; to come off in fumes; to be in a rage. — *vt* to treat with fumes; to give off; to offer incense to. — *n* **fūm'age** hearth-tax. — *n* **fumatō'rium** (*pl* **fumato'riums** or **fumato'ria**) or **fūm'atory** a place for smoking or fumigation. — *n* **fūmos'ity** (*archaic*) a fuming condition; an exhalation; breath stinking of food or drink. — *adj* **fūm'ous** or **fūm'y**. — **fume'-cham'ber** or **fume'-cup'board** a case for laboratory operations that give off fumes; **fumed oak** oak darkened by ammonia fumes; **fuming sulphuric acid** see **oleum** under **oleate**. [L *fūmus* smoke]

fumet[1] or **fewmet** *fū'mit*, (*archaic*, *usu* in *pl*) *n* the dung of deer, hares, etc. [Appar Anglo-Fr, from L *fimāre* to defecate]

fumet[2] or **fumette** *fū-met'*, *n* the scent of game when high. [Fr *fumet*]

fumetto *fo͞o-met'to*, (*Ital*) *n* a cartoon or comic-strip; a balloon in a cartoon: — *pl* **fumetti** (*-tē*).

fumigate *fūm'i-gāt*, *vt* to expose to fumes, *esp* for purposes of disinfecting, or destroying pests; to perfume (*archaic*). — *n* **fūm'igant** a source of fumes, *esp* a substance used for fumigation. — *n* **fūmigā'tion**. — *n* **fūm'igator** a fumigating apparatus. — *adj* **fūm'igatory**. [L *fūmigāre*, *-ātum*]

fumitory *fūm'i-tər-i*, *n* any plant of the genus *Fumaria*, *esp* one formerly used to treat scurvy. — Also (*Shakesp*) **fem'iter**, or **fen'itar** or **fem'etary**. [OFr *fume-terre*, literally earth-smoke, from L *fūmus* smoke, and *terra* earth; so called because its rapid growth was thought to resemble the dispersal of smoke]

fun *fun*, *n* a hoax or trick (*obs*); pleasure, enjoyment, merriment; frivolity or sport; a source of merriment or amusement. — *vt* (*obs*) to trick. — *vi* to play: — *pr p* **funn'ing**. — *adj* providing amusement; enjoyable or full of fun. — **fun'fair** a fair with side-shows, rides and other amusements; **fun fur** an artificial or inexpensive (sometimes dyed) fur, *esp* for casual wear; **fun park** an outdoor place of entertainment with various amusements; **fun run** a long-distance race, not *usu* covering the full distance of a marathon, undertaken for amusement, or for charitable fund-raising, rather than serious athletic competition; **fun runner**. — **all the fun of the fair** all the amusements of the occasion; **be great fun** to be very amusing; **in fun** as a joke, not seriously; **like fun** (*colloq*) rapidly or frenziedly; not at all; **make fun of** or **poke fun at** to ridicule. [Prob a form of obs *fon* to befool]

funambulist *fū-nam'bū-list*, *n* a rope-walker or rope-dancer. — *vi* **fūnam'būlate**. — *n* **fūnambūlā'tion**. — *n* **fūnam'būlātor**. — *adj* **fūnam'būlatory**. [L *fūnambulus* a rope-walker, from *fūnis* rope, and *ambulāre* to walk]

function *fungk'shən* or *fung'shən*, *n* the doing of a thing (*obs*); performance (*obs*); activity (*obs*); an activity appropriate to any person or thing; duty peculiar to any office or job; faculty or the exercise of faculty; the peculiar office of anything; a profession (*obs*); a solemn service; a ceremony; a social gathering; a variable so connected with another that for any value of the one there is a corresponding value for the other (*math*); a correspondence between two sets of variables such that each member of one set can be related to one particular member of the other set (*math* or *logic*); an event, etc dependent on some other factor or factors; the technical term for the vital activity of an organ, tissue, or cell (*physiol*); the part played by a linguistic form in a construction, or by a form or form class in constructions in general (*linguistics*). — *vi* to perform a function; to act; to operate, *esp* to expected standards; to work. — *adj* **func'tional** pertaining to or performed by functions (*math*); (of disease) characterized by impairment of function, not of organs; designed with special regard to purpose and practical use, often to the detriment of decorative qualities; serving a function. — *n* **func'tionalism** the theory or practice of adapting method, form, materials, etc primarily with regard to the purpose in hand. — *n* **func'tionalist**. — *adv* **func'tionally**. — *n* **func'tionary** a person who discharges any duty; a person who holds an office. — *vi* **func'tionate** (*obs*) to perform a function. — *adj* **func'tionless** having no function. — **functional group** (*chem*) the group of atoms in a compound that determines its chemical behaviour; **function word** (*linguistics*) a word, such as an article or auxiliary, which has little or no meaning apart from the grammatical concept it expresses. [OFr, from L *functiō*, *-ōnis*, from *fungī*, *functus* to perform]

functus officio *fungk'təs of-ish'i-ō*, *fo͝ongk'to͞os of-ik'i-ō*, (*L*) *adj* having fulfilled an office, or out of office; no longer having official power to act; (of a power) that can no longer be exercised.

fund *fund*, *n* a sum of money on which some enterprise is founded or financially supported; a supply or source (of money); a store laid up; a supply; (in *pl*) permanent government debts paying interest; (in *pl*) money available to an organization for a project, etc, or (*colloq*; *usu facetious*) available to an individual. — *vt* to convert into a long-term debt at a fixed rate of interest; to place in a fund; to provide (an organization, project, etc) with money. — *adj* **fund'able** capable of being converted into a fund or into bonds; capable of being funded. — *adj* **fund'ed** invested in public funds; existing in the form of bonds. — *n* **fund'er** a person who provides money for a project, etc; a financial backer. — *n* **fund'ing** the action of providing money for a project, etc; financial backing or funds. — *adj* **fund'less** completely lacking supplies or money. — **fund'-holder** a person who has money in public funds. — *n* **fund'-raising** the raising of money for an organization, project, etc. — Also *adj*. [L *fundus* the bottom]

fundamental *fun-də-men'tl*, *adj* basic; serving as foundation; essential; primary; important. — *n* anything which serves as a basis; an essential; the root of a chord or of a system of harmonics (*music*). — *n* **fund'ament** (*-mənt*; *facetious*) the buttocks or anus. — *n* **fundamen'talism** belief in the literal truth of the Bible, against evolution, etc; adherence to strictly orthodox religions or (*fig*) other, eg political, doctrines. — *n* **fundamen'talist** a person who professes such a belief or (*fig*) other, eg political, beliefs considered fundamental. — Also *adj*. — *n* **fundamental'ity**. — *adv* **fundamen'tally**. — **fundamental particle** same as **elementary particle**; **fundamental unit** any of a number of arbitrarily defined units in a system of measurement, such as metre, second or candela, from which the other quantities in the system are derived. [L *fundāmentum* foundation, from *fundāre* to found]

fundamentum relationis *fun-də-men'təm ri-lā-shi-ōn'is* or *fŏŏn-dä-men'tŏŏm re-lä-ti-ōn'is*, (*LL*) the basis of relation, the principle or nature of the connection.

fundi *fŏŏn'dē*, (*SAfr*) *n* an expert. [Nguni (SAfr language) *umfundisi* a teacher]

fundie or **fundy** *fun'dē*, (*colloq*) *n* a member of the radical wing of the German Green Party (cf **realo**).

fundus *fun'dəs*, *n* the bottom of anything; the upper end of the uterus in pregnant women (*med*); the rounded bottom of a hollow organ (*anatom*): — *pl* **fun'di** (*-ī*). [L]

funèbre *fü-ne-br'*, (*Fr*) *adj* mournful.

funebral and **funebrial** See under **funeral**.

funeral *fū'nər-əl*, *n* disposal of the dead, with related ceremonies or observances; the appropriate ceremony; a procession to the place of burial or cremation, etc; death (*Spenser* and *Shakesp*); tomb (*Spenser*). — *adj* pertaining to the disposal of the dead or to funerals. — *adj* **fūnē'bral** or **fūnē'brial** funereal. — *adj* **fū'nerary** pertaining to or suiting a funeral. — *n* **fūnē'real** pertaining to a funeral; dismal; mournful. — *adv* **funē'really**. — **funeral director** an undertaker; **funeral home** (*US*) an undertaker's place of business with facilities for funerals; **funeral parlour** a room that can be hired for funeral ceremonies; a funeral home. — **it's your, my**, etc **funeral** it's your, my, etc affair or look-out. [LL *fūnerālis* and L *fūnerārius*, *fūnebris*, *fūnereus*, from L *fūnus*, *fūneris* a funeral procession]

funest *fū-nest'*, (*obs*) *adj* deadly; lamentable. [Fr, from L *fūnestus* destructive]

fung *fung* or **fum** *fum*, *n* a fabulous Chinese bird, sometimes called the phoenix. [Chin *fung*, *fêng*]

fungibles *fun'ji-blz*, *n pl* movable effects which are consumed by use, and which are estimated by weight, number and measure (*law*); oil products which are interchangeable and can therefore be mixed during transport (*min ext*). [LL *fungibilis*, from L *fungī* to perform; see **function**]

fungus *fung'gəs*, *n* a plant of one of the lowest groups, thallophytes lacking chlorophyll and reproducing by spores, including mushrooms, toadstools, mould, yeasts, etc; a soft, morbid growth (*pathol*): — *pl* **fungi** (*fun'jī*, *-ji*, *-gī*) or **fung'uses**. — *adj* **fung'al** pertaining to, caused by, or resembling fungus. — *adj* **fungicīd'al** fungi-destroying; pertaining to a fungicide. — *n* **fungicide** (*fun'ji-sīd*) a substance which kills fungi. — *adj* **fungiform** (*fun'ji-förm*) mushroom-shaped. — *adj* **fung'oid** (*-goid*) or **fungoid'al** fungus-like; of the nature of a fungus. — *n* **fungos'ity** the quality of being fungous. — *adj* **fung'ous** of or like fungus; soft; spongy; growing suddenly; ephemeral (*obs*). — **fung'us-gall** a malformation in a plant caused by a fungal attack. [L *fungus* a mushroom; cf Gr *sphongos*, *spongos* a sponge]

funicle *fū'ni-kl*, *n* a small cord or ligature (*esp anatom*); a fibre; the stalk of an ovule (*bot*). — *adj* **fūnic'ūlar** relating to a funicle; relating to a string or cable. — *adj* **fūnic'ūlate**. — *n* **fūnic'ūlus** the umbilical cord; a funicle. — **funicular railway** a railway on which the carriages are pulled along a cable. [L *fūniculus*, dimin of *fūnis* a rope]

funk[1] *fungk*, (*colloq*) *n* a state of fear; panic; shrinking or shirking from loss of courage; a person who funks. — *vi* to flinch; to draw back or hold back in fear. — *vt* to balk at or shirk from fear. — *n* **funk'iness**. — *adj* **funk'y**. — **funk'hole** (*slang*, *orig military*) a place of refuge, a dug-out; a place to which one can retreat for shelter, etc (*fig*); a job that enables one to avoid military service. — **blue funk** see under **blue**[1]. [Poss Flem *fonck*]

funk[2] *fungk*, *n* decayed wood used for tinder, touchwood; a spark. [Cf Du *vonk*]

funk[3] *fungk*, *vt* to stifle with smoke. — *vi* to smoke and/or cause a strong unpleasant smell. — *n* a strong unpleasant smell, *esp* of smoke (*obs* or *US dialect*); funky music (*slang*). — *adj* **funk'y** with a strong, musty, or bad smell (*US dialect*); (of jazz, pop music, etc) unsophisticated, earthy and soulful, like early blues music in style, emotion, etc (*slang*); in the latest fashion, trendy (*slang*); kinky (*slang*); odd or quaint (*slang*). [Ety dubious]

funkia *fungk'i-ə*, *n* any plant of an E Asiatic genus allied to the day-lilies formerly called *Funkia*, now Hosta (see **hosta**). [From the German botanist, H C *Funck* (1771–1839)]

funky. See under **funk**[1] and **funk**[3].

funnel[1] *fun'l*, *n* a utensil, *usu* a cone ending in a tube, for pouring fluids into narrow-necked bottles or other containers; a passage for the escape of smoke, etc, *esp* on a ship. — *vt* to pour, pass, transfer, etc through, or as if through, a funnel. — *adj* **funn'elled** having a funnel; funnel-shaped. — **funn'el-net** a net shaped like a funnel; **funn'el-web** or **funnel-web spider** a venomous spider (genus *Atrax*) of E Australia which constructs a tube-shaped or funnel-shaped lair. [Prob through Fr or Port from L *infundibulum*, from *fundere* to pour]

funnel[2] *fun'l*, (*dialect*) *n* the offspring of a stallion and a she-ass. [Origin unknown]

funny[1] *fun'i*, *adj* full of fun; droll; amusing, mirth-provoking; queer or odd (*colloq*). — *n* a joke (*colloq*); (in *pl*) comic strips, or the comic section of a newspaper (*esp NAm*). — *adv* **funn'ily**. — *n* **funn'iness**. — **funny bone** (*colloq*) the bone at the elbow with the comparatively unprotected ulnar nerve which, when struck, shoots a tingling sensation down the forearm to the fingers (a pun on its medical name *humerus*); **funny business** tricks or deception (*slang*); amusing behaviour, joke-telling, etc (*colloq*); **funny farm** (*slang*) a mental hospital or asylum; **funny man** (*colloq*) a comedian; **funny money** (*colloq*) any currency or unit of account considered in some way less real or solid than 'ordinary' money, or a sum of money similarly regarded as in some way unreal; **funny paper** (*US*) the comic section of a newspaper, the funnies; **funny stuff** funny business. — **funny ha-ha** funny meaning 'amusing' (opposed to *funny peculiar*); **funny peculiar** funny meaning 'queer or odd' (opposed to *funny ha-ha*). [**fun**]

funny[2] *fun'i*, *n* a light racing-boat, with a pair of sculls. [Perh from **funny**[1]]

funster *fun'stər*, *n* a person who causes merriment; a joker or prankster. [**fun**]

Funtumia *fun-tū'mi-ə, n* an African genus of tree related to dogbane, yielding a type of rubber. [From a Ghanaian name]

fur[1] *fûr, n* the thick, soft, fine hair of certain animals; the skin with this hair attached; a garment of fur; furred animals (opposed to *feather*); a patched or tufted tincture (*heraldry*); a coating on the tongue; a crust formed by hard water in boilers, etc; a strengthening piece nailed to a rafter (*archit*). — *vt* to clothe, cover, coat, trim or line with fur; to coat. — *vi* to become coated: — *pr p* **furr'ing**; *pa t* and *pa p* **furred**. — *adj* **furred**. — *n* **furr'ier** a dealer or worker in furs. — *n* **furr'iery** furs in general; trade in furs. — *n* **furr'iness**. — *n* **furr'ing** fur trimmings; a coating on the tongue; (also **firr'ing**) strips of wood fastened to joists, etc; a lining to a wall to carry laths, provide an air-space, etc. — *adj* **furr'y** consisting of, like, covered with or dressed in fur. — **fur fabric** a fabric with a fur-like pile; **fur'-seal** a sea-bear, an eared seal with dense fur under its long hairs. [OFr *forrer* (Fr *fourrer*) to line or encase, from *forre, fuerre* a sheath]

fur[2] or **furr** *fûr*, (*Scot*) *n*. A form of **furrow**.

fur. *abbrev*: furlong.

furacious *fū-rā'shəs*, (*obs*) *adj* thievish. — *n* **fūrā'ciousness** or **fūracity** (*-ras'i-ti*). [L *fūrāx, -ācis*, from *fūr* thief]

fural. See under **furfur**.

furan *fū'ran* or *fū-ran'*, *n* a colourless liquid heterocyclic compound, C_4H_4O, obtained from wood-tar or synthesized, and used in tanning and nylon production (also **fur'furan** *-fū-* or *-fə-*); any of a group of heterocyclic compounds derived from furan. — Also **fūr'ane** (*-ān*). [L *furfur* bran]

furbelow *fûr'bi-lō*, (*archaic*) *n* a plaited border or flounce; a superfluous ornament. — *vt* to decorate with a furbelow. [Fr, Ital, and Sp *falbala*; of unknown origin]

furbish *fûr'bish*, *vt* to purify or polish; to rub up until bright; to renovate. — *n* **fur'bisher**. [OFr *fourbir, fourbiss-*, from OHGer *furban* to purify]

furcate *fûr'kāt* or *-kit* or **fur'cated** *-kā-tid*, *adj* forked. — *adj* **fur'cal**. — *n* **furcā'tion**. — *adj* **furciferous** (*-sif'*) bearing a forked appendage; rascally (*facetious*; in allusion to the *furca* or yoke of criminals). — *n* **fur'cūla** the joined clavicles of a bird, the wishbone. — *adj* **fur'cūlar** furcate; shaped like a fork. [L *furca* fork]

Furcraea *fûr-krē'ə* or **Fourcroya** *fōōr-kroi'ə*, *n* a tropical American genus of plants related to Agave, yielding Mauritius hemp. [After A F de *Fourcroy* (1755–1800), French chemist]

furder *fûr'dər*. An *obs* form (*Milton*) of **further**[1].

fureur *fū-rœr*, (Fr) *n* extravagant admiration.

furfur *fûr'fûr* or *-fər* (*Browning*, **furfair**), *n* dandruff or scurf. — *adj* **furfuraceous** (*fûr-fū-rā'shəs*) branny; scaly; scurfy. — *n* **furfural** (*fûr'fū-ral* or *-fə-ral*) or in full **furfural'dehyde**, also called **fūr'al**, **fur'fūrol**, **furfurole**, **fūr'ol** or **furole**, a liquid ($C_4H_3O{\cdot}CHO$) obtained by heating bran with dilute sulphuric acid. — *adj* **furfurous** (*fûr'fū-rəs* or *-fə-rəs*) furfuraceous. [L *furfur* bran]

furfuran. See **furan**.

furibund *fū'ri-bund*, (*obs*) *adj* raging. [L *furibundus*, from *furia* rage]

furioso *fōō-ri-ō'sō, fū-*, *n* a furious or mad person: — *pl* **furiō'sōs**. — *adj* and *adv* (*music*) with fury. [Ital; cf **furious**]

furious. See under **fury**.

furl *fûrl*, *vt* to roll up. [Perh **fardel**[2]]

furlana *fōōr-lä'nə*. Same as **forlana**.

furlong *fûr'long*, *n* a measure of distance, 40 poles, one-eighth of a mile, now little used except in horse-racing. [OE *furlang*, from *furh* furrow, and *lang* long]

furlough *fûr'lō*, *n* leave of absence, *esp* from military duty. — *vt* to grant furlough to. [Du *verlof*; cf Ger *Verlaub*]

furmenty, **furmety** and **furmity**. See **frumenty**.

furnace *fûr'nis*, *n* an enclosed structure in which great heat is produced for any of a number of industrial processes; a time or place of great affliction or torment (*fig*). — *vt* to exhale like a furnace; to subject to the heat of a furnace. [OFr *fornais*, from L *fornāx, -ācis*, from *fornus* an oven]

furniment *fûr'ni-mənt*, (*Spenser*) *n* furnishing.

furnish *fûr'nish*, *vt* to equip (a house, etc) with furniture, carpets, curtains, etc; to fit up or supply completely, or with what is necessary; to supply or provide; to equip. — *n* paper pulp, with any added ingredients, before it goes into the paper-making process. — *adj* **fur'nished** equipped; stocked with furniture. — *n* **fur'nisher** — *n pl* **fur'nishings** fittings of any kind, *esp* articles of furniture, etc within a house; any incidental part (*Shakesp*). — *n* **fur'nishment**. [OFr *furnir, furniss-*; of Gmc origin; cf OHGer *frummen* to further]

furniture *fûr'ni-chər*, *n* movables, either for use or ornament, with which a house is equipped; equipment (*Shakesp*); the trappings of a horse; decorations (*Shakesp*); the necessary equipment in some arts or trades; accessories; metal fittings for doors and windows; the piece of wood or metal put round pages of type to make margins and fasten the type in the chase (*printing*). — **furniture van** a long, high-sided van for transporting furniture, etc, eg when moving house. [Fr *fourniture*]

furol and **furole**. See under **furfur**.

furor *fū'rör*, *n* fury; excitement or enthusiasm. — **furor loquendi** (*fū'rör lok-wen'dī* or *fōō'ror lok-wen'dē*) a passion for speaking; the urge to speak; **furor poeticus** (*pō-et'ik-əs* or *po-āt-ik-ōōs*) poetic frenzy; a passion for writing poetry; **furor scribendi** (*skri-ben'dī* or *skrē-ben'dē*) a passion for writing; the urge to write. [L]

furore *fū'rōr, -rör* or *fōō-rōr'ā*, *n* a craze; wild enthusiasm; wild excitement. [Ital]

furphy *fûr'fi*, (*Austr*) *n* a water cart; a rumour or false report. [John *Furphy*, an Australian water cart manufacturer]

furr. See **fur**[2].

furrier and **furring**. See under **fur**[1].

furrow *fur'ō*, *n* the trench made by a plough; a groove; a wrinkle. — *vt* to form furrows in; to groove; to wrinkle. — *adj* **furr'owy**. — **furr'ow-weed** (*Shakesp*) a weed common on ploughed land. [OE *furh*; cf Ger *Furche*, L *porca* ridge]

furry. See under **fur**[1].

furth *fûrth*, (*Scot*) *adv* forth; outside of. — **furthcom'ing** (*Scots law*) an action brought by an arrester against the arrestee and the common debtor after an arrestment in order that the arrested money or property be delivered to the arrester. — **furth of** outside; beyond the bounds of. [Variant of **forth**]

further[1] *fûr'dhər*, *adv* at or to a greater distance or degree; in addition. — *adj* more distant; additional, more or other. — *adv* **fur'thermore** in addition to what has been said, moreover or besides. — *adj* **fur'thermost** most remote. — *adv* **fur'thest** at or to the greatest distance. — *adj* most distant. — **further education** post-school education other than at university, polytechnic, etc; **further outlook** (*meteorol*) a general forecast given for a longer or more distant period than that covered by a more detailed forecast. — **see someone further** to see someone hanged, or similar. [OE *furthor* (adv), *furthra* (adj), from *fore* or *forth* with compar sfx *-ther*]

further[2] *fûr'dhər*, *vt* to promote or help forward. — *n* **fur'therance** a helping forward. — *n* **fur'therer** a promoter or advancer. — *adj* **fur'thersome** (*obs*) helpful; advantageous; rash. [OE *fyrthran*]

furtive *fûr'tiv*, *adj* stealthy; secret. — *adv* **fur'tively**. — *n* **fur'tiveness**. [L *fūrtīvus*, from *fūr* a thief]

furuncle *fū'rung-kl*, (*pathol*) *n* a boil. — *adj* **fūrun'cūlar** or **fūrun'cūlous**. — *n* **fūruncūlō'sis** the condition of having many boils; a highly infectious disease of salmon and related fish. [L *fūrunculus* literally, a little thief]

fury *fū'ri*, *n* rage; violent passion; madness; (with *cap*; *mythol*) any one of the three goddesses of vengeance, the Erinyes, or *euphem* Eumenides, namely Tisiphone, Alecto and Megaera (in *Milton* a Fate); hence, a passionate, violent woman. — *n* **fūrios'ity** madness. — *adj* **furious** (*fū'ri-əs*) full of fury or extremely angry;

violent or raging. — *adv* **fū'riously**. — *n* **fū'riousness**. — **fast and furious** see under **fast**[2]; **like fury** (*colloq*) furiously. [Fr *furie*, from L *furia*, from *furere* to be angry]

furze *fûrz*, *n* whin or gorse. — *adj* **furz'y** overgrown with furze. [OE *fyrs*]

fusain *fū-zān'*, *n* an important constituent of coal, resembling charcoal and consisting of plant remains from which the volatiles have been eliminated (also *fū'zān*); artists' fine charcoal; a drawing done with this. [Fr, the spindle-tree, or charcoal made from it]

fusarole or **fusarol** *fū'sə-rōl* or *-zə-*, (*archit*) *n* an astragal moulding, a semicircular moulding round a column, etc. [Fr *fusarolle*, from Ital *fusaruolo* spindle-whorl, from L *fūsus* spindle]

fuscous *fus'kəs*, *adj* brown; dingy. — Also (*Lamb*) **fusc**. [L *fuscus*]

fuse[1] *fūz*, *vt* to melt; to liquefy by heat; to join by, or as if by, melting together; to cause to fail by the melting of a fuse (*elec*). — *vi* to be melted; to be reduced to a liquid; to melt together; to blend or unite; (of an electric appliance) to fail by the melting of a fuse. — *n* a piece of fusible metal, with its mounting, inserted as a safeguard against overloading in an electric circuit. — *n* **fūsibil'ity** the degree of ease with which a substance can be fused. — *adj* **fūs'ible** able to be fused or easily fused. — *adj* **fū'sil** (*fū'zil*; *Milton*) cast; fusible; molten. — Also **fūsile** (*fū'zīl*, *-sīl* or *-zil*). — **fuse box** a box containing the switches and fuses for an electrical system; **fusible metal** any of numerous alloys containing bismuth, lead and tin (sometimes with mercury or cadmium) with low melting-points, *esp* in the range 60° to 180°C; **fū'sing-point** melting-point. [L *fundere*, *fūsum* to melt]

fuse[2] or (*esp US*) **fuze** *fūz*, *n* a train of combustible material in a waterproof covering, used with a detonator to initiate an explosion; any device used to explode a mine, bomb, etc under specified circumstances or at a specified time. — **burn** or **have a short fuse** to be quick-tempered. [Ital *fuso*, from L *fūsus* a spindle]

fusee[1] or **fuzee** *fū-zē'*, *n* the spindle in a watch or clock on which the chain is wound; a match with a long, oval head, for outdoor use; a fuse for firing explosives. [OFr *fusée* a spindleful, from L *fūsus* a spindle]

fusee[2]. Same as **fusil**[2].

fuselage *fū-zə-läzh'* or *fū'zil-ij*, *n* the body of an aeroplane. [Fr *fuseler* to shape like a spindle, from L *fūsus* a spindle]

fusel-oil *fū'zl-oil*, *n* a nauseous mixture of alcohols in spirits distilled from potatoes, grain, etc. [Ger *Fusel* bad spirits]

fushion and **fushionless**. See **foison**.

fusidic acid *fū-sid'ik a'sid*, *n* an antibiotic steroid, $C_{31}H_{48}O_6$. [From the fungus *Fusidium coccineum*, from which it was first isolated]

fusiform *fū'zi-förm*, *adj* spindle-shaped. [L *fūsus* a spindle, and *fōrma* shape]

fusil[1] *fū'zil*, (*heraldry*) *n* an elongated rhomboidal figure. [OFr *fusel*, from L *fūsus* a spindle]

fusil[2] *fū'zil*, *n* a flintlock musket. — *n* **fusilier'** or **fusileer'** formerly a soldier armed with a fusil, now simply a historical title borne by a few regiments; a member of such a regiment. — *n* **fusillade** (*-ād'*) a simultaneous or continuous discharge of firearms; anything assaulting one in a similar way, a barrage (*lit* and *fig*). — *n* **fusillā'tion** (*obs*) death by shooting. [OFr *fuisil* a flint-musket, same as Ital *focile*, from LL *focile* steel (to strike fire with), dimin of L *focus* a fireplace]

fusil[3] and **fusile**. See under **fuse**[1].

fusilli *fū-zil'i*, *n pl* pasta in the form of short, thick spirals. (Ital)

fusion[1] *fū'zhən*, *n* fusing; melting; the state of fluidity from heat; a close union of things, as if melted together; coalition (*US*); nuclear fusion (see under **nucleus**). — *n* **fū'sionism** a policy that favours union or coalition. — *n* **fū'sionist**. — **fusion bomb** one deriving its energy from the fusion of atomic nuclei, eg the hydrogen bomb; **fusion cones** same as **Seger cones**; **fusion energy** energy released by the process of nuclear fusion; **fusion music** music in which two or more different styles are combined; **fusion reactor** a nuclear reactor operating by nuclear fusion; **fusion welding** a process in which the weld is carried out solely by the melting of the metals to be joined, without any mechanical pressure. [Ety as for **fuse**[1]]

fusion[2] and **fusionless**. See **foison**.

fuss *fus*, *n* a bustle; flurry; (a) commotion, *esp* over trifling matters; petty ostentatious activity or attentions. — *vi* to be in a fuss or agitate about trifling matters. — *vt* to agitate or flurry. — *n* **fuss'er**. — *adv* **fuss'ily**. — *n* **fuss'iness**. — *adj* **fuss'y** given to making a fuss; finicky; requiring careful attention; over-elaborate. — **fuss'-pot** or (*US*) **fuss'-budget** a person who fusses. — **make a fuss of** to give much (genuinely or apparently) affectionate or amicable attention to. [Origin obscure]

fuss-ball. See under **fuzz**.

fust *fust*, *n* a mouldy or musty smell; the shaft of a column. — *vi* to mould; to smell mouldy; (of wine, etc) to taste of the cask. — *n* **fustilā'rian**, **fustilir'ian** or **fustillir'ian** (*Shakesp*) a term of abuse. — *n* **fust'ilugs** (*obs*) a gross overgrown person, *esp* a woman. — *adv* **fust'ily**. — *n* **fust'iness**. — *adj* **fust'y** (of wine) smelling of the cask; musty; stale; stuffy; old-fashioned; lacking freshness. [OFr *fust* (Fr *fût*) cask, from *fūstis* a cudgel]

fustanella *fus-tə-nel'ə*, *n* a white kilt worn by Greek and Albanian men. [Mod Gr *phoustanella*, dimin of *phoustani*, Albanian *fustan*, from Ital *fustagno* fustian]

fustet *fus'tət*, *n* the Venetian sumach tree or shrub (*Rhus cotinus*) or its wood, source of the dye called *young fustic*. [Fr, from Provençal *fustet*, from Ar *fustuq*; see **fustic**]

fustian *fus'chən*, *n* a kind of coarse, twilled cotton fabric including the varieties moleskin, velveteen, corduroy, etc; a pompous and unnatural style of writing or speaking; bombast; an alcoholic drink made of white wine with egg yolks, lemon, spices, etc. — *adj* made of fustian; bombastic. — *n* **fust'ianist** a person who writes bombast. — *vi* **fust'ianize** or **-ise** (*Holmes*) to write bombastically. [OFr *fustaigne* (Fr *futaine*), from Ital *fustagno*, from LL *fustāneum*, prob from *El-Fustāt* (Old Cairo) where it may have been made]

fustic *fus'tik*, *n* formerly, fustet (now called **young fustic**); now, the wood of a tropical American tree (*Chlorophora tinctoria*), yielding a yellow dye (also **old fustic**); this yellow die. — Also **fus'toc**. [Fr *fustoc*, from Sp *fustoc*, from Ar *fustuq*, from Gr *pistakē* pistachio]

fustigate *fus'ti-gāt*, (*obs*) *vt* to cudgel. — *n* **fustigā'tion**. [L *fūstīgāre*, *-ātum*, from *fūstis* a stick]

fustilugs, **fustily**, **fusty**, etc. See under **fust**.

fustoc. See **fustic**.

Fusus *fū'səs*, *n* a genus of gasteropods related to whelks, the spindle-shells. [L *fūsus* a spindle]

fut. *abbrev*: future.

futchel *fuch'əl*, *n* a piece of timber lengthwise in a carriage, supporting the splinter-bar and the pole.

futhork or **futhorc** *fōō'thörk* or **futhark** *-thärk*, *n* the Runic alphabet. [From the first six letters, *f*, *u*, *þ*(*th*), *o* or *a*, *r*, *k*]

futile *fū'tīl*, (*US*) *-təl*, *adj* ineffectual; trifling; tattling (*obs*). — *adv* **fu'tilely**. — *n* **futilitā'rian** a person who devotes himself or herself to profitless pursuits; a person who believes everything to be futile. — *n* **futil'ity** (*-til'iti*) uselessness. [L *fūtilis* leaky or futile, from *fundere* to pour]

futon *fōō'ton*, *n* a type of sofa bed of Japanese design, a simple low frame with a mattress laid loosely on top; more properly, the mattress alone. [Jap]

futtock *fut'ək*, (*naut*) *n* one of the curved timbers of a wooden ship, a rib. — **futt'ock-plate** an iron plate with dead-eyes, for the topmast or topgallant rigging. — *n pl* **futt'ock-shrouds** short pieces of rope or chain securing the futtock-plates to a band round a lower mast. [Perh for **foot-hook**]

future *fū'chər*, *adj* about to be; that is to come; expressive of time to come (*gram*). — *n* time to come; life, fate or condition in time to come; prospects or likelihood of future success; the future tense (*gram*); (in *pl*) commodities or securities traded at an agreed price, to be delivered and paid for at a specified future date. — *adj* **fut'ureless** without prospects. — *n* **fut'urism** (*art*) a movement claiming to anticipate or point the way for the future, *esp* a 20c revolt against tradition. — *n* **fut'urist** a person whose chief interests are in what is to come; a believer in futurism. — *adj* **futurist'ic** of or relating to futurism; so modern (in design, concept, etc) as to appear to belong to some future time. — *n* **futurit'ion** future existence; accomplishment; futurity. — *n* **futurity** (*fū-tū'ri-ti*) time to come; an event, or state of being, yet to come. — *adj* **futurolog'ical**. — *n* **futurol'ogist**. — *n* **futurol'ogy** the science and study of sociological and technological developments, values and trends, with a view to planning for the future. — *adj* **future perfect** (*gram*) expressive of action viewed as past in reference to an assumed future time, in English formed using *will have* or *shall have*. — *n* the future perfect tense; a verb in that tense. — **future studies** futurology. [Fr *futur*, from L *futūrus*, used as future participle of *esse* to be]

fu yung *fōō yōōng*, *n* a Chinese omelette-like dish with bean sprouts, onion, meat, etc. — Also **foo yung** or **foo yong** (*yong*). [Chin, hibiscus]

fuze. See **fuse**[2].

fuzee. See **fusee**[1].

fuzz *fuz*, *n* light fine particles or fibres, eg of dust; fluff; blurr; police (*slang*). — *vi* to disintegrate in fuzz. — *adv* **fuzz'ily**. — *n* **fuzz'iness**. — *adj* **fuzz'y** covered with fuzz; fluffy; with many small tight curls; blurred. — **fuzz'-ball** or **fuss'-ball** a puff-ball fungus. — *adj* **fuzz'y-haired'**. — **fuzzy logic** a computerized form of logic used in machines where finer than usual interpretative distinctions need to be made, rather than coarse binary ones; **fuzz'y-wuzz'y** (*offensive*) a Sudanese soldier (*old colloq, esp military*); a coloured native of any of various countries, *esp* if fuzzy-haired (*slang*). [Origin doubtful]

fuzzle *fuz'l*, (*dialect*) *vt* to fuddle.

fwd *abbrev*: forward; four-wheel drive; front-wheel drive.

FX *abbrev*: (sound or special) effects.

fy *fī*, *interj*. Same as **fie**[1].

fya *abbrev*: first-year allowance.

fyke[1]. Same as **fike**.

fyke[2] *fīk*, (*US*) *n* a bag-net for keeping fish in. [Du *fuik*]

fyle. A Spenserian form of **file**[1,2].

fylfot or **filfot** *fil'fot*, *n* a swastika, *esp* one turned counter-clockwise. [Prob from misunderstanding of a manuscript, *fylfot* = fill-foot, really meaning a device for filling the foot of a painted window]

fynbos *fān'bös*, (*Afrik*) *n* (an area of) low shrubs. [Afrik, from Dutch *fijn* fine or delicate, and *bosch* bush]

fyrd *fûrd* or *fērd*, *n* any of the local militia of Anglo-Saxon times, in which service was compulsory for many. [OE *fyrd* army]

fytte. See **fit**[3].

fz (*music*) *abbrev*: sforzando.

FZS *abbrev*: Fellow of the Zoological Society.

G

G or **g** *jē*, *n* the seventh letter of the modern English alphabet, and of the Roman; *orig* a form of C, inserted in the place of the disused Z, its ordinary sound (as in Latin) a voiced guttural stop, but in some words in English the same as J; the fifth note of the diatonic scale of C major — also called *sol* (*music*); the scale or key having that note for its tonic (*music*). — **G'-clef** a clef, the treble clef, on the second line of the treble stave, marking G; **G'-string** the lowest string on the violin, tuned to the note of G, or a string tuned to G on another instrument (*music*); same as **gee-string**.

G or **G**. *abbrev*: Gauss; German (as in **G-agents**); giga- (10^9); good; gourde; Government (as in **G-man**). — **G'-agents** highly effective poisonous gases developed by the Nazis for possible military use; **G'-man** (*US*) an agent of the Federal Bureau of Investigation.

G *symbol*: (or ***G***) the constant of gravitation, the factor linking force with mass and distance; (or ***G***) conductance (*phys*); 400 (as a medieval Roman numeral; $\bar{G}$ = 400 000); general intelligence.

g or **g**. *abbrev*: gallon(s); good; gram(s) or gramme(s).

g symbol: acceleration due to gravity. — **g'-suit** a close-fitting suit with cells that inflate to prevent flow of blood away from the head, worn by airmen as a defence against blackout due to high acceleration and resultant great increase in weight.

G5, **G7**, **G10**, etc or (*US*) **G-5**, **G-7**, **G-10**, etc *abbrev*: Group of Five, Seven, Ten, etc (qv under **group**).

GA *abbrev*: General Assembly; general average; Georgia (US state; also **Ga**.).

Ga (*chem*) *symbol*: gallium.

gab[1] *gab*, (*colloq*) *vi* to chatter or prate: — *pr p* **gabb'ing**; *pa t* and *pa p* **gabbed**. — *n* idle or fluent talk; the mouth. — *n* **gabb'er** a chatterer. — *adj* **gabb'y** garrulous. — **gab'fest** (*slang*; chiefly *US*) a gathering characterized by much talk or gossip; a prolonged conversation, discussion, etc. — **the gift of the gab** a talent (or propensity) for talking. [Origin doubtful; possibly variant of **gob**[1]]

gab[2] *gab*, (*obs*) *n* mockery; a jest; a vaunt or boast. — *vi* to brag. [OFr *gabber* to mock]

gab[3] *gab*, *n* a Scots form of **gob**[1].

gabardine. See **gaberdine**.

gabbart *gab'ərt*, (*esp Scot*) *n* a barge. — Also **gabb'ard**. [Fr *gabare*, from Provençal and Ital *gabarra*]

gabble *gab'l*, *vi* to talk inarticulately; to chatter; to cackle like geese. — *n* **gabb'le** a noise as of unintelligible chatter. — *n* **gabb'ler**. — *n* **gabb'ling** or **gabb'lement**. [Perh frequentative of **gab**[1], perh MDu *gabbelen*; imit]

gabbro *gab'rō*, *n* a coarsely crystalline igneous rock composed of labradorite or similar plagioclase and pyroxene, often with olivine and magnetite: — *pl* **gabb'ros**. — *adj* **gabbro'ic** or **gabbroitic** (*-it'ik*). — *adj* **gabb'roid** resembling gabbro. [Ital]

gabelle *gab-el'*, *n* a tax, *esp* formerly in France, on salt. — *n* **gabell'er** a collector of gabelle. [Fr *gabelle*, from LL *gabella*, *gablum*; of Gmc origin]

gaberdine or **gabardine** *gab'ər-dēn*, *n* a loose cloak, *esp* a Jew's (*hist*); a closely woven twill fabric, *esp* of cotton and wool; a coat of this material. [OFr *gauvardine*; perh MHGer *wallevart* pilgrimage, whence also Sp *gabardina*, etc]

gaberlunzie *gab-ər-lün'i* or *-yi*, and later *-lun'zi*, (*Scot*) *n* a beggar's pouch; a strolling beggar, *orig* a bluegown.

gabfest. See under **gab**[1].

gabion *gā'bi-ən*, *n* a wickerwork or wire basket of earth or stones used for embankment work, etc in fortification and engineering; a small curiosity (*Scott*). — *n* **gā'bionade** (*fortif*) a work formed of gabions. — *n* **gā'bionage** gabions collectively. — *adj* **gā'bioned** furnished with gabions. [Fr, from Ital *gabbione* a large cage, from *gabbia*, from L *cavea* a cage]

gable *gā'bl*, (*archit*) *n* the triangular part of an exterior wall of a building between the top of the side-walls and the slopes on the roof; a gable-shaped structure over a window or door. — Also (*Scot*) **gā'vel**. — *adj* **gā'bled**. — *n* **gā'blet** (*dimin*) a small gable over a niche, buttress, tabernacle, etc. — **gable end** the end-wall of a building on the side where there is a gable; **gable window** a window in a gable end; a window with its upper part shaped like a gable. [The northern form *gavel* is prob ON *gafl*; Swed *gafvel*, Dan *gavl*; the southern form *gable* is prob through OFr *gable*, from ON *gafl*]

gabnash *gab'nash*, (*Scot*) *n* prattle; chatter; a pert prattler. [Cf **nashgab**]

gaby *gā'bi*, (*dialect*) *n* a simpleton. [Origin unknown]

gad[1] *gad*, *n* a metal spike or pointed bar (*obs*); a miner's wedge or chisel; a spear (*obs*; also **gade** or **gaid** *gād*); an engraver's stylus (*Shakesp*); a rod or stick (*obs*); a goad (*dialect*); the bar across a Scottish condemned cell, on which the iron ring ran which fastened the shackles (*hist*). — *n* **gad'ling** (*obs*) one of the spikes on the knuckles of a gauntlet. — **upon the gad** (*Shakesp*) on the spur of the moment. [ON *gaddr* a spike; confused with OE *gād*; see **goad**]

gad[2] *gad*, *interj* a minced form of **God**. — *interj* **gadzooks'** (*archaic*) an *obs* minced oath (*appar* for *God's hooks*; see **gadso**).

gad[3] *gad*, *vi* to rush here and there in a wayward uncontrolled manner (*obs*); to wander about, often restlessly, idly or in pursuit of pleasure (often with *about*); to straggle: — *pr p* **gadd'ing**; *pa t* and *pa p* **gadd'ed**. — *n* wandering, gadding about. — *n* **gadd'er**. — **gad'about** a person who wanders restlessly from place to place, or who goes about idly looking for amusement, etc. [Back-formation from OE *gædeling* companion, later vagabond]

Gadarene *gad'ə-rēn*, *adj* indicative of mass panic and headlong flight towards disaster. [From the swine of *Gadara*, Matthew 8.28]

gade. See **gad**[1] and **Gadus**.

gadfly *gad'flī*, *n* a bloodsucking fly (Tabanus) that distresses cattle; sometimes applied to a botfly; a mischievous gadabout; someone who provokes and irritates, *esp* deliberately. [**gad**[1] or OE *gād* (see **goad**) and **fly**]

gadge *gaj*, (*Browning*) *n* an instrument of torture.

gadget *gaj'it*, *n* any small ingenious device; a what-d'you-call-it. — *n* **gadgeteer'** someone who delights in gadgets. — *n* **gad'getry** gadgets; the making of gadgets. [Origin obscure]

gadgie or **gadje** *gaj'i*, **gaudgie** or **gauje** *gö'ji*, (*dialect*; usu *derog*) *n* a fellow. [Orig variants of **gorgio**]

Gadhel *gad'əl*, *n* a Gael, a Celt of the branch to which the Irish, the Scottish Highlanders, and the Manx belong. — *adj* **Gadhelic** (*-el'ik*, *-ēl'ik*, or *gad'*) relating to the Gaels (the Celts of Ireland, the Highlands of Scotland, and the Isle of Man) or their languages. — *n* the Q-Celtic language of this group; the Celtic language group to which Irish, Scottish Gaelic and Manx belong. See also **Gael** and **Goidel**. [Ir *Gaedheal* (pl *Gaedhil*)]

gadi *gäd'ē* or *gud'ē*, *n* an Indian throne. [Marathi *gādī*, Bengali *gadī*]

Gadidae. See **Gadus**.

gadje. See **gadgie**.

gadling[1] *gad'ling*, (*obs*) *n* a vagabond. [OE *gædeling*, orig companion]

gadling[2]. See **gad**[1].

gado-gado *gä'dō-gä'dō*, *n* a Malaysian dish of mixed vegetables, hard-boiled egg and peanut sauce.

gadoid. See under **Gadus**.

gadolinite *gad'ə-lin-īt*, *n* a silicate of yttrium, beryllium and iron. — *n* **gadolin'ium** a metallic element of the rare earths (symbol **Gd**; atomic no 64). [From the Finnish chemist *Gadolin* (1760–1852)]

gadroon or **godroon** *gə-drōōn'*, *n* an embossed, cable- or bead-like decoration used as an edging on silverware, etc. — *adj* **gadrooned'** or **godrooned'**. — *n* **gadroon'ing** or **godroon'ing**. [Fr *godron*]

gadsman *gadz'mən*, (*obs Scot*) *n* a person who drives horses at the plough. [**gad**[1], or OE *gād* (see **goad**), and **man**]

gadso *gad'sō*, (*archaic*) *interj* expressing surprise: — *pl* **gad'sos**. [Ital *cazzo* the penis, assimilated to **gad**[2]]

Gadus *gā'dəs*, *n* the cod genus, typical of the family **Gadidae** (*gad'i-dē*). — *n* **gade** or **gad'oid** a fish of the genus Gadus, to which the cod and hake belong. — *adj* **gad'oid** belonging to, or resembling, this genus. [Latinized from Gr *gados* the hake or similar fish]

gadwall *gad'wöl*, *n* a northern freshwater duck. [Origin unknown]

gadzooks. See **gad**[2].

gae[1] *gā*, a Scots form of **go**: — *pr p* **gaun**; *pa t* **gaed**; *pa p* **gane**.

gae[2]. See **gie**[1].

Gaea *gī'ə* or *jē'ə*, **Gaia** *gī'ə* or *gā'ə*, or **Ge** *gā* or *jē*, *n* in Greek mythology the goddess or personification of Earth, mother of Uranus and (by him) of Oceanus, Cronus and the Titans; (*usu* **Gaia**) Earth apprehended as a living entity within the solar system. — **Gaea** or **Gaia hypothesis** the hypothesis stating that natural life systems find their own balances. [Gr]

Gaekwar, **Gaikwar** or **Guicowar** *gīk'wär*, *n* the title given to the ruler of the former Indian state of Baroda. [Marathi *gāekwār* cowherd]

Gael *gāl*, *n* a Celt of the Scottish Highlands, Ireland or the Isle of Man, *esp* one who speaks Gaelic. — *n* **Gael'dom**. — *adj* **Gaelic** (*gāl'ik* or *gal'ik*) pertaining to the Gaels or their languages; relating to sports, such as shinty and hurling, played especially in, or originating in, Ireland and the Scottish Highlands. — *n* any of the Celtic languages of Ireland, the Scottish Highlands and the Isle of Man, *esp* (*usu gal'ik*) that of the Scottish Highlands. — *n* **gael'icism** (*-sizm*). — *vt* **gael'icize or -ise** (*-sīz*). — **Gaelic coffee** same as **Irish coffee**; **Gaelic football** a form of football, played mainly in Ireland, between teams of 15 players, using a round ball which may be kicked, bounced or punched, but not thrown or run with. — See also **Goidel**. [Scottish Gaelic *Gaidheal*]

Gael. *abbrev*: Gaelic.

Gaeltacht *gāl'tähht*, *n* the Irish-speaking districts of Ireland. [Ir *gaedhealtacht*]

gaff[1] *gaf*, *n* a hook used *esp* for landing large fish; the spar to which the head of a fore-and-aft sail is fastened (*naut*). — *vt* to hook or bind by means of a gaff. — *adj* **gaff'-rigged** (of a vessel) having a gaff. — **gaff sail** a sail attached to the gaff; **gaff'-topsail** a small sail, the head of which is extended on a small gaff which hoists on the top mast, and the foot on the lower gaff. [Fr *gaffe*]

gaff[2] *gaf*, (*slang*) *n* a low-grade or cheap theatre; a fair; a house or other building, *orig* as the site of a burglary; one's private accommodation, apartment, flat, room, pad, etc. [Origin obscure]

gaff[3]. See **gaffe**.

gaff[4] *gaf*, (*slang*) *vi* to gamble. — *n* **gaff'er**. — *n* **gaff'ing**. [Origin obscure]

gaff[5] *gaf*, (*slang*) *n* humbug, nonsense. — **blow the gaff** to disclose a secret, to blab. [Prob connected with **gab**[2] or **gaff**[3]; cf OE *gegaf-sprǣc* scurrility]

gaffe or (*rare*) **gaff** *gaf*, *n* a blunder. [Fr *gaffe*]

gaffer[1] *gaf'ər*, *n orig* a word of respect applied to an old man, now *archaic*, *dialect* or *derog* in this sense (*fem* **gammer**); the foreman of a squad of workmen; (*orig US*) the senior electrician responsible for the lighting in a television or film studio; a master glass-blower. [**grandfather** or **godfather**]

gaffer[2], **gaffing**. See **gaff**[4].

gag[1] *gag*, *vt* to stop up the mouth of forcibly; to silence; to prevent free expression by (the press, etc); to choke up. — *vi* to choke; to retch: — *pr p* **gagg'ing**; *pa t* and *pa p* **gagged**. — *n* something put into the mouth or over it to enforce silence (also *fig*), or to distend jaws during an operation; the closure applied in a debate; a nauseous mouthful, boiled fat beef (*Lamb*). — *n* **gagg'er** a person who gags. — **gag'-bit** a powerful bit used in breaking horses; **gag'-rein** a rein arranged so as to make the bit more powerful. [Prob imitative of sound made in choking]

gag[2] *gag*, (*slang*) *vt* to deceive. — *vi* to practise deception or fraud. — *n* a made-up story, lie. [Possibly **gag**[1]]

gag[3] *gag*, (*colloq*) *n* a joke; a hoax; an actor's (*esp* comic) interpolation or improvisation of his or her part. — *vi* to introduce a gag; to joke, make gags. — *vt* to introduce a gag into: — *pr p* **gagg'ing**; *pa t* and *pa p* **gagged**. — *n* **gag'ster** (*colloq*) a person who tells jokes, a comedian. — **gag'man** a person who writes gags; a comedian. [Poss **gag**[1]]

gaga *gä'gä*, (*slang*) *adj* fatuous; in senile dotage. [Fr]

gagaku *gä-gä'kōō*, or *gä'gä-*, *n* a type of Japanese classical music played mainly on ceremonial occasions at the Japanese court. [Jap, from *ga* graceful, noble, and *gaku* music]

gage[1] *gāj*, *n* a pledge (*archaic*); something thrown down as a challenge, *esp* a glove (*hist*). — *vt* to bind by pledge or security (*obs*); to offer as a guarantee (*obs*); to stake, wager (*obs* or *archaic*). [OFr *guage*; Gmc; see **wage**, **wed**]

gage[2]. See **gauge**.

gage[3] *gāj*, *n*. Same as **greengage**.

gage[4] *gāj*, (*drug-taking slang*) *n* marijuana. — Also **gauge**.

G-agent. See under **G**.

gaggle *gag'l*, *n* a flock of geese on water, in contrast to a *skein* in the air; a group or knot, *usu* of garrulous or animated people. — *vi* to cackle. — *n* **gagg'ling** cackling. — *adj* garrulous. [Prob imit]

gag-tooth *gag'-tōōth*, *n* a projecting tooth. — *adj* **gag'-toothed**.

gahnite *gän'īt*, *n* a zinc spinel. [J G *Gahn* (1745–1818), Swedish chemist]

Gaia. See **Gaea**.

gaid. See **gad**[1].

Gaidhealtachd *gä'yal-tähht*, *n* the Gaelic-speaking districts of Scotland. [Gaelic]

gaiety, **gaily**. See under **gay**.

gaijin *gī'jēn* or *-jin*, (*Jap*) *n* a foreigner: — *pl* **gaijin**.

Gaikwar. See **Gaekwar**.

gaillard or **gaillarde** *gal'yərd*. *Obs* spellings of **galliard**.

gain[1] *gān*, *vt* to obtain to one's advantage; to earn; to win; to be successful in; to increase (eg speed, weight, height, momentum); to draw to one's own party; to reach. — *vi* to profit; to become or appear better, to progress; (of a clock, etc) to go fast by so much in a given time. — *n* that which is gained; profit; an instance of gaining, a win; ratio of actual power delivered to that which would be delivered if an amplifier were not used (*telecomm*); ratio of output and input voltages (*telecomm*); volume control in amplifier or receiving set, *usu* a potentiometer (*telecomm*; also **gain control**). — *adj* **gain'able**. — *n* **gain'er**. — *adj* **gain'ful** lucrative; profitable; engaged in for pay, paid. — *adv* **gain'fully**. — *n* **gain'fulness**. — *n pl* **gain'ings**. — *adj* **gain'less**. — *n* **gain'lessness**. — **gain ground** to grow in influence, become more widely accepted; **gain on** or **upon** to get closer to, catch up on; to overtake by degrees; to increase one's advantage against; **gain time** to contrive a delay by temporizing, etc. [OFr *gain*, *gaain*, *gaigner*, *gaaignier*, from Gmc, as in OHGer *weidenen* to graze, to seek forage, and *weida* pasture]

gain[2] *gān*, (*dialect*) *adj* near, straight; convenient. [ON *gegn*]

gaingiving *gān'giv-ing*, (*Shakesp*) *n* misgiving.

gainly *gān'li*, (*dialect*) *adj* shapely; comely; graceful. [**gain**[2]]

gainsay *gān-sā'* or *gān'sā*, *vt* to contradict; to deny; to dispute: — *prp* **gainsay'ing** (or *gān'*); *pat* and *pap* **gainsaid** (*gān-sād'*, *-sed'*, or *gān'*); *3rd pers sing present indicative* **gainsays** (*-sāz*). — *n* **gain'say** (or *-sā'*) denial. — *n* **gainsay'er** (*Bible*) an opposer. — *n* **gainsay'ing**. [OE *gegn* against, and **say**]

gainst or **'gainst** *genst*. A poetic abbreviation of **against**.

gainstrive *gān-strīv'*, (*obs*) *vt* to strive against. — *vi* to resist.

gair *gār*, (*Scot*) *n* a gore (of cloth or land). [See **gore**[2]]

gairfowl. Same as **garefowl**.

gait[1] *gāt*, *n* way of walking; the pattern of leg-movements used by a horse in trotting, cantering, galloping, etc. — *vt* to teach (a horse) its gaits. — *combining form* **-gait'ed** having a particular gait, eg *slow-gaited*. [**gate**[2]]

gait[2] *gāt*, (*dialect*) *n* a sheaf of corn set on end.

gait[3] or **gaitt** (*Scott*) spellings of **get** (a child) and **gyte**[2].

gaiter *gāt'ər*, *n* a covering for the (lower leg and) ankle, fitting over the upper of the shoe. [Fr *guêtre*]

gajo. See **gorgio**.

Gal. (*Bible*) *abbrev*: (the Letter to the) Galatians.

gal[1] *gal*, *dialect* for **girl**.

gal[2] *gal*, (*phys*) *n* an unit of acceleration, one centimetre per second per second. [*Gal*ileo; see **Galilean**[1]]

gal. *abbrev*: gallon(s).

gala *gä'lə* or *gā'lə*, *n* a festivity; a sporting occasion, with competitions, etc. — *adj* of the nature of, or suitable for, a great occasion or festivity. — **ga'la-dress** festive costume for a gala day. [Fr *gala* show, from Ital *gala* finery]

galabiah, **galabiyah**. See **gallabea**.

galactic[1] *gə-lak'tik*, *adj* relating to or obtained from milk (*med*). — *n* **galac'tagogue** (*-tə-gog*; Gr *agōgos* bringing) a medicine that promotes secretion of milk. — *n* **galactom'eter** (Gr *metron* measure) an instrument for finding the specific gravity of milk. — *adj* **galactoph'orous** (Gr *phoros* bringing; *zool*) milk-carrying. — *adj* **galactopoiet'ic** (Gr *poiētikos* productive) milk-producing. — *n* **galactorrhoea** (*-rē'ə*; Gr *rhoiā* a flow; *med*) a too abundant flow of milk. — *n* **galac'tose** a sugar, ($C_6H_{12}O_6$), obtained by hydrolysis from lactose. — *n* **galactosaemia** (*-sēm'i-ə*; *med*) the presence of galactose in the blood. [Gr *gala*, *galaktos* milk]

galactic[2]. See **Galaxy**.

galage *gəl-āj'*. An obsolete form of **galosh** (*n*).

galago *gä-lā'gō*, *n* a large-eared, long-tailed nocturnal African lemur of the genus *Galago*, a bushbaby: — *pl* **gala'gos**. [Perh Wolof *golokh* monkey]

galah *gə-lä'*, *n* an Australian cockatoo with a grey back and pink underparts; a fool (*Austr slang*). [Aboriginal]

Galahad *gal'ə-had*, *n* a person notable for nobility and integrity of character. [From Sir *Galahad* in Arthurian legend, the noblest knight of the Round Table]

Galam butter *gä-läm' but'ər*, *n* shea butter. [*Galam*, a district in Senegal]

galanga, **galangal**. See **galingale**.

galant *gə-länt'*, *adj* of a musical style, current in the 18c, characterized by lightness, elegance and technical accomplishment. [Fr]

galantine *gal'ən-tēn* or *-tin*, *n* a dish of poultry, veal, etc served cold in jelly. [Fr; see **gelatine**]

galanty show *gəl-an'ti shō*, *n* a shadow pantomime. [Prob Ital *galanti*, pl of *galante*; see **gallant**]

galapago *gə-lap'ə-gō*, *n* a tortoise: — *pl* **galap'agos**. [Sp]

galatea *gal-ə-tē'ə*, *n* a cotton fabric *usu* with coloured stripe. [19c HMS *Galatea*]

Galaxy *gal'ək-si*, *n* the disc-shaped system, composed of spiralling arms of stars, that contains our solar system near its edge; (without *cap*) any similar system or 'universe'; (without *cap*) a splendid assemblage. — *adj* **galac'tic** relating to a galaxy or galaxies. — **galactic plane** the plane that passes through the centre of the bulging disc formed by the spiral arms of the Galaxy. [Through Fr and L, from Gr *galaxias* the Milky Way (*orig* also the meaning of **galaxy**), from *gala*, *-aktos* milk]

galbanum *gal'bə-nəm*, *n* an aromatic gum-resin obtained from several umbelliferous Asian plants. [L, from Gr *chalbanē*, prob an Eastern word]

galdragon *gal'drə-gən*, (*Scott*) *n* an obsolete Shetland word for a sorceress or witch. [ON *galdra-kona*, from *galdr* crowing, incantation, witchcraft, and *kuna* woman]

gale[1] *gāl*, *n* a strong wind of between about 30 and 60 mph, force 8 on the Beaufort scale; a gentle wind (*old poetic*); a wafted smell (*old poetic*); an outburst (*fig*). [Origin obscure]

gale[2] *gāl*, *n* (*usu* **sweet'-gale**) bog-myrtle. [Prob OE *gagel*; cf Ger *Gagel*]

gale[3] *gāl*, *n* a periodic payment of rent; a mining licence; the piece of land for which the licence is granted. [Perh **gavel**[2]]

galea *gal'i-ə* or *gāl'i-ə*, (*biol*) *n* a helmet-shaped structure. — *adj* **gal'eate** or **gal'eated**. [L *galea* a helmet]

galena *gə-lē'nə*, *n* lead sulphide, the commonest ore of lead, occurring as grey cubic crystals. — Also **galē'nite**. — *adj* **galē'noid**. [L *galēna* lead-ore]

galengale. See **galingale**.

Galenic *gə-len'ik*, *adj* relating to *Galen* (*Galēnos*), the 2c Greek physician, or to his methods and theories. — *adj* **Galen'ical**. — *n* a remedy such as Galen prescribed, a vegetable simple. — *n* **Galenism** (*gā'lən-izm*). — *n* **Gā'lenist**.

galenite, **galenoid**. See **galena**.

Galeopithecus *gā-li-ō-pi-thē'kəs*, or *-pith'*, *n* the so-called flying lemur. — *adj* **galeopithē'cine** (*-sīn*) or **galeopithē'coid**. [Gr *galeē* weasel, marten, and *pithēkos* ape]

galère *ga-ler'*, *n* a group of (*esp* undesirable) people; an unpleasant situation. [Fr, literally galley]

galette *gə-let'*, *n* a round, flat, sweet or savoury cake. [Fr]

Galician *gə-lith'i-ən*, or *-lish'*, *adj* of or relating to the former kingdom, now an autonomous region, of *Galicia* in NW Spain; (not *-lith'*) of or relating to *Galicia*, a region in E central Europe, now partly in Poland, partly in Ukraine. — *n* a native or citizen of Galicia; the dialect language of Galicia in NW Spain, closely related to Portuguese.

Galilean[1] *gal-i-lē'ən*, *adj* of or pertaining to *Galileo*, the great Italian mathematician (1564–1642).

Galilean[2] *gal-i-lē'ən*, *adj* of or pertaining to *Galilee* (L *Galilaea*, Gr *Galilaiā*), one of the Roman divisions of Palestine. — *n* a native of Galilee; a Christian (*archaic*).

galilee *gal'i-lē*, (*archit*) *n* a porch or chapel at the west end of some churches, in which penitents were placed, and where ecclesiastics met women who had business with them. — **galilee porch** a galilee in direct communication with the exterior. [Perh suggested by Mark 16.7, or Matthew 4.15]

galimatias *gal-i-mā'shi-əs* or *-mat'i-äs*, (*rare*) *n* nonsense; any confused mixture of unrelated things. [Fr]

galingale *gal'ing-gāl*, *n* the aromatic rootstock of certain E Indian plants of the ginger family (*Alpinia* and *Kaempferia*), formerly much used like ginger; the rootstock of a sedge (*Cyperus longus*), of ancient medicinal repute; also the whole plant. — Also **gal'angal** (*gal'ən-gal*), **gal'engale** or **galang'a**. [OFr *galingal*, from Ar *khalanjān*, from Chin *ko-liang-kiang*, from *Ko* a district near Canton, *liang* mild, and *kiang* ginger]

galiongee *gal-yən-jē'*, *n* a Turkish sailor. [Turk *qālyūnjī*, derivative of *qālyūn*, from Ital *galeone* galleon]

galiot. See **galliot**.

galipot *gal'i-pot*, *n* the turpentine that exudes from the cluster pine. [Fr]

gall[1] *göl*, *n* bile, the greenish-yellow fluid secreted from the liver (*old*); bitterness; malignity; assurance, presumption, impudence. — *adj* **gall'-less** without gall; mild;

free from rancour. — **gall bladder** a muscular sac close to or at the edge of the liver in vertebrates, which stores and concentrates bile, and releases it into the intestine; **gall duct** a tube for conveying bile or gall; **gall'sickness** or **gall'-sickness** (*SAfr*) a tick-borne disease affecting the livers of cattle, sheep and goats (Du *galziekte*); **gall'stone** a concretion in the gall bladder or biliary ducts. [OE *galla*, *gealla* gall; cf Ger *Galle*, Gr *cholē*, L *fel*]

gall[2] *göl*, *n* an abnormal growth on a plant caused by a parasite such as an insect or fungus, or by bacteria. — *n* **gallate** (*gal'āt*) a salt of gallic acid. — **gallfly** (*göl'*-) or **gall wasp** an insect of the hymenopterous family Cynipidae that causes galls by depositing its eggs in plants; **gall midge** a Cecidomyia or similar gall-making midge; **gall'nut** a nutlike gall produced on an oak by a gall wasp, used *esp* formerly for making ink. [Fr *galle*, from L *galla* oak-apple]

gall[3] *göl*, *n* a painful swelling, *esp* in a horse; a sore due to chafing; a state or cause of irritation; a chafed place; a bare place (*archaic*); a flaw (*archaic*; *Scot*); a fault or a dyke (*mining*). — *vt* to fret or hurt by rubbing; to irritate. — *vi* to become chafed; to scoff (*Shakesp*). — *adj* **gall'ing** irritating. — *adv* **gall'ingly**. [OE *galla*, *gealla* a sore place]

gall. *abbrev*: gallon(s).

gallabea(h), **gallabia(h)**, **gallabieh**, **gallabiya(h)**, **gallabiyeh**, also **galabea(h)**, **galabia(h)**, etc, *gal-ä'bi-ya* or *-bē'a*, *n* a loose-fitting cloak worn *esp* by Arabs; a djellaba. [See **djellaba**]

gallant *gal'ənt*, *adj* brave; noble; gay, splendid, magnificent (*rare*); attentive (*esp* formally or obsequiously) to ladies; amorous (sometimes *gə-lant'* in the last two senses). — *n* a dashing, debonair young man; a man (*archaic*; woman *obs*) of fashion; a lover (also *gə-lant'* in this sense). — *adv* **gall'antly**. — *n* **gall'antness**. — *n* **gall'antry** bravery; intrepidity; attention or devotion to ladies; a chivalrous attention or remark; amorous intrigue; gallants collectively (*Shakesp*). — **the honourable and gallant member** a mode of referring in parliament to a member who is an officer in the fighting services. [Fr *galant*, from OFr *gale* a merrymaking; prob Gmc; cf **gala**]

galleass *gal'i-as*, (*hist*) *n* a vessel of the same construction as a galley, but larger and heavier. — Also **gall'iass**. [OFr *galeace*, from Ital *galeazza*, augmentative from *galea* galley]

galleon *gal'i-ən*, *n* a large vessel with a high stem and stern, mostly used formerly by Spaniards for carrying treasure. [Sp *galeón*; cf **galley**]

galleria *gal-ə-rē'ə*, *n* a shopping-arcade. [Ital, arcade]

gallery *gal'ə-ri*, *n* a covered walk; a long balcony; a long passage; a long, narrow room; an upper floor of seats, *esp* in a theatre, *usu* the highest; the occupants of the gallery; a body of spectators; a room or building for the exhibition of works of art; a photographer's studio; in a television studio, a soundproof room overlooking the action, for the director or lighting engineer; an underground passage, drift or level. — *vt* to tunnel. — *adj* **gall'eried** furnished with, or made in the form of, a gallery or arcade. — *n* **gall'eryite** a person who frequents the gallery in the theatre. — **play to the gallery** to play for the applause of, or seek popularity with, the least cultured and least sophisticated section of one's audience. [OFr *galerie* (Ital *galleria*)]

gallet *gal'ət*, (*building*, etc) *n* a small pebble or stone chip. — *vt* to fill in mortar joints with gallets: — *pr p* **gall'eting**; *pa t* and *pa p* **gall'eted**. [Fr *galet* a pebble, from OFr *gal*]

galley *gal'i*, *n* a long, low-built ship with one deck, propelled by oars and sails; a Greek or Roman warship; a large open rowing-boat; the cooking area on board a ship, boat or aircraft; a flat oblong tray for type that has been set up (*printing*); a galley proof (*printing*). — **gall'ey-foist** (*obs*) a state barge; **galley proof** the first proof taken after text has been typeset (traditionally from type on a galley) and before it is made up into pages, a slip-proof; in photocomposition, an early proof before make-up; **galley slave** a person condemned to work as a slave at the oar of a galley (*hist*; also *fig*); a drudge; **gall'ey-worm** a myriapod. [OFr *galie*, *galee*, from LL *galea*]

galley-west *gal-i-west'*, (*US slang*) *adv* into confusion or unconsciousness. [Eng dialect *collywest*, perh from Northamptonshire village *Collyweston*]

galliambic *gal-i-am'bik*, *adj* in or of a metre (⏑⏑—⏑— ⏑——|⏑⏑—⏑) said to have been used by the Phrygian priests of Cybele, best known from the *Attis* of Catullus. — *n pl* **galliam'bics** galliambic verses. [Gr *galliambikos*, from Gallos a priest of Cybele, and *iambos* an iamb]

galliard *gal'yərd*, *adj* (*archaic*) brisk, lively. — *n* a spirited dance for two, in triple time, common in the 16c and 17c; a lively, fashionable fellow (*archaic*). — *n* **gall'iardise** (*archaic*; *-ēz* or *-īz*) gaiety; a merry trick. [OFr *gaillard*]

galliass. See **galleass**.

galli-bagger, **-beggar**, etc. See **gally**.

Gallic *gal'ik*, *adj* relating to Gaul or the ancient Gauls; relating to France or the French. — *adj* **Gall'ican** of or relating to Gallicanism; *esp* relating to the Roman Catholic Church in France, regarded as national and more or less independent. — *n* a person holding Gallican doctrines. — *n* **Gall'icanism** the spirit of nationalism within the French Church — as opposed to *Ultramontanism*, or the absolute subjection of everything to the personal authority of the pope. — *adv* **Gallice** (*gal'i-sē*; L *gal'i-kā*) in French. — (All the following also without *cap*) *n* **Gall'icism** an expression or idiom peculiar to French occurring as a use in another language. — *vt* and *vi* **Gall'icize** or **-ise** to assimilate or conform to French habits, etc. [L *Gallus* a Gaul; *Gallicus*, Gaulish]

gallic *gal'ik*, *adj* of, from, relating to, occurring in, etc plant galls. — **gallic acid** a crystalline substance present in gallnuts, tea, and various plants, and obtained by hydrolysis from tannin, used as a tanning agent, and for making inks and dyes. [Fr *gallique*, from *galle* **gall**[2]]

galligaskins *gal-i-gas'kinz*, *n pl* wide hose or breeches worn in the 16c and 17c; leggings. [OFr *garguesque*, from Ital *grechesco* Greekish, from L *graecus* Greek]

gallimaufry *gal-i-mö'fri*, *n* any inconsistent or absurd medley; a miscellaneous gathering. [Fr *galimafrée* a ragout, hash]

gallinaceous *gal-in-ā'shəs*, *adj* of or relating to the order of birds that includes grouse, pheasants and the domestic fowl. [L *gallīna* a hen, from *gallus* a cock]

gallinazo *gal-i-nä'zō*, *n* a turkey buzzard or other vulture: — *pl* **gallina'zos**. [Sp, from *gallina*, from L *gallīna* hen]

galling. See **gall**[3].

gallinule *gal'i-nūl*, *n* a waterhen, moorhen. [L *gallīnula* a chicken, from *gallīna* a hen]

Gallio *gal'i-ō*, *n* a person who keeps himself or herself free from trouble and responsibility: — *pl* **Gall'ios**. [From *Gallio*, Acts 18.12–17]

galliot or **galiot** *gal'i-ət*, *n* a small galley; an old Dutch cargo-boat. [Fr *galiote*, from LL *galea* galley]

gallipot *gal'i-pot*, *n* a small glazed pot, *esp* for medicine. [Prob a **pot** brought in **galleys**]

gallise, **gallisize**. See **gallize**.

gallium *gal'i-əm*, *n* a metallic element (symbol **Ga**; atomic no 31), as gallium arsenide an important semiconductor. [L *gallus* a cock, from the discoverer's name, *Lecoq* de Boisbaudran, or *Gallia* Gaul, France, his country]

gallivant *gal-i-vant'*, *vi* to spend time frivolously, *esp* in flirting; to gad about. [Perh **gallant**]

gallivat *gal'i-vat*, *n* a large two-masted Malay boat. [Port *galeota*; see **galliot**]

galliwasp *gal'i-wosp*, *n* a W Indian lizard.

gallize or **-ise** *gal'īz*, *vt* (in wine-making) to bring to standard proportions by adding water and sugar to inferior must. — Also **gall'isize** or **-ise**. [Ger *gallisieren*, from the name of the inventor, Dr L *Gall*]

gallnut. See **gall**[2].

Gallo- *gal-ō-*, *combining form* signifying France or Gaul, as in *Gallo-Roman*. — *n* **Galloma'nia** a mania for French ways. — *n* **Gall'ophil** or **Gall'ophile** a person who is friendly to, or has a fondness for, France or what is French. — *n* **Gall'ophobe** a person who dislikes or fears France or what is French. [**Gallic**]

galloglass or **gallowglass** *gal'ō-glas*, *n* a soldier or armed retainer of a chief in ancient Ireland and other Celtic countries. [Ir *gallóglach*, from *gall* foreign, and *óglach* soldier]

gallon *gal'ən*, *n* a unit of capacity, in Britain equal to 4.546 litres (277.4 cubic inches), also called **imperial gallon**, in the US equal to 3.785 litres (231 cubic inches). — *n* **gall'onage** an amount in gallons; the rate of use in gallons. [ONFr *galun*, *galon* (OFr *jalon*)]

galloon[1] *gə-lo͞on'*, *n* a kind of lace; a narrow tapelike trimming or binding material, sometimes made with gold or silver thread. — *adj* **gallooned'** adorned with galloon. [Fr *galon*, *galonner*; prob cognate with **gallant**]

galloon[2] *gə-lo͞on'*, (*obs*) *n* a variant of **galleon**.

gallop *gal'əp*, *vi* to go at a gallop; to ride a galloping animal; to move very fast. — *vt* to cause to gallop. — *n* the fastest pace of a horse, etc, at each stride of which all four feet are off the ground; a ride at a gallop; a fast pace (*fig*); a track for galloping or exercising horses. — *n* **gall'oper** someone who, or that which, gallops; an aide-de-camp (*old military*); (*esp* in *pl*) a fairground merry-go-round with wooden horses that rise and fall in imitation of galloping. — *adj* **gall'oping** proceeding at a gallop; advancing rapidly, as in *galloping consumption* (*fig*). — **galloping inflation** hyperinflation. — **Canterbury gallop** a moderate gallop of a horse (see **canter**). [OFr *galoper*, *galop*; prob Gmc; cf **wallop**]

gallopade *gal-əp-ād'*, *n* a quick kind of dance; the music appropriate to it; a sideways gallop. — *vi* to move briskly; to perform a gallopade. [Fr]

Gallophil, **Gallophile**, **Gallophobe**, etc. See under **Gallo-**.

Gallovidian *gal-ō-vid'i-ən*, *adj* belonging to Galloway. — *n* a native thereof. [*Gallovidia*, Latinized from Welsh *Gallwyddel*]

gallow *ga'lō*, (*Shakesp*) *vt* to frighten. [OE *āgælwan* to frighten, to astonish]

Galloway *gal'ō-wā*, *n* a small strong horse, 13–15 hands high; a breed of large black hornless cattle, *orig* from *Galloway* in Scotland.

Gallowegian. See **Galwegian**.

gallowglass. See **galloglass**.

gallows *gal'ōz*, or (*old-fashioned*) *gal'əs*, *n sing* (*orig pl*) a wooden frame for hanging criminals; a person who deserves the gallows (*Shakesp* and *literary*); the look of someone destined to hang (*Shakesp* and *literary*); any contrivance with posts and a crossbeam for suspending things (*obs*); a rest for the tympan of a hand printing-press (*obs*); the main frame of a beam-engine; (or **gallows frame**) a headframe; one of a pair of trouser braces (*dialect*): — *pl* (really double *pl*) **gall'owses** or **galowses** (used by *Shakesp*, in first sense above; used *Scot* and *dialect*, with various spellings — **gall'uses**, etc for trouser braces). — *adj* (often **gall'us**) deserving the gallows; villainous (*Scot* and *dialect*); mischievous, wild, unmanageable (*Scot* and *dialect*); impudent, saucy, tiresome (*Scot* and *dialect*); plucky, daring (*Scot* and *dialect*); perky, spirited, sprightly (*Scot* and *dialect*); in some dialects, a mere intensive. — *adv* (often **gall'us**) (*dialect*) damnably, confoundedly. — *n* **gall'owsness** (*dialect*) recklessness, perversity. — **gall'ows-bird** a person who deserves hanging or has been hanged; **gall'ows-foot** the space at the foot of the gallows. — *adj* **gall'ows-free** free from the danger of hanging. — **gallows humour** grim, sardonic humour; **gall'ows-lee** the place of hanging; **gall'ows-maker**. — *adj* **gall'ows-ripe'** ready for the gallows. — **gallows'-tree** a gallows. — **cheat the gallows** to deserve but escape hanging. [ME *galwes* (pl), from OE *galga*; Ger *Galgen*]

gallstone. See under **gall**[1].

gallumph. See **galumph**.

Gallup poll *gal'əp pōl*, *n* a method of gauging public opinion by questioning suitably distributed sample individuals, devised by George Horace *Gallup* (1901–84).

gallus *gal'əs*. An old, Scottish or dialect spelling of **gallows**.

gally *gal'i*, (*dialect* or *whaling*) *vi* to scare, daze. — **gall'y-bagger**, **-beggar** or **-crow** (*dialect*; also **galli-**) a scarecrow. [**gallow**]

galoche. See **galosh**.

galoot *gə-lo͞ot'*, (*slang*, orig and esp *US*) *n* a clumsy or inept fellow; an inexperienced soldier or marine. [Orig nautical slang]

galop *gal'əp* or *gə-lop'*, *n* a lively dance or dance tune in double time; a lively sideways slipping step used in dancing. — *vi* to dance a galop; to perform a lively sideways slipping step. [Fr; cf **gallop**]

galopin *gal'ə-pin*, (*obs*) *n* an errand boy (*Scott*); a kitchen boy. [Fr]

galore *gə-lōr'* or *-lör'*, *adv* in abundance. [Ir *go* (an adverbializing particle) and *leōr* sufficient]

galosh, **golosh** or **galoche** *gə-losh'*, *n* a rustic shoe, sandal or clog (*obs*); a piece running round a shoe or boot above the sole; an overshoe. — *vt* to provide (a shoe, etc) with a galosh. [Fr *galoche*, from prob LL *gallicula* small Gaulish shoe]

galowses. Same as **gallowses**.

galravage, **galravitch**. See **gilravage**.

galtonia *göl-tō'ni-ə*, or *gal-*, *n* any of several bulbous plants of the lily family (genus *Galtonia*) native to Southern Africa, esp *G. candicans*, the Cape hyacinth. [Named after Sir Francis *Galton* (1822–1911), British scientist]

galumph or **gallumph** *gə-lumf'*, *vi* to stride along exultantly; to bound about in a noisy, ungainly way. — *n* **galum'pher**. [A coinage of Lewis Carroll]

galut or **galuth** *gä-lo͞ot'* or *gō'ləs*, *n* (often with *cap*) a forced exile of Jews, *esp* (diaspora) from Palestine. [Heb *gālūth* exile]

galvanism *gal'vən-izm*, *n* current electricity (*obs*); medical treatment by electric currents; the production of an electric current by chemical means, as in a battery. — *adj* **galvanic** (*-van'*) relating to the production of an electric current by chemical means, *esp* the action of an acid on a metal; (of a response, behaviour, etc) sudden, startling or convulsive, as though produced by an electric shock; of, producing or produced by galvanism (*obs*). — *adv* **galvan'ically**. — *n* **gal'vanist**. — *n* **galvanīzā'tion** or **-s-**. — *vt* **gal'vanize** or **-ise** to subject to the action of an electric current; to stimulate to spasmodic action by, or as if by, an electric shock; to confer a false vitality upon; to coat with metal by an electric current; to coat with zinc without using a current. — *n* **gal'vanizer** or **-s-**. — *n* **galvanom'eter** an instrument for measuring electric currents. — *adj* **galvanomet'ric**. — *n* **galvanom'etry**. — *adj* **galvanoplas'tic** (*obs*). — *n* **galvanoplas'ty** (*obs*) electrodeposition. — *n* **galvan'oscope** an instrument for detecting electric currents. — **galvanic battery** or **cell** (*obs*) an electric battery or cell; **galvanic belt** (*obs*) a belt supposed to benefit the wearer by producing an electric current; **galvanic skin response** a change in the electrical conductivity of the skin, recorded by a polygraph, due to any of various emotional stimuli; **galvanized iron** iron coated with zinc to deter rust. [From Luigi *Galvani*, of Bologna (1737–98), the discoverer of galvanism]

Galwegian *gal-wē'ji-ən*, *adj* belonging to Galloway in Scotland (also **Gallowē'gian**), or of Galway in Ireland. — *n* a native of either place. [On the analogy of *Norwegian*]

gam[1] *gam*, *n* a collective noun for whales, a school; social intercourse or a visit (*esp* between whalers) at sea (*US old*). — *vi* to associate in a gam. — *vt* (*US old*; *specif* of whalers) to call on, exchange courtesies with. [Ety dubious]

gam[2] *gam*, (*Scot*) *n* a tooth or tusk; the mouth.

gam[3] *gam*, (*slang*) *n* a human leg, *esp* female. [Perh Fr dialect *gambe* leg]

gam[4] *gam*, (*vulg*) *n* and *vi* (to practise) oral sex. [Fr *gam*ahuche or *gam*aruche, term popularized through the Services]

-gam- *-gam-*, or **gamo-** *gam'ō-* or *gam-o'-* *combining form* signifying: marriage; union; reproduction or fertilization. — *n* **gamogen'esis** sexual reproduction. — *adj* **gamopet'alous** with petals united. — *adj* **gamophyll'ous** with perianth leaves united. — *adj* **gamosep'alous** with sepals united. — *adj* **gamotrop'ic**. — *n* **gamot'ropism** the tendency of gametes to attract each other. — *adj combining form* **-gamous** having a stated number of spouses, as in *bigamous*; pertaining to a stated means of fertilization or reproduction, as in *allogamous*. — *n combining form* **-gamy** marriage, or supposed marriage, to a stated number of spouses; a stated means of fertilization or reproduction. [Gr *gamos* marriage]

gama grass *gä'mə gräs*, *n* a tall N American forage grass (*Tripsacum dactyloides*). [Perh Sp *grama*]

gamash *gəm-ash'*, (*archaic* and *dialect*) *n* a kind of legging. — Also **gramash'** and **gramoche'** (*-osh'*; *Scott*). [Fr (now *dialect*) *gamache*, Provençal *garamacha*, apparently from *Ghadames*, famous for leather]

gamay *ga-mā'*, also *gam'ā*, *n* a variety of red grape used in making dry red wine, *esp* of the Beaujolais district; a wine made from this grape. [*Gamay* village in the Beaune district, Côte d'Or, France]

gamb *gamb*, (*heraldry*) *n* a beast's whole foreleg. [LL *gamba* a leg]

gamba *gam'bə*, (*music*) *n* short for **viola da gamba**; an organ stop of stringlike quality. — *n* **gam'bist** a gamba-player. [From *viola da gamba* a cello-like instrument]

gambado[1] *gam-bā'dō*, *n* a leather covering or boot attached to a saddle: — *pl* **gambā'does** or **gambā'dos**. [Ital *gamba* leg]

gambado[2] *gam-bā'dō*, *n* a bound or spring of a horse (*dressage*); a fantastic movement, a caper: — *pl* **gambā'does** or **gambā'dos**. — *vi* to frolic, caper. [Sp *gambada*; cf **gambol**]

gambeson *gam'bi-sən*, (*hist*) *n* an ancient leather or quilted cloth coat worn under the habergeon. [OFr, from OHGer *wamba* belly]

gambet *gam'bit* or **gambetta** *gam-bet'ə*, (*ornithol*) *n* the redshank. [Ital *gambetta* ruff; *gambetta fosca* spotted redshank]

gambier or **gambir** *gam'bēr*, *n* an astringent substance prepared from the leaves of *Uncaria gambir*, a rubiaceous climbing shrub of the East Indies, used in tanning and dyeing. [Malay]

gambist. See **gamba**.

gambit *gam'bit*, *n* the (offer of a) sacrifice of a piece for the sake of an advantage in timing or position in the opening stages of a game (**gam'bit-pawn** or **-piece** one so offered; *chess*); an initial move in any strategy or battle of wits, *esp* one with an element of trickery. — *vt* to sacrifice or offer for sacrifice in a gambit (*chess*). [Sp *gambito*, from Ital *gambetto* a tripping up, from *gamba* leg]

gamble *gam'bl*, *vi* to play for money, *esp* for high stakes; to take a chance (with *on*); to engage in wild financial speculations; to take great risks for the sake of possible advantage. — *vt* to squander or lose by staking. — *n* a transaction depending on chance. — *n* **gam'bler** a person who gambles, *esp* one who makes it his or her business. — *n* **gam'bling**. — **gam'bling-house** or (now *rare*) **-hell** a house kept for the accommodation of people who play at games of chance for money. [Frequentative of **game**[1]]

gamboge *gam-bōōzh'*, *-bōj'* or *-bōōj'*, *n* a yellow gum resin, obtained from any number of Asian trees, chiefly *Garcinia morella*, used as a pigment and in medicine. — *adj* **gambogian** (*-bōj'* or *-bōōj'*) or **gambogic** (*-bōj'*). [From *Cambodia*, whence it was brought about 1600]

gambo (*Welsh* and *dialect*) *n* a simple farm cart or hay-wagon.

gambol *gam'bl*, *vi* to leap; to frisk playfully: — *prp* **gam'bolling**; *pa t* and *pa p* **gam'bolled**. — *n* a playful frisk; a frolic. [Formerly *gambold*, from OFr *gambade*, from Ital *gambata* a kick, from LL *gamba* leg]

gambrel *gam'brəl*, *n* the hock of a horse; a crooked stick used by butchers for hanging carcasses on; a gambrel roof. — **gambrel roof** in the UK, a hipped roof in which the upper parts of the hipped ends take the form of a small vertical gable end; in the US, a roof with the lower part at a steeper pitch than the upper (called a *mansard* roof in the UK). [OFr *gamberel*; cf Fr *gambier* a hooked stick; connection with **cambrel** obscure]

gambroon *gam-brōōn'*, *n* a twilled cloth of worsted and cotton, or linen. [Prob *Gambrun*, in Persia]

game[1] *gām*, *n* a sport of any kind; (in *pl*) (an event consisting of competitions in) athletic sports; a contest for recreation; a competitive amusement played according to a system of rules; the state of a game; manner of playing a game; form in playing; the requisite number of points to be gained to win a game; a bout or contest in a series; a spell or set period of playing a game; a bit of fun, a jest; any object of pursuit; a scheme or method of seeking an end, or the policy that would be most likely to attain it; business, activity, operation; fighting spirit (*archaic*); gallantry (*Shakesp*); (*usu* **the game**) prostitution (*slang*); **the game**) thieving (*slang*); the spoil of the chase; wild animals hunted for sport; the flesh of such animals; a flock of swans (formerly of other animals) kept for pleasure. — *adj* of or belonging to animals hunted as game; having the spirit of a fighting cock (*colloq*); plucky, courageous (*colloq*); having the necessary spirit and willingness for some act (*colloq*). — *vi* to gamble. — *adv* **game'ly**. — *n* **game'ness**. — *adj* **game'some** playful. — *n* **game'someness**. — *n* **game'ster** a gambler; a lewd person (*Shakesp*); a merry, playful person, a maker of sport (*obs*). — *adj* **game'sy** keen on sports. — *n* **gā'miness** or **gā'myness** the condition or quality of being gamy. — *n* **gam'ing** gambling. — *adj* **gā'my** or **gā'mey** having the flavour of game, *esp* that kept till tainted; savouring of scandal, sensational; spirited, plucky, lively (*colloq*). — **game bag** a bag for holding a hunter's game; **game ball** see **game point**; **game bird** a bird hunted for sport; **game call** (*bridge*) a bid (and contract) which, if successful, will win a game; **game'-chicken** or **game'cock** a cock of a breed trained to fight, a fighting cock; **game chips** thinly-cut (*usu* disc-shaped) potato chips served with game; **game'-dealer**; **game fish** any freshwater fish of the salmon family except the grayling (*opp* to *coarse fish*); **game fishing**; **game'keeper** a person who has the care of game on an estate, etc (also *fig*); **game laws** laws relating to the protection of game; **game licence** a licence to kill, or to sell, game; **game plan** the strategy or tactics used by a football team, etc; any carefully devised strategy; **game point** or **game ball** the stage at which the next point wins the game; **game preserve** a tract of land stocked with game preserved for sport or with protected wild animals; **game preserver** a person who preserves game on his or her land; **games'manship** (*facetious*; coined by Stephen Potter) the art of winning games or, generally, of scoring points by talk or conduct aimed at putting one's opponent off; **game** (or **games**) **theory** (*math*) the theory concerned with analysing the choices and strategies available in a game or eg business conflict in order to choose the optimum course of action (used eg in training and selection procedures); **game tenant** a person who rents the privilege of shooting or fishing over a particular area; **game warden** a person who looks after game, *esp* in a game preserve; **gaming contract** a wager upon any game (eg a horse-race or football match); **gam'ing-house** a gambling-house; **gam'ing-table** a table used for gambling. — **big game** the larger animals hunted; **die game** to keep up courage to the last; **give the game away** to disclose a secret; to give up, to abandon (a game or contest) (*Austr*); **have a game with** or **make game of** to make sport of, to ridicule; **off one's game** playing badly; **on one's game** playing well; **on the game** (*colloq*) earning one's living as a prostitute; **play a waiting game** see under **wait**; **play the game** to act in a fair, sportsmanlike, straightforward manner; **red game** grouse; **round game** a game, eg at cards, in which the number of players is not fixed; **the game is not worth the candle** see under **candle**; **the game is up** the scheme has failed, all is revealed. [OE *gamen* play; ON *gaman*, Dan *gammen*]

game[2] *gām*, *adj* lame. [Origin obscure]

gamelan *gam'ə-lan*, *n* an instrument resembling a xylophone; an orchestra of SE Asia consisting of percussion (chiefly), wind instruments and stringed instruments. [Javanese]

gamete *gam'ēt* or *gam-ēt'*, *n* a sexual reproductive cell; an egg-cell or sperm-cell. — *adj* **gam'etal** (or *-ēt'*) or **gametic** (*-et'* or *-ēt'*). — *n* **gametangium** (*gam-it-an'ji-əm*) a cell or organ in which gametes are formed: — *pl* **gametan'gia**. — *n* **gametogen'esis** the formation of gametes. — *n* **gamē'tophyte** (or *gam'*; Gr *phyton* plant) in alternation of generations, a plant of the sexual generation, producing gametes. — **gamete intra-Fallopian transfer** an infertility treatment involving direct transfer of eggs and sperm into the woman's Fallopian tubes, where conception may occur (*abbrev* **GIFT**). [Gr *gametēs* husband, *gametē* wife, from *gameein* to marry]

Gamgee tissue® *gam'jē tish'ōō*, *-ū*, or *tis'ū*, *n* (sometimes without *cap*) a type of wound-dressing consisting of cotton-wool between two layers of gauze. [After its inventor, J S *Gamgee* (1828–86), English surgeon]

gamic *gam'ik*, *adj* sexual; sexually produced. [Gr *gamikos*, from *gamos* marriage]

gamin *gam'in* or *ga-mẽ*, *n* a street urchin, a precocious and mischievous imp of the pavement: — *fem* **gamine** (*-mēn'*) a girl of a pert, boyish, impish appearance and disposition. — *adj* boyish or impish. — *n* **gaminerie** (*gam'in-ri* or *gam-ēn-(ə-)rē*). — *adj* **gaminesque'** like or resembling a gamin or gamine. [Fr]

gamma *gam'ə*, *n* the third letter of the Greek alphabet (Γ, γ = G, g); as a numeral γʹ = 3, ͵γ = 3000; in classification, the third or one of the third grade, (one of) the grade below beta. — **gamma camera** a device which detects gamma radiation and which is used to produce images of parts of the body into which radioactive material has been introduced; **gamma globulin** any of a group of globulins occurring in blood plasma which contain antibodies that protect against various diseases; **gamma rays** or **radiation** a penetrating radiation given off by radium and other radioactive substances; **gamma securities** or **stocks** (*stock exchange*) stocks which are relatively inactive, as of small companies rarely traded (cf **alpha** and **beta securities**). [Gr]

gammadion, *gam-ā'di-on*, also **gammation** *-ā'ti-on*, *n* a figure composed of Greek capital gammas, *esp* a swastika: — *pl* **gammā'dia**. [Late Gr, little gamma]

gamme *gam*, (*obs*) *n* a musical scale; range, spectrum, gamut. [Fr, from Gr *gamma*; cf **gamut**]

gammer *gam'ər*, (*archaic* or *dialect derog*) *n* an old woman (*masc* **gaffer**). [**grandmother** or **godmother**]

gammerstang *gam'ər-stang*, (*dialect*) *n* a tall, awkward person, *esp* a woman; a wanton girl. [Perh **gammer** and **stang**[1]]

Gammexane® *gam-eks'ān*, *n* a powerful insecticide. [γ-hexachlorocyclo*hexane*]

gammock *gam'ək*, (*dialect*) *n* a frolic, fun. — *vi* to frolic, to lark.

gammon[1] *gam'ən*, *n* backgammon (*archaic*); a double game at backgammon, won by bearing all one's men before one's opponent bears any; patter, chatter, *esp* that of a thief's accomplice to divert attention, as in *to give gammon* (*slang*); nonsense, humbug. — *vt* to defeat by a gammon at backgammon; to hoax, impose upon. — *vi* to talk gammon; to feign or cheat (*obs*). — *n* **gamm'oner**. — *n* **gamm'oning**. [Prob OE *gamen* a game]

gammon[2] *gam'ən*, *n* the cured meat from the hindquarters and leg of a pig; the back part of a side of bacon. [ONFr *gambon*, *gambe* leg]

gammon[3] *gam'ən*, (*naut*) *n* the lashing of the bowsprit. — *vt* to lash (the bowsprit).

gammy *gam'i*, (*slang*) *adj* lame; maimed. [Cf **game**[2]]

gamo-, **-gamous**. See **-gam-**.

gamp *gamp*, (*colloq*) *n* a large, untidily furled umbrella; an umbrella. — *adj* **gamp'ish** (of an umbrella) bulging. [From Mrs Sarah *Gamp*, in Dickens's *Martin Chuzzlewit*]

gamut *gam'ət*, *n* the note G on the first line of the bass stave (*hist music*); Guido of Arezzo's scale of six overlapping hexachords, reaching from that note up to E in the fourth space of the treble (*hist music*); any recognized scale or range of notes; the whole compass of a voice or instrument; the full range or compass of anything, eg the emotions. [From *gamma*, the Gr letter G, adopted when it was required to name a note added below the A with which the old scale began, and *ut* the Aretinian (qv) syllable]

gamy. See under **game**[1].

-gamy. See under **-gam-**.

gan *gan*, *pa t* of **gin**[5].

ganch *gänsh* or *-ch*, or **gaunch** *gönsh* or *-ch*, *vt* (*obs*) to impale; to lacerate. — *n* impaling apparatus (*hist*); a wound from a boar's tusk (*archaic*). [OFr *gancher*, from Ital *gancio* a hook]

gander *gan'dər*, *n* the male of the goose; a simpleton (*colloq*); a look or glance (*slang*); a man living apart from his wife (*US archaic*). — *n* **gan'derism** behaviour of or suited to a gander. — **gan'der-moon** or **-month** the month of a wife's lying-in, confinement to bed prior to childbirth (*old US dialect*); **gan'der-mooner** a husband during his gander-moon (*old US dialect*). — **take a gander at** (*slang*) to have a quick look at. [OE *ganra*, *gandra*; Du and LGer *gander*]

Gandhian *gand'i-ən*, *adj* of, pertaining to or representative of (the policies, etc) of Mohandâs K *Gandhi*, Indian leader (1869–1949). — *n* **Gandh'i-ism** or **Gandh'ism**. — *n* and *adj* **Gandh'ist**.

G and S or **G & S** *abbrev*: Gilbert and Sullivan.

g and t *abbrev*: gin and tonic.

gandy dancer *gan'di dän'sər*, *n* (*US colloq*) a railway labourer; any manual labourer; an itinerant or seasonal labourer. [Prob from the *Gandy* Manufacturing Company, which made tools used by railway workmen]

gane *gān*, *pa p* of **gae**[1].

Ganesa or **Ganesha** *gən-ā'sha*, *n* the elephant-headed Hindu god of wisdom and success.

gang[1] *gang*, *n* a band of roughs or criminals; a number of people or animals (*esp* elk) associating together; a number of labourers working together; a set of boys who habitually play together; a set of tools, etc used together. — *vt* and *vi* to associate in a gang or gangs. — *vt* to adjust in co-ordination; to arrange or connect (electric components) so that they can be operated by a single control; to attack as a gang (*NAm colloq*). — *n* **ganger** (*gang'ər*) the foreman of a gang of labourers. — *n* **gang'ing**. — *n* **gang'ster** a member of a gang of roughs or criminals. — *n* **gang'sterdom**. — *n* **gang'sterism**. — **gang'-bang** (*slang*) successive sexual intercourse with one, *usu* unwilling, female by a group of males. — *vt* to subject (a woman) to a gang-bang. — **gang'buster** (*US*) a special police agent working to combat criminal gangs, typically by means of strong, swift, effective operations (**like gangbusters** (*US colloq*) with great speed, impact or effectiveness); **gang'busting**; **gang'-land** or **gang'sterland** the domain of gangsters, the world of (*esp* organized) crime; **gang mill** a sawmill with gang saws; **gang plug** an electrical adaptor with a row of sockets. — *vt* **gang'-punch** (*comput*) to punch (the same information) in a number of cards, or to punch (a number of cards) with the same information. — **gang rape** a number of successive rapes committed by members of a group on one victim on one occasion. — *vt* **gang'-rape**. — **gang saw** a saw fitted in a frame with others; **gangs'man** the foreman of a gang; **gang switches** a number of electrical switches connected so that they can be operated simultaneously. — **Gang of Four** a term applied to a group of four of Chairman Mao's leading advisers after their political downfall; (also without *caps*; sometimes *facetious*) any similar group in politics, etc; **gang up on** to make a concerted attack on; **gang up with** to join in the (doubtful) activities of. [OE *gang* (Dan *gang*, Ger *Gang*), from *gangan* to go]

gang[2] *gang*, *vi* and *vt* (*Scot*) to go: — *pr p* **gang'ing** (*rare*); *pa p* and *pa t* not in use. — *n* (*Scot*) the range of pasture allowed to cattle. — *n* **gang'er** a walker (*Scot*); a fast horse (*dialect*). — *n* **gang'rel** (*Scot*) a vagrant; a child beginning to walk (*rare*). — Also *adj*. — **gang'board** (*naut*) a gangway, plank or platform for walking on; **gang'-bye** (*Scot*) the go-by; **Gang Days** (*obs Scot*) Rogation Days; **gang'plank** a wooden board used to form a bridge to give access on to or out of a ship, or on to another ship. — *adj* **gang'-there-out** (*archaic Scot*) vagrant. — **gang'way** (OE *gangweg*) a gangplank, *usu* with sides for the protection of users, giving access on to or out of a ship; an opening in a ship's side to take a gangway; any passageway on a ship; an aisle between rows of seats, *esp* the cross-passage about halfway down the House of Commons (ministers and ex-ministers with their immediate followers sitting *above the gangway*). — *interj* make way; make room to pass. [OE *gangan* to go]

gang[3]. See **gangue**.

gangling *gang'gling*, *adj* loosely-built, lanky. — Also **gangly** (*gang'gli*). [Orig Scot and Eng dialect; OE *gangan* to go]

ganglion *gang'gli-ən*, *n* a tumour in a tendon sheath (*pathol*); a nerve-centre, collection of nerve cells (*anatom*): — *pl* **gang'lia** or **gang'lions**. — *adj* **gang'liar** or **ganglionic** (*-on'ik*) relating to a ganglion. — *adj* **gang'liate** or **gang'liated** having a ganglion or ganglia. — *adj* **gang'liform**. [Gr]

gangrel. See under **gang**[2].

gangrene *gang'grēn*, (*pathol*) *n* necrosis of part of the body, with decay of body tissue, resulting from a failure in the blood supply to the part. — *vt* to mortify; to cause gangrene in. — *vi* to become gangrenous. — *adj* **gangrenous** (*gang'grin-əs*) mortified, affected with gangrene. [Gr *gangraina* gangrene]

gangster, etc. See under **gang**[1].

gangue or **gang** *gang*, *n* rock in which ores are embedded. [Fr, from Ger *Gang* a vein]

gangway. See under **gang**[2].

ganister or **gannister** *gan'is-tər*, *n* a hard, close-grained siliceous stone, found in the Lower Coal Measures of N England. [Origin uncertain; poss from quarries at *Gannister*, Cheshire]

ganja *gän'jə*, *n* an intoxicating preparation, the female flowering tops of Indian hemp, ie marijuana. [Hindi *gājā*]

gannet *gan'ət*, *n* a large white sea-bird of the family *Sulidae*, with black-tipped wings; a greedy person (*colloq*). — See also **solan**. — *n* **gann'etry** a breeding-place of gannets. [OE *ganot* a sea-fowl; Du *gent*]

gannister. See **ganister**.

ganoid *gan'oid*, *adj* (of fish scales) having a hard glistening outer layer over bone; (of fishes) belonging to an order **Ganoid'ei** (*-i-ī*) in which such scales are a common feature, and which includes the sturgeon and many fossil forms. — *n* a ganoid fish. — *n* **ganoin** or **ganoine** (*gan'ō-in*) a calcareous substance, forming an enamel-like layer on ganoid scales. [Gr *ganos* brightness, and *eidos* appearance]

gansey *gan'zi n* a woollen sweater, a jersey. [From the island of *Guernsey*]

gant *gänt*, or **gaunt** *gönt*, (*Scot*) *vi* to yawn. — *n* a yawn. [Prob frequentative of OE *gānian* to yawn]

gantlet (*obs*). Same as **gauntlet**[1,2].

gantline *gant'līn*, (*naut*) *n* a rope used in a single-block hoist. [Variation of **girt** or **girth**[2] and **line**[2]]

gantlope *gant'lōp*. See **gauntlet**[2].

gantry *gan'tri*, *n* a stand for barrels; the shelving, racks, etc in which drinks are displayed in a bar; a platform or bridge for a travelling crane, railway signals, etc; the servicing tower beside a rocket on its launching pad. — Also (in first sense) **gauntry** (*gön'tri*) or **gaun'tree**. — **gantry crane** a crane in bridge form with vertical members running on parallel tracks. [Perh OFr *gantier*, from L *cantērius* a trellis, from Gr *kanthēlios* a pack-ass]

Gantt chart *gant chärt*, *n* a form of bar chart used to show progress in a production system, showing predicted production figures over a fixed period of time, and updated with actual figures for comparison. [Henry L *Gantt*, US management consultant (1861–1919)]

Ganymede *gan'i-mēd*, *n* a cupbearer or pot-boy; a catamite. [From *Ganymēdēs*, the beautiful youth who succeeded Hebe as cupbearer to Zeus]

GAO *abbrev*: General Accounting Office (*US*).

gaol, etc. See **jail**, etc.

gap *gap*, *n* an opening or breach; a cleft; a passage; a notch or pass in a mountain ridge; a gorge (*US*); a breach of continuity; an unfilled space, a lack; a divergence, disparity; the space between discharge electrodes, over which a spark can jump (also **spark gap**; *elec eng*); a break in the magnetic circuit of the recording or erasing head of a tape-recorder, which allows the signal to interact with the oxide film (*electronics*). — *vt* to make a gap in; to notch (*rare*, *dialect*). — *adj* **gapp'y** full of gaps. — **gap analysis** (*marketing*) a method of discovering gaps in the market for possible new products, by checking off consumer wants against qualities of products available and noting where these do not coincide; **gap junction** (*biol*) a junction of two cells at which there is direct communication through a channel spanning the narrow gap between them; **gap site** a piece of land in a built-up area lying empty because the building which once stood on it has been demolished. — *adj* **gap'-toothed** with teeth set wide apart. — **bridge, close, fill** or **stop the gap** to supply the deficiency. [ON *gap*]

gape *gāp*, *vi* to open the mouth wide; to yawn; to stare with open mouth; to be wide open; to bawl (*Shakesp*). — *n* act of gaping; the extent to which the mouth can be opened; the angle of the mouth; a wide opening, parting, fissure, chasm, or failure to meet; in a fish-hook, the width between the point and the shank; (in *pl*) a yawning fit; (in *pl*) a disease of birds of which gaping is a symptom, caused by a threadworm (*Syngamus*, or **gape'worm**) in the windpipe and bronchial tubes. — *n* **gā'per** a person who gapes; a mollusc (Mya) with a shell gaping at each end; a sea-perch (Serranus); an easy catch (*cricket*). — *n* and *adj* **gā'ping**. — *adv* **gā'pingly**. — **gape'seed** (*dialect*) an imaginary commodity that the gaping starer is supposed to be seeking or sowing; hence, the act of staring open-mouthed, or the object stared at. [ON *gapa* to open the mouth; Ger *gaffen* to stare]

gapó *gä-pō'*, *n* riverside forest periodically flooded: — *pl* **gapós'**. [Port (*i*)*gapó*, from Tupí *igapó*, *ygapó*]

GAR *abbrev*: Grand Army of the Republic (*US*), an association of Union veterans of the Civil War.

gar[1]. See **garfish**.

gar[2] *gär*, (chiefly *Scot*) *vt* to cause, to compel: — *pa t* and *pa p* **garred** or **gart**. — Also (*Spenser*) **garre**. [Norse *ger(v)a* to make; cf **yare**]

garage *gar'äzh*, *gə-räzh'* or *gar'ij*, *n* a building for housing motor vehicles; an establishment where motor vehicles are tended, repaired, bought and sold. — *vt* to put into or keep in a garage. — *adj* (of music) of the kind played by a garage band. — *n* **gar'aging** accommodation for cars, etc. — *n* **gar'agist** or **gar'agiste** a garage proprietor or owner; a garage employee. — **garage band** an unsophisticated rock group; **garage sale** a sale of various items held on the seller's premises, *esp* in the garage. [Fr, from *garer* to secure; cf **ware**³]

garam masala *gar'əm mə-sä'lə*, *n* a spice mixture used in making curry. [Hindi, hot mixture]

Garamond *gar'ə-mənd*, *n* a form of typeface like that designed by Claude *Garamond* (died 1561).

Garand rifle *gar'ənd* or *gə-rand' rī'fl*, *n* a semi-automatic, gas-operated, clip-fed, .30 calibre, US army rifle; also called **M1**. [After US inventor J C *Garand* (1888–1974)]

garb¹ *gärb*, *n* external appearance (*obs*); fashion of dress; dress, clothing; semblance, appearance (*fig*). — *vt* to clothe, array. [Ital *garbo* grace; of Gmc origin; cf **gear**]

garb² or **garbe** *gärb*, (*heraldry*) *n* a sheaf of wheat. [OFr *garbe*; of Gmc origin]

garbage *gär'bij*, *n* refuse, such as (*orig*) animal offal; any worthless matter; household food and other refuse; extraneous matter or invalid data (*comput*). — **gar'-bageman** (*US*) a dustman; **garbage can** (*US*) a bin for food-waste, etc, a dustbin. — **garbage in, garbage out** (*comput*, etc) see **GIGO**. [Of doubtful origin]

garbanzo *gär-ban'zō*, *n* a chick-pea: — *pl* **garban'zos**. [Sp]

garble *gär'bl*, *vt* to cleanse, sift (*obs*); to select what may serve one's own purpose from, *esp* in a bad sense (*rare*); to misrepresent or falsify by suppression and selection; to mangle, mutilate, distort, jumble. — *adj* **gar'bled**. — *n* **gar'bler**. — *n* **gar'bling**. [Ital *garbellare*, from Ar *ghirbāl* a sieve, perh from LL *crībellum*, dimin of *crībrum* a sieve]

garbo *gär'bō*, (*Austr colloq*) *n* a dustman, garbage-collector; rubbish: — *pl* **gar'bos**. [*garb*age]

garboard *gär'börd*, (*naut*) *n* the first range of planks or plates laid on a ship's bottom next to the keel. — Also **garboard strake**. [Du *gaarboord*]

garboil *gar'boil*, (*obs*) *n* disorder, uproar. [OFr *garbouil*, from Ital *garbuglio*, connected with L *bullīre* to boil]

garbologist *gär-bol'ə-jist*, (*US facetious*) *n* a dustman, garbage-collector. — *n* **garbol'ogy**. [**garbage**]

garbure *gär-būr'*, *n* a substantial type of soup made with vegetables, pulses, ham or other meat, and *usu* served with bread. [Fr]

garcinia *gär-sin'i-ə*, *n* a tropical evergreen tree of the *Garcinia* genus of Guttiferae, yielding gamboge, kokum butter, and mangosteen. [After the French botanist Laurent *Garcin*]

garçon *gär-sɔ̃*, *n* a boy; a male servant, now *usu* a waiter in a restaurant (*usu* used *vocatively*). [Fr]

garda *gör'də*, *n* an Irish policeman or guard: — *pl* **gardai** (*gör'də-ē*). — **Garda Siochana** (*shē'hhə-nə*; *literally* guard of peace; Ir *síochάin* peace) the Irish police force. [Ir *gárda*]

gardant (*heraldry*). *Obs* spelling of **guardant** (see under **guard**).

garden *gär'dən*, *n* a piece of ground on which flowers, etc are cultivated, adjoining a house; (often in *pl*) a *usu* public area laid out with walks, flowerbeds, lawns, trees, etc; a pleasant spot; a fertile region; (in *pl* with *cap*) used in street-names. — *adj* of, used in or grown in a garden or gardens. — *vi* to cultivate or work in a garden. — *n* **gar'dener** a person who gardens, or is skilled in gardening; a person employed to tend a garden. — *n* **gar'dening** the laying out and cultivation of gardens. — **garden centre** an establishment where plants, gardening equipment, etc are sold; **garden city**, **suburb** or **village** a model town, suburb or village, laid out with broad roads, trees, and much garden ground between the houses; **gardener's garters** variegated garden ribbon-grass; **gar'den-glass** a bell-glass for covering plants; **gar'den-house** a summerhouse (*Shakesp* and *literary*); a house in a garden; a house kept for sensual indulgence (*obs*); **garden party** a social gathering held in the garden of a house; **garden patch** a plot of ground to be used for a garden (*US*); **garden path**; **garden seat**; **garden stuff** garden produce for the table (*archaic*); **garden warbler** a warbler (*Sylvia borin*) common to European woodlands, the beccafico. — **everything in the garden is lovely** all is, or appears to be, well; **hanging garden** a garden formed in terraces rising one above another; **lead someone up the garden path** to mislead someone, *esp* to make someone the victim of an elaborate scheme of deception; **market garden** a garden in which vegetables, fruits, etc are raised for sale; **market gardener**; **philosophers of the garden** followers of Epicurus, who taught in a garden. [OFr *gardin* (Fr *jardin*); from Gmc; cf **yard**² and **garth**]

gardenia *gär-dē'ni-ə*, *n* (with *cap*) a genus of the madder family, Old World tropical and subtropical trees and shrubs with fragrant, *usu* white flowers of a waxy appearance; a member of the genus. [Named from the American botanist Dr Alex *Garden* (c.1730–91)]

garderobe *gärd'rōb*, (*hist*) *n* a wardrobe or its contents; an armoury; a private room; a privy. [Fr; cf **wardrobe**]

gardyloo *gär'di-lōō*, *interj* the old warning cry in Edinburgh before throwing slops out of the window into the street. — *n* the slops so thrown, or the act of throwing. [Recorded in this form by Smollett; supposed to be would-be Fr *gare de l'eau* for *gare l'eau* beware of the water; Sterne has *garde d'eau* (*Sentimental Journey*), for Paris]

gare *gār*, (*Scot*) *adj* greedy, miserly. [ON *gerr*; cf **yare**]

garefowl *gār'fowl*, *n* the great auk. [ON *geirfugl*]

garfish *gär'fish*, *n* a pike-like fish (*Belone*) with a long slender beaked head; the bony pike, an American ganoid river-fish (Lepidosteus); any of various similar Australian fish. — Also called **gar** and **gar'pike**. [OE *gār* spear]

garganey *gär'gə-ni*, *n* a small duck of Europe and Asia, the male having a curved white stripe over the eye. [Ital *garganello*]

Gargantuan *gär-gan'tū-ən*, *adj* like or worthy of Rabelais's hero *Gargantua*, a giant of vast appetite; (without *cap*) enormous, prodigious. — *n* **Gargan'tuism**. — *n* **Gargan'tuist**.

gargarism *gär'gə-rizm*, (*obs*) *n* a gargle. — *vt* and *vi* **gar'garize** or **-ise**.

garget *gär'git*, *n* inflammation of the throat or udder in cows, swine, etc (*vet*); (also **garget plant**) pokeweed (*US*). — *adj* **gar'gety** affected by, or pertaining to, garget (*vet*). [Appar from (*obs*, *rare*) *garget* throat, from ME, from MFr *gargate*; ult echoic]

gargle *gär'gl*, *vt* and *vi* to swill (a liquid) round the back of one's throat, *usu* for medicinal purposes, avoiding swallowing it by breathing out through it. — *n* a liquid for gargling; an act of gargling. [OFr *gargouiller*, from *gargouille* the throat]

gargoyle *gär'goil*, *n* a spout, *usu* grotesquely carved, projecting from a roof-gutter; any grotesque figure or person (*fig*). — Also **gur'goyle**. — *n* **gar'goylism** (*med*, *old-fashioned*) a rare condition characterized by grotesque physical deformity and severe mental disablement. [OFr *gargouille*, from LL *gurguliō* throat]

garial. See **gavial**.

garibaldi *gar-i-böl'di* or *-bal'di*, *n* a woman's loose blouse, an imitation of the red shirts worn by followers of the Italian patriot *Garibaldi* (1807–1882); a garibaldi biscuit. — **garibaldi biscuit** a biscuit with a layer of currants. [After G Garibaldi, Italian patriot (1807–82), appar arbitrarily for the biscuit]

garigue. See **garrigue**.

garish¹ *gär'ish*, *adj* showy; gaudy; (of colours) glaring. — *adv* **gar'ishly**. — *n* **gar'ishness**. [Formerly also *gaurish*, *gawrish*, perh from obs *guare* to stare, perh a frequentative of obs *gaw* to stare; cf ON *gā* to heed]

garish². See **guarish**.

garjan. See **gurjun**.

garland *gär'lənd*, *n* a crown (*obs*); a wreath of flowers or leaves; a book of selections in prose or poetry; ornament, glory (*Spenser*; *Shakesp*); (*usu* in *pl*) a rope (or iron, etc) band used for various purposes, such as for retaining shot in a ship's hold, etc (*naut*, also *military*). — *vt* to deck with a garland. — *n* **gar'landage** (*Tennyson*) a decoration of garlands. — *adj* **gar'landless**. — *n* **gar'landry** (*rare*) garlands collectively. [OFr *garlande*]

garlic *gär'lik*, *n* a bulbous liliaceous plant (*Allium sativum*) having a pungent taste and very strong smell; extended to others of the genus, such as **wild garlic** (ramsons). — *adj* **gar'licky** like garlic. — **gar'lic-mus'tard** a tall cruciferous hedge plant (*Sisymbium alliaria*) with a garlicky smell. [OE *gārlēac*, from *gār* a spear, and *lēac* a leek]

garment *gär'mənt*, *n* any article of clothing; a covering. — *vt* to clothe or cover. — *adj* **gar'mented**. — *adj* **gar'mentless**. — *n* **gar'menture** clothing. [OFr *garniment*, from *garnir* to furnish]

garner *gär'nər*, (*literary*) *n* (*old* or *poetic*) a granary; a store of anything. — *vt* to (gather up and) store. — *vi* (*Tennyson*) to accumulate. [OFr *gernier* (Fr *grenier*), from L *grānārium* (usu in pl) a granary]

garnet[1] *gär'nit*, *n* a mineral, in some varieties a precious stone, generally red, crystallizing in dodecahedra and icositetrahedra, a silicate of di- and trivalent metals. — *adj* **garnetif'erous**. — **gar'net-paper** abrasive paper similar to glass paper; **gar'net-rock** a rock composed of garnet with hornblende and magnetite. [OFr *grenat*, from LL *grānātum* pomegranate; or LL *grānum* grain, cochineal, red dye]

garnet[2] *gär'nit*, (*naut*) *n* a hoisting tackle. [Origin obscure]

garnet[3] *gär'nit*, *n* a T-shaped hinge (now only as **cross-garnet**). [Possibly OFr *carne*, from L *cardō*, *-inis* hinge]

garni *gär-nē*, (Fr; *cookery*) *adj* trimmed, garnished.

garnierite *gär'ni-ər-īt*, *n* a green hydrated nickel, magnesium silicate. [Jules *Garnier*, who discovered it in New Caledonia]

garnish *gär'nish*, *vt* to adorn, decorate, trim; to furnish, kit out, supply (*obs*); to add herbs, etc to a dish for flavour or decoration; to garnishee (*law*). — *n* a gift of money, *esp* that formerly paid to fellow-prisoners on entering prison or sometimes by workmen on starting a new job (*hist*); something placed round a principal dish at table, whether for embellishment or relish; decoration, embellishment. — *n* **gar'nishee** (*law*) a person warned not to pay money owed to another, because the latter is indebted to the garnisher who gives the warning. — *vt* to attach (a debt) in this way (*law*); to serve (a debtor) with a garnishment. — *n* **garnishee'ment**. — *n* **gar'nisher** a person who garnishes. — *n* **gar'nishing**. — *n* **gar'nishment** that which garnishes or embellishes; ornament; a garnisheement. — *n* **gar'nishry** (*Browning*) adornment. — *n* **gar'niture** that which garnishes or embellishes; trimming, decoration (on clothes); apparel; ornamentation, *esp* (*obs*) a set of ornaments, eg vases; a set of armour. — **garnishee order** (*law*) a court order which creates a charge over a debtor's bank account in favour of a creditor who has sued and obtained a court judgement against that debtor. [OFr *garniss-*, stem of *garnir* to furnish (old form *warnir*), from a Gmc root seen in OE *warnian*, Ger *warnen*; cf **warn**[1]]

garotte. See **garrotte**.

garpike. See **garfish**.

garran. Same as **garron**.

garre. See **gar**[2].

garret *gar'it*, *n* a turret or watchtower (*obs*); a room just under the roof of a house, an attic room. — *adj* **garr'eted** provided with garrets; lodged in a garret (*rare*, *literary*). — *n* **garreteer'** (*archaic*) a person who lives in a garret, *esp* a poor author. — **garr'et-master** a cabinetmaker, locksmith, etc working on his own account for the dealers. [OFr *garite* a place of safety, *guarir*, *warir* to preserve (Fr *guérir*), from the Gmc root seen in **ware**[1]]

garrigue or **garigue** *ga-rēg'*, *n* uncultivated open scrubland of the Mediterranean region; the scrub growing on it. [Fr, from Provençal *garriga* stony ground]

garrison *gar'i-sn*, *n* a body of troops stationed in a town, fortress, etc to defend it; a fortified place. — *vt* to furnish (a town, etc) with a garrison; to station (troops) as a garrison; to defend by fortresses manned with troops. — **garrison town** a town in which a garrison is stationed. [OFr *garison*, from *garir*, *guerir* to furnish; Gmc; see **garret**]

garron or **garran** *gar'ən*, *n* a small type of horse. [Ir *gearran*]

garrot[1] *gar'ət*, *n* a name for various ducks, but *esp* the golden-eye. [Fr]

garrot[2] *gar'ət*, (*surg*) *n* (also **garr'otte** or **gar'otte**) a tourniquet. [Fr; see **garrotte**]

garrotte, **garotte** or (*US*) **garrote** *gä-rot'* or *gə-rot'*, *n* a Spanish mode of putting criminals to death; the apparatus for the purpose, *orig* a string round the throat tightened by twisting a stick, later a brass collar tightened by a screw, whose point enters the spinal marrow. — *vt* to execute by the garrotte; suddenly to render unconscious by semi-strangulation in order to rob: — *pr p* **garrott'ing** or **garott'ing**; *pa t* and *pa p* **garrott'ed** or **garott'ed**. — *n* **garrott'er** or **garott'er**. — *n* **garrott'ing** or **garott'ing**. [Sp *garrot(t)e*; cf Fr *garrot* a stick]

garrulous *gar'ōō-ləs*, also *-ə-*, or *ū-*, *adj* talkative; loquacious; wordy, voluble. — *n* **garrulity** (*-ōō'li-ti*, or *-ū'*) loquacity. — *adv* **garr'ulously**. — *n* **garr'ulousness**. [L *garrulu*, from *garrīre* to chatter]

garrya *gar'i-ə*, *n* a North American ornamental catkin-bearing evergreen shrub of the genus *Garrya*. [Named after N *Garry* (1781–1856) of the Hudson's Bay Company]

garryowen *ga-ri-ō'ən*, (*Rugby football*) *n* a high kick forward together with a rush towards the landing-place of the ball. [Named after the *Garryowen* Rugby Club in Limerick]

gart. See **gar**[2].

garter *gär'tər*, *n* a band used to support a stocking; a suspender (*NAm*); (with *cap*) (the badge of) the highest order of knighthood in Great Britain. — *vt* to put a garter on; to support, bind, decorate, or surround with a garter. — **gar'ter-snake** in N America, any snake of the genus *Eutaenia*, non-venomous, longitudinally striped; in S Africa applied to two venomous snakes, with black and red rings (see **Elaps**); **gar'ter-stitch** a plain stitch in knitting; horizontally ribbed knitting made by using plain stitches only. — **Garter King-of-Arms** the chief herald of the Order of the Garter. [OFr *gartier* (Fr *jarretière*), from OFr *garet* (Fr *jarret*) ham of the leg, prob Celtic, as Breton *gar* shank of the leg]

garth *gärth*, *n* an enclosure or yard (now *dialect*); a garden (now *dialect*); a courtyard within a cloister; (or **fish'-garth**) a weir in a river for catching fish. [ON *garthr* a court; cf **yard**[2], **garden**]

garuda *gur'ōō-dä*, *n* (also with *cap*) a Hindu demigod, part man, part bird. [Sans]

garum *gā'rəm*, (*hist*) *n* a thick sauce prepared from pickled fish, very popular amongst the ancient Romans. [L, from Gr *garos*, *garon*]

garvie *gär'vi*, (*Scot*) *n* a sprat. — Also **gar'vock**. [Gaelic *garbhag* is perh from Scots]

gas *gas*, *n* a substance in a condition in which it has no definite boundaries or fixed volume, but will fill any space; often restricted to such a substance above its critical temperature; a substance or mixture which is in this state in ordinary terrestrial conditions; coal-gas, or other gas for lighting or heating, or one used for attack in warfare; gaslight; laughing gas (see under **laughing**); empty, boastful, frothy, garrulous, or pert talk (*colloq*); something delightful, impressive, exciting (*colloq*); short for gasoline (petrol) (*NAm*, *Austr* and *NZ*): — *pl* **gas'es**. — *vt* to supply, attack, light, inflate or treat with gas; to poison or asphyxiate with gas; to deceive, impose on by talking gas (*old US slang*); to impress or thrill (*US slang*). — *vi* to emit gas; to chatter, *esp* vapidly (*colloq*): — *pr p* **gass'ing**; *pa t* and *pa p* **gassed**. — *n* **gasalier'**, **gaselier'** or **gasolier'** a hanging frame with branches for gas-jets (formed on false analogy after *chandelier*). — *n* **gasē'ity** gaseous state, character or condition. — *adj* **gaseous** (*gāz'*, *gās'*; *gas'* or *gaz'i-əs*, also *gā'shəs* or *gash'əs*) in the form of gas; of, or relating to, gas. — *n* **gas'eousness**. — *n* **gasificā'tion** conversion into gas. — *adj* **gas'iform**. — *vt* **gas'ify** to convert into gas. — *n* **gas'ifier**. — *n* **gas'ogene** see **gazogene**. — *n* **gas'ohol** or **gas'ahol** a mixture of 8 or 9 parts petrol and 1 or 2 parts alcohol, used as a fuel. — *n* **gas'olene** or **gas'oline** (*-ə-lēn*) a low-boiling petroleum distillate; the ordinary word for petrol (*NAm*). — *n* **gasom'eter** a storage tank for gas. — *adj* **gasomet'ric** or **gasomet'rical** relating to the measurement of gas. — *n* **gasom'etry** the measurement of amounts of gas. — *n* **gass'er** an oil well that produces natural gas; something exceptional or remarkable, very successful or funny (*US slang*). — *n* **gassi'ness**. — *n* **gass'ing** poisoning by gas; idle or vapid chattering. — *adj* **gass'y** full of gas; abounding in or emitting gas; gaseous; given to vain and boastful talk (*slang*). — **gas'bag** a bag for holding gas, *esp* in a balloon or airship; a talkative person (*colloq*); **gas black** soot produced by burning natural gas; **gas'-bottle** a steel cylinder for holding compressed gas; **gas'-bracket** a gas pipe projecting from the wall of a room for lighting purposes; **gas'-buoy** a floating buoy carrying a supply of gas to light a lamp fixed on it; **gas'-burner** the perforated part of a gas-fitting where the gas issues and is burned; **gas cap** gas found in the highest part of oil-containing rock; **gas-car'bon** a hard dense carbon deposited in coal-gas retorts; **gas centrifuge** a centrifuge for separating gases; **gas chamber** an enclosed place designed for killing by means of gas (also **gas oven**); **gas chromatography** a widely used form of chromatography in which a gas is passed down the column which contains the mixture to be separated and a solvent; **gas'-coal** any coal suitable for making gas; cannel coal; **gas'-coke** coke made in gas retorts; **gas'-condenser** an apparatus for freeing coal-gas from tar; **gas cooker** a cooking-stove using gas as fuel. — *adj* **gas'-cooled** cooled by a flow of gas. — **gas-discharge tube** any tube in which an electric discharge takes place through a gas; **gas engine** an engine worked by the explosion of gas; **gaseous diffusion** (*nuc eng*) an isotope separation process based on the principle of molecular diffusion; **gaseous diffusion enrichment** (*phys*) the enrichment of uranium isotopes using gaseous uranium hexafluoride passing through a porous barrier; **gas escape** a leakage of gas; **gas'field** a region in which natural gas occurs. — *adj* **gas'-filled** filled with gas. — **gas fire** a room-heating apparatus in which gas is burned. — *adj* **gas'-fired** fuelled, or heated, by gas(es). — **gas'-fitter** a person whose job is to fit up the pipes, etc for gas appliances; **gas'-fittings** gas-pipes, etc for lighting and heating by gas; **gas'-furnace** a furnace of which the fuel is gas; **gas gangrene** gangrene resulting from infection of a wound by certain bacteria which form gases in the flesh; **gas'-globe** a glass used to enclose and shade a gaslight; **gas gun** a gun in which gas is the fuel or propellant; **gas'-guzzler** (*US colloq*) a car that consumes large amounts of petrol. — *adj* **gas'-guzzling** (*colloq*; esp *US*) consuming large amounts of petrol. — **gas heater** any heating apparatus in which gas is used; **gas helmet** a gas mask in the form of a helmet completely covering the head; **gas'holder** a storage tank for storing gas; a gasometer; **gas jar** a tall, narrow, cylindrical glass vessel for collecting and holding a gas in chemical experiments; **gas jet** a jet of gas; a gas-flame; the perforated part of a gas-fitting where the gas issues and is burnt, a burner; **gas lamp** a lamp that burns gas; **gas lift** a method of extracting oil from the bottom of an oil well by injecting compressed liquid gas there; **gas'light** light produced by combustion of gas; a gas jet, burner or lamp. — *adj* of, concerned with, or for use by, gaslight. — **gas'-lime** lime that has been used in purifying gas; **gas'-liquor** a solution of ammonia and ammonium salts derived from gas-making. — *adj* **gas'lit** lighted by gas. — **gas main** a principal gas pipe from the gasworks; **gas'man** a man employed in gas-making, in repairing or installing gas-fittings, or in the reading of meters; **gas mantle** a gauze covering, chemically prepared, enclosing a gas-jet, and becoming incandescent when heated; **gas mask** a respiratory device (covering nose, mouth and eyes) as a protection against poisonous gases; **gas meter** an instrument for measuring gas consumed; **gas'-motor** a gas engine; **gas oil** a petroleum distillate, intermediate between kerosine and lubricating oil, used as (*esp* heating) fuel; **gas oven** the oven of a gas cooker; a gas chamber. — *adj* **gas-per'meable** (of hard contact lenses) allowing oxygen to penetrate through to the eye. — **gas pipe** a pipe for conveying gas; **gas'-plant** dittany (see **burning bush**); **gas plasma display** (*comput*) a type of screen used on portable microcomputers, in which electronic signals form illuminated characters on a flat screen; **gas poker** a poker-shaped gas appliance with gas jets, that can be inserted into fuel to kindle a fire; **gas'-retort** a closed heated chamber in which gas is made; **gas ring** a hollow ring with perforations serving as gas jets; **gas shell** an artillery shell that gives off a poisonous gas or vapour on bursting; **gas stove** an apparatus in which coal-gas is used for heating or cooking, a gas cooker; **gas tank** a reservoir for coal-gas; **gas tap**; **gas'-tar** coal-tar. — *adj* **gas'-tight** impervious to gas. — **gas trap** a trap in a drain to prevent escape of foul gas; **gas turbine** a machine consisting of a combustion chamber, to which air is supplied by a compressor and in which the air is heated at constant pressure, and a turbine driven by the hot expanding gases; **gas'-water** water through which coal-gas has been passed in scrubbing; gas- or ammoniacal liquor; **gas well** a boring from which natural gas issues; **gas'-works** a factory where gas is made. — **gas and gaiters** nonsense; **ideal gas** see under **idea**; **natural gas** see **natural**; **step on the gas** (ie gasoline) (*colloq*) to press the accelerator pedal of a motor-car; to speed up, hurry. [A word invented by J B van Helmont (1577–1644); suggested by Gr *chaos*]

gasahol, **gasalier**. See under **gas**.

Gascon *gas'kən*, *n* a native of Gascony; (without *cap*) a boaster (*literary*). — *adj* of Gascony. — *n* **gasconade'** (*literary*) boasting talk. — *vi* (*literary*) to boast extravagantly. — *n* **gasconād'er**. — *n* **gas'conism** boastfulness. [Fr]

gaseity, **gaselier**, **gaseous**. See under **gas**.

gash[1] *gash*, *vt* to cut deeply into. — *n* a deep, open cut. [Formerly *garse*, from OFr *garser* to scarify, from LL *garsa* scarification, poss from Gr *charassein* to scratch]

gash[2] *gash*, (*Scot*) *adj* talkative. — *vi* to tattle.

gash[3] *gash*, (chiefly *Scot*) *adj* ghastly, hideous. — Also **gash'ful** or **gash'ly**. — *n* **gash'liness**. — *adv* **gash'ly**. [Perh **ghastful** or **ghastly**]

gash[4] *gash*, *adj* spare, extra (*slang*). — *n* rubbish, waste (*slang*, orig and esp *naut*).

gasification, **gasify**, etc. See under **gas**.

gasket *gas'kit*, *n* a canvas band used to bind the sails to the yards when furled (*naut*); a strip of tow, etc for packing a piston, etc; a layer of packing material, *esp* a flat sheet of asbestos compound, sometimes between thin copper sheets, used for making gas-tight joints between engine cylinders and heads, etc. — Also rarely **gas'kin**. [Cf Fr *garcette*, Ital *gaschetta*; ety dubious]

gaskins *gas'kinz*, (*obs*; *literary*) *n*. Same as **galligaskins**.

gasohol, **gasolene**, **gasoline**, **gasolier**, **gasometer**, etc. See under **gas**.

gasp *gäsp*, *vi* to pant, or breathe in a distressed manner (often *gasp for breath*); to breathe in sharply, in astonishment, horror, etc; to desire eagerly (with *for*). — *vt* (sometimes with *out*) to breathe, pant; to utter with gasps. — *n* the act of gasping; a sharp, noisy intake of breath (in astonishment, horror, etc). — *n* **gasp'er** a person who gasps; a cheap cigarette (*slang*). — *n* **gasp'iness**. — *n* and *adj* **gasp'ing**. — *adv* **gasp'ingly**. — *adj* **gasp'y**. — **the last gasp** the point of death. [ON *geispa* to yawn; cf *geip* idle talk]

gaspereau *gas'pə-rō* (*Can*) *n* the alewife (qv), a type of herring. [Fr *gasparot* a kind of herring]

gasser *gas'ər*, *n* a well, etc that yields natural gas.

gast *gäst*, *vt* (*Shakesp*) to make aghast, to frighten or terrify. — *adj* **gastfull** (*Spenser*; see **ghastful**). — *n* **gast'ness** or **gast'nesse** (*Shakesp*) dread. [OE *gǣstan*; cf **aghast**]

Gastarbeiter *gast'ar-bī-tər*, *n* a migrant worker, *esp* one who does menial work. [Ger, literally guest-worker]

gaster (*entomol*) *gas'tər*, *n* in hymenopterous insects, the abdomen proper, to the rear of the first (often constricted) abdominal segment. [Gr *gastēr* belly]

gastero- *gas'tər-ō-*, *combining form* denoting stomach or belly. — *n pl* **Gasteromycetes** (*gas'tər-ō-mī-sē'tez*; Gr *mykētes*, pl of *mykēs* mushroom) an order of fungi that includes puffballs, stinkhorns, etc. — **gasteropod**, **Gasteropoda**, **gasteropodous** see **gastropod**, **Gastropoda**, **gastropodous** under **gastro-**. [Gr combining form of *gastēr* belly]

Gasthaus *gast'hows* or **Gasthof** *-hōf*, (*Ger*) *n* a hotel, guest-house.

gastr- *combining form*. See **gastro-**.

gastraea *gas-trē'ə*, (*zool*) *n* Haeckel's hypothetical ancestor of the Metazoa, like a gastrula. [New L, from Gr *gastēr* belly]

gastraeum *gas-trē'əm*, (*zool*) *n* the under-surface of the body, *esp* in birds. [Gr *gastēr* belly]

gastralgia ... to ... **gastrectomy**. See under **gastro-**.

gastric *gas'trik*, *n* belonging to, pertaining to, or in the region of, the stomach. — **gastric fever** typhoid; **gastric flu** a popular term for any of several disorders of the stomach and intestinal tract, with symptoms of nausea, diarrhoea, abdominal cramps and fever; **gastric juice** a thin clear acid fluid secreted by the stomach to effect digestion; **gastric mill** in Malacostraca, a digestive organ sometimes known as the stomach, provided with muscles and ossicles for trituration of food. [Gr *gastēr* belly]

gastrin *gas'trin*, (*biol*) *n* a hormone which stimulates production of gastric juice. [**gastr-** and **-in**(1)]

gastritis *gas-trī'tis*, (*med*) *n* inflammation of the stomach. [Gr *gastēr* belly, and sfx *-itis* inflammation.]

gastro- *gas-trō-*, or often before a vowel **gastr-** *combining form* denoting (of or like) the stomach or belly. — *n* **gastral'gia** (Gr *algos* pain; *med*) pain in the stomach. — *n* **gastrec'tomy** (Gr *ek* out, and *tomē* cutting) surgical removal of the stomach, or part of it. — *n* **gastrocnemius** (*gas-trok-nē'mi-əs*; Gr *knēmē* lower leg) the muscle that bulges the calf of the leg: — *pl* **gastrocne'mī**. — *adj* **gastroenter'ic** gastrointestinal. — *n* **gastroenterī'tis** (*med*) inflammation of the lining of the stomach and intestines. — *n* **gastroenterol'ogist**. — *n* **gastroenterol'ogy** (*med*) the study of the stomach and intestines. — *adj* **gastrointest'inal** (or *-īn'l*) of, relating to, or consisting of, the stomach and intestines. — *n* **gastrol'oger**. — *adj* **gastrolog'ical**. — *n* **gastrol'ogy** cookery, good eating. — *n* **gastromancy** (*gas'trō-man-si*; Gr *manteiā* soothsaying) divination by sounds from the belly, ie ventriloquism; divination by large-bellied glasses. — *n* **gastronome** (*gas'trə-nōm*; Gr *nomos* law) or **gastronomer** (*-tron'ə-mər*) a lover and connoisseur of good food and wines, an epicure. — *adj* **gastronomic** (*-nom'ik*) or **gastronom'ical**. — *n* **gastron'omist**. — *n* **gastron'omy** the art or science of good eating. — *n* **gas'tropod** or **gas'teropod** (Gr *pous*, *podos* foot; *zool*) any of the **Gastrop'oda** or **Gasterop'oda**, a class of asymmetrical molluscs, including the limpets, whelks, snails and slugs, in which the foot is broad and flat, and the shell, if any, in one piece and conical. — *adj* **gastrop'odous** or **gasterop'odous**. — *n* **gas'troscope** an instrument for inspecting the interior of the stomach. — *n* **gas'trosoph** (Gr *sophos* wise) a person skilled in matters of eating. — *n* **gastros'opher**. — *n* **gastros'ophy**. — *n* **gastros'tomy** (Gr *stoma* mouth) the making of an opening to introduce food into the stomach. — *n* **gastrot'omy** (Gr *tomē* a cut) the operation of cutting open the stomach or abdomen. [Gr *gastēr* belly]

gastrula *gas'trŏŏ-lə*, (*zool*) *n* an embryo at the stage in which it forms a two-layered cup by the invagination of its wall. — *n* **gastrulā'tion** formation of a gastrula. [New L, a little stomach]

gat[1] *gat*, (*slang*, chiefly *US*) *n* a gun, revolver. [**gatling gun**]

gat[2] *gat*, (*Bible*) *pa t* of **get**.

gat[3] *gat*, *n* an opening between sandbanks; a strait. [Perh ON]

gat[4] *gät*, *n* in Indian music, the second and *usu* final section of a raga. — Also **gath**. [Sans *gāth*]

gate[1] *gāt*, *n* a passage into a city, enclosure, or any large building; a narrow opening or defile; a frame for closing an entrance; an entrance, passage or channel; an obstacle consisting of two posts, markers, etc between which competitors in a slalom, etc must pass; (at an airport) any of the numbered exits from which to board an aircraft; the people who pay to see a game, hence, the number attending; the total amount of money paid for entrance (also **gate'-money**); a starting gate; an electronic circuit which passes signals when permitted by another independent source of similar signals; an electronic circuit with one or more inputs and one output (*comput*); the part of a projector, printer or camera which holds the film flat behind the lens; an H-shaped series of slots for controlling the movement of a gear lever in a gearbox. — *vt* to supply with a gate; to punish (students or schoolchildren) by imposing a curfew or by confinement to school precincts for a time. — *adj* **gāt'ed** having a gate or gates (also in combination, as **hun'dred-gated**); punished by gating. — *adj* **gate'less**. — *n* **gāt'ing**. — *vi* and *vt* **gate'crash** to enter without paying or invitation. — **gate'crasher**; **gate fever** (*prison slang*) a neurotic or restless condition affecting long-term prisoners near the end of their prison sentence; **gate'-fine** the fine imposed upon the gated for disobedience; **gate'fold** an oversize page in a book, etc that has to be folded in on both sides, and opened out like a gate, a fold-out; **gate'house** (*archit*) a building over or at a gate; **gate'keeper** a person who watches over a gate and supervises the traffic through it (also **gate'man**); any of several large butterflies with brown or orange wings. — *adj* **gate'-legged** or **gate'leg** (of a table) having a hinged and framed leg that can swing in to let down a leaf. — **gate-money** see **gate** above; **gate net** a net hung across a gateway for catching hares; **gate of horn** see **ivory gate** below; **gate'post** a post from which a gate is hung or against which it shuts; **gate'-tower** a tower beside or over a gate; **gate valve** (in a pipeline) a valve with a movable barrier or gate for regulating the flow; **gate'vein** (*obs* or *fig*) the great abdominal vein; **gate'way** the way through a gate; a structure at a gate; a connection between computer networks, or between a computer network and a telephone line; any entrance or means of entrance (also as *adj*; often *fig*). — **break gates** (at Oxford and Cambridge) to enter college after the prescribed hour; **gate of justice** a gate eg of a city, temple, etc, where a sovereign or judge sat to dispense justice; **ivory gate** or **gate of horn** (or in *Spenser* **silver**) in Greek legend and poetical imagery, the gates through which false and true dreams respectively come; **stand in the gate** (*Bible*) to occupy a position of defence. [OE *geat* a way; Du *gat*, ON *gat*]

gate[2] *gāt*, (*Scot* and *NEng dialect*) *n* a way, path, street (often in street names, such as *Cowgate*, *Kirkgate*); manner of doing. See also **gait**[1]. [ON *gata*; Dan *gade*, Ger *Gasse*]

gate[3] *gāt*, (*Spenser*) *n* an *obs* Northern form of **goat**.

-gate *-gāt*, *sfx* attached to the name of a person or place to denote (on the analogy of **Watergate** (qv)) a scandal connected with that person or place.

gateau or **gâteau** *gat'ō* or *gä-tō*, *n* a rich cake, filled with cream, decorated with icing, etc: — *pl* **gateaus** (*gat'ōz*) or **gâteaux** (*gat'ōz* or *gä-tō*). [Fr]

gath. See **gat**[4].

gather *gadh'ər*, *vt* to collect; to assemble; to amass; to cull; to pick up; to draw together; (in sewing) to draw into puckers by passing a thread through and pulling it tight; to arrange (signatures of a book) in sequence for binding; to learn by inference; to have increase in (eg speed). — *vi* to assemble or muster; to increase; to suppurate; to make way (*naut*); to arrange signatures of a book in correct sequence for binding. — *n* a pleat or fold in cloth, made by drawing threads through; (in *pl*) that part of the dress which is gathered or drawn in. — *n* **gath'erer** a person who collects, amasses, assembles or culls; a worker who collects molten glass on the end of a rod preparatory to blowing. — *n* **gath'ering** the action of someone who or something that gathers; a crowd or assembly; a narrowing; a number of leaves of paper folded one within another; the assembling of the sheets of a book; a suppurating swelling, boil or abscess (*colloq*). — **gath'ering-coal** or **-peat** a coal, or peat, put into a fire to keep it alive till morning; **gath'ering-cry** a summons to assemble for war; **gath'ering-ground** catchment area. — **gather breath** to recover wind; **gather ground** to gain ground; **gather oneself together** to collect all one's powers, like one about to leap; **gather to a head** to ripen; to come into a state of preparation for action or effect; **gather way** (*naut*) to begin to make headway by sail or steam so as to answer the helm. [OE *gaderian*, *gæderian*; (*tō*)*gædere* together; *geador* together, and *gæd* fellowship]

gatling gun *gat'ling gun*, *n* a machine gun invented by R J *Gatling* about 1861.

GATT *gat*, *abbrev*: General Agreement on Tariffs and Trade, an international treaty to promote trade and economic benefits, and to simplify and standardize international trading procedures, signed in 1947.

gau *gow*, *n* a territorial district of ancient Germany; (under the Nazi régime) a German political district. — *n* **gauleiter** (*gow'lī-tər*) a chief official of a district under the Nazi régime; an overbearing wielder of petty authority (*colloq*, *fig*). [Ger *Gau* district, and *Leiter* leader]

gauche *gōsh*, *adj* clumsy; tactless; awkward. — *n* **gaucherie** (*gōsh'ə-rē* or *-rē'*) clumsiness; (an instance of) social awkwardness. [Fr, left]

Gaucher's disease *gō'shāz diz-ēz'*, *n* a rare hereditary disease characterized by the accumulation of certain fats in the liver and spleen. [P *Gaucher* (1854–1918), French physician]

gaucho *gow'chō*, *n* a cowboy of the pampas, *usu* of mixed Spanish and Indian descent; (in *pl*) women's knee-length wide trousers: — *pl* **gau'chos**. — *adj* **gauches'co** of a type of Spanish poetry inspired by the life, language and customs of the gauchos. [Sp]

gaucie, **gaucy**, **gawcy** or **gawsy** *gö'si*, (*Scot*) *adj* portly, jolly. [Origin unknown]

gaud *göd*, *n* a large ornamental bead on a rosary (*obs*); a prank (*obs*); an ornament; a piece of finery; showy ceremony; festivity (*obs*). — *vi* (*obs*) to make merry. — *vt* to adorn with gauds (*obs*); to paint, eg the cheeks (*obs*; *Shakesp*) — *n* **gaudeā'mus** (in Scotland *gow-di-ä'mōōs*; *L*, let us be glad; opening word of a students' song) a joyful celebration among students. — *n* **gaud'ery** finery. — *adv* **gaud'ily**. — *n* **gaud'iness**. — *n* **gaud'y** an entertainment or feast, *esp* in certain English colleges. — *adj* showy; merry, gay; vulgarly bright. — **gaud'y-day**; **gaud'y-night**. [In part appar from OFr *gaudir*, from L *gaudēre* to be glad, or *gaudium* joy; in part directly from L]

gaudeamus igitur *gö-di-äm'əs ij'i-tər* or *gow-de-äm'ōōs ig'i-tōōr*, (*L*) let us therefore rejoice.

gaudgie. See **gadgie**.

gaudium certaminis *gö'di-əm sûr-tam'in-is* or *gow'di-ōōm ker-täm'in-is*, (*L*) joy of combat.

gaudy. See under **gaud**.

gaudy-green *gö'di-grēn*, (*obs*) *n* and *adj* yellowish green. [OFr *gaude* weld, dyer's-rocket]

gaufer, **gaufre**. See **gofer**.

gauffer, **gauffering**. See **goffer**.

gauge, also **gage**, *gāj*, *n* a measuring apparatus; a standard of measure; a means of limitation or adjustment to a standard; a measurement, such as the diameter of a wire, calibre of a tube, or width of a row of slates; the distance between a pair of wheels or rails; a means of estimate; relative position of a ship to another vessel and the wind (in this sense *usu* **gage**; see **lee**[1], **weather**). — *vt* to measure; to estimate; to adjust to a standard. — *vi* to measure the contents of casks. — *adj* **gauge'able** capable of being gauged. — *n* **gaug'er** a person who gauges; a person who works in excise. — *n* **gaug'ing** the measuring of casks holding excisable liquors. — **gauge boson** (*phys*) a type of particle that mediates the interaction between two fundamental particles; **gauge glass** a tube to show height of water; **gauge theory** any one of the theories in particle physics that attempts to describe the various types of interaction between fundamental particles; **gaug'ing-rod** an instrument for measuring the contents of casks. — *adj* **broad'-** or **narr'ow-gauge** in railroad construction respectively greater or less than **standard gauge**, in Britain 1·435 metres (56½ inches). [OFr *gauge* (Fr *jauge*)]

gauje. See **gadgie**.

Gaul *göl*, *n* a name given to ancient France; an inhabitant of Gaul. — *adj* **Gaul'ish**. — *n* the Celtic (Brythonic) language of the Gauls. [Fr *Gaule*, from L *Gallia*, *Gallus*; perh connected with OE *wealh* foreign]

gauleiter. See **gau**.

Gaullist *gōl'ist*, *n* a follower of the French soldier and statesman General Charles de *Gaulle* (President of the Fifth Republic 1958–69). — Also *adj*. — *n* **Gaull'ism** the principles and policies of Gaullists.

Gault *gölt*, *n* a series of beds of clay and marl between the Upper and the Lower Greensand (*geol*); (**gault**) brick earth; a brick of gault clay. — *n* **gault'er** a person who digs gault. [Origin obscure]

gaultheria *göl-thē'ri-ə*, *n* a plant of the *Gaultheria* genus of evergreen aromatic plants of the heath family, which includes the American wintergreen and salal. [From the Swedish–Canadian botanist Hugues *Gaulthier*]

gaum[1] *göm* or **gorm** *görm*, (now *dialect*) *vt* to smear; to daub; to clog; to handle clumsily (*obs*). — *n* a smear; a daub; a shiny lustre as on new varnish; stickiness; a sticky mass. — *adj* (*rare*) **gaum'y** or **gorm'y** dauby. [Ety doubtful, perh variant of **gum**[2]]

gaum[2] *göm* or **gorm** *görm*, (*dialect*) *n* notice, heed, regard, attention; understanding. — *vt* to pay attention to, to heed; to understand. — *adj* **gaum'less** or **gorm'less** stupid, witless, vacant. [ON *gaumr* heed, attention]

gaun *gön*, *n*. Scots for **going** (see **gae**[1]).

gaunch. See **ganch**.

gaunt[1]. See **gant**.

gaunt[2] *gönt*, *adj* thin; of a pinched appearance; haggard; grim. — *adv* **gaunt'ly**. — *n* **gaunt'ness**. [ME, poss from Scand; cf Norw dialect *gand* thin stick, lanky person; OFr *gauntet* yellowish, also suggested]

gauntlet[1] *gönt'lit*, *n* the iron glove of armour, formerly thrown down in challenge and taken up in acceptance; a heavy glove with a long, wide cuff covering the wrist; the cuff of such a glove, covering the wrist. — *adj* **gaunt'leted** wearing a gauntlet or gauntlets. — **gaunt'let-guard** a guard of a sword or dagger, protecting the hand very thoroughly. — **throw down** and **take up the gauntlet** respectively to give and to accept a challenge. [Fr *gantelet*, dimin of *gant* glove, of Gmc origin; cf Swed *vante* a mitten, glove, ON *vöttr* a glove, Dan *vante*]

gauntlet[2] *gönt'lit* or (now *rare*) **gantlope** *gant'lōp*, *n* the former military (or naval) punishment of having to run through a lane of soldiers (or sailors) who strike one as one passes. — **run the gauntlet** to undergo the punishment of the gauntlet; to expose oneself to hostile treatment, harsh criticism or public disgrace. [Swed *gatlopp*, from *gata* lane (cf **gate**[2]), and *lopp* course (cf **leap**); confused with **gauntlet**[1]]

gauntree, **gauntry**. See **gantry**.

gaup, **gauper**, **gaupus**. See **gawp**.

gaur *gowr*, *n* a species of large, wild ox inhabiting some mountainous parts of India. [Hindustani]

gauss *gows*, *n* the CGS unit of magnetic flux density (formerly used for other magnetic units). — *adj* **Gauss'ian** (also without *cap*) of or due to Johann Karl Friedrich *Gauss* (1777–1855), German mathematician and physicist. — **Gaussian distribution** (*statistics*) normal distribution (qv).

gauze *göz*, *n* a thin, transparent fabric; an openwork fabric or fine mesh. — *n* **gauz'iness**. — *adj* **gauz'y**. — **gauze'-tree** a W Indian tree, the lacebark. — *adj* **gauze'-winged** having gauzy wings. [Fr *gaze*, dubiously referred to *Gaza* in Palestine]

gavage *gä-väzh'*, *n* feeding by stomach-tube (*med*); force-feeding of poultry. [Fr *gaver*, from *gave* bird's crop]

gave *gāv*, *pa t* of **give**.

gavel[1] *gā'vl*. A dialect form of **gable**.

gavel[2] *gav'l*, (*hist*) *n* tribute or rent. — **gav'elkīnd** a tenure long prevailing in Kent by which lands descended from the father to all sons (or, failing sons, to all daughters) in equal portions, and not by primogeniture; **gav'elman** a tenant holding land in gavelkind. [OE *gafol* tribute; connected with *giefan* to give]

gavel[3] *gav'l*, *n* a mallet; a chairman's, auctioneer's or judge's hammer. [Orig US; origin uncertain]

gavelock *gav'ə-lək*, (*hist* or *dialect*) *n* a javelin; a crow-bar. [OE *gafeluc*]

gavial *gā'vi-əl*, **garial** or **gharial** *gur'i-əl*, *n* an Indian crocodile (*Gavialis*) with a very long slender muzzle. [Hindi *ghariyāl* crocodile]

gavotte *gä-vot'*, *n* a dance, somewhat like a country-dance, *orig* a dance of the *Gavots*, people of the French Upper Alps; the music for such a dance in common time, often occurring in suites.

gawcy. Same as **gaucie**.

gawd *göd*, (*Shakesp*) *n*. Same as **gaud**.

gawk *gök*, *n* a person who is awkward or ungainly, *esp* from tallness, shyness or simplicity; a person who stares and gapes. — *vi* to stare and gape. — *n* **gawker**. — *n* **gawk'ihood**. — *n* **gawk'iness**. — *adj* **gawk'y** awkward; ungainly. — *n* a tall awkward person; a gawk. [Ety obscure: perh altered from (obs) *gaw* to gape, stare; prob not Fr *gauche* left]

gawp or **gaup** *göp*, (*colloq*) *vi* to gape in astonishment. — *n* **gawp'er** or **gaup'er**. — *n* **gaup'us** or **gawp'us** (*dialect*) a silly person. [From obs *galp*; cognate with **yelp**]

gawsy. Same as **gaucie**.

gay *gā*, *adj* (*compar* **gay'er**, *superl* **gay'est**) lively; bright, colourful; playful, merry; pleasure-loving, dissipated (as in *gay dog* a rake) (*archaic*); of loose life, whorish (*obs*); showy; spotted, speckled (*dialect*); in modern use, homosexual (orig *prison slang*); relating to or frequented by homosexuals (as *gay bar*); great, considerable (*Scot*; usu **gey** *gī*); often by hendiadys instead of an adv, as in *gey and easy*, easy enough; unduly familiar (*old US*). — *adv* (*Scot*; **gey**) rather, fairly, considerably. — *n* a homosexual; a gallant (*obs*). — *n* **gai'ety** gayness (but not used in sense of homosexuality). — *adv* **gai'ly**. — *n* **gay'ness**. — *adj* **gay'some** (*rare*) gladsome. — **gay'-bashing** (*colloq*) violent victimization of homosexuals by heterosexuals; **gay deceiver** (*old-fashioned*) a libertine; (in *pl*) a foam-padded brassière (*slang*); **Gay Gordons** a traditional Scottish dance that involves a walking movement and a polka alternately; **gay liberation** the freeing of homosexuals from social disadvantages and prejudice; **gay science** (*hist*) a rendering of *gai saber*, the Provençal name for the art of poetry. [OFr *gai*, perh from OHGer *wâhi* pretty]

gayal or **gyal** *gī'al*, *n* an Indian domesticated ox, related to the gaur, with curved horns. [Hindi]

Gay-Lussac's law. See under **law**[1].

gay-you *gī'ū* or *gā'ū*, *n* a narrow flat-bottomed Vietnamese boat with outrigger and masts. [Vietnamese *ghe hâu*]

gaz. *abbrev*: gazette; gazetteer.

gazal. See **ghazal**.

gazania *gə-zā'ni-ə*, *n* any plant of the genus *Gazania* of the southern hemisphere with bright yellow or orange composite flowers. [Theodore of *Gaza* (1398–1478), who translated the botanical works of Theophrastus]

gaze *gāz*, *vi* to look fixedly, or long and steadily, *esp* in admiration or abstraction. — *n* a fixed or long steady look; the object gazed at. — *n* **gaze'ment** (*Spenser*). — *adj* **gaze'ful** (*Spenser*) looking intently. — *n* **gā'zer**. — *adj* **gā'zy** (*rare*) affording a wide prospect; given to gazing. — **gaze'-hound** (*usu hist*) a hound that pursues by sight; **gaz'ing-stock** a object or person exposed to public view, generally unpleasantly. — **at gaze** (*obs*) in the attitude of gazing. [Prob cognate with obs *gaw* to stare; cf ON *gā* to heed; Swed dialect *gasa* to stare]

gazebo *gə-zē'bō*, *n* a summerhouse or other small structure giving a commanding view of the landscape, a belvedere: — *pl* **gazē'bos** or **gazē'boes**. [Perh connected with **gaze**, as a sham-Latin construction (after model of *videbo* I shall see)]

gazelle *gə-zel'*, *n* any of various small, large-eyed antelopes (specif *Gazella dorcas*) of N Africa and SW Asia. [Fr, from Ar *ghazāl* a wild goat]

gazette *gə-zet'*, *n* (with *cap*) an official newspaper containing lists of government appointments, legal notices, despatches, etc; a title used for some newspapers. — *vt* to publish or mention in a gazette; to announce or confirm (a person's appointment or promotion), *esp* in an official gazette: — *pr p* **gazett'ing**; *pa t* and *pa p* **gazett'ed**. — *n* **gazetteer'** (*gaz-*) a geographical dictionary, a reference book containing alphabetical entries for places of the world, with maps, etc; *orig* a writer for a gazette, an official journalist. — *vt* to describe in a gazetteer. — *adj* **gazetteer'ish**. — **gazetted officer** one of a higher grade who is listed in an official gazette. — **appear** (or **have one's name**) **in the Gazette** to be mentioned in one of the official newspapers, *esp* of bankrupts. [Fr, from Ital *gazzetta* a small coin; or from Ital *gazzetta*, dimin of *gazza* magpie]

gazogene *gaz'ə-jēn* or **gasogene** *gas'ə-*, *n* an apparatus for carbonating water, etc. [Fr *gazogène*, from *gaz* gas, and Gr sfx *-genēs*, from root of *gennaein* to generate]

gazon or **gazoon** *gə-zōōn'*, (*obs*) *n* a sod in fortification; used erroneously by Hogg for a compact body of men. [Fr, turf]

gazoo, **gazooka**. See **kazoo**.

gazpacho *gas-päch'ō*, or *gəz-*, *n* a spicy Spanish vegetable soup, served cold: — *pl* **gazpach'os**. [Sp]

gazump *gə-zump'*, (*colloq*) *vt* and *vi* (of a seller) to raise the price of property, etc, after accepting an offer from (a buyer), but before the contract has been signed. [Prob Yiddish *gezumph* to swindle; cf thieves' slang *gessump*, *gazumph* etc to rob by deception]

gazunder[1] *gə-zun'dər*, (*colloq*) *vt* and *vi* (of a buyer) to lower the sum offered to (the seller of a property) just before contracts are due to be signed. [*gaz*ump and **under**.]

gazunder[2] *gə-sun'dər*, (*Austr colloq*) *n* a chamberpot; a low ball in cricket. [*goes under*, contracted as in colloq speech]

gazy. See under **gaze**.

GB *abbrev*: Great Britain (also IVR).

Gb (*phys*) *abbrev*: gilbert.

GBA *abbrev*: (Great Britain) Alderney, Channel Islands (IVR).

GBE *abbrev*: (Knight or Dame) Grand Cross of the British Empire.

GBG *abbrev*: (Great Britain) Guernsey, Channel Islands (IVR).

GBH or **gbh** *abbrev*: grievous bodily harm.

GBJ *abbrev*: (Great Britain) Jersey, Channel Islands (IVR).

GBM *abbrev*: (Great Britain, Isle of) Man (IVR).

GBZ *abbrev*: (Great Britain) Gibraltar (IVR).

GC *abbrev*: George Cross (qv).

GCA *abbrev*: ground control (or controlled) approach system, or ground control apparatus (*aeronautics*); Guatemala, Central America (IVR).

GCB *abbrev*: (Knight or Dame) Grand Cross of the (Order of the) Bath.

GCE *abbrev*: General Certificate of Education (qv). — *n* a subject studied or certificate gained for a GCE examination.

GCH *abbrev*: (Knight) Grand Cross of Hanover.

GCHQ *abbrev*: Government Communications Headquarters.

G-clef. See under **G**.

GCM *abbrev*: General Court-martial; (or **gcm**) greatest common measure.

GCMG *abbrev*: (Knight or Dame) Grand Cross of (the Order of) St Michael and St George.

GCSE *abbrev*: General Certificate of Secondary Education (qv).

GCVO *abbrev*: (Knight or Dame) Grand Cross of the (Royal) Victorian Order.

Gd (*chem*) *symbol*: gadolinium.

Gde *abbrev*: gourde (Haitian currency).

Gdns *abbrev*: Gardens (in street-names, etc.).

GDP *abbrev*: gross domestic product (qv).

GDR *abbrev*: German Democratic Republic (the former East Germany).

Ge. See **Gaea**.

Ge (*chem*) *symbol*: germanium.

geal *jēl*, (*obs* or *dialect*) *vt* and *vi* to congeal. [Fr *geler*]

gealous, **gealousy** (*Spenser*). Same as **jealous**, **jealousy**.

gean *gēn*, *n* the European wild cherry. [OFr *guigne*]

geanticline *jē-an'ti-klīn*, *n* an anticline on a great scale. — *adj* **geanticlī'nal**. [Gr *gē* earth, and **anticline**]

gear *gēr*, *n* equipment; accoutrements; tackle; clothes, *esp* (*colloq*) young people's fashion clothes; personal belongings (*colloq*); illicit drugs (*slang*); armour (*obs*); harness; apparatus; a set of tools or a mechanism for some particular purpose; household stuff; stuff, matter (*archaic*); affair, business, doings (often contemptuous) (*obs*); any moving part or system of parts for transmitting motion, eg levers, gearwheels; connection by means of such parts; the actual gear ratio in use, or the gearwheels involved in transmitting that ratio, in an automobile gearbox, eg first gear (**low gear**), fourth gear (**high gear**); working connection; working order; the diameter in inches of a wheel whose circumference equals the distance a bicycle would go for one turn of the pedals. — *vt* to harness; to put (eg machinery) in gear; to connect in gear; to adjust in accordance with the requirements of a particular plan, etc (with *to*). — *vi* to be in gear. — *adj* (*slang*) unusually good, or (later) very up to date. — *adj* **geared**. — *n* **gear'ing** harness; working implements; means of transmission of motion, *esp* a series of toothed wheels and pinions; (in a company's capital) the ratio of ordinary shares to shares with fixed interest, or (*loosely*) the ratio of equity to loans (*econ*). — *adj* **gear'less**. — **gear'box** the box containing the apparatus for changing gear; (in a motor vehicle) the apparatus itself; **gear'-case** a protective case for the gearing of a bicycle, etc; **gear'-change** or **gear'change** a change of gear; the mechanism with which one changes gear; **gear-lever**, **gear'-stick** or (*NAm*) **gear'shift** a device for selecting or engaging and disengaging gears; **gear ratio** the ratio of the driving to the driven members of a gear mechanism; **gear train** two or more gearwheels, transmitting motion from one shaft to another; **gear'wheel** a wheel with teeth or cogs which impart or transmit motion by acting on a similar wheel or a chain. — *adj* **high'-gear** and **low'-gear** geared to give a high and a low number respectively of revolutions of the driven part relative to the driving part. — Also *n*. — **change gear** to select a higher or lower gear; **gear down** to make the speed of the driven part lower than that of the driving part; **gear up** to make the speed of the driven part higher than that of the driving part; to prepare for increased production, new demands, etc; to raise the gearing of (a company); **highly geared** (of a company or its capital) having a high ratio of fixed-interest shares to ordinary shares, or of loans to equity; **high gear** and **low gear** see **gear** above; **high gear** (*fig*) maximum speed and efficiency, peak performance; **multiplying gearing** a combination of cogwheels for imparting motion from wheels of larger to wheels of smaller diameter, by which the rate of revolution is increased; **straight gear** the name given when the planes of motion are parallel (opposite to **bevelled gear** (see **bevel**)); **three-speed gear**, **two-speed gear** and **variable gear** a contrivance for changing gear at will; see also **synchromesh**. [ME *gere*, prob ON *gervi*; cf OE *gearwe*, OHGer *garawi*; **yare**, **gar**[2]]

geare (*Spenser*). Same as **gear**, **jeer**.

geason *gē'zn*, (*obs*) *adj* rare; out of the way; wonderful. [OE *gǣne*, *gēsne* wanting, barren]

geat *jēt*, *n* the hole in a mould through which the metal is poured in casting. [**jet**]

gebur *gə-bōōr'* or *yə-bōōr'*, (*hist*) *n* a tenant-farmer. [OE *gebūr*]

GEC *abbrev*: General Electric Company.

geck *gek*, (*Scot* and *N Eng dialect*) *n* a dupe; object of scorn; a derisive gesture; scorn. — *vt* to mock. — *vi* to scoff; to toss the head; to show disdain. [Prob LGer *geck*; Du *gek*, Ger *Geck*]

gecko *gek'ō*, *n* any lizard of the genus **Gecko** or the subclass **Geckō'nēs**, mostly thick-bodied, dull-coloured animals with adhesive toes and vertebrae concave at both ends: — *pl* **geck'os** or **geck'oes**. [Malay *gēkoq*; imit of its cry]

ged *ged*, (*Scot* and *N Eng dialect*) *n* the pike or luce. [ON *gedda*]

geddit *ged'it*, (*slang*) *interj* (do you) get it?, do you see (the joke, point, etc)?; *usu* used in speech, or as though in speech, to reinforce or draw attention to a preceding pun, joke or irony. [**get it**? (colloq, esp US, pronunciation expressed phonetically)]

gee[1] *jē*, *n* the seventh letter of the alphabet (G or g).

gee[2] *gē*, (*Scot* and *N Eng dialect*) *n* a fit of perversity.

gee[3] *jē*, *vi* (of horses) to move to the right, to move on, or move faster. — *n* **gee'-gee** a child's word for a horse. — **gee up** to proceed faster, chiefly used as a command to horses (also **gee hup**); to encourage, stimulate, buck up. — *interj* a command to a horse to move on or go faster.

gee[4] *jē*, (*US dialect* or *slang*) *vi* to go, to suit, to get on well.

gee[5] *jē*, *n* a radio-navigation system in which three ground stations A (master), B and C (slave), give for AB and AC two sets of intersecting hyperbolas which, charted, give an equipped aircraft its geographical position over a few hundred miles' range from A. [*G*round *e*lectronics *e*ngineering]

gee[6] *jē*, (*NAm*) *interj* expressing surprise, sarcasm, enthusiasm, etc; sometimes used only for emphasis. — **gee whiz** *interj* expressing surprise, admiration, etc. [Perh **Jesus**]

geebung *jē'bung*, *n* an Australian proteaceous tree (*Persoonia*) or its fruit. [Aboriginal]

geechee *gē'chē*, (*US slang*, chiefly *Black*) *n* Gullah dialect; a Gullah; a rural Southern Black. [Origin uncertain]

gee-gee. See under **gee**[3].

geegaw. Same as **gewgaw**.

geek[1] *gēk*, (*NAm slang*) *n* a circus or carnival freak; a strange or eccentric person, a creep or misfit. — *adj* **geek'y**. [British dialect *geck* a fool]

geek[2] *gēk*, (*Austr colloq*) *n* a look, *esp* a good long look. [British dialect, a peep or peer]

geep *gēp*, *n* a creature produced by artificially combining DNA from a goat and sh*eep*.

geese, *pl* of **goose**.

gee-string or **G-string** *jē'-string*, *n* a string or strip worn round the waist supporting a strip worn between the legs; the strip itself or any similar covering for the genitals. [Origin obscure]

Geëz *gē-ez'*, *gē'ez* or *gēz* or **Giz** *gēz*, *n* the ancient language of Ethiopia, a Semitic tongue closely related to Arabic.

geezer *gēz'ər*, (*slang*) *n* a strange elderly person; a man. **[guiser]**

GEF *abbrev*: Global Environment Facility, an international environmental organization.

gefilte fish or **gefüllte fish** *gə-fil'tə fish*, *n* a cooked mixture of fish, eggs, breadcrumbs or matzo meal, and seasoning, served as balls or cakes or stuffed into a fish. [Yiddish, literally, filled fish]

gefuffle *gə-fuf'l*. Form of **carfuffle**.

gefüllte fish. See **gefilte fish**.

gegenschein *gā'gən-shīn*, (*astron*) *n* a glow of zodiacal light seen opposite the sun. [Ger *gegen* opposite, and *schein* glow, shine]

Gehenna *gi-hen'ə*, *n* the valley of Hinnom, near Jerusalem, in which the Israelites sacrificed their children to Moloch, and to which, at a later time, the refuse of the city was conveyed to be slowly burned; hence hell (*New Testament*); a place of torment. [Heb *Ge-hinnōm* valley of Hinnom]

Geiger counter *gī'gər kown'tər*, or **Geiger-Müller counter** *-mül'ər*, *n* an instrument for detecting and measuring radioactivity by registering electrical output pulses caused by ionization of particles in a gas-filled tube. [Hans *Geiger* and W *Müller*, German physicists]

geisha *gā'shə*, *n* a Japanese girl trained to provide entertainment (eg conversation, performance of dances, etc) for men: — *pl* **gei'sha** or **gei'shas**. [Jap]

Geissler tube *gīs'lər tūb*, (*chem*) *n* a gas-filled discharge tube, characterized by a capillary section for concentrated illumination. [Heinrich *Geissler* (1814–79), the inventor]

geist *gīst*, *n* spirit, any inspiring or dominating principle. [Ger]

geit. Same as **get**, a child, and **gyte**².

geitonogamy *gī-tən-og'ə-mi*, (*bot*) *n* pollination from another flower on the same plant. — *adj* **geitonog'amous**. [Gr *geiton* neighbour, and *gamos* marriage]

gel¹ *jel*, *n* a jelly-like apparently solid colloidal solution; a transparent substance, or a sheet of this, used in theatre and photographic lighting to produce light of different colours (short for **gelatine**); an inert matrix in which molecules can be separated by electrophoresis. — *vi* to form a gel; to come together, to begin to work, take shape (*colloq*; also **jell**): — *pr p* **gell'ing**; *pa t* and *pa p* **gelled**. — *n* **gelā'tion** see separate article. **[gelatine]**

gel² *gel*, *n* a facetious rendering of an upper-class pronunciation of **girl**.

gelada *jel'ə-də* or *gel'*, *ji-läd'ə* or *gi-*, *n* an Ethiopian baboon, with a long mane. [Poss from Ar *qilādah* collar, mane]

gelastic *jel-as'tik*, (*rare*) *adj* relating to or provoking laughter. [Gr *gelastikos*, from *gelaein* to laugh]

gelati. See **gelato**.

gelatine or **gelatin** *jel'ə-tēn* or *-tin*, *n* a colourless, odourless and tasteless glue, prepared from albuminous matter, eg bones and hides, used for foodstuffs, photographic films, glues, etc. — *vt* **gelatinate** (*ji-lat'i-nāt*), **gelat'inize** or **-ise** to make into gelatine or jelly; to coat with gelatine or jelly. — *vi* to be converted into gelatine or jelly. — *n* **gelatinā'tion**, **gelatinizā'tion** or **-s-**. — *n* **gelat'inizer** or **-s-**. — *n* **gelat'inoid** a substance resembling gelatine. — Also *adj*. — *adj* **gelat'inous** resembling or formed into jelly. — **blasting gelatine** a violently explosive rubbery substance composed of nitroglycerine and nitrocotton. [Fr, from Ital *gelatina*, *gelata* jelly, from L *gelāre* to freeze]

gelation *jel-ā'shən*, *n* a solidification by cooling; the formation of a gel from a sol. [Partly L *gelātiō*, *-ōnis*, from *gelāre* to freeze; partly **gel**¹]

gelato *je-lä'tō*, (*esp Austr*) *n* a type of whipped ice-cream made from cream, milk and/or water and flavoured with fruit or nuts: — *pl* **gela'ti** (*-tē*). [Ital]

geld¹ *geld*, (*Eng hist*) *n* a tax paid by landholders to the crown, in late Anglo-Saxon and Norman times. — *vt* to tax. [OE *geld*, *gyld* payment; ON *giald* money; cf **yield]**

geld² *geld*, *vt* to emasculate, castrate; to spay; to deprive of anything essential, to enfeeble, to deprive; to expurgate (*obs*): — *pa t* and *pa p* **geld'ed** or **gelt** (*archaic* or *dialect*). — *n* **geld'er**. — *n* **geld'ing** the act of castrating; a castrated animal, *esp* a horse. [ON *gelda*; Dan *gilde*]

gelder-rose. *Obs* form of **guelder-rose**.

gelid *jel'id*, *adj* icy cold; chilly, icy. — *adv* **gel'idly**. — *n* **gel'idness** or (*obs*) **gelid'ity**. [L *gelidus*, from *gelū* frost]

gelignite *jel'ig-nīt*, *n* a powerful explosive used in mining, made from nitroglycerine, nitrocotton, potassium nitrate and wood-pulp. [**gelatine** and L *ignis* fire]

gelliflowre (*Spenser*). Same as **gillyflower**.

gelly¹ *jel'i*, (*obs*) *adj* jellied.

gelly² *jel'i*, (*colloq*) *n* gelignite. — Also **jelly**.

gelosy (*Spenser*). Same as **jealousy**.

gelsemium *jel-sē'mi-əm*, *n* the so-called yellow or Carolina jasmine, an American climbing-plant of the Loganiaceae. — *n* **gel'semine** (*-səm-ēn*) and **gelseminine** (*-sem'*) two alkaloids yielded by the gelsemium rhizome and rootlets. [Ital *gelsomino* jasmine]

gelt¹ *gelt*, (*archaic* or *dialect*) *pa t* and *pa p* of **geld**².

gelt² *gelt*, (*Spenser*) *n* a madman. [Ir *geilt*]

gelt³ *gelt*, (*US slang*) *n* money; profit. [Yiddish, from Ger *Geld*, Du *geld*]

gelt⁴ *gelt*, an obsolete erroneous form of **geld**¹; same as **gilt**¹ (*Spenser*).

gem *jem*, *n* any precious stone, *esp* when cut (also **gem'stone**); a person or thing regarded as extremely admirable or flawless; an old size of type smaller than diamond (*printing*); a bud (*obs*). — *vt* (*obs*) to bud; to adorn with gems; to bespangle: — *pr p* **gemm'ing**; *pa t* and *pa p* **gemmed**. — *vt* **gemm'ate** (*obs*) to deck with gems. — *vi* (*bot*) see under **gemma**. — *adj* **gemm'eous** (*-i-əs*) relating to gems; like a gem. — *n* **gemm'ery** (*rare*) gems generally. — *adj* **gemolog'ical** or **gemmolog'ical**. — *n* **gemol'ogist** or **gemmol'ogist** a person with special knowledge of gems. — *n* **gemol'ogy** or **gemmol'ogy** the science of gems. — *adj* **gemm'y** full of gems; brilliant. — **gem'-cutting** the art of cutting and polishing precious stones; **gem'-engraving** the art of engraving figures on gems. [OE *gim*; OHGer *gimma*, from L *gemma* a bud; later remodelled on L or reintroduced]

Gemara *gə-mä'rə*, (*Judaism*) *n* the second part of the Talmud, consisting of a commentary on and complement to the first part, the Mishnah. [Aramaic, completion]

gematria *gə-mā'tri-ə*, *n* a cabbalistic method of interpreting the Hebrew Scriptures by interchanging words whose letters have the same numerical value when added. [Rabbinical Heb *gēmatriyā*, from Gr *geōmetriā* geometry]

Gemeinschaft *gə-mīn'shäft*, (Ger) *n* a social group held together by ties such as friendship, kinship, etc.

gemel *jem'əl*, *n* a twin (*obs*); a gimmal (type of ring) (*hist*); a hinge (*obs*); a pair of bars placed close together (*heraldry*). — **gem'el-ring** same as **gimmal ring**. [OFr *gemel* (Fr *jumeau*), from L *gemellus*, dimin of *geminus* twin]

gemfish *jem'fish*, *n* an edible marine fish (*Rexea solandri*) found off the S Australian and New Zealand coasts, formerly known as **kingfish** or **hake**.

geminate *jem'in-āt*, *vt* to double; to arrange in pairs. — *adj* (*bot*) in pairs. — *n* **geminā'tion** a doubling. — *adj* **gem'inous** (*bot*) double, in pairs. — *n* **gem'iny** (*Shakesp*) a pair, *esp* of eyes. — *interj* (perhaps a separate word) expressing surprise, spelt also **gemini** (*obs*), **gemony** (*obs*) and (the sole current form) **jiminy**. [L *gemināre* to double, from *geminus* twin]

Gemini *jem'in-ī*, *n pl* the twins, a constellation containing the two bright stars Castor and Pollux; the third sign of the zodiac, associated with this; (*sing* in construction; also **Geminī'an**) a person born between 22 May and 22 June, under the sign of Gemini (*astrol*; *pl* **Gem'inis**). — *n* **Gem'inid** a meteor of a swarm whose radiant is in the constellation Gemini. [L, pl of *geminus* twin]

gemma *jem'ə*, *n* a small multicellular body produced vegetatively, capable of separating and becoming a new individual (*bot*); a bud or protuberance from the body that becomes a new individual (*zool*); a plant bud, *esp* a leaf-bud (*rare*): — *pl* **gemm'ae** (*-ē*). — *adj* **gemmā'ceous** bud-like; relating to gemmae. — *adj* **gemm'ate** having or reproducing by buds or gemmae. — *vt* see under **gem**. — *vi* to reproduce by gemmae. — *n* **gemmā'tion** budding or gemma-formation. — *adj* **gemm'ative** pertaining to gemmation. — *adj* **gemmif'erous** bearing gemmae. — *adj* **gemmip'arous** reproducing by gemmae. — *n* **gemmūlā'tion** (*biol*) formation of gemmules. — *n* **gemm'ule** Darwin's hypothetical particle produced by each part of the body, as a vehicle of heredity; a plumule (*bot*); an internal bud in sponges (*zool*). — **gemm'a-cup** a liverwort cupule. [L, a bud]

gemman *jem'ən*, (*archaic colloq*) *n* a corruption of **gentleman**: — *pl* **gemmen** (*jem'ən*). [**gentleman**]

gemmate, **gemmation**, etc. See **gem**, **gemma**.

gemmeous, **gemmery**. See **gem**.

gemmiferous, **gemmiparous**. See **gemma**.

gemmologist, etc. See **gem**.

gemmulation, **gemmule**. See **gemma**.

gemmy[1]. See **gem**.

gemmy[2]. See **jemmy**[2].

gemologist, etc. See **gem**.

gemony. See **geminate**.

gemot *gə-mōt'* or *yə-mōt'*, (*Eng hist*) *n* a meeting or assembly; *specif* an Anglo-Saxon legislative or judicial assembly. [OE *gemōt*; cf **moot**]

Gems *jemz*, *abbrev*: Global Environment Monitoring System (set up by the United Nations Environment Programme).

gemsbok *hhemz'bok* (*SAfr*), or *gemz'bok*, *n* a S African antelope (*Oryx gazella*) about the size of a stag, with long straight horns. [Du, male chamois, from Ger *Gemsbock*]

gemshorn *gemz'hörn*, (*music*) *n* a chamois horn, as an early wind instrument; an organ stop made with conical metal pipes, having a soft fluty tone. [Ger, chamois horn]

gemütlich *gə-müt'lēhh*, (*Ger*) *adj* amiable; comfortable; cosy. — *n* **Gemütlichkeit** (*-kīt*) kindness; comfort; cosiness.

Gen. *abbrev*: General; (the Book of) Genesis (*Bible*).

gen *jen*, (*slang*) *n* general information; the low-down or inside information. — **gen up** to learn (with *on*): — *pr p* **genning up**; *pa t* **genned up**.

-gen *-jən*, or **-gene** *-jēn*, *combining form* used to denote: (1) producing or produced, as in *oxygen*, *phosgene* (*chem*); (2) growth, as in *endogen* (*bot*). [Gr *-genēs* born]

gena *jē'nə*, (*anatom* and *zool*) *n* the cheek or side of the head. — *adj* **gē'nal**. [L]

genappe *jə-nap'*, *n* a smooth worsted yarn used with silk in fringes, braid, etc. [*Genappe* in Belgium]

gendarme *zhā'därm*, *n orig* a man-at-arms, a horseman in full armour; since the French Revolution, a member of a corps of French military police; a similar policeman elsewhere; a rock-pillar on a mountain: — *pl* **gen'darmes**, occasionally **gens'darmes**. — *n* **gendarm'erie** (*-ə-rē*) an armed police force; a police station or barracks. [Fr *gendarme*, sing from pl *gens d'armes* men-at-arms, from *gens* people, *de* of, and *armes* arms]

gender[1] *jen'dər*, *n* kind, sort (*obs*); a distinction of words roughly answering to sex (*gram*); (*loosely* or *joc*) sex. — *adj* **gen'derless** not having or indicating gender; not indicating differences in sex, suitable for either sex. — **gender bender** (*colloq*) a person who for deliberate effect, publicity or amusement adopts a sexually-ambiguous public image and style (in dress, hairstyle, make-up, etc); **gen'der-bending** (*colloq*) the blurring of the distinctions between the sexes through sexual ambiguity or bisexuality in behaviour or dress; **gender role** (*behav*) the set of attitudes and behaviour considered appropriate by a given culture for each sex. — *adj* **gender-specif'ic** belonging to or limited to either males or females. [Fr *genre*, from L *genus* kind]

gender[2] *jen'dər*, *vt* to beget (*archaic*); to generate (*obs*). — *vi* (*obs*) to copulate. [Fr *gendrer*, from L *generāre*]

gene *jēn*, (*biol*) *n* one of the units of DNA, arranged in linear fashion on the chromosomes, responsible for passing on specific characteristics from parents to offspring. — *adj* **gen'ic** of or relating to a gene. — **gene flow** the passing of genes to succeeding generations; **gene frequency** (*biol*) the frequency of a particular allele of a gene in a population; **gene locus** the site on a chromosome occupied by a gene; **gene mapping** see **mapping**; **gene splicing** the artificial introduction of DNA from one organism into the genetic material of another, in order to produce a desired characteristic in the recipient; **gene therapist**; **gene therapy** the treatment or prevention of (*esp* heritable) diseases by genetic engineering. [Ger *Gen*, from Gr *-genēs* born]

gêne *zhen*, (Fr) *n* embarrassment. — Also **gene**.

-gene. See **-gen**.

genealogy *jē-ni-al'ə-ji*, or *jen'i-*, *n* history of the descent of families; the pedigree of a particular person or family. — *adj* **genealogical** (*-ə-loj'i-kl*) or **genealog'ic**. — *adv* **genealog'ically**. — *n* **geneal'ogist** a person who studies or traces genealogies or descents. — *vi* **geneal'ogize** or **-ise** to investigate or discuss genealogy. — **genealogical tree** a table of descent in the form of a tree with branches. [Gr *geneālogiā*, from *geneā* race, and *logos* discourse]

genera, *pl* of **genus**.

generable. See **generate**.

general *jen'ə-rəl*, *adj* relating to a genus or whole class; including various species; not special; not restricted or specialized; relating to the whole or to all or most; universal; nearly universal; common; prevalent; widespread; public; vague; (after an official title, etc) chief, of highest rank, at the head of a department (as in *director-general*, *postmaster-general*); socially accessible and familiar with all (*obs*). — *adv* (*Shakesp*) generally. — *n* the total (*obs*); the most part, majority (*obs*); the universal as opposed to the particular; an army officer between a field marshal and lieutenant-general in rank; the head of a religious order, such as the Jesuits; the chief commander of an army in service; a person acting as leader, planning tactics or management; the head of the Salvation Army; a general servant (*obs*); the public, the vulgar (*archaic* and *Shakesp*). — *vt* to act as general of: — *pr p* **gen'eralling**; *pa t* and *pa p* **gen'eralled**. — *n* **gen'eralate** the office of a general; the district or domain under the charge of a general. — *n* **generā'lē** (L *gen-er-ä'le*) general principles, *esp* in *pl* **generā'lia**. — *n* **generaliss'imo** (Ital *superl*) supreme commander of a great or combined force: — *pl* **generaliss'imos**. — *n* **gen'eralist** a person whose knowledge and skills are not restricted to one particular field (*opp* of *specialist*). — *adj* **gen'eralīzable** or **-s-**. — *n* **generalīzā'tion** or **-s-**. — *vt* **gen'eralize** or **-ise** to make general; to include under a general term; to reduce to a general form; to comprehend as a particular case within a wider concept, proposition, definition, etc; to represent or endow with the common characters of a group without the special characters of any one member; to bring to general use or knowledge; to infer inductively. — *vi* to make general statements; to form general concepts; to depict general character; to reason inductively. — *n* **general'ity** a statement having general application; the state of being general; broadness or vagueness; the majority; the general public. — *adv* **gen'erally** in a general or collective manner or sense; in most cases; on the whole. — *n* **gen'eralship** the position of a military commander; the art of manipulating armies; tactical management and leadership. — **General Assembly** see under **assemble**; **general delivery** (*US*) poste restante; **general election** an election of all the members of a body (eg House of Commons, House of Representatives) at once; **general epistles** see under **catholic**; **general journal** (*bookkeeping*) same as **journal proper**; **general ledger** (*bookkeeping*) a book which contains nominal accounts; **general line** the party line;

general officer (*military*) an officer above the rank of colonel; **general paralysis of the insane** general paresis (qv under **paresis**); **general post** formerly, dispatch of mail to all parts (*opp* to local *twopenny* or *penny post*); the first morning delivery of letters; a general change of positions, etc (from a parlour game); **general practice** the work of a **general practitioner** (*abbrev* **GP**), a doctor who treats patients for most illnesses or complaints, referring other cases to specialists; **general principle** a principle to which there are no exceptions within its range of application. — *adj* **gen'eral-purpose** generally useful, not restricted to a particular function. — **general reserve** (*accountancy*) profits which have been set aside for retention in the business but not for any specified purpose; **general servant** a servant whose duties embrace domestic work of every kind; **general staff** military officers who advise senior officers on policy, administration, etc; **General Synod** see under **synod**. — **General Certificate of Education** in secondary education in England and Wales, a certificate obtainable at Ordinary (*formerly*), Advanced, and Scholarship levels for proficiency in one or more subjects; **General Certificate of Secondary Education** in England and Wales, a certificate based on coursework as well as examinations, designed to suit a wide range of academic ability; **general post office** (*formerly*) an office receiving letters for the general post; (*now*) the head post office of a town or district. — **in general** as a generalization; mostly, as a general rule. [OFr, from L *generālis*, from *genus*]

generate *jen'ər-āt*, *vt* to produce; to bring into life or being; to evolve; to originate; to trace out (*geom*). — *adj* **gen'erable** that may be generated or produced. — *n* **gen'erant** a begetter, producer, parent (*obs*); a line, point or figure that traces out another figure by its motion (*geom*). — *n* **gen'erātor** a begetter or producer; an apparatus for producing gases, etc; an apparatus for turning mechanical into electrical energy; a fundamental tone, the first or lowest in a chord or harmonic series (*music*): — *fem* **gen'erātrix** a mother (*obs*); a generant (*geom*): — *pl* **gen'erātrices** (*-tri-sēz*). — **generating station** a plant where electricity is generated. [L *generāre*, *-ātum*, from *genus* a kind]

generation *jen-ə-rā'shən*, *n* production or originating; a single stage of natural descent; the people of the same age or period; descendants removed by the same number of steps from a common ancestor; the ordinary time interval between the births of successive generations (*usu* reckoned at 30 or 33 years); any of a number of stages, levels or series, generally in which each stage, etc is seen as a development of or improvement on the preceding one; a term used in describing the development of computers (see **first generation**, **fifth generation**); any series of files, each one an amended and updated version of the previous one (*comput*); offspring or progeny (*obs*); race, kind, class, family (*obs*); (in *pl*) genealogy, history (*Bible*). — *n* **generā'tionism** traducianism. — **generation gap** lack of communication and understanding, or the observable differences in attitudes, ideals or outlook, between one generation and the next. — **alternation of generations** see under **alternate**; **spontaneous generation** the origination of living fron non-living matter. [L *generātiō*, *-iōnis*, from *generāre* (see **generate**)]

generative *jen'ər-ət-iv*, *adj* having the power of, or concerned with, generating or producing. — **generative grammar** (*linguistics*) a description of the language as a finite set of grammatical rules able to generate an infinite number of grammatical sentences. — **motion generative** (*Shakesp*) a male puppet, or perhaps someone who is a mere puppet so far as engendering is concerned. [**generate**]

generic *jə-ner'ik*, *adj* general, applicable to any member of a group or class; of or belonging to a genus; (of a drug, etc) not patented or sold as a proprietary name; (of the name of a brand) that has come to be used as a general name for that type of product (eg *Biro* for ballpoint pen, *Hoover* for vacuum cleaner). — *n* a generic drug, etc; a product sold without a brand-name, in plain packaging, and with no promotion or advertising; a generic brand-name. — *adj* **gener'ical** general, applicable to any of a group or class; of or belonging to a genus. — *adv* **gener'ically**. — **generic name** the name of the genus, placed first in naming the species, thus *Equus caballus* (horse), *Equus asinus* (ass), *Equus zebra*, etc are species of the genus Equus, and Equus is the generic name (*biol*); the name of a generic drug, product, etc. [Fr *générique*, from L *genus* (see **genus**)]

generous *jen'ə-rəs*, *adj* of a noble nature (*archaic*); courageous (*obs*); liberal; bountiful; ample; (of eg wine) invigorating in its nature; nobly born (*obs*). — *adv* **gen'erously**. — *n* **generos'ity** or **gen'erousness** liberality of nature, the quality of being free and unstinting with one's possessions, money, time; nobleness of nature, magnanimity; a generous act; nobility of birth (*archaic*). [L *generōsus* of noble birth, from *genus* birth]

genesis *jen'i-sis*, *n* generation, creation, development or production; (with *cap*) the first book of the Bible, telling of the Creation: — *pl* **gen'esēs**. — *combining form* **-gen'esis**, as in *pathogenesis* development of disease, *parthenogenesis* virgin birth. — *adj* **Genesiac** (*ji-nē'si-ək*), **Genē'siacal** or **Genesitic** (*jenə-sit'ik*) relating to Genesis. [Gr]

genet[1]. See **jennet**.

genet[2] *jen'it*, or **genette** *ji-net'*, *n* a carnivorous animal (genus *Genetta*) related to the civet; its fur, or an imitation. [Fr *genette*, from Sp *gineta*, from Ar *jarnait*]

genethliac *ji-neth'li-ək*, *adj* (*obs*) relating to a birthday or to the casting of horoscopes. — *n* (*obs*) a caster of horoscopes; a genethliacon. — *adj* **genethliacal** (*jen-ith-lī'ə-kl*) genethliac. — *adv* **genethlī'acally**. — *n* (L, from Gr) **genethlī'acon** a birthday ode. — *adj* **genethlialog'ic** or **genethlialog'ical**. — *n* **genethlial'ogy** (Gr *genethliālogiā*) the art of casting horoscopes. [Gr *genethlē* birth]

genetic *ji-net'ik* or **genetical** *-əl*, *adj* causal, relating to origin; of or relating to genes or genetics. — *combining form* **-genet'ic**, as in *pathogenetic* productive of disease. — *adv* **genet'ically**. — *n* **genet'icist** (*-i-sist*) a student of genetics. — *n sing* **genet'ics** the branch of biology dealing with heredity and variation; inherited characteristics of an organism; origin; development. — **genetic code** the system by which genes pass on instructions that ensure transmission of hereditary characters; **genetic counselling** advice, based on chromosomal and amniotic fluid investigation, etc, given to prospective parents on possible heritable defects in their children; **genetic engineering** a biological science whose aims include the control of hereditary defects by the modification or elimination of certain genes, and the mass production of useful biological substances (eg insulin) by the transplanting of genes; **genetic fingerprint** the particular DNA configuration exclusive to an individual human or animal or its offspring; **genetic fingerprinting** the identification of genetic fingerprints (eg in forensic science, to identify or eliminate a specific individual); **genetic manipulation** the alteration of natural genetic processes, *usu* for the purposes of research; **genetic parents** the 'natural' parents, those whose genes the child carries; **genetic spiral** (*bot*) the line through insertions of successive leaves on a stem. — **genetically significant dose** (*radiol*) the dose of radiation that, if given to every member of a population prior to conception of children, would produce in the children the same genetic or hereditary damage as the actual doses received by the various individuals would in the individuals. [**genesis**]

genetotrophic *jen-ət-ō-trō'fik*, or *-trof'*, *adj* denoting deficiency diseases which have an underlying genetic, and a direct nutritional, cause and which are treatable by dietary means. [*geneto-*, combining form from **genetic**, and **trophic**]

genetrix. See **genitor**.

genette. See **genet**[2].

geneva *ji-nē'və*, *n* a spirit distilled from grain and flavoured with juniper berries, a gin, made chiefly in the Netherlands. — Also called **Hollands** or **Hollands gin**; see **gin**[1]. — *n* **genevrette** (*jen-əv-ret'*) a wine made from wild fruits flavoured with juniper-berries. [ODu *genever*, OFr *genevre*, from L *jūniperus* juniper; confused with town of *Geneva*]

Genevan *ji-nē'vən*, *adj* pertaining to *Geneva*, in Switzerland. — *n* an inhabitant of Geneva; an adherent of Genevan or Calvinistic theology. — *adj* and *n* **Genevese** (*jen'i-vēz*). — *n* **Genē'vanism** (*obs*) Calvinism. — **Geneva bands** the two strips of white linen hanging down from the neck of some clerical robes; **Geneva Bible** a version of the Bible, long popular, produced by English exiles in Geneva in 1560; **Geneva Convention** an international agreement of 1864, with subsequent revisions, concerning the status and treatment in wartime of the sick and wounded, prisoners of war, etc; **Geneva cross** a red cross on a white background displayed for protection in war of people serving in hospitals, etc; **Geneva gown** the long dark preaching gown of the early Geneva reformers, and still the common form of pulpit-gown among Presbyterians; **Geneva movement**, **mechanism**, etc (*eng*) a mechanism which converts continuous into intermittent motion by means of slots on the driven wheel; **Genevan theology** Calvinism, the theology of Calvin or his followers, so called from Calvin's residence in Geneva and the establishment of his doctrines there.

genevrette. See **geneva**.

genial[1] *jē'ni-əl*, *adj* relating to marriage and procreation (*archaic*); (of a climate) mild, pleasant, favouring growth; cheering; kindly; sympathetic; healthful. — *n* **gēniality** (*-al'i-ti*) or **gē'nialness**. — *vt* **gē'nialize** or **-ise** to impart geniality to. — *adv* **gē'nially**. [L *geniālis*, from *genius* the tutelary spirit]

genial[2] *jə-nī'əl*, (*anatom*) *adj* of or relating to the chin. [Gr *geneion* chin, from *genys* jaw]

genic. See **gene**.

-genic *combining form* signifying: (1) productive of, generating, as in *pathogenic*, *carcinogenic*; (2) ideal or suitable for, as in *photogenic*; (3) caused by, as in *iatrogenic*. [**-gen** and sfx *-ic*]

geniculate *jə-nik'ū-lāt*, or **geniculated** *-id*, *adj* bent like a knee; jointed; knotted. — *vt* **genic'ulate** to form joints in. — *adv* **genic'ulately**. — *n* **geniculā'tion**. [L *geniculātus*, from *geniculum* a little knee, from *genū* the knee]

genie *jē'ni*, *n* a jinnee (see **jinn**); a magical being who carries out a person's wishes. [Fr *génie*, from L *genius*, adopted because of its similarity to the Arabic word]

genii. See **genius**.

genipap *jen'i-pap*, *n* a large West Indian tree (*Genipa americana*; Rubiaceae); its orange-sized, wine-flavoured fruit. — Also **gen'ip**. [From Tupí]

genista *jə-nis'tə*, *n* a plant belonging to the *Genista* genus of shrubby, papilionaceous plants, with simple leaves and yellow flowers, eg green-weed and petty whin. [L *genista* broom]

genital *jen'i-təl*, *adj* belonging to biological generation or the act of reproducing; of, pertaining to, or affecting, the genitals, or genital area. — *n pl* **gen'itals** or **genitā'lia** the organs of generation, the (*esp* external) sexual organs. — *adj* **genital'ic** or **genitā'lial**. [L *genitālis*, from *gignere*, *genitum* to beget]

genitive *jen'i-tiv*, *adj* of or belonging to a case expressing origin, possession, or similar relation (*gram*); relating to procreation (*obs*). — *n* (*gram*) the genitive case; a word in the genitive case. — *adj* **genitī'val**. — *adv* **genitī'vally** or (*rare*) **gen'itively**. [L *genitīvus* (from *gignere*, *genitum* to beget) for Gr *genikē* (*ptōsis*), properly, generic (case), from *genos* a class]

genito- *jen-i-tō*, *combining form* denoting genital. — *adj* **genito-ūr'inary** relating to genital and urinary organs or functions.

genitor *jen'i-tər*, *n* (now *rare*) a father; a parent; a progenitor: — *fem* **gen'etrix** or **gen'itrix**. — *n* **gen'iture** engendering; birth (*astrol*; *obs*). [L]

genius *jēn'yəs* or *jē'ni-əs*, *n* the special inborn faculty of any individual; special taste or natural disposition (*obs*); consummate intellectual, creative, or other power, more exalted than talent; a person endowed with this; a good or evil spirit, supposed to preside over every person, place and thing, and *esp* to preside over a person's destiny from his or her birth; a person who exerts a power, influence (whether good or bad) over another; prevailing spirit or tendency; type or generic exemplification: — *pl* **ge'niuses** or, in sense of spirit, **genii** (*jē'ni-ī*). [L *genius*, from *gignere*, *genitum* to beget]

genius loci *jē'ni-əs lō'sī* or *gen'i-ōōs lo'kē*, (*L*) *n literally* the spirit of the place; a local presiding spirit or deity; the distinctive atmosphere or aura of a place.

genizah *gə-nēz'ə*, *n* a room adjoining a synagogue for the safe-keeping of old or damaged books, documents or valuables. [Heb]

Genl *abbrev*: General.

genlock *jen'lok*, (*image technol*) *n* a device for synchronizing locally-generated signals with those transmitted from a distance.

gennel. See **ginnel**.

gennet. See **jennet**.

genoa or **Genoa** *jen'ō-ə* or *jə-nō'ə*, *n* (*naut*) a large jib which overlaps the mainsail. — **Genoa cake** a rich cake containing fruit, with almonds on the top. [*Genoa* in Italy]

genocide *jen'ō-sīd*, *n* the deliberate extermination of a racial, national, religious or ethnic group; a person who exterminates, or approves extermination of, a race, etc. — *adj* **genocī'dal**. [Gr *genos* race, and L *caedere* to kill]

Genoese *jen'ō-ēz* or *-ēz'*, or **Genovese** *-vēz*, *adj* relating to *Genoa*, seaport in NW Italy. — *n* an inhabitant, citizen or native of Genoa: — *pl* **Genoese'** or **Genovese'**. [L *Genua*, Ital *Genova* Genoa]

genome *jē'nōm*, *n* the full set of chromosomes of an individual; the total number of genes in such a set. — Also (formerly) **genom**. — **genomic library** a DNA library derived from a whole, single genome. [*gene* and chromos*ome*]

genophobia *jen-ō-fō'bi-ə*, *n* pathological fear of sex. [*geno-* (combining form, from Gr *genos* begetting, producing) and **-phobia**]

genotype *jen'ō-tīp*, *n* genetic or factorial constitution of an individual; a group of individuals all of whom possess the same genetic constitution. — *adj* **genotyp'ic**. — *adv* **genotyp'ically**. — *n* **genotypic'ity**. [**gene**, *-o-* (linking element in compounds) and **type**]

genouillère *zhə-nōō-yer*, *n* the jointed knee-piece in armour. [Fr]

genre *zhã-r n* kind; a literary or artistic type or style; a style of painting scenes from familiar or rustic life. — Also *adj*. [Fr, from L *genus*]

Genro *gen-rō'*, (*hist*) *n pl* the Japanese Elder Statesmen. [Jap]

gens[1] *jenz* (L *gāns*), *n* (in ancient Rome) a clan including several families descended from a common ancestor; tribe or clan, group of families (*anthropol*): — *pl* **gen'tēs**. — *adj* **gen'tile** (qv). — **gens togata** (*tō-gä'tə*) the toga-wearing nation, ie the Romans. [L *gēns*, *gentis*]

gens[2] *zhã*, (Fr) *n pl* people. — **gens de bien** (*də byɛ̃*) honest, respectable people; **gens de condition** (*də kɔ̃-dēs-yɔ̃*) people of rank; **gens d'église** (*dā-glēz*) churchmen; **gens de lettres** (*də letr'*) men of letters; **gens de loi** (*də lwa*) lawyers; **gens de guerre** (*də ger*) military men; **gens de peu** (*də pø*) people of humble condition; **gens du monde** (*dü mɔ̃d*) people of fashion.

gensdarmes. See under **gendarme**.

gent[1] *jent*, (*Spenser*) *adj* noble; gentle. [OFr, from L *genitus* born]

gent[2] *jent*, *n* short for **gentleman**; a man who apes the gentleman (*old colloq*): — *pl* **gents**. — *n* **gents'** a public lavatory for men.

genteel *jen-tēl'*, *adj* well-bred; graceful in manners or in form; fashionable (*archaic*); now used mainly with mocking reference to a standard of obsolete snobbery or false refinement. — *adj* **genteel'ish**. — *n* **genteel'ism** a word or phrase used in place of an accustomed one, where this is felt to be coarse or vulgar. — *vt* **genteel'ize** or **-ise** to make genteel or falsely refined. — *adv* **genteel'ly**. — *n* **genteel'ness**. [Fr *gentil*, from L *gentīlis*; see **gentle**]

gentes. See **gens**[1].

gentian *jen'shən*, *n* any plant of the genus *Gentiana*, herbs, *usu* blue-flowered, abounding chiefly in alpine regions, typical of the family **Gentianā'ceae** (sympetalous dicotyledons with corolla twisted in bud and unilocular ovary); the root and rhizome of the yellow gentian used as a tonic and stomachic. — *adj* **gentianā'ceous** of, relating to or belonging to the Gentianaceae. — *n* **gentianell'a** a name for several species of gentian, *esp* *Gentiana acaulis*, with deep-blue flowers. — **gentian violet** in the British pharmacopoeia, crystal violet; sometimes, methyl violet; now generally a mixture of crystal violet, methyl violet and methyl rosaniline, used as a fungicide and anthelmintic. [L *gentiāna*, according to Pliny from *Gentius*, king of Illyria, who introduced it in medicine (2nd century BC)]

Gentile or **gentile** *jen'tīl*, *n* anyone not a Jew (*Bible*), or not a Christian (now *rare*), or not a Mormon; a heathen or pagan. — *adj* **gen'tile** of or belonging to a *gens* or clan (*rare*); belonging to the Gentiles; denoting a race or country (*gram*). — *adj* **gentilic** (*-til'ik*) tribal. — *adj* **gen'tīlish** (*obs*) heathenish. — *n* **gen'tilism** (*-til-* or *-tīl-*) paganism, or the quality of being a Gentile. — *adj* **gentilitial** (*jen-ti-lish'l*), **gentili'tian** or **gentili'tious** pertaining to a *gens*. [L *gentīlis*, from *gēns* a nation, clan]

gentilesse *jen-til-es'*, (*obs*) *n* the quality of being gentle, courtesy. [Fr, from *gentil* (see **genteel**)]

gentilhomme *zhã-tē-yom*, (*Fr*) *n* a nobleman; a gentleman.

gentility *jen-til'i-ti*, *n* good birth or extraction; good breeding; respectability; courtesy; signs or characteristics of any of these; genteel people. [OFr *gentilite* (Fr *gentilité*), from L *gentīlitās*, from *gentīlis*; see **gentle**]

gentilize or **-ise** *jen'til-īz*, (*archaic*) *vt* to raise to the class of gentleman. [OFr (Fr) *gentil*; see **gentle**]

gentle *jen'tl*, *adj* well-born, from a good family (*archaic*); mild and refined in manners; mild in disposition or action; amiable; soothing; moderate; gradual. — *vt* to ennoble (*obs*); to make gentle; to handle gently. — *n* a well-born person (*obs*); a trained falcon; hence a peregrine falcon (*masc* **ter'cel-gen'tle**; *fem* **fal'con-gen'tle**); a soft maggot used as bait in angling. — *n* **gen'tlehood** (*archaic*) position or character attaching to gentle birth. — *n* **gen'tleness**. — *n* **gen'tlenesse** (*obs*) same as **gentilesse**. — *adv* **gent'ly**. — *n pl* **gen'tlefolk** people of good family. — *adj* **gentle-heart'ed** having a gentle or kind disposition. — **gen'tleman** a man of good birth or high social standing; a man of refined manners; a man of good feeling and instincts, courteous and honourable; a well-to-do man of no occupation; a polite term used for man in general; a man who without a title bears a coat of arms (*hist*); more generally every man above the rank of yeoman, including the nobility (*hist*); a body servant (*Shakesp*): — *pl* **gen'tlemen** — also a word of address to a group of men: — *fem* **gen'tlewoman** a personal attendant on a lady of rank (*hist*); a woman of good breeding and refinement, a lady (*archaic*): — *pl* **gen'tlewomen**. — *adj* **gen'tlewomanly** like, or characteristic of, a refined and well-bred woman. — *n* **gen'tlewomanliness**. — **Gen'tleman-at-arms** a member of the royal bodyguard, instituted in 1509, and now composed of military officers of service and distinction only; **gen'tleman-cadet'** a student in a military college; **gen'tleman-comm'oner** (formerly) at Oxford and Cambridge, an undergraduate with special privileges; **gentleman farmer** a landowner who lives on his estate superintending the cultivation of his own soil; a gentleman who owns a farm and employs a farm manager and other staff to work it on his behalf; **gen'tlemanhood** or **gen'tlemanship** the condition or character of a gentleman. — *adj* **gen'tlemanlike** like or characteristic of a gentleman. — *adj* **gen'tlemanly** befitting a gentleman; well-bred, refined, generous. — *n* **gen'tlemanliness**. — **gentleman's** (or **-men's**) **agreement** an agreement resting on honour, not on formal contract; a contract made by word of mouth and without drawing up any legal documents, ie not legally binding but resting on honour alone (*business*); **gentleman's gentleman** a valet; **Gentleman's Relish**® a savoury paste for spreading on sandwiches, etc; **gentleman usher** (*pl* **gentlemen ushers**) a gentleman who serves as an usher at court, or as an attendant on a person of rank; **gentle reader** courteous reader, an old-fashioned phrase common in the prefaces of books; **gentlewoman**, etc see after **gentleman**. — **the gentle craft** shoemaking (*obs*); angling; **Gentleman of the Chapel Royal** a lay singer who assists the priests in the choral service of the royal chapel. [OFr (Fr) *gentil*, from L *gentīlis* belonging to the same *gens* or clan, later, well-bred; see **genteel**]

Gentoo *jen'tōō* or *jen-tōō'*, *n* Telugu, a Telugu-speaker (*obs*); a pagan of India, a Hindu (*hist*); (without *cap*) a Falkland Island penguin. — Also *adj*. [Port *gentio* a Gentile]

gentry *jen'tri*, *n* the class of people next below the rank of nobility; nobility, aristocracy; people of a particular, *esp* an inferior, sort (*colloq*); rank by birth (*archaic*); the rank of gentleman (*archaic*); good manners and courtesy (*Shakesp*). — *n* **gen'trice** (*-tris*; *archaic*) gentle birth; good breeding. — *n* **gentrificā'tion** the move of middle-class people into a formerly working-class area with the consequent change in the character of the area; the modernizing of old, badly-equipped property, *usu* with a view to increasing its value. — *n* **gen'trifier**. — *vt* **gen'trify**. [OFr *genterise*, *gentelise*, formed from adj *gentil* gentle]

genty *jen'ti*, (*Scot*) *adj* neat, dainty; graceful.

genu *jen'ōō* or *jen'ū*, (*anatom*) *n* the knee; a knee-like bend or structure. [L, knee]

genuflect *jen'ū-flekt*, *vi* to bend the knee in worship or respect. — *n* **genūflex'ion** or **genūflec'tion**. [L *genū* the knee, and *flectere*, *flexum* to bend]

genuine *jen'ū-in*, *adj* natural; native; not spurious; real; pure; sincere; of a horse, running consistently up to full ability (*horse-racing*). — *adv* **gen'uinely**. — *n* **gen'uineness**. — **genuine material difference** (*law*) (in an equal pay claim) a defence brought by an employer to show that on a balance of probabilities the variation in terms and conditions is due to a genuine material difference other than sex (eg grading scheme, age, experience); **genuine occupational qualification** an attribute of a person of a particular sex or racial origin which makes them more suited to a particular job, allowing an employer to choose them for the job in preference to someone of another sex or race. [L *genuīnus*, from *gignere* to beget]

genus *jē'nəs* or *jen'əs*, *n* a taxonomic group of lower rank than a family, consisting of closely related species, in extreme cases of one species only (*biol*); a class of objects comprehending several subordinate species (*logic*): — *pl* **genera** (*jen'ə-rə*) or **gē'nuses**. [L *genus*, *generis* birth; cognate with Gr *genos*]

-geny *-jəni*, *combining form* signifying production, development, origin. [Gr *-geneia*, from *-genēs* born]

Geo. *abbrev*: George.

geo or **gio** *gyō*, (*Orkney* and *Shetland*) *n* a gully, creek: — *pl* **geos** or **gios**. [ON *gjá*]

geo- *jē'ō-*, *combining form* denoting the earth. [Gr *gē* the earth]

geocarpy *jē-ō-kär'pi*, (*bot*) *n* the production, or ripening, of fruit underground. — *adj* **geocarp'ic**. [Gr *gē* earth, and *karpos* fruit]

geocentric *jē-ō-sen'trik*, *adj* having the earth for centre; as viewed or reckoned from the centre of the earth (*astron*); taking life on earth as the basis for evaluation.

— Also **geocen'trical**. — *adv* **geocen'trically**. — *n* **geocen'tricism** (*-sizm*) belief that the earth is the centre of the universe. [Gr *gē* the earth, and *kentron* point, centre]

geochemistry *jē-ō-kem'is-tri, n* the chemistry of the crust of the earth. — *adj* **geochem'ical**. — *adv* **geochem'ically**. — *n* **geochem'ist**. [geo-]

geochronology *jē-ō-kron-ol'ə-ji, n* the science of measuring geological time. — *adj* **geochronolog'ical**. — *n* **geochronol'ogist**. [geo-]

geode *jē'ōd, n* a rock cavity lined with crystals that have grown inwards, a druse (*geol*); a rock or stone having this (*geol*); a rounded hollow nodule of ironstone (*mining*). — *adj* **geod'ic**. [Fr *géode*, from Gr *geōdēs* earthy, from *gē* earth, and *eidos* form]

geodesy *jē-od'i-si, n* earth measurement on a large scale; surveying with allowance for the earth's curvature. — Also *n sing* **geodetics** (*jē-ō-det'iks*). — *adj* **geodesic** (*jē-ō-des'ik* or *-dē'sik*) pertaining to or determined by geodesy. — *n* a geodesic line (see below). — *adj* **geodes'ical** geodesic. — *n* **geod'esist** someone skilled in geodesy; a geodesic surveyor. — *adj* **geodet'ic** or **geodet'ical** geodesic. — *adv* **geodet'ically**. — **geodesic dome** a light strong dome made by combining a grid of triangular or other straightline elements with a section of a sphere; **geodesic** (or **geodetic**) **line** the shortest line on a surface between two points on it; **geodetic surveying** geodesy, surveying large areas with allowance for the earth's curvature. [Gr *geōdaisiā*, from *gē* the earth, and *daisis* division]

Geodimeter® *jē-ō-di'mi-tər, n* an instrument which measures distances by means of a beam of light, calculating on the basis of the speed of light.

geodynamics *jē-ō-dī-nam'iks, n sing* the study of the dynamic processes and forces within the earth. — *adj* **geodynam'ic** or **geodynam'ical**. [geo-]

geofact *jē'ō-fakt*, (*archaeol*) *n* a rock or other object altered (eg chipped) by the action of nature in such a way that it looks like an artefact. [**geo-** and arte*fact*]

geog. *abbrev*: geographic, geographical; geography.

geogeny *jē-oj'ə-ni, n* the science or theory of the formation of the earth's crust [**geo-** and **-geny**]

geognosy *jē-og'nə-si, n* knowledge of the general structure, condition and materials of the earth. — Also (*rare*) **geognosis** (*jē-əg-nō'sis*). — *n* **gē'ognost**. — *adj* **gēognostic** (*-nos'tik*) or **gēognost'ical**. — *adv* **gēognost'ically**. [Fr *géognosie*, from Gr *gē* the earth, and *gnōsis* knowledge]

geogony *jē-og'ə-ni, n* the science or theory of the formation of the earth. — *adj* **geogonic** (*jē-ō-gon'ik*). [Gr *gē* the earth, and *gonē* generation, production]

geography *jē-og'rə-fi, n* the science of the surface of the earth and its inhabitants; the features or the arrangement of a place; a book containing a description of the earth. — *n* **geog'rapher**. — *adj* **geographic** (*jē-ō-graf'ik*) or **geograph'ical**. — *adv* **geograph'ically**. — **geographical concentration** (*marketing*) the degree to which the market for a particular product or service is limited to one geographical area; **geographical distribution** the branch of science concerned with the range and dispersal of animals and plants around the world; **geographical filing** (eg in a company sales or transport department) a filing classification system where files are kept according to geographical district; **geographical mile** see under **mile**. — **physical** and **political geography** see under **physic** and **politic**. [Gr *geōgraphiā*, from *gē* earth, and *graphein* to write]

geoid *jē'oid, n* the figure of the earth's mean sea-level surface assumed to be continued under the land, approximately an oblate ellipsoid of revolution. — *adj* **geoid'al**. [Gr *geōdēs*, *geoeidēs* earth-like, from *gē* earth, and *eidos* form]

geol. *abbrev*: geologic, geological; geology.

geolatry *jē-ol'ə-tri*, (*rare*) *n* earth-worship. [Gr *gē* earth, and *latreiā* worship]

geolinguistics *jē-ō-ling-gwins'tiks, n sing* the study of language in relation to geography. [geo-]

geology *jē-ol'ə-ji, n* the science relating to the history and development of the earth's crust, with its successive floras and faunas. — *adj* **geologic** (*-loj'ik*) or **geolog'ical**. — *adv* **geolog'ically**. — *n* **geol'ogist**, also (now *rare*) **geologian** (*jē-ə-lō'ji-ən*) or **geol'oger**. — *vi* **geol'ogize** or **-ise** to work at geology in the field. — *vt* to investigate the geology of. — **geological column** a diagram showing the subdivisions of part or all of geological time or the stratigraphical sequence in a particular area; **geological time** time before written history, divided into epochs in each of which one of the great rock systems was formed. — **dynamical** or **dynamic geology** the study of the work of natural agents in shaping the earth's crust (wind, frost, rivers, volcanic action, etc); **structural geology** the study of the arrangement and structure of rock masses. [Fr *géologie*, from Gr *gē* earth, and *logos* a discourse]

geomagnetism *jē-ō-mag'nət-izm, n* the magnetism of the earth, earth's magnetic field; the study of this. — *adj* **geomagnet'ic**. — *n* **geomag'netist**. [geo-]

geomancy *jē'ō-man-si, n* divination by shapes formed, eg when earth is thrown down on to a surface; divination by shapes formed by linking random dots made on paper. — *n* **gē'omancer**. — *n* **gē'omant** (*rare*). — *adj* **geoman'tic**. [Gr *gē* earth, and *manteiā* divination]

geomedicine *jē-ō-med'sin, n* the study of diseases as influenced by geographical environment. — *adj* **geomed'ical**. [geo-]

geometry *jē-om'i-tri, n* that part of mathematics which deals with the properties of points, lines, surfaces and solids, either under classical Euclidean assumptions, or (in the case of *elliptic*, *hyperbolic*, etc *geometry*) involving postulates not all of which are identical with Euclid's; any study of a mathematical system in which figures undergo transformations, concerned with discussion of those properties of the figures which remain constant; a textbook of geometry (*archaic*). — *n* **geom'eter** a geometrician; a geometrid caterpillar or moth. — *adj* **geometric** (*-met'*) or **geomet'rical** relating to or according to geometry; (eg of a pattern, design or composition) consisting of or using simple figures such as geometry deals with. — *adv* **geomet'rically**. — *n* **geometrician** (*-me-trish'ən*) a person skilled in geometry. — *n* **geom'etrid** any moth of the family or superfamily **Geomet'ridae** whose caterpillars are loopers. — *n* **geom'etrist**. — *n* **geometrīzā'tion** or **-s-**. — *vt* and *vi* **geom'etrize** or **-ise** to work geometrically; to show in geometric form. — **geometrical progression** a series of quantities each of which has the same ratio to its predecessor; **geometric mean** see under **mean**[2]. [Gr *geōmetriā*, from *gē* earth, and *metron* a measure]

geomorphogeny *jē-ō-mör-foj'ən-i, n* the scientific study of the origins and development of land forms. — *adj* **geomorphogē'nic**. — *n* **geomorphog'enist**. [geo-]

geomorphology *jē-ō-mör-fol'ə-ji, n* the morphology and development of land forms, including those under the sea; the study of this. — *adj* **geomorpholog'ic** or **geomorpholog'ical**. — *adv* **geomorpholog'ically**. — *n* **geomorphol'ogist**. [geo-]

Geomys *jē'ō-mis, n* the typical genus of **Geomyidae** (*-mī'i-dē*), the pouched rats, a family of American burrowing rodents with outward-opening cheek-pouches. — *adj* **geomy'oid**. [Gr *gē* earth, and *mȳs* mouse]

geophagy *jē-of'ə-ji*, (*biol*) *n* earth-eating, the practice of feeding on soil. — Also **geoph'agism**. — *n* **geoph'agist**. — *adj* **geoph'agous** (*-gəs*). [Gr *gē* earth, and *phagein* to eat]

geophilous *jē-of'il-əs*, (*biol*) *adj* living in or on the ground; geocarpic; having a short stem with leaves at ground-level. — *adj* **geophil'ic**. [Gr *gē* earth, and *phileein* to love]

geophone *jē'ə-fōn, n* (*usu* in *pl*) a device for detecting sound waves, shock waves, etc in the ground. [Gr *gē* earth, and *phōnē* voice, sound]

geophysics *gē-ō-fiz'iks, n sing* the physics of the earth, the study of the earth's physical properties. — *adj* **geophys'ical**. — *n* **geophys'icist** (*-i-sist*). [geo-]

geophyte *jē'ō-fīt*, (*bot*) *n* a plant that survives the winter by having subterranean buds, eg bulbs, corms or rhizomes. — *adj* **geophytic** (*-fit'ik*). [Gr *gē* earth, and *phyton* plant]

geopolitics *jē-ō-pol'it-iks*, *n sing* a science concerned with problems of states, such as frontiers, as affected by their geographical environment; the special combination of geographical and political considerations in a particular state; a Nazi doctrine justifying expansion by necessity for Lebensraum, etc. — *adj* **geopolit'ical**. — *adv* **geopolit'ically**. — *n* **geopoliti'cian**. [Ger *Geopolitik*; see **geo-**]

geoponic *jē-ō-pon'ik* or **geoponical** *-əl*, *adj* agricultural. — *n sing* **geopon'ics** the science of agriculture. [Gr *geōponikos*, from *gē* earth, and *ponos* labour]

Geordie *jör'di*, *n* a native of Tyneside; the dialect of Tyneside; a Scotsman (*Austr* and *NZ*); a coal-miner; a coal-carrying boat; a guinea, from the figure of St *George*; a safety-lamp for miners invented by *George* Stephenson. — *adj* pertaining to Tyneside, its people, dialect, accent or culture. [Dimin of **George**]

George *jörj*, *n* a jewelled figure of St *George* slaying the dragon, worn by Knights of the Garter; a guinea or Geordie (qv) (*obs*); the automatic pilot of an aircraft (*airmen's slang*). — **George Cross** an award (instituted during World War II) for outstanding courage or heroism given in cases where a purely military honour is not applicable; **George Medal** an award for gallantry given to civilians and members of the armed forces. — **St George's cross** the Greek cross of England, red on a white background.

georgette *jör-jet'*, *n* a thin silk fabric. [From *Georgette* de la Plante, French dressmaker]

Georgian *jör'ji-ən*, *adj* relating to or contemporary with any of the various *Georges*, kings of Great Britain, *esp* the first four, who ruled from 1714 to 1830; belonging to *Georgia* (*Gurjestan*, *Gruzia*) in the Caucasus, its people, language, etc; of or relating to the American State of *Georgia*; relating to or following Henry *George*, Lloyd *George*, or other of the name. — Also *n*. — **Georgian planet** (*obs*) Uranus, named after George III by its discoverer, Sir William Herschel.

georgic *jör'jik*, *adj* (*obs*) relating to agriculture or rustic affairs. — *n* a poem on husbandry or rural affairs, after Virgil's poetic work in four books on that theme, the *Georgics*. [L *geōrgicus*, from Gr *geōrgikos*, from *geōrgiā* agriculture, from *gē* earth, and *ergon* work]

geoscience *jē'ō-sī-əns*, *n* any of the scientific disciplines, such as geology or geomorphology, which deal with the earth, or all of these collectively. — *adj* **geoscientif'ic**. [**geo-**]

geosphere *jē'ō-sfēr*, *n* the solid part of the earth, distinguished from *atmosphere* and *hydrosphere*. [Gr *gē* earth, and *sphaira* sphere]

geostatic *jē-ō-stat'ik*, *adj* (of a construction) capable of sustaining the pressure of earth from all sides. — *n sing* **geostat'ics** the statics of rigid bodies. [Gr *gē* the earth, and *statikos* causing to stand]

geostationary *jē-ō-stā'shən-ə-ri*, *adj* (of a satellite, etc) orbiting the earth in time with the earth's own rotation, ie circling it once every 24 hours, so remaining above the same spot on the earth's surface. [**geo-**]

geostrategy *jē-ō-strat'ə-ji*, *n* global strategy, strategy dealing with geopolitical concerns. — *adj* **geostratē'gic** or **geostratē'gical**. [**geo-**]

geostrophic *jē-ō-strof'ik*, *adj* of a virtual force used to account for the change in direction of the wind relative to the surface of the earth arising from the earth's rotation; of a wind whose direction and force are partly determined by the earth's rotation. [Gr *gē* earth, and *strophē* a turn]

geosynchronous *jē-ō-sing'krə-nəs*, *adj* (of a satellite, etc) geostationary. [**geo-**]

geosyncline *jē-ō-sin'klīn*, (*geol*) *n* a syncline on a great scale. — *adj* **geosynclī'nal**. [**geo-**]

geotaxis *jē-ō-taks'is*, (*biol*) *n* response of an organism to the stimulus of gravity. — *adj* **geotact'ic** or **geotact'ical**. — *adv* **geotact'ically**. [Gr *gē* earth, and *taxis* arrangement]

geotechnics *jē-ō-tek'niks*, *n sing* the application of scientific and engineering principles to the solution of civil-engineering and other problems created by the nature and constitution of the earth's crust. — *adj* **geotech'nic** or **geotech'nical**. — *n* **geotechnol'ogy** the application of science and technology to the extraction and use of the earth's natural resources. — *adj* **geotechnolog'ical**. [**geo-**]

geotectonic *jē-ō-tek-ton'ik*, *adj* relating to the structure of rock masses. — *n sing* **geotecton'ics** structural geology. [Gr *gē* earth, and *tektōn* a builder]

geothermic *jē-ō-thûr'mik* or **geothermal** *-thûr'məl*, *adj* pertaining to or heated by the internal heat of the earth. — *n* **geothermom'eter** an instrument for measuring subterranean temperatures. — **geothermal energy** energy extracted from the earth's natural heat, ie from hot springs and certain kinds of rock; **geothermal gradient** the rate at which the temperature of the earth's crust increases with depth. [Gr *gē* earth, and *thermē* heat]

geotropism *jē-ot'rop-izm*, (*bot*) *n* geotaxis (*positive* downwards, towards the centre of the earth, *negative* upwards, away from the centre of the earth). — *adj* **geotrop'ic**. — *adv* **geotrop'ically**. [Gr *gē* earth, and *tropos* a turning]

Ger. *abbrev*: German; Germany.

ger. *abbrev*: gerund; gerundive.

gerah *gē'rä*, (*antiq*; *Bible*) *n* the smallest Hebrew weight and coin, 1/20 of a shekel. [Heb *gērāh*]

geraniol *gə-rān'i-ol*, or *-rän'*, *n* an alcohol ($C_{10}H_{18}O$) forming a constituent of many of the esters used in perfumery. [Ger; *geranium* and chem sfx *-ol*, representing alcoh*ol*]

geranium *ji-rān'yəm*, *n* a plant of the genus *Geranium* with seed-vessels like a crane's bill, typical of the family **Geraniaceae** (*-i-ā'si-ē*); (loosely) any cultivated plant of the genus *Pelargonium*. [L, from Gr *geranion*, from *geranos* a crane]

gerbe *jûrb*, *n* a wheatsheaf (*obs* or *heraldry*); a fountain or firework resembling a wheatsheaf (*obs*). [Fr *gerbe*; cf **garb**[2]]

gerbera *gûr'bə-rə*, or *jûr'*, *n* a plant belonging to the **Ger'bera** genus of composite plants of S Africa, etc. [T *Gerber*, German naturalist]

gerbil *jûr'bil*, *n* a small desert-dwelling rodent capable of causing great damage to crops but often kept as a pet. — Also **jer'bil** and (*esp* formerly) **ger'bille**. [Fr *gerbille*]

gere (*Spenser*). Same as **gear**.

gerent *jē'rənt*, or *jer'*, (*rare*) *n* a controller, ruler. [L *gerēns*, *-entis*, pr p of *gerere* to manage]

gerenuk *ge'rə-nōōk*, *n* a long-legged, long-necked antelope of East Africa (*Litocranius walleri*). [From the Somali name]

gerfalcon. See **gyrfalcon**.

geriatrics *jer-i-at'riks*, *n sing* medical care of the old. — *adj* **geriat'ric** of, for, or relating to old people; (*loosely* and *facetiously*) ancient, worn-out, past it (used eg of objects or machines, etc) (*colloq*). — *n* (*colloq*) an old person. — *n* **geriatrician** (*-ə-trish'ən*) or **geriatrist** (*-at'rist*). [Gr *gēras* old age, and *iātros* physician]

gerle (*Spenser*). Same as **girl**.

germ *jûrm*, *n* a rudimentary form of a living thing, whether plant or animal; a shoot; that from which anything springs, the origin or beginning; a first principle; that from which a disease springs; a micro-organism, *esp* a harmful one; a plant ovary (*obs*). — *vi* to put forth buds, sprout. — *n* **germ'icide** a substance which kills germs. — *adj* **germicī'dal** or **germ'icide**. — *adj* **germ'inable** that can be germinated. — *adj* **germ'inal** pertaining to a germ or rudiment; in germ, or (*fig*) in the earliest stage of development; seminal (*fig*). — *adj* **germ'inant** sprouting; budding; capable of developing. — *vi* **germ'inate** (*esp* of a seed or spore) to begin to grow. — *vt* to cause to sprout. — *n* **germinā'tion**. — *adj* **germ'inative** — **germ cell** a gamete, a sperm or ovum, or a cell from which it springs; **germ layer** a primary cell-layer in an embryo, ie ectoderm, mesoderm, or endoderm; **germ line** (*biol*) the cells whose descendants give rise to the gametes; **germ plasm** that part of the nuclear protoplasmic material which, according to early theories of inheritance, is the vehicle of heredity, and maintains its continuity from generation to generation; **germ theory** the theory that all living organisms can be produced only from living organisms, by the growth and development of germ cells; the theory that micro-organisms cause all infectious diseases; **germ warfare** warfare in which bacteria are used as weapons. [Partly through Fr *germe*, from L *germen*, *-inis* a sprout, bud, germ, from *germināre*, *-ātum* to sprout]

germain, **germaine** (*Shakesp*). See **germen**.

German *jûr'mən*, *n* a native or citizen of *Germany*, or one of the same linguistic or ethnological stock (*pl* **Ger'mans**); the German language, *esp* High German. — *adj* of or from Germany, or the Germans; German-speaking. — *adj* **Germanesque'** marked by German characteristics. — *adj* **Germanic** (*-man'ik*) of Germany; of the linguistic family to which German, English, Norwegian, etc belong, Teutonic. — *n* an extinct Indo-European language which differentiated into **East Germanic** (Gothic and other extinct languages), **North Germanic** or Scandinavian (Norwegian, Danish, Swedish, Icelandic) and **West Germanic** (English, Frisian, Dutch, Low German, High German). — *adv* **German'ically**. — *adj* **Ger'manish** somewhat German. — *n* **Ger'manism** a German idiom; German ideas and ways. — *n* **Ger'manist** an expert in German philology or other matters relating to Germany. — *adj* **Germanis'tic** pertaining to the study of German. — *n* **Germanizā'tion** or **-s-**. — *vt* **Ger'manīze** or **-ise** to make German. — *vi* to become German; to adopt German ways. — *n* **German'ophil** a lover of the Germans and things German, now *usu* **German'ophile**. — *n* **Germanophil'ia**. — *n* **German'ophobe** a person who fears or hates the Germans and things German. — **German band** street-musicians, *orig* from Germany; **German flute** the ordinary modern flute; **German measles** rubella; **German Ocean** (*archaic*) the North Sea; **German silver** an alloy of copper, nickel and zinc, white like silver, and first made in Germany; **German sixth** (*music*) a chord with major third, perfect fifth, and augmented sixth; **German shepherd** or **German shepherd dog** the Alsatian dog. — **High German** the literary language throughout Germany, *orig* the speech of High or Southern Germany; **Low German** Platt-Deutsch, the language or dialects of Low or Northern Germany; formerly applied to all the West Germanic dialects except High German. [L *Germānus* German]

german *jûr'mən*, *adj* of the first degree, full (see **brother**, **cousin**); closely related (*obs*); germane, relevant (*obs*). — *n* (*obs*) a full brother or sister; a near relative. [OFr *germain*, from L *germānus* having the same parents or kin]

germander *jər-man'dər*, *n* a labiate herb (*Teucrium*) with aromatic, bitter and stomachic properties. — **germander speedwell** a bright blue-flowered veronica (*V chamaedrys*). [LL *germandra*, from Late Gr *chamandrya*, from Gr *chamaidrȳs*, from *chamai* on the ground, and *drȳs* oak]

germane *jer-mān'*, *adj* closely related (to); relevant, appropriate (to). — *adv* **germane'ly**. — *n* **germane'ness**. [Ety as for **german**]

Germanic, etc. See **German**.

Germanice *jûr-man'i-sē* or *ger-man'ik-e*, (*L*) *adv* in German.

Germanish . . . to . . . **Germanistic**. See **German**.

germanium *jər-mā'ni-əm*, *n* a metallic element (symbol **Ge**; atomic no 32), much used in diodes, transistors and rectifiers for its properties as a semiconductor. [Discovered and named by a *German* chemist, C A Winkler (1838–1904)]

Germanize, etc. See German.

germen *jer'mən*, or **germin** *jer'min*, (*Shakesp* **ger'main** or **ger'maine**) *n* a rudiment, germ; a shoot (*obs*); the ovary in a flower (*obs*). [L *germen*, *-inis*; see **germ**]

germicide, **germinal**, **germinate**, etc. See **germ**.

Germinal *zher-mē-nal'*, (*hist*) *n* the seventh month of the French revolutionary calendar, about 21 March to 19 April. [See **germ**]

gerne *gûrn*, (*Spenser*) *vi* to grin or gape. [**grin**[1]]

Geronimo *jə-ron'i-mō*, (*orig* and *esp US*) *interj* a paratroopers' war cry used on jumping into action; used facetiously as a stirring shout at the moment of attack upon some venture or activity (*colloq*). [*Geronimo*, Apache chieftain (1829–1909) who campaigned against US troops to preserve tribal lands]

gerontic *ger-* or *jer-on'tik*, *adj* (*biol*) pertaining to the senescent period in the life-history of an individual. — *n* **gerontoc'racy** government by old men. — *adj* **gerontocrat'ic**. — *adj* **gerontolog'ical**. — *n* **gerontol'ogist**. — *n* **gerontol'ogy** scientific study of the processes of growing old. — *n* **geron'tophil** or **geron'tophile** (*-fil* or *-fīl*) a person who experiences **gerontophilia** (*-fil'i-ə*), a sexual attraction towards old people. — *n* **geron'tophobe** (*-fōb*) a person who experiences **gerontophō'bia**, an irrational fear of old people and old age. — *n sing* **gerontotherapeut'ics** the science of medical treatment of the diseases of old age. [Gr *gerōn*, *-ontos* old man]

geropiga *jer-ō-pē'gə*, *n* a port substitute, a mixture consisting chiefly of grape-juice and brandy, sometimes illicitly mixed with real port. [Port]

Gerry. See **Jerry**.

gerrymander *jer'i-man-dər*, also *ger'*, *vt* to rearrange (voting districts) in the interests of a particular party or candidate; to manipulate (facts, arguments, etc) so as to reach undue conclusions. — *n* an arrangement of the above nature. — *n* **gerryman'derer**. [Formed from the name of Governor Elbridge *Gerry* (1744–1814) and sala*mander*, from the likeness to that animal of the gerrymandered map of Massachusetts in 1811]

gertcha *gûr'chə*, (*slang*) *interj* get away (along, off) with you!, come off it!; clear off!, get out of that (or there). [Corruption and contraction of spoken phrase]

gerund *jer'ənd*, *n* a part of a Latin verb with the value of a verbal noun, such as *amandum* loving; in English, a noun with the ending *-ing* formed from a verb and having some of the qualities of a verb, such as the possibility of governing an object, etc; often preceded by a possessive (eg *My leaving her was unwise*). — *adj* **gerundial** (*ji-rund'i-əl*), **gerundival** (*jer-ən-dī'vl*) or **gerundive** (*ji-rund'iv*). — *n* **gerund'ive** a Latin verbal adjective expressing necessity, such as *amandus*, *-a*, *-um* deserving or requiring to be loved. — **ger'und-grinder** a pedantic teacher. [L *gerundium*, from *gerere* to bear]

Gesellschaft *gə-zel'shäft*, (*Ger*) *n* an association of people, eg a commercial company, united by individual commitment to a common cause.

gesneria *jes-nē'ri-ə*, *n* a plant of the tropical America genus **Gesnē'ria**, typical of the **Gesneriā'ceae**, a family closely related to the Scrophulariaceae. [Named after Konrad von *Gesner* (1516–65), Swiss botanist and scholar]

gessamine (*Milton*). Same as **jasmine**.

gesse (*Spenser*). Same as **guess**[1].

gesso *jes'ō*, *n* plaster of Paris; a plaster surface prepared as a ground for painting: — *pl* **gess'oes**. [Ital, from L *gypsum*; see **gypsum**]

gest[1] *jest*, (*Shakesp*) *n* time fixed for a stay in a place. [OFr *giste* a stopping-place]

gest[2] or **geste** *jest*, (*obs*) *n* an exploit; a tale of adventure, a romance. [OFr *geste*, from L *gesta* things done, from *gerere*, *gestum* to bear, behave; cf **jest**]

gest[3] or **geste** *jest*, *n* (*obs*) bearing; gesture. — *adj* **gest'ic** of or relating to movement or gesture of the body, *esp* in dance. [Fr *geste*, from L *gestus*, from *gerere*, *gestum* to bear, behave]

Gestalt or **gestalt** *gə-shtält'*, (*Ger*) *n* form, shape, pattern; an organized whole or unit; Gestalt therapy. — *n*

gestalt'ism Gestalt psychology. — *n* **Gestalt'ist**. — **Gestalt psychology** the outlook or theory based on the concept that the organized whole is something more than the sum of the parts into which it can be logically analysed (a revolt from the atomistic outlook of the orthodox school); **Gestalt therapy** or **psychotherapy** a therapy that works towards self-discovery and liberation through a combination of existentialism, realism, self-expression, self-acceptance and regular self-analysis. [Ger]

gestant. See **gestate**.

Gestapo *gə-stä'pō*, *n* the secret police in Nazi Germany; (without *cap*) any such secret police organization associated with harsh and unscrupulous methods: — *pl* **gesta'pos**. — Also *adj*. [From Ger *Ge*heime *Sta*ats*po*lizei, secret state police]

gestate *jes-tāt'*, *vt* to carry in the womb during the period from conception to birth; to conceive and develop slowly in the mind. — *vi* to be in the process of gestating. — *adj* (*rare*) **ges'tant** laden (also *fig*). — *n* **gestation** (*jes-tā'shən*) the process of gestating (*biol* and *fig*); being carried in a vehicle, a boat, etc (*archaic*). — *adj* **gestā'tional** or **gest'ative** of carriage, *esp* in the womb. — *adj* **gestatō'rial** or **ges'tatory** pertaining to carrying (*archaic*). — **gestatorial chair** a ceremonial chair on which the pope is carried in procession. [L *gestāre*, *-ātum* to carry, from *gerere* to bear]

gesticulate *jes-tik'ū-lāt*, *vi* to make vigorous gestures. — *n* **gesticulā'tion**. — *n* **gestic'ulātor**. — *adj* **gestic'ulative** or **gestic'ulatory**. [L *gesticulāri*, *-ātus*, from *gesticulus*, dimin of *gestus* gesture, from *gerere* to carry, behave]

gesture *jes'chər*, *n* a posture, or movement of the body (*obs*); an action, *esp* of the hands, expressive of sentiment or passion or intended to show inclination or disposition; the use of such movements; an action dictated by courtesy or diplomacy, or by a desire to impress or create an impression, eg of willingness (also *adj*); behaviour (*Shakesp*). — *vi* to make a gesture or gestures. — *vt* to express by gesture(s). — *adj* **ges'tural**. [LL *gestūra*, from L *gestus*, from L *gerere* to carry, behave]

Gesundheit *gə-zōōnt'hīt*, (*Ger*) *interj* your health (said to someone who has just sneezed). — **auf Ihre Gesundheit** (*owf ē'rə*; said to a drinking companion) here's to your health.

get *get*, *vt* to obtain; to acquire; to procure; to receive; to attain; to come to have; to catch; to answer (a door or telephone) (*colloq*); to grasp or take the meaning of (often in the colloqial phrase **get it**?, of a joke, irony, etc); to learn; to commit to memory; to hit (*colloq*); to descry, discern, make out; to succeed in making contact with (eg a radio station); to have the better of, gain a decisive advantage over (*colloq*); to baffle (*colloq*); to irritate (*colloq*); to grip emotionally, take, captivate, hit the taste of exactly; to induce; to cause to be, go, or become; to betake, take (oneself); to beget (*archaic* except when used of animals, *esp* horses); to attack or injure, *esp* in revenge (*colloq*). — *vi* (with preposition, adverb, infinitive, etc) to arrive, to bring or put oneself (in any place, position or state); (with adjective, etc) to become; to become richer (*obs*); to clear out (*colloq*; orig *US*): — *pr p* **gett'ing**; *pa t* **got**, *obs* **gat**; *pa p* **got**, *archaic*, *Scot* and *US* **gott'en**. — *n* that which is got (*obs*); a (*usu* difficult) shot successfully reached and returned (*tennis*); output (*obs*); (of animals) offspring; (also **gait**, **gaitt**, **geit** (*get*); see also **git**, and **gyte**[2]) a child, brat (*Scot contemptuously*); begetting (*obs*). — *adj* **gett'able**. — *n* **gett'er** (*esp* in combination) someone who, or something which, gets, attains, collects; a material used, when evaporated by high-frequency induction currents, for evacuation of gas left in vacuum valves after sealing during manufacture (*electronics*). — *vt* to evacuate (a valve) using a getter; to remove (gas) using a getter. — *vi* to use a getter. — *n* **gett'ering** evacuation using a getter. — *n* **gett'ing** the action of the verb; a gaining, anything gained (*archaic*); procreation (*archaic*). — *adj* **get-at'-able** easily accessible. — **get'away** an escape; a start; breaking cover. — *adj* used in a getaway. — **get'-out** (*colloq*) a way of escape or avoidance (also *adj*); the dismantling, packing up and moving of props, scenery, costumes, etc at the end of a production run (*theat*); the total cost of a production for one week (*theat*). — *adj* **get'-rich'-quick'** (*colloq*) wanting, or leading to, easy prosperity. — **get'-together** a social gathering; an informal conference; **get'-up** (style of) equipment, outfit, make-up; **get'-up-and-go'** (*colloq*) energy. — **get about** or **around** to travel, go visiting; to be mobile and active; **get across** (*colloq*) to communicate successfully; **get ahead** to make progress, advance; **get along** to get on (see below); **get around** see **get about**; **get at** to reach, attain; to poke fun at (*slang*); to mean (*colloq*); to begin (*colloq*; *orig US*); to attack verbally (*slang*); to influence by underhand or unlawful means (*colloq*); **get away** to escape, make a successful departure; (as *imperative*) go away, be off, get back; (as *interj*) an expression of disbelief, never!, you don't say!; **get away with (something)** to pull something off; to carry a thing through successfully or with impunity; **get back at** to have one's revenge on; **get by** to succeed in passing; to elude notice and come off with impunity, manage satisfactorily, be sufficiently good (*colloq*); **get down** to alight; to depress (*colloq*); to complete the hole (*golf*); **get down to** to set to work on, tackle seriously; **get in** to (manage to) enter; to be elected; to gather; to send for; to manage, succeed in doing (as in *We got the gardening in before the rain*); **get in on** (*colloq*) to join in, become a participant in; **get it on** or **off** (**with**; *slang*) to have sexual intercourse (with); to get high (on a drug); **get off** to escape; to go, to set off (on a journey); to fall asleep (*colloq*); to learn, memorize; to gain the affection of, or have a sexual encounter with, someone of the opposite sex (with *with*; *colloq*); **get off on** (*slang*) to get excitement from; **get on** to proceed, advance; to prosper; to agree, associate harmoniously; to fare, manage; **get one's own back** (*colloq*) to have one's revenge (on); **get out** to produce; to extricate oneself (with *of*); to take oneself off; **get over** to surmount; to recover from; to make an impression on an audience; **get (something) over with** to accomplish (an unpleasant task, etc) as quickly as possible; **get round** to circumvent; to persuade, talk over; **get round to** to bring oneself to do (something); **get there** (*slang*) to achieve one's object, succeed; **get through** to finish; to reach a destination; to receive approval, or to obtain it for (something); to obtain a connection by telephone; to communicate with, reach the comprehension of (with *to*); **get together** to meet socially or for discussion; **get up** to rise, *esp* from bed; to ascend; to arrange, dress, prepare (oneself); to learn up for an occasion; to commit to memory; **have got** (*colloq*) to have; **have got to** to be obliged to; **tell someone where to get off** (*colloq*) to deal summarily or dismissively with someone; **you've got me there** (*colloq*) I don't know the answer to your question. [ON *geta*; cognate with OE *-gietan* (in compounds)]

geta *gā'tə*, *n* a Japanese wooden sandal with a thong between the big toe and the other toes: — *pl* **ge'ta** or **ge'tas**. [Jap]

geum *jē'əm*, *n* an avens, a plant of the **Ge'um** genus of the rose family. [L]

GeV (*phys*) *abbrev*: giga-electron-volt, a unit of particle energy (in *US* sometimes **BeV**).

gewgaw *gū'gö*, *n* a toy; a trifling object, a bauble. — *adj* showy without value. [Origin unknown]

Gewürztraminer *gə-vōōrtz'trə-mē-nər*, *n* a variety of white grape grown *esp* in the Alsace region: a wine, typically medium-dry, aromatic and with a spicy flavour, made from this grape. [Ger, from *Gewürz* spice, and *Traminer* a grape variety (after *Tramin* wine-growing region in S Tirol)]

gey (*Scot*). See **gay**. — *adv* **geyan** (*gī'ən*) for **gey and**.

geyser *gā'*, *gē'* or *gī'zər*, *n* a spring that periodically spouts hot water and steam into the air; (*usu gē'*) an apparatus that heats domestic water as the tap is turned on. — *n* **gey'serite** sinter. [*Geysir* a geyser in Iceland, from Icel *geysa*, ON *göysa* to gush]

GFOF *abbrev*: Geared Futures and Options Funds.

GH *abbrev*: Ghana (IVR).

Ghanaian *gä-nā'yən*, or *-nä'*, *adj* of or pertaining to *Ghana*, a W African republic. — *n* a native or citizen of Ghana.

gharial. Same as **gavial**, **garial**.

gharri or **gharry** *ga'ri*, *n* (*esp* in India) a wheeled vehicle, generally for hire. [Hindi *gārī* a cart]

ghast *gäst*, *vt* (*Shakesp*) to cause to be aghast; to frighten. — *adj* **ghast'ful** or **ghast'full** (*Spenser*) dreary, dismal. — *adv* **ghast'fully** (*obs*) frightfully. — *n* **ghast'liness**. — *adj* **ghast'ly** death-like; hideous; deplorable (*colloq*). — Also *adv* (*archaic*). — *n* **ghast'ness** (*Shakesp* **gastness** qv). [OE *gǣstan*; cf **gast**]

ghat or **ghaut** *göt*, *n* (in India) a mountain pass; a landing-stair on a riverside; a place of cremation (*burning ghat*). [Hindi *ghāt* descent]

ghazal *gaz'al*, *n* a Persian and Arabic verse-form, of not more than 18 couplets, the first two lines and the even-numbered lines thereafter rhyming together, used *esp* for poems of an amatory or bacchanalian nature. — Also **gazal**, **ghazel**. [Ar *ghazal*]

ghazi *gä'zē*, *n* a veteran Muslim warrior, slayer of infidels; a high Turkish title. [Ar *ghāzi* fighting]

Gheber or **Ghebre** *gā'bər* or *gē'bər*, *n*. Same as **Guebre**.

ghee or **ghi** *gē* or *ghē*, *n* clarified butter, *esp* made with milk from the Asiatic buffalo. [Hindi *ghī*]

gherao *ge-row'*, *n* (in India) the surrounding or trapping of a person (eg an employer) in a room, building, etc until he or she meets one's demands: — *pl* **gheraos'**. — Also *vt*. [Hindi, siege, from *gherna* to surround, besiege]

gherkin *gûr'kin*, *n* a small cucumber used for pickling. [From an earlier form of Du *augurk(je)* a gherkin; appar from Slavonic]

ghesse (*Spenser*). Same as **guess**[1]: — *pa t* and *pa p* **ghest** or **ghessed**.

ghetto *get'ō*, *n* the Jews' quarter in an Italian or other city, to which they used to be confined; a quarter, *esp* poor, inhabited by any racial or other identifiable group; a section marked out as distinct, set apart to contain some group regarded as non-mainstream (*fig*): — *pl* **ghett'oes** or **ghett'os**. — *vt* **ghett'oïze** or **-ise** to make into a ghetto; to confine to, put into, a ghetto. — **ghett'o-blaster** (*colloq*) a *usu* fairly large portable radio and cassette-recorder unit with built-in speakers. [Ital *ghetto* foundry, after one which previously occupied the site of the Venetian Jewish ghetto]

ghi. See **ghee**.

Ghibelline or **Ghibeline** *gib'ə-lēn*, *-līn* or *-lin*, *n* a member of a medieval Italian party, *orig* supporters of Hohenstaufen emperors against the Guelfs and the pope. [Ital *Ghibellino*, appar from *Waiblingen* a Hohenstaufen town]

ghilgai. See **gilgai**.

ghillie. Same as **gillie**.

ghost *gōst*, *n* a spirit; the soul of a person; a spirit appearing after death; a dead body (*Shakesp*); a person who writes (eg speeches) on behalf of another credited as author; a faint or false appearance; a semblance; a person on the payroll who does no actual work (*industry*, etc); a person counted on an attendance register who is not actually present; a duplicated image due to additional reception of a delayed similar signal which has covered a longer path (*TV*). — *vt* to haunt as or like a ghost; to transfer (a prisoner) quickly and secretly overnight. — *vi* to be a ghost (qv; *industry*); to fail to declare income from a job; to disappear, vanish like a ghost; to progress by sail despite very little wind (*naut*). — *vi* and *vt* to work, *esp* write, on behalf of another person credited as the creator or author. — *n* **ghost'ing**. — *adj* **ghost'like**. — *n* **ghost'liness**. — *adj* **ghost'ly** spiritual (*obs*); religious (*obs*); pertaining to apparitions; ghostlike. — *adj* faint. — *adj* **ghost'y**. — **ghost gum** an Australian tree (*Eucalyptus papuana*) with smooth white bark; **ghost moth** a moth (*Hepialus humuli*), the male of ghostly white appearance, the caterpillar destructive to hop-gardens; **ghost story** a story in which ghosts figure; **ghost town** one which once flourished owing to some natural resource in the vicinity but which is now deserted since the natural resource has been exhausted; **ghost word** a word that has originated in a copyist's or printer's error. — *vi* and *vt* **ghost'-write** to write for another as a ghost. — **ghost'-writer**. — **give up the ghost** to die; **Holy Ghost** the Holy Spirit, the third person in the Christian Trinity; **not to have a ghost (of a chance)** not to have the least chance of success; **the ghost walks** (*theat slang*) money is available, the wages can be paid (quotation from *Shakesp*). [OE *gāst*; Ger *Geist*; the *h* from Caxton (Flemish *gheest*)]

ghoul *gōōl*, now often *gowl*, *n* an Eastern demon that preys on the dead; a gruesome fiend; a person of gruesome or revolting habits or tastes. — *adj* **ghoul'ish**. — *adv* **ghoul'ishly**. — *n* **ghoul'ishness**. [Ar *ghūl*]

GHQ *abbrev*: General Headquarters.

ghubar numeral. Same as **gobar numeral**.

ghyll *gil*, *n*. See **gill**[4].

GHz *abbrev*: gigahertz.

GI *jē-ī'*, *n* a regular soldier in the US Army. [Abbrev for government (or general) issue.]

gi. See **gie**[2].

giambeux (*Spenser*). Same as **jambeaux**. See under **jamb**.

giant *jī'ənt*, *n* a huge mythical being of more or less human form; a person of abnormally great stature; anything much above the usual size of its kind; someone with much greater powers than the average person: — *fem* **gī'antess**. — *adj* **gī'ant** gigantic. — *n* **gī'anthood** the quality or character of a giant; the race of giants. — *n* **gī'antism** the occurrence of giants; gigantism. — *adj* **gī'antly** giant-like. — *n* **gī'antry** giants collectively; giant stories or mythology. — *n* **gī'antship**. — **giant fibres** the enlarged nerve fibres in the ventral nerve cord of many invertebrates which transmit impulses very rapidly and initiate escape behaviour; **gi'ant-killer** someone who defeats a far superior opponent; **gi'ant-killing**; **giant panda** see **panda**; **giant powder** a kind of dynamite. — *adj* **giant rude** (*Shakesp*) enormously rude or uncivil. — **giant's-kett'le** a large pot-hole believed to have been formed by subglacial water; **giant star** (*astron*) a star of great brightness and low mean density; **giant** (or **giant's**) **stride** a gymnastic apparatus enabling one to take great strides around a pole. [OFr *geant* (Fr *géant*), from L *gigās*, from Gr *gigās*, *gigantos*]

giaour *jowr*, *n* an infidel, a term applied by the Turks to all who are not of their own religion. [Through Turk, from Pers *gaur*; see **Guebre**]

Giardia *jē-är'di-ə*, *n* a genus of parasitic protozoa which commonly infect the small intestine of mammals, including man. — *n* **giardī'asis** intestinal infestation with protozoa of the Giardia genus, a disease, often with diarrhoea, nausea, etc, contracted through drinking contaminated water. [Fr biologist, A *Giard* (1846–1908)]

Gib *jib*, (*colloq*) *n* Gibraltar.

gib[1] *jib* or *gib*, *n* a wedge-shaped piece of metal holding another in place, etc. — *vt* to fasten with a gib: — *pr p* **gibb'ing**; *pa t* and *pa p* **gibbed**. [Origin obscure]

gib[2] *gib*, *n* (*obs*) a tom-cat, *esp* a castrated one; a term of reproach. — Also (*archaic* and *dialect*) **gib'-cat**. [From the name *Gilbert*]

gibber[1] *jib'ər*, *vi* to utter senseless or inarticulate sounds. [Imit]

gibber[2] *gib'ər*, (*Austr*) *n* a stone; a boulder. [Aboriginal]

Gibberella *jib-ər-el'ə*, *n* a genus of fungi found *esp* on grasses, eg wheat scab. — *n* **gibberell'in** any of several plant-growth regulators produced by a fungus of the genus. — **gibberellic** (*-el'ik*) **acid** an acid having similar effects.

gibberish *gib'ər-ish*, or *jib'*, *n* rapid, gabbling talk; meaningless words. — *adj* meaningless, nonsensical. [Imit]

gibbet *jib'it*, *n* a gallows, *esp* one on which criminals were suspended after execution; the projecting beam of a crane. — *vt* to expose on, or as on, a gibbet. [OFr *gibet* a stick; origin unknown]

gibble-gabble *gib'l-gab'l*, *n* senseless chatter. [**gabble**]

gibbon *gib'ən*, *n* an East Indian anthropoid ape (of several species) with very long arms. [Fr, used by Buffon, supposedly from an Indian word]

Gibbonian *gi-bō'ni-ən*, *adj* of, like or pertaining to the English historian Edward *Gibbon* (1734–94).

gibbous *gib'əs*, *adj* hump-backed; humped; swollen or pouched; (of the moon or a planet) between half and full, unequally convex on two sides. — Also **gibb'ose**. — *n* **gibbos'ity** or **gibb'ousness**. — *adv* **gibb'ously**. [L *gibbōsus*, from *gibbus* a hump]

gibbsite *gib'zīt*, *n* hydroxide of aluminium, $Al(OH)_3$, an important constituent of bauxite. [From George *Gibbs*, American mineralogist (died 1833)]

gibe or **jibe** *jīb*, *vi* to scoff; to flout, jeer. — *vt* to scoff at; to taunt. — *n* a flout; a taunt. — *n* **gī'ber** or **jī'ber**. — *adv* **gī'bingly**. [Origin obscure]

gibel *gib'əl*, *n* a common European and North Asian carp, without barbules, similar to a wild form of goldfish, also called *Prussian* or *Crucian carp*.

Gibeonite *gib'i-ən-īt*, (*Bible*) *n* a slave's slave (from Joshua 9).

giblets *jib'lits*, *n pl* the internal eatable parts of a fowl, etc; entrails. — *adj* **gib'let** made of giblets. [OFr *gibelet* a game stew; origin uncertain]

Gibraltarian *jib-röl-tā'ri-ən*, *n* and *adj* (an inhabitant) of Gibraltar. — **Gibraltar board**® (*NZ*) a type of plasterboard.

gibus *jī'bəs*, *n* an opera-hat. [Fr, from the maker's name.]

gid *gid*, *n* sturdy, a disease of sheep. [**giddy**]

giddap *gid-ap'* or *gid'ap*, **giddup** *gid-up'* or *gid'up*, or **giddy-up** *gid-i-up'* or *gid'i-*, (*colloq*) *interj* used to urge on a horse or other animal; hurry up, get along (often used *playfully* or *jocularly*). [From colloq pronunciation of **get up**]

giddy *gid'i*, *adj* unsteady, dizzy; causing giddiness; whirling; light-headed; flighty. — *vi* and *vt* to make or become giddy. — *adv* **gidd'ily**. — *n* **gidd'iness**. — *adj* **gidd'y-headed** thoughtless, frivolous. — *adj* **gidd'y-paced** (*Shakesp*) moving irregularly. — **play the giddy goat** to act the fool. [OE *gidig*, *gydig* insane, possessed by a god]

giddy-up see **giddap**.

Gideon *gid'i-ən*, *n* a member of an organization of Christian businessmen, founded in the United States in 1899, best known for putting Bibles (**Gideon Bibles**) in hotel rooms, etc. [Named after *Gideon*, the judge of Israel (Judges 6 ff)]

gidgee or **gidjee** *gi'jē*, (*Austr*) *n* a small acacia tree, the foliage of which at times emits an unpleasant odour. [Aboriginal]

gie[1] *gē*, *v* a Scots form of **give**[1]: — *pa t* **gied** (*gēd*) or **gae** (*gā*); *pa p* **gien** (*gēn*).

gie[2] or **gi** *gē*, *n* judo or karate costume. [Jap *ki* clothing]

gien. See **gie**[1].

gier-eagle *jēr'ē'gl*, (*Bible*) *n* a vulture. [Du *gier*]

gif *gif*, *conj* an obsolete form of **if**.

Giffen good *gif'ən good*, (*econ*, etc) *n* a foodstuff of relatively low quality which forms an important part of the diet of low-income households, demand for which (contrary to the normal rule) increases when its price rises and decreases when it falls. [Sir Robert *Giffen* Scottish economist (1837–1910) noted this effect in regard to potatoes]

giff-gaff *gif'-gaf'*, (*Scot*) *n* give and take. [**give**[1]]

GIFT *abbrev*: gamete intra-Fallopian transfer, an infertility treatment involving direct transfer of eggs and sperm into the woman's Fallopian tubes, where conception may occur.

gift *gift*, *n* a thing given; a bribe (*obs*); a quality bestowed by nature, a talent; the act of giving; something easily obtained, understood, etc (*slang*). — *vt* to endow, *esp* with any power or faculty; to present, give as a gift (*esp Scot*). — *adj* **gift'ed** highly endowed by nature with talents, abilities, etc; (*esp*) of a child, exceptionally clever. — *adv* **gift'edly**. — *n* **gift'edness**. — **gift'-book** a book suitable or intended for presentation; **gift horse** a horse given as a present (see phrase below); **gift'shop** a shop selling articles suitable for presents; **gift token** or **voucher** a printed card that can be used in payment or exchange for buying certain products to the value of the amount shown. — *vt* **gift'-wrap** to wrap (a present) in coloured paper, with ribbons, etc. — **look a gift horse in the mouth** to criticize, delay or niggle over a gift or lucky opportunity, (*orig* to look at a gift horse's teeth to tell its age). [See **give**[1]]

gig[1] *gig*, *n* a whipping-top (*obs*); a flighty girl (*obs*); a light, two-wheeled carriage; a long, light boat; a machine for raising the nap on cloth (in full, **gig mill**); sport, fun (*dialect*). — *vt* and *vi* **gigg'it** (*archaic US*) to convey or move rapidly. — **gig'-lamps** the lamps fixed on either side of a gig (carriage); spectacles (*old slang*); **gig'man** a man who drives or keeps a gig; a narrow middle-class philistine (*Carlyle*). — *n* **gigman'ity**. [ME *gigge* a whirling thing (cf **whirligig**); origin obscure]

gig[2] *gig*, *n* a pronged spear for fishing, a fishgig. [**fizgig**]

gig[3] *gig*, (*slang*) *n* an engagement, *esp* of a band or pop group for one performance only. — *vt* to play a gig: — *pr p* **gigg'ing**; *pa t* and *pa p* **gigged**. [Ety unknown]

giga. See **gigue**.

giga- *gī'gə*, *gig'ə*, *jī'gə* or *jig'ə*, *pfx* meaning ten to the ninth power (10^9), a thousand million or in US a billion. — *n* **giga-elec'tron-volt** a unit equal to a thousand million electron-volts. — *n* **gi'gahertz**. — *n* **gi'gawatt**. [Gr *gigas* giant]

gigantic *jī-gan'tik*, *adj* of, like or characteristic of a giant; huge. — Also **gigantē'an**. — *adj* **gigantesque'** befitting or suggestive of a giant. — *adv* **gigan'tically**. — *n* **gigan'ticide** the act of killing a giant. — *n* **gigant'ism** (of a business concern, etc) hugeness; excessive overgrowth, usually owing to overactivity of the pituitary gland (*med*); abnormal increase in size, often associated with polyploidy (*bot*). — *n* **gigantol'ogy** giant-lore. — *n* **giganto'machy** (*-ki*) or **gigantomachia** (*-tō-māk'i-ə*) a war of giants, *esp* against the gods (Gr *machē* fight). [L *gigās*, *gigantis*, Gr *gigās*, *-antos* a giant]

giggle *gig'l*, *vi* to laugh with short catches of the breath, or in a silly manner. — *n* a laugh of this kind; an amusing person or thing, a laugh (*colloq*). — *n* **gigg'ler**. — *n* **gigg'ling**. — *adj* **gigg'lesome** or **gigg'ly** inclined to giggle. [Echoic]

giglet or **giglot** *gig'lit* or *-lət*, (*obs*) *n* a giddy girl; a wanton person. — *adj* (*Shakesp*) inconstant. [Perh connected with **gig**[1]; later associated with **giggle**]

GIGO *gig'ō*, *gī'gō* or *gē'gō*, (*comput*, etc) *abbrev*: garbage in, garbage out, ie incorrect input results in incorrect output.

gigolo *jig'ō-lō*, *n* a professional male dancing partner or escort; a young man living at the expense of an older woman, *esp* one to whom he gives sexual favours in return: — *pl* **gig'olos**. [Fr]

gigot *jig'ət*, *n* a leg of mutton, etc; a leg-of-mutton sleeve. [Fr]

gigue *zhēg* or (Ital) **giga** *jē'ga*, (*music*) *n* a lively dance form *usu* in 6/8 or 12/8 time, often used to complete 18c dance suites. [Fr; cf **jig**]

gila *hhē'lə*, (in full **gila monster**) *n* either of the two *Heloderma* species, the only venomous lizards known. [*Gila* River, Arizona]

gilbert *gil'bərt*, *n* the CGS unit of magnetomotive force. [From the English physician and physicist William *Gilbert* (1540–1603)]

Gilbertian *gil'bûrt'i-ən*, *adj* whimsically or paradoxically humorous. [Sir W S *Gilbert* (1836–1911), librettist, playwright, poet, etc]

Gilbertine *gil'bûrt-īn* or *-in*, (*hist*) *n* a member of the order of canons and nuns founded (c. 1148) by St *Gilbert* of Sempringham. — Also *adj*.

gilcup. See **giltcup** under **gilt**[1].

gild[1] *gild*, *vt* to cover or overlay with gold or with any goldlike substance; to gloss over, give a specious appearance to; to adorn with lustre; to smear with blood (*obs*); to flush, redden, suffuse with colour (*obs*); to supply with gold or money (*obs*): — *pr p* **gild'ing**; *pa t* and *pa p* **gild'ed or gilt**. — *n* **gild'er** a person who coats articles with gold. — *n* **gild'ing** the task or trade of a gilder; gold or imitation gold laid on a surface. — **Gilded Chamber** the House of Lords; **gilded spurs** an emblem of knighthood; **gilded youth** rich young people of fashion. — **gild the lily** to embellish, decorate, etc unnecessarily; **gild the pill** to make a disagreeable thing seem less so. [OE *gyldan*, from *gold*; see **gold**[1]]

gild[2]. See **guild**.

gilder[1]. See **guilder**.

gilder[2]. See **gild**[1].

gilden or **gylden** *gil'dən*, (*obs*) *orig adj* golden, adopted later (as *Spenser*) as a *pa p* of **gild**[1]. [OE *gylden*]

gilet *zhē-lā*, *n* a waistcoat; in a woman's dress, a front part shaped like a waistcoat; in ballet dress, a bodice shaped like a waistcoat. [Fr]

gilgai or **ghilgai** *gil'gī*, (*Austr*) *n* a saucer-shaped depression forming a natural reservoir. [Aboriginal]

gilgie or **jilgie** *jil'gi*, (*Austr*) *n* a yabby, a small freshwater crayfish. [Aboriginal]

gill[1] *gil*, *n* a membranous organ for breathing in water, *usu* in the form of a thin platelike or branched filamentous structure (*zool*); the wattle below the bill of a fowl; one of the radiating plates on the underside of the cap of a mushroom or toadstool; a projecting rib of a heating surface; the flesh round a person's jaw, as in *green* or *white round the gills* (ie sickly-looking). — *vt* to gut (fish); to catch (fish) by the gills in a net. — **gill arch** (in fish) the incomplete jointed skeletal ring supporting a single pair of gill slits; **gill cover** a fold of skin, *usu* with bony plates, protecting the gills; **gill net** a type of fishing-net in which fish are caught by their gills; **gill pouch** one of a pair of outgrowths on the wall of the pharynx, found in cyclostomes and present at the embryonic stage in all vertebrates, developing, in fish, into openings (**gill slits**) containing the gills. [Cf Dan *gælle*; Swed *gäl*]

gill[2] *jil*, *n* a small measure, having various values; in recent times = $\frac{1}{4}$ pint. — **gill'-house** (*obs*) a dram-shop. [OFr *gelle*]

gill[3] *jil*, *n* a girl (also **jill** *obs*); a female ferret (*colloq* or *dialect*; also **jill**); a policewoman (*slang*); ground ivy (*dialect*); beer with an infusion of ground ivy (also **gill ale**, **gill beer** *obs*). — *n* **gill'et** or **jill'et** (*Scot*) a skittish, flighty, or loose young woman. — **gill'flirt** or **jill'flirt** (*archaic*) a wanton girl. [*Gillian* or *Juliana* (from *Julius*), a woman's name]

gill[4] or **ghyll** *gil*, *n* a small ravine, a wooded glen; a brook. [ON *gil*]

gill[5] *jil*, (*dialect*) *n* a two- or four-wheeled cart for carrying timber. — Also **jill**. [Origin uncertain]

gillaroo *gil-ə-ro͞o'*, *n* an Irish trout with a thickened muscular stomach. [Ir *giolla ruadh* red lad]

Gilles de la Tourette's syndrome *zhēl də la to͞or-et' sin'drōm*, *n* Tourette's syndrome (qv).

gillet. See **gill**[3].

gillie, **ghillie** or **gilly** *gil'i*, *n* a Highland chief's attendant (*hist*); an attendant on or guide of hunting and fishing sportsmen. — *vi* to act as gillie. — **gillie-wet'foot** (*obs*) or **-white'-foot** (*obs*) a barefoot Highland lad, *esp* a messenger or chief's attendant. [Gaelic *gille* a lad, Ir *giolla*]

gillion *jil'yən*, or *gil'*, *n* (in Britain) a thousand millions, 10^9, equivalent of a US billion. [**giga-** and **million**]

gillravage, **gillravitch**. See **gilravage**.

gilly. See **gillie**.

gillyflower *jil'i-flowr* (*Shakesp* **gill'yvor** *-vər*), *n* a flower that smells like cloves, *esp* **clove'-gillyflower** and **stock'-gillyflower** (see **clove**[4] and **stock**[1]). [OFr *girofle*, from Gr *karyophyllon* the clove-tree, from *karyon* a nut, and *phyllon* a leaf]

gilpy or **gilpey** *gil'pi*, (*Scot*) *n* a boisterous girl or (*formerly*) boy.

gilravage, **gillravage**, **galravage**, or **gilravitch**, **gillravitch**, **galravitch** *gəl-rav'ij*, or *rāv'*, (*Scot*) *n* a noisy frolic; riotous merrymaking. — *vi* to behave riotously. — *n* **gilrav'ager**.

gilsonite. See **uintaite**.

gilt[1] *gilt*, *pa t* and *pa p* of **gild**[1]. — *adj* gilded; gold-coloured. — *n* gilding; money (*old slang*); a gilt-edged security; glitter, glamour, superficial attractiveness. — **gilt'cup** or **gil'cup** (*dialect*) a buttercup. — *adj* **gilt'-edged** having the edges gilt; of the highest quality (**gilt-edged securities**, also called **gilts**, those stocks (such as government stocks) regarded as very safe investments, having a comparatively low fixed rate of interest but guaranteed repayment). — *n* **gilt'-edged** or (in *pl*) **gilts**. — **gilt'-head** a name for several fishes, *esp* a sparoid fish with a half-moon-shaped gold spot between the eyes; **gilt'-tail** a yellow-tipped worm (*Dendrobaena subrubicunda*) found in old dung-hills. — *adj* **gilt'wood** made of wood and covered with gilt.

gilt[2] *gilt*, (*dialect*) *n* a young sow (in various conditions locally). [ON *gyltr*; cf OE *gilte*]

gimbal *jim'bl*, *n* a gimmal (*obs*); (in *pl*) a contrivance with self-aligning bearings for keeping eg hanging objects, nautical instruments, etc horizontal (*sing* in combination, eg **gimbal ring**). [See **gemel**]

gimcrack or **jimcrack** *jim'krak*, *n* a dodge, trick; a trivial mechanism; a worthless knick-knack; a paltry, poorly made, flimsy article. — *adj* worthless, shoddy. — *n* **gimcrack'ery**. [ME *gibecrake* possibly inlay]

gimlet *gim'lit*, *n* a small hand tool with a pointed screw-tip for boring holes in wood; a cocktail made of gin or vodka, with lime-juice. — *vt* to pierce as with a gimlet; to turn like a gimlet. — *adj* **gim'let-eyed** very sharp-sighted. [OFr *guimbelet*, from Gmc; cf **wimble**[1]]

gimmal *jim'l*, *n* a ring (also **gimmal ring**) that can be divided into two (or three) rings; a joint or part in any mechanism (also *obs* or *dialect* **gimm'er**; *Shakesp* **gimm'or**). — *adj* **gimm'alled** (*Shakesp* **jymold**) jointed, hinged. [See **gemel**]

gimme *gi'mi*, (*slang*) contracted form of **give me**. — *n* (*colloq*) in golf, a short putt that one's opponent is sportingly excused from playing, there being little likelihood of missing it; (*usu* in *pl*, as **the gimmes**) avarice (*US slang*). — **gimme cap** or **hat** (*US slang*) a peaked cap printed with a company logo or a trademark, distributed among the public as advertising.

gimmer[1] *gim'ər*, (*Scot*) *n* a young ewe; (*contemptuously*) a woman. [ON *gymbr*; cf Swed *gimmer*, Dan *gimmer*]

gimmer[2]. See **gimmal**.

gimmick *gim'ik*, *n* a secret device for performing a trick; a device (often peculiar to the person adopting it) to catch attention or publicity; an ingenious mechanical device. — *vt* to provide, use or devise gimmick(s) for or in, to accomplish by means of gimmick(s). — *n* **gimm'ickry** gimmicks in quantity; use of gimmick(s). — *adj* **gimm'icky** pertaining to a gimmick; designed to catch attention or publicity; (loosely) of little worth or importance. [Orig US slang; origin unknown]

gimmor (*Shakesp*). See **gimmal**.

gimp[1] *gimp*, *n* a yarn with a hard core; a trimming made of this; a fishing-line bound with wire; a coarse thread in lace-making. — *vt* to make or furnish with gimp. — Also **guimp** or **gymp**. [Fr *guimpe*, appar from OHGer *wimpal*; cf **wimple**; perhaps confused with Fr *guipure*; see **guipure**]

gimp[2] *jimp*, (*rare* or *dialect*) *vt* to scallop, notch; to corrugate.

gimp[3] (*slang*, chiefly *US*) *n* a lame person; a limp. — *vi* to limp. — *adj* **gimp'y**. [Ety uncertain; Norw dialect *gimpa* to tip over, has been suggested, or perh a corruption of **gammy**]

gin[1] *jin*, *n* geneva; a spirit distilled from grain or malt and flavoured with juniper berries or other aromatic substances, made chiefly in Britain and the US. — *adj* **ginn'y** flavoured with, under the influence of, containing or pertaining to gin. — **gin fizz** a drink of gin, lemon juice, carbonated water, etc; **gin palace** (*derog*) a showily pretentious public house; **gin'shop** (*archaic*) a bar or shop selling mostly gin; **gin sling** an iced gin and water, sweetened and flavoured, with *usu* lemon or lime. — **gin and it** gin and *It*alian vermouth. [Contracted from **geneva**]

gin[2] *jin*, *n* a scheme, artifice, contrivance (*Spenser*); a snare or trap; a machine, *esp* one for hoisting (*eng*, *mining*, etc); a cotton-gin; an instrument of torture (*Spenser*). — *vt* to trap or snare; to clear of seeds by a cotton-gin: — *pr p* **ginn'ing**; *pa t* and *pa p* **ginned**. — *n* **ginn'er** a person who gins cotton. — *n* **ginn'ery** or **gin'house** a place where cotton is ginned. — **gin trap** a powerful spring trap fitted with teeth. [**engine**]

gin[3] *jin*, (*Austr*) *n* an Australian Aboriginal woman. [Aboriginal]

gin[4] *jin*, or **gin rummy** *rum'i*, *n* a type of rummy in which a player whose unmatched cards count ten or less may stop the game. [Origin uncertain]

gin[5] *gin*, (*archaic*) *vt* and *vi* to begin: — *pa t* **gan**, used poetically in the sense of *did*. [Aphetic from OE *beginnan* or *onginnan* to begin]

gin[6] *gin*, (*Scot*) *prep* by (the time of). [ME *gain*, appar from ON *gegn* against]

gin[7] *gin*, (*Scot*) *conj* if. [Perh pa p of **give** as a substitute for **gif**; perh from **gin**[6]]

ging *ging*, (*obs*) *n* a gang or company. See **gang**[1].

gingal, **gingall**. See **jingal**.

gingelly. See **gingili**.

ginger *jin'jər*, *n* the rootstock of *Zingiber officinale*, or another species of the genus (family Zingiberaceae) with a hot taste, used as a condiment, etc, *esp* dried and ground, or preserved eg in syrup as a sweet; ginger beer; stimulation (*slang*); mettle (*slang*). — *adj* (*esp* of hair) sandy, reddish. — *vt* to put ginger into; to make spirited, to enliven (often with *up*). — *adj* **gin'gerous** (*Dickens*) sandy, reddish. — *adj* **gin'gery** of or like ginger; sandy in colour. — **gingerade'** or **ginger ale** a carbonated soft drink flavoured with ginger; **ginger beer** a mildly alcoholic sparkling drink made with fermenting ginger; **ginger beer plant** a symbiotic association of a yeast and a bacterium, by which ginger beer can be prepared, also called *Californian bees*; **ginger cordial** a cordial made of ginger, lemon peel, raisins, water, and sometimes spirits; **ginger group** a group within eg a political party seeking to inspire the rest with its own enthusiasm and activity; **ginger nut** a small thick gingersnap; **ginger pop** weak ginger beer (*colloq*); **gin'gersnap** a gingerbread biscuit; **ginger wine** an alcoholic drink made by fermenting sugar and water, and flavoured with various spices, chiefly ginger. [ME *gingivere*, from OFr *gengibre*, from LL *gingiber*, from L *zingiber*, from Gr *zingiberis*, from Prakrit, from Sans *śrnga* horn, and *vera* body; Malayalam *inchiver*]

gingerbread *jin'jər-bred*, *n* a cake flavoured with treacle and *usu* ginger; (with *cap*) a self-help support group for one-parent families. — *adj* (of ornamental work) cheap and tawdry, over-elaborate. — **take the gilt off the gingerbread** to destroy the glamour. [OFr *gingimbrat*, from LL *gingiber*; see ety for **ginger**; confused with **bread**]

gingerly *jin'jər-li*, *adv* with soft steps; with extreme wariness and delicate gentleness. — Also *adj*. [Possibly OFr *gensor*, compar of **gent**; see **gent**[1]]

gingham *ging'əm*, *n* a kind of cotton cloth, woven from coloured yarns into stripes or checks; an umbrella (*obs colloq*). [Fr *guingan*, orig from Malay *ginggang* striped]

gingili, **gingelly** or **jinjili** *jin'ji-li*, *n* a species of sesame; an oil obtained from its seeds. [Hindi *jinjalī*, prob from Ar *juljulān*]

gingival *jin-jī'vl*, *adj* pertaining to the gums. — *n* **gingivec'tomy** the cutting back of inflamed or excess gum. — *n* **gingivī'tis** inflammation of the gums. [L *gingīva* gum]

gingko. See **ginkgo**.

gingle. *Obs* variant of **jingle**.

ginglymus *jing'gli-məs* (or *ging'-*), *n* a joint that permits movement in one plane only, a hinge joint: — *pl* **ging'lymī**. — *adj* **ging'limoid**. [Latinized from Gr *ginglymos*]

gink *gingk*, (*slang*) *n* a fellow. [Origin unknown]

ginkgo *gingk'gō*, *n* the maidenhair tree, an ornamental Chinese fan-leaved tree, holy in Japan, the only species in the **Ginkgoā'les** of Gymnosperms. — Also **ging'ko**: — *pl* **gink'goes** or **ging'koes**. [Jap *ginkyo*, from Chin *yin* silver, and *hing* apricot]

ginn. See **jinn**.

ginnel *gin'əl*, (*Northern dialect*) *n* a narrow alley or path between high walls or buildings. — Also **genn'el**. [A voiced form of **kennel**[2]]

ginny. See **gin**[1].

ginormous *jī-nör'məs*, (*colloq*) *adj* huge, altogether enormous. [*gi*gantic and e*normous*]

ginseng *jin'seng*, *n* a plant of the araliaceous genus Panax, cultivated *esp* in the Far East; its root, believed to have important restorative and curative properties. [Chin *jên-shên* perh image of man, from the shape of the root]

gio. See **geo**.

giocoso *jok-ō'sō*, (*music*) *adj* played in a lively or humorous manner. [Ital]

Giorgi system *jör'jē sis'tim*, *n* see **metre-kilogram-second system**. [After Giovanni *Giorgi*, Italian physicist (died 1950)]

gip *jip*, *n*. Same as **gyp**[1,3].

gippo or **gyppo** *jip'ō*, (*offensive slang*) *n* an Egyptian, *esp* a native Egyptian soldier; a gypsy: — *pl* **gipp'os** or **gypp'os**. — Also **gipp'y**, **gypp'ie** or **gypp'y**. — **gippy** (or **gyppy**) **tummy** (*colloq*) diarrhoea, severe upset stomach, thought of as a hazard of holidaying in hot countries. [*Egyp*; see also ety for **gypsy**]

gippy. See **gippo**.

gipsen *jip'sən*, (*Spenser*) *n* an *obs* form of **gypsy**.

gipsy. See **gypsy**.

giraffe *ji-räf'*, *n* an African ruminant mammal with a remarkably long neck and forelegs and a brown-patched gingery coat, the camelopard. — *adj* **giraff'id**, **giraff'īne** or **giraffoid**. [Ar *zarāfah*]

girandole *jir'ən-dōl* or **girandola** *-and'ə-lə*, *n* a branched chandelier or similar structure; a pendant, etc with small jewels attached around it; a rotating firework; a number of linked mines (*military*). [Fr, from Ital *girandola*, from *girare*, from L *gȳrāre* to turn round, from *gȳrus*, from Gr *gȳros* a circle]

girasol *jir'ə-sol*, or **girasole** *-sōl*, *n* a fire-opal or other stone that seems to send a firelike glow from within in certain lights; the plant heliotrope (*obs*); the sunflower (*obs*). [Ital, from *girare* (see ety for **girandole**) and *sole*, from L *sōl* the sun]

gird[1] *gûrd*, (*Northern dialect*) *vi* to gibe, jeer (with *at*). — *vt* (*obs*) to taunt. — *n* a blow, stroke (*obs*); a taunt, dig or gibe (*archaic*). [Origin obscure; not from OE *gyrd*, *gierd* rod]

gird[2] *gird*, (*Scot*) *n* a hoop. — Also **girr** (*gir*). [A form of **girth**[1]]

gird[3] *gûrd*, *vt* to bind round; to secure by a belt or girdle; to encompass; to surround; to clothe, furnish: — *pa t* and *pa p* **gird'ed** and **girt**. — *n* **gird'er** a large beam, simple or built up, of wood, iron or steel, to take a lateral stress, eg to support a floor, wall, or the roadway of a bridge; a strip of strengthening tissue (*bot*). — *n* **gird'ing** that which girds. — **girder bridge** a bridge whose load is sustained by girders resting on supports. — **gird oneself** to tuck up loose garments under the girdle (so as to be better able to run or act quickly); to brace the mind for any trial or effort; see also **loin**. [OE *gyrdan*; cf Ger *gürten*]

girdle[1] *gûrd'l*, *n* a waistbelt; a cord worn around the waist by a monk, etc; anything that encloses like a belt; a woman's lightweight, close-fitting undergarment, a form of corset, reaching from waist to thigh; a bony arch to which a limb is attached (*anatom*); a worm's clitellum; a ring-shaped cut around a tree; the rim of a brilliant-cut gem. — *vt* to bind or enclose with a girdle, or as if with a girdle; to cut a ring round (a tree, etc); to cut a circular outline around (a gemstone). — *adj* **gird'led**. — *n* **gird'ler** a person who or thing which girdles; a maker of girdles. — **girdle'stead** (*obs*) the waist. [OE *gyrdel*, from *gyrdan* to gird]

girdle[2]. See **griddle**.

girkin *gûr'kin*, (*obs*) *n*. Same as **gherkin**.

girl *gûrl*, *n* a female child; a daughter; a young unmarried woman; a woman irrespective of age (*colloq*); a girlfriend, sweetheart (*colloq*); a maidservant. — *n* **girl'hood** the state or time of being a girl. — *adj* **girl'ie** or **girl'y** (of magazines, photographs etc) showing nude or scantily clad young women. — Also *n*. — *adj* **girl'ish** of or like a girl. — *adv* **girl'ishly**. — *n* **girl'ishness**. — **Girl Friday** a young female general office worker; **girl'friend** a sweetheart, or a girl who is one's regular companion; (**girl friend**) a girl's or woman's female friend; **Girl Guide** formerly the name for a Guide (see **guide**); **Girl Scout** a member of a similar American organization. — **old girl** a female former pupil; an amicably disrespectful mode of address or reference to a female of any age or species. [ME *gerle*, *girle*, *gurle* boy or girl, perhaps related to LGer *gör*, *göre* child]

girlond. Obsolete form of **garland**.

girn *girn*, (*dialect*) *vi* to grin, snarl; to grimace, make a grotesque face; to complain peevishly. — *n* an act or manner of girning. — *n* **girn'er**. — *adj* **girn'ie** ill-tempered, peevish. [**grin**]

girnel *gir'nl*, (*Scot*) *n* a granary (*obs*); a large chest or vat for storing grain. [Variant of **garner**]

giro *jī'rō*, *n* (also with *cap*) a banking system, organized by the National Girobank, by which money can be transferred direct from the account of one holder to that of another person (or to those of others); a social security payment by giro cheque (*colloq*); — *pl* **gī'ros**. — **giro cheque**, **order**, etc one issued through the giro system. [Ger, transfer, from Gr *gyros* ring]

giron, **gironic**. See **gyron**.

Girondist *ji-rond'ist*, (*hist*) *n* a member of the moderate republican party during the French Revolution, so called because its earliest leaders were deputies for the *Gironde* department. — Also **Giron'din**. — *n* **Giron'dism**.

girosol. Same as **girasol**.

girr. See **gird**[2].

girt *gûrt*, *pa p* of **gird**[3] in all senses; (of a ship) moored so taut by her cables to two oppositely placed anchors as to be prevented from swinging to the wind or tide. — *vt* to gird; to girth. — *vi* to girth.

girth[1]. See **grith**.

girth[2] *gûrth*, *n* the belly-band of a saddle; a circumferential measure of thickness. — *vt* to put a girth on; to measure the girth of. — *vi* to measure in girth. — Also (now *obs* or *dialect* as *n*, *rare* as *v*) **girt**. — **girth'line** or **girt'line** (*naut*) a gantline. [ON *gjörth*]

gisarme *jē-zärm'*, also *zhē-* or *gē-*, (*hist*) *n* a type of long-staffed battle-axe carried by foot-soldiers. [OFr *guisarme*, prob OHGer *getan* to weed, and *īsarn* iron]

gism. See **jism**.

gismo or **gizmo** *giz'mō*, (*colloq*) *n* a gadget, thingumajig: — *pl* **gis'mos** or **giz'mos**. — *n* **gismol'ogy** or **gizmol'ogy** gadgetry, technology involving (strange, baffling or daunting) devices generally. [Origin unknown]

gist *jist*, *n* the main point or pith of a matter. [OFr *gist* (Fr *gît*), from OFr *gesir* (Fr *gésir*) to lie, from L *jacēre*]

git *git*, (*slang*) *n* a person (used *contemptuously*); a fool; a bastard. — See also under **get** (noun). [**get** offspring, brat]

gitano *jē-tän'ō*, or *hhē-*, (Sp) *n* a male gypsy: — *pl* **gitan'os**: — *fem* **gitan'a**.

gite or **gîte** *zhēt*, *n* a resting-place (*archaic*); in France, a farmhouse, cottage, etc; simple holiday accommodation in such a farmhouse, etc. [Fr *gîte*, from OFr *giste*; see **gest**[1]]

gittern *git'ərn*, *n* a kind of guitar, a cithern. — *vi* (*obs*) to play on the gittern. [OFr *guiterne*, connected with Gr *kitharā*; see **cithern**, **guitar**, **zither**]

giust *just*, (*Spenser*, *Scott*) *n* and *vi*. Same as **joust**.

giusto *jōōs'tō*, (*music*) *adj* suitable; regular; strict. — *adv* in strict time; at a reasonable speed. [Ital, from L *jūstus* just]

give[1] *giv*, *vt* to bestow; to impart; to yield; to grant; to donate; to permit; to afford, provide; to pay or render (thanks, etc); to pronounce (a judgement or decision); to show (a result); to apply (oneself); to allow or admit. — *vi* to yield to pressure; to begin to melt or soften; to grow soft; to open, or give an opening or view, to lead (with *upon*, *on* or *into*, a gallicism): — *pr p* **giv'ing**; *pa t* **gāve**; *pa p* **given** (*giv'n*). — *n* yielding; elasticity. — *adj* **giv'en** bestowed; specified; addicted, disposed; granted; admitted. — *n* **giv'enness**. — *n* **giv'er** a person who or thing which gives or bestows. — *n* **giv'ing** the act of bestowing; the thing given. — *adj* that gives; generous, liberal. — **give'away** a betrayal, revelation, *esp* if unintentional; something given free or at a greatly reduced price, *esp* something offered with a product or service with the aim of increasing sales; **give-away programme** a TV, radio or theatrical programme in which members of the audience seek to gain prizes; **given name** the name given to the individual, not that of the family, ie the first or Christian name, distinguished from the *surname*. — **give and take** reciprocity in concession; mutually compensatory variations; fair exchange of repartee; **give away** to give for nothing; to betray; to bestow ceremonially (eg a bride); **give birth to** to bring forth, produce; to originate, begin, generate; **give chase** to pursue; **give ear** (*archaic*) to listen (to); **give forth** to emit; to publish; to expatiate, talk at length (*colloq*); **give ground** or **place** to give way, yield; **give head** see under **head**; **give in to** (*obs* **give into**) to yield to; **give it to (someone)** (*colloq*) to scold or beat (someone) severely; **give line**, **head**, **rein** etc, to give more liberty or scope (the metaphors from angling and horse-riding); **give me** (*colloq*) I would choose if I had the choice; **give off** to emit (eg a smell); **give oneself away** to betray one's secret unawares; **give out** to report, announce; to emit; to distribute to individuals; to run short; to relinquish (*Shakesp*); **give over** to transfer; to desist from, to cease (*Northern dialect*); **give the lie to** to accuse openly of falsehood; to prove wrong; **give tongue** (*archaic*) to bark; to utter, expound (with *to*); **give up** to abandon; to surrender; to desist from; **give way** to fall back, to yield, to withdraw; to break, snap or collapse, under strain; to begin rowing (usually as a command to a crew); to allow traffic in a direction crossing one's path to proceed first; **give way to** to yield to, submit to; to allow to take precedence, give priority to; to succumb to (eg grief). [OE *gefan* (WSax *giefan*), the back *g* prob owing to Scand influence; ON *gefa*, Swed *gifva*, Dan *give*, Gothic *giban*, Ger *geben*]

give[2]. Same as **gyve**.

Giz. Same as **Geëz**.

gizmo, **gizmology**. See **gismo**.

gizz or **jiz** *jiz*, (*Scot*) *n* a wig. [Origin unknown]

gizzard *giz'ərd*, *n* a muscular stomach, *esp* the second stomach of a bird. — **stick in someone's gizzard** to be more than someone can accept or tolerate. [ME *giser*, from OFr *guiser*, supposed to be from L *gigeria* (pl), cooked entrails of poultry]

gizzen *giz'n*, (*Scot*) *vi* to shrink from dryness so as to leak; to wither. — *adj* leaky; shrivelled. [ON *gisna*]

gju. See **gue**.

Gk *abbrev*: Greek.

glabella *glə-bel'ə*, (*anatom*) *n* the part of the forehead between the eyebrows and just above their level: — *pl* **glabell'ae** (*-bel'ē*). — *adj* **glabell'ar**. [L *glaber* bald, smooth]

glabrous *glā'brəs* or **glabrate** *glā'brāt* or *-brət*, (*med*, *zool*, *bot*) *adj* hairless, smooth. [L *glaber*]

glacé *gla'sā*, *adj* frozen, or with ice; iced with sugar; candied; glossy, lustrous, *esp* of a thin silk material or kid leather. — *vt* to ice with sugar; to candy: — *pr p* **glac'éing**; *pa t* and *pa p* **glac'éed**. [Fr]

glacial *glās'yəl, glā'si-əl* or *-shəl, adj* icy; frozen; readily or ordinarily solidified (as **glacial acetic acid** practically pure acetic acid; *chem*); pertaining to ice or its action; (of progress) ponderously slow, like that of a glacier; (of manner, etc) distant, hostile. — *n* a glacial period, an ice age. — *n* **glā'cialist** or **glaciol'ogist** a person who studies the geological action of ice. — *vt* **glaciate** (*glās'* or *glāsh'*) to polish by ice action; to subject to the action of land ice; to freeze. — *n* **glaciā'tion**. — *adj* **glaciolog'ical**. — *n* **glaciol'ogy** the study of the geological nature, distribution and action of ice. — **Glacial Period** the Ice Age, or any ice age; **glacial deposits** rock material deposited by glaciers or glacier-associated streams and lakes. [L *glaciālis* icy, *glaciāre*, *-ātum* to freeze, from *glaciēs* ice]

glacier *glas'yər* or *-i-ər, glās'yər* or *glā'shər, n* a mass of ice, fed by snow on a mountain, slowly creeping downhill to where it melts or breaks up into icebergs. [Fr, from *glace* ice, from L *glaciēs* ice]

glaciology. See under **glacial**.

glacis *glās-ē, glas'is* or *glās'is, n* a gentle slope, *esp* in fortification: — *pl* **glacis** (*glās-ē, glas'iz* or *glās'iz*) or **glac'ises**. [Fr, orig a slippery place, from L *glaciēs* ice]

glad[1] *glad, adj* pleased, happy; cheerful; giving pleasure; bright (*obs*). — *vt* (*archaic*) to make glad, gladden: — *pr p* **gladd'ing**; *pa t* and *pa p* **gladd'ed**. — *vt* **gladd'en** to make glad; to cheer. — *adj* **glad'ful** (*archaic*; *Spenser*). — *n* (*archaic*) **glad'fulness**. — *adv* **glad'ly**. — *n* **glad'ness**. — *adj* **glad'some** (*archaic*) glad; joyous. — *adv* (*archaic*) **glad'somely**. — *n* (*archaic*) **glad'someness**. — **glad eye** (*slang*) an ogle (*esp* in the phrase *to give someone the glad eye*, to ogle someone); **glad hand** (*US*) the hand of welcome or of effusive or excessive greeting. — *vi* and *vt* (**glad'-hand**) to extend the glad hand to; to behave in this manner. — **glad'-hander** (*US*) a person who is out to make up to all and sundry (*esp* of a vote-seeking politician); **glad rags** (*colloq*) best clothes, dress clothes. — **glad of** glad to have; glad because of. [OE *glæd*; Ger *glatt* smooth, ON *glathr* bright, Dan *glad*]

glad[2] *glad* or **gladdie** *glad'i*, (*colloq*) *n* short for **gladiolus**.

gladdon *glad'ən*, (*dialect*) *n* an iris. [Origin obscure]

glade *glād, n* an open space in a wood. — *adj* **glā'dy** having glades. [Ety obscure; poss connected with **glad**]

gladiate *glad'i-ət* or *-āt*, also *glād'*, (*bot*) *adj* sword-shaped. [New L *gladiatus*, from L *gladius* sword]

gladiator *glad'i-āt-ər, n* in ancient Rome, a professional combatant with men or wild animals in the arena; a fierce or contentious fighter or debater (*fig*). — *adj* **gladiator'ial**, (*obs*) **gladiator'ian** or **glad'iatory**. — *n* **glad'iātorship**. [L, from *gladius* sword]

gladiolus *glad-i-ō'ləs*, rarely *glə-dī'o-ləs, n* any plant of a genus (*Gladiolus*) of the iris family, with sword-shaped leaves and long spikes of brightly-coloured flowers; the middle part of the sternum (*anatom*): — *pl* **gladiō'lī** or **gladiō'luses**. — Also **glad'iole**: — *pl* **glad'ioles**. [L, dimin of *gladius* sword]

gladius *glad'i-əs* or *glād'i-əs, n* a cuttlefish pen; a sword (*rare*). [L, sword]

Gladstonian *glad-stō'ni-ən, adj* pertaining to W E *Gladstone* (1809–98), four times prime minister. — *n* a follower of Gladstone. — **Gladstone bag** a travelling bag or small portmanteau, opening out flat, named in his honour; **Gladstone sherry** (*hist*) cheap sherry (referring to reduction in duty, 1860).

glady. See **glade**.

Glagolitic *glag-ō-lit'ik, adj* of or pertaining to *Glagol*, an ancient Slavonic alphabet, apparently derived from the cursive Greek of the 9c. [Old Slav *glagolu* a word]

glaik *glāk, n* (*obs Scot*; *usu* in *pl*) a flash; dazzling; mocking deception; a trick; a puzzle-game. — *adj* (*Scot*) **glaik'it** or sometimes **glaik'et** giddy; foolish; stupid, daft. — *n* (*Scot*) **glaik'itness** levity, giddiness; stupidity, ineptitude. — **fling the glaiks in folk's een** (*obs Scot*) to throw dust in people's eyes, dazzle or deceive. [Origin obscure]

glair *glār, n* the clear part of an egg used as a varnish or adhesive; any viscous, transparent substance. — *vt* to varnish with white of egg. — *adj* **glair'y** (*med, pathol*, etc), **glair'eous** (*archaic*) or **glār'eous** (*archaic*) of or like glair; slimy, viscous. — *n* **glair'in** organic matter in mineral waters. [Fr *glaire*, perh from LL *clāra* (*ōvī*) white (of egg), from L *clārus* clear]

glaive *glāv*, (*obs*) *n* a sword; a spear; a long-shafted weapon like a halberd, its edge on the outer curve; a pronged fish-spear (*dialect*; also **gleave** *glēv*). — *adj* **glaived**. [OFr *glaive*]

glam[1]. See **glamour**.

glam[2] *glam*, (*colloq*) *n* a greying, *l*eisured, *a*ffluent *m*arried person, a class of woopie (qv).

glamour or *US* **glamor** *glam'ər, n* allure, magnetism; an excitingly or fascinatingly attractive quality; groomed beauty and studied charm; the supposed influence of a charm on the eyes, making them see things as fairer than they are (*archaic*); enchantment; witchery (*archaic*). — *vt* (*archaic*) to enchant, betwitch, cast a spell over; (with *up*) to glamorize. — *adj* **glam** (*slang*) glamorous. — *n* **glamorīzā'tion** or **-s-**. — *vt* **glamor'ize** or **-ise** to make glamorous; to romanticize. — *adj* **glam'orous** full of glamour; bewitching, alluring. — *adv* **glam'orously**. — **glamour boy** or **girl** (*colloq*) a man or woman considered to be very glamorous (often *derog*); **glam'ourpuss** (*colloq*) a glamorous person, *esp* female. — *adj* and *n* **glam'-rock** or **glam rock** (of or relating to) the glamorized side of the rock music scene or industry. **[gramary]**

glance[1] *glāns, vi* to fly (off) obliquely on striking; to make a passing allusion, *esp* unfavourable (with *at*); to snatch a momentary view (with *at*); to dart a reflected ray, to flash. — *vt* to catch a glimpse of; to cause (eg a ball or other object) to glance; to direct glancingly; to deflect; to glance at (*obs*). — *n* an oblique impact or movement; a sudden shoot of reflected light; a darting of the eye; a momentary look; a stroke by which the ball is allowed to glance off an upright bat to fine leg (*cricket*); a passing allusion, *esp* satirical (*obs*). — *n* and *adj* **glanc'ing**. — *adv* **glanc'ingly**. — **at a glance** immediately, at a first look. [ME *glenten*, poss nasalized form of *glace* to glance, from OFr *glacier* to slip, slide]

glance[2] *glāns, n* a black or grey mineral with metallic lustre, usually a sulphide, selenide or telluride, eg redruthite or **copp'er-glance**, galena or **lead'-glance**, argentite or **sil'ver-glance**. — **glance'-coal** anthracite. [Ger *Glanz* glance, lustre]

gland[1] *gland*, (*biol*) *n* a secreting structure in plants and animals. — *adj* **glandif'erous** bearing acorns or nuts. — *adj* **glan'diform** resembling a gland; acorn-shaped. — *adj* **gland'ūlar** or rarely **gland'ūlous** containing, consisting of, or pertaining to glands. — *adv* **gland'ūlarly** or **gland'ūlously**. — *n* **glan'dūle** a small gland. — *adj* **glandūlif'erous**. — **glandular fever** infectious mononucleosis, a disease characterized by slight fever, enlargement of glands, and increase in the white cells of the blood. [L *glans*, *glandis* an acorn]

gland[2] *gland*, (*eng*) *n* a device for preventing leakage at a point where a rotating or reciprocating shaft emerges from a vessel containing fluid under pressure; a sleeve or nut used to compress the packing in a stuffing-box (qv). [Origin unknown]

glanders *gland'ərz, n sing* a malignant, contagious and fatal disease of the horse and ass (also communicable to man), showing itself *esp* on the mucous membrane of the nose, on the lungs, and on the lymphatic system. — *adj* **gland'ered** or **gland'erous** affected with glanders. [OFr *glandre* a gland]

glandiferous, **glandular**, **glandule**, etc. See under **gland**[1].

glans *glanz, n* an acorn or similar fruit; a glandular structure of similar shape (*anatom*): — *pl* **glan'des** (*-dēz*). — **glans clitoris** and **glans penis** respectively the extremity of the clitoris and of the penis. [L, acorn]

glare *glār*, *n* an oppressive or unrelieved dazzling light (also *fig*); excessive luminance emitted from a VDU screen, or by light reflecting off a terminal (*comput*); overpowering lustre (*archaic*); cheap or showy brilliance; a fierce stare; a glassy or icy surface (*US*). — *adj* (*US*) glassy (of ice). — *vi* to emit a hard, fierce, dazzling light; to be obtrusively noticeable, intense or strong, eg to shine dazzlingly; to stare fiercely. — *vt* to send out or express with a glare. — *adj* **glar'ing** bright and dazzling; flagrant. — *adv* **glar'ingly**. — *n* **glar'ingness**. — *adj* **glar'y** glaring; shining harshly. [ME *glāren* to shine; cf **glass**, OE *glær* amber, LGer *glaren* to glow]

glareous *glā'ri-əs*, *adj* gravelly (*obs*); growing on gravel (*bot*). — *adj* **glā'real** (*bot*) growing on dry exposed ground. See also **glair**. [L *glārea* gravel]

glasnost *glas'* or *glaz'nost*, *n* the policy of openness and forthrightness followed by the former Soviet government under the premiership of Mikhail Gorbachev. — *adj* **glasnos'tian** or **glasnos'tic** of, relating to, or in the spirit of, glasnost. [Russ, speaking aloud]

glass *gläs*, *n* a hard, amorphous, brittle substance, a bad conductor of electricity, usually transparent, made by fusing together one or more of the oxides of silicon, boron or phosphorus with certain basic oxides (eg sodium, magnesium, calcium, potassium), and cooling the product rapidly to prevent crystallization; an article made of or with glass, *esp* a drinking-vessel, a mirror, a lens, the cover of a watch-face, a weather-glass, a telescope, etc; the quantity of liquid a glass holds; any fused substance like glass, with a vitreous fracture; a rock, or portion of rock, without crystalline structure; (in *pl*) spectacles. — *adj* made of glass. — *vt* to furnish or fit with glass; to reflect in glass; to put in, under, or behind glass (*rare*); to glaze, cover with a glassy surface (*obs*); to polish highly (*rare*). — *adj* **glass'en** (*archaic*) of or like glass. — *n* **glass'ful** as much as a glass will hold: — *pl* **glass'fuls**. — *vt* and *vi* **glass'ify** to become glass or like glass; to cause to become glass or like glass. — *adv* **glass'ily**. — *n* **glassine** (*-ēn'*) a transparent, glazed, greaseproof paper, used for book-covers. — *n* **glass'iness**. — *adj* **glass'y** like glass; (of eyes) expressionless. — **glass'-blower**; **glass'-blowing** the process of making glassware by inflating a viscid mass; **glass ceiling** an indistinct yet unmistakable barrier on the career ladder, through which certain categories of employees (*usu* women) find they can see but not progress; **glass chin** or **glass jaw** a chin or jaw exceptionally vulnerable to punches, used chiefly of boxers; **glass'-cloth** a cloth for drying glasses; a material woven from glass threads; a polishing cloth covered with powdered glass; **glass'-coach** (*obs*) a coach (*esp* one for hire) having glazed windows; **glass cockpit** an aircraft cockpit in which an array of glass-screened displays presents computer-generated information; **glass'-crab** the transparent larva of the spiny lobster; **glass'-cutter** a tool for cutting sheets of glass; a person who does cut-glass work; **glass'-cutting** the act or process of cutting, shaping and ornamenting the surface of glass; **glass eye** an artificial eye made of glass; (in *pl*) spectacles (*obs*); a form of blindness in horses. — *adj* **glass'-faced** (*Shakesp*) reflecting the sentiments of another, as in a mirror. — **glass fibre** glass melted and then drawn out into extremely fine fibres, which are later to be spun, woven, etc (also called **fibreglass**); **glass'-gall** a scum formed on fused glass. — *adj* **glass'-gazing** (*Shakesp*) addicted to looking in a mirror; **glass'-grinding** the ornamenting of glass by rubbing with sand, emery, etc; **glass harmonica** the musical glasses (see **harmonica**); **glass'house** a house made of glass or largely of glass, *esp* a greenhouse; military detention barracks (from one with a glass roof at Aldershot; *slang*); a glass factory. — *adj* **glass'like**. — **glass jaw** see **glass chin**; **glass'man** a maker or seller of glass; a beggar hawking glass as a pretext (*hist*); **glass'-painting** the art of producing pictures on glass by means of staining it chemically; **glass paper** paper coated with finely pounded glass, used like sandpaper; **glass'-rope** a silicious sponge (Hyalonema) with a long anchoring tuft; **glass snake** a legless lizard (*Ophisaurus*) with a brittle tail; **glass soap** manganese dioxide or other substance used by glass-makers to remove colouring from glass; **glass'ware** articles made of glass; **glass wool** glass spun into woolly fibres; **glass'work** furnishings or articles made of glass; (*usu* in *pl*) a glass factory; **glass'worker**; **glass'wort** a name for plants of the genera Salicornia and Salsola yielding soda, once used in making glass. — *adj* **glass'yheaded** (*Tennyson*) with a shiny pate. — **live in a glass house** to be open to attack or retort; **musical glasses** see **harmonica**; **water** or **soluble glass** sodium or potassium silicate. [OE *glæs*]

Glassite *gläs'īt*, *n* a Sandemanian, or follower of John *Glas* (1695–1773), who was deposed in 1730 from the ministry of the Church of Scotland for maintaining that a congregation with its eldership is, in its discipline, subject to no jurisdiction but that of Jesus Christ.

Glaswegian *glas-* or *gläs-wēj'(y)ən*, *n* a native or citizen of *Glasgow*. — Also *adj*. [Modelled on *Norwegian*]

glauberite *glö'bər-īt*, *n* a greyish-white mineral, sodium calcium sulphate, found chiefly in rock salt, named after the German chemist Johann Rudolf *Glauber* (1604–68). — **Glauber** (or **Glauber's**) **salt** (*glow'bər* or *glö'bər*) hydrated sodium sulphate, discovered by him.

glaucescence, etc. See **glaucous**.

glaucoma *glö-kō'mə*, *n* an insidious disease of the eye, marked by increased pressure within the eyeball and growing dimness of vision. — *adj* **glaucomatous** (*-kōm'ə-təs*, or *-kom'*). [Gr *glaukōma* cataract; see **glaucous**]

glauconite *glök'ə-nīt*, *n* a mineral now forming in the sea, a hydrated potassium iron and aluminium silicate, which gives a green colour to some of the beds of the Greensand. — *adj* **glauconitic** (*-nit'ik*). — *n* **glauconītīzā'tion** or **-s-** conversion into glauconite. [Gr *glaukos* bluish-green]

glaucous *glö'kəs*, *adj* sea-green; greyish-blue; covered with a powdery greenish or bluish bloom (*bot*). — *n* **glaucescence** (*-ses'əns*). — *adj* **glaucesc'ent** (*bot*) somewhat glaucous. [L *glaucus*, from Gr *glaukos* bluish-green or grey (*orig* gleaming)]

Glaucus *glö'kəs*, *n* a genus of translucent blue nudibranch gasteropods of warm seas. [Gr *glaukos* bluish-green]

glaum *glöm*, (*Scot*) *vi* to clutch or grab (with *at*).

glaur *glör*, (*Scot*) *n* mire. — *adj* **glaur'y**. [Origin unknown]

Glaux *glöks*, *n* the generic name of sea-milkwort or black saltwort, a fleshy seaside plant of the primrose family, with pink sepals and no petals, once used in soda-making. [Gr *glaux* wart-cress]

glaze *glāz*, *vt* to furnish or set with glass; to cover with a thin surface of glass or something glassy; to cover with a layer of thin semitransparent colour; to give a glassy surface to; to apply a thin wash containing eg milk, eggs, or sugar to (eg pastry), to give a shiny appearance. — *n* the glassy coating applied to pottery; a thin coat of semitransparent colour; any shining exterior; a thin wash of eggs, milk, sugar, etc for glazing food. — *vi* to become glassy. — *adj* **glazed**. — *adj* **glā'zen** (*obs*) glassy; glazed. — *n* **glā'zer** a workman who glazes pottery, paper, etc. — *n* **glā'zier** (*-zyər*) a person who sets glass in window-frames, etc. — *n* **glā'zing** the act or art of setting glass; the art of covering with a vitreous substance; semitransparent colours put thinly over others to modify the effect (*painting*). — *adj* **glā'zy**. [ME *glasen*, from *glas* glass; see **glass**]

GLC *abbrev*: Greater London Council (abolished in 1986, the residue of its responsibilities being wound up by the London Residuary Body).

Gld *abbrev*: guilder (the Dutch unit of currency).

gleam *glēm*, *vi* to glow or shine, *usu* not very brightly. — *vt* to flash. — *n* a faint or moderate glow; a small stream of light; a beam; brightness; often used figuratively, as in *a gleam of hope*, *a gleam of understanding*. — *n* and *adj* **gleam'ing**. — *adj* **gleam'y** casting gleams or rays of light; in or of gleams. [OE *glǣm* gleam, brightness; see **glimmer**[1]]

glean *glēn*, *vt* to follow the harvester(s) gathering any residue; to collect (what is thinly scattered, neglected or overlooked); to pick up (facts or information); to learn by laboriously scraping together pieces of information. — *vi* to gather the corn left by a reaper or anything that has been left by others; to gather facts bit by bit. — *n* (*obs* or *dialect*) that which is gleaned; the act of gleaning. — *n* **glean'er**. — n **glean'ing**. [OFr *glener* (Fr *glaner*), through LL *glenāre*; origin unknown]

gleave. See **glaive**.

glebe *glēb*, *n* the soil (*archaic* or *poetic*); a clod (*obs*); a field (*archaic* or *poetic*); (also **glebe land**) the land attached to a parish church. — *adj* **glē'bous** (*rare*) or **glē'by** (*archaic*) cloddy, turfy. — **glebe'-house** a manse. [L *glēba* a clod]

glede *glēd* or **gled** *gled*, (*Bible*; now *Scot* or *N Eng*) *n* the common kite. [OE *glida*, from *glīdan* to glide]

gledge *glej*, (*Scot*) *vi* to squint; to cast an eye around; to look cunningly. — *n* a knowing look; a side-glance; a glimpse. [Cf **gley**[1]]

glee[1] *glē*, *n* joy; mirth and gaiety; impish enjoyment; a form of short part-song, strictly one without an accompaniment, popular from the mid-17c to the 19c (*music*); apparently glitter (proverbially coupled with *gold*; *Spenser*). — *adj* **glee'ful** or (*archaic*) **glee'some** merry. — **glee club** (chiefly *NAm*) a club or choir for singing glees, part-songs, etc; **glee'maiden** (*obs*) a female minstrel; **glee'man** (*obs*) a minstrel. [OE *glēo*, *glīw* mirth; ON *glȳ*]

glee[2]. See **gley**[1].

gleed[1] *glēd*, (*archaic* or *dialect*) *n* a hot coal or burning ember. [OE *glēd*; cf Du *gloed*, Ger *Glut*, Swed *glöd*]

gleed[2]. See **gley**[1].

gleek[1] *glēk*, (*obs*) *n* a jest or gibe, a trick. — *vi* to gibe (with *at*); to jest. — *vt* to play a trick upon. [Cf **glaik**]

gleek[2] *glēk*, (*hist*) *n* a card game for three players, each having twelve cards, and eight being left for the stock. [OFr *glic*, *ghelicque*, possibly from MDu *ghelic* alike]

gleet *glēt*, (*med* and *pathol*) *n* a viscous, transparent discharge from a mucous surface. — *vt* to discharge gleet. — *adj* **gleet'y**. [OFr *glette*, *glecte* a flux]

gleg *gleg*, (*Scot* and *N Eng*) *adj* clever; apt; alert; keen, sharp. [ON *gleggr* clever; cf OE *glēaw* wise, Ger *glau* clear]

glei. See **gley**[2].

Gleichschaltung *glīhh'shäl-tōōng*, *n* elimination of all opposition, enforcement of strict conformity, in politics, culture, etc. [Ger, co-ordination, from *gleich* like, and *schalten* to govern]

glen *glen*, *n* a narrow valley with a stream, often with trees; a depression, *usu* of some extent, between hills. [Gaelic *gleann*; cf Welsh *glyn*]

glendoveer *glen-dō-vēr'*, (*Southey*) *n* a heavenly spirit. [Fr *grandouver*]

glengarry *glen-gar'i*, (*Scot*) *n* a Highlander's cap of thick-milled woollen cloth, generally rising to a point in front, with ribbons hanging down behind. [*Glengarry* in Inverness-shire]

Glenlivet® *glen-liv'it*, *n* proprietary name for a noted whisky. [*Glenlivet*, a valley in Banffshire]

glenoid *glē'noid* or **glenoidal** *-əl*, (*anatom*) *adj* socket-shaped; slightly cupped. — Also *n*. [Gr *glēnoeidēs*, from *glēnē* a socket]

glent *glent*, *vt*, *vi*, and *n* an earlier form of **glint**.

gley[1] *glī*, *glē* or **glee** *glē*, (*Scot*) *vi* to squint. — *adj* **gleyed** or **gleed** squint-eyed. [Origin obscure; cf **gledge**]

gley[2] or **glei** *glā*, *n* a bluish-grey sticky clay found under some types of very damp soil. [Russ *gley* clay]

glia *glī'ə* or *glē'ə*, *n* (*anatom*) neuroglia. — *adj* **gli'al**. — *n* **gli'adin** or **gli'adine** prolamine, a protein in gluten. — *n* **gliō'ma** (*med*) a tumour of the neuroglia in the brain and spinal cord: — *pl* **gliō'mata** or **gliō'mas**. — *adj* **gliō'matous**. — *n* **gliomatō'sis** (*med*) diffuse overgrowth of neuroglia in the brain or spinal chord. — *n* **gliō'sis** (*med*) excessive growth of fibrous tissue in the neuroglia. [Gr *gliā* glue]

glib[1] *glib*, *adj* smooth, slippery (*archaic* or *dialect*); easy; facile; fluent and plausible. — *adv* (*archaic*) glibly. — *vt* (*archaic*) to make glib. — *adj* **glibb'ery** (*obs*) slippery. — *adv* **glib'ly**. — *n* **glib'ness**. [Cf Du *glibberig* slippery]

glib[2] *glib*, (*hist*) *n* a bush of matted hair hanging over the brow and eyes, a style formerly common in Ireland. [Ir]

glib[3] *glib*, (*Shakesp*) *vt* to castrate. [Cf **lib**[1]]

glidder *glid'ər*, (*dialect*) *adj* slippery. — Also **glid** (*Scot*; *obs*) or **glidd'ery**. [OE *glidder*]

glide *glīd*, *vi* to slide smoothly and easily; to flow gently; to pass smoothly or stealthily; to travel through the air without expending power; to travel by glider; to play a glide stroke. — *n* act of gliding; a transitional sound produced in passing from one position to another (*phonetics*); a glance stroke (*cricket*); a smooth and sliding dance-step; an inclined plane or slide; stretch of shallow gliding water. — *n* **glīd'er** someone who, or that which, glides; an aircraft like an aeroplane without an engine (a *powered glider* has a small engine); a hydroplane. — *n* **glīd'ing** the action of the verb in any sense; the sport of flying in a glider. — *adv* **glīd'ingly**. — **glide slope** or **path** the slope along which aircraft are assumed to come in for landing, marked out eg by a radio beam; **gliding plane** (*crystallog*) in minerals, a plane of molecular weakness along which movement can take place without actual fracture. [OE *glīdan* to slip; Ger *gleiten*]

gliff *glif*, (*Scot*) *n* a fright, a scare; a glimpse or other transient experience; a moment. — Also (now *obs*) **glift**. — *n* **gliff'ing** a moment. [Ety dubious]

glike *glīk*, (*Shakesp*) *n*. Same as **gleek**[1].

glim *glim*, *n* a glimpse (*Scot*); a scrap (*Scot*); a light or lantern (*slang*); an eye (*slang*). [Cf **gleam**, **glimmer** and Ger *Glimm* a spark]

glimmer[1] *glim'ər*, *vi* to burn or shine faintly or intermittently. — *n* a faint light; feeble rays of light; an inkling, faint perception. — *n* **glimm'ering** a glimmer; an inkling. — *adv* **glimm'eringly**. — *adj* **glimm'ery**. — **glimm'er-gowk** (*dialect*; *Tennyson*) an owl. [ME *glemern*, frequentative from root of **gleam**]

glimmer[2] *glim'ər*, *n* mica. [Ger]

glimpse *glimps*, *n* a short gleam (*archaic*); a passing appearance; a momentary view. — *vi* (*archaic*) to glimmer; to appear by glimpses. — *vt* to get a glimpse of. [ME *glymsen* to glimpse]

glint *glint*, *vi* to flash with a glittering light. — *vt* to reflect. — *n* a gleam; a momentary flash. [Earlier *glent*; prob Scand]

glioblastoma *glī-ō-blas-tō'mə*, (*pathol*) *n* a very malignant tumour of the central nervous system. [**glia** and **blastoma**]

glioma, etc. See **glia**.

Glires *glī'rēz*, *n pl* a division of mammals including the typical rodents (eg the genus **Glis**, Old World dormice), etc. [L *glis*, *glīris* dormouse]

glisk *glisk*, (*Scot*) *n* a glimpse. [Perhaps from the same root as OE *glisian* to shine]

glissade *glēs-äd'*, *vi* to slide or glide down. — *n* the act of sliding down a slope in a standing or squatting position, often with the aid of an ice axe; a gliding movement in dancing. [Fr]

glissando *glēs-än'dō*, (*music*) *n* the effect produced by sliding the finger along keyboard or strings; a similar effect on the trombone, etc: — *pl* **glissan'dos** or **glissan'di**. — Also *adj* and *adv*. [19c Ital, formed from Fr *glissant* sliding]

glisten *glis'n*, *vi* to gleam or shimmer as a wet or oily surface does. — *n* gleam. [ME *glistnen*, from OE *glisnian* to shine; cf Du *glisteren*]

glister *glis'tər*, (*archaic*) *vi* to sparkle, glitter. — *adj* **glis'tering**. — *adv* **glis'teringly**. [ME *glistren*; cf **glisten** and Du *glisteren*]

glit *glit*, (*obs*) *n* sticky, slimy or greasy material; gleet. [**gleet**]

glitch *glich*, *n* an instance of imperfect functioning in a spacecraft or other equipment, *esp* a minute change in voltage on an electronic circuit; any minor error or mishap, hiccup or temporary difficulty (*colloq*).

glitter *glit'ər*, *vi* to sparkle with light; to be splendid, brilliantly ornamented (*usu* with *with*); to be showy. — *n* sparkle; showiness. — *adj* **glitt'erand** (*Spenser*) glittering. — *n* and *adj* **glitt'ering**. — *adv* **glitt'eringly**. — *adj* **glitt'ery**. [ME *gliteren*; cf ON *glitra*, Ger *glitzern*]

glitterati *glit-ər-ä'tē*, (*colloq*) *n pl* the society lions of the day, ie famous, fashionable, rich and beautiful people.

glittery. See **glitter**.

glitzy *glits'i*, (*slang*, *orig NAm*) *adj* (*compar* **glitz'ier**, *superl* **glitz'iest**) showy, garish or gaudy; glittering. — *n* **glitz** (a back-formation) showiness, garishness. — *adv* **glitz'ily**. — *n* **glitz'iness**. [Perh from Ger *glitzern* to glitter]

gloaming *glōm'ing*, (*poetic*) *n* twilight, dusk. [Apparently from a short-vowelled derivative of OE *glōmung*, from *glōm* twilight]

gloat *glōt*, *vi* to eye with intense, *usu* malicious, satisfaction (*esp* with *over*); generally, to exult (over). — *n* an act of gloating. — *n* **gloat'er**. — *adv* **gloat'ingly**. [Perh ON *glotta* to grin]

glob *glob*, (*colloq*) *n* a roundish drop, dollop, etc of a semi-liquid substance. — *adj* **globb'y**. [Uncertain, possibly **globe** and **blob**]

globe *glōb*, *n* a ball, a round body, a sphere; the earth; a sphere representing the earth (terrestrial globe), or one representing the heavens (celestial globe); an orb, emblem of sovereignty; a light bulb (*esp Austr* and *NZ*); a nearly spherical glass vessel; a group, body (of people) (*obs*). — *vt* and *vi* to form into a globe. — *adj* **glōb'al** spherical; worldwide; affecting, or taking into consideration, the whole world or all peoples; (of products or companies) having a name that is recognized throughout the world (*marketing*); comprehensive; involving a whole file of data (*comput*). — *n* **glō'balism** the opinion or position that puts worldwide, international concerns above national or local; globalization. — *n* **glōbalizā'tion** or **-s-**. — *vt* **glō'balize** or **-ise** to make global. — *adv* **glōb'ally**. — *adj* **glōb'ate** or **glōbat'ed** globe-shaped. — *adj* **glōbed** globe-shaped; having a globe. — *adj* **glōb'y** (*Milton*, etc) round. — **global exchange** or **global search and replace** (*comput*) same as **search and replace**; **Global Positioning System** (*aeronautics*) a system for providing, worldwide, velocity information and an extremely accurate three-dimensional position; **global search** (*comput*) a word-processing feature which activates the cursor to find every occurrence of a pre-determined character, word or phrase in a file; **global variable** (*comput*) a variable which applies for the whole of a program, including any subroutine; **global village** the world, in reference to its apparent smallness due to improved communications, and the way in which changes in one area are likely to affect the rest of the world; **global warming** the slow increase in the earth's surface air temperature caused by man-made carbon dioxide in the atmosphere trapping excessive amounts of solar radiation which would otherwise be reflected back into space (also called the **greenhouse effect**); **globe fish** any fish of the families *Diodontidae* and *Tetrodontidae*, capable of blowing itself up into a globe; **globe'flower** any ranunculaceous plant of the genus *Trollius* with a globe of large showy sepals enclosing small inconspicuous petals; **globe thistle** see **Echinops**. — *vi* **globe'-trot** (back-formation). — **globe'trotter** a person who goes sightseeing around the world; **globe'trotting**. [L *globus*]

globigerina *glob-i-jə-rī'nə*, *n* a minute marine invertebrate of the genus **Globerigī'na**, with a calcareous shell of globose chambers in a spiral; a shell of this type: — *pl* **globigerinae** (*-ī'nē*). — **globigerina ooze** a deep-sea deposit of globigerina shells. [L *globus* globe, and *gerere* to carry]

globin *glōb'in*, (*biochem*) *n* a protein constituent of haemoglobin, a histone. [L *globus* globe, sphere, and **-in**(1)]

globoid *glōb'oid* or **globose** *glōb-ōs'* or *glōb'ōs*, *adj* globate. — *n* a globosity. — *n* **glōbosity** (something having) the quality of being globate. — *adj* **glō'bous** (*rare*) globoid or globose. [**globe**; L *globus*]

globular *glob'ū-lər*, *adj* spherical; made up of globules. — *n* **globularity**. — *adv* **glob'ūlarly**. — **globular cluster** (*astron*) symmetrical clusters into which many thousands of stars are gathered. [L *globulus* (see **globule**) and adj suffix *-ar*]

globule *glob'ūl*, *n* a little globe or round particle; a drop; a small pill. — *n* **glob'ūlet** a tiny globule. — *adj* **globulif'erous** producing or having globules. — *adj* **glob'ūlous**. [Fr, from L *globulus*, dimin of *globus* globe]

globulin *glob'ū-lin*, (*biochem*) *n* any one of a class of proteins soluble in dilute salt solutions but not in pure water. [**globule** and **-in**(1)]

globulite *glob'ū-līt*, (*geol*) *n* a minute spheroidal crystallite occurring *esp* in glassy rocks. [**globule** and **-ite**(3)]

globy. See **globe**.

glockenspiel *glok'ən-shpēl*, *n* an orchestral instrument consisting of a set of bells or metal bars struck by hammers, with or (more usually) without a keyboard. [Ger *Glocke* bell, and *Spiel* play]

glode *glōd*, (*Spenser*) *pa t* of **glide**.

glogg *glog*, *n* a Swedish hot spiced drink, of wine, a spirit and fruit, often served at Christmas. [Swed *glögg*]

gloire *glwär*, (Fr) *n* glory.

glom[1] *glom*, (*US slang*) *vt* to snatch; to steal: — *pr p* **glomm'ing**; *pa t* and *pa p* **glommed**. — **glom on to** to appropriate; to catch on to. [Variant of esp Scot dialect *glaum* to grab, from Gaelic *glàm* to seize, devour]

glom[2] *glom*, (*US slang*) *vt* to look at, to eye: — *pr p* **glomm'ing**; *pa t* and *pa p* **glommed**. [Origin uncertain]

glomerate *glom'ər-āt*, (*bot* and *anatom*) *vt* to gather into a ball. — *adj* balled; clustered in heads. — *n* **glomerā'tion**. — *adj* **glomer'ūlar** of a glomerulus. — *adj* **glomer'ūlate** of a glomerule. — *n* **glom'erule** (*-ōōl*; *bot*) a little ball of spores; a cluster of short-stalked flowers. — *n* **glomer'ūlus** (*anatom*) a cluster or mass of small organisms, *esp* of capillaries in the kidneys: — *pl* **glomer'ūlī**. [L *glomerāre*, *-ātum*, from *glomus*, *glomeris* a ball of yarn]

glonoin *glo-nō'in*, (*chem*) *n* a name for nitroglycerine, as used in medicine. [*gly*cerine, *O* (oxygen), NO_3 (nitric anhydride)]

gloom *glōōm*, *n* partial darkness; cloudiness; a dark place (*poetic*); heaviness of mind; hopelessness; sullenness; a scowl, a sullen look (*Scot*). — *vi* to be or look sullen or dejected; to be or become cloudy, dark or obscure; to scowl (*obs*); to dusk (*archaic*). — *vt* (*archaic*) to fill with gloom. — *adj* **gloom'ful**. — *adv* **gloom'ily**. — *n* **gloom'iness**. — *adj* **gloom'ing** (*Spenser*) shining obscurely. — *n* twilight, gloaming (*poetic*); scowling (*obs*). — *adj* **gloom'y** dim or obscure; dimly lit; depressed in spirits; dismal. — **gloom'-monger**. [ME *gloumbe*; see **glum**]

gloop *glōōp*, (*colloq*) *vi* (of a thick viscous substance) to bubble or plop slowly and heavily, *esp* with a soft thick plopping or popping sound; to fall, drip or lie in a thick viscous dribble or drop. — *n* thick viscous liquid, *esp* a glob, splodge or slow drip or dribble of such; sentimentality, mush or pulp. — *adj* **gloop'y** consisting of, falling, bubbling or dripping in gloops; soppy, gooey, mawkish. [Imit]

glop *glop*, (*US slang*) *n* a soft, gooey or sloppy semi-liquid substance or mush; unpalatable bland food of this consistency; schmaltz. [Perh a combination of **glue** and **slop**]

gloria[1] *glō'* or *glö'ri-ə*, *n* an aureole; a halo; a type of very closely-woven fabric, *usu* of a mixture of silk or nylon and wool or cotton, often used for umbrellas. [L]

gloria[2] *glō'ri-a* or *glö'ri-ə*, (L) *n* glory; any doxology beginning with the word "Gloria". — **gloria in excelsis**

(*in ek-* or *ik-sel'sis, eks-chel'sis,* or *eks-kel'sēs*) glory (to God) on high; **gloria Patri** (*pat'rī, 'ri,* or *pät'rē*) glory (be) to the Father.

glorify *glö'ri-fī, vt* to make glorious; to cast glory upon; to honour; to worship; to exalt to glory or happiness; to ascribe honour to; to ascribe great charm, beauty, etc to, *usu* to a markedly exaggerated extent; to add undeserved prestige to, *esp* under a euphemistic or overblown title: — *pr p* **glo'rifying**; *pa t* and *pa p* **glo'rified**. — *n* **glorificā'tion** an act of glorifying; a doxology; riotous festivity (*colloq*); something that has been or is glorified above its due or customary status (*colloq*). [L *glōria* glory, and *facere* to make]

gloriole *glö'ri-ōl, n* a halo or glory, aureola. [Fr, from L dimin *glōriola* little glory]

gloriosa *glö-ri-ō'sə, n* any plant of the tropical genus *Gloriosa*, leaf-climbers of the lily family, with showy colourful flowers. [New L, from L *gloriosus* full of glory]

glorious, etc. See under **glory**.

glory *glö'ri, n* renown; exalted or triumphant honour; widespread praise; an object of supreme pride; splendour, beauty; resplendent brightness; summit of attainment, prosperity or gratification; (in religious symbolism) a combination of the nimbus and the aureola, but often erroneously used for the nimbus; a ring or glow of light around the moon, the Brocken spectre, or other similar object or phenomenon; boastful or self-congratulatory spirit (*obs*); the presence of God; the manifestation of God to the blessed in heaven; a representation of the heavens opened; heaven. — *vi* to boast (*obs*); to exult proudly; to rejoice. — *vt* (*obs*) to glorify: — *pr p* **glo'rying**; *pa t* and *pa p* **glo'ried**. — *interj* (*old-fashioned*) expressing surprise. — *adj* **glō'rious** noble; splendid; conferring renown; wonderful, delightful, intensely enjoyable (*colloq*); elated, tipsy (*archaic*; *colloq*); boastful (*obs*). — *adv* **glo'riously**. — *n* **glo'riousness**. — **Glorious Twelfth** see under **twelfth**; **glory box** (*Austr* and *NZ*) a box in which a young woman keeps her trousseau, etc, a bottom drawer; **glo'ry-pea** the papilionaceous genus *Clianthus*, consisting of Sturt's desert pea (in Australia) and the parrot-bill (in New Zealand). — **glory be** a devout ascription of glory to God; hence, an ejaculation of exultation; an interjection expressing surprise; **glory of the snow** the plant chionodoxa; **Old Glory** the Stars and Stripes. [OFr *glorie* and L *glōria*]

glory hole *glö'ri hōl, n* a room, cupboard or receptacle for miscellaneous odds and ends (*colloq*); a steward's room on a ship; a hiding-place or enclosed space; a glass-maker's supplementary furnace; a hole for viewing the inside of a furnace; an excavation (*NAm*). [Perh ME *glory* to defile, or **glaury** or **glory** and **hole**]

Glos. *glos, abbrev*: Gloucestershire.

gloss[1] *glos, n* brightness or lustre, as from a polished surface; external show; superficial appearance. — *vt* to make glossy; to give a superficial lustre to; to render plausible; to palliate. — *n* **gloss'er**. — *adv* **gloss'ily**. — *n* **gloss'iness**. — *adj* **gloss'y** smooth and shining; highly polished. — *n* (*colloq*) a glossy magazine. — **gloss paint** paint containing varnish, giving a hard, shiny finish; **glossy magazine** a magazine of an expensive, luxury type, printed on glossy paper, with many colour photographs, illustrations and advertisements. — **gloss over** to explain away, render more acceptable. [Cf ON *glossi* blaze, *glōa* to glow; see **glass**]

gloss[2] *glos, n* a marginal or interlinear explanation, eg of an obscure or unusual word; a deceptive or intentionally misleading explanation; a collection of explanations of words, a glossary. — *vt* to give a gloss on; to explain away. — *vi* to comment or make explanatory remarks. — *n* **glossā'tor** or **gloss'er** a writer of glosses or comments, a commentator. [Gr *glōssa, glōtta* tongue, a word requiring explanation]

gloss- *glos-* or **glosso-** *glosō-, glos-ə-* or *glə-so'*, sometimes **glotto-**, *combining form* denoting: the tongue; a gloss (see **gloss**[2]). — *n* **glossec'tomy** surgical removal of the tongue. — *n* **glossī'tis** inflammation of the tongue. — *n* **glossodynia** (*-ō-din'i-ə*; Gr *odynē*, pain) pain in the tongue. — *n* **glossog'rapher**. — *adj* **glossograph'ical**. — *n* **glossog'raphy** the writing of glosses or comments. — *n* **glossolā'lia** (Gr *laleein* to talk) the 'gift of tongues', the speaking of wholly or partly unintelligible utterances thought to form part of an unknown language or languages and considered by (*esp* Early) Christians to be a manifestation of the Holy Spirit. — *adj* **glossolog'ical**. — *n* **glossol'ogist**. — *n* **glossol'ogy** (*obs*) comparative philology (also called **glottol'ogy**); terminology. — *n* **glottochronol'ogy** a statistical study of vocabulary to determine the degree of relationship between particular languages and the chronology of their independent development. — *adj* **glottogon'ic** relating to the origin of language. [Gr *glōssa* tongue]

glossa *glos'ə,* (*anatom* and *zool*) n the tongue; in insects, one of an inner pair of lobes in the labium. — *adj* **gloss'al**; of, or relating to, the tongue. [Gr *glossa* tongue]

glossary *glos'ə-ri, n* a collection or list of explanations of words; a dictionary of terms used in a specialized subject area; frequently-used words, phrases or paragraphs which can be stored by a word processor and recalled rapidly and easily; a collection of glosses. — *adj* relating to a glossary; of the nature of a glossary; containing explanation. — *adv* **glossārially**. — *n* **glossarist** a writer of a gloss or of a glossary. [L *glossārium* glossary, from *glossa* tongue, a word requiring explanation]

glossator. See **gloss**[2].

glosseme *glos'ēm,* (*linguistics*) *n* a unit or feature of a language that in itself carries significance and cannot be further analysed into meaningful units. [**gloss** and *-eme* (after phon*eme*), rather than Gr *glossēma* a word needing explanation]

Glossic *glos'ik, n* a phonetic alphabet devised by A J Ellis (1814–90). [Gr *glossa* tongue]

glossina *glos-ī'nə, n* an insect of the genus *Glossina*, the tsetse fly genus. [New L; named for its long proboscis (see **gloss-**)]

glossitis ... to ... **glossology**. See under **gloss-**.

-glot *-glot, combining form* denoting speaking or written in a language or languages, as in *monoglot, polyglot*. [Gr *glōtta* tongue, language]

glottal. See **glottis**.

glottis *glot'is,* (*anatom* and *zool*) *n* the opening of the larynx or entrance to the windpipe: — *pl* **glott'ises** or **glott'ides** (*-i-dēz*). — *adj* **glott'al** of the glottis. — *adj* **glott'ic** pertaining to the glottis or to the tongue; linguistic. — *adj* **glottid'ean**. — **glottal stop** a consonant sound produced by closing and suddenly opening the glottis, occurring as a phoneme in some languages, eg Arabic, and as a feature of others, and sometimes heard as a substitute for *t* in English. [Gr *glōttis*, from *glōtta* the tongue]

glottochronology, **glottogonic**, **glottology**. See under **gloss-**.

glout *glowt,* (*archaic*) *vi* to be sulky. — *n* a sulky look, the sulks. [Perh a variant of **gloat**]

glove *gluv, n* a covering for the hand, with a sheath for each finger; a boxing-glove; a baseball glove; a protective covering that is shaped to fit over a particular object exactly. — *vt* to cover with, or as if with, a glove. — *adj* **gloved**. — *n* **glov'er** a person who makes or sells gloves. — *n* **glov'ing** putting on gloves; the practice of making gloves; a glove-maker's craft. — Also *adj*. — **glove box** a closed compartment in which radioactive or toxic material may be manipulated by the use of gloves attached to the walls; a glove compartment; **glove compartment** a small compartment in the front of a car, *usu* part of the dashboard, in which gloves, etc can be kept; **glove'-fight** (*archaic*) a boxing-match in which the hands are gloved; **glove'-money** (*hist*) a gratuity given to servants, officers of a court, etc; **glove puppet** a puppet worn on the hand like a glove and manipulated by the fingers; **glove'-shield**

(*hist*) a shield worn by a knight on the left-hand gauntlet to parry blows; **glove'-stretcher** a scissors-shaped instrument for stretching the fingers of gloves. — **fit like a glove** to fit exactly; **the gloves are off** (*colloq*) now the fight, argument, etc is about to begin in earnest, without qualification or reservation (*adj* **gloves'-off**). [OE *glōf*, perh connected with **loof**[2]]

glow *glō*, *vi* to shine with an intense heat; to burn without flame; to emit a steady light; (*esp* of the complexion) to flush; to tingle with bodily warmth or with emotion; to be ardent. — *n* a shining with heat; a luminous appearance; a redness of complexion; a feeling of warmth; brightness of colour; warmth of feeling. — *adj* **glow'ing**. — *adv* **glow'ingly**. — **glow discharge** a luminous electrical discharge in gas at low pressure; **glow'lamp** an incandescent lamp, usually electric; **glow plug** an electric plug fitted in a diesel engine to make starting easier in cold weather; a similar device that can be switched on to re-ignite the flame in a gas turbine automatically; **glow'-worm** a beetle (*esp Lampyris noctiluca*) whose larvae and wingless females have luminous organs *usu* near the tip of the abdomen, emitting a greenish glow. [OE *glōwan*, to glow; Ger *glühen*, ON *glōa* to glow]

glower *glow'ər* or *glowr*, *vi* to stare frowningly; to scowl. — *n* a fierce or threatening stare. [Origin obscure]

gloxinia *glok-sin'i-ə*, *n* a plant of the tropical American genus of Gesneriaceae, *Gloxinia*, with bright bell-shaped flowers; generally applied to related plants of the genus Sinningia. [*Gloxin*, a German botanist]

gloze *glōz*, (*archaic*; *rare*) *vi* to flatter; to comment. — *vt* to make glosses on, explain; to palliate by specious explanation; to flatter; to deceive with smooth words. — *n* **glō'zing** flattery, deceit. — **gloze over** to explain away speciously. [OFr *glose*, from L *glōssa*, from Gr *glōssa*; see **gloss**[2]]

glucagon *glōō'kə-gon*, (*biochem*) *n* a polypeptide hormone secreted by the pancreas which accelerates glycogen breakdown in the liver, so increasing blood glucose levels. [Gr *glykys* sweet]

glucinum *glōō-sī'nəm*, also **glucinium** *glōō-sin'i-əm*, (*chem*) *n* former names for beryllium. — *n* **glucī'na** beryllia. [Gr *glykys* sweet, from the taste of its salts]

glucocorticoid *glōō-kō-kör'ti-koid*, (*biochem*) *n* any of a group of steroid hormones which affect glucose metabolism, having an anti-inflammatory effect. [Gr *glykys* sweet, and **corticoid**]

gluconeogenesis *glōō-kō-nē-ō-jen'ə-sis*, (*biochem*) *n* the conversion of non-carbohydrate substances, eg amino-acids, into glucose. — *adj* **gluconeogen'ic**. [Gr *glykys* sweet, **neo-**, and **genesis**]

glucoprotein. See **glycoprotein**.

glucose *glōō'kōs*, *n* any of several forms of naturally occurring sugar, *esp* dextrose; a yellowish syrup containing glucose, produced by the incomplete hydrolysis of starch, used in confectionery, etc. — *adj* **glucos'ic** (*kos'*). — *n* **glu'coside** any of the vegetable products making up a large group of the glycosides, which, on treatment with acids or alkalis, yield glucose or a similar substance. — *n* **glucosū'ria** sugar in the urine, glycosuria. — *adj* **glucosū'ric**. [Gr *glykys* sweet]

glue *glōō*, *n* an impure gelatine produced by boiling animal refuse (hoofs, hides, bones), used as an adhesive; any of several synthetic substances used as adhesives. — *vt* to join with, or as if with, glue or some other adhesive: — *pr p* **glu'ing**; *pa t* and *pa p* **glued**. — *n* **glu'er** — *adj* **glu'ey** containing glue; sticky; viscous. — *n* **glu'eyness**. — *adj* **glu'ish** (*obs*) having the nature of glue. — **glue ear** a condition of the ear where middle ear fluid fails to drain down the Eustachian tube, collecting instead behind the eardrum and causing deafness, infection and discharge; **glue'-pot** a vessel for melting or holding glue; a sticky place (*colloq*); **glue'-sniffer** a person who inhales the fumes of certain types of glue to achieve hallucinatory effects, etc; **glue'-sniffing** the practice (sometimes fatal) of doing this. — **marine glue** not a glue, but a composition of rubber, shellac and oil, that resists seawater. [Fr *glu*, from LL *glus*, *glūtis*]

glug *glug*, *n* a word representing the sound of liquid being poured from a bottle, down one's throat, etc. — *vi* (of liquid) to flow making this sound. — *vt* to drink in large draughts: — *pr p* **glugg'ing**; *pa t* and *pa p* **glugged**. [Imit]

glühwein or **Glühwein** *glü'vīn*, *n* hot, sweetened, spiced red wine, mulled wine as prepared in Germany, Austria, etc. [Ger, from *glühen* to glow, and *Wein* wine]

glum *glum*, *adj* sullen; gloomy. — *adv* **glum'ly**. — *n* **glum'ness**. — *adj* **glump'ish** (*archaic* or *dialect*) glum. — *n pl* **glumps** (*archaic* or *dialect*) the sulks. — *adj* **glump'y** (*archaic* or *dialect*) sulky. [ME *glombe*, *glome* to frown]

glume *glōōm*, (*bot*) *n* an outer sterile bract which, alone or with others, encloses the spikelet in grasses and sedges. — *adj* **glumā'ceous** like a glume, thin, brownish and papery. — *n* **glumell'a** a palea. — *adj* **glumif'erous** having glumes. — *n pl* **Glumiflō'rae** an order of monocotyledons consisting of grasses and sedges. [L *glūma* husk, from *glūbere* to peel]

glumpish, etc. See **glum**.

gluon *glōō'on*, (*phys*) *n* the name given to a hypothetical particle thought of as passing between quarks and so signifying the force that holds them together. [**glue**]

glut *glut*, *vt* to gorge; to feed beyond capacity; to saturate; to block or choke up: — *pr p* **glutt'ing**; *pa t* and *pa p* **glutt'ed**. — *n* a glutting; a surfeit; an oversupply; an excess quantity of a particular item on the market (*business*). [L *gluttīre* to swallow]

glutaeus. See **gluteus**.

gluten *glōō'tən*, *n* the nitrogenous part of the flour of wheat and other grains, insoluble in water. — *n* **glu'tamate** a salt of glutamic acid. — *n* **glutam'inase** an enzyme used in cancer treatment. — *n* **glu'tamine** (*-min* or *-mīn*) an amino-acid found in proteins. — *n* **glu'telin** any of various simple proteins, found in cereals and soluble only in dilute acids and alkalis. — *adj* **glu'tenous** containing, made from, etc gluten. — **glutam'ic** or **glutamin'ic acid** an important amino-acid, HOOC·CH_2·CH_2·CH(NH_2)·COOH. [L *glūten*, *-inis* glue; cf **glue**]

gluteus or **glutaeus** *glōō'ti-əs* or *glōō-tē'əs*, (*anatom*) *n* any of three muscles of the buttock and hip: — *pl* **glu'tēī** or **glutae'ī**. — *adj* **glutē'al** or **glutae'al**. [Gr *gloutos* the rump]

glutinous *glōō'tin-əs*, *adj* gluey; sticky. — *adv* **glu'tinously**. [L *glūten*, *glutinis* glue]

glutton[1] *glut'n*, *n* a person who eats to excess; someone who is extremely eager (for something, eg hard work). — *vi* **glutt'onize** or **-ise** to eat to excess. — *adj* **glutt'onous** or (*rare*) **glutt'onish** given to, or consisting in, gluttony. — *adv* **glutt'onously**. — *n* **glutt'ony** excess in eating. — **glutton for punishment** a person who seems indefatigable in seeking and performing strenuous or unpleasant work, etc. [Fr *glouton*, from L *glūtō*, *-ōnis*, from *glūtīre*, *gluttīre* to devour]

glutton[2] *glut'n*, *n* a N European carnivore (*Gulo gulo*) of the Mustelidae, 60–90cm (2–3ft) long, having dark, shaggy fur; a related animal (*Gulo luscus*) of N America, the wolverine. [Transl of Ger *Vielfrass*, literally large feeder, a popular imitation of Norw *fjeldfross*, literally mountain-cat]

glyceria *glis-ēr'i-ə*, *n* any plant of the genus *Glyceria* (family Gramineae) of aquatic and marsh-growing grasses. [New L, from Gr *glykeros* sweet]

glycerine *glis'ə-rēn*, **glycerin** *-in* or **glycerol** *-ol*, *n* a trihydric alcohol, a colourless, viscous, neutral, inodorous fluid, of a sweet taste, soluble in water and alcohol. — *adj* **glycer'ic**. — *n* **glyc'eride** an ester of glycerol. — *n* **gly'ceryl** a radical of which glycerine is the hydroxide. — **glyceryl trinitrate** same as **nitroglycerine**. [Gr *glykeros* sweet, from *glykys*]

glycin *glis'in* or *glī'sin*, or **glycine** *-sēn* or *-sēn'*, *n* amino-acid or glycocoll, $CH_2(NH_2)$·COOH, present in proteins, a sweetish colourless crystalline solid first prepared from glue. [Gr *glykys* sweet]

glycocoll *glik'ō-kol*, or *glīk'*, *n* glycin. [Gr *glykys* sweet, and *kolla* glue]

glycogen *glik'ō-jən*, or *glīk'*, *n* animal starch, a starch found in the liver, yielding glycose on hydrolysis. — *n* **glycogen'esis** the synthesis of glycogen; the synthesis of sugar from glycogen. — *adj* **glycogenet'ic**. — *adj* **glycogen'ic**. [Gr *glykys* sweet, and the root of *gennaein* to produce]

glycol *glik'ol* or *glīk'ol*, *n* the type of a class of compounds with two hydroxyl groups on adjacent carbon atoms, and so intermediate between alcohol and glycerine. — *adj* **glycol'ic** or **glycoll'ic**. [From *gly*cerine and alcoh*ol*]

glycolysis *glī-kol'i-sis*, *n* the breaking down of glucose into acids, with the release of energy. — *adj* **glycolyt'ic**. [*glyco*se and **-lysis**]

glyconic *glī-kon'ik*, (*Gr prosody*) *adj* consisting of four feet, one a dactyl, the others trochees. — *n* a glyconic verse. [The Greek poet *Glycon*]

glycoprotein *glī-kō-prō'tēn* or **glucoprotein** *glōō-kō-*, *n* any of the compounds formed by the conjugation of a protein with a substance containing a carbohydrate group other than a nucleic acid. [Gr *glykys* sweet, and **protein**]

glycose *glī'kōs*, *n* glucose. — *n* **gly'coside** any of a group of compounds derived from monosaccharides, yielding, on hydrolysis, a sugar and *usu* a non-carbohydrate. — *adj* **glycosid'ic**. — *n* **glycosū'ria** (Gr *ouron* urine) the presence of sugar in the urine. — *adj* **glycosū'ric**. [Gr *glykys* sweet]

glycosyl *glī'kə-sil*, (*biochem*) *n* a radical derived from glucose. — *vt* **glycos'ylate**. — *n* **glycosylā'tion** the process that attaches sugar to proteins to make glycoproteins.

glyph *glif*, *n* (*archit*) an ornamental channel or fluting, *usu* vertical; a sculptured mark. — *adj* **glyph'ic** carved. — *n* **glyph'ograph** a plate formed by glyphography. — *n* **glyphog'rapher**. — *adj* **glyphograph'ic**. — *n* **glyphog'raphy** a process of taking a raised copy of an engraved plate by electrotype. [Gr *glyphē*, from *glyphein* to carve]

glyptal resins *glip'təl rez'inz*, *n pl* almost colourless, tacky, adhesive resins made by heating glycerol or another polyhydric alcohol with a polybasic acid, used as bonding materials for mica, and (modified) in the paint and varnish trades.

glyptic *glip'tik*, *adj* pertaining to carving, *esp* gem-carving. — *n sing* **glyp'tics** the art of gem-engraving. — *adj* **glyptograph'ic**. — *n* **glyptog'raphy** the art of engraving on precious stones. — *n* **glyptothē'ca** (Gr *thēke* receptacle) a place for keeping sculpture. [Gr *glyptos* carved]

Glyptodon *glip'tō-don*, *n* an extinct genus of S American mammals of the Edentata, with fluted teeth. — *n* **glyp'todont** a mammal of this genus. [Gr *glyptos* carved, and *odous*, *odontos* tooth]

GM *abbrev*: (or **G-M**) Geiger-Muller (counter); general manager; General Motors; George Medal; Grand Master.

gm *abbrev*: gram(s) or gramme(s).

G-man. See under **G** (*abbrev*).

GMBATU *abbrev*: General, Municipal, Boilermakers and Allied Trades Union.

GmbH *abbrev*: *Gesellschaft mit beschränkter Haftung* (Ger), a limited liability company.

GMC *abbrev*: General Medical Council.

Gmc *abbrev*: Germanic.

gmelinite (*g*)*mel'in-īt*, (*mineralogy*) *n* a sodium aluminium zeolite. [After C G *Gmelin* (1792–1860), German chemist]

GMT *abbrev*: Greenwich Mean Time.

GMWU *abbrev*: General and Municipal Workers Union.

gnamma hole *nam'ə hōl*, (*Austr*) *n* a rock hollow in a desert area, perhaps containing water. [Aboriginal]

gnaphalium *na-fā'li-əm*, *n* any plant of the *Gnaphalium* genus of composites, to which cudweed belongs. [Latinized from Gr *gnaphallion* cottonweed]

gnar[1] *när*, *vi* to snarl or growl. — Also **gnarr**, **knar**, **gnarl**. [Onomatopoeic; cf OE *gnyrran* to grind the teeth, creak, Ger *knurren*, Dan *knurre* to growl]

gnar[2]. See **knar**[1].

gnarl[1] or **knarl** *närl*, *n* a lump or knot in a tree. — *adj* **gnarled** or **gnarl'y** knotty; contorted; rugged, weatherbeaten; ill-natured, bad-tempered. [After Shakespeare's *gnarled* for **knurled**]

gnarl[2], **gnarr**. See **gnar**[1].

gnash *nash*, *vt* and *vi* to strike (the teeth) together in rage or pain; to bite with a snap or clash of the teeth. — *n* a snap of the teeth. — *n* **gnash'er** someone who, or that which, gnashes; (*usu* in *pl*) a tooth (*facetious*). — *adv* **gnash'ingly**. [ME *gnasten*; prob from ON, ultimately onomatopoeic]

gnat *nat*, *n* any small fly of the family Culicidae, of which the females are commonly bloodsuckers; a mosquito; extended to other small insects. — *n* **gnat'ling** a little gnat; an insignificant person. — **gnat'catcher** any of the insectivorous American songbirds of the genus *Polioptila*. [OE *gnæt*]

gnathic *nath'ik* or **gnathal** *nath'* or *nā'thəl*, (*zool* and *anatom*) *adj* of, or relating to, the jaws. — *n* **gnath'ite** (or *nā'*) in arthropods, an appendage used as a jaw. — *n pl* **Gnathobdell'ida** (Gr *bdella* leech) an order of leeches with (*usu*) jaws but no proboscis. — *adj combining form* **-gnathous**. [Gr *gnathos* jaw]

gnathonic *na-thon'ik* or **gnathonical** *-əl*, (*obs*) *adj* flattering. — *adv* **gnathon'ically**. [From *Gnathō*, a character in Terence's *Eunuchus*, from Gr *gnathos* jaw]

gnaw *nö*, *vt* and *vi* (with *at*) to bite with a scraping or nibbling movement; to wear away; to bite in agony or rage; to distress persistently (*fig*): — *pa t* **gnawed**; *pa p* **gnawed** or **gnawn**. — *n* **gnaw'er** a person who gnaws; a rodent. [OE *gnagan*; cf **nag**[2]; Du *knagen*, Mod Icel *naga*]

gneiss *nīs*, (*geol*) *n* coarse-grained foliated metamorphic rock, *usu* composed of quartz, feldspar and mica. — *adj* **gneiss'ic** or **gneissit'ic** of the nature of gneiss. — *adj* **gneiss'oid** like gneiss. — *adj* **gneiss'ose** having the structure of gneiss. [Ger *Gneis*]

Gnetum *nē'təm*, *n* a tropical genus of trees and shrubs constituting, with Ephedra and Welwitschia, the family **Gnetā'ceae** and order **Gnetā'lēs**, gymnosperms differing from conifers in having a perianth, vessels in secondary wood, and no resin canals. [Said to be from *gnemon*, a name used in the island of Ternate]

gnocchi *no'kē*, *nö'kē* or *nyök'kē*, *n* a dish of small dumplings made from flour, semolina or potatoes, sometimes with the addition of cheese, and served with a sauce. [Ital]

gnome[1] *nōm* or *nō'mē*, *n* a pithy and sententious saying, generally in verse, embodying some moral sentiment or precept: — *pl* **gnomes** (*nōmz* or *nō'mēz*) or **gnomae** (*nō'mē*). — *adj* **gnō'mic** relating to or characterized by gnomes; (of writers) expressing themselves in gnomes. — *n* **gnō'mist** a writer of gnomes. — **gnomic aorist** (*gram*) a past tense of the Greek verb, used in proverbs, etc, for what once happened and is generally true. [Gr *gnōmē* an opinion, maxim]

gnome[2] *nōm*, *n* a sprite guarding the inner parts of the earth and its treasures; a dwarf or goblin; a statue of a gnome, *esp* in a garden as an ornament; an obscure but powerful international financier or banker (*facetious*). — *adj* **gnōm'ish**. — **the gnomes of Europe**, **Zürich**, etc, the big bankers. [New L *gnomus*, dwarf, pigmy, coined by Paracelsus, 16c scientist]

gnomon *nō'mon*, *n* the pin of a sundial, whose shadow points to the hour; an upright rod for taking the sun's altitude by its shadow; that which remains of a parallelogram when a similar parallelogram within one of its angles is taken away (*geom*); a geometrical figure which, added to or subtracted from another, gives a figure similar to the original one; an index or indicator (*obs*); the nose (*obs*; *joc*). — *adj* **gnomonic** or **gono-**

monical (*-mon'*) pertaining to a gnomon or to the art of gnomonics. — *adv* **gnomon'ically**. — *n sing* **gnomon'ics** (*hist*) the art of measuring time by the sundial. — *n* **gnomonol'ogy** (*rare*) a treatise on gnomonics. [Gr *gnōmōn* a gnomon, a carpenter's square, from *gnōnai* (aorist) to know]

gnosis *nō'sis*, *n* knowledge, *esp* spiritual: — *pl* **gnō'sēs**. — *n combining form* **-gno'sis** (-(*g*)*nō'sis*) denoting knowledge or recognition: — *pl* **-gnō'sēs**. — *adj combining form* **-gnos'tic**. — *adv combining form* **-gnos'tically**. — *n* **gnōseol'ogy** or **gnōsiol'ogy** the philosophy of knowledge. — *adj* **gnos'tic** (*nos'*) having knowledge; knowing, shrewd; (with *cap*) pertaining to Gnosticism. — *n* (with *cap*) an adherent of Gnosticism. — *adj* **gnos'tical** having knowledge. — *adv* **gnos'tically**. — *n* **Gnos'ticism** the eclectic doctrines of the Gnostics, whose philosophy, *esp* in early Christian times, taught the redemption of the spirit from matter by spiritual knowledge, and believed creation to be a process of emanation from the original essence or Godhead. — *vi* **Gnos'ticize** or **-ise** to profess or believe in Gnosticism. [Gr *gnōsis* knowledge, adj *gnōstikos*, from *gignōskein* to know]

gnotobiology *nō-tō-bī-ol'ə-ji*, *n* the study of life under germ-free conditions, gnotobiotics. — *adj* **gnotobiolog'ical**. — *n* **gnotobiō'sis** the condition of being germ-free, or germ-free and then inoculated with known micro-organisms only; the rearing of animals in such a germ-free environment, or in one in which all the living micro-organisms are known. — *n* **gnotobiote** (*-bī'ōt*) a gnotobiotic animal. — *adj* **gnotobiot'ic** in the condition of gnotobiosis. — *adv* **gnotobiot'ically**. — *n sing* **gnotobiot'ics** the study of gnotobiotic animals. [Gr *gnōtos* known, and **biology**]

GNP *abbrev*: gross national product.

gnu *nōō* or *nū*, *n* a large African antelope (*Connochaetes* or *Catoblepas*), superficially like a horse or buffalo: — *pl* **gnu** or **gnus**. — Also called **wildebeest**. [From Hottentot]

go[1] *gō*, *vi* to pass from one place to another; to be in motion; (of a path, etc) to lead or give access (to); to proceed; to run (in words or notes); (of verse) to flow smoothly; to walk (*obs*); to depart; to work, to be in operation; (of eg a bell or gun) to sound; to make a (specified) noise, as in *go bang, go moo*; to take a direction, turn, follow a course; to extend; (with *to*) to attend habitually (school, church, etc); (of a rumour, story, etc) to be current; to be valid, hold true; to be reckoned, to be regarded (as); to be known (*by* or *under* a name); to be on the whole or ordinarily; to tend, serve as a means; to be or continue in a particular state (as in fear, in rags); to elapse; to be sold; to be spent, consumed; to move or act in a way shown or specified; to be assigned or awarded (to); (of colours, etc) to harmonize; to die; (with *by* or (*up*)*on*) to be directed by, to act according to; (with *on*) to become chargeable to (an account, etc); (with *to*) to subject oneself (to expense, trouble, etc); (of a female) to be (eg a specific number of months) pregnant (*with* child, young, foal, etc); (of a female animal) to copulate (with *to*); to become, or become as if; to be considered generally as a concept; to be compared or ranked with others; to change to a new system, as in *go decimal, go metric*; to happen in a particular way; to be accepted as ultimately authoritative; to turn out; to fare; to contribute (to or towards a whole, purpose or result); to be contained; to be able to pass; to be finished or done away with; to give way; (with an infinitive without *to*) to move off with the intention of doing something, as in *go see* (*NAm*; see also **go and** below). — *vt* to pass through or over; to stake, bet; to call, bid or declare (*cards*); to eat or drink (a specific thing, *usu* in the phrase *I could go a ...*; *colloq*); to say (used when reporting speech; *dialect*): — *pr p* **gō'ing**; *pa p* **gone** (*gon*) (see separate articles); *pa t* **went** (supplied from **wend**); *3rd sing present indicative* **goes**. — *n* a going; success (*colloq*); energy, activity (*colloq*); a spell, turn, bout (*colloq*); a portion supplied at one time (*colloq*); an attempt (*colloq*); affair, matter (*colloq*; *archaic*); (with *the*) current fashion (*colloq*; *archaic*); a bargain, deal (*colloq*; *archaic*); failure to play (*cribbage*); a score for an opponent's failure to play (*cribbage*): — *pl* **goes**. — *adj* (*colloq*) ready; in perfect condition. — *interj* (called to start a race, etc) begin. — *n* **gō'er** a lively, energetic person; a sexually promiscuous person, *esp* a woman; used in combination, denoting a person who regularly goes to or attends a particular place, institution, etc, as in *cinema-goer*. — *adj* **gō'ey** (*colloq*) enterprising, go-ahead. — *n* **gō'ing** see separate article. — *adj* **go'-ahead** dashing, energetic; enterprisingly progressive. — *n* permission to proceed. — **go'-around** an act or instance of going, taking a route, around something (as in air traffic control, etc); an evasion, runaround; a round, cycle, sequence (that is repeated). — *adj* **go'-as-you-please** not limited by rules; informal. — **go'-between** an intermediary; **go'-by** any intentional disregard, as in *give (someone) the go-by*; (in coursing) the act of passing by or ahead in motion; escape by artifice; evasion; **go'-cart** a wheeled apparatus for teaching children to walk (*archaic*); a form of child's carriage (*archaic*); same as **go-kart**; **go'-devil** (*oil industry*) a cylindrical plug with brushes, scrapers and rollers able to move, under the oil pressure, through a pipeline to clean it; **go'-down** a cutting in the bank of a stream allowing animals to get to the water (*US*); see also **godown** (separate entry); **go-faster stripes** (*colloq*; *facetious*) matching horizontal stripes painted along the sides of a car for sporty effect, which unaccountably give (*esp* young male) drivers of cars bearing them a sense of superior power and road skill; **go'-getter** (*colloq*) a forceful aggressive person who sets about getting what he or she wants. — *adj* **go'-getting** forcefully ambitious. — **go'-kart** a low racing vehicle consisting of a frame with wheels, engine, and steering gear (now often simply **kart**); **go'-off** (*colloq*; *old*) start; **go-slow** see **go slow** below. — *adj* **go-to-meeting** see under **Sunday**. — **all systems go** everything in the spacecraft is operating as it should; everything in readiness; **all the go** (*colloq*; *old*) very fashionable; **a pretty go** (*archaic colloq*; *ironic*) an awkward turn of events; **at one go** in a single attempt or effort, simultaneously; **from the word go** from the very beginning; **give it a go** (*colloq*) to try, make an attempt at something; **go about** to pass from place to place; to busy oneself with; to seek, endeavour to (with *gerund*); (of a rumour, etc) to circulate; (of a ship) to change course; **go about one's business** to attend to one's own affairs; to be off, to leave or depart; **go abroad** to go to a foreign country or (*old-fashioned*) out of doors; (of rumour, etc) to circulate; **go against** to turn out unfavourably for; to be repugnant to; to be in conflict with; **go ahead** to proceed at once; **go along with** to agree with, support; **go along with you** (*colloq*) none of that!, away with you!, get away!; **go and** (*colloq*) to be so stupid or unfortunate as to (eg hurt oneself); to go in order to (do something); **go aside** to err (*archaic*); to withdraw, retire; **go at** to attack vigorously; **go back on** to betray, fail to keep (a promise, etc); **go bail** to give security (for); **go down** to sink, decline; to deteriorate; to be swallowed, believed, received or accepted (*esp* with pleasure); (of a computer or other electronic system) to break down; to fail to fulfil one's contract (*bridge*); to leave a university; to happen (*US slang*); to be sent to prison (*slang*); **go down on** (*vulg slang*) to perform fellatio or cunnilingus on; **go down the drain** (*colloq*) to be wasted; to become valueless; **go down with** (*colloq*) to contract (an illness); **go Dutch** see under **Dutch**; **go far** to go a long way (*lit* and *fig*); to achieve success; **go for** to assail; to set out to secure; to go to get or fetch; to be attracted by (*colloq*); to be true of; **go for broke** (*slang*; orig *US*) to risk everything one has in an attempt to win or succeed; to make an all-out, maximum effort; **go for nothing** to have no value; **go halves** to share (the substance or the expense of something) equally between two; **go hang** (*slang*) to be forgotten, neglected; to be no longer of concern; **go hard (with)** to prove difficult or unfortunate (for); **go in** to enter; (of the sun or moon) to become concealed behind cloud; to take the batting (*cricket*); **go in and out** to come and go freely; **go in for** to make a practice of; to take up as a career or special interest; to take part in (a competition, etc); **go into** to enter; to examine thoroughly, investigate; to adopt as a profession, etc; **go in unto** (*Bible*) to have sexual intercourse with; **go in with** to enter into partnership with; to join, combine with; **go it** to act in a striking or dashing manner (often in *impererative* by way of encouragement); **go it alone** to undertake a *usu* difficult or dangerous task alone; to manage by oneself; **go live** (*līv*) (*colloq*; of a radio station, automation equipment, etc) to go into operation; **go native** to assimilate oneself to an alien culture or to the way of life of a foreign country (*usu* less advanced than one's own); **go off** to leave; to explode; to deteriorate; (of food) to become rotten and inedible; to proceed to an expected conclusion; to cease to like or be fond of (a person, etc) (*colloq*); to experience orgasm (*slang*); to scold, reprimand (with *at*; *Austr slang*); to be raided by the police (*Austr slang*); to get married (*Austr slang*); to cease to operate; to die (*Shakesp*); **go off with** to go away with; to remove, take away (*colloq*); **go on** to continue, to proceed; an exclamation expressing disbelief (*colloq*); to behave, conduct oneself (*colloq*); to talk at length (*colloq*); to take the bowling, begin to bowl (*cricket*); to be capable of being fitted on to; to appear on stage; to fare; to begin to function; to proceed from (as in *nothing to go on*); **go one better** in some card games, to take a bet and increase the stake (also **go better**); **go one better (than)** to outdo, excel; to cap a performance; to achieve something more impressive, effective, etc (than someone or something); **go one's own way** to act independently; **go one's way** to depart; **go out** to become extinguished; to become unfashionable; to mingle in society (*old-fashioned*); **go over** to pass in review; to recall; to revise; **go over to** to transfer allegiance to; **go places** to travel widely; to go far in personal advancement; **go round** to be enough for all; **go slow** (of workers) deliberately to restrict output or effort in order to obtain concessions from employers (*adj* and *n* **go-slow'**); **go slow with** to be sparing with; **go steady** to court romantically, date regularly (with *with*); **go the whole hog** see under **whole**; **go through** to perform to the end, often perfunctorily; to examine in order; to undergo; **go through fire and water** to undertake any trouble or risks (from the usage in ancient ordeals); **go through with** to carry out; **go to** (*archaic*) come now (a kind of interjection, like the L *agedum*, the Gr *age nyn*); **go to pieces** see under **piece**; **go to the country** see under **country**; **go to the wall** see under **wall**; **go under** to become submerged, overwhelmed or ruined, eg (of a business) to fail, fold; to die (*archaic*); **go up** to ascend; to be erected; to be destroyed by fire or explosion; (of costs, prices, etc) to increase; to enter a university; **go with** to accompany; to agree with, accord with; to court romantically; **go without** to suffer the lack of; **go without saying** to be self-evident (a Gallicism; Fr *cela va sans dire*); **great go** at Cambridge University, a degree examination, contrasted with **little go** (last held in 1961), a preliminary examination; at Oxford University, Greats (*obs*); **have a go** (*colloq*) to make an attempt; (of a member of the public) to tackle a criminal; **have a go at** (*colloq*) to criticize severely; to attack physically; to tease or pick on; **have something going for one** (*colloq*) to enjoy the advantage of something; **I could go** (*colloq*) I could do with, I wouldn't mind (a drink, rest, etc); **let go** see under **let**[1]; **no go** not possible; futile; in vain; **no-go area** a part of a city, etc to which normal access is prevented by the erection of barricades, *esp* by local militants, a paramilitary group, etc; **on the go** very active; **to be going on with** (*colloq*) for the moment, in the meantime. [OE *gān* to go; cf Ger *gehen*, Du *gaan*]

go[2] *gō*, *n* a Japanese game for two, played with black and white stones (or counters) on a board, the object being to capture one's opponent's stones and be in control of the larger part of the board. [Jap]

Goa *gō'ə*, *n* a former Portuguese overseas territory on the west coast of India, part of the modern Indian republic since 1961. — *adj* **Gō'an** of Goa or its people. — *n* a native of Goa. — *adj* **Goanese** (*gō-ə-nēz'*) Goan. — *n* a Goan; the people of Goa. — **Goa bean** a papilionaceous plant (*Psophocarpus*) of tropical Asia and Africa, grown for its beans and root; its bean; **Goa butter** kokum butter; **Goa powder** araroba.

goa *gō'ə*, *n* a grey-brown gazelle of Tibet, with backward-curving horns. [Tibetan *dgoba*]

goad *gōd*, *n* a sharp-pointed stick, often tipped with iron, for driving oxen; a stimulus. — *vt* to drive with a goad; to urge forward; to incite; to provoke (with *into*). — *n* **goads'man** or rarely **goad'ster** a man who uses a goad. [OE *gād*]

goaf[1] *gōf*, (*E Anglian dialect*) *n* a rick in a barn. [ON *gōlf* floor]

goaf[2] *gōf*, (*mining*) *n* the space left by the extraction of a coal seam, into which waste is packed. [Origin obscure]

goal (*Milton* **gole**) *gōl*, *n* the structure or station into which the ball is driven in some games (eg *soccer*); the sending of the ball between the goalposts or over the crossbar; a score for doing so; an end or aim; (or **goals**) a name given to various outdoor games, eg early versions of hockey and football; a limit, boundary (*obs*); a competition, race (*obs*); the finishing point of a race; the winning-post or a similar marker; sometimes used for the starting-post (*obs*); a pillar marking the turning-point in a Roman chariot race (*antiq*); the target in archery (*obs*). — *vt* (*Rugby football*) to convert (a try) into a goal. — *adj* **goal'less** with no goals scored; without goals in life, unambitious. — **goal'ball** a game developed specifically for the blind, played by two teams on a rectangular indoor court using a ball containing bells, the object being to roll the ball past the opposing team into their goal; **goal'keeper** a player whose task is to defend goal (*colloq* **goal'ie**); **goal kick** (*soccer*) a free kick awarded to a defending player when an opponent has sent the ball over the goal line but not between the posts; **goal'kicker** a player who kicks a goal, or does a goal kick; **goal'kicking**; **goal line** the boundary marking each end of the field, on which the goals are situated; **goal'mouth** the space between the goalposts and immediately in front of the goal; **goal'post** one of the upright posts forming the goal; **goal'-tender** (in some games, *esp* ice-hockey) a goal-keeper; **goal'-tending**. — **change, move** or **shift the goalposts** to alter the rules of a game, conditions of an agreement, etc after proceedings have begun, or the agreement has been entered into; **own goal** a goal scored against one's own side by a player from one's own team; any self-inflicted disadvantage. [Origin obscure]

goalie *gō'li*, (*colloq*) *n* a goalkeeper.

Goan, Goanese. See **Goa**.

goanna *gō-an'ə*, *n* in Australia, any large monitor lizard. **[iguana]**

goary. Milton's spelling of **gory**.

goat *gōt*, *n* a horned ruminant animal (genus *Capra*) of Europe, Asia and N Africa, related to the sheep; a lecher (*fig*); a foolish person (*colloq*); (in *pl*) the wicked (*Bible*); (with *cap*) the zodiacal sign or the constellation Capricorn. — *adj* **goat'ish** resembling a goat, *esp* in smell; lustful; foolish. — *n* **goat'ishness**. — *n* **goat'ling** a young goat in its second year. — *adj* **goat'y**. — **goat'-antelope** a goatlike antelope, or an animal intermediate between goat and antelope, such as the chamois and the goral; **goat'-fig** the wild fig; **goat'fish** (*NAm*) the red mullet; **goat fuck** (*US vulg slang*) a chaotic situation, thoroughly confused muddle; **goat'-god** Pan; **goat'herd**

a person who tends goats; **goat'-moth** a large moth whose larva, feeding on willow-wood, etc, exudes a goatlike smell; **goat'-sallow** or **-willow** the great sallow (*Salix caprea*); **goat's'-beard** a composite plant of the genus *Tragopogon*, John-go-to-bed-at-noon; a herbaceous perennial with ornamental foliage (*Aruncus sylvester*); **goat's'-hair** cirrus clouds; **goat's'-rue** a papilionaceous border and fodder plant (*Galega officinalis*); **goat'skin** the skin of the goat; leather, or a wine-skin, made from it; **goat'sucker** (chiefly *NAm*) the nightjar, a bird similar to the swift, falsely thought to suck goats for milk; **goat's'-thorn** an Astragalus shrub; **goat'weed** goutweed. — **get someone's goat** to enrage someone; **play** or **(act) the (giddy) goat** see under **giddy**. [OE *gāt*; Ger *Geiss*, Du *geit*]

goatee *gō-tē'*, *n* a tuft on the chin, resembling a goat's beard. — *adj* **goateed'**. [**goat** and *-ee*, sfx of uncertain meaning]

gob[1] *gob*, *n* the mouth (*slang*); spittle (*slang*); a mouthful, lump (*dialect* or *vulg*); a lump or measured portion of molten glass; a space left in a mine by extraction of coal; waste packed into it. — *vi* (*slang*) to spit. — *adj* **gob'smacked** (*slang*) shocked; taken aback; astounded. — **gob'stopper** a very large hard round sweet for prolonged sucking. [OFr *gobe* mouthful, lump; cf Gaelic *gob* mouth; perh partly from **goaf**[2]]

gob[2] *gob*, (*US slang*) *n* a sailor in the US Navy. [Origin obscure]

gobang *gō-bang'*, *n* a game played on a board of 256 squares, with fifty counters, the object being to get five in a row. — Also **gomoku** (*go-mō'kōō*). [Jap *goban*]

gobar numeral *gō'bär nū'mər-əl*, *n* any of a set of numerals forming the stage between ancient Hindu numerals and present-day Arabic numerals. [Ar *ghubār* sanded board]

gobbeline *gob'ə-lēn*, (*Spenser*) *n*. Same as **goblin**.

gobbet *gob'it*, *n* a mouthful (*obs*); a lump to be swallowed; a clot (*obs*); a lump, *esp* of meat hacked or vomited; an extract, *esp* for translation or comment. [OFr *gobet*, dimin of *gobe*; see **gob**[1]]

gobble *gob'l*, *vt* to swallow in lumps; to swallow hastily (often with *up*); to snatch, seize eagerly (often with *up*; *colloq*); to play with a gobble (*golf*); to fellate (*vulg*). — *vi* to eat greedily; (of a turkey) to make a noise in the throat. — *n* (*golf*) a rapid straight putt so strongly played that if the ball had not gone into the hole, it would have gone a good way past. — *n* **gobb'ler** a turkey-cock. [OFr *gober* to devour]

gobbledegook or **gobbledygook** *gob'əl-di-gōōk*, (*orig US slang*) *n* unintelligible official jargon; rubbish, nonsense. [Imit of pompous utterance]

gobbo *gob'bō*, (Ital) *n* a hunchback; a hunchbacked figure: — *pl* **gob'bi** (*-bē*).

Gobelin *gōb'ə-lin*, *gob'*(*ə*)- or *go-blɛ̃'*, or **Gobelins** *-lin*, *-linz* or *-blɛ̃*, *n* a rich French pictorial tapestry. — Also *adj*. [From the *Gobelins*, a famous family of French dyers settled in Paris as early as the 15c]

gobe-mouches *gob-mōōsh*, (*Fr*) *n* a flycatcher (bird); an insectivorous plant; a credulous person.

gobiid, gobioid. See **goby**.

goblet *gob'lit*, *n* a large drinking-cup, properly one without a handle; a kind of saucepan with a straight handle and (*usu*) bulging sides (*Scot*). [OFr *gobelet*, dimin of *gobel*, of doubtful origin]

goblin *gob'lin*, *n* an unpleasant sprite; a bogy or bogle. [OFr *gobelin*, from LL *gobelīnus*, perh from *cobālus*, from Gr *kobālos* a mischievous spirit]

gobo *gō'bō*, (chiefly *US*) *n* a device used to protect a camera lens from light; a device for preventing unwanted sound from reaching a microphone: — *pl* **gō'boes** or **gō'bos**. [Origin obscure]

gobony *gob-ō'ni*, *adj*. Same as **compony**.

gobsmacked, gobstopper. See **gob**[1].

goburra *gō-bûr'ə*, *n*. Same as **kookaburra**.

goby *gō'bi*, *n* any fish of the genus *Gobius* or the family **Gobī'idae** small fishes with ventral fins forming a sucker. — *adj* **go'biid** of the Gobiidae. — *n* a goby. — *adj* **gō'bioid**. [L *gōbius*, from Gr *kōbios* a fish of the gudgeon kind]

GOC *abbrev*: General Officer Commanding.

god *god*, *n* a superhuman being, an object of worship (*fem* **godd'ess**); (with *cap*) the Supreme Being of monotheist religions, the Creator; an idol (*fem* **godd'ess**); an object of excessive devotion (*fem* **godd'ess**); a man of outstandingly fine physique; an extremely influential or greatly admired man (*fem* **godd'ess**); (in *pl*) the (occupants of the) gallery (*theat*). — *vt* to deify, treat as a god (*Spenser*, *Shakesp*, etc); (with *it*) to act as God or a god: — *pa t* **godd'ed**. — *n* **godd'ess-ship** the state or quality of a goddess. — *n* **god'head** (ME *-hēd*, *-hēde*, variant of *-hōd*) the state of being a god; divine nature; (with *cap* and *the*) God; a person idolized by the public (*colloq*). — *n* **god'hood** (OE *-hād*, ME *-hōd*) the position or state of being divine; a deity (*obs*). — *adj* **god'less** without a god; living without God; ungodly. — *adv* **god'lessly**. — *n* **god'lessness**. — *adj* **god'like** like a god; divine. — *adv* (*archaic*) **god'lily**. — *n* **god'liness** the quality of being godly. — *n* **god'ling** (*literary*; *Dryden*) a little god. — *adj* **god'ly** like God in character; pious; according to God's laws. — Also *adv* (*archaic*). — *n* **god'ship** the rank or character of a god; a divinity. — *adj* and *adv* **god'ward** towards God. — *adv* **god'wards**. — *adj* **God'-almighty** (*colloq*) enormous, excessive, inordinate; god-awful. — Also *adv*. — *interj* **God'-a-mercy** (*archaic*) thank God; many thanks to. — *n* (*obs*) an expression of thanks. — *adj* **god-aw'ful** (*colloq*) very bad; unpleasant, distasteful. — **god'child** a person to whom one is a godparent. — *adj* (*colloq*) **godd'am**, **godd'amn** or **god'damned** damned, accursed, hateful; utter, complete. — Also *adv*. — **god'daughter** a female godchild; **god'father** a male godparent; a sponsor (*fig*); the head of a criminal organization, *esp* the mafia (*colloq*); any influential leader or powerful figure (*colloq*). — *adj* **God'-fearing** reverencing God, religious. — *adj* **god'-forgotten** or **god'-forsaken** (or with *cap*) remote; miserable; behind the times. — *adj* **God'-gifted**. — *adj* **God'-given**. — **god'-king** a king considered to be a god, or thought to possess godlike powers; **god'mother** a female godparent; **god'parent** a person who, at baptism, guarantees a child's religious education or who (loosely) undertakes to bring up the child in the event of the death of its parents; **God's acre** a burial-ground (imitated from Ger *Gottesacker*); **god'send** a very welcome piece of unexpected good fortune; a person who or thing that provides unexpected but much needed support or help; **God slot** (*colloq*) a regular spot during the week's, day's, etc broadcasting reserved for religious exhortation, exposition or discussion; **god'-smith** (*Dryden*) a maker of idols; **god'son** a male godchild; **god'speed** (also with *cap*) a wish for good fortune, expressed at parting. — **for God's sake** an expression of urgent entreaty; (as *interj*) expressing eg annoyance or disgust; **God knows** God is my (his, etc) witness that; (*flippantly*) it is beyond human understanding; I don't know, I have no idea (*colloq*); **God's country** or **God's own country** a particularly well-favoured (*esp* scenically beautiful) region; one's homeland or native region (*esp US*); **God's truth** an absolute truth (a solemn and emphatic declaration; **God willing** if circumstances permit; **household gods** among the ancient Romans, the special gods presiding over the family; anything bound up with home interests. [OE *god*; Ger *Gott*, Gothic *guth*, Du *god*; all from a Gmc root *guth-* God, and quite distinct from *good*]

god day *god dā*, (*Spenser*) for **good-day**.

god-den or **godden** *god-en'*, a dialect variant of **good-even**.

Gödel's theorem *gōō'dəlz thē'ə-rəm*, *n* the theorem first demonstrated by Kurt Gödel, Austrian mathematician, in 1931, that in logic and mathematics there must be true statements that cannot be proved or disproved within the system, also that there can be no proof of the consistency of such a system from within itself.

godet *gō'dā* or *-det'*, *n* a triangular piece of cloth inserted in a skirt, etc, eg to make a flare. [Fr]

godetia *gə-* or *gō-dē'sh(y)ə*, *n* any plant of the American genus *Godetia*, closely related to the evening primrose. [C H *Godet*, Swiss botanist (died 1879)]

godown *gō-down'*, *n* a warehouse, or a storeroom, in the East. [Malay *gudang*]

godroon. See **gadroon**.

godso (*obs*) *interj*. Same as **gadso**.

godwit *god'wit*, *n* a bird (genus *Limosa*) of the plover family, with a long slightly up-curved bill and long slender legs, with a great part of the tibia bare. [Origin obscure]

goe[1] *gō*, (*Spenser*). Same as **go**[1], **gone**.

goe[2]. An earlier variant of **geo** (gully, creek).

goel *gō'el* or *-āl*, (*Jewish hist*) *n* the avenger of blood among the Hebrews, the nearest relative, whose duty it was to hunt down the murderer. [Heb]

goer, goes. See **go**[1].

goethite or **göthite** *gōō'tīt*, *n* a mineral, hydrated ferric oxide. [Named in honour of the poet *Goethe*]

goety *gō'ə-ti*, (*obs*) *n* black magic. — *adj* **goetic** (*-et'*). [Gr *goēteiā* witchcraft]

gofer[1], **gopher**, **gaufer** or **gaufre** *gō'* or *gö'fər*, (*dialect*) *n* a waffle with a pattern of crossed lines. [Fr *gaufre* honeycomb, waffle]

gofer[2] *go'fər*, (*NAm slang*) *n* a junior employee who is given errands to run by other members of the staff. [Alteration of *go for*]

goff *gof*. An archaic variant of **golf**.

goffer or **gauffer** *gŏf'ər*, *gof'*, or *gōf'ər*, *vt* to pleat, crimp, make wavy (paper or material). — *n* **goff'ering** or **gauff'ering** plaits or ruffles, or the process of making them; indented tooling on the edge of a book. [Fr *gaufrer*, from *gaufre* a waffle (see **gofer**[1])]

Gog *gog*, (*obs*) *n* for **God** (in oaths).

Gog and Magog *gog' ənd mā'gog*, *n pl* the nations represented in the Apocalypse as the forces of Satan at Armageddon (Revelation 10.8); the last two survivors of a mythical race of giants inhabiting ancient Britain.

goggle *gog'l*, *vi* to strain or roll the eyes; to stare wide-eyed, in amazement, etc; (of the eyes) to protrude. — *vt* to roll (the eyes). — *adj* (of the eyes) rolling; staring; prominent. — *n* a stare or affected rolling of the eyes; (in *pl*) spectacles with projecting eye tubes; (in *pl*) protective spectacles, as worn eg by motorcyclists, skiers, underwater divers, welders, etc; (in *pl*) spectacles, *esp* with round lenses (*colloq*); the eyes (*colloq*). — *adj* **gogg'led** wearing goggles. — *n* **gogg'ler** a person with goggle eyes (*colloq*); an eye (*slang*); an assiduous television-viewer (*colloq*). — *n* **gogg'ling**. — Also *adj*. — *adj* **gogg'ly**. — **gogg'le-box** (*colloq*) a television-set. — *adj* **gogg'le-eyed** having bulging, staring or rolling eyes. — Also *adv*. [Poss related to Ir and Gaelic *gog* to nod]

goglet *gog'lit*, (*Anglo-Ind*) *n* a water-cooler. [Port *gorgoleta*]

go-go or **gogo** *gō'gō*, used loosely as *adj* active, alert to seize opportunities; full of energy, lively; (of dancing, music, etc) rhythmic, exotic, vigorous; (of clubs, discotheques) featuring go-go dancers and/or music. — **go-go dancer** or **girl** a girl, *usu* scantily dressed, employed to dance (*usu* erotically) to a musical accompaniment in nightclubs or discothèques. [**à gogo** influenced by English **go**]

Goidel *goi'dəl*, (*hist*) *n* a Gael in the general sense (**Gadhel** (qv) now has the same meaning). — *adj* **Goidelic** (*-del'*) Gadhelic. [OIr *Góidel*]

going[1] *gō'ing*, *n* the act of moving; departure; condition of the ground for eg, walking, racing; progress; course of life (*Bible*); gait (*obs*). — *adj* (for earlier **a-go'ing**) in motion or activity; about, to be had; in existence; current. — **going-away dress**, **outfit** etc that worn by a bride when leaving on the honeymoon; **going concern** a business in actual activity (*esp* successfully), one currently operating normally and expected to continue to do so; **going concern concept** (*accountancy*) a concept which requires the accounts to reflect the state of a business that is expected to continue trading in future years; **going forth** (*Bible*) an outlet or exit; **going-o'ver** (*colloq*) a thorough check, examination; a complete treatment; a beating; **going rate** the current prevailing price that is being charged at the time for a service or product; **goings-on'** behaviour, activities, now *esp* if open to censure; **goings-out'** (*obs*) expenditure. — **be hard, heavy, tough**, etc **going** to prove difficult to do, etc. [**go**[1]]

going[2] *gō'ing*, *pr p* of **go**[1], in any sense; about or intending (to). — Used in combination meaning regularly attending, as in *the cinema-going public*. — **going on (for)** approaching (an age or time); **going strong** in full activity, flourishing.

goitre or (*esp NAm*) **goiter** *goi'tər*, (*pathol*) *n* abnormal enlargement of the thyroid gland, producing a swelling in front of the throat, sometimes accompanied by exophthalmus. — *adj* **goi'tred**. — *adj* **goi'trous**. [Fr *goître*, from L *guttur* the throat]

go-kart. See under **go**[1].

Golconda *gol-kon'də*, (*literary*) *n* a rich source of wealth. [Ruined city near Hyderabad, India, once famous for diamond-cutting]

gold[1] *gōld*, *n* a heavy yellow element (symbol **Au**; atomic no 79), one of the precious metals, used for coin, etc; articles made of it; money in the form of gold coins; a standard of money value which varies with the price of the metal; the gold standard; riches; anything very precious; the centre of an archery target; a gold medal; yellow, the colour of gold. — *adj* made of or like gold; golden in colour; (in modern marketing, often used to designate a product, service, etc) superior in quality to, improved upon or more sophisticated than the standard version. — *adj* **gold'ish** somewhat golden. — *adj* **gold'less**. — *adj* **gold'y** somewhat like gold. — **gold'-beater** a person whose trade is to beat gold into gold leaf; **gold-beater's skin** the outer coat of the caecum of an ox, used for separating sheets of gold being beaten into gold leaf; **gold'-beating**; **gold beetle** (*US*) a beetle of the family *Chrysomelidae* or of the *Cassididae*; **gold brick** a block of gold or (*orig US slang*) of pretended gold, hence a sham or swindle; a person who shirks duties or responsibilities. — Also *vt* **gold-brick'**. — **gold'-bug** (*US*) a gold beetle; a plutocrat; a person who favours a gold standard; a person who invests in gold bullion; **gold card** a special-privilege credit card available only to customers in the higher-income bracket; **gold certificate** or **note** (*US*) formerly, a US treasury note issued on gold reserves; **gold'-cloth** cloth of gold; **gold'crest** a golden-crested bird of the genus *Regulus* (also **golden-crested wren**); **gold'-digger** a person who digs for gold, *esp* a placer-miner; a person who treats an intimate relationship chiefly as a source of material gain; **gold'-digging**; **gold disc** a long-playing record that has sold 250 000 copies (500 000 in the US) or a single that has sold 500 000 (one million in US); a gold replica of such a record, presented to the composer, performer, etc; **gold dust** gold in fine particles, as found in some rivers; something very rare and precious, much sought-after (*fig*; *colloq*); **gold-end'-man** (*obs*) a dealer in **gold-ends'** (*archaic*), broken remnants of gold; **gold-exchange standard** a monetary system by which a country whose government is not on the gold standard is linked in its exchange rate to another's which is; **gold'eye** a N American freshwater fish (*Hyodon*); **gold-fe'ver** a mania for seeking gold; **gold'-field** a gold-producing region; **gold'finch** a European finch of the genus *Carduelis*, black, red, yellow and white, fond of eating thistle seeds; any of several Americal finches of the genus *Spinus*, the male being yellow with black wings, tail and crown; **gold'finny** a kind of small European wrasse, a corkwing; **gold'fish** a Chinese and Japanese freshwater fish closely related to the carp, golden or (*silverfish*) pale in its domesticated state, brownish when wild; **goldfish bowl** a spherical glass aquarium for goldfish; a situation entirely lacking in privacy; **gold foil** gold beaten into thin sheets, but not as thin as gold leaf; **gold'ilocks** a golden-haired person; a species of buttercup (*Ranunculus auricomus*); a composite European plant (*Aster linosyris*) with clustered bright yellow flowers; **gold ink** a writing fluid in which gold or an imitation is in suspension; **gold lace** lace made from gold thread. — *adj* **gold'-laced.** — **gold leaf** gold beaten extremely thin; **gold medal** in athletics competitions, etc, the medal awarded as first prize; **gold mine** a mine producing gold; a source of great profit; **gold'miner**; **gold note** see **gold certificate**; **gold=of-pleas'ure** a cruciferous plant (*Camelina sativa*), yellow-flowered, once much cultivated for its oil-rich seeds; **gold paint** bronze powders mixed with transparent varnish or amyl acetate; **gold plate** vessels and utensils of gold collectively; metal, *esp* silver, plated with gold. — *vt* **gold-plate'** to coat (another metal) with gold. — **gold point** (*finance*) in international transactions, an exchange rate at which it is advisable to export (**gold export point**) or import (**gold import point**) gold bullion rather than settle by bills of exchange; **gold record** a gold disc (qv above); **gold reserve** the stock of gold held by a country's central bank, etc, to finance any calls that may be made from overseas creditors for the settlement of debt; **gold rush** a rush of prospectors to a new goldfield; **gold'sinny** same as **goldfinny**; **gold'size** an adhesive, of various kinds, used to attach gold-leaf to a surface; **gold'smith** a worker in gold and silver; **goldsmith beetle** a beetle with wing-covers of a gold colour; **gold'smithry** or **gold'smithery**; **gold'spink** (chiefly *Scot*, also **gowd'spink**) the goldfinch; **gold standard** a monetary standard or system according to which the unit of currency has a precise value in gold; **gold'stick** a colonel of the Life Guards, who carries a gilded wand before the sovereign; the wand or rod so carried; **gold'stone** see **aventurine**; **gold thread** gold wire used in weaving; silk wound with gilded wire; an evergreen perennial ranunculaceous plant (genus *Coptis*) with slender yellow roots and white flowers; **gold'-washer** someone who obtains gold from sand and gravel by washing; a cradle or other implement for washing gold; **gold'-wasp** any wasp of a family (*Chrysididae*) with brilliant metallic colouring and telescopic abdomen, whose larvae feed on those of wasps and bees, known also as cuckoo-fly, ruby-tail or ruby-wasp; **gold wire** wire made of or covered with gold. — **as good as gold** behaving in an exemplary manner (*usu* of children); (**on** or **off**) **the gold standard** using (or not using) gold as standard. [OE *gold*, ON *gull*, Ger *Gold*, Gothic *gulth*]

gold[2] *gōld*, *n* the marigold (*obs*); the corn-marigold (*dialect*). — Also (*Scot*) **gool** or **gule** (*go͞ol*), also (*Spenser*) **goold** (*go͞old*). [OE *golde*, apparently related to **gold**[1], **gollan** and **gowan**; cf **marigold**]

goldarn *gol'därn*, (*US colloq*) *adj* and *adv* a euphemistic alteration of **goddamn**.

Goldbach's conjecture *gōld'bahhs kən-jek'chər*, (*math*) *n* the theory that every even number greater than 2 is the sum of two prime numbers. [After C *Goldbach*, 18c German mathematician.

golden *gōld'ən*, *n* of gold; of the colour of gold; bright, shining like gold; most valuable; happy; most favourable; of outstanding excellence. — *vt* (*rare*) to gild, make golden. — *vi* (*rare*) to become golden in colour. — *adv* **gold'enly**. — **golden age** an imaginary past time of innocence and happiness; any time of highest achievement; **gold'enberry** the Cape gooseberry; **golden bough** (*classical mythol*) the bough plucked by Aeneas before visiting the underworld; **golden bowler** (*slang*) dismissal from the Army followed by a job in Whitehall; **golden boy** or **girl** a young man or woman of outstanding talents, good looks, popularity, etc likely to win renown; **golden bull** (L *bulla aurea*) an edict issued by the Emperor Charles IV in 1356, mainly for the purpose of settling the law of imperial elections; **golden calf** see under **calf**[1]; **golden chain** laburnum. — *adj* **gold'en-crested**. — **Golden Delicious** a kind of sweet eating-apple; **golden eagle** a large eagle found in mountainous regions in Northern countries, so called from a slight golden gleam about the head and neck; **gold'en-eye** a northern sea-duck (genus *Clangula*); the lacewing fly; **golden fleece** (*Gr mythol*) the fleece of the ram Chrysomallus, the recovery of which was the object of the famous expedition of the Argonauts, and which gave its name to a celebrated order of knighthood in Austria and Spain, founded in 1429; **golden girl** see **golden boy**; **golden goodbye** see **golden handshake**; **golden goose** the fabled layer of golden eggs, killed by its over-greedy owner; a source of profit (*fig*; also **the goose that lays the golden eggs**); **golden handcuffs** (*colloq*) a substantial personal financial incentive or stake specifically designed by a company to constrain a valued employee into remaining on its staff; **golden handshake** (*colloq*) a large sum of money, or some equivalent, given to an employee or member who retires or is otherwise forced to leave a firm, etc. — Also **golden goodbye**. — **golden hello** (*colloq*) a large sum given in gratitude to a much-wanted new employee on joining a firm; **Golden Horde** the Kipchaks, a Turkic people, whose empire was founded in central and southern Russia by Batu in the 13c; **golden hour** (*med*) the time that passes between serious injury and skilled hospital treatment of that injury; **golden jubilee** a fiftieth anniversary; **Golden Legend** (L *Legenda Aurea*) a celebrated medieval collection of saints' lives, by Jacobus de Voragine (1230–98); **golden mean** the middle way between extremes; moderation; golden section; **golden mole** a bronze-coloured S African insectivore (*Chrysochloris*) and related genera superficially like a mole; **golden number** a number marking the position of a year in the Metonic Cycle of nineteen years; **golden oldie** (*colloq*) a song, recording, motion picture, etc issued some considerable time ago and still popular; **golden opportunity** a very favourable one; **golden parachute** (*colloq*) an unusually lavish cash payment to a senior member of a firm on his or her dismissal; **golden pheasant** a golden-crested Chinese pheasant; **golden plover** a plover with yellow-speckled feathers; **golden rectangle** one in which the ratio of width to length is the same as that of length to the sum of width and length; **gold'enrod** any plant of the composite genus *Solidago*, with rodlike stems and yellow heads crowded along the branches; **golden rose** an ornamental spray of roses made of wrought gold, blessed by the Pope on the fourth Sunday in Lent, sometimes presented to a dignitary or monarch in recognition of a special service; **golden rule** the precept that one should do as one would be done by; a rule of the first importance, a guiding principle; a rule of statutory interpretation, which allows the court to depart from a strict and literal interpretation of a statute where this would lead to an absurd result (*law*); **golden salmon** the S American dorado; **golden saxifrage** a greenish-yellow plant (genus *Chrysoplenium*) of the saxifrage family; **golden scoop** a system (judged to be illegal) according to which winners in bingo games in separate clubs can qualify for prizes offered by a large group of clubs acting together; **golden seal** a N American ranunculaceous plant (*Hydrastis canadensis*); its yellow rhizome, used in medicine; **golden section** division of a line so that one segment is to the other as that to the whole; **golden share** a large share in a company etc held by an institution or (often) a government, which prevents take-over by another company; **golden syrup** see under **syrup**; **golden thistle** and **tulip** a top award respectively in film-making and advertising; **golden wattle** any of various kinds of yellow-flowered Australian acacia, *esp Acacia pycnantha*; **golden wedding** see under **wed**. [**gold**[1] and adj-forming sfx *-en* like, made of]

gole. *Obs* (*Milton* etc) spelling of **goal**.

golem *gō'lem* or *-ləm*, *n* in Jewish folklore, a human image brought to life; a robot; a dolt. [Yiddish *goylem*, from Heb *gōlem*, a shapeless thing, an embryo]

golf *golf* (sometimes *gof*), *n* a game played with a club or set of clubs over a prepared stretch of land, the aim being to propel a small ball into a series of holes. — *vi* to play golf. — *n* **golf'er**. — *n* **golfia'na** (*-i-ä'nə*) a collector's or dealer's term for items of golfing interest. — *n* **golf'ing**. — **golf bag** a bag for carrying golf clubs; **golf ball** a small ball used in golf; in certain typewriters, printers, etc a small detachable metal sphere or hemisphere with the type characters moulded on to its surface; **golf club** a club used in golf; a golfing society; **golf course** an area of specially prepared, often landscaped, ground on which golf is played; **golf links** a golf course, *esp* by the sea, typically open and undulating. [Origin uncertain; Du *kolf* a club, has been suggested]

Golgi bodies *gōl'jē bod'iz*, (*biol*) *n pl* easily stained bodies around the centrosome in animal cells, studied by Camillo *Golgi* (1843–1926).

Golgotha *gol'gə-thə*, *n* a burial-ground; a charnel-house; a place littered with bones. [See under **Calvary**]

goliard *gō'li-ärd* or *-lyərd*, (*hist*) *n* any of a band of medieval wandering students and scholars noted for their riotous behaviour and *esp* their satirical Latin poems lampooning the Church, most of which were credited to a mythical Bishop *Golias*. — *adj* **goliardic** (*-ärd'ik*). — *n* **gō'liardy** or **goliard'ery**. — *vi* **gō'lias** (*Tennyson*) to play Golias, that is, perhaps, to behave riotously, irreverently or irreligiously. [OFr, glutton, from L *gūla* gluttony]

Goliath *gō-lī'əth*, or *gə-*, *n* a giant; a person or organization of enormous stature or power. — *vi* **golī'athize** or **-ise** to play Goliath, exaggerate extravagantly. — **goliath beetle** a tropical beetle (genus *Goliathus*) reaching four inches in length; **goliath frog** the largest kind of frog, living in central and west Africa. [From *Goliath*, the Philistine giant in 1 Samuel 17]

gollan or **golland** *gol'ən(d)*, also **gowlan** or **gowland** *gow'lənd*, (*dialect*) *n* a Northern name for various yellow flowers (marigold, corn-marigold, globeflower, etc). [Perh connected with **gold**[2]; see **gowan**]

gollar or **goller** *gol'ər*, (*Scot*) *n* a loud inarticulate gurgling sound; a thick or guttural bawl. — Also *vi*. [Imit]

golliwog. See **gollywog**.

gollop *gol'əp*, *vt* and *vi* to gulp greedily or hastily. [Perh **gulp**]

golly[1] *gol'i*, *interj* expressing surprise. [Thought to be orig a Negro modification of **God**]

golly[2], *gol'i*, *n*. A short form of **gollywog**.

gollywog or **golliwog** *gol'i-wog*, *n* a fantastical doll with a black face, staring eyes, and bristling hair; a person who has fuzzy hair or is in some way grotesque (*derog*). [*Golliwogg*, a doll in certain US children's books, the first of which, by Florence Upton, was published in 1895]

golomynka *go-lo-ming'kə*, *n* a very oily fish found in Lake Baikal, resembling the gobies. [Russ]

golosh. Same as **galosh**.

goloshoes. An *obs* spelling of **galoshes**.

golp or **golpe** *golp*, (*heraldry*) *n* a purple roundel. [Perh from Sp *golpe* bruise]

goluptious *gol-up'shəs*, or **goloptious** *-op'*, (*slang*; *joc*) *adj* delicious; voluptuous.

GOM *abbrev*: Grand Old Man (*orig* W E Gladstone), used of an elderly and venerated person, *esp* in a particular field of endeavour.

gombeen *gom'bēn'*, (*Ir*) *n* usury. — **gombeen'-man** a grasping usurer; a moneylender. [Ir *gaimbín*]

gombo, gombro. Same as **gumbo**.

gomeril or **gomeral** *gom'ər-əl*, (*Scot*) *n* a simpleton; a dunderhead. [Origin obscure]

gomoku. See **gobang**.

gompa *gom'pə*, *n* a Buddhist temple or monastery in Tibet. [Tibetan *gömpa* a place of seclusion, a hermitage]

gomphosis *gom-fō'sis*, (*anatom* and *zool*) *n* an immovable articulation, as of the teeth in the jaw: — *pl* **gompho'ses**. [Gr *gomphōsis*, from *gomphos* a bolt]

gomuti *gō-mōō'ti*, *n* a palm, *Arenga saccharifera*; the black fibre it yields. — Also **gomu'to** (*pl* **gomu'tos**). [Malay *gumuti*]

gon *gon*, (*geom*) *n* a grade. [Gr *gonia* angle]

-gon *-gon* or *-gən*, *combining form* used of a figure having a certain number of angles as in *hexagon*, *polygon*. [Gr *gōniā* angle]

gonad *gon'ad*, (*biol*) *n* an organ that produces sex-cells. — *adj* **gonadal** (*-ā'dəl*), **gonadial** (*-ā'di-əl*) or **gonadic** (*-ad'*). — *adj* **gonadotroph'ic** or **gonadotrop'ic** stimulating the gonads. — *n* **gonadotroph'in** or **gonadotrop'in** a substance that does this, used as a drug to promote fertility. [Gr *gonē* generation]

gondelay. See **gondola**.

gondola *gon'də-lə*, *n* a long, narrow boat used chiefly on the canals of Venice; a lighter, large open boat (*US*); a flat railway wagon (*US*); the car suspended from an airship or balloon; a car resembling this suspended from an earth-supported structure, *esp* on a ski-lift or aerial tramway, etc; a (free-standing) shelved unit for displaying goods in a supermarket, etc. — *n* (*Spenser*) **gon'delay**. — *n* **gondolier** (*-lēr*) a man who rows or propels a gondola. [Venetian dialect; origin obscure]

Gondwana *gond-wä'na* (formerly called **Gondwanaland** *gond-wä'nä-land*), *n* an ancient continent believed to have connected India with S Africa, S America, Antarctica and Australia from Carboniferous to Jurassic times. [*Gondwana* district in India, ie forest of the Gonds]

gone *gon*, *pa p* of **go**[1]; in an advanced stage (*esp* in *far gone*); lost, passed beyond help; departed; dead; over the hill, past one's peak; weak, faint, feeling a sinking sensation; pregnant (with specified time, eg *six months gone*); (of the time) past, as in *gone six*; (of an arrow) wide of the mark; enamoured of (with *on*; *slang*); in an exalted, delirious or inspired state (*slang*). — *n* **gone'ness** a sinking sensation. — *n* **gon'er** (*slang*) a person or animal dead or ruined beyond recovery; a thing beyond hope of recovery. — **gone goose** or **gosling** (*colloq*, *esp US*) a hopeless case. — **gone under** ruined beyond recovery.

gonfalon *gon'fə-lon*, *n* an ensign or standard with streamers, hung from a horizontal bar, used *esp* in certain medieval Italian republics. — *n* **gonfalonier** (*-ēr'*) a person who carries a gonfalon; the chief magistrate in some medieval Italian republics. — *n* **gon'fanon** (*hist*) a gonfalon; a pennon. [Ital *gonfalone* and OFr *gonfanon*, from OHGer *gundfano*, from *gund* battle, and *fano* (Ger *Fahne*) a flag; cf OE *gūthfana*]

gong *gong*, *n* a metal disc, *usu* rimmed, that sounds when struck or rubbed with a drumstick; an instrument used to sound a call, *esp* to meals; a steel spiral for striking in a clock; a flat bell sounded by a hammer; a medal (*slang*). — *vt* to summon, or call upon to stop, by sounding a gong. — *n* **gong'ster** a person who gongs. — **gong'-stick**. [Malay]

Gongorism *gong'gor-izm*, *n* a florid, inverted and pedantic style of writing, introduced by the Spanish poet Luis de *Góngora* y Argote (1561–1627), some of whose distinctive features reappeared in Euphuism. — *n* **Gong'orist**. — *adj* **Gongoris'tic**.

gonia. See **gonion**.

goniatite *gō'ni-ə-tīt*, (*palaeontol*) *n* a fossil cephalopod of a group with comparatively simple angular septa. — *n* and *adj* **goniatī'toid**. [Gr *gōniā* an angle]

gonidium *gon-id'i-əm*, (*bot*) *n* an algal cell in a lichen: — *pl* **gonid'ia**. — *adj* **gonid'ial** or **gonid'ic**. [Gr *gonē* generation, seed]

gonimoblast *gon'i-mō-bläst*, (*bot*) *n* in the red seaweeds, a spore-bearing filament that springs from the fertilized carpogonium. [Gr *gonimos* productive, and *blastos* a shoot]

goniometer *gōn-* or *gon-i-om'i-tər*, *n* an instrument for measuring angles, *esp* between crystal-faces; a direction-finding apparatus. — *adj* **goniometric** (*-ə-met'rik*) or **goniomet'rical**. — *adv* **goniomet'rically**. — *n* **goniom'etry**. [Gr *gōniā* an angle, and *metron* measure]

gonion *gō'ni-ən*, (*anatom*) *n* the point of the angle on either side of the lower jaw: — *pl* **gō'nia** (*-i-ə*). [Gr *gōniā* angle]

gonk *gongk*, *n* (**Gonk®**) a cushion-like soft toy, *usu* with arms and legs; a prostitute's client (*derog slang*). [Nonsense word]

gonna *gon'ə*, (*esp NAm*) a *colloq* contraction of **going to**.

gonococcus *gon-ō-kok'əs*, (*med*) *n* the bacterium that causes gonorrhoea: — *pl* **gonococci** (*-kok'sī*). — *adj* **gonococc'al** or **gonococcic** (*-kok'sik*). — *adj* **gonococc'oid**. [Gr *gonos* seed, and *kokkos* a berry]

gonocyte *gon'ō-sīt*, (*biol*) *n* an oocyte or spermatocyte. [Gr *gonos* seed, and **-cyte**]

gonophore *gon'ə-fōr*, *n* a prolongation of the axis bearing stamens or carpels (*bot*); a reproductive zooid of a hydrozoan, similar to a medusa but remaining fixed (*zool*). [Gr *gonos* seed, and *phoreein* to bear]

gonorrhoea *gon-ō-rē'ə*, (*med*) *n* a contagious infection of the mucous membrane of the genital tract. — *adj* **gonorrhoe'al** or **gonorrhoe'ic**. — Also (*esp NAm*) **gonorrhē'a**, **gonorrhē'al**, **gonorrhē'ic**. [Gr *gonorroia*, from *gonos* seed, and *rheein* to flow, from a mistaken notion of its nature]

gonys *gon'is*, (*ornithol*) *n* the ridge along and towards the tip of the lower mandible, formed by the junction of its two halves or rami (as in gulls). [New L, prob from Gr *genys* jaw]

gonzo *gon'zō*, (*US slang*) *adj* bizarre, crazy, absurd (*orig* and *esp* used in reference to journalism of a subjective eccentric nature). [Perh from Ital *gonzo* simpleton, or Sp *gonso*, literally goose]

goo *goo͞*, (*slang*) *n* any sticky substance; sentimentality. — *adj* **goo'ey**. [Origin uncertain]

goober *goo͞'bər*, *n* (also **goober pea**) peanut. [African]

good *good*, *adj* (*compar* **bett'er**, *superl* **best**) having suitable or desirable qualities; promoting health, welfare or happiness; virtuous; pious; kind; benevolent; well-behaved; not troublesome; of repute; doughty, able; worthy; commendable; suitable; adequate; thorough; competent; sufficient; valid; sound; serviceable; beneficial; genuine; pleasing; favourable; of a shot or play in tennis, golf, etc, made accurately; ample, moderately estimated; considerable, as in *a good deal, a good mind*; able to be counted on; financially or commercially safe or advisable; (from a range) of the better or best quality; used in patronizing address or reference, as in *my good man, your good lady* (ie wife). — *n* that which is morally or ethically right; prosperity; welfare; advantage, temporal or spiritual; benefit; avail; virtue; possessions (*archaic*); (*usu* in *pl*) moveable property, chattels, merchandise, freight; things bought and sold (eg machinery, clothing, foodstuffs, furniture), excluding currency, livestock, minerals, crops, land, buildings and services (*business*); the subject matter of a contract of sale of goods, which excludes money or choses in action (qv) (*law*); tangible items produced by firms and in demand by individuals for consumption, or by firms as an input to their production processes (*econ*). — *interj* well; right; be it so. — *adv* (now mainly *US colloq*, or *dialect*) well. — *n* **good'iness** weak, priggish or canting goodness. — *adj* **good'ish** pretty good, of fair quality or quantity. — *n* **good'liness**. — *adj* (*compar* **good'lier**, *superl* **good'liest**) **good'ly** comely, good-looking (*archaic*); fine; excellent; ample. — *adv* (*Spenser*) graciously; excellently, kindly. — *n* **good'lyhead** or **good'lihead** (*Spenser*) goodness. — *n* **good'ness** virtue; excellence; benevolence; substituted for God in certain expressions, such as *for goodness sake*, and as *interj*. — *n* **good'y** (*usu* in *pl*) a delicacy or sweetmeat; (*usu* in *pl*) something pleasant or desirable (usu *facetious*); the hero of a book, film, or any character on the side of justice and fair play, etc (*colloq*); a goody-goody; short for **goodwife** (*archaic*). — *interj* expressing (*esp* childish) pleasure. — *adj* goody-goody. — *n* and *interj* **good afternoon** a salutation on meeting or parting in the afternoon. — **good-breed'ing** polite manners formed by a good bringing-up; **good-broth'er**, **-fath'er**, **-moth'er**, **-sis'ter**, **-son'** (*Scot*; *archaic* or *dialect*; also **gude-**) a brother-in-law, father-in-law, etc. — *n* or *interj* **good-bye'** farewell, a form of address at parting (formed from *God be with you*). — *adj* **good'-cheap** (*archaic*) cheap (literally good-bargain). — *adj* **good-condi'tioned** in a good state. — **good-dame'** (*obs Scot*; also **gude-dame'** *güd-* or *gid-*) a grandmother. — *n* or *interj* **good-day'** a traditional salutation at meeting or parting, now rather *formal* or *archaic*, but in Australia a common greeting. — *n* or *interj* **good-den'** (*obs*; from *good-e'en*), **good-e'en'** (*archaic*), **good-e'ven** (*archaic*) or **good-eve'ning** a salutation on meeting or parting in the evening. — *adj* **good'faced** (*Shakesp*) having a handsome face. — **good faith** see **in good faith** below; **good'fellow** a jolly or boon companion; a reveller; **goodfell'owship** merry or pleasant company; conviviality; **good folk** good people. — *adj* **good'-for-nothing** worthless, useless. — *n* an idle or worthless person. — **Good Friday** see under **Friday**. — *interj* **good grief** an exclamation of surprise, dismay or exasperation. — *interj* **good heavens** an exclamation of surprise. — **good-hu'mour** cheerful, tolerant mood or disposition. — *adj* **good-hu'moured**. — *adv* **good-hu'mouredly**. — **good-hu'mouredness**; **good-King-Hen'ry** a goosefoot used in cooking and sometimes grown as a pot-herb. — *interj* **good-lack'** (*obs*) an expression of surprise or pity (*prob* a variation of *good Lord*, under the influence of **alack**). — *adj* **good'-liking** see under **like**[2]. — *adj* **good-look'ing** handsome, attractive. — **good-look'er** (*colloq*); **good looks** attractive appearance; **good'man** a yeoman (*obs*); (*usu* with *cap*) formerly prefixed to name of a man of yeoman's rank (*fem* **good'wife**; *obs*); (*good-man'*, chiefly *Scot*; *archaic*; also **gude-**) a householder or husband (*fem* **goodwife'**) or euphemistically the devil; **goodman's croft** a patch once left untilled in Scotland to avert the malice of the devil from the crop. — *n* and *interj* **good-morn'ing** or (*archaic*) **good-morr'ow** a salutation at meeting or parting early in the day. — **good-na'ture** natural goodness and mildness of disposition. — *adj* **good-na'tured**. — *adv* **good-na'turedly**. — **good-na'turedness**; **good neighbour policy** a US policy, presented by President Roosevelt in 1933, for co-operation in all fields between all the countries of North, South and Central America. — *n* and *interj* **goodnight'** a common salutation on parting at night or well on in the day. — *interj* **good'-now** (*obs* or *dialect*) an exclamation of wonder, surprise or entreaty. — *interj* **good'-o** or **good'-oh** expressing pleasure. — *adv* (*Austr*) well; thoroughly. — **good offices** mediation; instrumentality; **good people** or **good folk** (*euphem*) the fairies; **good sailor** a person who tends not to suffer from seasickness; **good Samaritan** see **Samaritan**; **goods engine** an engine used for drawing goods trains; **good sense** sound judgement; **goodsire'**, also **gudesire'** (*güd-* or *gid-*) and **gutcher** (*gut'shər*) (*obs Scot*) a grandfather. — *adj* **good'-sized** (fairly) large. — *n* and *interj* **good-speed'** (*archaic*) a contraction of *I wish you good speed* (ie success). — **goods train** a train of goods wagons. — *adj* **good-tem'pered** of a kindly disposition; not easily made angry. — **Good Templar** a member of a temperance society, modelled on the Freemasons. — *adj* **good'time** pleasure-seeking. — **good turn** something done for someone in a kind and helpful spirit or manner; **goodwife'** (or *good'*) the *fem* of **goodman**; **goodwill'** benevolence; well-wishing; the established trade, reputation, efficiency, popularity, and valuable personal relationships with customers, of a business or trade, often appearing as one of its (intangible) assets, with a marketable money value. — *adj* **good'will** or (*obs Scot*) **good-will'y** well-wishing; expressive of goodwill. — **good works** acts of charity. — *adj* **good'y-good'y** mawkishly good; weakly benevolent or pious. — Also *n*. — **as good as** the same as, no less than; virtually; **be as good as one's word** to fulfil one's promise; **for good** or **for good and all** permanently; irrevocably; **good and** (*colloq*) very; **goodies and baddies** characters in a drama regarded respectively as definitely good and definitely bad; **good for anything** ready for any kind of work; **good for you** *interj* expressing approval (*Austr colloq* **good on you**); **goods and chattels** see under **chattel**; **goods for own use** (*bookkeeping*) stock taken by the owner of a business for his or her own private purposes, the sale price of which is debited to the owner's drawings account and credited to the sales account; **goods on approval** (*marketing*) goods delivered and examined for a trial period before a decision to buy them is made; **goods on consignment** (*marketing*) goods delivered to an agent by a principal and sold on behalf of the principal; **goods received department** (*business*) one that deals with the reception of goods, and is responsible for checking condition of goods on delivery, etc; **goods received note** (*business*) a document completed by the storekeeper upon receipt of materials or goods from an outside supplier; **in good faith** honestly and without any intention to deceive (also *adj* **good faith**); **in someone's good books** in favour with someone; **make good** to fulfil, perform; to compensate; to come to success, *esp* unexpectedly; to do well, redeeming an unpromising false start; to repair; to justify; **no good** useless; unavailing; worthless; **not, hardly**, etc, **good enough** not sufficiently good; mean, unfair, very different from what was expected or promised; **stand good** to be lastingly good; to remain; **the Good Book** the Bible; **the goods** (*slang*) the real thing; that which is required, promised, etc; **think good** (*obs*) to be disposed, to be willing; **to the good** for the best; on the credit or advantage side. [OE *gōd*; Du *goed*, Ger *gut*, ON *gōthr*, Gothic *gōths*]

goodyear *good'yēr*, or **goodyears** (*Shakesp*) *n* the devil, the plague, or the like (a meaningless imprecation). [Of obscure origin. Perh orig 'as I hope for a *good year*']

gooey. See **goo**.

goof *gōōf*, (*slang*) *n* a stupid or awkward person; a blunder. — *vi* to make a blunder; to mess (about or around); to waste time, behave idly, etc (*NAm*; with *off*). — *vt* to make a mess of (often with *up*). — *adv* **goof'ily**. — *n* **goof'iness**. — *adj* **goof'y** foolish or stupid; (of teeth) protruding. — **goof'ball** (*NAm slang*) a barbiturate pill used as an exhilarant; a goofy person. [Perh Fr *goffe*]

googly *gōōg'li*, (*cricket*) *n* an off-breaking ball with an apparent leg-break action on the part of a right-arm bowler to a right-handed batsman, or conversely for a left-arm bowler. — Also *adj*. — *vi* **goog'le** to behave or bowl in such a manner. [Ety dubious]

googol *gōō'gol*, *n* 1 followed by a hundred zeros, 10^{100}. — *n* **goo'golplex** 1 followed by a googol of zeros, 10 to the power of a googol. [Coined by E Kasner, US mathematician (1878–1955)]

gook *gōōk*, (*offensive slang*) *n* someone of Asiatic race, *esp* a Japanese, Korean or Vietnamese soldier; *esp* formerly in Rhodesia, a guerrilla or terrorist; a tramp or anyone considered offensively dirty or stupid. [Origin uncertain]

gool, **goold**. See **gold**².

gooly, **gooley** or **goolie** *gōō'li*, *n* a small stone (*Austr colloq*); (in *pl*) testicles (*slang*; *humorous*) [Perh Hindi *goli* a bullet, ball]

goon *gōōn*, *n* a hired thug (*US slang*); a stupid person. [After 'Alice the *Goon*', a character created by American cartoonist E C Segar (1894–1938)]

goonda *gōōn'da* or *gōōn'də*, *n* (in India and Pakistan) a hired thug, *esp* one in the pay of a political party. [Hindi *goonda* a scoundrel]

gooneybird *gōō'nē-bûrd*, *n* an (*esp* black-footed) albatross. — Also **goon'ey**. [Prob dialect, simpleton, from obs *gony*]

goop¹ *gōōp*, (*slang*) *n* a fool; a fatuous person; a rude, ill-mannered person (*NAm*). — *adj* **goop'y**. [Cf **goof**]

goop² *gōōp*, (*US slang*) *n* an unpleasantly sticky or gooey substance. — *adj* **goop'y**. — *adj* **gooped up** clogged or stuck up with goop. [Connected with **goo**, **glop**, etc; imit]

goor, **Goorkha**, **gooroo**. Alternative spellings of **gur**, **Gurkha**, **guru**.

goosander *gōōs-an'dər*, *n* a large duck of the merganser genus. [Perh *goose*, and ON *önd*, pl *ander* duck]

goose *gōōs*, *n* any one of a group of birds of the duck family, intermediate between ducks and swans; a domesticated member of the group, descended mainly from the greylag; the female of such a bird (*masc* **gander**); a tailor's smoothing-iron, from the likeness of the handle to the neck of a goose; a stupid, silly person; a game of chance once common in England, in which the players moved counters on a board, with the right to a double move on reaching a picture of a goose (*obs*): — *pl* **geese** (*gēs*) or, of a tailor's goose, **goos'es**. — *vt* (*slang*) to hiss off the stage (*theat*); to prod (someone) between the buttocks from behind; to grab or poke (a male) in the genitals from behind. — *n* **goos'ery** a place for keeping geese; stupidity. — *n* **goos'ey** or **goos'y** a goose; a blockhead. — *adj* like a goose; affected with gooseflesh. — **goose-barnacle** see under **barnacle**¹; **goose bumps** (*colloq*) gooseflesh; **goose'-cap** (*obs*) a silly person; **goose'-club** (*old*) an association for saving to buy geese for Christmas, or to raffle for a goose; **goose'-egg** the egg of a goose; a zero score (*US*); **goose'-fish** (*US*) the angler-fish; **goose'flesh** a knobbly, pimply condition of the skin, like that of a plucked goose or other fowl due to erection of hairs through cold, horror, etc; the bristling feeling in the skin caused by this condition; **goose'-flower** the pelican-flower, a gigantic Aristolochia; **goose'foot** any plant of the genus Chenopodium of the beet family, so named because of the shape of the leaf; also applied to any member of the family Chenopodiaceae: — *pl* **goose'foots**; **goose'-girl** a girl who herds geese; **goosegog**, **goosegob** see under **gooseberry**; **goose'-grass** cleavers, a Eurasian plant (*Galium aparine*) with a bristly stem and fruits that cling to clothes, etc; silverweed; **goose'herd** a person who herds geese; **goose'-neck** a hook, bracket, pipe, etc bent like a goose's neck; **goose'-pimples** gooseflesh; **goose'-quill** one of the quills or large wing-feathers of a goose, *esp* one used as a pen; **goose'-skin** gooseflesh, horripilation; **goose step** (*military*) a method of marching (resembling a goose's walk) with knees stiff and soles brought flat on the ground. — *vi* **goose'-step**. — **goose'-wing** (*naut*) one of the clews or lower corners of a ship's mainsail or foresail when the middle part is furled or tied up to the yard. — *adj* **goose'-winged** (*naut*) having only one clew set; in fore-and-aft rigged vessels, having the mainsail on one side and the foresail on the other, so as to sail wing-and-wing. — **the goose that lays the golden eggs** see **golden goose** under **golden**. [OE *gōs* (pl *gēs*); ON *gās*, Ger *Gans*, L *anser* (for *hanser*), Gr *chēn*]

gooseberry *gōōz'bə-ri*, or *gōōs'*, *n* the small oval fruit (*usu* green) of the **goose'berry-bush** (*Ribes grossularia*), a prickly shrub of the saxifrage family; a fermented effervescing drink (in full **goose'berry-wine**) made from gooseberries; an imitation champagne (*jocular*); an unwanted third person in the company of a couple or group of couples, *esp* in the phrase **play gooseberry**. — **goose'berry-caterpillar** a creamy looper with orange spots and black dots, feeding on gooseberry leaves, the larva of the **goose'berry-moth** or magpie moth (*Abraxas grossulariata*) a yellow-bodied moth with black-spotted white wings; **gooseberry-fool**' see **fool**²; **goose'berry-stone** grossular, a mineral of the garnet group; **goose'-gog** or **goose'gob** (*colloq* and *dialect*) a gooseberry. — **Cape gooseberry** or **gooseberry tomato** see under **cape**²; **Chinese gooseberry** a subtropical vine (*Actinidia chinensis*) with brown, hairy, edible fruit, the kiwi fruit; **Coromandel gooseberry** carambola (qv). [Perh **goose** and **berry**¹; or *goose* may be from MHGer *krus* (Gr *kraus* crisp, curled); cf OFr *groisele*, *grosele* gooseberry, Scot *grossart*]

gopak *gō'pak*, *n* a high-leaping folk-dance from the Ukraine. [From Russ]

gopher[1] *gō'fər*, *n* a name in America applied to various burrowing animals, including the pouched rat, the ground squirrel, the land tortoise of the Southern States, and a burrowing snake. — *vi* to burrow; to mine in a small way. [Perh Fr *gaufre* honeycomb]

gopher[2] *gō'fər*, *n* a kind of wood, generally supposed to be cypress (*Bible*); yellow-wood (*Cladastris lutea*) (*US*). [Heb]

gopher[3]. See **gofer**.

gopura *gō'pōō-rə* or **gopuram** *gō'pōō-rəm*, *n* in Southern India, a pyramidal tower over the gateway of a temple. [Sans *gopura*]

goral *gō'rəl* or *gö'rəl*, *n* a Himalayan goat-antelope.

goramy. See **gourami**.

gor-belly *gör'bel-i*, (*obs*) *n* a big belly; a big-bellied person. — *adj* (*Shakesp*) **gor'-bellied**. [Perh OE *gor* filth, and **belly**]

gorblimey or **gorblimy** *gö-blī'mi*, (*Cockney*) *interj* expressing surprise. — Also as *adj* loud, coarse, vulgar. [Altered from *God blind me*]

Gorbymania *gör-bi-mān'i-ə*, (*colloq*) *n* mass, extreme enthusiasm and admiration for Mikhail *Gorbachev*, one-time leader of the former Soviet Union, and his initiatives of glasnost and perestroika, warmly welcomed by the West in the mid and late 1980s.

gorcock *gör'kok*, *n* the red grouse cock. [Origin obscure]

gorcrow *gör'krō*, (*dialect*) *n* the carrion-crow. [OE *gor* filth, and **crow**]

Gordian *görd'yən*, *adj* pertaining to *Gordium* the capital, or *Gordius* the king, of ancient Phrygia, or to the intricate knot he tied which could not be untied; intricate; difficult. — *vt* (*Keats*) to tie up, knot. — *n* **Gor'dius** a genus of hairworms. — **cut the Gordian knot** to overcome a difficulty by violent measures, as Alexander the Great cut the Gordian knot with his sword.

Gordon Bennett *gör'dən ben'it*, *interj* expressing mild surprise, annoyance, etc.

Gordon setter *gör'dən set'ər*, *n* an (*orig*) Scottish breed of setter with a black and tan coat. [Alexander *Gordon*, 19c Scottish nobleman.]

gore[1] *gōr* or *gör*, *n* filth (*obs*); clotted blood; blood. — *adv* **gor'ily**. — *n* **go'riness**. — *adj* **gor'y** like gore; covered with gore; bloody. — **gore'-blood** (*Spenser*); **gory dew** a dark-red slimy film sometimes seen on damp walls, etc, a simple form of vegetable life (*Porphyridium cruentum*). [OE *gor* filth, dung; ON *gor* cud, slime]

gore[2] *gōr* or *gör*, *n* a triangular piece of land (now *dialect*); a triangular piece let into a garment to widen it; a sector of a curved surface; a sector-like section of a parachute canopy; a skirt (*obs*). — *vt* to shape like or provide with gores; to pierce with anything pointed, such as a spear or horn. — *n* **gor'ing** an angular, tapering or obliquely-cut piece. — *adj* forming a gore. [OE *gāra* a pointed triangular piece of land, and *gār* a spear]

Gore-Tex® *gör'-teks*, *n* a water-repellent synthetic fibre which allows air and moisture to permeate out through its pores.

gorge *görj*, *n* the throat; a ravine; the entrance to an outwork (*fortif*); a hawk's crop; the maw; the contents of the stomach; a gluttonous feed; a fish-catching device, to be swallowed by the fish. — *vt* to swallow greedily; to glut. — *vi* to feed gluttonously. — *adj* **gorged** having a gorge or throat; glutted; having a crown or coronet around the neck (*heraldry*). — **heave the gorge** to retch; **one's gorge rises** one is filled with loathing or revulsion (with *at*). [OFr]

gorgeous *gör'jəs*, *adj* showy; splendid; magnificent; (loosely) pleasant, good, beautiful etc. — *adv* **gor'geously**. — *n* **gor'geousness**. [OFr *gorgias* gaudy]

gorgerin *gör'jə-rin*, (*archit*) *n* same as **necking**. [Fr, from *gorge* throat]

gorget (*hist*) *n* a piece of armour for the throat; a wimple; a neck ornament. [OFr, from *gorge* throat]

gorgia *gör'jə*, *n* an improvised virtuoso passage in 16c and 17c singing. [Obs Ital *gorgia* throat]

gorgio *gör'jō* or *gör'ji-ō*, *n* a gypsy word for a non-gypsy. — Also **gajo** (*gö'jō*): — *pl* **gor'gios**, **ga'jos**. [Romany]

Gorgon *gör'gən*, *n* one of three fabled female monsters (Stheno, Euryale and Medusa), of horrible and petrifying aspect, winged, and with hissing serpents for hair (*Gr mythol*); (*usu* without *cap*) anybody, *esp* a woman, who is very ugly or formidable. — Also *adj*. — *n* **gorgoneion** (-*ī'on*) a mask of a gorgon: — *pl* **gorgonei'a**. — *adj* **gorgō'nian**. — *vt* **gor'gonize** or **-ise** to turn to stone. [Gr *Gorgō*, pl *-ones*, from *gorgos* grim]

Gorgonia *gör-gō'ni-ə*, *n* a genus of sea-fans or horny corals. — *adj* **gorgo'nian**. — *n* a horny coral. [L *gorgonia* coral, from *Gorgō* Gorgon (because of its appearance after petrifying in the air)]

Gorgonzola *gör-gən-zō'lə*, *n* a blue cheese made from cow's milk. [From *Gorgonzola*, a small Italian town near Milan]

gorilla *gor-il'ə*, *n* a great African ape, the largest anthropoid; a thug (*slang*). — *adj* **gorill'ian** or **gorill'ine**. — *adj* **gorill'oid**. [Gr *Gorillai* (pl), reported by Hanno the Carthaginian as a tribe of hairy women; supposed to be an African word]

goring. See **gore**[2].

gorm, **gormless**, etc. See **gaum**[1,2].

gormand *gör'mənd*, *n* older form of **gourmand**. — *n* **gor'mandise** (-*dīz*) gourmandise; gluttony; gormandizing. — *n* **gor'mandism** gluttony. — *vi* **gor'mandize** or **-ise** to eat hastily or voraciously. — *n* **gor'mandīzer** or **-s-**. — *n* **gor'mandizing** or **-s-**. [See **gourmand**]

gorp[1] *görp*, (*US*) *n* a mixture of raisins, nuts, etc providing a high-energy snack for eg hikers. [Origin uncertain]

gorp[2]. A variant (*dialect*) spelling of **gawp**.

gorse *görs*, *n* any prickly papilionaceous shrub of the genus *Ulex*, with yellow flowers. — Also **gosse** (*Shakesp*). — *adj* **gors'y**. [OE *gorst*]

gorsedd *gor'sedh*, *n* (often with *cap*) a meeting of bards and druids, *esp* such an assembly prior to an eisteddfod. [Welsh, throne]

gorsoon. See **gossoon**.

gory. See **gore**[1].

gosh *gosh*, (*colloq*) *interj* a mild substitute or euphemism for **God**.

goshawk *gos'hök*, *n* a short-winged hawk, once used for hunting wild geese and other fowl, not having a toothed bill like the falcons proper. [OE *gōshafoc*, from *gōs* goose, and *hafoc* hawk]

Goshen *gō'shən*, *n* a happy place of light and plenty. [From the abode of the Israelites during the plague of darkness in Egypt, Exodus 10.23]

gosht *gosht*, (*Ind cookery*) *n* meat. [Hindi and Urdu]

goslarite *gos'lər-īt*, *n* a rare mineral, hydrated zinc sulphate, found at *Goslar* in the Harz Mts, central Germany.

gosling *goz'ling*, *n* a young goose. — *n* **gos'let** an Eastern dwarf goose (*Nettapus*). [OE *gōs* goose, with double dimin *-l-ing*]

gospel *gos'pəl*, *n* the teaching of Christ; a narrative of the life of Christ, *esp* one of those included in the New Testament, Matthew, Mark, Luke and John; the principles set forth in these gospels; the stated portion of these read at a religious service; any strongly advocated principle or system; absolute truth (*colloq*); a type of ardently religious jazz music (*esp* songs) originating amongst the Black population of the southern US. — *vt* (*Shakesp*) to instruct in the gospel. — *vt* **gos'pelize** or **-ise** to evangelize (*rare*); to square with the gospel (*obs*). — Also **gos'pellize** or **-ise**. — *n* **gos'peller** a preacher; an evangelist; a Wycliffite, Protestant or Puritan (often in derision; *hist*); a person who reads the gospel in church. — **gospel side** the north side or gospeller's side of the altar. [OE *godspel(l)*, a translation of L *evangelium*, from *gōd* good (with shortened vowel being understood as *God* God) and *spel(l)* story]

Gosplan *gos'plan*, *n* the former Soviet state economic planning department. [Russ, *Gos*udarstvennaya *plan*ovaya Comissiya, state planning committee]

gospodar. See **hospodar**.

Goss *gos*, (*antiques*) *n* white china vessels and trinkets bearing the crest of a town, etc, much sold as holiday mementos. [From W H *Goss* (1833–1906), manufacturer, of Stoke-on-Trent]

gossamer *gos'ə-mər*, *n* very fine spider-threads that float in the air or form webs on bushes in fine weather; any very thin material. — *adj* light, flimsy. — *adj* **goss'amery** like gossamer; flimsy. [ME *gossomer*; perh *goose-summer*, a St Martin's summer, when geese are in season and gossamer abounds; cf Ger *Sommerfäden*, summer-threads, also *Mädchensommer* maiden-summer]

gossan or **gozzan** *gos'ən*, *n* decomposed rock, largely quartz impregnated with iron compounds, at the outcrop of a vein *esp* of metallic sulphides. [Cornish miner's term; origin unknown]

gosse *gos*, (*Shakesp*) *n obs* spelling of **gorse**.

gossip *gos'ip*, *n* idle talk; tittle-tattle; scandalous rumours; easy familiar writing; someone who goes about telling and hearing news, or idle, malicious and scandalous tales; a familiar friend (*archaic*; *Spenser* **goss'ib**); a woman friend who comes to attend a birth (*archaic*); a sponsor at baptism (in relation to child, parent, or other sponsor) (*archaic* or *dialect*). — *vi* to run about telling idle or malicious tales; to talk a lot, prattle; to chat. — *vt* to tell or spread as gossip; to stand godfather or gossip to (*obs*; *Shakesp* and *Milton*): — *pa t* **goss'iped**. — *n* and *adj* **goss'iping**. — *n* **goss'ipry**. — *adj* **goss'ipy**. — **gossip column** the newspaper column written by a gossip-writer; **gossip columnist**; **goss'ip-monger** a person who spreads gossip and rumours; **goss'ip-writer** a journalist who writes articles about the lives and loves of well-known people. [OE *godsibb* godfather, one who is **sib in God**, ie spiritually related]

gossoon *go-sōōn'*, or **gorsoon** *gör'*, *n* a boy or boy-servant. [Anglo-Ir, from Fr *garçon* boy]

Gossypium *go-sip'i-əm*, *n* a tropical genus of the mallow family, yielding cotton. — *adj* **goss'ypine** cottony. — *n* **goss'ypol** a poisonous principle in cotton-seed. [L *gossypion*]

got. See under **get**.

Goth *goth*, *n* a member of an ancient Germanic people, originally settled on the southern coasts of the Baltic, migrating to Dacia in the 3c, and later founding kingdoms in Italy, southern France and Spain; a rude or uncivilized person, a barbarian; a Gothicist (*hist*); a performer or fan of Gothic music, or the style of music itself. — *adj* **Goth'ic** of the Goths or their language; barbarous; romantic; denoting the 12–16c style of architecture in churches, etc, with high-pointed arches, clustered columns, etc (*orig* applied in reproach at the time of the Renaissance); generally, the style, related to this, favoured in all the fine arts during this time; black-letter (*printing*); a square-cut type without serifs (*US*); *orig* applied to 18c tales or novels of mystery with gloomy sinister backgrounds, now denoting psychological horror-tales (also **Gothick** or **goth'ic**); lurid, extravagantly macabre, grotesque (*slang*); (of a music and fashion cult of the late 1980s, etc) characterized by a blend of punk and heavy metal styles, dark melancholy themes, severe black dress and white make-up. — *n* the language of the Goths, an East Germanic tongue; Gothic architecture. — *n* **Goth'icism** (*-sizm*) a Gothic idiom or style of building; rudeness of manners. — *n* **Goth'icist** an adherent or scholar of Gothic style or idiom. — *vt* **goth'icize** or **-ise** (*-sīz*) to make Gothic. — *n* and *adj* **Goth'ick** (denoting) a style of architecture (c. 1720–1840) in which the Gothic style of the middle ages was imitated; (of 18c and modern tales, etc) Gothic. — **Gothic revival** the more serious revival of the Gothic style of architecture which followed the Gothick, in Britain and the USA mid-18c to mid-19c. [The native names *Gutans* (sing *Guta*) and *Gutōs* (sing *Guts*), and *Gutthiuda* people of the Goths; Latinized as *Gothī*, *Gotthī*; Gr *Gothoi*, *Gotthoi*; OE *Gotan* (sing *Gota*)]

Gothamite *gōt'* or *got'əm-īt*, *n* a simpleton; a wiseacre; (*goth'* or *gōth'*) a New Yorker (*US*). — *n* **Goth'amist** (*obs*; *gōt'* or *got'*) a simpleton. [From *Gotham*, a village in Nottinghamshire, with which name are connected many of the simpleton stories of immemorial antiquity]

Gothic, **Gothicism**, **Gothick**, etc. See **Goth**.

göthite. See **goethite**.

gotta *got'ə*, (*colloq*) a contraction of **got to**.

gotten. See under **get**.

Götterdämmerung *gœ-tər-dem'ə-rōōng*, (*Ger mythol*) *n* the ultimate defeat of the gods by evil, literally the twilight of the gods.

gouache *gōō-äsh* or *gōō'äsh*, or (chiefly *NAm*) *gwäsh*, *n* watercolour painting with opaque colours, mixed with water, honey and gum, presenting a matt surface; work painted according to this method; watercolour paint made opaque in such a way. [Fr]

Gouda *gow'də*, *n* a kind of mild cheese *orig* from *Gouda* in the Netherlands.

gouge[1] *gowj*, also *gōōj*, *n* a chisel with a hollow blade for cutting grooves or holes. — *vt* to scoop out, as with a gouge; to force out (eg the eye with the thumb). [OFr, from LL *gubia* a kind of chisel]

gouge[2] *gōōj*, (*obs*; *Scott*) *n* a wench. [OFr]

gougère *gōō-jer'*, *n* a kind of choux pastry, the dough of which has been mixed with grated cheese prior to baking. [Fr]

goujeers (*obs*) an editor's would-be improvement upon **goodyear** (qv) from a spurious Fr *goujère*, supposedly venereal disease.

goujons *gōō-zhɔ̃*, *n pl* small strips of fish coated in flour and deep-fried. [Fr]

gouk. See **gowk**.

goulash *gōō'lash*, *n* a stew of beef, vegetables, *esp* onions, and paprika; a re-deal of cards that have been arranged in suits and order of value, so many (as eg five) cards at a time (*bridge*). [Hung *gulyás* (*hús*) herdsman (meat)]

goura *gow'rə*, *n* (with *cap*) a New Guinea genus of beautifully crested, ground-loving pigeons; a pigeon of the genus. [From a native name]

gourami *gōōr-äm'i*, *n* a large freshwater food fish (*Osphomenus olfax*) of SE Asia; any of a variety of often colourful, smaller fishes, popular as aquarium fishes. — Also **goram'y**, **guram'i**. [Malay *gurāmī*]

gourd *gōōrd*, *gōrd* or *görd*, *n* a large hard-rinded fleshy fruit characteristic of the cucumber family; the rind of one used as a bottle, cup, etc; a gourd-bearing plant. — **gourd'-worm** a fluke-worm resembling a gourd-seed, *esp* the liver-fluke. [OFr *gourde*, contracted from *cougourde*, from L *cucurbita* a gourd]

gourde *gōōrd*, *n* the standard monetary unit of Haiti (100 centimes). [Fr fem of *gourd*, from L *gurdus* dull, stupid]

gourds *gōrdz*, *gördz* or *gōōrdz*, (*obs*) *n pl* a kind of false dice. [Cf OFr *gourd* swindle]

gourdy *gōrd'i*, also *görd'* or *gōōrd'*, *adj* (of a horse) swollen in the legs. — *n* **gourd'iness**. [OFr *gourdi* swollen]

gourmand *gōōr'mənd* or *-mã*, *n* a person who eats greedily; a glutton; a lover of good fare. — *adj* voracious; gluttonous. — *n* **gourmandise** (*gōōr'mən-dīz* or *gōōr-mã-dēz*) indulgence in good eating; a discerning appreciation of good food and wines; voracious greed (*Spenser*). — *n* **gour'mandism**. [Fr; cf **gormand**]

gourmet *gōōr'mā* or *-me*, *n* a connoisseur of good food and wines, an epicure. — *adj* of, for or befitting the gourmet or the gourmet's taste. [Fr, a wine-merchant's assistant]

goustrous *gows'trəs*, (*Scot*) *adj* boisterous, rude.

gousty *gows'ti*, (*Scot*) *adj* dreary; desolate; empty.

gout[1] *gowt*, *n* a drop, spot (*archaic*); a disease in which excess of uric acid in the blood is deposited as urates in the joints, etc, with swelling *esp* of the big toe; a related disease of poultry affecting the viscera; a swelling of the stalk in wheat and other grasses, caused by goutfly larvae. — *n* **gout'iness**. — *adj* **gout'y** relating to gout;

diseased with or subject to gout. — **gout'fly** a fly (*Chlorops*) whose larvae cause gout by boring in wheat, etc; **gout'weed** or **gout'wort** an umbelliferous weed, (*Aegopodium podagraria*), long supposed to be good for gout, also called bishop('s)weed or goatweed. [OFr *goutte*, from L *gutta* a drop, the disease once supposed to be caused by a defluxion of humours]

gout² or properly **goût** *gōō*, *n* taste; relish. [Fr *goût*, from L *gustus* taste]

goutte *gōōt*, (*Fr*) *n* a drop (of liquid); a droplet shape (*heraldry*). — **goutte à goutte** drop by drop.

gouvernante *gōō-ver-nät*, *n* a female ruler (*obs*); a housekeeper (*archaic*); a duenna (*archaic*); a governess (*archaic*). [Fr]

Gov. *abbrev*: Governor; (or **Govt**) Government.

gov. See **governor** under **govern**.

govern *guv'ərn*, *vt* to direct; to control; to rule with authority; to determine; to determine the case of (*gram*); to require as the case of a noun or pronoun (*gram*). — *vi* to exercise authority; to administer the laws. — *adj* **gov'ernable**. — *n* **gov'ernall** (*Spenser*) government, management. — *n* **gov'ernance** government; control; direction; behaviour (*obs*). — *n* **gov'ernante** (*obs*) a gouvernante. — *n* **gov'erness** a female governor (*archaic*; *fig*, *Milton*); a woman entrusted with the care and education of a child or children, *esp* one employed in a private household (**nursery governess** one having charge of young children only, tending as well as teaching them). — *vi* to act as governess. — *vt* to be governess to. — *adj* **gov'ernessy** like a governess, *esp* prim. — *adj* **gov'erning** having control. — *n* **government** (*guv'ər(n)-mənt*) a ruling or managing; control; system of governing; the body of persons authorized to administer the laws, or to govern a state (often with *cap*, *esp* if applied to that of a specific country); tenure of office of someone who governs; an administrative division (*archaic*); territory (*archaic*); the power of one word in determining the case of another (*gram*); conduct (*Shakesp*). — *adj* of or pursued by government. — *adj* **governmental** (*-ment'l*) pertaining to government. — *n* **gov'ernor** a real or titular ruler, *esp* of a state, province or colony; the head of an institution or a member of its ruling body; the commander of a fortress; (usu *guv'nər'*) a father, chief or master, applied more generally in kindly, usually ironically respectful, address (sometimes shortened to **gov** or **guv** *guv*; *slang*); a regulator, or contrivance for maintaining uniform velocity with a varying resistance (*machinery*); a tutor (*obs*); a pilot (of a vessel) (*obs*; *Bible*). — *n* **gov'ernorship**. — **governess car** or **cart** (*hist*) a light low two-wheeled vehicle with face-to-face seats at the sides; **governing-bod'y** a board in whom is vested the authority to supervise and regulate the affairs of an establishment or of a particular field of activity; **governmental atonement** see **Grotian**; **government broker** a stockbroker who buys and sells gilt-edged securities on the stock exchange on behalf of the Bank of England; **government expenditure** that part of public expenditure incurred by central government (as opposed to local government authorities and non-government public offices); **government stock** consols, savings bonds and other gilt-edged securities; **governor-gen'eral** *orig* the supreme governor of a country, etc, with deputy governors under him; the representative of the British crown in Commonwealth countries which recognize the monarch as head of state: — *pl* **governors-gen'eral**; **governor-gen'eralship**. [OFr *governer*, from L *gubernāre*, from Gr *kybernaein* to steer]

Govt. See **Gov**.

gowan *gow'ən*, (*Scot* and *NEng dialect*) *n* the wild daisy; the ox-eye daisy (also **horse'-gowan**). — *adj* **gow'aned**. — *adj* **gow'any**. — **luck'engowan** the globeflower. [Apparently a form of **gollan(d)**]

gowd, **gowdspink**. Scots form of **gold¹**, **goldspink**.

gowf *gowf*, (*Scot*) *vt* to strike, cuff. — *vi* to golf. — *n* golf. — *n* **gowf'er** golfer. — **gowf'-ba'** golf-ball. [See **golf**]

gowk or **gouk** *gowk*, (*Scot and NEng dialect*) *n* a cuckoo; a fool; an April fool. [ON *gaukr*; OE *gēac*]

gowl *gowl*, (*Scot and NEng dialect*) *vi* to cry or howl. [ON *gaula*]

gowlan(d). See **gollan**.

gown *gown*, *n* a loose flowing outer garment; a woman's dress; an academic, clerical or official robe; the members of a university as opposed to the townspeople (see under **town**). — *vt* and *vi* to dress in a gown. — *vt* to invest or provide with a gown. — *adj* **gowned**. — **gown'boy** a school foundationer (as of Charterhouse), wearing a gown; **gown'man** or **gowns'man** someone who wears a gown, eg a divine or lawyer, or *esp* a member of an English university; a civilian (as distinct from a soldier) (*hist*). [OFr *goune*, from LL *gunna*; origin unknown]

gowpen *gowp'ən*, (*Scot*) *n* the hollow of the two hands held together; a double handful (now *usu* used in *pl*). — *n* **gow'penful**. [ON *gaupn*]

goy *goi*, *n* a non-Jew, a Gentile: — *pl* **goy'im** (*goi'im*) or **goys**. — *adj* **goy'ish** or **goyisch** (*goi'ish*). [Heb, (non-Jewish) nation]

gozzan. See **gossan**.

GP *abbrev*: Gallup Poll; General Practitioner; *Gloria Patri* (*L*) glory to the Father; graduated pension; Grand Prix.

GPI *abbrev*: general paralysis of the insane.

GPO *abbrev*: General Post Office.

GR *abbrev*: (*L*) Georgius Rex (see **GRI**); Greece (IVR).

Gr. *abbrev*: Greek.

gr. *abbrev*: grain(s); gram(s) or gramme(s); grey; gross.

Graafian *grä'fi-ən*, *adj* pertaining to the Dutch anatomist Regnier de *Graaf* (1641–73) who discovered the **Graafian follicles** in which the ova are contained in the ovaries of higher vertebrates.

graal. See **grail³**.

grab¹ *grab*, *n* an Eastern coasting vessel. [Ar *ghurāb*]

grab² *grab*, *vt* to seize or grasp suddenly; to lay hands on; to impress or interest (*slang*). — *vi* to clutch: — *pr p* **grabb'ing**; *pa t* and *pa p* **grabbed**. — *n* a sudden grasp or clutch; unscrupulous seizure; a mechanical double scoop hinged like a pair of jaws, used in excavating, etc; anything similar; a simple card-game depending upon prompt claiming. — *n* **grabb'er** a person who or thing which grabs; an avaricious person. — **grab'-bag** a bag or other receptacle for miscellaneous articles; one from which gifts are drawn (*US*). — Also *fig*. — **grabbing crane** an excavator consisting of a crane and a large grab, so hinged as to scoop into the earth as it is lifted. — **how does that grab you**? (*slang*) what's your reaction to that?; **up for grabs** (*slang*) (ready) for the taking, for sale, etc. [Cf Swed *grabba* to grasp]

grabble *grab'l*, *vt* and *vi* to grope; to scramble; to struggle with (somebody or something). — *n* **grabb'ler**. [Frequentative of **grab²**]

graben *grä'bən*, (*geol*) *n* a rift valley (qv). [Ger, ditch]

GRACE *grās*, (*telecomm*) *abbrev*: group routing and charging equipment (an automatic telephone system by which all calls, trunk as well as local, can be dialled directly by subscribers, and by which all STD calls are charged).

grace *grās*, *n* easy elegance in form or manner; any unassumingly attractive or pleasing personal quality; favour; kindness; pardon (*archaic*); the undeserved mercy of God; divine influence; eternal life or salvation; a short prayer before or after a meal; an ornament (eg trill, turn, acciacciatura) consisting of notes additional to the melody or harmony (*music*); an act or decree of the governing body of an English university; a ceremonious title in addressing a duke or duchess, an archbishop, or formerly a king or queen (*usu* with *cap*, as *Your Grace*, *His/Her Grace*); a short period of time in hand before a deadline is reached (see **days of grace** below); (in *pl*) favour, friendship (with *good*); (with *cap* in *pl*) the three sister goddesses in whom beauty was deified (the Greek Charites), Euphrosyne, Aglaia and Thalia (*classical mythol*). — *vt* to mark with favour; to adorn. — *adj* **graced** (*Shakesp*, etc) favoured, endowed with grace or graces, virtuous, chaste. — *adj* **grace'ful** elegant and easy; marked by propriety or fitness, becoming; having or conferring grace, in any sense. — *adv* **grace'fully**. — *n* **grace'-fulness**. — *adj* **grace'less** lacking grace or excellence; without mercy or favour (*obs*); depraved (*archaic*); indecorous. — *adv* **grace'lessly**. — *n* **grace'lessness**. — *adj* **grace-and-fa'vour** (of a residence) belonging to the British sovereign and granted rent-free to a person of importance (also with *caps*). — **grace cup** a cup or health drunk at the end of a feast or meal, after the final grace; **grace note** (*music*) a note introduced as an embellishment, not being essential to the harmony or melody. — **airs and graces** affectedly elegant and refined manners and behaviour; **days of grace** days allowed for the payment of a note or bill of exchange after it falls due (in England before 1972 legally three days); such an allowable period after which an insurance premium becomes due; **fall from grace** to backslide, to lapse from the state of grace and salvation, or from favour; **saving grace** divine grace so bestowed as to lead to salvation (*Christian theol*); a compensating virtue or quality (*colloq*); **take heart of grace** (*archaic*) to pluck up courage (origin of 'of grace' uncertain); **with (a) good** (or **bad**) **grace** in amiable (or ungracious) fashion; **year of grace** year of the Christian era, AD. [Fr *grâce*, from L *grātia* favour, from *grātus* agreeable]

grâce à Dieu *gräs a dyø*, (*Fr*) thanks to God.

gracile *gras'īl* or *-il*, *adj* slender; gracefully slight in form. — *n* **gracil'ity**. [L *gracilis* slender]

graciosity. See under **gracious**.

gracioso *grā-shi-ō'sō* or (Sp) *grä-thyō'sō*, *n* a favourite (*obs*); a clown in Spanish comedy: — *pl* **graciō'sos**. [Sp, gracious]

gracious *grā'shəs*, *adj* full of, or characterized by, grace and kindness; affable; of becoming demeanour; used as an epithet of royal acts or inclination; elegant, tasteful, *esp* classically so; favourable (*archaic*); acceptable (*obs*); proceeding from divine favour (*obs*). — *n* used as a substitute for God. — *adv* **grā'ciously**. — *n* **grā'ciousness** or **gracios'ity**. — **gracious living** (living in) conditions of ease, plenty, and good taste. — **good gracious** or **gracious me** exclamations of surprise. [L *grātiōsus*, from *grātia* favour]

grackle *grak'l*, *n* a myna (hill myna) or similar bird; an American 'blackbird' of the family Icteridae. — Also (now rarely) **grak'le**. [L *grāculus* jackdaw]

grad *grad*, (*colloq*) *n* a graduate.

gradate, etc. See **grade**.

graddan *grad'ən*, (*Scot*) *n* parched grain. — *vt* to parch in the husk. [Gaelic *gradan*]

grade *grād*, *n* a degree or step in quality, rank or dignity; a stage of advancement; rank; a yearly stage in education (*NAm*); a pupil's mark of proficiency (*orig US*); (in *pl*, with *the*) elementary school, grade school (*NAm*); position in a scale; a class, or position in a class, according to value, merit, quality; position in an ablaut series (*philol*); one-hundredth part of a right angle (*math*); gradient or slope (chiefly *US*); an inclined or level stretch of road or railway (*US*); a class of animals produced by crossing a breed with one purer. — *vt* to arrange according to grade; to assign a grade to; to adjust the gradients of. — *vi* to change gradually from one grade, level, value, etc to another; (of produce, etc) to take or fall within a (specified) grade (sometimes with *out*). — *adj* of improved stock. — *adj* **grā'dable** able to be graded; of or relating to a word depending on a standard, eg *clever*, *narrow* (*linguistics*; also *n*). — *vt* and *vi* **gradate** (*grə-dāt'*) to shade off, change grade, values, etc imperceptibly. — *vt* to arrange according to grades. — *adv* **gradā'tim** (L *gradä'tim*) step by step. — *n* **gradā'tion** a degree or step; a rising step by step; progress from one degree or state to another; position attained; state of being arranged in ranks; a gradual shift in grade, etc; a diatonic succession of chords (*music*); a gradual shading off; ablaut (*philol*). — *adj* **gradā'tional**. — *adv* **gradā'-tionally**. — *adj* **gradā'tioned** formed by gradations or stages. — *adj* **gradatory** (*grad'ət-ə-ri*) proceeding step by step; adapted for walking. — *n* **grād'er** a person who, or thing which, grades; a machine used to create a flat surface for road-building; (in combination, as eg *sixthgrader*) a school pupil in a specified grade (*NAm*). — **grade crossing** (*NAm*) a level crossing; **graded-index fibre** a fibre in an optical-fibre cable, in which the refractive index of the glass decreases gradually or in small steps from the central core to the periphery; **graded post** (in British schools) a post with some special responsibility, and so extra payment; **grade school** (*NAm*) elementary school corresponding broadly to the British primary school, often with a nursery school element; **grade separation** (*US*) a crossing at which one road, etc, is an underpass or an overpass; **grading system** a system to establish the rate at which an employee will be paid on a company's incremental payscales (taking eg qualifications, experience and age into account). — **at grade** (*US*) on the same level; **make the grade** *orig* to succeed in climbing a steep hill; to overcome obstacles; to succeed; to be up to standard. [L *gradus* a step, from *gradī* to step]

gradely *grād'li*, (*dialect*) *adj* decent; proper; fit; fine. — *adv* properly; readily (*obs*); very. — Also **graith'ly**. [See **graith**]

Gradgrind *grad'grīnd*, *n* a person who regulates all human things by rule and compass and the mechanical application of statistics, allowing nothing for sentiment, emotion and individuality. — *n* **Gradgrind'ery**. [From Thomas *Gradgrind* in Dickens's *Hard Times*]

gradient *grād'i-ənt*, *n* the degree of slope as compared with the horizontal; rate of change in any quantity with distance (eg in barometer readings); an incline. — *adj* rising or falling by degrees; walking, taking steps with the feet; sloping uniformly. — *n* **grād'ienter** (*US*; *surveying*) an instrument for determining grades. [L *gradīens*, *-entis*, pr p of *gradī* to step]

gradin *grād'in*, or **gradine** *grə-dēn'*, *n* a rising tier of seats, as in an amphitheatre; a raised step or ledge behind an altar. — *n* **gradino** (*grə-dēn'o*; *Ital*) a decoration for an altar gradin: — *pl* **gradin'i** (*-dēn'ē*). [Ital *gradino*, dimin of *grado* step]

gradiometer *grād-i-om'ə-tər*, *n* a magnetometer for measuring the gradient of a magnetic field, etc. [*gradi*ent and **-meter**]

gradual *grad'ū-əl*, *adj* advancing or happening by grades or degrees; (of a slope) gentle and slow. — *n* (in the RC church) the portion of the mass between the epistle and the gospel, formerly always sung from the steps of the altar; a book containing the sung parts of the mass, also called a **grail**. — *n* **grad'ūalism** the principle, policy or phenomenon of proceeding by degrees. — *adj* and *n* **grad'ūalist**. — *adj* **gradualis'tic**. — *n* **gradūality**. — *adv* **grad'ually**. [Med L *graduālis*, from L *gradus* a step]

graduate *grad'ū-āt*, *vt* to divide into regular intervals; to mark by degrees; to proportion; to confer a university, etc degree upon (*archaic*, except *NAm*). — *vi* to pass by grades; to receive a degree from a higher-education institution. — *n* (*grad'ū-ət*) a person who has obtained a degree from a university, college or polytechnic; a person who has completed a course in any educational or training institution (*NAm*). — *n* **grad'uand** a person about to receive a degree from a higher-education institution. — *adj* **grad'ūated** (of a thermometer, etc) marked with degrees. — *n* **grad'ūateship**. — *n* **gradu-ā'tion** division into proportionate or regular sections, for measurement, etc; a mark or all the marks made for this purpose; the gaining or (*US*) conferring of a degree from a higher-education institution; the ceremony marking this. — *n* **grad'ūātor** an instrument for dividing lines at regular intervals; someone who or something which graduates. — **graduated pension scheme** a government pension scheme in addition to the basic old age pension, to which employees make contributions in relation to their earnings, and employers contribute corresponding sums. [Med L *graduāri*, *-ātus* to take a degree, from *gradus* a step]

gradus *grād'əs*, *n* a dictionary of Greek or Latin prosody, the term taken from *Gradus ad Parnassum* a step, or stairs, to Parnassus. [L]

Graeae or **Graiae** *grī'ī*, (*Gr mythol*) *n pl* three sea-goddesses, sisters of the Gorgons, having the form of old women who shared between them a single eye and a single tooth. [Gr *graia* old woman]

Graecize or **-ise** or (*esp NAm*) **grecize** *grē'sīz*, *vt* to make Greek; to hellenize. — *vi* to become Greek; to conform to Greek ways or idioms; to use the Greek language. — *n* **Grae'cism** or (*esp NAm*) **Gre'cism** a Greek idiom; the Greek spirit; a following of the Greeks. — *adj* **Graeco-Ro'man** or (*esp NAm*) **Greco-** (*grē'kō-*) of or pertaining to both Greece and Rome, *esp* the art of Greece under Roman domination; applied to a mode of wrestling imagined to be that of the Greeks and Romans. [L *Graecus*, from Gr *Graikos*, Greek; *graikizein* to speak Greek]

Graf *gräf*, (*Ger*) *n* a count, earl: — *fem* **Gräfin** (*grā'fin*).

graff[1] *gräf*, (*Scot*; now *obs*) *n* a variant of **grave**[1].

graff[2] *gräf*, *n* and *v* an older, now *archaic*, form of **graft**[1].

graffito *gräf-fē'tō*, *n* a mural scribbling or drawing, as by schoolboys and idlers at Pompeii, Rome, and other ancient cities (*antiq*); sgraffito (*art*). — *n pl* or (loosely) *n sing* **graffi'ti** (*-tē*) scribblings or drawings, often indecent, found on public buildings, in lavatories, etc. — *n* **graffi'tist**. — **graffiti artist**. [Ital, from Gr *graphein* to write]

graft[1] *gräft*, *n* a small piece of a plant or animal inserted in another individual or another part so as to come into organic union; any transplanted organ or tissue (*med*); the act of inserting a part in this way; the place of junction of stock and scion (*bot*); the double plant composed of stock and scion; a sucker, branch or plant (*obs*). — *vt* to insert a graft in; to insert (an organ, piece of tissue, plant) as a graft; to cuckoldize (*obs*). — *vi* to insert grafts. — *n* **graft'er**. — *n* **graft'ing** the action of the verb; correction of a section of a stencil by cutting it to remove the unwanted section, and replacing it with a slightly larger piece of new stencil using stencil correcting fluid to glue it to the original; lengthening a timber by jointing another piece on to it. — **graft chimera** (*bot*) a chimera in which the genetically distinct cell types derive from different species; **graft hybrid** a hybrid form produced, as some have believed, by grafting; a patchwork compound of two species propagated from the junction of tissues in a graft, each part retaining the specific character proper to the cells from which it arose; **graft-versus-host disease** a graft-versus-host reaction of transposed or transplanted lymphocytes against antigens belonging to the host, a major complication of bone marrow grafting (*abbrev* **GVHD**); **graft-versus-host reaction** the reaction occurring when lymphocytes in a tissue graft (*esp* bone marrow) respond to antigens present in the recipient, resulting in attack and destruction of the host tissue (*abbrev* **GVH**). [From older **graff**, from OFr *graffe* (Fr *greffe*), from L *graphium*, from Gr *graphion*, *grapheion* a style, pencil, from *graphein* to write]

graft[2] *gräft*, *n* a ditch, excavation (*dialect*); a spade's depth; a ditching spade. — *vi* to dig (*dialect*). — *n* **graft'er**. [Cf ON *gröftr* digging]

graft[3] *gräft*, *n* hard work (*colloq*); a criminal's special branch of practice (*slang*); illicit profit by corrupt means, *esp* in public life (*slang*); corruption in official life (*slang*). — *vt* to work hard (*colloq*); to engage in graft or corrupt practices (*slang*). — *n* **graft'er**. [Perh **graft**[2] or an extended use of **graft**[1] for something inserted, supplementary]

graham flour *grā'əm flowr*, (mainly *US*) *n* a type of wheat flour similar to whole-wheat flour. — **graham bread** or **crackers** a type of bread, or crackers, made with graham flour. [After S *Graham* (1794–1851), US dietician]

Graiae. See **Graeae**.

grail[1] *grāl*, (*poetic*) *n* gravel. — Also (*Spenser*) **graile** or **grayle**. [Perh **gravel**; or OFr *graile* (Fr *grêle*) hail, from L *gracilis* slender]

grail[2]. See **gradual** (*n*).

grail[3] *grāl*, *n* (often **holy grail** or **Holy Grail**) in medieval legend, the platter (sometimes supposed to be a cup) used by Christ at the Last Supper, in which Joseph of Arimathaea caught his blood at the cross, said to have been brought by Joseph to Glastonbury, and the object of quests by King Arthur's Knights; a cherished ambition or goal. — Also (*archaic*) **graal** or **grayle**. [OFr *graal* or *grael* a flat dish, from LL *gradālis* a flat dish, ultimately from Gr *krātēr* a bowl]

grain[1] *grān*, *n* a single small hard seed; corn, in general; a hard particle; a very small quantity; the smallest British weight (the average weight of a seed of corn) = $\frac{1}{7000}$ of a pound avoirdupois; (in *pl*) refuse malt after brewing or distilling; the arrangement, size and direction of the particles, fibres, or plates of stone, wood, etc; texture; a granular surface; the particles in a photographic emulsion which go to compose the photograph; dried bodies of kermes or of cochineal insects, once thought to be seeds (*hist*); the red dye made from these (*hist*); any fast dye (to *dye in grain* is to dye deeply, also to *dye in the wool*; *hist*); dye in general (*obs*); innate quality or character. — *vt* to form into grains, cause to granulate; to paint in imitation of grain; to dye in grain; (in tanning) to take the hair off. — *n* **grain'age** duties on grain. — *adj* **grained** granulated; subjected to graining; having a grain; rough; furrowed. — *n* **grain'er** a person who grains; a paint-brush for graining. — *n* **grain'ing** (*specif*) painting to imitate the grain of wood; a process in tanning in which the grain of the leather is raised. — *adj* **grain'y** having grains or kernels; having large grains, so indistinct (*photog*). — **grain alcohol** alcohol made by the fermentation of grain; **grain amaranth** see **amarant**. — **against the grain** against the fibre of the wood; against the natural temper or inclination; **grains of Paradise** the aromatic and pungent seeds of an African Amomum; **in grain** in substance, in essence; **take with a grain of salt** see under **salt**[1]. [Fr *grain*, collective *graine*, from L *grānum* seed and *grāna* (orig pl); similar to **corn**[1]]

grain[2] *grān*, *n* a branch, prong or fork (*dialect*); (in *pl*, used as *sing*) a kind of pronged harpoon. [ON *grein*]

graine *grān*, *n* silkworm eggs. [Fr]

graining[1] *grān'ing*, *n* (in Lancashire) dace, though once thought a separate species. [Origin unknown]

graining[2], **grainy**, etc. See **grain**[1].

graip *grāp*, (*Scot* and *N Eng dialect*) *n* a three- or four-pronged fork used for lifting dung or digging potatoes. [A form of **grope**; cf Swed *grep*, Dan *greb*]

graith *grath*, (*Scot*) *n* apparatus; equipment. — *vt* (*obs*) to make ready, to dress. — *adj* and *adv* **graith'ly** an older form of **gradely**. [ON *greithr* ready; cf OE *gerǣde* ready]

grakle. See **grackle**.

Grallae *gral'ē* or **Grallatores** *-ə-tō'rēz*, or *-tö'*, *n pl* in old classifications, an order of wading birds. — *adj* **grallatō'rial**. [L *grallātor* a stilt-walker, from *grallae* stilts, from *gradī* to step]

gralloch *gral'əhh*, *n* a deer's entrails. — *vt* to disembowel (deer). [Gaelic *grealach*]

gram[1] *gram* or **grame** *grām*, (*obs*) *n* anger; grief, trouble. [OE *grama*, anger]

gram[2] *gram*, *n* the chick-pea; a pulse generally. — **black gram** see **urd**. [Port *grão* (sometimes *gram*), from L *grānum* a grain]

gram[3] or **gramme** *gram*, *n* a unit of mass in the metric system, formerly that of a cubic centimetre of water at 4°C, now a thousandth part of the International Prototype Kilogram (see **kilogram**). — **gram-at'om** or **gram-atomic weight**, and **gram-mol'ecule** or **gram-molecular weight** the quantity of an element, or a compound, whose mass in grams is equal to its atomic weight and molecular weight respectively (a now discarded concept: see **mole**[1]); **gram-equiv'alent** or **gram-equivalent weight** the quantity of a substance whose mass in grams is equal to its equivalent weight. [Fr *gramme*, from L *gramma*, from Gr *gramma* a letter, a small weight]

gram[4] *gräm*, *n* an Indian village. [Hindi]

-gram *-gram*, *combining form* denoting something written or drawn to form a record; a greetings message delivered by a messenger in a particular costume and in an appropriately absurd, amusing or humorous manner (eg *gorillagram*, *kissogram*, *strippagram*, *Tarzanogram*) to surprise and embarrass the recipient on a special occasion. [Gr *gramma* letter; later use follows 'singing tele*gram*']

grama *grä'mə* or **grama grass** (*gräs*), *n* an American pasture grass (*Bouteloua*) with spikelets ranged unilaterally. [Sp, from L *grāmen* grass]

gramary or **gramarye** *gram'ə-ri*, (*archaic*) *n* magic; enchantment. [ME *gramery* skill in grammar, hence magic; see **grammar**, **glamour**]

gramash. See **gamash**.

grame. See **gram**[1].

gramercy *grə-mûr'si*, (*obs*) *interj* great thanks. — *n* thanks. [OFr *grant merci* great thanks]

gramicidin *gram-i-sī'din*, *n* an antibiotic obtained from certain bacteria, used against Gram-positive bacteria. — Also **gramicidin D**. — *adj* **Gram-neg'ative** (also **gram-**) losing a stain of methyl violet and iodine on treatment with alcohol. — *adj* **Gram-pos'itive** (also **gram-**) retaining the stain. [H J C *Gram*, deviser of the method, and L *caedere* to kill]

Gramineae *grə-*, *gra-* or *grā-min'i-ē*, *n pl* the grass family. — *adj* **graminā'ceous** (*grā-* or *gra-*) or **gramin'eous** of, or relating to, the grass family; grasslike, grassy. — *adj* **graminiv'orous** (*gra-*) feeding on grass, cereals, etc. [L *grāmen*, *grāminis* grass]

gramma. Same as **grama**.

grammalogue *gram'ə-log*, *n* a word represented by a single sign, a logogram; a sign for a word in shorthand. [Gr *gramma* a letter, and *logos* a word]

grammar *gram'ər*, *n* the science of language, from the points of view of pronunciation, inflexion, syntax and historic development; the art of the right use of language by grammatical rules; a book that teaches these subjects; any elementary work; a grammar school (*colloq*). — *n* **grammā'rian** a person who has made a study of grammar, a teacher of or writer on grammar. — *adj* **grammat'ical** belonging to, or according to the rules of, grammar (also *formerly* **grammat'ic**). — *adv* **grammat'ically**. — *n* **grammat'icaster** (*archaic*; see **-aster**) a piddling grammarian. — *n* **grammat'icism** (*rare*) a point of grammar. — *vt* **grammat'icize** or **-ise** (*-sīz*) to make grammatical. — *vi* to act the grammarian, hold forth on grammatical matters. — *n* **gramm'atist** a strict grammarian. — *n* **grammatol'ogy** the science or study of systems of writing. — **grammar school** *orig* a school in which grammar, *esp* Latin grammar, was taught; now a secondary school in which academic subjects predominate; **grammatical meaning** the functional significance of a word, etc within the grammatical framework of a particular sentence, etc. [Gr *gramma*, *-atos* a letter; partly through OFr *gramaire*]

gramme. See **gram**[3].

Grammy *gram'i*, (*US*) *n* an award (corresponding to the cinema Oscar) awarded by the National Academy of Recording Arts and Sciences. [From *gram*ophone]

Gram-negative. See under **gramicidin**.

gramoche *gra-mosh'*, *n*. See **gamash**.

gramophone *gram'ə-fōn*, *n* (with *cap*, ® in US) an instrument (invented by E Berliner, 1887) for reproducing sounds by means of a needle moving along the grooves of a revolving disc, a record-player; (loosely) any record-player (now *facetiously* or *archaic*). — *adj* **gramophonic** (*-fon'ik*). — *adv* **gramophon'ically**. — *n* **gramophonist** (*obs*; *gram-of'ə-nist* or *gram'ə-fōn-ist*). — *n* **gramoph'ony** (*obs*). [Improperly formed from Gr *gramma* letter, record, and *phōnē* sound]

Gram-positive. See under **gramicidin**.

grampus *gram'pəs*, *n* technically, Risso's dolphin (*Grampus griseus*); a popular name for many whales, *esp* the killer; someone who puffs and blows (*archaic*). [16c *graundepose*, earlier *grapays*, from OFr *graspeis*, from L *crassus* fat, and *piscis* fish, confused with Fr *grand* big]

gran[1] *gran*, (*Ital*) *adj* great. — **gran turismo** (*tōō-rēz'mō*) (a motor car) designed for touring in luxury and at high speed (term sometimes used loosely). — Abbrev **GT**.

gran[2] *gran*, (*colloq*) *n* short for **granny**.

granadilla *gran-ə-dil'ə* or **grenadilla** *gren'*, *n* the edible, oblong, fleshy fruit of *Passiflora quadrangularis*, a tropical American passion-flower; the edible fruit of various other passion-flowers. — **granadilla tree** the cocus-wood tree. [Sp]

granary *gran'ə-ri*, *n* a storehouse for grain or threshed corn; a rich grain-growing region; (**Granary**®) a make of bread with a special nutty flavour, made with malted wheat flour (also *adj*). — *adj* (loosely, of bread) containing whole grains of wheat. [L *grānārium*, from *grānum* seed]

grand[1] *grand*, *adj* exalted; magnificent; dignified; sublime; imposing; would-be-imposing; on a great scale; pre-eminent; supreme; chief; main; in complete form; in full proportions; very good (*colloq*). — *n* a grand piano; a thousand dollars or pounds (*slang*). — *adv* **grand'ly**. — *n* **grand'ness**. — *adj* **grand-du'cal** relating to a grand duke. — **grand duke** a title of sovereignty over a **grand duchy**, first created by the Pope in 1569 for the rulers of Florence and Tuscany, later assumed by certain German and Russian imperial princes (*fem* **grand duchess**); **grand juror** a member of a **grand jury**, a special jury in the US (and until 1933 in Britain) which decides whether there is sufficient evidence to put an accused person on trial; **grand larceny** see **larceny**; **grand march** the processional opening of a ball; **grandmas'ter** *orig* the title given to a chess-player winning a major international tournament, now given generally to exceptionally skilled players; any such player; **Grand Master** the head of a religious order of knighthood (Hospitallers, Templars, and Teutonic Knights), or of the Freemasons, etc; **Grand Mufti** the head of the Muslim community in Jerusalem; the former head of the state religion in Turkey; **Grand National** a steeplechase held annually at Aintree in Liverpool; **grand old man** (*colloq*) a person commanding great respect and veneration; **grand opera** see under **opera**[1]; **grand piano** a large harp-shaped piano, with horizontal strings; **grand slam** the winning of every trick (*bridge*); the winning of all major championships in a season (*sport*, eg *tennis*, *golf*); **grand'stand** an elevated structure on a race-course, etc, with tiered seating, affording a good view for spectators. — *vi* (*US colloq*) to show off. — **grandstand finish** a close and rousing finish to a sporting contest; a supreme effort to win at the close of a sporting contest; **grand style** a style adapted to lofty or sublime subjects; **grand total** the sum of all subordinate sums; **Grand Tour** see under **tour**; **grand touring** same as **gran turismo**; **Grand Unified Theory** a unified quantum field theory of the electromagnetic, strong and weak interactions of elementary particles (*abbrev* **GUT**). [Fr *grand*, from L *grandis* great]

grand[2] *grã*, (*Fr*) *adj* great. — **grand amateur** (*da-ma-tœr*) a collector of beautiful objects on a large scale; **grand atelier** (*dat-əl-yā*) a top-ranking fashion house; **grand coup** (*kōō*) a successful stroke; in bridge or whist, the trumping of a trick that could have been trumped by the winner's partner; **grand cru** (*krü*; of a wine) from a famous vineyard or group of vineyards; **Grand Guignol** see **Guignol**; **grand luxe** (*lüks*) great luxury; **grand mal** (*mal*) a violently convulsive form of epilepsy (see also **petit mal**); **Grand Marnier**® an orange-flavoured liqueur, often with a cognac base; **grand merci** (*mer-sē*) many thanks; **grand monde** (*mɔ̃d*) high society; **grand prix** (*prē*) literally chief prize; (with *cap*) any of several international motor races; any competition of similar importance in other sports (*orig Grand Prix de Paris*, a famous horse race): — *pl* **grands prix**; **grand seigneur** (*sen-yœr*) a dignified aristocratic gentleman or noble (now *usu ironic*); **(le) Grand Siècle** (*syekl'*) the great century, ie the Classical age of French literature during the reign of Louis XIV.

grand- *grand-*, *combining form* signifying (a person) of the second degree of parentage or descent. — *n* **gran'dam** (*archaic*) or **grann'am** (*archaic*) an old dame or woman; a grandmother. — *n* **grand'-aunt** a great-aunt. — *n* **grand'child** a son's or daughter's child. — *n* **grand'dad** or **gran'dad** (*colloq*) old man; grandfather. — *n* **grand'daddy** or **gran'daddy** (*colloq*) a grandfather; a person or thing considered the oldest, biggest, first, etc of its kind. — *n* **grand'daughter** a son's or daughter's daughter. — *n* **grand'father** a father's or mother's father. — *vt* (*US colloq*) to exempt (an activity, person, etc) from a new piece of legislation, restriction or the like (see **grandfather clause** below). — *adj* **grand'fatherly** like a grandfather, kindly. — *n* **grand'ma**, **grand'mama** or **grand'mamma** (*colloq*) a grandmother; old woman. — *n* **grand'mother** a father's or mother's mother. — *adj* **grand'motherly** like a grandmother; over-anxious, fussy. — *n* **grand'-nephew** a great-nephew. — *n* **grand'-niece** a great-niece. — *n* **grand'pa** or **grand'papa** (*colloq*) a grandfather. — *n* **grand'parent** a grandfather or grandmother. — *n* **grand'sire** a grandfather (*archaic*); any ancestor (*archaic*); a method of ringing changes (*bell-ringing*). — *n* **grand'son** a son's or daughter's son. — *n* **grand'-uncle** a great-uncle. — **granddad collar** a round collar, not folded over (*orig* intended to take a detachable stud-fastened collar); **granddad shirt** one with a granddad collar; **grandfather clause** (*US colloq*) a qualifying clause within a piece of legislation exempting those already involved in the activity with which the legislation deals; **grandfather** (or **grandfather's**) **clock** an old-fashioned clock (longcase clock) standing on the ground, or a new clock of this style (larger than a **grandmother('s) clock**). [**grand**[1]]

grande *grãd*, (Fr) *adj fem* of **grand**[2]. — **grande amoureuse** (*a-mōō-rœz*) a woman greatly involved in love affairs; **(la) Grande Armée** (*ar-mā*; *hist*) the great army, ie that led by Napoleon to invade Russia in 1812; **grande cocotte** (*ko-kot*) a high-class prostitute, *usu* one kept by a rich lover; **grande dame** (*däm*) a great and aristocratic lady, or a socially important and very dignified one (now, as for *masc* **grand seigneur**, often *ironic*); **grande école** (*ā-kol*) a prestigious French higher-education college, to which entry is competitive, specializing *esp* in applied science, engineering and other technical subjects; **grande entrée** (*ã-trā*) admission to Court, etc, on occasions of state; **grande marque** (*märk*) of motor cars, etc, a famous make; **grande passion** (*pas-yɔ̃*) a serious love affair or intense attachment; **grande tenue** (*tə-nü*) full dress, *esp* military, etc; **grande toilette** (*twa-let*) full dress, *esp* women's evening dress; **grande vedette** (*və-det*) a leading film or theatre star.

grandee *gran-dē'*, *n* (in Spain and Portugal from the 13c) a noble of the most highly privileged class, the members of the royal family being included; a man of high rank or station. — *n* **grandee'ship**. [Sp *grande*]

grandeur *grand'yər*, *n* vastness; splendour of appearance, magnificence; loftiness of thought or deportment. — **delusions of grandeur** a mistaken belief in one's own importance. [Fr, from *grand* great]

grandiloquent *gran-dil'ə-kwənt*, *adj* speaking, or expressed, bombastically. — Also (*archaic*) **grandil'oquous**. — *adv* **grandil'oquently**. [L *grandiloquus* from *grandis* great, and *loquens*, *-entis* speaking]

grandiose *gran'di-ōz* or *-ōs*, *adj* grand or imposing; bombastic. — *adv* **gran'diosely**. — *n* **grandios'ity**. [Ital *grandioso*, from *grande* great]

Grandisonian *gran-di-sō'ni-ən*, *adj* beneficent, polite and chivalrous, like the novelist Richardson's hero, Sir Charles *Grandison*.

granfer *gran'fər*, (*dialect*) *n* contraction of **grandfather**.

grange *grānj*, *n* a farmhouse or country house with its stables and other buildings; a granary or barn (*archaic*; *Milton*); a country house (*obs*); a dwelling (*Spenser*); a lodge of the order of Patrons of Husbandry (*US*). — *n* **gran'ger** the keeper of a grange; a member of a grange. [OFr *grange* barn, from LL *grānea*, from L *grānum* grain]

Grangerism *grān'jər-izm*, *n* the practice of cutting plates and title-pages out of many books to illustrate one book. — *n* **grangerizā'tion** or **-s-**. — *vt* **gran'gerize** or **-ise** to practise Grangerism on. [From James *Granger* (1716–76), whose *Biographical History of England* (1769) included blank pages for illustrations]

granita *gra-nē'ta*, *n* a grainy-textured flavoured water ice. [Ital *granito* grainy]

granite *gran'it*, *n* a coarse-grained igneous crystalline rock, composed of quartz, feldspar and mica; hardness, resilience or resolution (of character); a curling-stone. — *adj* of granite; hard like granite; unyielding, resolute. — *adj* **granit'ic** pertaining to, consisting of, or like granite. — *n* **granitificā'tion**. — *adj* **granit'iform**. — *n* **gran'itite** biotite granite. — *n* **granitizā'tion** or **-s-**. — *vt* **gran'itize** or **-ise**. — *adj* **gran'itoid** of the form of or resembling granite. — *n* **granodī'orite** a rock resembling diorite but containing quartz. — *adj* **granolith'ic** (Gr *lithos* stone) composed of cement and granite chips. — Also *n*. — *n* **gran'ophyre** (*-fīr*; with *-phyre* after *porphyry*) a quartz-porphyry with graphic intergrowth of quartz and orthoclase for groundmass. — *adj* **granophyric** (*-fir'ik* or *-fīr'ik*). — **graniteware** (*gran'it-wār*) a kind of speckled pottery resembling granite; a type of enamelled ironware. [Ital *granito* granite, literally grained, from L *grānum* grain]

granivorous *gran-iv'ər-əs*, (*zool*) *adj* grain-eating; feeding on seeds. — *n* **gran'ivore**. [L *grānum* grain, and *vorāre* to devour]

grannam. See under **grand-**.

granny or **grannie** *gran'i*, *n* a grandmother (*colloq*); an old woman (*colloq*); an old-womanish person (*colloq*); a midwife (*US dialect*); a revolving cap on a chimney-pot. — *vt* (*Scot*) to defeat totally, whitewash (in a contest). — **granny bonds** a former name of index-linked National Savings certificates, before 1981 only available to people over 50 years old; **granny flat**, **annexe**, etc a self-contained flat, bungalow, etc built on to, as part of, or close to a house, for a grandmother or other elderly relative; **granny glasses** small, round, gold or steel-rimmed spectacles; **granny knot** a knot like a reef knot, but unsymmetrical, apt to slip or jam; **Granny Smith** a crisp, green, flavoursome, Australasian variety of apple (after Maria Ann *Smith* of New South Wales, the first cultivator of this variety). [**grannam** (under **grand-**)]

granodiorite. See under **granite**.

granola *grə-nō'lə*, (*NAm*) *n* a type of crunchy breakfast cereal made with mixed grain, oats, dried fruit, nuts, etc, and honey or brown sugar. [Orig a trademark]

granolithic, **granophyre**, etc. See under **granite**.

grant *gränt*, *vt* to bestow; to admit as true; to concede. — *n* something bestowed, an allowance; a gift; conveyance of property by deed (*Eng law*); a granting. — *vi* (*Shakesp*) to consent. — *adj* **grant'able**. — *pa p* or *conj* **grant'ed** (often with *that*) (it is) admitted or accepted. — *n* **grantee'** (*law*) the person to whom a grant, gift or conveyance is made. — *n* **grant'er** or **grant'or** (*law*) the person by whom a grant or conveyance is made. — **grant'-in-aid'** an official money grant for a particular purpose, *esp* from the government to a lesser department, or local authority, for its programme or to ensure high standards; **grant of arms** (*heraldry*) provision of an achievement to a petitioner by a king-of-arms, in exchange for a fee. — **take for granted** to presuppose, or assume, *esp* tacitly or unconsciously; to treat casually, without respect

[OFr *graanter*, *craanter*, *creanter* to promise, from L *crēdere* to believe]

Granth *grunt* or **Granth Sahib** *grunt sä'ib*, *n* the holy book of the Sikhs (also **Adi'-Granth**). — *n* **Gran'thi** (*-ē*) the guardian of the Granth Sahib and of the gurdwara. [Hindi *granth* a book]

granule *gran'ūl*, *n* a little grain; a fine particle; (of eg a dehydrated foodstuff) a pellet, crumb-like particle (as opposed to powder). — *adj* **gran'ūlar** or (*archaic*) **gran'ūlary**, also **gran'ūlose** or **gran'ūlous** consisting of or like grains or granules; containing or marked by the presence of grains or granules. — *n* **granūlar'ity**. — *adv* **gran'ūlarly**. — *vt* **gran'ūlate** to form or break into grains or small masses; to make rough on the surface. — *vi* to be formed into grains. — *adj* granular; having the surface covered with small elevations. — *n* **granū-lā'tion** the act of forming into grains, *esp* of metals by pouring them through a sieve into water while hot; a granulated texture; (*specif*) applied decoration made up of grains of metal (*esp* gold); (in *pl*) granulation tissue (qv). — *adj* **gran'ūlative**. — *n* **gran'ūlātor** or **gran'ulāter**. — *adj* **granūlif'erous**. — *adj* **gran'ūliform**. — *n* **gran'ūlīte** (*geol*) a schistose but sometimes massive aggregate of quartz and feldspar with garnets; a granular-textured metamorphic rock. — *adj* **granūlit'ic** of the texture of granulite. — *n* **granūlītizā'tion** or **-s-** (*geol*) reduction of the components of a rock to crystalline grains by regional metamorphism. — *n* **gran'ūlōcyte** (*-sīt*) a blood cell of the leucocyte division. — *adj* **granūlocytic** (*-sit'ik*). — *n* **granūlō'ma** (*pathol*) a localized collection of granulation tissue, caused by infection or invasion by a foreign body: — *pl* **granulō'mas** or **granulō'mata**. — *adj* **granūlō'matous**. — **granulated sugar** white sugar in fairly coarse grains; **granulation tissue** (*med*) a new formation of connective tissue which grows in small rounded masses in a wound or on an ulcerated surface, and tends to leave a white scar. [L *grānulum*, dimin of *grānum* grain]

grape[1] *grāp*, (*Scot*) *vi* a dialect variant of **grope**.

grape[2] *grāp*, *n* the small, green- or dark purple-skinned fruit of the grapevine, growing in bunches, used to make wine, dried to make raisins, or eaten raw; a mangy tumour on the legs of horses, or the form of tuberculosis it is indicative of (*vet*); grapeshot. — *adj* **grape'less** (of wine) without the flavour of the grape. — *n* **grā'pery** a building or place where grapes are grown. — *adj* **grā'pey** or **grāpy** made of or like grapes. — **grape'fruit** a large, round, yellow-skinned citrus fruit, so called because it grows in large bunches like grapes; **grape hyacinth** any of several plants of the genus *Muscari* closely related to the hyacinths, with clusters of small grapelike flowers; **grape ivy** an evergreen climbing vine (*Rhoicissus rhomboidea*), popular as a houseplant for its glossy foliage; **grape'-louse** the Phylloxera; **grape'seed** the seed of the vine; **grape'seed-oil** an oil pressed from it; **grape'shot** clustered iron shot that scatters when fired; **grape'stone** the pip of the grape; **grape sugar** glucose or dextrose; **grape'tree** a tropical American tree (*Coccoloba uvifera*) of the dock family, or its edible fruit; **grape'vine** *Vitis vinifera* or other species of Vitis; the bush telegraph, rumour (from its far-stretching branches) (*colloq*). — **sea-grape** see **Ephedra**; **sour grapes** saying or pretending that something is not worth having because one cannot have it oneself (from Aesop's fable of the fox and the grapes); **the grape** (*usu facetious*) wine. [OFr *grape*, *grappe* a cluster of grapes, from *grape* a hook; orig Gmc]

graph *gräf*, *n* a symbolic diagram; a drawing depicting the relationship between two or more variables (sets of numbers or quantities) *usu* with reference to two axes. — *vt* to plot on a graph. — *combining form* **-graph** denoting a device that writes, records, etc (eg *telegraph*, *seismograph*), or the thing written (eg *autograph*, etc). — *adj* **graphic** (*graf'ik*) or **graph'ical** pertaining to writing, descriptive, delineative, or diagrammatic representation; picturesquely described or describing; vivid. — *n* **graph'ic** a painting, print, illustration or diagram, an example of the graphic arts. — *n* **graph'icacy** accurate understanding of and use of visual information. — *adv* **graph'ically** or **graph'icly**. — *n sing* **graph'icness**. — *n sing* **graph'ics** graphic means of presenting, or means of reproducing, informational material; designs containing illustrations or drawings; visual data as distinct from text or numbers; the visual arts concerned with representation, illusion, typography, printing, etc on a flat surface; and the methods associated with these techniques; the art or science of mathematical drawing, and of calculating stresses, etc, by geometrical methods. — *n* **graphol'ogy** the art of estimating and analysing character, etc from handwriting. — *adj* **grapholog'ic** or **grapholog'ical**. — *n* **graphol'ogist** a person skilled in, or who practises, graphology. — *n* **graphoman'ia** obsession with writing. — *n* **graphopho'bia** fear of writing. — **graphic arts** painting, drawing, engraving (as opposed to music, sculpture, etc); **graphic equalizer** a device for boosting or cutting frequencies of an audio signal, using faders; **graphic formula** a chemical formula in which the symbols for single atoms are joined by lines representing valency bonds; **graphic granite** (*geol*) a granite with markings like Hebrew characters, owing to intergrowth of quartz and feldspar; **graphic novel** a novel in comic-book picture form, aimed mainly at adults; **graphics character** (*comput*) a pictorial character that appears on the screen; **graphics tablet** (*comput*) a peripheral input device which digitizes the movements of a pen over the sensitive pad (tablet), so that a traced pattern will appear on the screen; **graph paper** squared paper suitable for drawing graphs; **graph** (or **graphics**) **plotter** (*comput*) a device similar to a printer, which provides hard copy output of computer graphics, using a special pen control mechanism under software direction. [Gr *graphē* writing, from *graphein* to write]

grapheme *graf'ēm*, (*linguistics*) *n* a letter of an alphabet; all the letters or combinations of letters together that may be used to express one phoneme. — *adj* **graphēm'ic**. — *n sing* **graphē'mics** the study of systems of representing speech sounds in writing. [Gr *graphēma* a letter]

graphic, etc. See **graph**.

Graphis *graf'is*, *n* a genus of lichens, with fructifications that resemble writing, found on bark. [New L, from L; ult Gr *graphein* to write]

graphite *graf'īt*, *n* a soft black or grey mineral composed of carbon, with many commericial and industrial uses, notably as the 'lead' in lead pencils (also called *plumbago* or *blacklead*). — *adj* **graphit'ic**. — *adj* **graph'itoid** with the appearance of graphite. — *n* **graphitizā'tion** or **-s-**. — *vt* **graph'itize** or **-ise** to convert wholly or partly into graphite. — **graphite reactor** (*nuc eng*) a reactor in which fission is produced principally or substantially by slow neutrons moderated by graphite. [Ger *Graphit*, from Gr *graphein* to write, and **-ite**(3)]

graphium *graf'i-əm* *n* a stylus. [L]

graphology, etc, **graphomania**, **graphophobia**. See under **graph**.

-graphy *-grə-fi*, *combining form* denoting either a particular style of writing, drawing, etc (eg *photography*, *lithography*) or a method of arranging and recording data within a particular discipline (eg *seismography*, *biography*). [L *-graphia*, from Gr, from *graphein* to write]

graple. See **grapple**.

grapnel *grap'nəl*, *n* a small anchor with several claws or arms; a grappling-iron; a hooking or grasping instrument. [Dimin of OFr *grapin*, from *grape* a hook; of Gmc origin]

GRAPO or **Grapo** *grä'pō*, (*Sp*) *abbrev*: First of October Anti-Facist Resistance Groups, a left-wing terrorist organization.

grappa *gra'pə*, *n* a brandy (*orig* Italian) made from the residue from a wine-press. [Ital, grape stalk]

grapple *grap'l*, *n* an instrument for hooking or holding; a grasp, grip, hold or clutch; a state of being held or clutched. — *vt* to seize; to lay fast hold of, grasp or grip. — *vi* to contend in close fight; to wrestle mentally (with). — Also (*Spenser*) **graple**. — *n* **grap'lement** (*Spenser*) a close fight. — **grapp'le-plant** a S African herbaceous plant (*Harpagophytum procumbens*) of the sesame family, with woody hook-like growths on its fruits; **grapp'ling-iron** or **-hook** an instrument for grappling; a large grapnel for seizing hostile ships in naval engagements (*hist*). [Cf OFr *grappil*, from *grape* a hook]

graptolite *grap'tə-līt*, (*geol*) *n* one of a group of fossil Hydrozoa with one or two rows of hydrothecae on a simple or branched polypary, characteristic Silurian fossils with an appearance almost like writing upon shales. — *adj* **graptolit'ic**. [Gr *graptos* written, from *graphein* to write, and *lithos* stone]

GRAS *gras*, (*US*) *abbrev*: generally recognized as safe (used to designate an officially approved food additive).

grasp *gräsp*, *vt* to seize and hold; to take eagerly; to comprehend. — *vi* to endeavour to seize (with *at* or *after*); to seize or accept eagerly (with *at*). — *n* grip; power of seizing; mental power of apprehension. — *adj* **grasp'able**. — *n* **grasp'er**. — *adj* **grasp'ing** seizing; avaricious. — *adj* **grasp'ingly**. — *n* **grasp'ingness**. — *adj* **grasp'less** feeble, relaxed. — **grasp the nettle** see under **nettle**[1]. [ME *graspen*, *grapsen*, from the root of *grāpian* to grope]

grass[1] *gräs*, *n* any plant of the monocotyledonous family Gramineae, the most important to man in the vegetable kingdom, with long, narrow leaves and tubular stems, including wheat and other cereals, reeds (but not sedges), bamboo and sugar-cane; common herbage; pasture grasses; an area planted with or growing such grasses, eg a lawn or meadow; pasturage; an informer (*esp* to the police on a fellow criminal) (*slang*); marijuana (*slang*); temporary or casual work in a printing office (*archaic*); the time of new growth of grass, spring and early summer (*archaic* or *dialect*); the surface, ground level, at a mine. — *vt* to cover, sow or turf with grass; to feed with grass; to bring (eg a fish or game bird) on or down to the grass or ground; to inform on (*slang*). — *vi* to inform (on) (*slang*); to do temporary or casual work in a printing office (*archaic*). — *n* **grass'er** a grass, informer (*slang*); an extra or temporary printing worker (*archaic*). — *n* **grass'iness**. — *n* **grass'ing** bleaching by exposure on grass. — *adj* **grass'y** covered with or resembling grass, green. — **grass box** a receptacle attached to some lawnmowers to catch the grass cuttings; **grass carp** a breed of fish, native to the South China Sea, imported into other areas to control various kinds of weed which it eats in great quantities; **grass cloth** a name for various coarse cloths (rarely made of grass), *esp* rami; **grass'cloth plant** the plant (rami); **grass court** a grass-covered tennis court; **grass'-cutter** a mowing machine; (in India) a person who provides fodder for baggage cattle (perhaps really Hindustani *ghāskatā*). — *adj* **grass'-green** green with grass; green as grass. — *adj* **grass'-grown** grown over with grass. — **grass'hook** another name for **sickle**[1]; **grass'hopper** a name for various herbivorous jumping insects of the Orthoptera, related to locusts and crickets, that chirp by rubbing their wing-covers; **grasshopper mind** a mind which is desultory or unable to concentrate on any one object for long; **grasshopper warbler** a songbird (*Locustella naevia*) whose song resembles a grasshopper's stridulation); **grass'land** permanent pasture; **grass line** a sisal rope, used on boats, that floats on the surface of the water. — Also **grass rope**. — **grass moth** a small light-coloured moth that frequents grass, a veneer-moth; **grass'-oil** a name for several volatile oils derived from widely different plants, some of them grasses; **grass'-plot** a plot of grassy ground; **grass'-roots** (*orig US*) the ordinary people, the rank and file in a country, political party, etc, thought of as voters; the rural areas of a country; foundation, basis, origin, primary aim or meaning. — Also *adj*. — **grass'-rooter**; **grass rope** see **grass line**; **grass sickness** a disease of the bowels affecting horses; **grass snake** the harmless common ringed snake; **grass style** a form of Chinese calligraphy in which the shapes of characters (**grass characters**) are greatly simplified for artistic effect; **grass tree** an Australian plant (*Xanthorrhoea*) of the lily family, with shrubby stems, tufts of long wiry foliage at the summit, and a tall flower-stalk, with a dense cylindrical spike of small flowers; **grass widow** a wife temporarily separated from or deserted by her husband: — *masc* **grass-wid'ower**; **grass'wrack** eelgrass. — **go** (or **be put out**) **to grass** to be turned out to pasture, *esp* of a horse too old to work; to go into retirement or to live in the country; (of a boxer) to fall violently, be knocked down (*slang*); **grass of Parnassus** see under **Parnassus**; **grass (someone) up** (*slang*) to inform on (someone); **hear the grass grow** to have exceptionally acute hearing; to be exceptionally alert; **let the grass grow under one's feet** to loiter or linger, and so lose one's opportunity. [OE *gærs*, *græs*; ON, Du and Gothic *gras*, Ger *Gras*; prob related to **green**[1] and **grow**]

grass[2] *gräs*, (*old slang*) *n* for **sparrow-grass**, a corruption of **asparagus**.

grassum *gräs'əm*, (*Scots law*) *n* a lump sum paid (in addition to rent or other periodic payment) by a person taking a lease of landed property, called in England 'premium' or 'fine'. [OE *gærsum* treasure, rich gift, etc]

graste *grāst*, (*Spenser*) *pa p* of **grace**.

grat. See **greet**[2].

grate[1] *grāt*, *n* a framework of bars with spaces between, *esp* one for holding a fire or for looking through a door, etc; a cage; a grid. — *adj* **grāt'ed** having a grating. — *n* **grāt'ing** the bars of a grate; a perforated cover for a drain or the like; a partition or frame of bars; a surface ruled closely with fine lines to give a diffraction spectrum (*phys*). [LL *grāta* a grate, from L *crātis* a hurdle; see **crate**]

grate[2] *grāt*, *vt* to reduce (*esp* food) to small particles or slivers by rubbing against a rough surface; to rub hard, scrape or wear away with anything rough; to grind (the teeth); to emit or utter jarringly. — *vi* to make a harsh sound; to jar or rasp (on or against); to fret or irritate (*usu* with *on* or *upon*). — *n* **grāt'er** an instrument with a rough surface for rubbing (eg cheese) down to small particles. — *adj* **grāt'ing** rubbing harshly; harsh; irritating. — *adv* **grāt'ingly**. [OFr *grater*, through LL, from OHGer *chrazzōn* (Ger *kratzen*) to scratch, related to Swed *kratta*]

grateful *grāt'f(ŏŏ)l*, *adj* thankful; having a due sense of benefits one has received; expressing gratitude; (of a thing) causing pleasure, or acceptable. — *adv* **grate'fully**. — *n* **grate'fulness**. — *n* **gratificā'tion** (*grat-*) a pleasing or indulging; that which gratifies; delight, feeling of satisfaction; a recompense, tip or bribe (*archaic*). — *n* **grat'ifier**. — *vt* **grat'ify** to please; to satisfy; to indulge; to do what is agreeable to: — *pr p* **grat'ifying**; *pa t* and *pa p* **grat'ified**. — *adj* **grat'ifying**. — *adv* **grat'ifyingly**. [OFr *grat*, from L *grātus* pleasing, thankful]

graticule *grat'i-kūl*, (*surveying*) *n* a ruled grating for the identification of points on a map or on the field of a telescope, etc, a reticle. — *n* **graticulā'tion** the division of a design into squares for convenience in making an enlarged or diminished copy. [L *crātīcula*, dimin of *crātis* wickerwork]

gratillity *grə-til'i-ti*, (*Shakesp*) *n* a small gratuity.

gratin *grat'ɛ̃*, (*cookery*) *n* the golden brown crust covering a gratinated food or dish; see **au gratin**. — *vt* **grat'inate** to cook with a topping of buttered breadcrumbs and/or cheese browned until crisp, to cook au gratin. — *adj* **gratiné** *grat-ē-nā*, (*Fr*) cooked or served au gratin: —*fem* **gratinée** (*-nā*). [Fr *gratin* cheese, *gratiner* to cook au gratin]

gratis *grā'* or *grä'tis*, *adv* for nothing; without payment or recompense. — **gratis dictum** (*dik'təm* or *-tōōm*) mere assertion. [L *grātis*, contraction of *grātiīs*, ablative pl of *grātia* favour]

gratitude *grat'i-tūd*, *n* warm and friendly feeling towards a benefactor; thankfulness. [Fr, from LL *grātitūdō*, from L *grātus* thankful]

grattoir *grat-wär*, (*archaeol*) *n* a scraper made of flint. [Fr]

gratuity *grə-tū'i-ti*, *n* a gift, *usu* of money, separate from and additional to payment made for a service; a tip or present; a bounty, a payment to a soldier, etc on discharge. — *adj* **gratū'itous** done or given for nothing; voluntary; benefiting one party only (*law*); without reason, ground or proof; uncalled for. — *adv* **gratū'itously**. — **gratuitous promise** (*law*) a promise (not legally binding) made by one person to another when the latter has not provided any consideration in return (eg a promise of a gift). [Fr *gratuité*, from LL *grātuitās,-ātis*, from L *grātus* grateful]

gratulate *grat'ū-lāt*, (*archaic*) *vt* to congratulate; to welcome; to express joy at. — *adj* (*Shakesp*) gratifying. — *adj* **grat'ulant** congratulatory. — *n* **gratulā'tion** congratulation. — *adj* **grat'ulatory** congratulatory.

graunch *grönch*, (*colloq*) *vi* to make a grinding or crunching noise (*usu* of a mechanism). — *vt* to grind or crunch (a mechanism). — *n* **graunch'er** a clumsy, incompetent mechanic; someone who graunches. [Imit]

graupel *grow'pəl*, *n* frozen rain or snowflakes. [Ger *graupeln* to sleet]

gravadlax. See **gravlax**.

gravamen *grəv-ā'men*, *n* grievance; the substantial or chief ground of complaint or accusation (*law*); a statement of abuses, grievances, etc in the Church sent by the Lower to the Upper House of Convocation: — *pl* **gravā'mina**. [L *gravāmen*, from *gravis* heavy]

grave[1] *grāv*, *n* a pit dug out, *esp* one to bury the dead in; any place of burial; the abode of the dead (*Bible*); death, destruction (*fig*); a deadly place. — *vt* to dig (*obs*); to engrave on a hard substance (*archaic*); to fix deeply (eg on the mind) (*archaic*); to bury (*obs*). — *vi* (*archaic*) to engrave: — *pa p* **graved** or **grav'en**. — *adj* **grave'less** (*Shakesp*). — *n* **grāv'er** a burin; an engraver (*archaic*). — *n* **grāv'ing**. — *n pl* **grave'-clothes** the clothes in which the dead are buried. — **grave'-digger**; **grave goods** (*archaeol*) artefacts (eg pottery, jewellery, weapons) put into a grave along with the corpse; **grave'-maker** (*Shakesp*) a grave-digger; **grave'stone** a stone placed as a memorial at a grave; **grave'-wax** (*obs*) adipocere; **grave'yard** a burial-ground; **graveyard shift** (*US slang*) a work shift starting at midnight or during the night. — **turn in one's grave** (of a dead person) to be disturbed from one's rest by an occurrence that would have been particularly distressing to one's living self; **with one foot in the grave** on the brink of death; very ill and/or old. [OE *grafan* to dig, *græf* a cave, grave, trench; Du *graven*, Ger *graben*]

grave[2] *grāv*, *vt* to clean (by burning, etc) and seal with tar (a wooden ship's bottom). — **graving dock** a dry-dock for the cleaning and repair of ships. [Perh Fr *grave*, *grève* beach]

grave[3] *grāv*, *adj* of importance; serious, not gay or showy; sedate; solemn; weighty; calling for anxiety; low in pitch; marked with a grave accent. — *n* (also *gräv*) grave accent. — *adv* **grave'ly**. — *n* **grave'ness**. — **grave accent** (*UK gräv*) a mark (\`), originally indicating a pitch falling somewhat, or failing to rise, now used for various special purposes (as in French). [Fr, from L *gravis*]

grave[4] *grāv*, *n* a count, prefect, a person holding office (now *obs* except in compounds, such as *landgrave*, *margrave*, *burgrave*). [Du *graaf*, Ger *Graf*]

gravel *grav'l*, *n* a mass of small rounded mixed stones or rock fragments, often with sand; small collections of gravelly matter in the kidneys or bladder (*pathol*). — *vt* to cover with gravel; to run aground on gravel (*obs*); to puzzle, perplex; to irritate (*colloq*, *esp US*): — *pr p* **grav'elling**; *pa t* and *pa p* **grav'elled**. — *adj* **grav'elly** of, full of, or like, gravel; (of sound) harsh, rough. — *adj* **grav'el-blind** (*orig Shakesp* **high'-grav'el-blind'**) after Shakespeare, punningly, in a state somewhere between sand-blind and stone-blind. — **grav'el-pit** a pit from which gravel is dug. — *adj* **grav'el-voiced** harsh- or rough-voiced. — **grav'el-walk** a footpath covered with gravel. [OFr *gravele* (Fr *gravier*); prob Celtic, as in Breton *grouan* sand, Welsh *gro* pebbles]

graven *grāv'n*, *pa p* of **grave**[1]; engraved (*archaic*); deeply fixed (eg on the mind or memory). — **graven image** a sculpted (or engraved) idol; a solemn person (*fig*).

graveolent *grəv-ē'ō-lənt*, or *grav'i-*, (*obs* except *bot*) *adj* rank-smelling, fetid. [L *graveolēns*, *-entis*, from *gravis* heavy, and *olēns*, pr p of *olēre* to smell]

graver *n*. See under **grave**[1].

Graves *gräv*, *n* a white (or red) table wine from the *Graves* district in the Gironde department of France.

graves. See **greaves**.

Graves' disease *grāvz' di-zēz'*, (*med*) *n* exophthalmic goitre, caused by excessive secretion of thyroid hormone. [After R J *Graves*, 19c Irish physician]

Gravettian *grə-vet'i-ən*, (*archaeol*) *adj* relating to the Upper Palaeolithic culture of La *Gravette* in SW France, characterized by the narrow pointed blades with blunted back edges that were found there.

gravid *grav'id*, (*med* and *zool*) *adj* pregnant. — *n* **gravid'ity**. [L *gravidus*, from *gravis* heavy]

gravimeter *grə-vim'i-tər*, *n* an instrument for measuring variations in gravity at points on the earth's surface. — *adj* **gravimetric** (*grav-i-met'rik*) or **gravimet'rical** pertaining to measurement by weight. — *n* **gravim'etry**. — **gravimetric analysis** the chemical analysis of materials by the separation of the constituents and their estimation by weight. [L *gravis* heavy, and Gr *metron* measure]

gravitas *grav'i-täs* or *-tas*, *n* seriousness; weight, importance. [L; see ety for **gravity**]

gravitate, etc, **gravitometer, graviton**. See **gravity**.

gravity *grav'i-ti*, *n* weightiness; gravitational attraction or acceleration; graveness, solemnity; lowness of pitch. — *vi* **grav'itāte** to be acted on by gravity; to tend towards the earth or other body; to be attracted, or move, by force of gravitation; to sink or settle down; to be strongly attracted or move (towards; *fig*). — *n* **gravitā'tion** the act of gravitating; the force of attraction between bodies, this being directly proportional to the product of the masses and inversely to the square of the distances (the Newtonian *constant of gravitation* (symbol **G**) is $6{\cdot}67 \times 10^{-11}$ MKS units) (*phys*). — *adj* **gravitā'tional** of, pertaining to, etc gravity; of the weakest type of interaction between nuclear particles (*phys*). — *adv* **gravitā'tionally**. — *adj* **grav'itātive**. — *n* **gravitom'eter** an instrument for measuring specific gravities. — *n* **grav'iton** (*phys*) a hypothetical quantum of gravitational field energy. — **gravitational field** that region of space in which appreciable gravitational force exists; **gravity cell** an electric cell having electrolytes of different specific gravities, so that they form separate layers. — *adj* **grav'ity-fed** (of a boiler, plant, system, etc) to which fuel, etc is supplied under the force of gravity alone. — *vt* and *n* **grav'ity-feed**. — **gravity platform** a drilling platform, used in the oil industry, made from concrete and steel, the weight of which enables it to hold its position on the seabed; **gravity waves** liquid surface waves controlled by gravity and not by surface tension; hypothetical progressive energy-carrying waves whose existence was postulated by Einstein in 1916. — **acceleration due to gravity** (symbol **g**) the acceleration of a body falling freely under the action of gravity in a vacuum, about 9·8 metres (32·174) feet per second per second; **specific gravity** see under **specify**. [L *gravitās*, *-ātis*, from *gravis* heavy]

gravlax *gräv'läks, grav'laks*, also **gravadlax** *grav'ad-laks*, *n* a Scandinavian dish of salmon dry-cured with spice (*usu* dill), sugar, salt and pepper, sliced on the slant to serve. [Swed *gravlax*, Norw *gravlaks*, literally buried salmon]

gravure *grə-vūr'*, *n* any process of making an intaglio printing plate, including photogravure; the plate, or an impression from it. [Fr, engraving]

gravy *grāv'i*, *n* the juices exuded from meat while cooking; a sauce made by thickening and seasoning these juices; money, profit or pleasure, unexpected or in excess of what one might expect (*colloq*); money or profit obtained by corrupt practices or graft (*slang*). — **gravy boat** a container for gravy; **grav'y-soup** soup like gravy, made from fresh meat; **gravy train** (*colloq*) a position in which one can have excessive profits or advantages in contrast to other people. [Perh *gravé* a copyist's mistake for OFr *grané*, from *grain* a cookery ingredient]

gray[1]. See **grey**. — **gray'fly** (*Milton*) an unknown insect.

gray[2] *grā*, *n* the SI unit (symbol **Gy**) of absorbed dose of ionizing radiation, equivalent to one joule per kilogram (or 100 rads). [Louis H *Gray* (1905–65), British radiobiologist]

grayle. See **grail**[1,3].

grayling *grā'ling*, *n* a silvery-grey fish (genus *Thymallus*) of the salmon family, with a smaller mouth and teeth, and larger scales; a grey satyrid butterfly. [**gray**[1] and **-ling**]

graywacke. Same as **greywacke**.

graze[1] *grāz*, *vt* to eat or feed on (growing grass or pasture); to feed or supply with grass. — *vi* to eat grass; to supply grass; to eat on one's feet and on the move, eg without stopping work, or (straight from the shelves) in a supermarket (*slang*); to browse, skim along or through reading matter, TV or radio programmes, etc (*slang*). — *n* **grāz'er** an animal that grazes; a person who eats on his or her feet and on the move (*slang*); a person who browses in or skims through (books, TV programmes, etc). — *n* **grāz'ier** a person who pastures cattle and rears them for the market. — *n* **grāz'ing** the action of the verb in any sense; the act of feeding on grass; the feeding or raising of cattle. [OE *grasian*, from *græs* grass]

graze[2] *grāz*, *vt* to pass lightly along the surface of; to damage or scrape the top surface of (the skin, etc). — *n* a passing touch or scratch. [Ety doubtful; perhaps only a special use of **graze**[1]; perh from *rase* (Fr *raser*), the *g* due to the analogy of *grate*]

grazioso *grä-tsē-ō'sō*, (*music*) *adj* and *adv* graceful, gracefully. [Ital]

grease *grēs*, *n* a soft thick animal fat; oily matter of any kind; condition of fatness; an inflammation in the heels of a horse, marked by swelling, etc (*vet*). — *vt* (in UK sometimes pronounced *grēz*) to smear with grease; to lubricate; to bribe (*slang*); to facilitate. — *n* **greaser** (*grēz'ər* or *grēs'ər*) a person who greases; a member of a gang of young, long-haired motorcyclists (*slang*); a ship's engineer (*slang*); a Mexican or a Spanish American or Mediterranean person (*US*; *offensive slang*). — *adv* **greas'ily**. — *n* **greas'iness**. — *adj* **greas'y** (in UK sometimes *grēz'i*) of or like grease or oil; smeared with grease; having a slippery coating; fatty; oily; obscene; unctuous or ingratiating. — *n* (*Austr* and *NZ colloq*) a shearer; a camp-cook in the outback; (in *pl* **greas'ies**) fish and chips. — **grease'ball** (*US derog slang*) a person of Latin racial origin, *esp* Mediterranean or Latin American, with dark hair and skin; someone with oily, slicked-back hair; a loose derogatory term, *esp* for someone dirty or unkempt; **grease'-band** (*hortic*) a band of sticky or greasy material put around eg a tree-trunk to prevent insects from climbing further up it; **grease cup** a lubricating device which stores grease and feeds it into a bearing; **grease gun** a lubricating pump. — *n sing* **grease'-heels** (*vet*) grease (in horses). — **grease monkey** (*slang*) a mechanic; **grease paint** a tallowy substance used by actors in making up. — *adj* **grease'proof** resistant or impermeable to grease. — **grease'wood** a name for various oily American shrubs of the goosefoot family; **greasy spoon** (*slang*) a cheap, shabby, often grubby cafe. — **grease someone's palm** see under **palm**[1]; **grease the wheels** (*fig*) to make things go smoothly; **hart of grease** (*archaic*) a fat hart; **like greased lightning** extremely quickly. [OFr *gresse* fatness, *gras* fat, from L *crassus*]

great *grāt*, *adj* big; large; of a high degree of magnitude of any kind; (of a letter) capital (*archaic*); elevated in power, rank, station, etc; pre-eminent in genius; highly gifted; chief; sublime; weighty; outstanding; (with *on*) devoted to or obsessed by a certain thing; much given to, or excelling in the thing in question; favourite; habitual; in high favour or intimacy; in a high degree; on a large scale; excellent (*colloq*, often *ironic*); in combination, indicating one degree more remote in the direct line of descent (as in **great'-grand'father**, **great'-grand'son** and similarly **great'-great'-grandfather** and so indefinitely); pregnant, teeming (*archaic*); swelling with emotion (*archaic*). — *n* someone who has achieved lasting fame; used collectively for those people who have achieved lasting fame; bulk, mass (*obs*); whole (*obs*); wholesale (*obs*). — *adv* (*colloq*) very well. — *vt* **great'en** to make great or greater. — *vi* (*obs*) to become great. — *adj* **great'er** comparative of **great**; (with geographical names) in an extended sense (eg *Greater London*). — *adv* **great'ly**. — *n* **great'ness**. — *n pl* **Greats** the final honours examinations of the School of Literae Humaniores (*Classical Greats*) or of Modern Philosophy (*Modern Greats*) at Oxford University; the course leading to these. — **great ape** any of the larger anthropoid apes, such as the chimpanzee, gibbon, gorilla and orang-utan; **great auk** a large, flightless auk once common in North Atlantic areas, now extinct; **great'-aunt** a grandparent's sister or a grandparent's brother's wife. — *adj* **great'-bellied** (*archaic*; *Shakesp*) pregnant. — **Great Bear** Ursa Major; **Great Britain** England, Scotland and Wales; **great circle** a circle on the surface of a sphere whose centre is the centre of the sphere; **great'coat** an overcoat; **Great Dane** one of a breed of very large smooth- (and short-)haired dogs; **great'-grand'child** the child of a grandchild; **great'-grand'father** (and **-grand'mother**) the father (and mother) of a grandparent; **great gross** a unit of quantity equal to 12 gross (1728). — *adj* **great'-hearted** having a great or noble heart; high-spirited; magnanimous. — **great'-heartedness**; **great'-nephew** and **-niece** the grandson and granddaughter respectively of one's own or one's spouse's brother or sister; **great primer** see **primer**; **great schism** (*hist*) great Eastern schism, Western schism (see under **schism**); **great Scott** an exclamation of surprise; **Great Sea** (*archaic*) the Mediterranean; **great tit** a kind of tit (see **tit**[3]), *Parus major*, with yellow, black and white markings; **great toe** see under **toe**; **great'-uncle** a grandparent's brother or a grandparent's sister's husband; **Great War** a term applied *esp* to the war of 1914–18; **Great White Way** a nickname for Broadway in New York; any brightly-lit street with theatres, etc; **great year** (*astron*) the length of time (about 25 800 years) it takes for the equinoctial points to make a complete revolution. — **the Great and the Good** (an assembly of) eminent, worthy and respected public figures (often somewhat *ironic* in use); **the greatest** (*slang*) a wonderful, marvellous person or thing; **the great unwashed** a contemptuous term for the general populace. [OE *great*; Du *groot*, Ger *gross*]

greave[1] *grēv*, (*obs*) *n* a thicket. [OE *grǣfa*, *grǣfe*; cf **grove**]

greave[2]. Same as **grieve**[1,2].

greave[3] *grēv*, *n* armour for the leg below the knee. [OFr *greve* shin, greave]

greaves *grēvz* or (*obs*) **graves** *grāvz*, *n pl* dregs of melted tallow. [LGer *greven*; cf Ger *Griebe* greaves; OE *grēofa* pot]

grebe *grēb*, *n* a short-winged almost tailless freshwater diving bird (*Podiceps*). [Fr *grèbe*]

grece. See **gree**[2].

Grecian *grēsh'(y)ən*, *adj* Greek. — *n* a Greek; a scholar of Greek language and literature; a hellenizing Jew (*Bible*); a senior boy of Christ's Hospital; an Irish labourer recently arrived in England (*old slang*). — **Grecian bend** a mode of walking with a slight bend forward, at one time affected by a few women who fondly thought to imitate the pose of a figure such as the Venus of Milo; **Grecian nose** a straight nose which forms a continuous line with the forehead. [L *Graecia* Greece, from Gr *Graikos* Greek]

grecian. See under **gree**[2].

Grecize or **-ise**, **Grecism**, **Greco-Roman**. See **Graecize** or **-ise**, etc.

grecque *grek*, (*archit*) *n* a fret pattern. [Fr (*fem*), Greek]

gree[1] *grē*, *n* (*Spenser*) goodwill, favour. — *vi* (*Shakesp*, *archaic* or *Scot*) to agree. [OFr *gré*, from L *grātus* pleasing; the verb may be from OFr *gréer* or aphetic from **agree**]

gree[2] *grē*, *n* degree, rank (*obs*); a step (*obs*); superiority (*dialect*); victory (*dialect*); the prize for such (*dialect*). — *n* **grece** (*grēs*; *obs* or *dialect*; from the Fr *pl*) a flight of steps; a step. — Also spelt **grees**, **grese**, **greece**, **greese**, **grice**, **griece**, **gris**, **grise**, **grize** (**grees'ing**, **gress'ing** and even **grē'cian**, are *obs* forms). — *adj* **grieced** (*heraldry*) having or placed on steps. [OFr *gré*, from L *gradus*; see **grade**]

greedy *grēd'i*, *adj* having a voracious appetite; craving or longing eagerly, *esp* too eagerly; eager to increase, or to obtain or keep more than, one's own share; covetous, grasping. — *n* **greed** an eager desire or longing; gluttony; eagerness or longing for more than one's share; covetousness, *esp* excessive. — *adv* **greed'ily**. — *n* **greed'iness**. — **greedy guts** (*colloq*) a glutton. [OE *grǣdig*; Du *gretig*]

greegree. See **grisgris**.

Greek *grēk*, *adj* of Greece, its people, or its language. — *n* a native or citizen of Greece, of a Greek state, or of a colony elsewhere of a Greek state; the language of Greece; any language of which one is ignorant, jargon, anything unintelligible (*colloq*); a member of the Greek Church; a hellenizing Jew (*Bible*); a cunning rogue, a merry fellow (*archaic*); an Irishman (*old slang*). — *n* **Greek'dom** the Greek world; a Greek community. — *n* **Greek'ing** or **greek'ing** (as in desktop publishing, advertising, etc) representation of text and graphics as straight lines, random characters or other graphic convention, to give an overall impression of the page layout. — *adj* **Greek'ish**. — *adj* **Greek'less** without knowledge of Greek. — *n* **Greek'ling** (*archaic*) a contemptible Greek. — **Greek architecture** the style of architecture developed in ancient Greece (Corinthian, Doric, Ionic); **Greek Church** or **Greek Orthodox Church** see **Eastern Church**; **Greek cross** an upright cross with arms of equal length; **Greek fire** a substance (of unknown composition) that took fire when wetted, used in war against enemy ships, long a secret of the Byzantine Greeks; **Greek gift** a treacherous gift (from Virgil's *Aeneid* 2.49); **Greek key (pattern)** a fret pattern; **Greek letter society** (or **Greek-letter**) (in US universities) a social, professional or honorary fraternity or sorority, using a combination of Greek letters as a title, such as Phi Beta Kappa; **Greek love**, **style** or **way** (*US slang*) anal sex; **Greek nose** a Grecian nose. — **the Greek calends** never (the Greeks having no calends). [OE *Grēcas*, *Crēcas* Greeks, or L *Graecus*, from Gr *Graikos* Greek]

green[1] *grēn*, *adj* of the colour usual in leaves, between blue and yellow in the spectrum; growing; vigorous, flourishing; new; young; unripe; fresh; undried; raw; incompletely prepared; immature; unseasoned; inexperienced; jealous or envious; easily imposed on, gullible; relating to currency values expressing EC farm prices (eg *green pound*, *green franc*, *green rate*, etc); concerned with care of the environment or conservation of natural resources, *esp* as a political issue; (of goods etc) environment-friendly; (of people) environment-conscious. — *n* the colour of green things; a grassy plot, *esp* that common to a village or town, or for bowling, drying of clothes, etc; the prepared ground (*putting-green*) round a golf hole; a member of the Green Party, or an environmentalist generally; a green pigment; greenness, stage of vigorous growth (of plants, as *in the green*); the green colour as a symbol of the Irish republic; (in *pl*) fresh leaves; (in *pl*) green vegetables for food, *esp* of the cabbage kind; (in *pl*) money, *esp* dollar bills (*slang*); (in *pl*) sexual intercourse (*slang*); (in *pl*) low-grade marijuana (*slang*); (*pl* with *cap*) a political party at Constantinople, under Justinian, opposed to the Blues. — *vt* and *vi* to make or become green; to introduce trees and parks into urban areas. — *vi* to become environmentally conscious. — *n* **green'er** (*slang*) a newly-arrived immigrant. — *n* **green'ery** green plants or boughs; fresh, green growth. — *n* **green'ie** (*Austr*) an environmentalist. — Also *adj*. — *n* **green'ing** a becoming or making green; a becoming or making politically green, ecologically and environmentally conscious, or conservationist; a kind of apple green when ripe. — *adj* **green'ish**. — *n* **green'ishness**. — *n* **green'let** any of several greenish song-birds of the American family Vireonidae. — *adv* **green'ly** immaturely, unskilfully. — *n* **green'ness**. — *n* **greenth** (*obs*) greenness, verdure. — *adj* **green'y**. — *n* (*slang*) (also **green'ie**) a £1 note; (in *pl* **green'ies**) money, cash in notes. — **green algae** or **seaweeds** the Chlorophyceae; **green audit** an assessment of an investigation into a company's green, ie environment-conscious, claims, methods, policies, etc; **green'back** (*colloq*) an American note (often printed in green on the back), first issued in 1862; a dollar bill; a plant condition in which fruits (eg tomatoes) remain green around the stalk; **green'-bag** a lawyer's bag for documents, etc (formerly of green material); a lawyer (*old slang*); **green ban** (*Austr*) the refusal of trade unions to work on environmentally and socially objectionable projects; **green bean** a French bean, the immature pod of the kidney-bean; **green belt** a strip of open land surrounding a town; **Green Beret** (*colloq*) a British or American commando; **green'-bone** a garfish; a viviparous blenny; **green'bottle** a metallic-green fly (*Lucilia*); **green card** international motorists' insurance document; an official US work and residence permit (*orig* green) issued to foreign nationals; a card issued by the Manpower Services Commission certifying that the holder is registered disabled under the terms of the Disabled Persons (Employment) Act 1944, and is thus entitled to certain assistance in gaining and carrying out paid work; **green'cloth** a gaming-table (*colloq*); a department of the royal household chiefly concerned with the commissariat (from the green cloth on the table round which its officials sat); **green corn** same as **sweet-corn**; **green crop** a crop of green vegetables, such as grasses, turnips, etc; **Green Cross Code** a code of road-safety rules for children issued in 1971; **green dragon** a European aroid plant (Dracunculus); dragon-root (*US*); **green'-drake** a mayfly; **green earth** any green earthy mineral used as a pigment, *usu* a silicate of iron. — *adj* **green'ery-yall'ery** (*colloq*) in or favouring greens and yellows, hence decadently aesthetic; **green'-eyed** having green eyes; jealous (**the green-eyed monster** jealousy). — *adj* **green'field** applied to a site, separate from existing developments, which is to be developed for the first time); **green'finch** or **green linnet** a finch of a green colour, with some grey; **green fingers** (or **thumb**) a knack of making plants grow well; **green flash** or **ray** a flash of green light sometimes seen at the moment of sunrise or sunset; **green'fly** a plant louse or aphid; **green gland** one of a pair of glands on the head of certain crustaceans; **Green Goddess** a type of fire-engine operated by the army in civil emergencies, etc; **green goose** a young goose (*dialect*); a simpleton (*old slang*); **green gown** (*archaic*) a roll on the grass (sometimes but not always understood to imply loss of virginity); **green'grocer** a dealer in fresh vegetables and fruit; a large green cicada (*Austr*); **green'grocery** the produce sold by a greengrocer; **green'hand** an inferior sailor; **green'heart** bebeeru (*Nectandra rodiei*), a S American tree of the laurel family with very hard wood; **green'horn** a raw, inexperienced youth; **green'-house** a glasshouse for plants, *esp* one with little or no artificial heating; the cockpit of an aircraft, having transparent sides (*airmen's slang*); **greenhouse effect** the warming-up of the earth's surface due to the trapping of long-wave radiation by carbon dioxide (produced by the burning of fossil fuels, chlorofluorocarbons, natural methane emissions, etc) and other greenhouse gases; **greenhouse gas** a gas (*esp* carbon dioxide, also ozone, methane, nitrous oxide and chlorofluoro-carbons) that contributes to the greenhouse effect; **Green** (or **Emerald**) **Isle** Ireland; **green'-keeper** a person who has the care of a golf course or bowling-green; **green label**, **green labelling** same as **eco-lable**, **eco-labelling**; **green leek** any of various Australian parrots with green plumage; **green light** a traffic signal indicating that vehicles may advance; permission to go ahead; any signal or indication of consent or encouragement (*colloq*; as in *get the green light*); **green'-mail** a form of business blackmail whereby a company buys a strategically significant block of shares in another company, sufficient to threaten takeover and thus to force the parent company to buy back the shares at a premium; **green manuring** growing one crop (**green manure**) and digging it under to fertilize its successor; **green monkey** a West African long-tailed monkey, *Cercopithecus aethiops* (**green monkey disease** a sometimes fatal virus disease with fever and haemorrhaging, *orig* identified among technicians handling green monkeys in Marburg, Germany (also called *Marburg disease*)); **green paper** a statement of proposed government policy, intended as a basis for parliamentary discussion; **Green Party** a party principally concerned with resource conservation and the decentralization of political and economic power; **Greenpeace** an environmental pressure group which campaigns *esp* against nuclear power and dumping, and also whaling; **green plover** the lapwing; **green pound** the agreed value of the pound used to express EC farm prices in sterling and to measure the level of Britain's contribution under the Common Agricultural Policy; **green revolution** agricultural advances in developing countries; **green road** or **way** a grassy country track used by walkers; **green'room** in a theatre, a room for actors to relax or entertain guests in, etc backstage, traditionally and typically having the walls coloured green; **green'sand** a sandstone containing much glauconite; (with *cap*) two divisions (Lower and Upper) of the Cretaceous system, separated by the Gault (*geol*); **green'shank** a large sandpiper with long, somewhat greenish legs; **green sickness** chlorosis; **green snake** a harmless colubrine snake common in southern USA; **green'speak** ecological jargon, the terminology of green issues, or that used by green activists and supporters; **greenstick** see **greenstick fracture** under **fract**; **green stocks** (*commerce*) those of an organization engaged in combating pollution, or professing to avoid it in the manufacture of its products; **green'stone** a vague name for any basic or intermediate igneous rock (*geol*); nephrite; **green'stuff** green vegetables, *esp* of the cabbage kind; **green'sward** sward or turf green with grass; **green tea** tea made from leaves that have been dried without fermentation and retain a light colour; **green turtle** a tropical and subtropical sea turtle (*Chelonia mydas*) with a greenish shell (see **turtle**[2]); **green vitriol** ferrous sulphate; **green'wash** (*facetious*) a specious overlay, or ineffectual display, of concern for the environment. — Also *vt*. — **green'weed** a name given to certain half-shrubby species of Genista. — *adj* **green-well'ie** of, belonging to or relating to the British upper-class country-dwelling set (represented stereotypically as wearing a certain kind of heavy green wellingtons). — **green'wood** a leafy wood or forest. — Also *adj*. — **green woodpecker** a kind of European woodpecker with green and red plumage. — **something green in one's eye** (*colloq*) a sign that one is gullible. [OE *grēne*; Ger *grün*, Du *groen* green; ON *grœnn*]

green[2] or (*obs*) **grein** *grēn*, (*Scot*) *vi* to long, yearn. [Cf ON *girna*]

greengage *grēn'gāj*, *n* a green and very sweet variety of plum. [Said to be named from Sir W *Gage* of Hengrave Hall, near Bury St Edmunds, before 1725]

Greenland seal *grēn'lənd sēl*, *n* the harp seal, found in arctic and north Atlantic waters. — **Greenland whale** the arctic right whale (*Balaena mysticetus*). [*Greenland*, in the Arctic Ocean]

greenockite *grēn'ək-īt*, *n* a rare mineral, cadmium sulphide, discovered by Lord *Greenock* (1783–1859).

Greenwich Mean Time *grin'ij* (also *gren'* or *-ich*) *mēn tīm*, *n* mean solar time for the meridian of *Greenwich*. — Also called **Greenwich time**.

grees, **greese**, **greesing**. See **gree**[2].

greet[1] *grēt*, *vt* to acknowledge upon meeting with formal, familiar or customary words, or a customary or friendly gesture; to meet, receive; to become evident to (the eye or ear); to send kind wishes to; to congratulate (*obs*); to offer congratulations on (*Spenser*). — *vi* (*obs*) to meet and salute: — *pr p* **greet'ing**; *pa t* and *pa p* **greet'ed**. — *n* **greet'er** a person who greets, *specif* someone employed to greet visitors eg to a theatre or club. — *n* **greet'ing** expression of acknowledgement, good wishes, kindness or joy; salutation. [OE *grētan* to greet, to meet; Du *groeten*, Ger *grüssen* to salute]

greet[2] *grēt*, (*Scot*; *Spenser* **greete**) *vi* to weep (*pa t*, *obs Scot* **grat**; *pa p*, *obs Scot* **grutt'en**). — *n* weeping; a spell of weeping. — **greeting meeting** the last meeting of a town-council before an election. [OE (Anglian) *grētan*; Gothic *grētan*]

greffier *gref'yā*, (*Channel Is*, etc) *n* a registrar; a notary. [Fr]

gregale *grā-gä'lā*, *n* a north-east wind in the Mediterranean. [Ital, from L *graecus* Greek]

gregarian, etc. See **gregarious**.

Gregarina *greg-ə-rī'nə*, *n* a genus of Protozoa, typical of the **Gregarinida**, a group of parasitic insects, molluscs and crustaceans. — *n* **greg'arine** a member of the Gregarinida. — *adj* of or pertaining to the Gregarinida. [New L, after L *gregārius* (see next entry)]

gregarious *gri-gā'ri-əs*, *adj* associating in flocks and herds; fond of the company of others (*fig*); growing together but not matted (*bot*). — *adj* (*rare*) **gregā'rian** (of a soldier) of the common rank. — *n* **gregā'rianism** gregariousness. — *adv* **gregā'riously**. — *n* **gregā'riousness**. [L *gregārius*, from *grex*, *gregis* a flock]

gregatim *gri-gā'tim* or *gre-gä'tim*, (*L*) *adv* literally in flocks.

grège. See **greige**.

grego *grā'gō* or *grē'gō*, *n orig* a Levantine hooded jacket or cloak; an overcoat, *esp* a thick hooded seaman's coat: — *pl* **gre'gos**. [Port *grego* or other derivative of L *Graecus* Greek]

Gregorian *gri-gō'ri-ən*, or *-gö'*, *adj* belonging to or established by *Gregory* — such as the **Gregorian chant** or **tones** plainsong, introduced by Pope Gregory I (6c), the **Gregorian calendar** the calendar reformed by Gregory XIII (1582), the **Gregorian telescope**, the reflecting telescope of James Gregory (1638–75) and the **Gregorian wig**, a 16c or 17c type of wig attributed to a barber Gregory. — *n* a follower of any Gregory; a member of an 18c English brotherhood. — *n* **Gregory** (*greg'ər-i*; *colloq*) or **Gregory's mixture** or **powder** a laxative powder of rhubarb, magnesia and ginger, formulated by Dr James *Gregory* (1753–1821), great-grandson of James Gregory above.

greige *grāzh*, *adj* of cloth, undyed; of a greyish-beige colour. — Also **grège**. [Fr (*soie*) *grège* raw silk]

grein. See **green**[2].

greisen *grī'zən*, *n* a rock composed of quartz and mica, often with topaz, formed from granite by fluorine exhalations. — *n* **greisenīzā'tion** or **-s-** the process by which granite is converted to greisen. — *vt* **greis'enize** or **-ise**. [Ger]

greisly (*Spenser* and *Milton*). Same as **grisly**.

gremial *grē'mi-əl, adj* pertaining to the lap or bosom (*obs*); intimate (*obs*); resident (*hist*); in full membership (*hist*). — *n* a full or resident member (*hist*); a cloth laid on a bishop's knees to keep his vestments clean from oil at ordinations. [L *gremium* the lap]

gremlin *grem'lin, n orig* a goblin accused of vexing airmen, causing mischief and mechanical trouble to aircraft; any imaginary mischievous agency. [Origin uncertain; RAF slang, with a poss connection with *Fremlin's* Ale; prob modelled on **goblin**]

gremolata *grem-o-lä'ta*, (*cookery*) *n* a colourful, flavoursome garnish, as of chopped parsley, lemon or orange peel, garlic, etc. [Ital]

gren *gren*, (*Spenser*) *vi*. Same as **grin**[1].

grenade *gri-nād'*, *n* a small bomb thrown by hand or shot from a rifle; a glass projectile containing chemicals for putting out fires, testing drains, dispensing poison gas or tear gas, etc. — *n* **grenadier** (*gren-ə-dēr'*) *orig* a soldier who threw grenades; then, a member of the first company of every battalion of foot-soldiers; now used as the title (Grenadier Guards) of part of the Guards Division of infantry; any of various African weaver birds with red and black plumage; a deep-sea fish of the *Macrouridae* family. [Fr, from Sp *granada* pomegranate, from L *grānātus* full of seeds (*grāna*)]

grenadilla. Same as **granadilla**.

grenadine[1] *gren-ə-dēn'*, *n* a pomegranate syrup, or similar, used in certain drinks. [Ety as for **grenade**]

grenadine[2] *gren'ə-dēn, n* a thin silk or mixed fabric. [Fr, perh *Granada*]

Grenzgänger *grents'geng-ər*, (*Ger*) *n* a person who crosses a national or political border, *esp* (*hist*) from the communist countries to the West: — *pl* **Grenz'gänger**.

grese. See **gree**[2].

Gresham's law. See under **law**[1].

gressing. See **gree**[2].

gressorial *gres-ö'ri-əl*, (*zool*) *adj* adapted for walking. — Also **gresso'rious**. [L *gressus*, pa p of *gradī* to walk]

greve. An *obs* variant of **greave**[1,3].

grew[1] *groo͞, pa t* of **grow**.

grew[2]. See under **gruesome**.

grew[3] *groo͞* or **grewhound** *groo͞'hownd*, (*Scot* or *N Eng dialect*) *n* a greyhound. [By confusion with obs *Grew* Greek]

grex venalium *greks ven-āl'iəm* or *wen-äl'i-oo͞m*, (*L*) *n* the venal crowd or throng. [Literally the herd of hirelings]

grey or (*esp NAm*) **gray** *grā, adj* of a mixture of black and white with little or no hue; dull, dismal; neutral, anonymous; intermediate in character, condition, etc; grey-haired, old, mature; belonging or relating to the elderly. — *n* a grey colour; a grey or greyish animal, *esp* a horse; grey clothing; a middle-aged or old person (*slang*); a dry, colourless, restrained or uninteresting person (*slang*). — *vt* to make grey or dull. — *vi* to become grey or dull. — *n* **grey'ing** the process of becoming grey; (of population) the process or phenomenon of having a growing elderly or retired sector. — *adj* **grey'ish** somewhat grey. — *adv* **grey'ly**. — *n* **grey'ness**. — **grey area** an area between two extremes, having (mingled) characteristics of both of them; a situation in which there are no clear-cut distinctions; an area relatively high in unemployment but not classed as a development area (qv); **grey'beard** a person whose beard is grey; an old man; a stoneware jar for liquor, a bellarmine; **grey'-coat** a person who wears a grey coat, *esp* a pupil in certain schools; a Confederate soldier. — Also *adj*. — *adj* **grey'-coated**. — **grey eminence** see **eminence grise**. — *adj* **grey'-eyed**. — **grey'-fish** a dogfish (*US*); a young coalfish (*Scot*); **Grey Friar** (also without *caps*) a Franciscan; **grey goose** the common wild goose (*Anser anser*); **grey-goose quill, shaft** or **wing** (*archaic*) an arrow. — *adj* **grey'-haired** or **grey'-headed**. — **grey'hen** the female of the blackcock; **grey'-lag** the grey goose (perhaps from its lateness in migrating), also **grey-lag goose**; **grey literature** material published non-commercially, eg government reports; **grey mare** see **mare**; **grey market** the unofficial and often secret, but not necessarily illegal, selling of goods, etc alongside or in addition to an official or open market; a financial market trading in shares not yet officially listed; **grey matter** the ashen-grey active part of the brain and spinal cord; **grey'-out** a mild or less severe (physical) blackout (*aeronautics*); **grey owl** the tawny owl; **grey parrot** a red-tailed grey African parrot; **grey seal** a type of seal that populates N Atlantic coastal waters; **grey squirrel** a N American squirrel naturalized in Britain; **grey'stone** a grey volcanic rock; **grey-weth'er** a grey-coloured, rounded block of sandstone or quartzite, a relic of denudation, looking at a distance like a grazing sheep; **grey wolf** the N American timber wolf. — **the Greys** the Scots Greys (see under **Scots**). [OE *græg*; cf Ger *grau*]

greyhound *grā'hownd, n* a tall, slender dog of an ancient breed bred for their great speed and keen sight. [OE *grīghund* (cf ON *greyhundr*, or *grey*)]

greywacke *grā-wak'i*, (*geol*) *n* an indurated sedimentary rock composed of grains (round or angular) and splinters of quartz, feldspar, slate, etc in a hard matrix. — **greywacke-slate'** a fine-grained fissile greywacke. [Ger *Grauwacke*, partly translated, partly adopted]

grey-wether. See under **grey**.

GRI (*hist*) *abbrev*: *Georgius Rex Imperator* (*L*), George, King and Emperor.

gribble *grib'l, n* a small marine isopod (genus *Limnoria*) that bores into timber under water. [Perh from *grub*]

grice[1] *grīs*, (*dialect* or *archaic*) *n* a little pig: — *pl* **grices** or **grice**. — Also **gryce**. [ON *grīss*]

grice[2]. See **gree**[2].

gricer *grī'sər, n* a train-spotter or railway enthusiast. — *n* **grī'cing**. [Origin uncertain]

Grid *grid, abbrev*: the Global Resource Information Database (of the United Nations).

grid *grid, n* a grating; a gridiron; a framework; a network; a network of power transmission lines; a network of lines for finding places on a map, or for some other purpose; a framework above a theatre stage from which scenery and lights may be suspended; a perforated screen or spiral of wire between the filament and the plate of a thermionic valve (*electronics*). — *n* **gridd'er** (*US*) an American football player. — **grid'lock** (*US*) a traffic jam; a situation in which no progress is possible, a standstill. — *adj* **grid'locked**. [Back-formation from **gridiron**]

griddle *grid'l, n* a flat iron plate placed over heat for making eg drop scones; a flat, heated, metal cooking surface. — Also (*Scot*) **gird'le** (*gûr'dl, gir'dl*). — **gridd'le-cake** a drop scone; a thick pancake (*US*); **griddle car** (now *old*) a coach on a train where simple cooked meals can be obtained. [Anglo-Fr *gridil*, from a dimin of L *crātis* a hurdle]

gride or **gryde** *grīd*, (*poetic* or *archaic*) *vt* and *vi* to pierce; to cut, *esp* with a grating sound; to graze; to grate. — *n* a harsh grating sound. **[gird]**

gridelin *grid'ə-lin, n* and *adj* violet-grey. [Fr *gris de lin* flax grey]

gridiron *grid'ī-ərn, n* a frame of iron bars for broiling over a fire; a frame to support a ship during repairs; a network; an American-football field. — *vt* to cover with parallel bars or lines. — **gridlock** see under **grid**. [ME *gredire* a griddle; from the same source as **griddle**, (but the *-ire* ending became confused with ME *ire* iron]

griece, grieced. See **gree**[2].

grief *grēf, n* sorrow; distress; great mourning; affliction; a cause of sorrow; trouble, bother (*slang*); bodily pain (*Shakesp*). — *adj* **grief'ful** full of grief. — *adj* **grief'less**. — *adj* **grief'-shot** (*Shakesp*) pierced with grief. — *adj* **grief'-stricken** crushed with sorrow. — **come to grief** to meet with serious setback, disaster or mishap. [OFr, from L *gravis* heavy]

griesie, **griesy**, **griesly**. Spenserian forms of **grisy** (see under **gris**, **grise**) and **grisly**.

grieve[1] *grēv*, *vi* to feel grief; to mourn. — *vt* to cause grief, distress or pain of mind to; to make sorrowful; to vex; to inflict bodily pain on or do bodily harm to (*obs*); to show grief for, regret bitterly (*poetic*). — *n* **griev'ance** a cause or source of grief; a ground of complaint; a condition felt to be oppressive or wrongful; a burden or hardship; distress (*obs*); injury (*obs*); grief (*obs*). — *n* **griev'er**. — *adv* **griev'ingly**. — *adj* **griev'ous** causing grief or distress; burdensome; painful; severe; hurtful (*obs*). — *adv* **griev'ously**. — *n* **griev'ousness**. [OFr *grever*, from L *gravāre*, from *gravis* heavy]

grieve[2] *grēv*, *n* a farm overseer (*Scot*); a governor or sheriff (*hist*). [Old Northumbrian *grǣfa* (WSax *gerēfa*); cf **reeve**]

griff[1] or **griffe** *grif*, *n* a claw (*rare*); (**griffe**) a clawlike architectural ornament; a mulatto, or person of mixed Negro and mulatto or Negro and American Indian blood (*US dialect*); a steep narrow valley (*dialect*). [Fr *griffe*]

griff[2] *grif*, (*UK* and *NZ slang*) *n* (with *the*) the true facts, accurate information. [Shortened from earlier *griffin*; origin uncertain]

griffe. See **griff**[1].

griffin, **griffon**, **gryfon** or **gryphon** *grif'in* or *-ən*, *n* an imaginary animal with a lion's body and an eagle's beak and wings; a newcomer in the East, a greenhorn (*Anglo-Ind*); a pony never before entered for a race; a grimly or fiercely watchful guardian, *esp* over a young woman, a duenna (*obs*); a tip, a signal or warning (*slang*). — *adj* **griff'inish**. — *n* **griff'inism**. — **griffon vulture** a European vulture, *Gyps fulvus*. [Fr *griffon*, from L *grȳphus*, from Gr *gryps* a bird (probably the lammergeier), also a griffin, from *grȳpos* hook-nosed]

griffon[1] *grif'ən*, *n* a dog like a coarse-haired terrier. — **Brussels griffon** a toy dog with a rather snub nose. [Prob from **griffin**]

griffon[2]. See **griffin**.

grift *grift*, (*US slang*) *vi* to swindle. — Also *n*. — *n* **grif'ter** a con man, swindler. [Perh from **graft**[2]]

grig *grig*, *n* a cricket (*dialect*); a grasshopper (*dialect*); a small, lively eel, the sand-eel; a small, lively person. — *vt* to tease, irritate. — *vi* to fish for grigs (eels). — **merry as a grig** very merry and lively. [Origin obscure]

grigri. See **grisgris**.

grike or **gryke** *grīk*, *n* a fissure in limestone rock formed or widened by the dissolvent effect of rain (*geol*); a deep valley, ravine (*dialect*). [ON *kriki* a crack]

grill[1] *gril*, *vt* to cook on a gridiron, under a grill, etc by radiant heat; to brand or mark with a gridiron; to cross-examine harassingly; to torment (as though with burning heat); to scallop (oysters, etc). — *vi* to undergo grilling. — *n* a grating; a gridiron; the part of a cooker on which meat, etc is grilled; a grill room; a grilled dish; an act of grilling. — *n* **grillade'** (*obs*; *cookery*) anything grilled. — *n* **grill'age** (*building* and *eng*) a foundation of crossbeams, eg on marshy ground. — *adj* **grilled** cooked under a grill or on a gridiron; embossed with small rectangular indentations as those on certain late 19c postage stamps of the United States and Peru. — *n* **grill'ing**. — **grill room** part of a restaurant where beefsteaks, etc, are served grilled to order; **grill'steak** a large steak-shaped burger of seasoned minced beef, lamb, etc *usu* stored frozen and grilled without preliminary defrosting. — **mixed grill** a dish of several grilled meats *usu* with mushrooms, tomatoes, etc. [Fr *griller*, from *gril* a gridiron, from a dimin of L *crātis* a grate]

grill[2] or **grille** *gril*, *n* a lattice, grating, screen or openwork of metal, generally used to enclose or protect a window, car radiator, shrine, etc, or on a helmet to protect the face; a grating in a convent or jail door, etc; (in real tennis) a square opening in the corner of an end wall of the court. — **grill'work** or **grille'-work**. [Fr; see **grill**[1]]

grilse *grils*, *n* a young salmon on its first return from salt water. [Origin unknown]

grim *grim*, *adj* forbidding; stern; ghastly, grisly; sullen, dismal; repellent, unappealing; unyielding, harsh; unpleasant; ferocious (*obs*). — *adv* **grim'ly**. — *n* **grim'ness**. — *adj* **grim'looked** (*Shakesp*) having a grim or dismal aspect. [OE *grim(m)*; Ger *grimmig*, from *Grimm* fury, Du *grimmig*, ON *grimmr*]

grimace *gri-mās'*, *n* a distortion of the face, in fun, disgust, etc; a smirk. — *vi* to make grimaces. [Fr]

grimalkin *gri-mal'kin* or *-möl'kin*, *n* an old (*esp* female) cat; a cat generally; a bad-tempered or tyrannical old woman (*archaic*). [**grey** and **Malkin**, a dimin of *Maud*]

grime *grīm*, *n* ingrained dirt; sooty or coaly dirt. — *vt* to soil deeply; to cover with grime. — *adv* **grīm'ily**. — *n* **grīm'iness**. — *adj* **grīm'y**. [ME, from MDu *grīme*]

Grimm's law. See under **law**[1].

grimoire *grē-mwär'*, *n* a magician's book for calling up spirits. [Fr; cf **gramary**]

grin[1] *grin*, *vi* to give a broad smile; to set the teeth together and withdraw the lips in pain, derision, etc. — *vt* to express by grinning; to set (the teeth) in a grin (*obs*): — *pr p* **grinn'ing**; *pa t* and *pa p* **grinned**. — *n* an act of grinning. — *n* **grinn'er**. [OE *grennian*; ON *grenja*, Ger *greinen*, Du *grijnen* to grumble, Scot **girn**; related to **groan**]

grin[2] *grin*, (*dialect*) *n* a snare or trap. — Also *vt*. [OE *grīn*]

grind[1] *grind*, (*Spenser*) *pa t* of **grin**[1].

grind[2] *grīnd*, *vt* to reduce to powder or small particles by friction or crushing; to wear down, sharpen, smooth or roughen by friction; to rub together harshly; to force (in, into; *lit* and *fig*); to produce by great effort, or by working a crank (with *out*); to oppress or harass; to work by a crank. — *vi* to be moved or rubbed together; to jar or grate; (with *on* or *away*) to continue (to work, etc) relentlessly and doggedly, *esp* at something tedious; to read or study hard; (with *on*; *colloq*) to drone or harp on: — *pr p* **grīnd'ing**; *pa t* **ground** (*grownd*) or (*obs*) **grind'ed**; *pa p* **ground** or (*obs*) **ground'en**. — *n* the act, sound or jar of grinding; the specific fineness of particles in a ground powder, *esp* coffee; drudgery, a hard, tedious task; laborious study for a special examination, etc; a bore, bother (*colloq*); a student who gives all his or her time to study (*US*). — *n* **grind'er** someone who, or that which, grinds; a tooth that grinds food; a coach or crammer of students for examination; a hard-working student or dogged worker. — *n* **grind'ery** a place where knives, etc are ground; shoemakers' materials. — *n* **grind'ing** an act or process of the verb to grind; reducing to powder. — *adj* for grinding; wearing down; very severe; extortionate; (of sound) harsh; giving a harsh sound. — *adv* **grind'ingly**. — *adj* (*archaic*) **ground'en** sharpened. — **grind'stone** a circular revolving stone for grinding or sharpening tools; **ground beef** (*NAm*) minced beef; **ground glass** glass obscured by grinding, sandblast or etching. — **grind the face** (or **faces**) **of** to oppress, *esp* by taxation; **grind to a halt** to move more and more slowly until finally coming to a standstill (*lit* and *fig*); **keep one's** (or **someone's**) **nose to the grindstone** to subject oneself (or someone) to severe continuous toil; **take a grinder** (*Dickens*) to put the left thumb to the nose and to work an imaginary coffee-mill round it with the right hand (a gesture of derision). [OE *grindan*]

gringo *gring'gō*, *n* in Spanish-speaking America, someone whose language is not Spanish, *esp* an English speaker: — *pl* **grin'gos**. [Sp, gibberish, prob from *Griego* Greek]

griot *grē-ō'*, *n* in parts of Africa (*esp* W Africa), a tribal teller of legends and history, a poet, singer and musician; a member of the caste or class of such troubadours, considered of low social status. [Fr, of uncertain origin]

grip[1] *grip*, *n* a small ditch, gutter or trench to carry away surface water, a drain. — *vt* to trench or ditch. — Also (*dialect*) **gripe** (*grīp*). [OE *grȳpe*; cf LGer *gruppe*, *grüppe*]

grip[2] *grip*, *n* a grasp or firm hold, *esp* with the hand or mind; strength of grasp; the handle or part by which anything is grasped; a method or style of grasping; a particular mode of grasping hands for mutual recognition, a secret handshake; a gripsack, travelling bag (*orig US*); a holding or clutching device, eg a clasp for the hair, or a cable-car braking device; power, mastery; a twinge, spasm, pinch of distress; grasp, or power of holding the mind or commanding the emotions; grippe; a stagehand who moves scenery, etc, or a member of a camera crew responsible for manoeuvring the camera (also **grips**). — *vt* to take or keep a firm hold of; to hold fast the attention or interest of; to command the emotions of. — Also *vi*: — *pr p* **gripp'ing**; *pa t* and *pa p* **gripped** (*gript*). — *n* **gripp'er** someone who, or that which, grips; a clutch, claw, or similar device. — *adj* **gripp'y** inclining to avarice (*Scot*); having grip; tenacious. — **grip'sack** (*US*) a bag for travel, a grip; **grip'tape** a rough adhesive tape, as used on skateboarding equipment to provide extra grip. — **come** or **get to grips (with)** to tackle at close quarters, or (*fig*) seriously and energetically; **the grip** (*Scot*) the lump (qv under **lump**). [OE *gripe* grasp, *gripa* handful]

gripe[1] *grīp*, *vt* to cause a painful stomach spasm in; to grasp (*obs*); to seize and hold fast (*archaic*); to squeeze or pinch; to afflict, oppress. — *vi* to cause, or to suffer, a painful stomach spasm; to keep on complaining (*colloq*); to clutch (*obs*). — *n* fast hold, grasp; a grumble (*colloq*); a lashing for a boat on deck; a pain, pang (*obs*); (*esp* in *pl*) severe spasmodic pain in the intestines; forcible retention (*obs*); a usurer (*obs slang*). — *n* **grīp'er**. — *adj* **grīp'ing** avaricious, grasping; (of a pain) seizing acutely; (of a person) constantly complaining. — *adv* **grīp'ingly**. — **gripe'-water** or *specif* **Gripe Water**® a carminative solution given to infants to relieve colic and minor stomach ailments. [OE *grīpan* (*grāp*, *gripen*); ON *grīpa*, Ger *greifen*, Du *grijpen*]

gripe[2] or **grype** *grīp*, (*obs*) *n* a griffin; a vulture. — **gripe's egg** a large oval cup. [Gr *gryps*]

gripe[3]. Same as **grip**[1].

griple. See **gripple**.

grippe *grēp*, *n* (an old term for) influenza. [Fr, from *gripper* to seize]

gripple *grip'l*, (*Spenser* **grip'le**) *adj* gripping, grasping; greedy. — *n* (*obs*) a grip, grasp; a hook. [OE *gripul*, from stem of *grīpan* (see **gripe**[1])]

Griqua *grēk'wä*, *n* one of a people of Griqualand, in South Africa; one of a mixed Hottentot and European race (Hottentot prevailing), living chiefly in Griqualand.

gris[1] *gris* or **grise** *grīs*, *adj* (*obs*) grey. — *n* (*obs*) a grey fur. — *adj* **griseous** (*griz'* or *gris'i-əs*; *zool*, *bot*, etc) grey; blue-grey or pearl-grey. — *adj* **grisy** (*Spenser* **griesie** or **gryesy**; all *grī'zi*) grey (*obs*). [Fr]

gris[2]. See **gree**[2].

grisaille *grē-zāl'* or *-zä'ē*, *n* a style of painting on walls or ceilings, in greyish tints in imitation of bas-reliefs; a similar style of painting on pottery, enamel or glass; a work in this style. — Also *adj*. [Fr, from *gris* grey]

gris-amber *gris-am'bər*, (*obs*) *n* ambergris. — *adj* **gris-amb'er-steam'd'** (*Milton*) flavoured by steam from melted ambergris.

grise[1] *grīz*, (*obs*) *vt* to shudder at; to terrify. — *vi* to shudder with fear. — *adj* **grī'sy** (*Spenser* **griesy** or **grysie**) grim; horrible; grisly. [From the verb of which OE *āgrīsan* is a compound; cf **agrise**]

grise[2]. See **gree**[2].

grise[3]. See **gris**[1].

Griselda *griz-el'də*, *n* a woman of excessive meekness and patience, from the heroine of an old tale retold by Boccaccio, Petrarch and Chaucer.

grisely. See **grisly**.

griseofulvin *griz-i-ō-fōōl'vin*, (*med*) *n* an oral antibiotic used as a treatment for fungus infections of the skin and hair. [Isolated from the fungus *Penicillium griseofulvum dierckx*; L *griseus* grey, and *fulvus* reddish yellow]

griseous. See **gris**[1].

grisette *gri-zet'*, *n* (*esp* formerly) a young French working girl; a name given to varieties of eg birds, moths, fungi. [Fr *grisette* grey dress fabric, the usual garb of such girls, from *gris* grey]

grisgris, **grigri** or **greegree** (also **gris-gris**, etc) *grē'grē*, *n* an African charm, amulet or spell: — *pl* **gris'gris**, **gri'gris** or **gree'grees**. [Fr; prob of African origin]

griskin *gris'kin*, (*dialect*) *n* lean meat from a loin of pork. [**grice**[1]]

grisled *griz'ld*. Same as **grizzled**.

grisly *griz'li*, *adj* frightful, ghastly (*Spenser* and *Milton* **greisly**; *Spenser* **griesly**, **grisely**, **grysely** or **gryesly**). — Also *adv* (*rare*). — *n* **gris'liness**. [OE *grislic*; cf **grise**]

grison *griz'ən*, *grīz'ən*, or *-on*, *n* a grey, carnivorous S American mammal similar to a large weasel (*Galactis vittata*); a grey carnivorous mammal of a related species (*Galactis cuja*). [Fr, from *gris* grey]

grist *grist*, *n* corn for grinding, or ground; corn for grinding, or ground, at one time; malt for one brewing; supply, portion, quantity (*old US*); a measure of the thickness of rope or yarn; profit (*fig*). — **grist'-mill** a mill for grinding grain. — **grist to the mill** raw material for feeding a process; matter that can be turned to profit or advantage. [OE *grīst*; cf **grind**[2]]

gristle *gris'l*, *n* cartilage, *esp* when present in meat. — *n* **grist'liness**. — *adj* **grist'ly**. [OE]

grisy. See **grise**[1], **gris**[1].

grit[1] *grit*, *n* small hard particles of sand, stone, etc; gravel (*obs*); a coarse sandstone, often with angular grains (also **grit'stone**); texture of stone; strength of character, toughness, indomitability; small woody particles in the flesh of a pear. — *vt* and *vi* to grind or clench (one's teeth); to make a grating sound; to spread (eg icy roads, to prevent skidding) with grit. — *n* **gritt'er** a person who, or apparatus or vehicle that, applies grit. — *n* **gritt'iness**. — *adj* **gritt'y** having or containing hard particles; of the nature of grit; determined, plucky. — **grit blasting** a process used in preparation for metal spraying which cleans the surface and gives it the roughness required to retain the sprayed metal particles; **grit'stone** see **grit** above. [OE *grēot*; Ger *Griess* gravel]

grit[2] *grit*, a Scottish form of **great** (*compar* **gritt'er**, *superl* **gritt'est**). — *adj* (*agric*) (of a ewe) in lamb.

grith *grith*, or **girth** *girth*, (*hist*) *n* sanctuary, asylum. — **grith'-stool** a seat in which a fugitive was in sanctuary. [OE *grith*]

grits *grits*, *n pl* coarsely ground grain, *esp* oats or (*US*) hominy; a boiled dish of this. [OE *grytta*; cf **groats**]

grivet *griv'it*, *n* a north-east African guenon monkey (*Cercopithecus aethiops*), a vervet monkey. [Fr; origin unknown]

grize. See **gree**[2].

grizzle[1] *griz'l*, *n* a grey colour. — *adj* **grizz'led** (*esp* of hair or a beard) grey, or mixed with grey. — *adj* **grizz'ly** of a grey colour. — *n* (*mineral ext*) a set of parallel bars or a grating used for the coarse screening of ores, rocks, etc; the **grizzly bear** (*Ursus horribilis*) of the Rocky Mountains, a fierce brown bear with white-tipped fur. [ME *grisel*, from Fr *gris* grey]

grizzle[2] *griz'l*, *vi* to grumble; to whimper; to fret. — *n* a bout of grizzling. — *n* **grizz'ler**. [Origin unknown]

Gro. *abbrev*: Grove (in street names).

groan *grōn*, *vi* to utter a sustained, deep-toned sound expressive of distress, disapprobation, etc; to creak loudly; to be weighed down (with *under*, *beneath* or *with*; *esp* of a table *with* food); to be oppressed, suffer (with *under* or *beneath*). — *vt* to utter or express through a groan. — *n* a deep moan; the sound, or an act, of groaning; a grinding rumble. — *n* **groan'er**. — *adj* **groan'ful** (*archaic*; *Spenser* **grone'full**). — *n* and *adj* **groan'ing**. — **groaning board** (*archaic*) a table weighed down with very generous supplies of food. [OE *grānian*]

groat *grōt* (formerly *gröt*), *n* an obsolete English silver coin, worth fourpence (4d) and after 1662 coined only as Maundy money (the silver fourpenny-piece, coined 1836–56, was not officially called a groat); a very small sum, proverbially. — *n* **groats'worth** (*obs*). [MDu *groot*, literally great, ie thick]

groats *grōts*, *n pl* hulled (and crushed) grain, *esp* oats. [OE *grotan* (pl)]

Grobian *grō'bi-ən*, *n* a boorish rude sloven. — *n* **Gro'bianism**. [Ger *Grobianus*, a character in German satire of the 15c and 16c, from *grob* coarse]

grocer *grōs'ər*, *n* a dealer in staple foods and general household supplies. — *n* **grō'cery** the trade or business of a grocer; (*usu* in *pl*) articles sold by grocers; a grocer's shop or food and liquor shop (*US*). — *n* **grocetē'ria** (*NAm*) a self-service grocery store. [Earlier *grosser* a wholesale dealer; OFr *grossier*, from LL *grossārius*, from *grossus*; cf **gross**]

grockle *grok'l*, (*colloq derog*) *n* a tourist or incomer in an (*esp* holiday) area. [Origin unknown]

grody *grō'di*, (*US slang*) *adj* (*compar* **grō'dier**, *superl* **grō'diest**) sleazy, grotty, inferior; revolting, offensive, disgusting. [Perh a blend of **gross** and **mouldy**]

grog *grog*, *n* (formerly) a mixture of spirits and water; any alcoholic drink, *esp* beer (*Austr* and *NZ colloq*); bricks or waste from a clayworks broken down and added to clay to be used for brick manufacture (*building*). — *vi* to drink grog; (*Austr colloq* with *on*) to drink steadily. — *vt* to extract the spirit from the wood of empty spirit-casks by soaking with hot water. — *n* **grogg'ery** (*US*; *old*) a low public-house. — *n* **grogg'iness** the state of being groggy. — *adj* **grogg'y** affected by grog, partially intoxicated (*archaic*); dazed, unsteady from illness or exhaustion; weak and staggering from blows (*boxing*); applied to a horse that bears wholly on its heels in trotting. — **grog'-blossom** a redness of the nose due to drinking; **grog'-on** or **grog'-up** (*Austr colloq*) a drinking party or drinking session; **grog'-shop** a dram-shop, cheap bar (now *rare*); a shop selling alcoholic liquor (*Austr* and *NZ*). [From Old *Grog*, the nickname (apparently from his *grogram* cloak) of Admiral Vernon, who in 1740 ordered that rum (until 1970 officially issued to sailors) should be mixed with water]

grogram *grog'rəm*, *n* a kind of coarse cloth of silk and mohair. [OFr *gros grain* coarse grain]

groin[1] *groin*, *n* the fold between the belly and the thigh; the genitals, *esp* the testicles (*euphem*); the line of intersection of two vaults, also a rib along the intersection (*archit*). — *vt* to form into groins, to build in groins. — *adj* **groined**. — *n* **groin'ing**. — **groin'-centring** the centring of timber during construction. [Early forms *grind*, *grine*, perh from OE *grynde* abyss]

groin[2]. US spelling of **groyne** (qv).

groin[3] *groin*, (*obs*) *vi* to grunt, to growl; to grumble. [OFr *grogner*, from L *grunnīre* to grunt]

Grolier *grō'lyā*, *n* a book or a binding from the library of the French bibliophile Jean *Grolier* (1479–1565). — *adj* **Grolieresque** (*grō-lyər-esk'*) after the style of Grolier's bindings, with geometrical or arabesque figures and leaf-sprays in gold lines.

groma *grōm'ə*, *n* a surveying instrument used by the Romans, in which plumb-lines suspended from the arms of a horizontal cruciform frame were used to construct right angles. [L *grōma* a surveyor's pole, measuring rod]

grommet or **grummet** *grum'it*, *n* a ring of rope or metal; a hole edged with rope; a washer of hemp and red-lead putty, paint or some other substance; a metal ring lining an eyelet; an eyelet; a washer to protect or insulate electrical wire passing through a hole; (*usu* **grommet**) a small tube passed through the eardrum to drain the middle ear (*med*); a ring of stiffener inside a (*esp* novice) seaman's or serviceman's cap; (**grommet**) a young or novice surfer (or skateboarder) (*slang*). — Also (rarely) **grom'et**. — **grumm'et-hole**. [Perh 15c Fr *grom(m)ette* (Fr *gourmette*) curb of a bridle]

gromwell *grom'wəl*, *n* any plant of the genus *Lithospermum*, of the borage family, with smooth, stonelike seeds formerly used medicinally; the oyster-plant (*Mertensia*), also of the borage family. [OFr *gromil*]

grone. *Obs* form of **groan**.

groof *grōōf*, (*Scot*) *n* the front of one's body, one's face. — Also (*obs*) **grouf**, **grufe**. [ON *á grúfu* face downwards; cf **grovelling**]

groo-groo. See **gru-gru**.

grooly *grōōl'i*, (*slang*) *adj* gruesome. [*grue*some and gris*ly*]

groom *grōōm* or *grŏŏm*, *n* a boy or young man, *esp* a servant (*obs*); a person who has the charge of horses; a title of several officers in a noble or royal household (groom of the stole, grooms-in-waiting); a bridegroom. — *vt* to tend (*esp* a horse); to smarten; of an animal, to clean and maintain (all aspects of its own body surface, or of that of another member of the same species); to prepare for a particular, often political office, stardom, or success in any sphere. — **grooms'man** the attendant on a bridegroom. [Origin obscure; cf Du *grom* fry, offspring, OFr *gromet* boy (see **gourmet**, **grummet**[2]); encroaching on OE *guma* (as in bride*groom*) a man]

groove *grōōv*, *n* a furrow, or long hollow, *usu* one cut with a tool; the track cut into the surface of a record, along which the needle of the record-player moves; a set routine; an exalted mood, one's highest form (*dated slang*); a pleasurable or groovy experience (*slang*). — *vt* to grave or cut a groove or furrow in. — *vi* (*dated slang*) to experience great pleasure; to be groovy. — *n* **groov'er**. — *adj* **groov'y** in top form, or in perfect condition, up to date in style, or generally, pleasant or delightful (*dated slang*); following a set routine (as though set in grooves) (*old colloq*); passé, outmoded (*mod slang*). — **in the groove** (*dated slang*) in excellent form; up to date, fashionable. [Prob Du *groef*, *groeve* a furrow; cognate with Ger *Grube* a pit, ON *grōf*, Eng **grave**[1]]

grope *grōp*, *vi* to search, feel about, as if blind or in the dark (often with *for*). — *vt* to find (one's way) by feeling; to fondle (someone) lasciviously (*colloq*). — *n* **grop'er**. — *adv* **grop'ingly**. [OE *grāpian*; related to **grab**[2], **gripe**[1]]

groper[1]. Same as **grouper**.

groper[2]. See **grope**.

grosbeak *grōs'bēk*, *n* any of various more or less related birds, such as the cardinal and the rose-breasted grosbeak but *esp* the hawfinch, or other finch of the same subfamily, with thick, heavy, seed-crushing bill. [Fr *grosbec*, from *gros* thick, and *bec* beak]

groschen *grō'shən*, *n* an Austrian coin, a 100th part of a schilling; in Germany, a ten-pfennig piece; a small silver coin current in the north of Germany from the 13c to the late 19c, varying in value between 1/24 and 1/36 of a thaler. [Ger]

groser *grō'zər*, **grosert** or **grossart** *-zərt*, also **groset** *-zit*, (*Scot*) *n* a gooseberry. [Fr *groseille*]

grosgrain *grō'grān*, *n* a heavy corded silk used especially for ribbons and hat bands. [Fr]

gros point *grō point*, *n* a large cross-stitch or tent stitch, covering two vertical and two horizontal threads of the canvas; embroidery composed of this stitch. [Fr]

gross *grōs*, *adj* total, including everything, without deductions; extremely fat, obese; enormous, bulky; stupid, dull, slow; coarse, sensual; obscene; extreme; flagrant, glaring, palpable; crass, boorish; coarse in mind; dense in growth, rank; solid, earthbound, not ethereal; disgusting, repulsive (*NAm colloq*); (of pay) before the deduction of income tax, National Insurance, superannuation and other voluntary deductions; (of a horse) naturally large-girthed, as opposed to overweight (*racing*). — *n* the main bulk; the whole taken together, sum total (revived from *obs*); twelve dozen, 144; the total profit: — *pl* **gross**. — *vt* to make as total income or revenue. — *adv* **gross'ly**. — *n* **gross'ness**. — **gross capital employed** (*accounting*) the capital and other finance used by a business, which is the total value of assets as shown on the balance sheet; **gross circulation** the total sales of a magazine or newspaper before mistakes or the number of unsold copies have been taken into consideration; **gross domestic product** the gross national product less income from foreign investments, the total value of goods and services produced within a country; **gross earnings** a person's total income received from all sources; **gross investment** (*econ*) spending on replacement of worn-out and obsolescent buildings, machinery and equipment and on increasing stock of such capital assets; **gross loss** (*bookkeeping*) loss made when the cost of goods exceeds their sales value; **gross margin** or **profit** (*business*) the difference between the selling price of an article and the cost of the materials and labour needed to produce the article; **gross national product** the total value of all goods and services produced in a specified period (*usu* annually) within a country (ie the gross domestic product) plus the income from property held in foreign countries and incomes of domestic residents received from abroad as salaries, dividends or interest, minus similar payments made to residents of other countries; **gross'-out** (*US slang*) something offensive, disgusting, sickening (see also **gross out** below); **gross output** total selling value of (a firm's) output within a given period, *incl* the value of necessary materials bought to produce that output; **gross profit** see **gross margin**; trading profit before any allowance has been deducted for any other overhead or liabilities; **gross profit margin** gross profit expressed as a percentage of sales; **gross profit mark-up** gross profit expressed as a percentage of the cost price of goods; **gross weight** (business) the combined weight of an article and its packaging. — **great gross** a dozen gross; **gross out** (*US slang*) to disgust, shock, offend with indecency or sickening behaviour; **gross up** to convert a net figure into a gross one for the purpose of tax calculation, etc; **in gross** in bulk, wholesale. [Fr *gros*, from L *grossus* thick]

grossart. See **groser**.

grossièreté *gros-yer-tā*, (*Fr*) *n* grossness, rudeness, coarseness.

grossular *gros'ū-lər* or **grossularite** *-īt*, *n* gooseberry-stone, a lime alumina garnet, often green. [Fr *groseille* gooseberry, Latinized as *grossulāria*]

grot *grot*, (*poetic*) *n* a grotto.

grotesque *grō-tesk'*, *adj* extravagantly formed; fantastic; bizarre; ludicrous, absurd. — *n* an extravagant ornament, containing animals, plants, etc, in fantastic or incongruous forms (*art*); a bizarre figure or object. — *adv* **grotesque'ly**. — *n* **grotesque'ness**. — *n* **grotesqu'ery** or **grotesqu'erie**. [Fr *grotesque*, from Ital *grottesca*, from *grotta* a grotto]

Grotian *grō'shi-ən*, *adj* of or pertaining to Hugo *Grotius*, Latin name of Huig van *Groot* (1583–1645), founder of the science of international law. — **Grotian theory** the theory that man is essentially a social being, and that the principles of justice are of perpetual obligation and in harmony with man's nature. — **Grotian** or **governmental (theory of the) Atonement** the theory that Christ paid the penalty of human sin in order that God might for His sake forgive sinners while preserving the law that punishment should follow sin.

grotto *grot'ō*, *n* a cave; an imitation cave, *usu* fantastic or fanciful in appearance: — *pl* **grott'oes** or **grott'os**. — **grott'o-work**. [Ital *grotta* (Fr *grotte*), from L *crypta*, from Gr *kryptē* a crypt, vault]

grotty *grot'i*, (*slang*) *adj* ugly, in bad condition, or useless. [**grotesque**]

grouch *growch*, *vi* to grumble. — *n* a spell of grumbling; sulks; a grumbler. — *adv* **grouch'ily**. — *n* **grouch'iness**. — *adj* **grouch'y**. [See **grutch**, **grudge**]

grouf. See **groof**.

grough *gruf*, *n* a deep gully or channel eroded in upland peat moor areas such as the Peak District. [Perh from obs or dialect *groff* rough, coarse; see **gruff**]

ground[1], **grounden**. See **grind**[2].

ground[2] *grownd*, *n* the solid surface of the earth; a portion of the earth's surface; land; soil; the floor, etc; the solid land underlying an area of water (*naut*); earth (*elec*; *NAm*); position; an area associated with some activity (such as *football ground, playground, battleground*); distance to be covered; matter to be dealt with; that on which something is raised (*lit* or *fig*); foundation; sufficient reason; bottom, *esp* sea-bottom (*obs*); the surface on which a work is represented (*art*); a first coat of paint or colour; surrounding rock (*mining*); the space behind the popping-crease with which the batsman must be in touch by bat or person if he is not to be stumped or run out (*cricket*); (in *pl*) an area of land attached to or surrounding a building; (in *pl*) dregs or sediment (eg of coffee); (in *pl*) basis of justification. — *vt* to fix on a foundation or principle; to put or rest on the ground; to cause to run aground; to instruct in first principles; to cover with a preparatory layer or coating, as a basis for painting, etching, etc; to earth (*elec*; *NAm*); to keep on the ground, prevent from flying (*aeronautics*); to suspend from usual activity (eg as a punishment). — *adj* of, relating to, situated or operating on or near the ground. — *vi* to come to the ground; to strike the sea-bottom, etc and remain fixed. — *n* **ground'age** a charge on a ship in port. — *adj* **ground'ed**. — *adv* **ground'edly** on good grounds. — *n* **ground'er** someone who, or something that, grounds; a ball that keeps low. — *n* **ground'ing** foundation; sound general knowledge of a subject; the background of embroidery, etc; the act or process of preparing or laying a ground; the act of laying or of running aground. — *adj* **ground'less** without ground, foundation or reason. — *adv* **ground'lessly**. — *n* **ground'lessness**. — *n* **ground'ling** a fish that keeps near the bottom of the water, *esp* the spinous loach; a person on the ground in contrast to one in an aircraft, etc; formerly a spectator in the pit of a theatre, and hence a person of the common herd. — *adj* (*Lamb*, etc) base. — **ground'-angling** fishing without a float, with a weight placed a few inches from the hook, bottom-fishing; **ground annual** (*Scots law*) an annual payment forming a burden on land; **ground'-ash** a sapling of ash; a stick made of an ash sapling; **ground'bait** bait dropped to the bottom to bring fish to the neighbourhood (also *fig*); **ground'-bass** a bass part constantly repeated with varying melody and harmony (*music*); **ground'-beetle** any beetle of the Carabidae, a family related to the tiger-beetles; **ground'breaking** (*esp US*) the breaking of ground at the beginning of a construction project. — *adj* innovative, breaking new ground. — **ground'burst** the explosion of a bomb on the ground (as opposed to in the air); **ground cherry** any of the European dwarf cherries; any of several plants of the genus Physalis, also called husk-tomato, Cape gooseberry, etc; the fruit of these plants; **ground control** control, by information radioed from a ground installation, of aircraft observed by radar; **ground cover** low plants and shrubs growing among the trees in a forest; various low herbaceous plants used to cover an area instead of grass; **ground crew** see **ground staff**; **ground'-cuckoo** a name for several ground-running birds of the cuckoo family, such as the chaparral cock and the coucal; **ground'-dove** or **-pigeon** various small American pigeons of terrestrial habits; **ground effect** the extra aerodynamic lift, exploited by hovercraft, etc and affecting aircraft flying near the ground, caused by the cushion of trapped air beneath the vehicle; **ground elder** another name for goutweed; **ground'-feeder** a fish that feeds at the bottom; **ground floor** or **storey** the floor on or near a level with the ground; **ground frost** frost on the surface of the ground; a temperature of 0° C or less registered on a horizontal thermometer in contact with the shorn grass tips of a turf surface; **ground game** hares, rabbits, etc, as distinguished from winged game; **ground'hog** the woodchuck; the aardvark; **ground'-hold** (*Spenser* and *naut*) ground-tackle; **ground ice** the ice formed at the bottom of the water; **ground ivy** a British labiate creeping-plant (genus *Nepeta*) whose leaves when the edges curl become ivy-like; **ground** (or **grund**) **mail** (*Scot*) payment for right of burial; **ground'mass** (*geol*) the fine-grained part of an igneous rock, glassy or minutely crystalline, in which the larger crystals are embedded; **ground**

moraine a mass of mud, sand and stones dragged along under a glacier or ice-sheet; **ground'nut** the peanut or monkey-nut (Arachis); the earth-nut; **ground oak** a sapling of oak; various species of *Teucrium*; **ground'-officer** an officer in charge of the grounds of an estate; **ground plan** a plan of the horizontal section of the lowest or ground storey of a building; first plan, general outline; **ground plate** the bottom horizontal timber to which the frame of a building is secured; **ground'plot** the plot of ground on which a building stands; a method of calculating the position of an aircraft by relating the ground speed and time on course to the starting position; **ground-position indicator** an instrument which continuously displays the dead-reckoning position of an aircraft; **ground'prox** a device, fitted to large passenger aircraft, which warns the pilot when altitude falls below a given level (*ground proximity* warning system); **ground rent** rent paid to a landowner for the right to use of the ground for a specified term, usually in England ninety-nine years; **ground'-robin** the chewink, or towhee; **ground rule** a basic rule of procedure; a modifying (sports) rule for a particular place or circumstance; **ground'sel, ground'sill** or (*obs*) **ground'sell** the lowest timber of a structure, a ground plate, sleeper or sole plate; **ground'sheet** a waterproof sheet spread on the ground by campers, etc; **ground'-sloth** a heavy extinct ground-going sloth; **grounds'man** or sometimes **ground'man** a person whose job is to take care of a cricket ground or a sportsfield, etc; an aerodrome mechanic; **ground'speed** (*aeronautics*) speed of an aircraft relative to the ground; **ground squirr'el** the chipmunk or hackee, or any of several burrowing rodents; **ground staff** aircraft mechanics, etc, whose work is on the ground (also **ground crew**); a paid staff of players (*cricket*); people employed to look after a sportsfield; **ground state** the state of a nuclear system, atoms, etc, when at their lowest (or normal) energy; **ground stroke** (*tennis*) a return played after the ball has bounced; **ground'swell** a broad, deep undulation of the ocean caused by a distant gale or earthquake; a gathering movement, as of public or political opinion or feeling, which is evident although the cause or leader is not known; **ground tackle** tackle for securing a vessel at anchor. — *adj* **ground'-to-air'** (of a missile) aimed and fired from the ground at a target in the air. — **ground water** water naturally in the subsoil or occupying space in rocks; **ground'work** that which forms the ground or foundation of anything; the basis; essential preparatory work; the first principle; the ground of painting (*art*); **ground zero** the point on the ground directly under the explosion of a nuclear weapon in the air. — **break ground** to begin working untouched ground; to take the first step in any project; **break new** (or **fresh**) **ground** to be innovative; **cover a lot of ground** to make good progress; **cover the ground** to treat a topic, etc adequately; **cut** or **take the ground from under someone** or **from under someone's feet** to anticipate someone's arguments or actions and destroy their force; **down to the ground** see under **down**[3]; **fall to the ground** to come to nothing; **forbidden ground** an unmentionable topic; **gain ground** to advance; to become more widely influential; to spread; **give ground** to fall back, retreat (*lit* and *fig*); **hold** or **stand one's ground** to stand firm; **home ground** familiar territory; **into the ground** to the point of exhaustion; (**let in**) **on the ground floor** (to admit) on the same terms as the original promoters, or at the start (of a business venture, etc); **lose ground** to fall back; to decline in influence, etc; **off the ground** started, under way; **on firm ground** in a strong position, or one of confidence; **on one's own** (or **home**) **ground** in circumstances with which one is familiar; **prepare the ground** to ease the way for, facilitate the progress of, something (with *for*); **run to ground** to hunt out, track down; **shift one's ground** to change one's standpoint in a situation or argument; **to ground** into hiding. [OE *grund*; cognate with Ger *Grund*, ON *grunnr*]

groundsel[1] *grown(d)'sl*, *n* a very common yellow-flowered composite weed of waste ground (*Senecio vulgaris*). [OE *gundeswilge*, appar from *gund* pus, and *swelgan* to swallow, from its use in poultices, influenced by *grund* ground]

groundsel[2], **groundsell**, **groundsill**. See under **ground**[2].

group *grōōp*, *n* a number of people or things together; a number of individual things or people related in some definite way differentiating them from others; a clique, school, section of a party; a number of commercial companies combined under single ownership and central control; a division of an air force made up of a number of wings; a division of the US air force subordinate to a wing; a US military unit formed of two or more battalions; a scientific classification; a combination of figures forming a harmonious whole (*art*); a system of elements having a binary operation that is associative, an identity element for the operation, and an inverse for every element (*math*); a vertical column of the periodic table containing elements with similar properties, etc (*chem*); a number of atoms that occur together in several compounds (also **radical**; *chem*); a division in the Scout organization; a pop group. — *vt* to form into a group or groups. — *vi* to fall into harmonious combination; to cluster, mass. — *adj* **group'able**. — *n* **group'age** the collection of objects or people into a group or groups. — *n* **group'er** (*hist*) a member of the Oxford group. — *n* **group'ie** or **group'y** (*slang*) a (*usu* female) fan who follows pop groups, or other celebrities, wherever they appear, often in the hope of having sexual relations with them. — *n* **group'ing** (*art*) the act of disposing and arranging figures in a group. — *n* **group'ist** an adherent of a group. — Also *adj*. — *n* **group'let** (often *derog*) a small group, a clique or faction. — *n* **group'uscule** (*-əs-kūl*; from Fr; often *derog*) a grouplet. — **group calling** (with operator-connected extensions) automatic re-routing of incoming telephone calls to other extensions in a pre-determined order until the call has been taken; **group'-captain** an air force officer of equivalent rank to a colonel or naval captain; **group discussion** a meeting in which a group of people share their opinions on a particular subject (eg as a market research method, etc); **group dynamics** (*psychol*) the interaction of human behaviour within a small social group; **group insurance** insurance issued on a number of people under a single policy; **group marriage** a hypothetical primitive relationship by which every man of a group is husband to every woman of a group; **group practice** a medical practice in which several doctors work together as partners; **group selection** a form of natural selection proposed to explain the evolution of behaviour which apparently is to the long-term good of a group or species, rather than to the immediate good of the individual; **group sex** sexual activity in which several people take part simultaneously; **group theory** (*math*) the investigation of the properties of groups; **group therapy** therapy in which a small group of people with the same psychological or physical problems discuss their difficulties under the chairmanship of eg a doctor; **group trading** (*business*) the practice by a number of traders of joining up, eg to improve distribution, cut administration costs, etc. — **Group of Five, Seven, Ten**, etc (also **G5**, **G7**, **G10** or **G-5**, **G-7**, **G-10**, etc) (*econ*) during the 1960s, '70s and '80s (committees representing) groups of countries with common economic interests, the *Five* comprising the major Western-style economies, ie United States, Japan, West Germany, Britain and France, the *Seven* these with the addition of Italy and Canada, and the *Ten* the main industrial members of the International Monetary Fund; **pop group** see **pop**[2]. [Fr *groupe*, from Ital *groppo* a bunch, knot, from Gmc; cf Ger *Kropf* protuberance]

grouper[1] *grōōp'ər* (*US* and *UK*) or **groper** *grōp'ər* (*Austr*), *n* any one of many fishes, *esp* various kinds resembling bass: — *pl* **group'ers** or **grop'ers**, or (collectively) **group'er** or **grop'er**. [Port *garoupa*]

grouper[2]. See under **group**.

grouse[1] *grows*, *n* a plump reddish game bird (*Lagopus scoticus*) with a short curved bill, short legs, and feathered feet, found on Scottish moors and hills and in certain other parts of Britain, also called **red grouse**; extended to other birds of the family *Tetraonidae*, including the *black grouse* or blackcock, the *willow-grouse* and various birds of North America: — *pl* **grouse**. — **grouse'-disease** a nematode infection of grouse; **grouse moor** a tract of moorland on which grouse live, breed, and are shot for sport. [Origin uncertain]

grouse[2] *grows*, *vi* to grumble. — *n* a grumble. — *n* **grous'er**. [Cf **grutch**]

grouse[3] *grows*, (*Austr colloq*) *adj* very good. [Origin unknown]

grout[1] *growt*, *n* (*orig*) coarse meal; a thin coarse mortar for filling cracks, etc (also called *cement grout*); a fine plaster for finishing ceilings, filling between tiles, etc; the sediment of liquor; lees. — *vt* to fill and finish with grout. — *n* **grout'er**. — *n* **grout'ing** filling up or finishing with grout; the material so used. — *adj* **grout'y** (*dialect*) thick, muddy; sulky (*US archaic*). [OE *grūt* coarse meal; or perh in part Fr *grouter* to grout]

grout[2] *growt*, *vi* to root or grub with the snout. [Perh connected with OE *grēot* grit]

grove *grōv*, *n* a wood of small size, generally of a pleasant or ornamental character; an avenue of trees; (with *cap*) used in street names; an erroneous translation of *Asherah*, the wooden image of the goddess Ashtoreth, also of Hebrew *eshel* tamarisk, in Genesis 21.33 (*Bible*); a lodge of a benefit society called Druids. [OE *grāf*, possibly tamarisk]

grovel *grov'l*, *vi* to humble oneself, behave abjectly, eg in apologizing; to behave obsequiously or sycophantically; to lie face downwards, or crawl, in abject fear, etc: — *pr p* **grov'elling** or (*US*) **grov'eling**; *pa t* and *pa p* **grov'elled** or (*US*) **grov'eled**. — *n* **grov'eller** or (*esp US*) **grov'eler**. — *adj* **grov'elling** abject, cringing, servile. [Back-formation from ME *groveling*, *grofling* prone, from ON *grūfa* and sfx *-ling*]

grovet *grov'ət*, (*wrestling*) *n* a hold (from the kneeling position) in which the opponent's head is gripped and his (or her) shoulders are forced to the floor using the other arm.

grow *grō*, *vi* to have life; to have a habitat; to become enlarged by a natural process; to advance towards maturity; to increase in size; to tend in a certain direction while growing; to develop; to become greater in any way; to extend; to pass from one state to another; to become; to come by degrees (to love, like, hate, etc) — *vt* to cause or allow to grow; to produce or to cultivate; (in *passive*) to cover with growth: — *pa t* **grew** (*grōō*); *pa p* **grown** (*grōn*). — *adj* **grow'able**. — *n* **grow'er**. — *n* and *adj* **grow'ing**. — *n* the production of semiconductor crystals by slow crystallization from the molten state. — *adj* (sometimes in combination) **grown** having reached full, or a certain degree of, growth, as in *full-grown*, *half-grown*. — *n* **growth** a growing; gradual increase; progress, development; that which has grown; a diseased, abnormal formation; increase in value (**growth-orientated** providing increased capital rather than high interest). — Also *adj*. — *n* **growth'ist** a person who is committed to or who is an advocate of growth, *esp* economic. — Also *adj*. — **grow'-bag** or sometimes **grow'ing-bag** a large plastic bag containing compost in which seeds can be germinated and plants grown to full size; **grow'ing-pains** neuralgic pains sometimes experienced in growing children; initial problems in the establishment and running of an enterprise, etc; **grow'ing-point** (*bot*) the meristem at the apex of an axis, where active cell-division occurs and differentiation of tissues begins; **grown'-junction** a semiconductor junction produced by changing the types and amounts of acceptor and donor impurities added during growing; **grown'-up** an adult. — Also *adj*. — **growth area** (*business* and *marketing*) a region with rapidly increasing industrial and commercial activity, *usu* resulting from incentives offered to employers; **growth hormone** a hormone secreted by the anterior lobe of the pituitary gland, that promotes growth in vertebrates; any of several natural or artificial substances that promote growth in plants; **growth industry** an industry or branch of industry which is developing and expanding (also *fig*); **growth market** (*marketing*) a market in which demand for a product is greatly increasing; **growth promoter** any of various substances which promote growth in plants, such as cytokinin; any of various hormonal substances used to boost the fattening of livestock; **growth ring** a recognizable increment of wood in a cross-section of a branch or trunk, *usu* but not necessarily an annual ring (qv under **annual**); **growth-share matrix** (*marketing*) a diagrammatic analysis of a company's portfolio of businesses, arranged according to their rate of market growth and their relative market share; **growth substance** one of a number of substances (sometimes called *plant hormones*) formed in plants or synthetically, that at low concentrations have specific effects on plant growth or development. — **grow into** to grow big enough to fill comfortably; **grow like Topsy** (*colloq*) simply to grow, apparently from nothing (as Topsy in Harriet Beecher Stowe's *Uncle Tom's Cabin* assumed she did); (loosely) to grow in a random, indiscriminate or unplanned way; **grow on** to gain a greater hold on; to gain in the estimation of, become ever more acceptable to; (of seedlings) to (be stimulated to) develop into mature plants by suitable positioning, treatment, etc; **grow out of** to issue from, result from; to pass beyond in development; to become too big for; **grow to** to advance to, come to (*archaic*); (of milk) to stick to the pan and develop a bad taste in heating (so *prob* Shakesp *Merchant of Venice*, II.2; *obs*); **grow together** to become united by growth; **grow up** to advance in growth, become full-grown, mature or adult; to spring up. [OE *grōwan*; ON *grōa*]

growl *growl vi* (of a dog) to utter a deep rough murmuring sound in the throat expressive of hostility; (of thunder, etc) to make a sound similar to this; to speak or grumble surlily, snarl. — *vt* to utter or express by growling. — *n* a murmuring, snarling sound, as of an angry dog; a surly grumble. — *n* **growl'er** someone who or something that growls; a N American river fish, the large-mouthed black bass, so named from the sound it emits; a small iceberg; a four-wheeled horse-drawn cab (*old slang*); a jug or pitcher used for carrying beer (*US colloq*). — *n* **growl'ery** (*archaic*) a retreat for times of ill-humour. — *n* and *adj* **growl'ing**. — *adv* **growl'ingly**. — *adj* **growl'y**. [Cf Du *grollen* to grumble: allied to Gr *gryllizein* to grunt]

grown, **growth**. See **grow**.

groyne *groin*, *n* a breakwater, of wood or other material, to check erosion and sand-drifting. [Prob OFr *groin* snout, from L *grunnīre* to grunt, but perhaps the same as **groin**[1]]

GRT or **grt** *abbrev*: gross registered tonnage, (in shipping) a measurement of cubic capacity.

GRU *abbrev*: the military intelligence organization of the former Soviet Union. [Russ *Glavnoye Razvedyvatelnoye Upravleniye* Chief Intelligence Directorate]

grub *grub*, *vi* to dig, work or search in the dirt (with *about* or *around*); to be occupied meanly, toil, slog (with *about* or *around*); to eat (*slang*); (of a horse) to take its feed. — *vt* to dig or root out of the ground (generally followed by *up* or *out*); to dig up the surface of (ground) to clear it for agriculture, etc; to supply with victuals (*slang*): — *pr p* **grubb'ing**; *pa t* and *pa p* **grubbed**. — *n* an insect larva, *esp* one thick and soft; food (*colloq*); a ball bowled along the ground (*cricket*). — *n* **grubb'er** someone who, or that which, grubs; an implement for grubbing or stirring the soil; a grub (*cricket*); a grub-kick. — *adj* **grubb'y** dirty, soiled, grimy; infested with grubs. — **grub kick** (*Rugby football*) a kick where the ball moves along the ground;

grub screw a small headless screw; **grub shop** (*colloq*) a restaurant; **grub'stake** (*US*) outfit, provisions, etc given to a prospector for a share in finds. — *vt* to provide with such. — **Grub Street** a former name of Milton Street, Moorfields, London, once inhabited by booksellers' hacks and shabby writers generally; the milieu of hack writers or activity of hack writing. — Also (*usu* **Grub'street**) *adj*. [ME *grobe*; origin uncertain]

grubble *grub'l*, an *obs* variant of **grabble**.

grudge *gruj*, *vt* to envy (a person something); to give or allow (something to a person) unwillingly; to resent (doing something); to murmur at (*obs*). — *vi* to murmur, to show discontent (*obs*). — *n* an old cause of quarrel or resentment; a feeling of enmity or envy. — *adj* **grudge'ful** (*rare*; *Spenser*). — *n* and *adj* **grudg'ing**. — *adv* **grudg'ingly**. — **grudge a thought** (*Shakesp*) to thank resentfully or grudgingly. [**grutch**]

grue. See **gruesome**.

gruel *grōō'əl*, *n* a thin food made by boiling oatmeal in water; punishment, severe treatment (*archaic colloq*). — *vt* to subject to any severe or exhausting experience. — *n* and *adj* **gru'elling** or (*US*) **gruel'ing** (an experience, ordeal, encounter, defeat, etc that is) punishing, backbreaking, exhausting. [OFr *gruel* (Fr *gruau*) groats, from LL *grūtellum*, dimin of *grūtum* meal, of Gmc origin; cf OE *grūt*]

gruesome *grōō'səm*, *adj* horrible; grisly; macabre. — *n* **grue** or **grew** (*Scot*) a creeping of the flesh; a shiver; a shudder; a pellicle of ice. — *vi* **grue** or **grew** (*Scot*) to shudder; to feel the flesh creep; (of the flesh) to creep; (of the blood) to curdle. — *adv* **grue'somely**. — *n* **grue'someness**. [Cf Du *gruwzaam*, Ger *grausam*]

gruff *gruf*, *adj* rough, or abrupt in manner or sound. — *adj* **gruff'ish**. — *adv* **gruff'ly**. — *n* **gruff'ness**. [Du *grof*; cognate with Swed *grof* and Ger *grob* coarse]

grufted *gruft'id*, (*dialect*) *adj* dirty, begrimed. [Dialect *gruft* particles of soil]

gru-gru or **groo-groo** *grōō'-grōō*, *n* a name for several tropical American palms related to the coconut palm, yielding oil-nuts; an edible weevil grub (also **gru-gru worm**) found in their pith.

grum *grum*, *adj* morose; surly; (of a sound) deep in the throat (*obs*). — *adv* **grum'ly**. — *n* **grum'ness**. [Cf Dan *grum*]

grumble *grum'bl*, *vi* to murmur with discontent; to express discontent; to mutter, mumble, murmur; to growl, rumble. — *n* the act of grumbling; an instance or spell of grumbling; a cause or occasion for grumbling. — *n* **grum'bler**. — *n* **Grumbletō'nian** (*hist*; *derog*) a member of the country party as opposed to the court party, after 1689. — *n* and *adj* **grum'bling**. — *adv* **grum'blingly**. — *adj* **grum'bly** inclined to grumble. [Cf Du *grommelen*, frequentative of *grommen* to mutter; Ger *grummeln*]

grume *grōōm*, *n* (*med*) a thick, viscous fluid; a clot. — *adj* **grum'ous** or **grum'ose** of or like grume; clotted, lumpy; composed of grains (*bot*). [OFr *grume* a bunch, from L *grūmus* a little heap]

grummet[1]. See **grommet**.

grummet[2] *grum'it*, (*hist*) *n* a cabin-boy. [OFr *gromet*; see ety of **gourmet**]

grumose, **grumous**. See **grume**.

grumph *grumf*, (*Scot*) *n* a grunt. — *vi* to grunt. — *n* **grumph'ie** (*Scot*) a pig. [Imit]

grump *grump*, (*colloq*) *n* a bad-tempered, surly person; (in *pl*) a fit of bad temper, the sulks. — *vi* to grumble, complain. — *adv* **grum'pily**. — *n* **grum'piness**. — *adj* **grum'py** surly. [Obs *grump* snub, sulkiness]

grund mail. See **ground mail** under **ground**[2].

Grundyism *grun'di-izm*, *n* conventional prudery, from the question 'But what will Mrs *Grundy* say?' in Thomas Morton's play, *Speed the Plough* (1798).

grunge *grunj*, (*orig US*) *n* dirt, grime, trash; any unpleasant, nasty substance; thrift-shop fashion; its designer equivalent. — *adj* **grung'y** dirty, messy; unattractive, unappealing. [Prob an imit coinage]

grunion *grun'yən*, *n* a small Californian sea-fish which spawns on shore. [Prob Sp *gruñon* grunter]

grunt *grunt*, *vi* (of a pig) to make a gruff snorting noise; to produce a short gruff noise in the throat. — *vt* to utter with a grunt. — *n* a sound made by a pig; any similar sound made by a person or animal; a tropical spiny-finned fish (*Haemulon*, etc) of a family related to the snappers, that grunts when taken from the sea; an infantry soldier (*military slang*); a labourer, drudge (*US slang*). — *n* **grunt'er** a person who or animal that grunts; a pig; any of several kinds of grunting fish. — *n* and *adj* **grunt'ing**. — *adv* **grunt'ingly**. — *vi* **grunt'le** (*dialect*) to grunt, keep grunting. — *n* (*Scot*) a grunt; a snout. [OE *grunnettan*, frequentative of *grunian*]

gruntled *grun'tәld*, (*facetious*) *adj* happy, pleased, in good humour. [Back-formation from **disgruntled**]

gruppetto *grōō-pet'ō*, (*music*) *n* a turn: — *pl* **gruppett'i** (-*ē*). [Ital, a small group]

grutch *gruch*, (*Spenser*) *vt* or *vi* to grudge or complain. — *n* a grudge; a complaint. [OFr *groucher*, *grocher*, *gruchier* to grumble]

grutten. See **greet**[2].

Gruyère *grü'* or *grōō'yer*, or -*yer'*, *n* a whole-milk cheese, made at *Gruyère* (Switzerland) and elsewhere.

gr. wt. *abbrev*: gross weight.

gryce; **gryde**; **gryesly**, **grysely**; **gryesy**; **gryfon**; **gryphon**; **gryke**; **grype**. See **grice**[1]; **gride**; **grisly**; **gris**[1]; **griffin**; **grike**; **gripe**.

grypt *gript*, (*Spenser*) *prob* for **griped** or **gripped** in the sense of bitten, pierced.

grysbok *hhrās'bok* (*SAfr*) or *grīs'bok*, *n* a small S African antelope, ruddy chestnut with white hairs. [Du, greybuck, from *grys* grey, and *bok* a buck]

grysie. See **grise**[1].

GS *abbrev*: General Secretary; General Staff; Grammar School.

gs *abbrev*: gauss; guineas.

GSA *abbrev*: Girls' School Association (UK).

GSM *abbrev*: gram(me)s per square metre; *Groupe Spéciale Mobile*, the standard European digital cellular system (*telecomm*); Guildhall School of Music and Drama.

GSO *abbrev*: General Staff Officer.

GSR *abbrev*: galvanic skin response.

G-string. See **gee-string**.

g-suit. See under *g*.

GT *abbrev*: gran turismo (see **gran**[1]).

Gt or **gt** *abbrev*: Great or great.

gt. (*med*) *abbrev*: gutta, a drop.

GTC *abbrev*: General Teaching Council (Scotland); (on an order for goods, securities, etc) good till cancelled.

gtd *abbrev*: guaranteed.

gu. See **gue**.

guacamole *gwa-kə-mō'li*, *n* a dish of mashed avocado with tomatoes, onions and seasoning. [Am Sp, from Nahuatl *ahuacamolli*, from *ahuacatl* avocado, and *molli* sauce]

guacharo *gwä'chä-rō*, *n* the oil-bird, a S American nocturnal fruit-eating bird (*Steatornis*) that roosts in caves, similar to the nightjars: — *pl* **gua'charos**. [Sp *guácharo*]

guaco *gwä'kō*, *n* a tropical American name for plants reputedly antidotal against snakebite, *esp* species of *Mikania* (climbing composites), and of Aristolochia; the medicinal substance obtained from them: — *pl* **gua'cos**. [Am Sp]

guaiacum *gwī'ə-kəm*, *n* any of a family of tropical American trees of the genus *Guai acum* some yielding lignum vitae; their greenish resin, used in medicine. [Sp *guayaco*, from a Haitian word]

guan *gwän*, *n* a large noisy American arboreal game bird. [Am Sp]

guana *gwä'nä*, *n* any large lizard. [For **iguana**]

guanaco *gwä-nä'kō*, *n* a wild llama. — Also **huana'co** (*wä*-): — *pl* **guana'co** or **guana'cos**, **huana'co** or **huana'cos**. [Quechua *huanaco*]

guanazolo *gwä-nä-zō'lō, n* a synthetic substance (amino-hydroxy-triazolo-pyrimidine) closely resembling guanine, used experimentally in controlling cancer by the starving of tumours.

guango *gwang'gō, n* the rain tree or saman: — *pl* **guan'gos**. [Sp, prob from Quechua]

guanine *gwä'nēn, n* a yellowish-white, amorphous substance, found in guano, liver, pancreas, and other organs of animals, and germ cells of plants, forming a constituent of nucleic acids. [**guan(o)** and **-ine**[1]]

guano *gwä'nō, n* the dung of sea-fowl, used as manure; artificially produced fertilizer, *esp* made from fish: — *pl* **gua'nos**. — *adj* **guanif'erous**. [Sp *guano, huano*, from Peruv *huanu* dung]

guar *gwär, n* a legume grown for forage and for its seeds which yield guar gum; guar gum. — **guar gum** a powder ground from guar seeds, used in the food industry as a thickening agent and stabilizer, as a sizing for paper, etc. [Hindi]

guaraná *gwä-rä-nä', n* a Brazilian liana (*Paullinia cupana*, of the family Sapindaceae); a paste made from its seeds which are high in caffeine (**guaraná bread**); a drink or drug made from this, with stimulant and astringent properties, etc. [Tupí]

Guaraní *gwä-rä-nē', n* an Indian of a group of tribes of southern Brazil and Paraguay (*pl* **Guaraní**); their language, cognate with Tupí. — Also *adj*.

guarani *gwä'rə-ni, n* the standard monetary unit of Paraguay (100 céntimos): — *pl* **guaranis'**, **guarani'** or **guaranies'**. [**Guaraní**]

guarantee *gar-ən-tē', n* a formal promise that something will be done, *esp* one in writing by the maker of a product to replace or repair it if it proves faulty within a stated period; generally, a promise or assurance; a legally binding agreement to take responsibility for another person's obligation or undertaking; a pledge or surety; someone to whom a guarantee is given, who gives a guarantee, or who acts as guarantor. — *vt* to issue a guarantee in respect of (eg an article or product); to secure (with *against* or *from*); to ensure, make certain or definite; to engage or undertake; to undertake as surety for another person: — *pr p* **guarantee'ing**; *pa t* and *pa p* **guaranteed'**. — *n* **guar'antor** (or *-tör'*) a person who makes a guaranty; a person in a guarantee contract who agrees to answer for a debt or default of another. — *n* **guar'anty** a securing, guaranteeing; a written undertaking to be responsible; a person who guarantees; a security. — *vt* (now *rare*) to guarantee. — **guarantee company** a company in which the members undertake to contribute money up to a certain amount if the company is wound up; **guarantee payment** a payment ordered by statute to be paid to an employee by his or her employer where the employee has been laid off or put on short-time working; **guarantee society** a joint-stock company on the insurance principle, which becomes security for the integrity of employees, eg cashiers. [Anglo-Fr *garantie*, from *garant* warrant, and prob Sp *garante*; see **warrant**[1]]

guard *gärd, vt* to ward, keep watch over; to take care of; to protect from danger or attack; to control passage through (a doorway, etc); in any of several games, to make a move to protect (a piece, etc); to escort (*archaic*); to protect the edge of, as by an ornamental border; to provide with guards; to trim (*lit* and *fig*; *Shakesp*). — *vi* to watch; to be wary; to take precautions. — *n* ward, keeping; protection; watch; that which guards from danger; a person or contingent stationed to keep watch, protect, or keep in custody; a person in charge of a railway train, or formerly a stagecoach; state of caution; posture of defence; either of two defensive players (*basketball*); (**left** and **right guard**) a lineman positioned immediately to the left, and right, respectively, of center (*Am football*); this position; the position in which a batsman grounds his bat in facing the bowling (*cricket*); part of a sword hilt; a watch-chain; a cricketer's or other sportsperson's protective pad or shield; (in a book) a strip for attachment of a plate, map or additional leaf; a trimming, or a stripe (*obs*); (in *pl*) household troops (Foot, Horse, and Life Guards). — *adj* **guard'able**. — *n* **guard'age** (*Shakesp*) wardship. — *adj* **guard'ant** or **gard'ant** (*heraldry*) having the face turned towards the viewer. — *n* (*Shakesp*) protector. — *adj* **guard'ed** wary; cautious; uttered with caution; trimmed, or striped (*obs*). — *adv* **guard'edly**. — *n* **guard'edness**. — *n* **guardee'** (*colloq*) a guardsman, *esp* in reference to elegant or dashing appearance. — *adj* **guard'less** without a guard; defenceless. — **guard'book** a blank book with guards; **guard cell** (*bot*) one of the lips of a stoma, a pair of specialized epidermal cells; **guard dog** a watchdog; **guard hair** one of the long coarse hairs which form the outer fur of certain mammals; **guard'house** a building for the accommodation of a military guard, and where prisoners are confined; **guard of honour** see under **honour**; **guard'rail** a rail (on a ship, train, etc, or beside a road) acting as a safety barrier; an additional rail fitted to a railway track to improve a train's stability; **guard ring** a keeper, or finger ring that serves to keep another from slipping off; **guard'room** a room having the same function as a guardhouse; **guard'-ship** or **guard'ship** a ship of war that superintends marine affairs in a harbour and protects it; guardianship (*archaic*; *Swift*); **guards'man** a soldier of the Guards, or (*US*) National Guard; **guard's van** (on a railway train) the van in which the guard travels. — **mount guard** to go on guard; **on** (or **off**) **one's guard** on (or not on) the alert for possible danger; wary (or unwary) about what one says or does; **run the guard** to get past a guard or sentinel without detection; **stand guard** to keep watch, act as sentry. [OFr *garder*, from OHGer *warten*; OE *weardian*, mod Eng **ward**]

guardian *gär'di-ən, n* a person who guards or takes care of someone or something; a person who has the care of the person, property and rights of another (eg a minor; *law*); (in England till 1930) a member of a board administering the poor laws. — *adj* protecting. — *n* **guard'ianship**. — **guardian angel** an angel supposed to watch over a particular person; a person specially devoted to the interests of another; (in *pl*, with *caps*) vigilantes patrolling New York's subway (and active elsewhere) to prevent crimes of violence. [Anglo-Fr *gardein*]

guarish or **garish** *gār'ish*, (*obs*) *vt* to heal. [OFr *guarir* (Fr *guérir*) to heal]

guava *gwä'və, n* a small tropical American myrtaceous tree of the genus *Psidium*; its yellow, pear-shaped fruit, often made into jelly. [Sp *guayaba* guava fruit; of S American origin]

guayule *gwä-ū'lā, n* a silvery-leaved shrub of the daisy family (*Parthenium argentatum*), native to Mexico and south-west USA; the rubber yielded by it. [Sp; of Nahuatl origin]

gub *gub*, or **gubbah** *gub'ə*, (*Austr colloq*; *derog*) *n* a white man. [Aboriginal term, meaning white demon]

gubbins *gub'inz*, (*colloq*) *n sing* a trivial object; a device, gadget; a silly person, fool: — *pl* **gubb'inses**. — *n sing* or *pl* rubbish. [From obs *gobbon* portion, perh connected with **gobbet**]

gubernaculum *gū-bər-nak'ū-ləm, n* in mammals, the cord supporting the testes in the scrotal sac. — *adj* **gubernac'ular**. [Ety as for **gubernator**]

gubernator *gū'bər-nā-tər, n* (*rare*) a governor. — *n* (*rare*) **gubernā'tion** control, rule. — *adj* **gubernatorial** (*esp US*; *-nə-tö'ri-əl*) of, or relating to, a governor. [L *gubernātor* a steersman]

guck *guk*, (*esp US*; *slang*) *n* slimy, gooey muck; anything unpleasant or unappealing. — *adj* **guck'y** slimy, gooey, mucky; slushy, sloppy, sentimental. [Prob *goo* or *gunk* and *muck*]

guddle *gud'l*, (*Scot*) *vt* and *vi* to fish with the hands by groping under the stones or banks of a stream. — *vi* to dabble in, play messily with, something liquid. — *n* a mess, muddle, confusion. [Origin uncertain]

gude or **guid** *güd* or *gid*, Scottish forms of **good**. — **gudeman**, **gudesire**, etc, see under **good**.

gudgeon[1] *guj'ən*, *n* an easily caught small carp-like freshwater fish (*Gobio*); a person easily cheated. — *adj* (*archaic*) foolish. — *vt* (*archaic*) to impose on, cheat. [OFr *goujon*, from L *gōbiō*, *-ōnis* a kind of fish, from Gr *kōbios*; see **goby**]

gudgeon[2] *guj'ən*, *n* the bearing of a shaft, *esp* when made of a separate piece; a metallic journal piece let into the end of a wooden shaft; a metal pin into which the pintle of a small craft's rudder fits; a pin. — **gudgeon pin** in an internal combustion engine, a pin fastening the piston to the connecting rod. [OFr *goujon* the pin of a pulley]

gue, **gu** or **gju** *gōō* or *gū*, *n* a kind of viol formerly used in Shetland. [ON *gigja*]

Guebre or **Gueber** *gā'bər* or *gē'bər*, *n* a Zoroastrian in Iran. [Fr *guèbre*, from Pers *gabr*; see **giaour**]

guelder rose *gel'dər rōz*, *n* a shrub of the genus *Viburnum*, with large white balls of flowers. [From *Geldern* or from *Gelderland*]

Guelf or **Guelph** *gwelf*, (*hist*) *n* a member of a papal and popular party in medieval Italy, opposed to the Ghibellines and the emperors. — *adj* **Guelf'ic** pertaining to the Guelf family or party. [*Guelfo*, Italian form of the German family name *Welf*, said to have been the war cry of Henry the Lion at the battle of Weinsberg (1140) against the Emperor Conrad III]

guenon *gen'ən* or *gə-nɔ̃*, *n* any species of the genus *Cercopithecus*, long-tailed African monkeys. [Fr]

guerdon *gûr'dən*, (*esp poetic*) *n* a reward or recompense. — *vt* to reward. [OFr *guerdon*, *gueredon* (Ital *guidardone*), from LL *widerdonum*, from OHGer *widarlōn* (OE *witherlēan*), from *widar*, against, and *lōn* reward; or more prob the latter part of the word is from L *dōnum* a gift]

guereza *ger'ə-zə*, *n* a large, long-haired, black-and-white African monkey, with a bushy tail; any species of the same genus (*Colobus*). [Appar of Somali origin]

guerilla. See **guerrilla**.

guéridon *gā-rē-dɔ̃* or *ger'i-dən*, *n* a small ornate table or stand. [Fr]

guérite *ge-rēt'*, *n* a turret or sentry box (*hist*); a type of chair with a back that is elongated and curves over to form a hood. [Fr, from OFr *garite*; see **garret**]

guernsey *gûrn'zi*, *n* (sometimes with *cap*) a close-fitting knitted woollen jersey, *esp* worn by sailors; a *usu* sleeveless football shirt (*Austr*); (with *cap*) one of a breed of dairy cattle from *Guernsey*, in the Channel Islands; (with *cap*) Channel Island patois derived from Norman-French. — *adj* (sometimes with *cap*) in the style of a guernsey. — **Guernsey lily** a Nerine (qv). — **get a guernsey** (*Austr*) to be selected for a team; to win approval.

guerre à mort *ger a mor*, (*Fr*) war to the death; **guerre à outrance** (*ōō-trãs*) war to the uttermost, to the bitter end.

guerrilla or **guerilla** *gər-il'ə*, *n* a member of an irregular force engaging in warfare or in the harassment of an army, etc, *usu* operating in small bands, and often politically motivated. — Also *adj*. — *n* **guerrillero** (*-yā'ro*) a guerrilla, someone who takes part in guerrilla warfare: — *pl* **guerriller'os**. — **guerrilla strike** a sudden and brief industrial strike; **guerrilla tactics**; **guerrilla warfare**. [Sp *guerrilla*, dimin of *guerra* war, from OHGer *werra*; cf **war**; Fr *guerre*]

guess[1] *ges*, *vt* to judge on the basis of inadequate knowledge or none at all; to conjecture; to hit on or solve by conjecture; to think, believe, suppose (*archaic* or *esp NAm*). — *vi* to make a conjecture or conjectures. — *n* a judgement made or opinion formed without sufficient evidence or grounds; a random surmise; a riddle, conundrum (*Scot*). — *adj* **guess'able**. — *n* **guess'er**. — *n* and *adj* **guess'ing**. — *adv* **guess'ingly**. — **guess'work** the process or result of guessing. — **anybody's guess** purely a matter for individual conjecture, impossible for anyone to know. [ME *gessen*; cognate with Du *gissen*; Dan *gisse*, Mod Icel *giska*, *gizka*, for *gitska*, from *geta* to get, think; see **get, forget**]

guess[2]. See **othergates**.

guesstimate *ges'ti-mət*, *n* (*orig facetious*) a *guess*ed *estimate*, or one based on very little knowledge. — *vt* to estimate using a rough guess.

guest *gest*, *n* a visitor received and entertained gratuitously or for payment; a person visiting one's home by invitation, to stay, for a meal, etc; a person paying for accommodation in a hotel, etc; a person honoured with hospitality by a government, organization, etc; an animal inhabiting or breeding in another's nest (*zool*). — *adj* and *n* (an artist, conductor, etc) not a regular member of a company, etc, or not regularly appearing on a programme, but taking part on a special occasion. — *vi* to be a guest artist, etc. — *vt* to have as a guest artist on a show. — *vi* **guest'en** (*obs*; *Scott*) to stay as a guest. — *adv* **guest'wise** (*obs*) in the manner or capacity of a guest. — **guest'-chamber** (*archaic*; *Bible*) or **guest'-room** a room for the accommodation of a guest; **guest'-house** a small boarding-house; a hospice (*archaic*); **guest'-night** a night when non-members of a society are entertained; **guest rope** a rope hanging over the side of a vessel to help other vessels drawing alongside, etc; **guest worker** a foreign worker employed temporarily in a country, a Gastarbeiter (qv). [OE (Anglian) *gest* (WSax *giest*), perh influenced by ON; related to Du *gast* and Ger *Gast*, L *hostis* stranger, enemy]

Gueux *gø*, *n pl* the name assumed by the confederation (1565) of nobles and others to resist the introduction of the Inquisition into the Low Countries by Philip II of Spain. [Fr, beggars]

guff *guf*, *n* nonsense, humbug (*colloq*); a smell, stink (*Scot*). — *n* **guff'ie** (*Scot*) a pig. [Perh imit; cf Norwegian *gufs* a puff]

guffaw *guf-ö'*, *vi* to laugh vociferously. — *n* a loud, boisterous laugh. [From the sound]

guga *gōō'gə*, (*Scot*) *n* a young gannet, eaten as a delicacy, *esp* in the Hebrides. [Gaelic]

guggle *gug'l*, *vi* to gurgle. — *n* a gurgle. [Cf **gurgle**]

guichet *gē'shā*, *n* a hatch or other small opening in a wall, door, etc; a ticket-office window. [Fr; cf **wicket**]

Guicowar. See **Gaekwar**.

guid. See **gude**.

guide *gīd*, *vt* to lead, conduct or direct; to regulate, steer, control; to influence. — *vi* to act as a guide. — *n* a person who, or thing which, guides; a person who conducts travellers, tourists, mountaineers, etc; someone who directs another in their course of life; a soldier or other employed to obtain information for an army; (with *cap*) a member of an organization for girls analogous to the Scout Association (also formerly **Girl Guide**); a guidebook; anything serving to direct, show the way, determine direction of motion or course of conduct. — *adj* **guid'able**. — *n* (*obs*) **guid'age** guidance. — *n* **guid'ance** direction; leadership. — *n* **guid'er** a person who guides; a device for guiding; (with *cap*) a captain or lieutenant in the Guides. — *adj* **guide'less**. — *n* **guide'ship**. — *adj* **guid'ing**. — *n* the action of the verb; (*usu* with *cap*) the activities of a Guide. — **guide'book** a book of information for tourists; **guide card** (in a card index file) a card, *usu* with a protruding tab on its upper edge, used as a divider, eg to indicate the beginning of an alphabetic or numeric division; **guided atmospheric flight** any unpiloted aeronautical flight, as of guided missiles, remotely piloted military aircraft, drones, and radio-controlled model aircraft; **guided missile** a jet- or rocket-propelled projectile carrying a warhead and electronically directed to its target for the whole or part of the way by remote control; **guide dog** a dog trained to lead a blind person; **guide'line** a line drawn, or a rope, etc fixed, to act as a guide; an indication of the course that should be followed, or of what future policy will be (*fig*); **guide'post** a post to guide the traveller; **guide rail** an additional rail to keep rolling-stock on the rails at a bend; a rail designed to guide the movement of any object; **guide rope** a rope for guiding the movement of a thing hoisted, towed or hauled; **guiding light** or **star** a person or thing adopted as a guide or model. [OFr *guider*; prob from a Gmc root, as in OE *witan* to know, *wīs* wise, Ger *weisen* to show, connected with **wit**, **wise**]

guidon *gīd'ən*, *n* a pennant, *usu* with a rounded outer edge, carried by certain cavalry companies or mounted batteries; the officer who carries it. [Fr, from Ital *guidone*, appar from *guida* guide]

Guignol *gē-nyol*, *n* the chief puppet in traditional French puppet shows. — **Grand** (*grã*) **Guignol** a small theatre in Paris that specialized in short plays of horror; horror plays of this type; (without *caps*) something intended to horrify people. [Name originated in Lyons in 18c; said to be that of a local 'character']

guild or **gild** *gild*, *n* an association for mutual aid; a corporation; a medieval association looking after common (*esp* trading) interests, providing mutual support and protection, and masses for the dead (*hist*); the hall or meeting-place of a guild (*obs*; *Spenser* **gyeld**); a group of plants distinguished by their way of life (eg saprophytes, or parasites; *ecol*). — *n* **guild'ry** (*Scot*) the corporation of a royal burgh; membership of it (*obs*). — **guild'-brother** a fellow-member of a guild; **guild'hall** the hall of a guild; a town hall; **guilds'man** a male member of a guild; **Guild Socialism** a form of socialism that would make trade unions or guilds the authority for industrial matters; **guilds'-woman** a female member of a guild. [OE *gield*, influenced by ON *gildi*]

guilder or **gilder** *gild'ər*, *n* an old Dutch and German gold coin; a modern Dutch gulden; a coin vaguely (*Shakesp*). [Du *gulden*]

guile *gīl*, *n* cunning; deceit; wile, jugglery (*obs*). — *vt* (*Spenser*) to beguile. — *adj* **guiled** (*obs*) armed with deceit; treacherous. — *adj* **guile'ful** crafty; deceitful. — *adv* **guile'fully**. — *n* **guile'fulness**. — *adj* **guile'less** without deceit; artless. — *adv* **guile'lessly**. — *n* **guile'lessness**. — *n* **guil'er** or **guyl'er** (*Spenser*) a deceiver. [OFr *guile* deceit, perh Gmc; cf **wile**]

Guillain-Barré syndrome *gē-yɛ̃'ba-rā' sin'drōm*, (*med*) *n* an acute polyneuritis causing weakness or paralysis of the limbs. [Georges *Guillain* and Jean *Barré*, French neurologists]

guillemot *gil'i-mot*, *n* a diving bird of the genus *Uria* with a long pointed bill, a member of the auk family. [Fr, dimin of *Guillaume* William, perh suggested by Breton *gwelan* gull]

guilloche *gi-lōsh'*, (*art* or *archit*) *n* an ornamental border or moulding formed of interlacing curved bands enclosing roundels. — *vt* to decorate with intersecting curved lines. [Fr, a guilloching tool; said to be named from one *Guillot*]

guillotine *gil'ə-tēn* or *-tēn'*, also *gē'yə-*, *n* an instrument for beheading, by descent of a heavy oblique blade, adopted during the French Revolution, and named after Joseph Ignace *Guillotin* (1738–1814), a physician, who first proposed its adoption; a machine (either manually or electrically operated) with a single heavy blade for cutting or trimming, *esp* a piece of office equipment used for paper or card; a surgical instrument for cutting the tonsils; a specially drastic rule or closure for shortening discussion. — *vt* to behead, crop, or cut short by guillotine.

guilt[1] *gilt*, *n* the state of having done wrong; sin, sinfulness, or consciousness of it; the painful or uncomfortable emotion or state of mind caused by the awareness or feeling of having done wrong; the state of having broken a law; liability to a penalty (*legal*). — *adv* **guilt'ily**. — *n* **guilt'iness**. — *adj* **guilt'less** free from crime; innocent. — *adv* **guilt'lessly**. — *n* **guilt'lessness**. — *adj* **guilt'y** justly chargeable; blameworthy, responsible; wicked, criminal; involving, indicating, burdened with, or relating to guilt. — *adv* **guilt'y-like** (*Shakesp*) guiltily. — **guilt complex** a mental preoccupation with one's (real or imagined) guilt; **guilty party** a person, organization, etc that is guilty. — **guilty of** or (*Shakesp*) **to** having committed (an evil or injudicious act); to blame for (a happening; *archaic*); (sometimes in *Bible*) deserving of (*obs*). [Orig a payment or fine for an offence; OE *gylt*]

guilt[2] (*Spenser*). Same as **gilt**[1].

guimbard *gim'bärd*, *n* a Jew's-harp. [Perh from Provençal *guimbardo* a kind of dance, from *guimba* to leap, gambol]

guimp. See **gimp**[1].

guinea *gin'i*, *n* an obsolete English gold coin first made of gold brought from *Guinea*, in Africa; its value (now £1.05), a unit still favoured by certain professionals in charging fees. — *adj* priced at a guinea. — **Guinea** (or **guinea**) **corn** durra (*Sorghum vulgare*); pearl millet (*Pennisetum typhoideum*), a cereal; **guinea fowl** a native African bird (family *Numidae*) of the pheasant family, ground-dwelling, dark-grey with white spots; **Guin'ea** (or **guinea**) **grass** a tall African grass of the millet genus (Panicum); **guinea hen** a guinea fowl, *esp* a female; a turkey (*obs*); a courtesan (*Shakesp*); **guin'ea-pig** a small S American rodent, the cavy; (also **human guinea pig**) a person used as the subject of an experiment (as the cavy commonly is in the laboratory); a do-nothing, token company director, etc (*slang*); **Guinea** (or **guin'-ea**) **worm** a very slender threadlike parasitic nematode worm (*Filaria*), common in tropical Africa.

guipure *gē-pōōr'*, *n* a kind of lace having no ground or mesh, the pattern sections fixed by interlacing threads; a type of gimp. [Fr *guipure*, from OFr *guiper*, prob Gmc; cf Gothic *weipan* to weave]

guiro *gwē'rō*, *n* a notched gourd used as a percussion instrument in Latin America: — *pl* **gui'ros**. [Sp, gourd]

guise *gīz*, *n* semblance, pretence or mask; external appearance, shape, likeness; dress (*archaic*); manner, behaviour (*obs*); custom (*obs*). — *vt* (*archaic*) to dress. — *vi* to act as a guiser. — *n* **guis'er** or **guis'ard**, also **guizer** (chiefly *Scot*) a person in disguise, dressed up in costume; a Christmas (or now *usu* Hallowe'en and, in Shetland, Up-Helly-Aa) mummer; someone who goes guising. — *n* **gui'sing** *esp* in Scotland, a survival of mumming, whereby children dress up and go from house to house collecting cash in return for some musical performance, etc. [OFr *guise*; cf OHGer *wīsa* (Ger *Weise*) a way, guise, OE *wīse* way, *wīs* wise]

guitar *gi-tär'*, *n* a fretted musical instrument, now six-stringed with a waisted body, like the lute, but flat-backed. — *n* **guitar'ist**. [Fr *guitare*, from L *cithara*, from Gr *kitharā*; see **cithara**]

guizer. See **guiser**.

Gujarati or **Gujerati** *gōōj-ə-rä'tē*, *n* an Indic language spoken in the region and state of *Gujarat* in north-western India. — Also **Gujara'thi** or **Gujera'thi**. [Hindi, from Sans *Gurjara* Gujarat]

gula *gū'lə*, (*zool*) *n* the upper part of the throat; the gullet; in some insects, a plate on the underside of the head. — *adj* **gū'lar**. [L *gula* throat]

gulag *gōō'lag*, *n* formerly (one of) the system of *esp* political prisons and forced labour camps in the Soviet Union; any camp or system for the detention and silencing of political prisoners. [Russ acronym of the title of the body administering the system, popularized by A Solzhenitsyn, Russ author (1918–), in *The Gulag Archipelago*]

gulch *gulch* or *gulsh*, *n* (*US*) a ravine or narrow rocky valley, a gully. — *vt* (*dialect*) to swallow greedily. [Origin doubtful]

gulden *gōōl'dən*, *n* a Dutch coin, the guilder or florin; a gold or silver coin in Germany in the Middle Ages; the old unit of account in Austria (before 1892). [Ger, literally golden]

gule (*Scot*). See **gold**[2].

gules *gūlz*, (*heraldry*) *n* a red colour, marked in engraved figures by vertical lines. — *adj* **gū'ly** (*obs*). [OFr *gueules*, perh from L *gula* the throat]

gulf (or *obs* **gulph**) *gulf*, *n* a large indentation in the coast; the area of sea or ocean enclosed by it; a deep place; an abyss; a whirlpool (*archaic* or *poetic*); anything insatiable, or too large to be bridged (*fig*); a wide separation, eg between opponents' viewpoints; (with *cap* and **the**) the Arabian or Persian Gulf, or (loosely) the region of and surrounding this, or the Gulf States; in Oxford and Cambridge examinations, the place of those candidates for honours who are allowed a pass without honours. — *vt* to engulf. — *vi* to flow like a gulf. — *adj* (with *cap*) of or relating to the Gulf. — *adj* **gulf'y** full of gulfs or whirlpools. — **Gulf States** the small Arab states, rich in oil, bordering the Arabian Gulf, ie Bahrain, Kuwait, Qatar and the United Arab Emirates; **Gulf Stream** the warm ocean current which flows north from the Gulf of Mexico, eventually to merge into the North Atlantic Drift, having a warming influence on NW Europe; **gulf'weed** a large olive-brown seaweed (*Sargassum*) that floats unattached in great 'meadows' at the branching of the Gulf Stream and elsewhere in tropical oceans. [OFr *golfe*, from Late Gr *kolphos*, from Gr *kolpos* the bosom]

gull[1] *gul*, *n* a common large or medium-sized sea-bird of the family Laridae, *esp* of the genus *Larus*, with grey, white and black plumage, a sea-mew. — *n* **gull'ery** a place where gulls breed. — *adj* **gull'-wing** (of a motor-car door) opening upwards; (of an aircraft wing) having an upward-sloping short inner section and a long horizontal outer section. [Prob Welsh *gwylan*]

gull[2] *gul*, (*dialect*; *Shakesp*) *n* an unfledged bird. [Perh ON *gulr* yellow]

gull[3] *gul*, *n* a dupe or fool; an easily duped person; a hoax (*obs*). — *vt* to dupe, deceive, cheat, hoax. — *n* **gull'er**. — *n* **gull'ery** (*archaic*) deception. — *n* **gullibil'ity**. — *adj* **gull'ible** easily deceived or tricked, credulous (also (*archaic*) **gull'able**). — *adj* **gull'ish** simple; like a gull. — **gull'-catcher** (*Shakesp*) a cheat. [Perh from **gull**[1] or **gull**[2]]

Gullah *gu'lə* or *goo'lə*, *n* a member of a Negro people living in islands and coastal districts of the south-eastern United States; their language, a creolized English.

gullet *gul'it*, *n* the passage in the neck by which food is taken into the stomach; the throat; a narrow trench, passage, water channel, or ravine (*dialect*). [OFr *goulet*, dimin of *goule* (Fr *gueule*), from L *gula* the throat]

gullible, etc. See **gull**[3].

gully[1] or **gulley** *gul'i*, (chiefly *Scot*) *n* a big knife.

gully[2] or sometimes **gulley** *gul'i*, *n* a channel worn by running water, as on a mountain-side; a ravine; a ditch; a narrow channel or gutter, eg at the side of a tenpin bowling lane, or as a street drain, etc; a grooved rail, as for a tramway; the fielding position between point and slips, or a fielder in this position (*cricket*): — *pl* **gull'ies** or **gull'eys**. — *vt* to wear a gully or channel in. — *adj* **gull'ied**. — **gull'y-hole** a passage by which a gutter discharges into a drain; **gull'y-hunter** a person who picks up things from gutters; **gull'y-raker** (*Austr*) a cattle-thief. [Prob **gullet**]

gulosity *gū-los'i-ti*, (*archaic*) *n* gluttony. [L *gulōsus* gluttonous, from *gulō* glutton, from *gula* throat]

gulp *gulp*, *vt* to swallow spasmodically, in large draughts, or with effort; to stifle or suppress (with *back* or *down*). — *vi* to make a swallowing movement, eg in surprise, fright, or when drinking or eating hastily. — *n* a spasmodic or copious swallow; a movement as if of swallowing; a quantity swallowed at once; capacity for gulping (*rare*). — *n* **gulp'er**. [Cf Du *gulpen* gulp]

gulph. See **gulf**.

guly. See **gules**.

gum[1] *gum*, *n* the firm fleshy tissue that surrounds the bases of the teeth; insolence (*old slang*); nonsense, humbug (*old US dialect*). — *vt* to deepen and widen the gaps between the teeth of (a saw) to make it last longer (*US*); to chew with (toothless) gums; to talk nonsense, to jaw (*old US dialect*); to dupe, cheat, deceive (*US slang*). — *adj* **gumm'y** toothless. — **gum'boil** a small abscess on the gum; **gum'shield** a soft pad worn by boxers and others to protect the teeth and gums. [OE *gōma* palate; ON *gōmr*, Ger *Gaumen* palate]

gum[2] *gum*, *n* a substance that collects in or exudes from certain plants, and hardens on the surface, dissolves or swells in water, but does not dissolve in alcohol or ether; a plant gum or similar substance used as an adhesive, a stiffener, or for other purposes; any gumlike or sticky substance; chewing-gum; a gumdrop (qv); a gum tree; gummosis; a rubber overshoe (*US colloq*); a beehive, or trough, *orig* and *esp* one made from a hollow gum tree (*US dialect*). — *vt* to smear, coat, treat or unite with gum; to spoil, wreck (*esp* with *up*; *slang*, orig *US*). — *vi* to become gummy; to exude gum: — *pr p* **gumm'ing**; *pa t* and *pa p* **gummed**. — *adj* **gummif'erous** producing gum. — *n* **gumm'iness**. — *n* **gumm'ing** the act of fastening with gum; the application of gum in solution to a lithographic stone; gummosis; the process of becoming gummy. — *n* **gummos'ity** gumminess. — *adj* **gumm'ous** or **gumm'y** consisting of or resembling gum; producing or covered with gum. — **gum ammoniac** ammoniac, a gum resin; **gum arabic** a gum obtained from various acacias, used in the production of inks and food-thickeners; **gum benjamin** see **benjamin**[2]; **gum'boot** a rubber boot; **gum'-digger** a person who digs up fossilized kauri-gum (*NZ*); a dentist (*Austr colloq*); **gum dragon** or **tragacanth** tragacanth; **gum'-drop** a gelatinous type of sweet containing gum arabic; **gum elastic** rubber; **gum juniper** sandarac; **gum'nut** the woody fruit of the eucalyptus; **gum resin** a resin mixed with gum; **gum'shoe** (*US*) a rubber overshoe; a shoe with rubber sole, a sneaker; a detective or policeman (*slang*, orig *US*). — Also *vi* (*slang*, orig *US*) to snoop, pry. — **gum tree** a tree that exudes gum, or gum resin, kino, etc, *esp* a eucalyptus tree, or an American tree of the cornel family (*Nyssa*). — **gum up the works** (*colloq*) to make (eg a machine, or a scheme) unworkable; **up a gum tree** in a difficult situation (from the opossum's refuge). [OFr *gomme*, from L *gummi*, from Gr *kommi*; prob from Egyptian *kemai*]

gum[3] *gum*, *n* material that gathers in the corner of the eye. — **gum rash** a skin disease, red-gum. [Perh OE *gund* matter, pus]

gum[4] *gum*, (*dialect*) *n* used in oaths for **God**.

gumbo *gum'bō*, *n* the okra or its mucilaginous pods, lady's fingers; a soup of which okra is an ingredient; a dish of okra pods seasoned; a fruit conserve (*US colloq*); in central USA, a fine soil which becomes sticky or soapy when wet; (with *cap*) a patois spoken by Blacks and Creoles in Louisiana, etc: — *pl* **gum'bos**. [Bantu (*ki*)*ngombo*]

gumma *gum'ə*, (*pathol*) *n* a syphilitic tumour: — *pl* **gumm'ata**. — *adj* **gumm'atous**. [New L, from L *gummi* gum]

gummiferous, gumminess, gumming. See **gum**[2].

gummite *gum'īt*, *n* a hydrated oxide of uranium and lead, like gum in appearance. [L *gummi* gum, and **-ite**(3)]

gummosis *gum-ō'sis*, (*bot*) *n* pathological conversion of cell walls into gum; the diseased condition of plants caused by this, with conspicuous secretion of gum. [New L, from L *gummi* gum, and **-osis**]

gummosity, gummous, gummy[1]. See **gum**[2].

gummy[2]. See **gum**[1].

gump[1] *gump*, (*Scot*) *vt* and *vi* to guddle.

gump[2] *gump*, (*dialect*) *n* a foolish person.

gumphion *gum'fi-ən*, (*obs Scot*) *n* a kind of banner formerly carried in funeral processions. [**gonfanon**]

gumple-foisted *gum'pl-foist-id*, (*Scott*) *adj* sulky. [*gumps* sulks (**gump**[2]); the second element appears in other words as *-faced*, *-feist*, etc]

gumption *gum(p)'shən*, *n* sense; shrewdness; courage, enterprise; commonsense; art of preparing painters' colours (*obs*). — *adj* **gump'tious**. [Poss connected with ON *gaumr* heed]

gun *gun*, *n* a tubular weapon from which projectiles are discharged, *usu* by explosion; a cannon, rifle, revolver, etc; a device for spraying, squirting, or otherwise propelling material; a signal by gun; a person who carries a gun, a member of a shooting-party; a professional killer (*US slang*); the throttle of an aircraft (*slang*); the accelerator of a car (*slang*); an expert or champion, *esp* in shearing (*Austr* and *NZ colloq*). — *vt* to shoot; to shoot at; to provide with guns; to open the throttle of, to increase speed (*slang*; also **give the gun**); to rev up (the engine of a stationary car) noisily (*slang*). — *vi* to shoot; to go shooting. — *adj* (*Austr* and *NZ*) expert, pre-eminent. — *n* **gunn'age** the number of guns carried by a warship. — *n* **gunn'er** a person who works a gun; a private in the artillery; a branch officer in charge of naval ordnance (*naut*). — *n* **gunn'ery** the art of managing guns, or the science of artillery. — *n* **gunn'ing**. — *adj* **gun'less**. — **gun barrel** the tube of a gun; **gun'boat** a small vessel of light draught, fitted to carry one or more guns (**gunboat diplomacy** the show or threat of (*orig* naval) force in international negotiation); **gun carriage** a carriage on which a cannon is mounted; **gun'cotton** an explosive prepared by saturating cotton with nitric and sulphuric acids; **gun deck** a deck in old warships carrying guns below the main deck (earlier below spar deck); **gun dog** a dog trained to work with a shooting-party; **gun'fight** a fight involving two or more people with guns, *esp* formerly in the old American West. — Also *vi*. — **gun'fighter**; **gun'fire** the firing of guns; the hour at which the morning or evening gun is fired (*military* and *naut*); an early cup of tea (*military slang*); **gun'flint** a piece of flint fitted to the hammer of a flintlock musket; **gun'house** a protective shelter for a gun, and gunner, on a warship; **gun'layer** a person who sets the sights of a ship's gun; **gun'lock** the mechanism in some guns by which the charge is exploded; **gun'maker**; **gun'man** a man who carries a gun, *esp* an armed criminal; **gun'metal** an alloy of copper and tin or zinc in the proportion of about 9 to 1, once used in making cannon; any of various metals used in imitation of this; any of various colours with a metallic sheen; **gun moll** (*slang*) a woman who associates with criminals; a gangster's moll; **gun'play** the use of guns, *esp* in a fight or display of skill; **gun'point** the muzzle, or directed aim, of a gun (**at gunpoint** see below); **gun'port** a porthole or similar opening for a gun; **gun'powder** an explosive mixture of saltpetre, sulphur and charcoal; **gun'room** a room where guns are kept; on board ship, *orig* the gunner's apartment, now a mess-room for junior officers; **gun'runner**; **gun'-running** smuggling guns into a country; **gun'ship** an armed ship, helicopter, etc; **gun'shot** the shot fired from a gun; the distance to which shot can be thrown from a gun, the range of a gun. — *adj* caused by the shot of a gun. — *adj* **gun'-shy** frightened by guns or by the sound of guns. — **gun'slinger** (*colloq*) a gunfighter; **gun'smith** a smith or workman who makes or repairs guns or small-arms; **gun'stick** a ramrod; **gun'stock** the piece on which the barrel of a gun is fixed; **gun'stone** (*Shakesp*) a stone shot. — **as sure as a gun** quite sure, certainly; **at gunpoint** under, or using, the threat of injury or death from a gun; **beat the gun** to jump the gun (see under **jump**); **blow great guns** (of wind) to blow tempestuously; **go great guns** (*colloq*) to function, be carried out, etc with great success, speed, efficiency, etc; **great gun** a cannon (*obs*); a person of great importance (*colloq*; also **big gun**); **gun for** to seek, try to obtain; to seek to ruin or destroy; **hired gun** (*colloq*) a gunman hired to kill for a fee; a mercenary, professional fighter or killer; a person hired to destroy the opposition, or some unwelcome party, on behalf of another; **kiss the gunner's daughter** to be tied to a gun for a flogging; **son of a gun** a soldier's bastard son (*obs*); a rogue, rascal (*slang*); used as an affectionate greeting; also *interj* (*NAm*); **spike someone's guns** see under **spike**²; **stick** (or **stand**) **to one's guns** to maintain one's position staunchly. [ME *gonne*, prob from *Gunna* used as a pet name for a war engine, poss from the woman's name *Gunhild* (ON *gunnr* war, and *hildr* war)]

gundy *gun'di*, (*Scot*) *n* a toffee made of treacle and spices. [Perh variant of **candy**]

gunge *gunj*, (*colloq*) *n* any dirty, messy or sticky substance. — *adj* **gun'gy**. [Perh a combination of **goo** and **sponge**]

gung-ho *gung-hō'*, (*slang*; *orig US*) *adj* (excessively or irrationally) enthusiastic, eager or zealous. [Chin *kung* work and *ho* together]

gunite *gun'īt*, *n* a finely-graded cement concrete (a mixture of cement and sand) sprayed into position under air pressure by a cement gun. [Orig a trademark]

gunk *gungk*, (*colloq*) *n* any unpleasant, dirty, sticky material, or semi-solid, *usu* valueless, residue from a chemical process. [Orig the trademark of a grease-solvent]

gunnage. See under **gun**.

gunnel¹ *gun'l*, *n*. See **gunwale**.

gunnel² *gun'l*, *n* the butter-fish (genus *Centronotus*), a small eel-like coast fish of the blenny family. [Origin unknown]

gunnera *gun'ər-ə*, *n* any plant of the *Gunnera* genus of very large-leaved ornamental herbs of the mare's-tail family. [After J E *Gunner* (1718–73), Norwegian botanist]

gunnery. See **gun**.

gunny *gun'i*, *n* a strong coarse jute fabric. [Hindi *ganī*, *gonī* sacking, from Sans *gonī* a sack]

gunsel *gun'səl*, (*US slang*) *n* a stupid or inexperienced youth; a boy kept for homosexual purposes, a catamite; a gunman. [Yiddish *genzel* gosling, from MHGer *gensel*, dimin of *gans* goose; *gunman* meaning influenced by **gun**]

gunter *gun'tər*, *n* a Gunter's scale; a rig with topmast sliding on rings (from its resemblance to a sliding variety of Gunter's scale) (*naut*). — **Gunter's chain** a surveyor's chain of 100 links, 66 feet long (10 chains = 1 furlong; 10 sq chains = 1 acre); **Gunter's scale** a scale graduated in several lines for numbers, logarithmic sines, etc, so arranged that trigonometrical problems can be roughly solved by use of a pair of compasses, or in another form by sliding. [From the inventor, Edmund *Gunter* (1581–1626), astronomer]

gunwale or **gunnel** *gun'l*, *n* the *wale* or upper edge of a ship's side next to the bulwarks, so called because the upper *guns* were pointed from it. — **full** or **packed to the gunwales** (*colloq*) absolutely full; **gunwales to** or **under** (*naut*) with gunwales at or below the surface of the water.

gunyah *gun'yə*, (*Austr*) *n* an Australian Aborigine's hut; a roughly-made shelter in the bush. [Aboriginal]

Günz *günts*, *n* the first (Pliocene) stage of glaciation in the Alps. — *adj* **Günz** or **Günz'ian**. [From a Bavarian tributary of the Danube]

gup¹ *gup*, (*obs*) *interj* expressing remonstrance or derision. [Prob **go up**]

gup² *gup*, (*slang*; *orig Anglo-Ind colloq*) *n* gossip; prattle. [Urdu *gap*]

guppy *gup'i*, *n* a small brightly-coloured West Indian fish (genus *Lebistes*) that multiplies very rapidly and feeds on mosquito larvae, algae, etc: — *pl* **gupp'ies** (also called *millions*). [From R J L *Guppy*, who first sent a specimen of it to the British Museum]

gur or **goor** *gûr* or *gōōr*, *n* an unrefined sweet cane sugar. [Hindi, coarse sugar, from Sans *guḍa*]

gurami. See **gourami**.

gurdwara *gûr'dwär-ə*, *n* a Sikh place of worship which includes a place where the scripture is housed. [Punjabi *gurduārā*, from Sans *guru* teacher, and *dvāra* door]

gurge *gûrj*, (*literary*; *Milton*) *n* a whirlpool. [L *gurges*]

gurgitation *gûr-ji-tā'shən*, *n* surging. [L *gurges*, *-itis* whirlpool]

gurgle *gûr'gl*, *vi* to flow in an irregular noisy current; to make a bubbling sound; (of a baby, etc) to make a low gargle-like bubbling sound in the throat; to utter with a gurgle. — *n* the sound of gurgling. [Imit; cf Ital *gorgogliare*]

gurgoyle. See **gargoyle**.

gurjun *gûr'jun*, *n* an East Indian tree (genus *Dipterocarpus*) yielding timber and a balsamic liquid used to treat leprosy. — Also **gar'jan**. [Hindi *garjan*]

Gurkha or **Goorkha** *go͞or'kə* or *gûr'kə*, *n* a member of the dominant people of Nepal, claiming Hindu origin, but Mongolized, from whom regiments in the British and Indian armies were formed. — *n* **Gurkhali** (*go͞or-kä'lē* or *gûr-kä'lē*) the Indo-European language spoken by Gurkhas.

gurl *gûrl*, (*Scot*) *n* a growl. — *vi* to growl. — *adj* **gur'ly** grim; lowering; rough; surly. [Cf **growl**]

gurlet *gûr'lit*, *n* a pickaxe with a head pointed at one end, bladed at the other. [Fr]

Gurmukhi *go͞or'mo͞o-kē*, *n* the script in which the sacred texts of the Sikhs are written, which is used also for modern secular writing and printing. [Punjabi *Gurmukhī*, literally from the mouth of the *guru* or teacher]

gurn *gûrn*, (*dialect*) a variant of **girn**.

gurnard *gûr'nərd* or **gurnet** *-nit*, *n* a fish (genus *Trigla*; of many species) with a large, bony-plated angular head and three finger-like walking rays in front of the pectoral fin. [OFr *gornard*, related to Fr *grogner* to grunt, from L *grunnīre* to grunt; from the sound they emit when caught]

gurney *gûr'ni*, (*NAm*) *n* a wheeled stretcher or cart (as used in a hospital, etc). [Origin uncertain; perh from the personal name]

gurrah *gur'ə*, *n* a coarse Indian muslin. [Hindi *gārhā* thick]

gurry *gur'i*, (chiefly *US*) *n* whale offal; fish offal. [Origin unknown]

guru *go͞o'ro͞o*, *n* in Hinduism, a spiritual teacher; (often *facetious*) a revered instructor, mentor or pundit. — Also (now *obs*) **goo'roo**. — *n* **gu'rudom**, **gu'ruism** or **gu'ruship** the state of being a guru. [Hindi *gurū*, from Sans *guru* venerable]

GUS *abbrev*: Great Universal Stores.

gush *gush*, *vi* to flow out with violence or copiously; to be over-effusive, or highly sentimental. — *vt* to pour forth copiously. — *n* that which flows out; a sudden, violent issue of a fluid; sentimentality, effusiveness. — *n* **gush'er** a person who or thing that gushes; an oil well that does not have to be pumped. — *adj* **gush'ing**. — *adv* **gush'ingly**. — *adj* **gush'y** effusively sentimental. [ME *gosshe*, *gusche*; the connection, if any, with ON *gusa*, *gjōsa*, and Du *gudsen*, is not clear]

gusla *go͞os'lə*, **gusle** *-le* or **gusli** *-lē*, *n* a one-stringed Balkan musical instrument; a Russian instrument with several strings. — *n* **guslar'** a performer on it. [Bulgarian *gusla*, Serb *gusle*, Russ *gusli*]

gusset *gus'it*, *n* an angular piece inserted in a garment to strengthen or enlarge some part of it or give freedom of movement; a strengthening bracket or plate at a joint where two plates meeet, or between connecting members of a structure (*civ eng*); the piece of chainmail covering a join in armour, as at the armpit. — *vt* to make with a gusset; to insert a gusset into. [OFr *gousset*, from *gousse* pod, husk]

gussie *gus'i*, (*Austr colloq*) *n* an effeminate man. [From dimin of the personal name *Augustus*]

gussy up *gus'i up*, (*slang*) *vi* to put one's best clothes on; to smarten up. [Poss connected with **gussie**]

gust[1] *gust*, *n* a sudden blast of wind; a burst of smoke, fire, etc; a violent burst of passion, outburst. — *vi* to blow in gusts. — *adj* **gust'ful** (*rare*) or **gust'y** blowing in gusts, squally; stormy; fitfully irritable or emotional. — *n* **gust'iness**. — **gust'-lock** a mechanism on an aeroplane which prevents damage to the elevators by gusts of wind when the aeroplane is stationary. [ON *gustr* blast]

gust[2] *gust*, *n* the sense of pleasure of tasting (*archaic*); relish (*archaic*); gratification (*archaic*); taste experience (*obs*); flavour (*archaic*). — *adj* and *n* **gust'able** (*archaic*). — *n* **gustā'tion** the act of tasting; the sense of taste. — *adj* **gust'ative** or **gust'atory** of or pertaining to the sense of taste. — *adj* **gust'ful** (*archaic*) savoury, tasty; enjoyable. — *adj* **gust'ie** or **gust'y** (*Scot*) savoury; appetizingly flavoured. [L *gustus* taste; cf Gr *geuein* to make to taste]

gusto *gus'tō*, *n* exuberant enjoyment, zest. [Ital, from L *gustus* taste]

gusty. See **gust**[1,2].

GUT (*phys* and *astron*) *abbrev*: Grand Unified Theory.

gut *gut*, *n* the alimentary canal, *esp* the lower part; sheep's or other intestines or silkworm's glands prepared for use as violin-strings, etc; the belly, paunch (*slang*); (in *pl*) the viscera; (in *pl*) the inner or essential parts; (in *pl*) stamina, toughness of character, tenacity, staying power, endurance, forcefulness (*colloq*); a narrow passage; a strait or channel; a lane. — *adj* (*colloq*) (of feelings or reactions) strong, deeply personal, basic or instinctive; (of issues, etc) having immediate impact, arousing strong feelings. — *vt* to take out the guts of; to remove the contents of; to reduce to a shell (by burning, dismantling, plundering, etc); to extract what is essential from: — *pr p* **gutt'ing**; *pa t* and *pa p* **gutt'ed**. — **gut'ful** or **guts'ful** (*Austr* and *NZ colloq*) one's fill, more than enough. — *adj* **gut'less** cowardly, lacking strength of character. — *vi* and *vt* **guts** (*colloq*) to eat greedily: — *pr p* **gut'sing**; *pa p* and *pa t* **gut'sed**. — *n* **gutser** see **gutzer**. — *n* **gutsful** see **gutful**. — *n* **guts'iness** (*Scot* and *slang*). — *adj* **guts'y** having pluck or nerve (*slang*); lusty, passionate (*slang*); gluttonous (*Scot*). — *adj* **gutt'ed** (*colloq*) extremely shocked, upset or disappointed. — *n* **gutt'er**. — *vt* and *vi* **gutt'le** to eat greedily. — *n* **gut'zer** or **gut'ser** (*Austr* and *NZ*) a glutton; a heavy fall (**come a gutser** to take a heavy fall; to fail or crash). — **gutbucket** (*gut'buk-it*) a rhythmically simple, raucous, earthy and emotional style of playing jazz; **gut'rot** (*colloq*) rough, cheap alcohol; **gut'-scraper** (*facetious*) a fiddler, violinist. — **bust a gut** (*slang*) to make a great deal of strenuous effort; **hate someone's guts** (*colloq*) to have a violent dislike for someone; **have had a gutful (of)** (*slang*) to be thoroughly fed up with, have had as much as, or more than, one is prepared to tolerate; **have someone's guts (for garters)** (*slang*) to inflict severe and horrible punishment or harm on someone (*usu* used as a threat); **work**, **sweat** or **slog one's guts out** (*slang*) to work extremely hard. [OE *guttas* (pl); cf *geotan* to pour; dialect Eng *gut*, Ger *Gosse* a drain]

gutcher. See **goodsire** under **good**.

gutta[1] *gut'ə*, *n* a drop (*med*); a small droplike ornament on the underside of a mutule or a regula of the Doric entablature (*archit*); a small round colour-spot (*zool*): — *pl* **gutt'ae** (*-ē*). — *adj* **gutt'ate** or **guttā'ted** containing drops; having droplike markings; spotted. — *n* **guttā'tion** the exudation of drops of liquid from an uninjured part of a plant (whence *vi* **gutt'ate** to exude liquid by guttation). — *n pl* **Guttif'erae** (*bot*) a family of archichlamydeous dicotyledons with abundant oil-glands and passages, and entire exstipulate opposite leaves, including mangosteen, mammee apple, and (according to some) St John's wort. — *adj* **guttif'erous** exuding drops (of sap, gum, etc); belonging to the Guttiferae. — **gutta serena** (*med*) amaurosis. [L *gutta* drop]

gutta[2] *gut'ə*, *n* the coagulated milky latex of sapotaceous and other tropical trees, *esp* gutta-percha; a hydrocarbon (empirically $C_{10}H_{16}$) found in gutta-percha; a solid gutta-percha golf ball, as used in the 19c, also called (*colloq*) **gutt'y**. — **gutta-percha** (*-pûr'chə*) a highly resistive, waterproof substance, like rubber but harder and not extensible, obtained chiefly from the latex of Malaysian trees of the Sapotaceae (*Palaquium*, *Payena*, etc). — Also *adj*. [Malay *getah* gum, and *percha* a tree producing it]

guttate, **guttation**, etc. See under **gutta**[1].

gutter[1] *gut'ər*, *n* a channel for conveying away water, *esp* at the roadside or at the eaves of a roof; a furrow, groove; the blank strip separating the two halves of a sheet of stamps (*philat*); a grooved piece, used to separate pages of type in a forme (*printing*); (sometimes in *pl*) the space comprising the fore-edges of pages lying together internally in a forme (*printing*); the blank space (ie the inner margins) between two facing pages in a book, magazine, etc; (with *the*) slum-life, social degradation or sordidness; (in *pl*) mud, dirt (*Scot*). — *vt* to cut or form into small hollows. — *vi* (of a candle) to run down in a stream or channel of drops; (of a flame) to be blown downwards, or threaten to go out; to become hollowed; to trickle or stream. — *n* **gutt'ering** gutters collectively; material for gutters. — **gutt'erblood** (*Scot*) a low-born person; **gutter board** same as **snow board**; **gutter broadcasting**, **gutter** (or **gutter press) journalism** sensationalistic reporting in the popular press; **gutt'er-man** or **-merchant** a pavement-side seller of cheap trifles; **gutter pair** (*philat*) a pair of stamps separated by the gutter; **gutter press** that part of the press which specializes in sordid sensationalistic journalism; **gutt'ersnipe** a street urchin; a neglected child from a slum area. [OFr *goutiere*, from *goute*, from L *gutta* a drop]

gutter[2]. See under **gut**.

guttiferous, Guttiferae. See under **gutta**[1].

guttle. See under **gut**.

guttural *gut'ər-əl*, *adj* pertaining to the throat; formed in the throat; throaty in sound. — *n* a sound pronounced in the throat or (loosely) by the back part of the tongue (*phonetics*); a letter representing such a sound. — *vt* **gutt'uralize** or **-ise** to sound gutturally; to make guttural. — *adv* **gutt'urally**. [L *guttur* the throat]

gutty[1]. See **gutta**[2].

gutty[2] *gut'i*, (*US colloq*) *adj* (*compar* **gutt'ier**, *superl* **gutt'iest**) forceful, powerful; gritty, gutsy, spirited, plucky. [**gut** and **-y**[1]]

gutzer. See under **gut**.

guv. See **governor** under **govern**.

GUY *abbrev*: Guyana (IVR).

guy[1] *gī*, *n* a rope, rod, etc used to steady anything, or hold it in position. — *vt* to keep in position by a guy or guys. — **guy'-rope**. [OFr *guis*, *guie*; Sp *guia* a guide]

guy[2] *gī*, *n* an effigy of *Guy* Fawkes, dressed up grotesquely on the anniversary of the Gunpowder Plot (5 Nov); an oddly dressed figure; a fellow (*colloq*); a person generally (eg, as plural **guys**, used in referring to or addressing any group of people; *colloq*, *orig* and *esp US*); a joke, lark (*archaic* or *dialect*); flight, decamping (*archaic* or *dialect*). — *vt* (*slang*) to turn to ridicule, make fun of. — *vi* to decamp (*archaic* or *dialect*).

guyle, guyler. Spenserian forms of **guile**, **guiler**.

guyot *gē'ō*, *n* a flat-topped underwater mountain. [A H *Guyot*, Swiss-born American geologist]

guyse. A Spenserian form of **guise**.

guzzle *guz'l*, *vt* and *vi* to swallow (food, or *esp* drink) greedily or immoderately. — *n* a bout of guzzling. — *n* **guzz'ler**. [Perh connected with Fr *gosier* throat]

GVH *abbrev*: graft-versus-host (reaction) (qv under **graft**[1]).

GVHD *abbrev*: graft-versus-host disease (qv under **graft**[1]).

GW or **Gw** *abbrev*: gigawatts.

GWR *abbrev*: Great Western Railway (now incorporated into **BR**).

gwyniad or **gwiniad** *gwin'i-ad*, *n* a whitefish (*Coregonus pennanti*), found *esp* in Bala Lake in Wales. [Welsh *gwyniad*, from *gwyn* white]

Gy *symbol*: gray (**gray**[2]).

gyal. See **gayal**.

gybe or sometimes **jibe** *jīb*, *vi* (of a sail) to swing over from one side to the other; to alter course in this way. — *vt* to cause to gybe. — *n* an act or the action of gybing. — **gybe mark** a marker on a yacht-race course indicating a turning-point at which yachts must gybe. [Origin obscure; see **jib**]

gyeld. A Spenserian form of **guild**.

gylden. See **gilden**.

gym *jim*, *n* and *adj* a familiar shortening of **gymnasium**, **gymnastic** and **gymnastics**. — **gym shoe** a plimsoll; **gym slip** or **tunic** a pinafore dress worn (*esp* formerly) by schoolgirls.

gymbal. Same as **gimbal**.

gymkhana *jim-kä'nə*, *n* a public meeting in which (*esp* amateur) riders compete against each other in various equestrian sports; (formerly) a public place providing athletics facilities, etc (*Anglo-Ind*); a meeting for athletic sports, etc; another name for autocross (*US*). [Hindi *gend-khāna* (ball-house), racket-court, remodelled on *gym*nastics]

gymmal. Same as **gimmal**.

gymnasium *jim-nā'zi-əm*, *n* a place, hall, building or school for gymnastics; *orig*, in ancient Greece, a public place or building where the Greek youths exercised themselves, with running and wrestling grounds, baths, and halls for conversation; (*usu gim-nä'zi-o͞om*) a top-grade secondary school in many European countries, *esp* Germany, which prepares pupils for higher education, *esp* in academic rather than vocational subjects: — *pl* **gymnā'siums** or **gymnā'sia**, also for continental schools **gymnasien** (*gim-nä'zi-ən*). — *adj* **gymnā'sial**. — *n* **gymnā'siarch** (*-ärk*; Gr *archos* chief) the head of a gymnasium. — *n* **gymnā'siast** a pupil in a gymnasium; a gymnast (*archaic*). — *adj* (*rare*) **gymnā'sic**. — *n* **gym'nast** (*-nast*) a person skilled in gymnastics. — *n* **gymnas'tic** a system of training by exercise (*archaic*); (in *pl* used as *n sing*) exercises and activities devised to strengthen the body and improve agility and co-ordination, including exercises using apparatus and floor; (in *pl*) feats or tricks of agility. — *adj* **gymnas'tic** or (*archaic*) **gymnas'tical** pertaining to athletic exercises or (*specif*) gymnastics; athletic, vigorous. — *adv* **gymnas'tically**. [Latinized from Gr *gymnasion*, from *gymnos* naked]

gymnic *jim'nik*, (*archaic*; *Milton*) *adj* gymnastic. [Gr *gymnikos*, from *gymnos* naked]

gymno- or (before a vowel) **gymn-** *gim'n(ō)-*, *jim'n(ō)'-*, or *-no'*, *combining form* denoting (*esp* in biological terms) naked. — *adj* **gymnorhi'nal** (Gr *rhīs*, *rhīnos* nose) with unfeathered nostrils. — *n* **gym'nosoph** (*rare*) or **gymnos'ophist** (Gr *sophos* wise) an ancient Hindu philosopher who wore little or no clothing, and lived solitarily in mystical contemplation. — *n* **gymnos'ophy**. — *n* **gym'nosperm** (Gr *sperma* seed) any of the lower or primitive group of seed-plants whose seeds are not enclosed in any ovary. — *adj* **gymnosper'mous**. [Gr *gymnos* naked]

gymp. Same as **gimp**[1,2].

gyn-. See **gyno-**.

gynae, also **gynie** or **gyny** *gī'ni*. A colloquial shortening of **gynaecology** or **gynaecological**.

gynaeceum. See **gynoecium**.

gynaeco- or (*US*) **gyneco-** *gīn-*, *jīn-*, *gin-*, *jin-ē'kō-*, or *-i-ko'-*, *combining form* denoting woman, female. — *n* **gynaeco'cracy** (Gr *kratos* power) government by women or a woman; a country with such a government. — *adj* **gynaecocrat'ic**. — *adj* **gyn'aecoid** woman-like. — *adj* **gynaecolog'ical** or **gynaecolog'ic**. — *n* **gynaecol'ogist**. — *n* **gynaecol'ogy** the science of, or branch of medicine dealing with women's physiology and diseases. — *n* **gynaecomas'tia** or sometimes **gynaecomas'ty** the abnormal enlargement of a man's breast. — *n* **gyn'aecomast** a man suffering from gynaecomastia. [Gr *gynē*, *gynaikos* woman]

gynney, gynny. Shakespearian spellings of **guinea(-hen)**.

gyno- *gīnō-*, *gī-nə-*, *gī-no'-*, *jī-* or *ji-*, also **gyn-**, *combining form* denoting female, woman or (*bot*) the female reproductive organ. — *n* **gynandrism** see **gynandry**. — *n* **gynan'dromorph** (Gr *morphē* form) an organism that combines male and female physical characteristics. — *adj* **gynandromor'phic** or **gynandromor'phous**. — *n* **gynandromor'phism** or **gynandromor'phy**. — *adj* **gynand'rous** with stamen concrescent with the carpel, as in orchids (*bot*); hermaphroditic. — *n* **gynan'dry** or **gynand'rism** (Gr *anēr*, *andros* man, male). — *n* **gyniol'atry** extreme devotion to or regard for women. — *n* **gynoc'racy** gynaecocracy, female rule. — *adj* **gynocrat'ic**. — *adj* **gynodioe'cious** (*bot*) having hermaphrodite and female flowers on different plants. — *n* **gynodioe'cism**. — *adj* **gynomonoe'cious** (*bot*) having hermaphrodite and female flowers on the same plant. — *n* **gynomonoe'cism**. — *n* **gynophō'bia** the fear or dislike of women. — *adj* and *n* **gynophō'bic**. — **gy'nophore** (*bot*; Gr *phoros* carrying) an elongation of the receptacle of a flower carrying carpels only. — *n* **gynostē'mium** (Gr *stēma* stamen) a united gynoecium and androecium, such as the column of an orchid. [Gr *gynē* woman]

gynoecium, **gynaecium** or (*US*) **gynecium** *jī* or *gī-ni-sē'əm*, *n* the female organs of a flower (*bot*); (chiefly **gynaeceum**) the women's quarters in an ancient Greek or Roman house. [Gr *gynaikeion* women's apartments]

gynomonoecious ... to ... **gynostemium**. See under **gyno-**.

-gynous. See under **-gyny**.

gyny. See **gynae**.

-gyny *-ji-ni*, *combining form* denoting: female, woman, as in *misogyny*; the female organs (*bot*). — *adj combining form* **-gynous**. [Gr *gynē* woman]

gyp[1] *jip*, *n* a college servant at Cambridge and Durham. [Perh **gypsy**; or perh obs *gippo* a short jacket, a varlet, from obs Fr *jupeau*]

gyp[2] *jip*, (*slang*; *orig US*) *n* a swindle; a cheat. — *vt* to swindle: — *pr p* **gypp'ing**; *pa t* and *pa p* **gypped**.

gyp[3] *jip*, (*slang*) *n* pain, torture. — **give someone gyp** to cause someone pain. [**gee up**]

gyppie, **gyppo**, **gyppy**. See **gippo**.

gypseous, **gypsiferous**. See **gypsum**.

gypsophila *jip-sof'i-lə*, *n* any plant of the genus *Gypsophila*, hardy perennials related to the pinks, but of more chickweed-like appearance, with small white or pink flowers. [Gr *gypsos* chalk, and *phileein* to love]

gypsum *jip'səm* or *gip'səm*, *n* a soft mineral, hydrated calcium sulphate, source of plaster of Paris and other plasters. — *adj* **gyp'seous**. — *adj* **gypsif'erous** producing or containing gypsum. — **gypsum block** a building block (*usu* hollow) made of gypsum plaster; **gypsum plasterboard** (or simply **plasterboard**) building-board consisting of a core of gypsum or anhydrous gypsum plaster between two sheets of paper. [L, from Gr *gypsos* chalk]

gypsy or **gipsy** *jip'si*, *n* a Romany, a member of a wandering people of Indian origin, living mainly in Europe and the US; (loosely) a person who lives, or looks, like a gypsy; the Romany language; a cunning rogue (*obs*). — *adj* of, or characteristic of, the gypsies; out-of-door (eg of meals, etc); unconventional; operating independently or illegally (*US colloq*). — *vi* (now *rare*) to live like a gypsy, camp out, or picnic. — *n* **gyp'sydom** or **gyp'syism**. — **gypsy moth** a kind of tussock-moth, having whitish wings with dark line markings; **gyp'sywort** a labiate plant (*Lycopus europaeus*) with which gypsies were reputed to stain their skin. [**Egyptian**, because once thought to have come from Egypt]

gyrate, etc. See under **gyre**.

gyre *jīr*, *n* (*literary*) a ring, circle; a circular or spiral turn or movement. — *vt* and *vi* (in Lewis Carroll pronounced *gīr*) to spin round, gyrate. — *adj* **gyr'al** or **gyr'ant**. — *adv* **gyr'ally**. — *vi* **gyrate'** to revolve, spin, whirl. — *adj* **gyr'ate** curved round in a coil. — *n* **gyrā'tion** a whirling motion; a whirl or twist (also *fig*); a whorl. — *adj* **gyrā'tional**. — *adj* **gyr'atory** revolving; spinning round; (of traffic) revolving in one-way lines, or (of traffic systems) designed or working on this principle. — *adj* **gyroid'al** spiral; rotatory. — *adj* **gyr'ose** having a folded surface; marked with wavy lines or ridges. — *adj* **gyr'ous**. [L *gīrus*, from Gr *gȳros* a circle, ring]

gyre-carline *gīr'-kär-lin*, (*Scot*) *n* a witch. [ON *gȳgr* a witch, ogress, and **carline**]

gyrfalcon or **gerfalcon** *jûr'fö(l)-kn*, *n* a large northern and arctic falcon. — Also **jer'falcon**. [OFr *gerfaucon*, from LL *gyrofalcō*, most prob from OHGer *gîr* a vulture (Ger *Geier*); see **falcon**]

gyro *jī'rō*, (*colloq*) *n* a gyrocompass; a gyroscope.

gyro- *jī-rō*, *combining form* denoting: spiral, ring, circle; gyrating; gyroscope. — *n* **gyr'ocar** a monorail car balanced by a gyroscope. — *n* **gyrocom'pass** a compass which indicates direction by the freely moving axis of a rapidly spinning wheel, owing to the earth's rotation, the axis assuming and maintaining a north and south direction. — *n* **gyr'odyne** a rotorcraft in which the rotor(s) are power-driven for take-off, climb, landing, etc, but unpowered for cruising flight. — *n* **gyr'olite** a mineral, a hydrated calcium silicate. — *adj* **gyromagnet'ic** pertaining to magnetic properties of rotating electric charges. — *n* **gyromag'netism**. — *n* **gyr'omancy** (Gr *manteiā* divination) divination by walking in a circle and falling from giddiness. — *n* **gyr'oplane** or **gyrocop'ter** a rotorcraft with unpowered rotor(s) on a vertical axis, eg an autogiro. — *n* **gyr'oscope** an apparatus in which a heavy flywheel or top rotates at high speed, the turning movement resisting change of direction of axis, used as a toy, an educational device, a compass, etc. — *adj* **gyroscop'ic**. — *n* **gyrostābilīzā'tion** or **-s-**. — *n* **gyrostā'bilizer** or **-s-** a gyroscopic device for countering the roll of a ship, etc. — *n* **gyr'ostat** a gyroscope, *esp* one fixed in a rigid case. — *adj* **gyrostat'ic**. — *n sing* **gyrostat'ics** the science of rotating bodies. — *n* **gyr'ovague** (Med L *gyrovagus*, *pl gyrovagi*) a wandering monk of the Middle Ages. — **gyromagnetic compass** a compass used in aircraft in which, in order to eliminate errors caused by changes of course and speed (greater in an aircraft than in a ship), a gyroscope is combined with a magnet system. [Ety as for **gyre**]

gyron or (*Fr*) **giron** *jī'ron*, (*heraldry*) *n* two lines drawn from the edge of the escutcheon and meeting at right angles in the fesse-point. — *adj* **gyron'ic** or **giron'ic**. — *adj* **gyronn'y**. [Fr *giron*, older *geron*; OHGer *gêro*; cf **gore**[2]]

gyrose, **gyrous**. See under **gyre**.

gyrus *jīr'əs*, (*med* and *zool*) *n* a convoluted ridge between two grooves; a convolution on the surface of the brain. [Ety as for **gyre**]

gyte[1] *gīt*, (*Scot*) *adj* crazy, mad.

gyte[2] *gīt*, (*Scot*) *n* a child; a brat; a first-year boy at Edinburgh Royal High School or (in the Upper School of) Edinburgh Academy. — Also **gait**, **geit**. [**get** (offspring)]

gytrash *gī'trash*, (*dialect*) *n* a ghost or apparition.

gyve *jīv*, earlier (*archaic*) *gīv*, *vt* to fetter. — *n* a shackle; a fetter. [ME *gives*, *gyves*]

H

H or **h** *āch*, sometimes spelt out **aitch**, *n* the eighth letter of the modern English alphabet, representing in Old English a guttural sound, gradually softened down to a spirant, and now often silent; in German notation = B natural (*music*); in medieval Roman notation = 200, $\bar{H}$ = 200 000; something shaped like an H. — **H'-beam** a metal girder H-shaped in section.

H *abbrev*: hearts (*cards*); height; heroin (*slang*); hospital; Hungary (IVR); hydrant.

H *symbol*: hard (on lead pencils); henry or henries (*electronics*); hydrogen (*chem*). — **H'-bomb** a hydrogen bomb.

2H *symbol*: same as **HH** (on lead pencils).

h *abbrev*: hecto-; hot; hour.

h (*phys*) *symbol*: Planck('s) constant.

Ha (*chem*) *symbol*: hahnium.

ha[1] *hä*, *interj* denoting various emotions or responses, eg surprise, joy, exultation, dismay, enquiry, scepticism, encouragement, hesitation, and when repeated, laughter. [Spontaneous utterance]

ha[2] *abbrev*: hectare; *hoc anno* (*L*) in this year.

ha'[1] *hā* or *hə*, a shortened form of **have**.

ha'[2] *hö*, *n* Scots form of **hall**.

haaf *häf*, (*Orkney* and *Shetland*) *n* a deep-sea fishing-ground. — **haaf'-fishing**. [ON *haf* sea]

haaf-net. See under **halve-net**.

haanepoot. See **hanepoot**.

haar *här*, (*East Coast*) *n* a raw sea-mist. [ON *hārr* hoary; MDu *hare* bitter cold; Fris *harig* misty; cf **hoar**]

Hab. (*Bible*) *abbrev*: (the Book of) Habakkuk.

habanera *hä-bä-nā'rə*, *n* a Cuban dance or dance-tune in 2-4 time. [*Habana* or Havana, in Cuba]

habdabs *hab'dabz*, (*colloq*) *n pl* a state of extreme nervousness. — Also **ab'dabs**. — **screaming habdabs** (*colloq*) a bad case of this involving hysterical crying. [Origin uncertain]

habeas corpus *hā'bi-əs kör'pəs*, *n* a writ to a jailer to produce a prisoner in person, and to state the reasons of detention. [L, literally have the body (*ad subjiciendum* to be brought up before the judge)]

haberdasher *hab'ər-dash-ər*, *n* a seller of small sewing articles, such as ribbons, tape, etc; a men's outfitter (*NAm*). — *n* **hab'erdashery** (or *-dash'*) a haberdasher's goods, business or shop. [OFr *hapertas*; origin unknown]

haberdine *hab'ər-dēn*, *-dīn* or *-din*, *n* dried salt cod. [Old Du *abberdaen*, also *labberdaen*; prob from Le *Labourd*, or *Lapurdum*, Bayonne]

habergeon *hab'ər-jən* (*Milton hab'ûr'ji-on*), (*hist*) *n* a sleeveless coat of mail, *orig* lighter than a hauberk. [OFr *haubergeon*, dimin of *hauberc*]

habile *hab'il*, *adj* fit, suitable (*obs*); competent (*obs*); dexterous, adroit (*rare*). [ME variant of **able**, later associated more closely with Fr *habile*, L *habilis*]

habiliment *hə-bil'i-mənt*, *n* attire (*esp* in *pl*). — *adj* **hab'ilable** (*Carlyle*) capable of being clothed. — *adj* **habil'atory** of clothes or dressing. [Fr *habiller* to dress, from L *habilis* fit, ready, from *habēre*]

habilitate *hə-bil'i-tāt*, *vt* to qualify; to equip or finance (eg a mine); to attire. — *vi* to qualify, *esp* as a German university lecturer (Ger *habilitieren*). — *n* **habilitā'tion**. — *n* **habil'itātor**. [LL *habilitāre* to enable, from L *habilis* able]

habit *hab'it*, *n* ordinary course of behaviour; tendency to perform certain actions; custom; accustomedness; familiarity; bodily constitution; characteristic mode of development; the geometric form taken by a crystal (*crystallog*); outward appearance; official or customary dress, *esp* the costume of a nun or monk; a garment, *esp* a riding-habit; an addiction to a drug, etc. — *vt* to dress; to inhabit (*archaic*). — *n* **hab'itaunce** (*Spenser*) dwelling-place. — *adj* **hab'ited** clothed. — *adj* **habit'ūal** customary; usual; confirmed by habit. — *n* someone who has a habit; a habitual drunkard, drug-taker, frequenter, etc. — *adv* **habit'ūally**. — *n* **habit'ūalness**. — *vt* **habit'ūāte** to accustom; to settle (in), or to frequent (*archaic*). — *n* **habitūā'tion** the act of accustoming; the process of becoming accustomed; acquired tolerance for a drug, which thereby loses its effect; development of psychological, without physical, dependence on a drug. — *n* **hab'itūde** constitution; characteristic condition; habit; relation (*obs*); familiar acquaintance (*obs*). — *adj* **habitū'dinal**. — *n* **habitué** (*hab-it'ū-ā*; *Fr a-bē-tü-ā*) a habitual frequenter. — *n* **hab'itus** physical type, *esp* as predisposing to disease (*med*); characteristic appearance, manner of growth, etc of a plant or animal. — **hab'it-cloth** a light broadcloth. — *adj* **hab'it-forming** (of a drug) such as a taker will find it difficult or impossible to give up using. — **hab'it-maker** a maker of riding-habits. — **be in the habit of** or **make a habit of** to do regularly or usually; **habit and repute** (*Scots law*) public knowledge that affords strong and generally conclusive evidence of fact. [L *habitus* state, dress, from *habitāre* to dwell]

habitable *hab'i-tə-bl*, *adj* able to be lived in; fit to live in. — *n* **habitabil'ity** or **hab'itableness**. — *adv* **hab'itably**. — *n* **hab'itant** an inhabitant; (*ab-ē-tã*; *Fr*) a native of *esp* Canada or Louisiana of French descent (*pl* in this sense sometimes **habitans**). — *n* **habita'tion** the act of inhabiting; a dwelling or residence; a lodge of a society. — *adj* **habita'tional**. [L *habitāre* to dwell]

habitat *hab'i-tat*, *n* the normal abode or locality of an animal or plant (*biol*); the physical environment of any community; the place where a person or thing can usually be found (*facetious* or *colloq*); a capsule on the sea bed, in which men can live for a prolonged period and from which they can explore their surroundings, the capsule being at the same pressure as the water around it. — **habitat module** living accommodation for the crew on a space mission. [L, (it) dwells]

habitation. See **habitable**.

habitual etc, **habituate** etc, **habitude**, **habitué**, **habitus**. See under **habit**.

hable *hā'bl*, (*Spenser*) *adj*. Same as **able**.

haboob *hä-bōōb'*, *n* a sandstorm. [Ar *habūb*]

haček *hä'chek*, *n* in Slavonic languages, the diacritic (ˇ) placed over a letter to modify its sound. [Czech]

hachis *hä-shē* or *ä-shē*, *n* hash. [Fr]

hachure *hash'ūr* or *ä-shür*, *n* shading, in the form of lines, showing a hill or slope on a map. — *vt* to shade with hachures. [Fr]

hacienda *as-i-en'də*, (*Sp Am*) *n* a landed estate; a ranch or farm; a main dwelling-house on an estate; a country house; a stock-rearing, manufacturing or mining establishment in the country. [Sp, from L *facienda* things to be done]

hack[1] *hak*, *vt* to cut with rough blows; to chop or mangle; to notch; to roughen with a hammer; to kick or strike the shins of (in some sports, illicitly); to put up with or bear (*slang*). — *vi* to slash, chop; to cough; to use a computer with great skill; to gain unauthorized access to other computers (often with *into*). — *n* an act of hacking; a gash; a notch; a chap in the skin; a kick on the shin; a mattock or pick. — *n* **hack'er** a person who hacks; a skilled and enthusiastic computer operator, *esp* an amateur (*colloq*); an operator who uses his or her skill to break into commercial or government computer or other electronic systems. — *n* **hack'ing**. — *adj* short and interrupted, used eg of a broken, troublesome cough. — **hack'-log** a chopping-block; **hack'-saw** a saw for metals. — **hack someone off** (*slang*) to make someone thoroughly fed up, disgusted. [Assumed OE *haccian*, found in combined form *tō-haccian*; cf Du *hakken*, Ger *hacken*]

hack[2] *hak*, *n* a horse (or formerly, and still in the USA, a vehicle) kept for hire, *esp* one in a sorry condition; an ordinary riding-horse; any person overworked on hire; a literary or journalistic drudge; anything hackneyed (*obs*). — *adj* hired; mercenary; hackneyed. — *vt* to make a hack of; to use as a hack; to hackney; to hire out (a horse); to ride (a horse) in the countryside for recreation. — *vi* to work as a hack; to journey on horseback; to ride on horseback in the countryside for recreation. — *n* **hackette'** (*slang*) a woman journalist. — *n* **hack'ing**. — **hack'ing-jacket** or **-coat** a waisted jacket with slits in the skirt and flapped pockets on a slant; **hack'-work** literary drudgery for publishers. [**hackney**]

hack[3] *hak*, *n* a grating or rack, eg for feeding cattle; a rack on which food is placed for a hawk; a bank for drying bricks. [OE *hæce*, *hæc* grating, hatch; cf **hatch**[1] and **heck**[1]]

hack[4] *hak*, (*Shakesp*) *vi* meaning unknown — possibly to take to the highway (or the street), or to have spurs hacked off.

hackamore *hak'ə-mōr*, *n* a halter used *esp* in breaking in foals, consisting of a single length of rope with a loop to serve instead of a bridle; a bridle without a bit, exerting pressure on the horse's muzzle, not its mouth. [Sp *jáquima*]

hackberry *hak'ber-i*, *n* the hagberry; an American tree (*Celtis occidentalis*) related to the elm; its wood. [See **hagberry**]

hackbolt *hak'bōlt*, *n* the greater shearwater. — Also **hag'bolt**, **hag'den**, **hag'don** or **hag'down** (*hag'dən*). [Origin obscure]

hackbut *hak'but* or **hagbut** *hag'but*, (*hist*) *n* an arquebus. — *n* **hackbuteer'**. [OFr *haquebute*, from ODu *hakebus*; see **arquebus**]

hackee *hak'ē*, *n* the chipmunk. [Imit of its cry]

hacker. See **hack**[1].

hackery *hak'ər-i*, *n* an Indian ox-drawn cart for transporting goods. [Perh Bengali *hākārī* shouting]

hackette. See **hack**[2].

hacking. See **hack**[1,2].

hackle *hak'l*, *n* a comb for flax or hemp; a cock's neck feather; this worn as a decoration in a cap, etc; (in *pl*) the hair of a dog's neck; (in *pl*) hair, whiskers; an angler's fly made of a cock's hackle, or its frayed-out part. — *vt* to comb with a hackle. — *n* **hack'ler**. — *adj* **hack'ly** rough and broken, as if hacked or chopped; jagged and rough (*mining*). — **make someone's hackles rise** to make someone angry. [Cf **hatchel**, **heckle**; Du *hekel*; Ger *Hechel*; perh partly from OE *hacele*, *hæcele* cloak, vestment]

hacklet *hak'lit* or **haglet** *hag'lit*, *n* the kittiwake; also perhaps the shearwater. [Origin unknown]

hackmatack *hak'mə-tak*, *n* an American larch; its wood. [Indian word]

hackney *hak'ni*, *n* a horse for general use, *esp* for hire; a horse with a high-stepping action, bred to draw light carriages; a person hired for drudgery (*obs*). — *vt* to carry in a hackney-coach; to use to excess; to make commonplace. — *adj* **hack'ney** let out for hire. — *adj* **hack'neyed** devoted to common use; trite; dulled by excessive use. — **hackney cab**, **carriage** or **coach** (formerly) any horse-drawn vehicle serving as a taxi; (only **hacking carriage**) the official term used to describe a *usu* black London-style taxi; **hackney-coach'man**; **hack'neyman** someone who keeps hackney horses. [OFr *haquenée* an ambling nag; poss from *Hackney* in East London, where horses were pastured]

hac lege *hak lē'jē* or *lā'ge*, (*L*) with this law, under this condition.

hacqueton. Same as **acton**.

had[1] *had*, *pa t* and *pa p* of **have**.

had[2] *häd*, *höd* or *hud*, a Scots form of **hold**[1]: — *pa p* **hadden** (*häd'n* or *hud'n*).

hadal. See **Hades**.

haddock *had'ək*, *n* a N Atlantic sea fish (*Melanogrammus aeglefinus*) of the cod family. — Also (*Scot*) **hadd'ie**. [ME *haddok*; ety unknown]

hade *hād*, (*mining*) *n* the angle between the plane of a fault, etc, and a vertical plane. — *vi* to incline from the vertical. [Origin obscure]

Hades *hā'dēz*, *n* the underworld roamed by the souls of the dead (*Gr mythol*); the abode of the dead; hell (*New Testament*). — *adj* **hā'dal** forming or belonging to the levels of the ocean deeper than 6000 metres. [Gr *Aidēs*, *Haidēs* the god of the underworld; the abode of the dead]

Hadith *had'ith* or *hä-dēth'*, *n* the body of traditions about Mohammed, supplementary to the Koran. [Ar *hadīth*]

had-I-wist *had-ī-wist'*, (*obs*) *n* vain regret; remorse. [**had I wist**]

hadj, **haj** or **hajj** *häj*, *n* a Muslim pilgrimage to Mecca. — *n* **hadj'i**, **haj'i** or **hajj'i** (*-i*) someone who has performed a hadj; a Christian who has visited Jerusalem. [Ar *hajj* effort, pilgrimage]

hadn't *had'ənt*, contracted form of **had not**.

hadrome *had'rōm*, (*bot*) *n* xylem. [Gr *hadros* thick]

hadron *had'ron*, *n* one of a class of subatomic particles, including baryons and mesons. — *adj* **hadron'ic**. [Gr *hadros* heavy, with *-on* as in **proton**, etc]

hadrosaur *had'rə-sör*, *n* the name of a group of herbivorous, bird-hipped, Cretaceous dinosaurs of the ornithopod class, having webbed hands and feet, a duckbill-shaped jaw and a bony crest. [Gr *hadros* thick, and *sauros* a lizard]

hadst. See **have**.

hae *hā*, *vt* a form of **have**, *esp* Scots.

haecceity *hek-sē'i-ti* or *hēk-*, (*philos*) *n* Duns Scotus's word for that element of existence on which individuality depends, hereness-and-nowness. [Literally thisness, L *haec*]

haem- *hēm-* or *hem-*, **haemat-** *-ət-* or **haemo-** *-o-* (or *US* **hem-**, **hemat-** and **hemo-**) *combining form* denoting blood. — *n* **haem** (also **hem** and **heme**) the pigment combined with the protein (globin) in haemoglobin. — *adj* **haemal** or **hemal** (*hē'məl*) of the blood or blood-vessels; ventral (*opp* to *dorsal* or *neural*; *old*). — *n* **haemangioma** or (*esp US*) **hemangioma** (*hi-man-ji-ō'mə*) an angioma containing blood vessels. — *n* **Haeman'thus** (Gr *anthos* flower) blood-flower, a S African amaryllid. — *n* **haematem'esis** (Gr *emesis* vomiting) vomiting of blood from the stomach. — *adj* **haemat'ic** pertaining to blood. — *n* **hae'matin** a brown substance containing ferric iron obtainable from oxyhaemoglobin or from dried blood. — *adj* **haematin'ic** having the effect of increasing the haemoglobin or of stimulating production of red blood cells. — *n* a substance having this effect. — *n* **hae'matite** a valuable iron ore, Fe_2O_3, often blood-red, with red streak. — *n* **hae'matoblast** (Gr *blastos* a germ) a blood platelet. — *n* **hae'matocele** (Gr *kēlē* a tumour) a cavity containing blood. — *n* **hae'matocrit** a graduated capillary tube in which the blood is centrifuged, to determine the ratio, by volume, of blood cells to plasma (Gr *kritēs* judge). — *n* **haematogen'esis** blood formation. — *adj* **haematogenous** (*-oj'in-əs*) producing blood; produced by or arising in the blood; spread through the bloodstream. — *adj* **hae'matoid** bloodlike. — *n* **haematol'ogist**. — *n* **haematol'ogy** the study of blood, diseases of blood, and blood-forming tissues. — *n* **haematol'ysis** haemolysis (qv below). — *n* **haematō'ma** a swelling composed of blood effused into connective tissue. — *n* **haematopoiesis** (*-poi-ē'sis*; Gr *poieein* to make) the formation of blood. — *adj* **haematopoiet'ic**. — *n* **haematō'sis** the formation of blood; conversion of venous into arterial blood. — *n* **haematox'ylin** a dye obtained from logwood. — *n* **Haematox'ylon** (Gr *xylon* wood) the logwood genus. — *n* **haematū'ria** (Gr *ouron* urine) presence of blood in the urine. — *adj* **haem'ic** haematic (qv above). — *n* **hae'min** the chloride of haematin. — *n* **haemochromato'sis** (see ety for **chroma**, and **-osis**) a disease of the liver characterized by an excessive accumulation of iron and the development of fibrous tissue, and accompanied by bronzing of the skin. — *n* **haem'ocoel** (LL *coel*, Gr *koilos* hollow) the central body cavity of many invertebrates, including arthropods and molluscs. — *n* **haemoco'nia** (Gr *koniā* dust) blood-dust, small colourless granules in the blood. — *n* **haemocy'anin** (Gr *kyanos* blue) a blue respiratory pigment with functions similar to haemoglobin, in the blood of crustaceans and molluscs. — *n* **hae'mocyte** a blood cell, *esp* a red one. — *n* **haemodial'ysis** (Gr *dia* through, and *lysis* dissolution) the purifying of the blood (in eg cases of kidney failure) by circulating it through an apparatus containing a semi-permeable membrane that blocks the passage of waste products. — *n* **haemoglō'bin** (L *globus* a ball) the red oxygen-carrying pigment in the red blood corpuscles. — *n* **haemoglobinop'athy** any of various blood disorders caused by changes in the molecular structure of haemoglobin. — *n* **haemol'ysis** (Gr *lysis* dissolution) breaking up of red blood-corpuscles. — *adj* **haemolyt'ic** pertaining to haemolysis. — *n* **hae'mony** (prob Gr *haimōnios* blood-red) a plant with sovereign properties against magic, etc in Milton's poem *Comus*. — *n* **haemophil'ia** (Gr *phileein* to like) a hereditary disease causing excessive bleeding when any bloodvessel is even slightly injured. — *n* **haemophil'iac** someone who suffers from haemophilia. — *n* **haemop'tysis** (Gr *ptysis* a spitting) the spitting or coughing up of blood from the lungs. — *n* **haemorrhage** (*hem'ər-ij*; Gr *haimorrhagiā*, from *rhēgnynai* to burst) a discharge of blood from the bloodvessels; a steady and persistent draining away (*fig*). — Also *vi*. — *adj* **haemorrhagic** (*-raj'ik*). — *n* **haemorrhoid** (*hem'ər-oid*; Gr *haimorrhois*, *-idos*, from *rheein* to flow; *usu* in *pl*) dilatation of a vein around the anus, piles. — *adj* **haemorrhoid'al**. — *n* **haemo'stasis** stoppage of bleeding or the circulation. — *n* **hae'mostat** an instrument for stopping bleeding. — *n* and *adj* **haemostat'ic** (Gr *statikos*, or hypothetical *states* causing to stand) styptic. — **haemolytic disease of the newborn** disease of the newborn in which maternal antibodies cause haemolysis of the foetal red blood cells, often resulting in stillbirth, anaemia or jaundice. [Gr *haima*, *-atos* blood]

haeremai *hī'rə-mī*, (*NZ*) *interj* welcome. [Maori, come hither]

haet, ha'it or **hate** *hāt*, (*Scot*) *n* a whit. [From the phrase *deil ha' it* devil have it]

haff *haf*, *n* a lagoon separated from the sea by a long sandbar. [Ger *Haff* bay]

haffet or **haffit** *haf'it* or *häf'it*, (*Scot*) *n* the side of the head; the temple; locks of hair on the temple. [**half**= **head**; cf OE *healf-hēafod* the sinciput]

hafflin *häf'lin* (*Scot*) *n*. Same as **halfling** (see under **half**).

hafnium *haf'ni-əm*, *n* an element (symbol **Hf**; atomic no 72) discovered in 1922 by Profs Coster and Hevesy of Copenhagen. [L *Hafnia* Copenhagen]

haft *häft*, *n* a handle, *esp* of an axe or knife; a winged leaf-stalk. — *vt* to set in a haft; to establish firmly. [OE *hæft*; Ger *Heft*]

Hag. (*Bible*) *abbrev*: (the Book of) Haggai.

hag[1] *hag*, *n* an ugly old woman, *orig* a witch; an eel-like cyclostomous marine vertebrate, related to the lamprey (also **hag'fish**). — *adj* **hagg'ed** haglike; haggard. — *adj* **hagg'ish**. — *adv* **hagg'ishly**. — *adj* **hag'-ridden** tormented by nightmares or driven by obsessions, as though possessed by a witch; henpecked, harried by women (*facetious*). — *vt* **hag'-ride**. — **hag'-seed** a witch's offspring; **hag'-taper** mullein; **hag'-weed** the common broom-plant (a broomstick being a witch's supposed mode of transport). [Perh OE *hægtesse* a witch; cf Ger *Hexe*]

hag[2] *hag*, (*Scot*) *vt* and *vi* to hack, hew. [ON *höggva*]

hag[3] or **hagg** *hag*, (*Scot* and *NEng dialect*) *n* any broken ground in a moss or bog; a place from which peat has been dug; a pool or hole in a bog; a relatively high and firm place in a bog; the rough overhanging edge of a peat-hole or stream-bank; brushwood to be cut down. [ON *högg* a gash, ravine, a cutting of trees]

Hagberg falling number test *hag'bərg-*, *n* a test by which the milling quality of wheat can be determined, a low falling number indicating that the enzyme *alpha amylase* has begun to break down the starch in the grain, making it less suitable for bread making. — **hagberg value**.

hagberry *hag'ber-i*, *n* the bird-cherry, a small Eurasian tree with white flowers; the American hackberry tree or its cherry-like fruit. [Cf ON *heggr* bird-cherry]

hagbolt, hagden, hagdon, hagdown. See **hackbolt**.

hagbut. See **hackbut**.

hagfish. See **hag**[1].

hagg. See **hag**[3].

Haggadah *hä-gä'də*, *n* the homiletical and illustrative part of the authoritative book of Jewish civil and religious law and tradition, the Talmud, recited at a ceremonial meal, the Seder, on the first two nights of the Passover; the Passover ritual. — Also **Haggad'a** and **Aga'dah**. — *adj* **Haggad'ic**, **Haggadist'ic** or **Aga'dic**. — *n* **Hagga'-dist**. [Heb]

haggard *hag'ərd*, *adj* untamed; intractable; lean; hollow-eyed and gaunt, from weariness, hunger, etc. — *n* an untamed hawk, or one caught when adult, *esp* a female. — *adv* **hagg'ardly**. — *n* **hagg'ardness**. [OFr *hagard*]

hagged. See **hag**[1].

haggis *hag'is*, *n* a Scottish dish made of the heart, lungs and liver of a sheep or calf, etc, chopped up with suet, onions and oatmeal, etc, seasoned and boiled in a sheep's stomach-bag or a substitute. [ME *hageys*, poss from Anglo-Fr *hageis*, from *haguer* to cut up]

haggish. See **hag**[1].

haggle *hag'l*, *vi* to bargain contentiously or wranglingly; to raise trifling objections; to cavil, quibble. — *vt* to cut unskilfully; to mangle. — *n* **hagg'ler**. [ON *heggra* to hew]

hagi- *hag'i-* (sometimes *haj'i-*) and **hagio-** *-ō-*, *-o-* or *-ə-*, *combining form* signifying holy or denoting saint. — *n* **hag'iarchy** rule or order of saints or holy persons. — *n* **hagioc'racy** government by holy men. — *n pl* **Hagiog'-rapha** those books which with the Law and the Prophets make up the Old Testament. — *n* **hagiog'rapher** a writer of the Hagiographa; a writer of saints' lives. — *adj* **hagiograph'ic** or **hagiograph'ical**. — *n* **hagiog'raphist**. — *n* **hagiog'raphy** a biography of a saint; a biography which over-praises its subject. — *n* **hagiol'ater** a worshipper of saints. — *n* **hagiol'atry** (Gr *latreiā* worship). — *adj* **hagiolog'ic** or **hagiolog'ical**. — *n* **hagiol'ogist** a writer of or someone versed in saints' legends. — *n* **hagiol'ogy**. — *n* **hag'ioscope** a squint in a church, giving a view of the high altar. — *adj* **hagioscop'ic**. [Gr *hagios* holy]

haglet. Same as **hacklet**.

hah *hä*, *interj*. Same as **ha**[1].

ha-ha[1] *hä-hä*, *interj* in representation of a laugh. — *n* the sound of laughter. — *vi* to laugh. — *interj* **ha-ha'** an expression of triumph, eg on discovering something. [Imit]

ha-ha[2] *hä'-hä* or **haw-haw** *hö'-hö*, *n* a ditch or vertical drop often containing a fence, eg between a garden and surrounding parkland, forming a barrier without interrupting the view. [Fr *haha*]

hahnium *hä'ni-əm*, *n* an artificially-produced transuranic element (symbol **Ha**; atomic no 105). [Otto *Hahn* (1879–1968), Ger physicist]

haick. See **haik**[1].

haiduk or **heyduck** *hī'do͝ok*, *n* a brigand; a guerrilla warrior; a liveried servant. [Hung *hajduk*, pl of *hajdú*]

haik[1], **haick**, **haique** or **hyke** *hīk*, *n* an oblong cloth worn by Arabs on the head and body. [Ar *hayk*]

haik[2]. See **heck**[1].

haikai. See **haiku**.

Haikh *hīhh*, *n* and *adj* Armenian. [Armenian]

haiku *hī'ko͞o*, *n* a Japanese poem in three lines of 5, 7 and 5 syllables, *usu* comical, developed in the 17c, incorporating a word or phrase that symbolizes one of the seasons. — Also **haikai** (*hī'kī*) *orig* a linked series of haiku forming one poem (short for *haikai no renga* linked comic verse), and **hokku** (*hö'ko͞o*) *orig* the first half-line of a linked series of haiku. [From Jap]

hail[1] *hāl*, *n* health (*obs*); a call from a distance; a greeting; earshot (*esp* in the phrase *within hail*). — *adj* (*obs*) sound, hale. — *vt* to greet; to address, accost; to call to from a distance; to summon to stop or come. — *interj* of greeting or salutation. — *n* **hail'er**. — *adj* **hail'-fellow(-well-met')** readily or overly friendly and familiar. — Also *n* and *adv*. — **hail Mary** (a recital of) the English version of the ave Maria. — **hail from** to belong to, come from (a particular place). [ON *heill* health, (*adj*) sound; cf **hale**[1] and **heal**[1]]

hail[2] *hāl*, *n* frozen rain, or grains of ice falling from the clouds; a shower or bombardment of missiles, abuse, etc. — *vi* and *vt* to shower hail; to shower vigorously or abundantly. — *adj* **hail'y**. — **hail'shot** small shot that scatters like hail; **hail'stone** a ball of hail; **hail'-storm**. [OE *hægl* (*hagol*); Ger *Hagel*]

hail[3] *hāl*, (*Scot*) *n* (in ball-games) a goal; a score. — *vt* to score (a goal); to put into the goal. [Appar from **hail**[1], from the shout with which the player claimed a goal]

hain *hān*, (*Scot*) *vt* to save, preserve; to spare. — *adj* **hained**. — *n* **hain'ing** an enclosure. [ON *hegna* to enclose, protect; cf Swed *hägna*; Dan *hegne*]

hainch *hānsh* or *hānch*. Scots form of **haunch**[1].

haique. See **haik**[1].

hair *hār*, *n* a filament growing from the skin of an animal; an outgrowth of the epidermis of a plant; a fibre; a mass or aggregate of hairs, *esp* that covering the human head; anything very small and fine; a hair's-breadth; type or character (*obs*); a locking spring or other safety contrivance in a firearm. — *vt* to free from hair; to provide hair for. — *adj* **haired** (*usu* as *combining form*) signifying having hair (of a specified type, length, etc). — *n* **hair'iness**. — *adj* **hair'less** having no hair; very angry (*slang*); desperate (*slang*). — *n* **hair'lessness**. — *adj* **hair'like**. — *adj* **hair'y** of or like hair; covered with hair; dangerous, risky (*colloq*). — **hair'-ball** a concretion of hair in the stomach, eg in cats as a result of swallowing fur, etc during grooming; **hair'-band** a band, *usu* of or incorporating elastic material, worn over the hair to confine it, or for decoration; **hair'bell** same as **harebell**. — *adj* **hair'-brained** same as **hare-brained**. — **hairbreadth** see **hair's-breadth** below; **hair'-brush** a brush for the hair; **hair'cloth** coarse cloth made from horsehair, used in upholstery, etc; **hair'cut** a cutting of the hair or the style in which this is done; **hair'do** (*colloq*) process or style of hairdressing: — *pl* **hair'dos**; **hair'dresser** someone whose occupation is the cutting, colouring, arranging, etc of hair; a barber; **hair'dressing** a lotion, etc for the hair; the art or occupation of a hairdresser; **hair'dryer** or **hair'drier** any of various types of hand-held or other apparatus producing a stream of warm air for drying the hair; **hair'-eel** a hair-worm; **hair'-grass** a genus (*Aira*) of narrow-stemmed coarse grasses (perhaps only a modification of the generic name); **hair grip** or **hair'grip** a short, narrow band of metal, bent double, worn in the hair, to keep it in place; **hair'line** a line made of hair; a very fine line in writing, type, etc; a finely striped cloth; the edge of the hair on the forehead. — *adj* (of eg a crack) very thin; also *fig*. — **hair'net** a net for keeping (*usu* a woman's) hair in place; **hair oil** a scented oil for dressing the hair; **hair'-pencil** a fine paint-brush; **hair'piece** a length of false hair, or a wig covering only part of the head; **hair'pin** a U-shaped pin for fastening up the hair. — *adj* narrowly U-shaped, as a sharp bend on a road. — **hair'-powder** powdered starch formerly dusted on the hair or wig; **hair'-raiser** a tale of terror. — *adj* **hair'-raising** very exciting, terrifying. — **hair restorer** a preparation claimed to make hair grow on bald places; **hair's'-breadth** or **hair'breadth** the breadth of a hair; a minute distance. — *adj* (of an escape, etc) extremely narrow. — **hair seal** a sea-lion, or eared seal with coarse hair only; **hair shirt** a penitent's garment of haircloth; an intimate or secret affliction (*fig*); **hair slide** a hinged clasp, often decorative, worn in the hair, *esp* by young girls; **hair space** (*printing*) the thinnest metal space used by compositors, or its equivalent in photocomposition; **hair'-splitter** a maker of over-fine distinctions. — *n* and *adj* **hair'-splitting**. — **hair'spray** lacquer sprayed on the hair to hold it in place; **hair'spring** a slender spring regulating a watch balance; **hair'streak** any butterfly of several genera with a fine white band under the wing; **hair stroke** a hairline in penmanship; **hair'style** a particular way of cutting and arranging the hair; **hair'stylist**; **hair'-tail** a fish of the family Trichiuridae, with a whiplike tail; **hair trigger** a trigger, responding to very light pressure, that releases the hair of a gun. — *adj* **hair'-trigger** having a hair trigger; responding to the slightest stimulus. — **hair'-wave** a wavelike appearance artificially given to hair; **hair'-waver**; **hair'-waving**; **hair'-work** work done or something made with (*esp* human) hair; **hair'-worm** a worm, like a horse-hair, which when young lives in the bodies of insects. — **against the hair** (*archaic*) against the grain; contrary to inclination; **a hair of the dog (that bit him** or **her**, etc) a smaller dose of that which caused the trouble; a morning drink of the alcohol that caused the hangover as a cure for it — a homeopathic dose; **by the short hairs** or (*colloq*) **by the short and curlies** in a powerless position, at someone's mercy; **get in someone's hair** (*colloq*) to become a source of irritation to someone; **keep one's hair on** (*colloq*) to keep calm; **let one's hair down** to forget reserve and speak or behave freely; **lose one's hair** to grow angry; **make someone's hair curl** to shock someone extremely; **make someone's hair stand on end** to frighten or astonish someone greatly; **not turn a hair** (of a horse) to show no sweat; not to be ruffled or disturbed; **put up the hair** to dress the hair up on the head instead of wearing it hanging — once the mark of passage from girlhood to womanhood; **split hairs** to make superfine distinctions; **tear one's hair (out)** to display frenzied grief or (*colloq*) great irritation; **to a hair** or **to the turn of a hair** exactly, with perfect nicety. [OE *hǣr*, Ger *Haar*, Du and Dan *haar*, etc; vowel perhaps influenced by Fr *haire* a hair shirt]

hairst *hārst*, a Scottish form of **harvest**. — **hairst-rig'** a harvest-field or a section of it, formerly cut in competition.

ha'it. See **haet**.

haith *hāth*, (*Scot*) *interj* by my faith. [**faith**]

Haitian *ha-ē'shən* or *hā'shən*, *n* a native or citizen of Haiti; the creolized form of French spoken in Haiti. — *adj* of or from Haiti, or the Haitians; Haitian-speaking.

haj, **haji**, **hajj**, **hajji**. See **hadj**.

haka *hä'kä*, *n* a Maori ceremonial war-dance; a similar dance performed by New Zealanders, eg before a rugby match. [Maori]

hakam *häk'äm*, *n* a sage; a rabbinical commentator, *esp* one during the first two centuries AD. [Heb *hākhām* wise]

hake[1] *hāk*, *n* a gadoid fish resembling the cod. [Prob Scand; cf Norw *hake-fisk*, literally hook-fish]

hake[2]. See **heck**[1].

Hakenkreuz *hä'kən-kroits*, *n* the swastika. [Ger, hook-cross]

hakim[1] *hä-kēm'*, *n* a Muslim physician. [Ar *hakīm*]

hakim[2] *hä'kim*, *n* a judge, governor or official in Pakistan. [Ar *hakim*]

Halachah, **Halakah** or **Halacha** *hä-lä'hhä* or *-kä*, *n* the legal element in the Jewish book of civil and religious obedience, the Talmud. — *adj* **Halach'ic**. [Heb, from *hālak* to walk]

halal or **hallal** *häl-äl'*, *vt* to slaughter according to Muslim law: — *pr p* **halall'ing** or **hallall'ing**; *pa t* and *pa p* **halalled'** or **hallalled'**. — *n* meat from animals that have been so slaughtered, that may lawfully be eaten by Muslims. — Also *adj*. [Ar *halāl* lawful]

halation *hə-lā'shən*, *n* blurring in a photograph by reflection and dispersion of light; a bright area around a bright spot on a fluorescent screen. [**halo**]

halavah. See **halva**.

halberd *hal'bərd*, *n* a long-shafted axe-like weapon with a hook or pick on its reverse side, used in the 15 and 16c, and in the 18c denoting the rank of sergeant. — Also **hal'bert**. — *n* **halberdier** (*-dēr'*) a person armed with a halberd. [OFr *halebard*, from MHGer *helmbarde* (Ger *Hellebarde*), from *Halm* stalk, or *Helm* helmet, and OHGer *barta* (Ger *Barte*) axe]

Halbstarker *halp'shtärk'ər*, (*Ger*) *n* a juvenile delinquent.

halcyon *hal'si-ən*, *n* the kingfisher, once believed to make a floating nest on the sea, which remained calm during hatching. — *adj* calm; peaceful; happy and carefree. — **halcyon days** a time of peace and happiness. [L *halcyōn*, from Gr *alkyōn*, fancifully changed to *halkyōn* as if from *hals* sea, and *kyōn* conceiving]

hale[1] *hāl*, *adj* healthy; robust; sound of body; whole (*Scot*; also *n*, with definite article). — *n* **hayle** (*Spenser*) welfare. — *n* **hale'ness**. — **hale and hearty** in good health. [Northern, from OE *hāl*; see **whole**; cf **hail**[1], **heal**[1]]

hale[2] *hāl*, *vt* to drag. [OFr *haler*; Germanic in origin]

haler *hä'lər*, *n* a coin of Czechoslovakia, worth 1/100 of a koruna. — Also **heller** (*hel'ər*). [See **heller**[1]]

half *häf*, *n* one of two equal parts; a half-year or term; half-fare, on a bus, train, etc; a half back; a halved hole in golf; half a pint, *usu* of beer (*colloq*); a measure of an alcoholic spirit, *esp* whisky (*Scot*): — *pl* **halves** (*hävz*) or **halfs** (except for the first definition). — *adj* having or consisting of one of two equal parts; partial; incomplete, as measures. — *adv* to the extent of one-half; in part; imperfectly. — *adj* **half'en** (*Spenser*) half. — *adv* **half'endeale** (*Spenser*) half. — *n* (*Scot*) **half'lin** or **half'ling** a half-grown (*esp* male) person; half a silver penny. — *adj* half-grown. — *adv* **half'lings** or **half'lins** (*Scot*) half; partially. — *adj* half-grown. — **half'-adder** (*comput*) a circuit having two inputs and outputs, which can add two binary digits and give the sum and the carry digit; **half'-and-half'** a mixture of two things in equal proportions, traditionally beer or stout and ale. — *adj* and *adv* in the proportion of one to one, or approximately; in part one thing, in part another. — **half'-ape** a lemur; **half back** (in football) a player or position directly behind the forwards — (in Rugby) (*scrum* half and *stand-off* half), a link between forwards and three-quarters. — *adj* **half'-baked'** underdone; incomplete; crude; immature; half-witted. — **half'-ball** (*billiards*, etc) a shot in which the cue ball is aimed at the edge of the object ball. — *vt* **half'-baptize** or **-ise** to baptize privately and hastily. — **half'-beak** a fish (Hyporhynchus, etc) with a spearlike under-jaw; **half'-binding** a bookbinding with only backs and corners of leather or a similar material; **half'-blood** relation between those who have only one parent in common; a half-breed. — *adj* **half'-blooded**. — **half'-blue** (at university) a substitute for a full blue, or the colours awarded him or her; **half board** (in hotels, etc) the providing of bed, breakfast and one main meal per day, demi-pension; a manoeuvre by which a sailing-ship gains distance to windward by luffing up into the wind (*naut*); **half'-boot** a boot reaching halfway to the knee. — *adj* **half'-bound** bound in half-binding. — *adj* **half'-bred** poorly bred or trained; mongrel, of mixed breed. — **half'-breed** a person or animal of mixed breed (of people, *usu* with one white and one non-white parent; *offensive*); **half'-brother** and **half'-sister** a brother or sister with whom one has only one parent in common; **half'-butt** (*billiards*, etc) a cue longer than the standard snooker cue; **half'-cap** (*Shakesp*) a cap only partly taken off, a slight salute; **half'-caste** a person whose parents are from different races, *esp* a Eurasian; **half-cen'tury** (in eg cricket) a score of fifty. — *adj* **half'-checked** (*Shakesp*) with reins attached halfway up the side-piece of the bit, giving little leverage. — **half'-cheek** (*Shakesp*) a face in profile; **half'-close** (*music*) an imperfect cadence; **half-cock'** the position of the cock of a gun drawn back halfway and retained by the first notch (**at half-cock** only partially prepared); a stroke made by playing neither forward nor back (*cricket*). — *adv* in that position. — *adj* **half'-cocked'**. — **half-crown'** a coin worth **half-a-crown'** or two shillings and sixpence, from 1970 no longer legal tender; a sum of money equivalent to this (also *adj*). — *adj* **half-cut'** (*colloq*) drunk. — **half-day'** a holiday of half a working day. — *adj* **half-dead'** (*colloq*) very weary, exhausted. — **half-doll'ar** an American coin worth 50 cents (also *adj*). — *adj* **half'-done** partly done; partly cooked. — **half'-door** the lower part of a divided door. — *n* and *adj* **half-doz'en** six. — *adj* **half-dū'plex** (*comput*, *teleg*, etc) allowing communication or transmission in both directions, but not simultaneously. — *adj* **halfe-hors'y** (*Spenser*) (of the Centaurs) partly of the nature of horses. — *adj* **half-ev'ergreen** having foliage that persists during part of winter; tending to be evergreen in mild areas but deciduous where the climate is more rigorous. — **half'-face** profile. — *adj* **half'-faced** (*Shakesp*) showing only part of the face; thin-faced. — *adj* **half'-frame** (of a photograph) taking up half the normal area of a frame. — *adj* **half'-hardy** able to grow in the open air except in winter. — *adj* **half-heart'ed** lacking in zeal. — *adv* **half-heart'edly**. — **half-heart'edness**; **half'-hitch** a simple knot tied around an object; **half-hol'iday** half of a working day for recreation; **half-hose** see **hose**; **half-hour'** a period of 30 minutes. — Also *adj*. — *adj* and *adv* **half-hour'ly** at intervals of 30 minutes. — **half-hunter** see **hunter** under **hunt**; **half-in'teger** a number formed by the division of an odd integer by two. — *adj* **half-in'tegral**. — **half'-kirtle** a kind of jacket worn by women in the 16 and 17c; **half'-landing** a small landing at the bend of a staircase; **half'-leather** a half-binding for a book, with leather on back and corners; **half'-length** a portrait showing the upper part of the body. — *adj* of half the whole or ordinary length. — **half'-life** the period of time in which activity of a radioactive substance falls to half its original value; **half'-light** dim light; twilight; **half'-loaf** a loaf of half the standard weight; **half-mar'athon** a foot-race just over half the length of a marathon (21·243km, 13 miles 352 yards); **half-mast'** the position of a flag partly lowered, in respect for the dead or in signal of distress. — Also *adv* and *vt*. — **half-meas'ure** (often in *pl*) any means inadequate for the end proposed; **half-mil'er** a runner specializing in races of half a mile; **half-moon'** the moon at the quarters when half the disc is illuminated; anything semicircular; **half-mourn'ing** mourning attire less than deep or full mourning; the condition of having one black eye (*slang*); **half nelson** see **nelson**; **half'-note** (*music*; *NAm*) a minim; **half-one'** (*golf*) a handicap of one stroke every second hole (see also **half past one** below); **half-pay'** reduced pay, as for an officer not on active service. — *adj* **half'-pay** on half-pay. — **halfpenny** (*hāp'ni*) a coin worth half a penny, withdrawn from circulation in 1985; its value; anything very small (*Shakesp*): — *pl* **halfpence** (*hā'pəns*), or **halfpennies** (*hāp'niz*). — *adj* valued at a halfpenny. — **halfpennyworth** (*hāp'ni-wûrth*; also **hap'orth** *hāp'ərth*) as much as is sold for a halfpenny or is worth a halfpenny; **half'-pike** a short-shafted pike; a spontoon; **half'-pint** (*slang*) a very small person; **half'-plate** see **plate**; **half'-pound** half a pound. — *adj* weighing half a pound. — **half-pound'er** a fish or other thing weighing half a pound; a gun that fires a half-pound shot; **half-price'** a charge reduced to half. — *adj* and *adv* at half the usual price. — **half-round'** a semicircle. — *adj* (*Milton*) semicircular. — **half-roy'al** a kind of millboard. — *adj* and *adv* **half-seas-o'ver** halfway across the sea: half-drunk (*colloq*). — **half'-**

shell one shell or valve of a bivalve; **half-shift'** a position of the hand in violin-playing giving notes a semitone above the open-string position. — **half-size'** any size in clothes, etc halfway between two full sizes; **half'-sole** the part of a shoe-sole from the instep to the toe; **half-sove'reign** a gold coin worth **half-a-sov'ereign** or ten shillings. — *adj* **half-starved'** very inadequately fed. — **half'-step** (*music*; *NAm*) a semitone; **half'-sword** fighting within half a sword's length, close fighting; **half-term'** (a holiday taken at) the mid point of an academic term; **half'-text** handwriting half the size of text. — Also *adj*. — **half'-tide** the stage midway between flood and ebb. — *adj* uncovered at half-tide. — *adj* **half-tim'bered** built of a timber frame, with spaces filled in. — **half-time'** half of full or whole time; the middle of the whole time; a short break halfway through a game (*sport*); (in industry) half the time usually worked. — *adj* **half'-time** at or for half-time. — **half-tim'er** someone who works half the full time; **half'-tint** intermediate tone, between light and dark; **half-ti'tle** a short title preceding the title page or before a section of a book. — *adj* **half'-tone** representing light and shade photographically by dots of different sizes. — *n* (*music*) a semitone. — **half'-track** a motor vehicle with wheels in front and caterpillar tracks behind. — Also *adj*. — **half'-truth** a belief containing an element of truth; a statement conveying only part of the truth; **half-voll'ey** see **volley**. — *adv* **halfway'** (sometimes *häf'wā*) midway; at half the distance; imperfectly; slightly, barely (*colloq*). — *adj* **half'way** equidistant from two points. — **halfway house** an inn, etc situated midway between two towns or points on a journey, etc; a midway point or state; a centre offering accommodation and rehabilitation to eg released prisoners, people recovering from mental illness, etc; **half-wellingtons** see **wellingtons**; **half'wit** a would-be wit (*obs*); an idiot. — *adj* **halfwitt'ed** mentally defective (*obs*); foolish, stupid. — **half'-year** half of a year, six months. — *adj* **half-year'ly** occurring or appearing every half-year. — *adv* twice a year. — *n* a half-yearly publication. — **by half** by a long way; **by halves** incompletely; half-heartedly; **cry halves** to claim half; **go halves** to share equally; **half past one, two**, etc, **half after one, two**, etc (*NAm*), or **half one, two**, etc (*colloq*) thirty minutes after one o'clock, two o'clock, etc; **how the other half lives** (*facetious*) other (*esp* richer or poorer) people's way of life; **not half** (*slang*) not moderately; not even half; not at all; very much, exceedingly; **one's other** (or **better**) **half** one's spouse. [OE (Anglian) *half* (WSax *healf*) side, half; cf Ger *halb*; Dan *halv*]

halfa *hal'fə* or **alfa** *al'fə*, *n* a N African esparto grass. [Ar *halfā*]

halfpace *häf'pās*, *n* a landing or broad step; a raised part of a floor. [OFr *halt* (Fr *haut*) high, and *pas* step]

halibut *hal'i-bət*, *n* a large flatfish, more elongated than flounder or turbot. — Also **hol'ibut**. [Appar **holy butt** as much eaten on holy days; see **holy** and **butt**[5]; cf Du *heilbot*, Ger *Heilbutt*]

halicore *hal-ik'o-rē*, *n* the dugong. [Gr *hals* sea, and *korē* girl]

halide *hal'īd*, *n* a compound of a halogen with a metal or radical — a chloride, bromide, etc. [Gr *hals* salt]

halidom *hal'i-dəm*, (*archaic*) *n* holiness; a holy place or thing, *esp* in an oath. [OE *hāligdōm*, from *hālig* holy]

halieutic *hal-i-ū'tik*, *adj* pertaining to fishing. — *n sing* **halieu'tics** the art of fishing; a treatise on fishing. [Gr *halieutikos*, from *halieus* fisher, from *hals* sea]

halimot or **halimote** *hal'i-mōt*, *n* an erroneous form of **hall-moot** (as if a holy or church court).

haliotis *hal-i-ō'tis*, *n* any gasteropod of the family **Halio'tidae**, with a perforated ear-shaped shell lined with mother-of-pearl; (with *cap*) the genus to which they belong: — *pl* **haliō'tis**. [Gr *hals* sea, and *ous*, *ōtos* ear]

halite *hal'īt*, *n* rocksalt. [Gr *hals* salt]

halitus *hal'i-təs*, *n* a vapour. — *n* **halitō'sis** foul breath. — *adj* **halitō'tic**. — *adj* **hal'itous** vaporous. [L]

hall *höl*, *n* the main room in a great house; a building containing such a room; a manor-house; the main building of a college; in some cases the college itself; an unendowed college; a licensed residence for students; a college dining-room; hence, the dinner itself; a place for special professional education, or the conferring of diplomas, licences, etc; the headquarters of a guild, society, etc; a servants' dining-room and sitting-room (*servants' hall*); a building or large chamber for meetings, concerts, exhibitions, etc; a large room entered immediately by the front door of a house; a passage or lobby at the entrance of a house; a clear space (*archaic*). — **hall-bed'room** (*US*) a bedroom partitioned off at the end of an entrance hall; **hall'-door** front-door; **hall'mark** the authorized stamp impressed on gold, silver or platinum articles at Goldsmiths' Hall or some other place of assaying, indicating date, maker, fineness of metal, etc; any mark of authenticity or good quality. — *vt* to stamp with such a mark. — **hall'-moot** the court of the lord of a manor; the court of a guild; **hall'stand** a tall piece of furniture fitted with hooks on which hats, coats and umbrellas can be left; **hall'way** an entrance hall. — **a hall, a hall** (*archaic*) a cry at a masque for room for the dance, etc; **bachelor's hall** any place in which a man is free from the restraining presence of a wife; the state of having such freedom, often in the phrase *to keep bachelor's hall*; **hall of fame** a gallery of busts, portraits, etc of celebrated people; the ranks of the great and famous; **hall of residence** a building providing residential accommodation for students at a university, etc; **Liberty Hall** a place where everyone may do as they please; **the halls** music halls. [OE *hall* (*heall*); Du *hal*, ON *höll*, etc]

hallal. See **halal**.

hallali *hal'ə-lē*, *n* a bugle-call.

hallaloo *hal-ə-lōō'*, (*Fielding*) *n* halloo.

hallan *häl'ən*, (*Scot*) *n* a partition or screen between the door and fireplace in a cottage. — **hallan-shāk'er** (or *-shäk'ər*) a beggar; a vagrant; a shabby, sorry creature. [Perh **hall**]

hälleflinta *hel'ə-flin-tə*, *n* a very compact rock composed of minute particles of quartz and feldspar. [Swed, hornstone]

hallelujah or **halleluiah** *hal-ə-lōō'yə*, *n* and *interj* the exclamation 'Praise Jehovah'; a song of praise to God; a musical composition based on the word. — Also **allelu'ia**. [Heb *hallelū* praise ye, and *Jāh* Jehovah]

hallian. See **hallion**.

halliard. See **halyard**.

halling *hal'ing* or *höl'ing*, *n* a Norwegian country dance in 2-4 time, or its tune. [Perh *Hallingdal*, NW of Oslo]

hallion, **hallian** or **hallyon** *hal'yən*, *n* a lout; a lazy rascal. [Origin unknown]

hallo *hə-* or *ha-lō'*, **hello** *hə-* or *he-lō'*, or **hullo** *hə-* or *hu-lō'*, *interj* expressing surprise, discovery, becoming aware; used also in greeting, accosting, calling attention. — *n* a call of hallo: — *pl* **hallōs'**, **hellos'** or **hullos'**. — *vi* to call hallo. — Also **hullo'**. [Variant of MFr *hola*, *ho*, a cry drawing attention, and *la* there]

halloo *hə-lōō'* or **halloa** *hə-lō'*, *n* a cry to urge on a chase or to call attention. — *vi* to urge on a pack of hounds; to raise an outcry. — *vt* to encourage with halloos; to hunt with halloos. — **don't halloo till you're out of the wood** keep quiet till you are sure you are safe. [Imit]

halloumi *hal'ōō-mi*, *n* a Greek dish of fried goat's cheese, eaten as a starter.

hallow *hal'ō*, *vt* to make holy; to consecrate (*archaic*); to reverence. — *n* (*archaic*) a saint. — *adj* **hall'owed** holy, revered. — *n* **Hallowe'en'** the eve of or the evening before All Saints Day, celebrated by masquerading and the playing of pranks by children. — *n* **Hall'owmas** the feast of All Hallows or All Saints, 1 November. [OE *hālgian* to hallow, *hālga* a saint, from *hālig* holy]

halloysite *hal-oiz'īt*, *n* a clayey mineral, a hydrated aluminium silicate. [Omalius d'*Halloy* (1783–1875), Belgian geologist]

Hallstatt *häl'shtät, adj* relating to a European culture transitional between Bronze Age and Iron Age. [From finds at *Hallstatt* in upper Austria]

hallucinate *həl-ōō'sin-āt* or *həl-ū'sin-āt, vt* to affect with hallucination. — *vi* to experience hallucination. — *n* **hallucinā'tion** a perception without objective reality; (loosely) delusion. — *adj* **hallu'cinative** or **hallu'cinatory**. — *n* **hallu'cinogen** (*-nə-jən*) a drug producing hallucinatory sensations. — *adj* **hallucinogen'ic** causing hallucinations. — *n* **hallucino'sis** a mental disorder characterized by the repeated occurrence of hallucinations. [L *hallūcinārī* (better *ālūcinārī*), *-ātus* to wander in the mind]

hallux *hal'uks, n* the innermost digit of the hind-limb of a bird, mammal, reptile or amphibian; the human big toe; a bird's hind-toe: — *pl* **halluces** (*-ū'sēz*). [Wrong form of L (*h*)*allex, -icis*]

hallyon. See **hallion**.

halm *häm*. Same as **haulm**.

halma *hal'mə, n* in the Greek pentathlon, a long jump with weights in the hands (*hist*); a game played on a board of 256 squares, in which the pieces are moved into vacant squares immediately behind an opponent's pieces. [Gr, a jump]

halo *hā'lō, n* a ring of light or colour, *esp* one round the sun or moon caused by refraction by ice-crystals; (in paintings, etc) such a ring round the head of a holy person; an ideal or sentimental glory or glamour attaching to anything: — *pl* **hā'loes** or **hā'los**. — *vt* to surround with a halo (*literally* and *fig*): — *pa p* **hā'loed** or **hā'lo'd**. — **halo effect** (*psychol*) the tendency to judge a person (well or ill) on the basis of one or only a few characteristics. [Gr *halōs* a threshing-floor, disc, halo]

halobiont. See **haloid**.

halocarbon *hal'ō-kär-bən*, (*chem*) *n* a compound consisting of carbon and one or more halogens.

halogen *hal'ə-jən, n* any one of certain elements in the seventh group of the periodic table — fluorine, chlorine, bromine, iodine and astatine (the first four defined in the 19c as forming salts by direct union with metals; astatine discovered in 1940). — *vt* **halogenate** (*oj'*) to combine with a halogen. — *adj* **halog'enous**. [Gr *hals* salt, and **-gen**[1]]

haloid *hal'oid, n* a halide. — *adj* having the composition of a halide. — *n* **halobiont** (*hal-ō-bī'ont*) an organism living or growing in a saline habitat. — *adj* **halobion'tic** or **halobiotic** (*-bī-ot'ik*) living in the sea. — *n* **hal'ophile** (*-fil* or *-fīl*) an organism that thrives in very salty conditions, eg the Dead Sea. — *adj* tolerant of salt; capable of living in salt water. — *adj* **haloph'ilous** halophile. — *n* **haloph'ily** adaptation to life in the presence of much salt. — *n* **hal'ophobe** (*bot*) a plant that cannot survive in salty soil. — *n* **halophyte** (*hal'ō-fīt*) a plant adapted to life in soil or water containing much salt. — *adj* **halophytic** (*-fit'ik*). [Gr *hals* salt]

halon *hal'on, n* any one of a class of halogenated hydrocarbons, used *esp* in fire extinguishers, and considered detrimental to the ozone layer. [Gr *hals* salt]

Haloragis *hal-ə-rā'jis, n* the sea-berry, an Australasian genus of plants giving its name to the family **Haloragidā'ceae**, a reduced offshoot of the evening primrose family, including mare's-tail and water milfoil. [Gr *hals* sea, and *rhāx, rhāgos* a berry]

halothane *hal'ə-thane, n* a general, inhalation anaesthetic known proprietarily as Fluothane.

halse[1] *höls, Scot* and *NEng dialect* **hause** or **hawse** *hös*, (*obs* or *dialect*) *n* the neck; the throat; a pass, defile, or connecting ridge. — *vt* to embrace: — *pa t* **halsed** or (*Spenser*) **haulst**. — **hause'-bane** (*Scot*) collar-bone; **hause'-lock** (*Scot*) the wool of a sheep's neck. [OE *hals* (*heals*) neck; Ger *Hals*]

halse[2] *häls* or *hös*, (*obs*) *vt* to salute, greet. [OE *halsian*]

halser *höz'ər, n*. Same as **hawser**.

halt[1] *hölt, vi* to come to a standstill; to make a temporary stop. — *vt* to cause to stop. — *n* a standstill; a stopping-place; a railway station not fully equipped. — **call a halt (to)** to stop, put an end (to). [Ger *Halt* stoppage]

halt[2] *hölt, vi* to be lame, to limp (*archaic*); to walk unsteadily; to vacillate; to proceed lamely or imperfectly, to be at fault (eg in logic, rhythm, etc). — *adj* (*Bible*; *archaic*) lame, crippled, limping. — *n* a limp (*archaic*); foot-rot (*dialect*); an impediment in speech (*Scot*). — *n* and *adj* **halt'ing**. — *adv* **halt'ingly**. [OE *halt* (*healt*) lame; Dan *halt*]

halter *hölt'ər, n* a rope for holding and leading an animal, or for hanging criminals; a woman's backless bodice held in place by straps round the neck and across the back. — *vt* to put a halter on. — **halter neck** a neckline on a dress, etc in the style of a halter. — *adj* **halt'er-necked**. [OE *hælftre*; Ger *Halfter*]

halteres *hal-tēr'ēz*, (*entomol*) *n pl* the rudimentary hind-wings of flies, used to maintain balance in flight. [Gr *haltēres* dumbbells held by jumpers, from *hallesthai* to jump]

halva, halvah or **halavah** *häl'və, n* a sweetmeat, *orig* Turkish, containing sesame seeds, honey, nuts and saffron. [Yiddish *halva*; ult from Ar]

halve *häv, vt* to divide in half; to reduce by half; (in golf) to draw, be equal in; (in carpentry) to join by cutting away half the thickness of each. — *n* **halv'er** someone who halves; a half-share. — *interj* **halv'ers** used in claiming half a find. [**half**]

halve-net *häv'-net* or **haaf-net** *häf'-net*, (*dialect*) *n* a net held or set to catch fish as the tide ebbs, now only used in the Solway Firth. [Older Scots *half* such a net; cf Norw dialect *haav*, Swed *håf*, Dan *hov*, ON *háfr*]

halyard or **halliard** *hal'yərd, n* a rope or purchase for hoisting or lowering a sail, yard, or flag. [For *halier*, from **hale**[2], by association with **yard**[1]]

ham[1] *ham, n* the back of the thigh or hock; the thigh of an animal, *esp* of a pig salted and dried; the meat from this part. — *adj* **hamm'y**. — *adj* **ham-fist'ed** or **ham-hand'ed** clumsy. [OE *hamm*; cf dialect Ger *hamme*]

ham[2] *ham*, (*colloq*) *n* an actor who rants and overacts; overacting; a part that lends itself to this; an inexpert boxer; an amateur, *esp* an amateur radio operator. — *adj* given to overacting or ranting; amateur; clumsy, coarse, inexpert. — *vi* and *vt* to overact. — *adj* **hamm'y**. — *adv* **hamm'ily**. [Prob **hamfatter**]

hamadryad *ham-ə-drī'ad, n* a wood-nymph who died with the tree in which she dwelt (*classical mythol*); a large poisonous Indian snake, *Naja hamadryas*; a large baboon of Abyssinia: — *pl* **hamadry'ads** or **hamadry'ades** (*-ēz*). [Gr *hamadryas*, from *hama* together, and *drȳs* (oak) tree]

hamal. See **hammal**.

hamamelis *ham-ə-mē'lis, n* a shrub of the American witch-hazel genus, giving name to a family, **Hamamelidā'ceae**, related to the planes; (with *cap*) the genus itself. [Gr *hamamēlis* medlar, from *hama* together with, and *mēlon* an apple]

hamarthritis *ham-är-thrī'tis, n* gout in all the joints. [Gr *hama* together, and *arthrītis* gout]

hamartia *ha-mär'tē-ə, n* (in a literary work) the flaw or defect in the character of the hero which leads to his downfall (*orig* and *esp* in ancient Greek tragedy; see Aristotle's *Poetics*). — *n* **hamartiol'ogy** that section of theology which deals with sin. [Gr *hamartiā* failure, error of judgment, sin]

hamate *hā'māt, adj* hooked. [L *hāmātus*, from *hāmus* hook]

hamble *ham'bl, vt* to mutilate, make (a dog) useless for hunting (by cutting the balls of its feet). — *vi* to limp, to stumble (*dialect*). [OE *hamelian*]

Hamburg or **Hamburgh** *ham-bûrg* or *b(ə)-rə, n* a black variety of grape (often *black Hamburg*); a small blue-legged domestic fowl. — *n* **ham'burger** or **ham'burgher** Hamburg steak, finely chopped meat; (*usu* **hamburger**, often shortened to **burger**; a bread roll containing) a flat round cake of finely chopped meat fried; a large sausage. [*Hamburg* in Germany]

hame[1] *hām*, *n* one of the two curved bars of a draught-horse's collar. [Cf Du *haam*, LGer *ham*]

hame[2] *hām*, Scots form of **home**. — *adv* **hame'with** homewards.

hamesucken *hām'suk-n*, (*Scots law*) *n* the assaulting of a man in his own house. [OE *hāmsōcn*, from *hām* home, and *sōcn* seeking, attack; cf Ger *Heimsuchung* affliction]

hamfatter *ham'fat-ər*, *n* a third-rate minstrel, variety artist or actor. — *vt* and *vi* to act badly or ineffectively. [Perh from an old Negro minstrel song, The *Hamfat* Man]

Hamiltonian *ham-il-tō'ni-ən*, *adj* pertaining to: James *Hamilton* (1769–1829), or his method of teaching languages without grammar; to the philosopher Sir William *Hamilton* (1788–1856); to Sir William Rowan *Hamilton* (1805–65), Irish mathematician; or any other of the name.

Hamite *ham'īt*, *n* a descendant or supposed descendant of *Ham*, son of Noah; a member of a dark-skinned long-headed race of NE Africa (*Galla*, *Hadendoa*, etc), sometimes understood more widely to cover much of N Africa; a speaker of any language of a N African family distantly related to Semitic (ancient Egyptian, Berber, etc). — *adj* **Hamitic** (*-mit'ik*).

hamlet *ham'lit*, *n* a cluster of houses in the country; a small village. [OFr *hamelet*, dimin of *hamel* (Fr *hameau*), from Gmc; cf **home**]

hammal or **hamal** *hum-äl'*, *n* an Eastern porter. [Ar *hammāl*]

hammam *hum-äm'*, *hum'um* or *ham'am*, *n* an Oriental bathing establishment, a Turkish bath. — Also **humm'aum** or **humm'um**. [Ar *hammām*]

hammer *ham'ər*, *n* a tool for beating metal, breaking rock, driving nails, etc; a striking-piece in the mechanism of a clock, piano, etc; the apparatus that causes explosion of the charge in a firearm; the mallet with which an auctioneer announces that an article is sold; a small bone of the ear, the malleus; a metal ball weighing about 7kg, attached to a long handle of flexible wire, for throwing in competition (*athletics*); a trouncer. — *vt* to beat, drive, shape, or fashion with or as if with a hammer; to contrive or think out by intellectual labour (with *out*); to arrive at (a conclusion) or settle (differences) after much argument (with *out*); to trounce or criticize severely (*colloq*); to teach by frequent and energetic reiteration (with *in* or *into*); to declare a defaulter on the Stock Exchange; to beat down the price of (a stock), to depress (a market). — *vi* to use a hammer; to make a noise as of a hammer; to persevere doggedly (with *away*). — *n* **hamm'erer**. — *n* and *adj* **hamm'ering**. — *adj* **hamm'erless**. — **hammer beam** a horizontal piece of timber in place of a tie-beam at or near the feet of a pair of rafters; **hamm'er-brace** a curved brace supporting a hammer beam; **hammer drill** a rock drill in which the piston is independent and strikes blows against the boring part; **hamm'erhead** a shark with a hammer-shaped head (also **hamm'er-fish** and **hammer-headed shark**); the umbrette, a crested thick-billed African wading bird (also (*Du*) **hamm'erkop**). — *adj* **hamm'er-headed** with a head shaped like a hammer; dull in intellect, stupid. — **hamm'erlock** (*wrestling*) a hold in which the opponent's arm is twisted upwards behind his (or her) back; **hamm'erman** someone who wields a hammer, such as a blacksmith, goldsmith, etc; **hamm'er-pond** an artificial pond at a water-mill; **hamm'er-toe** a condition in which a toe is permanently bent upwards at the base and doubled down upon itself. — **bring to the hammer** to sell, or cause to sell, by auction; **(come) under the hammer** (come up for sale) by auction; **give** (or **take**) **a hammering** to beat (or be beaten) severely, to defeat (or be defeated) comprehensively; **hammer and sickle** the crossed hammer and sickle emblem of the former Soviet Union, or of Communism; **hammer and tongs** with great noise and violence; **hammer home** to impress (a fact) strongly and effectively on someone. [OE *hamor*; Ger *Hammer*, ON *hamarr*]

hammercloth *ham'ər-kloth*, *n* a cloth covering a coach-box. [Origin unknown]

Hammerklavier *ham-ər-kla-vēr'*, (*Ger*) *n* a pianoforte.

hammerkop. See **hammer**.

hammock *ham'ək*, *n* a cloth or netting hung by the ends, for use as a bed or couch. [Sp *hamaca*, from Carib]

Hammond organ® *ham'ənd ör'gən*, *n orig* a two-manual organ, with tones electromagnetically generated by means of rotating wheels controlled by the keys; (loosely) any two-manual digital organ. [Invented by L *Hammond*, 20c US mechanical engineer]

hamose *hā'mōs*, *adj* hooked. — Also **hā'mous**. — *adj* **hamular** (*ham'ū-lər*) like a small hook. — *adj* **ham'ūlate** tipped with a small hook. — *n* **ham'ūlus** a small hook or hook-like process: — *pl* **ham'uli** (*-lī*). [L *hāmus* hook]

hamper[1] *ham'pər*, *vt* to impede the progress or movement of; to distort; to curtail. — *n* a shackle; that which impedes; essential but somewhat cumbrous equipment on a vessel (*naut*). [First, about 1350, in Northern writers; cf ON and Mod Icel *hemja* to restrain, Ger *hemmen*]

hamper[2] *ham'pər*, *n* a large basket, *usu* with a cover; the basket and its contents, *usu* food; a laundry basket (*NAm*). — *vt* to give a hamper to, to bribe. [**hanapier** (see under **hanap**)]

hampster. See **hamster**.

hamshackle *ham'shak-l*, *vt* to shackle by tying head to foreleg; to fetter, restrain. [**shackle**; otherwise obscure]

hamster or **hampster** *ham'stər*, *n* a small Eurasian rodent (genus *Cricetus*) with cheek-pouches reaching almost to the shoulders. [Ger]

hamstring *ham'string*, *n* (in humans) one of the five tendons at the back of the knee; (in a horse, etc) the large tendon at the back of the knee or hock of the hindleg. — *vt* to lame by cutting the hamstring; to make powerless: — *pa t* and *pa p* **ham'stringed** or **ham'strung**. [**ham**[1] and **string**[1]]

hamular, **hamulate**, **hamuli**, **hamulus**. See **hamose**.

hamza or **hamzah** *häm'zä* or *ham'zə*, *n* in Arabic, the sign used to represent the glottal stop. [Ar *hamzah* a compression]

Han *han*, *n* and *n pl* (a member of) the native Chinese people, as opposed to the Mongols, Manchus, etc. [Chin]

han *han*, an old *pl* (*Spenser*) of **have**.

hanap *han'əp*, *n* an ornate medieval drinking goblet, often having a cover. — *n* **han'aper** a case for a hanap; a receptacle for treasure, paper, etc; a former department of Chancery. [OFr *hanap* drinking-cup; cf OHGer *knapf*; OE *hnæpp* a bowl]

hance *häns* or *hans*, *n* a curved rise from a lower to a higher part (*naut*); the arc of smaller radius at the springing of an elliptical or many-centred arch (*archit*). — Also **haunch**. [OFr *hauce*, *haulce* rise: cf **enhance**]

hanch[1] *hänsh*, (*Scot*) *vi* and *vt* to snap (at) with the jaws. [Obs Fr *hancher*]

hanch[2]. See **haunch**[1].

hand *hand*, *n* (in humans) the extremity of the arm below the wrist; any corresponding member in the higher vertebrates; the forefoot of a quadruped; the extremity of the hind-limb when it is prehensile; a pointer or index; a measure of four inches; a division of a bunch of bananas; side, direction, quarter; a worker, *esp* in a factory or on a ship; a performer; a doer, author or producer; instrumentality; influence; share in performance; power or manner of performing; style; skill; handiwork; touch; stroke; control; (often in *pl*) keeping, custody; possession; assistance; style of handwriting; a signature, *esp* of a sovereign; pledge; consent to or promise of marriage, or fulfilment of such promise; feel, handle (of a textile); the set of cards held by a player at one deal; the play of a single deal of cards; (loosely) a game of cards; a turn, round or innings in a game; in various games, (possession of) service; a round of applause; (in *pl*) skill in handling a horse's reins. — *vt* to lay hands on, set hand to, manipulate, handle (*obs*); to join hands with (*rare*); to pass with the hand; to lead, escort or help (eg *into* a vehicle) with the hands; to transfer or deliver (often with *over*); to furl or lower (a (*esp* a square) sail) (*naut*). — **hand-** (in combination) denoting: by hand, or direct bodily operation (**hand'-held, hand'-knitted, hand'-made, hand'-painted, hand'-sewn, hand'-weeded**); for the hands (**hand'-lotion, hand'towel**); operated by hand (**hand'-punch**); held in the hand (**hand'-basket**). — *adj* **hand'ed** having hands; with hands joined (*Milton*). — **-hand'ed** used in combination to signify: using one hand in preference to the other (as in *left-handed*); having a hand or hands as stated (as in *one-handed* or *neat-handed*). — *n* **hand'edness** the tendency to use one hand rather than the other; inherent asymmetry in particles, etc, eg causing twisting in one direction (*phys*). — **-hand'edness** noun combining form. — *n* **hand'er** someone who hands; a blow on the hand. — **-hander** used in combination to signify: a blow, etc with the hand or hands as stated (eg *right-hander, back-hander*); a play with a specified number of characters (eg *two-hander*). — *n* **hand'ful** enough to fill the hand; a small number or quantity; someone or something that taxes one's powers: — *pl* **hand'fuls**. — *adv* **hand'ily**. — *n* **hand'iness**. — *adj* **hand'less** without hands; awkward; incompetent. — *adj* **hand'y** (*compar* **hand'i-er**; *superl* **hand'iest**) dexterous; near to hand; convenient; near. — **hand'bag** a bag for small articles, carried *esp* by women; a light travelling-bag. — *vt* (*colloq*; of a woman, *orig* of Margaret Thatcher, British prime minister 1979–90) to attack, destroy, wreck, undermine (unity). — **hand'bagging**; **handbag diplomacy**; **hand'-ball** a game between goals in which the ball is struck with the palm of the hand; a game similar to fives in which a ball is struck with the gloved hand against a wall or walls (*usu* four); (also **hand ball**; *football*) the offence of touching or striking the ball with one's hand; **hand'-barrow** a wheelless barrow, carried by handles; a handcart; **hand'-basket**; **hand'bell** a small bell with a handle, rung by hand; **hand'bill** a light pruning-hook; a bill or loose sheet bearing an announcement; **hand'book** a manual; a bookmaker's book of bets (*US*); **hand'brake** a brake applied by hand-operated lever; **handbrake turn** a sharp U-turn on the spot in a motor car, achieved by applying the handbrake at speed; **hand'-breadth** or **hand's breadth** the breadth of a hand; **hand'car** (*US*) a workman's small, open-sided railway car, motorized or propelled by hand-pumping a lever; **hand'cart** a light cart drawn by hand; **hand'clap** a clap of the hands; **hand'clasp** (*US*) a handshake; **hand'craft** handicraft; **hand'cuff** (*esp* in *pl*) a shackle locked on the wrist. — *vt* to put handcuffs on. — **hand'fast** (*archaic*) a firm grip; custody; a handle (*dialect*); a contract, *esp* a betrothal. — *adj* (*archaic*) bound; espoused; tight-gripping. — *vt* (*archaic*) to betroth; to join by handfasting. — **hand'-fasting** (*archaic*) betrothal; probationary marriage; private marriage; **hand'-feeding** feeding of animals or machinery by hand; **hand'-gallop** an easy gallop, restrained by the bridle-hand; **hand'-glass** a glass or glazed frame to protect plants; a mirror or a magnifying glass with a handle; **hand grenade** a grenade to be thrown by hand; **hand'grip** a grasp with the hand; something for the hand to grasp; (in *pl*) close struggle; **hand'gun** a gun which can be held and fired in one hand. — *adj* **hand'-held** held in the hands rather than mounted on some support. — **hand'hold** a hold by the hand; a place or part that can be held by the hand; **hand'-horn** an early form of musical horn without valves. — *n pl* **hand'icuffs** fisticuffs. — **hand'-in** (*badminton*, etc) the player who is serving. — *n* and *adj* **hand'-knit** (a garment) knitted by hand. — *vt* **hand'-knit'**. — **hand line** a fishing-line without a rod. — *vi* to fish with such a line. — **hand'list** a list without detail, for handy reference; **hand'-loom** a hand-worked weaving loom; **hand'-lotion**. — *adj* **hand'made**. — **hand'maid** or **hand'maiden** (*archaic*) a female servant or attendant; **hand mating** (*agric*) a system in which the stockman supervises the mating of a specific female to a specific male. — *adj* **hand'-me-down** (of garments) formerly ready-made, usually cheap, now *usu* second-hand, *esp* formerly belonging to a member of one's own family. — *n* a cheap ready-made garment; a second-hand garment. — **hand'-mill** a quern; a coffee-mill, pepper-mill, etc worked by hand; **hand'-off** act or manner of pushing off an opponent (*Rugby football*); **hand organ** a barrel-organ; **hand'out** a portion handed out, *esp* to the needy; an issue; a prepared statement issued to the press; a *usu* free leaflet containing information, propaganda, etc; **hand'-out** (*badminton*, etc) a player whose side is receiving the service; the situation when the first player on the serving side loses his service; **hand'over** a transfer, handing over. — *adj* **hand'-painted**. — **hand'-paper** paper with a hand for watermark. — *vt* **hand'-pick** to pick by hand; to select carefully for a particular purpose. — **hand'play** dealing of blows; **hand'-post** a finger-post; **hand'-press** a printing or other press worked by hand; **hand-prom'ise** (*Irish*) formerly a solemn form of betrothal; **hand puppet** a glove puppet; **hand'rail** a rail to hold for safety, support, etc, as on stairs; **hand relief** (*colloq*) masturbation. — *adv* **hand-runn'ing** (*dialect*) consecutively. — **hand'saw** a saw worked by hand, *specif* with a handle at one end; in Shakespeare, perhaps mistakenly written or copied in place of **heronshaw** (see also **know a hawk from a handsaw** under **hawk**[1]); **hand'-screen** a screen against fire or sun, held in the hand; **hand'-screw** a clamp; a jack for raising weights; **hand'set** on a telephone, the part held by the hand, containing the mouthpiece and earpiece; **hand'-sewing**. — *adj* **hand'-sewn**. — *adj* **hands'-free** not involving manual operation, eg of a telephone apparatus that incorporates a microphone and speaker so that the user need not hold the handset when making a call. — **hand'shake** a shaking of hands in greeting, etc (also **hand'shaking**); a golden handshake or the like; an exchange of signals (on a separate line) between two or more devices, which synchronizes them in readiness for the transfer of data (*comput*); **hand'shaking** (*comput*) the process of performing a handshake. — *adj* **hands-off'** not touching with the hands; operated by remote control; that cannot be touched; not interfering. — *adj* **hands-on'** operated by hand; involving practical rather than theoretical knowledge, experience, method of working, etc; (of museums, etc) with exhibits that can be handled. — **hand'spike** a bar used as a lever; **hand'spring** a cartwheel or somersault with hands on the ground; **hand'staff** a staff-like handle, eg of a flail; a staff as a weapon; a javelin: — *pl* **hand'staves** or **hand'staffs**; **hand'stand** an act of balancing one's body on the palms of one's hands with one's trunk and legs in the air; **hands'turn** or **hand's turn** (*usu* with a negative) a single or least act of work; **hand'towel**. — *adj* **hand'-weeded**. — **hand'work** work done by hand. — *adj* **hand'worked** made or done by hand. — **hand'writing** writing, script; style of writing; individual style discernible in one's actions. — *adj* **hand'written** written by hand, not typed or printed. — *adj* **hand'wrought** handworked. — **hand'yman** a man employed to carry out, or skilled in doing, odd jobs; a bluejacket. — **at any hand** or **in any hand** (*Shakesp*) at any rate, in any case; **at first hand** directly from the source; **at hand** conveniently near; within easy reach; near in time; at the beginning (*Shakesp*); **at the hand** (or **hands**) **of** by the act of; **bear a hand** to take part, give aid; **bloody** or **red hand** (*heraldry*) the arms of Ulster, a sinister hand erect couped at the wrist gules, borne by baronets in a canton or inescutcheon; **by hand** by use of the hands, or tools worked by the hand, not by machinery or other indirect means; by personal delivery, not by post; **by the strong hand** by force; **change hands** to pass to other ownership or keeping; **come to hand** to arrive; to be received; **come to one's hand** to be found easy; to come to close quarters; **for one's own hand** to one's own account; **get one's hand in** to get control of the play so as to turn one's cards to good use; to get into the way or knack; **good hands** a trustworthy source; good keeping; care of those who may be trusted to treat one well; **hand and foot** *orig* with respect to hands and feet; with assiduous attention; **hand and** (or **in**) **glove** on very intimate terms; in close co-operation; **hand down** or **on** to transmit in succession or by tradition; **hand in hand** with hands mutually clasped; with one person holding the hand of another; in close association; conjointly (*adj* **hand'-in-hand'**); **hand it to someone** (*slang*) to admit someone's superiority, *esp* as shown by his or her success in a difficult matter; **hand of glory** see separate entry; **hand of God** unforeseen and unavoidable accident, such as lightning or storm; **hand out** to distribute, pass by hand to individuals (see also **handout** above); **hand over** to transfer; to relinquish possession of; **hand over fist** with steady and rapid gain; **hand over hand** by passing the hands alternately one before or above another, as in climbing a rope or swimming with a certain stroke; progressively; with steady and rapid gain; **hand over head** headlong; **hands down** with utter ease (as in winning a race); **hands off** (as a command) keep off; do not touch or strike; **hands up** (as a command) hold the hands above the head in surrender; **hand to hand** at close quarters (*adj* **hand'-to-hand'**); **hand to mouth** with provision for immediate needs only (*adj* **hand'-to-mouth'**); **handwriting on the wall** see under **write**; **have one's hands full** to be preoccupied, very busy; **hold hands** see under **hold**[1]; **in hand** as present payment; in preparation; under control; of a ball that has to be played from balk (*billiards*); **keep one's hand in** see under **keep**; **lay hands on** to seize; to obtain or find; to subject physically to rough treatment; to bless, or to ordain by touching with the hand(s) (also **lay on hands**); **laying on of hands** the touch of a bishop or presbyters in ordination; **lend a hand** to give assistance; **lift a hand** (*usu* with a negative) to make the least effort (to help, etc); **off one's hands** no longer under one's responsible charge; **old hand** see under **old**; **on all hands** or **on every hand** on all sides; by everybody; **on hand** ready, available; in one's possession; **on one's hands** under one's care or responsibility; remaining as a burden or encumbrance; **on the one hand ... on the other hand** phrases used to introduce opposing points in an argument, etc; **out of hand** at once, immediately, without premeditation; out of control; **poor hand** an unskilful person or way of handling (*usu* with *at*); **raise one's hand to** (often with a negative) to strike, behave violently towards; **set** or **put one's hand to** to engage in, undertake; to sign; **shake hands with** see under **shake**; **show of hands** a vote by holding up hands; **show one's hand** to expose one's purpose; **sit on one's hands** to take no action; **slow handclap** slow rhythmic clapping showing disapproval; **stand one's hand** (*colloq*) to buy a drink for someone else; **take in hand** to undertake; to take charge of in order to educate, discipline, etc; **take off someone's hands** to relieve someone of; **throw in one's hand** to give up a venture or plan; to concede defeat; **tie someone's hands** to render someone powerless; **to (one's) hand** in readiness; within easy reach; (of a letter) received; **try one's hand at** to attempt; test one's prowess at; **under one's hand** with one's proper signature attached; **upper hand** mastery; advantage; **wash one's hands (of)** to disclaim responsibility (for) (Matthew 27.24). [OE *hand*; in all Gmc tongues, perh related to Gothic *hinthan* to seize]

h and c *abbrev*: hot and cold (water laid on).

handicap *hand'i-kap*, *vt* to impose special disadvantages or impediments upon, in order to offset advantages and make a better contest; to place at a disadvantage. — *n* any contest so adjusted, or the condition imposed; an amount added to or subtracted from one's score in stroke competitions (*golf*); any physical, mental or social disability; a disadvantage. — *adj* **hand'icapped** suffering from some physical or mental disability; disadvantaged in some way. — *n* **hand'icapper** an official in some sports who fixes the handicaps of competitors; a punter (*US horse racing*). [Appar *hand i' cap*, from the drawing from a cap in an old lottery game]

handicraft *hand'i-kräft*, *n* a manual craft or art; objects produced by such craft. — *n* **hand'icraftsman** or *fem* **hand'icraftswoman** a man or woman skilled in a manual art. [OE *handcræft*, from **hand**, and *cræft* craft, assimilated to **handiwork**]

handiwork or **handywork** *hand'i-wûrk*, *n* work done by the hands, performance generally; work of skill or wisdom; creation; doing. [OE *handgewerc*, from *hand* and *gewerc* (*geweorc*) work.

handjar or **hanjar** *han'jär*, *n* a Persian dagger. — Also **khan'jar**. [Pers and Ar *khanjar*]

handkerchief *hang'kər-chif* or *-chēf*, *n* a cloth or paper for wiping the nose, etc; a neckerchief: — *pl* **hand'kerchiefs** and sometimes **hand'kerchieves**. — Also (now *illiterate*) **hand'kercher**. — **throw the handkerchief** to summon to pursuit, call upon to take one's turn — as in children's games and royal harems. [**hand** and **kerchief**]

handle *hand'l*, *vt* to hold, move about, feel freely, etc with the hand; to make familiar by frequent touching; to manage (*esp* successfully); to discuss; to deal with, treat; to cope with, take in one's stride (*colloq esp NAm*); to pass through one's hands; to trade or do business in. — *vi* to respond to control (in a specified way). — *n* a part by which a thing is held, opened or picked up; anything affording an advantage or pretext to an opponent; feel, as of a textile; the total takings from betting on a horse race, etc; one's name (*slang*). — *adj* **hand'led** having a handle. — *n* **hand'ler** someone who handles; a boxer's trainer or second; someone who trains, holds, controls, incites, or shows off an animal at a show, fight, etc; someone who trains and uses a dog or other animal which works for the police or an armed service. — *n* **hand'ling**. — **hand'lebar** the steering-bar of a cycle, or one half of it; **handlebar moustache** a wide, thick moustache with curved ends thought to resemble handlebars. — **a handle to one's name** a title; **fly off the handle** see under **fly**. [OE *handle*, *handlian* from *hand*]

hand of glory *hand əv glō'ri*, *n* a charm made originally of mandrake root, afterwards of a murderer's hand from the gallows. [A translation of Fr *main de gloire*, from OFr *mandegloire* mandrake, from *mandragore*]

handsel or **hansel** *han'səl*, *n* an inaugural gift, eg a present on Handsel Monday, a coin put in the pocket of a new coat, or the like; something thought of as an inauguration or beginning, such as the first money taken, earnest-money, a first instalment, the first use of anything; apparently payment or penalty (*Spenser*). — *vt* to give a handsel to; to inaugurate; to make a beginning on; to cut off, kill (*Chatterton*, from a blundering reading of a dictionary explanation, 'to cut off a first slice'): — *pr p* **hand'selling** or **han'selling**; *pa p* and *pa t* **hand'selled** or **han'selled**. — **Handsel Monday** (*Scot*) the first Monday after New Year's Day, when handsels were given. [OE *handselen* hand-gift, giving; or ON *handsal*]

handsome *han'səm*, *adj* convenient, handy (*obs*); suitable, becoming, gracious (*archaic*); good-looking; well-proportioned; dignified; liberal or noble; generous; ample. — *adv* **hand'somely** graciously (*archaic*); generously, amply; carefully (*naut*). — *n* **hand'someness**. [**hand** and sfx **-some**; cf Du *handzaam*]

handy. See under **hand**.

handy-dandy *hand'i-dand'i*, *n* a children's game of guessing which hand a thing is in. — *interj* (*Shakesp*) the formula used in the game. [**hand**]

handywork. See **handiwork**.

hanepoot *hän'ə-pōōt*, (*SAfr*) *n* a kind of grape. — Also **haan'epoot** and **hon'eypot**. [Du *haane-poot*, from *haan* cock, and *poot* foot]

hang *hang*, *vt* to support from above against gravity; to suspend; to decorate (eg a wall) with pictures, tapestry, etc; to fasten, to stick (wallpaper, etc); to exhibit pictures, etc; to fix, to fit (a door, etc); to put to death by suspending by the neck; to cause to be brought to justice; to prevent (a jury) from coming to a decision; to suspend (meat and game) until mature; (in the *imperative* and *passive*) a euphemism for damn. — *vi* to be suspended, so as to allow free sideways motion; to be put to death by suspending by the neck; to be brought to justice; to weigh down, to oppress (with *on* and *over*); to cling (with *on* or *onto*); to drape (well, badly, etc); to be exhibited; (of a jury) to be undecided; to be in suspense; to hover; to impend; to linger; to hold back; to depend for outcome (on); to have things hanging; to be in a state of paying extremely close attention (with *on*): — *pa t* and *pa p* **hung** (*hung*) (in all senses) or **hanged** (by the neck). — *n* the action or mode of hanging; principle of connection, plan; knack of using; meaning; a declivity; a slackening of motion; a hanging mass; a euphemism for *damn*. — *n* **hangabil'ity**. — *adj* **hang'able** liable to be hanged; punishable by hanging. — *n* **hang'er** someone who hangs; that on which anything is hung; (in placenames) a wood on a hillside (*OE hangra*); a short sword. — *adj* **hang'ing** suspending; suspended; drooping; downcast; deserving or involving death by hanging. — *n* death by the noose; (*esp* in *pl*) that which is hung, eg drapery or decorations. — *adj* **hung** (of a vote, election, etc) not decisive, producing no viable majority for any one party; (of a parliament, etc) having no party with a working majority; (of a jury) unable to agree on a verdict; (of a situation) unable to be settled or solved; (of a man) genitally endowed in a specified way, as in *well-hung* (*colloq*). — **hang'bird** a Baltimore oriole (from its pensile nest); **hang'dog** a contemptible person. — *adj* with a cowed, dejected or guilty look. — **hanger-on'** a person who hangs around or sticks to a person or place for personal gain; an importunate acquaintance; a dependant; **hang'fire** delay in explosion. — *vi* **hang'-glide**. — **hang'-glider** an apparatus for hang-gliding, or the person using it; **hang'-gliding** a sport in which one glides from a cliff-top, etc hanging in a harness from a large kite; **hanging buttress** a buttress supported by a corbel or the like; **hanging committee** a committee which chooses the works of art to be shown in an exhibition; **hanging drop preparation** a preparation for a microscope in which the specimen, in a drop of medium on the lower surface of the coverslip, is suspended over the depression in a hollow-ground slide; **hanging garden** see under **garden**; **hanging matter** a crime leading to capital punishment; a serious matter (*colloq*); **hanging valley** a tributary valley not graded to the main valley, a product of large-scale glaciation (*geog*); **hang'man** a public executioner; a word-guessing game involving the drawing of a gibbet with victim. — *adj* rascally. — **hangnail** see separate entry; **hang'nest** a hangbird; **hang'out** a haunt (*colloq*); **hang'over** a survival (from another time); after-effects, *esp* of drinking alcohol (see also **hung over** below); **hang'-up** (*slang*) a problem about which one is obsessed or preoccupied; an inhibition (see also **hung up** below); **hung'-beef** beef cured and dried; **hung jury** a jury that fails to agree. — **get the hang of** (*colloq*) to grasp the principle or meaning of; **hang about** or **around** to loiter; to associate habitually (*with* someone; *colloq*); to stay, remain, persist; **hang a left** or **right** (*US colloq*) to turn left or right (*esp* when driving); **hang back** to show reluctance; to lag behind; **hang by a thread** to depend upon very precarious conditions, a most slender chance, etc (from the sword of Damocles); **hang, draw, and quarter** to hang (a person), cut them down while still alive, disembowel and cut them into pieces for exposure at different places (earlier, **draw, hang, and quarter** to drag on a hurdle or otherwise to the place of execution, then hang and quarter); **hang fire** to be a long time in exploding or discharging; to be slow in taking effect; to hesitate, delay; **hang in** (*slang*) to wait; to persist (also **hang in there**); **hang in the balance** to be in doubt or suspense; **hang loose** (*slang*) to do nothing; to be relaxed; **hang off** to let go; to hold off; **hang on** (*colloq*) to wait; **hang on someone's lips** or **words** to give close, admiring attention to someone; **hang one's head** to look ashamed or sheepish; **hang out** to hang up outside; to display (eg a sign); to put outside on a clothes-line; to lodge or reside (*slang*); **hang out for** to insist on; **hang out with** (*colloq*) to associate habitually with; **hang over** to project over or lean out from; (of an unresolved problem, decision, etc) to overshadow, threaten; **hang together** to keep united; to be consistent; to connect; **hang tough** (*US*) to stay resolute or determined; **hang up** to suspend; to delay; to replace a telephone receiver and so break off communication; **hang up one's hat** to take up one's abode; **hung over** suffering from a hangover; **hung up** (*colloq*) in a state of anxiety, obsessed (with *about* or *on*); **let it all hang out** (*colloq*) to be completely uninhibited, relaxed. [OE *hangian*, pa t *hangode*, pa p *hangod* (intransitive) and *hōn*, pa t *heng*, pa p *hangen* (transitive), and ON *hanga* and *hengja*; cf Du and Ger *hangen*]

hangar *hang'ər* or *hang'gär*, *n* a large shed or building for aircraft, carriages, etc. [Fr]

hangnail *hang'nāl*, *n* a torn shred of skin beside the fingernail. — Also **ag'nail**. [OE *angnægl*, corn, from *ange*, *enge* compressed, painful, and *nægl* nail (for driving in), confused with *hang* and (finger)*nail*]

Hang Seng index *hang seng in'deks*, *n* the indicator of relative prices of stocks and shares on the Hong Kong stock exchange.

hanjar. See **handjar**.

hank *hangk*, *n* a coil or skein of a specified length, varying with the type of yarn; a loop; a tuft or handful, eg of hair; a ring for attaching a luff to a sail (*naut*); a restraining hold (*dialect*). — *vt* to catch, as on a loop. — *vi* to catch, be entangled. [ON *hanki* a hasp]

hanker *hangk'ər*, *vi* to yearn (with *after* or *for*); to linger about (*dialect*). — *n* a yearning. — *n* **hank'ering**. [Perh connected with **hang**; cf Du *hunkeren*]

hankie or **hanky** *hangk'i*, (*colloq*) *n* dimin of **handkerchief**.

hanky-panky *hangk'i-pangk'i*, *n* funny business, underhand trickery, jugglery; goings on; faintly improper (*esp* sexual) behaviour. [Arbitrary coinage]

Hanoverian *han-ə-vē'ri-ən*, *adj* pertaining to *Hanover* (Ger *Hannover*); pertaining to the dynasty that came from Hanover to the British throne in 1714. — *n* a native of Hanover; a supporter of the house of Hanover (opp of a *Jacobite*).

Hansa. See **Hanseatic league**.

Hansard *han'särd*, *n* the printed reports of debates in parliament, from Luke *Hansard* (1752–1828), whose descendants continued to print them down to 1889. — *vt* **han'sardize** or **-ise** to confront (someone) with his or her former recorded opinions.

Hanseatic league *han-si-at'ik lēg*, **Hanse** *hans* or **Hansa** *han'sə*, or *-zə*, *n* a league of German commercial cities, operating in the 14c and 15c. [OHGer *hansa* a band of men (MHGer *hanse* merchants' guild)]

hansel. See **handsel**.

hansom *han'səm*, *n* a light two-wheeled horse-drawn cab with the driver's seat raised behind. — Also **han'som-cab**. [From the inventor, Joseph A *Hansom* (1803–82)]

ha'n't *hänt*, a colloq contraction of **have not** or **has not**.

hantle *han'tl* or *hän'tl*, (*Scot*) *n* a good many; a good deal. [Poss **hand** and **tale** number]

Hants *hants*, *abbrev*: Hampshire. [*Hantsharing*, orig name of county]

Hanukkah, **Chanukah** or **Chanukkah** *hä'nə-kə*, *hä-nōō-kä* or *hhä'nōō-kä*, *n* the Jewish festival of lights commemorating the re-dedication of the temple in 165 BC. [Heb, consecration]

hanuman *han-ōō-män'*, *n* a long-tailed sacred monkey of India — the entellus monkey. [*Hanumān* Hindu monkey god]

haoma *how'ma*, *n* a drink prepared from the haoma vine, used in Zoroastrian ritual; (with *cap*) a deity, personification of haoma. [Avestan; see **soma**[1]]

hap[1] *hap*, *n* chance; fortune; accident. — *vi* to chance, happen: — *pr p* **happ'ing**; *pa t* and *pa p* **happed**. — *n* and *adj* **haphaz'ard** random; chance. — *adv* at random. — *adv* **haphaz'ardly**. — *n* **haphaz'ardness**. — *adj* **hap'less** unlucky; unhappy. — *adv* **hap'lessly**. — *n* **hap'lessness**. — *adv* **hap'ly** by hap; perhaps; it may be. [ON *happ* good luck]

hap[2] *hap*, (*Scot* and *E Anglian*) *vt* to cover up; to wrap up. — *n* a wrap. [Origin unknown]

hapax legomenon *hap'aks leg-om'ən-on*, (Gr) *n* (literally) said once; a word or phrase that is found once only.

ha'pence *hā'pəns*, short for **halfpence** (see under **half**).

ha'penny *hāp'ni*, short for **halfpenny** (see under **half**).

haphazard, hapless. See under **hap**[1].

haplo- *hap-lō-*, *hap-lə-* or *hap-lo'-*, *combining form* denoting single. — *n* **haplography** (*hap-log'rə-fi*) the inadvertent writing once of what should have been written twice. — *adj* **hap'loid** (*biol*) having the reduced number of chromosomes characteristic of the species in question, as in germ-cells (*opp* of *diploid*). — *n* **haploid'y**. — *n* **haplol'ogy** omission in an utterance of a word of a sound resembling a neighbouring sound (as *idolatry* for *idololatry*). — *adj* **haplostē'monous** (Gr *stēmōn* thread; *bot*) with one whorl of stamens. [Gr *haploos* single, simple]

haply. See **hap**[1].

hap'orth *hā'pərth*, short for **halfpennyworth** (see under **half**).

happen *hap'ən*, *vi* to turn out; to come to pass; to take place, occur; to chance. — *adv* (*NEng*) perhaps. — *n* **happ'ening** an event, occurrence; a performance consisting of discrete events, in which elements from everyday life are put together in a non-realistic way, *usu* demanding audience participation (*theatre*); one such event in the theatre or in other activities including those of everyday life. — *adj* (*colloq*) fashionable, up to the minute. — *n* **happ'enstance** chance; a chance circumstance. — **happen into, on** or **upon** to meet or come across by chance. [**hap**[1]]

happy *hap'i*, *adj* lucky; fortunate; expressing, full of, or characterized by content, well-being, pleasure, or good; apt; felicitous; carefree; confident; mildly drunk (*slang*); used in combination to signify drunk with, delighted by the possession of or use of, as in *power-happy, bomb-happy* — *usu* implying irresponsibility — or dazed as result of. — *vt* (*Shakesp*) to make happy. — *adv* **happ'ily** in a happy manner; in happiness; contentedly; by chance; perhaps; I'm glad to say, luckily. — *n* **happ'iness**. — *adj* **happ'y-go-luck'y** easy-going, carefree; taking things as they come. — *adv* in any way one pleases. — **happy dispatch** a euphemism for hara-kiri; **happy event** (usu *facetious* or *joc*) a euphemism for the birth of a baby; **happy hour** (in a club, bar, etc) a time, *usu* in the early evening, when drinks are sold at reduced prices; **happy hunting-ground** (also in *pl*) the Paradise of the N American Indian; any place that one frequents, *esp* to make acquisitions or to profit in any way; **happy medium** a prudent or sensible middle course. — **happy as Larry** (*colloq*) completely happy. [**hap**[1]]

hapten *hap'tən*, (*immunol*) *n* a substance, *usu* a small molecule, that can combine with an antibody but can initiate an immune response only when it is attached to a carrier molecule. [Gr *haptein* to fasten, grasp]

hapteron *hap'tər-on*, (*biol*) *n* a holdfast or attachment organ of a plant thallus. — *adj* **haptotrop'ic** curving in response to touch, as a tendril. — *n* **haptot'ropism**. [Gr *haptein* to fasten, and *tropos* turning]

haptic *hap'tik*, *adj* pertaining to the sense of touch. — *n sing* **hap'tics** the science of studying data obtained by means of touch. [Gr *haptein* to fasten]

haqueton *hak'tən*. Same as **acton**.

hara-kiri *ha-rä-kē'rē*, *n* ceremonial Japanese suicide by ripping open the belly with a sword. [Jap *hara* belly, and *kiri* cut]

haram. See **harem**.

harambee *hä-räm-bē'*, *n* and *interj* a rallying cry used in Kenya, meaning 'let's organize together'. [Swahili]

harangue *hə-rang'*, *n* a loud, aggressive speech addressed to a crowd; a pompous or wordy address. — *vi* to deliver a harangue. — *vt* to address by a harangue: — *pr p* **haranguing** (*-rang'ing*); *pa t* and *pa p* **harangued** (*-rangd'*). — *n* **harangu'er**. [OFr *arenge, harangue*, from OHGer *hring* (Ger *Ring*) ring (of listeners)]

harass *har'əs* or *hər-as'*, (similarly in derivatives), *vt* to distress, wear out; to beset or trouble constantly; to annoy, pester. — *adj* **har'assed** (or *hə-rasd'*). — *adv* **harass'edly**. — *n* **harass'er** (or *har'*). — *n* and *adj* **harass'ing** (or *har'*). — *adv* **harass'ingly** (or *har'*). — *n* **harass'ment** (or *har'*). [OFr *harasser*; prob from *harer* to incite a dog]

harbinger *här'bin-jər*, *n* a host (*obs*); someone sent ahead to provide lodging (*obs*); a forerunner, a thing which tells of the onset or coming (of something); a pioneer. — *vt* to precede as harbinger. [ME *herbergeour*; see **harbour**]

harbour or *NAm* **harbor** *här'bər*, *n* a refuge or shelter; a shelter, natural or artificial, for ships; a haven. — *vt* to lodge, shelter, entertain, or give asylum to; to have or keep in the mind (feelings, *esp* unfriendly ones); to put (a ship) into harbour; to trace to its lair. — *vi* to take shelter. — *n* **har'bourage** or (*NAm*) **har'borage** a place of shelter; the act of harbouring. — *n* **har'bourer** or (*NAm*) **har'borer**. — *adj* **har'bourless**. — **harbour-bar'** a sandbank at a harbour's mouth. — *n pl* **har'bour-dues** charges for the use of a harbour. — **har'bour-light** a guiding light into a harbour; **har'bour-master** an officer who has charge of a harbour; **harbour seal** a small seal, *Phoca vitulina*, found in Atlantic waters. — **harbour of refuge** a harbour constructed to give shelter to ships; protection in distress. [ME *herberwe*, from OE *here-beorg*, from *here* army, and *beorg* protection; cf Ger *Herberge*, ON *herbergi*]

hard[1] *härd*, *adj* not easily penetrated or broken; unyielding to pressure; firm, solid; difficult to scratch (*mining*); difficult; strenuous; laborious; vigorous; bodily fit; coarse and scanty; stingy, niggardly; difficult to bear or endure; difficult to please; unfeeling; insensitive; severe; rigorous; stiff; tough; constrained; intractable; obdurate; troublesome; (of coal) anthracitic; (of water) difficult to lather owing to calcium or magnesium salt in solution; harsh; brilliant and glaring; over-sharply defined; live, reverberating; lacking in finer shades; used as a classification of pencil-leads to indicate durability in quality and faintness in use; (of drink) alcoholic or extremely so; (of a drug) habit-forming; (of news) definite, substantiated; (of consonants) representing a guttural, not a sibilant sound; voiceless (*obs phonetics*); (of radiation) penetrating; (of photographic paper) giving a high degree of image contrast; (of a person) tough; (of spaces or hyphens in typesetting or word processing) orthographically necessary, not merely the fortuitous requirement of a particular piece of text-setting, as, for instance, is the hyphen used to break a word at the end of a justified line (*opp* of *soft*). — *n* hardship; hard state; hard ground; a firm beach or foreshore; a layer of gravel or similar material laid down on swampy or wet ground to provide passage on foot; hard labour; an erection of the penis (*colloq*). — *adv* with urgency, vigour, etc; earnestly, forcibly; uneasily; in excess; severely; to the full extent (as **hard aport**); with difficulty; harshly; close, near, as in **hard by**. — *vt* **hard'en** to make hard, harder or hardy; to make firm; to strengthen; to confirm in wickedness; to make insensitive. — *vi* to become hard or harder (*lit* or *fig*). — *adj* **hard'ened** made hard; unfeeling; obdurate. — *n* **hard'ener**. — *n* **hard'ening** the act or fact of making or becoming hard; a substance added to harden anything; sclerosis of the arteries. — *adj* **hard'ish** somewhat hard.

— *adv* **hard'ly** with difficulty; scarcely, not quite; severely, harshly. — *interj* I shouldn't think so, it seems unlikely. — *n* **hard'ness** the quality of being hard; power of, and resistance to, scratching (*mining*). — *n* **hard'ship** a thing, or conditions, hard to bear; privation; an instance of hard treatment (*obs*). — *adv* **hard-a-lee'** close to the lee-side, etc. — *adj* **hard-and-fast'** (of a rule, etc) rigidly laid down and adhered to. — **hard-and-fast'ness**; **hard'back** a book with rigid covers. — Also *adj*. — *adj* **hard'backed**. — **hard'bake** almond toffee; **hard'ball** no-nonsense, tough tactics used for (*esp* political) gain; **hard'beam** the hornbeam. — *adj* **hard'-billed** having a hard bill or beak. — *adj* **hard'-bitten** given to hard biting, tough in fight; ruthless, callous. — **hard'board** compressed board made from wood fibre. — *adj* **hard-boiled'** (of eggs) boiled until solid; (of a person) callous, brazen or cynical (*colloq*); practical. — **hard bop** a type of jazz, developed in the late 1950s, with less complex rhythms than bop; **hard card** (*comput*) a hard disk on a card that can be used with a personal computer; **hard case** a person difficult to deal with or reform (*slang*); **hard cash** coin; ready money; **hard cheese** (chiefly as *interj*, often insincere; *slang*) bad luck; **hard coal** anthracite; **hard copy** (*comput*) output printed on paper, legible to the human reader, as distinct from material which is coded or stored on disk. — *adj* **hard'-copy**. — **hard core** a durable, unyielding central part; (*usu* **hard'-core**) the rubble and other material used in the foundation of roadways; something very resistant to change, as, eg the most loyal or the most die-hard members of a group. — *adj* **hard'-core** pertaining to a hard core; blatant; (of pornography) explicit, very obscene. — **hard court** a tennis court laid with asphalt or concrete, etc, not grass. — *adj* **hard'-cured** (of fish) thoroughly cured by drying in the sun. — **hard currency** metallic money; a currency with a high, stable or improving exchange rate, not subject to depreciation; a currency backed by bullion; **hard disk** (*comput*) a metal disc with a magnetic coating, in a sealed rigid container, *usu* having a higher recording density than a floppy disk. — *adj* **hard'-drawn** (of wire, etc) drawn when cold to give the required thickness. — **hard drinker** someone who drinks alcohol persistently and excessively. — *adj* **hard'-earned** earned through hard work or with difficulty. — **hard ecu** (or **Ecu**) see **ecu**. — *adj* **hard edge** (of a style of abstract painting) using bright areas of colour with sharply defined edges. — **hard'face** a soullessly relentless person; **hard facts** undeniable, stubborn facts. — *adj* **hard-fav'oured** or **hard-feat'ured** having hard, coarse, or forbidding features. — **hard'-fav'ouredness**; **hard-feat'uredness**; **hard feelings** hostility, resentment; **hard'-fern** the northern fern (*Lomaria* or *Blechnum*). — *adj* **hard-fist'ed** having hard or strong fists or hands; close-fisted; niggardly. — *adj* **hard'-fought** sorely contested. — *adj* **hard'-got** or **hard'-gotten** obtained with difficulty. — *adj* **hard'-grained** having a close firm grain; forbidding. — **hard'grass** cocksfoot or other coarse grass; **hard'hack** an American spiraea. — *adj* **hard-hand'ed** having hard hands; rough; severe. — **hard hat** a bowler hat; a protective helmet worn by building workers, etc; an obstinately conservative person; **hard'head** knapweed; a fish of various kinds (eg gurnard, menhaden, father-lasher). — *adj* **hard-head'ed** shrewd. — *adj* **hard-heart'ed** unfeeling; cruel. — *adv* **hard-heart'edly**. — **hard-heart'edness**. — *adj* **hard-hit'** seriously hurt, as by a loss of money, the death of a loved one, etc; deeply smitten with love. — *adj* **hard-hitt'ing** duly condemnatory; frankly condemnatory, pulling no punches. — **hard labour** physical labour as an additional punishment to imprisonment, abolished in 1948; **hard landing** one made by a spacecraft, etc in which the craft is destroyed on impact; **hard left** or **hard right** the extremes of political thought, allegiance, etc, favouring the left (socialist) or right (conservative) views; **hard line** a hardline attitude or policy. — *adj* **hard'line** (of an attitude or policy) definite and unyielding; having such an attitude or policy. — **hardlin'er**; **hard lines** a hard lot; bad luck (*usu* as *interj*); **hard luck** hard lines, bad luck; **hard-luck story** a person's (*esp* false or exaggerated) account of his or her own bad luck and suffering, *usu* intended to gain sympathy; **hard man** (*colloq*) a criminal specializing in acts of violence; generally, a tough man; **hard'-metal** sintered tungsten carbide, used for the tip of high-speed cutting tools; **hard money** coin. — *adj* **hard'mouthed** (of a horse) with a mouth insensible to the bit; not easily managed. — *adj* **hard'nosed** (*colloq*) tough, unsentimental. — **hard on** or **hard'-on** (*vulg slang*) an erection of the penis; **hard pad** once considered to be a neurotropic virus disease of dogs, now recognized as a symptom of distemper, causing hardness of the pads of the feet; **hard'-pan** a hard layer often underlying the superficial soil; the lowest level; **hard'parts** the skeletal material in an organism. — *adj* **hard'-paste** (of porcelain) made of china-clay and altered granite; **hard'-pressed** or **hard'-pushed** in difficulties. — **hard radiation** the more penetrating types of X-, beta- and gamma-rays. — *adj* **hard-rid'ing** strenuously riding. — **hard right** see **hard left** above; **hard rock** a form of rock and roll, *usu* structurally and rhythmically simple and highly amplified; **hard-rock geology** (*colloq*) the geology of igneous and metamorphic rocks; **hard roe** see **roe**[1]; **hard rubber** ebonite. — *adj* **hard'-ruled** (*Shakesp*) ruled with difficulty. — *adj* **hard'-run** greatly pressed. — **hard sauce** a sauce made with butter and sugar, and flavoured with rum or other liquor; **hard science** any of the physical or natural sciences. — *adj* **hard-sec'tored** (*comput*; of a floppy disk) formatted by a set of holes punched near the hub of the disk, each hole marking the start of a sector. — **hard sell** an aggressive and insistent method of promoting, advertising or selling. — *adj* **hard'-set** beset by difficulty; rigid; obstinate. — *adj* **hard'shell** having a hard shell; rigidly orthodox; uncompromising. — **hard shoulder** a surfaced strip forming the outer edge of a motorway, used when stopping in an emergency; **hard-stand'ing** a hard (concrete, etc) surface on which cars, aircraft, etc may be parked; **hard stocks** bricks that, though sound, are overburnt and of bad shape or colour; **hard stuff** (*slang*) strong alcohol, spirits; important information; **hard swearing** persistent and reckless swearing (by a witness); (often) perjury; **hard'tack** ship's biscuit, a hard biscuit formerly used as food on sailing ships; **hard'top** a rigid roof on a motor car; a motor car with such a roof. — *adj* **hard-up'** short of money, or of anything else (with *for*). — *adj* **hard-vis'aged** of a hard, coarse or forbidding face. — **hard'ware** domestic goods (*esp* tools, etc) made of the baser metals, such as iron or copper; mechanical equipment including war equipment; mechanical, electrical or electronic components of a computer (*opp* of *software*); **hard'-wareman**. — *adj* **hard-wear'ing** lasting well in use, durable. — **hard wheat** wheat having a hard kernel with a high gluten content. — *adj* **hard'-wired** (*comput*) having or being a circuit built in, whose function therefore cannot be altered. — *adj* **hard'-won** won with toil and difficulty. — **hard'wood** timber of deciduous trees, whose comparatively slow growth produces compact hard wood; **hard words** words that give difficulty to a half-educated reader; harsh words; angry words. — *adj* **hardwork'ing** diligent, industrious. — **be hard going** see under **going**[1]; **die hard** to die only after a desperate struggle for life; to survive obstinately; to die impenitent (*obs*); **go hard but** will not easily fail that; **go hard with** turn out badly for; **hard as nails** very hard; callous; very tough; **hard at it** working hard, very busy; **hard done by** badly treated; **harden off** to accustom (a plant) to outdoor conditions by gradually increasing exposure to the weather; **hard of hearing** somewhat deaf; **hard on the heels of** following immediately after; **hard put to it** in dire straits or difficulty; **hold hard** to stop; **Mohs's scale of hardness** a series of minerals each of which will scratch the one before it: (1) talc, (2) gypsum, (3) calcite, (4) fluorite, (5) apatite, (6) orthoclase, (7) quartz, (8) topaz, (9) corundum, (10) diamond; **no hard feelings** no offence taken, no animosity (as a result of a defeat, etc); **put the hard word on** (*Austr*) to ask, particularly for a loan or (*esp* sexual) favour; **the hard way** through personal endeavour or salutary experience. [OE *hard* (*heard*); Du *hard*, Ger *hart*, Gothic *hardus*; allied to Gr *kratys* strong]

hard[2] *härd*, (*Spenser* and *Scot*) form of **heard** (see under **hear**).

harden[1], etc, **hardish**, **hardly**, **hardness**. See **hard**[1].

harden[2]. See **hards**.

hardoke *här'dok*, (*Shakesp*, King Lear, folio) *n* perhaps burdock. — The quartos have **hor'dock**. [Prob OE *hār* hoary, and **dock**[1]]

hards *härdz* or **hurds** *hûrdz*, *n pl* coarse or refuse flax or hemp; tarred rags used as torches (*Scott*). — *n* **hard'en**, **herd'en** or **hurd'en** a coarse fabric made from hards. [OE *heordan*]

hardship. See **hard**[1].

hardy *härd'i*, *adj* daring, brave, resolute; confident; impudent; able to bear cold, exposure, or fatigue. — *n* **hard'ihead** (*archaic*) or **hard'ihood** boldness; audacity; robustness (*rare*). — *adv* **hard'ily**. — *n* **hard'iment** (*archaic*) hardihood; an act of hardihood. — *n* **hard'iness**. — **hardy annual** an annual plant which can survive frosts; a story or topic of conversation which comes up regularly (*facetious*). [OFr *hardi*, from OHGer *hartjan* to make hard]

Hardy-Weinberg Law *här-di-wīn'bûrg lö*, *n* the law stating that, provided mating is random and there is no selection, migration or mutation, the gene frequencies in a large population remain constant from generation to generation. [G H *Hardy*, Eng mathematician (1877–1947), and W *Weinberg*, Ger physician (1862–1937), who independently of one another formulated the law]

hare *hār*, *n* a common very timid and very swift mammal of the order Rodentia or in some classifications the order Lagomorpha (*esp* of the genus *Lepus*), in appearance like, but larger than, a rabbit. — *vi* (*slang*) to run like a hare, hasten (with *along*, etc). — *adj* **har'ish** somewhat like a hare. — **hare-and-hounds'** a paper-chase; **hare'bell** a slender-stemmed plant with a hanging blue bell-shaped flower, the Scottish bluebell (*Campanula rotundifolia*). — *adj* **hare'-brained**, sometimes **hair'-brained** giddy, silly, stupid; heedless; headlong. — *adj* **hare'-foot** swift of foot. — **hare'-lip** a cleft upper lip like that of a hare. — *adj* **hare'-lipped**. — **hare's'-ear** an umbelliferous plant (*Bupleurum*, various species) with yellow flowers; **hare's'-foot** or **hare's-foot trefoil** a variety of clover with long soft fluffy heads; **hare-stane** see **hoar-stone** under **hoar**. — **first catch your hare** make sure you have a thing first before you think what to do with it — from a direction in Mrs Glasse's cookery-book, where catch was a misprint for *case* meaning to skin; **hold with the hare and run with the hounds** run with the hare and hunt with the hounds (qv below); **raise** or **start a hare** to introduce an irrelevant topic, line of inquiry, etc; **run with the hare and hunt with the hounds** to play a double game, to be on both sides at once. [OE *hara*; Du *haas*, Dan *hare*, Ger *Hase*]

hareem. See **harem**.

Hare Krishna *hä'rā krish'nə*, *n* the chant used by members of a sect of the Hindu religion called Krishna Consciousness; the sect itself; a member of the sect. [Hindi *hare* O god, and *Krishna* an incarnation of the god Vishnu]

hareld *har'ld*, *n* the long-tailed duck, *Clangula hyemalis*. [Mod Icel *havella*, from *hav* sea]

harem *hā'rəm* or *hä-rēm'*, *n* women's quarters in a Muslim house; a set of wives and concubines; the equivalent in the society of certain animals; any Muslim sacred place. — Also **haram'**, **hareem'** and **harim** (*-ēm'*). — **harem skirt** an early 20c divided skirt in imitation of Turkish trousers. [Ar *harīm*, *haram*, anything forbidden, from *harama* to forbid]

harewood *hār'wŏŏd*, *n* stained sycamore wood, used for making furniture. [Ger dialect *Ehre*, from L *acer* maple]

haricot *har'i-kō* or *-kot*, *n* a kind of ragout or stew of mutton and beans or other vegetables; (usu **haricot bean**) the kidneybean or French bean (plant or seed). [Fr *haricot*]

harigalds or **harigals** *har'i-glz*, (*Scot*) *n pl* viscera.

Harijan *ha'rē-jən*, *n* one of the caste of untouchables, the name proposed by Gandhi. [Sans *Hari* a name of Vishnu, and *jana* person]

hari-kari *här'ē-kär'ē*, an incorrect form of **hara-kiri**.

harim. See **harem**.

hariolate *har'i-ō-lāt*, *vi* to divine. — *n* **hariolā'tion**. [L *hariolārī*, *-ātus*]

harish. See **hare**.

hark *härk*, *vi* to listen; to listen (to; also with *at*); to go (away, forward, etc); to go in quest, or to follow (with *after*). — *vt* to listen to (*archaic*). — *n* a whisper (*Scot*). — **hark'-back** a going back again (*lit* and *fig*). — **hark away**, **back** or **forward** cries to urge hounds and hunters; **hark back** to revert to, or be reminiscent of (an earlier topic, etc). [See **hearken**]

harken *här'kən*, *vi*. Same as **hearken**.

harl[1] *härl* or **herl** *hûrl*, *n* a fibre of flax, etc; a barb of a feather, *esp* one used in making an artificial fly for angling. [ME *herle*, from LGer]

harl[2] *härl*, (*Scot*) *vt* to drag along the ground; to roughcast. — *vi* to drag oneself; to troll for fish. — *n* the act of dragging; a small quantity, a scraping of anything; a haul; roughcast. — *n* **har'ling**.

Harleian *här-lē'ən* or *här'li-ən*, *adj* pertaining to Robert *Harley*, Earl of Oxford (1661–1724), and his son Edward, or the library collected by them. — **Harley Street** in London, a favourite abode of consultant or specialist physicians and surgeons, hence symbolically.

harlequin *här'lə-kwin*, *n* a pantomime character, in tight spangled dress, with visor and magic wand; a buffoon; a breed of small spotted dogs. — *adj* brightly-coloured; variegated. — *vi* to play the harlequin. — *n* **harlequināde'** part of a pantomime in which the harlequin plays a chief part. — **harlequin duck** a variegated northern sea-duck, *Histrionicus histrionicus*. [Fr *harlequin*, *arlequin* (Ital *arlecchino*), prob the same as OFr *Hellequin* a devil in medieval legend, perh of Gmc origin]

harlot *här'lət*, *n* a general term of opprobrium applied to a man or woman (*obs*); a whore; a prostitute. — *adj* lewd; base. — *n* **har'lotry** prostitution; unchastity; meretriciousness; a harlot (*obs*). — *adj* (*obs*) base, foul. [OFr *herlot*, *arlot* base fellow; ety dubious]

harm *härm*, *n* injury, physical, mental or moral. — *vt* to injure. — *adj* **harm'ful** hurtful. — *adv* **harm'fully**. — *n* **harm'fulness**. — *adj* **harm'less** not harmful or objectionable, innocent; unharmed. — *adv* **harm'lessly**. — *n* **harm'lessness**. — **harm'doing**. — **out of harm's way** in a safe place. [OE *herm* (*hearm*); Ger *Harm*]

harmala *här'mä-lə*, *n* the so-called African or Syrian rue (*Peganum harmala*) of the bean caper family. — Also **har'mel**. — *n* **har'malin**, **har'maline**, **har'min** or **har'mine** alkaloids derived from its seeds. [Gr, from Semitic; cf Ar *harmil*]

harman *här'mən*, (*old thieves' slang*) *n* a constable; (in *pl*) the stocks. — **har'man-beck** a constable. [Origin obscure; see **beak**]

harmattan *här-mä-tan'* or *här-mat'ən*, *n* a dry, dusty NE wind from the desert in W Africa. [Fanti *harmata*]

harmel, **harmin**, **harmine**. See **harmala**.

harmonic *här-mon'ik*, *adj* in harmony; in aesthetically pleasing proportion; pertaining to (good) harmony; musical; concordant; in accordance with the physical relations of sounds in harmony or bodies emitting such sounds (*math*). — *n* a component of a sound whose frequency is an integral multiple of the fundamental frequency; an overtone; a flutelike sound produced on a violin, etc, by lightly touching a string at a node and bowing; one of the components of what the ear hears as a single sound; (in television broadcasting) a reflected signal received on a different channel from that on which the main signal is received; (see also **harmonics** below). — *n* **harmon'ica** the musical glasses, an instrument consisting of drinking-glasses (or revolving glass basins in Benjamin Franklin's mechanized version) filled to different levels with water, and touched on the rim with a wet finger to produce sounds of different pitch; an instrument composed of a sound-box and hanging strips of glass or metal, struck by a hammer; a mouth-organ. — *adj* **harmon'ical**. — *adv* **harmon'ically**. — *n* **harmon'ichord** a keyboard instrument of violin tone, in which the strings are rubbed by rosined wheels. — *n* **harmon'icon** a harmonica; an orchestrion; a pyrophone (as in *chemical harmonicon*). — *n sing* **harmon'ics** the science or study of musical acoustics. — *adj* **harmonious** (*-mō'ni-əs*) in, having or producing harmony; in agreement; aesthetically pleasing to the ear or eye; concordant; congruous. — *adv* **harmōn'iously**. — *n* **harmōn'iousness**. — *n* **harmoniphone** or **harmoniphon** (*-mon'i-fōn* or *-fon*) a keyboard wind instrument with reeds. — *n* **harmonization** or **-s-** (*här-mən-ī-zā'shən*, or *-i-*) any action of the verb *harmonize*; (in the EC) the progressive introduction of norms and standards applicable in all EC countries. — *vi* **har'monize** or **-ise** to be or get in harmony; to sing in harmony; to agree; to be compatible (orally, visually, or *fig*). — *vt* to bring into harmony; to reconcile (eg points of view); to provide non-unison parts to (eg a song or tune) (*music*). — *n* **har'monizer** or **-s-**. — *n* **har'monist** a person skilled in harmony (in theory or composition); a reconciler; a person who seeks to reconcile apparent inconsistencies; (with *cap*) a member of a Second Adventist celibate sect (also **Har'monite**) founded by George Rapp (died 1847), from its settlement at *Harmony*, Pennsylvania. — *adj* **harmonist'ic**. — *n* **harmōn'ium** a reed-organ, *esp* one in which the air is forced (not drawn) through the reeds. — *n* **harmōn'iumist**. — *n* **harmonogram** (*-mon'*) a curve drawn by a harmonograph. — *n* **harmon'ograph** an instrument for tracing curves representing vibrations. — *n* **harmonom'eter** an instrument for measuring the harmonic relations of sounds. — *n* **harmony** (*här'mən-i*) a fitting together of parts so as to form a connected whole; agreement in relation; in any art, a normal and satisfying state of completeness and order in the relations of things to each other; a simultaneous and successive combination of aesthetically agreeable sounds (*music*); the whole chordal structure of a piece, as distinguished from its melody or its rhythm (*music*); concord, agreement; music in general; a collation of parallel passages to demonstrate agreement — eg of Gospels. — **harmonic conjugates** two points dividing a line internally and externally in the same ratio; **harmonic division** division by such conjugates; **harmonic mean** the middle term of three in harmonic progression (qv); **harmonic minor** a minor scale with minor sixth and major seventh, ascending and descending; **harmonic motion** (*math*) the motion along a diameter of a circle of the foot of a perpendicular from a point moving uniformly round the circumference; **harmonic pencil** (*math*) a pencil of four rays that divides a transversal harmonically; **harmonic progression** a series of numbers whose reciprocals are in arithmetical progression, such numbers being proportional to the lengths of strings that sound harmonics; **harmonic proportion** the relation of successive numbers in harmonic progression; **harmonic range** a set of four points in a straight line such that two of them divide the line between the other two internally and externally in the same ratio; **harmonic receiver** a receiver for electric waves, in harmony with the impulses producing them; **harmonic triad** (*music*) the common chord; **harmonic wave** (*phys*) a wave whose profile is a sine curve. — **harmony of the spheres** see under **sphere**; **pre-established harmony** the divinely established relation, according to Leibniz, between body and mind — the movements of monads and the succession of ideas being in constant agreement like two clocks. [Gr *harmoniā*, from *harmos* a joint fitting]

harmony. See under **harmonic**.

harmost *här'most*, *n* a Spartan governor of a subject city or province. — *n* **har'mosty** the office of harmost. [Gr *harmostēs*]

harmotome *här'mə-tōm*, *n* a zeolite, hydrated silicate of aluminium and barium. [Gr *harmos* joint, and *tomē* a cut]

harn *härn*, *n* a coarse linen fabric. [See **harden** under **hards**]

harness *här'nis*, *n* tackle; gear; equipment, *esp* now the reins of a draught animal; armour for man or horse (*archaic*); an arrangement of straps, etc for attaching a piece of equipment to the body, such as a parachute harness, a child's walking reins, a seat belt, etc; the wiring system of a car, etc when built separately for installing as a unit. — *vt* to equip with armour; to put (a) harness on; to attach by harness; to control and make use of. — **har'ness-cask** (*naut*) a cask for salt meat for daily use; **harnessed antelope** any antelope of the striped genus *Tragelaphus*; **har'ness-maker**; **harness racing** trotting or pacing races between specially bred horses harnessed to sulkies (two-wheeled, one-person light carriages); **har'ness-room**. — **in harness** occupied in the routine of one's daily work, not on holiday or retired. [OFr *harneis* armour]

harns *härnz*, (*Scot*) *n pl* brains. — **harn'-pan** the cranium. [OE *hærn*, prob from ON *hjarne*; cf Ger *Hirn*; Gr *krānion*]

haro. See **harrow**[2].

haroset, **haroseth**, **charoset** or **charoseth** *ha-rō'set*, *-seth*, or *hha-*, *n* (in Judaism) a mixture of finely chopped apples, nuts, spices, etc mixed with wine, and eaten with bitter herbs at the Passover meal, and symbolizing the clay from which the Israelites made bricks in Egypt. [Heb, from *charsit* clay]

harp *härp*, *n* a musical instrument played by plucking strings stretched from a curved neck to an inclined sound-board; a harmonica, mouth-organ (*colloq*); term of abuse for an Irish American Roman Catholic. — *vi* to play on the harp. — *vt* to render on or to the harp; to lead, call, or bring by playing the harp; to give voice to (*archaic*); to guess at (*obs*). — *n* **harp'er** or **harp'ist** a player on the harp. — *n pl* **harp'ings** (*naut*) the foreparts of the wales at the bow. — **harp'-seal** the Greenland seal, a grey animal with dark bands curved like an old harp; **harp'-shell** a genus (*Harpa*) of gasteropods with ribs suggesting harp-strings. — **harp on about** (*colloq*) to dwell tediously or repeatedly on in speech or writing; **harp on one string** to dwell constantly on one topic. [OE *hearpe*; Ger *Harfe*]

harpoon *här-pōōn'*, *n* a barbed dart or spear, *esp* for killing whales. — *vt* to strike, catch or kill with a harpoon. — *n* **harpoon'er** or **harpooneer'**. — **harpoon'-gun**. [Fr *harpon* a clamp, from L *harpa*, from Gr *harpē* sickle]

harpsichord *härp'si-körd*, *n* a keyboard instrument in which the strings are plucked by quills or leather plectrum-like devices. [OFr *harpechorde*; see **harp** and **chord**]

harpy *här'pi*, *n* a rapacious and filthy monster, part woman, part bird (*mythol*); a large South American eagle (also **har'py-eagle**); a grasping, greedy woman. [Gr *harpyia* literally snatcher, in Homer a personification of the storm-wind, from *harpazein* to seize]

harquebus, **harquebuse**, **harquebuss** *här'kwi-bus*, *n*. Same as **arquebus**.

harridan *har'i-dən*, *n* a sharp-tongued, scolding or bullying old woman. [Prob OFr *haridelle* a lean horse, a jade]

harrier[1] *har'i-ər*, *n* a medium-sized keen-scented dog for hunting hares; a cross-country runner. [**hare** or **harry**]

harrier[2]. See **harry**.

Harrovian *har-ō'vi-ən, adj* pertaining to *Harrow* town or school. — *n* a person educated at Harrow school.

harrow[1] *har'ō, n* a spiked frame or other contrivance for breaking up or levelling soil, covering seeds, etc. — *vt* to draw a harrow over; to distress or harass. — *adj* **harr'owing** acutely distressing. — *adv* **harr'owingly**. — **harrowing** (or **harrying**) **of hell** Christ's delivery of the souls of patriarchs and prophets. [ME *harwe*]

harrow[2] or **haro** (*pl* **haros**) *har'ō* or *har-ō', interj* alas (*archaic*); out upon it (*archaic*); (in the Channel Islands) a cry announcing a claim to legal redress. [OFr *haro, harou*; not an appeal to *Rou* or Rollo]

harrumph *hə-rumf', vi* to make a noise as of clearing the throat, *esp* self-importantly; to disapprove. [Imit]

harry *har'i, vt* to plunder; to ravage; to destroy; to harass: — *pr p* **harr'ying**; *pa t* and *pa p* **harr'ied**. — *n* **harr'ier** someone who, or something which, harries; a kind of hawk (*Circus*) that preys on small animals. — **harrying of hell** see **harrow**[1]. [OE *hergian*, from *here* army; Ger *Heer*]

harsh *härsh, adj* rough; jarring on the senses or feelings; rigorous, severe. — *vt* **harsh'en**. — *adv* **harsh'ly**. — *n* **harsh'ness**. [ME *harsk*, a Northern word; cf Swed *härsk* and Dan *harsk* rancid, Ger *harsch* hard]

harslet. See **haslet**.

hart[1] *härt, n* a male deer (*esp* red deer) *esp* over five years old, when the crown or surroyal antler begins to appear: — *fem* **hind** (*hīnd*). — **harts'horn** the antler of the red deer; a solution of ammonia in water, *orig* a decoction of the shavings of hart's horn (*spirit of hartshorn*); **hart's'-tongue** a fern (*Scolopendrium vulgare*) with strap-shaped leaves. [OE *heort*]

hart[2] (*Spenser*) for **heart**.

hartal *här'tal* or *hûr'täl*, (*India*) *n* a stoppage of work in protest or boycott. [Hindi *hartāl*]

hartebeest *här'tə-bēst* or (*Afrik*) **hartbees** *härt'bēs, n* a large South African antelope. — **bastard hartebeest** the sassaby. [SAfr Du, hart-beast]

hartely, harten, hartlesse, (*Spenser*) for **heartly, hearten, heartless** all under **heart**.

hartie-hale. See under **heart**.

hartshorn. See **hart**[1].

harum-scarum *hā'rəm-skā'rəm, adj* scatty, disorganized; rash, reckless. — *n* a giddy, rash person. [Prob from obs *hare* to harass, and **scare**]

haruspex *ha-rus'peks, n* a person (among the Etruscans) who foretold events from inspection of the entrails of animals: — *pl* **harus'pices** (*-pi-sēz*). — *n* **haruspication** (*-kā'shən*) or **harus'picy** (*-si*). — *adj* **harus'pical** or **harus'picate**. — *vi* **harus'picate**. [L, perhaps from an Etruscan word and L *specere* to view]

Harvard classification *här'vəd klas-i-fi-kā'shən*, (*astron*) *n* a method of classifying stars according to their spectra, *orig* used at *Harvard* University, and now universally.

harvest *har'vist, n* autumn (*obs* and *dialect*); the time of gathering in crops; crops gathered in; fruits; the product or result of any labour or act. — *vt* to reap and gather in (crops); to gather or reap (benefits, etc). — *vi* to gather a crop. — *n* **har'vester** a person who harvests; a reaping-machine; any member of the Opiliones, a class of Arachnida with very long legs (also **har'vestman** or **harvest spider**). — **har'vest-bug, -louse, -mite** or **-tick** a minute larval form of mites of species *Trombiculidae* and *Tetranychidae* abundant in late summer, a very troublesome biter; **har'vest-feast**; **harvest-fes'tival** a church service of thanksgiving for the harvest; **har'vest-field**; **har'vest-fly** (in the USA) a cicada of various kinds; **har'vest-goose** a goose eaten at a harvest-home feast; **har'vest-home** (a celebration of) the bringing home of the harvest; **harvest lady** and **harvest lord** the head reapers at the harvest; **har'vestman** a harvester; **harvest moon** the full moon nearest the autumnal equinox, rising nearly at the same hour for several days; **harvest mouse** a very small mouse that nests in the stalks of corn; **harvest queen** the corn-maiden; the harvest lady; **harvest spider** a harvester. [OE *hærfest*; Ger *Herbst*, Du *herfst*]

Harvey Smith *här'vi smith', n* a V-sign (qv) with palm inwards, signifying derision or contempt. — Also **Harvey Smith salute, wave**, etc. [From the showjumper *Harvey Smith*, who made such a gesture during a show]

has *haz*. See **have**. — **has'-been** a person or thing no longer as popular, influential, useful, etc as before: — *pl* **has'-beens**.

hash[1] *hash, vt* to hack; to mince; to chop small. — *n* something which is hashed; a mixed dish of meat and vegetables in small pieces; a mixture and preparation of old matter; a mess; a stupid person (*Scot*). — *adj* **hash'y**. — **hash browns** or **hash brown potatoes** pre-cooked potatoes, diced or mashed, mixed with chopped onion, seasoned, and fried until brown. — **make a hash of** (*colloq*) make a mess of; **settle someone's hash** (*slang*) to silence or subdue someone. [Fr *hacher*, from *hache* hatchet]

hash[2] *hash*, (*slang*) *n* short for **hashish**.

hash[3] *hash* or **hashmark** *hash'märk, n* the symbol #, used to mean: (1) number, eg apartment number (*esp NAm*); (2) space, eg in proofreading and marking up copy for printing. [Cf **hatch**[3] and **hachure**]

hashish or **hasheesh** *hash'ish* or *-ēsh, n* leaves, shoots or resin of hemp, smoked or swallowed as an intoxicant. [Ar *hashīsh*]

Hasid *has'id* or *hhäs'id, n* a very pious Jew; a member of any of a number of extremely devout and often mystical Jewish sects existing at various times throughout history: — *pl* **Hasidim** (*has'id-im* or *hhä-sē'dim*). — Also **Hass'id, Chas'id** or **Chass'id**. — *adj* **Hasid'ic, Hassid'ic, Chasid'ic** or **Chassid'ic**. — *n* **Has'idist**. — *n* **Has'idism, Hass'idism, Chas'idism** or **Chass'idism**. [Heb *hāsid* (someone who is) pious]

hask *hask*, (*Spenser*) *n* a fish-basket. [Cf **hassock**]

haslet *hāz'lit*, also *hās'* or *häs'*, or **harslet** *härs'lit, n* edible entrails, *esp* of a pig, shaped into a loaf and cooked. [OFr *hastelet* roast meat, from *haste* spit, from L *hasta* a spear]

hasn't *haz'ənt*, contracted form of **has not**.

hasp *häsp, n* a clasp; a slotted part that receives a staple, eg for a padlock; a fourth part of a spindle (*dialect*); a skein of yarn (*dialect*). — *vt* to fasten with a hasp. [OE *hæpse*; Ger *Haspe*, Dan *haspe*]

hassar *has'ər, n* a South American nest-building land-walking catfish (in the American sense). [Am Indian origin]

Hassid, Hassidic, etc. See **Hasid**.

hassle *has'l*, (*colloq*) *vt* to harass, annoy persistently; to argue with, bother, make trouble with. — *vi* to be involved in a struggle or argument. — *n* bother, fuss; a difficulty, problem; something requiring trouble or effort; a struggle; an argument. [Ety dubious]

hassock *has'ək, n* a tuft or tussock of grass, rushes, etc; a firmly stuffed cushion for kneeling on in church; (in Kent) a soft calcareous sandstone. — *adj* **hass'ocky**. [OE *hassuc*]

hast *hast*. See **have**.

hasta *äs'tä*, (Sp) *prep* and *conj* until. — **hasta la vista** (*lä vē'stä*) until we meet again; **hasta luego** (*lōō-ā'gō*) see you later; **hasta mañana** (*män-yän'ä*) see you tomorrow. (All three common terms of farewell).

hastate *hast'āt* or **hastated** *hast'āt-id, adj* spear-shaped; with basal lobes turned outward (*bot*). [L *hastātus*, from *hasta* spear]

haste *hāst, n* urgency calling for speed; hurry; inconsiderate or undue speed. — *vt* **haste** or **hasten** (*hās'n*) to speed up; to hurry on; to drive forward. — *vi* to move with speed; to hurry; (**hasten**) to be quick to, make an immediate move to (do something), as in *I hasten to say that ...*. — *n* **hastener** (*hās'n-ər*). — *adv* **hastily** (*hāst'i-li*). — *n* **hast'iness** hurry; rashness; irritability. — *n pl* **hast'ings** (*dialect*) early fruit or vegetables, *esp* peas. — *adj* **hast'y** speedy; quick; rash; eager; irritable. — **hasty pudding** a simple porridge of flour or oatmeal and water. — *adj* **hast'y-witted** (*obs*) rash. — **make haste** to hasten. [OFr *haste* (Fr *hâte*), from Gmc; cf OE *hǣst*, Du *haast*, Ger *Hast*]

hat *hat*, *n* any covering for the head, *esp* one with a crown and brim; the office of cardinal, from the red hat formerly worn; a salutation by lifting the hat (*Scot* or *obs*). — *vt* to provide with or cover with a hat; to lift one's hat to (*archaic*). — *vi* (*Austr*) to work alone: — *pa t* and *pa p* **hatt'ed**. — *n* **hat'ful** as much as will fill a hat: — *pl* **hatfuls**. — *adj* **hat'less**. — *n* **hat'lessness**. — *adj* **hatt'ed** provided or covered with a hat. — *n* **hatt'er** a maker or seller of hats; a miner or other who works by himself, one whose 'hat covers his family' (*Austr*). — *n* **hatt'ing**. — *n* **hatt'ock** (*archaic Scot*) a little hat. — **hat'band** a ribbon round a hat; **hat'box**; **hat'brush**; **hat'guard** a string for keeping a hat from being blown away; **hat'peg** a peg on which to hang a hat; **hat'pin** a long pin for fastening a hat to the hair; **hat'-plant** the sola plant, used for making topees; **hat'rack** a set of hatpegs; **hat'stand** a piece of furniture with hatpegs; **hat trick** a conjurer's trick with a hat; (in cricket) the taking of three wickets by consecutive balls (deserving a new hat); a corresponding feat (such as three goals scored by the same player) in other games; three successes in any activity. — **a bad hat** (*slang*) a rascal, an unscrupulous person; **hang up one's hat** see **hang**; **hats off to** (give) all honour to; **horse and hattock** to horse (traditionally a signal of witches or fairies); **mad as a hatter** completely mad (*poss* from the odd behaviour of some hatters due to mental and physical disorders caused by the mercury in the chemicals used in the making of felt hats); **my hat**! an exclamation of surprise or disbelief; **pass** or **send round the hat** to take up a collection, solicit contributions; **take off one's hat to** to acknowledge in admiration (*fig*); to praise; **talk through one's hat** to talk wildly or nonsensically; **throw one's hat into the ring** see under **ring**[1]; **under one's hat** in confidence; **wear several hats, another hat, etc** to act in several capacities, another capacity, etc. [OE *hæt*; Dan *hat*]

hatch[1] *hach*, *n* a half-door; a small gate (*dialect*); the covering of a hatchway; a hatchway. — *vt* to close as with a hatch. — **hatch'back** (a car with) a sloping rear door which opens upwards; **hatch beams** timber balks across a hatch on which the hatch covering planks rest; **hatch boat** a kind of half-decked fishing-boat; **hatch coamings** same as **coamings**; **hatch'way** an opening with a hinged or sliding door in a deck, floor, wall or roof. — **down the hatch** (*colloq*) your health, cheers — said when about to drink something, *esp* alcohol; **under hatches** below deck, *esp* in confinement; hidden, out of sight; in servitude or a depressed state; dead. [OE *hæcc*, *hæc* grating, half-gate, hatch; cf **hack**[3], **heck**[1]; Du *hek* gate]

hatch[2] *hach*, *vt* to bring out from egg; to breed; to originate, develop or concoct (eg a plan). — *vi* to bring young from the egg; to come from the egg; to develop into young. — *n* the act of hatching; brood hatched. — *n* **hatch'er**. — *n* **hatch'ery** a place for artificial hatching, *esp* of fish eggs. — *n* **hatch'ling** a bird or reptile newly hatched. — **count one's chickens before they are hatched** to rely too much on some uncertain future event; **hatches, matches, and dispatches** (*colloq*) newspaper announcements of births, marriages, and deaths. [Early ME *hacchen*, from an assumed OE *hæccean*]

hatch[3] *hach*, *vt* to mark with fine (*usu* diagonal) lines, incisions, or inlaid or applied strips. — *n* **hatch'ing** shading in fine lines. [OFr *hacher* to chop]

hatchel *hach'əl*, *n* and *v*. Same as **hackle**.

hatchet *hach'it*, *n* a small axe for use in one hand. — *adj* **hatch'ety** like a hatchet. — *adj* **hatch'et-faced** having a narrow face with a sharp profile like a hatchet. — **hatchet job** (*colloq*) the (attempted) destruction of a person's reputation or standing; a severely critical attack; a severe reduction; **hatchet man** (*colloq*) a gunman; a severely critical journalist; a person who does illegal, unpleasant or destructive work for a politician or political party or other boss or company; a person who destroys or attempts to destroy another's reputation or standing. — **bury the hatchet** to end a war or dispute (from a habit of North American Indians). [Fr *hachette*, from *hacher* to chop]

hatchettite *hach'it-īt*, *n* mountain tallow, a natural waxy hydrocarbon. [After Charles *Hatchett* (died 1847), English chemist]

hatchment *hach'mənt*, (*heraldry*) *n* the arms of a deceased person within a black lozenge-shaped frame, formerly placed on the front of his house. [**achievement**]

hate[1] *hāt*, *vt* to dislike intensely. — *n* extreme dislike; hatred; an object of hatred. — *adj* **hāt'able** or **hate'able** deserving to be hated. — *adj* **hate'ful** provoking hate; odious; detestable; feeling or manifesting hate. — *adv* **hate'fully**. — *n* **hate'fulness**. — *adj* **hate'less**. — *n* **hate'lessness**. — *n* **hāt'er**. — *n* **hate'rent** (*Scot*) hatred. — *adj* **hate'worthy**. — *n* **hāt'red** extreme dislike; enmity; malignity. — **hate mail** correspondence containing anything from insults to death threats, etc; **hate'-monger** someone who stirs up hatred. [OE *hete* hate, *hatian* to hate; Ger *Hasz*]

hate[2]. Same as **haet**.

hath. See under **have**.

hatha yoga. See under **yoga**.

hatred. See under **hate**[1].

hatter[1]. See under **hat**.

hatter[2] *hat'ər*, *vt* to trouble, annoy (*archaic*); to batter (*dialect*).

Hatteria *hat-ē'ri-ə*, (*zool*) *n* the Sphenodon genus of reptiles. [Origin unknown]

hatting. See under **hat**.

hatti-sherif *ha'ti-she-rēf'*, (*hist*) *n* a decree signed by the Sultan of Turkey. [Pers *khatt-i-sharīf* noble writing, from Ar]

hattock. See under **hat**.

hauberk *hö'bərk*, *n* a long coat of chain-mail sometimes ending in short trousers; *orig* armour for the neck. [OFr *hauberc*, from OHGer *halsberg*, from *hals* neck, and *bergan* to protect]

haud *höd*, *n* and *v* a Scottish form of **hold**[1]: — *pa p* **hudd'en**.

haugh *höhh* or *hähh*, (*esp* in place names) *hö* or *hä*, (*Scot*) *n* a riverside meadow or flat. [OE *halh* (WSax *healh*) corner]

haughty *hö'ti*, *adj* proud; arrogant; contemptuous; bold (*archaic*); high (*Spenser*). — *adj* **haught**, **hault** or **haut** (*höt*; *Shakesp*, *Spenser*, *Milton*) haughty; exalted. — *adv* **haught'ily**. — *n* **haught'iness**. [OFr *halt*, *haut* high, from L *altus* high]

haul *höl*, *vt* to drag; to pull with violence or effort; to transport by road. — *vi* to tug, to try to draw something; to alter a ship's course; (of a ship) to change direction. — *n* an act of pulling, or of pulling in; the contents of a hauled-in net or nets; a take, gain, loot (from a robbery); a hauled load; distance (to be) covered in hauling or travelling. — *n* **haul'age** the act of hauling; the business of transporting goods, *esp* by heavy road transport; charge for hauling. — *n* **haul'er**. — *n* **haulier** (*höl'yər*) a man who conveys coal from the workings to the foot of the shaft; a person or firm employed in transporting goods, *esp* by road. — **haul over the coals** see under **coal**; **haul round** or **off** to turn a ship's course away from an object; **haul up** to come or bring to rest after hauling; to call to account. — **long haul** a long distance to travel; a difficult objective gained only after a lengthy process. [A variant of **hale**[2]]

hauld *höld*, *n* a Scottish form of **hold**[1], as in the *dialect* phrase *out of house and hauld* homeless.

haulm or **halm** *höm* or *häm*, *n* a strawy stem; a culm; straw, or stems of plants collectively. [OE *halm* (*healm*)]

haulst. See **halse**[1].

hault. See **haughty**.

haunch[1] *hönch* or *hönsh*, also (*old-fashioned*) **hanch** *hänsh*, *n* the expansion of the body at and near the pelvis; the hip and buttock taken together; the leg and loin (of venison, etc); the side or flank of an arch between the crown and the springing (*archit*); the rear (*Shakesp*); a jerked underhand throw (*dialect*). — *vt* to throw with an underhand movement (*dialect*). — **haunch bone** the innominate bone. [OFr *hanche*, prob of Gmc origin; cf OHGer *anchâ* leg]

haunch[2]. See **hance**.

haunt *hönt*, *vt* to frequent, visit frequently; to associate a great deal with; to intrude upon continually; (of a ghost) to inhabit or visit; to cling or keep coming back into the memory of. — *vi* to be often around, to visit frequently (with *about*, etc). — *n* a place frequently visited; resort, habit of frequenting (*Shakesp*); a ghost (*US dialect*). — *adj* **haunt'ed** frequented or infested, *esp* by ghosts or apparitions; obsessed; worried. — *n* **haunt'er**. — *n* and *adj* **haunt'ing**. — *adv* **haunt'ingly**. [OFr *hanter*]

haurient or **hauriant** *hö'ri-ənt*, (*heraldry*) *adj* rising as if to breathe. [L *hauriēns*, *-entis*, pr p of *haurīre* to draw up, drink]

Hausa *how'sə* or *-zə*, *n* a Negroid people living mainly in N Nigeria; a member of this people; their language, widely used in commerce throughout W Africa.

hause. See **halse**[1].

hausfrau *hows'frow*, *n* a housewife, *esp* a woman exclusively interested in domestic matters. [Ger]

haussmannize or **-ise** *hows'mən-īz*, *vt* to open out, generally to rebuild, as Baron *Haussmann* did in Paris as prefect of the Seine (1853–70). — *n* **haussmannīzā'tion** or **-s-**.

haustellum *hös-tel'əm*, *n* a sucking proboscis or its sucking end, as in flies: — *pl* **haustell'a**. — *adj* **haus'tellate** having a haustellum. — *n* **haustō'rium** the part by which a parasitic plant fixes itself and derives nourishment from its host: — *pl* **haustō'ria**. [L *haurīre*, *haustum* to draw up, drink]

haut[1]. See under **haughty**.

haut[2] *ō*, (Fr) *adj* high. — **haut monde** (*mɔ̃d*) high society; **haut pas** (*pä*) a dais; **haut relief** (*rə-lyef*) high relief; **haut ton** (*tɔ̃*) high fashion. — **de haut en bas** (*də ō tā bä*) downwards, or from top to bottom (*literary*); with an air of superiority, contemptuously.

hautboy *hō'boi* or *ō'boi*, *n* an *archaic* name for **oboe**; a large kind of strawberry (also **haut'bois**). [Fr *hautbois*, from *haut* high, and *bois* wood]

haute *ōt*, (*Fr*) *adj* fem of **haut**[2]. — **haute bourgeoisie** (*bōōr-zhwä-zē*) the richer, more influential part of the middle class; **haute couture** (*kōō-tür*) fashionable, expensive dress-designing and dressmaking; **haute cuisine** (*kwē-zēn*) cookery of a very high standard; **haute école** (*ā-kol*) horsemanship of the most difficult kind; **haute époque** (*ā-pok'*; in relation to architecture, furniture, etc) the period during which Louis XIV, XV and XVI reigned in France; **haute politique** (*po-lē-tēk*) the higher reaches of politics; **haute vulgarisation** (*vül-gar-ēz-as-yɔ̃*) popularization of scholarly subjects.

hauteur *ō'tər* or *ō-tœr*, *n* haughtiness; arrogance. [Fr]

haüyne *hö'in* or *hä'win*, *n* a blue mineral, in composition like nosean, with calcium. [After the French mineralogist René J *Haüy* (1743–1822)]

Havana *hə-van'ə*, *n* a fine quality cigar, made in *Havana* or Cuba generally.

have *hav*, *vt* to hold; to keep; to possess; to own; to hold in control; to bear; to be in a special relation to (analogous to, if not quite ownership; eg *to have a son, an assistant*, or *no government*); to be characterized by; to be given the use or enjoyment of; to experience; to know; to entertain in the mind; to grasp the meaning or point of; to hold as information; to put, assert or express; to suffer, endure, tolerate; to hold or esteem; to cause or allow to (do something; *esp NAm*); to convey, take, cause to go; to accept, take; to remove (with *off* or *out*); to cause to be removed; to get; to obtain; to give birth to; to get the better of, hold at a disadvantage or in one's power in a dilemma; to take in, deceive (*usu* in *passive*); to entertain in one's home (with *back*, *in*, *round*, etc; *colloq*); to ask to do a job in one's house, etc (with *in*, *round*, etc; *colloq*); as an auxiliary verb, used with the *pa p* in forming the perfect tenses: — *2nd pers sing* (*archaic* and *dialect*) **hast**; *3rd pers sing* **has** or (*archaic*) **hath**; *pl* **have**; *pres subjunctive* **have**; *pa t* and *pa p* **had**; *2nd pers pa t* (*archaic* or *dialect*) **hadst**; *pa subjunctive* **had**; *pr p* **hav'ing**. — *n* a person who has possessions: — *pl* **haves**. — *n* **hav'er** a person who has or possesses, a holder; the person in whose custody a document is (*Scots law*). — *n* **hav'ing** act of possessing; possession, estate; (*esp* in *pl hāv'ingz*) behaviour, good manners (*Scot*). — *adj* greedy. — *adj* **have-a-go'** willing to attempt something, *esp* to stop a criminal in the act. — **have-at'-him** (*Shakesp*) a thrust; **have'-not** a person who lacks possessions: — *pl* **have'-nots**; **have-on'** a deception, a hoax; a piece of humbug or chaff. — **had as good** (*archaic*) might as well; **had as lief** (*archaic*) would as willingly; **had better** or **had best** would do best to; **had like** see under **like**[1]; **had rather** would prefer; **have at** (let me) attack; here goes; **have done** see under **do**[1]; **have had it** (*colloq*) to be ruined; to have missed one's opportunities; to be doomed, beyond hope; to have been killed; (also **have had that**) not to be going to get or do (something); **have it** to prevail; to exceed in any way; to get punishment, unpleasant consequences; **have it away** (*slang*) to escape; to have it off; **have it coming (to one)** (*colloq*) to deserve the bad luck, punishment, etc that one is getting or will get; **have it in for (someone)** (*colloq*) to have a grudge against (someone); **have it in one** to have the courage or ability within oneself (to do something); **have it off** or **away (with)** (*vulg slang*) to have sexual intercourse (with); **have it out** to discuss a point of contention, etc explicitly and exhaustively; **have on** to wear; to take in, hoax, chaff; to have as an engagement or appointment; **have to** to be obliged to; **have to be** (*colloq*) to surely be; **have to do with** see under **do**[1]; **have up** to call to account (before a court of justice, etc); **have what it takes** to have the necessary qualities or capabilities (to do something); **have with you** (*archaic*) I am ready to go with you; **I have it** I have found the answer (to a problem, etc); **let (someone) have it** to attack (someone) with words, blows, etc; **not be having any (of that)** to be unwilling to accept, tolerate, etc the thing proposed or mentioned. [OE *habban*, pa t *hæfde*, pa p *gehæfd*; Ger *haben*, Dan *have*]

havelock *hav'lək*, *n* a white cover for a military cap, with a flap over the neck. [From General Henry *Havelock* (1795–1857)]

haven *hā'vn*, *n* an inlet affording shelter to ships; a harbour; any place of retreat, protection, peace or asylum. — *vt* to shelter. — *adj* **hā'vened**. [OE *hæfen*; Du *haven*, Ger *Hafen*]

haven't *hav'ənt*, contracted form of **have not**.

haveour. See **haviour**.

haver[1] *hāv'ər*, *vi* to talk nonsense or foolishly (*Scot* and *N Eng dialect*); to waver, to be slow or hesitant in making a decision. — *n* (*usu* in *pl*; *Scot* and *N Eng dialect*) foolish talk; nonsense. — *n* **hav'erel** (*Scot* and *N Eng dialect*) a foolish person. — *n pl* **haver'ings** (*Scot* and *N Eng dialect*) havers.

haver[2] *hav'ər*, *n* (*Northern*) oats; the wild oat (grass). — *n* **hav'ersack** a bag worn over one shoulder for carrying provisions, etc (*orig* horse's oats) on a journey. [ON (pl) *hafrar*; cf Ger *Hafer*, *Haber* oats]

haver[3]. See under **have**.

Haversian canals *hav-vûr'shən kə-nalz*, (*zool*) *n pl* small channels containing blood vessels and pervading compact bone. [C *Havers* (1650–1702), Eng physician and anatomist]

haversine *hav'ər-sīn*, *n* half the *versine*.

havildar *hav'il-där*, *n* an Indian sergeant. [Pers *hawāl-dār*]

having. See under **have**.

haviour or **haveour** *hāv'yər*, *n* possession (*obs*); behaviour (*Spenser*). [Partly OFr *aveir* possession, partly **be-haviour**]

havoc *hav'ək*, *n* general destruction; devastation; chaos. — *vt* to lay waste: — *pr p* **hav'ocking**; *pa t* and *pa p* **hav'ocked**. — *interj* an ancient war cry, a signal for plunder. — **play havoc with** see under **play**. [Anglo-Fr *havok*, from OFr *havot* plunder; prob Gmc]

haw[1] *hö*, *n* a hedge (*hist*); an enclosure (*hist*); a messuage (*hist*); the fruit of the hawthorn. — **haw'buck** a bumpkin; **haw'finch** the common grosbeak (*Coccothraustes coccothraustes*); **haw'thorn** a small tree of the rose family, widely used for hedges. [OE *haga* a yard or enclosure, a haw; Du *haag* a hedge, Ger *Hag* a hedge, ON *hagi* a field]

haw[2] *hö*, *vi* to speak with hesitation or drawl, natural or affected; to make indecisive noises, as in *hum and haw* (qv under **hum**[1]). — *adj* **haw'-haw'** affectedly superior in enunciation. — *n* a hesitation or affectation of superiority in speech; loud vulgar laughter. — *vi* to guffaw, to laugh boisterously. [Imit]

haw[3] *hö*, (*zool*) *n* the nictitating membrane; a disease of the nictitating membrane. [Origin unknown]

Hawaiian *ha-wī'(y)ən*, *adj* pertaining to *Hawaii*, to its citizens, or to its language. — *n* a citizen or native of Hawaii. — **Hawaiian goose** the nene (qv); **Hawaiian guitar** a guitar, *usu* held horizontally, on which the required notes and *esp* glissandos are produced by sliding a metal bar or similar object along the strings while plucking.

haw-haw. See **ha-ha**[2] and **haw**[2].

hawk[1] *hök*, *n* a name given to many birds of prey of the family Accipitridae (related to the falcons) which includes the eagles and buzzards, *esp* to those of the sparrow-hawk and goshawk genus (Accipiter); (in the USA) applied also to some falcons; (in *pl*) all members of the Accipitridae (*biol*); a hawk-moth; a predatory or a keen-sighted person; (in politics, industrial relations, etc) a person who advocates war, aggressiveness or confrontation rather than peace and conciliation (opp to *dove*). — *vt* and *vi* to hunt with trained hawks; to hunt on the wing. — *n* **hawk'er** a person who hunts with a hawk. — *n* **hawk'ing** falconry. — *adj* practising falconry; hawklike, keen (*Shakesp*). — *adj* **hawk'ish**. — *adv* **hawk'ishly**. — *n* **hawk'ishness**. — *adj* **hawk'like**. — *adj* **hawk'-beaked** or **-billed** with a beak, or nose, like a hawk's bill. — **hawk'bell** a small bell attached to a hawk's leg; **hawk'bit** a plant (Leontodon) closely related to the dandelion. — *adj* **hawk'-eyed** sharp-sighted. — **hawk'-moth** any member of the Sphinx family, heavy moths with hovering flight. — *adj* **hawk'-nosed** having a hooked beak or nose. — **hawks'beard** a plant (*Crepis*) very like hawkweed; **hawks'bill** a hawk-beaked turtle; **hawk'weed** (*bot*) a genus (Hieracium) of yellow-headed ligulate-flowered composites. — **know a hawk from a handsaw** (prob for *heronshaw*) to be able to judge between things pretty well. [OE *hafoc*; Du *havik*, Ger *Habicht*, ON *haukr*]

hawk[2] *hök*, *vt* to force up (phlegm, etc) from the throat. — *vi* to clear the throat noisily. — *n* the act of doing so. [Prob imit]

hawk[3]. See under **hawker**.

hawk[4] *hök*, *n* a plasterer's slab with a handle underneath. [Origin uncertain; a connection with **hawk**[1] has been suggested, because of how the slab is held]

hawked *hökt*, or (*Scot*) **hawk'it**, *adj* streaked; white-faced. — *n* **hawk'ey** or **hawk'ie** a cow with a white-striped face.

hawker[1] *hök'ər*, *n* a person who goes round houses or streets offering goods for sale — now confined to someone who uses a beast of burden or vehicle (distinguished from a pedlar, who carries his wares bodily). — *vt* **hawk** to carry around for sale; to cry one's wares while doing this. [Cf LGer and Ger *Höker*, Du *heuker*]

hawker[2]. See under **hawk**[1].

hawkey. See under **hockey**[2], **hawked**.

hawkie. See under **hawked**.

hawking, **hawkish**. See under **hawk**[1].

hawkit. See under **hawked**.

hawklike. See under **hawk**[1].

hawm *höm*, (*dialect*) *vi* to lounge about. [Ety dubious]

hawse[1] *höz*, *n* part of a vessel's bow in which the hawseholes are cut. — **hawse'hole** a hole for a ship's cable; **hawse'pipe** a tubular casting, fitted to a ship's bows, through which the anchor chain or cable passes. [ON *hāls* neck]

hawse[2]. See **halse**[1].

hawser *hö'zər*, *n* a small cable, a large rope used in tying a ship to a quayside, etc; a hawser-laid rope. — *adj* **haw'ser-laid** composed of strands with a left-handed twist twisted together to the right hand. [OFr *haucier*, *haulser* to raise, from LL *altiāre*, from L *altus* high]

hawthorn. See **haw**[1].

hay[1] *hā*, *n* grass, etc, cut down and dried for fodder or destined for that purpose. — *vt* and *vi* to make hay. — *n* **hay'ing** the making or harvesting of hay. — *n* **hay'sel** the hay season (OE *sǣl* season). — **hay'band** a rope of twisted hay; **hay'box** an airtight box of hay used to continue the cooking of dishes already begun; **hay'cock** a conical pile of hay in the field; **hay fever** irritation by pollen of the nose, throat, etc, with sneezing and headache — also (*rare*) **hay asthma**; **hay'field** a field where hay is made; **hay'fork** a long-handled fork used in turning and lifting hay; **hay knife** a broad knife with a handle set crosswise at one end, used for cutting hay from a stack; **hay'loft** a loft in which hay is kept; **hay'maker** someone who makes hay; a wild swinging blow (*slang*); (in *pl*) a kind of country-dance; **hay'-making**; **hay'mow** a rick of hay; a mass of hay stored in a barn; **hay'rick** a haystack; **hay'ride** a pleasure ride in a hay wagon; **hay'seed** grass seed dropped from hay; a rustic, traditionally a stupid person (*colloq*); **hay'stack**; **hay'wire** wire for binding hay. — *adj* (*slang*), tangled; crazy; all awry. — Also *adv*. — **hit the hay** (*slang*) to go to bed; **make hay** to toss and turn cut grass; to throw things into confusion (with *of*); **make hay while the sun shines** to seize an opportunity while it lasts. [OE *hīeg*, *hīg*, *hēg*; Ger *Heu*, Du *hooi*; ON *hey*]

hay[2] *hā*, (*archaic*) *n* a hedge, fence. — **hay'-bote** hedge-bote; **hay'ward** a person who had charge of fences and enclosures and prevented cattle from breaking through; a person who herded the common cattle of a town. [OE *hege*, from *haga* a hedge]

hay[3] *hā*, (*obs*) *interj* used on hitting in fencing. — *n* (*Shakesp*) a hit or home-thrust. [Ital *hai* thou hast (it), from *avere*, from L *habēre* to have]

hay[4]. See **hey**[2].

hayle (*Spenser*). See **hale**[1].

hazard *haz'ərd*, *n* an old dice game; chance; accident; risk; the thing risked; the pocketing of the object ball (*winning* hazard), or of the player's own ball after contact (*losing* hazard; *billiards*); the side of the court into which the ball is served (*real tennis*); any difficulty on a golf course — bunker, long grass, road, water, whins, etc; anything which might cause an accident, create danger, etc. — *vt* to expose to chance; to risk; to venture; to venture to say or utter; to jeopardize. — *adj* **haz'ardable**. — *n* **haz'ardize** (*Spenser*) hazard. — *adj* **haz'ardous** dangerous; perilous; uncertain. — *adv* **haz'ardously**. — *n* **haz'ardousness**. — *n* **haz'ardry** (*Spenser*) playing at games of hazard or chance; rashness. [OFr *hasard*; prob through Sp from Ar *al zār* the die; according to William of Tyre from *Hasart*, a castle in Syria, where the game was invented during the Crusades]

haze[1] *hāz*, *n* vapour, mist or shimmer due to heat, often obscuring vision; mistiness; lack of definition or precision. — *vt* to make hazy. — *vi* to form a haze. — *adv* **hā'zily**. — *n* **hā'ziness**. — *adj* **hā'zy** thick with haze; ill-defined; not clear; (of the mind) confused. [Appar not OE *hasu*, *haswe* grey]

haze[2] *hāz*, *vt* to vex with needless or excessive tasks, rough treatment, practical jokes; to rag; to bully. — *n* **hā'zer**. — *n* **hā'zing**. [OFr *haser* to annoy]

hazel *hā'zl*, *n* a tree (Corylus) of the birch family; its wood. — *adj* made or consisting of hazel; light-brown, like a hazelnut. — *adj* **hā'zelly**. — **hazel grouse** or **hen** the ruffed grouse; **hā'zelnut** the edible nut of the hazel tree. [OE *hæsel*; Ger *Hasel*, ON *hasl*, L *corulus*, *corylus*]

Hb *symbol*: haemoglobin.

HB *abbrev*: hard black (on lead pencils).

HBM *abbrev*: Her (or His) Britannic Majesty.

HBO *abbrev*: hyperbaric oxygen.

H-bomb. See under **H** (symbol).

HC *abbrev*: Heralds' College; Holy Communion; House of Commons.

HCF *abbrev*: highest common factor (also **hcf**); Honorary Chaplain to the Forces.

HCFCs *abbrev*: hydrocholorofluorocarbons.

HCM *abbrev*: Her (or His) Catholic Majesty.

HDL *abbrev*: high-density lipoprotein.

HDTV *abbrev*: high definition television, an advanced TV system in which the image is formed by a much greater number of scanning lines than in standard TV, giving much improved picture quality.

HE *abbrev*: High Explosive; His Eminence; His Excellency.

He (*chem*) *symbol*: helium.

he *hē* (or when unemphatic *hi*, *ē* or *i*), *nominative* (irregularly, in dialect, or ungrammatically *accusative* or *dative*) *masc pron* of the 3*rd pers sing* the male (or thing spoken of as if male) named before, indicated, or understood (*pl* **they**). — *n* (*nominative*, *accusative* and *dative*) a male (*pl* **hēs**). — *adj* and *combining form* signifying male, as in *he-goat*, *he-pigeon*. — **he'-man** a man of exaggerated or extreme virility, or what some women consider to be virility. [OE *hē*, *he*]

HEA *abbrev*: Health Education Authority.

head *hed*, *n* the uppermost part of the human body, or the uppermost or foremost part of an animal's body, in which reside the brain, mouth and principal sense organs; the brain; the understanding; self-possession; a chief or leader; a headteacher, principal; the place of honour or command; the front, upper end or top of anything; a rounded or enlarged end or top; a capitulum; a mass of leaves, flowers, hair, etc; a headdress or dressing for the head (*archaic*); a headache (*colloq*); the peg-box and scroll of a violin, etc; the membrane of a drum; the essential part of an apparatus; in a bicycle, the tube in which the front-fork is socketed; an individual animal or person as one of a group; a title, heading; a topic or chief point of a discourse; a source; energy of a fluid owing to height, velocity and pressure; pressure; strength (*archaic*); insurrectionary force (*archaic*); the highest point of anything; culmination; a cape, headland; a froth on liquor (*esp* beer) poured out; a point where pus gathers on the surface of the skin; headway; the length or height of an animal's or person's head; a mine tunnel; (in *pl*) the obverse of a coin; someone who takes hallucinogenic drugs (*slang*; often in combination as in **acid-head**); (often in *pl*) a ship's toilet (*naut slang*); an electromagnetic device in tape recorders, etc for converting electrical signals into the recorded form or vice versa, or erasing recorded material. — *adj* of or pertaining to the head; for the head; chief, principal; at or coming from the front. — *vt* to remove the head or top from (*obs*); to behead (*obs*); to supply with a head, top or heading; to be the head, or at the head of (also **head up**); to go round the head of; to face; to meet in the face; to cause to face or front; to strike with the head; to be ahead of. — *vi* to form a head; to face, front; to direct one's course, make (for). — *n* **head'age** a subsidy payable to farmers, based on the number of animals kept. — *adj* **head'ed** (*usu* as combining form) having a head; come to a head (*Shakesp*). — *n* **head'er** a person who or a machine which removes heads from or supplies heads for casks, etc; a dive head foremost; a brick or stone with the short side showing on the wall surface; the act of heading a ball; a heading for a chapter or article, etc; a heading at the top of a microfiche, etc, readable with the naked eye; an optional piece of coded information preceding a collection of data, giving certain details about the data (*comput*); a card attached to the top of a dumpbin giving information such as the name(s) and author(s) of the book(s) displayed; (also **header tank**) a reservoir, etc that maintains an apparatus or system relying on pressure (eg plumbing) or gravity feed. — *adv* **head'ily**. — *n* **head'iness**. — *n* **head'ing** the action of the verb *head* in any sense; a part forming a head; a small passage to be enlarged into a tunnel; words placed at the head of a chapter, paragraph, etc. — *adj* **head'less**. — *adv* **head'long** with the head foremost or first; head over heels; without thought, rashly; precipitately, at full speed. — *adj* rash; precipitate, at full speed; precipitous. — *adj* **head'most** most advanced or furthest forward. — *n* **head'ship** the position or office of head or chief. — *adj* **head'y** affecting the brain; intoxicating; inflamed; rash; violent; exciting. — **head'ache** a pain in the head; a source of worry (*colloq*). — *adj* **head'achy**. — **head'band** a band (eg of ribbon, or elastic or rigid material) for wearing around the head; a band round the top of trousers, etc; a band of cloth attached to each end of the spine of a book to strengthen it, or for decoration; a thin slip of iron on the tympan of a printing-press; **head'-banger** (*colloq*) a person who is crazy, foolish, fanatical, etc; a fan of heavy metal rock music; **head'-banging** the act of shaking the head extremely vigorously in time with (*usu*) heavy metal rock music; **head'board** an often ornamental board or panel at the head of a bed; **head'=boom** a jib-boom or a flying jib-boom; **head'borough** (*hist*) the head of a frank-pledge, tithing, or decennary; a petty constable; **head boy** the senior boy in a school; **head-bummer** see under **bum**[2]; **head'-butt** to strike (a person) violently with the head. — Also *n*. — **head'case** (*colloq*) a person who is mad or crazy; **head-centre** see **centre**; **head'chair** a high-backed chair with a headrest; **head'cheese** (*US*) brawn; **head'cloth** a kerchief worn instead of a hat; **head cold** a cold which affects parts of the sufferer's head, such as the eyes or nasal passages; **head count** (*colloq*) a count of people, bodies, etc; **head'-crash** (*comput*) the accidental contact of a computer head with the surface of a hard disk in a disk drive, damaging the disk and wiping out the data stored on it; **head-down display** (*aeronautics*) a display, *usu* visual, mounted inside the cockpit to supplement the head-up display; **head'dress** a (sometimes ceremonial) covering for the head; a mode of dressing the hair (*archaic*); **head'fast** a mooring rope at the bows of a ship; **head'frame** the structure over a mine-shaft supporting the winding machinery; **head'gear** anything worn on the head; apparatus at the head of a mine-shaft; **head girl** the senior girl in a school; **head'-hugger** a woman's close-fitting headgear of kerchief type. — *vi* **head'hunt** (*colloq*) to (attempt to) deprive a political opponent of power and influence (*US*); (also *vt*) to seek out and recruit (executives, etc) for a business or organization, *esp* to do so professionally as eg a management consultant. — **head'hunter**; **head'hunting** the practice of collecting human heads; the practice of trying to undermine one's opponent's power (*US*); the seeking out of senior staff for one's organization; **headlamp** see **headlight** below; **head'land** a point of land running out into the sea; a cape; the border of a field where the plough turns, ploughed separately afterwards; **head'lease** a main or original lease, which can be divided into subleases; **head'light** or **head'lamp** a strong light on the front of a vehicle; **head'line** a line at the top of a page containing title, folio, etc (*printing*); the title of an article, *esp* a main article, in a newspaper, a caption; a news item given very briefly (*radio* and *TV*); (in *pl*) the sails and ropes next to the yards. — *adj* (likely to be) published or broadcast as a headline. — *vt* to give as a headline, mention in a headline; to add a headline to; to publicize. — *vi* to be a headliner. — **head'liner** the person whose name is made most prominent in a playbill or programme; **head'lock** a wrestling hold made by putting one's arm round one's opponent's head and tightening the grip by interlocking the fingers of both hands. — *adj* **head'-lugged** (*Shakesp*) dragged by the head. — **head'man** a chief, a leader (in primitive societies); **head'mark** a peculiar characteristic; **headmas'ter** the principal master of a school; **headmas'tership**; **headmis'tress**; **headmis'tress-ship**; **head money** a poll tax; a sum of money paid for each prisoner taken, or each slave delivered; a reward for a proscribed outlaw's head; **head'note** a note placed at the head of a chapter or page, *esp* a condensed statement of points of law involved introductory to the report of a legal decision; a tone produced in the head register (*music*). — *adj* and *adv* **head-on'** head to head, *esp* (of a collision) with the front of one vehicle, etc hitting the front of another, or (rarely) a stationary object; with head pointing directly forward; directly opposed, confronting each other. — **head'phone** (usu in *pl*) an audio receiver worn in pairs over the ears, *esp* for listening to a radio, cassette player, etc; a hairdressing style of similar form; **head'piece** a helmet; a hat; head, skull (*archaic*; *Spenser* **head'peace**); a brain; a man of intelligence; a top part; a decorative engraving at the beginning of a book, chapter, etc (*printing*). — *adj* **headquar'tered** having one's headquarters (in a specified place). — *n pl* and *n sing* **headquar'ters** the quarters or residence of a commander-in-chief or general; a central or chief office of a company, etc. — **head'race** the channel leading to a water-wheel or other hydraulically-operated machine; **head'rail** one of the rails at a ship's head; **head'reach** the distance made to windward in tacking. — *vi* to shoot ahead, in tacking. — **head register** (*music*) high register; of the voice in which nose and head cavities vibrate sympathetically; (in male voice) falsetto; **head rent** rent payable to the freeholder; **head'rest** a support for the head; (also **head restraint**) a cushioned frame fitted to the top of a seat in a car, etc to prevent the head jerking back in a collision; **head'-rhyme** alliteration; **head'rig** (*Scot*) a headland in a ploughed field; **head'ring** a palm-leaf hair ornament worn by S African native men after marriage; **head'room** uninterrupted space below a ceiling, bridge, etc; space overhead, below an obstacle, etc; **head'rope** a rope for tying or leading an animal; part of the boltrope at the top of a rectangular sail; **head'scarf** a scarf worn over the head, a headsquare: — *pl* **head'scarves**; **head sea** (*naut*) a sea running directly against a ship's course; **head'set** a set of headphones, often with a microphone attached; **head'shake** a significant shake of the head; **head'sheets** the forepart of a small vessel or craft; **head'shot** a photograph or television picture of someone's head (and shoulders) only; **head'shrinker** a headhunter who shrinks the heads of his victims; a psychiatrist (*colloq*); **heads'man** an executioner who cuts off heads; **head'square** a square of material worn as a covering for the head; **head'stall** the part of a horse's bridle round the head; a choir-stall with its back to the choir-screen (*obs*); **head start** boost or advantage intended to overcome a disadvantage or give a better chance of success; **head'-station** the dwelling-house, etc, on an Australian sheep or cattle station; **head'stick** (*printing*) formerly a straight piece of furniture placed at the head of a form, between the chase and the type; **head'stock** (*machinery*) a device for supporting the end or head of a member or part; **head'stone** the principal stone of a building; the main principle; cornerstone; gravestone; **head'-stream** a head-water; a high tributary; the stream forming the highest or remotest source (of a river). — *adj* **head'-strong** obstinately self-willed. — **head teacher** a headmaster or headmistress; **head'-tire** (*obs*) a head-dress; **head-up display** the presentation of data on the windscreen of an aircraft or car, etc enabling the pilot or driver to see the information without having to look down at the instrument panel (*abbrev* **HUD**); **head voice** tones in the head register; **head waiter** the most senior waiter of a restaurant or hotel; **head'-water** the highest part of a stream or river before receiving tributaries; **head'way** motion ahead, *esp* of a ship; progress; the time interval or distance between buses, trains, etc travelling on the same route in the same direction; **head wind** a wind blowing directly against one's course; **head-wo'man** a female leader or chief; **head'word** a word forming a heading eg of an entry in a dictionary or encyclopedia; a word under which other related words are grouped, as in a dictionary; **head'work** mental work; **head'worker**. — **above one's head** beyond one's capacity for understanding; **against the head** (of the ball in a rugby scrum, or the scrum itself) won by the team not putting the ball in; **bring** or **come to a head** to (cause to) reach a climax or crisis; **eat one's head off** see under **eat**; **get it into one's head** to conceive the (*esp* wrong or foolish) notion, to believe (with *that*); **give head** (*vulg slang*) to perform oral sex; **give a horse his** or **her head** to let him or her go as they choose; **give someone his** or **her head** to increase someone's scope for initiative; **go by the head** (*naut*) to sink head foremost; **go over someone's head** to take a problem, complaint, etc directly to a person more senior than someone; **go to someone's head** to make someone vain or conceited; to make someone confused or dizzy; to make someone drunk; **have a (good**, etc) **head on one's shoulders** to have ability and balance; **have one's head screwed on (the right way)** to be sensible, bright, etc; **head and shoulders** very much, as if taller by a head and shoulders; violently (*archaic*); **head first** or **head foremost** with the head in front; **head off** to get ahead of so as to turn back; to deflect from a path or intention; **head over heels** as in a somersault; completely; **heads or tails** an invitation to guess how a coin will fall; **head to head** in direct competition (*adj* **head-to-head'**); **hit the headlines** to get prominent attention in the press or other media; **hold up one's head** see under **hold**[1]; **keep** (or **lose**) **one's head** to keep (or lose) one's self-possession, calmness, control; **keep one's head above water** see under **water**; **lay** or **put heads together** to confer and co-operate; **off** or **out of one's head** (*colloq*) crazy; **off the top of one's head** see under **top**[1]; **on one's (own) head be it** one must, or will, accept responsibility for any unpleasant or undesirable consequences of one's actions; **out of one's (own) head** spontaneously; of one's own invention; crazy, mad (*colloq*); **over head and ears** deeply submerged or engrossed; **over one's head** beyond one's capacity for understanding; beyond one's control; **put one's head on the block** (*colloq*) to stick one's neck out, run the risk of censure, etc; **put heads together** see **lay heads together** above; **put one's head on the block** (*colloq*) to stick one's neck out, run the risk of censure, etc; **show one's head** to allow oneself to be seen; **take it into one's head** to conceive the (*esp* wrong or foolish) notion, believe (with *that*); to conceive the (*esp* misguided) intention of (with *to*); **turn one's head** see under **turn**. [OE *hēafod*; cf Du *hoofd*, Ger *Haupt*]

-head. See **-hood**.

heal[1] *hēl*, *vt* to make whole and healthy; to cure; to restore to health or good condition (physical or mental); to remedy, amend. — *vi* to grow sound or healthy again. — *n* (*archaic* and *Scot*) health; soundness; welfare. — *adj* **heal'able**. — *n* **heal'er**. — *n* and *adj* **heal'ing**. — *adv* **heal'ingly**. — *adj* **heal'some** (*Scot*) wholesome. — **heal'-all** allheal. [OE *hǣlan* (verb), *hǣlu* (n), from *hāl* whole; cf Ger *heil*, Du *heel*; ON *heill*; **hail**[1], **hale**[1], **whole**]

heal[2]. See **hele**.

heald *hēld*, the same as **heddle**. — Also an old form of **heel**[2].

health *helth*, *n* sound physical or mental condition; soundness; condition of wholesomeness; well-being; state with respect to soundness; a toast. — *adj* **health'ful** enjoying, indicating, or conducive to health. — *adv* **health'fully**. — *n* **health'fulness**. — *adv* **health'ily**. — *n* **health'iness**. — *adj* **health'less**. — *n* **health'lessness**. — *adj* **health'some** healthy, wholesome. — *adj* **health'y** in good health; morally or spiritually wholesome;

economically sound; conducive to or indicative of good health. — **health camp** (*NZ*) a camp intended to improve the physical and emotional condition of children who attend it; **health'care** the care of one's own or others' health; **health centre** a centre for clinical and administrative health welfare work. — *adj* **health'-conscious** anxious to maintain (*esp* one's own) good health. — **health farm** a place, *usu* in the country, where people go to improve their health by dieting, exercise, etc; **health food** food thought to be particularly good for one's health, *esp* that grown and prepared without artificial fertilizers, chemical additives, etc; **health resort** a place noted for its health-giving conditions, *esp* its salubrious climate; **health stamp** (*NZ*) a stamp, part of the cost of which goes to supporting health camps; **health visitor** a nurse concerned mainly with health education and advice and preventive medicine rather than the treatment of disease, who visits *esp* mothers with young children and the elderly in their own homes. [OE *hǣlth*, from *hāl* whole]

heame *hēm*, (*Spenser*) *adv* form of **home**.

heap *hēp*, *n* a mass of things resting one above another; a mound; a company (*Shakesp*); a great number, a great deal (often in *pl*), a collection (*colloq*); an old dilapidated motor car; a ruin (*Bible*). — *vt* to throw into a heap; to amass; to load with a heap or heaps; to pile high, or above the rim or brim (also *vi*). — *adj* **heap'ing** (*US*; of a spoonful, etc) heaped. — *adv* **heaps** (*colloq*) very much. — *adj* **heap'y** full of heaps. — **heap'stead** the buildings and works around a mine-shaft. — **knock** or **strike all of a heap** to confound utterly, dumfound. [OE *hēap*; cf ON *hōpr*, Ger *Haufe*, Du *hoop*]

hear *hēr*, *vt* to perceive by the ear; to accede to; to listen to; to listen to for the purpose of witnessing ability (or otherwise) to recite lines learned; to try judicially; to be informed; to be a hearer of; to be called (*Milton*, a Latinism). — *vi* to have or exercise the sense of hearing; to listen; to have news (of or from); to be spoken of (*Spenser*, a Graecism): — *pa t* and *pa p* **heard** (*hûrd*). — *adj* **heard** (*hûrd*). — *n* **hear'er**. — *n* **hear'ing** power or act of perceiving sound; an opportunity to be heard; audience; audition; judicial investigation and listening to evidence and arguments, *esp* without a jury; earshot; news; a scolding (*dialect*). — **hear'ing-aid** any device, electrical or other, for enabling the deaf to hear or to hear better; **hearing-impair'ed** (now a preferred term for) deaf or hard of hearing; **hear'say** common talk; report; rumour. — *adj* of the nature of or based on report given by others. — **hear, hear!** an exclamation of approval from the hearers of a speech; **hear out** to listen (to someone) until they have said all they wish to say; **hear tell of** to hear someone speak of; **hear things** see under **thing**; **will** or **would not hear of** will or would not allow or tolerate. [OE (Anglian) *hēran* (WSax *hīeran*, *hȳran*); Du *hooren*, ON *heyra*, Ger *hören*, Gothic *hausjan*]

heard[1]. See under **hear**.

heard[2], **heare** (*her*) and **hearie**, (*Spenser*) forms of **herd**, **hair**, and **hairy** respectively.

hearken *härk'n*, (*archaic* or *literary*) *vi* to hear attentively; to listen. — *vt* to listen to, pay attention to, heed (*poetic*); to seek by enquiry (*obs*). — *n* **heark'ener**. [OE *hercnian* (*heorcnian*); cf **hark**, **hear**; Ger *horchen*]

hearse or (*Spenser*) **herse** *hûrs*, *n orig* a canopy or frame over a bier, designed to hold candles; a funeral service (*Spenser*); a bier (*obs*); a vehicle for carrying the dead. — *vt* to put on or in a hearse. — *adj* **hearse'-like**. — *adj* **hears'y**. — **hearse'-cloth** a pall. [OFr *herse* (Ital *erpice*), from L *hirpex*, *-icis* a harrow]

heart *härt*, *n* the organ that circulates the blood through the body; the stomach (*obs*); the innermost part; the core; the chief or vital part; the breast, bosom; the (imagined) place of origin of the affections, understanding, and thought, as opposed to the head, the seat of reason; courage; innermost feelings or convictions; vigour, spirit; cordiality; compassion; a term of endearment or encouragement; a heart-shaped figure or object; a playing-card with heart-shaped pips; the centre of cabbage, lettuce, etc; a diseased state of the heart. — *vt* to hearten (*archaic*); to fill up a centre space with rubble (*building*). — *vi* (of a lettuce) to form a compact head or inner mass. — *adj* **hart'ie-hale** (*Spenser*) good for the heart, healthy. — *adj* **heart'ed** used in combination to signify having a heart, *esp* of a specified kind (eg *hard-hearted*, etc); seated or fixed in the heart, stored up in the heart. — *vt* **heart'en** to encourage, stimulate; to add strength to; to give courage to. — *vi* to take courage. — *n* **heart'ikin** (*obs*) a little heart (used euphemistically in an old oath). — *adv* **heart'ily** lustily, vigorously; completely (sick, tired, etc). — *n* **heart'iness**. — *adj* **heart'less** without heart, courage, consideration or feeling; callous. — *adv* **heart'lessly**. — *n* **heart'lessness**. — *n* **heart'let** a little heart, a nucleus. — *n* **heart'ling** (*Shakesp*) little heart, used euphemistically in the oath *ods heartlings*, God's heart. — *adv* **heart'ly** or (*Spenser*) **harte'ly** heartily. — *adj* **heart'some** exhilarating; merry. — *adj* **heart'y** full of heart; heartfelt; sincere; cordial; robust; lusty; enthusiastic; unrestrained; in or indicating good spirits, appetite or condition; sound; in good heart. — *n* a hearty person, *esp* one who goes in for sports, outdoor pursuits, etc, distinguished from an *aesthete*; (in *pl*) an old form of address to fellow sailors. — **heart'ache** sorrow; anguish; **heart attack** an occurrence of coronary thrombosis, with the death of part of the heart muscle, or some other sudden malfunction of the heart; **heart'beat** a pulsation of the heart; a throb; **heart'-block** a condition in which the ventricle does not keep time with the auricle; **heart'-blood** or **heart's'-blood** blood of the heart; life, essence; **heart'-bond** (in masonry) a bond in which two headers meet in the middle of a wall and one header overlaps them; **heart'break** a crushing sorrow or grief. — *vt* (*Burns*) to break the heart of. — **heart'breaker** a fickle or unfaithful lover; a flirt; a curl, lovelock. — *adj* **heart'breaking**. — *adj* **heart'broken**. — **heart'burn** a burning, acrid feeling in throat or breast, severe indigestion, cardialgia; **heart'burning** discontent; secret grudging; **heart cam** a heart-shaped cam in a stop-watch, etc; **heart cockle** or **heart shell** a mollusc (*Isocardia*) or its shell, like a cockle coiled at the bosses. — *adj* **heart'-dear** (*Shakesp*) dear to the heart, sincerely beloved. — **heart disease** any morbid condition of the heart. — *adj* **heart'-easing** bringing peace of mind. — **heart'-failure** stoppage or inadequate functioning of the heart; shock producing faintness. — *adj* **heart'felt** felt deeply; sincere. — *adj* **heart'-free** having the affections disengaged. — **heart'-grief** deep-seated affliction; **heart-heav'iness** depression of spirits; **heart'land** an area of a country that is centrally situated and/or vitally important; **heart-lung machine** a machine used in chest surgery to take over for a time the functions of the heart and lungs; **heart murmur** an abnormal sound from the heart indicating a structural or functional abnormality; **heartpea** see **heartseed**; **heart'-quake** trembling, fear. — *adj* **heart'-rending** agonizing. — **heart'-rot** decay in the hearts of trees, caused by various fungi; **heart's-blood** see **heart-blood**; **heart'-searching** examination of one's deepest feelings; **heart's'-ease** or **hearts'ease** the pansy; **heart'seed** or **heart'pea** the balloon-vine, from the heart-shaped scar left by the seed; **heart'-service** sincere devotion, as opposed to *eye-service*. — *adj* **heart'-shaped** shaped like the conventional representation of the human heart. — **heart shell** see **heart cockle**. — *adj* **heart'-sick** despondent; greatly depressed. — **heart'-sickness**. — *adj* **heart'-sore** sore at heart; greatly distressed, very sad; caused by soreness of heart (*Shakesp*). — *n* grief; a cause of grief (*Spenser*). — **heart'-spoon** (*dialect*) the depression in the breastbone; the breastbone; the pit of the stomach. — *adj* **heart'-stirring** rousing; exhilarating. — *vt* **heart'-strike** (*archaic*) to strike to the heart; to dismay; to drive into the heart: — *pa p* **heart'-stricken** or **heart'-struck** (*obs* **-strook**). — **heart'-string** *orig* a nerve or tendon imagined to brace and sustain the heart; (in *pl*) affections; **heart'-throb** a sentimental emotion for a person of the opposite sex (*colloq*); a person who is the object of great romantic affection from afar (*colloq*). — *adj* **heart'-to-heart'** candid, intimate and unreserved. — *n* a conversation of this sort. — **heart'-urchin** a sea-urchin of the order Spatangoidea, typically heart-shaped. — *adj* **heart'warming** emotionally moving; very gratifying, pleasing. — **heart'water** a fatal tick-borne viral disease of cattle, sheep and goats, with accumulation of fluid in the pericardium and pleural cavity. — *adj* **heart'-whole** whole at heart; sincere; with affections disengaged; undismayed; out-and-out. — **heart'wood** the duramen or hard inner wood of a tree. — **after one's own heart** exactly to one's own liking; **at heart** in one's real character; substantially; **break one's heart** to die of, or be broken down by, grief or disappointment; **break someone's heart** to cause deep grief to someone; (loosely) to disappoint someone romantically; **by heart** by rote; in the memory; **change of heart** see under **change**; **cross one's heart** an expression used to emphasize the truth of a statement (often literally, by making the sign of the cross over one's heart); **cry one's heart out** see under **cry**; **dear** or **near to one's heart** whom or which one feels a warm interest in or concern or liking for; **eat one's heart out** see under **eat**; **find it in one's heart** to be able to bring oneself; **from the bottom of one's heart** most sincerely; **have a heart** (*usu* in *imperative*) to show pity or kindness; **have at heart** to cherish as a matter of deep interest; **have one's heart in it** (often in *neg*) to have enthusiasm for what one is doing; **have one's heart in one's boots** to feel a sinking of the spirit; **have one's heart in one's mouth** to be in trepidation, great fear or anxiety; **have one's heart in the right place** to be basically decent or generous; **have one's heart set on** to desire earnestly; **have the heart** (*usu* in *neg*) to have the courage or resolution (to do something unpleasant); **heart and hand** or **heart and soul** with complete sincerity; with complete devotion to a cause; **heart of hearts** the inmost feelings or convictions; deepest affections; **heart of oak** heartwood of the oak-tree; a brave, resolute person; **in good heart** in sound or fertile condition; in good spirits or courage; **lay** or **take to heart** to store up in the mind for future guidance; to be deeply moved by something; **lose heart** to become discouraged; **lose one's heart to** to fall in love with; **near to one's heart** see **dear to one's heart** above; **set one's heart on** or **upon** to come to desire earnestly; **set someone's heart at rest** to render someone easy in mind, to reassure someone; **speak to the heart** (*Bible*) to comfort, encourage; **take heart** to be encouraged; **take heart of grace** see under **grace**; **take to heart** to lay to heart; to come to feel in earnest; **take to one's heart** to form an affection for; **to one's heart's content** as much as one wishes; **wear one's heart on one's sleeve** to show one's feelings openly; **with all one's heart** most willingly. [OE *heorte*; cf Du *hart*, Ger *Herz*; L *cor*, *cordis*; Gr *kardiā*]

hearth *härth*, *n* the floor of a fireplace or the area of floor surrounding it; the fireside; the house itself; the home circle; the lowest part of a blast-furnace; a brazier, chafing-dish, or fire-box. — **hearth'-brush** a brush for sweeping the hearth; **hearth'-money**, **-penny** or **-tax** (*hist*) a tax on hearths; **hearth'-rug** a rug laid over the hearth-stone or in front of the hearth or fireplace; **hearth'-stone** a stone forming a hearth; a soft stone used for whitening hearths, doorsteps, etc. [OE *heorth*; Du *haard*, Ger *Herd*]

heast or **heaste** *hēst* (*Spenser*) *n*. Same as **hest**.

heat *hēt*, *n* that which excites the sensation of warmth; the sensation of warmth, *esp* in a high degree; degree of hotness; exposure to intense heat; a high temperature; the hottest time; redness of the skin, *esp* when irritated; vehemence, passion; sexual excitement in animals, or its period, *esp* in the female, corresponding to *rut* in the male; a single eliminating round in a race; a division of a contest from which the winner goes on to a final test; animation; pressure intended to coerce (*colloq*); period of intensive search, *esp* by the police for a criminal after a crime has taken place (*colloq*); trouble (*orig* with the police; *colloq*); the police (*US slang*); a firearm (*US slang*). — *vt* to make hot; to agitate; *perh* to run over, as in a race (*Shakesp*). — *vi* to become hot. — *adj* **heat'ed** having become or been made hot; angry, agitated or impassioned. — *n* **heat'er** someone who, or that which, heats; an apparatus for heating a room or building; a gun, pistol (*esp US*; *slang*) — *n* and *adj* **heat'ing**. — **heat'-apoplexy** sunstroke; **heat barrier** difficulties caused by a thin envelope of hot air which develops round aircraft at high speeds and causes structural and other problems; **heat death** the final state of the universe (if it is a closed system) predicted by the Second Law of Thermodynamics, in which heat and energy are uniformly distributed throughout the substance of the universe; **heat engine** an engine that transforms heat into mechanical work; **heat'er-shield** a triangular shield, like the heated plate of an iron; **heat exchanger** a device for transferring heat from one fluid to another without allowing contact between them; **heat pump** a device (on the refrigerator principle) for drawing heat from water, air, or the earth, and giving it out to warm, eg a room. — *adj* **heat'-resistant**. — **heat shield** an object or substance designed to protect against excessive heat, *esp* that which protects a spacecraft re-entering the earth's atmosphere; **heat sink** something into which unwanted heat can be directed; **heat'spot** an area of skin with nerve-ends sensitive to heat; a spot or blotch on the skin caused by heat; a freckle; **heat'stroke** exhaustion, illness, or prostration due to exposure to heat; sunstroke; **heat unit** see **British thermal unit**; **heat wave** a heated state of atmosphere passing from one locality to another; a hot spell. — **heat of formation** (*chem*) the net quantity of heat evolved or absorbed during the formation of one mole of a substance from its component elements in their standard states; **in heat** or **on heat** (of a female animal) ready to mate; **latent heat** the heat required to change solid to liquid, or liquid to gas, without change of temperature; **mechanical equivalent of heat** the energy required to produce one heat unit; **specific heat** see under **specify**; **take the heat out of** to lessen the vehemence, intensity of emotion, or acrimony of (a situation, etc); **turn on the heat** (*slang*) to use brutal treatment, mental or physical, *esp* in order to coerce. [OE *hǣtu* heat; *hāt* hot; Ger *Hitze*]

heath *hēth*, *n* barren open country, *esp* covered with ericaceous and other low shrubs; any shrub of genus Erica, sometimes extended to Calluna (heather) and others of the family Ericaceae; a butterfly of the Satyridae family. — *adj* **heath'y** abounding with heath. — **heath bell** heather bell; harebell; **heath'bird** or **heath'-fowl** the black grouse; **heath'cock** the male black grouse; **heath'-hen** the grey-hen or female black grouse; an extinct American bird related to the prairie-chicken; **heath'-poult** the black grouse, *esp* the female or young. [OE *hǣth*; Ger *Heide*, Gothic *haithi* a waste]

heathen *hē'dhn*, *n* someone who is not a Christian, Jew or Muslim but who follows another form of religion, *esp* polytheistic; a pagan; someone who has no religion; someone who is ignorant or unmindful of religion; an uncivilized person (*colloq*): — *pl* **hea'then** (collectively) or **hea'thens** (individually). — *adj* pagan; irreligious. — *n* **hea'thendom** or **hea'thenesse** (*archaic*) heathenism; the condition of a heathen; those regions of the world where heathenism prevails. — *adj* **hea'thenish** relating to the heathen; rude; uncivilized; cruel. — *adv* **hea'thenishly**. — *n* **hea'thenishness**. — *n* **hea'thenism** any religious system of the heathens; paganism; barbarism. — *n* **hea'thenry** heathenism; heathendom. — *vt* **hea'thenize** or **-ise** to make heathen or heathenish. [OE *hǣthen*; Du *heiden*]

heather *hedh'ər*, *n* ling, a common low-growing evergreen shrub (*Calluna vulgaris*) of the heath family that grows in carpet-like thickets on exposed ground; sometimes extended to the heaths (*Erica*); an expanse of heather plants. — *adj* of the purple colour of (red) heather; composed of or from heather. — *adj* **heath'ery**. — **heather ale** a famous liquor traditionally brewed in Scotland from the bells of heather — a lost art; **heather bell** the flower of the cross-leaved heath (*Erica tetralix*) or of the common heath (*Erica cinerea*); **heath'er-mixture** a woollen fabric speckled in colours like heather. — **set the heather on fire** to create a disturbance or a sensation; **take to the heather** to become an outlaw. [Older Scots *hadder*; origin unknown; prob influenced by **heath**]

heather-bleat *hedh'ər-blēt'*, or **heather-bleater** *-blēt'ər*, (*Scot*) *n* a snipe. — Also **heather-bluiter**, **heather-blutter** (*-blüt'* or *-blut'*). [OE *haefer-blǣte*, from *hæfer* goat, and *blǣtan* to bleat, from its cry; influenced by **heather**; cf also Scots *bluiter* bittern]

Heath(-)Robinson *hēth(-)rob'in-sən*, *adj* used to describe an over-ingenious, ridiculously complicated or elaborate mechanical contrivance. — *adj* **Heath-Robinsonesque'**, **Heath-Robinsō'nian** or **Heath-Rob'insonish**. [*Heath Robinson* (1872–1944), an artist who drew such contraptions]

heaume *hōm*, (*archaic*) *n* a massive helmet. [Fr]

heave *hēv*, *vt* to lift up, *esp* with great effort; to throw; to haul; to swell or puff out; to force (a sigh) from the chest; to displace (a vein) (*mining*). — *vi* to be raised; to rise like waves; to retch; to strive or strain to lift or move something; to move into a certain position, *orig* of a ship, now also *fig*: — *pa t* and *pa p* **heaved**, (*naut*) **hōve**; *pa p* in sense of swollen **hōv'en**. — *n* an effort upward; a throw; a swelling; an effort to vomit; a sigh (*Shakesp*); horizontal displacement (*mining*); the lifting up of soil and rocks, eg because of the freezing of water below the surface of the ground; (in space flight) motion perpendicular to the surge (qv); (in *pl*) broken wind in horses. — *n* **heav'er**. — *n* **heav'ing**. — **heave'-ho** (*colloq*) dismissal, rejection (see also below); **heave'-offering** and **heave'-shoulder** (*Bible*) an offering, an animal's shoulder, elevated in sacrifice. — **give** (or **get**) **the heave** or **the heave-ho** (*colloq*) to dismiss, reject or snub (or be dismissed, rejected or snubbed); **heave ho**! an *orig* sailors' call to exertion, as in heaving the anchor; **heave in sight** to come into view; **heave the lead** to take a sounding with a lead, to determine the depth of water (*naut*); **heave the log** to cast the log into the water in order to ascertain the ship's speed; **heave to** to bring a vessel to a standstill, to make her lie to. [OE *hebban*, pa t *hōf*, pa p *hafen*; Ger *heben*]

heaven *hev'n* or *hevn*, *n* the vault of sky overhanging the earth (commonly in *pl*); the upper regions of the air; a very great and indefinite height; any one of the concentric revolving spheres imagined by the old astronomers; (often with *cap*) the dwelling-place of God or the gods, and the blessed; (often with *cap*) the Deity as inhabiting heaven; supreme happiness, contentment or pleasure. — *interj* (in *pl*) expressing surprise, disbelief, dismay, etc. — *n* **heavenliness** (*hev'n-*). — *adj* **heavenly** (*hev'n-*) of or inhabiting heaven; of or from God or the angels or saints; celestial; pure; supremely blessed; excellent (*colloq*). — *adv* divinely, exceedingly (*archaic*); by the influence of heaven (*Milton*). — *adj* **heav'enward**. — *adv* **heav'enward** or **heav'enwards**. — *adj* **heav'en-born** descended from heaven. — *adj* **heav'en-bred** (*Shakesp*) bred or produced in heaven. — *adj* **heav'en-directed** pointing to the sky; divinely guided. — *adj* **heaven-fallen** (*hevn-föln'*; *Milton*) fallen from heaven. — *adj* **heaven-gift'ed** bestowed by heaven. — *adj* **heav'en-kissing** (*Shakesp*) as it were, touching the sky. — **heavenly bodies** the sun, moon, planets, comets, stars, etc; **heavenly host** a multitude of angels. — *adj* **heav'enly-minded** with the mind set upon heavenly things; pure. — **heavenly-mind'edness**. — *adj* **heav'en-sent** sent by heaven; very timely. — **good heavens** or **heavens above** expressing surprise, disbelief, dismay, etc; **heaven forbid** or (*archaic*) **forfend** may it not happen (that); **heaven knows** God knows (qv); it is beyond human knowledge; it is anyone's guess; **heaven of heavens** (*Bible*) the highest heavens, abode of God; **in (the) seventh heaven** in a state of the most exalted happiness (from the Cabbalists, who divided the heavens into seven in an ascending scale of happiness up to the abode of God); **move heaven and earth** to do everything possible; **the heavens opened** there was a very heavy shower of rain; **tree of heaven** ailanto. [OE *heofon*]

Heaviside layer. See **Kennelly-Heaviside layer**.

heavy *hev'i*, *adj* weighty; ponderous; laden; abounding; of high specific gravity; not easy to bear; grievous; oppressive; grave; dull, lacking brightness and interest; lacking sprightliness; pedantic; pompous; laborious; sad; in low spirits; drowsy; with great momentum; deep-toned; massive; thick; not easily digested; doughy; impeding the feet in walking; (of the ground) very wet and soft (*horse-racing*, etc); heavy-armed (*military*); (of liquor) strong; dark with clouds; gloomy; pertaining to grave or serious roles (*theat*); (of newspapers) serious, highbrow; tense, emotional, strained (*slang*); serious, important (*slang*); (of a market) with falling prices (*commerce*): — *compar* **heav'ier**; *superl* **heav'iest**. — *adv* heavily. — *n* the villain on stage or screen; a large, strong man employed for purposes of a violent and often criminal nature or to deter others (*slang*); (in Scotland) a type of beer similar to, but not as strong as, export; anything particularly large or heavy. — *adv* **heav'ily**. — *n* **heav'iness**. — *adj* **heav'ier-than-air'** of a greater specific gravity than the air it displaces, *esp* (of an aircraft) not sustained by a gas-filled bag. — *adj* **heav'y-armed** bearing heavy armour or arms. — **heavy breather**; **heavy breathing** loud and laboured breathing due to exertion, excitement, etc, or *esp* sexual arousal, sometimes associated with anonymous obscene telephone calls; **heavy chemicals** those produced on a large scale for use in industry (eg sulphuric acid and sodium carbonate) (*opp* of *fine chemicals*). — *adj* **heav'y-duty** made to withstand very hard wear or use. — *adj* **heav'y-hand'ed** clumsy, awkward; oppressive. — *adj* **heav'y-head'ed** having a heavy or large head; dull; stupid; drowsy. — *adj* **heavy-heart'ed** weighed down with grief. — **heavy hydrogen** deuterium; also tritium; **heavy industry** see under **industry**. — *adj* **heavy-lad'en** with a heavy burden. — **heavy metal** a metal of high specific gravity, *usu* above 5; guns or shot of large size; great influence or power; a person to be reckoned with; a particularly loud, simple and repetitive form of hard rock (*music*); **heavy particle** a baryon; **heavy rock** hard rock (*music*); **heavy spar** barytes; **heavy swell** a rough sea; **heavy water** water in which deuterium takes the place of ordinary hydrogen, or a mixture of this and ordinary water; **heav'yweight** a person or thing well above the average weight; someone important or very influential (*colloq*); a competitor in the heaviest class (*sport*); a weight category variously applied in boxing and wrestling; a sportsman of the specified weight for the category (eg in professional boxing above middleweight, **light-heav'yweight** (maximum 79kg/175 lb), **jun'ior-heavy-weight** or **cruis'erweight** (maximum 88kg/195 lb), and **heav'yweight** any weight above these). — Also *adj*. **heavy wet** (*old slang*) a drink of strong ale, or ale and porter mixed. — **be heavily into** (*colloq*) to be keen on or an enthusiastic practitioner of; **be heavy going** see under **going**[1]; **heavy marching order** the condition of troops fully equipped for field service; **the heavies** the heavy cavalry (*military*); those who play heavy parts (*theat*); the more serious, highbrow newspapers and journals, etc (*colloq*); (shares in) the heavy industries. [OE *hefig*, from *hebban* to heave; OHGer *hebîg*]

Heb. or **Hebr.** *abbrev*: Hebrew; (the Letter to the) Hebrews (*Bible*).

hebdomad *heb'dō-mad*, *n* a set of seven; a week; in some Gnostic systems, a group of superhuman beings. — *adj*

hebdomadal (*-dom'ə-dl*) weekly. — *adv* **hebdom'adally**. — *n* **hebdom'adar** or **hebdom'ader** (in Scottish Universities) a senior member appointed weekly for the supervision of student discipline. — *adj* **hebdom'adary** weekly. — *n* a member of a chapter or convent taking his or her weekly turn to officiate. — **hebdomadal council** an administrative board of Oxford University, meeting weekly. [Gr *hebdomas*, *-ados* a set of seven, a week, from *hepta* seven]

Hebe *hē'bē*, *n* a daughter of Zeus and Hera, cup-bearer of Olympus, a personification of youth (*Gr mythol*); a genus of Australasian and S American shrubby plants with spikes of showy flowers, belonging to the family Scrophulariaceae, in some classifications included in the genus Veronica; (without *cap*) a member of the genus. — *n* **hebephrenia** (*hē-bi-frē'ni-ə*) a form of insanity beginning in late childhood, arresting intellectual development, and ending in complete dementia. — *adj* and *n* **hebephrē'niac** or **hebephrenic** (*-fren'ik*). [Gr *hēbē* youth, puberty (*Hēbē* the goddess), and *phrēn* mind]

heben *heb'n*, *n* and *adj*. Obs form of **ebony**.

hebenon *heb'ə-non* and **hebona** *-nə*, (*Shakesp*) *n* anything (eg a plant or fruit) with a poisonous juice. [Perh **ebony** or **henbane**, or Ger *Eibenbaum* yew-tree]

hebephrenia. See under **Hebe**.

hebetate *heb'i-tāt*, *vt* to dull or blunt. — *vi* to become dull. — *adj* dull; blunt; soft-pointed. — *adj* **heb'etant** making dull. — *n* **hebetā'tion**. — *n* **heb'etude**. — *n* **hebetūdinos'ity**. — *adj* **hebetū'dinous**. [L *hebetāre*, *-ātum*, from *hebes*, *-etis* blunt]

hebona. See **hebenon**.

Hebrew *hē'broo*, *n* a Jew; the Semitic language of the Hebrews; unintelligible speech (*colloq*). — *adj* of the Hebrews or their language. — *adj* **Hebraic** (*hē-brā'ik*) or **Hebra'ical** relating to the Hebrews or to their language. — *adv* **Hebrā'ically** after the manner of the Hebrew language; from right to left. — *n* **Hebrā'icism**. — *n* **Hē'brāism** a Hebrew idiom. — *n* **Hē'brāist** a person skilled in Hebrew. — *adj* **Hebrāist'ic** or **Hebrāist'ical** of or like Hebrew. — *adv* **Hebrāist'ically**. — *vt* **Hē'brāīze** or **-īse** to make Hebrew. — *vi* to use a Hebrew idiom; to conform or incline to Hebrew ways or ideals. — *n* **Hē'brāīzer** or **-s-**. — *n* **Hē'brewess** (*Bible*) a Jewess. — *n* **Hē'brewism**. — **Hebrew year** see under **year**. [OFr *Ebreu* and L *Hebraeus*, from Gr *Hebraios*, from Aramaic *'ebrai* (Heb *'ibrī*), literally one from the other side (of the Euphrates)]

Hebridean *heb-ri-dē'ən* or **Hebridian** *-rid'i-ən*, *adj* of the Hebrides (*heb'ri-dēz*), islands off the west coast of Scotland. — *n* a native of the Hebrides. — *adj* **He'brid** (*rare*). [Due to a misprint of L *Hebudēs*, from Gr *Heboudai*]

Hecate *hek'ə-tē* or (*Shakesp*) **Hecat** or **Hecate** *hek'ət*, *n* a mysterious goddess, in Hesiod having power over earth, heaven and sea — afterwards identified with Artemis, Persephone, and other goddesses (*Gr mythol*); in Shakespeare, etc, the chief or goddess of witches. [Gr *Hekatē*]

hecatomb *hek'ə-tom* or *-tōm* (sometimes *-toom*), *n* a great public sacrifice; any large number of victims. [Gr *hekatombē*, from *hekaton* a hundred, and *bous* an ox]

hech *hehh*, (*Scot*) *interj* an exclamation of surprise, weariness, etc.

hecht *hehht*. Scottish form of the verb **hight**.

heck[1] *hek*, **haik** or **hake** *hāk*, (*dialect*) *n* the lower part of a door; an inner door; a grating, *esp* in rivers or streams; a rack for animal fodder; a rack or frame for drying cheese, etc; a piece of spinning machinery, for guiding the yarn to the reels. — **heck and manger** rack and manger. [OE *hec* (*hæc*) grating, hatch; cf **hack**[3] and **hatch**[1]; Du *hek* gate]

heck[2] *hek*, *n* and *interj* euphemism for **hell**.

heckelphone *hek'l-fōn*, *n* an instrument of the oboe family, invented by W *Heckel* (1856–1909), between the cor anglais and the bassoon in pitch.

heckle *hek'l*, *vt* to comb out (flax or hemp fibres). — *vt* and *vi* (*orig Scot*) to ply (someone) with embarrassing questions, or shout or jeer abusively or disruptively at (as at an election hustings or public lecture). — *n* a hackle. — *n* **heck'ler**. — *n* **heck'ling**. [Cf **hackle** and **hatchel**]

hecogenin *hek'ō-jen-in*, *jen'-* or *hek-oj'ən-in*, *n* a chemical obtained from various plants, eg *Hechtia texensis*, and *esp* from sisal waste, used in the manufacture of cortisone, etc. [*Hec*(htia texensis), and suffixes *-gen* and *-in*]

hectare. See under **hecto-**.

hectic *hek'tik*, *adj* relating to the constitution or habit of body (*old*); relating to hectic fever (*old*); feverish, agitated, rushed (*colloq*); flushed (*Shelley*). — *n* a hectic fever or flush; a consumptive. — *adj* **hec'tical**. — *adv* **hec'tically**. — **hectic fever** (*old*) fever occurring in connection with certain wasting diseases of long duration, *esp* tuberculosis, typically producing a flush in the cheeks. [Gr *hektikos* habitual, from *hexis* habit]

hecto- *hek'tō-* or *hek'tə-* or **hect-** *combining form* denoting (*esp* in the metric system) 100 times. — *n* **hectare** (*hek'tär* or *-tār*) 100 ares or 10 000 sq metres. — *n* **hec'togram** or **-gramme** 100 grams. — *n* **hec'tograph** a gelatine pad for printing copies. — *vt* to reproduce in this way. — *adj* **hectograph'ic**. — *n* **hec'tolitre** 100 litres. — *n* **hec'tometre** 100 metres. — *n* **hec'tostere** 100 cubic metres or steres. [Fr contraction of Gr *hekaton* a hundred]

hector *hek'tər*, *n* a bully, a blusterer. — *vt* to treat insolently; to annoy. — *vi* to play the bully; to bluster. — *n* **hec'torer**. — *n* and *adj* **hec'toring**. — *n* **hec'torism**. — *adj* **hec'torly**. — *n* **hec'torship**. [Gr *Hektōr* the Trojan hero]

he'd *hēd*, a contraction of **he had** or **he would**.

heddle *hed'l*, (*weaving*) *n* a series of vertical cords or wires, each having in the middle a loop (**hedd'le-eye**) to receive a warp-thread, and passing round and between parallel bars. — *vt* to draw through heddle-eyes. — Also **heald**. [An assumed OE *hefedl*, earlier form of *hefeld*]

Hedera *hed'ər-ə*, *n* the ivy genus of the Aralia family. — *adj* **hed'eral**. — *adj* **hed'erated** crowned with a wreath of ivy. [L]

hedge *hej*, *n* a close row of bushes or small trees serving as a fence; a barrier, protection (*fig*); an act of securing, or something that secures, protection against (*esp* financial) loss. — *vt* to enclose with a hedge; to obstruct; to surround; to guard; to protect oneself from loss on, by compensatory transactions, eg bets on the other side. — *vi* to make hedges; to shuffle, be evasive, eg in an argument; to be shifty; to buy or sell something as a financial hedge. — *adj* living in or frequenting hedges; wayside; used by, or only fit for, vagrants; low; debased. — *n* **hedg'er** a person who hedges or dresses hedges. — *n* **hedg'ing** the work of a hedger; the action of the verb *hedge*. — *adj* **hedg'y**. — **hedge'-accen'tor** the hedge-sparrow; **hedge'bill** or **hedg'ing-bill** a bill for dressing hedges, a kind of long-handled hatchet. — *adj* **hedge'-born** born under a hedge, low-born. — **hedge'-bote** a tenant's right to cut wood for repairing hedges or fences; **hedge'-creep'er** a sneaky rogue; **hedge'hog** a small prickly-backed insectivorous animal that lives in hedges and bushes, thought to have a pig-like snout; a prickly fruit, or prickly-fruited plant; someone whose manners keep others at a distance; an offensive person; a small, strongly fortified, defensive position (*military slang*). — *vi* **hedge'-hop** (*airmen's slang*) to fly low as if hopping over hedges. — **hedge'-hyssop** a plant (*Gratiola*) of the figwort family; **hedge'-marriage** a clandestine marriage; **hedge'-mustard** a tall stiff cruciferous roadside weed (*Sisymbrium officinale*) with small yellow flowers, or a related species; **hedge'-parsley** an umbelliferous roadside weed (*Torilis* or *Caucalis*) with leaves somewhat like parsley; **hedge'-parson** or **hedge'-priest** a disreputable, vagrant, or illiterate parson or priest; **hedge'pig** a hedgehog; **hedge'row** a line of hedge, often with trees; **hedge'-school** an open-air school, common in Ireland in 17c and 18c during the ban on Catholic education; a poorly equipped school; **hedge'-school-master**; **hedge'-sparrow** or formerly also **hedge'-warbler** the dunnock (*Prunella modularis*), a small bird that frequents hedges, superficially like a sparrow but with a more slender bill; **hedge'-writer** a Grub Street author, a hack. [OE *hecg*; Du *hegge*, Ger *Hecke*]

hedonism *hē'dən-izm* or *hed'*, *n* (in ethics) the doctrine that pleasure is the highest good; the pursuit of pleasure; a lifestyle devoted to pleasure-seeking. — *adj* **hēdonic** (*-don'*) or **hēdonist'ic**. — *n sing* **hēdon'ics** that part of ethics or of psychology that deals with pleasure. — *n* **hē'donist**. [Gr *hēdonē* pleasure]

hedyphane *hed'i-fān*, *n* a white variety of green lead ore, arsenate, phosphate, and chloride of lead and calcium with barium. [Gr *hēdys* sweet, pleasant, and the root of *phainein* to show]

heebie-jeebies or **heeby-jeebies** *hē'bi-jē'biz*, *n pl* (with *the*; *slang*) a fit of nerves; irritation or depression; the creeps. [A coinage]

heed *hēd*, *vt* to observe; to look after; to attend to. — *vi* to mind, care. — *n* notice; caution; attention. — *adj* **heed'ful** attentive; cautious. — *adv* **heed'fully**. — *n* **heed'fulness**. — *n* **heed'iness**. — *adj* **heed'less**. — *adv* **heed'lessly**. — *n* **heed'lessness**. — *adj* **heed'y** (*Spenser*) heedful, careful. [OE *hēdan*; Du *hoeden*, Ger *hüten*]

heehaw *hē'hö*, *vi* (of a donkey, etc) to bray. — *n* a bray. [Imit]

heel[1] *hēl*, *n* the hind part of the foot below the ankle; the whole foot (*esp* of animals); the part of a shoe, etc that covers or supports the heel; a spur; the hinder part of anything, such as a violin bow; a heel-like bend, as on a golf-club; a knob; the top, bottom or end of a loaf or a cheese; a despicable person, often someone who lets others down (*slang*). — *vt* to execute or perform with the heel; to strike with the heel; to supply with a heel; to arm with a spur, as a fighting cock; to seize by the heels; to tie by the heels; to follow at the heels of; to supply with a weapon, money, etc. — *vi* (of a dog) to follow well; to move one's heels to a dance rhythm; to kick the ball backwards out of the scrum with the heel (*Rugby football*). — *adj* **heeled** provided with a heel, shod; (as **-heeled**) in combination, signifying (of shoes) having a heel of a specified type (as in *high-heeled*), and used *fig* in *well-heeled* comfortably off. — *n* **heel'er** someone who heels, in any sense; a person who follows at heel, such as an unscrupulously faithful follower of a party boss; a dog which herds livestock by following and barking at their heels (*Austr*). — *n* **heel'ing** a heel-piece (*Spenser*); the act of making or attaching a heel. — **heel'-ball** a black waxy composition for blacking the edges of heels and soles of shoes and boots, and for taking brass rubbings, etc; **heel'-piece** a piece or cover for the heel; **heel'-tap** a layer of material in a shoe-heel; a small quantity of liquor left in the glass after drinking. — **Achilles' heel** see under **Achillean**; **at** (or **on** or **upon**) **the heels of** following close behind; **back on one's heels** driven back by an opponent; on the defensive; **bring to heel** to cause or persuade to come to heel; **clap by the heels** see **lay by the heels** below; **come to heel** to come in behind; to obey or follow like a dog; to submit to authority; **cool** or **kick one's heels** to be kept waiting for some time; **dig in one's heels** to behave stubbornly; **down at heel** having the heels of one's shoes trodden down; slovenly; in poor circumstances; **heel and toe** with strict walking pace, as opposed to running. — *vi* to use the heel and toe of one foot to operate both the brake and accelerator pedals, eg when driving a racing car. — **heel in** to cover the roots of (plants, etc) temporarily with earth to keep them moist (also **hele in**); **heel of Achilles** see under **Achillean**; **heels o'er gowdy** (*Scot*) or **heels over head** (*archaic*) upside down; **kick up one's heels** to gambol or frisk; **lay, set** or **clap by the heels** to fetter; to put in confinement; **out at heel** having one's heels showing through holes in the socks or stockings; shabby; **set (one) back on one's heels** to surprise, astonish one; **set by the heels** see **lay by the heels** above; **show a clean pair of heels** to run off; **take to one's heels** to flee; **tread on someone's heels** to come crowding behind; **trip up someone's heels** to trip up or overthrow someone; **turn on** (or **upon**) **one's heel** to turn sharply round, to turn back or away; **two for his heels** (in cribbage) a score for turning up the knave; **under the heel** crushed, ruled over tyrannically; **walk to heel** (of a dog) to walk obediently at the heels of the person in charge of it, under control. [OE *hēla*; Du *hiel*]

heel[2] *hēl*, *vi* to incline, slope; (of a ship) to lean on one side. — *vt* to tilt. [Earlier *heeld*, *hield*; OE *hieldan* to slope; cf Du *hellen*]

heel[3]. Same as **hele**.

heeze *hēz*, (*Scot*) *vt* a form of **hoise**. — *n* a lift; a heave upward. — *n* **heez'ie** a lift.

heft[1] *heft*, *n* heaving (*obs*); retching (*Shakesp*); weight (*US*); the greater part (*archaic*). — *vt* to lift; to feel or judge the weight of. — *adv* **hef'tily**. — *n* **hef'tiness**. — *adj* **heft'y** rather heavy; muscular; sizeable; vigorous; violent; abundant. — *adv* very. **[heave]**

heft[2] and **hefte** (*Spenser*), obsolete forms of **heaved**.

heft[3] *heft* (*Scot*) *vt* to restrain; to retain (milk or urine). [Cf ON *hefta* to bind]

heft[4] *heft*, *n* a number of sheets fastened together; an instalment of a serial publication. [Ger]

heft[5] *heft*. A Scots form of **haft**.

hefty, etc. See under **heft**[1].

Hegelian *hā-gēl'i-ən*, *adj* of or pertaining to Wilhelm Friedrich *Hegel* (1770–1831) or his philosophy. — *n* a follower of Hegel. — *n* **Hegel'ianism**.

hegemony *hi-gem'ən-i*, *n* leadership; preponderant influence, *esp* of one state over others. — *adj* **hegemō'nial**, **hegemon'ic** or **hegemon'ical**. — *n* **hegem'onism**. — *n* **hegem'onist**. [Gr *hēgemoniā*, from *hēgemōn* leader, from *hēgeesthai* to lead]

hegira, **hejira**, **hejra**, **hijra** or **hijrah** *hej'*, *hij'(i)-rə* or *hi-jī'rə*, *n* the flight of Mohammed from Mecca, AD 622, from which is dated the Muslim era; any flight. [Ar *hijrah* flight, from *hajara* to leave]

he-he *hē-hē*, *interj* representing a high-pitched or gleeful laugh. — *n* such a laugh. — *vi* to laugh so. [Imit]

heich-how. See under **heigh**.

heid *hēd*, (*Scot*) *n* a head. [See **head**]

heifer *hef'ər*, *n* a young cow. [OE *hēahfore*, *hēahfru*, *-fre*; literally prob high-goer, from *faran* to go]

heigh *hā* (or *hī*), *interj* a cry of enquiry, encouragement or exultation. — *interj* **heigh'-ho** an exclamation expressive of weariness. — *n* (*Scot* also **heich-how** *hēhh'-how'*) routine; familiar jog-trot. [Imit]

height *hīt*, *n* the condition of being high; degree of highness; distance upwards; angle of elevation; that which is elevated; a hill; a high place; elevation in rank or excellence; utmost degree. — *vt* and *vi* **height'en** to make or become higher; to make or become brighter or more conspicuous, or (*fig*) stronger or more intense; to elate (*obs*). — **height of land** a watershed, *esp* if not a range of hills; **height to paper** (*printing*) the standard height of type, blocks, etc from foot to face (*approx* 0·918 in). [From **highth**, from OE *hīehtho*, *hēahthu*, from *hēah* high]

heil! *hīl*, (*Ger*) *interj* hail!

Heimweh *hīm'vā*, (*Ger*) *n* home-sickness.

heinous *hā'nəs* or sometimes *hē'nəs*, *adj* outrageously wicked, odious, atrocious. — *adv* **hei'nously**. — *n* **hei'nousness**. [OFr *haïnos* (Fr *haineux*), from *haïr* to hate]

heir *ār*, *n* (in law) a person who actually succeeds to property, title, etc on the death of its previous holder; (popularly) a person entitled to succeed when the present possessor dies; a child, *esp* a first-born son; a successor to a position, eg of leadership; inheritor of qualities, or of social conditions, or the past generally. — *vt* (*dialect*) to inherit. — *n* **heir'dom**. — *n* **heir'ess** a female heir; a woman who has succeeded or is likely to succeed to a considerable fortune. — *adj* **heir'less** without an heir. — *n* **heir'ship**. — **heir'-appa'rent** the one by law acknowledged to be heir, no matter who may subsequently be born; a person expected to succeed the leader of a party, etc; **heir'-at-law'** an heir by legal right; **heir'-by-cus'tom** a person whose right as heir is determined by customary modes of descent, such as gavelkind, etc; **heir'loom** any piece of furniture or personal property which descends to the heir-at-law by special custom; any object which is passed down through a family from generation to generation; **heir'-por'tioner** (*Scots law*) a joint-heiress or her representative; **heir'-presump'tive** a person who will be heir if no nearer relative should be born (also *fig*). — **fall heir to** to inherit (also *fig*). [OFr *heir*, from L *hērēs* (vulgar accusative *hērem*) an heir]

Heisenberg (or **Heisenberg's**) **uncertainty principle** *hī'zən-bûrg(z) un-sûr'tən-ti prin'si-pl*, *n* a more formal name for **uncertainty principle** (see under **un-**).

heist *hīst*, (*slang*) *vt* to steal or rob in a heist. — *n* a robbing or theft, *esp* an armed hold-up, or a particularly clever or spectacular theft; a person who robs or steals. — *n* **heist'er**. [Variant of **hoist**]

hejab or **hijab** *hi-jab'* or *he-jäb'*, *n* a covering for a Muslim woman's head and face, sometimes reaching the ground. [Ar and Pers]

hejira or **hejra**. See **hegira**.

Hel *hel*, *n* in Northern mythology, the goddess of the dead, sister of the wolf Fenrir, and daughter of Loki.

helcoid *hel'koid*, *adj* ulcerous. [Gr *helkos* an ulcer]

held *pa t* and *pa p* of **hold**[1].

Heldentenor *held'ən-ten'ər* or *held'ən-te-nör'*, *n* (a man with) a powerful tenor voice, particularly suitable for heroic roles in (*esp* Wagnerian) operas: — *pl* **Heldenten'ors** or **Heldentenöre** (*-te-nø'rə*). [Ger, hero tenor, from *Held* hero]

hele, **heel** or **heal** *hēl*, *vt* (*Spenser*; now *dialect*) to hide, conceal; to cover. — **hele in** (*dialect*; *gardening*) to heel in. [OE *helian* from *hellan* (weak verb) blended with *helan* (strong), both meaning to hide; Ger *hehlen*; L *celāre*; Gr *kalyptein*]

helenium *hə-lē'ni-əm*, *n* any plant of the genus *Helenium*, commonly with yellow or variegated daisy-like flowers. [L, from Gr *helenion*]

heli- *hel-i-*, *combining form* denoting helicopter (as in **hel'ibus**; **hel'idrome**; **hel'iman**; **hel'ipilot**, etc). — *adj* **hel'iborne**. — *n* **hel'icopter** (Gr *pteron* wing) a flying-machine sustained by rotating blades revolving on a vertical axis above the machine. — *vt* to take or carry by helicopter. — *n* **hel'ideck** a landing deck for helicopters on a ship, drilling platform, etc. — *n* **hel'ipad** a landing-place for a helicopter. — *n* **hel'iport** the equivalent of an aerodrome for helicopters, *usu* for commercial services. — *n* **hel'iscoop** a net let down from a helicopter to rescue people in difficulty. — *n* **heli-ski'er**. — *n* **heli-ski'ing** the use of helicopters to transport skiers to remote slopes; a form of extreme skiing (qv) in which the skier is dropped by helicopter at the top of a mountain, and skis down to the treeline. — *n* **hel'istop** a landing-place for a helicopter. [Gr *helix*, *-ikos* screw]

heliac *hē'li-ak* or **heliacal** *hē-lī'ək-əl*, *adj* solar; coincident with that of the sun, or as nearly as could be observed. — *adv* **helī'acally**. — **heliacal rising** the emergence of a star from the light of the sun; **heliacal setting** its disappearance in it. [Gr *hēliakos*, from *hēlios* the sun]

Helianthemum *hē-li-anth'ə-məm*, *n* the rock-rose genus. [Gr *hēlios* sun, and *anthemon* flower]

Helianthus *hē-li-an'thəs*, *n* the sunflower genus. [Gr *hēlios* sun, and *anthos* flower]

heliborne. See under **heli-**.

helical, etc, **helices**. See under **helix**.

Helichrysum *he-li-krī'zəm*, *n* a genus of composite plants, the flowers of which keep their colour and shape when dried; (without *cap*) a plant of this genus. [Gr *helix* spiral, and *chrysos* gold]

Helicidae, **helicograph**, **helicoid**, etc. See under **helix**.

helicon *hel'i-kon*, *n* a bass tuba. [Poss from Gr *helix* spiral]

Heliconian *hel-i-kō'ni-ən*, *adj* pertaining to *Helicon* (Gr *Helikōn*), a mountain-range in Boeotia, favourite seat of the Muses, described as a fountain by some poets.

helicopter. See under **heli-**.

helictite *hel'ik-tīt*, *n* a twisted, branching stalactite. [Gr *heliktos* twisted, and **stalactite**]

helideck. See under **heli-**.

helio- *hē'li-ō-*, *hē-li-o'-* or *hē-li-ə-*, *combining form* denoting sun. — *adj* **heliocentric** (*-sen'trik*; Gr *kentron* centre; *astron*) having the sun as centre. — *adv* **heliocen'trically**. — *n* **he'liochrome** (*-krōm*; Gr *chrōma* colour) a photograph in natural colours. — *adj* **heliochrō'mic**. — *n* **he'liochrōmy**. — *n* **he'liograph** (Gr *graphē* a drawing) an apparatus for signalling by flashing the sun's rays; an engraving obtained photographically; an apparatus for photographing the sun; an instrument for measuring intensity of sunlight. — *vt* and *vi* to communicate by heliograph. — *n* **heliog'rapher**. — *adj* **heliograph'ic** or **heliograph'ical**. — *adv* **heliograph'ically**. — *n* **heliog'raphy**. — *n* **heliogravure** (*-grəv-ūr'* or *-grāv'yər*; Fr *héliogravure*) photo-engraving. — *n* **heliol'ater** a sun-worshipper. — *adj* **heliol'atrous**. — *n* **heliol'atry** (Gr *latreiā* worship) sun-worship. — *n* **heliol'ogy** the science of the sun. — *n* **heliom'eter** an instrument for measuring angular distances, eg the sun's diameter. — *adj* **heliomet'ric** or **heliomet'rical**. — *adj* **helioph'ilous** (Gr *phileein* to love) fond of the sun. — *adj* **heliopho'bic** (Gr *phobos* fear) fearing or shunning sunlight. — *n* **he'liophyte** (Gr *phyton* a plant) a plant that can live in full exposure to sunlight. — *n* **heliosciophyte** (*hē-li-ō-sī'ō-fīt*; Gr *skiā* shadow) a plant that can live in shade but does better in the sun. — *n* **he'lioscope** (*-skōp*; Gr *skopeein* to look at) an apparatus for observing the sun without injury to the eye. — *adj* **helioscopic** (*-skop'ik*). — *n* **heliō'sis** (Gr *hēliōsis*) (over-)exposure to the sun; the spotting of leaves by raindrops, or by greenhouse glass flaws, etc acting as burning-glasses. — *n* **he'liostat** (Gr *statos* fixed) an instrument on the principle of the coelostat by means of which a beam of sunlight is reflected in an invariable direction, for study of the sun or for signalling. — *n* **heliotax'is** (Gr *taxis* arrangement) response of an organism to the stimulus of the sun's rays. — *n* **heliother'apy** (Gr *therapeiā* healing) medical treatment by exposure to the sun's rays. — *n* **heliotrope** (*hē'li-ō-trōp* or *hel'i-ō-trōp*; Gr *hēliotropion*) any plant of the genus *Heliotropium* of the borage family, many species with fragrant flowers, *esp* the *Peruvian heliotrope*, with small fragrant lilac-blue flowers; the colour of its flowers; a kind of perfume imitating that of the flower; a bloodstone (*mining*); a surveyor's heliograph. — *adj* **heliotropic** (*-trop'ik*) or **heliotrop'ical**. — *adv* **heliotrop'ically**. — *n* **heliot'ropin** piperonal. — *n* **heliotropism** (*-ot'rə-pizm*) or **heliot'ropy** the tendency of stem and leaves to bend towards (*positive heliotropism*), and roots from (*negative heliotropism*), the light. — *n* **he'liotype** (Gr *typos* impression) a photograph by heliotypy. — *adj* **heliotypic** (*-tip'ik*). — *n* **he'liotypy** (*-tī-pi*) a photo-mechanical process in which the gelatine relief is itself used to print from. — *n pl* **Heliozō'a** (Gr *zōion* an animal) sun-animalcules, an order of Protozoa, spherical with radiating processes of living matter. — *adj* and *n* **heliozō'an**. — *adj* **heliozō'ic**. [Gr *hēlios* the sun]

heliodor *hel'i-ə-dōr* or *-dör*, *n* a variety of clear yellow beryl occurring in SW Africa. [Ger]

heliograph, etc. See under **helio-**.

helipad, **heliscoop**, **heliskiing**. See under **heli-**.

helispheric, **helispherical**. See under **helix**.

helistop. See under **heli-**.

helium *hē'li-əm*, *n* an element (symbol **He**; atomic no 2), a very light inert gas, discovered (1868) by Lockyer in the sun's atmosphere, isolated (1895) by Ramsay from cleveite, and found in certain natural gases. — **helium speech** distorted speech such as occurs in a helium atmosphere. — **liquid helium** helium in liquid form (below 4·22K), which has remarkable qualities, undergoing a striking change at 2·19K (see **superfluidity**). [Gr *hēlios* sun]

helix *hē'liks*, *n* a screw-shaped coil; a curve on a developable surface (*esp* a right circular cylinder) which becomes a straight line when the surface is unrolled into a plane — distinguished from a *spiral*, which is a plane curve (*math*); the rim of the ear (*anatom*); a small volute or twist in the capital of a Corinthian column (*archit*); a screw-propeller; (with *cap*; *zool*) a genus of molluscs including the best-known land-snails; one of the genus: — *pl* **hē'lixes** or **helices** (*hel'i-sēz*). — *adj* **helical** (*hel'ik-əl*). — *adv* **hel'ically**. — *n pl* **Helicidae** (*-is'i-dē*) a large family of terrestrial, air-breathing gasteropods, including the common snails. — *n* **hel'icograph** a drawing instrument for describing spirals on a plane. — *adj* **hel'icoid** or **hel'icoidal** like a helix, screw-shaped. — *adj* **helispher'ic** or **helispher'ical** loxodromic. — **helicoid cyme** a bostryx. [Gr *helix* a spiral, from *helissein* to turn round]

Hell *hel*, *n* the place of the dead in general; the place or state of punishment of the wicked after death; the abode of evil spirits; the powers of Hell; (the following meanings without *cap*) any place of vice or misery; a place of turmoil; (a state of) supreme misery or discomfort; anything causing misery, pain or destruction; ruin, havoc; commotion, uproar; severe censure or chastisement; used in various colloq phrases expressing displeasure, emphasis, etc (as in *what in hell?*, *get the hell out of here*, *I wish to hell he'd go away*); a gambling-house; a space under a tailor's board, or other receptacle for waste; the den in certain games. — *interj* (*colloq*) expressing displeasure or used for mildly shocking effect. — *vi* to live or act in a wild or dissolute fashion (usu with *around*). — *n* **hell'er** an obstreperous troublesome person. — *n* **hellion** (*hel'yən*) a troublesome, mischievous child, or other troublesome person (*esp US*; *colloq*; poss related to **hallion** qv); someone given to diabolical conduct. — *adj* **hell'ish** pertaining to or like hell; very bad, severe, etc; often used to express displeasure (*colloq*). — *adv* **hell'ish** or **hell'ishly** in the manner of hell; often used intensively (*colloq*). — *n* **hell'ishness**. — *adj* (*colloq*) **hell'ova** or **hell'uva** hell of a (see below). — *adv* very. — *adj* and *adv* **hell'ward** towards hell. — *adv* **hell'wards**. — **hell'bender** a large American salamander; a reckless or debauched person. — *adj* **hell'-bent** (with *on*) recklessly determined. — *adv* with reckless determination. — *adj* **hell'-black** (*Shakesp*) black as hell. — *adj* **hell'-born** born in hell; of hellish origin. — **hell'-box** a receptacle for broken type. — *adj* **hell'-bred**. — **hell'-broth** (*Shakesp*) a concoction boiled up for malignant purposes; **hell'-cat** a malignant hag; a violent-tempered woman; **hell'-fire** or **hell'fire** the fire of hell; punishment in hell; **hell'-gate** the entrance into hell. — *adj* **hell'-hated** (*Shakesp*) hated or abhorred as hell. — **hell'-hole** the pit of hell; an evil, frightening place; **hell'hound** a hound of hell; an agent of hell; **hell'-kite** (*Shakesp*) a kite of infernal breed; **hell's angel** (often with *cap*) a member of any gang of motorcyclists who indulge in violent or antisocial behaviour. — *interj* (*colloq*) **hell's bells**, **teeth**, etc expressions of irritation, surprise, etc. — (The following phrases all *colloq*) **all hell breaks** (or **is let**) **loose** there is chaos or uproar; **as hell** absolutely; very; **beat**, **kick**, **knock**, etc (**the**) **hell out of** to beat, etc severely; **come hell or high water** no matter what difficulties may be encountered; **for the hell of it** for fun or adventure; **give someone hell** to punish, castigate or rebuke someone severely; to cause someone pain or misery; **hell for leather** at a furious pace; **hell of a** great, terrific, very, as in *at a hell of a speed*, *a hell of a row*; **hell to pay** serious trouble, unpleasant consequences; **like hell** very much, very hard, very fast, etc; (also **the hell** or **hell**) used to express strong disagreement or refusal (as in *like hell I will!*, *the hell I will!*, *will I hell!*); **not have a cat in hell's chance** see under **cat**[1]; **not have a hope in hell** to have no hope at all; **play hell with** see under **play**; **raise hell** see under **raise**[1]; **to hell with** an expression of angry disagreement with or intention to ignore, etc (someone or something); **what the hell** it does not matter, who cares? [OE *hel*, *hell*; ON *hel*, Ger *Hölle*; cf **Hel**]

hell[1] *hel*, *vt* obs form of **hele**. — *n* (*dialect*) **hell'ier** a slater; a tiler; a thatcher. [See **hele**]

hell[2]. See **Hell**.

he'll *hēl*, contraction for **he will** and **he shall**.

Helladic *hel-ad'ik*, *adj* Greek; of the Greek mainland Bronze Age, answering roughly to Minoan. [Gr *Helladikos* Greek, from *Hellas* Greece]

hellbender. See under **Hell**.

hellebore *hel'i-bör*, *n* any plant of the genus *Helleborus*, of the buttercup family (such as *black hellebore* or Christmas rose, *stinking hellebore*, *green hellebore*); any plant of the genus *Veratrum* of the lily family (*American*, *false*, or *white hellebore*, known also as Indian poke or itchweed); the winter aconite (*winter hellebore*); the rhizome and roots of these prepared as a drug. — *n* **hell'eborine** (*-īn* or *-in*) an orchid of the genus Epipactis. [Gr *helleboros*]

Hellene *hel'ēn*, *n* a Greek. — *adj* **Hellēn'ic** (or *-en'*) Greek. — *n* **Hell'enism** a Greek idiom; the Greek spirit; Greek nationality; conformity to Greek ways, *esp* in language. — *n* **Hell'enist** someone skilled in the Greek language; a person who adopted Greek ways and language, *esp* a Jew. — *adj* **Hellenist'ic** or **Hellenist'ical** pertaining to the Hellenists; pertaining to the Greeks, the Greek language and Greek culture, affected by foreign influences after the time of Alexander. — *adv* **Hellenist'ically**. — *vi* **hell'enize** or **-ise** (*-in-īz*; often with *cap*) to conform, or tend to conform, to Greek usage. — *vt* to make Greek. [Gr *Hellēn* a Greek; also the son of Deucalion]

heller[1] *hel'ər*, *n* a small coin probably first made at *Hall* in Swabia, formerly used in Austria (worth a hundredth part of a crown) and Germany (worth half a pfennig), and still in use in Czechoslovakia (see **haler**).

heller[2]. See under **Hell**.

hellgrammite or **hellgramite** *hel'grə-mīt*, *n* a large American neuropterous larva, used as bait by bass-fishers. [Origin unknown]

hellicat *hel'i-kat*, (*Scot*) *adj* giddy-headed; flighty. — *n* a wicked creature. [Origin obscure]

hellier. See under **hell**[1].

hellion, hellish, etc, **hell-kite**. See under **Hell**.

hello. See **hallo**.

hellova, helluva, hellward, etc. See under **Hell**.

helm[1] *helm*, *n* steering apparatus. — *vt* to direct, steer. — *adj* **helm'less**. — **helms'man** a steersman. [OE *helma*; ON *hjālm* a rudder, Ger *Helm* a handle]

helm[2]. See under **helmet**.

helmet *hel'mit*, or (*archaic* or *poetic*) **helm**, *n* a covering of armour for the head; any similar protective covering for the head; anything resembling a helmet, such as a cloud on a mountain top, the top of a guinea-fowl's head, the hooded upper lip of certain flowers. — *adj* **hel'meted** or (*archaic* or *poetic*) **helmed**. — **hel'met-shell** a gasteropod of the genus Cassis, having a thick heavy shell with bold ridges. [OE *helm*; Ger *Helm*; cf **hele**]

helminth *hel'minth*, *n* a worm. — *n* **helminthī'asis** infestation with worms. — *adj* **helmin'thic**. — *adj* **helmin'thoid** worm-shaped. — *adj* **helminthologʹic** or **helminthologʹical**. — *n* **helminthol'ogist**. — *n* **helminthol'ogy** the study of worms, *esp* parasitic ones. — *adj* **helminth'ous** infested with worms. [Gr *helmins*, *-inthos* a worm]

Helodea. Same as **Elodea**.

helot *hel'ət*, *n* one of a class of serfs among the ancient Spartans, deliberately humiliated and liable to massacre (*hist*); a serf (*hist*); a plant or animal living symbiotically with another in a subject relationship (*biol*). — *n* **hel'otage** the state of a helot. — *n* **hel'otism**. — *n* **hel'otry** the whole body of the helots; any class of slaves. [Gr *Heilōtēs*, also *Heilōs*, *-ōtos*]

help *help*, *vt* to contribute towards the success of, aid or assist; to give means for doing anything; to relieve the wants of; to provide or supply with a portion; to deal out; to remedy; to mitigate; to prevent, to keep from. — *vi* to give assistance; to contribute: — *pa t* **helped** or (*archaic*) **hōlp**; *pa p* **helped** or (*archaic*) **hōlp'en**. — *n* means or strength given to another for a purpose; assistance; relief; someone who assists; a hired servant, *esp* domestic; an employee. — *adj* **help'able**. — *n* **help'er** someone who helps; an assistant; an assistant minister (*archaic*). — *adj* **help'ful** giving help; useful. — *n* **help'fulness**. — *adj* **help'ing** giving help or support. — *n* a portion served at a meal. — *adj* **help'less** without ability to do things for oneself; wanting assistance; destitute of (*obs*); giving no help (*Shakesp*); that cannot be helped (*Spenser*). — *adv* **help'lessly**. — *n* **help'lessness**. — **helper T lymphocyte** or **helper T cell** (*immunol*) a thymus-derived lymphocyte which co-operates with B lymphocytes to enable them to produce an antibody when stimulated by an antigen; **helping hand** assistance; a long-handled device used for reaching and gripping objects that one cannot reach by hand; **help'line** an often free telephone line by means of which people with a particular problem may contact advisers who will help them deal with it; **help'mate** (a modification of **help'meet**, itself formed from the phrase in Genesis 2. 18, 'an help meet for him') a helper, *specif* a wife. — **cannot help** (or **be helped**) cannot avoid (or be avoided); **help off with** to aid in taking off, disposing or getting rid of; **help oneself (to)** to take for oneself without waiting for offer or authority; **help on with** to help to put on; **help out** to eke out; to supplement; to assist; **more than one can help** (illogically but idiomatically) more than is necessary; **so help me (God)** a form of solemn oath; on my word. [OE *helpan*, pa t *healp* (pl *hulpon*), pa p *holpen*; ON *hjālpa*; Ger *helfen*]

helter-skelter *hel'tər-skel'tər*, *adv* in a confused hurry; tumultuously. — *n* a confused medley; disorderly motion; a fairground or playground spiral slide. — *adj* confused. — *n* **hel'ter-skel'teriness**. [Imit]

helve *helv*, *n* the handle of an axe or similar tool. — *vt* to provide with a helve. — **helve'-hammer** a tilt-hammer. [OE *helfe* (*hielfe*) a handle]

Helvetic *hel-vet'ik* or **Helvetian** *hel-vē'shən*, *adj* Swiss. — *n* **helvē'tium** a superseded name for astatine. — **Helvetic Confessions** two confessions of faith drawn up by the Swiss theologians in 1536 and 1566. [L *Helvētia* Switzerland]

hem[1] *hem*, *n* an edge or border; a border doubled down and sewed. — *vt* to form a hem on; to edge: — *pr p* **hemm'ing**; *pa t* and *pa p* **hemmed**. — **hem'-line** the height or level of the hem of a dress, skirt, etc; **hem'-stitch** the ornamental finishing of the inner side of a hem, made by pulling out several threads adjoining it and drawing together in groups the cross-threads by successive stitches. — *vt* to embroider with such stitches. — **hem in** to surround. [OE *hemm* a border]

hem[2] *hem* or *hm*, *n* and *interj* a sort of half-cough to draw attention. — *vi* to utter this sound: — *pr p* **hemm'ing**; *pa t* and *pa p* **hemmed**. [Sound of clearing the throat]

hem[3] *əm* or *həm*, (*obs*) them; to them. [See **'em**]

hem[4]. See **haem** under **haem-**.

hem-. See under **haem-**.

hemal. See **haemal** under **haem-**.

he-man. See under **he**.

hemat- and **hemato-**. See under **haem-**.

heme[1] *hēm*, (*Spenser*) *adv*. Same as **home**.

heme[2]. See **haem** under **haem-**.

hemeralopia *hem-ər-ə-lō'pi-ə*, *n* day-blindness; vision requiring dim light; sometimes misapplied to night-blindness. [Gr *hēmerā* day, *alaos* blind, and *ōps* eye]

Hemerobaptist *hem-ər-ō-bap'tist*, *n* a member of an ancient Jewish sect that practised daily baptism; also a Mandaean. [Gr *hēmerā* day, and *baptistēs* a baptizer]

Hemerocallis *hem-ər-ō-kal'is*, *n* a day-lily. [Gr *hēmerokalles*, from *hēmerā* day, and *kallos* beauty]

hemi- *hem'i-*, *combining form* used to denote half. — *n* **hemial'gia** (Gr *algos* pain) pain confined to one side of the body. — *n* **hemianops'ia** (Gr *an-*, privative, and *opsis* sight) blindness in half of the field of vision. — Also **hemianō'pia**, **hemiō'pia** or **hemiop'sia**. — *adj* **hemianop'tic** or **hemiop'ic**. — *n* **hemicellulose** (*-sel'ū-lōs*) a type of polysaccharide, found in plant cell walls, which can be more easily broken down than cellulose. — *n pl* **Hemichordata** (*-kör-dā'tə*) or **Hemichorda** (*-kör'də*) a group of wormlike marine animals with rudimentary notochord, including Balanoglossus, believed by many to represent the ancestors of the vertebrates. — *n* **hemicrania** (*-krā'ni-ə*; Ger *hēmikrāniā*, from *krānion* skull, head) headache confined to one side. — *adj* **hemicrys'talline** (*petrology*) consisting of crystals in a glassy or partly glassy groundmass. — *n* **hem'icycle** (Gr *kyklos* wheel) a semicircle; a semicircular structure. — *adj* **hemicy'clic** (*bot*) having some parts in whorls, some in spirals. — *n* **hemidemisem'iquaver** (*music*) a note equal in time to half a demisemiquaver. — *n* **hemihē'drism** or **hemihē'dry** (*-dri*; Gr *hedrā* a seat) a property of crystals of being **hemihē'dral**, or having half the number of symmetrically arranged planes occurring on a holohedron. — *n* **hemihē'dron**. — *adj* **hemimorph'ic** (Gr *morphē* form) having a polar axis, dissimilar at the two ends. — *n* **hemimorph'ism**. — *n* **hemimorph'ite** the mineral electric calamine, hydrous zinc silicate, which forms crystals whose ends are different in form and pyroelectric property. — *n* **hemiō'lia** or **hemiō'la** (Gr *hēmiolios* half as much again, from *holos* whole) (in medieval music) a perfect fifth; also, a triplet. — *adj* **hemiolic** (*-ol'*) in or based on the ratio of 3 to 2, as the paeonic foot. — *n* **hemionus** (*hi-mī'on-əs*) or **hemione** (*hem'i-ōn*; Gr *hēmionos* mule, from *onos* an ass) an Asiatic wild ass, the kiang or the dziggetai. — *n* **hemipar'asite** an organism that is partly parasitic, partly independent; a saprophyte capable of living parasitically. — *adj* **hemiparasit'ic**. — *adv* **hemiparasit'ically**. — *n* **hemiplegia** (*-plē'ji-ə* or *-gi-ə*; Gr *plēgē* a blow) paralysis of one side only. — *adj* **hemiplegic** (*-plej'* or *-plēj'*). — Also *n*. — *n pl* **Hemip'tera** (Gr *pteron* a wing) an order of insects, variously defined, with wings (when present) often half leathery, half membranous, ie the bugs, cicadas, greenfly, cochineal insect, etc. — *adj* **hemip'teral**, **hemip'teran** or **hemip'terous**. — *n* **hem'ispace** the area to one side, either left or right, of the body. — *n* **hem'isphere** (Gr *hēmisphairion*, from *sphaira* a sphere) a half-sphere divided by a plane through the centre; half of the globe or a map of it; one of the two divisions of the cerebrum. — *adj* **hemispher'ic** or **hemispher'ical**. — *n* **hemisphē'roid** the half of a spheroid. — *adj* **hemisphēroi'dal**. — *n* **hemistich** (*hem'i-stik*; Gr *hēmistichion*, from *stichos* a line) one of the two divisions of a line of verse; half a line, an incomplete or unfinished line; an epodic line or refrain. — *adj* **hem'istichal** (or *-is'*). — *n* **hem'itrope** (Gr *tropos* a turn) a form of twin crystal in which one twin is as if rotated through two right angles from the position of the other. — *adj* **hem'itrope**, **hemitropal** (*hem-it'rə-pl*), **hemitropic** (*-trop'*) or **hemit'ropous**. — *adj* **hemizy'gous** (see **zygote**) having only one representative of a gene or chromosome, as male mammals, which have only one X-chromosome. — **Eastern and Western hemispheres** the eastern and western halves of the terrestrial globe, the former traditionally including Europe, Asia and Africa and the latter, the Americas; **Northern and Southern hemispheres** the northern and southern halves of the terrestrial globe divided by the equator. [Gr *hēmi-* half]

hemina *hi-mī'nə*, (*obs*) *n* a measure for liquids, about half a pint; a measure for corn, of varying amount. [L, from Gr *hēmina*, from *hēmi-* half]

hemlock *hem'lok*, *n* a poisonous spotted umbelliferous plant (*Conium maculatum*); the poison obtained from it; extended to other umbelliferous plants, eg water hemlock (Cicuta); a N American tree (hemlock spruce or Tsuga) whose branches are fancied to resemble hemlock leaves. [OE *hymlīce* (Kentish *hemlīc*)]

hemo-. See **haemo-** under **haem-**.

hemp *hemp*, *n* a plant (*Cannabis sativa*), classified by some as belonging to the mulberry family, *Moraceae*, but by many now placed in a separate family, *Cannabinaceae*, yielding a coarse fibre, a narcotic drug, and an oil; the fibre itself; the drug; a similar fibre derived from various other plants (eg *Manila*, *sisal*, *sunn hemp*). — *adj* **hemp'en** made of hemp; pertaining to the hangman's noose or hanging (*archaic*). — *adj* **hemp'y** like hemp; roguish; romping. — *n* (*Scot*) a rogue; a romp; a tomboy. — **hemp'-ag'rimony** a composite plant (*Eupatorium cannabinum*) with hemp-like leaves; **hempen caudle** see under **caudle**; **hempen widow** the widow of a man who has been hanged; **hemp'-nettle** a coarse bristly labiate weed (*Galeopsis*); **hemp'-palm** a palmetto (yielding fibre); **hemp'-seed** the oil-yielding seed of hemp, a bird's food; gallows-bird (*Shakesp*). [OE *henep*, *hænep*; cf **cannabis**]

hen *hen*, *n* a female bird; a female domestic fowl; applied (loosely) to any domestic fowl; the female of certain fishes and crustaceans; (facetiously, disrespectfully, or endearingly) a woman or girl; a faint-hearted person. — *vi* (*Scot*) to lose courage or resolution; to balk. — *vt* (*Scot*) to challenge to an act of daring. — *adj* female; composed of women. — *n* **henn'er** (*Scot*) a challenge to an act of daring. — *n* **henn'ery** a place where fowls are kept. — *n* **henn'y** a hen-like cock. — *adj* hen-like. — **hen'-and-chick'ens** a name for various plants, *esp* a garden daisy with small heads surrounding the main head; **hen'bane** a poisonous plant (*Hyoscyamus niger*) of the nightshade family; **hen'-bit** the ivy-leaved speedwell; a species of dead-nettle; **hen'-coop** a coop for a hen; **hen'-court** an enclosure for fowls; **hen'-driver** a hen-harrier; **hen'-flesh** gooseflesh; **hen'-harrier** a bird of prey, the common harrier. — *adj* **hen'-hearted** faint-hearted; timid. — **hen'-house** a house for fowls; **hen'-hussy** a man who meddles with women's affairs; **hen'-pad(d)le** or **hen-paidle** see under **paddle**[2]; **hen'-party** (*colloq*) a gathering of women only. — *vt* **hen'peck** (of a wife) to domineer over (her husband). — Also *n*. — *adj* **hen'pecked**. — **henpeck'ery**; **hen'-pen** (*Scot*) manure from a hen-house; **hen'-roost** a roosting-place for fowls; **hen'-run** an enclosure for fowls. — *adj* **hen'-toed'** with toes turned in. — **hen'-wife** a woman in charge of poultry. — *adj* **hen'-witted** brainless, silly. — **hen on a hot girdle** (chiefly *Scot*) someone who is in a jumpy or nervous state. [OE *henn*, fem of *hana* a cock; Ger *Henne* (*Hahn* cock)]

hence *hens*, (*formal* or *archaic*) *adv* from this place; from this time onward; in the future; from this cause or reason; from this origin. — *interj* away!, begone! — *adv* **hence'forth** or **hencefor'ward** from this time forth or forward. [ME *hennes*, formed with genitive ending from *henne*, from OE *heonan*, from the base of **he**; Ger *hinnen*, *hin* hence: so L *hinc* hence, from *hīc* this]

henchman *hench'mən* or *hensh'mən*, *n* a servant; a page; a right-hand man; an active political partisan, *esp* from self-interest; a thick-and-thin supporter: — *pl* **hench'-men**. — Also **hench'person**; (*fem*) **hench'woman**: — *pl* **hench'women**. [OE *hengest* a horse (Ger *Hengst*), and *man*; not connected with **haunch**]

hend[1] *hend*, (*obs*) *adj* convenient; skilful; gracious; courteous. [Appar OE *gehende* handy, from *hand*]

hend[2] *hend*, (*Spenser*) *vt* to seize, to grasp. [OE *gehendan* or ON *henda*; cf **hand**]

hendecagon *hen-dek'ə-gon*, *n* a plane figure of eleven angles and eleven sides. — *adj* **hendecagonal** (*-ag'ən-l*). [Gr *hendeka* eleven, and *gōniā* an angle]

hendecasyllable *hen'dek-ə-sil'ə-bl*, *n* a metrical line of eleven syllables. — *adj* **hendecasyllabic** (*-ab'ik*). [Gr *hendeka* eleven, and *syllabē* a syllable]

hendiadys *hen-dī'ə-dis*, *n* a rhetorical figure in which a notion, normally expressible by an adjective and a noun, is expressed by two nouns joined by *and* or another conjunction, as *clad in cloth and green* for *clad in green cloth*. [Medieval L, from Gr *hen dia dyoin*, literally one by two]

henequen *hen'ə-kən*, *n* a Mexican agave; its leaf-fibre, sisal-hemp, used for cordage. — Also **hen'equin** and **hen'iquin**. [Sp *henequén*, *jeniquén*]

henge[1] *henj*, (*Spenser*) *n* axis. [**hinge**]

henge[2] *henj*, *n* a circular or oval area enclosed by a bank and internal ditch, often containing burial chambers, or a circular, oval or horseshoe-shaped construction of large upright stones or wooden posts. [Back-formation from *Stonehenge*, a famous example, in OE *Stānhengist* hanging stones]

heniquin. See under **henequen**.

henna *hen'ə*, *n* a small Oriental shrub (*Lawsonia*) of the loosestrife family, with fragrant white flowers; a red or reddish-orange pigment made from its leaves, used for dyeing the nails and hair and for skin decoration. — *adj* **hennaed** (*hen'əd*) dyed with henna. [Ar *hinnā'*]

henner, etc. See under **hen**.

hennin *hen'in*, *n* a steeple-hat with a veil hanging from it, worn by French women in the 15c. [Obs Fr]

henny. See under **hen**.

henotheism *hen'ō-thē-izm*, *n* belief in one god, supreme or specially venerated as the god of one's household or tribe, etc, but not the only god — a stage between polytheism and monotheism. — *n* **henothē'ist**. — *adj* **henotheist'ic**. [Gr *heis*, *henos* one, and *theos* god]

henotic *hen-ot'ik*, *adj* tending to unify or reconcile. [Gr *henōtikos*, from *heis*, *henos* one]

henpeck, etc. See under **hen**.

henry *hen'ri*, (*electricity*) *n* the unit of inductance, such that an electromotive force of one volt is induced in a circuit by current variation of one ampere per second: — *pl* **hen'ries** or **hen'rys**. [Joseph *Henry*, American physicist (1797–1878)]

hent *hent*, (*obs*) *vt* to grasp; to take; to snatch away, carry off; to reach: — *pa t* and *pa p* **hent**. — *n* a grasp (*obs*); perhaps a conception, intention, perhaps an opportunity (*Shakesp*). [OE *hentan* to seize]

heortology *hē-ört-ol'ə-ji*, *n* the study of religious feasts. — *adj* **heortological** (*-ə-loj'i-kl*). — *n* **heortol'ogist**. [Gr *heortē* a feast, and *logos* discourse]

hep[1] *hep*, *n*. See under **hip**[2].

hep[2] *hep*, (*slang*) *adj* knowing, informed or well abreast of fashionable knowledge and taste, *esp* in the field of jazz. — **hep'-cat** or **hep'ster** (*slang*) a hipster (qv under **hip**[4]). — **be** (or **get**) **hep to** to be (or become) informed about. [Perh *hep* left (command in drilling), with ideas of being in step]

hepar *hē'pär*, *n* an old name for liver-coloured compounds of sulphur. — *n* **heparin** (*hep'ə-rin'*) a complex substance formed in tissues of liver, lung, etc that delays clotting of blood, used in medicine and surgery. — *n* **hepatec'tomy** excision of the liver. — *adj* **hepatic** (*hi-pat'ik*) pertaining to or acting on the liver; pertaining to liverworts; liver-coloured. — *n* a liverwort; a hepatic medicine. — *n* **Hepat'ica** a genus of plants with three-lobed leaves, once classed as a section of the Anemone genus; the common liverwort *Marchantia polymorpha*; (in *pl*) **Hepat'icae** (*-sē*) liverworts. — *adj* **hepat'ical**. — *adj* **hepaticolog'ical**. — *n* **hepaticol'ogist** a student of liverworts. — *n* **hepaticol'ogy**. — *n* **hep'atite** a variety of barytes with a sulphureous stink. — *n* **hepatī'tis** inflammation of the liver usually referring to **viral hepatitis** which can be divided into: (1) **hepatitis A** which is caused by a virus encountered in contaminated food and drink (also *colloq* **jaundice**); (2) **hepatitis B** or **serum hepatitis** which is caused by a virus introduced by contaminated blood products or hypodermic syringes, etc; (3) **hepatitis Non-A, Non-B** or **Non-A, Non-B hepatitis** which is caused by a virus transmitted in contaminated blood products. All these diseases cause fever, jaundice, and general weakness. — *n* **hepatization** or **-s-** (*-ə-tī-zā'shən*) a liver-like solidification of tissue as of the lungs in pneumonia. — *vt* **hep'atize** or **-ise** to convert into a substance resembling liver; to impregnate with sulphuretted hydrogen (*obs*). — *n* **hepatol'ogist** a specialist in liver diseases. — *n* **hepatol'ogy**. — *n* **hepatomeg'aly** abnormal enlargement of the liver. — *n* **hepatos'copy** divination by inspection of the livers of animals. [Gr *hēpar*, *hēpatos* liver]

hephthemimer *hef-thi-mim'ər*, (*Gr* and *Latin prosody*) *n* seven half-feet. — *adj* **hephthemim'eral** (of a caesura) occurring in the middle of the fourth foot. [Gr *hepta* seven, *hēmi-* half, and *meros* part]

Hepplewhite *hep'l-wīt*, *adj* belonging to a school of graceful furniture design typified by George *Hepplewhite* (died 1786), who favoured the use of curves, *esp* in shield-shaped chair-backs.

hepster. See under **hep**[2].

hept *hept*, (*Spenser*) for **heaped**.

hepta- *hep'tə-* or *hep-ta'-*, *combining form* denoting seven. — *n* **hep'tachlor** (*-klör*) a very toxic pesticide, $C_{10}H_5Cl_7$, which forms the even more toxic **heptachlor epoxide**, $C_{10}H_5Cl_7O$, in the soil and in animal and plant tissue. — *n* **hep'tachord** (Gr *chordē* string) in Greek music, a diatonic series of seven tones, containing five whole steps and one half-step; an instrument with seven strings; an interval of a seventh. — *n* **hep'tad** (Gr *heptas*, *heptados*) a group of seven; an atom, radical or element having a combining power of seven (*chem*). — *adj* **hep'taglot** (Gr *heptaglōttos*, from *glōtta* tongue) in seven languages. — *n* a book in seven languages. — *n* **hep'tagon** (Gr *heptagōnos*, from *gōniā* an angle) a plane figure with seven angles and seven sides. — *adj* **heptag'onal**. — *n pl* **Heptagynia** (*-jin'i-ə*; Gr *gynē* woman, female) in Linnaean classification, an order of plants (in various classes) having seven styles. — *adj* **heptag'ynous**. — *n* **Heptam'eron** (Gr *hēmerā* a day) a book containing the transactions of seven days, *esp* the collection of stories told in seven days bearing the name of Queen Margaret of Navarre (1492–1549). — *adj* **heptam'erous** (Gr *meros* part) having parts in sevens. — *n* **heptam'eter** (Gr *metron* measure) a verse of seven measures or feet. — *n pl* **Heptan'dria** (Gr *anēr*, *andros* a man, male) a Linnaean class of plants having seven stamens. — *adj* **heptan'drous** with seven stamens. — *n* **hep'tane** a hydrocarbon (C_7H_{16}), seventh of the methane series. — *adj* **heptapod'ic**. — *n* **heptap'ody** (Gr *pous*, *podos* foot) a verse of seven feet. — *n* **hep'tarch** or **hep'tarchist** a ruler in a heptarchy. — *adj* **heptar'chic**. — *n* **heptarchy** (*hep'tär-ki*; Gr *archē* sovereignty) a government by seven persons; a country governed by seven; a misleading term for a once supposed system of seven English kingdoms — Wessex, Sussex, Kent, Essex, East Anglia, Mercia, and Northumbria. — *adj* **heptasyllab'ic** seven-syllabled. — *n* **Hep'tateuch** (*-tūk*; Gr *teuchos* instrument, volume) the first seven books of the Old Testament. — *n* **heptath'lon** (Gr *athlon* contest) since 1984, a seven-event contest consisting of 100 metres hurdles, shot-put, javelin, high jump, long jump, 200 metres sprint and 800 metres race at the Olympic games. — *adj* **heptaton'ic** (Gr *tonos* tone; *music*; of a scale) consisting of seven notes. [Gr *hepta* seven]

her[1] *hûr*, *pron*, *genitive* (or *possessive adj*), *dative* and *accusative* of the *pron* **she**; herself (*reflexive*; *poetic* or *dialect*); she (*colloq nominative*). [OE *hire*, genitive and dative sing of *hēo* she]

her[2] *hûr*, (*obs*; *Spenser*) *pron* or *possessive adj* their. [OE *hiera*, *hira*, *heora*, genitive pl of **he**]

her. *abbrev*: heraldry; *heres* (L) heir.

Heraclean or **Heracleian** *her-ə-klē'ən*, *adj* pertaining to *Heracles* (Gr *Hēraklēs*), also known as *Hercules*. — *adj* **Heracli'dan** or **Heraclei'dan** pertaining to the Heracleidae or descendants of Heracles, the aristocracy of Sparta. — *n* **Her'aclid** a person claiming such descent.

Heraclitean or **Heracleitean** *her-ə-klī'shē-ən*, *adj* pertaining to *Heraclitus*, a Greek philosopher of the 5c BC, who held that all things are in a state of flux, continually entering a new state of being.

herald *her'əld*, *n* (in ancient times) an officer who made public proclamations and arranged ceremonies; (in medieval times) an officer who had charge of all the etiquette of chivalry, keeping a register of the genealogies and armorial bearings of the nobles; an officer whose duty is to read proclamations, blazon the arms of the nobility, etc; a proclaimer; a forerunner; a name given to many newspapers; the red-breasted merganser, usually **her'ald-duck**. — *vt* to usher in; to proclaim. — *adj* **heraldic** (*her-* or *hər-al'dik*) of or relating to heralds or heraldry. — *adv* **heral'dically**. — *n* **her'aldry** the art or office of a herald; the science of recording genealogies and blazoning coats of arms. — *n* **her'aldship**. [OFr *herault*; of Gmc origin]

herb *hûrb* (old-fashioned *ûrb*), *n* a plant with no woody stem above ground, distinguished from a tree or shrub; a plant used in medicine; an aromatic plant used in cookery. — *adj* **herbā'ceous** pertaining to, composed of, containing, or of the nature of, herbs; like ordinary foliage leaves; *usu* understood to refer to tall herbs that die down in winter and survive in underground parts (*hortic*). — *n* **herb'age** herbs collectively; herbaceous vegetation covering the ground; right of pasture. — *adj* **herb'aged** covered with grass. — *adj* **herb'al** composed of or relating to herbs; pertaining to the use of plants, eg medicinally. — *n* a book containing descriptions of plants with medicinal properties, *orig* of all plants. — *n* **herb'alism** herbal medicine, the use of (extracts of) roots, seeds, etc for medicinal purposes. — *n* **herb'alist** a person who studies, collects or sells herbs or plants; a person who practises herbalism; an early botanist. — *n* **herb'ar** (*Spenser*) a herb-garden, arbour (qv). — *n* **herbā'rian** a herbalist. — *n* **herbārium** (a room, building, etc for) a classified collection of preserved plants: — *pl* **herbā'riums** or **herbā'ria**. — *n* **herb'ary** a garden of herbs. — *adj* **herbicīd'al**. — *n* **herb'icide** (*-i-sīd*) a substance for killing weeds, etc, *esp* a selective weed-killer. — *n* **herb'ist** a herbalist. — *n pl* **herbiv'ora** (*-ə-rə*) grass-eating animals, *esp* ungulates. — *n* **herb'ivore** (*-vör*). — *adj* **herbiv'orous** eating or living on grass or herbage. — *n* **herbiv'ory**. — *adj* **herb'less**. — *n* **herb'let** or **herb'elet** (*Shakesp*) a small herb. — *n* **herb'orist** a herbalist. — *n* **herborīzā'tion** or **-s-**. — *vi* **herb'orize** or **-ise** to botanize. — *adj* **herb'ose** or **herb'ous** abounding with herbs. — *adj* **herb'y** of or pertaining to herbs. — **herbal tea** see **herb tea** below; **herb'-beer** a substitute for beer made from herbs; **herb-benn'et** (L *herba benedicta* blessed herb) avens; **herb-Chris'topher** baneberry; **herb'-garden**; **herb-(of-)grace'** or **herb-of-repent'ance** the common rue; **herb-Par'is** a tetramerous plant (*Paris quadrifolia*) of the lily family; **herb-Pe'ter** cowslip; **herb-Rob'ert** stinking cranesbill (*Geranium robertianum*), a plant with small reddish-purple flowers; **herb tea** or **herbal tea** a drink made by infusing aromatic herbs; **herb-trin'ity** the pansy. [Fr *herbe*, from L *herba*]

Herbartian *hər-bärt'i-ən*, *adj* of Johann Friedrich *Herbart* (1776–1841), German philosopher and paedagogic psychologist.

hercogamy or **herkogamy** *hər-kog'ə-mi*, (*bot*) *n* the prevention of self-pollination in flowers by the presence of some physical obstacle. — *adj* **hercog'amous**. [Gr *herkos* fence, and *gamos* marriage]

Herculean *hûr-kū-lē'ən* or *-kū'li-ən*, *adj* of or pertaining to *Hercules* (*hûr'kū-lēz*; Greek *Hēraklēs*); (without *cap*) extremely difficult or dangerous, as the twelve labours of Hercules; (without *cap*) of extraordinary strength and size. — **Hercules beetle** a gigantic S American lamellicorn beetle (*Dynastes hercules*), over 6 inches long, with a long horn on the thorax of the male and a smaller one on the head; (loosely) a related species, such as the *Dynastes gideon* of SE Asia; **Hercules' choice** toil and duty chosen in preference to ease and pleasure — from a famous story in Xenophon's *Memorabilia*; **Hercules' club** a stick of great size and weight; a West Indian tree (Xanthoxylum); a kind of gourd; a species of Aralia. — **Pillars of Hercules** two rocks flanking the entrance to the Mediterranean at the Strait of Gibraltar.

Hercynian *hûr-sin'i-ən*, *adj* of or pertaining to the forest-covered mountain region between the Rhine and the Carpathians or the mountain chains running NW and SE between Westphalia and Moravia, of Upper Carboniferous to Cretaceous date. — *n* **her'cynite** black spinel, aluminate of ironic. [L *Hercynia* (*silva*), the Hercynian (forest)]

herd[1] *hûrd*, *n* a collective term for a company of animals, *esp* large animals, or of birds that habitually keep together; a group of domestic animals, *esp* cows or pigs, with or without a guardian; a stock of cattle; the people regarded as a mass, as acting from contagious impulse, or merely in contempt; the rabble. — *vi* to associate (as if) in herds; to live like an animal in a herd. — *vt* to put in a herd; to drive together. — **herd'-book** a pedigree book of cattle or pigs; **herd instinct** the instinct that urges men or animals to act upon contagious impulses or to follow the herd; **herds'man** keeper of a herd. [OE *heord*; Ger *Herde*; cf **herd**[2]]

herd[2] *hûrd*, *n* (*esp* in combination) a keeper of a herd or flock (of a particular animal, as in *goatherd*, *swineherd*, etc). — *vt* to tend; to harbour. — *vi* to act as herd. — *n fem* **herd'ess** (*rare*). — **herd'boy** a boy who acts as shepherd, cowherd, etc; a cowboy; **herd'-groom** (*archaic*) a herdsman; shepherd boy; **herd'man** (*obs*) a herdsman. [OE *hirde*, *hierde*; Ger *Hirte*; cf **herd**[1]]

herden *hûrd'ən*. See under **hards**.

herd grass or **herd's grass** *hûrd*(*z*) *gräs*, (*US*) *n* timothy; redtop. [From John *Herd*, who observed timothy in New Hampshire, 1700]

herdic *hûr'dik*, *n* a low-hung two- or four-wheeled carriage with a back entrance and side seats. [From the inventor, P *Herdic* (1824–88), of Pennsylvania]

herdwick *hûrd'wik*, *n* a grazing ground (*obs*); a breed of Lake District sheep. [**herd**[2] and **wick**[2]]

here *hēr*, *adv* in, at or to this place; in the present life or state; at this point or time. — *interj* calling attention to one's presence, or to what one is going to say. — *adv* **here'about** or **here'abouts** around or near this place; in this area. — *adv* **hereaf'ter** after this, in some future time, life or state. — *n* a future state; the after-life. — *adv* **hereat'** (*archaic*) at or by reason of this. — *adv* **here'away** (*colloq*) hereabout. — *adv* **hereby'** not far off; by this. — *adv* **herefrom'** from this; from this place. — *adv* **herein'** (*formal*) contained in this letter, document, etc; in this respect. — *adv* **hereinaf'ter** (*formal*) afterward in this (document, etc; *opp* of **hereinbefore'**). — *n* **here'ness** the fact of being here. — *adv* **hereof'** (*formal*) of or concerning this. — *adv* **hereon'** (*formal*) on or upon this. — *adv* **hereto'** to this (*formal*); till this time (*Shakesp*); for this object. — *adv* **heretofore'** (*formal*) before this time; formerly. — *adv* **hereund'er** (*formal*) under this; below; following; by the authority of this (document, etc). — *adv* **here'unto** (also *-un'*) (*formal*) to this point or time. — *adv* **hereupon'** on this; immediately after this. — *adv* **herewith'** with this; enclosed with this letter, etc. — **here and there** in this place, and then in that; in various places; thinly; irregularly; **here goes!** an exclamation indicating that the speaker is about to proceed with some proposed act or narration, etc; **here's to** I drink the health of; **here today, gone tomorrow** a comment on the transient, ephemeral nature of things; **here we are** (*colloq*) this is what we are looking for; we have now arrived (at); **here we go again** (*colloq*) the same undesirable situation is recurring; **here you are** (*colloq*) this is what you want; this is something for you; this way; **neither here nor there** of no special importance; not relevant; **the here and now** the present time. [OE *hēr*, from base of *hē* he; Du and Ger *hier*, Swed *här*]

heredity *hi-red'i-ti*, *n* the transmission of recognizable characteristics to descendants; the sum of such characteristics transmitted; heritability. — *n* **hereditabil'ity**. — *adj* **hered'itable** that may be inherited. — *n* **hered'it'ament** (*her-id-*) any property that may pass to an heir. — *n* **heredita'rian** (also **heredita'rianist**) an adherent of **heredita'rianism**, the view that heredity is the major factor in determining human and animal behaviour. — *adv* **hered'itarily**. — *n* **hered'itariness** the quality of being hereditary. — *adj* **hered'itary** descending or coming by inheritance; transmitted to offspring; succeeding by inheritance; according to inheritance. — *n* **hered'itist** a hereditarian. [L *hērēditās*, *-ātis*, from *hērēs*, *-ēdis* an heir]

Hereford *her'i-fərd*, *adj* of a breed of white-faced red cattle, originating in *Hereford*shire. — Also *n*.

herefrom ... to ... **hereon**. See under **here**.

Herero *hə-re'rō* or *he'rə-rō*, *n* a Bantu people of South West Africa; a member of this people; its language: — *pl* **Hereros** or **Hereroes**. — *adj* of or pertaining to the Herero or their language.

heresy *her'i-si*, *n* belief contrary to the authorized teaching of the religious community to which one ostensibly belongs; an opinion opposed to the usual or conventional belief; heterodoxy. — *n* **heresiarch** (*he-rē'zi-ärk*) a leader of a heretical movement. — *n* **heresiog'rapher** a person who writes about heresies. — *n* **heresiog'raphy**. — *n* **heresiol'ogist** a student of, or writer on, heresies. — *n* **heresiol'ogy**. — *n* **heretic** (*her'ə-tik*) the upholder of a heresy; a person whose views are at variance with those of the majority. — *adj* **heretical** (*hi-ret'i-kl*). — *adv* **heret'ically**. — *vt* **heret'icate** to denounce as heretical. — **her'esy-hunt** vexatious pursuit of a supposed heretic; **her'esy-hunter**. [OFr *heresie*, from L *haeresis*, from Gr *hairesis* the act of taking, choice, set of principles, school of thought, from *haireein* to take]

hereto ... to ... **herewith**. See under **here**.

heriot *her'i-ət*, (*hist*) *n* a fine due to the lord of a manor on the death of a tenant — originally their best beast or chattel. — *adj* **her'iotable**. [OE *heregeatu* a military preparation, from *here* an army, and *geatwe* equipment]

herisson *her'i-sən*, *n* a freely revolving beam fitted with spikes, erected for defence (*hist*); a hedgehog (*heraldry*). — *adj* **hérissé** (*her'is-ā* or *ā'rē-sā*; *heraldry*) bristled. [Fr; see **urchin**]

heritable *her'i-tə-bl*, *adj* that may be inherited. — *n* **heritabil'ity**. — *adv* **her'itably**. — *n* **her'itor** a person who inherits; (in Scotland) a landholder obliged to contribute to the upkeep of the parish, *esp* the church: — *fem* **her'itress** or **her'itrix** (*pl* **her'itrixes** or **heritrī'cēs**). — *n* **heritage** (*her'it-ij*) that which is inherited; inherited lot, condition of one's birth; anything transmitted from ancestors or past ages, *esp* historical buildings and the natural environment; the children (of God; *Bible*). — **heritable property** (*Scots law*) real property, as opposed to movable property or chattels; **heritable security** (*Scots law*) same as English mortgage. [OFr (*h*)*eritable*, (*h*)*eritage*, from LL *hērēditāre* to inherit, from *hērēditas*; see **heredity**]

herkogamy. See **hercogamy**.

herl. Same as **harl**[1].

herling or **hirling** *hûr'ling*, (*dialect*) *n* a young sea-trout, a finnock.

herm *hûrm* or **herma** *hûrm'ə*, *n* a head or bust (originally of *Hermes*) on a square base, often double-faced: — *pl* **herms** or **hermae** (*-ē*).

hermandad *ûr-män-däd'*, *n* a confederation of the entire burgher class of Spain for police and judicial purposes, formed in 1282, and formally legalized in 1485. [Sp, brotherhood, from *hermano* brother, from L *germānus*]

hermaphrodite *hûr-maf'rəd-īt*, *n* a human being, animal or plant with the organs of both sexes, whether normally or abnormally; a compound of opposite qualities. — *adj* uniting the characters of both sexes; combining opposite qualities. — *n* **hermaph'rodītism** the union of the two sexes in one body. — *adj* **hermaphrodit'ic** or **hermaphrodit'ical**. — *adv* **hermaphrodit'ically**. — **hermaphrodite brig** a brig square-rigged forward and schooner-rigged aft. [Gr *Hermaphrodītos*, the son of *Hermēs* and *Aphroditē*, who grew together with the nymph Salmacis into one person]

hermeneutic *hûr-mə-nū'tik* or **hermeneutical** *-nū'tik-l*, *adj* interpreting; concerned with interpretation, *esp* of Scripture. — *adv* **hermeneu'tically**. — *n sing* **hermeneu'tics** the science of interpretation, *esp* of Scriptural exegesis; the study of human beings in society (*philos*).

— *n* **hermeneu'tist**. [Gr *hermēneutikos*, from *hermēneus* an interpreter, from *Hermēs*]

Hermes *hûr'mēz*, *n* the herald of the Greek gods, patron of herdsmen, arts, eloquence, and thieves (*Gr mythol*); the Egyptian god Thoth, identified with the Greek Hermes; a herm. [Gr *Hermēs*, identified by the Romans with Mercury]

hermetic *hûr-met'ik* or **hermetical** *-met'ik-l*, *adj* belonging in any way to the beliefs current in the Middle Ages under the name of *Hermes*, the Thrice Great; belonging to magic or alchemy, magical; perfectly closed, completely sealed; obscure, abstruse. — *adv* **hermet'ically**. — *n* **hermetic'ity**. — *n sing* **hermet'ics** the philosophy contained in the **hermetic books**, esoteric science; alchemy. — **hermetically sealed** closed completely; made airtight by melting the glass. [Medieval L *hermēticus*, from *Hermēs Trismegistos* Hermes the thrice-greatest, the Greek name for the Egyptian Thoth, god of science, *esp* alchemy]

hermit *hûr'mit*, *n* a solitary religious ascetic; a person who lives a solitary life; a beadsman; a kind of humming-bird; a hermit-crab. — *n* **her'mitage** a hermit's cell; a retreat, a secluded abode; a secluded place; a wine produced near Valence (Drôme) in France, where there was a supposed hermit's cell. — *n* **her'mitess** a female hermit. — *adj* **hermit'ical**. — **her'mit-crab** a soft-bodied crustacean that inhabits a mollusc shell. [ME *eremite*, through Fr and L from Gr *erēmītēs*, from *erēmos* solitary]

hern[1] *hûrn*. Same as **heron**.

hern[2] *ûrn*, a dialect form for **hers**. [Appar from **her**, on the analogy of **mine**, **thine**]

hernia *hûr'ni-ə*, *n* a protrusion of an organ through the wall of the cavity containing it, *esp* of part of the viscera through the abdominal cavity; a rupture. — *adj* **her'nial**. — *adj* **her'niated**. — *n* **hernior'rhaphy** (Gr *rhaphē* stitching, suture) the surgical repair of a hernia by an operation involving suturing. — *n* **herniot'omy** (Gr *tomē* a cut) a cutting operation for the repair of a hernia. [L]

hernshaw *hûrn'shö*, *n*. See **heronshaw**.

Hero *hē'rō*, *n* acronym for *H*azards of *E*lectro-Magnetic *R*adiation to *O*rdnance, the danger that a missile warhead might explode, due to the accidental triggering of the electrical fuse by some form of electro-magnetic discharge.

hero *hē'rō*, *n* a man of distinguished bravery; any illustrious person; a person reverenced and idealized; the principal male figure, or the one whose life is the thread of the story, in a history, work of fiction, play, film, etc; *orig* a man of superhuman powers, a demigod: — *pl* **hē'roes** (formerly, as in *Spenser*, who never uses the singular, **hērō'ēs**, from which a singular form, **hērō'ē**, was formed). — *adj* **heroic** (*hi-rō'ik*) befitting a hero; of or pertaining to heroes; epic; supremely courageous; using extreme or elaborate means to obtain a desired result, such as the preserving of life; on a superhuman scale, larger-than-life. — *n* a heroic verse; (in *pl*) extravagant phrases, bombast; (in *pl*) unduly bold behaviour. — *adj* **herō'ical**. — *adv* **herō'ically** (or *Milton* **herō'icly**). — *n* **herō'icalness**. — *n* **herō'icness**. — *n* **heroism** (*her'ō-izm*) the qualities of a hero; courage; boldness. — *vt* **hē'rōize** or **-ise** to treat as a hero, make a hero of; to glorify. — *n* **hērō'on** a temple dedicated to a hero; a temple-shaped tomb or monument. — *n* **hē'roship** the state of being a hero. — **heroic age** any semi-mythical period when heroes or demigods were represented as living among men; **heroic couplet** a pair of rhyming lines of heroic verse. — *adj* **herō'i-comic** or **hero'i-comical** consisting of a mixture of heroic and comic; high burlesque. — **heroic poem** an epic; a compromise between epic and romance which flourished in the 16c and 17c; **heroic remedy** treatment that may kill or cure; **heroic size** (in sculpture) larger than life, but less than colossal; **heroic verse** the form of verse in which the exploits of heroes are celebrated (in classical poetry, the hexameter; in English, the iambic pentameter, *esp* in couplets; in French, the alexandrine); **he'ro-worship** the worship of heroes; excessive admiration of great men, or of anybody. — Also *vt*. [Through OFr and L from Gr *hērōs*; poss related to L *vir*, OE *wer* a man, Sans *vīra* a hero]

heroin *her'ō-in*, *n* a derivative of morphine used in medicine and by drug-addicts. [Said to be from Gr *hērōs* a hero, from its effect]

heroine *her'ō-in*, *n* a woman of heroic character, a female hero; a woman admired and idealized; the central female character in a story, play, film, etc. [Fr *héroïne*, from Gr *herōinē*, fem of *hērōs* hero]

heroism, **heroise**, **heroize**. See under **hero**.

heron *her'ən*, *n* a large long-legged, long-necked wading bird, commonly grey or white in colour (Ardea or related genus). — *n* **her'onry** a place where herons breed. [OFr *hairon*, from OHGer *heigir*]

heronshaw, **heronsew** or **hernshaw** *her'ən-*, *hern'-* or *hûrn'-shö* or *-shōō*, *n* a young heron; (*esp dialect*) a heron. [OFr *herounçel*, confounded with **shaw** (wood)]

heroon, **heroship**. See under **hero**.

herpes *hûr'pēz*, *n* a skin disease of various kinds, with spreading clusters of vesicles, or watery blisters, on an inflamed base — *esp herpes simplex* a sexually transmitted disease, and *herpes zoster* or shingles. — *adj* **herpetic** (*-pet'ik*) relating to or resembling herpes; creeping. [Gr *herpēs*, from *herpein* to creep]

Herpestes *hər-pes'tēz*, *n* the ichneumon or mongoose genus. [Gr *herpēstēs*, from *herpein* to creep]

herpetology *hûr-pi-tol'ə-ji*, *n* the study of reptiles and amphibians. — *n* **her'petofauna** reptiles and amphibians. — *adj* **her'petoid** reptile-like. — *adj* **herpetolog'ic** or **herpetolog'ical**. — *adv* **herpetolog'ically**. — *n* **herpetol'ogist**. [Gr *herpeton* a reptile, from *herpein* to creep]

Herr *her*, *n* lord, master, the German term of address equivalent to sir, or (prefixed) Mr: — *pl* **Herr'en**. — *n* **Herrenvolk** (*her'en-fōlk*) literally 'master race', who believe themselves to be fitted and entitled by their superior qualities to rule the world. [Ger]

herring *her'ing*, *n* a small silvery sea-fish (*Clupea harengus*) of great commercial value, found moving in great shoals in northern waters. — *n* **herr'inger** (*-ing-ər*) a man or boat employed in herring fishing. — *adj* **herr'ing-bone** like the spine of a herring, applied to a kind of masonry in which the stones slope in different directions in alternate rows, to a zigzag stitch crossed at the corners, and to a crossed strutting, etc; (in skiing) of a method of climbing a slope, the skis being placed at an angle and leaving a herring-bone-like pattern in the snow. — *vt* to make in herring-bone work; to make or mark with a herring-bone pattern. — *vt* and *vi* to climb (a slope) on skis by herring-bone steps. — **herr'ing-buss** (*hist*; see under **buss**[2]); **herr'ing-fishery**; **herr'ing-gull** a large white gull with black-tipped wings; **herr'ing-pond** (*facetious*) the ocean, *esp* the Atlantic. — **dead as a herring** quite certainly dead — a herring out of water soon dies; **neither fish nor flesh nor good red herring** see under **fish**[1]; **packed like herring (in a barrel)** very closely packed; **red herring** see under **red**[1]. [OE *hǣring*, *hēring*; cf Ger *Hering*]

Herrnhuter *hûrn'hōōt-ər*, *n* one of the Moravians or United Brethren, so called from their settlement in 1722 at *Herrnhut* in Saxony.

herry[1]. See **hery**.

herry[2] *her'i*, (*Scot*) *vt* to harry. — *n* **herr'iment** or **herr'yment** spoliation; plunder. [**harry**]

hers *hûrz*, *pron* possessive of **she** (used without a noun).

hersall *hûr'səl*, (*Spenser*) *n* rehearsal.

herse *hûrs*, (*obs*) *n* a harrow; a spiked portcullis; a form of battle-array; a hearse in various senses. — *adj* **hersed** arranged in harrow form. [**hearse**]

herseems, **herseemed**. See under **seem**.

herself *hûr-self'*, *pron* an emphatic form for **she** or **her**; in her real character; the reflexive form of **her**; predicatively (or *n*) a woman when in command of her faculties, sane, in good form or normal condition, or

(*Scot*) alone, by herself; the mistress of a house, owner of an estate, etc (*Scot*). [See **her** and **self**]

hership *hûr'ship*, (*Scot*) *n* plundering; plunder. [OE *here* army, or *hergan* to harry; cf ON *herskapr* warfare]

Herts *härts*, *abbrev*: Hertfordshire.

hertz *hûrts*, *n* the unit of frequency, that of a periodic phenomenon of which the periodic time is one second — sometimes called **cycle per second** in the UK. — *adj* **Hertz'ian** connected with Heinrich *Hertz* (see below). — **Hertzian waves** electromagnetic waves used in communicating information through space. [After Heinrich *Hertz* (1857–94), German physicist]

Hertzsprung–Russell diagram *hûrts'proŏng rus'l dī'ə-gram*, (*astron*) *n* a graphical representation of the correlation between spectral type and luminosity for a sample of stars. [E *Hertzsprung* (1873–1967) Danish astronomer, and H Norris *Russell* (1877–1957) American astronomer]

hery, **herye** or **herry** *her'i*, (*Spenser*) *vt* to praise, to regard as holy. [OE *herian* to praise]

hes *hēz*, *n pl* plural of **he**.

he's *hēz*, a contraction of **he is** or **he has**.

Heshvan. See **Hesvan**.

hesitate *hez'i-tāt*, *vi* to hold back or delay in making a decision; to be in doubt; to stammer. — *vt* (*rare*) to express or utter with hesitation. — *n* **hes'itance**, **hes'itancy** or **hesitā'tion** wavering; doubt; stammering; delay. — *adj* **hes'itant** hesitating. — *adv* **hes'itantly**. — *adv* **hes'itātingly**. — *adj* **hes'itātive** showing hesitation. — *n* **hes'itātor**. — *adj* **hes'itātory** hesitating. — **hesitā'tion-form** (*linguistics*) a sound used in speech when stammering or pausing, such as *er*, *eh* or *um*; **hesitation waltz** a kind of waltz into which a pause and gliding step are introduced at intervals. [L *haesitāre*, *-ātum*, frequentative of *haerēre*, *haesum* to stick]

hesp *hesp*, a Scots form of **hasp**.

Hesper *hes'pər* or **Hesperus** *-əs*, *n* Venus as the evening star. — *adj* **Hesperian** (*-pē'ri-ən*) western (*poetic*); Italian (from the Greek point of view); Spanish (from the Roman); of the Hesperides; of the skipper butterflies. — *n* a westerner; a skipper butterfly. — *n* **hes'perid** (*-pər-id*) one of the Hesperides; a skipper butterfly. — *n pl* **Hesperides** (*-per'i-dēz*) the sisters who guarded in their delightful gardens in the west the golden apples which Hera, on her marriage with Zeus, had received from Gaea (*Gr mythol*). — *n* **hesperid'ium** (*bot*) a fruit of the orange type. — *n pl* **Hesperiidae** (*-ī'i-dē*) a family of moth-like butterflies, the skippers. — *n* **Hes'peris** the dame's-violet genus of Cruciferae, generally fragrant in the evening. [Gr *hesperos* evening, western]

Hessian *hes'i-ən*, sometimes *hesh'(i)ən*, *adj* of or pertaining to *Hesse* in Germany; mercenary (from the use of German mercenaries by the British Army in the American War of Independence) (*US*). — *n* a native or citizen of Hesse; (without *cap*) a cloth made of jute; short for **Hessian boot**, a kind of long boot first worn by Hessian troops. — **Hessian fly** a midge whose larva attacks wheat stems in America, once believed to have been introduced in straw for the Hessian troops.

hessonite. An amended form of **essonite**.

hest *hest*, (*archaic*) *n* behest, command; vow. — Also (*Spenser*) **heast** or **heaste** (*hēst*). [OE *hǣs* a command, from *hātan* to command]

hesternal *hes-tûr'nəl*, *adj* of yesterday. [L *hesternus*]

Hesvan *hes'vän* or **Heshvan** *hesh'-*, or *hhes(h)'-*, *n* the second month of the Jewish civil year and the eighth month of the Jewish ecclesiastical year. — Also **Chesh'van** or **Ches'van**. [Heb]

Hesychast *hes'i-kast*, *n* a member of a 14c quietist sect of the Greek Church. — *n* **Hes'ychasm** their doctrines and practice. — *adj* **Hesychas'tic** keeping silence. [Gr *hēsychastēs*, from *hēsychos* quiet]

het[1] *het*, *adj* a Scots form of **hot**[1]. [OE *hāt*]

het[2] *het*, (*UK* and *NAm dialect*) *pa p* for **heated**. — **het up** agitated.

het[3] *het*, (*slang*) *n* a heterosexual. — Also *adj*.

hetaera *hi-tē'rə* or **hetaira** *he-tī'rə*, *n* in ancient Greece, a woman employed in public or private entertainment, for flute-playing, dancing, etc; a paramour; a prostitute or courtesan, *esp* of a superior class: — *pl* **hetae'rae** (*-rē*), **hetai'rai** (*-rī*) or **hetai'ras**. — *n* **hetai'ria** (*hist*) a club or society. — *n* **hetae'rism** or **hetai'rism** concubinage; the system of society that admitted hetairai; a supposed primitive communal marriage. — *adj* **hetaeris'mic** or **hetairis'mic**. — *n* **hetai'rist**. [Gr *hetairā*, fem of *hetairos* companion; *hetair(e)iā* a club]

hete. See **hight**.

heter- *het'ər-* or **hetero-** *het-ə-rō-*, *het-ə-rə-* or *-ro'-*, *combining form* signifying other, different; one or other (often opposed to *homo-* or *auto-*). — *n* **heterauxē'sis** (Gr *auxēsis* growth; *bot*) unsymmetrical growth. — *n* and *adj* **het'ero** (*slang*) heterosexual. — *adj* **heteroblast'ic** (Gr *blastos* bud, germ) derived from different kinds of cells; showing indirect development. — *n* **het'eroblasty** heteroblastic condition. — *adj* **heterocarp'ous** (Gr *karpos* fruit) bearing fruit of more than one kind. — *n pl* **Heterocera** (*-os'ər-ə*; Gr *keras* horn) a loose term for moths, distinguished from *Rhopalocera* (butterflies). — *adj* **heterocercal** (*-sûr'kl*; Gr *kerkos* tail) having the vertebral column passing into the upper lobe of the tail, which is usually larger than the lower, as in sharks. — *n* **heterocercal'ity** or **het'erocercy**. — *adj* **heterochlamydeous** (*-klə-mid'i-əs*; Gr *chlamys*, *-ydos* mantle) having calyx and corolla distinctly different. — *adj* **heterochromat'ic** or **heterochromous** (*-krō'məs*; Gr *chrōma* colour) having different or varying colours. — *adj* **heterochron'ic**. — *n* **heteroch'ronism**. — *adj* **heterochronist'ic**. — *adj* **heteroch'ronous**. — *n* **heterochrony** (*ok'rə-ni*; Gr *chronos* time; *biol*) divergence from the normal time sequence in development. — *adj* **het'eroclite** (*-klīt*; Gr *heteroklitos*, from *klitos* inflected, from *klīnein* to inflect; *gram*) irregularly inflected; irregular; having forms belonging to different declensions. — *n* a word irregularly inflected; anything irregular. — *adj* **heteroclit'ic** or **heteroc'litous**. — *n* **heterocont** see **heterokont** below. — *adj* **heterocyclic** (*-sī'klik*; Gr *kyklos* a wheel) having a closed chain in which the atoms are not all alike (*chem*); having different numbers of parts in different whorls (*bot*). — *n* **heterodactyl** (*-dak'til*; Gr *daktylos* toe) a heterodactylous bird. — *adj* **heterodac'tylous** having the first and second toes turned backwards (as in trogons — not the first and fourth as in parrots). — *adj* **het'erodont** (Gr *odous*, *odontos* a tooth) having different kinds of teeth. — *adj* **het'erodox** (Gr *heterodoxos* from *doxa* opinion, from *dokeein* to think) holding an opinion other than or different from the one generally received, *esp* in theology; heretical. — *n* **het'erodoxy** heresy. — *adj* **het'erodyne** (*-ō-dīn*; Gr *dynamis* strength) in radio communication, applied to a method of imposing on a continuous wave another of slightly different length to produce beats. — *adj* **heteroecious** (*-ē'shəs*). — *n* **heteroecism** (*-ē'sizm*; Gr *oikos* a house; *biol*) parasitism upon different hosts at different stages of the life-cycle. — *adj* **heterog'amous**. — *n* **heterog'amy** (Gr *gamos* marriage) alternation of generations (*biol*); reproduction by unlike gametes (*biol*); the presence of different kinds of flower (male, female, hermaphrodite, neuter, in any combination) in the same inflorescence (*bot*); indirect pollination (*bot*). — *n* **heterogenē'ity**. — *adj* **heterogeneous** (*-jē'ni-əs*; Gr *heterogenēs*, from *genos* a kind) different in kind; composed of parts of different kinds (opp of *homogeneous*). — *adv* **heteroge'neously**. — *n* **heteroge'neousness**. — *n* **heterogenesis** (*-jen'i-sis*; Gr *genesis* generation; *biol*) spontaneous generation; alternate generation. — *adj* **heterogenetic** (*-ji-net'ik*). — *n* **heterogeny** (*-oj'ən-i*) a heterogeneous assemblage; heterogenesis. — *adj* **heterogonous** (*og'ə-*; Gr *gonos* offspring, begetting) having flowers differing in length of stamens (*bot*); having alternation of generations (*biol*). — *n* **heterog'ony**. — *n* **het'erograft** a graft of tissue from a member of one species to a member of another species. — *n* **het'erokont** or **het'erocont** (Gr *kontos* a punting pole) any member of the **Hetero-**

cont'ae or yellow-green algae (eg the common Conferva), a class usually characterized by the pair of unequal cilia on the motile cells. — *adj* **heterokont'an**. — *adj* **heterologous** (*-ol'ə-gəs*) not homologous; different; of different origin; abnormal. — *n* **heterol'ogy** lack of correspondence between apparently similar structures due to different origin. — *adj* **heterom'erous** (Gr *meros* part) having different numbers of parts in different whorls (*bot*); (of lichens) having the algal cells in a layer (*bot*); having unlike segments (*zool*). — *adj* **heteromor'phic** (Gr *morphē* form) deviating in form from a given type; of different forms — also **heteromor'phous**. — *n* **heteromor'phism** or **het'eromorphy**. — *adj* **heteron'omous** (Gr *nomos* law) subject to different laws; subject to outside rule or law (opp of *autonomous*). — *n* **heteron'omy**. — *n* **het'eronym** a word of the same spelling as another but of different pronunciation and meaning. — *adj* (often with *cap*) **heteroousian** (*het-ər-ō-o͞o'si-ən*, or *-ow'*; Gr *ousiā* being) or **heterousian** (*-o͞o'*, *-ow'*, or *-ō-o͞o'*) of unlike essence; believing the Father and Son to be of different substance. — *n* (often with *cap*) a holder of such belief. — *adj* **heterophyllous** (*-fil'əs*; Gr *phyllon* a leaf) having different kinds of foliage leaf. — *n* **het'erophylly**. — *n* **heteroplasia** (*plā'z(h)i-ə* or *-si-ə*; Gr *plasis* a forming) development of abnormal tissue or tissue in an abnormal place. — *adj* **heteroplastic** (*-plas'tik*). — *n* **het'eroplasty** heteroplasia; grafting of tissue from another person. — *n* **het'eropod**. — *n pl* **Heterop'oda** (Gr *pous, podos* a foot) pelagic gasteropods in which the foot has become a swimming organ. — *n pl* **Heterop'tera** (Gr *pteron* a wing) a suborder of insects, the bugs, Hemiptera with fore and hind wings (when present) markedly different. — *adj* **heterop'terous**. — *n* **heteroscian** (*het-ər-osh'i-ən*; Gr *skiā* a shadow) a dweller in a temperate zone, whose noon-shadow is always thrown one way, either north or south. — *n* **heterosex'ism** the belief that homosexuality is a perversion, used as grounds for discrimination against homosexuals. — *n* **heterosex'ist** someone who discriminates against homosexuals. — Also *adj*. — *adj* **heterosex'ūal** having or pertaining to sexual attraction towards the opposite sex. — Also *n*. — *n* **heterosexual'ity**. — *n* **heterō'sis** (*biol*) cross-fertilization; the increased size and vigour (relative to its parents) often found in a hybrid. — *n pl* **Heterosō'mata** (Gr *sōma* (pl *sōmata*) a body) the flat-fishes. — *adj* **heterosō'matous**. — *adj* **heterospecif'ic** (of blood or serum) belonging to different groups; derived from different species. — *adj* **heterosporous** (*-os'por-əs*, or *-pōr'* or *-pör'*) having different kinds of asexually produced spores. — *n* **heteros'pory**. — *adj* **heterostroph'ic** (Gr *strophē* a turning) consisting of unequal strophes; coiled contrary to the usual direction. — *n* **heteros'trophy**. — *adj* **het'erostyled** or **heterosty'lous** having styles of different length in different flowers. — *n* **heterostyl'ism**. — *n* **het'erostyly**. — *adj* **heterotact'ic**. — *n* **heterotax'is** or **het'erotaxy** (Gr *taxis* arrangement) anomalous arrangement of eg parts of the body, etc. — *adj* **heterothall'ic** (Gr *thallos* a shoot; *bot*) (of certain fungi) having two physiologically different types of mycelium, called plus and minus, comparable to male and female. — *n* **heterothall'ism** or **het'erothally**. — *adj* **heterother'mal** (Gr *thermos* heat) taking the temperature of the surroundings. — *adj* **heterot'ic** pertaining to or showing heterosis. — *n* **heterotō'pia** displacement of an organ of the body. — *adj* **heterotop'ic**. — *n* **het'erotroph** a heterotrophic organism. — *adj* **heterotroph'ic**. — *n* **heterot'rophy** (Gr *trophē* livelihood; *bot*) dependence (immediate or ultimate) upon green plants for carbon (as in most animals, fungi, etc). — *adj* **heterotyp'ic** differing from the normal condition; pertaining to the first (reductional) cell division in meiosis (*biol*), see also **homotypic** under **homo-**. — *adj* **heterousian** see **heteroousian** above. — *n* **heterozygos'ity** the mixed ancestry of heterozygotes. — *n* **heterozygote** (*-zī'gōt*; Gr *zygōtos* yoked, from *zygon* yoke) a zygote or individual formed from gametes differing with respect to some pair of alternative characters (one dominant and one recessive). — *adj* **heterozy'gous**. — **heteroduplex DNA** double-stranded DNA made by annealing two single DNA strands from different sources. [Gr *heteros* other, one or other]

hetero *het'ə-rō*, (*colloq*) *n* and *adj* short for (a) heterosexual: — *pl* **het'eros**.

hether and **hetherward** (*Spenser*). Same as **hither** and **hitherward**.

hetman *het'man*, (*hist*) *n* a Polish officer; the head or general of the Cossacks: — *pl* **het'mans**. — *n* **het'manate**. — *n* **het'manship**. [Pol, from Ger *Hauptmann* captain]

heuch or **heugh** *hūhh*, (*Scot*) *n* a crag; a ravine or steep-sided valley; a quarry-face; an excavation, *esp* for coal. [OE *hōh* heel; cf **hoe**[2]]

heulandite *hū'lan-dīt*, *n* a zeolite like stilbite. [After H *Heuland*, an English mineralogist]

heureka. See **eureka**.

heuristic *hū-ris'tik*, *adj* serving or leading to find out; encouraging the desire to find out; (of method, argument, etc) depending on assumptions based on past experience; consisting of guided trial and error. — *n* the art of discovery in logic; the method in education by which the pupil is set to find out things for himself; (in *pl*) principles used in making decisions when all possibilities cannot be fully explored. — *adv* **heuris'tically**. — *n* **heuret'ic** (*logic*) heuristic. — *n* **heur'ism** the heuristic method or principle in education. [Irreg formed from Gr *heuriskein* to find; cf **eureka**]

hevea rubber *hē'vē-ə rub'ər*, *n* rubber from the S American tree **hevea** (*Hevea brasiliensis*), used in electrical insulators for its good electrical and mechanical properties.

hew[1] *hū*, *vt* to cut with blows; to shape, fell or sever with blows of a cutting instrument. — *vi* to deal blows with a cutting instrument: — *pa t* **hewed**; *pa p* **hewed** or **hewn**. — *n* (*Spenser*) hacking. — *n* **hew'er** a person who hews. — *n* and *adj* **hew'ing**. — *adj* **hewn**. [OE *hēawan*; Ger *hauen*]

hew[2] (*Spenser*). See **hue**[1].

hewgh *hū*, (*Shakesp*) *interj* imitating the whistling of an arrow.

hex[1] *heks*, *n* a witch; a wizard; a spell; something which brings bad luck. — *vt* to bring misfortune, etc to by a hex; to bewitch. — *n* **hex'ing**. [Pennsylvania Dutch *hex*, from Ger *Hexe* (*fem*), *Hexer* (*masc*)]

hex[2] *heks*, *n* colloq for *uranium hexafluoride*, a compound used in separating uranium isotopes by gaseous diffusion.

hex- *heks-* or **hexa-** *heks'ə-* or *heks-a'-*, *combining form* denoting six. — *n* **hex'achord** (*-körd*) a diatonic series of six notes having a semitone between the third and fourth. — *n* **hexachlō'rophene** or **hexachlō'rophane** (or *-ör'*) a bactericide, $CH_2(C_6HCl_3OH)_2$ used in antiseptic soaps, deodorants, etc. — *adj* **hex'act** (*-akt*; Gr *aktīs, -īnos* ray) six-rayed. — *n* a six-rayed sponge spicule. — *adj* **hexactī'nal** (or *-ak'ti-nl*) six-rayed. — *n* and *adj* **hexactinell'id**. — *n pl* **Hexactinell'ida** a class of sponges whose spicules have three axes and therefore (unless some are suppressed) six rays. — *n* **hexad** (*heks'ad*; Gr *hexas, -ados*) a series of six numbers; a set of six things; an atom, element, or radical with a combining power of six units (*chem*). — *adj* **hexadactyl'ic** or **hexadact'ylous** (Gr *daktylos* finger, toe) six-fingered; six-toed. — *adj* **hexad'ic** pertaining to a hexad. — *n* and *adj* **hexadec'imal** (of) a number system with 126 as its base, having a radix of 16 (also *n* **hexadecimal notation**). — *n* **hexaëmeron** (*heks-ə-ē'mer-on*; Gr *hēmerā* day) a period of six days, *esp* that of the creation, according to Genesis; a history of the six days of creation. — *n* **hex'afoil** a pattern with six leaf-like lobes or sections. — Also *adj*. — *adj* **hex'aglot** (Gr *glōtta* tongue) in six languages. — *n* **hex'agon** (Gr *hexagōnon*, from *gōniā* an angle) a figure with six sides and six angles. — *adj* **hexagonal** (*-ag'ən-l*) of the form of a hexagon; of the

hexagonal system, a crystal system with three axes at 60° to each other and a fourth perpendicular to their plane (*crystalog*). — *adv* **hexag'onally**. — *n* **hex'agram** (Gr *gramma* figure) a figure of six lines, *esp* a stellate hexagon. — *n pl* **Hexagynia** (*-jin'i-ə*; Gr *gynē* woman) a Linnaean order of plants (in various classes) having six styles. — *adj* **hexagyn'ian** or **hexagynous** (*-aj'i-nəs*). — *adj* **hexahē'dral**. — *n* **hexahē'dron** (Gr *hedrā* a base) a solid with six sides or faces, *esp* a cube: — *pl* **hexahē'drons** or **hexahē'dra**. — *adj* **hexam'erous** (Gr *meros* part) having six parts, or parts in sixes. — *n* **hexam'eter** (Gr *metron* measure) a verse of six measures or feet; (in Greek and Latin verse) such a line where the fifth is almost always a dactyl and the sixth a spondee or trochee, the others dactyls or spondees. — *adj* having six metrical feet. — *adj* **hexamet'ric** or **hexamet'rical**. — *n* **hexam'etrist** a writer of hexameters. — *vi* **hexam'etrize** or **-ise** to write hexameters. — *n pl* (*bot*) **Hexan'dria** (Gr *anēr*, *andros* a man, male) a Linnaean class of plants having six stamens. — *adj* **hexan'drian**. — *adj* **hexan'drous** having six stamens. — *n* **hexane** (*heks'ān*) a hydrocarbon (C_6H_{14}), sixth member of the methane series. — *n* **hex'apla** (Gr *hexaplā*, contracted pl neuter of *hexaploos* sixfold) an edition (*esp* of the Bible) in six versions. — *adj* **hex'aplar**. — *adj* **hexaplār'ian**. — *adj* **hexaplar'ic**. — *adj* **hex'aploid** of or having six times the ordinary number of chromosomes. — *n* a hexaploid cell, individual, species, etc. — *n* **hex'apod** (Gr *pous*, *podos* a foot) an animal with six feet; an insect. — *n pl* **Hexap'oda** insects. — *n* **hexap'ody** a line or verse of six feet. — *adj* **hexarch** (*heks'ärk*; Gr *archē* beginning; *bot*) having six vascular strands. — *n* **hexastich** (*heks'ə-stik*; Gr *hexastichos*, adj, from *stichos* a line) a poem or stanza of six lines. — *adj* **hexastichal** (*-as'tik-l*) having six lines or rows. — *adj* **hexastyle** (*heks'ə-stīl*; Gr *hexastȳlos*, from *stȳlos* a pillar) having six columns. — *n* a building or portico having six columns in front. — *n* **Hexateuch** (*heks'ə-tūk*; Gr *teuchos* tool, afterwards book) the first six books of the Old Testament. — *adj* **hexateuch'al**. — *n* **hex'ose** a sugar (of various kinds) with six carbon atoms to the molecule. — *n* **hexylene** (*heks'i-lēn*; Gr *hȳlē* matter) or **hex'ene** an unsaturated hydrocarbon (C_6H_{12}) of the ethylene series. — **hexagonal chess** a kind of chess played on hexagonal boards. [Gr *hex* six; cf L *sex*, and **six**]

hexobarbitone sodium *heks-ō-bär'bi-tōn sō'di-əm*. See **Evipan**®.

hey[1] *hā*, *interj* expressing joy or interrogation, or calling attention. — *interj* **hey'day** (*archaic*) expressive of frolic, exultation or wonder. — *interj* **hey'-go-mad** (*dialect*) expressing a high degree of excitement. — Also *n*, as **like hey-go-mad** helter-skelter. — *interj* and *n* **hey-pres'to** or (*old*) **hey'-pass** a conjuror's command in passing objects. — **hey for** now for; off we go for. [Imit]

hey[2] or **hay** *hā*, *n* a winding country-dance. — *vi* to dance this dance. — *n* **hey'-** or **hay'-de-guy** (*-gī*), **-guise** or **-guyes** such a dance popular in the 16c and 17c. [Obs Fr *haye*]

heyday *hā'dā*, *n* high spirits (*archaic*); culmination or climax of vigour, prosperity, gaiety, etc; flush or full bloom. [Origin obscure]

heyduck. See **haiduk**.

HF *abbrev*: high frequency.

Hf (*chem*) *symbol*: hafnium.

hf *abbrev*: half.

HG *abbrev*: High German; His or Her Grace.

Hg (*chem*) *symbol*: mercury.

HGH *abbrev*: human growth hormone.

HGV *abbrev*: heavy goods vehicle.

HH *abbrev*: His or Her Highness; His Holiness.

HH *symbol*: very hard (on lead pencils).

hh *abbrev*: hands.

HI *abbrev*: Hawaii (US state); Hawaiian Islands.

hi *hī*, *interj* calling attention; hey; hello. [Cf **hey**[1]]

hiant *hī'ənt*, *adj* gaping. [L *hiāns*, *-antis*, pr p of *hiāre* to gape]

hiatus *hī-ā'təs*, *n* a gap; an opening; a break in continuity, a defect; a concurrence of vowel sounds in two successive syllables (*phonetics*): — *pl* **hiā'tuses**. — **hiatus hernia** a hernia in which a part of a viscus protrudes through a natural opening, *esp* part of the stomach through the opening in the diaphragm intended for the oesophagus. [L *hiātus*, *-ūs*, from *hiāre*, *hiātum* to gape]

hibachi *hib-ä'chi*, *n* a portable barbecue for cooking food out of doors: — *pl* **hiba'chi** or **hiba'chis**. [Japanese *hi* fire, and *bachi* bowl]

hibakusha *hib-ä'ko͞o-shə*, *n* a survivor of the 1945 atomic bombings of Hiroshima and Nagasaki: — *pl* **hiba'kusha**. [Japanese]

hibernate *hī'bər-nāt*, *vi* to winter; to pass the winter in a dormant state; to be inactive. — *n* **hī'bernacle** winter quarters; a hibernaculum. — *n* **hībernac'ūlum** a winter retreat; a bud in Polyzoa that regenerates the colony after winter (*zool*); a winter-bud, bulb, etc by which a plant survives the winter (*bot*): — *pl* **hībernac'ūla**. — *adj* **hīber'nal** belonging to winter; wintry. — *n* **hībernā'tion**. — **hibernation anaesthesia** freezing-down. [L *hībernāre*, *-ātum*, from *hībernus* wintry, from *hiems* winter]

Hibernian *hī-bûr'ni-ən*, *adj* relating to *Hibernia*, an ancient and poetic name for Ireland; Irish; characteristic of Ireland. — *n* an Irishman. — *n* **Hiber'nianism** or **Hiber'nicism** (*-sizm*) an Irish idiom or peculiarity; a bull in speech. — *adv* **Hiber'nically**. — *vt* **hiber'nicize** or **-ise** (*-sīz*; often with *cap*) to render Irish. — *n* **hibernīzā'tion** or **-s-**. — *vt* **hi'bernize** or **-ise** to hibernicise. [L *Hibernia* Ireland]

Hibiscus *hib-is'kəs*, *n* a genus of malvaceous plants, mostly tropical trees or shrubs with large colourful flowers; (without *cap*) a plant of this genus. [L, from Gr *ibiskos* marsh-mallow]

hic[1] *hik*, *interj* representing a hiccup.

hic[2] *hik* or *hēk*, (L) this (*demonstrative pron*). — **hic et ubique** (*et ū-bī'kwē* or *o͞o-bē'kwe*) here and everywhere; **hic jacet** (*jā'set* or *yä'ket*) here lies (frequently preceding the name of the dead person on older grave monuments); **hic sepultus** (*sə-pul'tus* or *se-po͞ol'to͞os*) here buried (frequently preceding the name of the dead person on older grave monuments).

hiccatee or **hicatee** *hik-ə-tē'*, *n* a West Indian freshwater tortoise. [From a native name]

hiccough. See under **hiccup**.

hiccup *hik'up*, *n* the involuntary contraction of the diaphragm while the glottis is spasmodically closed; the sound caused by this; a temporary (and *usu* minor) difficulty or setback (*fig*). — *vi* to produce a hiccup (*lit* and *fig*); to falter or malfunction (*colloq*). — *vt* to say with a hiccup: — *pr p* **hicc'uping**; *pa t* and *pa p* **hicc'uped**. — *adj* **hicc'upy** marked by hiccups. — Also spelt **hiccough**, etc. [Imit; an early form was *hicket*; cf Du *hik*, Dan *hik*, Bret *hik*. The spelling *hiccough* is due to a confusion with *cough*]

hick *hik*, *n* (*derog*) a person from the country; any unsophisticated or unintelligent person. — *adj* pertaining to, or suggestive of, a hick; rural and uncultured. [A familiar form of *Richard*]

hickery-pickery *hik'ər-i-pik'ər-i*. See **hiera-picra**.

hickey *hik'i*, (*NAm colloq*) *n* a gadget; a doodah; a thingummy; a love-bite. [Origin obscure]

hickory *hik'ər-i*, *n* a North American genus (Carya) of the walnut family, yielding edible nuts and heavy strong tenacious wood. [Earlier *pohickery*; of Indian origin]

hickwall *hik'wöl*, (*dialect*) *n* the green woodpecker. [Origin obscure]

hid, hidden. See under **hide**[1].

hidage. See under **hide**[3].

hidalgo *hi-dal'gō*, *n* a Spanish nobleman of the lowest class; a gentleman: — *pl* **hidal'gōs**; *fem* **hidal'ga**: — *pl* **hidal'gas**. — *adj* **hidal'gōish**. — *n* **hidal'gōism**. [Sp *hijo de algo* son of something]

HIDB *abbrev*: Highlands and Islands Development Board (now **HIE**).

hiddenite *hid'ən-īt*, *n* a green spodumene, discovered by W E *Hidden* (1853–1918).

hidder *hid'ər*, (*Spenser*) *n* a young male sheep: — *fem* **shidd'er**. [Perh **he** and **deer**]

hide[1] *hīd*, *vt* to conceal; to keep in concealment; to keep secret or out of sight. — *vi* to go into, or to stay in, concealment: — *pa t* **hid** (*hid*); *pa p* **hidden** (*hid'n*) or **hid**. — *n* a hiding-place; a concealed place from which to observe wild animals, etc. — *adj* **hidd'en** concealed; kept secret; unknown. — *adv* **hidd'enly** in a hidden or secret manner. — *n* **hidd'enness**. — *adj* **hidd'enmost** most hidden. — *n* **hi'der**. — *n* **hid'ing** concealment; a place of concealment. — **hidden economy** see **black economy** under **black**; **hide-and-seek'** or **hide'-and-go-seek'** a game in which one person seeks the others, who have hidden themselves; **hide'-away** a fugitive; a place of concealment; a refuge. — *adj* that hides away. — **hide'out** a retreat; **hid'ing-place**; **hid'y-hole** or **hid'ey-hole** (*Scot* and *US*) a hiding-place. — **hide one's head** (*colloq*) to hide or keep out of sight, from shame, etc (usu *fig*). [OE *hȳdan*; cf MLGer *hûden*, and (doubtfully) Gr *keuthein*]

hide[2] *hīd*, *n* the skin of an animal, *esp* the larger animals, sometimes used derogatorily or facetiously for human skin. — *vt* to flog or whip (*colloq*); to skin. — *n* **hīd'ing** (*colloq*) a thrashing. — *adj* **hide'-bound** (of animals) having the hide attached so closely to the back and ribs that it is taut, not easily moved, as a result of incorrect feeding; (in trees) having the bark so close that it impedes the growth; stubborn, bigoted, obstinate (*derog*). — **hide nor** (or **or**) **hair of** the slightest trace of (something or someone). — **on a hiding to nothing** (*colloq*) in a situation in which one is bound to lose, in spite of all one's efforts; **tan someone's hide** (*colloq*) to whip or beat someone. [OE *hȳd*; Ger *Haut*, L *cutis*]

hide[3] *hīd*, *n* (in old English law) a variable unit of area of land, enough for a household. — *n* **hīd'age** a tax once assessed on every hide of land. [OE *hīd*, contracted from *hīgid*; cf *hīwan*, *hīgan* household]

hide[4] *hīd*, (*Spenser*) *pa t* of **hie**[1].

hideous *hid'i-əs*, *adj* frightful; horrible; ghastly; extremely ugly; huge (*obs*). — *n* **hideos'ity** or **hid'eousness**. — *adv* **hid'eously**. [OFr *hideus*, *hisdos*, from *hide*, *hisde* dread, poss from L *hispidus* rough, rude]

hiding. See under **hide**[1,2].

hidlings, **hidlins** or **hidling** *hid'lin(g)* or *-s* (*Scot*) *adv* in secrecy. — *adj* secret. — *n* a hiding-place or hiding-places; secrecy. [**hid**, and adv sfx *-ling*]

hidrosis *hid-rō'sis*, (*med*) *n* sweating, *esp* in excess. — *n* and *adj* **hidrotic** (*-drot'ik*) sudorific. [Gr *hidrōs*, *-ōtos* sweat]

HIE *abbrev*: Highland and Islands Enterprise.

hie[1] *hī*, (*archaic* or *poetic*) *vi* to hasten. — *vt* to urge (on); to pass quickly over (one's way): — *pr p* **hie'ing** or **hy'ing**; *pa t* and *pa p* **hied**. — *n* (*obs*) haste. [OE *hīgian*]

hie[2] or **high** *hī*, (*Scot*) *n* and *interj* the call to a horse to turn to the left (*opp* of *hup*). — *vt* and *vi* to turn to the left (of or to a horse or plough-ox).

hielaman *hē'lə-man*, *n* an Australian Aboriginal narrow shield of bark or wood. [Native word *hīlaman*]

Hieland *hēl'ən(d)* or *-ənt*, *adj* a Scots form of **Highland** (see under **high**) — sometimes used with pejorative meanings, eg foolish, clumsy, etc, *esp* in *neg*, as in **no sae Hieland** not altogether absurd; not so bad as might be. — Also **Hielan'** or **Hielant**.

hiems *hī'emz*, (*Shakesp*) *n* winter. — *adj* **hī'emal**. [L *hiems*]

hieracium *hī-ər-ā'shi-əm*, *n* any plant of the genus *Hieracium*, the hawkweed genus of Compositae. [Latinized from Gr *hierākion* hawkweed, from *hierāx* hawk]

hiera-picra *hī'ər-ə-pik'rə*, *n* a purgative drug made from aloes and canella bark. — Also **hick'ery-pick'ery** or **hig'ry-pig'ry**. [Gr *hierā* (fem), sacred, and *pikrā* (fem), bitter]

hierarch *hī'ər-ärk*, *n* a ruler in holy things; a chief priest; a prelate; an archangel (*Milton*); any senior person in a hierarchy. — *adj* **hī'erarchal**, **hīerarch'ic** or **hīerarch'ical**. — *adv* **hierarch'ically**. — *n* **hī'erarchism**. — *n* **hī'erarchy** a body or organization classified in successively subordinate grades; (loosely) in an organization so classified, the group of people who control that organization; classification in graded subdivisions; graded government amongst priests or other religious ministers; the collective body of angels, grouped in three divisions and nine orders of different power and glory: (1) seraphim, cherubim, thrones; (2) dominations or dominions, virtues, powers; (3) principalities, archangels, angels; each of the three main classes of angels. [Gr *hierarchēs*, from *hieros* sacred, and *archein* to rule]

hieratic *hī-ər-at'ik*, *adj* priestly; applying to a certain kind of ancient Egyptian writing which consisted of abridged forms of hieroglyphics; also to certain styles in art bound by religious convention. — *n* **hīerat'ica** the finest papyrus. [L *hierāticus*, from Gr *hierātikos*, from *hieros* sacred]

hierocracy *hī-ər-ok'rə-si*, *n* government by priests or other religious ministers. — *n* **hī'erocrat**. — *adj* **hīerocrat'ic**. [Gr *hieros* sacred, and *krateein* to rule]

hierodule *hī'ər-ō-dūl*, *n* in ancient Greece and Rome, any of various groups of slaves in the service of a temple, including female prostitutes obliged to give up some or all of their gains. [Gr *hieros* sacred, and *doulos* a slave]

hieroglyph *hī'ər-ō-glif*, *n* a sacred character used in ancient Egyptian picture-writing or in picture-writing in general. — *vt* to represent by hieroglyphs. — *adj* **hīeroglyph'ic** or **hīeroglyph'ical**. — *n* **hīeroglyph'ic** a hieroglyph; (in *pl*) hieroglyphic writing; (in *pl*) writing that is difficult to read. — *adv* **hīeroglyph'ically**. — *n* **hīeroglyphist** (*-og'*) a person skilled in hieroglyphics. [Gr *hieroglyphikon*, from *hieros* sacred, and *glyphein* to carve]

hierogram *hī'ər-ō-gram*, *n* a sacred or hieroglyphic symbol. — *n* **hīerogramm'at** or **hīerogramm'ate** a writer of sacred records. — *adj* **hīerogrammat'ic** or **hīerogrammat'ical**. — *n* **hīerogramm'atist**. — *n* **hī'erograph** a sacred symbol. — *n* **hīerog'rapher** a sacred scribe. — *adj* **hīerograph'ic** or **hīerograph'ical** pertaining to sacred writing. — *n* **hīerog'raphy** a description of sacred things. [Gr *hieros* sacred, and *gramma* a character, from *graphein* to write]

hierolatry *hī-ər-ol'ə-tri*, *n* the worship of saints or sacred things. [Gr *hieros* sacred, and *latreiā* worship]

hierology *hī-ər-ol'ə-ji*, *n* the science of sacred matters, *esp* ancient writing and Egyptian inscriptions. — *adj* **hīerologic** (*-ə-loj'ik*) or **hierolog'ical** (*-kəl*). — *n* **hīerol'ogist**. [Gr *hieros* sacred, and *logos* discourse]

hieromancy *hī-ər-ō-man'si*, *n* divination by observing the objects offered in sacrifice. [Gr *hieros* sacred, and *manteiā* divination]

Hieronymic *hī-ər-on-im'ik*, *adj* of or pertaining to St Jerome. — Also **Hieronym'ian**. — *n* **Hieron'ymite** a member of any of a number of hermit orders established in the 13c and 14c. [L *Hierōnymus*, Gr *Hierōnymos* Jerome]

hierophant *hī'ər-ō-fant*, *n* a person who shows or reveals sacred things; a priest; an expounder. — *adj* **hīerophant'ic**. [Gr *hierophantēs*, from *hieros* sacred, and *phainein* to show]

hierophobia *hī-ər-ō-fō'bi-ə*, *n* fear of sacred objects. — *adj* **hieropho'bic**. [Gr *hieros* sacred, and *phobos* fear]

hieroscopy *hī-ər-os'kə-pi*, *n* hieromancy. [Gr *hieros* sacred, and *skopeein* to look at]

Hierosolymitan *hī-ə-rō-sol'i-mī-tən*, *adj* of or pertaining to Jerusalem. [L and Gr *Hierosolyma* Jerusalem]

hierurgy *hī'ər-ûr-ji*, *n* a sacred performance. — *adj* **hīerur'gical**. [Gr *hierourgiā*, from *hieros* sacred, and *ergon* work]

hi-fi or (*rare*) **Hi-Fi** *hī'-fī*, *n* *high-fi*delity sound reproduction; equipment for this, eg tape-recorder, record-player, etc; the use of such equipment, *esp* as a hobby. — Also *adj*.

higgle *hig'l*, to make difficulties in bargaining; to chaffer. — Also **higg'le-hagg'le** (reduplicated variant). — *n* **higg'ler** a person who higgles; in Jamaica, a market trader dealing in hand-crafted wares. — *n* and *adj* **higg'ling**. [Prob a form of **haggle**]

higgledy-piggledy *hig'l-di-pig'l-di*, (*colloq*) *adv* and *adj* haphazard; in confusion. [Origin obscure]

high[1] *hī*, *adj* elevated; lofty; tall; far up from a base, such as the ground, sea-level, low-tide, the mouth of a river, the zero of a scale, etc; advanced in a scale, *esp* the scale of nature; reaching far up; expressible by a large number; of a height specified or to be specified; of advanced degree of intensity; advanced, full (in time, eg *high season* or *high summer*); (of a period) at its peak of development, as in *High Renaissance* or *high drama*; of grave importance; advanced; exalted; excellent; eminent; dignified; chief (as in *high priestess*); noble; haughty; arrogant; extreme in opinion; powerful; angry; loud; violent; tempestuous; acute in pitch; luxurious (as in *the high life*); elated; drunk; over-excited, nervy; under the influence of a drug; standing out; difficult, abstruse; (of a price) dear; for heavy stakes; remote in time; (of meat, etc) slightly tainted or decomposed, or, in the case of game, ready to cook; pronounced with some part of the tongue well raised in the mouth (*phonetics*); (of latitude) far from the equator; (of an angle) approaching a right angle; (of facial colouring) florid. — *adv* at or to an elevated degree; in or into a raised position; aloft; shrilly; arrogantly; eminently; powerfully; extremely; luxuriously; dear; for heavy stakes. — *n* that which is high; an elevated region; the highest card; a high level; the maximum, highest level; a euphoric or exhilarated frame of mind (*esp drug-taking slang*); a high school (*colloq*). — *adj* **high'er**, *compar* of **high**. — *n* (with *cap*; also **Higher grade**) (in Scotland, a pass in) an examination generally taken at the end of the 5th year of secondary education, more advanced than Standard grade. — Also *adj*. — *vt* to raise higher; to lift. — *vi* to ascend. — *adj* **high'ermost** (*rare*) or **high'est** *superl* of **high**. — *adj* **high'ish** somewhat high. — *adv* **high'ly** in or to a high degree; in a high position. — *adj* **high'most**. — *n* **high'ness** the state of being high; dignity of rank; (with *cap*) a title of honour given to princes, princesses, royal dukes, etc. — *n* **hight** (*hīt*) or **highth** (*hīth*) obsolete forms of **height**. — **high admiral** a high or chief admiral of a fleet; **high altar** see under **altar**; **high-alumina cement** a type of quick-hardening cement, made of bauxite and chalk or limestone, found to lose strength through time under certain conditions; **high bailiff** an officer who serves writs, etc in certain franchises, exempt from the ordinary supervision of the sheriff; **high'ball** (*NAm*) whisky (or other alcoholic spirit) and soda with ice in a tall glass. — *vi* to go at great speed. — *vt* to drive very fast. — *adj* **high'-battled** (also **hye-battel'd**; *Shakesp*) *appar* in command of proud battalions. — **high'binder** (*US*) a member of a Chinese criminal secret society; a conspirator; a rowdy, ruffian or blackmailer. — *adj* **high-blest'** (*Milton*) supremely blest or happy. — *adj* **high'blooded** of noble lineage. — *adj* **high'-blown** swelled with wind; inflated, as with pride (*orig Shakesp*). — *adj* **high'-born** of noble birth. — **high'boy** (*NAm*) a tallboy. — *adj* **high'-bred** of noble breed, training or family. — **high'brow** an intellectual. — Also *adj*. — **high'browism**; **high camp** see under **camp**[3]; **high'chair** a baby's or young child's tall chair, *usu* fitted with a tray, used *esp* at mealtimes. — *adj* **High Church** of a section within the Church of England that exalts the authority of the episcopate and the priesthood, the saving grace of sacraments, etc; of similar views in other churches. — **High-Church'ism**; **High-Church'man**. — *adj* **high'-class** superior; typical of or belonging to an upper social class. — *adj* **high-col'oured** having a strong or glaring colour; (of a complexion) ruddy; over-vivid. — **high comedy** comedy set in refined sophisticated society, characterized more by witty dialogue, complex plot and good characterization than by comical actions or situations; **high command** the commander-in-chief of the army together with his staff, or the equivalent senior officers of any similar force; **High Commission** and **High Commissioner** see under **commission**; **high court** a supreme court; **high cross** a town or village cross; **high day** a holiday or festival; (*dā'*) broad daylight; (*hī'*) heyday (erroneously). — *adj* befitting a festival. — **high definition television** see **HDTV**. — *adj* **high-den'sity** (*comput*) (of a disk) having very compact data-storage capacity. — *adj* **high'-dried** brought to an advanced stage of dryness; of fixed and extreme opinions. — **High Dutch** High German (see below); pure Dutch of Holland (opp to former *Cape Dutch*); **high-energy physics** (*phys*) same as **particle physics**; **higher criticism** see under **critic**; **higher education** education beyond the level of secondary education, eg at a university or college; **Higher grade** see **Higher** above; **high'er-up** (*colloq*) a person occupying an upper position; **high explosive** a detonating explosive (eg dynamite, TNT) of great power and exceedingly rapid action. — Also *adj*. — **highfalutin** or **highfaluting** (*-lōōt'*) bombastic discourse. — *adj* affected; pompous. — **high feather** high spirits; happy state. — *adj* **high'-fed** fed highly or luxuriously; pampered. — **high'-feeding**; **high fidelity** good reproduction of sound. — *adj* **high-fidel'ity**. — See also **hi-fi**. — **high five** or **high-five'-sign** a sign of greeting or celebration, *esp* popular in N America, consisting of the slapping of raised right palms. — *vi* and *vt* **high-five'**. — **high'-flī'er** or **high-fly'er** a bird that flies high; someone prone to extravagance of opinion or action; an ambitious person, or one naturally equipped to reach prominence; (with *cap*; *hist*) a High-Churchman, or, in Scotland, an Evangelical. — *adj* **high'-flown** extravagant; elevated; turgid. — *adj* **high'-fly'ing** extravagant in conduct or opinion. — **high frequency** see under **frequent**. — *adj* **high'-gear** see under **gear**. — **High German** of upper or southern Germany; the standard form of the German language, as it is written and spoken amongst educated people; that form of Germanic language affected by the second consonant shift, including the literary language of Germany. — *adj* **high'-grade** superior; rich in metal. — *vt* to steal rich ore from. — *adj* **high'-grown** (*Shakesp*) covered with a high growth. — **high hand** arbitrary arrogance. — *adj* **high'-hand'ed** overbearing; arbitrary. — **high'-hand'edness**; **high'-hat'** *orig* a wearer of a top-hat; a snob or aristocrat (*colloq*); a person who puts on airs (*colloq*); (**high'-hat**) a pair of cymbals on a stand, the upper one operated by a pedal so as to strike the lower one (also **hi'-hat**). — *adj* affectedly superior. — *vi* to put on airs. — *vt* to adopt a superior attitude towards or to ignore socially. — *adj* **high'-heart'ed** full of courage. — *adj* **high'-heeled'** having or wearing high heels. — **High Holidays** or **High Holy Days** the Jewish festivals of Rosh Hashanah and Yom Kippur; **highjack** and **highjacker** see under **hijack**; **high jinks** boisterous play, jollity; an old Scottish tavern game in which people played various parts under penalty of a forfeit; **high jump** (a field event consisting of) a jump over a high bar; punishment, a severe reproof, *esp* in the phrase *be for the high jump*. — *adj* **high'-key** (of paintings and photographs) having pale tones and very little contrast. — **high kick** a dancer's kick high in the air, *usu* with a straight leg. — *adj* **high'-kilt'ed** having the skirt tucked up high; indecorous. — **high'land** a mountainous district; (with *cap*; in *pl*) the north-west of Scotland, bordered geologically by the great fault running from Dumbarton to Stonehaven, or, ethnologically, the considerably narrower area in which Gaelic is, or was till recently, spoken. — *adj* belonging to or characteristic of a highland, *esp* (*usu* with *cap*) the Highlands, of Scotland. — **high'lander** an inhabitant or native of a mountainous region, *esp* (with *cap* or **High'landman**) of the Highlands of Scotland; **Highland cattle** a shaggy breed of cattle with very long horns; **Highland dress** or **costume** kilt, plaid and sporran; **Highland fling** a lively solo dance of the Scottish Highlands. — *adj* **high'-lev'el** at a high level, *esp* involving very important people. — **high-level language** (*comput*) a computer programming language which allows a user to employ instructions close to his or her own familiar language rather than machine code; **high-level waste** nuclear waste requiring continuous cooling to remove the heat produced by radioactive decay; **high life** the life of fashionable society; the people of this society; a blend of traditional West African music and North American jazz, popular in West Africa; **high'light** an outstanding feature; (in *pl*) the most brightly lit spots; the most memorable moments; (*usu* in *pl*) a portion or patch of the hair which reflects the light or which is artificially made lighter than the rest of the hair. — *vt* to throw into relief by strong light; to draw attention to or point out; to overlay (parts of a text) with a bright colour, for special attention: — *pa t* and *pa p* **high'lighted**. — **high'lighter** a broad-tipped felt pen for highlighting parts of a text, etc; **high living** luxurious living. — *adv* **high'-lone** (*Shakesp*) quite alone. — **high'-low** (*archaic*; often *pl*) an ankle-high shoe fastened in front. — *adj* **highly-strung'** nervously sensitive, excitable. — *adj* **highly tried** (*horse racing*) tested in experienced company. — **high'man** a loaded die: — *pl* **high'men**; **high mass** a mass celebrated with music, ceremonies and incense. — *adj* **high'-mett'led** high-spirited, fiery. — *adj* **high'-mind'ed** having a high, proud or arrogant mind (*rare*); having lofty principles and thoughts. — **high'-mind'edness**; **high-muck-a-muck** see separate entry. — *adj* **high'-necked'** (of a garment) covering the shoulders and neck. — **high noon** exactly noon; the peak (*fig*). — *adj* **high'-oc'tane** (of petrol) of high octane number and so of high efficiency (also *fig*). — *adj* **high'-pitched'** acute in sound, tending towards treble; (of a roof) steep; lofty-toned. — **high'-place** (*Bible*) an area of high ground on which idolatrous rites were performed by the Jews, hence the idols, etc themselves. — *adj* **high'-placed** having a high place; placed high. — **high places** positions of importance and *usu* influence; **high point** the most memorable, pleasurable, successful, etc moment or occasion; a high spot; **high polymer** a polymer of high molecular weight. — *adj* **high'-pow'ered** very powerful; very forceful and efficient. — *adj* **high'-press'ure** making or allowing use of steam or other gas at a pressure much above that of the atmosphere; involving intense activity. — *adj* **high'-priced'** costly. — **high priest** a chief priest; **high priestess**; **high'-priest'hood**. — *adj* **high'-priest'ly**. — *adj* **high'-prin'cipled** of high, noble or strict principle. — **high profile** a conspicuous position. — *adj* **high'-pro'file** prominent, public. — *adj* **high'-proof** proved to contain much alcohol; highly rectified. — *adj* **high'-raised** or **-reared** raised aloft; elevated. — **high'-ranker**. — *adj* **high'-ranking** senior; eminent. — *adj* **high'-reach'ing** reaching upwards; ambitious. — **high relief** bold relief, standing out well from the surface. — *adj* **high'-rise** (of modern buildings) containing a large number of storeys. — *adj* **high'-risk'** vulnerable to some sort of danger; potentially dangerous. — **high'-road** one of the public or chief roads; a road for general traffic; **high'-roll'er** a plunging spendthrift; a person who gambles for high stakes; **high'-roll'ing**; **high school** a secondary school, often one which was formerly a grammar school; **high seas** the open ocean; **high season** the peak tourist period. — *adj* **high'-sea'soned** or **high'ly-sea'soned** made rich or piquant with spices or other seasoning. — *adj* **high'-set** placed or pitched high. — **high shoe** (*archaic*) a boot not reaching far above the ankle. — *adj* **high'-sight'ed** (*Shakesp*) looking upwards, supercilious. — **high society** fashionable, wealthy society. — *adj* **high'-souled** having a high or lofty soul or spirit. — *adj* **high'-sound'ing** pompous; imposing. — *adj* **high spec** of a high standard of design and workmanship. — *adj* **high'-speed** working, or suitable for working, at a great speed. — **high-speed steel** an alloy that remains hard when red-hot, suitable for metal-cutting tools. — *adj* **high'-spir'ited** having a high spirit or natural fire; bold; daring. — **high spirits** a happy, exhilarated frame of mind; **high spot** see under **spot**; **high'-stepp'er** a horse that lifts its feet high from the ground; a person of imposing bearing or fashionable pretensions. — *adj* **high'-stepp'ing**. — *adj* **high'-stom'ached** (*Shakesp*) proud-spirited, lofty, obstinate. — **High Street** (sometimes without *cap*) a common name for the main, or former main, shopping street of a town; (with *the*) shops generally, the everyday marketplace. — *adj* **high'-street** typical of or readily found in high streets. — *adj* **high'-strung** (*esp NAm*) highly-strung. — **high table** the dons' table in a college dining-hall. — *vi* **high'tail** to hightail it (see below). — **high'-tap'er** hag-taper, the great mullein. — *adj* **high'-tast'ed** having a strong, piquant taste or relish. — **high tea** an early-evening meal comprising a hot dish followed by cakes, etc and tea; **high tech** or **hi tech** a style or design of furnishing, etc imitative of or using industrial equipment. — *adj* **high'-tech** or **hi'-tec**. — **high technology** advanced, sophisticated technology in specialist fields, eg electronics, involving high investment in research and development. — *adj* **high'-ten'sion** high-voltage. — *adj* **high'-test** (of petrol) boiling at comparatively low temperature and so of high performance. — **high tide** high water; a tide higher than usual; a great festival (*rare*); **high time** quite time (that something were done); a time of jollity; **high toby** (*thieves' slang*) see under **toby**. — *adj* **high'-toned** high in pitch; morally elevated; superior, fashionable. — **high'-top** (*Shakesp*) a mast-head; **high treason** treason against the sovereign or state; **high'-up** someone in high position (also *adj*). — *adj* **high-vac'uum** (*electronics*) (of a system) so completely evacuated that the effect of ionization on its subsequent operation may be neglected. — *adj* **high'-veloc'ity** (of shells) propelled at high speed with low trajectory. — *adj* **high'-viced** (*Shakesp*) enormously wicked. — *adj* **high'-vol'tage** of or concerning a high voltage, one great enough to cause injury or damage. — **high water** the time at which the tide or other water is highest; the greatest elevation of the tide; **high'-wa'ter mark** the highest line so reached; a tide-mark; **high'way** a public road on which all have right to go; the main or usual way or course; a road, path or navigable river (*law*); see **bus** (*comput*); **Highway Code** (the booklet containing) official rules and guidance on correct procedure for road-users; **high'wayman** a robber who attacks people on the public way; **highway patrol** (*NAm*); **high-wing monoplane** an aircraft with the wing mounted on or near the top of the fuselage; **high wire** a tightrope stretched exceptionally high above the ground; **high words** angry altercation. — *adj* **high'-wrought** wrought with exquisite skill; highly finished; elaborate; worked up, agitated. — **for the high jump** (*colloq*) about to be reprimanded or chastised; about to be hanged; **from on high** from a high place, heaven, or (*facetiously*) a position of authority; **high and dry** up out of the water; stranded, helpless; **high and low** rich and poor; up and down; everywhere; **high and mighty** (*ironic*) exalted; arrogant; **high as a kite** (*colloq*) over-excited, drunk, or very much under the influence of drugs; **high life below stairs** servants' imitation of the life of their employers; **high old time** (*colloq*) a time of special jollity or enthusiasm; **hightail it** (*colloq*, *esp NAm*) to hurry away; **hit the high spots** to go to excess; to reach a high level; **on high** aloft; in heaven; **on one's high horse** in an attitude of fancied superiority; very much on one's dignity; **on the high ropes** (*colloq*) in an elated or highly excited mood; **running high** see under **feel**. [OE *hēah*; Gothic *hauhs*, ON *hār*, Ger *hoch*]

high[2]. See **hie**[2].

high-muck-a-muck *hī-muk-ə-muk'*, (*NAm colloq*) *n* an important, pompous person. [Chinook Jargon *hiu* plenty, and *muckamuck* food]

hight *hīt*, *Scot* **hecht** *hehht* and *obs* **hete** *hēt*, *vt* to command (*obs*); to promise, assure, vow (*Scot*); to call, name (*archaic*); to mention (*Spenser*); to commit (*Spenser*); to direct, determine, intend (*Spenser*): — *Spenser* senses not found elsewhere. — *vi* (*archaic*, and only in pa t; *orig passive*) to be called or named, to have as a name: — *pa t* (*archaic*) **hight**, (*Scot*) **hecht**, (*Spenser*) **hot** or **hote**; *pa p* (*archaic*) **hight**, (*Scot*) **hecht**, (*obs*) **hō'ten**. [OE *hēht* (*hēt*), reduplicated pa t of *hātan* (pa p *hāten*) substituted for the present and for the last surviving trace of the inflected passive in English, *hātte* is or was called; cf Ger *ich heisse* I am named, from *heissen* to call, be called, command]

highty-tighty *hī'ti-tī'ti*. Same as **hoity-toity**.

higry-pigry *hig'ri-pig'ri*. See **hiera-picra**.

HIH *abbrev*: His or Her Imperial Highness.

hijab. See **hejab**.

hijack or **highjack** *hī'jak*, *vt* to stop and rob (a vehicle); to steal in transit; to force a pilot to fly (an aeroplane) to a destination of the hijacker's choice; to force the driver to take (a vehicle or train) to a destination of the hijacker's choice (also *fig*). — Also *vi*. — *n* **hi'jacker** or **high'jacker** a highwayman (*hist*); a robber or blackmailer of rum-runners and bootleggers; a person who hijacks. [Origin obscure]

hijinks. Same as **high jinks**.

hijra, hijrah. Same as **hegira**.

hike *hīk*, *vi* to tramp; to go walking, *esp* wearing boots and carrying camping equipment, etc in a backpack; to hitch; (of shirts, etc) to move up out of place (with *up*). — *vt* (*usu* with *up*; *colloq*) to raise up with a jerk; to increase (eg prices), *esp* sharply and suddenly (*NAm*). — *n* a walking tour, outing or march; an increase (in prices, etc; *NAm*). — *n* **hi'ker**. [Perh **hitch**]

hila, hilar. See under **hilum**.

hilarious *hi-lā'ri-əs*, *adj* extravagantly merry; very funny. — *adv* **hilā'riously**. — *n* **hilarity** (*hi-lar'*) gaiety; pleasurable excitement. [L *hilaris*, from Gr *hilaros* cheerful]

Hilary term *hil'ər-i tûrm*, *n* the Spring term or session of the High Court of Justice in England; also the Spring term at Oxford and Dublin universities — from St *Hilary* of Poitiers (died c. 367; festival Jan 13).

hilch *hilsh*, (*Scot*) *vi* to hobble. — *vt* to lift. — *n* a limp.

hild *hild* (*Shakesp*, *Spenser*). Same as **held**.

Hildebrandism *hil'də-brand-izm*, *n* the spirit and policy of *Hildebrand* (Pope Gregory VII, 1073–1085), unbending assertion of the power of the Church, etc. — *adj* **Hildebrand'ic**.

hilding *hild'ing*, (*archaic*) *n* a mean, cowardly person, a dastard; a worthless beast. — *adj* cowardly, spiritless. [Prob connected with **heel**[2]]

hill *hil*, *n* a high mass of land, smaller than a mountain; a mound; an incline on a road. — *vt* to form into a hill; to bank up (sometimes for **hele**). — *adj* **hilled** having hills. — *n* **hill'iness**. — *n* **hill'ock** a small hill. — *adj* **hill'ocky**. — *adj* **hill'y** full of hills. — **hill'-billy** (*NAm*) a rustic of the hill country; any unsophisticated person; country-and-Western music. — Also *adj*. — **hill'-digger** a rifler of sepulchral barrows, etc. — *n pl* **hill'folk** or **hill'men** people living or hiding among the hills; the Scottish sect of Cameronians; the Covenanters generally. — **hill'-fort** a fort on a hill; a prehistoric stronghold on a hill; **hill'-pasture**; **hill'side** the slope of a hill; **hill station** a government station in the hills, *esp* of Northern India; **hill'top** the summit of a hill; **hill'walker**; **hill'walking**. — **hill and dale** (*obs*; of a gramophone record) with vertical groove undulations; **old as the hills** (*colloq*) immeasurably old; **over the hill** (*colloq*) past one's highest point of efficiency, success, etc; on the downgrade; past the greatest difficulty; **up hill and down dale** vigorously and persistently. [OE *hyll*; cf L *collis* a hill, *celsus* high]

hillo (*archaic*). Same as **hallo**.

hilt *hilt*, *n* the handle, *esp* of a sword or dagger (sometimes in *pl*). — *vt* to provide with a hilt. — **up to the hilt** completely, thoroughly, to the full. [OE *hilt*; MDu *hilte*; OHGer *helza*; not connected with **hold**]

hilum *hī'ləm*, *n* the scar on a seed where it joined its stalk (*bot*); the depression or opening where ducts, vessels, etc enter an organ (*anatom*): — *pl* **hī'la**. — *adj* **hī'lar**. — *n* **hī'lus** a hilum (*anatom*): — *pl* **hī'lī**. [L *hīlum* a trifle, 'that which adheres to a bean']

HIM *abbrev*: His or Her Imperial Majesty.

him *him*, *pron* the dative and accusative (objective) case of **he**; the proper character of a person (as in *that's not like him*). [OE *him*, dative sing of *hē*, he and *hit* it]

Himalaya *him-ə-lā'ə* or *hi-mäl'yə*, or **Himalayan** *-n*, *adj* pertaining to the Himalayas, the mountain range along the border of India and Tibet.

himation *hi-mat'i-on*, *n* the ancient Greek outer garment, a rectangular cloak thrown over the left shoulder, and fastened either over or under the right. [Gr]

himseems, himseemed. See under **seem**.

himself *him-self'*, *pron* the emphatic form of **he** or **him**; the reflexive form of **him** (*dative* and *accusative*); predicatively (or *n*) a man in his real character; having command of his faculties; sane; in normal condition; in good form; alone, by himself (*Scot*); the head of an institution or body of people (eg a husband; *Scot*). [See **him** and **self**]

Himyarite *him'yär-īt*, *n* a member of an ancient South Arabian people. — *n* and *adj* **Himyaritic** (*-it'ik*). [*Himyar* a traditional king of Yemen]

hin *hin*, *n* a Hebrew liquid measure containing about four or six English quarts. [Heb *hīn*]

Hinayana *hin-ə-yä'nə*, *n* Theravada, one of the two main systems of practice and belief into which Buddhism split, the 'Little or Lesser Vehicle' (*orig* so called derogatorily by Mahayana (qv) Buddhists), the form of Buddhism found in Ceylon and SE Asia, holding more conservatively than Mahayana Buddhism to the original teachings of the Buddha and the practices of the original Buddhist communities. — Also *adj*. [Sans *hīna* little, lesser, and *yāna* vehicle]

Hind. *abbrev*: Hindustani.

hind[1] *hīnd*, *adj* placed in the rear; pertaining to the part behind; backward (opp of *fore*). — *adj* **hinder** (*hīn'dər*; *Scot hin'ər*) hind; last (*Scot*; as in *this hinder nicht* last night). — *n pl* **hind'erlings**, **hind'erlins**, or less correctly **hinderlands** or **hinderlans** (*hin'ər-lənz*; *Scot*) the buttocks. — *adj* **hīnd'ermost** or **hīnd'most** (superlative of **hind**) farthest behind. — *adj* and *adv* **hīnd'ward**. — **hīnd'brain** the cerebellum and medulla oblongata; **hin'der-end** (*Scot*; *hin'ər-en'* or *-end'*) the latter end; buttocks; **hīnd'foot**. — *adv* **hīndfore'most** with the back part in the front place. — **hīnd'-gut** the posterior part of the alimentary canal; **hīnd'head** the back of the head, the occiput; **hīnd'leg**. — *n pl* **hīndquar'ters** the rear parts of an animal. — **hīnd'sight** the ability or opportunity to understand and explain an event after it has happened; the rear sight on a gun, etc; **hīnd'-wheel**; **hīnd'wing**. [OE *hinder* backwards; Gothic *hindar*, Ger *hinter* behind; cf OE *hindan* (adv), back; **behind**]

hind[2] *hīnd*, *n* the female of the red deer. — *n* **hind'berry** the raspberry. [OE *hind*; Du *hinde*, Ger *Hinde*]

hind[3] *hīnd*, (now *Scot*) *n* a farm-servant, with a cottage on the farm, formerly bound to supply the landowner with a female field-worker (*bondager*); a rustic. [OE *hīna*, *hīwna*, genitive pl of *hīwan* members of a household]

hindberry. See under **hind**[2].

hindbrain. See under **hind**[1].

hinder[1] *hin'dər*, *vt* to keep back; to stop, or prevent, progress of. — *vi* to be an obstacle. — *n* **hin'derer**. — *adv* **hin'deringly**. — *n* **hin'drance** act of hindering; that which hinders; prevention; obstacle. — Also **hin'derance**. [OE *hindrian*; Ger *hindern*]

hinder[2], **hinderend**. See under **hind**[1].

hinderland *hin'dər-land*, an Anglicized form of **hinterland**. [See also under **hind**[1]]

hinderlands, hinderlans, hinderlings, hinderlins, hindermost. See under **hind**[1].

Hindi *hin'dē, n* a group of Indo-European languages of Northern India, including Hindustani; a recent literary form of Hindustani, with terms from Sanskrit, one of the official languages of India. — Also *adj.* [Hindi *Hindī*, from *Hind* India]

hindleg... to... **hindquarters**. See under **hind**[1].

hindrance. See under **hinder**[1].

hindsight. See under **hind**[1].

Hindu or *formerly* **Hindoo** *hin-dōō'* or *hin'dōō, n* a member of any of the races of Hindustan or India (*archaic*); *specif* an adherent of Hinduism; a believer in a form of Brahmanism. — Also *adj.* — *n* **Hindu'ism** (or *hin'*) the aggregation of religious values and beliefs and social customs dominant in India, including the belief in reincarnation, the worship of several gods and the arrangement of society in a caste system. — *vt* and *vi* **Hin'duize** or **-ise**. [Pers *Hindū*, from *Hind* India]

Hindustani or *formerly* **Hindoostanee** *hin-dōō-stä'nē, n* a form of Hindi containing elements from other languages, used as a lingua franca in much of India and Pakistan. — Also *adj.*

hindward... to... **hindwing**. See under **hind**[1].

hing *hing, n* asafoetida. [Hindi *hīg*, from Sans *hiṅgu*]

hinge *hinj, n* the hook or joint on which a door or lid turns; a joint as of a bivalve shell; the earth's axis (*Milton*); a small piece of gummed paper used to attach a postage-stamp to the page of an album (also **stamp'-hinge**); a cardinal point; a principle or fact on which anything depends or turns. — *vt* to provide with hinges; to bend. — *vi* to hang or turn as on a hinge; to depend (with *on*): — *pr p* **hinging** (*hinj'ing*); *pa t* and *pa p* **hinged** (*hinjd*). — *adj* **hinge'-bound** unable to move easily on a hinge. — **hinge'-joint** (*anatom*) a joint that allows movement in one plane only. — **off the hinges** disorganized; out of gear. [Related to **hang**]

hinny[1] *hin'i, n* the offspring of a stallion and a female ass or donkey. [L *hinnus*, from Gr *ginnos*, later *hinnos* a mule]

hinny[2] *hin'i, n* a Scot or N Eng variant of **honey** (the term of endearment).

hinny[3] *hin'i, vi* to neigh, whinny. [Fr *hennir*, from L *hinnīre*]

hint *hint, n* moment, opportunity (*obs*); a distant or indirect indication or allusion; slight mention; insinuation; a helpful suggestion or tip. — *vt* to intimate or indicate indirectly. — *vi* to give hints. — *adv* **hint'ingly**. — **hint at** to give a hint, suggestion, or indication of. [OE *hentan* to seize]

hinterland *hint'ər-land* or (*Ger*) *-länt, n* a region lying inland from a port or centre of influence. [Ger]

hip[1] *hip, n* the haunch or fleshy part of the thigh; the hip-joint; the external angle formed by the sides of a roof when the end slopes backwards instead of terminating in a gable (*archit*). — *vt* to sprain or hurt the hip of; to throw over the hip; to carry on the hip (*US*); to construct with a hip (*archit*): — *pr p* **hipp'ing**; *pa t* and *pa p* **hipped** or **hipt**. — *adj* **hipped** having a hip or hips; of a roof, sloping at the end as well as at the sides. — *n* **hipp'ing** (*Scot*) a baby's nappy (wrapped around the hips). — *adj* **hipp'y** having large hips. — *n pl* **hip'sters** (or *US* **hip'-huggers**) trousers (for men or women) designed to fit on the hips, not the waist. — **hip'-bath** a bath to sit in; **hip'-belt** the 14c sword-belt, passing diagonally from waist to hip; **hip'-bone** the innominate bone; **hip'-flask** a flask, *esp* one containing alcoholic spirit, carried in a hip-pocket; **hip'-girdle** the pelvic girdle; a hip-belt; **hip'-gout** sciatica; **hip-huggers** see **hipsters** above; **hip'-joint** the articulation of the head of the thigh-bone with the ilium; **hip-joint disease** a disease of the hip-joint with inflammation, fungus growth, caries, and dislocation; **hip'-knob** an ornament placed on the apex of the hip of a roof or of a gable; **hip'-lock** in wrestling, a form of cross-buttock; **hip-pock'et** a trouser pocket behind the hip; **hip replacement** operative replacement of the hip-joint, performed *esp* in cases of severe osteo-arthritis; **hip-roof'** a hipped roof. — *adj* **hip'-shot** having the hip out of joint. — **have or catch on the hip** to get an advantage over someone (from wrestling). [OE *hype*; Gothic *hups*, Ger *Hüfte*]

hip[2] *hip*, or **hep** *hep, n* the fruit of the dog-rose or other rose. [OE *hēope*]

hip[3] or **hyp** *hip, n* (*archaic*) hypochondria. — *vt* to render melancholy or annoyed; to offend. — *adj* **hipped** melancholy; peevish, offended, annoyed; obsessed. — *adj* **hipp'ish**. [**hypochondria** (see under **hypo-**)]

hip[4] *hip, interj* an exclamation to invoke a united cheer — **hip'-hip'-hurrah'** or **hip'-hip'-hooray'**.

hip[5] *hip,* (*colloq*) *adj* knowing, informed about, or following the latest trends in music, fashion, political ideas, etc. — *n* **hip'ness**. — *n* **hipp'ie** or **hipp'y** one of the hippies, successors of the beatniks as rebels against the values of middle-class society, who stress the importance of love, organize to some extent their own communities, and wear colourful clothes. — *n* **hipp'iedom** or **hipp'ydom** the lifestyle or community of hippies. — *n* **hipster** (*hip'stər*) a person who knows and appreciates up-to-date jazz; a member of the beat generation (1950s and early 1960s). — **hip'-hop** a popular culture movement developed in the US in the early 1980s and comprising rap music, breakdancing and graffiti, and whose adherents typically wear baggy clothes and loosely tied or untied training shoes or boots. — Also *adj.* [A later form of **hep**[2]]

hip-bath... to... **hip-gout**. See under **hip**[1].

hip-hip-. See under **hip**[4].

hip-huggers... to... **hip-lock**. See under **hip**[1].

hipness. See under **hip**[5].

hipp- *hip-* or **hippo-** *hip-o-, combining form* denoting a horse. — *n* **hipp'ophile** a lover of horses. — *n* **hipp'ophobe** a hater of horses. [Gr *hippos* a horse]

hipparch *hip'ärk, n* in ancient Greece, a cavalry commander. [Gr *hipparchos*]

Hipparion *hi-pā'ri-on, n* a fossil genus of Equidae. [Gr *hipparion*, dimin of *hippos* a horse]

hippeastrum *hip-i-as'trəm, n* any plant of the S American genus *Hippeastrum*, bulbous, with white or red flowers. [Gr *hippeus* horseman, and *astron* star]

hipped. See under **hip**[1,3].

hippety-hoppety *hip'ə-ti-hop'ə-ti, adv* hopping and skipping. — *n* and *adv* **hipp'ety-hop'**.

hippiatric *hip-i-at'rik, adj* relating to the treatment of the diseases of horses. — *n sing* **hippiat'rics**. — *n* **hippiatrist** (*-ī'ət-rist*). — *n* **hippiatry** (*-ī'ət-ri*). [Gr *hippiātrikos*, from *hippos* horse, and *iātros* a physician]

hippic *hip'ik, adj* relating to horses. [Gr *hippikos*, from *hippos* horse]

hippie, hippiedom. See **hip**[5].

hipping. See under **hip**[1].

hippish. See under **hip**[3].

hippo *hip'ō, n* a shortened form of **hippopotamus**: — *pl* **hipp'os**.

hippo-. See **hipp-**.

hippocampus *hip-ō-kam'pəs, n* a fish-tailed horse-like sea-monster (*mythol*); a genus of small fishes (family Syngnathidae) with horse-like head and neck, the sea-horse; a raised curved trace on the floor of the lateral ventricle of the brain (*anatom*): — *pl* **hippocamp'ī**. — *adj* (*anatom*) **hippocamp'al**. [Gr *hippokampos*, from *hippos* a horse, and *kampos* a sea-monster]

Hippocastanaceae *hip-ō-kast-ə-nā'si-ē, n pl* the horse-chestnut family. [**hippo-**, and Gr *kastanon* chestnut tree]

hippocentaur *hip-ō-sent'ör, n.* Same as **centaur**. [Gr *hippokentauros*, from *hippos* a horse, and *kentauros*]

hippocras *hip'ō-kras, n* an old English drink of spiced wine, formerly much used as a cordial. [ME *ypocras* Hippocrates]

Hippocratic *hip-ō-krat'ik, adj* pertaining to the Greek physician *Hippocrates* (*Hippokratēs*; born about 460 BC). — *n* **Hippoc'ratism**. — *vi* **Hippocratize** or **-ise** (*-ok'rə-tīz*) to imitate or follow Hippocrates. — **Hippocratic face, look**, etc, sunken, livid appearance, eg near death, described by Hippocrates; **Hippocratic oath** an oath taken by a doctor binding him or her to observe the code of medical ethics contained in it — first drawn up (perhaps by Hippocrates) in the 4th or 5th century BC.

Hippocrene *hip-ō-krē'nē* or *hip'ō-krēn*, (*mythol*) *n* a fountain on the northern slopes of Mount Helicon, sacred to the Muses and Apollo, attributed to a kick of Pegasus. [Gr *hippokrēnē*, from *hippos* a horse, and *krēnē* a fountain]

hippocrepian *hip-ō-krē'pi-ən*, *adj* horseshoe-shaped. [**hippo-** and Gr *krēpis* a shoe]

hippodame *hip'ō-dām*, *n* (*Spenser*, wrongly) the sea-horse. — *n* **hippodamist** (*hip-od'ə-mist*) a horse-tamer. — *adj* **hippod'amous** horse-taming. [**hippo-** and Gr *damaein* to tame]

hippodrome *hip'ə-drōm*, *n* (in ancient Greece and Rome) a racecourse for horses and chariots; a circus; a variety theatre. — *adj* **hippodromic** (*-drom'ik*). [Gr *hippodromos*, from *hippos* a horse, and *dromos* a course]

hippogriff or **hippogryph** *hip'ō-grif*, *n* a fabulous medieval animal, a griffin-headed winged horse. [Fr *hippogriffe*, from Gr *hippos* a horse, and *gryps* a griffin]

hippology *hip-ol'ə-ji*, *n* the study of horses. — *n* **hippol'ogist**. [**hippo-** and Gr *logos* discourse]

hippomanes *hip-om'ən-ēz*, *n* an ancient philtre obtained from a mare or foal. [**hippo-** and Gr *maniā* madness]

hippophagy *hip-of'ə-ji* or *-gi*, *n* feeding on horse-flesh. — *n* **hippoph'agist** an eater of horse-flesh. — *adj* **hippoph'agous** (*-gəs*) horse-eating. [**hippo-** and Gr *phagein* (aorist) to eat]

hippophile, hippophobe. See under **hipp-**.

hippopotamus *hip-ō-pot'ə-məs*, *n* a large African artiodactyl ungulate of aquatic habits, with very thick skin, short legs, and a large head and muzzle: — *pl* **hippopot'amus, hippopot'amuses** or **hippopot'ami** (*-mī*). — *adj* **hippopotamian** (*-tām'*) or **hippopotamic** (*-tam'*, also *-pot'*) like a hippopotamus, clumsy. [L, from Gr *hippopotamos*, from *hippos* a horse, and *potamos* a river]

hippuric *hip-ū'rik*, *adj* denoting an acid, first obtained from the urine of horses, occurring in the urine of many animals, particularly in that of herbivores and rarely in that of human beings. [**hippo-** and Gr *ouron* urine]

Hippuris *hi-pū'ris*, *n* the mare's-tail genus of Haloragidaceae. — *n* **hipp'ūrite** a Cretaceous fossil lamellibranch (**Hippurī'tes**) with one conical valve and one flat one. — *adj* **hippurit'ic**. [**hippo-** and Gr *ourā* a tail]

hippus *hip'əs*, *n* clonic spasm of the iris. [New L, from Gr *hippos* a horse]

hippy. See under **hip**[1,5].

hippydom. See under **hip**[1,5].

hipster, hipsters. See under **hip**[1,5].

hipt. See under **hip**[1].

hirable. See under **hire**.

hiragana *hēr-ə-gä'nə*, *n* the more widely used of the two Japanese systems of syllabic writing (the other being **katakana**; both based on Chinese ideograms). [Jap, flat kana]

hircine *hûr'sīn*, *adj* goat-like; having a strong goatish smell. — *n* **hircosity** (*-kos'i-ti*) goatishness. — **hircocervus** (*hûr-kō-sûr'vəs*) a fabulous creature, half goat, half stag. [L *hīrcus* a he-goat]

hirdy-girdy *hûr'di-gûr'di*, (*Scot*) *adv* in confusion or tumult.

hire *hīr*, *n* wages for service; the price paid for the use of anything; an arrangement by which use or service is granted for payment. — *vt* to procure the use or service of, at a price; to engage for wages; to grant temporary use of for payment (often with *out*). — *adj* **hir'able** or **hire'able**. — *n* **hir'age** or **hire'age** (*NZ*) the fee for hiring something. — *adj* **hired**. — *n* **hire'ling** (*derog*) a hired servant; a mercenary; a person activated solely by material considerations. — Also *adj*. — *n* **hir'er** a person who obtains use or service for payment; (now *Scot* or *obs*) a person who lets out something on hire. — *n* **hir'ing** the act or contract by which an article or service is hired; (also **hiring fair**) a fair or market where servants are engaged (*archaic*). — Also *adj*. — **hire car** a rented car, *usu* one rented for a short period; **hire-pur'chase** a system by which a hired article becomes the hirer's property after a stipulated number of payments. — Also *adj*. — **on hire** for hiring; for hire. [OE *hȳr* wages, *hȳrian* to hire]

hirling. See **herling**.

hirple *hûr'pl* or *hir'pl*, (*Scot*) *vi* to walk or run as if lame. — *n* a limping gait.

hirrient *hir'i-ənt*, *adj* roughly trilled. — *n* a trilled sound. [L *hirriēns*, *-entis*, pr p of *hirrīre* to snarl]

hirsel *hûr'sl* or *hir'sl*, (*Scot*) *n* a stock of sheep; a multitude; the ground occupied by a hirsel of sheep. — *vt* to put in different groups. [ON *hirzla* safe-keeping, from *hirtha* to herd]

hirsle *hûr'sl* or *hir'sl*, (*Scot*) *vi* to slide or wriggle on the buttocks; to shift or fidget in one's seat; to move forward with a rustling sound. [Cf ON *hrista* to shake]

hirstie *hirs'ti* or *hûrs'ti*, (*obs Scot*) *adj* dry; barren.

hirsute *hûr'sūt*, or *hər-sūt'*, *adj* hairy; rough; shaggy; having long, stiffish hairs (*bot*). — *n* **hirsute'ness**. — *n* **hirsut'ism**. [L *hirsūtus*, from *hirsus*, *hirtus* shaggy]

hirudin *hir-ōōd'in*, *n* a substance present in the salivary secretion of the leech which prevents blood-clotting. — *n pl* **Hirudinea** (*-in'i-ə*) a class of worms, the leeches. — *n* and *adj* **hirudin'ean**. — *adj* **hirud'inoid**. — *adj* **hirud'inous**. [L *hirūdō*, *-inis* a leech]

hirundine *hi-run'dīn* or *-din*, *adj* of or pertaining to the swallow. [L *hirundō*, *-inis* a swallow]

his *hiz*, *pron*, *genitive* of **he**, or (*obs*) of **it** (or *possessive adj*). — **hisn** or **his'n** dialectal forms on the analogy of **mine, thine**. [OE *his*, genitive of *hē*, *he* he, and of *hit* it]

hish *hish*, a by-form of **hiss**.

Hispanic *his-pan'ik*, *adj* Spanish; of Spanish origin, eg Mexican. — Also *n*. — *adv* **Hispan'ically**. — *n* **hispan'icism** a Spanish phrase. — *vt* **hispan'icize** or **-ise** (*-i-sīz*; often with *cap*) or **hispan'iolize** or **-ise** to render Spanish. [L *Hispānia* Spain]

Hispano- *his-pā'nō-*, *combining form* denoting Spanish, as in *Hispano-American* Spanish-American. [L *hispānus*]

hispid *his'pid*, (*bot* and *zool*) *adj* rough with, or covered with, strong hairs or bristles. — *n* **hispid'ity**. [L *hīspidus*]

hiss *his*, *vi* to make a sibilant sound like that represented by the letter *s*, the sound made by a goose, snake, gas escaping from a narrow hole, a disapproving audience, etc. — *vt* to condemn by hissing; to drive by hissing. — *n* a sibilant; a hissing sound. — *n* and *adj* **hiss'ing**. — *adv* **hiss'ingly**. [Imit]

hist *hist* or *st*, *interj* demanding silence and attention; hush; silence. — *vt* (*hist*) to urge or summon, as by making the sound. — *vi* to be silent. [Imit]

hist. *abbrev*: histology; historian; history.

hist- *hist-*, **histio-** *hist-(i-)ō-* or **histo-** *hist-o'-*, *combining form* denoting: animal or plant tissue; sail. — *n* **histaminase** (*-am'i-nās*) an enzyme which helps to break down histamine, often used in the treatment of allergies. — *n* **hist'amine** (*-ə-mēn*) a base used in medicine, obtained from ergot, from histidine, etc; present also in all tissues of the body, being liberated into the blood, eg when the skin is cut or burnt. — *n* **hist'idine** (*-i-dēn*) an amino-acid derived from proteins. — *n* **histiocyte** (*-i-ō-sīt'*) a macrophage. — *adj* **histiocyt'ic**. — *adj* **hist'ioid** or **hist'oid** like ordinary tissue. — *n* **histiol'ogy** same as **histology** (see below). — *n* **Histioph'orus** or **Istioph'orus** (Gr *phoros* bearer) a genus of sword-fishes with a sail-like dorsal fin. — *adj* **histioph'oroid**. — *n* **hist'oblast** a cell or group of cells, forming the primary element or unit of tissue. — *n* **histochem'ist**. — *n* **histochem'istry** the chemistry of living tissues. — *n* **histocompatibil'ity** (*genetics*) the factor determining the acceptance or rejection of cells. — *n* **hist'ogen** (*bot*) a more or less well-defined region within a plant where tissues undergo differentiation. — *n* **histogenesis** (*-jen'i-sis*) the formation or differentiation of tissues (*biol*). — *adj* **histogenetic** (*-ji-net'ik*). — *adv* **histogenet'ically** or **histogen'ically**. — *adj* **histogen'**-

ic. — *n* **histogeny** (*his-toj'i-ni*) histogenesis. — *n* **hist'ogram** a statistical graph in which frequency distribution is shown by means of rectangles. — *adj* **histolog'ic** or **histolog'ical**. — *adv* **histolog'ically**. — *n* **histologist** (*-tol'*). — *n* **histol'ogy** the study of the minute structure of the tissues of organisms. — *n* **histol'ysis** (Gr *lysis* loosing) the breakdown of organic tissues. — *adj* **histolytic** (*-ō-lit'ik*). — *adv* **histolyt'ically**. — *n* **his'tone** any of a group of simple proteins, strongly basic and of quite low molecular weights, present in chromosomes and believed to act as gene inhibitors. — *n* **histopathol'ogist** a pathologist who studies the effects of disease on tissues of the body. — *adj* **histopatholog'-ical**. — *n* **histopathol'ogy**. — *n* **histoplasmō'sis** a disease of animals and man due to infection by the fungal organism *Histoplasma capsulatum*. [Gr *histos* and *histion* a web]

histie. Same as **hirstie**.

history *hist'ər-i*, *n* an account of an event; a systematic account of the origin and progress of the world, a nation, an institution, a science, etc; the knowledge of past events; the academic discipline of understanding or interpreting past events; a course of events; a life-story; an eventful life, a past of more than common interest; a drama representing historical events. — *vt* to record (*Shakesp*). — *n* **historian** (*his-tö'ri-ən*) a writer of history (*usu* in the sense of an expert or an authority on). — *adj* **histo'riāted** decorated with elaborate ornamental designs and figures (also **sto'riated**). — *adj* **historic** (*-tor'ik*) famous or important in history. — *adj* **histor'ical** pertaining to history; containing history; derived from history; associated with history; according to history; authentic. (Formerly *historic* and *historical* were often used interchangeably.) — *adv* **histor'ically**. — *n* **histor'icism** or **hist'orism** a theory that all sociological phenomena are historically determined; a strong or excessive concern with and respect for the institutions of the past. — *n* and *adj* **histor'icist**. — *n* **historicity** (*hist-ər-is'i-ti*) historical truth or actuality. — *vt* **histor'icize** or **-ise** (*-sīz*) to make or represent as historic. — *n* **historiette'** a short history or story. — *vt* **histor'ify** to record in history. — *n* **historiog'rapher** a writer of history (*esp* an official historian). — *adj* **historiograph'ic** or **historiograph'ical**. — *adv* **historiograph'ically**. — *n* **historiog'raphy** the art or employment of writing history. — *n* **historiol'ogy** the knowledge or study of history. — **historism** see **historicism** above. — **historic** (or **historical**) **cost** the actual price paid; **historical materialism** the Marxist theory that all historic processes and forms of society are based on economic factors; **historical method** the study of a subject in its historical development; **historical novel** a novel having as its setting a period in history and involving historical characters and events; **historical painting** the painting of historic scenes in which historic figures are introduced; **historical present** the present tense used for the past, to add life and reality to the narrative; **historical school** those scholars, *esp* in the fields of economics, legal philosophy and ethnology, who emphasize historical circumstance and evolutionary development in their researches and conclusions. — **be history** (*colloq*) to be finished, gone, dead, etc, as in *he's history*; **make history** to do that which will mould the future or have to be recognized by future historians; to do something never previously accomplished. [L *historia*, from Gr *historiā*, from *histōr* knowing]

histrionic *his-tri-on'ik* or **histrionical** *his-tri-on'ik-əl*, *adj* relating to the stage or actors; stagy, theatrical; affected; melodramatic; hypocritical. — *adv* **histrion'-ically**. — *n* (*archaic*) **his'triō** (from L; *pl* **his'trios**) or **his'trion** (from Fr) an actor. — *n* **histrion'icism** or **his'trionism** acting; theatricality. — *npl* **histrion'ics** play-acting; stagy action or speech; insincere exhibition of emotion. [L *histriōnicus*, from *histriō* an actor]

hit *hit*, *vt* to strike; to reach with a blow or missile (also *fig*); to come into forceful contact with; to knock (eg oneself, one's head); to inflict (a blow); to drive by a stroke; to move on to (a road), reach (a place); (of news) to be published in (*colloq*); to light upon or attain by chance; to imitate exactly; to suit, fit or conform to; to hurt, affect painfully (*fig*); to make a request or demand of (*NAm colloq*). — *vi* to strike; to make a movement of striking; to come in contact; to arrive suddenly and destructively; to come, by effort or chance, luckily (upon); to suit (with) (*obs*); (of an internal combustion engine) to ignite the air and fuel mixture in the cylinders; to inject a dose of a hard drug (*slang*); to murder (*slang*): — *pr p* **hitt'ing**; *pa t* and *pa p* **hit**. — *n* an act or occasion of striking; a successful stroke or shot; a lucky chance; a surprising success; an effective remark, eg a sarcasm, witticism; something that pleases the public or an audience; at backgammon, a move that throws one of the opponent's men back to the entering point, or a game won after one or two men are removed from the board; a murder by a gang of criminals (*slang*); a dose of a hard drug (*slang*). — *n* **hitt'er**. — *adj* **hit'-and-miss'** hitting or missing, according to circumstances; **hit'-and-run'** (eg of an air raid) lasting only a very short time; (of a driver) causing injury and driving off without reporting the incident; (of an accident) caused by a hit-and-run driver. — Also *n*. — **hit list** (*slang*) a list of people to be killed by gangsters or terrorists; *generally* a list of targeted victims; **hit'-man** (*slang*) someone employed to kill or attack others (also *fig*). — *adj* **hit'-or-miss'** random. — **hit'-parade** a list of currently popular songs (*old*); a list of the most popular things of any kind (*fig*). — *adj* **hitt'y-miss'y** random, haphazard. — **a hit or a miss** a case in which either success or complete failure is possible; **hard hit** gravely affected by some trouble, or by love; **hit a blot** in backgammon, to capture an exposed man; to find a weak place; **hit at** to aim a blow, sarcasm, jibe, etc at; **hit below the belt** see under **belt**; **hit it** to find, often by chance, the right answer; **hit it off** to agree, be compatible and friendly (sometimes with *with*); **hit it up** (*slang*) to inject a drug; **hit off** to imitate or describe aptly (someone or something); **hit on** or **upon** to come upon, discover, devise; to single out; **hit out** to strike out, *esp* with the fist; to attack strongly (absolute or with *at*); **hit the bottle** (*slang*) to drink excessively; **hit the ceiling** or **roof** to be seized with or express violent anger; **hit the ground running** (*colloq*) to react instantly, functioning at full speed and efficiency immediately; **hit the hay** or **sack** (*slang*) to go to bed; **hit the high spots** see under **high**[1]; **hit the nail on the head** see under **nail**; **hit the road** (*slang*) to leave, go away; **hit the sack** see **hit the hay** above; **hit wicket** the act, or an instance, of striking the wicket with the bat or part of the body (and thus being out; *cricket*); **make** or **score a hit with** to become popular with; to make a good impression on. [OE *hyttan*, appar ON *hitta* to light on, to find; Swed *hitta* to find, Dan *hitte* to hit upon]

hitch *hich*, *vi* to move jerkily; to hobble or limp; to catch on an obstacle; to connect with a moving vehicle so as to be towed (*orig NAm*); to travel by getting lifts, to hitch-hike. — *vt* to jerk; to hook; to catch; to fasten; to tether; to harness to a vehicle; to make fast; to throw into place; to bring in (to verse, a story, etc), *esp* with obvious straining or effort; to obtain (a lift) in a passing vehicle. — *n* a jerk; a limp or hobble; a catch or anything that holds; a stoppage owing to a small or passing difficulty; a type of knot by which one rope is connected with another, or to some object (*naut*); a means of connecting a thing to be dragged; a mode or act of harnessing a horse or horses, a team, or a vehicle with horses (*US*); a lift in a vehicle; a slight fault or displacement in a bed of sedimentary rock (*mining*); a recess cut in rock to support a timber (*mining*). — *n* **hitch'er**. — *adv* **hitch'ily**. — *adj* **hitch'y**. — *vi* **hitch'-hike** to hike with the help of lifts in vehicles. — **hitch'-hike**; **hitch'-hiker**; **hitching post** a post, etc to which a horse's reins can be tied. — **clove hitch** a type of knot by which a rope is attached to a pole, spar or rope thicker than itself; **get hitched** (*slang*) to get married; **hitch and kick** a technique in high jumping whereby the athlete springs from, kicks with, and lands on the same foot; **hitch up** to harness a horse to a vehicle; to jerk up; to marry (*slang*); **timber hitch** a knot for tying a rope round a log, etc for hauling. [Ety obscure]

hi tech. See **high tech** under **high**.

hithe *hīdh*, *n* a small haven or port, *esp* a landing-place on a river. Now *obs* except in historical use or in place names. [OE *hȳth*]

hither *hidh'ər*, *adv* to this place. — *adj* on this side or in this direction; nearer. — *vi* to come — chiefly in the phrase *to hither and thither*, ie to go to and fro. — *adj* **hith'ermost** nearest on this side. — **hith'erside** the nearer side. — *adv* **hith'erto** up to this time; to this point or place (*archaic*). — *adv* **hith'erward** or **hith'erwards** (*archaic*) towards this place. — **hither and thither** to and fro; this way and that. [OE *hider*; Gothic *hidrē*, ON *hethra*]

Hitler *hit'ler*, (*colloq*) *n* a person similar in character to Adolf *Hitler* (1889–1945), German Nazi dictator, overbearing or despotic (also (*contemptuous*) **little Hitler**). — *n* **Hitlerism** (*hit'lər-izm*) the principles, policy, and methods of Adolf Hitler, ie militant anti-Semitic nationalism, subordinating everything to the state. — *n* and *adj* **Hit'lerist** or **Hit'lerite**.

Hitopadesa *hē-tō-pä-dā'shə*, *n* a collection of fables and stories in Sanskrit literature, a popular summary of the *Panchatantra*. [Sans *Hitopadeśa*]

Hittite *hit'īt*, *n* one of the Khatti or Heth, an ancient people of Syria and Asia Minor; an extinct language belonging to the Anatolian group of languages and discovered from documents in cuneiform writing. — Also *adj*. [Heb *Hitti*; Gr *Chettaios*]

hitty-missy. See under **hit**.

HIV *abbrev*: human immunodeficiency virus. — *adj* **HIV positive** or (*colloq*) **positive** carrying the virus. — **HIV test**; **HIV testing**; **HIV-1** and **HIV-2** the two identified strains of the virus.

hive *hīv*, *n* a box or basket in which bees live and store up honey; a colony of bees; a scene of great industry; a teeming multitude or breeding-place; a hat of plaited straw shaped like an old beehive (*obs*). — *vt* to collect into a hive; to lay up in store (often with *away* or *up*). — *vi* (of bees) to enter or take possession of a hive; to take shelter together; to reside in a body. — *adj* **hive'less**. — *adj* **hive'like**. — *n* **hīv'er** someone who hives. — *adj* and *adv* **hive'ward**. — *adv* **hive'wards**. — **hive'-bee** the common honey-producing bee, *Apis mellifica*; **hive'-honey**; **hive'-nest** a large nest built and occupied by several pairs of birds in common. — **hive off** to withdraw as if in a swarm; to assign (work) to a subsidiary company; to divert (assets or sections of an industrial concern) to other concerns (*n* **hive'-off**). [OE *hȳf*]

hives *hīvz*, *n* a popular term for nettlerash and similar diseases or for laryngitis. [Origin unknown]

hiya *hī'yə*, (*slang*) *interj* a greeting developed from **how are you**.

Hizbollah or **Hizbullah** *hiz-bə-lä'*, *n* an organization of militant Shiite Muslims. [Ar, party of God]

Hizen *hē-zen'*, (also without *cap*) *adj* of a type of richly decorated Japanese porcelain. — Also *n*. [*Hizen* province in Kyushu, Japan]

hizz *hiz*, (*Shakesp*) *vi* to hiss. [Echoic]

HO *abbrev*: hostilities only, used to designate service in the Royal Navy during wartime.

HK *abbrev*: Hong Kong (IVR); House of Keys (the Manx parliament).

HKJ *abbrev*: Hashemite Kingdom of Jordan (IVR).

hl *abbrev*: hectolitres.

HM *abbrev*: (His or) Her Majesty.

hm *abbrev*: hectometre.

HMAS *abbrev*: (His or) Her Majesty's Australian Ship.

HMC *abbrev*: (His or) Her Majesty's Customs; Headmasters' Conference.

HMCS *abbrev*: (His or) Her Majesty's Canadian Ship.

HMG *abbrev*: (His or) Her Majesty's Government.

HMI *abbrev*: (His or) Her Majesty's Inspector or Inspectorate.

HMP *abbrev*: (*L*) *hoc monumentum posuit* erected this monument.

HMIP *abbrev*: Her Majesty's Inspectorate of Pollution.

HMS *abbrev*: (His or) Her Majesty's Service or Ship.

HMSO *abbrev*: (His or) Her Majesty's Stationery Office

HNC *abbrev*: Higher National Certificate (a qualification awarded by BTEC).

HND *abbrev*: Higher National Diploma.

Ho (*chem*) *symbol*: holmium.

ho (*old*), **hoa** or **hoh** *hō*, *interj* a call to excite attention, to announce destination or direction, to express exultation, surprise, or (*esp* if repeated) derision or laughter; hullo; hold; stop. — *n* cessation; moderation: — *pl* **hos, hoas** or **hohs**. — *vi* (*obs*) to stop. [Cf ON *hō*, Fr *ho*]

ho. *abbrev*: house.

hoa. See under **ho**.

hoactzin. See under **hoatzin**.

hoar *hör*, *adj* white or greyish-white, *esp* with age or frost (*poetic*); mouldy (*obs*). — *n* hoariness; age. — *vi* (*Shakesp*) to become mouldy. — *vt* (*Shakesp*) to make hoary. — *adv* **hoar'ily**. — *n* **hoar'iness**. — *adj* **hoar'y** white or grey with age; ancient; covered with short, dense, whitish hairs (*bot*, *entomol*). — **hoar'-frost** rime or white frost, the white particles formed by the freezing of the dew; **hoar'head** a hoary-headed old man. — *adj* **hoar'-headed**. — **hoar'-stone** (*Scot* **hare'-stane**) an old hoary stone; a standing-stone or ancient boundary stone. [OE *hār* hoary, grey; ON *hārr*]

hoard[1] *hörd*, *n* a store; a hidden stock; a treasure; a place for hiding anything (*obs*). — *vt* to store, *esp* in excess; to treasure up; to amass and deposit in secret. — *vi* to store up; to collect and form a hoard. — *n* **hoard'er**. [OE *hord*; ON *hodd*, Ger *Hort*]

hoard[2] *hörd*, (*old*) *n* a hoarding. [OFr *hurdis*, from *hurt*, *hourt*, *hourd* a palisade]

hoarding *hörd'ing*, *n* a screen of boards, *esp* for enclosing a place where builders are at work, or for display of bills, advertisements, etc. [**hoard**[2]]

hoarhound. See **horehound**.

hoarse *hörs*, *adj* rough and husky; having a rough husky voice, as from a cold; harsh; discordant. — *adv* **hoarse'ly**. — *vt* and *vi* **hoars'en**. — *n* **hoarse'ness**. [ME *hors*, *hoors*, from OE *hās*, inferred *hārs*]

hoast *hōst*, (*dialect*) *n* a cough. — *vi* to cough. [ON *hōste*; cf OE *hwōsta*; Du *hoest*]

hoastman *hōst'man*, *n* a member of an old merchant guild in Newcastle, with charge of coal-shipping, etc. [OFr *hoste*, from L *hospes* stranger, guest]

hoatzin *hō-at'sin* or **hoactzin** *-akt'*, *n* a S American bird (*Opisthocomus*), forming an order by itself, with an occipital crest, large crop, peculiar sternum, and, in the tree-climbing and swimming young, clawed wings. — Also **stink'-bird**. [Nahuatl *uatsin*]

hoax *hōks*, *n* a deceptive trick played as a practical joke or maliciously. — Also *adj*. — *vt* to trick, by a practical joke or fabricated tale, for fun or maliciously. — *n* **hoax'er**. [Appar **hocus** (see under **hocus-pocus**)]

hob[1] *hob*, *n* a hub; a surface beside a fireplace, on which anything may be laid to keep hot; the flat framework or surface on top of a gas, etc cooker on which pots are placed to be heated; a game in which stones are thrown at coins on the end of a short stick — also the stick used; a gear-cutting tool. — **hob'nail** a nail with a thick strong head, used in horseshoes, heavy workshoes, etc. — *vt* to furnish with hobnails; to trample upon with hobnailed shoes. — *adj* **hob'nailed**. [Cf **hub**]

hob[2] *hob*, *n* a rustic; a lout; a fairy or brownie (as Robin Goodfellow); a clownish fellow; a male ferret; mischief. — *adj* **hobb'ish** clownish. — *n* **Hobb'inoll** a rustic (from Spenser's *Shepheards Calender*). — *n* **hob'goblin** a mischievous fairy; a frightful apparition. — *n* **hobgob'linism** or **hobgob'linry**. — **play hob** or **raise hob** to cause confusion. [For *Robert*]

hob-a-nob and **hob-and-nob**. Same as **hobnob**.

Hobbesian *hobz'i-ən* or **Hobbian** *hob'i-ən*, *adj* relating to Thomas *Hobbes* (1588–1679) or his political philosophy. — *n* a follower of Hobbes. — *n* **Hobbes'ianism**, **Hobb'ianism** or **Hobb'ism**. — *n* **Hobb'ist** a Hobbesian. — *adj* **Hobb'ist** or **Hobbist'ical**.

hobbit *hob'it*, *n* one of a race of imaginary beings, half human size, hole-dwelling and hairy-footed, invented by J R R Tolkien in his novel *The Hobbit* (1937). — *n* **hobb'itry**.

hobble *hob'l*, *vi* to walk with short unsteady steps; to walk awkwardly; (of action, verse, speech, etc) to move irregularly. — *vt* to fasten the legs of (a horse) loosely together; to hamper; to perplex. — *n* an awkward hobbling gait; a difficulty, a scrape (*archaic*); anything used to hamper the feet of an animal, a clog or fetter. — *n* **hobb'ler** someone who hobbles; an unlicensed pilot, a casual labourer in docks, etc; a man who tows a canal-boat with a rope. — *n* **hobb'ling**. — *adv* **hobb'lingly**. — **hobb'le-bush** the N American wayfaring-tree (*Viburnum alnifolium*), a small shrub with white flowers and straggling branches that impede movement among them; **hobble skirt** a narrow skirt that hampers walking. [Cf Du *hobbelen*, *hobben* to toss, and **hopple**]

hobbledehoy *hob'l-di-hoi'*, *n* an awkward youth, a stripling, neither man nor boy. — *n* **hobbledehoy'dom**, **hobbledehoy'hood** or **hobbledehoy'ism**. — *adj* **hobbledehoy'ish**. [Origin obscure]

hobbler *hob'lər*, (*obs*) *n* a person required to keep a hobby (horse) for military service; a horseman employed for light work, such as reconnoitring, etc; a horse. [OFr *hobeler*, from *hobin* a small horse]

hobby[1] *hob'i*, *n* a small or smallish strong, active horse; a pacing horse; a favourite pursuit followed as an amusement; a hobby-horse; an early form of bicycle. — *n* **hobb'yism**. — *n* **hobb'yist** someone who rides or pursues a hobby. — *adj* **hobb'yless**. — **hobb'y-horse** a stick or figure of a horse straddled by children; one of the chief parts played in the ancient morris-dance; the wooden horse of a merry-go-round; a rocking-horse; a dandy-horse; a loose and frivolous person, male or female (*Shakesp*); a hobby; a favourite topic or obsession, *esp* in the phrase *to be on one's hobby-horse*. — *adj* **hobby-hors'ical** whimsically given to a hobby. [ME *hobyn*, *hoby*, prob *Hob*, a by-form of the name *Rob*, for *Robert*. OFr *hobin*, *hobi* (Fr *aubin*), is from the English]

hobby[2] *hob'i*, *n* a small species of falcon. [OFr *hobé*, *hobet*, from LL *hobētus*; prob OFr *hober* to move]

hobday *hob'dā*, *vt* to cure a breathing impediment in (a horse) by surgical operation. — *adj* **hob'dayed**. [After Sir Frederick *Hobday* (1869–1939)]

hobgoblin. See **hob**[2].

hobjob *hob'job*, (*dialect*) *n* an odd job. — *vi* to do odd jobs. — *n* **hob'jobber**. — *n* **hob'jobbing**.

hobnail. See **hob**[1].

hobnob *hob'nob*, *adv* at random; hit-or-miss; with alternate or mutual drinking of healths. — *vi* to associate or drink together familiarly; to talk informally (with): — *pr p* **hob'nobbing**. — *n* a sentiment in drinking (*obs*); mutual healthdrinking; a familiar private talk. — *adj* **hob'nobby**. [Prob *hab nab* have or have not (ne have); cf Shakespeare's *Twelfth Night*, III. 4 'Hob, nob, is his word; give 't or take 't']

hobo *hō'bō*, *n* an itinerant workman, *esp* unskilled (*NAm*); a homeless, penniless person; a tramp: — *pl* **ho'boes** or **ho'bos**. — *vt* to travel as a hobo. — *n* **ho'bodom** or **ho'boism**. [Origin unknown]

Hobson-Jobson *hob'sən-job'sən*, *n* festal excitement, *esp* at the Moharram ceremonies; the modification of names and words introduced from foreign languages, which the popular ear assimilates to already familiar sound, as in the case of the word Hobson-Jobson itself. [Ar *Yā Hasan*, *Yā Hosain* a typical phrase of Anglo-Indian argot at the time adopted as an alternative title for Yule and Burnell's *Glossary of Anglo-Indian Colloquial Words and Phrases* (1886)]

Hobson's choice. See under **choice**.

hoc *hok* or *hōk*, (*L*) *adj*, *pron* this. — **hoc anno** (*an'ō*) in this year; **hoc genus omne** (*jēn'əs* or *gen'ōōs om'ne*) all that sort; **hoc loco** (*lōk'* or *lok'ō*) in this place; **hoc tempore** (*tem'pə-rē* or *-po-re*) at this time.

hock[1] *hok* or **hough** *hok* or (*Scot*) *hohh*, *n* a joint on the hindleg of a quadruped, between the knee and fetlock, and sometimes on the leg of a domestic fowl, corresponding to the ankle-joint in humans; a piece of meat extending from the hock-joint upward; in humans, the back part of the knee-joint; the ham. — *vt* to hamstring. — *n* **hock'er**. [OE *hōh* the heel]

hock[2] *hok*, (*slang*) *vt* to pawn. — *n* the state of being in pawn. — **in hock** in debt; in prison; having been pawned, in pawn (*colloq*). [Du *hok* prison, hovel]

hock[3] *hok*, *n* properly, the wine made at *Hochheim*, on the Main, in Germany; now applied to all white Rhine wines. [Obs *Hockamore*, from Ger *Hochheimer*]

hock[4] *hok*, *vt* to subject to Hock-tide customs. — *vi* to observe Hock-tide. — **Hock'-day** or **Hock Tuesday** an old English festival held on the second Tuesday after Easter Sunday, one of the chief customs being the seizing and binding of men by women until they gave money for their liberty; (in *pl*) Hock Tuesday and the preceding day (**Hock Monday**) on which the men seized the women in the same way; **Hock'-tide** the two Hock-days. [Origin unknown]

hockey[1] *hok'i*, *n* a ball game played by two teams of eleven players, each with a club or stick curved at one end, a development of shinty; a hockey stick (*NAm*); ice hockey. — Also (*old*) **hook'ey**. [Prob OFr *hoquet* a crook]

hockey[2] *hok'i*, (*dialect*) *n* harvest-home, the harvest-supper. — Also **hawk'ey** or **hork'ey**. — **hock'-cart** the cart that brings home the last load of the harvest. [Origin unknown]

hockey[3]. See **oche**.

hocus-pocus *hō'kəs-pō'kəs*, *n* a juggler (*obs*); a juggler's trick or formula; skill in conjuring; deception; mumbo-jumbo. — *vi* to juggle. — *vt* to play tricks on. — *vt* **hoc'us** to cheat; to stupefy with drink; to drug (drink): — *pr p* **hō'cusing** or **hōcussing**; *pa t* and *pa p* **hō'cused** or **hō'cussed**. [Conjuror's sham Latin, once conjectured to be a corruption of *hoc est corpus* this is my body, Christ's words used in the communion service at the consecration of the bread]

hod[1] *hod*, *n* a V-shaped stemmed trough for carrying bricks or mortar on the shoulder; a coal-scuttle; a pewterer's blowpipe. — **hod carrier** or **hod'man** a man who carries a hod; a bricklayer's or mason's labourer. [Cf dialect *hot*, *hott*, MHGer *hotte*, obs Du *hodde*, Fr *hotte* a basket]

hod[2] *hod*, (*Scot*) *vi* to bob; to jog. — *vi* **hodd'le** (*Scot*) to waddle.

hodden *hod'n*, *n* coarse, undyed homespun woollen cloth, made from a mixture of black and white wool and so grey in appearance. — *adj* of or clad in hodden; rustic. — **hodd'en-grey** hodden; a homely unpretentious person. — Also *adj*. [Origin unknown]

hoddy-doddy. See under **hodmandod**.

Hodge *hoj*, *n* a countryman, rustic. [For *Roger*]

hodgepodge. See **hotchpotch**.

hodge-pudding *hoj'-pōōd-ing*, (*Shakesp*) *n* a pudding made of a mass of ingredients mixed together.

Hodgkin's disease *hoj'kinz diz-ēz'*, *n* a disease in which the spleen, liver and lymph nodes become enlarged, and progressive anaemia occurs. [After Thomas *Hodgkin*, 19c British physician]

hodiernal *hō-di-ûrn'əl*, *adj* of or pertaining to the present day. [L *hodiernus*, from *hodiē* today = *hōc diē* on this day]

hodja. See **khoja**.

hodmandod *hod'mən-dod*, *n* a shelled snail. — *n* **hodd'y-dodd'y** (*obs*) a dumpy person; a duped husband; a simpleton. [Cf **dodman**]

hodograph *hod'ə-gräf*, (*math*) *n* a curve whose radius vector represents the velocity of a moving point. [Gr *hodos* a way, and *graphein* to write]

hodometer, hodometry. See under **odometer**.

hodoscope *hod'ə-skōp*, (*phys*) *n* any apparatus for tracing the paths of charged particles. [Gr *hodos* a way, and *skopeein* to see]

hoe[1] *hō*, *n* a long-handled instrument with a narrow blade used for scraping or digging up weeds and loosening the earth. — *vt* to scrape, remove or clean with a hoe; to weed. — *vi* to use a hoe: — *pr p* **hoe'ing**; *pa t* and *pa p* **hoed**. — *n* **hō'er**. — **hoe'-cake** (*US*) a thin cake of Indian meal (*orig* baked on a hoe-blade); **hoe'down** (*esp US*) a country-dance, *esp* a square dance; hillbilly or other music for it; a party at which such dances are performed. [OFr *houe*, from OHGer *houwâ* (Ger *Haue*) a hoe]

hoe[2] *hō*, *n* a promontory or projecting ridge (now only in place names). [OE *hōh* heel; cf **heuch**]

Hof *hof* or *hōf*, (*Ger*) *n* yard; manor; court.

hog[1] *hog*, *n* a general name for swine; a castrated boar; a pig reared for slaughter; a yearling sheep not yet shorn (also **hogg**); the wool from such a sheep; a yearling of other species; a shilling (*old slang*); a low filthy fellow; a greedy person; an inconsiderate boor; a person of coarse manners; a frame or brush which is hauled along a ship's bottom to clean it. — *vt* and *vi* to eat hoggishly; to arch or hump like a hog's back, *esp* of the hull of a ship. — *vt* to cut like a hog's mane; to behave like a hog or a road-hog towards; to take or use selfishly: — *pr p* **hogg'ing**; *pa t* and *pa p* **hogged**. — *adj* **hogged** (*hogd*). — *n* **hogg'erel** a yearling sheep. — *n* **hogg'ery** hogs collectively; hoggishness of character; coarseness. — *n* **hogg'et** a yearling sheep or colt. — *adj* **hogg'ish**. — *adv* **hogg'ishly**. — *n* **hogg'ishness**. — *n* **hog'hood** the nature of a hog. — **hog'back** or **hog's'back** a hill-ridge, an ancient monument, or other object, shaped like a hog's back, ie curving down towards the ends; **hog'-cholera** swine-fever; **hog'-deer** a small Indian deer; **hog'-fish** a fish of N Atlantic waters, with bristles on its head; **hog'-frame** a frame built to resist vertical flexure; **hog'-mane** a mane clipped short or naturally short and upright. — *adj* **hog'-maned**. — **hog'-nose** any of various species of short-bodied, harmless American snakes (*Heterodon*); **hog'-pen** a pig-sty; **hog'-plum** a West Indian tree (*Spondias*) of the cashew family, the fruit of which is relished by pigs; **hog'-rat** the hutia, a West Indian rodent (*Capromys*); **hog'-reeve** or **hog'-constable** an officer whose duty was to round up stray swine; **hog'-ringer** a person who puts rings into the snouts of hogs. — *vt* **hog'-shouther** (*-shōō'dhər*; *Scot*) to jostle with the shoulder. — **hog'skin** leather made of the skin of pigs, pigskin; **hog's pudding** a hog's entrails stuffed with various ingredients. — *vt* **hog'tie** to tie (a person) up so as to prevent any movement of the arms or legs; to thwart, stymie, frustrate, impede. — **hog'ward** (*-wörd*) a swine-herd; **hog'wash** the refuse of a kitchen, brewery, etc given to pigs; thin worthless stuff; insincere nonsense; **hog'weed** the cow-parsnip; applied also to many other coarse plants. — **bring one's hogs to a fine market** to make a complete mess of something; **go the whole hog** see under **whole**; **hog in armour** a boor in fine clothes; **hog it** (*slang*) to eat greedily; to live in a slovenly fashion. [OE *hogg*]

hog[2] *hog*, *n* (in curling) a stone that does not pass the hog-score. — *vt* to play a hog. — **hog'-line** or **hog'-score** a line drawn across the rink short of which no stone counts. [Perh **hog**[1]]

hog[3] *hog*, (*dialect*) *n* a mound of earth and straw in which potatoes, etc, are stored. — *vt* to store (potatoes, etc) in such a heap. [Origin obscure]

hogan[1] *hō'gən*, *n* a log hut, *usu* covered with earth, built by the Navaho tribe of North American Indians. [Navaho]

hogan[2]. See under **hogen-mogen**.

hogen-mogen *hō'gən-mō'gən*, (*obs*) *n* haughtiness; (*usu* in *pl*) the Dutch States General. — *adj* high and mighty; Dutch; (of liquor) strong. — *n* **ho'gan** or **ho'gen** strong liquor. [Du *hoog en mogend* high and mighty]

hogg, hogged. See under **hog**[1].

hogger *hog'ər*, (*Scot*) *n* a footless stocking worn as a gaiter; a short connecting-pipe. [Origin obscure]

hoggerel, hoggery, hogget. See under **hog**[1].

hoggin or **hogging** *hog'in*, *n* sifted gravel; a mixture containing gravel. [Origin uncertain]

hoggish. See under **hog**[1].

hogh. A Spenserian spelling of **hoe**[2].

Hogmanay *hog-mə-nā'*, (*Scot*) *n* the last day of the year, New Year's Eve; something to eat and/or drink or a gift begged or bestowed then. [Prob from North Fr dialect *hoginane*, from 16c *aguillanneuf* (*-l'an neuf*) a gift at the New Year]

hogmane. See under **hog**[1].

hogshead *hogz'hed*, *n* a large cask (*Shakesp*); a measure of capacity = 52$\frac{1}{2}$ imperial gallons, or 63 old wine gallons; *of beer* = 54 gallons; *of claret* = 46 gallons; *of tobacco* (*US*) = 750 to 1200 lb. [Appar **hog's**, and **head**; reason unknown]

hogtie, hogward, hogwash, hogweed. See **hog**[1].

hoh *hō*. See **ho**.

ho-hum *hō'-hum'*, (*colloq*) *adj* dull, apathetic; boring, routine.

hoi *hoi*, (*colloq*) *interj* used to attract attention.

hoick or **hoik** *hoik*, *n* a jerk. — *vt* and *vi* to hitch up; (*esp* of aeroplanes) to jerk upwards. [Poss a variant of **hike**]

hoicks *hoiks*, *interj* a cry to urge hounds. — *vt* to urge on with cries. — *vi* to shout hoicks; to hark back.

hoiden. See **hoyden**.

hoik. See **hoick**.

hoi polloi *hoi'-pə-loi'*, (*derog*) *n* the many; the masses; the rabble, the vulgar. [Gr]

hoise *hoiz*, (*archaic*) *vt* to hoist: — *pa t* and *pa p* **hoised** or **hoist**. [Perh Old Du *hijssen*, Du *hijschen* to hoist]

hoist *hoist*, *vt* to lift; to heave upwards; to raise or move with tackle; to steal (*slang*). — *n* act of lifting; the height of a sail; that part of a flag next to the mast; a set of signal flags flying on a single line; tackle for lifting heavy objects. — *n* **hoist'er** someone who or that which lifts; a shoplifter (*slang*). — **hoist'man** a person who works a hoist; **hoist'way** a hoist shaft. — **hoist with one's own petard** caught in one's own trap. [Pa t and pa p of **hoise** (qv)]

hoisting *hōst'ing* (*Scott*). Same as **hosting** (see under **host**[2]).

hoity-toity *hoi'ti-toi'ti*, *interj* an exclamation of surprise or disapprobation. — *adj* giddy, noisy; huffy; superciliously haughty. [From *hoit* (*obs*) to romp; origin uncertain]

hoke, hokey. See **hokum**.

hokey cokey *hō'ki kō'ki*, *n* a Cockney song whose lyrics dictate a pattern of accompanying movements, *usu* performed by several people in a circle; these dance-type movements.

hokey-pokey. See **hoky-poky**.

hoki *hō'ki*, *n* a food-fish with white flesh found in the waters of the southern hemisphere, eg around the Falkland Islands and around New Zealand. — Also **whiptail hake**.

hokku. See **haiku**.

hokum *hō'kəm*, (*NAm slang*) *n* something done for the sake of applause; claptrap; pretentious or over-sentimental rubbish. — Also **hoke**. — *vt* **hoke** (*hōk*) to overact (a part in a play); to give an impressive facade or appearance to (*usu* with *up*). — *adj* **hokey** (*hōk'i*) overdone, contrived; phoney. [Appar **hocus-pocus** combined with **bunkum**]

hoky-poky or **hokey-pokey** *hō'ki-pō'ki*, *n* hocus-pocus; a kind of ice-cream sold on the streets.

Holarctic *hol-ärk'tik*, *adj* of the north temperate and Arctic biological region, including Palaearctic and Nearctic. [Gr *holos* whole, and *arktikos* northern, from *arktos* a bear, the Great Bear constellation]

hold[1] *hōld*, *vt* to keep; to have; to grasp; to have in one's possession, keeping or power; to sustain; to defend successfully; to maintain; to assert authoritatively; to think, believe; to occupy; to pass on a title to; to bind; to contain; to have a capacity of; to enclose; to confine; to restrain; to detain; to retain; to reserve; to keep the attention of; to catch; to stop; to continue; to persist in; to celebrate, observe; to conduct; to carry on; to convoke and carry on; to esteem or consider; to aim, direct; to endure; to bet (*archaic*). — *vi* to grasp; to remain fixed; to be true or unfailing; to continue unbroken or unsubdued; to remain valid; to continue, to persist; to adhere; to derive right; when making a telephone call, to wait, without replacing the receiver, eg to be connected to a person one wants to speak to (also **hold the line**): — *pr p* **hōld'ing**; *pa t* **held**; *pa p* **held**, and *obs* **hōld'en**. — *n* an act or manner of holding; grip; power of gripping; tenacity; a thing held; a place of confinement; custody; stronghold; (a sign for) a pause (*music*); an order to keep in reserve (a room, etc) or to suspend (operations) (*NAm*); a means of influencing or controlling. — *n* **hold'er**. — *n* **hold'ing** anything held; a farm managed for its owner; hold; influence; intensive embracing and prolonged eye-contact as a technique for developing intimacy between parent (*esp* mother) and child, claimed by some to be a cure for autism (*psychiatry*); stacking (of aircraft waiting to land); tenure (*Scots law*); the burden of a song (*Shakesp*); (in *pl*) property owned (eg land or investments). — **hold'-all** an accommodating receptacle for clothes, etc, *esp* a canvas bag; **hold'back** a check; a strap joining the breeching to the shaft of a vehicle (see also **hold back** below); **hold'erbat** (*building*) a metal collar formed from two semicircular parts which can be clamped together round a pipe, with a projecting piece for fixing to a wall; **hold'fast** that which holds fast; a long nail; a catch; a plant's fixing organ other than a root; **holding company** an industrial company that owns and controls part or all of one or more other companies, *usu* without having a direct hand in production; **holding ground** any part of the sea bed where an anchor will hold; **holding operation** a course of action designed to preserve the status quo; **holding pattern** a specific course which aircraft are instructed to follow when waiting to land; **hold'over** (*NAm*) someone or something held over; a leftover, relic; **hold'-up** an attack with a view to robbery; a highwayman; an act or state of holding up; a stoppage. — **get hold of** to obtain; to get in touch with; **hold against** (*colloq*) to remember as a failing or as a misdemeanour on the part of; **hold back** to restrain; to hesitate; to keep in reserve (*n* **hold'back**); **hold by** to believe in; to act in accordance with; **hold a call** or **put a call on hold** to delay completing a direct connection between a caller and the telephone number or person that they are trying to reach, keeping the caller waiting, eg until the line is clear, or the person sought can come to a telephone; **hold down** to restrain; to keep (a job) by carrying out its duties efficiently, *esp* in spite of difficulties; **hold forth** to put forward; to show; to speak in public, to declaim; **hold good** to remain the case; **hold hands** (of two people) to be hand in hand or clasping both of each other's hands; (of several people) each to clasp the hand of the person on either side, thus forming a line, circle, etc; **hold hard**! stop!; **hold in** to restrain, check; to restrain oneself; **hold it**! keep the position exactly!; stop!; **hold of** (*Prayer Bk*) to regard; **hold off** to keep at a distance; to refrain (from); **hold on** to persist in something; to continue; to cling; to keep (with *to*); stop (*imperative*); to wait a bit; **hold (someone) in hand** to amuse in order to gain some advantage; **hold one's own** to maintain one's position; (in the course of an illness) not to fail or lose strength; **hold one's peace** or **one's tongue** to keep silence; **hold out** to endure, last; to continue resistance; to offer; **hold out for** to wait determinedly for something one wants or has asked for; **hold out on** (*colloq*) to keep information from; **hold over** to postpone; to keep possession of (land or a house beyond the term of agreement); **hold the line** see **hold** *vi* above; **hold the road** (of a vehicle) to remain stable and under the driver's control, eg in wet weather, at high speeds or on bends; **hold to** or **hold someone to** to keep, or make someone keep (a promise), adhere to (a decision), etc; **hold together** to remain united; to cohere; **hold up** to raise; to keep back; to endure; to bring to, or keep at, a standstill; to stop and rob; to rob by threatening assault; **hold up one's head** to face the world with self-respect; **hold water** see under **water**; **hold with** to take sides with, support; to approve of; **no holds barred** not observing any rules of fair play (*adj* **no'-holds-barred'**); **on hold** postponed; in abeyance; waiting to be connected. [OE *haldan* (WSax *healdan*); OHGer *haltan*, Gothic *haldan*]

hold[2] *hōld*, *n* the interior cavity of a ship used for the cargo. [**hole**[1], with excrescent *d*]

hole[1] *hōl*, *n* a hollow place; a cavity; an aperture; a gap; a breach; a pit; a subterfuge; a means of escape; a difficult situation; a scrape; a place of hiding, a mean lodging, a secret room for some disreputable business; an animal's excavation or place of refuge; a miserable or contemptible place; a cavity $4\frac{1}{4}$ inches in diameter, into which golf-balls are played; the distance, or the part of the game, between tee and hole (*golf*); the score for playing a hole in fewest strokes (*golf*); a vacancy in an energy band, caused by removal of an electron, which moves and is equivalent to a positive charge (*electronics*). — *vt* to form holes in; to put, send or play into a hole. — *vi* to go or play into a hole. — *adj* **holey** (*hōl'i*) full of holes. — *n* and *adj* **hol'ing**. — *adj* **hole'-and-cor'ner** secret; underhand; in obscure places. — **hole card** (in stud poker) the card dealt face down in the first round. — *adj* **hole'-in-the-wall'** (*colloq*) small, insignificant, difficult to find. — **hol'ing-axe** a narrow axe for cutting holes in posts; **hol'ing-pick** a pick used in under-cutting coal. — **a hole in one's coat** a stain on a person's reputation; **hole in one** (in golf) a shot from the tee that goes into the hole, and so completes the hole with a single stroke; **hole in the heart** imperfect separation of the left and right sides of the heart; **hole out** (*golf*) to play the ball into the hole; **hole up** (*colloq*) to go to earth, hide (also *fig*); **in holes** full of holes; **make a hole in** (eg **one's pocket**) to use up a large amount of (eg money); **pick holes in** see under **pick**[1]; **toad in the hole** meat, *esp* sausages, baked in batter. [OE *hol* a hole, cavern; Du *hol*, Dan *hul*, Ger *hohl* hollow; connected with Gr *koilos* hollow]

hole[2] an earlier (and etymological) spelling (*Spenser*) of **whole**. — *adj* **hole'som(e)** wholesome.

holey. See under **hole**[1].

Holi *hō'lē*, *n* a Hindu spring festival characterized by boisterous revelry. [Hind *holī*, from Sans *holikā*]

holibut. See **halibut**.

holiday *hol'i-dā*, *n orig* a religious festival; a day or (*esp* in *pl*) a season of rest and recreation; (often in *pl*) a period of time spent away from home, for recreation. — *vi* to go away from home for a holiday. — *adj* befitting a holiday; cheerful. — **holiday camp** an area, often at the seaside, with chalets, hotels, entertainments, etc for holidaymakers; **hol'idaymaker** someone on holiday away from home; a tourist. — **holiday of obligation** (*esp* in the Roman Catholic church) an important religious festival, on which attendance in church is obligatory. [**holy** and **day**]

holing, etc. See under **hole**[1].

holism *hol'izm* or *hōl'izm*, *n* the theory that the fundamental principle of the universe is the creation of wholes, ie complete and self-contained systems from the atom and the cell by evolution to the most complex forms of life and mind; the theory that a complex entity, system, etc, is more than merely the sum of its parts. — *n* **hol'ist**. — *adj* **holist'ic**. — *adv* **holist'ically**. — **holistic medicine** a form of medicine which considers the whole person, physically and psychologically, rather than treating merely the diseased part. [Gr *holos* whole; coined by General Smuts]

holla *hol'a, interj* ho, there!, attend!, the usual response to *ahoy*! (*naut*). — *n* a loud shout. — *interj* **holl'a-ho**! or **holl'a-hoa**!. [Fr *hola*, from **ho** and *là*, from L *illāc* there]

holland *hol'ənd, n* a coarse linen fabric, unbleached or dyed brown, which is used for covering furniture, etc; *orig* a fine kind of linen first made in *Holland*. — *n* **Holl'ander** a native or citizen of *Holland*; a Dutch ship. — *adj* **Holl'andish**. — *n* **Holl'ands** gin made in Holland. — **sauce hollandaise** (*sōs ol-ã-dez*; Fr) or **hollandaise sauce** (*hol-ən-dāz'* or *hol'ən-dāz sōs*) a sauce made of the yolk of an egg with melted butter and lemon juice or vinegar.

holler *hol'ər*, (*NAm* and *dialect*) *n*, *vi* and *vt*. Same as **hollo**.

Hollerith code *hol'ər-ith kōd*, (*comput*) *n* a code for transforming letters and numerals into a pattern of holes, for use in punched cards. [H *Hollerith* (1860–1929), US inventor]

hollidam. See under **holy**.

hollo *hol'ō, n* and *interj* a shout of encouragement or to call attention; a loud shout: — *pl* **holl'oes** or **holl'os**. — *vt* and *vi* to shout. [Cf **holla** and **hallo**]

holloa *hol-ō'*. Same as **hallo**.

hollow *hol'ō, n* a hole; a cavity; a depression; a vacuity; an emptiness; a groove; a channel. — *adj* having an empty space within or below, not solid; concave; sunken; unsound, unreal, fleeting, deceptive; insincere; echoing, as if coming from a hollow. — *vt* (often with *out*) to make a hole or cavity in; to make hollow; to excavate. — *adv* completely, as in *beat* (ie defeat) *someone hollow*; clean. — *adv* **holl'owly** with a hollow sound; in a hollow or insincere manner. — *n* **holl'owness** the state of being hollow; a cavity; insincerity; treachery. — *adj* **holl'ow-eyed** having sunken eyes. — *adj* **holl'ow-ground** ground so as to have concave surface(s). — **hollow-ground slide** a microscope slide having a depression in the centre, used in hanging drop preparations. — *adj* **holl'ow-heart'ed** having a hollow heart; faithless; treacherous. — **holl'ow-ware** or **holl'oware** hollow articles of iron, china, etc, eg pots and kettles. [OE *holh* a hollow place, from *hol*; see **hole**[1]]

holly *hol'i, n* an evergreen shrub (*Ilex aquifolium*; family Aquifoliaceae) having leathery, shining, spinous leaves and scarlet or yellow berries, much used for Christmas decorations. — **holl'y-fern** a spiny-leaved fern; **holl'y-oak** the holm-oak. [OE *holegn*; cf Welsh *celyn*, Ir *cuileann*]

hollyhock *hol'i-hok, n* a plant (*Althaea*) of the mallow family, with flowers of many colours, brought into Europe from the Holy Land. [ME *holihoc*, from *holi* holy, and OE *hoc* mallow]

Hollywood *hol'i-wŏŏd, adj* of or belonging to *Hollywood*, a suburb of Los Angeles in California and the centre of American cinema; typical of or resembling films made there, brash and romantic, presenting the image of an affluent and often artificial society. — *vt* **Holl'ywoodize** or **-ise** to refurbish or trivialize in the Hollywood manner.

holm[1] *hōm, n* (in place names) an islet, *esp* in a river; rich flat land beside a river. [OE *holm*; Ger *Holm*, etc]

holm[2] *hōm*, (*Spenser*) *n* holly; the holm-oak. — **holm'-oak** the evergreen oak (*Quercus ilex*), not unlike holly. [ME *holin*; see **holly**]

Holmesian *hōm'zi-ən, adj* relating to, or in the manner of, the detective Sherlock *Holmes*, in the stories by A Conan Doyle (1859–1930). — *n* a devotee of Holmes.

holmium *hōl'mi-əm, n* a metallic element (symbol **Ho**; atomic no 67). — *n* **hol'mia** its oxide. — *adj* **hol'mic**. [New L *Holmia* Stockholm]

holo- *hol'ō-, hol'ə-* or *hə-lo'-* or **hol-** *hol-, combining form* denoting: whole; wholly. — *adj* **holobenth'ic** (*zool*) passing the whole life-cycle in the depths of the sea. — *adj* **holoblast'ic** (Gr *blastos* a shoot, bud) (of egg) segmenting completely. — *adj* **hol'ocrine** (Gr *krinein* to separate, decide) producing a secretion of disintegrated cells. — *adj* **holocrys'talline** wholly crystalline in structure, without glass. — *n* **holodisc'us** a genus of deciduous shrubs (family Rosaceae) grown for their summer flowers. — *n* **holoen'zyme** an enzyme which has a protein and non-protein component. — *adj* **holohē'dral** (Gr *hedrā* base). — *n* **holohēd'rism** (*math*) the property of having the full number of symmetrically arranged planes crystallographically possible. — *n* **holohē'dron** a geometrical form possessing this property. — *adj* **holometabol'ic**. — *n* **holometab'olism** (of an insect) complete metamorphosis. — *adj* **holometab'olous**. — *adj* **holophōt'al** (Gr *phōs*, *phōtos* light). — *n* **hol'ophote** an apparatus by which all the light from a lighthouse is thrown in the required direction. — *n* **hol'ophrase** a single word expressing a sentence or phrase. — *adj* **holophras'tic**. — *n* **hol'ophȳte** (*-fīt*). — *adj* **holophytic** (*-fit'ik*; Gr *phyton* a plant) obtaining nutriment wholly in the manner of a green plant. — *n* **holophytism** (*-fīt'izm*). — *n* **holoplank'ton** organisms which remain as plankton throughout their life-cycle. — *adj* **holop'tic** having the eyes meeting in front. — *n pl* **Holostei** (*hol-os'ti-ī*; Gr *osteon* bone) an order of fishes including Lepidosteus. — *adj* **holosteric** (*-ster'ik*; Gr *stereos* solid) wholly solid; having no liquids (eg an aneroid barometer). — *n* **hol'otype** (*zool*) the original type specimen from which the description of a new species is established. — *adj* **holotypic** (*-tip'ik*). — *adj* **holozoic** (*-zō'ik*; Gr *zōion* an animal) obtaining nutrition wholly in the manner of an animal, ie from other organisms live or dead. [Gr *holos* whole]

holocaust *hol'ə-kōst, n* a huge slaughter or destruction of life; the cause of such, eg a major fire; a disaster (*colloq*); (with *cap*) the mass murder of Jews by the Nazis during World War II; a sacrifice, in which the whole of the victim was burnt. — *adj* **holocaust'al** or **holocaust'ic**. [Gr *holokauston*, from *kaustos* burnt]

Holocene *hol'ə-sēn*, (*geol*) *n* the most recent period of geological time, following the Quaternary period, and approximating to the period since the last glaciation. [**holo-** and Gr *kainos* new]

holocrine, **holocrystalline**, **holodiscus**, **holoenzyme**. See under **holo-**.

hologram *hol'ə-gram, n* a photograph made without use of a lens, by means of interference between two parts of a split laser beam, the result appearing as a meaningless pattern until suitably illuminated, when it shows as a 3-D image (a number of pictures can be stored on the same plate or film). — *n* **hol'ograph** (*-gräf*) a document wholly written by the person from whom it comes. — Also *adj*. — *vt* to make a hologram of. — *adj* **holographic** (*-graf'ik*). — *n* **holog'raphy** (the technique or process of) making or using holograms. [**holo-** and **-graph**]

holohedron ... to ... **holosteric**. See under **holo-**.

holothurian *hol-ō-thōō'ri-ən, n* any member of the genus **Holothu'ria** or family **Holothuroid'ea**, a class of worm-like unarmoured echinoderms, the sea-cucumbers. — Also *adj*. [Gr *holothourion* a kind of sea animal]

holotype ... to ... **holozoic**. See under **holo-**.

holp *hōlp* and **holpen** *-ən*, (*old*) *pa t* and *pa p* of **help**.

hols *holz*, (*schoolchildren's slang*) *n pl* holidays.

holster *hōl'stər, n* a pistol-case, slung on a saddle or belt; a similar case for a tool, eg a torch or an axe used in mountaineering. — *adj* **hol'stered**. [Perh Du *holster* pistol-case; cf OE *heolster* hiding-place]

Holstein *hōl'stīn*, (*NAm*) *adj* and *n* same as **Friesian**. [Region of Germany]

holt[1] *hōlt, n* (in place names) a wood or woody hill; an orchard. [OE *holt* a wood; ON *holt* a copse, Ger *Holz*]

holt[2] *hōlt, n* a hold, grasp (*UK* and *US dialect*); a stronghold (*obs*); a refuge; an otter's den. [**hold**[1]]

holus-bolus *hōl'əs-bōl'əs, adv* all at once; altogether. [Sham L; perh from Eng *whole bolus* or Gr *holos* and *bōlos* lump, bolus]

holy *hō'li, adj* perfect in a moral sense; pure in heart; religious; associated with God or gods; set apart for a sacred use; regarded with awe (often *ironic*); saintly sanctimonious, simulating holiness. — *n* a holy object, place or (*obs*) person. — *adv* **ho'lily**. — *n* **ho'liness** sanctity; (with *cap*) a title of the pope and of patriarchs in Eastern Churches. — *n* **holydam**, **holydame** or **hollidam** (*Shakesp*), used for **halidom**. — *adj* **ho'lier-than-thou'** offensively sanctimonious and patronizing. — *n* such an attitude; someone who has such an attitude. — **ho'ly-ale** (conjectured in Shakespeare's *Pericles*, Prologue 6, for rhyme's sake) a church festival; **Holy Alliance** a league formed after the fall of Napoleon (1815) by the sovereigns of Austria, Russia and Prussia, professedly to regulate all national and international relations in accordance with the principles of Christian charity; **holy city** depending upon religion: Jerusalem; Rome; Mecca; Benares; Allahabad, etc; **holy coat** the seamless coat of Jesus, claimed to be kept at Trier. — *adj* **ho'ly-cru'el** (*Shakesp*) cruel through holiness. — **holy day** a religious festival (see also **holiday**); **Holy Family** the infant Christ with Joseph, Mary, etc; **Holy Ghost** or **Holy Spirit** the third person of the Christian Trinity; **holy grail** see under **grail**[3]; **holy grass** a sweet-smelling grass sometimes strewed on church floors on festival days; **holy Joe** (*slang*) a parson; a pious person; **Holy Land** Biblical Palestine; **Holy Office** the Inquisition; **Holy One** God; Christ; the one who is holy, by way of emphasis; a person, eg a monk, living a cloistered life in the service of God; **holy orders** see under **order**; **ho'ly-rood** (as a place name *hol'*) Christ's cross; a cross, *esp* in RC churches over the entrance to the chancel (for **Holy-rood Day** see under **rood**); **Holy Roller** (*derog*) a preacher or follower of an extravagantly emotional religious sect; **Holy Roman Empire** the unification of Europe with papal blessing, under a Christian emperor, AD 800–814 and AD 926–1806; **Holy Saturday** the Saturday before Easter Sunday; **Holy See** the Roman Catholic bishopric of Rome, ie the Pope's see; **Holy Spirit** see **Holy Ghost** above; **ho'lystone** a sandstone used by seamen for cleansing the decks, said to be named from cleaning the decks for Sunday, or from kneeling in using it. — *vt* to scrub with a holystone. — **holy terror** (*colloq esp jocular*) a formidable person, or someone given to causing commotion or agitation; **Holy Thursday** Maundy Thursday; Ascension Day (*rare*); **holy war** a war waged for the eradication of heresy or a rival religion; a Crusade; **holy water** water blessed for religious uses; **Holy Week** the week before Easter; **Holy Willie** a religious hypocrite (after Burns's poem); **holy writ** the Scriptures; **Holy Year** in the RC church, a jubilee year. — **holy of holies** the inner chamber of the Jewish tabernacle. [OE *hālig*, literally whole, from *hāl* sound; connected with **hail**[1], **heal**[1], **whole**]

homage *hom'ij*, *n* a vassal's acknowledgement that he is the man of his feudal superior (*hist*); a body of vassals or tenants; anything done or rendered as an acknowledgement of superiority; reverence, *esp* shown by outward action. — *vt* to do or pay homage to. — *n* **hom'ager** a person who does homage. [OFr *homage*, from LL *homināticum*, from L *homō* a man]

homaloid *hom'əl-oid*, *n* Euclidean space, analogous to a plane. — *adj* **homaloid'al** flat; of the nature of a plane. [Gr *homalos* even, and *eidos* form]

hombre *om'brā*, (Sp) *n* man.

Homburg *hom'bûrg* or **Homburg-hat** (*-hat'*), *n* a man's hat, of felt, with a narrow brim and crown, and a depression in the top. [First worn at *Homburg*, town in western Germany]

home *hōm*, *n* a habitual dwelling place, or the place felt to be such; the residence of one's family; the scene of domestic life, with its emotional associations; a separate building occupied by a family, a house; one's own country; the mother-country; seat; habitat; natural or usual place of anything; the den or base in a game; the goal; the inner table in backgammon; the plate in baseball (also **home plate**); an institution affording refuge, asylum or residence for strangers, the afflicted, poor, etc; a private hospital; a place where cats, dogs, etc are received and boarded; in football pools, a match won by a team playing on their own ground; a home signal. — *adj* pertaining or belonging to, or being in, one's own dwelling, country, playing-ground, etc; domestic; near the dwelling or headquarters; coming or reaching home; effective, searching; made or done at home, not in a factory, abroad, etc. — *adv* to one's home; at home; to the innermost, most significant or final place or position; effectively. — *vi* to go home; to find the way home; to dwell; to be guided to a target or destination (*usu* with *in*). — *vt* to send home; to provide with a home; to guide to a target or destination (*usu* with *in on*). — *adj* **home'less** without a home; of or pertaining to people who, having no permanent place of residence, live and sleep rough in public places, or in squats or doss-houses. — Also *n* (with *the*; *collectively*). — *n* **home'lessness**. — *adj* **home'like** like a home; familiar; easy; comfortable. — *adv* **home'lily** (*-li-li*). — *n* **home'liness**. — *adj* **home'ly** pertaining to home; familiar; plain; unpretentious; (*usu* of people) ugly (*NAm*). — *n* **hom'er** a pigeon of a breed that can readily be trained to find its way home from a distance; any person or animal so skilled; a home-run (*baseball*). — *adv* **home'ward** or **home'wards**. — *adj* **home'ward** in the direction of home. — *adj* **home'y** or **hom'y** home-like; homely. — *adj* **hom'ing** returning home; (*esp* of pigeons) trained to return home; guiding home; (of a navigational device on a missile, etc) guiding itself to the target or destination. — Also *n*. — *adj* **home'-and-home'** or **home'-and-away'** (of sports events) played alternately on one's own and one's opponents' home grounds. — **home banking** or **home and office banking system** a system offered by some banks allowing a person at home, in an office, etc to gain access to information about their own account(s), transfer funds, etc, by means of a computer linked to the system employed by the bank; **home base** (*baseball*) the plate at which the batter stands when batting and which must be touched by a runner in order to score a run; **home bird** or **home body** a person who likes to stay at home, whose interests are in the home. — *adj* **home'-born** originating at home or in the home; native, not foreign. — *adj* **home'bound** homeward bound; fixed to the home. — *adj* **home'-bred** bred at home; native; domestic; plain; unpolished. — *adj* **home'-brewed** brewed at home or for home use (*n* **home'-brew'**); also *fig*. — **home'buyer** a person in the process of arranging to buy their own home; **home circuit** the south-eastern circuit of Assize with boundaries changed at various times; **home'-comer**; **home'-coming** arrival at home; return home. — Also *adj*. — **home counties** the counties over and into which London has extended, ie Middlesex, Essex, Kent, Surrey (and sometimes also Herts and Sussex); **home'craft** household skills; skills practised at home or concerned with home life; **home'-croft** a cottage with a small piece of land for an industrial worker to grow his or her own food; **home'-crofter**; **home'-crofting**; **home-defence'** defence of a country by a force of its own people within it; **Home Department** the official title, now rarely used, of the government department commonly known as the **Home Office**, whose head, the **Home Secretary**, is broadly responsible for the domestic civil affairs of the United Kingdom as a whole; **home economics** domestic science, household skills and management; **home economist**; **home'-farm** the farm attached to and near a large house. — *adj* **home'felt** felt in one's own breast; inward; private. — **home'-fire** the domestic hearth, with its activities and connections. — *adj* **home'-grown** produced in one's own country, or garden. — **home-guard'** a member of a volunteer force for the defence of a country; a force of this kind (first formed in Britain in the war of 1939–45, **Home Guard**); **home help** a person employed by the local authority to help the handicapped or the aged with domestic work. — *adj* **home'-keeping** staying at home. — **home'land** native land, fatherland; mother-country; in South Africa, the formal name for an area reserved for Black African peoples (also **Bantustan**); **home'-life** domestic life; **home loan** a mortgage. — *adj* **home'-made** made at home; made in one's own country; plain. — **home'-maker** a housewife or house-husband; **home market** the market for goods in the country that produces them; **home movie** a motion picture made at home, *usu* by an amateur; **home nurse** a district nurse; **home'-owner**; **home plate** (*baseball*) the final point which a batter must reach in order to score a run; **home port** the port at which a boat is registered. — *adj* **home'-produced'** produced within the country in question, not imported. — **Home Rule** self-government, such as that claimed by Irish, Scottish and Welsh Nationalists, including a separate parliament to manage internal affairs; **home'-rul'er** an advocate of Home Rule; **home run** (in baseball) a hit which goes far enough to allow the batter to make a complete circuit of all four bases; the score made in this way. — *adj* **home'sick** pining for home. — **home'sickness**; **home'-sig'nal** a signal at the beginning of a section of railway line showing whether or not the section is clear. — *adj* **home'spun** spun or made at home; not made in foreign countries; plain, unadorned; simple, artless, rustic; inelegant. — *n* cloth made at home; an unpolished person (*Shakesp*). — **home'stall** (*obs*) a homestead; a farmyard; **home'stead** a dwelling-house with outhouses and enclosures immediately connected with it; a piece of public land allotted under special laws to a settler (*US* and *Austr*); **home'steader**; **home'steading** (*orig US*) a scheme by which people are permitted to buy, or live rent-free in, semi-derelict buildings and improve them with the help of Government grants, etc; **home'-straight'** or **home'-stretch'** the last stretch of a racecourse; the final or winning stage of anything; **home'-thrust** in fencing, a hit that goes home where it is aimed; a pointed remark that goes home; **home time** the end of the formal school day at a day school; **home'-town** the town where one's home is or was; **home'-truth** a pointed, *usu* unanswerable, typically wounding, statement made direct to the person concerned; **home unit** (*Austr* and *NZ*) a flat or apartment; **home video** a home movie made with a video camera. — *adj* **home'ward-bound'** bound homeward or to one's native land. — **home'work** work or preparation to be done at home, *esp* for school; paid work, *esp* piece-work, done at home. — *n* **home'worker** a person who works from home, *esp* someone who is linked to an office by computer, and under terms and conditions similar to conventional office-workers; **home'working**. — **at home** in one's own house; ready to receive a visitor; feeling the ease of familiarity with a place or situation (*n* **at-home'** a reception); **bring home to** to prove to, in such a way that there is no way of escaping the conclusion; to impress upon; **do one's homework** (*colloq*) to prepare oneself, eg for a discussion by acquainting oneself with the relevant facts; **eat someone out of house and home** (*colloq*) to live at the expense of another person so as to ruin him or her; **go** or **strike home** (of a remark, etc) to impress itself duly on the mind of the person addressed; **home and dry** having arrived or achieved one's aim, etc; safe, successful, secure; **home from home** a place where one feels comfortable and at ease; **long home** the grave; **make oneself at home** to be as free and unrestrained as in one's own house; **not at home** out of one's house; not receiving visitors; **nothing to write home about** (*colloq*) not very exciting or attractive; **pay home** to strike to the quick; to retaliate. [OE *hām*; Du *heim*, Ger *Heim*, Gothic *haims*]

homelyn *hom'əl-in* or *hōm'lin*, *n* the spotted ray. [Origin unknown]

homeo-. See under **homo-**.

homer[1] *hō'mər*, *n* a Hebrew measure of capacity, roughly 11 bushels. [Heb *khōmer* heap, from *khāmar* to swell up]

homer[2]. See under **home**.

Homeric *hō-mer'ik*, *adj* pertaining to *Homer*, the great poet of Greece (who flourished c. 850 BC); attributed to Homer; resembling Homer or his poetry; worthy of Homer; in the heroic or epic manner. — *n* **Homerid** (*hō'mər-id*) one of the **Homer'idae** (*-i-dē*), Chian reciters of the Homeric poems, claiming descent from him. — **Homeric laughter** loud inextinguishable laughter (Gr *asbestos gelos*, the Iliad, 1.599); **Homeric question** the question of Homer's authorship of the *Iliad* and the *Odyssey*, disputed by Wolf (1795). [Gr *homērikos*, from *Homēros* Homer]

homey. See under **home**.

homicide *hom'i-sīd*, *n* manslaughter or murder; a person who kills another. — *adj* **homicī'dal** pertaining to homicide; murderous; bloody. [L *homicīdium* manslaughter, and *homicīda* a man-slayer, from *homō* a man, and *caedere* to kill]

homily *hom'i-li*, *n* a plain explanatory sermon, practical rather than doctrinal; a talk giving advice and encouragement. — *adj* **homilet'ic** or **homilet'ical**. — *adv* **homilet'ically**. — *n sing* **homilet'ics** the art of preaching. — *n* **hom'ilist**. [Gr *homīliā* an assembly, a lecture or sermon, from *homos* the same, and *īlē* a company]

homing. See under **home**.

hominid *hom'in-id*, (*zool*) *n* an animal of the family **Homin'idae**, comprising man and his close, now extinct, bipedal ancestors (also *adj*). — *n* and *adj* **hom'inoid**. [L *homō*, *-inis* man]

hominoid *hom'in-oid*, (*zool*) *n* a member of the superfamily **Hominoid'ea**, comprising man and modern apes and their extinct ancestors (also *adj*). [L *homō*, *inis* man]

hominy *hom'i-ni*, *n* maize hulled, or hulled and crushed; a kind of porridge made by boiling this. [Am Ind origin]

homme *om*, (*Fr*) *n* man. — **homme d'affaires** (*da-fer*) a business man; an agent, steward; **homme de bien** (*də byẽ*) a man of worth, a good man; **homme de lettres** (*də letr'*) a man of letters; **homme d'épée** (*dā-pā*) a military man; **homme d'esprit** (*des-prē*) a man of wit; **homme d'état** (*dā-tä*) a statesman; **homme du monde** (*dü mɔ̃d*) a man of fashion; **homme moyen sensuel** (*mwa-yẽ sã-sü-el*) the ordinary man; the man in the street; **homme sérieux** (*sā-ryø*) a serious, earnest man.

hommock. See **hummock**.

homo[1] *hō'mō*, *n* man generically; (with *cap*; *zool*) the human genus. — **Homo erectus** (formerly known as Pithecanthropus erectus) a name given to a type of erect hominid between Australopithecus and Homo sapiens, represented by Java man and Peking man; **Homo habilis** a name given to a much earlier hominid, thought also to walk upright; **Homo neanderthalensis** see under **Neanderthal**; **Homo sapiens** the one existing species of man. [L *homō*, *-inis* man, human being]

homo[2] *hō'mō*, (*usu derog*; now *old slang*) *n* and *adj* short for homosexual. — *n pl* **ho'mos**. [**homo-**]

homo- *hom-ō-*, *hom-ə-*, *hə-mo* or *hō-*, *combining form* denoting: same. — **homoeo-** or **homeo-** *hom-i-ō-*, *hom-i-ə-*, *hom-i-o-*, or *hō-*, or **homoio-** *-moi-*, *combining form* denoting: like, similar. — *adj* **homoblast'ic** (Gr *blastos* a germ; *zool*) derived from similar cells; showing direct embryonic development. — *n* **hom'oblasty**. — *adj* **homocentric** (*-sen'trik*; Gr *homokentros*, from *kentron* centre, point) concentric; proceeding from or diverging to the same point; (of rays) either parallel or passing through one focus (*phys*). — *adj* **homocercal** (*-sûr'kəl*; Gr *kerkos* tail) (of fishes) having the upper and lower lobes of the tail-fin alike. — *adj* **homochlamydeous** (*-klə-mid'i-əs*; Gr *chlamys*, *-ydos* cloak; *bot*) with calyx and corolla similar. — *adj* **homochromat'ic** monochromatic. — *adj* **homochromous** (*-krō'məs*; Gr *chrōma* colour) alike in colour; of the same colour. — *n* **homochromy** (*-ok'*, or *-krōm'*) protective coloration. — *adj* **homocyclic** (*-sīk'lik*; Gr *kyklos* a ring; *chem*) having a closed chain of similar atoms. — *adj* **homodont** (*hom'ə-dont*; Gr *odous*, *odontos* tooth) having teeth all alike. — *adj* **homodyne** (*hom'ə-dīn*; Gr *dynamis* power; *radio telephony*) applied to the reception of waves strengthened by the imposition of a locally generated wave of the same length. — *adj* **hom'oeobox** or **hom'eobox** (of genes) that regulate the development of multicellular animals and plants. — *adj* **homoeom'erous**, **homeom'erous** or **homoiom'erous** (Gr *meros* part) composed of similar parts; (of lichens) having the algal cells distributed throughout the thallus; (in metameric animals) having all the somites alike — also **homoeomeric** or **homeomeric** (*-mer'ik*). — *n* **homoeom'ery** or **homeom'ery**. — *n* **hom'oeomorph** or **hom'eomorph** (Gr *morphē* form) a thing similar in form to another but essentially different, *esp* a different chemical substance with similar crystalline form. — *adj* **homoeomorph'ic** or **homeomorph'ic** of or pertaining to a homoeomorph; of two geometrical figures, such that one can be converted into the other by distortion (*math*). — *n* **homoeomorph'ism** or **homeomorph'ism**. — *adj* **homoeomorph'ous** or **homeomorph'ous**. — *n* **homoeomorph'y** or **homeomorph'y**. — *n* **homoeopath** or **homeopath** (*hom'* or *hōm'i-ə-path*; Gr *pathos* feeling) or **homoeopathist** or **homeopathist** (*-op'ə-thist*) a person who believes in or practises homoeopathy. — *adj* **homoeopathic** or **homeopathic** (*-path'*). — *adv* **homoeopath'ically** or **homeopath'ically**. — *n* **homoeopathy** or **homeopathy** (*-op'ə-thi*) the system of treating diseases by small quantities of drugs that excite symptoms similar to those of the disease. — *n* **homoeosis** or **homeosis** (*hom-i-ō'sis*; Gr *homoiōsis* a becoming like; *biol*) assumption of the character of a corresponding member of another whorl or somite. — *n* **homoeostasis** or **homeostasis** (*hom-i-os'tə-sis*; Gr *stasis* a standing still) the tendency for the internal environment of the body to remain constant in spite of varying external conditions; a tendency towards health or stable physical conditions. — *adj* **homoeostat'ic** or **homeostat'ic**. — *n* **homoeoteleuton** or **homeoteleuton** (*hom-i-ō-tel-ū'ton*; Gr *homoioteleuton*, from *teleutē* ending) the use or occurrence of similar endings. — *adj* **homoeotherm'al**, **homeotherm'al**, **homoeotherm'ic**, **homeotherm'ic**, **homoeotherm'ous** or **homeotherm'ous** homothermal (qv below). — Also **homoi'other'mal**, etc. — *adj* **homoeot'ic** or **homeot'ic** showing, depending on, or characterized by homoeosis; (of a mutant) effecting large-scale changes in development, eg in Drosophila, the substitution of a leg for a wing). — *n* **homoerot'icism** or **homoerot'ism** orientation of the libido towards someone of the same sex. — *adj* **homoerot'ic**. — *n* **homogamic** (*-gam'ik*) or **homogamous** (*hom-og'ə-məs*). — *n* **homogamy** (*hom-og'ə-mi*; Gr *gamos* marriage) breeding of like with like; inbreeding; the condition of having all the flowers of an inflorescence sexually alike (*bot*); simultaneous ripening of stamens and stigmas (*bot*). — *n* **homogenate** (*-oj'ə-nāt*) a substance produced by homogenizing (see **homogenize** below). — *n* **homogeneity** (*hom-ō-ji-nē'i-ti*) the state or fact of being homogeneous. — *adj* **homogeneous** (*hom-ō-jēn'i-əs*, also *hōm-* or *-jen'*; Gr *homogenēs*, from *genos* kind) of the same kind or nature; having the constituent elements similar throughout; of the same degree or dimensions in every term (*math*); (of radiation) of constant wavelength or constant quantum energy. — *n* **homogē'neousness**. — *n* **homogenesis** (*-jen'i-sis*; Gr *genesis* birth; *biol*) a mode of reproduction in which the offspring is like the parent, and passes through the same cycle of existence. — *adj* **homogenet'ic** or **homogenet'ical** homogenous. — *vt* **homog'enize** or **-ise** (or *hom'o-jən-īz*) to make homogeneous; to make (milk) more digestible by breaking up fat globules, etc; to produce (milk) synthetically by mixing its constituents. — *n* **homogeniza'tion** or **-s-**. — *n* **homog'enizer** or **-s-**. — *adj* **homogenous** (*hom-oj'ən-əs*) similar owing to common descent. — *n* **homog'eny** similarity owing to common descent or origin. — *n* **homograft** (*hom'ō-gräft*) a graft from one individual to an unrelated member of the same species (*med*). — *n* **homograph** (*hom'ə-gräf*; Gr *graphein* to write) a word of the same spelling as another, but of different meaning, pronunciation or origin. — *adj* **homoiousian** (*hom-oi-ōō'si-ən*, or *-ow'*; Gr *ousiā* being) of similar (as distinguished from identical) essence; believing God the Father and God the Son to be of similar (not identical) essence. — *n* a holder of such belief, a semi-Arian. — *vt* **homol'ogate** (LL *homologāre*, *-ātum*, from Gr *homologeein* to agree, from *logos* speech) to confirm; to approve; to consent to; to ratify. — *vi* to agree. — *n* **homologā'tion** (*Scots law*) confirming and ratifying by subsequent act. — *adj* **homological** (*-loj'*). — *adv* **homolog'ically**. — *vt* and *vi* **homol'ogize** or **-ise** (*-jīz*). — *adj* **homologous** (*hom-ol'ə-gəs*) agreeing; of the same essential nature, corresponding in relative position, general structure, and descent (*med* or *biol*); (of chromosomes) pairing with each other during meiosis, so that one member of each pair is carried by every gamete. — *n* **hom'ologue** or (*US*) **hom'olog** (*-ə-log'*) anything which is homologous to something else, such as a man's arm, a whale's flipper and a bird's wing. — *n pl* **homologoumena** or **homologumena** (*hom-ol-o-gōō'mi-nə*; Gr *homologoumena* things granted, neuter pl of pr p passive (contracted) of *homologeein*) the books of the New Testament whose authenticity was universally acknowledged in the early Church (opp of *antilegomena*). — *n* **homol'ogy** (*-ə-ji*; Gr *homologos*) the quality of being homologous; affinity of structure and origin, apart from form or use. — *n* **hom'omorph** (Gr *morphē* form) a thing having the same form as another. — *adj* **homomorph'ic** or **homomorph'ous** alike in form, *esp* if essentially different otherwise; uniform. — *n* **homomorph'ism**. — *n* **homomorphō'sis** regeneration of a lost part in the original form. — *n* **hom'onym** (Gr *homōnymos*, from *onyma*, *onoma* name) a word having the same sound and perhaps the same spelling as another, but a different meaning and origin; a name rejected as already used for by another genus or species (*biol*); a namesake. — *adj* **homonym'ic** pertaining to homonyms. — *adj* **homon'ymous** having the same name; having different significations and origins but the same sound; ambiguous; equivocal. — *adv* **homon'ymously**. — *n* **homon'ymy**. — *n* **homonym'ity**. — *adj* **homoousian** or **homousian** (*hom-ō-ōō'si-ən*, *ho-mōō'* or *-ow'*; Gr *ousiā* being) of the same essence; believing God the Son to be of the same essence as God the Father. — *n* a holder of such belief (according to the Nicene Creed). — *n* **hom'ophile** (*rare*) a homosexual. — *n* **hom'ophobe** (*-fōb*; Gr *phobos* fear) a person with a strong antipathy to homosexuals. — *n* **homophō'bia**. — *adj* **homophō'bic**. — *n* **homophone** (*hom'-ə-fōn*; Gr *phōnē* sound) a character representing the same sound as another; a word which is pronounced the same as another but is different in spelling and meaning. — *adj* **homophonic** (*-fon'*) sounding alike in unison; in the monodic style of music, where one voice only carries the melody. — *adj* **homophonous** (*-of'*). — *n* **homoph'ony**. — *n* **homophyly** (*-of'i-li*; Gr *phȳlon* a race; *biol*) resemblance due to common ancestry. — *n* **hom'oplasmy** (*-plaz-mi*) or **homop'lasy** the quality or fact of being homoplastic. — *adj* **homoplast'ic** (Gr *plastikos* plastic, *plasma* a mould; *biol*) similar in structure and development owing to parallel or convergent evolution but not descended from a common source. — *adj* **homopō'lar** (*chem*) having an equal distribution of charge, as in a covalent bond. — *n* **homopolar'ity**. — *n* **homopol'ymer** a DNA or RNA strand whose nucleotides are all of the same kind. — *n pl* **Homoptera** (*-op'*; Gr *pteron* a wing) an order of insects (or suborder of Hemiptera) having wings of a uniform texture, eg cicadas, frog-hoppers, green-fly, scale-insects, etc. — *adj* **homop'terous**. — *n* **Homorelaps** see under **Elaps**. — *adj* **homosex'ūal** having or pertaining to sexual attraction to members of one's own sex. — *n* a person sexually attracted only to others of their own sex. — *n* **homosex'ualism**. — *n* **homosex'ualist**. — *n* **homosexual'ity**. — *adj* **homosporous** (*-os'por-əs*, or *-ō-spō'rəs* or *-spö'*; Gr *sporos* seed; *bot*) having spores all of one kind. — *adj* **homotax'ial** or **homotax'ic**. — *n* **homotax'is** (Gr *taxis* arrangement;

geol) coincidence in order of organic succession but not necessarily in time; similarity in geological age, while not necessarily strict contemporaneity. — *adj* **homothall'ic** (*bot*) having only one type of mycelium (opp of *heterothallic*). — *n* **homothall'ism** or **hom'othally**. — *adj* **homotherm'al, homotherm'ic** or **homotherm'ous** (Gr *thermē* heat) keeping the same temperature, warm-blooded. — *adj* **homotonic** (*-ton'*) or **homot'onous** (Gr *tonos* tone) of the same tenor or tone. — *n* **homot'ony**. — *adj* **homotypal** (*-tīp'l*) or **homotypic** (*-tip'ik*) conforming to normal type; (**homotypic**; *biol*) pertaining to the second (equational) cell-division in meiosis (cf **heterotypic** under **heter**). — *n* **hom'otype** (*-ō-tīp*; Gr *typos* type) that which has the same fundamental structure as something else. — *n* **homotypy** (*hom'ō-tī-pi* or *hom-ot'i-pi*). — *n* **homousian** see **homoousian** above. — *n* **homozygōs'is** the condition of having inherited a given genetic factor from both parents, so producing gametes of only one kind as regards that factor; genetic stability as regards a given factor. — *n* **homozy'gote** a zygote which is formed as a result of homozygosis. — *adj* **homozygot'ic**. — *adj* **homozy'gous**. [Gr *homos* same, *homoios* like, similar]

homunculus *hō-mung'kū-ləs*, *n* a tiny man capable of being produced artificially according to Paracelsus, endowed with magical insight and power; a dwarf, manikin; a dwarf of normal proportions (*med*); a minute human form believed by the spermatist school of preformationists to be contained in the spermatozoon: — *pl* **homunc'ulī**. — Also **homunc'ūle** or **homunc'le**. — *adj* **homunc'ūlar**. [L, dimin of *homō* a man]

homy. See under **home**.

Hon. See **honourable** under **honour**.

hon *hun*, (*colloq*) *n* short for **honey** as a term of endearment.

honcho *hon'cho*, (*US slang*) *n* a boss, a leader, a manager. [Jap *han'cho* squad leader]

hond *hond*, *n* an obs form of **hand**.

Honduras bark *hon-dūr'əs bärk*, *n* cascara amarga.

hone[1] *hōn*, *n* a smooth stone used for sharpening instruments. — *vt* to sharpen on or as if on a hone. — *n* **ho'ner**. — **hone'-stone** a hone; any hard fine-grained stone suitable for honing, *esp* novaculite. [OE *hān*; ON *hein*; allied to Gr *kōnos* a cone]

hone[2] *hōn*, (*dialect*) *vi* to pine, moan, grieve (for or after). [Perh Fr *hogner* to grumble]

honest *on'ist* or *-əst*, *adj* truthful; full of honour; honourable; just; fair-dealing; upright, upstanding; the opposite of thieving; free from fraud or trickery; candid, frank; ingenuous; seemly; respectable (now *patronizing*); chaste (*archaic*). — *adv* **hon'estly** in an honest way; in truth. — *interj* expressing annoyance, disbelief, etc. — *n* **hon'esty** the state of being honest; integrity; candour, frankness, truthfulness; a cruciferous garden-plant (*Lunaria biennis*) with shining silver or satiny white dissepiments; decorum (*obs*); chastity (*Shakesp*). — **honest broker** an impartial mediator in a dispute. — *adj* **hon'est-to-God'** or **hon'est-to-good'ness** genuine, out-and-out, complete. — Also *adv*. — **honest Injun** (*colloq*) upon my honour; **make an honest woman of** (now *usu facetious*) to marry, where the woman has first been seduced. [OFr *honeste*, from L *honestus*, from *honor*]

honewort *hōn'wərt*, *n* a name given to various umbelliferous plants. [Poss obs *hone* a tumour, and **wort**[1]]

honey *hun'i*, *n* a sweet, thick fluid elaborated by bees from the nectar of flowers; its colour, golden brown; nectar of flowers; anything sweet like honey; a term of endearment; a thing which is pleasant or delightful (*colloq*). — *vt* to sweeten; to make agreeable. — *vi* (*Shakesp*) to talk endearingly: — *pr p* **hon'eying**; *pa t* and *pa p* **hon'eyed** (*-id*). — *adj* (*Shakesp*) sweet. — *adj* **hon'eyed** or **hon'ied** covered with honey; (often falsely) sweet; seductive; flattering. — *adj* **hon'eyless**. — **hon'ey-ant** one of several types of ant, *esp* of the genus *Myrmecocystus*, that feed on honey, and store it in the worker-ants, who disgorge it as necessary; **hon'ey-badger** the ratel, a badger-like animal from India and Africa; **hon'ey-bag** an enlargement of the alimentary canal of the bee in which it carries its load of honey; **hon'ey-bear** the kinkajou, which robs the nests of wild bees; the sloth-bear; the Malayan bear; **hon'ey-bee** any of the varieties of bee living in hives and producing honey; **hon'ey-bird** a honey-guide; a honey-sucker; **hon'ey-blob** (*dialect*) a sweet yellow gooseberry; **hon'eybun** or **hon'eybunch** terms of endearment; **hon'ey-buzzard** a hawk (*Pernis apivora*) that feeds on the larvae and honey of bees, wasps, etc; **hon'ey-cart, hon'ey-waggon** or **-wagon** a truck for offensive refuse; **hon'ey-chile** (*US dialect*) a term of endearment; **hon'eycomb** (*-kōm'*) a comb or mass of waxy cells formed by bees in which they store their honey; anything like a honeycomb; a bewildering maze (of rooms, cavities, etc). — *vt* to make like a honeycomb; to spread into all parts of. — *adj* **hon'eycombed** (*-kōmd*). — *n* **hon'eycombing** honeycomb stitch. — **hon'eycomb-moth** a bee-moth; **honeycomb stitch** an embroidery stitch used to hold the gathers made when smocking; **honey creeper** any of several kinds of small, brightly-coloured S American birds which feed on nectar; **hon'ey-crock** a crock or pot of honey; **hon'ey-dew** a sugar secretion from aphids or plants; ambrosia; a fine sort of tobacco moistened with molasses; **honeydew melon** a sweet-flavoured melon with smooth green or orange rind; **hon'ey-eater** any bird of a large Australian family, the *Meliphagidae*, which feeds on nectar; **honey fungus** a kind of honey-coloured edible mushroom (*Armillaria mellea*), a parasite on the roots of trees and shrubs, which it can kill; **hon'ey-guide** a species of bird of a mainly African family (*Indicatoridae*) which guides men and ratels to honey-bees' nests by hopping from tree to tree with a peculiar cry; a marking on a flower said to show the way to the nectaries; **hon'ey-lōcust** an ornamental N American tree (*Gleditsia*); **hon'eymoon** (*obs* **hon'eymonth**) the first weeks after marriage, commonly spent on holiday, before settling down to the business of life; such a holiday; a holiday reminiscent of a honeymoon (also **second honeymoon**); a period of (unusual) harmony at the start of a new business relationship, term of office, etc (*fig*). — *vi* to spend one's honeymoon (with *in*). — **hon'eymooner**; **hon'ey-mouse** (*obs*) the honey possum. — *adj* **hon'ey-mouthed** having a honeyed mouth or speech; soft or smooth in speech. — **honey possum** a long-snouted Australian marsupial (*Tarsipes*) that feeds on honey and insects (also **phalanger**); **hon'eypot** a container for honey; anything that attracts people in great numbers (*fig*); (in *pl*) a children's game; see also **hanepoot** (*SAfr*); **hon'ey-sac** a honey-bag (see above); **hon'ey-stalk** (*Shakesp*) probably the stalk or flower of the clover; **hon'ey-stone** mellite, a very soft yellow mineral found with lignite; **hon'ey-sucker** a honey-eater; **hon'eysuckle** a climbing shrub (*Lonicera*) with mainly cream-coloured flowers, so named because honey is readily sucked from the flower (by long-tongued insects only); applied also to clover and many other plants; the rewarewa (*NZ*). — *adj* **hon'ey-suckle** or **hon'y-suckle** and *adj* and *n* **hon'ey-seed** or **hon'y-seed** (*Shakesp*; *Henry IV part* 2) the Hostess's blunders for **homicidal, homicide**. — *adj* **hon'ey-sweet** sweet as honey. — *adj* **hon'ey-tongued** soft, pleasing, persuasive, or seductive in speech; eloquent. — **hon'ey-trap** a scheme used to entrap someone, involving seduction or some other sexual act that could shame the person involved if the subsequent threat of exposure were carried out; **honey-wagon** see **honey-cart** above. — **virgin honey** honey that flows of itself from the comb; **wild honey** honey made by wild bees. [OE *hunig*; Ger *Honig*; ON *hunang*]

honeypot *hun'i-pot*. See under **honey** and **hanepoot**.

hong[1] *hong*, *n* a Chinese warehouse; a foreign mercantile house in China; one of the multinational trading and financial companies based in Hong Kong. [Chin *hang* row, range]

hong² *hong*, obs form of **hang, hung**.
hongi *hong'i*, *n* a traditional Maori greeting involving touching nose to nose. [Maori]
honied. See **honeyed** under **honey**.
Honiton *hon'i-tən* or (locally) *hun'-*, *adj* of a kind of pillow lace with sprigs, made at *Honiton*, Devon. — *n* such lace.
honk *hongk*, *n* the cry of the wild goose; the noise of a motor horn. — *vi* to make such a sound; to smell unpleasantly (*slang*); to vomit (*slang*). — *n* **honk'er**. — *adj* **honk'ing**. [Imit]
honky or **honkie** *hongk'i*, (*derog slang, orig US*) *n* a white man. — Also *adj*. [Origin uncertain]
honky-tonk *hongk'i-tongk*, (*slang*) *n* a low drinking haunt (*NAm*); cheap entertainment; a style of jangly piano music. — Also *adj*. [Ety dubious]
honor. See **honour**.
honorand *on'ə-rand*, *n* a person receiving an honour, *esp* an honorary degree. [L *honōrandus*, gerundive of *honōrāre* to honour, from *honor*, *-ōris* honour]
honorarium *on-ə-rā'ri-əm*, *n* a voluntary fee paid, *esp* to a professional person for their services: — *pl* **honorā'ria** or **honorā'riums**. [L *honōrārius*, *honōrārium* (*dōnum*) honorary (gift), from *honor*, *-ōris* honour]
honorary *on'ə-rə-ri*, *adj* conferring honour; (holding a title or office) without performing services or without reward. — *n* an honorarium. [Ety as for **honorarium**]
honorific (*h*)*on-ə-rif'ik*, *adj* attributing or giving honour or respect. — *n* an honorific form of title, address or mention. — *adj* **honorif'ical**. — *adv* **honorif'ically**. [L *honōrificus*, from *honor*, *-ōris* honour, and *facere* to do, make]
honorificabilitudinity *hon-or-if-ik-əb-il-i-tū-din'i-ti*, *n* honourableness. [LL *honōrificābilitūdinitās*, preserved in the ablative pl *honōrificābilitūdinitātibus* as a superlatively long word, in *Love's Labour's Lost*, V.1.44 and elsewhere; the genitive sing is used by Albertino Mussato (early 14c)]
honoris causa *hon-ōr'is* or (*-ör'*) *kö'zə* or *kow'zä*, or **honoris gratia** *grā'shi-ə* or *grä'ti-ä*, (*LL*) as an honour, as a token of respect.
honour or *US* **honor** *on'ər*, *n* the esteem due or paid to a worthy person, body, etc; respect; high estimation; veneration; that which rightfully attracts esteem; that which confers distinction or does credit; integrity; a fine and scrupulous sense of what is right; chastity; virginity; distinction; exalted rank; any mark of esteem; privilege; a title or decoration; a title of respect in addressing or referring to judges, etc (in Ireland quite generally); a prize or distinction; (in *pl*) privileges of rank or birth; an ornament or decoration (*poetic*); (in *pl*) civilities, respects paid; (in *pl*; in universities, etc) a higher grade of distinction for meritorious, advanced or specialized work; the right to play first from the tee (*golf*); any one of four (in whist) or five (in bridge) best trumps, or an ace in a no-trump hand; (in *pl*) a score for holding these; a group of manors held by one lord. — *vt* to hold in high esteem; to respect; to adorn (*obs*); to exalt; to do honour to; to confer honour(s) upon; to grace (eg with one's presence); to accept and pay when due. — *adj* **hon'ourable** worthy of honour; illustrious; governed by principles of honour, good, honest, etc; conferring honour; befitting people of exalted rank; (with *cap*; written **Hon.**) prefixed to the names of various people as a courtesy title. — *n* **hon'ourableness** eminence; conformity to the principles of honour; fairness. — *adv* **hon'ourably**. — *adj* **hon'oured**. — *adj* **hon'ourless**. — *n* **hon'ourer**. — *adj* **hon'our-bound'** same as **in honour bound** (below). — **hon'or-guard** (*US*) a guard of honour; **hon'our-point** (*heraldry*) the point just above the fesse-point; **honours list** a list of people who have received or are to receive a knighthood, order, etc from the monarch for eg service to their community or country; **hon'ours-man** (*old*) one who has taken a university degree with honours. — **affair of honour** a duel; **birthday honours** honours granted to mark the monarch's birthday; **Companions of Honour** an order instituted in 1917 for those who have rendered conspicuous service of national importance; **Court of Honour** a court regulating affairs of honour; **debt of honour** see under **debt**; **do the honours** (*colloq*) to perform a task, *esp* the duties of a host; **guard of honour** a body of soldiers serving as a ceremonial escort; **guest of honour** the most important or distinguished guest (at a party, etc); **honour bright** (*old schoolchildren's slang*) an oath or appeal to honour; **honours easy** see under **ease**; **honours of war** the privileges granted to a surrendering force of marching out with their arms, flags, etc; **in honour bound** (or *adj* **hon'our-bound'**) obliged by duty, conscience, etc (to); **in honour of** out of respect for; celebrating; **last honours** funeral rites; **laws of honour** the conventional rules of honourable conduct, *esp* in the conduct of duels; **maid of honour** a lady in the service of a queen or princess; a small almond-flavoured cake, or a kind of cheese-cake; a bridesmaid (*NAm*); **matron of honour** a married woman in the service of a queen or princess; a married woman performing the duties of a bridesmaid, *esp* the chief bridesmaid; **military honours** ceremonial tokens of respect paid by troops to royalty, or at the burial of an officer, etc; **person of honour** (*obs*) a titled person; **point of honour** any scruple caused by a sense of duty, honour, self-respect, etc; the obligation to demand and to receive satisfaction for an insult, *esp* by duelling; **upon my honour** an appeal to one's honour in support of a statement; **word of honour** a promise which cannot be broken without disgrace. [Anglo-Fr (*h*)*onour*, from L *honor*, *-ōris*]
hony-seed, hony-suckle. See **honeysuckle** under **honey**.
hoo *hōō*, (*Shakesp*) *interj* expressing boisterous emotion. — Also **hoo-oo'**.
hooch¹ *hōōhh*, *interj* a Highland dancer's shout.
hooch² *hōōch*. See **hootch**.
hood¹ *hŏŏd*, *n* a flexible covering for the head and back of the neck; a covering for a hawk's head; a distinctively coloured ornamental fold of material, derived from a hood, worn on the back over an academic gown; a folding roof for a car, carriage, etc; a chimney-cowl; an overhanging or protective cover; the expansion of a cobra's neck; a hood-moulding; a motor-car bonnet (*NAm*). — *vt* to cover with a hood; to blind. — *adj* **hood'ed**. — *n* **hood'ie** a hoodie crow. — *adj* **hood'less** having no hood. — **hooded seal** a large seal (*Cystophora cristata*) of the N Atlantic, which has an inflatable sac over the nose region; **hood'ie-crow** the hooded crow (*Corvus cornix*); **hood'man** (*obs*) the person blindfolded in blindman's buff; **hood'man-blind** (*Shakesp*) blindman's buff; **hood'-mould** or **hood'-moulding** an uppermost projecting moulding over a door, window or arch. [OE *hōd*; Du *hoed*, Ger *Hut*]
hood² *hŏŏd*, (*slang*) *n* a hoodlum, a violent criminal.
hood³ *hŏŏd*, (*Spenser*) *n* condition. [OE *hād*]
-hood *-hŏŏd*, *n sfx* indicating: state or nature, as in *hardihood, manhood* (also **-head** (*-hed*) as in *Godhead*); a group of people, as in *priesthood, sisterhood*. [OE *hād*, Ger *-heit* state]
hoodlum *hōōd'ləm*, *n* a rowdy, street bully; a small-time criminal or gangster.
hoodman. See under **hood**¹.
hoodoo *hōō'dōō*, *n* voodoo; a bringer of bad luck; a jinx; foreboding of bad luck; bad luck; a rock-pinnacle (*geol*). — *vt* to bewitch; to bring bad luck to: — *pr p* **hoo'dooing**; *pa t* and *pa p* **hoo'dooed**. [Appar **voodoo**]
hoodwink *hŏŏd'wingk*, *vt* to blindfold; to cover up, hide (*Shakesp*); to deceive, cheat. [**hood**¹ and **wink**]
hooey *hōō'i*, (*slang*) *n* nonsense.
hoof *hōōf*, *n* the horny part of the feet of certain animals, eg horses; a hoofed animal; a foot (*colloq*): — *pl* **hooves** or **hoofs**. — *vt* to strike with the hoof, to kick; to expel; (with *it*) to walk (*slang*); (with *it*) to dance (*slang*). — *adj* **hoofed**. — *n* **hoof'er** (*slang*) a professional dancer. — *adj* **hoof'less**. — **hoof'beat** the sound of a hoof striking *esp* a hard road. — *adj* **hoof'-bound** having a contraction of the hoof causing lameness. — **hoof'=**

mark or **hoof'print** the mark of a hoof on the ground, etc; **hoof'rot** foot-rot. — **on the hoof** (of animals) still alive, *esp* (of cattle) not yet slaughtered; on the move, moving (*colloq*). [OE *hōf*; Ger *Huf*; ON *hōfr*]

hoo-ha or **hoo-hah** *hōō'-hä'*, (*slang*) *n* a noisy fuss. [Imit]

hook *hŏŏk*, *n* an object bent so that it can catch or hold something; a sharply bent line; a snare, trap, attraction, etc; an advantageous hold; a curved instrument for cutting grain, branches, etc; a spit of land with a hooked end; a boxer's blow made with the elbow bent; the curve of a ball in flight (*sport*); a particular way of striking the ball which makes it curve in a convex shape (*golf*) or in the direction of the swing (*cricket*); an act of hooking; in pop-music, a catchy phrase. — *vt* to catch, fasten, or hold with or as if with a hook; to form into a hook; to make with a hook; to make (a **hooked rug**) by drawing yarn through a prepared backing with a hooked tool; to ensnare, trap; to attract; to pull the ball abruptly to one's left if right-handed, or right if left-handed (*golf* and *cricket*); to obtain possession of (the ball) in the scrum (*Rugby football*). — *vi* to bend; to be curved; to pull abruptly; to act as hooker (*Rugby*); to curve in a particular direction (*golf*): — *pa p* or *adj* **hooked** (*hŏŏkt*) physically dependent (on drugs); (with *on* or *by*) addicted (to a drug, activity or indulgence); enthralled. — *n* **hook'edness**. — *n* **hook'er** someone who hooks; the person whose task it is to hook the ball (*Rugby football*); a prostitute (*slang*). — *adj* **hook'y**. — **hook'-climber** a climbing plant that clings to its support by means of hooks. — *adj* **hook'-nosed**. — **hook'-pin** an iron pin with a hooked head used for pinning the frame of a floor or roof together; **hook'-up** a connection; a temporary linking up of separate broadcasting stations for a special transmission; **hook'-worm** a parasitic nematode with hooks in the mouth; the disease it causes, ankylostomiasis or miner's anaemia. — **by hook or by crook** by one method or another; **hook and eye** a contrivance for fastening garments by means of a hook that catches in a loop or eye; **hook it** (*slang*) to decamp, make off; **hook, line and sinker** complete or completely; **off the hook** ready-made; out of difficulty or trouble; (of a telephone handset) not on its rest, so that incoming calls cannot be received; **off the hooks** out of gear; superseded; dead; **on one's own hook** on one's own responsibility, initiative or account; **sling** or **take one's hook** (*slang*) to get out, run away, make off. [OE *hōc*; Du *hoek*]

hookah or **hooka** *hŏŏk'ə*, *n* the tobacco-pipe of Arabs, Turks, etc with which smoke is inhaled through water. [Ar *huqqah* bowl, casket]

hooker[1] *hŏŏk'ər*, *n* a two-masted Dutch or Irish fishing vessel; a small fishing-smack. [Du *hoeker*]

hooker[2]. See under **hook**.

hookey[1] or **hooky** *hŏŏk'i*, (*US*) *n* truant (in the phrase *play hookey*). — **blind hookey** a gambling card-game; **Hookey Walker** see under **walk**.

hookey[2]. See under **hockey**[1].

hooky. See under **hook, hookey**[1].

hoolachan *hōō'lə-hhən*, or **hoolican** *hōō'li-kən*, (*Scot*) *n* a Highland reel, *esp* the reel of Tulloch. [Gaelic (*ruidhle*) *Thulachain* the reel of Tulloch, in Strathspey]

hooley *hōō'li*, (chiefly *Irish*) *n* a boisterous party, *usu* with singing and dancing. [Origin unknown]

hooligan *hōōl'i-gən*, *n* a street tough, vandal; a (young) violent, rude person. — *n* **hool'iganism**. [Said to be the name of a leader of a gang, poss *Houlihan* or *Hooley's gang*]

hoolock *hōō'lək*, *n* a small Assamese gibbon. [Said to be a native name, *hulluk*]

hooly *hül'i* or *hûl'i*, (*Scot*) *adv* softly, carefully. — Also *adj*. — **hooly and fairly** fair and soft, gently. [Perh ON *hōfliga* fitly, or *hōgliga* gently]

hoo-oo. See under **hoo**.

hoon *hōōn*, (*Austr slang*) *n* a lout, yob; a pimp.

hoop[1] *hōōp*, *n* a ring or circular band, *esp* for holding together the staves of casks, etc; any large ring, eg for a child to roll, for leaping through, for holding wide a skirt; a ring; a croquet arch. — *vt* to bind with hoops; to encircle. — *n* **hoop'er** a person who hoops casks; a cooper. — **hoop'-ash** a kind of ash used for making hoops; the nettle-tree (Celtis); **hooped'-pot** a drinking-pot with hoops to mark the amount each man should drink. — *interj* **hoop'-la** *orig* used at a circus when a performer jumped through a hoop. — *n* a fairground game in which small hoops are thrown over prizes; great activity, excitement or disturbance; pointless activity, nuisance, nonsense (*US slang*). — **hoop'-snake** any of several harmless snakes, once erroneously believed to be capable of forming themselves into a hoop and rolling over the ground. — **go through the hoop** to suffer an ordeal, undergo punishment. [OE *hōp*; Du *hoep*]

hoop[2], **hooper**[1] and **hooping-cough**. See under **whoop**.

hooper[2]. See under **hoop**[1].

hoopoe *hōōp'ōō*, *n* a crested bird with salmon-coloured plumage (*Upupa epops*), an occasional visitor to Britain. [Earlier *hoop*, from OFr *huppe*, partly remodelled on L *upupa*; cf Gr *epops*]

hooray[1] or (*old*) **hoorah**. Same as **hurrah**. — **Hooray** (or **Hoorah**) **Henry** a young middle- or upper-class man with an affectedly ebullient manner and an ostentatiously materialistic or self-seeking outlook.

hooray[2] *hōō-rā'* or **hooroo** *-rōō'*, (*Austr*) *interj* goodbye, cheerio.

hoord. An obs form of **hoard**[1].

hoosegow or **hoosgow** *hōōs'gow*, (*US slang*) *n* a prison, jail. [Sp *juzgado* tribunal, courtroom, from *juzgar* to judge, from L *jūdicāre*]

hoosh[1] *hōōsh*, *interj* used in driving away animals. — *vt* to drive or shoo away. [Imit]

hoosh[2] *hōōsh*, *n* a thick soup.

hoot *hōōt*, *vi* (of an owl) to give a hollow cry; to make a sound like an owl, *usu* expressing hostility or scorn; to laugh loudly; to sound a motor-horn, siren, or the like (also *vi*). — *vt* to greet or drive with such sounds. — *n* the sound of hooting; the note of an owl, motor-horn, etc; a whit, a care (often *two hoots*); a hilarious performance, escapade, situation, etc (*colloq*). — *interj* (*sing* or *pl*; *Scot*) expressing incredulity, irritation, annoyance, etc (also **hoot'-toot'** or **hoots'-toots'**). — *n* **hoot'er** someone who hoots; a siren or steam-whistle at a factory, mine, etc; a nose, *esp* a large or ugly one (*slang*). [Imit, prob immediately Scand; cf Swed *hut* begone]

hootch or **hooch** *hōōch*, *n* whisky or any strong liquor, *esp* if illicitly made or acquired; *orig* a drink made by the Indians of NW America from fermented dough and sugar. [Said to be from *Hooch*ino, an Alaskan Indian tribe]

hootenanny, **hootananny** or **-ie** *hōōt'ə-nan-ē*, or **hootnanny** or **-ie** *hōōt'nan-ē*, *n* thingummy (*US dialect*); a party with folk-singing and sometimes dancing, *esp* an informal concert with folk music (*NAm colloq*).

hoove[1] *hōōv*, *n* a disease of cattle and sheep, marked by distension of the abdomen by gas — also **wind-dropsy** or **drum-belly**. — *adj* **hoov'en** or **hō'ven**. [Cf **heave**]

hoove[2]. See **hove**[2].

Hoover® *hōō'vər*, *n* a vacuum-cleaner (also without *cap*). — *vt* and *vi* (*usu* without *cap*) to clean with (or suck up, etc as if with) a vacuum-cleaner.

hooves. See under **hoof**.

hop[1] *hop*, *vi* to leap on one leg; to move in jumps like a bird; to walk lame; to limp; to move smartly (in or out); to fly (in aircraft) (*colloq*). — *vt* to cause to hop; to jump or fly over; to jump from; to board when in motion (*US*): — *pr p* **hopp'ing**; *pa t* and *pa p* **hopped**. — *n* a leap on one leg; a jump; a spring; a dance, dancing-party (*slang*); one stage in a journey by aeroplane. — *n* **hopp'er** someone who hops; a hopping or leaping animal, *esp* (*US*) a grasshopper; a jack or sticker of a piano; a shaking or moving receiver, funnel or trough (*orig* a shaking one) in which something is placed to be conveyed or fed, as to a mill; a barge with an opening in its bottom for discharging refuse; a railway wagon with an opening in the bottom for discharging its cargo; a container in which seed-corn is carried for sowing; a device which holds and passes on punched cards to a feed mechanism (*comput*). — *n* **hopp'ing**. — *combining form* **-hopping** denoting: making quick journeys between, *usu* by air, as in *island-hopping*; (of an aircraft) skimming, as in *hedge-hopping*. — **hop-off'** the start of a flight; **hop'-o'-my-thumb** (ie on my thumb) a pygmy. — *adj* **hopp'ing(-)mad'** (*colloq*) extremely angry. — **hop'scotch** a game in which children hop over lines scotched or scored on the ground. — **hop it** (*slang*) to take oneself off, go away; **hop, skip** (or **step**) **and jump** a leap on one leg, a skip, and a jump with both legs as an athletic event, the triple jump; **hop the twig** (*slang*) to escape one's creditors; to die; **on the hop** in a state of restless activity; in the act, unawares, at the very moment. [OE *hoppian* to dance; Ger *hopfen*, *hüpfen*]

hop[2] *hop*, *n* a plant (*Humulus lupulus*) of the mulberry family with a long twining stalk; (in *pl*) its bitter catkin-like fruit-clusters used for flavouring beer and in medicine; opium (*old US slang*); any narcotic (*old slang*). — *vt* to mix or flavour with hops. — *vi* to gather hops: — *pr p* **hopp'ing**; *pa t* and *pa p* **hopped**. — *adj* **hopped** impregnated with hops. — *n* **hopp'er** or **hop'-picker** a person who picks hops; a mechanical contrivance for stripping hops from the bines. — *n* **hopp'ing** the act of gathering hops; the time of the hop harvest. — *adj* **hopp'y** tasting of hops. — **hop'bind** or **hop'bine** the stalk of the hop; **hop'-bitters** a drink like ginger-beer, flavoured with hops; **hop'dog** the tussock-moth caterpillar; a tool for pulling out hop-poles; **hop'-flea** a small beetle injurious to hops; **hop'-fly** a greenfly injurious to hops; **hop'-garden** a field of hops; **hop'-head** (*derog slang*) a drug addict; **hop'-oast** a kiln for drying hops. — *adj* **hopped'-up** (*US slang*) drugged; under an exhilarating drug; excited, agitated; artificially stimulated; made to seem exciting; given added power. — **hop'-picker** a hopper; **hop pillow** a pillow stuffed with hops, said to aid sleep; **hop'-pocket** coarse sack for hops; an amount of hops equal to approximately 75 kilos or 1 ½ cwt; **hop'-pole** a pole supporting a hop-bine; **hop'-sack** or **hop'sack** a sack for hops; **hop'sack** or **hop'-sacking** sacking for hops; coarse fabric of hemp and jute, or woollen fabric with a roughened surface; **hop'-tree** an American rutaceous shrub (*Ptelea trifoliata*) with bitter fruit, a substitute for hops; **hop'-tre'foil** a yellow clover; **hop'-vine** hop-plant; its stem; **hop'-yard** a field where hops are grown. — **hop up** (*old slang*) to excite, artificially stimulate; to drug. [Du *hop*]

hope[1] *hōp*, *vi* to cherish a desire (that something good will happen), with some expectation of success or fulfilment; to have confidence; to be hopeful. — *vt* to desire, with belief in the possibility of fulfilment; to expect, fear (*obs*). — *n* a desire for something good, with a certain expectation of obtaining it; confidence; anticipation; that on which hopes are grounded; an embodiment of hope; the event, object, etc which is hoped for. — *adj* **hope'ful** full of hope; having qualities which excite hope; promising good or success. — *n* a promising young person; a (*usu* young) person of ambition. — *adv* **hope'fully** in a hopeful manner; if all goes well (*colloq*). — *n* **hope'fulness**. — *adj* **hope'less** without hope; giving no reason to expect good or success; incurable; unhoped-for (*Spenser*). — *adv* **hope'lessly**. — *n* **hope'lessness**. — *n* **hōp'er**. — *adv* **hōp'ingly** (*archaic*). — **hope'-chest** (*NAm*) a place, often a trunk or chest, for things stored by a woman for her marriage, a bottom drawer. — **hope against hope** to continue to hope when there is no (longer any) reason for hope; **it is hoped** (*colloq*) if all goes well; **no'-hop'er** (*slang*) a racehorse that is not good enough to have a chance of winning; any thing or person that has absolutely no chance of success (*adj* **no'-hope'**); **some hope**, **what a hope** or **not a hope** (*ironic*) that will never happen. [OE *hopian*, from *hopa* hope; Du *hopen*, Ger *hoffen*]

hope[2] *hōp*, *n* an enclosure; the upper end of a narrow mountain-valley; a combe — common in Border place names (*usu* pronounced *-əp*); an inlet. [OE *-hop* (in compounds), or ON *hōp*]

hope[3]. See **forlorn hope**.

hoplite *hop'līt*, *n* a heavily-armed Greek foot-soldier. [Gr *hoplītēs*]

hoplology *hop-lol'ə-ji*, *n* the study of weapons. — *n* **hoplol'ogist**. [Gr *hoplon* tool, weapon]

hopped, hopped-up. See under **hop**[2].

hopper, hopping. See under **hop**[1], **hop**[2].

hopple *hop'l*, *vt* to restrain by tying the feet together. — *n* (chiefly in *pl*) a fetter for horses, etc when left to graze. [Cf obs Flem *hoppelen*; also **hop**[1] and **hobble**]

hoppus (cubic) foot *hop'əs* (*kū'bik*) *fŏŏt*, *n* a unit of volume for round timber. [Edward *Hoppus*]

hoppy. See under **hop**[2].

hopscotch. See under **hop**[1].

horae canonicae *hō'* or *hö'rē kən-on'i-kē*, or *hō'rī kan-on'i-kī*, (*L*) *n pl* the canonical hours.

horal *hö'rəl*, *adj* relating to hours; hourly. — *adj* **ho'rary** pertaining to an hour; noting the hours; hourly; continuing for an hour. [L *hōra* an hour]

Horatian *hor-ā'shən*, *adj* pertaining to *Horace*, the Latin poet (65–8 BC), or to his manner or verse.

horde *hörd*, *n* a migratory or wandering tribe or clan; a multitude. — *vi* to live together as a horde; to come together to form a horde. — **Golden Horde** see under **gold**[1]. [Fr, from Turk *ordu* camp]

Hordeum *hör'di-əm*, *n* the barley genus. — *n* **hordein** (*hör'di-in*) a protein found in barley grains. — *n* **hordeolum** (*-dē'*) a sty on the eyelid. [L, barley]

hordock. See under **hardoke**.

hore (*Spenser*). Same as **hoar**.

horehound or **hoarhound** *hör'hownd*, *n* a hoary labiate plant (*Marrubium vulgare*) once popular as a remedy for coughs. — Also called **white horehound**. — **black horehound** or **stinking horehound** a darker-coloured related weed (*Ballota nigra*); **water horehound** gypsywort. [OE *hār* hoar, and *hūne* horehound]

horizon *hər-ī'zən*, *n* the line at which earth and sky seem to meet (called the *sensible*, *apparent* or *visible horizon*); a plane through the earth's centre parallel to the sensible horizon (called the *rational horizon*), or the great circle in which it meets the heavens (*astron*); a horizontal reflecting surface, eg of mercury, used as a substitute for the horizon in taking an observation (an *artificial horizon*); a stratigraphical level, characterized generally by some particular fossil or fossils (*geol*), by a different physical property of the soil (*soil science*), or by artefacts characteristic of a particular culture or period (*archaeol*); a level line or surface (*anatom*); the limit of one's experience or mental vision. — *adj* **horizontal** (*hor-i-zont'l*) pertaining to the horizon; parallel to the horizon; level; near the horizon; measured in the plane of the horizon; applying equally to all members of a group, aspects of an activity, etc; of relationships between separate groups of equal status or stage of development. — *n* a horizontal line, position or object; a large Tasmanian shrub, whose stem and branches ascend and then grow horizontally to form a dense mass of boughs and foliage — also **horizontal scrub**. — *n* **horizontal'ity**. — *adv* **horizon'tally**. — **horizontal bar** (*gymnastics*) a steel bar used for swinging and vaulting exercises. [Fr, from L, from Gr *horizōn* (*kyklos*) bounding (circle); *horizōn*, *-ontos*, pr p of *horizein* to bound, from *horos* a limit]

horkey. See under **hockey**[2].

horme *hör'mē*, (*psychol*) *n* goal-directed or purposive behaviour. — **hormic theory** theory stressing the importance of instinctive impulses and purposive striving. [Gr *hormē* animal impulse]

hormone *hör'mōn*, *n* an internal secretion which, on reaching some part of a plant or animal body, exercises a specific physiological action. — *adj* **hormon'al**. — *adj*

hormon'ic (or *-mōn'*). — **hormone replacement therapy** a treatment for post-menopausal women involving the artificial provision of a hormone which is no longer produced naturally after the menopause, thereby reducing the risk of brittle bones in later life. [Gr *hormōn*, contracted pr p of *hormaein* to stir up]

horn *hörn*, *n* a hard outgrowth on the head of an animal, sometimes confined to the hollow structure on an ox, sheep, goat, etc, sometimes extended to a deer's antler, the growth on a giraffe's head, on a rhinoceros's snout, etc; a beetle's antenna; a snail's tentacle; any projection resembling a horn; a cusp; a crescent tip; either of the pair of outgrowths supposed to spring from a cuckold's forehead; the material of which horns are composed, keratin; an object made of or like a horn, eg a drinking vessel; a funnel-shaped mouthpiece; a primitive musical instrument consisting of an animal's horn, blown through to produce sound; any of various musical instruments consisting of a brass tube tapering to a mouthpiece; an apparatus on motor vehicles for making a noise warning of approach; a Jewish symbol of strength; (*cap*; with *the*) Cape Horn, in S America; an erection of the penis (*vulgar slang*); the telephone (*US slang*); see also **horn balance** below. — *adj* made of horn. — *vt* to furnish with horns, real or cuckold's; to dishorn; to outlaw (*obs Scots law*); to gore; to butt or push. — *vi* to play or blow the horn; to butt. — *adj* **horned** having a horn or horns; curved like a horn. — *n* **horn'er** a person who works or deals in horns; a horn-player; a cuckold-maker (*obs*). — *n* **horn'ful**. — *n* **Horn'ie** (*Scot*) the devil, *usu* represented with horns. — *n* **horn'iness**. — *n* **horn'ing** appearance of the moon when in its crescent form; a mock serenade with tin horns and any discordant instruments, a shivaree (*US dialect*); putting to the horn (*obs Scots law*; see below); cuckold-making (*obs*). — *adj* **horn'ish** like horn; hard. — *n* **horn'ist** a horn-player. — *adj* **horn'less** without horns. — *n* **horn'let** a little horn. — *adj* **horn'y** like horn; of horn; hard; callous; sexually aroused (*slang*); lecherous, lustful (*slang*). — **horn balance** a forward extension of an aircraft control surface to assist its operation; **horn'beak** (*dialect*) the garfish; **horn'beam** a tree (*Carpinus*) resembling a beech, with hard tough wood; **horn'bill** a bird (of family Bucerotidae) with a horny excrescence on its bill; **horn'book** (*hist*) a first book for children, which consisted of a single leaf set in a frame, with a thin plate of semitransparent horn in front to preserve it; **horn'bug** (*US*) a stag-beetle; **horned cairn** (*archaeol*) a long barrow with a pair of curved projecting arms at one end, or at both; **horned horse** the gnu; **horned owl** or **horn owl** an owl with hornlike tufts of feathers on its head; **horned poppy** a poppy (*Glaucium*) with a horned seed-vessel; **horned toad** a spiny American lizard (*Phrynosoma*); a S American toad (*Ceratophrys*) with a bony shield on the back. — *adj* **horn'-footed** hoofed. — **horn gate** gate of horn (see under **gate**[1]); **horn'geld** (*hist*) cornage. — *adj* **horn'-mad** (*archaic*) mad to the point of goring anybody; enraged like a cuckold. — **horn'-madness** (*Browning*); **horn'-maker** (*Shakesp*) a cuckold-maker; **horn mercury** native mercurous chloride or calomel; **horn'-nut** water-chestnut; **horn-pout, horned-pout** see under **pout**[2]. — *adj* **horn'-rimmed** (*esp* of spectacles) having rims of horn, or material resembling horn. — **horn'-rims** spectacles with rims of dark horn, or material resembling horn; **horn silver** cerargyrite; **horn spoon** a spoon made of (*usu* a sheep's) horn; **horn'stone** (*mineralogy*) a flinty chalcedony; hornfels; **horn'tail** a hymenopterous insect, often with a stout ovipositor; **horn'work** an outwork having angular points or horns, and composed of two demi-bastions joined by a curtain (*fortif*); work in horn; cuckoldry (*obs*); **horn'worm** a hawk-moth caterpillar; **horn'wort** a rootless water-plant (*Ceratophyllum*) with much-divided submerged leaves that turn translucent and horny; **horn'wrack** the sea-mat. — *adj* **horn'y-hand'ed** with hands hardened by toil. — **horn'yhead** an American cyprinoid fish with hornlike processes on its head. — **horn in** (*slang*) to interpose, butt in (on); **horn of plenty** see **cornucopia**; a trumpet-shaped edible fungus, *Craterellus cornucopoides*; **horns of a dilemma** see under **dilemma**; **horns of the altar** the projections at the four corners of the Hebrew altar; **letters of horning** (*Scots law*) letters running in the sovereign's name, and passing the signet, instructing messengers-at-arms to charge the debtor to pay, on his failure a caption or warrant for his apprehension being granted; **make a spoon or spoil a horn** to attempt something at the risk of failure; **pull** or **draw in one's horns** to abate one's ardour or pretensions; to curtail or restrict one's activities, spending, etc; **put to the horn** (*obs Scots law*) to outlaw by three blasts of the horn at the Cross of Edinburgh. [OE *horn*; Scand *horn*, Ger *Horn*, Gaelic and Welsh *corn*, L *cornū*, Gr *keras*]

hornblende *hörn'blend*, *n* a rock-forming mineral, one of the amphiboles, essentially silicate of calcium, magnesium and iron, generally green to black, with a cleavage angle of about 56°. — *adj* **hornblend'ic**. [Ger; cf **horn** and **blende**]

horned, horner. See under **horn**.

hornet *hörn'it*, *n* a large kind of wasp. — **stir up a hornet's** (or **hornets'**) **nest** to do something which causes a violent reaction. [OE *hyrnet*, appar from *horn* horn]

hornfels *hörn'fels*, (*mineralogy*) *n* a compact type of rock composed of lime silicates. [Ger, from *Horn* horn, and *Fels* rock]

hornful, horngeld, Hornie, horniness, horning, hornish, hornist. See under **horn**.

hornito *hör-nē'tō*, *n* a low oven-shaped fumarole: — *pl* **horni'tos**. [Sp, dimin of *horno*, from L *furnus* an oven]

hornless, hornlet. See under **horn**.

hornpipe *hörn'pīp*, *n* an old Welsh musical instrument like a clarinet, probably sometimes having a horn mouthpiece or bell; a lively English dance, usually by one person, traditionally popular amongst sailors; a tune for the dance. [**horn** and **pipe**[1]]

hornstone. See under **horn**.

hornswoggle *hörn'swog-l*, (*slang*; *orig* and *esp US*) *vt* to trick, deceive; to cheat. [Ety unknown]

horntail . . . to . . . **hornwrack, horny**. See under **horn**.

horography *hor-og'rə-fi*, *n* the art of constructing sundials, clocks, etc. — *n* **horog'rapher**. [Gr *hōrā* an hour, and *graphein* to describe]

horologe *hor'ə-loj*, *n* any instrument for telling the time. — *n* **horologer** (*-ol'ə-jər*) or **horol'ogist** a maker of clocks, etc. — *adj* **horolog'ic** or **horolog'ical**. — *n* **horolog'ium** a horologe (*obs*); (with *cap*) a southern constellation (*astron*). — *n* **horol'ogy** the science of the measurement of time; the art of clock-making; the office-book of the Greek Church for the canonical hours (also **horologium**). [L *hōrologium*, from Gr *hōrologion*, from *hōrā* an hour, and *legein* to tell]

horometry *hor-om'it-ri*, *n* time measurement. — *adj* **horometrical** (*-met'*). [Gr *hōrā* an hour, and *metron* a measure]

horoscope *hor'ə-skōp*, *n* a map of the heavens at the hour or on the day of a person's birth, by which an astrologer predicts the events of a person's life; such a prediction; a representation of the heavens for this purpose; any similar prediction about the future. — *adj* **horoscopic** (*-skop'*). — *n* **horoscopist** (*-os'kə-pist*) an astrologer. — *n* **horos'copy** the art of predicting the events of a person's life from his or her horoscope; the aspect of the stars at the time of birth. [Gr *hōroskopos*, from *hōrā* an hour, and *skopeein* to observe]

horrendous *hor-en'dəs*, (*colloq*) *adj* dreadful; frightful; horrible. — *adv* **horren'dously**. — *n* **horren'dousness**. [L *horrendus*, gerundive of *horrēre* to bristle]

horrent *hor'ənt*, *adj* bristling. [L *horrēns*, *-entis*, pr p of *horrēre* to bristle]

horrible *hor'i-bl*, *adj* producing horror; dreadful; detestable, foul (*colloq*). — *n* **horr'ibleness**. — *adv* **horr'ibly**. [L *horribilis*, from *horrēre* to shudder]

horrid *hor'id*, *adj* shaggy, bristling, rough (*archaic* or *poetic*); horrible (*archaic*); nasty, repellent, detestable (*colloq*). — *adv* **horr'idly**. — *n* **horr'idness**. [L *horridus*, from *horrēre* to bristle]

horrify *hor'i-fī*, *vt* to produce a reaction of horror in (a person): — *pr p* **horr'ifying**; *pa t* and *pa p* **horr'ified**. — *adj* **horrif'ic** producing horror; frightful, awful. — *adv* **horrif'ically**. — *adv* **horr'ifyingly**. [L *horrificus*, from root of *horrēre* to shudder, with *facere* to make]

horripilation *hor-i-pi-lā'shən*, *n* a contraction of the cutaneous muscles causing erection of the hairs and goose-flesh. — *adj* **horrip'ilant**. — *vt* and *vi* **horrip'ilate**. [L *horripilātiō*, *-ōnis*, from root of *horrēre* to bristle, and *pilus* a hair]

horrisonant *hor-is'ən-ənt*, *adj* dreadful-sounding. — Also **horris'onous** (*archaic*). [From root of L *horrēre* to bristle, and *sonāns*, *-antis* sounding]

horror *hor'ər*, *n* shagginess, raggedness (*obs*); a shuddering (*obs*); intense repugnance or fear; the power of producing such feelings; a source of such feelings; any person or thing that is mildly objectionable, ridiculous, grotesque or distasteful (*colloq*). — **horror comic**, **horror film**, **horror novel**, etc a comic (ie strip cartoon), film, novel, etc having gruesome, violent, horrifying, or bloodcurdling themes. — **horror story** a story (often true) of one disaster after another; such a sequence of events, a chapter of accidents. — *adj* **horr'or-stricken** or **horr'or-struck**. — **the horrors** extreme depression, frightening thoughts; delirium tremens. [L *horror* a shudder, bristling, etc]

hors *or*, (*Fr*) *prep* out of, outside. — **hors concours** (*kɔ̃-kōōr*) not in competition; **hors de combat** (*də kɔ̃-ba*) unfit to fight, disabled; **hors de saison** (*də se-zɔ̃*) out of season; **hors d'œuvre** (*pl* **d'œuvre** or **d'œuvres**; *dœ-vr'*) a savoury snack, eg olives, sardines, etc to whet the appetite before a meal; **hors la loi** (*la lwa*) in outlawry, outlawed; **hors série** (*sā-rē*) excluded from a series, added later; **hors texte** (*tekst*) an illustration inset separately into a book.

horse *hörs*, *n* a solid-hoofed ungulate (*Equus caballus*) with flowing tail and mane, widely domesticated for riding and as a draught animal; any member of the genus Equus (horse, ass, zebra, etc) or the family Equidae; a male adult of the species; cavalry (*collectively*); a wooden frame on which soldiers used to be mounted as a punishment — also *timber-mare*; a gymnastic apparatus for vaulting over, etc; a horselike apparatus or support of various kinds (such as *sawhorse*, *clothes-horse*); a crib or translation, a pony (*US slang*); a mass of barren country interrupting a lode (*mining*); heroin (*slang*): — *pl* **horses**, or sometimes **horse**. — *vt* to mount or set on, or as if on, a horse; to provide with a horse; to sit astride; to carry on the back; (of a stallion) to copulate with (a mare); to urge to work tyrannically. — *vi* to get on horseback; to travel on horseback; to charge for work before it is done (with *it*). — *adj* **horse'less** without a horse; mechanically driven, motorized. — *adj* **hors'ey** or **hors'y** of or pertaining to horses; horselike, *esp* in appearance (*derog* of people); devoted to horses, horse-racing or breeding; (*esp* of a woman) affectedly refined in speech or manner, in a way stereotypically associated with the upper classes, traditionally fond of equestrian pursuits. — *n* **hors'iness**. — *n* **hors'ing** (*archaic*) birching of a person mounted on another's back. — *adj* **horse'-and-bugg'y** hopelessly out of date. — **horse artillery** field artillery with comparatively light guns and the gunners mounted; **horse'back** the back of a horse; **horse bean** a variety of broad bean; applied also to other beans; **horse block** a mounting block; **horse boat** a boat for carrying horses, or towed by a horse; **horse bot** a botfly; **horse box** a road trailer or railway car designed to carry horses; a stall or compartment on a ship; a high-sided church pew (*facetious*); **horse'-boy** a stable boy; **horse brass** a *usu* brass ornament of a kind hung on the harness of a horse; **horse'-bread** a coarse bread for feeding horses; **horse'-breaker** or **horse-tamer** a person who breaks or tames horses, or teaches them to pull or carry; a courtesan who appears on horseback (*obs*); **horse'car** (*US*) a streetcar drawn by horses; **horse chestnut** a smooth, brown, bitter seed or nut, perhaps so called from its coarseness contrasted with the edible chestnut; the tree that produces it (*Aesculus hippocastanum*); **horse'-cloth** a cloth for covering a horse; **horse'-collar** a stuffed collar for a draught-horse, carrying the hames; **horse'-coper** or (*Scot*) **horse'-couper** (*kow* or *kōō*) or **horse'-dealer** a person who deals in horses; **horse'-courser** (*obs*) a jobbing dealer in horses; **horse'-dealing** horse-trading; **horse'-doctor** a veterinary surgeon; **horse'-drench** a dose of medicine for a horse. — *adj* **horse'-faced** having a long horselike face. — **horse fair** a fair or market for sale of horses. — *n pl* and *interj* **horse'feathers** (*US*) nonsense. — **horse'-flesh** the flesh of a horse, *esp* when eaten as meat, or traded on the hoof; horses collectively. — *adj* of a reddish-bronze colour. — **horseflesh ore** bornite or erubescite (from its colour); **horse'fly** the forest-fly or other large fly that stings or bites horses; **horse'-foot** coltsfoot (*obs*); a kingcrab; **horse-god'mother** (*dialect*) a fat clumsy woman; **horse'-gowan** (*Scot*) the ox-eye daisy. — *n pl* **horse guards** cavalry soldiers employed as guards; (with *cap*) the cavalry brigade of the British household troops, *esp* the *Royal Horse Guards*, or *Blues*, a regiment raised in 1661; (with *cap*) their headquarters in Whitehall, London, once the seat of the departments of the army commander-in-chief; the military authorities. — **horse'hair** a hair from a horse's mane or tail; a mass of such hairs; a fabric woven from horsehair. — *adj* made of or stuffed with horsehair. — **horse'hide**; **horse hoe** a hoe drawn by horses; **horse'-knacker** someone who buys and slaughters worn-out horses; **horse latitudes** two zones of the Atlantic Ocean (about 30°N and 30°S, *esp* the former) noted for long calm periods; **horse'laugh** a harsh, boisterous laugh; **horse'-leech** a horse-doctor (*obs*); a large species of leech, supposed to fasten on horses; a bloodsucker (Proverbs 30.15); **horseless carriage** (*archaic*) a motor car; **horse'-litter** a litter or bed borne between two horses; bedding for horses; **horse mackerel** the scad or any related fish; the tunny; applied to various other fishes; **horse'man** a rider; a person skilled in managing a horse; a mounted soldier; a person who has charge of horses; a kind of carrier pigeon; a kind of land-crab; **horse'manship** the art of riding and of training and managing horses; **horseman's word** (*Scot hist*) a ploughman's secret word to control horses; a magic word used against one's enemy, imparted by the devil in exchange for service in hell; **horse marine** a person quite out of his element; a member of an imaginary corps; **horse'meat** food for horses; horseflesh used as food; **horse mill** a mill turned by horses; **horse'-milliner** (*archaic*) someone who provides the trappings for horses; **horse'mint** any wild mint; the American *Monarda punctata*, or any of several other species of *Monarda*; (**sweet horsemint**) the common dittany; **horse mushroom** a large coarse mushroom; **horse mussel** a mollusc (*Modiolus*) similar to the common mussel but much bigger; **horse nail** a nail for fastening a horseshoe to the hoof; **horse opera** a Wild West film (*facetious*); **horse pistol** a large pistol formerly carried in a holster by horsemen; **horse'play** rough, boisterous play; **horse'pond** a pond for watering horses at; **horse'power** the power a horse can exert, or its conventional equivalent (taken as 745–7 watts, or **metric horsepower** taken as 735.5 watts); **horse race** a race by horses; **horse'-racing** the practice of racing or running horses in matches; **horse'radish** a plant related to scurvy-grass with a pungent root, used in the preparation of a sharp-tasting condiment; the condiment itself (also **horseradish sauce**); **horse'radish tree** a tree (*Moringa pterygosperma*) cultivated in tropical countries for its edible capsules and its seeds, ben-nuts, which yield oil of ben — the roots tasting like horseradish; an Australian tree, (*Codonocarpus cotinifolius*) with leaves of horseradish flavour; **horse rake** a rake pulled by horses; **horse'-rider**; **horse'-riding**; **horse**

sense (*colloq*) plain common sense; **horse'shoe** a metal plate for horses' feet, consisting of a curved piece of iron nailed to the underside of the hoof; anything of similar shape; a representation of it, *esp* as a symbol of good luck. — *adj* shaped like a horseshoe. — **horse'-shoer** (*-shōō'ər*) a person who makes or fits horseshoes; **horse'shoeing**; **horse'-sickness** or **African horse-sickness** a serious disease of horses, due to a virus; **horse soldier** a cavalry soldier; **horse'tail** a horse's tail; a Turkish standard, marking rank by number; any plant of the genus Equisetum (scouring-rush) with hollow rush-like stems, constituting with related fossils a class of fern-allies, Equisetinae; **horse'-thief**; **horse'-trading** hard bargaining; **horse'-trainer** a person who trains horses for racing, etc; **horse'way** a road along which a horse may pass; **horse'whip** a whip for driving horses. — *vt* to thrash with a horsewhip; to lash. — **horse'-woman** a woman who rides on horseback, or who rides well; **horse-wrangler** see under **wrangle**. — **dark horse** see under **dark**; **flog a dead horse** to try to work up excitement about a subject in which others have lost interest; **from the horse's mouth** see **straight from the horse's mouth** below; **gift horse** see under **gift**; **high horse** see **on one's high horse** (under **high**[1]); **hold your horses** not so fast; wait a moment; **horse and hattock** see under **hat**; **horse around** (*slang*) to fool about, play boisterously; **horses for courses** phrase expressing the view that each racehorse will do best on a certain course which peculiarly suits it (also *fig* of people); **horse of a different colour** another thing altogether; **metric horsepower** see under **horsepower** above; **put the cart before the horse** see under **cart**; **straight from the horse's mouth** from a very trustworthy source (of information); **take horse** to mount on horseback; **white horse** see under **white**; **willing horse** a willing, obliging worker. [OE *hors*; ON *hross*; OHGer *hros* (Ger *Ross*)]

horson (*Shakesp*). Same as **whoreson** at **whore**.

horst *hörst*, (*geol*) *n* a block of the earth's crust that has remained in position while the ground around it has either subsided or been folded into mountains by pressure against its solid sides. [Ger]

horsy. See under **horse**.

hortative *hört'ə-tiv*, *adj* inciting; encouraging; giving advice. — Also **hort'atory**. — *adv* **hort'atively** or **hort'atorily**. — *n* **hortā'tion**. [L *hortārī*, *-ātus* to incite]

horticulture *hör'ti-kul-chər*, *n* the art of gardening. — *adj* **horticul'tural**. — *n* **horticul'turist** an expert in the art of cultivating gardens. [L *hortus* a garden, and *cultūra*, from *colere* to cultivate]

hortus siccus *hör'təs sik'əs* or *hor'tōōs sik'ōōs*, (*L*) *n* a collection of dried plants; a herbarium.

Horus *hō'rəs* or *hör'əs*, *n* the Egyptian sun-god, son of Isis and Osiris, *usu* depicted with a falcon's head. [Egyp *hur* hawk]

Hos. (*Bible*) *abbrev*: (the Book of) Hosea.

hosanna *hō-zan'ə*, *n* an exclamation of praise to God. [Gr *hōsanna*, from Heb *hōshī 'āh nnā*, *hōshīā'* save, and *nā* I pray]

hose *hōz*, *n* an old-fashioned covering for the legs or feet; stockings; socks (also **half-hose**); close-fitting breeches or drawers (*obs*); a flexible pipe for conveying water, etc, so called from its shape; a socket for a shaft: — *pl* **hose** or (*archaic*) **hos'en**; in sense of pipe, *pl* **hos'es**. — *vt* to provide with hose (*archaic*); to direct a hose at; to wash (*down*) with water from a hose. — *adj* **hosed**. — *n* **hosier** (*hōzh'(y)ər* or *hōz'yər*) a dealer in or a maker of hosiery. — *n* **hō'siery** hose collectively; knitted goods, *esp* underwear. — **hose'man** a fireman who directs the stream of water; **hose'-net** (*Scot*) a stocking-shaped net; **hose'pipe**; **hose'-reel** a large revolving drum for carrying hoses. [OE *hosa*, pl *hosan*, Du *hoos*, Ger *Hose*]

hospice *hos'pis*, *n* a house of entertainment for strangers, *esp* one kept by monks; a hostel; a home of refuge; a home for the care of the terminally ill. [Fr, from L *hospitium*, from *hospes*, *-itis* a stranger, guest]

hospitable *hos'pit-ə-bl* or *hos-pit'ə-bl*, *adj* kind to strangers; welcoming and generous towards guests. — *n* **hos'pitableness** (or *-pit'*). — *adv* **hos'pitably** (or *-pit'*). — *n* **hospitage** (*hos'pit-ij*; *Spenser*) behaviour expected of a guest. [LL *hospitāgium*, from L *hospes*, *-itis* stranger, guest]

hospital *hos'pit-l*, *n* a hostel for travellers (*obs*); formerly a charitable institution for the old or destitute, or for taking in (and educating) the needy young; any institution for the treatment of the sick or injured; a building for any of these purposes. — *n* **hos'pitale** (*-āl*; *Spenser*) lodging. — *n* **hospitalizā'tion** or **-s-**. — *vt* **hos'pitalize** or **-ise** to send to hospital; to injure so badly that hospital treatment is needed. — *n* **hos'pitaller** or (*US*) **hos'pitaler** a member of a charitable brotherhood for the care of the sick in hospitals; one of the Knights of St John (otherwise called Knights of Rhodes, and afterwards Knights of Malta), an order which built a hospital for pilgrims at Jerusalem. — **hos'pital-ship** a ship fitted out exclusively for the treatment and transport of the sick and wounded, *esp* in time of war. [OFr *hospital*, from LL *hospitāle*, from *hospes*, *-itis* a guest]

hospitality *hos-pi-tal'i-ti*, *n* (friendly welcome and) entertainment of guests (also *fig*); a room or suite where guests, delegates, etc are welcomed and entertained, *usu* being offered free drinks (also **hospitality suite**). [Ety as for **hospital**]

hospitium *hos-pish'i-əm*, *n* a hospice: — *pl* **hospi'tia**. [L; cf **hospice**]

hospodar *hos'po-där*, (*hist*) *n* a prince or governor, *esp* of Moldavia or Wallachia. — Also **gos'podar**. [Rom *hospodár*, of Slav origin]

hoss *hos*, (*esp US colloq* and *dialect*) *n* a horse.

host[1] *hōst*, *n* a person who entertains a stranger or guest at his or her house without (or with) reward; an innkeeper or publican; a person who introduces performers or participants, who chairs discussions, etc on a programme or show; a place acting as the venue for (an event), *usu* implying some involvement in the organization of the event and the welcoming of the participants; an organism on which another lives as a parasite (also *fig*); a person or animal that has received transplanted tissue or a transplanted organ; a host computer (see below). — *vt* to receive and entertain as one's guest; to act as or be the chairperson, compère, etc of (a show, programme, event, etc). — *vi* (*Spenser*, *Shakesp*) to lodge, to be a guest. — *n* **hōst'ess** a female host; a paid female partner at a dance-hall, nightclub, etc; a prostitute (*euphem*). — Also *vt* (*obs* and *US*) and *vi* (*obs*). — *n* **hōst'ess-ship** the character or office of a hostess. — *adj* **hōst'lesse** (*Spenser*) inhospitable. — *n* **hōst'ry** (*Spenser*) lodging. — **host computer** a computer attached to and in control of a multi-terminal computer system, or one attached to a multi-computer network and able eg to provide access to a number of databases. — **air'-hōstess** see under **air**; **lie at host** (*Shakesp*) to be lodged; **reckon** or **count without one's host** to count up one's bill without reference to the landlord; to fail to take account of some important possibility, such as the action of another. [OFr *hoste*, from L *hospes*, *hospitis*]

host[2] *hōst*, *n* an army (*archaic*); a great multitude. — *n* **hōst'ing** a battle (*Milton*); a muster, a military expedition (*Spenser*). — **a host in himself** a man of great strength, skill or resources within himself; **heavenly host** (*Bible*) the angels and archangels; **Lord of hosts** a favourite Hebrew term for Jehovah, considered as head of the hosts of angels, the hosts of stars, etc. [OFr *host*, from L *hostis* an enemy]

host[3] *hōst*, *n* a sacrificial victim (*obs*); (often with *cap*) in the RC Church, the consecrated wafer of the eucharist. [L *hostia* a victim]

hosta *hōst'ə*, *n* any plant of the *Hosta* genus of decorative perennial herbaceous plants (family *Liliaceae*) from Asia with ribbed basal leaves and blue, white and lilac flowers. [After Austrian botanist N T *Host*]

hostage *hos'tij*, *n* a person kept prisoner by an enemy as security. — **hostages to fortune** the people and things one values most (Bacon's *Essays*: Of Marriage and Single Life); hence, things of which the loss would be particularly painful. [OFr *hostage* (Fr *ôtage*), from L *obses, obsidis* a hostage]

hostel *hos'təl*, *n* an inn; in some universities, an extra-collegiate hall for students; a residence for students or for some class or society of people, *esp* one run charitably or not for profit; a youth hostel. — *n* **hos'teler** or **hos'teller** hospitaller (*archaic*); the keeper of a hostel; a person who lives in or uses a hostel, *esp* a youth hostel. — *n* **hos'telling** holidaying in youth hostels. — *n* **hos'telry** (now *esp jocularly*) an inn. [OFr *hostel, hostellerie*, from L *hospitāle*; cf **hospital**]

hostess. See under **host**[1].

hostile *hos'tīl* or (*US*) *-təl*, *adj* pertaining to an enemy; showing enmity or unfriendliness, or angry opposition; resistant (*esp* to new ideas, changes, etc); (of a place or conditions) inhospitable, harsh; engaged in hostilities; pertaining to hostilities. — *adv* **hos'tilely**. — *n* **hostility** (*-til'*) enmity, unfriendliness: — *pl* **hostil'ities** (acts of) warfare. — **hostile bid** (*commerce*) a bid not welcomed by the company whose shares are to be bought; **hostile witness** (*legal*) a witness who gives evidence against the party he or she was called by. [L *hostīlis* from *hostis*]

hostler *hos'lər* or (*obs*) *os'ler*, *n* an ostler (now *US*); a maintenance worker who services railway wagons, locomotives, etc (*US*).

hostlesse, hostry. See under **host**[1].

hot[1] *hot*, *adj* (*compar* **hott'er**; *superl* **hott'est**) having a high temperature; very warm; fiery; pungent; powerful; giving a feeling suggestive of heat; animated; ardent; vehement; violent; passionate; sexually excited (*slang*); lustful; dangerously charged with electricity; dangerous; near the object sought (eg in the game of hide-and-seek); (of news) fresh, exciting; (of jazz, etc) intensely played with complex rhythms and exciting improvisations; skilful (*colloq*); currently fashionable, sought-after, most wanted (*colloq*); recently stolen or obtained dishonestly (*colloq*); highly radioactive (*colloq*). — *adv* hotly. — *vt* (*colloq*) to heat: — *pr p* **hott'ing**; *pa t* and *pa p* **hott'ed**. — *adv* **hot'ly**. — *n* **hot'ness**. — *n* **hott'er** (*colloq*) a (*usu* young) car thief who attempts displays of dangerous stunts in powerful cars. — *n* **hott'ie** (*colloq*) a hot-water bottle. — *n* **hott'ing** (*colloq*) attempting high-speed stunts in stolen powerful cars, often as a display. — *adj* **hott'ish**. — **hot air** empty talk. — *adj* **hot'-air** making use of heated air; boastful, empty. — **hot-air balloon** one containing air which is heated by a flame to maintain or increase altitude. — *adj* **hot'-and-hot'** cooked and served up at once in hot dishes. — Also *n*. — **hot'bed** a glass-covered bed heated by a layer of fermenting manure for bringing forward plants rapidly; a place, or conditions, favourable to rapid growth or development, *usu* of a bad kind (*fig*); **hot blast** a blast of heated air. — *adj* **hot'-blood'ed** having hot blood; homothermous; passionate; ardent; high-spirited; irritable. — **hot'-brain** (*archaic*) a hothead. — *adj* **hot'-brained** (*archaic*). — **hot button** (*orig US*; *politics*) an emotive topic, a sensitive issue; **hot-cock'les** an old game in which a person with eyes covered guesses who strikes him or her; **hot coppers** see under **copper**[1]; **hot dog** a hot sausage sandwich; (**hot'-dog**) a person who performs clever manoeuvres, such as spins and turns, while skiing, surfing or skate-boarding (*colloq*; *esp US*) — *vi* **hot'-dog** (*colloq*; *esp US*). — **hot'-dogger**; **hot'-dogging**; **hot favourite** (in sports, races, etc) the one (considered) most likely to win (also *fig*); **hot flue** (*obs*) a drying-room. — *adv* **hot'foot** in haste (**hotfoot it** (*colloq*) to rush). — **hot gospeller** a loud, forceful proclaimer of a vigorously interactive kind of religious faith; a fanatical propagandist; **hot gospelling**; **hot hatch** (*colloq*) a powerful sports hatchback model (often designated **GT**, etc) of certain prestigious makes of car. — *adj* **hot'-hatch**. — **hot'head** an impetuous headstrong person. — *adj* **hot'headed**. — **hot'house** a greenhouse kept hot for the rearing of tropical or tender plants; any heated chamber or drying-room, *esp* that where pottery is placed before going into the kiln; a hot-bathing establishment (*obs*); a brothel (*Shakesp*); any establishment promoting the development of skills, etc (*fig*). — *adj* (of a plant) suitable for rearing only in a greenhouse; (too) delicate, unable to exist in tough, or even normal, conditions (*fig*). — **hot line** or **hot'line** a special telephone and teleprinter link, *orig* one between the Kremlin and Washington; any line of speedy communication ready for an emergency. — *adj* **hot'-liv'ered** (*Milton*) hot-tempered. — **hot melt**, **hot-melt glue** or **hot-melt adhesive** an adhesive that is applied hot and which sets as it cools; **hot metal** (*printing*) used to describe machines or methods using type made from molten metal. — Also *n*. — **hot money** funds transferred suddenly from one country to another because conditions make transfer financially advantageous. — *adj* **hot'-mouthed** (*obs*) (of a horse) restive, as when the bit hurts. — **hot pants** women's very brief shorts; sexual desire (for) (*slang*); **hot plate** the flat top surface of a stove for cooking; a similar plate, independently heated, for keeping things hot; **hot'pot** a dish of chopped mutton, beef, etc seasoned and stewed together with sliced potatoes; **hot potato** see under **potato**. — *vt* **hot'-press** to press (paper, cloth, etc) between hot plates to produce a glossy surface. — **hot property** (*colloq*) a person regarded as a great asset or success; **hot rod** a motor car converted for speed by stripping off non-essentials and heightening in power; **hot rodder** the owner of a hot rod; a reckless youth; **hot seat** the electric chair (*US slang*); any uncomfortable or tricky situation (*fig*); a position of responsibility; **hot shoe** a socket on a camera for attaching flash or other apparatus (also **accessory shoe**). — *adj* **hot'-short** brittle when heated. — **hot'shot** (*esp US*) a person who is (*esp* showily) successful, skilful, etc. — Also *adj*. — *adj* **hot-spir'ited** having a fiery spirit. — **hot spot** an area of (too) high temperature in an engine, etc; a region of the earth where there is evidence of isolated volcanic activity due to hot material rising through the earth's mantle; a popular nightclub (*colloq*); an area of potential trouble, *esp* political or military; a place of very high radioactivity; **hot spring** a spring of water which has been heated underground, occurring *esp* in volcanic regions; **Hot'spur** a violent, rash man like Henry Percy (1364–1403), so nicknamed; **hot stuff** (*slang*) any person, thing, or performance that is outstandingly remarkable, excellent, vigorous or attractive. — *adj* **hotted-up** see **hot up** below. — *adj* **hot-tem'pered** having a quick temper. — **hot'-trod** (*Scot*) the hot pursuit (see below) in old Border forays; **hot wall** a wall enclosing passages for hot air, affording warmth to fruit-trees; **hot war** real war, not cold war; **hot water** (*colloq*) a state of trouble; **hot-water bottle** a (now *usu* rubber) container for hot water, used to warm a bed, or sometimes parts of the body; **hot well** a spring of hot water; in a condensing engine, a reservoir for the warm water drawn off from the condenser; **hot'-working** (*eng*) the process of shaping metals by rolling, extrusion, forging, etc at elevated temperatures. — **go** or **sell like hot cakes** to sell off or disappear promptly; **have the hots for** (*vulg slang*) to be sexually attracted to, desire sexually; **hot cross bun** a bun bearing a cross, customarily eaten on Good Friday; **hot on** (*colloq*) very fond of, interested in; good at, well-informed about; **hot on the heels (of)** (*colloq*) following or pursuing closely; **hot under the collar** (*colloq*) indignant; embarrassed; **hot up** (*colloq*) to increase in excitement, energy, performance, etc (*adj* **hotted-up'**); **in hot pursuit** pursuing at full speed; **make it hot for** (*colloq*) to make it unpleasant or impossible for. [OE *hāt*; Ger *heiss*, Swed *het*]

hot[2] *hot* or **hote** *hōt*, (*Spenser*) named; was called. [Pa t active and passive of **hight**]

hotch *hoch*, (*Scot*) *vt* and *vi* to hitch, jog; to fidget with eagerness. — **hotch with** to swarm, seethe with. [Cf Du *hotsen*, Fr *hocher*]

hotchpotch *hoch'poch*, **hotchpot** *hoch'pot* or **hodgepodge** *hoj'poj*, *n* a confused mass of ingredients shaken or mixed together in the same pot; a kind of mutton-broth with vegetables of many kinds; a jumble; (**hotchpot**) a commixture of property in order to secure an equable division amongst children. [Fr *hochepot*, from *hocher* to shake, and *pot* a pot; cf Du *hutspot*]

hote, hoten. See **hight**.

hotel *hō-tel'* (or old-fashioned *ō-tel'*), *n* a commercial building with rooms for the accommodation of the paying public; an inn; in France, also a public office, a private townhouse, a palace. — *n* **hotelier** (*hō-tel'yər*; Fr *hôtelier*; *ōt-ə-lyā*) a person who owns or runs a hotel. — **hôtel de ville** (Fr *ō-tel də vēl*) a town hall; **hôtel-Dieu** (Fr *ō-tel-dyø*) a hospital. — **hotel'-keeper**. [Fr *hôtel*, from L *hospitālia* guest-chambers, from *hospes*]

hoten. See under **hight**.

hotly. See under **hot**[1].

HOTOL *hō'tol*, (*aeronautics*) *abbrev*: *ho*rizontal *t*ake-*o*ff and *l*anding, a proposed single-stage-to-orbit launch vehicle burning oxygen and hydrogen propellants. [Cf **VTOL**]

Hotspur, hotted. See under **hot**[1].

Hottentot *hot'n-tot*, *n* one of a dwindling, nomad, pastoral, pale-brown-skinned race in SW Africa (resembling Bushmen and Bantu), calling themselves *khoi-khoin* (men of men); their language; a barbarian; a member of any black or coloured people (*old derog*); (without *cap*) a small fish (*Pachymetopon blochii*). — Also *adj*. — **Hottentot fig** the edible fruit of a Mesembrianthemum; **Hottentot's bread** elephant-foot; **Hottentot** (or **Hottentot's**) **god** praying mantis. [Du imit; the language was unintelligible to them and sounded staccato]

hotter[1] *hot'er*, (*Scot*) *vi* to vibrate; to tremble; to clatter; to totter; to jolt; to swarm. — *n* vibration; commotion; swarming. [Cf Flem *hotteren*]

hotter[2], **hottest**. See under **hot**[1].

hottie, hotting, hottish. See under **hot**[1].

houdah. See under **howdah**.

houdan *hōō'dən*, *n* a black and white five-toed domestic fowl of a breed *orig* from *Houdan* in Seine-et-Oise.

houf, houff. See **howf**.

hough *hok* or (*Scot*) *hohh*. See **hock**[1].

hoummos, houmus. See **hummus**.

hound[1] *hownd*, *n* a dog (*colloq*); a dog of a kind used in hunting; a pursuer in a paper-chase; a contemptible scoundrel; a hunter, tracker or assiduous seeker of anything; an addict or devotee (often as combining form). — *vt* to set on in chase; to drive by harassing. — **hound'-fish** a dog-fish; **hounds'-berry** dogwood; **hounds'-foot** (*obs*; Ger *Hundsfott*, *-futt* vulva canina) a scoundrel. — *adj* (*Scott*) scoundrelly. — **hound's'-tongue** a plant (*Cynoglossum*) of the borage family (from its leaf); **hound's'-tooth** a textile pattern of broken checks. — Also *adj*. — **hound'-trailing** speed competition between hounds trained to follow an aniseed trail. — **Gabriel** (or **Gabriel's**) **hounds** (*colloq*) the yelping noise made by flights of wild-geese, ascribed to damned souls whipped on by the angel Gabriel; **master of hounds** the person responsible for looking after a pack of hunting hounds, associated hunting equipment, etc; **ride to hounds** to hunt foxes (on horseback). [OE *hund*; Gr *kyōn*, *kynos*, L *canis*, Sans *sva*]

hound[2] *hownd*, *n* one of a pair of bars supporting and strengthening the chassis of a horse-drawn vehicle; either of a pair of supports for the topmast (*naut*). [ME *hune*, *hownde* related to ON *hunn* knob, cube]

hour *owr*, *n* 60 minutes, or the 24th part of the day; the time as indicated by a clock, etc; an hour's journey, or (*old*) three miles; a time or occasion; an angular unit (15°) of right ascension; (in *pl*) the goddesses of the seasons and the hours (*mythol*); (in *pl*) set times of prayer, the *canonical hours*, the offices or services prescribed for these, or a book containing them, often illustrated (also **book of hours**); (in *pl*) the prescribed times for doing business. — *adj* **hour'ly** happening or done every hour; frequent. — *adv* every hour; frequently. — **hour'-angle** (*astron*) the angle (*usu* measured as time) between the declination circle of a body observed and the observer's meridian; **hour'-circle** (*astron*) a great circle passing through the celestial poles; the equivalent of a meridian; the circle of an equatorial which shows the right ascension; **hour'-glass** an instrument for measuring the hours by the running of sand through a narrow neck. — *adj* having the form of an hour-glass; constricted; slim-waisted. — **hour hand** the hand which shows the hour on a clock, etc. — *adj* and *adv* **hour'long'** lasting an hour. — **hour'plate** a timepiece dial. — **at all hours** at irregular hours, *esp* late hours; **at the eleventh hour** at the last moment (Matthew 20.6 and 9); **in a good** (or **evil**) **hour** under a fortunate (or an unfortunate) impulse — from the old belief in astrological influences; **keep good hours** to go to bed and to rise early; to lead a quiet and regular life; **on the hour** at exactly one, two, etc o'clock. [OFr *hore* (Fr *heure*), from L *hora*, from Gr *hōrā*]

houri *hōō'ri* or *how'ri*, *n* a nymph of the Muslim paradise; a voluptuously alluring woman. [Pers *hūrī*, from Ar *hūriya* a black-eyed girl]

house *hows*, *n* a building for living in; a building in general; a dwelling-place; an inn; a public house; a household; a family in line of descent; kindred; a trading establishment; one of the twelve divisions of the heavens in astrology; a legislative or deliberative body or its meeting-place; a convent; a school boarding-house; the pupils belonging to it (*collectively*); a section of a school; an audience, auditorium or performance; the workhouse (*old colloq*); the circle around the tee within which stones must lie to count (*curling*); (**the House**) at Oxford, Christ Church (*Aedes Christi*), in London, the Stock Exchange or the Houses of Parliament; bingo, *esp* when played for money or (*esp army slang*); (*usu* with *cap*) House music (see below; *colloq*): — *pl* **houses** (*howz'iz*). — *adj* domestic; of a restaurant, hotel, etc or its management, as in *house rules*; (of wine) unnamed and cheaper than those listed on a menu, etc by name or region. — *vt* **house** (*howz*) to protect by covering; to shelter; to store; to provide houses for. — *vi* to take shelter; to reside. — *n* **house'ful**: — *pl* **house'fuls**. — *adj* **house'less** without a house or home; having no shelter. — *n* **housing** (*how'zing*) houses, accommodation or shelter, or the provision of any of these; a cavity into which a timber fits; anything designed to cover, protect or contain machinery, etc; a housing joint (see below). — Also *adj*. — **house agent** a person who arranges the buying, selling and letting of houses; **house arrest** confinement, under guard, to one's house, or to a hospital, etc instead of imprisonment; **house'boat** a barge with a deck-cabin that may serve as a dwelling-place; **house'-bote** a tenant's right to wood to repair his or her house (*law*). — *adj* **house'bound** confined to one's house, eg because of illness, responsibilities towards young children, etc. — **house'boy** a male domestic servant, *esp* in Africa or India; **house'-breaker** a person who breaks into and enters a house for the purpose of stealing; someone whose work is demolishing old houses; **house'-breaking**. — *adj* **house'-broken** house-trained. — **house call** a visit made by a professional person, *esp* a doctor, to a client or patient at home; **house'-carl** (*hist*) a member of a king's or noble's bodyguard; **house church** or **house group** a group of Christians meeting, *usu* in a house, for worship, prayer, Bible study, etc, *usu* in addition to Sunday church worship; **house'coat** a woman's *usu* long coatlike dressing-gown, worn at home; **house'craft** skill in domestic activities; **house'-dog** a dog kept in a house; a watchdog; **house'-dūty** or **house'-tax** a tax laid on inhabited houses; **house'-factor** (*Scot*) a house agent; **house'-father** the male head of a household or community; a man in charge of children in an institution; **house flag** the distinguishing flag of a shipowner or shipping company; **house'fly** the common fly; **house group** see **house church**; **house guest** a guest in a private house; **house'hold** those who are held together in the same house, and compose a family; a single person living alone or a group of people living together (*econ*). — *adj* pertaining to the house and family; well-known to the general public, as in *household name*, *household word*. — **house'holder** the holder or tenant of a house; **household gods** see under **god**, **lar**, **penates**; **household suffrage** or **franchise** the right of householders to vote for members of parliament; **household troops** Guards regiments whose particular duty is to attend the sovereign and defend the metropolis; **household word** a familiar saying or name. — *vi* **house'-hunt** to look for a house to live in. — **house'-hunter**; **house'-hunting**; **house'-husband** a married man or live-in male partner who looks after the house and family and does not have a paid job; **house'keeper** a person employed to run a household; a person who has the chief care of a house; someone who stays much at home (*archaic*); a dispenser of hospitality (*obs*); a watchdog (*obs*); **house'keeping** the keeping or management of a house or of domestic affairs; the money used for this; hospitality (*obs*); operations carried out on or within a computer program or system to ensure the efficient functioning of the program or system. — *adj* domestic. — **house'-leek** a plant (*Sempervivum tectorum*) of the stonecrop family with succulent leaves, often growing on roofs; **house lights** (*theat*) the lights illuminating the auditorium; **house'-line** (*naut*) a small line of three strands, for seizings, etc; **house'maid** a maid employed to keep a house clean, etc; **housemaid's knee** an inflammation of the sac between the knee-cap and the skin, to which those whose work involves frequent kneeling are especially liable; **house'man** a recent graduate in medicine holding a junior resident post in a hospital; **house martin** a kind of black and white swallow with a slightly forked tail (*Delichon urbica*); **house'master** or **house'mistress** (in schools) the male or female head of a (boarding-)house, *esp* in connection with a public school; **house'-mate** one person sharing a house with another; **house'-mother** the mother of a family, the female head of a family; a woman in charge of children in an institution; **House music** or **House** a type of disco music, popular during the late 1980s, produced electronically incorporating edited fragments of other recordings; **house'parent** a man or woman in charge of children in an institution; **house'-party** a company of guests spending some days in a private house, *esp* one in the country; **house plant** a plant that can be grown indoors as decoration. — *adj* **house'-proud** taking a pride (often an excessive and fussy pride) in the condition of one's house. — **house'room** room or place in a house (also *fig*); **house'-sitting** looking after a house by living in it while the owner is away, on holiday, etc. — *vi* **house'-sit**. — **house sparrow** see under **sparrow**; **house'-steward** a steward who manages the household affairs of a great family; **house surgeon** a resident surgeon in a hospital — so also **house physician**; **house-tax** see **house-duty** above. — *adj* **house'-to-house'** performed or conducted by calling at house after house. — **house'top** the top or roof of a house. — *adj* **house'-trained** (of animals) taught to urinate and defecate outdoors, or in a place provided for the purpose; (of human beings) clean and well-mannered (*colloq*). — **house'-warming** a party given after moving into a new house; **housewife** (*hows'wīf*, formerly *huz'if*) the mistress and manager of a house; a married woman who looks after the house and family and does not have a paid job; (*huz'if*) a pocket sewing-outfit. — *adj* **house'wifely**. — **housewifery** (*hows'wif-ri*, *-wīf-ri* or *huz'if-ri*); **house'wifeship** or (*Scot*) **house'-wifeskep**; **house'work** domestic work; **house'y-house'y** a game in which numbers are drawn at random and marked off on players' boards until one is clear — now *usu* called **bingo**; **housing estate** a planned residential area, *esp* one built by a local authority; **housing joint** a joint where the end of one board fits into a groove cut across another board; **housing scheme** a plan for the designing, building and provision of houses, *esp* by a local authority; sometimes applied to an area coming under such a plan. — **bring the house down** to evoke very loud applause in a place of entertainment; **full house** see under **full**[1]; **house longhorn beetle** see under **long**[3]; **house of call** a house where the journeymen of a particular trade call when out of work; a house that one often visits; **house of cards** a situation, etc that is as unstable as a pile of playing cards; **House of Commons** see under **common**; **house of correction** a jail; **house of God**, **house of prayer** or **worship** a place of worship; **house of ill-fame** or **house of ill repute** a brothel; **House of Lords** see under **lord**; **House of Keys** see under **Keys**; **House** or **Council of States** the upper house of the Indian parliament; **House of Peers** see under **peer**[1]; **House of the People** the lower house of the Indian parliament; **House of Representatives** see under **represent**; **Inner House** the higher branch of the Court of Session, its jurisdiction chiefly appellate (**Outer House** the lower branch of the Court of Session); **keep a good house** to keep up a plentifully supplied table; **keep house** to maintain or manage an establishment; **keep open house** to give entertainment to all comers; **keep the house** to remain indoors; to take charge of the house or be on watch for the time being; to be confined to the house; **like a house on fire** (or **afire**) with astonishing rapidity; very well or successfully; **on the house** (of drinks) at the publican's expense; free, with no charge; **put** or **set one's house in order** to settle one's affairs; **set up house** to start a domestic life of one's own; **the Household** the royal domestic establishment. [OE *hūs*; Gothic *hūs*, Ger *Haus*]

housel *howz'əl*, *n* the eucharist; the act of taking or administering it. — *vt* to administer the eucharist to: — *pap* **hous'elled**. — *n* **hous'elling**. — *adj* (*Spenser*) **hous'ling** sacramental. [OE *hūsel* sacrifice]

housing[1] *how'zing*, *n* an ornamental covering for a horse; a saddle-cloth; (in *pl*) the trappings of a horse. [OFr *houce* a mantle, of Gmc origin]

housing[2]. See under **house**.

hout, **hout-tout**, **houts-touts**. Same as **hoot**, etc.

houting *how'ting*, *n* a European food-fish with white flesh. [Du, MDu *houtic*]

Houyhnhnm *hwin'əm* or *win'əm*, *n* one of the noble and rational race of horses in Swift's *Gulliver's Travels*. [Perh **whinny**]

Hova *huv'ə* or *hōv'ə*, *n* a member of the dominant race in Madagascar, *esp* of the middle class: — *pl* **Hov'a** or **Hov'as**.

hove[1] *hōv* or *hōōv* or (*Scot*) *hüv*, *vt* to swell. — *vi* to swell; to rise (*Spenser*). [Perh a form of **heave**]

hove[2] or **hoove** *hōōv*, (*Spenser*) *vi* to hover; to loiter, linger. [Origin unknown]

hove[3] *pa t* and *pa p* of **heave**.

hovel *hov'əl* or *huv'əl*, *n* a small or wretched dwelling; a shed; a framework for a corn-stack (*dialect*). — *vt* to put in a hovel; to shelter; to build like a hovel or shed, as a chimney with a side opening: — *pa t*, *pa p* **hov'elled** or (*US*) **hov'eled**. — **hov'el-post** a post for supporting a corn-stack. [Origin doubtful]

hoveller *hov'ə-lər*, *hov'lər*, *huv'ə-lər* or *huv'lər*, *n* a boatman acting as an uncertificated pilot or doing any kind of occasional work on the coast; a small coasting-vessel. [Ety dubious]

hoven[1] *hō'vən*. See under **hoove**[1].

hoven[2]. See under **heave**.

hover *hov'ər* or *huv'ər*, *vi* to remain aloft flapping the wings; to remain suspended; to remain undecided (with *between*); to linger, *esp* nervously or solicitously; to move about nearby. — *vt* to brood over. — *n* an act or state of hovering; a helicopter (*US*); an apparatus for keeping chicks warm. — Used in combination to describe vessels, vehicles, or stationary objects, which move or rest on a cushion of air, eg **hov'ercraft** (a craft able to move at a short distance above the surface of sea or land supported by a down-driven blast of air), **hov'er-barrow, hov'er-bus, hov'er-car, hov'er-mower**. — *adv* **hov'eringly**. — **hov'er-bed** a bed which supports a patient on a film of warm air; **hov'er-fly** a syrphid or other wasp-like fly that hovers and darts; **hov'erport** a port for hovercraft; **hov'ertrain** a train which moves supported by a cushion of air, like a hovercraft. [Perh from **hove**[2]]

how[1] *how*, *adv* and *conj* in what manner; to what extent; by what means; in what condition; for what reason; to what extent, in what degree; that. — *n* manner, method. — *adj* **how'-to** (of books, etc) showing how to do things. — Also *n*. — **and how!** (*orig NAm colloq*) yes, certainly; very much indeed; I should think so indeed; **how about** what do you think of; would you like (something); are you interested in (doing something); **how are you?** a conventional greeting to an acquaintance; sometimes specifically referring to his or her state of health; **how come?** (*colloq*) how does that come about; **how-do-you-do** see under **do**[1]; see also under **howdy**; **how now** what is this?; why is this so?; **how so?** (*archaic*) how can this be so?, why?; **how's that** (*how-zat'*; sometimes written **howzat'**; *cricket*) the appeal of the fielding side to the umpire to give the batsman out; **how's your father** (*facetious*) amorous frolicking; sexual intercourse; nonsense, foolish activity; **the how and the why** the manner and the cause. [OE *hū*, prob an adverbial form from *hwā* who]

how[2] or **howe** *how*, (*Scot*) *n* a hollow. [**hole**[1]]

how[3] *how*, (*dialect*) *n* a low hill; a tumulus or barrow. [ON *haugr*; cf OE *hēah* high]

how[4] *how*, *interj* a greeting thought to have been used by North American Indians. [From Sioux, related to Dakota *háo*]

howbeit *how-bē'it*, (*archaic* or *formal*) *conj* be it how it may; notwithstanding; yet; however. — (*Spenser*) **howbe'**. [**how**[1], **be** and **it**[1]]

howdah or **houdah** *how'dä*, *n* a pavilion or seat fixed on an elephant's back. [Ar *haudaj*]

howdie or **howdy** *how'di*, (*Scot*) *n* a midwife. [Poss OE *hold* gracious]

howdy *how'di*, *interj* a colloquial form of the common greeting, *How do you do?*. — **how'-d'ye-do'** or **how'dy-do'** a troublesome state of affairs.

howe. See **how**[2].

however *how-ev'ər*, *adv* and *conj* in whatever manner or degree; nevertheless; at all events. — *poetic abbrev* **howe'er** (*how-ār'*). [**how**[1] and **ever**]

howff, howff, houf or **houff** *howf*, (*Scot*) *n* a place in which one is often to be found, a haunt, often a public house. — *vi* to go often to a place. [Poss OE *hof* a house]

howitzer *how'its-ər*, *n* a short, squat gun, used for shelling at a steep angle, *esp* in siege and trench warfare. [Ger *Haubitze*, from Czech *houfnice* a sling]

howk *howk*, (*Scot*) *vt* and *vi* to dig, burrow. [Earlier *holk*; cf LGer *holken*]

howker *how'kər*, *n*. Same as **hooker**[1].

howl *howl*, *vi* to yell or cry, like a wolf or dog; to utter a long, loud, whining sound; to wail; to roar; to laugh (*colloq*); to cry (*colloq*). — *vt* to utter through a shriek or wail: — *pr p* **howl'ing**; *pa t* and *pa p* **howled**. — *n* a loud, prolonged cry of distress; a mournful cry; a loud sound like a yell, made by the wind, a radio, etc. — *n* **howl'er** someone who howls; a S American monkey, with prodigious power of voice; a glaring and amusing blunder (*colloq*). — *adj* **howl'ing** filled with howlings, as of the wind, or of wild beasts; tremendous (*colloq*). — *n* a howl. — **howl down** to drown out (a speaker) with angry cries. [OFr *huller*, from L *ululāre* to shriek or howl, from *ulula* an owl; cf Ger *heulen*, Eng **owl**]

Howleglass. See under **owl**.

howlet *how'lit*, *n* an owlet; (*Scot hōōl'it*) an owl. [**owlet**]

howre. An *obs* form of **hour**.

howso *how'sō*, (*obs*) *adv* howsoever.

howsoever *how-sō-ev'ər*, *adv* in what way soever; although; however. — Provincial forms are **howsomev'er** and **howsomdev'er**. [**how**[1], **so**[1] and **ever**; and ME *sum* as]

how-to. See under **how**[1].

howtowdie *how-tow'di*, (*Scot*) *n* a dish of boiled chicken. [OFr *hetoudeau*, *estaudeau* a young chicken prepared for eating]

howzat. See **how's that** under **how**[1].

hox *hoks*, (*Shakesp*) *vt* to hock or hamstring. [OE *hōhsinu* hock-sinew]

hoy[1] *hoi*, *n* a large one-decked boat, commonly rigged as a sloop. [MDu *hoei*; Du *heu*, Flem *hui*]

hoy[2] *hoi*, *interj* ho!, stop!. — *vt* to incite, drive on.

hoya *hoi'ə*, *n* a plant of the Australasian *Hoya* genus of plants of the Asclepiadaceae, including the wax plant. [Thomas *Hoy*, died 1821, English gardener]

hoyden or (*old*) **hoiden** *hoi'dən*, *n* a tomboy, a romp (formerly also *masc*). — *n* **hoy'denhood**. — *n* **hoy'denism**. — *adj* **hoy'denish**. [Perh Du *heiden* a heathen, a gypsy, from *heide* heath]

HP *abbrev*: half-pay; high pressure; High Priest; hire purchase; Houses of Parliament.

hp *abbrev*: horsepower.

HQ or **hq** *abbrev*: headquarters.

HR *abbrev*: Home Rule; House of Representatives (*US*).

hr *abbrev*: hour.

HRE *abbrev*: Holy Roman Emperor or Empire.

HRH *abbrev*: His or Her Royal Highness.

HRT *abbrev*: hormone replacement therapy.

HS *abbrev*: High School; Home Secretary.

hs *abbrev*: *hoc sensu* (L), in this sense.

Hse *abbrev*: House (in addresses or place names).

HSH *abbrev*: His or Her Serene Highness.

HSM *abbrev*: His or Her Serene Majesty.

HT *abbrev*: high tension.

ht *abbrev*: height.

HTLV *abbrev*: human T-cell lymphotrophic virus.

huanaco. Same as **guanaco**.

huaquero *wä-kā'rō*, *n* a person who steals antiquities and relics from tombs in Latin America. [Am Sp, from Quechua *huaca* holy place]

hub *hub*, *n* the centre of a wheel, the nave; a mark at which quoits, etc are thrown; an important centre or focus of activity, as applied (*archaic* and *facetious*) to Boston, USA, *esp* in the phrases *hub of the universe* or *hub of the solar system*; the focal point (of a discussion, problem, etc). — **hub'-brake** a brake acting on the hub of a wheel; **hub'-cap** a metal covering over the hub of a wheel. [Prob a form of **hob**[1]; origin unknown]

hubble-bubble *hub'l-bub'l*, *n* a bubbling sound; tattle; confusion; a crude kind of hookah. [Reduplication from **bubble**]

Hubble constant *hub'l kon'stənt* or **Hubble's constant** (*hub'lz*), (*astron*) *n* the constant factor in **Hubble's law** that the velocity of a galaxy is proportional to its distance from us, giving the rate of increase of velocity with distance in the expanding universe. [From E P *Hubble* (1889–1953), US astronomer]

hubbub *hub'ub* or (*Shakesp*) **whoobub** *hōōb'ub*, *n* a confused sound of many voices; riot; uproar. — Also **hubb'uboo**. [*Appar* of Irish origin]

hubby *hub'i*, (*colloq*) *n* husband. [Dimin of **husband**]

hubris *hū'bris* or **hybris** *hī'bris*, *n* insolence; over-confidence; arrogance, such as invites disaster or ruin (*classical Gr theat*); overweening. — *adj* **hubris'tic**. — *adv* **hubris'tically**. [Gr *hybris*]

huck. See under **huckle**.

huckaback *huk'ə-bak*, *n* a coarse linen or cotton fabric with a raised surface, used for towels, etc. [Origin unknown]

huckle *huk'l*, *n* the haunch; the hip. — Also **huck**. — *adj* **huck'le-backed** having a rounded back; humpbacked. — *adj* **huck'le-shoul'dered** round-shouldered. — **huckle'-bone** the hip-bone; the astragalus, the talus or ankle-bone of a quadruped. [Poss connected with **hook**]

huckleberry *huk'l-bər-i* or *-ber-i*, *n* a N American shrub (*Gaylussacia*) related to the whortleberry; its fruit; extended to species of whortleberry. — *n* **huck'leberrying**. [Appar for *hurtleberry* whortleberry]

huckster *huk'stər*, *n* a retailer of smallwares, a hawker or pedlar; an aggressive seller; a mercenary person. — *vi* to hawk or peddle; to haggle meanly or sell aggressively. — *n* **huck'sterage**. — *n* **huck'steress** or **huck'stress**. — *n* **huck'stery**. [Origin obscure]

HUD *abbrev*: head-up display.

hudden. See under **haud**.

huddle *hud'l*, *vt* to hustle out of sight, hush up (*obs*); to jumble; to hustle, bundle; to drive, draw, throw or crowd together in disorder; to put hastily; to perform perfunctorily and hastily. — *vi* to crowd in confusion; to crowd closely together, eg because of cold (sometimes with *up*); to form or gather into a huddle (*Am football*). — *n* a confused mass; a jumble; confusion; perfunctory haste; a gathering together of the team behind their line of scrimmage so as to receive instructions, signals, etc before the next play (*Am football*); a secret conference (*colloq*); a period of deep consideration of a problem. — *adj* **hudd'led** jumbled; crowded closely together; in a heap; crouching. [Poss connected with **hide**[1]]

huddup *hud-up'*, (*US*) *interj* get up (to a horse).

Hudibrastic *hū-di-bras'tik*, *adj* similar in style to *Hudibras*, a metrical burlesque on the Puritans by Samuel Butler (1612–80); mock-heroic. — *n pl* **Hudibras'tics** verses of the form used in *Hudibras*, a burlesque cacophonous octosyllabic couplet with extravagant rhymes.

hue[1] or (*Spenser*) **hew** *hū*, *n* appearance; colour; tint; dye. — *adj* **hued** having a hue, often in combination, as in *dark-hued*. — *adj* **hue'less**. [OE *hīow*, *hēow* (WSax *hīw*, *hīew*); Swed *hy* complexion]

hue[2] *hū*, *n* a shouting, clamour. — *n* **hu'er** a pilchard fishermen's lookout man. — **hue and cry** an outcry calling upon all to pursue someone who is to be made prisoner (*hist*); a proclamation or publication to the same effect (*hist*); the pursuit itself; a loud clamour about something. [Imit; perh Fr *huer*]

huff *huf*, *n* a puff of wind (*obs*); bluster (*obs*); a blusterer, bully (*obs*); a fit of anger, sulks or offended dignity, *esp* in the phrase *in a huff* (*colloq*); an act of huffing (*draughts*). — *vt* to puff up (*obs*); to hector; to give offence; to remove from the board for failing to make a possible capture (*draughts*). — *vi* to blow, puff, swell (*obs*); to take offence; to bluster. — *adj* **huff'ish** or **huff'y** given to huff; touchy; ready to take offence. — *adv* **huff'ishly** or **huff'ily**. — *n* **huff'ishness** or **huff'iness**. — *n* **huff'kin** (*local*) a type of muffin or bun. — *adj* **huff'-cap** (*obs*) (of liquor) heady; blustering. — **huffing and puffing** loud talk, noisy objections. [Imit]

hug *hug*, *vt* to clasp close with the arms; to embrace; to cherish; to keep close to or skirt: — *pr p* **hugg'ing**; *pa t* and *pa p* **hugged**. — *n* a close embrace; a particular grip in wrestling. — *adj* **hugg'able**. — **hug'-me-tight** a close-fitting knitted garment. — **hug oneself** to congratulate oneself. [Ety obscure]

huge *hūj*, *adj* vast; enormous. — *adv* **huge'ly**. — *n* **huge'ness**. — *adj* **huge'ous** (*archaic*) huge. — *adv* **huge'ously** (*archaic*). — *n* **huge'ousness** (*archaic*). — *adj* **hu'gy** (*archaic*). [OFr *ahuge*]

hugger-mugger *hug'ər-mug'ər*, *n* secrecy; confusion. — *adj* secret; disorderly. — *adv* in secrecy or disorder. [Origin obscure]

HUGO *hū'gō*, *abbrev*: *H*uman *G*enome *O*rganization.

Huguenot *hū'gə-not* or *-nō*, (*hist*) *n* a French Protestant. — Also *adj*. [Fr, from earlier *eiguenot*, from Ger *Eidgenoss* confederate, assimilated to the name *Hugues* Hugh]

huh *hu*, *interj* expressing disgust, disbelief, enquiry, etc. [Imit]

hui *hoo'i*, (*NZ*) *n* a Maori gathering; any social gathering (*colloq*): — *pl* **hu'ies**. [Maori]

huia *hōō'yə* or *hōō'ē-ə*, *n* a New Zealand bird (*Heteralocha acutirostris*) related to the crows and starlings, now *prob* extinct. [Maori; imit]

huissier *wē-syā*, (Fr) *n* a doorkeeper, usher; a bailiff.

huitain *wē-tān'*, *n* a group of eight lines of verse. [Fr, from *huit* eight]

hula-hula *hōō'lə-hōō'lə*, *n* a Hawaiian dance. — Also **hu'la**. — **hu'la-hoop** a light hoop used in the game of keeping the hoop in motion around the waist by a swinging movement of the hips; **hula skirt** a grass skirt as worn by hula dancers. [Hawaiian]

hule. Same as **ule**.

hulk *hulk*, *n* an unwieldy ship; a dismantled ship; a big ungainly or awkward person (*derog slang*); anything unwieldy; often by confusion, a hull; (in *pl* with *the*) old ships formerly used as prisons. — *adj* **hulk'ing** or **hulk'y** big and clumsy. [OE *hulc*, cf Gr *holkas* a towed ship, from *helkein* to draw]

hull[1] *hul*, *n* a husk or outer covering. — *vt* to separate from the hull; to husk. — *adj* **hull'y** having husks or pods. [OE *hulu* a husk, as of corn, from *helan* to cover; Ger *Hülle* a covering, from *hehlen* to cover]

hull[2] *hul*, *n* the frame or body of a ship; part of a flying-boat in contact with the water; the heavily-armoured body of a tank, missile, rocket, etc. — *vt* to pierce the hull of. — *vi* (*Shakesp*) to float or drift, as a mere hull, to float about. — *adj* (of a ship, etc) floating and moving on the hull, as opposed to being raised on hydrofoils, etc. — *adv* and *adj* **hull'-down'** so far away that the hull is below the horizon. [Perh same word as above, modified in meaning by confusion with Du *hol* a ship's hold, or with **hulk**]

hullabaloo *hul-ə-bə-lōō'*, *n* an uproar. [Perh **halloo** or possibly rhyming on Scot *baloo* lullaby]

hullo *hu-lō'*, *v*, *n* and *interj*. Same as **hallo**.

Hulsean *hul'si-ən*, *adj* of or pertaining to John *Hulse* (1708–90), founder of the Hulsean divinity lectures at Cambridge.

hum[1] *hum*, *vi* to make a sound like bees or that represented by *m*; to sing with closed lips without words or articulation; to pause in speaking and utter an inarticulate sound; to stammer through embarrassment; to be audibly astir; to have a strong, unpleasant smell (*slang*); to be busily active. — *vt* to render by humming; to applaud (*obs*): — *pr p* **humm'ing**; *pa t* and *pa p* **hummed**. — *n* the noise of bees; a murmurous sound; an inarticulate murmur; the sound of humming. — *adj* **humm'able**. — *n* **humm'er** a person or thing that hums, such as a bee, a humming-bird, or a top; a person who makes things hum (see below). — *n* and *adj* **humm'ing**. — **humming ale** ale that froths up well, or that makes the head hum; **humm'ing-bird** any member of the tropical family Trochilidae, very small birds of brilliant plumage and rapid flight (from the humming sound of the wings); **humm'ing-top** a top that produces a humming sound as it spins. — **hum and haw** or **hum and ha** to make inarticulate sounds when at a loss; to shilly-shally; **make things hum** to set things going briskly. [Imit; cf Ger *hummen*, *humsen*]

hum[2] *hum*, *vt* to impose on; to hoax. — *n* an imposition; a hoax. [Contraction of **humbug**]

hum[3] *hum*, *interj* expressing doubt or reluctance to agree.

huma *hōō'mə*, *n* a fabulous restless bird. [Pers *humā* phoenix]

human *hū'mən*, *adj* belonging to, relating to, or of the nature of, man or mankind; having the qualities of a person or the limitations of people; humane; not invidiously superior; genial, kind. — *n* a human being. — *adj* **humane** (*hū-mān'*) having the feelings proper to man; kind; tender; merciful; humanizing, as *humane letters*, classical, elegant, polite. — *adv* **humane'ly**. — *n* **humane'ness**. — *n* **hū'manism** literary culture; classical studies; any system which puts human interests and the mind of man paramount, rejecting the supernatural, belief in a god, etc; pragmatism (*philos*); a critical application of the logical method of pragmatism to all the sciences. — *n* **hū'manist** student of polite literature; at the Renaissance, a student of Greek and Roman literature; a student of human nature; advocate of any system of humanism; a pragmatist. — Also *adj.* — *adj* **hūmanist'ic** of or pertaining to humanism; emphasizing observation of one's own feelings and reactions to others as a basis for a greater understanding of the self (*psychol* and *psychiatry*). — *vt* **humanize** or **-ise** (*hū'mən-īz*) to render human or humane; to soften; to impart human qualities to, to make like that which is human or of mankind. — *vi* to become humane or civilized. — *n* **humanīzā'tion** or **-s-**. — *n* **hū'mankind** the human species. — *adj* **hū'manlike**. — *adv* **hū'manly** in a human manner; by human agency; having regard to human limitations; humanely. — *n* **hū'manness**. — *n* **hū'manoid** any of the earlier creatures from which modern man is directly descended and to which he is immediately related, more closely than to *anthropoid* creatures; any creature with the appearance or characteristics of a human being. — Also *adj.* — **human being** any member of the human race; a person; **humane society** a society promoting humane behaviour, *usu* to animals; **human immunodeficiency virus** (*abbrev* **HIV**) a virus which breaks down the human body's natural immune system, often causing Aids; **human interest** (in newspaper articles, broadcasts, etc) reference to people's lives and emotions; **human nature** the nature of man; the qualities of character common to all men that differentiate them from other species; irrational or less than saintly behaviour (often *facetious*); **human rights** the right each human being has to personal freedom, justice, etc; **human shield** a person or people (civilian, POW, etc) deliberately deployed in strategic sites (during hostilities) to deter enemy attack upon them; this use of people, as a tactic in war. [Fr *humain*, from L *hūmānus*, from *homō* a human being]

humanity *hū-man'it-i*, *n* the nature peculiar to a human being; humanness; humaneness; the kind feelings of man; mankind collectively; (in Scottish universities) Latin language and literature; (in *pl*) grammar, rhetoric, Latin, Greek and poetry, so called from their humanizing effects. — *n* **humanitarian** (*hū-man'i-tā'ri-ən*) someone who denies Christ's divinity, and holds him to be a mere man; a philanthropist. — *adj* of, belonging to, or worthy of humanity or human beings, *esp* benevolent. — *n* **humanitā'rianism**. [Fr *humanité*, from L *hūmānitās*, from *hūmānus*, from *homō* a man]

humble[1] *hum'bl* (old-fashioned *um'bl*), *adj* low; lowly; modest; unpretentious; having a low opinion of oneself or of one's claims; abased. — *vt* to bring down to the ground; to lower; to abase; to mortify; to degrade. — *n* **hum'bleness**. — *n* **hum'blesse** (*Spenser*). — *adj* and *n* **hum'bling**. — *adv* **hum'blingly**. — *adv* **hum'bly**. — *adj* **hum'ble-mouthed** humble in speech. — **your humble servant** an old formula used in subscribing a letter. [Fr, from L *humilis* low, from *humus* the ground]

humble[2] *hum'bl*. Same as **hummel**.

humble-bee *hum'bl-bē*, *n* the bumble-bee (genus *Bombus*). [Perh from *humble*, frequentative of **hum**[1]; cf Ger *Hummel*]

humbles *hum'blz*, *n pl.* Same as **umbles**. — **humble-pie'** a pie made from the umbles of a deer. — **eat humble-pie** (*punningly*) to humble or abase oneself, to eat one's words, etc.

humbug *hum'bug*, *n* hollowness, pretence, fraud, deception; an imposter; a lump of toffee; a peppermint drop, or the like. — *vt* to deceive; to hoax; to cajole. — *vi* to potter about: — *pr p* **hum'bugging**; *pa t* and *pa p* **hum'bugged**. — *adj* **humbugg'able**. — *n* **hum'bugger**. — *n* **hum'buggery**. [Appears about 1750; origin unknown]

humbuzz *hum'buz*, (*dialect*) *n* a cockchafer; a bull-roarer. [**hum**[1] and **buzz**[1]]

humdinger *hum-ding'ər*, (*slang*) *n* an exceptionally excellent person or thing; a smooth-running engine; a swift vehicle or aircraft. [Prob **hum**[1] and **ding**[1]]

humdrum *hum'drum'*, *adj* dull; droning; monotonous; commonplace. — *n* a stupid fellow; monotony; tedious talk. [**hum**[1] and perh **drum**[1]]

humdudgeon *hum-duj'ən*, *n* an unnecessary outcry (*Scot*); low spirits (*dialect*). [**hum**[1] and **dudgeon**[1]]

Humean or **Humian** *hū'mi-ən*, *adj* pertaining to David *Hume*, or his philosophy. — *n* a follower of Hume. — *n* **Hūm'ism**. — *n* **Hūm'ist**.

humect *hū-mekt'*, *vt* and *vi* to make or become moist. — Also **humect'ate**. — *adj* and *n* **humect'ant**. — *n* **humectā'tion**. — *adj* and *n* **humect'ive**. [L (*h*)*ūmectāre*, from *ūmēre* to be moist]

humefy. See **humify**[1].

humerus *hū'mər-əs*, *n* the bone of the upper arm: — *pl* **hū'merī**. — *adj* **hū'meral** belonging to the shoulder or the humerus. — *n* (also **humeral veil**) an oblong vestment worn on the shoulders. [L (*h*)*umerus* shoulder]

humf. See **humph**[2].

humgruffin *hum-gruf'in* or **humgruffian** *-i-ən*, *n* a terrible person. [Appar **hum**[1] and **griffin**]

humhum *hum'hum*, *n* a kind of plain, coarse cotton cloth used in the East Indies.

Humian. See **Humean**.

humic. See under **humus**[1].

humid *hū'mid*, *adj* moist; damp; rather wet. — *n* **humidificā'tion**. — *n* **humid'ifier** a device for increasing or maintaining humidity. — *vt* **humid'ify** to make humid. — *n* **humid'istat** a device for controlling humidity. — *n* **humid'ity** moisture, *esp* in the air; a moderate degree of wetness. — *adv* **hu'midly**. — *n* **hu'midness**. — *n* **hum'idor** a box or a chamber, etc for keeping anything moist, such as cigars; a contrivance for keeping the air moist. [L (*h*)*ūmidus*, from (*h*)*ūmēre* to be moist]

humify[1] *hū'mi-fī*, *vt* to moisten. — Also (*obs*) **hu'mefy**. — *n* **humificā'tion**. [L (*h*)*ūmificāre*]

humify[2] *hū'mi-fī*, *vt* and *vi* to make or turn into humus. — *n* **humificā'tion**. [**humus**[1]]

humiliate *hū-mil'i-āt*, *vt* to humble; to mortify, injure the self-respect or pride of. — *adj* **humil'iant** humiliating. — *adj* **humil'iāting**. — *n* **humiliā'tion**. — *adj* **humil'iative**. — *n* **humil'iātor**. — *adj* **humil'iatory** (*-ə-tər-i*). [L *humiliāre*, *-ātum*]

humility *hū-mil'i-ti*, *n* the state or quality of being humble; lowliness of mind; modesty. [OFr *humilite*, from L *humilitās*, from *humilis* low]

Humism, **Humist**. See under **Humean**.

humite *hū'mit*, (*mineralogy*) *n* an orthorhombic magnesium orthosilicate also containing magnesium hydroxide, found in impure marbles. [Sir Abraham *Hume*, 19c mineral collector]

humlie. See under **hummel**.

hummable. See under **hum**[1].

hummaum. See **hammam**.

hummel *hum'l* or **humble** *hum'bl* or *hum'l* (*Scot*), *adj* hornless; awnless. — *n* a hornless stag. — *vt* to make hummel. — *n* **hum'lie** (*Scot*) a polled or hornless cow, ox, etc. — *n* **humm'eller** (*dialect*) a machine for removing barley awns. — **hummel bonnet** (or *usu* **hummle bonnet** a type of Scottish cap worn by Highland regiments before the introduction (1851) of the glengarry. [Cf LGer *hummel*, *hommel*]

hummer, **humming**. See under **hum**[1].

hummock *hum'ək* or (*archaic*) **hommock** *hom'ək*, *n* a hillock; a pile or ridge of ice. — *adj* **humm'ocked**. — *adj* **humm'ocky**. [Origin unknown: at first nautical]

hummum. Same as **hammam**.

hummus *hum'əs* or *hōō'məs*, *n* a Middle Eastern hors d'oeuvre of puréed chick-peas and sesame oil with garlic and lemon. — Also **houmm'os**, **houm'us**. [Turk]

humogen *hū'mō-jən*, *n* a fertilizer composed of peat treated with a culture of nitrogen-fixing bacteria. [L *humus* soil, and Gr *gennaein* to produce]

humongous or **humungous** *hū'* or *ū'mung-gəs*, (*slang*, *orig NAm*) *adj* huge, enormous; exceptionally bad. [Uncertain]

humour or in US **humor** *hū'mər* or *ū'mər*, *n* moisture (*archaic*); a fluid (*med*); a fluid of the animal body, *esp* formerly any one of the four that in old physiology were held to determine temperament; temperament or disposition of mind; state of mind (as in *good humour*, *ill humour*); disposition; caprice; in Corporal Nym's vocabulary in *The Merry Wives* and *Henry V* (also as *adj* and *vt*, and *adj* **hū'moured**) a word of any meaning, down to no meaning at all (*Shakesp*); a mental quality which apprehends and delights in the ludicrous and mirthful; that which causes mirth and amusement; the quality of being funny; playful fancy. — *vt* to go along with the humour of; to gratify by compliance. — *adj* **hū'moral** pertaining to or proceeding from a body fluid. — *n* **hū'moralism** the state of being humoral; the old doctrine that diseases have their seat in the humours. — *n* **hū'moralist** someone who favoured the doctrine of humoralism. — *adv* **hū'morally**. — *n* **hūmoresk'** or **hūmoresque'** a musical caprice. — *n* **hū'morist** someone possessed of a sense of humour; a writer of comic stories; a person whose conduct and conversation are regulated by humour or caprice (*archaic*); a person who studies or portrays the humours of people. — *adj* **hūmoris'tic** humorous. — *adj* **hū'morous** full of humour; exciting laughter; governed by humour (*archaic*); capricious (*archaic*); irregular (*archaic*). — *adv* **hū'morously**. — *n* **hū'morousness**. — *adj* **hū'mourless** or (*US*) **hu'morless**. — *adj* **hū'moursome** capricious, petulant. — *n* **hū'moursomeness**. — **humoral immunity** an acquired immunity in which antibodies circulating in body fluids play the major part. — **comedy of humours** the comedy of Ben Jonson and his school in which the characters, instead of being conceived as rounded individuals, are little more than personifications of single qualities; **out of humour** displeased, in a bad mood. [OFr *humor* (Fr *humeur*), from L (*h*)*ūmor*, from (*h*)*ūmēre* to be moist]

humous. See under **humus**[1].

hump *hump*, *n* a rounded projection in the back due to spinal deformity; a protuberance; a rounded mass, eg of earth; a long walk with one's possessions in a bundle on one's back (*Austr obs*); despondency or annoyance, *esp* in the phrase **have** (or **give someone**) **the hump** (*slang*); the sulks (*slang*). — *vt* to bend in a hump; to hunch; to exert oneself (*slang*); to hurry (*slang*); to vex or annoy (*slang*); to shoulder, to carry on the back (*orig Austr*); to carry, to heave (heavy loads) (*colloq*); to have sexual intercourse with (someone) (*slang*). — *vi* to put forth effort; to have sexual intercourse (*slang*). — *adj* **humped** having a hump. — *n* **hum'per** (*colloq*) someone who carries heavy loads, eg a porter in a market. — *adj* **hump'y** full of humps or protuberances; having a hump or humps; sulky, irritable (*colloq*). — **hump'back** a back with a hump or hunch; a person with a humpback; a Pacific species of salmon; a whale with a humplike dorsal fin. — *adj* **hump'-back** or **hump'-backed** having a humpback. — **humpback bridge** a bridge with a sharp rise in the middle. — **hump the bluey** (*Austr*) to travel on foot, carrying a bundle of possessions; **over the hump** (*colloq*) past the crisis or difficulty. [Origin obscure]

humpen or **Humpen** *hŏŏm'pən*, *n* a type of *usu* cylindrical enamelled or painted glass drinking-vessel made in Germany from the 17c. [Ger]

humper. See under **hump**.

humph[1] *hmh*, *huh* or *hmf*, *interj* expressive of reserved doubt or dissatisfaction.

humph[2] or **humf** *humf*, (*Scot*) *n* a hump. — *vt* to carry (something cumbersome, heavy or awkward). [**hump**]

Humphrey, dine with Duke. See under **dine**.

humpty *hump'ti* or *hum'ti*, *n* a low padded seat, a pouffe. [*humpty* hunchbacked; perh connected with **Humpty-dumpty**]

Humpty-dumpty *hump'ti-dump'ti* or *hum'ti-dum'ti*, *n* a short, squat, egg-like character of nursery folklore; a gypsy drink, ale boiled with brandy. — *adj* short and broad.

humpy[1] *hum'pi*, (*Austr*) *n* an Aboriginal hut. [Aboriginal *oompi*]

humpy[2]. See under **hump**.

humstrum *hum'strum*, (now *dialect*) *n* a hurdy-gurdy or other musical instrument. [**hum**[1] and **strum**, with imit effect]

humungous. See **humongous**.

humus[1] *hūm'əs*, *n* decomposed organic matter in the soil. — *adj* **hū'mic** or **hū'mous**. — *adj* **hum'usy** having much humus. [L *humus*; cf Gr *chamai* on the ground]

humus[2]. Same as **hummus**.

Hun *hun*, *n* a member of a powerful squat, swarthy and savage nomad race of Asia who moved westwards, and under Attila (433–453) overran Europe; in US formerly a Hungarian (*derog*); a barbarian; a German (*orig war slang* of 1914, now *derog slang*). — *adj* **Hunn'ic** or **Hunn'ish**. [OE (pl) *Hūne*, *Hūnas*; L *Hunnī*; Gr *Ounnoi*, *Chounnoi*]

hunch *hunch* or *hunsh*, *n* a hump; a lump; a premonition; a hint; an intuitive feeling. — *vt* to hump, bend. — **hunch'back** a person whose spine is convexly curved to an abnormal degree. — *adj* **hunch'backed**. — **play one's hunch** to act on one's hunch (as a gambler might). [Origin obscure]

hundred *hun'drəd*, *n* the number of ten times ten; a set of a hundred things; a hundred pounds, dollars, etc; (in *pl*) an unspecified large number; a division of a county in England *orig* supposed to contain a hundred families (chiefly *hist*): — *pl* **hundreds** or, when preceded by a numeral, **hundred**. — *adj* to the number of a hundred; hundredth (*obs* or *dialect*); also used indefinitely, very many (*colloq*). — *n* **hun'dreder** or **hun'dredor** (*hist*) the bailiff or an inhabitant of a hundred. — *adj*, *adv* and *n* **hun'dredfold** folded a hundred times; in a hundred divisions; a hundred times as much. — *adj* **hun'dredth** last of a hundred; next after the ninety-ninth; equal to one of a hundred equal parts. — *n* one of a hundred equal parts; a person or thing in hundredth position. — *adj* **hun'dred-per-cent'** out-and-out; thorough-going (**not a hundred-per-cent** not in perfect health). — **hun'dred-percent'er** (*US*) an uncompromising patriot; **hun'dreds-and-thou'sands** little sweets used as decoration; **hun'dredweight** 1/20 of a ton, or 112 lb avoirdupois (50.80kg; also called **long hundredweight**); *orig* and still in US, 100 lb (45.3kg; also called **short hundredweight**); 50kg (also called **metric hundredweight**) — *abbrev* **cwt** (*c* standing for L *centum*, *wt* for weight). — **Chiltern Hundreds** a district of Buckinghamshire, whose stewardship is a nominal office under the Crown, the temporary acceptance of which by a member of parliament enables him or her to vacate his or her seat; **great** or **long hundred** usually six score; sometimes some other number greater than ten tens (eg of herrings, 132 or 126); **Hundred Years' War** the struggle between England and France, from 1337 down to 1453; **not a hundred miles from** (*colloq*) at, very near; **Old Hundred** see under **old**; **one, two**, etc **hundred hours** one, two, etc o'clock (from the method of writing hours and minutes 1.00, 2.00, etc); **the Hundred Days** the time between Napoleon's return from Elba and his final downfall after Waterloo (the reign lasted exactly 95 days, March 20–June 22, 1815). [OE *hundred*, from old form *hund* a hundred, with the suffix *-red* a reckoning]

Hung. *abbrev*: Hungarian; Hungary.

hung *pa t* and *pa p* of **hang** (qv).

Hungarian *hung-gā'ri-ən*, *adj* pertaining to *Hungary* or its inhabitants. — *n* a person of Hungarian birth, descent or citizenship; the Magyar or Hungarian language. — **Hungary** (*hung'gə-ri*) **water** oil of rosemary distilled with alcohol (said to have been used by a queen of Hungary). [Cf **Ugrian**]

hunger *hung'gər*, *n* craving for food; need or lack of food; strong desire for anything. — *vi* to crave food; to long (*for*). — *adj* **hung'erful** hungry. — *adj* **hung'erly** (*Shakesp*) hungry. — *adv* (*Shakesp*) hungrily. — *adv* **hung'rily**. — *adj* **hung'ry** having an eager desire for food (or anything else); greedy, desirous, longing (with *for*); stingy, mean (*Austr*); lean; poor; used in combination to signify eager for, in need of (as in *land-*

hungry). — *adj* **hung'er-bitten** bitten, pained or weakened by hunger. — **hunger march** a procession of unemployed or others in need, as a demonstration; **hunger'-marcher**; **hunger strike** prolonged refusal of all food by a prisoner, etc as a form of protest, or a means to ensure release. — *vi* **hung'er-strike**. — **hung'er-striker**. — **go hungry** to remain without food. [OE *hungor* (n), *hyngran* (verb); cf Ger *Hunger*, Du *honger*, etc]

hung over, **hung up**, etc. See under **hang**.

hunk[1] *hungk*, *n* a lump; a strong or sexually attractive man (*colloq*). — *adj* **hunk'y** (*colloq*; of a man) strong or sexually attractive. [Same as **hunch**]

hunk[2] *hungk*, *n* (*US*) goal or base in boys' games. — *adj* safe, secure. — *adj* **hunk'y** (*US*) or **hunk'y-do'ry** (*orig US*) (*colloq*) in good position or condition; excellent; all right. [Du *honk*]

hunker[1] *hungk'ər*, (*US*) *n orig* a member of the conservative section of the New York Democratic party (1845–8); a conservative person. [Origin obscure]

hunker[2] *hungk'ər*, *vi* to squat (often with *down*). — *n pl* **hunk'ers** the hams or haunches. [Origin obscure; perh connected with ON *hūka* to squat]

hunks *hungks*, *n sing* a miserly curmudgeon. [Ety dubious]

hunky[1] *hungk'i*, (*NAm*) *n* a derogatory name for a person of East European descent, *esp* an unskilled workman. [For **Hungarian**]

hunky[2,3]. See under **hunk**[1,2].

hunky-dory. See under **hunk**[2].

Hunnic, **Hunnish**. See under **Hun**.

hunt *hunt*, *vt* to chase or go in quest of for prey or sport; to seek or pursue game over (land, etc); to ransack; to use in the hunt; to search for; to pursue; to hound or drive; to drive away, dismiss (*Austr*). — *vi* to go out in pursuit of game; to search; to oscillate or vary in speed (*mech*); (of a bell) to move its order of ringing through a set of changes (**hunt up** to be rung progressively earlier; **hunt down** to be rung progressively later). — *n* a chase of wild animals; a search; a pack of hunting hounds; an association of huntsmen; the district hunted by a pack; game killed in a hunt (*Shakesp*); a huntsman (*obs*). — *n* **hunt'er** a person or animal that hunts (*fem* **hunt'ress**); a horse used in hunting, *esp* fox-hunting; a watch whose face is protected with a metal case (a **half-hunt'er** if that case has a small circle of glass let in). — *n* **hunt'ing** the pursuit of wild game, the chase. — Also *adj*. — **hunt ball** a ball given by the members of a hunt; **hunt'-counter** (*Shakesp*) perhaps one who hunts counter (qv below); **hunt'er-gath'erer** (*anthropol*) a member of a society which lives by hunting and gathering fruit, etc, as opposed eg to cultivating crops; **hunt'er-kill'er** a surface craft or submarine designed to hunt down and destroy enemy vessels; **hunt'er's-moon'** full moon following harvest-moon; **hunt'ing-box**, **-lodge** or **-seat** temporary accommodation for hunters; **hunt'ing-cap** a form of cap often worn in the hunting-field; **hunt'ing-cat** a cheetah; **hunt'ing-cog** an extra cog in one of two geared wheels, by means of which the order of contact of cogs is changed at every revolution; **hunt'ing-crop** or **-whip** a short whip with a crooked handle and a loop of leather at the end, used in the hunting-field; **hunt'ing-field** the scene or sphere of hunting, *esp* fox-hunting; the assemblage of huntsmen; **hunt'ing-ground** a place or region for hunting (**happy hunting-ground** see under **happy**); **hunt'ing-horn** a horn used in hunting, a bugle; **hunt'ing-knife** or **-sword** a knife or short sword used to dispatch the game when caught, or to skin and cut it up; **hunt'ing-leopard** a cheetah; **hunt'ing-mass** (*hist*) a hasty and abridged mass said for impatient hunters; **hunt'ing-song**; **hunt'ing-spider** a wolf-spider; **hunt'ing-tide** the season of hunting; **hunting-whip** see **hunting-crop** above; **hunt saboteur** a person opposed to all blood sports, *esp* fox-hunting, who *usu* as part of an organized group, takes action to thwart the activities of hunters; **hunts'man** a person who hunts; a person who manages the hounds during the chase; **hunts'manship** the qualifications of a huntsman; **huntsman spider** (*Austr*) any spider of the many varieties belonging to the *Heteropodidae* (*Sparassidae*) family, *esp* those of the genus *Isopoda*, typically large and flat-bodied, inhabiting tree-bark; **hunt's'-up** (*Shakesp*) a tune or song intended to arouse huntsmen in the morning; hence, anything calculated to arouse; **hunt'-the-gowk** the making of an April fool; (also **hunt'iegowk**) a fool's errand, a deception or a hoax, appropriate to the First of April. — Also *adj*. — *vt* to make an April fool of. — **hunt'-the-slipp'er** a game in which a person in the middle of a ring of people tries to catch a shoe passed around surreptitiously by the others. — *interj* **good hunting**! good luck! (*colloq*). — **hunt after** or **for** to search for; **hunt counter** to follow the scent backwards; **hunt down** to pursue to extremities; to persecute out of existence; see also at **hunt** above; **hunt out** or **up** to seek out; **hunt the letter** to affect alliteration; **hunt up** see **hunt** above. [OE *huntian*; prob connected with *hentan* to seize]

Hunterian *hun-tē'ri-ən*, *adj* of or pertaining to the surgeon John *Hunter* (1728–93), to his anatomical collection, nucleus of the Hunterian Museum in London, or to the annual Hunterian Oration at the Royal College of Surgeons; of or pertaining to his elder brother, William *Hunter* (1718–83), anatomist and obstetrician, or his museum in Glasgow.

huntiegowk, **hunting**. See under **hunt**.

Huntingdonian *hun-ting-dō'ni-ən*, *n* a member of the Countess of Huntingdon's Connection, a denomination of Calvinistic Methodists founded by Whitefield with Selina, Countess of *Huntingdon* (1707–91). — Also *adj*.

Huntington's chorea *hunt'ing-tənz ko-rē'ə* or **Huntington's disease** (*diz-ēz'*), *n* an inherited and fatal disease, marked by progressive mental deterioration. [Dr G *Huntington* (died 1916), who described it]

huntress, **huntsman**, **huntsmanship**. See under **hunt**.

Huon pine *hū'on pīn*, *n* a Tasmanian conifer (*Dacrydium*, or *Lagerostrobus*, *franklinii*), found first on the *Huon* river.

hup *hup*, *vi* to shout 'hup'; (of a horse) to go on, to go faster; to turn to the right. — *vt* to turn (a horse) to the right. — *n* a cry of 'hup'. — *interj* (to a horse) to go faster or to turn to the right. — **neither hup nor wind** (*Scot*) to do neither one thing nor another, be unmanageable.

hupaithric *hū-pāth'rik*, *adj* hypaethral.

hurcheon *hûr'chən*, Scots form of **urchin**.

hurden. See **hards**.

hurdies *hûr'diz*, (*Scot*) *n pl* the buttocks; the thighs. [Origin unknown]

hurdle *hûr'dl*, *n* a frame of twigs or sticks interlaced; a movable frame of timber or iron for gates, etc (*agric*); (in certain races) a portable barrier over which runners jump; a rude sledge on which criminals were drawn to the gallows (*hist*); an obstacle to be surmounted, difficulty to be overcome; (in *pl*) a hurdle-race. — *vt* to enclose with hurdles; to jump over (a hurdle, an obstacle, etc). — *vi* to jump as over a hurdle; to run a hurdle-race. — *n* **hurd'ler** a maker of hurdles; an athlete who takes part in hurdles events. — *n* **hur'dling**. — **hur'dle-race** a race in which hurdles have to be cleared; **hur'dle-racer**; **hur'dle-racing**. [OE *hyrdel*; Ger *Hürde*]

hurds. See **hards**.

hurdy-gurdy *hûr'di-gûr'di*, *n* a stringed musical instrument, whose strings are sounded by the turning of a wheel; a barrel-organ. [Imit]

hurl *hûrl*, *vt* to fling with violence; to wheel (*Scot*); to convey in a wheeled vehicle (*Scot*). — *vi* to dash; to travel in a wheeled vehicle (*Scot*); to play hurley. — *n* act of hurling; a trip or journey in a wheeled vehicle (*Scot*). — *n* **hurl'er**. — *n* **hurl'ey** or **hurl'ing** a game similar to hockey, of Irish origin, played by teams of 15, with broad-bladed sticks (**hurl'eys**) and a hide-covered cork ball. — *n* **hurl'y** (*Scot*) a large two-wheeled barrow. — **hurl'barrow** (*Scot*) a wheelbarrow; **hurl'bat** see **whirlbat** under **whirl**; **hurl'ey-house** (*Scott*) a house in a state of disrepair; **hurl'y-hacket** (*Scot*) a carriage, gig; an improvised sledge; sledging. [Cf LGer *hurreln* to hurl, precipitate; influenced by **hurtle** and **whirl**]

hurly[1] *hûr'li*, *n* commotion; tumult. — *n* **hurly-burly** (*hûr'li-bûr'li*) tumult; confusion. — Also *adj* and *adv*. [Perh from **hurl**]

hurly[2]. See under **hurl**.

Huronian *hū-rō'ni-ən*, (*geol*) *n* and *adj* upper Pre-Cambrian of Canada, well exemplified north of lake *Huron*.

hurrah, **hurra** *hŏŏr-ä'* or *hur-ä'* or now usually **hurray** or **hooray** *hoo-ā'*, *interj* an exclamation of approbation or joy. — Also *n* and *vi*. [Cf Norw, Swed, Dan *hurra*, Ger *hurrah*, Du *hoera*]

hurricane *hur'i-kin* or *-kān*, *n* a West Indian cyclonic storm of great violence; a wind of extreme violence (over 75mph (120km/h)); anything tempestuous, a tumult, commotion; a social party, a rout (*obs*); (with *cap*) a type of fighting aeroplane used in World War II. — *n* **hurricā'nō** (*obs*) a hurricane; a waterspout (*Shakesp*): — *pl* **hurricā'noes**. — **hurr'icane-deck** a light partial deck over the saloon of some steamers; **hurr'icane-lamp** an oil lamp encased so as to defy strong wind; a protected electric lamp. [Sp *huracán*, from Caribbean]

hurry *hur'i*, *vt* to urge forward; to hasten. — *vi* to move or act with haste, *esp* perturbed or impatient haste: — *pr p* **hurr'ying**; *pa t* and *pa p* **hurr'ied**. — *n* a driving forward; haste; flurried or undue haste; commotion; a rush; need for haste; a tremolo passage for strings, or a drum roll, in connection with an exciting situation (*music*). — *adj* **hurr'ied**. — *adv* **hurr'iedly**. — *n* **hurr'iedness**. — *n* and *adj* **hurr'ying**. — *adv* **hurr'yingly**. — **hurr'y-scurr'y** or **-skurr'y** confusion and bustle. — *adv* confusedly. — **in a hurry** in haste, speedily; soon; easily; willingly; **hurry up** to make haste. [Prob imit; cf Old Swed *hurra* to whirl round]

hurst *hûrst*, *n* a wood, a grove; a sand bank. [OE *hyrst*]

hurt *hûrt*, *vt* to cause pain to; to damage; to injure; to wound (a person's feelings, etc). — *vi* to give pain; to be the seat or source of pain; to be injured (*colloq esp NAm*): — *pa t* and *pa p* **hurt**. — *n* a wound; injury. — *adj* injured; pained in body or mind. — *n* **hurt'er** that which hurts; a beam, block, etc to protect a wall from wheels; the shoulder of an axle against which the hub strikes. — *adj* **hurt'ful** causing hurt or loss; harmful, *esp* emotionally. — *adv* **hurt'fully**. — *n* **hurt'fulness**. — *adj* **hurt'less** without hurt or injury, harmless. — *adv* **hurt'lessly**. — *n* **hurt'lessness**. [OFr *hurter* (Fr *heurter*) to knock, to run against]

hurtle *hûrt'l*, *vt* to dash; to hurl; to brandish (*Spenser*). — *vi* to clash (*archaic*); to rattle; to move rapidly with a clattering sound. [Frequentative of **hurt** in its original sense]

hurtleberry *hûrt'l-ber-i*, *n*. Same as **whortleberry**.

husband *huz'bənd*, *n* a man to whom a woman is married; a husbandman (*obs*); a manager; a thrifty manager. — *vt* to supply with a husband (*archaic*); to become, be or act as a husband to (*archaic*); to manage with economy; to conserve; to cultivate (*archaic*). — *n* **hus'-bandage** allowance or commission of a ship's husband. — *adj* **hus'bandless**. — *adj* **hus'bandlike**. — *adj* **hus'-bandly** frugal, thrifty, pertaining to or befitting a husband. — *n* **hus'bandry** the business of a farmer; tillage; economical management; thrift. — **hus'-bandland** (*hist*) a manorial tenant's holding; two oxgangs; **hus'bandman** a working farmer; a man who labours in tillage. — **ship's husband** an owner's agent who manages the affairs of a ship in port. [OE *hūsbonda*, ON *hūsbōndi*, from *hūs* a house, and *būandi* inhabiting, pr p of ON *būa* to dwell; cf **boor**, **bower**[1] and Ger *bauen* to till]

hush *hush*, *interj* or *imperative* silence; be still. — *n* a silence, *esp* after noise; a rush of water or its sound (*dialect*); the washing away of surface soil to lay bare bedrock (*mineralogy*). — *adj* silent (*archaic*); quiet (*archaic*); for the purpose of concealing information (eg *hush money*) (*colloq*). — *vi* to become silent or quiet. — *vt* to make quiet; to calm; to procure silence or secrecy about (sometimes with *up*); to pour in a stream (*dialect*); to wash away or to pour in order to expose bedrock (*mining*). — *n* **hush'aby** (*-ə-bī*) a lullaby used to soothe babies to sleep. — Also *vt* and *interj*. — *adj* **hushed** silent, still. — *adj* **hush'-hush** or **hush'y** (*colloq*) secret. — **hush'-boat** (1920s) a mystery-ship; **hush kit** (*colloq*) a device fitted to the jet engine of an aeroplane to reduce noise; **hush puppy** (*US*; *usu* in *pl*) a ball or balls of maize dough, deep-fried (from its occasional use as dog food); a light, soft (*esp* suede) shoe for men. — **hush up** to stifle, suppress; to be silent. [Imit; cf **hist** and **whist**[1]]

husher *hush'ər*. Another spelling of **usher**.

husk *husk*, *n* the dry, thin covering of certain fruits and seeds; a case, shell or covering, *esp* one that is worthless or coarse; (in *pl*) refuse, waste; huskiness; bronchitis in cattle caused by parasitic nematodes; a supporting frame. — *vt* to remove the husk or outer integument from. — *adj* **husked** covered with a husk; stripped of husks. — *n* **husk'er** someone who husks maize, *esp* at a husking-bee; apparatus (such as a glove) for the same purpose. — *adv* **husk'ily**. — *n* **husk'iness**. — *n* **husk'ing** the stripping of husks; a festive gathering to assist in husking maize (also **husk'ing-bee**). — *adj* **husk'y** full of husks; of the nature of husks; like a husk; dry; sturdy like a corn-husk; (of a voice) dry and almost whispering, as if there were husks in the throat; (of words) spoken in a husky voice. — *n* (*NAm*) a big strong man. [Perh connected with **house**]

husky[1]. See under **husk**.

husky[2] *hus'ki*, *n* an Eskimo sledge-dog; an Eskimo; the Eskimo language. [Appar from *Eskimo*]

huso *hū'sō*, *n* the great sturgeon: — *pl* **hu'sos**. [OHGer *hûso*]

huss *hus*, *n* any of various kinds of dogfish, when used as food. [ME *husk*, *huske*]

hussar *hŏŏ-zär'* or *hə-*, *n* a soldier of a light cavalry regiment; *orig* a soldier of the national cavalry of Hungary in the 15c. [Hung *huszar*, through Old Serb, from Ital *corsaro* a freebooter]

hussif *hus'if*. Dialect form of **housewife**, in the sense of pocket sewing-kit.

Hussite *hus'īt* or *hŏŏs'īt*, *n* a follower of the Bohemian reformer John *Hus*, martyred in 1415.

hussy *hus'i* or *huz'i*, *n* an impudent girl; a promiscuous or worthless girl or woman; a housewife (*obs*); a hussif (*obs*). [**housewife**]

hustings *hus'tingz*, *n sing* the principal court of the city of London; formerly the booths where the votes were taken at an election of an MP, or the platform from which the candidates gave their addresses; electioneering. [OE *hūsting* a council (used in speaking of the Danes), from ON *hūsthing*, from *hūs* a house, and *thing* an assembly]

hustle *hus'l*, *vt* to shake or push together; to crowd with violence; to jostle; to thrust hastily; to hasten roughly; to exert pressure on; to sell (*esp* aggressively); to obtain (money) illicitly (*slang*). — *vi* to act strenuously or aggressively; to earn money illicitly (eg as a prostitute; *slang*). — *n* frenzied activity; a type of lively disco dance with a variety of steps. — *n* **hus'tler** a lively or energetic person; a swindler (*slang*); a prostitute (*slang*). — *n* **hus'tling**. [Du *hutselen* to shake to and fro; cf **hotchpotch**]

huswife *hus'if*. Obs form of **housewife**.

hut *hut*, *n* a small, mean or crudely built house; a small temporary dwelling or similar structure. — *vt* to quarter (troops) in or furnish with a hut or huts. — *vi* to dwell in a hut or huts: — *pr p* **hutt'ing**; *pa t* and *pa p* **hutt'ed**. — *n* **hut'ment** an encampment of huts (*military*) lodging in huts. — *n* **hutt'ing** material for making huts. — **hut'-cir'cle** (*antiq*) the remains of a prehistoric circular hut, a pit lined with stones, etc. [Fr *hutte*, from OHGer *hutta* (Ger *Hütte*); cf **hide**[1]]

hutch *huch*, *n* a box, a chest; a coop or cage for small animals, *esp* for rabbits; a small, cramped house (*colloq*); a baker's kneading-trough; a trough used with some ore-dressing machines; a low wagon in which coal is drawn up out of the pit. — *vt* (*Milton*) to hoard up. [Fr *huche* a chest, from LL *hūtica* a box; prob Gmc]

Hutchinsonian *huch-in-sōn'i-ən*, *n* a follower of John *Hutchinson* (1674–1737), who held that the Hebrew Scriptures contain typically the elements of all rational philosophy, natural history and true religion.

hutia *hōō-tē'ə*, *n* the hog-rat. [Sp *hutia*, from Taino]

Huttonian *hut-ō'ni-ən*, *adj* relating to the teaching of James *Hutton* (1726–97), *esp* expounding the importance of geological agencies still at work, and the igneous origin of granite and basalt. — *n* a follower of Hutton.

huzoor *huz-ōōr'*, *n* an Indian potentate, or (loosely) any person of rank or importance. [Ar *hudūr* the presence]

huzza *hōōz-ä'* or *huz-ä'*, *interj* and *n* hurrah; a shout of joy or approbation. — *vt* to attend with shouts of joy. — *vi* to utter shouts of joy or acclamation: — *pr p* **huzza'ing**; *pa t* and *pa p* **huzzaed** or **huzza'd** (*-zäd'*). [Perh Ger *hussa*; cf **hurrah**]

huzzy *huz'i*, dialect variant of **hussy**.

HV or **hv** *abbrev*: high voltage.

HWM *abbrev*: high water mark.

hwyl *hū'il*, *n* divine inspiration in oratory; emotional fervour. [Welsh]

hyacine *hī'ə-sīn*, (*Spenser*) *n* hyacinth (the stone).

hyacinth *hī'ə-sinth*, *n* a flower (a bluebell or blue larkspur) that sprang from the blood of Hyacinthus, a youth accidentally killed by Apollo (*Gr mythol*); a bulbous genus (*Hyacinthus*) of the lily family, cultivated; extended to others of the family, such as **wild hyacinth** (the English bluebell), **grape hyacinth** (*Muscari*), and **Cape hyacinth** a species of Galtonia (*G. candicans*) with white flowers; a blue stone of the ancients (*perh* aquamarine); a red, brown or yellow zircon — jacinth; cinnamon-stone; a purple colour, of various hues. — *adj* **hyacin'thine** consisting of or resembling hyacinth; very beautiful, like Hyacinthus; of a colour variously understood as golden, purple-black, or a blue or purple of some kind. [Gr *hyakinthos* a species of Scilla, blue larkspur, or a blue stone; cf **jacinth**]

Hyades *hī'ə-dēz* or **Hyads** *hī'adz*, *n pl* a cluster of five stars in the constellation of the Bull, supposed by the ancients to bring rain when they rose with the sun. [Gr *Hyades*, *Hȳades*, explained by the ancients as from *hyein* to rain; more prob little pigs, from *hȳs* a pig]

hyaena. See **hyena**.

hyaline *hī'ə-lin* or *-līn*, *adj* glassy; of or like glass; clear; transparent; free from granules (*biol*). — *n* (*Milton*) a glassy transparent surface. — *n* **hyaliniza'tion** or **-s-**. — *vt*, *vi* **hy'alinize** or **-ise** (*med*) (of tissue) to change to a firm, glassy consistency. — *n* **hy'alite** transparent colourless opal. — *adj* **hy'aloid** (*anatom*) hyaline, transparent. — *n* **hyalom'elane** or **hyalom'elan** (*-ān* or *-an*; Gr *melās*, *-anos* black) tachylite. — *n* **hyalonē'ma** (Gr *nēma* thread) the glass-rope sponge. — *n* **hy'alophane** (root of Gr *phainesthai* to seem) a feldspar containing barium. — *n* **hy'aloplasm** the clear fluid part of protoplasm. — **hyaline cartilage** a translucent bluish-white cartilage, eg covering bones at points of articulation; **hyaline degeneration** hyalinization; **hyaloid membrane** the transparent membrane which encloses the vitreous humour of the eye. [Gr *hyalos* glass]

Hyblaean *hi-blē'ən*, *adj* pertaining to ancient *Hybla* in Sicily, noted for its honey.

hybrid *hī'brid*, *n* an organism which is the offspring of a union between different races, species, genera or varieties; a mongrel; a word formed of elements from different languages. — *adj* **hy'brid** or **hyb'ridous** produced from different species, etc; mongrel; (of a circuit) consisting of transistors and valves; (of an integrated circuit) having integrated circuit(s) and other components attached to a ceramic base. — *n* **hy'bridism** or **hybrid'ity** the state of being hybrid. — *adj* **hybridīz'able** or **-s-**. — *n* **hybridīzā'tion** or **-s-** a technique for determining the similarity of two DNA or RNA strands from different sources by annealing them to form hybrid molecules, whose stability is a measure of their relatedness. — *vt* **hy'bridize** or **-ise** to cause to interbreed. — *vi* to interbreed. — *n* **hybridīz'er** or **-s-**. — *n* **hybridō'ma** a hybrid cell produced from a cancer cell and an antibody-producing cell. — **hybrid bill** (*politics*) a parliamentary public bill which affects certain private interests; **hybrid computer** one which combines features of digital and analog computers; **hybrid vigour** heterosis. [L *hibrida* offspring of a tame sow and wild boar; with associations of Gr *hybris* insolence, overweening]

hybris. See under **hubris**.

hydathode *hī'dəth-ōd*, (*bot*) *n* an epidermal water-excreting organ. [Gr *hydōr*, *hydatos* water, and *hodos* way]

hydatid *hī'də-tid*, *n* a water cyst or vesicle in an animal body, *esp* one containing a tapeworm larva; the larva itself; hydatid disease. — *adj* **hydatid'iform** resembling a hydatid. — **hydatid disease** an infection, *esp* of the liver, caused by tapeworm larvae, giving rise to expanding cysts; **hydatidiform mole** (*med*) an affection of the vascular tufts of the foetal part of the placenta whereby they become greatly enlarged. [Gr *hydatis*, *-idos* a watery vesicle, from *hydōr*, *hydatos* water]

hydatoid *hī'də-toid*, *adj* watery. [Gr *hydōr*, *-atos* water, and *eidos* form]

Hydnocarpus *hid-nō-kär'pəs*, *n* a genus of trees related to the chaulmoogra, yielding an oil containing chaulmoogric acid. [Gr *hydnon* truffle, and *karpos* fruit]

hydr-. See **hydro-**.

Hydra *hī'drə*, *n* a water-monster with many heads, which when cut off were succeeded by others (*mythol*); a large southern constellation; (without *cap*) any manifold evil; (without *cap*) a freshwater hydrozoon of the genus *Hydra*, remarkable for power of multiplication on being cut or divided. — *adj* **hy'dra-headed** difficult to root out, springing up vigorously again and again. [Gr *hydrā*, from *hydōr* water, related to Sans *udra* an otter]

hydraemia, **hydragogue**, **hydrangea**, etc. See under **hydro-**.

hydrargyrism *hī-drär'jir-izm*, *n* mercurial poisoning. — *adj* **hydrar'gyral**. — *n* **hydrar'gyrum** mercury. [Gr *hydrargyros* mercury, from *argyros* silver; *hydrargyrum* is modern L on analogy of *argentum*, etc, L *hydrargyrus*]

hydrate, **hydration**. See under **hydro-**.

hydraulic *hī-dröl'ik* or *-drol'ik*, *adj* relating to hydraulics; conveying water; worked by water or other liquid in pipes; setting in water. — *vt* (*mining*) to excavate and wash out by powerful jets of water: — *pr p* **hydraul'icking**; *pa t* and *pa p* **hydraul'icked**. — *adv* **hydraul'ically**. — *n sing* **hydraul'ics** the science of hydrodynamics in general, or its practical application to water-pipes, etc. — **hydraulic belt** an endless belt of absorbent material for raising water; **hydraulic brake** a brake in which the force is transmitted by means of a compressed fluid; **hydraulic cement** a cement which will harden under water; **hydraulic jack** a lifting apparatus in which oil, etc, is pumped against a piston; **hydraulic mining** hydraulicking; **hydraulic press** a press operated by forcing water into a cylinder in which a ram or plunger works; **hydraulic ram** a device whereby the pressure head produced when a moving column of water is brought to rest is caused to deliver some of the water under pressure; **hydraulic seeding** sowing seed by spraying it, mixed with nutrients, etc, on the ground; **hydraulic suspension** a system of car suspension using hydraulic units. [Gr *hydōr* water, and *aulos* a pipe]

hydrazine *hī'drə-zēn*, *n* a fuming corrosive liquid, $H_2N{\cdot}NH_2$, a powerful reducing agent, used as a rocket fuel; any of a class of organic bases derived from it. —

n pl **hy'drazides** a class of chemical compounds derived from hydrazine. — **hydrazoic** (*-zō'ik*) **acid** HN_3, a colourless, foul-smelling liquid that combines with lead and other heavy metals to produce explosive salts (azides). [From **hydr-** and **azo-**]

hydria *hī'dri-ə* or *hid'ri-ə*, *n* a large Greek water-vase. [Gr *hydriā*]

hydro *hī'drō*, *n* short form of **hydroelectric** or **hydropathic establishment** (see under **hydro-**): — *pl* **hy'dros**.

hydro- *hī'drō-*, *hī-drə-* or *hī-dro'-*, also **hydr-** *combining form* denoting of, like or by means of water (see also **hydrogen**). — *n* **hydraemia** or (*esp NAm*) **hydremia** (*hī-drē'mi-ə*; Gr *haima* blood) wateriness of the blood. — *adj* **hydragogue** (*hī'drə-gog*, *-gōg*; Gr *agōgos* bringing; *med*) removing water or serum. — *n* a drug with that effect. — *n* **hydrangea** (*hī-drān'jə* or *hī-drān'jyə*; Gr *angeion* vessel) a plant of the *Hydrangea* genus of shrubby plants of the family **Hydrangeā'ceae**, with large globular clusters of showy flowers, natives of China and Japan. — *n* **hydrant** (*hī'drənt*) a connection for attaching a hose to a water-main or a fire-plug. — *n* **hydranth** (*hī'dranth*; Gr *anthos* flower) a nutritive polyp in a hydroid colony. — *n* **hydrarthrō'sis** (*med*) swelling of a joint caused by the accumulation in it of watery fluid. — *n* **hy'drate** a compound containing water which is chemically combined and which can be expelled without affecting the composition of the other substance; an old word for a *hydroxide* (see under **hydrogen**). — *vt* to combine with water; to cause to absorb water. — *n* **hydrā'tion**. — *n* **hydrē'mia** mainly *NAm* form of **hydraemia**. — *adj* **hy'dric** pertaining to an abundance of moisture; see also under **hydrogen**. — *adv* **hy'drically**. — *n* **hydride** see under **hydrogen**. — *n* **hydro-ae'roplane** (*NAm* **hydro-air'plane**) a seaplane. — *adj* **hydrobiolog'ical**. — *n* **hydrobiol'ogist**. — *n* **hydrobiol'ogy** the biology of aquatic animals and plants. — *n* **hy'drocele** (*-sēl*; Gr *kēlē* a swelling; *med*) a swelling containing serous fluid, *esp* in the scrotum. — *n* **hydrocell'ūlose** a gelatinous material obtained by hydration of cellulose, used in paper- making, etc. — *adj* **hydrocephal'ic** or **hydroceph'alous**. — *n* **hydrocephalus** (*-sef'ə-ləs*, or *-kef'*; Gr *kephalē* head) an accumulation of serous fluid within the cranial cavity, either in the subdural space or the ventricles; water in the head; dropsy of the brain. — *n* **Hydrocharis** (*hī-drok'ə-ris*; Gr *charis*, *-itos* grace) the frogbit genus, giving name to the **Hydrocharitā'ceae**, a family of water-plants related to the pondweeds. — *n* **hydrochlorofluorocar'bon** a chlorofluorocarbon that contains hydrogen and is therefore more easily broken down. — Abbrev **HCFC**. — *n* **hy'drochore** (*-kōr*; Gr *chōreein* to make room, spread about) a plant disseminated by water. — *adj* **hydrochoric** (*-kor'ik*). — *n pl* **Hydrocorallī'nae** an order of Hydrozoa, massive reef-builders, the millepores, etc. — *n* and *adj* **hydrocor'alline**. — *adj* **hydrodynamic** (*-dīn-am'ik*; Gr *dynamis* power) or **hydrodynam'ical**. — *n* **hydrodynam'icist**. — *n sing* **hydrodynam'ics** the science of the motions and equilibrium of a material system partly or wholly fluid (called *hydrostatics* when the system is in equilibrium, *hydrokinetics* when it is not). — *adj* **hydroelast'ic** see **hydroelastic suspension** below. — *adj* **hydroelec'tric**. — *n* **hydroelectric'ity** electricity produced by means of water, *esp* by water-power. — *n* **hydroextract'or** a drying-machine that works centrifugally. — *n* **hydrofluorocar'bon** an alkane in which some of the hydrogen atoms, are substituted by fluorine atoms (cf fluorocarbon). — *Abbrev* **HFC**. — *n* **hy'drofoil** a device on a boat for raising it from the water as its speed increases; a boat fitted with this device; a corresponding device on a seaplane to aid its take-off (also **hy'drovane**); a seaplane with hydrofoils. — *n* **hydrogeol'ogist**. — *n* **hydrogeol'ogy** the branch of geology dealing with ground water. — *n* **hy'drograph** a graph showing seasonal variations in level, force, etc of a body of water. — *n* **hydrog'rapher** (Gr *graphein* to write). — *adj* **hydrographic** (*-graf'ik*) or **hydrograph'ical**. — *adv* **hydrograph'ically**. — *n* **hydrog'raphy** the investigation of seas and other bodies of water, including charting, sounding, study of tides, currents, etc. — *adj* **hy'droid** like a Hydra; polypoid. — *n* a hydrozoan; a hydrozoan in its asexual generation. — *adj* **hydrokinet'ic** pertaining to hydrokinetics; pertaining to the motion of fluids; pertaining to fluids in motion; operated or operating by the movement of fluids. — *n sing* **hydrokinet'ics** a branch of **hydrodynamics** (qv above). — *adj* **hydrolog'ic** or **hydrolog'ical**. — *adv* **hydrolog'ically**. — *n* **hydrol'ogist**. — *n* **hydrol'ogy** the study of water resources in land areas of the world — (*US*) *esp* underground water. — *n* **hydrol'ysate** (*-i-sāt*) a substance produced by hydrolysis. — *vt* **hydrolyse** or (*esp US*) **-yze** (*hī'drō-līz*) to subject to hydrolysis. — Also *vi*. — *n* **hydrolysis** (*hī-drol'i-sis*; Gr *lysis* loosing) chemical decomposition or ionic dissociation caused by water. — *n* **hy'drolyte** (*-līt*) a body subjected to hydrolysis. — *adj* **hydrolytic** (*-lit'ik*). — *adj* **hydromagnet'ic**. — *n sing* **hydromagnet'ics** magnetohydrodynamics. — *n* **hy'dromancy** (Gr *manteiā* divination) divination by water. — *n* **hydromā'nia** a craving for water. — *adj* **hydromant'ic**. — *n sing* **hydromechan'ics** hydrodynamics. — *n* **hydromedū'sa** a hydrozoan in its sexual generation: — *pl* **Hydromedū'sae** the class Hydrozoa. — *adj* **hydromedū'san** or **hydromedū'soid** (also *n*). — *n* **hy'dromel** (Gr *hydromeli*, from *meli* honey) a beverage made of honey and water; mead. — *n* **hydromet'allurgy** (or *-met-al'ər-ji*) the extraction of metal from ore by treatment with water or other fluids. — *n* **hydromē'teor** (Gr *meteōron* a meteor) any weather phenomenon depending on the moisture content of the atmosphere. — *n* **hydrometeorol'ogy**. — *n* **hydrom'eter** (Gr *metron* a measure) a float for measuring specific gravity. — *adj* **hydrometric** (*-met'*) or **hydromet'rical**. — *n* **hydrom'etry** the science of the measurement and analysis of water, including the methods, techniques and instrumentation used in hydrology. — *n* **Hydromys** (*hī'drō-mis*; Gr *mȳs* mouse) an Australasian genus of aquatic rodents. — *n* **hy'dronaut** a person trained to work in an underwater vessel, eg a submarine. — *n* **hydronephrō'sis** distension of the kidney with urine held up as a result of obstruction in the urinary tract. — *adj* **hydronephro'tic**. — *adj* **hydropathic** (*hī-drō-path'ik* or *hī-drə-*) of, for, relating to or practising hydropathy. — *n* (in full **hydropathic establishment**; *colloq* **hy'dro**, *pl* **hy'dros**) a hotel (with special baths, etc, and often situated near a spa) where guests can have hydropathic treatment. — *adj* **hydropath'ical**. — *adv* **hydropath'ically**. — *n* **hydrop'athist** a person who practises hydropathy. — *n* **hydrop'athy** (Gr *pathos* suffering) the treatment of disease by water, externally and internally. — *n* **hydrophane** (*hī'drō-fān*; Gr *phānos* bright) a translucent opal transparent in water. — *adj* **hydrophanous** (*-drof'ən-əs*) transparent on immersion. — *n pl* **Hydrophidae** (*hī-drof'i-dē*; Gr *ophis* snake) a family of venomous sea-snakes. — *adj* **hydrophil'ic** (*chem*) attracting water. — *n* **hydroph'ilite** native calcium chloride (a very hygroscopic mineral). — *adj* **hydroph'ilous** water-loving; pollinated by agency of water (*bot*). — *n* **hydroph'ily** (Gr *phileein* to love) water-pollination. — *n* **hydrophō'bia** (Gr *phobos* fear) horror of water; inability to swallow water owing to a contraction in the throat, a symptom of rabies; rabies itself. — *adj* **hydrophō'bic** (or *-fob'*) pertaining to hydrophobia; repelling water (*chem*). — *n* **hydrophobic'ity**. — *adj* **hydrophobous** (*-drof'ə-bəs*) (*obs*). — *n* **hy'drophone** (*-fōn*; Gr *phōnē* voice) an apparatus for listening to sounds conveyed by water. — *n* **hy'drophyte** (*-fīt*; Gr *phyton* plant) a plant growing in water or in very moist conditions. — *adj* **hydrophytic** (*-fit'ik*). — *n* **hydrophyton** (*hī-drof'i-ton*) the coenosarc of a hydroid colony. — *adj* **hydroph'ytous**. — *adj* **hydrop'ic** (*erroneously* **hydrop'tic**; see **hydropsy**) dropsical; thirsty; charged or swollen with water. — *n* **hy'droplane** a light, flat-bottomed motor-boat which, at high speed, skims along the surface of the water; (erroneously) a hydro-aeroplane or seaplane. — *vi* (of a boat) to skim like a hydroplane; (of a vehicle) to skid on a wet road. — *adj* **hydropneumat'ic** using water and air acting together. — *n* **hydropol'yp** a hydrozoan polyp. — *adj* **hydropon'ic**. — *adv* **hydropon'ically**. — *n sing* **hydroponics** (*hī-drō-pon'iks*; Gr *ponos* toil) the art or practice of growing plants in (sand or gravel containing) a chemical solution without soil. — *n* **hy'dropower** hydroelectric power. — *n* **hy'dropsy** (Gr *hydrōps* dropsy; *archaic*) dropsy. — *n pl* **Hydropterid'eae** (*-i-ē*; Gr *pteris*, *-idos* male-fern) the water-ferns or heterosporous ferns. — **hydroptic** see **hydropic** above. — *n* **hy'dropult** (modelled on **catapult**) a hand force-pump. — *n* **hydroquinone** (*-kwin-ōn'*, or *kwin'*, or *-kwīn'*) quinol. — *n* **hy'droscope** (Gr *skopeein* to view) a kind of water-clock, a graduated tube, from which the water escaped (*hist*); an instrument for viewing under water. — *n* **hy'droski** (*-skē*) a kind of hydrofoil used on seaplanes as a source of hydrodynamic lift, and on aeroplanes to make them amphibious. — *n* **hydrosō'ma** or **hy'drosome** (*-sōm*; Gr *sōma* body) a hydroid colony: — *pl* **hydrosō'mata** or **hy'drosomes**. — *adj* **hydrosō'mal** or **hydrosō'matous**. — *n* **hy'drospace** or **hydrosphere** (*hī'drō-sfēr*; Gr *sphaira* sphere) the water on the surface of the earth — the seas and oceans. — *n* **hy'drostat** (Gr *-statēs* causing to stand) a contrivance for indicating the presence of water. — *adj* **hydrostat'ic** or **hydrostat'ical**. — *adv* **hydrostat'ically**. — *n sing* **hydrostat'ics** a branch of **hydrodynamics** (qv above). — *adj* **hydrotac'tic**. — *n* **hydrotax'is** (Gr *taxis* arrangement) response of an organism to the stimulus of water. — *n* **hydrothē'ca** (Gr *thēkē* case) the horny cup of a hydranth. — *adj* **hydrotherapeu'tic**. — *n sing* **hydrotherapeu'tics** or *n* **hydrother'apy** treatment of disease by the external use of water, eg treatment of disability by developing movement in water. — *adj* **hydrother'mal** pertaining to or produced by the action of heated or super-heated water, *esp* in dissolving, transporting and redepositing mineral matter. — *n* **hydrothorax** (*-thö'*; Gr *thōrax* chest) dropsy in the chest. — *adj* **hydrotrop'ic**. — *n* **hydrot'ropism** (Gr *tropos* a turn) the turning of a plant root towards (*positive*) or away from (*negative*) moisture. — *adj* **hydrous** (*-hī'drəs*; *chem* and *mineralogy*) containing water. — *n* **hydrovane** see **hydrofoil** above. — *n* **hydrozincite** (*-zingk'īt*) basic zinc carbonate. — *n pl* **Hydrozō'a** (Gr *zōion* an animal) a class of Coelenterata, chiefly marine organisms in which alternation of generations typically occurs, the hydroid phase colonial, giving rise to the medusoid phase by budding — eg the zoophytes, millepores, etc; sometimes extended to include the true jellyfishes; (without *cap*) hydrozoans: — *n* and *adj* **hydrozō'an**. — *n* **hydrozō'on** a coelenterate of the Hydrozoa: — *pl* **hydrozō'a**. — **hydrated electron** a very reactive free electron released in aqueous solutions by the action of ionizing radiations; **hydrated ion** an ion surrounded by molecules of water which it holds in a degree of orientation; **hydroelastic suspension** a system of car suspension in which a fluid provides interconnection between the front and rear suspension units; **hydrostatic balance** a balance for weighing bodies in water to determine their specific gravity; **hydrostatic drive** or **transmission** (in a vehicle) drive consisting of system transmitting power through oil, under pressure; **hydrostatic extrusion** (*metallurgy*) a form of extrusion in which the metal to be shaped is preshaped to fit a die forming the lower end of a high-pressure container which is filled with a pressure-transmitting liquid, the pressure being built up in the liquid by a plunger until the metal is forced through the die; **hydrostatic paradox** the principle that — disregarding molecular forces — any quantity of fluid, however small, may balance any weight, however great; **hydrostatic press** a hydraulic press; **hydrostatic transmission** see **hydrostatic drive** above. [Gr *hydōr* water]

hydrogen *hī'drō-jən*, *n* a gas (symbol **H**; atomic no 1) which in combination with oxygen produces water, is the lightest of all known substances, and very inflammable, and is of great importance in the moderation (slowing down) of neutrons. — *adj* **hy'dric** of or containing hydrogen. — *n* **hy'dride** a compound of hydrogen with an element or radical. — *adj* **hydriodic** (*hī-dri-od'ik*) of an acid composed of hydrogen and iodine, hydrogen iodide. — **hydro-** (*hī-drō-*, *hī-drə-* or *hī-dro'-*) *combining form* denoting hydrogen in a chemical compound. — *adj* **hydrobrō'mic** applied to an acid composed of hydrogen and bromine, hydrogen bromide. — *n* **hydrocar'bon** a compound of hydrogen and carbon with nothing else, occurring notably in oil, natural gas and coal. — *adj* **hydrochloric** (*-klor'ik* or *-klōr'*) applied to an acid composed of hydrogen and chlorine, hydrogen chloride, still sometimes called *muriatic acid*. — *n* **hydrochlor'ide** a compound of hydrochloric acid with an organic base. — *n* **hydrocor'tisone** one of the corticosteroids, 17-hydroxycorticosterone, a synthesized form of which is used to treat rheumatoid arthritis, etc. — *n* **hy'drocracking** cracking of petroleum, etc in the presence of hydrogen. — *adj* **hydrocyanic** (*-sī-an'ik*) denoting an acid (*prussic acid*) composed of hydrogen and cyanogen. — *adj* **hydroferricyanic** (*-fer-i-sī-an'ik*) and **hydroferrōcyan'ic** applied to two acids composed of hydrogen, iron and cyanogen, hydroferricyanic acid, $H_3Fe(CN)_6$, having an atom of hydrogen less than hydroferrocyanic, $H_4Fe(CN)_6$. — *adj* **hydrofluor'ic** applied to an acid composed of fluorine and hydrogen, hydrogen fluoride. — *n* **hydrogasificā'tion** production of methane from coal by treatment with hydrogen at high temperature and pressure. — *vt* **hydrogenate** (*hī'drō-jən-āt* or *hī-droj'ən-āt*) to (cause to) combine with hydrogen, as in the hardening of oils by converting an olein into a stearin by addition of hydrogen in the presence of a catalyst such as nickel or palladium. — *adj* **hydrog'enated**. — *n* **hydrogenā'tion**. — *vt* **hydrog'enize** or **-ise** to hydrogenate. — *adj* **hydrog'enous**. — *n* **hydrosul'phide** a compound formed by action of hydrogen sulphide on a hydroxide. — *n* **hydrosul'phite** a hyposulphite (*esp* sodium hyposulphite). — *adj* **hydrosulphū'ric** formed by a combination of hydrogen and sulphur. — *n* **hydrox'ide** a chemical compound which contains one or more hydroxyl groups. — *adj* **hydrox'y** (of a compound) containing one or more hydroxyl groups (also *combining form* **hydrox'y-**). — *n* **hydrox'yl** (Gr *hȳlē* matter) a compound radical consisting of one atom of oxygen and one of hydrogen; sometimes loosely applied to *hydrogen peroxide*. — *n* **hydroxyl'amine** a basic substance composed of a hydroxyl group and an amino group (NH_2OH). — **hydrogen bomb** or **H-bomb** a bomb in which an enormous release of energy is achieved by converting hydrogen nuclei into helium nuclei — a fusion, not fission, process started by great heat (the first H-bomb was exploded by the USA in November 1952); **hydrogen bond** a strong inter- or intra-molecular force, important in water molecule self-association and in polypeptide chain arrangement in proteins, resulting from the interaction of a hydrogen atom bonded to an electronegative atom with a lone-pair of electrons on another electronegative atom; **hydrogen ion** an atom or molecule of hydrogen having a positive charge, *esp* an atom formed in a solution of acid in water — strong acids being highly ionized and weak acids only slightly; **hydrogen peroxide** see under **peroxide**; **hydrogen sulphide** a compound of hydrogen and sulphur, H_2S; **hydronium ion** a hydrated hydrogen ion, such as H_3O^+. — **heavy hydrogen** see under **heavy**; **hydrogenation of coal** conversion of coal to liquid fuels by hydrogenation. [Coined by Cavendish (1766) from Gr *hydōr* water, and *gennaein* to produce]

hydyne *hī'dīn*, *n* an American rocket-launching fuel.

hye. An *obs* form of **hie** and **high**.

hyena or **hyaena** *hī-ē'nə*, also **hyen** *hī'en* (*Shakesp*), *n* a carrion-feeding carnivore (genus *Hyaena*, constituting a family **Hyaenidae**) with a long thick neck, coarse mane and sloping body. — **hyena dog** an African wild dog, with blotched markings like that of a hyena. — **spotted hyena** an animal (*Crocuta*) resembling a hyena, that produces a sound like a hysterical laugh. [L *hyaena*, from Gr *hyaina*, from *hȳs* a pig]

hyetal *hī'i-tl*, *adj* rainy; pertaining to rain or rainfall. — *n* **hy'etograph** a rain chart; a self-registering rain-gauge. — *adj* **hyetograph'ic** or **hyetograph'ical**. — *adv* **hyetograph'ically**. — *n* **hyetog'raphy**. — *n* **hyetol'ogy** a branch of meteorology dealing with rainfall. — *n* **hyetom'eter** a rain-gauge. — *n* **hyetomet'rograph** a self-registering rain-gauge, hyetograph. [Gr *hyetos* rain]

Hygeian *hī-jē'ən*, *adj* relating to Hygieia or to health and its preservation. [Gr *Hygieia*, later *Hygeia* goddess of health, daughter of Asklēpios (Aesculapius)]

hygiene *hī'jēn*, *n* the science or art of preserving health; sanitary principles and practices. — *adj* **hygienic** (*hī-jēn'ik*). — *adv* **hygien'ically**. — *n sing* **hygien'ics** principles of hygiene. — *n* **hygien'ist** (*hī'jēn-ist*) a person skilled in hygiene; a dental hygienist. [Fr *hygiène*, from Gr *hygieinē* (*technē*) hygienic (art), from *hygieia* health, *hygiēs* healthy]

hygristor *hī-gris'tər*, *n* an electronic component whose resistance varies with humidity. [**hygro-** and res*istor*]

hygro- *hī-grō-*, *hī-grə-* or *hī-gro'-*, *combining form* signifying wet, moist. — *n* **hygrochasy** (*hī-grok'ə-si*; Gr *chasis* a gape) dehiscence on moistening. — *adj* **hygrochas'tic**. — *n* **hy'grodeik** (*-dīk*; Gr *deiknynai* to show) a psychrometer with an index and scale. — *n* **hy'grograph** an instrument, a development of a hygroscope, for recording the humidity of the air. — *adj* **hygrograph'ic** or **hygrograph'ical**. — *n* **hygrol'ogy** the study of the humidity of the air or other gases. — *n* **hygrom'eter** an instrument for measuring the humidity of the air or of other gases. — *adj* **hygrometric** (*-met'rik*) or **hygromet'rical** belonging to hygrometry: hygroscopic. — *n* **hygrom'etry** measurement of the humidity of the air or of other gases. — *adj* **hy'grophil** or **hygrophilous** (*-grof'*; Gr *phileein* to love) moisture-loving; living where there is much moisture. — *adj* **hy'grophobe** (Gr *phobeein* to fear) growing best where moisture is scanty. — *n* **hy'grophyte** (*-fīt*; Gr *phyton* plant) a plant adapted to plentiful water-supply. — *adj* **hygrophytic** (*-fit'ik*). — *n* **hy'groscope** an instrument that shows, without measuring, changes in the humidity of the air. — *adj* **hygroscopic** (*-skop'ik*) or **hygroscop'ical** relating to the hygroscope; readily absorbing moisture from the air; (of eg some movements of plants) indicating or caused by absorption or loss of moisture. — *n* **hygroscopicity** (*-skop-is'i-ti*). — *n* **hy'grostat** an apparatus which produces constant humidity. — **hygroscopic salt** a salt, *esp* calcium chloride, which absorbs moisture from other substances. [Gr *hygros* wet]

hying *hī'ing*, *pr p* of **hie**[1,2].

hyke *hīk*, *n*. See **haik**[1].

Hyksos *hik'sos* or *-sōs*, *n* a foreign line of kings (the xv and xvi dynasties, called the shepherd kings) who ruled Egypt for centuries. [Gr *Hyksōs*, from Egyptian *Hiku-khasut* princes of the desert, appar misunderstood as shepherd princes]

hylding (*Spenser*). Same as **hilding**.

hyle *hī'lē*, *n* wood, matter. — *adj* **hy'lic** material; corporeal. — *n* **hy'licism** or **hy'lism** materialism. — *n* **hy'licist** or **hy'list** (also *wrongly* **hy'loist**). — *n* **hy'lobate** a gibbon (genus **Hylob'atēs**; from the root of Gr *bainein* to go). — *n* **hylogen'esis** the origin of matter. — *adj* **hylomor'phic**. — *n* **hylomor'phism** (*philos*) the doctrine that matter is the first cause of the universe. — *n* **hylop'athism** (Gr *pathos* feeling) the doctrine that matter is sentient. — *n* **hylop'athist**. — *adj* **hyloph'agous** (Gr *phagein* to eat) wood-eating. — *n* **hy'lophyte** (Gr *phyton* plant) a woodland plant. — *n* **hy'lotheism** (Gr *theos* god) the doctrine that there is no God but matter and the universe. — *n* **hy'lotheist**. — *adj* **hylot'omous** (Gr *tomē* a cut) wood-cutting. — *adj* **hylozō'ical** or **hylozoist'ic**. — *n* **hylozō'ism** (Gr *zōē* life) the doctrine that all matter is endowed with life. — *n* **hylozō'ist**. [Gr *hȳlē* wood, matter]

hyleg *hī'leg*, *n* the ruling planet at the hour of birth. [Origin obscure; cf Pers *hailāj* nativity]

Hymen *hī'men*, *n* the god of marriage (*mythol*); marriage (*archaic*). — *adj* **hymenē'al** or **hymenē'an** (also **hymenae'al** or **hymenae'an**). — *n* **hymenē'al** wedding hymn; (in *pl*) nuptials (*archaic*). [Gr wedding-cry, perh also a god]

hymen *hī'men*, *n* a membrane; a thin membrane partially closing the vagina of a virgin. — *adj* **hy'menal** pertaining to the hymen. — *adj* **hymē'nial** pertaining to the hymenium. — *n* **hymē'nium** the spore-bearing surface in fungi. — *n pl* **Hymenomycetes** (*hī-mən-ō-mī-sē'tēz*) an order of fungi with exposed hymenium from an early stage eg toadstools, etc. — *n pl* **Hymenophyllā'ceae** the filmy ferns. — *adj* **hymenophyllā'ceous**. — *n pl* **Hymenop'tera** an order of insects with four transparent wings eg ants, bees, wasps, etc. — *n* and *adj* **hymenop'teran**. — *adj* **hymenop'terous**. [Gr *hymēn* membrane]

hymn *him*, *n* a song of praise, *esp* to God, but also to a nation, etc. — *vt* to celebrate in song; to worship by hymns. — *vi* to sing in adoration: — *pr p* **hymning** (*him'ing* or *him'ning*); *pa t* and *pa p* **hymned** (*himd* or *him'nid*). — *n* **hym'nal** or **hym'nary** a hymn-book. — Also *adj*. — *adj* **hym'nic**. — *n* **hym'nist** or **hym'nodist** a person who composes hymns. — *n* **hym'nody** hymns collectively; hymn-singing; hymnology. — *n* **hymnog'rapher**. — *n* **hymnog'raphy** the art of writing hymns; the study of hymns. — *n* **hymnol'ogist**. — *n* **hymnol'ogy** the study or composition of hymns. — **hymn'-book** a book of hymns. [Gr *hymnos*]

hynde. A Spenserian spelling of **hind**[2].

hyoid *hī'oid*, *adj* having the form of the Greek letter upsilon (υ), applied to a bone at the base of the tongue. [Gr *hyoeidēs*, from *hȳ*, the letter upsilon, and *eidos* form]

hyoplastron *hī-ō-plas'tron*, *n* in a turtle's plastron, a plate between the hypoplastron and the entoplastron: — *pl* **hyoplas'tra**. — *adj* **hyoplas'tral**. [Gr *hȳ* the letter upsilon]

Hyoscyamus *hī-ō-sī'ə-məs*, *n* the henbane genus. — *n* **hy'oscine** (*-sēn* or *-sən*; also called **scopolamine**; used as a truth drug, for travel sickness, etc) and **hyoscy'amine** two poisonous alkaloids similar to atropine, obtained from henbane. [Gr *hyoskyamos*]

hyp. *abbrev*: hypotenuse; hypothesis; hypothetical.

hyp. See **hip**[3].

hypabyssal *hip-ə-bis'l*, (*petrology*) *adj* moderately deep-seated, not quite abyssal, intermediate between plutonic and eruptive. [Gr *hypo* beneath]

hypaethral *hi-pē'thrəl* or (*esp NAm*) *hī-*, *adj* roofless, open to the sky. — *n* **hypae'thron** an open court. [Gr *hypo* beneath, and *aithēr* upper air, sky]

hypalgesia *hip-al-jē'si-ə* or *-zi-ə*, or *hīp'*, *n* diminished susceptibility to pain. — Also **hypal'gia**. — *adj* **hypalgē'sic**. [Gr *hypo* under, and *algēsis*, *algos* pain]

hypallage *hi-pal'ə-je* or *hī-*, (*rhetoric*) *n* a figure in which the relations of words in a sentence are mutually interchanged. — *adj* **hypallact'ic**. [Gr *hypo* under, and *allassein* to exchange]

hypanthium *hi-* or *hī-pan'thi-əm*, *n* the flat or concave receptacle of a perigynous flower. [Gr *hypo* under, and *anthos* flower]

hypate *hi'pə-tē*, (*Gr music*) *n* the lowest string of the lyre, or its tone. [Gr *hypatē* highest (fem), prob as having the longest string]

hype *hīp*, (*slang*) *n* a hypodermic needle; a drug addict; something which stimulates artificially; intensive or artificially induced excitement about or enthusiasm for something or someone; a sales gimmick, etc; a publicity stunt; the person or thing promoted by such a stunt; a deception. — *vi* (*esp* with *up*) to inject oneself with a drug. — *vt* (often with *up*) to stimulate artificially; to promote or to advertize extravagantly. — *n* **hyp'er** someone who or that which hypes. — *adj* over-stimulated. — **hyped up** (or **hyped'-up** when *attrib*) artificially stimulated; highly excited; artificial, fake. [Abbrev of **hypodermic** (under **hypo-**)]

hyper- *hī'pər-* or *hī-pûr'-*, *combining form* signifying: over; excessive; more than normal. — *n* **hyperacid'ity** excessive acidity, *esp* in the stomach. — *adj* **hyperact'ive** (*med*) abnormally or pathologically active. — *n* **hyperactiv'ity**. — *n* **hyperacusis** (*-ə-kū'sis*; Gr *akousis* hearing) abnormally increased power of hearing. — *adj* **hyperacute'**. — *n* **hyperacute'ness**. — *n* **hyperadrē'nalism** excessive activity of the adrenal gland. — *n* **hyperaemia** or (*NAm*) **hyperemia** (*-ē'mi-ə*; Gr *haima* blood) congestion or excess of blood in any part. — *adj* **hyperae'mic** or (*NAm*) **hypere'mic**. — *n* **hyperaesthesia** (*-ēs-thē'zi-ə*) or (*NAm*) **hyperesthesia** (*-is-thē'*; Gr *aisthēsis* perception) excessive sensitivity to stimuli; an abnormal extension of the bodily senses assumed to explain telepathy and clairvoyance; exaggerated aestheticism. — *adj* **hyperaesthē'sic**, **hyperaesthetic** or (*NAm*) **hyperesthetic** (*-thet'ik*) overaesthetic; abnormally or morbidly sensitive. — *n* **hyperalgē'sia** (*-si-ə* or *-zi-ə*; Gr *algēsis* pain) heightened sensitivity to pain. — *adj* **hyperalgē'sic**. — *adj* **hyperbar'ic** having specific gravity greater than that of cerebrospinal fluid (*spinal anaesthesia*); pertaining to conditions of high atmospheric pressure with a greater concentration of oxygen than normal, as in a **hyperbaric chamber**, a chamber containing oxygen at high pressure. — *adj* **hyperbat'ic**. — *adv* **hyperbat'ically**. — *n* **hyper'baton** (Gr, from the root of *bainein* to go; *rhetoric*) a figure of speech in which the customary order of words is reversed. — *n* **hyper'bola** (Gr *hyperbolē* overshooting, from *ballein* to throw; *pl* usually **hyper'bolas**; *geom*) one of the conic sections, the intersection of a plane with a cone when the plane cuts both branches of the cone. — *n* **hyperbole** (*hī-pûr'bə-lē*) a rhetorical figure which produces a vivid impression by extravagant and obvious exaggeration. — *adj* **hyperbol'ic** or **hyperbol'ical** of a hyperbola or hyperbole. — *adv* **hyperbol'ically**. — *vi* to speak hyperbolically or with exaggeration. — *n* **hyper'bolism**. — *vt* **hyper'bolize** or **-ise** to represent hyperbolically. — *n* **hyper'boloid** a solid figure in which some of the plane sections are hyperbolas. — *adj* **hyperborean** (*-bö'*; Gr *Hyperboreoi* a people supposed to live in sunshine beyond the north wind, from *Boreas* the north wind) belonging to the extreme north. — *n* an inhabitant of the extreme north. — *n* **hypercalcae'mia** or **hypercalce'mia** abnormal rise in the calcium content of the blood. — *adj* **hypercatalect'ic** (*prosody*) having an additional syllable or half-foot after the last complete dipody. — *n* **hypercatalex'is**. — *n* **hy'percharge** the strangeness of a particle plus its baryon number. — *vt* (*-chärj'*) to charge excessively, to overload. — *n* **hypercholesterolae'mia** a condition characterized by an abnormally high level of blood cholesterol. — *adj* **hypercon'scious** more than normally aware (of). — *adj* **hypercorrect'** over-correct; very critical; due to or showing hypercorrection. — *n* **hypercorrec'tion** a correction made in the mistaken belief that nonstandard linguistic usage is being thus avoided, eg the erroneous use of *I* in the place of *me* in phrases such as *Between you and I*. — *n* **hypercorrect'ness**. — *n* **hypercrit'ic** someone who is over-critical; a carper. — *adj* **hypercrit'ic** or **hypercrit'ical** excessively critical, *esp* of very small faults. — *adv* **hypercrit'ically**. — *n* **hypercrit'icism**. — *vt* **hypercrit'icize** or **-ise** (*-sīz*). — *n* **hy'percube** (*math*) a theoretical solid in four or more dimensions, all sides being equal and all angles right angles. — *adj* **hyperdac'tyl** (Gr *daktylos* finger, toe). — *n* **hyperdac'tyly** possession of more than five fingers or toes. — *adj* **hyperdorian** (*-dö'*; Gr *hyperdōrios*; *music*) above the Dorian mode; applied in ancient Greek music to a mode having as its lower tetrachord the upper tetrachord of the Dorian (as: *b c d e*; *e f g a*; *b*). — *n* **hyperdulia** (*-doo-lī'ə*) see under **dulia**. — *n* **hyperem'esis** (Gr *emesis* vomiting) excessive vomiting. — *adj* **hyperemet'ic**. — *n* **hyperemia**, **hyperesthesia** see **hyperaemia**, **hyperaesthesia** above. — *adj* **hypereutec'tic** (of a compound) containing more of the minor component than an eutectic compound. — *adj* **hyperfō'cal** (*photog*) referring to the minimum distance from a lens to the point from which all objects can be focused clearly. — *adj* **hyper'gamous** pertaining to hypergamy. — *n* **hypergamy** (*hī-pûr'gə-mi*; Gr *gamos* marriage) a custom that allows a man but forbids a woman to marry a person of lower social standing; now sometimes more generally marriage of one person with another of higher social rank. — *n* **hyperglycaemia** or (*NAm*) **hyperglycemia** (*-glī-sē'mi-ə*) abnormal rise in the sugar content of the blood. — *adj* **hypergolic** (*-gol'ik*) (of two or more liquids) spontaneously explosive on mixing. — *n* **hyperhidrō'sis** or **hyperidrō'sis** excessive sweating. — *n* **hyperinflā'tion** (*econ*) rapid inflation uncontrollable by normal means. — *n* **hyperinō'sis** (Gr *īs*, *īnos* strength, fibre) excess of fibrin in the blood. — *adj* **hyperinot'ic**. — *n* **hyperlink'** a form of cross-reference in computer-readable text which allows instant access to related material. — *adj* **hyperlydian** (*-lid'i-ən*; Gr *hyperlȳdios*) above the Lydian mode; applied in ancient Greek music to a mode having as its lower tetrachord the upper tetrachord of the Lydian (as: *g a b c*; *c d e f*; *g*). — *n* **hyperman'ia** (*psychiatry*) an extreme form of mania. — *adj* **hyperman'ic**. — *n* **hy'permarket** or **hy'permart** a very large self-service store with a wide range of goods. — *adj* **hypermet'rical** (*prosody*) beyond or exceeding the ordinary metre of a line; having or being an additional syllable. — *n* **hypermetrō'pia** (Gr *metron* measure, and *ōps* eye) long-sightedness. — Also **hyperō'pia**. — *adj* **hypermetrop'ic**. — *n* **hypernatraemia** (*-nə-trē'mi-ə*; *natrium* (see **natron**) and Gr *haime* blood) an abnormally high concentration of sodium chloride (salt) in the blood, *esp* in infants. — *n* **hy'pernym** (Gr *onyma* name) a superordinate word representing a class or family of which several other words can be members, as *flower* is a hypernym of *rose* and *daisy*. — *n* **hyper'nymy**. — *n* **hy'peron** any baryon that is not a neutron. — *n* **hyperopia** see **hypermetropia** above. — *n* **hyperpar'asite** a parasite living on another parasite. — *n* **hyperphagia** (*-fā'ji-ə*) bulimia. — *adj* **hyperphrygian** (*-frij'i-ən* or *-frij'ən*; Gr *hyperphrygios*) above the Phrygian; applied to a mode of ancient Greek music having as its lower tetrachord the upper tetrachord of the Phrygian (as: *a b c d*; *d e f g*; *a*). — *adj* **hyperphys'ical** beyond physical laws; supernatural. — *n* **hyperplasia** (*-plā'zi-ə* or *-zhə*; Gr *plasis* a forming; *pathol*) overgrowth of a part due to excessive multiplication of its cells. — *adj* **hyperplastic** (*-plas'*). — *adj* **hyperpyretic** (*-pir-et'ik*; Gr *pyretikos* feverish). — *n* **hyperpyrex'ia** abnormally high body temperature. — *n* **hypersarcō'ma** or **hypersarcō'sis** (Gr *hypersarkōma*, *hypersarkōsis*, from *sarx* flesh; *pathol*) proud or fungous flesh. — *adj* **hypersens'itive** excessively sensitive. — *n* **hypersens'itiveness**. — *n* **hypersensitiv'ity**. — *n* **hypersensitizā'tion** or **-s-**. — *vt* **hypersens'itize** or **-ise** to increase the sensitivity of. — *adj* **hypersen'sūal** beyond the scope of the senses. — *n* **hypersom'nia** (L *somnus* sleep) a pathological tendency to sleep excessively. — *adj* **hyperson'ic** (L *sonus* sound) (of speeds) greater than Mach 5; (of aircraft) able to fly at such speeds; (of sound waves) having a frequency greater than 1000 million Hz. — *n pl* **hyperson'ics**. — *n* **hy'perspace** (*math*) space having more than three dimensions; (in science fiction) a theoretical fourth dimension. — *n* **hypersthene** (*hī'pər-sthēn*; Gr *sthenos* strength, because harder than hornblende) rock-forming orthorhombic pyroxene, anhydrous silicate of magnesium and iron, generally dark green, brown, or raven-black with a metallic lustre. — *n* **hypersthē'nia** (*pathol*) a morbid condition marked by excessive excitement of all the vital phenomena. — *adj* **hypersthenic** (*-sthen'ik*) of hypersthene or of hypersthenia. — *n* **hypersthē'nite** a rock consisting almost entirely of hypersthene; an aggregate of labradorite and hypersthene (*obs*). — *n* **hy'perstress** excessive stress. — *n* **hyperten'sion** blood pressure higher than normal; a state of great emotional tension. — *adj* **hyperten'sive**. — *n* a victim of hypertension. — *n* **hy'pertext** computer-readable text which allows very extensive cross-referencing. — Also *adj*. — *adj* **hyper-therm'al**. — *n* **hypertherm'ia** (dangerous) overheating of the body. — *n* **hyperthyroidism** (*-thī'roid-izm*) overproduction of thyroid hormone by the thyroid gland, and the resulting condition. — *adj* **hyperton'ic** (of muscles) having excessive tone; tensed to an abnormally high degree; (of a solution) having a higher osmotic pressure than a specified solution. — *adj* **hypertroph'ic, hypertroph'ical, hyper'trophied** or **hyper'-trophous** (Gr *trophē* nourishment). — *n* **hyper'trophy** overnourishment (of an organ, etc) causing abnormal enlargement. — *n* **hyperveloc'ity** very great speed, as of nuclear particles. — *vi* **hyperven'tilate**. — *n* **hyper-ventilā'tion** abnormally increased speed and depth of breathing. — *n* **hypervitaminō'sis** the condition resulting from too much of any vitamin (*esp* vitamin D). — **hyperbolic functions** (*math*) a set of six functions (sinh, cosh, tanh, etc) analogous to the trigonometrical functions; **hyperbolic geometry** that involving the axiom that through any point in a given plane there can be drawn more than one line that does not intersect a given line; **hyperbolic logarithms** natural logarithms; **hyperbolic paraboloid** a saddle-shaped surface represented by the equation $x^2/a - y^2/b = z$; **hyperbolic spiral** a spiral of polar equation $\rho\theta = k^2$; **hyperfine structure** (*phys*) the splitting of spectrum lines into two or more very closely spaced components. [Gr *hyper* over]

hyperb. *abbrev*: hyperbolically.

Hypericum *hī-per'i-kəm*, *n* the St John's wort genus of plants, shrubs with yellow five-petalled flowers, giving name to the family **Hypericā'ceae**. [Gr *hyperikon* or *hypereikos*, from *hypo* under, and *ereikē* heath]

Hyperion *hī-pēr'i-on*, (*Gr mythol*) *n* a Titan, son of Uranus and Ge, and father of Helios, Selene and Eos; Helios himself, the incarnation of light and beauty; a satellite of Saturn. [Gr *Hyperiōn*]

hypha *hī'fə*, *n* a thread of fungus mycelium: — *pl* **hy'phae** (*-fē*). — *adj* **hy'phal**. [Gr *hyphē* web]

hyphen *hī'fən*, *n* a short stroke (-) joining two syllables or words. — *vt* to hyphenate. — *vt* **hy'phenate** to join or separate by a hyphen. — *adj* hyphened; hyphenated. — *n* a hyphenated American. — *adj* **hy'phenated** hyphened; of mixed nationality, expressed by a hyphened word, such as *Irish-American* (*NAm*); of divided or alien national sympathies. — *n* **hyphena'tion**. — *adj* **hy'phened** containing a hyphen. — *adj* **hyphenic** (*-fen'ik*). — *n* **hy'phenism** state of being a hyphenate. — *n* **hyphenīzā'tion** or **-s-** hyphenation. — *vt* **hy'phenize** or **-ise**. [Gr *hyphen*, from *hypo* under, and *hen* one]

hypinosis *hip-i-nō'sis*, *n* a deficiency of fibrin in the blood; opposite of **hyperinosis** (see under **hyper-**). [Gr *hypo* under, and *īs*, *īnos* fibre]

hypnagogic, hypnogogic image. See under **hypno-**.

hypno- *hip-nō-*, *hip-nə-* or *hip-no'-*, or **hypn-** *combining form* denoting: sleep; hypnosis. — *adj* **hypnagogic** (*-goj'ik* or *-gog'ik*; Gr *agōgos* bringing) sleep-bringing; ushering in sleep; pertaining to a state of drowsiness preceding sleep. — *adj* **hyp'nic** pertaining to or inducing sleep. — *n* a soporific. — *n* **hypno-anaesthē'sia** hypnotic sleep. — *n* **hypno-anal'ysis** analysis of a patient's psychological troubles by obtaining information from him or her while in a state of hypnosis. — *n* **hypnogen'esis** or **hypnogeny** (*-noj'i-ni*) production of the hypnotic state. — *adj* **hypnogenet'ic, hypnog'enous** or **hypnogen'ic** inducing the hypnotic state, or sleep. — *adj* **hyp'noid** or **hyp'noidal** like sleep; like hypnosis; *esp* of a state between hypnosis and waking. — *vt* **hyp'-noidize** or **-ise** to put in the hypnoidal state. — *n* **hypnol'ogy** the scientific study of sleep. — *n* **hyp'none** an aromatic ketone used in medicine as a hypnotic. — *n* **hypnopae'dia** learning or conditioning, by repetition of recorded sound during sleep (or semiwakefulness). — *adj* **hypnopomp'ic** (Gr *pompē* a sending) dispelling sleep; pertaining to a state between sleep and wakefulness. — *n* **hypnō'sis** a sleeplike state in which the mind responds to external suggestion and can recover forgotten memories. — *n* **hypnotee'** a person who has been hypnotized. — *n* **hypnother'apy** the treatment of illness by hypnotism. — *adj* **hypnot'ic** of or relating to hypnosis; soporific. — *n* a soporific; a person subject to hypnotism or in a state of hypnosis. — *adv* **hypnot'ically**. — *n* **hyp'notism** the science of hypnosis; the art or practice of inducing hypnosis; hypnosis. — *n* **hyp'notist** a person skilled in hypnotism. — *adj* **hypnotist'ic**. — *n* **hypnotizabil'ity** or **-s-**. — *adj* **hypnotīz'able** or **-s-**. — *n* **hypnotīzā'tion** or **-s-**. — *vt* **hyp'notize** or **-ise** to put in a state of hypnosis; to fascinate, dazzle, overpower the mind of. — *n* **hyp'-notīzer** or **-s-**. — *adj* **hyp'notoid** like hypnosis. — **hypnagogic** (or **hypnogogic**) **image** hallucination experienced when falling asleep or fatigued; **hypnotic suggestion** suggestion (qv) made to a person under hypnosis. [Gr *hypnos* sleep]

Hypnos *hip'nos*, (*Gr mythol*) *n* the god of sleep.

hypnum *hip'nəm*, *n* any moss of the large *Hypnum* genus (often divided), with capsules on special lateral branches. [Latinized from Gr *hypnon* a kind of lichen]

hypo *hī'po*, (*colloq*) *n* short for **hyposulphite**, in the sense of sodium thiosulphate, used as a fixing agent (*photog*); short for **hypodermic syringe** or **injection** (see also **hype**); short for (an attack of) **hypoglycaemia**: — *pl* **hy'pos**. — *adj* short for **hypodermic**; short for **hypo-glycaemic**.

hypo- *hī-pō-*, *hī-pə-* or *hī-po'-* or occasionally *hip-ō-* or *hi-po'-*, *combining form* signifying: under; defective; inadequate. — *adj* **hypoaeolian** (*hī-pō-ē-ō'li-ən*) below the Aeolian mode; applied in old church music to a plagal mode extending from *e* to *e*, with *a* for its final. — *adj* **hypoallergen'ic** specially formulated in order to minimize the risk of allergy. — *n* **hypoblast** (*-bläst*; Gr *blastos* bud; *zool*) the inner germ-layer of a gastrula. — *adj* **hypoblast'ic**. — *n* **hypobole** (*hip-ob'ə-lē*; Gr *hypobolē* throwing under, suggestion, from *ballein* to throw; *rhetoric*) anticipation of objections. — *n* **hypocaust** (*-köst*; Gr *hypokauston*, from *hypo* under, and *kaiein* to burn) a space under a floor for heating by hot air or furnace gases, *esp* in ancient Roman villas. — *n* **hy'pocentre** the point on the centre of the earth directly below the centre of explosion of a nuclear bomb. — *n* **hypochlorite** (*-klö'rīt*) a salt of **hypochlo'rous acid**, an acid (HClO) with less oxygen than chlorous acid. — *n* **hypochondria** (*-kon'dri-ə*) *orig* the *pl* of **hypochondrium** (see below); morbid anxiety about health; imaginary illness; a nervous malady, often arising from indigestion, and tormenting the patient with imaginary fears (once supposed to have its seat in the abdomen) (*obs*). — *adj* **hypochon'driac** relating to or affected with hypochondria; melancholy. — *n* a sufferer from hypochondria. — *adj* **hypochondrī'acal**. — *n* **hypo-chondrī'asis, hypochondrī'acism** or **hypochon'driasm** hypochondria. — *n* **hypochon'driast** someone suffering from hypochondria. — *n* **hypochon'drium** (Gr *hypo-chondrion*, from *chondros* cartilage; *anatom*) the region of the abdomen on either side, under the costal cartilages and short ribs. — *n* **hypocist** (*hī'pō-sist*; Gr *hypokistis*, from *kistos* cistus) an inspissated juice from the fruit of *Cytinus hypocistis* (Rafflesiaceae), a plant parasitic on cistus roots. — *n* **hypocorism** (*hī-pok'ə-rizm*) or **hypocorisma** (*-iz'mə*; Gr *hypokorisma*, from *hypokorizesthai* to use child-talk, from *koros* boy, *korē* girl) a pet-name; a diminutive or abbreviated name. — *adj* **hypocorist'ic** or **hypocorist'ical**. — *adv* **hypocorist'-ically**. — *n* **hypocotyl** (*-kot'il*) that part of the axis of a plant which is between the cotyledons and the primary root. — *adj* **hypocotylē'donary**. — *n* **hypocrisy** (*hi-pok'ri-si*; Gr *hypokrisiā* acting, playing a part) a feigning to be better than one is, or to be what one is not; concealment of true character or belief (not necessarily conscious); an instance or act of hypocrisy. — *n* **hypocrite** (*hip'ə-krit*; Gr *hypokritēs* actor) a person who practises hypocrisy. — *adj* **hypocrit'ical** (also

hypocrit'ic) practising hypocrisy; of the nature of hypocrisy. — *adv* **hypocrit'ically**. — *n* **hypocycloid** (*-sī'kloid*) a curve generated by a point on the circumference of a circle which rolls on the inside of another circle. — *adj* **hypocycloid'al**. — *n* **hypoderm** (*-dûrm*), **hypoder'ma** or **hypoder'mis** (Gr *derma* skin; *bot* and *anatom*) the tissue next under the epidermis. — *adj* **hypoderm'al**. — *adj* **hypoderm'ic** pertaining to the hypodermis; under the epidermis; under the skin, subcutaneous, *esp* of a method of injecting a drug in solution under the skin by means of a fine hollow needle to which a small syringe is attached. — *n* a hypodermic injection; a drug so injected; a syringe for the purpose. — *adv* **hypoder'mically**. — *adj* **hypodorian** (*-dō'ri-ən*; Gr *hypodōrios*) below the Dorian; applied in ancient Greek music to a mode whose upper tetrachord is the lower tetrachord of the Dorian (as: *a*; *b c d e*; *e f g a*), and in old church music to a plagal mode extending from *a* to *a*, with *d* as its final. — *adj* **hypoeutec'tic** (of a compound) containing less of the minor component than a eutectic compound. — *adj* **hypogastric** (*-gas'trik*; Gr *gastēr* belly) belonging to the lower median part of the abdomen. — *n* **hypogas'trium** the hypogastric region. — *adj* **hypogeal** or **hypogaeal** (*-jē'əl*), **hypoge'an** or **hypogae'an** (*-jē'ən*), **hypoge'ous** or **hypogae'ous** (*-je'əs*) (Gr *hypogeios*, *-gaios*, from *gē* or *gaia* the ground; *bot*) underground; germinating with cotyledons underground. — *adj* **hypogene** (*-jēn*; Gr *gennaein* to engender; *geol*) of or pertaining to rocks formed, or agencies at work, under the earth's surface; plutonic (opposite of *epigene*). — *n* **hypogeum** or **hypogaeum** (*-jē'əm*) an underground chamber; a subterranean tomb: — *pl* **hypoge'a** or **hypogae'a**. — *adj* **hypoglossal** (*-glos'əl*; Gr *glōssa* the tongue) under the tongue. — *n* **hypoglycaemia** or **hypoglycemia** (*hī-pō-gli-sē'mi-ə*; *med*) abnormal reduction of sugar content of the blood. — *adj* **hypoglycae'mic** or **hypoglyce'mic**. — *n* **hypog'nathism**. — *adj* **hypognathous** (*hīp-* or *hip-og'nə-thəs*) having the lower jaw or mandible protruding. — *adj* **hypogynous** (*hī-poj'i-nəs*; Gr *gynē* a woman, female; *bot*) growing from beneath the ovary; having the other floral parts below the ovary. — *n* **hypog'yny**. — *adj* **hy'poid** of a type of bevel gear in which the axes of the driving and driven shafts are at right angles but not in the same plane. — *n* **hypolim'nion** (Gr *limnion*, dimin of *limnē* lake) a lower and colder layer of water in a lake. — *adj* **hypolydian** (*hī-pō-lid'i-ən*) below the Lydian mode; applied in ancient Greek music to a mode having as its upper tetrachord the lower tetrachord of the Lydian (as: *f*; *g a b c*; *c d e f*) and in old church music to a plagal mode extending from *c* to *c* with *f* as its final. — *n* **hypomagnesaemia** (*hī-pō-mag-nə-zē'mi-ə*) a condition, *esp* in cattle, characterized by an abnormally low level of magnesium in the blood. — *n* **hypomania** (*-mā'ni-ə*; *med*) a milder form of mania, a condition marked by overexcitability. — *adj* **hypomā'nic** (or *-man'ik*). — *n* **hypomenorrhea** or **hypomenorrhoea** (*-men-ə-rē'ə*; *med*) the condition in which the interval between two menstrual periods is increased to between 35 and 42 days. — *adj* **hypomixolydian** (*hī-pō-mik-sō-lid'i-ən*) applied in old church music to a mode extending from *d* to *d* with *g* as its final. — *n* **hyponasty** (*-nas-ti*; Gr *nastos* pressed close; *bot*) increased growth on the lower side causing an upward bend (opposite to *epinasty*). — *n* **hyponī'trite** a salt or ester of **hyponī'trous acid**, a crystalline acid, $H_2N_2O_2$, an oxidizing or reducing agent. — *n* **hyponym** (Gr *onyma* = *onoma* a name) one of a group of terms whose meanings are included in the meaning of a more general term, eg *spaniel* and *puppy* in the meaning of *dog*. — *n* **hypon'ymy**. — *n* **hypophosphite** (*-fos'fīt*) a salt of **hypophosphorous acid**, an acid (H_3PO_2) with less oxygen than phosphorous acid. — *adj* **hypophrygian** (*-frij'i-ən*) below the Phrygian mode; applied in ancient Greek music to a mode having as its upper tetrachord the lower tetrachord of the Phrygian (as: *g*; *a b c d*; *d e f g*), and in old church music to a plagal mode extending from *b* to *b*, with *e* for its final. — *adj* **hypophyseal** or **hypophysial** (*-fiz'i-əl*). — *n* **hypophysec'tomy** surgical removal of the pituitary gland. — *n* **hypophysis** (*hī-pof'i-sis*; Gr *hypophysis* an attachment underneath, from *phyein* to grow: — *pl* **hypophysēs**) a down-growth (*zool*); the pituitary gland; an inflated part of the pedicel under the capsule, in mosses (*bot*); (in flowering plants) a cell between the suspensor and the embryo proper. — *n* **hypopitū'itarism** underproduction of growth hormones by the pituitary gland. — *n* **hypoplasia** (*-plā'zi-ə* or *-zhə*; Gr *plasis* a forming; *pathol*) underdevelopment or immaturity of an organ. — *adj* **hypoplastic** (*-plas'-*). — *n* **hypoplastron** (*-plas'tron*; *zool*) the plate behind the hyoplastron in a turtle's plastron. — *n* **hypostasis** (*hip-* or *hīp-os'tə-sis*; Gr *hypostasis*, from *stasis* setting; *pl* **hypostasēs**) *orig* basis, foundation; substance, essence (*metaphys*); the essence or real personal subsistence or substance of each of the three divisions of the Trinity; Christ as the union of human and divine qualities (*theol*); sediment, deposit; passive hyperaemia in a dependent part owing to sluggishness of circulation (*med*). — *vt* **hypostasize** or **-ise** same as **hypostatize** below. — *adj* **hypostatic** (*-stat'ik*) or **hypostat'ical**. — *adv* **hypostat'ically**. — *vt* **hypos'tatize** or **-ise** to treat as hypostasis; to personify. — *n* **hyp'ostress** insufficient stress. — *n* **hypostrophe** (*hip-* or *hīp-os'trə-fi*; Gr *hypostrophē* turning back) relapse (*med*); reversion after a parenthesis (*rhetoric*). — *adj* **hypostyle** (*hip'* or *hīp'ō-stīl*; Gr *stȳlos* a pillar; *archit*) having the roof supported by pillars. — Also *n*. — *n* **hyposul'phate** a dithionate. — *n* **hyposul'phite** a salt of **hyposulphurous acid** ($H_2S_2O_4$; also, in older usage $H_2S_2O_3$). — *adj* **hyposulphūr'ic** dithionic. — *adj* **hypotac'tic**. — *n* **hypotaxis** (*-tak'sis*; Gr *taxis* arrangement; *gram*) dependent construction; subordination of one clause to another (*opp* of *parataxis*). — *n* **hypoten'sion** low blood-pressure. — *adj* **hypoten'sive** characterized by low blood-pressure; reducing blood-pressure. — *n* a person with low blood-pressure. — *n* **hypotenuse** (*hīp-* or *hip-ot'ən-ūs*, or *-ūz*) or **hypothenuse** (*-oth'*; Fr *hypoténuse*, from L *hypotēnūsa*, from Gr *hypoteinousa* fem participle, subtending or stretching under, from *teinein* to stretch) the side of a right-angled triangle opposite to the right angle. — *n* **hypothalamus** (*-thal'ə-məs*; LL; *med*) the part of the brain which makes up the floor and part of the lateral walls of the third ventricle. — *adj* **hypothalam'ic**. — *n* **hypothec** (*hip-* or *hīp-oth'ik*; Gr *hypothēkē* a pledge) in Scots law, a lien or security over goods in respect of a debt due by the owner of the goods (**the hale** (or **whole**) **hypothec** (*Scot*) the whole affair, collection, concern — everything). — *adj* **hypoth'ecary** pertaining to hypothecation or mortgage. — *vt* **hypoth'ecate** to place or assign as security under an arrangement; to mortgage; to hypothesize (*NAm*). — *n* **hypothecā'tion**. — *n* **hypoth'ecātor**. — *adj* **hypotherm'al**. — *n* **hypothermia** (*-thûr'mi-ə*; Gr *thermē* heat) subnormal body temperature, caused by exposure to cold or induced for purposes of heart and other surgery (see **freeze down**). — *n* **hypothesis** (*hī-poth'i-sis*; Gr *hypothesis*, from *thesis* placing) a supposition: a proposition assumed for the sake of argument; a theory to be proved or disproved by reference to facts; a provisional explanation of anything: — *pl* **hypoth'esēs**. — *vt* and *vi* **hypoth'esize**, **-ise**, **hypoth'etize** or **-ise**. — *adj* **hypothet'ic** or **hypothet'ical**. — *adv* **hypothet'ically**. — *adj* **hypothy'roid** pertaining to or affected by hypothyroidism. — *n* **hypothy'roidism** insufficient activity of the thyroid gland; a condition resulting from this, cretinism, etc. — *n* **hypotōn'ia** a hypnotic condition. — *adj* **hypoton'ic** (of muscles) lacking normal tone; (of a solution) having lower osmotic pressure than a specified solution. — *n* **hypotrochoid** (*-trō'koid*; Gr *trochos* wheel, and *eidos* form) the curve traced by a point on the radius, or radius produced, of a circle rolling within another circle. — *n* **hypotyposis** (*-tīp-ō'sis*; *rhetoric*) vivid description of a scene. — *n* **hypoventilā'tion** abnormally decreased speed and depth of breathing. — *n* **hypoxaemia** or (*NAm*) **hypoxemia** (*-ē'mi-ə*) deficiency of oxygenation of the blood. — *adj* **hypoxaem'ic** or **hypoxem'ic**. — *n* **hypox'ia** deficiency of oxygen reaching the body tissues. — *adj* **hypox'ic**. [Gr *hypo* under]

hypso- *hipsō-*, *hip-sə-* or *hip-so'-* *combining form* signifying height. — *n* **hypsography** (*-sog'rə-fi*; Gr *graphein* to write) the branch of geography dealing with the measurement and mapping of heights above sea-level; a map showing topographic relief; a method of making such a map. — *n* **hypsometry** (*hip-som'ə-tri*; Gr *metron* a measure) the art of measuring the heights of places on the earth's surface. — *n* **hypsom'eter** an instrument for doing this by taking the boiling point of water. — *adj* **hypsomet'ric**. — *n* **hyp'sophobe** a person suffering from **hypsophobia** (*hip-sō-fō'bi-ə*; Gr *phobos* fear) fear of (falling from) high places. — *n* **hypsophyll** (*hip'sō-fil*; Gr *phyllon* leaf; *bot*) a bract. — *adj* **hypsophyll'ary**. [Gr *hypsos* height]

hypural *hī-pū'rəl*, *adj* situated beneath the tail. [Gr *hypo* under, and *ourā* tail]

Hyrax *hī'raks*, *n* a genus (also called **Procavia**) of mammals superficially like marmots but really more closely related to the ungulates, living among rocks in Africa and Syria, ie the daman, the dassie or rock-rabbit, the cony of the Bible, constituting the order **Hyracoid'ea**; (without *cap*) any animal of this genus: — *pl* **hy'raxes** or **hy'races** (*-sēz*). — *adj* **hy'racoid**. [Gr *hyrax* a shrew]

hyson *hī'son*, *n* a very fine sort of green tea. — **hy'son-skin** the refuse of hyson tea removed by winnowing. [From Chin]

hyssop *his'əp*, *n* an aromatic labiate (*Hyssopus officinalis*) used in perfumery and folk-medicine; an unknown wall-plant used as a ceremonial sprinkler (*Bible*); a holy-water sprinkler. [L *hyssōpus*, *-um*, from Gr *hyssōpos*, *-on*; cf Heb *'ēzōb*]

hyster- *his-tər-* or **hystero-** *his-tə-rō-*, *his-tə-rə-* or *his-tə-ro'-* *combining form* signifying womb. — *vt* **hysterec'tomize** or **-ise**. — *n* **hysterec'tomy** (Gr *ektomē* a cutting out) surgical removal of the uterus. — *n* **hysterī'tis** inflammation of the uterus. — *n* **hysterot'omy** (Gr *tomē* a cut) surgical incision of the uterus. [Gr *hysterā* the womb]

hysteranthous *his-tər-an'thəs*, *adj* having the leaves appearing after the flowers. [Gr *hysteros* later, and *anthos* flower]

hysteresis *his-tə-rē'sis*, *n* the retardation or lagging of an effect behind the cause of the effect; the influence of earlier treatment of a body on its subsequent reaction. — *adj* **hysterēs'ial**. — *adj* **hysteret'ic**. — **high-hysteresis rubber** rubber with less than normal bounce. [Gr *hysterēsis* a deficiency, coming late, from *hysteros* later]

hysteria *his-tē'ri-ə*, *n* a psychoneurosis in which repressed complexes become split off or dissociated from the personality, forming independent units, partially or completely unrecognized by consciousness, giving rise to hypnoidal states (eg amnesia, somnambulisms), and manifested by various physical symptoms (such as tics, paralysis, blindness, deafness, etc), general features being an extreme degree of emotional instability and an intense craving for affection; (loosely) an outbreak of wild emotionalism. — *adj* **hysteric** (*his-ter'ik*) or **hyster'ical** pertaining to, of the nature of, or affected with, hysterics or hysteria; like hysterics; fitfully and violently emotional; (**hyster'ical**) extremely funny (*colloq*). — *n* **hyster'ic** a hysterical person. — *adv* **hyster'ically**. — *adj* **hyster'icky** (*colloq*). — *n pl* **hyster'ics** hysteric fits; (popularly) fits of uncontrollable laughter or crying, or of both alternately. — *adj* **hysterogen'ic** inducing hysteria. — *n* **hysterogeny** (*-oj'ə-ni*). — *adj* **hys'teroid** or **hys'teroidal** like hysteria. — *n* **hysteromān'ia** hysterical mania, often marked by erotic delusions and an excessive desire to attract attention. — **hysterical pregnancy** pseudocyesis; **hysteroid dysphoria** pathological depression typical of women. [Gr *hysterā* the womb, with which hysteria was formerly thought to be connected]

hysteron-proteron *his'tər-on-prot'ər-on*, *n* a figure of speech in which what would ordinarily follow comes first; an inversion. [Gr, literally latter-former]

hythe. Same as **hithe**.

Hz *symbol*: hertz.

I

I[1] or **i** *ī*, *n* the ninth letter of the modern English alphabet; any of various sounds represented by this letter (as in *dip*, *mind*, *bird*, *machine*). — **I'-beam** a metal girder I-shaped in section.

I[2] *ī*, *pronoun* the nominative singular of the first personal pronoun; the word used in mentioning oneself. — *n* the object of self-consciousness, the ego. — *pronoun* **I'=and-I'** Rastafarian for **we** or **us**. [ME *ich*, from OE *ic*; Ger *ich*, ON *ek*, L *ego*, Gr *egō*]

I[3] *ī*, *adv* same as **ay**.

I or **I**. *abbrev*: independence; independent; institute; island or isle; Italy (*IVR*).

I *symbol*: iodine (chem); (Roman numeral) the number one, 1.

I (*phys*) *symbol*: electric current.

i (*math*) *symbol*: the imaginary square root of -1.

i' *i*, *prep* a form of **in**.

IA or **Ia** *abbrev*: Iowa (US state).

IA *abbrev*: Institute of Actuaries; International Ångström.

-ia *-ē'ə* or *-yə*, *sfx* used in naming: (1) a pathological condition; (2) a genus of plants or animals; (3) (as *L* or *Gr neut pl*) a taxonomic division; (4) (as *pl*) things pertaining to (something specified).

IAA *abbrev*: indoleacetic acid.

IAAF *abbrev*: International Amateur Athletic Federation.

IAEA *abbrev*: International Atomic Energy Agency.

Iai-do *ē-ī'dō*, *n* Japanese swordsmanship as a martial art. [From Jap]

IAL (*comput*) *abbrev*: International Algebraic Language (see **ALGOL**).

iambus *ī-am'bəs*, *n* (*prosody*) a foot of two syllables, a short followed by a long, or an unstressed by a stressed: — *pl* **iam'buses** or **iam'bī**. — Also **i'amb**. — *adj* **iam'bic** consisting of iambuses; of the nature of an iambus; using iambic verse. — *n* an iambus; (in *pl*) iambic verse. — *adv* **iam'bically**. — *n* **iam'bist**. — **iambic pentameter** a verse form comprising lines each of five feet, each foot containing two syllables, used in blank or heroic verse in English. [L *iambus*, from Gr *iambos*, from *iaptein* to assail, this metre being first used by satirists]

-ian. See **-an**.

-iana. See **-ana**.

ianthine *ī-an'thīn*, *adj* violet-coloured. [Gr *ianthinos*, from *ion* violet, and *anthos* flower]

IAS or **i.a.s.** *abbrev*: immediate access storage (*comput*); indicated air speed (*aeronautics*); instrument approach system.

-iasis *-ī-ə-sis*, (*med*) *sfx* denoting a diseased condition, as in *pityriasis*, *psoriasis*. [Gr sfx meaning state or condition]

Iastic *ī-ast'ik*, (*music*) *adj* Ionian. — **Iastic mode** the Ionian, hypophrygian or hyperdorian mode of ancient Greek music. [Gr *Iastikos* Ionian]

IATA *abbrev*: International Air Transport Association.

-iatric *-ī-at'rik*, *adj combining form* relating to care or treatment within a particular specialty, as in *paediatric*, *psychiatric*. — *n sing combining form* **-iat'rics**. — *n combining form* **-i'atry**. [Gr *iātros* physician]

iatrochemistry *ī-at-rō-kem'i-stri*, *n* an application of chemistry to medical theory introduced by Franciscus Sylvius (1614–72) of Leyden. — *adj* **iatrochem'ical**. — *n* **iatrochem'ist**. [Gr *iātros* physician, and **chemistry**]

iatrogenic *ī-at-rō-jen'ik*, *adj* (of a disease or symptoms) induced in a patient by the treatment or comments of a physician. — *n* **iatrogenic'ity**. — *n* **iatro'geny**. [Gr *iātros* a physician, and *-genēs* born]

IB *abbrev*: International Baccalaureate.

ib. or **ibid.** *abbrev*: *ibidem* (*L*), in the same place.

IBA *abbrev*: Independent Broadcasting Authority, to be replaced by **ITC**.

Iberian *ī-bē'ri-ən*, *adj* of Spain and Portugal; formerly, of Iberia (now Georgia) in the Caucasus; of the ancient inhabitants of either of these, or their later representatives; of a Mediterranean people of Neolithic culture in Britain, etc. — *n* a member of any of these peoples. [L *Ibēria*, from Gr *Ibēriā*]

iberis *ī-bē'ris*, *n* any plant of the *Iberis* genus of Cruciferae, including the candytuft (*I. sempervirens*). [Gr *ibēris* pepperwort]

ibex *ī'beks*, *n* any of various wild mountain-goats of Europe, N Africa and Asia, with large, ridged, backward-curving horns: — *pl* **i'bex**, **i'bexes** or **ibices** (*ī'bi-sēz*). [L *ibex*, *-icis*]

ibidem *ib-ī'dəm*, *ib'i-dəm* or *i-bē'dem*, (*L*) *adv* (used in referring to a book, chapter, passage, etc already cited) in the same place (*abbrev* **ib.** or **ibid.**)

ibis *ī'bis*, *n* a wading bird of the family *Threskiornithidae*, typically having long, thin down-curved bills, long broad wings and short tails, and including the sacred ibis (*Threskiornis aethiopica*) worshipped by the ancient Egyptians. See also **wood ibis**. [L and Gr *ībis*, prob Egyptian]

-ible *-ə-bl*, *adj sfx* having similar uses to those of **-able** (qv), *esp* the passive 'capable of being', as in *audible*, *permissible*, *visible*. — *n sfx* **-ibility**. — *adv sfx* **-ibly**. [L *-ibilis*, from *-bilis* as used with a 2nd-, 3rd- or 4th-conjugation verb]

Iblis. See **Eblis**.

Ibo *ē'bō*, *n* a Negro people of SE Nigeria; a member of this people; their language, widely used in southern Nigeria: — *pl* **I'bo** or **I'bos**. — Also *adj*. — Also **Igbo** (*ē'bō*).

IBRD *abbrev*: International Bank for Reconstruction and Development (ie the World Bank, qv).

IBS (*med*) *abbrev*: irritable bowel syndrome.

Ibsenism *ib'sən-izm*, *n* the dramatic qualities and type of social criticism characteristic of the plays of the Norwegian dramatist, Henrik *Ibsen* (1828–1906). — *adj* **Ibsen'ian** of or in the style of Ibsen. — *n* **Ib'senite** a champion or follower of Ibsen.

ibuprofen *ī-bū-prō'fən*, *n* a non-steroidal anti-inflammatory drug used *esp* in the treatment of arthritis and rheumatic pain. [From its full name, *i*so*bu*tyl*phen*yl *pro*pionic acid]

IC *abbrev*: integrated circuit (*electronics*); internal-combustion.

i/c *abbrev*: in charge; in command.

ICA *abbrev*: Institute of Contemporary Arts; Invalid Care Allowance.

ICAO *abbrev*: International Civil Aviation Organization.

ICBM *abbrev*: intercontinental ballistic missile.

ICD *abbrev*: International Classification of Diseases.

ICE *abbrev*: Institution of Civil Engineers; internal combustion engine.

ice *īs*, *n* frozen water; any substance resembling this, *esp* any liquid or gaseous substance reduced to a solid state by freezing; a portion of ice-cream or water ice; reserve, formality; coldness of manner; diamond(s) or other precious stone(s) (*slang*); an illicit drug, a highly synthesized form of methamphetamine (*drug-taking slang*). — *adj* of ice. — *vt* to cool with ice; to cover with icing; to kill (*US underworld slang*). — *vi* to freeze; to become covered with ice (with *up*, *over*, etc): — *pr p* **ic'ing**; *pa t* and *pa p* **iced**. — *adj* **iced** (*īst*) covered with or cooled with ice; coated or topped with icing. — *n* **i'cer** a person who makes or applies icing. — *adv* **ic'ily**. — *n* **ic'iness**. — *n* **ic'ing** (a coating of) concreted sugar; the formation of ice, eg on roads, aircraft, ships, etc. — *adj* **ic'y** composed of, covered with, or like ice; frosty; cold; chilling; (of manner) without warmth, distant, hostile. — Also *adv*. — **ice'-action** the action of glaciers and land ice on the earth's surface; **ice age** (*geol*) any time when a great part of the earth's surface has been covered with ice, *esp* (often with *caps*) that in the Pleistocene period; **ice anchor** an anchor with a single arm for mooring to an ice floe, etc; **ice apron** a structure on the upstream side of a bridge pier to break or ward off floating ice; **ice axe** an axe used by mountain-climbers to cut footholds in ice or compacted snow; **ice bag** a waterproof bag filled with or for carrying ice; **iceball** a game, similar to basketball, played by two teams of players on ice; **ice'berg** (from Scand or Du) a huge mass of ice, floating in the sea, which has broken away from a glacier, ice barrier, etc; a cold and unemotional person (*esp US colloq*); a type of crisp lettuce with tightly-packed light-green leaves (also **iceberg lettuce**); **ice'blink** a glare in the sky caused by light reflected from distant masses of ice; **ice block** (*Austr* and *NZ*) an ice lolly. — *adj* and *n* **ice'-blue** (a) very pale blue. — **ice'boat** a boat for forcing a way through ice, an icebreaker; a craft mounted on runners for moving over ice (also **ice yacht**). — *adj* **ice'bound** covered, surrounded or immobilized by ice. — **ice'box** the freezing compartment of a refrigerator; a refrigerator (*old US*); an insulated box packed with ice, used for storing and carrying cold food and drink; **ice'-breaker** a ship for breaking channels through ice; anything for breaking ice; something or someone that breaks down reserve between a group or gathering of people. — *adj* **ice'breaking**. — **ice bucket** an insulated container for holding ice cubes to be used in drinks; a receptacle partially filled with ice, used for cooling bottles of wine; **ice'cap** a permanent covering of ice over the polar regions of a planet, a mountain-top, etc. — *adj* **ice'-cold** cold as, or like, ice. — **ice colours** (*chem*) dyestuffs produced on cotton fibre by a solution of diazo-salt cooled with ice interacting with a second component; **ice cream** a sweet frozen food containing cream, or one of various substitutes, and flavouring (**ice'-cream soda** carbonated water with ice cream added); **ice cube** a small cube of ice used for cooling drinks, etc; **ice dance** or **dancing** a form of ice-skating based on the movements of ballroom dancing; **iced water** drinking water chilled with ice; **ice fall** a fall of ice; a steep broken place in a glacier; **ice'field** a large flat area of land covered with ice or an area of sea covered with floating ice; **ice fish** the capelin; **ice floe** a large sheet of ice floating in the sea; **ice'-foot** a belt of ice forming round the coast in Arctic regions. — Also **ice'-belt** or **ice'-ledge**. — *adj* **ice'-free** without ice. — **ice hockey** a game played by two teams on an ice rink, in which players equipped with skates and long sticks try to drive a flat puck into their opponent's goal; **ice house** (*esp* formerly) a building for storing ice in; **ice lolly** a lollipop consisting of water-ice on a stick; **ice machine** a machine for making ice in large quantities; **ice man** (*esp US*) a man who sells or delivers ice; a jewel thief (*slang*); a professional killer, a hit man (*underworld slang*); **ice'pack** drifting ice packed together, pack ice; an ice-filled bag for applying to a part of the body to reduce swelling (*med*); a gel-filled pack that remains frozen for long periods, for use in a cool box, etc; **ice pick** a tool with a pointed end used for splitting ice; **ice plant** a flowering plant (*Mesembrianthemum* or *Dorotheanthus*) whose succulent leaves are covered with fine hairs which give them a glistening, sugary appearance; **ice point** the temperature (0°Celsius or 32°Fahrenheit) at which ice is at equilibrium with water in liquid form at a pressure of one atmosphere; **ice rink** a skating rink of ice; **ice sheet** a thick sheet of ice covering a large area of land, *esp* an entire region, as in ice ages; **ice show** an entertainment or exhibition provided by skaters on ice; **ice skate** a skate for moving on ice (see **skate**[1]). — Also *vi* **ice'-skate**. — **ice'-skater**; **ice'-skating**; **ice spar** a clear glassy orthoclase; **ice'stone** see **cryolite**; **ice water** water formed from melted ice; **ice worm** a species of oligochaete stated by some to be found on glaciers in Alaska, etc; **ice yacht** see **ice boat**; **icing sugar** sugar in the form of a very fine powder, for icing cakes, etc. — **break the ice** to break through the barrier of reserve or inhibition on first meeting; to move to restore friendly relations after a period of hostility; **cut no ice** to count for nothing; to have no effect; **dry ice** solid carbon dioxide, which changes directly into vapour at -78·5° Celsius, and is chiefly used for refrigeration, but is also exploited in the theatre, the dense, swirling, floor-level white cloud it produces on evaporation creating a spectacular stage-effect — *adj* **dry'-iced**); **ice contact slope** (*geol*) the steep slope of material deposited at the ice front of a glacier and in contact with it; **ice out** (*fig*) to exclude (someone) from one's company by ignoring him or her; **icing on the cake** anything that is a desirable addition to something already satisfactory; **on ice** (*fig*) kept, or waiting in readiness; postponed; in prison, *esp* in solitary confinement (*US prison slang*); **put on ice** to put into abeyance, to suspend; **(skate) on thin ice** (to be) in a delicate, difficult or potentially embarrassing situation; **tip of the iceberg** the top of an iceberg, visible above the water, most of it being invisible below the surface; hence, the small obvious part of a much larger problem, etc (*fig*). [OE *īs*; ON *īss*; Ger *Eis*, Dan *is*]

Iceland *īs'lənd*, *adj* of, belonging to, or originating in, *Iceland*. — *n* **Ice'lander** (or *īs-land'ər*) a native or citizen of Iceland. — *adj* **Icelandic** (*īs-land'ik*) of Iceland. — *n* the modern language of the Icelanders; Old Norse. — **Ice'land-dog'** a shaggy white dog with sharply pointed ears originally from Iceland; **Iceland falcon** a white gerfalcon of Iceland; **Iceland moss** a lichen (*Cetraria islandica*) of northern regions, used as a medicine and for food; **Iceland poppy** a dwarf poppy (*Papaver nudicaule*) with grey-green pinnate leaves and flowers varying from white to orange-scarlet; **Iceland spar** a transparent calcite with strong double refraction.

Iceni *ī-sē'nī*, *n pl* an ancient British tribe that, led by Queen Boudicca, rebelled against the Romans in AD 61.

ICFTU *abbrev*: International Confederation of Free Trade Unions.

ich[1] *ich*, (*Shakesp*) *vt*. Same as **eche**.

ich[2]. See **ch**.

ichabod *ik'ə-bod*, *interj* the glory is departed. [From Heb; see 1 Sam 4, 21]

I.Chem.E. *abbrev*: Institution of Chemical Engineers.

ich dien *ihh dēn*, (*Ger*) I serve (the motto of the Prince of Wales).

I Ching *ī* or *ē ching*, *n* an ancient Chinese system of divination, consisting of a set of symbols, 8 trigrams and 64 hexagrams, and the text, the *I Ching*, used to interpret them. [Chin, book of changes]

ichneumon *ik-nū'mən*, *n* any animal of the mongoose genus (*Herpestes*) of the civet family, *esp* the Egyptian species that destroys crocodiles' eggs; (in full **ichneumon fly**) any insect of a large family of Hymenoptera whose larvae are parasitic in or on other insects and their larvae. [Gr *ichneumōn* literally tracker, *ichneuein* to hunt after, from *ichnos* a track]

ichnite *ik'nīt* or **ichnolite** *ik'nə-līt*, *n* a fossilized footprint. — *n* **ichnol'ogy** the science of fossilized footprints. [Gr *ichnos* a track, footprint]

ichnography *ik-nog'rə-fi*, *n* a ground plan; the art of drawing ground plans. — *adj* **ichnograph'ic** or **ichnograph'ical**. — *adv* **ichnograph'ically**. [Gr *ichnos* a track, footprint, and *graphein* to write]

ichor *ī'kör*, *n* the ethereal juice in the veins of the gods (*mythol*); colourless matter oozing from an ulcer or wound (*med*). — *adj* **ī'chorous**. [Gr *īchōr*]

ICSH *abbrev*: interstitial-cell-stimulating hormone.

ichthyic *ik'thi-ik or* **ichthic** *ik'thik*, *adj* of, resembling or relating to fish. [Gr *ichthȳs* fish]

ichthyo- *ik'thi-ō-* or **ichthy-** *ik'thi- combining form* signifying fish. — *n* **ichthyocoll'a** (Gr *kolla* glue) fish glue; isinglass. — *n* **ichthyodor'ūlite** or **ichthyodor'ylite** (*-i-līt*; Gr *dory* a spear, and *lithos* a stone) a fossilized fish spine. — *adj* **ichthyol'atrous**. — *n* **ichthyol'atry** (Gr *latreiā* worship) the worship of fish. — *n* **ich'thyolite** (Gr *lithos* a stone) a general term for any fossil fish. — *adj* **ichthyolitic** (*-lit'ik*). — *adj* **ichthyolog'ical**. — *n* **ichthyol'ogist**. — *n* **ichthyol'ogy** the study of fishes, their natural history, distribution, etc. — *adj* **ichthyoph'agous** (*-ə-gəs*; Gr *phagein* to eat) feeding on fish. — *n* **ichthyoph'agy**. — *n* **ichthyor'nis** (Gr *ornis* a bird) an extinct Cretaceous sea bird of the genus *Ichthyornis* with reptilian teeth set in sockets. — *n* **ichthyosaur** (*ik'thi-ō-sör*; Gr *sauros* lizard) any Mesozoic extinct marine reptile of the order *Ichthyosauria*, with a fish-shaped body and elongated snout similar to dolphins. — *adj* **ichthyosaur'ian**. — *n* **ichthyō'sis** a rare inherited condition in which the skin becomes thickened, scaly and rough, due to an abnormality in the production of keratin (also called **fish skin disease**). — *adj* **ichthyot'ic**. [Gr *ichthȳs* fish]

ichthyoid *ik'thi-oid* or **ichthyoidal** *-əl*, *adj* fishlike. — *n* **ich'thyoid** a fishlike vertebrate. [Gr *ichthȳs* fish]

ichthys *ik'this*, *n* a fish symbolizing Christ or an emblem or motto (*ΙΧΦΥΣ*), believed to have mystical qualities, being the first letters of the Greek words *J*esous *Ch*ristos, *Th*eou *U*ious, *S*oter (Jesus Christ, Son of God, Saviour). [Gr *ichthȳs* fish]

ICI *abbrev*: Imperial Chemical Industries.

icicle *īs'i-kl*, *n* a hanging, tapering piece of ice formed by the freezing of dropping water. [OE *īsesgicel*, from *īses*, genitive of *īs* ice, and *gicel* icicle]

icing. See under **ice**.

-icism. See **-ism**.

icker *ik'ər*, (*Scot*) *n* an ear of corn. [OE (Northumbrian) *eher*, *æhher* (WS *ēar*)]

icky *ik'i*, (*colloq*) *adj* sickly-sweet, cloying; repulsive, distasteful, unpleasant (also **icky poo**). [Perh from **sickly**]

ICL *abbrev*: International Computers Ltd.

icon or **ikon** *ī'kon*, *n* in the Eastern Churches, a figure representing Christ, the Virgin Mary or a saint, in painting, mosaic, or low relief sculpture; a symbol, image, picture or representation; anybody or anything venerated or uncritically admired; a picture or symbol in a graphic display, representing a particular facility or operation available to the user, *usu* activated by means of a mouse (*comput*). — *adj* **icon'ic**. — *adv* **icon'ically**. — *vt* and *vi* **icon'ify** to reduce (a window) on a computer screen to an icon. — *vt* **i'conize** or **-ise** to venerate or admire uncritically. — *n* **icon'oclasm** (Gr *klaein* to break) the act of destroying images that are the object of veneration; opposition to image-worship. — *n* **icon'oclast** a destroyer of images; a person opposed to image-worship, *esp* those in the Eastern Church, from the 8c; a person who attacks traditional or established beliefs, principles, ideas, institutions, etc. — *adj* **iconoclast'ic**. — *n* **iconog'raphy** (Gr *graphiā* a writing) the study of the subjects depicted in paintings, etc; pictorial representation of subjects; the symbols used in paintings, etc and their conventional significance; a description, catalogue or collective representation of portraits. — *n* **iconol'ater** an image-worshipper. — *n* **iconol'atry** (Gr *latreiā* worship) image-worship. — *n* **iconol'ogist**. — *n* **iconol'ogy** the study of icons; icons collectively; the study of artistic symbolism. — *n* **iconomachist** (*-om'ə-kist*) a person who contends against the use of icons in worship. — *n* **iconom'achy** (Gr *machē* fight) opposition to image-worship. — *adj* **iconomat'ic** using pictures of objects to represent not the things themselves but the sounds of their names, as in a transitional stage of writing between pictorial representation and a phonetic system. — *n* **iconomat'icism** (*-i-sizm*). — *n* **iconom'eter** an instrument for inferring distance from size or size from distance of an object, by measuring its image; a direct photographic viewfinder. — *n* **iconom'etry**. — *n* **iconoph'ilism** a taste for pictures, etc. — *n* **iconoph'ilist** a connoisseur of pictures, etc. — *n* **icon'oscope** an early form of electron camera. — *n* **iconos'tasis** or **icon'ostas** (Gr *eikonostasis*, from *stasis* placing) in Eastern churches, a screen separating the sanctuary from the nave, on which the icons are placed. — **iconic memory** the persistence of a sense impression after the disappearance of the stimulus. [L *īcōn*, from Gr *eikōn* an image]

icosahedron *ī-kos-ə-hē'drən*, (*geom*) *n* a solid with twenty plane faces: — *pl* **icosahē'dra**. — *adj* **icosahē'dral**. — *n* **icositetrahē'dron** (Gr *tetra* four) a solid figure with twenty-four plane faces: — *pl* **icositetrahe'dra**. [Gr *eikosi* twenty, and *hedrā* a seat]

Icosandria *ī-kos-an'dri-ə*, (*bot*) *n pl* a Linnaean class of plants with twenty or more free stamens. — *adj* **icosan'drian**. — *adj* **icosan'drous**. [Gr *eikosi* twenty, and *anēr*, *andros* a man (male)]

ICR (*comput*) *abbrev*: intelligent character recognition.

ICRF *abbrev*: Imperial Cancer Relief Fund.

-ics *-iks*, *n sing* or *n pl sfx* denoting: (1) the study, practice, art or knowledge of a particular subject or type of activity, as in *aeronautics*, *paediatrics*, *gymnastics*, *politics*; (2) the procedures, functions or phenomena involved in, or relating to, a specific activity, as in *mechanics*, *acoustics*, *graphics*; (3) the actions, behaviour, etc characteristic of a particular state or condition, as in *hysterics*, *histrionics*. [Gr *-ika*, neuter pl adj ending]

icterus *ik'tər-əs*, *n* jaundice. — *adj* **icteric** (*-ter'ik*) or **icter'ical** relating to or suffering from jaundice. — *n* a medicine for jaundice. — *n* and *adj* **ic'terid** (of or resembling) a member of a family of American orioles (**Icter'idae**), mostly yellow and black passerine birds, including the Baltimore oriole, bobolinks, cowbirds and grackles. — *adj* **ic'terine** (*-tər-īn* or *-in*) of or resembling the family Icteridae; yellowish or marked with yellow. — *adj* **icteritious** (*ik-tər-ish'əs*) jaundiced; yellow. [Gr *ikteros* jaundice, also a yellowish bird (according to Pliny the golden oriole) the sight of which supposedly cured jaundice]

ictus *ik'təs*, *n* rhythmical or metrical stress in contradistinction to the usual stress of a word in prose, etc (*prosody*); a stroke or sudden attack, *esp* an epileptic fit (*med*): — *pl* **ic'tuses** (or *L pl* **ic'tūs** *-tōōs*). — *adj* **ic'tal** or **ic'tic**. [L, a blow]

ICU (*med*) *abbrev*: intensive care unit.

ID *abbrev*: Idaho (US state); identification; infectious diseases (*med*); inner diameter (also **i.d.**); intelligence (or information) department. — **ID card** a card which identifies a person, often including a photograph, details of age, membership, etc.

I'd *īd*, contracted from *I would*, or *I had*; also used for *I should*.

id[1] *id* or **ide** *īd*, *n* a fish (*Idus idus*) of the same family as the carp, inhabiting fresh water in Northern Europe. [Swed *id*]

id[2] *id*, *n* in psychoanalytic theory, one of the three parts of the personality, being the unconscious mass of primitive energies from which come instincts for the gratification of basic desires for food, sex, etc, and for the avoidance of pain, modified by the ego and the superego. [L *id* it]

-id[1] *-id*, *adj sfx* as in *fluid*, *stupid*, *solid*, *tepid*, *turgid*, *gelid*, etc. [L *-idus*]

-id[2] *-id*, *n* and *adj sfx* used in the names of a particular zoological or racial group, or dynastic line, as in *arachnid*, *hominid*, *Fatimid*. [Gr *-idēs* son of]

-id[3] *-id*, *n sfx* used in names of bodies, formations, particles, etc, as *hydatid*, *energid*; used in the names of meteors coming from a particular constellation, as in *Perseid*, *Orionid*. [Gr *-is*, *-idos* daughter of]

-id[4]. See **-ide**.

IDA *abbrev*: International Development Association.

Ida. *abbrev*: Idaho (US state).

-idae *-i-dē, n sfx* used in names of zoological families, as in *Boridae*, *Canidae*. [L, from Gr *-idai*, pl of *-idēs*]

Id al-Adha *ēd al ad'ha, n* the Muslim 'Feast of Sacrifice', celebrating Abraham's sacrifice of his son. [*'Id al-Adha*]

Id al-Fitr *ēd al fē'tər, n* the Muslim 'Feast of Breaking Fast', celebrated on the first day after Ramadan. [*'Id al-Fitr*]

IDB (*esp SAfr*) *abbrev*: illicit diamond buying.

IDD (*telecomm*) *abbrev*: International Direct Dialling.

iddy-umpty *id'i-ump'ti* or *-um'ti*, (*forces' slang*) *n* Morse code. [From a phrase used in India to teach morse to the native troops]

ide. See **id**[1].

-ide *-īd* or **-id** *-id, n sfx* indicating: (1) a chemical compound composed of two chemical elements, as in *potassium iodide*; (2) a chemical compound derived from another or belonging to a class of compounds, as in *hydroperoxide*, *amide*. [From Ger *-id* (Fr *-ide*), from its first use in *oxide*]

idea *ī-dē'ə, n* an image of an external object formed by the mind; a notion, thought, impression, conception, any product of intellectual action, of memory and imagination; a plan; in Plato, an archetype of the manifold varieties of existence in the universe, belonging to the supersensible world, in Kant, one of the three products of the reason (the Soul, the Universe, and God) transcending the conceptions of the understanding, and in Hegel, the ideal realized, the absolute truth of which everything that exists is the expression (*philos*). — *vt* **idē'ate** to form or have an idea of; to imagine; to preconceive. — *vi* to form ideas. — *adj* produced by an idea. — *n* the correlative or object of an idea. — *n* **idēā'tion** the power of the mind for forming ideas or images; the exercise of such power. — *adj* **idēā'tional** or **idē'ative**. — *adv* **idēā'tionally**. — **get** or **have ideas** (*slang*) to become or be overambitious; to have undesirable ideas; **have no idea** to be unaware of what is happening; to be ignorant or naive; **not my idea of** (*colloq*) the opposite of my (or the accepted and familiar) conception of; **put ideas into someone's head** to fill someone with unsuitable or over-exalted aspirations; **that's an idea** that plan, suggestion, etc is worth considering; **the very idea** the mere thought; (as an ejaculation) that's absurd, outrageous; **what an idea!** that's preposterous; **what's the big idea?** (*slang, usu ironic*) what's the intention, purpose? [L *idea*, from Gr *ideā*; cf *idein* (aorist) to see]

ideal *ī-dēl'* or *ī-dē'əl, adj* conceptual; existing in imagination only; highest and best conceivable; perfect, as opposed to the real or the imperfect; theoretical, conforming absolutely to theory. — *n* the highest conception of anything, or its embodiment; a standard of perfection; that which exists in the imagination only; a subring of a ring, any member of which when multiplied by any member of the ring, whether in the subring or not, results in a member of the subring (*math*). — *n* **idē'alism** a tendency towards the highest conceivable perfection, love for or the search after the best and highest; the habit or practice of idealizing; impracticality; the doctrine that in external perceptions the objects immediately known are ideas, that all reality is in its nature psychical. — *n* **idē'alist** a person who strives after the ideal; an impractical person; a person who holds the doctrine of idealism. — *adj* **idēalist'ic** pertaining to idealists or to idealism. — *adv* **idēalist'ically**. — *n* **idēality** (*-al'i-ti*) an ideal state; ability and disposition to form ideals of beauty and perfection. — *n* **idēalizā'tion** or **-s-**. — *vt* **idē'alize** or **-ise** to regard or represent as ideal. — *vi* to form ideals; to think or work idealistically. — *n* **id'ealizer** or **-s-**. — *adj* **idē'alless** having no ideals. — *adv* **idē'ally** in an ideal manner; in ideal circumstances; mentally. — *n* **idē'alogue** a misspelling of **ideologue**. — *vt* **idē'ate** to form or have in idea of; to imagine; to preconceive. — *vi* to form ideas. — *adj* produced by an idea. — *n* the correlative or object of an idea. — *n* **idēā'tion** the power of the mind for forming ideas; the exercise of such power. — *adj* **idēā'tional** or **idē'ative**. — *adv* **idēā'tionally**. — **ideal crystal** (*crystallog*) a crystal in which there are no imperfections or alien atoms; **ideal gas** (*chem*) a hypothetical gas which obeys physical laws under all conditions (also **perfect gas**); **ideal point** (*math*) a hypothetical point where two parallel lines join at infinity; **ideal transducer** (*elec eng*) a transducer which converts without loss all the power supplied to it. [LL *idealis*, from Gr *idea*, from *idein* to see]

idée *ē-dā*, (*Fr*) *n* an idea. — **idée fixe** (*fēks*) a fixed idea, an obsession or monomania; **idée reçue** (*rə-sü*) an accepted idea; conventional outlook.

idem *ī'dem* or *i'dem*, (*L*) *pronoun* the same (*abbrev* **id**). — **idem quod** the same as (*abbrev* **iq**); **idem sonans** (*sō'nanz* or *so'näns*) sounding the same (used of a word in a legal document which, though misspelt, can be accepted as that for which it clearly stands).

idempotent *ī'dəm-pō-tənt* or *i-dem'pə-tənt*, (*math*) *adj* and *n* (of) a quantity which does not change value when multiplied by itself. Cf **nilpotent**. — *n* **ī'dempotency** (or *i-dem'*). [L *idem* the same, and **potent**]

identic *ī-den'tik*, (*diplomacy*) *adj* identical, as in **identic note** or **identic action** an identical note sent by, or identical action taken by, two or more governments in dealing with another, or others. [Med L *identicus*, from L *idem* the same]

identical *ī-den'ti-kl, adj* the very same; not different; exactly alike; expressing or resulting in identity (*logic* or *math*). — *adv* **iden'tically**. — *n* **iden'ticalness**. — **identical twins** twins who are the same sex and look very alike, having developed from one zygote. [Med L *identicus*, from L *idem* the same]

identify *ī-den'ti-fī, vt* to ascertain or establish the identity of; to assign (a plant, animal, etc) to a species; to associate closely (eg one concept with another, a person with a group, movement, etc); to regard (oneself) as in sympathy (with a group, movement etc); to see clearly, pinpoint (a problem, etc). — *vi* to be emotionally in sympathy (with eg a character in a book, play, etc): — *pr p* **iden'tifying**; *pa t* and *pa p* **iden'tified**. — *adj* **iden'tifīable**. — *adv* **identifī'ably**. — *n* **identificā'tion** the act of identifying, eg in establishing a person's name and individuality; the state of being identified; something which proves one's identity; a process by which a person adopts the behaviour, ideas, etc of someone else, particularly someone whom he or she admires (*psychol*). — *n* **identifier** someone or something that identifies; a name or label used to identify a program or file (*comput*). — **identification card, disc**, etc a card, disc, etc carried on one's person, with one's name, etc on it; **identification parade** a group of people assembled by the police, from among whom a witness tries to identify a suspect. [LL *identificāre*, from *idem* the same, and *facere* to make]

identikit *ī-den'ti-kit*, (*orig US* **Identi-Kit**) *n* a device for building up a composite portrait from a large number of different features shown on transparent slips, by means of which a witness is assisted in producing a likeness of someone sought by the police. [*identi*ty and **kit**]

identity *ī-den'ti-ti, n* the state of being the same; sameness; individuality; personality; who or what a person or thing is; (also **old identity**) a long-standing and well-known inhabitant of a place (*Austr* and *NZ colloq*); an equation true for all values of the symbols involved (*math*). — **identity bracelet** a bracelet consisting of a flat metal bar, on which the owner's name may be engraved, joined to a chain; **identity card, disc** etc, a card, disc, etc bearing the owner's or wearer's name, etc, used to establish his or her identity; **identity crisis** psychological confusion caused by inability to reconcile differing elements in one's personality; **identity element** (*math*) an element (e) in a system of elements such that $e*x = x*e = x$, for every value of x — where $*$ denotes a binary operation (in the ordinary number system, for addition *e* = O, for multiplication *e* = 1). [LL *identitās, -ātis*, from L *idem* the same]

ideo- *id-* or *īd-i-ō-*, *combining form* signifying the mind or mental activity, idea. [Fr *idéo-*, from Gr *ideā*]

ideogram *id'i-ō-gram* or *īd'* or **ideograph** *-gräf*, *n* a character or symbol in writing that stands not for a word or sound but for a concept, idea or the thing itself; any sign or symbol used to represent a word. — *adj* **ideographic** (*-graf'ik*) or **ideograph'ical**. — *adv* **ideograph'ically**. — *n* **ideography** (*-og'rə-fi*). [Gr *ideā* idea, and *gramma* a drawing, or *graphein* to write]

ideology *īd-* or *id-i-ol'ə-ji*, *n* the science of ideas, metaphysics; abstract speculation; visionary speculation; a body of ideas, *usu* political and/or economic, forming the basis of a national or sectarian policy; way of thinking. — *adj* **ideolog'ic** (*-loj'*) or **ideolog'ical** of or relating to an ideology; arising from or concerned with rival ideologies. — *n* **ideol'ogist** a person occupied with ideas or an idea; a theorist or visionary; a supporter of a particular ideology. — *n* **id'eologue** (*usu derog*) a doctrinaire adherent of an ideology. [Gr *ideā* idea, and *logos* discourse]

ideomotor *id-i-ō-mō'tər*, *adj* describing or relating to a muscular action that is evoked by an idea. [**ideo-** and **motor**]

ideophone *id'i-ō-fōn*, *n* a word or phrase that is spoken but not written, *usu* one that is only fully comprehensible in the context in which it is spoken. [Gr *ideā* idea, and *phōnē* sound]

ideopraxist *id-* or *īd-i-ō-prak'sist*, *n* someone who is impelled to carry out an idea. [Gr *ideā* idea, and *prāxis* doing]

Ides *īdz*, *n pl* (also without *cap*) in ancient Rome, the 15th day of March, May, July, October, and the 13th of the other months. [Fr *ides*, from L *īdūs* (pl)]

id est *id est*, (*L*) that is, that is to say (*abbrev* **ie** or **i.e.**)

idio- *id-i-ō-*, *combining form* signifying peculiarity to the individual, separateness, isolation. [Gr *idios* own, private]

idioblast *id'* or *ī'di-ə-bläst*, *n* a plant cell that differs from neighbouring cells in the same tissue. — *adj* **idioblast'ic**. [Gr *idios* own, private, and *blastos* sprout]

idiocy. See under **idiot**.

idioglossia *id-i-ō-glos'i-ə*, *n* a condition in which pronunciation is so bad as to be quite unintelligible; a private language developed between two or more children, *esp* twins, etc. [Gr *idios* own, private, and *glōssa* tongue]

idiogram. See **karyogram**.

idiograph *id'i-ō-gräf*, *n* a private mark; a trademark. — *adj* **idiographic** (*-graf'ik*) relating to an individual or to anything unique. [Gr *idios* own, private, and *graphein* to write]

idiolect *id'i-ō-lekt*, *n* an individual's own distinctive form of speech. — *adj* **idiolec'tal** or **idiolec'tic**. [Gr *idios* own, and dia*lect*]

idiom *id'i-əm*, *n* a mode of expression peculiar to a language; a distinctive expression whose meaning is not determinable from the meanings of the individual words; a form or variety of language; a dialect; a characteristic mode of artistic expression of a person, school, etc. — *adj* **idiomat'ic**. — *adv* **idiomat'ically**. — *n* **idioticon** (*-ot'i-kon*) a vocabulary of a particular dialect or district. — *n* **id'iotism** (*-ə-tizm*) an idiom (*obs*); idiocy (*archaic*). [Gr *idiōma*, *idiōtikon*, from *idios* own]

idiomorphic *id-i-ō-mör'fik*, *adj* (of minerals) having the faces belonging to its crystalline form, as a mineral that has had free room to crystallize out. [Gr *idios* own, and *morphē* form]

idiopathic *id-i-ō-path'ik*, *adj* (of a state or experience) peculiar to the individual; (of a disease, etc) arising spontaneously from some unknown cause, primary. — *adv* **idiopath'ically**. [Gr *idios* own, and *pathos* suffering]

idiophone *id'i-ō-fōn*, (*music*) *n* a percussion instrument made entirely of a naturally resonant material. [Gr *idios* own, and *phōnē* voice]

idioplasm *id'i-ō-plazm*, *n* that part of the protoplasm that was once thought to determine hereditary character. [Gr *idios* own, private, and *plasma* mould]

idiorrhythmic or **idiorhythmic** *id-i-ō-ridh'mik*, or *-rith'*, *adj* self-regulating; allowing each member to regulate his or her own life. [Gr *idios* own, and *rhȳthmos* order]

idiosyncrasy *id-i-ō-sing'krə-si*, *n* peculiarity of temperament or mental constitution; any characteristic of a person; hypersensitivity exhibited by an individual to a particular food, drug, etc (*med*). — *adj* **idiosyncratic** (*-krat'ik*). — *adv* **idiosyncrat'ically**. [Gr *idios* own, and *synkrāsis* a mixing together, from *syn* together, and *krāsis* a mixing]

idiot *id'i-ət* or *id'yət*, *n* a person afflicted with the severest degree of intellectual subnormality, ie having an intelligence quotient of less than 20 (now *obs*); a foolish or unwise person. — *adj* afflicted with idiocy; idiotic. — *n* **id'iocy** (*-ə-si*) or (*rare*) **id'iotcy** the state of being an idiot; imbecility; folly. — *adj* **idiotic** (*-ot'ik*) or **idiot'ical** relating to or like an idiot; foolish. — *adv* **idiot'ically**. — *adj* **id'iotish** idiotic. — *n* **id'iotism** the state of being an idiot (*archaic*); an idiom (*obs*). — **idiot board** a mechanical device used to prompt a speaker or performer on television, an autocue; **idiot box** (*slang*) a television set; **idiot card** a large card with words, etc, for the same purpose as an idiot board. — *adj* **id'iot-proof** (of a tool, device, machine, method of working, etc) so simple that even an idiot cannot make a mistake. — **idiot tape** (*comput*) a tape that prints out a continuous flow of characters, without breaks. [Fr, from L *idiōta*, from Gr *idiōtēs* a private person, ordinary person, one who holds no public office or has no professional knowledge, from *idios* own, private]

idiothermous *id-i-ō-thûr'məs*, *adj* warm-blooded, ie having a body temperature of one's own, independent of surroundings. [Gr *idios* own, and *thermē* heat]

idioticon. See under **idiom**.

idiot savant *ē-dyō sa-vã* or *id'i-ət sav'ənt*, *n* a mentally subnormal individual who demonstrates remarkable talent in some restricted area such as memorizing or rapid calculation. [Fr, literally, knowing idiot]

idle *ī'dl*, *adj* vain; baseless, without foundation; trifling; unemployed; disliking work, lazy; not occupied; not in use or operation; useless; unimportant; unedifying. — *vt* to pass or spend in idleness. — *vi* to be idle or unoccupied; (of machinery) to run without doing work; (of an engine) to run slowly when disengaged from the transmission. — *n* **i'dlehood** (*archaic*). — *n* **i'dleness**. — *n* **i'dler** a person who wastes time or is reluctant to work; an idle pulley or idle wheel. — *n* **id'lesse** (*poetic*) idleness. — *adv* **i'dly**. — **idle money** (*econ*) that part of the total money supply that is neither being used to finance current transactions nor being lent out on the money market; **idle pulley** a pulley which rotates freely and guides, or controls the tension of, a belt (also **i'dler**); **idle time** a period or periods when a machine, eg a computer, is able to function properly but is not being used for productive work; **idle wheel** a wheel placed between two others for transferring the motion from one to the other without changing the direction (also **i'dler**). [OE *īdel*; Du *ijdel*, Ger *eitel*]

IDN *abbrev*: *in Dei nomine* (*L*), in the name of God.

Ido *ē'dō*, *n* an auxiliary international language developed (since 1907) from Esperanto. — *n* **Id'ist** or **I'doist**. [Ido, offspring, from Gr *-idos* daughter of]

idocrase *īd'* or *id'ō-krās*, or *-krāz*, *n* another name for the mineral vesuvianite. [Gr *eidos* form, and *krāsis* mixture]

idol *ī'dl*, *n* an image of a god; an object of worship; an object of love, admiration or honour in an extreme degree; an idolum; a fantasy, a phantom (*archaic*) ; an impostor, a sham (*obs*); an image or semblance (*obs*); a figure or effigy (*obs*). — *n* **i'dolism** the worship of idols; great reverence or admiration; a fallacy (*Milton*).

— *n* **i'dolist**. — *vt* **i'dolize** or **-ise** to worship as an idol; to admire or revere greatly. — *vi* to worship idols. — *n* **i'dolizer** or **-s-**. — *n* **idoloclast** (*-dol'*) a destroyer of idols. [L *īdōlum*, from Gr *eidōlon*, from *eidos* form, from *idein* (aorist) to see]

idolater *ī-dol'ə-tər*, *n* a worshipper of idols; a besotted admirer: — *fem* **idol'atress**. — *vt* and *vi* **idol'atrize** or **-ise** to worship as an idol; to adore. — *adj* **idol'atrous**. — *adv* **idol'atrously**. — *n* **idol'atry** the worship of an image held to be the abode of a superhuman personality; excessive adoration of or devotion to someone or something. [Fr *idolâtre*, from Gr *eidōlolatrēs*, from *eidōlon* idol, and *latreuein* to worship]

idolize. See under **idol**.

idolum *ī-dō'ləm*, *n* a mental image; a fallacy (*logic*). [L, from Gr *eidolon* phantom]

idoxuridine *ī-doks-ū'ri-dēn*, *n* a drug containing iodine used to treat viral infections of the eye.

IDP (*comput*) *abbrev*: integrated data processing.

idyll or sometimes *US* **idyl** *id'il*, *īd'il* or *-əl*, *n* a short pictorial poem, chiefly on pastoral subjects; a story, episode, or scene of happy innocence or rustic simplicity; a work of art of this character in any medium. — *adj* **idyll'ic** or (*rare*) **idyll'ian**. — *adv* **idyll'ically**. — *n* **id'yllist**. [L *īdyllium*, from Gr *eidyllion*, dimin of *eidos* image]

IE *abbrev*: Indo-European.

ie or **i.e.** *abbrev*: *id est* (*L*), that is, that is to say.

-ie *-ē* or *-i*, (*esp Austr*) *sfx* variant of, and forming nouns in the same way as, **-y**, as in *nightie*, *hippie*, *movie*, *barbie*, *tinnie*.

IEE *abbrev*: Institution of Electrical Engineers.

IF *abbrev*: intermediate frequency (also **i.f.**).

if *if*, *conj* on condition that; provided that; supposing that; whether; though; whenever; in surprise or irritation, as in *if it isn't John!*, *if that isn't the doorbell again!* — *n* a condition; a supposition; an uncertainty. — *adj* **iff'y** (*colloq*) dubious, uncertain, risky. — *n* **iff'iness**. — **as if** as it would be if; even supposing that, although, accepting that; **if only** see under **only**; **if only to** if for no other reason than to; **ifs and buts** objections; **if you like** if you want, if you approve; to use another expression, to put it a different way. [OE *gif*; cf Du *of*, ON *ef*]

Ifad or **IFAD** *abbrev*: International Fund for Agricultural Development.

-iferous. See **-ferous**.

iff *if*, (*logic*) *conj* used to express *if and only if*.

iffy. See under **if**.

-iform. See **-form**.

IFS *abbrev*: Institute for Fiscal Studies; Irish Free State (*hist*).

IG *abbrev*: Indo-Germanic.

igad *i-gad'*. Same as **egad**.

igapó. Same as **gapó**.

igarapé *ē-gä-rä-pā'*, *n* a canoe waterway in Brazil. [Tupí]

Igbo. See **Ibo**.

igloo *ig'lōō*, *n orig* a dome-shaped hut made of blocks of hard snow; now *usu* a dwelling made of other materials; a dome-shaped place of storage or container for goods; a hollow in the snow made by a seal over its breathing hole in the ice. [Eskimo *igdlu*, *iglu* house]

ign. *abbrev*: *ignotus* (*L*), unknown.

ignaro *ig-nä'rō* or *ēn-yä'rō*, *n* (*archaic*) an ignorant person: — *pl* **igna'roes** or **igna'ros**. [Prob from Spenser's character (*Faerie Queene*, I, viii) whose only answer is 'He could not tell', from Ital *ignaro*, from L *ignārus* ignorant]

Ignatian *ig-nā'shən*, *adj* of or pertaining to St *Ignatius*, first-century bishop of Antioch (applied to the Epistles attributed to him), or Saint *Ignatius* Loyola, the Spanish founder of the Society of Jesus. — *n* a Jesuit. — **St Ignatius's bean** see under **Saint**.

igneous *ig'ni-əs*, *adj* of or like fire; produced by solidification of the earth's internal molten magma (*geol*). [L *igneus* fiery, from *ignis* fire]

ignescent *ig-nes'ənt*, *adj* emitting sparks when struck. — *n* an ignescent substance. [L *ignēscēns*, *-entis*, pr p of *ignēscere* to catch fire]

ignimbrite *ig'nim-brīt*, *n* a hard rock formed by fusion of the volcanic fragments and dust of a nuée ardente. [L *ignis* fire, from *imber*, *imbris* a shower of rain, and **-ite**]

ignipotent *ig-nip'ə-tənt*, (*poetic*) *adj* presiding over fire. [L *ignipotens* powerful in fire, from *ignis* fire, and *potens* powerful]

ignis fatuus *ig'nis fat'ū-əs* or *fat'ōō-ōōs*, *n* will-o'-the-wisp, the light produced by combustion of marsh-gas, which may lead a traveller into danger; any delusive ideal or hope that may lead one astray: — *pl* **ignes fatui** (*ig'nēz fat'ū-ī* or *ig'nās fat'ōō-ē*). [L *ignis* fire, and *fatuus* foolish]

ignite *ig-nīt'*, *vt* to set on fire; to heat to the point at which combustion occurs. — *vi* to catch fire. — *adj* **ignīt'able** or **ignīt'ible**. — *n* **ignītabil'ity** or **ignītibil'ity**. — *n* **ignīt'er** someone who or something that ignites, eg an apparatus for firing an explosive or explosive mixture. — *n* **ignition** (*-nish'ən*) an act of igniting; a means of igniting; the state of being ignited; the firing system of an internal-combustion engine. — *n* **ig'nitron** (or *ig-nī'tron*) a device for conducting current in which an electrode dips into a pool of mercury and draws up an arc to start ionization. — **ignition key** in a motor vehicle, the key which is turned to operate the ignition system. [L *ignīre*, *ignītum* to set on fire, to make red-hot, from *ignis* fire]

ignoble *ig-nō'bl*, *adj* of low birth; mean or worthless; unworthy; base; dishonourable. — *n* **ignōbil'ity** or **ignō'bleness**. — *adv* **ignō'bly**. [Fr, from L *ignōbilis*, from *in-* not, and (*g*)*nōbilis* noble]

ignominy *ig'nə-min-i*, or *-nō-*, *n* loss of good name; public disgrace; humiliation; dishonour, infamy. — Also **ig'nomy** (*Shakesp*). — *adj* **ignomin'ious** disgraceful; humiliating. — *adv* **ignomin'iously**. [L *ignōminia*, from *in-* not, and (*g*)*nōmen*, *-inis* name]

ignoramus *ig-nō-rā'məs* or *-nə-*, *n* an ignorant person: — *pl* **ignorā'muses**. [L *ignōrāmus* we are ignorant, in legal use, we ignore, take no notice, 1st pers pl pres indicative of *ignōrāre*]

ignorant *ig'nər-ənt*, *adj* lacking knowledge, ill-educated; uninformed; having no understanding or awareness (with *of*); showing or arising from lack of knowledge; discourteous, rude, ill-bred; keeping back knowledge (*Shakesp*); unknown (*obs*). — *n* (*rare*) an ignorant person. — *n* **ig'norance** lack of knowledge, awareness, education or enlightenment; the state of being ignorant. — *adv* **ig'norantly**. [Fr, from L *ignōrāns*, *-antis*, pr p of *ignōrāre*; see **ignore**]

Ignorantine *ig-nō-ran'tīn*, *-nö-* or *-tin*, (*RC*) *n* a member of a religious congregation of men devoted to the instruction of the poor (inaccurately applied to *Brethren of the Christian Schools*).

ignoratio elenchi *ig-nə-rā'shō il-eng'kī* or *ig-nō-rät'i-ō el-eng'kē*, (*logic*) *n* the fallacy of appearing to refute a proposition by proving a proposition that is irrelevant to the point at issue. [L, literally ignorance of proof, from Gr *elenchou agnoia*]

ignore *ig-nōr'* or *-nör'*, *vt* to disregard; to refuse to take notice of; to pay no heed or attention to; to waive or set aside. — *adj* **ignor'able**. — *n* **ignorā'tion**. — *n* **ignor'er**. [L *ignōrāre* not to know, from *in-* not, and the root of (*g*)*nōscere*, to know]

iguana *i-gwä'nə*, *n* a large thick-tongued grey-green arboreal lizard of tropical America, having a row of spines along its back; loosely extended to others of the same family *Iguanidae* (also **iguanid**); in South Africa, a monitor lizard of the genus *Varanus*. [Sp, from Arawak *iwana*]

iguanid. See **iguana**.

iguanodon *i-gwä'nə-don*, *n* a large, bipedal, bird-hipped herbivorous dinosaur of the Jurassic and Cretaceous periods, with teeth like those of the iguana. [**iguana**, and Gr *odous*, *odontos* tooth]

IHC or **IHS** *abbrev*: *Iesous* (*Gr*), Jesus, using Greek capital iota, capital eta, and capital sigma (**C** or **S**), the first two and last letters of the name (used as a Christian symbol).

ihram *ē-räm* or *ēhh'räm*, *n* the scanty white cotton garment worn by Muslim pilgrims to Mecca; the holy state it betokens or bestows. [Ar *ihrām*]

ijtihad *ij-tə-häd'*, *n* the use of reasoning in Islamic law. [Ar, exerting oneself]

ikat *ik'at*, *n* a technique of dyeing yarn and tying it prior to weaving, resulting in a fabric with a geometric pattern of colours; this fabric. [Malay-Indonesian *mengikat* to tie]

IKBS (*comput*) *abbrev*: intelligent knowledge-based system.

ikebana *ē'ke-bä'nə*, *n* the Japanese art of flower arranging. [Jap, living flowers, arranged flowers]

ikon. Same as **icon**.

IL *abbrev*: Illinois (US state); Israel (*IVR*).

il- *il*, *pfx* same as **in-**, the form used with words beginning with *l*, as in *illegible*.

ilang-ilang. Same as **ylang-ylang**.

Ilchester cheese *il'chəs-tər chēz*, *n* Cheddar cheese flavoured with beer, spices, etc. [*Ilchester*, in Somerset, where it was first made]

ileac. See **ileum**.

ileo- *il-* or *īl-i-ō-*, or **ile-** *il-i-* or *īl-i-*, *combining form* denoting the ileum.

ileum *il'* or *īl'i-əm*, *n* the lowest part of the small intestine, between the jejunum and the ileocaecal valve: — *pl* **il'ea**. — *adj* **il'eac**. — *n* **ileitis** (*il-* or *īl-i-ī'tis*) inflammation of the ileum. — *n* **ileos'tomy** a surgical operation in which the ileum is brought through an artificial opening in the abdominal wall through which the contents of the intestine may be discharged. [LL *īleum*, L *īlia* (pl) the groin, flank, intestines]

ileus *il'* or *īl'i-əs*, *n* obstruction of the intestine with severe pain, vomiting, etc: — *pl* **il'euses**. [L *īleos*, from Gr *īleos* or *eileos* colic]

ilex *ī'leks*, *n* the holm-oak (*Quercus ilex*); a shrub or tree of the genus *Ilex*, to which the holly belongs: — *pl* **i'lexes** or **ilices** (*ī'li-sēz*). [L *īlex* holm-oak]

Iliac and **iliac**. See **Ilium** and **ilium**.

iliacus *il-ī'ə-kəs*, (*anatom*) *n* a triangular muscle in the groin which, acting with psoas muscle, flexes the thigh. [New L, from L *īlia* (pl); see **ileum**]

Iliad *il'i-ad* or *-əd*, *n* a Greek epic ascribed to Homer, on the siege of Troy; a long story or series of woes. [Gr *Īlias*, *-ados*, from *Īlios* or *Īlion* Ilium, Troy]

ilices. See **ilex**.

ilio- *il-i-ō-* or **ili-** *il-i-*, *combining form* denoting the ilium.

Ilium *il'i-əm*, or *īl'*, *n* Troy. — *adj* **Il'iac** or **Il'ian**. [L *Īlium*, from Gr *Īlion* Troy]

ilium *īl'* or *il'i-əm*, *n* a wide bone that is fused with the ischium and pubis to form the hip (or innominate) bone; the haunch bone: — *pl* **il'ia**. — *adj* **il'iac**. [L *īlium* (in classical L only in pl *īlia*); see **ileum**]

ilk[1] *ilk*, *n* type, kind. — *adj* (*Scot*) same. — **of that ilk** of that same, ie of the estate of the same name as the family (*Scot*); of that class, type or kind (*erron*). [OE *ilca* same]

ilk[2] *ilk*, (*Scot*) *adj* each, *usu* combined with the article as **ilk'a** (*-ə* or *-a*). — *n*, *adj* and *adv* **ilk'aday** every day, every day but Sunday. [OE *ǣlc* each, and *ān* one]

I'll *īl*, a contraction of **I will** or **I shall**.

Ill. *abbrev*: Illinois (US state).

ill *il*, *adj* (*compar* **worse**; *superl* **worst**) ailing, sick; evil, bad, wicked; producing evil; hurtful; unfortunate; unfavourable; difficult; reprehensible; incorrect, incompetent; (of temper, etc) peevish; grieved, distressed (*Scot*); severe (*Scot*). — *adv* (*compar* **worse**; *superl* **worst**) badly; not well; not rightly; wrongfully; unfavourably; amiss; with hardship; with difficulty. — *n* evil; wickedness; misfortune; harm; ailment. — *n* **ill'ness** sickness; disease. — *n* **illth** (*Ruskin*, etc) the contrary of wealth or well-being. — *adv* **illy** (*il'li*; *rare*) ill. — *adj* **ill-advised'** imprudent; ill-judged. — *adj* **ill-affect'ed** not well disposed. — *adj* **ill-assort'ed** incompatible; not matching. — *adj* **ill-behaved'** behaving badly, ill-mannered. — **ill'-being** the state of being poor or in bad health. — *adj* **ill-beseem'ing** (*Shakesp*) unbecoming. — **ill blood** or **ill feeling** resentment, enmity. — *adj* **ill-bod'ing** (*literary*) inauspicious. — *adj* **ill-bred'** badly brought up or badly educated; uncivil. — **ill breeding**. — *adj* **ill-condit'ioned** in bad condition; churlish (*archaic*). — *adj* **ill-consid'ered** badly thought out; misconceived. — *adj* **ill-deed'ly** (*Scot*; *archaic*) mischievous. — *adj* **ill-defined'** having no clear outline; vague, imprecise, hazy. — *adj* **ill-disposed'** unfriendly; unsympathetic. — *adj* **ill'-faced** (*poetic*; *Spenser* **ill-faste**) ugly-faced. — **ill fame** disrepute — *adj* **ill-fa'ted** unlucky. — *adj* **ill-fa'voured** (*Scot* **ill-faurd'**) unattractive, ugly. — *adv* **ill-fā'vouredly**. — **ill-fā'vouredness**. — **ill feeling** resentment, animosity, bad feeling; **ill fortune** bad luck. — *adj* **ill-found'ed** without foundation, baseless. — *adj* **ill'-gotten** or (*archaic*) **ill'-got** procured by dishonest or unworthy means. — *adj* **ill-haired'** (*Scot*) cross-grained. — *adj* **ill-head'ed** (*archaic*; *Spenser* **ill-hedd'ed**) not clear in the head. — **ill health** poor health; **ill-hu'mour**. — *adj* **ill-hu'moured** bad-tempered. — *adj* **ill-informed'** ignorant. — *adj* **ill-judged'** folish, unwise, ill-timed. — *adj* **ill-look'ing** having an evil look; ugly. — **ill luck** bad luck. — *adj* **ill-manned'** (*archaic*) provided with too few men. — *adj* **ill-mann'ered** rude, discourteous; boorish, uncouth. — *adj* **ill-matched'** not suited to one another; not matching well. — **ill nature**. — *adj* **ill-na'tured** bad-tempered; spiteful, malevolent, mean. — *adv* **ill-na'turedly**. — *n* **ill-na'turedness**. — *adj* **ill-off'** (*rare*) in bad circumstances, badly off. — *adj* **ill-o'mened** unfortunate, unlucky; inauspicious, doomed. — *adj* **ill-spent'** misspent, wasted, squandered. — *adj* **ill-starred'** born under the influence of an unlucky star; unlucky, ill-fated. — **ill success** lack of success, failure; **ill temper**. — *adj* **ill-tem'pered** bad-tempered; morose. — *adj* **ill-timed'** said or done at an unsuitable time; inappropriate, ill-judged. — *vt* **ill-treat'** to treat badly or cruelly; to abuse. — **ill-treat'ment**; **ill turn** an act of unkindness or enmity; **ill-u'sage** or **ill-use'**. — *vt* **ill-use'** to ill-treat. — *adj* **ill-used'** badly treated. — *adj* **ill-versed'** having scanty knowledge or skill (with *in*). — **ill-will'** unkind feeling; enmity, hostility; **ill'-wisher** a person who wishes harm to another. — *adj* **ill-wrest'ing** (*Shakesp*) misinterpreting to disadvantage. — **go ill with** to result in danger or misfortune to; **ill at ease** uneasy; embarrassed; **take it ill** to be offended; **with an ill grace** ungraciously. [ON *illr*; not connected with OE *yfel*, evil, but formerly confused with it, so that *ill* is often (esp in Scots) to be read where *evil* is written]

illapse *il-aps'*, *n* a sliding in. — *vi* to glide in. [L *illābī*, *illāpsus*, from *il-*(*in-*) in, and *lābī* to slip, to slide]

illaqueate *i-lak'wi-āt*, *vt* to ensnare. — *adj* **illaq'ueable**. — *n* **illaqueā'tion**. [L *illaqueāre*, *-ātum*, from *il-*(*in-*) into, and *laqueus* a noose]

illation *il-ā'shən*, *n* the act of inferring from premises; inference; conclusion. — *adj* **illative** (*il'ə-tiv* or *il-ā'tiv*) relating to, of the nature of, expressing, or introducing an inference; denoting a case in some Finno-Ugric languages expressing direction into or towards (*gram*). — *n* the illative case; a word in this case. — *adv* **ill'atively** (or *-ā'*). [L *illātiō*, *-ōnis*, from *illātus*, used as pa p of *inferre* to infer, from *il-*(*in-*) in, and *lātus* carried]

illaudable *il-ö'də-bl*, *adj* not praiseworthy. — *adv* **illau'd-ably**. [**il-** (**in-** (2))]

Illecebrum *il-es'i-brəm*, *n* a genus of plants of one species found in Devon and Cornwall, for which the name **Illecebrā'ceae** is used for its family in some classification systems, whilst in others it is regarded as belonging to the Paronychiaceae, the Corregiolaceae or the Caryophyllaceae families. [Said to be from L *illecebra* allurement, 'as enticing the simpler into bogs and marshes']

illegal *il-ē'gl*, *adj* prohibited by law, unlawful. — *n* **illēgality** (*-gal'i-ti*) the quality or condition of being illegal. — *vt* **illē'galize** or **-ise**. — *adv* **illē'gally**. [**il-** (**in-** (2))]

illegible *il-ej'i-bl, adj* impossible or very difficult to read. — *n* **illegibil'ity** or **illeg'ibleness**. — *adv* **illeg'ibly**. [**il-** (**in-** (2))]

illegitimate *il-i-jit'i-mit, adj* born of parents not married to each other at the time; (of a birth) happening outside marriage; unlawful, improper; not properly inferred or reasoned (*logic*); not recognized by authority or good usage. — *n* a person born outside marriage. — *vt* (*-māt*) to pronounce or render illegitimate. — *n* **illegit'imacy** (*-mə-si*) or **illegit'imateness**. — *adv* **illegit'imately**. — *n* **illegitimā'tion**. — **illegitimate pollination** in dimorphic flowers, pollination of long style from short stamen, or short from long; **illegitimate recombination** recombination, facilitated by the casual presence of duplicate sequences, between species whose DNA shows little or no homology. [**il-** (**in-** (2))]

illiad. A Shakespearian form of **oeillade**.

illiberal *il-ib'ər-əl, adj* narrow-minded, intolerant or prejudiced; niggardly, ungenerous; narrow in opinion or culture, unenlightened. — *n* **illiberality** (*-al'i-ti*). — *vt* **illib'eralize** or **-ise**. — *adv* **illib'erally**. [**il-** (**in-** (2))]

illicit *il-is'it, adj* not allowable; unlawful; unlicensed. — *adv* **illic'itly**. — *n* **illic'itness**. — **illicit process of the major** or **minor** (*logic*) the fallacy of distributing the major or minor term in the conclusion when it is not distributed in the premise. [L *illicitus*, from *il-* (*in-*) not, and *licitus*, pa p of *licēre* to be allowed]

illimitable *il-im'it-ə-bl, adj* limitlessly infinite. — *n* **illim'itability** or **illim'itableness**. — *adv* **illim'itably**. — *n* **illimitā'tion**. — *adj* **illim'ited**. [**il-** (**in-** (2))]

illinium *il-in'i-əm*, (*chem*) *n* former name for **promethium**. [*Illinois* University, where its discovery was claimed]

illipe *il'ip-i* or **illupi** *il-ōō'pi, n* the mahwa tree (family Sapotaceae), producing **illipe nuts** and **illipe oil**. [Tamil *illuppai*]

illiquation *il-i-kwā'shən, n* the melting of one thing into another. [**il-** (**in-** (1))]

illiquid *il-ik'wid, adj* (of assets, etc) not readily converted into cash; deficient in liquid assets. — *n* **illiquid'ity**. [**il-** (**in-** (2))]

illision *il-izh'ən, n* the act of striking against something. [L *illīsiō, -ōnis*, from *illīdere*, from *in* into, and *laedere* to strike]

illit. *abbrev*: illiterate.

illite *il'īt*, (*mineralogy*) *n* a white or pale clay mineral found in shales and sediments, having a similar structure to the micas. [US state of *Ill*inois, and **-ite**[3]]

illiterate *il-it'ər-it, adj* unable to read and write; ignorant, uneducated; displaying ignorance of, or contravening the accepted standards of, writing and speech; ignorant in a particular field or subject, as in *mathematically illiterate*. — *n* an illiterate person. — *n* **illit'eracy** (*-ə-si*) or **illit'erateness**. — *adv* **illit'erately**. [**il-** (**in-** (2))]

illocution *il-ə-kū'shən*, (*philos*) *n* an act which is performed by a speaker actually speaking the words, as an order or a promise (cf **perlocution**). — *adj* **illocū'tionary**. [**il-** (**in-** (1))]

illogical *il-oj'i-kəl, adj* contrary to the rules of logic; regardless or incapable of logic; senseless, unreasonable, crazy. — *n* **illog'ic**. — *n* **illogicality** (*-kal'i-ti*) or **illog'icalness**. — *adv* **illog'ically**. [**il-** (**in-** (2))]

illude *il-ōōd'* or *-ūd', vt* to trick. [L *illūdere*, from *in* on, and *lūdere, lūsum* to play]

illume *il-ūm'* or *-ōōm', vt* a shortened poetic form of **illumine**.

illuminance *il-ū'min-əns* or *-ōō'*, (*phys*) *n* the luminous flux incident on a given surface per unit area, expressed in lux. — Also **illuminā'tion**.

illuminate *il-ū'min-āt* or *-ōō', vt* to light up; to make bright, fill with light; to enlighten, clarify; to illustrate, elucidate; to adorn with coloured lettering or illustrations. — *adj* (*-āt* or *-it*) enlightened; claiming special enlightenment; made bright or clear with light. — *n* a person who claims to have special enlightenment. — *adj* **illu'minant** enlightening; giving off light. — *n* a means of lighting. — *n* **illuminā'tion** the act or state of illuminating or being illuminated; an act of lighting up; a source of light; the strength or intensity of light; intellectual or spiritual enlightenment; clarification, elucidation; (in *pl*) a decorative display of lights; the adorning of books with coloured lettering or illustrations; illuminance (*phys*). — *adj* **illu'minating**. — *adj* **illu'minative** (*-ə-tiv* or *-ā-tiv*). — *n* **illu'minātor** a decorator of manuscripts, etc; a person who provides clarification or enlightenment. [L *illūmināre, -ātum*, from *lumen* light]

Illuminati *il-lōō-mi-nä'tē, n pl* the enlightened, a name given to various religious sects, and *esp* to a society of German Free-thinkers at the end of the 18c; (without *cap*) people who claim to have special enlightenment, *esp* in philosophical or religious matters. [L, pl of *illiminatus*]

illumine *il-ū'min* or *-ōō', vt* a literary form of **illuminate**. — *adj* **illu'minable**. — *n* **illu'miner**. [L *illūmināre*, from *in* in, upon, and *lūmināre* to cast light]

illuminism *il-ū'min-izm* or *-ōō', n* the doctrines or principles of the Illuminati; belief in or claim to an inward spiritual light. — *n* **illu'minist**.

illupi. See **illipe**.

illusion *il-ōō'zhən* or *-ū', n* deceptive appearance; an apparition; a false conception or notion; delusion; a false perception due to misinterpretation of stimuli from an object (*psychol*; cf **hallucination**); a very fine transparent gauze or tulle used for veils, dresses, trimmings, etc; a mocking (*obs*). — *n* **illu'sionism** the doctrine that the external world is illusory (*philos*); the production of illusion, *esp* the use of artistic techniques, such as perspective, etc, to produce an illusion of reality. — *n* **illu'sionist** a believer in or practitioner of illusionism; a person who produces illusions, a conjurer, prestidigitator. — *adj* **illu'sive** (*-siv*) or **illu'sory** (*-sər-i*) misleading by false appearances; false, deceptive, unreal. — *adv* **illu'sively**. — *n* **illu'siveness**. [L *illūsio, -ōnis*, from *illūdere* to mock, make sport of]

illustrate *il'əs-trāt, vt* to elucidate and amplify by pictures, examples, etc; to execute pictures for (a book, etc); to demonstrate, show clearly; to make bright, adorn (*obs*); to enlighten (*archaic*); to show in a favourable light (*obs*); to give distinction or honour to (*obs*). — *vi* to provide an example, etc. — *adj* (*-lus'*; *archaic*) illustrious; renowned. — *adj* **ill'ustrated** (or *-us'*) having pictorial illustrations. — *n* an illustrated periodical. — *n* **illustrā'tion** the act of illustrating or process of being illustrated; something that serves to illustrate; exemplification; an example; a picture or diagram elucidating or accompanying text. — *adj* **illustrā'tional**, **illustrative** (*il'əs-trā-tiv* or *-trə-*, or *il-us'trə-tiv*) or **illus'tratory** serving to clarify, explain or adorn. — *adv* **ill'ustratively** (or *il-us'*). — *n* **ill'ustrātor**. [L *illūstrāre* to light up, prob from *lūx* light]

illustrious[1] *il-us'tri-əs, adj* distinguished, renowned; noble, glorious; luminous (*obs*). — *adv* **illus'triously**. — *n* **illus'triousness**. [L *illūstris* lustrous, or renowned; see also **illustrate**]

illustrious[2] *il-us'tri-əs*, (*Shakesp*) *adj* dull (*perh* for *illustrous*, not lustrous).

illustrissimo *ēl-lōōs-trē'sē-mō*, (*Ital*) *adj* most illustrious.

illuvium *il-ōō'vi-əm, n* material, including mineral salts, fine clay and silt particles, dissolved or suspended in water and transported from one layer of soil to a lower layer where they are deposited. — *adj* **illu'vial**. — *n* **illuviā'tion** the process of deposition of illuvium. [New L, from pfx **il-** (*in-*) in, into, and **-luvium** (see **alluvium**), from L *luēre* to wash]

Illyrian *il-ir'i-ən, adj* of or pertaining to *Illyria*, an ancient region to the east of the Adriatic Sea, its inhabitants, or their (*prob* Indo-European) language. — Also *n*.

illy whacker *il'i whak'ər* or *wak'ər*, (*Austr slang*) *n* a conman, a trickster. [Origin unknown]

ilmenite *il'mən-īt, n* a black mineral $FeTiO_3$, composed of iron, titanium and oxygen. [From the *Ilmen* Mountains in the Urals]

ILO *abbrev*: International Labour Organization.
il penseroso *ēl pen-se-rō'zō*, (Ital *pensieroso*) *n* the pensive (or melancholy) man.
ILS *abbrev*: instrument landing system.
IM *abbrev*: intramuscular(ly).
im- *im-*, *pfx* same as **in-**, but the form used with words beginning with *b*, *m* or *p*, as in *imbalance*, *immodest*, *implant*.
I'm *īm*, a contraction of **I am**.
image *im'ij*, *n* a likeness or representation of a person or thing; a statue, an idol; a person or thing that closely resembles another; a representation in the mind, an idea; a mental picture or representation resulting from thought or memory rather than sensory perception (*psychol*); (a person who is) the epitome or personification of a quality; the figure of any object formed by rays of light reflected or refracted (*real* if the rays converge upon it, *virtual* if they appear to diverge from it) (*optics*); an analogous figure formed by other rays (*optics*); the element of a set which is associated with an element in a different set when one set is a function or transformation of the other (*math*); a figure of speech, *esp* a metaphor or simile (*rhetoric*); the character or attributes of a person, institution, business, etc as regarded by the general public; a favourable self-representation created by a public figure, corporation, etc; an exact copy of an area of store held either in another storage device or in another area of the same device (*comput*). — *vt* to form an image of; to form a likeness of in the mind; to mirror; to imagine; to portray; to typify; to produce a pictorial representation of (a part of the body) for diagnostic medical purposes. — *adj* **im'ageable**. — *adj* **im'ageless**. — *n* **imagery** (*im'ij-ri* or *-ə-ri*) the products of the imagination; mental pictures; figures of speech; images in general or collectively. — *n* **im'aging** image formation. — *n* **im'agism** (sometimes with *cap*) an early 20c school of poetry aiming at concentration, clear and simple language, and freedom of form and subject. — *n* and *adj* **im'agist**. — *adj* **imagist'ic**. — **image converter** an instrument which converts infrared or other invisible images into visible images; **image intensifier** an electronic device for increasing the brightness of an optical image, such as the fluoroscopic image in X-ray examinations; **image orthicon** a television camera tube which converts the images it receives into electronic impulses which are transmitted as television signals; **image printer** a printer which will print a copy of a complete page on paper from an image composed by optical technology from digital input; **im'age-worship**. [OFr, from L *imāgō* image; cf *imitārī* to imitate]
imaginal. See under **imago**.
imagine *im-aj'in*, *vt* to form a mental image of; to conceive; to think; to believe falsely, to fancy; to conjecture, suppose; to contrive or devise. — *vi* to form mental images; to exercise imagination. — *adj* **imag'inable**. — *n* **imag'inableness**. — *adv* **imag'inably**. — *adj* **imag'inary** existing only in the imagination; not real, illusory; of or containing an imaginary number (*math*); non-existent. — *n* **imag'inariness**. — *n* **imaginā'tion** the act of imagining; the faculty of forming mental images; the creative power of the mind; resourcefulness, contrivance. — *adj* **imag'inative** (*-ə-tiv* or *-ā-tiv*) full of or endowed with imagination; done or created with, or showing, imagination. — *adv* **imag'inatively**. — *n* **imag'inativeness**. — *n* **imag'iner**. — *n* **imag'ining** (in *pl*) things imagined. — *n* **imag'inist** (*Jane Austen*) a person with an active imagination and a tendency to speculate or wonder. — **imaginary numbers** or **quantities** non-existent quantities involving the square roots of negative quantities. [OFr *imaginer*, from L *imāginārī*, from *imāgō* an image]
imagism and **imagist**. See under **image**.
imago *i-mā'gō*, or *-mä'*, *n* the last or perfect stage of an insect's development; an image or optical counterpart of a thing; an elaborated representation of an important or influential person (*esp* a parent) in an individual's life, persisting in the unconscious (*psychol*): — *pl* **imagines** (*i-mā'jin-ēz*, *-mā'gin-* or *-mä'*), **ima'gos** or **ima'goes**. — *adj* **imaginal** (*i-maj'*). [L *imāgō*, *-inis* image]
imam *i-mäm'* or **imaum** *i-mōm'*, *n* the officer who leads the devotions in a mosque; (with *cap*) a title for various Muslim potentates, founders and leaders. — *n* **imam'ate** the (period of) office of an imam; the territory under the jurisdiction of an imam. [Ar *imām* chief]
IMarE *abbrev*: Institute of Marine Engineers.
imaret *im-ä'ret* or *im'ə-ret*, *n* (in Turkey) an inn or hospice for travellers. [Turk, from Ar *'imārah* building]
Imari *ē-mä'ri*, (also without *cap*) *n* and *adj* (of) a type of Japanese porcelain, richly decorated in red, green and blue. [*Imari*, seaport in Japan from where such porcelain was exported]
imaum. See **imam**.
imbalance *im-bal'əns*, *n* a lack of balance, as between the ocular muscles or between the activities of the endocrines, or between the parts of the involuntary nervous system, or between the elements of a diet (*med*); temporary lack of balance in a self-adjusting system; lack of balance between any two corresponding things; lack of balance in the sphere of a nation's economy or in the economics of, or trade between, two nations. [**im-** (**in-** (2))]
imbar, etc. See **embar**, etc.
imbark *im-bärk'*, (*poetic*) *vt* to enclose in bark. [**im-** (**in-** (1))]
imbecile *im'bi-sēl*, *-sīl* or *-sil*, *n* a person of moderate to severe intellectual subnormality (from birth or an early age) whose mental defectiveness is of a lesser degree than idiocy, but who is incapable of managing adequately his or her own affairs (now *obs*); (loosely) a foolish, unwise or stupid person. — *adj* extremely feeble-minded; foolish, fatuous. — *adj* **imbecilic** (*im-bi-sil'ik*). — *n* **imbecil'ity**. [Fr *imbécille* (now *imbécile*), from L *imbēcillus* weak, feeble]
imbed. Same as **embed**.
imbibe *im-bīb'*, *vt* to drink; to absorb, drink in; to receive into the mind, assimilate. — *vi* to drink. — *n* **imbīb'er**. — *n* **imbibition** (*im-bib-ish'ən*) the absorption or adsorption of a liquid by a solid or gel (*chem*); the uptake of water by germinating seeds (*bot*); the transfer of dye to an absorbing layer, eg gelatine, to produce a dye image (*image technol*). — *adj* **imbibit'ional**. [L *imbibere*, from *in* in, into, and *bibere* to drink]
imborder. See **emborder**.
imbosk and **imboss**. See **emboss**[2].
imbrast (*Spenser*). Same as **embraced** (see **embrace**[1]).
imbrex *im'breks*, *n* in Roman buildings, one of a series of *usu* curved tiles fixed over the joins of flat tiles: — *pl* **im'brices** (*-bri-sēz*). [L]
imbricate *im'bri-kāt*, *vt* to lay one overlapping another, as tiles on a roof. — *vi* to be so placed. — *adj* (*-kit* or *-kāt*) (of fish-scales, leaves, layers of tissue, teeth, etc) overlapping like roof tiles. — *adv* **im'bricately**. — *n* **imbricā'tion**. [L *imbricāre*, *-ātum* to cover with overlapping tiles, from *imbrex* a pantile]
imbroccata *im-bro-kä'tə*, (*fencing*) *n* a thrust. [Ital]
imbroglio *im-brōl'yō*, *n* a confused mass or heap; an intricate or perplexing situation, a tangle; an embroilment; an ordered confusion (*music*): — *pl* **imbro'glios**. — Also **embro'glio**: — *pl* **embro'glios**. [Ital, confusion, from *imbrogliare* to confuse, embroil]
imbrue or **embrue** (*Spenser* **embrewe'**) *im-broo'*, (*literary*) *vt* to wet or moisten; to soak; to drench; to stain or dye. — *n* **imbrue'ment** or **embrue'ment**. [OFr *embreuver*, from *bevre* (Fr *boire*), from L *bibere* to drink]
imbrute or **embrute** *im-broot'*, (*archaic*) *vt* or *vi* to degrade, or sink, to the state of a brute. [**im-** (**in-** (1))]
imbue *im-bū'*, *vt* to fill, permeate, inspire (eg the mind) (with *with*); to moisten; to tinge deeply. [OFr *imbuer*, from L *imbuere*, from *in*, and root of *bibere* to drink]

imburse *im-bûrs'*, (*rare*) *vt* to put in a purse or in one's purse; to pay, refund. [**im-** (**in-** (1)), and L *bursa* a purse]
IMechE *abbrev*: Institute of Mechanical Engineers.
IMF *abbrev*: International Monetary Fund.
imidazole *im-id'ə-zōl*, (*chem*) *n* any of a group of heterocyclic compounds produced by substitution in a five-membered ring containing two nitrogen atoms on either side of a carbon atom. — Also called **gloxaline**. [**imide** and **azole**]
imide *im'īd*, (*chem*) *n* any of a class of organic compounds formed from ammonia or a primary amine by replacing two hydrogen atoms by a metal or acid radical. — *adj* **imid'ic**. [Alteration of **amide**]
imine *im'īn* or *i-mīn'*, *n* a highly reactive nitrogen-containing organic substance having a carbon-to-nitrogen double bond. [Alteration of **amine**]
imipramine *i-mip'rə-mēn*, *n* an antidepressant drug also used in the treatment of enuresis. [From d*im*ethyl-*pr*opyl*amine*]
imit. *abbrev*: imitation; imitative.
imitate *im'i-tāt*, *vt* to strive to be like or produce something like; to copy or take as a model; to mimic. — *n* **imitability** (*-ə-bil'i-ti*). or **im'itableness**. — *adj* **im'itable**. — *adj* **im'itancy** (*Carlyle*) the tendency to imitate. — *n* **im'itant** (*rare*) an imitation. — *n* **imitā'tion** the act of imitating; that which is produced as a copy, or counterfeit; a performance in mimicry; the repeating of the same passage, or the following of a passage with a similar one in one or more of the other parts (*music*). — *adj* sham, counterfeit; produced as a substitute, by a cheaper method in cheaper materials, etc. — *adj* **im'itātive** inclined to imitate; formed after a model; mimicking; (of words) onomatopoeic. — *adv* **im'itātively**. — *n* **im'itātiveness**. — *n* **im'itātor**. [L *imitārī*, *-ātus*]
immaculate *im-ak'ū-lit*, *adj* clean, spotless; perfectly groomed; flawless; unstained; pure. — *n* **immac'ulacy**. — *adv* **immac'ulately**. — *n* **immac'ulateness**. — **Immaculate Conception** the RC dogma that the Virgin Mary was conceived without original sin, first proclaimed as an article of faith in 1854 (not the same as the Virgin Birth). [L *immaculātus*, from *in-* not, and *maculāre* to spot]
immanacle *im-an'ə-kl* or *im-man'*, (*Milton*) *vt* to put in manacles, to fetter or confine. [**im-** (**in-** (1))]
immanation *im-ə-nā'shən*, *n* a flowing in. [L *in* in, and *mānāre*, *-ātum* to flow]
immane *im-ān'*, (*archaic*) *adj* huge; cruel, savage. — *adv* **immane'ly**. — *n* **immanity** (*im-an'i-ti*) monstrous cruelty. [L *immānis* huge, savage]
immanent *im'ə-nənt*, *adj* dwelling within; pervading; inherent. — *n* **imm'anence** or **imm'anency** the pervasion of the universe by the intelligent and creative principle, a fundamental conception of pantheism. — *adj* **immanental** (*-ent'l*). — *n* **imm'anentism** belief in an immanent God. — *n* **imm'anentist**. [L *in* in, and *manēre* to remain]
immanity. See under **immane**.
Immanuel. See **Emmanuel**.
immarcescible *im-är-ses'i-bl*, *adj* unfading; imperishable. [L *in-* not, and *marcēscere* to languish]
immarginate *im-är'jin-āt*, (*bot*) *adj* without a distinct margin. [**im-** (**in-** (2))]
immask *im-mäsk'*, (*Shakesp*) *vt* to mask or disguise. [**im-** (**in-** (1))]
immaterial *im-ə-tē'ri-əl*, *adj* not consisting of matter; incorporeal; unimportant. — *n* **immatē'rialism** (*philos*) the doctrine that there is no material substance, that material things do not exist outside the mind. — *n* **immatē'rialist**. — *n* **immatēriality** (*-al'*) the quality of being immaterial or of not consisting of matter. — *vt* **immatē'rialize** or **-ise** to separate from matter, to make immaterial. — *adv* **immatē'rially**. [**im-** (**in-** (2))]
immature *im-ə-tyŏŏr'* or *-chŏŏr'*, *adj* not fully grown; not yet ripe; not fully developed (mentally, physically, etc); (of behaviour, attitudes, etc) childish. — *adv* **immature'ly**. — *n* **immature'ness** or **immatur'ity**. [**im-** (**in-** (2))]
immeasurable *im-ezh'ər-ə-bl*, *adj* to great to be measured. — *n* **immeas'urableness**. — *adv* **immeas'urably**. — *adj* **immeas'ured** (*Spenser*) immeasurable. [**im-** (**in-** (2))]
immediate *im-ē'di-it*, *-dyət*, *-dyit* or *-jət*, *adj* done or happening without delay; direct, with nothing intervening; next, nearest or closest; involving, or resulting from, nothing other than direct knowledge or intuitive understanding (*philos*). — *n* **immē'diacy** the state of being immediate; directness or freshness of appeal. — *adv* **immē'diately**. — *conj* as soon as. — *n* **immē'diateness**. — *n* **immē'diatism** the policy of action at once, *esp* (*US hist*) in abolition of slavery. — **immediate access store** (*comput*) the part of the central processing unit which provides the working memory store of a computer (*abbrev* **IAS**); **immediate constituent** any meaningful constituent forming part of a linguistic construction which may be used to analyse structure, eg in a sentence the subject and predicate are immediate constituents. [**im-** (**in-** (2))]
immedicable *im-med'i-kə-bl* or *im-ed'*, (*formal*) *adj* incurable. [**im-** (**in-** (2))]
Immelmann turn *im'əl-mən tûrn*, (*aeronautics*) *n* a manoeuvre involving a half loop and a half roll, carried out to achieve greater height and reverse the direction of flight. [Named after Max *Immelmann* (1890–1916), German aviator]
immemorial *im-i-mōr'i-əl*, or *-mör'*, *adj* ancient beyond the reach of memory. — *adv* **immemō'rially**. [**im-** (**in-** (2))]
immense *i-mens'*, *adj* vast in extent or degree; very large, enormous; fine, very good (*slang*). — *adv* **immense'ly**. — *n* **immense'ness** or **immens'ity** a measureless expanse; vastness. [Fr, from L *immēnsus*, from *in-* not, and *mēnsus*, pa p of *metīrī* to measure]
immensurable *im-men'shŏŏr-ə-bl*, *im-en'*, *-syŏŏr-*, or *-syər-*, *adj* too great to be measured, immeasurable. — *n* **immensurabil'ity**. [**im-** (**in-** (2))]
immerge *im-mûrj'* or *im-ûrj'*, (*rare*) *vt* and *vi* to dip or plunge in to liquid, to immerse. [**im-** (**in-** (1))]
immeritous *im-mer'it-əs*, (*archaic*) *adj* undeserving. [L *immeritus*, from *in-* not, and *meritus* deserving]
immerse *im-ûrs'* or *im-mûrs'*, *vt* to dip or plunge under the surface of a liquid; to baptize by immersion; to engage or involve deeply, to engross. — *adj* **immersed'** embedded in another part (*bot* or *zool*); growing entirely submerged in water (*bot*). — *n* **immer'sion** the act of immersing; the process or state of being immersed; deep absorption or involvement; baptism by immersing all or part of a person's body in water; the disappearance of a celestial body eg in eclipse or occultation (*astron*); a method of teaching a foreign language by giving the learner intensive practice in a situation in which all communication is in the language concerned. — *n* **immer'sionism**. — *n* **immer'sionist** a person who favours or practises baptism by immersion. — **immersion foot** another name for **trench foot**; **immersion heater** an electrical apparatus directly immersed in the liquid, used for heating water; **immersion lens** a microscope object-glass that works with a drop of oil or water between it and the cover-glass. [See **immerge**]
immesh. See **enmesh**.
immethodical *im-mi-thod'ik-əl* or *im-i-*, *adj* without method or order, disorganized; irregular. — *adv* **immethod'ically**. [**im-** (**in-** (2))]
immew. See **emmew**.
immigrate *im'i-grāt*, *vi* to migrate into a country with the intention of settling in it. — *n* **imm'igrant** a person who immigrates; an animal or plant living or growing in an

imb- for many words see **emb-**.

area to which it has migrated. — *n* **immigrā'tion**. [L *immigrāre*, from *in* into, and *migrāre*, *-ātum* to remove]

imminent *im'i-nənt*, *adj* impending, approaching, forthcoming; looming, threatening; jutting, overhanging (*obs*). — *n* **imm'inence** imminency; impending evil (*Shakesp*). — *n* **imm'inency**. — *adv* **imm'inently**. [L *imminēns*, *-entis*, from *in* upon, and *minēre* to project, jut]

immingle *im-ming'gl* or *im-ing'*, (*rare*) *vt* and *vi* to mingle together, to mix. [**im-** (**in-** (1))]

imminute *im'i-nūt*, (*archaic*) *adj* lessened. — *n* **imminū'tion** lessening. [L *imminutus*, pa p of *imminuere*, from *in-* (intensive), and *minuere* to lessen]

immiscible *im-mis'i-bl* or *im-is'*, *adj* not capable of being mixed, eg as oil and water. — *n* **immiscibil'ity**. [**im-** (**in-** (2))]

immiseration *im-iz-ər-ā'shən*, *n* progressive impoverishment or degradation. — Also **immiserīzā'tion** or **-z-**. — *vt* **immis'erize** or **-ise**. [**im-** (**in-**(1)), and *misery*]

immit *im-mit'* or *im-it'*, (now *obs*) *vt* to insert, infuse; to introduce; to inject: — *pr p* **immitt'ing**; *pa t* and *pa p* **immitt'ed**. — *n* **immission** (*-ish'ən*). [L *immittere*, from *in* into, and *mittere*, *missum* to send]

immitigable *im-it'i-gə-bl*, *adj* incapable of being mitigated. — *n* **immitigabil'ity**. — *adv* **immit'igably**. [**im-** (**in-** (2))]

immix *im-miks'* or *im-iks'*, (*archaic*) *vt* to mix in (with *with*); to commingle. — *n* **immix'ture**. [**im-** (**in-** (1))]

immobile *im-ō'bīl*, *im-mō'*, *-bēl*, or *US -bil*, *adj* immovable; not readily moved; unable to move; motionless; stationary. — *n* **immob'ilism** a political policy characterized by extreme lack of action. — *n* **immobil'ity**. — *n* **immobilīzā'tion** or **-s-**. — *vt* **immob'ilize** or **-ise** to render immobile; to put or keep out of action or circulation. [**im-** (**in-** (2))]

immoderate *im-od'ər-it*, *adj* excessive; extravagant; unrestrained. — *adv* **immod'erately**. — *n* **immoderā'tion**, **immod'erateness** or **immod'eracy**. [**im-** (**in-** (2))]

immodest *im-od'ist*, *adj* shameless indecent, improper; too self-assertive, boastful. — *adv* **immod'estly**. — *n* **immod'esty**. [**im-** (**in-** (2))]

immolate *im'ō-lāt* or *im'əl-āt*, *vt* to offer or kill as a sacrifice; to give up or sacrifice (something highly valued) in exchange for, or for the sake of, something else. — *n* **immolā'tion**. — *n* **imm'olātor**. [L *immolāre*, *-ātum* to sprinkle meal (on a victim), hence, to sacrifice, from *in* upon, and *mola* meal]

immoment *im-mō'mənt*, (*Shakesp*) *adj* of no value, trifling. — *adj* **immome'ntous**. [**im-** (**in-** (2))]

immoral *im-or'əl* or *im-mor'*, *adj* inconsistent with accepted moral principles or standards, wrong; evil, unscrupulous; sexually improper; promiscuous, licentious, dissolute. — *n* **immor'alism** the denial or rejection of morality. — *n* **immor'alist** a person who practises or advocates immorality. — *n* **immorality** (*im-or-* or *im-ər-al'i-ti*) the quality or state of being immoral, *esp* promiscuity or licentiousness; an immoral act or practice. — *adv* **immor'ally**. [**im-** (**in-** (2))]

immortal *im-ör'tl*, *adj* exempt from death; living in perpetuity without fading or decaying; imperishable; never to be forgotten, famous or remembered throughout time. — *n* a being who will never cease to exist; a person whose greatness will never fade, or whose genius will be revered for all time; (in *pl*; often with *cap*) a god, *esp* of the ancient Greeks and Romans; (in *pl*; *usu* with *cap*) the forty members of the French Academy. — *n* **immortality** (*im-ör-* or *im-ər-tal'i-ti*). — *adv* **immor'tally**. — *n* **immortalīzā'tion** or **-s-**. — *vt* **immor'talize** or **-ise** to make immortal; to give everlasting fame to. — **the Immortal Memory** a toast in memory of the Scottish poet, Robert Burns, *usu* on the anniversary of his birth, 25 January. [**im-** (**in-** (2))]

immortelle *im-ör-tel'*, *n* an everlasting flower; a china replica of flowers, as a graveyard monument. [Fr (*fleur*) *immortelle* immortal (flower)]

immovable *im-o͞ov'ə-bl*, *adj* impossible to move; steadfast; unyielding; impassive; motionless; unalterable; not liable to be removed (*law*; commonly **immove'able**); real, not personal (*law*). — *n* (*law*; *usu* in *pl* **immove'ables**) immoveable property. — *n* **immov'ableness** or **immovabil'ity**. — *adv* **immov'ably**. [**im-** (**in-** (2))]

immune *im-ūn'*, *adj* exempt (with *from*); free from obligation (with *from*); not liable to danger, protected (with *to*); protected against a disease or infection because of the presence of specific antibodies which act against the antigens concerned; unaffected, not susceptible (with *to*). — *n* someone who, or something that, is immune. — *adj* **immunifā'cient** producing immunity. — *n* **immun'ity** the condition of being immune. — *n* **immunīzā'tion** or **-s-**. — *vt* **imm'unize** or **-ise** to render immune, *esp* to make immune from a disease by injecting or exposing to disease germs or their poisons (either active or rendered harmless). — **immuno-** (*i-mū'no-* or *im'*) *combining form* denoting immune, immunity. — *n* **immunoass'ay** (or *ə-sā'*) any of the various methods used to determine levels of antibody and antigen in a tissue. — *n* **immunoblot'** a technique used to transfer the pattern of proteins separated by electrophoresis to a medium in which they can be further analysed (also called **western blotting**). — *adj* **immunochem'ical**. — *adv* **immunochem'ically**. — *n* **immunochem'istry** the chemistry of antibodies, antibody reactions, etc. — *adj* **immunocom'promised** (*med*) having an impaired immune system. — *adj* **immunocytochem'ical**. — *adv* **immunocytochem'ically**. — *n* **immunocytochem'istry** the study of the chemical aspects of cellular immunity. — *n* **immuno defi'ciency** deficiency in immune response due to depletion or inactivity of lymphoid cells. — *n sing* **immunodiagnos'tics** diagnostics relating to immunology. — *n* **immunofluoresc'ence** a technique used to detect antibodies or antigens in which the antibodies or antigens are marked with a fluorescent dye. — *n* **immū'nogen** same as **antigen**. — *n sing* **immunogenet'ics** the study of inherited characteristics of immunity. — *adj* **immunogen'ic** capable of producing an immune response. — *n* **immunogenic'ity**. — *n* **immunoglō'bulin** one of a group of proteins found in blood plasma, acting as antibodies. — *adj* **immunolog'ical**. — *adv* **immunolog'ically**. — *n* **immunol'ogist**. — *n* **immunol'ogy** the scientific study of immunity and the defence mechanisms of the body. — *adj* **immunopatholog'ical**. — *adv* **immunopatholog'ically**. — *n* **immunopathol'ogy** the study of immune factors associated with disease. — *n* **immunophorē'sis** a technique for identifying an (unknown) antigen or testing for a specific antibody in serum, which makes use of the precipitin reaction of known antibodies. — *vt* and *vi* **immunosuppress'**. — *n* **immunosuppress'ant** a drug which inhibits the body's immune response, used to ensure that transplanted organs are not rejected, and in the treatment of various autoimmune diseases. — *n* **immunosuppress'ion**. — *adj* **immunosuppress'ive**. — *n* **immunother'apy** the treatment or prevention of disease, *esp* cancer, by the use of agents which stimulate the patient's own natural immunity. — *adj* **immunotox'ic**. — *n* **immunotox'in** a toxin with immunosuppressive effects. — *n* **immunotransfū'sion** the transfusion of blood or plasma containing in high concentration the appropriate antibodies for the infection from which the patient is suffering. — **immune body** an antibody; **immune response** the production of antibodies in the body as a defensive response to the presence of antigens, foreign tissue, etc; **immune system** the process within an organism whereby antigenic or foreign matter is distinguished and neutralized through antibody or cytoxic action; **immunological memory** the ability of the immune system to mount a larger and more rapid response to an antigen that has already been encountered, mediated by long-lived cells stimulated on first exposure to the antigen; **immunological tolerance** the failure of the body to recognize antigens with consequent absence of antibody production. [L *immūnis*, from *in-* not, and *mūnis* serving]

immure *im-ūr'*, *vt* to enclose as if within walls, to wall in; to shut up; to imprison; to confine. — *n* (*obs*; *Shakesp*

emure') an enclosing wall. — *n* **immure'ment**. [L *in* in, and *mūrus* a wall]

immutable *im-ūt'ə-bl, adj* unchangeable; changeless. — *n* **immūtabil'ity** or **immūt'ableness**. — *adv* **immūt'ably**. [**im-** (**in-** (2))]

IMO *abbrev*: International Maritime Organization; International Miners' Organization.

Imp. *abbrev*: *Imperator* (*L*), Emperor; *Imperatrix* (*L*), Empress; Imperial.

imp *imp, n* a mischievous child; a little devil or wicked spirit; a shoot, scion, graft (*obs*); a scion of a family (*obs*). — *vt* to graft, engraft (*obs*); to engraft (a hawk or falcon's wing or tail) with new feathers in order to repair broken feathers or improve flight (*falconry*). — *adj* **imp'ish** like or characteristic of an imp, teasingly mischievous. — *adv* **imp'ishly**. — *n* **imp'ishness**. [OE *impa*, from LL *impotus* a graft, from Gr *emphytos* engrafted]

impacable *im'pak-ə-bl*, (*rare*) *adj* not to be quieted or appeased, implacable. [L *in-* not, and *pācāre* to quiet]

impact *im-pakt', n* the blow of a body in motion impinging on another body; the impulse resulting from collision; the impulse resulting from a new idea or theory; strong effect, influence, eg (*marketing*) the effect of an advertisement, promotion, etc on a potential customer. — *vt* to drive (an object) with force into something else; to drive or press (two objects) together with force; to have an impact or effect on. — *n* **impac'tion** the act of pressing together, or of fixing a substance tightly in a body cavity; the condition so produced. — *n* **impact'ite** a glassy type of rock formed as a result of the impact (and heat) of a meteorite on the earth's surface. — *adj* **impact'ive**. — **impact adhesive** a glue which forms a bond when two surfaces, each coated with the adhesive, are brought together; **impacted faeces** faeces that are so hard or dry that they cannot be evacuated through the anus; **impacted fracture** a fracture in which the broken ends of bone are driven into each other; **impacted tooth** a tooth, *esp* a wisdom tooth, wedged between the jawbone and another tooth and thus unable to erupt through the gum; **impact parameter** (*nuc phys*) the distance at which two particles which collide would have passed if no interaction had occurred between them; **impact printer** any device in which printed characters are formed on the paper by means of a hammer striking the ribbon, eg dot matrix printers, line printers. [L *impactus*, pa p of *impingere*; see **impinge**]

impaint *im-pānt'*, (*Shakesp*) *vt* to paint or depict. [**im-** (**in-** (1))]

impair[1] *im-pār', vt* to diminish in quantity, value, or strength; to injure, damage or spoil; to weaken. — *vi* (*obs*; *Spenser* **empaire'** or **empare'**) to become worse; to decay. — *adj* **impaired** damaged, weakened; (of a driver or driving) under the influence of drugs or alcohol (*Can*). — *n* **impair'er**. — *n* **impair'ing**. — *n* **impair'ment**. [OFr *empeirer* (Fr *empirer*), from L *im-* (intensive), and *pējōrāre* to make worse, from *pējor* worse]

impair[2] *im-pār'*, (*Shakesp*) *adj* perhaps unsuitable, unfit, inferior. [Fr, from L *impār*, *from in-* not, and *par* equal]

impala *im-pä'lə, n* an African antelope (*Aepyceros melampus*), with horns curved in the shape of a lyre and capable of prodigious leaps: — *pl* **impa'la** or **impa'las**. [Zulu *i-mpālaj*]

impale or **empale** *im-pāl', vt* to pierce with something pointed, eg a sharp stake; to fix on a sharp stake thrust through the body; to transfix; to juxtapose (two coats of arms) on a single vertically divided shield (*heraldry*); to shut or fence in, to surround with pales (*archaic*). — *n* **impale'ment** or **empale'ment** the act or punishment of impaling; the marshalling side by side of two escutcheons combined in one (*heraldry*); an enclosed space (*archaic*). [Fr *empaler*, from L *in* in, and *pālus* a stake]

impalpable *im-pal'pə-bl, adj* not perceivable or detectable by touch; not capable of being comprehended or grasped; extremely fine-grained. — *n* **impalpabil'ity**. — *adv* **impal'pably**. [**im-** (**in-** (2))]

impaludism *im-palū'-dizm, n* a disease carried by insects, affecting inhabitants of marshy areas. [L *in* in, and *palus, palūdis* a marsh]

impanation *im-pə-nā'shən* or *-pā-, n* a local union of the body of Christ with the consecrated bread in the Eucharist; later specially used of Luther's consubstantiation. — *adj* **impanate** (*im-pān'āt* or *im'pən-āt*) embodied in bread. [From LL *impānāre, -ātum*, from *in* in, and *pānis* bread]

impanel and **impannel**. See **empanel**.

imparadise *im-par'ə-dīs*, (chiefly *literary*) *vt* to transport to a state of blissful happiness, as if in paradise; to enrapture; to make a paradise of (a place). — Also **empar'adise**. [**im-** (**in-** (1))]

impar- *im-par-*, or **impari-** *im-par-i-*, *combining form* signifying unequal. — *n* **imparity** (*im-par'i-ti*) inequality, disparity. — *adj* **imparidigitate** (*-dij'i-tāt*; *zool*) having an odd number of fingers or toes on each limb. — *adj* **imparipinn'ate** (*bot*) (of pinnate leaves) with a terminal unpaired leaflet. — *adj* **imparisyllab'ic** (of a noun or verb) having differing numbers of syllables in different inflected forms. [L *impār*, from *in-* not, and *pār* equal]

impark *im-pärk'*, (*archaic*) *vt* to enclose in, or as, a park. — *n* **imparkā'tion**. [**im-** (**in-** (1))]

imparl or **emparl** *im-pärl'*, (*obs* except *law*) *vi* to hold a consultation; to parley. — *vt* to talk over. — *n* **imparl'ance** (*Spenser* **emparl'aunce**) parleying, conference; delay in pleading, ostensibly for amicable adjustment. [Obs Fr *emparler*, from *em-* (L *in-*), and *parler* to talk]

impart or (*Spenser*) **empart** *im-pärt'*, *vt* to give (something abstract); to communicate, make known, relate. — *adj* **impart'able**. — *n* **impartā'tion**. — *n* **impart'er**. — *n* **impart'ment**. [OFr *empartir*, from L *impartīre*, from *in* on, and *pars, partis* a part]

impartial *im-pär'shl, adj* not favouring one more than another, unbiased; fair, just; partial (*Shakesp*; *erron*). — *n* **impartiality** (*-shi-al'i-ti*) or **impar'tialness**. — *adv* **impar'tially**. [**im-** (**in-** (2))]

impartible *im-pärt'i-bl*, (now chiefly *law*) *adj* not partible; incapable of, or not subject to, partition; indivisible. — *n* **impartibil'ity**. — *adv* **impart'ibly**. [**im-** (**in-** (2))]

impassable *im-päs'ə-bl, adj* not capable of being passed, traversed or travelled through. — *n* **impassabil'ity** or **impass'ableness**. — *adv* **impass'ably**. [**im-** (in- (2))]

impasse *am-pas'* or *ɛ̃-pas, n* a situation from which further progress is impossible; a deadlock, stalemate. [Fr, from *in* in, and *passer* to pass]

impassible *im-pas'i-bl*, (*rare*) *adj* incapable of suffering or experiencing pain, unfeeling; incapable of emotion, impassive. — *n* **impassibil'ity** or **impass'ibleness**. — *adv* **impass'ibly**. [Church L *impassibilis*, from *in-* not, and *patī, passus* to suffer]

impassion *im-pash'ən, vt* to arouse the passions of; to make passionate. — *adj* **impass'ionate** (*Spenser* **empass'ionate**) impassioned; dispassionate (rare). — *adj* **impass'ioned** (*Spenser* **empass'ioned**) moved by or filled with passion; fiery; ardent. [Ital *impassionare*, from L *in* in, and *passiō, -ōnis* passion]

impassive *im-pas'iv, adj* not showing feeling or emotion; imperturbable; not capable of feeling or emotion; having no sensation. — *adv* **impass'ively**. — *n* **impass'iveness** or **impassiv'ity**. [**im-** (**in-** (2))]

impaste *im-pāst'*, *vt* to lay paint or colours thickly on. — *n* **impastation** (*im-pas-tā'shən*). — *adj* **impāst'ed**. — *n* **impasto** (*im-päs'tō*) in painting, paint or pigment applied thickly, *esp* when used to achieve surface texture; the technique of laying paint on thickly in this

imp- for words beginning thus see also **emp-**.

way: — *pl* **impast'os**. — *adj* **impast'oed** or **impast'o'd**. [LL *impastāre*, from *in* into, and *pasta* paste]

impatiens *im-pā'shi-enz*, *n* any of various plants of the genus *Impatiens*, including busy lizzie, touch-me-not and balsam. [L, impatient, because the ripe seed capsules burst at a touch]

impatient *im-pā'shənt*, *adj* not able to endure or to wait; fretful; restless; intolerant (of). — *n* **impā'tience**. — *adv* **impā'tiently**. [L *impatiēns*, *-entis* impatient, from *in* not, and *patiēns* patient]

impave *im-pāv'*, (*Wordsworth*) *vt* to depict or set in pavement, as mosaic. [Pfx **im-** (**in-** (1))]

impavid *im-pav'id*, (*rare*) *adj* fearless, undaunted. — *adv* **impav'idly**. [L *impavidus*, from *im-* (*in-*) not, and *pavidus* fearing]

impawn *im-pön'*, (*archaic*) *vt* to put in pawn; to pledge; to risk. [**im-** (**in-** (1))]

impeach or (*Spenser*) **empeach** *im-pēch'*, *vt* to disparage; to find fault with; to call in question or cast doubt on; to arraign (*esp* when a lower legislative house charges a high officer with grave offences before the upper house as judges); to turn king's evidence against (*law*); to bring an accusation against; to charge (a public official) with an offence committed in office (*esp NAm*); to hinder, impede, prevent (*obs*); to impair (*obs*). — *n* hindrance, prevention (*obs*); damage, impairment, detriment (*obs*); calling in question (*Shakesp*). — *adj* **impeach'able**. — *n* **impeach'er**. — *n* **impeach'ment**. [OFr *empech(i)er* to hinder (Fr *empêcher*), from L *impedicāre* to fetter]

impearl *im-pûrl'*, (*poetic*) *vt* to decorate with, or as if with, pearls; to make pearl-like. [**im-** (**in-** (1))]

impeccable *im-pek'ə-bl*, *adj* faultless; without flaw or error; incapable of sin. — *n* **impeccabil'ity**. — *adv* **impecc'ably**. — *n* **impecc'ancy**. — *adj* **impecc'ant** free from sin. [**im-** (**in-** (2))]

impecunious *im-pi-kū'ni-əs* or *-nyəs*, *adj* without money, penniless; short of money. — *adv* **impecun'iously**. — *n* **impecunios'ity** or **impecun'iousness**. [**im-** (**in-** (2))]

impede *im-pēd'*, *vt* to hinder or obstruct. — *n* **impē'dance** hindrance; the measurement, in ohms, of opposition to an alternating current (*elec*); a similar measurement of resistance to vibrations of alternating effects as in sound (*acoustic impedance*) or as caused by applied forces (*mechanical impedance*). — *n* **impediment** (*-ped'*) an obstacle; a defect preventing fluent speech. — *n pl* **impediment'a** (L *impedīmenta*) military baggage; baggage or luggage generally; encumbrances. — *adj* **impedimen'tal** or **imped'itive** hindering. [L *impedīre*, from *in* in, and *pēs*, *pedis* a foot]

impel *im-pel'*, *vt* to urge forward; to excite to action; to instigate: — *pr p* **impell'ing**; *pa t* and *pa p* **impelled'**. — *adj* **impell'ent** impelling or driving on. — *n* an impelling agent or power. — *n* **impell'er** someone who, or something that, impels; a rotor for transmitting motion in a compressor, centrifugal pump, etc. [L *impellere*, *impulsum*, from *in* on, and *pellere* to drive]

impend *im-pend'*, *vi* to threaten; to be about to happen; to overhang (*obs*). — *n* (*obs*) **impend'ence** or **impend'ency**. — *adj* **impend'ing** or (now *rare*) **impend'ent**. [L *impendēre*, from *in* on, and *pendēre* to hang]

impenetrable *im-pen'i-trə-bl*, *adj* incapable of being penetrated; impervious; inscrutable; occupying space exclusively (*phys*). — *n* **impenetrabil'ity**. — *adv* **impen'etrably**. [**im-** (**in-** (2))]

impenetrate *im-pen'i-trāt*, *vt* to permeate; to penetrate thoroughly. — *n* **impenetrā'tion**. [**im-** (**in-** (1))]

impenitent *im-pen'i-tənt*, *adj* not repenting. — *n* someone who does not repent; a hardened sinner. — *n* **impen'itence**. — *n* **impen'itency**. — *adv* **impen'itently**. [**im-** (**in-** (2))]

impennate *im-pen'ət*, *adj* (of birds) featherless, wingless (applied to birds with small wings adapted for swimming, such as penguins). [**im-** (**in-** (2))]

imper. *abbrev*: imperative.

imperative *im-per'ə-tiv*, *adj* expressive of command, advice or request; urgently necessary; calling out for action; obligatory; authoritative; peremptory. — *n* that which is imperative; the imperative mood (*gram*); a verb in the imperative mood. — *adv* **imper'atively**. — **imperative mood** the form of a verb expressing command, advice or request. — **categorical imperative** see under **category**. [L *imperātīvus*, from *imperāre* to command, from *in* in, and *parāre* to prepare]

imperator *im-pər-ā'tər*, or *im-per-ä'tor*, *n* a commander; a ruler; an emperor. — *adj* **imperatorial** (*im-per-ə-tō'ri-əl* or *-tö'*). [L *imperātor* a general, later an emperor, from *imperāre* to command]

imperceable. See **impierceable**.

imperceptible *im-pər-sep'ti-bl*, *adj* not discernible by the senses; very small, slight or gradual. — *n* **imperceptibil'ity**. — *n* **impercep'tibleness**. — *adv* **impercep'tibly**. — *adj* **impercep'tive** or **impercip'ient** not perceiving; having no power to perceive. [**im-** (**in-** (2))]

imperf. *abbrev*: imperfect.

imperfect *im-pûr'fikt*, *adj* incomplete, deficient; defective, faulty; falling short of perfection; lacking any normal part, or the full normal number of parts; lacking some necessary sanction, formality, etc and therefore incapable of being legally enforced (*law*); expressing continued or habitual action in past time (*gram*); of or relating to the intervals of the third and sixth (*music*); (in mensural notation) a note value containing two of the next lower note values (*med music*). — *n* the imperfect tense; a verb in the imperfect tense. — *n* **imperfectibil'ity**. — *adj* **imperfect'ible** — *n* **imperfection** (*-fek'shən*) the state of being imperfect; a defect. — *adj* **imperfec'tive** (*gram*) denoting the aspect of the verb which indicates that the action described is in progress. — *adv* **imperfec'tively** (*gram*). — *adv* **imper'fectly**. — *n* **imper'fectness**. — **imperfect cadence** (*music*) a cadence which is not resolved to the tonic key, *esp* one passing from tonic to dominant chord; **imperfect competition** (*econ*) the market condition that exists between the extremes of perfect competition and absolute monopoly; **imperfect flower** a flower in which stamens or carpels are lacking or non-functional; **imperfect fungus** a fungus of the order *Fungi Imperfecti* of which no sexual stage is known. [**im-** (**in-** (2))]

imperforate *im-pûr'fə-rit* or **imperforated** *-rā-tid*, *adj* not pierced through or perforated; having no opening; lacking an opening, *esp* as a result of abnormal development, as in *imperforate anus* (*med*); without perforations as a means of separation, as a sheet of postage stamps. — *adj* **imper'forable**. — *n* **imperforā'tion**. [**im-** (**in-** (2))]

imperial *im-pē'ri-əl*, *adj* pertaining to, or of the nature of, an empire or emperor; sovereign, supreme; commanding, imperious, august; (of products, etc) of superior quality or size. — *n* an emperor or empress or a member of an imperial family; a supporter of an emperor; a small beard or tuft of hair under the lower lip as popularized by Napoleon III; a domed roof shaped to a point at the top (*archit*); the top of a coach or carriage, or a trunk designed to be carried there; a size of paper, in Britain 22 × 30in (56 × 76cm), in US 23 × 33in (58 × 78cm); a size of slates, 33 × 24in (838 × 610mm); a stag with fourteen points on its antlers; an obsolete Russian gold coin. — *n* **impē'rialism** the power or authority of an emperor; the policy, practice or advocacy of extension of a nation's power or influence over other territories; the spirit or character of an empire. — *n* **impē'rialist** a soldier or partisan of an emperor; a believer in, or advocate of, imperialism. — *adj* **impērialist'ic**. — *n* **impēriality** (*-al'i-ti*) imperial power, right or privilege. — *vt* **impē'rialize** or **-ise** to make imperial. — *adv* **impē'rially**. — *adj* **impē'rious** assuming command; haughty; tyrannical; overbearing, domineering, dictatorial; imperial (*obs*). — *adv* **impē'riously**. — *n* **impē'riousness**. — **imperial city** Rome; **imperial measure** or **weight** non-metric standard of measure or weight (**imperial gallon**, **yard** and **pound**) as fixed by parliament for the United Kingdom (final act 1963); **imperial octavo** a book size, in Britain

$7\frac{1}{2} \times 11$in, in US $8\frac{1}{4} \times 11\frac{1}{2}$in; **imperial preference** (*hist*) the favouring of trade within the British Empire by discriminating tariffs. [L *imperium* sovereignty]

imperil *im-per'il*, (*formal*) *vt* to endanger: — *pa p* **imper'illed**. — *n* **imper'ilment**. [**im-** (**in-** (1))]

imperious, etc. See under **imperial**.

imperishable *im-per'ish-ə-bl*, *adj* not perishable, not subject to decay or deterioration, indestructible; everlasting, enduring. — *n* **imperishabil'ity**. — *n* **imper'ishableness**. — *adv* **imper'ishably**. [**im-** (**in-** (2))]

imperium *im-pēr'i-əm* or *-per'*, *n* absolute sovereignty, the power to command; the area, or extent, of absolute sovereignty: — *pl* **imper'ia**. — **imperium in imperio** (*in im-pēr'i-ō*, or *-per'*) absolute authority within the sphere of higher authority. [L *imperium*]

impermanence *im-pûr'mən-əns*, *n* lack of permanence, transitoriness. — *n* **imper'manency**. — *adj* **imper'manent**. — *adv* **imper'manently**. [**im-** (**in-** (2))]

impermeable *im-pûr'mi-ə-bl*, *adj* (of a substance, membrane, etc) not permitting passage, *esp* of fluids or gases; impervious. — *n* **impermeabil'ity**. — *n* **imper'meableness**. — *adv* **imper'meably**. [**im-** (**in-** (2))]

impermissible *im-pər-mis'i-bl*, *adj* not permissible; not allowed. — *n* **impermissibil'ity**. — *adv* **impermiss'ibly**. [**im-** (**in-** (2))]

impers. *abbrev*: impersonal.

imperseverant *im-pər-sev'ər-ənt*, *adj* lacking the power to perceive; lacking perseverance. [**im-** (**in-** (2)), and **perceive** or **persevere**]

impersistent *im-pər-sis'tənt*, *adj* not persistent; not enduring. [**im-** (**in-** (2))]

impersonal *im-pûr'sən-əl*, *adj* having no personality, or personal touches; (of a verb) used only in the third person singular (in English *usu* with *it* as subject; *gram*); without reference to any particular person; objective, uncoloured by personal feeling, cold. — *n* **impersonality** (*-al'i-ti*). — *vt* **imper'sonalize** or **-ise**. — *adv* **imper'sonally**. [**im-** (**in-** (2))]

impersonate *im-pûr'sən-āt*, *vt* to assume the character of (another person); to pretend to be (another person); to personify (*archaic*); to embody, incarnate (*obs*). — *n* **impersonā'tion**. — *n* **imper'sonātor**. [L *in* in, and *persōna* person; see **personate**]

impertinent *im-pûr'ti-nənt*, *adj* saucy, impudent; intrusive, presumptuous; not pertinent (*archaic* or *legal*). — *n* **imper'tinence** or **imper'tinency** that which is impertinent; impudence, disrespectful behaviour; intrusion, presumptuousness; matter introduced into an affidavit, etc not pertinent to the matter (*law*). — *adv* **imper'tinently**. [**im-** (**in-** (2))]

imperturbable *im-pər-tûr'bə-bl*, *adj* that cannot be disturbed or agitated; serene, unruffled. — *n* **imperturbabil'ity**. — *adv* **impertur'bably**. — *n* **imperturbā'tion**. [L *imperturbābilis*, from *in-* not, and *perturbāre* to disturb; see **perturb**]

impervious *im-pûr'vi-əs* or **imperviable** *-pûr'vi-ə-bl*, *adj* not able to be penetrated; not easily influenced by ideas, arguments, etc, or moved or upset (with *to*). — *n* **imperviabil'ity**. — *n* **imper'viableness**. — *adv* **imper'viously**. — *n* **imper'viousness**. [**im-** (**in-** (2))]

impeticos *im-pet'i-kos*, (*Shakesp*) *vt* a word coined by the fool in *Twelfth Night* II.3, perhaps meaning **impocket**, or perhaps to bestow on (the wearer of) a petticoat.

impetigo *im-pi-tī'gō*, *n* a contagious bacterial skin infection characterized by clusters of small pustules which join to form crusty yellow sores: — *pl* **impetigines** (*-tij'i-nēz*) or **impetī'gos**. — *adj* **impetiginous** (*-tij'*). [L *impetigō*, from *impetere* to rush upon, attack]

impetrate *im'pi-trāt*, *vt* to obtain by entreaty or request, *esp* by prayer. — *n* **impetrā'tion**. — *adj* **im'petrātive** or **im'petrātory**. [L *impetrāre*, *-ātum*, from *in* on, and *patrāre* to bring about]

impetuous *im-pet'ū-əs*, *adj* rushing on with great force or violence (*poetic*); tending to act in a rash or impulsive manner or without due consideration; (of an action) rash, impulsive. — *n* **impetuosity** (*-os'i-ti*). — *adv* **impet'uously**. — *n* **impet'uousness**. [L *impetus* (pl *impetūs*), from *in* into, on, and *petere* to seek]

impetus *im'pi-təs*, *n* momentum; impulse; incentive: — *pl* **im'petuses**. [Ety as for **impetuous**]

imp. gal. or **imp. gall.** *abbrev*: imperial gallon(s).

impi *im'pi*, (*SAfr*) *n* a group of armed southern African native warriors: — *pl* **im'pis** or **im'pies**. [From Zulu]

impictured *im-pik'chərd*, (*Spenser*) *adj* painted. [**im-** (**in-** (1))]

impierceable *im-pērs'ə-bl*, (*obs*; *Spenser* **imperceable** *im'pərs-ə-bl*) *adj* not pierceable. [**im-** (**in-** (2))]

impiety *im-pī'ə-ti*, *n* lack of piety or veneration; any impious act. [L *impietās*, *-ātis*, from *in* not; cf **piety**]

impignorate *im-pig'nər-āt*, (*formal* and *Scot*) *vt* to pledge, pawn or mortgage. — Also *adj*. — *n* **impignorā'tion**. [L *in* in, into, and *pignus*, *-oris*, *-eris* pledge]

impinge *im-pinj'*, *vi* (with *on*, *upon* or *against*) to encroach, infringe; to strike, collide with; to make an impression on (the mind, senses, etc). — *vt* to strike, drive or fix upon or against something else: — *pr p* **imping'ing**. — *n* **impinge'ment**. — *adj* **imping'ent**. [L *impingere*, from *in* against, and *pangere* to fix, drive in]

impious *im'pi-əs* (also, *esp US*, *im-pī'əs*), *adj* irreverent, lacking respect; lacking veneration, as for gods, etc. — *adv* **imp'iously**. [L *impius*, from *im-* (*in-*) not, and *pius*; cf **pious**]

impish. See under **imp**.

implacable *im-plak'ə-bl*, or *-plāk'*, *adj* incapable of being placated or appeased; inexorable. — *n* **implacabil'ity** or **implac'ableness**. — *adv* **implac'ably**. [**im-** (**in-** (2))]

implacental *im-plə-sen'tl*, *adj* aplacental, having no placenta. [**im-** (**in-** (2))]

implant *im-plänt'*, *vt* to engraft; to plant firmly, to embed; to fix in; to insert; to instil or inculcate; to plant (ground, etc with). — *n* (*im'*) anything implanted or inserted which has a specialized function; something implanted in body tissue, such as a graft, a pellet containing a hormone, an artificial pacemaker, etc. — *n* **implantā'tion** the act or process of implanting; the attachment of an embryo to the lining of the uterus (also **nidation**). [**im-** (**in-** (1))]

implate *im-plāt'*, *vt* to put a plate or covering on; to sheathe. [**im-** (**in-** (1))]

implausible *im-plöz'i-bl*, *adj* not plausible. — *n* **implausibil'ity** or **implaus'ibleness**. — *adv* **implaus'ibly**. [**im-** (**in-** (2))]

impleach or **empleach** *im-plēch'*, (*poetic*) *vt* to intertwine. [**im-** (**in-** (1))]

implead *im-plēd'*, (*law*, now *rare*) *vt* to take legal action against, to sue. — *n* **implead'er**. [**im-** (**in-** (1))]

impledge *im-plej'*, *vt* to pledge. [**im-** (**in-** (1))]

implement *im'pli-mənt*, *n* a piece of equipment, a requisite; something that serves to achieve a purpose; a tool or instrument of labour; the fulfilment of an obligation (*Scots law*). — *vt* (often *-ment'*) to give effect to, to carry out; to fulfil, complete or perform. — *adj* **implemen'tal** instrumental; effective. — *n* **implementā'tion** performance, fulfilment; the various steps involved in producing a functioning data-processing or control system from a design (*comput*). [LL *implēmentum*, from L *in* in, and *plēre* to fill]

implete *im-plēt'*, (*archaic*) *vt* to fill. — *adj* filled up, replete. — *n* **impletion** (*-plē'shən*) filling; fullness; fulfilment. [L *implēre*, *-ētum*, from *in* in, and *plēre* to fill]

implex *im'pleks*, *adj* not simple; involved, complicated. — *n* (*zool*) in arthropods, an in-turning of the integument where muscles are attached. — *n* **implexion** (*im-plek'shən*). — *adj* **implex'ūous**. [L *implexus*, from *in* into, and *plectere* to twine]

implicate *im'pli-kāt*, *vt* to involve; to entangle; to imply; to show to be, or to have been, a participator; to entwine together; to enfold. — *n* a thing implied. — *adj* (*-kit*) intertwined. — *n* **implicā'tion** the act of implicating or implying; that which is implied; the relation between two propositions in a sentence or statement such that the sentence or statement is only true when both propositions are true, or, if the first proposition is true the second proposition must be true (*logic*). — *adj* **im'plicātive** (or *im-plik'ə-tiv*) tending to implicate. — *adv* **im'plicatively**. — *adj* **implicit** (*im-plis'it*) not explicit; implied but not expressly stated; absolute, relying entirely, unquestioning; present without being visible or realized (with *in*); entangled, intertwined (*obs*). — *adv* **implic'itly**. — *n* **implic'itness**. [L *implicāre*, *-ātum*, also *-itum*, from *in* in, and *plicāre*, *-ātum* or *-itum* to fold]

implied, etc. See **imply**.

implode *im-plōd'*, *vt* and *vi* to (cause to) collapse inwards suddenly and violently; to pronounce or sound by implosion (*phonetics*). — *n* **implōd'ent** an implosive sound. — *n* **implosion** (*-plō'zhən*) a collapsing inwards; in the formation of voiceless stops, compression of enclosed air by simultaneous stoppage of the mouth parts and the glottis (*phonetics*); inrush of air in a suction stop (*phonetics*); (in behaviour therapy) a method of treating phobias in which the patient is exposed intensively to the object of fear (also called **flooding**; *psychol*). — *adj* **implosive** (*-plōs'iv*, or *-plōz'*). — *n* (*phonetics*) an implosive consonant; a suction stop or (sometimes) a click. [L *in* in, and *plōdere* (*plaudere*) to clap]

implore *im-plōr'* or *-plör'*, *vt* to ask or beg earnestly; to entreat. — Also *vi*. — *n* **implorā'tion**. — *n* **implor'ator** (*Shakesp*). — *adj* **imploratory** (*-plor'ə-tə-ri*). — *n* **implōr'er**. — *adv* **implōr'ingly**. [L *implōrāre* to invoke with tears, from *in* in, and *plōrāre* to weep]

implosion and **implosive**. See under **implode**.

implunge *im-plunj'*, *vt* to plunge, submerge. — Also (*Spenser*) **emplonge'**. [**im-** (**in-** (1))]

impluvium *im-plōō'vi-əm*, *n* in ancient Roman houses, the square basin in the atrium that received the rainwater from the open space in the roof: — *pl* **implu'via**. [L *impluvium*, from *in* in, into, and *pluere* to rain]

imply *im-plī'*, *vt* to express indirectly; to insinuate, to hint; to signify, to mean; to include in reality; to enfold (*obs*): — *pr p* **imply'ing**; *pa t* and *pa p* **implied'**. — *adv* **implī'edly**. [OFr *emplier*, from L *implicāre* to involve]

impocket *im-pok'it*, (*archaic*) *vt* to put in one's pocket. [**im-** (**in-** (1))]

impolder or **empolder** *im-pōl'dər*, *vt* to make a polder of. [Du *impolderen*; see **polder**]

impolite *im-pə-līt'*, *adj* having rough manners; bad-mannered, rude. — *adv* **impolite'ly**. — *n* **impolite'ness**. [**im-** (**in-** (2))]

impolitic *im-pol'i-tik*, *adj* not politic; inexpedient. — Also (*obs*) **impolit'ical**. — *n* **impol'icy** an act or instance of being impolitic. — *adv* **impolit'ically** (*rare*). — *adv* **impol'iticly**. — *n* **impol'iticness**. [**im-** (**in-** (2))]

imponderable *im-pon'dər-ə-bl*, *adj* not able to be weighed or evaluated. — Also *n*. — *n* **imponderabil'ity** or **impon'derableness**. — *n pl* **impon'derables** formerly, supposed fluids without sensible weight, such as heat, light, electricity, magnetism; factors in a situation whose influence cannot be gauged or evaluated. — Also (*L*) **imponderabil'ia**. — *adj* **impon'derous** weightless; very light. [**im-** (**in-** (2))]

impone *im-pōn'*, *vt* and *vi* to impose. — *vt* to stake as a wager (*Shakesp*; *perh* an error for *impawn*). — *adj* **impōn'ent** that which imposes, or is competent to impose, an obligation. — *n* a person who imposes an obligation, duty, etc. [L *impōnere*, from *in* on, and *pōnere* to place]

import *im-pōrt'* or *-pört'*, *vt* to bring in from an outside source; to bring in from abroad; to convey, as a word; to signify; to portend; to load (a file) into an application package other than the one in which it was created (*comput*); to be of consequence to (*archaic*); to behove (*archaic*). — Also *vi*. — *n* **im'port** (formerly *-pōrt'* or *-pört'*) something which is brought from abroad; importing; meaning; importance; tendency. — *adj* **import'able**. — *n* **import'ance** the fact of being important; extent of value or significance; weight, consequence; appearance of dignity; import, significance (*archaic*); importunity (*obs*). — Also (*Shakesp*; *obs*) **import'ancy**. — *adj* **import'ant** of great import or consequence; momentous; significant; pompous. — *adv* **import'antly**. — *n* **importā'tion** the act of importing; a commodity or service imported. — *n* **import'er**. — **import duty** a tax levied on goods which enter one country from another; **import licence** an official licence which permits the trader, etc to import certain goods which are otherwise restricted from entry into a country. — **invisible imports** services bought from foreign countries, such as money spent by tourists abroad, etc (cf **invisible exports** under **export**); **visible imports** goods and raw materials bought from foreign countries. [L *importāre*, *-ātum*, from *in* in, and *portāre* to carry]

importune *im-pör-tūn'* or *-pör'*, *vt* to press or urge with repeated requests; to harass with troublesome insistence; to solicit for immoral purposes, make improper advances to; to annoy (*obs*); to import, signify (*Spenser*; *erron*). — *vi* to press, urge or solicit importunately. — *adj* importunate; inopportune, untimely (*obs*); burdensome (*obs*); urgent, resistless (*obs*). — *n* **impor'tunacy** (*Shakesp -tūn'*) or **import'unateness**. — *adj* **impor'tunate** (*-it* or *-āt*) troublesomely persistent or demanding; pressing, insistent; annoying; inopportune (*obs*); burdensome (*obs*). — *adv* **impor'tunately**. — *adv* **importune'ly** (or *-pör'*). — *n* **importun'er**. — *n* **importun'ing**. — *n* **importun'ity**. [L *importūnus* inconvenient, from *im-* (*in-*) not, and *portus* a harbour; cf **opportune**]

impose *im-pōz'*, *vt* to place upon something; to lay on; to lay (the hands) on the head of a candidate for ordination or in certain sacraments; to enjoin; to set as a burden or task; to set up in, or by, authority; to pass off unfairly or deceptively; to arrange or place in a chase, as pages of type (*printing*). — *vi* (with *on* or *upon*) to mislead, deceive; to burden by taking undue advantage of one's good nature; to act with constraining effect. — *n* (*Shakesp*) command, charge. — *adj* **impos'able**. — *n* **impos'er**. — *adj* **impos'ing** commanding, impressive; adapted to impress forcibly; specious, deceptive (now *rare*). — *adv* **impos'ingly**. — *n* **impos'ingness**. — **imposing stone** or **table** (*printing*) a heavy table upon which metal type is imposed. [Fr *imposer*; see **compose**]

imposition *im-pəz-ish'ən*, *n* an act or instance of imposing or laying on; the act of laying on hands in ordination and certain sacraments; something imposed, a burden; a punishment task; the assembling of pages and locking them into a chase (*printing*). [L *impositiō*, *-ōnis*, from *in* on, and *pōnere*, *positum* to place]

impossible *im-pos'i-bl*, *adj* that cannot be; that cannot be done or dealt with; that cannot be true; out of the question; hopelessly unsuitable or difficult to deal with (*colloq*); beyond doing anything with. — *n* a person or thing that is impossible. — *n* **imposs'ibilism** belief in or advocacy of an impracticable policy. — *n* **imposs'ibilist**. — *n* **impossibil'ity**. [**im-** (**in-** (2))]

impost[1] *im'pōst*, *n* a tax, *esp* on imports; the weight carried by a horse in a handicap race (*colloq*). [OFr *impost* (Fr *impôt*), from L *impōnere*, *impositum* to lay on]

impost[2] *im'pōst*, (*archit*) *n* the upper part of a pillar in vaults and arches, on which the weight of the building is laid; a horizontal block resting on uprights. [Fr *imposte*, from Ital *imposta*, from L *impōnere*, *impositum*]

imposter. See **impostor**.

imposthume. See **impostume**.

impostor or **imposter** *im-pos'tər*, *n* someone who assumes a false character or impersonates another. — *n* **impos'ture** (*-chər*) an imposition, fraud. [LL, from L *impōnere*, *impositum* to impose]

impostume or **imposthume** *im-pos'tūm*, (*archaic*) *n* an abscess. — *vt* and *vi* **impos'tumate** or **impos'thumate** to affect with or form into an impostume. — *n* **impostumā'tion** or **imposthumā'tion**. — *adj* **impos'tumed** or **impos'thumed**. [OFr *empostume* from *apostème*, from

Gr *apostēma* abscess, from *apo* from, and the root of *histanai* to set; the form due to confusion with *posthumous*, which itself is due to confusion]

imposture. See **impostor**.

impot *im'pot*, (*school slang*) *n* an imposition.

impotent *im'pə-tənt*, *adj* powerless; helpless; incapable of having sexual intercourse, owing to inability to achieve or maintain an erection; unable to control (with *of*; *obs*); without self-control, unrestrained (*poetic*; *obs*). — *n* **im'potence** or **im'potency**. — *adv* **im'potently**. [**im-** (**in-** (2))]

impound *im-pownd'*, *vt* to confine, as within a pound; to restrain within limits; to take legal possession of; to hold up in a reservoir. — *adj* **impound'able**. — *n* **impound'age**. — *n* **impound'er**. — *n* **impound'ment**. [**im-** (**in-** (1)) and **pound**[2]]

impoverish *im-pov'er-ish*, *vt* to make poor (*lit* or *fig*). — *n* **impov'erishment**. [From OFr *empovrir*, *-iss-*, from L *in* in, and *pauper* poor]

impracticable *im-prak'tik-ə-bl*, *adj* not able to be done or put into practice; not able to be used; unmanageable (*archaic*). — *n* **impracticabil'ity**. — *n* **imprac'ticableness**. — *adv* **imprac'ticably**. [**im-** (**in-** (2))]

impractical *im-prak'ti-kl*, *adj* not practical. — *n* **impracticality** (*-kal'*). — *adv* **imprac'tically**. — *n* **imprac'ticalness**. [**im-** (**in-** (2))]

imprecate *im'pri-kāt*, *vt* to call down by prayer (*esp* something evil); to invoke evil upon, to put a curse on. — *vi* to curse or blaspheme. — *n* **imprecā'tion** the act of imprecating; a curse. — *adj* **im'precatory** (*-kə-tə-ri*, *-kā-* or *kā'*). [L *imprecārī*, from *in* upon, and *precārī*, *-ātus* to pray]

imprecise *im-pri-sīs'*, *adj* not precise; inexact. — *adv* **imprecise'ly**. — *n* **imprecis'ion**. [**im-** (**in-** (2))]

impregn *im-prēn'*, (*poetic*; *archaic*) *vt* to impregnate. — *adj* **impregnant** (*im-preg'nənt*) impregnating (*archaic*); impregnated (*obs*). [Ety as for **impregnate**]

impregnable *im-preg'nə-bl*, *adj* that cannot be captured, broken into or taken by force; which cannot be overcome, unassailable. — *n* **impregnabil'ity**. — *adv* **impreg'nably**. [Fr *imprenable*, from L *in-* not, and *prendere*, *prehendere* to take]

impregnate *im'preg-nāt* or *-preg'*, *vt* to make pregnant; to fecundate; to fill, saturate or imbue (with the particles or qualities of another substance); to saturate (also *fig*). — *n* **impregnā'tion**. [LL *impraegnāre*, *-ātum*, from *in* in, and *praegnāns* pregnant]

impresa *im-prā'zə*, or **imprese** *im'prēz* or (*Milton*) *im-prēz'*, (*obs*) *n* an emblematic device, often with a motto; a motto. [Ital *impresa*]

impresario *im-pre-sä'ri-ō* or *-zä'*, *n* the manager of an opera company, etc; a producer or organizer of entertainments; a showman: — *pl* **impresa'rios** or **impresa'ri** (*-rē*). [Ital, from *impresa* undertaking, enterprise]

imprescriptible *im-pri-skrip'ti-bl*, (*legal*) *adj* not liable to be lost by prescription or lapse of time; inalienable. — *n* **imprescriptibil'ity**. [**im-** (**in-** (2))]

imprese. See **impresa**.

impress[1] *im-pres'*, *vt* to press; to apply with pressure, *esp* so as to leave a mark; to mark by pressure; to produce by pressure; to stamp or print; to fix deeply in the mind; to affect the mind; to produce a profound effect upon, or upon the mind of. — *vi* to be impressive, make a good impression. — *n* **im'press** that which is made by pressure; stamp; distinctive mark. — *n* **impressibil'ity**. — *adj* **impress'ible** susceptible, easily impressed. — *n* **impression** (*im-presh'ən*) the act or result of impressing; pressure; a difference produced in a thing by action upon it; a single printing of a book, or a reprint from the same plates or type setting; the effect of anything on the mind; a profound effect on the emotions; a vague uncertain memory or inclination to believe; belief, generally ill-founded; (the mould formed by) the pressing of an elastic substance, eg wax or silicone, on the teeth and/or gums, which is then used in the making of dentures, etc (*dentistry*); an impersonation. — *n* **impressionabil'ity**. — *adj* **impress'ionable** able to receive an impression; very susceptible to impressions. — *n* **impress'ionism** (often with *cap*) a 19c movement in painting, originating in France, aiming at the realistic representation of the play of light in nature, purporting to render faithfully what the artist actually saw, dispensing with the academic rules of composition and colouring; any similar tendency in other arts. — *n* and *adj* **impress'ionist** an exponent of impressionism (often with *cap*); an entertainer who impersonates people. — *adj* **impressionis'tic**. — *adv* **impressionist'ically**. — *adj* **impressive** (*-pres'*) exerting or tending to exert pressure; likely to impress others; solemn. — *adv* **impress'ively**. — *n* **impress'iveness**. — *n* **impressure** (*im-presh'ər*; *archaic*) impression. — **be under the impression** to think or believe without certainty. [L *imprimere*, *-pressum*, from *in premere*; see **press**[1]]

impress[2] *im-pres'*, *vt* to force into service, *esp* government service; to pressgang. — *n* **im'press** (Shakesp *im-pres'*) or **impress'ment** the act of impressing or seizing for service, *esp* government service. [**im-** (**in-** (1)), and cf **press**[2]]

impress[3] or **impresse** *im'pres*, (*obs*) *n* an impresa.

impress[4]. Obsolete variant of **imprest**.

imprest *im'prest*, *n* a loan or advance of money, *esp* from government funds for some public purpose; formerly, an advance of wages to soldiers and sailors. — **imprest system** (*commerce*) a method of maintaining a cash fund, eg petty cash, in which a fixed amount or float is regularly topped up from central funds, reimbursing the fund for incidental expenses. [**im-** (**in-** (1)) and **prest**[2]]

imprimatur *im-pri-mā'tər*, *n* a licence or permission to print a book, etc. [L *imprımātur*, let it be printed, subjunctive passive of *imprimere*, from *in* on, and *premere* to press]

imprimis *im-prī'mis*, *adv* in the first place. [L *imprīmīs*, from *in prīmīs* (ablative pl), *in* in, and *prīmus* first]

imprint *im-print'*, *vt* to print; to stamp; to impress; to fix in the mind; to cause (a young animal) to undergo imprinting (*usu* with *on*). — *n* (*im'print*) that which is imprinted; any characteristic mark, stamp, etc; the name of the publisher, time and place of publication of a book, etc, printed *usu* on the back of the title page or at the end of the book; the printer's name on the back of the title page or at the end of the book. — *n* **imprint'ing** a learning process in young animals in which their social preferences become restricted to their own species, or a substitute for this. [**im-** (**in-** (1))]

imprison *im-priz'n*, *vt* to put in prison; to shut up; to confine or restrain. — *adj* **impris'onable** liable to be, or capable of being, imprisoned; (of an offence) likely to lead to imprisonment. — *n* **impris'onment**. [**im-** (**in-** (1))]

improbable *im-prob'ə-bl*, *adj* unlikely. — *n* **improbabil'ity**. — *adv* **improb'ably**. [**im-** (**in-** (2))]

improbation *im-prō-bā'shən*, (*Scots law*) *n* an action for the purpose of declaring some instrument false or forged. [**im-** (**in-** (2))]

improbity *im-prōb'i-ti* or *-prob'*, *n* lack of probity; dishonesty or unscrupulousness. [**im-** (**in-** (2))]

impromptu *im-promp'tū*, *adj* improvised, spontaneous, unrehearsed; makeshift. — *adv* without preparation; on the spur of the moment. — *n* an extempore witticism or speech; an improvised composition; a musical composition with the character of an extemporization. [L *impromptū* for *in promptū* (ablative), *in* in, and *promptus* readiness]

improper *im-prop'ər*, *adj* not strictly belonging; not properly so called; not suitable; unfit; unbecoming; unseemly; indecent. — *adv* **improp'erly**. — *n* **imprō-prī'ety**. — **improper fraction** a fraction in which the numerator has a greater value or degree than the denominator. [L *im-* (*in-*) not, and *proprius* own]

impropriate *im-prō'pri-āt*, *vt* to appropriate to private use; to place (ecclesiastical property) into the hands of a layman. — *adj* (*-it*) transferred into the hands of a layman. — *n* **imprōpriā'tion**. — *n* **imprō'priātor** a layman who is in possession of a benefice or its revenues. [LL *impropriātus*, from L *in* in, and *proprius* one's own]

impropriety. See under **improper**.

improv *im'prov*, (*colloq*) *n* improvisation. [Abbrev]

improve *im-proōv'*, *vt* to make better; to make more valuable (*esp* by cultivating or building); to make good use of (*archaic*); to make use of (land, etc), to occupy (*US*; *archaic*); to increase (*obs*). — *vi* to become better; to make progress; to make improvements; to grow in price or value; to follow up with something better (with *on* or *upon*); to increase (*obs*). — *n* **improvabil'ity** or **improv'ableness**. — *adj* **improv'able**. — *adv* **improv'ably**. — *n* **improve'ment** the act of improving; a change for the better; a thing changed, or introduced in changing, for the better; a better thing substituted for, or following, one not so good (often with *on*). — *n* **improv'er**. — *pr p* and *adj* **improv'ing** tending to cause improvement; instructive; edifying; uplifting. — *adv* **improv'ingly**. — **on the improve** (*Austr*) improving. [Anglo-Fr *emprower*, from OFr *en prou*, *preu* into profit]

improvident *im-prov'i-dənt*, *adj* not provident or prudent; lacking foresight; thoughtless. — *n* **improv'idence**. — *adv* **improv'idently**. [**im-** (**in-** (2))]

improvise *im-prō-vīz'*, *-prə-* or *im'*, *vt* to compose and recite, or perform, without preparation; to bring about suddenly; to make or contrive without preparation or in emergency. — *vi* to perform extempore; to do anything without proper materials or preparation. — Also (*obs*) **improvisate** (*im-prov'i-zāt*). — *n* **improvīsā'tion** (or *-prov'iz-*) the act of improvising; something (eg a performance) which is improvised. — *n* **improvisator** (*im-prov'iz-ā-tər* or *im'prov-īz-*; *Ital* **improvvisatore** *im-prov-vē-sä-tō'rā*) someone, *esp* a performer, who improvises: — *fem* (*archaic*) **improv'isātrix** (*Ital* **improvvisatrice** *-trē'chā*). — *adj* **improvisatō'rial** (*-iz-ə-*). — *adj* **improvisatory** (*-iz'* or *-īz'*). — *n* **improvīs'er**. [Fr *improviser*, from L *in-* not, and *prōvīsus* foreseen; see **provide**]

imprudent *im-proō'dənt*, *adj* lacking foresight or discretion; incautious; inconsiderate. — *n* **impru'dence**. — *adv* **impru'dently**. [**im-** (**in-** (2))]

impsonite *imp'sən-īt*, (*mineralogy*) *n* an organic compound of the asphaltite group. [*Impson* valley, Oklahoma, where it is chiefly found, and **-ite** (3)]

impudent *im'pū-dənt*, *adj* shamelessly bold; impertinent; disrespectful; insolent; immodest (*obs*). — *n* **im'pudence**. — *adv* **im'pudently**. — *n* **impudicity** (*-dis'i-ti*) (*rare*) immodesty. [L *im-* (*in-*) not, and *pudēns*, *-entis*, pr p of *pudēre* to be ashamed; and *pudīcus* modest]

impugn *im-pūn'*, *vt* to oppose; to attack by words or arguments; to call in question, criticize. — *adj* **impugnable** (*-pūn'*). — *n* **impugā'tion**. — *n* **impugn'er**. — *n* **impugn'ment**. [L *impugnāre*, from *in* against, and *pugnāre* to fight]

impuissant *im-pū'is-ənt*, *-pū-is'*, *-pwis'* or *-pwēs'*, (*archaic*) *adj* powerless, feeble, impotent. — *n* **impuiss'ance** (or *-pū'*). [**im-** (**in-** (2))]

impulse *im'puls*, *n* the act of impelling; the effect of an impelling force; force suddenly and momentarily communicated; a beat; a single blow, thrust or wave; a disturbance travelling along a nerve (**nerve impulse**) or a muscle; an obsolete term for **pulse** (*electronics*); an outside influence on the mind; a sudden inclination, whim or desire. — *vt* to give an impulse to. — *n* **impul'sion** (*-shən*) a driving or impelling force; the act of impelling or state of being impelled. — *adj* **impuls'ive** having the power of impelling; acting or actuated by impulse; not continuous; tending or likely to act on impulse. — *adv* **impuls'ively**. — *n* **impuls'iveness**. — **impulse buyer**; **impulse buying** the buying of goods on a whim rather than because of previous intent. [L *impulsus* pressure, from *impellere*; see **impel**]

impundulu *im-poōn'doō-loō*, (*SAfr*) *n* a mythical bird with magical powers, often identified with the secretary bird. [Bantu *mpundulu*]

impunity *im-pūn'i-ti*, *n* freedom or safety from punishment or recrimination. [L *impūnitās*, *-ātis*, from *in* not, and *poena* punishment]

impure *im-pūr'*, *adj* mixed with something else; containing some unclean or extraneous substance; tainted, adulterated; unchaste, lewd; unclean ritually or ceremonially. — *adv* **impure'ly**. — *n* **impure'ness**. — *n* **impur'ity** an impure or unclean thing or constituent; the quality or state of being impure. — **impurity level** (*electronics*) an abnormal energy level arising from slight impurities, resulting in conduction in semiconductors. [**im-** (**in-** (2))]

impurple *im-pûr'pl*. Same as **empurple**.

impute *im-pūt'*, *vt* to ascribe (*usu* something evil, dishonest, etc); to charge; to attribute (grief, righteousness, etc) vicariously to (*theol*); to reckon or take into account. — *adj* **imput'able** capable of being imputed or charged; open to accusation; ascribable, attributable. — *n* **imputabil'ity**. — *n* **imput'ableness**. — *adv* **imput'ably**. — *n* **imputā'tion** the act of imputing or charging; censure; reproach; the reckoning as belonging. — *adj* **imput'ative** imputed. — *adv* **imput'atively**. — *n* **imput'er**. — **imputation system** a method of taxation whereby some or all of the corporation tax on a company is offset by the income tax paid by shareholders on dividends. [Fr *imputer*, from L *imputāre*, *-ātum*, from *in* in, and *putāre* to reckon]

IMRO *abbrev*: Investment Management Regulatory Organization.

imshi or **imshy** *im'shi*, (*old military slang*) *interj* go away. [Ar]

IMunE *abbrev*: (former) Institution of Municipal Engineers (now merged with **ICE**).

IN *abbrev*: Indiana (US state).

In (*chem*) *symbol*: indium.

in[1] *in*, *prep* expressing the relation of a thing to that which surrounds, encloses, includes or conditions it, with respect to place, time or circumstances, or to that which is assumed, held, maintained, or the relation of a right or possession to the person who holds or enjoys it; at; among; into; within; during; consisting of; by way of; because of; by or through; by the medium or method of; among the characteristics or possibilities of; wearing; belonging to; concerned or involved with; being a member of; with (*obs*). — *adv* within; not out; at home or at one's place of business; on the spot; in or into a position within or inward; in or into a centre or central point; in or into office, parliament, etc; in favour; in a position of assured success; in intimacy, on good terms (with); in or into fashion; in the market; in season; into concealment; having innings (*cricket*); as an addition or inclusion; alight; in pocket. — *n* a member of the party in office or (*cricket*) the side that is having its innings; a reflex angle; a turning in of anything upon itself. — *adj* inward; proceeding inwards; that is fashionable, much in use, as in **in'-word**, **in'-thing**; within a small group. — *vt* to take in; to enclose; to gather in harvest. — *n combining form* **-in** indicating a (public) gathering of a group of people in one room, building, etc, *orig* as a form of protest (as in *sit-in*, *work-in*), now for any joint purpose (as in *love-in*, *teach-in*). — *adj* and *adv* **in'-and-in'** (of breeding) carried out repeatedly within a closely related group of individuals of the same species to ensure continuity of certain characteristics, etc; with constant and close interaction. — *adj* **in'-built** built in, integral. — *adj* **in'-car** existing, situated or operating within a car, as *in-car entertainment*. — *adj* **in'-depth** (of a survey, research, etc) detailed or penetrating; thorough, comprehensive, not superficial. — **in'-fighting** fighting or bitter rivalry, between individuals or within a group, that is kept secret from, or is not apparent to, outsiders (see also separate entry **infighting**). — *adj* **in'-flight** provided during an aeroplane flight. — **Ingathering, Feast of** see **Feast of Tabernacles** under **tabernacle**; **in'group** a social group of people having the same interests and attitudes. — *adj* and *adv* **in'-house'** within a particular company, establishment, etc. — **in'-joke** a joke to be fully appreciated only by members of a particular limited group; **in-line skate** and **in-line skating** same as **roller-blade** and **rollerblading** (see under **roll**); **in'-off** (*billiards*) a losing hazard; **in'-patient** a patient living and being treated in a hospital (cf **out-patient**). — *adj* **in'-service** carried out while continuing with one's ordinary employment, eg *in-service training*. — *adj* **in'shore** close to the shore; moving towards the shore. — *adj* **in'-store** provided within a shop. — **in'-tray** a shallow container for incoming letters, etc still to be dealt with. — **be in it** to participate (*Austr colloq*); to be involved (*esp* in dishonest or illegal activities); **in as far as, in so far as** or **insofar as** to the extent that; **in as much as** or **inasmuch as** considering that; **in for** doomed to receive (*esp* unpleasant consequences); involved to the extent of; entered for; (see also **go in for** under **go**[1]); **in for it** in for trouble; committed to a certain course; **in it** enjoying success; in the running; **in itself** intrinsically, apart from relations; **in on** (*slang*) participating in; privy to; **ins and outs** (or **outs and ins**) turnings this way and that; nooks and corners; the complete details of any matter; those who repeatedly enter and leave; **in that** for the reason that; **in with** friendly with, associating much with; enjoying the favour of; **nothing in it** no truth, no importance, no difficulty in the matter; no important difference, no significant gap, six of one and half a dozen of the other; **on the in** (*slang*) on the inside, ie in prison. [OE *in*; Du, Ger *in*, ON *ī*; Welsh *yn*, L *in*, Gr *en*; OE also had *innan* within; cf OHGer *inanna*, Swed *innan*]

in[2] *in*, (*obs*) *n*. See **inn**.

in. *abbrev*: inch(es).

-in *-in*, (*chem*, etc) noun-forming *sfx usu* indicating: (1) a neutral substance such as a protein, fat or glycoside, eg *albumin*, *stearin*, *insulin*; (2) certain enzymes, eg *pepsin*; (3) an antibiotic or other pharmaceutical production, eg *penicillin*, *aspirin*. [Variant of **-ine**[1]]

in- *in-*, *pfx* (1) in words derived from Latin and Old English, used to form verbs with the sense in, into; sometimes used to form other parts of speech with this sense; sometimes used as an intensive or almost meaningless prefix; (2) in words derived from Latin, used to form negatives. — See also **il-**, **im-** and **ir-**.

inability *in-ə-bil'i-ti*, *n* lack of sufficient power or means; incapacity. [**in-** (2)]

in absentia *in ab-sensh'yə* or *ab-sent'i-ä*, (*L*) in (his, her, their, etc) absence.

inabstinence *in-ab'sti-nəns*, *n* lack of abstinence. [**in-** (2)]

in abstracto *in ab-strak'tō*, (*L*) in the abstract.

inaccessible *in-ak-ses'i-bl* or *-ək-*, *adj* not able to be reached, obtained or approached. — *n* **inaccessibil'ity** or **inaccess'ibleness**. — *adv* **inaccess'ibly**. [**in-** (2)]

inaccurate *in-ak'ūr-it*, *adj* not accurate; incorrect; erroneous. — *n* **inacc'uracy** (*-ə-si*) the state or condition of being inaccurate; an error or mistake. — *adv* **inacc'urately**. — *n* **inacc'urateness**. [**in-** (2)]

inactive *in-akt'iv*, *adj* not active; (of personnel or equipment) not in active service (*military*); not functioning; dormant; inert; having no power to move; sluggish; idle; lazy; having no effect; having no reactivity (*chem*); optically neutral in polarized light. — *n* **inac'tion**. — *vt* **inact'ivate** to render inactive. — *n* **inactivā'tion**. — *adv* **inact'ively**. — *n* **inactiv'ity** inaction; inertness; idleness. [**in-** (2)]

inadaptable *in-ə-dap'tə-bl*, *adj* that cannot be adapted. — *n* **inadaptā'tion** (*-ad-*). — *adj* **inadap'tive**. [**in-** (2)]

inadequate *in-ad'i-kwit*, *adj* insufficient; short of what is required; incompetent. — Also *n*. — *n* **inad'equacy** (*-kwə-si*) or **inad'equateness** insufficiency. — *adv* **inad'equately**. [**in-** (2)]

inadmissible *in-əd-mis'i-bl*, *adj* not allowable. — *n* **inadmissibil'ity**. — *adv* **inadmiss'ibly**. [**in-** (2)]

inadvertent *in-əd-vûrt'ənt*, *adj* unintentional; inattentive. — *n* **inadvert'ence** or **inadvert'ency** negligence; oversight. — *adv* **inadvert'ently**. [**in-** (2)]

inadvisable *in-ad-vī'zə-bl*, *adj* not advisable, unwise; another form of **unadvisable** which is still the form preferred by some. — *n* **inadvisabil'ity** or **inadvis'ableness**. [**in-** (2)]

inaidable *in-ād'ə-bl*, (*Shakesp*) *adj* that cannot be aided. [**in-** (2)]

inalienable *in-āl'yən-ə-bl* or *-i-ən-ə-bl*, *adj* not capable of being transferred or removed. — *n* **inalienabil'ity**. — *adv* **inal'ienably**. [**in-** (2)]

inalterable *in-öl'tə-rə-bl*, *adj* not alterable. — *n* **inalterabil'ity**. — *n* **inal'terableness**. — *adj* **inal'terably**. [**in-** (2)]

inamorata *in-am-o-rä'tə* and **inamorato** *-tō*, *n* respectively, a woman and man in love or beloved: — *pl* **inamora'tas** and **inamora'tos**. [Ital *innamorata*, *-to*, from LL *inamorāre* to cause to love, from L *in* in, and *amor* love]

inane *in-ān'*, *adj* empty, void; vacuous; senseless; characterless. — *adv* **inane'ly**. — *n* **inane'ness**. — *n* **inanition** exhaustion due to lack of nutrients in the blood, resulting from starvation or intestinal disease. — *n* **inanity** (*in-an'i-ti*) senselessness; mental vacuity; emptiness; an insipid frivolous utterance. [L *inānis*]

inanimate *in-an'i-mit*, *adj* without animation; without life; dead; spiritless; dull. — *adv* **inan'imately**. — *n* **inan'imateness**. — *n* **inanimā'tion**. [**in-** (2)]

inappeasable *in-ə-pēz'ə-bl*, *adj* that cannot be appeased. [**in-** (2)]

inappellable *in-ə-pel'ə-bl*, *adj* incapable of being appealed against or challenged. [**in-** (2); see **appeal**]

inappetent *in-ap'i-tənt*, *adj* lacking desire or appetite. — *n* **inapp'etence** or **inapp'etency**. [**in-** (2)]

inapplicable *in-ap'lik-ə-bl* or *in-əp-lik'ə-*, *adj* not applicable. — *n* **inapplicabil'ity** or **inapplicableness**. — *adv* **inapplicably**. [**in-** (2)]

inapposite *in-ap'ə-zit*, *adj* not apposite, suitable or pertinent. — *adv* **inapp'ositely**. — *n* **inapp'ositeness**. [**in-** (2)]

inappreciable *in-ə-prē'shə-bl* or *-shyə-bl*, *adj* too small or slight to be noticed or to be important; negligible; priceless (*obs*). — *n* **inappreciation** (*-shi-ā'shən*). — *adj* **inapprē'ciative** (*-shi-ə-tiv* or *-shi-ā-tiv*) not valuing justly or at all. — *adv* **inapprē'ciatively**. — *n* **inapprē'ciativeness**. [**in-** (2)]

inapprehensible *in-ap-ri-hen'si-bl*, *adj* not apprehensible; that cannot be grasped by the intellect or senses. — *n* **inapprehen'sion**. — *adj* **inapprehen'sive** not apprehensive; untroubled; without apprehension. — *n* **inapprehen'siveness**. [**in-** (2)]

inapproachable *in-ə-prōch'ə-bl*, *adj* unapproachable; inaccessible. — *n* **inapproachabil'ity**. — *adv* **inapproach'ably**. [**in-** (2)]

inappropriate *in-ə-prō'pri-it*, *adj* not appropriate, not suitable. — *adv* **inappro'priately**. — *n* **inappro'priateness**. [**in-** (2)]

inapt *in-apt'*, *adj* not apt; unfit or unqualified. — *n* **inapt'itude** or **inapt'ness** unfitness, awkwardness. — *adv* **inapt'ly**. [**in-** (2)]

inarable *in-ar'ə-bl*, *adj* not arable. [**in-** (2)]

inarch *in-ärch'*, (*rare*) *vt* to graft (a plant) by uniting without separating from the original stem. — Also **enarch'**. [**in-** (1)]

inarm *in-ärm'*, *vt* to embrace. [**in-** (1)]

inarticulate *in-är-tik'ū-lit*, *adj* not jointed or hinged; not uttered with the distinct sounds of spoken language; indistinctly uttered or uttering; incapable of clear and fluent expression. — *n* **inartic'ulacy**. — *adv* **inartic'ulately**. — *n* **inartic'ulateness** or **inarticulā'tion** indistinctness of sounds in speaking. [**in-** (2)]

in articulo mortis *in ärt-ik'ū-lō mör'tis*, or *ärt-ik'ŏŏ-lō*, (*L*) at the point (or moment) of death.

inartificial *in-ärt-i-fish'əl*, *adj* not artificial; simple. — *adv* **inartific'ially**. [**in-** (2)]

inartistic *in-är-tis'tik*, *adj* not artistic; deficient in appreciation of art. — *adv* **inartis'tically**. [**in-** (2)]

inasmuch *in-az-much'* or *-əz-*. See under **in**.

inattentive *in-ə-ten'tiv, adj* careless; not paying attention; neglectful. — *n* **inatten'tion**. — *adv* **inatten'tively**. — *n* **inatten'tiveness**. [**in-** (2)]

inaudible *in-öd'i-bl, adj* not loud enough to be heard. — *n* **inaudibil'ity**. — *n* **inaud'ibleness**. — *adv* **inaud'ibly**. [**in-** (2)]

inaugurate *in-ö'gūr-āt, vt* to induct formally into an office; to cause to begin; to make a public exhibition of for the first time. — *adj* **inau'gural** pertaining to, or done at, an inauguration. — *n* an inaugural address. — *n* **inaugurā'tion**. — *n* **inau'gurātor**. — *adj* **inau'guratory** (*-ə-tər-i*). [L *inaugurāre, -ātum* to inaugurate with taking of the auspices; see **augur**]

inaurate *in-ö'rāt*, (*rare*) *adj* gilded; having a golden lustre. [L *inaurāre, -ātum* to gild, from *in* in, on, and *aurum* gold]

inauspicious *in-ö-spish'əs, adj* not auspicious; ill-omened; unlucky. — *adv* **inauspic'iously**. — *n* **inauspic'iousness**. [**in-** (2)]

inauthentic *in-ö-then'tik, adj* not authentic; not genuine; untrue. [**in-** (2)]

in banco *in bang'kō*, (*LL*; *law*) in full court. — **in banco regis** (*rē'jis* or *rā'gis*) in the King's Bench.

inbd *abbrev*: inboard.

inbeing *in'bē-ing, n* inherent existence; inherence; inner nature. [**in-** (1)]

inbent *in'bent, adj* bent inwards. [**in-** (1)]

in-between *in-bi-twēn', adj* intervening; intermediate. — *n* an interval; an intermediary; any thing or person that is intermediate.

in bianco *in byang'kō* or *bē-äng'kō*, (*Ital*) in blank, in white.

inboard *in'bōrd* or *-börd, adv* and *adj* within the hull or interior of a ship; between the wingtip and fuselage (of an aircraft). [**in-** (1)]

in-bond *in'-bond, adj* (of goods, raw materials, etc) not subject to import/export duties, held in bond. — **in-bond shop** (*Caribbean*) a duty-free shop. [**in-** (1)]

inborn *in'börn, adj* born in or with one; innate; implanted by nature. [**in-** (1)]

inbound *in'bownd, adj* coming in. [**in-** (1)]

inbreak *in'brāk*, (*rare*) *n* a violent rush in; irruption. [**in-** (1)]

inbreathe *in-brēdh'* or *in'brēdh, vt* to breathe in, inhale; to imbue. [**in-** (1)]

inbreed *in'brēd* or *in-brēd', vt* to breed or generate within; to breed from closely related parents: — *pa p* and *adj* **in'bred** innate; bred from closely related parents. — *n* **in'breeding**. — **inbred line** (*biol*) a strain that has been inbred over many generations. [**in-** (1)]

inbring *in-bring'*, (*obs*) *vt* to bring in; to bring into court: — *pa p* and *adj* **inbrought'**. — *n* **in'bringing**. [**in-** (1)]

inburning *in-bûrn'ing*, (*Spenser*) *adj* burning within. [**in-** (1)]

inburst *in'bûrst*, (*rare*) *n* an irruption. [**in-** (1)]

inby or **inbye** *in-bī'*, (*Scot*) *adv* toward the interior; near; near the house. — Also *adj*. [**in-** (1)]

inc. *abbrev*: including: inclusive; incorporated.

Inca *ing'kə, n* a member of a S American Indian people of Peru before the Spanish conquest in the 16c, who had a complex civilization and empire; the language of the Incas; a member of the Incan royal family; a king or emperor of the Incas. — Also *adj*. — *adj* **In'can**. [Sp, from Quechua *inka* ruler, king]

incage. See **encage**.

incalculable *in-kal'kū-lə-bl, adj* not calculable or able to be reckoned; too great to calculate; unpredictable. — *n* **incalculabil'ity**. — *n* **incal'culableness**. — *adv* **incal'culably**. [**in-** (2)]

incalescent *in-ka-les'ənt* or *-kə-*, (*chem*) *adj* growing warm. — *n* **incalesc'ence**. [L *incalēscēns, -entis*, pr p of *incalēscere*, from *in* in, and *calēscere*, inceptive of *calere* to be warm]

in-calf *in-käf'*, *adj* pregnant (with calf). [**in**[1] and **calf**[1]]

in camera. See under **camera**.

incandesce *in-kan-des', vi* to be luminous by heat. — *n* **incandesc'ence** a white heat. — *adj* **incandesc'ent** white-hot. — **incandescent lamp** one whose light is produced by heating something to white heat, such as a filament resisting an electric current or a mantle heated by a flame. [L *in* in, and *candēscere*, from *candēre* to glow]

incantation *in-kan-tā'shən, n* a formula of words said or sung for purposes of enchantment, a magic spell; recitation of magic spells. — *adj* **incantā'tional**. — *n* **in'cantātor**. — *adj* **incan'tatory** (*-tə-tə-ri*). [L *incantāre* to sing a magical formula over]

incapable *in-kā'pə-bl, adj* not capable; unable (with *of*); incompetent; helplessly drunk; disqualified; unable to receive or keep (with *of*; *obs*). — *n* an incompetent person; a person who is helplessly drunk. — *n* **incapabil'ity**. — *adv* **incā'pably**. [**in-** (2)]

incapacious *in-kə-pā'shəs, adj* not large, narrow; of small capacity. — *n* **incapā'ciousness**. — *vt* **incapacitate** (*-pas'*) to disable; to make unfit (for); to disqualify legally. — *n* **incapacitā'tion** (a) disqualifying. — *n* **incapac'ity** lack of capacity; inability; disability; legal disqualification. [L *incapāx, -ācis*]

Incaparina *in-kap-ər-ē'nə, n* a high-protein dietary supplement developed by the *I*nstitute of *N*utrition of *C*entral *A*merica and *P*anama. [*I.N.C.A.P* and *-arina*, from Sp *fariña* powdered manioc, from L *farina* flour]

in capite *in kap'it-ē* or *kap'it-e*, (*LL*) in chief; holding directly from the Crown (*feudal law*).

incapsulate *in-kap'sūl-āt, vt* to enclose as in a capsule; to enclose (a modifying element) between other elements of a word. [**in-** (1)]

incarcerate *in-kär'sər-āt, vt* to imprison; to confine. — *n* **incarcerā'tion** imprisonment; obstinate constriction or strangulation (*surg*). [L *in* in, and *carcer* a prison]

incardinate *in-kär'di-nāt, vt* to attach or transfer (a priest, etc) to the jurisdiction of a (new) bishop. — *adj* Sir Andrew Aguecheek's blunder for *incarnate* (Shakesp, *Twelfth Night* V.1). — *n* **incardinā'tion** the official acceptance of a priest or member of the clergy into a new diocese. [LL *incardināre* to ordain as chief priest]

incarnadine *in-kär'nə-dīn* or *-din, vt* to dye red. — *adj* carnation-coloured; flesh-colour; blood-red. [Fr *incarnadin*, from Ital *incarnadino* carnation, flesh-colour]

incarnate *in-kär'nāt*, or *in'*, *vt* to embody in flesh, give human form to; to personify (*fig*). — *vi* to form flesh, heal. — *adj* (*-kär'nit* or *-nat*) invested with flesh; personified. — *n* **incarnā'tion** the act of embodying in flesh, *esp* of Christ (often with *cap*); an incarnate form; manifestation, visible embodiment; the process of healing, or forming new flesh (*surg*). [LL *incarnāre, -ātum*, from L *in* in, and *carō, carnis* flesh]

incarvillea *in-kär-vil'i-ə*, any plant of the genus *Incarvillea*, of the family *Bignoniaceae* typically having trumpet-shaped flowers borne in clusters on erect stems. [After Pierre d'*Incarville* (1706–57), French missionary to China]

incase and **incasement**. See **encase** and **encasement**.

incatenation *in-kat-i-nā'shən, n* harnessing; chaining together; linking. [L *in* in, and *catēna* chain]

incautious *in-kö'shəs, adj* not cautious or careful. — *n* **incau'tion**. — *adv* **incau'tiously**. — *n* **incau'tiousness**. [**in-** (2)]

incave. See **encave**.

incavo *in-kä'vō, n* the incised part in an intaglio: — *pl* **inca'vi** (*-vē*). [Ital, from L *in* in, and *cavus* hollow]

incede *in-sēd'*, (*rare*) *vi* to advance majestically. — *adv* **incēd'ingly**. [L *incēdere*; see Virgil, *Aeneid* I.46]

incendiary *in-sen'di-ər-i, n* a person who maliciously sets fire to property; a person who inflames passions or stirs up trouble; an incendiary bomb. — *adj* relating to incendiarism; adapted or used for setting buildings, etc on fire; tending to stir up trouble. — *n* **incen'diarism**. — **incendiary bomb** a bomb containing a highly inflammable substance and designed to burst into flames on striking its objective. [L *incendiārius*, from *incendium*, from *incendere* to kindle]

incendivity *in-sen-div'i-ti, n* the power of causing ignition. [L *incendere* to set on fire]

incense[1] *in-sens'*, *vt* to inflame with anger, to enrage; to incite, urge; to kindle (*obs*). — *n* **incense'ment**. — *n* **incen'sor** (*obs*) an instigator or inciter. [OFr *incenser*, from L *incendere*, *incēnsum* to kindle]

incense[2] *in'sens*, *n* material burned or volatilized to give fragrant fumes, *esp* in religious rites, *usu* a mixture of resins and gums, etc (eg olibanum, benzoin, styrax, cascarilla bark); the fumes so obtained; any pleasant smell; homage, adulation (*fig*). — *vt* to perfume or fumigate with incense; to offer incense to. — *n* **incensā'tion**. — *n* **in'censer** or **in'censor** (or *-sens'*) a burner or offerer of incense; a flatterer. — *n* **in'censory** (or *-sens'*) a censer or thurible. — **in'cense-boat** a boat-shaped vessel for feeding a censer with incense. — *adj* **in'cense-breathing** (*Gray*) exhaling fragrance. — **in'-cense-burner** a stationary vessel for burning incense. [OFr *encens*, from L *incēnsum*, from *incendere* to set on fire]

incentive *in-sent'iv*, *adj* inciting, encouraging; igniting (*Milton*). — *n* that which incites to action, a stimulus. — *n* **incentivizā'tion** or **-s-**. — *vi* **incent'ivize** or **-ise** to have or be given an incentive, *esp* to work more efficiently, productively, etc. [L *incentīvus* striking up a tune, from *incinere*, from *in* in, and *canere* to sing]

incentre *in'sen-tər*, *n* the centre of an inscribed circle or sphere. [**in-** (1)]

incept *in-sept'*, *vt* to take into the body, ingest; to begin (*obs*). — *vi* formerly, to complete the taking of a master's or doctor's degree at a university. — *n* **incep'tion** beginning. — *adj* **incep'tive** beginning or marking the beginning; inchoative (*gram*). — *n* (*gram*) an inchoative verb. — *n* **incep'tor**. [L *incipere*, *inceptum* to begin, from *in* in, on, and *capere* to take]

incertain *in-sûr'tən*, (*obs*) *adj* uncertain. — *n* **incer'tainty** (*obs*) or **incer'titude** (*archaic*). [**in-** (2)]

incessant *in-ses'ənt*, *adj* uninterrupted; continual. — *n* **incess'ancy**. — *adv* **incess'antly** unceasingly; immediately (*obs*). — *n* **incess'antness**. [L *incessāns*, *-antis*, from *in-* not, and *cessāre* to cease]

incest *in'sest*, *n* sexual intercourse between people who are so closely related that marriage is prohibited. — *adj* **incest'ūous** pertaining to, or characterized by, incest; turned inward on itself, or of, or within, a small closely-knit group (*fig*). — *adv* **incest'uously**. — *n* **incest'uousness**. — **incest taboo** (*behav*) a strong negative social sanction that forbids sexual relations between members of the same immediate family. [L *incestum*, from *in-* not, and *castus* chaste]

inch[1] *inch* or *insh*, *n* the twelfth part of a foot, equal to 2·54cm; the amount of eg rainfall that will cover a surface to the depth of one inch (now measured in millimetres); the amount of atmospheric pressure needed to balance the weight of a column of mercury one inch high (now measured in millibars); proverbially, a small distance or degree; (in *pl*) stature. — *vt* and *vi* to move by slow degrees. — *adj* **inched** marked with inches. — **inch'-tape** a measuring tape divided into inches; **inch'-worm** a looper caterpillar. — **at an inch** (*Shakesp*) ready at hand; **by inches** or **inch by inch** by small degrees; **every inch** entirely, thoroughly; **within an inch of** very close to; **within an inch of someone's life** to the point where there is danger of death. [OE *ynce* an inch, from L *uncia* a twelfth part; cf **ounce**[1]]

inch[2] *insh*, (*Scot* and *Irish*) *n* an island; a low-lying meadow beside a river. [Gaelic *innis* island]

incharitable *in-char'it-ə-bl*, *adj* an old form of **uncharitable**. [**in-** (2)]

inchase *in-chās'*. Same as **enchase**.

inchmeal *inch'mēl* or *insh'mēl*, *adv* inch by inch; little by little. [**inch**[1] and ME *-mele*, from OE *maelum* measure or quantity taken at one time]

inchoate *in-kō'āt* or *in'kō-āt*, *adj* only begun; unfinished, rudimentary; not established. — *vt* (*in'*) to begin. — *adv* **inchoately** (*-kō'* or *in'*). — *n* **inchoā'tion** beginning; rudimentary state. — *adj* **inchoative** (*in-kō'ə-tiv* or *in-kō-ā'tiv*) incipient; denoting the beginning of an action, inceptive (*gram*). — *n* (*gram*) an inchoative verb. [L *inchoāre* (for *incohāre*), *-ātum* to begin]

inchpin *inch'* or *insh'pin*, (*obs*) *n* a deer's sweetbread. [Perh **inch**[1] and **pin**]

incident *in'si-dənt*, *adj* falling (on something); liable to occur; naturally belonging (to); consequent. — *n* that which happens; an event; a subordinate action; an episode; that which naturally belongs to or is consequent on something else; a minor event showing hostility and threatening more serious trouble; a brief violent action, eg a bomb explosion. — *n* **in'cidence** the frequency or range of occurrence; the fact or manner of falling; the falling of a ray on a surface; the falling of a point on a line, or a line on a plane (*geom*). — *adj* **incidental** (*-dent'l*) incident; striking or impinging; liable to occur; naturally attached; accompanying; concomitant; occasional, casual. — *n* anything that occurs incidentally. — *adv* **incident'ally** in an incidental way; (*loosely*) by the way, parenthetically, as a digression. — *n* **incident'alness**. — **incidental music** music accompanying the action of a play, film, television programme, etc; **incident centre**, **office** or **room** a temporary establishment set up near the scene of a crime, disaster or unrest, etc by the police or army in order to collect information and monitor the situation. — **angle of incidence** (*phys*) the angle between an incident ray and the normal to the surface it falls on. [L *incidēns*, *-entis*, from *in* on, and *cadere* to fall]

incinerate *in-sin'ər-āt*, *vt* to reduce to ashes. — *n* **incinerā'tion**. — *n* **incin'erātor** a furnace for burning anything to ashes. [L *incinerāre*, *-ātum*, from *in*, in, and *cinis*, *cineris* ashes]

incipient *in-sip'i-ənt*, *adj* beginning, coming into existence; nascent. — *n* **incip'ience**. — *n* **incip'iency**. — *adv* **incip'iently**. [L *incipiēns*, *-entis*, pr p of *incipere* to begin]

incipit *in-sip'-it* or *in-kip'it*, (*L*) (here) begins (commonly used as an introduction in medieval manuscripts).

incise *in-sīz'*, *vt* to cut into; to cut or gash; to engrave. — *adj* **incised'** cut; engraved; cut to about the middle (*bot*). — *adj* **incīs'iform** (*zool*) shaped like an incisor tooth. — *n* **incision** (*in-sizh'ən*) the act of cutting in, *esp* (*surg*) into the soft tissues of the body; a cut; a gash; a notch; trenchancy. — *adj* **incisive** (*-sīs'*) having the quality of cutting in; trenchant; acute; sarcastic. — *adv* **inci'sively**. — *n* **inci'siveness**. — *n* **incisor** (*-sīz'ər*) a tooth at the front of the mouth, a cutting tooth. — *adj* **incisorial** (*-sis-ō'ri-əl*, *-sīz-* or *-ö'*) or **incisory** (*-sīs'* or *-sīz'ər-i*). — *n* **incisure** (*-sizh'ər*) a cut, incision. [Fr *inciser*, from L *incīdere*, *incīsum*, from *in* into, and *caedere* to cut]

incite *in-sīt'*, *vt* to move or provoke to action; to instigate. — *n* **incitant** (*in'sit-ənt* or *in-sīt'ənt*) that which incites; a stimulant. — *n* **incitā'tion** (*-sit-* or *-sīt-*) the act of inciting or rousing; an incentive. — *adj* and *n* **incitative** (*-sīt'ə-tiv*). — *n* **incite'ment**. — *n* **incit'er**. — *adv* **incit'ingly**. [Fr, from L *incitāre*, from *in* in, and *citāre* to rouse, from *ciēre* to put in motion]

incivil *in-siv'il*, *adj* an old form of **uncivil**. — *n* **incivil'ity** lack of civility or courtesy; impoliteness; an act of discourtesy (often in *pl* **incivil'ities**). [**in-** (2)]

incivism *in'siv-izm*, *n* neglect of duty as a citizen, conduct unbecoming a good citizen. [Fr *incivisme*]

inclasp *in-kläsp'*. Same as **enclasp**.

incle. See **inkle**[1].

inclement *in-klem'ənt*, *adj* severe; stormy; harsh. — *n* **inclem'ency**. — *adv* **inclem'ently**. [**in-** (2)]

inclinable *in-klī'nə-bl*, *adj* leaning, capable of being tilted or sloped; tending; somewhat disposed; favourably disposed. — *n* **inclīn'ableness**. [**incline**]

inclination *in-klin-ā'shən*, *n* the act of inclining; a bend or bow; a slope or tilt; a deviation; an angle with the horizon or with any plane or line; tendency; disposition, *esp* favourable; natural aptness; preference, affection. — *adj* **inclinā'tional**. [**incline**]

incline *in-klīn'*, *vi* to lean forward or downward; to bow or bend; to deviate or slant; to slope; to tend; to be disposed; to have some slight desire. — *vt* to cause to bend downwards; to turn; to cause to deviate; to slope; to tilt; to direct; to dispose. — *n* (*in'klīn* or *in-klīn'*) a slope; a sloping tunnel or shaft (*mining*). — *adj* **inclīn'atory**. — *adj* **inclined'** bent; sloping; oblique; having a tendency; disposed. — *n* **inclīn'ing** inclination; party, following (*Shakesp*). — *n* **inclinom'eter** (*-klin-*) an instrument for measuring slopes or the inclination of the axis of an aeroplane. — **inclined plane** one of the mechanical powers, a slope or plane up which one can raise a weight one could not lift. [L *inclīnāre* to bend towards, from *in* into, and *clīnāre* to lean]

inclip *in-klip'*, (*archaic*) *vt* to embrace, enfold. [**in-** (1)]

inclose and **inclosure**. See **enclose**.

include *in-kloōd'*, *vt* to enclose; to comprise as a part, contain; to classify, or reckon as part; to take in; to conclude (*Shakesp*). — *adj* **includ'able** or **includ'ible**. — *adj* **includ'ed** enclosed; comprised; not protruding (*bot*). — *prep* (or *pr p* merging into *prep*) **includ'ing** with the inclusion of. — *n* **inclusion** (*-kloō'zhən*) the act of including; that which is included; a foreign body (gas, liquid, glass or mineral) enclosed in a mineral groundmass; a particle, etc distinct from the substance surrounding it (*biol*). — *adj* **inclusive** (*-kloō'siv*) enclosing; comprehensive; including everything; including the stated limits or extremes (with *of*); included. — *adv* **inclu'sively**. — **inclusion bodies** (*pathol*) particles found in the nucleus and cytoplasm of cells infected with a virus; **inclusive fitness** see under **fitness**; **inclusive reckoning** a system of counting in which both the first and the last terms are included (ie Monday–Wednesday is 3 days); **inclusive transcription** any phonetic transcription allowing more than one pronunciation of the transcribed words. — **include in** or **out** (*colloq*) to include or exclude. [L *inclūdere*, *inclūsum*, from *in* in, and *claudere* to shut]

incoagulable *in-kō-ag'ū-lə-bl*, *adj* incapable of coagulation. [**in-** (2)]

incoercible *in-kō-ûrs'i-bl*, *adj* that cannot be coerced; that cannot be liquefied by pressure. [**in-** (2)]

incog. *abbrev*: incognito.

incogitable *in-koj'i-tə-bl*, *adj* unthinkable. — *n* **incogitabil'ity**. — *n* **incog'itancy**. — *adj* **incog'itant** unthinking; thoughtless. — *adj* **incog'itātive**. [L *in-* not, and *cōgitāre* to think]

incognisable, incognisant, incognisance. See **incognizable**.

incognito *in-kog'ni-tō* or *in-kog-nē'tō*, *adj* unknown, unidentified; disguised; under an assumed name or title. — *adv* under an assumed name; with concealment of identity. — *n* a person concealing his or her identity; an assumed identity: — *pl* **incognitos**. [Ital, from L *incognitus*, from *in-* not, and *cognitus* known, from *cognōscere* to recognize, come to know]

incognizable or **incognisable** *in-kog'niz-ə-bl*, *adj* that cannot be known or distinguished. — *n* **incog'nizance** or -**s**- failure to recognize. — *adj* **incog'nizant** or -**s**- unaware (with *of*). [See **cognition** and **recognize**]

incoherent *in-kō-hēr'ənt*, *adj* not coherent; loose; rambling. — *n* **incohēr'ence** or **incoherency**. — *adv* **incohēr'ently**. [**in-** (2)]

incombustible *in-kəm-bust'i-bl*, *adj* incapable of combustion; incapable of being burnt. — *n* **incombustibil'ity** or **incombust'ibleness**. — *adv* **incombust'ibly**. [**in-** (2)]

income *in'kum*, *in'kəm* or *ing'kəm*, *n* profit, or interest from anything; revenue; that which comes in, inflow; arrival, entrance (*archaic*); a disease, tumour, etc without known cause (*Scot* and *NEng dialect*). — *n* **incomer** (*in'kum-ər*) a person who comes in, *esp* one who comes to live in a place, not having been born there. — *adj* **in'coming** coming in; accruing; ensuing, next to follow. — *n* the act of coming in; revenue. — **income bond** a type of savings bond paying monthly or annual interest (without deducting tax at source); **income group** a group within a population having incomes within a certain range, eg *middle income group*; **incomes policy** a government policy of curbing inflation by controlling wages; **income support** in Britain, a social security payment made to people on low incomes and the unemployed; **income tax** a tax directly levied on income or on income over a certain amount; **income unit** a type of unit trust in which a regular dividend is paid to the holder instead of accumulating in the capital fund. — **negative income tax** a type of Government subsidy in which low-paid workers are paid an additional sum instead of having tax deducted from their wages. [**in-** (1)]

in commendam. See **commend**.

incommensurable *in-kə-men'shə-rə-bl* or *-shoō-*, *adj* having no common measure; not reaching the same standard; disproportionate. — *n* (*math*) a quantity that has no common factor with another, *esp* with rational numbers. — *n* **incommensurabil'ity** or **incommen'surableness**. — *adv* **incommen'surably**. [**in-** (2)]

incommensurate *in-kə-men'shə-rət*, *adj* disproportionate; inadequate; incommensurable. — *adv* **incommen'surately**. — *n* **incommen'surateness**. [**in-** (2)]

incommiscible *in-kəm-is'i-bl*, *adj* that cannot be mixed together. [L *in-* not, and *commiscēre* to mix]

incommode *in-kəm-ōd'*, *vt* to cause trouble or inconvenience to. — *adj* **incommō'dious** inconvenient; (of eg a house) cramped, poky; troublesome (*obs*); unsuitable (with *to* or *for*; *obs*). — *adv* **incommō'diously**. — *n* **incommō'diousness**. — *n* **incommodity** (*-od'*) inconvenience; anything that causes inconvenience. [Fr *incommoder*, from L *incommodāre*, from *in-* not, and *commodus* commodious]

incommunicable *in-kəm-ūn'i-kə-bl*, *adj* that cannot be communicated or passed on to others. — *n* **incommunicabil'ity** or **incommun'icableness**. — *adv* **incommun'icably**. — *adj* **incommun'icative** uncommunicative. — *adv* **incommun'icatively**. — *n* **incommun'icativeness**. [**in-** (2)]

incommunicado *in-kəm-ūn-i-kä'dō*, *adj* and *adv* without means of communication; in solitary confinement. — Also **incomunica'do**. [Sp *incomunicado*]

incommutable *in-kəm-ūt'ə-bl*, *adj* that cannot be commuted or exchanged. — *n* **incommutabil'ity** or **incommut'ableness**. — *adv* **incommut'ably**. [**in-** (2)]

incomparable *in-kom'pər-ə-bl*, *adj* not admitting comparison; matchless. — *n* **incomparabil'ity** or **incom'parableness**. — *adv* **incom'parably**. — *adj* **incompared** (*in-kom-pā'red*; *Spenser*) peerless. [**in-** (2)]

incompatible *in-kəm-pat'i-bl*, *adj* not consistent; contradictory; incapable of existing together in harmony, or at all; incapable of combination, co-operation, or functioning together; mutually intolerant or exclusive; irreconcilable. — *n* a thing incompatible with another; (in *pl*) things which cannot co-exist. — *n* **incompatibil'ity** the state of being incompatible; an incompatible feature, element, etc; a difference, *usu* physiological, which prevents completion of fertilization (*bot*); a difference in physiological properties between a host and parasite which limits the development of the latter (*bot*). — *n* **incompat'ibleness**. — *adv* **incompat'ibly**. [**in-** (2)]

incompetent *in-kom'pi-tənt*, *adj* unable to function; without the proper legal qualifications; lacking ability or skill for one's work. — *n* an incompetent person. — *n* **incom'petence** the state or condition of being incompetent; (in the veins, heart, etc) a condition in which the proper function of the valves is impaired, allowing blood to leak backwards (*med*). — *n* **incom'petency**. — *adv* **incom'petently**. [**in-** (2)]

incomplete *in-kəm-plēt'*, *adj* imperfect; unfinished; lacking calyx, corolla, or both (*bot*). — *adv* **incomplete'ly**. — *n* **incomplete'ness**. — *n* **incomplē'tion**. — **incomplete reaction** (*chem*) a process in which a reversible reaction is allowed to reach equilibrium and from which a mixture of reactants and reaction products is obtained. [**in-** (2)]

incompliance *in-kəm-plī'əns*, *n* refusal to comply; an unaccommodating disposition; inflexibility. — *adj* **incomplī'ant**. [**in-** (2)]

incomposed *in-kəm-pōzd'*, (*poetic*; *obs*) *adj* discomposed. [**in-** (2)]

incomposite *in-kom'pəz-it*, *adj* simple; ill-constructed. — **incomposite numbers** prime numbers. [**in-** (2)]

incompossible *in-kəm-pos'i-bl*, (*rare*) *adj* incapable of co-existing. — *n* **incompossibil'ity**. [**in-** (2)]

incomprehensible *in-kom-pri-hens'i-bl*, *adj* not capable of being understood; not to be contained within limits, limitless (*archaic* and *theol*). — *n* **incomprehensibil'ity** or **incomprehens'ibleness**. — *adv* **incomprehens'ibly**. — *n* **incomprehen'sion**. — *adj* **incomprehens'ive**. — *n* **incomprehens'iveness**. [**in-** (2)]

incompressible *in-kəm-pres'i-bl*, *adj* incapable of being compressed into smaller bulk. — *n* **incompressibil'ity** or **incompress'ibleness**. [**in-** (2)]

incomputable *in-kəm-pūt'ə-bl* or *in-kom'*, *adj* that cannot be computed or reckoned. [**in-** (2)]

incomunicado. See **incommunicado**.

inconceivable *in-kən-sēv'ə-bl*, *adj* that cannot be conceived by the mind; incomprehensible; involving a contradiction in terms; physically impossible; taxing belief or imagination (*colloq*). — *n* (*rare*) an inconceivable thing. — *n* **inconceivabil'ity** or **inconceiv'ableness**. — *adv* **inconceiv'ably**. [**in-** (2)]

inconcinnity *in-kən-sin'i-ti*, *n* lack of congruousness or proportion. — *adj* **inconcinn'ous**. [**in-** (2)]

inconclusive *in-kən-kloo͞s'iv*, *adj* not settling a point in debate; indeterminate, indecisive. — *n* **inconclusion** (*-kloo͞'zhən*). — *adv* **inconclus'ively**. — *n* **inconclus'iveness**. [**in-** (2)]

incondensable *in-kən-dens'ə-bl*, *adj* incapable of being condensed. [**in-** (2)]

incondite *in-kon'dit* or *-dīt*, *adj* not well put together, poorly constructed, irregular, unfinished. [L *inconditus*, from *in-* not, and *condere*, *conditum* to build]

incongruous *in-kong'groo͝-əs*, *adj* inconsistent; out of keeping; unsuitable. — Also **incong'ruent**. — *n* **incongruity** (*-kong-* or *-kən-groo͞'*) the fact of being incongruous; an incongruous thing. — *adv* **incong'ruously**. — *n* **incong'ruousness**. [**in-** (2)]

inconie. See **incony**.

inconnu *ɛ̃-ko-nü*, (*Fr*) *n* an unknown person (fem **inconnue**); a large food fish (*Stenodus mackenziei*) of NW Canada.

inconscient *in-kon'shyənt* or *-shənt*, *adj* unconscious; abstracted; not controlled by, or arising from, consciousness. — *adv* **incon'sciently**. — *adj* **incon'scious** unconscious. [**in-** (2)]

inconscionable *in-kon'shən-ə-bl*, *adj* unconscionable. [**in-** (2)]

inconsecutive *in-kən-sek'ū-tiv*, *adj* not succeeding or proceeding in regular order; not consecutive. — *n* **inconsec'utiveness**. [**in-** (2)]

inconsequent *in-kon'si-kwənt*, *adj* not following from the premises (*logic*); illogical; irrelevant; disconnected; unrelated; unimportant. — *n* **incon'sequence**. — *adj* **inconsequential** (*-kwen'shl*) not following from the premises (*logic*); of no consequence or value. — *adv* **inconsequen'tially**. — *adv* **incon'sequently**. [**in-** (2)]

inconsiderable *in-kən-sid'ər-ə-bl*, *adj* not worthy of notice; unimportant; of no great size. — *n* **inconsid'erableness**. — *adv* **inconsid'erably**. [**in-** (2)]

inconsiderate *in-kən-sid'er-it*, *adj* without care or regard for others; thoughtless; rash, imprudent. — *adv* **inconsid'erately**. — *n* **inconsid'erateness** or **inconsiderā'tion**. [**in-** (2)]

inconsistent *in-kən-sist'ənt*, *adj* not consistent; not suitable or agreeing; intrinsically incompatible; self-contradictory; changeable, fickle. — *n* **inconsist'ence** or **inconsist'ency**. — *adv* **inconsist'ently**. [**in-** (2)]

inconsolable *in-kən-sōl'ə-bl*, *adj* not able to be comforted. — *n* **inconsol'ability** or **inconsol'ableness**. — *adv* **inconsol'ably**. [**in-** (2)]

inconsonant *in-kon'sən-ənt*, *adj* not agreeing or in harmony with. — *n* **incon'sonance**. — *adv* **incon'sonantly**. [**in-** (2)]

inconspicuous *in-kən-spik'ū-əs*, *adj* not conspicuous. — *adv* **inconspic'uously**. — *n* **inconspic'uousness**. [**in-** (2)]

inconstant *in-kon'stənt*, *adj* subject to change, variable; fickle. — *n* **incon'stancy**. — *adv* **incon'stantly**. [**in-** (2)]

inconstruable *in-kən-stroo͞'ə-bl*, *adj* which cannot be construed; impossible to interpret or understand. [**in-**(2)]

inconsumable *in-kən-sūm'ə-bl*, *adj* that cannot be consumed or wasted. — *adv* **inconsum'ably**. [**in-** (2)]

incontestable *in-kən-test'ə-bl*, *adj* too clear to be called in question; undeniable. — *n* **incontestabil'ity**. — *adv* **incontest'ably**. [**in-** (2)]

incontiguous *in-kən-tig'ū-əs*, *adj* not adjoining or touching. — *adv* **incontig'uously**. — *n* **incontig'uousness**. [**in-** (2)]

incontinent[1] *in-kon'ti-nənt*, *adj* unable to control urination or defecation; lacking self-restraint, *esp* in sexual matters; lacking control over (with *of*). — *n* **incon'tinence** or **incon'tinency**. — *adv* **incon'tinently**. [L *incontinēns*, *-entis*, from *in* not, and *continēns*; see **continent**]

incontinent[2] *in-kon'ti-nənt*, (*archaic*) *adv* straight away, immediately. — Also **incon'tinently**. [Fr, from LL *in continenti* (*tempore*), in unbroken (time)]

incontrollable *in-kən-trōl'ə-bl*, *adj* uncontrollable. — *adv* **incontroll'ably**. [**in-** (2)]

incontrovertible *in-kon-trə-vûrt'i-bl*, *adj* incontestible; indisputable. — *n* **incontrovertibil'ity**. — *adv* **incontrovert'ibly**. [**in-** (2)]

inconvenient *in-kən-vēn'yənt*, *adj* not convenient, unsuitable; inopportune; causing trouble, difficulty or uneasiness; incommodious. — *vt* **inconvēn'ience** to trouble or incommode. — *n* the state of being inconvenient; something causing difficulty or giving trouble. — *adv* **inconvēn'iently**. [**in-** (2)]

inconversable *in-kən-vûrs'ə-bl*, *adj* indisposed to conversation, unsocial. [**in-** (2)]

inconversant *in-kon'vər-sənt*, or (*rare*) *-kən-vûr'*, *adj* not versed (with *with* or *in*). [**in-** (2)]

inconvertible *in-kən-vûrt'i-bl*, *adj* that cannot be changed or exchanged. — *n* **inconvertibil'ity**. — *adv* **inconvert'ibly**. [**in-** (2)]

inconvincible *in-kən-vin'si-bl*, *adj* not capable of being convinced. [**in-** (2)]

incony or **inconie** *in-kun'i*, (*Shakesp*) *adj* fine, delicate, pretty. [Origin unknown]

inco-ordinate *in-kō-örd'i-nit* or *-örd'nit*, *adj* not co-ordinate. — *n* **inco-ordination** (*-i-nā'shən*) lack or failure of co-ordination, eg the inability to combine the muscular movements necessary to perform an action. — Also **incoor-** in both words. [**in-** (2)]

incoronate *in-kor'ə-nāt* or *-nit* or **incoronated** *-nāt-id*, (*formal*) *adj* crowned. — *n* **incoronā'tion**. [**in-** (1)]

incorporal or **incorporall** *in-kör'pər-əl*, (*archaic*) *adj* incorporeal. [L *incorporālis* bodiless, from *in-* not, and *corporālis*, from *corpus*, *-oris* body]

incorporate[1] *in-kör'pər-āt*, *vt* to form into a body; to combine into one mass; to merge; to absorb; to form into a corporation; to admit to a corporation. — *vi* to unite into one mass; to form a corporation. — *adj* **incorporate** (*-it*) or **incor'porated** united in one body; constituted as an incorporation. — *adj* **incor'porāting** (*linguistics*) combining the parts of a sentence in one word, polysynthetic. — *n* **incorporā'tion** the act of incorporating; the state of being incorporated; the formation of a legal or political body; an association; an incorporated society. — *adj* **incor'porative** (*-ə-tiv* or *-ā-tiv*). — *n* **incor'porātor** a person who incorporates; a member, or original member, of an incorporated company (*US*); a member of a university admitted to membership of another. [L *incorporāre*, *-ātum*, from *in* in, into, and *corpus*, *-oris* body]

incorporate[2] *in-kör'pər-it* or *-āt*, *adj* without a body; incorporeal. [L *incorporātus*, from *in-* not, and *corporātus*, from *corpus*, *-oris* body]

incorporeal *in-kör-pör'i-əl*, *adj* having no material form or body; spiritual or metaphysical; intangible; of, pertaining to, or constituting a legal right which attaches to something without a physical existence (eg copyright, patents, easement). — *n* **incorporeal'ity** or **incorpore'ity**. — *adv* **incorpo'really**. [L *incorporeus*, from *in-* not, and *corpus*, *-oris* body]

incorpse *in-körps'*, (*archaic*) *vt* to incorporate. [**in-** (1)]

incorrect *in-kər-ekt'*, *adj* containing faults; not accurate; not correct in manner or character, improper; not regulated or corrected (*obs*). — *adv* **incorrect'ly**. — *n* **incorrect'ness**. [**in-** (2)]

incorrigible *in-kor'i-ji-bl*, *adj* beyond correction or reform. — Also *n*. — *n* **incorrigibil'ity** or **incorr'igibleness**. — *adv* **incorr'igibly**. [**in-** (2)]

incorrosible *in-kə-rō'si-bl* or **incorrodible** *in-kə-rō'di-bl*, *adj* incapable of being corroded; not readily corroded. [**in-** (2)]

incorrupt *in-kər-upt'*, *adj* free from corruption; pure; not decayed; not depraved or defiled; free from error; not able to be influenced by bribes. — *n* **incorruptibil'ity** or **incorrupt'ibleness**. — *adj* **incorrupt'ible** incapable of corruption; not capable of decay; that cannot be bribed; honest; just. — *adv* **incorrupt'ibly**. — *n* **incorrup'tion** or **incorrupt'ness**. — *adj* **incorrupt'ive**. — *adv* **incorrupt'ly**. [**in-** (2)]

incrassate *in-kras'āt*, *vt* and *vi* (*obs*) to thicken. — *adj* **incrass'ate** or **incrass'ated** (*esp biol*) thickened or swollen. — *n* **incrassā'tion**. — *adj* **incrass'ative** (*-ə-tiv*). [LL *incrassāre*, *-ātum*, from L *in* in, and *crassus* thick]

increase *in-krēs'*, *vi* to grow in size, number or (*archaic*) wealth; to have a syllable more in the genitive than in the nominative (*L gram*). — *vt* to make greater in size, number or (*archaic*) wealth. — *n* (*in'*) growth; increment; addition to the original stock; profit; produce; progeny (*archaic*). — *adj* **increas'able**. — *adj* **increase'ful** (*Shakesp*) fruitful, productive. — *n* **increas'er**. — *n* and *adj* **increas'ing**. — *adv* **increas'ingly**. [ME *encressen*, from Anglo-Fr *encresser*, from L *incrēscere*, from *in*, *crēscere* to grow]

increate *in-krē-āt'*, (*archaic*) *adj* uncreated, never having been created. [**in-** (2)]

incredible *in-kred'i-bl*, *adj* unbelievable; difficult to believe in; very great; unusually good, amazing (*colloq*). — *n* **incredibil'ity** or **incred'ibleness**. — *adv* **incred'ibly**. [**in-** (2)]

incredulous *in-kred'ū-ləs*, *adj* unwilling to believe, sceptical; unbelieving; expressing disbelief; unbelievable (*obs*). — *n* **incredū'lity** (*-krid-*) or **incred'ūlousness**. — *adv* **incred'ūlously**. [**in-** (2)]

incremate *in'kri-māt*, (*obs*) *vt* to burn; to cremate. — *n* **incremā'tion**. [**in-** (1)]

increment *ing'* or *in'kri-mənt*, *n* increase; the amount of increase, eg in wages and salaries; an amount or thing added; the finite increase of a variable quantity (*math*); (in computer programming) to add 1 to the value in a storage location (cf **decrement**); an adding of particulars towards a climax (*rhetoric*); a syllable in excess of the number of the nominative singular or the second person singular present indicative (*gram*). — *adj* and *n* **incremental** (*-ment'l*). — **incremental plotter** (*comput*) a device in which graphs are produced on paper from data specifying increments up to the current positon, rather than from data specifying coordinates (cf **digital plotter**). — **unearned increment** any exceptional increase in the value of land, houses, etc not due to the owner's labour or outlay. [L *incrēmentum*, from *incrēscere* to increase]

increscent *in-kres'ənt*, (*esp heraldry*) *adj* (of the moon) waxing. [**in-** (1)]

incretion *in-krē'shən*, (*physiol*) *n* secretion directly into the bloodstream, eg of a hormone from an endocrine gland. [**in-** and *secretion*]

incriminate *in-krim'in-āt*, *vt* to charge with a crime or fault; to implicate, involve in a charge. — *adj* **incrim'inatory**. [**in-** (1)]

incross *in'kros*, *n* a plant or animal produced by crossing two inbred individuals of different lineage but of the same breed. — Also *vt*. — *n* **incross'bred** a plant or animal produced by crossing two inbred individuals of different breeds. — *vt* **incross'breed**. [**in-** (1)]

incrust and **incrustation**. See **encrust** and **encrustation**.

incubate *in'* or *ing'kū-bāt*, *vi* to brood eggs; to hatch; to undergo incubation; to brood, foment (*fig*). — *vt* to hatch; to foster the development of (as bacteria, etc); to brood or ponder over (*fig*). — *n* **incubā'tion** the act of sitting on eggs to hatch them; hatching (natural or artificial); fostering (as of bacteria, etc); brooding or fomenting (*fig*); the period between infection with disease and the appearance of symptoms (*med*; also **incubation** or **latent period**). — *adj* **in'cubātive** or **in'cubātory**. — *n* **in'cubātor** an apparatus for hatching eggs by artificial heat, for rearing prematurely born babies, or for developing bacteria; a brooding hen. — *adj* **in'cubous** (*bot*) (of a liverwort) having the upper leaf-margin overlapping the leaf above. [L *incubāre*, *-ātum* (or usu *-itum*), from *in* on, and *cubāre* to lie, recline]

incubus *in'* or *ing'kū-bəs*, *n* a devil supposed to assume a male body and have sexual intercourse with women in their sleep (cf **succubus**); a nightmare; any oppressive person, thing or influence. — *pl* **in'cubuses** or **in'cubi** (*-bī*). [L *incubus* nightmare, from *in* on, and *cubāre* to lie]

incudes. See **incus**.

in cuerpo. See **en cuerpo**.

inculcate *in'kul-kāt* or *-kul'*, *vt* to instil by frequent admonitions or repetitions. — *n* **inculcā'tion**. — *adj* **inculc'ative** (*-ə-tiv*). — *n* **in'culcātor**. — *adj* **inculc'atory**. [L *inculcāre*, *-ātum*, from *in* into, and *calcāre* to tread, from *calx* heel]

inculpable *in-kul'pə-bl*, *adj* free from guilt; blameless. — *adv* **incul'pably**. [L *inculpābilis*, from *in-* not, and *culpābilis*; see **culpable**]

inculpate *in'kul-pāt* or *-kul'*, *vt* to blame; to incriminate; to charge. — *n* **inculpā'tion**. — *adj* **incul'patory** (*-pə-tə-ri*). [LL *inculpāre*, *-ātum*, from L *in* in, and *culpa* a fault]

incult *in-kult'*, (*rare*) *adj* uncultivated; coarse, uncultured. [**in-** (2)]

incumbent *in-kum'bənt*, *adj* lying, resting or weighing on something; overlying (*geol*); leaning over (*archaic*); overhanging (*archaic*); imposed on, or laid on or upon, someone as a duty; obligatory; lying along a surface, as a moth's wings at rest; (of a radicle) lying along the back of one cotyledon (*bot*). — *n* a person who holds an ecclesiastical benefice, or any office. — *n* **incum'bency** the state or fact of being incumbent or an incumbent; a duty or obligation; the holding of an office; an ecclesiastical benefice. — *adv* **incum'bently**. [L *incumbēns*, *-entis*, pr p of *incumbere* to lie upon]

incunabula *in-kū-nab'ū-lə*, *n pl* early printed books, *esp* those printed before the year 1501; the cradle, birthplace, origin of a thing: — *n sing* **incūnab'ūlum**. — Also **incūn'able** (*n sing*) and **incūn'ables** (*n pl*). — *adj* **incūn'able**. — *adj* **incūnab'ūlar**. — *n* **incūnab'ūlist** a student or collector of incunabula. [L *incūnābula* swaddling-clothes, infancy, earliest stage, from *in* in, and *cūnābula*, dimin of *cūnae* a cradle]

incur *in-kûr'*, *vt* to become liable to; to bring upon oneself; to suffer: — *pr p* **incurr'ing**; *pa t* and *pa p* **incurred'**. — *adj* **incurr'able**. — *n* **incurr'ence**. [L *incurrere*, *incursum*, from *in* into, and *currere* to run]

incurable *in-kūr'ə-bl*, *adj* unable to be cured or remedied. — *n* someone beyond cure or who does not respond to treatment. — *n* **incurabil'ity** or **incur'ableness**. — *adv* **incur'ably**. [**in-** (2)]

incurious *in-kū'ri-əs*, *adj* not curious or inquisitive; inattentive; uninterested; indifferent; not fastidious, uncritical (*obs*); not exquisite (*obs*); uninteresting (*archaic*). — *n* **incurios'ity**. — *adv* **incū'riously**. — *n* **incū'riousness**. [**in-** (2)]

incurrent *in-kur'ənt*, *adj* running or flowing in or inward; carrying an inflowing current. [L *in* into, and *currēns*, *-entis*, pr p of *currere* to run]

incursion *in-kûr'shən, n* a hostile inroad; the action of leaking or running in; a sudden attack, invasion; an intrusion. — *adj* **incur'sive** making inroads; aggressive; invading; intruding. [L *incursiō, -ōnis*, from *incurrere* to run into]

incurve *in-kûrv', vt* and *vi* to curve; to curve inward. — *n* **in'curve** a curve inwards; a ball that curves in, or towards the batsman (*baseball*). — Also *adj.* — *vt* and *vi* **incur'vate** (or *in'*) to bend, *esp* inwards. — *adj* curved, *esp* inward (also **incur'vāted**). — *n* **incurvā'tion** bending; bowing, kneeling, etc; an inward bend or growth. — *n* **incur'vature** a curve or curvature, *esp* inward. — *adj* **incurved'** (or *in'*) curved; curved inward. — *n* **incur'vity**. [L *incurvāre* to bend in, and *incurvus* bent]

incus *ing'kəs, n* one of the small bones in the middle ear articulated with the malleus and the stapes, so called because it is considered to resemble an anvil in shape: — *pl* **incudes** (*ing-kū'dēz* or *ing'*). — *adj* anvil-shaped. [L *incūs, incūdis* an anvil; see **incuse**]

incuse *in-kūz', vt* to impress (eg a coin) with a design, or a design on a coin, etc, by stamping. — *adj* hammered. — *n* an impression, a stamp. [L *incūsus*, pa p of *incūdere*, from *in* on, and *cūdere* to strike, to work on the anvil]

incut *in'kut, adj* set in by, or as if by, cutting; inserted in spaces left in the text (*printing*). [**in**[1] and **cut**]

IND *abbrev*: *in nomine Dei* (*L*), in the name of God; India (IVR).

Ind *ind* or *īnd*, (*poetic*) *n* India.

Ind. *abbrev*: Independent; India; Indian; Indiana (US state).

indaba *in-dä'bə, n* an important tribal conference; an international Scout conference; a problem, a matter of concern (*SAfr colloq*). [Zulu]

indagate *in'də-gāt*, (*archaic*) *vt* to search out. — *n* **indagā'tion**. — *adj* **in'dagātive**. — *n* **in'dagātor**. — *adj* **in'dagātory**. [L *indāgāre, -ātum* to trace]

indamine *in'də-mēn, n* any organic base whose salts are unstable blue or green dyes. [From *ind*igo and **amine**]

indapamide *in-dap'ə-mīd, n* a synthetic thiazide drug used in the treatment of high blood pressure and oedema. [From *ind*ole and **amide**]

indart. See **endart**.

indebted *in-det'id, adj* owing money; owing gratitude to another for something received, obligated. — *n* **indebt'edness**. [**in-** (1)]

indecent *in-dē'sənt, adj* offensive to common modesty; unbecoming; gross, obscene. — *n* **indē'cency** the quality of being indecent; anything violating modesty or seemliness. — *adv* **indē'cently**. — **indecent assault** a sexual assault not involving rape; **indecent exposure** the offence of indecently exposing part of one's body (*esp* the genitals) in public. [**in-** (2)]

indeciduous *in-di-sid'ū-əs, adj* not deciduous. — *adj* **indecid'uate** not deciduate. [**in-** (2)]

indecipherable *in-di-sī'fər-ə-bl, adj* incapable of being deciphered; illegible. [**in-** (2)]

indecision *in-di-sizh'ən, n* lack of decision or resolution; hesitation; wavering. — *adj* **indecisive** (*-sī'siv*) inconclusive; undecided; vacillating; hesitant. — *adv* **indecī'sively**. — *n* **indecī'siveness**. [**in-** (2)]

indeclinable *in-di-klīn'ə-bl*, (*gram*) *adj* not varied by inflection. — *adv* **indeclin'ably**. [**in-** (2)]

indecomposable *in-dē-kəm-pōz'ə-bl, adj* that cannot be decomposed. [**in-** (2)]

indecorous *in-dek'ə-rəs*, sometimes *-di-kō'* or *-kö'*, *adj* unseemly; violating good manners. — *adv* **indec'orously**. — *n* **indec'orousness** or **indecō'rum** improper or impolite behaviour; a breach of decorum. [L *indecōrus*]

indeed *in-dēd', adv* (emphasizing an affirmation, marking a qualifying word or clause, a concession or admission, or, as an *interj*, expressing surprise, interrogation, disbelief or mere acknowledgement) in fact, in truth, in reality. [**in**[1] and **deed**[1]]

indef. *abbrev*: indefinite.

indefatigable *in-di-fat'i-gə-bl, adj* untiring; unflagging; unremitting in effort. — *n* **indefat'igableness**. — *adv* **indefat'igably**. [Fr (obs), from L *indēfatīgābilis*, from *in-* not, *dē* from, and *fatīgāre* to tire]

indefeasible *in-di-fēz'i-bl, adj* not to be annulled, forfeited or made void. — *n* **indefeasibil'ity**. — *adv* **indefeas'ibly**. [**in-** (2)]

indefectible *in-di-fekt'i-bl, adj* incapable of defect, flawless; unfailing. [**in-** (2)]

indefensible *in-di-fens'i-bl, adj* untenable, that cannot be defended (*lit* or *fig*); that cannot be excused or justified. — *n* **indefensibil'ity** or **indefens'ibleness**. — *adv* **indefens'ibly**. [**in-** (2)]

indefinable *in-di-fīn'ə-bl, adj* that cannot be defined; hard to identify or describe. — *n* **indefin'ableness**. — *adv* **indefin'ably**. [**in-** (2)]

indefinite *in-def'i-nit, adj* without clearly marked outlines or limits; not clearly distinguished in character; not precise, unclear; undetermined; (of a determiner or pronoun) not referring to a particular person or thing (*gram*; see also **article**); not distinguishing between complete and incomplete active, as the Greek aorist (*gram*); not fixed in number (*bot*); not terminating in a flower (*bot*); racemose or centripetal (*bot*). — *adv* **indef'initely**. — *n* **indef'initeness**. [**in-** (2)]

indehiscent *in-di-his'ənt*, (*bot*) *adj* not dehiscent; (of fruits) not opening when mature. — *n* **indehisc'ence**. [**in-** (2)]

indelible *in-del'i-bl, adj* unable to be erased or blotted out; (of ink, etc) making an indelible mark. — *n* **indelibil'ity** or **indel'ibleness**. — *adv* **indel'ibly**. [L *indēlēbilis*, from *in-* not, and *dēlēre* to destroy]

indelicate *in-del'i-kit, adj* immodest or verging on the immodest; tactless; in poor taste; coarse. — *n* **indel'icacy**. — *adv* **indel'icately**. [**in-** (2)]

indemnify *in-dem'ni-fī, vt* to secure (with *against*); to compensate; to free, exempt (with *from*): — *pr p* **indem'nifying**; *pa t* and *pa p* **indem'nified**. — *n* **indemnification** (*-fi-kā'shən*) the act of indemnifying; the state of being indemnified; the amount paid as compensation. [L *indemnis* unhurt (from *in-* not, and *damnum* loss), and *facere* to make]

indemnity *in-dem'ni-ti, n* security from damage or loss; compensation for loss or injury; legal exemption from incurred liabilities or penalties. — **Act of Indemnity** an act or decree for the protection of public officers from any technical or legal penalties or liabilities they may have been compelled to incur. [Fr *indemnité*, from L *indemnis* unharmed, from *damnum* loss]

indemonstrable *in-dem'ən-strə-bl*, or *in-di-mon'*, *adj* that cannot be demonstrated or proved. — *n* **indemonstrabil'ity**. — *adv* **indemon'strably**. [**in-** (2)]

indene *in'dēn, n* a liquid hydrocarbon (C_9H_8) obtained from coal tar and used in making resins. [**indigo**]

indent *in-dent', vt* to cut into zigzags; to divide along a zigzag line; to notch; to indenture, apprentice; to draw up (as a deed, contract, etc) in exact duplicate; to begin farther in from the margin than the rest of a paragraph; to impress; to make a dent or dint in. — *vt* and *vi* to make out a written order with counterfoil or duplicate; to order (*esp* from abroad); to requisition; (of a coastline, etc) to penetrate, form recesses. — *vi* to move in a zigzag course (*archaic*); to bargain (*obs*); to make a compact (*obs*). — *n* (*in'dent*, also *in-dent'*) a cut or notch; a recess like a notch; the amount of space left at the beginning of a line, indentation; an indenture; an order for goods (*esp* from abroad); an (*orig* Indian) official requisition for goods; a dent or dint. — *n* **indentā'tion** a hollow or depression; the act or process of indenting or notching; a space left at the beginning of a line; the act or process of creating or leaving such a space; a notch; a recess. — *adj* **indent'ed** having indentations; serrated; zigzag. — *n* **indent'er**. — *n* **inden'tion** indentation; a blank space left at the beginning of a line. [Two different words fused together: (1), from LL *indentāre*, from L *in* in, and *dēns, dentis* a tooth; (2), from Eng **in** and **dint**, **dent**]

indenture *in-den'chər*, *n* the act of indenting, indentation; a deed under seal, with mutual covenants, where the edge is indented to enable authenticity to be confirmed (*law*); a written agreement between two or more parties, *esp* (in *pl*) between an apprentice and an employer; a contract. — *vt* to bind by indentures; to indent. [Anglo-Fr *endenture*, from LL *indentāre*; see **indent**]

independent *in-di-pend'ənt*, *adj* not dependent or relying on others (with *of*); not subordinate or subject to control by others; completely self-governing, autonomous; (of a business, etc) not affiliated or merged with a larger organization; capable of thinking or acting for oneself; too self-respecting to accept help; not subject to bias; having or affording a comfortable livelihood without necessity of working or help from others; (of a quantity or function) not depending on another for its value (*math*); (with *cap*) belonging to the Independents. — *n* (with *cap*) a person who in ecclesiastical affairs holds that every congregation should be independent of every other and subject to no superior authority, a Congregationalist; a person not committed to any group or (*esp* political) party. — *n* **independ'ence** the state of being independent; a competency (*law*). — *n* **independ'ency** the state of being independent, independence; a sovereign state; an independent income; (with *cap*) Congregationalism. — *adv* **independ'ently**. — **Independence Day** (see **Declaration of Independence** below) a day when a country becomes self-governing or the anniversary of this event (often celebrated with an annual national holiday); **independent clause** see under **clause**; **independent financial adviser** (*abbrev* **IFA**) a professional adviser on life insurance, pensions and investment who is not employed by an institution selling such services; **independent particle model** (*phys*) a model of a nucleus in which each nucleon is assumed to act quite separately in a common field to which they all contribute; **independent school** a public school, a school not part of the state education system; **independent suspension** (*autos*) a suspension system in which the wheels are mounted independently on the chassis, so as to be incapable of independent movement. — **Declaration of Independence** the document proclaiming with reasons the secession of the thirteen colonies of America from the United Kingdom, reported to the Continental Congress on 4 July 1776, the anniversary of this being observed in the US as a national holiday, **Independence Day**. [**in-** (2)]

in deposito *in də-poz'it-ō* or *dā-pos'ēt-ō*, (*LL*) on deposit, as a pledge.

indescribable *in-di-skrīb'ə-bl*, *adj* that cannot be described; that is too bad, severe or extreme to be satisfactorily described. — *n* (*old slang*; in *pl*) trousers. — *n* **indescribabil'ity** or **indescrib'ableness**. — *adv* **indescrib'ably**. [**in-** (2)]

indesignate *in-dez'ig-nāt*, (*logic*) *adj* without any indication of quantification. [**in-** (2)]

indestructible *in-di-struk'ti-bl*, *adj* that cannot be destroyed. — *n* **indestructibil'ity** or **indestruc'tibleness**. — *adv* **indestruc'tibly**. [**in-** (2)]

indetectable *in-di-tekt'ə-bl*, *adj* which cannot be detected. — Also **indetect'ible**. [**in-** (2)]

indeterminable *in-di-tûr'min-ə-bl*, *adj* incapable of being ascertained or fixed; (of an argument, etc) that cannot be settled. — *n* **indeter'minableness**. — *adv* **indeter'minably**. — *n* **indeter'minacy**. — *adj* **indeter'minate** not determinate or fixed; uncertain; having no defined or fixed value. — *adv* **indeter'minately**. — *n* **indeter'minateness** or **indeterminā'tion** lack of determination; absence of fixed direction. — *adj* **indeter'mined** not determined; unsettled. — *n* **indeter'minism** (*philos*) the theory that denies determinism. — *n* **indeter'minist**. — **indeterminacy principle** another name for **uncertainty principle**. [**in-** (2)]

indew (*obs*). Same as **endue**.

index *in'deks*, *n* the forefinger (also **in'dex-finger**), or the corresponding digit in animals; a pointer or hand on a dial or scale, etc; a moving arm, as on a surveying instrument; the gnomon of a sundial; the finger of a fingerpost; a figure of a pointing hand, used to draw attention (*printing*); the nose (*old slang*); anything giving an indication; a table of contents or other preliminary matter in a book (*obs*); hence a preface, prologue, introduction (*Shakesp*; *fig*); an alphabetical register of subjects dealt with in the text of a book, etc, *usu* located at the end, with page or folio references; a similar list of other things; a list of prohibited books; a direct, or indication of the first notes of the next page or line (*music*; *obs*); a symbol denoting a power (*math*); a number, commonly a ratio, expressing some relation (as *refractive index*, the ratio of sines of angles of incidence and refraction or *cranial index*, the breadth of a skull as a percentage of its length); a numerical scale showing the relative changes in the cost of living, wages, etc, with reference to some predetermined base level; the reciprocal of intercept with parameter as unit (*crystallog*): — *pl* of a book *usu* **in'dexes**; other senses **indices** (*in'di-sēz*). — *vt* to provide with or place in an index; to link to an index, index-link. — *adj* **index'al**. — *n* **indexā'tion** or **in'dexing** a system by which wages, rates of interest, etc are directly linked (**index-linked'**) to changes in the cost of living index. — *n* **in'dexer**. — *adj* **index'ical**. — *adj* **in'dexless**. — **index auctorum** (*L*) index of authors; **Index Expurgatorius** (*L*; *RC*) formerly, a list of books from which certain passages must be expurged before the books may be read by Roman Catholics; **index fossil** a fossil species that characterizes a particular geological horizon; **Index Librorum Prohibitorum** (*L*; *RC*) (until 1966) a list of books prohibited to Roman Catholic readers. — *vt* **index-link'**. — **index=link'ing** indexation; **index locorum** (*L*) an index of places; **index mineral** (*geol*) a mineral whose appearance marks a particular grade of metamorphism in progressive regional metamorphism; **index number** a figure showing periodic movement up or down of a variable compared with another figure (*usu* 100) taken as a standard; **index rerum** (*L*) an index of matters or subjects; a reference notebook; **index verborum** (*L*) an index of words. [L *index*, *indicis*, from *indicāre* to show]

indexterity *in-deks-ter'i-ti*, *n* lack of dexterity. [**in-** (2)]

Indian *in'di-ən*, *adj* of or belonging to India (with various boundaries) or its native population, or to the Indies (East or West), or to the aborigines of America, or to the Indians of South Africa. — *n* a member of one of the races of India; formerly a European long resident in India; a member of any of the aboriginal peoples of America; in South Africa, a person belonging to the Asian racial group; a person who carries out orders, a worker, etc, as opposed to a leader or organizer, as in *chiefs and Indians*. — *n* **In'dianist** a person who has a scholarly knowledge of Indian languages, history, etc. — *n* **Indianizā'tion** or **-s-**. — *vt* **In'dianize** or **-ise** to make Indian; to assimilate to what is Indian; to cause to be done, controlled, etc by Indians. — *vi* to become Indian or like an Indian. — **In'diaman** a large ship employed in trade with India; **Indian agent** in US and Canada, an official who represents the government in the administration of native Indian affairs, *esp* on reservations; **Indian berry** the fruit of *Anamirta cocculus* (see **cocculus indicus** under **coccus**); **Indian bread** maize bread; a Virginian fungus said to have been eaten by the Indians; **Indian club** a bottle-shaped block of wood, swung in various motions by the arms to develop the muscles; **Indian corn** maize, so called because brought from the West Indies; **Indian cress** a garden plant (*Tropaeolum majus*, popularly nasturtium) from Peru, with orange flowers; **Indian fig** the banyan-tree; the prickly pear; **Indian file** see under **file**[1]; **Indian fire** a firework used as a signal light, consisting of sulphur, realgar, and nitre; **Indian gift** (*NAm colloq*) a gift that is given and then taken back, or for which a return gift is expected; **Indian giver**;

Indian giving; **Indian hemp** *Cannabis sativa* (*Cannabis indica* is a variety), source of the drug variously known as hashish, marihuana, etc; a perennial American plant (*Apocynum cannabinum*) formerly used to make rope; **indian ink** or (*NAm*) **india ink** see under **ink**; **Indian liquorice** the jequirity or crab's-eye plant (*Abrus precatorius*) whose root is used as a substitute for liquorice; **Indian mallow** a tall N American weed (*Abutilon theophrasti*) with small yellow flowers; **Indian meal** ground maize; **Indian millet** durra; **Indian pink** see under **pink**[3]; **Indian pipe** a woodland plant (*Monotropa uniflora*) of N America, with a solitary drooping flower, not unlike a tobacco-pipe; **Indian poke** an American liliaceous plant, white hellebore; **Indian red** red ochre, or native ferric oxide, formerly imported from the East as a red pigment, also made artificially; **Indian rice** see **Zizania**; **Indian rope-trick** the supposed Indian trick of climbing an unsupported rope; **Indian runner** a breed of domestic duck; **Indian shot** a cosmopolitan tropical plant of the genus Canna, much cultivated for its flowers; **Indian summer** (*orig* in America) a period of warm, dry, calm weather in late autumn; a time of particular happiness, success, etc towards the end of a life, era, etc (*fig*); **Indian tobacco** an American flowering plant (*Lobelia inflata*) with inflated seed pods; **Indian turnip** an American araceous plant with a starchy tuber; **Indian wrestling** a trial of strength in which contestants lie on their backs side by side, head to toe, with one leg and arm interlocking, the object being to turn the opponent on his face; a trial of strength with contestants standing face to face with one arm interlocking and outsides of corresponding feet braced against each other, the object being to unbalance the opponent; arm wrestling; **India paper** a thin soft absorbent paper, of Chinese or Japanese origin, used in taking the finest proofs (**India proofs**) from engraved plates; a thin tough opaque paper used for printing Bibles; **india-rubb'er** or **India rubber** an elastic gummy substance, the inspissated juice of various tropical plants; a piece of this material, *esp* one used for rubbing out pencil marks; **India shawl** a Kashmir shawl. — **East India Company** a great chartered company formed for trading with India and the East Indies, the English Company, incorporated in 1600 and (having lost its power by 1858) dissolved in 1874; **East Indian** an inhabitant or native of the East Indies, *usu* applied to a Eurasian; **East Indies** the Indian subcontinent, south-east Asia, and the Malay archipelago (*hist*); Sumatra, Borneo, Java and the other islands of Indonesia, by some, but not generally, taken to include the Philippines and New Guinea; **Red Indian** (now considered *offensive*) an (*esp* North) American Indian, a Native American; **West Indian** a native or an inhabitant of the West Indies; **West Indies** an archipelago stretching from Florida to Venezuela. [L *India*, from *Indus* (Gr *Indos*), the Indus (Pers *Hind*, Sans *sindhu* a river)]

Indic *in'dik*, *adj* originating or existing in India; of the Indian branch of Indo-European languages.

indic. *abbrev*: indicative.

indican *in'di-kən*, *n* a glucoside, $C_{14}H_{17}NO_6$, that occurs in the indigo plant and is a source of the dye indigo; a compound, $C_8H_7NO_4S$, excreted in the urine of mammals as a detoxification product of indoxyl. [L *indicum* indigo, and **-an**]

indicate *in'di-kāt*, *vt* to point out; to show; to give some notion of; to be a mark or token of; to give ground for inferring; to point to as suitable treatment (*med*), also (*usu* in *passive*) as a desirable course of action in any sphere. — *adj* **in'dicant** indicating. — *n* something which indicates. — *n* **indicā'tion** the act of indicating; a mark; a token; suggestion of treatment; a sign; a symptom. — *adj* **indicative** (*in-dik'ə-tiv*) pointing out; giving intimation; applied to the mood of the verb that expresses fact (*gram*). — *n* the indicative mood; a verb in the indicative mood. — *adv* **indic'atively**. — *n* **in'dicātor** someone who or that which indicates; something that provides an indication; a pointer; a diagram showing names and directions of visible objects, as on a mountain top; a substance showing chemical condition by change of colour; a measuring contrivance with a pointer or the like; any device for exhibiting condition for the time being; (with *cap*) a genus of birds, the honey-guides. — *adj* **in'dicatory** (or *dik'*). — **indicator diagram** a graphical representation of the pressure and volume changes undergone by a fluid in performing a work-cycle in the cylinder of an engine on compression, the area representing, to scale, the work done during the cycle; **indicated horsepower** (of a reciprocating engine) the horsepower developed by the pressure-volume changes of the working agent within the cylinder, exceeding the useful or brake horsepower at the crankshaft by the power lost in friction and pumping. [L *indicāre*, *-ātum*, from *in* in, and *dicāre* to proclaim]

indices. See **index**.

indicia *in-dish'i-ə* or *in-dik'i-a*, *n pl* indicating marks or signs, symptoms: — *n sing* **indicium**. — *adj* **indic'ial**. [L *indicium* sign, notice]

indicolite *in-dik'ə-līt* or **indigolite** *-dig'*, (*mineralogy*) *n* a pale blue or bluish black variety of tourmaline. [**indigo** and **-ite**]

indict *in-dīt'*, *vt* to charge with a crime formally or in writing. — *adj* **indict'able**. — *n* **indictee'** a person who is indicted. — *n* **indict'ment** a formal accusation; the written accusation against someone who is to be tried by jury; the form under which one is put to trial at the instance of the Lord Advocate (*Scots law*). — **find an indictment** of a grand jury, to be satisfied that there is a *prima facie* case, and endorse the bill *a true bill*. [With Latinized spelling (but not pronunciation) from Anglo-Fr *enditer*, from L *in* in, and *dictāre* to declare, frequentative of *dicere* to say]

indiction *in-dik'shən*, *n* a proclamation; a decree of the emperor, fixing land-tax valuation (*Roman hist*); the tax itself (*Rom hist*); a recurring period of fifteen years, instituted by Constantine the Great for fiscal purposes, and adopted by the popes as part of their chronological system; a year bearing a number showing its place in a fifteen years' cycle, reckoning from 24 September (or other day), AD 312 (*Roman hist*). [L *indictiō*, *-ōnis*, from *indīcere* to appoint]

indie *in'di*, (*informal*) *n* an independent record company, *esp* one that produces music outside the mainstream of popular music; also, an independent film or television production company. — Also *adj*. [**independent**]

indifferent *in-dif'ər-ənt*, *adj* without importance; uninteresting; of a middle quality; not very good, inferior; in poor health (*dialect*); apathetic; neutral; unconcerned. — *n* (*now rare*) a person who is indifferent, apathetic or neutral; that which is indifferent. — *n* **indiff'erence** or **indiff'erency**. — *n* **indiff'erentism** indifference; the doctrine that religious differences are of no importance (*theol*); the doctrine of absolute identity, ie that to be in thought and to exist are one and the same thing (*metaphys*). — *n* **indiff'erentist**. — *adv* **indiff'erently** in an indifferent manner; tolerably; passably; without distinction, impartially. [**in-** (2)]

indigenous *in-dij'in-əs*, *adj* native born; originating or produced naturally in a country, not imported (opposite to *exotic*). — *adj* and *n* **in'digene** (*-jēn*) native, aboriginal. — *n* **indigenizā'tion** or **-s-**. — *vt* **indi'genize** or **-ise** to adapt or subject to native culture or influence; to increase the proportion of indigenous people in administration, employment, etc. — *adv* **indig'enously**. [L *indigena* a native, from *indu-* in, and *gen-*, root of *gignere* to produce]

indigent *in'di-jənt*, *adj* impoverished; in need, *esp* of means of subsistence. — *n* a person so poor as to lack means of subsistence. — *n* **in'digence** or **in'digency**. — *adv* **in'digently**. [Fr, from L *indigēns*, *-entis*, pr p of *indigēre*, from *indu-* in, and *egēre* to need]

indigest *in-di-jest'*, *adj* not digested; shapeless. — *n* a crude mass; a disordered state of affairs. — *adj*

indigest'ed not digested; unarranged; not methodized. — *n* **indigestibil'ity**. — *adj* **indigest'ible** not digestible; not easily digested (*lit* and *fig*). — *adv* **indigest'ibly**. — *n* **indigestion** (*in-di-jes'chən*) difficulty in digesting, or inability to digest, food; pain, flatulence, etc caused by this. — *adj* **indigest'ive** dyspeptic. [L *indīgestus* unarranged, from *in* not, and *dīgerere* to arrange, digest]

indign *in-dīn'*, (*archaic* or *poetic*) *adj* unworthy; disgraceful, unseemly. [L *in-* not, and *dīgnus* worthy]

indignant *in-dig'nənt*, *adj* feeling or showing justifiable anger (often mixed with scorn). — *n* **indig'nance** (*archaic*) indignation; contemptuous impatience. — *adv* **indig'nantly**. — *n* **indignā'tion** righteous anger at injustice, etc; feeling caused by an unjustified slight, etc to oneself; a thing, *eg* a weapon, indicating anger (*Shakesp*). — *vt* **indig'nify** to treat insultingly (*archaic*); to disgrace (with inadequate praise) (*obs*). — *n* **indig'nity** unworthiness (*obs*); disgrace; dishonour; unmerited contemptuous treatment; incivility with contempt or insult; indignation (*archaic*). [L *indīgnus* unworthy, from *in-* not, and *dīgnus* worthy]

indigo *in'di-gō*, *n* a violet-blue dye obtained from the leaves of the indigo plant, from woad, or produced synthetically; the colour of this dye; indigotin; the indigo plant, any of various species of *Indigofera*, a tropical genus of Papilionaceae: — *pl* **in'digos** or **in'digoes**. — *adj* deep blue. — *n* **in'digotin** (or *in-dig'*) or **indigo blue** the blue colouring matter of indigo obtained from indican by hydrolysis. — *n* **indirubin** (*in-di-ro͞o'bin*) or **indigo red** an isomer of indigotin, obtained from natural indigo. — **indigo bird**, **bunting** or **finch** an American finch (*Passerina cyanea*) of which the male is blue; **indigo carmine** a blue dye administered by injection to test kidney function. [Sp *índico*, *índigo*, from L *indicum*, from Gr *Indikon* Indian (neuter adj)]

indigolite. See **indicolite**.

indigotin. See under **indigo**.

indirect *in-di-rekt'*, or *-dī-*, *adj* not direct or straight; not lineal or in direct succession; not related in the natural way, oblique; not straightforward or honest. — *n* **indirec'tion** (*Shakesp*) indirect course or means, dishonest practice. — *adv* **indirect'ly**. — *n* **indirect'ness**. — **indirect address** (*comput*) an instruction which specifies a location which contains the required address; **indirect evidence** or **testimony** circumstantial or inferential evidence; **indirect immunofluorescence** a technique for detecting the presence of an antigen in which a specific antibody is first bound to the antigen, the antibody and hence the antigen then being detected by fluorescence microscopy; **indirect lighting** a system of lighting in which the light emitted from the fittings is reflected upwards or diffused; **indirect object** (*gram*) a noun, pronoun or noun phrase affected by the action of the verb but not itself directly acted upon, as *the man* in *Give the man your seat*; **indirect speech** a person's words reported with adjustment of the necessary person and time, as in *He said he was leaving*; **indirect tax** one collected not directly from the taxpayer but through an intermediate agent, as eg a customs duty or sales tax; **indirect taxation**. [**in-** (2)]

indirubin. See under **indigo**.

indiscernible *in-di-sûrn'i-bl*, or *-zûrn'*, *adj* not discernible. — *n* **indiscern'ibleness** or **indiscernibil'ity**. — *adv* **indiscern'ibly**. [**in-** (2)]

indiscerptible *in-di-sûrp'ti-bl*, *adj* not able to be separated or disunited; not discerptible. — *n* **indiscerptibil'ity**. [**in-** (2)]

indiscipline *in-dis'i-plin*, *n* lack of discipline. — *adj* **indisc'iplinable**. [**in-** (2)]

indiscoverable *in-dis-kuv'ər-ə-bl*, *adj* not discoverable. [**in-** (2)]

indiscreet *in-dis-krēt'*, *adj* not discreet; imprudent; injudicious. — *adv* **indiscreet'ly**. — *n* **indiscreet'ness**. — *n* **indiscretion** (*-kresh'ən*) lack of discretion; rashness; an indiscreet act, or one apparently so; (*esp* formerly) an imprudent or immoral act. [**in-** (2)]

indiscrete *in-dis-krēt'* or *-dis'*, *adj* not separated or distinguishable in parts; homogeneous. — *adv* **indiscrete'ly**. — *n* **indiscrete'ness**. [**in-** (2)]

indiscriminate *in-dis-krim'i-nit*, *adj* lacking discrimination; choosing or chosen at random; promiscuous. — *adv* **indiscrim'inately**. — *n* **indiscrim'inateness**. — *adj* **indiscrim'ināting** undiscriminating. — *n* **indiscriminā'tion**. — *adj* **indiscrim'inative** (*-ə-tiv*) not discriminative. [**in-** (2)]

indispensable *in-dis-pens'ə-bl*, *adj* that cannot be dispensed with; absolutely necessary; (of a law, etc) that cannot be set aside. — *n* **indispensabil'ity** or **indispens'ableness**. — *adv* **indispens'ably**. [**in-** (2)]

indispose *in-dis-pōz'*, *vt* to render indisposed, averse, unwilling or unfit. — *pa p* and *adj* **indisposed'** averse, unwilling; unwell, sick. — *n* **indispos'edness**. — *n* **indisposition** (*-pə-zish'ən*) the state of being indisposed; disinclination; the state of being unwell or unfit. [**in-** (2)]

indisputable *in-dis-pū'tə-bl*, also *-dis'*, *adj* beyond doubt or question. — *n* **indisputabil'ity** or **indisput'ableness**. — *adv* **indisput'ably**. [**in-** (2)]

indissociable *in-dis-ō'shyə-bl* or *-shə-bl*, *adj* incapable of being separated. [**in-** (2)]

indissoluble *in-dis-ol'ū-bl* or *-dis'əl-*, *adj* that cannot be broken or dissolved; inseparable; binding permanently. — *n* **indissol'ubleness** or **indissolubility** (*-ol-ū-bil'*). — *adv* **indissol'ubly**. [**in-** (2)]

indissolvable *in-di-zol'və-bl*, (*archaic*) *adj* that cannot be dissolved. [**in-** (2)]

indissuadable *in-dis-wād'ə-bl*, *adj* not able to be dissuaded. — *adv* **indissuad'ably**. [**in-** (2)]

indistinct *in-dis-tingkt'*, *adj* not distinct; not plainly marked; confused; not clear to the mind or senses; dim. — *adj* **indistinct'ive** not constituting a distinction; not discriminating. — *adv* **indistinct'ively** indiscriminately. — *n* **indistinct'iveness**. — *adv* **indistinct'ly**. — *n* **indistinc'tion** (*rare*) confusion; absence of distinction, sameness. — *n* **indistinct'ness**. [**in-** (2)]

indistinguishable *in-dis-ting'gwish-ə-bl*, *adj* that cannot be told apart, identical; indiscernible. — *n* **indistinguishabil'ity** or **indistin'guishableness**. — *adv* **indistin'guishably**. [**in-** (2)]

indistributable *in-dis-trib'ū-tə-bl*, *adj* not distributable. [**in-** (2)]

indite *in-dīt'*, (*archaic*) *vt* to compose or write; to dictate. — *n* **indite'ment**. — *n* **indit'er**. [OFr *enditer*; see **indict**]

indium *in'di-əm*, *n* a soft malleable silver-white metallic element (symbol **In**; atomic no 49). [From two *indi*go-coloured lines in the spectrum]

indiv. *abbrev*: individual.

indivertible *in-di-vûrt'i-bl*, *adj* not capable of being turned aside. [**in-** (2)]

individable *in-di-vīd'ə-bl*, (*archaic*) *adj* indivisible. [**in-** (2)]

individual *in-di-vid'ū-əl*, *adj* not divisible without loss of identity; subsisting as one; pertaining to one only or to each one separately of a group or kind; single, separate; distinctive; inseparable (*obs*). — *n* a single person, animal, plant or thing considered as a separate member of its species or as having an independent existence; a person (*colloq*). — *n* **individ'ualism** individual character; independent action as opposed to cooperation; that theory which opposes interference of the state in the affairs of individuals (opposite to *socialism* or *collectivism*); the theory that looks to the rights of individuals, not to the advantage of an abstraction such as the state; the doctrine that individual things alone are real; the doctrine that nothing exists but the individual self. — *n* **individ'ualist** a person who thinks and acts with independence; someone who advocates individualism. — Also *adj*. — *adj* **individualist'ic**. — *n* **individuality** (*-al'i-ti*) separate and distinct existence; oneness; distinctive character. — *n* **individualīzā'tion** or **-s-**. — *vt* **individ'ualize** or **-ise** to stamp with individual character; to particularize. — *adv* **individ'ually**. — *vt* **individ'uate** to individualize; to give individuality to. — *adj* undivided; inseparable; individuated. — *n* **indivi-**

duā'tion the act or process of individuating or individualizing; individual existence; essence; continued identity; the sum of the processes of individual life; synthesis into a single organic whole. — *n* **individ'uum** an indivisible entity; an individual person or thing; a member of a species. [L *indīviduus*, from *in-* not, and *dīviduus* divisible, from *dīvidere* to divide]

indivisible *in-di-viz'i-bl, adj* not divisible, incapable of being divided. — *n* (*math*) an indefinitely small quantity. — *n* **indivisibil'ity** or **indivis'ibleness**. — *adv* **indivis'ibly**. [**in-** (2)]

Indo- *in'dō-, combining form* denoting Indian.

Indo-Chinese *in'dō-chī-nēz', adj* of or pertaining to Indo-China, the south-eastern peninsula of Asia.

Indocid® *in'do-sid, n* a proprietary name for **indomethacin**.

indocile *in-dō'sīl* or *in-dos'il, adj* not docile; not willing to be instructed or disciplined. — Also **indō'cible**. — *n* **indocil'ity**. [**in-** (2)]

indoctrinate *in-dok'trin-āt, vt* to instruct in any doctrine; to imbue with any opinion. — *n* **indoctrinā'tion**. — *n* **indoc'trinātor**. [**in-** (1)]

Indo-European *in'dō-ū-rō-pē'ən*, (*philol*) *adj* of the family of languages, also called **In'do-German'ic** and sometimes Aryan, whose great branches are Aryan proper or Indian, Iranian, Armenian, Greek or Hellenic, Italic, Celtic, Tocharian, Balto-Slavic, Albanian, Germanic, and probably Anatolian. — *n* the hypothetical parent-language of this family (also called **Proto-Indo-European**).

Indo-Germanic *in-dō-jûr-man'ik*, (*philol*) *adj* Indo-European. — Also *n*.

Indo-Iranian *in'dō-ir-ān'i-ən, -īr-* or *-än', adj* of the Indic and Iranian languages, constituting a subfamily of Indo-European. — *Also n.*

indole or **indol** *in'dōl*, (*chem*) *n* a crystalline chemical compound (C_8H_7N), forming the basis of the indigo molecule and found in some plants, coal tar, and present in urine and faeces of mammals (being a product of decomposition of the amino acid tryptophan). — **indoleacetic acid** a naturally-occurring plant growth hormone ($C_8H_6NCH_2CO_2H$), the commonest of the auxin type; **indolebutyric acid** a synthetic plant growth regulator ($C_8H_6N(CH_2)_3COOH$), with auxin-like action, used in rooting compounds. [**indigo** and L *oleum* oil]

indolent *in'dəl-ənt, adj* disliking activity; lazy; causing little or no pain (*med*). — *n* **in'dolence** or **in'dolency**. — *adv* **in'dolently**. [L *in-* not, and *dolēns, -entis*, pr p of *dolēre* to suffer pain]

indomethacin *in-dō-meth'ə-sin, n* a non-steroidal, anti-inflammatory, anti-pyretic and analgesic drug, used in the treatment of arthritic conditions. [*indo*le, *meth*yl, *a*cetic (acid) and **-in** (3)]

in Domino *in dom'i-nō*, (*LL*) in the Lord.

indomitable *in-dom'it-ə-bl, adj* not to be overcome, unconquerable. — *n* **indomitabil'ity** or **indom'itableness**. — *adv* **indom'itably**. [**in-** (2)]

Indonesian *in-dō-nē'zi-ən, in-də-* or *-zhən, adj* of the East Indian or Malay Archipelago, *specif* of the Republic of Indonesia, covering much of this territory; of a short, mesocephalic, black-haired, light-brown race distinguishable in the population of the East Indian Islands; of a branch of the Austronesian family of languages chiefly found in the Malay Archipelago and Islands (Malay, etc). — *n* an Indonesian national, a member of the race or a speaker of one of the languages; the official language of the Republic of Indonesia, a form of Malay also known as Bahasa Indonesia. [Gr *Indos* Indian, and *nēsos* island]

indoor *in'dör, adj* practised, used, or being within a building; (of a game or sport) adapted for playing indoors. — *adv* **indoors'** inside a building. — **indoor relief** (*hist*) support given to paupers in the workhouse or poorhouse, as opposed to *outdoor relief*, or help given them at their own homes. [**in-** (1)]

indorse. See **endorse**[1].

Indra *in'drə, n* the Hindu god of the firmament and of rain. [Sans]

indraught or **indraft** *in'dräft, n* a drawing in; an inward flow of current or air. [**in**[1] and **draught**]

indrawn *in'drön* or *in-drön', adj* drawn in. [**in**[1] and **drawn**]

indrench *in-drench'* or *-drensh'*, (*obs*) *vt* to submerge in water. [**in-** (1)]

indris *in'dris* or **indri** *in'dri, n* a short-tailed lemur (*Indri indri*) found in the forests of eastern and central Madagascar. [Fr, from Malagasy *indry*! look! (mistakenly thought to be the animal's name)]

indubious *in-dū'bi-əs*, (*archaic*) *adj* not dubious; certain. [**in-** (2)]

indubitable *in-dū'bit-ə-bl, adj* that cannot be doubted; certain. — *n* **indūbitabil'ity** or **indū'bitableness**. — *adv* **indū'bitably** without doubt, certainly. [**in-** (2)]

induce *in-dūs', vt* to bring in (*obs*); to draw on; to prevail on, make, cause, encourage (to do something); to bring into being; to initiate or speed up (labour of childbirth) artificially, as by administering drugs (also *vi*) (*med*); to cause, as an electric state, by mere proximity (*phys*); to infer inductively (*logic*). — *vi* to reason or draw inferences inductively. — *n* **induce'ment** the act of inducing or that which induces; a means of persuasion; incentive, motive; a statement of facts introducing other important facts (*law*). — *n* **induc'er** someone who, or that which, induces; an agent which increases the transcription of specific genes (*biol*). — *adj* **indu'cible**. — **induced current** (*elec*) a current set in action by the influence of the surrounding magnetic field, or by the variation of an adjacent current; **induced radioactivity** radioactivity induced in non-radioactive elements by neutrons in a nuclear reactor, or protons or deuterons in a cyclotron or linear accelerator; **inducible enzyme** (*bot*) an enzyme produced only in response to an inducing agent, often its substrate. — See also **induct** and **induction** below. [L *indūcere, inductum*, from *in* into, and *dūcere* to lead]

indoxyl *in-dok'sil*, (*chem*) *n* a crystalline chemical compound (C_8H_7NO), derived from indole, occurring in plants and the urine of mammals and as an intermediate stage in the manufacture of indigo dye.

induciae *in-dū'si-ē*, (*Scots law*) *n sing* the time limit within which (after a citation) the defendant must appear in court or reply. [L *indūciae, -tiae* truce, delay]

induct *in-dukt', vt* to introduce; to put in possession, as of a benefice, to install; to enlist into military service, to conscript (*NAm*). — *n* **induct'ance** the property of inducing an electromotive force by variation of current in a circuit; a device having inductance. — *n* **inductee'** (*NAm*) a person enlisted into military service, a conscript. — *n* **induc'tion** a bringing or drawing in; installation in office, benefice, etc; a prelude; an introductory section or scene; the act of inducing (*archaic*); magnetizing by proximity without contact; the production by one body of an opposite electric state in another by proximity; production of an electric current by magnetic changes in the neighbourhood; reasoning from particular cases to general conclusions (*logic*). — *adj* **induc'tional**. — *adj* **induct'ive**. — *adv* **induct'ively**. — *n* **inductiv'ity**. — *n* **induct'or**. — **induction coil** an electrical machine consisting of two coils of wire, in which every variation of the current in one induces a current in the other; **induction heating** the heating of a conductive material by means of an induced current passing through it; **induction lighting** a form of lighting that uses long-life, energy-saving, phosphorus-coated **induction lamps** containing not filaments but a magnetic coil and mercury gas; **induction loop system** a method of sound distribution in which signals fed into a wire loop are received via headphones or hearing-aids by those inside the area enclosed by the loop; **induction motor** an electric motor in which currents in the primary winding set up an electromagnetic flux which induces currents in the secondary winding, interaction of these currents with the flux producing rotation; **induction port** or **valve** a port or valve by which steam, or an explosive mixture, is admitted to the cylinder of an engine. — **induction by simple enumeration** logical induction by enumeration of all the cases singly. [See ety for **induce**]

inductile *in-duk'tīl* or *til*, *adj* not ductile. — *n* **inductility** (*-til'i-ti*). [**in-** (2)]

indue. See **endue**.

indulge *in-dulj'*, *vt* to yield to the wishes of; to favour or gratify; to treat with favour or undue favour; not to restrain; to grant an indulgence to or on; to grant some measure of religious liberty to (*hist*). — *vi* to gratify one's appetites freely, or permit oneself any action or expression (with *in*); to partake, *esp* of alcohol (*colloq*). — *n* **indulg'ence** gratification; excessive gratification; favourable or unduly favourable treatment; a grant of religious liberty; forbearance of present payment; (in the RC Church) a remission, to a repentant sinner, of the temporal punishment which remains due after the sin and its eternal punishment have been remitted (*plenary* indulgences, which remit all, *partial*, which remit a portion of the temporal punishment due, *temporal*, those granted only for a time, *perpetual* or *indefinite*, those which last till revoked, *personal*, those granted to a particular person or confraternity, *local*, those gained only in a particular place); exemption of an individual from an ecclesiastical law. — Also **indulg'ency**. — *adj* **indulg'ent** ready to gratify the wishes of others; compliant; not severe. — *adv* **indulg'ently**. — *n* **indulg'er**. — **Declaration of Indulgence** a name given to proclamations of Charles II and *esp* James II declaring laws restraining religious liberty suspended by the king's will. [L *indulgēre* to be kind to, indulge, from *in* in, and prob *dulcis* sweet]

induline or **indulin** *in'dū-lin*, *-lēn* or *-līn*, *n* any one of a class of coal tar dyestuffs, giving blues, etc. [**indigo**]

indult *in-dult'*, *n* a licence granted by the Pope, authorizing something to be done which the common law of the church does not sanction. [Ety as for **indulge**]

indumentum *in-dū-men'təm*, (*biol*) *n* a total covering of hair, feathers, etc: — *pl* **indumen'ta** or **indumen'tums**. [L *indūmentum* garment, from *induere* to put on]

induna *in-dōō'nə*, (*SAfr*) *n* a tribal councillor or leader, *esp* of an impi; a Black African foreman or overseer. [Zulu *nduna* person of rank]

induplicate *in-dū'pli-kit* or **induplicated** *-kāt-id*, (*bot*) *adj* folded inwards. — *n* **induplicā'tion**. [**in-** (1)]

indurate *in'dū-rāt*, *vt* to make hard; to make hardy; to make callous, unfeeling or obdurate. — *vi* to harden; to become hardy. — *adj* **in'durate** or **in'durated** — *n* **indurā'tion**. — *adj* **in'durative**. [L *indūrāre*, *-ātum*, from *in* in, and *dūrāre* to harden]

indusium *in-dū'zi-əm*, (*biol*) *n* a protective membrane or scale, eg that covering a fern sorus; an insect larva case: — *pl* **indu'sia**. — *adj* **indu'sial** containing fossil insect indusia. — *adj* **indu'siate** having indusia. [L *indūsium* an undergarment, tunic, from *induere* to put on]

industry *in'dəs-tri*, *n* the quality of being diligent; assiduity; steady application; habitual diligence; any branch of manufacture and trade, *heavy* industry relating to such basic industries as coalmining, steel-making, shipbuilding, etc, involving heavy equipment, *light* industry to smaller factory-processed goods, eg knitwear, glass, electronics components, etc; all branches of manufacture and trade collectively. — *adj* **industrial** (*-dus'*) relating to, characteristic of or used in industry. — *n* an industrial worker (*rare*); (in *pl*) stocks and shares in industrial concerns. — *n* **indus'trialism** devotion to labour or industrial pursuits; that system or condition of society in which industrial labour is the chief and most characteristic feature. — *n* **indus'trialist** a person who owns, or holds a powerful position in, an industrial concern or concerns. — *adj* of or characterized by industry. — *n* **industrialīzā'tion** or **-s-**. — *vt* **indus'trialize** or **-ise** to give an industrial character, or character of industrialism, to. — *adv* **indus'trially**. — *adj* **indus'trious** diligent or active in one's work or in a particular pursuit; skilful (*obs*). — *adv* **indus'triously**. — **industrial action** any action, such as a strike or go-slow, taken by workers as a means of forcing employers to meet demands, as a protest, etc; **industrial archaeology** the study of industrial machines and buildings of the past; **industrial democracy** a form of management in which workers' representatives are appointed to the board of a company, or actively participate in the management in some other capacity; **industrial diamond** small diamonds, not of gemstone quality and often synthesized from carbon, used to cut rock in borehole drilling and in abrasive grinding; **industrial disease** a disease or condition caused by one's occupation, eg pneumoconiosis; **industrial engineer**; **industrial engineering** the application of scientific principles to the various factors affecting an industrial or manufacturing process in order to develop the most efficient method of production; **industrial espionage** the practice of obtaining or attempting to obtain trade secrets or other confidential information by underhand or dishonest means; **industrial estate** a planned industrial area, with factories organized to provide varied employment; **industrial melanism** melanism (eg in moths) developed as a response to blackening of trees, etc by industrial pollution; **industrial relations** relations between management and workers or labour in general; **industrial revolution** the economic and social changes arising out of the change from industries carried on in the home with simple machines to industries in factories with power-driven machinery — *esp* such changes (from about 1760) in Britain, the first country to be industrialized; **industrial tribunal** a tribunal set up to hear complaints and make judgements in disputes between employers and employees on matters such as industrial relations and alleged unfair dismissal. — **Industrial Injuries Disablement Benefit** in Britain, a National Insurance weekly payment for injury sustained while at work (also **injury benefit**). [L *industria*, perhaps from the old word *indu* in, within, and *struere* to build up]

induviae *in-dū'vi-ē*, (*bot*) *n pl* withered leaves persistent on the stems of some plants. — *adj* **indū'vial**. — *adj* **indū'viate**. [L *induviae* clothes]

indwell *in-dwel'*, (*literary*) *vi* and *vt* to dwell or abide in: — *pr p* **indwell'ing**; *pa t* and *pa p* **indwelt'**. — *n* **in'dweller** an inhabitant. — *adj* **in'dwelling** dwelling within, abiding permanently in the mind or soul. — *n* residence within, or in the heart or soul. [**in-** (1)]

-ine[1] *-īn* or *-in*, (*chem*) noun-forming *sfx* indicating: (1) a basic organic compound containing nitrogen, such as an amino-acid or alkaloid; (2) a halogen, such as *chlorine* and *fluorine*; (3) a mixture of compounds, such as *kerosine*, *benzine*. [L fem adjectival ending *-īna*]

-ine[2] *īn*, adjectival *sfx* meaning: (1) belonging to, characteristic of, as in *elephantine*; (2) like, similar to, or being, as in *adamantine*, *crystalline*. [L adjectival ending *-īnus*]

inearth *in-ûrth'*, (*archaic*) *vt* to inter. [**in-** (1)]

inebriate *in-ē'bri-āt*, *vt* to make drunk, to intoxicate; to exhilarate greatly. — *adj* (*-it* or *-ət*) drunk; intoxicated. — *n* a drunk person; a drunkard. — *adj* **inē'briant** intoxicating. — Also *n*. — *n* **inēbriā'tion** or **inebriety** (*in-ē-brī'i-ti*, or *in-i-*) drunkenness; intoxication. — *adj* **inē'brious** drunk; causing intoxication (*obs*). [L *inēbriāre*, *-ātum*, from *in* (intens) and *ēbriāre* to make drunk, from *ēbrius* drunk]

inedible *in-ed'i-bl*, *adj* not good to eat; not suitable for eating (eg because poisonous or indigestible). — *n* **inedibil'ity**. [**in-** (2)]

inedited *in-ed'it-id*, *adj* not edited; unpublished. [**in-** (2)]

ineducable *in-ed'ū-kə-bl*, *adj* incapable of being educated or of learning. — *n* **ineducabil'ity**. [**in-** (2)]

ineffable *in-ef'ə-bl*, *adj* not able to be described, inexpressible. — *n* **ineffabil'ity** or **ineff'ableness**. — *adv* **ineff'ably**. [L *ineffābilis*, from *in-* not, and *effābilis* expressible]

ineffaceable *in-i-fās'ə-bl, adj* that cannot be rubbed out, indelible. — *n* **ineffaceabil'ity**. — *adv* **inefface'ably**. [**in-** (2)]

ineffective *in-i-fek'tiv, adj* not effective; not capable of performing competently, useless. — *adv* **ineffec'tively**. — *n* **ineffec'tiveness**. — *adj* **ineffec'tual** not producing, or not capable of producing, the proper effect; futile; ineffective, weak. — *n* **ineffectual'ity** or **ineffec'tualness**. — *adv* **ineffect'ually**. [**in-** (2)]

inefficacious *in-ef-i-kā'shəs, adj* not having the power to produce an effect, or the desired effect. — *adv* **inefficā'ciously**. — *n* **inefficacy** (*-ef'i-kə-si*) lack of efficacy. [**in-** (2)]

inefficiency *in-i-fish'ən-si, n* lack of the power or skill to do or produce something in the best, most economical, etc way. — *adj* **ineffic'ient** not efficient. — *adv* **ineffic'iently**. [**in-** (2)]

inegalitarian *in-i-gal-i-tä'ri-ən, adj* not egalitarian. [**in-** (2)]

inelaborate *in-il-ab'ər-it* or *-āt, adj* not elaborate; simple, *esp* in workmanship. — *adv* **inelab'orately**. [**in-** (2)]

inelastic *in-i-las'tik, adj* not elastic; incompressible; unyielding. — *n* **inelasticity** (*in-el-əs-tis'i-ti*). — **inelastic collision** or **scattering** see under **collide**. [**in-** (2)]

inelegance *in-el'i-gəns, n* lack of grace or refinement. — Also **inel'egancy**. — *adj* **inel'egant**. — *adv* **inel'egantly**. [**in-** (2)]

ineligible *in-el'i-ji-bl, adj* not qualified for election; not suitable to be available for choice or to be chosen; unsuitable. — Also *n*. — *n* **ineligibil'ity**. — *adv* **inel'igibly**. [**in-** (2)]

ineloquent *in-el'ə-kwənt, adj* not eloquent. — *n* **inel'oquence**. — *adv* **inel'oquently**. [**in-** (2)]

ineluctable *in-i-luk'tə-bl, adj* not able to be escaped from or avoided. [L *inēluctābilis*, from *in-* not, *ē* from, and *luctārī* to struggle]

inenarrable *in-en'ər-ə-bl* or *in-ē-nar'ə-bl, adj* incapable of being narrated or told, indescribable. [L *inēnarrābilis*, from *in-* not, *ē-* out, and *narrāre* to tell]

inept *in-ept', adj* foolish, silly; awkward, clumsy; unsuitable; irrelevant and futile; void (*law*). — *n* **inept'itude** or **inept'ness**. — *adv* **inept'ly**. [L *ineptus*, from *in-* not, and *aptus* apt]

inequable *in-ek'wə-bl* or *-ēk', (rare) adj* not equable; uneven, not uniform. [**in-** (2)]

inequality *in-ē-kwol'i-ti* or *in-i-*, *n* lack of equality; disparity; difference; inadequacy; incompetence; unevenness; dissimilarity; an uneven place; a statement that two quantities or expressions are not equal (*math*); a departure from uniformity in orbital motion (*astron*). [**in-** (2)]

inequation *in-ə-kwā'shən* or *-zhən, n* a mathematical sentence which expresses an inequality. [**in-** (2)]

inequipotent *in-ek-wi-pō'tənt, (zool) adj* having different potentialities for development and differentiation. [**in-** (2)]

inequitable *in-ek'wi-tə-bl, adj* unfair, unjust. — *n* **ineq'uitableness**. — *adv* **ineq'uitably**. — *n* **ineq'uity** lack of equity or fairness; an unjust action. [**in-** (2)]

ineradicable *in-i-rad'i-kə-bl, adj* not able to be got rid of, removed completely, or rooted out. — *n* **inerad'icableness**. — *adv* **inerad'icably**. [**in-** (2)]

inerasable *in-i-rāz'ə-bl, adj* impossible to erase. — Also **ineras'ible**. — *adv* **ineras'ably** or **ineras'ibly**. [**in-** (2)]

inerm *in-ûrm', (bot) adj* unarmed; without thorns. — *adj* **ine'rmous**. [L *inermis*, from *in-* not, and *arma* (pl) arms]

inerrable *in-er'ə-bl*, or *-ûr', adj* incapable of erring, infallible. — *n* **inerrabil'ility** or **inerr'ableness**. — *adv* **inerr'ably**. — *n* **inerr'ancy** the quality of being inerrant. — *adj* **inerr'ant** unerring; (of a star) fixed (*astron*). [**in-** (2)]

inert *in-ûrt', adj* without inherent power of moving, or of active resistance to motion; passive; chemically inactive; not readily changed by chemical means; sluggish; disinclined to move or act. — *n* **inertia** (*in-ûr'shi-ə, -shyə* or *-shə*) inertness; the inherent property of matter by which it continues, unless constrained, in its state of rest or uniform motion in a straight line. — *adj* **iner'tial** of or pertaining to inertia. — *adv* **inert'ly**. — *n* **inert'ness**. — **inert gas** any of a group of elements whose outer electron orbits are complete, rendering them inert to all the usual chemical reactions; **inertial confinement** in fusion studies, short-term containment of plasma arising from inertial resistance to outward forces, achieved mainly by using a powerful laser; **inertial control guidance** or **navigation** an automatic gyroscopic guidance system for aircraft, missiles, etc using data computed from acceleration and the physical properties of the earth, but dispensing with the magnetic compass and independent of ground-based radio aids; **inertia-reel seat belt** a type of self-retracting seat belt in which the wearer is constrained only when violent deceleration of the vehicle causes the belt to lock; **inertia selling** sending unrequested goods to householders and attempting to charge for them if they are not returned. [L *iners*, *inertis* unskilled, idle, from *in-* not, and *ars*, *artis* art]

inerudite *in-er'ū-dīt* or *ŏŏ-*, *adj* not erudite; unlearned. [**in-** (2)]

inescapable *in-is-kā'pə-bl, adj* unescapable; inevitable. [**in-** (2)]

inesculent *in-es'kū-lənt, (archaic) adj* inedible. [**in-** (2)]

inescutcheon *in-is-kuch'ən, (heraldry) n* a small shield borne as a charge on a larger escutcheon. [**in**[1] and **escutcheon**]

in esse. See **esse**.

inessential *in-is-en'shl, adj* not essential; not necessary; immaterial. [**in-** (2)]

inessive *in-es'iv, (gram) adj* (in Finnish and related languages) denoting a case in nouns indicating 'place in which'. — *n* the inessive case. [L *inesse* to be in, on, or at]

inestimable *in-es'tim-ə-bl, adj* not able to be estimated or valued; priceless. — *n* **inestimabil'ity** or **ines'timableness**. — *adv* **ines'timably**. [**in-** (2)]

inevitable *in-ev'it-ə-bl, adj* not able to be evaded or avoided; certain to happen; exactly right, giving the feeling that the thing could not have been other than it is. — *n* **inevitabil'ity**. — *n* **inev'itableness**. — *adv* **inev'itably**. [L *inēvītābilis*, from *in-* not, *ē* from, and *vītāre* to avoid]

inexact *in-ig-zakt', adj* not precisely correct or true; lax. — *n* **inexact'itude** lack of exactitude, or an example of this. — *adv* **inexact'ly**. — *n* **inexact'ness**. [**in-** (2)]

in excelsis *in ek-sel'sis, ik-, eks-, iks-chel'sis, -kel'sis* or *-sēs*, (*LL*) on the heights; on high; in the highest degree.

inexcitable *in-ik-sīt'ə-bl, adj* not excitable; from which one cannot be roused (*obs*). [**in-** (2)]

inexcusable *in-ik-skūz'ə-bl, adj* which cannot be excused; not justifiable; unpardonable. — *n* **inexcusabil'ity**. — *n* **inexcus'ableness**. — *adv* **inexcus'ably**. [**in-** (2)]

inexecrable *in-eks'i-krə-bl, (Shakesp) adj* perhaps a misprint for *inexorable*, though interpreted by some as an intensive form of *execrable*.

inexecutable *in-ig-zek'ūt-ə-bl, in-ek-sek', -ik-* or *in-eks-i-kūt'ə-bl, adj* incapable of being executed or carried out. — *n* **inexecū'tion** the fact or state of not being executed. [**in-** (2)]

inexhausted *in-ig-zös'tid, adj (archaic)* unexhausted, not used up or spent. — *n* **inexhaustibil'ity**. — *adj* **inexhaust'ible** not able to be exhausted or spent; unfailing, tireless; endless. — *adv* **inexhaust'ibly**. — *adj* **inexhaust'ive** unfailing (*archaic*); not exhaustive. [**in-** (2)]

inexistence[1] *in-ig-zist'əns, (now rare) n* non-existence. — *adj* **inexist'ent**. [**in-** (2)]

inexistence[2] *in-ig-zist'əns, (archaic) n* inherence. — *adj* **inexist'ent** or **inexist'ant** indwelling; inherent. [**in-** (1)]

inexorable *in-eks'ər-ə-bl, adj* not to be moved by entreaty or persuasion; unrelenting; unyielding. — *n* **inexorabil'ity** or **inex'orableness**. — *adv* **inex'orably**. [LL *inexōrābilis*, from *in-* not, and *exōrāre*, from *ex* out of, and *ōrāre* to entreat]

inexpansible *in-ik-span'si-bl, adj* incapable of being expanded. [**in-** (2)]

inexpectant *in-ik-spek'tənt, adj* not expecting; without expectation. — *n* **inexpec'tancy**. — *n* **inexpecta'tion**. [**in-** (2)]

inexpedient *in-ik-spē'di-ənt, adj* contrary to expediency; not in accordance with good policy, impolitic. — *n* **inexpe'dience** or **inexpe'diency**. — *adv* **inexpe'diently**. [**in-** (2)]

inexpensive *in-ik-spens'iv, adj* not costing much; cheap in price. — *adv* **inexpens'ively**. — *n* **inexpens'iveness**. [**in-** (2)]

inexperience *in-ik-spē'ri-əns, n* lack of experience. — *adj* **inexpe'rienced** not having experience; unskilled or unpractised. [**in-** (2)]

inexpert *in-eks'pûrt* or *in-ik-spûrt', adj* not expert; unskilled. — *n* **inexpertness**. [**in-** (2)]

inexpiable *in-eks'pi-ə-bl, adj* that cannot be expiated or atoned for; that cannot be appeased. — *n* **inex'piableness**. — *adv* **inex'piably**. [**in-** (2)]

inexplainable *in-eks-plān'ə-bl, (rare) adj* inexplicable.

inexplicable *in-eks'pli-kə-bl* or *-ik-splik', adj* incapable of being explained or accounted for, inexplainable; that cannot be disentangled, inextricable (*obs*). — *n* **inexplicabil'ity** or **inexplic'ableness**. — *adv* **inexplic'ably**. [**in-** (2)]

inexplicit *in-ik-splis'it, adj* not explicit; not clear. [**in-** (2)]

inexpressible *in-ik-spres'i-bl, adj* that cannot be expressed; unutterable; indescribable. — *n* (in *pl*; *archaic, facetious*) trousers. — *adv* **inexpress'ibly**. — *adj* **inexpress'ive** inexpressible (*archaic*); unexpressive. — *n* **inexpress'iveness**. [**in-** (2)]

inexpugnable *in-ik-spug'nə-bl, adj* not able to be attacked or captured; unassailable, impregnable. — *n* **inexpugnabil'ity** or **inexpugn'ableness**. — *adv* **inexpug'nably**. [**in-** (2)]

inexpungible *in-ik-spun'ji-bl, adj* incapable of being wiped out or effaced. [**in-** (2)]

inextended *in-ik-stend'id, adj* not extended; without extension. — *n* **inextensibil'ity**. — *adj* **inexten'sible** that cannot be extended or stretched. — *n* **inexten'sion**. [**in-** (2)]

in extenso *in ik-sten'sō* or *ek-sten'*, (*LL*) at full length.

inextinguishable *in-ik-sting'gwish-ə-bl, adj* that cannot be extinguished, quenched, or destroyed. — *n* **inextin'guishableness**. — *adv* **inextin'guishably**. [**in-** (2)]

inextirpable *in-ik-stûrp'ə-bl, adj* not able to be destroyed, exterminated or rooted out. [**in-** (2)]

in extremis *in ik-strē'mis* or *ek-strā'mēs*, (*LL*) in the last extremity; at the point of death; at the last gasp; in desperate circumstances.

inextricable *in-eks'tri-kə-bl* or *-ik-strik', adj* not able to be escaped from; from which one cannot extricate oneself; not able to be extricated or disentangled; intricately involved, confused. — *adv* **inex'tricably**. [L *inextrīcābilis*]

INF *abbrev*: intermediate-range nuclear forces.

inf. *abbrev*: infantry; informal; *infra* (*L*), below.

in facie curiae *in fāsh'ē-ē kū'ri-ē, fāsh'ē* or *fak'i-ā*, (*LL*) in the presence of, or before, the court.

infall *in'fōl, n* an inroad; a falling in; a confluence, inlet or junction. [**in**[1] and **fall**[1]]

infallible *in-fal'i-bl, adj* incapable of error; incapable of making a mistake; incapable of failure, or not liable to fail; inevitable. — *n* **infall'ibilism** (*RC*) the doctrine of the Pope's infallibility. — *n* **infall'ibilist**. — *n* **infallibil'ity**. — *adv* **infall'ibly**. — **the doctrine of infallibility** (*RC*) (defined in 1870) the doctrine that the Pope, when speaking *ex cathedra*, is kept from error in all that regards faith and morals. [**in-** (2)]

infame *in-fām', (archaic) vt* to defame. — *vt* **in'famize** or **-ise** to defame, to brand with infamy. — Also **infam'onize** or **-ise**. [Ety as for **infamous**]

infamous *in'fə-məs*, formerly *in-fā'məs, adj* having a very bad reputation; publicly declared guilty; notoriously vile; disgraceful. — *adv* **in'famously**. — *n* **in'famy** ill repute; public disgrace; an infamous act or happening; extreme vileness. [L *īnfāmāre*, from *in-* not, and *fāma* fame]

infancy. See under **infant**.

infangthief *in'fang-thēf*, (*OE law*) *n* the right of taking and fining a thief within the boundary of one's own jurisdiction. [OE *infangenethēof*, from *in* in, the root of *fōn* to seize, and *thēof* thief]

infant *in'fənt, n* a baby; a person under the age of legal maturity (*Eng law*); a young schoolchild; an infante or infanta; an aristocratic youth (*obs*). — *adj* of or belonging to infants; of or in infancy; at an early stage of development. — *n* **in'fancy** the state or time of being an infant; childhood; the beginning or an early stage of anything; speechlessness, silence (*Milton*). — *n* **in'fanthood**. — *adj* **infantile** (*in'fən-tīl*, US *-til*, also *-fant'*) pertaining to infancy or to an infant; having characteristics of infancy; no better than that of an infant, childish; undeveloped. — *n* **infant'ilism** the persistence of infantile characteristics; a childish utterance or characteristic. — *adj* **in'fantine** (*-īn*) infantile. — **infantile paralysis** poliomyelitis; **infant mortality (rate)** (the rate of) deaths in the first year of life; **infant school** a school for children up to about the age of seven. [L *infāns*, *infantis*, from *in-* not, and *fāns*, pr p of *fārī* to speak; cf Gr *phanai*]

infante *in-fan'tā*, (*hist*) *n* a prince of the royal family of Spain or Portugal, *esp* a son of the king other than the heir-apparent: — *fem* **infant'a** a princess similarly defined; the wife of an infante. [Sp and Port from the root of **infant**]

infanticide *in-fan'ti-sīd, n* the killing of newborn children, practised in some societies; the killing of a child, *esp* by its mother, within twelve months of its birth; loosely, the murder of an infant; someone, *esp* a mother, who kills an infant. — *adj* **infanticī'dal** (or *-fant'*). [L *īnfanticīdium* child-killing, *īnfanticīda* child-killer, from *infāns* an infant, and *caedere* to kill]

infantry *in'fənt-ri, n* foot-soldiers; a part of an army composed of such soldiers; infants or children collectively (*archaic*). — Also *adj*. — *n* **in'fantryman** a soldier of the infantry: — *pl* **in'fantrymen**. [Fr *infanterie*, from Ital *infanteria*, from *infante* youth, servant, foot-soldier, from L *īnfāns*, *-antis*, a youth]

infarct *in-färkt', n* a portion of tissue that is dying because blood supply to it has been cut off. — *n* **infarc'tion**. [Med L *īnfarctus*, from *in* in, and *far(c)tus*, from *farcīre* to cram, stuff]

infare *in'fār, n* entrance (*obs*); the act of going in (*obs*); a house-warming after a wedding (*Scot* and *US*). [OE *innfær*; cf **in**[1] and **fare**]

infatuate *in-fat'ū-āt, vt* to inspire with foolish or unreasoning passion; to cause to behave foolishly or unreasonably; to deprive of judgement. — *adj* (*archaic*) infatuated. — *n* a person who is infatuated. — *pa p* and *adj* **infat'uated** filled with foolish or unreasoning passion; besotted; deprived of judgement. — *n* **infatuā'tion**. [L *īnfatuāre*, *-ātum*, from *in* in, and *fatuus* foolish]

infaust *in-fōst', (rare) adj* unlucky; ill-omened. [L *īnfaustus*, from *in-* not, and *faustus* propitious]

infeasible *in-fēz'i-bl, adj* not feasible. — *n* **infeasibil'ity** or **infeas'ibleness**. [**in-** (2)]

infect *in-fekt', vt* to taint, *esp* with disease; to introduce pathogenic microorganisms into; to corrupt; to spread to; to affect successively. — *adj* (*obs*) tainted. — *n* **infec'tion** (*-shən*) the act of infecting; that which infects or taints; an infectious disease. — *adj* **infec'tious** (*-shəs*) or **infec'tive** (*-tiv*) (of a disease) able to be transmitted by infection; caused by infection; corrupting; apt or likely to spread to others. — *adv* **infec'tiously**. — *n* **infec'tiousness**. — *n* **infect'iveness**. — *n* **infect'or**. — **infectious mononucleosis** glandular fever. [L *inficere*, *īnfectum*, from *in* into, and *facere* to make]

infecundity *in-fi-kun'di-ti, n* lack of fecundity or fertility; unfruitfulness. — *adj* **infecund** (*-fek'* or *-fēk'*). [**in-** (2)]

infeft *in-feft'*, (*old Scots law*) *vt* to invest with heritable property: — *pa p* **infeft'** or (*rare*) **infeft'ed**. — *n*

infeft'ment the symbolical giving possession of land in completion of the title. **[enfeoff]**

infelicitous *in-fi-lis'i-təs, adj* not felicitous or happy; inappropriate, inapt. — *n* **infelic'ity** something that is inappropriate or inapt. **[in-** (2)**]**

infelt *in'felt, adj* inwardly felt, heartfelt. **[in-** (1)**]**

infer *in-fûr', vt* to bring on (*Spenser* and *Shakesp*); to render (*Milton*); to derive from what has gone before; to arrive at as a logical conclusion, to deduce; to conclude; (*usu* of a thing or statement) to entail or involve as a consequence, to imply — often condemned as a misuse, but generally accepted for over four centuries: — *pr p* **inferr'ing**; *pa t* and *pa p* **inferred'**. — *adj* **in'ferable** (*-fûr'*; also **inferr'able**) or **inferr'ible** that may be inferred or deduced. — *n* **in'ference** that which is inferred or deduced; the act of drawing a conclusion from statements of fact; consequence; conclusion. — *adj* **inferential** (*-en'shl*) relating to inference; deducible or deduced by inference. — *adv* **inferen'tially**. [L *īnferre*, from *in* into, and *ferre*, to bring]

infere *in-fēr', (obs) adv* for **in fere**, together. [See **fere**[1]]

inferiae *in-fē'ri-ē* or *ēn-fe'ri-ī, (L) n pl* offerings to the spirits of the dead.

inferior *in-fē'ri-ər, adj* lower in any respect; subordinate; poor or poorer in quality; set slightly below the line (*printing*); (of an ovary) having the other parts above it (*bot*); (of the other parts) below the ovary (*bot*); (of a planet) revolving within the earth's orbit (*astron*). — *n* a person who is lower in rank or station. — *n* **inferiority** (*-or'*). — *adv* **infe'riorly** in an inferior manner. — **inferior conjunction** (*astron*) a conjunction when a celestial body, such as a planet, passes between the sun and the earth; **inferiority complex** a complex involving a suppressed sense of personal inferiority (*psychol*); popularly, a feeling of inferiority. [L *īnferior*, comparative of *īnferus* low]

infernal *in-fûr'nəl, adj* belonging to the regions below the earth, the underworld; resembling or suitable to hell; outrageous, very unpleasant (*colloq*); extremely annoying (*colloq*). — *n* **infernality** (*-nal'*). — *adv* **infer'nally**. — *n* **infer'no** (also with *cap*) hell (*Ital*); a place or situation of horror and confusion, *esp* a conflagration: — *pl* **infer'nos**. — **infernal machine** a contrivance made to resemble some ordinary harmless object, but charged with a dangerous explosive. [L *īnfernus*, from *īnferus*]

infertile *in-fûr'tīl* or (*US*) *-til, adj* not fertile; not capable of producing offspring, sterile; not productive; barren. — *n* **infertility** (*-til'*). **[in-** (2)**]**

infest *in-fest', vt* to swarm over, cover or fill, in a troublesome, unpleasant or harmful way; to invade and live on or in as a parasite; to disturb or harass. — *adj* (*obs*) hostile; troublesome. — *n* **infestā'tion** molestation (*obs*); attack, or the condition of being attacked, *esp* by parasites. [L *īnfestāre*, from *īnfestus* hostile]

infeudation *in-fū-dā'shən, n* the putting of an estate in fee, enfeoffment; a deed of enfeoffment; the granting of tithes to laymen. **[in-** (1) and **feud**[2]**]**

infibulate *in-fib'ū-lāt, vt* to fasten with a clasp. — *n* **infibulā'tion** the act of confining or fastening, *specif* the fastening or partial closing-up of the prepuce or the labia majora by a clasp, stitches or the like to prevent sexual intercourse. **[in-** (1) and L *fibula* a clasp]

inficete *in-fi-sēt', (rare) adj* not facetious; rudely jesting. [L *īnficētus*, from *in-* not, and *facētus* courteous, witty]

infidel *in'fi-dl, n* someone who rejects a religion, *esp* Christianity or Islam; loosely, someone who disbelieves in a particular theory, etc. — *adj* unbelieving; sceptical; disbelieving a religion. — *n* **infidel'ity** lack of faith or belief; disbelief in religion; unfaithfulness, *esp* in marriage; treachery. [OFr *infidèle*, from L *īnfidēlis*, from *in-* not, and *fidēlis* faithful, from *fidēs* faith]

infield *in'fēld, n* the space enclosed within the base-lines (*baseball*); the part of the field near the wicket (*cricket*); the players stationed in the infield; formerly, land near a farmhouse, kept constantly manured and under tillage (also *adj*). — *n* **in'fielder** a player on the infield. **[in**[1] and **field]**

in fieri *in fī'ə-rī, (L; law)* in course of completion; pending.

infighting *in'fīt-ing, n* boxing at close quarters when blows from the shoulder cannot be given. — See also under **in**[1]. **[in**[1] and **fighting]**

infilling *in'fil-ing, n* filling up or in; something used to fill up or in; material used to fill up or level (*building*); infill housing. — *vt* **in'fill** to fill in. — *n* material for infilling. — **infill housing** or **development** new houses, buildings, etc built in the gaps between existing ones. **[in**[1] and **fill**[1]**]**

infiltrate *in'fil-trāt*, or *-fil', vt* to cause to filter; to cause to filter into; to sift into; to permeate. — *vi* to permeate gradually; to sift or filter in. — *vt* and *vi* (of troops, agents, etc) to enter (a hostile area) secretly and for subversive purposes. — *n* **infiltrā'tion** the process of infiltrating; gradual permeation or interpenetration; gradual accession or introduction of a new element, as of population or troops; a deposit or substance infiltrated. — *adj* **in'filtrative**. — *n* **in'filtrator** someone who becomes accepted as a member of a group towards which he or she has hostile or subversive intentions. **[in-** (1)**]**

infima species *in'fi-mə spē'shēz* or *ēn'fi-ma spe'ki-ās, (LL) n* the lowest species included in a genus or class: — *pl* **infimae** (*-ē*) **species**.

infimum *in-fī'məm, (math) n* (*abbrev* **inf**) the greatest lower bound (cf **supremum**). [L, neuter of *infimus*, superlative of *inferus* lower]

infin. *abbrev*: infinitive.

infinite *in'fin-it*, in church singing also *in'fi-nīt, adj* without end or limit; greater than any quantity that can be assigned (*math*); extending to infinity; vast; in vast numbers; inexhaustible; infinitated (*logic*); (of part of a verb) not limited by person or number. — *n* something that has no determinate bounds, and for which there is no possible bound or limit; the Absolute, the Infinite Being or God. — *adj* **infin'itant** (*logic*) denoting merely negative attribution. — *adj* **infin'itary** pertaining to infinity. — *vt* **infin'itate** to make infinite; to turn into a negative term (*logic*). — *adv* **in'finitely**. — *n* **in'finiteness**. — *adj* **infinitesimal** (*-es'*) infinitely small; (loosely) extremely small; (of a variable) having values that are close to zero (*math*). — *n* an infinitely small quantity; an infinitesimal variable (*math*). — *adv* **infinites'imally**. — *n* **infin'itude** infinity. — *n* **infin'ity** the state or quality of having no limits or bounds; an infinite quantity or distance; vastness, immensity; a countless or indefinite number. — **infinite canon** (*music*) a canon that can be repeated indefinitely; **infinite set** (*math*) a set that can be put into a one-one correspondence with part of itself; **infinitesimal calculus** differential and integral calculus. **[in-** (2)**]**

infinitive *in-fin'it-iv, (gram) adj* expressing, or in the mood that expresses, the verbal idea without reference to person, number or time, as *stop* in Make him *stop*, or, in English, the *to* + *verb* form generally. — *n* the infinitive mood; a verb in the infinitive mood. — *adj* **infinitī'val**. — *adv* **infin'itively**. — **infinitive marker** a word that is used with a verb in the infinitive, such as *to* in *to sing*. [L *infīnītīvus*, from *in-* not, and *fīnīre* to limit]

infinity. See under **infinite**.

infirm *in-fûrm', adj* sickly; weak; frail; unstable. — *n* **infirm'ity**. — *adv* **infirm'ly**. — *n* **infirm'ness**. [L *īnfirmus*, from *in-* not, and *firmus* strong]

infirmarian *in-fər-mā'ri-ən, (hist) n* an officer in a medieval monastery who was in charge of the infirmary. — Also **infirm'arer**. [See **infirmary**]

infirmary *in-fûr'mə-ri, n* a hospital or place for the treatment of the sick. [Med L *infirmaria*; see **infirm**]

infix *in-fiks', vt* to fix in; to drive or fasten in; to set in by piercing; to insert an affix within (a root) (*philol*). — Also **enfix** (*archaic*). — *n* **in'fix** (*philol*) an element or affix inserted within a root or word, as *m* in the Gr *lambanō*, from the root *lab*. [L *īnfīxus*, from *in* in, and *fīgere*, *fīxum* to fix]

infl. *abbrev*: influenced.

in flagrante delicto *in flə-gran'ti di-lik'tō* or *flä-gran'te dā-lik'tō*, (*L*) in the very act of committing the crime, red-handed.

inflame *in-flām'*, *vt* to cause to burn; to make hot; to make red; to cause inflammation in; to arouse strong emotions in; to anger; to exacerbate. — *vi* to burst into flames; to become hot, painful, red, excited or angry; to suffer inflammation. — *adj* **inflamed'**. — *n* **inflām'er**. [OFr *enflammer*, from L *īnflammāre*; see ety for **inflammable**]

inflammable *in-flam'ə-bl*, *adj* capable of being set on fire (see **flammable**); easily kindled or excited. — *n* an inflammable substance. — *n* **inflammabil'ity**. — *n* **inflamm'ableness**. — *adv* **inflamm'ably**. — *n* **inflammation** (*-flə-mā'shən*) the state of being in flames or inflamed; heat of a part of the body, with pain, redness, and swelling; arousal of the passions. — *adj* **inflamm'atory** tending to inflame; inflaming; exciting, tending to stir up trouble. [L *īnflammāre*, from *in* into, and *flamma* a flame]

inflate *in-flāt'*, *vt* to cause to swell up with air or gas; to puff up; to expand unduly; to increase excessively; to elate. — *vi* to become full of air or gas; to distend. — *adj* and *n* **inflat'able** (any object) that can be inflated. — *adj* **inflat'ed** swollen or blown out; turgid; pompous; hollow, filled with air (*bot*). — *adv* **inflat'ingly**. — *n* **inflation** (*in-flā'shən*) the act of inflating; the condition of being inflated; undue increase in quantity of money in proportion to buying power, as on an excessive issue of fiduciary money; a progressive increase in the general level of prices; turgidity of style; afflatus, inspiration (*rare*). — *adj* **infla'tionary**. — *n* **infla'tionism** the policy of inflating currency. — *n* **infla'tionist**. — *adj* **inflat'ive** causing inflation; tending to inflate. — *n* **inflat'or** someone who, or something that, inflates; a cycle pump. — *n* **inflat'us** (*L*) inspiration. — **inflationary universe** (*astron*) model of the very early universe (10^{-44} seconds after the Big Bang) in which the universe expands momentarily much faster than the speed of light. — *adj* **infla'tion-proof** (of investments, etc) protected, *esp* by indexation, against inflation. — **infla'tion-proofing**. [L *īnflāre*, *-ātum*, from *in* into, and *flāre* to blow]

inflect *in-flekt'*, *vt* to bend in; to turn from a direct line or course; to modulate (eg the voice); to vary the endings of (a word) (*gram*). — *n* **inflec'tion** or **inflex'ion** a bending or deviation; modulation of the voice; variation in word-ending to express the relations of case, number, gender, person, tense, etc (*gram*). — *adj* **inflec'tional** or **inflex'ional**. — *adj* **inflec'tionless** or **inflex'ionless**. — *adj* **inflect'ive** subject to inflection. — *adj* **inflexed'** (*esp biol*) bent inward; bent; turned. — *n* **inflexure** (*in-flek'shər*) an inward bend or fold. [L *īnflectere*, from *in* in, and *flectere*, *flexum* to bend, *flexiō*, *-ōnis* a bend]

inflexible *in-flek'si-bl*, *adj* not flexible; incapable of being bent; unyielding; rigid; obstinate; unbending. — *n* **inflexibil'ity** or **inflex'ibleness**. — *adv* **inflex'ibly**. [**in-** (2)]

inflexion and **inflexional**. See under **inflect**.

inflict *in-flikt'*, *vt* to lay on (a blow, etc); to impose (eg punishment or pain; *usu* with *on* or *upon*); to afflict (*Shakesp*). — *n* **inflic'ter** or **inflic'tor**. — *n* **inflic'tion** the act of inflicting or imposing; something inflicted. — *adj* **inflict'ive**. [L *īnflīgere*, *īnflīctum*, from *in* against, and *flīgere* to strike]

inflorescence *in-flor-es'əns* or *-flər-*, (*bot*) *n* a specialized branching stem or axis of a plant bearing a flower or flowers; the arrangement of flowers on an axis, a flower cluster; the process of producing flowers, blossoming. [L *īnflōrēscere* to begin to blossom]

inflow *in'flō*, *n* the act of flowing in, influx; the rate of flowing in; something that flows in. — *n* and *adj* **in'flowing**. [**in-** (1)]

influence *in'flōō-əns*, *n* the power of producing an effect, *esp* unobtrusively; the effect of power exerted; something having such power; someone exercising such power; domination, often hidden or inexplicable; exertions of friends who have useful connections and are able to secure advantages for one; the occult power or virtue supposed to flow from stars and planets, thought to affect a person's personality, actions, future, etc (*astrol*); a spiritual influx; inflow (*obs*). — *vt* to have or exert influence upon: to affect. — *adj* **in'fluent** flowing in; exerting influence. — *n* a tributary stream; an organism that has a major or modifying effect on an ecological community. — *adj* **influential** (*-en'shl*) of the nature of influence; having a great deal of influence; effectively active (in bringing something about). — *adv* **influen'tially**. — **under the influence** (*informal*) suffering from the effects of (too much) alcohol, drunk. [OFr, from LL *īnfluentia*, from L *in* into, and *fluere* to flow]

influenza *in-flōō-en'zə*, *n* a highly contagious virus infection characterized by headache, fever, muscular aches and pains and inflammation of the respiratory passages; any of several diseases of *esp* domestic animals which attack the respiratory system. — *adj* **influen'zal**. [Ital, influence, influenza (as a supposed astral visitation), from LL *īnfluentia*; see **influence**]

influx *in'fluks*, *n* a flowing in, *esp* of a large number of people or things; accession; that which flows in, eg a river or stream. — *n* **influxion** (*in-fluk'shən*). — **influx control** formerly in South Africa, a government control which prevented Black Africans entering urban areas without permits (cf **pass laws**). [L *īnfluxus*, from *īnfluere*]

info *in'fō*, *n colloq* short form of **information**. — *n* **infomer'cial** a short film which is in fact an advertising medium. — *adj* **infopreneur'ial** of or relating to the industry concerned with the development, manufacture and sale of *esp* computerized or electronic equipment for the distribution of information. — *n* **infotain'ment** the presentation of serious subjects or current affairs as entertainment.

in-foal *in-fōl'*, *adj* pregnant (with foal). [**in**[1] and **foal**]

infold[1]. See **enfold**.

infold[2] *in'fold'*, *n* a fold inwards. [**in-** (1)]

infomercial and **infopreneurial**. See under **info**.

inforce. Same as **enforce**.

inform[1] *in-förm'*, *vt* to pass on knowledge to; to tell; to animate or inspire; to give a quality to; to direct or educate (*obs*); to give form to (*obs*). — *vi* to give information, make an accusation (with *against* or *on*); to take shape or form (*obs*). — *n* **inform'ant** someone who informs or communicates information. — *n* **informati'cian** someone engaged in informatics. — *n sing* **informa'tics** information science; information technology. — *n* **information** (*in-fər-mā'shən*) the act of informing; intelligence given; knowledge; an accusation made before a magistrate or court; data (*comput*). — *adj* **informāt'ional**. — *adj* **inform'ative** having the power to form; instructive. — *adj* **inform'atory** instructive; giving information. — *adj* **informed'** knowing, intelligent, educated. — *n* **inform'er** a person who gives information; a person who informs against another; an animator or inspirer (*literary*). — **information retrieval** the storage, classification, and subsequent tracing of (*esp* computerized) information; **information science** (the study of) the processing and communication of data, *esp* by means of computerized systems; **information scientist**; **information technology** the (*esp* computerized or electronic) technology related to the gathering, recording and communicating of information; **information theory** mathematical analysis of the efficiency with which communication channels are employed. [OFr *enformer*, from L *īnfōrmāre*, from *in* into, and *fōrmāre* to form, *fōrma* form]

inform[2] *in-förm'*, (*archaic*) *adj* formless, unformed; misshapen, deformed. [Ety as **informal**]

informal *in-för'məl*, *adj* not of a formal or conventional nature; characterized by lack of ceremony or formality; relaxed, friendly, unceremonious; (*esp* of clothes) appropriate to everyday or casual use; (of speech or writing) having vocabulary, idiom, etc characteristic of conversational speech; (of a vote) invalid (*Austr*). — *n* **informal'ity**. — *adv* **inform'ally**. [L *in-* not, and *fōrma* form; *infōrmis* formless, misshapen]

in forma pauperis *in fŏr'mə pö'pər-is* or *fōr'mä powp'er-is*, (*L*) as a pauper; as a poor person, not liable to costs (*law*).

informidable *in-fŏr'mi-də-bl*, (*rare*) *adj* not formidable. [**in-** (2)]

in foro conscientiae *in fō'rō kon-shi-en'shi-ē* or *kōn-ski-en-ti-ī*, (*L*) in the court of conscience; judged by one's own conscience.

infortune *in-fŏr'tūn*, *n* misfortune (*rare*); a malevolent influence or planetary aspect (*astrol*). [**in-** (2)]

infotainment. See under **info**.

infra *in'frə* or *ēn'frä*, (*L*) *adv* below; lower down on the page, or further on in the book. — **infra dignitatem** (*dig-ni-tā'təm* or *-tä'tem*) beneath one's dignity; unbecoming (*colloq* short form **infra dig**).

infra- *in'frə-*, *pfx* signifying: (1) below, as in *infrastructure*; (2) within, as in *infraspecific*.

infracostal *in-frə-kos'tl*, (*anatom*) *adj* beneath the ribs. [L *īnfrā* below, and *costa* a rib]

infraction *in-frak'shən*, *n* violation, *esp* of law; a breach. — *vt* **infract'** to infringe. — *adj* **infract'ed** broken; interrupted; bent in. — *n* **infrac'tor**. [L *īnfringere*, *īnfrāctum*, from *in* in, and *frangere*, *frāctum* to break]

infra dig. See **infra**.

infragrant *in-frā'grənt*, *adj* not fragrant, malodorous. [**in-** (2)]

infrahuman *in-frə-hū'mən*, *adj* lower than human. — Also *n*. [L *īnfrā* below]

Infralapsarian *in-frə-lap-sā'ri-ən*, *n* a believer in Infralapsarianism. — Also *adj*. — *n* **Infralapsār'ianism** the common Augustinian and Calvinist doctrine, that God for his own glory determined to create the world, to permit the fall of man, to elect some to salvation and leave the rest to punishment, distinct both from *Supralapsarianism* and *Sublapsarianism*; also sometimes used as equivalent to Sublapsarianism. [L *īnfrā* below, after, and *lāpsus* a fall]

inframaxillary *in-frə-mak'si-lə-ri*, *adj* situated under the jaw; belonging to the lower jaw. [L *īnfrā* below, and *maxilla* jaw]

infrangible *in-fran'ji-bl*, *adj* not able to be broken; not to be violated. — *n* **infrangibil'ity** or **infran'gibleness**. — *adv* **infran'gibly**. [L *in-* not, and *frangere* to break]

infraorbital *in-frə-ör'bi-tl*, *adj* situated below the orbit of the eye. [L *īnfrā* below]

infraposed *in'frə-pōzd*, *adj* placed below something else (cf **superposed**). — *n* **infraposi'tion**.

infrared *in'frə-red'*, *n* infrared radiation. — *adj* between the red end of the visible spectrum and microwaves; using infrared radiation; sensitive to this radiation. — **infrared astronomy** the study of radiation from celestial bodies, such as nascent stars, in the infrared wavelength range; **infrared photography** photography using film specially sensitized to infrared radiation, with applications in conditions without visible light, camouflage and forgery detection, and aerial surveys; **infrared radiation** electromagnetic radiation between the visible and microwave regions of the spectrum, ie in the range from 0·75 to 1000 micrometres. [L *īnfrā* below]

infrasonic *in-frə-son'ik*, (*acoustics*) *adj* (of frequencies) below the usual audible limit; of, using or produced by infrasonic vibrations or pressure waves. — *n* **in'frasound**. [L *infrā* below]

infraspecific *in-frə-spə-sif'ik*, (*biol*) *adj* included within or affecting a species.

infrastructure *in'frə-struk-chər*, *n* inner structure, structure of component parts; a system of communications and services as backing for military, commercial, etc operations. — *adj* **infrastruc'tural**. [L *īnfrā* below]

infrequent *in-frē'kwənt*, *adj* seldom occurring; rare; uncommon. — *n* **infre'quency** or **infrē'quence**. — *adv* **infrē'quently**. [**in-** (2)]

infringe *in-frinj'*, *vt* to violate, *esp* a law; to neglect to obey. — *vi* to encroach or trespass (with *on* or *upon*). — *n* **infringe'ment**. [L *īnfringere*, from *in* in, and *frangere* to break]

infructuous *in-fruk'tū-əs*, *adj* not fruitful (*lit* and *fig*). — *adv* **infruc'tuously**. [L *īnfrūctuōsus*, from *in-* not, and *frūctūosus* fruitful]

infula *in'fū-lə*, *n* a white-and-red band of woollen cloth, worn on the forehead by the ancient Romans in religious rites; one of the lappets in a bishop's mitre: — *pl* **in'fulae** (*-ē*). [L *īnfula*]

infundibulum *in-fun-dib'ū-ləm*, *n* a funnel or funnel-shaped part, *esp* the funnel-shaped stalk that connects the pituitary gland to the brain: — *pl* **infundib'ula**. — *adj* **infundibular** (*in-fun-dib'ū-lər*), funnel-shaped; having an infundibulum. — Also **infundib'ulate**. — *adj* **infundib'uliform**. [L, a funnel, from *in* in, and *fundere* to pour]

infuriate *in-fū'ri-āt*, *vt* to enrage, anger; to madden. — *adj* (*-it* or *-āt*) enraged, furiously angry; mad. — *adj* **infur'iating**. — *adv* **infur'iatingly**. — *n* **infuria'tion**. [L *in* in, and *furiāre*, *-ātum* to madden, from *furere* to rave]

infuscate *in-fus'kāt* or *-kit*, *adj* clouded or tinged with brown. [L *in* in, and *fuscus* brown]

infuse *in-fūz'*, *vt* to pour in; to instil; to soak in liquid without boiling; to imbue; to shed or pour (*obs*). — *vi* to undergo infusion. — *n* (*Spenser*) infusion. — *n* **infus'er** a device for making an infusion, *esp* of tea. — *adj* **infus'ible**. — *n* **infusion** (*in-fū'zhən*) pouring in; something poured in or introduced; the pouring of water over any substance in order to extract its active qualities; a solution in water of an organic, *esp* a vegetable, substance; the liquid so obtained; inspiration; instilling. — *adj* **infusive** (*-fū'siv*) having the power of infusion, or of being infused. [L *īnfundere*, *īnfūsum*, from *in* into, and *fundere*, *fūsum* to pour]

infusible *in-fūz'i-bl*, *adj* that cannot be fused; having a high melting-point. — *n* **infusibil'ity**. [**in-** (2)]

infusoria *in-fū-zō'ri-ə*, *-zö*, *-sō'ri-ə* or *-sö'*, (*obs*) *n pl orig* minute organisms found in stagnant infusions of animal or vegetable material; (with *cap*) the Ciliophora, a former class of Protozoa with cilia throughout life (Ciliata) or in early life (Suctoria). — *adj* **infūsō'rial** or **infū'sory** composed of or containing infusoria. — *n* and *adj* **infūsō'rian**. — **infusorial earth** diatomite. [Neuter pl of New L *īnfūsorius*; see **infuse**]

-ing[1] *-ing*, *sfx* forming: (1) the present participle of verbs, as in *jumping*, *waiting*, *talking*; (2) adjectives from participles, as in *a crying baby*, *a moving vehicle*; (3) adjectives not derived from verbs, as in *sodding*, *swashbuckling*. [ME *-ing*, *inde*, from OE *-ende*]

-ing[2] *-ing*, *sfx* forming: (1) nouns, signifying something consisting of, made from, or used in making, as in *wiring*, *matting*, *scaffolding*; (2) *sing* and *pl* nouns from verbs, signifying a result of an action or process, as in *etching*(*s*), *drawing*(*s*); (3) nouns, signifying an activity or area of activity as a whole, as in *skiing*, *banking*, *mining*, *engineering*.

-ing[3] *-ing*, *sfx* forming nouns, denoting a person or thing of a specified quality or kind, as in *sweeting*.— See also **-ling**. [ME, from OE, related to OHGer *-ing* belonging to]

ingan *ing'ən*, *n* a Scots and dialect form of **onion**.

ingate[1] *in'gāt*, *n* an inlet for molten metal in founding. [**in**[1] and **gate**[1]]

ingate[2] *in'gāt*, (now *Scot* and *NEng dialect*) *n* a way in, (an) entrance. [**in**[1] and **gate**[2]]

ingather *in-gadh'ər*, *vt* to gather in; to harvest. — *n* **ingathering** (*in'gadh-ər-ing*) collection; securing of the fruits of the earth; harvest. — **Feast of Ingathering** see **Feast of Tabernacles** under **tabernacle**. [**in-** (1)]

ingeminate *in-jem'in-āt*, (*formal*) *vt* to reiterate; to redouble. — *n* **ingeminā'tion**. [L *ingemināre*, *-ātum*, from *in* in, and *geminus* twin]

ingener *in'jən-ər*, (*Shakesp*) *n*. Same as **engineer**.

ingenerate[1] *in-jen'ər-āt*, *vt* to generate or produce within. — *adj* (*-it*) inborn; innate. [**in-** (1)]

ingenerate[2] *in-jen'ər-it* or *-āt*, *adj* not generated, self-existent. [**in-** (2)]

ingenious *in-jē'nyəs* or *-ni-əs*, *adj* skilful in invention or contriving; skilfully contrived; of good natural abilities, *esp* having or displaying great intelligence (*obs*). — *adv* **ingē'niously**. — *n* **ingē'niousness** great inventiveness and imagination; skill in combining ideas; cleverly contrived or unconventional design. — *n* **ingē'nium** (*obs*) mentality; talent or genius. [L *ingenium* mother-wit]

ingénue *ɛ̃-zhā-nü*, (*Fr*) *n* an artless, naïve or inexperienced young woman, *esp* an actress portraying such a type: — *masc* **ingénu**.

ingenuity *in-ji-nū'i-ti*, *n orig* ingenuousness; now (by confusion with **ingenious**) ingeniousness. [L *ingenuitās, -ātis*; see ety for **ingenuous**]

ingenuous *in-jen'ū-əs*, *adj* candid, frank; honourable; free from deception, artless; free-born (*obs*). — *adv* **ingen'uously**. — *n* **ingen'uousness**. — *n* **ingenu'ity** (see previous entry). [L *ingenuus* free-born, ingenuous]

ingest *in-jest'*, *vt* to take (eg food) into the body. — *n pl* **ingest'a** nourishment taken into the body through the alimentary canal via the mouth. — *adj* **ingest'ible**. — *n* **ingestion** (*in-jes'chən*). — *adj* **ingest'ive**. [L *ingerere, ingestum* to carry in, from *in* in, and *gerere* to carry]

ingine *in-jīn'*, (*obs*) *n* ability; genius. [L *ingenium*]

ingle[1] *ing'gl*, (*Scot* and *dialect ing'l*) *n* a fire in a room; a fireplace. — **ing'le-cheek** the jamb of a fireplace; **ing'lenook** or (*Scot*) **ing'leneuk** an alcove by a large open fire, a chimney corner; **ing'le-side** a fireside. [Poss Gaelic *aingeal*; or L *igniculus*, dimin of *ignis* fire]

ingle[2] *ing'gl*, (*obs*) *n* a catamite; a friend (*Scott*; *erron*). [Origin obscure]

inglobe *in-glōb'*, (*Milton*) *vt* to englobe, form into a sphere. [**in-** (1)]

inglorious *in-glō'ri-əs* or *-glö'*, *adj* not glorious; unhonoured; shameful, disgraceful. — *adv* **inglo'riously**. — *n* **inglo'riousness**. [**in-** (2)]

ingluvies *in-gloo'vi-ēz*, *n* the crop or craw of birds. — *adj* **inglu'vial**. [L *ingluviēs*]

ingo *in'gō*, (*Scot*) *n* an entrance; a reveal, the inner sides of a recess or opening, eg a doorway; entry into or taking on of a new tenancy: — *pl* **in'goes**. [**in**[1] and **go**[1]]

ingoes. See **ingo**.

ingoing *in'gō-ing*, *n* a going in; an entrance; a reveal (*Scot*). — *adj* going in; entering as an occupant; thorough, penetrating. [**in**[1] and **go**[1]]

ingot *ing'gət* or *-got*, *n* a mass of unwrought metal, *esp* gold or silver, cast in a mould. [Perh OE *in* in, and the root *got*, as in *goten*, pa p of *gēotan* to pour; Ger *giessen*, Gothic *giutan*]

ingraft. See **engraft**.

ingrain *in-grān'*, *vt* same as **engrain**. — *adj* (*in'grān* when *attrib*) dyed in the yarn or thread before manufacture; deeply fixed; through and through. — *adj* **ingrained'** (attrib *in'grānd*). [**in-** (1)]

ingram or **ingrum** *ing'rəm*, (*obs*) *adj* ignorant. [**ignorant**]

ingrate *in-grāt'* or *in'grāt*, (*archaic*) *adj* ungrateful; unpleasing (*obs*). — *n* an ungrateful person. — *adj* **ingrate'ful**. — *adv* **ingrate'ly**. [L *ingrātus*, from *in-* not, and *grātus* pleasing, grateful]

ingratiate *in-grā'shi-āt*, *vt* to commend (*usu* oneself) persuasively to someone's favour (followed by *with*). — *adj* **ingra'tiating**. — *adv* **ingra'tiatingly**. — *n* **ingratia'tion**. [L *in* into, and *grātia* favour]

ingratitude *in-grat'i-tūd*, *n* lack of gratitude or thankfulness. [LL *ingrātitūdō*, from L *ingrātus* unthankful]

ingravescent *in-grə-ves'ənt* or *ing-grə-*, *adj* (of a disease or medical condition) becoming more severe. [L *ingravescere* to become heavier, from L *gravis* heavy]

ingredient *in-grē'di-ənt*, *n* something that is put into a mixture or compound; a component. [L *ingrediēns, -entis*, pr p of *ingredī*, from *in* into, and *gradī* to walk]

in gremio *in grēm'* or *grem'i-ō*, (*LL*) in the bosom. — **in gremio legis** (*lē'jis*) in the bosom of the law; under the protection of the law.

ingress *in'gres*, *n* entrance; power, right or means of entrance. — *n* **ingression** (*in-gresh'ən*). — *adj* **ingress'ive** (*phonetics*) (of speech sounds) pronounced with inhalation rather than exhalation of breath. [L *ingressus*, from *ingredī*; see ety for **ingredient**]

ingroove. See **engroove**.

ingross *in-grōs'*, (*archaic*) *vt*. Same as **engross**.

ingroup. See under **in**[1].

ingrowing *in'grō-ing*, *adj* growing inwards; growing into the flesh; growing in or into. — *adj* **in'grown**. — *n* **in'growth** growth within or inwards; a structure formed in this way. [**in-** (1)]

ingrum. See **ingram**.

inguinal *ing'gwin-əl*, *adj* in, of or relating to the groin. [L *inguinālis*, from *inguen, inguinis* the groin]

ingulf and **ingulph**. See **engulf**.

ingurgitate *in-gûr'ji-tāt*, *vt* to swallow up (food) greedily. — *n* **ingurgitā'tion**. [L *ingurgitāre, -ātum*, from *in* into, and *gurges, -itis* a whirlpool]

inhabit *in-hab'it*, *vt* to dwell in; to occupy. — *vi* (*archaic*) to dwell. — *adj* **inhab'itable** capable of being inhabited; fit to live in (see also separate entry **inhabitable** below). — *n* **inhab'itance** or **inhab'itancy** the act of inhabiting; abode or residence. — *n* **inhab'itant** a person who or an animal which inhabits a particular place; a resident. — *adj* resident. — *n* **inhabitā'tion** the act of inhabiting; dwelling-place; population (*archaic*); *perh* the inhabited world (*Milton*). — *n* **inhab'iter** an inhabitant (*rare*); a colonist, settler (*obs*). — *n* **inhab'itiveness** (*phrenology*) love of locality and home. — *n* **inhab'itress** (*archaic*) a female inhabitant. [L *inhabitāre*, from *in* in, and *habitāre* to dwell]

inhabitable *in-hab'it-ə-bl*, (*obs*) *adj* not habitable, uninhabitable. — See also under **inhabit**. [L *inhabitābilis*, from *in-* not, and *habitābilis*]

inhale *in-hāl'*, *vt* and *vi* to breathe in; to draw in. — *adj* **inhā'lant** inhaling; drawing in. — *n* a medicinal preparation to be inhaled; an inhaling organ, structure or apparatus. — *n* **inhalation** (*in-hə-lā'shən*) the act of drawing into the lungs; something to be inhaled. — *n* **inhalator** (*in'hə-lā-tər*, or *-lā'*) an apparatus for enabling one to inhale a gas, vapour, etc. — *n* **inhā'ler** a person who inhales; a smoker who fully inhales tobacco smoke; a device for administering a medicinal preparation by inhalation, eg to relieve asthma, etc; a respirator or gas mask. [L *in* upon, and *hālāre* to breathe (L *inhālāre* means to breathe upon)]

inharmonious *in-här-mō'ni-əs*, *adj* discordant, unmusical; disagreeing; marked by disagreement and discord. — *adj* **inharmonic** (*in-här-mon'ik*) or **inharmon'ical** lacking harmony; inharmonious. — *n* **inharmonic'ity** (*-nis'*) the quality or phenomenon of being inharmonious. — *adv* **inharmō'niously**. — *n* **inharmō'niousness**. — *n* **inharmony** (*in-här'mən-i*). [**in-** (2)]

inhaul *in'höl* or **inhauler** *-ər*, (*naut*) *n* a rope or line for hauling in something, eg a sail. [**in**[1] and **haul**]

inhaust *in-höst'*, (*archaic*) *vt* to drink in. [L *in* in, and *haurīre, haustum* to draw]

inhearse or **inherce** *in-hûrs'*, (*Shakesp*) *vt* to enclose as in a hearse; to bury. — Also **enhearse'**. [**in-** (1)]

inhere *in-hēr'*, *vi* (with *in*) to stick, remain firm in something; to be inherent. — *n* **inhēr'ence** or **inhēr'ency** a sticking fast; existence in something else; a fixed state of being in another body or substance; the relation between a quality or attribute and its subject (*philos*). — *adj* **inhēr'ent** sticking fast (*archaic*); existing in and inseparable from something else; innate; natural. — *adv* **inhēr'ently**. — **inherent floatability** (*min ext*) the natural tendency of some mineral species to repel water and to become part of the float (*opp* to the froth) in the froth flotation process. [L *inhaerēre, inhaesum*, from *in* in, and *haerēre* to stick]

inherit *in-her'it*, *vt* to make heir (*Shakesp*); to be the heir of, succeed as heir (*archaic*); to get possession of as heir; to possess by transmission from past generations;

to have at secondhand from anyone (*colloq*); to have by genetic transmission from ancestors. — *vi* to succeed. — *adj* **inher'itable** same as **heritable**. — *n* **inher'itance** that which is or may be inherited; hereditary descent. — *n* **inher'itor** someone who inherits or may inherit; an heir: — *fem* **inher'itress** or **inher'itrix**. — **inheritance tax** a tax (replacing **death duty**) levied on inheritors according to their relationship to the testator (with exemption for spouses in the UK) when the estate exceeds a specified allowance. [OFr *enhériter* to put in possession as heir, from LL *inhērēditāre* to inherit, from L *in* in, and *hērēs, hērēdis* an heir]

inhesion *in-hē'zhən*. Same as **inherence**.

inhibit *in-hib'it, vt* to hold in or back; to keep back; to restrain or check; to restrict or prevent. — *n* **inhibi'tion** the act of inhibiting or restraining; the state of being inhibited; something that restricts, prevents or debars; a writ from a higher court to an inferior judge to stop, suspend or postpone proceedings (*obs*); a restraining action of the unconscious will; the blocking of a mental or psychophysical process by another set up at the same time by the same stimulus; stoppage or retardation of a physical process by some nervous influence. — *adj* **inhib'itive**. — *n* **inhib'itor** something which inhibits (also **inhib'iter**); a substance that interferes with a chemical or biological process. — *adj* **inhib'itory** prohibitory. [L *inhibēre, -hibitum*, from *in* in, and *habēre* to have]

inholder *in-hōld'ər*, (*obs*) *n* an inhabitant (*Spenser*); a container. [**in-** (1)]

inhomogeneous *in-hom-ō-jēn'i-əs, adj* not homogeneous. — *n* **inhomogeneity** (*-jən-ē'i-ti*). [**in-** (2)]

inhoop *in-hōōp'*, (*Shakesp*) *vt* to confine, as in a hoop or enclosure. [**in-** (1)]

inhospitable *in-hos'pit-ə-bl* or *-pit'*, *adj* not kind or welcoming to strangers; (of a place) barren, not offering shelter, food, etc. — *n* **inhos'pitableness** or **inhospital'ity**. — *adv* **inhosp'itably**. [**in-** (2)]

inhuman *in-hū'mən, adj* not human; brutal; cruel; without human feeling. — *n* **inhumanity** (*in-hū-man'i-ti*) the state of being inhuman or inhumane; brutality; cruelty. — *adv* **inhū'manly**. [**in-** (2)]

inhumane *in-hū-mān'*, *adj* lacking humane feelings, cruel. — *adv* **inhumane'ly**. [**in-** (2)]

inhume *in-hūm'*, *vt* to bury in the earth, to inter. — Also **inhumate** (*in'* or *-hūm'*). — *n* **inhumā'tion** the act or process of depositing in the ground; burial. — *n* **inhum'er**. [L *inhumāre*, from *in* in, and *humus* the ground]

inia. See **inion**.

inimical *in-im'i-kl, adj* unfriendly; hostile; unfavourable; opposed. — *adv* **inim'ically**. — *n* **inim'icalness** or **inimical'ity**. — *adj* **inimicitious** (*-sish'əs*; *Sterne*) unfriendly. [L *inimīcālis*, from *inimīcus* enemy, from *in-* not, and *amīcus* friend]

inimitable *in-im'it-ə-bl, adj* that cannot be imitated; exceptionally good or remarkable. — *n* **inimitabil'ity** or **inim'itableness**. — *adv* **inim'itably**. [**in-** (2)]

inion *in'i-ən*, (*anatom*) *n* the external occipital protuberance: — *pl* **in'ia**. [Gr *īnion* the occiput]

iniquity *ī-nik'wi-ti, n* lack of fairness and justice; gross injustice; wickedness, sin; a crime; (with *cap*) one of the names of the Vice, the established buffoon of traditional medieval morality plays (*hist*). — *adj* **iniq'uitous** unjust; scandalously unreasonable; wicked, sinful. — *adv* **iniq'uitously**. — *n* **iniq'uitousness**. [Fr *iniquité*, from L *inīquitās, -ātis*, from *inīquus* unequal, from *in-* not, and *aequus* equal]

inisle. Same as **enisle**.

initial *in-ish'l, adj* beginning; of, at, or serving as the beginning; original. — *n* the letter beginning a word, *esp* a name. — *vt* to put the initials of one's name to, *esp* when acknowledging or agreeing to something: — *pr p* **init'ialling** or *NAm* **init'ialing**; *pa t* and *pa p* **init'ialled** or *NAm* **init'ialed**. — *n* **initializa'tion** or **-s-**. — *vt* **init'ialize** or **-ise** to assign initial values to variables, eg in a computer program; to return a device (eg a computer or a printer) to its initial state. — *adv* **init'ially**. — **initial cell** (*bot*) a cell that remains meristematic and gives rise to many daughter cells from which permanent tissues are formed; **Initial Teaching Alphabet** a 44-character alphabet in which each character corresponds to a single sound or phoneme of English, sometimes used in the teaching of reading. [L *initiālis*, from *initium* a beginning, from *inīre, initum*, from *in* into, and *īre, itum* to go]

initiate *in-ish'i-āt, vt* to begin, start; to introduce (to) (eg knowledge); to admit, *esp* with rites, (eg to a secret society, a mystery). — *vi* to perform the first act or rite. — *n* (*-it*) someone who is initiated. — *adj* initiated; belonging to someone newly initiated. — *n* **initiā'tion**. — *adj* **init'iative** (*-i-ə-tiv*) serving to initiate; introductory. — *n* the lead, first step, often considered as determining the conditions for oneself or others; the right or power of beginning; energy and resourcefulness enabling one to act without prompting from others; the right to originate legislation, or a constitutional method of doing so. — *n* **init'iātor** someone who or something which initiates; a substance that starts a chain reaction (*chem*). — *adj* **init'iatory** (*-i-ə-tə-ri*) tending or serving to initiate; introductory. — *n* an introductory rite. — **initiator codon** (*biochem*) the first codon of the coding region in messenger RNA and the point at which translation *usu* starts. [L *initiāre* to originate or initiate, from *initium* a beginning; see ety for **initial**]

inject *in-jekt'*, *vt* to force in; to inspire or instil; to fill or introduce into by injection. — *adj* **injec'table** able to be injected. — Also *n*. — *n* **injec'tion** (*-shən*) the act of injecting, introducing or forcing in, *esp* a liquid; something injected, *esp* a liquid injected into the body with a syringe or similar instrument; a magma injected into a rock (*geol*); the spraying of fuel into the cylinder of a compression-ignition engine by an injection pump (*autos*); an amount of money added to an economy in order to stimulate production, expansion, etc; a mapping function in which each element in a set corresponds to only one element in another set (*math*). — *n* **injec'tor** a person who injects; something used for injecting, *esp* an apparatus for forcing water into a boiler. — **injection moulding** the moulding of thermoplastics by squirting the material from a heated cylinder into a water-chilled mould; **injection string** (*min ext*) a pipe run in addition to the production string in the borehole to allow the passage of additives or of drilling mud to stop the well (also called **kill string**). [L *injicere, injectum*, from *in* into, and *jacere* to throw]

injelly *in-jel'i*, (*Tennyson*) *vt* to place as if in jelly. [**in-** (1)]

injera *in-jer'ə*, *n* a type of Ethiopian bread made from soured tef flour.

injoint *in-joint'*, (*Shakesp*) *vi* to join. [**in-** (1)]

injudicious *in-jōō-dish'əs, adj* not judicious; ill-judged, imprudent. — *adj* **injudic'ial** not according to legal forms. — *adv* **injudic'ially**. — *adv* **injudic'iously**. — *n* **injudic'iousness**. [**in-** (2)]

Injun *in'jən*, (*colloq*) *n* an American Indian. — Also *adj*. — **honest Injun** see under **honest**.

injunction *in-jungk'shən, n* the act of enjoining or commanding; an order, command; a precept; an exhortation; an inhibitory writ by which a superior court stops or prevents some inequitable or illegal act being carried out, called in Scotland an *interdict*; conjunction (*Milton*). — *vt* **injunct'** to prohibit, restrain by means of an injunction. — *adj* **injunc'tive**. — *adv* **injunc'tively**. [LL *injunctiō, -ōnis*, from *in* in, and *jungere, junctum* to join]

injure *in'jər, vt* to wrong; to harm; to damage; to hurt. — *n* **in'jurer**. — *adj* **injurious** (*in-jōō'ri-əs*) tending to injure; wrongful; hurtful; damaging to reputation. — *adv* **inju'riously**. — *n* **inju'riousness**. — *n* **injury** (*in'jər-i*) that which injures; wrong; physical damage, a wound; hurt; impairment; annoyance; insult, offence (*obs*). — **injury benefit** see **Industrial Injuries Disablement Benefit**; **injury time** (in ball games) extra time allowed for play to compensate for time lost as a result of injury stoppages during the game. [L *injūria* injury, from *in-* not, and *jūs, jūris* law]

injustice *in-jus'tis*, *n* the violation or withholding of another's rights or dues; the fact or an act of being unjust; wrong; iniquity. [**in-** (2)]

ink *ingk*, *n* a black or coloured liquid used in writing, printing, etc; a dark liquid ejected by cuttlefishes, etc. — *vt* to daub, cover, blacken or colour with ink. — *n* **ink'er** someone who inks; a pad or roller for inking type, etc. — *n* **ink'iness** — *adj* **ink'y** consisting of or resembling ink; very black; blackened with ink; drunk (*esp Austr slang*; also **inked**). — **ink'-bag** or **ink'-sac** a sac in some cuttlefishes, containing a black viscid fluid; **ink'berry** (the fruit of) any of various N American shrubs, *esp Ilex glabra* of the holly family and *Phytolacca americana*, pokeweed; **ink'-blot** (*psychol*) a standardized blot of ink used in the Rorschach test to test personality traits and disorders; **ink'-bottle** a bottle for holding ink; **ink'-cap** any mushroom of the genus *Coprinus*, such as the *shaggy ink-cap* (*C. comatus*); **ink'-eraser** an eraser of india-rubber treated with fine sand, used for rubbing out ink marks; **ink'-feed** the passage by which ink is fed to the nib of a fountain-pen; **ink'-fish** a cuttlefish or squid; **ink'holder** a container for ink; the reservoir of a fountain-pen; **ink'horn** formerly an ink-holder, made of horn; a portable case for ink, etc. — *adj* pedantic, bookish, obscure. — **ink'-horn-mate** (*Shakesp*; *contemptuous*) a bookish person, a scribbler; **ink'ing-roll'er** a roller covered with a substance for inking printing type; **ink'ing-ta'ble** a table or flat surface used for supplying the inking-roller with ink during the process of printing; **ink jet printer** a printer which produces characters on paper by squirting a fine jet of ink which is vibrated, electrically charged and deflected by electrostatic fields; **ink pencil** a copying-pencil, a pencil made from a substance whose marks when moistened look like ink and can be copied by a printing-press; **ink plant** a European shrub (*Coriaria myrtifolia*) or a related species native to New Zealand (*C. thymifolia*); **ink'pot** an ink-bottle, or pot for dipping a pen in; **ink'-slinger** or *US* **ink'-jerker** (*contemptuous slang*) a professional author or journalist; a scribbler; a controversialist; **ink'spot** a small ink stain. — *adj* **ink'-stained**. — **ink'stand** a stand or tray for ink bottles and (*usu*) pens; **ink'stone** a kind of stone containing sulphate of iron, used in making ink; **ink'well** a container for ink fitted into, or standing on, a desk, etc. — **China ink**, **Chinese ink** or **Indian ink**, (*US*) **India ink** (sometimes without *caps*) a mixture of lamp-black and size or glue, *usu* kept in solid form and rubbed down in water for use; a liquid suspension of the solid ink; **ink-blot test** see **Rorschach test**; **ink in** to fill in (eg a pencil drawing) in ink; to apply ink to (a printing roller); **invisible** or **sympathetic ink** a kind of ink that remains invisible on the paper until it is heated; **marking-ink** see under **mark**[1]; **printing-ink** see under **print**; **sling ink** (*contemptuous slang*) to write; to earn one's living by writing; to engage in controversy. [OFr *enque* (Fr *encre*), from LL *encaustum* the purple-red ink used by the later Roman emperors, from Gr *enkauston*, from *enkaiein* to burn in; see **encaustic**]

Inkatha *in-kä'tə*, *n* a S African Zulu cultural and political movement, *orig* a paramilitary organization, seeking liberation from white minority rule. [Zulu, a plaited grass coil used for carrying loads on the head]

inkle[1] *ingk'l*, (*obs*) *n* a kind of broad linen tape. — Also **inc'le**. [Poss Du *enkel* single]

inkle[2]. See **inkling**.

inkling *ingk'ling*, *n* a slight hint; an intimation; a faint notion or suspicion. — *vi* **ink'le** to have or give a hint of. [ME *inclen* to hint at; origin unknown]

in-kneed *in'-nēd'*, *adj* bent inward at the knees; knock-kneed. [**in-** (1)]

INLA *abbrev*: Irish National Liberation Army.

inlace. Same as **enlace**.

inlaid. See **inlay**.

inland *in'land* or *in'lənd*, *n* the interior part of a country; the populated part of a country, or part near the capital (*archaic*). — *adj* of the interior of a country, remote from the sea; operating or produced within a country; confined to a country; sophisticated, refined (*Shakesp*). — *adv* (also *in-land'*) landward; away from the sea; in an inland place. — *n* **in'lander** a person who lives inland. — **inland bill** a bill of exchange that is (designated as being) payable in the same country, state, etc as it is drawn (cf **foreign bill**); **inland navigation** the passage of boats or vessels on rivers, lakes, or canals within a country; **inland revenue** internal revenue, derived from direct taxes such as income tax and stamp duty; (with *caps*) the government department responsible for collecting such taxes. [OE *inland* a domain, from *in* and *land*]

in-law *in'-lö*, (*colloq*) *n* a relative by marriage, eg mother-in-law, brother-in-law: — *pl* **in'-laws**.

inlay *in'lā'* or *in-lā'*, *vt* to insert, embed; to insert a page of text, an illustration, etc into a space cut in a larger page; to ornament by laying in or inserting pieces of metal, ivory, etc; to insert (a substance or piece of tissue) to replace or correct a defect in tissue (*med*); to mix images electronically, using masks (*TV*): — *pr p* **inlaying**; *pa t* and *pa p* **inlaid**. — *n* (*in'*) inlaying; inlaid work; material inlaid. — *adj* **inlaid'** (or *in'lād*, or *in-lād'*) inserted by inlaying; decorated with inlay; consisting of inlay; having a pattern set into the surface. — *n* **inlayer** (*in'lā-ər* or *in-lā'ər*). — *n* **inlaying**. [**in-** (1)]

inlet *in'let* or *-lət*, *n* a small bay or opening in a coastline; a piece let in or inserted; an entrance; a passage by which anything is let in; a place of entry. [**in**[1] and **let**[1]]

inlier *in'lī-ər*, (*geol*) *n* an outcrop of older rock surrounded by younger. [**in**[1] and **lie**[2]]

in limine *in li'mi-nē* or *lē'mi-ne*, (*L*) on the threshold.

inlock *in-lok'*, *vt*. Same as **enlock**.

in loc. *abbrev*: *in loco* (*L*), in its place.

in loc. cit. *abbrev*: *in loco citato* (*L*), in the place cited.

in loco parentis *in lō'kō* (or *lok'ō*) *pə-* or *pä-ren'tis*, (*L*) in the place of a parent.

inly *in'li*, (*poetic*) *adv* inwardly; in the heart; thoroughly, entirely. [**in**[1]]

inlying *in'lī-ing*, *adj* situated inside or near a centre. [**in**[1] and **lying**]

in malam partem *in mā'ləm pär'təm* or *ma'lam pär'tem*, (*L*) in an unfavourable manner.

inmarriage *in'mar-ij*, *n* endogamy (qv under **endo-**). [**in-** (1)]

INMARSAT *abbrev*: International Maritime Satellite.

inmate *in'māt*, *n* a person who lodges in the same house with others (*obs*); a person confined in an institution, *esp* a prison. — *adj* (*obs*) dwelling in the same place. [**in**[1] or **inn** and **mate**[1]]

in medias res *in mē'di-əs rēz*, or *mā'di-* or *me'di-äs rās*, (*L*) into the midst of things.

in memoriam *in me-mö'ri-am*, *mō'*, (*L*) in memory of. [L, into memory]

inmesh. Same as **enmesh**.

inmost. See **innermost** under **inner**.

inn *in*, *n* a small hotel open to the public for food, drink and accommodation; a hotel; loosely, a public house; a dwelling-place, abode (*obs*; often in *pl*; *Spenser* **in**). — *vt* and *vi* (*archaic*) to lodge, put up. — **inn'keeper** a person in charge of an inn; **inn sign** a painted or otherwise decorated panel outside an inn, illustrating its name; **inn'yard** the courtyard round which an old-fashioned inn was built. — **Inns of Court** the buildings of four voluntary societies that have the exclusive right of calling to the English bar (Inner Temple, Middle Temple, Lincoln's Inn and Gray's Inn); hence, the societies themselves; the **Inns of Chancery** were the buildings of minor societies, residences of junior students of law. [OE *inn* an inn, house, from *in*, *inn* within (adv), from the prep *in* in]

innards *in'ərdz*, (*colloq*) *n pl* entrails; internal parts of a mechanism; interior. [**inwards**]

innate *in'āt* or *i-nāt'*, *adj* inborn; instinctive; inherent; (of an anther) attached by the base to the tip of the filament (*bot*). — *adv* **inn'ately** (or *-nāt'*). — *n* **inn'ateness** (or *-nāt'*). — *adj* **innā'tive** (*archaic*) native. [L *innātus*, from *in-* in, and *nāscī*, *nātus* to be born]

innavigable *in-nav'i-gə-bl*, *adj* unnavigable. — *adv* **innav'igably**. [**in-** (2)]

inner *in'ər*, *adj* (*compar* of **in**) farther in; interior. — *n* (*archery*) (a hit on) that part of a target next to the bull's-eye. — *adj* **inn'ermost** or **in'most** (*superl* of **in**) farthest in; most remote from the outside. — **inner bar** (*law*) Queen's or King's counsel as a whole; **inner city** the central part of a city, *esp* with regard to its special social problems, eg poor housing, poverty. — **inner dead-centre** the piston position, when the crank pin is nearest to the centre, at the beginning of the outstroke of a reciprocating engine or pump (also **top dead-centre**). — *adj* **inner-direc'ted** (*psychol*) guided by one's own principles, values, etc rather than by external influences. — **inner-direc'tion**; **inner ear** (*anatom*) the internal structure of the ear, encased in bone and filled with fluid, consisting of the cochlea, the semicircular canals and the vestibule; **inner light** (often with *caps*) a divine presence in the soul believed, *esp* by Quakers, to guide one and unite one with Christ; **inner man** or **inner woman** the soul; the mind; the stomach or appetite (*facetious*); **inner part** or **voice** (*music*) a voice part intermediate between the highest and the lowest; **inner space** the undersea region regarded as an environment; the unconscious human mind; **inner tube** the rubber tube inside a tyre, which is inflatable; **inn'erwear** underwear; **inner woman** see under **inner man** above. [OE *in*, compar *innera*, superl *innemest*]

innervate *in'ər-vāt* or *in-ûr'vāt*, *vt* to supply (an area or organ of the body) with nerves or nervous stimulus. — Also **innerve'**. — *n* **innervā'tion**. [**in-** (1)]

inning *in'ing*, *n* ingathering, *esp* of crops; (in *pl*; *US* sometimes in *sing*) a team's turn of batting in cricket, etc, or a turn of batting for both teams in baseball, etc; hence, the time during which a person or a party is in possession of anything, a spell or turn; (in *pl*) lands recovered from the sea. — **a good innings** (*colloq*) a long life. [**in**[1] or **inn**]

innocent *in'ə-sənt*, *adj* not hurtful; inoffensive; pure; harmless; guileless; simple-minded; ignorant of evil; imbecile (*dialect*); not legally guilty; not responsible or to blame; devoid (with *of*); not malignant or cancerous, benign (*med*). — *n* someone having no fault; someone having no knowledge of evil; a child; a foolish, simple-minded person; an idiot. — *n* **inn'ocence** harmlessness; blamelessness; guilelessness; simplicity; freedom from legal guilt. — *n* **inn'ocency** (*archaic*) the quality of being innocent. — *adv* **inn'ocently**. — **Innocents' Day** see **Childermas**. [OFr, from L *innocēns*, *-entis*, from *in-* not, and *nocēre* to hurt]

innocuous *in-ok'ū-əs*, *adj* harmless. — *adv* **innoc'uously**. — *n* **innocū'ity** or **innoc'uousness**. [L *innocuus*, from *in-* not, and *nocuus* hurtful, from *nocēre* to hurt]

innominate *i-nom'i-nāt* or *-nit*, *adj* having no name. — *adj* **innom'inable** unnamable. — *n* (in *pl*; *obs facetious*) trousers. — **innominate artery** the first large artery rising from the arch of the aorta, dividing at the lower neck to form the right common carotid and right subclavian arteries (also called **branchiocephalic artery**); **innominate bone** the hipbone, formed by fusion in the adult of the ilium, ischium, and pubis; **innominate vein** one of two large veins on either side of the lower part of the neck formed by the union of the external jugular and subclavian veins (also called **branchiocephalic vein**). [L *in-* not, and *nōmināre*, *-ātum* to name]

innovate *in'ō-vāt* or *in'ə-vāt*, *vt* to introduce as something new; to renew, alter (*rare*). — *vi* to introduce novelties; to make changes. — *n* **innovā'tion** the act of innovating; a thing introduced as a novelty; revolution (*Shakesp*); substitution of one obligation for another (*Scots law*); a season's new growth (*bot*). — *n* **innovā'tionist**. — *adj* **inn'ovative**. — *n* **inn'ovātor**. — *adj* **inn'ovatory**. [L *innovāre*, *-ātum*, from *in* in, and *novus* new]

innoxious *in-ok'shəs*, *adj* not noxious. — *adv* **innox'iously**. — *n* **innox'iousness**. [**in-** (2)]

innuendo *in-ū-en'dō*, *n* insinuation; an indirect reference or intimation; a part of a pleading in cases of libel and slander, pointing out what and who was meant (*law*): — *pl* **innuen'dos** or **innuen'does**. — *vt* to insinuate by innuendo; to interpret as innuendo. — *vi* to make insinuations. [L *innuendō* by nodding at (ie indicating, to wit, from its use in old legal documents to introduce a parenthetic indication), ablative gerund of *innuere* to nod to, indicate, from *in* to, and *nuere* to nod]

Innuit or **Inuit** *in'ū-it* or *in'o͞o-it*, *n* the Eskimo people, *esp* those of Greenland, Canada and Northern Alaska; a member of this people; their language. [Eskimo, people, *pl* of *inuk* a person]

innumerable *i-nū'mər-ə-bl* or *in-nū'*, *adj* too many to be numbered; countless. — *n* **innūmerabil'ity**. — *n* **innū'merableness**. — *adv* **innū'merably**. — *adj* **innū'merous** (*archaic*) without number; innumerable. [**in-** (2)]

innumerate *i-nū'mər-it* or *in-nū'*, *adj* having little or no knowledge or understanding of mathematics, *esp* calculating or arithmetic. — Also *n*. — *n* **innum'eracy**. [Coined 1959 by Sir Geoffrey Crowther (on analogy of *illiterate*), from L *numerus* number]

innutrition *in-nū-trish'ən* or *i-nū-*, *n* lack of nutrition; the failure to give proper nourishment. — *adj* **innū'trient** not nutrient. — *n* **innūtritious** (*-trish'əs*) not nutritious. [**in-** (2)]

ino- *ī-nō-*, *combining form* denoting fibrous tissue or muscle, as in *inotopic*. [Gr *is*, *inos* muscle, fibre]

inobedient *in-ō-bē'dyənt*, *adj* disobedient. — *n* **inobe'dience**. — *adv* **inobe'diently**. [**in-** (2)]

inobservant *in-əb-zûr'vənt*, *adj* unobservant; heedless. — *adj* **inobser'vable** incapable of being observed. — *n* **inobser'vance** lack of observance. — *n* **inobservā'tion** (*-ob-*). [**in-** (2)]

inobtrusive *in-əb-tro͞o'siv*, *adj* unobtrusive. — *adv* **inobtru'sively**. — *n* **inobtru'siveness**. [**in-** (2)]

inoccupation *in-ok-ū-pā'shən*, *n* lack of occupation. [**in-** (2)]

inoculate *in-ok'ū-lāt*, *vt* to introduce (eg bacteria, a virus) into an organism; to give a mild form of a disease to in this way, *esp* for the purpose of safeguarding against subsequent infection; to insert as a bud or graft; to graft; to imbue. — *vi* to practise inoculation. — *n* **inoculabil'ity**. — *adj* **inoc'ulable**. — *n* **inoculā'tion** the act or practice of inoculating; the communication of disease by the introduction of a germ or virus, *esp* that of a mild form of the disease to produce immunity; the analogous introduction of anything, eg nitrogen-fixing bacteria into soil or seed, or a crystal into a supersaturated solution to start crystallization; the insertion of the buds of one plant into another. — *adj* **inoc'ulative** (*-ə-tiv* or *-ā-tiv*). — *n* **inoc'ulātor**. — *adj* **inoc'ulatory**. — *n* **inoc'ulum** any material used for inoculating. [L *inoculāre*, *-ātum*, from *in* into, and *oculus* an eye, a bud]

inodorous *in-ō'dər-əs*, *adj* having no smell. — *adv* **ino'dorously**. — *n* **ino'dorousness**. [**in-** (2)]

inoffensive *in-ə-fen'siv*, *adj* giving no offence; harmless. — *adv* **inoffen'sively**. — *n* **inoffen'siveness**. [**in-** (2)]

inofficious *in-ə-fish'əs*, *adj* disobliging (*obs*); regardless of duty (*law*); inoperative. — *adv* **inoffi'ciously**. — *n* **inoffi'ciousness**. [**in-** (2)]

inoperable *in-op'ər-ə-bl*, *adj* that cannot be operated on successfully, or without undue risk (*med*); not workable. — *n* **inoperabil'ity** or **inop'erableness**. — *adv* **inop'erably**. — *adj* **inop'erative** not in action; producing no effect. — *n* **inop'erativeness**. [**in-** (2)]

inoperculate *in-o-pûr'kū-lāt*, (*esp zool*) *adj* without an operculum or lid. [**in-** (2)]

inopinate *in-op'in-āt*, (*obs*) *adj* not thought of; unexpected. [L *inopīnatus*]

inopportune *in-op'ər-tūn* or *-tūn'*, *adj* badly timed; inconvenient. — *adv* **inopp'ortūnely** (or *-tūn'*). — *n* **inopp'ortuneness** (or *-tūn'*) or **inopportun'ity**. [**in-** (2)]

inorb *in-örb'*, (*poetic*) *vt* to set in an orb; to encircle. [**in-** (1)]

inordinate *in-örd'i-nit* or *-örd'nit*, *adj* unrestrained; excessive; immoderate. — *n* **inor'dinacy** or **inor'dinateness**. — *adv* **inor'dinately**. — *n* **inordinā'tion** deviation from rule; irregularity. [L *inordinātus*, from *in-* not, and *ordināre*, *-ātum* to arrange, regulate]

inorganic *in-ör-gan'ik*, *adj* not organic, not of animal or vegetable origin; of or relating to compounds which do not contain carbon (*chem*); not belonging to an organism; of accidental origin, not normally developed. — *adv* **inorgan'ically**. — *n* **inorganizā'tion** or **-s-** lack of organization. — *adj* **inor'ganized** or **-ised** unorganized. — **inorganic chemistry** the chemistry of all substances except carbon compounds, generally admitting a few of these also (such as oxides of carbon and carbonates). [**in-** (2)]

inornate *in-ör-nāt'* or *-ör'nit*, *adj* not ornate; simple. [**in-** (2)]

inosculate *in-os'kū-lāt*, (*physiol*) *vt* and *vi* to join together by interconnecting ducts or openings, so as to allow a flow from one into the other, as a connection between blood vessels; to anastomose. — *n* **inosculā'tion**. [L *in* in, and *osculārī*, *-ātus* to kiss]

inositol *in-os'i-tol*, *n* a member of the vitamin B complex, occurring in practically all plant and animal tissues. [Gr *īs*, *īnos* a sinew, muscle, and suffixes *-ite* and *-ol*]

inotropic *in-ə-trop'ik* or *īn-*, (*med*) *adj* affecting or controlling muscular contraction, *esp* in the heart. [Gr *īs*, *īnos* tendon, and *tropos* a turn]

in pace *in pā'sē*, *pä'chā* or *pä-ke*, (*L*) in peace.

in partibus infidelium *in pär'ti-bəs in-fi-dē'li-əm* or *pär'ti-bōōs ēn-fi-dā'li-ōōm*, (*L*) in the lands of the unbelievers, a phrase applied to titular bishops in countries where no Catholic hierachy had been set up, or to those bearing the title of an extinct see.

in-patient. See under **in**[1].

inpayment *in'-pā'mənt*, *n* the payment of money into a bank account; the amount paid in. [**in**[1] and **payment**]

in pectore *in pek'to-rē* or *pek'to-re*, (*L*) in secret; undisclosed; in reserve; in petto.

in personam *in pər-sō'nam* or *per-*, (*L*; *law*) against a specific person, used of a proceeding, enforceable rights, etc (see also **in rem**).

in petto *ēn* or *in pet'tō*, (*Ital*) within the breast; in one's own mind but not yet divulged; in secret; in reserve.

inphase *in-fāz'*, *adj* in the same phase. [**in**[1] and **phase**[1]]

in pleno *in plē'nō* or *plā'nō*, (*L*) in full.

in posse *in pos'i*, (*L*) potentially; in possibility (see also **in esse** under **esse**).

inpouring *in'pör-ing*, *-pör'* or *-pōr-*, *n* a pouring in; addition. [**in**[1] and **pouring**]

in principio *in prin-sip'i-ō* or *-kip'*, (*L*) in the beginning.

in propria persona *in prō-pri-ə pûr-sō'nə* or *pro'pri-ä per-sō'nä*, (*LL*) in person; personally.

in puris naturalibus *in pū'ris na-tūr-āl'i-bəs* or *pōō'rēs* (*LL*) stark naked.

input *in'pōōt*, *n* amount, material or energy, that is put in; power, or energy, or coded information, stored or for storage; information available in a computer for dealing with a problem; the process of feeding in data; contribution (*Scot*). — *adj* relating to computer input. — *vt* to feed (data, etc) into eg a computer: — *pr p* **inputt'ing**; *pa t* and *pa p* **input'**. — *n* **inputt'er**. — **input area** or **block** (*comput*) an area of memory reserved for data input from a backing store or peripheral; **input device** (*comput*) a piece of equipment used to transfer data into memory, eg a keyboard, light pen, etc; **input-output analysis** (*econ*) a method of studying an economy as a whole by analysing the relationship between the input and output of each industry; **input program** or **routine** (*comput*) part of a program that controls transfer of data to an input area. [**in**[1] and **put**[1]]

inqilab *in'ki-läb*, *n* (in India, Pakistan, etc) revolution. [Urdu]

inquere *in-kwēr'*, (*Spenser*) *vi* and *vt* to inquire. [**inquire**]

in querpo. See **en cuerpo**.

inquest *in'kwest*, formerly *in-kwest'*, *n* a judicial inquiry before a jury into any matter, *esp* any case of violent or sudden death; the body of people appointed to hold such an inquiry; an inquiry or investigation. [OFr *enqueste*, from LL *inquesta*, from L *inquīsīta* (*rēs*), from *inquīrere* to inquire]

inquietude *in-kwī'i-tūd*, *n* uneasiness; disturbance. — *adj* **inquī'et** (*archaic*) unquiet, disturbed. — *vt* (*rare*) to disturb. — *adv* **inquī'etly**. [**in-** (2)]

inquiline *in'kwi-līn*, *adj* living in the home of or in close association with another. — *n* an animal living in this way. — *adj* and *n* **inquilin'ic**. — *n* **in'quilinism** or **inquilin'ity**. — *adj* **inquilī'nous**. [L *inquilīnus* tenant, lodger, from *incola* inhabitant, from *in* in, and *colere* to inhabit]

inquinate *in'kwin-āt*, *vt* to defile or corrupt. — *n* **inquinā'tion**. [L *inquināre*, *-ātum* to defile]

inquire or **enquire** *in-kwīr'*, *vi* to ask a question; to make an investigation. — *vt* to ask; to seek (*obs*); to make an examination regarding (*obs*); to call (*archaic*). — *n* (*archaic*) inquiry. — *n* **inquirā'tion** (*Dickens*) or **enquirā'tion** (*dialect*) inquiry. — *n* **inquir'er** or **enquir'er**. — *adj* **inquir'ing** tending to inquire; eager to acquire information; (of eg a look) expressing inquiry. — *adv* **inquir'ingly**. — *n* **inquir'y** or **enquir'y** (or *ing'kwi-ri*, esp *US*) the act of inquiring; a search for knowledge; (an) investigation; a question. — **inquire after** to ask about the health, etc of; **writ of inquiry** a writ appointing an inquest. [OFr *enquerre* (Fr *enquérir*), from L *inquīrere*, from *in* in, and *quaerere*, *quaesītum* to seek]

inquirendo *in-kwī-ren'dō*, (*law*) *n* authority to inquire into something, eg for the benefit of the Crown: — *pl* **inquiren'dos**. [L, by inquiring]

inquisition *in-kwi-zish'ən*, *n* a searching examination; an investigation; a judicial inquiry; a Roman Catholic tribunal established from 1232 to 1820 to preserve the supremacy of Catholicism in Europe by suppressing heresy, notably in Spain (the **Spanish Inquisition**) where the torture and execution of disbelievers was not uncommon. — *adj* **inquisit'ional** searching, often unduly vexatiously, in inquiring; relating to inquisition or the Inquisition. — *adj* **inquisitive** (*-kwiz'i-tiv*) eager to know; apt to ask questions, *esp* about other people's affairs; curious. — *adv* **inquis'itively**. — *n* **inquis'itiveness**. — *n* **inquis'itor** someone who inquires, *esp* with undue pertinacity or searchingness; an official inquirer; a member of the Inquisition tribunal. — *adj* **inquisitō'rial** (or *-tör'*) pertaining to an inquisitor or inquisition; unduly pertinacious in interrogation; used of criminal proceedings in which the prosecutor is also judge, or in which the trial is held in secret (*law*). — *adv* **inquisito'rially**. — *n* **inquisito'rialness**. — *n* **inquis'itress** (*archaic*) a female inquisitor. — *adj* **inquisitū'rient** (*Milton*) eager to act as inquisitor. — **Grand Inquisitor** the head of a court of Inquisition. [L *inquīsītiō*, *-ōnis*; see ety for **inquire**]

inquorate *in-kwör'it*, *adj* not making up a quorum. [**in-** (2) and **quorum**]

in re *in rē* or *rā*, (*L*) in the matter (of); concerning.

in rem *in rem*, (*L*; *law*) against a thing or property, used of a proceeding, an enforceable right, etc against all persons or against property, such as the arrest of a ship in the enforcement of a maritime lien (see also **in personam**).

INRI *abbrev*: *Jesus Nazarenus Rex Judaeorum* (*L*), Jesus of Nazareth, King of the Jews.

in rerum natura *in rē'rəm nə-tū'rə* or *rā'rōōm na-tōō'rä*, (*L*) in the nature of things.

in rixa *in rik'sə*, (*L*; *law*) in a quarrel; (said) in the heat of the moment, used as a defence in cases of defamation.

inro *in'rō*, *n* a small Japanese container for pills and medicines, once part of traditional Japanese dress: — *pl* **in'rō**. [Jap, seal-box]

inroad *in'rōd*, *n* an incursion into an enemy's country; a raid; encroachment. — **make inroads into** to make progress with; to use up large quantities of. [**in**[1] and **road** in sense of riding; cf **raid**]

inrush *in'rush*, *n* an inward rush. — *n* and *adj* **in'rushing**. [**in**[1] and **rush**[1]]

INS *abbrev*: Immigration and Naturalization Service (*US*); inertial navigation system; International News Service.

ins. *abbrev*: insurance.

in saecula saeculorum *in sek'yŏŏ-lə sek-yŏŏ-lōr'əm* or *-lör'əm*, or *sī'kŏŏ-lä sī'kŏŏ-lō'rŏŏm*, (*L*) for ever and ever.

insalivate *in-sal'i-vāt*, *vt* to mix with saliva. — *n* **insalivā'tion**. [**in-** (1)]

insalubrious *in-sə-lōō'bri-əs* or *-lū'*, *adj* not salubrious; unhealthy. — *adv* **insalu'briously**. — *n* **insalu'brity**. [**in-** (2)]

insalutary *in-sal'ū-tər-i*, *adj* unwholesome. [**in-** (2)]

insane *in-sān'*, *adj* not sane or of sound mind; crazy; mad; utterly unwise; senseless; causing insanity (*Shakesp* **insane root** probably a root mentioned by Plutarch, *Life of Antony*, *perh* hemlock, henbane or belladonna). — *adv* **insane'ly**. — *n* **insane'ness** insanity; madness. — *n* **insan'ie** (*Shakesp*; an emendation of the reading *infamie*) insanity. — *n* **insanity** (*in-san'i-ti*) lack of sanity; a degree of mental illness causing one to act against the social or legal demands of society or in which one is held to be not responsible for one's actions under law; madness. [L *īnsānus*]

insanitary *in-san'i-tər-i*, *adj* not sanitary; dirty and unhealthy. — *n* **insan'itariness**. — *n* **insanitā'tion**. [**in-** (2)]

insatiable *in-sā'shə-bl* or *-shi-ə-bl*, *adj* not capable of being satiated or satisfied. — *n* **insātiabil'ity** or **insa'tiableness**. — *adv* **insā'tiably**. — *adj* **insā'tiate** not sated; insatiable. — *adv* **insā'tiately**. — *n* **insā'tiateness**. — *n* **insatiety** (*in-sə-tī'i-ti*) the state of not being, or of being incapable of being, sated. [**in-** (2)]

inscape *in'skāp*, *n* (in poetry, literature, etc) the essential inner nature or distinctive form of a person, object, etc. — See also **instress**. [Coined by Gerard Manley Hopkins, from **in**[1] and **scape**[4]]

inscient[1] *in'shənt* or *-shi-ənt*, (*archaic*) *adj* having little or no knowledge, ignorant. — *n* **in'science**. [L *īnsciēns*, *-entis*, from *in-* not, and *scīre* to know]

inscient[2] *in'shənt* or *-shi-ənt*, (*archaic*) *adj* having insight or inward knowledge. [L *in* in, and *sciēns*, *-entis*, pr p of *scīre* to know]

insconce (*Shakesp*). Same as **ensconce**.

inscribe *in-skrīb'*, *vt* to engrave or mark in some other way; to engrave or mark on; to enter in a book or roll; to dedicate; to describe within another figure so as either to touch all sides or faces of the bounding figure or to have all angular points on it (*geom*); to rewrite (data on a document) in a form which may be read by a character recognition device (*comput*). — *adj* **inscrīb'able**. — *n* **inscrīb'er**. — *n* **inscription** (*in-skrip'shən*) the act of inscribing; that which is inscribed; a dedication; a record inscribed on stone, metal, clay, etc. — *adj* **inscrip'tional** or **inscrip'tive**. — *adv* **inscrip'tively**. [L *īnscrībere*, *īnscrīptum*, from *in* upon, and *scrībere* to write]

inscroll *in-skrōl'*, (*Shakesp*) *vt* to write on a scroll.

inscrutable *in-skrōōt'ə-bl*, *adj* that cannot be scrutinized or searched into and understood; mysterious, enigmatic, inexplicable. — *n* **inscrutabil'ity** or **inscrut'ableness**. — *adv* **inscrut'ably**. [L *īnscrūtābilis*, from *in-* not, and *scrūtārī* to search into]

insculp *in-skulp'*, *vt* to engrave, to cut or carve upon something (*Shakesp*); to carve; to form by carving (*archaic*). — *adj* **insculpt'** engraved (*Shakesp*); having depressions in the surface (*bot*). — *n* **insculp'ture** anything engraved (*Shakesp*); an inscription (*archaic*). — *vt* (*archaic*) to carve on something. [L *īnsculpere*, from *in* in, and *sculpere* to carve]

in se *in sā*, (*L*) in itself.

inseam[1] *in'sēm*, *n* an inner seam in a shoe or garment.

inseam[2]. Same as **enseam**[3].

insect *in'sekt*, *n* a word loosely used for a small invertebrate creature, *esp* one with a body divided into sections; a member of the Insecta (*zool*); a small, wretched, insignificant person (*fig*). — *adj* of insects; like an insect; small, insignificant. — *n pl* **Insec'ta** a subphylum of arthropods having a distinct head, thorax and abdomen, with three pairs of legs attached to the thorax, usually winged in adult life, breathing air by means of tracheae, and commonly having a metamorphosis in the life-history. — *n* **insectār'ium** or **in'sectary** a vivarium for insects. — *n* **insec'ticide** (*-i-sīd*) a substance that kills insects. — *adj* **insec'tiform**. — *n* **insec'tifuge** a substance that drives away insects. — *adj* **insec'tile**. — *n pl* **Insectiv'ora** an order of mammals, mostly terrestrial, insect-eating, nocturnal in habit, and small in size, including shrews, moles, hedgehogs, etc. — *n* **insect'ivore** a member of the Insectivora. — *adj* **insectiv'orous** feeding on insects; of or relating to the Insectivora. — *n* **insectol'ogist**. — *n* **insectol'ogy** the study of insects. — **insect net** a light hand-held net for catching insects; **insect powder** powder for stupefying and killing insects; an insecticide or insectifuge; **insect repellant** a substance which keeps off (*esp* biting) insects. [L *īnsectum*, pa p of *īnsecāre*, from *in* into, and *secāre* to cut]

insection *in-sek'shən*, *n* an incision; a notch; divison into segments. [L *insecare*]

insecure *in-si-kūr'*, *adj* apprehensive of danger or loss; anxious because not well-adjusted to life; exposed to danger or loss; unsafe; uncertain; not fixed or firm. — *adv* **insecure'ly**. — *n* **insecur'ity**. [**in-** (2)]

inseem (*Shakesp*). Same as **enseam**[2].

inselberg *in'zəl-bûrg* or *in'səl-berg*, (*geol*) *n* a steep-sided round-topped mount, *usu* of granite or gneiss, rising above the general level of plain eroded bedrock, often found in the semi-arid regions of tropical countries: — *pl* **in'selberge** (*-gə*). [Ger, island mountain]

inseminate *in-sem'in-āt*, *vt* to sow; to implant; to introduce (ideas, philosophies, attitudes, etc) into people's minds; to impregnate (a female) *esp* artificially. — *n* **inseminā'tion**. — *n* **insem'inator**. [L *īnsēmināre*, from *in* in, and *sēmen*, *-inis* seed]

insensate *in-sen'sāt* or *-it*, *adj* without sensation, inanimate; having little or no sensibility or moral feeling; having little or no good sense. — *adv* **insen'sately**. — *n* **insen'sateness**. [L *īnsēnsātus*, from *in-* not, and *sēnsātus* intelligent, from *sēnsus* feeling]

insensible *in-sen'si-bl*, *adj* not having feeling; not capable of emotion; callous; dull; unconscious; not capable of being sensed. — *n* **insensibil'ity** or **insen'sibleness**. — *adv* **insen'sibly**. [**in-** (2)]

insensitive *in-sen'si-tiv*, *adj* not sensitive; unfeeling, inconsiderate, crass. — *adv* **insen'sitively**. — *n* **insen'sitiveness** or **insensitiv'ity**. [**in-** (2)]

insensuous *in-sen'sū-əs* or *-shŏŏ-əs*, *adj* not sensuous. [**in-** (2)]

insentient *in-sen'shənt* or *-shi-ənt*, *adj* not having perception; incapable of sensation. — *n* **insen'tience** or **insen'tiency**. [**in-** (2)]

inseparable *in-sep'ər-ə-bl*, *adj* incapable of being separated; (of eg friends or siblings) unwilling to be separated; (of a prefix) not existing as a separate word (*gram*). — *n* (*usu* used in *pl*) an inseparable companion. — *n* **insep'arableness** or **inseparabil'ity**. — *adv* **insep'arably**. — *adj* **insep'arate** (*archaic*) not separate or separable. [**in-** (2)]

insert *in-sûrt'*, *vt* to put in; to introduce (into). — *n* **in'sert** something inserted; a loose sheet placed within the folds of a newspaper or periodical, as a supplement or containing advertising material. — *adj* **insert'able**. — *adj* **insert'ed** (*bot*) attached to or growing out of another member. — *n* **insert'er**. — *n* **insertion** (*in-sûr'shən*) the act of inserting; something inserted; the mode or condition of being inserted; the part of a muscle by which it is attached to the part to be moved, eg the point or place of attachment to a bone (*anatom*); a piece of embroidery, lace, etc inserted in a dress, etc; the putting of a man-made craft or satellite into orbit (also **injection**). — *adj* **inser'tional**. [L *īnserere*, *īnsertum*, from *in* in, and *serere* to join]

in-service. See under **in**[1].

insessorial *in-ses-ōr'i-əl, adj* (of eg birds' claws) adapted for perching; (of a bird) having claws of this type. [L *īnsessor*, pl *-ōrēs*, besetter (of the roads), highwayman, adopted with the meaning percher, from *īnsidēre*, from *in* on, and *sedēre* to sit]

inset *in'set, n* something set in, an insertion or insert, *esp* a loose sheet inserted between the pages of a magazine, book, etc; a small map or figure inserted in a spare corner of another; a piece let in to a garment, etc; the setting in of a current. — *vt* **inset'** to set in, to infix or implant: — *pa t* and *pa p* **inset'**. [**in** and **set**]

inseverable *in-sev'ər-ə-bl, adj* that cannot be severed or separated. [**in-** (2)]

inshallah *in-shä'lä, interj* (among Muslims) if Allah wills, equivalent to 'God willing'. [Ar *in shā'llāh*]

insheathe. See **ensheathe**.

inshell *in-shel'*, (*Shakesp*) *vt* to draw in or withdraw, as into a shell. [**in-** (1)]

inshelter *in-shel'tər, vt* to place in shelter. [**in-** (1)]

inship *in-ship'*, (*Shakesp*) *vt* to ship, to embark. [**in-** (1)]

inshore *in'shōr'* or *-shör', adv* and *adj* near or towards the shore from the water. — *adj* (*in'shōr* or *-shör*) situated, carried on, or operating on the water close to the shore, as fishing-grounds, fishing, or fishermen.

inshrine *in-shrīn'*. Same as **enshrine**.

inside *in'sīd'* or *in'sīd, n* the side, space or part within; (often in *pl*) the entrails; inner nature; that which is not visible at first sight; (in *pl*) the inner quires of a ream of paper. — *adj* being within; interior; indoor; working indoors; from within; from a secret or confidential source; (of a criminal 'job') carried out by, or with the help of, someone trusted and/or employed by the victim (*colloq*). — *adv* in, to or near the interior; indoors; on the inner side; in or into prison (*colloq*). — *prep* within; into; on the inner side of. — *n* **insi'der** a person who is inside; someone within a certain organization, etc; someone possessing some particular advantage. — **in'side-car** an Irish horse-drawn buggy in which the passengers face one another; **inside centre** in some games, *esp* rugby, (a player in) the central position nearer the stand-off half; **inside edge** see under **edge**; **inside left** or **inside right** in some games, a forward between the centre and outside; **insider dealing** or **trading** the criminal offence of using information not publicly available to deal on the Stock Exchange; **inside track** the inner side of a race-track, being the most advantageous position (*also fig*). — **inside of** (*esp US*) in less than, within; **inside out** with the inner side turned outwards; **know (something) inside out** (*colloq*) to know (something) thoroughly. [**in**[1] and **side**[1]]

insidious *in-sid'i-əs, adj* deceptively attractive; developing or advancing gradually and imperceptibly; cunning and treacherous. — *adv* **insid'iously**. — *n* **insid'iousness**. [L *īnsidiōsus*, from *īnsidiae* an ambush, from *īnsidēre*, from *in* in, and *sedēre* to sit]

insight[1] *in'sīt, n* the power of discerning and understanding things; imaginative penetration; practical knowledge; enlightenment; a view into anything; awareness, often of one's own mental condition (*psychol*); the apprehension of the principle of a task, puzzle, etc (*psychol*). — *adj* **insight'ful**. — **insight learning** direct learning without the process of trial and error. [**in**[1] and **sight**[1]]

insight[2] *in'sīt* or *in'sihht*, (*Scot*) *n* household goods, furniture. — Also *adj*. [Origin unknown]

insignia *in-sig'ni-ə, n pl* (in US treated as *sing*) signs or badges of office, honour, membership, occupation, etc; marks by which anything is known. — Also rarely **insigne** (*in-sig'ni*). [L, neuter pl of *īnsignis*, from *in* in, and *signum* a mark]

insignificant *in-sig-nif'i-kənt, adj* having no meaning; having no effect; unimportant; small in size, amount, etc; petty. — *n* **insignif'icance** or **insignif'icancy**. — *adv* **insignif'icantly**. — *adj* **insignif'icative** not significative or expressing by external signs. [**in-** (2)]

insincere *in-sin-sēr', adj* not sincere, hypocritical. — *adv* **insincere'ly**. — *n* **insincerity** (*-ser'i-ti*). [**in-** (2)]

insinew *in-sin'ū, vi* (*Shakesp*) to be joined as with sinews. [**in-** (1)]

insinuate *in-sin'ū-āt, vt* to hint or indirectly suggest (*usu* something unpleasant); to introduce or insert gently or artfully (with *into*); (with *into*) to work (*esp* oneself) into (someone's favour). — *adj* **insin'uating**. — *adv* **insin'uatingly**. — *n* **insinuā'tion**. — *adj* **insin'uative** insinuating; using insinuation. — *n* **insin'uator**. — *adj* **insin'uatory** (*-ə-tər-i*). [L *īnsinuāre, -ātum*, from *in* in, and *sinus* a curve]

insipid *in-sip'id, adj* without a satisfying or definite flavour, tasteless; lacking spirit or interest; dull. — *adv* **insip'idly**. — *n* **insip'idness** or **insipid'ity**. [LL *īnsipidus*, from L *in-* not, and *sapidus* well-tasted, from *sapere* to taste]

insipience *in-sip'i-əns*, (*archaic*) *n* lack of wisdom. — *adj* **insip'ient**. — *adv* **insip'iently**. [L *īnsipientia*, from *in-* not, and *sapiēns* wise]

insist *in-sist', vi* (often with *on*) to maintain very firmly; to persist in demanding; to take no refusal. — *vt* to maintain persistently. — *n* **insist'ence** or **insist'ency**. — *adj* **insist'ent** urgent; compelling attention; insisting; (of a bird's hind-toe) touching the ground with the tip only. — *adv* **insist'ently**. [L *īnsistere*, from *in* upon, and *sistere* to stand]

in situ *in sī'tū* or *si'too*, (*L*) in the original, intended or designated position; in position; (of a cancer) not having undergone metastasis to invade surrounding tissue (*med*). — **in-situ hybridization** (*biol*) a technique, using a radioactive nucleic acid probe and autoradiography, for locating the position of a specific DNA sequence on a chromosome.

insnare. Same as **ensnare**.

insobriety *in-sō-brī'ə-ti, n* lack of sobriety, drunkenness. [**in-** (2)]

insociable *in-sō'shə-bl, adj* unsociable; incompatible (*obs*). — *n* **insociabil'ity**. [**in-** (2)]

insofar. See under **in**[1].

insolate *in'sō-lāt* or *in-sō'lāt, vt* to expose to the sun's rays; to treat by exposure to the sun's rays. — *n* **insolā'tion** exposure to the sun's rays; solar radiation falling upon a given surface. [L *īnsōlāre, -ātum*, from *in* in, and *sōl* the sun]

insole *in'sōl, n* the inner sole of a boot or shoe; a sole of some material placed inside a shoe for warmth, dryness or comfort. [**in**[1] and **sole**[1]]

insolent *in'səl-ənt, adj* disrespectful and rude; impudent. — *n* **in'solence**. — *adv* **in'solently**. [L *īnsolēns, -entis*, from *in-* not, and *solēns*, pa p of *solēre* to be wont]

insolidity *in-so-lid'i-ti, n* lack of solidity. [**in-** (2)]

insoluble *in-sol'ū-bl, adj* not capable of being dissolved; not capable of being solved or explained. — *n* **insolubil'ity** or **insol'ubleness**. — *vt* **insol'ubilize** or **-ise** to make insoluble. — *adv* **insol'ubly**. [**in-** (2)]

insolvable *in-solv'ə-bl, adj* not solvable. — *n* **insolvabil'ity**. — *adv* **insol'vably**. [**in-** (2)]

insolvent *in-solv'ənt, adj* not able to pay one's debts; bankrupt; concerning insolvent people. — *n* a person unable to pay his or her debts. — *n* **insolv'ency** bankruptcy. [**in-** (2)]

insomnia *in-som'ni-ə, n* sleeplessness; prolonged inability to sleep. — *n* **insom'niac** a person who suffers from insomnia. — *adj* suffering from, causing, or caused by, insomnia. — *adj* **insom'nious**. — *n* **insom'nolence**. [L *īnsomnis* sleepless]

insomuch *in-sō-much', adv* to such a degree (with *as* or *that*); inasmuch (with *as*); so.

insooth *in-sooth'*, (*archaic*) *adv* in sooth, indeed. [**in** and **sooth**]

insouciant *in-soo'si-ənt* or *ɛ̃-soo-sē-ã, adj* indifferent, unconcerned, nonchalant; heedless; apathetic. — *n* **insouciance** (*in-soo'si-əns* or *ɛ̃-soo-sē-ãs*). — *adv* **insouciantly** (*in-soo'si-ənt-li* or *ɛ̃-soo-sē-ãt'li*). [Fr, from *in-* not, and *souciant*, pr p of *soucier*, from L *sollicitāre* to disturb]

insoul. See **ensoul**.

inspan *in-span'* or *in'span*, (*esp SAfr*) *vt* to yoke to a vehicle; to bring or force into service. — *vi* to prepare to depart: — *pr p* **inspann'ing**; *pa t* and *pa p* **inspanned'**. [Du *inspannen* to yoke, from *in* in, and *spannen* to tie]

inspect *in-spekt'*, *vt* to look into; to examine; to look at closely, officially or ceremonially. — *n* **in'spect** (*obs*) inspection. — *adv* **inspect'ingly**. — *n* **inspec'tion** the act of inspecting or looking into; careful or official examination. — *adj* **inspec'tional**. — *adj* **inspec'tive**. — *n* **inspec'tor** a person who inspects; an examining officer; a police officer ranking below a superintendent; an officer in any of several charities or humane societies. — *n* **inspec'torate** a district for which an inspector is responsible; the office of inspector; a body of inspectors. — *adj* **inspectō'rial**. — *n* **inspec'torship** the office of inspector. — **inspector general** the head of an inspectorate; a military officer who conducts investigations. [L *īnspectāre*, frequentative of *īnspicere*, *īnspectum*, from *in* into, and *specere* to look]

insphere and **insphear'd**. See **ensphere**.

inspire *in-spīr'*, *vt* to breathe in or blow in (air, etc); to draw or inhale into the lungs; to infuse into (the mind), *esp* with an encouraging or exalting influence; (of divine influence, etc) to instruct or guide; to instruct or affect with a particular emotion; to bring about, cause to occur; to animate. — *vi* to draw in the breath. — *adj* **inspīr'able** able to be inhaled. — *n* **inspirā'tion** (*in-spər-*, *-spir-* or *-spīr-*) the act of inspiring or breathing in; a breath; instruction, dictation, or stimulation by a divinity, a genius, an idea or a passion; an inspired condition; an object or person that inspires; an inspired thought or idea. — *adj* **inspirā'tional**. — *adv* **inspirā'tionally**. — *n* **inspirā'tionism**. — *n* **inspirā'tionist** a person who maintains that the writers of the Scriptures were directly and divinely inspired. — *adj* **inspirative** (*in-spīr'ə-tiv* or *in'spir-ā-tiv*) tending to inspire. — *n* **inspirator** (*in'spir-ā-tər*) an inspirer; an apparatus for injecting or drawing in vapour, liquid, etc. — *adj* **inspiratory** (*in-spir'ə-tər-i*, *in-spīr'*, or *in'spir-*) belonging to or aiding inspiration or inhalation. — *adj* **inspīred'** actuated or directed by divine influence; influenced by elevated feeling; prompted by superior, but not openly declared, knowledge or authority; actually authoritative; (of a guess, etc) unexpectedly accurate. — *n* **inspīr'er**. — *adv* **inspīr'ingly**. [L *īnspīrāre*, from *in* in, into, and *spīrāre* to breathe]

inspirit *in-spir'it*, *vt* to infuse spirit into, encourage. — *adj* **inspir'iting**. — *adv* **inspir'itingly**. [**in-** (1)]

inspissate *in-spis'āt*, *vt* to thicken, condense. — *adj* **inspiss'ate** or **inspiss'ated** thickened or hardened by absorption or evaporation. — *n* **inspissā'tion**. — *n* **in'spissātor**. [L *in* in, and *spissāre*, from *spissus* thick]

Inst. *abbrev*: Institute; Institution.

inst. *abbrev*: instant, ie the present month (used in formal correspondence).

instability *in-stə-bil'i-ti*, *n* lack of stability, physical or mental. — *adj* **instā'ble** unstable. [**in-** (2)]

install (also **instal**) *in-stöl'*, *vt* to set up and put in use; to place in an office or order; to place in a certain position; to invest with any charge or office with the customary ceremonies: — *pr p* **install'ing**; *pa t* and *pa p* **installed'**. — *n* **install'ant** someone who installs another in an office, etc. — *n* **installā'tion** the act of installing; the act of fitting something in position for use; apparatus placed in position for use; the complete apparatus for electric lighting, or the like; a military base, etc. — *n* **install'ment** instalment (*US*); a knight's stall (*Shakesp*); installation (*archaic*). [LL *īnstallāre*, from *in* in, and *stallum* a stall, from OHGer *stal* (Ger *Stall*, Eng **stall**[1])]

instalment or *US* **installment** *in-stöl'mənt*, *n* one of a series of partial payments; a portion (eg of a serial story) supplied or completed at one time. [Anglo-Fr *estaler* to fix, set; prob influenced by **install**]

instance *in'stəns*, *n* an example; an occurrence; an occasion; solicitation, urging; process, suit (*law*); the quality of being urgent (*archaic*); motive, cause (*archaic*); evidence, proof (*Shakesp*). — *vt* to mention as an example. — *n* **in'stancy** insistency; urgency; imminence. — *adj* **in'stant** immediate; instantaneous; without delay; present, current; of the current month (used in formal correspondence); (*esp* of food or drink) pre-prepared so that little has to be done to it before use; urgent (*archaic*). — *n* the present moment of time; a very brief period of time, a moment; a particular moment or point of time; the present month (used in formal correspondence). — *n* **instantaneity** (*in-stant-ə-nē'i-ti*). — *adj* **instantaneous** (*in-stənt-ā'ni-əs*) done in an instant; momentary; occurring or acting at once or very quickly; for the instant; at a particular instant. — *adv* **instantān'eously**. — *n* **instantān'eousness**. — *adj* **instantial** (*in-stan'shl*; *rare*). — *vt* **instan'tiate** to be or provide an example of. — *n* **instantiā'tion**. — *adv* **in'stantly** at once; at this very time (*Shakesp*); importunately, zealously (*Bible*). — **instant photography** a system which rapidly produces, sometimes by processing within the camera itself, a positive picture from the original exposed material. — **at the instance of** at the urging or request of; **court of first instance** a lower court in which a legal case is first heard, from which it may be referred to a higher court; **for instance** as an example; **in the first instance** firstly, originally; **on the instant** immediately; **this instant** immediately. [L *īnstāns*, *īnstantis*, pr p of *īnstāre* to be near, press upon, urge, from *in* upon, and *stāre* to stand]

instar[1] *in-stär'*, (*poetic*; *archaic*) *vt* to adorn with stars; to place as a star. [**in-** (1)]

instar[2] *in'stär*, *n* the form of an insect between moult and moult. [L *īnstar* image]

instar omnium *in'* or *ēn'stär om'ni-əm* or *-ŏŏm*, (*L*) worth all of them, as Cicero described Plato in relation to all other men.

instate *in-stāt'*, *vt* to put in possession; to install. — *n* **instate'ment**. [**in-** (1) and **state**]

in statu pupillari *in stāt'ū pū-pi-lā'rī* or *stat'ŏŏ pŏŏ-pi-lä'rē*, (*LL*) in a state of wardship; as a pupil.

in statu quo *in stāt'ū* or *stat'ŏŏ kwō*, (*L*) in the same state as formerly; in the same state as at present, unchanged.

instauration *in-stör-ā'shən*, (*rare*) *n* restoration; renewal. — *n* **in'staurātor**. [L *īnstaurātiō*, *-ōnis*]

instead *in-sted'*, *adv* in the stead, place or room (of); as an alternative or substitute. [**in**[1] and **stead**]

instep *in'step*, *n* the prominent arched part of the human foot, between the ankle and the toes; the corresponding part of a shoe, stocking, etc; (in horses) the hindleg from the ham to the pastern joint. [Origin obscure]

instigate *in'sti-gāt*, *vt* to urge on, incite; to initiate, bring about. — *adv* **in'stigātingly**. — *n* **instigā'tion** the act of inciting, *esp* to do wrong or cause trouble. — *adj* **in'stigātive**. — *n* **in'stigātor** an inciter, generally in a bad sense. [L *īnstīgāre*, *-ātum*]

instil *in-stil'*, *vt* to drop in; to infuse slowly into the mind: — *pr p* **instill'ing**; *pa t* and *pa p* **instilled'**. — Also **instill'**. — *n* **instillā'tion** or **instil'ment** the act of instilling or pouring in by drops; the act of infusing slowly into the mind; the application of medication drop by drop; that which is instilled or infused; a medication applied drop by drop. [L *īnstillāre*, from *in* in, and *stillāre* to drop]

instinct *in'stingkt*, formerly *in-stingkt'*, *n* impulse; an involuntary prompting to action; intuition; the natural impulse by which animals are guided apparently independently of reason or experience; a complex coordination of reflex actions by which an organism successfully adapts to its environment without foresight or experience. — *adj* (*in-stingkt'*) instigated or incited; moved; animated; charged; imbued. — *adj* **instinct'ive** prompted by instinct; involuntary; acting according to or determined by natural impulse. — *adv* **instinc'tively**. — *n* **instinctiv'ity** (*rare*). — *adj* **instinc'tual** concerning instincts. — *adv* **instinc'tually**. [L *īnstinctus*, from *īnstinguere* instigate]

institorial *in-sti-tō'ri-əl* or *-tö'ri-*, (*law*) *adj* pertaining to an agent or factor. [L *īnstitōrius*, from *īnstitor* an agent, broker]

institute *in'sti-tūt*, *vt* to set up, establish; to originate, inaugurate; to order (*obs*); to educate (*obs*). — *n* anything instituted or formally established; an institution; a literary and philosophical society or organization for education, research, etc; the building in which such an organization is housed; a foundation for further education, *esp* in technical subjects; established law; precept or principle; a brief course of instruction, *esp* for teachers (*US*); the person first nominated as heir (distinguished from the *substitutes* who follow) (*Scots law*); (in *pl*) a book of precepts, principles or rules; the act of instituting (*obs*). — *n* **institution** (*-tū'shən*) the act of instituting or establishing; that which is instituted or established; foundation; established order; enactment; a society or organization established for some object, *esp* cultural, charitable or beneficent, or the building housing it; a custom or usage, *esp* one familiar or characteristic; the act by which a bishop commits a cure of souls to a priest; appointment of an heir; a system of principles or rules (*obs*); that which institutes or instructs (*obs*). — *adj* **institū'tional** concerning an institution, institutions or institutes; being, or of the nature of, an institution; depending on or originating in institution; associated with, or typical of, institutions, routine, uninspiring. — *n* **institū'tionalism** the system or characteristics of institutions or institution life; belief in the merits of institutions and institution life. — *n* **institū'tionalist** a writer on institutes; a person who sets a high value on institutionalism. — *n* **institutionaliz'ation** or **-s-**. — *vt* **institū'tionalize** or **-ise** to make an institution of; to confine to an institution; (*usu* in *passive*) as a result of such confinement, to cause to become apathetic and dependent on routine. — *adv* **institū'tionally**. — *adj* **institū'tionary** institutional; educational (*obs*). — *n* **in'stitūtist** a writer of institutes or elementary rules. — *adj* **in'stitūtive** able or tending to establish; depending on an institution. — *adv* **institū'tively**. — *n* **in'stitūtor** or **in'stitūter** a person who institutes; an instructor (*obs*). — **institutional church** one that is active through social organizations. [L *īnstituere*, *-ūtum*, from *in* in, and *statuere* to cause to stand, from *stāre* to stand]

instreaming *in'strēm-ing*, *n* an influx. — Also *adj*. [**in**[1] and **streaming**]

instress *in'stres*, *n* the force or energy which sustains an inscape, the sensation of inscape. — Also *vt*. [Coined by Gerard Manley Hopkins, from **in**[1] and **stress**]

instruct *in-strukt'*, *vt* to inform; to teach; to direct; (of a judge) to give (a jury) guidance concerning the legal issues of a case; to give (a lawyer) the facts concerning a case; to order or command; to prepare (*obs*). — *adj* (*Milton*; *obs*) instructed, taught. — *adj* **instruct'ible**. — *n* **instruc'tion** (the art of) instructing or teaching; information; direction; command; an element in a computer program or language that activates a particular operation; (in *pl*) special directions for performing a specific task. — *adj* **instruc'tional** relating to instruction; educational. — *adj* **instruc'tive** providing instruction; conveying knowledge; denoting, as in Finnish, 'by means of' (*gram*). — *adv* **instruc'tively**. — *n* **instruc'tiveness**. — *n* **instruc'tor** a teacher; a college or university lecturer, below assistant professor in rank (*NAm*): — *fem* **instruc'tress**. [L *īnstruere*, *īnstructum*, from *in* in, and *struere* to pile up]

instrument *in'strə-mənt*, *n* a tool or utensil; a contrivance for producing musical sounds; a document constituting or containing a contract; a formal record; a person or thing used as a means or agency; a term generally employed to denote an indicating device but also other pieces of small electrical apparatus. — *vt* (*-ment'*) to score (a piece of music) for instruments; to equip with indicating, measuring or control, etc apparatus. — *adj* for instruments; by means of instruments (as *instrument flight*). — *adj* **instrumental** (*-ment'l*) acting as an instrument or means; serving to promote an object; helpful; of, for, belonging to, or produced by, musical instruments; denoting a type of learning process in which a particular response is always associated with a reinforcement, the response then intensifying (*psychol*); serving to indicate the instrument or means (*gram*). — *n* the instrumental case (*gram*); a piece of music for instruments only, ie without a vocal part. — *n* **instrument'alism** (*philos*) a form of pragmatism associated with John Dewey. — *n* **instrument'alist** a person who plays on a musical instrument; a person skilled in the making of instruments; a person who believes in or advocates instrumentalism. — *n* **instrumentality** (*-ment-al'i-ti*) agency. — *adv* **instrument'ally**. — *n* **instrumentā'tion** the use or provision of instruments; the arrangement of a composition for performance by different instruments, orchestration (*music*). — *adj* **instrumen'ted** equipped with electronic, etc instruments. — **instrument flying** and **landing** navigation of aircraft by means of instruments only and landing of aircraft by means of instruments and ground radio devices only, when visibility is poor; **instrument panel** a panel, eg in a car, on which instruments, dials, etc are mounted. [L *instrūmentum*, from *īnstruere* to instruct; see **instruct**]

insubjection *in-səb-jek'shən*, *n* lack of subjection. [**in-** (2)]

insubordinate *in-səb-örd'i-nit* or *-örd'nit*, *adj* refusing to submit to authority; disobedient, rebellious. — *adv* **insubord'inately**. — *n* **insubordinā'tion**. [**in-** (2)]

insubstantial *in-səb-stan'shəl*, *adj* not substantial; tenuous, flimsy; not real. — *n* **insubstantiality** (*-shi-al'i-ti*). — *adv* **insubstan'tially**. [**in-** (2)]

insucken *in'suk-n*, (*Scots law*; *hist*) *adj* pertaining to a sucken. [**in**[1] and **sucken**]

insufferable *in-suf'ər-ə-bl*, *adj* not able to be endured; detestable. — *adv* **insuff'erably**. [**in-** (2)]

insufficient *in-səf-ish'ənt*, *adj* not sufficient; inadequate; lacking (*obs*). — *n* **insuffic'iency** the state of being insufficient (also *rare* **insuffic'ience**); the inability of an organ or part to function normally (*med*). — *adv* **insuffic'iently**. [**in-** (2)]

insufflate *in'suf-lāt* (or *-suf'*), *vt* to blow in; to breathe on. — *n* **insufflā'tion** the act of breathing on anything, *esp* in baptism or exorcism; the act of blowing air, power, etc into a cavity or on a surface; the act of blowing gas or a medication in powder form into a body cavity. — *n* **in'sufflātor** an instrument or device for insufflation. [L *īnsufflāre*, from *in* in, on, and *sufflāre* to blow]

insula *in'sū-lə* (L *ēn'soo-la*), *n* a block of buildings (*Roman antiq*); an apartment house (*Roman antiq*); Reil's island, a small lobe of the cerebrum hidden in the fissure of Sylvius (*anatom*). [L, an island]

insular *in'sū-lər*, *adj* belonging to an island; surrounded by water; standing or situated alone; remaining, *esp* seeking to remain, isolated, detached or aloof; hence, narrow, prejudiced. — *n* **in'sūlarism**. — *n* **insūlarity** (*-lar'i-ti*) the state of being insular. — *adv* **in'sūlarly**. [LL *insulāris*, from L *insula* an island]

insulate *in'sū-lāt*, *vt* to cut off from connection or communication; to prevent the passing of heat, sound, electricity, etc from (a body, area, etc) to another; to place in a detached situation. — *n* **insūlā'tion** material which insulates or is a non-conductor of electricity; the process of insulating. — *n* **in'sūlātor** someone who, or that which, insulates; a non-conductor of electricity; a device for insulating a conductor; a stand for a piano leg. — **insulating board** (*building*) fibreboard of low density to reduce heat loss and give a degree of soundproofing; **insulating tape** or (*NAm*) **friction tape** a *usu* adhesive tape made from, or impregnated with, water-resistant insulating material, used for covering joins in electrical wires, etc. [L *insulātus* made into an island, from *insula* island]

insulin *in'sū-lin*, *n* a protein hormone produced in the islets of Langerhans in the pancreas of animals, important in the regulation of glucose in the blood, and used in the treatment of diabetes mellitus. — *n*

in'sulinase an enzyme, present in the tissues of the liver and kidneys, which breaks down insulin in the body. — **insulin shock** or **reaction** a state of collapse produced by an overdose of insulin. [New L *insula* islet, and **-in**]

insulse *in-suls'*, (*rare*) *adj* lacking wit; dull, stupid; tasteless, insipid. — *n* **insul'sity** stupidity. [L *īnsulsus*, from *in-* not, and *salere* to salt]

insult *in-sult'*, *vt* to triumph insolently or exultantly over; to treat with indignity or contempt; to affront; to attack physically, assault (*obs*). — *vi* (*obs*) to make an attack; to behave with boastful insolence. — *n* **in'sult** an offensive remark or action; abuse; an affront; injury, damage (*med, esp US*). — *adj* **insult'able**. — *adj* **insult'ant** (*rare*) insulting. — *n* **insult'er**. — *adj* **insult'ing**. — *adv* **insult'ingly**. — *n* **insult'ment** (*Shakesp*) insult. [L *īnsultāre*, from *insilīre* to spring at, from *in* upon, and *salīre* to leap]

insuperable *in-sū'pər-ə-bl* or *-sōō'*, *adj* not capable of being overcome or surmounted. — *n* **insuperabil'ity** or **insu'perableness**. — *adv* **insu'perably**. [L *īnsuperābilis*, from *in-* not, and *superāre* to pass over, from *super* above]

insupportable *in-səp-ōrt'ə-bl* or *-ört'*, *adj* unbearable, intolerable, insufferable; not sustainable or defensible; irresistible (*Spenser*). — *n* **insupport'ableness**. — *adv* **insupport'ably**. [**in-** (2)]

insuppressible *in-sə-pres'i-bl*, *adj* not capable of being suppressed or concealed. — *adv* **insuppress'ibly**. [**in-** (2)]

insure *in-shōōr'*, *vt* to make an arrangement for the payment of a sum of money in the event of loss or injury to; to guarantee; to make sure or secure. — *vi* to effect or undertake insurance. — *n* **insurabil'ity**. — *adj* **insur'able** capable of being insured. — *n* **insur'ance** the act, practice or business of insuring; a contract of insurance, a policy; the premium paid for insuring; the sum to be received; means of avoiding risk, loss, damage, etc. — *n* (*obs*) **insur'ancer**. — *n* **insur'ant** someone who obtains or holds an insurance policy. — *n* **insur'ed** an insured person or organization. — *n* **insur'er** either party to a contract of insurance (now, strictly the insurance company). [OFr *enseurer*, from *en*, and *seur* sure; see **ensure** and **sure**[1]]

insurgent *in-sûr'jənt*, *adj* rising in revolt; rising; rushing in. — *n* a person who rises in opposition to established authority; a rebel. — *n* **insur'gence** or **insur'gency** a rising up or against; rebellion; insurrection. [L *īnsurgēns, -entis*, from *in* upon, and *surgere* to rise]

insurmountable *in-sər-mownt'ə-bl*, *adj* not surmountable; not capable of being overcome. — *n* **insurmountabil'ity** or **insurmount'ableness**. — *adv* **insurmount'ably**. [**in-** (2)]

insurrection *in-sər-ek'shən*, *n* a rising or revolt. — *adj* **insurrec'tional** or **insurrec'tionary**. — *n* **insurrec'tionary** or **insurrec'tionist**. — *n* **insurrec'tionism**. [L *īnsurrēctiō, -ōnis*, from *īnsurgere*; see **insurgent**]

insusceptible *in-səs-ep'ti-bl*, *adj* not susceptible. — Also **insuscep'tive**. — *n* **insusceptibil'ity**. — *adv* **insuscep'tibly** or **insuscep'tively**. [**in-** (2)]

inswathe. Same as **enswathe**.

inswing *in'swing*, *n* an inward swing or swerve. — *n* **inswinger** (*in'swing-ər*) a ball bowled so as to swerve to leg (*cricket*); a ball kicked so as to swing in towards the goal or the centre of the pitch (*football*). [**in**[1] and **swing**]

Int. *abbrev*: International.

int. *abbrev*: interest; interior.

intact *in-takt'*, *adj* untouched; unimpaired; whole; undiminished. — *n* **intact'ness**. [L *intactus*, from *in-* not, and *tangere, tactum* to touch]

intaglio *in-täl'yō*, *n* a figure cut into any substance; a stone or gem in which the design is hollowed out (opposite to *cameo*); the production of such figures, stones or gems; a countersunk die; a method of printing in which the image area is sunk into the surface of the plate (opposite to *relief*): — *pl* **intagl'ios**. — Also *vt*. — *adj* **intagl'iated** incised, engraved. — See also **cavo-rilievo**. [Ital, from *in* into, and *tagliare* to cut, from L *tālea* a cutting, layer]

intake *in'tāk*, *n* amount, quantity, etc taken in; an airway in a mine; a place where water, gas, etc is taken in; a narrowing in a pipe; decrease by knitting two stitches together; the place where contraction occurs; the setting back of a wall-face; a body of people taken into an organization, eg new recruits, or new pupils at a school; the point at which the fuel mixture enters the cylinder of an internal-combustion engine; a cheat or cheater (*dialect*). [**in**[1] and **take**]

Intal® *in'tal*, *n* a drug (*sodium cromoglycate*), *usu* administered by inhaler and used to control certain types of asthma and allergic bronchitis.

intangible *in-tan'ji-bl*, *adj* not tangible or perceptible to touch; insubstantial; eluding the grasp of the mind. — *n* something intangible, eg a supplementary asset such as goodwill. — *n* **intangibil'ity** or **intan'gibleness**. — *adv* **intan'gibly**. [**intact**]

intarsia *in-tär'si-ə*, *n* a form of decorative wood inlay work, developed in Italy during the 15c; coloured geometrical patterning in knitting, reminiscent of this. — Also **tar'sia**. — Also *adj*. [Ital *intarsio*]

integer *in'ti-jər*, *n* a whole; any positive whole number, any negative whole number, or zero (*arith*). [L, from *in* not, and root of *tangere* to touch]

integral *in'tə-grəl*, also *in-teg'rəl*, *adj* entire or whole; not fractional; not involving fractions; relating to integrals; unimpaired, intact; intrinsic, belonging as a part to the whole. — *n* a whole; the whole as made up of its parts; the value of the function of a variable whose differential coefficient is known (*math*). — *n* **integral'ity**. — *adv* **in'tegrally**. — **integral calculus** see under **calculus**; **integral function** (*algebra*) a function which does not include the operation of division in any of its parts. [LL *integralis*; see ety for **integer**]

integrand *in'ti-grand*, (*math*) *n* a function to be integrated. [L *integrandus* gerundive of *integrare*]

integrant *in'ti-grənt*, *adj* making part of a whole; necessary to form an integer or an entire thing. [Fr *intégrant*]

integrate *in'ti-grāt*, *vt* to make up as a whole; to make entire; to combine, amalgamate; to incorporate (one person or thing) into another; to desegregate; to find the integral of (*math*); to find the total value of. — *vi* to become integral; to perform integration. — *adj* made up of parts; complete; whole. — *adj* **in'tegrable** capable of being integrated. — *n* **integrā'tion** the act or process of integrating (*math*); unification into a whole, eg of diverse elements (such as racial variety) in a community; the state of being integrated; the formation of a unified personality (*psychol*). — *n* **integrā'tionist** someone who favours racial and/or cultural integration. — Also *adj*. — *adj* **in'tegrātive** integrating; tending to integrate. — *n* **in'tegrātor** a person who integrates; an instrument for finding the results of integrations (*math*). — **integrated circuit** a circuit consisting of an assembly of electronic elements in a single structure which cannot be subdivided without destroying its intended function. — **monolithic integrated circuit** an integrated circuit formed in or on a single crystal of semiconductor, *usu* silicon. [L *integrare* to make whole]

integrity *in-teg'ri-ti*, *n* entireness, wholeness; the unimpaired state of anything; uprightness; honesty; purity. [**integer**]

integument *in-teg'ū-mənt*, *n* an external covering; either of the two coats of an ovule (*bot*); a covering layer of tissue, such as the skin, exoskeleton, etc (*zool*). — *adj* **integumentary** (*-ment'ər-i*). [L *integumentum*, from *in* upon, and *tegere* to cover]

intellect *int'i-lekt*, *n* the mind, in reference to its rational powers; the thinking principle. — *adj* **in'tellected** (*Cowper*) endowed with intellect. — *n* **intellec'tion** the act of understanding; apprehension or perception (*philos*). — *adj* **intellec'tive** able to understand; produced or perceived by the understanding. — *n* **intellectual** (*-lek'tū-əl*) of or relating to the intellect;

perceived or performed by the intellect; having the power of understanding; endowed with a superior intellect; appealing to, or (thought to be) intended for, intellectuals; intelligible only to a person with a superior intellect. — *n* a person of superior intellect or enlightenment (often used to suggest doubt as to common sense or practical skills); a person who uses his or her intellect to earn a living, *esp* a writer, philosopher, etc; a member of the intelligentsia; (in *pl*) intellectual matters (*archaic*); (in *pl*) mental powers (*archaic*); intellect (*obs*). — *n* **intellect'ualism** the doctrine that derives all knowledge from pure reason; the culture (*esp* exclusive or unbalanced) of the intellect. — *n* **intellect'ualist**. — *n* **intellectuality** (*-al'i-ti*) intellectual power. — *vi* **intellect'ualize** or **-ise** to reason intellectually. — *vt* to endow with intellect; to give an intellectual character to. — *adv* **intellect'ually**. — **intellectual property** (*law*) property such as copyright, trademarks and patents, having no tangible form but representing the product of creative work or invention. [L *intellēctus*, *-ūs*, from *intelligere*, *intellēctum* to understand, from *inter* between, and *legere* to choose]

intelligent *in-tel'i-jənt*, *adj* endowed with the faculty of reason; capable of performing some of the functions of a computer (*automation*); having or showing highly developed mental faculties; alert, bright, quick of mind; well-informed; knowing, aware (with *of*; *archaic*); communicative (*Shakesp*). — *n* **intell'igence** intellectual skill or knowledge; mental brightness; information communicated; news; intelligence department. — *n* **intell'igencer** (*archaic*) a spy; a source of information or news, an informant; a newspaper (*usu* as a title). — *adj* **intelligential** (*-jen'shl*) concerning the intelligence. — *adv* **intell'igently**. — **intelligence department** or **service** a department of state or armed service for securing and interpreting information, *esp* about an enemy; **intelligence quotient** the ratio, commonly expressed as a percentage, of a person's mental age to his or her chronological age (*abbrev* **IQ**); **intelligence test** a test by questions and tasks to determine a person's mental capacity, or the age at which his or her capacity would be normal; **intelligent terminal** (*comput*) a terminal incorporating a microprocessor, capable of performing simple tasks independently of the larger computer to which it is connected. [L *intelligēns*, *-entis*, pr p of *intelligere* ; see ety for **intellect**]

intelligentsia or (formerly) **intelligentzia** *in-tel-i-jent'si-ə* or (formerly) *-gent'*, *n* the intellectual or cultured classes, *orig* in Russia, the intellectual elite. [Russ, from L *intelligentia* intelligence]

intelligible *in-tel'i-jə-bl*, *adj* capable of being understood, comprehensible; easy to understand, clear; capable of being apprehended by the understanding only, not by senses (*philos*). — *n* **intelligibil'ity** or **intell'igibleness**. — *adv* **intell'igibly**. [L *intelligibilis*]

Intelsat *in'tel-sat*, *n* a worldwide satellite service dealing with communications such as television exchange, business messages, etc. [*In*ternational *Tel*ecommuncations *Sat*ellite Consortium]

intemerate *in-tem'ər-it*, (now *rare*) *adj* pure; undefiled; inviolate. — *adv* **intem'erately**. [L *intemerātus*, from *in-* not, and pa p of *temerāre* to violate]

intemperance *in-tem'pər-əns*, *n* lack of due restraint; excess of any kind; habitual overindulgence in alcoholic liquor. — *n* **intem'perant** a person who is intemperate. — *adj* **intem'perate** indulging to excess in any appetite or passion; given to an immoderate use of alcoholic liquors; exceeding the usual degree; immoderate. — *adv* **intem'perately**. — *n* **intem'perateness**. [L *intemperans* intemperate]

intempestive *in-tem-pest'iv*, (*literary*) *adj* unseasonable; untimely, inopportune. — *adv* **intempest'ively**. — *n* **intempestiv'ity**. [L *intempestīvus*, from *in-* not, and *tempestās* season, from *tempus* time]

intenable *in-ten'ə-bl*, (*obs*) *adj* untenable. [**in-** (2)]

intend *in-tend'*, *vt* to have as a purpose, plan; to mean or express; to design or destine; to direct or turn (the attention, etc) (*archaic*); to stretch out, extend (*obs*); to expand (*obs*); to strain (*obs*); to intensify (*obs*). — *vi* to set out for or proceed towards a particular destination (with *for*; *obs*); to be present, attend (*obs*); to listen (with *to*; *obs*). — *adj* **intend'ed** planned. — *n* (*colloq*) a fiancé or fiancée. — *adv* **intend'edly** with intention or design. — *n* **intend'ment** the true meaning or intention of something, *esp* a law. [OFr *entendre*, from L *intendere*, *intentum* and *intensum*, from *in* towards, and *tendere* to stretch]

intendant *in-ten'dənt*, *n* an administrative official (eg a provincial or colonial governor) of France, Portugal and Spain (*hist*); an official who superintends some public business in certain countries; a superintendent, director or manager. — *n* **intend'ancy** the office, term of office, or sphere of an intendant; a body of intendants; management, superintendence (also **intend'ance**). [Fr, from L *intendens*, *-dentis*, pr p of *intendere*; see ety for **intend**]

intender. See **entender**.

intenerate *in-ten'ər-āt*, (*rare*) *vt* to make tender; to soften. — *n* **intenerā'tion**. [L *in* in, to, and *tener* tender]

intenible *in-ten'i-bl*, *adj* incapable of holding or retaining. [L *in-* not, and *tenēre* to hold]

intensative. See under **intensive**.

intense *in-tens'*, *adj* strained; concentrated, dense; extreme in degree; (of person, manner, etc) earnestly or deeply emotional, or affecting to have deep feeling; (of a photographic negative) opaque. — *vt* **intens'ate** (*rare*) to intensify. — *adv* **intense'ly**. — *n* **intense'ness** or **intens'ity**. — *n* **intensificā'tion** the act of intensifying. — *n* **intens'ifier** an utterance that lends force and emphasis. — *vt* **intens'ify** to make more intense. — *vi* to become intense: — *pr p* **intens'ifying**; *pa t* and *pa p* **intens'ified**. [OFr *intens*, from L *intensus*]

intension *in-ten'shən*, *n* straining; intentness; intensity; intensification; the sum of the qualities by which a general name is determined (*logic*). — *adj* **inten'sional**. [Ety as for **intend**]

intensitive. See under **intensive**.

intensive *in-ten'siv*, *adj* concentrated, intense; strained; unremitting; relating to intensity or to intension; using large amounts of capital or labour to increase production; intensifying; intensified; giving force or emphasis (*gram*). — Also (*rare*) **intens'ative** or **intens'itive**. — *n* an intensifier. — Used in combination to signify having, using or requiring a great deal of something, as in *labour-intensive*, *capital-intensive*. — *adv* **intens'ively**. — *n* **intens'iveness**. — **intensifying screen** (*radiol*) a layer or screen of fluorescent material adjacent to a photographic surface that augments, by local fluorescence, registration by incident X-rays; **intensive care** specialized, closely-monitored health care for the critically ill in a specially designed hospital unit (**intensive care unit**); **intensive culture** or **intensive farming** obtaining the maxiumum yield from the soil of a limited area. [**intend**]

intent *in-tent'*, *adj* fixed with close attention; diligently applied; concentrating on a particular aim or purpose. — *n* the thing aimed at or intended; purpose, intention, design; meaning or connotation; intentness (*obs*). — *adj* **inten'tive** (*archaic*) attentive. — *adv* **intent'ly** earnestly; diligently. — *n* **intent'ness**. — **to all intents (and purposes)** in every important aspect; virtually; **with intent** (*law*) deliberately, with the intention of doing the harm, etc that is or was done. [Ety as for **intend**]

intention *in-ten'shən*, *n* design; purpose, aim; application of thought to an object; a concept; (in *pl*) purpose with respect to marriage (*colloq*); a plan of treatment (*med*); a process of healing (see also phrases below); application or direction of the mind (*obs*). — *adj* **inten'tional** with intention; intended; designed; directed towards, or pertaining to the mind's capacity to direct itself towards, objects and states of affairs (*philos*). — *n* **intentional'ity**. — *adv* **inten'tionally** with intention; on purpose. — *adj* **inten'tioned** having a certain intention. — **intention tremor** a tremor that occurs when an individual with a chronic disease affecting the central nervous system (eg multiple sclerosis) tries to touch an object. — **first intention healing** healing by which the edges of a wound are brought together directly and granulation occurs; **second intention healing** healing in which the edges of a wound are separated and the gap is filled first by granulation tissue and then covered by epithelial tissue from the wound edges; **third intention healing** healing in which ulceration occurs and scar tissue is formed at the wound site; **well-** (or **ill-**) **intentioned** having good (or evil) intentions; meaning well (or meaning harm). [**intend**]

inter *in-tûr'*, *vt* to bury: — *pr p* **interr'ing**; *pa t* and *pa p* **interred'**. — *n* **inter'ment** burial. [Fr *enterrer*, from LL *interrāre*, from L *in* into, and *terra* the earth]

inter- *in'tər-* or *in-tûr'-*, *pfx* denoting: between, among, in the midst of; mutual, reciprocal; together. [L *inter*]

interact[1] *in'tər-akt*, *n* an interlude; an entr'acte; the interval between acts. [**inter-**]

interact[2] *in-tər-akt'*, *vi* to act on one another. — *n* **interac'tant** a substance, etc which interacts. — *n* **interaction** (*-ak'shən*) mutual action. — *n* **interac'tionism** (*philos*) the theory that mind and body act on each other (as distinct from *psychophysical parallelism* and *epiphenomenalism*). — *n* **interac'tionist**. — *adj* **interac'tive** allowing, or capable of, mutual action; allowing continuous two-way communication, eg between a computer and its user. — **interactive television** a television system in which the viewer can choose, from a range of options, what is shown on the screen, eg camera angle, action replay, etc. [**inter-**]

inter alia *in'tər* or *-ter ā'li-ə* or *a'li-a*, (*L*) among other things; **inter alios** (*ā'li-ōs* or *a'li-ōs*) among other people.

interallied *in-tər-al'īd* or *-īd'*, *adj* between or among allies. [**inter-**]

interambulacrum *in-tər-am-bū-lā'krəm*, *n* (in sea urchins) a radial band between two ambulacra: — *pl* **interambulā'cra**. — *adj* **interambulā'cral**. [**inter-**]

inter-arts *in'tər-ärts'*, *adj* belonging to the examination between matriculation and BA of London University. [For **intermediate arts**]

interatomic *in-tər-ə-tom'ik*, *adj* existing, happening, etc between atoms. [**inter-**]

interbank *in'tər-bangk*, *adj* between or among banks. [**inter-**]

interbedded *in-tər-bed'id*, (*geol*) *adj* interstratified. — *n* **interbedd'ing**. [**inter-**]

interbrain *in'tər-brān*, *n* the diencephalon.

interbreed *in-tər-brēd'*, *vt* and *vi* to breed together, *esp* of different races: — *pa t* and *pa p* **interbred'**. — *n* **interbreed'ing**. [**inter-**]

intercalate *in-tûr'kə-lāt*, *vt* to insert between others (eg a day in a calendar); to interpolate. — *adj* **inter'calar** (*-lər*; *obs*) or **inter'calary** inserted between others. — *adj* **inter'calated**. — *n* **intercalā'tion**. — *adj* **inter'calative** (*-lā-tiv* or *-lə-tiv*). [L *intercalāre*, *-ātum*, from *inter* between, and *calāre* to proclaim; see **calends**]

intercede *in-tər-sēd'*, *vi* to act as peacemaker between two parties, mediate; to plead (for). — *adj* **intercēd'ent**. — *n* **intercēd'er**. [L *intercēdere*, *-cēssum*, from *inter* between, and *cēdere* to go]

intercellular *in-tər-sel'ū-lər*, (*biol*) *adj* placed, situated or occurring between cells. [**inter-**]

intercensal *in-tər-sen'səl*, *adj* between censuses. [Irregularly formed from L *inter* and **census**]

intercept *in-tər-sept'*, *vt* to stop and seize on the way from one place to another; to cut off; to stop, alter, or interrupt the progress of; to take or comprehend between (*math*). — *n* (*in'*) (*math*) that part of a line that is intercepted. — *n* **intercep'ter** or **intercep'tor** a person or thing which intercepts; a light, swift aeroplane for pursuit. — *n* **intercep'tion**. — *adj* **intercep'tive**. [L *intercipere*, *-ceptum*, from *inter* between, and *capere* to seize]

intercession *in-tər-sesh'ən*, *n* the act of interceding or pleading on behalf of another. — *adj* **intercess'ional**. — *n* **intercessor** (*-ses'ər*) a person who intercedes; a bishop who acts during a vacancy in a see. — *adj* **intercessōrial** (*-ōr'* or *-ör'*) or **intercess'ory** interceding. — **intercession of saints** prayer offered on behalf of Christians on earth by saints. [**intercede**]

interchain *in-tər-chān'*, *vt* to chain together. [**inter-**]

interchange *in-tər-chānj'*, *vt* to give and take mutually; to exchange. — *vi* to succeed alternately. — *n* (*in'*) mutual exchange; alternate succession; a road junction or series of junctions designed to prevent streams of traffic crossing one another. — *adj* **interchange'able** capable of being interchanged; following each other in alternate succession (*obs*). — *n* **interchange'ableness** or **interchangeabil'ity**. — *adv* **interchange'ably**. — *n* **interchange'ment** (*Shakesp*) exchange, mutual transfer. — *n* **interchang'er**. — **interchange fee** one charged by the issuer of a debit or credit card for processing a transaction made with it. [**inter-**]

interchapter *in'tər-chap-tər*, *n* an intercalary chapter in a book, not numbered in the general sequence. [**inter-**]

intercipient *in-tər-sip'i-ənt*, (*obs*) *adj* intercepting. — *n* the person or thing that intercepts. [L *intercipiēns*, *-entis*, pr p of *intercipere*; see **intercept**]

intercity *in-tər-sit'i*, *adj* between cities. [**inter-**]

interclude *in-tər-klōōd'*, *vt* to block; to enclose; to cut off. — *n* **interclusion** (*-klōō'zhən*). [L *interclūdere*, from *inter* between, and *claudere* to shut]

intercollegiate *in-tər-kə-lē'ji-āt* or *-ət*, *adj* between colleges. [**inter-**]

intercolline *in-tər-kol'īn*, *adj* lying between hills. [**inter-**]

intercolonial *in-tər-kə-lō'ni-əl*, *adj* between colonies. — *adv* **intercolo'nially**. [**inter-**]

intercolumniation *in-tər-kə-lum-ni-ā'shən*, (*archit*) *n* the spacing of, or distance between, columns, measured in terms of the lower diameter. — *adj* **intercolum'nar** placed between columns. [**inter-**]

intercom *in'tər-kom*, *n* a telephone system within a building, aeroplane, tank, etc. [*Inter*nal *com*munication]

intercommune *in-tər-kə-mūn'*, *vi* to commune mutually or together; to hold discussions, have dealings. — *adj* **intercomm'unal** existing between communities. — *n* **intercommun'ion** or **intercommunica'tion** mutual communion or relation, *esp* between churches; the permitting of members of one denomination to receive Holy Communion in the churches of another denomination. — *n* **intercommun'ity** the state of being or having in common. — **letters of intercommuning** an ancient writ issued by the Scottish Privy Council warning people not to harbour or have any dealings with those named, on pain of being held accessory. [**inter-**]

intercommunicate *in-tər-kə-mū'ni-kāt*, *vt* and *vi* to communicate mutually or together; to have free passage from one to another. — *adj* **intercommun'icable**. — *n* **intercommunicā'tion**. [**inter-**]

interconnect *in-tər-kə-nekt'*, *vt* to connect (things) with each other. — *vi* to be mutually connected. — *n* **interconnec'tedness**, **interconnec'tion** or **interconnex'ion**. — *n* **interconnec'tor** a device or feeder by which electricity generated in an area or country may be exported to another area or country. [**inter-**]

intercontinental *in-tər-kon-ti-nen'tal*, *adj* between or connecting different continents. — **intercontinental ballistic missile** a ballistic missile capable of carrying a nuclear bomb over 5500km (*abbrev* **ICBM**). [**inter-**]

interconversion *in-tər-kən-vûr'shən*, *n* the conversion of two things or more into one another, mutual conversion. — *vt* (back-formation) **interconvert'** to convert (two or more things) into one another. — *adj* **interconvert'ible** mutually convertible; interchangeable; exactly equivalent. [**inter-**]

intercooler *in'tər-ko͞o-lər*, *n* a heat exchanger in a turbo-charger, used eg in supercharged internal-combustion engines. — *adj* **intercool'ed**. [**inter-** and **cool**]

intercostal *in-tər-kost'əl*, *adj* between the ribs or the leaf-veins. [L *inter* between, and *costa* a rib]

intercourse *in'tər-kōrs* or *-körs*, *n* connection or dealings between people; communication; commerce; communion; coition, sexual intercourse. [OFr *entrecours*, from L *intercursus* a running between, from *inter* between, and *currere*, *cursum* to run]

intercrop *in-tər-krop'*, *vt* and *vi* to grow or cultivate in alternate rows: — *pr p* **intercropp'ing**; *pa t* and *pa p* **intercropped'**. — *n* **in'tercrop** a crop grown in the rows between another crop. [**inter-**]

intercross *in-tər-kros'*, *vt* and *vi* to cross and recross; to cross mutually; to place or lie crosswise; to crossbreed. — *n* **in'tercross** a crossing of breeds. [**inter-**]

intercrural *in-tər-kro͞or'əl*, *adj* situated or pertaining to (the area) between the crura or legs. [**inter-**]

intercurrent *in-tər-kur'ənt*, *adj* running between, intervening; going on at the same time; supervening. — *n* **intercurr'ence**. [L *inter* between, and *currere* to run]

intercut *in-tər-kut'*, (*cinema*) *vt* to alternate (contrasting shots) within a sequence by cutting. [**inter-**]

interdash *in-tər-dash'*, *vt* to intersperse with dashes. [**inter-**]

interdeal *in'tər-dēl*, (*archaic*) *n* mutual dealings; negotiations. — Also (*Spenser*) **enterdeale**. — *vi* to have mutual dealings. — *n* **interdeal'er**. [**inter-**]

interdenominational *in-tər-di-nom-i-nā'shə-nl* or *-nāsh'nl*, *adj* common to, or with the participation of, various religious denominations; independent of denomination. [**inter-**]

interdental *in-tər-dent'l*, *adj* between the teeth; pertaining to the surfaces of the teeth where they adjoin (*dentistry*); pronounced with the tip of the tongue between upper and lower teeth (*phonetics*). — *adv* **interdent'ally**. [**inter-**]

interdepartmental *in-tər-dē-pärt-ment'l*, *adj* between departments. — *adv* **interdepartment'ally**. [**inter-**]

interdepend *in-tər-di-pend'*, *vi* to depend on one another. — *n* **interdepend'ence**. — *adj* **interdepend'ent**. [**inter-**]

interdict *in-tər-dikt'*, *vt* to prohibit; to forbid; to forbid (someone) to take communion (*RC*). — *n* prohibition; a prohibitory decree; a prohibition of the pope restraining the clergy from performing divine service. — *n* **interdic'tion** (*-shən*). — *adj* **interdic'tive** or **interdic'tory** containing interdiction; prohibitory. [L *interdīcere*, *-dictum*, from *inter* between, and *dīcere* to say]

interdigital *in-tər-dij'i-tl*, *adj* between digits. — *vt* and *vi* **interdig'itate** to interlock by finger-like processes, or in the manner of the fingers of clasped hands; to interstratify or be interstratified. — *n* **interdigitā'tion**. [**inter-**]

interdine *in-tər-dīn'*, (*rare*) *vi* to eat together. [**inter-**]

interdisciplinary *in-tər-di-si-plin'ə-ri*, *adj* involving two or more fields of study. [**inter-**]

interess or **interesse** *in'tər-es* or *-es'*, (*obs*) *n* interest. — *vt* to interest: — *pa p* (*Shakesp*) **interest'**. [Anglo-Fr *interesse*, from LL *interesse* compensation, interest, from L *interesse* (infinitive) to concern]

interest *int'ə-rest*, *int'rəst* or *-rist*, *n* advantage, benefit; premium paid for the borrowing of money; any increase; concern, importance; personal influence; a right to some advantage; claim to participate or be concerned in some way; stake, share; partisanship or side; the body of people whose advantage is bound up in anything; regard to (*esp* personal) advantage; a state of engaged attention and curiosity; disposition towards such a state; the power of arousing it; a subject or activity to which one willingly devotes time and attention, a hobby. — *vt* to concern deeply; to cause to have an interest; to engage the attention of; to awaken concern in; to excite the curiosity of. — *adj* **in'terested** having an interest or concern; affected or biased by personal considerations, self-interest, etc. — *adv* **in'terestedly**. — *n* **in'terestedness**. — *adj* **in'teresting** (old-fashioned *-est'*) engaging or apt to engage the attention or regard; exciting emotion or passion. — *adv* **in'terestingly**. — *n* **in'terestingness**. — **interest group** a number of people grouped together to further or protect a common interest. — **compound interest** see under **compound**; **in an interesting condition**, **state** or **situation** old-fashioned euphemisms for pregnant; **in the interest(s) of** with a view to furthering or to helping; **make interest for** (*obs*) to secure favour for; **simple interest** see under **simple**. [From *interess*, influenced by OFr *interest*, L *interest*, it concerns, 3rd person singular present indicative of *interesse*, from *inter* between, among, and *esse* to be]

interface *in'tər-fās*, *n* a surface forming a common boundary; a meeting-point or area of contact between objects, systems, subjects, etc; the connection or junction between two systems or two parts of the same system (*comput*); the surface of separation between phases (*chem*). — *vt* to connect by means of an interface. — *vi* (*comput*) to interact or operate compatibly (with). — *adj* **interfacial** (*-fā'shl*) between plane faces; of an interface. [**inter-**]

interfacing *in'tər-fās-ing*, *n* firm material sewn between layers of fabric to shape and stiffen a garment. [**inter-**]

interfaith *in'tər-fāth*, *adj* occurring, carried out or organized between (members, representatives, etc of) different religious faiths. [**inter-**]

interfascicular *in-tər-fə-sik'ū-lər*, *adj* between vascular bundles. [**inter-**]

interfemoral *in-tər-fem'ər-əl*, *adj* situated between the thighs, connecting the hind limbs. [**inter-**]

interfenestration *in-tər-fen-is-trā'shən*, *n* spacing of windows. [L *inter* between, and *fenestra* a window]

interfere *in-tər-fēr'*, *vi* to intervene; to come in the way, obstruct; to interpose; to meddle; (of a horse) to strike a foot against the opposite leg in walking; (of waves, rays of light, etc) to act reciprocally. — *n* **interfēr'ence** the act of interfering; the effect of combining similar rays of light, etc (*phys*); the spoiling of a wireless or television signal by others or by natural disturbances. — *adj* **interferential** (*-fər-en'shl*). — *n* **interfēr'er**. — *adv* **interfēr'ingly**. — *n* **interfēr'ogram** (*phys*) a photographic or diagrammatic record of interference. — *n* **interfērom'eter** an instrument which, by observing interference fringes, makes precision measurements of wavelengths, wave speeds, angles, distances, etc; a radio telescope (**radio interferometer**) using two or more antennas spaced at known intervals and linked to a common receiver, one of its applications being the precise determination of the position of sources of radio waves in space. — *adj* **interfēromet'ric**. — *n* **interfērom'etry**. — *n* **interfēr'on** any of several proteins produced by cells infected with a virus and having the ability to inhibit viral growth. — **interference figure** a figure observed when a crystal section is viewed between crossed nicols; **interference fringes** alternate light and dark bands seen when similar beams of light interfere; **interference microscopy** a method of microscopy that measures the optical retardation of a specimen. — **interfere with** to meddle in; to get in the way of, hinder; to assault sexually. [OFr *entreférir*, from L *inter* between, and *ferīre* to strike]

interfertile *in-tər-fûr'tīl* or (*US*) *-təl*, *adj* capable of interbreeding. [**inter-**]

interflow *in'tər-flō*, *n* intermingling. — *vi* to flow into one another or between. [**inter-**]

interfluent *in-tûr'flo͞o-ənt*, *adj* flowing between or together. — Also **inter'fluous**. — *n* **inter'fluence**. [L *interfluēns*, *-entis*, from *inter* between, and *fluere* to flow]

interfold *in-tər-fōld'*, *vt* to fold one into the other [**inter-**]

interfoliate *in-tər-fō'li-āt*, *vt* to interleave. [L *inter* between, and *folium* a leaf]

interfretted *in-tər-fret'id*, (*heraldry*) *adj* interlaced. [**inter-**]

interfrontal *in-tər-frun'tl* or *-fron'tl*, *adj* between the frontal bones. **[inter-]**

interfuse *in-tər-fūz'*, *vt* to cause to mix or fuse. — *vi* to mix or fuse, mingle; — *n* **interfusion** (*-fū'zhən*). **[inter-]**

intergalactic *in-tər-gal-ak'tik*, *adj* between, or among, galaxies. **[inter-]**

interglacial *in-tər-glā'si-əl* or *-glā'shəl*, (*geol*) *adj* occurring between two periods of glacial action. — *n* a retreat of ice between glaciations. **[inter-]**

Interglossa *in-tər-glos'ə*, *n* an international language based on well-known Greek and Latin roots, devised by Lancelot Hogben (1943). [L *inter* between, and Gr *glōssa* tongue]

intergrade *in-tər-grād'*, *vi* to merge in or shade off into something else through a series of intermediate forms. — *n* **in'tergrade** an intermediate grade. — *n* **intergradation** (*-grə-dā'shən*). **[inter-]**

intergrow *in-tər-grō'*, *vt* to grow into or among each other. — *adj* **intergrown'**. — *n* **in'tergrowth**. **[inter-]**

interim *in'tər-im*, *n* the time between or intervening; the meantime; (with *cap*) in the history of the Reformation, the name given to certain edicts of the German emperor for the regulation of religious and ecclesiastical matters, till they could be decided by a general council, such as the Augsburg Interim (1548). — *adj* temporary, provisional. — *adv* (*rare*) meanwhile. — **interim dividend** (*finance*) a dividend distributed part of the way through a company's financial year. [L]

interior *in-tē'ri-ər*, *adj* inner; remote from the frontier or coast; inland; domestic rather than foreign; situated within or further in (sometimes with *to*); devoted to mental or spiritual life. — *n* the inside of anything; the inland part of a country; a picture of a scene within a house; the home affairs of a country; inner nature or character. — *n* **interiority** (*-or'i-ti*). — *adv* **inter'iorly**. — **interior angle** the angle between two adjacent sides of a polygon; **interior decoration** or **design** the construction and furnishing of the interior of a building; **interior decorator** or **designer** a person or company that specializes in the design and furnishing of interiors; **interior grate** an open grate with built-in boiler; **interior monologue** a literary representation of a person's inner thoughts and feelings before they take coherent grammatical form. — *adj* **inter'ior-sprung** (of a mattress, etc) containing springs. [L, comparative of assumed *interus* inward]

interj. *abbrev*: interjection.

interjacent *in-tər-jā'sənt*, *adj* lying between; intervening. — *n* **interjā'cency**. [L *interjacēns*, *-entis*, pr p of *interjacēre*, from *inter* between, and *jacēre* to lie]

interjaculate *in-tər-jak'ū-lāt*, *vt* to ejaculate in interruption. — *adj* **interjac'ulatory** (*-ū-lə-tə-ri*). [L *inter* between, and *jaculārī* to throw]

interject *in-tər-jekt'*, *vt* to throw between; to interpose; to exclaim in interruption or parenthesis; to insert. — *vi* to throw oneself between. — *n* **interjec'tion** (*-shən*) an act of interjecting; a syntactically independent word or phrase of an exclamatory nature, an ejaculation or exclamation (*gram*). — *adj* **interjec'tional**, **interjec'tionary** or **interjec'tural**. — *adv* **interjec'tionally**. — *n* **interjec'tor**. [L *inter(j)icere*, *interjectum*, from *inter* between, and *jacere* to throw]

interjoin *in-tər-join'*, (*Shakesp*) *vt* to join together. **[inter-]**

interkinesis *in-tər-kīn-ē'sis* or *-kin-*, (*biol*) *n* the resting stage between two divisions of meiosis. — See also **interphase**.

interknit *in-tər-nit'*, *vt* to knit into each other. **[inter-]**

interlace *in-tər-lās'*, *vt* to lace, weave or entangle together. — *vi* to intermix. — *n* **interlace'ment**. — **interlaced scanning** in television, the alternate scanning of an image in two sets of alternate lines. **[inter-]**

interlaminate *in-tər-lam'in-āt*, *vt* to insert between layers; to arrange or apply in alternate layers. — *adj* **interlam'inar**. — *n* **interlaminā'tion**. **[inter-]**

interlard *in-tər-lärd'*, *vt* to mix in, as fat with lean; to diversify by mixture, to intersperse. **[inter-]**

interlay *in-tər-lā'*, *vt* to lay between; to interpose. — *n* **in'terlay** layers of tissue, etc placed between a printing plate and its base to achieve the correct type height or printing pressure (*printing*). **[inter-]**

interleave *in-tər-lēv'*, *vt* to put a leaf or page between; to insert blank leaves or pages in. — *n* **in'terleaf** a leaf or page so inserted: — *pl* **in'terleaves**. **[inter-]**

interleukin *in-tər-lū'kin*, *n* any of a group of proteins that control the production of blood cells and play an important part in the combating of infection. — **interleukin 2** (*abbrev* **IL-2**) an interleukin that stimulates production of T-lymphocytes, used as an experimental treatment for cancer.

interline[1] *in-tər-līn'*, *vt* to write in alternate lines; to insert between lines; to write between the lines of. — *adj* **interlinear** (*-lin'i-ər*) written between lines. — *n* **interlineation** (*-lin-i-ā'shən*) or **interlin'ing**. **[inter-]**

interline[2] *in-tər-līn'*, *vt* to supply (a part of a garment, eg the collar) with an additional lining to reinforce or stiffen it. — *n* **interlin'ing**.

interline[3] *in-tər-līn'*, *vi* to join an airline route at a point other than its starting-point; to change from one plane (and airline route) during the course of a journey. — *adj* **in'terline** involving or relating to more than one transport (eg air) line or route. **[inter-]**

interlinear and **interlineation**. See under **interline**[1].

Interlingua *in-tər-ling'gwə*, *n* an international language based on the living Latin roots in European languages; (without *cap*) any artificially devised international language. — *adj* **interlin'gual**. — *adv* **interlin'gually**. [L *inter* between, and *lingua* tongue]

interlink *in-tər-lingk'*, *vt* and *vi* to link together. **[inter-]**

interlobular *in-tər-lob'ū-lər*, *adj* between lobes. **[inter-]**

interlocation *in-tər-lō-kā'shən*, *n* a placing between. **[inter-]**

interlock *in-tər-lok'*, *vt* to lock or clasp together; to connect so as to work together. — *vi* to be locked together. — *n* **in'terlock** an interlocked condition; any synchronizing mechanism. **[inter-]**

interlocution *in-tər-lo-kū'shən*, *n* dialogue, conversation; an intermediate decree before a final decision. — *n* **interlocutor** (*-lok'ū-tər*) a person who speaks in dialogue; a judge's decree (*Scots law*). — *adj* **interloc'utory**. — *n* **interloc'utress**, **interloc'utrice** or **interloc'utrix** a female interlocutor. [L *interlocūtiō*, *-ōnis*, from *inter* between, and *loquī*, *locūtus* to speak]

interloper *in'tər-lō-pər*, *n* an intruder; a person who meddles in another's affairs, *esp* for profit. — *vi* and *vt* **interlope'** (or *in'*) to intrude into any matter in which one has no fair concern. [Prob L *inter* between, and **lope**[1]]

interlude *in'tər-lo͞od* or *-lūd*, *n* an interval between acts of a play, etc; a short dramatic or comic piece, formerly often performed during this interval; a short piece of music played between the parts of a drama, opera, hymn, etc; an interval, any period of time or any happening different in character from what comes before or after. — *vt* and *vi* to interrupt, as an interlude. — *adj* **interlu'dial**. [L *inter* between, and *lūdus* play]

interlunar *in-tər-lo͞o'nər* or *-lū'*, *adj* belonging to the moon's monthly time of invisibility. — Also **interlu'nary**. — *n* **interlunā'tion** (*-lo͞o-*) the dark time between old moon and new. [L *inter* between, and *lūna* the moon]

intermarry *in-tər-mar'i*, *vi* to marry within one's own family or group; (of groups, races, etc) to mingle by marriage; (of a couple) to marry (*legal*); to marry (with *with*; *legal*). — *n* **intermarr'iage**. **[inter-]**

intermaxilla *in-tər-maks-il'ə*, *n* the premaxilla. — *adj* **intermax'illary** (or *-il'*) of the intermaxilla; between the maxillaries. — *n* the intermaxilla. [L *inter* between, and *maxilla* a jawbone]

intermeddle *in-tər-med'l*, *vi* to meddle; to interfere improperly. — *n* **intermedd'ler**. **[inter-]**

intermediate *in-tər-mē'dyit* or *-di-it*, *adj* placed, occurring or classified between others, or between extremes, limits or stages; (of igneous rocks) between acid and basic in composition; intervening. — *n* that which is intermediate; any compound manufactured from a primary that serves as a starting material for the synthesis of some other product (*chem*). — *vi* (*-di-āt*) to mediate; to act as an agent or go-between. — *n* **intermē'diacy** (*-ə-si*) the state of being intermediate. — *adj* **intermē'dial** (*rare*) intermediate; intermediary. — *adj* **intermē'diary** acting as an intermediate; intermediate. — *n* an intermediate agent. — *adv* **intermē'diately**. — *n* **intermēdiā'tion** the act of intermediating. — *n* **intermē'diātor**. — *adj* **intermē'diatory** (*-ə-tə-ri*). — *n* **intermē'dium** an intervening agent or instrument; a small bone in the wrist and ankle. — **intermediate frequency** (*electronics*) the output carrier frequency of a frequency changer in a superheterodyne receiver, adjusted to coincide with the frequency band of the intermediate amplifier; **intermediate host** (*zool*) an animal that acts as a secondary host to a parasite but in which it does not become sexually mature; **intermediate level waste** nuclear waste which is mixed with concrete and stored in steel drums in deep mines or under the seabed in concrete chambers (cf **high level** and **low level waste**); **intermediate school** (*NZ*) a school for children aged between eleven and thirteen; **intermediate technology** technology which combines simple, basic materials with modern sophisticated tools and methods; **intermediate vector boson** (*phys*) any of three elementary particles that mediate weak reactions between particles. [**inter-**]

interment. See under **inter**.

intermetallic *in-tər-mə-tal'ik*, *adj* (of an alloy or compound) formed from two or more metallic elements. [**inter-**]

intermezzo *in-tər-met'sō*, sometimes *-med'zō*, *n* a short dramatic or musical entertainment as entr'acte; a short intermediate movement separating sections of a symphonic work (*music*): — *pl* **intermez'zi** (*-sē*) or **intermezz'os**. [Ital, from L *intermedius*]

intermigration *in-tər-mī-grā'shən*, *n* reciprocal migration. [**inter-**]

interminable *in-tûr'min-ə-bl*, *adj* without termination or limit; boundless; endless; tediously long. — *n* **inter'minableness**. — *adv* **inter'minably**. — **interminate decimal** a decimal fraction that runs to an infinity of places. [**in-** (2)]

intermingle *in-tər-ming'gl*, *vt* and *vi* to mingle or mix together. [**inter-**]

in terminis *in tûr'min-is*, (*L*) definitely; in express terms.

intermit *in-tər-mit'*, *vt* and *vi* to stop for a time. — *vt* (*obs*) to interpose. — *n* **intermission** (*-mish'ən*) an act of intermitting; an interval; music played during the interval at a theatre, etc; pause; a respite; *perh* a temporary occupation or recreation (*Shakesp*). — *adj* **intermissive** (*-mis'iv*) coming and going; intermittent. — *n* **intermitt'ence** or **intermitt'ency**. — *adj* **intermitt'ent** intermitting or ceasing at intervals. — *adv* **intermitt'ently**. [L *intermittere*, *-missum*, from *inter* between, and *mittere* to cause to go]

intermix *in-tər-miks'*, *vt* and *vi* to mix together. — *n* **intermix'ture** a mass formed by mixture; something added and intermixed. [L *intermiscēre*, *-mixtum*, from *inter* among, and *miscēre* to mix]

intermodal *in-tər-mō'dəl*, *adj* (of a vehicle, container, system, etc) employing, suitable for, or able to adapt to or be conveyed by, two or more modes of transport. [**inter-**]

intermodulation *in-tər-mod-ū-lā'shən*, (*electronics*) *n* unwanted mutual interference between electronic signals, affecting the amplitude of each. [**inter-**]

intermolecular *in-tər-mol-ek'ū-lər*, *adj* between molecules. [**inter-**]

intermontane *in-tər-mon'tān*, (*geol*) *adj* (of a basin) lying between mountain ranges, often associated with a graben. [**inter-**]

intermundane *in-tər-mun'dān*, *adj* between worlds. [**inter-**]

intermure *in-tər-mūr'*, (*obs*) *vt* to wall in. [L *inter* within, and *mūrus* a wall]

intern *in-tûrn'*, *n* an inmate, eg of a boarding-school; a resident assistant surgeon or physician in a hospital, hence also a trainee gaining practical experience in any profession (*NAm*; also **in'terne**). — *vt* to confine to a prescribed area, or imprison (eg an enemy ship or alien, a suspected terrorist), as a precautionary measure. — *n* **internee'** a person interned. — *n* **intern'ment** confinement of this kind. — *n* **in'ternship** (*NAm*) the position or period of being an intern. [Fr *interne*, from L *internus* inward]

internal *in-tûr'nəl*, *adj* in the interior; domestic as opposed to foreign; intrinsic; pertaining to the inner nature or feelings; inner; taking place within, or involving those inside, an organization or institution. — *n* (in *pl*) inner parts. — *n* **internality** (*-nal'i-ti*). — *n* **internalizā'tion** or **-s-**. — *vt* **inter'nalize** or **-ise** to assimilate (an idea, etc) into one's personality; to withdraw (an emotion, etc) into oneself (rather than express it). — *participial adj* **inter'nalized** or **-s-**. — *adv* **inter'nally**. — **internal-combustion engine** an engine in which the fuel is burned within the working cylinder; **internal evidence** evidence afforded by the thing itself; **internal rhyme** a rhyme occurring within a line of verse; **internal student** one who has studied at the university that examines him or her. [L *internus*, from *inter* within]

international *in-tər-nash'ən-l*, *adj* between nations or their representatives; transcending national limits; extending to several nations; pertaining to the relations between nations. — *n* (with *cap*) an international socialist organization, the **First International** formed in London in 1864 with the aim of economic emancipation for the working classes of the world, the **Second International** formed in Paris in 1889 as a successor to it, the **Third International** founded by the Bolsheviks in 1919 to encourage World revolution, the **Fourth International** formed in 1938 as a rival to the Third, by that time dominated by Stalin; a game or contest between players chosen to represent different nations (*colloq*); a player who takes (or has taken) part in an international match. — *n* **Internationale** (*ɛ̃-ter-na-syō-näl'*) international communist song, first sung in France in 1871; the Second International. — *n* **interna'tionalism**. — *n* **interna'tionalist** someone who favours the common interests, or action, of all nations; someone who favours the principles of the International; a player who represents his or her country in international contests; a specialist in international law. — *adj* **internationalis'tic**. — *n* **internationalizā'tion** or **-s-**. — *vt* **interna'tionalize** or **-ise** to make international; to put under international control. — *adv* **interna'tionally**. — **International Atomic Energy Agency** an organization for promoting the peaceful uses of atomic power (*abbrev* **IAEA**); **International Atomic Time** an international standard of time synchronized by atomic clocks (*abbrev* **TAI**); **International Baccalaureate** (a school-leaving examination giving) an international qualification for higher education; **International Bible Students' Association** see **Russellite**; **International Classification of Diseases** a list of all known diseases published by the World Health Organization (*abbrev* **ICD**); **International Court of Justice** the World Court; **International Date Line** the line east and west of which the date differs, being the 180th meridian with deviations; **International Development Association** an organization founded in 1960 to lend money at low interest rates to developing countries; **international law** the law regulating the relations of states (**public international law**) or that determining which nation's law shall in any case govern the relations of private persons (**private international law**); **international master** (also with *caps*) (a person holding) the second highest international chess title; **international match point** a scoring unit in tournament contract bridge, often shortened to **imp** or **i.m.p.**; **international modern** or **style** a 20c architectural style characterized by the use of modern building materials and techniques, lack of ornament and simple geometric shapes; **International**

Monetary Fund an organization, established in 1945 to promote international trade through increased stabilization of currencies, which maintains a pool of money on which member countries can draw (*abbrev* **IMF**); **International Phonetic Alphabet** the alphabet of the International Phonetic Association, a series of symbols representing human speech sounds (*abbrev* **IPA**); **international (concert) pitch** since 1939, 440 cycles per second at 20°C for A in the treble clef; **International Space Station** the former name for 'Freedom', the space station developed by NASA, ESA, Japan and Canada; **international standard atmosphere** a standardized atmosphere adopted internationally for comparing aircraft performance; **international standard book number** see under **standard**; **international system of units** see **SI units**; **International Telecommunication Union** a UN agency promoting international telecommunications collaboration in order to improve worldwide service (*abbrev* **ITU**); **international units** internationally recognized units in terms of which pure, or impure, vitamin material can be assayed. [**inter-**]

interne. See **intern**.

internecine *in-tər-nē'sīn, adj* deadly; murderous; (loosely) mutually destructive; involving conflict within a group. — Also **internē'cive**. [L *internecīnus, -īvus*, from *internecāre*, from *inter* between (used intensively), and *necāre* to kill]

internee. See under **intern**.

internetting *in-tər-net'ing*, (*comput*) *n* (an) interconnection of computer networks. — Also **in'ternet**.

interneural *in-tər-nū'rəl*, (*anatom*) *adj* situated between the neural spines or spinous processes of successive vertebrae. [**inter-**]

internist *in-tûr'nist, n* a specialist in internal diseases; a physician rather than a surgeon. [*internal* and **-ist**]

internment. See under **intern**.

internode *in'tər-nōd, n* the space between two nodes, eg in a plant stem or nerve fibre. — *adj* **internō'dal** or (*obs*) **internō'dial**. [L *internōdium*, from *inter* between, and *nōdus* a knot]

inter nos *in'tər* or *-ter nōs*, (*L*) between ourselves.

internuncio *in-tər-nun'shi-ō, n* a messenger between two parties; the Pope's representative at minor courts: — *pl* **internun'cios**. — *adj* **internun'cial** relating to an internuncio; interconnecting, as the neurone linking the afferent and efferent neurones of the central nervous system. [Ital *internunzio*, Sp *internuncio*, L *internuntius*, from *inter* between, and *nuntius* a messenger]

interoceanic *in-tər-ō-shi-an'ik, adj* between oceans. [**inter-**]

interoceptor *in-tər-ō-sep'tər*, (*physiol*) *n* a sensory receptor that responds to changes within the body, such as the acidity of the blood. — *adj* **interocep'tive**. [*interior* and *receptor*]

interocular *in-tər-ok'ū-lər, adj* between the eyes. [**inter-**]

interorbital *in-tər-ör'bit-əl, adj* between orbits. [**inter-**]

interosculation *in-tər-os-kū-lā'shən, n* interconnection by, or as if by, osculation; possession of characters common to different groups; dovetailing into one another. — *adj* **interos'culant**. — *vt* **interos'culate**. [**inter-**]

interosseous *in-tər-os'i-əs, adj* situated between bones. — Also **inteross'eal**. [**inter-**]

interpage *in-tər-pāj', vt* to print on intermediate pages; to insert (intervening pages). [**inter-**]

interparietal *in-tər-pə-rī'ə-təl, adj* situated between the right and left parietal bones of the skull. [**inter-**]

inter partes *in'tər* or *-ter pär'tēz* or *pär'tās*, (*L; law*) between parties.

interpellation *in-tər-pel-ā'shən, n* a question raised during the course of a debate, *esp* in parliament; interruption (*obs*); intercession (*obs*); a summons (*obs*). — *adj* **interpell'ant** causing an interpellation. — *n* a person who interpellates. — *vt* **inter'pellate** (or *-pel'*) to question by interpellation. [Fr, from L *interpellāre, -ātum* to disturb by speaking, from *inter* between, and *pellere* to drive]

interpenetrate *in-tər-pen'i-trāt, vt* to penetrate thoroughly; to pervade. — *vt* and *vi* to penetrate each other. — *adj* **interpen'etrable**. — *adj* **interpen'etrant**. — *n* **interpenetrā'tion**. — *adj* **interpen'etrātive**. [**inter-**]

interpersonal *in-tər-pûr'sən-əl, adj* between persons. — *adv* **interper'sonally**. [**inter-**]

interpetiolar *in-tər-pet'i-ō-lər*, (*bot*) *adj* between petioles. [**inter-**]

interphase *in'tər-fāz, n* an interface (*chem*); the period of the cell cycle between one mitosis and the next (*biol*; also **interkinesis**). [**inter-**]

interphone *in'tər-fōn, n* an intercom. [Gr *phōnē* voice]

interpilaster *in-tər-pil-as'tər*, (*archit*) *n* a space between two pilasters. [**inter-**]

interplanetary *in-tər-plan'it-ə-ri, adj* between planets. [**inter-**]

interplant *in-tər-plänt', vt* to plant among another crop. [**inter-**]

interplay *in'tər-plā, n* mutual action; interchange of action and reaction. [**inter-**]

interplead *in-tər-plēd'*, (*law*) *vi* to discuss adverse claims to property by bill of interpleader. — *n* **interplead'er** a person who interpleads; a form of process in the English courts, by a bill in equity, intended to protect a defendant who claims no interest in the subject matter of a suit, but has reason to know that the plaintiff's title is disputed by some other claimant. [**inter-**]

interpleural *in-tər-ploo͞'rəl, adj* situated between the right and left pleural cavities. [**inter-**]

inter pocula *in'tər* or *-ter pok'ū-lə* or *pō'ko͞o-la*, (*L*) literally, over one's cups, hence, in the course of drinking, over drinks.

Interpol *in'tər-pol*, the *Inter*national Criminal *Pol*ice Commission, directed to international cooperation in the suppression of crime.

interpolable. See **interpolate**.

interpolar *in-tər-pō'lər, adj* between or connecting the poles. [**inter-**]

interpolate *in-tûr'pō-lāt* or *-pə-lāt, vt* to insert a word or passage in a book or manuscript, *esp* in order to mislead; to tamper with or to corrupt by spurious insertions; to insert, interpose, interject; to fill in as an intermediate term of a series (*math*). — *adj* **inter'polable**. — *n* **interpolā'tion**. — *adj* **inter'polātive**. — *n* **inter'polātor** or **inter'polater** someone who or that which interpolates; an apparatus for regenerating and retransmitting signals (*telecomm*). [L *interpolāre, -ātum*, from *inter* between, and *polīre* to polish]

interpone *in-tər-pōn'*, (*Scots law*) *vt* to interpose. [L *interpōnere*]

interpose *in-tər-pōz', vt* to place between; to thrust in; to offer (eg aid or services); to put in by way of interruption. — *vi* to come between; to mediate; to interfere. — *n* **interpos'al**. — *n* **interpos'er**. — *n* **interposition** (*in-tər-poz-ish'ən*) the act of interposing; intervention; mediation; the right of a state to oppose the federal government for encroachment on the prerogatives of the state (*US*); anything interposed. [Fr *interposer*, from L *inter* between, and Fr *poser* to place; see **pose**[1]]

interpret *in-tûr'prit, vt* to explain the meaning of, to elucidate, unfold, show the significance of; to translate into intelligible or familiar terms. — *vi* to practise interpretation. — *adj* **inter'pretable** capable of being explained. — *vt* and *vi* (*archaic*) **inter'pretate**. — *n* **interpretā'tion** the act of interpreting; the sense given by an interpreter; the representation of a dramatic part, performance of a piece of music, etc, according to one's conception of it. — *adj* **inter'pretative** (*-āt-iv* or *-ət-iv*) or **inter'pretive** inferred by or containing interpretation. — *adv* **inter'pretatively** or **inter'pretively** — *n* **inter'preter** a person who translates orally for the benefit of two or more parties speaking different languages; an expounder; a machine which prints out on punched cards fed into it the data contained in the patterns of holes in the cards (*comput*); a program which executes other programs (*comput*; cf **compiler** under **compile**); a translator of written texts (*obs*). — *n* **inter'pretership**. — *n* **inter'pretress** or (*obs*) **inter'pretess** a female interpreter. [L *interpretārī*, *-ātus*, from *interpres*, *-etis*]

interprovincial *in-tər-prə-vin'shl*, *adj* between provinces. [**inter-**]

interproximal *in-tər-prok'si-məl*, (*dentistry*) *adj* pertaining to the surfaces of teeth where they adjoin. [**inter-**]

interpunction *in-tər-pungk'shən*, *n* the insertion of punctuation marks in writing.. — Also **interpunctūā'tion**. — *vt* **interpunc'tūate**. [**inter-**]

interracial *in-tər-rā'shəl* or *-shi-əl*, *adj* between races. [**inter-**]

interradial *in-tər-rā'di-əl*, *adj* between radii or rays; of or relating to an interradius. — *adv* **interrā'dially**. — *n* **interrā'dius** an interradial part; a radius midway between primary radii or perradii. [**inter-**]

interramal *in-tər-rā'məl*, *adj* situated between the rami or branches, *esp* of the lower jaw. — *n* **interramificā'tion** (*-ram-*) interweaving of branches. [L *inter* between, and *rāmus* a branch]

interregal *in-tər-rē'gəl*, *adj* between kings. [**inter-**]

interregnum *in-tər-reg'nəm*, *n* the time between two reigns; the time between the cessation of one and the establishment of another government; any breach of continuity in order, etc: — *pl* **interreg'na** or **interreg'nums**. [L *inter* between, and *regnum* rule]

interrelation *in-tər-ri-lā'shən*, *n* reciprocal relation. — *n* **interrelā'tionship**. [**inter-**]

interrex *in'tər-reks*, *n* someone who rules during an interregnum; a regent: — *pl* **interreges** (*-rē'jēz*). [L *inter* between, and *rēx* a king]

interrog. *abbrev*: interrogate; interrogation; interrogative; interrogatively.

interrogate *in-ter'ə-gāt*, *vt* to question; to examine by asking questions; (of a radar set, etc) to send out signals to (a radio-beacon) in order to ascertain position. — *vi* to ask questions. — *adj* **interr'ogable**. — *n* **interr'ogant** a questioner. — *n* **interrogatee'** someone who is interrogated. — *n* **interrogā'tion** the act of interrogating; a question put; the mark placed after a question (?) (also **interrogation mark**). — *adj* **interrogative** (*in-tər-og'ə-tiv*) denoting a question; expressed as a question. — *n* a word used in asking a question. — *adv* **interrog'atively**. — *n* **interr'ogator**. — *n* **interrog'atory** a question or inquiry. — *adj* expressing a question. [L *interrogāre*, *-ātum*, from *inter* between, and *rogāre* to ask]

in terrorem *in te-rōr'em* or *-rör'*, (*L*) as a warning.

interrupt *in-tər-upt'*, *vt* to break in between; to stop or hinder by breaking in upon; to break continuity in. — *vi* to make an interruption. — *adj* interrupted (*obs*); gaping apart (*Milton*). — *n* (*comput*) a signal that causes a break in the current routine, control passing to another routine in such a way that the original one may later be resumed. — *adj* **interrupt'ed** broken in continuity; irregular in spacing or size of parts (*biol*). — *adv* **interrupt'edly** with interruptions; irregularly. — *n* **interrup'ter** or **interrup'tor** a person who interrupts; an apparatus for interrupting, eg for breaking an electric circuit. — *n* **interrup'tion** the act of interrupting; hindrance; temporary cessation. — *adj* **interrup'tive** tending to interrupt. — *adv* **interrup'tively**. — **interrupted cadence** (*music*) a cadence in which some other chord (often the submediant) replaces the expected tonic. [L *interrumpere*, *-ruptum*, from *inter* between, and *rumpere* to break]

interscapular *in-tər-ska'pū-lər*, (*anatom*) *adj* between the shoulder blades. [**inter-**]

interscholastic *in-tər-skə-las'tik*, *adj* between schools; representative of several schools. [**inter-**]

inter-science *in-tər-sī'əns*, *adj* belonging to the examination between matriculation and BSc of London University. [**inter-**]

interscribe *in-tər-skrīb'*, (*obs*) *vt* to write between. [L *interscrībere*, from *inter* between, and *scrībere* to write]

inter se *in'tər* or *-ter sē* or *sā*, (*L*) between or among themselves.

intersect *in-tər-sekt'*, *vt* to cut across; to cut or cross mutually; to divide into parts. — *vi* to cross each other. — *n* **in'tersect** a point of intersection. — *n* **intersec'tion** intersecting; the point or line on which lines or surfaces cut each other (*geom*); the set of elements which two or more sets have in common (*math*); a crossroads. — *adj* **intersec'tional**. [L *inter* between, and *secāre*, *sectum* to cut]

interseptal *in-tər-sep'tl*, *adj* between septa. [**inter-**]

intersert *in-tər-sûrt'*, *vt* (*obs*) to insert between other things, interpolate. — *adj* **intersert'al** (*petrology*) having interstitial crystalline or glassy matter between feldspar laths. [L *interserere*, *-sertum* to interpose, from *inter* between, and *serere* to plant]

interservice *in-tər-sûr'vis*, *adj* between the armed forces. [**inter-**]

intersex *in'tər-seks*, (*biol*) *n* an individual developing anatomical characteristics of both sexes; the condition of being intersexual. — *adj* **intersex'ūal** between the sexes; intermediate between the sexes. — *n* **intersexūal'ity**. [**inter-**]

intersidereal *in-tər-sī-dē'ri-əl*, (*rare*) *adj* interstellar. [**inter-**]

interspace *in'tər-spās*, *n* an interval. — *vt* (*-spās'*) to put intervals between. — *adj* **interspatial** (*-spā'shl*). — *adv* **interspa'tially**. [**inter-**]

interspecific *in-tər-spis-if'ik*, *adj* between species. [**inter-**]

intersperse *in-tər-spûrs'*, *vt* to scatter or set here and there; to diversify. — *n* **interspers'al** (*rare*). — *n* **interspersion** (*-spûr'shən*). [L *interspergere*, *-spersum*, from *inter* among, and *spargere* to scatter]

interspinal *in-tər-spī'nəl*, *adj* between the vertebrae. — Also **interspī'nous**. [**inter-**]

interstadial *in'tər-stā'di-əl*, (*geol*) *n* a retreat of ice during a glacial period, less extensive than an interglacial. — *adj* belonging to an interstadial.

interstate *in'tər-stāt* or *-stāt'*, *adj* pertaining to relations, *esp* political and commercial, between states; between or involving two or more states. — *adv* (*Austr*) into or to another state. — *n* (*US*) (*in'*) an interstate highway. [**inter-**]

interstellar *in-tər-stel'ər*, *adj* beyond the solar system or among the stars; in the intervals between the stars. — Also **interstell'ary**. [L *inter* between, and *stella* a star]

interstice *in-tûr'stis*, *n* a small space between things closely set, or between the parts which compose a body; the time interval required by canon law before receiving higher orders (*RC*); a space between atoms in a lattice where other atoms can be located. — *adj* **interstitial** (*-stish'l*) occurring in an interstice or interstices; containing interstitial atoms or ions (*chem*); pertaining to the surfaces of teeth where they adjoin (*dentistry*). — *n* an extra atom in a crystal lattice, causing a defect. — **interstitial cells** (*anatom*) the cells between the seminiferous tubules of the testis, that secrete androgens. [L *interstitium*, from *inter* between, and *sistere*, *statum* to stand, set]

interstratification *in-tər-strat-i-fi-kā'shən*, *n* the state of lying between, or alternating with, other strata. — *adj* **interstrat'ified**. — *vt* and *vi* **interstrat'ify**. [**inter-**]

intersubjective *in-tər-sub-jek'tiv* or *-səb-*, *adj* between subjects; between points of view. — *adv* **intersubjec'tively**. — *n* **intersubjectiv'ity**. [**inter-**]

interswitchboard line *in-tər-swich'bōrd* or *-börd līn*, (*telecomm*) *n*. Same as **tie line** (see under **tie**).

intertangle *in-tər-tang'gl*, *vt* and *vi* to tangle together. — *n* **intertang'lement**. [**inter-**]

intertarsal *in-tər-tär'sl*, (*anatom*) *adj* between tarsal bones. [**inter-**]

intertentacular *in-tər-ten-tak'ū-lər*, *adj* between tentacles. [**inter-**]

interterritorial *in-tər-ter-i-tō'ri-əl* or *-tö'*, *adj* between territories. [**inter-**]

intertexture *in-tər-teks'chər*, *n* interwoven state. [**inter-**]
intertidal *in-tər-tī'dl*, *adj* between low-water and high-water mark. [**inter-**]
intertie *in'tər-tī*, *n* (in roofing, etc) a short timber binding together upright posts. [**inter-**]
intertissued *in-tər-tish'ūd*, *adj* interwoven. — Also (*Shakesp*) **entertiss'ued**. [**inter-**]
intertraffic *in-tər-traf'ik*, (*obs*) *n* traffic between two or more people or places. [**inter-**]
intertribal *in-tər-trī'bl*, *adj* between tribes. [**inter-**]
intertrigo *in-tər-trī'gō*, *n* an inflammation of the skin from chafing or rubbing: — *pl* **intertri'gos**. [L *intertrīgō*, from *inter* between, and *terere*, *trītum* to rub]
intertropical *in-tər-trop'i-kl*, *adj* between the tropics. [**inter-**]
intertwine *in-tər-twīn'*, *vt* and *vi* to twine or twist together. — *n* **in'tertwine** intertwining. — *n* **intertwine'ment**. — *n* and *adj* **intertwīn'ing**. — *adj* **intertwīn'ingly**. [**inter-**]
intertwist *in-tər-twist'*, *vt* to twist together. — *adv* **inter-twist'ingly**. [**inter-**]
interunion *in-tər-ūn'yən*, *n* a blending together. [**inter-**]
interurban *in-tər-ûr'bən*, *adj* between cities. [L *inter* between, and *urbs*, *urbis* a city]
interval *in'tər-vəl*, *n* time or space between; a break between lessons, acts of a play, etc; difference of pitch between any two musical tones (*music*); a set of real numbers or points between two given numbers or points (*math*). — *adj* **intervallic** (*-val'ik*). [L *intervallum*, from *inter* between, and *vallum* a rampart]
intervale *in'tər-vāl*, (*US*) *n* a low level tract of land along a river. [**inter-**]
intervallum *in-tər-val'əm*, *adj* (of fortifications, etc) between the ramparts. — *n* (*obs*) an interval. [Ety as for **interval**]
intervein *in-tər-vān'*, *vt* to intersect, as with veins. [**inter-**]
intervene *in-tər-vēn'*, *vi* to come or be between; to occur between points of time; to interrupt; to step in so as to affect the outcome of a situation; to interpose in an action to which one was not at first a party (*law*). — *vt* (*obs*) to separate. — *n* **interven'er** a person who intervenes. — Also (*law*) **interven'or**. — *adj* **intervenient** (*-vē'ni-ənt*; *archaic*) being or passing between, intervening. — *adj* **interven'ing** coming in between. — *n* **intervention** (*-ven'shən*) intervening; interference; mediation; interposition; a system of removing surplus produce from the market and storing it until prices rise. — *n* **interven'tionism**. — *n* **interven'tionist** someone who advocates interference, *esp* by a government in economic matters, or in the affairs of a foreign government (also *adj*). — *n* **interven'tor** a mediator in ecclesiastical controversies. — **intervening sequence** (*biol*) an intron; **intervention price** the market price at which intervention occurs; **intervention stock** the total stock of surplus produce removed from the market by intervention. [L *inter* between, and *venīre* to come]
interview *in'tər-vū*, *n* a formal meeting; a meeting between an employer, board of directors, etc and a candidate to ascertain by questioning and discussion the latter's suitability for a post, etc; a meeting between a journalist, or radio or TV broadcaster, and a notable person to discuss the latter's views, etc for publication or broadcasting; an article or programme based on such a meeting; a mutual view or sight (*obs*). — *vt* and *vi* to conduct an interview (with). — *n* **interviewee'** a person who is interviewed. — *n* **in'terviewer** a person who interviews. [OFr *entrevue*, from *entre* between, and *voir* to see]
intervital *in-tər-vī'təl*, *adj* between lives, between death and resurrection. [L *inter* between, and *vīta* life]
inter vivos *in'tər* or *-ter vīvōs* or *wē'wōs*, (*L*; *law*) from one living person to another, among the living.
intervocalic *in-tər-vō-kal'ik*, *adj* between vowels. [**inter-**]
intervolve *in-tər-volv'*, *vt* and *vi* to entwine or roll up one with or within another. [L *inter* within, and *volvere* to roll]
interwar *in-tər-wör'*, *adj* between wars. [**inter-**]
interweave *in-tər-wēv'*, *vt* and *vi* to weave together; to intermingle. [**inter-**]
interwind *in-tər-wīnd'*, *vt* and *vi* to wind together or around and among one another: — *pa t* and *pa p* **interwound** (*-wownd'*). [**inter-**]
interwork *in-tər-wûrk'*, *vt* and *vi* to work together; to work into another or one another. — *adj* **interwrought** (*-röt'*). [**inter-**]
interwreathe *in-tər-rēdh'*, *vt* to wreathe together or into one another. [**inter-**]
interzone *in-tər-zōn'* or **interzonal** *-zōn'əl*, *adj* between zones (eg of occupied country). — *n* **in'terzone**. [**inter-**]
intestate *in-tes'tāt* or *-tit*, *adj* dying without having made a valid will; (of property) not disposed of by will. — *n* a person who dies without making a valid will. — *n* **intes'tacy** (*-tə-si*) the state of someone dying without having made a valid will. [L *intestātus*, from *in-* not, and *testārī*, *-ātus* to make a will]
intestine *in-tes'tin*, *n* (commonly in *pl*) a part of the digestive system extending from the stomach to the anus, divided into the *small intestine* (comprising duodenum, jejunum and ileum) and the *large intestine* (comprising caecum, colon and rectum). — *adj* **intes'tinal** (also *-tīn'*) pertaining to the intestines. — **intestinal flora** bacteria normally present in the intestine. [L *intestīnus*, from *intus* within]
inthral, inthrall. See **enthrall**.
inti *in'ti*, *n* the standard unit of currency of Peru (100 centavos). [Quechua]
intifada *in-ti-fä'də*, *n* the uprising in 1987 and continued resistance by Palestinians to Israeli occupation of the Gaza Strip and West Bank of the Jordan. [Ar, shaking off]
intil *in-til'*, (*Scot*) *prep* into, in, or unto. [**in** and **till**[2]]
intima *in'tim-ə*, (*anatom*) *n* the innermost coat or membrane of an organ or part, *esp* a blood or lymphatic vessel: — *pl* **in'timae** (*-mē*). [L, short for *tunica intima* innermost coat]
intimate *in'ti-mit* or *-māt*, *adj* innermost; internal; close; deep-seated; private; personal; closely acquainted; familiar; in a sexual relationship; engaging in sex; encouraging informality and closer personal relations through smallness, exclusiveness. — *n* a close friend. — *vt* (*-māt*) to hint; to announce. — *n* **in'timacy** (*-mə-si*) the state of being intimate; close familiarity; sexual intercourse. — *adv* **in'timately**. — *n* **intimā'tion** an indication; a hint; an announcement. — *n* **intim'ity** (*archaic*) intimacy. [L *intimāre*, *-ātum*, from *intimus* innermost, from *intus* within]
intime *ɛ̃-tēm'*, *adj* intimate; small and cosy. [Fr]
intimidate *in-tim'i-dāt*, *vt* to strike fear into; to influence by threats or violence. — *n* **intimidā'tion** the act of intimidating; the use of violence or threats to influence the conduct or compel the consent of another; the state of being intimidated. — *adj* **intim'idatory**. [L *in* into, and *timidus* fearful]
intimism *in'ti-mizm*, *n* a genre of French impressionist painting of the early 20c, based on subject matter from everyday life. — *n* and *adj* **in'timist** (*Fr* **intimiste** *ɛ̃-tē-mēst*). [Fr *intime*; see ety for **intimate**]
intinction *in-tingk'shən*, (*Christianity*) *n* a mode of administering communion by dipping the bread into the wine. [LL *intinctiō*, *-ōnis*, from L *intingere*, *intinctum* to dip in]
intine *in'tin*, *-tēn* or *-tīn*, (*bot*) *n* the inner membrane of a pollen grain or spore. [L *intus* within]
intire *in-tīr'*. An obsolete form of **entire**.
intitule *in-tit'ūl*, *vt* same as **entitle**, now used only to mean give a title to (a Parliamentary Act, etc). [OFr *intituler*, from L *titulus* title]
into *in'too*, *prep* to a position within; to a state of; used to indicate the dividend in dividing (*math*); in contact or collision with; interested in or enthusiastic about (*colloq*); to part of (*math*). — *adj* (*math*) describing a mapping of one set to a second set, involving only some of the elements of the latter. — **multiply into** (*rare*) to

multiply (one quantity) by (another quantity) to find the product. [**in** and **to**]

intoed or **in-toed** *in'tōd'*, *adj* having the toes more or less turned inwards. [**in-** (1)]

intolerable *in-tol'ər-ə-bl*, *adj* too bad, severe, etc to be tolerated; insufferable. — *n* **intolerabil'ity** or **intol'erableness**. — *adv* **intol'erably**. — *n* **intol'erance** the state of being intolerant; inability to tolerate, *esp* a drug. — *adj* **intol'erant** not able or willing to endure; not accepting opinions different from one's own; persecuting; easily irritated or angered by the faults of others. — *n* someone opposed to toleration. — *adv* **intol'erantly**. — *n* **intolera'tion**. [**in-** (2)]

intomb *in-tōōm'*, obsolete form of **entomb**.

intonaco *in-tō'nə-kō*, (*Ital*) *n* in fresco painting, the finishing coat of lime plaster on which the paint is applied.

intonate[1] *in'tōn-āt*, (*obs*) *vt* and *vi* to thunder. [L *intonāre*, *-ātum* to thunder; cf **intonate**[2]]

intonate[2] *in'tōn-āt* or *-tən-*, *vt* and *vi* to intone. — *n* **intonā'tion** modulation or rise and fall in pitch of the voice; the opening phrase of any plainsong melody, sung *usu* either by the officiating priest alone, or by one or more selected choristers; pitching of musical notes; intoning. — *n* **in'tonātor** a monochord. — *vt* and *vi* **intone** (*in-tōn'*) to chant, read or utter in musical tones, singsong, or monotone; to begin by singing the opening phrase; to utter with a particular intonation. — *n* **intōn'er**. — *n* and *adj* **intōn'ing**. — *adv* **intōn'ingly**. [LL *intonāre*, *-ātum*, from L *in* in, and *tonus* tone]

intorsion or **intortion** *in-tör'shən*, *n* a twist; a twine. — *adj* **intort'ed** twisted inwards; involved. [Fr *intorsion*, L *intortiō*, *-ōnis*, from *in* in, and *torquēre*, *tortum* to twist]

in totidem verbis *in tot'i-dem ver'bēs* or *wer'bēs*, (*L*) in so many words.

in toto *in tō'tō*, (*L*) entirely.

intown *in'tōōn*, (*Scot*) *adj* infield, near the farmhouse. — **intown multure** (*hist*) payment to the miller by those who are compelled to have their grain ground at the mill. [**in** and **town**]

intoxicate *in-toks'i-kāt*, *vt* to make drunk; to excite to enthusiasm or madness; to elate excessively; to poison (*obs*). — *adj* **intox'icant** intoxicating. — *n* an intoxicating agent. — *adj* **intox'icāting**. — *n* **intoxicā'tion** poisoning (*med*); the state of being drunk; high excitement or elation. [LL *intoxicāre*, *-ātum*, from *in* in, and *toxicum*, from Gr *toxikon* arrow-poison, from *toxon* a bow]

Intoximeter® *in-tok'si-mē-tər*, *n* a device for measuring the amount of alcohol in the blood of a person who breathes into it, and showing this measurement on a printout. — Also without *cap*.

intra *in'trə* or *in'trä*, (*L*) within. — **intra muros** (*mū'rōs* or *mōō'rōs*) within the walls; **intra vires** (*vī'rēz*, *wē'* or *vē'rās*) within the legal power of; **intra vitam** (*vē'tam*, *vī'tam* or *wē'täm*) during life.

intra- *in'trä-* or *-trə-*, *pfx* signifying within. — *adj* **intra-abdom'inal** situated within the cavity of the abdomen. — *adj* **intra-artē'rial** within an artery. — *adj* **intra-artic'ular** in or within a joint. — *adj* **intracap'sular** lying within a capsule. — *adj* **intracar'diac** within the heart. — *adj* **intracav'itary** (*radiol*) applied within or through body cavities, as radium applied in the uterus, or irradiation through natural or artificial body cavities. — *adj* **intracell'ular** inside a cell or cells. — *adj* **intracrā'nial** within the skull. — *adj* **intraderm'al** within the skin. — *adj* **intrafallō'pian** within, or introduced into, (either of) the Fallopian tubes. — *adj* **intramed'ullary** within the bone marrow. — *adj* **intramercū'rial** within Mercury's orbit. — *adj* **intramolec'ūlar** within the limits of the molecule; formed by a reaction between different parts of a molecule. — *adj* **intramun'dane** within the world. — *adj* **intramū'ral** within walls; taking place within, or between groups within, a single (*esp* educational) establishment or institution. — *adj* **intramus'cūlar** within a muscle. — *adv* **intramus'cularly**. — *adj* **intranat'ional** within a nation. — *adj* **intraparī'etal** within walls, private; situated in the parietal lobe of the brain. — *adj* **intrapet'iolar** between petiole and stem. — *adj* **intrasex'ual** within or between members of the same sex. — *adj* **intraterritō'rial** within a territory. — *adj* **intrathē'cal** within, or introduced into, the sheath of the spinal cord or brain. — *adj* **intravas'cular** within the blood vessels. — *adj* **intravē'nous** within, or introduced into, a vein or veins. [L *intrā* within]

intractable *in-trakt'ə-bl*, *adj* unmanageable; obstinate. — *n* **intractabil'ity** or **intract'ableness**. — *adv* **intract'ably**. [**in-** (2)]

intrada *in-trä'də*, (*music*) *n* an introductory piece, prelude. [Ital]

intradermal. See under **intra-**.

intrados *in-trā'dos*, (*archit*) *n* the soffit or under surface of an arch or vault: — *pl* **intra'dos** or **intra'doses**. [Fr, from L *intrā* within, and *dorsum* the back]

intrafallopian... to ... **intranational**. See under **intra-**.

in trans. *abbrev*: *in transitu* (L), in transit.

intrans. *abbrev*: intransitive.

intransigent *in-tran'si-jənt*, *-trän'* or *-zi-*, *adj* refusing to come to any understanding, irreconcilable; obstinate. — *n* an intransigent person. — *n* **intran'sigence** or **intran'sigency**. — *n* **intran'sigentism**. — *n* **intran'sigentist**. — *adv* **intran'sigently**. — Also (now *rare*) **intransigeance**, **intransigeant**, etc. [Fr *intransigeant*, from Sp *intransigente*, from L *in-* not, and *transigēns*, *-entis*, pr p of *transigere* to transact; see **transact**]

intransitive *in-tran'si-tiv*, *-trän'* or *-zi-*, *adj* not passing over or indicating passing over; representing action confined to the subject of the verb, ie having no object (*gram*). — *adv* **intran'sitively**. [**in-** (2)]

in transitu *in tran'* or *trän'si-tōō*, (*L*) in passage, in transit, on the way.

intransmissible *in-trans-mis'i-bl*, *-tranz-* or *-tränz-*, *adj* that cannot be transmitted. [**in-** (2)]

intransmutable *in-trans-mūt'ə-bl*, *-tranz-* or *-tränz-*, *adj* that cannot be changed into another substance. — *n* **intransmutabil'ity**. [**in-** (2)]

intrant *in'trənt*, *adj* entering; penetrating. — *n* a person who enters, *esp* on membership, office or possession. [L *intrāns*, *-antis*, from *intrāre* to enter]

intraparietal and **intrapetiolar**. See under **intra-**.

intrapreneur *in-trə-prə-nœr'*, *n* a person who initiates commercial ventures within a large organization. — *adj* **intrapreneur'ial**. [**intra-** and entre*preneur*]

intrasexual... to ... **intrathecal**. See under **intra-**.

intrauterine *in-trə-ū'tə-rīn*, *adj* within the uterus. — **intrauterine contraceptive device** see **IUCD**. [**intra-**]

intravasation *in-tra-və-zā'shən*, *n* the entrance of extraneous matter into blood or lymph vessels. [L *intrā* within, and *vās* a vessel]

intravascular and **intravenous**. See under **intra-**.

intra vires and **intra vitam**. See under **intra**.

intreat, etc *in-trēt'*, etc. Archaic form of **entreat**, etc.

intrench and **intrenchment**. See **entrench**.

intrenchant *in-trensh'ənt*, or *-trench'*, (*Shakesp*) *adj* not able to be cut or wounded, indivisible. [**in-** (2)]

intrepid *in-trep'id*, *adj* without trepidation or fear; undaunted; brave. — *n* **intrepid'ity** firm, unshaken courage; daring. — *adv* **intrep'idly**. [L *intrepidus*, from *in-* not, and *trepidus* alarmed]

intricate *in'tri-kit* or *-kāt* (also *-trik'it*), *adj* involved; entangled; complex. — *n* **in'tricacy** (*-kə-si*; also *-trik'*) or **in'tricateness**. — *adv* **in'tricately**. [L *intrīcātus*, from *in-* in, and *trīcāre* to make difficulties, from *trīcae* hindrances]

intrigue *in'-trēg*, *n* indirect or underhand scheming or plotting; a private scheme; the plot of a play or romance; a secret illicit love affair. — *vi* (*treg'*) to engage in intrigue. — *vt* to puzzle, to fascinate. — *n* **intrigant** or **intriguant** (*in'tri-gant* or *ɛ̃-trē-gā̃*; *archaic*) a person who intrigues (also *adj*): — *fem* **intrigante** or **intriguante**. — *n* **intrigu'er**. — *adj* **intrigu'ing**. — *adv* **intrigu'ingly**. [Fr; see **intricate**]

intrince *in-trins'*, (*Shakesp*) *adj* intricate. [See **intrinsicate**]

intrinsic *in-trin'sik* or **intrinsical** *-əl*, *adj* inward; genuine; inherent; essential, belonging to the point at issue; (of muscles) entirely contained within the limb and girdle. — *n* **intrinsicality** (*-al'i-ti*; *rare*). — *adv* **intrin'sically**. — *n* **intrin'sicalness** (*rare*). — **intrinsic factor** a protein secreted in the stomach, essential in the absorption of vitamin B_{12}. [Fr *intrinsèque*, from L *intrīnsecus*, from *intrā* within, sfx *-in*, and *secus* following]

intrinsicate *in-trins'i-kāt*, (*Shakesp*) *adj* intricate. [Apparently Ital *intrinsecato* familiar, confused with **intricate**]

intro *in'trō*, (*colloq*) *n* contraction of **introduction**, used *esp* of the opening passage of a jazz or popular music piece: — *pl* **in'tros**.

intro- *in'trō-* or *in-tro'-*, *pfx* within, into. [L *intrō*]

introd. *abbrev*: introduction.

introduce *in-trə-dūs'*, *vt* to bring in, establish; to conduct into a place; to put in, add, insert or inject; formally to make known or acquainted; to give (a person) his or her first experience of, to acquaint with (with *to*); to preface; to present to an audience (eg a radio broadcast, a theatre entertainment). — *n* **introduc'er**. — *adj* **introduc'ible**. — *n* **introduction** (*-duk'shən*) (an) act of introducing; formal presentation; preliminary matter serving to introduce the text of a book; a preliminary passage or section leading up to a movement (*music*); a text serving to acquaint the reader with the fundamental principles of a subject or course of study; something introduced. — *adj* **introductive** (*-duk'tiv*) promoting introduction. — *adv* **introduc'torily**. — *adj* **introduc'tory** serving to introduce; preliminary; prefatory. [L *intrōdūcere*, *-ductum*, from *intrō* inward, and *dūcere* to lead]

introgression *in-trə-gresh'ən*, *n* the introduction of the genes of one species into another species. [L *intrō* inwards, and pa p of *gradī* to step]

introit *in-trō'it*, *in'* or *-troit*, *n* the anthem sung at the beginning of Mass, immediately after the *Confiteor*, and when the priest has ascended to the altar (*RC*); in other churches, an introductory hymn, psalm or anthem. — *n* **intrō'itus** an entrance to a cavity or hollow organ, eg the vagina (*anatom*); an introit. [L *introitus*, from *introīre*, from *intrō* inwards, and *īre*, *itum* to go]

introjection *in-trō-jek'shən*, *n* the endowment of inanimate objects with the attributes of living creatures; the taking into the self of persons or things from the outer world so as to experience a oneness with them and to feel personally touched by their fate; the process of believing one possesses the qualities of another person (*psychol*). — *vt* and *vi* **introject'**. [L *intrō* within, and *jacere* to throw]

introld. See **entrold**.

intromit *in-trō-mit'* or *-trə-*, *vt* to introduce; to admit; to permit to enter; to insert. — *vi* to have dealings (*Scots law*); to interfere, *esp* with the effects of another (esp *Scots law*): — *pr p* **intromitt'ing**; *pa t* and *pa p* **intromitt'ed**. — *n* **intromission** (*-mish'ən*) introduction; insertion; in Scots law, the assumption of authority to deal with another's property (*legal*, where the party is expressly or impliedly authorized to interfere, *vicious*, where an heir or next of kin, without any authority, interferes with a deceased person's estate); the proceeds of such interference. — *adj* **intromiss'ive** pertaining to intromission; intromitting. — *n* **intromitt'ent** intromitting; adapted for insertion, *esp* (*zool*) in copulation. — *n* **intromitt'er**. [L *intrō* inward, and *mittere*, *missum* to send]

intron *in'tron*, (*biol*) *n* any of the segments of a eukaryotic gene that do not carry coded information for the synthesis of proteins (cf **exon**[2]). — Also known as **intervening sequence**. [Perh *intervening* sequence and **-on** as in **codon** and **exon**]

introrse *in-trörs'*, *adj* turned or facing inward; (of an anther) opening towards the centre of the flower. — *adv* **introrse'ly**. [L *introrsus* toward the middle, inward, from *intrō* inward, and *versus*, from *vertere* to turn]

introspection *in-trō-spek'shən*, *n* a viewing of the inside or interior; the observation and analysis of the processes of one's own mind. — *vi* **introspect'** to practise introspection. — *n* **introspec'tionist**. — *adj* **introspec'tive**. [L *intrō* within, and *specere* to look at]

introsusception *in-trō-sə-sep'shən*, *n* intussusception. [L *intrō* inwards]

introvert *in-trō-vûrt'* or *-trə-*, *vt* to turn inwards; to turn in upon itself; to turn inside out; to withdraw part within the rest of. — *n* (*in'*) anything introverted; a person interested mainly in his or her own inner states and processes rather than the outside world (*opp* to *extrovert* or *extravert*) (*psychol*); loosely, a shy or reflective person. — *adj* **introvers'ible**. — *n* **introver'sion** (*-shən*). — *adj* **introver'sive** or **introver'tive**. [L *intrō* inwards, and *vertere*, *versum* to turn]

intrude *in-trōōd'*, *vi* to thrust oneself in; to enter uninvited or unwelcome. — *vt* to force in. — *n* **intrud'er** a person or thing that intrudes; a military aircraft which raids enemy territory alone; a person who enters premises secretly or by force, with criminal intentions. — *n* **intrusion** (*-trōō'zhən*) (an) act of intruding; encroachment; an injection of rock in a molten state among and through existing rocks; a mass so injected. — *n* **intru'sionist** a person who intrudes, *esp* of those who, before the Scottish Disruption of 1843, refused a parish the right of objecting to the settlement of an obnoxious minister by a patron. — *adj* **intru'sive** (*-siv*) tending or apt to intrude; intruded; inserted without etymological justification; entering without welcome or right; (of a rock) which has been forced while molten into cracks and fissures in other rocks. — *n* an intrusive rock. — *adv* **intru'sively**. — *n* **intru'siveness**. [L *in* in, and *trūdere*, *trūsum* to thrust]

intrust. A variant of **entrust**.

intubate *in'tū-bāt*, *vt* to insert a tube in; to treat or diagnose by insertion of a tube into, eg the larynx (*med*). — *n* **intūbā'tion** the act or process of inserting a tube. [L *in* in, and *tubus* a tube]

intuition *in-tū-ish'ən*, *n* the power of the mind by which it immediately perceives the truth of things without reasoning or analysis; a truth so perceived, immediate, instinctive knowledge or belief. — *vt* and *vi* **intuit** (*in'tū-it*) to know intuitively. — *adj* **intu'ited**. — *adj* **intuitional** (*-ish'ən-əl*). — *n* **intuit'ionalism** or **intuit'ionism** the doctrine that the perception of truth is by intuition; a philosophical system which stresses intuition and mysticism as opposed to the idea of a logical universe. — *n* **intuit'ionalist** or **intuit'ionist**. — *adj* **intu'itive** perceived or perceiving by intuition; received or known by simple inspection and direct apprehension. — *adv* **intu'itively**. — *n* **intu'itivism**. [L *in* into or upon, and *tuērī*, *tuitus* to look]

intumesce *in-tū-mes'*, *vi* to swell up. — *n* **intumesc'ence** a swelling or increase in volume, eg of an organ in the body. — *adj* **intumesc'ent**. — **intumescent paint** fire-retardant paint that on exposure to heat swells to form an insulating barrier that protects the underlying surface. [L *in* in, and *tumēscere* to swell]

inturbidate *in-tûr'bi-dāt*, *vt* to render turbid. [L *in* in, and *turbidāre*, *-ātum* to trouble]

intuse *in'tūs*, (*Spenser*) *n* a bruise. [L *in* in, and *tundere*, *tūsum* to thump]

intussusception *in-təs-sə-sep'shən*, *n* the passing or telescoping of part of a tube (*esp* the bowel) within the adjacent part (*med*); growth by intercalation of particles. — *vt* **intussuscept'**. — *adj* **intussuscept'ed**. — *adj* **intussuscep'tive**. [L *intus* within, and *susceptiō*, *-ōnis*, from *suscipere* to take up]

intwine and **intwist**. Same as **entwine** and **entwist**.

Inuit. See **Innuit**.

Inuktitut *in-ōōk'ti-tōōt*, *n* the Innuit language. [**Innuit**]

inula *in'ū-lə*, *n* a plant of the genus *Inula* of the Compositae, including the elecampane *I. helenium*. —

n **in'ulase** (*-lās*) an enzyme that forms fructose from inulin. — *n* **in'ulin** a carbohydrate present in the roots of certain plants. [L *inula*, prob from Gr *helenion* elecampane]

inumbrate *in-um'brāt*, *vt* to cast a shadow upon; to shade. [L *inumbrāre*, *-ātum*, from *in* on, and *umbrāre* to shade, from *umbra* a shadow]

inunction *in-ungk'shən*, *n* anointing; smearing or rubbing with an ointment or liniment. [L *inunctiō*, *-ōnis*, from *inunguere* to anoint, from *in* in, on, and *ung(u)ere* to smear]

inundate *in'un-dāt*, formerly *in-un'dāt*, *vt* (of water) to flow upon or over in waves; to flood; to overwhelm, swamp (*fig*); to fill with an overflowing abundance. — *adj* **inun'dant** overflowing. — *n* **inundā'tion**. [L *inundāre*, *-ātum*, from *in* in, and *undāre* to rise in waves, from *unda* a wave]

inurbane *in-ûr-bān'*, *adj* not urbane. — *adv* **inurbane'ly**. — *n* **inurbanity** (*-ban'i-ti*). [**in-** (2)]

inure[1] or **enure** *in-ūr'*, *vt* to accustom; to habituate; to harden; to use or practise (*obs*); to put into operation (*Spenser* and *Milton* **enure**; *obs*); to commit (*obs*). — *vi* (*law*) to come into operation or effect; to serve to one's use or benefit. — *n* **inured'ness** or **enured'ness**. — *n* **inure'ment** or **enure'ment** the act of inuring; the state of being inured; habituation. [**in-** (1) and **ure**[1]]

inure[2] *in-ūr'*, (*obs*) *vt* to burn in. [L *inūrere*, from *in* in, and *urere* to burn]

inurn *in-ûrn'*, *vt* to place in an urn; to entomb. [**in-** (1)]

inusitate *in-ū'zi-tāt*, (*obs*) *adj* unwonted. — *n* **inusitation** (*-ā'shən*) disuse. [L *inūsitātus*, from *in* not, and *ūsitātus* familiar]

inust *in-ust'*, (*obs*) *adj* burned in. — *n* **inustion** (*inus'chən*) burning in; cauterization. [L *inūrere*, *inūstum*; see **inure**[2]]

in usum Delphini *in ūz'əm del-fī'nī* or *o͞os'o͞om del-fē'nē*, (*L*) literally, for the use of the Dauphin; toned down to suit the young, expurgated.

in utero *in ū'tər-ō* or *o͞o'ter-ō*, (*L*) in the womb.

inutility *in-ū-til'i-ti*, *n* lack of utility; uselessness; unprofitableness; something useless. [**in-** (2)]

in utroque iure *in o͞o'trō-kwā yo͞o'rā*, (*L*) under both laws (civil and canon).

in utrumque paratus *in ū-tro͞om'kwi pə-rā'təs*, or *o͞o-tro͞om'kwe pa-rä'to͞os*, (*L*) prepared for either event.

inutterable *in-ut'ər-ə-bl*, *adj* unutterable. [**in-** (2)]

inv. *abbrev*: *invenit* (*L*), designed it; invented; invoice.

in vacuo *in vak'ū-ō*, *vak'o͞o-ō* or *wak'*, (*L*) in a vacuum; unrelated to a context, without specific application.

invade *in-vād'*, *vt* to enter by military force; to attack; to encroach upon; to violate; to overrun; to enter; to penetrate; to rush into. — *n* **invad'er**. [L *invādĕre*, from *in* in, and *vādĕre* to go]

in vadio *in väd'i-ō*, (*LL*) in pledge.

invaginate *in-vaj'in-āt*, *vt* to ensheath; to dint inwards, push or withdraw within, introvert. — *vi* to be introverted; to form a hollow cavity by infolding. — *n* **invaginā'tion**. [**in-** (1) and L *vāgīna* a sheath]

invalid *in-val'id*, *adj* without validity, efficacy, weight or cogency; having no effect; void; null. — *adj* (*in'və-lid* or *-lēd*) disabled through injury or chronic sickness; suitable for invalids. — *n* (*-id*, *-ēd* or *-ēd'*) a feeble, sickly or disabled person; a person disabled during, and no longer fit for, active service, *esp* a soldier or sailor. — *vt* (*-id*, *-ēd* or *-ēd'*) to disable or affect with disease; to enrol or discharge as an invalid. — *vi* (*archaic*) to become an invalid; to be discharged as an invalid. — *vt* **invalidate** (*-val'*) to render invalid or ineffective. — *n* **invalidā'tion**. — *n* **invalidhood** (*in'və-lid-ho͝od*, *-lēd-* or *-lēd'*). — *n* **in'validing** the sending or return home, or to a more healthy climate, of those rendered incapable of active duty by wounds, sickness, etc. — *n* **in'validism** (*-id-*, *-ēd-* or *-ēd'*). — *n* **invalid'ity** the state of being an invalid; lack of validity. — *adv* **inval'idly**. — *n* **inval'idness** lack of cogency or force. — **invalidity benefit** an allowance paid by the government to someone who has been unable to work through illness for more than 28 weeks. [**in-** (2)]

invaluable *in-val'ū-ə-bl*, *adj* that cannot have a value set upon it; priceless. — *adv* **inval'uably**. [**in-** (2)]

Invar® *in'vär* or *in-vär'*, *n* an alloy of iron, nickel and carbon, very slightly expanded by heat, used in the making of scientific instruments. [From **invariable**]

invariable *in-vā'ri-ə-bl*, *adj* not variable; without alteration or change; unalterable; constantly in the same state. — *n* **invāriabil'ity** or **invā'riableness**. — *adv* **invā'riably**. — *n* **invar'iance** invariableness: the theory of the constancy of physical laws. — *n* **invā'riant** that which does not change; an expression or quantity that is unaltered by a particular procedure (*math*). — Also *adj*. [**in-** (2)]

invasion *in-vā'zhən*, *n* the act of invading; an attack; incursion; an attack on the rights of another; encroachment; penetration; a violation. — *adj* **invasive** (*-vā'ziv*) invading; aggressive; encroaching; infringing another's rights; entering; penetrating. [Ety as for **invade**]

inveagle. Same as **inveigle**.

invecked *in-vekt'*, *adj* invected.

invected *in-vek'tid*, (*heraldry*) *adj* having or consisting of a borderline of small convex curves (opposite to *engrailed*). [L *invehere*, *invectum* to enter]

invective *in-vek'tiv*, *n* a severe or reproachful accusation or denunciation; an attack with words; abusive language; sarcasm or satire. — *adj* sarcastic; abusive; satirical. [L *invectīvus* attacking, from *invehi* to assail; see **inveigh**]

inveigh *in-vā'*, *vi* to make an attack in speech or writing; to rail; to revile. [L *invehi* to assail, launch oneself at]

inveigle *in-vē'gl* or *in-vā'gl*, *vt* to entice; to persuade by cajolery; to wheedle. — Older forms **invea'gle** and **envei'gle**. — *n* **invei'glement**. — *n* **invei'gler**. [Prob altered from Anglo-Fr *enveogler* (Fr *aveugler*) to blind, from L *ab* from, and *oculus* the eye]

invendible *in-ven'di-bl*, *adj* unsaleable. — *n* **invendibil'ity**. [**in-** (2)]

invenit *in-vēn'it*, *in-wān'it* or *-vān'*, (*L*) he or she devised or designed (this).

invent *in-vent'*, *vt* to devise or contrive; to design for the first time, originate; to form or compose by imagination; to fabricate (something false); to find (*obs*). — *adj* **inven'tible** or **inven'table**. — *n* **inven'tion** that which is invented; a contrivance; a deceit; the faculty or power of inventing; ability displayed by any invention or effort of the imagination; a short piece working out a single idea (*music*). — *adj* **inven'tive** able to invent, devise or contrive; showing imaginative skill. — *adv* **inven'tively**. — *n* **inven'tiveness**. — *n* **inven'tor**: — *fem* **inven'tress**. — **Invention of the Cross** a festival observed on 3 May in commemoration of the alleged discovery of the true cross at Jerusalem in AD 326 by Helena, mother of Constantine the Great. [L *invenīre*, *inventum*, from *in* upon, and *venīre* to come]

inventory *in'vən-tər-i*, *n* a list or schedule of articles, eg furniture in a rented house, items of property comprised in an estate; a catalogue; stock, equipment; stock of a commodity (*US*); stocktaking (*US*); the total quantity of material in a nuclear reactor. — *vt* to make an inventory of; to amount to. — *vi* to sum up. — *adj* **inventō'rial**. — *adv* **inventō'rially**. [LL *inventōrium* for L *inventārium* a list of things found, from *invenīre* to find]

in ventre *in vent'rā*, (*L*; *law*) in the womb.

inveracity *in-vər-as'i-ti*, *n* lack of veracity; an untruth. [**in-** (2)]

Inverness *in-vər-nes'* or *in'vər-nes*, *adj* of or named after the town of *Inverness*, eg of a cloak or overcoat with a cape or tippet. — Also *n*.

inverse *in'vûrs* or *in-vûrs'*, *adj* inverted; upside down; in the reverse or contrary order; opposite; opposite in effect, as subtraction to addition, etc (*math*); related by inversion. — *n* an inverted state; the result of inversion; a direct opposite; a proposition formed by immediate inference from another, its subject being the negative of the original subject (*logic*); a point so related to another point that the rectangle contained by their distances from a fixed point collinear with them is constant, or related in some analogous manner (*geom*). — *adv* **in'versely** (or *-vûrs'*). — *n* **inver'sion** (*-shən*) the act of inverting; the state of being inverted; a change or reversal of order or position; that which results from inverting; a mutation of chromosomes in which certain genes are in reverse order. — *adj* **inver'sive**. — **inverse proportion** (*math*) a process by which one quantity decreases while another increases, their product remaining constant; **inverse ratio** the ratio of reciprocals; **inverse square law** (*phys*) a law in which the force, magnitude, etc of a phenomenon is inversely proportional to the square of the distance from the source. [L *inversus*, pa p of *invertere*, *inversum*, from *in* in, and *vertere* to turn]

invert *in-vûrt'*, *vt* to turn in or round; to turn upside down; to reverse; to change the customary order or position of; to form the inverse of; to change by placing the lowest note an octave higher (*music*); to modify by reversing the direction of motion; to break up (cane-sugar) into dextrose and laevulose, thereby (the laevulose prevailing) reversing the direction of rotation of polarized light (*chem*). — *n* (*in'*) an inverted arch; invert sugar; a homosexual or transsexual (*psychol*). — *n* **in'vertase** (or *-vûr'*) an enzyme that inverts cane-sugar. — *adj* **inver'ted** turned inwards; upside down; reversed; pronounced with tip of tongue turned up and back (as *r* in SW England). — *adv* **inver'tedly**. — *n* **inver'ter** or **inver'tor**. — *n* **inver'tin** invertase. — **inverted arch** an arch with its curve turned downwards; **inverted commas** see under **comma**; **inverted mordent** see **mordent**; **inverted pleat** a box pleat with the folded edges on the right side of the fabric; **inverted snob** a person who prefers (the attitudes and conventions of) the lower classes to (those of) the upper classes; **invert sugar** the mixture obtained by hydrolysis of cane-sugar. [L *invertere*, *inversum*, from *in* in, and *vertere* to turn]

invertebrate *in-vûrt'i-brit* or *-brāt*, *adj* without a vertebral column or backbone; weak, irresolute, spineless; characterless; formless. — *n* a member of the Invertebrata; an indecisive person. — *npl* **Invertebrā'ta** a collective name for all animals other than vertebrates. [**in-** (2)]

invest *in-vest'*, *vt* to clothe with insignia of office; to place in office or authority (with *with* or *in*); to give rights, privileges or duties to; to lay out for profit, as by buying property, shares, etc; to put on (*archaic*); to adorn, clothe, cover (*archaic*); to surround, besiege (*military*). — *vi* (*colloq*) to make a purchase (with *in*). — *adj* **inves'titive**. — *n* **inves'titure** investing; the ceremony of investing; in feudal and ecclesiastical history, the act of giving corporal possession of a manor, office, or benefice, accompanied by a certain ceremonial, such as the delivery of a branch, a banner, etc, to signify the authority which it is supposed to convey. — *n* **invest'ment** the act of investing; investiture; any placing of money to secure income or profit; that in which money is invested; a blockade (*military*); (in *pl*) clothes (*archaic*). — *n* **inves'tor** a person who invests, *esp* money. — **investment trust** see under **trust**. [L *investīre*, *-ītum*, from *in* on, and *vestīre* to clothe]

investigate *in-vest'i-gāt*, *vt* to search or inquire into with care and accuracy. — *vi* to make a search, examination or inquiry. — *adj* **invest'igable** able to be investigated. — *n* **investigā'tion** the act of examining; a search, examination or inquiry; research. — *adj* **invest'igātive** or **invest'igātory**. — *n* **invest'igātor**. — **investigative journalism** journalism involving the investigation and exposure of corruption, crime, inefficiency, etc. [L *investīgāre*, *-ātum*, from *in* in, and *vestīgāre* to track]

inveterate *in-vet'ər-it*, *adj* firmly established by usage or custom; deep-rooted, confirmed in any habit; stubborn; rootedly hostile. — *n* **invet'eracy** or **invet'erateness**. — *adv* **invet'erately**. [L *inveterātus* stored up, long continued, from *in* in, and *vetus*, *veteris* old]

invexed *in-vekst'*, (*heraldry*) *adj* arched; concave. [L *in* in, and the root of *vehere* to carry]

inviable *in-vī'ə-bl*, *adj* not viable; unable to survive. — *n* **inviabil'ity**. [**in-** (2)]

invidious *in-vid'i-əs*, *adj* likely to incur or provoke ill-will or resentment; likely to excite envy, enviable; offensively discriminating. — *adv* **invid'iously**. — *n* **invid'iousness**. [L *invidiōsus*, from *invidia* envy]

invigilate *in-vij'i-lāt*, *vt* and *vi* to supervise, *esp* at examinations. — *n* **invigilā'tion**. — *n* **invig'ilātor**. [L *in* on, and *vigilāre*, *-ātum* to watch]

invigorate *in-vig'ər-āt*, *vt* to give vigour to; to strengthen; to animate or enliven. — *n* **invig'orant** an invigorating agent. — *n* **invigorā'tion**. — *n* **invig'orātor**. [**in-** (1)]

invincible *in-vin'si-bl*, *adj* that cannot be defeated or overcome; insuperable. — *n* **invincibil'ity** or **invin'cibleness**. — *adv* **invin'cibly**. — **invincible ignorance** see under **ignorant**. [**in-** (2)]

in vino veritas *in vī'nō ver'it-as*, *wē'nō wār'it-äs* or *vē'nō vār'it-äs*, (*L*) literally, in wine is truth, hence, truth is told under the influence of alcohol.

inviolable *in-vī'ə-lə-bl*, *adj* that must not be profaned; that cannot be injured. — *n* **invīolabil'ity** or **invī'olableness** the quality of being inviolable. — *adv* **invī'olably**. — *adj* **invī'olate** (*-lit* or *-lāt*) or **inviolated** (*-lāt-id*) not violated; unprofaned; uninjured. — *adv* **invī'olately**. — *n* **invī'olateness**. [**in-** (2)]

invious *in'vi-əs*, (*rare*) *adj* impassable; trackless. [L *invius*, from *in-* not, and *via* a way]

invis'd *in'vīzd*, (*Shakesp*) *adj* probably, unseen or inscrutable. [L *invīsus* unseen]

invisible *in-viz'i-bl*, *adj* incapable of being seen; unseen; relating to services rather than goods (*econ*); not shown in regular statements, as *invisible assets* (see also under **export** and **import**; *finance*). — *n* an invisible export, etc; (in *pl*) invisible imports and exports collectively. — *n* **invisibil'ity** or **invis'ibleness**. — *adv* **invis'ibly**. — **invisible earnings** profits from invisibles, *esp* invisible exports; **invisible ink** see under **ink**. [**in-** (2)]

invite *in-vīt'*, *vt* to ask hospitably or politely to come; to express affable willingness to receive or to have done; to request formally or publicly; to encourage or tend to bring on; to offer inducement; to attract. — *n* (*in'*) (*colloq*) an invitation. — *n* **invitation** (*in-vi-tā'shən*) the act of inviting; a request or solicitation; the written or verbal form with which a person is invited; an enticement; the brief exhortation introducing the confession in the Anglican communion office. — *adj* **invitatory** (*in-vīt'ə-tə-ri*) using or containing invitation. — *n* a form of invitation to worship, *esp* the antiphon to the Venite or 95th Psalm. — *n* **invitee'** (or *-vīt'*; *rare*) someone who is invited, a guest. — *n* **invite'ment** (*Lamb*) allurement, temptation. — *n* **invīt'er**. — *adj* **invīt'ing** alluring; attractive. — *n* (*archaic*) invitation. — *adv* **invīt'ingly**. — *n* **invīt'ingness** attractiveness. [L *invītāre*, *-ātum*]

in vitro *in vīt'rō*, *wit'rō* or *vit'*, (*L*) in glass; in the test tube (*opp* to *in vivo*; *med*). — **in vitro fertilization** (*abbrev* **IVF**) fertilization of an ovum by mixing wih sperm in a culture medium, after which the fertilized egg is implanted in the uterus to continue normal development; **in vitro transcription** the use of a laboratory medium without the presence of intact cells to obtain specific messenger RNA production from a DNA sequence (also called **cell-free transcription**); **in vitro translation** the use of pure messenger RNA, ribosomes and other cell extracts to obtain a specific protein product without the presence of intact cells (also called **cell-free translation**).

in vivo *in vī'vō*, *wē'wō* or *vē'vō*, (*L*) in the living organism.

invocation *in-vō-kā'shən*, *n* the act or the form of invoking or addressing in prayer or supplication; an appellation under which a divinity, etc is invoked; any formal invoking of the blessing or help of a god, a saint, etc; an opening prayer in a public religious service or in the

Litany (*eccles*); a call for inspiration from a Muse or other deity eg at the beginning of a poem; an incantation or calling up of a spirit; a call or summons, *esp* for evidence from another case (*law*). — *adj* **invocatory** (*in-vok'ə-tə-ri*) making an invocation. [L *invocātio*, from *invocāre* to invoke]

invoice *in'vois*, *n* a letter of advice of the despatch of goods, with particulars of their price and quantity. — *vt* to list (goods) on an invoice; to send an invoice to (a customer). [Prob pl of Fr *envoi*]

invoke *in-vōk'*, *vt* to call upon earnestly or solemnly; to implore to assist or give assistance; to address in prayer; to conjure up; to resort to. [Fr *invoquer*, from L *invocāre*, *-ātum*, from *in* on, and *vocāre* to call]

involucre *in'və-lōō-kər* or *-lū-*, *n* an envelope (*anatom*); a ring or crowd of bracts around a capitulum, umbel, etc (*bot*). — *n* **involucel** (*in-vol'ū-sel*) the group of bracts below a partial umbel. — *adj* **involūcell'ate** having an involucel. — *adj* **involu'cral** of the nature of, or pertaining to, an involucre. — *adj* **involu'crate** having an involucre. — *n* **involū'crum** an involucre; a growth of new bone enclosing a mass of infected or dead bone in osteomyelitis (*med*). [L *involūcrum*, from *involvere* to involve]

involuntary *in-vol'ən-tər-i*, *adj* not voluntary; not having the power of will or choice; not under control of the will; not done voluntarily. — *adv* **invol'untarily**. — *n* **invol'untariness**. [**in-** (2)]

involute *in'vol-ōōt* or *-ūt*, *adj* involved; rolled inward at the margins (*bot*); turned inward; closely rolled; (of gear teeth) having the profile of an involute curve. — *n* that which is involved or rolled inward; a curve traced by the end of a string unwinding itself from another curve (the *evolute*). — *vt* and *vi* to make or become involute. — *adj* **in'voluted**. [Ety as for **involve**]

involution *in-və-lū'shən* or *lōō'*, *n* the action of involving; the state of being involved or entangled; complicated grammatical construction; raising to a power (*math*); the condition satisfied by a system of pairs of points in a straight line such that the rectangle contained by their distances from a fixed point in that line (the *centre of involution*) is constant (*geom*); degeneration; return to normal size, as the uterus after birth (*zool*); atrophy of an organ, eg in old age. — *adj* **involu'tional**. — **involutional psychosis** or **melancholia** a psychosis occurring in middle life, with feelings of anxiety, futility, guilt, and, in some cases, with delusions of persecution. [Ety as for **involve**]

involve *in-volv'*, *vt* to entangle; to complicate; to implicate; to comprehend; to entail or imply, bring as a consequence; to be bound up with; to concern; to raise to a power (*math*); to make (oneself) emotionally concerned (in or with); to engage the emotional interest of; to engage in a romantic or sexual relationship (with). — *n* **involve'ment**. [L *involvere*, from *in* in, and *volvere*, *volūtum* to roll]

invulnerable *in-vul'nər-ə-bl*, *adj* that cannot be wounded; not vulnerable. — *n* **invulnerabil'ity** or **invul'nerableness**. — *adv* **invul'nerably**. [**in-** (2)]

invultuation *in-vul-tū-ā'shən*, *n* the making or using of an image of a person for the purposes of witchcraft. [LL *invultuātiō*, *-ōnis*, from L *in* in, and *vultus* the face]

inwall. See **enwall**.

inward *in'wərd*, *adj* placed or being within; internal; seated in the mind or soul, not perceptible to the senses; uttered as if within, or with closed mouth; confidential (*archaic*); secret, private (*archaic*). — *n* inside (*Shakesp*); interior (*obs*); an intimate friend (*Shakesp*); (in *pl*; often *in'ərdz*) entrails (also **inn'ards**). — *adv* toward the interior; into the mind or thoughts. — *adv* **in'wardly** within; in the heart; privately; toward the centre. — *n* **in'wardness** internal state; inner meaning or significance; intimacy, familiarity (*Shakesp*). — *adv* **in'wards** same as **inward**. — **inward investment** investment in production, manufacturing, distribution, etc in an area or country by business organizations based elsewhere, *esp* in foreign countries. [OE *inneweard* (adv)]

inweave *in-wēv'*, *vt* to weave in; to complicate: — *pa t* **inwove'**; *pa p* **inwo'ven** (*Milton*, etc **inwove'**). [**in-** (1)]

inwick *in'wik*, (*curling*) *n* a stroke in which the stone glances off the edge of another stone, and then slides close to the tee. — *vi* to make an inwick. [**in**[1] and **wick**[4]]

inwind. See **enwind**.

inwit *in'wit*, (*obs* or *literary archaism*) *n* inward knowledge; conscience. [**in**[1] and **wit**[2]]

inwith *in'with* or *in-widh'*, (*Scot*) *prep* and *adv* within. [**in**[1] and **with**[2]]

inwork *in-wûrk'*, *vt* and *vi* to work in. — *n* **in'working** energy exerted inwardly. — *adj* **in'wrought** (as pa p *in-röt'*) wrought in or among other things; adorned with figures. [**in-** (1)]

inworn *in'wōrn*, *in-wōrn'* or *-wörn*, *adj* worn or worked in, inwrought. [**in-** (1)]

inwove, etc. See **inweave**.

inwrap. Same as **enwrap**.

inwreathe. Same as **enwreathe**.

inyala *in-yä'lə* or **nyala** *n-yä'lə*, *n* a South African antelope. [Bantu]

io *ī'ō*, *interj* of invocation, or expressing joy or triumph or grief. — *n* a cry of 'Io': — *pl* **ī'os**. [Gr *iō*]

IOB *abbrev*: Institute of Building.

IOC *abbrev*: International Olympic Committee.

iodine *ī'ə-dēn* or *or ī'ō-dēn*, also *-dīn* or *-din*, *n* a halogen element (symbol **I**; atomic no 53) giving a violet-coloured vapour. — *n* **i'odate** a salt of iodic acid. — *adj* **iodic** (*ī-od'ik*) pertaining to or caused by iodine; applied to an acid (HIO_3) and its anhydride (I_2O_5). — *n* **i'odīde** a salt of hydriodic acid. — *n* **i'odism** iodine poisoning. — *vt* **i'odize** or **-ise** to treat with iodine. — *n* **iodoform** (*ī-od'* or *-ōd'ə-förm*) a lemon-yellow crystalline compound of iodine (CHI_3) with a saffron-like odour, used as an antiseptic. — *adj* **iodomet'ric** (*chem*) measured by iodine. — *adj* **iod'ophile** (*-fil* or *-fīl*) staining intensely with iodine. — *adj* **i'odous** of, containing, or resembling iodine. — *n* **iod'ūret** (*obs*) an iodide. — **iodine-131** a short-lived radioactive isotope of iodine present in fall-out, widely used in medicine. [Gr *ioeidēs* violet-coloured, from *ion* a violet, and *eidos* form]

iodyrite *ī-od'ir-īt*, *n* a mineral, silver iodide. [**iodine** and **argyrite**]

IoJ *abbrev*: Institute of Journalists.

iolite *ī'ō-līt*, *n* cordierite or dichroite, a strongly dichroic transparent gem, a silicate of aluminium, magnesium and iron, violet-blue, grey or yellow according to direction of view by transmitted light. [Gr *ion* violet, and *lithos* stone]

IOM *abbrev*: Isle of Man.

ion *ī'ən* or *ī'on*, *n* an electrically charged particle formed by loss or gain of electrons by an atom, effecting by its migration the transport of electricity. — *adj* **ionic** (*ī-on'ik*). — *n* **ionīzā'tion** or **-s-** — *vt* **ionize** or **-ise**. (*ī'ən-īz*) to produce ions in; to turn into ions. — *n* **ī'onizer** or **-s-**. — *n* **ion'omer** the product of ionic bonding action between long-chain molecules, characterized by toughness and a high degree of transparency. — *n* **i'onone** either of, or a mixture of, two isomeric ketones extracted from certain plants, with an intense odour of violets, used in making perfumes. — *n* **ion'opause** the region of the earth's atmosphere at the outer limit of the ionosphere. — *n* **ionophore** (*ī'ə-nə-för*) a chemical compound able to combine with an ion and enable it to pass through a cell membrane, etc. — *n* **ionophorē'sis** electrophoresis, *esp* of small ions. — *n* **ion'osphere** the region of the upper atmosphere that includes the highly ionized Appleton and Kennelly-Heaviside layers. — *adj* **ionospher'ic**. — *n* **iontophorē'sis** the migration of charged particles, eg of a drug, into body tissue through electric currents; electrophoresis. — *adj* **iontophoret'ic**. — **ion engine** a space engine in which the thrust is produced by a stream of ionized particles; **i'on-exchange** transfer of ions from a solution to a solid or another liquid, used in water-softening and many industrial processes; **ionic bond** a bond within a chemical compound achieved by transfer of electrons, the resulting ions being held together by electrostatic attraction; **ion implantation** the introduction of ions into a crystalline material by subjecting the material to bombardment with a stream of ions, an important element in the production of integrated circuits; **ion implanter**; **ionization chamber** an instrument used to detect and measure ionizing radiation, consisting of an enclosure containing electrodes between which ionized gas is formed; **ionization potential** the energy, in electronvolts, required to detach an electron from an atom, molecule or radical; **ionizing radiation** any electromagnetic or particulate radiation which can cause ionization. [Gr *ion*, neuter pr p of *ienai* to go]

Ionian *ī-ō'ni-ən, adj* Ionic; of or relating to an area off the west coast of Greece, as in *Ionian Islands, Ionian Sea.* — *n* an Ionic Greek. [Gr *Iōnios*]

Ionic *ī-on'ik, adj* relating to the Ionians, one of the main divisions of the ancient Greeks, to their dialect, to Ionia, the coastal district of Asia Minor settled by them, to a metrical foot of two long and two short syllables (*Ionic a majore*) or two short and two long (*Ionic a minore*), to verse characterized by the use of that foot, to an order of Greek architecture characterized by the volute of its capital, to a mode of ancient Greek music (the same as the Iastic, Hypophrygian, or Hyperlydian), or to an old ecclesiastical mode extending from C to C with C for its final. — *n* the Ionic dialect; an Ionic foot or verse; an Ionic philosopher. — *vt* and *vi* **Ionicize** or **-ise** (*ī-on'i-sīz*) or **Ionize** or **-ise** (*ī'ən-īz*) to make or become Ionian; to use the Ionic dialect. — *n* **I'onism**. — *n* **I'onist**. — **Ionic dialect** the most important of the three main branches (Ionic, Doric and Aeolic) of the ancient Greek language, the language of Homer and Herodotus, of which Attic is a development; **Ionic school** the representative philosophers of the Ionian Greeks, such as Thales, Anaximander, Heraclitus, Anaxagoras, who debated the nature of the primordial constitutive principle of the cosmic universe. [Gr *Iōnikos*, *Iōnios*]

ionium *ī-ōn'i-əm, n* a radioactive isotope of thorium. [**ion**]

ionomer... to ... **iontophoretic**. See under **ion**.

iopanoic acid *ī-ō-pə-nō'ik as'id, n* a compound containing iodine, opaque to X-rays and used in X-ray examination of the gall bladder.

IOPCW *abbrev*: International Organization for the Prohibition of Chemical Weapons.

iota *ī-ō'tə, n* the Greek letter *I*, *ι*, corresponding to I; as a numeral *ι'* = 10, *͵ι* = 10,000; a jot, a very small amount. [Gr *iōta* the smallest letter in the alphabet, *I*, *ι*; Heb *yōd*]

IOU *ī-ō-ū', n* a signed slip of paper or other document acknowledging a debt (*esp* of money) to a specified person, stating the date and nature of the debt. [Pronunciation of *I owe you*]

IOW *abbrev*: Isle of Wight.

IPA *abbrev*: Institute of Practitioners in Advertising; International Phonetic Alphabet; International Phonetic Association; International Publishers' Association.

IPC *abbrev*: International Publishing Corporation.

IPCC *abbrev*: Intergovernmental Panel on Climate Change.

IPCS *abbrev*: Institution of Professional Civil Servants (now **IPMS**).

ipecacuanha *ip-i-kak-ū-an'ə, n* the dried root of various South American plants, used as a purgative, emetic and expectorant; a plant from which this is obtained, chiefly *Cephaelis* or *Uragoga* (family *Rubiaceae*). — Sometimes shortened to **ipecac'**. [Port, from Tupí]

IPM *abbrev*: Institute of Personnel Management.

IPMS *abbrev*: Institution of Professionals, Managers and Specialists (*formerly* **IPCS**).

ipomoea *ip-ō-mē'ə, n* a plant of the jalap and morning-glory genus (*Ipomoea*) of the Convolvulus family; [Gr *īps*, *īpos* a worm, and *homoios* like]

IPPF *abbrev*: International Planned Parenthood Federation.

ippon *ip'on*, (*judo* and *karate*) *n* a winning point awarded for a perfectly executed move. [Jap, one point]

ipratropium *ip-rə-trō'pi-əm, n* a bronchodilator drug used in the treatment of certain types of asthma and bronchitis.

iprindole *ip-rin'dōl, n* an antidepressant drug.

ipse dixit *ip'sē dik'sit* or *ip'se dēk'sit*, (*L*) he himself said it; a dogmatic pronouncement; dictum.

ipsilateral or **ipselateral** *ip-si-lat'ə-rəl, adj* belonging to or affecting the same side of the body (cf **contralateral**). [Irregularly formed from L *ipse* and **lateral**]

ipsissima verba *ip-sis'ə-mə vûr'bə* or *ip-sis'i-ma ver'* or *wer'ba*, (*L*) the very word. — **ipsissimis verbis** quoted exactly.

ipso facto *ip'sō fak'tō*, (*L*) by that very fact; thereby.

IQ *abbrev*: intelligence quotient.

iq *abbrev*: *idem quod* (*L*), the same as.

Ir. *abbrev*: Irish.

Ir (*chem*) *symbol*: iriduium.

ir *abbrev*: infrared.

ir- *ir-*, *pfx* same as **in-**, the form used with words beginning with *r*, as in *irradiate.*

IRA *abbrev*: Irish Republican Army.

iracund *ī'rə-kund, adj* inclined to become angry, easily angered. — *n* **iracund'ity**. — *adj* **iracund'ulous** somewhat iracund. [L *īrācundus*, from *īra* anger]

irade *i-rä'de*, (*hist*) *n* a written decree of the Sultan of Turkey. [Turk, from Ar *irādah* will]

Iranian *i-*, *ī-rān'i-ən*, or *-rän'*, *n* a native or inhabitant of Iran; the modern Persian language; the branch of Indo-European which includes Persian. — *adj* of or relating to Iran, its people or language; of or relating to this branch of Indo-European. [Pers *Irān* Persia]

Iraqi *i-rä'kē, n* a native of Iraq; the form of Arabic spoken in Iraq. — *adj* pertaining to the country of Iraq, its inhabitants or language. [Ar *'Irāqī*]

irascible *ir-as'i-bl*, or *īr-*, *adj* quick-tempered; irritable. — *n* **irascibil'ity**. — *adv* **irasc'ibly**. [Fr, from L *īrāscibilis*, from *īrāscī* to be angry, from *īra* anger]

irate *ī-rāt', adj* enraged, angry. — *adv* **irate'ly**. [**ire**]

IRBM *abbrev*: intermediate range ballistic missile.

ire *īr, n* anger; rage; keen resentment. — *adj* **ire'ful** full of ire or wrath; resentful. — *adv* **ire'fully**. — *n* **ire'fulness**. [L *īra* anger]

irenic *ī-rēn'ik* or *-ren'*, or **irenical** *-əl, adj* tending to create peace; pacific. — *adv* **iren'ically**. — *n* **iren'icism**. — *n* **iren'icon** same as **eirenicon**. — *n sing* **iren'ics** irenical theology, promoting peace between Christian churches (*opp* to *polemics*). — *n* **irenology** (*ī-rən-ol'ə-ji*) the study of peace. [Gr *eirēnē* peace]

IRFB *abbrev*: International Rugby Football Board.

irid *ī'rid, n* the iris of the eye; any plant of the iris family. — *n pl* **Iridā'ceae** (*i-rid-ā'si-ē, ī-*) the iris family, distinguished from lilies by their inferior ovary and single whorl of stamens. — Also **Irid'eae**. — *adj* **iridaceous** (*i-rid-ā'shəs* or *ī-*) or **irid'eal** belonging to the Iridaceae. — *adj* **i'ridal**, **irid'ial** or **irid'ian** pertaining to the iris of the eye. [Ety as for **iris**]

irid- *i-rid-* or *ī-rid-*, or **irido-** *-dō-* or *-do'*, *combining form* denoting the iris (of the eye). — *n* **iridec'tomy** surgical removal of part of the iris. — *n sing* **iridodiagnos'tics** or *n* **iridol'ogy** diagnosis by examination of the iris. — *n* **iridol'ogist**. — *n* **iridot'omy** surgical incision into the iris of the eye. [Ety as for **iris**]

iridescence *ir-i-des'əns, n* play of rainbow colours, caused by interference, as on bubbles, mother-of-pearl, some feathers. — *adj* **iridesc'ent** coloured like the rainbow; glittering with changing colours. — *adv* **iridesc'ently**. [Ety as for **iris**]

iridic *ī-rid'ik* or *i-*, *adj* containing or consisting of iridium; of or relating to the iris of the eye. [Ety as for **iris**]

iridium *ī-rid'i-əm*, a very heavy steel-grey metallic element (symbol **Ir**; atomic no 77), with very high melting-point. [Ety as for **iris**]

iridize or **-ise** *īr'* or *ir'id-īz*, to make iridescent; to tip with iridium. — *n* **iridization** or **-s-** (*ī-rid-īz-ā'shən*, *ir-id-*, or *-iz-*) iridescence. [Ety as for **iris**]

iridosmine *ir-id-oz'min*, *īr-*, or *-os'* or **iridosmium** *ir-id-oz'mi-əm*, *īr-*, or *-os*, *n* a native alloy of iridium and osmium used for pen-points, also called *osmiridium*.

iris *ī'ris*, *n* an appearance resembling the rainbow; the contractile curtain perforated by the pupil, and forming the coloured part of the eye; a plant of the genus *Iris* with tuberous roots, long tapering leaves and large showy flowers; an iris diaphragm: — *pl* **irides** (*ī'rid-ēz*, or *i'*) or **i'rises**. — *vt* **ī'risate** to make iridescent. — *n* **irisation** (*ī-ri-sā'shən*). — *adj* **irised** (*ī'rist*) showing colours like the rainbow. — **iris diaphragm** an adjustable stop for a lens, giving a continuously variable hole. [Gr *Īris*, *-idos* the rainbow goddess]

iriscope *ī'ri-skōp*, *n* an instrument for exhibiting the prismatic colours. [Gr *īris*, and *skopeein* to see]

Irish *ī'rish*, *adj* relating to, produced in, derived from, or characteristic of, Ireland; self-contradictory, ludicrously inconsistent (as Irish thought and speech is traditionally supposed to be; *facetious, rather offensive*). — *n* the Celtic language of Ireland; an Irish commodity, *esp* whiskey; (as *pl*) the natives or people of Ireland. — *n* **I'rishism** an Irish phrase, idiom or characteristic, *esp* an apparently nonsensical one. — *n* **I'rishman** or **I'rishwoman**. — *n* **I'rishness** the qualities or characteristics of Ireland or the Irish. — **Irish bridge** a ford or watersplash treated so as to be permanent; **Irish car** a lightweight horse-drawn buggy; **Irish coffee** a beverage made of sweetened coffee and Irish whiskey and topped with cream; **Irish elk** see under **elk**; **Irish Guards** a regiment formed in 1900 to represent Ireland in the Foot Guards; **Irish moss** carrageen; **Irish Republican Army** a militant organization seeking to bring about union between the Republic of Ireland and Northern Ireland, and independence from Britain; **Irish stew** mutton, onions and potatoes stewed with flour; **Irish terrier** a breed of dog with rough, wiry, reddish-brown coat.

iritis *īr-ī'tis*, *n* inflammation of the iris of the eye. — *adj* **irit'ic** having iritis; affecting the iris.

irk *ûrk*, *vt* (now *usu* used impersonally) to weary; to disgust; to distress; to annoy, gall. — *adj* **irk'some** tedious; burdensome. — *adv* **irk'somely**. — *n* **irk'someness**. [ME *irken*]

IRL *abbrev*: Ireland (IVR).

IRO *abbrev*: Inland Revenue Office.

iroko *i-rō'kō*, *n* either of the two timber trees of the genus *Chlorophora* of central and western Africa; the hard wood of these trees, often used as a substitute for teak: — *pl* **irō'kos**. [Yoruba]

iron *ī'ərn*, *n* an element (symbol **Fe**; atomic no 26), the most widely used of all the metals; a weapon, instrument or utensil made of iron; an appliance for smoothing cloth; a pistol or revolver (*slang*); a golf club with a metal head; strength; a medicinal preparation of iron; (in *pl*) fetters, chains; a theatre safety curtain (*archaic*; *orig* short for **iron curtain**, see below); a stirrup. — *adj* formed of iron; resembling iron; harsh, grating; stern; not to be broken; robust; insensitive; inflexible. — *vt* to smooth with an iron; to arm with iron; to hit (a golf ball) with an iron; to fetter; to smooth, clear up (with *out*; *fig*). — *n* **i'roner** a person who irons; an iron for pressing clothes. — *n* **i'roning** the act or process of smoothing with hot irons; clothes, etc that are to be, or have been, ironed. — *adj* **i'rony** made, consisting of, rich in iron; like iron; hard. — **Iron Age** the stage of culture of a people using iron as the material for their tools and weapons (*archaeol*); **i'ronbark** any of several eucalyptus trees. — *adj* **i'ron-bound** bound with iron; rugged, as a coast. — *adj* **i'ron-cased**. — *adj* **i'ron-clad** clad in iron; covered or protected with iron. — *n* a ship defended by iron plates. — **i'ron-clay** clay ironstone; **Iron Cross** a Prussian war medal instituted in 1813, revived in 1870 and 1914 and reinstated by Hitler as a German war medal in 1939; **Iron Crown** the crown of Lombardy, so named from a thin band of iron said to be made from one of the nails of the Cross; **iron curtain** the safety curtain in a theatre, *orig* made of iron (*archaic*); an impenetrable barrier to observation or communication, *esp* (with *caps*) between the former Soviet bloc and the West. — *adj* **iron-fis'ted** exercising strict, despotic control. — **i'ron-founder** a person who founds or makes castings in iron; **i'ron-foundry**; **i'ron-glance** specular iron. — *adj* **iron-gray'** or **-grey'** of a grey colour like that of iron freshly cut or broken. — *n* this colour. — **iron hand** strict, despotic control (the iron hand is sometimes hidden in the *velvet glove*, qv). — *adj* **iron-hand'ed**. — *adj* **iron-heart'ed** having a heart as hard as iron; unfeeling. — **iron horse** a worn-out circumlocution for a railway engine; **i'roning-board** a smooth board covered with cloth, *usu* on a stand, on which clothes, etc are ironed; **iron-liq'uor** iron acetate, a dyers' mordant; **iron lung** an apparatus consisting of a chamber that encloses a patient's chest, the air pressure within the chamber being varied rhythmically so that air is forced into and out of the lungs, a respirator; **iron maiden** an old instrument of torture, consisting of a box lined with iron spikes in which a prisoner was fastened; **iron man** a man of extraordinary strength (*esp Austr*); (the winner of) a test of endurance at a surf carnival, comprising swimming, surfing and running events (*Austr*); a pound note (*orig Austr colloq*) or a dollar (*US colloq*); **i'ronmaster** a proprietor of an ironworks; **i'ron-mine**; **i'ron-miner**; **i'ron-mining**; **i'ronmonger** a dealer in ironmongery or, loosely, in household goods and equipment generally; **i'ronmongery** articles made of iron; domestic hardware; **iron ore**; **iron-pan'** a hard layer in sand or gravel, due to percolation of water precipitating iron salts; **iron pyrites** common pyrites, sulphide of iron; **iron ration** a ration of concentrated food, *esp* for an extreme emergency; **i'ron-sand** sand containing particles of iron ore; steel filings used in fireworks. — *adj* **i'ron-sick** (*naut*) having the iron bolts and spikes much corroded. — **I'ronside** or **I'ronsides** a nickname for a man of iron resolution (eg Oliver Cromwell); a Puritan cavalryman; a Puritan; (in *pl*) a name given to Cromwell's cavalry. — *adj* **iron-sid'ed** having a side of, or as hard as, iron; rough; hardy. — **i'ronsmith** a worker in iron, blacksmith; **i'ronstone** any iron-ore, *esp* carbonate; **i'ronware** wares or goods of iron. — *adj* **iron-willed'** firmly determined. — *adj* **iron-witt'ed** (*Shakesp*) unfeeling, insensible. — **i'ronwood** timber of great hardness, and many kinds of trees producing it. — *adj* **iron-word'ed** (*Tennyson*) expressed in strong terms. — **i'ronwork** the parts of a building, etc, made of iron; anything of iron, *esp* artistic work; (often in *pl*) an establishment where iron is smelted or made into heavy goods. — **rule with a rod of iron** to rule with stern severity; **strike while the iron is hot** to seize one's opportunity while the circumstances are favourable to one; **too many irons in the fire** too many responsibilities, undertakings, etc to cope with at once. [OE *īren* (*īsern*, *īsen*); Ger *Eisen*]

irony[1] *ī'rən-i*, *n orig* the Socratic method of discussion by professing ignorance; conveyance of meaning (generally satirical) by words whose literal meaning is the opposite, *esp* words of praise used as a criticism or condemnation; a situation or utterance (eg in a tragedy) that has a significance unperceived at the time, or by the persons involved (cf **dramatic irony** under **drama**); a condition in which one seems to be mocked by fate or the facts. — *adj* **ironic** (*ī-ron'ik*) or **iron'ical**. — *adv* **iron'ically**. — *n* **i'ronist**. — *vt* and *vi* **i'ronize** or **-ise**. [L *īrōnīa*, from Gr *eirōneiā* dissimulation, from *eirōn* a dissembler]

irony[2]. See under **iron**.

Iroquoian *ir-ə-kwoi'ən*, *adj* of or belonging to the *Iroquois*, a group of *orig* five, later six, N American Indian peoples, now mainly in the north-east US and eastern Canada, who constitute the Iroquois Confederacy (cf **Five Nations** and **Six Nations** under **five** and **six**); of a group of N American Indian languages including those spoken by the Iroquois, and also Cherokee. — Also *n*.

IRQ *abbrev*: Iraq (IVR).

irradiate *ir-ā'di-āt*, *vt* to shed light or other rays upon or into; to treat by exposure to rays; to expose (perishable food) to electromagnetic radiation to kill bacteria and slow down decomposition; to light up; to brighten; to radiate. — *vi* to radiate; to shine. — *adj* adorned with rays of light or with lustre. — *n* **irra'diance** or **irra'diancy**. — *adj* **irra'diant**. — *n* **irradiā'tion** the act of irradiating; exposure to rays; the therapeutic application of electromagnetic radiation; that which is irradiated; brightness; apparent enlargement of a bright object by spreading of the excitation of the retina, or in a photograph by reflections within the emulsion; spread of a nervous impulse beyond the usual area affected; intellectual light. — *adj* **irra'diative**. [**ir-** (**in-**(1))]

irradicate *ir-ad'i-kāt*, *vt* to fix firmly. [**ir-** (**in-** (1))]

irrational *ir-ash'ən-əl*, *adj* not rational; not commensurable with natural numbers; long treated as short, or having such a syllable (indicated > ; *prosody*) — *n* an irrational syllable or number. — *n* **irra'tionalism** an irrational system; irrationality. — *n* **irra'tionalist**. — *adj* **irrationalist'ic**. — *n* **irrational'ity**. — *vt* **irra'tionalize** or **-ise** to make irrational. — *adv* **irra'tionally**. [**ir-** (**in-** (2))]

irrealizable or **irrealisable** *ir-ē-ə-līz'ə-bl*, *adj* not realizable. — *n* **irreality** (*-al'i-ti*) unreality. [**ir-** (**in-** (2))]

irrebuttable *ir-i-but'ə-bl*, *adj* which cannot be rebutted. [**ir-** (**in-** (2))]

irreceptive *ir-i-sep'tiv*, *adj* not receptive. [**ir-** (**in-** (2))]

irreciprocal *ir-i-sip'rə-kəl*, *adj* not reciprocal. — *n* **irreciprocity** (*ir-es-i-pros'i-ti*). [**ir-** (**in-** (2))]

irreclaimable *ir-i-klām'ə-bl*, *adj* that cannot be claimed back, brought into cultivation, or reformed; incorrigible. — *n* **irreclaimabil'ity** or **irreclaim'ableness**. — *adv* **irreclaim'ably**. [**ir-** (**in-** (2))]

irrecognizable or **irrecognisable** *ir-ek-əg-nīz'ə-bl* or *ir-ek'*, *adj* unrecognizable. — *n* **irrecognition** (*-nish'ən*) lack of recognition. [**ir-** (**in-** (2))]

irreconcilable *ir-ek-ən-sīl'ə-bl* or *ir-ek'*, *adj* incapable of being brought back to a state of friendship or agreement; inconsistent. — *n* an irreconcilable opponent; an intransigent; any of two or more opinions, desires, etc that cannot be reconciled. — *n* **irreconcīlabil'ity** or **irreconcī'lableness**. — *adv* **irreconcīl'ably**. — *adj* **irrec'onciled** not reconciled, *esp* (*Shakesp*) with God; not brought into harmony. — *n* **irreconcile'ment**. [**ir-** (**in-** (2))]

irrecoverable *ir-i-kuv'ər-ə-bl*, *adj* irretrievable; not reclaimable; beyond recovery. — *n* **irrecov'erableness**. — *adv* **irrecov'erably**. [**ir-** (**in-** (2))]

irrecusable *ir-i-kū'zə-bl*, *adj* that cannot be rejected. — *adv* **irrecūs'ably**. [Fr, from LL *irrecūsābilis*]

irredeemable *ir-i-dēm'ə-bl*, *adj* not redeemable; not subject to be paid at the nominal value. — *n* **irredeemabil'ity** or **irredeem'ableness**. — *n pl* **irredeem'ables** undated government or debenture stock. — *adv* **irredeem'ably**. [**ir-** (**in-** (2))]

Irredentist *ir-i-den'tist*, *n* a member of an Italian party formed in 1878, its aims to gain or regain for Italy various regions claimed on language and other grounds; (without *cap*) a person who advocates the redeeming of territory from another state. — Also *adj*. — *n* **Irredent'ism** the programme of the Irredentist party; (without *cap*) the doctrine of 'redeeming' territory from another state, *esp* where there is some historical claim to the territory or when an ethnic group seeks to rejoin the major part of the ethnic group in another state. [Ital (*Italia*) *irredenta* unredeemed (Italy), from L *in-* not, and *redemptus* pa p of *redimere* to redeem]

irreducible *ir-i-dūs'i-bl*, *adj* that cannot be reduced or brought from one degree, form, or state to another; not to be lessened; not to be overcome; unable to be replaced in a normal position by manipulation, as a hernia, etc. — *n* **irreducibil'ity** or **irreductibility** (*-duk-ti-bil'i-ti*). — *n* **irreduc'ibleness**. — *adv* **irreduc'ibly**. — *n* **irreduction** (*-duk'shən*). [**ir-** (**in-** (2))]

irreflective *ir-i-flek'tiv*, *adj* not reflective. — *n* **irreflec'tion** or **irreflex'ion**. [**ir-** (**in-** (2))]

irreformable *ir-i-fōrm'ə-bl*, *adj* not reformable; not subject to revision or improvement. — *adv* **irreform'ably**. [**ir-** (**in-** (2))]

irrefragable *ir-ef'rə-gə-bl*, *adj* that cannot be refuted; unanswerable. — *n* **irrefragabil'ity** or **irref'ragableness**. — *adv* **irref'ragably**. — **the Irrefragable Doctor** Alexander of Hales (died 1245) who prepared a system of instruction for the schools of Christendom. [L *irrefrāgābilis*, from *in-* not, *re-* backwards, and *frangere* to break]

irrefrangible *ir-i-fran'ji-bl*, *adj* incapable of refraction. — *n* **irrefrangibil'ity** or **irrefran'gibleness**. — *adv* **irrefran'gibly**. [**ir-** (**in-** (2))]

irrefutable *ir-ef'ūt-ə-bl*, also *-ūt'*, *adj* that cannot be refuted. — *n* **irrefutabil'ity** or **irref'utableness** (or *-ūt'*). — *adv* **irref'utably** (also *-ūt'*). [**ir-** (**in-** (2))]

irreg. *abbrev*: irregular; irregularly.

irregular *ir-eg'ū-lər*, *adj* not regular; not conforming to rule or to the ordinary rules; disorderly; uneven; unsymmetrical; variable; (of troops) not trained under the authority of a government; (of a marriage) not celebrated by a minister after proclamation of banns or of intention to marry. — *n* an irregular soldier. — *n* **irregularity** (*-lar'i-ti*) a rough place or bump on an even surface; an instance of action, behaviour, etc not conforming to rules or regulations. — *adv* **irreg'ularly**. [**ir-** (**in-** (2))]

irrelative *ir-el'ə-tiv*, *adj* not relative; irrelevant. — *adj* **irrelated** (*ir-i-lā'tid*). — *n* **irrelā'tion** or **irrel'ativeness**. — *adv* **irrel'atively**. [**ir-** (**in-** (2))]

irrelevant *ir-el'ə-vənt*, *adj* not relevant. — *n* **irrel'evance** or **irrel'evancy**. — *adv* **irrel'evantly**. [**ir-** (**in-** (2))]

irreligious *ir-i-lij'əs*, *adj* destitute of religion; regardless of religion; opposed to religion; false in religion (*Shakesp*); ungodly. — *n* **irrelig'ion** lack of religion; hostility to or disregard of religion. — *n* **irrelig'ionist**. — *adv* **irrelig'iously**. — *n* **irrelig'iousness**. [**ir-** (**in-** (2))]

irremeable *ir-em'i-ə-bl*, or *-ēm'*, *adj* which cannot be returned. — *adv* **irrem'eably**. [L *irremeābilis*, from *in-* not, *re-* back, and *meāre* to go, come]

irremediable *ir-i-mē'di-ə-bl*, *adj* beyond remedy or redress. — *n* **irremē'diableness**. — *adv* **irremē'diably**. [**ir-** (**in-** (2))]

irremissible *ir-i-mis'i-bl*, *adj* not to be remitted or forgiven. — *n* **irremissibil'ity** or **irremiss'ibleness**. — *n* **irremission** (*-mish'ən*). — *adj* **irremiss'ive** unremitting. [**ir-** (**in-** (2))]

irremovable *ir-i-mo͞ov'ə-bl*, *adj* not removable; not liable to be displaced. — *n* **irremovabil'ity** or **irremov'ableness**. — *adv* **irremov'ably**. [**ir-** (**in-** (2))]

irrenowned *ir-i-nown'id*, (*Spenser*) *adj* inglorious. [**ir-** (**in-** (2))]

irrepairable *ir-i-pār'ə-bl*, (*archaic*) *adj* beyond repair, irreparable. [**ir-** (**in-** (2))]

irreparable *ir-ep'ər-ə-bl*, *adj* that cannot be made good or rectified; beyond repair. — *n* **irreparabil'ity** or **irrep'arableness**. — *adv* **irrep'arably**. [**ir-** (**in-** (2))]

irrepealable *ir-i-pēl'ə-bl*, *adj* that cannot be repealed or annulled. — *n* **irrepealabil'ity** or **irrepeal'ableness**. — *adv* **irrepeal'ably**. [**ir-** (**in-** (2))]

irreplaceable *ir-i-plās'ə-bl*, *adj* whose loss cannot be made good; without possible substitute. — *adv* **irreplace'ably**. [**ir-** (**in-** (2))]

irrepleviable *ir-i-plev'i-ə-bl* or **irreplevisable** *ir-i-plev'isə-bl*, (*law*) *adj* unable to be replevied. [**ir-** (**in-** (2))]

irreprehensible *ir-ep-ri-hens'i-bl*, *adj* beyond blame. — *n* **irreprehens'ibleness**. — *adv* **irreprehens'ibly**. [**ir-** (**in-** (2))]

irrepressible *ir-i-pres'i-bl, adj* not able or willing to be restrained, subdued or (loosely) kept out of the limelight. — *n* **irrepressibil'ity** or **irrepress'ibleness**. — *adv* **irrepress'ibly**. [**ir-** (**in-** (2))]

irreproachable *ir-i-prōch'ə-bl, adj* free from blame; faultless. — *n* **irreproachabil'ity** or **irreproach'ableness**. — *adv* **irreproach'ably**. [**ir-** (**in-** (2))]

irreproducible *ir-ē-prō-dūs'i-bl, adj* that cannot be reproduced. [**ir-** (**in-** (2))]

irreprovable *ir-i-prōōv'ə-bl, adj* blameless. — *n* **irreprov'ableness**. — *adv* **irreprov'ably**. [**ir-** (**in-** (2))]

irresistance *ir-i-zist'əns, n* lack of resistance; passive submission. — *adj* **irresist'ible** not capable of being successfully opposed; resistless; overpowering; overmastering; fascinating, enticing. — *n* **irresistibil'ity** or **irresist'ibleness**. — *adv* **irresist'ibly**. [**ir-** (**in-** (2))]

irresoluble *ir-ez'əl-ū-bl* or *-ōō-bl, adj* that cannot be resolved into parts; that cannot be solved; that cannot be got rid of (*archaic*). — *n* **irresolubil'ity**. — *adv* **irres'olubly**. [**ir-** (**in-** (2))]

irresolute *ir-ez'əl-ūt* or *-ōōt, adj* not firm in purpose. — *adv* **irres'olutely**. — *n* **irres'oluteness** or **irresolution** (*-ū'shən* or *-ōō'shən*) lack of resolution. [**ir-** (**in-** (2))]

irresolvable *ir-i-zolv'ə-bl, adj* that cannot be resolved. — *n* **irresolvabil'ity** or **irresolv'ableness**. — *adv* **irresol'vably**. [**ir-** (**in-** (2))]

irrespective *ir-i-spek'tiv, adj* not having regard (with *of*). — Also *adv*. — *adv* **irrespec'tively**. [**ir-** (**in-** (2))]

irrespirable *ir-es'pir-ə-bl* or *-is-pīr', adj* unfit for respiration. [**ir-** (**in-** (2))]

irresponsible *ir-i-spons'i-bl, adj* not responsible; without sense of responsibility; feeling no burden of responsibility, light-hearted, carefree; reprehensibly careless; done without feelings of responsibility. — *n* **irresponsibil'ity** or **irrespon'sibleness**. — *adv* **irrespons'ibly**. — *adj* **irrespons'ive** not responding; not readily responding. — *adv* **irrespons'ively**. — *n* **irrespons'iveness**. [**ir-** (**in-** (2))]

irrestrainable *ir-i-strān'ə-bl, adj* not restrainable. [**ir-** (**in-** (2))]

irresuscitable *ir-i-sus'i-tə-bl, adj* incapable of being resuscitated or revived. — *adv* **irresusc'itably**. [**ir-** (**in-** (2))]

irretention *ir-i-ten'shən, n* absence of retention or power to retain. — *adj* **irreten'tive**. — *n* **irreten'tiveness**. [**ir-** (**in-** (2))]

irretrievable *ir-i-trēv'ə-bl, adj* not able to be recovered; irreparable. — *n* **irretrievabil'ity** or **irretriev'ableness**. — *adv* **irretriev'ably**. [**ir-** (**in-** (2))]

irreverent *ir-ev'ər-ənt, adj* not reverent; proceeding from irreverence. — *n* **irrev'erence** lack of reverence or veneration, *esp* for God. — *adj* **irreverential** (*-en'shəl*). — *adv* **irrev'erently**. [**ir-** (**in-** (2))]

irreversible *ir-i-vûrs'i-bl, adj* not reversible; that cannot proceed in the opposite direction or in both directions; incapable of changing back; not alike both ways; that cannot be recalled or annulled; (involving damage which is) permanent (*med*). — *n* **irreversibil'ity** or **irrevers'ibleness**. — *adv* **irrevers'ibly**. [**ir-** (**in-** (2))]

irrevocable *ir-ev'ək-ə-bl, adj* that cannot be recalled or revoked. — *n* **irrevocabil'ity** or **irrev'ocableness**. — *adv* **irrev'ocably**. [**ir-** (**in-** (2))]

irrigate *ir'i-gāt, vt* to wet or moisten; to water by means of canals or watercourses; to cause a stream of liquid to flow upon. — *vi* (*slang*) to drink. — *adj* **irr'igable**. — *n* **irrigā'tion** the act or process of irrigating; the washing out of a wound, the eye, or a hollow organ with a flow of water or solution, as in *colonic irrigation* (*med*). — *adj* **irrigā'tional**. — *adj* **irr'igative**. — *n* **irr'igātor** someone who, or something which, irrigates; an appliance for washing a wound, etc. — *adj* **irrig'ūous** watered; wet; irrigating. [L *irrigāre*, *-ātum* to water, and *irriguus* watering, watered, from *in* upon, and *rigāre* to wet]

irrision *ir-izh'ən, n* the act of laughing at another — *adj* **irrisory** (*ir-ī'sər-i*) mocking, derisive. [L *irrīsiō*, *-ōnis*, from *in* on, at, and *rīdēre*, *rīsum* to laugh]

irritate[1] *ir'i-tāt, vt* to excite or stimulate; to rouse; to provoke; to make angry or fretful; to excite a painful, uncomfortable, or unhealthy condition (eg heat and redness) in. — *n* **irritabil'ity** the quality of being easily irritated; the peculiar susceptibility to outside stimuli possessed by living matter. — *adj* **irr'itable** that may be irritated; easily annoyed; susceptible to excitement or irritation. — *n* **irr'itableness**. — *adv* **irr'itably**. — *n* **irr'itancy**. — *adj* **irr'itant** irritating. — *n* that which causes irritation. — *n* **irritā'tion** the act of irritating or exciting; anger, annoyance; stimulation; the term applied to any discomfort in the vital organs not amounting to inflammation but often leading to it (*med*). — *adj* **irr'itātive** tending to irritate or excite; accompanied with or caused by irritation. — *n* **ir'ritātor**. — **irritable bowel syndrome** a condition in which abdominal pain, constipation and/or diarrhoea occurs, often recurring over a period of years, without there being any significant deterioration in health or underlying disease. [L *irrītāre*, *-ātum* to annoy, vex]

irritate[2] *ir'i-tāt*, (*Scots law*) *vt* to make void. — *n* **irr'itancy**. — *adj* **irr'itant** rendering void. [L *irritāre*, from *in-* not, and *ratus* valid]

irrupt *ir-upt', vi* to break in; to carry out a sudden invasion or incursion. — *n* **irruption** (*ir-up'shən*) a breaking or bursting in; a sudden invasion or incursion. — *adj* **irrup'tive** rushing suddenly in. — *adv* **irrup'tively**. [L *irrumpere*, *irruptum*, from *in* in, and *rumpere* to break]

IRS *abbrev*: Internal Revenue Service (*US*).

Irvingite *ûr'ving-īt, n* a popular name for a member of the Catholic Apostolic Church. — Also *adj*. — *n* **Ir'vingism** the doctrine and practice of the Irvingites. [From Edward *Irving* (1792–1834)]

IS *abbrev*: Iceland (IVR); independent suspension (*mech*); information science; internal security.

Is.[1] or **Isa.** (*Bible*) *abbrev*: (the Book of) Isaiah.

Is.[2] *abbrev*: Island(s) or Isle(s).

is *iz*, used as 3rd *pers sing pres* indicative of **be**. [OE *is*; Ger *ist*, L *est*, Gr *esti*, Sans *asti*]

is-. See **iso-**.

isabel *iz'ə-bel, n* and *adj* dingy yellowish-grey or drab. — Also **isabell'a** or **isabell'ine** (*-in* or *-īn*). [Origin unknown: too early in use to be from *Isabella*, daughter of Philip II, who did not change her linen for three years until Ostend was taken; an etymological connection with Isabella of Castile, to whom a similar legend is ascribed, is chronologically possible but by no means certain]

isagogic *ī-sə-goj'ik* or *-gog'ik, adj* introductory. — *n* **isagoge** (*ī'sə-gō-ji*, or *-gō'*) an academic introduction to a subject. — *n sing* **isagog'ics** that part of theological study introductory to exegesis. [Gr *eisagōgē* an introduction, from *eis* into, and *agein* to lead]

isallobar *īs-* or *īz-al'-ə-bär*, (*meteorol*) *n* the contour line on a weather chart, connecting those places experiencing equal changes in atmospheric pressure over a specified period. [Gr *isos* equal, *allos* other, different, and *baros* weight]

isapostolic *īs-ap-əs-tol'ik, adj* equal to the apostles, as bishops of apostolic creation, the first preachers of Christ in a country, etc. [Gr *isos* equal, and *apostolikos* apostolic]

Isatis *ī'sə-tis, n* the woad genus of Cruciferae. — *n* **ī'satin** or **ī'satine** a substance ($C_8H_5O_2N$) obtained by oxidizing indigo. [Gr *isatis* woad]

ISBN *abbrev*: International Standard Book Number.

ISCh. *abbrev*: Incorporated Society of Chiropodists.

ischaemia or **ischemia** *is-kē'mi-ə, n* inadequate flow of blood to a part of the body. — *adj* **ischaem'ic** or **ischemic**. [Gr *ischein* to restrain, and *haima* blood]

ischium *is'ki-əm, n* a posterior bone of the pelvic girdle: — *pl* **is'chia**. — *adj* **ischiad'ic**, **is'chial** or **ischiat'ic**. [Latinized from Gr *ischion* the hip-joint]

ischuria *is-kū'ri-ə, n* a suppression or retention of urine. — *adj* and *n* **ischuretic** (*is-kū-ret'ik*). [Gr *ischein* to hold, and *ouron* urine]

ISD *abbrev*: international subscriber dialling.
ISDN *abbrev*: integrated services digital network, an advanced telecommunications network.
-ise. See **-ize**.
isenergic *īs-en-ûr'jik*, (*phys*) *adj* denoting equal energy. [Gr *isos* equal, and *energeia* energy]
Isengrim *i'zən-grim* or **Isegrim** *ī'zə-grim*, *n* the wolf in the beast epic of *Reynard the Fox*.
isentropic *ī-sen-trop'ik*, (*phys*) *adj* of equal entropy. [Gr *isos* equal, and *entropē* a turning about, from *en* in, and *trepein* to turn]
ish *ish*, (*Scots law*) *n* issue, liberty of going out; expiry. [OFr *issir* to go out, from L *exīre*, from *ex* out of, and *īre* to go]
-ish *-ish*, *sfx* signifying somewhat, as in *brownish*, *oldish*; like or similar to (sometimes implying deprecation), as in *outlandish*, *childish*; roughly, approximately, as in *sixish*. [OE *-isc*]
Ishmael *ish-mā'əl*, *n* someone like Ishmael (Genesis 16.12), at war with society. — *n* **Ish'maelīte** a descendant of Ishmael; a Bedouin; an Ishmael. — *adj* **Ishmaelīt'ish**.
Ishtar. See **Astarte**.
Isidorian *is-* or *iz-i-dō'* (or *-dö'*) *-ri-ən*, *adj* of or pertaining to St *Isidore* of Seville (c.560–636), or the collection of canons and decretals adopted by him; but *esp* applying to the forged *Pseudo-Isidorian* or *False Decretals*, published (c.845) by *Isidore* Mercator, and ascribed to St Isidore.
isinglass *ī'zing-gläs*, *n* a material, mainly gelatine, obtained from sturgeons' air-bladders and other sources. [Appar from obs Du *huizenblas*, from *huizen* a kind of sturgeon, and *blas* a bladder; Ger *Hausenblase*; cf **huso**]
ISIS or **Isis** *abbrev*: Independent Schools Information Service.
Isl. *abbrev*: Island.
Islam *iz'läm*, *is'läm* or *-läm'*, *n* the Muslim religion (also **Is'lamism**); the whole Muslim world. — *adj* **Islamic** (*-lam'ik*). — *n* **Islam'icist** a person who studies Islam, Islamic law, Islamic culture, etc. — *vt* **Islam'icize** or **-ise** to Islamize. — *n* **Is'lamite**. — *adj* **Islamitic** (*-lə-mit'ik*). — *n* **Islamīzā'tion** or **-s-**. — *vt* and *vi* **Is'lamize** or **-ise** to convert or (cause to) conform to Islam. [Ar *islām* surrender (to God)]
island *ī'lənd*, *n* a mass of land (not a continent) surrounded with water; anything isolated, detached, or surrounded by something of a different nature; a small raised traffic-free area in a street, *esp* for pedestrians; tissue or cells detached and differing from their surroundings. — *adj* of an island; forming an island. — *vt* to cause to appear like an island; to isolate; to dot as with islands. — *n* **islander** (*ī'lənd-ər*) an inhabitant of an island. — **island-hopping** see under **hop**[1]; **island universe** a spiral nebula regarded as forming a separate stellar system. — **islands of Langerhans** same as **islets of Langerhans** (see under **isle**); **Islands of the Blest** (*Gr mythol*) the abode of the blessed dead, situated somewhere in the far west; **Reil's island** see **insula**. [ME *iland*, from OE *īegland*, *īgland*, *ēgland*, from *īeg*, *īg*, *ēg* island (from a root which appears in Angles-*ea*, Aldern-*ey*, etc, OE *ēa*, L *aqua* water) and *land*; the *s* is due to confusion with *isle*]
isle *īl*, *n* an island. — *vt* to make an isle of; to set in an isle. — *vi* to dwell in an isle. — *n* **islet** (*ī'lit*) a little isle. — **isles'man** or **isle'man** an islander, *esp* an inhabitant of the Hebrides. — **Isle of Wight disease** a disease of bees caused by a mite in the spiracles, that appeared in the Isle of Wight in 1906, and spread to other regions; **islets of Langerhans** (*läng'ər-häns*) groups of epithelial cells discovered by Paul *Langerhans*, a German pathologist (1847–88), in the pancreas, that secrete the hormones insulin and glucagon. [ME *ile*, *yle*, from OFr *isle* (Fr *île*), from L *īnsula*]
ism *izm*, *n* any distinctive doctrine, theory or practice — *usu* in disparagement. — *adj* **ismat'ic** or **ismat'ical** addicted to isms or faddish theories. — *n* **ismat'icalness**. [From the suffix *-ism*]
-ism *-izm*, **-asm** *-azm*, or **-icism** *-i-sizm*, *sfx* forming abstract nouns signifying condition, system, as ego*ism*, de*ism*, Calvin*ism*, lacon*ism*, pleon*asm*, Angl*icism*, wit*ticism*. [L *-ismus*, *-asmus*, from Gr *-ismos*, *-asmos*]
Ismaili *is-mä-ē'lē* or *is-mā'i-li*, *n* one of a sect of Shiite Muslims whose imam or spiritual head is the Aga Khan. — Also *adj*. — *n* and *adj* **Ismailian** (*is-mā-il'i-ən*). — *n* **Is'mailism**. — *adj* **Ismailit'ic**.
isn't *iz'ənt*, contraction of **is not**.
ISO *abbrev*: Imperial Service Order; International Standards Organization.
iso *ī'sō*, (*film* and *TV*) *n* short for **isolated replay**, a facility whereby a section of film can be isolated and the action replayed.
iso- *ī-sō-*, *-so'*, also **is-** *īs-*, *combining form* signifying equal; denoting an isomeric substance, as in **iso-oc'tane** one of the isomers of normal octane. [Gr *isos* equal]
isoagglutination *ī-sō-ə-gloo-ti-nā'shən*, *n* the agglutination of red blood corpuscles within the same blood group. — *n* **isoagglu'tinin** an antibody that causes the agglutination of red blood corpuscles in animals of the same species from which it was derived. [**iso-**]
isoaminile *ī-sō-am'in-īl*, *n* an antitussive drug *usu* administered in capsules or linctus.
isoantibody *ī-sō-an'ti-bod-i*, *n* an antibody that occurs naturally against foreign tissue from an individual of the same species.
isoantigen *ī-sō-an'ti-jən*, *n* an antigen that stimulates antibody production in different members of the same species.
isobar *ī'sō-bär*, *n* a curve running through places of equal pressure; *esp* one connecting places, or their representations on a map, of equal barometric pressure (*meteorol*); same as **isobare** (*chem*). — *adj* **isobaric** (*-bar'ik*). — *adj* **isobaromet'ric**. [**iso-** and Gr *baros* weight]
isobare *ī'sō-bār* or **isobar** *ī'sō-bär*, *n* either of two atoms of different chemical elements but of identical atomic mass (eg an isotope of titanium and an isotope of chromium both of atomic mass 50). [Ety as for **isobar**]
isobase *ī'sō-bās*, (*geol*) *n* a contour line of equal upheaval of the land. [**iso-** and Gr *basis* step]
isobath *ī'sō-bäth*, *n* a contour line connecting points of equal underwater depth. — *adj* **isobath'ic**. [**iso-** and Gr *bathos* depth]
isobilateral *ī-sō-bī-lat'ər-əl*, *adj* bilaterally symmetrical with upper and under surfaces alike; symmetrical about two planes (*bot*). [**iso-**]
isobront *ī'sō-bront*, *n* a contour line marking simultaneous development of a thunderstorm. [**iso-** and Gr *brontē* thunder]
isochasm *ī'sō-kazm*, *n* a contour line of equal frequency of auroral displays. — *adj* **isochasm'ic**. [**iso-** and Gr *chasma* a gap, expanse]
isocheim or **isochime** *ī'sō-kīm*, *n* a contour line of mean winter temperature. — *adj* and *n* **isocheim'al**, **isocheim'enal** or **isochī'mal**. — *adj* **isocheim'ic**. [**iso-** and Gr *cheima* winter weather, *cheimainein* to be stormy]
isochor or **isochore** *ī'sō-kōr* or *-kör*, *n* a curve representing variation of some quantity under conditions of constant volume. — *adj* **isochoric** (*-kor'ik*). [**iso-** and Gr *chōrā* space]
isochromatic *ī-sō-krō-mat'ik*, *adj* having the same colour (*optics*); orthochromatic (*photog*). [**iso-** and Gr *chrōma*, *-atos* colour]
isochronal *ī-sok'rən-əl* or **isochronous** *-əs*, *adj* of equal time; performed in equal times; in regular periodicity. — *adv* **isoch'ronally** or **isoch'ronously**. — *n* **i'sochrone** a line on a chart or map joining points associated with a constant time difference, eg in reception of radio signals. — *n* **isoch'ronism**. — *vt* **isoch'ronize** or **-ise**. [**iso-** and Gr *chronos* time]
isoclinal *ī-sō-klī'nəl*, *adj* (of stratified rock) folded with nearly the same dip in each limb (*geol*); in terrestrial magnetism, having the same magnetic dip. — *n* a

contour line of magnetic dip. — *n* **ī'socline** an area of rock strata with isoclinal folds; an isoclinal. — *adj* and *n* **isoclinic** (*-klin'ik*) isoclinal. [**iso-** and Gr *klīnein* to bend]

isocracy *ī-sok'rə-si*, *n* (a system of government in which all people have) equal political power. — *adj* **isocrat'ic**. [**iso-** and Gr *krateein* to rule]

isocryme *ī'sō-krīm*, *n* a contour line of equal temperature during the coldest time. — *adj* and *n* **isocrȳm'al**. [**iso-** and Gr *krȳmos* cold]

isocyanide *ī-sō-sī'ən-īd*, *n* a salt or ester of **isocyanic acid**, a hypothetical acid only known in its compounds. [**iso-**]

isocyclic *ī'sō-sī-klik*, *adj* homocyclic. [**iso-**]

isodiametric *ī-sō-dī-ə-met'rik* or **isodiametrical** *-əl*, *adj* of equal diameters; about as broad as long. [**iso-**]

isodiaphere *ī-sō-dī'ə-fēr*, *n* one of two or more nuclides with the same difference between the totals of neutrons and protons. [**iso-** and Gr *diapherein* to differ, carry across]

isodicon *ī-sod'i-kon*, (*Gr Church*) *n* a troparion or short anthem sung while the Gospel is being carried through the church. [Dimin of Gr *eisodos* entrance]

isodimorphism *ī-sō-dī-mörf'izm*, (*crystallog*) *n* isomorphism between each of the two forms of a dimorphous substance and the corresponding forms of another dimorphous substance. — *adj* **isodimorph'ic**. — *adj* **isodimorph'ous**. [**iso-**]

isodomon *ī-sod'o-mon*, *n* masonry of uniform blocks in courses of equal height, the vertical joints placed over the middle of the blocks below. — Also (Latinized) **isod'omum**: — *pl* **isod'oma**. — *adj* **isod'omous**. [Gr, neuter of *isodomos* equal-coursed, from *isos* equal, and *domos* a course, from *demein* to build]

isodont *ī'sō-dont* or **isodontal** *-əl*, (*zool*) *adj* having all the teeth similar in size and form. — *n* an isodontal animal. [Gr *isos* equal, and *odous*, *odontos* tooth]

isodynamic *ī-sō-dīn-am'ik* or *-din-*, *adj* of equal strength, *esp* of magnetic intensity. — *n* an isodynamic line on the earth or the map, a contour line of magnetic intensity. [**iso-** and Gr *dynamis* strength]

isoelectric *ī-sō-i-lek'trik*, *adj* having the same potential. — **isoelectric point** the pH-value at which the ionization of an ampholyte is at a minimum. [**iso-**]

isoelectronic *ī-sō-el-ik-tron'ik*, *adj* having an equal number of electrons, or similar electron patterns. [**iso-**]

isoetes *ī-sō'ə-tēz*, *n* a plant of the quillwort genus (*Isoetes*) constituting a family (**Isoetā'ceae**) of pteridophytes, with short stem, a bunch of quill-shaped leaves in which the sporangia are sunk, and branching roots: — *pl* **iso'etes**. [Gr *isoetes* houseleek (an evergreen), from *isos* equal, and *etos* a year]

isogamy *ī-sog'ə-mi*, (*biol*) *n* the conjugation of two gametes of similar size and form. — *n* **isogamete** (*ī-sō-gam'ēt* or *ēt'*). — *adj* **isogamet'ic**, **isogam'ic** or **isog'amous**. [**iso-** and Gr *gamos* marriage]

isogeny *ī-soj'ə-ni*, *n* likeness of origin. — *adj* **isogenetic** (*ī-sō-ji-net'ik*). — *adj* **isog'enous**. [**iso-** and Gr *genos* kind]

isogeotherm *ī-sō-jē'ō-thûrm*, *n* a subterranean contour of equal temperature. — *adj* **isogeotherm'al** or **isogeotherm'ic**. — *n* an isogeotherm. [**iso-** and Gr *gē* the earth, and *thermē* heat, from *thermos* hot]

isogloss *ī'sō-glos*, *n* a line separating one region from another region which differs from it in a particular feature of dialect. — *adj* **isogloss'al**, **isoglott'al** or **isoglott'ic**. [**iso-** and Gr *glōssa* tongue]

isogonic *ī-sō-gon'ik* or **isogonal** *ī-sog'ən-əl*, *adj* of equal angles, *esp* of magnetic declination. — *n* an isogonic line or contour line of magnetic declination. — *n* **i'sogon** an equiangular polygon. [**iso-** and Gr *gōniā* an angle]

isogram *ī'sō-gram*, *n* a line drawn on a map or diagram showing all points which have an equal numerical value with respect to a given climatic or other variable. — See also **isopleth**. [**iso-** and Gr *gramma* a letter]

isohel *ī'sō-hel*, *n* a contour line of equal amounts of sunshine. [**iso-** and Gr *hēlios* sun]

isohyet *ī-sō-hī'ət*, *n* a contour line of equal rainfall. — *adj* **isohy'etal**. — *n* an isohyet. [**iso-** and Gr *hȳetos* rain, from *hȳein* to rain]

isoimmunization *ī-sō-im-ū-nī-zā'shən*, *n* the development of antibodies within an individual against antigens from another individual of the same species. [**iso-**]

isokinetic *ī-sō-kin-et'ik*, *adj* (of the withdrawal of a fluid sample) accomplished without disturbance to the speed and direction of flow. [**iso-** and Gr *kīneein* to move]

Isokontae *ī'sō-kont'ē*, *n pl* the green algae, whose zoospores *usu* have equal cilia. — *n* **i'sokont**. — *adj* and *n* **isokont'an**. [**iso-** and Gr *kontos* a (punting) pole]

isolate *ī'sō-lāt*, *vt* to place in a detached situation, like an island; to detach; to insulate; to separate (*esp* those with an infectious disease) (*med*); to seclude; to segregate; to obtain in a pure, uncombined state; to establish a pure culture of (a microorganism). — *n* (*-lit* or *lāt*) something isolated, *esp* for individual study or experiment. — Also *adj*. — *n* **isolabil'ity**. — *adj* **i'solable**. — *n* **isolā'tion**. — *n* **isolā'tionism** the policy of avoiding political entanglements with other countries. — *n* **isolā'tionist**. — *adj* **i'solātive** tending towards isolation; occurring without influence from outside. — *n* **i'solātor** someone who or something that isolates; a transparent plastic bag in which a patient is kept free of contamination by infective agents (*med*). — **isolated replay** see **iso**; **isolating languages** those in which each word is a bare root, not inflected or compounded. [Ital *isolare*, from *isola*, from L *īnsula* an island]

isolecithal *ī-sō-les'i-thəl*, *adj* (of the ova of mammals and some other vertebrates) having the yolk distributed evenly through the protoplasm. [**iso-** and Gr *lekithos* egg-yolk]

isoleucine *ī-sō-lū'sīn*, *n* an essential amino acid. [**iso-**]

isoline *ī'sō-līn*. Same as **isopleth**.

isologue *ī'sō-log*, *n* an organic compound with similar molecular structure to another, but containing different atoms of the same valency. — *adj* **isol'ogous**. [**iso-** and Gr *logos* ratio]

isomagnetic *ī-sō-mag-net'ik*, *adj* having equal magnetic induction or force. — *n* (also **isomagnetic line**) an imaginary line joining places at which the force of the earth's magnetic field is constant. [**iso-**]

isomer *ī'sō-mər*, (*chem*) *n* a substance, radical, or ion isomeric with another; an atomic nucleus having the same atomic number and mass as another or others but a different energy state. — *n* **i'somēre** (*zool*) an organ or segment corresponding to or homologous with another. — *adj* **isomeric** (*-mer'ik*; *chem*) identical in percentage composition and molecular weight but different in constitution or the mode in which the atoms are arranged; (of nuclei) differing only in energy state and half-life. — *n* **isom'erism** the property of being isomeric; the existence of isomers. — *n* **isomerīzā'tion** or **-s-**. — *vt* and *vi* **isomerize** or **-ise** (*ī-som'ər-īz*) to change into an isomer. — *adj* **isom'erous** (*bot*) having the same number of parts (*esp* in floral whorls). [**iso-** and Gr *meros* part]

isomerase *ī-som'ə-rāz* or *-rās*, *n* an enzyme which speeds up the conversion of one isomeric compound to another isomeric form.

isometric *ī-sō-met'rik* or **isometrical** *-əl*, *adj* having equality of measure; pertaining to isometrics; having the plane of projection equally inclined to three perpendicular axes; of the cubic system, or referable to three equal axes at right angles to one another (*crystallog*). — *n* **isomet'ric** (also **isometric line**) a line on a graph showing variations of pressure and temperature at a constant volume. — *adv* **isomet'rically**. — *n sing* **isomet'rics** a system of strengthening the muscles and tuning up the body by opposing one muscle to another or to a resistant object. — *n* **isom'etry** equality of measure. [**iso-** and Gr *metron* measure]

isomorph *ī'sō-mörf*, *n* that which shows isomorphism. — *adj* **isomorph'ic** showing isomorphism. — *n* **isomorph'-**

ism similarity in shape or structure in unrelated forms (*biol*); close similarity in crystalline form combined with similar chemical constitution (*crystallog*); a one-to-one correspondence between the elements of two or more sets and between the sums or products of the elements of one set and those of the equivalent elements of the other set or sets (*math*). — *adj* **isomorph'ous**. — **isomorphous mixture** a mixed crystal or solid solution in which isomorphous substances are crystallized together by vicarious substitution. [**iso-** and Gr *morphē* form]

isoniazid *ī-sō-nī'ə-zid* or **isoniazide** *-zīd*, *n* a drug, a pyridine derivative, used, *usu* with streptomycin, in the treatment of tuberculosis (sold under several proprietory names). [*isoni*cotinic acid hydr*azide*]

isonomy *ī-son'ə-mi*, *n* equal law, rights or privileges. — *adj* **isonom'ic** or **ison'omous**. [Gr *isonomiā*, from *isos* equal, and *nomos* law]

isoperimeter *ī-sō-pər-im'i-tər*, *n* a figure with perimeter equal to another. — *adj* **isoperimetrical** (*ī-sō-per-i-met'ri-kəl*). — *n* **isoperim'etry**. [**iso-** and Gr *perimetron* circumference]

isopleth *ī'sō-pleth*, *n* an isogram, *esp* one on a graph showing variations of a climatic element as a function of two variables; cf **nomogram**. [**iso-** and Gr *plēthos* great number]

isopod *ī'sō-pod*, *n* a member of the Isopoda. — *n pl* **Isopoda** (*ī-sop'ə-də*) an order of Crustacea with no carapace, depressed body, sessile eyes, seven pairs of nearly equal thoracic legs, and *usu* lamellar uropods — woodlice, fishlice, etc. — *adj* **isop'odan** or **isop'odous**. [**iso-** and Gr *pous*, *podos* a foot]

isopolity *ī-sō-pol'i-ti*, *n* reciprocity of rights of citizenship in different communities. [**iso-** and Gr *polīteiā* citizenship]

isoprene *ī'sō-prēn*, (*chem*) *n* a hydrocarbon of the terpene group, which may be polymerized into synthetic rubber. [**iso-**, *pro*pyl and **-ene**]

isoprenaline *ī-sō-pren'ə-lēn*, *n* a drug used to stimulate the heart and to dilate the air passages in asthma and bronchial conditions.

isopropyl *ī-sō-prop'il*, *n* the radical $(CH_3)_2CH$, derived from propane. [**iso-** and **propane**]

Isoptera *ī-sop'tər-ə*, *n pl* an order of insects having the two pairs of wings (when present) closely alike — the termites. — *adj* **isop'terous**. [**iso-** and Gr *pteron* a wing]

isorhythmic *ī-sō-ridh'mik* or *-rith'mik*, *adj* (in ancient prosody) equal in the number of time-units for thesis and arsis, as dactyl, spondee, anapaest; (in medieval motets) having a strict scheme of repeated rhythm independent of melodic repetition. [**iso-** and Gr *rhythmos* rhythm]

isosceles *ī-sos'i-lēz*, (*geom*) *adj* (of a triangle) having two equal sides. [Gr *isoskelēs*, from *isos* equal, and *skelos* a leg]

isoseismal *ī-sō-sīz'məl*, *n* a curve or line connecting points at which an earthquake shock is felt with equal intensity. — *adj* **isoseis'mal** or **isoseis'mic**. [**iso-** and Gr *seismos* a shaking]

isospin *ī'sō-spin*, *n* (in particle physics) a quantum number applied to members of closely related groups of particles to express and explain the theory that such particles (eg protons and neutrons) are in fact states of the same particle differing with regard to electric charge. — Also **isotopic spin**. [*iso*topic *spin*]

isosporous *ī-sos'pər-əs*, *ī-sō-spō'rəs*, or *-spö'*, (*bot*) *adj* having spores of one kind only (opposite to **heterosporous**). — *n* **isos'pory**. [**iso-** and Gr *sporos* seed]

isostasy *ī-sos'tə-si*, (*geol*) *n* a condition of equilibrium held to exist in the earth's crust, equal masses of matter underlying equal areas, whether of sea or land down to an assumed level of compensation. — *adj* **isostatic** (*ī-sō-stat'ik*) in hydrostatic equilibrium from equality of pressure; in a state of isostasy; pertaining to isostasy. — *adv* **isostat'ically**. [Gr *isos* equal, and *stasis* setting, weighing, *statikos* pertaining to weighing]

isostemonous *ī-sō-stēm'ən-əs*, (*bot*) *adj* having as many stamens as petals. [**iso-** and Gr *stēmōn* a thread]

isosteric *ī-sō-ster'ik*, *adj* (of two different molecules) having the same number of atoms, and the same number and arrangement of valency electrons. [**iso-**]

isotactic *ī-sō-tak'tik*, *adj* of or concerning a polymer with its attached groups of atoms in a regular order on one side of the central chain. [**iso-**]

isothenuria *ī-sō-then-ū'ri-ə*, *n* a condition which occurs in the final stages of renal failure, in which the kidneys are unable to produce urine.

isothere *ī'sō-thēr*, *n* a contour line of equal mean summer temperature. — *adj* **isotheral** (*ī-soth'ər-əl* or *ī-sō-thēr'əl*). — *n* an isothere. [**iso-** and Gr *theros* summer, from *therein* to make warm]

isotherm *ī'sō-thûrm*, *n* a contour line of equal temperature. — *adj* **isotherm'al** at constant temperature; pertaining to isotherms. — *n* an isothermal line, isotherm. — *adv* **isotherm'ally**. [**iso-** and Gr *thermē* heat, from *thermos* hot]

isotone *ī'sō-tōn*, *n* one of a number of nuclides having the same number of neutrons in the nucleus with differing numbers of protons. [**iso-** and prob Gr *tonos* tension]

isotonic *ī-sō-ton'ik*, *adj* having the same tone, tension or osmotic pressure. — *n* **isotonic'ity**. [**iso-** and Gr *tonos* tension, tone]

isotope *ī'sō-tōp*, *n* one of a set of chemically identical species of atom which have the same atomic number but different mass numbers (a natural element is made up of isotopes, always present in the same proportions). — *adj* **isotopic** (*-top'ik*). — *n* **isotopy** (*ī-sot'ə-pi*) the fact or condition of being isotopic. — **isotope separation** the process of altering the relative abundance of isotopes in a mixture; **isotopic number** the excess number of neutrons over protons in a nuclide; **isotopic spin** same as **isospin**. — **stable isotope** a non-radioactive isotope found in nature. [**iso-** and Gr *topos* place (ie in the periodic table)]

isotretinoin *ī-sō-trə-tin'ō-in*, *n* a drug derived from Vitamin A, used in the treatment of severe acne.

isotron *ī'sō-tron*, *n* a device for separating isotopes by accelerating ions by means of an electric field — the velocities attained are in inverse proportion to the masses. [**iso(tope)** and **-tron**]

isotropic *ī-sō-trop'ik*, *adj* having the same properties irrespective of direction; without predetermined axes (*biol*). — Also **isotropous** (*ī-sot'rə-pəs*). — *n* **isot'ropism** or **isot'ropy**. [**iso-** and Gr *tropos* turn, direction]

isotype *ī'sō-tīp*, *n* a presentation of statistical information by a row of diagrammatic pictures each representing a particular number of instances. [**iso-** and Gr *typos* form]

isoxsuprine *ī-sok'sə-prēn*, *n* a drug which dilates blood vessels, used to inhibit contractions in premature labour and in the treatment of arteriosclerosis.

I-spy *ī'-spī'*, *n* a word-game, in which one guesses objects in view, whose names begin with a certain letter of the alphabet; a children's game of hide-and-seek, so called from the cry when someone is spied. [**I** and **spy**]

Israeli *iz-rā'lē*, *n* a citizen of the modern state of Israel. — Also *adj*. [See **Israelite**]

Israelite *iz'ri-əl-īt*, or *-rə-*, *n* a descendant of Israel or Jacob (*Bible*); a Jew (*Bible*); one of the elect (*fig*); a member of a Christian sect that observes the Jewish law. — *adj* **Israelit'ic** or **Israelīt'ish**. [Gr *Isrāēlītēs*, from *Isrāēl*, Heb *Yisrāēl*, perhaps contender with God, from *sara* to fight, and *El* God]

ISS *abbrev*: International Social Services.

issei *ēs'sā'*, *n* a Japanese immigrant in the US, *orig* one to the USA or Canada after 1907, who did not qualify for citizenship till 1952 (cf **nisei** and **sanei**). [Jap, first generation]

ISSN *abbrev*: International Standard Serial Number.

issue *ish'ū* or *-ōō*, also *is'ū*, *n* a going or flowing out; an outlet; (an) act of sending out; that which flows or passes out; fruit of the body, children; produce, profits; a fine (*obs*); a putting into circulation, giving out for use, as of banknotes; publication, as of a book; a set of things put forth at one time; a single thing given out or supplied (chiefly *military*); an act or deed (*Shakesp*); ultimate result, outcome; upshot; lucky or successful outcome (*Shakesp*); critical determination; a point in dispute; a point on which a question depends; a question awaiting decision or ripe for decision; a discharge or flux (*archaic med*); an ulcer produced artificially. — *vi* (in *Spenser usu* **issue'**) to go, flow or come out; to proceed, as from a source; to spring; to be produced; to come to a point in fact or law (*law*); to turn out, result, terminate. — *vt* to send out; to put forth; to put into circulation; to publish; to give out for use; to supply (*military*). — *adj* **iss'uable**. — *adv* **iss'uably**. — *n* **iss'uance** the act of giving out, promulgation. — *adj* **iss'uant** (*heraldry*) issuing or coming up from another, as a charge or bearing. — *adj* **iss'ueless** without issue; childless. — *n* **iss'uer**. — **at issue** in disagreement; in dispute; **feigned issue** (*law*) an issue made up for trial by agreement of the parties or by an order of court, instead of by the ordinary legal procedure; **force the issue** to hasten or compel a final decision on a matter; **general issue** (*law*) a simple denial of the whole charge, as 'Not guilty', instead of a **special issue**, an issue taken by denying a particular part of the allegations; **immaterial issue** (*law*) an issue which is not decisive of any part of the litigation, as opposed to a **material issue**, one which necessarily involves some part of the rights in controversy; **join** (or **take**) **issue** to take an opposite position, or opposite positions, in dispute; to enter into dispute; to take up a point as basis of dispute; **side issue** a subordinate issue arising from the main business. [OFr *issue*, from *issir* to go or flow out, from L *exīre*, from *ex* out, and *īre* to go]

-ist *-ist*, *sfx* denoting the person who is an advocate or believer in a doctrine or practises an art, as Calvin*ist*, chem*ist*, novel*ist*, art*ist*, royal*ist*. [L *-ista*, from Gr *-istēs*]

ISTC *abbrev*: Iron and Steel Trades Confederation.

isthmus *is'məs* or *isth'məs*, *n* a narrow neck of land connecting two larger portions; a narrow part of a structure connecting two larger parts (*anatom*); a constriction. — *adj* **isth'mian** pertaining to an isthmus, *esp* the Isthmus of Corinth. — **Isthmian Games** (*Gr hist*) games held on the Isthmus of Corinth, near the Saronic Gulf shore. [L, from Gr *isthmos*, from root of *ienai* to go]

Istiophorus. Same as **Histiophorus** (see under **hist-**).

istle *ist'li* or **ixtle** *ikst'li*, *n* a valuable fibre obtained from Agave, Bromelia, and other plants. [Mexican Sp *ixtle*, from Nahuatl *ichtli*]

IT *abbrev*: Information Technology.

It. *abbrev*: Italian; Italian vermouth.

it[1] *it*, *pronoun* the neuter of **he** or **she** and **him** or **her** applied to a thing without life, a lower animal, a young child, rarely (except as an antecedent or in contempt) to a man or woman; used as an impersonal, indefinite, or anticipatory or provisional subject or object, as the object of a transitive verb that is normally an intransitive, or a noun; (in children's games) the player chosen to oppose all others; the *ne plus ultra*, that which answers exactly to what one is looking for (*colloq*); an indefinable crowning quality, personal magnetism; sex-appeal (*slang*); sexual intercourse, or matters sexual (*euphem*). — *genitive* **its**; *pl* **they** and **them**. [OE *hit*, neuter (nominative and accusative) of *hē*; Du *het*, Gothic *hita*, this; related to Gothic *ita*, Ger *es*, L *id*, Sans *i*]

it[2] *it*, (*colloq*) *n* Italian vermouth.

ita *ē'tə*, *it'ə*, *n* the miriti palm. [Arawak *ité*]

i.t.a. or **ITA** *abbrev*: initial teaching alphabet.

itacism *ē'tə-sizm*, *n* the pronunciation of Greek **ēta** as in Modern Greek, like English long *e* (opposite to *etacism*); iotacism in pronunciation of various vowels and diphthongs. [Gr *ēta* eta, *η*]

itacolumite *it-ə-kol'ūm-īt*, *n* a schistose quartzite containing scales of mica, talc and chlorite, often having a certain flexibility. [*Itacolumi* a Brazilian mountain]

itaconic acid *it-ə-kon'ik*, or *īt-*, *as'id*, a white crystalline solid obtained by fermentation of sugar with Aspergillus mould, used in plastics manufacture. [Anagram of *aconitic*]

ita est *ē'tə est*, (*L*) it is so.

Ital. *abbrev*: Italian.

ital. *abbrev*: italic.

Itala. See **Italic version** under **Italian**.

Italian *i-tal'yən*, *adj* of or relating to *Italy* or its people or language. — *n* a native or citizen of Italy, or a person of the same race; the language of Italy. — *adj* **Ital'ianate** Italian in style. — Also *vt*. — *n* **Ital'ianism** or **Ital'icism** (*-sizm*) an Italian idiom or habit; Italian sympathies. — *n* **Ital'ianist** a person who has a scholarly knowledge of Italian; a person of Italian sympathies. — *n* **Italianīzā'tion** or **-s-**. — *vt* **Ital'ianize** or **-ise** to make Italian; to give an Italian character to. — *vi* to become Italian; to play the Italian; to speak Italian; to use Italian idioms; to adopt Italian ways. — *adj* **Ital'ic** pertaining to Italy, *esp* ancient Italy; of or pertaining to the Italic branch of languages; (without *cap*) of a sloping type introduced by the Italian printer Aldo Manuzio in 1501, used *esp* for emphasis or other distinctive purpose, indicated in manuscripts by single underlining. — *n* a branch of Indo-European *usu* considered to comprise Oscan, Umbrian, Latin and related languages, but sometimes applied to either the Latin group or the Osco-Umbrian group alone; (without *cap*, *usu* in *pl*) an italic letter. — *n* **italicīzā'tion** or **-s-**. — *vt* **ital'icize** or **-ise** to put in, or mark for, italics. — *n* **Ital'iot** or **Ital'iote** a Greek of ancient Italy. — Also *adj*. — **Italian architecture** the style practised by Italian architects of the 15th to 17th centuries, which originated in a revival of the ancient architecture of Rome; **Italianate Englishman** an Englishman of the Renaissance, full of Italian learning and vices, proverbially equivalent to a devil incarnate; **Italian garden** a formal garden with statues; **Italian iron** a smoothing iron for fluting; **Italian sixth** (*music*) a chord of a note with its major third and augmented sixth; **Italian sonnet** same as **Petrarch(i)an sonnet** (see under **sonnet**); **Italian vermouth** a sweet vermouth; **Italian warehouseman** a dealer in such groceries as macaroni, olive oil, dried fruits, etc; **Italic version** or **It'ala** a translation of the Bible into Latin, based on the 'Old Latin' version, and made probably in the time of Augustine. [L *Ītaliānus* and Gr *Ītalikos*, from L *Ītalia*, Gr *Ītaliā* Italy]

Italic, **italic**, etc. See under **Italian**.

Italo- *i-tal'ō-* or *it'ə-lō-*, *combining form* signifying Italy or Italian, as in *Italophile*.

ITC *abbrev*: Independent Television Commission (replacing **IBA**).

itch *ich*, *n* an irritating sensation in the skin; scabies, an eruptive disease in the skin, caused by a parasitic mite; a constant teasing desire. — *vi* to have an uneasy, irritating sensation in the skin; to have a constant, teasing desire. — *n* **itch'iness**. — *adj* **itch'y** pertaining to or affected with an itch or itching. — **itching palm** a greed for gain. — *adj* **itch'y-palmed**. — **itch'-mite** a mite (*Sarcoptes scabiei*) that burrows in the skin causing severe itching leading to scabies; **itch'weed** Indian poke. [OE *giccan* to itch; Scot *youk*, *yuck*, Ger *jucken* to itch]

-ite *-īt*, *sfx* used to form: (1) names of people, indicating their origin, place of origin, affiliations, loyalties, etc (eg *Semite*, *Durhamite*, *Jacobite*, *Thatcherite*); (2) names of fossil organisms (eg *ammonite*); (3) names of minerals (eg *calcite*); (4) names of salts of acids with sfx **-ous** (eg *sulphite* salt of sulphurous acid); (5) names of bodily parts (eg *somite*). The nouns may be used also as adjs.

item *ī'təm*, *n* a separate article or particular in an enumeration; a piece of news or other matter in a newspaper, magazine, television programme, etc. — *vt* to set down in enumeration; to make a note of. — *adv* (*archaic*) likewise; also. — *vt* **i'temize** or **-ise** to give or list by items. [L *item* likewise]

iterate *it'ər-āt, vt* to do again; to say again, repeat. — *n* **it'erance** or **iterā'tion** repetition. — *adj* **it'erant** or **it'erative** (*-ə-tiv* or *-ā-tiv*) repeating. — *adv* **it'erātively**. [L *iterāre, -ātum*, from *iterum* again]

iterum *it'ə-rəm* or *-e-rōōm*, (*L*) *adv* again; anew.

ithyphallus *ith-i-fal'əs, n* an erect phallus; (with *cap*) the stinkhorn genus of fungi. — *adj* **ithyphall'ic** of or with an ithyphallus; pertaining to the processions in honour of Dionysos in which an ithyphallus was carried, or to the hymns sung or the metres used; shameless. [Gr *īthyphallos*, from *īthys* straight, and *phallos* a phallus]

itinerant *i-tin'ər-ənt*, also *ī-, adj* making journeys from place to place; travelling. — *n* someone who travels from place to place, *esp* a judge, a Methodist preacher, a strolling musician, or a pedlar; a wanderer. — *n* **itin'eracy** (*-ə-si*) or **itin'erancy**. — *adv* **itin'erantly**. — *adj* **itin'erary** travelling; relating to roads or journeys. — *n* a plan or record of a journey; a road-book; a route; an itinerant. — *vi* **itin'erate** to travel from place to place, *esp* for the purpose of judging, preaching or lecturing. [L *iter, itineris* a journey]

-itis *-ī'tis, combining form* denoting: an inflammatory disease, as in bronch*itis*; jocularly extended to conditions considered disease-like, as in jazz*itis*. [Gr *-ītis*]

it'll *it'l*, a contraction of **it will**.

ITN *abbrev*: Independent Television News.

ITO *abbrev*: International Trade Organization.

its *its*, possessive or genitive of **it**[1]. (The old form was *his*, *its* not being older than the end of the 16c. *Its* does not occur in the English Bible of 1611 (in Leviticus 25.5 the possessive *it* was amended to *its* for the 1660 edition) or in Spenser, rarely in Shakespeare, and is not common until the time of Dryden.) — *pronoun* **itself** (*it-self'*) the emphatic and reflexive form of **it**. — **by itself** alone, apart; **in itself** by its own nature.

it's *its*, a contraction of **it is** or **it has**.

itsy-bitsy *it'si-bit'si*, (*colloq*) *adj* tiny. [Prob a childish reduplicated form of **little** influenced by **bit**[1]]

ITT *abbrev*: International Telephone and Telegraph Corporation.

ITU *abbrev*: International Telecommunication Union.

ITV *abbrev*: Independent Television.

IU *abbrev*: international unit.

IUCD or **IUD** *abbrev*: intrauterine (contraceptive) device, a plastic or metal spiral or T-shaped device inserted in the uterus to prevent conception.

iure *yōō're*, (*L*) by right or by law. — **iure coronae** (*ko-rō'nē*) by right of the crown; **iure divino** (*di-vī'nō*) by divine law; **iure humano** (*hū-mā'nō*) by human law; **iure mariti** (*ma-rē'tē*) by a husband's right; **iure propinquitatis** (*prō-ping-kwi-tä'tis*) by right of relationship; **iure sanguinis** (*sang'gwi-nis*) by right of blood.

IV *abbrev*: intravenous; intravenous drip; intravenously.

IVB *abbrev*: Invalidity Benefit.

I've *īv*, a contraction of **I have**.

IVF *abbrev*: in-vitro fertilization.

Ivorian *ī-vö'ri-ən, adj* of or relating to the Ivory Coast, now officially Côte d'Ivoire, a W African republic. — *n* a native or citizen of the Ivory Coast.

ivory *ī'və-ri, n* dentine, *esp* the hard white substance composing the tusks of the elephant, walrus, hippopotamus and narwhal; (in *pl*) objects of, or resembling, ivory, eg piano-keys, dice, teeth, and formerly billiard balls and dominoes (*slang*). — *adj* made of, resembling, or of the colour of, ivory. — *adj* **i'voried** made like ivory; supplied with teeth (*slang*). — *n* **i'vorist** a worker in ivory. — **i'vory-black** a black powder, *orig* made from burnt ivory, but now from bone; **ivory gate** see under **gate**[1]; **i'vory-nut** the nut of the S American palm *Phytelephas* or other palm, yielding **vegetable ivory** a substance like ivory; **i'vory-palm**; **ivory-por'celain** a fine ware with an ivory-white glaze; **ivory tower** (*fig*) a place of retreat from the world and one's fellows; a life style remote from that of most ordinary people, leading to ignorance of practical concerns, problems, etc. — *adj* **ivory-tow'ered**. — **i'vory-tree** the palay. — **show one's ivories** (*slang*) to show the teeth. [OFr *ivurie* (Fr *ivoire*), from L *ebur, eboris* ivory; Coptic *ebu* elephant, ivory]

IVR *abbrev*: International Vehicle Registration.

ivresse *ē-vres*, (*Fr*) *n* drunkenness.

ivy *ī'vi, n* an araliaceous evergreen plant (*Hedera helix*) that climbs by roots on trees and walls. — *adj* **i'vied** (also **i'vy'd**) overgrown or covered with ivy. — **i'vy-bush** a bush or branch of ivy, *esp*, formerly, one hung at a tavern-door, the ivy being sacred to Bacchus; **Ivy League** a name given to eight eastern US universities of particular academic and social prestige. — *adj* **i'vy-leaved** having five-lobed leaves like ivy (as the *ivy-leaved* toadflax). — *adj* **i'vy-man'tled** (*poetic*) ivied. — **ground-ivy** and **poison-ivy** see under **ground**[2] and **poison** respectively. [OE *īfig*, OHGer *ebah*]

IW *abbrev*: Isle of Wight.

IWC *abbrev*: International Whaling Commission.

iwis or **ywis** *i-wis'*, (*archaic*) *adv* certainly, sometimes erroneously written *I wis*, as if 'I know'. [ME *ywis, iwis*, from OE *gewis* certain; Ger *gewiss* (adv)]

ixia *ik'si-ə, n* any plant of the iridaceous genus *Ixia*, found in Southern Africa. [New L, from Gr *ixos* mistletoe, birdlime]

ixodiasis *iks-ō-dī'ə-sis, n* a disease caused by or transmitted by ticks. [From New L *Ixodes* the tick genus, and **-iasis**]

ixtle. See **istle**.

Iynx. A spelling of the generic name **Jynx**.

Iyyar *ē'yär, n* the eighth month of the Jewish year (second of the ecclesiastical year). [Heb]

izard *iz'ərd, n* the Pyrenean ibex. [Fr *isard*]

-ize or **-ise** *-īz*, also **-icize** or **-icise** *-is-īz, sfx* forming verbs from adjectives (meaning to (cause to) become as specified), eg *equalize*, or from nouns (meaning to practise, or subject to, the thing specified), eg *botanize* or *satirize*. [L *-izare*, from Gr *-izein*; Fr *-iser*]

izvestiya or **izvestia** *iz-ves'ti-ə*, (*Russ*) *n* news; information.

izzard *iz'ərd*, (*archaic* or *dialect*) *n* the letter Z.

izzat *iz'ət, n* public esteem; honour, reputation, prestige. [Urdu, from Ar *'izzah* glory]

J

J or **j** *jā* or (*Scot*) *jī*, *n* the tenth letter in the modern English alphabet, developed from I, specialized to denote a consonantal sound (*dzh* in English, *y* in German and other languages, *zh* in French, an open guttural in Spanish), I being retained for the vowel sound (a differentiation not general in English books till about 1630); as numeral, used in old MSS and in medical prescriptions instead of *i* final, eg *vj*, six; used equally with *i* for $\sqrt{-1}$; **J** represents the mechanical equivalent of heat. — **J'-curve** (*econ*) a small initial deterioration, decrease, etc followed by a larger sustained improvement, increase, etc, appearing on a graph as a J-shaped curve; **J'-pen** a pen with a short broad nib.

J or **J.** *abbrev*: Japan (IVR); joint (of marijuana) (*colloq*); joule; Journal; Judge; Justice.

JA *abbrev*: Jamaica (IVR).

jab *jab*, *vt* and *vi* to poke, stab. — *n* a sudden thrust or stab; a short straight punch; an injection (*colloq*). [Orig Scot variant of **job**[1]]

jabber *jab'ər*, *vi* to gabble or talk rapidly. — *vt* to say indistinctly. — *n* rapid indistinct speaking. — *n* **jabb'erer**. — *n* and *adj* **jabb'ering**. — *adv* **jabb'eringly**. [Imit]

jabberwock *jab'ər-wok*, *n* a fabulous monster created by Lewis Carroll in his poem *Jabberwocky*; (also **jabb'erwocky**) nonsense, gibberish.

jabble *jab'l*, (*Scot*) *n* an agitation in liquid; a rippling; a quantity of liquid enough to dash about or splash. — *vt* and *vi* to splash; to ripple; to dash; to jumble (*fig*). [Imit]

jabers *jā'bərz*, *n* in the Irish oath *be jabers* prob for **Jesus**.

jabiru *jab'i-roo* or *-roo'*, *n* a large Brazilian stork; also applied to other kinds of stork. [Tupí *jabirú*]

jaborandi *jab-ə-ran'di* or *jab-ö-*, *n* a sweat- and saliva-inducing Brazilian drug, obtained from the leaflets of rutaceous shrubs (Pilocarpus) and other sources; the leaflets or plants themselves. [Tupí]

jabot *zha'bō*, *n* a frill of lace, etc, worn in front of a woman's dress or on a man's shirt-front, *esp* (now) as part of full Highland dress. [Fr]

jacamar *jak'ə-mär*, *n* any one of a S American family (*Galbulidae*) of long-billed insect-catching birds with reversible fourth toe and *usu* metallic green or bronze plumage. [Fr, from Tupí *jacamá-ciri*]

jaçana *zhä-sə-nä'* or **jacana** *jak'ə-nə*, *n* a long-toed swamp bird of the tropics. [Port, from Tupí]

jacaranda *jak-ə-ran'də*, *n* a tropical American, etc tree of the Bignoniaceae, with lilac-coloured flowers, fernlike leaves and hard, heavy, fragrant brown wood; any similar tree or its wood. [Port and Tupí *jacarandá*]

jacchus *jak'əs*, *n* a S American marmoset (*Callithrix*). [L *Iacchus*, from Gr *Iakchos* Bacchus]

jacent *jā'sənt*, (*obs*) *adj* lying flat; sluggish. [L *jacēns*, *-entis*, pr p of *jacēre* to lie]

jacinth *jas'inth* or *jās'*, *n orig* a blue gemstone, *perh* sapphire; a reddish-orange variety of transparent zircon, hyacinth (*mineralogy*); a variety of garnet, topaz, quartz, or other stone (*jewellery*); a reddish-orange colour; a slaty-blue fancy pigeon. [**hyacinth**]

jack[1] *jak*, *n* (with *cap*) a familiar form or diminutive of John; (with *cap*) the common man (*obs*); (with *cap*) contemptuously, a fellow (*obs*); (*usu* with *cap*) an ill-mannered, vulgar or boorish fellow (*obs*); (sometimes with *cap*) an attendant, servant or labourer; (often with *cap*) a sailor; (with *cap*) used in addressing a man whose name is unknown to the speaker (*US slang*); a detective (*slang*); money (*US slang*); a machine or device which *orig* took the place of a servant, such as a boot-jack for taking off boots, a contrivance for turning a spit (*smoke-jack*, *roasting-jack*), an apparatus for raising heavy weights; a winch; a socket whose connections operate either to complete or break the circuit only when a jack plug is inserted (*telecomm*, etc); a figure that strikes the bell in clocks; the male of some animals; a jackass (also **jack donkey**); a jack-rabbit; a jackdaw; a young pike; (in keyboard instruments) part of the action that moves the hammer or carries the quill or tangent; the key itself (*Shakesp*); a contrivance for guiding threads in a loom; a saw-horse; a jack-crosstree (*naut*); a small flag indicating nationality, flown by a ship, *usu* at the bow or the bowsprit; a leather pitcher or bottle; a knave (*cards*); (in *pl*) the game of dibs; a piece used in this game; the small white ball aimed at in bowls; (with *cap*) a Jacqueminot rose. — *vt* to raise with, or as if with, a jack (with *up*); to act upon with a jack; to throw up or abandon (*usu* with *in* or, formerly, *up*; *slang*); to increase (eg prices) (with *up*). — *vi* to give up (with *up*) (*old slang*); (with *off*) to masturbate (*slang*); (with *up*) to inject oneself, take a fix (*drug-taking slang*); (with *up*) to refuse, resist (*Austr slang*). — *adj* (*Austr*) tired, fed up. — *n* **Jack'een** or **jack'een** a pushy lower-class Dubliner. — *n* **Jack'y** or **Jack'y-Jacky** (*Austr* contemptuous *slang*) a nickname for an Aborigine. — **Jack-a-dan'dy** a dandy or fop, *esp* if diminutive; **Jack-a-lan'tern** a Jack-o'-lantern; **Jack'-a-Lent** (*Shakesp*) a boy (for **Jack of Lent** a kind of puppet formerly used as an Aunt Sally in Lent); **jack'-bean** a subtropical American climbing bean (genus *Canavalia*); **jack'-block** a block of pulleys used for raising and lowering topgallant-masts; **jack'boot** a large boot reaching above the knee, to protect the leg, *orig* covered with iron plates and worn by cavalry; military rule, *esp* when brutal (*fig*). — *vi* (with *around*; also *vt* with *it*) to behave in an oppressive or brutally authoritarian way, to domineer, throw one's weight around. — *adj* **jack'booted**. — **jack'-by-the-hedge** (also with *cap*) garlic-mustard; **jack-cross'tree** (*naut*) the crosstree at the head of a topgallant-mast. — *adj* **jack easy** indifferent, not caring one way or the other. — **Jack'-fool** a fool; **Jack Frost** frost or freezing weather personified; **Jack'-go-to-bed-at-noon** the plant goat's-beard; **jack'hammer** a hand-held compressed-air hammer drill for rock-drilling. — *adj* and *adv* **jack'-high** (in bowls) as far as the jack. — **Jack'-in-office** (also without *cap*) a vexatiously self-important petty official; **Jack'-in-the-box** (also without *cap*) a toy figure that springs up from a box when the lid is released; **Jack'-in-the-green** a May-Day dancer enclosed in a green shrubby framework; **Jack'-in-the-pulpit** a N American plant (*Arisaema triphyllum*) like cuckoo-pint; also applied to various other plants, *esp* of the genus *Arisaema*; **Jack Ketch** (*archaic*) a public hangman, from one so named under James II; **jack'knife** a large clasp-knife; a dive in which the performer doubles up in the air and straightens out again. — *vi* and *vt* to double up as a jackknife does; (of articulated vehicles or parts) through faulty control, to form, or cause to form, an angle of 90° or less. — **Jack Mormon** (*US*) a non-Mormon living amicably in a Mormon community; an inactive, lapsed or nominal Mormon; **Jack-of-all'-trades** someone who can turn a hand to anything; **jack-o'-lan'tern** a will-o'-the-wisp; a lantern made from a hollowed-out pumpkin, turnip, etc with holes cut to resemble eyes, mouth and nose; **jack'-pine** any of several N American species of pine; **jack'-plane** a large strong plane used by carpenters; **jack plug** (*telecomm*, etc) a one-pronged plug used to introduce an apparatus quickly into a circuit; **jack'pot** a poker game, played for the pot or pool (consisting of equal stakes from all the players), which must be opened by a player holding two jacks or better; a money pool in card games, competitions, etc that can be won only on certain conditions being fulfilled and accumulates till such time as they are (see also **hit the jackpot** below); a prize-money fund; a mess, an awkward situation (*US slang*); **Jack'-priest** (*contemptuous*) a parson; **Jack'-pudding** (*archaic*) a merry-andrew, buffoon; **jack'-rabbit** a long-eared American hare; **jack'-rafter** a rafter shorter than the rest, as in a hip-roof; **Jack Russell** or **Jack Russell terrier** a breed of small terrier, introduced by *John Russell*, 19c parson; **Jack'-sauce** (*Shakesp*) an impudent fellow; **jack shaft** or **jack'shaft** (*eng*) an intermediate shaft, eg between a motor and the wheels it drives; **Jack'-slave** (*Shakesp*) a low servant, a vulgar fellow; **jack'smith** (*obs*) a maker of roasting-jacks; **jack'-snipe** any of various small species of snipe; **Jack Sprat** a diminutive fellow; **jack'-staff** the staff on which the jack (flag) is hoisted; **jack'-stays** ropes or strips of wood or iron stretched along the yards of a ship to bind the sails to; **Jack'-straw** or **jack'-straw** a straw effigy; a man of straw, a lightweight; a straw or slip used in the game of **jack'-straws** or spillikins; **Jack tar** (also without *cap*) a sailor; **jack towel** a continuous towel passing over a roller; **jack'-up** an offshore oil rig or accommodation platform, etc secured by legs that are lowered from the platform to the sea bed (also **jack'-up rig**); an act of non-co-operation or resistance (*Austr slang*); **Jacky-Jacky** see **Jacky** above. — **before you can** or **could say Jack Robinson** very quickly; **cheap Jack** see under **cheap**; **every man Jack** one and all; **hit the jackpot** to win a jackpot; to have a big success or stroke of good fortune; **I'm all right, Jack** an expression of selfish or indifferent complacency at the misfortunes or difficulties of others; **Jack the lad** a flashy, cocksure young man; **steeplejack** see under **steeple**; **Union Jack** (not properly a jack) see under **union**[1]; **yellow Jack** (*slang*) yellow fever. [Appar Fr *Jacques*, the most common name in France, hence used as a substitute for *John*, the most common name in England; really = *James* or *Jacob*, from L *Jacōbus*; but possibly partly from *Jackin*, *Jankin*, dimin of *John*]

jack[2] *jak*, *n* a medieval defensive coat, *esp* of leather. — **jack'man** a soldier wearing a jack; a retainer. [Fr *jaque*, perh from *Jacques* James]

jack[3] or **jak** *jak*, *n* a tree of the East Indies of the breadfruit genus (*Artocarpus*); its fruit. — **jack'-fruit**; **jack'-tree**. [Port *jaca*, from Malayalam *chakka*]

jackal *jak'öl* or *jak'l*, *n* a wild, carnivorous, gregarious African or Asian animal closely related to the dog, which feeds on the kill of other animals, though erroneously supposed to act as a lion's provider or hunting scout; someone who does another's dirty work; someone who wants to share the spoil but not the danger. — *vi* to play the jackal: — *pa p* **jack'alled**. [Pers *shaghāl*]

jackanapes *jak'ə-nāps*, *n* an ape or monkey (*archaic*); a cocky, impudent fellow; a cheeky child. [Origin uncertain]

jackaroo or **jackeroo** *jak-ə-rōō'*, (*Austr colloq*) *n* a newcomer, or other person, gaining experience on a sheep- or cattle-station: — *fem* **jillaroo'**. — *vi* to be a jackaroo. [Aboriginal]

jackass *jak'as*, *n* a male ass; a blockhead, fool. — **laughing jackass** the kookaburra. [**jack**[1] and **ass**]

jackdaw *jak'dö*, *n* a daw, a small species of crow with greyish neck. [**jack**[1] and **daw**[2]]

jackeen. See under **jack**[1].

jackeroo. See **jackaroo**.

jacket *jak'it*, *n* a short coat; an animal's coat; the skin (of potatoes); a loose paper cover (of a book, etc); a paper or cardboard envelope to protect a gramophone record (*US*); a document folder (*US*); the outer casing of a boiler, pipe, etc, eg a steam-jacket or water-jacket; the steel lattice structure which supports a steel offshore oil platform; the aluminium or zirconium alloy covering of the fissile elements in a reactor. — *vt* to provide or cover with a jacket; to beat (*old slang*). — *adj* **jack'eted** wearing a jacket. — **jacket potato** a potato cooked in its skin. — **dust someone's jacket** (*old slang*) to beat someone. [OFr *jaquet*, dimin of *jaque*; see ety for **jack**[2]]

jacksie or **jacksy** *jak'si*, (*slang*) *n* the posterior; the anus. [Perh **jack**[1]]

Jacky. See under **jack**[1].

Jacob *jā'kəb*, *n* (also **Jacob sheep**) a kind of sheep, piebald in colour, with 2 or 4 horns, *orig* imported to Britain from Spain. [From Gen 30. 40]

Jacobean *jak-ō-bē'ən*, *adj* of or characteristic of the period of James I of England (1603–25). — *n* a person who lived in the reign of James I. — **Jacobean lily** (*Sprekelia formosissima*) a Mexican bulbous plant named after St James. [L *Jacōbus* James]

Jacobethan *jak-ō-bē'thən*, *adj* consisting of a mixture of *Jacob*ean and Eliza*bethan* styles.

Jacobian *jə-kō'bi-ən*, (*math*) *n* the matrix or determinant formed from the first partial derivatives of several functions of several variables (also **Jacobian determinant**). [From K G J *Jacobi*, 19c German mathematician]

Jacobin *jak'ō-bin*, *n* a French Dominican monk, their order being *orig* established at St *Jacques*, Paris; one of a society of revolutionists in France, so called from their meeting in the hall of the Jacobin convent (*hist*); an extremist or radical, *esp* in politics; (also without *cap*) a hooded pigeon. — Also *adj*. — *adj* **Jacobin'ic** or **Jacobin'ical**. — *adv* **Jacobin'ically**. — *n* **Jac'obinism** the principles of the Jacobin revolutionists. — *vt* **Jac'obinize** or **-ise**. [Fr, from L *Jacōbus* James]

Jacobite *jak'ō-bīt*, *n* an adherent of James II of England and his descendants; a Syrian monophysite, named after the 6c monk *Jacobus* Baradaeus (*Ch hist*). — Also *adj*. — *adj* **Jacobit'ic** or **Jacobit'ical**. — *n* **Jac'obītism**. [L *Jacōbus* James]

Jacob's ladder *jā'kəbz lad'ər*, *n* a ladder of ropes with wooden steps (*naut*); a wild or garden plant (Polemonium) with ladder-like leaves; an endless chain of buckets used as an elevator. [From the *ladder* seen by *Jacob* in his dream, Gen 28. 12]

Jacob's staff *jā'kəbz stäf*, *n* a pilgrim's staff (*obs*); any of several different surveying instruments of different periods; a sword-stick (*obs*). [From its likeness to a pilgrim's staff, prob from the pilgrimage to St James (L *Jacōbus*) of Compostela]

jacobus *jə-kō'bəs*, (*hist*) *n* a gold coin of James I worth 20 to 25 shillings. [L *Jacōbus* James, from Gr *Iakōbos*, from Heb *Ya'aqōb*]

jaconet *jak'ə-net*, *n* a cotton fabric, rather stouter than muslin, different from the fabric *orig* so named which was imported from *Jagannāth* (Puri) in India; a thin material with waterproof backing used for medical dressings. [See also **Juggernaut**]

jacquard *jak'ärd* or *jak-ärd'*, (often with *cap*) *n* an apparatus with perforated cards for controlling the movement of the warp threads in weaving intricate designs; a fabric woven by this method. — **Jacq'uard-loom** a loom with jacquard, which produces jacquard. [Joseph Marie *Jacquard* (1752–1834), the French inventor]

Jacqueminot *jak'mi-nō*, *n* a deep-red hybrid perpetual rose. — Also **Jacque** and **Jack**. [From General *Jacqueminot* of Paris]

Jacquerie *zhäk'rē*, *n* the revolt of the French peasants in 1358; any peasant revolt. [From *Jacques* Bonhomme, Goodman Jack, a name applied in derision to the peasants]

jactation *jak-tā'shən*, *n* act of throwing; jactitation (*pathol*); boasting. [L *jactātiō*, *-ōnis* tossing, boasting, from *jactāre* to throw]

jactitation *jak-ti-tā'shən, n* restless tossing in illness (*pathol*); bodily agitation, twitching, jerking, etc (*pathol*); tossing or bandying about of words (*obs*); bragging; public assertion, *esp* if ostentatious and false. — **jactitation of marriage** pretence of being married to another. [LL *jactitātiō, -ōnis*, from L *jactitāre, -ātum* to toss about, put about, make a display of, frequentative of *jactāre* to throw]

jaculation *jak-ū-lā'shən, n* the act of throwing or hurling, eg a dart. — *vt* **jac'ulate** to throw. — *n* **jac'ulātor** someone who throws eg a javelin; an archer-fish. — *adj* **jac'ulatory** (*-ət-ər-i*) throwing out suddenly; ejaculatory. [L *jaculārī, -ātus* to throw eg a dart, from *jaculum* a dart, from *jacere* to throw]

Jacuzzi® *jə-kōō'zi, n* a type of bath or small pool equipped with a mechanism that agitates the water to provide extra invigoration; (*usu* without *cap*) a bathe in such a bath or pool. [From its Italian inventor Candido *Jacuzzi* (1902–86)]

jade[1] *jād, n* a pitiful, worn-out horse; a worthless nag; a woman, *esp* perverse, ill-natured, or not to be trusted (often *ironic*). — *vt* to exhaust or cause to flag from overwork; to satiate or weary from excess. — *vi* to become weary. — *adj* **jā'ded**. — *adv* **jā'dedly**. — *n* **jā'dery** (*obs*) the tricks of a jade. — *adj* (*obs*) **jā'dish**. [Origin unknown; cf ON *jalda* a mare, Scot *yaud*]

jade[2] *jād, n* a hard ornamental stone of varying shades of green and sometimes almost white, *nephrite* (silicate of calcium and magnesium) and **jade'ite** (silicate of aluminium and sodium), once believed to cure side pains. — *adj* made of jade; of the colour of jade. [Fr, from Sp *ijada* the flank, from L *ilia*]

j'adoube *zha-dōōb*, (*Fr*; *chess*) a warning that only an adjustment is intended, not a move, literally I adjust.

Jaeger® *yā'gər, n* woollen material used in making clothes, *orig* containing no vegetable fibre. [Dr Gustav *Jaeger*, the original manufacturer]

jaeger. See **jäger**.

Jaffa *jaf'ə, n* (also **Jaffa orange**) an orange from *Jaffa* in Israel.

Jag *jag*, (*colloq*) *n* a Jaguar car. [Short form]

jag[1] *jag, n* a notch, slash or dag in a garment, etc; a ragged protrusion; a cleft or division (*bot*); a prick (*Scot*); an inoculation, injection (chiefly *colloq Scot*). — *vt* to cut unevenly or into notches; to prick or pierce: — *pr p* **jagg'ing**; *pa p* **jagged** (*jagd*). — *adj* **jagg'ed** notched, rough-edged, uneven. — *adv* **jagg'edly**. — *n* **jagg'edness**. — *n* **jagg'er** a brass wheel with a wavy edge for cutting and decorating the edges of pastry (also **jagg'ing-iron**). — *adj* **jagg'y** notched; slashed; prickly (*Scot*). [Origin unknown]

jag[2] *jag, n* a load (*dialect*); a saddlebag or other bag (*obs*); a quantity (*US*); a spree, bout of indulgence; one's fill of liquor or narcotics; a spell, fit. — *vt* (*dialect*) to cart; to transport by pack-horse. — *adj* **jagged** (*jagd*; *US*) drunk. — *n* **jagg'er** (*dialect*) a carter; a pack-horseman; a pedlar.

Jagannath *jug-ən-ät', n* a corrected form of **Juggernaut**.

jäger or **jaeger** *yā'gər, n* a (German) huntsman; a German or Austrian rifleman or sharpshooter; an attendant upon an important or wealthy person, dressed in huntsman's costume; (**jaeger**) a skua that chases and robs other seabirds (*NAm*). [Ger, hunter, from *jagen* to hunt]

jaggery *jag'ə-ri, n* a coarse, dark sugar made from palm-sap. [Hindi *jāgrī*, Sans *śarkarā*; cf **sugar**, **Saccharum**]

jaghir, **jaghire** or **jagir** *jä-gēr'*, (*Ind, Pak*) *n* the government revenues of a tract of land assigned with power to administer. — *n* **jaghir'dar** the holder of a jaghir. [Hindi and Pers *jāgīr*]

jaguar *jag'wär*, also *jag'ū-är* or *-ər, n* a powerful feline beast of prey, related to the leopard, native to S America. [Tupí *jaguāra*]

jaguarundi or **jaguarondi** *jä-gwə-run'dē* or *-ron'dē, n* a S American wild cat. [Tupí, from Guaraní]

Jah *yä* or *jä, n* Jehovah, the Hebrew God. — *n* **Jah'veh** same as **Yahweh**. — *n* **Jah'vism** the (system of) religion of Yahweh. — **Jah'vist**. [Heb *Yah*]

jai alai *hī'(ə-)lī* or *-lī', n* a game resembling handball but played with a long curved basket strapped to the wrist, a type of pelota. [Sp, from Basque *jai* festival, and *alai* merry]

jail or **gaol** *jāl, n* a prison. — *vt* to imprison. — *n* **jail'er**, **jail'or** or **gaol'er** a person in charge of a jail or of prisoners: — *fem* **jail'eress**, etc. — **jail'-bait** (*slang*) a girl who has not reached the legal age of consent (also *adj*); **jail'-bird** or **gaol'-bird** (*colloq*) someone who often is, has been, or should be in jail; **jail'-break** or **gaol'-break** see **break jail** below; **jail'-delivery** or **gaol'-delivery** the clearing of a jail by sending all prisoners to trial; deliverance from jail; **jail'-fēver** or **gaol'-fēver** typhus fever, once common in jails; **jail'house** (*US*) a prison. — **break jail** or **gaol** to force one's way out of prison (*n* **jail'-break** or **gaol'-break**); **Commission of Jail Delivery** one of the commissions formerly issued to judges of assize and judges of the Central Criminal Court in England to try all prisoners. [OFr *gaole* (Fr *geôle*), from LL *gabiola* a cage, from L *cavea* a cage, from *cavus* hollow]

Jain *jīn* or *jān* or **Jaina** *jī'na, n* an adherent of an ascetic Indian religion related to Buddhism. — Also *adj*. — *n* **Jain'ism**. — *n* and *adj* **Jain'ist**. [Hindi *jina* conquerer, title of the Jain teachers]

jak *jak, n*. Same as **jack**[3].

jake[1] *jāk*, (*US*) *n* a country lout; a yokel. [Perh from the name, short form of *Jacob*]

jake[2] *jāk*, (*colloq*, *orig US*, now also *Austr* in sense of 'fine') *adj* honest; correct; fine, OK, first-rate.

jakes *jāks*, (*Shakesp*) *n* a privy. [Origin unknown]

JAL *abbrev*: Japan Air Lines.

jalap *jal'ap, n* the purgative root of an Ipomoea or *Exogonium*, first brought from *Jalapa* (or Xalapa), in Mexico. — *adj* **jalap'ic**. — *n* **jal'apin** a glucoside resin, one of the purgative principles of jalap. — **false jalap** marvel of Peru (qv under **marvel**), formerly used as a substitute for jalap.

jalapeño *hä-lə-pān'yō* or **jalapeño pepper** (*pep'ər*) (chiefly *US*) *n* an especially hot type of Capsicum pepper, used in Mexican cooking. [Mex Sp]

jalopy or **jaloppy** *jə-lop'i, n* an old motor car or aeroplane. [Origin obscure]

jalouse *jə-lōōz'*, (*Scot*) *vt* to suspect. — Also **jealouse**, by conflation with **jealous**.

jalousie *zhal-ōō-zē'*, or *zhal', n* an outside shutter with slats. — *adj* **jal'ousied**. [Fr, from *jalousie* jealousy]

jam[1] *jam, n* a conserve of fruit boiled with sugar. — *vt* to spread with jam; to make into jam. — *adj* **jamm'y** smeared or sticky with jam; like jam; lucky, excellent (*colloq*). — **jam'pot** a jar for jam (also **jam'jar**); a high collar, *esp* a clergyman's. — **jam tomorrow** better things promised for the future that always remain in the future; **want jam on it** (*colloq*) to expect or want too much. [Perh from **jam**[2]]

jam[2] *jam, vt* to press or squeeze tight; to push forcefully or violently (*on* or *in*); to crowd full; to block by crowding; to bring to a standstill by crowding or interlocking; to interfere with by emitting signals of similar wavelength (*radio*); to interfere or block (signals generally). — *vi* to become stuck, wedged, etc; to become unworkable; to press or push (eg into a confined space); (in jazz) to play enthusiastically, interpolating and improvising freely: — *pr p* **jamm'ing**; *pa t* and *pa p* **jammed**. — *n* a crush or squeeze; a block or stoppage due to crowding or squeezing together; a jammed mass (eg of logs in a river); a jamming of radio messages; a difficult or embarrassing situation (*colloq*). — *n* **jamm'er** a person or thing that jams something. — *adj* **jam-packed'** completely full, crowded, etc. — **jam session** a gathering of jazz musicians (*orig* an informal one) at which jazz (as described at *vi* above) is played. [Poss onomatopoeic; connected with **champ**[1]]

jamadar. Same as **jemadar**.

jamahiriya or **jumhouriya** *ja-mä'hē-rē'ya*, *n* (in Arab socialist countries) the people's or proletariat's state. [Ar, connected with *jumhūrīya* republic, from *jumhūr* people]

Jamaica *jə-mā'kə* or **Jamaican** *-kən*, *adj* of the island of Jamaica. — *n* **Jamai'can** a native or inhabitant of Jamaica. — **Jamaica bark** Caribbee bark (qv under **Carib**); **Jamaica cedar** bastard Barbados cedar (see **cedar**); **Jamaica ebony** cocus-wood; **Jamaica pepper** allspice; **Jamaica plum** hog-plum (qv under **hog**[1]); **Jamaica rum** a slowly-fermented, full-bodied pungent rum.

jamb *jam*, *n* the sidepiece or post of a door, fireplace, etc; a greave (in this sense also **jambe** *jam*). — *n* **jambeau** (*jam'bō*; *obs*) a greave; legging: — *pl* **jam'beaux** or **jam'beux** (*Spenser* **giambeux**). — *n* **jam'ber** or **jam'bier** (*obs*) a greave. [Fr *jambe* leg; cf **gamb**]

jambalaya *jum-bə-lī'ə*, (*US*) *n* a Creole or Cajun dish made with rice mixed with seafood or chicken, seasonings, etc; a mixture generally. [Provençal *jambalaia*]

jambee *jam-bē'*, *n* an 18c light cane. [*Jambi* in Sumatra]

jamber, jambeux, jambier. See **jamb**.

jambiya or **jambiyah** *jam-bē'yä*, *n* a type of Middle Eastern curved, double-edged dagger. [Ar]

jambo *jam'bō*, *interj* an E African salutation: — *pl* **jam'bos**. [From Swahili]

jambok. Same as **sjambok**.

jambolan, jambolana. See **jambu**.

jambone *jam'bōn*, *n* a lone hand in euchre, played only by agreement, in which the player lays his or her cards on the table and must lead one chosen by their opponent, scoring 8 points if he or she takes all the tricks. [Origin unknown]

jambool. See **jambu**.

jamboree *jam-bə-rē'*, *n* a boisterous frolic, a spree (*slang*); a large Scout rally; in euchre, a lone hand of the five highest cards, by agreement scoring 16 points for the holder. [Origin uncertain]

jambu *jum'*, *jam'bōō*, (*Malaysia*, etc) *n* the rose-apple tree or other eugenia. — Also **jambul**, **jambool** (*jum-bōōl'*), **jam'bolan** and **jambolana** (*-bō-lä'nə*). [Sans *jambu*, *jambū*, *jambūla*]

jamdani *jäm'dä-nē*, *n* a variety of Dacca muslin woven in a flowery design. [Pers *jāmdānī*]

james. Same as **jemmy**[1].

Jamesian *jāmz'ī-ən*, *adj* relating to William *James* (1842–1910), American psychologist, or Henry *James* (1843–1916), his brother, the writer.

Jamesonite *jim'i-sən-īt* or *jām'sən-īt*, *n* a mineral compound of lead, antimony and sulphur. [Robert *Jameson* (1772–1854), Scottish mineralogist]

Jamestown-weed. See **jimson-weed**.

jammy. See **jam**[1].

jampan *jam'pan*, *n* an Indian sedan chair. — *n* **jampanee'** or **jampani** (*-ē'*) its bearer. [Bengali *jhāmpān*]

Jan. *abbrev*: January.

jandal® *jan'dəl*, (*NZ*) *n* a thong, a type of sandal.

jane[1] *jān*, *n* a small silver Genoese coin (*Spenser*); jean (cloth). [LL *Janua*, L *Genua* Genoa]

jane[2] *jān*, (*slang*, *orig* and chiefly *US*) *n* a woman. [The name, *Jane*]

Janeite *jān'īt*, *n* a devotee of *Jane* Austen.

JANET *jan'ət*, *abbrev*: Joint Academic Network, a computer network linking UK universities, research councils, etc.

jangle *jang'gl*, *vt* and *vi* to sound with an unpleasant irritating tone, such as a harsh, dissonant metallic or ringing noise. — *vt* to upset, irritate. — *vi* (*obs*) to wrangle or quarrel. — *n* dissonant clanging; contention. — *n* **jang'ler**. — *n* **jang'ling**. — *adj* **jang'ly**. [OFr *jangler*]

Janian, Janiform. See **Janus**.

janissary. See **janizary**.

janitor *jan'i-tər*, *n* a doorkeeper; an attendant or caretaker: — *fem* **jan'itrix** or **jan'itress**. — *adj* **janitorial** (*-tö'*). — *n* **jan'itorship**. [L *jānitor*, from *jānua* a door]

janizary *jan'i-zər-i*, *n* a soldier of the old Turkish footguards (c. 1330–1826), formed *orig* of renegade prisoners and of tributary Christian children; a Turkish soldier acting as an escort for travellers in the East (*hist*); a follower, supporter. — Also **jan'issary** (*-zər-i* or *-sər-i*) or **jan'izar**. — *adj* **janizā'rian**. — **janizary music** military music with a great deal of percussion. [Fr *Janissaire*, supposed to be from Turk *yeni* new, and *çeri* soldiery]

janker *jang'kər*, (*Scot*) *n* a long pole on wheels for transporting large logs suspended from it. [Origin unknown]

jankers *jang'kərz*, (*military slang*) *n pl* defaulters. — *n sing* punishment, detention, etc for defaulting. [Ety unknown]

jann *jän*, *n pl* the least powerful order of jinn; (*sing*) a jinni. [Ar *jānn*]

jannock[1] *jan'ək*, (*dialect*) *adj* straightforward, on the level. [Origin obscure]

jannock[2] *jan'ək*, (*N Eng*) *n* oaten bread. [Origin obscure]

Jansenism *jan'sən-izm*, (*Christian relig*) *n* a system of evangelical doctrine deduced from Augustine by Cornelius *Jansen* (1585–1638), Roman Catholic Bishop of Ypres, essentially a reaction against the ordinary Catholic dogma of the freedom of the will, maintaining that human nature is corrupt, and that Christ died only for the elect, all others being irretrievably condemned to hell. — *n* **Jan'senist** a believer in Jansenism. — Also *adj*.

jansky *jan'ski*, (*astron*) *n* the unit of strength of radio wave emission, $10^{-26}W^{-2}Hz^{-1}$: — *pl* **jan'skys**. [Named after Karl G *Jansky*, the American radio engineer who first discovered radio interference coming from the stars]

jantee. See **jaunty**[1].

janty. See **jaunty**[1], **jonty**.

January *jan'ū-ər-i*, *n* the first month of the year, dedicated by the Romans to Janus. [L *Jānuārius*]

Janus *jā'nəs*, *n* the ancient Roman two-faced god, guardian of doors, whose temple in Rome was closed in time of peace. — *adj* **Jān'iform** (wrongly **Jān'uform**) Janus-faced. — *adj* **Jān'ian** or **Jān'us-faced** two-faced, facing in two directions; hypocritical, deceitful. [L *Jānus*]

Jap *jap*, (*derog colloq*) *n* and *adj* Japanese. — **Jap**. *abbrev*: Japanese. — **Jap'-silk** a thin kind of silk.

jap. See **jaup**.

japan *jə-pan'*, *adj* of Japan; japanned. — *n* Japanese ware or work; a glossy black varnish or lacquer; a liquid used for paint-grinding and -drying; japanned work. — *vt* to varnish with japan, *esp* in imitation of Japanese work; to make black; to ordain (a clergyman) (*old slang*): — *pr p* **japann'ing**; *pa t* and *pa p* **japanned'**. — *adj* **Japanese** (*jap-ə-nēz'*, or *jap'*) of Japan, its people, or their language. — *n* a native or citizen of Japan; the language of Japan: — *pl* **Japanese** (formerly **Japaneses**). — *n* **Japanēs'ery** Japanese decoration; a Japanese ornament; Japanese bric-à-brac. — *n* **Japanesque** (*-esk'*) a design in Japanese style. — *adj* (also **Japanēs'y**) savouring of the Japanese. — *vt* **Jap'anize** or **-ise** to make Japanese. — *n* **japann'er**. — *combining form* **Jap'ano-** Japanese (*esp* in combination with another nationality, eg **Jap'ano-Chinese**). — *adj* **Jap'anophile** a lover of Japan or the Japanese. — **Japan Current** Kuroshio; **japan'-earth** terra-japonica, gambier; **Japanese beetle** a small scarabaeid beetle (*Popillia japonica*) introduced accidentally into the Eastern US and now a major plant pest there; **Japanese cedar** a very tall Japanese conifer (*Cryptomeria japonica*) often dwarfed by Japanese gardeners; **Japanese garden** a formal garden with water, bridges, rocks, raked gravel and shrubs but without bright flowers; **Japanese maple** a decorative foliage tree (*Acer palmatum* or *Acer japonicum*); **Japanese medlar** the loquat; **Japanese paper** a fine soft paper handmade from paper-mulberry bark; **Japanese vellum** a heavier weight of Japanese paper; **Japan lacquer** Japan varnish; **Japan laurel** a shrub (*Aucuba japonica*) of the dogwood family, with spotted yellow leaves; **japanned leather** patent leather (see under **patent**); **Japan varnish** a varnish obtained from a species of sumach (*Rhus vernicifera*), extended to various other similar varnishes; **Japan wax** or **tallow** a fat obtained from the berries of species of sumach.

jape *jāp*, *vi* to jest, joke. — *vt* to mock; to seduce (*obs*). — *n* a jest, joke, trick. — *n* **jāp'er**. — *n* **jāp'ing**. [OFr *japer* to yelp]

Japhetic *jə-fet'ik*, (*obs*) *adj* of European race; pertaining to a number of European and near-Eastern non-Indo-European languages formerly thought to be related and to belong to some pre-IE grouping. [From supposed descent from *Japheth*]

Japonic *jə-pon'ik*, *adj* Japanese. — *n* **japon'ica** the Japanese quince (*Chaenomeles japonica*), camellia, or other Japanese plant. [New L *japonicus*, fem *japonica* Japanese]

japonaiserie *zha-pə-nez-ri*, (*Fr*) Japanesery.

jar[1] *jär*, *vi* to make a harsh discordant sound; to vibrate from an impact; to give an unpleasant shock; to grate (on); to be discordant or distasteful; to clash; to quarrel; to be inconsistent; to tick (*Shakesp*). — *vt* to cause to vibrate or shake; to cause to vibrate painfully; to grate on; to make dissonant: — *pr p* **jarr'ing**; *pa t* and *pa p* **jarred**. — *n* a harsh sudden vibration; a dissonance; a grating sound or feeling; clash of interests or opinions; conflict; a tick of a clock (*Shakesp*). — *n* **jarr'ing** the act of jarring; severe reproof. — Also *adj*. — *adv* **jarr'ingly**. [Imit]

jar[2] *jär*, *n* a wide-mouthed wide vessel; as much as a jar will hold; a Leyden jar (qv); a unit of electrical capacitance (*obs*); a drink (of an alcoholic beverage) (*colloq*). — *vt* to put in jars. — *n* **jar'ful**: — *pl* **jar'fuls**. [Fr *jarre* or Sp *jarra*, from Ar *jarrah*]

jar[3] *jär*, *n* a turn, used only in the phrase *on the jar* ajar. [Earlier *char*, from OE *cerr*; cf **char**[3], **ajar**]

jararaca or **jararaka** *jär-ər-äk'ə*, *n* a venomous S American snake of the family *Crotalidae*. [Tupí, from Guaraní]

jardinière *zhär'dē-nyer'*, *n* a container for the display of flowers, growing or cut; a style of drapery (eg curtains) with raised centre and full-length ends; a mixture of diced or sliced cooked vegetables, *usu* as a garnish for meat; a lappet forming part of an old headdress. [Fr, gardener (fem)]

jargon[1] *jär'gən*, *n* the terminology of a profession, art, group, etc; an artificial or barbarous language; a pidgin; unintelligible talk, gibberish; chatter, twittering. — *vi* to twitter, chatter; to speak jargon. — *n* **jargoneer'** or **jar'gonist** a person who uses jargon. — *n* **jargonīzā'tion** or **-s-** — *vt* **jar'gonize** or **-ise** to express in jargon. — *vi* to speak jargon. [Fr]

jargon[2], **jargonelle**. See **jargoon**.

jargoon *jär'gōōn'* or **jargon** *jär'gən*, *n* a brilliant colourless or pale zircon. — *n* **jargonelle'** an early pear (*orig* a gritty kind). [Fr *jargon*; prob connected with **zircon**]

jark *järk*, (*old cant*) *n* a seal on a (*usu* counterfeit) document; a pass, safe-conduct. — **jark'man** a swindling beggar, a begging-letter writer.

jarl *yärl*, (*hist*) *n* a Scandinavian noble or chief. [ON; related to **earl**]

jarool. See **jarul**.

jarosite *jar'ō-sīt*, *n* a hydrous sulphate of iron and potassium forming hexagonal crystals. [From Barranco *Jaroso*, an area in Spain]

jarrah *jar'ə*, *n* a Western Australian timber-tree, *Eucalyptus marginata*. [Aboriginal]

jarta or **yarta** *yär'tə*, (*Shetland*) *n* used as an endearment, literally, heart. Also *adj*. — Also (*Scott*) **yar'to**. [ON *hjarta* heart]

jarul or **jarool** *jə-rōōl'*, *n* the Indian bloodwood (genus *Lagerstroemia*), a lythraceous tree. [Bengali *jarūl*]

jarvey or **jarvie** *jär'vi*, (*obs slang*) *n* a hackney-coach driver; a jaunting-car driver. [Earlier *Jarvis*, poss from St *Gervase*, whose emblem is a whip]

Jas. *abbrev*: James; (the Letter of) James (*Bible*).

jasey, **jasy** or **jazy** *jā'zi*, (*old colloq*) *n* a wig, *orig* of worsted. [**jersey**]

Jasher or **Jashar** *jäsh'ər*, *n* one of the lost books of the ancient Hebrews, quoted twice (Joshua 10. 13, and 2 Samuel 3. 18), most probably a collection of heroic ballads.

jasmine *jas'min* or *jaz'*, also **jessamine** *jes'ə-min*, *n* a genus (*Jasminum*) of oleaceous shrubs, many with very fragrant flowers. — **red jasmine** frangipani (*Plumeria rubra*), a tropical American shrub related to periwinkle. [Fr *jasmin*, *jasemin*, from Ar *yāsmin*, *yāsamīn*, from Pers *yāsmīn*]

jasp *jasp* (*Spenser*) or **jasper** *jas'pər*, *n* a precious stone (*obs*); an opaque quartz containing clay or iron compounds, used in jewellery or ornamentation and red, yellow, brown or green in colour; a fine hard porcelain (also **jas'perware**). — *adj* made of jasper. — *adj* **jaspe** or **jaspé** (*jasp* or *jas'pā*) mottled, variegated or veined. — *n* cotton or rayon cloth with a shaded effect used for bedspreads, curtains, etc. — *vt* **jasp'erize** or **-ise** to turn into jasper. — *adj* **jasp'erous** or **jasp'ery**. — *n* **jas'pis** (now *rare*) jasper. — *adj* **jaspid'ean** or **jaspid'eous**. [OFr *jaspe*, *jaspre*, from L *iaspis*, *-idis*; and directly from Gr *iaspis*, *-idos*, of Eastern origin]

jasy. See **jasey**.

Jat *jät*, *n* a member of a people inhabiting NW India and Pakistan. — Also *adj*. [Hindi *jāt*]

jataka *jä'tə-kə*, *n* a nativity, the birth-story of Buddha. [Sans *jātaka*, from *jāta* born]

jato *jā'tō*, (*aeronautics*) *n* a *j*et-*a*ssisted *t*ake-*o*ff, using a **jato unit** consisting of one or more rocket motors, *usu* jettisoned after use: — *pl* **jā'tos**.

jaunce or **jaunse** *jöns* or *jäns*, *vi* (*Shakesp*) to prance. — *vt* to cause (a horse) to prance. — *n* prancing (*Shakesp*); a wearisome journey (*dialect*). [Perh from a doubtful OFr *jancer* to cause to prance]

jaundice *jön'dis* (rarely *jän'dis*), *n* a disease in which there is yellowing of the eyes, skin, etc, by excess of bile pigment, the patient in rare cases seeing objects as yellow; any of various diseases with some similar features; the state of taking an unfavourable, prejudiced view. — *vt* to affect with jaundice, in any sense. — *adj* **jaun'diced** affected with jaundice; feeling or showing prejudice, distaste or jealousy. [Fr *jaunisse*, from *jaune* yellow, from L *galbinus* yellowish, from *galbus* yellow]

jaunse. See **jaunce**.

jaunt *jönt* (also *jänt*) *vi* to go from place to place, *esp* for pleasure; to make an excursion. — *n* an excursion; a ramble. — *adj* **jaunt'ing** strolling; making an excursion. — **jaunt'ing-car** a low-set, two-wheeled, open vehicle used in Ireland, with side-seats either back to back or facing each other. [Origin obscure, though early meanings correspond with **jaunce**]

jauntie. See **jonty**.

jaunty[1] or **janty** *jön'ti* (also *jän'ti*), *adj* gentlemanly (*formerly* **jantee** or **jauntee**) (*obs*); having an airy or sprightly manner approaching a swagger. — *adv* **jaunt'ily**. — *n* **jaunt'iness**. [Fr *gentil*]

jaunty[2]. See **jonty**.

jaup *jöp* or *jäp*, or **jap** *jäp*, (*Scot*) *vt* and *vi* to spatter; to splash. — *n* a splash; a spattering. [Origin unknown]

Java *jä'və*, *adj* of the island of Java. — *adj* and *n* **Ja'van** or **Javanese'**. — **Java man** the early man formerly known as Pithecanthropus erectus, later re-designated Homo erectus; **Java plum** the jambolana (*Eugenia jambolana*); **Java sparrow** a kind of weaver bird.

javel *jav'əl*, (*Spenser*) *n* a worthless fellow. [Origin unknown]

javelin *jav'(ə)-lin*, *n* a throwing-spear. — **jav'elin-man** (*hist*) an armed member of a sheriff's retinue or a judge's escort at assizes; a soldier armed with a javelin. [Fr *javeline*; prob Celtic]

Javel water (or **Javelle**) *zha-* or *zhə-vel' wö'tər*, also **eau de** (*ō də*) **Javel** or **Javelle**, *n* a solution of potassium chloride and hypochlorite used for bleaching, disinfecting, etc. [After *Javel*, former town, now part of the city of Paris]

jaw[1] *jö*, *n* a mouth-structure for biting or chewing; one of the bones of a jaw; one of a pair of parts for gripping, crushing, cutting, grinding, etc; (in *pl*) a narrow entrance; (in *pl*) a dangerous position, on the point of being devoured (*fig*); talkativeness, a chat, a long talk or lecture (*slang*). — *vt* (*slang*) to scold, lecture. — *vi* to talk, *esp* at excessive length, chat, lecture. — *adj* **jawed** having jaws. — *n* **jaw'ing** (*slang*) talk, *esp* if unrestrained, abusive or reproving. — **jaw'bone** the bone of the jaw. — *vt* and *vi* (*US slang*) to engage in jawboning, to lecture or scold. — **jaw'boning** (*US slang*) governmental urging of industry to restrict wage increases, accept restraints, etc; **jaw'-breaker** a heavy-duty rock-breaking machine with hinged jaws (also **jaw'-crusher**); a word hard to pronounce (*slang*; also **jaw'-twister**). — *adj* and *n* **jaw'breaking**. — *adv* **jaw'breakingly**. — *adv* **jaw'droppingly** (*colloq*) amazingly. — **jaw'fall** a falling of the jaw (*archaic*); depression of spirits (*rare*). — *adj* **jaw'-fallen** (*rare*) depressed in spirits; dejected. — **jaw'-foot** a foot-jaw, maxilliped; **jaw lever** an instrument for opening the mouth of a horse or cow to admit medicine; **jaw'-tooth** a molar. — **his**, etc **jaw dropped** his, etc mouth fell open in amazement; **hold one's jaw** (*colloq*) to stop talking or scolding. [Perh **chaw**[1], modified by Fr *joue* cheek]

jaw[2] *jö*, (*Scot*) *n* a dash or surge of liquid; a portion of liquid so dashed. — *vt* and *vi* to pour suddenly in a body. — **jaw'box** a sink; **jaw'hole** a cesspool; an entrance to a sewer. [Origin unknown]

jawan *jə-wän'*, *n* an Indian common soldier. [Urdu *javān*]

jawari. See **jowar**.

jawbation *jö-bā'shən*, *n* variant of **jobation** (see under **Job**). [Influenced by **jaw**[1]]

Jawi *jä'wi*, *n* the Arabic script used to write Malay; Malay written in Arabic script. [Malay]

ja wohl *ya vōl'*, (*Ger*) yes indeed.

jay[1] *jā*, *n* a bird of the crow family with colourful plumage; a flashy, immoral woman (*archaic slang*); a stupid, awkward or easily duped person (*US slang*). — *adj* (*US slang*) stupid, unsophisticated. — *vi* **jay'walk**. — **jay'walker** a careless pedestrian whom motorists are expected to avoid running down; **jay'walking**. [OFr *jay*]

jay[2] *jā*, *n* the tenth letter of the modern English alphabet (J or j); an object or mark of that shape.

jazerant. See **jesserant**.

jazy. See **jasey**.

jazz or (*hist*) **jass** *jaz*, *n* any of various styles of music with a strong rhythm, syncopation, improvisation, etc, originating in American Negro folk music; an art form and also various types of popular dance music derived from it; garish colouring, lively manner, vivid quality; insincere or lying talk, nonsense (*slang*, esp *US*); sexual intercourse (*US Black slang*). — Also *adj*. — *vt* to impart a jazz character to (often with *up*). — *vt* and *vi* (*US Black slang*) to have sexual intercourse (with). — *n* **jazz'er** a jazz musician. — *adv* **jazz'ily**. — *n* **jazz'iness**. — *adj* **jazz'y**. — **jazz age** the decade following World War I, *esp* in America; **jazz-funk'**, **-pop'** and **-rock'** music which is a blend of jazz and funky, pop and rock music respectively; **jazz'man** a jazz musician. — **and all that jazz** (*colloq*) and all that kind of thing, and all that palaver. [Origin uncertain]

JC *abbrev*: Jesus Christ; Julius Caesar.

JCB *jā-sē-bē'*, *n* a type of mobile excavator used in the construction industry. [Abbrev for *J C B*amford, the manufacturer's name]

JCR *abbrev*: junior common or combination room (see under **junior**).

jealous *jel'əs*, *adj* suspicious of, or upset or angered by, rivalry; envious; solicitous, anxiously heedful; mistrustfully vigilant; unable to tolerate unfaithfulness, or the thought of it. — *adv* **jeal'ously**. — *n* **jeal'ousy**, **jeal'oushood** (*Shakesp*) or **jeal'ousness**. [OFr *jalous*, from L *zēlus*, from Gr *zēlos* emulation]

jealouse *jə-lōōz'*, (*obs* except *Scot*) *vt* see **jalouse**.

Jeames *jēmz*, *n* a flunkey. [From Thackeray's *Jeames* (James) de la Pluche]

jean *jēn*, or (*esp* formerly) *jān*, *n* a twilled-cotton cloth (also in *pl*); (in *pl*) trousers or overalls made *orig* of jean; (in *pl*) casual trousers made *esp* of denim, and also of corduroy or other similar material. — *n* **jeanette** (*ja-net'*) a light or coarse jean. — **satin jean** a smooth, glossy twilled cotton. [OFr *Janne*, from L *Genua* Genoa]

jeat *jet* (*obs*). Same as **jet**[1,2].

jebel or **djebel** *jeb'əl*, *n* in Arab countries, a hill or a mountain. [Ar, mountain]

Jebusite *jeb'ū-zīt*, *n* one of a Canaanitish people, predecessors of Israelites at Jerusalem; 17c nickname for a Roman Catholic. — *adj* **Jebusitic** (*-zit'ik*).

Jeddart *jed'art* or **Jethart** *jedh'ərt*, (*Scot*) *n* Jedburgh, in SE Scotland. — **Jeddart justice** hanging first and trying afterwards; **Jeddart staff** (*hist*) a sort of battle-axe with a long head. [OE *Gedwearde*]

jee[1]. Same as **gee**[1,3].

jee[2] *jē*, (*Scot*) *vi* to stir; to budge. — *vt* to disturb; to set on one side or ajar. — *n* a displacement to the side; a condition of being ajar. — **jee** or **jow one's ginger** to bestir onself, show perturbation.

jeel *jēl*, (*Scot*) *vi* to congeal; to set. — *n* extreme cold; jelly. — *n* **jee'lie** or **jee'ly** jelly; jam. — *vi* to set, to jelly. — **jeely nose** (*colloq*) a bleeding nose; **jeely piece** a jam sandwich.

Jeep *jēp*, *n* (®) a light, strong, four-wheel-drive, military vehicle suitable for rough terrain; any similar model of car. [From GP, for *g*eneral *p*urpose (vehicle)]

jeepers *jē'pərz* or **jeepers creepers** *krē'pərz*, (*US slang*) *interj* expressing surprise. [Euphemism for *Jesus* (*Christ*)]

jeepney *jēp'ni*, *n* (in the Philippines) a jitney constructed from a jeep. [*jeep* and jit*ney*]

jeer *jēr*, *vi* (*usu* with *at*) to scoff; to deride; to mock. — *vt* to mock; to treat with derision. — *n* a derisive remark; a sarcastic or satirical jest; mockery (*obs*). — *n* **jeer'er**. — *n* and *adj* **jeer'ing**. — *adv* **jeer'ingly**. [Origin unknown]

Jeez or **Jeeze** *jēz*, (*slang*) *interj* expressing surprise, enthusiasm or emphasis. [Euphem for **Jesus**]

jeff[1] *jef*, (*obs printers' slang*) *vi* to gamble with quadrats thrown like dice.

jeff[2] *jef*, (*orig circus slang*) *n* a rope.

Jeffersonian *jef-ər-sōn'i-ən*, *adj* pertaining to Thomas *Jefferson* (1743–1826), US President 1801–09; holding Jeffersonian, ie Democratic, political principles. — *n* a Democrat.

jehad. See **jihad**.

Jehovah *ji-hō'və*, *n* Yahweh, the name of the Hebrew God revealed to Moses, a name used also by Christians. — *n* **Jehō'vist** a person who held that the vowel-points attached by the Masoretes to the Hebrew word *YHWH* are the proper vowels of the word (*obs*); a writer of passages in the Pentateuch in which the name applied to God is Yahweh, a Yahwist. — *adj* **Jehovist'ic**. — **Jehovah's Witnesses** a Christian fundamentalist sect which rejects all other religions and denominations, believes in the imminent end of the world, and refuses to accept civil authority where it clashes with its own principles, *orig* called the International Bible Students' Association (see **Russellite**). [Heb; for *Yehōwāh*, ie *Yahweh* with the vowels of *Adōnāi*]

Jehu *jē'hū*, (*colloq*) *n* any fast and furious coachman or driver. [The King of Israel renowned for his furious chariot driving, from 2 Kings 9. 20]

jeistiecor *jēs'ti-kör*, (*obs Scot*) *n* a close-fitting garment. [Fr *juste au corps* close-fitting to the body]

jejune *ji-jōōn'*, *adj* naïve, immature, callow; showing lack of information or experience; spiritless, meagre, arid. — *adv* **jejune'ly**. — *n* **jejune'ness** or **jeju'nity**. — *n* **jeju'num** the part of the small intestine between the duodenum and the ileum. [L *jejūnus* hungry]

Jekyll and Hyde *jek'il* (or *jēk'il*) *ənd hīd*, a split personality exemplifying both good and evil. [From R L Stevenson, *The Strange Case of Dr Jekyll and Mr Hyde* (1886)]

jelab. See **djellaba**.

jell. See **jelly**[1].

jellaba. See **djellaba**.

jelly[1] *jel'i*, *n* anything gelatinous; the juice of fruit boiled with sugar; a conserve of fruit, jam (*US* and formerly *Scot* (see also **jeely** under **jeel**)); a clear, gelatinous, fruit-flavoured dessert (in NAm **jell'o**, formerly a trademark: — *pl* **jell'os**); a savoury gelatinous food obtained by boiling bones or by setting stock with gelatin; a jellyfish. — *vi* to set as a jelly; to congeal. — *vt* to make into a jelly. — *vi* and *vt* **jell** to jelly; to take distinct shape (*colloq*). — *adj* **jell'ied** in a state of jelly; enclosed in jelly. — *adj* **jell'iform**. — *vt* **jell'ify** to make into a jelly. — *vi* to become gelatinous. — **jelly baby** a kind of gelatinous sweet in the shape of a baby; **jelly bag** a bag through which fruit juice is strained for jelly; **jell'ybean** a kind of sweet in the shape of a bean with a sugar coating and jelly filling; **jell'yfish** a marine coelenterate with jelly-like body; a person who lacks firmness of purpose (*colloq*); **jell'ygraph** a former device for copying that used a plate of jelly. — *vt* to copy by this means. — **jell'y-pan** (*Scot*) a preserving-pan. [Fr *gelée*, from *geler*, from L *gelāre* to freeze; cf **gel**]

jelly[2] *jel'i*, (*colloq*) *n* short form of **gelignite**.

jelutong *jel'o͞o-tong*, *n* pontianac, a substitute for gutta-percha; the Bornean apocynaceous tree (*Dyera costulata*) producing it. [Malay]

jemadar *jem'ə-där*, (*Ind*) *n* a native Indian army officer below a subahdar; an officer of police, customs, etc. — Also **jamadar** (*jum'*) or **jem'idar**. [Urdu *jamaʻdār*]

jemima *ji-mī'mə*, (*colloq*) *n* an elastic-sided boot. [The female name]

jemmy[1] *jem'i*, *n* a burglar's short crowbar; a baked sheep's head (*slang*); an overcoat (*dialect*). — *vt* (*usu* with *open*) to force open with a jemmy or similar: — *pr p* **jemm'ying**; *pa t* and *pa p* **jemm'ied**. [A form of the name *James*]

jemmy[2] *jem'i*, (*dialect*) *adj* neat, smart, handy. — Also **gemm'y**. — *n* **jemm'iness** neatness. [Cf **jimp**]

Jena glass *yā'nə gläs*, *n* a special type of glass containing borates and free silica, resistant to chemical attack. [From *Jena* in Germany]

je ne sais quoi *zhə nə se kwa*, a special unknown ingredient or quality. [Fr, I don't know what]

Jenkins *jengk'inz*, (*colloq*) *n* a society reporter; a toady.

jennet *jen'it*, *n* a small Spanish horse; a jenny donkey. — Also **genn'et** or **gen'et**. [OFr *genet*, from Sp *jinete* a light horseman, perh of Ar origin]

jenneting *jen'it-ing*, *n* a kind of early apple. [Prob St John's apple, from Fr *Jeannet*, dimin of *Jean* John; not from *June-eating*]

Jenny *jen'i*, *n* generic name for a country lass (*Scot*); a womanish man (*Scot*); (the following meanings *usu* without *cap*) a wren or owl regarded as female; a female-ass (also **jenny donkey**); a travelling crane; a spinning-jenny; an in-off into a middle pocket from near the cushion (*billiards*). — **Jenny-long'-legs** (*Scot*) or **Jenn'y-spinner** (*dialect*) a crane-fly; **Jenny-wren** a wren. [The female name]

jeofail *jef'āl*, (*obs*) *n* an error in pleadings, or the acknowledgement of a mistake. [Anglo-Fr *jeo fail* I mistake]

jeopardy *jep'ər-di*, *n* hazard, danger; the danger of conviction and punishment faced by the accused on a criminal charge (*US law*). — *vt* **jeop'ard** (*rare* and *US archaic*), **jeop'ardize** or **-ise** or **jeop'ardy** (*rare*) to put in jeopardy, risk losing or damaging. — *n* **jeop'arder**. — *adj* **jeop'ardous** (*obs*) dangerous; daring. — *adv* **jeop'ardously** (*obs*). [Fr *jeu parti* a divided or even game, from LL *jocus partītus*, from L *jocus* a game, and *partītus* divided, from *partīrī* to divide]

jequirity *jə-kwir'i-ti*, *n* the tropical shrub Indian liquorice, the seeds of which are used ornamentally and medicinally, and its root for a liquorice substitute; (also **jequirity bean**) its seed. [Origin obscure]

Jer. (*Bible*) *abbrev*: (the Book of) Jeremiah.

jerbil. See **gerbil**.

jerboa *jûr-bō'ə*, *n* a desert rodent (family *Dipodidae*) that jumps on long hind legs like a kangaroo. [Ar *yarbūʻ*]

jereed. See **jerid**.

jeremiad *jer-i-mī'ad*, *n* a lamentation; a tale of grief, a doleful story. — *n* **Jeremī'ah** a person who continually prophesies doom. [From *Jeremiah*, reputed author of the *Book of Lamentations*]

jerfalcon. Same as **gerfalcon**.

Jericho *jer'i-kō*, (*humorous*) *n* a remote out-of-the way place, to which one is consigned. [Supposed to refer to 2 Samuel 10. 4, 5]

jerid or **jereed** *jer-ēd'*, *n* a wooden Oriental javelin; a tournament in which it is used. [Ar *jarīd*]

jerk[1] *jûrk*, *n* a stroke (*obs*); a short movement begun and ended suddenly; a twitch; an involuntary spasmodic contraction of a muscle; a movement in physical exercises; a short burst of bird-song (*obs*); a useless or stupid person (*slang*); (in weightlifting) a movement lifting the barbell from shoulder height to a position on outstretched arms above the head; (also **clean and jerk**) a weightlifting competition involving such a lift (cf **clean**). — *vt* to throw or move with a jerk; to utter abruptly (*usu* with *out*); to thrash (*obs*). — *vi* to move with a jerk. — *n* **jerk'er** a person who, or thing that, jerks; a hornyhead (fish) (*US*). — *n* **jerk'iness**. — *adj* **jerk'y** moving or coming by jerks or starts, spasmodic. — **jerk'water** (*US*) a train on a branch line. — *adj* not on a main line; small, insignificant, hick (*colloq*). — **jerk off** (*vulg*) to masturbate. [Imit, related to **yerk**]

jerk[2], etc. See **jerque**, etc.

jerk[3] *jûrk*, *vt* to make into charqui. — *n* charqui (also **jerked'-meat** or **jerk'y**). [**charqui**]

jerkin *jûr'kin*, *n* a sleeveless jacket, a short coat or close-fitting waistcoat. — *n* **jirkinet'** (*Scot*) a woman's bodice. [Origin unknown]

jerkinhead *jûr'kin-hed*, (*archit*) *n* the combination of a truncated gable with a lipped roof. [Perh from **jerk**[1]]

jeroboam *jer-ō-bō'əm*, *n* a very large drinking bowl, a jorum; a large bottle, *esp* one for wine holding the equivalent of 6 normal bottles, or for champagne, the equivalent of 4 normal bottles. [Allusion to 1 Kings 9. 28]

jerque or **jerk** *jûrk*, *vt* to search (eg a vessel) for concealed or smuggled goods; to examine (eg a ship's papers). — *n* **jerqu'er** or **jerk'er**. — *n* **jerqu'ing** or **jerk'ing**. [Poss Ital *cercare* to search]

Jerry or **Gerry** *jer'i*, (*war slang*) *n* a German; *collectively* the Germans. — *n* **jerrican** or **jerrycan** *jer'i-kan*, a kind of petrol-can, *orig* a German one.

jerry[1] *jer'i* (*slang*) *n* a chamberpot. [**jeroboam**]

jerry[2] *jer'i*, (*colloq*) *n* a jerry-builder. — *adj* constructed hastily and with bad materials. — **jerr'y-builder** someone who builds flimsy houses cheaply and hastily; **jerr'y-building**. — *adj* **jerr'y-built**. — **jerr'y-come-tum'ble** (*dialect*) a tumbler, circus performer; **jerr'y-shop** a pub. [Prob the personal name]

jerrymander. A mistaken form of **gerrymander**.

jersey *jûr'zi*, *n* the finest part of wool; combed wool; a knitted (*usu* woollen) garment for the upper body; a fine knitted fabric in cotton, nylon, etc; (with *cap*) a cow of Jersey breed. — *adj* made of knitted fabric; (with *cap*) of or pertaining to the Jersey breed of cows. — *n* **Jer'sian** a hybrid obtained by mating a Jersey bull and a Friesian cow. [The island of *Jersey*]

Jerusalem artichoke *jər-o͞os'ə-ləm är'ti-chōk*, see **artichoke**; **Jerusalem cross** (*heraldry*) a cross potent; **Jerusalem letters** (*hist*) letters or symbols tattooed on someone who has made a pilgrimage to Jerusalem; **Jerusalem pony** a donkey; **Jerusalem sage** a perennial plant (*Phlomis fruticosa*) found in S Europe, with dense yellow flowers.

jess *jes*, (*falconry*) *n* a short strap round the leg of a hawk. — *adj* **jessed** having jesses on. [OFr *ges*, from L *jactus* a cast, from *jacere* to throw]

jessamine. See **jasmine**.

jessamy *jes'ə-mi*, (*obs*) *n* jasmine; a dandy. [Altered from **jessamine**]

jessant *jes'ənt*, (*heraldry*) *adj* overlying; also *appar* for **issuant**. [Appar OFr *gesant*, pr p of *gesir*, from L *jacēre* to lie]

Jesse *jes'i*, *n* a genealogical tree of Christ's descent from *Jesse*; a large branched church candlestick. — **Jesse window** one showing Christ's genealogy in stained glass or carved on the mullions.

jesserant *jes'ə-rənt* or **jazerant** *jaz'*, (*hist*) *n* splint armour. [OFr *jaseran(t)*, *jazeran*, from Sp *jacerina*]

Jessie *jes'i*, (*Scot colloq*) *n* (also without *cap*) an effeminate or namby-pamby man or boy.

jest *jest*, *n* something spoken in fun; joke; fun; a taunt or jeer; something ludicrous, an object of laughter. — *vi* to make a jest; to joke. — *vt* to jeer at, ridicule; to utter as a jest. — *n* **jestee'** (*Sterne*) the object of a jest. — *n* **jest'er** a person who jests; a buffoon; a court-fool; a reciter of romances (*archaic*). — *adj* **jest'ful** given to jesting. — *n* and *adj* **jest'ing**. — *adv* **jest'ingly**. — **jest'book** a collection of funny stories; **jest'ing-stock** (*obs*) a butt for jests. [ME *geste* a deed, a story, from OFr *geste*, from L *gesta* things done, doings, from *gerere* to do]

Jesuit *jez'ū-it*, *n* a member of the religious order, the Society of *Jesus*, founded in 1534 by Ignatius Loyola; (*derog*) a crafty person, an intriguer, a prevaricator. — *adj* **Jesuit'ic** or **Jesuit'ical**. — *adv* **Jesuit'ically**. — *n* **Jes'uitism** or **Jes'uitry** the principles and practices of, or ascribed to, the Jesuits. — **Jesuits' bark** cinchona (brought to Rome by Jesuit missionaries).

Jesus *jē'zəs*, *n* the founder of Christianity, acknowledged by Christians as the Son of God and Saviour of mankind. — Also **Jesus Christ**, **Jesus of Nazareth** and (in hymns, etc, *esp* in the vocative) **Jesu** (*jē'zū*). — *interj* a loose profanity expressing anger, surprise, etc. — **Jesus wept** (*slang*) *interj* expressing amazement, horror, etc. [Gr *Iēsous* (vocative and oblique cases *Iēsou*), from Heb *Yēshūa'*, short form of *Yehōshūa'* Joshua]

jésus *zhā'zü*, *n* a size of paper in France, *approx* super-royal. — **grand jésus** imperial size.

JET *abbrev*: Joint European Torus, a large Tokomak experiment designed to use deuterium and tritium to produce energy by a fusion process.

jet[1] *jet*, *n* a rich black variety of lignite, taking a high polish, used for ornaments; jet-black. — *adj* made of jet; jet-black. — *n* **jett'iness**. — *adj* **jett'y** of the nature of jet, or black as jet. — *adj* **jet'-black** black as jet. — Also *n*. [OFr *jaiet*, from L and Gr *gagātēs*, from *Gagas* or *Gangai*, a town and river in Lycia, where it was obtained]

jet[2] *jet*, *n* a narrow spouting stream; a spout, nozzle or pipe emitting a stream or spray of fluid; a jetplane; a strutting movement (*obs*). — *vt* and *vi* to spout. — *vi* to travel by jetplane; to jut (*obs*); to encroach (*Shakesp*); to strut (*obs*): — *pr p* **jett'ing**; *pa t* and *pa p* **jett'ed**. — **jet boat** (*NZ*) a power boat propelled by a pressurized jet of water. — *adj* **jet'-driven** driven by the backward emission of a jet of gas, etc. — **jet engine** a gas turbine, *esp* one fitted to an aircraft, which uses jet propulsion to provide thrust; **jet'foil** a hydrofoil powered by a jet of water; **jet'-lag** exhaustion, discomfort, etc resulting from the body's inability to adjust to the rapid changes of time zone caused by high-speed long-distance air travel. — *adj* **jet'-lagged**. — **jet'liner** an airliner powered by a jet engine; **jet'plane** or **jet'-plane** a jet-driven aeroplane. — *adj* **jet'-propelled**. — **jet'-propulsion**; **jet'-setter** a member of the jet set (see below). — *adj* **jet'-setting** living in the style of the jet set. — **jet'-ski** a powered craft comparable to a motorbike adapted to plane across water on a ski-like keel. — *vi* to ride a jet-ski (as a water sport or recreation). — **jet'-skier**; **jet'stream** or **jet'-stream** a narrow band of very high-velocity, westerly winds more than 30 000 feet (c. 10 000 m) above the earth (*meteorol*); the exhaust of a jet engine or rocket motor. — **the jet set** a wealthy social set whose members frequently travel for pleasure to fashionable resorts around the world. [OFr *jetter*, from L *jactāre* to fling]

jet d'eau *zhe dō*, (*Fr*) *n* a jet of water, eg in an ornamental fountain.

jeté *zhə-tā*, (*ballet*) *n* a leap from one foot to the other in which the free leg *usu* finishes extended forward, backward or sideways. [Fr, thrown]

Jethart. See **Jeddart**.

jeton. See **jetton**.

jetsam *jet'səm*, *n* goods jettisoned from a ship and washed up on shore; according to some, goods from a wreck that remain under water (cf **flotsam**); jettison (*obs*). — Also (*archaic*) **jet'som** and **jet'son**. — **flotsam and jetsam** often, unclaimed odds and ends. [Contraction of **jettison**]

jettatura *jet-ə-tōō'rə*, *n* the evil eye. [Ital *iettatura*, a Neapolitan word, from L *ējectāre*, from *jactāre*, frequentative of *jacere* to throw]

jettiness. See **jet**[1].

jettison *jet'i-sən*, *n* the act of throwing goods overboard. — *vt* to throw overboard (goods in time of danger); to abandon, reject. [Anglo-Fr *jetteson*, from L *jactātiō*, *-ōnis* a casting, from *jactāre*, frequentative of *jacere* to throw]

jetton or **jeton** *jet'ən*, *n* a piece of stamped metal used as a counter in card-playing, casting accounts, etc; a (*usu* metal) token for operating a machine, *esp* a pay telephone. [Fr *jeton*, from *jeter* to throw, from L *jactāre*, frequentative of *jacere* to throw]

jetty[1] *jet'i*, *n* a pier, or similar projecting structure. — *vi* (*archit*) to project, jut out: — *pa t* and *pa p* **jett'ied**. [OFr *jettee* thrown out; see **jet**[2]]

jetty[2]. See **jet**[1].

jeu *zhø*, (*Fr*) *n* a game. — **jeu de mots** (*də mō*) a play on words, a pun: — *pl* **jeux de mots**; **jeu d'esprit** (*des-prē*) a witticism: — *pl* **jeux d'esprit**; **jeu de paume** (*pōm*) real tennis.

jeune *zhœn*, (*Fr*) *adj* young. — **jeune amour** (*a-mōōr*) young love; **jeune fille** (*fē-y'*) a girl; **jeune premier** (*prə-myā*; *theat*) a juvenile lead: — *fem* **jeune première** (*prə-myer*).

jeunesse dorée *zhœ-nes do-rā*, (*Fr*) *n* luxurious, stylish, sophisticated young people, literally gilded youth.

Jew *jōō*, *n* a person of Hebrew descent or religion; an Israelite; (*offensive*) a usurer, miser, someone who drives a hard bargain: — *fem* (*offensive* when used by non-Jews) **Jew'ess**. — *adj* (*derog* or *offensive*) Jewish. — *vt* (*offensive*; also without *cap*) to cheat or get the better of in a bargain. — *adj* **Jew'ish** of the Jews or their religion; extortionate, money-grubbing (*offensive*). — *adv* **Jew'ishly**. — *n* **Jew'ishness**. — *n* **Jew'ry** see separate article. — **Jew'-baiting** the persecuting of Jews; **jew'fish** a name for several very large American and Australian fishes; **Jew's'-ear** an ear-like fungus (Auricularia) parasitic on elder and other trees; **Jew's eye** something of very high value (*Shakesp* 'worth a Jewe's eye'; from the practice of torturing Jews for money); **Jew's-frank'incense** benzoin; **Jew's** or **Jews'-harp'** or **-trump'** (also without *cap*) a small lyre-shaped instrument played against the teeth by plucking a metal tongue with the finger; **Jews' houses** or **leavings** in Cornwall, remains of prehistoric miners' dwellings, mine refuse, and tin furnaces; **Jew's mallow** a yellow-flowered plant, *Kerria japonica* (family Rosaceae); (**Jews' mallow**) jute, *Corchorus olitorius*; **Jew's-myr'tle** butcher's broom; **Jew's'-pitch** asphalt; **Jew's'-stone** a large fossil sea-urchin spine; **Jews' thorn** Christ's thorn. — **wandering Jew** see under **wander**. [OFr *Jueu*, from L *Jūdaeus*, from Gr *Ioudaios*, from Heb *Yehūdāh* Judah]

jewel *jōō'əl*, *n* a precious stone; a personal ornament of precious stones, gold, etc; a hard stone (ruby, etc) used for pivot bearings in a watch; an imitation of a gemstone; an ornamental glass boss; anything or anyone highly valued. — *vt* to adorn with jewels; to fit with a jewel: — *pr p* **jew'elling**; *pa t* and *pa p* **jew'elled**. — *n* **jew'eller** someone who deals in, or makes, jewels. — *n* **jewellery** (*jōō'əl-ri*) or **jew'elry** jewels in general. — **jew'el-case** a casket for holding jewels; **jew'elfish** an African cichlid (*Hemichromis bimaculatus*) popular in aquaria for its bright colours; **jew'el-house** a room in the Tower of London where the crown-jewels are kept; **jeweller's rouge** finely powdered ferric oxide, used for polishing metal; **jew'el-weed** any plant of the genus Impatiens. — **jewel in the crown** *orig* (in *pl*) any or all of the countries of the British Empire, *esp* (in *sing*) India; the best, most highly prized, most successful, etc of a number or collection. [OFr *jouel* (Fr *joyau*); either a dimin of Fr *joie* joy, from L *gaudium* joy, from *gaudēre* to rejoice, or derived through LL *jocāle*, from L *jocārī* to jest]

Jewry *jōō'ri*, *n* the Jewish world, community or religion; Judaea (*archaic*); a district inhabited by *Jews* (*hist*).

jezail *jez'īl* or *-āl'*, *n* a heavy Afghan musket (*hist*). [Pers *jazā'il*]

Jezebel *jez'ə-bəl*, *n* a wicked scheming woman; (formerly often) a shameless painted woman. [From Ahab's wife, see eg 1 Kings 21, 2 Kings 9. 30]

jhala *jä'lə*, (*Hindu music*) *n* part of the second movement of a raga. [Sans]

jiao *jow*, *n* a unit of Chinese currency, equal to 10 fen or $\frac{1}{10}$ of a yuan. [Chin]

jib[1] *jib*, *n* a triangular sail stretched in front of the foremast in a ship; the boom of a crane or derrick; the underlip, the face (*dialect*); a jibbing horse; an act of jibbing, a standstill. — *vt* to cause to gybe. — *vi* (*usu* with *at*) to gybe; (of a horse) to balk or shy; to refuse, show objection, boggle: — *pr p* **jibb'ing**; *pa t* and *pa p* **jibbed**. — *n* **jibb'er** a jibbing horse. — **jib'-boom** a boom or extension of the bowsprit, on which the jib is spread; **jib'-crane** a crane with an inclined, pivoted arm fixed to the foot of a rotating vertical post, the upper ends connected by a chain, etc, to allow raising and lowering of the arm; **jib'-sail**; **jib'-sheet** a rope for trimming the jib. — **the cut of someone's jib** (*colloq*) someone's appearance. [Origin obscure; perh several different words; cf **gibbet** and **gybe**; the j sound precludes connection with Dan *gibbe*, Du *gijpen*]

jib[2] *jib*, (*Scot*) *vt* to milk closely, strip; to fleece (*obs*). — *n pl* **jibb'ings** the last milk drawn from a cow.

jibbah *jib'ə*. See **jubbah**.

jibber[1]. Same as **gibber**[1].

jibber[2]. See **jib**[1].

jib-door *jib'-dör*, *n* a disguised door, flush with the wall. [Origin unknown]

jibe[1]. See **gybe**.

jibe[2], **jiber**. See **gibe**.

jibe[3] *jīb* (chiefly *US*) *vi* to agree, accord (with). [Poss related to **chime**[1]]

jickajog. See **jig-jog**.

JICTAR or **Jictar** *jik'tär*, *abbrev*: Joint Industry Committee for Television Advertising Research, now superseded by BARB.

jiffy *jif'i*, (*colloq*) *n* an instant (sometimes shortened to **jiff**). — **Jiffy bag**® a stout padded envelope in which to post books, etc. [Origin unknown]

jig *jig*, *n* a jerky movement; a lively dance, *usu* in 6–8 time; a dance-tune for such a dance; a lure which moves jerkily when drawn through the water (*angling*); an appliance for guiding or positioning a tool; an appliance of various kinds in mechanical processes, eg a jigger in mining; a mocking ballad (*obs*); a jingle or piece of doggerel (*obs*); a farcical afterpiece or interlude sung and danced to popular tunes (*obs*); a jest, a prank (*obs*). — *vt* and *vi* to jerk; to perform as a jig. — *vt* to work upon with a jig; to equip with jigs: — *pr p* **jigg'ing**; *pa t* and *pa p* **jigged**. — *n* **jigamaree'** or **jigg'umbob** (*colloq*) a what's-its-name; a gadget. — *n* **jigg'er** a person or thing that jigs in any sense; any of various kinds of subsidiary appliance, *esp* with reciprocating motion, such as an oscillation transformer, an apparatus for separating ores by jolting them in sieves in water, a simple potter's wheel or a template or profile used with it, and a type of warehouse crane; a golf club, used *esp* formerly, with narrow lofted iron head; a light hoisting tackle (*naut*); a small aft sail on a ketch, etc (*naut*); a boat with such a sail (*naut*); a jigger-mast (*naut*); a sail on a jigger-mast (*naut*); a what's-its-name (*NAm colloq*); a small measure for alcoholic drinks. — *vt* to jerk or shake; to form with a jigger; to ruin (sometimes with *up*); to damn, blast (*colloq*). — *vi* to tug or move with jerks. — *adj* **jigg'ered** (*colloq*) exhausted; surprised; bewildered; damned. — *n* **jigg'ing**. — *adj* **jigg'ish**. — *vt* and *vi* **jigg'le** to move with vibratory jerks. — *n* a jiggling movement. — *adj* **jigg'ly**. — **jig borer** an adjustable precision machine-tool for drilling holes; **jigg'er-mast** a four-masted ship's aftermost mast; a small mast astern; **jig'saw** a narrow reciprocating saw for cutting awkward shapes; a jigsaw puzzle. — *vt* and *vi* to cut with a jigsaw: — *pa t* and *pa p* **jig'sawed**. — **jigsaw puzzle** a picture mounted on wood or card and cut up into pieces (as by a jigsaw) to be fitted together. — **the jig is up** (*colloq*) the game is up, the trick is discovered, etc. [Origin obscure; Fr *gigue* is from the English word]

jigajig, etc. See **jig-jog**.

jigamaree. See under **jig**.

jigger[1] *jig'ər*, *n* a variant of **chigoe**.

jigger[2], **jiggered**. See **jig**.

jiggery-pokery *jig'ə-ri-pō'kə-ri*, (*colloq*) *n* trickery; deception. [Cf **joukery-pawkery**]

jiggety-jog. See **jig-jog**.

jiggle, **jiggumbob**. See under **jig**.

jig-jog *jig'-jog*, *adv* with a jolting, jogging motion. — *n* a jolting motion; a jog. — Also **jick'ajog**, **jig'jig'**, **jig'ajig'**, **jig'ajog'**, **jigg'ety-jog**. — **jig'-a-jig** or **jig'-jig** (*slang*, used *esp* in pidgins) sexual intercourse. — Also *vi*. [**jig** and **jog**]

jigot. Same as **gigot**.

jihad or **jehad** *jē-had'*, *n* a holy war (for the Muslim faith); a fervent crusade. [Ar *jihād* struggle]

jilgie. See **gilgie**.

jill[1], etc. See **gill**[3].

jill[2]. See **gill**[5].

jillaroo. See **jackaroo**.

jillet. See **gill**[3].

jillion *jil'yən*, (*US*) *n* an indefinite but extremely large number. — Also *adj*. [Coinage based on **million**; cf **zillion**]

jilt *jilt*, *n* a person, *orig* and *esp* a woman, who encourages and then rejects a lover. — *vt* to discard abruptly (a lover one had previously encouraged). [Poss **jillet** (see under **gill**[3])]

jimcrack. See **gimcrack**.

Jim Crow *jim krō*, (*derog slang*, *orig US*) *n* a generic name for the Negro; racial discrimination against Negroes. — **jim'-crow** a tool for bending or straightening iron rails or bars; a plane or other tool that works in both directions. — **Jim Crow car**, **school** etc, one for Negroes only. [From a Negro minstrel song with the refrain 'Wheel about and turn about and jump *Jim Crow*']

jim-dandy *jim'-dan'di*, (*US colloq*) *n* a fine or excellent example. — *adj* fine, excellent, superb. [Prob *Jim* and **dandy**[1]]

jiminy *jim'in-i*. See under **geminate**.

jimjam *jim'jam*, (*colloq*) *n* a knick-knack, a gadget; an oddity, peculiarity; (in *pl*) delirium tremens (*slang*); (in *pl*) the fidgets; (in *pl*; *child's word*) pyjamas. [Origin unknown]

jimmy *jim'i*, (chiefly *US*) *n* a burglar's jemmy. — *vt* to force open, *esp* with a jimmy.

Jimmy[1] *jim'i*, (*slang*) *n* an act of urinating. — Also **Jimmy Riddle**. [Rhyming slang for *piddle*]

Jimmy[2] (*Scot colloq*) *n* term of address for a male stranger.

jimmy-o'goblin *jim'i-ō-gob'lin*, (*slang*) *n* (also with *cap(s)*) a pound sterling or Irish punt. [Rhyming slang for *sovereign*]

Jimmy Riddle. See **Jimmy**.

Jimmy Woodser *jim'i wood'sər*, (*Austr* and *NZ colloq*) *n* a solitary drinker; a drink taken on one's own.

jimp *jimp*, (*Scot*) *adj* slender; elegant; scant. — *adv* **jimp** or **jimp'ly** neatly; hardly; scant. — *n* **jimp'ness**. — *adj* **jimp'y** neat. [Origin unknown]

jimson-weed, **jimpson-weed** or (*obs*) **Jamestown-weed** *jim'sən-wēd*, (*NAm*) *n* the thorn-apple (*Datura stramonium*). [*Jamestown*, Virginia, where it established itself]

jingal, **gingall** or **gingal** *jin(g)'göl* or *-göl'*, *n* a large Chinese or Indian swivel-musket. [Hindi *janjāl*]

jingbang *jing-bang'* or *jing'bang*, (*slang*) *n* company; collection; lot. [Origin unknown]

jingle *jing'gl*, *n* a succession of clinking, tinkling sounds; something which makes a tinkling sound, *esp* a metal disc on a tambourine; a catchy, pleasant-sounding arrangement of words which may have very little meaning; a short, simple verse, *usu* with music, or sometimes a short catchy tune on its own, used to advertise a product, etc; a covered two-wheeled vehicle (*obs*). — *vt* and *vi* to sound with a jingle. — *n* **jing'ler**. — *n* **jing'let** a ball serving as the clapper of a sleigh-bell. — *adj* **jing'ly**. — **jing'le-jangle** a dissonant continued jingling; a jingling ornament; **jingling Johnny** a Chinese pavilion, or musical percussion instrument with little bells; **jingling match** (*obs*) a game in which blindfolded players try to catch a player who is holding or wearing bells. [Imit]

jingo or **Jingo** *jing'gō*, *n* used in the mild oaths 'By jingo', 'By the living jingo' (*Scot* 'By jing', 'By jings'); from its occurrence in a music-hall song of 1878 that conveyed a threat against Russia, a chauvinistic, sabre-rattling patriot: — *pl* **jing'oes**. — *adj* **jing'o** or **jing'oish** chauvinist, sabre-rattling. — *n* **jing'oism**. — *n* **jing'oist**. — *adj* **jingois'tic** characteristic of jingoism. — *adv* **jingois'tically**. [Appears first as a conjurer's summoning call; poss from Basque *Jinkoa*, *Jainko(a)* God]

jingo-ring *jing'gō-ring*, *n* a children's game in which the players dance round one of their number singing 'Here we go round the jingo-ring'. [Connected with **jink**]

jinjili. See **gingili**.

jink *jingk*, (*orig Scot*) *vi* to dodge nimbly; to make a sudden evasive turn (*aeronautics*). — *vt* to elude; to cheat. — *n* (*esp aeronautics* and *Rugby football*) a quick, deceptive turn. — **high jinks** see under **high**. [Imit of the movement]

jinker *jing'kər*, (*Austr*) *n* a janker; a sulky or other light horse-drawn passenger vehicle. [**janker**]

jinn *jin*, *n pl* (*sing* **jinnee**, **jinni**, **djinni** or **genie** (*jēn'i* or *jin-ē'*) a class of spirits in Muslim theology and folklore, assuming various shapes, sometimes as enormous monstrous men with supernatural powers. — Also **djinn**, or **ginn**. The *jinn* are often called **genii** by a confusion and **jinns** is sometimes erroneously used as a *pl*. [Ar *jinn* (pl), *jinnī* (sing)]

jinricksha, **jinrickshaw**, **jinrikisha**. See **ricksha**.

jinx *jingks*, *n* a bringer of bad luck; an unlucky influence. — *vt* to bring bad luck to, or put an unlucky spell on. — *adj* **jinxed** beset with bad luck. [Appar from **Jynx**, the bird being used in spells, and the name itself coming to mean 'a spell or charm']

jipyapa or **jippi-jappa** *hē-pi-hä'pə*, *n* a palm-like tree (*Carludovica palmata*) of tropical America, the fibre from whose leaves is used for panama hats, etc. [Name of a town in Ecuador)

jirble *jir'* or *jûr'bl*, (*Scot*) *vt* and *vi* to pour splashingly or unsteadily. [Imit)

jird *jûrd*, *n* a N African gerbil of the genus *Meriones*. [Berber *(a)gherda*]

jirga *jēr'gə*, *n* in Afghanistan, a council of tribal headmen. [Pushtu]

jirkinet. See **jerkin**.

jism, **gism** *jiz'əm* or **jissom** *jis'əm*, *n* energy, force (*colloq*, chiefly *US*); semen (*vulg*). [Origin unknown]

JIT (*business*) *abbrev*: just-in-time (qv).

jitney *jit'ni*, (*US slang*) *n* five-cent piece, a nickel; a bus or other, smaller, passenger vehicle, *usu* with low fares. — *adj* cheap; paltry. [Perh Fr *jeton* counter]

jitter *jit'ər*, (*orig US*) *vi* to behave in a flustered way. — *n pl* **jitt'ers** a flustered state (*usu* with *the*, *esp* as in **have the jitters** to be on edge, nervous or flustered). — *adj* **jitt'ery**. — **jitt'erbug** (*US*) a type of two-step to jazz music, the standard movements allowing for energetic improvisation; someone who performs this dance; (in Britain, by misunderstanding or extension) a scaremonger, alarmist. — *vi* to dance the jitterbug, *esp* wildly.

jiu-jitsu. See **ju-jitsu**.

jive *jīv*, *n* a lively style of jazz music, swing; the style of fast dancing done to this music; jargon, *specif* of Harlem and of jazz musicians (*slang*). — *vi* to play or dance jive; to talk jive (also **jive talk**; *slang*). — *n* **jī'ver**. — *n* and *adj* (*US colloq*) **jive'-ass** term of contempt.

jiz. See **gizz**.

jizz *jiz*, *n* the characteristic features which distinguish a bird, animal or plant from other species which resemble it. [Ety uncertain]

jnana *jə-nä'nə*, (*Hinduism*) *n* spiritual knowledge. [Sans *jñāna*, for *jñā* to know]

Jnr or **jnr** *abbrev*: Junior or junior.

jo or **joe** *jō*, (*Scot*) *n* a beloved one: — *pl* **joes**. [An old form of **joy**]

joanna *jō-an'ə*, (*slang*) *n* a piano. [Rhyming slang]

joannes. See **johannes**.

Job *jōb*, *n* a person of great patience. — *n* **jōbā'tion** (also **jawbā'tion**) a tedious scolding. — *vt* **jobe** (*jōb*) to reprimand tediously. — **Job's comforter** someone who aggravates the distress of the unfortunate person they have come to comfort; **Job's news** bad news; **Job's post** the bearer of bad news; **Job's tears** the involucres of an Indian grass (*Coix lachryma*) used as beads; round grains of chrysolite. [From *Job* in the *Book of Job*]

job[1] *job*, *n* a sudden thrust with anything pointed, such as a beak. — *vt* and *vi* to prod or peck suddenly. — *vt* to punch (*Austr colloq*): — *pr p* **jobb'ing**; *pa t* and *pa p* **jobbed**. [Appar imit; cf **jab**]

job[2] *job*, *n* any individual piece of work; any undertaking or employment done for payment or profit; an occupation or post; someone's proper business or responsibility; a state of affairs (*colloq*); an item or example of a specified kind (*colloq*); a transaction in which private gain is sought under pretence of public service; an end accomplished by intrigue or wire-pulling; a criminal enterprise, *esp* theft (*colloq*); a hired horse or carriage (*obs*); a job-lot. — *adj* employed, hired or used by the job or for jobs; bought or sold lumped together. — *vi* to work at jobs; to buy and sell, as a broker; to practise jobbery. — *vt* to perform as a job; to put or carry through by jobbery; to deal in, as a broker; to hire or let out (*esp* horses). — *n* **jobb'er** a person who jobs; a person who buys and sells, as a broker; a stock-jobber; someone who turns official actions to private advantage; a person who engages in a mean lucrative affair; a wholesale merchant, *esp* if selling to retailers (*US*); as *combining form* with *first*, *second*, etc, someone in, or seeking, their first, second, etc job. — *n* **jobb'ery** jobbing; unfair means employed to secure some private end. — *n* **jobb'ie** (*colloq*) a lump of excrement. — *adj* **jobb'ing** working by the job. — *n* the doing of jobs; miscellaneous printing-work other than books or newspapers; buying and selling as a broker; stock-jobbing; jobbery. — *adj* and *collective n* **job'less** (people) having no job. — *n* **job'lessness**. — **job centre** or **Jobcentre** (also without *cap*) a government-run employment office, *esp* one where information about available jobs is displayed; **job club** or **Job'club** an association directed towards helping the jobless to find employment for themselves through learning and using the required skills, motivation, etc; **job description** a detailed listing of all the duties, responsibilities, tasks, etc necessary to a specific job; **job evaluation** a method of working out the relative postion and appropriate salary for the different jobs in an organization by allocating points for the various aspects of each job as listed in the job description; **job'-hopping** changing job frequently; **job-lot'** a collection of odds and ends, *esp* for sale as one lot; any collection of inferior quality; **job'-master** a livery-stable keeper who jobs out horses and carriages; **job share**, **job'share** or **job sharing** the practice of dividing one job between two part-time workers. — **a bad** (or **good**) **job** a piece of work badly (or well) done; an unlucky (or lucky) fact; **have a job to** (*colloq*) to have difficulty in; **job off** to sell (goods) cheaply to get rid of them; **job of work** a task, bit of work; **job out** to divide (work) among contractors, etc; **jobs for the boys** jobs given to or created for friends or supporters; **just the job** (*colloq*) exactly what is wanted; **odd jobs** see under **odd**; **on the job** at work, in activity, busy. — *adj* **on'-the-job** happening while one is at work. [Origin unknown]

jobation, **jobe**. See **Job**.

jobernowl *job'ər-nōl*, (*old colloq*) *n* a stupid head; a stupid person. [Appar Fr *jobard* a noodle, and **nowl**, **noll**]

jobsworth *jobz'wûrth*, (*derog slang*) *n* a minor official, *esp* one who adheres rigidly and unco-operatively to petty rules. [From 'It's more than my *job's worth* to let you ... ']

Jock *jok*, *n* a Scottish soldier (*slang*); a Scotsman (*slang*); Jack (*Scot*); the jack or knave in cards (*Scot*); a male yokel (*Scot*). [Scots variant of **Jack**]

jock *jok*, *n* a jockstrap; a male athlete or sportsman (*US slang*); a macho young man whose clothes accentuate and display his physique; a disc-jockey (*slang*). [**jock-strap**]

jockey *jok'i*, *n* a person who rides (*esp* professionally) in horse-races; a horse-dealer (*obs*); someone who takes undue advantage in business. — *vt* to jostle by riding against; to manoeuvre; to trick by manoeuvring. — *vi* (often with *for*) to seek advantage by manoeuvring. — *n* **jockette'** (*facetious*) a female jockey. — *n* **jock'eyism**. — *n* **jock'eyship** the art or practice of a jockey. — **Jockey Club** an association for the promotion and ordering of horse-racing; a perfume composed of rose, orris, cassia, tuberose, bergamot, etc; **jockey strap** see **jockstrap**. [Dimin of **Jock**, ie a lad, jockeys orig being boys]

jocko *jok'ō*, *n* a chimpanzee: — *pl* **jock'os**. [Fr, from a W African word *ncheko*]

Jock Scott *jok skot*, (*angling*) *n* a kind of artificial fly.

jockstrap *jok'strap*, *n* a genital support worn by men participating in athletics. — Also **jock** or **jockey strap**. [Dialect *jock* the penis, and **strap**]

jockteleg *jok'tə-leg*, (*Scot*) *n* a large clasp-knife. [The suggested *Jacques de Liège*, supposedly a famous cutler, lacks confirmation]

joco *jō-kō'*, (*Scot*) *adj* cheerful; pleased with oneself. [**jocose**]

jocose *jō-kōs'*, *adj* full of jokes; facetious; merry. — *adv* **jocose'ly**. — *n* **jocose'ness** or **jocosity** (*-kos'i-ti*) the quality of being jocose. — *adj* **jocosē'rious** half in jest, half in earnest. [L *jocōsus*, from *jocus* a joke]

jocular *jok'ū-lər*, *adj* given to or inclined to joking; of the nature of, or intended as, a joke. — *n* **jocularity** (*-lar'i-ti*). — *adv* **joc'ularly**. [L *joculāris*, from *jocus*]

joculator *jok'ū-lā-tər*, *n* a professional jester or minstrel. [L, from *joculārī* to jest]

jocund *jōk'und* or *jok'und*, or *-ənd*, *adj* mirthful; merry; cheerful; pleasant. — *n* **jocundity** (*-kund'i-ti*) or **joc'undness**. — *adv* **joc'undly**. [OFr, from LL *jocundus* for L *jūcundus* pleasant, modified by association with *jocus*]

jodel *yō'dl*. Same as **yodel**.

jodhpurs *jod'pûrz*, *n pl* riding-breeches, loose round the hip and tight-fitting from the knee to the ankle. — Also **jodhpur breeches**. — **jodhpur boots** ankle-high boots worn with jodhpurs for riding. [*Jodhpur* in India]

Joe *jō*, (*slang*) *n* a man, an ordinary fellow, *esp* (*US*) a soldier. — *n* **Joey** (*jō'i*) a circus clown, *esp* in the English tradition (*Joseph* Grimaldi); a fourpenny bit (*obs*) (*Joseph* Hume, MP, 1836); (sometimes without *cap*) a threepenny bit. — **Joe Bloggs** or (*US* and *Austr*) **Joe Blow** the average man in the street. — **Joe Miller** an old or stale jest; a joke-book; **Joe Millerism** the habit of telling old jokes (*Joe Miller* (1684–1738), a comedian after whom a joke-book was named); **Joe Public** the average man in the street; **Joe Soap** or merely **Joe** (*airmen's rhyming slang* for *dope*) someone imposed on to perform unpleasant tasks. — **not for Joe** see under **Joseph**.

joe. See **jo**.

joey[1] *jō'i*, (*Austr colloq*) *n* a young animal, *esp* a kangaroo; an opossum (*NZ*). [Aboriginal]

joey[2]. See **Joe**.

jog *jog*, *vt* to shake; to push with the elbow or hand; to stimulate, stir up (eg the memory). — *vi* to move by jogs; (with *on* or *along*) to move along or progress slowly, steadily, unremarkably; to run at a slow, steady pace, as a form of exercise: — *pr p* **jogg'ing**; *pa t* and *pa p* **jogged**. — *n* a slight shake; a push or nudge; a spell of jogging. — *n* **jogg'er** a person who moves slowly and heavily (*Dryden*); a person who jogs for exercise; a piece of mechanical equipment which shakes sheets of paper into alignment ready for stapling, binding, etc; (in *pl*) jog pants. — *n* **jogg'ing** running at a slow, steady pace, *esp* for exercise. — Also *adj*. — **jogger's nipple** (*colloq*) painful inflammation of a runner's nipple caused by friction against clothing; **jogging bottoms** jog pants; **jog pants** or **jog'pants** loose-fitting trousers of jersey fabric, elasticated at waist and ankles, such as are worn for jogging; **jog'trot** a slow jogging trot; a humdrum routine. [Appar imit; perh related to **shog**]

joggle[1] *jog'l*, *n* a tooth, notch or pin to prevent surfaces in contact with each other from slipping; a joint made for this purpose. — *vt* to join with a joggle. [Perh connected with **jag**[1]]

joggle[2] *jog'l*, *vt* to jog or shake slightly; to jostle. — *vi* to shake: — *pr p* **jogg'ling**; *pa t* and *pa p* **jogg'led**. — *n* the act of joggling; a slight jog. [Appar dimin or frequentative of **jog**]

johannes *jō-(h)anēz*, *n* a gold coin of *John V* of Portugal. — Also **joann'es**. — *adj* **Johann'ean** or **Johann'ine** of or pertaining to John, *esp* the Apostle. [L *Jōhannēs*, from *Jōannēs*, from Gr *Iōannēs*, from Heb *Yōchānān* John]

Johannisberger *jō-han'is-bûrg-ər*, *n* a white Rhenish wine produced at *Johannisberg* ('St John's Mountain'), near Wiesbaden.

John *jon*, *n* a male proper name; (without *cap*) a lavatory (*slang*, *esp US*); a prostitute's client (*slang*). — *n* **Johnian** (*jōn'i-ən*) a member of St *John's* College, Cambridge. — *n* **Johnn'y** (or **Johnn'ie**) (*slang*) a simpleton, an empty-headed man-about-town; a fellow or chap generally. — *n* **johnn'ie** or **johnn'y** (*slang*) a condom. — **John'-a-dreams** (*Shakesp*) a dreamy fellow; **John a-Nokes** or **John a-Stiles** or **-Styles** (*obs*) a fictitious name for a person in a law-suit, or generally; **John'-apple** a kind of apple, apple-John; **John Barleycorn** malt spirits personified; **John Bircher** (*US*) a member of the extreme right-wing anti-communist **John Birch Society**; **John Bull** a generic name for an Englishman, from Arbuthnot(t)'s *History of John Bull*, 1712; **John Bullism** the typical English character, or any act or word expressive of it; **John Canoe** see separate entry; **John Chinaman** (*derog*) a Chinaman; *collectively* the Chinese; **John Citizen** a typical citizen; **John Collins** an alcoholic long drink based on gin; **John Company** (*obs*) the East India Company; **John Doe** see **Doe**; **John Dory** see **dory**[1]; **John'-go-to-bed-at-noon** the goat's-beard (because it closes early in the day); **John Hancock** (*US colloq*) a signature (from *John Hancock*, signatory of the Declaration of Independence); **John Hop** (*Austr* and *NZ rhyming slang* for *cop*) a policeman; **John Kanoo** see **John Canoe**; **Johnn'y-cake** a flat cake made from maize flour (*US*) or wheat flour (*Austr*); **Johnny-come-late'ly** a bumptious newcomer; **Johnny-head'-in-air** or **John o'dreams** a dreamy, impractical person; **Johnn'y-raw** a beginner; a greenhorn; **John Thomas** (*slang*) the penis. [L *Jōhannēs*; see **johannes**]

John Canoe *jon kə-no͞o'*, (*W Indies*) *n* a boisterous rhythmic dance performed *esp* as part of Christmas celebrations; the celebrations themselves; any of, or *esp* the leader of, the dancers; the mask or headdress of such a dancer. — Also **John Kanoo, joncanoe, junkanoo,** etc. [From a W African language]

Johnsonian *jon-sō'ni-ən*, *adj* of or in the manner of Dr Samuel *Johnson*, the lexicographer (1709–84). — *n* **Johnsō'nianism** or **John'sonism** (*-sən-izm*). — *n* **John'sonese** Johnsonian style, idiom, diction, or an imitation of it, ponderous English, full of antitheses, balanced triads, and words of classical origin. — *n pl* **Johnsōniana** (*-ä'nə* or *-ā'nə*) matters or miscellaneous items connected with Johnson.

joie de vivre *zhwa də vē-vr'*, (*Fr*) *n* exuberance, literally joy of living.

join *join*, *vt* to connect; to unite; to associate; to add or annex; to become a member of; to come into association with or the company of; to go to and remain with, in, or on; to draw a straight line between (*geom*). — *vi* to be connected; to combine, unite; to run into one; to grow together; to be in, or come into, close contact. — *n* a joining; a place where things have been joined; a mode of joining. — *n* **joind'er** (*esp law*) joining, uniting. — *n* **join'er** a worker in wood, *esp* one who makes smaller structures than a carpenter; someone who joins or unites; someone who joins many societies. — *n* **join'ery** the art of the joiner; a joiner's work. — *n* **join'ing** the act of joining; a seam; a joint. — *n* **joint** a joining; the place where, or mode in which, two or more things join; a place where two things (*esp* bones) meet, allowing a hingelike movement; a node, or place where a stem bears leaves, *esp* if swollen; a segment; a piece of an animal's body as cut up for serving at the table; the flexible hinge of cloth or leather connecting the back of a book with its sides; a crack intersecting a mass of rock (*geol*); the place where adjacent surfaces meet; the condition of adjustment at a joint (in the phrase *out of joint*); a disreputable bar or other meeting-place (*US slang*); a public meeting-place, a place in general (*colloq*); a cigarette containing marijuana (*colloq*); see also **the joint** below. — *adj* joined, united or combined; shared among more than one; done or made by more than one; sharing with another or others. — *vt* to unite by joints; to provide with joints or an appearance of joints; to fill the joints of with mortar, etc; to divide into joints. — *vi* to fit closely together. — *adj* **joint'ed** having a joint or joints; composed of segments; constricted at intervals. — *n* **joint'er** a jointer plane; a bricklayer's tool for putting mortar in joints. — *adj* **joint'less.** — *adv* **joint'ly** in a joint manner; unitedly or in combination; together. — *n* **joint'ness.** — **joined-up writing** (*child's word*) or **join'-hand** (*obs*) cursive handwriting; **joint account** a bank or building-society account held in the name of two or more people, any of whom can deposit or withdraw money; **jointed cactus** a plant (*Opuntia pusilla*) of the prickly-pear genus, a serious pest in S Africa; **joint'er-plane** or **jointing plane** the largest kind of plane used by a joiner; **joint'-fir** any plant of the family Gnetaceae; **joint'-heir** a person who inherits jointly with another or others; **joint'ing-rule** a long straight-edged rule used by bricklayers; **joint'-oil** synovia; **joint resolution** (*US*) one passed by both Houses of Congress; **joint'-stock** stock held jointly (**joint'-stock company** one in which each shareholder can transfer shares without consent of the rest); **joint'-stool** (*Shakesp*) a stool made of parts inserted in each other; **joint-ten'ancy**; **joint-ten'ant** a person who is owner of land or goods along with others; **joint venture** a business activity undertaken by two or more companies acting together, sharing costs, risks and profits; **joint'-worm** or **joint'worm** (*US*) a hymenopterous larva that attacks grain-stalks near the first joint. — **join battle** see under **battle**; **join in** to (begin to) take part; **join issue** to begin to dispute; to take up the contrary view or side; **joint and several liability** (*law*) the responsiblity of any one member of a group for the actions or debts of any or all of the others, and the responsibiltiy of the group as a whole for the actions or debts of any one member; **Joint European Torus** see **JET**; **join up** to enlist, *esp* as part of a general movement; **out of joint** dislocated; disordered, awry; **put someone's nose out of joint** to supplant someone in another's love or confidence; to disconcert, rebuff or offend someone; **second joint** the middle piece of a fly-fishing rod; the thigh of a fowl (*opp* to the leg or drumstick, the first joint); **universal joint** a device one part of which is able to move freely in all directions, as in the ball-and-socket joint. [OFr *joindre*, from L *jungere*, *junctum* to join]

jointure *join'tyər*, *n* property settled by a husband on his wife at their marriage for her use after her husband's death. — *vt* to settle a jointure upon, arrange a jointure for. — *n* **joint'uress** or **joint'ress** a woman on whom a jointure is settled. [OE, from OFr, from L *junctūra* a joining]

joist *joist*, *n* a beam supporting the boards of a floor or the laths of a ceiling. — *vt* to fit with joists. [OFr *giste*, from *gesir*, from L *jacēre* to lie]

jojoba *hō-hō'bə*, *n* a desert shrub of the box family, native to Mexico, Arizona and California, whose edible seeds yield a waxy oil chemically similar to spermaceti, used in cosmetic preparations, etc. [Mex Sp]

joke *jōk*, *n* an amusing quip or story; a witticism; anything said or done for fun; anything that or anyone who provokes a laugh; an absurdity. — *vi* to jest; to tell jokes; to be humorous; to make fun. — *vt* to poke fun at; to chaff. — *n* **jok'er** a person who jokes or jests; a fifty-third card in the pack, used at euchre, poker, etc; an innocent-looking clause insidiously introduced to cripple the effect of a bill or document (*US*); an unforeseen factor affecting a situation; a fellow, often one viewed with mild, *usu* amicable, amusement (*slang*). — *adj* **joke'some, jō'key** or **jō'ky.** — *adv* **jok'ingly** in a joking manner. — **joke'smith** (*archaic*) a maker of jokes. — **joking apart** if I may be serious, seriously; **no joke** a serious or difficult matter. [L *jocus*]

jokol *yō'köl*, (*Shetland*; *obs*) *adv* yes, literally yes carl. — Also **yo'kul.** [Shetland Norn *jo* yes, and (inferred) *koll*, from ON *karl* carl]

jole. See **jowl**[1,2].

jolie laide *zho-lē led*, (*Fr*) *n* a woman whose ugliness is part of her charm: — *pl* **jol'ies laides.**

joll. See **jowl**[1,2].

jolley *jol'i*, (*pottery*) *n* a kind of jigger to which the mould for making plates, etc is fixed. — *n* **joll'eyer** or **joll'yer.** — *n* **joll'eying** or **joll'ying.**

jollies *jol'ēz*, (*slang*; *usu* with *cap*) *n pl* *J*et-setting *o*lder people with *l*ots of *l*oot. [Coined in imitation of **woopie, yuppie**]

jolly *jol'i*, *adj* merry; expressing, providing or provoking fun and gaiety, entertaining, festive, jovial; healthy, plump; splendid, very agreeable (*colloq*). — *vt* to make fun of; (*esp* with *along*) to put or keep in good humour, amuse. — *adv* (*colloq*) very. — *n* a royal marine (*slang*); a jollification (*colloq*); an outing, a trip, *esp* at someone else's expense (*colloq*). — *n* **jollificā'tion** an occasion of merrymaking or being jolly; noisy festivity and merriment. — *vi* **joll'ify.** — *adv* **joll'ily.** — *n* **joll'iment** (*Spenser*) merriment. — *n* **joll'iness, joll'ity** or (*Spenser*) **joll'yhead.** — **Jolly Roger** a black flag with white skull and crossbones, flown by pirate ships. [OFr *jolif*, *joli*, perh connected with ON *jōl* Yule]

jollyboat *jol'i-bōt*, *n* a small boat kept hoisted at the stern of a ship. [Origin obscure]

jolt *jōlt* or *jolt*, *vi* to jostle or proceed with sudden jerks. — *vt* to jostle or knock against; to shake with a sudden shock. — *n* a sudden jerk; a shock; a surprising or activating shock. — *n* **jolt'er.** — *adv* **jolt'ingly** in a jolting manner. — *adj* **jolt'y.** [Ety obscure]

jolterhead *jōlt'ər-hed* or **jolthead** *jōlt'hed*, (*archaic*) *n* a large clumsy head; a blockhead. [Ety obscure]

jomo. See **zho**.

Jonah *jō'nə*, *n* a bringer of bad luck on shipboard or elsewhere. — **Jonah word** a word with which a chronic stutterer has difficulty. [From the biblical prophet *Jonah*, whose disobedience to God provoked a storm at sea, to put an end to which he was thrown overboard]

Jonathan *jon'ə-thən*, *n* the people of the United States, collectively, or a typical specimen (often *Brother Jonathan*) (*archaic*); an American variety of apple. [The male personal name, orig of the son of Saul, king of Israel]

joncanoe. See **John Canoe**.

jongleur *zhɔ̃-glœr'*, *n* a wandering minstrel; a mountebank. [Fr, from OFr *jogleor*, from L *joculātor*; cf **juggler**]

jonquil *jong'kwil*, formerly *jung-kwil'*, *n* a name given to certain species of narcissus with rush-like leaves. [Fr *jonquille*, from L *juncus* a rush]

Jonsonian *jon-sō'ni-ən*, *adj* of or characteristic of the English dramatist Ben *Jonson* (1572–1637) or his works.

jonty *jon'ti*, **jaunty**, **jauntie** or **janty** *jön'ti* or *jän'ti*, (*slang*) *n* a naval master-at-arms.

jook, etc. See **jouk**.

jor *jör*, (*Hindu music*) *n* the second movement of a raga. [Sans]

joram. See **jorum**.

Jordan[1] *jör'dn*, *n* a country in SW Asia. — Also *adj*. — *adj* **Jordan'ian** (*-dān'*). — *n* a native or citizen of Jordan. [See **Jordan**[2]]

Jordan[2] *jör'dn*, *n* the great river of Palestine; death (as a passage into the Promised Land, from Num 33. 51); (*usu* without *cap*) a chamberpot (*Shakesp*).

jordeloo *jör-di-loo'*. Same as **gardyloo**.

jorum or **joram** *jör'əm*, *n* a large drinking-bowl; a large drink. [Poss from *Joram* in 2 Samuel 8. 10]

Joseph *jō'zif*, *n* someone whose chastity is above temptation (from the story of *Joseph* and Potiphar's wife in Gen 39); (without *cap*) a caped overcoat worn by women in the 18c for riding (possibly in allusion to *Joseph's* coat, Gen 37). — **not for Joseph** (or **Joe**) not on any account (*prob* from the refrain of a 19c music-hall song).

josephinite *jo'zə-fēn-īt*, *n* a mineral found only in *Josephine* Creek, in Oregon, USA, and believed to have originated at the outer edge of the earth's core and been carried up nearly 2 000 miles to the surface.

Josephson junction *jō'zif-sən jung'shən*, (*electronics*) *n* a junction formed from two superconducting metals separated by a thin insulating layer, allowing the unimpeded passage of a current and generating microwaves when subjected to a certain voltage. [B D *Josephson* (1940-), English physicist]

josh *josh*, (*slang*) *vt* to ridicule; to tease. — *vi* to banter, joke — *n* a hoax; a derisive joke. — *n* **josh'er**.

Josh. (*Bible*) *abbrev*: (the Book of) Joshua.

joskin *jos'kin*, (*old slang*) *n* a clown, yokel. [Thieves' cant]

joss *jos*, *n* a Chinese idol; luck or fate. — *n* **joss'er** (*slang*) a clergyman (*Austr*); a fellow; a blunderer, a fool. — **joss'-house** a temple; **joss'-stick** a stick of gum which gives off a perfume when burned, used as incense *esp* in India, China, etc. [Port *deos* god, from L *deus*]

joss-block *jos'-blok*, (*dialect*) *n* a mounting-block.

jostle *jos'l* or **justle** *jus'l*, *vi* to tilt, joust (*obs*). — *vt* and *vi* to shake or jar by collision; to hustle; to elbow. — *n* an act of jostling. — *n* **jos'tlement** or **jos'tling**. [Frequentative of **joust**, **just**]

jot *jot*, *n* an iota, a whit, a tittle. — *vt* to set down briefly; to make a memorandum of: — *pr p* **jott'ing**; *pa t* and *pa p* **jott'ed**. — *n* **jott'er** someone who jots; a book or pad for notes. — *n* **jott'ing** a memorandum; a brief note. [L *iōta* (read as *jōta*), from Gr *iōta* the smallest letter in the alphabet, equivalent to *i*; Heb *yōd*]

jota *hhō'tä*, *n* a Spanish dance in triple time. [Sp]

jotun *yō'tən* or **jötunn** *yœ'tən*, (*Scand mythol*) *n* a giant. [ON *jötunn*]

joual *zhoo-al'* or *-äl'*, (*Can*) *n* a non-standard, chiefly urban, variety of Canadian French. [Can Fr dialectal variant of Fr *cheval* horse]

jougs *joogz* or *jugz*, (*Scot hist*) *n pl* an instrument of punishment consisting of an iron collar attached to a wall or post and put round an offender's neck. [Prob OFr *joug* a yoke, from L *jugum*]

jouisance or **jouysaunce** *joo'is-əns*, (*Spenser*) *n* joyousness. [Fr *jouissance*, from *jouir* to enjoy, from L *gaudēre* to rejoice]

jouk or **jook** *jook*, (*Scot*) *vi* to duck; to dodge; to bow. — *n* an elusive duck or dodging movement; a bow. — *n* **jouk'ery**, **jook'ery** or **jouk'ery-pawk'ery** (*Scot*) trickery, roguery. [Ety obscure]

joule[1] *jool*, *n* a unit of energy, work and heat in the MKS and SI systems, equal to work done when a force of 1 newton advances its point of application 1 metre (1 joule = 10^7 ergs). [After the physicist J P *Joule* (1818–89)]

joule[2]. See **jowl**[2].

jounce *jowns*, *vt* and *vi* to jolt, bump. [Ety uncertain]

jour *zhoor* (*Fr*) *n* a day. — **jour de fête** (*də fet*) a feast day, *esp* a saint's day.

journal[1] *jûr'nəl*, *n* a daily register or diary; a book containing a record of each day's transactions; a newspaper published daily (or otherwise); a magazine; the transactions of any society. — *adj* (*Shakesp*) diurnal. — *n* **journalese'** the jargon of bad journalism. — *n* **journ'alism** the profession of collecting, writing, editing, publishing, etc news reports and other articles for newspapers, journals, television, radio and related media; the style of writing associated with the reporting of news, current affairs and popular interest subjects via a transitory medium; the material produced in this way. — *n* **jour'nalist** a person who writes for or manages a newspaper, magazine, or other news-related medium; a person who keeps a journal (*obs*). — *adj* **journalist'ic**. — *adv* **journalist'ically**. — *vi* **jour'nalize** or **-ise** to write for or in a journal. — *vt* to enter in a journal. — *n* **jour'no** (*Austr colloq*) a journalist: — *pl* **jour'nos**. [Fr, from L *diurnālis*; see **diurnal**]

journal[2] *jûr'nəl*, (*mech*) *n* that part of a shaft or axle which is in contact with and supported by a bearing. — *vt* to provide with or fix as a journal. — **jour'nal-box** a box or bearing for a journal. [Origin unexplained]

journal intime *zhoor-nal ɛ̃-tēm*, (*Fr*) *n* a diary.

journey *jûr'ni*, *n* any travel from one place to another; a tour or excursion; movement from end to end of a fixed course; a day's work or travel (*obs*); a campaign (*obs*); the weight of finished coins delivered at one time to the Master of the Mint (also **jour'ney-weight**); a set of colliery trucks: — *pl* **jour'neys**. — *vi* to travel: — *pr p* **jour'neying**; *pa t* and *pa p* **jour'neyed** (*-nid*). — *n* **jour'neyer**. — *adj* **jour'ney-bated** (*Shakesp*) travelworn. — **jour'neyman** a hired workman, *orig* one hired by the day; a worker whose apprenticeship is completed; someone who is competent at his trade; an electrically controlled clock or dial; **jour'ney-work** work done by a journeyman or for hire; necessary, routine work. [Fr *journée*, from *jour* a day, from L *diurnus*]

joust or **just** *jowst* (less commonly *just* or *joost*), *n* an encounter between two lance-bearing knights on horseback at a tournament. — *vi* to take part in such a tournament, to tilt. — *n* **joust'er**. [OFr *juste*, *jouste*, *joste*, from L *juxtā* near to]

jouysance. See **jouisance**.

Jove *jōv*, *n* another name for the god Jupiter. — *adj* **Jō'vian** of the god or planet Jupiter. — **by Jove** an exclamation of surprise, admiration, etc. [Early L *Jovis* (in the nominative usu *Juppiter*, *Jupiter* father Jove) the god Jove or Jupiter, or the planet Jupiter, an auspicious star]

jovial *jō'vi-əl*, *adj* joyous; full of jollity and geniality; (with *cap*) of the god or planet or influenced by Jupiter. — *n* **joviality** (*-al'i-ti*) or **jō'vialness**. — *adv* **jō'vially**. [**Jove**]

Jovian. See **Jove**.

jovysaunce. A misreading of **jouysaunce**. See **jouisance**.

jow *jow*, (*Scot*) *vt* and *vi* to ring, toll; to rock. — *n* a stroke of a bell. — *n* and *adj* **jowing-in'** ringing-in. — **jow one's ginger** see **jee one's ginger** under **jee**[2]. [**jowl**[2]]

jowar *jow-är'*, **jowari** or **jawari** *-ē*, *n* durra. [Hindi *jawār*, *jawārī*]

jowl[1] *jowl* or *jōl* (*obs* **jole** or **joll** *jōl*), *n* the jaw; the cheek; a pendulous double chin; (in animals) a dewlap or wattle; a head; the head and shoulders of a salmon, sturgeon or ling. — *adj* **jowled**. — *n* **jowl'er** a heavy-jawed hound. — *adj* **jow'ly** having noticeable heavy or droopy jaws. [Prob several different words. The development and relations of ME *chaul*, OE *ceafl* jaw, ME *chol*, OE *ceolu*, *ceolur*, etc, and the modern forms with *j* are difficult to make out. Fr *joue* cheek, or some other word may have added to the confusion]

jowl[2], **joll**, **jole** or **joule** *jōl*, (*dialect*) *vt* and *vi* to bump; to beat; to toll. — *n* a stroke; a knock. [Ety obscure]

joy *joi*, *n* intense gladness; rapture, delight; rejoicing; a cause of joy; a beloved person, a dear. — *vi* (*obs*) to rejoice; to be glad; to exult. — *vt* (*obs*) to give joy to; to enjoy (*Milton*): — *pr p* **joy'ing**; *pa t* and *pa p* **joyed**. — *n* **joy'ance** (*poetic*, *orig Spenser*) gaiety, festivity. — *adj* **joy'ful** full of joy; feeling, expressing or giving joy. — *adv* **joy'fully**. — *n* **joy'fulness**. — *adj* **joy'less** without joy; not giving joy. — *adv* **joy'lessly**. — *n* **joy'lessness**. — *adj* **joy'ous** joyful. — *adv* **joy'ously**. — *n* **joy'ousness**. — *vi* **joy'-pop** (*slang*) to take addictive drugs from time to time without forming an addiction. — **joy'-ride** (*slang*) a pleasure-drive, *esp* if reckless or surreptitious and in a stolen car. — Also *vi*. — **joy'-rider**; **joy'-riding**; **joy'-stick** the control-lever of an aeroplane, invalid car, video game, etc; a lever controlling the movement of the cursor on a VDU screen (*comput*); **joy'-wheel** a huge fairground wheel that carries passengers round its axis. — (**get** or **have**) **any joy** (*colloq*) (to achieve) satisfaction or success (in an attempt, etc); **no joy** (*colloq*) no news, reply, information, luck or success. [Fr *joie* (cf Ital *gioia*), from L *gaudium*]

Joycean *joi'sē-ən*, *adj* of, or in the manner of, James *Joyce* (1882–1941), Irish writer. — *n* a student or imitator of James Joyce.

JP *abbrev*: Justice of the Peace.

Jr or **jr** *abbrev*: Junior or junior.

juba *jōō'bə*, *n* a Negro breakdown or rustic dance, in which the participants clap hands, slap their thighs, and sing verses with *juba* as a refrain.

jubate *jōō'bāt*, (*zool*, etc) *adj* maned. [L *jubātus*, from *juba* mane]

jubbah *jōōb'ə* or *jub'ə*, *n* a long loose outer garment worn by Muslims. — Also **jibbah** or **djibbah**. [Ar *jubbah*]

jube[1] *jōō'bē*, *n* a rood-loft or screen and gallery. [L, imperative of *jubēre* to command, the first word of the prayer said on or beside it by the deacon]

jube[2] *jōōb*. An *Austr colloq* shortening of **jujube** (the sweet).

jubilant *jōō'bi-lənt*, *adj* rejoicing, feeling or expressing great joy; singing or shouting in joy or truimph. — *n* **ju'bilance** or **ju'bilancy** exultation. — *adv* **ju'bilantly**. — *vi* **ju'bilate** to exult, rejoice. — *n* **jubilā'tion** rejoicing, the expression of joy; joyful or triumphal shouting or singing. [L *jūbilāre* to shout for joy. Not connected with *jubilee*]

jubilate *jōō-bi-lä'tē* or *yōō-bi-lä'te*, *n* the third Sunday after Easter, so called because the church service began on that day with the 66th Psalm (*RC*); (*usu* with *cap*) the 100th Psalm, used as a canticle, or a setting of this (*Ch of Eng*, *RC*). [The opening word of both psalms in L, imperative pl of *jūbilāre* to shout for joy]

jubilee *jōō'bi-lē*, *n* a time, season or circumstance of great joy and festivity; jubilation; the celebration of a 50th or 25th anniversary, eg of a king's accession; a year (every 25th year, *ordinary jubilee*) of indulgence for pilgrims and others, an *extraordinary jubilee* being specially appointed by the Pope (*RC*); every 50th year, a year of release of slaves, cancelling of debts, and return of property to its former owners (*Jewish hist*). — **jubilee clip** a metal loop with a screw fitting, placed round a tube, hose, etc, and tightened to form a watertight connection. — **silver**, **golden** and **diamond jubilee** respectively a 25th, 50th and 60th anniversary. [Fr *jubilé*, from L *jūbilaeus*, from Heb *yōbēl* a ram, ram's horn]

JUD *abbrev*: *Juris Utriusque Doctor* (*L*), Doctor of both laws (ie Canon and Civil).

Jud. (*Bible*) *abbrev*: (the Book of) Judges (also **Judg**.); (the Apocryphal Book of) Judith.

jud *jud*, (*mining*) *n* a mass of coal holed or undercut ready for final removal. [Origin unknown]

Judaean or **Judean** *jōō-dē'ən*, *adj* of Judaea or the Jews. — *n* a native of Judaea; a Jew. [L *Judaea*]

Judaeo- *jōō-dā'ō-* or *US* **Judeo-** *jōō-dē'ō-*, *combining form* denoting Judaic, as in *Judaeo-Spanish* Jewish-Spanish, Ladino. [L *Judaea*]

Judaic *jōō-dā'ik*, *adj* pertaining to the Jews or Judaism. — *n pl* **Judā'ica** the culture of the Jews, their literature, customs, etc, *esp* as described in books, articles, etc. — *adj* **Judā'ical** Judaic. — *adv* **Judā'ically**. — *n* **Ju'dāism** the doctrines and rites of the Jews; conformity to the Jewish rites; the Jewish way of life. — *n* **Ju'dāist** someone who holds the doctrines of Judaism. — *adj* **Judāist'ic**. — *adv* **Judāist'ically**. — *n* **Judāīzā'tion** or **-s-**. — *vi* **Ju'dāīze** or **-īse** to conform to, adopt or practise Jewish customs or Judaism. — *vt* to imbue with Jewish principles or beliefs. — *n* **Ju'dāīzer** or **-s-**. [L *Jūdaicus*, from *Jūda* Judah, a son of Israel]

Judas *jōō'dəs*, *n* a traitor; (also without *cap*) a Judas-hole; *attrib* (as in *Judas goat*) denoting an animal or bird used to lure others. — *adj* **Ju'das-coloured** (of hair) red (*Judas* traditionally being red-haired). — **Ju'das-hole** or **Ju'das-window** (also without *caps*) a spy-hole in a door, etc; **Ju'das-kiss** any act of treachery under the guise of kindness (from Matt 26. 48, 49); **Ju'das-tree** a tree (genus *Cercis*) of the Caesalpinia family, with rose-coloured flowers that appear before the leaves (*Judas* being traditionally believed to have hanged himself on one); also the elder (for the same reason). [*Judas* Iscariot]

judder *jud'ər*, *n* a strong vibration in an aircraft or other mechanical apparatus; an intense, jerking motion; in singing, a vibratory effect produced by alternations of greater or less intensity of sound. — Also *vi*. [Prob **jar**[1] and **shudder**]

Judenhetze *yōō'dən-het-sə*, (*Ger*) *n* Jew-baiting.

Judeo-. See **Judaeo-**.

Judg. See under **Jud**.

judge *juj*, *vi* to act in the capacity of a judge; to point out or declare what is just or law; to try cases and decide questions of law, guiltiness, etc; to pass sentence; to compare facts to determine the truth; to form or pass an opinion; to distinguish. — *vt* to hear and determine authoritatively; to sit in judgement on; to pronounce on the guilt or innocence of; to sentence; to decide the merits of; to find fault with, to censure, condemn; to decide; to award; to estimate; to form an opinion on; to conclude; to consider (to be). — *n* a person who judges; a person appointed to hear and settle causes, and to try accused persons; someone chosen to award prizes, to decide doubtful or disputed points in a competition, etc; an arbitrator; someone who can decide upon the merit of anything; (in Jewish history) a supreme magistrate having civil and military powers; someone capable of discriminating well; (with *cap*; in *pl*) the title of the 7th book of the Old Testament. — *n* **judge'ment** or **judg'ment** the act of judging; the comparing of ideas to find out the truth; the faculty by which this is done, the reason or discernment; the mental act of establishing a relationship between two terms (*logic*); an opinion formed; an estimate; discrimination, good taste; a legal verdict or sentence; condemnation, doom; a misfortune thought to be sent as a punishment from God. — *adj* **judgement'al** or **judgment'al** involving judgement; apt to pass judgement. — *n* **judge'ship** the office or function of a judge. — **judge-ad'vocate** the crown-prosecutor at a court-martial. — *adj* **judge'-made** (of law) based on decisions of judges. — **judge'ment-day** (also **Judgment Day**) the day of God's final judgement on mankind; **judge'ment-debt** a debt validated by a legal judgement; **judge'ment-hall** a hall where a court of justice meets; **judge'ment-seat** the seat or bench in a court from which judgement is pronounced; **Judges' Rules** (formerly) in English law, a system of rules governing the behaviour of the police towards suspects, eg the cautioning of a person about to be charged. — **Judge Advocate General** the civil adviser to the crown on military law, *esp* courts-martial: — *pl* **Judge Advocates General** or **Judge Advocate Generals**; **judgement of Solomon** a judgement intended to call the bluff of the false claimant, like that of Solomon in 1 Kings 3. 16–28; **judgement reserved** a decision delayed after the close of a trial (in Scotland, 'avizandum made'); **judgement respited** execution of sentence delayed. [Anglo-Fr *juger*, from L *jūdicāre*, from *jūs* law, and *dīcere* to say, to declare]

Judica *jōō'di-kə*, (*Christian relig*) *n* Passion Sunday. [From the opening words of the introit, '*Judica* me, Deus' (43rd Psalm)]

judicature *jōō'di-kə-chər*, *n* the power of dispensing justice by legal trial; jurisdiction; the office of judge; the body of judges; a court or system of courts. — *adj* **ju'dicable** that may be judged or tried. — *n* **judicā'tion** judgement. — *adj* **ju'dicative** having power to judge. — *n* **ju'dicātor** a person who judges. — *n* **ju'dicatory** (*-kə-tər-i*) judicature; a court. — *adj* pertaining to a judge or judgment. [L *jūdicāre*, *-ātum* to judge]

judicial *jōō-dish'əl*, *adj* pertaining to a judge, a court of justice or the administration of justice; established by decision of a court; arising from process of law; having the authority to make judgements; of the nature of judgement; forming or expressing judgement; judge-like, impartial; inclined to pass judgement, critical. — *adj* **judic'ially**. — **judicial astrology** (*hist*) the study of the influence of the planets, etc on human affairs; **judicial combat** trial by battle; **judicial murder** a death sentence which is deemed unjust although passed in accordance with legal procedure; **judicial precedent** the system whereby a court is bound to declare the law in accordance with previous rulings by equivalent or higher courts; **judicial separation** the separation of two married people by order of court; **judicial trustee** (or (*Scot*) **factor**) an administrator appointed by the courts to manage the estate of someone in need of such. — **Judicial Committee of the Privy Council** the final court of appeal for certain Commonwealth countries, and for UK medical tribunals and ecclesiastical courts. [L *jūdiciālis*, from *jūdicium*]

judiciary *jōō-dish'ər-i* or *-i-ər-i*, *adj* pertaining to judgement, judges, or courts of law. — *n* a body of judges; a system of courts. [L *jūdiciārius*]

judicious *jōō-dish'əs*, *adj* according to sound judgement; possessing sound judgement, discreet. — *adv* **judic'iously**. — *n* **judic'iousness**. [Fr *judicieux*, from L *jūdicium*]

judo *jōō'dō*, *n* a sport and physical discipline based upon unarmed self-defence techniques, a modern variety of ju-jitsu. — *n* **judogi** (*jōō'dō-gi* or *-dō'gi*) the costume (jacket and trousers) worn by a **ju'dōist** or **judoka** (*jōō'dō-kə* or *-dō'kə*), a person who practises, or is expert in, judo. [Jap *jiu* gentleness, and *do* way]

Judy *jōō'di*, *n* Punch's wife in the street puppet-show 'Punch and Judy'; a frump, an odd-looking woman (*obs*); (often without *cap*) a girl (*Austr* and *UK slang*). [From the personal name *Judith*]

jug[1] *jug*, *n* a vessel for pouring liquids, *usu* with a spout or lip and a handle; a jugful; a container, *esp* a tankard or glass (of beer, etc). — *vt* to boil or stew in a closed pottery jar, or similar: — *pa t* and *pa p* **jugged**. — *n* **jug'ful** as much as a jug will hold: — *pl* **jug'fuls**. — *n* **jugg'ing**. — *n* **jug'let** (*archaeol*) a small juglike vessel. — **jug band** a band using jugs and other utensils as musical instruments; **jug'-ears** (*derog colloq*) a name for someone with protruding ears; **jugged hare** hare cut in pieces and stewed with wine and other seasoning. [Origin unknown]

jug[2] *jug*, (*slang*) *n* prison. [Cf **jougs**]

jug[3] *jug*, *n* the note or sound of the nightingale. — Also **jug'-jug**. — *vi* to utter the sound. [Imit]

juga. See **jugum**.

jugal *jōō'gəl*, *adj* relating to a yoke, *esp* that of marriage; malar. — *n* the malar bone. [L *jugālis*, from *jugum* a yoke]

Jugarnath. See under **Juggernaut**.

jugate *jōō'gāt*, *adj* paired (*bot*); having the leaflets in pairs (*bot*); side by side or overlapping, like heads shown on a coin, etc. [L *jugāre*, *-ātum* to join, from *jugum* a yoke]

Jugendstil *yōō'gənd-shtēl*, *n* the German term for art nouveau. [Ger *Jugend* youth (the name of a magazine first appearing in 1896), and *Stil* style]

Juggernaut *jug'ər-nöt*, *n* (without *cap*) a very large lorry; (often without *cap*) any relentless destroying force or object of devotion and sacrifice; an incarnation of Vishnu, whose idol at Puri is traditionally drawn on a processional chariot, beneath which devotees were once believed to throw and crush themselves. — Also **Jugannath** (*jug'u-nät*). [Sans *Jagannātha* lord of the world]

juggins *jug'inz*, (*slang*) *n* a simpleton. [Origin unknown]

juggle *jug'l*, *vi* to throw and manipulate balls or other objects in the air with great dexterity (also *fig*); to conjure, practise sleight-of-hand; to perform as an entertainer (*obs*); to practise trickery or deception; to tamper. — *vt* to keep (several different items, activities, etc) in motion, progress or operation simultaneously, *esp* with dexterity; to manipulate or alter by trickery or cheating. — *n* an act of juggling; a fraudulent trick. — *n* **jugg'ler**. — *n* **jugg'lery** (*-lə-ri*) the art or act of a juggler; legerdemain; trickery. — *n* and *adj* **jugg'ling**. — *adv* **jugg'lingly** in a deceptive manner. [OFr *jogler*, from L *joculārī* to jest, from *jocus* a jest]

jughead *jug'hed*, (*US slang*) *n* an idiot, fool, mindless person. [**jug**[1] and **head**]

Juglans *jōō'glanz*, *n* the walnut genus, giving the name to the family **Juglandaceae** (*-glən-dā'si-ē*). — *adj* **juglandaceous** (*-dā'shəs*). [L *jūglāns*, from *Jovis glāns* Jove's acorn]

Jugoslav. Same as **Yugoslav**.

jugular *jug'ū-lər*, also *jōōg'*, *adj* pertaining to the neck or throat; having or denoting ventral fins situated in front of pectoral fins. — *n* one of the large veins on each side of the neck. — *vt* **jug'ūlate** to cut the throat of; to check (a disease, etc) by drastic means. — **go for the jugular** to attack someone at the place at which they are most vulnerable and liable to greatest harm. [L *jugulum* the collar-bone, from *jungere* to join]

jugum *jōō'gəm*, *n* in certain insects, a process on the back edge of the forewing that unites it to the hindwing in flight; a pair of opposite leaves (*bot*): — *pl* **ju'ga**. [L, yoke]

juice *jōōs*, *n* the liquid in fruit and vegetables; the fluid part of animal bodies; characteristic essence, interesting flavour, tasty nourishment (*fig*); vitality, piquancy; electric current, petrol, or other source of power (*slang*); alcoholic drink (*US slang*). — *vt* to squeeze juice from (a fruit); (with *up*) to enliven (*US*). — *adj* **juiced** or **juiced up** (*slang*) drunk. — *adj* **juice'less**. — *n* **juic'er** (*esp US*) a juice extractor. — *n* **juic'iness**. — *adj* **juic'y** full of juice; of popular interest, *esp* of a scandalous or sensational kind; profitable. — **juice extractor** a kitchen appliance for extracting the juice from fruit, etc. — **step on the juice** (*slang*) to accelerate a motorcar. [Fr *jus*]

ju-jitsu or **jiu-jitsu** *jōō-jit'sōō*, *n* a system of fighting without weapons, developed by the samurai in Japan; a martial art founded on it. [Jap *jū-jutsu*]

ju-ju or **juju** *jōō'jōō*, *n* an object of superstitious worship in W Africa; a fetish or charm; the supernatural power or taboo of a ju-ju. [Appar Fr *joujou* a toy]

jujube *jōō'jōōb*, *n* a spiny shrub or small tree (Zizyphus) of the buckthorn family; its dark red fruit, which is dried and eaten as a sweetmeat; a chewy, fruit-flavoured lozenge, sweet or lolly made with sugar and gum or gelatine (also shortened to **jube** (*Austr*). [Fr *jujube* or LL *jujuba*, from Gr *zizyphon*]

juke *jōōk*, (*slang*) *vi* to dance. — **juke'-box** (*orig US*) a slot machine that plays gramophone records; a device that selects computer tapes or optical disks for reading; **juke'-joint** a place for dancing and drinking. [Gullah *juke* disorderly, from W African *dzug* to lead a careless life]

jukskei *yŏŏk'skay*, (*SAfr*) *n* an outdoor game similar to quoits, in which bottle-shaped pegs are thrown at stakes fixed in the ground; one of these pegs. [Afrik *yuk* yoke, and *skei* pin (orig yoke pins were thrown)]

julep *jōō'ləp*, *n* a sweet drink, often medicated; an American drink of spirits, sugar, ice and mint (also **mint-jul'ep**). [Fr, from Sp *julepe*, from Ar *julāb*, from Pers *gulāb*, from *gul* rose, and *āb* water]

Julian *jōōl'yən*, *adj* pertaining to *Julius* Caesar (100–44 BC). — **Julian calendar** that in which a year was set at 365 days with a leap year every 4 years (from which the Gregorian calendar later evolved), instituted by Julius Caesar in 46 BC; **Julian year** see under **year**.

julienne *jōō-li-en'* or *zhü-lyen*, *n* a clear soup, with shredded vegetables; any foodstuff which has been shredded. — *vt* to shred or cut into thin strips. [Fr personal name]

juliet cap *jōō'i-et kap*, *n* a round close-fitting skullcap worn by women. [Prob *Juliet*, in Shakespeare's *Romeo and Juliet*]

July *jōō-lī'*, *n* the seventh month of the year. [L *Jūlius*, from Gaius Julius Caesar, who was born in it]

July-flower. A mistaken form of **gillyflower**.

jumar *jōō'mär*, (*mountaineering*) *n* a clip which grips the rope when weight is applied, and runs freely along the rope when the weight is taken off (also **jumar clamp**); a climb using these. — *vi* to climb using jumars. [Swiss name]

jumart *jōō'märt* or *-mərt*, (*obs*) *n* the supposed offspring of a bull and a mare, or stallion and cow. [Fr]

jumbal or **jumble** *jum'bl*, *n* a thin, crisp, sweet cake, formerly made in the shape of a ring. [Perh **gimmal** or **gimbal**]

jumbie. See **jumby**.

jumble[1] *jum'bl*, *vt* to mix confusedly; to confuse mentally; to throw together without order; to shake up, jolt (*obs*). — *vi* (*obs*) to be mixed together confusedly; to flounder about. — *n* a confused mixture; confusion; things offered for sale at a jumble sale; a jolting. — *n* **jum'bler**. — *adv* **jum'blingly** in a confused or jumbled manner. — *adj* **jum'bly**. — **jumble sale** a sale of miscellaneous articles, second-hand or home-made, etc, to raise money for a charity or other body. [Origin obscure]

jumble[2]. See **jumbal**.

jumbo *jum'bō*, *n* anything very big of its kind; an elephant (after a famous large one so named); a jumbo jet: — *pl* **jum'bos**. — *adj* huge; colossal; extra-large. — *vt* **jum'boize** or **-ise** (*-bō-īz*) to enlarge (a ship) by adding a prefabricated section, eg amidships. — **jumbo jet** a large jet airliner. [Prob mumbo-*jumbo*; earlier than Jumbo the elephant]

jumbuck *jum'buk*, (*Austr colloq*) *n* a sheep. [Origin unknown]

jumby or **jumbie** *jum'bi*, (*W Indian Black*) *n* a ghost or evil spirit. [Kongo *zumbi*; cf **zombie**]

jumelle *jōō-mel'* or *zhü-mel*, *n* a paired or twinned article, *esp* opera-glasses. [Fr, twin; cf **gemel**, **gimmal**]

jumhouriya. See **jamahiriya**.

jump[1] *jump*, *vi* to spring or leap; to move suddenly or quickly; to move with a jerk, to start, eg with fright; (of a parachutist) to leap out of a plane; to bounce; to rise suddenly; to change or move abruptly or out of sequence from one thing, state, etc to another; to throb, flicker; to be lively or exciting; to agree, coincide (*with*). — *vt* to cause or help to leap; to leap over, from, or on to; to skip over; to drive through (a (red) traffic light) (*colloq*); to fall off or out of (rails, a groove, etc); (eg of game) to spring or start; to appropriate (a claim), on the grounds that the owner has failed to satisfy conditions or has abandoned it; to seize suddenly, catch unawares, ambush (*slang*); (of a male) to have sexual intercourse with (*vulg*); to make up hastily (*obs*); to risk (*Shakesp*). — *n* an act of jumping; a bound; an obstacle to be jumped over; a height or distance jumped; a descent by a parachutist; a sudden rise or movement; a jerk or start; (in *pl*) convulsive movements, chorea, delirium tremens, or the like (*slang*); a bounce; an abrupt change; a jump-cut; a branch (*comput*); venture, hazard (*Shakesp*). — *adv* (*Shakesp*) exactly. — *adj* **jump'able**. — *n* **jump'er** a person, animal or thing that jumps; a jump-shot or a player of such (*basketball*); a heavy drill with a jumping motion, used in quarrying, etc; a short section of overhead transmission line conductor forming an electrical connection between two sections of a line (*elec eng*); a multi-core flexible cable connection between the coaches of a multiple-unit train; one of a group of Welsh Methodists (c. 1760) who jumped about in worship. — *adv* **jump'ily**. — *n* **jump'iness**. — *adj* **jump'y** nervy, on edge, liable to jump or start. — **jump'-ball** (*basketball*) a ball thrown up between opposing players by the referee to restart the game; **jump'-cut** (*films*) an abrupt change from one scene or subject to another, across an interval of time. — *adj* **jumped'-up** (*colloq*) upstart. — **jump'ing-bean** the seed of a Mexican euphorbiaceous plant (*esp* genus *Sebastiania*), containing a moth larva which causes it to move or jump; **jump'ing-deer** the black-tailed American deer; **jump'ing-hare** a S African rodent related to the jerboa; **jump'ing-jack** a jointed toy figure whose limbs can be moved by pulling a string; a firework that jumps along the ground; **jump'ing-mouse** a genus (*Zapus*) of jumping rodents; **jump'ing-spider** any member of the spider family *Salticidae* that leap upon their prey; **jump'-jet** a fighter plane able to land and take off vertically; **jump'-jockey** (*horse-racing*) a jockey who rides in steeplechases; **jump leads** two electrical cables for supplying power to start a car from another battery; **jump'-off** (*US*) the start; starting-place; see **jump off** below; **jump'-rope** (*NAm*) a skipping rope; **jump'-seat** a movable seat in a car or aircraft; a carriage with a movable seat (*obs*); a folding seat; **jump'-shot** (*basketball*) a shot at a basket made when the player is in mid-air; **jump suit** a one-piece garment for either sex, combining trousers and jacket or blouse; **jump'-up** (*Caribb*) a social dance. — **for the high jump** see under **high**; **jump at** to accept eagerly; **jump down someone's throat** to berate or snap at someone angrily and suddenly; **jumping-off place** the terminus of a route, a destination; a starting-point; a place from which one sets out into the wilds, the unknown, etc; somewhere very remote (*US*); **jump off** (*showjumping*) to compete in another, more difficult round, when two or more competitors have an equal score after the first round (*n* **jump'-off**); **jump on** to jump so as to come down heavily upon; to censure promptly and vigorously; **jump (one's) bail** to abscond, forfeiting one's bail; **jump ship** (*colloq*) (of a sailor) to leave one's ship while still officially employed, in service, etc; **jump start** to start (a car) by using jump leads; to bump start (a car). — Also *n* **jump'-start**. — **jump the gun** (ie the starting-gun in a race) to get off one's mark too soon, act prematurely, take an unfair advantage; **jump the queue** to get ahead of one's turn (*lit* and *fig*); **jump to conclusions** come to a decision prematurely, based upon insufficient facts or consideration; **jump to it**! hurry!; **one jump ahead of** in a position of advantage over. [Prob onomatopoeic]

jump[2] *jump*, (*obs*) *n* a short coat; (in *pl*) a kind of female under-bodice. [Perh from Fr *juppe*, now *jupe* a petticoat]

jumper *jump'ər*, *n orig* a type of overall, slipped over the head; a knitted upper garment, *orig* one loose at the waist; a pinafore dress (*NAm*). [Prob **jump**[2]]

Jun. *abbrev*: June; Junior.

Juncaceae, juncaceous. See **Juncus**.

juncate (*Spenser*). A variant of **junket**.

junco *jung'kō*, *n* the reed-bunting (*obs*); a N American snow-bird: — *pl* **junc'oes** or **junc'os**. [Sp *junco*, from L *juncus* rush]

junction *jung'shən* or *jungk'shən*, *n* a joining, a union or combination; a place or point where eg roads, railway lines or wires meet; the contact area between semi-conductor material of different electrical properties (*electronics*). — **junction box** a casing for a junction of electrical wires. [L *junctiō*, *-ōnis*; see ety of **join**]

juncture *jungk'chər*, *n* a joining, a union; a critical or important point of time; a feature of pronunciation which marks the beginning or ending of an utterance or the transition between elements within it (*linguistics*). [L *junctūra*; see ety of **join, jointure**]

juncus *jungk'əs*, *n* any plant of the genus *Juncus*, the typical genus of rushes, giving name to the **Juncā'ceae**, the rush family. — *adj* **juncā'ceous**. [L *juncus* a rush]

June *jo͞on*, *n* the sixth month of the year. — **June'berry** the fruit of the shadbush; **June drop** a falling of immature fruit through a variety of causes, at its height around June. [L *Jūnius*]

juneating. An erroneous form of **jenneting**.

Jungermanniales *yo͝ong-ər-man-i-ā'lēz*, (*bot*) *n pl* one of the main divisions of the Hepaticae, with thallus or leafy stem, and *usu* a capsule opening by four valves. [Ludwig *Jungermann* (1572–1653), German botanist]

Jungian *yo͝ong'i-ən*, *adj* of or according to the theories of the Swiss psychologist, Carl Gustav *Jung* (1875–1961).

jungle *jung'gl*, *n* a dense tropical growth of thickets, brushwood, etc; dense tropical forest; a jumbled assemblage of large objects; a confusing mass eg of regulations; a place or situation where there is ruthless competition, or cruel struggle for survival. — *adj* **jungli** (*jung'gli*; *Ind*) inhabiting a jungle; wild and boorish. — *n* an inhabitant of a jungle; an uneducated peasant. — *adj* **jung'ly**. — **jungle fever** a severe malarial fever; **jungle fowl** any of several Asiatic fowl of the genus *Gallus*, thought to be the wild ancestor of the domestic fowl; the mound-bird (*Austr*). — *adj* **jun'gle-green** very dark green. — **jungle gym** (*US*) a climbing-frame; **jungle juice** (*slang*) alcoholic liquor, *esp* if very strong, of poor quality, or home-made. [Hindi *jangal* waste ground, Sans *jāngala* desert]

junior *jo͞on'yər*, *adj* younger; less advanced; of lower standing; (of a product) smaller (and often simpler) than the standard; (of boxing weights) lighter than the standard for that weight. — *n* someone younger, less advanced, or of lower standing; (often with *cap*) the young boy in a family (*US*); a bridge-player on the declarer's right; an American student in his or her third year (of four); a British junior school-pupil. — *n* **juniority** (*-i-or'i-ti*). — **junior college** (*NAm*) a college offering only (the first) two years of a university education; **junior common room** or (*Cambridge*) **junior combination room** (*abbrev* **JCR**) in some universities, a common room for the use of (*esp* undergraduate) students, as opposed to a *senior common* or *combination room* for the use of staff and sometimes also a *middle common* or *combination room* for postgraduates; **junior high school** or **junior high** (*NAm*) a school between elementary and senior high, for 12- to 14-year-olds; **junior miss** (*fashion*) a (clothing size or range suitable for the) teenage girl or young woman; **junior optime** see **optime**; **junior school** (*UK*) a school for 7- to 11-year-olds; **junior service** the Army; **junior soph** a second-year undergraduate at Cambridge (*hist*). [L *jūnior*, compar of *juvenis* young]

juniper *jo͞o'ni-pər*, *n* an evergreen coniferous shrub (genus *Juniperus*) whose berries are used in making gin; any of various other coniferous trees, or, in the Bible, other shrubs. [L *jūniperus*]

junk[1] *jungk*, *n* an E Asian flat-bottomed sailing vessel, with high forecastle and poop, and large squarish sails internally supported by battens. [Port *junco*, appar from Javanese *djong*]

junk[2] *jungk*, *n* rubbish generally; nonsense; a narcotic, *esp* heroin (*slang*); an old or useless piece of rope (*archaic*); a chunk; salt meat, *perh* because it becomes as hard as old rope (*obs*; *orig naut*). — *vt* to treat as junk; to discard or abandon as useless (*slang*); to cut into junks. — *n* **junk'er** (*US obs*), **junk'ie** or **junk'y** a narcotics addict (*colloq*); (**junkie** or **junky**; loosely) someone hooked on something, an addict (*colloq usu* as *combining form*, as in *art junkie*, *coffee junkie*). — *n* **junk'iness**. — *adj* **junk'y** rubbishy; worthless. — **junk bond** a bond offering a high yield but with high risk; **junk'-bottle** (*US*) a thick strong bottle of green or black glass; **junk'-dealer** or **junk'man** a dealer in junk; **junk fax** unsolicited material (as **junk mail**) sent by fax; **junk food** food of little nutritional value, *usu* easily available and quick to prepare; **junk jewellery** fun jewellery, of little value but often quite showy; **junk mail** unsolicited mail such as advertising circulars, etc; **junk'-ring** a metal ring confining the packing of a piston; **junk'-shop** a shop where assorted second-hand bric-à-brac is sold; **junk'-yard** a yard in which junk is stored or collected for sale. [Origin obscure]

junkanoo. See **John Canoe**.

Junker *yo͝ongk'ər*, *n* a young German noble or squire; an overbearing, narrow-minded, reactionary aristocrat. — *n* **Junk'erdom**. — *n* **Junk'erism**. [Ger, from *jung* young, and *Herr* lord]

junker. See **junk**[2].

junket *junk'it*, *n* curds mixed with cream, sweetened and flavoured; a feast or merrymaking, a picnic, an outing, a spree, now (*esp NAm*) one enjoyed by officials using public funds; a cream cheese; any sweetmeat or delicacy (*obs*); a rush-basket (*dialect*). — *vi* to feast, banquet, or take part in a convivial entertainment or spree; to go on a junket (chiefly *NAm*). — *vt* to feast, regale, entertain: — *pr p* **junk'eting**; *pa p* **junk'eted**. — *n* **junketeer'**. — *n* (often in *pl*) **junk'eting** merry feast or entertainment, picnicking. [Anglo-Fr *jonquette* rush-basket, from L *juncus* a rush]

junkie, junky. See **junk**[2].

Juno *jo͞o'nō*, *n* the wife of Jupiter, identified with the Greek Hera, special protectress of marriage and guardian of women (*Roman mythol*); a queenly woman. — *adj* **Junō'nian** pertaining to Juno. — *adj* **Junoesque** (*-esk'*; of a woman) large, buxom, and (*usu*) beautiful. [L *Jūnō*, *-ōnis*]

junta *jun'tə* or *ho͝on'ta*, *n* a government formed by a *usu* small group of military officers following a coup d'état; a meeting or council; a Spanish grand council of state; (in the following meanings also **junto**, *pl* **jun'tos**) a body of men joined or united for some secret intrigue, a confederacy, a cabal or faction. [Sp, from L *jungere*, *junctum* to join]

jupati *jo͞o'pə-tē* or *-tē'*, *n* a species of raphia palm. [Tupí]

Jupiter *jo͞o'pi-tər*, *n* the chief god, the counterpart of the Greek Zeus (also **Jove**; *Roman mythol*); the largest and, next to Venus, the brightest of the planets, fifth in outward order from the sun. — **Jupiter's beard** the house-leek; a kidney-vetch; a fungus (*Hydnum barba-jovis*). [L *Jūpiter*, *Juppiter* Father (*pater*) Jove]

jupon *jo͞o'pən*, *n* a sleeveless jacket or close-fitting coat, extending down over the hips (*hist*); a petticoat. [Fr]

jura. See **jus**[1].

Jura. See **Jurassic**.

jural *jo͞o'rəl*, *adj* pertaining to law; pertaining to rights and obligations. — *adv* **ju'rally**. [L *jūs*, *jūris* law]

jurant *jo͞o'rənt*, *adj* taking an oath. — *n* someone who takes an oath. — *adj* **ju'ratory** pertaining to an oath. [L *jūrāre*, *-ātum* to swear]

Jurassic *jo͞o-ras'ik*, (*geol*) *adj* of the middle division of the Mesozoic rocks, well developed in the *Jura* Mountains. — *n* the Jurassic period or system. — Also **Ju'ra**. [Fr *jurassique*, from *Jura*]

jurat[1] *jo͞o'rat*, (*law*) *n* the official memorandum at the end of an affidavit, showing the time when and the person before whom it was sworn. [L *jūrātum* sworn, from *jūrāre* to swear]

jurat[2] *jo͞o'rat*, *n* a sworn officer, *esp* (*Fr* and *Channel Is*) a magistrate. [Fr, from Med L *jūrātus* a sworn man, from L *jūrāre* to swear]

juratory. See **jurant**.

jure *jo͞o'rē* or *yo͞o're*, (*L*) *adv* by law. — **jure divino** (*di-vī'nō* or *dē-wē'nō*) by divine law; **jure humano** (*hū-mā'nō* or (*h*)*o͞o-mä'nō*) *by human law*. [Cf **iure**]

juridical *jo͞o-rid'ik-əl* or **juridic** *-rid'ik*, *adj* relating to the administration of justice; pertaining to a judge; used in courts of law. — *adv* **jurid'ically**. — **juridical days** days on which law courts are in session. [L *jūridicus*, from *jūs*, *jūris* law, and *dīcere* to declare]

jurisconsult *jo͞oris-kon-sult'*, *n* someone who is consulted on the law; a lawyer who gives opinions on cases put to him or her; a person knowledgeable in law. [L *jūris consultus*, from *jūs*, *jūris* law, and *consulere*, *consultum* to consult]

jurisdiction *jo͞o-ris-dik'shən*, *n* the distribution of justice; legal authority; extent of power; the district over which any authority extends. — *adj* **jurisdic'tional** or **juris-dic'tive**. [L *jūrisdictiō*, *-ōnis*]

jurisprudence *jo͞o-ris-pro͞o'dəns*, *n* knowledge of law; the science or philosophy of law; a body or branch of law. — *adj* **jurispru'dent** knowledgeable in jurisprudence. — *n* a person who is knowledgeable in jurisprudence. — *adj* **jurisprudential** (*-den'shl*). — **medical jurisprudence** forensic medicine (see **forensic**). [L *jūrisprūdentia*, from *jūs*, *jūris* law, and *prūdentia* knowledge]

jurist *jo͞o'rist*, *n* a person versed in the science of law, *esp* Roman or civil law; a student or graduate of law; a lawyer (*US*). — *adj* **jurist'ic** or **jurist'ical**. — *adv* **jurist'ically**. [Fr *juriste*]

juris utriusque doctor *jo͞o'ris ū-tri-us'kwē* (or *yo͞o'ris o͝o-tri-o͝os'kwe*) *dok'tör*, (*L*) doctor both of canon and of civil law.

jury *jo͞o'ri*, *n* a group of people sworn to reach a just verdict on the basis of the evidence before them; a committee of adjudicators or examiners. — *n* **ju'ror** a person who serves on a jury (also **ju'ryman** and **ju'rywoman**: — *pl* **ju'rymen** and **ju'rywomen**). — **ju'ry-box** the place in court in which the jury sits during a trial; **jury duty**; **jury-pro'cess** a writ summoning a jury; **jury room** the room in which the jury deliberates and comes to a verdict; **jury service**. — **jury of matrons** (*obs*) a jury of women empanelled to give a decision in a case of alleged pregnancy. [Anglo-Fr *juree*, from *jurer*, from L *jūrāre* to swear]

jurymast *jo͞o'ri-mäst* or *-məst*, (*naut*) *n* a temporary mast raised instead of one lost. — *n* **jury rig** a temporary, makeshift rig. — *adj* **ju'ry-rigged** rigged in a temporary way. — **ju'ry-rudder** a temporary replacement rudder. [Not *injury-mast*, but perh OFr *ajurie* aid, from L *adjūtāre* to aid]

jus[1] *jus* or *yo͞os*, (*L*) *n* law; a legal right: — *pl* **jura** (*jo͞o'rə* or *yo͞o'ra*). — **jus canonicum** (*kə-non'i-kəm* or *ka-non'iko͞om*) canon law; **jus civile** (*si-vī'lē*, *kē-wē'le* or *-vē'*) civil law; **jus divinum** (*di-vī'nəm*, *di-wē'no͞om* or *-vē'*) divine right; **jus gentium** (*jen'shi-əm* or *gen'ti-o͞om*) law of nations; **jus mariti** (*ma'ri-tī* or *-rē'tē*) the right of a husband; **jus naturale** (*nat-ū-rā'lē* or *nat-o͞o-rä'le*) natural law; the fundamental shared human conception of what constitutes justice; **jus primae noctis** (*prī'mē* or *prē'mī*, *nok'tis*) the formerly alleged right of a feudal superior to take the virginity of a vassal's bride; **jus sanguinis** (*sang'gwi-nis*) the principle that a person's nationality is that of their natural parents; **jus soli** (*sō'lī* or *sō'lē*) the principle that a person's nationality is that of the country in which they were born.

jus[2] *zhüs*, or (*Fr*) *zhü*, (*cookery*) *n* juice; gravy. [Fr]

jusqu'au bout *zhüs-kō bo͞o*, (*Fr*) to the very end. — *n* **jusqu'auboutisme** (*-tēz-m'*) the practice of carrying on to the bitter end. — *n* **jusqu'auboutiste** (*-tēst*; also anglicized as **jusqu'aubou'tist** *bo͞o'tist*).

jussive *jus'iv*, (*gram*) *adj* expressing a command. — *n* a grammatical form or construction expressing a command. [L *jubēre*, *jussum* to command]

just[1] *just*. See **joust**.

just[2] *just*, *adj* righteous (*Bible*); fair, impartial; according to justice; due, deserved; in accordance with facts, valid; well-grounded; accurately true; exact; normal (*obs*); close-fitting (*obs*). — *adv* precisely, exactly; so much and no more; barely; barely a moment ago; at this very moment; only, merely; quite, absolutely, indeed (*colloq*). — *adv* **just'ly** in a just manner; equitably; accurately; by right. — *n* **just'ness** equity; fittingness; exactness. — **just intonation** (*music*) observance of the true mathematical theoretical pitch, without compromise or temperament. — **just about** nearly; more or less; **just about to** see **about to** under **about**; **just now** precisely at this moment; a little while ago; very soon; **just so** exactly, I agree; in a precise, neat manner. [Fr *juste*, or L *justus*, from *jūs* law]

juste milieu *zhüst mēl-yø*, (*Fr*) *n* the just mean, the happy medium.

justice *jus'tis*, *n* the quality of being just; integrity; impartiality; rightness; the awarding of what is due; the administration of law; a judge; a magistrate. — *n* **jus'ticer** (*obs*) a maintainer or administrator of justice. — *n* **jus'ticeship** the office or dignity of a justice. — *adj* **justiciable** (*jus-tish'i-ə-bl*) liable to trial. — *n* **justiciar** (*-tish'i-ər*; *hist*) a judge or administrator of justice; a supreme judge. — *n* **justiciary** (*-tish'i-ə-ri*) a justiciar (*hist*); the jurisdiction of a justiciar (*Scot*). — *adj* pertaining to the administration of justice. — **justices' justice** (*ironic*) the (unsatisfactory) kind of justice to be expected from the unpaid and amateur magistracy of England. — **bring to justice** to bring to trial and (*usu*) to punish (someone believed to be guilty); **chief justice** in the Commonwealth, a judge presiding over a supreme court; in the US, a judge who is chairman of a group of judges in a court; **do justice to** to give full advantage to; to treat fairly; to appreciate (a meal, etc) fully by eating heartily (*colloq*); **do oneself justice** to show one's abilities to best advantage; **European Court of Justice** an EC institution whose function is to ensure that the laws embodied in the EC treaties are observed, and to rule on alleged infringements; **High Court of Justice** a section of the English Supreme Court, comprising Chancery and Queen's (or King's) Bench Divisions; **High Court of Justiciary** the supreme criminal court in Scotland; **Justice of the Peace** (*abbrev* **JP**) a person commissioned to perform certain minor judicial and other functions within a specified locality, in England and Wales (but not in Scotland) called a magistrate; **Lord Chief Justice** the chief judge of the Queen's (or King's) Bench Division of the High Court of Justice; **Lord Justice-Clerk** the Scottish judge ranking next to the Lord Justice-General, presiding over the Second Division of the Inner House of the Court of Session, vice-president of the High Court of Justiciary; **Lord Justice-General** the highest criminal judge in Scotland, called also the Lord President of the Court of Session. [Fr, from L *justitia*]

Justicialism *jus-tish'əl-izm*, *n* (also without *cap*) the political ideology of Juan Domingo Perón (1895–1974), President of Argentina, which combined Fascism and Socialism. [Sp *justicialismo*, from *justicia* justice]

justify *jus'ti-fī*, *vt* to prove or show to be just, right or reasonable; to vindicate; to show adequate reason or grounds for (one's action) (*law*); to absolve; to punish, *esp* to hang (*obs*); to adjust by spacing to fill the required line length and to form an even right margin (*printing*; *comput*): — *pr p* **jus'tifying**; *pa t* and *pa p* **jus'tified**. — *n* **justifiabil'ity**. — *adj* **jus'tifiable** (or *-fī'*) that may be justified or defended. — *n* **jus'tifiableness** (or -*fī'*). — *adv* **jus'tifiably** (or -*fī'*). — *n* **justification** (*jus-ti-fi-kā'shən*) the act of justifying; something which justifies; vindication; absolution; a plea showing sufficient reason for an action (*law*). — *adj* **jus'tificātive** or **justificatory** (*jus-tif'i-kə-tə-ri* or *jus'ti-fi-kā-tə-ri*, or -*kā'*) having power to justify. — *n* **jus'tificātor** or **jus'tifier** a person who defends or vindicates; a person who pardons and absolves from guilt and punishment. — **justifiable homicide** the killing of a person in execution of sentence of death, in self-defence, or to prevent an atrocious crime. — **justification by faith** the doctrine that mankind is absolved from sin by faith in Christ. [Fr *justifier* and LL *jūstificāre*, from *justus* just, and *facere* to make]

just-in-time *just-in-tīm'*, (*business*) *n* a method of stock control in which little or no warehoused stock is kept at the production site, supplies being produced and delivered just in time for use. — Also *adj*.

justle. See **jostle**.

jut *jut*, *vi* to project or protrude from the main body, *esp* sharply: — *pr p* **jutt'ing**; *pa t* and *pa p* **jutt'ed**. — *n* a projection; a jerking movement (*obs*). — *adj* **jutt'ing**. — *adv* **jutt'ingly**. — **jut'-window** a bay window. [A variant of **jet**[2]]

Jute *jōōt*, (*hist*) *n* a member of a Germanic people *orig* from Jutland, who with the Angles and Saxons invaded Britain in the 5c. [ME, from LL *Jutae* Jutes]

jute *jōōt*, *n* the fibre of *Corchorus capsularis* or *C. olitorius* (family Tiliaceae), plants of Bangladesh, etc, used for making sacks, mats, etc; the plant itself. — Also *adj*. — **China jute** a species of Abutilon; its fibre. [Bengali *jhūṭo*, from Sans *jūṭa* matted hair]

jutty *jut'i*, *n* a projecting part of a wall; a pier, a jetty. — *vt* (*Shakesp*) to project beyond. — *vi* (*archaic*) to jut. [Cf **jetty**]

juv. *abbrev*: juvenile.

juve *jōōv*, (*theat*) *n* a juvenile lead. — Also **juve lead**.

juvenal[1] *jōō'vən-əl*, (*Shakesp*) *n* a youth. [L *juvenālis* belonging to youth, from *juvenis* young]

juvenal[2]. See **juvenile**.

Juvenalian *jōōv-i-nā'li-ən*, *adj* of the Roman satirist *Juvenal* (Decimus Junius Juvenalis, 1c-2c AD); bitterly sarcastic and denunciatory rather than humorous.

juvenescent *jōō-vən-es'ənt*, *adj* becoming youthful. — *n* **juvenesc'ence**. [L *juvenēscere* to grow young]

juvenile *jōō'və-nīl*, *adj* young; pertaining or suited to youth or young people; having or retaining characteristics of youth; childish; (of plants and animals) immature; (of a bird) having its first plumage of true feathers but sexually immature. — Also (*NAm*) **ju'venal** of the plumage of such a bird; originating beneath the surface of a planet, *esp* Earth, and now appearing at the surface for the first time (*geol*). — *n* a young person, *esp* (*law*) one under the age of seventeen; a book written for the young; an actor who plays youthful parts. — *adv* **ju'venilely**. — *n* **ju'venileness**. — *n pl* **juvenilia** (-*il'yə*) writings or works produced in the childhood or youth of the author, artist, etc. — *n* **juvenility** (-*il'i-ti*) juvenile character; juveniles as a group; (in *pl*) juvenile behaviour. — **juvenile court** a special court for the trial of children and young persons aged under seventeen; **juvenile delinquency** criminal or antisocial behaviour by a juvenile; **juvenile delinquent** or **juvenile offender** a young law-breaker, in the UK under the age of seventeen; **juvenile hormone** a hormone necessary to an insect in immature stages, which must be absent when it changes to adult form. [L *juvenīlis*, from *juvenis* young]

juxtaposition *juks-tə-pə-zish'ən*, *n* a placing or being placed close together. — *vt* **jux'tapose** (or -*pōz'*) to place side by side. — *adj* **juxtaposi'tional**. — **juxtaposition twins** (*mineralogy*) crystals joined together face to face without interpenetration. [L *juxtā* near, and **position**, **pose**[1]]

Jy *abbrev*: jansky (*astron*); July.

jymold. See **gimmal**.

Jynx *jingks*, (*obs*) *n* the wryneck genus; (without *cap*) a wryneck. [L *iynx*, from Gr *iynx* or *īynx*]

K

K or **k** *kā*, *n* the eleventh letter in the modern English alphabet, derived from Greek kappa, representing a back voiceless stop, formed by raising the back of the tongue to the soft palate. — **the five Ks** the symbols of a Sikh's spiritual and cultural allegiance to Sikhism (**kaccha**, **kangha**, **kara**, **kesh** and **kirpan**), worn by baptized Sikhs.

K or **K.** *abbrev*: Kampuchea (IVR); kaon (*phys*); kelvin, (a degree on) the Kelvin scale; kina (Papua New Guinea currency); king (*cards* and *chess*); Kirkpatrick (catalogue of Domenico Scarlatti's works); knight; Köchel (catalogue of Mozart's works); krona (Swedish currency); króna (Icelandic currency); krone (Danish and Norwegian currency); kwacha (Zambian currency).

K *symbol*: *kalium* (L), potassium (*chem*); a thousand; a unit of 1024 words, bytes or bits (*comput*); as a medieval numeral, 250.

k or **k.** *abbrev*: karat or carat; kilo or kilo-.

k symbol: Boltzmann constant (*phys*); velocity constant (*chem*).

ka[1] *kä*, (*ancient Egyp relig*) *n* the spirit or soul within a person, a god, or a statue of a dead person. [Egyp]

ka[2] or **kae** *kā*, (*obs*) *vt* serve (in the phrase *ka me, ka thee* one good turn deserves another). [Origin unknown]

ka[3]. See **kae**[1].

Kaaba *kä'bə*, *n* the cube-shaped holy building at Mecca into which the Black Stone is built, which Muslims face towards when they pray. [Ar *ka'bah*, from *ka'b* cube]

kaama *kä'mə*, *n* the hartebeest. [Of Hottentot or Bantu origin]

kabab. See **kebab**.

kabaddi *ka-bä'di*, *n* an *orig* Asian version of tag played barefoot by two teams of seven, in which the players in turn make 'raids' into the opposing team's court, ie, for as long as they can hold their breath while chanting 'kabaddi', they try to touch a member of the opposing team and escape to safety without being captured.

kabala. See **cabbala**.

kabaya *kä-bä'yə*, *n* a loose tunic. [Malay, from Pers or Ar]

kabbala, kabbalah. See **cabbala**.

kabele. See **kebele**.

kabeljou or **kabeljouw** *kob'* or *kub'l-yō*, *n* a large S African fish, *Johnius hololepidotus*. [Afrik]

kabob. See **kebab**.

kabuki *kä-bōō-kē'* or *-bōō'kē*, *n* a popular, traditional, stylized form of Japanese drama, with singing and dancing, in which men play all the roles. [Jap, from *ka* song, *bu* dance, and *ki* skill]

Kabyle *ka-bīl'*, *n* one of a branch of the great Berber people of N Africa; a dialect of Berber. [Fr, from Ar *qabā'il*, pl of *qabīlah* a tribe]

kaccha *kuch'ə*, *n* the short trousers traditionally worn by Sikhs. [Punjabi]

kacha or **kachcha**. Same as **cutcha**.

kachahri or **kacheri** *kuch'ə-ri* or *kuch-er'i*, *n* an Indian magistrate's office or courthouse. — Also **cutcherr'y**. [Hindi *kachahrī*]

kachina *kə-chē'nə*, *n* any of the ancestral spirits invoked by the Pueblo Indians of N America at ritual ceremonies; a dancer who impersonates the ancestral spirits at these ceremonies. — **kachina doll** a doll representing a kachina given to children by the dancers at these ceremonies. [Hopi *qachina* supernatural]

kack-handed. See **cack-handed**.

Kaddish *kad'ish*, (*Judaism*) *n* a liturgical prayer used during the mourning period. — **say Kaddish** to be a mourner. [Aramaic *qaddīsh*]

kade. See **ked**.

kadi *kä'di*, *n*. Same as **cadi**.

kae[1] *kā*, (*Scot*) *n* a jackdaw. — Also **ka**. [Cf MDu *ka*, Dan *kaa*]

kae[2]. See **ka**[2].

Kaffir or **Kaffer** *kaf'ər* or *kuf'ər*, *n* a black African (*SAfr*; *offensive*) a name applied to certain indigenous peoples of S Africa including the Xhosa, and to the languages spoken by them (*hist*); (in *pl*) S African mining shares (*stock exchange slang*). — Also (*formerly*) **Caffre** or **Kafir** (*ka'* or *kä'fər*). — Also *adj*. — **kaff'ir-boom** (Du *boom* tree) the coral-tree (*Erythrina caffra*); **kaffir bread** the pith of S African cycads (*Encephalartos*); **kaffir corn** sorghum. **[Kafir]**

kaffiyeh *käf-ē'ye*, **keffiyeh** or **kufiyah** *kə-fē'yə*, *n* an Arab headdress of cloth, folded and held by a cord around the head. [Ar *kaffīyah*]

kafila. See **cafila**.

Kafir *käf'ər*, *n* an infidel (*offensive*); a native of Kafiristan (in Afghanistan; also **Caffre**); a Kaffir. [Ar *kāfir* unbeliever]

Kafkaesque *kaf-kə-esk'*, *adj* in the style of, or reminiscent of, the ideas, work, etc of the Czech novelist Franz *Kafka* (1883–1924), *esp* in his vision of man's isolated existence in a dehumanized world.

kaftan. Same as **caftan**.

kago *käg'ō*, *n* a Japanese basketwork palanquin: — *pl* **kag'os**. [Jap]

kagool, kagoul, kagoule. See **cagoul**.

kahal *kä'hal*, *n* any of the Jewish communities scattered across Europe; the local governing body of any of these communities. [Heb *kāhal* congregation, community]

kahawai *ka'ha-wī* (*Austr* and *NZ*) *n* a large marine fish (*Arripis trutta*) of the perch family but resembling a salmon. [Maori]

kai *kä'ē* or *kī*, (*NZ*, etc) *n* food; a meal. — *n* **kai'kai** food; a feast. [Maori; also in other Polynesian languages]

kaiak. Same as **kayak**.

kaid *kä-ēd'* or *kād*, *n* a N African chief. [Ar *qā'īd*; cf **alcaide**]

kaie *kā*, an obsolete form of **key**[1,2].

kaif. See **kef**.

kail[1] *kāl*, *n* a ninepin; (in *pl*) the game of ninepins; (in *pl*) skittles. [Cf Du *kegel*, Ger *Kegel*, Fr *quille*]

kail[2], **kaim**. See **kale, kame**.

kaimakam *kī-mä-käm'*, *n* a Turkish lieutenant-colonel or lieutenant-governor. [Turk *kaymakam*, from Ar *qā'i-maqām*]

kain. See **cain**.

kainite *kī'nīt*, *kā'nīt* or *kä'in-īt*, *n* hydrous magnesium sulphate with potassium chloride, found in salt deposits, used as a fertilizer. [Ger *Kainit*, from Gr *kainos* new, recent]

kainogenesis. See **caenogenesis**.

Kainozoic. Same as **Cainozoic**.

kaisar-i-Hind *kī'sär-i-hind'*, *n* title from 1876 to 1947 of the British monarch as emperor of India. [Pers *qaysari-Hind*, from L *Caesar*]

kaiser *kī'zər*, *n* an emperor, *esp* a German emperor. — Also (*obs*) **kesar** or **keasar** (*kē'zər*). — *n* **kai'serdom**. — *n* **kai'serin** the wife of a kaiser. — *n* **kai'serism**. — *n* **kai'sership**. — **the Kaiser's war** the war of 1914–18 (Kaiser Wilhelm II). [Ger, from L *Caesar*]

kajawah *kä-jä'wä*, *n* a camel saddle or pannier. [Pers]

kaka *kä'kə*, *n* a green New Zealand parrot (*Nestor meridionalis*). — *n* **kaka beak** or **bill** the New Zealand glory-pea (*Clianthus*). — *n* **ka'kapō** the rare New Zealand owl-parrot, nocturnal and flightless: — *pl* **ka'kapōs**. [Maori *kaka* parrot, and *po* night]

kakemono *kak-i-mō'nō*, *n* a Japanese wall-picture or calligraphic inscription on a roller: — *pl* **kakemō'nos**. [Jap *kake* to hang, and *mono* thing]

kaki *kä'kē*, *n* the Japanese persimmon, or Chinese date-plum. [Jap]

kakiemon *kä-ki-ā'mon*, *n* a Japanese porcelain, first made by Sakaida *Kakiemon* in the 17c, recognizable from its characteristic use of iron-red.

kakistocracy *kak-is-tok'rə-si*, *n* government by the worst. [Gr *kakistos*, superl of *kakos* bad, and *kratos* power]

kakodyl. Same as **cacodyl**.

kala-azar *kä'lä-ä-zär'*, *n* an often fatal tropical fever, characterized by acute anaemia, etc, caused by a protozoan parasite and *usu* transmitted by sandfly bites. [Assamese *kālā* black, and *āzār* disease]

Kalamazoo® system *ka-lə-mə-zoo' sis'təm*, *n* a book-keeping system which uses simultaneous recording, with different forms placed on top of each other interleaved with carbon sheets.

kalamdan *kal'am-dan*, *n* a Persian writing-case. [Pers *qalamdān*, from *qalam* a pen, and *dān* holding]

kalamkari *kal-am-kä'rē*, *n* a method of colouring and decorating by several dyeings or printings; a chintz fabric treated in this way. [Pers *qalamkārī* writing, painting, etc, from *qalam* pen]

kalanchoe *kal-ən-kō'ē*, *n* a succulent plant which bears red, yellow or pink clusters on long stems. [Fr, from Mandarin]

kalashnikov *kə-lash'ni-kof*, *n* a sub-machine gun made in the former USSR. [Russ]

kale or **kail** *kāl*, *n* a variety of cabbage with open curled leaves; cabbage generally; broth of which kale is a chief ingredient, *hence* a meal, dinner (*Scot*); money (*US slang*). — *n* **kail'-pot** (*Scot* **-pat'**); **kail'-runt** a cabbage stem; **kail'yard** or (*Scot*) **-yaird** a cabbage-patch, kitchen garden; **Kailyard school** a late 19c to early 20c group of Scottish writers of sentimental stories (one of whom, Ian Maclaren, used the title *Beside the Bonnie Brier Bush*, 1894, in allusion to the Jacobite song 'There grows a bonnie brier bush in our kailyard'). — **give someone his kale through the reek** (*Scot*) to reprimand someone severely. [Northern form of **cole**]

kaleidophone *kə-lī'də-fōn*, *n* an instrument for demonstrating sound waves by lines of light on a screen. [Gr *kalos* beautiful, *eidos* form, and *phōnē* voice]

kaleidoscope *kə-lī'də-skōp*, *n* an optical toy in which one sees an ever-changing variety of beautiful colours and forms; a delightfully diverse and unpredictable sequence of sights, events, etc. — *adj* **kaleidoscopic** (*-skop'ik*) pertaining to a kaleidoscope; showing constant change. — *adv* **kaleidoscop'ically**. [Gr *kalos* beautiful, *eidos* form, and *skopeein* to look]

kalendar, kalends. Same as **calendar, calends**.

Kalevala *kä'le-vä-lə*, *n* the great Finnish epic, in eight-syllabled trochaic verse (from which Longfellow's *Hiawatha* is imitated) pieced together from oral tradition by Dr Elias Lönnrot from 1835–49. [Finnish *kaleva* a hero, and *-la* denoting place]

Kali *kä'lē*, *n* a Hindu goddess, Durga, wife of Siva, as goddess of destruction. [Sans]

kali[1] *kal'i* or *kā'lī*, *n* the prickly saltwort or glasswort (*Salsola kali*); its ash (*obs*); an alkali, *esp* potash (*obs*). — *n* **kalinite** (*kal'in-īt*) native potash alum. — *n* **kā'lium** potassium. [Ar *qili*, as in root of **alkali**]

kali[2] *kä'lē*, *n* a carpet with long nap; the large carpet covering the centre of a Persian room. [Pers *kālī*]

kalian *käl'yän'*, *n* a Persian hookah. [Pers]

kalif. See **caliph**.

Kaliyuga *käl-i-yoo'gə*, (*Hindu mythol*) *n* the present (fourth) age of the world, of universal degeneracy. [Sans]

Kallima *kal'i-mə*, *n* an Oriental genus of butterflies, mimicking dead leaves. [Gr *kallimos* beautiful]

kallitype *kal'i-tīp*, *n* a former photographic process in which ferric salts are reduced to ferrous salts. [Gr *kallos* beauty, and *typos* type]

kalmia *kal'mi-ə*, *n* any shrub of the N American *Kalmia* genus of evergreen shrubs of the heath family, including the mountain laurel or calico-bush. [From Peter *Kalm* (1715–79), pupil of Linnaeus]

Kalmuck *kal'muk*, *n* a member of a Mongolian race in China and Russia; their language. — Also *adj*. — Also **Cal'muck**. [Turki and Russ]

kalong *kä'long*, *n* a large fruit-bat. [Malay *kālong*]

kalotype. Same as **calotype**.

kalpa *kal'pə*, (*Hinduism*) *n* a day of Brahma, a period of 4320 million years. — Also **cal'pa**. [Sans, formation]

kalpak *käl'päk* or *-päk'*, *n* a triangular Turkish or Tatar felt cap. — Also **calpac** or **calpack**. [Turk *kālpāk*]

kalpis *kal'pis*, *n* a water-jar. [Gr]

kalsomine® or **calcimine** *kal'sə-mīn* or *-min*, *n* a kind of whitewash or colour wash for walls. — *vt* to cover with kalsomine. [From L *calx*, *calcis* lime]

kalumpit *kä-loom-pēt'*, *n* a Philippine tree of the myrobalan genus; its edible fruit. [Tagálog]

kalyptra *ka-lip'trə*, *n* a veil worn by Greek women. [Gr; see also **calyptra**]

kam, kamme or **cam** *kam*, (*Shakesp*) *adj* and *adv* awry. [Cf Welsh, Gaelic and Ir *cam*]

Kama *kä'mä*, (*Hinduism*) *n* the god of love in the Puranas; (without *cap*) earthly desire. — Also **Ca'ma** or **Ka'madeva** (*-dā-vä*). [Sans *Kāma*]

kamacite *kam'ə-sīt*, *n* a variety of nickeliferous iron, found in meteorites. [Ger *Kamacit* (obs), from Gr *kamax*, *kamakos* vine-pole, shaft]

kamala *kä'mä-lä*, *n* an orange dyestuff obtained from the fruit-hairs of an E Indian tree of the spurge family (*Mallotus philippinensis*); the tree itself. — Also **kamela** or **kamila** (*kä-mā'lä* or *-mē'lä*). [Sans *kamala*; Hindi *kamēlā*, *kamīlā*]

Kamasutra or **Kama Sutra** *kä-mə-soo'trə*, *n* an ancient Sanskrit text on sexual love. [Sans, from *kama* love, and *sūtra* a string, rule]

kame or **kaim** *kām*, *n* a comb (*Scot*); a steep irregular ridge like a cock's comb; an esker, a bank or ridge of gravel, sand, etc, eg as associated with the glacial deposits of Scotland (*geol*); a fortified site (*Scott*). [Northern form of **comb**[1]]

kamees *ka-mēs'*. Same as **camise**.

kameez *kə-mēz'*, *n* (in S Asia) a loose tunic with tight sleeves, worn by women. — See also **shalwar-kameez** under **shalwar**. [Urdu *kamis*, from Ar *qamīs* (see **camise**)]

kamela. See **kamala**.

kamelaukion *ka-me-lö'ki-ən*, *n* the tall cylindrical hat worn by Orthodox priests. [Mod Gr]

kamerad *kam-ər-äd'*, *interj* a German shout of surrender. — *vi* to surrender. [Ger, comrade, from Fr *camarade*]

kami *kä'mi*, (*Jap*) *n* a lord; a divine being or object of worship (*Shinto*). [Jap, superior, lord, god]

kamichi *kä'mē-shē*, *n* the horned screamer, a S American bird. [Fr, from Carib]

kamik *kä'mik*, *n* a knee-length sealskin boot. [Eskimo]

kamikaze *kä-mi-kä'zē*, *n* (a Japanese airman, or plane, making) a suicidal attack. — *adj* of, or pertaining to, a kamikaze attack or someone who carries it out; of, or of someone or something engaged upon, an act of certain or deliberate self-destruction in pursuit of a particular cause; reckless, foolhardy (*colloq*). [Jap, divine wind]

kamila. See **kamala**.

kamis *ka-mēs'*. Same as **camise**.

kamme. See **kam**.

kampong *kam'pong* or *kam-pong'*, *n* (in Malaysia) an enclosed space or village. [Malay]

kamseen, kamsin. See **khamsin**.

Kan. *abbrev*: Kansas (US state).

kana *kä'nä*, *n* Japanese syllabic writing (either **hiragana** or **katakana**), as distinguished from Japanese written in Chinese characters (**kanji**). [Jap]

Kanak *kən-ak'*, *n* a Melanesian; a member of the Melanesian population of New Caledonia seeking its independence from France. [Hawaiian *kanaka* a man]

Kanaka *kən-ak'ä* or *kan'ə-kä*, *n* a Hawaiian; (sometimes without *cap*) a South Sea Islander, *esp* an indentured or forced labourer in Australia (*derog*); the Hawaiian language. [Hawaiian, a man]

Kanarese or **Canarese** *kan-ər-ēz'*, *adj* of *Kanara* in W India. — *n* one of the people of Kanara; their Dravidian language, now called *Kannada*, related to Telugu.

kandy *kan'di*, *n*. See under **candy**².

kaneh or **caneh** *kä'ne*, *n* a Hebrew measure of 6 cubits in length. [Heb *qāneh* reed, cane]

kang *kang*, *n* a Chinese sleeping-platform that can be warmed by a fire underneath. [Chin]

kanga or **khanga** *kang'gə*, *n* (in E Africa) a piece of cotton cloth, *usu* brightly decorated, wound around the body as a woman's dress. [Swahili]

kangaroo *kang-gə-rōō'*, *n* a large Australian herbivorous marsupial (family *Macropodidae*), with short fore-limbs, very long hindlegs and great leaping power; an early type of safety bicycle; (in *pl*; with *cap*) the Australian national Rugby league team; (in *pl*; *UK stock exchange*) Australian mining shares. — *vi* (*colloq*) (of a car) to move forward in jerks, because of the driver's poor clutch control. — **kangaroo'-apple** the edible fruit of a species of Solanum; the plant that yields it; **kangaroo closure** the method of allowing the chairman to decide which clauses shall be discussed and which passed or leapt over; **kangaroo court** a court operated by a mob, by prisoners in jail, or by any improperly constituted body; a tribunal before which a fair trial is impossible; a comic burlesque court; **kangaroo'-grass** a valuable fodder grass of the southern hemisphere (*Anthistiria* or *Themeda*). — *vi* **kangaroo'=hop** to move forward jerkily. — **kangaroo justice** the kind of justice dispensed by a kangaroo court; **kangaroo paw** (*Austr*) a plant of the genus *Anigozanthus*, the flower of which resembles a paw in shape; **kangaroo'=rat** a N American rodent (*Dipodomys*) related to the jerboa; a rat-kangaroo; **kangaroo'-thorn** a prickly Australian acacia (*Acacia armata*); **kangaroo vine** an evergreen climber (*Cissus antarctica*). [Aboriginal]

kangha *kung'hə*, *n* the comb traditionally worn by Sikhs in their hair. [Punjabi]

kanji *kan'ji*, *n* in the Japanese writing system, the set of characters derived from Chinese ideographs; one of these characters: — *pl* **kan'ji** or **kan'jis**. [Jap, from Chin, a Chinese work; cf **kana**]

Kannada *kun'ə-də*, *n* an important Dravidian language. [Kanarese]

kans *käns*, *n* an Indian grass related to sugar-cane. [Hindi *kās*]

kant. See **cant**².

kantar or **cantar** *kan-tär'*, *n* a varying unit of weight in Turkey, Egypt, etc, *approx* a hundredweight. [Ar *qintār*; see **quintal**]

kantele *kan'tə-lā*, *n* a Finnish zither. — Also **kan'tela**. [Finn *kantele*]

kanten *kan'tən*, *n* agar-agar jelly. [Jap]

kantha *kän'thə*, *n* an embroidered cloth quilt. [Beng]

Kantian *kant'i-ən*, *adj* pertaining to the German philosopher Immanuel *Kant* (1724–1804) or his philosophy. — *n* **Kan'tianism** or **Kant'ism** the doctrines or philosophy of Kant. — *n* **Kant'ist** a disciple or follower of Kant.

kantikoy, **canticoy** *kan'ti-koi*, or **cantico** (*-kō*; *pl* **can'ticos**) *n* an American Indian religious dance; a dancing-match. — *vi* to dance as an act of worship. [From Algonquian]

KANU *kä'nōō*, *abbrev*: Kenya African National Union.

Kanuck. Same as **Canuck**.

kanzu *kan'zōō*, *n* a long white garment worn by men in central E Africa. [From Swahili]

kaoliang *kä-ō-li-ang'*, *n* sorghum grain of several varieties; an alcoholic drink made from it. [Chin, tall grain]

kaolin or **kaoline** *kā'ō-lin*, *n* China clay, *esp* that composed of kaolinite. — *n* **ka'olinite** a hydrated aluminium silicate occurring in minute monoclinic flakes, a decomposition product of feldspar, etc. — *adj* **kaolinit'ic**. — *vt* and *vi* **ka'olinize** or **-ise** to turn into kaolin. — *n* **kaolinō'sis** a disease caused by inhaling kaolin dust. [From the mountain *Kao-ling* (high ridge) in China]

kaon *kā'on*, (*phys*) *n* one of several types of subatomic particle of smaller mass than a proton. — See **meson**. [*K* (pronounced *kā*) and meso*n*]

kapellmeister *kə-pel'mīs-tər*, *n* the director of an orchestra or choir, *esp* formerly in the household of a German prince. [Ger *Kapelle* chapel, orchestra, and *Meister* master]

kapok *kāp'* or *käp'ok*, *n* very light, waterproof, oily fibre covering the seeds of a species of silk-cotton tree, used for stuffing pillows, life-belts, etc. [Malay *kāpoq*]

Kaposi's sarcoma *kap-ō'sēz* (or *kap'ə-sēz*) *sär-kō'mə*, *n* a form of cancer characterized by multiple malignant tumours, *esp* of the skin of the feet and legs, first described by Hungarian-born dermatologist Moritz *Kaposi* (1837–1902), a common feature of AIDS.

kappa *kap'ə*, *n* the tenth (earlier eleventh) letter of the Greek alphabet (Κ, κ); as a numeral κ' = 20, ͵κ = 20 000.

kaput or **kaputt** *kə-pōōt'*, (*slang*) *adj* ruined; broken; not working; smashed. [Ger]

kara *kur'ə*, *n* the steel bangle, signifying the unity of God, traditionally worn by Sikhs. [Punjabi]

karabiner *ka-rə-bēn'ər*, (*mountaineering*) *n* a steel link with a spring clip in one side. — Also **carabin'er**. [Ger]

karait *kär-īt'*. Same as **krait**.

Karaite *kā'rä-īt*, *n* a member of a strict sect of Jews adhering to the literal interpretation of Scripture as against oral tradition. — *n* **ka'raism**. [Heb *qārā* to read]

karaka *kə-ra'kə*, *n* a New Zealand tree with edible orange fruit whose seeds are poisonous until treated. [Maori]

karakul or **caracul** *kär'ə-kōōl* or *-kōōl'*, *n* (often with *cap*) an Asiatic breed of sheep; a fur prepared from the skin of very young lambs of the Karakul or Bukhara breed, or of kids; a cloth imitating it. [Russ *Kara Kul*, a lake near Bukhara, Uzbekistan]

karaoke *kar-i-ō'kē*, *n* the (*orig* and *esp* Japanese) practice and entertainment, popular at public venues and parties, of singing personally-selected hit pop songs to accompanying backing music provided (from a large pre-recorded selection similar to a juke-box system) by a **karaoke machine**, which also enables the singer, using a microphone, to follow the words on a screen. — **karaoke bar** a bar equipped with a karaoke machine, providing karaoke entertainment. [Jap, literally empty orchestra]

karat. NAm spelling of **carat**.

karate *ka-rä'ti*, *n* a traditional Japanese form of unarmed self-defence using blows and kicks, now a popular combative sport. — *n* **kara'teist**. — *n* **kara'teka** an expert in karate. — **karate chop** a sharp downward blow with the side of the hand. [Jap, literally empty hand]

Karen *kə-ren'*, *n* a member of a Thai people of E and S Burma; the language of the Karens. — Also *adj*. — *n* **Karenn'i** (one of) a group of eastern Karen peoples whose women stretch their necks by wearing brass collars.

karite *kar'i-ti*, *n* the shea-tree. [Native African name]

Karling *kär'ling*, *n* and *adj* Carlovingian. [Ger *Karl* Charles, and patronymic suffix *-ing*]

karma *kär'mə* or *kur'mə*, (*Hinduism* and *Buddhism*) *n* the moral quality of a person's (or animal's) actions regarded as determining the nature of a future existence or incarnation; the concept of such transcendental retribution; the theory of inevitable consequence generally; fate, destiny. — *adj* **kar'mic**. [Sans *karma* act]

Karman vortex street *kär'mən vör'teks strēt*, (*acoustics*) *n* the regular vortex pattern behind an obstacle in a flow where vortices are generated and travel away from the object. [T von Karman (1881–1963), Hungarian-born American engineer]

Karmathian *kär-mā'thi-ən*, *n* a member of a pantheistic socialistic Muslim sect which arose in Turkey about the close of the 9c. [*Karmat*, its founder]

karmic. See under **karma**.

Karoo or **Karroo** *kä-roō'*, *n* a high inland pastoral tableland (*SAfr*); a series of strata in S Africa of the Permian and Triassic periods (*geol*). [Believed to be of Hottentot origin]

kaross *kä-ros'*, *n* a S African garment of animal skins. [Perh a Hottentot modification of Du *kuras* cuirass]

karri *kar'ē*, *n* a Western Australian gum-tree (*Eucalyptus diversicolor*); its red timber. [Aboriginal]

Karroo. See **Karoo**.

karsey. See **kazi**.

karst *kärst*, (*geol*) *n* rough limestone country with underground drainage. — Also *adj*. — *adj* **karst'ic**. — *n* **karstificā'tion** the development of karstic features. — *vt* **karst'ify**. [From the *Karst* district, near Trieste]

karsy. See **kazi**.

kart *kärt*, *n* a go-kart (qv). — *n* **kart'er**. — *n* **kart'ing** go-kart racing.

Kartell *kär-tel'*, *n* a German spelling of **cartel**.

kary- *ka-ri-* or **karyo-** *ka-ri-ō-* or *ka-ri-o'-*, (*biol*) *combining form* denoting nucleus. — *n* **karyog'amy** the fusion of cell nuclei during fertilization. — *n* **karyokinesis** (*-kin-ē'sis*; Gr *kinēsis* movement) mitosis. — *n* **karyol'ogy** the study of cell nuclei, and *esp* of chromosomes. — *n* **kar'yolymph** a colourless, watery fluid, occupying most of the space inside the nuclear membrane; nuclear sap. — *n* **karyol'ysis** the dissolution of the nucleus by disintegration of the chromatin; the gradual disappearance of the nucleus in a dead cell; the liquefaction of the nuclear membrane in mitosis. — *n* **kar'yon** the cell nucleus. — *n* **kar'yoplasm** the protoplasm of a cell nucleus. — *n* **kar'yosome** a nucleus; an aggregation of chromatin; a type of nucleolus. — *n* **kar'yotin** chromatin. — *n* **kar'yotype** the appearance, number and arrangement of the chromosomes in the cells of an individual; a diagram or photograph of the chromosomes of a cell or cells. — *vt* to investigate or determine the karyotype of. — *adj* **karyotyp'ic**. [Gr *karyon* kernel]

karzy. See **kazi**.

kasbah or **casbah** *kaz'bä*, *n* a castle or fortress in a N African town or the area round it, *esp* in Algiers. [Ar dialect *kasba*]

kasha *kash'ə*, *n* a porridge or gruel-like dish made from crushed cereal, *usu* buckwheat. [Russ]

Kashmir *kash-mēr'*, *n* a region in the north-west of the Indian subcontinent; (without *cap*; *obs*; also *kash'-*) same as **cashmere**. — *adj* **Kashmiri** (*kash-mēr'i*) belonging to Kashmir.

Kashrut, **Kashruth** *kash-roōt'* or **Kashrus** *kash-roōs'*, *n* (also without *cap*) the Jewish system of dietary laws relating to the fitness and preparation of food. [Heb, fitness, from *kāshēr* (see **kosher**)]

kat[1]. See **khat**.

kat[2] or **khat** *kät*, *n* the chief ancient Egyptian unit of weight, 1/50 lb avoirdupois.

kata *kat'a*, (*karate*) *n* a formal sequence of practice exercises and movements. [Jap]

katabasis *kat-ab'ə-sis*, *n* a going down; a military retreat. — *adj* **katabatic** (*-ə-bat'ik*; of a wind) blowing down a slope, because of air density differences resulting from overnight cooling, etc. [Gr]

katabolism. See **catabolism**.

katabothron *kat-ə-both'ron* or **katavothron** *kat-av'oth-ron*, *n* an underground water-channel. [Mod Gr *katabothron*, from Gr *kata* down, and *bothros* hole]

katadromous. Same as **catadromous**.

katakana *kat-ä-kä'nä*, *n* one of the two syllabic writing systems in Japanese, based on cursive Chinese ideograms, and used for loan words from languages other than Chinese. [Jap; cf **kana**]

katana *kä-tä'nä*, (*Jap*) *n* a long single-edged samurai sword, slightly curved towards the tip. [Jap]

katathermometer *ka-tə-thər-mom'i-tər*, *n* an alcohol thermometer for measuring the cooling power of the air. [Gr *kata* down, and **thermometer**]

katavothron. See **katabothron**.

kathak *kəth-äk'*, *n* a classical dance of N India in which brief passages of mime alternate with rapid, rhythmic dance. [Sans, a professional storyteller, from *katha* story]

kathakali *käth-ə-kä'li*, *n* a classical dance drama of S India. [Malayalam, drama]

katharevousa *ka-thə-rev'oō-sə*, *n* a formal archaizing written form of Modern Greek, based on Ancient Greek. [Mod Gr *kathareuousa*, fem pr p of Ancient Gr *kathareuein* to be pure, from *katharos* pure]

katharometer *ka-thə-rom'i-tər*, *n* an instrument for analysing the concentration of gases by measuring heat loss. [Gr *katharos* pure, and **-meter**]

katharsis, **kathode**. Same as **catharsis**, **cathode**.

kati. See **catty**.

kation. See **cation**.

katipo *ka'ti-pō*, *n* a venomous NZ spider. [Maori]

katorga *kä'tər-gə*, (*Russ*) *n* penal servitude, hard labour, *esp* in the labour camps of Joseph Stalin.

katti. See **catty**.

katydid *kā'ti-did*, *n* a N American insect related to the grasshopper. [Imit of its distinctive sound]

katzenjammer *kat'sən-jam-ər*, or *-jam'*, (*NAm*) *n* a hangover; a similar state of emotional distress; an uproar, clamour. [Ger, literally cats' misery]

kaugh. See under **kiaugh**.

kauri *kow'ri*, or **kauri-pine** (*-pīn*), *n* a tall coniferous forest-tree of New Zealand (*Agathis australis*), source of **kau'ri-gum**, a resin used in making varnish. [Maori]

kava *kä'və*, *n* an aromatic plant of the pepper family (*Piper methysticum*); a narcotic drink prepared from its root and stem. — Also **a'va**. [Polynesian]

kavass *kä-väs'*, *n* an armed servant in Turkey. — Also **cavass'**. [Ar *qawwās*]

kaw. See **caw**.

kay[1] *kā*, *n* the eleventh letter of the modern English alphabet (K or k).

kay[2]. See **quay**.

kayak *kī'ak*, *n* an Eskimo seal-skin canoe; a canvas, fibreglass, etc canoe built in this style. — *vi* to travel or race in a kayak. [Eskimo]

kayle. Same as **kail**[1].

kayo or **KO** *kā-ō'*, (*slang*) *n* and *vt* knockout, knock out: — *pl* **kayos'**, **kayoes'** or **KOs**; *pa t* and *pa p* **kayoed'** or **Ko'd'**. — *n* **kayo'ing**.

Kazak or **Kazakh** *kaz-äk'*, *n* a member of a Turko-Tatar people of central Asia; the Turkic dialect spoken by Kazaks. [Russ]

kazatzka *kəz-at'skə*, *n* a Slavic folk-dance performed by a man and a woman. [Russ *kazachki* Cossack dances]

kazi, **karzy**, **karsey** or **karsy** *kä-zi*, (*slang*) *n* a lavatory. [Said to be from Ital *casa* house or perh Ar *kursi* chair]

kazoo *kä-zoō'*, *n* a musical instrument consisting of a tube with a strip of catgut, plastic, etc, that makes a buzzing sound when hummed into. — Also **gazoo'** or **gazoo'ka**. [Prob imit]

KB *abbrev*: kilobyte (*comput*); King's Bench; king's bishop (*chess*); knight bachelor.

KBE *abbrev*: Knight Commander of the (Order of the) British Empire.

kbyte (*comput*) *abbrev*: kilobyte.

KC *abbrev*: Kennel Club; King's Counsel.

kcal *abbrev*: kilocalorie.

KCB *abbrev*: Knight Commander of the (Order of the) Bath.

KCMG *abbrev*: Knight Commander of (the Order of) St Michael and St George.

Kčs *abbrev*: *koruna československá* (*Czech*), koruna (Czechoslovakian currency).

KCVO *abbrev*: Knight Commander of the (Royal) Victorian Order.

KD *abbrev*: knocked down (*commerce*); Kuwaiti dinar (unit of currency, = 1000 fils).

kea *kē'ə* or *kē'a*, *n* a large New Zealand parrot. [Maori]

keasar. See **kaiser**.

keavie. See **cavie**.

keb *keb*, (*Scot*) *vi* to give birth to a premature or stillborn lamb. — *n* a ewe giving birth to such a lamb. [Cf Ger *Kibbe*, *Kippe* ewe]

kebab *kə-bab'*, *n* (also used in *pl*) small pieces of meat cooked with vegetables, etc, *esp* (from Turkish **shish kebab**) when on a skewer. — Also **kabob** (*-bob'*), **kabab**, **kebob** or **cabob**. — *vt* (*lit* and *fig*) to skewer. — **doner kebab** (*dō'nər* or *don'ər*) a Middle Eastern dish, thin slices cut from a block of minced and seasoned lamb grilled on a spit, eaten in a split piece of unleavened bread. [Ar *kabab*]

kebbie *keb'i*, (*Scot*) *n* a shepherd's crook; a crook-handled walking-stick.

kebbock or **kebbuck** *keb'ək*, (*Scot*) *n* a cheese. [Origin unknown; Gaelic *cabag* (a cheese) may be derived from this word]

kebele *kə-bā'lā*, *n* a self-governing local district association found in Ethiopia. — Also **kabe'le** (*kä-*). [From Amharic]

keblah. See **kiblah**.

kebob. See **kebab**.

keck[1] *kek*, *vi* to retch, feel sick; to feel disgust or loathing. — *n* a retching. [Imit]

keck[2]. See **kex**.

keckle[1] *kek'l*, *vt* to protect by binding with rope, etc. — *n* **keck'ling** rope, etc used to keckle cables or hawsers. [Origin unknown]

keckle[2] *kek'l*, (chiefly *Scot*) *vi* a variant of **cackle**.

kecks, **kecksy**, **kecksye**. See **kex**.

ked *ked* or **kade** *kād*, *n* a wingless fly (*Melophagus ovinus*) that infests sheep. [Origin unknown]

keddah. See **kheda**.

kedge[1] *kej*, (*naut*) *n* a small anchor for keeping a ship steady, and for warping (qv) the ship. — *vt* to move by means of a kedge, to warp. — *n* **kedg'er** a kedge. [Origin doubtful]

kedge[2] *kej*, (*dialect*) *adj* brisk, lively; pot-bellied. — Also **kedg'y** or **kidge**. [Cf **cadgy**]

kedgeree *kej'ə-rē*, *n* an Indian dish of rice, cooked with butter and dal, flavoured with spice, shredded onion, etc; a similar British dish made with rice, cooked fish and hard-boiled eggs. [Hind *khichrī*]

keech *kēch*, (*Shakesp*) *n* a lump of fat. [Perh connected with **cake**]

keek *kēk*, (*Scot* and *NEng*) *vi* to peep. — *n* a peep. — *n* **keek'er** someone who peeps or spies; an inspector of coal; an eye; a black eye. — **keek'ing-glass** a mirror. [ME *kyke*; cf Du *kijken*, Ger *kucken*]

keel[1] *kēl*, *n* the part of a ship extending along the bottom from stem to stern, and supporting the whole frame; a ship (*poetic*); a longitudinal member running along the underside of an airship's hull; any similar structure functioning like a ship's keel (*biol*); any narrow prominent ridge. — *vt* or *vi* to turn keel upwards. — *n* **keel'age** dues for a keel or ship in port. — *adj* **keeled** keel-shaped (*bot*); having a ridge on the back. — **keel'boat** a type of yacht with a heavy external keel providing weight to offset that of the sails; see also under **keel**[2]. — *vt* **keel'haul** to punish by hauling under the keel of a ship by ropes from the one side to the other; to rebuke severely. — **keel'hauling**. — **keel over** to stagger or fall over; **on an even keel** calm, or calmly. [ON *kjölr*]

keel[2] *kel*, *n* a low flat-bottomed boat, a barge. — Also **keel'boat**. — *n* **keel'er** or **keel'man** someone who works on a barge. [MDu *kiel* ship, cognate with OE *cēol* ship]

keel[3] *kēl*, (*Shakesp*) *vt* to cool. [OE *cēlan* to chill]

keel[4] *kēl*, (*Scot*) *n* red ochre, ruddle. — *vt* to mark with ruddle. [Origin obscure; Gaelic *cílic* (ruddle) may be from this word]

keelie *kē'li*, (*Scot*) *n* the kestrel or other hawk; an urban tough, *esp* from Glasgow; a boorish lower-class youth or man. [Of uncertain origin; some connect with **gillie**]

keeling *kē'ling*, (*Scot*) *n* a codfish. [Origin unknown]

keelivine or **keelyvine** *kē'li-vīn*, (*Scot*) *n* a lead pencil. [Perh **keel**[4], but ety uncertain]

keelson *kel'* or *kēl'sən*, or **kelson** *kel'sən*, *n* a ship's inner keel, which binds the floor-timbers to the outer keel. [LGer *kielswīn* keel swine]

keelyvine. See **keelivine**.

keen[1] *kēn*, *adj* eager; sharp, having a fine edge; piercing; having an acute or penetrating mind; intense; competitive, low (eg of prices); very good, wonderful (*slang*, *esp NAm*). — *vt* to sharpen. — *adv* **keen'ly**. — *n* **keen'ness**. — **keen on** (*colloq*) devoted to; fond of; very interested in, *esp* romantically or sexually; very desirous of. [OE *cēne* bold, fierce, keen; cf Ger *kühn* bold, and ON *kœnn* expert]

keen[2] *kēn*, *n* a lamentation over the dead. — *vi* to wail over the dead. — *n* **keen'er** a professional mourner. — *n* **keen'ing** wailing, lamentation. [Ir *caoine*]

keep *kēp*, *vt* to tend, look after; to have or take care or charge of; to guard; to maintain; to manage, conduct, run; to attend to the making of records in; to retain; to retain as one's own; to have in one's custody; to store customarily in a specified place; to have habitually in stock for sale; to support financially, or otherwise supply with necessaries; to have in one's service; to remain in or on (a place or position); to adhere to; to associate with; to continue to follow or hold to; to continue to make; to maintain a hold on or of; to restrain from leaving, to hold back; to prevent; to reserve or withhold; not to divulge (a secret); to be faithful to (a promise); to preserve or cause to remain in a certain state; to observe, celebrate; to conform to the requirements of, to fulfil. — *vi* to remain; to continue to be or go; to be or remain in a specified condition; to remain fresh or good; to last or endure; to be capable of being reserved; to continue; to lodge or reside (*Cambridge University* and *US*); to refrain; to confine or restrict oneself; to keep wicket: — *pr p* **keep'ing**; *pa t* and *pa p* **kept** (*kept*). — *n* something kept, one's charge (*Spenser*); something which keeps, contains or protects; food, means of subsistence, board; the innermost and strongest part of a castle, the central tower; a stronghold. — *n* **keep'er** someone or something that keeps, in any sense; an attendant in charge of animals in captivity; a custodian of a museum or gallery; a prison guard; a gamekeeper; the title of certain officials, such as *Lord Keeper* (*of the Great Seal*), whose office since 1757 has been merged in that of Lord Chancellor; a wicket-keeper; a goalkeeper; a man who keeps a mistress (*obs*); the socket that receives the bolt of a lock; the armature of a magnet; a guard ring. — *adj* **keep'erless**. — *n* **keep'ership** the office of a keeper. — *n* **keep'ing** care, custody, charge; preservation; reservation; retention; observance, compliance; just proportion; harmonious consistency; maintenance of, or as, a mistress; maintenance, support (*Shakesp*). — **keep fit** a programme of physical exercises designed to keep the muscles, circulation and respiratory system in good condition. — Also *adj*. — **keep'ing-room** (*dialect*) a sitting-room, parlour; **keep'-net** a cone-shaped net suspended in a river, etc, in which fish caught by anglers can be kept alive; **keep'sake** something given, or kept, as a reminder of the giver, or a certain event, time, etc; an annual gift-book (such as *The Keepsake* itself, 1827–56). — *adj* (also **keep'saky**) vapidly pretty. — **kept man** and **kept woman** a man or woman maintained financially by a romantic or sexual partner. — **for keeps** for good; permanently; with serious intent; defensively (*cricket*); **how are you keeping**? how are you?; **in keeping with** in accord with, suitable to; **keep an act** formerly, to hold an academic debate; **keep an eye on** see under **eye**; **keep at** to persist in (anything); to nag, badger (someone to do something) (*colloq*); **keep back** to withhold; to keep down, repress; **keep body and soul together** to stay alive; **keep chapel**, **company**, **counsel** and **distance** see under the nouns; **keep down** to remain low or out of sight; to restrain, repress; to retain (food) in the stomach, not to vomit; to set in lower-case type, avoiding capitals; **keep from** to abstain from; to remain away from; **keep hours**, **keep house** see under the nouns; **keep in** to prevent from escaping; to confine in school after school hours; to conceal; to restrain; **keep in with** to maintain the confidence or friendship of; **keep off** to hinder or prevent from approaching or making an attack, etc; to stay away or refrain from; (of rain, etc) not to start; **keep on** to continue; to retain, continue to employ; **keep on about** to continue talking about; **keep on at** (*colloq*) to nag, badger; **keep one's breath to cool one's porridge** to hold one's peace when further talk is clearly in vain; **keep one's countenance** to avoid showing one's emotions; **keep oneself to oneself** to avoid the company of others; **keep one's hand in** to retain one's skill by practice; **keep one's head down** to avoid attracting attention to oneself; **keep one's mind on** to concentrate on; **keep the peace** see under **peace**; **keep one's powder dry** see under **powder**; **keep someone going in something** to keep someone supplied with something; **keep tabs on** to keep a check on, to keep account of; **keep a term** see under **term**; **keep time** to observe rhythm accurately, or along with others; (of a clock or watch) to go accurately; **keep to** to stick closely to; to confine oneself to; **keep under** to hold down in restraint; **keep up** to retain (one's strength or spirit); to support, prevent from falling; to continue, to prevent from ceasing; to maintain in good condition; to continue to be in touch (with); to keep pace (with); to stop, stay (*obs*); **keep up with the Joneses** to keep on an equal social footing with one's neighbours, eg by having possessions of the same quality in the same quantity; **keep wicket** to act as a wicket-keeper. [OE *cēpan*]

keeshond *kās'hond* or *-hont*, *n* a medium-sized dog of the spitz type. [Du, from *kees* terrier, and *hond* dog]

keeve or **kieve** *kēv*, *n* a large tub. [OE *cȳf* vat]

kef *käf*, *n* a state of dreamy repose; a drug such as marijuana, smoked to produce this state. — Also **kaif** (*kīf*) or **kif** (*kif* or *kēf*). [Ar *kaif* pleasure]

keffel *kef'l*, (*dialect*) *n* a horse, nag. [Welsh *ceffyl*; cf **caple**]

keffiyeh. See **kaffiyeh**.

kefir or **kephir** *ke'fər*, *n* an effervescent drink made from fermented cow's milk. [Native name in the Caucasus]

kefuffle. See **carfuffle**.

keg *keg*, *n* a small cask; a metal cask in which beer is kept under gas pressure. — **keg beer** any of various types of beer kept in and served from pressurized kegs. [Earlier *cag*, from ON *kaggi*]

keight *kīt*, (*Spenser*) *vt* for **caught** (*pa t* of **catch**).

keir. See **kier**.

keister *kē'stər*, (*US slang*) *n* the buttocks, arse; a safe or strong-box; a case or box. [Prob Ger *Kiste* chest, case]

keitloa *kāt'lō-ə*, *n* a two-horned rhinoceros. [Tswana *kgetlwa*]

keksye. See under **kex**.

kelim. See **kilim**.

kell *kel*, (*Scot* and *NEng*) *n* a woman's headdress or hairnet; a film or membrane; a caul. **[caul]**

kellaut. See **killut**.

kelly *kel'i*, *n* (in drilling processes) the top pipe of a rotary string of drill pipes, with which is incorporated a flexibly attached swivel through which mud is pumped to the bottom of the hole. [Origin uncertain]

keloid or **cheloid** *kē'loid*, *n* a hard growth of scar tissue in skin that has been injured. — *adj* **keloid'al** or **cheloid'al**. [Gr *chēlē* claw]

kelp *kelp*, *n* any large brown seaweed, wrack; the calcined ashes of seaweed, a source of soda, iodine, etc. — Also **kilp**. — *n* **Kel'per** (also without *cap*) an inhabitant of the Falkland Islands. — *adj* of or pertaining to the Falkland Islands. [ME *culp*; origin unknown]

kelpie or **kelpy** *kel'pi*, *n* a malignant water-sprite haunting fords in the form of a horse (*Scot*; *folklore*); an Australian breed of sheep-dog. [Origin uncertain]

kelson. See **keelson**.

kelt[1] *kelt*, *n* a salmon, etc that has just spawned. [Origin unknown]

kelt[2] *kelt*, (*Scot*) *n* coarse cloth *usu* made of black and white wool mixed and not dyed. — *n* and *adj* **kelt'er**. [Origin obscure]

Kelt, **Keltic**. See under **Celt**.

kelter[1]. See **kilter**.

kelter[2]. See **kelt**[2].

keltie or **kelty** *kel'ti*, (*Scot*) *n* a bumper or glass filled to the brim, *esp* one imposed as a penalty on someone who does not drain his glass completely.

Kelvin *kel'vin*, *adj* applied to a thermometer scale with absolute zero for zero and centigrade degrees. — *n* **kel'vin** (in SI units) the unit of temperature (formerly known as 'degree Kelvin'); a kilowatt-hour (*rare*). [Sir William Thomson, Lord *Kelvin* (1824–1907), physicist]

kemb *kem*, (*obs* and *dialect*) *vt* to comb. — *adj* **kempt** (*kemt* or *kempt*) combed, tidy. [OE *cemban*]

kembo. Same as **kimbo**.

kemp[1] *kemp*, *n* a coarse, rough strand of wool; (in *pl*) knotty hair that will not felt. [ON *kampr* beard]

kemp[2] *kemp*, (*Scot* and *NEng*) *n* a champion (*archaic*); a contest in reaping or other work. — *vi* to strive for mastery. — *n* **kem'per** or **kem'pery-man** a champion, a knight-errant. — *n* **kemp'ing**. [OE *cempa* a warrior; cf **champion**]

kemple *kem'pl*, (*Scot*) *n* forty bundles of hay or straw. [Origin obscure]

kempt. See under **kemb**.

Ken. *abbrev*: Kentucky (US state).

ken[1] *ken*, *vt* to know (chiefly *Scot*); to see and recognize at a distance (*archaic*); to cause to know, direct (*obs*): — *pa t* and *pa p* **kenned** or **kent**. — *n* range of sight or knowledge. — *n* **kenn'er**. — *n* **kenn'ing** range of vision; a small portion, a little bit (*Scot*); a periphrastic formula in Old Norse or other old Germanic poetry. — *n* **ken-no** (*ken'ə*; *Scot*, literally know not) a cheese prepared in ostensible secrecy for the gossips at a birth. — *adj* **kent** known. — **beyond one's ken** outside the limits of one's knowledge. [OE *cennan*, causative of *cunnan*, and ON *kenna*; cf **can**[1], **con**[2]]

ken[2] *ken*, (*slang*) *n* a house, *esp* a disreputable one. [Perh Pers *khān* a caravanserai, or **kennel**; or connected with preceding word]

kenaf *kə-naf'*, *n* a tropical Asian herbaceous plant, the jute-like fibres of which can be used as a substitute for wood-pulp in paper-making. [Pers]

Kendal-green *ken'dl-grēn*, *n* green cloth for foresters made at *Kendal* in Cumbria.

kendo *ken'dō* or *-dō'*, *n* the Japanese art of swordsmanship practised with bamboo staves, in 18c-style armour, and observing strict ritual. [Jap *kendō* way of the sword]

kennel[1] *ken'l*, *n* a house for a dog or dogs; a pack of hounds; the hole of a fox, etc; a hovel; (in *pl*) an establishment where dogs are boarded. — *vt* to put or keep in a kennel. — *vi* to live in a kennel: — *pr p* **kenn'elling**; *pa t* and *pa p* **kenn'elled**. — **kenn'el-maid** or **kenn'el-man** a female or male attendant who looks after dogs. [From an ONFr form corresponding to Fr *chenil*, from L *canīle*, from *canis* a dog]

kennel[2] *ken'l*, *n* a street gutter. [ME *canel*, from ONFr *canel*, from L *canālis*; see **canal**]

kennel-coal. Same as **cannel-coal**.

Kennelly-Heaviside layer or **region** *ken'ə-li-hev'i-sīd lā'ər* or *rē'jən*, *n* a strongly ionized region of the upper atmosphere about 60 miles up, in which wireless waves are deflected. — Also **Heaviside layer** and **E'-layer**.

[From A E *Kennelly* and O *Heaviside*, who inferred its existence]

kenner. See under **ken**[1].

kennet *ken'it*, (*obs*) *n* a small hunting dog. [ONFr *kennet* (dimin) from L *canis* dog]

Kennick *ken'ik*, *n* a name given to the jargon used by some vagrant tinkers.

kenning, ken-no. See under **ken**[1].

keno *kē'nō*, (*NAm*, *Austr*) *n* a gambling game similar to bingo. [Fr *quine* five winning numbers]

kenophobia *ken-ō-fō'bi-ə*, *n* a morbid fear of empty spaces. [Gr *kenos* empty, and **phobia**]

kenosis *ken-ō'sis*, (*Christian theol*) *n* Christ's renunciation of divine attributes in order to identify with humanity. — *adj* **kenotic** (*-ot'ik*). — *n* **kenot'icist** (*-i-sist*) a believer in kenosis. [Gr *kenōsis* emptying, from Philem 2.7]

Kensington *ken'zing-tən*, *adj* (of people) interested exclusively in an artificial city life and in material values. [Part of a London borough]

kenspeckle *ken'spek-l*, (*Scot* and *NEng*) *adj* easily recognized; conspicuous. — Also **ken'speck**. [Appar ult from ON *kennispeki* power of recognition]

kent[1] *kent*, (*Scot*) *n* a leaping or punting pole. — *vt* and *vi* to punt or pole. [Cf **quant**]

kent[2]. See **ken**[1].

kent-bugle *kent'-bū'gl*, *n* an obsolete keybugle. [Supposed to be named after a Duke of Kent]

kente cloth *ken'ti kloth*, *n* a silk cloth made in Ghana by sewing together long narrow handwoven strips. [Origin uncertain]

Kentia *kent'i-ə*, *n* (also without *cap*) a name formerly applied to many pinnate varieties of palm, but now only to the Howea feather palm. [From W *Kent* (died in 1820s), Dutch botanist]

Kentish *kent'ish*, *adj* of *Kent*. — *n* the dialect of Kent, Essex, etc. — **Kentish fire** synchronized volleys of applause (probably from anti-Catholic demonstrations in Kent, 1828–9); **Kent'ish-man** a native of W Kent (one born east of the Medway being a *Man of Kent*); **Kentish-rag'** a rough limestone from the Lower Greensand of Kent.

kentledge *kent'lij*, *n* pig-iron in a ship's hold for ballast. — Also **kint'ledge**. [Origin unknown]

Kenyapithecus *kēn'yə-pith'ə-kəs* or *ken'yə-*, *n* a lower Pliocene genus of fossil anthropoid ape; an example of this genus, first discovered by L S B Leakey in Kenya in 1961. [*Kenya*, and Gr *pithēkos* ape]

kep *kep*, (*Scot* and *NEng*) *vt* to catch (an approaching object or falling liquid): — *pa t* and *pa p* **kepp'it**. — *n* a catch; an act or opportunity of catching. **[keep]**

kephalic *ki-fal'ik*. Same as **cephalic**.

kephir. See **kefir**.

kepi *kāp'ē*, *n* a flat-topped French military cap with a straight peak. [Fr *képi*]

Keplerian *kep-lē'ri-ən*, *adj* pertaining to the German astronomer Johann *Kepler*. — See under **law**[1].

keppit. See **kep**.

kept *pa t* and *pa p* of **keep**.

keramic *ki-ram'ik*. See under **ceramic**.

keratin *ker'ə-tin*, *n* a nitrogenous compound, the essential ingredient of horny tissue, the substance of horns, nails, etc. — *n* **keratinizā'tion** or **-s-** the formation of keratin; a becoming horny. — *vt* and *vi* **ker'atinize** or **-ise** to make or become horny. — *adj* **keratinous** (*kə-rat'i-nəs*) horny. — *n* **keratī'tis** inflammation of the cornea. — *adj* **keratogenous** (*-oj'i-nəs*) producing horn or keratin. — *adj* **ker'atoid** resembling horn or keratin. — *n* **keratom'eter** an instrument for measuring the curvature of the cornea. — *n* **ker'atōplasty** grafting of part of a healthy cornea to replace a piece made opaque by disease, etc. — *adj* **ker'atose** (*esp* of certain sponges) having a horny skeleton. — *n* **keratō'sis** a horny growth on or over the skin, eg a wart; a skin condition producing this: — *pl* **keratoses** (*-sēz*). — *n* **keratot'omy** surgery of the cornea. [Gr *keras*, *-atos* a horn]

keratophyre *ker'ət-ō-fīr*, (*petrology*) *n* a fine-grained soda trachyte. [Gr *keras*, *-atos* horn, and *-phyre* from **porphyry**]

keraunograph *kə-rön'ō-gräf*, *n* an instrument for recording distant thunderstorms. [Gr *keraunos* a thunderbolt, and *graphein* to write]

kerb, or (*esp NAm*) **curb** (qv), *kûrb*, *n* a kerbstone, pavement edge; a kerb market; an edging or margin of various kinds. — *adj* (of a market, of dealing, etc) unofficial, outside official trading hours. — **kerb'-crawler** someone who drives along slowly with the intention of enticing people into the car, *usu* for sexual purposes; **kerb'-crawling**; **kerb drill** the procedure for crossing a road safely, recommended for pedestrians; **kerb'-market** a market in stocks operating separately from the stock exchange, *orig* on the pavement; **kerb'-merchant**, **-trader** or **-vendor** a person who sells on or beside the pavement; **kerb'side** (also *adj*); **kerb'stone** a stone placed edgeways as an edging to a path or pavement; **kerb'stone-broker** one outside the stock exchange; **kerb weight** the weight (of a car) without passengers and luggage. [Fr *courbe*, from L *curvus* bent]

kerchief *kûr'chif*, *n* a square piece of cloth worn to cover the head, neck, etc; a handkerchief. — *vt* to cover with a kerchief. — *adj* **ker'chiefed**. [OFr *cuevrechief* (Fr *couvrechef*), from *covrir* to cover, and *chef* the head]

kerf *kûrf*, *n* a cut; a notch; the groove made by a saw; a cut place, the face of a cut; a quantity cut at once, as of wool, etc; a single layer of hay, turf, etc cut. [OE *cyrf* a cut]

kerfuffle. See **carfuffle**.

Kerguelen cabbage *kûr'gə-lən kab'ij*, *n* a wind-pollinated plant (*Pringlea antiscorbutica*) related to the cabbage, growing on Kerguelen and nearby islands in the S Indian Ocean.

kermes *kûr'mēz*, *n* the female bodies of a coccus insect (*Kermes* (or *Coccus*) *ilicis*), used as a red dyestuff; the oak (**kermes oak**; *Quercus coccifera*) on which they breed; a cherry-red mineral, antimony oxysulphide (also **kermes mineral** or **ker'mesite**). [Pers and Ar *qirmiz*]

kermesse *kûr'mis*, *n* a cycle-race held in an urban area. [Flem *kermesse* kermis]

kermis or **kirmess** *kûr'məs*, *n* a fair in the Low Countries; in N America, an indoor fair, *usu* for charity. [Du *kermis*, from *kerk* church, and *mis* mass]

kern[1]. See **kirn**[1].

kern[2] *kûrn*, *vi* to granulate. [Cf **corn**[1]]

kern[3] *kûrn*, (*printing*) *n* part of a type that projects beyond the body and rests on an adjoining letter. — *vt* to give (a typeface) a kern; to adjust (*esp* by reduction) the space between characters in (a typeface or piece of writing). — *n* **kern'ing**. [Fr *carne* a projecting angle, from L *cardō*, *-inis*]

kern[4] or **kerne** *kûrn*, *n* an Irish or highland foot-soldier (*hist*); a troop of such (*hist*); a peasant, a boor (*obs*). — *adj* **ker'nish**. [From Ir, from OIr; see **cateran**]

kernel *kûr'nl*, *n* a seed within a hard shell; the edible part of a nut; a gland (*rare*); a nucleus; the important, central part of anything. — *vi* (*rare*) to form kernels. — *adj* **ker'nelly** full of, or resembling, kernels. [OE *cyrnel*, from *corn* grain, and dimin suffix *-el*; Ger *Kern* a grain]

kernicterus *kûr-nik'tər-əs*, (*pathol*) *n* a condition of acute neural dysfunction linked with high levels of bilirubin in the blood. [Ger *Kern* nucleus, and Gr *ikteros* jaundice]

kernish. See under **kern**[4].

kernite *kûrn'it*, *n* hydrated oxide of sodium and boron. [*Kern* County, California, where it was discovered]

kerogen *ker'ō-jen*, *n* the organic matter in oil-shale that yields oil on distillation. [Gr *kēros* wax, and root of *gennaein* to generate]

kerosine *ker'ō-sēn*, *n* paraffin-oil obtained from shale or by distillation of petroleum; paraffin (*NAm*). — This spelling is now used commercially; **kerosene** is the older spelling. [Gr *kēros* wax]

Kerr effect *ker i-fekt'*, (*phys*) *n* one of two effects relating to the optical properties of matter in electric and magnetic fields, the *electro-optical effect* causing some liquids and gases to become double refracting in certain circumstances, the *magneto-optical effect* producing an elliptic polarization in certain circumstances. [J Kerr (1824-1907), Scottish physicist]

Kerria *ker'i-ə*, *n* a plant genus comprising a single species, the deciduous yellow-flowering shrub, Jew's mallow; (without *cap*) a plant of this genus. [From William *Kerr*, late 18c–early 19c English gardener]

Kerry blue terrier *ke'ri bloo ter'i-ər*, *n* a breed of Irish terrier with a long, silky, bluish coat.

kersantite *kûr'sən-tīt*, *n* a dyke-rock of black mica and plagioclase. [From *Kersanton*, in Brittany]

kersey *kûr'zi*, *n* a coarse woollen cloth. [Perh from *Kersey* in Suffolk]

kerseymere *kûr'zi-mēr* or *-mēr'*, *n* a twilled cloth of very fine wool. [For **cassimere**, **cashmere**]

kerve *kûrv'*, (*Spenser*) *vt* a variant of **carve**.

kerygma *kə-rig'mə*, (*theol*) *n* (preaching of) the Christian gospel, *esp* in the way of the early Church. — *adj* **kerygmat'ic**. [Gr *kērygma* proclamation, preaching]

kesar. See **kaiser**.

kesh *kāsh*, *n* the uncut hair and beard traditionally worn by Sikhs. [Punjabi]

kest *kest*, an *obs* variant of **cast**.

kestrel *kes'trəl*, *n* a small species of falcon. [OFr *cresserelle*]

ket[1] *ket*, (*Scot*) *n* carrion. [ON *kjöt*]

ket[2] *ket*, (*Scot*) *n* matted wool. [Anglo-Fr *cot*]

ket-. See **keto-**.

keta *kē'tə*, *n* a Pacific salmon, the dog-salmon. [Russ *keta*]

ketamine *ket'ə-mēn*, *n* an anaesthetic and analgesic drug (*med*), in recreational misuse often referred to as *Special K*. [**ket-**]

ketch[1] *kech*, *n* a small two-masted sailing vessel, the foremast being the taller. [Earlier *catch*, perh from the verb **catch**]

ketch[2] *kech*, an *obs* variant of **catch**.

ketchup *kech'əp*, *n* a smooth, thick sauce made from tomatoes, mushrooms, etc. — Also **catch'up** or **cat'sup**. [Malay *kēchap*, perh from Chinese]

keto- *kē-tō-* or **ket-** *kēt-*, *combining form* denoting a ketone compound or derivative.

ketone *kē'tōn*, *n* an organic compound consisting of a carbonyl group united to two like or unlike alkyl radicals. — *n* **kē'tose** any of a class of monosaccharide sugars which contain a ketone group. — *n* **ketō'sis** the excessive formation in the body of ketone or acetone bodies, due to incomplete oxidation of fats, as occurs in eg diabetes. [Ger *Keton*, from *Aketon* acetone]

kettle[1] *ket'l*, *n* a container for boiling water, with a spout, a lid and a handle, for domestic use; a metal container for heating liquids; a kettle hole (*geol*); a kettledrum (*Shakesp*). — *n* **kett'leful**. — **kett'ledrum** (*music*) a percussion instrument, consisting of a hollow metal hemisphere with a parchment head, tuned by screws which adjust the tension; **kett'ledrummer**; **kett'le-holder** a little cloth, etc for lifting a hot kettle; **kettle hole** (*geol*) a circular hollow in rock caused by the melting of a trapped block of ice; **kett'lestitch** (*bookbinding*) the stitch which is made at the head and tail of each section of a book to interlock the sections. — **a kettle of fish** a riverside picnic at which new-caught salmon are cooked on the spot (*obs*); a situation, set of circumstances; (often *ironically*) **a fine** or **pretty kettle of fish** an awkward mess or situation. [ON *ketill*; OE *cetel*, Ger *Kessel*, Gothic *katils*; all perh from L *catillus*, dimin of *catīnus* a deep cooking-vessel]

kettle[2]. See **kiddle**.

kettle-pins. See **kittle-pins**.

Ketubah *ke-too-vä'*, *n* a formal Jewish marriage contract which couples sign before their wedding. [Heb *kethū-bhāh* document]

Keuper *koi'pər*, (*geol*) *n* the uppermost division of the Trias. — Also *adj*. [Ger miners' term]

kevel *kev'l*. Same as **cavel**.

Kevlar® *kev'lär*, *n* a lightweight synthetic fibre of exceptionally high strength and heat resistance, used in aerospace, fire-fighting equipment, etc.

kewpie doll *kū'pi dol*, *n* a plump baby doll with a topknot of hair. [**Cupid**]

kex *keks*, *n* a dry, often hollow, herbaceous (*usu* umbelliferous) stalk; any tall umbelliferous plant. — Also **kecks**, and (false singulars) **keck**, **kecks'y** or **keks'ye**. [Origin unknown]

key[1] *kē*, formerly *kā*, *n* an instrument for locking or unlocking, winding up, turning, tuning, tightening or loosening; (in musical instruments) a lever or piston-end pressed to produce the sound; a similar lever for other purposes in machines, as in a typewriter or calculating machine; a system of tones definitely related to one another in a musical scale; a keynote (*obs*); something which gives command of anything or upon which success turns; a scheme or diagram of explanation or identification; a taxonomic system for distinguishing similar species (*biol*); a set of answers to problems; a crib translation; a field or group of characters in each record used for sorting and retrieving (*comput*); that which leads to the solution of a problem; a leading principle; general tone of voice, emotion, morals, etc; a wedge; a peg inserted into eg a key-way to prevent relative motion; a tapered piece of metal for fixing the boss of a wheel, etc to a shaft; a spanner; the middle stone of an arch; a piece of wood let into another piece crosswise to prevent warping; a lever to close or break an electrical circuit; a dry winged fruit, eg of ash or maple, often hanging with others in bunches; a fret pattern; the preparation of a surface to take plaster, glue, etc. — *vt* to provide with a key; to lock or fasten with a key (*obs*); to mark the position on the layout of (something to be printed), using symbols (*printing*); to keyboard; to stimulate (to a state of nervous tension and excitement), raise (in pitch or standard), or increase (with *up*). — *vt* and *vi* to attune (with *to*); to prepare (a surface) eg for plastering; to give (an advertisement) a feature that will enable replies to it to be identified. — *adj* vital, essential, crucial. — *adj* **keyed** equipped with a key or keys; set to a particular key (*music*); in a state of tension or readiness. — *adj* **key'less** without a key or keys; not requiring a key. — **key'board** the manually operated range of keys or levers in a musical instrument, computer, etc (also *adj*); (in *pl*) *usu* in pop groups, etc, a musical instrument, *esp* electronic, incorporating a keyboard. — *vi* and *vt* to type text, etc by means of a keyboard, *esp* into a computer. — **key'boarder** someone who types text on a keyboard; **key'bugle** a bugle with keys, having a chromatic scale of two octaves. — *adj* **key'-cold** (*Shakesp*) cold as a key, lifeless. — **key'-desk** the frame enclosing the keyboards, stops, etc of an organ; **key'-fruit** a winged fruit of a tree; **key'hole** the hole in which a key of a lock is inserted; any small hole similar in shape or purpose; **keyhole limpet** a mollusc (*Fissurella*) with a perforated conical shell; **keyhole saw** a padsaw (qv under **pad**[2]); **keyhole surgery** (*colloq*) surgery using miniature instruments, etc, performed through tiny holes in the outer tissue instead of making major incisions; **key industry** an industry indispensable to others and essential to national economic welfare and independence; **key'line** (*printing*) an outline drawing showing the shape, size, position, etc of an illustration; **key man** an indispensable worker, essential to the continued conduct of a business, etc; **key money** a premium, fine or sum additional to rent, demanded for the grant, renewal or continuance of a tenancy; **key'note** the fundamental note or tonic (*music*); any central principle or controlling thought. — *adj* of fundamental importance; (of a speech, etc) expounding the central principle, or setting the tone for a conference, etc. — *vt* and *vi* to give the keynote; to put forward the central principle in an opening address at a convention. — **key'pad** a small device with push-button controls, eg a TV remote control unit or pocket calculator; a small keyboard with push-button controls for a specific purpose, eg a numeric keypad (*comput*); **key'-plate** a keyhole escutcheon; **key punch** (*comput*) a device operated by a keyboard, which transfers data on to punch-cards, etc. — *vt* **key'punch**. — **key'-ring** a ring for holding a bunch of keys; **key'-seat** a groove for receiving a key, to prevent one piece of machinery from turning on another; **key signature** (*music*) the indication of key by marking sharps, flats or naturals where the key changes or at the beginning of a line; **key stage** (*UK educ*) any of the four age-based levels of the National Curriculum; **key'stone** the stone at the apex of an arch; the chief element; something on which all else depends. — *vt* and *vi* to produce a **keystone effect** ie the distortion of a television picture in which a rectangular pattern is transformed into a trapezoidal pattern. — **key'stroke** a single operation of a key on a typewriter or other machine using keys; **key'stroking**; **key'-way** a groove cut in a shaft or boss to accommodate a key which interlocks with another component so as to prevent relative motion; **key'word** a headword; a word serving as a key in an index, etc; a word that encapsulates the passage in which it appears. — *adj* **key'word-in-context** applied to electronic concordances or indexes which supply the keywords alphabetically in a fixed position in the line, preceded and followed by a fixed amount of context. — **have the key of the door** (*colloq*) to have reached the age of 21; **have the key of the street** (*colloq*) to be locked out; to be homeless; **key in** (*comput*) to enter (data) by operating a keyboard; **out of key** out of tune; out of place, incongruous; **power of the keys** the power to loose and to bind, conferred by Christ on Peter (Matt 16.19), and claimed by the Popes. [OE *cæg*]

key[2]. An old spelling of **quay**.

key[3] or **cay** *kē*, *n* a low island or reef. [Sp *cayo*]

Keynesian *kānz'i-ən*, *adj* relating to John Maynard *Keynes* (1883–1946) or to his economic teaching, *esp* his advocacy of a measure of public control, within capitalism, of the unrestricted play of economic forces both national and international. — *n* **Keynes'ianism**.

Keys *kēz*, *n pl* in full **House of Keys** the lower house of the Manx Court of Tynwald. [Appar **key**[1], not Manx *kiare-as-feed* four-and-twenty]

KG *abbrev*: Knight of the (Order of the) Garter.

kg *abbrev*: keg(s); kilogram(s), kilogramme(s).

KGB *abbrev*: *Komitet Gosudarstvennoi Bezopasnosti* (Russ), Committee of State Security, the Soviet secret police.

kgotla *hhö'tlə* or *kgot'lə*, *n* an assembly of tribal elders in Botswana; the place of such assembly. [Bantu]

kgy *abbrev*: kilogray(s).

khaddar *kud'ər*, or **khadi** *kud'i*, *n* (in India) hand-spun, hand-woven cloth. [Hind *khādar*, *khādī*]

khaki *kä'ki*, *adj* dust-coloured, dull brownish or greenish yellow; militaristically imperialist (*hist*). — *adv* (*hist*) with war-spirit. — *n* a cloth of this colour used for military uniforms, etc. — **khaki election** an election called immediately after a war, or at a time of patriotic military fervour. [Urdu and Pers *khākī* dusty]

khalat. See **killut**.

khalif. See **caliph**.

khalifa or **khalifah** *kä-lē'fä*, *n* a caliph; a Senussi leader; the Mahdi's successor. — *n* **khalifat** (*käl'i-fat*) or **khalifate** (*-fāt*) the caliphate. [Ar *khalīfah*]

Khalka *kal'kə*, *n* a dialect of Mongolian. [Native word]

Khalsa *kal'sə*, *n* the order of baptized Sikhs who wear the five Ks. [Hindi, pure]

khamsin, **kamsin** or **kamseen** *kam'sin* or *-sēn'*, *n* a hot S or SE wind in Egypt, which blows for about fifty days from mid-March. [Ar *khamsīn*, from *khamsūn* fifty]

khan[1] *kän*, *n* an Eastern inn, a caravanserai. [Ar *khan*]

khan[2] *kän*, *n* in Central Asia, (a title for) a prince or chief; in ancient Persia, (a title for) a governor. — *n* **khan'ate** the rank of a khan; a region governed by a khan. — *n* **khan'um** (*-ōōm*; *Middle Eastern*) (a title for) a lady of rank; Mrs. [Turki (and thence Pers) *khān* lord or prince]

khanga. See **kanga**.

khanjar. See **handjar**.

khansamah or **khansama** *kän'sä-mä*, *n* a house-steward or butler in India. [Hindi *khānsāmān*, from Pers *khān* lord, and *sāmān* household stores]

kharif *kə-rēf'*, (*India*, etc) *n* a crop sown before the monsoon to ripen in autumn. [Hindi *kharīf*, from Ar, gathered]

khat[1], **kat** or **qat** *kat*, *n* a shrub of E Africa, Arabia, etc, or *specif* its leaves, chewed or taken as tea for their stimulant effect. [Ar *qat*]

khat[2]. See **kat**[2].

khaya *kā'yə*, *n* any tree of the African genus *Khaya*, related to mahogany. [Wolof *khaye*]

kheda or **keddah** *ked'ə*, *n* an enclosure for catching wild elephants; the operation of catching wild elephants. [Hindi *khēdā*]

khedive *ke-dēv'*, *n* the title (1867–1914) of the viceroy of Egypt. — *n* **khedi'va** his wife. — *n* **khedi'vate** or **khedi'viate** the khedive's office or territory. — *adj* **khedi'val** or **khedi'vial**. [Fr *khédive*, from Turk *khidīv*, *hudîv*, from Pers *khidīw* prince]

khidmutgar *kid'mut-gär*, or **khitmutgar** *kit'*, *n* a table-servant. [Urdu, from Pers *khidmat* service, and agent suffix *-gār*]

khilafat *kil'ä-fat* or *kil-ä'fat*, *n* caliphate. — *adj* of an anti-British agitation among Muslims in India after the Treaty of Sèvres, 1920. [Ar *khilāfat*; cf **caliph**]

khilat. See **killut**.

khilim. See **kilim**.

khitmutgar. See **khidmutgar**.

Khmer *kmûr* or *kmer*, *n* a member of a people inhabiting Cambodia; their language, the official language of Cambodia. — Also *adj*. — **Khmer Rouge** (*rōōzh*) the Communist guerrilla movement in Cambodia. — See also **Mon-Khmer**.

Khoikhoi *koi'koi*, *n* the Hottentot people; their language. — Also *adj*. [Hottentot]

khoja or **khodja** *kō'ja* or **hodja** *hō'ja*, (*Middle-Eastern*) *n* a title of respect; a professor or teacher in a Muslim school; a member of a sect of converts to Islam from Hinduism. [Turk and Pers *khōjah*, *khwājah*]

khor *kōr* or *kör*, *n* a dry watercourse; a ravine. [Ar *khurr*, *khorr*]

khotbah, **khotbeh**. See **khutbah**.

khud *kud*, (*Ind*) *n* a pit, hollow; a ravine. [Hindi *khad*]

khurta. See **kurta**.

khuskhus. Same as **cuscus**[2].

khutbah *kōōt'bä*, *n* a Muslim prayer and sermon delivered in the mosques on Fridays. — Also **khot'bah** or **khot'beh**. [Ar]

kHz *abbrev*: kilohertz.

kiang or **kyang**, *kyang* or *ki-ang'*, *n* a Tibetan wild ass. [Tibetan *rkyang*]

kia-ora *kē'ä-ö'rə*, (*NZ*) *interj* good health. [Maori]

kiaugh *kyöhh* or *kyähh* or **kaugh** *köhh* or *kähh*, (*Scot*) *n* care, trouble.

kibble[1] *kib'l*, *n* the bucket of a well. — **kibb'le-chain** the chain for drawing up a bucket. [Cf Ger *Kübel* bucket]

kibble[2] *kib'l*, *vt* to grind cereal, etc fairly coarsely. [Origin obscure]

kibbutz *ki-bōōts'*, *n* a Jewish communal agricultural settlement in Israel: — *pl* **kibbutzim** (*ki-bōōts-ēm'*). — *n* **kibbutz'nik** a person who lives and works on a kibbutz. [Heb]

kibe *kīb*, *n* a chilblain, *esp* on the heel. [Prob Welsh *cibi*]

kibitka *ki-bit'kə*, *n* a Russian covered wagon or sledge; a Central Asian felt tent. [Russ]

kibitzer *kib'it-sər*, (*NAm slang*) *n* an onlooker (at cards, etc) who gives unwanted advice; an interferer. — *vi* **kib'itz** to give unwanted advice, to meddle, comment out of turn. [Yiddish]

kiblah *kib'lä*, *n* the point toward which Muslims turn in prayer, the direction of Mecca. — Also **keb'lah**. [Ar *qiblah*]

kibosh or **kybosh** *kī'bosh* or *ki-bosh'*, (*colloq*) *n* nonsense, rot. — *vt* to dispose of finally. — **put the kibosh on** to kibosh. [Ety obscure]

kick *kik*, *vt* to hit with the foot; to put or drive by blows with the foot; to start or work by foot on a pedal; to achieve by a kick or kicking; to free oneself from (eg a habit) (*slang*). — *vi* to thrust out the foot with violence; to raise the leg high, eg in dancing; to show opposition or resistance; (of a gun, etc) to recoil or jerk violently; (of a ball, etc) to rear up unexpectedly; to move suddenly as if kicked; to put on an extra spurt of speed (*athletics*); to be exposed to kicking, lie around (often with *about*); to be full of vitality (*usu* in *pr p*). — *n* a blow or fling with the foot; the recoil of a gun; an unexpected rearing up of a ball; kicking power; resistance; resilience; an extra spurt of speed (*athletics*); stimulus, pungency (*colloq*); a thrill (*colloq*); an enthusiastic but short-lived interest; a phase of such interest; the fashion (*archaic slang*); the depression in the bottom of a bottle; dismissal (*esp* with *the*; *slang*); sixpence (*obs slang*). — *adj* **kick'able**. — *n* **kick'er** someone or something that kicks, eg a horse; (in some sports) a player whose function is to take (*esp* set-piece) kicks; an outboard motor (*NAm*). — **kick'back** part of a sum received paid to another by confidential agreement for favours past or to come; money paid in return for protection; loose material thrown up from the track by a galloping horse (*horse-racing*); a strong reaction; **kick'ball** a game played by children, similar to baseball but using a much larger ball which is kicked not batted; **kick boxing** a martial art in which the combatants kick with bare feet and punch with gloved fists; **kick'down** a method of changing gear in a car with automatic gear transmission, by pressing the accelerator pedal right down; **kick'ing-strap** a strap behind a draught-horse's hindquarters to prevent kicking; **kick'-off** the first kick in a game of football; the start of the game; the start of any activity (*colloq*); **kick pleat** a pleat in a narrow skirt from knee-level to hem, which allows the wearer to walk easily; **kick'-sorter** (*telecomm*) a device which selects and counts electrical pulses of specified amplitudes; **kick'stand** a piece of metal attached to a motorcycle, etc, which is kicked into position to hold the machine upright when parked; **kick'-start** the starting of an engine by a pedal. — *vt* to start (an engine) thus; to get (something) moving, to give a sudden (advantageous) impulse to (*fig*). — **kick turn** a skiing or skateboarding turn through 180°; **kick'-up** a disturbance; a dance; a depression in the bottom of a bottle. — **for a kick-off** for a start; **for kicks** for thrills; **kick about** or **around** to consider; to discuss; to treat harshly (*colloq*); (of a person) to wander around doing nothing in particular; (of an object) to lie about serving no useful purpose; **kick back** (of a machine, *esp* a gun) to react strongly, to recoil; to pay as a kickback (*colloq*); **kick in** (*slang*) to contribute, pay one's share; **kick in the pants** a sharp telling-off intended to make the recipient put in more effort; **kick in the teeth** a mortifying repulse; **kick off** to start a game of football; to open a discussion (*colloq*); to die (*slang*); **kick oneself** to reproach oneself; **kick one's heels** see under **heel**[1]; **kick out** (*colloq*) to eject with force; to dismiss; **kick over the traces** to throw off control; **kick** or **strike the beam** to be of little weight or importance (*fig* from the lighter scale in a balance rising so as to strike against the beam); **kick the bucket** see under **bucket**; **kick up a dust, fuss** or **row** to create a disturbance; **kick upstairs** to promote (*usu* to a less active or less powerful position). [ME *kiken*; origin unknown; Welsh *cicio* (to kick) comes from Eng]

kickie-wickie *kik'i-wik-i*, (*Shakesp*) *n* a wife. [Altered by editors to **kicksy-wicksy**; perh connected with **kickshaws**]

kickshaws *kik'shöz* or **kickshaw** *-shö*, *n* a trinket, a cheap, worthless article; a delicacy (*archaic*). [Fr *quelque chose* something]

kid[1] *kid*, *n* a young goat; a young antelope or other related animal; a child or young person (*colloq*); leather made of kidskin, or a substitute; a glove, shoe or boot made of kid (*archaic*). — *adj* made of kid leather or imitation kid leather; young, still a child, as in *kid sister* (*colloq*). — *vt* and *vi* (of a goat) to give birth to a kid or kids: — *pr p* **kidd'ing**; *pa t* and *pa p* **kidd'ed**. — *n* **kidd'o** (*colloq*) term of address for a young man or woman. — *n* **kidd'y** dimin of **kid**, a little child; a flashy thief (*thieves' slang*): — *pl* **kidd'ies**. — *n* **kiddy'wink**, **kidd'iewink** or **kiddie-wink'ie** (*facetious*) extended forms of **kiddy**, a child. — *n* **kid'let** dimin of **kid**, a little child. — *n* **kid'ling** a young kid. — **kid'-fox** (*Shakesp*) a young fox; **kid-glove'** a glove made of kid leather. — *adj* as if done by someone wearing kid-gloves; overnice, delicate; extremely tactful. — **kid'skin** kid leather, typically soft and smooth; **kids' stuff** (*colloq*) something only suitable for young children, *usu* because very tame or very easy. — **handle**, etc **with kid gloves** to treat carefully and gently; to deal with very tactfully. [ON *kith*; cf Dan *kid*; Ger *Kitze* a young goat]

kid[2] *kid*, (*colloq*) *vt* and *vi* to hoax; to pretend, *esp* as a joke; to tease, delude, deceive as a joke. — Also **kidd'y**. — *n* a deception. — *n* **kidd'er**. — *n* **kidol'ogist** (*-jist*; *colloq*). — *n* **kidology** (*kid-ol'ə-ji*; *colloq*) the art of kidding, sometimes to gain a psychological advantage. — **kid'stakes** (*Austr colloq*) nonsense, humbug. — **kid on** to kid (*n* **kid'-on**). [Perh connected with **kid**[1] a child]

kid[3] *kid*, *n* a small tub. [Perh a variant of **kit**[1]]

kid[4] *kid*, *n* a faggot. [Origin unknown; Welsh *cedys* (faggots) is prob from Eng]

kidder *kid'ər* or **kiddier** *-i-ər*, *n* a forestaller; a huckster. [Origin obscure]

Kidderminster *kid'ər-min-stər*, *n* a two-ply or ingrain carpet formerly made at *Kidderminster*. — Also *adj*.

kiddle *kid'l*, (*hist*) *n* a stake-fence set in a stream for catching fish. — Also **kid'el** or **kett'le**. [OFr *quidel*; cf Breton *kidel*]

kiddush *kid'əsh*, *n* a Jewish blessing which is uttered over wine and bread on holy days. [Heb *qiddūsh* sanctification]

kiddy, etc. See under **kid**[2].

kidel. See **kiddle**.

kidge. See **kedge**[2].

kidgie. See **cadgy**.

kidling. See under **kid**[1].

kidnap *kid'nap*, *vt* to steal (a human being), often for ransom: — *pr p* **kid'napping**; *pa t* and *pa p* **kid'napped**. — *n* an instance of this. — *n* **kid'napper**. [**kid**[1] a child, and **nap**[4]]

kidney *kid'ni*, *n* either of two rounded flattened glands, in the anterior abdominal area in man, that filter waste from the blood and secrete it as urine; temperament, humour, disposition; sort, kind. — **kid'ney-bean** the French bean; any kidney-shaped variety of bean, *esp* the red variety of runner bean; **kidney machine** an apparatus used, in cases where the kidney functions badly, to remove harmful substances from the blood by dialysis; **kid'ney-ore** haematite in kidney-shaped masses; **kidney-potā'to** a kidney-shaped variety of potato; **kid'ney-stone** nephrite; a septarian nodule; a hard deposit formed in the kidney; **kidney vetch** any plant of the papilionaceous genus Anthyllis, including lady's fingers. [ME *kidenei* (pl *kideneiren*), perh a compound of *ei* (pl *eiren*) egg, confused sometimes with *nere* kidney]

kidologist, kidology. See under **kid**[2].

kie-kie *kē'-kē*, *n* a New Zealand climbing plant (*Freycinetia banksii*) of the screw-pine family. [Maori]

kier or **keir**, *kēr*, *n* a bleaching vat. [Cf ON *ker* tub]

kierie *kē'rē*, (*SAfr*) *n* a stick. [Prob Hottentot]

kieselguhr *kē'zl-gōōr*, *n* diatomite. [Ger, from *Kiesel* flint, and *Guhr* fermentation]

kieserite *kēz'ər-īt*, *n* a mineral, hydrated magnesium sulphate ($MgSO_4H_2O$), a source of Epsom salts. [After D G *Kieser* (1779–1862) of Jena]
kieve. See **keeve**.
kif. See **kef**.
kight (*Spenser*). Same as **kite**[1].
kike *kīk*, (*offensive slang*; *esp NAm*) *n* and *adj* Jew. [Possibly from the *-ki* ending of many E European Jewish immigrants' names in US at the end of the 19c]
kikoi *kē'koi*, *n* (in E Africa) a piece of striped cloth wound round the waist. [Swahili]
kikumon *kik'ōō-mon*, *n* the chrysanthemum badge of the Japanese imperial family. [Jap *kiku* chrysanthemum, and *mon* badge]
Kikuyu *ki-* or *kē-kōō'ū*, *n* an agricultural Negroid people of Kenya; a member of this people; their language. — **kikuyu** (or **kikuyu grass**) an African grass (*Pennisetum clandestinum*) grown also in Australia and S America.
kild *kild*, (*Spenser*). Variant of **killed**.
kilderkin *kil'dər-kin*, (*obs*) *n* a small cask; a liquid measure of 18 gallons. [MDu *kindeken, kinneken* (Scot *kinken*), dimin of *kintal*, from LL *quintāle* quintal]
kilerg *kil'ûrg*, *n* a thousand ergs. [Gr *chīlioi* thousand, and **erg**]
kiley. See **kylie**.
kilfud-yoking *kil-fud-yōk'ing*, (*Scot*) *n* a fireside disputation. [Scot *kilfuddie* the aperture for feeding a kiln, and **yoking**]
kilim *ki-lēm'*, *n* a pileless woven rug traditionally made in the Middle East. — Also **kelim** or **khilim**. [Turk, from Pers *kilīm*]
kill[1] *kil*, *vt* to put to death, to murder or execute; to deprive of life; to destroy; to nullify or neutralize, to make inactive, to weaken or dilute; to reject, discard, defeat; to overwhelm with amazement, admiration, laughter, etc (*colloq*); to injure seriously (*Ir*); to spoil; to muffle or still; to extinguish (a light, etc) (*colloq*); to stop the flow of oil in (a well) by pumping in mud or other liquid (*oil industry*); to cause to stop, to turn off (machinery, etc); to exhaust, to overexert (*colloq*); to cause severe pain to (*colloq*); to consume completely (*colloq*); to mark for cancellation, to cut (*printing*); to cancel or suppress (a story) (*journalism*); to bring (a loose ball) under control (*football*, etc); to play (a shot) so hard that one's opponent cannot play it back again (*lawn tennis*, etc). — *vi* to commit murder or manslaughter. — *n* an act or instance of killing, etc; prey or game killed; an act or instance of destroying an enemy plane, tank, etc; the plane, tank, etc so destroyed; a shot impossible to return (*lawn tennis*, etc). — *n* **kill'er** a person, creature, organism, chemical, etc that kills; someone who murders readily or habitually; the grampus or killer whale, a ferocious, black-and-white, toothed, marine whale; an instrument for killing; a neutralizing agent; an animal intended for slaughter (*Austr* and *NZ colloq*); a gruelling task or activity (*colloq*). — *adj* (*slang*) spectacularly impressive, stupendous. — *adj* **kill'ing** depriving of life; destructive; deadly, irresistible; exhausting; fascinating; irresistibly funny (*colloq*). — *n* the act of causing death, slaughter; a large financial gain, *esp* sudden (*colloq*); a severe handling. — **kill-court'esy** (*Shakesp*) a discourteous person; **kill'cow** (*obs*) a bully, a swaggerer; **killing time** (*Scot hist*) the days of the persecution of the Covenanters in the 17c; **kill'joy** a spoilsport; **kill line** (*mineral ext*) one of the small-bore pipelines, connected through the blow-out preventer stack, that allow denser mud to be pumped into a borehole which has to be shut down because of the danger of a blow-out; **kill string** see **injection string**. — *adj* austere, disapproving. — **dressed to kill** dressed so as to dazzle, attract and impress others; **in at the kill** (*fig*) present at the culminating moment; **kill by inches** to kill gradually, eg by torture; **kill off** to exterminate; **kill the fatted calf** to prepare an elaborate feast, etc for a homecoming or welcome (also *fig*); **kill time** to occupy oneself with amusements, etc, in order to pass spare time or to relieve boredom (also *n* **kill'-time** an occupation of this sort); **kill two birds with one stone** to accomplish one thing by the same means as, or by accomplishing, another; **kill up** (*Shakesp*) to exterminate; **make a killing** (*colloq*) to make a lot of money, a large profit. [ME *killen* or *cullen*]
kill[2] *kil*, (*US dialect*) *n* a stream, brook; a river; a channel (used chiefly in place names, *esp* in areas *orig* settled by Dutch). — **kill'ifish** any of several small freshwater fish used as bait and to control mosquitoes, a topminnow. [Du *kil*, from MDu *kille* a channel]
killadar *kil'ə-där*, (*India*, etc) *n* the commandant of a fort or garrison. [Hind (Pers) *qil'adār*]
killas *kil'əs*, (*geol*) *n* clay slate. [Cornish miners' term]
killcrop *kil'krop*, *n* a greedy, insatiable baby; a changeling. [LGer *kîlkrop*; Ger *Kielkropf*]
killdeer *kil'dēr*, *n* the largest N American ring-necked plover: — *pl* **kill'deer** or **kill'deers**. — Also **kill'dee**. [Imit]
killick *kil'ik* or **killock** *-ək*, *n* a small anchor; its fluke or barb; in the Royal Navy, a leading seaman (from his badge, bearing the symbol of an anchor). [Origin obscure]
killifish. See under **kill**[2].
killikinick. See **kinnikinick**.
killogie *ki-lō'gi*, (*Scot*) *n* the space in front of the fireplace of a kiln. [**kiln** and **logie**]
killut *kil'ut*, *n* (in India) a robe of honour or other ceremonial present. — Also **kell'aut, khal'at** or **khil'at**. [Hind and Pers *khil'at*]
Kilmarnock *kil-mär'nək*, *n* a kind of closely woven broad cap for men, *orig* made at *Kilmarnock* in Scotland. — **Kilmarnock cowl** a kind of nightcap.
kiln *kiln* or (now *dialect*) *kil*, *n* a large oven for drying, baking or calcining corn, hops, bricks, pottery, limestone, etc. — *vt* to dry, fire, etc in a kiln. — *vt* **kiln'-dry** to dry in a kiln: — *pa p* and *adj* **kiln'-dried**. — **kiln'-hole** the mouth of a kiln. [OE *cyln, cylen*, from L *culīna* a kitchen]
Kilner jar® *kil'nər jär*, *n* a glass jar with an airtight lid, used for preserving fruit and vegetables.
kilo *kēl'ō*, *n* a short form of **kilogram** or sometimes of another word with the prefix **kilo-**: — *pl* **kil'os**.
kilo- *kil-ə-*, *kil-ō-*, *kē-lə-*, *kē-lō-* or *ki-lo'-*, *pfx* denoting 1000 times the unit to which it is attached, eg **kil'obar** = 1000 bars. — *n* **kil'obit** (*comput*) 1024 bits. — *n* **kil'obyte** (*comput*) 1000 bytes; 2^{10} (1024) bytes. — *n* **kil'ocalorie** 1000 calories, a Calorie, used to measure energy content of food (see also **calorie**). — *n* **kil'ocycle** or **kilocycle per second** kilohertz (qv). — *n* **kil'ogram** or **kil'ogramme** the SI base unit of mass, the mass of a platinum-iridium cylinder kept as the standard (International Prototype Kilogram) in Paris, 2·205 lb. — *n* **kil'ogram-calorie** same as **kilocalorie**. — *n* **kil'ogray** 1000 grays (see **gray**[2]), used to measure the absorbed dose of radiation, eg in food irradiation. — *n* **kil'ohertz** 1000 cycles of oscillation per second, used to measure frequency of sound and radio waves. — *n* **kil'ojoule** 1000 joules, used to measure energy, work and heat. — *pfx* **kil'omega-** one thousand million times (now replaced by **giga-**). — *n* **kil'ometre** (also *-om'-*) 1000 metres, 0·6214 or about $\frac{5}{8}$ mile. — *n* **kil'oton** a measure of explosive force equivalent to that of 1000 tons of TNT. — *n* **kil'ovolt** 1000 volts. — *n* **kil'owatt** 1000 watts, the power used by one bar of the average electric fire. — **kilowatt hour** the energy consumed by a load of one kilowatt in one hour of use (3·6 megajoules), the unit by which electricity is charged to the consumer. [Gr *chīlioi* a thousand]
kilp *kilp*. See **kelp**.
kilt[1] *kilt*, *n* a man's short pleated skirt, *usu* of tartan, forming part of Highland dress; any similar garment. — *vt* to tuck up (skirts); to pleat vertically; to hang, string up (*archaic*). — *vi* (*archaic*) to move lightly and quickly, to trip. — *adj* **kilt'ed** dressed in a kilt; tucked up; vertically pleated. — *n* **kilt'y** or **kilt'ie** (*colloq*) a

wearer of a kilt. [Scand; cf Dan *kilte* to tuck up; ON *kilting* a skirt]

kilt[2] *kilt*, (*Spenser* and *Ir*, *esp* hyperbolically) *pa p* of **kill**[1].

kilter *kil'tər*, (*esp US*) *n* good condition. — Also **kelter** (*kel'tər*; *dialect*). — **out of kilter** or **off kilter** out of order, not functioning properly; out of correct condition or shape. [Origin unknown]

Kimball tag *kim'bl tag*, *n* a punched tag detached from retail goods when sold, and used as computer input for information on sales, stock control, etc.

kimberlite *kim'bər-līt*, *n* a mica-peridotite, an intrusive igneous rock, in which the diamonds at *Kimberley* and elsewhere in S Africa were found.

kimbo *kim'bō*, *vt* to set akimbo: — *adj* **kim'boed**.

kimchi *kim'chi*, *n* a very spicy Korean dish made with a variety of raw vegetables, *esp* cabbage, radish, cucumber, garlic, ginger, etc. [Korean]

Kimeridgian or **Kimmeridgian** *kim-ə-rij'i-ən*, (*geol*) *adj* of the lowest division of the Upper Jurassic, named from a clay well developed at *Kimmeridge* in Dorset. — Also *n*.

kimmer. See **cummer**.

kimono *ki-mō'nō*, *n* a loose robe with wide sleeves, fastening with a sash, a traditional outer garment in Japan; a dressing-gown of similar form: — *pl* **kimō'nos**. — **kimono sleeve** a magyar sleeve. [Jap]

kin[1] *kin*, *n* people belonging to the same family; one's relatives; relationship; affinity. — *adj* related. — *adj* **kin'less** without relatives. — *n* **kinsfolk** (*kinz'fōk*) folk or people kindred or related to one another (also, chiefly *NAm*, **kin'folk** or **kins'folks**). — *n* **kin'ship** relationship. — *n* **kins'man** a man of the same kin or race as another: — *fem* **kins'woman**. — **next of kin** one's closest relatives, among whom one's personal property is distributed if one dies intestate; the person or persons most closely related to an individual by blood, marriage, or a legal ruling; **of kin** related. [OE *cynn*; ON *kyn*, Gothic *kuni* family, race; cognate with L *genus*, Gr *genos*]

kin[2] *kin*, *n* a Japanese and Chinese weight, the catty. [Jap *kin*, Chin *chin*]

-kin *-kin*, *sfx* denoting a diminutive, eg lamb*kin* and mani*kin*; also in proper names, eg Jen*kin* (from *John*), Wil*kin* (from *William*). [Prob Du or LGer; cf Ger *-chen*]

kina[1], **kinakina**. See **quina**.

kina[2] *kē'nə*, *n* the standard monetary unit of Papua New Guinea (100 *toea*). [Native name]

kinaesthesis or (*NAm*) **kinesthesis**, *kīn-ēs-thē'sis*, *kin-* or *-es-*, *n* sense of the body's movement or of muscular effort. — Also **kinaesthē'sia** or (*NAm*) **kinesthe'sia** (*-zi-ə* or *-zyə*). — *adj* **kinaesthetic** or (*NAm*) **kinesthetic** (*-thet'ik*) pertaining to kinaesthesis. [Gr *kīneein* to move, and *aisthēsis* sensation]

kinase *kī'nāz* or *kin'āz*, *n* an enzyme which catalyses the phosphorylation of its substrate by adenosine triphosphate (ATP). [*kin*etic, and **-ase**]

kinchin *kin'chin*, (*thieves' slang*) *n* a child. — **kin'chin-cove** (*obs*) a boy; **kin'chin-lay** the robbing of children; **kin'chin-mort** (*obs*) a girl. [Appar Ger *Kindchen* little child]

kincob *king'kəb*, *n* a rich silk fabric embroidered with gold or silver thread, made in India. [Urdu and Pers *kimkhāb*]

kind[1] *kīnd*, *n* related people, a race; sort or species, a particular variety; an individual belonging to a specific variety; fundamental qualities (of a thing); produce, as distinguished from money; either of the eucharistic elements; nature, the material universe (*archaic*); innate character (of a person) (*archaic*); sex (*obs*). — *adj* disposed to do good to others; benevolent; helpful; agreeable; having or springing from the feelings natural for those of the same family (*obs*). — *adv* **kind'a** (*colloq*) short for **kind of**, somewhat, sort of. — *adj* **kind'less** (*Shakesp*) unnatural, destitute of kindness. — *adv* **kind'ly** in a kind manner; a (rather peremptory) substitute for 'please' (for the *adj* see separate entry). — *n* **kind'ness** the quality or fact of being kind; a kind act. — *adj* **kind-heart'ed**. — *adv* **kind-heart'edly**. — **kind-heart'edness**. — *adj* **kind-spok'en** spoken kindly; given to speaking kindly. — **after (its) kind** according to (its) nature; **do one's kind** (*Shakesp*) to act according to one's nature; **in a kind** (*archaic*) in a way, to some extent; **in kind** in goods instead of money; tit for tat; **kind of** (*colloq*) of a kind, somewhat, sort of, to some extent, as it were, used adjectivally and adverbially. [OE (*ge*)*cynde*, from *cynn* kin]

kind[2] *kīnd*, (*obs*) *vt* to beget: — *pa p* (*Spenser*) **kynd'ed**.

kindergarten *kin'dər-gär-tn*, *n* a school or class for pre-primary children on Froebel's principle (1826), in which object-lessons and games figure largely. — Also in short forms **kin'der** (*Austr*) and **kin'dy** (*Austr* and *NZ*). — *n* **kindergart'ener** a teacher in a kindergarten; a pupil of a kindergarten (*US*). — Also **kindergärtner** (*-gert'nər*). [Ger, from *Kinder* children, and *Garten* garden]

kinderspiel *kin'dər-spēl*, *n* a children's cantata or play. [Ger, children's sport, child's play, from *Kinder* children, and *Spiel* game, play]

kindle[1] *kin'dl*, *vt* to set fire to; to light; to inflame (eg the passions); to provoke, incite. — *vi* to catch fire; to begin to be excited; to be roused. — *n* **kin'dler**. — *n* **kin'dling** the act of causing to burn; materials for starting a fire, such as twigs, dry wood. [Cf ON *kyndill* a torch, from L *candēla* candle]

kindle[2] *kin'dl*, (*Shakesp*) *vt* and *vi* to bring forth young. — *n* brood, litter. — **in kindle** with young. [ME *kindlen*; cf **kind**[1]]

kindless. See under **kind**[1].

kindly *kīnd'li*, *adj* inclined to kindness; benign; genial; comfortable; natural (*obs*); native (*obs*); native-born (*archaic*). — *adv* in a kind or kindly manner (see also under **kind**[1]). — *adv* **kind'lily** (*rare*). — *n* **kind'liness**. — *adj* **kind'ly-nā'tured**. — **kindly tenant** (*Scot hist*) a tenant whose family has held lands in succession, from father to son, for several generations. — **take it kindly** to feel it as a kindness; **take kindly to** (often in *neg*) to take a favourable view of, or to adopt (a practice) with enthusiasm. [OE *gecyndelic*; cf **kind**[1]]

kindred *kin'drid* (*Spenser* **kin'red**), *n* relationship by blood, or (less properly) by marriage; relatives; a group of relatives, family, clan; similarity, affinity. — *adj* related; cognate; congenial. — *n* **kin'dredness**. — *n* **kin'dredship**. [ME *kinrede*, from OE *cynn* kin, and the suffix *-rǣden* expressing mode or state]

kine *kīn*, (*Bible*) *n pl* cows. [ME *kyen*, a double plural of OE *cū* a cow, the plural of which is *cȳ*; cf Scots **kye**]

kinema. See **cinema**.

kinematics *kin-i-mat'iks* or *kīn-*, *n sing* the science of motion without reference to force. — *adj* **kinemat'ic** or **kinemat'ical**. [Gr *kīnēma* motion, from *kīneein* to move]

kinematograph. See **cinematograph**.

kinescope *kin'is-kōp*, (*NAm*) *n* a cathode-ray tube for a television.

kinesi- *kīn-ēs-i-* or (before a vowel) **kines-** *kīn-ēs-* (*med*) *combining form*, denoting movement, motion. — *adj* **kinesiat'ric** or **kinesipath'ic**. — *n* **kinesiat'rics**, **kinesip'athy** or **kinesither'apy** a method of treating disease by means of exercises or gymnastic movements. — *n* **kinesiol'ogist**. — *n* **kinesiol'ogy** the scientific study of human movement and posture, relating mechanics and anatomy. — *n* **kines'ipath** or **kinesip'athist**. [Gr *kīnēsis* movement]

kinesis *kī-nē'sis* or *ki-*, *n* a movement, change of position, *specif* (*biol*) under stimulus, and with the direction not precisely determined. — *n sing* **kinē'sics** (the study of) body movements which convey information in the absence of speech. [Gr *kīnēsis* movement]

kinesthesis, etc. *NAm* spelling of **kinaesthesis**, etc.

kinetheodolite *kin-* or *kīn-i-thi-od'ə-līt*, *n* an improved form of theodolite used in tracking missiles and artificial satellites.

kinetics *kī-net'iks* or *ki-*, *n sing* the science of the action of force in producing or changing motion. — *adj* **kinet'ic** or **kinet'ical** pertaining to motion or to kinetics; due to motion. — *n* **kinetochore** (*kin-et'ə-kōr*) (*biol*) a densely staining region within the centromere of a chromosome to which spindle microtubules attach during meiosis and mitosis. — *n* **kinet'ograph** an early form of cinematograph camera. — *n* **kinet'oscope** an early form of cinematograph projector; an instrument for the production of curves by combination of circular movements. — **kinetic art** or **sculpture** art or sculpture in which movement (produced by air currents, or electricity, or sound, etc) plays an essential part; **kinetic energy** the energy possessed by a body by virtue of its motion. [Gr *kīnetikos*, from *kīneein* to move]

kinfolk. Same as **kinsfolk**, under **kin**[1].

king *king*, *n* a male hereditary chief ruler or titular head of a nation; a male monarch; a queen bee (*obs*); a playing-card having the picture of a king; the most important piece in chess; a piece that has been crowned (*draughts*); a man or other male animal who is pre-eminent among his fellows: — *fem* **queen**. — *vt* to make king; to provide with a king (*obs*). — **king-** *combining form* denoting most important. — *n* **king'dom** the state or attributes of a king; a monarchical state; a region that was once a monarchical state; the spiritual sovereignty of God; one of the three major divisions of natural history (animal, vegetable, mineral); an area in which a specified quality or attribute is paramount. — *adj* **king'domed** (*Shakesp*) provided with or constituted like a kingdom. — *adj* **king'domless**. — *n* **king'hood** kingship; kingliness. — *adj* **king'less**. — *n* **king'let** a little or petty king; the golden-crested wren (*NAm*). — *n* **king'lihood**. — *adj* **king'-like**. — *n* **king'liness**. — *n* **king'ling** a petty king. — *adj* **king'ly** belonging or suitable to a king; royal; king-like. — Also *adv*. — *n* **Kings** the title of two historical books of the Old Testament. — *n* **king'ship** the state, office or dignity of a king. — **king'-apple** a large red variety of apple; **king'-archon** the second of the nine archons in Athens, successor to the abolished kings in religious functions; **king'-bird** an American flycatcher; **king'-bolt** or **king'-rod** a metal rod in a roof connecting the tie-beam and the ridge; **king-co'bra** a large Asiatic species of cobra; **king'-crab** Limulus, a large marine arachnid, with a convex horseshoe-shaped armoured body; **king'craft** the art of governing (*obs*); **king'-crow** a kind of drongo; **king'cup** the buttercup; the marsh-marigold; **King Edward** a popular English variety of potato; **king'fish** the opah; any of various fish notable for their size or value (*NAm* and *Austr*); **king'fisher** a European fish-eating bird with very brilliant blue-green and chestnut plumage, formerly known as the halcyon; any bird of the same family, most species of which are not fish-eating; a brilliant blue colour (also *adj*); **king'-hit** (*Austr slang*) a knockout blow. — Also *vt*. — **king'klip** (*SAfr*) any of several marine food fishes; **King Log** a do-nothing king, as opposed to **King Stork**, one who devours his frog-subjects (from Aesop's fable); **king'-maker** a person who has the power to create kings or other high officials; **king mob** the vulgar multitude; **king-of-arms'** (sometimes **king-at-arms'**) a principal herald (those of England having the designations Garter, Clarencieux, and Norroy and Ulster (includes N Ireland), of Scotland, Lyon); **king penguin** a large penguin, smaller than the emperor; **king'-pin** a tall pin, or one prominently placed; a pin on which an axle swivels, like that on an automobile front wheel; the most important person of a group engaged in an undertaking; the key issue; **king'post** a perpendicular beam in the frame of a roof rising from the tie-beam to the ridge; **king prawn** a large prawn, *esp* of the genus *Penaeus*, found around Australia; **king salmon** the largest Pacific salmon, the quinnat; **King's Bench** see **Queen's Bench**; **king's bounty** see under **bounty**; **king's'-chair** or **king's -cush'ion** a seat formed by two people clasping wrists; **King's Counsel** see **Queen's Counsel**; **king's English** (or sometimes **queen's English**) correct standard speech; **king's evidence** see **queen's evidence**; **king's-e'vil** a scrofulous disease formerly supposed to be healed by the touch of the monarch; **King's Guide** see **Queen's Guide**; **king's highway** the public thoroughfare; **king's'-hood** the second stomach of a ruminant, sometimes humorously for the human stomach. — *adj* **king'-size** or **king'-sized** of large size. — **king's'-man** a royalist; a custom-house officer; **king's peace** (or **queen's peace**) *orig* the peace secured by the sovereign for certain people (eg those employed on the king's or queen's business); the peace of the kingdom generally; **King's Proctor** (or **Queen's Proctor**) a legal officer chiefly concerned with establishing collusion in divorce cases; **King's Regulations** see **Queen's Regulations**; **King's Scout** see **Queen's Scout**; **king's shilling** see under **shilling**; **king's'-spear** an asphodel; **King's Speech** see **Queen's Speech**; **king's-yell'ow** orpiment as a pigment; **king-vul'ture** a large brilliantly-coloured tropical American vulture; **king'wood** a beautiful Brazilian wood also called *violet-wood*: the papilionaceous tree yielding it, a species of Dalbergia. — **King Charles's head** a matter that persists in obtruding itself as did King Charles's head in the thoughts of Mr Dick in *David Copperfield*; **King Charles spaniel** see under **spaniel**; **kingdom come** (*slang*) the state after death; some inconceivably far-off time; **king it** to play king, act as superior to, or in authority over, others; **King James Bible** (or **Version**) the Authorized Version; **king of beasts** the lion; **king of birds** the eagle; **king of kings** a powerful monarch with other monarchs subject to him; (with *caps*) God, Christ; **king of metals** gold; **king of terrors** death; **king of the castle** (*orig* from a children's game) the most important, powerful person in a group; **king of the forest** the oak; **king of the herrings** the shad; the oarfish; applied also to various other fishes, such as the opah, the rabbit-fish or chimaera; **take the king's shilling** see under **shilling**; **three kings of Cologne** the three Wise Men of the East, Caspar, Melchior and Balthazar; **turn king's** or **queen's evidence** see under **evident**. [OE *cyning*, from *cynn* a tribe, with suffix *-ing*; cf ety of **kin**[1]]

kingle *king'l*, (*Scot*) *n* very hard rock, *esp* sandstone.

kinin *kī'nin*, (*biol*) *n* a plant hormone which promotes cell-division and is used commercially as a preservative for cut flowers; any of a group of polypeptides in the blood, causing dilation of the blood vessels and contraction of smooth muscles. [Gr *kīn(ēsis)* movement]

kink[1] *kingk*, *n* a twisted loop in a string, rope, etc; a mental twist or quirk; a crick; a whim; an imperfection; an unusual sexual preference, or a person who has one (*colloq*). — *vi* to form a kink. — *vt* to cause a kink in. — *n* **kink'le** a slight kink. — *adj* **kink'y** twisted; curly; eccentric (*colloq*); crazy (*colloq*); out of the ordinary in an attractive (*esp* provocative) way (*colloq*); with unusual or perverted sexual tastes (*colloq*). [Prob Du]

kink[2] *kingk*, (*Scot* and *NEng*) *vi* to cough loudly; to gasp for breath. — *n* a convulsive cough or gasp. — **kink'-cough** or **kink'-host** whooping-cough. [Northern form of **chink**[3]]

kinkajou *king'kə-joo*, *n* a S American tree-dwelling animal related to the raccoon. [Appar from a N Am Ind word misapplied]

kinkle, kinky. See under **kink**[1].

kinnikinick *kin-i-kin-ik'* or **killikinick** *kil-*, *n* a mixture used by American Indians as a substitute for tobacco; a species of cornel or other plant forming part of the mixture. [From Algonquian, mixture]

kino *kē'nō*, *n* an astringent resinous substance that exudes from various tropical trees: — *pl* **kin'os**. [Appar of W African origin]

kinone. See **quinol**.

kinred (*Spenser*). See **kindred**.

kinsfolk, kinship, etc. See under **kin**[1].

kintledge. See **kentledge**.

kiosk *kē'osk* or *ki-osk'*, *n orig* an Eastern garden pavilion; a small roofed stall for the sale of papers, sweets, etc, either out-of-doors or inside a public building; a bandstand; a public telephone box. [Turk *köşk*, *keushk*, from Pers *kūshk*]

kip[1] *kip*, *n* the skin of a young animal. — **kip'-skin** leather made from the skin of young cattle, intermediate between calfskin and cowhide. [Du, bundle of hides, is suggested]

kip[2] *kip*, (*slang*) *n* a nap; a bed; a lodging-house; a brothel (*Ir*). — *vi* to go to bed, sleep, nap. — **kip down** to go to bed. [Cf Dan *kippe* a low alehouse]

kip[3] *kip*, (*mining*) *n* a level or slight incline at the end of an underground passage, on which the tubs of coal stand till hoisted up the shaft.

kip[4] or **kipp** *kip*, *n* anything beaked (*Scot*); a pointed hill (*Scot*); (in gymnastics) a swinging movement which reverses the relative positions of body and legs. [Cf Ger, orig LGer, *Kippe* point, tip]

kip[5] *kip*, (*Scot*) *vi* to play truant. — **play kip** or **play the kip** to play truant. [Origin uncertain]

kip[6] *kip*, (*Austr*) *n* a short flat stick used to throw up pennies in the game of two-up. [Origin unknown]

kip[7] *kip*, *n* a unit of weight equal to 1000 pounds. [*ki*lo and *p*ound]

kip[8] *kip*, *n* the standard unit of currency in Laos (100 *at*). [Thai]

kipe *kīp*, (*dialect*) *n* an osier basket for catching pike. [OE *cȳpe*]

Kipp *kip*, *n* a form of generator for hydrogen sulphide or other gas. — Also **Kipp's apparatus**. [P J *Kipp* (19c), Dutch founder of a firm of manufacturers of scientific apparatus]

kipp. See **kip**[4].

kippa *ki'pa*, (*Judaism*) *n* a religious skullcap, the yarmulka. [Heb *kipa*]

kippage *kip'ij*, (*Scot*) *n* a state of displeasure or anger. [Fr *équipage*; see **equipage** under **equip**]

kipper *kip'ər*, *n* a male salmon during the spawning season after spawning; a salmon or (*esp*) herring split open and cured; a person, *esp* if young or small (*slang*); a British person (*Austr slang*). — *vt* to cure or preserve (eg a salmon or herring). — *n* **kipp'erer**. — **kipper tie** (*colloq*) a very wide, and often garish, necktie. [Perh OE *cypera* a spawning salmon; or perh from **kip**[4], from the beaked lower jaw of the male salmon after spawning]

kir *kēr*, *n* a drink made of white wine and blackcurrant syrup or liqueur. [F *Kir* (1876–1968), the Frenchman who is said to have invented it]

kirbeh *kir'be*, *n* a water container made from animal hide. [Ar *qirba*]

Kirbigrip®, **kirby-grip** or **kirbigrip** *kûr'bi-grip*, *n* a kind of hair-grip, a U-shaped piece of springy metal with one side ridged to prevent slipping. [From *Kirby*, the name of one of the original manufacturers]

kirimon *kē'ri-mon*, *n* one of the two imperial crests of Japan, bearing three leaves and three flowers of Paulownia. [Jap]

kirk *kirk* or *kûrk*, (*Northern*, *esp Scot*) *n* church, in any sense; sometimes specially applied to the Church of Scotland. — *vt* to church. — *n* **kirk'ing** or **kirk'in'** the first attendance at church of a couple after marriage, of a woman after giving birth, or of a magistrate after election. — *adj* and *adv* **kirk'ward**. — **kirk session** the lowest court in the Scottish Presbyterian church, minister or ministers and elders as the governing body of a particular congregation; **kirk'ton** or **kirk town** (*Scot*) the village in which the parish church stands; **kirkyard** or **kirkyaird** (*-yärd'* or *kirk'*) a churchyard. — **Auld Kirk** see under **auld**; **make a kirk or** (or **and**) **a mill of** do what one pleases or can with. [Northern form of **church**, from ON *kirkja*; OE *cirice*]

Kirlian photography *kûr'li-ən fə-tog'rə-fi*, *n* a process of directly recording on photographic film the electrical discharge emitted by an object placed in contact with the film, claimed by some to prove the existence o auras, and also used as a diagnostic tool in alternative medicine. [From S and V *Kirlian*, Soviet electricians who discovered the process in 1939]

Kirman *kûr'mən*, *adj* or *n* applied to a type of Persian rug or carpet with naturalistic designs. [*Kerman* in SE Iran, where they are made]

kirmess. See **kermis**.

kirn[1] *kirn* or **kern** *kern* or *kûrn*, (*Scot*) *n* the cutting of the last sheaf or handful of the harvest; a harvest-home. — **kirn'-ba'by**, **corn'-ba'by**, **kirn'-doll'ie**, **corn'-doll'ie** or **corn'-maiden** a dressed-up figure made of the last handful of corn cut; (*esp* **corn-dollie**) any of a number of straw decorations *usu* of traditional design. [Origin unknown]

kirn[2] *kirn*, *n* a *Scot* and *NEng* form of **churn**. — **kirn'-milk** buttermilk.

kirpan *kər-pän'*, *n* a small sword or dagger, worn by Sikh men as a symbol of religious loyalty. [Punjabi]

kirri. Older form of **kierie**.

kirsch *kērsh* or **kirschwasser** *kērsh'väs-ər*, *n* a liqueur made from the wild cherry. [Ger *kirschwasser* cherry water]

kirtle *kûr'tl*, (*hist*) *n* a women's gown or outer petticoat a man's tunic or mantle. — *adj* **kir'tled**. [OE *cyrtel* Dan *kjortel*; ON *kyrtill*; appar from L *curtus* short]

kisan *kē'sän*, (*Ind*) *n* a peasant. [Hindi *kisān*]

kish *kish*, *n* solid graphite which has separated from and floats on the top of, a molten bath of cast-iron or pig-iron which has a high carbon content. [Origin uncertain; poss Ger *Kies* gravel]

kishke *kish'kə*, (*Jewish*) *n* beef or chicken intestine stuffed with onion, flour meal and fat; (*esp* in *pl*) the guts [Yiddish]

Kislev, **Chislev** *kis'lef* or **Kisleu** *kis'li-o͞o*, *n* the third (ecclesiastically ninth) Jewish month, parts of November and December. [Heb]

kismet *kiz'met* or *kis'*, *n* fate, destiny. [Turk *qismet*, from Ar *qisma*]

kiss *kis*, *vt* to caress or greet by touching with the lips; (of an inanimate object) to touch gently. — *vi* to greet by touching with the lips; (of two people) to press their lips together, *esp* as an expression of affection or sexual love; to touch lightly; (of billiard balls) to touch gently while moving. — *n* a caress, greeting, etc by touching with the lips; a light touch, *esp* by a moving billiard ball on another; a melt-in-the-mouth biscuit, etc; a drop of sealing-wax. — *adj* **kiss'able**. — *n* **kiss'er** a person who kisses; the mouth (*slang*). — *n* **kiss'ogram** or **kiss'agram** a service whereby a kiss is delivered to a specific person (eg on their birthday) by a **kissogram girl** (or **man**) *usu* in glamorous or unusual costume. — **kiss'-curl** a flat circular curl at the side of the forehead; **kiss'ing-com'fit** a perfumed comfit for sweetening the breath; **kissing bug** any of several N and S American biting insects which attack victim's lips and cheeks; **kissing cousin** a more or less distant relation with whom one is on familiar enough terms to kiss on meeting; **kiss'ing crust** that part of the upper crust of a loaf which overhangs and touches another; **kissing disease** (*colloq*) glandular fever; **kissing gate** a gate set in a V- or U-shaped enclosure. — *n pl* **kiss'ing-strings** cap or bonnet strings tied under the chin. — **kiss-in-the-ring'** an old game in which one kisses another after a chase round a ring of players; **kiss'-me** or **kiss'-me-quick** the wild pansy or other plant; a short veil; a small bonnet. — **kiss'-off** (*slang*) a sudden, *usu* offensive dismissal. — **kiss and make up** (*colloq*) to become reconciled (also *adj* **kiss'-and-make-up**); **kiss and tell** (*colloq*) to give an exposé of one's sexual adventures (*adj* **kiss'-and-tell**); **kiss (someone's) arse** or (*US*) **ass** (*slang*) to be obsequious or sycophantic (towards someone); (in *imperative*; *offensive*) get lost, go away; **kiss hands** to kiss the sovereign's hands on acceptance of office; **kiss of death** (*colloq*) something that causes failure, destruction, etc; **kiss off** (*slang*) to dismiss; to kill; to die. **kiss of life** in first-aid, a mouth-to-mouth method of restoring breathing (cf **Schafer's method**); a means of restoring vitality or vigour (*fig*); **kiss of peace** a kiss of greeting between the members of the early, and some branches of the modern, Church; **kiss the book** to kiss a Bible or New Testament, in England, after taking a legal oath; **kiss the gunner's daughter** to get a flogging, tied to the breech of a cannon; **kiss the rod** to submit to punishment. [OE *cyssan* to kiss, from *coss* a kiss; Ger *küssen*, Dan *kys*; related to **choose** and **gust**[2]]

kissel *kis'l*, *n* a Russian dessert of thickened fruit purée. [Russ *kisel*]

kist *kist*, (*Scot* and *NEng*) *n* a chest; a coffin; a cist (*archaeol*). — *vt* to coffin. — **kist o' whistles** an organ. [OE *cist* chest, or ON *kista*]

kistvaen or **cistvaen** *kist'vīn*, (*archaeol*) *n* a cist. [Welsh *cist* chest, and *maen* stone, with lenition of *m*]

kit[1] *kit*, *n* an outfit; equipment; material, tools, instructions, assembled in a container for some specific purpose; the container itself; a container for fish, or the quantity held (10 stones or 63.6kg); a set of parts or pieces for assembly by the purchaser; a small wooden tub or pail (*dialect*). — *vt* (sometimes with *out*) to provide with kit. — **kit'-bag** a strong canvas bag for holding one's kit or outfit (*military*); a knapsack; a strong canvas grip; **kit'-boat** or **-car** a boat or car put together from standard components by an amateur builder. — **the whole kit** the whole set or lot (of things or people). [Prob MDu *kitte* a hooped container for beer]

kit[2] *kit*, (*hist*) *n* a small pocket violin. [Origin obscure; cf OE *cytere*, Gr *kithara*]

kit[3] *kit*, *n* a kitten; the young of various small fur-bearing mammals, eg the polecat, ferret, fox. — **kit'-cat** the game of tip-cat.

Kit-Cat *kit'kat*, *n* the name of a London Whig literary club, which existed from about 1688 or 1703 to about 1720, meeting for some time at the pie-shop of Christopher (*Kit*) *Cat* (or *Catling*); a portrait 36 by 28 inches in size, like those of the Kit-Cat Club painted by Kneller to fit their later low-ceilinged clubroom.

kitchen *kich'ən*, *n* a room or building in which food is cooked; the staff of such a room or building; a tea-urn (*obs Scot*); anything eaten as a relish with other food (*esp Scot*); the percussion section of an orchestra (*slang*). — *vt* to regale in the cook-room (*Shakesp*); to serve as relish to (*Scot*); to make palatable (*Scot*); to use sparingly, make to last (*Scot*). — *n* **kitch'endom** the domain of the kitchen. — *n* **kitch'ener** a person employed in the kitchen; a cooking-stove. — *n* **kitchenette'** a very small kitchen, or part of a room modified as such. — **kitchen cabinet** an informal, unelected group of advisers to a political office-holder; **kitchen Dutch** or **kitchen Kaffir** (*archaic SAfr*) a mixture of Dutch or Kaffir with English, used in speaking to native servants; **kitch'en-fee** (*obs*) the fat that falls from meat in roasting, a perquisite of the cook; **kitch'en-fur'niture** the furniture of a kitchen; the percussion instruments of an orchestra; **kitch'en-gar'den** a garden where vegetables are cultivated for the kitchen; **kitch'en-gar'dener**; **kitch'en-knave** (*obs*) a scullion; **kitch'en-maid** a maid or servant whose work is in the kitchen; **kitch'en-midd'en** (Dan *kjökkenmödding*) a domestic rubbish-heap found on an archaeological site; **kitchen physic** (*Milton*) feeding up; **kitch'en-range** an old-fashioned kitchen grate with oven, boiler, etc attached, for cooking. — *adj* **kitchen-sink'** (of plays, etc) dealing with banal or sordid real-life situations. — **kitch'en-stuff** material used in kitchens; kitchen refuse, *esp* fat from pots, etc; **kitchen tea** (*Austr*) a bride's shower, the gifts being kitchen utensils, etc; **kitchen unit** one of a set of fitted kitchen cupboards; **kitchen'ware** pots, pans, bowls, gadgets, utensils, etc such as are used in the kitchen; **kitch'en-wench** (*Shakesp*) a kitchen-maid. — **everything except** (or **but**) **the kitchen sink** every conceivable thing. [OE *cycene*, from L *coquīna*, from *coquere* to cook]

kite[1] *kīt*, *n* a long-tailed bird of prey of the hawk family (*Accipitridae*); a rapacious person; a light frame covered with paper or cloth for flying in the air; a more complicated structure built of boxes (*box-kite*), often for carrying recording instruments or a person in the air; a light additional sail, *usu* set high up; a rumour or suggestion given out to see how the wind blows, test public opinion, etc; an accommodation bill, *esp* a mere paper credit; an aircraft (*airmen's slang*). — *vt* to cause to fly like a kite; to write (a cheque) before one has sufficient money in one's bank to cover it (*slang*). — *vi* to fly like a kite; to rise sharply. — *n* **kit'ing** kite-flying. — **kite'-balloon** an observation-balloon designed on the principle of the kite to prevent revolving, etc; **kite'-flyer** a person who takes part in kite-flying; **kite'-flying** sending up and controlling a kite; the juggling of cheques between accounts so as to create a sham balance of funds on which to draw; testing public opinion by circulating rumours, etc; **Kite mark**, **Kite'-mark** or **kite'-mark** a kite-shaped mark on goods indicating conformity in quality, size, etc, with the specifications of the British Standards Institution. — *adj* **kite'-marked** bearing this mark. — **fly a kite** to take part in kite-flying (qv above). [OE *cyta*; cf Welsh *cud*, Breton *kidel* a hawk]

kite[2] or **kyte** *kīt*, (*Scot* and *NEng*) *n* a paunch, belly. [Ety uncertain]

kitenge *ki-ten'ge*, *n* (in E Africa) a length of brightly-coloured thick cotton cloth, worn *esp* as a woman's dress. [Swahili]

kith *kith*, *n* knowledge (*obs*); native land (*obs*); one's friends or acquaintances (*obs* except in **kith and kin** friends and relatives). [OE *cȳth*, from *cunnan* to know]

kithara *kith'ə-rə*. Same as **cithara**.

kithe. See **kythe**.

kitling. See under **kitten**.

kitsch *kich*, *n* trash; art, literature, fashion, etc dismissed as being of merely popular taste or appeal, vulgar, sentimental or sometimes pretentious. — Also *adj*. — *adv* **kitsch'ily**. — *adj* **kitsch'y**. [Ger]

kitten *kit'n*, *n* a young cat (*dimin* **kitt'y**); sometimes the young of another animal. — *vt* and *vi* (of a cat) to give birth (to). — *n* **kit'ling** (*Scot*) a kitten. — *adj* **kitt'enish** or **kitt'eny** frolicsome; skittish; affectedly playful. — *n* **kitt'enishness**. — *vt* and *vi* **kitt'le** (*Scot*) to kitten; to come or bring into being. — **kitt'en-moth** any of several smaller moths similar to the puss-moth. — **have kittens** to be in a state of great excitement or anger. [ME *kitoun*, from ONFr *caton*, dimin of *cat*, from LL *cattus* cat]

kittiwake *kit'i-wāk*, *n* a gull of the genus *Rissa* with long wings and rudimentary hind-toes. [Imit]

kittle[1] *kit'l*, (*esp Scot*) *adj* difficult to deal with, *esp* because touchy, obstinate or intractable; fickle, capricious. — *vt* to tickle; to offend; to puzzle. — *adj* **kitt'ly** (*Scot*) ticklish; easily offended, sensitive. — **kittle cattle** (*fig*) awkward customers; **kitt'ly-bend'ers** (*US*) running on thin bending ice. [Ety obscure]

kittle[2]. See under **kitten**.

kittle-pins *kit'l-pinz*, *n pl* skittles. — Also **kett'le-pins**. [Prob alteration of **kail**[1]]

kittly. See under **kittle**[1].

kittul *kit-ōōl'*, *n* the jaggery palm (*Caryota urens*); its fibre. [Sinhalese *kitūl*]

kitty[1] *kit'i*, *n* a pool or fund of money held in common; the jack (*bowls*); a jail (*archaic*).

kitty[2]. See **kitten**.

kitty-cornered *kit'i-kör-nərd*, (*NAm*) *adj* and *adv*. Same as **cater-cornered**.

kiva *kē'və*, *n* a partly or wholly underground chamber used for religious ceremonies by Pueblo Indians. [Hopi]

kiwi *kē'wē*, *n* the Apteryx; a New Zealander (*colloq*, esp *sport*); a non-flying member of an airfield staff (*colloq*); a kiwi fruit. — **kiwi fruit** the edible green fruit of the Chinese gooseberry (qv), with pale green flesh and a furry greyish-brown skin. [Maori, from its cry]

KKK *abbrev*: Ku-Klux Klan.

KL *abbrev*: Kuala Lumpur, the capital of Malaysia.

Klan, Klansman. See under **Ku-Klux Klan**.

klang *klang*, (*music*) *n* a complex tone, composed of fundamental and harmonics; timbre. — Also **clang**. — **klang'farbe** (*-fär-bə*) tone-colour, timbre. [Ger]

klavier *klä-vēr'*, *n* a clavier. [Ger, from Fr *clavier*]

klaxon or **Klaxon** *klaks'ən*, *n orig* a mechanical horn with a loud rasping sound, of a kind used on early motor vehicles; any electric horn. — *vi* to sound a klaxon. [Name of the manufacturer]

klebsiella *kleb'zi-el-ə*, *n* a genus of gram-negative rodlike bacteria, which cause various diseases in man and animals, including pneumonia. [E *Klebs* (died 1913), Ger pathologist]

Kleenex® *klē'neks*, *n* a kind of soft paper tissue used as a handkerchief.

Kleig light. See **Klieg light**.

Klein bottle *klīn bot'l*, (*math*) *n* a one-sided four-dimensional surface, which in three dimensions can be represented as a surface obtained by pulling the narrow end of a tapering tube through the wall of the tube and then stretching the narrow end and joining it to the larger end. [Felix *Klein*, Ger mathematician]

klendusic *klen-dū'sik*, *adj* (of plants) able to withstand disease by means of some protective mechanism. — *n* **klendū'sity**. [Gr *kleidoein* to lock up, from *kleis* a key, and *endusis* entry]

klepht *kleft*, *n* one of the Greeks who took to the mountains in patriotic resistance to the 15c Turkish conquest of Greece, or one of their descendants, by the 19c merely brigands. — *adj* **klepht'ic**. — *n* **klepht'ism**. [Mod Gr *klephtēs*, from ancient Gr *kleptēs* thief, from *kleptein* to steal]

kleptocracy *klep-tok'rə-si*, *n* government by thieves, a thieves' régime; a country with such a government; a body or order of thieves. — *adj* **kleptocrat'ic**. [Gr *kleptēs* thief, and **-cracy**]

kleptomania *klep-tō-mā'ni-ə*, *n* a mania for stealing; a morbid impulse to hide things away. — *n* **klepto-mā'niac**. [Gr *kleptein* to steal, and *maniā* madness]

Kletterschuhe *klet'ər-shōō-ə*, *n pl orig* felt-soled, now also vibram-soled, lightweight rock-climbing boots. [Ger, from *kletter-* climbing, and *Schuhe* shoes]

Klieg light or **Kleig light** *klēg līt*, *n* a type of incandescent floodlighting lamp for film studio use. — **klieg eyes** the effect of strain on the eyes caused by the brilliance of floodlights in film production. [From *Kliegl* brothers, the inventors]

Klinefelter's syndrome *klīn'felt-ərz sin'drōm*, *n* impaired gonadal development in a male with one or more extra X-chromosomes, resulting in underdeveloped testes, mixed (male and female) secondary sexual characteristics, sterility, and sometimes mild mental retardation. [H F *Klinefelter* (1912–), US physician]

klinker or **clinker** *klingk'ər*, *n* a very hard paving-brick. [Du]

klinostat *klī'nō-stat*, *n* a revolving stand for experimenting with growing plants. [Gr *klīnein* to incline, and *statos* standing]

klipdas *klip'dus*, *n* the Cape hyrax. [Du, literally rock-badger]

klipspringer *klip'spring-ər*, *n* a small S African antelope. [Du *klip* rock, and *springer* jumper]

KLM *abbrev*: *Koninklijke Luchtvaart Maatschappij* (*Du*), Royal Dutch Airlines.

Klondike or **Klondyke** *klon'dīk*, (also without *cap*) *n* a very rich source of wealth; a card game, a form of patience. — *vt* and *vi* to export (fresh fish, *esp* herring) direct from Scotland to the Continent; to trans-ship (fish) at sea. — *n* **klon'dyker** or **klon'diker** a factory-ship. [From the gold-rush to *Klondike* in the Yukon, in 1896, etc]

kloof *klōōf*, (*SAfr*) *n* a mountain ravine. [Du, cleft]

klootchman or **kloochman** *klōōch'mən*, (*NW NAm*) *n* an Indian woman, wife or squaw: — *pl* **-mans** or **-men**. — Also **klootch** or **klooch**. [Chinook, from Nootka *lhūtsma*]

kludge *kluj*, (*comput*; *colloq*) *n* a botched or makeshift device or program which is unreliable or inadequate in function.

klutz *kluts*, (*NAm slang*) *n* an idiot; an awkward, stupid person. [Ger *Klotz* idiot]

klystron *klis'* or *klīs'tron*, *n* any of a number of electron tubes (amplifiers, oscillators, etc) in which the velocity of the electron beam is modulated by an ultra-high frequency field and subsequently imparts energy to it or other UHF fields. [Gr *klystēr* syringe]

KM *abbrev*: Knight of Malta.

km *abbrev*: kilometre(s). — **km/h** *abbrev*: kilometres per hour.

kn. *abbrev*: knot(s) (the nautical, etc measure).

knack *nak*, *n* a special unfailing talent, learned or *esp* intuitive; a thing regularly (and *esp* unwittingly or unconsciously) done, a habit; a clever contrivance (*obs*); a toy, ornament or knick-knack (*obs*). — *n* **knack'iness**. — *adj* **knack'ish** or **knack'y** cunning; crafty. [Prob from (obs) *knack* a cracking sound (imit); cf Du *knak* a crack, Ger *knacken* to crack]

knacker[1] *nak'ər*, *n* anything that makes a snapping or cracking sound; (in *pl*) castanets or clappers, bones; (in *pl*) testicles (*slang*). [Imit]

knacker[2] *nak'ər*, *n* someone who buys and slaughters old horses; someone who buys and breaks up old houses, ships, etc; a worn-out horse. — *vt* to wear out, exhaust (*colloq*); to kill; to castrate. — *adj* **knack'ered** (*colloq*) exhausted, worn out. — *n* **knack'ery** a knacker's yard. — **knacker's yard** a place where horses are slaughtered; the scrap-heap (*fig*). [Origin obscure]

knackwurst *nak'wōōrst, -wûrst* or (*Ger*) *-vōōrst*, *n* a kind of highly seasoned sausage. — Also **knock'wurst**. [Ger *knacken* to crack, and *Wurst* sausage]

knag *nag*, *n* a knot in wood; a peg. — *n* **knagg'iness**. — *adj* **knagg'y** knotty; rugged. [Cf Dan *knag*, Ger *Knagge*]

knaidel *knā'dl*, (*Jewish cookery*; *esp* in *pl* **knaidloch** or **kneidlach** *knā'dlohh*) *n* a kind of dumpling *usu* eaten in clear soup. [From Yiddish]

knap[1] *nap*, *vt* to snap or break with a snapping noise; to break (eg stones) in pieces with repeated blows; to pronounce with a snapping effect; to rap; to bite off, nibble; to steal: — *pr p* **knapp'ing**; *pa t* and *pa p* **knapped**. — *n* **knapp'er** someone who breaks stones, *esp* flint-flakes for gun-flints. — *vi* **knapp'le** to nibble. — **knap'-bottle** the bladder-campion; **knapp'ing-hammer** (*Scot*) a hammer for breaking stones. [Du *knappen* to crack or crush]

knap[2] *nap*, (*obs* except *dialect*) *n* a protuberance; a hillock; a hill-crest. [OE *cnæpp*]

knapsack *nap'sak*, *n* a bag made of strong material, with straps for carrying on the back, eg when hiking; a rucksack. [Du *knappen* to crack, eat]

knapskull, **knapscull** or **knapscal** *nap'skəl*, (*Scot obs*) *n* a kind of helmet. [Origin unknown]

knapweed *nap'wēd*, *n* a composite plant of the genus *Centaurea*, like a spineless thistle. [Earlier *knopweed*; see **knop**]

knar[1] or **gnar** *när*, *n* a knot on a tree. — *adj* **knarred** or **gnarred** gnarled, knotty. [Cf LGer *knarre*, Du *knar*; also **knur**]

knar[2] *när*. See **gnar**[1].

knarl. See **gnarl**[1].

knave *nāv*, *n orig*, as in *Shakesp*, a boy; a serving-boy; a dishonest or deceitful man, a rogue (*old*); a playing card bearing the picture of a servant or soldier, a jack. — *n* **knav'ery** dishonesty. — *n* **knave'ship** (*Scot*) a certain quantity of grain, the due of the miller's servant. — *adj* **knav'ish** fraudulent; rascally. — *adv* **knav'ishly**. — *n* **knav'ishness**. — **knave'-bairn** (*Scot*) a male child. [OE *cnafa*, *cnapa* a boy, a youth; Ger *Knabe*, *Knappe*]

knawel *nö'əl*, *n* a cornfield weed (*Scleranthus*) of the chickweed family. [Ger *Knauel* or *Knäuel*]

knead *nēd*, *vt* to work and press together into a mass (eg flour into dough); to massage. — *n* **knead'er**. —

knead'ing-trough a trough in which to knead. [OE *cnedan*; cf ON *knotha*, Ger *kneten*]

knee *nē*, *n* the joint between the thigh and shin bones; in a horse's foreleg, the joint corresponding to the human wrist; in a bird, the joint corresponding to the ankle; the part of a garment covering the knee; a root upgrowth by which swamp-growing trees breathe; a piece of timber or metal shaped like a bent knee; a piece of machinery which operates like a knee; a genuflexion (*Shakesp*). — *vt* to provide with a knee; to press, strike or nudge with the knee; to make (trousers, etc) baggy at the knee; to kneel to (*Shakesp*); to achieve by kneeling, or crawl over on the knees (*Shakesp*). — *vi* (*obs*) to kneel. — *adj* **kneed** or **knee'd** having knees or angular joints: (of trousers) baggy at the knees. — **knee'-breeches** breeches extending to just below the knee; **knee'-cap** or **knee'cap** the patella, a flat round bone on the front of the knee-joint; a cap or strong covering for the knees, used chiefly for horses to save their knees in case of a fall. — *vt* to subject to knee-capping. — **knee'-capping** or **knee'capping** a form of torture or (terrorist) punishment in which the victim is shot or otherwise injured in the knee-cap; **knee'-cords** knee-breeches of corduroy. — *adj* **knee'-crooking** (*Shakesp*) obsequious, fawning. — *adj* **knee'-deep** rising or reaching to someone's knees; sunk to the knees; deeply involved (in). — **knee'-drill** directed devotional exercises. — *adj* **knee'-high** rising or reaching to someone's knees. — **knee'hole** the space beneath a desk or bureau for the knees; **knee'-holly** butcher's broom; **knee'-jerk** a reflex throwing forward of the leg when tapped below the knee-cap. — *adj* (of a reaction) automatic, unthinking, predictable. — **knee'-joint** the joint of the knee; a joint with two pieces at an angle, so as to be very tight when pressed into a straight line. — *adj* **knee'-length** reaching to the knee. — **knee'-pad** a protective cover for the knee; **knee'-pan** the knee-cap; **knee sock** a sock reaching to just below the knee; **knee'-stop** or **-swell** a lever worked by an organist's knee, for regulating the wind-supply of a reed-organ, etc; **knees'-up** (*colloq*) a riotous dance or party; **knee'-timber** timber bent into a shape suitable for a knee in shipbuilding, etc; **knee'-trembler** (*slang*) an act of sexual intercourse in a standing position; loosely, any sexual adventure; **knee'-tribute** (*Milton*) the homage of kneeling. — **bend** or **bow the knee** to kneel or submit; **bring someone to his** or **her knees** to make someone admit defeat; **give** or **offer a knee** (*Thackeray*, etc) to act as second in a fight, it being usual for the principal to rest on the second's knee between the rounds; **knee-high to a grasshopper** (*orig US*) very short, with connotation of extreme youth; **on the knees of the gods** awaiting the decision of fate (after Homer); **sit on someone's knee** to sit on the horizontal surface of a seated person's thighs. [OE *cnēow*, *cnēo*; Ger *Knie*, L *genu*, Gr *gony*]

kneel *nēl*, *vi* to rest or fall on the bended knee: — *pa t* and *pa p* **kneeled** or **knelt** (*nelt*). — *n* **kneel'er** a person who kneels; a flat cushion to rest the knees on while kneeling; a hassock. [OE *cnēowlian*]

kneidlach. See **knaidel**.

Kneipe *knī'pə*, (*Ger*) *n* a tavern, a students' beer-house or drinking party.

knell *nel*, *n* the sound of a bell, *esp* at a death or funeral. — *vi* to toll. — *vt* to summon or proclaim as by a tolling bell. [OE *cnyllan* to beat noisily; Du and Ger *knallen*]

knelt *pa t* and *pa p* of **kneel**.

Knesset *knes'it*, *n* the one-chamber parliament of Israel. [Heb, assembly]

knevell. A variant of **nevel**.

knew *nū*, *pa t* of **know**.

knicker. See **nicker**[3].

knickerbocker *nik'ər-bok-ər*, *n* (in *pl*) loose breeches gathered in at the knee; (with *cap*) a descendant of one of the original Dutch settlers of New York; (with *cap*) a New Yorker. — **knickerbocker glory** a large and opulent ice-cream sundae. [From the wide-breeched Dutchmen in Knickerbocker's (ie Washington Irving's) humorous *History of New York*]

knickers *nik'ərz*, *n pl* women's or girls' underpants (*colloq*); a woman's undergarment covering (and sometimes gathered in at) the thigh; knickerbockers (*US*). — *interj* (*slang*) now *usu* a mild expression of exasperation, etc. — *adj* **knick'ered** clad in knickers. — *n* **knicks** (*colloq*) knickers. — **get one's knickers in a twist** (*colloq*) to become harassed, anxious or agitated. [**knickerbocker**]

knick-knack *nik'-nak*, *n* a small, trifling, ornamental or would-be ornamental article. — *n* **knick-knack'atory** a collection of knick-knacks. — *n* **knick-knack'ery** knick-knacks collectively. — *n* **knick-knack'et** a knick-knack. — *adj* **knick'-knacky**. — Also **nick'-nack**, etc. [A doubling of **knack**]

knickpoint or **nickpoint** *nik'point*, (*geol*) *n* a discontinuity in a river profile, *esp* when caused by the intersection of a new curve of erosion. [Part-translating Ger *Knickpunkt*, from *knicken* to bend, and *punkt* point]

knife *nīf*, *n* an instrument with a blade for cutting or spreading: — *pl* **knives** (*nīvz*). — *vt* to cut; to apply with a knife; to stab; to try to defeat by treachery. — *vi* to cut (with *through*) or penetrate (with *into*) as if with a knife. — *adj* **knife'less** without a knife; without use of the knife. — *n* **knif'ing** the (criminal) act of putting a knife into someone. — **knife-and-fork'** (*Dickens*) a trencherman. — *adj* involving, or relating to, the use of a knife and fork. — **knife'-board** a board on which knives are cleaned; a bench running along the top of an old type of bus (*colloq*); **knife'-box** a box for keeping table cutlery in; **knife'-boy** a boy employed in cleaning knives; **knife'-edge** a sharp-edged ridge; a sharp piece of steel serving as the axis of a balance, etc (also *fig*, *esp* as *adj* or in phrase **on a knife edge** critically poised, in the balance); **knife'-grinder** someone who grinds or sharpens knives; **knife'-man** a man wielding or using a knife; **knife'-money** a knife-shaped bronze currency formerly used in China; **knife pleat** a narrow, flat pleat; **knife'-point** the sharp tip of a knife (**at knife-point** under threat of injury by a knife); **knife'-rest** a support for a carving knife or fork; **knife'-switch** a switch in an electric circuit, in which the moving element consists of a flat blade which engages with fixed contacts. — **at it like knives** continuously and eagerly occupied with it; **have one's knife in** to be persistently hostile or vindictive towards; **the knives are out for** people are out to get (someone); **under the knife** undergoing a surgical operation; **war to the knife** unrelenting conflict. [ME *knif*, from OE *cnīf*]

knight *nīt*, *n* in the Middle Ages, a man who performed mounted military service for his lord in exchange for land; a man of the rank immediately below baronet, with the title 'Sir'; a chessman, *usu* with a horse's head, that moves one square forward, backward, or to either side, and one diagonally, at each move; (in feudal times) a gentleman, bred to arms, admitted to a certain honourable military rank; a man devoted to the service of a lady, her champion; a member of the equestrian order in ancient Rome. — *vt* to make a knight. — *n* **knight'age** knights collectively. — *n* **knight'hood** the rank, title or status of knight; the order or fraternity of knights. — *adj* **knight'less** (*Spenser*) unbecoming to a knight. — *n* **knight'liness**. — *adj* **knight'ly** like a knight; befitting a knight; chivalrous; of a knight or knights. — Also *adv*. — **knight bachelor** a knight belonging to no special order of knighthood (the lowest form of knight in rank and earliest in origin): — *pl* **knights bachelors** or **knights bachelor**; **knight-bann'eret** a knight who carried a banner and who was superior in rank to the knight bachelor: — *pl* **knights bannerets**; **knight-err'ant** a knight who travelled in search of adventures; a man or boy who behaves adventurously or chivalrously: — *pl* **knights-err'ant**; **knight-err'antry**; **knighthood-err'ant** (*Tennyson*) the body of knights-errant; **knight-mar'shal** formerly an officer who had jurisdiction over offences within twelve miles of the king's abode; **knight'-service** tenure of land by a knight on condition of military service; **knight's fee** a holding of land for which knight-service was required; **knight's progress** (*chess*) a series of moves in which a knight may visit every square on the board; **Knights Templar** see under **temple**[1]. — **knight of the road** (*facetious*) a highwayman (*obs*); a commercial traveller; a lorry driver; a tramp; **knight of the shire** a member of parliament for a county; **Knights of Labor** (*US*) a secret 19c organization for workers; **Knights of Malta** see **hospitaller** under **hospital**. *The following are jocular titles used formerly*: — **knight of industry** a footpad, thief or sharper; **knight of St Crispin** a shoemaker; **knight of the pestle** an apothecary; **knight of the post** (ie possibly the whipping-post) a professional false witness and offerer of bail; **knight of the rainbow** a flunkey (from his livery); **knight of the shears** a tailor; **knight of the spigot** a tapster, a publican; **knight of the stick** a compositor; **knight of the whip** a coachman. [OE *cniht* youth, servant, warrior; Ger *Knecht* and Du *knecht* servant]

kniphofia *nip-hōf'i-ə* or *nī-fō'fi-ə*, *n* any plant of the African *Kniphofia* genus of the lily family, otherwise called *Tritoma*, the red-hot poker. [Named after J H *Kniphof* (1704–65), German botanist]

knish *knish*, *n* (in Jewish cookery) dough with a potato, meat, etc filling, baked or fried. [Yiddish, from Russ]

knit *nit*, *vt* to intertwine; to make (a garment, etc) by means of knitting-needles or a knitting-machine; to form (wool, etc) into network by needles or machinery; to do so in plain stitch (as opposed to **purl**[3]); to unite closely, to draw together; to contract (the brows, etc); to form into a knot (*archaic*); to tie together (*archaic*). — *vi* to knit something; (of the brows, forehead, etc) to contract in a frown; to grow together: — *pr p* **knitt'ing**; *pa t* and *pa p* **knitt'ed** or **knit**. — *n* a style of knitting (*Shakesp*); a knitted fabric or article. — *n* **knitt'er**. — *n* **knitt'ing** knitted work; the act or process of producing knitted work; union, junction. — Also *adj*. — **knitt'ing-machine** a machine for knitting; **knitt'ing-needle** a long needle or wire, without an eye, used for knitting; **knit'wear** knitted clothing. [OE *cnyttan*, from *cnotta* a knot]

knitch *nich*, (*dialect*) *n* a faggot, a bundle of wood, etc tied together. [OE *gecnycc* bond]

knittle *nit'l*, *n* a small line made of two or three yarns twisted with the fingers (*naut*); (in *pl*) the halves of two yarns in a rope, twisted for pointing. [OE *cnyttels* sinew, string]

knive *nīv*, *vt* (*rare*) to knife. — **knives** *pl* of **knife**.

knob *nob*, *n* a hard protuberance; a hard swelling; a round ornament or handle; the penis (*slang*); a small group (of wildfowl). — *adj* **knobbed** containing or set with knobs. — *n* **knobb'er** a stag in its second year. — *n* **knobb'iness**. — *n* **knobb'le** a little knob. — *adj* **knobb'ly** or **knobb'y** having, or full of, knobs; knotty. — **knob'-stick** a stick with knobbed head; a blackleg or scab (*obs slang*). — **with knobs on** (*colloq*) with interest, more so. [Cf LGer *knobbe*; **knop**]

knobble. See under **knob**, **knubble**.

knobkerrie *nob'ker-i*, *n* a round-headed stick used as a club and a missile by some S African tribes. [**knob** and **kierie**, on the model of Afrik *knopkierie*]

knock *nok*, *vi* to strike hard or heavily; to drive or be driven against something; to strike *esp* a door for admittance; to rap; to make a noise by, or as if by, striking; (of machinery) to rattle or clank regularly; (of an internal-combustion engine) to make the noise caused by detonation. — *vt* to strike; to drive against; to bring to a specified state or position by striking or pushing; to impress strongly, stun, daze, confound (*slang*); to disparage, criticize in a carping way (*colloq*). — *n* a sudden stroke; a rap; the noise of detonation in an internal-combustion engine; a reversal, shock, setback (*colloq*); a criticism (*colloq*); an innings, a spell at batting (*cricket*); a clock (*Scot*). — *n* **knock'er** someone who knocks; a device suspended on a door for making a knock; a carper or critic (*colloq*); (in *pl*) breasts (*slang*); someone who makes unsolicited door-to-door calls on domestic householders, eg hoping to buy valuables from them, or selling, etc; a goblin thought to inhabit a mine who points out the presence of ore by knocks (*dialect*). — *n* **knock'ing** a beating on a door; a rap; a noise as if of something that knocks; knock in an internal-combustion engine; the practice of making unsolicited calls on householders, eg hoping to buy valuables from them. — **knock'about** a boisterous performance with horseplay; a performer of such turns; a doer of odd jobs, *esp* on a station (*Austr*); a small yacht without a bowsprit (*NAm*); a small motor car suitable for doing short journeys. — *adj* boisterous (*orig theat*); suitable for rough use (*obs*). — **knock'-back** a setback; a refusal of parole from prison (*slang*); **knock'-down** an act or instance of knocking down; an introduction (*US*, *Austr* and *NZ colloq*). — *adj* such as to overthrow, powerful; adapted for being taken to pieces; (of prices) very low. — *adj* **knocked'-down** supplied in parts or kit form for assembly by the purchaser. — **knock'er-up** a person employed to rouse workers in the morning; **knocking copy** advertising material which denigrates competing products; **knock'ing-shop** or **knocking shop** (*slang*) a brothel; **knock'-knee** the state of being knock-kneed. — *adj* **knock-kneed'** having knees that knock or touch in walking; weak (*fig*). — **knock'-on** see **knock on** and **knock-on effect** below. — *adj* (*colloq*) causing or caused by a series of consequences. — **knock'out** the act of knocking out; a blow that knocks out; a conspiracy among dealers at an auction to keep prices artificially low; any person or thing of outstanding attraction or excellence (*colloq*); a knockout competition; **technical knockout** see under **technical**. — *adj* (of a competition) eliminating losers at each round; stunningly attractive or excellent (*colloq*). — **knockout auction** an auction at which the majority of bidders are dealers in league to keep prices artificially low; **knockout drops** (*slang*) a drug put in a drink to make the drinker unconscious; **knock'-rating** the measurement of freedom from knocking of a fuel in an internal-combustion engine, as compared with a standard fuel; **knock'-up** (in tennis, etc) practice immediately before a match. — **knock about** or **around** to mistreat physically; to discuss informally; to saunter, loaf about; to be around in the area; to travel about, roughing it and having varied experiences; to be a casual friend of, associate with (with *with*); **knock back** (*slang*) to drink or eat, *esp* swiftly; to cost; to shock, disconcert; to rebuff, reject, turn down; **knock cold** to knock (someone) out; to shock violently; **knock copy** to disparage a rival's products; **knock down** to fell with a blow; to demolish; to assign (an article) with a tap of the auctioneer's hammer (to); to reduce in price (*colloq*); to spend (one's resources) on a drinking binge (*Austr* and *NZ slang*); to misappropriate, filch (*US*) (*adj* **knock-down** see above); **knock-for-knock agreement**, **policy**, etc, an arrangement between motor insurance companies by which, after an accident involving two cars, each company settles the damage to the car it insures without considering which driver was to blame; **knock into a cocked hat** see under **cock**[1]; **knock into the middle of next week** (*colloq*) to hit (someone) very hard; **knock off** (*colloq*) to stop work; to stop, discontinue; to accomplish hastily; to deduct; to steal, rob (*slang*); to copy illegally, to pirate (*slang*); to kill (*slang*); to have sexual intercourse with (*slang*); **knock on** (*Rugby football*) to knock (the ball) forward with the hand or arm (an infringement of the rules; *n* **knock'-on**); **knock-on effect** the effect one action or occurrence has on one or more indirectly related matters or circumstances; **knock on the head** (*colloq*) to suppress, put an end to; **knock one's head against a brick wall** to meet with total resistance or refusal to compromise; **knock on wood** see **touch wood** under **touch**; **knock out** to dislodge by a blow; to strike unconscious or incapable of recovering in time (*boxing*); to overcome, demolish; to produce, *esp* quickly or roughly (*colloq*); to tire (oneself) out (*slang*); to overwhelm with amazement, admiration, etc (*slang*); **knock sideways** to put off one's usual course; **knock the bottom out of** to make, or show to be, invalid; to make ineffectual, bring to nothing; **knock the living daylights out of** see under **day**; **knock together** to get together or construct hastily; **knock under** (*archaic*) to give in, yield; **knock up** to rouse by knocking; to weary out; to be worn out; to construct or arrange hastily; to achieve (a certain score) (*games, esp cricket*); to practise immediately before a match (*tennis*, etc); to make pregnant (*slang*); **on the knocker** on credit (*slang*); immediately, on the nail (*Austr slang*); **up to the knocker** (*obs slang*) up to the required standard of excellence or fashion. [OE *cnocian*; perh imit]

knockwurst. See **knackwurst**.

knoll[1] *nōl* (*Scot* **knowe** *now*), *n* a round hillock; the top of a hill (*dialect*). [OE *cnol*; Ger *Knollen* a knob, lump]

knoll[2] *nōl*. Archaic form of **knell**.

knop *nop*, *n* a knob (*obs*); a bud (*archaic*); a loop or tuft in yarn. [Cf ON *knappr*; Du *knop*, Ger *Knopf*]

knosp *nosp*, *n* the unopened bud of a flower; an architectural ornament resembling this. [Ger *Knospe*]

knot[1] *not*, *n* a snipe-like shore bird (*Calidris canutus*) of the sandpiper family. [Origin unknown: the connection with King Cnut is a fancy of William Camden's]

knot[2] *not*, *n* an interlacement of parts of a cord or cords, rope, ribbon, etc, by twisting the ends around each other, and then pulling tight the loops thus formed; any of various specific methods of forming such an interlacement; a piece of ribbon, lace, etc folded or tied upon itself as an ornament, eg *shoulder-knot*, *breast-knot*, etc; anything like a knot in form; a bond of union; an elaborately designed flower-bed (*hist*); a tangle (in string, hair, etc); a difficulty; the main point or central part of a tangle, intricacy, problem or difficulty; a complex of lines, mountains, etc; the base of a branch buried in a later growth of wood; a cross-section of this joint, visible as a darker roundish mark, in a length of wood; a node or joint in a stem, *esp* of a grass; a hard lump; a concretion; a swelling; a knob; a boss; a bud; a hill (*dialect*); a clump or cluster; a specific quantity of yarn; a division of the knot-marked log-line; a nautical mile per hour, used in navigation and meteorology; loosely, a nautical mile. — *vt* to tie in a knot; to unite closely; to make knotty; to make by knotting; to remove knots from; to cover knots in (wood before painting). — *vi* to form a knot or knots; to knit knots for a fringe: — *pr p* **knott'ing**; *pa t* and *pa p* **knott'ed**. — *adj* **knot'less**. — *adj* **knott'ed** full of, or having, knots. — *n* **knott'er** a person or contrivance that makes or removes knots. — *n* **knott'iness**. — *n* **knott'ing** the formation or removal of knots; the covering of knots before painting; the sealer used for this; fancywork done by knitting threads into knots. — *adj* **knott'y** containing knots; hard, rugged; difficult; intricate. — **knot garden** a garden with intricate formal designs of shrubs, flower-beds, etc; **knot'grass** a much-jointed species of *Polygonum*, a common weed; applied also to various grasses; **knot'-hole** a hole in wood where a knot has fallen out; **knot'weed** any of various plants of the genus *Polygonum*; **knot'work** ornamental work made with knots; carving or decoration in interlaced forms. — **at a rate of knots** (*colloq*) very fast; **get knotted!** (*slang*) *interj* expressing anger, derision, defiance, etc; **porters' knot** (*obs*) a double shoulder-pad with loop fitting round the forehead, used to help market porters carry their load; **tie someone (up) in knots** to confuse or bewilder someone completely; **tie the knot** (*colloq*) to get married. [OE *cnotta*; Ger *Knoten*, Dan *knude*, L *nōdus*]

knotenschiefer *knō'tən-shē-fər*, *n* spotted slate or spotted schist, slightly altered argillaceous rock spotted with little concretions. [Ger, knot slate or schist]

knout *knōōt* or *nowt*, *n* a whip formerly used as an instrument of punishment in Russia; punishment inflicted by the knout. — *vt* to flog. [Fr spelling of Russ *knut*]

know *nō*, *vt* to be informed or assured of; to be acquainted with; to be familiar with from having learned or experienced; to recognize; to take notice of, approve (*Bible*); to have sexual intercourse with (*archaic*). — *vi* to possess knowledge, in general or of the matter in hand: — *pr p* **know'ing**; *pa t* **knew** (*nū* or *US nōō*); *pa p* **known** (*nōn*). — *n* possession of the relevant facts; knowledge (*Shakesp*). — *adj* **know'able** capable of being known, discovered or understood. — *n* **know'ableness**. — *n* **know'er**. — *adj* **know'ing** intelligent; skilful; cunning. — *adv* **know'ingly** in a knowing manner; consciously; intentionally. — *n* **know'ingness** the quality of being knowing or intelligent; shrewdness. — *adj* **known** widely recognized; identified by the police. — *n* a known fact; (with *the*) that which is known. — **know'-all** someone who thinks they know everything; **know'-how** or **know'how** the faculty of knowing the right thing to do in any contingency; specialized skill; **know'-nothing** someone who is totally ignorant; a member of the (Native) American Party (1854–56), *orig* secret. — *adj* completely ignorant. — **know'-nothingism**. — **I don't know** I disagree; **I know** or **I know what** I've got an idea; **in the know** (*colloq*) in possession of private information; initiated; **I wouldn't know** I am not in a position to know; **know all the answers** to be completely informed on everything, or to think one is; **know better** to be wiser, better instructed (than to do this or that); **know how many beans make five** to be sensible and aware, to have one's wits about one; **knowing to** (*obs*) aware or informed of; **known as** going by name of; **know the ropes** to understand the detail or procedure; **know what's o'clock** (*obs*) or **know what's what** to have one's wits about one, be on the ball; **know which side one's bread is buttered on** to be looking after one's own interests; **what do you know?** what is the news?; a greeting or expression of incredulity; **you know** (*colloq*) used as a conversation filler, marking a pause, sometimes for emphasis but often almost meaningless; **you never know** (*colloq*) perhaps. [OE *cnāwan*; ON *knā*, L *(g)nōscere*, Gr *gignōskein*]

knowe. See **knoll**[1].

knowledge *nol'ij*, *n* that which is known; information, instruction; enlightenment, learning; practical skill; assured belief; acquaintance; cognizance (*law*); (with *the*) the detailed information on which London taxi-drivers are tested before being licensed; sexual intimacy (*archaic*). — *vt* (*obs*) to acknowledge. — *n* **knowledgeabil'ity** or **knowledgabil'ity**. — *adj* **knowl'edgeable** or **knowl'edgable** possessing knowledge; intelligent. — *adv* **knowl'edgeably** or **knowl'edgably**. — **knowledge base** (*comput*) a collection of specialist knowledge formulated for use *esp* in expert systems. — *adj* **knowl'edge-based** of software systems that store and effectively utilize large amounts of such specialist knowledge. — **knowledge box** (*slang*) the head; **knowledge engineering** (*comput*) the application of artificial intelligence techniques in constructing expert systems. — **to one's knowledge** so far as one knows. [ME *knowleche*, where *-leche* is unexplained; see **know**]

knub or **nub** *nub*, *n* a knob; a small lump; the waste or refuse of silk-cocoons. — *n* **knubb'le** or **nubb'le** a small lump. — *adj* **knubb'ly**, **nubb'ly**, **knubb'y** or **nubby**. [Cf LGer *knubbe*]

knubble, **nubble** *nub'l* or **knobble** *nob'l*, *vt* to beat with the fists; to knock. [**knob**]

knuckle *nuk'l*, *n* any of the bones which protrude when a finger-joint is bent; a joint of veal or pork from the knee downwards (*cookery*). — *vi* to yield (*usu* with *down* or *under*); (in marbles) to touch the ground with the knuckles (*usu* with *down*); to bend the knee inward (*obs golf*). — *vt* to touch or press with the knuckle or knuckles; to shoot (a marble) from the thumb knuckle. — *adj* **knuck'ly**. — **knuck'le-bone** any bone with a rounded end; (in *pl*) the game of dibs; **knuck'le-bow** the curved part of a sword-guard that covers the fingers; **knuck'leduster** a metal covering for the knuckles, worn on the hand as a weapon in fist-fighting; **knuck'le-head** (*colloq*) an idiot. — *adj* **knuck'le-headed**. — **knuckle-head'edness**; **knuck'le-joint** any of the finger-joints; a hinged joint in which two pieces of machinery are joined by a pin through eyes at their ends, one piece being forked and enclosing the other (*mech*); **knuckle sandwich** (*slang*) a blow with the fist. — **knuckle down (to)** to set oneself to hard work (on); see also *vi* above; **knuckle under** to yield to authority, pressure, etc; **near the knuckle** on the verge of the indecent; **rap someone's knuckles** to reprimand someone. [ME *knokel*, not recorded in OE; cf Du *knokkel* (dimin of *knok*), Ger *Knöchel* ankle-bone, knuckle (dimin of *Knochen* bone)]

knur, knurr, nur or **nurr** *nûr*, *n* a knot on a tree; a hard ball or knot of wood. — **knur and spell** a game played with a knur, trap (*spell*), and stick, chiefly in N England. [ME *knurre*; cf Du *knor*, MHGer *knorre*, Ger *Knorren*]

knurl or **nurl** *nûrl*, *n* a small excrescence or protuberance; a ridge or bead, *esp* in series, eg in the milling of a screw-head; a dwarfish person (*Burns*). — *vt* to make knurls on, to mill. — *adj* **knurled** (spelt **gnarled** in *Shakesp*, Measure for Measure, folio 1623) covered with knurls. — *n* **knurl'ing** mouldings or other wood-work elaborated into a series of knobs. — *adj* **knurl'y** gnarled. [Prob a dimin of **knur**]

knut *knut* or *nut*, (*slang*). See **nut**.

KO or **k.o.** *abbrev*: kick-off; knockout; knock out. — *vt* (*kā'ō*; *colloq*) to knock out: — *pr p* **KO'ing** or **k.o.''ing**; *pa t* and *pa p* **KO'd'** or **k.o.'d'**. — *n* a knockout: — *pl* **KO''s** or **k.o.'s'**.

ko *kō*, (*NZ*) *n* a Maori digging-stick. [Maori]

koa *kō'ə*, *n* a Hawaiian acacia. [Hawaiian]

koala *kō-ä'lə*, *n* an Australian marsupial, like a small bear, called also **koala bear** or **native bear**. [Aboriginal *kūlā*]

koan *kō'än*, *n* (in Zen Buddhism) a nonsensical question given to students as a subject for meditation. [Jap, a public proposal or plan]

kob *kob*, *n* any of various species of African water-antelope or waterbuck. [Wolof]

koban *kō'ban* or **kobang** *kō'bang*, *n* an obsolete oblong gold Japanese coin, rounded at the corners. [Jap *koban*]

kobold *kō'bold*, (*Ger folklore*) *n* a spirit of the mines; a domestic brownie. [Ger]

Koch's postulates *kohhs pos'tū-lāts*, *n pl* criteria formulated by Koch for establishing that a micro-organism is the cause of a disease. [Robert Koch (1843–1910), German bacteriologist]

Kodak® *kō'dak*, *n* a make of camera. — *vt* and *vi* (*rare*) to photograph with a Kodak. [The trademark name of the Eastman *Kodak* Company]

Kodiak or **Kodiak bear** *kō'di-ak bār*, *n* the largest variety of brown bear (*Ursus arctos*), found in Alaska and the Aleutian Islands. [From *Kodiak* Island, Alaska]

koff *kof*, *n* a small Dutch sailing-vessel. [Du *kof*]

kofta *kof'tə*, (*Ind cookery*) *n* minced and seasoned meat or vegetables, shaped into balls and fried.

koftgar *koft'gär*, (*Ind*) *n* someone who inlays steel with gold. — *n* **koftgari** (*koft-gur-ē'*) or sometimes **koft'work** such work. [Urdu from Pers *koftgar*]

kohl *kōl*, *n* a fine powder of native stibnite (formerly known as antimony), black in colour, used (*orig* in the East) to darken the area around the eyes. [Ar *koh'l*]

kohlrabi *kōl-rä'bi*, *n* a variety of cabbage with a turnip-shaped stem. [Ger, from Ital *cavolo rapa*, from L *caulis* cabbage, and *rapa* turnip]

Koine *koi'nē*, *n* a Greek dialect developed from Attic, in use in the E Mediterranean in Hellenistic and Byzantine times; (often without *cap*) any dialect which has spread and become the common language of a larger area. [Gr *koinē* (*dialektos*) common (dialect)]

kokanee *kō-kan'ē*, *n* a small landlocked species of sockeye salmon. [From Salish]

koker *kōkər*, (*Guyana*) *n* a sluice-gate. [Du]

kokra *kok'rə*, *n* the wood of an Indian tree (*Aporosa*) of the spurge family, used for making flutes, clarinets, etc.

kok-saghyz *kok'-sä'gēz*, *n* a species of dandelion (*Taraxacum kok-saghyz*) from the Tien Shan, grown in Russia, etc for rubber-making. [Russ]

kokum *kō'kəm*, *n* an E Indian tree (*Garcinia indica*). — **kokum butter** an edible fat obtained from its nuts. [Marathi *kokamb* mangosteen]

kola. See **cola**.

Kolarian *kō-lā'ri-ən*, *n* the Munda group of languages.

kolinsky *ko-lin'ski*, *n* a species of mink (*Mustela sibirica*) found in E Asia, or its fur. [Russ *kolinski* of the Kola Peninsula]

kolkhoz *kol-hhoz'*, *n* a collective or co-operative farm in the former USSR. [Russ abbrev of *kollektivnoe khozyaistvo*]

kolo *kō'lō*, *n* a Serbian folk-dance or dance-tune: — *pl* **kō'los**. [Serbo-Croatian, wheel]

komatik *kom'ə-tik*, *n* an Eskimo sled with wooden runners. [Eskimo]

kombu *kom'bōō*, *n* an edible brown seaweed, used *esp* for making stock, a species of Laminaria. [Jap]

Kominform, Komintern. Alternative forms of **Cominform, Comintern**.

komissar. Same as **commissar**.

komitaji *kō-mē-tä'jē*, *n orig* a member of the Bulgarian Revolutionary Committee in Macedonia; any Balkan guerrilla. [Turk *qomitaji* committee-man, bandit, from *qomite*, from Fr *comité* committee]

Kommers *kom-ers'*, *n* a traditional gathering of a German student fraternity, with drinking and singing. — *n* **Kommers'buch** (*-bōōhh*) a songbook for such occasions. [Ger, from L *commercium* commerce]

Komodo dragon or **lizard** *kə-mō'dō drag'ən* or *liz'ərd*, *n* a large monitor lizard (*Varanus komodoensis*) of some Indonesian islands. [*Komodo* Island, Indonesia]

Komsomol *kom'sə-mol*, *n* the Communist youth organization in the former Soviet Union. [Russ abbrev of *Kommunisticheskii Soyuz Molodezhi* Communist Union of Youth]

kon (*Spenser*) variant of **con**[2]: — *pa t* **kond**.

konfyt *kon-fīt'*, (*SAfr*) *n* a preserve of fruit, in syrup or candied; jam. [Afrik, from Du *konfijt*]

konimeter *kon-im'i-tər*, *n* an instrument for measuring dust in air. — *n* **koniol'ogy** the study of dust in the air and its effects. — *n* **kon'iscope** an instrument for estimating the dustiness of air. [Gr *konis* dust, and *metron* measure, or *skopeein*, to look at]

konk. Same as **conk**[1,2].

koodoo. See **kudu**.

kook[1] *kōōk*, (*slang*) *n* a person who is mad, foolish, or eccentric and amoral. — *adj* **kook'ie** or **kook'y** with the qualities of a kook; (of clothes) smart and eccentric. [Prob from **cuckoo**]

kook[2]. See **cook**[3].

kookaburra *kōōk'ə-bur-ə*, *n* an Australian kingfisher (*Dacelo novaeguineae*) which has a discordant laughing call, the laughing jackass. [Aboriginal]

kookie, kooky. See under **kook**[1].

koolah *kōō'lə*, *n* an *obs* form of **koala**.

koori *kōō'ri*, (*Austr*) *n* an Aborigine; a young Aboriginal woman. [Aboriginal]

kop *kop*, *n* a hill (*SAfr*); (with *cap*) a bank of terracing at a football ground, *esp* (and *orig*) that at Liverpool's Anfield ground. — *n* **koppie** or **kopje** (*kop'i*; *SAfr*) a low hill. [Cape Du *kopje*; from Du *kop* head]

kopeck or **copeck** *kō-pek'* or *kō'pek*, *n* a Russian coin, the hundredth part of a rouble. [Russ *kopeika*]

koph *kof*, *kōf* or *kōf*, *n* the nineteenth letter of the Hebrew alphabet. [Heb *qōph*]

kopje. See under **kop**.

koppa *kop'ə*, *n* a Greek letter (Ϙ) between Pi and Rho in the alphabet, corresponding to Q in the Roman alphabet,

dropped by most Greek dialects but retained as a numeral ϙʹ = 90, ͵ϙ = 90 000. [Gr; cf Hebr *qōph*]
koppie. See under **kop**.
kora[1] *kō'rə* or *kö'rə*, *n* the water-cock (*Gallicrex*). [Origin uncertain]
kora[2] *kör'ə* or *kō'rə*, *n* a W African musical instrument similar to a harp. [Native word]
Koran *kō-rän'* or *kö-*, sometimes *kō'rən* or *kö'*, *n* the Muslim Scriptures in Arabic, believed by the faithful to be the true word of God as spoken by Mohammed. — Also **Qoran**, **Quran** and **Qur'an**. — *adj* **Koranic** (*-rän'ik*). [Ar *qurān* reading]
kore *kö'rā*, *n* an archaic Greek statue of a draped maiden. [Gr, maiden; cf **kouros**]
Korean *kə-rē'ən*, *adj* of or pertaining to N or S Korea in SE Asia, their people or language. — *n* an inhabitant or native of N or S Korea; their language. — **Korean chrysanthemum** a late-flowering hybrid chrysanthemum.
korero *ko-re'rō*, (*NZ*) *n* a talk, discussion. [Maori]
korfball *kōrf'böl* or *körf'böl*, *n* a game of Dutch origin resembling basketball played by teams of six men and six women a side. [Du *korfbal*, from *korf* basket, and *bal* ball]
korkir. See **corkir**.
korma *kör'mə*, *n* a mild-flavoured Indian dish, meat or vegetables braised in water, stock, yoghurt or cream.
korora *kō'rō-rə*, *n* the fairy penguin or little (blue) penguin (*Eudyptula minor*), smallest of all the penguins. [Maori]
Korsakoff's psychosis *kör'sə-kofs sī-kō'sis*, (*med*) *n* an illness in which damage to a small area of the brain results in disorientation and absolute loss of recent memory, often caused by alcoholism. [From S *Korsakoff* (1854–1900), Russian physician]
koruna *ko-ro͞o'nə*, *n* the standard unit of currency of the former Czechoslovakia (100 *halers*). [Czech, from L *corona* crown]
kos. Same as **coss**.
kosher *kō'shər*, *adj* pure or clean according to Jewish law; (of food) prepared according to Jewish dietary law; legitimate, proper, genuine (*colloq*). — *n* kosher food. — *vt* to prepare (food) in a kosher manner. [Heb *kāshēr* right]
kosmos. Same as **cosmos**.
koss. Same as **coss**.
koto *kō'tō*, *n* a Japanese musical instrument consisting of a long box with thirteen silk strings; — *pl* **kō'tos**. [Jap]
kotow *kō-tow'*. A less common form of **kowtow**.
kottabos *kot'ə-bos*. Same as **cottabus**.
kotwal or **cotwal** *kōt'wäl*, *n* a chief constable or magistrate of an Indian town. [Hind *kotwāl*]
Kotytto *kot-it'ō* or **Kotys** *kot'is*, *n* a Thracian goddess worshipped with wild orgies. [Gr *Kotyttō*, *Kotys*]
koulan, **koumiss**. See **kulan**, **kumiss**.
kouprey *ko͞o'prā*, *n* the very rare Indo-Chinese wild cow, believed to be closely related to the ancestors of modern domestic cattle. [Kampuchean native name]
kouros *ko͞o'ros*, *n* an archaic Greek statue of a nude youth. [Ionic Greek, boy; cf **kore**]
kouskous. See **couscous**.
kow. See **cow**[2].
kowhai *kō'hī*, *-hwī* or *-wī*, *n* a New Zealand tree or shrub of the genus *Sophora*, with golden flowers. [Maori]
kowtow *kow-tow'*, *n* the old Chinese ceremony of touching the forehead to the ground as a gesture of deference. — *vi* to perform that ceremony; to abase oneself before (with *to*); to grovel or fawn. — Also **kōtow'**. [Chin *k'o* knock, and *t'ou* head]
KP *abbrev*: Knight of (the Order of) St Patrick.
kpg *abbrev*: kilometres per gallon.
kph *abbrev*: kilometres per hour.
Kr (*chem*) *symbol*: krypton.
kr *abbrev*: krona (Swedish currency); króna (Icelandic currency); krone (Danish and Norwegian currency).
kraal *kräl*, *n* a S African village of huts surrounded by a fence; a corral. — *vt* to pen. [Du *kraal*, from Port *curral*, from L *currere* to run]
krab *krab*, (*mountaineering*) *n* short form of **karabiner**.
kraft *kräft*, *n* a type of strong brown wrapping paper made from pulp treated with a sulphate solution. — Also **kraft paper**. [Ger *Kraft* strength]
krait *krīt*, *n* a deadly S Asian rock snake (*Bungarus caeruleus*). [Hind *karait*]
kraken *krä'kən*, *n* a fabled sea-monster. [Norw; the *-n* is the definite article]
krakowiak. See **cracovienne** under **Cracovian**.
krameria *krä-mē'ri-ə*, *n* the shrub rhatany, a S American plant with thick roots from which an astringent is prepared; the astringent itself. [J G H and W H *Kramer*, 18c German botanists]
krang. See **kreng**.
krantz, **kranz** *kränts* or **krans** *kräns*, (*SAfr*) *n* a crown of rock on a mountain-top; a precipice. [Du *krans* a wreath]
krater. See under **crater**.
kraut *krowt*, (often with *cap*; *derog slang*) *n* a German. [From **sauerkraut**]
kreasote, **kreatine**. Same as **creosote**, **creatine**.
kreese. Same as **kris**.
kremlin *krem'lin*, *n* a citadel, *esp* (with *cap*) that of Moscow; (with *cap*) the Russian government, formerly the central government of the Soviet Union. — *n* **Kremlinol'ogist**. — *n* **Kremlinol'ogy** the study of the former Soviet government and its policies. [Russ *kreml'*]
kreng *kreng* or **krang** *krang*, *n* the carcass of a whale after the blubber has been removed. [Du]
kreosote. Same as **creosote**.
kreplach *krep'lähh*, *n pl* small dough dumplings filled with cheese, meat, etc, *usu* served in soup. [Yiddish]
kreutzer *kroit'sər*, *n* any of various former copper coins of Austria, S Germany, etc, 100 to the florin or gulden. [Ger *Kreuzer*, from *Kreuz* cross, because they were at one time stamped with a cross]
k'ri *krē*, *n* a marginal reading in the Hebrew Bible, intended as a substitute for the k'thibh (qv). [Heb *qerē* read (imperative)]
kriegspiel or **kriegsspiel** *krēg'spēl*, *n* a war-game played on a map to train officers; a form of chess in which the players use separate boards and are allowed only limited communication through an umpire. [Ger *Kriegsspiel*, from *Krieg* war, and *Spiel* game]
Krilium® *kril'i-əm*, *n* a substance added to soil to improve its structure, consisting of synthetic polymers.
krill *kril*, *n* a species of *Euphausia* (family *Euphausiaceae*), small shrimplike creatures eaten by whales, etc. [Norw *kril*]
krimmer or **crimmer** *krim'ər*, *n* tightly curled grey or black fur from a Crimean type of lamb. [Ger *Krim* Crimea]
kris *krēs*, *n* a Malay dagger with wavy scalloped blade: — *pl* **kris'es**. — *vt* to stab with a kris. — Also **crease**, **creese**, **kreese**. [Malay]
Krishna *krish'nə*, *n* a deity in later Hinduism, a form of Vishnu. — *n* **Krish'naism** (also called **Krishna Consciousness**) belief in, or worship of, Krishna. [Sans]
kromesky *krō-mes'ki* or *krə-*, also *krō'-* or *kro'-*, *n* a croquette wrapped in bacon or calf's udder, and fried. [Pol *kroméczka* little slice]
krone *krō'nə*, *n* (*pl* **kro'ner**) in Denmark and Norway, **krona** *kro͞o'na* (*pl* **kro'nor**) in Sweden, and **króna** *krō'na* (*pl* **krónur**) in Iceland, a silver coin and monetary unit equal to 100 öre, or in Iceland 100 *aurar*. — *n* **krone** (*krō'nə*; *pl* **kro'nen**) a former silver coin of Austria, equal to 100 heller; in Germany a former gold coin of 10 marks. [Cf **crown**]
Kronos *kron'os*, *n* a supreme god of the Greeks, son of Ouranos and Gaia, dethroned by his son Zeus.
krónur. See **krone**.
Kru or **Kroo** *kro͞o*, *n* one of a W African people of the coast of Liberia, noted as seamen. — Also *adj*. — **Kru'-** or **Kroo'-boy** or **-man**.

Krugerrand *krōō'gər-rand*, *n* a S African coin, used only for investment, containing one troy ounce of fine gold and bearing a portrait of President *Kruger*. — Also **Kruger Rand**, **rand**, or **krugerrand**. [**rand**[1]]

krummhorn, **krumhorn** or **crumhorn** *krōōm'hörn*, *n* an old double-reed wind instrument with a curved end; an organ reed-stop. [Ger, curved horn]

kryometer, etc. Same as **cryometer**, etc.

krypsis *krips'is*, *n* the 17c doctrine that Christ secretly exercised divine powers. [Gr, concealment]

krypton or **crypton** *krip'ton*, *n* an inert gas present in the air in extremely small quantity, used in fluorescent lights and lasers (symbol **Kr**; atomic no 36). [Gr *kryptein* to hide]

krytron *krī'tron*, (*tech*) *n* a sophisticated electronic timing device used for detonating nuclear and other explosive charges, and for varied industrial and scientific purposes.

KS *abbrev*: Kansas (US state); Kaposi's sarcoma.

ksar *ksär*, (*Milton*) *n* a variant of **tsar**.

Kshatriya *kshat'ri-ya*, *n* a member of the second or military caste among the Brahmanic Hindus. [Sans, from *kshatra* authority]

KT *abbrev*: Knight of the Thistle.

Kt *abbrev*: Knight.

kt *abbrev*: karat (carat); knot (*naut*).

k'thibh *kthēv*, *n* a traditional but erroneous reading retained in the main text of the Hebrew Scriptures. [Heb *kethībh* written; cf **k'ri**]

Ku (*chem*) *symbol*: kurchatovium.

kuchcha. Same as **cutcha**.

Kuchen *kōōhh'ən*, (Ger) *n* a cake or cakes.

kudos *kū'dos*, *n* credit, fame, renown, prestige. [Gr *kȳdos* glory]

kudu or **koodoo** *kōō'dōō*, *n* an African antelope with long spiral horns. [From Hottentot]

kudzu *kōōd'zōō*, *n* an ornamental papilionaceous plant of China and Japan (*Pueraria thunbergiana*) with edible root tubers and a stem yielding a fibre. [Jap]

kufiyah. See **kaffiyeh**.

Kufic or **Cufic** *kū'fik*, *adj* of Al *Kūfa*, south of Babylon, *esp* of the lettering of its coins, inscriptions and manuscripts, mainly early copies of the Koran.

Kuh-horn *kōō'hörn*, *n* an alpenhorn. [Ger]

Ku-Klux Klan *kōō' kluks klan*, or **Ku-Klux** or **the Klan**, *n* a secret organization in several Southern US states after the Civil War of 1861–5, to oppose Northern influence, and prevent Blacks from enjoying their rights as freemen, revived in 1916 to deal drastically with Jews, Catholics, Blacks, etc, and to preserve white Protestant supremacy. — *n* **Klan'sman** or **Ku-Klux Klansman** a member of this organization. [Gr *kyklos* a circle, and **clan**]

kukri *kōōk'rē*, *n* a sharp, curved Gurkha knife or short sword. [Hindi *kukṛī*]

kuku *kōō'kōō*, *n* a large fruit-eating pigeon of New Zealand (*Hemiphaga novaeseelandiae*), the wood-pigeon. [Maori]

kulak *kōō-lak'*, (*Russ*) *n* a rich peasant, in the Communist period regarded as an exploiter of others and a class traitor. [Russ, fist]

kulan or **koulan** *kōō'län*, *n* the onager, or a related wild ass of the Kirghiz Steppe. [Kirghiz]

Kultur *kōōl-tōōr'*, *n* culture, civilization, *esp* German civilization, regarded by outsiders as imperialist, militaristic and arrogant. — *n* **Kultur'geschichte** (*-gə-shēhh'tə*) the history of civilization; **Kultur'kampf** (*-kampf*) the war of culture (used by Virchow in 1873 of the conflict between Bismarck and the RC Church); **Kultur'kreis** (*-krīs*) an area regarded as a centre of diffusion of cultural elements. [Ger]

kumara *kōō'mə-rə*, *n* the sweet potato. [Maori]

kumari *kōō-mar'i*, (*Ind*) *n* Miss (as a title of respect).

kumiss or **koumiss** *kōō'mis*, *n* fermented mares' milk. [Russ *kumis*, from Tatar *kumiz*]

kümmel *küm'l*, *kim'l* or *kōōm'l*, *n* a liqueur flavoured with cumin and caraway seeds. [Ger, from L *cumīnum*, from Gr *kymīnon* cumin]

kumquat *kum'kwot*, *n* a very small Chinese variety of orange with a sweet rind. [Cantonese, gold orange]

kung fu *kung fōō*, *n* a martial art (of both armed and unarmed combat and self-defence) developed in ancient China. [Chin, combat skill]

kunkur *kung'kûr* or **kunkar** *kung'kər*, *n* a concretionary limestone in India; a laterite found in Ceylon. [Hindi *kaṅkar* stone]

Kunstlied *kōōnst'lēt*, (*Ger*) *n* an art-song.

kunzite *kun'zīt*, *n* a lilac-coloured variety of spodumene, used as a gemstone. [G F *Kunz* (1856–1932), US gemologist]

Kuomintang *kwō'min-tang* or *gwö'min-däng*, *n* the Chinese nationalist people's party. [Chin]

Kuo-yü *kwō'* or *gwö'yü*, *n*, a form of Mandarin taught all over China, literally national language.

Kupferschiefer *kōōp'fər-shē-fər*, *n* a shale rich in copper in the Permian of Germany. [Ger, copper shale]

kurbash or **kourbash** *kōōr'bash*, *n* a hide whip used in the East. — *vt* to whip with a kurbash. [Ar *qurbāsh*]

kurchatovium *kûr-chə-tō'vi-əm*, *n* the element (symbol **Ku**; atomic no 104) named by Russians (who claimed its discovery in 1966) after a Russian physicist (American name **rutherfordium**).

Kurd *kōōrd* or *kûrd*, *n* one of the Islamic people of Kurdistan, a mountainous region of Turkey, Iran and Iraq. — *adj* and *n* **Kurd'ish**.

kurgan *kōōr-gän'*, *n* a prehistoric burial mound. [Russ, from Tatar]

Kurhaus *kōōr'hows*, *n* a building in which a spa is housed. [Ger, literally cure-house]

kuri *kū'ri*, (*NZ*) *n* a mongrel; an extinct native dog. [Maori]

Kuroshio *kōō-rō'shi-ō*, *n* a warm current flowing north along the western edge of the Pacific. [Jap, black stream]

kurrajong or **currajong** *kur'ə-jong*, *n* a name for various Australian trees with fibrous bark. [Aboriginal]

kurre (*Spenser*). Same as **cur**.

kursaal *kōōr'zäl*, *n* the reception-room of a spa. [Ger, literally cure-room]

kurta or **khurta** *kōōr'tä*, *n* a loose-fitting collarless shirt or tunic worn in India. [Hindi]

kurtosis *kər-tō'sis*, (*statistics*) *n* the relative degree of sharpness of the peak on a frequency-distribution curve. [Gr *kurtōsis* bulging, swelling, from *kurtos* curved]

kuru *kōō'roo*, *n* a progressive and fatal brain disease, related to Creutzfeldt-Jakob disease, found only in certain parts of Papua New Guinea and thought to be transmissible by a slow virus. [Native word, meaning 'the trembles']

kurvey *kûr-vā'*, (*obs SAfr*) *vi* to transport goods by ox-wagon. — *n* **kurvey'or** a carrier. [Du *karwei* work, from Fr *corvée*; cf **corvée**]

Kushitic. Same as **Cushitic**.

kutch. Same as **cutch**[2].

kutcha. Same as **cutcha**.

kV *abbrev*: kilovolt.

kvass *kväs*, *n* an E European rye beer. [Russ *kvas*]

kvetch *kvech*, *vi* to complain, whine, *esp* incessantly. — *n* **kvetch** or **kvetch'er** a complainer, fault-finder. [Yiddish]

kW *abbrev*: kilowatt. — **kWh** *abbrev*: kilowatt-hour.

KWAC *kwak*, *abbrev*: keyword and context.

kwacha *kwach'ə*, *n* the basic unit of currency in Zambia (100 *ngwee*) and Malawi (100 *tambala*). [Native name, meaning 'dawn']

Kwakiutl *kwä-kē-ōōt'l*, *n* a N American Indian people of Vancouver Island and the mainland coastal area adjacent to it; a member of this people; their language.

kwanza *kwän'zə*, *n* the standard unit of currency of Angola (100 *lweis*).

kwashiorkor *kwä-shi-ör'kör* or *kwosh'*, *n* a widespread nutritional disease of newly weaned children in tropical and subtropical regions due to deficiency of protein. [Ghanaian name; perh derived from a reference to the displacement of a child on weaning and arrival of next child]

kwela *kwā'la*, *n* Zulu folk-music of jazz type. [Bantu, lift (from leaping upward in dancing to the music)]

kWh. See **kW**.

KWIC *kwik*, *abbrev*: keyword-in-context.

KWOC *kwok*, *abbrev*: keyword out of context.

Kwok's disease. Same as **Chinese restaurant syndrome** (under **China**).

KWT *abbrev*: Kuwait (IVR).

KY or **Ky** *abbrev*: Kentucky (US state).

ky. See **kye**.

kyang. See **kiang**.

kyanite *kī'ə-nīt* or **cyanite** *sī'*, *n* a mineral, an aluminium silicate, generally sky-blue. [Gr *kyanos* blue]

kyanize or **-ise** *kī'ə-nīz*, *vt* to preserve from dry-rot by injecting corrosive sublimate into the pores of (wood). [From John H *Kyan* (1774–1830)]

kyat *kyät*, *n* the standard unit of currency of Burma (100 *pyas*).

kybosh. See **kibosh**.

kydst (*Spenser*). See **kythe**.

kye or **ky** *kī*, (*Scot*) *n pl* cows. [See **kine**]

kyle *kīl*, *n* a narrow strait. [Gaelic *caol*]

kylie or **kiley** *kī'li*, (*Austr*) *n* a boomerang. [Aboriginal]

kylin *kē'lin*, *n* a mythical animal illustrated on Chinese and Japanese pottery. [From Chinese *ch'ī lin*]

kylix *kil'* or *kīl'iks*. See **cylix**.

kyllosis *kil-ō'sis*, *n* club-foot. [Gr *kyllōsis*]

kyloe *kī'lō*, *n* one of the small, long-haired cattle of the Scottish Highlands and Hebrides. [Origin unknown]

kymograph *kī'mō-gräf*, *n* an instrument for recording the pressure of fluids, *esp* of blood in a blood vessel. — *n* **ky'mogram** such a record. — *adj* **kymographic** (*-graf'ik*). — *n* **kymog'raphy**. [Gr *kȳma* a wave, and *graphein* to write]

kynd or **kynde** *kīnd*, (*Spenser*) *n*, *adj*, and *vt*. Same as **kind**[1,2].

kyne (*Spenser*). Same as **kine**.

kyogen *kyō-gen'*, *n* a comic interlude between Noh plays. [Jap, play, drama]

kyphosis *kī-fō'sis*, (*pathol*) *n* a hunchbacked condition. — *adj* **kyphotic** (*-fot'ik*). [Gr *kȳphōsis*, from *kȳphos* a hump]

Kyrie eleison *kēr'i-e el-ā'i-son*, *kir'* or *kīr'i-e el-e-ē'son*, or *el-e-ā'son*, etc, (in short **Kyrie**) *n* a form of prayer in all the ancient Greek liturgies, retained in the RC mass, following immediately after the introit (including both words and music); one of the responses to the commandments in the Anglican ante-communion service. [Gr *Kȳrie, eleēson* Lord, have mercy]

kyrielle *kēr-i-el'*, *n* a string of short lines in stanzas all ending with the same word or line. [Fr, litany, rigmarole, from Gr *Kȳrie eleēson*; see preceding]

kyte. See **kite**[2].

kythe or **kithe** *kīdh*, (*Scot*) *vt* to make known: — *2nd pers sing* **kydst** (*Spenser*) knowest. — *vi* to show oneself, to appear. [OE *cȳthan* to make known; see **uncouth**]

kyu *kū*, (*judo*) *n* one of the six novice grades, the least experienced being sixth kyu; a novice in one of these grades. [Jap]

L

L[1] or **l** *el, n* the twelfth letter in the modern English alphabet, the eleventh in the Roman alphabet, representing a lateral liquid sound, the breath passing the side or sides of the tongue; anything shaped like the letter L.

L[2] *el,* (*US colloq*) *n* an elevated railroad.

L or **L.** *abbrev*: Lake; lambert; Latin; learner (driver); lecturer; left; Liberal; *libra* (*L*), pound sterling (*usu* written £); Loch; Lough.

L *symbol*: (Roman numeral) 50.

L *symbol*: angular momentum (*phys*); inductance (*elec*); luminance (*phys*); molar latent heat (*chem*).

L- *el-, pfx* denoting: laevo (or levo-); laevorotatory. — ***L*-dopa** see **dopa**.

l or **l.** *abbrev*: laevorotatory (*chem*); latitude; league; left; length; *libra* (*L*), pound weight (*usu* written **lb**); line; lira or (*pl*) lire; litre.

l (*chem*) *symbol*: specific latent heat per gramme.

LA *abbrev*: Legislative Assembly; Library Association; Literate in Arts; Los Angeles; Louisiana (US state; also **La**).

La. *abbrev*: Lane (in street names, etc).

La (*chem*) *symbol*: lanthanum.

la[1] *lä, interj* lo! see! behold! ah! indeed! [Cf **lo** and **law**[5]]

la[2] *lä, n* the sixth note of the scale in sol-fa notation. — Also spelt **lah**. [See **Aretinian**]

laager *lä'gər,* (*Afrik* **laer**, not used in S African English) *n* in South Africa, a defensive ring of ox-wagons; any extemporized fortification; an encampment; a defensive group of people drawn together by similarity of opinion, etc (*fig*). — *vt* and *vi* to arrange or camp in a laager. [Afrik *lager*, from Ger *Lager* a camp; Du *leger*; cf **lair**[1], **layer** and **leaguer**]

Lab. *abbrev*: Labour; Labrador.

lab *lab, n* a familiar contraction of **laboratory**.

labanotation *lāb-ə-nō-tā'shən, n* the Laban system of ballet notation. — Also called **Laban system**. [Rudolf von *Laban*, who proposed it]

labarum *lab'ə-rəm, n orig* a Roman military standard, the imperial standard after Constantine's conversion, with a monogram of the Greek letters XP (ChR), for Christ; a similar ecclesiastical banner carried in processions; any moral standard or guide. [L, from Late Gr *labaron*, origin unknown]

labda, labdacism. See **lambda**.

labdanum. See **ladanum**.

labefactation *lab-i-fak-tā'shən* or **labefaction** *-fak'shən, n* a weakening decay; overthrow. [L *labefactātiō, -ōnis*, from *labāre* to totter, and *facere* to make]

label *lā'bl, n* a small slip of paper or other material placed on or near anything to denote its nature, contents, composition, ownership, destination, etc; a characterizing or classificatory designation (*fig*); a manufacturer's or retailer's tradename attached to goods to identify them; a strip of material with this or other information on it; the piece of paper on a record, cassette, compact disc, etc giving the maker's production company's tradename and identifying the recorded material; the tradename itself (*colloq*); a character or set of characters indicating the start of an instruction in a program and used elsewhere in the program to refer to that instruction (*comput*); a paper appended to a will, such as a codicil (*law*); a fillet with pendants (an eldest son's cadency mark; *heraldry*); a dripstone (*archit*); an attached band or strip (*archaic*). — *vt* to fix a label to; to describe by or on a label; to replace an atom in (a molecule or compound) by a radioactive isotope, for the purpose of identification (*phys*): — *pr p* **lā'belling**; *pa t* and *pa p* **lā'belled**. — **labelled atom** a tagged atom. [OFr *label*, perh from OHGer *lappa* (Ger *Lappen*) flap]

labellum *lə-bel'əm,* (*bot*) *n* the lower petal, morphologically *usu* the upper, of an orchid; applied also to other lip-like structures in flowers: — *pl* **labell'a**. — *adj* **labell'oid**. [L, dimin of *labrum* lip]

labial *lā'bi-əl, adj* of or formed by the lips; sounded by the impact of air on a lip-like projection, such as an organ flue-pipe (*music*). — *n* a sound formed by the lips. — *n* **lā'bialism, labializā'tion** or **-s-** a tendency to labialize. — *vt* **lā'bialize** or **-ise** to make labial; to pronounce with rounded lips. — *adv* **lā'bially**. — *n pl* **Lābiatae** (*-ā'tē*) a family of sympetalous dicotyledons with lipped flowers, four-cornered stems and opposite branches, comprising the dead-nettles, mints, etc. — *adj* **lā'biate** lipped; having a lipped corolla; belonging to the Labiatae. — *n* any plant of the Labiatae. — *n* **lā'bium** a lip or lip-like part; in insects, the underlip, formed by the partial fusion of the second maxillae: — *pl* **lā'bia**. — *adj* and *n* **lābiodent'al** (a sound) produced by the lips and teeth together, such as *f* and *v*. — **labia majora** and **labia minora** the two outer and inner folds of skin respectively surrounding the vaginal orifice in human females. [L *labium* lip]

labile *lā'bīl* or (*esp* in US) *lā'bəl, adj* unstable; apt to slip or change. — *n* **labil'ity**. [L *lābilis*, from *lābī* to slip]

labiodental. See under **labial**.

labis *lā'bis,* (*anatom*) *n* the cochlear or eucharistic spoon. [Gr *labis* handle, from root of *lambanein* to take]

labium. See **labial**.

lablab *lab'lab, n* a tropical bean (*Dolichos lablab*) with edible pods. [Ar *lablāb*]

labor. See **labour**.

laboratory *lə-bor'ə-tə-ri* or (*esp* in US) *lab'ə-rə-tə-ri, n* a place for experimental work or research; *orig* a chemist's workroom. [L *labōrāre*, from *labor* work]

labor improbus *lā'bör im-prō'bəs* or *la'bor im-pro'bŏŏs,* (*L*) *n* persistent, dogged labour.

laborious, etc. See under **labour**.

labour or (*esp* in NAm) **labor** *lā'bər, n* physical or mental toil; work, *esp* when done for money or other gain; pains; duties; a task requiring hard work; effort made toward the satisfaction of needs; workers collectively; supply or services of workers, *esp* physical workers; (with *cap*) the Labour Party or its cause, principles or interest (*politics*); the pains and physical efforts of childbirth; heavy pitching or rolling of a ship (*naut*); the outcome of toil (*archaic*); trouble taken (*archaic*); exertion of influence (*archaic*). — *adj* of labour or (with *cap*) the Labour Party. — *vi* to experience labour; to work; to take pains; to be oppressed or burdened; to move slowly and with difficulty; to undergo childbirth; to pitch and roll heavily (*naut*). — *vt* to strain, over-elaborate or repeat unnecessarily; to elaborate, work out in detail; to spend labour on (*archaic*); to cultivate (*dialect*). — *adj* **laborious** (*lə-bō'* or *-bö'ri-əs*) involving or devoted to labour; strenuous; arduous. — *adv* **labo'riously**. — *n* **labo'riousness**. — *adj* **lā'boured** showing signs of effort in execution; strained; over-elaborated, repeated unnecessarily; cultivated (*dialect*); worked (*archaic*). — *n* **lā'bourer** someone who labours; someone who does heavy physical work requiring little skill or training. — *n* **lā'bourism**. — *n* **lā'bourist** someone who supports or works for the rights of workers. — *n* **Lā'bourite** a member or supporter of the Labour Party. — *adj* **lā'boursome** (*Shakesp*) laborious. — **labor union** (*US*) a trade union;

labour camp a penal institution where the inmates are forced to work; temporary accommodation for workers; **Labour Day** a public holiday held in many countries on 1 May in celebration of labour and workers; in N America (**Labor Day**) a holiday held on the first Monday in September; **Labour Exchange** a former name for an **employment office**; **labour force** the number of workers employed in an industry, factory, etc; the part of the population which is employed or available for work. — *adj* **la'bour-intens'ive** requiring a relatively large number of workers for the capital invested (*opp* of *capital-intensive*). — **Labour Party** in Britain, a political party formed in 1900 by trade unions, etc to represent the working community and its interests; its representatives in parliament; a local organization of the party; a similar party in various countries, *esp* (as **Labor Party**) Australia. — *adj* **la'bour-sav'ing** intended to supersede or lessen labour. — **hard labour** compulsory work imposed in addition to imprisonment, abolished in the UK in 1948; **labour of love** work undertaken for its own sake and without hope of any tangible reward; **labour with** to take pains to convince. [OFr *labour*, *labeur*, from L *labor*]

labra. See **labrum**.

Labrador *lab'rə-dör* or *lab-rə-dör'*, *n* a mainland region of Newfoundland and Quebec; a Labrador dog. — Also *adj*. — *n* **lab'radorite** (or *-dör'*) a plagioclase feldspar with a fine play of colours found on the Labrador coast. — **Labrador dog** or **Labrador retriever** a sporting dog about 56cm in height, either black or (**yellow** or **golden Labrador**) from red to fawn in colour; **Labrador tea** a shrub of the heather family (genus *Ledum*) used in Labrador as a substitute for tea.

labrum *lā'brəm*, *n* a lip; a lip-like part: — *pl* **lā'bra**. — *n* **lā'bret** a lip ornament. — *adj* **lā'brose** thick-lipped. [L *labrum* a lip]

Labrus *lā'brəs*, *n* the wrasse genus of fishes, of the family **La'bridae**. — *adj* and *n* **la'brid** or **la'broid** (*la'* or *lā'*). [L *lābrus*, *lābros* a kind of fish]

labrys *lab'ris* or *lāb'ris*, *n* the double-headed axe, a religious symbol of ancient Crete, etc. [Gr, from Lydian; perh connected with **labyrinth**]

laburnum *lə-bûr'nəm*, *n* a small poisonous papilionaceous tree or shrub, a native of the Alps, bearing slim seed-pods and hanging clusters of yellow flowers. [L]

labyrinth *lab'i-rinth*, *n orig* a building with intricate passages; an arrangement of tortuous paths or alleys (*usu* between hedges) in which it is difficult to find the way out; a maze; a tangle of intricate ways and connections; a perplexity; the cavities of the internal ear (*anatom*). — *adj* **labyrinth'al**, **labyrinth'ian**, **labyrinth'ic**, **labrinth'ical** or **labyrinth'ine** (*-īn* or *-in*). — *n* **labyrinthī'tis** (*med*) inflammation of the inner ear. — *n* **labyrinth'odont** an extinct stegocephalian amphibian of Carboniferous, Permian, and *esp* Triassic times, so called from the mazy pattern of a section of the teeth (Gr *odous*, *odontos* tooth) in some. [Gr *labyrinthos*, perh connected with *labrys* the double axe; see **labrys**]

LAC *abbrev*: leading aircraft(s)man; Licentiate of the Apothecaries' Company.

lac[1]. Same as **lakh**.

lac[2] *lak*, *n* a dark-red transparent resin used in making shellac, secreted on the twigs of trees in Asia by certain coccid insects (**lac insects**). — **lac'-dye** and **lac'-lake** scarlet colouring matters obtained from it. [Hindi *lākh*, from Sans *lākṣā* 100 000, hence the (teeming) lac insect]

laccolith *lak'ō-lith* or **laccolite** *lak'ō-līt*, (*geol*) *n* a mass of igneous rock that has risen in a molten condition and bulged up the overlying strata to form a dome. — *adj* **laccolithic** (*-lith'ik*) or **laccolit'ic**. [Gr *lakkos* a reservoir, and *lithos* a stone]

lace *lās*, *n* a string or cord for passing through holes, eg to tie up a shoe or garment, etc; a delicate ornamental fabric made by looping, knotting, plaiting or twisting threads into definite patterns. — *vt* to fasten with a lace (often with *up*); to compress or pinch in by lacing; to trim or decorate with lace; to streak with colour (*fig*); to thrash; to reprimand severely (often with *into*); to intermingle, eg coffee with brandy, etc; to intertwine. — *vi* to have lacing as the means of fastening; to practise tight-lacing. — *adj* **laced**. — *n* **lacet** (*lās-et'*) a kind of braidwork. — *n* and *adj* **lac'ing**. — *adj* **lac'y** or (*rare*) **lac'ey** of or like lace; decorated with lace. — **lace'bark** a tall W Indian tree of the Daphne family, the inner bark like a coarse lace; **lace'-boot** a boot fastened by a lace; **laced mutton** (*Shakesp*) a prostitute; **lace'-frame** a machine used in lace-making; **lace glass** see **lacy glass** below; **lace'-leaf** see **lattice-leaf** under **lattice**; **lace'-man** a dealer in lace; **lace'-paper** paper stamped or cut like lace; **lace'-pill'ow** a cushion held on the knees by lacemakers, on which the lace is worked; **lace'-ups** boots or shoes tied with laces; **lace'wing** the golden-eye, a type of green or brown insect with two pairs of gauzy wings and brilliant golden eyes, which feeds on aphids, etc; **lacy glass** or **lace glass** an early form of pressed glass with a lacy design. [OFr *las* a noose, from L *laqueus*]

lacerate *las'ə-rāt*, *vt* to tear or rip; to rend; to wound; to afflict or distress severely. — *adj* **lac'erable**. — *adj* **lac'erant** harrowing. — *adj* **lac'erate** or **lac'erated** rent or torn; with edges cut into irregular segments (*bot*). — *n* **lacerā'tion**. — *adj* **lac'erative** tearing; having the power to tear. [L *lacerāre*, *-ātum* to tear, from *lacer* torn]

Lacerta *la-sûr'tə*, *n* a genus of lizards, including the common lizard; one of the northern constellations, the Lizard. — *adj* **lacertian** (*-sûr'shyən*) of lizards; lizard-like. — *n pl* **Lacertil'ia** the lizard order or suborder of reptiles. — *adj* **lacertil'ian**. — *adj* **lacer'tine**. [L]

lacet and **lacey**. See under **lace**.

laches *lach'iz*, (*law*) *n* negligence or undue delay in carrying out a legal duty, *esp* until the entitlement period (for a claim, remedy, etc) has expired. [Anglo-Fr *lachesse*]

Lachesis *lak'i-sis*, (*Gr mythol*) *n* that one of the three Fates who assigned to each mortal his or her destiny, and who spun the thread of life from the distaff held by Clotho; a genus of snakes including the bushmaster. [Gr]

lachrymal *lak'ri-məl*, *adj* of or for tears. — *n* a bone near the tear-gland; (in *pl*) lachrymal glands; (in *pl*) weeping fits; a tear-bottle. — *adj* **lach'rymary** or **lach'rymatory** lachrymal; causing tears to flow. — *n* a tear-bottle. — *n* **lachrymā'tion** the secretion of tears; (the act of) weeping. — *n* **lach'rymātor** a substance that causes tears to flow, as teargas; a contrivance for releasing such a substance. — *adj* **lach'rymose** shedding tears; tearful, given to weeping; lugubrious. — *adv* **lach'rymosely**. — *n* **lachrymos'ity**. — Also **lac'rymal**, **lac'rimal**, etc. — **lachryma Christi** (*lak'ri-mə kris'tē*; *L*, Christ's tear) a sweet but piquant wine from grapes grown on Vesuvius; **lachrymal duct** a duct that conveys tear-water from the inner corner of the eye to the nose; **lachrymal gland** a gland at the outer angle of the eye that secretes tears; **lachrymal urn** a tear-bottle. [From *lachryma*, a medieval spelling of L *lacrima* tear; cf Gr *dakry*; Eng **tear**; Gr *dakrȳma* may have influenced the spelling]

lacinia *lə-sin'i-ə*, *n* a long narrow lobe in a leaf, etc (*bot*); the inner lobe of the maxilla (*entomol*): — *pl* **lacin'iae** (*-ē*). — *adj* **lacin'iate** or **lacin'iated** cut into narrow lobes, slashed. — *n* **laciniā'tion**. [L, a lappet or tag]

lack[1] *lak*, *n* want, deficiency; something absent or in short supply. — *vt* to be without; to be short of or deficient in; to need; to miss (*obs*). — *vi* (now *usu* in *pr p*) to be wanting or absent; to be deficient; to be in want (*obs*). — *adj* **lack'ing**. — **lack'-all** (*archaic*) someone who is destitute; **lack'-beard**; **lack'-brain** (*Shakesp*) a fool; **lack'land**. — Also *adj*. — **lack'-Latin** (*obs*; often *Sir John Lack-Latin*) an ignorant priest. — *adj* uneducated, ignorant. — *adj* **lack'-linen** (*Shakesp*) without linen. — **lack'-love** someone who is deficient in love. — Also *adj*. — *adj* **lack'lustre** or in US **lack'luster** dull, without brightness, sheen or vitality. — Also *n*. [Cf MLGer and Du *lak* blemish]

lack[2] *lak*, *n*. See **good-lack** under **good**.

lackadaisical *lak-ə-dā'zi-kl*, *adj* affectedly pensive; shallowly sentimental; listless; languid and ineffectual; indolent. — *adv* **lackadai'sically**. — *n* **lackadai'sicalness**. — *interj* (*archaic*) **lack'adai'sy** or **lack'aday**. [See **alack-a-day**]

lacker. See **lacquer**.

lackey or (*rare*) **lacquey** *lak'i*, *n* a footman or valet; a servile follower: — *pl* **lack'eys** or **lacqu'eys**. — *vt* and *vi* to serve or attend as or like a footman or slavish servant. — **lackey moth** a moth (*Malacosoma neustria*) of the egger group with a gaudily striped caterpillar, like a footman in livery. [OFr *laquay* (Fr *laquais*), from Sp *lacayo* a lackey; perh Ar *luka'* servile]

lacmus *lak'məs*, *n* an *obs* form of **litmus**.

Laconian *lə-kō'nyən* or *-ni-ən* or **Laconic** *lə-kon'ik*, *adj* of Laconia or Lacedaemonia, Spartan. — *adj* **lacon'ic** or **lacon'ical** expressing or expressed in few words; sententiously brief. — *adv* **lacon'ically**. — *n* **laconism** (*lak'*) or **lacon'icism** a concise style; a short, pithy phrase. [Gr *lakōnikos* of Laconia, ie Spartan (in reference to the succinct style of Spartan speech)]

lacquer or **lacker** *lak'ər*, *n* a solution of film-forming substances in a volatile solvent, *esp* a varnish of lac and alcohol; a similar substance sprayed on the hair to hold it in place; the juice of the lacquer-tree (*Japan lacquer*) or a similar product; a covering of one of these; an article or ware so coated. — *vt* to cover with lacquer; to varnish. — *n* **lacqu'erer**. — *n* **lacqu'ering** varnishing with lacquer; a coat of lacquer varnish. — **lacqu'er-tree** a tree of the genus *Rhus*. [Fr *lacre*, from Port *lacre*, *laca*; *lacrymal*, see **lac**[2]]

lacquey. See **lackey**.

lacrimal, etc. Variants of **lachrymal**, etc.

lacrimoso *lak-ri-mō'sō* (*music*) *adj* and *adv* plaintive or plaintively. [Ital, from L *lacrimōsus* tearful, from *lacrima* a tear]

lacrosse *lə-* or *lä-kros'*, *n* a team sport (*orig* N American Indian) in which a long-handled, netted stick (**lacrosse stick** or **crosse**) is used to throw, catch and cradle (qv) the ball and drive it through the opponents' goal. — **min'i-lacrosse** and **pop'-lacrosse** simplified versions of lacrosse. [Can Fr]

lacteal *lak'ti-əl*, *adj* of milk; conveying chyle. — *n* a lymphatic vessel conveying chyle from the intestines to the thoracic ducts. — *n* **lactā'rian** a vegetarian whose diet includes milk and other dairy products. — *adj* of or designating such a person or diet. — *n* **lactase** (*lak'tās*) an enzyme that acts on lactose. — *n* **lac'tate** a salt of lactic acid. — *vi* (also *lak-tāt'*) to secrete milk. — *n* **lactā'tion** secretion or yielding of milk; the period of suckling. — *adj* **lac'teous** milky. — *n* **lactesc'ence**. — *adj* **lactesc'ent** turning to milk; producing milky juice. — *adj* **lac'tic** derived from or relating to milk. — *adj* **lactif'erous** conveying or producing milk or milky juice. — *adj* **lactif'ic** producing milk or milky juice. — *adj* **lactif'luous** flowing with milk. — *n* **lactobacill'us** any bacterium of the genus *Lactobacillus*, which converts certain carbohydrates to lactic acid. — *adj* **lactogen'ic** inducing lactation. — *n* **lactom'eter** a hydrometer for testing the relative density of milk. — *n* **lac'tone** a cyclic ester which can be formed by the reaction between the hydroxyl group and the carboxyl group in a hydroxycarboxylic acid molecule. — *n* **lactoprō'tein** any protein present in milk. — *n* **lac'toscope** an instrument for measuring the purity or richness of milk. — *n* **lac'tose** milk-sugar, $C_{12}H_{22}O_{11}H_2O$, a crystalline sugar obtained by evaporating whey. — *n* and *adj* **lactovegetā'rian** same as **lactarian** above. — **lactic acid** an acid obtained from milk, $CH_3CH(OH)\ COOH$, used as a preservative. [L *lac*, *lactis* milk; Gr *gala*, *galaktos* milk]

lactoflavin *lak-tō-flā'vin*, *n* an earlier name for **riboflavin**. [L *lac*, *lactis* milk, and *flāvus* yellow]

Lactuca *lak-tū'kə*, *n* the lettuce genus of composite plants, with milky juice. [L *lactūca*, from *lac*, *lactis* milk]

lacuna *lə-* or *la-kū'nə*, *n* a gap or hiatus; an intercellular space (*biol*); a cavity; a depression in a pitted surface: — *pl* **lacū'nae** (*-nē*). — *adj* **lacūn'al** lacunary. — *n* **lacū'nar** a sunken panel or coffer in a ceiling or a soffit; a ceiling containing these: — *pl* **lacū'nars** or **lacunaria** (*lak-ū-nā'ri-ə*). — Also *adj*. — *adj* **lacūn'ary** or **lacūn'ate** relating to or including lacunae. — *adj* **lacū'nose** having lacunae; pitted. [L *lacūna* hollow or gap, and *lacūnar*, *-āris* a fretted ceiling]

lacustrine *lə-kus'trīn*, *adj* relating to lakes; dwelling in or on lakes; formed in lakes. [L *lacus* a lake]

LACW *abbrev*: leading aircraft(s)woman.

lacy. See under **lace**.

lad[1] *lad*, *n* a boy; a youth; a male companion, workmate, etc (*colloq*); a stable-man or -woman; a dashing, high-spirited or extrovert man (*colloq*); a lover (*Scot*). — *n* **ladd'ie** a little lad; a boy (*N Eng*). — **lad's love** (*dialect*) the aromatic plant southernwood. [ME *ladde* youth or servant; origin obscure]

lad[2]. *Obs* form of **led**.

ladanum *lad'ə-nəm*, *n* a fragrant resin exuded from Cistus leaves in Mediterranean countries. — Also **lab'danum**. [L *lādanum*, *lēdanum*, from Gr *lādanon*, *lēdanon*, from *lēdon* the Cistus plant, prob from Pers *lādan*]

ladder *lad'ər*, *n* a piece of equipment, generally portable, with horizontal rungs between two vertical supports, used for going up and down; anything of similar form or pattern, such as a run in knitwear where the breaking of a thread gives an appearance of rungs; an arrangement which enables fish to ascend a waterfall (*fish-ladder* or *salmon-ladder*); a means of attaining a higher status (*fig*). — *vt* (*rare*) to provide with a ladder; to scale with a ladder. — *vi* of knitwear, fabric, etc, to develop a ladder. — *adj* **ladd'ered** or **ladd'ery**. — *n* **ladd'er-back** a chair with a back consisting of several horizontal bars between two long uprights. — Also *adj*. [OE *hlǣder*; Ger *Leiter*]

laddie. See **lad**[1].

lade[1] *lād*, *vt* to load; to burden; to put on board; to ladle or scoop (now *usu technical*); to empty or drain, as with a ladle. — *vi* to take cargo aboard: — *pa t* **lād'ed**; *pa p* **lād'en** or **lād'ed**. — *adj* **lād'en** loaded; burdened. — *n* **lād'ing** the act of loading; that which is loaded; cargo; freight. [OE *hladan*, pa t *hlōd*; pa p *hlæden*, *hladen* to load, draw water]

lade[2] or **laid** *lād*, Scots forms of **load**.

lade[3] *lād*, (*Scot*) *n* a millstream. [Perh OE *lād* way or course; cf **lode** and **lead**[1]]

laden. See **lade**[1].

la-di-da or **lah-di-dah** *lä-di-dä'*, (*slang*) *adj* affectedly elegant or superior, *esp* in speech or bearing.

ladies, etc. See **lady**.

Ladin *lä-dēn'*, *n* a Romance language spoken in the upper Inn valley in central Europe; a general name for the Rhaeto-Romanic languages or dialects. — Also **Ladi'no**. — *n* **Ladinity** (*-din'i-ti*). [L *Latīnus* Latin]

Ladino[1] *lä-dē'nō*, *n* the old Castilian language; the language, Spanish mixed with Hebrew, spoken by Jews in areas near the Eastern Mediterranean; a Latino (see under **Latin**): — *pl* **Ladin'os**. [Sp, from L *Latīnus* Latin]

Ladino[2]. See **Ladin**.

ladle *lād'l*, *n* a large, *usu* deep spoon for lifting liquid; the float-board of a millwheel; a long-handled pan or bucket for holding and conveying molten metal; a church collection-box on a long handle (*Scot*). — *vt* to transfer or distribute with a ladle. — *n* **lad'leful** as much as a ladle will hold: — *pl* **lad'lefuls**. — **ladle out** (*colloq*) to distribute generously. [OE *hlædel*, from *hladan* to lade]

ladrone *lə-drōn'*, (*archaic*) *n* a robber. [Sp *ladrón*, from L *latrō*, *-ōnis*]

lady *lā'di*, (with *cap* when used as a prefix) *n* the mistress of a house; used as the feminine of **lord** and of **gentleman**, and ordinarily as a less formal substitute for

dame; any woman with refined manners and instincts; a consort, a term formerly preferred to wife by some who liked to stand upon their dignity (*archaic*); a lady-love or object of chivalric devotion; a girlfriend, mistress, etc; a feminine prefix with various formal uses, eg for the wife of a knight, baron or baronet; a size of slates, *approx* 40.6 × 20cm, 16 × 8in. — *combining form* denoting a woman who performs a certain job, etc, such as *tea-lady*: — *pl* **ladies** (*lā'diz*); old genitive **la'dy**. — *n* **ladies'** a ladies' lavatory. — *adj* **la'dyfied** or **la'dified** inclined to affect over-refined manners. — *vt* **la'dyfy** or **la'dify** to make a lady of; to call My Lady or Your Ladyship. — *n* **la'dyhood** the condition or character of a lady. — *adj* **la'dyish** having the airs of a fine lady. — *n* **la'dyism** affectation of the airs of a fine lady. — *n* **la'dykin** (*archaic*) an endearing diminutive of **lady**. — *adj* **la'dylike** like a lady in manners; refined; soft, delicate; genteel. — *n* **la'dyship** the title of a lady. — **ladies' companion** a small bag used for a woman's needlework; **ladies' fingers** see **lady's finger(s)** below; **ladies' gallery** a gallery in the House of Commons, once screened off by a grille; **ladies' man** or **lady's man** a man who enjoys the company of women and being attentive to them; a (would-be) seducer of women; **la'dieswear** clothing for women; **la'dybird** any member of the family Coccinellidae, little round beetles, often brightly spotted, which prey on greenfly, etc (also **la'dybug** (*NAm*), **la'dycow** or **la'dyfly**); **Lady Bountiful** (also without *caps*; often *derog*; from a character in Farquhar's *The Beaux' Stratagem*) a rich and generous woman, often applied to one who is ostentatiously or offensively so; **lady chapel** a chapel dedicated to the Virgin Mary, usually behind the high altar, at the end of the apse; **Lady Day** 25 March, the day of the annunciation of the Virgin; **la'dy-fern** a pretty British fern (*Athyrium filix-foemina*), with long bipinnate fronds (imagined by the old herbalists to be the female of the male-fern); **la'dy-help** a woman paid to assist in housework, but treated more or less as one of the family; **lady-in-wait'ing** a female attendant to a lady of royal status; **la'dy-killer** a man who is, or fancies himself, irresistible to women; **la'dy-love** a beloved lady or woman; a sweetheart; **Lady Muck** see under **muck**; **lady's-cu'shion** the mossy saxifrage; **lady's finger** or **fingers** a name for many plants, *esp* the kidney-vetch; okra; a finger-shaped sponge cake; **la'dy's-maid** a lady's female attendant, responsible for her clothes, etc; **lady's-mant'le** a genus (*Alchemilla*) of plants of the rose family with small, yellowish-green flowers and leaves like folded drapery; **lady's-slipp'er** a genus (*Cypripedium*) of orchids with a large slipper-like lip; **la'dy's-smock** or **la'dy-smock** the cuckoo-flower (*Cardamine pratensis*), a cruciferous meadow-plant, with pale lilac-coloured flowers; **lady's-thist'le** the milk thistle; **lady's** (or **ladies'**) **tresses** (*sing* or *pl*) an orchid of the genus *Spiranthes* with small white flowers; **la'dy-trifles** (*Shakesp*) trifles befitting a lady. — **find the lady** see **three-card trick** under **three**; **her ladyship, your ladyship** and **my lady** forms of expression used in speaking of or to a person who has the title of Lady; **our Lady** the Virgin Mary; **(Our) Lady's bedstraw** see **bedstraw** under **bed**[1]. [OE *hlǣfdige*, literally appar the bread-kneader, from *hlāf* loaf, and a lost word from the root of **dough**]

Laender. See **Land**.

laeotropic *lē-ō-trop'ik*, *adj* turning to the left. [Gr *laios* left, and *tropos* a turn]

laer. See **laager**.

laesa majestas *lē'zə mə-jes'tas* or *lī'sa mä-yes'täs*, (*L*) *n* lese-majesty (qv), injured majesty.

laesie (*Spenser*) for **lazy**.

laetare *lē-tā'ri* or *lī-tär'e*, *n* the fourth Sunday in Lent. [*Laetāre* (the first word of the introit), imperative singular of L *laetārī* to rejoice, from *laetus* joyful]

laevigate a faulty spelling of **levigate**.

laevo- or **levo-** *lē-vō-*, *combining from* denoting on or to the left. [L *laevus* left]

laevorotatory or **levorotatory** *lē-vō-rō'tə-tə-ri* or *-rō-tā'*, *adj* counterclockwise; rotating the plane of polarization of light to the left (*optics*). — *n* **laevorotā'tion**. [L *laevus* left, and *rotāre* to rotate]

laevulose *lēv'ū-lōs* or *lev'*, *n* fructose, a laevorotatory sugar ($C_6H_{12}O_6$). — Also **lev'ulose**. [L *laevus* left]

Laffer curve *la'fər kûrv*, (*econ*) *n* a curve joining the points on a graph which shows the relationship between tax revenue received by the state and the percentage tax rate imposed by the state. [Arthur *Laffer*, born 1940, US economist]

LAFTA *laf'tə*, *abbrev*: Latin American Free Trade Association, which in 1981 became LAIA (qv).

lag[1] *lag*, *n* a retardation or falling behind; the amount by which one phenomenon is delayed behind another; delay; someone who, or something which, comes behind; the fag-end; (*esp* in *pl*) dregs (*obs*). — *vi* to fall behind; to move or walk slowly; to loiter; to string (*billiards*): — *pr p* **lagg'ing**; *pa t* and *pa p* **lagged**. — *adj* hindmost (*obs*); behindhand (*rare*); late (*rare*); tardy (*rare*). — *adj* **lagg'ard** lagging behind. — *n* **lagg'ard** or **lagg'er** a person who lags behind. — *n* and *adj* **lagg'ing**. — *adv* **lagg'ingly**. — **lag'-end** (*Shakesp*) the last or long-delayed end. — **lag of the tides** the progressive lengthening of the interval between tides as neap-tide is approached (opposed to *priming*). [Origin unknown]

lag[2] *lag*, *n* an insulating wooden or other lining; a non-conducting covering for pipes, etc; boarding; a wooden stave or lath; a wooden lining; a non-conducting covering; a perforated wooden strip used instead of a card in weaving. — *vt* to provide with a lag or lagging. — *n* **lagg'er** a person who insulates pipes, machinery, etc against heat loss. — *n* **lagg'ing** a non-conducting covering for pipes, etc to minimize loss of heat; boarding, as across the framework of a centre for an arch, or in a mine to prevent ore falling into a passage. [Prob ON *lögg* barrel-rim; cf Swed *lagg* stave]

lag[3] *lag*, (*slang*) *vt* to steal; to carry off; to arrest; to imprison; to transport or send to penal servitude. — *n* a convict; a former convict; a term of imprisonment or transportation. [Origin unknown]

lagan *lag'ən*, *n* wreckage or goods at the bottom of the sea; now *esp* such goods attached to a buoy with a view to recovery. — Also **ligan** (*lī'gən*). [OFr *lagan*, perh Scand from the root of **lay**[3] and **lie**[2]; falsely associated with L *ligāmen* a tying]

lagena *lə-jē'nə*, (*antiq*) *n* a narrow-necked bottle. — *adj* **lagē'niform** flask-shaped. [L *lagēna*, from Gr *lagȳna*]

lager *lä'gər*, *n* (in full **lager beer**) a light beer traditionally matured for up to six months before use. — **lager lout** a youth noted for his boorish, aggressive and unruly behaviour brought on by an excess of lager, beer, etc; **lager loutery** (*colloq*) the phenomenon or behaviour of lager louts. [Ger *Lager-bier*, from *Lager* a storehouse]

laggard. See under **lag**[1].

laggen or **laggin** *lag'* or *läg'ən*, (*Burns*) *n* the angle between the side and bottom of a wooden dish. — **lagg'en-gird** a hoop at the bottom of a wooden vessel. [Cf **lag**[2] and **leglin**]

lagger, lagging. See **lag**[1,2].

lagniappe or **lagnappe** *lan'yap*, *n* something given beyond what is strictly required; a gratuity. [Louisiana Fr, from Am Sp (Quechua *yápa* addition)]

lagomorph *lag'o-mörf*, *n* an animal of the order *Lagomorpha* of gnawing mammals having two pairs of upper incisors, eg hares and rabbits. — *adj* **lagomor'phic** or **lagomor'phous**. [Gr *lagōs* hare, and *morphē* form]

lagoon *lə-go͞on'*, *n* a shallow lake, *esp* one near or communicating with the sea or a river; an area of water separated from the sea by earth or sand banks, coral reefs, etc. — Also (*old-fashioned*) **lagune'**. — *adj* **lagoon'al**. [Ital *laguna*, from L *lacūna*]

Lagos rubber *lā'gos rub'ər*, *n* a high-grade rubber yielded by tropical African trees of the genus *Funtumia*. [*Lagos*, a state of Nigeria]

Lagrangian points *la-grān'ji-ən points*, (*astron* and *space tech*) *n pl* the five points associated with a binary system (*esp* Earth-Moon) where the combined gravitational forces are zero. [From J L *Lagrange* (1736–1813), Fr mathematician and astronomer]

lagrimoso *läg-ri-mō'sō*, (*music*) *adj* and *adv* plaintive or plaintively. [Ital from L *lacrimōsus* tearful, from *lacrima* a tear]

Lagting or **Lagthing** *läg'ting*, *n* the upper house of the Norwegian parliament; the parliament of the Faeroe Islands (also **Løg'ting**). [Norw *lag*, Faeroese *løg* law, and *ting* (*thing*) court, parliament]

lagune. See **lagoon**.

lah. Same as **la**[2].

lahar *lä'här*, *n* a mud-lava or other mud-flow.

lah-di-dah. See **la-di-da**.

LAIA *abbrev*: Latin American Integration Association (before 1981, LAFTA (qv)).

laic, laical, laicize and **laicity**. See under **lay**[6].

laid[1] *lād*, *pa t* and *pa p* of **lay**[3]. — *adj* put down or prostrate; pressed down; spread or set out; flattened by wind and rain. — *adj* **laid'-back'** or **laid back** (*colloq*) relaxed; easy-going; unhurried. — **laid paper** paper that shows the marks of the close parallel wires on which the pulp was laid (*opp* of *wove*); **laid work** in embroidery, the simplest kind of couching.

laid[2] *lād*, Scots form of **load**.

laidly *lād'li*, *adj* Northern (*esp Scot*) form of **loathly**.

laigh *lāhh*, *adj* and *adv* a Scots form of **low**[2]; low-lying; sunken. — *n* a tract of low-lying or sunken land.

laik. See **lake**[4].

laika *lī'kə*, *n* any of several similar breeds of small reddish-brown working dog, originating in Finland.

lain *pa p* of **lie**[2].

Laingian *lang'i-ən*, *adj* of or relating to the theories or practices of R D *Laing* (1927–89), British psychiatrist, *esp* his view that mental illness is a response to stress caused by a person's family life or by social pressures. — *n* a supporter of Laing's theories and practices.

lair[1] *lār*, *n* the den or retreat of a wild animal; an enclosure for beasts; the ground for one grave in a graveyard (*Scot*). — *vt* to put in a lair. — *vi* to lie in a lair; to go to a lair. — *n* **lair'age** a place or accommodation where cattle are housed or laired, *esp* at markets and docks. [OE *leger* a couch, from *licgan* to lie down; Du *leger*, Ger *Lager*]

lair[2] *lār*, (*Scot*) *vt* and *vi* to mire, cover with mud. — *n* mire. — *adj* **lair'y** (*Scot*). [ON *leir* mud]

lair[3] *lār*, *n* Scots form of **lore**[1].

lair[4] *lār*, (*Austr slang*) *n* a flashily dressed man. — *vi* **lai'rize** or **-ise** to act the lair. — *adj* **lair'y**. — **laired up** dressed flashily.

laird *lārd*, (*Scot*) *n* an estate landowner. — *n* **laird'ship**. [Northern form of **lord**]

lairy. See under **lair**[2,4].

laisse *les*, *n* a tirade or string of verses on one rhyme. [Fr]

laissez-aller *les-ā-al'ā*, *n* lack of constraint; relaxed freedom. — Also **laisser-all'er**. [Fr, let go]

laissez-faire *les-ā-fer'*, *n* a general principle of non-interference in the concerns of other people or parties. — Also **laisser-faire'**. [Fr, let do]

laissez-passer *les-ā-päs'ā*, *n* a pass, special passport or similar permit, to allow one to travel in a restricted area, etc. [Fr, let pass]

laitance *lā'təns*, *n* a milky accumulation of fine particles which forms on the surface of newly laid concrete if the concrete is too wet or is vibrated or tamped too much. [Fr, from *lait* milk]

laith *lāth*, *adj* a Scots form of **loth**. — *adj* **laithfu'** (*lāth'fə*) bashful.

laity. See under **lay**[6].

lake[1] *lāk*, *n* a reddish pigment originally derived from lac; a coloured substance derived by combining a dye with a metallic hydroxide; its colour; carmine. — *vt* and *vi* to make or become lake-coloured. — *adj* **lak'y**. [**lac**[2]]

lake[2] *lāk*, *n* a large or considerable body of water enclosed by land; a large quantity, an excess, eg of wine, etc (*econ*). — *n* and *adj* **Lake'land** (of or belonging to) the Lake District (qv); (without *cap*) (of or belonging to) any similar area of countryside. — *n* **lake'let** a little lake. — *n* **lāk'er** a fish found in lakes; a boat for lakes; a person who sails on lakes; a Lake poet; a visitor to the Lake District. — *adj* **lāk'ish** resembling or having the characteristics of the Lake school (see below). — *adj* **lāk'y**. — **lake'-basin** a hollow now or once containing a lake; the area drained by a lake; **Lake District** a picturesque and mountainous region in Cumbria (formerly Cumberland, Westmorland and Lancashire) with many lakes; **lake'-dweller**; **lake'-dwelling** a settlement, *esp* prehistoric, built on piles in a lake; **lake herring** see **cisco**; **lake'-law'yer** (*US*) the bowfin; the burbot; **Lake poets** or **Lake school** Wordsworth, Coleridge and Southey, who lived in the Lake District. — *n* and *adj* **lake'side**. [ME *lac*, either from OE *lacu* stream (see **lake**[3]), confused in sense with L *lacus* lake, or from *lacus* itself, directly or through Fr *lac*]

lake[3] *lāk*, (*obs*) *n* a small stream or water channel. [OE *lacu*]

lake[4] or **laik** *lāk*, (*N Eng*) *vi* to sport or play; to take a holiday from work; to be unemployed. — *n* **lak'er** or **laik'er**. [OE *lācan*]

lakh or **lac** *lak*, (*Ind* and *Pak*) *n* the number 100 000, *esp* in referring to rupees; an indefinitely vast number. [Hindi *lākh*, from Sans *lakṣa* 100 000]

lakin *lā'kin*, (*Shakesp*) *n* a short form of **ladykin**, *dimin* of **lady**.

Lakota *lə-kō'tə*, *n* (a member of) a N American Indian people comprising the westernmost branch of the Sioux (qv); the Siouan language of this people. — Also *adj.*

Lakshmi *luksh'mē*, *n* in Hindu mythology, Vishnu's consort. [Sans]

la-la *la'la* or *lä'lä*, *vi* to sing an accompaniment using syllables such as la-la. [Poss **la**[2]]

lalang *lä'läng*, *n* a coarse grass, *Imperata arundinacea*, of the Malay archipelago. [Malay]

lalapalooza. See **lallapalooza**.

laldie or **laldy** *lal'di*, (*Scot*) *n* a beating or thrashing (as punishment); vigorous action of any kind. — **get laldie** to receive a thrashing; **give it** or **give someone laldie** to do something or punish someone energetically and enthusiastically. [Perh connected with OE *læl* a whip, weal, bruise]

Lalique glass *lal-ēk' gläs*, *n* ornamental glassware, *esp* with bas-relief decoration of figures, flowers, etc. [Named after René *Lalique* (died 1945), Fr designer of jewellery and glassware]

lallan *lal'ən* or *läl'ən*, (*Scot*) *adj* and *n* a form of **lawland** or **lowland**. — *n* **Lall'ans** the Broad Scots language or dialect; a form of Scots developed by modern Scottish writers.

lallapalooza, **lalapalooza** *lal-ə-pə-lōō'zə* or **lollapalooza** *lol-ə-pə-lōō'zə*, (*US slang*) *n* something excellent or wonderful. [Ety unknown]

lallation *lal-ā'shən*, *n* in speech, the pronouncing of *r* like *l*; *orig* childish speech. — *n* **lall'ing** babbling. [L *lallāre* to sing lullaby]

l'allegro *lä-lā'grō*, (*Ital*) *n* the merry or cheerful man.

lallygag *lal'i-gag* or **lollygag** *lol'i-gag*, (*colloq*, *esp NAm*) *vi* to idle or loiter; to caress, *esp* publicly. [Ety uncertain]

Lam. (*Bible*) *abbrev*: (the Book of) Lamentations.

lam[1] *lam*, *vt* to beat. — *n* **lamm'ing** a thrashing. [Cf OE *lemian* to subdue or lame, ON *lemja* to beat, literally lame]

lam[2] *lam*, (*US slang*) *n* escape or hurried flight, *esp* from the police. — *vi* (with *it*, or *out*, *into*, etc) to escape or flee. — **on the lam** escaping, running away; **take it on the lam** to make an escape or flee. [Origin uncertain, perh from **lam**[1]]

lama *lä'mə*, *n* a Buddhist priest in Tibet. — *n* **Lamaism** (*lä'mə-izm*) the religion prevailing in Tibet and Mongolia, being Buddhism influenced by Tantrism, and by Shamanism or spirit-worship. — *n* **La'maist**. — *adj*

lamaist'ic. — *n* **la'masery** (or *lä-mä'sə-ri*) or **lamaserai** (*-rī*) a Tibetan monastery. [Tibetan *blama*, the *b* silent]

lamantin *lä-man'tin*, *n* the manatee. [Fr]

Lamarckism *lä-märk'izm*, *n* the theory of the French naturalist J B P A de Monet de *Lamarck* (1744–1829) that species have developed by the efforts of organisms to adapt themselves to new conditions. — Also **Lamarck'ianism**. — *adj* and *n* **Lamarck'ian**.

lamasery or **lamaserai**. See **lama**.

lamb *lam*, *n* the young of a sheep; its flesh eaten as a food; lambskin; someone simple, innocent, sweet or gentle as a lamb (*fig*); a dear (*colloq*). — *vt* and *vi* to give birth to (a lamb or lambs); to tend at lambing. — *n* **lamb'er** someone who tends lambing ewes; a lambing ewe. — *n* **lamb'kin**, **lamb'ling** (*rare*), or (*Scot*) **lamb'ie** a little lamb. — *adj* **lamb'-like** like a lamb; gentle. — **lamb'-ale** a feast at lamb-shearing; **lamb's ears** or **lamb's tongue** a labiate plant, *Stachys lanata*, with silver woolly leaves; **lamb'skin** the skin of a lamb dressed with the wool on; the skin of a lamb dressed as leather; a woollen cloth resembling this; a cotton cloth with raised surface and deep nap; **lamb's'-lett'uce** corn-salad; **lamb's'-tails** hazel catkins; **lamb's tongue** see **lamb's ears** above; **lamb's'-wool** fine wool, *specif* wool obtained from the first shearing of a (yearling) lamb; an old English beverage composed of ale and the pulp of roasted apples, with sugar and spices. — **like a lamb to the slaughter** meekly, innocently, without resistance; **the Lamb** or **Lamb of God** applied to Christ, in allusion to the paschal lamb and John 1.29. [OE *lamb*; Ger *Lamm*, Du *lam*]

lambada *lam-bä'də*, *n* a rhythmic and energetic dance originating in Latin America and popularized in the late 1980s.

lambast *lam-bast'* or **lambaste** *lam-bāst'*, *vt* to thrash; to reprimand severely. [Perh **lam**[1] and **baste**[1]]

lambda *lam'də*, also (more correctly) **labda** *lab'də*, *n* the Greek letter (Λ, λ) corresponding to Roman *l*; as a numeral, λ = 30, $_{,}\lambda$ = 30 000; used as a symbol for wavelength; used as a symbol for the lambda particle (*phys*); the meeting of the sagittal and lambdoid sutures of the skull (*anatom*). — *n* **lamb'dacism** or **lab'dacism** a too frequent use of words containing *l*-sounds; faulty pronunciation of the sound of *l*; a defective pronunciation of *r*, making it like *l*. — *adj* **lamb'doid** or **lambdoid'al** shaped like or relating to the Greek capital Λ, applied in anatomy to the suture between the occipital and the two parietal bones of the skull. — **lambda particle** a subatomic particle, the lightest of the hyperons (*phys*); a bacteriophage, an important vector in genetic manipulation, which can either grow in synchrony with its host (*Escherichia coli*) or exist as a multiplying virulent phage (*biol*). [Gr *lambda*, properly *labda*, from Heb *lāmedh*]

Lambeg drum *lam'beg drum*, *n* (also without *cap*) a large drum used *esp* on ceremonial occasions in Northern Ireland. — *n* **Lam'begger** someone who plays a Lambeg drum. [From the village of *Lambeg*, near Belfast]

lambent *lam'bənt*, *adj* moving about as if touching lightly like a flame; gliding or playing over; flickering; softly radiant, glowing; (*esp* of wit) light and brilliant; licking. — *n* **lam'bency** the quality of being lambent; a flicker. — *adv* **lam'bently**. — *adj* **lam'bitive** (*obs*) of a medicine, taken by licking. — *n* a medicine so taken. [L *lambere* to lick]

lambert *lam'bərt*, (*phys*) *n* a unit of brightness, one lumen per square centimetre. [After J H *Lambert* (1728–77), German scientist]

Lambeth degree *lam'bəth di-grē'*, *n* a degree conferred by the Archbishop of Canterbury, whose palace is at *Lambeth*.

Lambeth Walk *lam'bəth wök*, *n* a dance popularized in the 1930s, named after the London borough of Lambeth.

lambitive. See under **lambent**.

lambkin, lambling, etc. See under **lamb**.

lamboys *lam'boiz*, (*antiq*) *n pl* kilted flexible steel-plates worn skirt-like from the waist. [Perhaps Fr *lambeaux* flaps; or a blunder for *jambeaux*]

lambrequin *lam'bər-kin* or *-bri-kin*, *n* a veil over a helmet; a strip of drapery over a window, doorway, from a mantelpiece, etc; a stylized representation of such drapery in a coat-of-arms (*heraldry*). [Fr]

LAMDA *lam'də*, *abbrev*: London Academy of Music and Dramatic Art.

lame[1] *lām*, *adj* disabled, *specif* in the use of a leg; hobbling; unsatisfactory; imperfect; weak, implausible; conventional, unfashionable (*US slang*). — *n* (*US slang*) an old-fashioned person. — *vt* to make lame; to cripple; to make imperfect (*fig*). — *adv* **lame'ly**. — *n* **lame'ness**. — *adj* **lam'ish** a little lame; hobbling. — **lame brain** (*colloq*) a stupid person, an idiot; **lame duck** see under **duck**[3]. [OE *lama* lame; Du *lam*, Ger *lahm*]

lame[2] *lām*, *n* a thin plate *esp* of metal, as in armour. [Fr, from L *lāmina* a thin plate]

lamé *lä'mā*, *n* and *adj* (of) a fabric in which metallic (*usu* gold or silver) threads are interwoven. [Ety as for **lame**[2]]

lamella *lə-mel'ə*, *n* a thin plate or layer: — *pl* **lamell'ae** (*-ē*). — *adj* **lamell'ar** (or *lam'i-*). — *adj* **lam'ellate** (or *-el'*) or **lam'ellated**. — *adj* **lamell'iform**. — *adj* **lamell'-oid**. — *adj* **lamell'ose**. [L *lāmella*, dimin of *lāmina*]

lamellibranch *lə-mel'i-brangk*, *n* any member of the **Lamellibranchiā'ta**, Pelecypoda, or bivalve molluscs (eg the mussel, oyster or clam) with plate-like (nutritive) gills. — *adj* **lamellibranch'iate**. [New L, from L *lāmella* a thin plate, and *branchia* a gill]

lamellicorn *lə-mel'i-körn*, *n* a member of the **Lamellicorn'ia**, a group of beetles (eg the cockchafer) with flattened plates on the end of their antennae. [New L, from L *lamella* a thin plate, and *cornu* a horn]

lamellirostral *lə-mel-i-ros'trəl* or **lamellirostrate** *lə-mel-i-ros'trāt*, (*zool*) *adj* having transverse lamellae within the edge of the bill. [New L, from L *lamella* a thin plate, and *rostrum* beak]

lament *lə-ment'*, *vi* to cry out in grief; to wail; to mourn. — *vt* to mourn for; to deplore. — *n* sorrow expressed by crying out; an elegy or dirge; a musical composition of a similar character. — *adj* **lamentable** (*lam'ənt-ə-bl*) deserving or expressing sorrow; sad; pitiful; pitifully bad (*colloq*); worthless (*colloq*). — *adv* **lam'entably**. — *n* **lamentā'tion** the act of lamenting; the audible expression of grief; wailing. — *n* **Lamentā'tions** a book of the Old Testament traditionally attributed to Jeremiah. — *adj* **lament'ed**. — *n* and *adj* **lament'ing**. — *adv* **lament'ingly**. [L *lāmentārī*]

lameter or **lamiter** *lām'i-tər*, (*Scot*) *n* a cripple. [Obscurely derived from **lame**[1]]

lamia *lā'mi-ə*, *n* in Greek and Roman mythology, a blood-sucking serpent-witch. [Gr and L *lamia*]

lamiger or **lammiger** *lam'i-jər*, (*dialect*) *n* a cripple. [Cf **lameter**]

lamina *lam'i-nə*, *n* a thin plate or layer; a leaf blade; a thin plate of bone; a thin layer of rock (*geol*); a plate of sensitive tissue within a hoof: — *pl* **lam'inae** (*-nē*). — *adj* **lam'inable** suitable for making into thin plates. — *adj* **lam'inar**, **lam'inary** or **lam'inose** consisting of or like thin plates or layers; of or relating to a fluid, streamlined flow. — *n* **Laminā'ria** the tangle genus of brown seaweeds, with large expanded leathery fronds. — *adj* **laminār'ian**. — *vt* **lam'inarize** or **-ise** to make (a surface, etc) such that a flow over it will be laminar. — *adj* **lam'inate** or **lam'inated** in laminae or thin plates; consisting of scales or layers, over one another; made by laminating; covered by a thin layer (eg of protective material). — *vt* **lam'inate** to make into a thin plate; to separate into layers; to make by bonding layers together; to cover with a thin layer (eg of protective material). — *n* a laminated plastic, or other material similarly made. — *n* **laminā'tion** arrangement in thin layers; a thin layer; a thin, transparent protective coating, *usu* of plastic, *esp* one that covers a book-jacket, certificate, menu, etc. — *n* **lam'inator** someone who manufactures laminates. — *n* **laminī'tis** (*vet*) inflammation of a horse's lamina. — **laminar flow** viscous flow; a fluid flow in which the particles move smoothly without turbulence, *esp*, as in aircraft, such a non-impeding flow over a streamlined surface (*phys*); **laminated glass** safety glass; **laminated plastic** sheets of paper, canvas, linen or silk, impregnated with a resin, dried and bonded together, *usu* by means of heat and pressure. [L *lāmina* a thin plate]

lamington *lam'ing-tən*, (*Austr*) *n* a piece of sponge cake, coated in chocolate and coconut. [From Lord *Lamington*, Governor of Queensland (1895–1901)]

laminitis, laminose. See under **lamina**.

lamiter. See **lameter**.

Lammas *lam'əs*, *n* 1st August, an old feast day celebrating the first fruits of the harvest; a quarter-day in Scotland; the time of year of Lammas. — **Lamm'as-tide** the season of Lammas. [OE *hlāf-mæsse*, *hlāmmæsse*, from *hlāf* loaf, and *mæsse* feast]

lammer *läm'* or *lam'ər*, (*Scot*) *n* amber. [Fr *l'ambre* the amber]

lammergeier or **lammergeyer** *lam'ər-gī-ər*, *n* the great bearded vulture of southern Europe, etc. [Ger *Lämmergeier*, from *Lämmer* lambs, and *Geier* vulture]

lammiger. See **lamiger**.

lammy or **lammie** *lam'i*, *n* a thick quilted jumper or coat of blanket-like material worn in cold weather by sailors. [Perh **lamb**]

lamp[1] *lamp*, *n* any appliance or device containing a source of artificial light, *usu* an electric light bulb; a container with a wick for burning oil, paraffin, etc to give light; any source of light; an eye (*archaic* and *slang*). — *vi* (*Spenser*) to shine. — *vt* (*archaic*) to illumine; to supply with lamps. — *n* **lamp'ad** (*rare* or *poetic*) a lamp, candlestick or torch. — *n* **lamp'adary** in the Greek Church, someone who looks after the lamps and carries a lighted taper before the patriarch; a candelabrum. — *n* **lampaded'romy** or **lampadephor'ia** (Gr *lampadēdromiā*, *lampadēphoriā*) an ancient Greek torch-race. — *n* **lamp'adist** a runner in a torch-race. — *n* **lamp'adomancy** (Gr *manteiā* divination) divination by flame. — *adj* **lamp'ing** (*poetic*) shining. — *n* the hunting of ferrets, etc by using bright lights to lure them out of their holes. — *n* **lamp'ion** an oil lamp, often in a decorative coloured-glass pot. — **lamp'-black** soot obtained from a fuel-burning lamp, or from burning substances rich in carbon (eg mineral oil, turpentine, tar, etc) in a limited supply of air; a pigment made from it and used in chemical and industrial processes, etc. — *vt* to blacken with lamp-black. — **lampbrush chromosome** a chromosome observed during the early stages of meiosis in many eukaryotes, having a characteristic appearance due to the orderly series of lateral loops of chromatin arranged in pairs on either side of the chromosome axis; **lamp'-burner** the part of a lamp from which the flame rises; **lamp'-chimney** or **lamp'=glass** a glass funnel placed round the flame of a lamp; **lamp'-fly** (*Browning*) *perh* a glow-worm, or a firefly; **lamp'holder** a socket for an electric bulb; **lamp'hole** a shaft for lowering a lamp into a sewer; **lamp'-hour** the energy required to maintain a lamp for an hour; **lamp'light** the light shed by a lamp or lamps; **lamp'-lighter** a person employed to light street-lamps; a spill or other means of lighting a lamp (*US*); **lamp'post** or **lamp'-standard** the pillar supporting a street-lamp; **lamp'-room** a room in which miners' or other lamps are kept, tended, etc; the room at the top of a lighthouse, housing the lamp itself; **lamp'shade** a decorative or protective cover designed to moderate or direct the light of a lamp or light bulb; **lamp'-shell** a brachiopod, *esp* Terebratula or a similar genus, from its shell shaped like an antique lamp. — **smell of the lamp** to show signs of great elaboration or study. [Fr *lampe*, and Gr *lampas*, *-ados*, from *lampein* to shine]

lamp[2] *lamp*, (*Scot*) *vi* to run wild, to scamper; to go jauntily, stride along; to walk with long, heavy steps.

lampas[1] *lam'pas*, *n* a flowered material of silk and wool used in upholstery. [Fr]

lampas[2] *lam'pas* or **lampers** *lam'pərz*, (*vet*) *n* a swelling of the roof of the mouth in horses. — Also **lam'passe** (*Shakesp*). [Fr *lampas*]

lampern *lam'pərn*, *n* the European river lamprey. [OFr *lamprion*]

lampion. See under **lamp**[1].

lampoon *lam-po͞on'*, *n* a personal satire. — *vt* to attack or ridicule by personal satire. — *n* **lampoon'er** or **lampoon'ist**. — *n* **lampoon'ery**. [OFr *lampon*, perh from a drinking-song with the refrain *lampons* let us drink]

lamprey *lam'pri*, *n* a type of primitive fish-like vertebrate (genus *Petromyzon*) or cyclostome which fixes itself to the fish it preys on and to stones, etc by its sucking mouth: — *pl* **lam'preys**. [OFr *lamproie*, from LL *lamprēda*, *lampetra*, explained as from L *lambere* to lick, and *petra* rock, but found also as *naupreda*, *nauprida*]

lamprophyre *lam'prō-fīr*, (*mineralogy*) *n* a compact intrusive rock with phenocrysts of black mica, hornblende, etc, but not of feldspar. — *adj* **lamprophyric** (*-fir'ik*). [Gr *lampros* bright, and *-phyre* from **porphyry**]

lampuki *lam'po͞o-kē*, *n* an edible Mediterranean fish, the dolphin-fish (*Coryphaena*). — Also **lam'puka**. [Maltese]

LAN *lan*, (*comput*) *abbrev*: local area network.

lana *lä'nə*, *n* the wood of the genipap tree. [S American word]

lanate *lā'nāt* or **lanose** *lā'nōs* or *-nōz*, (*biol*) *adj* woolly. [L *lānātus*, from *lāna* wool]

Lancashire *lang'kə-shər* or *-shēr*, *n* a crumbly, white cheese made *orig* in the county of *Lancashire*.

Lancasterian *lang-kəs-tē'ri-ən*, (*educ*) *adj* of or relating to Joseph *Lancaster* (1778–1838), or his method of teaching by means of monitors.

Lancastrian *lang-kas'tri-ən*, *adj* of or relating to *Lancaster* or Lancashire, or to the dukes or (*hist*) house of Lancaster. — *n* a native of Lancaster or Lancashire; a supporter of the house of Lancaster (*hist*).

lance[1] *läns*, *n* a cavalry weapon with a long shaft, a spearhead, and a small flag; a similar weapon for other purposes, such as hunting; a surgeon's lancet; a blade in a cutting tool to sever the grain in advance of the main blade (*carpentry*); a lancer. — *vt* to pierce, as with a lance; to open or incise with a lancet in order to allow drainage (*med*); to shoot out or fling (*obs*). — *vi* to rush, dart or fling oneself (*obs*). — Also (*Spenser*) **launce**. — *n* **lance'let** any of the narrow, translucent, backboned marine animals of the genera *Amphioxus* and *Asymmetron*. — *n* **lanc'er** a light cavalry soldier armed with a lance, or a soldier of a regiment formerly so armed. — *n pl* **lanc'ers** a set of quadrilles, first popular in England about 1820, or its music. — *adj* **lanc'iform** shaped like a lance. — **lance'-corporal** (formed on **lance prisado** (qv)) acting corporal; the military rank between private and corporal, the lowest rank of non-commissioned officer in the British Army (*army slang* **lance'-jack**); **lance'-sergeant** a corporal acting as a sergeant; **lance'-wood** any of various W Indian, Australian and New Zealand trees with strong, elastic, durable wood. [Fr, from L *lancea*; Gr *lonchē* a lance; cf **launch**[1]]

lance[2]. See **launce**[3].

lancegay *läns'gā*, (*obs*) *n* a kind of spear. [OFr, from *lance* a lance, and *zagaye* a pike (as in **assegai**)]

lance-knight and **lance-knecht**. Erroneous forms of **landsknecht**.

lanceolate *län'si-ə-lāt* or **lanceolated** *län'si-ə-lāt-id*, *adj* shaped like a lance-head; lancet-shaped; tapering toward both ends and two or three times as long as broad (*bot*). — Also **lan'ceolar**. — *adv* **lan'ceolately**. [L *lanceolātus*, from *lanceola*, dimin of *lancea* lance]

lance prisado *läns pri-zä'dō*, **prisade** *pri-zäd'*, **pesade** *pi-zäd'* or **speisade** *spē-zäd'*, (*obs*) *n* a lance-corporal. [Ital *lancea spezzata* broken lance, as if meaning an experienced soldier]

lancet *län'sit*, *n* a surgical instrument used for opening veins, abscesses, etc; a lancet window; a lancet arch. — *adj* shaped like a lancet, narrow and pointed. — *adj* **lan'ceted**. — **lancet arch** a high and narrow pointed arch; **lancet window** a tall, narrow, acutely arched window. [OFr *lancette*, dimin of **lance**[1]; see **lance**[1]]

lanch. See **launch**[1].

lanciform. See under **lance**[1].

lancinate *län'sin-āt*, *vt* to lacerate; to pierce. — *adj* **lan'cinating** (of pain) shooting or darting. — *n* **lancinā'tion** sharp, shooting pain. [L *lancināre*, *-ātum* to tear]

Lancs. *langks*, *abbrev*: Lancashire.

Land *länt*, *n* a state or province in Germany and Austria functioning as a unit of local government: — *pl* **Länder**, sometimes **Laender** (*len'dər*). [Ger *Land* land]

land[1] *land*, *n* the solid portion of the surface of the earth; a country; a district; a nation or people; a constituent part of an empire or federation; ground; a piece of ground owned, real estate; soil; a group of dwellings or tenements under one roof and having a common entry (*Scot*); the high part of the bore of a gun that remains after the gun has been rifled. — *combining form* **-land** denoting a domain or district frequented or dominated by, as in *gangland*. — *vt* to set on land or on shore; to set down; to deposit, drop or plant; to cause to arrive; to bring ashore; to capture; to secure; to attach to one's interest; to earth up; (with *up*) to silt or to block with earth. — *vi* to come on land or on shore; to alight; to arrive, find oneself or end up being. — *adj* of or on the land; land-dwelling; terrestrial. — *adj* **land'ed** possessing land or estates; consisting in or derived from land or real estate. — *n* **land'er** someone who, or something which, lands; a heavy blow (*colloq*). — *n* **land'ing** disembarkation; a coming to ground; alighting; putting ashore; setting down; a place for getting on shore or on to the ground; the level part of a staircase between flights of steps or at the top. — *adj* relating to the unloading of a vessel's cargo, or to disembarking, or to alighting from the air. — *adj* **land'less**. — *adj* **land'ward** lying towards the land; inland; rural (*Scot*). — *adv* **land'ward** or **land'wards** towards the land; in the country (*Scot*). — **land'-agent** a person employed to let farms, collect rents, etc; an agent or broker for the buying and selling of land; **land'-army** a body of women organized for farm-work in wartime; **land bank** a bank which finances real estate transactions using the land as security; **land'-breeze** a breeze setting from the land towards the sea; **land'-bridge** a connection by land allowing terrestrial plants and animals to pass from one region to another (*geol*); a route by land allowing passage between countries or regions previously unconnected; **land'-crab** any crab that lives much or mostly on land; **landed interest** the combined interest of the land-owning class in a community; **land'fall** an approach to land after a journey by sea or air; the land so approached; **land'fill** the disposal of refuse by burying it under the soil; refuse disposed of in this way; a place where landfill is practised; **land'filling**; **land'-fish** (*Shakesp*) a fish on land, someone who is more fish than man; **land'-flood** an overflowing of land by water; inundation; **land'force** a military force serving on land; **land'form** a feature of the landscape such as a valley or escarpment; **land'-girl** a girl who does farm-work, *esp* in wartime; **land'-grabber** someone who acquires land by harsh and grasping means; someone who is eager to occupy land from which others have been evicted; **land'-grabbing**; **land grant** a grant of public land (to a college, etc). — *vt* **land'-haul** to haul (eg a boat) overland. — **land'-herd** a herd of land animals; **land'holder** a tenant or proprietor of land. — *adj* **land'holding**. — **land'-hunger** the desire to possess land; **land'ing-beam** a radio beam by which an aircraft is guided in to land; **land'ing-carriage** the wheeled structure on which an aeroplane runs when starting or landing; **land'ing-craft** a small, low, open vessel (or vessels) for landing troops and equipment on beaches; **land'ing-field** a field that allows aircraft to land and take off safely; **land'ing-gear** the wheels, floats, etc of an aircraft used in landing; **land'ing-ground** a piece of ground prepared for landing aircraft as required; **land'ing-net** a kind of scoop-net for landing a fish that has been hooked; **land'ing-place** a place for landing; **land'ing-ship** a ship whose forward part can be let down in order to put vehicles ashore; **land'ing-speed** the minimum speed at which an aircraft normally lands; **land'ing-stage** a platform, fixed or floating, for landing passengers or goods; **land'ing-strip** a narrow hard-surfaced runway; **land'-jobber** a speculator in land; **land'-jobbing**; **land'lady** a woman who has tenants or lodgers; the manageress or proprietress of a public house or hotel; a hostess (*obs*); **land'-law** (*usu* in *pl*) a law concerning property in land; **Land League** an association founded in Ireland in 1879 to procure reduction of rents and to promote peasant-proprietorship, suppressed in 1881; **land'-line** overland line of communication or transport. — *adj* **land'-locked** almost or entirely shut in by land; cut off from the sea. — **land'lord** a man who has tenants or lodgers; the manager or proprietor of a public house or hotel; **land'lordism** the authority, policy, behaviour or united action of the landowning class; the system of land-ownership; **land'-lubber** (*naut*; *contemptuous*) a landsman. — *adj* **land'-lubberly**. — **land'man** a countryman; a landsman; **land'mark** any land-boundary mark; any conspicuous object on land marking a locality or serving as a guide; an event of outstanding significance in history, thought, etc; **land'mass** a large area of land unbroken by seas; **land'-measure** a system of square measure used in measuring land; **land'-measuring** the determination of superficial extent of land; **land'-mine** a type of bomb laid on or near the surface of the ground, which explodes when trodden on or driven over; a large bomb dropped by parachute. — *vt* to lay with land-mines. — **land'-mining**; **land office** (*US*) an office dealing with the sale of public land; **land'owner** someone who owns land; **land'-ownership**. — *adj* **land'-owning**. — **land'-pilot** (*Milton*) someone skilled in finding his or her way by land; **land'-pirate** a highway robber; someone who swindles sailors in port; a piratical publisher (*obs*); **land'-plane** an aeroplane that takes off from and alights on land. — *adj* **land'-poor** (*US*) poor through owning much unprofitable land. — **land'race** a large white Danish breed of pig; any locally-developed breed of farm animal, *esp* pig or sheep; **land'rail** the corncrake; **land'-rat** a rat properly so called, not a water-rat; a thief by land, distinguished from a pirate; **land'-reeve** a land-steward's assistant; **Land Registry** in England and Wales, the official body which registers title to land; **land'-roll** a machine for breaking up clods of earth; **Land'-Rover**® a sturdy motor vehicle used for driving on rough ground; **land'-scrip** (*US*) a negotiable government certificate giving title to the acquisition of public land; **land set-aside** (also **set-aside**) the practice of taking arable land out of production, eg for environmental or national economic reasons; **land'-shark** a land-grabber; someone who robs sailors on shore; a lean breed of pig (*archaic US*); **land'-ship** a land vehicle having certain properties of a ship, eg a tank. — *adj* and *n* **land'side** (of, in or relating to) that part of an airport accessible to the general public, as opposed to airside (qv). — **land'skip** same as **landscape**; **land'slide** a landslip (*orig US*); an overwhelming victory in a political election; **land'slip** a fall of land or rock from a hillside or cliff; a portion of land fallen in this way; **lands'man** a man who lives or works on land; a man with no seafaring experience; **land'-spring** a shallow intermittent spring; **land'-steward** the manager of a landed estate; **land'-survey'ing** measurement and mapping of land; **land'-survey'or**; **land'-tax** a tax on land; **land'-val'ue** (*usu* in *pl*) the economic value of land as a basis of taxation; **land'-waiter** a customs officer who is present at the landing of goods from ships; **land'wind** a wind blowing off the land; **land-yacht** and **land-yachting** see under **yacht**. — **land of milk and honey** a land of great fertility promised to the Israelites by God (*Bible*); any region of great fertility, abundance, contentment, etc; **land of Nod** the land to which Cain went after killing Abel (*Bible*); sleep (*colloq*); **land with** to encumber with (a burden, difficult situation, etc); **see how the land lies** to find out in advance how matters stand. [OE *land*; Du *land*, Ger *Land*]

land[2] *land*, (*obs*) *n*. Same as **laund**.

land[3] *land*, (*US*) *n* and *interj* euphemism for **lord**.

landamman or **landammann** *land'am-an* (Ger *länt'äm-än*), *n* the chief magistrate in some Swiss cantons. [Ger *Landammann*, from *Land* land, and *Amtmann* bailiff, from *Amt* office, and *Mann* man]

landau *lan'dö*, *n* a horse-drawn carriage with a folding top. — *n* **landaulet'** or **landaulette'** a motor car with a folding top, a convertible; a small landau. [*Landau* in Germany, where the carriage is said to have been first made]

landdamne *land-dam'*, (*Shakesp*) *vt* said to mean to abuse with violence (*perh* a misprint for *lamdamn* or *lame-damn*).

landdros *lunt'dros* or **landdrost** *lunt'drost*, (*SAfr hist*) *n* a district magistrate or sheriff. [Du, from *land* land, and *drost* a bailiff]

lande *lãd*, *n* a heathy plain or sandy tract (now forested) along the coast in SW France. [Fr]

landgrave *land'grāv*, (*hist*) *n* a German count with jurisdiction over a territory; later a mere title: — *fem* **landgravine** (*land'grə-vēn*). — *n* **landgrā'viate** or **land'-gravate** the territory of a landgrave. [Ger *Landgraf*, from *Land* land, and *Graf* count]

ländler *lent'lər*, *n* a S German and Austrian dance, or the music for it, similar to a slow waltz. [Ger, from *Landl*, a nickname for Upper Austria]

landloper, **land-loper** *land'lōp-ər* or **land-louper** *land'lowp-ər*, (now *dialect*, *esp Scot*) *n* a vagabond or vagrant. [MDu *landlooper*, from *land* land, and *loopen* to ramble; cf Ger *Landläufer*]

landscape *land'skāp*, *n* the appearance of the area of land which the eye can view at once; the aspect of a country, or a picture or photograph representing it; the production of such pictures or photographs. — *vt* to improve by landscape-gardening or interior landscaping (also *fig*). — Also *vi*. — *adj* (of a page, illustration, etc) wider than it is deep (*opp* of *portrait*; *printing*). — **land'scape-gar'dening** the art of laying out grounds so as to produce the effect of a picturesque landscape; **land'scape-mar'ble** a limestone with dendritic markings; **land'scape-paint'er** or **land'scapist** a painter of landscapes; **land'scape-paint'ing**. — **interior landscaping** the supply and display of plants in order to landscape (*esp* office) interiors. [Du *landschap*, from *land* and *-schap*, suffix = *-ship*]

Landseer *land'sēr* or **Landseer Newfoundland** (*nū'fənd-lənd* or *nū-fownd'lənd*), *n* a type of black and white Newfoundland dog, as painted by Sir Edwin *Landseer* (1802–73).

landsknecht *länts'knehht*, (*hist*) *n* a mercenary foot-soldier of the 16c. [Ger, from *Lands*, genitive of *Land* country, and *Knecht* servant, soldier]

Landsmaal or **Landsmål** *läns'möl*, *n* a literary language based on Norwegian dialects, created by Ivar Aasen (1850), now called Nynorsk, new Norse. [Norw from *land* land, and *maal* speech]

Landsting or **Landsthing** *läns'ting*, *n* the upper house of the Danish Rigsdag or parliament; a Swedish provincial council. [Dan and Swed, from *land* land, and *t(h)ing* parliament]

Landsturm *länt'shtōōrm*, *n* conscription in time of national emergency; the force so called up. [Ger, from *Land* land, and *Sturm* alarm]

Landtag *länt'tähh*, *n* the legislative assembly of a German state or land; the Diet of the Holy Roman Empire, or of the German Federation; formerly the provincial assembly of Bohemia or Moravia. [Ger, from *Land* country, and *Tag* diet, day]

Landwehr *länt'vār*, *n* an army reserve. [Ger, from *Land* land, and *Wehr* defence]

lane[1] *lān*, *n* a narrow passage or road; a narrow street; a passage through a crowd or between obstructions; a division of a road for a single stream of traffic; a similar division of waterways or airspace; a channel; a sluggish stream (*Scot*); a prescribed course. — **lane'way** a lane. — **Red Lane** (*colloq*) the throat, gullet. [OE *lane*, *lone*]

lane[2] *lān*, *adj* a Scots form of **lone**. — **my lane**, **his** or **her lane**, etc alone.

lang *lang*, *adj* a Scots form of **long**. — *adv* **lang syne** (*sīn*) long since, long ago. — *n* time long past.

lang. *abbrev*: language.

langaha *läng-gä'hə*, *n* a Madagascan wood snake, with a long flexible snout. [Perh Malagasy]

Langerhans. See **islets of Langerhans** under **isle**.

langlauf *läng'lowf*, *n* cross-country skiing. [Ger *lang* long, and *Lauf* race, run or leap]

Langmuir trough *lang'mūr trof*, (*min ext*) *n* apparatus in which a rectangular tank is used to measure surface tension of a liquid. [I *Langmuir* (1881–1957), American chemist]

Langobard *lang'gō-bärd*. See **Lombard**.

langouste *lã-gōōst'*, *n* the spiny lobster. — *n* **langoustine** (-*ēn'*) the Norway lobster, spiny lobster or rock lobster (*Nephrops*: see **lobster**), larger than a prawn but smaller than a lobster. [Fr]

langrage, **langridge** *lang'grij* or **langrel** *lang'grəl*, (*naval warfare*) *n* shot consisting of a canister containing irregular pieces of iron, formerly used to damage sails and rigging. [Origin unknown]

Langshan *lang'shan*, *n* a small black Chinese hen. [From a place near Shanghai]

langspel *läng'spāl* or **langspiel** *läng'spēl*, *n* an old Shetland cithern. [Norw *langspill*, from *lang* long, and *spill* play or instrument]

language *lang'gwij*, *n* human speech; a variety of speech or body of words and idioms, *esp* that of a nation; mode of expression; diction; any manner of expressing thought or feeling; an artificial system of signs and symbols, with rules for forming intelligible communications, for use in eg a computer; a national branch of one of the religious and military orders, eg the Hospitallers; bad language, swearing (*colloq*). — *vt* (*archaic*) to express in language. — *adj* **lang'uaged** skilled, rich in or having language. — *adj* **lang'uageless** (*Shakesp*) speechless or silent. — **language laboratory** a room in a school, college, etc in which pupils sit in separate cubicles and are taught a language by means of material recorded on tapes. — **bad language** swearing; **dead language** a language no longer spoken, as opposed to **living language**; **speak the same language** to have the same tastes, understanding, background or way of thinking; to come within one's range of understanding. [Fr *langage*, from *langue*, from L *lingua* the tongue]

langue *lãg*, *n* language viewed as a general or abstract system, as opposed to *parole* (*linguistics*); a language (qv) of a religious or military order. [Fr, from L *lingua* tongue]

langued *langd*, (*heraldry*) *adj* having a tongue (of this or that tincture). [Fr *langue*, from L *lingua* tongue]

langue de chat *lãg-də-sha'*, *n* a very thin finger-shaped biscuit or piece of chocolate. [Fr, cat's tongue]

Langue d'oc *lãg dok*, *n* a collective name for the Romance dialects of southern France, the language of the troubadours, often used as synonymous with Provençal, one of its chief branches. The name itself survived in the province *Languedoc*, also giving its name to a class of wines. — *adj* **Languedocian** (*lang-gə-dō'shi-ən*). — **Langue d'oil** (*lãg do-ēl* or *doil*), also **Langue d'oui** (*dwē*) the Romance dialect of northern France, the language of the trouvères, the main element in modern French. [OFr *langue*, from L *lingua* tongue; *de* of;

Provençal *oc* yes, from L *hōc* this; OFr *oil*, *oui* yes, from L *hōc illud* this (is) that, yes]

languescent. See under **languid**.

languet or **languette** *lang'gwet*, *-get* or *-get'*, *n* a tongue-like object or part. [Fr *languette*, dimin of *langue* tongue]

languid *lang'gwid*, *adj* slack; flagging; inert; listless; faint; relaxed; spiritless. — *adj* **languescent** (*-gwes'ənt*; *rare*) growing languid. — *adv* **lang'uidly**. — *n* **lang'uidness**. [L *languidus*, from *languēre* to be weak]

languish *lang'gwish*, *vi* to become or be languid, inert or depressed; to lose strength and animation; to pine; to flag or droop; to look languishingly. — *n* (*Shakesp*) languishing; languishment. — *adj* **lang'uished** (*poetic*) overcome by languor. — *n* **lang'uisher**. — *n* **lang'uishing**. — *adj* expressive of languor, or merely sentimental emotion; lingering. — *adv* **lang'uishingly**. — *n* **lang'uishment** the act or state of languishing; tenderness of look. [Fr *languiss-* (serving as participial stem of *languir*), from L *languēscere*, from *languēre* to be faint]

languor *lang'gər*, *n* languidness; listlessness; weariness or weakness; dreamy inertia; tender softness; pining; affliction (*obs*). — *adj* **lang'uorous** full of or expressing languor; languishing. — *adv* **lang'uorously**. — *n* **lang'uorousness**. [L *languor*, *-ōris*]

langur *lung-gōōr'*, *n* the entellus monkey or another of its genus. [Hindi *lāgūr*]

laniard. See **lanyard**.

laniary *lā'ni-ər-i*, *adj* of teeth, claws, etc, designed for tearing. [L *laniārius* of a butcher, from *lanius* a butcher]

laniferous *lan-if'ər-əs* or **lanigerous** *lan-ij'ər-əs*, *adj* wool-bearing. [L *lānifer*, *lāniger*, from *lāna* wool, and *ferre*, *gerere* to bear]

lank *langk*, *adj* long and thin; drooping; flaccid; limp; thin; (of hair) long, straight and lifeless. — *vt* and *vi* (*Shakesp*) to make or become lank. — *adv* **lank'ily**. — *n* **lank'iness**. — *adv* **lank'ly**. — *n* **lank'ness**. — *adj* **lank'y** lean, tall and ungainly; long and limp. [OE *hlanc*]

lanner *lan'ər*, *n* a kind of falcon native to regions of Africa, SE Asia and the Mediterranean; the female of this species (*falconry*). — *n* **lann'eret** (*falconry*) the male lanner. [Fr *lanier*, poss from L *laniārius* tearing, or from *lānārius* a weaver (a medieval term of reproach)]

lanolin *lan'ō-lin* or **lanoline** *lan'ə-lin* or *lan'ə-lēn*, *n* fat from wool, a mixture of palmitate, oleate and stearate of cholesterol, used as a base for certain ointments. [L *lāna* wool, and *oleum* oil]

lanose. See **lanate**.

lansquenet *lans'kə-net*, *n* a landsknecht; a card game. [Fr, from Ger *Landsknecht*]

lant[1] *lant*, *n* stale urine, used in wool-scouring. [OE and ON *hland*]

lant[2] *lant*. Same as **launce**[3].

lantana *lan-tā'nə* or *-tä'*, *n* any plant of the *Lantana* genus, tropical American shrubs of the vervain family with flamboyant spikes of yellow or orange flowers.

lanterloo *lant'ər-lōō*, (*obs*) *n* a card game, ancestral form of loo. [Fr *lanturlu* (a meaningless refrain)]

lantern *lant'ərn*, *n* a case for holding or carrying a light; the light-chamber of a lighthouse; a magic lantern; an open structure like a lantern, *esp* one surmounting a building, giving light and air. — *vt* to provide with a lantern. — *n* **lant'ernist** a person who works a magic lantern. — **lantern fly** any insect of the homopterous family Fulgoridae, with a lantern-like proboscis, formerly thought to give out light. — *adj* **lan'tern-jawed** hollow-faced. — **lantern jaws** thin long jaws; **lantern slide** a transparent slide with a picture to be projected by a magic lantern or slide projector; **lan'tern-wheel** or **lan'tern-pinion** a type of cog-wheel consisting of pins fastened at each end to circular plates, somewhat like a lantern in appearance. — **lantern of the dead** a lighted tower, once common in French cemeteries. [Fr *lanterne*, from L *lanterna*, from Gr *lamptēr*, from *lampein* to give light]

lanthanum *lan'thə-nəm*, *n* a metallic element (atomic no 57; symbol **La**). — *n pl* **lan'thanides** the rare-earth elements. — **lanthanum glass** optical glass used for high-quality photographic lenses, etc. [Gr *lanthanein* to escape notice, because it lay hid in rare minerals till 1839]

lanthorn. *Obs* spelling of **lantern**, based on folk etymology, from the old use of horn for lanterns.

lantskip *lant'skip*, (*Milton*) *n*. Same as **landscape**.

lanugo *lan-ū'gō*, *n* down, fine hair; an embryonic woolly coat of hair: — *pl* **lanū'gos**. — *adj* **lanū'ginose** (*-jin-*) or **lanū'ginous** downy; covered with fine soft hair. [L *lānūgō*, *-inis* down, from *lāna* wool]

lanx *langks*, (*antiq*) *n* a platter: — *pl* **lances** (*lan'sēz*). [L]

lanyard or **laniard** *lan'yərd*, *n* a short rope used as a fastening or handle (*naut*); a cord for hanging a knife, whistle, etc around the neck. [Fr *lanière*, origin doubtful; confused with **yard**]

lanzknecht an erroneous form of **landsknecht** (as if from Ger *Lanze* lance).

LAO *abbrev*: Laos (IVR).

Lao or **Laotian** *la-ō'shən*, *adj* of Laos in SE Asia, or of its people. — *n* a native of Laos.

Laodicean *lā-od-i-sē'ən*, *adj* lukewarm or half-hearted, *esp* in religion, like the Christians of *Laodicea* (Revelations 3.14–16). — *n* **Laodicē'anism**. [Gr *Lāodikeia* Laodicea]

Laotian. See **Lao**.

lap[1] *lap*, *vt* to scoop up with the tongue (often with *up*); to take in greedily or readily (*usu* with *up*; *fig*); to wash or flow against. — *vi* to drink by licking up; to make a sound or movement as of lapping: — *pr p* **lapp'ing**; *pa t* and *pa p* **lapped**. — *n* a motion or sound of lapping; something which can be lapped; thin liquid food for animals. — *n* and *adj* **lapp'ing**. [OE *lapian*; LGer *lappen*; L *lambere* to lick; Gr *laptein*]

lap[2] *lap*, *n* the fold of the clothes and body from waist to knees of a person sitting down; part of a garment covering this area, *esp* arranged to hold or catch something; a fold; a single circuit of a race-track, or round of anything coiled; an overlap; the amount of overlap (in slating, over the next but one); a hollow; a place where one is nurtured or where one can rest secure (*fig*; in phrases); a flap; a lobe (of the ear); a polishing disc, cylinder, etc; the length of material needed to go round a drum, etc; a layer or sheet of (cotton, etc) fibres; in a steam-engine, the distance the valve has to move from mid position to open the steam or exhaust port; in euchre, etc, points carried over to another game. — *vt* to wrap, enfold or surround; to lay overlappingly; to get or be a lap ahead of; to traverse as a lap or in laps; to polish with a lap (*rare*); to unite accurately; to hold in the lap (*rare*). — *vi* to lie with an overlap; to overlap; to extend beyond some limit. — *n* **lap'ful**. — *n* **lapp'er** someone who wraps or folds; a machine that compacts scutched cotton into a fleece on a roller called a **lap'-roller**. — *n* and *adj* **lapp'ing**. — **lap'-board** a flat wide board resting on the lap, used by tailors and seamstresses; **lap'dog** a dog small enough to be petted in the lap; a pet dog (also *fig*); a devoted, docile, dependent person (*fig*; *usu derog*). — *adj* **lap'held** same as **laptop** (see below). — **lap'-joint** a joint formed by overlapping edges. — *adj* **lap'-joint'ed**. — **lap'stone** a stone held in the lap to hammer leather on; **lap'streak** or **lap'strake** a clinker-built boat. — Also *adj*. — *adj* **lap'top** (of a computer) somewhat smaller than a desktop computer, able to be carried in a briefcase, etc and set on one's lap. — *n* a laptop computer. — **lap'work** lap-jointed work. — **in the lap of luxury** in luxurious conditions; **in the lap of the gods** of a situation, such that the result cannot be predicted; **lap of honour** a ceremonial circuit of a field, track or show ring, made by the victor or victors in a contest. [OE *læppa* a loosely hanging part; Ger *Lappen* a rag]

lap[3] *läp* or *lap*, (*Scot*) *pa t* of **leap**[1].

lap[4] *lap* or **lappie** (formerly **lapje**) *lap'i*, (*SAfr*) *n* a rag or piece of cloth. [Afrik, from Du *lap* rag, patch]

laparoscopy *lap-ər-os'kəp-i*, *n* surgical examination by means of a **laparoscope** (*lap'ər-ə-skōp*), a tube-shaped optical instrument which permits examination of the internal organs from outside, also used in female sterilization procedures. [Gr *laparā* flank, and *skopeein* to see]

laparotomy *lap-ə-rot'ə-mi*, *n* surgical cutting of the abdominal wall. [Gr *laparā* flank, and *tomē* cutting]

lapel (*obs* **lappel**) *la-pel'* or *lə-pel'*, *n* part of a coat, jacket, etc folded back as a continuation of the collar. — *adj* **lapelled'**. [Dimin of **lap**[2]]

lapis *lap'is*, *n* a stone (the Latin word, used in certain phrases only, eg *lapis philosophicus* the philosophers' stone, and *lapis ollaris* potstone). — *adj* **lapidār'ian** relating to stones; inscribed on stones; knowledgeable about stones. — *n* **lap'idarist** (*-ə-rist*) an expert in gems. — *n* **lap'idary** (*-ə-ri*) a cutter of stones, *esp* gem-stones; a treatise on gems (*obs*); an expert in gems (*obs*). — *adj* relating to stones; of a bee, dwelling in stone-heaps; inscribed on stone; suitable for an inscription, eg on a monument; written in such a style, ie pithy, polished, impressive. — *vt* **lap'idate** (*archaic*) to pelt with stones. — *n* **lapidā'tion** (*archaic*) stoning. — *adj* **lapid'eous** stony. — *n* **lapidesc'ence** (*archaic*). — *adj* **lapidesc'ent** (*archaic*) becoming stone; petrifying. — *adj* **lapidic'olous** (L *colěre* to inhabit) living under or among stones. — *adj* **lapidif'ic** (*archaic*). — *n* **lapidificā'tion** (*archaic*). — *vt* and *vi* **lapid'ify** (*archaic*) to turn into stone: — *pr p* **lapid'ifying**; *pa t* and *pa p* **lapid'ified**. — *n pl* **lapilli** (*lä-pil'lē*) small fragments (in size from a pea to a walnut) of lava ejected from a volcano (*pl* of Ital *lapillo*; also of L *lapillus*). — *adj* **lapill'iform**. — **lapis laz'ūlī** a beautiful stone consisting of calcite and other minerals coloured ultramarine by lazurite, haüyne, and sodalite, commonly spangled with iron pyrites (see **azure**, **lazulite** and **lazurite**); **lapis lazuli blue** a deep blue, sometimes veined with gold, used in decoration and in porcelain; **lapis lazuli ware** a pebble ware veined with gold upon blue. [L *lapis*, *-idis* a stone]

Lapith *lap'ith*, (*Gr mythol*) *n* a member of a people of Thessaly who fought the Centaurs: — *pl* **lap'ithae** (*-ē*) or **lap'iths**.

lapje. See **lap**[4].

Lapp *lap* or **Laplander** *lap'lən-dər*, *n* a native or inhabitant of Lapland; a person of the race or people inhabiting Lapland. — *adj* **Lapp** or **Lap'landish**. — *n* **Lapp** or **Lapp'ish** the language of the Lapps.

lappel. See **lapel**.

lapper. See **lopper**[1].

lappet *lap'it*, *n* a little lap or flap. — *adj* **lapp'eted**. — **lapp'et-head** (*obs*) a headdress with lappets; **lappet moth** a moth of the *Lasiocampidae* whose caterpillar has lappets on its sides. [Dimin of **lap**[2]]

lappie. See **lap**[4].

lapsang *lap'sang* or **lapsang souchong** (*sōō-shong'* or *-chong'*), *n* (also with *caps*) a variety of souchong tea with a smoky flavour. [Chin]

lapse *laps*, *vi* to slip or glide; to pass by degrees; to fall away by ceasing or relaxing effort or cause; to fall from the faith; to fail in virtue or duty; to pass into disuse; to pass or fail owing to some omission or non-fulfilment; to become void. — *vt* to catch in a lapse (*Shakesp*; *perh* with associations of *lap* or *latch*); to allow to pass, fall away or become void. — *n* a slip; passage (of time); a falling away; a failure (in virtue, attention, memory, etc); a vertical gradient, eg of atmospheric temperature; a gliding (*archaic*). — *adj* **laps'able** liable to lapse. — *adj* **lapsed** having slipped or passed or been let slip; *esp* in the Christian Church, fallen away from the faith. — **lapse rate** (*meteorol*) rate of change in temperature in relation to height in the atmosphere. [L *lāpsāre* to slip, *lāpsus* a slip, from *lābi*, *lāpsus* to slip]

lapsus *lap'səs* or *lap'sōōs*, (*L*) *n* a slip. — **lapsus calami** (*kal'ə-mī* or *ka'la-mē*) a slip of the pen; **lapsus linguae** (*ling'gwē* or *-gwī*) a slip of the tongue; **lapsus memoriae** (*me-mōr'i-ē* or *mōr'*, or *-ri-ī*) a slip of the memory.

Laputa *lä-pū'tə*, *n* a flying island in Swift's *Gulliver's Travels*, inhabited by people who engaged in ridiculous projects. — *n* **Lapu'tan** or **Lapu'tian** (*-shən*) an inhabitant of Laputa. — *adj* absurd; chimerical.

lapwing *lap'wing*, *n* a bird of the plover family, the peewit. [ME *lappewinke*, from OE *læpewince*, *hlǣpewince*, *hlēapewince*; modified by folk etymology]

laquearia *lak-wi-ā'ri-ə* or *lak-we-ä'ri-a*, *n pl* a panelled ceiling. [L]

LAR *abbrev*: Libya (IVR; Libyan Arab Jamahiriya).

lar *lär*, *n* the god of a house (*orig prob* a field god): — *pl* **lares** (*lā'rēz* or *lä'rās*). — See also **lares et penates**. [L *lar*]

larboard *lär'bōrd*, *-börd* or *läb'ərd*, (*obs naut*) *n* and *adj* port or left. [ME *laddeborde*, influenced by **starboard**; origin unknown]

larceny *lär'sə-ni*, *n* the legal term in England and Ireland for stealing; theft. — *n* **lar'cener** or **lar'cenist** a thief. — *adj* **lar'cenous**. — *adv* **lar'cenously**. — **grand larceny** in England before 1827, larceny of property of the value of one shilling or more, as opposed to **petty larceny**, larceny of property less in value than one shilling; **simple larceny** as opposed to **compound larceny**, is larceny uncombined with aggravating circumstances. [OFr *larrecin* (Fr *larcin*), from L *latrōcinium*, from *latrō* a robber]

larch *lärch*, *n* any tree of the coniferous genus *Larix*, distinguished from cedar by the deciduous leaves. — *adj* (*rare*) **larch'en**. [Ger *Lärche*, from L *larix*, *-icis*]

lard *lärd*, *n* the clarified fat of the pig; a *usu* modified form of this, produced *esp* in a solid, white form for use in cookery. — *vt* to smear or enrich with lard; to stuff with bacon or pork; to fatten; to mix with anything; to stuff or load; to interlard, interpenetrate; to garnish or strew. — *vi* (*Shakesp*) to be intimately mixed. — *adj* **lardā'ceous**. — *n* **lar'don** or **lardoon'** a strip of bacon used for larding. — *adj* **lar'dy**. — **lar'dy-cake** *esp* in S England, a rich sweet cake made of bread dough, with lard, dried fruit, etc. [OFr, from L *lāridum*, *lārdum*; cf Gr *lārīnos* fat, and *lāros* pleasant to taste]

lardalite. See **laurdalite**.

larder *lärd'ər*, *n* a place where food is kept; a stock of provisions. — *n* **lard'erer** a person in charge of a larder. — **larder fridge** a type of refrigerator without a freezer compartment. [OFr *lardier* bacon-tub; see **lard**]

lardon, lardoon and **lardy**. See under **lard**.

lare *lār*, *n* a Northern form of **lore**[1]; also a Spenserian form of **lair**[1].

lares et penates *lā'rēz et pe-nā'tēz* or *lä'rās et pe-nä'tās*, (*L*) *n pl* household gods; valued personal or household objects.

Largactil® *lär-gak'til*, *n* a tranquillizing drug, chlorpromazine.

large *lärj*, *adj* great in size; extensive; bulky; broad; copious; abundant; generous; magnanimous; loftily affected or pretentious; diffuse (*obs*); (of language) free or licentious (*Shakesp*); (of the wind) having a favouring component (*naut*). — *adv* ostentatiously; prominently or importantly; before the wind (*naut*). — *n* (*music*) an obsolete note, equal to two (or in 'perfect' time three) longs. — *adv* **large'ly** in a large manner; in great measure; mainly, especially. — *vi* and *vt* **lar'gen** (*poetic*) to enlarge. — *n* **large'ness**. — *adj* **larg'ish** fairly large, rather big. — *adj* **large'-hand'ed** having large hands; grasping (*Shakesp*); profuse. — *adj* **large'-heart'ed** having a large heart; of liberal disposition or comprehensive sympathies; generous. — *adj* **large'-mind'ed** magnanimous; characterized by breadth of view. — **large paper edition** a special edition with wider margins. — *adj* **large'-scale** (of maps, models, etc) made in accordance with a series of larger measurements; (of enterprises, etc) extensive. — **large-scale integration** (*electronics*) production of an integrated circuit with more than 100 gates on an integratred chip. — **as large as life** actually, really; **at large** at liberty; at random; in general; in full; representing the whole area, not a division (*US*);— **larger than life** exaggerated. — *adj* **larg'er-than-life'**. [Fr, from L *largus* abounding]

largess or **largesse** *lär-jes'* or *lärj'es*, *n* a bestowal or distribution of gifts; generosity, magnanimous spirit or manner. — *n* **largition** (*lär-jish'ən*; *archaic*) giving of largess. [Fr *largesse* and L *largītiō*, *-ōnis*, from *largus*]

largo *lär'gō*, (*music*) *adj* broad and slow. — Also *adv*. — *n* a movement to be performed in this manner: — *pl* **lar'gos**. — *adj* **larghet'to** somewhat slow; not so slow as largo. — Also *adv*. — *n* a somewhat slow movement: — *pl* **larghet'tos**. [Ital, from L *largus*]

lariat *lar'i-ət*, *n* a lasso or picketing rope. [Sp *la* the, and *reata* picketing rope]

Laridae and **larine**. See under **Larus**.

lark[1] *lärk*, *n* a bird of the genus *Alauda*, well-known for flying high as it sings; extended to various similar birds. — *vi* to catch larks. — *adj* **lark'-heeled** having a long hind-claw. — **lark'ing-glass** an instrument with mirrors used by bird-catchers to dazzle larks; **lark's'-heel** the Indian cress; the larkspur. — **get up with the lark** to rise very early in the morning. [ME *laverock*, from OE *lǣwerce*, *lāwerce*; Ger *Lerche*]

lark[2] *lärk*, *n* a frolic; a piece of mischief; an activity, *esp* a mischievous one. — *vi* to frolic, play about, have fun (now *usu* with *about*). — *n* **lark'er**. — *n* **lark'iness**. — *adj* **lark'ish**. — *adj* **lark'y** (*colloq*). [Perh from the preceding (cf **skylarking**); some connect it with **lake**[4]]

larkspur *lärk'spûr*, *n* any plant of the genus *Delphinium*, from the spurred flowers. [**lark**[1] and **spur**]

larmier *lär'mi-ər*, *n* a corona or other course serving as a drip-stone (*archit*); a tear-pit (*zool*). [Fr, from *larme*, from L *lacrima* a tear]

larn *lärn*, (*dialect* or *facetious*) *vt* and *vi* to learn; to teach. [**learn**]

larnax *lär'naks*, *n* a chest, coffin, etc of ancient Greece, *usu* made of terracotta and frequently ornamented: — *pl* **larnakes** (*lär'nək-ēz*). [Gr, perh connected with late Gr *narnax* a chest]

laroid. See under **Larus**.

larrigan *lar'i-gən*, *n* a long boot made of oiled leather, worn by lumbermen, etc. [Origin unknown]

larrikin *lar'i-kin*, (*Austr*) *n* a rough or hooligan; someone who is careless of usual social conventions or behaviour. — Also *adj*. — *n* **larr'ikinism**. [Origin doubtful; a connection with '*larking* about' has been suggested but remains unsubstantiated; also perh Cornish *larrikin* a rowdy youth]

larrup *lar'əp*, (*colloq*) *vt* to flog or thrash. [Cf Du *larpen* thresh with flails]

larum *lar'əm*, (*archaic*) *n* alarm; a noise giving notice of danger. — **lar'um-bell**. [**alarm**]

Larus *lār'əs* or *lär'əs*, *n* the principal genus of the gull family (**Laridae** *lar'i-dē*). — *adj* **lar'ine**. — *adj* **lar'oid**. [L, from Gr *laros* a bird, prob a gull]

larva *lär'və*, *n* an animal in an immature but active state markedly different from the adult, eg a caterpillar; a spectre or ghost (*obs*): — *pl* **larvae** (*lär'vē* or *-vī*). — *adj* **lar'val**. — *adj* **lar'vate** or **lar'vated** masked, or covered as if masked. — *adj* **larvicī'dal** destroying larvae. — *n* **lar'vicide**. — *adj* **lar'viform**. — *adj* **larvip'arous** giving birth to larvae. [L *lārva*, *lārua* a spectre, a mask]

larvikite. See **laurvikite**.

larynx *lar'ingks*, *n* the upper part of the windpipe: — *pl* **larynges** (*lar'in-jēz* or *lar-in'jēz*) or **lar'ynxes**. — *adj* **laryngal** (*lar-ing'gl*) or **laryngeal** (*lar-in'ji-əl*). — *n* **laryngectomee** (*-jek'*) a person who has undergone a laryngectomy. — *n* **laryngectomy** (*-jek'*) surgical removal of the larynx. — *n* **laryngismus** (*-jiz'məs*) spasm of the larynx. — *adj* **laryngitic** (*-jit'ik*). — *n* **laryngitis** (*-jī'tis*) inflammation of the larynx. — *adj* **laryngological** (*-ing-gə-loj'*). — *n* **laryngol'ogist**. — *n* **laryngology** (*-gol'ə-ji*) the science of the larynx. — *n* **laryngophony** (*-gof'*) the sound of the voice as heard through the stethoscope applied over the larynx. — *n* **laryng'oscope** a mirror for examining the larynx and trachea. — *adj* **laryngoscop'ic**. — *n* **laryngos'copist**. — *n* **laryngos'copy**. — *n* **laryng'ospasm** spasmodic closure of the larynx. — *n* **laryngot'omy** the operation of cutting into the larynx. [Gr *larynx*, *-yngos*]

lasagne *lä-zän'yə*, *-sän'*, *la-* or *lə-*, *n pl* flat sheets of pasta; (*n sing*) a baked dish of this with tomatoes, cheese and *usu* meat. — Also **lasagn'a**. [Ital; sing *lasagna*]

lascar *las'kər*, *-kär* or *las-kär'*, *n* an Oriental (*orig* Indian) sailor or camp-follower. [Hindi and Pers *lashkar* army, or *lashkarī* a soldier]

lascivious *lə-siv'i-əs*, *adj* wanton; lustful; inclining or tending to lechery. — *adv* **lasciv'iously**. — *n* **lasciv'iousness**. [LL *lascīviōsus*, from L *lascīvus* playful]

laser[1] *lās'ər*, *n* the juice of laserwort; the plant silphium (*hist*). — *n* **Laserpicium** or **Laserpitium** (*las-ər-pish'i-əm*) a genus of umbelliferous perennial herbs of Europe, Asia and N Africa. — *n* **laserwort** (*lās'ər-wûrt*) any plant of the genus, *esp* herb frankincense (L *latifolium*); also applied to species of *Ferula* and *Thapsia*. [L *lāser* the juice of *lāserpīcium*, the silphium plant]

laser[2] *lāz'ər*, *n* a device which amplifies an input of light, producing an extremely narrow and intense monochromatic beam which can be used for a range of tasks, eg printing, optical scanning, surgical operations, etc. — Also *adj*. — *vi* **lase** (of a crystal, etc) to be, or become, suitable for use as a laser. — *adj* and *n* **lā'sing**. — **laser-beam machining** (*eng*) the use of a focused beam of high-intensity radiation from a laser to vaporize and so machine material; **laser disc** or **disk** a disc on which digitally recorded data, audio or video material is registered as a series of pits that are readable by laser beam, a compact disc; **laser disc** (or **disk**) **player**; **laser level** (*surveying*) an instrument for accurate single-handed levelling, using a laser beam narrowly confined in the vertical dimension and continuously rotated round an accurately-vertical axis; **laser printer** a fast, high quality printer using a laser beam to form characters on paper; **Laser Vision®** a video disc system for playing digitally-recorded audio-visual material through a TV or hi-fi; (without *caps*) a similar video disc system. [*l*ight *a*mplification by *s*timulated *e*mission of *r*adiation]

lash[1] *lash*, *n* loosely, the flexible part of a whip, but properly its terminal piece of whipcord; a scourge; an eyelash; a stroke with a whip or anything pliant; a sweep or flick; a stroke of satire. — *vt* to strike with, or as if with, a lash; to dash against; to drive, urge or work by blows of anything flexible (also *fig*); to whisk or flick with a sweeping movement; to secure with a rope or cord; to bind (rope) to prevent unravelling; to scourge with sarcasm or satire; to lavish or squander (*obs*). — *vi* to dash or rush; to make a rapid sweeping or flicking movement; to use the whip. — *n* **lash'er** a person who lashes or whips; a rope for binding one thing to another. — *n* **lash'ing** an act of whipping; a rope for making things secure; the binding preventing the unravelling of a rope; (*esp* in *pl*) an abundance of anything (*colloq*). — **lash'-up** (*slang*) an improvisation; a mess, fiasco. — **lash out** to kick out, fling out or hit out without restraint; to spend extravagantly. [Perh several different words, with possible connections with **latch**, **lash**[2] and **lace**]

lash[2] *lash*, (*obs* or *dialect*) *adj* slow or slack; soft; insipid. — *n* **lash'er** a weir; a waterfall from a weir; a pool below a weir. [ME *lasche* slack, from OFr *lasche* (Fr *lâche* cowardly), from L *laxus* lax]

lashkar *lash'kär*, *n* a camp of Indian soldiers (*obs*); a body of armed Indian tribesmen, a force. [Hindi, army, camp; cf **lascar**]

Lasiocampidae *lā-zi-ō-kamp'i-dē* or *lā-si-*, *n pl* a family of moths including eggers and lackey moths. [Gr *lasios* woolly, and *kampē* a caterpillar]

lasket *las'kit*, (*naut*) *n* a loop at the foot of a sail, to fasten an extra sail. [Perh **latchet**]

lasque *läsk*, *n* a flat thin diamond, common in India. [Perh Pers *lashk* a bit or piece]

lass *las*, *n* a girl, young woman; a sweetheart; a maid-servant (*Scot*). — *n* (*dimin*) **lassie** (*las'i*) the ordinary

Scots word for a girl. — *n* **lass'ock** (*dimin*). — *adj* **lass'lorn** (*Shakesp*) forsaken by one's mistress. [Origin obscure; the association with **lad**[1] may be accidental]

Lassa fever *la'sə fē'vər*, *n* an infectious tropical virus disease, often fatal, transmitted by rodents. [From *Lassa*, in Nigeria, where it was first recognized]

lassi *las'i*, or *lus'i*, (*Ind*) *n* a (sweet or savoury) flavoured cold drink made with yoghurt or buttermilk. [Hindi]

lassitude *las'i-tūd*, *n* faintness; weakness; weariness; languor. [L *lassitūdō*, from *lassus* faint]

lasslorn and **lassock**. See under **lass**.

lasso *la-sōō'* or *la'sō*, *n* a long rope with a running noose for catching wild horses, etc: — *pl* **lassoes'** or **lassos'** (or *las'*). — *vt* to catch with the lasso: — *pr p* **lasso'ing** (or *las'*); *pa p* **lassoed** (*las-ōōd'* or *las'*). [S American pronunciation of Sp *lazo*, from L *laqueus* a noose]

lassu *losh'ōō*, *n* the slow movement of a csárdás. [Hung]

last[1] *läst*, *n* a shoemaker's model of the foot on which boots and shoes are made or repaired. — *vt* to fit with a last. — *n* **last'er** someone who fits the parts of shoes to lasts; a tool for doing so. [OE *lǣste* last, *lāst* footprint]

last[2] *läst*, *vi* to continue, endure; to escape failure; to remain fresh or unimpaired; to hold out; to survive. — *n* **last'er** someone who has staying power; a thing that keeps well. — *adj* **last'ing** enduring; durable. — *n* endurance. — *adv* **last'ingly**. — *n* **last'ingness**. — **last out** to last as long as or longer than; to last to the end or as long as is required. [OE *lǣstan* to follow a track, keep on, suffice, last; see **last**[1]]

last[3] *läst*, *n* a load or cargo; a varying weight, generally about 4000 lb. — *n* **last'age** the lading of a ship; room for stowing goods in a ship; a duty formerly paid for the right of carrying goods, etc. [OE *hlæst*, from *hladan* to lade; Ger *Last*, ON *hlass*]

last[4] *läst*, *adj* latest; coming or remaining after all the others; final; immediately before the present; utmost; ending a series; most unlikely, least to be preferred. — Also *adv*. — *adv* **last'ly** finally. — *adj* **last'-ditch** (of an attempt, etc) made at the last moment or in the last resort. — *adj* **last'-gasp'** made, etc when almost at the point of death, defeat, etc. — **last heir** the person to whom lands escheat when other heirs are lacking. — *adj* **last'-minute** made, done or given at the latest possible time. — **last post** (*military*) the second of two bugle-calls denoting the time for retiring for the night; the farewell bugle-call at military funerals; **last rites** religious rites performed for a person close to death; **last straw** (ie the straw that breaks the camel's back) that small event or factor which, following a series of others, finally makes the situation intolerable or irreparable; **last word** the final remark in an argument; the final decision; the most up-to-date of its kind (*colloq*). — **at last** in the end; **at long last** after long delay; **breathe one's last** to die; **die in the last ditch** to fight to the bitter end; **first and last** altogether; **last thing** after doing everything else; finally before going to bed at night; **on one's last legs** on the verge of utter failure or exhaustion; **put the last hand to** to finish, put the finishing touch to; **see** (or **hear**) **the last of** to see (or hear) for the last time; **the Last Day** the Day of Judgment; **the Last Supper** the supper taken by Christ and his disciples on the eve of the crucifixion; **the last trump** the trumpet that will sound at the Last Day (1 Corinthians 15.52); **to the last** to the end; till death. [OE *latost*, superl of *læt* slow, late]

Lat. *abbrev*: Latin.

lat[1] *lät*, *n* in India, an isolated pillar. [Hindi *lat*]

lat[2] *lat*, (*colloq*) *n* short form of **latrine**.

lat. *abbrev*: lateral; latissimus dorsi, a muscle in the lower back (*anatom*); latitude.

Latakia *lat-ä-kē'ə*, *n* a Syrian tobacco from *Latakia*.

latch[1] *lach*, *vt* (*Shakesp*) probably to moisten, but possibly to fasten (see **latch**[2]). — *n* (*Scot*) a mire; a boggy water-channel. — Also **letch**. [**leach**[1]]

latch[2] *lach*, *n* a door catch lifted from the outside by a lever or string; a light door-lock, opened from the outside by a key. — *vt* (*obs*) to seize, take or receive. — *vt* and *vi* to fasten with a latch. — **latch'key** or **latch'-string** a key or string for opening a latched door; **latchkey child** a child who regularly returns home to an empty house. — **latch on to** (*colloq*) to attach oneself to; to gain comprehension of; **on the latch** not locked, but able to be opened by a latch. [OE *læccan* to catch]

latchet *lach'it*, (*obs*) *n* a loop; a thong or lace. [OFr *lachet*, a form of *lacet*, dimin of *laz*; see **lace**]

late *lāt*, *adj* tardy; behindhand; coming, remaining, flowering, ripening, producing, etc after the due, expected or usual time; long delayed; nearly at the end; deceased; departed; out of office; former; not long past; most recent; slow (*dialect*): — *compar* **lāt'er**; *superl* **lāt'est**. — Also *adv*. — *adj* **lāt'ed** (*Shakesp*) belated. — *adv* **late'ly** recently. — *vt* and *vi* **lāt'en** to make or grow late. — *n* **late'ness**. — *n* **lāt'est** (*colloq*; with *the*) the latest news, fashion, version, etc. — *adj* and *adv* **lāt'ish**. — **late'-comer** a person who arrives late; **late onset diabetes** diabetes occurring in older people, in which the insulin lack is only relative; **late wood** (*bot*) the wood formed in the later part of a growth ring, *usu* having smaller, thicker-walled cells than the early wood. — **at the latest** not later than (a stated time); **late in the day** (*fig*) at an unreasonably late stage of development, etc; **of late** recently. [OE *læt* slow; Du *laat*, ON *latr*, Ger *lass* weary; L *lassus* tired]

lateen *lə-tēn'*, *adj* applied to a triangular sail, common in the Mediterranean, the Lake of Geneva, etc; rigged with such a sail. — *n* a lateen sail; a boat with a lateen rig. [Fr (*voile*) *latine*, from L *Latīnus* Latin]

La Tène *la ten*, *adj* of a division of the Iron Age exemplified at *La Tène* near Neuchâtel in Switzerland, later than Hallstatt.

latent *lā'tənt*, *adj* hidden; concealed; not visible or apparent; dormant; undeveloped, but capable of development; in Freudian psychoanalysis, applied to that part of a dream's content that is repressed and transformed into the manifest content. — *n* **lā'tence** or **lā'tency**. — *adv* **lā'tently**. — *n* **lātesc'ence**. — *adj* **lātesc'ent** becoming latent. — **latent heat** see under **heat**; **latent image** (*photog*) the invisible image produced by the action of light on the sensitive chemicals on a film, etc, which becomes visible after development; **latent period** the time between stimulus and reaction (*psychol*); the time between the contracting of a disease and the appearance of symptoms (*med*). [L *latēns*, *-entis*, pr p of *latēre* to lie hidden; Gr *lanthanein* to be hidden]

lateral *lat'ə-rəl*, *adj* on, relating to, belonging to, or in the direction of the side or sides; (of a consonant) produced by air passing over one or both sides of the tongue (*phonetics*). — *n* a lateral part, movement, consonant, etc. — *n* **laterality** (*-ral'i-ti*) the state of belonging to the side; physical one-sidedness, either right or left. — *n* **lateralīzā'tion** or **-z-** the specialized development in one or other hemisphere of the brain of the mechanisms controlling some activity or ability. — *adv* **lat'erally**. — **lateral line** in fishes, a line along the side of the body, marking the position of a sensory organ; **lateral shift** (*geol*) the horizontal displacement of outcrops, as a consequence of faulting; **lateral thinking** thinking which seeks new ways of looking at a problem and does not merely proceed by logical steps from the starting-point of what is known or believed. [L *laterālis*, from *latus*, *lateris* a side]

Lateran *lat'ə-rən*, *adj* relating to the Church of St John *Lateran* at Rome, the Pope's cathedral church, on the site of the splendid palace or basilica of Plautius Lateranus (executed AD 66). — **Lateran Councils** five general councils of the Western Church, held in the Lateran basilica (1123, 1139, 1179, 1215, and 1512–17), regarded by Roman Catholics as ecumenical; **Lateran Treaty** the treaty that restored the independent papal state Vatican city in 1929. [L *Laterānus*]

laterigrade *lat'ə-ri-grād*, *adj* running sideways, like a crab. [L *latus*, *-eris* side, and *gradus* step]

laterite *lat'ə-rīt*, *n* a clay formed by weathering of rocks in a tropical climate, composed chiefly of iron and aluminium hydroxides. — *adj* **lateritic** (*lat-ə-rit'ik*) of laterite; similar to laterite in composition. — *n* **laterī-zā'tion** or **-s-** conversion into laterite. [L *later*, *lateris* a brick]

lateritious *lat-ə-rish'əs*, *adj* brick-red. [L *laterīcius*, from *later*, *lateris* a brick]

latewake *lāt'wāk*, *n* a mistaken form of **lykewake**.

latex *lā'teks*, (*bot*) *n* the milky juice of some plants, eg rubber trees; a synthesized form of such juice, widely used in the manufacture of rubber products: — *pl* **lā'texes** or **lā'ticēs**. — *adj* **laticiferous** (*lat-i-sif'ə-rəs*) containing or conveying latex. [L *latex*, *laticis*]

lath *läth*, *n* a thin strip of wood; a substitute for such a strip, used in slating, plastering, etc; anything long and thin: — *pl* **laths** (*lädhz* or *läths*). — *vt* to cover with laths. — *adj* **lathen** (*läth'ən*). — *n* **lath'ing** the act or process of covering with laths; a covering of laths. — *adj* **lath'y** like a lath. — *adj* **lath'like**. — **lath'-splitter** someone who splits wood into laths. — **dagger of lath** the Vice's weapon in the old morality plays. [OE *lætt*]

lathe[1] *lādh*, *n* a machine for turning and shaping articles of wood, metal, etc; the swing-frame of a loom carrying the reed for separating the warp threads and beating up the weft. — **capstan lathe** and **turret lathe** see under **capstan** and **turret** respectively. [Origin doubtful]

lathe[2] *lādh*, (*hist*) *n* a former division of Kent. [OE *lǣth* a district; ON *lāth* landed property]

lather *ladh'ər* or *lädh'ər*, *n* a foam made with water and soap; froth from sweat; a state of agitation (*colloq*). — *vt* to spread over with lather; to thrash (*colloq*). — *vi* to form a lather. — *adj* **lath'ery**. [OE *lēathor*; ON *lauthr*]

lathi or **lathee** *lä-tē'*, (*Ind*) *n* a long, heavy stick used as a weapon. [Hindi *lāthī*]

lathyrus *lath'i-rəs*, *n* any plant of the *Lathyrus* genus of Papilionaceae. — *n* **lath'yrism** a neurological disease producing stiffness and paralysis of the legs in humans and animals, apparently due to eating cultivated vetch made poisonous by a freak mixing with some unknown seed. [L, from Gr *lathyros* the chickling vetch]

latices and **laticiferous**. See under **latex**.

laticlave *lat'i-klāv*, (*hist*) *n* a broad stripe on a Roman senator's tunic. [L *lātus* broad, and *clāvus* a stripe]

latifundia *lat-i-fun'di-ə*, *n pl* great landed estates. — Also in *sing* **latifun'dium** and as *Ital pl* **latifondi** (*lä-tē-fon'dē*). [Pl of L *lātifundium*, from *lātus* wide, and *fundus* an estate]

Latin *lat'in*, *adj* relating to ancient Latium (*esp* Rome) or its inhabitants, or its language, or to those languages that are descended from Latin, or to the peoples speaking them, *esp* (popularly) the Spanish, Portuguese and Italians or the inhabitants of Central and S America of Spanish, etc extraction; of or denoting the temperament considered characteristic of the Latin peoples, passionate, excitable, volatile; written or spoken in Latin; Roman Catholic. — *n* an inhabitant of ancient Latium; the language of ancient Latium, and *esp* of Rome; a person belonging to a Latin people; a Roman Catholic. — *adj* **Latian** (*lā'shyən* or *-shən*) of Latium. — *adj* **Lat'inate** imitating Latin style; (of vocabulary) borrowed from Latin. — *n* **Lat'iner** (*obs*) someone who knows Latin; an interpreter. — *n* **Lat'inism** a Latin idiom; the use or inclination towards use of Latin idioms, words or ways. — *n* **Lat'inist** a person skilled in Latin. — *n* **Latin'ity** the (easy) use of Latin; the quality of one's Latin. — *vt* **Lat'inize** or **-ise** to turn into or make Latin or like Latin. — *vi* to use Latin idioms or derivatives. — *n* **Latino** (*la-tē'nō*) *esp* in N America, a person of Latin American descent: — *fem* **Latin'a**. — Also *adj*. — **Latin America** those parts of America where Spanish, Portuguese and French are the official languages, with the exception of French-speaking Canada. — *adj* and *n* **Lat'in-Amer'ican**. — **Latin Church** the Roman Catholic Church; **Latin cross** an upright cross with the lowest limb longest; **Latin Empire** that portion of the Byzantine Empire seized in 1204 by the Crusaders (French and Venetian), and overthrown by the Greeks in 1261; **Latin Kingdom** the Christian kingdom of Jerusalem ruled by French or Latin kings, and lasting from 1099 to 1187; **Latin Quarter** the educational and students' quarter of Paris around the Sorbonne (where Latin was spoken in the Middle Ages; Fr *quartier latin*), famous for its unconventional way of life; **Latin Union** a monetary union (1865–1926) of France, Belgium, Italy and Switzerland, with Greece from 1868. — **classical Latin** the Latin of the writers who flourished from about 75 BC to about AD 200; **dog Latin** see under **dog**[1]; **Late Latin** the Latin written by authors between AD 200 and *c.* 600; **Low Latin** Medieval, or Late and Medieval, Latin; **Middle** or **Medieval Latin** the Latin of the Middle Ages between AD 600 and 1500; **New** or **Modern Latin** Latin as written between 1500 and the present time, mostly used as a scientific medium; **Silver Latin** see under **silver**; **thieves' Latin** thieves' cant; **Vulgar Latin** colloquial Latin, *esp* that of the period under the emperors. [L *Latīnus* belonging to *Latium*, the district round Rome]

Latina and **Latino**. See under **Latin**.

latirostral *lat-i-ros'trəl*, (*ornithol*) *adj* broad-billed. — Also **latiros'trate**. [L *lātus* broad, and *rōstrum* beak]

latiseptate *lat-i-sep'tāt*, (*bot*) *adj* having a broad partition. [L *lātus* broad, and *saeptum* a fence (used in pl)]

latitant *lat'i-tənt*, *adj* lurking; lying in wait; hibernating; dormant. — *n* **lat'itancy**. — *n* **lat'itat** a writ based on the supposition that the person summoned is in hiding. — *n* **latitā'tion**. [L *latitāre*, *-ātum* (3rd pers sing present *latitat*), frequentative of *latēre* to be in hiding]

latitude *lat'i-tūd*, *n* angular distance from the equator (*geog*); a place of specified angular distance from the equator (*geog*); angular distance from the ecliptic (*celestial latitude*; *astron*); width (chiefly *humorous*); a wide extent; range; scope; allowance; breadth in interpretation; extent of meaning or importance; freedom from restraint; laxity. — *adj* **latitūd'inal** relating to latitude; in the direction of latitude. — *adj* **latitūdinā'rian** broad or liberal, *esp* in religious belief; lax. — *n* a member of a school of liberal and philosophical theologians within the English Church in the later half of the 17c; a person with latitudinarian views, *esp* one free from prejudice in religious or church matters. — *n* **latitūdinā'rianism**. — *adj* **latitūd'inous** broad or wide, *esp* in interpretation. [L *lātitūdō*, *-inis*, from *lātus* broad]

latke *lät'kə*, *n* a traditional Jewish pancake, *esp* one made with grated potato. [Yiddish, from Russ *latka* a pastry]

latration *lə-trā'shən*, (*usu facetious*) *n* barking. — *adj* **latrant** (*lā'trənt*). [L *lātrāre*, *-ātum* to bark]

la trenise. See **trenise**.

latria *lä-trī'ə*, *n* see under **dulia**. [Gr *latreiā*, from *latreuein* to serve]

latrine *lə-trēn'*, *n* a lavatory, *esp* in barracks, camps, etc. [L *lātrīna*, from *lavātrīna*, from *lavāre* to wash]

latrocinium *lat-rō-sin'i-əm* or **latrociny** *lat'rō-sin-i*, (*obs*) *n* highway-robbery; Pope Leo I's name for the 'Robber-Council' at Ephesus in AD 449, which upheld the doctrine of Eutych. [L *latrōcinium* robbery]

latron *lā'tron*, (*obs*) *n* a robber. [L *latrō*, *-ōnis*]

-latry *-lə-tri*, *combining form* denoting worship. [Gk *latreiā*, from *latreuein* to serve]

latten *lat'ən*, *n* brass or any similar alloy (*old*); tin-plate; metal in thin plates. [OFr *laton* (Fr *laiton*), prob from Old Provençal, from Ar *lātūn* copper, from Turkic; a Germanic origin for the word has also been postulated, cf **lath**]

latter *lat'ər*, *adj* later; coming or existing after; second-mentioned of two; modern; recent; last (*Shakesp*). — *adv* **latt'erly** towards the latter end; of late. — *adj* **latt'ermost** (OE *lætemest*) last. — *adj* **latt'er-born** (*Shakesp*) younger. — *adj* **latt'er-day** modern; recent. — **Latter-day Saint** a Mormon; **latter end** the final part; the end of life; **latt'ermath** (*dialect*) aftermath; **latt'er-mint** (*Keats*) apparently a late kind of mint;

latt'er-wit (*archaic US*) a witty thought after the occasion has passed. [OE *lætra*, compar of *læt* slow, late]

lattice *lat'is*, *n* a network of crossed laths or bars, called also **latt'ice-work**; anything of a similar pattern; a window with small, *esp* diamond-shaped panes set in lead, called also **lattice window**; the geometrically regular, three-dimensional arrangement of fissionable and non-fissionable material in an atomic pile; the regular arrangement of atoms in crystalline material; a system of lines for position-fixing overprinted on a navigational chart; a partially-ordered set in which any two elements have a least upper bound and a greatest lower bound (*math*); a space-lattice (qv). — *vt* to form into open work; to provide with a lattice. — **latt'ice-bridge** a bridge of lattice-girders; **latt'ice-gird'er** a girder composed of upper and lower members joined by a web of crossing diagonal bars; **latt'ice-leaf** the **lace-leaf** or ouvirandra (*Aponogeton fenestrale*), a water plant of Madagascar with leaves like open lattice-work. — **red lattice** (*Shakesp*) the sign of an ale-house. [Fr *lattis*, from *latte* a lath]

latticinio *la-ti-chē'ni-ō*, *n* a type of Venetian glassware containing decorative threads of milk-white glass; a piece of such glassware; the white glass itself: — *pl* **lattici'ni** (*-nē*). — Also *adj*. — Also **lattici'no**: — *pl* **lattici'ni**. [Ital, from L *lacticinium* food made with milk, from *lac*, *lactis* milk]

latus rectum *lā'təs rek'təm* or *la'tōōs rek'tōōm*, (*geom*) *n* a focal chord parallel to the directrix of a conic. [L, right or perpendicular side]

Latvian *lat'vi-ən*, *adj* of or relating to Latvia, Lettish. — *n* a native or citizen of Latvia; the language of Latvia, Lettish. [Lettish *Latvija* Latvia or Lettland]

lauch *löhh*, a Scots form of **law**[2] (*Scott*) and of **laugh**, *n* and *vb*: — *pa t* **leuch** or **leugh** (*lūhh*); *pap* **leuch'en** or **leugh'en**.

laud *löd*, *vt* to praise; to celebrate. — *n* praise; (in *pl*) in the RC Church, the prayers immediately following matins. — *adj* **laud'able** praiseworthy. — *n* **laud'ableness** or **laudabil'ity**. — *adv* **laud'ably**. — *n* **laudā'tion** praise; honour paid. — *adj* **laud'ative** or **laud'atory** containing praise; expressing praise. — *n* (*obs*) a eulogy. — *n* **laud'er**. [L *laudāre*, from *laus*, *laudis* praise]

laudanum *löd'ə-nəm* or *löd'nəm*, *n* tincture of opium. [Coined by Paracelsus; perh **ladanum**, transferred to a different drug]

lauf *lowf*, *n* a run in a bobsleigh contest. [Ger]

laugh *läf*, *vi* to express, by explosive inarticulate sounds of the voice, amusement, joy, scorn, etc, or a reaction to tickling, etc; to be entertained or amused by (with *at*); to make fun of (with *at*); to express scorn for (with *at*); to have a cheerful appearance (*fig*). — *vt* to have an effect on, affect or force into by laughing; to express by laughter; to laugh at, deride (*Spenser*). — *n* an act or sound of laughing. — *adj* **laugh'able** ludicrous. — *n* **laugh'ableness**. — *adv* **laugh'ably**. — *n* **laugh'er** someone who laughs; a breed of pigeon which makes a laughing sound. — *adj* **laugh'ful** mirthful. — *n* and *adj* **laugh'ing**. — *adv* **laugh'ingly**. — *adj* **laugh'some** (*archaic*) inclined to laugh; provoking laughter. — *n* **laugh'ter** the act or sound of laughing. — *adj* **laugh'y** (*rare*) inclined to laugh. — **laugh'ing-gas** nitrous oxide, which may excite laughter when breathed, used as an anaesthetic, *esp* in dentistry; **laughing hyena** the spotted hyena (*Crocuta crocuta*; see under **hyena**); **laughing jackass** the kookaburra; **laugh'ing-stock** an object of ridicule. — *adj* **laugh'worthy** deserving to be laughed at. — **be laughing** (*colloq*) to have no (further) problems, worries, etc; to be in a favourable or advantageous position; **don't make me laugh** (*colloq*) an expression of scornful disbelief; **have the last laugh** to triumph finally after one or more setbacks or defeats; to have one's actions, etc finally vindicated after being scorned; **have the laugh of** to get the better of; **laugh and lie** (or **lay**) **down** an old card-game in which a player lays down his or her cards when a winning hand is achieved; **laugh in someone's face** to scorn or mock a person openly; **laugh off** to treat (injuries, etc) as of no importance; **laugh on the other side of one's face** or (*rare*) **on the wrong side of one's mouth** to be made to feel disappointment or sorrow, *esp* after boasting, etc; **laugh someone out of court** to prevent someone getting a hearing by ridicule; **laugh to scorn** to deride or jeer at; **laugh up one's sleeve** or (*rare*) **in one's sleeve** to laugh inwardly; **no laughing matter** a very serious matter. [OE (Anglian) *hlæhhan* (WSax *hliehhan*); Ger *lachen*, Gothic *hlahjan*]

launce[1] *löns* or *läns* (*Spenser*). Same as **lance**[1].

launce[2] *löns* or *läns*, (*Spenser*) *n* a balance. [L *lanx*, *lancis* a plate, a scale of a balance]

launce[3] *löns* or *läns* or **lance** *läns*, *n* a sand eel (*Ammodytes*), an eel-like fish that buries itself in wet sand at ebb-tide. — Also **lant**. [Perh connected with **lance**[1]]

launcegaye *löns'gā* or *läns'gā*. Same as **lancegay**.

launch[1] *lönch* or *lönsh* (*obs* **lanch** *länch* or *länsh*) *vt* to throw or hurl; to dart; to send out; to set going; to initiate; to cause or allow to slide into water or to take off from land; to put (a book or other product) on the market, *esp* with attendant publicity, etc; to throw (oneself) freely, venturesomely, or enthusiastically (into some activity) (with *into*); to pierce (*Spenser*); to lance (*obs*). — *vi* to rush, dart, plunge or fling oneself; to be launched; to take off; to throw oneself freely, or in a spirit of adventure (into some activity) (with *out* or *into*); to begin a *usu* long story, speech, etc (with *into*). — *n* the act or occasion of launching; the introduction of a new product or service on to the market (*commerce*); a lancing (*Spenser*). — *n* **launch'er** a device for launching, *esp* for sending off a rocket. — **launch'ing-pad** a platform from which a rocket can be launched; a place, event, etc which gives a good start to a career, etc, or at which a project, campaign, etc is launched; **launch'ing-site**. — *n pl* **launch'ing-ways** the timbers on which a ship is launched. — **launch pad** and **launch site** same as **launching-pad** and **launching-site** above; **launch vehicle** see under **vehicle**; **launch window** the period of time during which the launching of a spacecraft must take place if the flight is to be successful. [OFr *lanchier*, *lancier* (Fr *lancer*); see **lance**[1]]

launch[2] *lönch*, *lönsh*, *länch* or *länsh*, *n* a large power-driven boat for pleasure or short runs; the largest boat carried by a man-of-war. [Sp *lancha*, perh from Malay *lanchār* swift]

laund *lönd*, (*Shakesp*) *n* a glade; a grassy place. [OFr *launde*, *lande*; prob Celtic; see **lawn**[2]]

launder *lön'dər*, *vt* to wash and iron (clothes, etc); to clean or cleanse generally (*fig*); to handle (the transfer of money, goods, etc or the movement of people) in such a way that the identity or illegality of the source, the illegality of the transfer, or the identity or criminality of the people remains undetected (*colloq*). — *vi* to wash and iron clothes, etc; to be able to be laundered. — *n* a washerwoman or washerman (*obs*); a trough for conveying water. — *n* **laun'derer**. — *n* **laun'dress** a woman who washes and irons clothes. — *n* **laun'dry** a place where clothes, etc are washed and ironed; clothes, etc for or from the laundry; a collection of articles for washing or that have been washed. — **laundry list** a list of items to be laundered; a list of items or matters to be achieved, produced, dealt with, prevented, etc (*fig*); **laun'dry-maid**; **laun'dry-man** or **laun'dry-woman** a worker in a laundry; a person who runs a laundry; a person who collects and delivers laundry. [ME *lavander*, from OFr *lavandier*, from L *lavandārius*, from the gerundive of *lavāre* to wash]

launderette *lön-dər-et'* or **laundrette** *-dret'*, *n* a shop where customers wash clothes in washing-machines. [Orig trademark]

Laundromat® *lön'drō-mat*, (*NAm*) *n* a launderette.

laura *lö'rə* or **lavra** *läv'rə*, *n* a group of recluses' cells. [Gr *laurā* (modern *labra*, with *b* as *v*) alley, lane, monastery]

lauraceous. See under **Laurus**.

Laurasia *lör-ā'shyə, -shə, -zhyə* or *-zhə, n* the ancient landmass thought to have existed in the northern hemisphere, and which subsequently split up to form N America, Greenland, Europe and northern Asia. — *adj* **Laurā'sian**. [*Laur*entia, the ancient N American landmass, from the Laurentian strata of the Canadian Shield, and Eur*asia*]

laurdalite *lör'dəl-īt* or **lardalite** *lär-*, (*mineralogy*) *n* a coarse nepheline syenite. [*Laurdal* or *Lardal* in Norway]

laureate *lö'ri-it, adj* crowned with laurel; honoured by a distinction. — *n* a person crowned with laurel; a person honoured by a distinction; a poet laureate. — *vt* (*-āt*) to crown with laurel, in token of literary merit; to confer a degree upon. — *n* **lau'reateship**. — *n* **laureā'tion** crowning with laurel; graduation. — **Poet Laureate** see under **poet**. [L *laureātus* laurelled, from *laurus* laurel]

laurel *lor'əl, n* the sweet bay tree (*Laurus nobilis*), used in ancient times for making wreaths of honour; another species of *Laurus* found in Madeira and the Canaries; the cherry-laurel; in America, any species of Rhododendron or of Kalmia; extended to various trees and shrubs of similar appearance; a crown of laurel; honours gained (often in *pl*). — *adj* **lau'rel**. — *adj* **lau'relled** crowned, adorned or covered with laurel. — **lau'rel-wa'ter** a sedative and narcotic water distilled from cherry-laurel leaves; **lauric acid** (*lör'ik*) an acid, $CH_3{\cdot}(CH_2)_{10}{\cdot}COOH$, occurring in the berries of *Laurus nobilis*, etc; **lauryl alcohol** (*lor'il* or *lör'*) a liquid made from coconut oil or its fatty acids, used in the manufacture of detergents; **lauryl thiocyanate** a salt of lauryl alcohol used as a disinfectant. — **cherry laurel**, **Japan laurel** and **spurge-laurel** see under **cherry**, **Japan** and **spurge** respectively. — **look to one's laurels** to be careful in case one loses one's pre-eminent position; **rest on one's laurels** (sometimes as a criticism) to be content with one's past successes and the honour they bring, without attempting any further achievements. [Fr *laurier*, from L *laurus*]

Laurentian *lö-ren'sh(y)ən, adj* of or relating to *Lorenzo* or *Laurentius* de' Medici (1449–92), or to the library founded by him at Florence; of or relating to, or in the style of, the English writer D H Lawrence (1885–1930; also **Lawren'tian**); of or relating to the St *Lawrence* river in SE Canada; applied to a series of Pre-Cambrian rocks covering a large area in the region of the Upper Lakes of N America.

lauric acid. See under **laurel**.

Laurus *lö'rəs, n* the laurel genus, giving its name to the family **Laurā'ceae**, leathery-leaved archichlamydeous dicotyledons. — *adj* **laurā'ceous**. [L]

laurustine, *lö'rəs-tīn* or **laurustinus** *lö-rəs-tī'nəs, n* a winter-flowering shrub (*Viburnum tinus*). [L *laurus* laurel, and *tīnus* laurustine]

laurvikite *lör'vik-īt* or **larvikite** *lär-*, (*mineralogy*) *n* a soda syenite composed mainly of feldspar with schiller structure. [*Laurvik* or *Larvik* in Norway]

lauryl. See under **laurel**.

laus Deo *lös dē'ō* or *lows dā'ō*, (*L*) praise to God.

LAUTRO *low'trō, abbrev*: Life Assurance and Unit Trust Regulatory Organization.

lauwine *lö'win*, (*Byron*) *n* an avalanche. [Ger *La(u)wine*, perh from *lau* tepid]

lav *lav*, (*colloq*) *n* short for **lavatory**.

lava *lä'və, n* molten material discharged in a stream from a volcano or fissure; such material subsequently solidified: — *pl* **la'vas**. — *adj* **la'vaform** in the form of lava. [Ital, poss from L *lavāre* to wash, or from L *lābes* a falling down, from *lābī* to slide, fall]

lavabo *ləv-ā'bō, n* in the mass, the ritual act of washing the celebrant's fingers while he says *Lavabo inter innocentes* (*RC*); a monastic lavatory; a fixed basin or washstand; a lavatory: — *pl* **lavā'bos** or **lavā'boes**. [L, I shall wash (from Psalm 26.6]

lavage. See under **lave**[1].

lava-lava *lä'və-lä'və, n* a rectangular piece of printed cloth worn by both sexes in Polynesia as a kind of skirt. [Samoan, clothing]

lavallière or **lavaliere** *la-va-lyer* or *lav'ə-lēr, n* a loosely-tied bow; a jewelled pendant worn round the neck on a chain. [After the Duchesse de *la Vallière* (1644–1710)]

lavatera *la-və-tē'rə* or *lə-vä'tə-rə, n* any plant of the genus *Lavatera* of herbs and shrubs (family *Malvaceae*) with large pink, white or purple mallow-like flowers. [The brothers *Lavater*, 17c and 18c Swiss physicians and naturalists]

lavatory *lav'ə-tər-i, n* a bowl, *usu* with a wooden or plastic seat and flushed by water, used for urination and defecation; a room containing a lavatory and often a wash-basin; *orig* a place, room, fixture or vessel for washing; a laundry (*obs*); a ritual washing; a lotion (*obs*). — *adj* **lavator'ial** of or characteristic of lavatories; of humour, etc, scatological (*usu derog*). — **lavatory paper** toilet-paper. [LL *lavatorium*, from *lavare, lavatum* to wash]

lave[1] *lāv*, (*archaic*) *vt* and *vi* to wash; to bathe. — *n* **lavage** (*lav'ij* or *läv-äzh'*; *med*) irrigation or washing out. — *n* **lavation** (*lav-ā'shən*) washing. — *n* **lavement** (*lāv'*) a washing; a lavage. — *n* **lāv'er** a large vessel for washing, *esp* ritual washing; the basin of a fountain (*Spenser*); an ablution (*Milton*). [L *lavāre, -ātum*; Gr *louein* to wash]

lave[2] *lāv*, (*Scot*) *n* remainder. [OE *lāf*; ON *leif*; see **leave**[2]]

lave[3] *lāv*, (*obs*) *vt* to pour out; to bale. [OE *lafian* to pour; fused with L *lavāre* to wash]

laveer *lä-vēr'*, (*archaic naut*) *vi* to beat to windward. [Du *laveeren*; cf **luff**]

lavender *lav'ən-dər, n* a labiate plant (*Lavandula vera*) with fragrant pale-lilac flowers, yielding an essential oil; sprigs of it used for perfuming clothes, linen, etc; the colour of its blossoms. — *adj* of the colour of lavender flowers. — *vt* to sprinkle with lavender. — **lav'ender-cott'on** a species of Mediterranean shrub, Santolina; **lav'ender-wa'ter** a perfume composed of spirits of wine, essential oil of lavender, and ambergris. — **lay in lavender** to lay by carefully, with sprigs of lavender; to pawn (*colloq*); **oil of lavender** an aromatic oil distilled from lavender flowers and stems, used as a stimulant and tonic. [Anglo-Fr *lavendre* (Fr *lavande*), from LL *lavendula*, earlier *livendula*, perh connected with *līvidus* livid]

laver[1]. See under **lave**[1].

laver[2] *lāv'ər, n* edible seaweed of various kinds, *esp* porphyra (*purple laver*) and Ulva (*green laver*). — **laver bread** or **laverbread** (*lā'vər* or *lä'vər bred*) a name for a food popular in Wales, the fronds of porphyra boiled, dipped in oatmeal and fried. [L *laver* a kind of water plant]

laverock *lav'ə-rək*, also (*Scot*) *lāv'ə-rək* or *lāv'rək*. An archaic and dialectal form of **lark**[1].

lavish *lav'ish, vt* to expend or bestow profusely; to waste. — *adj* generous or profuse in giving; prodigal or wasteful; extravagant; unrestrained. — *n* (*obs*) profusion; over-abundance; extravagant outpouring. — *adv* **lav'ishly**. — *n* **lav'ishment**. — *n* **lav'ishness**. [OFr *lavasse, lavache* deluge of rain, from *laver*, from L *lavāre* to wash]

lavolta *la-volt'ə* or **lavolt** *la-volt'*, (*Shakesp*) *n* an old dance in which there was much turning and high leaping. — *vi* to dance the lavolta. [Ital *la volta* the turn]

lavra. See **laura**.

law[1] *lö, n* a rule of action established by authority; a statute; the rules of a community or state; jurisprudence; established usage; that which is lawful; the whole body of persons connected professionally with the law; litigation; a rule or code in any department of action, such as morality, art, honour, arms (including heraldry), a game, etc; a theoretical principle extracted from practice or observation; a statement or formula expressing the constant order of certain phenomena; the Mosaic code or the books containing it (*theol*); an allowance of time, a start *esp* in hunting (*sport*);

indulgence (*obs*). — *vt* to take to court, go to law with (*obs*); to determine (*Burns*); to expeditate (*obs*). — *vi* (*obs*) to go to law. — *adj* **law'ful** allowed by law; rightful. — *adv* **law'fully**. — *n* **law'fulness**. — *n* **law'ing** going to law (*archaic*); expeditation (*obs*). — *adj* **law'less** not subject to or controlled by law; unruly. — *adv* **law'lessly**. — *n* **law'lessness**. — *n* **law'yer** a practitioner in the law, *esp* a solicitor; a person learned or skilled in law; an interpreter of the Mosaic law (*New Testament*); a brier, bramble, or other tenacious trailing or climbing plant (see also **Penang-lawyer**). — *adj* **law'yerly**. — *adj* **law'-abiding** having respect for and obedient to the law. — **law agent** (*Scots law*; *old*) a solicitor; **law'-book** a book dealing with the law or law cases; **law'-breaker** a person who does not observe or who abuses a law; **law'-burrows** (*Scots law*) a writ requiring a person to give security against doing violence to another; **law'-calf** a book-binding in smooth, pale-brown calf; **law centre** an office, *usu* in a socially deprived area, where free legal advice and assistance are given (also **neighbourhood law centre**); **Law Commission** a body of solicitors, barristers and academic lawyers, appointed by the Lord Chancellor to report to Parliament on areas of possible law reform; **law'-court** a court of justice; **law'-day** a day when court proceedings may be held in public, a day of open court; **lawful day** a day on which particular kinds of business may be legally done, not a Sunday or a public holiday; **law'-giver** a person who enacts or imposes laws. — *adj* **law'-giving**. — **law Latin** Latin as used in law and legal documents, being a mixture of Latin with Old French and Latinized English words; **law'-list** an annual book of information about lawyers, courts, etc; **Law Lord** a peer in parliament who holds or has held high legal office, also called **Lord of Appeal in Ordinary**; in Scotland, a judge of the Court of Session; **law'-maker** a legislator; **law'man** a sheriff or policeman (*US*; now chiefly *archaic* or *facetious*); **law'-man** (*hist*) a member of a select body with magisterial powers in some of the Danish towns of early England; **law'-mer'chant** the customs that have grown up among merchants in reference to mercantile documents and business, commercial law; **law'monger** a trivially contentious lawyer; **law'-officer** a legal official and adviser of the government, *esp* an Attorney-General, Solicitor-General, or Lord Advocate; **law reports** written records of previous case law which are used during court proceedings to make reference to established legal principles; **Law Society** the solicitors' governing body, which also administers the legal aid scheme; **law'-stā'tioner** a person who sells parchment, documents and other articles needed by lawyers; **law'suit** a suit or process in law; **law'-writer** a writer on law; a copier or engrosser of legal papers. — **be a law unto oneself** or **itself** to act in a way that does not follow established rules or conventions; **Bode's law** (*astron*) a rule popularized by Johann *Bode* (1747–1826, German astronomer) but first announced by Johann Titius (1729–96), which states that the distances of the planets from the sun in astronomical units is found by adding 4 to the series 0, 3, 6, 12, 24,... and dividing the number so obtained by 10; **Boyle's** or **Mariotte's law** the law that, for a gas at a given temperature, pressure varies inversely to volume, announced by Robert *Boyle* in 1662, and confirmed by Mariotte (1620–84, French physicist); **Charles's law** the law that all gases have the same value for the coefficient of expansion at constant pressure, stated by J A C *Charles* (1746–1823, French physicist), also called **Gay-Lussac's law** after J L Gay-Lussac (1778–1850, French chemist and physicist); **go to law with** to resort to litigation against; **Gresham's law** the law, formulated by Sir Thomas *Gresham* (1519–79), that of two forms of currency the inferior or more depreciated tends to drive the other from circulation, owing to the hoarding and exportation of the better form; **Grimm's law** the law formulating certain changes undergone by Indo-European stopped consonants in Germanic, stated by Jacob *Grimm* (1785–1863); **have** or **get the law on** (*colloq*) or **have the law of** (*archaic*) to enforce the law against; **Kepler's laws** three laws of planetary motion discovered by Johann *Kepler* (1571–1630): (1) the orbits of the planets are ellipses with the sun at one focus; (2) the areas described by their *radii vectores* in equal times are equal; (3) the squares of their periodic times vary as the cubes of their mean distances from the sun; **law of averages** see under **average**; **law of nations**, now **international law** (qv), *orig* applied to those ethical principles regarded as obligatory on all communities; **law of nature** the invariable order of nature; natural law; **law of octaves** see under **octave**; **law of supply and demand** the economic theory that the price of an item at a particular time is determined by conditions of supply and demand; **law of the jungle** the rules for surviving, succeeding, etc in a competitive or hostile situation by the use of force, etc; **law of the land** the established law of a country; **laws of motion** see under **motion**; **law of the Medes and Persians** see under **Median**; **lay down the law** to speak authoritatively or dictatorially; **Mariotte's law** see **Boyle's law** above; **Murphy's law** (*facetious*) the law which states that if anything can go wrong, it will; **Parkinson's law** see separate entry; **Snell's law** the law of refraction discovered by Willebrod *Snell* (1591-1626), a Dutch mathematician, which states that the sine of the angle of incidence divided by the sine of the angle of refraction is a constant, known as the refractive index; **Sod's law** see under **sod**[3]; **take the law into one's own hands** to obtain justice, or what one considers to be justice, by one's own actions, without recourse to the law, the police, etc; **the law** (*colloq*) the police; a policeman; **Verner's law** a law stated by Karl *Verner* in 1875, showing the effect of accent in the shifting of Indo-European stopped consonants and *s* in Germanic, and explaining the most important anomalies in the application of Grimm's law. [ME *lawe*, from late OE *lagu*, of ON origin, from the same root as **lie**[2] and **lay**[3]]

law[2] *lö*, (*obs*) *n* share of expense, score. — *n* **law'ing** or **law'in** (*Scot*) a bill or reckoning, *esp* in a bar or pub. [ON *lag* market-price]

law[3] *lö*, (*Scot*) *n* a hill, *esp* rounded or conical. [Northern form of **low**[3], OE *hlāw*]

law[4] *lö*, (*Scot*) *adj* low. — *n* and *adj* **law'land** lowland. [Northern form of **low**[2]]

law[5] *lö*, *interj* expressing asseveration (*obs*); expressing surprise (*dialect*). [Partly for **la** or **lo**, partly **lord** (qv)]

lawin and **lawing**. See **law**[2].

lawk *lök* or **lawks** *löks*, (*dialect*) *interj* expressing surprise. [**lord** or **lack**[2]]

lawn[1] *lön*, *n* a sort of fine linen or cambric; extended to some cottons. — *adj* made of lawn. — *adj* **lawn'y**. — **lawn sleeves** wide sleeves of lawn worn by Anglican bishops. [Prob from *Laon*, near Rheims]

lawn[2] *lön*, *n* a smooth space of ground covered with grass, generally beside a house; an open space between woods (*archaic*). — *adj* **lawn'y**. — **lawn'mower** a machine for cutting grass on a lawn; **lawn'-par'ty** (*US*) a garden-party; **lawn'-sprink'ler** a machine for watering a lawn by sprinkling; **lawn tennis** the modern game of tennis, played by one or two a side on an unwalled court (hard or of turf), the aim being to hit the ball over the net and within the court, if possible in such a way as to prevent its return. [**laund**]

lawrencium *lö-ren'si-əm*, *n* the name given to the element (symbol **Lr**; atomic no 103) first produced at Berkeley, California. [Ernest O *Lawrence* (1901–58), American physicist]

Lawrentian. See **Laurentian**.

lawyer, etc. See under **law**[1].

lax[1] *laks*, *adj* slack; loose; soft or flabby; not strict in discipline or morals; careless or negligent; loose in the bowels. — *adj* **lax'ative** stimulating loosening of the bowels; giving freedom (*archaic*); speaking or expressing itself freely (*obs*). — *n* a purgative or aperient medicine. — *n* **lax'ativeness**. — *n* **laxā'tor** a muscle that relaxes an organ or part. — *n* **lax'ism** the view that in morals an opinion only slightly probable may be safely followed. — *n* **lax'ist** a person holding loose notions of moral laws, or of their application. — *n* **lax'ity** or **lax'ness**. — *adv* **lax'ly**. [L *laxus* loose]

lax[2] *laks*, *n* a salmon (*usu* one caught in Swedish or Norwegian waters). [Revived use, from OE *leax*; OHGer *lahs*, ON *lax*; cf **lox**[2]]

lay[1] *lā*, *n* a form of **lea**[1,2,3].

lay[2] *lā*, *pa t* of **lie**[2].

lay[3] *lā*, *vt* to cause to lie; to place or set down; to beat down; to spread on a surface; to spread or set something on; to cover; to apply; to cause to subside; to exorcize; to deposit; to set on the table; to make (a bet), wager; to put forward; to cause to be; to set; to produce and deposit; to station; to locate; to put in (a particular) position; to waylay; to impose; to attribute or impute; to set material in position for making; to form (a rope, etc) by setting in position and twisting; to design or plan; to layer (*hortic*); to cause (a hedge) to grow more thickly by cutting some of the growth halfway through and pressing it diagonally towards the ground; to have sexual intercourse with (*slang*); to put below the horizon by sailing away; to give birth to a child (*obs*); to beset (*Shakesp*). — *vi* to produce eggs; to wager or bet; to deal blows; to lie (*archaic*, *naut* and *illiterate*): — *pr p* **lay'ing**; *pa t* and *pa p* **laid**. — *n* a situation, a place for lying; an oyster-bed; a way of lying; a disposition, arrangement or plan; a layer; a mode of twisting; laying activity; an act of sexual intercourse (*slang*); a partner, *usu* female, in sexual intercourse (*slang*); a bet (*Shakesp*); a share of profit, *esp* in whaling; a field or method of operation, *esp* in thieving (*slang*). — *n* **layer** (*lā'ər* or *lār*) someone who or something which lays, eg a hen, a bricklayer, etc; (*lār*) a course, bed or stratum; a distinctively coloured space between contour-lines on a map; a shoot bent down to earth in order to take root. — *vt* and *vi* to propagate by layers. — *vt* to put in layers; to cut (hair) in layers. — *vi* to be laid flat, lodge. — *adj* **lay'ered** in or with layers. — *n* **lay'ering**. — *n* **lay'ing** the first coat of plaster; the act or time of laying eggs; the eggs laid. — **lay'about** a lazy, idle person, a loafer; **lay'away** goods on which a deposit has been paid, kept for a customer until payment is completed (as *vt* **lay away**); **lay'back** in rock-climbing, a method of climbing a sharp-edged crack in a horizontal position. — Also *vi*. — **lay'-by** a widened area of a roadway to allow vehicles to draw up out of the stream of traffic: — *pl* **lay'-bys**; a deposit against future purchase (also **lay'-bye**; *SAfr*); **lay'-down** in card games, *esp* bridge, a hand which cannot fail to take the number of tricks required to win, and which therefore is sometimes exposed to view without any play taking place; the contract made by the holder of such a hand. — Also *adj*. — **lay'er-cake** a cake built up in layers; **lay'-off** a temporary suspension of work introduced by an employer as an economic measure; the act of laying off or period of time during which someone lays off or is laid off; **lay'out** something which is laid out; a display; an outfit; the disposition, arrangement, plan, *esp* of buildings or ground; the general appearance of a printed page, also called **format**; a set, unit or organization; **lay'-shaft** an auxiliary geared shaft in a machine, *esp* the secondary shaft in an automobile gearbox; **lay'stall** (*obs*) a place for depositing dung, rubbish, etc; **lay'-up** the time or condition of being laid up. — **lay aboard** to run alongside, *esp* in order to board; **lay about one** to deal blows vigorously or on all sides; **lay a course** (*naut*) to succeed in sailing to the place required without tacking; **lay aside** or **lay away** to discard; to put on one side for future use (see also **layaway** above); **lay at** to try to strike; **lay away** (*Scot*, etc) to lay eggs in out-of-the-way places; **lay bare** to show clearly, disclose; **lay before** to submit (eg plans) to; **lay by** to keep for future use; to dismiss; to put off; **lay by the heels** see under **heel**[1]; **lay down** to give up; to deposit, as a pledge; to apply (eg embroidery; *archaic*); to formulate; to assert (a law or rule); to store; to plant; to record; to lay on (*printing*); **lay hands on** see under **hand**; **lay heads together** (*archaic*) to confer together; **lay hold of** or **on** to seize; **lay in** to get in a supply of; **lay into** to beat thoroughly; **lay it on** to charge exorbitantly; to do anything, eg to exaggerate or flatter, excessively; **lay off** to mark off; to dismiss temporarily from employment as an economic measure; to cease (*colloq*); to doff (*archaic*); to harangue volubly; to hedge (*betting*); **lay on** to install a supply of; to provide; to deal blows with vigour; to arrange made-up pages in the correct order on the imposing surface (also **lay down**; *printing*); **lay on hands** see under **hand**; **lay oneself open to** to make oneself vulnerable to, or exposed to (criticism, etc); **lay oneself out to** (*archaic*) to make it one's professed object or practice, take great pains, to; **lay on load** (*Spenser*) to belabour; **lay on the table** see under **table**; **lay open** to make bare, to show or expose; to cut open; **lay out** to display; to spend (money); to plan; to arrange according to a plan; to prepare for burial; to knock unconscious; to take measures, seek; **lay siege to** to besiege; to importune; **lay the table** to put dishes, etc on the table in preparation for a meal; **lay to** to apply with vigour; to bring a ship to rest; **lay to heart** see under **heart**; **lay under** to subject to; **lay up** to store up, preserve; (*usu* in *passive*) to confine to bed or one's room; to put in dock for cleaning, repairs, etc or because no longer wanted for or fit for service; **lay upon** to wager upon; **lay wait** to lie in wait, or in ambush; **lay waste** to devastate; **on a lay** on shares instead of wages. [OE *lecgan* to lay, causative of *licgan* to lie; cf ON *leggja*, Ger *legen*]

lay[4] *lā*, *n* a short narrative poem; a lyric; a song. [OFr *lai*; origin obscure]

lay[5] *lā*, (*archaic*) *n* law; religious faith. [OFr *lei* (Fr *loi*), from L *lēx*, *lēgis* law]

lay[6] *lā*, *adj* of or relating to the people; not clerical; non-professional; not trumps (*cards*). — *n* the laity; a layman (*obs*). — *adj* **laic** (*lā'ik*) lay. — *n* a layman. — *adj* **lā'ical**. — *n* **lāic'ity** the state of being lay; the nature of the laity; the influence of the laity. — *n* **lāicizā'tion** or **-s-**. — *vt* **laicize** or **-ise** (*lā'i-sīz*) to make laical; to open to the laity. — *n* **lā'ity** the people as distinguished from some particular profession, *usu* the clerical; (*usu* with *cap*) *specif* one of the three divisions within the General Synod of the Church of England, the others being the Bishops and the Clergy. — **lay baptism** baptism administered by a layman; **lay brother** or **lay sister** a person under vows of celibacy and obedience, who serves a religious house, but is exempt from the studies and choir duties of monks or nuns; **lay clerk** a singer in the choir of an Anglican cathedral, etc; **lay communion** the state of being in the communion of the church as a layman; **lay impropriator** an impropriator who is a layman; **lay'man** one of the laity; a non-professional person; someone who is not an expert; **lay people**; **lay'person**; **lay reader** (in some branches of the Anglican communion) a man or woman who is not ordained but is licensed by a bishop to undertake a range of ecclesiastical duties; **lay sister** see **lay brother** above; **lay vicar** a layman who is vicar-choral in an Anglican cathedral; **lay'woman**. [OFr *lai*, from L *lāicus*, from Gr *lāikos*, from *lāos* the people]

lay-day *lā'-dā*, *n* one of a number of days allowed for loading and unloading of cargo (*commerce*); a day a vessel is delayed in port (*naut*). — **lay'time** the total time allowed. [Perh formed from **delay** and **day** combined with **time**]

layer. See under **lay**[3].

layette *lā-et'*, *n* a baby's complete set of clothing, etc. [Fr]

lay-figure *lā'-fig-ər*, *n* a jointed model used by painters; a living person or a fictitious character lacking in individuality. — Also (earlier) **lay'man**. [Du *leeman*, from *led* (now *lid*) joint, and *man* man]

laylock *lā'lək*, *n* an obsolete form of **lilac**.
layman. See under **lay**[6] and **lay-figure**.
lazar *laz'ər*, *n* a leper; a person with a pestilential disease such as leprosy. — *n* **Laz'arist** a member of the Roman Catholic Congregation of the Priests of the Mission, founded by St Vincent de Paul in 1624. — *adj* or *adv* **la'zar-like**. — **lazar house** a lazaretto. [From *Lazarus*, the beggar with leprosy, in the Bible (Luke 16. 20)]
lazaretto *laz-ə-ret'ō*, *n* a hospital for infectious diseases, *esp* leprosy; a place of quarantine; a place for keeping stores on a ship: — *pl* **lazarett'os**. — Also **laz'aret**. [Ital *lazzaretto*]
laze, lazily, etc. See under **lazy**.
lazo. Same as **lasso**.
lazuli *laz'ū-lī*. See **lapis lazuli** under **lapis**.
lazulite *laz'ū-līt*, *n* a blue mineral, hydrated phosphate of aluminium, magnesium, and iron. [LL *lazulum*, from Pers *lājward*; cf **azure**, **lapis lazuli** and **lazurite**]
lazurite *laz'ū-rīt*, *n* a blue cubic mineral, sodium aluminium silicate with some sulphur, a constituent of lapis lazuli. [LL *lazur*, from Pers *lājward*; cf **azure**, **lapis lazuli** and **lazulite**]
lazy *lā'zi*, *adj* reluctant to exert oneself; averse to work; sluggish. — *vi* **laze** (back-formation) to be idle. — *adv* **la'zily**. — *n* **la'ziness**. — **la'zy-bed** a bed for growing potatoes, the seed being laid on the surface and covered with earth dug out of trenches along both sides; **la'zy-bones** (*colloq*) a lazy or idle person; **lazy eye** an apparently healthy eye having, nevertheless, impaired vision; amblyopia; **la'zy-jack** a jack constructed of compound levers pivoted together; **lazy painter** (*naut*) see under **painter**[1]; **lazy Susan** a revolving tray, often with a number of separate dishes or sections for foods, intended to be placed on a dining-table, etc. — *n pl* **la'zy-tongs** a series of diagonal levers pivoted together at the middle and ends, capable of being extended by a movement of the scissors-like handles so as to pick up objects at a distance. — *adj* constructed on the model of lazy-tongs. [Origin unknown]
lazzarone *läd-zä-rō'nā* or *laz-ə-rō'ni*, *n* a Neapolitan beggar: — *pl* **lazzaro'ni** (*-nē*). [Ital]
lazzo *läd'dzō*, (*Ital*) *n* a piece of farce or comic dialogue in the commedia dell'arte: — *pl* **laz'zi** (*-ē*).
LB *abbrev*: Liberia (IVR).
lb *abbrev*: leg before (wicket) (*cricket*); leg bye (*cricket*); *libra* (*L*), pound weight.
LBC *abbrev*: London Broadcasting Company.
lbf *abbrev*: pound force.
LBS *abbrev*: London Business School.
lbw (*cricket*) *abbrev*: leg before wicket.
LC *abbrev*: Library of Congress (US).
lc *abbrev*: left centre; letter of credit; *loco citato* (*L*), in the place cited; lower case (*printing*).
LCC *abbrev*: London County Council (later **GLC**).
LCD *abbrev*: liquid crystal display; lowest common denominator (also without *caps*).
LCDT *abbrev*: London Contemporary Dance Theatre.
LCh or **LChir** *abbrev*: *Licentiatus Chirurgiae* (*L*), Licentiate in Surgery.
LCJ *abbrev*: Lord Chief Justice.
LCM or **lcm** (*math*) *abbrev*: least or lowest common multiple.
LCP *abbrev*: Licentiate of the College of Preceptors.
LCST *abbrev*: Licentiate of the College of Speech Therapists.
LD *abbrev*: Lady Day; lethal dosage; Low Dutch.
Ld *abbrev*: Lord.
LDC *abbrev*: less developed country.
LDL *abbrev*: low-density lipoprotein.
***L*-dopa**. See **dopa**.
Ldp or **Lp** *abbrev*: Lordship.
LDS *abbrev*: Latter-Day Saints; *laus Deo semper* (*L*), praise be to God always; Licentiate in Dental Surgery.
LDV *abbrev*: Local Defence Volunteers.
LEA *abbrev*: local education authority.
lea[1] *lē*, *n* open country, meadow, pasture, or arable. — Also **lay, lee, ley** (*lā* or *lē*). [OE *lēah*; dialect Ger *lohe*, *loh*; perh Flem *-loo* in place names, eg Water*loo*; confused with **lease**[4]]
lea[2] *lē*, *adj* and *n* fallow; (of) arable land under grass or pasture. — Also **lay** (*lā*) or **ley** (*lē* or *lā*). — **lea'-rig** an unploughed rig or grass field; **ley'-farm'ing** pasturing and cropping in alternating periods. [OE *lǣge*, found in *lǣghrycg* lea-rig]
lea[3] *lē*, **lay** or **ley** *lā*, *n* a measure of yarn, 80 yards of worsted, 120 of cotton, 300 of linen. [Perh connected with Fr *lier*, from L *ligāre* to bind]
leach[1] *lēch*, *vt* to allow (a liquid) to percolate through something; to subject (something) to percolation so as to separate the soluble constituent(s); to drain away by percolation. — *vi* to percolate through or out of; to pass out of by the action of a percolating liquid; to lose soluble elements by the action of a percolating liquid. — Also **letch**. — *n* **leach'ate** a liquid that has percolated through or out of some substance; a liquid that has been polluted or made toxic by percolating through rubbish; a solution obtained by leaching. — *n* **leach'ing**. — *adj* **leach'y** liable to be leached. — **leach'-trough** or **leach'tub** a trough or tub in which ashes are leached. — **bacterial leaching** the use of selected strains of bacteria to accelerate the acid leach of sulphide minerals. [OE *leccan* to water, irrigate or moisten]
leach[2] and **leachour**. Spenserian forms of **leech**[2] and **lecher**.
lead[1] *lēd*, *vt* to show the way by going first; to precede; to guide by the hand; to direct; to guide; to conduct; to convey; to cart (*dialect*); to induce; to live; to cause to live or experience; to adduce (*Scots law*); to have a principal or guiding part or place in; to play as the first card of a round (*cards*). — *vi* to be first or among the first; to be guide or chief; to act or play (a card) first; to cart crops to the farmyard (often with *in*); to afford a passage (to), or (*fig*) tend towards; of a newspaper, etc, to have as its main story, feature, etc (with *with*): — *pa t* and *pa p* **led**. — *n* first place; precedence; the amount by which one is ahead; direction; guidance; an indication; a precedent or example; a chief role; the player of a chief role; leadership; initiative; the act or right of playing first, or the play of whoever plays first; the first player of a side (*curling*, etc); a leash; a watercourse leading to a mill; a channel through ice; the course of a running rope from end to end; a main conductor in electrical distribution; the distance between successive contours on the same helix of a screw thread measured parallel to the axis of the screw. — *adj* chief; main; leading. — *n* **lead'er** a person who leads or goes first; a chief; in an orchestra, the principal first violin; the head of a party, expedition, etc; the leading editorial article in a newspaper (also **leading article**); the principal upward-growing shoot of a tree; a horse in a front place in a team; a tendon; a translucent connection between a fishing-line and bait; a line of dots to guide the eye (*printing*); the principal wheel in any machinery; an alternative name for a conductor (of an orchestra, etc) (*US*). — *n* **leaderette'** a brief newspaper leader. — *n* **lead'ership** the office of leader or conductor; those acting as leaders of a particular organization or group; ability to lead. — *n* **lead'ing** guidance; spiritual guidance; leadership; carting (crops, etc). — *adj* acting as leader; directing or controlling; principal; preceding. — **lead'er-ca'ble** a cable on the sea-bottom by which ships with induction-receiving apparatus can find their way into port; **lead'-in** the part of the groove on a record before the start of the recording (also **lead-in groove**; *opp* to *lead-out*); the cable connecting the transmitter or receiver to the elevated part of an aerial; the introduction to, or introductory passage of, a commercial, discussion, newspaper article, piece of music, etc. — Also *adj*. — **leading aircraftman** or **aircraftsman**, **aircraftwoman** or **aircraftswoman** the rank above aircraft(s)man or aircraft(s)woman; **leading business** (*rare*) the acting of the principal parts or roles in plays (by the **leading lady** and the **leading man**); **leading case** (*law*) a case serving as a precedent; **leading counsel** counsel who takes pre-

cedence over another in conducting a case; **leading edge** the edge first met; the foremost edge of an aerofoil or propeller blade; the rising amplitude portion of a pulse signal (*telecomm*); the forefront, *esp* in scientific or technical development (*fig*); **leading lady** or **leading man** the principle actress or actor in a play; **leading light** a very influential member; **leading note** (*music*) the seventh tone of a major or minor scale, which leads the hearer to expect the tonic to follow; **leading question** a question put in such a way as to suggest the desired answer; **lead'ing-strings** (*US*) children's walking reins; vexatious care or custody; **lead'-out** the part of the groove on a record after the recording has finished (also **lead-out groove**; *opp* to *lead-in*); a wire by which electric current can enter or leave an electronic instrument. — Also *adj*. — **lead time** (*orig US*) the time between the conception or design of a product, factory, alteration, etc and its production, completion, implementation, etc; the time taken for delivery of goods after an order has been placed. — **lead apes in hell** feigned to be the lot of old maids in after-life; **lead astray** to draw into a wrong course; to seduce from proper conduct; **lead by the nose** to make (someone) follow submissively; **Leader of the House of Commons** or **Lords** a senior member of the government in whom rests the primary authority for initiating the business of the House; **lead in** (*Scot*) to house the harvest; **lead in prayer** to lead the offering up of prayer in an assembly, uniting the prayers of others; **lead off** to begin or take the start in anything; **lead on** to persuade to go on, to draw on; to persuade to do something foolish; to trick or deceive in fun; **lead out** to conduct to execution or a dance; to bring out by preceding; to begin to play (*cards*); **leads and lags** (*commerce*) in international trade, the early payment of bills, dividends, etc to concerns abroad, and the delayed invoicing of foreign customers and delayed conversion of foreign currencies into sterling (in order to take advantage of expected changes in the rate of exchange), which have an effect on the balance of payments situation; **lead someone a dance** see under **dance**; **lead the way** to go first and guide others; **lead up to** to bring about by degrees, to prepare for by steps or stages; to play in challenge to, or with a view to weakness in (*cards*). [OE *lǣdan* to lead, *lād* a way; Ger *leiten* to lead]

lead[2] *led*, *n* a heavy soft bluish-grey metal (symbol **Pb**; atomic no 82); a plummet for sounding; a thin plate of lead separating lines of type (also **leading**); a pan or cauldron of lead, or of a kind once made of lead; a strip of lead, U- or H-shaped in cross-section, used to join pieces of stained glass or the panes of a lattice window, a came; blacklead graphite; the core of coloured material in a coloured pencil; a stick of graphite for a pencil; (in *pl*) sheets of lead for covering roofs, or a flat roof so covered. — *adj* made of lead. — *vt* to cover, weight or fit with lead; to join together (pieces of stained glass or a lattice window) with leads (often with *up*; also *vi*); to separate the lines of with leads (*printing*). — *adj* **lead'ed** fitted or weighted with or set in lead; separated by leads (*printing*). — *adj* **lead'en** made of lead; lead-coloured; inert; oppressive; depressing; heavy; dull. — *vt* and *vi* to make or become leaden. — *adv* **lead'enly**. — *n* **lead'enness**. — *n* **lead'ing** leads collectively; (also **lead**) the strip of lead separating lines of type (*printing*); the vertical space caused by such a strip. — *adj* **lead'less**. — *adj* **lead'y** like lead. — **lead'-arm'ing** (*naut*) tallow, etc placed in the hollow of a sounding-lead to ascertain the nature of the bottom of the sea, river, etc; **lead colic** see **lead poisoning** below. — *adj* **lead'en-stepp'ing** (*Milton*) moving slowly. — *adj* **lead'-free** see **unleaded**. — **lead glance** galena; **lead'-line** a sounding-line (*naut*); any of the lines on a stained glass cartoon indicating where the leads will lie in the finished work; **lead'-paint'** paint with red lead or white lead as its base; **lead'-pencil** a blacklead pencil for writing or drawing; **lead poisoning** plumbism, poisoning by the absorption of lead into the system, its commonest form being **lead colic**, or painter's colic; death by shooting (*slang*); **leads'man** a seaman who heaves the lead or plummet for sounding; **lead tree** tree of lead. — **eat lead** (*slang*) to be shot, be killed by shooting; **go down like a lead balloon** (*humorous*) to be conspicuously unsuccessful; **red lead** and **white lead** see under **red** and **white** respectively; **swing the lead** (*naut* and *military slang*) to invent specious excuses to evade duties; **tree of lead** Saturn's tree (qv). [OE *lēad*; Ger *Lot*]

leaf *lēf*, *n* one of the lateral organs developed from the stem or axis of a plant below its growing-point, *esp* one of those flat green structures that transpire and assimilate carbon; any similar structure, such as a scale or a petal; the condition of having leaves; leaves collectively; anything beaten thin like a leaf; two pages of a book on opposite sides of the same paper; a broad thin part, structure or extension, hinged, sliding or inserted at will, for folding doors, window-shutters, table-tops, drawbridges, etc; the tooth of a pinion; marijuana (*slang*): — *pl* **leaves** (*lēvz*). — *vt* and *vi* (with *through*) to turn the pages of (a book, etc). — *vi* (also **leave**) to produce leaves: — *pr p* **leaf'ing**; *pa p* **leafed**. — *adj* in the form of leaves. — *n* **leaf'age** foliage. — *adj* **leafed** (*lēft*) having leaves (also **leaved** *lēvd*). — *n* **leaf'ery** leafage. — *n* **leaf'iness**. — *adj* **leaf'less** having no leaves. — *n* **leaf'let** a little leaf; a division of a compound leaf; a single sheet of printed political, religious, advertising, etc matter, flat or folded, or several sheets folded together. — *vt* to distribute leaflets to. — *vi* to distribute leaflets: — *pr p* **leaf'leting**, or less correctly **leaf'letting**; *pa t* and *pa p* **leaf'leted** or less correctly **leaf'letted**. — *n* **leafleteer'**. — *adj* **leaf'like**. — *adj* **leaf'y** or **leav'y** covered with or having many leaves; leaflike. — **leaf'-base** the base of a leaf-stalk, where it joins the stem; **leaf'-bridge** a drawbridge with rising leaves swinging on hinges; **leaf'bud** a bud producing a shoot with foliage leaves only (not flowers); **leaf'-climb'er** a plant that climbs by means of its leaves (petioles or tendrils); **leaf'-curl** a plant disease of various kinds characterized by curling of the leaves; **leaf'-cushion** a swollen leaf-base; a pulvinus that serves as a hinge for leaf movements; a raised scar marking the position of a leaf; **leaf'-cutter** an insect (ant or bee) that cuts pieces out of leaves; **leaf'-cutt'ing** a leaf used as a cutting for propagation; **leaf'-fall** the shedding of leaves; the time of the shedding of leaves, *usu* autumn; premature fall of leaves; **leaf'-green** chlorophyll; **leaf'-hopper** a name for various hopping orthopterous insects that suck plant juices; **leaf'-in'sect** an orthopterous insect of the family Phasmidae with wing-covers like leaves; **leaf'-met'al** metal, *esp* alloys imitating gold and silver, in very thin leaves for decoration; **leaf'-mosa'ic** a name for various virus diseases of potato, tobacco, etc in which the leaf is mottled; the arrangement of leaves so as to avoid shading one another; **leaf'-mould** or **-soil** earth formed from decayed leaves, used with soil as a compost for plants. — *adj* **leaf'-nosed** having a leaflike structure on the nose, as certain bats. — **leaf'-roll** a potato disease; **leaf'-scar** a scar left by the fall of a leaf; **leaf'-sheath** a leaf-base more or less completely enveloping the stem; **leaf'-spring** a spring made up of narrow, curved strips of metal of increasing length; **leaf'-stalk** (*bot*) the petiole of a leaf; **leaf'-trace** a branch from the vascular system of the stem destined to enter a leaf. — **take a leaf out of someone's book** see under **book**; **turn over a new leaf** to begin a new and better course of conduct. [OE *lēaf*; Ger *Laub*, Du *loof* a leaf]

league[1] *lēg*, *n* a nautical measure, 1/20th of a degree, 3 international nautical miles, 5·556km (3·456 statute miles); an old measure of length, varying from the Roman league, 2·215km (1·376 modern English miles), to the French, 4·448km (2·764 miles), and the Spanish, 6·781km (4·214 miles), in general, eg in poetry, taken to be about 4·828km (3 miles). [LL *leuga*, *leuca* Gallic mile of 1500 Roman paces; poss Gaulish]

league[2] *lēg*, *n* a bond or alliance; a union for mutual advantage; an association or confederacy; an association of clubs for games; a class or group. — *vt* and *vi* to join in league. — *n* **lea'guer** a member of a league; (with *cap*) a member of the league against the Huguenots in the time of Henry III of France, of the Anti-Corn-Law League, or of the Irish Land League (*hist*). — **league match** a match between two clubs in the same league; **league table** a table in which clubs in a league are placed according to their performances, or (*fig*) any grouping made to reflect relative success, importance, etc. — **in league with** having made an alliance with, *usu* for a bad purpose; **in the big league** (*colloq*) among the most important, powerful, etc people, organizations, etc; **League of Nations** an international body, formed under a covenant drawn up in 1919, to secure peace, justice, scrupulous observance of treaties, and international cooperation generally, and superseded in 1945 by the United Nations; **not in the same league as** not of the same calibre, ability, importance, etc as; **top** or **bottom of the league** (*fig*) the highest or lowest in a particular field of achievement, or in quality. [Fr *ligue*, from LL *liga*, from L *ligāre* to bind]

leaguer[1] *lēg'ər*, (*archaic*) *n* a camp, *esp* of a besieging army; siege; (by confusion with **ledger**) an ambassador. — *vt* to beleaguer. — **lea'guer-la'dy** or **lea'guer-lass'** a female camp-follower. [Du *leger* a lair]

leaguer[2] *lēg'ər*, (*obs*) *n* an old Dutch liquid measure; a large cask. [Du *ligger* a tun]

leaguer[3]. See under **league**[2].

leak *lēk*, *n* a crack or hole in a vessel or container through which fluid may pass; passage through such an opening; an act of urination (*slang*); a place, means or instance of unintended or undesirable admission or escape (*lit* and *fig*); the *usu* unauthorized, but sometimes only apparently unauthorized, revealing of secret information; a piece of such information; a high resistance, *esp* serving as a discharging path for a condenser (*elec*). — *adj* (*obs*) leaky. — *vi* to have a leak; to pass through a leak. — *vt* to cause to leak; to let out or in by, or (*fig*) as if by, a leak; to divulge (secret information) without, or apparently without, authorization, or to cause this to be done. — *n* **leak'age** a leaking; something which enters, escapes or is revealed by leaking; an allowance for leaking. — *n* **leak'er**. — *n* **leak'iness**. — *adj* **leak'y**. — **leak out** (of air) to escape; (of secret information) to be divulged to the public without, or apparently without, authorization; **spring a leak** to become leaky; **take a leak** (*colloq*) to urinate. [OE *hlec* leaky; or perh reintroduced from Du or LGer *lek* leak; or ON *leka* to leak]

leal *lēl*, (*archaic* or *poetic*) *adj* true-hearted or faithful. — *adv* **leal'ly**. — *n* **lealty** (*lē'əl-ti*). — **Land o' the Leal** the home of the blessed after death, heaven. [OFr *leel*, *leiel*; doublet of **loyal**]

leam[1] or **leme** *lēm*, (*archaic*) *n* a gleam of light, a glow. — *vi* to shine. [OE *lēoma*]

leam[2] *lēm*. Same as **lyam**.

lean[1] *lēn*, *vi* to incline; to be or become inclined to the vertical; to rest sideways against something; to bend over; to swerve; to abut; to have an inclination; to rely. — *vt* to cause to lean: — *pa t* and *pa p* **leaned** (*lēnd*) or **leant** (*lent*). — *n* an act or condition of leaning; a slope; a thing to lean on (*archaic*). — *n* and *adj* **lean'ing**. — **lean'-to** a shed, greenhouse, conservatory, etc propped against another building or wall: — *pl* **lean'-tos**. — **lean on** (*slang*) to put pressure on, to use force on (a person); **lean over backwards** see under **backwards**. [OE *hlēonian*, *hlinian*, and causative *hlǣnan*; Du *leunen*]

lean[2] *lēn*, *adj* thin, without (much) flesh; not fat; without fat; unproductive; unprofitable, taking extra time (*printing*); (of ore) low grade, of marginal value (*min ext*). — *n* flesh without fat. — *adv* **lean'ly**. — *n* **lean'ness**. — *adj* **lean'y** (*Spenser*) lean. — *adj* **lean'-burn'** of, using or relating to a fuel-air mixture in which the fuel component is relatively low, so reducing the amount of fuel used and pollution produced. — **lean concrete** a non-load-bearing concrete of low cement content; **lean cuisine** cuisine minceur (qv). — *adj* **lean'-faced** having a thin face; slender and narrow, eg letters (*printing*). — *adj* **lean'-witt'ed** of little sense. [OE *hlǣne*; LGer *leen*]

LEAP *abbrev*: Life Education for the Autistic Person.

leap[1] *lēp*, *vi* to move with bounds; to spring upward or forward; to jump; to rush violently; to pass abruptly or over a wide interval. — *vt* to bound over; to cause to take a leap; of male animals, to mate with, cover: — *pr p* **leap'ing**; *pa t* and *pa p* **leaped** (*lēpt*) or **leapt** (*lept*). — *n* an act of leaping; a bound; the space passed or covered by leaping; a place of leaping; an abrupt transition; a wide gap or interval. — *n* **leap'er** a steeplechaser; someone who or something that leaps. — **leap day** an intercalary day in the calendar (29 February); **leap'-frog** a game in which two people, *esp* children, take turns in vaulting each other, the one stooping or crouching to become the other's vaulting-horse; any similar vault or jump (also *fig*); a method of advancing against an enemy force in which one part of an army engages with the enemy whilst the rear part advances (*military*). — *vt* and *vi* to jump (over) as in leap-frog (also *fig*); to go in advance of each other alternately (*military*; also *fig*): — *pr p* **leap'-frogging**; *pa t* and *pa p* **leap'-frogged**. — *adj* and *n* **leap'-frogging**. — **leap'ing-house** (*Shakesp*) a brothel; **leap'ing-time** (*Shakesp*) active youth; **leap second** a second added to or subtracted from one scale of time whenever necessary, to bring that scale into harmony with another scale or with the rotation of the earth; **leap year** a year with an intercalary day (*perh* because any anniversary after that day misses or leaps over a day of the week). — **by leaps and bounds** by a large amount or extent; very quickly; **leap in the dark** an act of which the consequences cannot be foreseen. [OE *hlēapan*; cf **lope**[1], **loup**[1], and Ger *laufen* to run]

leap[2] *lēp*, (*dialect*) *n* a basket; a wicker net. [OE *lēap*]

leaprous, **leaperous** and **leaporous**. Old spellings of **leprous**.

leapt. See **leap**[1].

lear[1], **leare**, **lere** or **leir** *lēr*, *vt* to teach (*archaic* and *Scot*); to learn (*Spenser*). — *n* something which is learned, a lesson; lore; learning (*Scot*). [OE *lǣran* to teach]

lear[2], **leer** or **lehr** *lēr*, *n* a glass-annealing oven. [Ety uncertain]

learn *lûrn*, *vt* to be informed; to get to know; to gain knowledge, skill or ability in; to teach (now *illiterate*). — *vi* to gain knowledge or skill: — *pa t* and *pa p* **learned** (*lûrnd*) or **learnt** (*lûrnt*). — *n* **learnabil'ity**. — *adj* **learn'able** that can be learned. — *adj* **learned** (*lûrn'id*) having learning; knowledgeable about literature, etc; skilful. — *adv* **learn'edly**. — *n* **learn'edness**. — *n* **learn'er** someone who learns; someone who is still in the early stages of learning. — *n* **learn'ing** what is learned; knowledge; scholarship; skill in languages or science (*obs*). — **learned helplessness** (*psychol*) the eventual passive acceptance of consistent violence, failure, oppression, etc, resulting in the cessation of all voluntary activity; **learning curve** a graph used in education and research to represent progress in learning; **learning support** in teaching, the term which has largely superseded *remedial* as relating to the education of pupils with learning difficulties. — **New Learning** the awakening to classical learning in the 16c, led (in England) by Colet, Erasmus, Warham, More, etc; **specific learning difficulty** dyslexia. [OE *leornian*; Ger *lernen*; cf OE *lǣran* (Ger *lehren*) to teach]

leary. Same as **leery** under **leer**[1].

lease[1] *lēs*, *n* a contract letting or renting a house, farm, etc for a term; tenure or rights under such a contract; the duration of such tenure; a hold upon, or prospect of continuance of, life, enjoyment, health, etc. — *vt* to grant or take under lease. — *adj* **leas'able**. — *n* **leas'er**

a lessee. — **lease'back** an arrangement whereby the buyer of a property leases it back to the seller (also called **sale and leaseback**); **lease'hold** land or property held by the occupier under a lease; a tenure by lease. — *adj* held by lease. — **lease'holder**. — *n* and *adj* **lease'-lend** same as **lend-lease** (see under **lend**). [Fr *laisser* to leave, from L *laxāre* to loosen, *laxus* loose]

lease[2] *lēz*, (*dialect*) *vi* to glean. — *n* **leas'ing** gleaning. [OE *lesan* to gather]

lease[3] *lēs*, *n* in weaving, a place or way of separating warp threads at the ends. — **lease'-band** or **lease'-rod** a band or rod above and below which the warp threads are placed. [Perh connected with **leash**]

lease[4] or **leaze** *lēz*, (*dialect*) *n* pasture. [See **leasow**]

leash *lēsh*, *n* a line for holding and controlling a dog, or a hawk; control by a leash, or (*fig*) as if by a leash; a set of three of anything, *esp* of animals. — *vt* to hold by a leash; to bind. [OFr *lesse* (Fr *laisse*) a thong to hold a dog by, from L *laxus* loose]

leasing *lēz'ing*, (*dialect*) *n* falsehood, lies; lying. — **leas'ing-mak'er** a speaker of seditious words; **leas'ing-mak'ing**. [OE *lēasung*, from *lēasian* to lie, from *lēas* false, loose; Gothic *laus*, OHGer *los*]

leasow or **leasowe** *lē'sō* or *-zō*, (*dialect*) *n* pasture. — *vt* and *vi* to pasture. [Same word as **lease**[4], from OE *lǣs* a meadow, in oblique cases *lǣswe*; cf **mead** and **meadow**]

least[1] *lēst*, *adj* (used as *superl* of **little**) little beyond all others; smallest. — *adv* in the smallest or lowest degree. — *n* the smallest amount; the lowest degree. — *adv* **least'aways**, **least'ways** (*dialect*) or **least'wise** (*rare* or *US*) at least; however (used to tone down a preceding statement). — **least energy principle** (*phys*) the principle stating that a system is in stable equilibrium only under those conditions for which its potential energy is a minimum (*phys*); **least time principle** see **principle of least time** under **principle**. — **at least** or **at the least** at the lowest estimate; at any rate. [OE *lǣst* (adj and adv); compar *lǣssa* (adj), *lǣs* (adv); no positive]

least[2] *lēst*, (*Spenser*) *conj* same as **lest**[1].

leasure (*Spenser*). An obsolete spelling of **leisure**.

leat or **leet** *lēt*, (*dialect*) *n* a trench for bringing water to a millwheel, etc. [OE *gelǣt*]

leather *ledh'ər*, *n* a tanned, tawed, or otherwise dressed skin; a strap or other piece of leather; the ball in certain games; human skin (*slang*); (in *pl*) clothes, *esp* riding breeches made from leather. — *adj* made of leather. — *vt* to apply leather to; to thrash (*colloq*). — *n* **leatherette'**® cloth or paper made to look like leather. — *n* **leath'ering** (*colloq*) a thrashing. — *adj* **leath'ern** of or like leather. — *adj* **leath'ery** resembling leather; tough. — **leath'er-back** a large variety of sea-turtle; **leath'er-cloth** a fabric coated on one face so as to resemble leather, also called **American cloth**; **leath'er-coat** (*Shakesp*) an apple with a rough coat, the golden russet; **leath'ergoods** objects and utensils made from leather; **leath'er-head** a blockhead; an Australian friarbird with a bare head; **leath'er-jacket** a name applied to various fishes; a grub of the crane-fly; **leath'er-knife** a curved knife for cutting leather. — *adj* **leath'er-lunged** (*-lungd*) strong-lunged, able to shout vigorously. — *adj* **leath'er-mouthed** (*-mowdhd*) of certain fish, having a mouth like leather, smooth and toothless. — **leath'er-neck** a sailors' name for a soldier or marine (from the leather stock once worn), *esp* now a US marine. — *adj* **leath'er-winged** (*Spenser*) having wings like leather. — **artificial leather** any of certain plastic materials treated so as to simulate leather; **fair leather** leather not artificially coloured; **morocco leather** see **morocco**; **patent leather**, also **japanned** or **lacquered leather** see under **patent**; **Russia leather** see under **Russia**; **split leather** leather split by a machine, for trunk-covers, etc; **white leather** tawed leather, having its natural colour. [OE *lether* leather; Du *leder*, Ger *Leder*]

leave[1] *lēv*, *n* permission; liberty granted; a formal parting; a farewell; permission to depart or be absent; permitted absence from duty; the time of this; holidays. — **leave'-taking** bidding farewell. — **French leave** see under **French**; **leave of absence** permission to be absent, or the (time of) permitted absence; **take leave** to assume permission; **take (one's) leave (of)** to depart (from), say farewell (to); **take leave of one's senses** to become irrational. [OE *lēaf* permission, cognate with *lēof* dear; see **lief**]

leave[2] *lēv*, *vt* to abandon or resign; to quit or depart from; to have remaining at death; to bequeath; to refer for decision, action, etc; to allow, or cause, to remain. — *vi* to desist; to cease; to depart: — *pr p* **leav'ing**; *pa t* and *pa p* **left**. — *n* **leav'er** someone who leaves, *esp* leaves school. — *n pl* **leav'ings** things left; relics; refuse. — **leav'ing-shop** an unlicensed pawnshop. — **be left with** to have remaining; **leave a little** or **leave much** (or **a lot**) **to be desired** to be slightly or very inadequate or unsatisfactory; **leave alone** to let remain undisturbed; **leave be** to leave undisturbed; **leave behind** to forget to bring, or leave intentionally or accidentally; to go away from (also *fig*); **leave go** (*colloq*) to let go; **leave it at that** to take no further action, make no further comment, etc; **leave off** to desist, to terminate; to give up using; **leave out** to omit; **leave unsaid** to refrain from saying. [OE *lǣfan*]

leave[3] *lēv*, (*Spenser*) *vt* to levy, to raise. [Fr *lever*]

leave[4], **leaved**, **leaves** and **leavy**. See under **leaf**.

leaven *lev'n*, *n* the ferment, eg yeast, that makes dough rise; anything that makes a general change. — *vt* to raise with leaven; to permeate with an influence. — *n* **leav'ening**. — *adj* **leav'enous** containing leaven. [Fr *levain*, from L *levāmen*, from *levāre* to raise, from *levis* light]

Leavisite *lē'vis-īt*, *n* a follower of the English literary critic and editor F R *Leavis* (1895–1978). — Also *adj*.

leaze. See **lease**[4].

Lebanese *ləb-ə-nēz'*, *adj* of (the) Lebanon or of its people. — *n* a native of (the) Lebanon.

lebbek *leb'ek*, *n* an Old World tropical mimosaceous timber tree (*Albizzia lebbek*). [Origin unknown]

Lebensraum *lāb'ənz-rowm*, (*Ger*) *n* space inhabited by living things; room to live (and, if necessary, expand); *specif* territory claimed as necessary for economic growth (as by the Nazis).

lecanora *lek-ə-nō'rə* or *-nö'*, *n* any lichen of the genus *Lecanora*, including the edible manna lichen of the steppes and deserts of Asia and Africa. [Gr *lekanē* a dish]

lecher *lech'ər*, *n* an excessively lewd man. — *vi* to practise lewdness. — *n* **lech** (*lech*; *slang*; back-formation from *lecher*) lust, a lewd desire; a lecher. — *vi* to lust. — *adj* **lech'erous** lustful; provoking lust. — *adv* **lech'erously**. — *n* **lech'erousness**. — *n* **lech'ery**. [OFr *lecheor*, from *lechier* to lick; OHGer *leccôn*, Ger *lecken*, Eng **lick**]

Lecher wires *lehh'ər wīrz*, *n pl* two insulated parallel stretched wires, forming a microwave electromagnetic transmission line. [Ernst *Lecher*, Austrian physicist (1856–1926)]

lechwe *lēch'wē* or *lech'wā*, *n* an African antelope, smaller than the water buck to which it is related. [Bantu; cf Sotho *letsa* antelope]

lecithin *les'i-thin*, *n* a very complex substance containing phosphorus, found in the yolk of an egg, in the brain, blood, etc. [Gr *lekithos* egg-yolk]

lect. *abbrev*: lecture; lecturer.

lectern *lek'tərn*, *n* a reading-desk (*esp* one from which the lessons are read in a church). — Also (*obs*) **lec'turn** or **lett'ern**. [LL *lectrīnum*, from *lectrum* a pulpit, from Gr *lektron* a couch]

lectin *lek'tin*, *n* any of a number of naturally occurring substances, *usu* proteins derived from plants, which act like antibodies but are not formed in response to an antigen. [L *lectus*, pa p of *legere* to choose, select]

lection *lek'shən*, *n* a reading; a lesson read in church. — *n* **lec'tionary** a book of church lessons for each day. [L *lectiō*, *-ōnis*, from *legere*, *lectum* to read]

lectisternium *lek-ti-stûr'ni-əm*, *n* an ancient Roman religious observance at which images of gods were placed on couches as if at a feast. [L, from *lectus* a couch, and *sternere* to spread]

lector *lek'tör* or *-tər*, *n* a reader, *esp* in a college; someone who has the duty of reading the Scripture lesson in a church service; an ecclesiastic in one of the minor orders, lowest in the Orthodox, second-lowest (next above doorkeeper) in the Roman Catholic. — *n* **lec'torate**. — *n* **lec'torship**. — *n* **lec'tress** a female reader. — **lector benevole** (*bi-nev'ə-li* or *be-nev'o-le*) kind reader. [L *lector*, *-ōris*, from *legere*, *lectum* to read]

lecture *lek'chər*, *n* a lesson or period of instruction; a discourse on any subject, *esp* a professorial or tutorial discourse; a long, formal, stern reproof; reading (*archaic*); an expository and discursive religious discourse; an endowed lectureship, eg the Bampton, Hulsean, etc. — *vt* to instruct by lectures; to instruct authoritatively; to reprove, scold lengthily and sternly. — *vi* to give a lecture or lectures. — *n* **lec'turer** a person who lectures; a college or university instructor of lower rank than a professor; one of a class of preachers in the Church of England, supported by voluntary contributions. — *n* **lec'tureship** the post or job of a lecturer; the foundation of a course of lectures. [L *lectūra*, from *legere*, *lectum* to read]

lecturn. See **lectern**.

lecythus *les'i-thəs*, *n* the Latinized form of **lekythos**. — *n* **Lec'ythis** the monkey-pot genus of **Lecythidā'ceae**, a family of tropical trees, including the Brazil-nut, cannonball-tree, and anchovy-pear. — *adj* **lecythidā'ceous**. [See **lekythos**]

LED *abbrev*: light-emitting diode (qv under **light**[1]).

led *led*, *pa t* and *pa p* of **lead**[1]. — *adj* under leading or control, *esp* of a farm or place held along with another by a non-resident. — **led captain** an obsequious attendant, a henchman; **led horse** a spare horse led by a servant; a sumpter-horse or pack-horse.

ledden *led'n*, (*Spenser*) *n* language, dialect or speech. [OE *lēden*, *lēoden*, language, from *lēode* people, confused with *lǣden* Latin, from L *Latīnum* Latin]

lederhosen *lā'dər-hōz-ən*, *n pl* short leather trousers with braces. [Ger, leather trousers]

ledge *lej*, *n* a shelf-like projection; a ridge or shelf of rocks; a lode or vein (of ore or rock); an attached strip; a raised edge (*obs*). — *adj* **ledg'y** having many ledges. [ME *legge*, prob from the root of **lay**[3]]

ledger *lej'ər*, formerly also **lidger** *lij'ər*, *n* the principal financial record-book of a company, in which details of all transactions, assets and liabilities are kept, and in which the records in all the other books are entered; a register or account book (*US*); a book that lies permanently in one place (*obs*); a horizontal timber in scaffolding; ledger-bait, ledger-tackle or ledger-line (*angling*); a flat grave-slab; (also **leidger**, **lieger** or **leiger**) a resident, *esp* an ambassador (*obs*). — *adj* resident or stationary. — *vi* to fish with a ledger-line. — **ledg'er-bait** (*angling*) fishing bait that is anchored to the bottom, the **ledg'er-tackle** being weighted; **ledg'er-line** a line fixed in one place (*angling*); a short line added above or below the stave where required (often **leg'er-line**; *music*). [Appar from OE *licgan* to lie, *lecgan* to lay]

ledum *lē'dəm*, *n* a plant of the Labrador tea genus (*Ledum*) of ericaceous plants. [Latinized from Gr *lēdon* ladanum]

lee[1] *lē*, *n* shelter; the sheltered side; the quarter toward which the wind blows; tranquillity (*obs*). — *adj* (*opp* of *windward* or *weather*) sheltered; on or towards the sheltered side. — *adj* **lee'ward** (also *naut* *lū'ərd* or *lōō'ərd*) relating to, or in, the direction towards which the wind blows. — *adv* towards the lee. — Also *n*. — **lee'-board** a board lowered on the lee side of a vessel, to lessen drift to leeward; **lee'-gage** or **lee'-gauge** position to leeward (*opp* of *weather-gage*); **lee shore** a shore on a ship's lee side; **lee side** the sheltered side; **lee tide** a tide moving in the same direction as the wind; **lee wave** (*meteorol*) a stationary wave, sometimes dangerous to aircraft, set up under particular conditions in an airstream to the lee of a hill or mountain range over which air is flowing; **lee'way** leeward drift; room to manoeuvre, latitude. — **lee licht of the mune** (in Scottish ballads) *perh* the pleasant moonlight; **make up leeway** to make up for lost time, ground, etc. [OE *hlēo*(*w*), genitive *hlēowes* shelter; ON *hlē*, LGer *lee*; see also **lew**[1]]

lee[2] *lē*, (*Spenser*) *n* a river. [Poss from the River *Lee*]

lee[3]. See **lea**[1], **lees** and **lie**[1]. — *n* **leear** (*lē'ər*) Scots form of **liar**.

leech[1] *lēch*, *n* the side edge of a sail. [Cf ON *līk*; Dan *lig*; Swed *lik* a bolt-rope]

leech[2] *lēch*, *n* a blood-sucking annelid worm, *usu* aquatic; someone who attaches himself or herself to another for personal gain; a physician (*archaic*). — *vt* to apply leeches to (a former medical treatment, drawing blood from a patient); to cling to like a leech; to drain. — *vi* (*usu* with *on*) to cling (to). — *n* **leech'craft** (*archaic*) the art of medicine. — *n* **leech'dom** (*archaic*) a remedy or prescription. [OE *lǣce*, perh orig two different words]

leechee. See **lychee**.

Lee Enfield *lē en'fēld*, *n* a type of rifle used by the British Army in the Boer War and World Wars I and II. [From J P *Lee*, US designer (1831–1904), and *Enfield*, the town where it was manufactured]

leek *lēk*, *n* a vegetable (*Allium porrum*) of the onion genus, with broad flat leaves and a slim white bulb which extends into a long stem, taken as the national emblem of Wales. — **eat the leek** (*Shakesp*) to be compelled to take back one's words or put up with insulting treatment. [OE *lēac* leek, plant; cf **charlock**, **garlic** and **hemlock**]

lee-lane *lē'lān'*, (*Scot*) *n* used only in phrases (**by**) **my**, **his**, **her** etc **lee-lane** quite alone. — Also **lee'some-lane**. [**lee** of obscure origin; see **lone**]

leep[1] *lēp*, *vt* to plaster with cow dung. [Hindi *līpnā*]

leep[2] *lēp*, (*dialect*) *vt* to boil, to scald. [Cf ON and Icel *hleypa* to curdle, from ON *hlaupa* to leap]

leer[1] *lēr*, *n* a sly, sidelong or lecherous look; complexion or colour (*Shakesp*). — *vi* to look lecherously; to glance sideways. — *n* and *adj* **leer'ing**. — *adv* **leer'ingly**. — *adj* **leer'y** cunning; wary (with *of* or *about*). [OE *hlēor* face, cheek]

leer[2]. See **lear**[2].

Leerie *lē'ri*, (*Scot*) *n* a nickname for a lamplighter, in full **Lee'rie-licht'-the-lamp**.

lees *lēz*, *n pl* sediment that forms during the fermentation or aging of an alcoholic liquor, eg wine. — *n sing* (*rare*) **lee**. [Fr *lie*, from LL *lia*]

leese *lēz*, (*Spenser* and *Shakesp*) *vt* to lose: — *pa t* **lore** (*lōr* or *lör*); *pa p* **lore** or **lorn** (in *Spenser*, in the sense of left). [OE *lēosan* (in compounds) to lose]

leesome-lane. See **lee-lane**.

leet[1] *lēt*, (*Scot*) *n* a selected list of candidates for a position. — **short leet** a select list for the final choice. [Origin uncertain, perh Anglo-Fr *litte* a list, or aphetic form of *élite*]

leet[2] *lēt*, (*hist*) *n* a court-leet; its jurisdiction or district; the right to hold it. [Anglo-Fr *lete* or Anglo-Latin *leta*, poss from OE *lǣth* lathe (of a county)]

leet[3]. See **leat**.

leet[4]. See **lite**[1].

leetle *lē'tl*, an old-fashioned affectation for **little**.

leeward and **leeway**. See under **lee**[1].

leeze. See under **lief**.

left[1] *left*, *pa t* and *pa p* of **leave**[2]. — *adj* **left'-off** laid aside or discarded. — *adj* **left'over** remaining over from a previous occasion. — *n* a thing left over; a survival; food uneaten at a meal (*usu* in *pl*). — **left-luggage office** a room at an airport or a railway or bus station where for a small fee one can safely leave one's luggage for a time.

left[2] *left*, *adj* on, for, or belonging to that side or part of the body, etc on that side which in man has normally the weaker and less skilful hand (*opp* to *right*); on that side from the point of view of a person looking downstream, a soldier looking at the enemy, a president looking at an assembly, an actor looking at the audience; on the west side from the point of view of a person looking north; in politics, relatively liberal, democratic, progressive, innovating; inclined towards socialism or communism. — *n* the left side; the region to the left side; the left hand; a blow with the left hand; a glove, shoe, etc for the left hand or foot, etc; the more progressive, democratic, socialist, radical or actively innovating party or wing (from its sitting in some legislatures to the president's left); a shot from the left barrel of a gun or a bird killed by this. — *adv* on or towards the left. — *adj* and *n* **left'ie** or **left'y** (often *derog*) (a) leftist. — *adj* **left'ish**. — *n* **left'ism** the principles of the political left. — *adj* and *n* **left'ist**. — *adj* and *adv* **left'ward** towards the left; on the left side; more left-wing. — Also *n* (*rare*). — *adv* **left'wardly** or **left'wards**. — **Left Bank** the artistic quarter of Paris on the south bank of the Seine. — *adj* **left'-bank**. — **left'field** in baseball, the area to the left facing from the plate; a player occupying this position. — *adj* (*slang, esp US*) out of the ordinary, bizarre. — *adj* **left'-footed** performed with the left foot; having more skill or strength in the left foot. — **left-foot'er** (*colloq*) a Roman Catholic. — *adj* **left'-hand** on the left side; towards the left; with thread or strands turning to the left; performed with the left hand. — **left-hand drive** a driving mechanism on the left side of a vehicle which is intended to be driven on the right-hand side of the road. — *adj* **left'-hand'ed** having the left hand stronger and readier than the right; for the left hand; counter-clockwise; forming a mirror-image of the right-handed form; awkward; unlucky; dubious (as in *a left-handed compliment*); of a marriage, morganatic. — *adv* **left'hand'edly**. — **left'-hand'edness**; **left'-hand'er** a blow with the left hand; a left-handed person; **left'-hand'iness** awkwardness. — *adj* **left'-of-centre** in politics, etc, towards the left, but only moderately so. — **left wing** the political left; the wing on the left side of an army, football pitch, etc. — *adj* **left'-wing** playing on the left wing; belonging to the more leftwardly inclined section; (having opinions which are) progressive, radical, socialist, etc. — **left'-wing'er** a person with left-wing views or who supports the left wing of a party, etc; a player on the left wing. — **have two left feet** to be clumsy or awkward, *esp* in dancing; **left, right and centre** in, from, etc all directions; everywhere; **over the left (shoulder)** (*obs slang*) contrariwise. [ME *lift, left*, from OE (Kentish) *left* weak, worthless; cf OE *lyftādl* paralysis]

lefte *left*, (*Spenser*) *pa t* lifted.

leg *leg*, *n* a limb for walking by; the human lower limb, or sometimes the part between knee and ankle; a long, slender support of eg a table; a branch or limb of anything forked or jointed, eg a pair of compasses; a single short trunk, as of a fruit bush not managed as a stool (qv), from which branches grow (*hortic*); the part of a garment that covers the leg; a distinct part or stage of a course or journey; in sports, one event or part in a contest consisting of two or more parts or events; in cricket, that part of the field, or that fielder, on or behind a line straight out from the batsman on the on side (also *adj*); a backward movement of the leg in making a bow (*archaic*); a swindler, *esp* at a race-course (for *blackleg*; *old slang*). — *vt* and *vi* to walk briskly, run or dash away (*vt* with *it*); to propel (a barge) through a canal tunnel by pushing with the feet on the wall or roof. — *adj* **legged** (*legd* or *leg'id*; *usu* as *combining form*) having (a certain type, number, etc of) legs. — *n* **legg'er** a bargeman who legs; a worker or machine that makes stocking-legs. — *n* **legg'iness**. — *n* **legg'ing** an outer and extra covering for the leg, eg (in *pl*) thick, footless tights, *usu* of wool or knitted fabric, or fashion varieties made in other, thinner materials; an outer and extra covering for the lower leg. — *n* **legg'ism** (*archaic*) the character of a blackleg. — *adj* **legg'y** having noticeably long slim legs. — *adj* **leg'less** having no legs; very drunk (*colloq*). — *n* **leg'lessness**. — *n* **leg'let** any object worn on the leg for decoration. — **leg bail** see **give leg bail** under **bail**[1]; **leg before** see **leg before wicket** below; **leg break** (*cricket*) a ball that breaks from the leg side towards the off side on pitching; a ball bowled to have this deviation; spin imparted to a ball to cause such a deviation; **leg'-bus'iness** (*slang*) ballet-dancing; **leg bye** (*cricket*) a run made when the ball touches any part of the batsman's person except his or her hand; **leg'-guard** a cricketer's pad; **leg'-iron** a fetter for the leg; **leg'-man** or **-woman** a person whose work involves journeys outside the office; an assistant who travels on errands or gathers information; a newspaper reporter. — *adj* **leg-of-mutt'on** shaped like a leg of mutton, eg a triangular sail; of a sleeve, tight on the lower arm and full between elbow and shoulder. — **leg'-over** (*vulg slang*) an act of sexual intercourse with a woman; **leg'-pull** a good-humoured hoax, bluff or practical joke; **leg'-puller**; **leg'-pulling**; **leg'-rest** a support for the legs; **leg'room** space for one's legs, as in a car; **leg'-show** an entertainment depending mainly on the exhibition of women's legs; **leg side** (or **the leg**; *cricket*) that half of the field nearest the batsman's legs (*opp* to *off side*). — *adj* **leg'-side**. — **leg slip** (*cricket*) a fielder or position on the leg side somewhat behind the batsman; **leg spin** (*cricket*) a leg break. — *adj* **leg'-spin**. — **leg spinner** (*cricket*) someone who bowls leg breaks; **leg theory** (*cricket*) the policy of bowling on the striker's legs with a trap of leg-side fielders; body-line; **leg warmers** long footless socks; **leg'wear** anything worn on the legs, eg socks, stockings, etc; **leg-woman** see **leg-man** above; **leg'work** (*colloq*) work involving much travelling, searching, etc. — **a leg up** a help or hoist in mounting, climbing, etc (also *fig*); **change the leg** (of a horse) to change the gait; **feel one's legs** to begin to support oneself on the legs; **find one's legs** to become familiar or accustomed; **fine, long, short** and **square leg** (*cricket*) fielding positions respectively fine from, far from, near to and square to the batsman on the leg side; **get one's leg over** (*vulg slang*; of a man) to have sex with a woman; **in high leg** (*archaic*) in great excitement; **leg before** or **leg before wicket** in cricket, a way of being given out as a penalty for stopping with the leg (or any part of the body except the hands) a straight or off-break ball that would have hit the wicket (*abbrev* **lbw**); **not have a leg to stand on** to have no case at all; **on one's last legs** see under **last**[4]; **on one's legs** standing, *esp* while speaking; **pull someone's leg** to make a playful attempt to hoax or deceive someone; **shake a leg** (*colloq*) to hurry up; **show a leg** to make an appearance; to get up; **upon one's legs** in an independent position. [ON *leggr* a leg; Dan *læg*, Swed *lägg*]

leg. *abbrev*: legal; legate; legato; legislation; legislative; legislature.

legacy *leg'ə-si*, *n* that which is left to one by will; a bequest of personal property. — *n* **leg'atary** a legatee. — *n* **legatee'** a person to whom a legacy is left. — *n* **legator** (*li-gā'tər*) a person who leaves a legacy. — **legacy duty** a duty levied on legacies, varying according to degree of relationship, abolished in 1950; **leg'acy-hunter** a person who courts those likely to leave legacies. — **cumulative legacy** an additional legacy to the same person; **demonstrative legacy** a general legacy with a particular fund named from which it is to be satisfied; **general legacy** a sum of money payable out of the assets generally; **residuary legatee** the person to whom the remainder of the property is left after all claims are discharged; **specific legacy** a legacy of a definite thing, such as jewels, pictures, a sum of stock in the funds, etc; **substitutional legacy** a second legacy to the same person instead of the first. [L *lēgāre, -ātum* to leave by will]

legal *lē'gl*, *adj* relating to, or according to, law; lawful; created by law; according to the Mosaic law or dispensation (*theol*). — *n* **lēgalese'** complicated legal jargon. — *n* **lē'galism** strict adherence to law; the doctrine that salvation depends on strict adherence to the law, as distinguished from the doctrine of salvation by grace (*theol*); the tendency to observe letter or form rather than spirit, or to regard things from the point of view of law. — *n* **lē'galist** someone inclined to legalism; someone knowledgeable about the law. — *adj* **lēgal-is'tic**. — *adv* **lēgalist'ically**. — *n* **lēgality** (*-gal'i-ti*). — *n* **lēgalizā'tion** or **-s-** a process whereby something previously unlawful is made lawful. — *vt* **lē'galize** or **-ise** to make lawful. — *adv* **lē'gally**. — **legal aid** financial assistance given to those unable to pay the full costs of legal proceedings; **legal eagle** (*colloq*) a bright, discerning lawyer; **legal fiction** a fact or point of law that is probably no longer true but is held to be so as a further point of law depends upon it; **legal tender** banknotes or coins which by law must be accepted as payment of a debt, or for a product or service; the currency of exchange, notes and coin, in a particular country; **legal year** see under **year**. [L *lēgālis*, from *lēx*, *lēgis* law]

legate *leg'it*, *n* an ambassador, *esp* from the Pope; a delegate deputy, *esp orig* a Roman general's lieutenant; the governor of a Papal province (*hist*). — *n* **leg'ateship**. — *adj* **leg'atine** (*-ə-tīn*) of or relating to a legate. — *n* **legation** (*li-gā'shən*) a diplomatic mission, body of delegates, or its official quarters; the office or status of legate; a Papal province (*hist*). [L *lēgātus*, from *lēgāre* to send with a commission]

legatee. See under **legacy**.

legato *le-gä'tō*, (*music*) *adj* and *adv* smooth or smoothly, the notes running into each other without a break (*superl* **legatis'simo**). — *n* a legato passage or manner: — *pl* **legat'os**. [Ital, bound, tied, from L *ligāre*, *-ātum* to tie]

legator. See under **legacy**.

legend[1] *lej'ənd*, *n orig* a story of a saint's life; a traditional story; an untrue or unhistorical story; a collection of such stories; a body of tradition; a person having a special place in popular opinion for their striking qualities or deeds, real or fictitious; the body of fact and fiction gathered round such a person; a motto, inscription, or explanatory words (with eg a picture); a book of readings from the Bible and saints' lives (*obs*). — *n* **leg'endary** a book or writer of legends. — *adj* relating to, of the nature of, consisting of, or described in, legend; romantic; fabulous. — *n* **leg'endist** a writer of legends. — *n* **leg'endry**. [Fr *légende*, from LL *legenda* to be read]

legend[2] *lej'ənd*, (*Shakesp*) *n* for **legion**.

leger *lej'ər*, (*obs cant*) *n* someone who sells short weight in charcoal; someone who swindles by scamping work, using bad materials. — *n* **leg'ering**. [Poss Fr *léger* light]

legerdemain *lej-ər-də-mān'*, *n* dexterous trickery or conjuring, sleight-of-hand; jugglery. — *adj* juggling; tricky. [Literally light of hand, from Fr *léger* light, *de* of, and *main* hand]

legerity *li-jer'i-ti*, *n* lightness; nimbleness. [Fr *légèreté*, from *léger* light, from assumed LL *leviārius*, from L *levis* light]

leger-line. See **ledger-line** under **ledger**.

legge *leg*, (*Shakesp*) *n* dregs of the people. [**lag**[1]]

legger, **leggism**, etc. See under **leg**.

leghorn *leg'hörn* or *li-görn'*, *n* fine straw plait made in Tuscany; a hat made of it; (*li-görn'*) a small breed of domestic fowl. [*Leghorn* (Ital *Legorno*, now *Livorno*, L *Liburnus*) in Italy]

legible *lej'i-bl*, *adj* clear enough to be deciphered; easy to read; readable (*rare*). — *n* **leg'ibleness** or **legibil'ity**. — *adv* **leg'ibly**. [L *legibilis*, from *legere* to read]

legion *lē'jən*, *n* in ancient Rome, a body of three to six thousand soldiers; a military force, applied *esp* to several in French history; a very great number. — *adj* (*rare*) multitudinous. — *adj* **le'gionary** of, relating to, or consisting of, a legion or legions; containing a great number. — *n* a member of a legion. — *adj* **le'gioned** set out in legions. — *n* **lēgionnaire** (*-nār'*; Fr *légionnaire*) a member of the British, Foreign, etc Legion. — **American Legion** an association of US war veterans; **British Legion** (in full **Royal British Legion**) an ex-servicemen's and -women's association; **Foreign Legion** a legion composed of foreigners, *esp* that in the French army organized in 1831; **Legionnaire's** or **Legionnaires' Disease** a severe, sometimes fatal, pneumonia-like disease caused by the bacterium *Legionella pneumophilia* (so named after an outbreak of the disease at an American Legion convention in Philadelphia in 1976); **Legion of Honour** a French order instituted in 1802 by Napoleon I; **their name is Legion** they are too many to number (from the Bible: Mark 5.9); **Thundering Legion** in Christian tradition, a body of soldiers under Marcus Aurelius, whose prayers brought down a thunderstorm and destroyed the enemy. [L *legiō*, *-ōnis*, from *legere* to levy]

legis. *abbrev*: legislation; legislative; legislature.

legislate *lej'is-lāt*, *vi* to make laws; to pass law in the form of an Act of Parliament or by delegated legislation. — *n* **legislā'tion**. — *adj* **leg'islātive** (or *-lə-tiv*) law-making; having the power to make laws; relating to legislation. — *n* a law-making power; a law-making body. — *adv* **leg'islatively**. — *n* **leg'islator** a lawgiver; a member of a legislative body: — *fem* (*rare*) **leg'islatress**. — *adj* **legislatorial** (*-lə-tö'ri-əl*) of or relating to, or of the nature of, a legislator, legislature or legislation. — *n* **leg'islatorship**. — *n* **leg'islature** a law-making body. [L *lēx*, *lēgis* law, *latum* serving as supine to *ferre* to bear]

legist *lē'jist*, *n* a person knowledgeable about the law. [Fr *légiste*]

legit *lij-it'*, (*colloq*) *adj* short form of **legitimate**.

legitim *lej'i-tim*, (*Scots law*) *n* that which children are entitled to out of a deceased father's moveable estate (also called **bairn's-part**). [L *lēgitima* (*pars*) lawful (part), from *lēx* law]

legitimate *li-jit'i-mit* or (*rare*) *-māt*, *adj* lawful; lawfully begotten, born in wedlock, or having the legal status of those born in wedlock; related, derived, or transmitted by birth in wedlock or subsequently legitimated; as used by believers in the theory of divine right, according to strict rule of heredity and primogeniture; logically inferred; following by natural sequence; genuine; conforming to an accepted standard; of or relating to legitimate drama (*theat*). — *vt* (*-māt*) to make lawful; to give the rights of a legitimate child to. — *n* **legit'imacy** (*-mə-si*) the fact or state of being legitimate. — *adv* **legit'imately**. — *n* **legit'imateness**. — *n* **legitimā'tion** the act of making legitimate, *esp* of conferring the privileges of legitimate birth. — *n* **legit'imism**. — *n* **legit'imist** a person who believes in the right of royal succession according to the principle of heredity and primogeniture. — *n* **legitimizā'tion** or **-s-**. — *vt* **legit'imize** or **-ise** to legitimate. — **legitimate drama** drama of typical form, normal comedy and tragedy, distinguished from opera, musicals, variety, etc, as well as cinema and television; drama of lasting relevance and value; **legitimate pollination** in heterostyled plants, pollination of long styles from long stamens, and short from short. [LL *lēgitimāre*, *-ātum*, from L *lēgitimus* lawful, from *lēx* law]

leglin, **leglan** or **leglen** *leg'lən*, (*Scot*) *n* a milking-pail. — **cast a leglin girth** to have an illegitimate child. [Cf **laggen**]

Lego® *leg'ō*, *n* a toy consisting of small interlocking plastic pieces, principally bricks for constructing model buildings, etc. — *adj* of buildings, simply and cheaply constructed, jerry-built (*fig*). — **Leg'oland** (*fig*) an area of buildings of this kind. [Dan *leg godt* play well, invented by Godfred Kirk Christiansen, *Legoland* from the model village in Jutland, made with these bricks]

legume *leg'ūm* or *li-gūm'*, *n* any plant of the pea or bean family, including lentils; the seed pod of such a plant, *esp* when eaten as a vegetable. — *n* **legū'min** a globulin obtained from peas, beans, lentils, etc. — *n pl* **Legūminō'sae** (*-sē*) an order of angiosperms characterized by the legume or seed pod, including Papilionaceae, Mimosaceae, and Caesalpiniaceae. — *adj* **legū'minous** relating to pulse vegetables; of or relating to the Leguminosae; bearing legumes. [L *legūmen* pulse, prob from *legere* to gather]

lehr. See **lear**[2].

Lehrjahre *lār'yä-rə*, *n* or *n pl* (also without *cap*) an apprenticeship (*usu fig*). [Ger, from *lehren* to teach, and *Jahre* years]

lei[1]. See **leu**.

lei[2] *lā'ē*, *n* a garland or wreath, *esp* of flowers, shells or feathers. [Hawaiian]

Leibnitzian or **Leibnizian** *līb-nit'si-ən*, *adj* relating to the great German philosopher and mathematician Gottfried Wilhelm *Leibniz* (1646–1716). — *n* **Leibnitz'ianism** or **Leibniz'ianism** the philosophy of Leibniz, the doctrine of primordial monads, pre-established harmony, and fundamental optimism on the principle of sufficient reason.

Leicester *les'tər*, *adj* of a long-woolled breed of sheep that originated in *Leicestershire*. — *n* a sheep of that breed. — **Leicester** (or **Leicestershire**) **plan** a comprehensive school system, started in Leicestershire in 1957, which avoids the use of very large schools and also makes full use of free modern methods of learning.

Leics. *abbrev*: Leicestershire.

leidger and **leiger**. See **ledger**.

leiotrichous *lī-ot'ri-kəs*, *adj* straight-haired. — *n* **leiot'richy** (*-ki*) straight-hairedness. [Gr *leios* smooth, and *thrix*, *trichos* hair]

Leip. *abbrev*: Leipzig.

leipoa *lī-pō'ə*, *n* any bird of the genus *Leipoa* of Australian mound-birds. [Gr *leipein* to leave, forsake, and *ōon* an egg]

Leipzig option *līp-tzig op'shən*, *n* the strategic possibility of toppling a government, regime, etc by mass demonstrations. [From the use of this method in defeating Communism in E Germany in 1989]

leir. See **lear**[1].

leish *lēsh*, (*Scot*) *adj* active, supple or athletic. [Origin uncertain]

leishmania *lēsh-mān'i-ə* or *-man'i-ə*, *n* any protozoon of the genus *Leishmania* of Protozoa (family Trypanosomidae), or any protozoon of the Trypanosomidae in a non-flagellated form: — *pl* **leishman'ia**, **leishman'iae** (*-i-ē*) or **leishman'ias**. — *n* **leishmaniasis** (*lēsh-mən-ī'ə-sis*) or **leishmaniō'sis** any of various diseases, such as kala-azar, due to infection with any protozoon of the genus *Leishmania*: — *pl* **leishmanī'ases** or **leishmanī'oses**. [Named after Sir William *Leishman* (1865–1926), who discovered the cause of kala-azar]

leisler *līz'lər*, *n* a small black bat (*Nyctalus leisleri*) named after the 19c zoologist T P *Leisler*. — Also **Leisler's bat**.

leister *lēs'tər*, (*Scot*) *n* a salmon-spear. — *vt* to spear with a leister. [ON *ljōstr*; Dan *lyster*]

leisure *lezh'ər* or (*US* and *old-fashioned*) *lēzh'ər*, *n* time away from work; freedom from occupation, free-time; convenient opportunity. — *adj* free from necessary business; for casual wear; for or relating to leisure, recreational time or pursuits. — *vi* (*archaic*) to have leisure. — *vt* (*archaic*) to make leisurely. — *adj* **leis'urable** leisured; leisurely. — *adv* **leis'urably**. — *adj* **leis'ured** having much leisure. — *adj* and *adv* **leis'urely** not hasty or hastily. — **leisure centre** a centre providing a variety of recreational facilities; **leisure suit** a loose-fitting garment comprising matching top and trousers made from a soft fabric; **leisure wear** comfortable, casual clothing worn on informal or recreational occasions. — **at leisure** or **at one's leisure** free from occupation; at one's ease or convenience. [OFr *leisir*, from L *licēre* to be permitted]

leitmotiv or **leitmotif** *līt'mō-tēf*, *n* (in opera, etc) a musical theme associated with a person or a thought, recurring when the person appears on the stage or the thought becomes prominent in the action; a recurring theme in literature; any recurring theme. [Ger, from *leiten* to lead, and *Motiv* a motif]

lek[1] *lek*, *n* the standard monetary unit of Albanian currency (100 *qintars*); a coin or note of this value.

lek[2] *lek*, *n* the piece of ground on which the blackcocks and cock capercailzies gather to display; the season during which this displaying takes place. — *vt* to gather and display at a lek. — *n* **lekk'ing**. [Appar from Swed *leka* to play]

leke. Spenserian form of **leak** (*adj*).

lekythos *lē'ki-thos*, (*antiq*) *n* a narrow-necked Greek flask. [Gr *lēkythos*]

LEM or **lem** *lem*, *abbrev*: Lunar Excursion Module.

leman *lem'ən* or *lēm'*, (*archaic*) *n* a lover; a sweetheart; a paramour; later chiefly applied *derog* to women: — *pl* **lem'ans**. [OE *lēof* lief, and *mann* man]

leme. See **leam**[1].

lemel or **limail** *lē'mel*, *n* the dust and filings of metal. [ME *lemaille*, from MFr *lemaille*, from OFr *limer* to file, from L *limāre* to file]

lemma *lem'ə*, *n* a preliminary proposition (*math*); a premise taken for granted (*math*); a theme, argument, heading or headword: — *pl* **lemm'as** or **lemm'ata**. — *vt* **lemm'atize** or **-ise** to organize (words in a text) so that inflected and variant forms are grouped under the appropriate lemma. [Gr *lēmma*, *-atos*, from the root of *lambanein* to take]

lemming *lem'ing*, *n* a northern rodent (of the genus *Lemmus* and others) closely related to voles; a fool, *esp* a person unthinkingly following others to disaster (from the rodent's reputed habit of rushing en masse into the sea to drown when migrating; *colloq*). [Norw *lemming*]

Lemna *lem'nə*, *n* the duckweed genus, giving its name to the family **Lemnā'ceae**, free-floating spathifloral monocotyledons. [Gr *lemna* water starwort]

Lemnian *lem'ni-ən*, *adj* relating to *Lemnos* in the Aegean Sea. — **Lemnian earth** an earthy clay from Lemnos; **Lemnian ruddle** a red ochre found in Lemnos.

lemniscate *lem-nis'kāt*, (*math*) *n* the locus of the foot of the perpendicular from the centre of a conic upon the tangent. [L *lēmniscātus* riboned, from Gr *lēmniskos* a ribbon or bandage]

lemon[1] *lem'ən*, *n* a pale yellow oval citrus fruit with sour-tasting flesh; the tree that bears it; a pale yellow colour; something or someone disappointing, worthless, unattractive or defective (*slang*). — *adj* flavoured with lemon; (coloured) pale yellow. — *vt* to flavour with lemon. — *n* **lemonade'** a drink (still or carbonated) made with lemon juice or more or less flavoured with lemon. — *adj* **lem'ony**. — **lemon balm** same as **balm** (*Melissa officinalis*); **lemon cheese** or **lemon curd** a soft cooked paste of lemons, eggs, butter and sugar, used as a spread. — *adj* **lem'on-coloured**. — **lemon drop** a hard lemon-flavoured sweet; **lem'onfish** (*NZ*) shark meat sold as food; **lem'on-grass** a fragrant perennial grass (*Cymbopogon* or *Andropogon*) of tropical climates, smelling like lemon and yielding an essential oil; **lemon peel** the skin of lemons, sometimes candied; **lemon squash** a concentrated lemon drink; **lemon squeezer** a small hand-press for extracting the juice of lemons; **lem'on-weed** sea-mat. — *n* and *adj* **lem'on-yell'ow**. — **hand someone a lemon** (*slang*) to swindle someone; **the answer is a lemon** (*colloq*) one is given an unsatisfactory answer or no answer at all. [Fr *limon* (now the lime); cf Pers *līmūn*; cf **lime**[2]]

lemon[2] *lem'ən*, *n* a species of sole differing in its markings from the common sole (also **lem'on-sole'** or **sand sole**); a kind of dab resembling a sole (**lem'on-dab'**, **lem'on-sole'**, also called **smear-dab** or **smooth dab**). [Fr *limande*]

lempira *lem-pē'rə*, *n* the standard monetary unit of Honduras (100 centavos). [*Lempira*, a department of Honduras named after a native chief]

lemur *lē'mər*, *n* any member of the **Lemuroidea** (*lem-ū-roid'i-ə*) or **Prosimiae**, a group of long-tailed mammals related to the monkeys, forest dwellers, mainly nocturnal, common in Madagascar (*pl* **lē'murs**); an ancient Roman ghost of the dead (*pl* **lemures** *lem'ū-rēz*). — *n*

Lemuria (*li-mū'ri-ə*; *pl*) an ancient Roman festival (9, 11, and 13 May) when ghosts were exorcized; (*sing*) a hypothetical vanished continent where the Indian Ocean now is, posited to explain the distribution of lemurs. — *n* and *adj* **lemurian** (*li-mū'ri-ən*), **lemurine** (*lem'ū-rīn*) or **lem'ūroid**. [L *lemurēs* ghosts]

lend *lend*, *vt* to give the use of for a time; to provide, grant or supply in general; to supply (money) at interest; to let for hire. — *vi* to make a loan: — *pr p* **lend'ing**; *pa t* and *pa p* **lent**. — *n* (*Scot*) a loan (often **len'**). — *n* **lend'er**. — *n* **lend'ing** the act of giving in loan; something which is lent or supplied (*Shakesp*). — **lend'-lease** in World War II, an arrangement authorized by Congress in 1941 by which the US President could supply war materials to other countries whose defence he considered vital to the United States. — Also *adj*. — **lend an ear** (*colloq*) to listen; **lend itself to** to be able to be used for. [OE *lǣnan*, from *lǣn*, *lān* a loan]

lenes. See **lenis**.

leng *leng*, (*obs*) *vi* to lengthen; to tarry; to long (*Spenser*). [OE *lengan*]

lenger *leng'gər*, *adj* and *adv* (*Spenser*) longer. — *adj* and *adv* **leng'est** (*obs*) longest. [OE *lengra*, compar of *lang* (adj), *lengest*, superl of *lang* and of *lange* (adv)]

length *length*, *n* the quality of being long; extent from end to end; the longest measure of anything; long duration; prolixity; time occupied in uttering a vowel or syllable (*phonetics*); the quantity of a vowel; any definite portion of a known extent; a stretch or extent; distance (chiefly *Scot*); a suitable distance for pitching a cricket ball; the lengthwise measurement of a horse, boat, etc (*racing*). — *combining form* **-length** stretching downwards, or sometimes along, as far as, eg *knee-length*, *arm's-length*. — *vt* and *vi* **length'en** to increase in length. — *adj* (*obs*) **length'ful**. — *adv* **length'ily**. — *n* **length'iness**. — *adv* **length'ways** or **length'wise** in the direction of the length. — *adj* **length'y** of great or tedious length; rather long. — **length'sman** someone responsible for the upkeep of a particular stretch of road or railway. — **at length** in full; fully extended; at last; **go the length of** to go as far as (also *fig*); **go to great lengths**, **all lengths**, **any length** or **lengths** to do everything possible (sometimes more than is ethical) to achieve a purpose; **length of days** prolonged life. [OE *lengthu*, from *lang* long]

lenient *lēn'yənt* or *lē'ni-ənt*, *adj* mild; tolerant; merciful; softening (*archaic*); soothing (*archaic*). — *n* (*med*; *archaic*) something which softens; an emollient. — *n* **lē'nience** or **lē'niency**. — *adv* **lē'niently**. — *vt* **lenify** (*len'* or *lēn'*; *archaic*) to mitigate or assuage. — *adj* **lenitive** (*len'*) soothing; mitigating; laxative. — *n* any palliative; an application for easing pain (*med*); a mild purgative (*archaic*). — *n* **lenity** (*len'*) mildness; clemency. [L *lēniēns*, *-entis*, pr p of *lēnīre* to soften, from *lēnis* soft]

Leninism *len'in-izm*, *n* the political, economic and social principles and practices of the Russian revolutionary leader, Vladimir Ilyich Ulyanov *Lenin* (1870–1924), *esp* his theory of government by the proletariat. — *n* and *adj* **Len'inist** or **Len'inite**.

lenis *lē'nis*, (*phonetics*) *adj* of a consonant, articulated with relatively little muscular effort and pressure of breath (*opp* to *fortis*). — Also *n*: — *pl* **lē'nes** (*-ēz*). — *n* **lenition** (*li-nish'ən*) a softening of articulation, common in Celtic languages. [L, soft]

lenitive and **lenity**. See under **lenient**.

leno *lē'nō*, *n* a thin muslin-like fabric: — *pl* **lē'nos**. [Perh Fr *linon*]

lenocinium *lē-nō-sin'i-əm*, (*Scots law*) *n* connivance at one's wife's adultery. [L *lēnōcinium* enticement, from *lēnō* a pander]

lens *lenz*, *n* a piece of transparent matter (glass, plastic, etc) with one or both surfaces curved to cause regular convergence or divergence of rays passing through it; the refracting structure (*crystalline lens*) between the crystalline and vitreous humours of the eye; a mechanical equivalent of the human lens on a camera, allowing the subject image to fall on the eye or (on the opening of the shutter) the film plane (see also **fisheye lens** under **fish**, **telephoto lens** under **telephoto**, and **wide-angle** under **wide**); a contact lens; a device to influence the direction of sound waves (*acoustic lens*); (with *cap*) the lentil genus: — *pl* **lens'es**. — **lens hood** a piece fitted around or over a camera lens to shield it from a direct source of light; **lens'man** (*colloq*) a cameraman. — **electron lens** any arrangement of electrodes designed to influence the direction of cathode rays. [L *lēns*, *lentis* lentil]

Lent *lent*, *n* in the Christian religion, the time from Ash Wednesday to Easter observed in the Western Churches (a longer period in the Eastern Churches) as a time of fasting in commemoration of Christ's fast in the wilderness (Matt 4.2); a similar observance in other religions; any period of fasting (*fig*); spring (*obs*). — *adj* **Lent'en** (also without *cap*) of Lent; meagre; fleshless. — **lenten rose** a herbaceous perennial, *Helleborus orientalis*, which flowers from February to April; **lent'-lil'y** the daffodil. [OE *lencten* the spring; Du *lente*, Ger *Lenz*]

lent *pa t* and *pa p* of **lend**.

lentamente, **lentando** and **lenti**. See under **lento**.

Lenten and **lenten**. See under **Lent**.

Lentibulariaceae *len-tib-ū-lā-ri-ā'si-ē*, *n pl* the bladderwort and butterwort family of tubifloral dicotyledons. [Origin obscure]

lentic *len'tik*, (*ecol*) *adj* associated with standing water; inhabiting ponds, swamps, etc. [L *lentus* slow]

lenticel *len'ti-sel*, (*bot*) *n* a breathing pore in bark. — *adj* **lenticell'ate**. [New L *lenticella*, from L *lenticula*, dimin of *lens*, *lentis* lentil]

lenticle *len'ti-kl*, *n* (*geol*) a lenticular mass. — *adj* **lenti'cūlar** shaped like a lens or lentil seed; double-convex. — *n* a three-dimensional picture made up of photographs of a scene which have been taken from several different angles, split into strips, juxtaposed, and laminated with corrugated plastic, the corrugations acting as lenses to create an illusion of depth. — *adv* **lentic'ūlarly**. — *adj* **lent'iform** or **lent'oid** lenticular. [L *lens*, *lentis* lentil]

lentiform. See under **lenticle**.

lentigo *len-tī'gō*, *n* a freckle or (as *sing*) freckles: — *pl* **lentigines** (*len-tij'i-nēz*). — *adj* **lentig'inose** or **lentig'inous** (*bot*) minutely dotted. [L *lentīgō*, *-inis* a freckle, from *lēns* a lentil]

lentil *len'til*, *n* a leguminous annual plant (*Lens esculenta*, or *Ervum lens*) common near the Mediterranean; its small, flattish, round seed, orange or brown, used for food. [OFr *lentille*, from L *lēns*, *lentis* the lentil]

lentisk *len'tisk*, *n* the mastic tree. [L *lentiscus*]

lentivirus *len'ti-vī-rəs*, *n* a slow virus. [New L, from L *lentus* slow, and **virus**]

lento *len'tō*, (*music*) *adj* slow. — *adv* slowly. — *n* a slow passage or movement: — *pl* **len'tos** or **len'ti** (*-tē*). — *adv* **lentamen'te** (*-tā*). — *adj* and *adv* **lentan'do** slowing. — *adj* and *adv* **lentiss'imo** very slow or slowly. [Ital, from L *lentus* slow]

lentoid. See under **lenticle**.

lentor *len'tör*, (*archaic*) *n* sluggishness; viscidity. — *adj* **len'tous**. [L *lentus* slow]

lenvoy *len-voi'*. Same as **envoy**[2]. [Fr *l'envoi* the envoy]

Leo *lē'ō*, *n* the Lion, a constellation between Cancer and Virgo; the 5th sign of the zodiac, in which it used to be (the constellation is now in the sign Virgo); a person born between 24 July and 23 August, under the sign of Leo. — *n* **Lē'onid** (*-ə-nid*) a meteor of a swarm whose radiant is in the constellation Leo. — *adj* **Lē'onine** relating to any of the Popes named *Leo*; of a kind of Latin verse, generally alternate hexameter and pentameter, rhyming at the middle and end (*prob* from some unknown poet named Leo, Leoninus, or Leonius); (without *cap*) lionlike. [L *leō*, *-ōnis* lion]

leone *lē-ō'nē*, *n* the standard monetary unit of Sierra Leone (100 Sierra Leone cents).

leontiasis *lē-ont-ī'ə-sis, n* a form of leprosy in which the face takes on a lionlike appearance. [Gr *leontiāsis*, from *leōn, -ontos* lion]

leopard *lep'ərd, fem* **leop'ardess** *lep'ərd-es, n* a large spotted animal of the cat family found in Africa and Asia, also called the panther; in N America, the jaguar or any similar large cat; a lion passant gardant (also *rarely*, **leop'ardess**; *heraldry*). — **leop'ard-cat** a spotted wild cat of the Indian subcontinent; **leop'ard-moth** a white moth (*Zeuzera pyrina*) with black spots on its wings and body; **leop'ard's-bane** a composite plant, *Doronicum*; **leop'ard-wood** letter-wood. — **hunting leopard** the cheetah; **snow leopard** a Central Asian relative of the leopard, with pale fur and dark markings, the ounce. — **the leopard cannot change its spots** personality traits cannot be changed. [OFr, from L *leopardus*, from Gr *leopardos* (for *leontopardos*), from *leōn* lion, and *pardos* pard]

leotard *lē'ə-tärd, n* a skin-tight garment worn by dancers, acrobats, etc, sleeveless or long-sleeved, with legs varying from none at all to ankle-length. [Jules *Léotard*, 19th-century French trapeze artist]

lep *lep, vi* (*dialect, esp Ir*) for **leap**[1]; also *dialect* for the *pa t*. — *pa t* (*Spenser*) **lepp'ed**.

leper *lep'ər, n* a person affected with leprosy; a spurned person (*fig*); an outcast; leprosy (*obs*). [OFr *lepre*, from L *lepra*, from Gr *leprā*: see ety for **lepra**]

lepid *lep'id, adj* pleasant or jocose. [L *lepidus*]

lepid- *lep'id-* or **lepido-** *lep-id-ō-* or *-o'*, *combining form* denoting scales. — *n* **Lepidoden'dron** (Gr *dendron* tree) a genus of fossil trees, mainly Carboniferous, of the **Lepidodendrā'ceae**, related to Lycopodiaceae, the stem covered with ovate leaf-scars arranged spirally. — *adj* and *n* **lepidoden'droid**. — *n* **lepid'olite** (Gr *lithos* stone) a lithia mica, *usu* pink. — *n* **lepidomelane'** (Gr *melās, -anos* black) a black mica rich in iron, occurring in scales. — *n pl* **Lepidop'tera** (Gr *pteron* wing) an order of insects, with four wings covered with fine scales, the butterflies and moths. — *n* **lepidop'terist** a person who studies butterflies and moths. — *n* **lepidopterol'ogy**. — *adj* **lepidop'terous**. — *n* **Lepidosī'ren** (Gr *Seirēn* a Siren) an Amazon mudfish. — *n* **Lepidos'teus** (Gr *osteon* a bone) a genus of fishes with rhomboid scales hard like bone, the bony pike. — *n* **Lepidos'trobus** (Gr *strobos* twist) the fossil fructification of Lepidodendron. — *adj* **lep'idote** (Gr *lepidōtos*) scaly; scurfy. [Gr *lepis, -idos* a scale]

leporine *lep'ə-rīn, adj* of or resembling the hare. [L *leporīnus*, from *lepus, leporis* the hare]

lepped. See **lep**.

LEPRA *lep'rə, abbrev*: Leprosy Relief Association.

lepra *lep'rə, n* leprosy (*med*); a scurfy, mealy substance on some plants (*bot*). — *adj* **lep'rose** (*-rōs*) scaly; scurfy. [Gr *leprā, fem* of *lepros* scaly, from *lepos* or *lepis* a scale, *lepein* to peel]

leprechaun *lep'rə-hhön*, (*folklore*) *n* a little brownie, who helps Irish housewives, mends shoes, grinds meal, etc. — Old form **lep'rechawn**. [Prob OIr *luchorpán*, from *lu* small, and *corpan, corp* a body]

leprose. See **lepra**.

leproserie or **leprosery** *lep'rə-sər-i, n* a leper hospital. [Fr *léproserie*]

leprosy *lep'rə-si, n* a chronic skin disease caused by a bacillus and occurring in two forms, tubercular, beginning with spots and thickenings of the skin, and anaesthetic, attacking the nerves, with loss of sensation in areas of skin; a name formerly widely applied to chronic skin diseases; corruption (*fig*). — *n* **leprosā'rium** a hospital for lepers. — *n* **leprosity** (*-ros'i-ti*) scaliness. — *adj* **lep'rous** of or affected with leprosy; scaly; scurfy. [Ety as for **leper**]

-lepsy *-lep-si*, (*med*) *combining form* denoting a seizing or seizure, as in *catalepsy*. — *adj combining form* **-leptic**. [Gr *lēpsis*, from *lambanein* to seize, take]

lepton *lep'ton, n* any of a group of subatomic particles with weak interactions, electrons, negative muons, tau particles and neutrinos (*opp* of *baryon*; *pl* **lep'tons**); a modern Greek coin, 1/100th of a drachma (*pl* **lep'ta**); the smallest ancient Greek coin, translated 'mite' in the New Testament (*pl* **lep'ta**). — *adj* **leptocephal'ic** (Gr *kephalē* head) narrow-skulled. — *n* **leptoceph'alus** the larva of an eel. — *adj* **leptocerc'al** (Gr *kerkos* tail) slender-tailed. — *n* **leptodac'tyl** (Gr *daktylos* finger, toe) a bird or other animal with long slender toes. — *adj* **leptodac'tylous** slender-toed. — *n* **lep'tome** (*bot*) phloem or bast. — *adj* **lepton'ic** of or relating to leptons. — *adj* **leptophyll'ous** (*bot*) with long slender leaves. — *adj* **lep'torrhine** (Gr *rhīs, rhīnos* nose) narrow-nosed. — *n* **lep'tosome** (Gr *sōma* body) a person with a slight, slender physical build; an asthenic. — *adj* **leptosō'mic** or **leptosomatic** (*-sə-mat'ik*). — *n* **leptospīrō'sis** (Gr *speira* a coil) a disease of animals or man caused by bacteria of the genus **Leptospī'ra**. — *adj* **leptosporan'giate** (*bot*) having each sporangium derived from a single cell (*opp* of *eusporangiate*). — *n* **lep'totene** (*-tēn*) the first stage of meiotic prophase in which long, slender, single-stranded chromosomes develop. [Gr *leptos*, neuter *lepton* slender]

lere. See **lear**[1].

Lerna *lûr'nə* or **Lerne** *lûr'nē*, (*Gr mythol*) *n* a swamp near Argos, supposed to be the home of the Hydra killed by Hercules. — *adj* **lernaean** or **lernean** (*lûr-nē'ən*).

lerp *lûrp, n* in Australia, a scalelike, waxy, protective, edible secretion produced on the leaves of certain plant louse larvae. [Aboriginal]

les. See **lez**.

Lesbian *lez'bi-ən, adj* of the island of *Lesbos*, or Mytilene, home of Alcaeus and Sappho; amatory or erotic; (without *cap*; of women) homosexual. — *n* (without *cap*) a female homosexual. — *n* **les'bianism**. — *adj* **les'bic** lesbian. — *n* **lesbo** (*lez'bō*; *slang*, often *offensive*) a lesbian (*pl* **les'bos**). — **Lesbian rule** (fig) an adaptable standard, from the pliable leaden rule *orig* used by Lesbian masons.

lese-majesty or **leze-majesty** *lēz'-maj'is-ti*, (also **-majesté** *-mazh-ə-stā*; *Fr*) *n* an offence against the sovereign power, treason. — **lese** or **leze**, treated as if it had verbal force, has also been used to form compounds such as **lese'-human'ity** and **leze'-lib'erty**. [Fr *lèse majesté*, transl of L *laesa mājestās* injured majesty, from *laedere* to hurt]

lesion *lē'zhən, n* an abnormal change in the structure of body tissue caused by disease or injury, *esp* an injury or wound (*med*); an injury or hurt. [Fr *lésion*, from L *laesiō, -ōnis*, from *laedere, laesum* to hurt]

less *les, adj* (used as *compar* of **little**) smaller (not now used of material things); in smaller quantity (not number); minor; fewer (*archaic* and *colloq*); inferior, lower in estimation; younger; more (*Shakesp*, with an expressed or implied negative). — *adv* not so much; in a lower degree. — *n* a smaller portion or quantity. — *conj* (*Milton*) unless (often written **'less**). — *prep* without; with diminution of, minus. — **much less** often used by confusion for much more; not to mention; **no less** (*usu ironically*) a phrase used to express admiration; **nothing less than** quite as much as; tantamount to; (formerly) anything rather than. [OE *lǣssa* less, *lǣs* (adv); apparently not connected with **little**]

-less *-les* or *-lis, adj sfx* free from or lacking, as in guilt*less* or god*less*. [OE *-lēas*, Ger *-los*, Gothic *-laus*]

lessee *les-ē'* or *les'ē, n* the person or business to which a lease is granted. [**lease**[1]]

lessen *les'n, vt* to make less, in any sense; to lower in estimation; to disparage; to belittle. — *vi* to become less, shrink. [**less**]

lesser *les'ər, adj* less; smaller; inferior; minor. — *adv* (*Shakesp*) less. [Double compar from **less**]

lesson *les'n, n* a portion of Scripture read during a religious service; a spell, instalment, or prescribed portion of instruction; a set exercise; an instructive or warning experience or example; a severe reproof; a piece or performance of music (*obs*). — *vt* (*archaic*) to instruct; to train; to rebuke. — *n* (*archaic*) **less'oning**. [Fr *leçon*, from L *lectiō, -ōnis*, from *legere* to read]

lessor *les'ör*, *n* the person or business which grants a lease. [**lease**[1]]

lest[1] *lest*, *conj* so that not; for fear that. [ME *leste*, from OE *thȳ lǣs the* the less that, from *thȳ* instrumental case; see **the**[2]]

lest[2] *lest*, (*Spenser*) *vi* for **list**[5], to listen.

let[1] *let*, *vt* to allow to go or come; to give leave or power to, to allow, permit, suffer (*usu* with infinitive without *to*); to grant to a tenant or hirer; in the imperative with accusative and infinitive without *to*, often used virtually as an auxiliary with imperative or optative effect; to leave (*Shakesp*); to omit (*Shakesp*); to allow to escape (*archaic*); to behave so as to give an impression, make it appear (*obs*; also *vi*): — *pr p* **lett'ing**; *pa t* and *pa p* **let**. — *n* a letting for hire. — *adj* **lett'able** able to be hired out, suitable for letting. — *n* **lett'er** a person who lets, *esp* on hire. — *n* **lett'ing**. — **let'-alone** (*Shakesp*) absence of restraint, freedom. — *adj* refraining from interference; leaving things to themselves. — **let'-down** an act or occasion of letting down; a disappointment; **let'-off** an act or occasion of letting off; a festivity; an outlet; (in games) a failure to take advantage of an opportunity; **let'-out** a chance to escape or avoid keeping an agreement, contract, etc; **lett'er-gae'** (*Scot*) someone who lets go, a precentor; **letting down** (*aeronautics*) the reduction of altitude from cruising height to that required for the approach to landing; **let'-up** end or ceasing; abatement; respite or relief. — **let alone** not to mention, much less; to refrain from interference with; (*imperative*) trust (*archaic*); **let be** (*dialect* **let-a-be**) to leave undisturbed; not to mention, to say nothing of (*Scot*); **let blood** to bleed; **let down** to allow to fall; to lower; to leave in the lurch, fail to back up when needed, betray trust, disappoint; **let drive** to aim a blow; to discharge a missile; **let fall** to drop; to mention or hint; **let fly** to fling, discharge, shoot; to deliver a blow (also *fig*); **let go** to cease holding; to finish the employment of; to slacken (*naut*); **let in** to allow to enter; to take in or swindle (*archaic*); (with *for*) to involve in or betray into anything unpleasant or troublesome; to insert; to leak inwards; **let in on** (*colloq*) to allow to take part in; **let into** to admit to the knowledge of; to throw into one with; **let loose** to set free; to let go of restraint, to indulge in unrestrained talk or conduct; **let off** to allow to go free or without exacting all; to fire off, discharge; to break wind from the anus (*slang*); **let on** (*colloq*) to allow to be believed, to pretend; to disclose awareness; to reveal, divulge; **let oneself go** (*colloq*) to allow one's appearance, lifestyle, etc to deteriorate; to act without restraint; **let out** to allow to get free, or to become known; to widen, slacken, enlarge; to put out to hire; to leak outwards; to strike out or kick out (*archaic*); **let someone know** to inform someone; **let up** (*colloq*) to become less; to abate; **let up on** (*colloq*) to cease to have to do with; **let well alone** to let things remain as they are from fear of making them worse; **to let** available for hire. [OE (Anglian) *lētan* (WSax *lǣtan*) to permit, pa t *lēt*; pa p *lǣten*; Ger *lassen*]

let[2] *let*, *vt* (*archaic*) to hinder; to prevent: — *pa t* and *pa p* **lett'ed** or **let**. — *adj* **let** (*archaic*) obstructed. — *n* hindrance, obstruction (*archaic*); delay (*archaic*); obstruction by the net, or other ground for cancelling a service (*lawn tennis*, etc); a service affected in such a way. — *n* **lett'er**. [OE *lettan* to hinder, from *lǣt* slow]

-let *-lit* or *-lət*, *n sfx* used to form diminutives, as in brace*let*, leaf*let* and stream*let*.

letch[1] *lech*, *vt* a variant of **leach**[1]. — *n* (*dialect*) a boggy patch of ground. — Also **latch**. [See **leach**[1]]

letch[2]. Same as **lech** under **lecher**. — *n* **letch'ing**.

lethal *lē'thəl*, *adj* deadly; mortal; vicious; death-dealing. — *n* **lethal'ity**. — *adv* **le'thally**. — *n* **le'thee** (*Shakesp*) *appar* life-blood, or death; *prob* with some reminiscence of Lethe (qv). — *adj* **lethif'erous** carrying death. [L *lēt(h)ālis*, from *lēt(h)um* death]

lethargy *leth'ər-ji*, *n* heavy unnatural slumber; torpor. — *adj* **lethargic** (*-är'*) or **lethar'gical** relating to lethargy; unnaturally sleepy; torpid. — *adv* **lethar'gically**. — *adj* **leth'argied**. — *vt* **leth'argize** or **-ise**. — **lethargy of neutrons** the natural logarithm of the ratio of initial and actual energies of neutrons during the moderation process. [Gr *lēthārgiā* drowsy forgetfulness, from *lēthē* forgetfulness, and *ārgos* idle]

Lethe *lē'thē*, *n* a river of the underworld causing forgetfulness in all who drank of it (*Gr mythol*); oblivion. — *adj* **lethē'an**. — *adj* **leth'ied** (*Shakesp*). [Gr *lēthē* forgetfulness (*lēthēs hydōr* the water or river of forgetfulness), from *lēthein*, a collateral form of *lanthanein* to be hidden]

lethee and **lethiferous**. See under **lethal**.

Letraset® *let'rə-set*, *n* a transfer lettering system of alphabets, symbols, etc which can be stripped into position on paper, film, etc.

Lett *let*, *n* a member of a people inhabiting **Lett'land** (now Latvia); a native or citizen of Latvia. — *adj* **Lett'ic** of the group (also called *Baltic*) of languages to which Lettish belongs, including Lithuanian and Old Prussian. — *adj* **Lett'ish**. — *n* the language of Letts. [Ger *Lette*, from Lettish *latvis* (now *latvietis*)]

letter[1] *let'ər*, *n* a conventional mark primarily used to express a sound of speech; often loosely applied to the sound itself; a written or printed message signed and sent, *usu* by post, to an addressee; literal meaning; printing-type; (in *pl*) learning, literary culture. — *vt* to stamp letters upon; to mark with a letter or letters. — *adj* **lett'ered** marked with letters; educated; knowledgeable in literature; literary. — *n* **lett'erer**. — *n* **lett'ering** the act of impressing or marking with letters; the letters impressed or marked; their style or mode of formation. — *adj* **lett'erless** without letters; illiterate. — **lett'er-board** a board on which material in type is placed for keeping or convenience in handling; **lett'er-bomb** a device inside an envelope which explodes when the envelope is opened; **lett'er-book** a book in which letters or copies of letters are kept; **lett'erbox** a box or slot for receiving mail. — *adj* (*cinematog*) of a film shown on television or video, etc, preserving the original widescreen cinematic format, not cut for a television screen. — *adj* **lett'erboxed**. — **lett'er-card** a card folded and gummed like a letter, with a perforated margin for opening; **lett'er-carrier** a postman; mail-carrier; **lett'er-clip** a device for gripping letters or papers to keep them together; **lett'er-file** an arrangement for holding letters for reference; **lett'er-founder** someone who casts type; **lett'erhead** a printed heading on notepaper, etc; a piece of notepaper with such a heading (also **lett'er-heading**). — *adj* **lett'er-perfect** (of an actor, etc) having the words of the part committed accurately to memory, word-perfect. — **lett'erpress** printed reading matter; a copying-press; a method of printing in which ink on raised surfaces is pressed on to paper; **letter quality** output from a printer where the printing is indistinguishable from the output of a good typewriter, and is acceptable for distribution outside an organization (*adj* **lett'er-quality**). — *n pl* **lett'ers-pat'ent** a document conferring a patent or privilege, so called because written on open sheets of parchment. — *n pl* **letters requisitory** or **letters rogatory** a legal instrument by which a court of one country asks that of another to take a certain evidence on its behalf. — **lett'er-stamp** an instrument for cancelling postage-stamps; a stamp for imprinting dates, etc; **lett'er-weight** a paperweight; **lett'er-wood** leopard-wood, a S American tree of the bread-nut genus, with dark brown mottled heart-wood; **lett'er-writer** someone who writes letters, *esp* for payment; a book of forms for imitation in writing letters. — **letter of credit** a letter authorizing credit or cash to a certain sum to be given to the bearer; **letter of indication** a banker's letter requesting foreign bankers to accept the bearer's circular notes; **letter-of-marque** see under **marque**[1]; **letter of the law** literal interpretation of the law; **letters of administration** see under **administer**; **letters of credence** or **letters credential** a diplomat's formal document accrediting him or her to a foreign government; **to the letter** exactly, in every detail. [Fr *lettre*, from L *littera*, *lītera*]

letter[2] and **letting**. See under **let**[1,2].

lettern *let'ərn* (*obs*). Same as **lectern**.

lettre *le-tr'*, (*Fr*) *n* a letter. — **lettre de cachet** (*də ka-she*) a letter under the royal signet; a royal warrant for arrest and imprisonment; **lettre de change** (*də shãzh*) a bill of exchange; **lettre de marque** (*də märk*) a letter of marque or of reprisal.

lettuce *let'is*, *n* a composite plant (*Lactuca sativa*) with milky juice, or one of many varieties, whose leaves are used for salad; extended to other (inedible) plants of the genus. — **frog's lettuce** a kind of pondweed; **lamb's lettuce** corn-salad. [Appar from some form (perh the pl) of AngloFr *letue* (Fr *laitue*), from L *lactūca*, from *lac* milk, from the milky juice of the leaves]

leu *lā'ōō*, *n* the standard monetary unit of Rumania (100 *bani*). — Also (*rare*) **ley** (*lā*): — *pl* **lei** (*lā*). [Rom, lion]

leuc- or **leuk-** *lūk-*, *lōōk-*, *lūs-* or *lōōs-*, also **leuco-** or **leuko-** *lū'kō-*, *lōō'ko-* or *-ko'-*, *combining form* denoting white. — **c** and **k** are in most cases interchangeable and, except in the first case, **-k-** forms have not been given below. — *n* **leucaemia**, or (*esp* in *US*) **leukemia** and, more strictly formed, **leuchaemia** (*lōō-kē'mi-ə*; Gr *haima* blood) a sometimes fatal cancerous disease in which too many leucocytes are accumulated in the body, associated with changes in the lymphatic system and enlargement of the spleen. — *adj* **leucae'mic**. — *n* **leucae'mogen** a substance that encourages the development of leucaemia. — *adj* **leucaemogen'ic**. — *n* **leu'co-base** or **leu'co-compound** a colourless reduction product of a dye that can be converted back to the dye by oxidation. — *n* **leu'coblast** an immature cell which will develop into a leucocyte. — *adj* **leucocrat'ic** of igneous rocks, light in colour, due to a low content of iron and magnesium. — *n* **leu'cocyte** (*-kō-sīt*; Gr *kytos* container, used as if cell) a white corpuscle of the blood or lymph. — *adj* **leucocytic** (*-sit'ik*). — *n* **leucocythaemia** (*-sī-thē'mi-ə*; Gr *haima* blood) leucaemia. — *n* **leucocytol'ysis** (Gr *lysis* dissolution) breaking down of the leucocytes. — *n* **leucocytopē'nia** (Gr *peniā* poverty) deficiency in leucocytes. — *n* **leucocytō'sis** the presence of an excessive number of white corpuscles in the blood. — *n* **leucoder'ma** or **leucoder'mia** (Gr *derma* skin) a condition in which white patches, surrounded by a pigmented area, appear in the skin. — *adj* **leucoder'mal** or **leucoder'mic**. — *n* **leucopē'nia** leucocytopenia. — *n* **leucoplakia** (*lū-* or *lōō-kō-plā'ki-ə*; Gr *plax*, *plakos* a flat surface) the stage of a chronically inflamed area at which the surface becomes hard, white and smooth. — *n* **leucoplast** (*lū'* or *lōō'kō-pläst*; Gr *plastos* formed, from *plassein* to form; *bot*) a starch-forming body in protoplasm (also **leucoplas'tid**). — *n* **leucopoiesis** (*lū-* or *lōō-kō-poi-ē'sis*; Gr *poieein* to make) the production of white blood cells. — *n* **leucorrhoea** (*lū-* or *lōō-kō-rē'ə*; Gr *rhoiā*, from *rheein* to flow) an abnormal mucous or muco-purulent discharge from the vagina, the whites. — *n* **leucotomy** (*lū-* or *lōō-kot'ə-mi*; Gr *tomē* a cutting) a surgical scission of the white association fibres between the frontal lobes of the brain and the thalamus to relieve cases of severe schizophrenia and manic-depressive psychosis. — *n* **leu'cotome** (*-kō-tōm*) a needle used for the purpose. [Gr *leukos* white]

leuch and **leuchen**. See under **lauch**.

leucin *lū'* or *lōō'sin* or **leucine** *lū'* or *lōō'sēn*, *n* an essential amino-acid, a product of protein hydrolysis. [Gr *leukos* white]

Leuciscus *lū-* or *lōō-sis'kəs*, *n* a genus of freshwater cyprinoid fishes, including the roach, dace, chub, minnow, etc. [Gr *leukiskos* white mullet]

leucite *lū'* or *lōō'sīt*, *n* a whitish mineral (silicate of aluminium and potassium). — *adj* **leucitic** (*-sit'ik*). — *n* **leucitohē'dron** the cubic icositetrahedron, simulated by typical leucite crystals. [Gr *leukos* white]

leuco-. See **leuc-**.

Leucojum *lū-* or *lōō-kō'jəm*, *n* the snowflake genus of amaryllids. [Gr *leukoïon* snowdrop, etc, from *leukos* white, and *ion* violet]

leucoma *lū-* or *lōō-kō'mə*, (*pathol*) *n* a white opacity of the cornea. [Gr *leukōma*, from *leukos* white]

leugh and **leughen**. See under **lauch**.

leuk- and **leuko-**. See **leuc-**.

Lev. or **Levit.** (*Bible*) *abbrev*: (the Book of) Leviticus.

lev or **lew** *lef*, *n* the standard monetary unit of Bulgaria (100 *stotinki*): — *pl* **leva** (*lev'ä*). [Bulg, lion]

Levant *li-vant'*, *n* the eastern Mediterranean and its shores; the East (*obs*); (without *cap*) the levanter wind; (without *cap*) a kind of morocco leather. — *adj* (without *cap*; *lev'ənt*) eastern. — *n* **Levant'er** an inhabitant of the Levant; (without *cap*) a boisterous easterly wind in the Levant. — *adj* **Levant'ine** (or *lev'ən-tīn*) of the Levant. — *n* (without *cap*) a closely-woven twilled silk cloth. [Fr *levant* or Ital *levante* east, literally rising, from L *levāre* to raise]

levant *li-vant'*, *vi* to decamp. — *n* **levan'ter** someone who absconds, *esp* with bets unpaid. [Sp *levantar* to move, from L *levāre* to raise]

levator *le-vā'tər* or *-tör*, (*anatom*) *n* a muscle that raises (*opp* of *depressor*). [L *levātor* a lifter, from *levāre* to raise]

leve. See under **lief**.

levee[1] *lev'i*, also *lev'ā* or *li-vē'*, (*hist* or *archaic*) *n* a morning (or comparatively early) reception of visitors, *esp* by a person of distinction; getting out of bed (*archaic*). — *vt* to attend the levee of. [Fr *levée*, *lever*, from L *levāre* to raise]

levee[2] *lev'i* or *li-vē'*, (*US*) *n* a natural or artificial riverside embankment, *esp* on the Lower Mississippi; a quay. [Fr *levée* raised; see ety for **levee**[1]]

levée en masse *lə-vā ã mas*, (*Fr*). See **levy in mass** under **levy**.

level *lev'l*, *n* a horizontal position; a condition of horizontality; a horizontal plane or line; a nearly horizontal surface or a region with no considerable inequalities; the horizontal plane, literal or figurative, that anything occupies or reaches up to; height; an instrument for testing horizontality; a horizontal mine-gallery; an ascertainment of relative elevation; a levelling survey; natural or appropriate position or rank; a condition of equality; a ditch or channel for drainage, *esp* in flat country; an area of flat, *usu* low-lying farming land that has been drained for agricultural use; the act of aiming (*Shakesp*); the thing aimed at (*Spenser*). — *adj* horizontal; even, smooth; even with anything else; uniform; well-balanced, sound of judgment; in the same line or plane; filled to a level with the brim; equal in position or dignity. — *adv* in a level manner; point-blank. — *vt* to make horizontal; to make flat or smooth; to lay low; to raze; to aim; to make equal; to direct; to survey by taking levels. — *vi* to make things level; to aim; to speak honestly, to be frank (*usu* with *with*; *colloq*); to guess, estimate. — *vt* and *vi* to change in spelling or pronunciation, making one word or form the same as another: — *pr p* **lev'elling**; *pa t* and *pa p* **lev'elled**. — *n* **lev'eller** someone who levels in any sense; someone who would like to remove all social or political inequalities, *esp* (with *cap*) one of an ultra-republican party in the parliamentary army, crushed by Cromwell in 1649. — *n* **lev'elling** the act of making level; a change in spelling or pronunciation making one word or form the same as another. — **level best** (*colloq*) one's utmost; **lev'el-cross'ing** a place at which a road crosses a railway at the same level. — *adj* **lev'el-head'ed** having sound common sense. — **lev'elling-rod** or **lev'elling-staff** a graduated rod used in surveying; **lev'el-pegg'ing** the equal state of two rivals, contestants, etc (often in the form **be level-pegging with**). — *adj* at the same level, equal (also **lev'el-pegg'ed**). — **level playing field** (*fig*) a position of equality, from which rivals may compete without either having an unfair advantage. — **find one's level** to settle in one's natural position or rank; **level**

down or **up** to lower or raise to the same level or status; **level off** to make flat or even; to reach and maintain equilibrium; **level with** (*slang*) to tell the truth; **on the level** fair; honestly speaking. [OFr *livel*, *liveau* (Fr *niveau*), from L *lībella* a plummet, dimin of *lībra* a balance]

level-coil *lev'l-koil*, (*archaic*) *n* an old Christmas game in which the players changed seats; a hubbub. [Fr *lever le cul* to lift the buttocks]

lever *lē'vər* or in US *lev'ər*, *n* a bar turning on a support or fulcrum for imparting pressure or motion from a source of power to a resistance. — *vt* to move with a lever. — *n* **le'verage** the mechanical power gained by the use of a lever; advantage gained for any purpose, eg (in *finance*) power gained over a resource greater than that one actually owns. — *vi* and *vt* (*finance*) to borrow necessary capital (*esp* for a management buy-out) counting on the profits from the deal to cover interest repayment. — *adj* **le'veraged** financed by borrowed capital. — **lever arch file** a file in the form of a large loose-leaf folder or book with arch-shaped metal rods on which the papers are secured; **le'ver-watch** a watch with a vibrating lever in the escapement mechanism. [OFr *leveor*, from *lever*, from L *levāre* to raise]

lever de rideau *lə-vā də rē-dō*, (*Fr*) *n* a curtain-raiser.

leveret *lev'ə-rit*, *n* a hare in its first year. [OFr *levrette* (Fr *lièvre*), from L *lepus*, *leporis* a hare]

leviable. See under **levy**.

leviathan *le-vī'ə-thən*, *n* (also with *cap*) a biblical sea-monster, described in Job 41, apparently a crocodile; a huge sea-monster; anything of huge size, *esp* a ship or a man; (after Hobbes's book, 1651) the state; Satan (*obs*). — *adj* gigantic, formidable. [Heb *livyāthān*]

levigate[1] *lev'i-gāt*, *vt* to smooth; to grind to a fine powder, *esp* with a liquid. — *adj* smooth. — *adj* **lev'igable**. — *n* **leviga'tion**. [L *lēvigāre*, *-ātum*, from *lēvis* smooth; Gr *leios*; related to **level**]

levigate[2] *lev'i-gāt*, *vt* to lighten. [L *levigāre*, *-ātum*, from *levis* light]

levin *lev'in*, (*archaic*) *n* lightning. [ME *leuen(e)*, prob from ON]

levirate *lēv'* or *lev'i-rāt*, *n* the (ancient Hebrew and other) custom of compulsory marriage with a childless brother's widow. — *adj* **lev'irate** or **leviratical** (*-rat'i-kl*). — *n* **levirā'tion**. [L *lēvir* a brother-in-law]

Levis® *lē'vīz*, *n pl* (also without *cap*) heavy, close-fitting denim, etc trousers, reinforced at points of strain with copper rivets. [From the US original manufacturer, *Levi* Strauss]

Levit. See **Lev**.

levitation *lev-i-tā'shən*, *n* the act of rising by virtue of lightness; the act of making light; the floating of heavy bodies in the air, according to spiritualists; raising and floating on a cushion of air. — *vt* and *vi* **lev'itate** to float or cause to float. [On the model of *gravitate*, from L *levis* light]

Levite *lē'vīt*, *n* a descendant of *Levi*, the third son of Jacob and Leah (*Old Testament*); a subordinate priest of the ancient Jewish Church; (also without *cap*) a clergyman (*slang*). — *adj* **levitic** (*li-vit'ik*) or **levit'ical**. — *adv* **levit'ically**. — *n* **Levit'icus** the third book of the Old Testament. — **Levitical degrees** the degrees of kindred within which marriage was forbidden in Leviticus 18.6–18.

levity *lev'it-i*, *n* lightness of temper or conduct; thoughtlessness; a trifling or frivolous tendency; vain quality; lightness of weight (*archaic*). [L *levitās*, *-ātis*, from *levis* light]

levo-. See **laevo-**.

levulose. See **laevulose**.

levy *lev'i*, *vt* to raise or collect (eg an army or tax); to call for; to impose; to begin to wage: — *pr p* **lev'ying**; *pa t* and *pa p* **lev'ied**. — *n* the act of levying; a contribution called for from members of an association; a tax; the amount collected; troops levied. — *adj* **leviable** (*lev'i-ə-bl*) able to be levied or assessed. — **levy in mass** (Fr **levée en masse**) a levy of all able-bodied men for military service, conscription; **levy war** to make war. [Fr *levée*, from *lever*, from L *levāre* to raise]

lew[1] *lū* or *lōō*, *adj* tepid, lukewarm. [OE *hlēow*]

lew[2]. See **lev**.

lewd *lōōd* or *lūd*, *adj* obscene; sensual; lustful; unchaste; ignorant (*obs*); bare (*Bible*); bad (*obs*). — *adv* **lewd'ly**. — *n* **lewd'ness**. — *n* **lewds'by** or **lewd'ster** (*archaic*) someone addicted to lewdness. [OE *lǣwede* ignorant]

lewis *lōō'is*, *n* a dovetail iron tenon for lifting blocks of stone (also **lew'isson**); a freemason's son. [Ety uncertain]

Lewis gun *lōō'is gun*, *n* a light machine-gun designed by the American Samuel McLean, *c.* 1908, and perfected by Colonel Isaac Newton *Lewis*.

lewisia *lōō-is'i-ə*, *n* a perennial herb with pink or white flowers, of the genus *Lewisia*. [American explorer Meriwether *Lewis* (1774–1809)]

Lewisian *lōō-iz'i-ən* or *-is'*, *adj* of *Lewis* in the Outer Hebrides; Pre-Cambrian (*geol*).

lewisite[1] *lōō'is-īt*, *n* a yellow cubic mineral, calcium titanium antimonate. [Named after W J *Lewis* (1847–1926), English mineralogist]

lewisite[2] *lōō'is-īt*, *n* a vesicant liquid, an arsine derivative, that causes blistering and other irritation, used in chemical warfare as a poison gas. [Named after W L *Lewis* (1878–1943), American chemist]

lewisson. See **lewis**.

lex *leks*, (*L*) *n* law. — **lex non scripta** (*non skrip'tə* or *nōn skrēp'tä*) unwritten law, ie the common law; **lex scripta** (*skrip'tə* or *skrēp'tä*) statute law; **lex talionis** (*ta-li-ō'nis* or *tä-*) the law of talion, or retaliation.

lex. *abbrev*: lexicon.

lexeme *lek'sēm*, (*linguistics*) *n* a word or other essential unit of vocabulary in its most abstract sense. [*lex*icon and *-eme*]

lexicon *leks'i-kən*, *n* a word-book or dictionary; a vocabulary of terms used in connection with a particular subject. — *adj* **lex'ical** belonging to a lexicon; relating to the words of a language as distinct from its grammar and constructions. — *adv* **lex'ically**. — *n* **lexicographer** (*-kog'rə-fər*). — *adj* **lexicographic** (*-kə-graf'ik*) or **lexicograph'ical**. — *n* **lexicog'raphist**. — *n* **lexicog'raphy** the writing and compiling of dictionaries. — *n* **lexicol'ogist**. — *n* **lexicol'ogy** the study of the history and meaning of words. — **lexical analysis** (*comput*) a stage during the compilation of a program in which standard components of a statement are replaced by internal codes (tokens) which identify their meaning; **lexical meaning** the meaning of the base word when not inflected. [Gr *lexikon* a dictionary, from *lexis* a word, *legein* to speak]

lexigram *lek'si-gram*, *n* a sign which represents a word. [Gr *lexis* a word, and **-gram**]

lexigraphy *leks-ig'rə-fi*, *n* a system of writing in which each sign represents a word. — *adj* **lexigraphic** (*-graf'ik*) or **lexigraph'ical**. [Gr *lexis* word, and *graphein* to write]

lexis *lek'sis*, *n* the way in which a piece of writing is expressed in words, diction; the total stock of words in a language. [Gr, word]

ley[1] *lā* or *lē*. See **lea**[1,2,3]. — **ley'-farming** see under **lea**[2].

ley[2]. See **leu**.

ley[3] *lā*, *n* any of the straight lines between features of the landscape, possibly pathways, or perhaps having scientific or magical significance in prehistoric times. — Also **ley line**. [Variant of **lea**[1]]

Leyden jar *lā'dən jär*, *n* a condenser for electricity, a glass jar coated inside and outside with tinfoil or other conducting material. [*Leyden* in Holland, where it was invented]

lez, lezz or **les** *lez* or **lezzy** *lez'i*, (*colloq*; often *offensive*) *n* short form of **lesbian**.

leze-majesty, leze-liberty, etc. See **lese-majesty**.

LF (*radio*) *abbrev*: low frequency.

LG. See **LGer**.

lg. or **lge** *abbrev*: large.

LGer or **LG** *abbrev*: Low German.
lgth *abbrev*: length.
LGU *abbrev*: Ladies' Golf Union.
LH *abbrev*: luteinizing hormone.
lh *abbrev*: left hand. — **lhd** *abbrev*: left-hand drive.
lhasa apso *lä'sə ap'sō*, *n* a Tibetan (breed of) small, long-haired terrier: — *pl* **lhasa apsos**. [*Lhasa*, the capital of Tibet]
LHD *abbrev*: *Litterarum Humaniorum Doctor* (*L*), Doctor of Humanities, literally Doctor of the Humaner Letters.
lhd. See **lh**.
lherzolite *lûr'zə-līt*, (*mineralogy*) *n* peridotite, consisting essentially of olivine with monoclinic and orthorhombic pyroxenes. [From Lake *Lherz* in the Pyrenees (Ariège)]
LI *abbrev*: Light Infantry; Long Island (US).
Li (*chem*) *symbol*: lithium.
li *lē*, *n* a Chinese unit of distance, about one-third of a mile. [Chin]
liable *lī'ə-bl*, *adj* subject to an obligation; exposed to a possibility or risk; responsible (for); tending (*usu* with *to*); apt; likely (to); subject (*Shakesp*); fitting, suitable (*Shakesp*). — *n* **liabil'ity** the state of being liable; that for which one is liable, a debt, responsibility, etc. — **employers' liability** responsibility of employers to their servants for the negligence of those to whom they have delegated their authority; **limited liability** a principle of modern statute law which limits the responsibilities of shareholders in a partnership, joint-stock company, etc by the extent of their personal interest therein. [Appar from Fr *lier*, from L *ligāre* to bind]
liaison *lē-ā'zn* or *-zɔ̃* or *lyez-ɔ̃*, *n* union, or bond of union; connection; a secret or illicit love affair; effective conjunction with another unit or force (*military*); in French, the linking in pronunciation of a final (and otherwise silent) consonant to a vowel beginning the next word. — *vi* **liaise** (*lē-āz'*; back-formation) to form a link (with); to be or get in touch (with). — **liaison officer** an officer forming a link with another unit or force. [Fr, from L *ligātiō*, *-ōnis*, from *ligāre* to bind]
liana *lē-ä'nə* or **liane** *lē-än'*, *n* any climbing plant, *esp* a twisted woody kind festooning tropical forests. — *adj* **lian'oid**. [Fr *liane*, Latinized or Hispanicized as *liana*, appar from *lier*, from L *ligāre* to bind]
liang *lyang*, *n* a Chinese ounce or tael, a unit of weight and of currency. [Chin]
liar. See under **lie**[1].
liard *lī'ərd*, *adj* grey; dapple-grey (*Scot* **lī'art** or **ly'art**). — *n* (*lyär*) an old French coin of low value. [OFr *liard*, *liart*]
Lias *lī'əs*, (*geol*) *n* and *adj* Lower Jurassic. — *adj* **Liassic** (*lī-as'ik*). [A Somerset quarryman's word, appar from OFr *liois* (Fr *liais*) a kind of limestone]
Lib. *lib*, *abbrev*: Liberal.
lib[1] *lib*, (now *dialect*) *vt* to geld. [Cf Du *lubben*]
lib[2] *lib* (*colloq*) *n* short form of **liberation** (see under **liberate**).
lib. *abbrev*: *liber* (*L*), book; librarian; library.
libation *lī-bā'shən* or *li-*, *n* the pouring forth of wine or other liquid in honour of a god or goddess, or (*facetiously*) for some other purpose; the liquid poured. — *adj* **lī'bant** (*archaic* or *poetic*) sipping; lightly touching. — *vt* **lī'bate** (*rare*) to make a libation to. — *adj* **lī'batory**. [L *lībāre*, *-ātum* to pour, sip, touch; Gr *leibein* to pour]
libbard *lib'ərd*, (*archaic*) *n*. Same as **leopard**.
libber *lib'ər*, (*colloq*) *n* short form of **liberationist** (see under **liberate**).
lib. cat. *abbrev*: library catalogue.
libeccio *li-bet'chō*, *n* the south-west wind. — Also (*Milton*) **libecchio** (*li-bek'i-ō*; *Ital*): — *pl* **libecc'ios** or **libecch'ios**. [Ital, from L *Libs*; Gr *Lips*, *Libos*]
libel *lī'bl*, *n* a written accusation; any malicious defamatory publication or statement; defamation, either written or made for general reception, eg by radio or television (*English law*; distinguished from *slander* or spoken defamation; in Scots law both are slander); the statement of a plaintiff's grounds of complaint. — *vt* to defame by libel; to satirize unfairly; to proceed against by producing a written complaint (*law*): — *pr p* **lī'belling** or (*US*) **lī'beling** (and in all such forms); *pa t* and *pa p* **lī'belled**. — *n* **lī'bellant** a person who brings a libel. — *n* **libellee'** a person against whom a libel is brought. — *n* **lī'beller** a defamer. — *n* **lī'belling**. — *adj* **lī'bellous** containing a libel; defamatory. — *adv* **lī'bellously**. [L *libellus*, dimin of *liber* a book]
liber *lī'bər*, (*bot*; *rare*) *n* phloem or bast. [L *liber* bast, book]
liberal *lib'ə-rəl*, *adj* generous; noble-minded; broad-minded; not bound by authority or traditional orthodoxy; looking to the general or broad sense rather than the literal; candid; free; free from restraint; ample; (with *cap*) of the Liberal Party (see below); of studies or education, directed towards the cultivation of the mind for its own sake, disinterested (*opp* of *technical* and *professional*); befitting a freeman or a gentleman (*archaic*); licentious in speech or action (*obs*). — *n* a person who advocates greater freedom in political institutions; (with *cap*) a member of the Liberal Party (see below); a person whose views are liberal. — *n* **lib'eralism** the principles of a liberal in politics or religion. — *n* and *adj* **lib'eralist**. — *adj* **liberalist'ic**. — *n* **liberality** (*-al'i-ti*) the quality of being liberal; generosity; magnanimity, broad-mindedness or nobleness of mind; candour; freedom from prejudice. — *n* **liberalīzā'tion** or **-s-**. — *vt* and *vi* **lib'eralize** or **-ise** to make or become liberal or enlightened. — *adv* **lib'erally**. — *n* **lib'eralness**. — **liberal arts** the studies that make up a liberal (qv) education; in the Middle Ages, the *trivium* and *quadrivium*; **liberal democracy** (*politics*) a state or system which combines the right to individual freedom with the right to representative government; **Liberal Democrat** a member of the **Liberal Democrats** (formerly called Social and Liberal Democrats), a UK political party formed in 1988 from the Liberal Party and the Social Democratic Party; **Liberal Party** in the UK, the political party which emerged, as successors to the Whigs, in the mid 19c, splitting into two factions in 1988, the larger and more influential group forming, together with the SDP, the Liberal Democrats; in Australia, one of the major political parties; generally, a party advocating democratic reform and individual liberty; **Liberal Unionists** a section of the Liberal Party that opposed Gladstone's Home Rule policy (1886) and joined the Conservatives. [L *līberālis* befitting a freeman, from *līber* free]
liberate *lib'ə-rāt*, *vt* to set free; to release from restraint, confinement or slavery; to steal or appropriate (*facetious*); to give off (*chem*). — *n* **liberā'tion** setting free, releasing; the first stage in ore treatment, in which comminution is used to detach valuable minerals from gangue (*min ext*); freeing, or seeking to free (a group) from social disadvantages, prejudices, injustice or abuse (*colloq abbrev* **lib**). — *n* **liberā'tionism**. — *n* **liberā'tionist** a person who supports the cause of social freedom and equality for sections of society believed to be underprivileged or discriminated against (*colloq abbrev* **libb'er**); a person who is in favour of church disestablishment. — Also *adj*. — *n* **lib'erātor**. — *adj* **lib'eratory** (*-ə-tə-ri*) tending to liberate. — **liberated woman** one who rejects the older ideas of woman as the weaker sex, a woman's place being in the home, etc, and believes in living and working on equal terms with men; **liberation theology** *esp* in S America, a development of Christian doctrine that demands a commitment to social revolution whenever injustice and exploitation are thought to exist. [L *līberāre*, *-ātum*, from *līber* free]
libero *lē'bə-rō*, (*football*) *n* a footballer who plays behind the backs, acting as the last line in the defence but able to move freely throughout the field, a sweeper: — *pl* **li'beros**. [Ital, free, free man]

liberty *lib'ər-ti*, *n* freedom from constraint, captivity, slavery or tyranny; freedom to do as one pleases; the unrestrained enjoyment of natural rights; power of free choice; privilege; permission; free range; leisure; disposal; the bounds within which certain privileges are enjoyed; (often in *pl*) a limited area outside a prison in which prisoners were allowed to live (*archaic*); presumptuous, improper or undue freedom of speech or action; speech or action violating ordinary civility. — *n* **libertā'rian** a believer in free-will; a person who believes in the maximum amount of freedom of thought, behaviour, etc. — Also *adj*. — *n* **libertā'rianism**. — *adj* **liberticī'dal**. — *n* **liber'ticide** a destroyer of liberty; destruction of liberty. — *n* **lib'ertinage** (also *-ûrt'*) debauchery. — *n* **lib'ertine** (*-tēn*, *-tin* or *-tīn*) a person who leads a licentious life, a rake or debauchee; *orig* a freedman; formerly a person who professed free opinions, *esp* in religion. — *adj* unrestrained; licentious; belonging to a freedman. — *n* **lib'ertinism**. — **lib'erty-boat** a boat for liberty-men (see below); **liberty bodice** an undergarment like a vest formerly often worn by children; **liberty cap** same as **cap of liberty** under **cap**[1]; a yellowish-brown conical-capped mushroom producing the drug psilocybin; **Liberty Hall** (*colloq*; also without *cap*) a place where one may do as one likes; **liberty horse** a circus horse that, as one of a group and without a rider, carries out movements on command; **lib'erty-man** a sailor with permission to go ashore; **liberty ship** a prefabricated all-welded cargo-ship mass-produced in the US during World War II. — **at liberty** not restrained or constrained, free; unoccupied; available; **civil liberty** freedom of an individual within the law; individual freedom as guaranteed by a country's laws; **liberty of indifference** freedom of the will; **liberty of the press** freedom to print and publish without government permission; **take liberties with** to treat with undue freedom or familiarity, or indecently; to falsify; **take the liberty** to venture or presume. [Fr *liberté*, from L *lībertās*, *-ātis* liberty; L *lībertīnus* a freedman, from *līber* free]

libido *li-bē'dō* or *li-bī'dō*, *n* vital urge, either in general or as of sexual origin (*psychol*); sexual impulse: — *pl* **libid'os**. — *adj* **libidinal** (*-bid'*) relating to the libido. — *n* **libid'inist** a lewd person. — *n* **libidinos'ity** or **libid'inousness**. — *adj* **libid'inous** lustful, lascivious, lewd. — *adv* **libid'inously**. [L *libīdō*, *-inis* desire, from *libet*, *lubet* it pleases]

libken *lib'ken*, (*old slang*) *n* a place of abode, a home. [Old slang *lib* to sleep, and **ken**[2]]

Lib-Lab *abbrev*: Liberal-Labour.

LIBOR or **Libor** *lī'bör*, (*finance*) *abbrev*: London Inter-Bank Offered Rate.

Libra *lē'brə*, *n* the Balance, a constellation between the Virgin and the Scorpion; the seventh sign of the zodiac in which it used to be (it is now in Scorpio); a person born between 24 Sep and 23 Oct, under the sign of Libra.

libra *lī'brə* or *lē'brə*, *n* a Roman pound (*antiq*; used contracted to **lb** for the British pound in weight and to £ for a pound in money). [L *lībra*]

libraire *lē-brer*, (*Fr*) *n* a bookseller. — *n* **librairie** (*lē-bre-rē*) book-trade; a bookshop.

library *lī'brə-ri*, *n* a collection of books; a building or room containing it; a publisher's series; also a collection of gramophone records, films, etc; a collection of computer programs. — *n* **librā'rian** the keeper of a library. — *n* **librā'rianship**. — **library edition** an edition of a book with high-quality binding, etc. — **lending library** one from which people may take books away on loan. [L *librārium* a bookcase, from *liber* a book]

librate *lī'brāt*, *vi* to oscillate; to be poised. — *vt* (*obs*) to poise; to balance. — *n* **lībrā'tion** balancing; a state of equipoise; a slight swinging motion. — *adj* **lībrā'tional**. — *adj* **lī'bratory**. — **libration of the moon** a slight turning of the moon to each side alternately so that more than half of its surface is visible at any one time. [L *lībrāre*, *-ātum*, from *lībra* balance]

libretto *li-bret'ō*, *n* the text or book of words of an opera, oratorio, ballet, etc: — *pl* **librett'i** (*-ē*) or **librett'os**. — *n* **librett'ist** a writer of libretti. [Ital dimin of *libro*, from L *liber* a book]

Librium® *lib'ri-əm*, *n* a proprietary name for chlordiazepoxide, a tranquillizer.

Libyan *lib'i-ən*, *adj* of *Libya* in N Africa. — *n* a native or citizen of Libya. [Gr *Libyē* Libya]

lice *līs*, *n pl*. See **louse**.

licence or (*US*) **license** *lī'səns*, *n* being allowed; leave; grant of permission, eg for manufacturing a patented article, developing an area or natural resource, selling intoxicants, driving a motor vehicle, piloting an aeroplane, using a television set, keeping a dog, owning a gun; the document by which authority is conferred; excess or abuse of freedom; licentiousness, libertinage or debauchery; a departure from a rule or standard for artistic or literary effect; tolerated freedom. — *vt* **li'cense** (also **li'cence**) to grant licence to; to issue with a licence; to permit to depart, dismiss; to authorize or permit. — *adj* **li'censable**. — *adj* **li'censed** holding a (valid) licence; permitted, tolerated. — *n* **licensee'** a person to whom a licence is granted, *esp* to sell alcoholic drink. — *n* **li'censer** or (chiefly *US*) **li'censor** a person who grants licence or permission; a person authorized to license. — *n* **li'censure** the act of licensing or granting of a licence, *esp* for professional practice. — *n* **licentiate** (*lī-sen'shi-āt*) a holder of an academic diploma of various kinds; in some European universities, a graduate ranking between bachelor and doctor; among Presbyterians, a person authorized by a Presbytery to preach. — *adj* **licentious** (*-sen'shəs*) indulging in excessive freedom; given to the indulgence of the animal passions; dissolute. — *adv* **licen'tiously**. — *n* **licen'tiousness**. — **license block** see under **block**; **licensed victualler** a person licensed to sell food and *esp* alcoholic drink, for consumption on the premises, a publican; **license plate** (*NAm*) a vehicle number plate. — **special licence** licence given by the Archbishop of Canterbury permitting the marriage of two specified people without banns, and at a place and time other than those prescribed by law, loosely used in Scotland in speaking of marriage by consent registered by warrant of the sheriff. [Fr *licence*, from L *licentia*, from *licēre* to be allowed]

licentia vatum *lī-sen'shyə vā'təm* or *li-ken'ti-ä wä'tŏŏm*, also *vä'*, (*L*) *n* poetic licence.

lich[1] *lich*, (*Spenser*) *adj* a Southern form of **like**[1].

lich[2] *lich*, *n* (*obs*) a body, living or dead. — **lich'gate** or **lych'gate** a roofed churchyard gate, *orig* to rest a bier under; **lich'-owl** a screech-owl, once thought to be a death-portent; **lich'wake** see **lykewake**; **lich'way** a path by which the dead are carried to burial. [ME *lich*, *liche* (Southern), *like* (Northern), from OE *līc*; Ger *Leiche* corpse]

lichanos *lik'a-nos*, (*ancient Gr music*) *n* the string or the note struck by the forefinger. [Gr *lichanos* forefinger, lichanos, from *leichein* to lick]

lichee. See **lychee**.

lichen *lī'kən* or *lich'ən*, *n* a compound plant consisting of a fungus and an alga living symbiotically, forming crusts and tufts on stones, trees, and soil; an eruption on the skin. — *adj* **li'chened** covered with lichens. — *n* **li'chenin** a starch obtained from Iceland moss. — *n* **li'chenism** the association of fungus and alga as a lichen. — *n* **li'chenist** or **lichenol'ogist** a specialist in **lichenol'ogy**, the study of lichens. — *adj* **li'chenoid**. — *adj* **li'chenose** or **li'chenous** relating to, of the nature of, or covered with, lichens or lichen. [L *līchēn*, from Gr *leichēn*, *-ēnos*]

lichgate, etc. See under **lich**[2].

lichi. See **lychee**.

licht *lihht*, the Scots form of **light**[1,2,3].

licit *lis'it*, *adj* lawful, allowable. — *adv* **lic'itly**. [L *licitus*]

lick *lik*, *vt* to pass the tongue over (eg to moisten or taste); to take in to the mouth using the tongue; to lap; to put or make by passing the tongue over; to pass over or play upon in the manner of a tongue; to flicker over or around; to smear; to beat (*slang*). — *vi* to go at full speed (*slang*); to smoke crack (*drug-taking slang*). — *n* an act of licking; a quantity licked up, or such (a small amount) as might be imagined to be licked up; a slight smearing or wash; a place where animals lick salt; a blow or flick (*esp Scot* in *pl* a thrashing); vigorous speed (*colloq*); a wag (*Scot*); in jazz music, a short instrumental passage or flourish (*US slang*). — *n* **lick'er**. — *n* **lick'ing** a thrashing. — **lick'er-in'** a toothed cylinder that takes in material to a carding engine; **lick'penny** (*obs*) something which licks up, or is a drain upon, one's money; **lick'spittle** or (*rare*) **lick'-platter** a toady; **lick'-trencher** (*archaic*) a parasite. — **a lick and a promise** a perfunctory wash; **lick into shape** to mould into satisfactory form, from the notion that the she-bear gives form to her shapeless young by licking them; **lick one's lips** to look forward, or (*archaic*) to recall, with pleasure; **lick one's wounds** to retire from a defeat, failure, etc, *esp* in order to try to recover one's strength, pride, etc; **lick someone's boots** to toady; **lick the dust** to be killed or finished off (*colloq*); to be abjectly servile. [OE *liccian*; Ger *lecken*, L *lingere*, Gr *leichein*]

lickerish or **liquorish** *lik'ər-ish*, (*obs*) *adj* dainty; tempting; eager to taste or enjoy; lecherous. — *adv* **lick'erishly**. — *n* **lick'erishness**. [Variant of **lecherous**]

lickety-split *lik'ə-ti-split'*, (*US colloq*) *adv* immediately; very quickly. [**lick** and **split**]

licorice. Another spelling (chiefly *US*) for **liquorice**.

lictor *lik'tör* or *-tər*, (*hist*) *n* an officer who attended a Roman magistrate, bearing the fasces. [L]

lid *lid*, *n* a cover, hinged or separate, for the opening of a receptacle; the movable cover of the eye; a temperature inversion in the atmosphere that prevents the mixing of the air above and below the inversion region (*meteorol*); an effective restraint (*fig*); a hat (*slang*). — *adj* **lidd'ed** having a lid or lids. — *adj* **lid'less**. — **flip one's lid** see under **flip**; **put the lid on it** (*colloq*) to end the matter; to be a culminating injustice, misfortune, etc; **take, lift** or **blow the lid off** to uncover, reveal (a scandal, etc). [OE *hlid* (Du *lid*), from *hlīdan* to cover]

Lide *līd*, (*obs* or *dialect*) *n* the month of March. [OE *hlȳda*, connected with *hlūd* loud]

lidger. See **ledger**.

lido *lē'dō*, *n* a bathing beach; an open-air swimming-pool: — *pl* **lid'os**. [From the *Lido* at Venice, from L *lītus* shore]

lidocaine *lī'də-kān*, *n* US name for **lignocaine**. [acetani*lid* and co*caine*]

LIE (*insurance*) *abbrev*: loss of independent existence.

lie[1] *lī*, *n* a false statement made with the intention of deceiving; anything misleading or of the nature of imposture; (with *the*) an accusation of lying. — *vi* to make a false statement with the intention to deceive; to give a false impression: — *pr p* **ly'ing**; *pa t* and *pa p* **lied**. — *n* and *vi* (*Scot*) **lee** (*lē*) often of an unintentional false statement. — *n* (*dialect*) **lig**. — *n* **lī'ar** a person who lies, *esp* habitually. — *adj* **ly'ing** addicted to telling lies. — *n* the habit of telling lies. — *adv* **ly'ingly**. — **lie detector** an instrument claimed to detect lying by recording abnormal involuntary bodily reactions in a person not telling the truth. — **give someone the lie** (*archaic*, **in his** or **her throat**) to accuse someone directly of lying; **give the lie to** to accuse of lying; to prove false; **lie in one's throat** or **through one's teeth** (*usu facetious*) to lie shamelessly; **white lie** a minor falsehood, *esp* one uttered for reasons of tact, etc. [OE *lyge* (noun), *lēogan* (strong verb); Du *liegen*, Gothic *liugan*, Ger *lügen* to lie]

lie[2] *lī*, *vi* to be in a horizontal or nearly horizontal position; to assume such a position; to lean; to press; to be situated; to have a position or extent; to remain; to be or remain passively; to abide; to be still; to be incumbent; to depend; to consist; to be sustainable (*law*); to be imprisoned (*Shakesp*); to lodge, pass the night (*archaic*): — *pr p* **ly'ing**; *pa t* **lay**; *pa p* **lain**, (*Bible*) **lī'en**; erroneously **laid**, by confusion with **lay**[3]. — *n* mode or direction of lying; slope and disposition; relative position; general situation; a spell of lying; an animal's lair or resting-place; a position from which a golfball is to be played; a layer (*archaic* or *dialect*); a railway siding. — *n* **lī'er**. — **lie'-abed'** someone who lies late in bed. — Also *adj*. — **lie-down** see **lie down** below; **lie'-in'** a longer than usual stay in bed in the morning; **ly'ing-in'** confinement during childbirth: — *pl* **ly'ings-in'**. — Also *adj*. — **lying-in hospital** (*archaic*) a maternity hospital. — **lie along** (*archaic*) to be extended at full length; **lie at someone's door** (of something untoward) to be directly attributable to someone; **lie at someone's heart** (*archaic*) to be an object of interest or affection to someone; **lie back** to lean back on a support; to rest after a period of hard work; **lie by** to be inactive; to keep out of the way; to lie to (*naut*); **lie by the heels** (*archaic*) to be in prison; **lie down** to place oneself in a horizontal position, *esp* in order to sleep or rest (*n* **lie'-down**); **lie hard** or **heavy on, upon** or **to** to oppress, burden; **lie in** to be in the state of giving birth to a child (*old*); to stay in bed later than usual; **lie in one** to be in one's power; **lie in the way** to be ready, at hand; to be an obstacle; **lie in wait** to lie in ambush (often with *for*); **lie low** to keep quiet or hidden; to conceal one's actions or intentions; **lie of the land** (*fig*) the current situation; **lie on** or **upon** to be incumbent on; **lie on one's hands** to remain unwanted, unclaimed or unused; **lie on one's oars** see under **oar**; **lie out of** to remain without the good of, without payment of; **lie over** to be deferred to a future occasion; **lie to** (*naut*) to be or become nearly stationary with head to the wind; **lie under** to be subject to or oppressed by; **lie up** to abstain from work; to take to or remain in bed; of a ship, to go into or be in dock; **lie with** to rest with as a choice, duty, etc; to have sexual intercourse with (*Bible* or *archaic*); to lodge or sleep with (*archaic*); **take it lying down** (*colloq*) to endure without resistance or protest. [OE *licgan*; Ger *liegen*; Gothic *ligan*]

Liebfraumilch *lēb'frow-milk* or *-milhh*, *n* a German white wine made with grapes from the Rhine region. [Ger *Liebfrau* the Virgin Mary (after the convent where originally made) and *Milch* milk]

Liebig *lē'big*, *n* a beef extract first prepared by the German chemist J von *Liebig* (1803–73). — **Liebig condenser** the ordinary water-cooled glass condenser used in laboratory distillations.

lied *lēt*, *n* a German lyric or song, *esp* an art-song: — *pl* **lieder** (*lē'dər*). — **lied ohne worte** (*ō'nə vör'tə*) a song without words. [Ger; cf OE *lēoth* a song]

lief *lēf*, (*archaic*) *adj* and *n* beloved, dear. — *adv* willingly. — Also *adj* and *adv* **lieve** or **leve** (*lēv*): — *compar* **lief'er** or **liev'er** (*Scot* **loor**); *superl* **lief'est** or **liev'est**. — **had as lief** should like as well to; **had liefer** or **liever** had rather; **leeze me** (*Scot*) for *lief is me*, an expression of affection (*usu* with *on*). [OE *lēof*; Ger *lieb*]

liege *lēj*, (*hist*) *adj* free except as within the relations of vassal and feudal lord; under a feudal tenure. — *n* a person under a feudal tenure; a vassal; a loyal vassal, a subject; a lord or superior (also in this sense, **liege'-lord**). — *n* **liege'dom** allegiance. — *adj* **liege'less** not subject to a superior. — **liege'man** a vassal; a subject. [OFr *lige*, prob from OHGer *ledic* free, and *līdan* to depart]

lieger. See **ledger**.

lien[1] *lē'ən* or *lēn*, (*law*) *n* a right to retain possession of another's property until the owner pays a debt or fulfils a contract. [Fr, from L *ligāmen* tie or band]

lien[2] *lī'ən*, (*Bible*) *pa p* of **lie**[2].

lien[3] *lī'ən*, (*obs*) *n* the spleen. — *adj* **lī'enal**. [L *liēn*]

lientery *lī'ən-tə-ri*, *n* a form of diarrhoea with liquid evacuations of undigested food. — *adj* **lienteric** (*-ter'ik*). [Gr *leios* smooth, and *enteron* an intestine]

lier. See under **lie**[2].

lierne *li-ûrn'*, (*archit*) *n* a cross-rib or branch-rib in vaulting. [Fr]

lieu *lū* or *lo͞o*, *n* place or stead, used chiefly in the phrase *in lieu of*. — *adj* in place of, substitute, as in *lieu day* or *lieu holiday*. [Fr, from L *locus* place]

Lieut. *abbrev*: Lieutenant.

lieutenant *lef-*, *lif-* or *ləf-ten'ənt*, also (*esp navy*) *le-*, *lə-* or *lo͞o-ten'-*, (*archaic*) *lo͞ot'nənt*, (*US*) *lo͞o-*, *n* a person representing, or performing the work of, a superior (formerly also *fig*); an officer holding the place of another in his or her absence; a commissioned officer in the army next below a captain, or in the navy next below a lieutenant-commander and ranking with captain in the army; an officer in the police or fire departments next below a captain (*US*); a person holding a place next in rank to a superior, as in the compounds **lieuten'ant-col'onel, lieuten'ant-command'er** and **lieuten'ant-gen'eral**. — *n* **lieuten'ancy** or **lieuten'antship**, (*Shakesp*) **lieuten'antry** the post or commission of a lieutenant; lieutenants as a group or class. — *n* **lieuten'ant-col'onelcy**. — *n* **lieuten'ant-command'ership**. — *n* **lieuten'ant-gen'eralship**. — *n* **lieuten'ant-gov'ernor** a State governor's deputy (*US* and *Austr*); a governor subordinate to a governor-general; a governor in the Isle of Man, Jersey and Guernsey. — *n* **lieuten'ant-gov'ernorship**. — **Lord Lieutenant** a permanent governor of a county, head of the magistracy and the chief executive authority; the title of the viceroy of Ireland (till 1922): — *pl* **Lords Lieutenant**, **Lord Lieutenants** or **Lords Lieutenants**. [Fr; see **lieu** and **tenant**]

lieve, etc. See under **lief**.

life *līf*, *n* the state of being alive; conscious existence; animate or vegetative existence; the sum of the activities of plants and animals; continuation or possession of such a state; continued existence, activity, vitality or validity of anything; the period of usefulness of machinery, etc; vitality; union of soul and body; the period between birth and death; any of a number of opportunities of remaining in a game; career; current state of existence; manner of living; moral conduct; animation; liveliness, vivacity; the appearance of being alive; a living being, *esp* human; living things (collectively); social state; social vitality; human affairs; a narrative of a life, a biography; eternal happiness; a quickening principle; that on which continued existence depends; a person who imparts animation; the living form and expression, living semblance; in wines, sparkle; in cut gems, reflection, sparkle; imprisonment for life (*colloq*); a person insured against death: — *pl* **lives** (*līvz*). — *interj* used as an oath, abbreviated from *God's life*. — *adj* and *combining form* for the duration of life; of life. — *adj* **life'ful** (*Spenser* **lyfull** or **lifull**) full of vital energy. — *adj* **life'less** dead; unconscious; without vigour or vivacity; of food or drink, insipid; sluggish. — *adv* **life'lessly**. — *n* **life'lessness**. — *adj* **life'like** of something inanimate, like a living person or the copied original. — *n* **līf'er** a person sentenced to imprisonment for life; a life sentence. — *adj* **life'some** (*archaic*) full of life; gay, lively. — *adj* **life'-and-death'** critical; determining or affecting whether someone lives or dies. — **life annuity** a sum paid to a person yearly during his or her life; **life assurance** or **life insurance** insurance providing a sum of money for a specified beneficiary in the event of the policy-holder's death, and sometimes for the policy-holder if he or she reaches a specified age; **life'belt** a buoyant circular belt for keeping a person afloat in water; any aid to survival (*fig*); **life'-blood** the blood necessary to life; anything which gives essential strength or life; a twitching, eg of the eyelid or lip (*archaic*); **life'boat** a boat for saving shipwrecked persons; a measure taken in an attempt to save a business, financial operation, etc (*fig*; also often as *adj*); **life'buoy** a float for supporting a person in the water till he or she can be rescued; **life class** an art class in which the students draw or paint the human body from a live model; **life'-cycle** the round of changes in the life and generations of an organism, from zygote to zygote (*biol*); the various stages in the life or development of anything, eg a manufactured product (*fig*); **life'-estate'** an estate held during the life of the possessor; **life'-expect'ancy** the length of time which any living organism can reasonably be expected to remain alive; **life'-force'** a directing principle supposed to be inherent in living things, turning their activities to nature's own purposes. — *adj* **life'-giving** imparting life; invigorating. — **life'guard** a person employed to rescue bathers in difficulties; a bodyguard; **Life Guards** two troops of cavalry, first so called in 1685, amalgamated in 1922 and forming, with the Royal Horse Guards, the Household Cavalry; **life'-his'tory** the history of a (person's, plant's, animal's, etc) life; the succession of changes from zygote to maturity and death; the life-cycle. — *adj* **life'hold** held for life. — **life insurance** see **life assurance** above; **life'-in'terest** an interest lasting during a life; **life'-jack'et** a buoyant jacket for keeping a person afloat in water, a lifebelt; **life'line** a rope for saving or safeguarding life; a vital means of communication. — *adj* **life'long** lasting throughout one's life. — **life'manship** (*facetious*; from the book by Stephen Potter) the art of making the other person feel inferior, of placing oneself at an advantage; **life'-mor'tar** a mortar for throwing a line to a ship in distress; **life peer** a peer whose title is not hereditary; **life peerage**; **life peeress** a woman who receives a peerage which cannot be handed down to heirs; **life'-preserv'er** an apparatus for saving from drowning; a club or cosh; **life'-raft** a raft kept on board a ship for use in an emergency. — *adj* **life'-ren'dering** (*Shakesp*) yielding up life. — **life'-rent** (*Scots law*) a right to use for life; **life'-renter** a person who enjoys a life-rent: — *fem* **life'-rentrix**; **life'-rock'et** a rocket for carrying a line to a ship in distress; **life'-saver** a person who saves another from death, *esp* from drowning; a lifeguard; something or someone that comes to one's aid at a critical moment (*colloq*). — *adj* **life'-sav'ing** designed to save life, *esp* from drowning. — **life school** a school where artists work from living models; **life sciences** those sciences (biology, medicine, etc) concerned with living organisms; **life sentence** a prison sentence to last for the rest of the prisoner's natural life (*usu* now lasting *approx* 15 years). — *adj* **life'-size** or **life'-sized** of the size of the object represented. — **life'span** the length of time for which a person or animal normally lives, or a machine, etc functions; **life story** a biography or autobiography, *esp* as recounted in the media or book form; **life'style** way of living, ie one's material surroundings, attitudes, behaviour, etc; the characteristic way of life of a group or individual; **life-support machine** or **system** a device or system of devices designed to maintain human life in adverse conditions, eg in space, during serious illness, etc; **life'-table** a table of statistics of probability of life; **life'-tenant** the holder of a life-estate; **life'time** the time during which one is alive. — *adj* **life'-wear'y** (*Shakesp*) weary of life; wretched. — **life'-work** the work to which one's life is, has been or is to be devoted. — **bring to life** to give life to, make alive; to animate; **come to life** to become alive; to become animated; **for life** for the whole period of one's existence; (as if) to save one's life; **for the life of me, him, her**, etc (*usu* with *can* and a *neg*) try as I, he, she, etc might; though it were to save my, his, her, etc life; **high life** fashionable society or its (glamorous) manner of living; **line of life** a crease in the palm in which palmists see a promise of longevity; **not on your life** (*colloq*) on no account, absolutely not; **see life** to see how other people live, *esp* the less well off or respectable; **take someone's life** to kill someone; **the life and soul** the person who is the chief source of fun, etc, *esp* at a party; **the life of Riley** (*rī'li*) an easy, carefree (and often irresponsible) life; **to the life** very closely like the original; exactly drawn. [OE *līf*; ON *līf*, Swed *lif*, Du *liif* body, life; Ger *Leib* body, *leben* to live, *Leben* life]

LIFFE *abbrev*: London International Financial Futures Exchange.

LIFO *lī'fō, abbrev*: last in, first out (a method of pricing goods, controlling stock, storing data in a computer, or determining the likely order of redundancies).

lift[1] *lift*, (*Scot*) *n* the air, heavens or sky. [OE *lyft*; Ger *Luft*, ON *lopt*, Gothic *luftus* the air]

lift[2] *lift*, *vt* to bring or take (often with *up*) to a higher or (with *down*) lower position; to elevate; to take up; to elate, encourage; to take and carry away; to hold up, support; to arrest (*slang*); to steal (*colloq*); to plagiarize; to remove or revoke; in a foundry, to remove a pattern from a mould; to take up for burial (*Scot*); to increase (in value, price, etc) (*esp US*). — *vi* to rise. — *n* an act of lifting; lifting power; vertical distance of lifting; the component of the aerodynamic force on an aircraft acting upwards at right angles to the drag; something which is to be raised; something which assists in lifting; an enclosed platform or cagelike structure moving in a vertical shaft to carry people or goods up and down; the shaft in which it works; one of the layers of material in a shoe heel, *esp* an extra one to increase the wearer's height; a mechanism for raising or lowering a vessel to another level of a canal; a step in advancement, promotion, etc; a boost to one's spirits; a feeling of elation; a (*usu* free) journey in someone else's vehicle. — *adj* **lift'able**. — *n* **lift'er** someone who, or something which, lifts; a thief (*Shakesp*). — **lift'back** a motor car with a sloping rear door lifting up from the bottom, a hatchback; **lift'-boy**, **lift'-girl** or **lift'-man** a person whose job is to operate a lift in a hotel, store, etc; **lift'ing-bridge** a bridge whose roadway can be raised bodily; **lift'-off** the take-off of an aircraft or rocket; the moment when this occurs; **lift'-pump** any pump that is not a force-pump. — **have one's face lifted** to undergo an operation for smoothing and firming the skin of one's face; **lift a finger** or **hand (to)** to make the smallest effort (to help, etc); **lift a** or **one's hand (to)** to raise it in hostility (to), to threaten physically; **lift off** of a rocket, etc, to take off, be launched. [ON *lypta*, from *lopt* the air]

lifull. See under **life**.

lig[1] *lig*, (*slang*) *vi* to lie about, to idle; to be a freeloader, *esp* in the entertainment industry. — *n* **ligg'er**. — *n* **ligg'ing**. [Orig dialect for **lie**[2]]

lig[2] or **ligge** *lig*, (*Spenser* and *N Eng dialect*) *vi* a form of **lie**[2]. — *infin* and *pl* (*Spenser*) also **ligg'en**.

lig[3]. Dialect form of **lie**[1].

ligament *lig'ə-mənt*, *n* anything that binds; the bundle of fibrous tissue joining bones or cartilages (*anatom*); a bond or tie. — *adj* **ligamental** (*-ment'l*), **ligament'ary** or **ligament'ous**. — *n* **ligand** (*lig'ənd* or *lī'*) an atom, molecule, radical or ion which forms a complex with a central atom. — *n* **ligase** (*lī'gāz*) an enzyme which seals nicks in one strand of a duplex DNA, often used to seal gaps resulting from the artificial insertion of one DNA sequence into another. — *vt* **ligate** (*lī'gāt*) to tie up. — *n* **līgā'tion** the act of binding; the state of being bound; the joining together, often facilitated by sticky ends, of two linear nucleic acid molecules (*biol*). — *n* **ligature** (*lig'ə-chər*) anything that binds; a bandage; a tie or slur (*music*); a character formed from two or more letters, eg *æ*, *ff* (*printing*); a cord for tying the blood vessels, etc (*med*); impotence produced by magic (*archaic*). — *vt* to bind with a ligature. [L *ligāre* to bind]

ligan. See **lagan**.

ligand, **ligase**, **ligate**, **ligation**, **ligature**, etc. See under **ligament**.

liger *lī'gər*, *n* the offspring of a *li*on and female ti*ger*.

ligge and **liggen**. See **lig**[2].

ligger[1] *lig'ər*, *n* the horizontal timber of a scaffolding; a lower millstone (cf **runner**); a plank bridge; a coverlet for a bed; a kelt or spent salmon; a night-line with float and bait for pike-fishing. [**lig**, Northern form of **lie**[2]]

ligger[2] and **ligging**. See under **lig**[1].

light[1] *līt*, *n* the agency by which objects are made visible; electromagnetic radiation capable of producing visual sensation; anything from which it originates, such as the sun or a lamp; a high degree of illumination; day; a gleam or shining from a bright source; a gleam or glow in the eye or on the face; the power of vision (*archaic*); an eye (*archaic*); the brighter part of a picture; a means of igniting or illuminating; a lighthouse; mental or spiritual illumination (*fig*); enlightenment; a hint, clue or help towards understanding; knowledge; open view; aspect; a conspicuous person; an aperture for admitting light; a vertical division of a window; in a crossword, the word (or sometimes an individual letter in the word) on the diagram that is the answer to a clue. — *adj* not dark; bright; whitish; well lit. — *vt* to shine light on, provide light in; to set fire to; to follow or precede (someone, or his or her path) with a light. — *vi* (*archaic*) to become light or bright: — *pr p* **light'ing**; *pa t* and *pa p* **light'ed** or **lit**. — *n* **light'er** a person who sets something alight; a means of igniting, *esp* a small device for lighting cigarettes. — *adj* **light'ful** (*archaic*) full of light. — *n* **light'ing** illumination; ignition, kindling; arrangement or quality of lights. — Also *adj*. — *adj* **light'ish**. — *adj* **light'less**. — *n* **light'ness**. — *adj* **light'some** (*archaic* and *poetic*) full of light. — **light'-ball** (*hist*) a combustible ball used to give light in warfare; **light'-box** a box-shaped device with an internal lamp to facilitate viewing through paper, negatives, etc placed on its translucent surface; **light bulb** a glass bulb containing a low-pressure gas and a metal filament which glows when an electric current is passed through it, one of the most common methods of electric lighting. — *n pl* **light'-dues** tolls from ships, for maintenance of lighthouses. — **light-emitting diode** a semiconducting device that emits light when an electric current passes through it, as used for alphanumeric displays in digital clocks, electronic calculators, etc (*abbrev* **LED**). — *adj* **light'-fast** (of colour in fabric, or coloured fabric) not liable to fade from prolonged exposure to light. — **light'house** a building with a powerful light to guide or warn off ships or aircraft; **light'houseman** or **light'housekeeper** the person in charge of a lighthouse. — *n* and *adj* **light'ing-up**. — **lighting-up time** the time of day from which vehicles must show lights; **light meter** (*photog*) a meter for measuring the level of light present, an exposure meter; **light'-mill** a radiometer; **light'-or'gan** a keyboard instrument that gives a play of light as an organ gives sound; **light pen** (*comput*) a pen-shaped photoelectric device that can communicate directly with a computer, entering or altering data on a visual display unit; a light-sensitive fibre-optic device shaped like a pen, used for reading bar-coded labels. — *adj* **light'-proof** impervious to light, light-tight. — **light'ship** a ship serving the purpose of a lighthouse; **light'-table** (*printing*) (a table incorporating) a ground-glass surface, illuminated from below, for use when working on lay-out with translucent materials. — *adj* **light'-tight** light-proof. — **light time** the time taken by light to travel from a heavenly body to the observer; **light'-tower**; **light'-year** the distance light travels in a year (about 6 000 000 000 000 miles). — **according to one's lights** as far as one's knowledge, spiritual illumination, etc enables one to judge; **between the lights** in the twilight; **between two lights** under cover of darkness; **bring to light** to reveal; **come to light** to be revealed; **fixed light** in lighthouses, an unchanging light; **floating light** a light at the masthead of a lightship; **hide one's light under a bushel** see under **bushel**[1]; **in a good** or **bad light** putting a favourable or unfavourable construction on something; **inner light** spiritual illumination, *esp* divinely inspired; **in one's** (or **the**) **light** between the speaker or the stated person and the source of illumination or chance of success, etc; **in the light of** considering, taking into account; **leading light** see under **lead**[1]; **light at the end of the tunnel** an indication that success, completion, etc is assured, if still distant; **light of nature** intellectual perception or intuition; man's capacity of discovering truth unaided by revelation (*theol*); **lights out** a bugle or trumpet call for the extinction of lights (*military*); the time at which lights are turned out for the night, in a boarding-school, barracks, etc; **light up** to light one's lamp, pipe, cigarette, etc; to turn on the light; to make or become light, bright, happy, etc; **lit (up)** drunk; **northern** and **southern lights** aurora borealis and australis respectively; **see the light** to come into view or being; to realize a fact, mistake, etc; to be religiously converted; **shed** or **throw light on** to clarify, help to explain; **stand in one's own light** to hinder one's own advantage; **strike a light** (*slang*) an exclamation expressing surprise. [ME *liht*, from OE (Anglian) *leht*, *lēht* (WSax *lēoht*); Ger *Licht*]

light[2] *līt*, *adj* not heavy; of incorrectly low weight; of work, easily suffered or performed; easily digested; containing little fat and/or sugar, and so healthier; containing little alcohol; of bread, well risen; not heavily armed; active; not heavily burdened or equipped; unimportant; not dense, copious or intense; slight; scanty; gentle; delicate; nimble; facile; frivolous; unheeding; gay or lively; amusing; unchaste; of soil, loose or sandy; giddy or delirious; idle; worthless; in the state of having given birth to a child (in *compar*; *obs*); falling short in the number of tricks one has contracted to make (*bridge*). — *adv* lightly. — *vt* (*obs*) to make lighter. — *vt* **light'en** to make lighter. — *vi* to become lighter. — *n* **light'er** a large open boat used in unloading and loading ships. — *n* **light'erage** loading, unloading and ferrying by lighters; the payment for such service. — *adj* **light'ish**. — *adv* **light'ly** in a light manner; slightly; easily, readily, unthinkingly (*Shakesp*); not improbably (*archaic*); promptly. — *vt* (*esp* in Scots form **lichtly** *lihht'li*) to slight or make light of. — *n* **light'ness**. — *n pl* **lights** the lungs of an animal (as lighter than the adjoining parts). — *adj* **light'some** light, gay, lively, cheering. — *n* **light'someness**. — *adj* **light'-armed** (*military*) armed in a manner suitable for activity. — **light engine** one without coaches or trucks attached; **light'erman** a person employed in lighterage. — *adj* **light'er-than-air** of aircraft, kept in the air by gas which is lighter than air. — *adj* **light'-faced** (*printing*) of type, having thin lines. — *adj* **light'-fing'ered** light or active with one's fingers; inclined to steal. — *adj* **light'-footed** (*archaic* **light'-foot**) nimble, active. — *adj* **light'-hand'ed** with a light, delicate, or dexterous touch; having little in the hand; empty-handed; insufficiently manned. — *adj* **light'-head'ed** giddy in the head; delirious; thoughtless; unsteady, *esp* through slight drunkenness. — **light'-head'edness**. — *adj* **light'-heart'ed** unburdened or merry of heart; free from anxiety; cheerful; inconsiderate (*archaic*). — *adv* **light'-heart'edly**. — **light'-heart'edness**; **light-heavyweight** see under **heavy**. — *adj* **light'-heeled** swift of foot; loose, unchaste (*obs*). — **light horse** light-armed cavalry; **light horseman**; **light industry** see under **industry**; **light infantry** light-armed-infantry. — *adj* **light'-legged** swift of foot. — **light literature, music**, etc, such as calls for little mental effort; **light-middleweight** see under **middle**. — *adj* **light'-mind'ed** frivolous or unstable; inconsiderate. — **light'-mind'edness**; **light'-o'-love** a fickle or wanton woman; in *Shakesp* the name of an old dance tune; **light railway** a railway of light construction. — *adj* **light'-spir'ited** having a cheerful spirit. — **light water** normal water (H_2O) as opposed to heavy water (qv); **light-water reactor** a reactor using normal water as moderator and coolant (*abbrev* **LWR**); **light'weight** a weight category applied in boxing and wrestling; a sportsman of the specified weight for the category (eg in professional boxing above featherweight, **jun'ior-lightweight** (maximum 59kg/130lb) and **light'weight** (maximum 61kg/135lb); an animal between middleweight and featherweight; a person of little importance, authority, etc; a light article of any kind, eg a motorcycle. — *adj* light in weight; lacking substance, earnestness, solemnity, etc (*fig*). — *adj* **light'-winged** having light wings; volatile. — **lighten up** (*US slang*) to relax, calm down; to become less serious, angry or otherwise emotional; **make light of** to treat as being of little consequence. [OE (Anglian) *līht* (WSax *līoht*, *lēoht*); Ger *leicht*, ON *lēttr*; L *levis*]

light[3] *līt*, *vi* to dismount; to come down eg from a horse or vehicle, or from a fall or flight; to alight; to settle; to rest; to come upon by chance (with *on* or *upon*): — *pr p* **light'ing**; *pa t* and *pa p* **light'ed** or **lit**. — Also (*Prayer Bk*) **light'en**. — **light into** (*colloq*) to attack, with blows or words; **light out** (*colloq*) to decamp. [OE *līhtan* to dismount, literally to make light; see **light**[2]]

lighten[1] *līt'n*, *vt* to make light, lighter or brighter; to illuminate. — *vi* to become light, lighter or brighter; to flash as lightning. — *n* **light'ening** a making or becoming lighter or brighter. [Ety as for **light**[1]]

lighten[2]. See under **light**[2,3].

lightning *līt'ning*, *n* a flash of light in the sky, caused by electricity being discharged from thunderclouds; a revival or exhilaration supposed to precede death (*Shakesp*). — *adj* characterized by speed and suddenness. — **light'ning-arrester** an apparatus for protecting electrical apparatus in thunderstorms; **light'ning-bug** a firefly; **light'ning-conductor** or **light'ning-rod** a metallic rod for protecting buildings from lightning; **lightning strike** an industrial or military strike without warning; **light'ning-tube** a fulgurite. [Ety as for **light**[1]]

lightsome. See under **light**[1,2].

lignage *līn'ij* (*Spenser*). Same as **lineage**.

lign-aloes or **lignaloes** *līn-al'ōz* or *lig-nal'ōz*, (*Bible*) *n* aloes-wood. [L *lignum* wood, and *aloēs*, genitive of L and Gr *aloē* aloe]

ligne *līn* (Fr *lēn-y'*), *n* a measure of watch movement (Swiss ligne = 2·256mm). [Fr]

ligneous, **lignite**, etc. See under **lignum**[1].

lignocaine *lig'nō-kān*, *n* a local anaesthetic used eg in dentistry and also to regulate an unsteady heartbeat. [L *lignum* wood, and *cocaine*]

lignum[1] *lig'nəm*, *n* wood. — *adj* **lig'neous** woody; wooden. — *n* **lignificā'tion**. — *adj* **lig'niform** resembling wood. — *vt* and *vi* **lig'nify** to turn into wood or make woody: — *pr p* **lig'nifying**; *pa t* and *pa p* **lig'nified**. — *n* **lig'nin** a complicated mixture of substances deposited in the thickened cell-walls of plants, making them rigid. — *adj* **ligniper'dous** (L *perdere* to destroy) destructive of wood. — *n* **lig'nite** (*-nīt*) brown coal, a stage in the conversion of vegetable matter into coal. — *adj* **lignitic** (*-nit'ik*). — *adj* **ligniv'orous** (L *vorāre* to devour) feeding on wood. — *adj* **lig'nose** ligneous. — *n* a constituent of lignin. — *n* **lignocell'ulose** any of several compounds of lignin and cellulose occurring in woody tissue. — **lignum vitae** (*vī'tē*, or *lig'nōōm wē'tī* or *vē'*; *L*, wood of life) the wood of a tropical American genus of trees, *Guaiacum*. [L *lignum* wood]

lignum[2] *lig'nəm*, (*Austr*) *n* a wiry shrub (*Muehlenbeckia cunninghamii*) or any other shrub of the Polygonum family, forming dense masses in swamps and plains in Australia. — **lig'num-scrub'**; **lig'num-swamp'**. [For **polygonum**]

ligroin *lig'rō-in*, *n* a petroleum fraction boiling between 80° and 120°C. [Origin unknown]

ligule *lig'ūl*, *n* (*bot*) a scale at the top of the leaf-sheath in grasses; a similar scale on a petal; a strap-shaped corolla in composite plants. — *n* **lig'ula** a tongue-like part or organ; the anterior part of an insect's labium or lower lip. — *adj* **lig'ular**. — *adj* **lig'ulate** (*bot*) like a strap; having ligules. — *n pl* **Liguliflo'rae** a division of the Compositae having all flowers ligulate. — *adj* **liguliflo'ral**. — *adj* **lig'uloid**. [L *ligula*, dimin of *lingua* a tongue]

Liguorian *li-gwō'ri-ən* or *-gwö'*, *n* and *adj* Redemptorist.

ligure *lig'ūr* or *-yər*, (*Bible*) *n* an unknown precious stone, jacinth or amber according to RV (the New English Bible says turquoise). [Gr *ligyrion*]

like[1] *līk*, *adj* identical, equal, or nearly equal in any respect; similar, resembling; suiting, befitting; characteristic of; used in requesting a description, as in *what is it like?*; used in combination to form adjectives from nouns, with the force 'resembling', 'suitable to', 'typical of', eg *cat-like*, *lady-like*; used in combination to form adjectives and adverbs from adjectives, with the force 'somewhat', 'kind of', eg *stupid-like* (*colloq*); inclined, likely or probable (*dialect*). — *n* one of the same kind; the same thing; a stroke bringing the total to the same as the other side's (*golf*); an exact resemblance. — *adv* in the same manner; probably (*dialect*); as it were (*dialect*); as if about (*dialect*); nearly (*colloq*); to some extent (*dialect*); sometimes used meaninglessly (*dialect*). — *conj* (*Shakesp*; another reading *as*; now *illiterate*) as; as if. — *prep* in the same manner as; to the same extent as. — *vt* (*Shakesp*) to compare or liken. — *vi* (*obs*) to be or seem likely (to), come near (to). — *n* **like'lihood** probability; promise of success or of future excellence; similitude (*obs*); semblance (*obs*); resemblance (*obs*). — *n* **like'liness** likelihood; likeness (*Spenser*). — *adj* **like'ly** like the thing required; promising; probable; credible; similar (*Spenser*); pleasing (*dialect*); comely (*dialect*). — *adv* (*colloq*) probably. — *vt* **lik'en** to represent as like or similar; to compare. — *n* **like'ness** a resemblance; semblance; guise; a person who or thing which has a resemblance; a portrait. — *adv* **like'wise** in the same or similar manner; moreover; too, also. — *adj* **like'-mind'ed** having similar opinions, values, etc. — **compare like with like** to compare only such things as are genuinely comparable; **feel like** to be disposed or inclined towards; used in requesting a description, as in *what does it feel like*?; **had like** (*archaic*) was likely, came near to; **look like** to show a probability of; to appear similar to; used in requesting a description, as in *what does it look like*?; **something like (a)** a fine specimen, a model of what the thing should be; around, approximately; **such like** of that kind, similar; **the like** (*colloq*) similar things; **the likes of** people such as. [OE *līc*, seen in *gelīc*; ON *līkr*, Du *gelijk*, Ger *gleich* (= *geleich*)]

like[2] *līk*, *vt* to be fond of; to be pleased with; to approve; to enjoy; to please (*obs*). — *n* a liking, chiefly in the phrase *likes and dislikes*. — *adj* **lik'able** or **like'able** lovable; amiable, pleasant. — *n* **līk'er** someone who likes. — *n* **līk'ing** affection, fondness; taste or preference; satisfaction; beloved (*Milton*); condition, plight (*obs*). — *adj* (*obs*) pleasing; in good condition (also (*archaic*) **good'-liking** or **well'-liking**). — **on liking** (*archaic*) on approval. [Orig impersonal, from OE *līcian* to please, to be suitable, from *līc* like, suitable, likely]

like[3] *līk*, (*Scot*) *n* a corpse; a lykewake. — **likewake** and **likewalk** see **lykewake**. [Northern form of **lich**[2]]

-like *-līk*, *adj sfx* combining with nouns to convey senses such as 'having the qualities of', 'similar to'. [**like**[1]]

likin *lē-kēn'*, *n* formerly, a Chinese transit duty. [Chin]

lilac *lī'lək*, *n* a European tree (*Syringa vulgaris*) of the olive family, with light-purple or white flowers, or other species of the genus; a light purple colour (also *adj*). [Fr (*obs*; now *lilas*) and Sp, from Ar *līlāk*, *līlak*, from Pers *līlak*, *nīlak* bluish]

lilangeni *lil-ən-gen'i*, *n* the standard unit of currency of Swaziland (100 cents): — *pl* **emalangeni** (*em-ə-lən-gen'i*).

liliaceous, **lilied**, etc. See under **lily**.

lill[1] *lil*, (*Spenser*) *vt* to loll (the tongue). [Cf **loll**]

lill[2] *lil*, (*Scot*) *n* a finger-hole of a wind instrument. [Cf Du *lul*]

Lillibullero *lil-i-bŏŏ-le'rō* or *-lē'rō*, *n* the famous ballad in mockery of the Irish Catholics, which 'sung James II out of three kingdoms'. — Also **Lilliburlē'ro**. [From the meaningless refrain]

Lilliputian *lil-i-pū'shən* or *-shyən*, *n* an inhabitant of **Lill'iput** (*-put* or *-pŏŏt*), an imaginary diminutive country described by Swift in *Gulliver's Travels*, inhabited by tiny people; a midget. — *adj* (also without *cap*) diminutive.

LILO *lī'lō*, *abbrev*: last in, last out (a rough guide to likely order of redundancies).

Lilo® *lī'lō*, *n* (also without *cap*) an inflatable mattress, often used in camping, etc.

lilt *lilt*, *vi* to sing or play, *esp* merrily, or vaguely and absent-mindedly, giving the swing or cadence rather than the structure of the melody; to hum; to do anything briskly or adroitly, eg to hop about (*dialect*). — *vt* to sing or play in such a manner. — *n* a cheerful song or air; cadence, movement of a tune, etc; a springy quality in gait, etc; a lill, a finger-hole (*obs*). [ME *lulte*; origin unknown]

lily *lil'i*, *n* any plant or flower of the genus **Lil'ium**, typical genus of **Liliā'ceae**, a family of monocotyledons differing from rushes chiefly in the large conspicuous flowers; extended to other plants of the same family, of the related family Amaryllidaceae, or unrelated; the fleur-de-lis; a person or thing of great purity or whiteness (*fig*). — *adj* white; pale. — *adj* **liliā'ceous**. — *adj* **lil'ied** adorned with lilies; resembling lilies. — *adj* **lil'y-liv'ered** white-livered; cowardly. — **lily pad** a leaf of a waterlily. — *adj* **lil'y-white** pure white; faultless, without blame. — **lily of the Nile** Richardia or Zantedeschia; **lily of the valley** Convallaria, with two long oval leaves and spikes of white bell-shaped flowers. [OE *lilie*, from L *līlium*, from *Gr leirion* lily]

lima *lē'mə*, *n* (in full **Lima bean**) a flattened, whitish, edible bean (*Phaseolus lunatus*), the seed of a tropical American plant related to the French bean, and of which the butter bean is a well-known variety. — **li'ma-wood** a kind of brazil-wood. [*Lima* in Peru]

limaces, etc. See **limax**.

limail. See **lemel**.

limation *lī-mā'shən*, *n* filing. [L *līma* a file]

limax *lī'maks*, *n* a slug of the common genus *Limax*, giving its name to the slug family **Limā'ceae**: — *pl* **limaces** (*lī-mā'sēz*). — *adj* **limaceous** (*lī-mā'shəs*). — *n* **limacel** (*lim-ə-sel'*) a slug's reduced, *usu* embedded, shell. — *adj* **limaciform** (*lim-as'* or *lī-mās'*) slug-like. — *adj* **limacine** (*lim'ə-sīn* or *lī'*, or *-sin*) of, resembling or relating to slugs. — *n* **limacol'ogist**. — *n* **limacol'ogy** the study of slugs. — *n* **limaçon** (*lim'ə-son*; Fr *lē-ma-sõ*) a curve whose polar equation is $r = a\cos\theta + b$. [L *līmāx* a slug]

limb[1] *lim*, *n orig* a member or organ of the body, now only an arm, leg or wing; a prudish euphemism for leg; a projecting part; a main branch of a tree, spur of a mountain, etc; a member of a body of people, as in *a limb of the law*; an imp or mischievous child, as in *a limb of Satan*. — *vt* to dismember (*archaic*); to supply with limbs (*Milton*). — *adj* **limbed** having limbs, *esp* used in combination, as in *long-limbed*. — *adj* **limb'less**. — *adv* **limb'meal** (*Shakesp*) limb by limb. — **limb'-girdle** a bony arch with which a limb articulates. — **out on a limb** in a hazardous position on one's own (*fig*). [OE *lim*; ON *limr*, Swed *lem*]

limb[2] *lim*, *n* an edge or border, eg of the sun, etc; the edge of a sextant, etc; the free or expanded part of a floral or other leaf (*bot*). — *adj* **lim'bate** bordered. — *adj* **lim'bous** overlapping. [L *limbus* a border]

limbeck or **limbec** *lim'bek*, (*Spenser* and *Shakesp*) *n* aphetic for **alembic**.

limber[1] *lim'bər*, *n* a detachable two-wheeled vehicle containing ammunition, preceding the gun carriage and forming with it part of a field gun unit (*military*); the shaft of a vehicle (*dialect*). — *vt* to attach to the limber. [Poss Fr *limonière*]

limber[2] *lim'bər*, *adj* pliant, flexible, supple. — *vt* to make limber. — **lim'ber-neck** botulism in birds. — **limber up** to loosen up the muscles in preparation for physical effort of some sort. [Origin uncertain]

limber[3] *lim'bər*, (*naut*) *n* (*usu* in *pl*) a channel or hole on either side of the inner keel for drainage. [Fr *lumière*, from L *lumināria* windows]

limbic *lim'bik*, (*anatom*) *adj* of or relating to the **limbic system** in the brain, the hypothalamus, etc, concerned with basic emotions. [L *limbicus*, from *limbus* border]

Limbo or **limbo** *lim'bō*, *n* the borderland of Hell, reserved for the unbaptized (*Limbus patrum* for the righteous who died before Christ, *Limbus infantum* for children); any unsatisfactory place of consignment or oblivion;

an uncertain or intermediate state; prison: — *pl* **Lim'bos** or **lim'bos**. — Also **Lim'bus** (*-bəs*): — *pl* **Lim'bi**. [From the Latin phrase *in limbo*, *in* in, and ablative of *limbus* border]

limbo *lim'bō*, *n* a W Indian dance in which the dancer bends backwards and passes under a bar which is progressively lowered: — *pl* **lim'bos**. [Perhaps **limber**[1]]

Limburger *lim'bûrg-ər*, *n* a white cheese from *Limburg* in Belgium, of strong taste and smell. — Also **Limberger cheese**.

limburgite *lim'bər-gīt*, *n* a volcanic rock composed of olivine and augite, etc, in a fine-grained or glassy groundmass. [*Limburg* in Baden, a typical locality]

Limbus patrum and **Limbus infantum**. See **Limbo**.

lime[1] *līm*, *n* bird-lime, a sticky substance for catching birds; any slimy or gluey material (*dialect*); the white caustic earth (calcium oxide, quicklime, or caustic lime) obtained by driving off water and carbon dioxide from calcium carbonate (eg in the form of limestone); calcium hydroxide (slaked lime) obtained by adding water to quicklime; loosely, limestone or calcium carbonate. — *adj* of lime. — *vt* to cover with lime; to treat with lime; to manure with lime; to ensnare, trap (also *fig*); to cement (*dialect*). — *vi* (*Shakesp*) to adulterate wine with lime. — *n* **līm'iness**. — *n* **līm'ing** in the preparation of leather, etc, the soaking of skins in limewater to remove hair; the application of lime. — *adj* **līm'y** glutinous, sticky (*dialect*); smeared with, containing, like or of the nature of, lime. — **lime'-burner** someone who calcines limestone, etc to form lime; **lime'kiln** a kiln or furnace in which calcium carbonate is reduced to lime; **lime'light** Drummond light, light produced by a blowpipe-flame directed against a block of quicklime; the glare of publicity (*fig*; from a type of lamp formerly used in theatre stage lighting, which used heated lime to provide light). — *vt* (*esp fig*) to illuminate by limelight, to subject to the glare of limelight: — *pa t* and *pa p* **lime'lit** or **lime'-lighted**. — **lime'pit** a lime-filled pit in which hides are steeped to remove hair; **lime'stone** a sedimentary rock of calcium carbonate, sometimes (*magnesian* limestone) with a high dolomite content; **limestone pavement** (*geol*) a surface of exposed limestone resembling a pavement; **lime'-twig** a twig smeared with bird-lime; a snare; **lime'wash** a milky mixture of slaked lime and water, used for coating walls, etc; **lime'water** a suspension of calcium hydroxide in water, sometimes used as an antacid. [OE *līm*; Ger *Leim* glue, L *līmus* slime]

lime[2] *līm*, *n* a tropical citrus tree, *Citrus aurantifolia*; its small nearly globular fruit, with acid-tasting flesh; the colour of the fruit, a yellowish green. — *n* **limeade** (*līm-ād'*) a non-alcoholic drink made from the juice of limes and water, often carbonated. — *n* **lime'y** (*NAm slang*) a British sailor or ship (from the use of lime juice on British ships to prevent scurvy); any British person. — **lime green** a bright, yellowish shade of green, the colour of limes (*adj* **lime'-green'**); **lime juice** the acid-tasting juice of the lime. [Fr, from Sp *lima*; cf **lemon**[1]]

lime[3] *līm*, *n* the linden tree (*Tilia europaea*), or any other tree of the genus, with heart-shaped leaves and small yellowish flowers. — **lime'-tree**; **lime'-wood**. [**lind**]

lime[4] and **lime-hound**. See **lyam**.

lime[5] *līm*, (*Caribbean slang*) *vi* to loiter, hang about. [Ety unknown]

limen *lī'men*, (*psychol*) *n* the threshold of consciousness; the limit below which a stimulus is not perceived. — *adj* **liminal** (*līm'* or *lim'in-əl*). [L *līmen*, *-inis* threshold]

limerick *lim'ə-rik*, *n* a form of humorous verse in a five-line jingle. [Said to be from a refrain formerly used, referring to *Limerick* in Ireland]

limes *lī'mēz* or *lē'mes*, *n* a boundary or boundary work, *esp* of the Roman Empire: — *pl* **limites** (*lī'mit-ēz* or *lē'mi-tās*). [L *līmes*, *-itis*]

limey. See under **lime**[2].

limicolous *lī-mik'ə-ləs*, *adj* living in mud. — *adj* **lī'mous** (*archaic*) muddy; slimy. [L *līmus* mud, and *colere* to dwell]

liminal. See under **limen**.

limit *lim'it*, *n* a boundary, *esp* one which may not be passed; a restriction; a predetermined price at which a broker is instructed to buy or sell (*stock exchange*); a value, position or figure that can be approached indefinitely (*math*); a prescribed time (*Shakesp*); something which is bounded, a region or division; (with *the*) the unspeakable extreme of what may be endured (*colloq*). — *vt* to confine within bounds; to restrict; to appoint or specify (*Shakesp*). — *adj* **lim'itable**. — *n* **limitā'rian** (*theol*) someone who limits salvation to part of mankind. — *adj* **lim'itary** (*-ə-ri*) of a boundary; placed at the boundary; confined within limits; licensed as a limiter (*hist*). — *n* **limitā'tion** a limiting; a lack of physical ability, talent, etc; a specified period within which an action must be brought, etc (*law*). — *adj* **lim'itātive** tending to limit. — *adj* **lim'ited** within limits; narrow; restricted. — *n* a limited company. — *adv* **lim'itedly**. — *n* **lim'itedness**. — *n* **lim'iter** a person, device or circumstance that limits or confines; a friar who had a licence to beg within certain bounds (*hist*). — *n* and *adj* **lim'iting**. — *adj* **lim'itless** having no limits; boundless; immense; infinite. — *adv* **lim'itlessly**. — *n* **lim'itlessness**. — **limited edition** an edition, *esp* of a book, of which only a certain number of copies is printed or made; **limited express** (*NAm*) an express railway train carrying a limited number of passengers; **limited liability** see under **liable**; **limited** (or **lim'ited-liabil'ity**) **company** one whose owners have liability for its debts, etc only according to their financial stake in it; **limited monarchy** one in which the monarch shares the supreme power with others, constitutional monarchy. — *adj* **lim'ited-o'ver** of a cricket match, in which the number of overs bowled by each side is restricted. — **limit gauge** (*eng*) a gauge used to verify that a part has been made to within specified dimensional limits. — **off limits** out of bounds; **statute of limitations** an act specifying the period within which certain action must be taken; **within limits** to a limited extent. [L *līmes*, *-itis* boundary]

limitrophe *lim'i-trōf*, *adj* near the frontier; border. [L *līmitrophus*, from *līmes*, *-itis* border, and Gr *trophos* feeder]

limma *lim'ə*, *n* a pause of one mora (*prosody*); in Pythagorean music, the difference between two whole tones and a perfect fourth; applied also to other minute intervals. [Gr *leimma* a remnant]

limmer *lim'ər*, (*Scot* and *N Eng dialect*) *n* a rogue or thief; a hussy, a jade. [Origin obscure]

limn *lim*, *vt* and *vi* (*archaic*) to draw or paint, *esp* in water-colours; *orig* to illuminate with ornamental letters, etc: — *pr p* **limning** (*lim'ing* or *lim'ning*). — *n* **limner** (*lim'nər*) a painter on paper or parchment; a portrait-painter. [OFr *luminer* or *enluminer*, from L *lūmināre* or *illūmināre* to cast light on]

Limnaea *lim-nē'ə*, *n* a genus of pond-snails. — *n* **limnae'id** any member of the family **Limnae'idae**, to which it belongs. — *adj* **limnetic** (*-net'ik*) living in fresh water. — *adj* **limnolog'ical**. — *n* **limnol'ogist**. — *n* **limnol'ogy** the scientific study (embracing physical, geographical, biological, etc characteristics) of lakes and other freshwater bodies. — *adj* **limnoph'ilous** living in ponds or marshes. [Gr *limnē* a pool or marsh]

limo *lim'ō*, (*colloq*; *esp US*) short form of **limousine**: — **lim'os**.

limonite *lī'mən-īt*, *n* brown iron ore, hydrated ferric oxide, a deposit in bogs and lakes (*bog-iron*) or a decomposition product in rocks. — *adj* **limonitic** (*-it'ik*). [Gr *leimōn* a meadow]

limosis *lī-mō'sis*, *n* an abnormally ravenous appetite. [Gr *līmos* hunger]

limous. See under **limicolous**.

Limousin *lē-mōō-zɛ̃*, *n* a breed of cattle. [*Limousin*, a district in France]

limousine *lim'ōō-zēn*, *n* a large closed motor car (*orig* with the driver's seat outside but covered by the roof) which has a partition separating driver and passengers; any large motor car (sometimes used *ironically*). [Fr, after a type of long cloak once worn in the *Limousin* district (see above)]

limp[1] *limp, adj* lacking stiffness; flaccid; drooping; of a cloth binding for books, not stiffened by boards. — *adv* **limp'ly**. — *n* **limp'ness**. — *adj* **limp-wrist'ed** (*slang*) of a man, effeminate. [Origin obscure]

limp[2] *limp, vi* to walk unevenly, *esp* when one leg is injured; to drag a leg; (of a damaged ship or aircraft) to proceed with difficulty. — *n* a limping gait. — *n* and *adj* **limp'ing**. — *adv* **limp'ingly**. [There is an OE adj *lemp-healt* halting]

limpet *lim'pit, n* a gasteropod (genus *Patella*, etc) with a conical shell, that clings to rocks; a person not easily got rid of. — **limpet mine** an explosive device designed to cling to a surface, *esp* one attached to a ship's hull by a magnet, etc. [OE *lempedu* lamprey]

limpid *lim'pid, adj* clear; transparent. — *n* **limpid'ity**. — *adv* **lim'pidly**. — *n* **lim'pidness**. [L *limpidus*]

limpkin *limp'kin, n* an American wading bird, *Aramus guarauna*, like a rail. [From its limping gait]

limulus *lim'ū-ləs, n* (without *cap*) a crab of the king-crab genus *Limulus*. [L *līmulus*, dimin of *līmus* looking sideways]

limy. See under **lime**[1].

lin[1] *lin, vi* (*Spenser*) to cease, to give over. — *vt* (*obs*) to cease from. [OE *linnan* to cease]

lin[2]. See **linn**.

lin. *abbrev*: lineal; linear.

linac *lin'ak, n* a linear accelerator (qv under **line**[2]).

linage. See under **line**[2].

linalool *lin-al'ō-ol* or *lin'ə-lōōl, n* a fragrant liquid alcohol, used as an ingredient of perfume, obtained from oil of rosewood and other essential oils. [Mex Sp *lináloe* a tree with aromatic wood, from L *lignum aloes* lignaloes]

linch *linch* or *linsh*, (*dialect*) *n* a boundary ridge or unploughed strip; a terrace or ledge. — Also **linch'et** or **lynch'et**. [OE *hlinc* ridge; cf **link**[3]]

linchpin *linch'* or *linsh'pin, n* a pin used to keep a wheel on its axle; a person or thing essential to a plan, organization, etc (*fig*). [OE *lynis* axle, and **pin**]

Lincoln green *lingk'ən grēn, n* a bright green cloth once made in *Lincoln*, England; its colour.

lincomycin *lingk-ō-mī'sin, n* an antibiotic used against streptococcal and staphylococcal infections, produced from the bacterium *Streptomyces lincolnensis*. [L *lincol*nensis and *-mycin*]

lincrusta *lin-krus'tə, n* a thick, embossed type of wall-paper. [L *līnum* flax, and *crusta* rind, on the analogy of **linoleum**]

Lincs. *lingks, abbrev*: Lincolnshire.

linctus *lingk'təs, n* a syrup-like medicine for coughs and sore throats: — *pl* **linc'tuses**. — *n* **linc'ture**. [L *linctus*, *-ūs* a licking]

lind *lind* or **linden** *lin'dən*. Same as **lime**[3]. [OE *lind*; cf ON *lind*, Ger *Linde*]

lindane *lin'dān*. Same as **Gammexane**.

lindworm *lind'wûrm*, (*mythol*) *n* a wingless dragon. [Adapted from Swed and Dan *lindorm*]

line[1] *līn, n* flax, its fibre, or its seed (*obs*); combed out or heckled flax; yarn spun from good flax; linen thread or cloth (*obs*). — *vt* to cover on the inside; to fill or stuff; to reinforce or strengthen (*esp* books); to be placed all along the side of; to serve as lining for. — *adj* **lined** having a lining. — *n* **lin'er** a person who lines; something which serves as a lining; a sleeve of metal, resistant to wear and corrosion, etc, fitted inside or outside a cylinder, tube, etc (*eng*); a sleeve for a gramophone record, or an insert inside it, or (*usu* **liner notes**) the text printed on either. — *n* **līn'ing** the action of a person who lines; material applied to a surface, *esp* material on the inner surface of a garment, etc; contents; (in *pl*) underclothing, *esp* drawers (*obs* or *dialect*). — **line one's pocket** or **pockets** to make a profit, *esp* dishonestly. [OE *līn* flax, cognate with or derived from L *līnum*; cf ety for **line**[2]]

line[2] *līn, n* a thread, string, cord or rope, *esp* one for fishing, sounding, hanging clothes, or guidance; something which has length without breadth or thickness (*math*); a long narrow mark; a streak, stroke, or narrow stripe; draughtsmanship; a row; a row of printed or written characters, ships, soldiers, etc; a verse, such as is *usu* written in one row; a series or succession, eg of descendants; a service of ships, buses, etc or a company running them; a course, route or system; a railway or tramway track or route; a stretch or route of telegraph, telephone, or power wires or cables; a connection by telephone; an order given to an agent for goods; such goods received; trade in, or the stock on hand of, any particular product; a lineament; a rank, column of figures, etc; a short letter or note; a wrinkle, *esp* on the face; a trench or other military position; a limit; method; policy; a rule or canon; (with *the*; often with *cap*) the equator; lineage, ancestry; direction; occupation; course; province or sphere of life, interest, or taste; the regular army; line of battle (see below); an old measurement, the twelfth part of an inch; relevant information (*colloq*); glib talk, not always honest (*slang*); in a TV, the path traversed by the electron beam or scanning spot in moving once from side to side (horizontal scanning) or from top to bottom (vertical scanning) of the picture; a queue (*NAm*); (*usu* **the line**) the odds, *esp* on football games, set by bookmakers (*NAm*); (in *pl*) a certificate of marriage or church membership; (in *pl*) the words of an actor's part; (in *pl*) one's lot in life (*rare*); (in *pl*) outlines; (in *pl*) military fieldworks; (in *pl*) rows of huts (*military*); (in *pl*) a school punishment of writing out a phrase or sentence a wearisome number of times; (in *pl*) fits of bad temper (*Shakesp*). — *vt* to mark out with lines; to cover with lines; to put in line; to form a line along; to give out (a hymn, etc) for public singing line by line; to delineate or sketch (sometimes verbally); to measure with a line (*archaic*). — *vi* to take a place in line. — *n* **linage** or **lineage** (*līn'ij*) the number of lines in a piece of printed matter; measurement or payment by the line, *eg* in newspapers; aligning (*archaic*). — *n* **lineage** (*lin'i-ij*), *obs* forms **linage**, **lignage** or **lynage** (*līn'ij*) ancestry. — *adj* **lineal** (*lin'i-əl*) of or belonging to a line or lines, or to one dimension; composed of lines; in the direction of a line; in, of, or transmitted by, direct line of descent, or legitimate descent. — *n* **lineality** (*-al'i-ti*). — *adv* **lin'eally**. — *n* **lineament** (*lin'i-ə-mənt*) a feature; a distinguishing mark in the form of anything, *esp* of the face. — *adj* **linear** (*lin'i-ər*) of or belonging to a line; in or of one dimension; consisting of, or having the form of, lines; long and very narrow, with parallel sides; capable of being represented on a graph by a straight line; of a system, in which doubling the cause doubles the effect. — *n* **linearity** (*lin-i-ar'i-ti*). — *adv* **lin'early**. — *adj* **lin'eate** or **lin'eated** marked with lines. — *n* **lineā'tion** marking with lines; arrangement of or in lines. — *adj* **lined** (*līnd*) marked with lines; having a line. — *adj* **lineolate** (*lin'i-ə-lāt*) marked with fine lines. — *n* **līn'er** a person who makes, marks, draws, paints, or writes lines; a paintbrush for making lines; a line-fisherman; a line-fishing boat; any large passenger-carrying vessel or aircraft of a particular company; cosmetic material used to outline the eyes or lips. — *n* **līn'ing** alignment; the making of a line; use of a line; marking with lines. — *adj* **līn'y** or **līn'ey**. — **line abreast** or **ahead** naval formation(s) in which all the vessels are side by side or one behind the other; **linear A** a script, essentially the same as linear B, used with an earlier Semitic language of Crete; **linear accelerator** an apparatus in which electrons are accelerated while travelling down a metal tube or tubes, eg by means of electromagnetic waves; **linear B** an ancient script (*c.* 1400 BC) found in Crete, deciphered with all but general acceptance as a form of Greek seven centuries earlier than any previously known; **linear equation** an equation with more than two terms, of which none is raised above the power one; **linear motor** an electric motor which produces direct thrust, without the use of gears; **linear perspective** that part of perspective which regards only the positions, magnitudes and forms of the objects delineated; **linear programming** programming which enables a computer to give an optimum result when fed with a number of unrelated variables, used in determining the most efficient arrangement of eg an industrial process; **line'backer** (*Am football*) a defensive player whose position is just behind the line of scrimmage; **line block** a printing block consisting of black and white only, without gradations of tone; **line drawing** a drawing in pen or pencil using lines only, without gradations of tone; **line'-engrav'er**; **line'-engrav'ing** the process of engraving in lines, steel or copperplate engraving; an engraving done in this way; **line feed** (*comput*) a facility of most printers to move the paper up through the printing mechanism automatically, one line at a time; **line'-fence'** (*US*) a farm-boundary fence; **line'-fish** one caught with a line rather than a net; **line'-fish'er** or **line-fish'erman**; **line'-fish'ing**; **line judge** (*sport*) an official whose job is to watch a line to see on which side of it the ball, etc falls; **line'man** a person who attends to the lines of a railway, telegraph, telephone, or electric-light wires, etc; a player in the forward line (*Am football*); **line'-of-batt'le-ship** a ship fit for the line of battle, a battleship; **line'-out** (*Rugby football*) a method of restarting play when the ball has gone into touch, the forwards of each team lining up behind each other facing the touch-line and trying to catch or deflect the ball when it is thrown in; **line'-print'er** a machine for rapid printing of computer output, a line at a time; **line'-shooter** (*slang*) someone who shoots a line (see **shoot**[1]); **line scanning** (*image technol*) a method of scanning in which the scanning spot repeatedly traverses the field of the image in a series of straight lines; **linesman** (*līnz'*) a lineman; a soldier in a regiment of the line; in Association football, an official who marks the spot at which the ball goes into touch; in lawn-tennis, an official whose job is to watch a line to see on which side of it the ball falls, a line judge; **line'-squall** one of a chain of squalls occurring along a travelling line, with rise and sudden change of wind, rise of pressure and fall of temperature; **line'-storm** (*US*) an equinoctial storm; **line'-up** arrangement in line; putting or coming into line; a queue; an identification parade; the bill of artistes appearing in a show; a list of team members. — **above the line** (of advertising) through the media and by poster; **all along the line** at every point (*lit* or *fig*); **below the line** (of advertising) by such means as free gifts, direct mailings to households, etc; **bring into line** to cause to conform; **down the line** of a shot, travelling parallel to and close to the side of the court (*tennis*); in the future (*colloq*); **draw the line** see under **draw**; **end of the line** (*fig*) a point beyond which it is useless or impossible to proceed; **fall into line** to conform; **Fraunhofer's lines** dark lines crossing the spectrum, from the Bavarian optician Joseph von *Fraunhofer* (1787–1826); **get a line on** (*slang*) to get information about; **give line** (*angling*) to allow apparent freedom in order to secure at last (also *fig*); **hold the line** see under **hold**[1]; **in line** in a straight line; in agreement or harmony (with *with*); in the running (with *for*); in contention (with *for*); in a line of succession (with *to*); **lay it on the line** (*colloq*) to speak out firmly and frankly; **lay** or **put on the line** to risk or stake (a reputation, etc); **line of battle** arrangement in line to meet the enemy; **line of beauty** a curve like a drawn-out S, so described by Hogarth; **line of country** one's field of study or interest; **line of sight** the straight line between the eye and the object on which it is focused, or between two objects along which they are visible from each other (also **line of vision**); the straight line along which the eye looks, in any direction; the straight line between a transmitter and the receiving antenna (*telecomm*); **line up** to bring into alignment; to make a stand (*in support of*, or *against*); to gather together in readiness; to secure or arrange (for a person); **on the line** (*painting*) hanging on the level of the eyes; **on** or **along the lines of** in a (specified) manner or direction; **read between the lines** to infer what is not explicitly stated; **shoot a line** see under **shoot**[1]; **toe the line** see under **toe**. [Partly from OE *līne* cord (from or cognate with L *līnum* flax), partly through Fr *ligne*, and partly directly from L *līnea*; cf **line**[1]]

line[3] *līn*, *vt* (*esp* of a dog or wolf) to copulate with. [Fr *ligner*]

line[4] *līn*, *n* a form of **lind**. — **line'-grove** (*Shakesp*).

lineage, lineal, linear, etc. See under **line**[2].

lined. See **line**[1,2].

linen *lin'ən*, *n* cloth made of lint or flax; underclothing, *orig* of linen; articles of linen, or of other materials generally, such as cotton, rayon, etc, eg *table-linen, bed-linen, body-linen*. — *adj* of or like linen. — **lin'en-draper** a dealer in linens; **lin'en-fold** or **lin'en-scroll** a decoration in mouldings like parallel folds of linen; **linen paper** paper made of flax fibres, or with a similar texture. — **wash one's dirty linen in public** or (*rare*) **at home** to expose, or (*rare*) keep secret, sordid family affairs. [OE *līnen* (adj), from *līn* flax; see **line**[1]]

lineolate. See under **line**[2].

ling[1] *ling*, *n* a fish (genus *Molva*) of the cod family. [Prob connected with **long**[3]]

ling[2] *ling*, *n* heather. — *adj* **ling'y**. [ON *lyng*]

ling[3] *ling*, *n* Scots form of **line**[2]. — **sting and ling** see under **sting**[2].

-ling[1] *-ling*, *sfx* forming nouns and denoting a diminutive, such as duck*ling*; hence expressing affection, as in dar*ling* (OE *dēorling*); sometimes implying depreciation, as in under*ling*.

-ling[2] *-ling*, *adv sfx* conveying the senses of direction, condition, position.

ling. *abbrev*: linguistics.

lingam *ling'gam*, *n* the Hindu phallus, a symbol of Siva. — Also **ling'a**. [Sans]

lingel or **lingle** *ling'gl* (chiefly *Scot*, *ling'l*), *n* a shoemaker's waxed thread. [OFr *lignoel*, from a dimin from L *līnea*]

linger *ling'gər*, *vi* to remain for long; to be left or remain behind; to delay, in reluctance to leave; to tarry; to loiter; to be protracted; to remain alive, although gradually dying. — *vt* to prolong or protract (*Shakesp*); to pass in tedium or dawdling. — *n* **ling'erer**. — *n* and *adj* **ling'ering**. — *adv* **ling'eringly**. [Frequentative from OE *lengan* to protract, from *lang* long]

lingerie *lẽzh'ə-rē*, *n* women's underclothing; *orig* linen goods. [Fr, from *linge* linen, from L *līnum* flax thread, linen]

lingle. See **lingel**.

lingo *ling'gō*, *n* a language, *esp* one poorly regarded or not understood; the jargon of a profession or class: — *pl* **ling'oes**. [Provençal *lengo*, *lingo*, or some other form of L *lingua* language]

lingoa geral *ling'gwä zher-äl'*, *n* a trade jargon used in Brazil based on Tupí-Guaraní. [Port, general language]

lingot *ling'gət*, (*obs*) *n* an ingot. [Fr *lingot*, from Eng **ingot**, with the definite article *l'*]

lingua *ling'gwə*, *n* the tongue (*anatom*); a tongue-like structure. — *adj* **ling'ual** relating to the tongue; pronounced using the tongue (*phonetics*); of a tooth-surface, facing towards the tongue (*dentistry*); relating to language (*rare*). — *adv* **ling'ually**. — *adj* **ling'uiform** tongue-shaped. — *n* **ling'uist** someone who has a good knowledge of languages; someone who studies linguistics; in W Africa, an intermediary between chief or priest and the people. — *n* **ling'uister** (*US*) an interpreter. — Also **link'ster** or **ling'ster**. — *adj* **linguist'ic** or **linguist'ical** relating to languages or knowledge or the study of languages. — *adv* **linguist'ically**. — *n* **linguistic'ian** a student of linguistics. — *n sing* **linguist'ics** the scientific study of language in its widest sense, in every aspect and in all its varieties. — *n* **ling'uistry**. — *n* **lingula** (*ling'gū-lə*) a little tongue-like part; (with *cap*; *zool*) a narrow-shelled genus of brachiopods; extended loosely to related genera, such as **Lingulell'a**, the characteristic fossil of the Upper Cambrian *Lingula Flags*. — *adj* **ling'ular** relating to a lingula. — *adj* **ling'ulate** tongue-shaped. — **lingua franca** (*ling'gwə frangk'ə*; Ital, Frankish language) *orig* a mixed Italian trade jargon used in the Levant; a language chosen as a medium of communication among speakers of different languages; any hybrid language used for the same purpose; the familiar conventions of any style, *esp* in music or the arts, readily recognized and understood by devotees: — *pl* **lingue franche** (*ling'gwā frangk'ā*) or **lingua francas**; **linguistic philosophy** a term loosely used to cover methods of analysis of philosophically puzzling concepts by the meticulous assembly and scrutiny of the widely-varying expressions of these concepts in ordinary discourse; later extended to a systematic study of the working of language itself. — Also **linguistic analysis**. [L *lingua* (for *dingua*) the tongue]

linguini *ling-gwē'nē* or **linguine** *-nā*, *n pl* a kind of pasta made in long thin flat pieces. [Ital, pl of *linguino*, *linguina*, dimins of *lingua* tongue]

linguist, etc, **lingula**, etc. See under **lingua**.

linhay, **linney** or **linny** *lin'i*, (*dialect*) *n* a shed, open in front. [Origin obscure]

liniment *lin'i-mənt*, *n* a thin ointment; an embrocation for relieving muscular stiffness. [L *linīmentum*, from *linīre*, *linĕre* to smear]

linin *lī'nin*, *n* a substance which forms the network of a cell nucleus. [L *līnum* thread, net]

lining. See under **line**[1,2].

link[1] *lingk*, *n* a ring of a chain, chain-mail, etc; anything that connects (also *fig*); a unit in a communications system; the 1/100th part of the surveyor's chain, 7·92 inches (*approx* 20cm); a segment or unit in a connected series; a winding of a river (*Scot*); a cuff-link. — *vt* to connect or join up. — *vi* to be or become connected; to go arm-in-arm. — *adj* **link'able**. — *n* **link'age** an act or mode of linking; the fact of being linked; a system of links, a connection; a chemical bond; product of magnetic flux by number of coils (*elec*); a system of lines pivoted together, describing definite curves (*math*); a tendency of genes, or characters, to be inherited together because the genes are on the same chromosome (*biol*). — *n* **link'er** (*comput*) a program enabling two or more different machine-language segments to be treated as a unit. — **linked verse** a form of Japanese verse alternating three lines of respectively 3, 7 and 5 syllables with two lines of 7 and 7 syllables, different poets supplying succeeding verses; **link man** a person who provides a connection, eg by passing on information, or by holding together separate items of eg a broadcast programme; **link'-mo'tion** reversing gear of a steam-engine; a system of pieces moving as a linkage; **link'-up** a connection, union; **link'work**. — **missing link** any point or fact needed to complete a series or a chain of thought or argument; an intermediate form in the evolution of man from his ape ancestors. [Prob from an ON form cognate with OE *hlencan* (pl) armour; Icel *hlekkr*, Ger *Gelenk* a joint]

link[2] *lingk*, (*hist*) *n* a torch of pitch and tow; burnt links used as blacking (*Shakesp*). — **link'boy** or **link'man** an attendant carrying a link to light the way in dark streets. [Origin doubtful]

link[3] *lingk*, *n* a bank (*obs*); (in *pl*, often treated as *sing*) a stretch of flat or gently undulating ground along a seashore; hence a golf course, *orig* one by the sea. [OE *hlinc* a ridge of land, a bank; cf **linch**]

link[4] *lingk*, (*Scot*) *vi* to move nimbly; to trip along briskly. [Cf Norw *linke* to hobble, limp]

linkster. See **linguister** under **lingua**.

Link trainer *lingk trān'ər*, *n* a flight-simulator training device for pilots and aircrew; a similar device for training motor vehicle drivers. [From E *Link* (1904–81), US inventor]

Linn. *lin*, *abbrev*: Linnaean; Linnaeus.

linn or **lin** *lin*, *n* a waterfall; a pool at the foot of a waterfall; a deep ravine. [OE *hlynn*, a torrent, combined with Gaelic *linne*, Ir *linn*, Welsh *llyn* pool]

Linnaean or **Linnean** *lin-ē'ən*, *adj* relating to *Linnaeus* or *Linné*, the Swedish botanist (1707–1778), or to his artificial system of classification.

linnet *lin'it*, *n* *Linota cannabina*, a common finch, feeding on flax seed. — **green linnet** the greenfinch. [OFr *linette*, *linot*, from *lin* flax, from L *līnum*; cf OE *līnece* or *līnete*, and **lintie**]

linney and **linny**. See **linhay**.

lino and **linocut**. See under **linoleum**.

linoleic *lin-ō-lē'ik* (or **linolenic** *lin-ō-lēn'ik* or *-len'*) **acid** *as'id*, *n* highly unsaturated fatty acid obtained from the glycerides of certain fats and oils, such as linseed oil, and constituting Vitamin F.

linoleum *lin-ō'li-əm*, or *-lyəm*, *n* stiff, hard-wearing floor-covering made by impregnating a fabric with a mixture of oxidized linseed-oil, resins, and fillers (*esp* cork). — Also *adj*. — Also (*colloq*) **lino** (*lī'nō*): — *pl* **lī'nos**. — **linocut** (*lī'nō-kut*) a design cut in relief in linoleum; a print made from such a block; **lino tile** a floor tile made of linoleum or a similar material. [L *līnum* flax, and *oleum* oil]

Linotype® *līn'ō-tīp*, *n* a machine for producing stereotyped lines of printer's type; a slug or line of printing-type cast in one piece by this method.

linsang *lin'sang*, *n* a civet-like animal of Borneo and Java; applied also to related animals of the Himalayas, Burma and W Africa. [Javanese *linsan*]

linseed *lin'sēd*, *n* lint or flax seed. — Also **lint'seed**. — **lin'seed-cake** the cake remaining when the oil is pressed out of lint or flax seed, used as a food for sheep and cattle; **lin'seed-meal** the meal of linseed, used for poultices and as a cattle-food; **lin'seed-oil** oil extracted from flax seed, having many industrial applications. [OE *līn* flax, and *sǣd* seed]

linsey *lin'zi*, *n* cloth made from linen and wool. — Also *adj*. — **lin'sey-woolsey** (*-wŏŏl'zi*) a thin coarse material of linen and wool mixed, or inferior wool with cotton; gibberish (*Shakesp*). — *adj* made of linen and wool; neither one thing nor another, presenting a confusing mixture. [Perh **line**[1] wool, and poss **say**[3]]

linstock *lin'stok*, (*hist*) *n* a staff to hold a lighted match for firing a cannon. — Also **lint'stock**. [Du *lontstok*, from *lont* a match (cf **lunt**), and *stok* a stick]

lint *lint*, *n* flax (*Scot*); scraped linen, or a cotton substitute, for dressing wounds; cotton fibre (*esp US*); raw cotton. — *n* **lin'ter** (*US*) a machine for stripping off short cotton fibre from the ginned seeds; (in *pl*) the fibre so removed. — *adj* **lint'y**. — **lint'seed** (*Scot*) flax seed for sowing. — *adj* **lint'white** flaxen. [ME *lynt*, *lynet* from L *linteus* of linen, from *līnum* flax]

lintel *lint'l*, *n* a timber or stone over a doorway or window. — *adj* **lint'elled**. [OFr *lintel* (Fr *linteau*), from a dimin of L *līmes*, *-itis* border]

linter, etc. See under **lint**.

lintie *lin'ti* or **lintwhite** *lint'hwīt* or *lint'wīt*, (now chiefly *Scot*) *n* a linnet. [OE *linetwige*, literally perh, flax-twitcher]

lintseed and **lintstock**. See **linseed** and **linstock** respectively.

lintwhite. See **lint** and **lintie**.

lion *lī'ən*, *n* a large, fierce, tawny, loud-roaring animal of the cat family, the male having a shaggy mane (*fem* **li'oness**); a person of unusual courage (*fig*); (with *cap*) the constellation or the sign Leo (*astron* and *astrol*); any object of interest, *esp* a famous or conspicuous person much sought after (from the lions once kept in the Tower, one of the sights of London); an old Scots coin, with a lion on the obverse, worth 74 shillings Scots (James VI); (with *cap*) a member of an international organization of professional people's clubs (**the Lions**), with charitable, etc aims. — *n* **li'oncel**, **li'oncelle** or **li'onel** (*heraldry*) a small lion used as a bearing. — *n* **li'onet** a young lion. — *n* **li'onism** lionizing; a lion-like appearance occurring in leprosy.

— *vt* **li'onize** or **-ise** to treat as a hero or celebrity; to go around the sights of; to show the sights to (*rare*). — *adj* **li'onlike** or **li'only**. — **li'on-cub** a young lion; **li'on-heart** a person with great courage. — *adj* **li'on-heart'ed**. — **li'on-hunt'er** a hunter of lions; a person who runs after celebrities; **lion's mouth** (*fig*) a dangerous position; **lion's provider** (*archaic*) the jackal, supposed to attend upon the lion, really his hanger-on; **lion's share** the whole or greater part; **li'on-tā'mer**. — **twist the lion's tail** to harass Great Britain. [Anglo-Fr *liun*, from L *leō*, *-ōnis*, from Gr *leōn*, *-ontos*]

lip *lip*, *n* either of the muscular flaps in front of the teeth, forming the opening to the mouth; any similar structure, such as either of the two divisions of a liplike flower corolla; the edge or rim of an orifice, cavity, deep geographical depression, vessel, etc; part of such a rim bent outwards like a spout; impudent talk, insolence or cheek (*slang*). — *vt* to touch with the lips; to kiss; to wash, overflow, or overrun the edge of; to lap or lave; to form a lip on; to edge; to turn or notch the edge of (*Scot*); (of a golfer or golf shot) to get the ball to the very edge of (the hole); to utter with the lips. — *vi* to use the lips in playing a wind-instrument; to lap at the brim; to have water lapping over: — *pr p* **lipp'ing**; *pa t* and *pa p* **lipped**. — *adj* of the lip; formed or sounded by the lips. — *combining form* **lip-** from the lips only, not sincere. — *adj* **lip'less**. — *adj* **lip'like**. — *adj* **lipped** (*lipt*) having a lip or lips; labiate. — *adj* **lipp'y** having a hanging lip; saucy, cheeky (*slang*). — **lip brush** a brush for applying colouring to the lips. — *adj* **lip'=deep** insincere; immersed to the lips. — **lip'-gloss** a substance applied to the lips to give them a glossy appearance; **lip liner** cosmetic material used to outline the lips. — *vi* **lip'-read**. — **lip'-reader**; **lip'-read'ing** gathering what a person says by watching the movement of his or her lips; **lip'-rounding** rounding of the lips, as in pronouncing *o* (*phonetics*); **lip'-salve** ointment for the lips, *esp* to prevent chapping; blandishment; **lip'-service** insincere praise or worship; professed, not real, respect or loyalty. — *adj* **lip'=smacking** (*colloq*) delicious, appetizing. — **lip'stick** a short stick of colouring for the lips. — *vt* and *vi* to paint with (a) lipstick. — **lip-sync** or **lip-synch** (*lip'singk*) the synchronization of lip movements with already recorded sound, *esp* by singers making television appearances; the synchronization of the voice with already filmed lip-movements (in dubbing; also *vt* and *vi*). — **bite one's lip** to do this to show annoyance or disappointment; to repress laughter, tears, an angry retort, etc; **hang on someone's lips** to listen eagerly to all that someone has to say; **in Lipsburie pinfold** (*Shakesp*) *perh* between the teeth; **(keep) a stiff upper lip** (to show) resolution, with no yielding to emotion; **make a lip** (*Shakesp*) to pout in sullenness or derision; **smack one's lips** to bring the lips together and part them with a smacking noise, as an indication of relish. [OE *lippa*; Du *lip*, Ger *Lippe*, L *labium*]

lip- *lip-* or **lipo-** *lip-ō-*, *lip-ə-* or *li-po'-*, also *lī-*, *combining form* denoting fat. — *n* **lip'ase** (*-ās* or *-āz*) an enzyme that breaks up fats. — *n* **lipec'tomy** (Gr *ektomē* a cutting out) surgical removal of fatty tissue. — *n* **lip'id**, sometimes **lip'ide** (*-īd*), any of a group of chemicals found in bodily tissues, including fats, oils and waxes (esters of fatty acids), derivatives of these such as phospholipids (qv under **phosphorus**), and other substances such as steroids and terpenes. — *n* **lip'ochrome** (*-krōm*; Gr *chrōma* colour) a pigment of butter fat, etc. — *adj* **lip'oid** fat-like. — *n* a fat-like substance; a lipid. — *n* **lipō'ma** a fatty tumour: — *pl* **lipō'mata**. — *n* **lipomatō'sis** the excessive growth of fat. — *adj* **lipō'-matous**. — *n* **lipoprō'tein** a water-soluble protein found in the blood, which carries cholesterol. — *adj* **liposō'mal**. — *n* **lip'ōsome** (Gr *sōma* body) a naturally occurring lipid globule in the cytoplasm of a cell; an artificial droplet of an aqueous substance surrounded by a lipid, used in the treatment of various diseases. — *n* **lip'ōsuction** a surgical process for the removal o excess, unwanted fat from the body. [Gr *lipos* fat]

liparite *lip'ə-rīt*, (*mineralogy*) *n* rhyolite. [From the *Lipar* Islands, where it occurs]

Lipizzaner *lip-it-sä'nər*, *n* a breed of horses (*usu* grey o white in colour) particularly suited and trained fo displays of dressage. — Also **Lippiza'ner**, **Lippizza'ner** **Lippiza'na** (*-nə*) or **Lippizza'na**. [*Lipizza* (*Lippiza* o *Lippizza*), near Trieste, where originally bred]

lipo-, etc. See **lip-**.

lipogram *lip'ō-gram* or *līp'*, *n* a piece of writing, *esp* i verse, from which all words are omitted which contai a particular letter. — *adj* **lipogrammat'ic**. — *n* **lipo gramm'atism**. — *n* **lipogramm'atist**. — *n* **lipog'raph** accidental omission of a letter or letters in writing. [G *leipein* to leave, and *gramma* a letter, *graphein* to write

lippen *lip'n*, (*Scot*) *vi* to trust, rely or depend (with *to* o *on*). — *vt* to expect. — *adj* **lipp'ening** (*Scott*) unguarded [Origin obscure]

Lippes loop. See under **loop**[1].

lippitude *lip'i-tūd*, (*archaic*) *n* soreness of the eyes. [*lippitūdō*, from *lippus* blear-eyed]

lippy[1] **or lippie** *lip'i*, *n* an old Scottish dry measure, th fourth part of a peck. [Dimin from OE *lēap* a basket cf **leap**[2]]

lippy[2]. See under **lip**.

liq. *abbrev*: liquid; liquor.

liquate *lik'wāt*, *vt* to melt; to subject to liquation. — *ac* **liq'uable**. — *n* **liquā'tion** melting; separation of meta with different melting-points. [L *liquāre*, *-ātum* t liquefy]

liquefy *lik'wi-fī*, *vt* to make liquid. — *vi* to become liquid to drink (*facetious*): — *pr p* **liq'uefying**; *pa t* and *pa* **liq'uefied**. — *n* and *adj* **liquefacient** (*-fā'shənt*). — **liquefaction** (*-fak'shən*). — *adj* **liq'uefiable**. — *n* **liq'ue fier**. — **liquefied petroleum gas** propane or butane unde moderate pressure, used in some vehicles in place c petrol or diesel fuel. [L *liquefacere*, from *liquēre* to b liquid, and *facere* to make]

liquesce *lik-wes'*, *vi* to become liquid; to merge. — **liquesc'ence** or **liquesc'ency**. — *adj* **liquesc'ent**. [*liquēscere*, from *liquēre* to be liquid]

liqueur *lik-ūr'*, or *lē-kœr'*, *n* a potent alcoholic preparatio flavoured or perfumed and sweetened, eg chartreuse cherry brandy, curaçao, benedictine, kümmel c maraschino. — *vt* to flavour with a liqueur. — *adj* (c brandy or whisky) that may be drunk as a liqueur. – **liqueur'-glass** a very small drinking-glass. [Fr, from *liquor*; see **liquor**]

liquid *lik'wid*, *adj* flowing; fluid; watery; in a stat between solid and gas, in which the molecules mov freely about one another but do not fly apart (*phys*) clear; moist; (of sound, etc) free from harshness indisputable; unfixed; (of assets) readily converte into cash. — *n* a fluid substance; a flowing consonan sound, such as *l* or *r* (*phonetics*). — *vt* **liq'uidate** to clea up or off (*esp* a debt); to wind up (a commercial firm etc), bringing its trading to an end; to turn (assets) int cash; to dispose of; to wipe out, do away with (*slang*) to kill off (*slang*). — *vi* to go into liquidation. — **liquidā'tion**. — *n* **liq'uidator**. — *n* **liquid'ity** the state c being liquid; the condition of having liquid assets; th amount of liquid assets a company has; a measure c the ease with which an asset can be turned into cash. – *vt* **liq'uidize** or **-ise** to make liquid; to purée (food). – *n* **liq'uidizer** or **-s-** a machine which purées foodstuff — *adv* **liq'uidly**. — *n* **liq'uidness**. — **liquid asse** (*finance*) assets which are already, or may be easi converted into, cash, such as shares, bank deposits, etc **liquid crystal** a liquid which, like a crystal, has differer optical properties depending on its polarity, over definite range of temperature above its freezing point **liquid crystal display** a display, *esp* in electroni instruments, based on the changes in reflectivity of liquid crystal cell when an electric field is applie switching it from an opaque to a transparent state. – **go into liquidation** (of a commercial firm, etc) to b wound up, cease trading. [L *liquidus* liquid, clear, from *liquēre* to be clear]

Liquidambar *lik-wid-am'bər*, *n* a genus of balsamiferous trees of the family *Hamamelidaceae*, found in N America and Asia. [L *liquidus* liquid, and LL *ambar* amber]

liquidus *lik'wi-dəs*, *n* (also **liquidus curve** or **freezing-point curve**) a curve plotted on a graph showing how temperature affects the composition of a melting or solidifying mixture, above which curve the mixture is entirely liquid. [L, liquid]

liquor *lik'ər*, *n* anything liquid, *esp* the product of cooking or a similar operation; a liquid secretion; a beverage, *esp* a strong alcoholic drink; any prepared solution, *esp* a strong one (*chem*). — *vt* to apply liquor or a solution to; to rub with oil or grease (*Shakesp*). — *vi* (*slang*) to drink (alcohol) (*esp* with *up*). — **in liquor**, also **liqu'ored** (*slang*), drunk; **liquor laws** laws controlling the sale of intoxicating drinks. [OFr *licur*, *licour* (Fr *liqueur*), from L *liquor*, *-ōris*]

liquorice or **licorice** *lik'ə-ris*, (*US* also *-rish*), *n* a butterfly-like plant (*Glycyrrhiza glabra*, or other species) of Europe and Asia; its long sweet root used in medicine; an extract from the root; confectionery having a laxative effect, made with the extract. — **liquorice allsorts** an assortment of sweets flavoured with liquorice. — **Indian liquorice** Abrus (also *liquorice-vine*); **wild liquorice** a kind of milk-vetch (*Astragalus glycyphyllus* also *liquorice-vetch*); rest-harrow. [Anglo-Fr *lycorys*, from LL *liquirītia*, a corruption of Gr *glykyrrīza*, from *glykys* sweet, and *rhīza* root]

liquorish. Another spelling of **lickerish**; also used to mean inclined towards liquor.

lira *lē'rə*, *n* the standard Italian monetary unit (100 *centesimi*); the standard monetary unit of Turkey (100 kurus): — *pl* **lire** (*lē'rā*) or **lir'as**. [Ital, from L *lībra* a pound]

liriodendron *lĭr-i-ō-den'dron*, *n* a tree of the tulip-tree genus *Liriodendron*. [Gr *leirion* a lily, and *dendron* a tree]

liripipe *lir'i-pīp* or **liripoop** *lir'i-po͞op*, (*obs*) *n* the long tail of a graduate's hood; a part or lesson committed to memory; a silly person. [LL *liripipium*; origin unknown]

lirk *lirk*, (*Scot*) *n* a fold; a wrinkle. — *vi* to wrinkle. [Origin unknown]

lis *lēs*, (*heraldry*) *n* a fleur-de-lis: — *pl* **lis** or **lisses** (*lēs'iz*). [Fr]

Lisbon *liz'bən*, *n* a light-coloured wine from Estremadura in Portugal, shipped from *Lisbon*.

lisk *lisk*, (*dialect*) *n* the groin; the flank or loin. [ME *leske*, prob Old Swed *livski* the joint of the groin]

lisle *līl*, *n* a long-stapled, hard-twisted cotton yarn. — Also *adj*. [Old spelling of *Lille*, France, where orig manufactured]

LISP *lisp*, (*comput*) *n* a high-level programming language, designed to create complex chains of operations and data, and used in artificial intelligence research. [*list* processor]

lisp *lisp*, *vi* to pronounce certain sounds with the tongue against the upper teeth or gums, as *th* for *s* or *z*; to articulate childishly; to utter imperfectly. — *vt* to utter with a lisp. — *n* the act or habit of lisping; a defect of speech causing one to lisp. — *n* **lisp'er**. — *adj* and *n* **lisp'ing**. — *adv* **lisp'ingly**. [OE *wlisp* (adj) stammering; Du *lispen*, Ger *lispeln*]

lispound or **lispund** *lis'pownd* or *-pōnd*, (*Orkney* and *Shetland*) *n* a varying weight, 12 to 34 pounds (*approx* 5·4 to 15·4kg). [LGer or Du *lispund*, for *livschpund* Livonian (*Livonia*, former Baltic province of Russia) pound]

lissencephalous *lis-en-sef'ə-ləs*, (*zool*) *adj* with smooth cerebral hemispheres. [Gr *lissos* smooth, and *enkephalon* brain]

lissome or **lissom** *lis'əm*, *adj* lithe, nimble, flexible. — *adv* **liss'omely** or **liss'omly**. — *n* **liss'omeness** or **liss'omness**. [**lithesome**]

lissotrichous *lis-ot'ri-kəs*, (*zool*) *adj* smooth-haired. [Gr *lissos* smooth, and *thrix*, *trichos* hair]

list[1] *list*, *n* the selvage on woven textile fabrics; a border; a stripe; a strip, *esp* one cut from an edge; a ridge or furrow made with a lister (also **lister ridge**; *archaic US*); material composed of cut-off selvages; a boundary (*obs*); a destination (*Shakesp*); (in *pl*) the boundary of a jousting-ground or similar area, hence the ground itself, combat. — *adj* made of strips of woollen selvage. — *vt* to border; to put a list on; to remove the edge from; to plough with a lister (*US*). — *adj* **list'ed** enclosed for jousting, etc; fought in lists. — *n* **list'er** (*US*) a double-mould-board plough. — **enter the lists** to come forward for contest or to do battle. [OE *līste*; Ger *Leiste*; affected in some senses by OFr *lisse* (Fr *lice*, Ital *lizza*), from LL *liciae* barrier]

list[2] *list*, *n* a catalogue, roll, or enumeration (of items). — *vt* to place in a list or catalogue; to make a list of; to enrol (eg soldiers). — *vi* to enlist (also **'list**, as if for **enlist**). — *n* **list'ing** a list; a position in a list; a print-out of all the data stored in a file or the commands in a program (*comput*); an official quotation for stock so that it can be traded on the Stock Exchange; (in *pl*) a guide to currently-running theatrical or other entertainments. — **List D schools** since 1969, the name given in Scotland to community homes for young offenders (formerly approved schools); **listed building** one officially listed as being of special architectural or historic interest, which cannot be demolished or altered without (local) government consent; **listed company** (*commerce*) a public company which obtains an official listing from the stock exchange; **list price** the recommended price of an article as shown in a manufacturer's catalogue or advertisement, ie before discounts, etc. — **active list** the roll of those liable for active service. [OFr *liste*, of Gmc origin, ultimately same word as **list**[1], from the sense of a strip of paper]

list[3] *list*, *n* a fillet (*archit*); a division of parted hair (*archaic* or *poetic*). — *n* **list'el** (*archaic*) a small fillet. [Ital *lista*, *listello*; ult the same as **list**[1] and **list**[2]]

list[4] *list*, *vt* to please (*impers*; *archaic*); to have pleasure in (*pers*; *archaic*); to desire (*archaic*); to like or please (*archaic*); to choose (*archaic*); to cause to heel or lean over (*naut*). — *vi* (*naut*) to heel over: — *pa t* **list'ed** or (*archaic*) **list**; *pa p* **list'ed**; *3rd pers sing pr t* **lists**, or (*archaic*) **list** or **list'eth**. — *n* the action or degree of heeling over; joy (*obs*); desire; inclination; choice. — *adj* **list'less** uninterested; languid; having no desire or wish (*archaic*). — *adv* **list'lessly**. — *n* **list'lessness**. [OE *lystan*, (impers) to please, from *lust* pleasure]

list[5] *list*, (*archaic* or *poetic*) *vi* to listen. — *vt* to listen to. — *adj* **list'ful** attentive. [OE *hlystan*]

listel. See under **list**[3].

listen *lis'n*, *vi* to attempt to hear something or pay attention (to what is being said or to the person saying it); to follow advice. — *n* an act or period of listening. — *adj* **list'enable** pleasant to listen to. — *n* **listener** (*lis'nər*) a person who listens. — *n* **list'enership** the estimated number of listeners to a radio broadcast. — **list'ener-in** (*pl* **list'eners-in**); **list'ening-in**; **list'ening-post** *orig* a post where soldiers are stationed to hear what the enemy is doing; a position advantageous for the gathering of information about the affairs of another country, etc. — **listen in** to listen (to a radio broadcast); to overhear intentionally a message intended for another person; **listen up** (*US colloq*) to pay attention, listen hard. [OE *hlysnan*, recorded in the Northumbrian form *lysna*]

lister. See under **list**[1].

listeria *lis-tē'ri-ə*, *n* a bacterium frequently found in certain foods (*esp* chicken, soft cheeses, etc), which if not killed in cooking can affect the central nervous system, causing meningitis, encephalitis, miscarriage and even death in the very young and elderly. — *adj* **Listerian** (*-tē'ri-ən*) relating to the English surgeon Lord Joseph *Lister* (1827–1912), surgeon and pioneer of antiseptics, or to his system (**Lis'terism**) of antiseptic treatment of surgical wounds. — *n* **listeriō'sis** the disease caused by listeria bacteria. — *vt* **Lis'terize** or **-ise** to treat by Listerism.

listful. See under **list**[5].

listless. See under **list**[4].

lit *pa t* and *pa p* of **light**[1,3].

lit. *abbrev*: literal; literally; (*lit*) literary; (*lit*) literature.

litany *lit'ə-ni*, *n* a prayer of supplication, *esp* in processions; an appointed form of responsive prayer in public worship in which the same thing is repeated several times; a long list or catalogue, evocative or merely boring. — **lit'any-desk** or **-stool** in the Anglican Church, a movable desk at which a priest kneels, facing the altar, while reciting the litany. — **lesser litany** the common formula, 'Kyrie eleison, Christe eleison, Kyrie eleison'. [LL *litanīa*, from Gr *litaneiā*, from *litesthai* to pray]

LitB. See **LittB**.

litchi. See **lychee**.

LitD. See **LittD**.

lit crit *lit krit*, *n* short for literary criticism.

lit de justice *lē də zhüs-tēs*, (*Fr*). See **bed of justice** under **bed**[1].

lite[1] or **lyte** *līt*, (*dialect*, also **leet**, otherwise *obs*) *n*, *adj* and *adv* little. [OE *lȳt*]

lite[2] (*Spenser*). Same as **light**[3]; also as **light**[2] in phrase *lungs and lites*.

lite[3] *adj* (of food and drink) low in calories, alcoholic content, etc. [Advertising simplification of **light**[2]]

lite pendente *lī'tē pen-den'tē* or *lē'te pen-den'te*, (*L*; *legal*) pending the suit.

liter. US spelling of **litre**.

literacy. See under **literate**.

literae (or **litterae**) **humaniores** *lit'ər-ē hū-mān-i-ōr'ēz* or *-ōr'*, or *lit'e-rī hōō-män-i-ōr'ās*, (*L*) *n* the humanities, Latin and Greek, literally the more humane letters; (as *sing*) the name of the school and examination at Oxford University.

literal *lit'ə-rəl*, *adj* relating to or consisting of letters of the alphabet; of the nature of a letter; according to the letter, following word for word; not figurative or metaphorical; inclined to use or understand words in a matter-of-fact sense. — *n* a wrong letter in printed or typed material; a misprint of a letter in a word (*printing*). — *n* **lit'eralism** strict adherence to the literal form; interpretation that is not figurative or metaphorical; exact and unimaginative rendering (*art*). — *n* **li'teralist**. — *adj* **literalist'ic**. — *adv* **literalist'ically**. — *n* **literality** (*-al'i-ti*). — *vt* **lit'eralize** or **-ise**. — *n* **lit'eralizer** or **-s-**. — *adv* **lit'erally** (often used by no means literally, merely to reinforce a metaphor). — *n* **lit'eralness**. [L *litterālis*, from *littera* (*lītera*) a letter]

literary *lit'ər-ər-i*, *adj* relating to letters of the alphabet (*obs*); epistolary (*obs*); relating to, of the nature of, knowledgeable about, or practising, literature or the writing of books; bookish; (of language) formal, such as found in (*esp* older) literature. — *adv* **lit'erarily**. — *n* **lit'erariness**. — *n* **lit'eraryism** a bookish expression. — **literary agent** a person who deals with the business affairs of an author; **literary criticism** (the art of making) qualitative judgments on literary works (short form **lit crit**); **literary executor** a person appointed to deal with unpublished material after an author's death; **literary source** (*legal*) in English law, a statute or law report, as the place where the law can be physically located. [L *lītterārius*, from *lītera* (*littera*) a letter]

literate *lit'ər-it* or *-ət*, *adj* able to read and write; learned, scholarly; having a competence in or with (often used as *combining form*, as in *computer-literate*). — *n* a person who is literate; an educated person without a university degree, *esp* a candidate for priestly orders, or formerly a woman holding a certificate from St Andrews University (**LLA** Lady Literate in Arts). — *n* **lit'eracy** the condition of being literate. — *n pl* **literati** (*-ä'tē*) men and women of letters, the learned: — *sing* **literā'tus** (or *-ä'*; *L*) or **literato** (*-ä'tō*; *Ital*). — *adv* **literā'tim** (*L -ä'*) letter for letter; without the change of a letter. — *n* **literā'tion** the representation of sounds by letters. — *n* **lit'erātor** a dabbler in learning; a person of letters, a literary person. — *adj* **lit'erose** affectedly or spuriously literary. — *n* **literos'ity**. [L *lītera*, *lītterātus*, *lītterātim*, *lītterōsus*, from *lītera* (*littera*) letter]

literature *lit'(ə-)rə-chər*, *n* the art of composition in prose and verse; the whole body of literary composition universally, or in any language, or on a given subject, etc; literary matter; printed matter; humane learning; literary culture or knowledge. — *adj* **lit'eratured** (*Shakesp*) learned, having literary knowledge. [L *lītterātūra*, from *lītera* (*littera*) a letter]

literose. See under **literate**.

Lith. *abbrev*: Lithuania; Lithuanian.

lith *lith*, (*archaic* and *Scot*) *n* a joint or segment. [OE *lith* a member; Ger *Glied*]

lith., **litho**. or **lithog**. *abbrev*: lithograph; lithography.

lith- *lith-* or **litho-** *lith-ō-*, *-ə-* or *-o-*, *combining form* denoting: stone; calculus (*med*). — *n* **lith'ate** (*obs*) a urate. — *n* **lithī'asis** (Gr *lithiāsis*) formation of calculi in the body. — *adj* **lith'ic** relating to or obtained from stone or calculi. — *n* **lithist'id** any of the **Lithist'ida**, hard stony sponges. — *n* **lith'ite** a calcareous body secreted in an animal cell, *esp* with a sensory function. — *adj* **lithochromatic** (*-ə-krō-mat'ik* or *-krə-*). — *n sing* **lithochromat'ics** the art or process of painting in oil on stone and taking impressions from the result. — *n* **lith'ochromy** (*-krō-mi*; Gr *chrōma*, *-atos* colour) painting on stone; chromolithography. — *n* **lith'oclast** (Gr *klaein* to crush) an instrument for crushing bladder-stones. — *n* **lith'ocyst** (*-ō-sist*; Gr *kystis* a bladder) a sac containing a lithite. — *adj* **lithodomous** (*-od'ə-məs*; Gr *lithodomos* a mason, from *domos* a dwelling) living in burrows in rocks. — *n* **Lithod'omus** the date-shell genus. — *adj* **lithogenous** (*-oj'i-nəs*) rock-building. — *n* **lith'oglyph** (*-ə-glif*; Gr *glyphein* to carve) an engraving on stone, *esp* a precious stone. — *n* **lith'ograph** (*-gräf*; Gr *graphein* to write) a print produced by lithography, from stone (**lithographic stone** or **slate** a fine-grained slaty limestone), or a substitute (such as zinc or aluminium), with greasy ink. — *vt* and *vi* to print in this way. — *n* **lithographer** (*-og'rə-fər*). — *adj* **lithographic** (*-ə-graf'ik*) or **lithograph'ical**. — *adv* **lithograph'ically**. — *n* **lithog'raphy** a method of printing from a stone or metal plate that makes use of the immiscibility of oil and water, the image to be printed being receptive to the oil-based ink, and the rest of the plate to moisture, so that when ink comes into contact with the dampened plate, only the image prints. — *adj* **lith'oid** or **lithoid'al** like stone. — *n* **lith'olapaxy** (Gr *lapaxis* evacuation) the operation of crushing stone in the bladder and working it out. — *adj* **lithol'atrous**. — *n* **litholatry** (*-ol'ə-tri*; Gr *latreiā* worship) stone-worship. — *adj* **litholog'ic** or **litholog'ical**. — *n* **lithol'ogist**. — *n* **lithol'ogy** the science of rocks as mineral masses; the department of medicine concerned with calculi. — *n* **lith'omancy** (*-man-si*; Gr *manteiā* divination) divination by stones. — *n* **lith'omarge** (*-ō-märj*; L *marga* marl) a compact china-clay. — *adj* **lithophagous** (*-of'ə-gəs*; Gr *phagein* to eat) stone-swallowing; rock-boring. — *n* **lith'ophane** (*-ō-fān*; Gr *phainesthai* to appear) porcelain with pictures showing through transparency. — *adj* **lithophilous** (*-of'i-ləs*; Gr *philos* friend) growing, living or sheltering among stones. — *n* **lithophysa** (*-ō-fī'sə*; Gr *phȳsa* bubble) a bladder-like spherulite (also **lith'ophyse**): — *pl* **lithophy'sae** (*-sē*). — *n* **lith'ophyte** (*-fīt*; Gr *phyton* plant) a plant that grows on rocks or stones; a stony organism, such as coral. — *adj* **lithophytic** (*-fit'ik*). — *n* **lith'opone** (*-ō-pōn*; Gr *ponos* work) a white pigment of barium sulphate and zinc sulphide. — *n* **lithoprint** (*lī'thō-*) a print made by lithography. — *n* **lith'osphere** (*-ō-sfēr*; Gr *sphaira* sphere; *geol*) the rocky crust of the earth. — *adj* **lithospheric** (*-sfer'ik*). — *n* **lith'otome** (*-ō-tōm*; Gr *tomia* the operation of cutting) an instrument for lithotomy. — *adj* **lithotomic** (*-tom'*) or **lithotom'ical**. — *n* **lithotomist** (*-ot'əm-ist*) a surgeon who practices lithotomy. — *adj* **lithot'omous** boring in rocks, as some molluscs. — *n* **lithot'omy** the surgical operation of removing a stone from a bodily organ, *esp* the bladder. — *n* **lithotripter**, **lithotrite**, **lithotrity**, etc see under **lithotripsy**. [Gr *lithos* stone]

litharge *lith'ärj, n* lead monoxide, such as is obtained in the process of refining silver. [Fr, from Gr *lithargyros*, from *lithos* a stone, and *argyros* silver]

lithate. See under **lith-**.

lithe[1] *līdh, adj* supple or limber. — *adv* **lithe'ly**. — *n* **lithe'ness**. — *adj* **lithe'some**. — *n* **lithe'someness**. [OE *līthe* soft, mild; Ger *lind* and *gelinde*]

lithe[2] *līdh*, (*obs*) *vi* to listen. [ON *hlȳtha* to listen]

lither *lidh'ər, adj* bad (*obs*); lazy (*obs*); soft, yielding (*Shakesp*). — *adj* **lith'erly** mischievous. — *adv* idly. [OE *lȳthre* bad; influenced by **lithe**[1]]

lithia *lith'i-ə, n* lithium oxide, a white crystalline substance that absorbs carbon dioxide and water vapour (from its mineral origin, unlike soda and potash); lithium in the form of salts, found in mineral waters. — Also *adj*. — *adj* **lith'ic** relating to or obtained from lithium. — *n* **lith'ium** (*-i-əm*) the lightest metallic element (symbol **Li**; atomic no 3), whose salts, *esp* lithium carbonate, are used to treat manic depression and other psychiatric illnesses. — **lithium driften silicon detector** a detector for ionizing radiation, used for low-energy X-ray and X-ray spectroscopy. [Gr *lithos* stone]

lithic. See under **lith-** and **lithia**.

lithium. See under **lithia**.

litho *lī'thō, n* short form of **lithograph** or **lithography** (see under **lith-**): — *pl* **lī'thos**. — *adj* short form of **lithographic** (see under **lith-**).

lithology, **lithophyte**, etc. See under **lith-**.

lithospermum *lith-ō-spûr'məm, n* any plant of the genus *Lithospermum* of the borage family. [Gr *lithospermon* gromwell, from *lithos* stone, and *sperma* seed]

lithospheric, **lithotome** etc. See under **lith-**.

lithotripsy *lith'ō-trip-si* or **lithotrity** *lith-ot'ri-ti, n* the surgical operation of crushing a stone in the bladder, kidney or gall bladder, so that its fragments may be passed naturally from the body. — *n* **lithotrip'ter** or **lithotrip'tor** a device that crushes stones in the bladder, etc by ultrasound (also **lith'otrite**, **lith'otrītor** or **lithontrip'tor**). — *adj* **lithotritic** (*-trit'ik*), **lithotrip'tic**, **lithontrip'tic** or **lithonthryp'tic**. — *n* a medicine producing a similar result. — *n* **lithot'ritist**, **lithotrip'tist** or **lithontrip'tist** a surgeon who performs the operation. — *vt* **lithot'ritize** or **-ise**. [Gr *lithōn* (genitive pl) *thryptika* breakers of stones; reconstructed as from Gr *tripsis* rubbing or L *trītus* rubbing]

Lithuanian *li-thū-ā'ni-ən, adj* relating to the republic of *Lithuania* on the Baltic Sea, or its people or their language. — *n* the Lithuanian language; a native or inhabitant of Lithuania.

lit. hum. *abbrev*: literae (or litterae) humaniores.

litigate *lit'i-gāt, vt* and *vi* to dispute, *esp* by a lawsuit. — *adj* **lit'igable**. — *adj* **lit'igant** contending at law; engaged in a lawsuit. — *n* a person engaged in a lawsuit. — *n* **litigā'tion**. — *adj* **litigious** (*-ij'əs*) relating to litigation; inclined to engage in lawsuits; disputable; open to contention; *perh* depending on results of negotiation (*Shakesp*). — *adv* **litig'iously**. — *n* **litig'iousness**. [L *lītigāre, -ātum*, from *līs, lītis* strife, and *agere* to do]

litmus *lit'məs, n* a substance obtained from certain lichens, turned red by acids, blue by alkalis. — **litmus paper** a test-paper dipped in litmus solution; **litmus test** (*fig*) an event seen as an indicator of underlying attitudes, factors, etc. [ON *litmosi* herbs used in dyeing, from *litr* colour, and *mosi* moss]

litotes *lī'* or *lit'ō-tēz*, (*rhetoric*) *n* meiosis or understatement; *esp* affirmation by negation of the contrary, as in *not a little angry* (= furious). [Gr *lītotēs* simplicity, from *lītos* plain]

litre *lē'tər, n* the metric unit of capacity, 1 cubic decimetre or 1000 cubic centimetres; until 1964, the volume of a kilogram of water at 4°C, under standard atmospheric pressure (1·000 028cu dm). — *combining form* **-litre** denoting the capacity of the cylinders of a motor vehicle engine (eg *three-litre*). [Fr, from LL *lītra*, from Gr *lītrā* a pound]

LittB or **LitB** *abbrev*: *Lit(t)erarum baccalaureus* (*L*), Bachelor of Letters or of Literature.

LittD or **LitD** *abbrev*: *Lit(t)erarum doctor* (*L*), Doctor of Letters or of Literature.

litten. See **loot**[2].

litter *lit'ər, n* rubbish, *esp* rejected food containers, wrappings, etc carelessly dropped in a public place; any scattered or confused collection of objects, *esp* of little value; a state of confusion and untidiness with things strewn about; a stretcher, or bed supported on poles, for transporting a sick person; a couch carried by men or animals (*hist*); a brood of young, born to eg a bitch or sow; an occasion of birth of animals; straw, bracken, hay, etc provided as bedding for animals (see also **cat litter** under **cat**); materials for a bed (*archaic*). — *vt* to scatter carelessly about; (of animals) to give birth to; to supply (animals) with litter. — *vi* to produce a litter or brood; to strew rubbish, etc untidily. — *adj* **litt'ered**. — *adj* **litt'ery** in a condition of litter; addicted to litter. — **litter basket** or **litter bin** a receptacle for rubbish; **litt'er-lout** or (*NAm*) **litt'er-bug** a person who wilfully drops litter; **litt'ermate** a fellow-member of a litter. [OFr *litiere*, from LL *lectāria*, from L *lectus* a bed]

litterae humaniores. See **literae humaniores**.

littérateur *lē-tā-rä-tœr', n* a literary man. [Fr]

little *lit'l, adj* small in size, extent, quantity or significance; petty; small-minded; young; resembling or reminiscent of something else, but on a small or smaller scale. — *n* (or *adj* with a noun understood) that which is small in quantity or extent; a small quantity; a small thing; not mûch. — *adv* in a small quantity or degree; not much; not at all. — **less** and **least** serve as *compar* and *superl* to the *adv* and to some extent, along with **lesser**, to the *adj*. — *n* **litt'leness**. — *n* **litt'ling** (*Scot* **litt'lin** or **litt'leane**; OE *lȳtling*) a child. — **Little Bear** or (*US*) **Little Dipper** Ursa Minor; **litt'le-ease** (*hist*) a confined space in which a prisoner can neither sit, stand nor lie; the pillory; the stocks; **little end** in an internal-combustion engine, the smaller end of the connecting rod; **Litt'le-end'ian** one of the Lilliputian party who opposed the *Big-endians*, maintaining that boiled eggs should be cracked at the little end (from Swift's *Gulliver's Travels*); **little Englander** an opponent of British imperialism and empire-building; **little finger** the fifth and smallest digit of the hand; **little go** see under **go**[1]; **little green men** a type of men imagined as originating in parts of the universe other than our earth; **little magazine** a small highbrow magazine; **little man** a man of no importance, an underdog; **little Mary** (*J M Barrie*) the stomach; **little office** a short service of psalms, hymns, collects, etc; **little people** the fairies, or other race of small supernatural beings; a traditional race of pygmies (*archaic*); **Little Russian** (*archaic*) Ukrainian; **little theatre** a small theatre, *usu* one in which experimental plays, and other plays not likely to be a great commercial success, are produced; **little toe** see under **toe**; **little woman** (*facetious*, mainly *old*) one's wife. — *adj* **litt'leworth** (*archaic*) worthless. — **little by little** or (*archaic*) **by little and little** by degrees; **in little** on a small scale; **make little of** to treat as of little consequence, to belittle; to comprehend only slightly; **twist, wind** or **wrap someone round one's little finger** see under **finger**. [OE *lȳtel*]

littoral *lit'ər-əl, adj* belonging or relating to the seashore or to the shore of a lake, to lands near the coast, the beach, the space between high and low tidemarks, or water a little below low-water mark; inhabiting the shore or shallow water in a lake or sea. — *n* the shore or coastal strip of land. [L *littorālis* for *lītorālis*, from *lītus, lītoris* shore]

liturgy *lit'ər-ji, n* the form of service or regular ritual of a church, strictly that used in the celebration of the eucharist; the form of service used in the Eastern Orthodox Church in the celebration of the Eucharist; in ancient Greece, personal service to the state. — *adj* **liturgic** (*-ûr'jik*) or **litur'gical**. — *adv* **litur'gically**. — *n sing* **litur'gics** the doctrine of liturgies. — *n* **liturgiol'ogist**. — *n* **liturgiol'ogy** the study of liturgical forms. — *n* **lit'urgist** a leader in public worship; a person who adheres to, or who studies, liturgies. [Gr *leitourgiā*]

lituus *lit'ū-əs*, *n* an augur's curved staff (*hist*); a J-shaped Roman trumpet (*hist*); a curve of similar form with the polar equation $r^2 \theta = a$ (*math*). [L *lituus*]

live[1] *liv*, *vi* to have, or continue in, life, temporal, spiritual, or figurative, to be alive; to enjoy life; to lead one's life in a certain way, eg *live well, loosely*, etc; to be supported, subsist, get a living; to survive, remain alive, escape death; to continue, last, escape destruction or oblivion; to reside or dwell. — *vt* to spend or pass; to act in conformity to; to express (eg a set of principles, a creed, etc) by one's life, make one's life the same thing as: — *pr p* **liv'ing**; *pa t* and *pa p* **lived** (*livd*). — *n* **livabil'ity** or **liveabil'ity**. — *adj* **liv'able** or **live'able** worth living, capable of being lived; (*usu* followed by *in*) habitable; (*usu* followed by *with* or *in*) such as one could endure to live with or in, bearable. — *n* **liv'er**. — *adj* **lived'-in** (of a room, etc) homely with the signs of habitation; (of a face) marked by life's experiences. — *adj* **live'-in'** (of an employee) living at the place of work; (of a sexual partner) sharing the same dwelling. — **live a lie** to conduct one's life in such a way as to deny or conceal some essential circumstance or aspect of one's character, *usu* shameful; **live and breathe** to be passionately enthusiastic about; **live and learn** to keep learning new and surprising things; **live and let live** to give and expect toleration or forbearance; **live by** to order one's life according to (a principle, etc); **live down** eventually to rehabilitate oneself in people's eyes after (a failure, mistake, etc); **live for** to attach great importance to; to make (something) the chief concern of one's life; to look forward longingly to; **live in** to reside at one's place of employment; **live it up** to go on the spree; to cram one's life with excitement and pleasure; **live off** to be financially supported by; to feed oneself exclusively on (particular foods); **live on** to live by feeding upon, or with expenditure limited to; **live on air** (*facetious*) to have no apparent means of sustenance; **live out** to live (one's life) entirely in a particular way or place; to survive; to fulfil (eg the destiny reserved for one); (of someone in domestic service) to live away from the workplace (*US*); (of eg a hotel worker, hospital doctor, etc) to live away from one's place of employment; (of a student) to have accommodation outside the college or university campus; **live out of** (*colloq*) to depend on the limited range of eg food offered by (tins) or clothes contained in (a suitcase); **live through** to experience at first hand and survive (*esp* an unpleasant event); **live to** to live long enough to, come at last to; **live together** to cohabit; **live under** (*archaic*) to be tenant to; **live up to** to rule one's life in a manner worthy of; to spend up to the scale of; **live well** to live luxuriously; **live with** to cohabit with; to accept and adapt to as an inescapable part of one's life; **the living theatre** the live theatre. [OE *lifian* (WSax *libban*)]

live[2] *līv*, *adj* having life; alive, not dead; of a volcano, active, not extinct; stirring; in operation or motion; current, applicable, relevant; unquarried or unwrought; charged with energy (eg from electricity, explosives or other chemicals, etc) and still capable of discharge; burning; vivid; of the theatre, etc, concerned with living performance as distinct from filming, broadcasting or televising; of a broadcast, made directly from the actual event, not from a recording; fully operational (*comput*); a fishmonger's word for very fresh. — *combining form* **-lived** (*-līvd*; sometimes *-livd*) denoting having life (eg *long-lived*). — *vt* **liv'en** to enliven. — *vi* to become lively. — *n* **liv'ener**. — **live'-ax'le** driving-axle; **live'-bait** a living animal as bait; **live birth** birth in a living condition (*opp* of *stillbirth*). — *adj* **live'-born**. — **live'-box** a glass box for examining living objects under the microscope; a box for live fish; **live cartridge** one containing a bullet, as opposed to a *blank* or a *spent* cartridge; **live centre** a rotating centre in the headstock of a lathe, turning with the workpiece; **live circuit** a circuit through which an electric current is flowing. — *n pl* **live'-feath'ers** those plucked from the living fowl. — **live load** a moving weight or variable force on a structure; **live'-oak** an American evergreen oak, with durable wood; **live'-rail** one carrying electric current (see also **live wire** below); **live shell** a shell still capable of exploding; **live steam** steam at full pressure, direct from a boiler; **live'stock** domestic animals, *esp* horses, cattle, sheep and pigs; domestic or body vermin (*slang*); **live'ware** (*colloq*) all the people working with a computer system, personnel as distinct from hardware or software; **live weight** weight of living animals; **live'-well** the well in a fishing-boat where fish are kept alive; **live wire** a wire charged with an electric current; a person of intense energy or alertness (*fig*). [**alive**]

livelihead. See under **lively**.

livelihood *līv'li-hŏŏd*, *n* means of living; occupation or employment as a means of support. — Also (*Spenser*) **live'lod** or **live'lood**. [OE *līflād*, from *līf* life, and *lād* course]

livelong[1] *liv'long*, also *līv'long*, (*poetic*) *adj* very long; protracted; enduring; of the day or night, complete, entire, in all its pleasant or tedious length. [**lief** dear, used intensively, and **long**[3]]

livelong[2] *liv'long*, *n* the orpine, a plant difficult to kill. [**live**[1] and **long**[3]]

livelood. See **livelihood**.

lively *līv'li*, *adj* brisk; active; sprightly; spirited; vivid; lifelike; vital (*obs*); oral (*obs*). — *adv* vivaciously; vigorously. — *n* **live'lihead** (*obs*) liveliness; life; living form; livelihood. — *adv* **live'lily**. — *n* **live'liness**. — **look lively**! make haste, hurry up. [OE *līflic*, from *līf*, life]

liven. See under **live**[2].

liver[1] *liv'ər*, *n* a large gland that secretes bile, stores and filters blood, converts sugar into glycogen and performs other metabolic functions, formerly regarded as the seat of courage, love, etc; this organ taken from an animal's body, used for food; a disordered state of the liver (*colloq*); in old chemistry, a sulphide or other liver-coloured substance (*liver of sulphur*, a mixture obtained by heating potassium carbonate with sulphur). — *adj* liver-colour. — *combining form* **-liv'ered** having a liver, eg in *white-livered* or *lily-livered* (literally, having a pallid, blood-starved liver), cowardly. — *adj* **liv'erish** or **liv'ery** (*old*) suffering from a disordered liver; irritable. — *n* and *adj* **liv'er-col'our** of the colour of liver, dark reddish brown. — *adj* **liv'er-coloured**. — **liver fluke** a trematode worm that infects the bile-ducts of sheep and other animals. — *adj* **liv'er-grown** having a swollen liver. — **liv'er-rot** a disease caused by liver-flukes. — *n pl* **liver salts** mineral salts taken to cure indigestion. — **liver sausage** a rich sausage made of liver; **liver spot** a liver-coloured mark on the skin appearing in old age; **liv'er-wing** a fowl's right wing, which is cooked with the liver; **liv'erwort** (*-wûrt*) any plant of the Hepaticae, forming with the mosses the Bryophyta, similar to a moss, growing in damp places and having leaves of a liverlike shape, some kinds having once been used medicinally in diseases of the liver; **liv'erwurst** (*-wûrst*) liver sausage. [OE *lifer*; Ger *Leber*, ON *lifr*]

liver[2]. See under **live**[1].

liver[3] *lī'vər*, *n* a fanciful bird on the arms of the city of Liverpool. [Formed from *Liverpool*]

Liverpudlian *liv-ər-pud'li-ən*, *adj* belonging to Liverpool. — *n* a native of Liverpool. [*Liverpool*, with *-puddle* facetiously substituted for *-pool*]

livery[1] *liv'ər-i*, *n* the feeding, care, and stabling of a horse at a certain rate; the distinctive dress or badge of a great man's household (*hist*); the distinctive dress or uniform of a person's servants, *esp* men-servants, or of a body, eg a trade guild; any characteristic garb; the distinctive decoration used for all its aircraft, etc by an airline, etc; the distinctive style of dress or consistent visual appearance of employees, vehicles, communications, etc of a company; a body of liverymen or of livery-servants; a livery-servant (*archaic*); a delivery or handing over (*obs*); a dispensing or allowance of food or clothes to servants and retainers (*hist*). — *adj* **liv'eried** clothed in livery. — **livery company** any of the trade guilds of the City of London which assumed a distinctive dress in the 14c; **livery cupboard** a small cupboard used for the temporary storage of food, etc; **liv'eryman** a man who wears a livery; a freeman of the City of London entitled to wear the livery and enjoy other privileges of his company; a person who keeps or works at a livery stable; **livery pot** a flask in which an allowance of wine was formerly given to a servant; **liv'ery-servant** a servant who wears a livery; **livery stable** a stable where horses are kept at livery and for hire. — **at livery** of a horse, kept at the owner's expense at a livery stable; **sue one's livery** (*Shakesp*) to ask for the writ delivering a freehold into the possession of its heir. [Anglo-Fr *liveré* literally handed over, from *livrer*, from L *līberāre* to free]

livery[2]. See under **liver**[1].

lives *līvz*, *n* plural of **life**.

livid *liv'id*, *adj* black and blue; of a lead colour; discoloured; pale, ashen; extremely angry (*colloq*). — *n* **livid'ity**, **liv'idness** or **livor** (*lī'vər* or *-vör*) lividness of colour. — *adv* **liv'idly**. — *n* **liv'idness**. [L *līvidus*, from *līvēre* to be of a lead colour]

living *liv'ing*, *adj* live; alive; having vitality; lively; of a likeness, strikingly exact; currently in existence, activity or use. — *n* means of subsistence; manner of life; a property; a benefice. — **living death** a life of unrelieved misery; **living fossil** an animal or a plant of a group of which most are extinct; **living memory** the memory of anybody or somebody still alive; **living rock** rock still forming part of the bedrock, not detached; **liv'ing-room** a sitting-room for the general use of a family, etc; **living wage** a wage on which it is possible for a wage-earner and family to live adequately; **living will** a document drawn up to state what kind of medical care the signatory would prefer if he or she became terminally ill. — **the living** those alive at present. [Pr p of **live**[1]]

Livingstone daisy *liv'ing-stən dā'zi*, *n* a South African annual succulent plant (*Dorotheanthus bellidiformis* or *Mesembryanthemum criniflorum*), with daisy-like flowers. [Ety unknown]

livor. See under **livid**.

livraison *lē-vrez-ɔ̃*, (*Fr*) *n* a number of a book published in parts.

livre *lēvr'*, *n* an old French coin, superseded by the franc in 1795; an old French weight about 1lb avoirdupois. [Fr, from L *lībra* a pound]

lixiviation *liks-iv-i-ā'shən*, *n* leaching. — *adj* **lixiv'ial** or **lixiv'ious**. — *vt* **lixiv'iate**. — *n* **lixiv'ium** lye. [L *lixīvium* lye]

lizard *liz'ərd*, *n* any member of the *Lacertilia*, an order of scaly reptiles, *usu* differing from snakes in having four legs, movable eyelids, and non-expansible mouths; (with *cap*) the constellation Lacerta (*astron*). — *adj* **liz'ard-hipped** (of dinosaurs) having a pelvis slightly similar to a lizard's, the pubis extending forwards and downwards from the limb socket, saurischian. [OFr *lesard* (Fr *lézard*), from L *lacerta*]

LJ *abbrev*: Lord Justice.

LL *abbrev*: Late Latin; Lord Lieutenant; Low Latin.

ll *abbrev*: lines.

'll *l*. Short form of **will** and **shall**.

LLA *abbrev*: Lady Literate in Arts (see under **literate**).

llama *lä'mə*, *n* a S American transport animal of the camel family, a domesticated guanaco; its wool; cloth made of this. [Sp, from Quechua]

llano *lyä'nō* or *lä'nō*, *n* one of the vast steppes or plains in the northern part of S America: — *pl* **lla'nos**. — *n* **llanero** (*lyä-nā'rō*) an inhabitant of the llanos: — *pl* **llaner'os**. [Sp, from L *plānus* plain]

LLB *abbrev*: *Legum baccalaureus* (*L*), Bachelor of Laws.

LLCM *abbrev*: Licentiate of the London College of Music.

LLD *abbrev*: *Legum doctor* (*L*), Doctor of Laws.

LLM *abbrev*: *Legum magister* (*L*), Master of Laws.

LLW *abbrev*: low-level waste.

LM *abbrev*: long metre; Lord Mayor; lunar module.

lm *symbol*: lumen, the SI unit of luminous flux.

LMS *abbrev*: local management of schools (in which a school's board of governors is responsible for managing its allocated budget).

LMVD (*NZ*) *abbrev*: Licensed Motor Vehicle Dealer.

LMX (*insurance*) *abbrev*: London Market Excess of Loss.

ln *abbrev*: (natural) logarithm.

LNE or **LNER** *abbrev*: London and North-Eastern (Railway), now incorporated in British Rail.

LNG *abbrev*: liquefied natural gas.

lo *lō*, (*archaic*) *interj* look; behold: — *pl* **lōs**. — **lo and behold** (often *facetious*) used to signal a startling revelation. [OE *lā*]

loach *lōch*, *n* a small river-fish of a family (*Cobitidae*) related to the carp, having a long narrow body and spines round its mouth. [Fr *loche*]

load *lōd*, *n* that which is carried; that which may or can be carried at one time or journey; a burden; a charge; a freight or cargo; a definite quantity, varying according to the goods; weight carried; power output of an engine, etc; work imposed or expected; power carried by an electric circuit; a large quantity borne; a burden sustained with difficulty; that which burdens or grieves; a weight or encumbrance; weight of blows (*Spenser*); abundance (*colloq*, *esp* in *pl*). — *vt* to lade or burden; to charge; to put a load on or in; to put on or in anything as a load; to put film in (a camera); to put on too much; to weigh down; to overburden; to supply, present, or assail overwhelmingly or lavishly; to weight or bias; to give weight or body to, by adding something; to mix (colour) with white (*painting*); to lay colour on in masses (*painting*); to add charges to (*insurance*); to doctor, drug, adulterate or fortify (wine); to transfer (data or a program) to the main memory (*comput*). — *vi* to put or take on a load; to charge a gun; to become loaded or burdened: — *pa t* **load'ed**; *pa p* **load'ed** or (*archaic*) **load'en**. — *combining form* **-load** denoting the goods or people conveyed in a vehicle (as in *busload*, *coachload*, *lorryload*). — *adj* **load'ed** rich, wealthy (*slang*); under the influence of drink or drugs (*slang*); weighted in discussion in a certain direction; (of dice, etc) illicitly weighted so as to produce a desired outcome. — *vt* **load'en** (*obs* or *dialect*) to load. — *n* **load'er**. — *n* **load'ing** the act of loading; that with which anything is loaded. — *n pl* **loads** (*colloq*) a lot, heaps. — *adv* very much, as in *loads nicer*. — *adj* **load'-bearing** of a wall, etc, supporting a structure, carrying weight. — **loaded question** a question designed to make an unwilling answerer commit himself or herself to some opinion, action or course; **load factor** the ratio of an external load to the weight of an aircraft; the actual payload on an aircraft as a percentage of the maximum permissible payload; the ratio of an average load to peak load over a period; **loading bay** see under **bay**[3]; **loading coil** a coil inserted in an electric circuit to increase inductance; **loading gauge** a suspended bar that marks how high a railway truck may be loaded; the maximum horizontal and vertical space that rolling stock may safely occupy above the track; **load line** a line on a ship's side to mark the depth to which her cargo may be allowed to sink her; **load'master** a member of an air-crew who is in charge of the cargo; **load shedding** temporarily reducing the amount of electricity sent out by a power station. — **a load of** a quantity of (something distasteful or senseless eg *a load of rubbish*, *a load of tripe*); **a load off one's mind** relief from anxiety; **get a load of** (*slang*) to listen to, look at, pay attention to; **have a load on** (*NAm*) to be drunk; **load the dice** to make one side heavier than the other so as to influence their fall for purposes of cheating; **load the dice against someone** (*fig*) to deprive someone of a fair chance of success. [OE *lād* course, journey, conveyance; meaning affected by the unrelated **lade**[3]; cf **lode** and **lead**[1]]

loadsa- *lōd-zə-*, (*slang*) *combining form* representing *loads of*, chiefly in (and originating as a back-formation from) **load'samoney**, (a person loaded with) wealth accumulated as a result of the Thatcherite economics of the 1980s. [*Loadsamoney*, grotesque character invented by comedian H Enfield, 1988]

loadstar and **loadstone**. Same as **lodestar** and **lodestone**.

loaf[1] *lōf*, *n* a portion of bread baked in one mass, *esp* of standard weight; a moulded portion of food, *esp* bread or meat; a conical mass of sugar; bread (formerly, still *Scot*); any lump (*obs*); a cabbage-head; the head, or brains (for *loaf of bread*; *Cockney rhyming slang*): — *pl* **loaves** (*lōvz*). — *vi* **loaf** or **loave** (*lōv*) to form a head, as in a cabbage. — **loaf'-bread** (*Scot*) ordinary plain bread; **loaf'-cake** (*US*) a plain cake like a loaf in form; **loaf sugar** refined sugar moulded into a large cone. — **half loaf** a loaf of half the standard weight; **loaves and fishes** temporal benefits, the main chance (from John 6.26). [OE *hlāf* bread]

loaf[2] *lōf*, *vi* to loiter or stand idly about, pass time idly. — *n* **loaf'er** someone who loafs; a casual shoe, *esp* one resembling a moccasin. — *adj* **loaf'erish**. — *n* and *adj* **loaf'ing**. [Poss from Ger *Landläufer* tramp, vagabond]

Loaghtan *lohh'tən*, *n* a breed of four-horned sheep with a soft brown fleece, native to the Isle of Man. [Manx *loaghtyn* brown, poss literally mouse-brown, from *lugh* mouse, and *dhoan* brown]

loam *lōm*, *n* a soil consisting of a natural mixture of clay and sand, with animal and vegetable matter; a composition basically of moist clay and sand used in making bricks. — *vt* to cover with loam. — *n* **loam'iness**. — *adj* **loam'y**. [OE *lām*; Ger *Lehm*; cf **lime**[1]]

loan[1] *lōn*, (*Scot*) *n* a lane; an open space for passage left between fields of corn; a place for milking cows. — Also **loan'ing**. [OE *lone*, *lane*; see **lane**[1]]

loan[2] *lōn*, *n* anything lent, *esp* money at interest; the act of lending; the condition of being lent; an arrangement for lending; permission to use. — *vt* to lend. — *adj* **loan'able**. — **loan'back** a facility available from some life-assurance companies whereby a person may borrow from the sum he or she has invested; **loan collection** privately-owned works of art lent by their owner for a public exhibition; **loan'-hold'er** a person who holds security for a loan; **loan'-office** a public office at which loans are negotiated, received, or recorded; a pawnshop; **loan shark** (*colloq*) a person who lends money at exorbitant rates of interest, a usurer; **loan'-sharking**; **loan'-society** a society organized to subscribe money to be lent; **loan translation** a compound, phrase, etc that is a literal translation of a foreign expression, such as English *motorway* from German *Autobahn*, German *Fernsehen* from English *television* (also called a **calque**: see under **calk**[3]); **loan word** a word taken into one's own language from another language, generally with slight adaptation. [ON *lán*; cf **lend**, OE *lǣnan*; Dan *laan*]

loast *lōst*, (*Spenser*). See **lose**[2]

loath. See **loth**.

loathe *lōdh*, *vt* to dislike intensely; to feel disgust at. — *adj* **loathed**. — *n* **loath'edness**. — *n* **loath'er**. — *adj* **loath'ful** exciting loathing or disgust; (*Spenser* **lothefull** or **lothfull**) loathsome; reluctant. — *n* **loath'fulness**. — *n* **loath'ing** extreme hate or disgust; abhorrence. — *adj* hating. — *adv* **loath'ingly**. — *n* **loath'liness**. — *adj* **loath'ly** (*archaic*) hideous; loathsome. — *adj* **loathsome** (*lōth'* or *lōdh'səm*) exciting loathing or abhorrence; detestable. — *adv* **loath'somely**. — *n* **loath'someness**. — *adj* **loathy** (*lōdh'i*; *archaic*). [OE *lāthian*; cf **loth**]

loave and **loaves**. See under **loaf**[1].

lob *lob*, *n* a lump; a clumsy person; a lout; something thick and heavy; a pollack; a lobworm; in cricket, a slow, high underhand ball; in lawn tennis, a ball high overhead, dropping near the back of the court. — *vt* to bowl or strike as a lob; to droop (*Shakesp*): — *pa t* and *pa p* **lobbed**. — **Lob'-lie'-by-the-fire** a brownie who works by night for his bowl of cream; a Puck; **Lob's pound** (*dialect*) prison; difficulty. [Cf Fris and Du *lob*]

lobar, **lobate**, etc. See under **lobe**.

lobby *lob'i*, *n* a small hall or waiting-room; a passage serving as a common entrance to several apartments; the ante-chamber of a legislative hall; a corridor into which members of parliament pass as they vote (also **divis'ion-lobb'y**); a group of people who campaign to persuade legislators to make regulations favouring their particular interests. — *vt* to seek to influence (public officials), *esp* in the lobby. — *vi* to frequent the lobby in order to influence members or to collect political intelligence; to conduct a campaign in order to influence public officials. — *n* **lobb'yer**. — *n* **lobb'ying**. — *n* **lobb'yist**. — **lobby correspondent** a reporter on parliamentary affairs; **lobb'y-member** (*US*) formerly, someone who frequented a lobby in the interest of some cause; **lobby system** the giving of political information to lobby correspondents on condition that the source is not revealed. [LL *lobia*, from MHGer *loube* (Ger *Laube*) a portico arbour, from *Laub* a leaf; cf **lodge**]

lobe *lōb*, *n* a broad, *esp* rounded, segmental division, branch, or projection; the soft lower part of the ear; a division of the lungs, brain, etc; a division of a leaf. — *adj* **lōb'ar** relating to or affecting a lobe. — *adj* **lōb'ate**, **lōbed** or **lōb'ose** having a lobe or lobes. — *n* **lōbā'tion** lobing. — *n* **lobec'tomy** (*med*) the surgical excision of a lobe of any organ or gland of the body. — *n* **lobe'let** or **lobule** (*lob'ūl*) a small lobe. — *n* **lōb'ing** division into lobes; formation of, possession of, or provision with, lobes. — *adj* **lobiped** see **lobe-footed** below. — *vt* **lobot'omize** or **-ise** to perform a lobotomy on; to render dull, bland or inoffensive (*fig*). — *n* **lobot'omy** surgical incision into a lobe of an organ or gland; (loosely) leucotomy. — *adj* **lob'ular**, **lob'ulate** or **lob'ulated**. — *n* **lobulā'tion**. — *n* **lob'ulus** a small lobe or lobe-like structure: — *pl* **lob'uli** (-*ī*). — *n* **lō'bus** a lobe: — *pl* **lō'bī**. — **lobar pneumonia** inflammation of a whole lobe of the lungs, as distinguished from **lobular pneumonia**, which attacks the lungs in patches; **lōbe'-foot** a phalarope. — *adj* **lōbe'-foot'ed** or **lō'biped** having lobate feet, ie with lobes along the sides of the toes, as a coot does. [Gr *lobos* lobe]

lobelia *lō-bē'lyə*, *n* a plant of the genus *Lobelia* giving its name to a family, **Lobeliāceae**, differing from Campanulaceae in having two carpels and zygomorphic flowers, twisted upside-down, including garden plants with red, white, blue, purple or yellow flowers. — *n* **lobeline** (*lō'bə-lēn* or *-lin*) a poisonous alkaloid obtained from *Lobelia inflata*, used as a respiratory stimulant and to discourage tobacco-smoking. [Named after the botanist Matthias de *Lobel* (1538–1616)]

loblolly *lob'lol-i*, *n* thick gruel, hence ship's medicine (*dialect*); a lout (*dialect*); a muddy swamp or mire (*US*); a name for various American pines (also **loblolly pine**). — **lob'lolly-bay** an American tree of the tea family (*Gordonia lasianthus*), the bark of which is used in tanning; **lob'lolly-boy** (*obs*) a ship-surgeon's attendant; **lob'lolly-tree** a name for several American leathery-leaved trees. [Perh **lob** and **lolly**]

lobo *lō'bō*, (*US*) *n* a timber wolf. [Sp, wolf, from L *lupus*]

lobose, **lobotomy**, etc. See under **lobe**.

lobscouse *lob'skows*, *n* a stew or hash with vegetables or biscuit, a sea dish. — Also **lob's course**. [Origin obscure; cf **lob** and **loblolly**]

lobster *lob'stər*, *n* a large strong-clawed edible crustacean (genus *Homarus*), red when boiled; any of several crustaceans resembling it, eg the **Norway lobster** (*Nephrops*), **spiny** or **rock lobster** (*Palinurus*); a British soldier (*obs slang*). — **lob'ster-pot** a basket for trapping lobsters. [OE *loppestre*, from L *locusta* a lobster; cf **locust**]

lobular, lobus, etc. See under **lobe**.

lobworm *lob'wûrm*, *n* a lugworm; sometimes an earthworm. [**lob** and **worm**]

local *lō'kl*, *adj* relating to position in space; of or belonging to a place; confined to a place or places; concerned with a particular place or area; (of a bus or train) serving the community of a particular area, stopping at every stop. — *n* a person belonging to a particular place, an inhabitant; one's nearest public-house; an examination (*US*); a local anaesthetic (qv below); a local train; a trade union branch (*US*); a news item of local interest (*NAm journalism*); a place. — *n* **lo'calism** the state of being local; affection for place; provincialism. — *n* **lo'calist** someone preoccupied with local concerns. — *n* **locality** (*lō-kal'i-ti*) place; position; district. — *n* **localīza'tion** or **-s-**. — *vt* **lo'calize** or **-ise** to assign or limit to a place. — *n* **lo'calizer** or **-s-** something that localizes, *esp* a radio transmitter used in effecting a blind landing. — Also *adj* as in *localizer beam*, etc. — *adv* **lo'cally**. — **local action** (*law*) a legal action that relates to a specific place and must be brought there; **local anaesthesia** anaesthesia affecting only a restricted area of the body; **local anaesthetic** a solution for injecting into any part of the body to anaesthetize it, or an injection of this; **local area network** (*comput*) a computer network operating over a small area such as an office or group of offices, in which a high rate of data transfer is possible (*abbrev* **LAN**); **local authority** the elected body for local government, eg town council, county council; **local call** a telephone call made to another number on the same exchange or group of exchanges; a call made within a certain radius (less than 56km); **local colour** faithful, characteristic details of particular scenery, manners, etc, giving verisimilitude in works of art and fiction; colour of individual items as apart from the general colour-scheme in a picture; **local education authority** the department of a local authority which administers state education (*abbrev* **LEA**); **local examinations** examinations of school pupils held in various local centres by universities; **local government** self-administration (in local affairs) by towns, counties, etc, as opposed to *national* or *central government*; a local authority (*US*); **local option** the right of a town or district to decide whether liquor licences shall be granted within its bounds, or to decide whether or not to enforce (locally) permissive laws and regulations; **local preacher** a Methodist layperson authorized to preach in his or her district; **local radio** radio (programmes) broadcast from a local station to a relatively small area, often on local themes; **local time** the time of a place as measured by the passage of the sun over the meridian passing through that place; **local veto** the power of a district to prohibit the sale of liquors in its own area. [L *locālis*, from *locus* a place]

locale *lō-käl'*, *n* the scene of some event, etc. [Fr *local*, with *e* to show stress]

locate *lō-kāt'*, *vt* to place; (often *passive*) to set in a particular position, situate; to designate or find the position of; to find or pinpoint. — *vi* (*orig NAm*) to establish oneself in residence or business in an area. — *adj* **locāt'able** or **locāte'able**. — *n* **locā'tion** the act of locating, or process of being located; a farm (*Austr*); in South Africa, under apartheid, any of the townships or other areas in which the Black or Coloured population were obliged to live; position, site; site for filming outside the studio (*cinema*); a leasing on rent (*law*); a position in a memory which can hold a unit of information, eg a word (*comput*); such a unit of information (*comput*). — *adj* **locative** (*lok'ə-tiv*) relating to location; denoting a case representing 'place where' (*gram*). — *n* the locative case; a word in the locative case. — **on location** outside the studio (of filming or sound-recording). [L *locāre* to place]

loc. cit. *lok sit*, *abbrev*: *loco citato* (*L*), in the passage or place just quoted.

locellate *lō-sel'āt*, (*bot*) *adj* divided into small compartments. [L *locellus*, dimin of *locus* a place]

loch *lohh*, (*Scot*) *n* a lake; an arm of the sea (also **sea loch**). — *n* **loch'an** (*Gaelic*) a little loch. [Gaelic *loch*; OE (Northumbrian) *luh*]

Lochaber-axe *lohh-ä'bər-aks*, *n* a long-handled Highland variety of halberd. [*Lochaber* district in Inverness-shire]

lochan. See under **loch**.

lochia *lok'i-ə* or *lōk'*, (*med*) *n pl* a discharge from the uterus after childbirth. — *adj* **lō'chial**. [Gr *lochia* (pl)]

loci *lō'sī* or *lō'kē*, pl of **locus** (qv).

lock[1] *lok*, *n* a fastening device, *esp* one in which a bolt is moved by mechanism, with or without a key; an immobilizing device that can be operated on machinery, etc; an enclosure on a canal in which water can be adjusted to allow boats to be raised or lowered; the part of a firearm by which it is discharged; a grapple in wrestling or a disabling hold generally; in Rugby football, one of the two inside players in the second row of a scrum (also **lock'-for'ward**); a state of being jammed or immovable; the state of being firmly interlocked or engaged; (*usu* **air'-lock**) a bubble blocking the flow of fluid through a pipe, etc; a number of things mutually engaged; a lockful; a lock-keeper; any narrow, confined place; a lock-hospital; locking up; the full extent of the turning arc of the front wheels of a motor vehicle. — *vt* to fasten (a door, chest, etc) with a lock; to fasten so as to impede motion; to engage; to jam; to shut up, secure; to close fast; to hold closely, eg in an embrace; to construct locks on (a canal). — *vi* to become fixed, to jam; to unite or engage firmly; to become or have the means of becoming locked. — *adj* **lock'able**. — *n* **lock'age** the locks of a canal; the difference in the levels of locks; materials used for locks; water lost by use of a lock; tolls paid for passing through locks. — *adj* **lock'fast** firmly fastened by locks. — *n* **lock'ful** enough to fill a lock. — **lock'away** (*finance*) a long-term security. — Also *adj*. — **lock'-chain** a chain for fastening the wheels of a vehicle by tying the rims to some part which does not rotate; **lock gate** a gate for opening or closing a lock in a canal, river, or dock-entrance; **lock'-hos'pital** (*archaic*) a hospital for venereal diseases (from one in Southwark, *orig* a lazar-house, probably since specially isolated); **lock'house** a lock-keeper's house; **lock'jaw** tetanus; loosely, trismus; **lock'-keeper** the attendant at a lock; **lock'man** a lock-keeper; a hangman (*Scot*; *obs*); an under-sheriff, or a coroner's summoner (*Isle of Man*); **lock'-nut** or **lock'ing-nut** a nut screwed on top of another one to prevent it loosening; a nut designed to lock itself when screwed tight; **lock'out** the act of locking out, *esp* used of the locking out of employees by the employer during an industrial dispute; **lock'pick** a picklock; **locks'man** a turnkey; a lock-keeper; **lock'smith** a person who makes and mends locks; **lock'step** a method of marching in tight formation, with minimum space between one marcher and the one behind; **lock'stitch** a sewing-machine stitch formed by the locking of two threads together; **lock'-up** a cell for locking up prisoners; a lockable shelter for a motor vehicle; a small shop; a locking up. — *adj* capable of being locked up. — **a shot in the locker** see under **shot**; **Davy Jones's locker** see under **Davy Jones**; **lock away** to hide, *usu* by locking up out of sight; **lock horns** to engage in combat, physical or otherwise; **lock in** to confine by locking doors; **lock on (to)** of a radar beam, to track (an object) automatically; **lock out** to keep out by locking doors; to exclude employees from a factory, etc; to prevent other users from accessing (a file) while one user is reading or updating it (*comput*); **lock, stock and barrel** the whole; altogether, entirely; **lock up** to confine; to lock securely; to lock whatever is to be locked; to make inaccessible or unavailable (*fig*); to invest (capital) so that it cannot be readily realized; **under lock and key** locked up; imprisoned. [OE *loc*]

lock[2] *lok, n* a piece, strand, tuft or ringlet of hair; a wisp of wool or cotton; a small quantity, as of hay; a quantity of meal, the perquisite of a mill-servant (*Scots law*); a lovelock (*Shakesp*); (in *pl*) hair; (in *pl*) dread-locks (qv). [OE *locc*; ON *lokkr*, Ger *Locke* a lock]

locker *lok'ər, n* a small cupboard that can be locked. — **locker room** a room for changing clothes and storing belongings in lockers. [**lock**[1]]

locket *lok'it, n* little ornamental case containing a miniature portrait, photograph or memento, worn on a chain, etc round the neck. [Fr *loquet* latch]

Lockian *lok'i-ən, adj* relating to the philosophy of John *Locke* (1632–1704). — *n* **Lock'ian** or **Lock'ist**.

lockram *lok'rəm, n* a coarse linen said to have been made at *Locronan* (Ronan's cell) in Brittany.

loco[1] *lō'kō*, (*US*) *adj* of cattle, suffering from loco disease; mad, crazy (*slang*). — *n* (also **lo'coweed** or **lo'coplant**) Astragalus or any other related leguminous plant: — *pl* **lō'cos** or (*rare*) **lō'coes**. — *adj* **locoed** (*lō'kōd*) poisoned by loco; mad (*slang*). [Sp *loco* mad]

loco[2] *lō'kō, n* a locomotive: — *pl* **lō'cos**. — **lō'coman** a railway engine driver.

loco citato *lō'kō si-tā'tō* or *lok'ō ki-tä'tō*, (*L*) in the passage cited (*abbrev* **loc. cit.**).

locofoco *lō-kō-fō'kō*, (*US*) *n* a match for striking, a friction match; (*usu* with *cap*) one of the extreme section of the Democratic party of 1835, known as the Equal Rights Party: — *pl* **lōcōfō'cos**. [Origin unknown]

locomotive *lō-kə-mō'tiv, n* a railway engine; a self-propelled engine running on rails, used for pulling trains, and driven by steam, electricity or diesel power; any machine or engine that converts power into movement. — *adj* moving from place to place; capable of, or assisting in, locomotion. — *adj* **locomo'bile** (*-bil*) having the power of changing place; self-propelling. — *n* a locomobile vehicle. — *n* **locomobil'ity**. — *vi* **lo'comote** to move from place to place (back-formation). — *n* **locomotion** (*-mō'shən*) the power of moving from place to place. — *n* **locomotiv'ity**. — *n* **locomo'tor**. — *adj* **locomo'tor** or **locomo'tory** relating to locomotion. — **locomotor ataxia** (*pathol*) tabes dorsalis, failure of muscle coordination in the late stages of syphilis, caused by degeneration of the nerve fibres [L *locus* a place, and *movēre, mōtum* to move]

locorestive *lō-kō-res'tiv*, (*Lamb*) *adj* staying in one place. [Humorously modelled on **locomotive**, from L *restāre* to stay still]

Locrian *lō'kri-ən, adj* of *Locris* in Greece, or its people, the *Locri*. — *n* one of the Locri. — **Locrian mode** in ancient Greek music, the same as the Hypodorian. [Gr *Lokros* Locrian]

loculus *lok'ū-ləs, n* a small compartment or chamber (*bot, anatom* and *zool*); in ancient catacombs, a small recess for holding an urn: — *pl* **loc'uli** (*-lī*). — Also **loc'ule** (*-ūl*): — *pl* **loc'ules**. — *n* **loc'ulament** (*bot*) a loculus. — *adj* **loc'ular** or **loc'ulate** having loculi. — *adj* **loculicidal** (*lok-ū-li-sī'dl*; L *caedere* to cut) dehiscing along the back of the carpel. [L *loculus*, dimin of *locus* a place]

locum *lō'kəm, n* a locum tenens or a locum-tenency: — *pl* **lō'cums**. — **locum tenens** (*lō'kəm tē'nenz* or *ten'enz*) a deputy or substitute, *esp* for a doctor or member of the clergy: — *pl* **lō'cum tenen'tes** (*-tēz*). — **lōcum-ten'ency**. [L *lŏcum*, accusative of *lŏcus* a place, *tĕnēns*, pr p of *tenēre* to hold]

locuplete *lok'ū-plēt, adj* well-stored. [L *locuplēs, -ētis*]

locus *lō'kəs* or *lok'ŏŏs, n* a place, locality, location; a passage in a book, piece of writing, etc; the line or surface constituted by all positions of a point or line satisfying a given condition (*math*); the position of a gene on a chromosome (*genetics*): — *pl* **loci** (*lō'sī* or *lok'ē*). — **locus classicus** (*klas'i-kəs* or *-kŏŏs*) the classical passage, the stock quotation; **locus paenitentiae** (*pē-ni-ten'shi-ē* or *pī-ni-ten'ti-ī*) room for penitence; time for repentance; **locus standi** (*stan'dī* or *-dē*) a place for standing; a right to interfere. [L *locus* place]

locust *lō'kəst, n* a name for several kinds of migratory winged insects of the family *Acrididiae*, related to grasshoppers, highly destructive to vegetation; extended to various similar insects; a devourer or devastator (*fig*); a locust bean; a locust tree. — *vi* (*rare*) to lay waste like locusts. — *n* **locust'a** a grass spikelet; (with *cap*) a genus of grasshoppers of the family **Locust'idae** (not *usu* classed as locusts): — *pl* **locust'ae** (*-ē*). — **locust bean** the carob-bean; **locust bird** any of several pratincoles that feed on locusts; **locust tree** the carob; the false acacia (*Robinia pseudo-acacia*) or its wood; a large W Indian tree (*Hymenaea courbaril*) of the Caesalpinia family, with buttress roots, valuable wood, and bark exuding resin; **lo'cust-years** years of poverty and hardship (used by Winston Churchill, after an expression in the Old Testament, Joel 2.25). [L *locusta* lobster, locust; cf **lobster**]

locution *lok-ū'shən, n* an act or mode of speaking; an expression, word or phrase. — *adj* **locū'tionary** of or relating to an utterance. — *n* **loc'utory** a room for conversation, *esp* in a monastery. [L *loquī, locūtus* to speak]

lode *lōd, n* a vein containing metallic ore; a reach of water; an open ditch. — **lodes'man** a pilot; **lode'star** or **load'star** the star that guides, the Pole Star, often used figuratively; **lode'stone** or **load'stone** a form of magnetite which exhibits polarity, behaving, when freely suspended, as a magnet; a magnet (often *fig*). [OE *lād* a course; cf **load**]

loden *lō'dən, n* a thick waterproof woollen cloth with a short pile; (also **loden coat**) a coat made of this cloth. [Ger]

lodge *loj, n* an abode, *esp* if secluded, humble, small or temporary; a house in the wilds for sportsmen; a gate-keeper's cottage; a college head's residence; a porter's room; the meeting-place of a branch of some societies, eg freemasons; the branch itself; a N American Indian dwelling, *esp* a teepee or longhouse (qv); the dwelling-place of a beaver, otter, etc; a retreat; a frequently used element in the name of a house or hotel; an accumulation (*obs*); a loggia; a box in a theatre. — *vt* to supply with temporary accommodation; to place; to deposit for safety, etc; to infix; to bring (a charge or accusation) against someone; to make (a complaint or objection) officially; to vest (a power, talent, etc) in someone; to settle, fix firmly; to prompt or force to take shelter; (of wind, etc) to blow (eg crops) flat, to lay flat. — *vi* to stay temporarily, rent accommodation as a lodger; to pass the night; to take shelter; to come to rest in a fixed position; (of crops, etc) be blown flat. — *n* **lodg'er** a person who lodges; a person who lives in a hired room or rooms. — *n* **lodg'ing** temporary accommodation; (often in *pl*) a room or rooms rented in another person's house; harbour. — *n* **lodg'ment** or **lodge'ment** the act of lodging, or state of being lodged; the depositing of monies in a bank account; an accumulation of something that remains at rest, or a blockage caused by it; the occupation and holding of a position within enemy territory by a besieging party, and the fortifications erected to maintain it (*military*); the position so occupied. — **lodge'-gate** a gate with a lodge; **lodge'-keeper**; **lodge'pole** a pole used in the construction of a N American Indian lodge; **lodgepole pine** either of two fast-growing N American pines (*Pinus contorta*); **lodging house** a house where lodgings are let; a house other than a hotel where travellers lodge; a house where vagrants may lodge; **lodging turn** a turn or shift of railway work that requires sleeping away from home. [OFr *loge*, from OHGer *lauba* shelter; cf **lobby** and **loggia**]

lodicule *lod'i-kūl*, (*bot*) *n* a small scale in a grass flower. — Also **lodic'ula**: — *pl* **lodic'ulae** (*-ē*). [L *lōdīcula*, dimin of *lōdīx, -īcis* coverlet]

lo'e *lōō*. Scots form of **love** (verb).
loess or **löss** *lœs* or *lō'is*, *n* a wind-blown loamy deposit found in river valleys. [Ger *Löss*]
L of C *abbrev*: line of communication.
lo-fi *lō'-fī*, (*colloq*) *adj* (of sound reproduction) of low quality; loosely applied to anything shoddy or inferior. [**low**[2]; modelled on **hi-fi**]
loft *loft*, *n* a room or space immediately under a roof; a gallery in a hall or church; an upper room; an attic or upper floor, *usu* unfurnished, for storage, etc, eg in a warehouse (*US*); a room for pigeons; a stroke that causes a golf ball to rise; a backward slope on a golf club head for the purpose of lofting; a lifting action; upper region, sky or height (*Spenser*); a floor or ceiling (*Spenser*); a layer (*Milton*). — *vt* to provide with a loft (*obs*); to put or keep in a loft (*obs*); to strike (the ball) so that it rises (*golf*); to toss; to propel high into the air or into space. — *adj* **loft'ed**. — *n* **loft'er** a golf iron for lofting. — *adv* **loft'ily**. — *n* **loft'iness**. — *adj* **loft'y** very high in position, character, sentiment, manner or diction; stately; haughty; (of wool) bulky, springy, supple and soft. — **lofted house** (*Scot*) a house of more than one storey. — **cock of the loft** the head or chief of a set. [Late OE *loft*, from ON *lopt* sky, an upper room; OE *lyft*, Ger *Luft* the air]
log[1] *log*, *n* short form of **logarithm**. — **log tables** a book of tables setting out logarithmic values.
log[2] *lōg* or *log*, *n* a Hebrew liquid measure, believed to be very nearly a British pint. [Heb *lōg*]
log[3] *log*, *n* a fallen tree trunk; a bulky piece of wood, used eg as firewood; a clog or impediment; an inert or insensitive person (*fig*); an apparatus (*orig* a block of wood), attached to the end of a line thrown overboard, for ascertaining a ship's speed; a record of a ship's, or other, performance and experiences, a logbook; a record produced by a mainframe computer of all the work done over a certain period of time. — *adj* consisting of or constructed of logs. — *vt* to cut or haul in the form of logs; to enter in a logbook, or record otherwise; to cover a distance of, according to the log; to record the name and punishment of; to punish or fine. — *vi* to fell timber: — *pr p* **logg'ing**; *pa t* and *pa p* **logged**. — *n* **logg'at** a small log or piece of wood; a stake; (in *pl*) the old game of throwing loggats at a stake. — *adj* **logged** (*logd*) reduced to the inactivity or helplessness of a log; waterlogged (*naut*); cleared of logs. — *combining form* **-logged** denoting saturated, permeated, impregnated, entirely filled, as in *waterlogged, smoke-logged*. — *n* **logg'er** a lumberman; (also **data logger**) a device which automatically records data. — *n* **logg'ing**. — **log'board** a hinged board for noting particulars for the logbook; **log'book** a book containing an official record of a ship's progress and proceedings on board, or of a journey made by an aircraft or car, or of any progress; a headteacher's record of attendances, school events, etc; a record of work done, studies followed, etc; the registration documents of a motor vehicle; **log cabin** a hut built of cut or uncut logs; **log'-canoe** a boat made by hollowing out the trunk of a tree; **log'-chip** the quadrant-shaped board attached to a logline; **logg'erhead** (*poss* from *logger* a block of wood for hobbling a horse) a blockhead; a dunce; a round piece of timber in a whale-boat, over which the line is passed (*naut*); (also **loggerhead turtle**) a large-headed type of sea-turtle (*Caretta caretta*); an implement consisting of a large metal ball attached to a shaft, heated for melting tar, etc. — *adj* **logg'erheaded**. — **log'-glass** a 14- or 28-second sand-glass, used with the logline to ascertain the speed of a ship; **log'-head** a blockhead; **log'-house** a log cabin; **log'-hut**; **log'-jam** jamming that brings floating logs to a standstill; congestion of events, etc, leading to a complete cessation of action (*fig*); such cessation of action, a deadlock, impasse; **log'juice** (*slang*) bad port wine, as if coloured with logwood; **log'line** (*naut*) the line fastened to the log, and marked for finding the speed of a vessel; **log'-man** a man who carries logs (*Shakesp*); someone who cuts and removes logs; **log'-reel** a reel on which the logline is wound. — *vt* and *vi* **log'-roll**. — **log'-roller**; **log'-rolling** a gathering of people to facilitate the collection of logs after the clearing of a piece of land, or for rolling logs into a stream; the sport of trying to dislodge another person standing on the same floating log; mutual aid among politicians, etc, *esp* trading in votes to secure the passage of legislation; **log'-saw** a bow-saw, a saw with a narrow blade stretched like a bowstring in a bow-like frame; **log'-slate** a double slate used as a logboard; **log'wood** a tropical American tree (*Haematoxylon campechianum*) of the Caesalpinia family, exported in logs; its dark-red heartwood; an extract from it used in dyeing. — **at loggerheads** at variance, quarrelling (with *with*); **log in** or **on** (*comput*) to gain access to a mainframe system, *usu* by means of a code; **log out** or **off** (*comput*) to exit from a mainframe system; **sleep like a log** to sleep very soundly. [Origin obscure]
-log *-log*, *combining form US* variant of **-logue**.
logan *log'ən*, *n* a rocking-stone. — Also **log'an-stone**, **logg'an-stone** or **logg'ing-stone**. [Dialect word *log* to rock; poss connected with Dan *logre* to wag the tail]
loganberry *lō'gən-ber-i* or *-bər-i*, *n* a supposed hybrid between a raspberry and a Pacific coast blackberry, obtained by Judge J H *Logan* (died 1928).
logania *lō-gā'ni-ə*, *n* any plant of the *Logania* genus of Australian plants giving name to the **Loganiā'ceae**, related to the gentians. [Named after James *Logan* (1674–1751), botanist, scholar and statesman]
logaoedic *log-ə-ē'dik*, (*ancient prosody*) *adj* combining dactyls with trochees. [Gr *logos* prose, and *aoidē* song]
logarithm *log'ə-ridhm* or *-rithm*, *n* the power of a fixed number (called the base of the system, *usu* 10 or *e*) that equals the number in question, used *esp* before electronic computing, to simplify multiplication and division (short form **log**). — *adj* **logarith'mic** or **logarith'mical**. — *adv* **logarith'mically**. — **logarithmic sine**, **cosine**, etc the logarithm of the sine, cosine, etc; **logarithmic spiral** the path of a point travelling along a radius vector with a velocity increasing as its distance from the pole increases, its polar equation being $r = a^{\theta}$, or $\theta = k \log r$. [Gr *logos* ratio, reckoning, and *arithmos* number]
loge *lozh*, *n* a box in the theatre or opera house.
loggan-stone. See **logan**.
loggat, **logger**, **loggerhead**, etc. See under **log**[3].
loggia *loj'(y)ə*, *n* a covered open arcade: — *pl* **loggie** (*loj'ā*) or **logg'ias**. [Ital; cf **lodge**]
logging-stone. See **logan**.
Loghtan or **Loghtyn**. Alternative spellings of **Loaghtan**.
logia *log'i-ə*, *n pl* sayings, *esp* early collections of those attributed to Christ: — *sing* **log'ion**. [Gr]
logic *loj'ik*, *n* the science and art of reasoning correctly; the science of the necessary laws of thought; the principles of any branch of knowledge; sound reasoning; individual method of reasoning; convincing and compelling force (eg of facts or events); basis of operation as designed and effected in a computer, comprising **logical elements** which perform specified elementary arithmetical functions. — *adj* **log'ical** of or according to logic; reasoning correctly; following necessarily from facts or events; of, or used in, logic circuits (*comput*). — *n* **logical'ity** or **log'icalness**. — *adv* **log'ically**. — *n* **logician** (*loj-ish'ən*) a person skilled in logic. — *n* **log'icism** (*log'i-sizm*) Frege's theory that underlying mathematics is a purely logical set of axioms, mathematics being thus a part of logic. — *n* **log'icist**. — *vi* **log'icize** or **-ise** (*-sīz*) to argue. — **logical analysis** (*philos*) analysis, the process of stating clearly what our concepts comprise and imply; **logical atomism** (*philos*) the theory that all propositions can be analysed into simple elements; **logical designer** one engaged in the scientific construction of computers; **logical positivism** (or **empiricism**) see under **positive**; **logic circuit** (*comput*) an electronic circuit with *usu* two or more

inputs and one output, which performs a logical operation, eg *and*, *not*; **logic diagram** (*comput*) a diagram showing logical elements and interconnections without engineering details. — **chop logic** see under **chop**[2]. [Gr *logikē* (*technē*) logical (art), from *logos* speech, reason]

logie *lō'gi*, (*Scot*) *n* the space in front of a kiln fire. [Origin unknown; cf **killogie**]

logion. See **logia**.

logistic *loj-is'tik* or **logistical** *loj-is'tik-əl*, *adj* relating to reasoning, to calculation, or to logistics or logistic; proportional. — *n* **logis'tic** the art of calculation; sexagesimal arithmetic. — *n* **logistician** (*-tish'ən*) a person skilled in logistics. — *n sing* or *n pl* **logis'tics** the art of movement and supply of troops; the handling of the practical detail of any large-scale enterprise or operation. — **logistic equation** (*ecol*) an equation describing the typical increase of a population towards an asymptotic value; **logistics vessel** a ship designed for the transport of troops and vehicles, and for their landing directly on to beaches. [Gr *logistikos*, from *logizesthai* to compute; influenced by Fr *loger* to lodge]

loglog *log'log*, *n* the *log*arithm of a *log*arithm. — Also **lō'log**.

LOGO *lō'gō*, (*comput*) *n* a simple programming language with list processing features and distinctive graphics.

logo *lō'gō*, *n* a small design used as the symbol of an organization, etc: — *pl* **lo'gos** (*lōg'ōz*). [Short for **logotype**]

logodaedalus *log-ō-dē'də-ləs*, *n* an artificer in words. — *adj* **logodaedal'ic**. — *n* **logodae'daly** verbal legerdemain. [Latinized from Gr *logodaidalos*, from *logos* word, and *Daidalos* Daedalus; see ety for **daedal**]

logogram *log'ō-gram* or **logograph** *-gräf*, (*shorthand*) *n* a single sign standing for a word, phrase or morpheme; a logogriph. [Gr *logos* word, and *gramma* letter]

logographer *log-og'rə-fər*, *n* in Greek literature, one of the earliest annalists, *esp* those before Herodotus; a professional speech-writer. — *adj* **logographic** (*-graf'ik*) or **logograph'ical**. — *adv* **logograph'ically**. — *n* **logog'raphy** a method of printing with whole words cast in a single type. [Gr *logos* word, and *graphein* to write]

logogriph *log'ō-grif*, *n* a riddle in which a word is to be found from other words made up of its letters, or from synonyms of these. [Gr *logos* word, and *grīphos* a net, riddle]

logomachy *log-om'ə-ki*, *n* contention about words or in words. — *n* **logom'achist**. [Gr *logomachiā*, from *logos* word, and *machē* fight]

logopedics or **logopaedics** *log-ə-pē'diks*, *n sing* speech therapy. — *adj* **logope'dic** or **logopae'dic**. [Gr *logos* word, and *paideiā* education]

logophile *log'ə-fīl*, *n* a lover of words. [Gr *logos* word, and **-phile**]

logorrhoea or **logorrhea** *log-ō-rē'ə*, *n* excessive flow of words, uncontrollable garrulity. [Gr *rhoiā* flow]

Logos *log'os*, *n* in the Stoic philosophy, the active principle living in and determining the world; the Word of God incarnate (*Christian theol*). [Gr *logos* word]

logothete *log'ō-thēt*, (*hist*) *n* a chancellor, *esp* in the Byzantine Empire and in Norman Sicily. [Gr *logothetēs* an auditor]

logotype *log'ō-tīp* or *lōg'ō-tīp*, (*printing*) *n* a piece of type representing a word or several letters cast in one piece; a single piece of type comprising a name and/or address, trademark or design; (*usu* **logo**) an identifying symbol consisting of a simple picture or design and/or letters. [Gr *logos* word, and *typos* an impression]

Løgting. See **Lagting**.

-logue or (*US*) **-log** *-log*, *combining form* denoting: speech or discourse, as in *monologue*, *dialogue*, *travelogue*; compilation, as in *catalogue*; student or enthusiast, as in *idealogue*.

logy *lō'gē*, (*chiefly US*) *adj* dull, lethargic. [Poss Du *log* heavy]

-logy *-lə-ji*, *combining form* indicating: science, theory; discourse, treatise. [Gr *logos* word, reason]

loid *loid*, (*slang*) *n* short for **celluloid**. — *vt* to open (a spring lock) with a strip of celluloid.

loin *loin*, *n* meat from the lower part of an animal's back; (*usu* in *pl*) the waist and lower part of the back or the hips and top of the legs; (in *pl*) the genital area, *esp* (*poetic*) as a source of new life. — **loin'cloth** a piece of cloth for wearing round the loins. — **gird up one's loins** to prepare for energetic action, as if by tucking up one's clothes. [OFr *loigne*, from L *lumbus* loin]

loipe *loi'pə*, *n* a track used for cross-country skiing: — *pl* **loi'pen**. [Dan *løjpe*]

loir *loir*, *n* a large European species of dormouse. [Fr, from LL *lis*, *liris*, from L *glīs*, *glīris*]

loiter *loi'tər*, *vi* to proceed lingeringly; to dawdle; to linger or lurk. — *n* **loi'terer**. — *n* and *adj* **loi'tering**. — *adv* **loi'teringly**. [Du *leuteren* to dawdle; Ger dialect *lottern* to waver]

loke *lōk*, (*dialect*) *n* a short, narrow lane; a cul-de-sac; a private road; a grass-covered track. [ME, from OE *loca* an enclosed place]

Loki *lō'ki*, *n* an evil god in Norse mythology.

Lok Sabha *lok sä'bə*, *n* the lower house of the Indian parliament. [Hindi *lok* people, and *sabha* assembly]

lokshen *lok'shən*, *n pl* noodles. — **lokshen pudding** a traditional Jewish pudding made with noodles, egg, sugar, dried fruit and cinnamon; **lokshen soup** a traditional Jewish noodle soup. [Yiddish, pl of *loksh* a noodle, from Russ *loksha*]

loligo *lō-lī'gō*, *n* the common squid or any other cephalopod mollusc of the *Loligo* genus or related genera. [L *lōlīgō*, *-inis*]

lolium *lō'li-əm*, *n* any plant of the *Lolium* genus of grasses, including darnel and rye-grass. [L *lōlium* darnel, 'tares']

loll *lol*, *vi* to lie lazily about, to lounge or sprawl; to dangle, hang (now mainly of the tongue). — *vt* to let hang out. — *n* **loll'er**. — *adv* **loll'ingly**. [Perh imitative; cf Du *lollen* to sit over the fire]

lollapalooza. See **lallapalooza**.

Lollard *lol'ərd*, (*hist*) *n* a follower of John Wycliffe, the 14c English religious reformer; an idler. — *n* **Loll'ardy**, **Loll'ardry**, or **Loll'ardism**. [MDu *lollaerd* mutterer or droner, from *lollen* to mew, bawl, mutter; combined with **loller** (see **loll**)]

lollipop *lol'i-pop*, *n* a large boiled sweet which has been allowed to solidify around a stick; a sweet made with sugar and treacle (*dialect*); (*usu* in *pl*) a sweet in general (also *fig*); (in *pl*; *old*) popular works of classical music. — **lollipop man**, **woman** or **lady** a person appointed to conduct children across a busy street, distinguished by carrying a pole with a disc on the end. [Perh Northern dialect *lolly* tongue]

lollop *lol'əp*, *vi* to bound about in an uncoordinated, puppylike manner; to lounge or idle: — *pr p* **loll'oping**; *pa t* and *pa p* **loll'oped**. [Poss from **loll**]

loll-shraub *lol'-shröb'* or **loll-shrob** *-shrob'*, (*India*) *n* red wine, claret. [Hindustani *lāl sharāb*, from Pers *lāl* red. and Ar *sharāb* wine]

lolly *lol'i*, (*colloq*) *n* a lollipop; money.

lollygag. See **lallygag**.

lolog. Same as **loglog**.

loma[1] *lō'mə*, (*zool*) *n* a membranous fringe or flap. [Gr *lōma*, *-atos*]

loma[2] *lō'mə*, (*US*) *n* in south-western states, a hill with a broad, flat top. [Sp, back, ridge]

Lombard *lom'bərd*, *lum'bərd* or *lom'bärd*, *n* an inhabitant of *Lombardy* in Northern Italy; (also **Langobard** *lang'gō-bärd* or **Longobard** *long'*) one of the Langobardi, or Longobardi, a Germanic tribe which founded a kingdom in Lombardy (568), overthrown by Charlemagne (774); a banker or moneylender, so called from the number of Lombard bankers in London (*obs*). — *adj* **Lom'bard** or **Lombardic** (*-bärd'ik*). — **Lombard architecture** the Romanesque style of Northern Italy, superseded by the Gothic in the 13c; **Lombardic script**

a medieval Italian style of handwriting; **Lombard Street** the chief centre of the banking interest in London; the British money market and banking scene (*fig*); **Lombardy poplar** a variety of black poplar with erect branches. [OFr, from L *Langobardus*, *Longobardus*]

lome. Same as **loam**.

lomentum *lō-ment'əm*, (*bot*) *n* a pod that breaks in pieces at constrictions between the seeds: — *pl* **loment'a**. — Also **lō'ment** (*-mənt*). — *adj* **lomentā'ceous**. [L *lōmentum* bean-meal (used as a cosmetic), from *lavāre*, *lōtum* to wash]

lompish (*Spenser*). Same as **lumpish**.

lon. or **long**. *abbrev*: longitude.

Lond. *abbrev*: London.

Londin. *abbrev*: *Londiniensis* (*L*), of London.

Londoner *lun'dən-ər*, *n* a native or citizen of *London*. — *adj* **Londonese'**, **Londonian** (*-dō'ni-ən*), **Lon'donish** or **Lon'dony**. — *n* **Londonese'** cockney speech. — *n* **Lon'donism** a mode of speech, etc peculiar to London. — *vt* and *vi* **Lon'donize** or **-ise**. — **London Clay** (*geol*) a Lower Eocene formation in south-eastern England; **London ivy** smoke; **London Pride** or **pride** a hardy perennial saxifrage (*Saxifraga ambrosa*), also *none-so-pretty* and *St Patrick's cabbage*; formerly applied to other plants. — **London Inter-Bank Offered Rate** (*abbrev* **LIBOR**) the rate of interest at which the major clearing banks lend money amongst themselves.

lone *lōn*, *adj* isolated; solitary; unfrequented, uninhabited; unmarried, or widowed. — *n* **lone'ness**. — *n* **lon'er** a lone wolf. — *adj* **lone'some** (*esp NAm*) solitary; feeling lonely. — Also *n*. — *adv* **lone'somely**. — *n* **lone'someness**. — **lone pair** (*chem*) a pair of valency electrons unshared by another atom; **lone wolf** (*fig*) a person who prefers to act on his or her own and not to have close friends or confidential relationships. [**alone**]

lonely *lōn'li*, *adj* unaccompanied; isolated; uninhabited, unfrequented; uncomfortably conscious of being alone. — *n* **lone'liness**. — **lonely heart** a *usu* unmarried person without close friends and consequently lonely and unhappy, *esp* one in search of a happy relationship. — *adj* **lone'ly-heart**. [**alone**]

long[1] *long*, (*Shakesp* and *dialect*) *adj* and *adv* on account. [**along**[2]]

long[2] *long*, (*archaic*) *vi* to belong, pertain or be fitting. [Not found as a verb in OE; perh *gelang* along, beside (as if to go along with)]

long[3] *long*, *adj* not short; of a specified (or to be specified) length; extended in space in the direction of greatest extension; far-extending; extended in time; of extended continuance; taking a considerable time to utter or do; distant in time (*rare*); of distant date; requiring much time in utterance or performance; (of a speech sound) of extended duration (*phonetics*); (of a syllable) loosely, accented; (of a vowel) loosely, in a long syllable; (of a dress, etc) coming down to the ankles, full-length; (of the memory) retentive; (of a word) abstruse or grandiose; numerically extensive; (of eg a suit of cards) of more than average number; exceeding the standard value, as in *long dozen*, *long hundred* (qv); having a large holding in a commodity or security, in expectation of a rise in prices (*finance*); (of a chance) remote; tedious: — *compar* **longer** (*long'gər*), *obs* **leng'er**; *superl* **longest** (*long'gist*), *obs* **leng'est**. — *n* a long time; a long syllable (*prosody*); the long summer university vacation (*colloq*); an obsolete note equal to two (in 'perfect' time three) breves (*music*; L *longa*); (in *pl*) long trousers; (in *pl*) long-dated securities. — *adv* for, during, or by, a great extent of time; throughout the whole time; far in space (*rare*): — *compar* and *superl* as for *adj*. — *vi* to yearn (with *for*). — *combining form* **-long** denoting eg of a specified length (as *year-long*, *mile-long*). — *n* **long'a** (*music*) a long. — *n* **long'ing** an eager desire, craving. — *adj* yearning. — *adv* **long'ingly**. — *adj* **longish** (*long'ish* or *-gish*). — *adv* **long'ly** (*Shakesp*) long. — *n* **long'ness** (*rare*). — *adj* **long'some** (*archaic* and *dialect*) long and tedious. — *adv* **long'ways** or (*NAm*) **long'wise** lengthways. — *adj* **long'-ago'** of the far past. — *n* the far past. — **long arm** far-reaching power; **long'boat** the largest and strongest boat of a ship; a longship; **long'bow** a bow drawn by hand as distinct from the crossbow. — *adj* **long'-breathed** (*bretht'*) able to continue violent exercise of the lungs for a long time. — **longcase clock** a grandfather clock. — *adj* **long'-chain** (*chem*) having a long chain of atoms in the molecule. — **long'cloth** a cotton made in long pieces. — *n pl* **long'-clothes** or (*obs*) **long'-coats** long garments for a baby. — *adj* **long'-da'ted** of securities, due for redemption in more than fifteen years. — **long-day plant** a plant that will only flower after being exposed to conditions of long days and short nights. — *adj* **long'-descend'ed** of ancient lineage. — *adj* **long'-dist'ance** going or extending to or over a long distance or time; (of a chance) remote. — **long division** (*math*) division in which the working is shown in full; **long dozen** thirteen. — *adj* **long'-drawn-out'** prolonged; unduly protracted. — **long drink** a large thirst-quenching drink (sometimes alcoholic) in a tall glass. — *adj* **long'-eared** with long ears or earlike feather-tufts. — **long face** a dismal expression. — *adj* **long'-faced** dismal-looking. — **long field** (*cricket*) a fielder or station near the boundary on the bowler's side, long off or long on; **long'-firm** a company of swindlers who obtain goods on pretence of being established in business, and then decamp without payment; **long'-hair** a highbrow. — Also *adj*. — *adj* **long'-haired** unconventional, hippy; highbrow. — **long'-hand** ordinary writing as distinct from *shorthand*; **long haul** a journey over a great distance; any activity requiring lengthy effort (*fig*). — *adj* **long'-haul**. — **long'-head** a dolichocephal. — *adj* **long'-headed** dolichocephalous; shrewd; sagacious. — **long'-head'edness**; **long home** the grave; **long hop** (*cricket*) a short-pitched, and so long-bounding, ball, easy to hit; **long'horn** an animal belonging to a breed of cattle with long horns; a longicorn beetle with long antennae (**house longhorn beetle**, a beetle whose larvae are very destructive to house timbers); a long-eared owl; **long'house** a long communal house, eg in SE Asia or among certain N American Indian peoples, *esp* the Iroquois; a large oblong hall or dwelling built by the Vikings (*archaeol*); **long hundred(weight)** see under **hundred**; **long johns** long underpants; **long jump** an athletic contest in which competitors jump as far as possible along the ground from a running start; **long'-leg** (*cricket*) a fielder, or a fielder's station, far out behind, and a little to the side of, the batsman. — *adj* **long'-legged** having long legs. — **long'-legs** a crane-fly. — *adj* **long'-life** (of foodstuffs) treated so as to prolong freshness. — *n* **long'-line** a long fishing line with many hooks attached. — *adj* (of clothing) long or lengthened in shape, as of a brassière or top extending over the ribcage. — *adj* **long'-lived** (*-livd'*; also *-līvd'*) having a long life. — **long mark** a macron; **long'-meas'ure** lineal measure; (also **long metre**) quatrains of eight-syllable lines; **long moss** a tropical American rootless epiphyte (*Tillandsia usneoides*) of the pineapple family, resembling bunches of hair; **long'-nine'** (*obs US*) a cheap cigar; **long odds** in betting, a remote chance, unfavourable odds in terms of risk, favourable in terms of potential gain; **long off** and **long on** (*cricket*) the fielders in the long field to the off and on of their positions. — *adj* **long-oil** see **oil length** under **oil**. — **long paddock** (*Austr*) the grass verge of a road, sometimes used for grazing animals on; **long-persistence screen** a cathode-ray tube coated with long afterglow (up to several seconds) phosphor; **long pig** (from a cannibal term) human flesh as food. — *adj* **long'-playing** of a gramophone record, giving length in reproduction because of the extremely fine groove. — **long'prim'er** (*printing*) a size of type (about 10-point) intermediate between small pica and bourgeois; **long'-pur'ples** the early purple orchis; purple loosestrife. — *adj* **long'-range** (of weapons) long in range, designed to reach remote targets of aircraft, etc, covering long distances without having to refuel; (of a forecast) extending well into the future. — **long robe** see under **robe**. — *n pl* **longs'-and-shorts'** Greek or Latin verses; masonry of alternate vertical and horizontal blocks, as in quoins and jambs. — **long sheep** a long-woolled sheep; **long'ship** (*hist*) a distinctive type of long vessel built by the Vikings; **long shot** (a bet, entry, venture, etc with) a remote chance of success; a shot taken at a distance from the object filmed. — *adj* **long'-sight'ed** able to see far but not close at hand; hypermetropic; presbyopic; having foresight; sagacious. — **long'-sight'edness**. — *n pl* **long'-six'es** (*archaic*) candles weighing six to a pound. — **long slip** (*cricket*) a fielder some distance behind the batsman on the off side. — *adj* **long'-spun** long-drawn, tedious. — *adj* **long'-stand'ing** of long existence or continuance. — *adj* **long'-sta'ple** having a long fibre. — *adj* **long'-stay** of eg patients in a hospital, staying permanently or semi-permanently. — **long stop** a fielder who stands to the rear of the wicket to stop balls missed by the wicket-keeper (*cricket*); a person or thing that acts as a final safeguard or check (*fig*). — *vi* to field as long-stop. — *adj* **long'suff'ering** enduring long and patiently. — *n* long endurance or patience. — **long suit** the suit with most cards in a player's hand; a particular talent, good quality, or advantage that one has; **long'-tail** an animal, *esp* a dog, with an uncut tail; a greyhound. — Also *adj*. — *adj* **long'-term** extending over a long time; of a policy, concerned with time ahead as distinct from the immediate present. — *adj* **long'-time** enduring for a long time. — **long-togs**, **long Tom** and **long ton** see under **tog**, **Tom** and **ton**[1] respectively. — *adj* **long'-tongued** having a long tongue; talkative, babbling. — **long-track** (**skating** or) **speedskating** speedskating in which contestants race against the clock; **long vacation** a long holiday during the summer, when schools, etc are closed; **long view** the taking into consideration of events, etc in the distant future. — *adj* **long'-vis'aged** long-faced; with a rueful countenance. — *adj* **long'-waist'ed** of a garment, having a deep or dropped waist; of a person, long from the armpits to the hips. — **long'wall** a long working face in a coalmine (**longwall system** or **working** a mining technique in which a seam is exposed along its length and then removed, layer by layer). — *adj* **long'-wave** (*radio*) of, or using, wavelengths over 1000 metres. — *adj* **longwear'ing** of clothes, that may be worn for a long time without wearing out, hard-wearing. — **long whist** see under **whist**[2]. — *adj* **long'-wind'ed** long-breathed; tediously wordy and circumlocutory. — **long'-wind'edness**. — **a long figure** (*slang*) a high price or rate; **a long purse** abundance of money; **as long as** provided only that; **before long** or (*poetic* or *facetious*) **ere long** soon; **draw the long bow** see under **bow**[2]; **go long** (*finance*) to acquire more holdings in commodities or securities in expectation of a rise in prices; **in the long run** see under **run**; **long on** well supplied with; **long since** a long time ago; **make a long arm** (*colloq*) to help oneself freely at table; **make a long nose** to cock a snook or put a thumb to the nose as a vulgar gesture; **no longer** not now as formerly; **not long for this world** near death; **so long** (*colloq*; *poss* from Ar *salaam* peace, used as a word of farewell) good-bye; **so long as** provided only that; **the long and the short (of it)** or (*esp Shakesp*) **the short and the long (of it)** the sum of the matter in a few words. [OE *lang*, *long* (adj), *lange*, *longe* (adv); Ger *lang*, ON *langr*; L *longus*]

long. (*abbrev*). See **lon**.

longa *long'gə*, *n*. See under **long**[3].

longaeval and **longaevous**. See **longevity**.

longan *long'gan*, *n* a tropical Asian tree (*Nephelium longana*) related to the lychee; its fruit. [Chin *lung-yen* dragon's eye]

longanimity *long-gə-nim'i-ti*, (*rare*) *n* forbearance. — *adj* **longanimous** (*-gan'*). [L *longanimitās*, *-ātis*, from *longus* long, and *animus* spirit]

longe. See **lunge**[2].

longeron *lon'jə-*, *lon'zhə-ron* or *lɔ̃-zhə-rɔ̃*, *n* a longitudinal member of an aeroplane. [Fr]

longevity *lon-jev'i-ti*, *n* great length of life. — *adj* **longaeval**, **longeval**, **longaevous** or **longevous** (*-jēv'*). [L *longaevitās*, *-ātis*, from *longus* long, and *aevum* age]

longicaudate *lon-ji-kö'dāt*, (*zool*) *adj* long-tailed. [L *longus* long, and *cauda* tail]

longicorn *lon'ji-körn*, *n* a longhorn beetle, any of several beetles of the family *Cerambycidae*, with very long antennae (the larvae feed on wood). — *adj* denoting, or having, long antennae. [L *longus* long, and *cornū* horn]

longinquity *lon-jingk'wi-ti*, *n* remoteness. [L *longinquitās*, *-ātis*, from *longus* long]

longipennate *lon-ji-pen'āt*, (*zool*) *adj* having elongated wings or feathers. [L *longus* long, and *penna* feather, wing]

longitude *lon'ji-tūd* or *long'gi-*, *n* the arc of the equator between the meridian of a place and a standard meridian (*usu* that of Greenwich) expressed in degrees East or West; the arc of the ecliptic between a star's circle of latitude and the first point of Aries or vernal equinox (21 March), measured eastwards (*astron*); length. — *adj* **longitūd'inal** relating to longitude; lengthways. — *adv* **longitūd'inally**. — **longitudinal wave** (*acoustics*) a wave in which the particles are displaced in the direction of advance of the wave. [L *longitūdō*, *-inis* length, from *longus* long]

Longobard. See under **Lombard**.

longshore *long'shōr* or *-shör*, *adj* existing or employed along the shore. — **long'shoreman** a stevedore; a person who makes a living along the shore by fishing, etc. [**along**[1] and **shore**[1]]

longueur *lɔ̃-gœr*, (*Fr*) *n* a tedious passage, eg in a book; prolixity, long-windedness; a period or instance of dullness or tedium. — Often in *pl*.

lonicera *lon-is'ər-ə*, *n* the honeysuckle, a shrub of the *Lonicera* genus. [A *Lonicerus* (died 1586), Ger botanist]

Lonrho *abbrev*: *Lon*don *Rho*desian (industrial conglomerate).

Lonsdale belt *lonz'dāl belt*, *n* an award in the form of a belt (qv) for gaining the same boxing title three times in succession. [Lord *Lonsdale*]

loo[1] *lōō*, (*colloq*) *n* a lavatory. — **loo roll** a roll of lavatory paper. [Ety uncertain; perh Fr *lieu*, *l'eau* (see **gardyloo**) or **Waterloo**]

loo[2] *lōō*, *n* a card game. — *vt* to subject to a forfeit at loo. — **loo'-table** a form of round table, *orig* one for playing loo. [See **lanterloo**]

loo[3] *lōō*, Scots form of **love** (verb).

looby *lōōb'i*, *n* a clumsy, clownish fellow. — *adj* clumsy, stupid. — *adv* **loob'ily** (*obs*). [Cf **lob**]

loof[1] *lōōf*. See **luff**.

loof[2] *lōōf* or *Scot lüf*, *n* the palm of the hand: — *pl* **loofs** or **looves**. — *n* **loof'ful** (*Scot lüf'fə*) an open handful. [ON *lōfi*]

loofah *lōō'fə*, *n* a tropical plant (genus *Luffa*) of the gourd family; the fibrous network of its fruit, used as a hard, rough sponge. — Also **loofa** or **luffa** (*luf'*). [Ar *lūfah*]

look *lŏŏk*, *vi* to direct one's eyes and attention; to give attention; to face; to seem or appear; to seem to be; to have an appearance; to take care (*archaic* or *dialect*). — *vt* to make sure; to see to it; to ascertain by a look; to look at; to expect; to seem likely; to render by a look; to express by a look; to refer to, turn (with *up*); to give (a look, as cognate object). — *n* an act of looking; view; air; appearance; (in *pl*) beauty, comeliness (also *good looks*). — *imperative* or *interj* see; behold. — *n* **look'er** a person who looks; an observer; a person who has good looks (*colloq*). — *combining form* **-looking** having a specified appearance or expression, as in *sad-looking*. — *n* **look'ism** a term formed on the analogy of *racism* and *sexism*, denoting an attitude of prejudice and discrimination against people who look different, eg because of some physical disability. — **look'-alike** a person who closely resembles another in personal appearance, a double; **look'er-in'** a television viewer; **look'er-on'** an onlooker; a (mere) spectator: — *pl* **look'ers-on'**; **look'-in'** a chance of doing anything effectively or of sharing; a short casual call; **look'ing-for** (*Bible*) expectation; **look'ing-glass** a mirror. — *adj* topsy-turvy (alluding to *Through the Looking-Glass* (1872) by Lewis Carroll). — **look'out** a careful watch; a place to observe from; a person given the task of watching or keeping watch; prospect; concern; **look'-round** inspection; **look'-see** (*slang*) a look around. — **be looking at** (*colloq*) to be able to expect (a possible price, length by time, etc); **look after** to take care of; to seek; to expect (*Bible*); **look alive** (*colloq*) to rouse oneself for action; **look and say** (*educ*) a method of teaching reading, whereby the pupil is trained to recognize words at a glance, and say them, rather than articulate the letters of the word one by one; **look down on** to despise; **look down one's nose at** to regard with contempt; **look for** to search for; to expect; **look forward to** to anticipate with pleasure; **look here**! used to draw attention to something, or as an angry response; **look in** to make a short visit; to watch television (*colloq*); **look into** to inspect closely; to investigate; **look like** to resemble; to promise or threaten (eg rain); used in requesting a description, as in *what does it look like*?; **look on** to regard, view or think; to be a spectator; **look out** to be watchful; to be on one's guard; to look for and select; to show or appear (*Shakesp*); **look over** to examine cursorily; to overlook or pass over; **look sharp** (*colloq*) be quick about it; **look small** to appear or feel foolish and ashamed; **look the part** to have, or assume, an appearance in keeping with one's role; **look to** to look at or towards; to watch; to take care of; to depend on (with *for*); to expect (to do); **look to be** (*colloq*) to seem to be; **look up** to search for, refer to; to take courage; to improve, take a turn for the better; to seek out and call upon, visit (*colloq*); **look up to** to feel respect or veneration for; **look you** (*archaic* and *Welsh*) observe, take notice of this; **not much to look at** (*colloq*) plain, unattractive. [OE *lōcian* to look]

loom[1] *lo͞om*, *n* a machine for weaving; the shaft of an oar; an electrical wiring assembly complete with insulating covering; a tool, implement (*obs*); a receptacle (*Scot*). [OE *gelōma* a tool]

loom[2] *lo͞om*, *vi* to appear indistinctly or as in a mirage, *esp* in an exaggerated or magnified form; (of an event) to impend, be imminent; to overhang threateningly (with *over*). — *n* an indistinct or mirage-like appearance. [Origin obscure]

loom[3]. See **loon**[2].

loon[1] *lo͞on*, also (*Shakesp*) **lown** or **lowne** *lown*, *n* a simple-minded or eccentric person (*colloq*); a low-born fellow (*archaic*); a rascal; a harlot; in the north-east of Scotland, a boy (also **loon'ie**); (in *pl*) casual trousers that flare widely from the knees (also **loon'-pants**). [Origin unknown]

loon[2] *lo͞on* or **loom** *lo͞om*, (*esp NAm*) *n* any of an order of northern diving birds, *esp* a sleek-bodied sharp-beaked bird of the genus *Gavia*. — *n* **loon'ing** their cry. [ON *lōmr*]

loony *lo͞on'i*, (*slang*) *adj* crazy, insane, lunatic. — *n* a mad person, a lunatic. — *n* **loon'iness**. — **loony bin** a lunatic asylum; **loony left** (the members of) the extreme left wing of the (*usu* British) political spectrum, whose policies and beliefs are popularly regarded as lunatic. [Short form of **lunatic**, and **-y**[1]]

loop[1] *lo͞op*, *n* the oval-shaped coil made in a piece of string, chain, etc as it crosses back over itself; any similar doubling in the shape or structure of anything; anything of similar form, eg an element in fingerprints; a branch of anything that returns to the main part; a series of instructions within a computer program which is performed repeatedly until a predetermined condition is met, when the computer will exit from the loop and carry on with the next instruction in the main program (*comput*); a closed circuit sound which a signal can pass (*electronics*); an aerobatic manoeuvre in which an aircraft climbs, from level flight, to describe a circle in the sky; any loop-shaped movement or manoeuvre; an intra-uterine contraceptive device shaped like a loop (also called **Lippes loop**). — *vt* to fasten in or with a loop; to ornament with loops; to make a loop of. — *vi* to travel in loops. — *adj* **looped**. — *n* **loop'er** a caterpillar of the Geometridae, so-called from its mode of walking by forming the body into a loop and planting its hinder legs close behind the six 'true' legs; someone who loops the loop in an aeroplane. — *n* and *adj* **loop'ing**. — *adj* **loop'y** having loops; crafty (*Scot*); slightly crazed (*slang*). — **loop'line** a branch railway that returns to the main line. — **loop the loop** to move in a complete vertical loop or circle, head downwards at the top of the curve. [Ety dubious]

loop[2] *lo͞op* or **loophole** *lo͞op'hōl*, *n* a vertical slit in a wall eg of a castle, for looking through, firing through or receiving light and air; a means of escape; a means of evasion, eg an ambiguity in a contract, etc. — *adj* **looped** (*Shakesp*) full of small openings. — *vt* **loop'hole** to make loopholes in. — **loop'-light** a small narrow window. [Perh MDu *lûpen* to peer]

loor. See under **lief**.

loord *lo͞ord*, (*Spenser*) *n* a lout. [Fr *lourd* heavy]

loos (*Spenser*). See **los**.

loose *lo͞os*, *adj* slack; free; unbound; not confined; not compact; unattached; untied; not close-fitting; not tight; relaxed; (of the joints) freely mobile; (of the bowels) affected by diarrhoea; inexact; indefinite; vague; not strict; unrestrained; lax; licentious; inattentive; dispersedly or openly disposed; not serried; (of the ball) not in the possession of any player (*football*); in Rugby football, denoting all play except for the set scrums and line-outs. — *adv* loosely. — *n* loose play (*Rugby football*); an act or mode of loosing, *esp* an arrow (*archaic*); the loose state (*archaic*); unrestraint (*archaic*); freedom (*archaic*); abandonment (*archaic*); an outbreak of self-indulgence; a course or rush (*obs*); event, upshot, end, as in *at the very loose* (*Shakesp*). — *vt* to make loose; to set free; to unfasten; to untie; to disconnect; to relax; to slacken; to discharge; to solve (*Spenser*). — *vi* to shoot; to weigh anchor (*archaic*). — *adv* **loose'ly**. — *vt* **loos'en** to make loose; to relax; to make less dense; to open or relieve (the bowels). — *vi* to become loose; to become less tight. — *n* **loos'ener** a laxative. — *n* **loose'ness** the state of being loose; diarrhoea. — *adj* **loose'-bod'ied** of clothes, flowing, loose-fitting; loose in behaviour. — **loose box** a part of a stable where horses are kept untied; **loose cannon** (*fig*) something or someone dangerously uncontrolled, like a cannon that may discharge unpredictably and cause damage to one's own side; **loose change** coins kept about one's person for small expenditures; **loose cover** a detachable cover, eg for an armchair; **loose'-cut** a disease of cereal crops caused by a parasitic fungus, *Ustilago nuda*, that reduces the grains to powder; **loose fish** a person of irregular, *esp* lax, habits; a prostitute; **loose forward** in Rugby union football, either of the two wing forwards or the number 8 at the back of the scrum; in Rugby league, the player at the back of the scrum; **loosehead prop** (*Rugby football*) the prop forward on the left of the front row in the scrum; **loose housing** a means of housing cattle whereby the animals have access to shelter but are free to move about in straw-covered yards. — *adj* **loose'-leaf** of a folder, binder, etc, having a cover designed so as to allow leaves to be inserted or removed. — *adj* **loose'-limbed'** or **loose'-joint'ed** having supple limbs. — **be at a loose end** to be disengaged, have nothing to do; **break loose** to escape from confinement; **give a loose to** to give rein or free vent to; **let loose** to set at liberty; **loosen up** to become less shy or taciturn; to exercise gently, eg in preparation for athletic effort; **on the loose** indulging in a bout of unrestraint; freed from confinement; **stay loose** (*slang*) keep cool, keep relaxed. [ON *lauss*; OE *lēas*; see **less**]

loosestrife *lo͞os'strīf*, *n* a plant (*Lysimachia vulgaris*) of the primrose family, or other member of the genus (eg yellow pimpernel, creeping Jenny); a tall waterside plant (*Lythrum salicaria*, purple loosestrife). [Intended as a translation of Gr *lȳsimacheion* common loosestrife (as if from *lyein* to loose, and *machē* strife), which may be from the personal name *Lȳsimachos*]

loot[1] *lo͞ot*, *n* plunder; stolen goods; money (*slang*). — *vt* and *vi* to plunder. — *n* **loot'er**. — *n* **loot'ing**. [Hindi *lūt*]

loot[2] *lüt* or *lo͞ot*, Scots *pa t* of **let**[1]: — *pa p* **loot'en**, **litt'en** or **lutt'en**.

loot[3] *lo͞ot*, (*colloq*) *n* short form of **lieutenant**.

looves. See **loof**[2].

lop[1] *lop*, *vi* to hang down loosely. — *n* lopgrass (see below). — *adj* **lop'-eared** of animals, having drooping ears. — **lop'grass** soft brome-grass. — *adj* **lopsid'ed** leaning to one side, off balance; heavier or bigger on one side than the other. [Perh connected with **lob**]

lop[2] *lop*, *vt* to cut off the top or ends of, *esp* of a tree; to cut away (eg superfluous parts): — *pr p* **lopp'ing**; *pa t* and *pa p* **lopped**. — *n* twigs or branches of trees cut off; an act of lopping. — *n* **lopp'er**. — *n* **lopp'ing** a cutting off; the part or parts cut off. [OE *loppian*]

lope[1] *lōp*, *vi* to run with a long stride; to leap. — *adj* **lō'ping**. [ON *hlaupa*; cf **leap**[1] and **loup**[1]]

lope[2] *lōp*, (*Spenser*) *pa t* of **leap**[1].

loper *lō'pər*, *n* one of *usu* a pair of sliding or hinged pieces of wood, metal, etc which act as supports for a desk top or the extended flap of a table. [Ety unknown]

lopho- *lōf-ō-* or *lof-ō-*, *combining form* signifying crested or tufted. — *n* **loph'obranch** (*-brangk*; Gr *branchia* gills) any fish of the seahorse and pipefish group, characterized by tufted gills. — Also *adj*. — *adj* **lophobranch'iate**. — *adj* **loph'odont** (*-dont*; Gr *odous*, *odontos* a tooth) having transversely ridged molar teeth. — *n* **loph'ophore** (*-fōr*; Gr *phoros* bearing) a ring of ciliated tentacles round the mouth of some sedentary marine animals. [Gr *lophos* a crest]

lopper[1] *lop'ər* (*dialect*; *Scot* **lapper** *läp'ər*), *vi* to curdle. — *vt* to curdle; to clot. — *n* a clot; slush. — *n* (*Scot*) **lapp'er-milk'** or **lapp'ered-milk**. [ON *hlöypa* to curdle]

lopper[2] and **lopping**. See under **lop**[2].

loq. *abbrev*: *loquitur* (*L*), see separate entry.

loquacious *lō-kwā'shəs*, *adj* talkative. — *adv* **loquā'ciously**. — *n* **loquā'ciousness** or **loquacity** (*-kwas'*). [L *loquāx*, *-ācis*, from *loquī* to speak]

loquat *lō'kwot* or *-kwat*, *n* a Chinese and Japanese ornamental tree (*Eriobotrya japonica*) of the rose family; its small, yellow edible fruit. [Chin *luh kwat*]

loquitur *lok'wi-tər* or *-to͞or*, (*L*) speaks (3rd pers present indicative), used with a person's name as stage direction, etc (*abbrev* **loq**.).

lor and **lor'**. See under **lord**.

loral and **lorate**. See under **lore**[2].

loran *lō'* or *lö'rän*, *n* a long-range radio-navigation system. [For *lo*ng-*ra*nge *n*avigation]

lorazepam *lo-raz'ə-pam*, *n* a benzodiazepine used as a sleeping drug and in the treatment of anxiety.

lorcha *lör'chə*, *n* a light vessel of European build, but rigged like a Chinese junk. [Port]

lord *lörd*, (with *cap* when used as a prefix) *n* a master; a feudal superior (also **lord'-supe'rior**; *hist*); a ruler; the proprietor of a manor (*hist*); a titled nobleman, duke (not prefixed), marquess, earl, viscount or (*esp*) baron; a peer; by courtesy, the son of a duke or marquess, or the eldest son of an earl; a bishop, *esp* if a member of the House of Lords; a judge of the Court of Session; used in various official titles, such as Lord Chief Justice; (with *cap*) God; (with *cap*) Christ; an owner (*archaic*); a dominant person; a husband (*archaic* or *facetious*, *esp* in the phrase **lord and master**). — *vt* (with *it*) to act like a lord, tyrannize; to address as lord; to make a lord (*archaic*). — *interj* expressing surprise (*colloq* **lor**, **lor'**, **law** or **lord'y**). — *n* **lord'ing** (*archaic*) sir (*usu* in *pl*, gentlemen); a petty lord. — *adj* **lord'less**. — *n* **lord'liness**. — *n* **lord'ling** a little lord; a would-be lord (also **lord'kin**). — *adj* **lord'ly** like, befitting, or in the manner of a lord; magnificent; lavish; lofty; haughty, proud; tyrannical. — Also *adv*. — *n* **lordol'atry** (*jocular*) worship of nobility. — *n* **lord'ship** state or condition of being a lord; the territory of a lord (*hist*); dominion; authority; used in referring to or addressing a lord (with *his* or *your*), or a woman sheriff or judge (with *her* or *your*). — **Lord Chancellor** see under **chancellor**; **Lord Chief Justice** see under **justice**; **Lord High Admiral** see under **admiral**; **Lord Lieutenant** see under **lieutenant**; **Lord Mayor** see under **mayor**; **Lord Muck** see under **muck**; **Lord Provost** see under **provost**; **Lord's Day** Sunday; **lords ordinary** the judges forming the Outer House of the Court of Session; **Lord's Prayer** the prayer that Christ taught his disciples (Matt 6. 9–13); **lords spiritual** the archbishops and bishops (and formerly mitred abbots) in the House of Lords; **Lord's Supper** holy communion; **Lord's table** the communion table; **lord-superior** see **lord** above; **lords temporal** the lay peers. — **drunk as a lord** extremely drunk; **House of Lords** upper house of British parliament; **live like a lord** to live in luxury; **Lord knows** (**who**, **what**, etc) I don't know, and I doubt if anybody knows; **Lord of Appeal in Ordinary** same as **Law Lord**; **Lord of Misrule** see under **misrule**; **Lord of Session** a judge of the Court of Session; **lords and ladies** (*bot*) common arum; **My Lord** (*mi-lörd'* or *mi-lud'*) used in addressing a judge or other lord; formerly also used as a prefix. [ME *lovered*, *laverd*, from OE *hlāford*, from *hlāf* bread, and *ward* (WSax *weard*) keeper, guardian]

lordosis *lör-dō'sis*, *n* abnormal curvature of the spinal column, the convexity towards the front. — *adj* **lordot'ic** affected with relating to lordosis. [Gr *lordōsis*, from *lordos* bent back]

lore[1] *lōr* or *lör*, *n* learning, *esp* of a special, traditional, or out-of-the-way miscellaneous kind, as in *folklore*, *plant-lore*; that which is learned; teaching (*archaic*); doctrine (*archaic*). — *n* **lor'ing** (*Spenser*) teaching. [OE *lār*]

lore[2] *lōr*, or (*zool*) *lör*, *n* the side of the head between eye and bill of a bird; the corresponding area of a reptile or fish; a thong (*obs*). — *adj* **lor'al**. — *adj* **lor'ate** strap-like. [L *lōrum* thong]

lore[3]. See **leese**.

lorel. See **losel**.

Lorelei *lor'ə-lī*, *n* in German legend, a siren of the Rhine who lured sailors to their death. [Ger *Lurlei* the name of the rock she was believed to inhabit]

Lorentz force *lō'rents fōrs*, (*phys*) *n* the force experienced by a point charge moving with a certain velocity in a field of magnetic induction and in an electric field. — **Lorentz transformations** the relations between the coordinates of space and time of the same event as measured in two inertial frames of reference moving with a uniform velocity relative to one another, and derived from the postulates of the special theory of relativity. [H A *Lorentz* (1853–1928), Dutch physicist]

lorette *lör-et'*, *n* a courtesan. [Fr, from the church of their district in Paris, Notre Dame de *Lorette*]

lorgnette *lörn-yet'*, *n* eyeglasses with a handle; an opera-glass. — *n* **lorgnon** (*lörn'yɔ̃*) an eyeglass; eyeglasses. [Fr *lorgner* to look sidelong at, to ogle]

lorica *lō-*, *lö-* or *lə-rī'kə*, *n* a leather corslet (*hist*); the case of a protozoan, rotifer, etc (*zool*): — *pl* **lori'cae** (*-sē*). — Also **loric** (*lō'* or *lö'rik*). — *vt* **loricate** (*lor'i-kāt*) to coat or armour protectively. — *adj* armoured with plates or scales. — *n* **loricā'tion**. [L *lōrīca* a leather corslet, from *lōrum* a thong]

lorikeet *lor-i-kēt'*, *n* a small lory. [From **lory**, on the analogy of para*keet*]

lorimer *lor'i-mər* or **loriner** *-nər*, *n* a maker of the metal parts of a horse-harness. [OFr *loremier*, *lorenier*, from L *lōrum* a thong]

loring. See under **lore**[1].

loriot *lō'ri-ət* or *lō'*, *n* the golden oriole. [Fr *loriot*, from *l'* the, and OFr *oriol*, from L *aureolus*, dimin of *aureus* golden, from *aurum* gold]

loris *lō'* or *lō'ris*, *n* the slender lemur of Sri Lanka; an E Indian lemur (*Nycticebus* or *Bradycebus tardigradus*, the *slow loris*). [Fr *loris*; said to be from Du]

lorn *lörn*, (*archaic*) *adj* lost; forsaken; left (*Spenser*). [OE *loren*, pa p of *lēosan* (found in compounds), to lose; see **leese**]

lorrell. See **losel**.

lorry *lor'i*, *n* a heavily-built motor vehicle for transporting heavy loads by road; a long (*esp* railway) wagon without sides, or with low sides. — *vi* (or *vt* with *it*) **lorr'y-hop** to travel by getting lifts on lorries. — **lorr'y-hopping**. [Origin uncertain]

lory *lō'* or *lō'ri*, *n* any parrot of a family with brushlike tongues, natives of New Guinea, Australia, etc; in South Africa, a touraco. [Malay *lūrī*]

los or **loos** *lōs*, (*obs*) *n* praise, reputation. [OFr, from L *laudēs*, pl of *laus* praise]

lose[1] *lōōz*, *vt* to fail to keep or obtain; to be deprived or bereaved of; to cease to have; to cease to hear, see or understand; to mislay; to waste (eg time); to miss; to be defeated in; to cause the loss or ruin of; to cause to perish; to bring to ruin. — *vi* to fail, to be unsuccessful; to suffer waste or loss; (of a clock or watch) to go slow: — *pr p* **los'ing**; *pa t* and *pa p* **lost** (*lost*). — *adj* **los'able**. — *n* **los'er**. — *n* and *adj* **los'ing**. — *adv* **los'ingly**. — *adj* **lost** (*lost*) parted with; no longer possessed; missing; not able to be found; thrown away; squandered, wasted; ruined; confused, unable to find the way (*lit* and *fig*). — **losing game** a game that is going against one; a game played with the aim of losing; **lost cause** a hopeless ideal or endeavour; **lost soul** a damned soul, an irredeemably evil person; **lost tribes** the tribes of Israel that never returned after deportation by Sargon of Assyria in 721 BC. — **get lost!** (*slang*) go away and stay away!; stop annoying or interfering!; **lose face** see under **face**; **lose oneself** to lose one's way; to become rapt or bewildered; to become totally engrossed; **lose out** (*colloq*) to suffer loss or be at a disadvantage; (also with *on*) to fail to acquire something desired; **lose way** (of a boat) to lose speed; **lost'-and-found'** relating to an office, official, etc whose function is to trace or take care of lost property, luggage etc; **lost to** insensible to. [OE *losian* to be a loss; apparently influenced in sense by **leese** and in pronunciation by **loose**]

lose[2] *lōz*, (*Spenser*) *vt*. Same as **loose**. — Also **los'en**: — *pa p* **loast** or **los'te** (both *lōst*).

losel *lō'zl* or *lōō'zl*, or **lorel** *lō'* or *lō'rəl* (*Spenser* **lozell** or **lorrell**), *n* a worthless fellow; a scamp. — *adj* good-for-nothing. [Appar from the pa p *losen*, *loren*, of **leese**]

losh *losh*, (*Scot*) *interj* **lord**.

loss *los*, *n* losing; diminution; default (*Shakesp*); bereavement; destruction; defeat; deprivation; detriment; something lost. — *adj* **loss'y** (*electronics* and *telecomm*) dissipating energy, said of a dielectric material or of a transmission line with high attenuation. — **loss adjuster** an assessor employed by an insurance company, *usu* in fire damage claims; **loss'-leader** something sold at a loss to attract other custom; **loss'maker** an organization, business, etc that makes a continual loss. — **at a loss** in, or resulting in, deficit; off the scent; at fault; nonplussed; perplexed. [OE *los*, influenced by **lost**]

löss. See **loess**.

lost. See under **lose**[1].

los'te *lōst*, a Spenserian *pa p* of **loose** and **lose**[2].

lot *lot*, *n* an object, such as a slip of wood or a straw, drawn or thrown out from among a number in order to reach a decision by chance; decision by this method; sortilege or divination; a prize won through divination; destiny; that which falls to anyone as his or her fortune; a separate portion; a patch of ground; a set; a set of things offered together for sale; the whole; a great deal, large amount; a plot of ground allotted or assigned to any person or purpose, *esp* for building; a turn (*obs*); a tax or due (*hist*; see **scot**) a large quantity or number; a batch of horses grouped for daily exercise (*horse-racing*). — *vt* to allot; to separate into lots; to divide (a property) into lots, *esp* for selling purposes; to cast lots for (*obs*): — *pr p* **lott'ing**; *pa t* and *pa p* **lott'ed**. — **across lots** (*US*) by short cuts; **bad lot** an unscrupulous person with a bad reputation; **cast** or **throw in one's lot with** to choose to share the fortunes of; **cast** or **draw lots** (of two or more people) to draw from a set of different but unseen or superficially indistinguishable objects as a means of singling out one person; **lots of** (*colloq*) many; **lots to blanks** (*Shakesp*) any odds; **the lot** the entire number or amount. [OE *hlot* lot, from *hlēotan* to cast lots]

lota or **lotah** *lō'tä*, *n* in India, a small brass or copper pot. [Hindi *loṭā*]

lote. See **lotus**.

loth or **loath** *lōth*, *adj* reluctant, unwilling; hateful, repulsive, ugly (*obs*). — **nothing loth** not at all unwilling. [OE *lāth* hateful; cf **loathe**]

Lothario *lō-thä'ri-ō* or *-thā'*, *n* a seducer, a rake: — *pl* **Lothar'ios**. [From *Lothario*, in Rowe's play, *The Fair Penitent*]

lothefull or **lothfull** (*Spenser*). See under **loathe**.

lotic *lō'tik*, *adj* associated with, or living in, running water. [L *lavāre*, *lōtum* to wash]

lotion *lō'shən*, *n* a liquid preparation for applying to the skin, medicinally or cosmetically; a washing (*obs*). [L *lōtiō*, *-ōnis* a washing, from *lavāre*, *lōtum* to wash]

loto. See under **lottery**.

Lotophagi and **lotos**. See under **lotus**.

lottery *lot'ər-i*, *n* an arrangement for the distribution of prizes by lot; a game of chance (not involving skill) in which prizes are distributed to purchasers of tickets chosen by lot; a matter of chance; a card game of chance. — *n* **lott'o** or (*rare*) **lō'to** a game played by covering on a card each number drawn till a line of numbers is completed (also called *housey-housey*, now *usu* **bingo**): — *pl* **lott'os** or **lō'tos**. [Ital *lotteria*, *lotto*, of Gmc origin; cf **lot**]

lotus *lō'təs*, *n* an Egyptian or Indian waterlily of various species of Nymphaea and Nelumbium; a N African tree (possibly the jujube), whose fruit induced in the eater a state of blissful indolence and forgetfulness (*Gr mythol*); an architectural ornament like a waterlily; (with *cap*) the bird's-foot trefoil genus. — Also **lote** (*lōt*; *archaic*) or **lō'tos**. — **lot'us-eat'er** an indolent person who enjoys the luxuries of life; **Lot'us-eat'ers** or **Lotophagi** (*lō-tof'ə-jī*; Gr *phagein* to eat) a people who ate the fruit of the lotus, among whom Ulysses lived for a time. — *adj* **lot'us-eat'ing**. — **Lo'tus-land** the country of the Lotus-eaters; **lotus position** a seated position used in yoga, cross-legged, with each foot resting on the opposite thigh. [Latinized Gr *lōtos*]

louche *lōōsh*, *adj* squinting; ambiguous; shady, sinister, shifty or disreputable. — *adv* **louche'ly**. [Fr]

loud *lowd*, *adj* making a great sound; noisy; obtrusive; flashy or showy in a vulgar way. — *adv* **loud** or **loud'ly**. — *vt* and *vi* **loud'en** to make or grow louder. — *adj* **loud'ish**. — *n* **loud'ness**. — **loudhail'er** a portable megaphone with microphone and amplifier. — *adj* **loud'-lunged**. — **loud'mouth** (*colloq*) someone who talks too much or offensively; a boaster. — *adj* **loud'-mouthed**. — **loud'speak'er** an electro-acoustic device which amplifies sound. — *adj* **loud'-voiced**. [OE *hlūd*; Ger *laut*; L *inclytus*, *inclutus*, Gr *klytos* renowned]

lough *lohh*, *n* the Irish form of **loch**.

louis *lōō'i*, *n* a French gold coin superseded in 1795 by the 20-franc piece: — *pl* **lou'is** (*-iz*). — *n* **lou'is-d'or'** a louis; a 20-franc piece: — *pl* **louis-d'or** (*lōō'i-dör'*). — *adj* **Lou'is-Quatorze** (*-kä-törz'*) characteristic of the reign (1643–1715) of Louis XIV, eg in architecture and decoration; **Lou'is-Quinze'** (*-kēz*) of that of Louis XV (1715–74); **Lou'is-Seize'** (*-sez*) of that of Louis XVI (1774–92); **Lou'is-Treize'** (*-trez*) of that of Louis XIII (1610–43).

loun or **lound**. See **lown**[2].

lounder *lōōn'dər* or *lown'dər*, (*Scot*) *vt* to beat, to bethump. — *n* a heavy blow. — *n* **loun'dering** a beating.

lounge *lownj*, *vi* to lie in a relaxed way; to idle. — *vt* to idle (away). — *n* a sitting-room in a private house; a room in a public building for sitting or waiting, often providing refreshment facilities; (also **lounge'-bar**) a more expensive and luxurious bar in a public house; an act, spell or state of lounging; an idle stroll; a resort of loungers; a kind of sofa, *esp* with a back and one raised end. — *n* **loung'er** someone who lounges; a woman's long loose dress for wearing indoors; an extending chair or light couch for relaxing on. — *n* and *adj* **loung'ing**. — *adv* **loung'ingly**. — **lounge'-liz'ard** a person who indolently spends time at social events and gatherings; **lounge suit** a man's matching jacket and trousers for (formal) everyday wear. [Origin doubtful]

loup[1] *lowp*, (*Scot*) *n* a leap. — *vi* to leap; to dance; to flee; to burst. — *vt* to leap over: — *pa t* **loup'it**; *pa p* **loup'en** or **loup'it**. — **loup'ing-ill** a disease causing sheep to spring up in walking, due to a virus transmitted by ticks, one of several diseases in sheep also called **staggers** (qv); **loup'ing-on'-stane'** a stone to mount a horse from. — *adj* **loup'-the-dyke** runaway; flighty; wayward. [ON *hlaup*; cf **lope**[1] and **leap**[1]]

loup[2]. A variant (*Scott*) of **loop**[1] and (*Spenser*) of **loop**[2].

loupe *lōōp*, *n* a jeweller's and watchmaker's small magnifying glass, worn in the eye-socket. [Fr]

lour or **lower** *lowr* or *low'ər*, *vi* to look sullen or threatening; to scowl. — *n* a scowl or glare; a gloomy threatening appearance. — *n* and *adj* **lour'ing** or **lower'ing**. — *adv* **lour'ingly** or **lower'ingly**. — *adj* **lour'y** or **lower'y**. [ME *louren*; cf Du *loeren*]

loure *lōōr*, *n* an old slow dance, or its tune, *usu* in 6–4 time, sometimes included in suites. [Fr, bagpipe]

louse *lows*, *n* a wingless parasitic insect (*Pediculus*), with a flat body and short legs; extended to similar animals related and unrelated (see **bird-louse** under **bird**, **fish-louse** under **fish**, etc; *pl* **lice** *līs*); a person worthy of contempt (*slang*; *pl* **lous'es**). — *vt* (*lowz*) to remove lice from; to spoil, make a mess of (with *up*; *slang*). — *adv* **lou'sily** (*-zi-*). — *n* **lous'iness**. — *adj* **lousy** (*low'zi*) infested with lice; swarming or full (with *with*; *slang*); inferior, bad or unsatisfactory (*slang*). — **louse'-wort** any plant of the genus *Pedicularis*, marsh-growing scrophulariaceous herbs popularly supposed to cause grazing animals to become lousy. [OE *lūs*, pl *lȳs*; Ger *Laus*]

lout[1] (*obs* **lowt**) *lowt*, *n* an ill-mannered, aggressive or awkward man or youth; a bumpkin. — *vt* (*Shakesp*) to treat with contempt, to flout. — *vi* to play the lout. — *adj* **lout'ish** clownish; awkward, ill-mannered and coarse. — *adv* **lout'ishly**. — *n* **lout'ishness**. [Perh connected with **lout**[2]]

lout[2] (*obs* **lowt**) *lowt*, (*archaic*) *vi* to bow; to stoop. — *n* a bow. [OE *lūtan* to stoop]

louvre or **louver** *lōō'vər*, *n* a louvre-board; a turret-like structure on a roof for the escape of smoke or for ventilation; an opening or shutter with louvre-boards; a dovecote (*obs*). — *adj* **lou'vred** or **lou'vered**. — **lou'vre-board** or **lou'ver-board** a sloping slat placed horizontally or vertically across an opening; **lou'vre-** (or **lou'ver-**)**-door** or **louvre-** (or **lou'ver-**)**win'dow** a door or open window crossed by a series of sloping boards. [OFr *lover*, *lovier*; origin obscure]

lovage *luv'ij*, *n* an umbelliferous salad plant (*Levisticum officinale*) of Southern Europe related to Angelica; a liquor made from its roots and seeds; any plant of the related genus *Ligusticum*, including *Scottish lovage*. [OFr *luvesche*, from LL *levisticum*, L *ligusticum*, literally, Ligurian]

lovat *luv'ət*, *n* a greyish- or bluish-green colour, *usu* in tweed or woollen cloth; cloth or wool of this colour (also **lov'at-green'**). — Also *adj*. [From *Lovat*, in Inverness-shire]

love *luv*, *n* fondness; charity; an affection for something that gives pleasure; strong liking; devoted attachment to another person; sexual attachment; a love affair; the object of affection; a term of address indicating endearment or affection (often spelled **luv** to represent *dialect* or *colloq* use); the god of love, Cupid, Eros, etc (*mythol*); a kindness, a favour done (*Shakesp*); the mere pleasure of playing, without stakes; in some games, no score. — *vt* to be fond of; to regard with pleasure and affection; to delight in with exclusive affection; to regard with benevolence. — *vi* to feel love and affection. — *adj* **lov'able** or **love'able** (*luv'ə-bl*) worthy of love; amiable; attracting affection. — *adj* **love'less**. — *n* **love'lihead** (*rare*) loveliness. — *adv* **love'lily** (*rare*). — *n* **love'liness**. — *adj* **love'ly** exciting admiration; attractive; extremely beautiful; delightful (*colloq*); loving, amorous (*Shakesp*). — *adv* delightfully, very well (*colloq*); lovingly (*Spenser*); beautifully (*obs*). — *n* (*colloq*) a beautiful woman, *esp* a showgirl or model. — *n* **lov'er** someone who loves, *esp* someone in a sexual relationship with another person; one of the partners in a love affair, a paramour; someone who is fond of anything; a friend (*Shakesp*). — *combining form* **-lover** denoting someone with a keen interest in, eg *animal-lover*, *bird-lover*. — *adj* **lov'ered** (*Shakesp*) having a love. — *adj* **lov'erless**. — *adj* **lov'erly** (*archaic*) like a lover. — *adj* **love'some** (*archaic*) lovely; loving. — *adj* **love'worthy** worthy of being loved. — *n* **lov'ey** (*colloq*) a term of endearment. — *n* and *adj* **lov'ing**. — *adv* **lov'ingly**. — *n* **lov'ingness**. — **love affair** a romantic sexual relationship, *esp* a short-lived one; **love'-apple** the tomato; **love'-arrow** a hair-like crystal of rutile enclosed in quartz (*mineralogy*); a calcareous dart protruded by a snail, supposed to have a sexual function; **love'bird** a small African parrot (*Agapornis*), strongly attached to its mate; extended to other kinds of bird; either of the (*esp* romantically demonstrative) partners in a sexual relationship (*facetious*); **love'bite** a temporary red patch left on the skin after sucking and biting during lovemaking; **love'-bro'ker** (*Shakesp*) a go-between in love affairs; **love'-charm** a magic spell intended to induce someone to fall in love, *esp* in the form of a philtre; **love'-child** an illegitimate child; **love'-day** (*Shakesp*) a day for settling disputes; **love'-drug** Indian hemp; **love'-favour** something given to be worn as a token of love; **love'-feast** the agape, or a religious feast in imitation of it; **love'-feat** an act of courtship; **love game** (*lawn tennis*) a game in which the loser has not scored (possibly from Fr *l'œuf* egg, cf **duck**[3] in cricket); **love-hate relationship** a relationship which alternates between emotional extremes, or in which both emotions exist concurrently; **love'-in** a gathering devoted to sexual activity, of idealistic rather than orgiastic nature; **love'-in-a-mist'** a fennel-flower (*Nigella damascena*); a W Indian passion-flower; **love'-in-i'dleness** the pansy; **love'-juice** a concoction dropped in the eye to induce someone to fall in love; **love'-knot** or **lov'er's-knot** an intricate knot, used as a token of love; **love'-letter** a letter written during the period of courtship; **love'-lies-bleed'ing** a kind of amaranth with a drooping red spike; **love life** a state of events in, or area of life concerning, romance or sexual attachments; **love'light** a lustre in the eye expressing love; **love'lock** a long or prominent lock of hair, *esp* one hanging at the ear, worn by men of fashion in the reigns of Elizabeth and James VI and I. — *adj* **love'lorn** forsaken by one's love; pining for love. — **love'lornness**; **love'maker**; **love'making** amorous courtship; sexual play and *usu* intercourse; **love'-match** a marriage for love, not money, status, etc; **love'-monger** (*rare*) someone who deals in affairs of love; **love'-nest** a place where lovers meet or live, *esp* when illicitly; **love'-potion** a philtre; **lover's knot** see **love-knot** above; **lovers' lane** a quiet path or road frequented by lovers; **love'-seat** an armchair for two; **love'-shaft** a dart of love from Cupid's bow. — *adj* **love'sick** sad, pining for love; languishing with love. — **love'-song** a song expressing or relating to love; **love'-story** a story with romantic love as its subject; **love'-suit** (*Shakesp*) courtship; **love'-**

token a gift in evidence of love. — *adj* **lovey-dovey** (*luv'i-duv'i*; *colloq*) sentimentally and (over-)demonstratively affectionate. — **lov'ing-cup** a cup passed round at the end of a feast for all to drink from; **lov'ing-kind'ness** (*Bible*) kindness full of love; tender regard; mercy. — **fall in love** to become in love (with); **for love or money** in any way or for any reason whatever; **for the love of it** for the sake of it; for the pleasure of it; **for the love of Mike** (*slang*) for any sake; **in love (with)** romantically and sexually attracted, devoted (to); **make love to** to have sexual intercourse with; to make romantic or sexual overtures or advances to, to woo (*old*); **of all loves** (*Shakesp*) for any sake, by all means; **play for love** to play without stakes; **there's no love lost between them** they have no liking for each other. [OE *lufu*, love; Ger *Liebe*; cf L *libet*, *lubet* it pleases]

Lovelace *luv'lās*, *n* a well-mannered libertine. [From *Lovelace*, in Richardson's *Clarissa*]

lover[1]. An obsolete form of **louver (louvre)**.

lover[2], etc. See under **love**.

low[1] *lō*, *vi* to make the noise of cattle. — *n* the sound made by cattle. — *n* **low'ing**. [OE *hlōwan*; Du *loeien*]

low[2] *lō*, *adj* occupying a position that is far down or not much raised; of no great upward extension; not reaching a high level; depressed; not tall; (of type or blocks) below the level of the forme surface (*printing*); reaching far down; (of clothes) cut so as to expose the neck and chest; quiet and soft, not loud; of deep pitch, as sounds produced by slow vibrations are; produced with part of the tongue low in the mouth (*phonetics*); nearly level or not much raised, in shallow relief; expressed in measurement by a small number; of numbers, small; of small value, intensity, quantity or rank; having little vitality, badly nourished; scanty, deficient; attributing lowness; for stakes of no great value; dejected; debased; base; mean; vulgar; humble; socially depressed; little advanced or backward in organization or culture; (of latitude) near the equator; (of dates) comparatively recent (*archaic*); attaching little value to priesthood, sacraments, etc: — *compar* **lower** (*lō'ər*); *superl* **lowest** (*lō'ist*) or **low'ermost**. — *n* that which is low or lowest; an area of low barometric pressure; a low or minimum level; low gear. — *adv* in or to a low position, state or manner; humbly; with a low voice or sound; at low pitch; at a low price; late (*archaic*); in small quantity or to a small degree. — *vt* **low'er** to make lower; to let or put down; to lessen; to dilute (*obs*). — *vi* to become lower or less. — *n* (*Scot*) (an examination at) the lower grade (qv). — *n* **low'ering** the act of bringing low, reducing or letting down. — *adj* letting down; sinking; degrading. — *adj* **low'ermost** lowest. — *n* **low'lihead** (*archaic*) humility. — *adv* **low'lily** (*-li-li*). — *n* **low'liness**. — *adj* **low'ly** humble; modest; low in stature or in organization. — *n* **low'ness**. — *adj* **low'-born** of humble birth. — **low'boy** a Low-Churchman (*obs*); a short-legged dressing-table with drawers (*US*). — *adj* **low'-bred** ill-bred; unmannerly. — **low'-brow** a person who is not intellectual or makes no pretensions to intellect. — Also *adj*. — **low'-cal** (*colloq*) low in calories. — *adj* **Low Church** of a party within the Church of England setting little value on sacerdotal claims, ecclesiastical constitutions, ordinances and forms, holding evangelical views of theology (*opp* to *High Church*). — **Low-Church'ism**; **Low-Church'man**; **low comedy** comedy of farcical situation, slapstick or low life. — *adj* **low'-cost'** cheap. — *adj* **low'-country** lowland (**the Low Countries** Holland and Belgium). — *adj* **low-cut'** (of a garment) with a low neck-line, revealing much of the chest. — *adj* **low'-down** (*colloq*) base; dishonourable. — *n* (*slang*) information, *esp* of a confidential or damaging nature. — **low-down'er** (*obs US*) a poor white; **Low Dutch** (*obs*) Low German including Dutch. — *adj* **low'er-brack'et** in a low grouping in a list. — *adj* **low'er-case** (*printing*) small as distinguished from capital, *orig* because kept in a lower case. — **lower chamber** see **lower house** below. — *adj* **low'er-class** relating to people of low social class. — **low'er-deck** the deck immediately above the hold; ship's crew (as opposed to officers). — Also *adj*. — **lower grade** (*Scot*; often with *cap*) formerly, the lower level of the Scottish Certificate of Education superseded in 1962 by the Ordinary grade, and by the Standard grade in 1989; an examination at this level; a pass in such an examination; **lower house** or **chamber** the larger, more representative, of two legislative chambers; **lower regions** Hades, hell; **lowest** (or **least**) **common denominator** see under **denominate**. — *adj* **low-fat'** containing only a small proportion of fat. — **low frequency**, **low-gear** and **Low German** see under **frequency**, **gear** and **German** respectively. — *adj* **low'-key'** (in painting or photography) in mostly dark tones or colours, with few if any highlights; undramatic, understated, restrained; (of a person) not easily excited, showing no visible reaction. — **low'land** land low in relation to higher land (also *adj*); **low'lander** (also with *cap*) a native of lowlands, *esp* the **Lowlands** of Scotland; **Low Latin** see under **Latin**; **low-level language** a computer-programming language using easily remembered words or letters, each instruction translating into one machine code instruction (*opp* of *high-level language*); **low level waste** (*nuc eng*) radioactive waste which, because of its low activity, does not require shielding during normal handling or transport; **low life** sordid social circumstances; people of low social class. — *adj* **low'-life**. — **low'light** (*usu* in *pl*) a portion of hair artificially brightened to enhance the natural colour of the hair. — Also *vt*. — *adj* **low'-lived** (*-livd*) vulgar; shabby. — **low'-loader** a low wagon without sides, used for very heavy loads; **low mass** mass celebrated without music and incense. — *adj* **low'-mind'ed** having crude or vulgar motives or interests; vulgar. — *adj* **low'-necked** (of a dress, blouse, etc) cut low in the neck and away from the shoulders, décolleté. — **low-noise converter** (*TV*) an aerial component that receives, magnifies and transmits by wire a satellite signal. — *adj* **low'-paid'** (of a worker) receiving or (of job) rewarded by low wages. — *adj* **low'-pitched** of sound, low in pitch; of a roof, gentle in slope; having a low ceiling. — *adj* **low'-press'ure** employing or exerting a low degree of pressure (ie less than 50 lb (*c*. 22·7 kg) to the sq in), said of steam and steam-engines; having low barometric pressure. — **low profile** a manner or attitude revealing very little of one's feelings, intentions, activities, etc. — *adj* **low-pro'file** (of people) having such a manner or attitude; (of a tyre) wide in proportion to its height (*autos*). — **low relief** same as **bas-relief**. — *adj* **low'-rise** (of buildings) having only a few storeys, in contrast to *high-rise* (qv). — *n* a building of this kind; **low side window** a narrow window (or lower part of a window) near the ground, sometimes found in old churches, *esp* in the chancel. — *adj* **low'-slung'** (of a vehicle, etc) with body close to the ground; generally, hanging low; (of a building) not tall. — *adj* **low'-spir'ited** downcast or depressed; not lively; sad. — **low'-spir'itedness**; **Low Sunday** the first Sunday after Easter, so called in contrast to the great festival whose octave it ends. — *adj* **low'-tar'** (of cigarettes) made of tobacco with a low tar content. — **low technology** or **low tech** simple, unsophisticated technology used in the production of basic commodities (also (with *hyphen*) *adj*); **low-temperature physics** the study of physical phenomena at temperatures near absolute zero. — *adj* **low'-ten'sion** using, generating or operating at a low voltage. — *adj* **low'-thought'ed** (*Milton*) having the thoughts directed to base or vulgar pursuits. — **low tide** or **low water** the lowest point of the ebbing tide; **low toby** see under **toby**; **Lowveld** (*lō'felt* or *-velt*; also without *cap*) the lower altitude areas of the eastern Transvaal in South Africa; **low'-wat'ermark** the lowest line reached by the tide; anything marking the point of greatest degradation, decline, etc (*fig*); **low wines** the weak spirit produced from the first distillation of substances containing alcohol. — **an all-time low** the lowest recorded level; **in low water** short of money; **lay**

low to overthrow, fell or kill; **lie low** see under **lie**[2]. [ON *lāgr*, Du *laag* low; allied to OE *licgan* to lie]

low[3] *lō*, (*archaic*, except in place names) *n* a hill; a tumulus. [OE *hlāw*; cf **law**[3]]

low[4] or **lowe** *low*, (*Scot*) *n* a flame. — *vi* to blaze. — **low-bell** (*low'*, *lō'* or *lo͞o'bel*; *dialect*) a small bell; a bell used by night along with a light, to frighten birds into a net. [ON *logi*; cf Ger *Lohe*]

lowan *lō'ən*. Same as **mallee-bird** or **mound-bird**.

lower[1] *lowr*, **lowering** and **lowery**. See **lour**.

lower[2] *lō'ər*. See under **low**[2].

lown[1] and **lowne** *lown*, *n* variants of **loon**[1].

lown[2] or **loun** *lown*, **lownd** or **lound** *lownd*, (*Scot*) *adj* sheltered; calm; quiet. — *adv* quietly. — *n* calm; quiet; shelter. — *vi* to calm. [ON *logn* (noun)]

Lowrie *low'ri*, (*Scot*) *n* a nickname for the fox. — Also **Low'rie-tod** or **Tod-low'rie**. [*Laurence*]

lowse *lows*, (*Scot*) *adj* loose. — *vt* (*lows* or *lowz*) to loose; to unyoke, set free; to redeem. — *vi* to unyoke the horses; to knock off work: — *pa t* and *pa p* **lows'it**. [See **loose**]

lowt. See **lout**[1,2].

lox[1] *loks*, *n* *l*iquid *ox*ygen, used as a rocket propellant. — Also **lox'ygen**.

lox[2] *loks*, *n* a kind of smoked salmon. [Yiddish *laks*, from MHGer *lahs* salmon]

loxodrome *loks'ə-drōm*, *n* a line on the surface of a sphere which makes equal oblique angles with all meridians, a rhumb-line. — Also called **loxodromic curve, line** or **spiral**. — *adj* **loxodromic** (*-drom'ik*) or **loxodrom'ical**. — *n sing* **loxodrom'ics** or *n* **loxod'romy** the art of sailing on rhumb-lines. [Gr *loxos* oblique, and *dromos* a course]

loxygen. See **lox**[1].

loy *loi*, (*Ir*) *n* a long, narrow spade with footrest on one side of the handle.

loyal *loi'əl*, *adj* faithful; true as a lover; firm in allegiance; personally devoted to a sovereign (or would-be sovereign), government, leader, etc; expressing or manifesting loyalty; legitimate (*Shakesp*). — *n* **loy'alist** a loyal adherent, *esp* of a king or of an established government; (also with *cap*) in Northern Ireland, a supporter of the British government; (also with *cap*) in British history, a partisan of the Stuarts; (also with *cap*) in the American war of Independence, a person siding with the British. — *adv* **loy'ally**. — *n* **loy'alty**. — **loyal toast** a toast to the sovereign, drunk at a formal dinner after which by tradition, the guests may smoke. [Fr, from L *lēgālis*, from *lēx*, *lēgis* law]

lozell. See **losel**.

lozenge *loz'inj*, *n* a diamond-shaped parallelogram or rhombus (*geom*); a small sweet, sometimes medicated, *orig* diamond-shaped; a diamond-shaped shield for the arms of a widow, spinster, or deceased person (*heraldry*). — *n* **loz'en** (*Scot*) a window-pane. — *adj* **loz'enged** divided into lozenges. — *adj* **loz'engy** (*heraldry*) divided into lozenge-shaped compartments. — *adj* **loz'enge-shaped**. [Fr *losange* (of unknown origin)]

LP *el-pē'*, (*colloq*) *n* a *l*ong-*p*laying record.

LP *abbrev*: Labour party; Lord or Lady Provost; low pressure.

LPG *abbrev*: liquefied petroleum gas.

L-plate *el'-plāt*, *n* a sign displayed on a motor vehicle driven by a learner-driver, a red 'L' on a white background. [*L*earner]

lpm (*comput*) *abbrev*: lines per minute.

LPO *abbrev*: London Philharmonic Orchestra.

L'pool *abbrev*: Liverpool.

LPS *abbrev*: Lord Privy Seal.

Lr (*chem*) *symbol*: lawrencium.

lr *abbrev*: lira (the Italian unit of currency; also **Lr**).

LRAM *abbrev*: Licenciate of the Royal Academy of Music.

LRB *abbrev*: London Residuary Body (see **GLC**).

LRCP *abbrev*: Licentiate of the Royal College of Physicians (**Edin**, of Edinburgh; **Lond**, of London; **Irel**, of Ireland).

LRCS *abbrev*: Licentiate of the Royal College of Surgeons (**Ed**, of Edinburgh; **Eng**, of England; **Irel**, of Ireland).

LS *abbrev*: Lesotho (IVR); Linnaean Society; (also **ls**) *loco sigilli* (*L*), in the place of the seal.

LSA *abbrev*: Licentiate of the Society of Apothecaries.

LSD *abbrev*: lysergic acid diethylamide (see under **lysis**).

LSD, £sd or **lsd** *abbrev*: *librae*, *solidae*, *denarii* (*L*), pounds, shillings and pence.

LSE *abbrev*: London School of Economics.

LSI *abbrev*: large-scale integration.

LSO *abbrev*: London Symphony Orchestra.

LT *abbrev*: Lithuania (IVR; provisional); low tension.

Lt *abbrev*: Lieutenant. — *abbrev*: **Lt Cdr** Lieutenant Commander. — *abbrev*: **Lt Col**. Lieutenant Colonel. — *abbrev*: **Lt Gen**. Lieutenant General. — *abbrev*: **Lt Gov**. Lieutenant Governor.

LTA *abbrev*: Lawn Tennis Association.

Ltd *abbrev*: limited company.

LTh *abbrev*: Licentiate in Theology.

LTOM (*commerce*) *abbrev*: London Traded Options Market.

Lu (*chem*) *symbol*: lutetium.

lu (*phys*) *abbrev*: lumen.

luau *lo͞o-ow'*, *n* a Hawaiian dish made of coconut, taro, octopus, etc; a Hawaiian feast or party. [Hawaiian *lu'au*]

Lubavitch *lub'ə-vich*, *n pl* a sect of Hasidic orthodox Jews. — *adj* **Lub'avitcher**.

lubber *lub'ər* or **lubbard** *lub'ərd*, *n* an awkward, big, clumsy man; a lazy, sturdy fellow. — *adj* lubberly. — *adj* and *adv* **lubb'erly**. — **lubber fiend** a beneficent goblin or drudging brownie, Lob-lie-by-the fire; **lubber hole** or **lubber's hole** (*naut*) a hole in a mast platform saving climbing round the rim; **lubber line** or **lubber's line** (*naut*) a line on the compass bowl marking the position of the ship's head. [Origin doubtful]

lubfish *lub'fish*, *n* a kind of stockfish. [**lob**]

lubra *lo͞o'brə*, (*Austr*) *n* an Aboriginal woman. [Aboriginal]

lubricate *lo͞o'* or *lū'bri-kāt*, *vt* to make smooth or slippery; to cover or supply with oil or other material to overcome friction; to supply with alcoholic drink (*colloq*); to bribe. — *adj* **lu'bric** or **lu'brical** (*archaic*) lubricious. — *adj* **lu'bricious** (*-brish'əs*) or **lu'bricous** (*-kəs*) slippery (*rare*); lewd (often *literary*). — *adj* **lu'bricant** lubricating. — *n* a substance used to reduce friction. — *n* **lubricā'tion**. — *adj* **lu'bricātive**. — *n* **lu'bricātor**. — *n* **lubricity** (*-bris'i-ti*) slipperiness; smoothness; instability; lewdness. — *n* **lubritō'rium** (chiefly *US*) a place in a garage or service station where motor vehicles are lubricated. — **lubricated water** water with certain additives which make it flow more smoothly. [L *lūbricus* slippery]

Lucan *lo͞o'kən* or *lū-*, *adj* of or relating to Luke or Luke's gospel.

lucarne *lo͞o-* or *lū-kärn'*, *n* a dormer window, *esp* in a church spire. [Fr (of unknown origin)]

luce *lo͞os* or *lūs*, *n* a freshwater fish, the pike. [OFr *lus*, from LL *lūcius*]

lucent *lo͞o'* or *lū'sənt*, *adj* shining; bright. — *n* **lu'cency**. [L *lūcēns*, *-entis*, pr p of *lūcēre* to shine, from *lūx*, *lūcis* light]

lucerne *lo͞o-* or *lū-sûrn'*, *n* purple medick, a plant resembling clover, also called alfalfa (*esp US*), valuable as fodder for cattle, etc. — Also **lucern'** (*Browning* **lu'zern**); formerly often **la lucerne**. [Fr *luzerne*]

luces. See **lux**.

lucid *lo͞o'* or *lū'sid*, *adj* shining; transparent; easily understood; intellectually bright; not confused, sane. — *n* **lucid'ity** or **lu'cidness**. — *adv* **lu'cidly**. — **lucid intervals** times of sanity in madness, of quietness in fever, turmoil, etc. [L *lūcidus*, from *lūx*, *lūcis* light]

Lucifer *lo͞o'* or *lū'si-fər*, *n* the planet Venus as morning star; Satan; (without *cap*) a match of wood tipped with a combustible substance to be ignited by friction (*archaic*). — Also **lucifer-match'**. — *n* **lucif'erase** an oxidizing enzyme in the luminous organs of certain animals that acts on luciferin to produce luminosity. — *adj* **Lucifē'rian** relating to Lucifer. — *n* **lucif'erin** a protein-like substance in the luminous organs of certain animals, *esp* glow-worms and fireflies. — *adj* **lucif'erous** light-bringing; light-giving. [L *lūcifer* light-bringer, from *lūx*, *lūcis* light, and *ferre* to bring]

lucifugous *lōō-* or *lū-sif'ū-gəs*, *adj* shunning or avoiding light. [L *lūx*, *lūcis* light, and *fugere* to flee]

lucigen *lōō'* or *lū'si-jən*, *n* a lamp burning oil mixed with air in a spray. [L *lūx*, *lūcis* light, and root of L *gignere*, *genitum* to beget]

Lucina *lōō-* or *lū-sī'nə*, *n* the Roman goddess of childbirth, Juno; also Diana; hence, the moon; a midwife (*archaic*). [L *Lūcīna*, thought by the Romans to be from *lūx*, *lūcis* light, as if the bringer to light]

Lucite® *lū'sīt*, *n* a kind of solid, transparent plastic, often used instead of glass.

luck *luk*, *n* fortune; good fortune; an object with which a family's fortune is supposed to be bound up. — *adv* **luck'ily** in a lucky way; I'm glad to say, fortunately. — *n* **luck'iness**. — *adj* **luck'less** without good luck; unhappy. — *adv* **luck'lessly**. — *n* **luck'lessness**. — *adj* **luck'y** having, attended by, portending or bringing good luck. — **luck'-penny** a small sum returned for luck to the customer by a seller; a coin carried for luck; **luck'y-bag** a bag sold without its contents being disclosed; a bag in which one may dip and draw a prize (also *US* **luck'y-dip**); a receptacle for lost property on board a man-of-war (*naut*); **lucky charm** an object which is supposed to bring good fortune; **lucky dip** a tub or container in which to dip and draw a prize; **luck'y-piece** a coin; the illegitimate child of a prosperous father (*colloq*); **lucky stone** a stone with a natural hole through it (carried for good fortune); **lucky strike** a stroke of luck. — **down on one's luck** (*colloq*) see under **down**[3]; **I should be so lucky** an ironic expression meaning loosely, 'that kind of luck does not happen to me'; **luck out** (*US*) to have a run or instance of good luck; **no such luck** unfortunately not; **push one's luck** (*colloq*) to try to make too much of an advantage, risking total failure; **touch lucky** (*colloq*) to have good luck; **tough luck** an expression of real or affected sympathy for someone's predicament; **try one's luck (at)** to attempt something; **worse luck** unfortunately. [Prob LGer or Du *luk*; cf Ger *Glück* prosperity]

lucken *luk'ən*, (*Scot*) *adj* closed. — **luck'enbooth** a booth or shop, *esp* of the type found in Edinburgh in the 18c (**Luckenbooth brooch** a *usu* silver and heart-shaped brooch, *orig* sold at such a booth); **luck'engow'an** the globe-flower. [OE *locen*, pa p of *lūcan* to lock]

lucky[1] or **luckie** (prefixed or vocative, **Lucky**) *luk'i*, (*Scot*) *n* an elderly woman; a woman who keeps an ale-house. — **luck'ie-dad** a grandfather. [Perh from adj **lucky** under **luck**]

lucky[2] *luk'i*, (*slang*) *n* departure. — **cut** or **make one's lucky** (*archaic*) to bolt.

lucky[3]. See under **luck**.

lucre *lōō'* or *lū'kər*, *n* sordid gain; riches. — *adj* **lu'crative** (*-krə-tiv*) profitable. — *adv* **lu'cratively**. [L *lucrum* gain]

luctation *luk-tā'shən*, (*obs*) *n* struggle. [L *luctātiō*, *-ōnis*]

lucubrate *lōō'* or *lū'kū-brāt*, *vi* to study by lamplight; to discourse learnedly or pedantically. — *n* **lucūbrā'tion** (*archaic* or *facetious*) study or composition protracted late into the night; a product of such study; a composition that smells of the lamp. — *n* **lu'cūbrātor**. [L *lūcubrāre*, *-ātum*, from *lūx* light]

luculent *lōō'* or *lū'kū-lənt*, *adj* bright; clear; convincing. — *adv* **lu'culently**. [L *lūculentus*, from *lūx* light]

Lucullan *lōō-* or *lū-kul'ən*, *adj* in the style of the Roman L Licinius *Lucullus*, famous for his banquets. — Also **Lucullē'an**, **Lucull'ian** or **Lucull'ic**.

lucuma *lōō'kū-mə*, *n* a tree of the *Lucuma* genus of sapotaceous trees with edible fruit, mostly found in S America. [Quechua]

lucumo *lōō'* or *lū'kū-mō*, *n* an Etruscan prince and priest: — *pl* **lu'cumos** or (*L*) **lucumōn'es** (*-ēz*). [L *lucumō*, from Etruscan]

Lucy Stoner *lōō'si stō'ner*, (*US*) *n* a woman who keeps her maiden name after marriage. [From *Lucy Stone*, an American suffragist (1818–93)]

lud *lud*, *n* a form of **lord** (trivial and forensic). — *n* **lud'ship**.

Luddite *lud'īt*, *n* one of a band of protesters against unemployment who destroyed machinery in northern England about 1812–18; hence, any opponent of technological innovation, etc. — Also *adj*. — *n* **Ludd'ism**. [Said to be from Ned *Ludd*, who had smashed stocking-frames (machines on which stockings were made) at a slightly earlier date]

ludic *lōō'dik*, *adj* playful, *esp* spontaneously and aimlessly. — *adv* **lu'dically**. [Fr *ludique*, from L *ludus* play]

ludicrous *lōō'* or *lū'di-krəs*, *adj* intended to excite, or exciting, laughter; ridiculous, absurd; laughable; sportive (*obs*); humorous (*obs*). — *adv* **lu'dicrously**. — *n* **lu'dicrousness**. [L *lūdicrus*, from *lūdere* to play]

ludo *lōō'* or *lū'dō*, *n* a game in which counters are moved on a board according to the numbers shown on thrown dice: — *pl* **lud'os**. [L *lūdō* I play]

lues *lōō'* or *lū'ēz*, *n orig* a pestilence; now syphilis (**lues venerea**). — *adj* **luetic** (*-et'ik*; an etymologically unjustifiable formation). [L *luēs*]

luff *luf*, *n* the windward side of a ship; the act of sailing a ship close to the wind; the after-part of a ship's bow where the planks begin to curve in towards the cut-water (also **loof**). — *vi* to turn a ship towards the wind. — *vt* to turn nearer to the wind; to move (the jib of a crane) in and out. — **luffing crane** or **luffing-jib crane** a jib crane with the jib hinged at its lower end to the crane structure so as to allow alteration of its radius of action. [ME *luff*, *lof(f)*, from OFr *lof*; poss from a conjectured MDu form *loef* (modern Du *loef*)]

luffa. See **loofah**.

luffer-board *luf'ər-bōrd* or *-börd*. Same as **louvre-board** under **louvre**.

Luftwaffe *lōōft'vä-fə*, (*Ger*) *n* air force.

lug[1] *lug*, *vt* to pull; to drag heavily; to carry (something heavy); of sailing-ships, to carry (too much sail). — *vi* to pull: — *pr p* **lugg'ing**; *pa t* and *pa p* **lugged**. — *adj* **lugg'able** (*esp* of computers) portable, but with some difficulty. — Also *n*. — **lug in** to introduce without any apparent connection or relevance. [Cf Swed *lugga* to pull by the hair; perh connected with **lug**[4]]

lug[2] *lug* or **lugsail** *lug'sāl* or *lug'sl*, *n* a square sail bent upon a yard that hangs obliquely to the mast. — *n* **lugg'er** a small vessel with lugsails.

lug[3] *lug*, *n* a pole or stick (*dialect*); a perch or rod of land (*Spenser*). [Origin obscure]

lug[4] *lug*, *n* the sideflap of a cap; the ear (*colloq*; chiefly *Scot*); an earlike projection or appendage; a handle; a loop; a chimney corner (*Scot*). — *adj* **lugged** (*lugd*) having lugs or a lug. — *n* **lugg'ie** (*Scot*) a hooped dish with one long stave. — **lug'-chair** an armchair with side headrests; **lug'hole** (*slang*) (the hole in) the ear. [Perh connected with **lug**[1]]

lug[5] *lug* or **lugworm** *lug'wûrm*, *n* a sluggish worm found in the sand on the seashore, often used for bait. [Origin doubtful]

luge *lōōzh* or *lüzh*, *n* a light toboggan. — *vi* to glide on such a sledge: — *pr p* and *n* **lug'ing** or **luge'ing**. — *n* **lug'er**. [Swiss Fr]

Luger® *lōō'gər*, (*Ger*) *n* a type of pistol.

luggage *lug'ij*, *n* the trunks, suitcases and other baggage of a traveller. — **lugg'age-carrier** a structure fixed to a bicycle, motor car, etc, for carrying luggage; **lugg'age-van** a railway wagon for luggage. [Ety as for **lug**[1]]

lugger. See under **lug**[2].

luggie. See under **lug**[4].

lugsail. See **lug**[2].

lugubrious *lōō-gōō'bri-əs* or *-gū'*, *adj* mournful; dismal. — *adv* **lugu'briously**. — *n* **lugu'briousness**. [L *lūgubris*, from *lūgēre* to mourn]

lugworm. See **lug**[5].

Luing cattle *ling kat'l*, *n* a breed of hardy beef cattle. [*Luing*, an island off West Scotland]

luit *lüt* or *lit*, also **luit'en**, (*Scot*) *pa t* and *pa p* of **let**[1].

lukewarm *lo͞ok'wörm*, *adj* moderately warm; tepid; half-hearted. — *adj* **luke** (*dialect*) lukewarm. — *adj* **luke'-warmish**. — *adv* **luke'warmly**. — *n* **luke'warmness** or **luke'warmth**. [ME *luek*, *luke*; doubtful whether related to **lew**[1], or to Du *leuk*]

lulibub. Early form of **lollipop**.

lull *lul*, *vt* to soothe; to compose; to quiet. — *vi* to become calm; to subside. — *n* an interval of calm; a calming influence. [Imit]

lullaby *lull'ə-bī*, *n* a song to lull children to sleep, a cradle-song. — *vt* to lull to sleep. [Ety as for **lull** and **bye**[2]; cf Swed *lulla*]

lulu *lo͞o'lo͞o*, (*slang*) *n* a thing or person that is outstandingly bad or impressive. [Origin obscure]

lum *lum*, (*Scot*) *n* a chimney; a chimney-pot hat (also **lum'-hat**). — **lum'-head'** the top of a chimney. [Origin obscure; OFr *lum* light, and Welsh *llumon* chimney, have been suggested]

lumbago *lum-bā'gō*, *n* rheumatic pain in the muscles or fibrous tissues in the lumbar region: — *pl* **lumbā'gos**. — *adj* **lumbaginous** (*-baj'i-nəs*). [L *lumbāgō* lumbago, from *lumbus* loin]

lumbang *lo͞om-bäng'*, *n* the candle-nut tree or other species of Aleurites, whose nuts yield **lumbang'-oil'**. [Tagálog]

lumbar *lum'bər*, *adj* of or relating to the section of the spine between the lowest rib and the pelvis. — **lumbar puncture** the process of inserting a needle into the lower part of the spinal cord to take a specimen of cerebrospinal fluid, inject drugs, etc. [L *lumbus* loin]

lumber[1] *lum'bər*, *n* furniture stored away out of use; anything cumbersome or useless; timber, *esp* sawn or split for use (*NAm*). — *vt* to fill with lumber; to heap together in confusion; to burden with something, eg a task or responsibility, that is unwanted or troublesome (*colloq*); to cut the timber from. — *vi* to work as a lumberjack. — *n* **lum'berer** a lumberjack. — *n* **lum'bering** felling, sawing and removal of timber. — **lum'ber-camp** a lumberman's camp; **lum'berjack** or **lum'berman** someone employed in the felling, sawing, etc of timber; **lum'ber-jacket** a man's longish, loose-fitting, sometimes belted jacket fastened right up to the neck and *usu* in bold-patterned heavy material; a woman's cardigan similarly fastened; **lum'ber-mill** a sawmill; **lum'ber-room** a room for storing things not in use; **lum'ber-yard** a timber-yard. [Perhaps from **lumber**[2] or from **lumber**[3] influenced by **lumber**[2]]

lumber[2] *lum'bər*, (*slang*) *n* pawn (*archaic*); a pawnshop (*archaic*); prison. — *vt* (*archaic*) to pawn; to imprison. — *n* **lum'berer** (*obs*) a pawnbroker. — **lum'ber-pie'** a pie of meat or fish, with eggs. — **in lumber** (*slang*) in trouble; in prison. [See **Lombard**]

lumber[3] *lum'bər*, *vi* to move heavily and clumsily; to rumble. — *n* **lum'berer**. — *adj* **lum'berly** or **lum'bersome**. — *n* **lum'bersomeness**. [ME *lomeren*, perh a frequentative formed from *lome*, a variant of **lame**[1]; but cf dialect Swed *lomra* to resound]

lumbricus *lum-brī'kəs*, *n* a worm of the very common genus of earthworms, *Lumbricus*, giving its name to the family **Lumbricidae** (*-bris'i-dē*) to which all British earthworms belong. — *adj* **lum'brical** (or *-brī'*) worm-like. — *n* (for **lumbrical muscle**), also **lumbricā'lis**, one of certain muscles of the hand and foot used in flexing the digits. — *adj* **lumbriciform** (*-bris'*) or **lum'bricoid** (or *-brī'*) worm-like. [L *lumbrīcus*]

lumen *lo͞o'* or *lū'men*, *n* a unit of luminous flux, the light emitted in one second in a solid angle of one steradian from a point that is a radiation source of uniform intensity of one candela (*abbrev* **lu**); the cavity of a tubular organ (*anatom*); the space within the cell-wall (*bot*): — *pl* **lu'mina** or **lu'mens**. — *adj* **lu'menal** or **lu'minal** of a lumen. — *n* **lu'minance** luminousness; the measure of brightness of a surface, measured in candela cm^2 of the surface radiating normally; the brightness of a television screen or visual display unit, adjustable to suit the operator. — *adj* **lu'minant** giving light. — *n* a means of lighting. — *n* **lu'minarism**. — *n* **lu'minarist** a person who paints luminously, or with skill in the creation of light and shade; an impressionist or plein-airist (qv). — *n* **lu'minary** a source of light, *esp* one of the heavenly bodies; someone who illustrates any subject or instructs mankind. — Also *adj*. — *n* **luminā'tion** a lighting up. — *vt* **lu'mine** (*-in*; *obs*) to illumine. — *vi* **luminesce'** to show luminescence. — *n* **luminescence** (*-es'əns*) emission of light otherwise than by incandescence and so at a relatively cool temperature; the light so emitted. — *adj* **luminesc'ent**. — *adj* **luminif'erous** giving, yielding, or being the medium of, light. — *n* **lu'minist** a luminarist. — *n* **luminosity** (*-os'i-ti*) luminousness; the measure of the quantity of light actually emitted by a star, irrespective of its distance. — *adj* **lu'minous** giving light; shining; lighted; clear; lucid. — *adv* **lu'minously**. — *n* **lu'minousness**. — **luminance signal** a signal controlling the luminance of a colour TV picture, ie its image brightness, as distinct from its chrominance; **luminous energy** energy emitted in the form of light; **luminous flux** a measure of the rate of flow of luminous energy; **luminous intensity** a measure of the amount of light radiated in a given direction from a point-source; **luminous paint** a paint that glows in the dark, those that glow continuously having radioactive additives. [L *lūmen*, *-inis* light, from *lūcēre* to shine]

luminaire *lū-min-er'*, *n* the British Standards Institution term for a light fitting. [Fr]

lumme or **lummy** *lum'i*, (*colloq*) *interj* expressing surprise or concern. [(Lord) love me]

lummox *lum'əks*, (*colloq*) *n* a stupid, clumsy person. [Origin unknown]

lummy[1] *lum'i*, (*slang*; *Dickens*) *adj* excellent.

lummy[2]. See **lumme**.

lump *lump*, *n* a shapeless mass; a bulge or protuberance; a swelling; a feeling as if of a swelling or tightening in the throat; a considerable quantity; the total as a whole; the gross; an inert, dull, good-natured or fair-sized person; a lumpfish. — *vt* to throw into a confused mass; to consider everything together; to include under one heading, *esp* regardless; to endure willy-nilly; to put up with regardless; to be lumpish about; to dislike. — *vi* to be lumpish; to gather or collect in a lump; to walk or move heavily. — *n* **lumpec'tomy** the surgical removal of a lump, caused by cancer, in the breast, *esp* as opposed to removal of the entire breast. — *n* **lump'er** someone who works on the lump (see **the lump** below); a militiaman (*dialect*); someone inclined to lumping in classification (*opp* of *hair-splitter*). — *adv* **lump'ily**. — *n* **lump'iness**. — *adj* **lump'ing** in a lump; heavy; bulky. — *adj* **lump'ish** like a lump; heavy; gross; dull; sullen. — *adv* **lump'ishly**. — *n* **lump'ishness**. — *n* **lump'kin** a lout. — *adj* **lump'y** full of lumps; like a lump. — **lump'fish** or **lump'sucker** a sea-fish (*Cyclopterus*), clumsy and with excrescences on its skin, with pectoral fins transformed into a sucker; **lump'-su'gar** loaf-sugar broken in small pieces or cut in cubes; **lump sum** a single sum of money in lieu of several; **lump'y-jaw'** actinomycosis affecting the jaw in cattle. — **in the lump** in gross; **like it or lump it** enjoy it or put up with it; **take one's lumps** (*colloq*) to be reprimanded or scolded; **the lump** the system of using self-employed workmen for a particular job, *esp* in order to evade tax and national insurance payments. [Origin doubtful; found in various Gmc languages]

lumpen *lum'pən*, *adj* relating to a dispossessed and/or degraded section of a social class, as in **lumpen proletariat** (also as one word), the poorest down-and-outs; stupid, boorish. — *adj* **lump'enly**. [From Ger *Lumpen* a rag]

luna *lo͞o'nə*, *n* a N American moth (*Actias luna*), with crescent-shaped markings on its blue-green, yellow and black wings. — Also **luna moth**. [L *luna* moon]

lunacy *lo͞o'nə-si*, *n* a form of insanity once believed to come with changes of the moon; insanity generally; extreme folly. — *n* **lun'anaut** same as **lunarnaut** under **lunar**. — *adj* **lunatic** (*lōō'nə-tik*) affected with lunacy. — *n* a person so affected; a madman or madwoman. — **lunatic asylum** a former, now offensive, name for a mental hospital; **lunatic fringe** the more nonsensical, extreme-minded, or eccentric members of a community or of a movement. [Ety as for **lunar**]

lunar *lōō'nər*, *adj* belonging to the moon; measured by the moon's revolutions; caused by the moon; like the moon; of silver (*old chem*). — *n* a lunar distance. — *n* **lunā'rian** (*archaic*) an inhabitant of the moon; a student of the moon. — *n* **lu'narist** someone who thinks the moon affects the weather. — *n* **lun'arnaut** an astronaut who travels or has travelled to the moon. — *n* **lu'nary** the moonwort fern; the plant honesty. — *adj* lunar. — *adj* **lu'nate** or **lu'nated** crescent-shaped. — *n* **lunā'tion** a synodic month. — *n* **lune** (*lōōn* or *lūn*) anything in the shape of a half-moon; a lunule; a fit of lunacy (*Shakesp*). — *n* **lunette'** a crescent-shaped ornament; a semicircular or crescent-shaped space where a vault intersects a wall or another vault, often occupied by a window or by decoration; an arched opening in a vault; a detached bastion (*fortif*); a small horseshoe; a watch-glass flattened more than usual in the centre; in the RC Church, a moon-shaped case for the consecrated host. — *adj* **lunisō'lar** relating to the moon and sun jointly (**lunisolar calendar** and **lunisolar year** a calendar or year divided according to the changes of the moon, but made to agree in average length with the solar year). — *adj* **lunitī'dal** relating to the moon and its influence on the tide (**lunitidal interval** the time interval between the moon's transit and the next high tide at a particular place). — *n* **lu'nūla** a lunule (*obs*); a crescent-like appearance, *esp* the whitish area at the base of a nail; a Bronze Age crescent-shaped gold ornament forming part of a necklace. — *adj* **lu'nūlar**. — *adj* **lu'nūlate** or **lu'nulated** shaped like a small crescent (*bot*); having crescent-shaped markings. — *n* **lu'nule** anything shaped like a small crescent; a geometrical figure bounded by two arcs of circles. — **lunar caustic** fused crystals of silver nitrate, applied to ulcers, etc; **lunar cycle** see **Metonic cycle** under **Metonic**; **lunar distances** a method of finding longitude by comparison of the observed angular distance of the moon from a star at a known local time, with the tabulated angular distance at a certain Greenwich time; **Lunar Excursion Module** (*abbrev* **LEM** or **lem**) a module for use in the last stage of the journey to land on the moon; **lunar month** see under **month**; **lunar theory** the *a priori* deduction of the moon's motions from the principles of gravitation; **lunar year** see under **year**. [L *lūna* the moon, from *lūcēre* to shine]

lunatic. See under **lunacy**.

lunch *lunch* or *lunsh*, *n* a midday meal; formerly a snack at any time of day, now a light midday meal (*US*); a thick slice, a lump (*dialect*); a slight repast between breakfast and midday meal (*archaic*). — *vi* to take lunch. — *vt* to provide lunch for. — *n* **lunch'eon** (*esp* a formal) lunch. — *vi* (*archaic*) to lunch (also *vt*). — *n* **luncheonette'** (*orig US*) a restaurant serving snacks and light meals. — *n* **lunch'er**. — **lunch box** a box or container in which one carries, *esp* to work, sandwiches, etc for lunch; **lunch'-eon-bar** a counter where luncheons are served; **lunch'-eon-basket** a basket for carrying lunch, with or without cutlery, etc; **lunch'eon-meat** a type of pre-cooked meat containing preservatives, *usu* served cold; **luncheon** (or **lunch**) **voucher** a ticket or voucher given by employer to employee to be used to pay for the latter's lunch; **lunch'-hour** or **lunch'-time** the time of, or time allotted to, lunch; an interval allowed for lunch; **lunch'-table**. — **out to lunch** (*slang*; *orig US*) slightly crazy, in a world of his or her own. [Short form of **luncheon**, from ME *none(s)chench* noon drink]

lung *lung*, *n* a respiratory organ in animals that breathe atmospheric air; an open space in a town (*fig*). — *adj* **lunged**. — *n* **lung'ful**. — **lung'-book** a breathing organ in spiders and scorpions, constructed like the leaves of a book; **lung'-fish** any of certain species of S America, Africa and Australia, of the subclass Dipnoi, able to breathe atmospheric air using 'lungs' or modified air-bladders, the Australian *Neoceratodus* having only a single such 'lung'. — *adj* **lung'-grown** having an adhesion of the lung to the pleura. — **lung'wort** a genus (*Pulmonaria*) of the borage family, once thought good for lung diseases because of its spotted leaves; a lichen (*Lobaria pulmonaria*) on tree-trunks, used as a domestic remedy for lung diseases. — **iron lung** see under **iron**. [OE *lungen*]

lunge[1] *lunj*, *n* a sudden thrust as in fencing; a forward plunge. — *vi* to make a lunge; to plunge forward. — *vt* to thrust with a lunge: — *pr p* **lunge'ing** or **lung'ing**. [Fr *allonger* to lengthen, from L *ad* to, and *longus* long]

lunge[2] or **longe** *lunj*, *n* a long rope used in horse-training; training with a lunge; a training-ground for horses. — *vt* to train or cause to go with a lunge. — **lunge** (or **longe** or **lunging**) **whip** a whip used with a lunge. [Fr *longe*, from L *longus* long]

lungi *lōōn'gē*, *n* a long cloth used as loincloth, sash, turban, etc. [Hindi and Pers *lungī*]

lungie[1] *lung'i*, (*Scot*) *n* the guillemot. [Norw dialect *longivie*]

lungie[2] *lung'i* or **lunyie** *lun'yi*, *n* Scots form of **loin**.

lunisolar, **lunitidal**, **lunulate**, **lunule**, etc. See under **lune**.

lunker *lung'kər*, (*colloq*, *esp US*) *n* a particularly large specimen of an animal, *esp* a fish. [Origin unknown]

lunkhead *lungk'hed*, (*colloq*, *esp US*) *n* a fool, blockhead. [Perh a form of **lump**, and **head**]

lunt *lunt*, (*Scot*) *n* a slow-match or means of setting on fire; a sudden flame, blaze; smoke. — *vt* to kindle; to smoke. — *vi* to blaze up; to send up smoke; to smoke tobacco. [Du *lont* a match; cf Ger *Lunte*]

lunyie. See **lungie**[2].

Lupercal *lōō'pər-kal* or *-kl*, or *lū'*, *n* the grotto, or the festival (15 February) of *the Lupercus*, Roman god of fertility and flocks. — Also (*pl*) **Lupercā'lia**. [Perh L *lupus* wolf, and *arcēre* to ward off]

lupin or (*esp US*) **lupine** *lōō'* or *lū'pin*, *n* a plant of the papilionaceous genus (*Lupinus*), with flowers on long spikes; its seed. [L *lupīnus*]

lupine[1] *lōō'* or *lū'pīn*, *adj* of a wolf; like a wolf; wolfish. [L *lupīnus*, from *lupus* a wolf]

lupine[2]. See **lupin**.

luppen *lup'n*, (*Scots*) *pa p* of **leap**[1].

lupulin *lōō'pū-lin*, *n* a yellow powder composed of glands from hop flowers and bracts, used as a sedative. — *adj* **lu'puline** or **lupulinic** (*-lin'ik*). [L *lupus* hop-plant]

lupus *lōō'* or *lū'pəs*, *n* a chronic tuberculosis of the skin, often affecting the nose, strictly **lupus vulgaris** (*med*); (with *cap*) a constellation in the southern hemisphere (*astron*). — **lupus erythematosus** (*med*) a disease of the connective tissue. [L *lupus* a wolf]

lur. See **lure**[2].

lurch[1] *lûrch*, *n* an old game, probably like backgammon; in various games, a situation in which one side fails to score at all, or is left far behind; a discomfiture. — *vt* to defeat by a lurch; to outdo so as to deprive of all chance (*Shakesp*); to leave in the lurch. — **leave someone in the lurch** to leave someone in a difficult situation without help. [OFr *lourche*]

lurch[2] *lûrch*, *n* (*archaic* or *dialect*) wait, ambush. — *vi* (*obs*) to lurk or prowl about. — *vt* (*archaic*) to get the start of, forestall; to defraud, to overreach; to filch. — *n* **lurch'er** someone who lurches (*archaic* or *dialect*); a glutton (*obs*); a dog with a distinct cross of greyhound, *esp* a cross of greyhound and collie. [Connection with **lurk** difficult; influenced appar by **lurch**[1]]

lurch[3] *lûrch*, *vi* to roll or pitch suddenly forward or to one side. — *n* a sudden roll or pitch. [Origin obscure]

lurdan, **lurdane** or **lurden** *lûr'dən*, (*archaic*) *n* a dull, heavy, stupid or sluggish person. — Also *adj*. [OFr *lourdin* dull, from *lourd* heavy]

lure[1] *lōōr* or *lūr*, *n* any enticement; bait; a decoy; a brightly-coloured artificial bait (*angling*); a bunch of feathers used to recall a hawk (*falconry*). — *vt* to entice; to decoy. [OFr *loerre* (Fr *leurre*), from MHGer *luoder* (Ger *Luder*) bait]

lure[2] or **lur** *lo͞or*, *n* a long curved Bronze Age trumpet of a style still used in Scandinavian countries for calling cattle, etc. [ON *lūthr*; Dan and Norw *lur*]

Lurex® *lū'reks*, *n* (fabric made from) a plastic-coated aluminium thread.

Lurgi *lo͞or'gi*, *adj* relating to a German plant that enables coal-gas to be made from low-grade coal.

lurgy or **lurgi** *lûr'gi*, (*esp facetious*) *n* a fictitious disease. [Popularized and prob invented by the cast of BBC Radio's *The Goon Show* (1949–1960)]

lurid *lo͞o'* or *lū'rid*, *adj* glaringly bright; dingily reddish-yellow or yellowish-brown (*bot*); gloomily threatening; pale or wan; ghastly; melodramatically sensational; brimstony. — *adv* **lu'ridly**. — *n* **lu'ridness**. [L *lūridus*]

lurk *lûrk*, *vi* to lie in wait; to be concealed; to skulk; to linger around furtively. — *n* a prowl; a lurking-place; a dodge or swindle (*esp Austr slang*). — *n* **lurk'er**. — *n* and *adj* **lurk'ing**. — **lurk'ing-place**. [Perh frequentative from **lour**]

lurry *lur'i*, (*Milton*) *n* any gabbled formula; confusion. [**liripipe**]

Lusation *loo-sā'shən*, *adj* of or belonging to *Lusatia*, a former region in eastern Germany between the Elbe and the Oder rivers. — *n* an inhabitant of the region; the language spoken there, a form of West Slavic.

luscious *lush'əs*, *adj* exceedingly sweet; delightful, pleasurable; (*esp* of musical sound or literary style) too rich, cloying, fulsome; attractive and voluptuous. — *adv* **lusc'iously**. — *n* **lusc'iousness**. [Origin unknown; **delicious**, influenced by **lush**[1], has been suggested]

lush[1] *lush*, *adj* rich, juicy and succulent; luxuriant; luxurious. — *adv* **lush'ly**. — *n* **lush'ness**. [Perh a form of **lash**[2]]

lush[2] *lush*, (*slang*, *esp NAm*) *n* a drinker or drunkard; alcohol; a drink; a drinking bout. — *vt* (*archaic*) to ply with alcohol. — *vt* and *vi* to overindulge in alcohol. — *n* **lush'er**. — *adj* **lush'y** tipsy. — **lush'-house** (*archaic*) a disreputable public house. [Perh from **lush**[1]]

Lusiad *lo͞o'* or *lū'si-ad*, *n* or **Lusiads** (*-adz*), *n pl* a Portuguese epic by Camoens, celebrating Vasco da Gama's voyage to India by the Cape. — *n* and *adj* **Lusitā'nian** Portuguese. — *n* and *adj* **Lusita'no-Amer'ican** Brazilian of Portuguese descent. — *pfx* **Luso-** Portuguese. — *n* **Lu'sophile** a lover of Portugal. [Port *Os Lusiadas* the Lusitanians; L *Lūsitānia*, approximately, Portugal]

lusk *lusk*, (*obs*) *n* a lazy fellow. — *adj* lazy. — *vi* to skulk; to lie about lazily. — *adj* **lusk'ish**. — *n* **lusk'ishness**. [Origin obscure]

lust *lust*, *n* strong sexual desire; passionate desire; eagerness to possess; longing; appetite; relish (*rare*); pleasure (*Spenser* and *Shakesp*). — *vi* to desire eagerly (with *after* or *for*); to have strong sexual desire; to have depraved desires. — *n* **lust'er**. — *adj* **lust'ful** having lust; inciting lust; sensual. — *adv* **lust'fully**. — *n* **lust'fulness**. — *adj* (*obs*) **lust'ick** or **lust'ique** (*Shakesp* 'as the Dutchman says'; for Du *lustig*) lusty, healthy, vigorous. — *n* **lust'ihead** (*archaic*), **lust'ihood** (*archaic*) or **lust'iness**. — *adv* **lust'ily**. — *adj* **lust'less** (*Spenser*) listless, feeble. — *adj* **lust'y** vigorous; healthful; stout; bulky; lustful (*Milton*); pleasing, pleasant (*obs*). — *adj* **lust'-breathed** (*-brēdh'id*; *Shakesp*) animated by lust. — *adj* **lust'-di'eted** (*Shakesp*) pampered by lust. [OE *lust* pleasure]

lustrate, etc. See under **lustre**[2].

lustre[1] or (*US*) **luster** *lus'tər*, *n* characteristic surface appearance in reflected light; sheen; gloss; brightness; splendour; renown, distinction (*fig*); a candlestick, vase, etc ornamented with pendants of cut-glass; a dress material with cotton warp and woollen weft, and highly finished surface; a metallic pottery glaze. — *vt* to impart a lustre to. — *vi* to become lustrous. — *adj* **lus'treless**. — *n* **lus'tring**. — *adj* **lus'trous** bright; shining; luminous. — *adv* **lus'trously**. — **lus'treware** pottery, etc with a metallic glaze. [Fr, from L *lūstrāre* to shine on]

lustre[2] *lus'tər* or **lustrum** *lus'trəm*, *n* a ceremonial purification of the Roman people made every five years, after the taking of the census; a period of five years: — *pl* **lus'tres**, **lus'tra** or **lus'trums**. — *adj* **lus'tral**. — *vt* **lus'trate** to purify by sacrifice; to perambulate (*obs*). — *n* **lustrā'tion** purification by sacrifice; an act of purifying. [L *lūstrum*, prob from *luere* to wash or purify]

lustring *lus'tring*, *n* a glossy silk cloth. — Also **lus'trine** or **lutestring** (*lo͞ot'* or *lūt'string*). [Fr *lustrine*, from Ital *lustrino*]

lustrum. See **lustre**[2].

lusty. See under **lust**.

lusus naturae *lo͞o'səs na-tū'rē* or *lo͞o'so͞os na-to͞or'ī*, (*L*) *n* a sport or freak of nature.

lute[1] *lo͞ot* or *lūt*, *n* an old stringed instrument shaped like half a pear. — *vi* to play on the lute. — *vt* and *vi* to sound as if on a lute. — *n* **lut'anist**, **lut'enist**, **lut'er** or **lut'ist** a player on the lute. — *n* **luthier** (*lūt'i-ər*) a maker of lutes, guitars, and other stringed instruments. — **lute'string** a string of lute (see also **lustring**). [OFr *lut* (Fr *luth*); like Ger *Laute*, from Ar *al* the, and *'ūd* wood, the lute]

lute[2] *lo͞ot* or *lūt*, *n* clay, cement or other material used as a protective covering, an airtight stopping, a waterproof seal, etc; a rubber packing-ring for a jar. — *vt* to coat or close with lute. — *n* **lut'ing**. [L *lutum* mud, from *luere* to wash]

lute[3] *lo͞ot* or *lūt*, *n* a straight-edge for scraping off excess clay in a brick mould. [Du *loet*]

luteal. See under **lutein**.

lutecium. Same as **lutetium**.

lutein *lo͞ot'ē-in* or *lūt'*, *n* a yellow pigment found in egg yolk. — *adj* **luteal** (*lo͞o'ti-əl*) relating to (the formation of) the corpus luteum. — *n* **luteinīzā'tion** or **-s-** the process of stimulation to the ovary, whereby ovulation occurs and a corpus luteum is formed. — *vt* and *vi* **lu'teinize** or **-ise**. — *n* **lutē'olin** the yellow pigment of weld or dyer's weed. — *adj* **lutē'olous** yellowish. — *adj* **lu'teous** (*-i-əs*) golden-yellow. — *adj* **lutescent** (*-es'ənt*) yellowish. — **luteinizing hormone** a hormone that, in females, stimulates ovulation and the formation of the corpus luteum (qv under **corpus**), and in males, the production of androgen. [L *lūteus* yellow, *lūteum* egg-yolk, and *lūtum* weld]

lutenist. See under **lute**[1].

lutestring. See **lustring** and under **lute**[1].

Lutetian *lū-tē'shən*, *adj* Parisian. [L *Lutetia Parīsiōrum*, the mud town of the Parisii, Paris, from *lutum* mud]

lutetium *lo͞o-tē'shi-əm* or *lū-*, *n* metallic element (symbol **Lu**; atomic no 71) first separated from ytterbium by Georges Urbain, a Parisian. [L *Lutetia* Paris]

Lutheran *lo͞o'thər-ən*, *adj* relating to Martin *Luther*, the great German Protestant reformer (1483–1546), or to his doctrines. — *n* a follower of Luther. — *n* **Lu'theranism** or **Lu'therism**. — *n* **Lu'therist**.

luthern *lo͞o'* or *lū'thərn*, *n* a dormer window. [Prob a variant of **lucarne**]

luthier. See under **lute**[1].

Lutine bell *lo͞o-tēn'* or *lo͞o'ten bel*, *n* a bell recovered from the frigate *Lutine*, and rung at Lloyd's of London before certain important announcements.

lutten. See **loot**[2].

lutz *lo͞ots*, *n* in figure-skating, a jump (with rotation) from the back outer edge of one skate to the back outer edge of the other. [Poss Gustave *Lussi* of Switzerland (born 1898) the first exponent]

luv. See **love**.

lux *luks*, *n* a unit of illumination, one lumen per square metre: — *pl* **lux**, **luxes** or **luces** (*lo͞o'sēs*). — **lux'meter** an instrument for measuring illumination. [L *lūx* light]

luxate *luks'āt*, (*med*) *vt* to put out of joint; to displace. — *n* **luxā'tion** a dislocation. [L *luxāre*, *-ātum*, from *luxus*, from Gr *loxos* slanting]

luxe *lŏŏks* or *luks*, Fr *lüks*, *n* luxury. — See also **de luxe**. [Fr, from L *luxus* a dislocation, extravagance or luxury]

luxmeter. See under **lux**.

lux mundi *luks mun'dī* or *lŏŏks mŏŏn'dē*, (*L*) *n* light of the world.

luxulyanite, **luxulianite** or **luxullianite** *luks-ūl'yən-īt*, *-ul'* or *-ŏŏl'*, *n* a tourmaline granite found at *Luxulyan*, Cornwall.

luxury *luk'shə-ri*, also *lug'zhə-ri*, *n* abundant provision of means of comfort, ease and pleasure; indulgence, *esp* in costly pleasures; anything delightful, often expensive, but not necessary; a dainty; wantonness (*Shakesp*). — *adj* relating to or providing luxury. — *n* **luxuriance** (*lug-zhŏŏ'ri-əns*, *-zū'*, *-zhū'*, or *luk-*, etc) or **luxu'riancy** growth in rich abundance or excess; exuberance; overgrowth. — *adj* **luxu'riant** exuberant in growth; overabundant; profuse; (erroneously) luxurious. — *adv* **luxu'riantly**. — *vi* **luxu'riate** to be luxuriant, grow profusely; to live luxuriously; to enjoy luxury; to enjoy or revel in indulgence. — *n* **luxuriā'tion**. — *adj* **luxu'rious** of luxury; enjoying or indulging in luxury; providing or aiming to provide luxury; provided with luxuries; softening by pleasure; luxuriant (*Milton*); lustful (*Shakesp*). — *adv* **luxu'riously**. — *n* **luxu'riousness**. — *n* **luxurist** (*luk'shə-rist* or *-sū-*) someone given to luxury. — **luxury good** (*econ*; *usu* in *pl*) a class of goods on which a consumer spends a greater share of his or her income as that income rises. [OFr *luxurie*, from L *luxuria* luxury, from *luxus* excess]

luz *luz*, *n* a bone supposed by Rabbinical writers to be indestructible, *prob* the sacrum.

luzern. See **lucerne**.

Luzula *lŏŏ'* or *lū'zū-lə*, *n* the wood-rush genus, with flat *usu* hairy leaves. [Old Ital *luzziola* (mod *lucciola*) firefly, glow-worm, from its shining capsules]

LV *abbrev*: luncheon voucher; Latvia (IVR; provisional).

LW (*radio*) *abbrev*: long wave.

Lw (*chem*) *symbol*: the former symbol for lawrencium, now **Lr**.

LWM or **lwm** *abbrev*: low water mark.

LWR *abbrev*: light-water reactor.

LWT *abbrev*: London Weekend Television.

LX *el-eks'*, (*theat*) *abbrev*: electrical or electricals; technical staff who work on lighting and sound.

lx (*phys*) *abbrev*: lux.

lyam *lī'əm*, **lime** or **lyme** *līm*, (*obs* or *dialect*) *n* a leash; a lyam-hound. — **ly'am-hound**, **lime'-hound** or **lyme'-hound** a bloodhound. [OFr *liem* (Fr *lien*), from L *ligāmen*, from *ligāre* to tie]

lyart. See **liard**.

Lycaena *lī-sē'nə*, *n* a genus of butterflies giving its name to the family **Lycae'nidae**, *usu* small and blue or coppery. [Gr *lykaina* she-wolf]

lycanthropy *lī-* or *li-kan'thrə-pi*, *n* the power of changing oneself into a wolf; a kind of madness, in which the patient has fantasies of being a wolf. — *n* **lycanthrope** (*lī'kan-thrōp*, or *-kan'*) or **lycan'thropist** a wolf-man or werewolf; a person suffering from lycanthropy. — *adj* **lycanthropic** (*-throp'*). [Gr *lykos* a wolf, and *anthrōpos* a man]

lycée *lē'sā*, *n* a state secondary school in France. [Fr, lyceum]

lyceum *lī-sē'əm*, *n* (with *cap*) a gymnasium and grove beside the temple of Apollo at Athens, in whose walks Aristotle taught; a college; a place or building devoted to literary studies, lectures, etc; an organization for instruction by lectures (*US*); a lycée: — *pl* **lyce'ums**. [L *Lycēum*, from Gr *Lykeion*, from *Lykeios*, an epithet of Apollo (perh wolf-slayer, perh the Lycian)]

lychee, **litchi**, **lichee** or **lichi** *lī'chē* or **leechee** *lē'chē*, *n* a Chinese fruit, a nut or berry with a fleshy aril; the tree (*Litchi chineasis*, family Sapindaceae) that bears it. [Chin *li-chi*]

lychgate. See under **lich**[2].

Lychnic *lik'nik*, *n* the first part of the vespers of the Greek Orthodox Church. — *n* **Lychnap'sia** (Gr *haptein* to touch or light) a series of seven prayers in the vespers of the Greek Orthodox Church. — *n* **lych'noscope** a low side window (named on the theory that it was intended to let lepers see the altar lights). [Gr *lychnos* a lamp]

lychnis *lik'nis*, *n* a plant of the campion genus *Lychnis* of the pink family. [Gr *lychnis* rose-campion]

lycopod *lī'kə-pod*, *n* a club moss, any plant of the genus *Lycopodium* or of the Lycopodiales. — *n pl* **Lycopōdiā'ceae** a homosporous family of Lycopodiales. — *n pl* **Lycopōdiā'lēs**, **Lycopodī'nae** or **Lycopodin'eae** one of the main branches of the Pteridophytes, *usu* with dichotomously branched stems and axillary sporangia, commonly in cones. — *n* **Lycopō'dium** the typical genus of Lycopodiaceae, club moss, or stag's horn; (without *cap*) a powder consisting of the spores of Lycopodium. [Gr *lykos* a wolf, and *pous*, *podos* a foot]

Lycosa *lī-kō'sə*, *n* a genus of hunting spiders, including the true tarantula, typical of the family **Lycosidae** (*-kos'i-dē*) or wolf-spiders. [Gr *lykos* a wolf, also a kind of spider]

Lycra® *lī'krə*, *n* (a fabric made from) a lightweight, synthetic, elastomeric fibre.

lyddite *lid'īt*, *n* a powerful explosive made in Kent, composed mainly of picric acid. [Tested at *Lydd*]

Lydford law *lid'fərd lö*, *n* the same kind of law as that called Jeddart or Jethart justice. [*Lydford* in Devon]

Lydian *lid'i-ən*, *adj* relating to *Lydia* in Asia Minor; (of music) soft and slow. — *n* native of Lydia; the language of ancient Lydia, apparently related to Hittite. — **Lydian mode** (in ancient Greek music) a mode of two tetrachords with a semitone between the two highest notes in each and a whole tone between the tetrachords (eg *c d e f*; *g a b c*; but reckoned downwards by the Greeks); (in old church music) an authentic mode, extending from *f* to *f*, with *f* for its final; **Lydian stone** touchstone. [Gr *Lȳdiā* Lydia]

lye[1] *lī*, *n* a short side-branch of a railway. [See **lie**[2]]

lye[2] *lī*, *n* a strong alkaline solution; a liquid used for washing; a solution obtained by leaching. [OE *lēah*, *lēag*; Ger *Lauge*; related to L *lavāre* to wash]

lyfull. See **lifefull** under **life**.

lying. See **lie**[1,2].

lykewake, **likewake** *līk'wāk*, **like'-walk** or **lyke'walk** *-wök*, (*Scot*; *Eng* **lichwake** *lich'*) *n* a watch over the dead, often involving festivities. [OE *līc*; Ger *Leiche* a corpse, and **wake**]

lym *lim*, *n* a conjectural Shakespearian form of **lyme**.

Lymantriidae *lī-man-trī'i-dē*, *n pl* the tussock-moths, a family related to the eggers. [Gr *lȳmantēr* destroyer]

lyme and **lyme-hound**. See **lyam**.

Lyme disease *līm di-zēz'*, *n* a viral disease transmitted to humans by ticks, affecting the joints, heart and nervous system. [First discovered in *Lyme*, Connecticut, US]

lyme-grass *līm'-gräs*, *n* a coarse sand-binding grass, *Elymus arenarius* or any other of the genus. [Origin unknown]

Lymeswold® *līmz'wōld*, *n* a kind of mild blue full-fat soft cheese.

lymiter (*Spenser*). Same as **limiter**.

Lymnaea. An erroneous form of **Limnaea**.

lymph *limf*, *n* a colourless or faintly yellowish fluid collected into the lymphatic vessels from the tissues in animal bodies, of a rather saltish taste, and with an alkaline reaction; a vaccine; pure water (*archaic*). — *n* **lymphadenop'athy** (Gr *adēn* a gland, and *pathos* suffering) a disease of the lymph nodes. — *adj* **lymphangial** (*-anj'əl*; Gr *angeion* vessel) relating to the lymphatic vessels. — *n* **lymphan'giogram** or **lymphangiog'raphy** same as **lymphogram** and **lymphography**. — *n* **lymphangitis** (*-an-jī'tis*) inflammation of a lymphatic vessel. — *adj* **lymphat'ic** relating to lymph; inclined to be sluggish and flabby, *orig* considered as the result of excess of lymph; mad (*obs*). — *n* a vessel that conveys lymph. — *adv* **lymphat'ically**. — *n* **lymph'ocyte** (*-ō-sīt*) a small white blood cell, one of many present in lymphoid tissues, circulating in blood and lymph and involved in antigen-specific immune reactions. — *n* **lymphog'raphy**

radiography of the lymph glands and lymphatic system, recorded on a **lymph'ogram**; the description of the lymphatic system (*rare* or *obs*). — *adj* **lymph'oid** of, carrying, or like lymph; relating to the lymphatic system. — *n* **lymph'okine** (Gr *kinein* to move; *immunol*) any of a number of substances secreted by lymphocytes activated by contact with an antigen and thought to play a part in cell-mediated immunity. — *n* **lymphō'ma** a tumour consisting of lymphoid tissue. — *adj* **lymphotroph'ic** (of a virus) preferentially infecting lymphocytes. — **lymphatic system** the network of vessels that conveys lymph to the venous system; **lymph gland** or **node** any of the small masses of tissue sited along the lymphatic vessels, in which lymph is purified, and lymphocytes are formed; **lymphoid tissue** (*immunol*) body tissue, eg lymph nodes, spleen, thymus and adenoids, in which the predominant cells are lymphocytes. [L *lympha* water; *lymphāticus* mad]

lymphad *lim'fad*, *n* a kind of large rowing boat (*esp* formerly) much used in the Scottish Highlands. [Gaelic *longfhada*]

lymphangial, lymphatic, lymphocyte, etc. See under **lymph**.

lynage (*Spenser*). Same as **lineage**.

lyncean. See under **lynx**.

lynch *linch* or *linsh*, *vt* to judge and put to death without the usual forms of law. — **lynch'-law**. [Thought to be after Captain William *Lynch* (1742–1820) of Virginia who set up and presided over tribunals outside the regular law]

lynchet. See **linch**.

lynchpin. A variant of **linchpin**.

lyne (*Spenser*). Same as **line**[1] (linen).

lynx *lingks*, *n* an animal of the *Lynx* genus of the cat family, high at the haunches, with long legs, a short tail and tufted ears (*pl* **lynx'es**); (with *cap*; Latin *genitive* **Lyncis** *lin'sis*) a constellation in the Northern Hemisphere. — *adj* **lyncean** (*lin-sē'ən*) lynx-like; sharp-sighted. — *adj* **lynx'-eyed**. [L, from Gr *lynx*, *lynkos*]

lyomerous *lī-om'ə-rəs*, *adj* relating to the **Lyom'erī**, soft-bodied fishes. [Gr *lyein* to loosen, and *meros* part]

Lyon *lī'ən*, *n* the chief herald of Scotland. — Also **Lord Lyon, Lyon King-of-arms** or **Ly'on-at-arms**. — **Lyon Court** the court over which he presides, having jurisdiction in questions of coat-armour and precedency. [From the heraldic *lion* of Scotland]

Lyonnaise *lī-* or *lē-on-ez'*, *adj* (also without *cap*) of food, cooked or served with (*usu* fried) onions. [Fr, *à la Lyonnaise* in the style of Lyons or the Lyonnais region]

lyophil *lī'ō-fil*, **lyophile** *lī'ō-fīl* or **lyophilic** *-fil'ik*, *adj* (of a colloid) readily dispersed in a suitable medium. — *n* **lyophilizā'tion** or **-s-** freeze-drying. — *vt* **lyoph'ilize** or **-ise** to dry by freezing. — *adj* **ly'ophobe** (*-fōb*) or **lyophobic** (*-fob'*) (of a colloid) not readily dispersed. [Gr *lyē* separation, *phileein* to love, and *phobeein* to fear]

lyre *līr*, *n* a musical instrument like the harp, used *esp* in ancient Greece as an accompaniment to poetry, consisting of a convex resonating box with a pair of curved arms connected by a cross-bar, from which the strings were stretched over a bridge to a tailpiece. — *n* **Ly'ra** (*astron*) one of the northern constellations. — *adj* **ly'rate** or **ly'rated** lyre-shaped; having the terminal lobe much larger than the lateral ones (*bot*). — *adv* **ly'ra-way** or **ly'ra-wise** according to lute tablature. — *adj* **lyric** (*lir'*) (of poems or their authors) expressing individual or private emotions; relating to the lyre; intended or suitable to be sung to the lyre. — *n* a lyric poem; a song; (in *pl*) the words of a popular song; a composer of lyric poetry (*obs*). — *adj* **lyrical** (*lir'*) lyric; song-like; expressive or imaginative; effusive. — *adv* **lyr'ically**. — *n* **lyricism** (*lir'i-sizm*) a lyrical expression; lyrical quality. — *n* **lyr'icist** the writer of the words of a song, musical, opera, etc; a lyric poet. — *n* **lyr'icon** an electronic wind instrument like a large flute (but played like a clarinet), used with a synthesizer. — *adj* **lyriform** (*lī'*) shaped like a lyre. — *n* **lyr'ism** (*līr'* or *lir'*) lyricism; singing. — *n* **lyrist** (*līr'* or *lir'*) a player on the lyre or harp; (*lir'*) a lyric poet. — **ly'ra-vi'ol** (also without *hyphen*) an obsolete instrument like a viola da gamba adapted for playing from lute tablature; **lyre'-bird** either of two Australian passerine ground-dwelling birds of the genus *Menura* about the size of a pheasant, the tail-feathers of the male arranged, in display, in the form of a lyre; **lyre guitar** a form of lyre with a fingerboard, at its greatest popularity in the late 18c and early 19c; **lyriform organs** (*zool*) patches of chitin on the legs and other parts of spiders, believed to be olfactory in function. — **wax lyrical** to become increasingly expressive or effusive in praise of something. [L *lyra*, from Gr *lyrā*]

lyse. See under **lysis**.

Lysenkoism *li-sen'kō-izm*, *n* the teaching of the Soviet geneticist T D *Lysenko* (1898–1976) that acquired characteristics are inheritable.

lysergic acid, lysin, etc. See under **lysis**.

lysis *lī'sis*, *n* the gradual abatement of a disease, as distinguished from *crisis*; breaking down, eg of a cell (*biol*); the action of a lysin. — *vt* **lyse** (*līz*) to cause to undergo lysis. — *v combining form* **-lyse** or **-lyze** (*-līz*) to break down or divide into parts. — *n combining form* **-lysis** (*-lis'is*) denoting the action of breaking down or dividing into parts. — *adj* **lysigenic** (*li-* or *lī-si-jen'ik*), **lysigenet'ic** or **lysigenous** (*-sij'i-nəs*) caused by the breaking down of cells. — *n* **lysim'eter** an instrument for measuring percolation of water through the soil. — *n* **lysin** (*lī'sin*) a substance that causes breakdown of cells. — *n* **lysine** (*lī'sēn*) an essential amino-acid, a product of protein hydrolysis. — *n* **ly'sol** a solution of cresol in soap, a poisonous disinfectant (a trademark in some countries). — *n* **ly'sosome** (Gr *soma* a body) any of the tiny particles present in most cells, containing enzymes that play a part in intracellular digestion. — *n* **ly'sozyme** (*-zīm*) a bacteriolytic enzyme present in some plants, animal secretions (eg tears), egg-white, etc. — *n combining form* **-lyst** (*-list*) or **-lyte** (*-līt*) denoting something that can be broken down or divided into parts. — *adj combining form* **-lytic** or **-lytical** (*-lit'*) denoting something that can be broken down or divided into parts. — **lysergic acid** (*lī-sûr'jik*) a substance, $C_{16}H_{16}O_2N_2$, derived from ergot, causing (in the form of lysergic acid diethylamide, **LSD** or **ly'sergide**) a schizophrenic condition, with hallucinations and thought processes outside the normal range. [Gr *lysis* dissolution, from *lyein* to loose]

lyssa *lis'ə*, (*pathol*) *n* rabies. [Gr, madness, rabies]

lyte. A form of **light**[3] or **lite**[1].

-lyte. See under **lysis**.

lythe[1] (*Spenser*). A form of **lithe**[1].

lythe[2] *līdh*, (*Scot*) *n* the pollack, a common fish of the cod family.

Lythrum *lith'rəm*, (*bot*) *n* the purple loosestrife genus, giving its name to a family of archichlamydeous dicotyledons, **Lythrā'ceae**, commonly hexamerous, heterostyled, with epicalyx. — *adj* **lythraceous** (*lith-rā'shəs* or *lī-*). [Latinized from Gr *lythron* gore, from the colour of its flowers]

-lytic and **-lytical**. See under **lysis**.

lytta *lit'ə*, (*zool*) *n* a cartilaginous or fibrous band on the under surface of the tongue in carnivores, *esp* the dog, in which it was once thought to cause lyssa, or rabies. [Gr, Attic form of *lyssa* (see **lyssa**)]

-lyze. See under **lysis**.

M

M or **m** *em, n* the twelfth letter of the Roman, the thirteenth of the modern English alphabet, representing a bilabial nasal consonant; an object or figure shaped like the letter. — **M1** a Garand rifle (qv); **M'-roof** a roof formed by the junction of two simple roofs, resembling the letter M in cross-section.

M or (except IVR) **M.** *abbrev*: Malta (IVR); mega-; Member (of); money; *mille* (*L*), a thousand; million(s); *Monsieur* (*Fr*), Mr (*pl* **MM**); Motorway (followed by a number). — **M'-way** a written contraction of **motorway**. — See also **em**.

M *symbol*: (Roman numeral) 1 000; followed by a number, used to designate the seven categories of money supply in the UK (see **M0**, **M1**, etc, below; *econ*); meta- or meso- (*chem*). — **M0** all notes and coins in current general circulation plus banks' till money and balances with the Bank of England; **M1** all notes and coins in current general circulation plus all instantly-withdrawable bank deposits; **M2** all notes and coins in current general circulation plus non-interest-bearing bank deposits, building society deposits, and National Savings accounts; **M3** M1 plus all privately-held bank deposits and certificates of deposit; **M3c** M3 plus all foreign currency bank deposits; **M4** M1 plus most privately-held bank deposits and holdings of money-market instruments; **M5** M4 plus building society deposits.

m or **m.** *abbrev*: maiden over (*cricket*); male; mark(s) (German currency); married; masculine; mass; medium; *meridiem* (*L*), noon; metre(s); mile(s); mille-; million(s).

'm *m*, a short form of **am**; a contraction of **madam**.

m' *m* or *mə*, a short form of **my** as in *m'lud* (see under **lud**).

M'. See **Mac**.

3M *abbrev*: Minnesota Mining and Manufacturing Company.

MA *abbrev*: Massachusetts (US state); Master of Arts; Morocco (IVR).

ma *mä, n* a childish contraction for **mamma**.

MAA *abbrev*: Motor Agents' Association.

maa *mä, vi* (of a goat) to bleat. [Imit]

ma'am *mäm, mam, məm, n* a contraction of **madam**, the pronunciation *mäm* being used as a form of address to female royalty. — Also (*colloq*) **marm** (*mäm*) or **mum**.

maar *mär, n* (*geol*) a crater that has been formed by a single explosion and so does not lie in a cone of lava. [Ger]

maatjes or **matjes** *mät'yəs, n* young herring before it has spawned, cured in brine, sugar, and spices, and served as an hors d'oeuvre. [Dan *maatjes*(*haring*) maiden herring]

MAB (*immunol*) *abbrev*: monoclonal antibody.

Mab *mab*, (*folklore*) *n* the name of a female fairy believed to be the bringer of dreams; the queen of the fairies.

Mabinogion *mab-i-nō'gi-on, n* a collective title for four tales in the *Red Book of Hergest*, a 14c Welsh manuscript; extended to refer to the whole collection in Lady Charlotte Guest's edition and translation of 1838. [Welsh, juvenilities]

MAC *abbrev*: Multiplex Analogue Components, designating a method of encoding television signals.

Mac[1] *mak, mək*, a Gaelic prefix in names, meaning *son* (of). — Also written **Mc** and **M'**. [Gaelic and Ir *mac* son; Welsh *mab*, OWelsh *map*]

Mac[2] *mak, n* (*esp US*) an informal term of address used to a man whose name is not known. [**Mac**[1]]

mac. See **mackintosh**.

macabre *ma-, mə-kä'br', ma-, mə-käbər, adj* gruesome, ghastly; resembling the dance of death (qv). — *adj* **macaberesque** (*-bər-esk'*). [Fr *macabre*, formerly also *macabré*, perh a corruption of *Maccabee* in reference to 2 Macc 12. 43–6, said to have been represented in medieval drama, or from Heb *meqabēr* grave-digger]

macaco *mə-kä'kō, n* any of various kinds of lemur: — *pl* **maca'cos**. [Fr *mococo*]

macadamia *mak-ə-dā'mi-ə, n* a tree of the *orig* Australian *Macademia* genus of evergreen trees (family *Proteaceae*). — **macadamia nut** (also **Queensland nut**) the edible nut of two species of macadamia, *Macadamia ternifolia* and *Macadamia integrifolia*; the tree bearing this nut. [John *Macadam* (1827–65), Scottish-born Australian chemist]

macadamize or **-ise** *mək-ad'əm-īz, vt* to cover (a road) with small broken stones, so as to form a smooth, hard surface. — *n* **macad'am** a macadamized road surface; material for macadamizing. — *n* **macadamīzā'tion** or **-s-**. [From John Loudon *McAdam* (1756–1836), Scottish engineer]

macahuba. See **macaw-tree**.

macallum *mə-kal'əm*, (*Scot*) *n* a dish of vanilla ice cream topped with raspberry sauce. [From the surname]

Macanese *mak-ə-nēz', n* a member of the Portuguese-Chinese population of Macau, a Portuguese province on the SE China coast. — *adj* relating to Macau or its people.

macaque *mə-käk', n* a monkey of genus *Macacus* or *Macaca*, to which the rhesus and the Barbary ape belong. [Fr, from Port *macaco* a monkey]

macarize or **-ise** *mak'ə-rīz, vt* to declare to be happy or blessed. — *n* **mac'arism** a beatitude. [Gr *makar* happy]

macaroni *mak-ə-rō'ni, n* pasta in the form of long thin tubes; a medley; something fanciful and extravagant; in the 18c, a dandy; a rock-hopper or crested penguin: — *pl* **macarō'nis** or **macarō'nies**. — *adj* **macaronic** (*-ron'ik*) used of poetry in which vernacular words are given Latin inflections and intermixed with genuine Latin for comic effect; written or including lines in more than one language. — *n* (often in *pl*) macaronic poetry. — *adv* **macaron'ically**. — **macaroni cheese** macaroni served with a cheese sauce. [Neapolitan dialect *maccaroni* (Ital *maccheroni*), pl of *maccarone*, prob from *maccare* to crush]

macaroon *mak-ə-rōōn', n* a sweet biscuit made with egg-white and ground almonds or coconut. [Fr *macaron*, from Ital *maccarone* (see **macaroni**)]

macassar oil *mə-kas'ər oil, n* an oil obtained *esp* from the seeds of the sapindaceous tree *Schleichera trijuga*, or from ylang-ylang flowers, formerly used as a hair oil (also **macass'ar**). [*Macassar* (now Ujung Pandang) in Indonesia]

macaw *mə-kö', n* any of the large, long-tailed, brightly-coloured tropical American parrots of the genus *Ara* or *Anodorhynchus*. [Port *macao*]

macaw-tree *mə-kö'trē* or **macaw-palm** *-päm, n* a S American palm (*Acrocomia*) whose nuts yield a violet-scented oil. — Also **maco'ya** or **macahuba** (*mä-kä-ōō'ba*). [Sp *macoya*, from Arawak; Port *macauba*, from Tupí]

Macc (*Bible*) *abbrev*: (the Apocryphal Books of) Maccabees.

Maccabaean or **Maccabean** *mak-ə-bē'ən, adj* relating to Judas *Maccabaeus*, or to his family the Hasmonaeans or **Macc'abees**, who freed the Jews from the persecution of Antiochus Epiphanes, king of Syria, c.166 BC (1 Macc, 2 Macc).

macchie *mak'kyā, n pl* Italian form of **maquis**, a thicket.

mace[1] *mās*, *n* a metal or metal-headed war-club, often spiked; a heavy, *usu* ornamented, staff carried as a mark of authority; a mace-bearer; a billiard cue (*obs*); a mallet used by a currier in dressing leather. — *n* **mā'cer** a mace-bearer; (in Scotland) an usher in a law court. — **mace'-bearer** a person who carries a mace in a procession or ceremony. [OFr *mace* (Fr *masse*), from hypothetical L *matea*, whence L dimin *mateola* a kind of tool]

mace[2] *mās*, *n* a spice which is ground from the dried layer immediately within a nutmeg drupe and outside shell and kernel. — **mace'-ale** ale flavoured with mace. [ME *macis* (mistakenly supposed to be a plural), from Fr; of uncertain origin]

Mace® *mās*, *n* a type of tear gas (also **Chemical Mace**). — *vt* (also without *cap*) to spray, attack or disable with Mace.

macédoine *ma-sā-dwän'*, *-sə-*, *n* a mixture of (*usu* diced) vegetables or fruit in syrup or jelly; a mixture or medley. [Fr, literally Macedonia]

maceranduba. Same as **massaranduba**.

macerate *mas'ər-āt*, *vt* to steep or soak; to soften, break up, or separate into pulp, by steeping; to emaciate, *esp* by fasting; to mortify. — *vi* to undergo maceration or softening; to become emaciated, waste away. — *n* **macerā'tion**. — *n* **mac'erātor** a person who macerates by fasting; a paper-pulping machine. [L *mācerāre*, *-ātum* to steep]

MacFarlane's buat. See **bowat**.

MacGuffin or **McGuffin** *mə-guf'in*, *n* the element of a film, book, etc that drives, or provides an excuse for, the action, of supreme importance to the main characters but largely ignored by the audience or reader. [Coined by Sir Alfred Hitchcock (1899–1980), film maker]

mach. *abbrev*: machinery.

machair *ma'hhər*, *n* a low-lying sandy beach or boggy links affording some pasturage. [Gaelic]

Machairodus *ma-kī'rə-dəs* or **Machaerodus** *-kē'*, *n* the prehistoric sabre-toothed tiger. — *n* and *adj* **machair'odont**. [Gr *machaira* a sword, and *odous*, *odontos* a tooth]

machan *ma-chän'*, (*Ind*) *n* a raised platform, *esp* built in a tree, to watch for game. [Hindi *macān*]

machete *ma-shet'ē*, *ma-chā'tā*, *n* a heavy knife or cutlass used in Central and South America as a tool and a weapon. [Sp]

Machiavellian *mak-i-ə-vel'yən*, *adj* ruled by (*esp* political) expediency rather than morality; crafty, perfidious in conduct or action. — *n* a follower of the political principles described by Niccolò *Machiavelli*, Florentine statesman and writer (1469–1527); any cunning and unprincipled politician. — *n* **Machiavell'ianism** or **Machiavell'ism** the political principles described by Machiavelli, or conduct based on them; cunning statesmanship.

machicolation *ma-chik-ō-lā'shən*, (*fortif*) *n* a space between the corbels supporting a parapet, or an opening in the floor of a projecting gallery, for dropping missiles, molten lead, etc, on an attacking enemy; a structure with such openings; the provision of such openings or structures. — *vt* **machic'olate** to provide or build with machicolations. — *adj* **machic'olated**. [Fr *mâchicoulis*]

machinate *mak'i-nāt*, *mash'i-*, *vi* to form a plot or scheme, *esp* for doing harm. — *n* **machinā'tion** the action of machinating; (often in *pl*) an intrigue or plot. — *n* **mach'inātor** a person who machinates. [L *māchinārī*, *-ātus*, from *māchina*, from Gr *mēchanē* contrivance]

machine *mə-shēn'*, *n* any artificial means or contrivance; any instrument for the conversion of motion; an engine; an engine-powered vehicle, *esp* a motorcycle; a person incapable of independent action; (in classical drama) a pulley-like device used for the entrance of an actor representing a god; a supernatural occurrence which furthers the action of a poem; an organized system of people or institutions; *orig* a political party organization (*US*; also **party machine**). — *vt* to use machinery for; to print, sew or make with a machine. — *n* **machin'ery** machines in general; the working parts of a machine; combined means for keeping anything in action, or for producing a desired result; supernatural occurrences within a poem. — *n* **machin'ist** a person who builds, operates or repairs machines. — **machine code** (*comput*) a binary code used to represent a machine language; **machine'gun** an automatic rapid-firing gun on a stable but portable mounting. — *vt* to shoot at with a machinegun. — *adj* with the speed or rhythm of a machinegun. — **machine'-gunner**; **machine hour method** (*business*) a method of calculating depreciation by dividing the cost of a machine by the estimated number of hours of its useful life, and applying the resultant rate to the actual running hours in each year; **machine intelligence** artificial intelligence; **machine language** instructions for processing data, put into a form that can be directly understood and obeyed by a specific computer. — *adj* **machine'-made** made by a machine. — **machine'man** a person who oversees the working of a machine; **machine'-pistol** a small sub-machine-gun. — *adj* **machine'-readable** (of data) in a form that can be directly processed by a computer. — **machine'-ruler** a machine for ruling lines on paper; **machine screw** a screw, *usu* not more than $\frac{1}{4}$ inch in diameter, with a machine-cut thread, used with a nut, or in tapped holes in metal parts; **machine'-shop** a workshop where metal, etc, is machined to shape; **machine tool** a power-driven machine, such as a lathe, drill, press, etc, for shaping metal, wood, or plastic material. — *adj* **machine'-washable** of a textile article that may be washed in a domestic washing-machine. — Also *n*. — **machine'-work** work done by a machine; **machining allowance** (*eng*) the material provided beyond the finished contours on a casting, forging, or roughly prepared component, which is subsequently removed in machining to size. [Fr, from L *māchina*, from Gr *mēchanē*, related to *mēchos* contrivance]

machismo. See under **macho**.

Mach number *mähh*, *mahh num'bər*, *n* the ratio of the air speed (ie speed in relation to the air) of an aircraft to the velocity of sound under the given conditions; the speed of sound. — *n* **mach'meter** an instrument for measuring Mach number. [Named after Ernst *Mach* (1838–1916), Austrian physicist and philosopher]

macho *mach'ō*, *adj* aggressively male; ostentatiously virile. — *n* a man of this type (*pl* **mach'os**); machismo. — *n* **machismo** (*ma-chiz'mō*, *-chēz'*, *-kiz'*, *-kēz'*) the cult of male virility and masculine pride. [Sp *macho* male, from L *masculus*]

machree *mə-hhrē'*, (*Anglo-Ir*) *n* an affectionate form of address, my dear, my love. [Ir *mo chroidhe* of my heart, from *mo* my, and genitive of *croi* heart]

Machtpolitik *mähht'pō-lē-tēk'* (*Ger*) *n* power politics, *esp* the doctrine that a state should use force to attain its ends.

machzor. See **mahzor**.

macintosh. See **mackintosh**.

mack[1] *mak*, *n* a mackintosh.

mack[2] *mak*, (*slang*) *n* a pimp. [Short form of obsolete **mackerel**]

mackerel *mak'ər-əl*, *n* an edible bluish-green N Atlantic fish (*Scomber*) with a silvery underside and wavy cross-streaks on its back; a pimp (*obs*). — **mackerel breeze** a strong breeze that ruffles the surface of the sea and so favours mackerel fishing; **mackerel guide** the common garfish, which visits the coasts just before the mackerel; **mackerel midge** a small rockling; **mackerel shark** the porbeagle; **mackerel sky** a sky streaked with long, parallel white masses of cloud. [OFr *makerel* (Fr *maquereau*)]

mackinaw *mak'in-ö*, *n* a kind of blanket formerly distributed by the US government to N American Indians; a short heavy woollen coat, *usu* double-breasted and belted; a flat-bottomed lake-boat. [*Mackinaw*, an island between Lakes Huron and Michigan]

mackintosh or **macintosh** *mak'in-tosh*, *n* a kind of waterproof rubberized cloth; a coat made with this material; any waterproof coat or raincoat: — *contraction* **mac** or **mack** (*mak*). — See also **McIntosh**. [From Charles *Macintosh* (1766–1843), a Scottish chemist, the patentee]

mackle *mak'l*, *n* a blur or other imperfection in printing, caused by a double impression, wrinkling, etc. — *vt* to print imperfectly, blur. [See **macle**]

macle *mak'l*, *n* a dark spot in a crystal; chiastolite; a twin crystal. — *adj* **macled** (*mak'ld*) (of a crystal or mineral) spotted. [Fr *macle*, from L *macula* spot]

Macleaya *mə-klā-ī'ə*, *n* a herbaceous Asiatic plant with pinnate leaves and cream-coloured, plume-like flowers. [Alexander *Macleay* (died 1848), British entomologist and statesman]

Macmillanite *mək-mil'ən-īt*, *n* a Cameronian or Reformed Presbyterian. [From Rev John *Macmillan* (1670–1753), one of the founders of the church]

Mâcon *mä-kɔ̃*, *n* a heavy red or white burgundy from the Mâcon district of Central France.

macon *mā'kn*, *n* smoked, salted mutton. [*m*utton and b*acon*]

maconochie *mə-kon'ə-hhi*, (*military*) *n* tinned meat and vegetable stew; any tinned food. [Packer's name]

macoya. See **macaw-tree**.

macramé or **macrami** *mə-krä'mi*, *n* a fringe or trimming of knotted thread; ornamental knotted threadwork. [Appar from Turk *maqrama* towel]

macro. See under **macro-**.

macro- *mak-rō-*, *-ro-*, *combining form* denoting long, great, sometimes interchanging with *mega-*. — *n* **mac'rō** (*comput*) a macroinstruction: — *pl* **mac'ros**. — *n* **macro-axis** (*mak'rō-aks'is*; *crystallog*) the longer lateral axis. — *adj* **macrō'bian** (Gr *bios* life) long-lived. — *n pl* **macrobiō'ta** the larger organisms in the soil. — *n* **macrobiote** (*-bī'ōt*) a long-living organism. — *adj* **macrobiotic** (*-bī-ot'ik*) prolonging life; long-lived; (of a seed) able to remain alive in dormant state for years; relating to longevity or to macrobiotics. — *n sing* **macrobiot'ics** the art or science of prolonging life; a cult partly concerned with diet, foods regarded as pure being vegetable substances grown and prepared without chemicals or processing. — *n* **macrocar'pa** an evergreen conifer of New Zealand, *Cupressus macrocarpa*, planted *esp* for ornamentation and as a windbreak. — *adj* **macrocephalic** (*-si-fal'ik*) or **macrocephalous** (*-sef'ə-ləs*). — *n* **macrocephaly** (*-sef'ə-li*; Gr *kephalē* head) largeness, or abnormal largeness, of the head. — *n* **mac'rocode** (*comput*) a macroinstruction. — *n* **mac'rocopy** an enlarged copy of printed material for use by people with weak sight. — *n* **mac'rocosm** (*-kozm*; Gr *kosmos* world) a large and complex structure considered a whole, of which smaller similar structures contained within it are microcosms; the whole universe. — *adj* **macrocos'mic**. — *adv* **macrocos'mically**. — *n* **mac'rocycle** a macrocyclic organic molecule or compound. — *adj* **macrocy'clic** being or having a ring structure with a large number of atoms. — *n* **mac'rocyte** (*-sīt*; Gr *kytos* a vessel, container) an abnormally large red blood cell associated with some forms of anaemia. — *adj* **macrodactyl** (*-dak'til*). — *adj* **macrodactylic** (*-til'ik*). — *adj* **macrodactylous** (*-dak'til-əs*; Gr *daktylos* finger, toe) long-fingered; long-toed. — *n* **macrodac'tyly** the condition of being macrodactylous. — *n* **macrodiag'onal** (*crystallog*) the longer lateral axis. — *n* **macrodome** (*crystallog*) a dome parallel to the macrodiagonal. — *n sing* **macroeconomics** (*-ēk-ən-om'iks*, *-ek'*) the study of economics on a large scale or of large economic units such as national income, international trade, etc. — *adj* **macroeconom'ic**. — *n* **macroevolū'tion** major evolutionary developments over a long period of time, such as have given rise to the taxonomic groups above the species level. — *n* **mac'rofauna** and **mac'roflora** animals and plants that are visible to the naked eye. — *n* **mac'rofossil** a fossil large enough to be seen with the naked eye. — *n* **macrogamete'** (*-gam'ēt*) a female gamete. — *n* **macroglob'ūlin** any globulin with a molecular weight above about 400 000. — *n* **mac'roinstruction** (*comput*) an instruction written in a programming language, *usu* in assembly language, which generates and is replaced by a series of microinstructions. — *n* **macrol'ogy** much talk with little to say. — *n* **mac'ro-marketing** marketing set in the context of the whole of a country's economy and social needs (cf **micro-marketing**). — *adj* **macromolec'ular**. — *n* **macromol'ecule** a large molecule, *esp* one formed from a number of simpler molecules. — *n* **mac'rophage** (*-fāj*) any of the large phagocytic cells sited in the walls of blood vessels and found in connective tissue, *usu* immobile but stimulated into mobility by inflammation. — *n* **macropin'akoid** and **mac'roprism** (*crystallog*) a pinakoid and prism parallel to the macrodiagonal. — *n* **mac'ropod** an animal of the **Macropod'idae** (*-ē*; Gr *pous*, *podos* foot), the family of marsupials comprising the kangeroos and related animals. — *adj* **macrop'terous** (Gr *pteron* a wing) long-winged; long-finned. — *adj* **macroscop'ic** visible to the naked eye (*opp* of *microscopic*). — *adv* **macroscop'ically**. — *n* **macrosporan'gium** (*pl* **-ia**) same as **megasporangium**. — *n* **mac'rospore** same as **megaspore**. — *n* **Macrozā'mia** (Gr *zamia* loss) a genus of Australian cycads; (without *cap*) a plant of this genus. — *n pl* **Macrura** (*mak-ro͞o'rə*; Gr *ourā* tail) a group of decapod crustaceans including lobsters, shrimps, prawns, etc. — *adj* **macru'ral** or **macru'rous** long-tailed. [Gr *makros* long, also great]

macron *mak'rən*, (*US*) *mā'krən*, *n* a straight line placed over a vowel to show it is long (as in *ē*), as opposed to *breve*, the mark of a short vowel (*ĕ*). [Gr *makros*]

mactation *mak-tā'shən*, *n* killing or slaughter, *esp* of a sacrificial victim. [L *mactātiō*, *-ōnis*]

macula *mak'ū-lə*, *n* a spot, eg on the skin, the sun or a mineral: — *pl* **maculae** (*-lē*). — *adj* **mac'ular** spotted; patchy; relating to the macula lutea. — *vt* **mac'ulate** to spot or stain; to defile. — *adj* (*-lit*) spotted, stained; defiled. — *n* **maculā'tion** the act of spotting or staining; a spot. — *n* **mac'ulāture** an impression taken to remove remaining ink from an engraved plate before re-inking. — *n* **mac'ule** a macula; a mackle. — *adj* **mac'ulose** spotted. — **macula lutea** (*lo͞o'ti-ə*; L *luteus* yellow) the yellow-spot (qv). [L *macula* a spot]

MAD *mad*, *abbrev*: mutual assured destruction, a theory of nuclear deterrence; magnetic anomaly detection, a technique for detecting submarines by checking levels of magnetism in seawater.

mad *mad*, *adj* (*compar* **madd'er**; *superl* **madd'est**) mentally disordered or deranged; insane; resulting from or caused by madness; extremely and recklessly foolish; extremely enthusiastic; infatuated; violently affected by pain, strong emotion, appetite, etc; furious with anger (*colloq*; *orig US*); extravagantly playful or exuberant; rabid. — *vt* (*Shakesp*) to drive mad. — *vi* (*archaic*) to be mad; to act madly or irrationally. — *vt* **madd'en** to make mad; to enrage. — *vi* to go mad; to act as if mad. — *adj* **madd'ening** driving to madness; making very angry; extremely annoying. — *adv* **madd'eningly**. — *adj* **madd'ing** (*archaic*) distracted, acting madly. — *adv* **madd'ingly** (*archaic*). — *n* **mad'ling** (*archaic*) a mad person. — *adv* **mad'ly** insanely, irrationally; frantically; extremely (*colloq*). — *n* **mad'ness**. — *adj* **mad'brain** or **mad'brained** (*Shakesp*) mentally disordered; rash; hot-headed. — *adj* **mad'=bred** (*Shakesp*) bred in madness or heat of passion. — **mad'cap** a person who acts madly; a wild, rash, or hot-headed person; an exuberantly playful person. — *adj* fond of wild and reckless or extravagantly playful behaviour. — **mad cow disease** bovine spongiform encephalopathy (see under **bovine**); **mad'-doctor** a person who studied and treated mental illness (*obs*); **Mad Hatter** a character in Lewis Carroll's *Alice in Wonderland* given to irrational behaviour and logic-chopping (see also **hatter** under **hat**); **mad'house** an insane asylum (*obs*); a place characterized by noise, confusion, and unpredictable behaviour; **mad'man** or **mad'woman** a man or woman who is insane; a foolish and reckless man or woman; **mad'wort** a plant believed to cure canine madness (*Alyssum*, *Asperugo*, etc). — **go mad** to go insane; to become very angry (*colloq*); **like mad** with great speed or energy, furiously; **mad as a hatter** see under **hat**. [OE *gemǣd(e)d*; OSax *gimēd* foolish]

Madagascar jasmine *mad-ə-gas'kər jaz'min*. Same as **stephanotis**.

madam *mad'əm*, *n* a courteous form of address to a woman, *esp* an elderly or married one, or any female customer in a shop, restaurant, etc; (with *cap*) the form of address to a woman in a formal letter; a woman of social rank or station; prefixed to an official title, as *Madam Chairman*, etc; the female head of a household (*archaic*); a formidable woman; a capricious or autocratic woman; a general term of reproach for a woman; a precocious young girl; a concubine (*obs*); the woman in charge of a brothel; (with *cap*) prefixed to a name instead of Mrs or Miss (in US to distinguish mother-in-law from daughter-in-law; *obs*): — *pl* **mad'ams**; in sense (2) above, **mesdames** (*mā-dām'*). — *vt* to address as madam. — *n* **madame** (*ma-dām'*, *mad'əm*; *usu* with *cap*) used instead of Mrs as a title for a Frenchwoman or French-speaking woman; extended to any woman in an artistic profession, or one regarded as exotic, such as a palm-reader: — *pl* **mesdames** (*mā-dām*, *-dam*). [Fr *ma* my, and *dame* lady, from L *mea domina*]

mad-apple *mad'-ap-l*, *n* an aubergine; the Dead Sea apple (see under **apple**); a gallnut produced by the Asiatic gall-wasp (*Cynips insana*). [From some form of mod L *melongēna*, Ital *melanzana*; *mālum insānum*, transl as mad apple]

madarosis *mad-ə-rō'sis*, (*pathol*) *n* abnormal loss of hair, *esp* of the eyebrows or eyelashes. [Gr *madarōsis*, from *madaros* bald, *madaein* to fall off]

madder *mad'ər*, *n* a herbaceous plant (*Rubia tinctorum*) whose root produces a red dye; any other species of *Rubia*. — **madd'er-lake** a pigment mixed with either oil or water, made from madder root. — **field madder** a minute, lilac-flowered plant (*Sherardia arvensis*) of the same family. [OE *mæddre*, *mædere*; ON *mathra*, Du *mede*, later *meed*, *mee*]

Maddock *mad'ək*, (*dialect*) *n*. Same as **mattock**.

made *mād*, *pa t* and *pa p* of **make**, and also *adj*. — **made dish** a dish composed of various ingredients, often recooked; **made ground** ground formed by artificial filling in; **made man** or **woman** a man or woman whose prosperity is assured; **made man** (*slang*) a man who has murdered, or is willing to murder, for the Mafia; **made road** a road with a surface constructed of tarmac, etc, not merely formed by traffic; a road with a metalled as opposed to a gravel surface; **made wine** wine fermented from the juice of imported grapes. — **be** or **have it made** (*colloq*) to have one's prosperity assured; **made to measure** or **order** made to individual requirements; **made up** put together, finished; parcelled up; dressed for a part, disguised; wearing cosmetic make-up; meretricious; artificial, invented, fictional; consummate (*Shakesp*).

madefy *mad'i-fī*, (*archaic*) *vt* to moisten or make wet. — *n* **madefac'tion**. [L *madefacere*, *-factum*, from *madēre* to be wet]

Madeira *mə-dē'rə*, *ma-dā'ra*, *n* a rich fortified white wine produced in *Madeira*. — **Madeira cake** a plain, rich sponge cake.

madeleine *mad-len'*, *n* a small, plain sponge cake, often baked in the shape of a shell. [Fr, prob named after *Madeleine* Paulmier, 19c French pastry cook]

Madelenian. Same as **Magdalenian**.

mademoiselle *mad-mwə-zel'*, *n* a form of address to, or (with *cap*) a title for, an unmarried Frenchwoman or French-speaking woman, Miss (*pl* **Mesdemoiselles** *mād-*); a French governess or teacher. — Contracted to **mamselle** (*mam-zel'*), *pl* **mamselles** (*-zelz'*). [Fr *ma* my, and *demoiselle*; see **damsel**]

maderize or **-ise** *mad'ə-rīz*, *vi* (of white wine) to become rusty in colour and flat in taste, as a result of absorbing too much oxygen during maturation. — *n* **maderizā'tion** or **-s-**. [Fr *maderiser*, from the colour of Madeira wine]

madge[1] *maj*, *n* a lead hammer. [Woman's name]

madge[2] *maj*, *n* the barn owl; the magpie. [Appar from the woman's name]

madid *mad'id*, *adj* wet, dank. [L *madidus*, from *madēre* to be wet; related to Gr *madaein*]

Madison Avenue *mad'i-sn av'ə-nū*, *n* the US advertising and public-relations industries; the characteristic methods or attitudes of these. [From the street in New York City which is their centre]

Madonna *mə-don'ə*, *n* as a form of address, my lady (*Shakesp*); the Virgin Mary, *esp* as represented in works of art. — *adj* **madonn'aish**. — *adv* **madonn'awise** after the fashion of the Madonna, *esp* in the arrangement of a woman's hair. — **Madonn'a-lily** the white Mediterranean lily (*Lilium candidum*), which produces trumpet-shaped flowers. [Ital, literally my lady, from L *mea domina*]

madoqua *mad'ō-kwə*, *n* a very small Abyssinian antelope. [Amharic *midaqua*]

madras *mə-dräs'*, *n* a large, *usu* brightly-coloured head-scarf, formerly exported from *Madras* in SE India; a fine cotton or silk fabric, often with a woven stripe; sunn; a kind of medium-hot curry.

madrasa, **madrassa**, **madrasah** or **madrassah** *ma-dras'a* or **medresseh** *mə-dres'ə*, *n* a Muslim college; a mosque school. [Ar *madrasah*]

madrepore *mad'ri-pōr*, *-pör*, *n* a coral (*Madrepora*) of the common reef-building type, occurring *esp* in tropical seas. — *adj* **madreporic** (*-por'ik*) or **madreporit'ic**. — *n* **mad'reporite** or **madreporic plate** in echinoderms, a perforated plate serving as opening to the stone canal. [Ital *madrepora* from *madre* mother, from L *māter*, and Gr *pōros* a soft stone, stalactite, etc, or L *porus* a pore]

madrigal *mad'ri-gəl*, *n* an unaccompanied song in several parts in counterpoint (*music*); a lyrical poem suitable for such treatment. — *adj* **madrigā'lian**. — *n* **mad'rigalist**. [Ital *madrigale*, prob from LL *mātricālis* primitive, simple (from L *mātrix*, see **matrix**), altered under the influence of Ital *mandria* a herd, from L *mandra*, from Gr *mandrā* a stall, stable, sty, etc]

madroño *ma-drō'nyō*, *n* an evergreen tree of the genus *Arbutus* of N California, with thick, shiny leaves and edible berries: — *pl* **madrō'ños**. — Also **madrō'ña** (*-nyə*) or **madro'ne**. [Sp *madroño*]

madzoon. See **matzoon**.

mae. See **mo**[1].

Maecenas *mē-sē'nas*, *n* a rich patron of art or literature. [L *Maecēnās*, a Roman knight who befriended Virgil and Horace]

maelid *mē'lid*, (*mythol*) *n* an apple nymph. [Gr *mēlon* apple, soft-skinned fruit]

maelstrom *māl'strom*, *n* a particularly powerful whirlpool; (with *cap*) a well-known whirlpool off the coast of Norway; a confused or disordered state of affairs; any resistless overpowering influence for destruction. [Du (now *maalstroom*), a whirlpool]

maenad *mē'nad*, *n* a female follower of Bacchus, a bacchante (*Gr mythol*); a woman beside herself with frenzy. — *adj* **maenad'ic** bacchanalian; furious. [Gr *mainas*, *-ados* raving, from *mainesthai* to be mad]

Maeonian *mē-ō'ni-ən*, *adj* and *n* Lydian. — *n* **Maeonides** (*mē-on'i-dēz*) Homer, as a supposed native of Lydia. [Gr *Maionia* an old name for Lydia]

maestoso *mä-es-tō'sō*, *mī-stō'sō*, (*music*) *adj* and *adv* with dignity or majesty. [Ital]

maestro *mī'strō*, *mä-es'trō*, *n* a master, *esp* an eminent musical composer or conductor: — *pl* **maestros** (*mī'strōz*) or **maestri** (*mä-es'trē*). [Ital]

Mae West *mā west*, *n* an airman's pneumatic life-jacket, used in WW II. [From its supposed resemblance, when inflated, to the figure of the American film star of that name (1892–1980)]

MAFF *maf*, *abbrev*: Ministry of Agriculture, Fisheries and Food.

Maffia. See **Mafia**.

maffick *maf'ik*, *vi* to celebrate exuberantly and boisterously. — *n* **maff'icker**. — *n* **maff'icking**. [By back-formation from *Mafeking* (now Mafikeng), South Africa, treated jocularly as a gerund or participle, from the scenes in the streets of London on the news of the relief of the town (1900)]

maffled *maf'ld*, (*colloq*) *adj* mentally confused, baffled. — *n* **maff'lin** or **maffling** a simpleton.

Mafia or **Maffia** *mä'fē-ə*, *n* a spirit of opposition to the law in Sicily, hence a preference for private and unofficial rather than legal justice; a secret criminal society originating in Sicily, controlling many illegal activities, eg gambling, narcotics, etc, in many parts of the world, and particularly active in the US (also called **Cosa Nostra**); (also without *cap*) any group considered to be like the Mafia in the criminal and unscrupulous use of power, fear, etc to gain its ends. — *n* **Mafioso** (*-fē-ō'sō*, *-zō*) a member of the Mafia (also without *cap* and as *adj*): — *pl* **Mafiosi** (*-sē*, *-zē*). [Sicilian Ital *mafia*]

mafic *maf'ik*, (*mineralogy*) *n* a mnemonic term for the ferromagnesian and other non-felsic minerals present in an igneous rock. [*ma*gnesian, *f*els*ic*]

ma foi *ma fwa*, (*Fr*) *interj* my goodness (literally, upon my faith).

mag[1] *mag*, **meg**, (*archaic slang*) *n* a halfpenny. — Also **maik** (now *Scot*) or **make** (*māk*).

mag[2] *mag*, (*dialect*) *vi* to chatter. — *vt* to tease; (*Scott* **magg**) to steal. — *n* chatter; the magpie; the long-tailed titmouse. — *n pl* **mags** or **maggs** (*Scot*; *perh* same as **mag**[1]) a gratuity; the free allowance granted to some workers, *esp* drinks for brewery employees. — **mags'-man** a street swindler. [From the name *Margaret*]

mag[3] *mag*, (*colloq*) *n*. Short form of **magazine** (periodical publication).

magalog *mag'ə-log*, (*colloq*) *n* a large mail-order catalogue in the form of a magazine. [*mag*azine and cat*alog*(ue)]

magazine *mag-ə-zēn'*, *mag'ə-*, *n* a storehouse; a place for military stores; a ship's powder-room; a compartment in a rifle for holding extra cartridges; a periodical publication containing articles, stories, etc, by various people, and often aimed at a specific group of readers; a television or radio programme containing a variety of news and factual reports. — **magazine'-gun** or **-rifle** a gun or rifle from which a succession of shots can be fired without reloading. [Fr *magasin*, from Ital *magazzino*, from Ar *makhāzin*, pl of *makhzan* a store-house]

Magdalen or **Magdalene** *mag'də-lən*, *-lēn*, (in the name of the Oxford college *möd'lin*) *n* (without *cap*) a repentant prostitute; an institution for receiving such persons (*abbrev* for *Magdalene hospital* or *asylum*). [From Mary *Magdalene*, ie (Gr) *Magdalēnē*, of Magdala (Luke 8. 2), on the assumption that she was the woman of Luke 7. 37–50]

Magdalenian *magd-ə-lē'ni-ən* or **Madelenian** *mad-*, (*archaeol*) *adj* belonging to an upper Palaeolithic culture that succeeded the Solutrean and preceded the Azilian. [La *Madeleine*, a cave in the Dordogne region of France]

Magdeburg hemispheres *mag'de-bûrg hem'i-sfērz*, *n pl* two hemispherical cups held together by atmospheric pressure when the air is pumped out from between them. [Invented at *Magdeburg* in Germany]

mage *māj*. See under **magus**.

Magellanic clouds *mag-el-an'ik*, *maj- klowdz*, *n pl* two galaxies in the southern hemisphere, appearing to the naked eye like detached portions of the Milky Way, the nearest galaxies to the earth.

Magen David *mä'gän dä'vēd*, *n* the Star of David. — Also **Mogen David** (*mö'gən dö'vid*). [Heb, shield of David]

magenta *mə-jen'tə*, *n* the dyestuff fuchsine; its colour, a reddish purple. — *adj* reddish purple. [From its discovery about the time of the battle of *Magenta* in N Italy, 1859]

magg. See **mag**[2].

maggot *mag'ət*, *n* a legless grub, *esp* of a fly; a fad or whim; a whimsical or improvised tune (*obs*). — *adj* **magg'oty** full of maggots; crotchety; very drunk (*slang*). — *n* **maggotorium** (*-tō'*, *-tö'*) a place where maggots are bred for sale to fishermen. [Poss a modification of ME *maddok*, *mathek*, dimin, see **mawk**]

maggot-pie. See **magpie**.

maggs. See **mag**[2].

Maghreb or **Maghrib** *mag'rəb*, *n* the countries of NW Africa collectively, sometimes including Libya. — Also *adj*. [Ar, the West]

magi and **magian**. See under **magus**.

magic *maj'ik*, *n* the art of producing marvellous results by compelling the aid of spirits, or by using the secret forces of nature, such as the power supposed to reside in certain objects as 'givers of life'; enchantment; sorcery; the art of producing illusions by sleight of hand; a secret or mysterious power over the imagination or will. — *vt* to affect by, or as if by, magic: — *pr p* **mag'icking**; *pa t* and *pa p* **mag'icked**. — *adj* relating to, used in, or done by, magic; causing wonderful or startling results; marvellous, exciting (*colloq*). — *adj* **mag'ical** relating to magic; wonderful, enchanting. — *adv* **mag'ically**. — *n* **magician** (*mə-jish'ən*) a person skilled in magic; a wizard or sorcerer; an enchanter; a conjuror; a wonder-worker. — **magic bullet** a drug, etc, which is capable of destroying bacteria, cancer cells, etc without adversely affecting the host; **magic carpet** one that, in fairy stories, can transport people magically through the air; **magic eye** a miniature cathode ray tube in a radio receiver which helps in tuning the receiver by indicating, by means of varying areas of luminescence and shadow, the accuracy of the tuning; a lightbeam focused on a photoelectric cell which activates an automatic door, security alarm, etc, when broken; **magic lantern** an apparatus for projecting pictures on slides on to a screen; **Magic Marker**® (also without *cap* or **magic-marker**) a thick fibre-tip pen used for writing on display boards, etc; **magic mushroom** any of various mushrooms, eg *Psilocybe mexicana*, which contain a hallucinogen; **magic pyramid** a puzzle resembling a Rubik's Cube® (qv), but in the shape of a tetrahedron with similarly shaped pieces; **magic** (or **magical**) **realism** a style of art, literature or cinema in which fantastical or surreal events or images are presented in a realistic or everyday context; **magic square** a square filled with rows of figures so arranged that the sums of all the rows will be the same, perpendicularly, horizontally or diagonally (as the square formed from the three rows 2, 7, 6; 9, 5, 1; 4, 3, 8); **magic circles**, **cubes**, **cylinders** and **spheres**, are similarly arranged. — **black magic** the black art, magic by means of evil spirits; **natural magic** the art of working wonders by a superior knowledge of the powers of nature; the power of investing a work of art with an atmosphere of imagination; sleight of hand; **sympathetic magic** magic aiming at the production of effects by mimicry, such as bringing rain by libations, injuring a person by melting or sticking pins in his or her image; **white magic** magic without the aid of the devil. [Gr *magikē* (*technē*) magic (art). See **magus**]

magilp. See **megilp**.

Maginot-minded *mä'zhē-nō-mīnd'id*, *adj* over-concerned with the defensive (*military*); static in ideas. [From the abortive French Maginot Line fortifications (1927–35) along the German border (war minister André *Maginot*; 1877–1932)]

magister *mə-jis'tər*, *n* a person licensed to teach in a medieval university; still used in the degree titles of *Magister Artium*, etc. — *adj* **magisterial** (*maj-is-tē'ri-əl*) relating or suitable to, or in the manner of, a teacher, master artist, or magistrate; of the rank of a magistrate; authoritative; dictatorial; of a magistery. — *adv*

magistē'rially. — *n* **magistē'rialness**. — *n* **magistē'rium** the philosopher's stone; teaching authority or function. — *n* **magistery** (*maj'is-tə-ri*) in alchemy, a transmuting agent, such as the philosopher's stone; a product of transmutation; a precipitate; any sovereign remedy; magisterium. — *adj* **magistral** (*mə-jis'trəl*, *maj'is-*) of or relating to a master; masterly; authoritative; specially prescribed for a particular case as a medicine; effectual; guiding or determining the other positions (*fortif*). — Also *n*. — *n* **magistrand** (*maj'*) at Scottish universities, an arts student ready to proceed to graduation, now only at St Andrews and Aberdeen. — **Magister Artium** (*mə-jis'tər är'shi-əm*) Master of Arts. [L *magister* master]

magistrate *maj'-is-trāt*, *n* a person with the power of putting the law in force, *esp* a justice of the peace, a provost, or a bailie. — *n* **mag'istracy** (*-trə-si*) the office or dignity of a magistrate; magistrates in general; a body of magistrates. — *adj* **magistratic** (*-trat'ik*) or **mag'istral**. — *n* **mag'istrature**. — **Magistrates' court** an inferior court composed of justices of the peace with both criminal and civil jurisdiction. [Ety as for **magister**]

Maglemosian *mag-li-mō'zi-ən*, (*archaeol*) *adj* of or designating a culture represented by finds at *Maglemose* in Denmark, transitional between Palaeolithic and Neolithic.

maglev *mag'lev*, *adj* of a railway, train, carriage, etc, operating by *mag*netic *lev*itation (qv); relating to this form of transport.

magma *mag'mə*, *n* a pasty or doughy mass; molten or pasty rock material; a glassy base of a rock: — *pl* **mag'mata** (*-mə-tə*) or **mag'mas**. — *adj* **magmatic** (*-mat'ik*). [Gr *magma*, *-atos* a thick unguent]

Magna Carta or **Magna Charta** *mag'nə kär'tə n* the Great Charter obtained from King John in 1215, the basis of English political and personal liberty (*hist*); any document establishing rights. [L]

magna cum laude *mag'nə kum lö'dē*, *mag'nä ko͝om low'de*, (*L*) with great distiction; used as the mark of the second level of excellence in N American universities (L *laus*, *laudis*, praise).

magnalium *mag-nā'li-əm*, *n* a light, strong, easily-worked and rust-resisting alloy of *magn*esium and *al*umin*ium*, used in aircraft construction, etc.

magnanimity *mag-nə-nim'i-ti*, *n* greatness of soul; that quality of mind which raises a person above all that is mean or unjust; generosity. — *adj* **magnanimous** (*-nan'*). — *adv* **magnan'imously**. [L *magnanimitās*, from *magnus* great, and *animus* mind]

magnate *mag'nāt*, *-nit*, *n* a noble; a person of rank or wealth, or of power. [L *magnās*, *-ātis*, from *magnus* great]

magnes *mag'nēz*, (*archaic*) *n* lodestone. — Also **mag'nes-stone** (*Spenser*). [L and Gr *magnēs*]

magnesium *mag-nē'z(h)i-əm*, *-z(h)yəm*, *-shi-əm*, *-shyəm*, *n* a metallic element (symbol **Mg**; atomic no 12) of a bright, silver-white colour, burning with a dazzling white light. — *n* **magnē'sia** an imagined substance sought by the alchemists (*obs*); manganese (*obs*); a light white powder, oxide of magnesium; basic magnesium carbonate, used as a medicine. — *adj* **magnē'sian** belonging to, containing, or resembling magnesia. — *n* **magnesite** (*mag'nəs-īt*) native magnesium carbonate. — **Magnesian Limestone** dolomite rock; a division of the Permian of England. [From *Magnesia*, in Thessaly, eastern Greece]

magnet *mag'nit*, *n* the lodestone (**natural magnet**); a bar or piece of metal, *esp* iron, to which the property of attracting other substances containing iron or some other metals has been imparted and which, when suspended, will point approximately north to south; anything or anyone that attracts (*fig*). — *adj* **magnetic** (*mag-net'ik*) or **magnet'ical** relating to magnets or to magnetism; having, or capable of acquiring, the properties of a magnet; attractive; strongly affecting others by personality; hypnotic. — *adv* **magnet'ically**. — *n* **magnetician** (*-ish'ən*) a magnetist. — *n sing* **magnet'ics** the science of magnetism. — *adj* **magnetīz'able** or **-s-**. — *n* **magnetīzā'tion** or **-s-**. — *vt* **mag'netize** or **-ise** to make magnetic; to attract as if by a magnet; to hypnotize (*archaic*); to convert (a school) into a magnet school (*US*). — *n* **mag'netīzer** or **-s-**. — *n* **mag'netism** the cause of the attractive power of the magnet; the phenomena connected with magnets; the science that deals with the properties of magnets; attraction; influence of personality. — *n* **mag'netist** a scientist specializing in magnetism. — *n* **mag'netite** magnetic iron ore (Fe_3O_4), called lodestone when polar. — *n* **magneto** (*mag-nē'tō*) short form of **magneto-electric machine**, a small generator with a permanent magnet, used for ignition in an internal-combustion engine, etc: — *pl* **magnē'tos**. — **magneto-** *combining form* denoting magnetic; relating to magnetism; magneto-electric. — *adj* **magneto-elas'tic** (of a material) that increases in elasticity when exposed to a magnetic field. — *adj* **magnē'to-elec'tric** or **-elec'trical** relating to or operated by magneto-electricity. — *n* **magnē'to-electric'ity** electricity produced by the action of magnets; the science concerned with this. — *n* **magnē'tograph** an instrument for recording the variations of the magnetic elements. — *adj* **magnē'tohydrodynam'ic**. — *n sing* **magnē'tohydrodynam'ics** a branch of mathematical physics dealing with interactions between an electricity-conducting fluid (such as an ionized gas) and a magnetic field; the practical application of such interactions to producing magnetohydrodynamic power by means of a **magnetohydrodynamic generator**. — *n* **magnetometer** (*mag-ni-tom'i-tər*) an instrument for measuring the strength or direction of a magnetic field, *esp* the earth's. — *n* **magnetom'etry**. — *adj* **magnētomō'tive** producing a magnetic flux. — *n* **magnē'ton** (*mag'ni-ton*) a natural unit of magnetic moment. — *n sing* **magnēto-op'tics** the study of the influence of magnetism on light. — *n* **magnet'osphere** that region surrounding the earth within which the behaviour of charged particles is influenced by the earth's magnetic field; any similar region surrounding another body. — *n* **magnētostric'tion** (or *-net'*; *phys*) the phenomenon of elastic deformation of certain ferromagnetic materials, eg nickel, on the application of magnetizing force. — *n* **mag'netron** a vacuum tube combined with a magnetic field to deflect electrons. — *n* **magnon** (*mag'non*) a quantum of spin wave energy in magnetic material. — **magnet (high) school** in the USA, a school which, in addition to providing a general education, specializes in teaching a particular subject such as science, languages or performing arts; **magnetic battery** several magnets placed with their like poles together, so as to act with great force; **magnetic board** a white enamelled metal board upon which material for display is mounted by means of magnetic strips; **magnetic bottle** the containment of a plasma during thermonuclear experiments by applying a specific pattern of magnetic fields; **magnetic bubble memory** or **store** (*comput*) same as **bubble memory**; **magnetic card** a piece of plastic or cardboard with a magnetizable surface on which data can be stored; **magnetic chuck** a chuck having a surface in which alternate steel elements, separated by insulating material, are polarized by electromagnets, allowing light flat work to be held securely; **magnetic confinement** (*nuc eng*) in fusion research, the use of shaped magnetic fields to confine a plasma; **magnetic curves** the curves formed by iron-filings around the poles of a magnet; **magnetic dip** or **inclination** the angle between the horizontal and the line of the earth's magnetic field; **magnetic disk** or **disc** (*comput*) a flat, circular sheet of material coated with a magnetic oxide, used to store programs and data; **magnetic diskette** (*comput*) same as **floppy disc**; **magnetic drum** (*comput*) a storage device consisting of a rotating cylinder with a magnetic coating; **magnetic equator** the line round the earth where the magnetic needle remains horizontal; **magnetic field** the space over which magnetic force is felt; **magnetic fluid** a hypothetical fluid formerly assumed to explain the phenomena of magnetism; **magnetic flux** the surface integral of the product of the permeability of the medium and the magnetic field intensity perpendicular to the surface; **magnetic flux density** the product of the field intensity and the permeability of the medium; **magnetic forming** use of magnetic fields to shape metal; **magnetic induction** induced magnetization in magnetic material; magnetic flux density; **magnetic ink** ink with magnetic quality, used eg in printing cheques that are to be sorted by machine; **magnetic ink character recognition** the reading by a computer of numbers printed in magnetic ink; **magnetic lens** the counterpart of an optical lens, in which a magnet or system of magnets is used to produce a field which acts on a beam of electrons in a similar way to a glass lens on light rays; **magnetic levitation** suspension of eg a train above a track by means of a magnetic field; **magnetic media** a collective term for all forms of magnetic recording media, such as magnetic disks, tape, etc; **magnetic meridian** the vertical plane through the magnetic needle; **magnetic mine** a mine sunk to the sea-bottom, detonated by a pivoted magnetic needle when a ship approaches; **magnetic mirror** (*nuc eng*) a device based on the principle, used in mirror machines, that ions moving in a magnetic field towards a region of considerably higher magnetic field strength are reflected; **magnetic monopole** see **monopole**; **magnetic needle** the light bar in the mariner's compass which, because it is magnetized, always points to the north; **magnetic north** the direction indicated by the magnetic needle; **magnetic poles** two nearly opposite points on the earth's surface, where the dip of the needle is 90°; **magnetic storm** a disturbance in the magnetism of the earth; **magnetic stripe** (also **mag'-stripe**) a horizontal stripe on the back of a credit card, etc, which is read electronically to identify the card; **magnetic tape** flexible plastic tape, coated on one side with magnetic material, used to register for later reproduction television images, or sound, or computer data; **magneto-optical effect** see **Kerr effect**. — **animal magnetism** Mesmer's name for hypnotism; the power to hypnotize; according to Christian Science, the false belief that mortal mind exists (and has power to transfer thoughts); sexual power of attraction due entirely to physical attributes; **artificial magnet** a magnet made by rubbing with other magnets; **bar magnet** a magnet in the form of a bar; **horse-shoe magnet** a magnet bent like a horseshoe; **permanent magnet** a magnet that keeps its magnetism after the force which magnetized it has been removed; **personal magnetism** the power of a personality to make itself felt and to exercise influence; **terrestrial magnetism** the magnetic properties possessed by the earth as a whole. [Through OFr or L, from Gr *magnētis* (*lithos*) Magnesian (stone), from *Magnēsiā*, in Lydia or Thessaly]

magnifiable. See under **magnify**.

magnific *mag-nif'ik* or **magnifical** *-ik-l*, (*archaic*) *adj* magnificent; exalted; pompous. — *adv* **magnif'ically**. — *n* **magnif'ico** (Ital *adj*) a Venetian noble; a grandee: — *pl* **magnif'icoes**. [L *magnificus*; cf **magnify**]

Magnificat *mag-nif'i-kat*, *n* the song of the Virgin Mary, Luke 1. 46–55, beginning in the Vulgate with this word; a song of praise or thanksgiving, a paeon. [L '(my soul) doth magnify', 3rd pers sing present indicative of *magnificāre*]

magnification. See under **magnify**.

magnificence *mag-nif'i-səns*, *n* well-judged liberality (*archaic*); the quality of being magnificent. — *adj* **magnif'icent** great in deeds or in show; noble; pompous; displaying greatness of size or extent; very fine, excellent (*colloq*). — *adv* **magnif'icently**. [L *magnificēns*, *-entis*, literally doing great things]

magnifico. See under **magnific**.

magnify *mag'ni-fī*, *vt* to make great or greater; to enlarge; to cause to appear greater; to exaggerate; to praise highly. — *vi* to signify (*archaic slang*): — *pr p* **mag'nifying**; *pa t* and *pa p* **mag'nified**. — *adj* **mag'nifiable** that may be magnified. — *n* **magnification** (*-fi-kā'shən*) the act or power of magnifying; state of being magnified; enlarged appearance, state or copy; extolling. — *n* **mag'nifier** (*-fī-ər*) a person who, or instrument which, magnifies or enlarges, *esp* a pocket-lens (**magnifying glass**); a person who extols. [L *magnificāre*, from *magnus* great, and *facere* to make]

magniloquent *mag-nil'ə-kwənt*, *adj* speaking in a grand or pompous style; bombastic. — *n* **magnil'oquence**. — *adv* **magnil'oquently**. [L *magnus* great, and *loquēns*, *-entis*, pr p of *loquī* to speak]

magnitude *mag'ni-tūd*, *n* greatness; size; extent; importance; a measure of the intensity of a star's brightness (*astron*; see also **of the first magnitude** below). — **absolute magnitude** see under **absolute**; **of the first magnitude** (of a star) of the first degree of brightness (*astron*); of a very important, significant or catastrophic kind (*fig*). [L *magnitūdō*, from *magnus* great]

magnolia *mag-nōl'i-ə*, *-yə*, *n* any tree of the N American and Asiatic genus *Magnolia*, with beautiful foliage, and large solitary flowers, giving name to the family **Magnoliā'ceae**, with a petaloid perianth and spirally arranged stamens and carpels; a light pinkish-white or purplish-white colour. — *adj* **magnoliā'ceous**. [From Pierre *Magnol* (1638–1715), a Montpellier botanist]

Magnox® *mag'noks*, (also without *cap*) *n* a material consisting of any of various magnesium-based alloys containing a small amount of aluminium, from which containers for the fuel of certain nuclear reactors are made; such a container or reactor. — Also *adj*. [*mag*nesium *no ox*idation]

magnum *mag'nəm*, *n* a two-quart bottle or other container; as a bottle-size of champagne or other wine, the equivalent of two ordinary bottles, containing *usu* $1\frac{1}{2}$ litres; two quarts of alcohol: — *pl* **mag'nums**. — **magnum bonum** a large good variety, *esp* of plums or potatoes: — *pl* **magnum bonums**. [L *magnum* (neuter) big, and *bonum* (neuter) good]

magnum opus *mag'nəm ōp'əs*, *mag'nŏŏm op'ŏŏs*, (*L*) *n* a great work, *esp* of literature or learning; a writer's greatest achievement or the culmination of his or her efforts.

Magnus effect *mag'nəs i-fekt'* or **Magnus force** *förs*, *n* the force which acts on a cylinder rotating in a stream of fluid flowing in a direction perpendicular to the cylinder's axis, the force thrusting in a direction perpendicular to both the axis and the direction of the flow. [HG *Magnus* (1802–70), German scientist]

Magog. See **Gog and Magog**.

magot *mag'ət*, *mä-gō'*, *n* the Barbary ape; a small grotesque figure, in Chinese or Japanese workmanship. [Fr]

magot-pie. See **magpie**.

magpie *mag'pī*, *n* the pie (*Pica rustica*), a black-and-white chattering bird of the same type as the crow; extended to other black-and-white or pied birds (in Australia, a piping crow); a chattering person; an Anglican bishop (*obs*); a hit on the penultimate outermost division of a target (*darts*); a person who hoards or steals objects (*fig*); a halfpenny (*obs slang*). — (*Shakesp*) **mag'ot-pie** or **magg'ot-pie**. — **magpie moth** the moth of the gooseberry caterpillar. [*Mag* or *Magot*, short form of *Margaret*, and **pie**[1]]

magsman. See under **mag**[2].

maguey *mag'wā*, *mä-gā'i*, *n* agave. [Sp]

magus *mā'gəs*, *n* (in ancient Persia) a priest or member of a priestly class; an Eastern magician; a magician; (with *cap*) any of the three wise men from the East who brought gifts to the infant Christ: — *pl* **mā'gi** (*-jī*). — *n* **mage** (*māj*) a magus or sorcerer. — *n* **mage'ship**. — *adj* **mā'gian** relating to the magi or to a sorcerer. — *n* a magus; a sorcerer. — *n* **mā'gianism** or **mā'gism** the philosophy or teaching of the magi. [L, from Gr *magos*, from OPers *magus*]

Magyar *mag'yär, mod'yor, n* a member of the majority ethnic group of Hungary; the Finno-Ugric language of Hungary. — *adj* (without *cap*) of a garment, cut with the sleeves in a piece with the rest. — *vt* and *vi* **Mag'yarize** or **-ise** to make or become Magyar. — *n* **Mag'yarism** Hungarian nationalism. [Magyar]

Mahabharata *mə-hä-bä'rə-tə, n* one of the great Sanskrit epics of ancient India, which describes the war between the descendants of Bharata. [Sans]

Mahadeva *mə-hä-dā'və, n* Siva. [Sans *mahat* great, and *deva* god]

maharaja or **maharajah** *mä-hä-rä'jä, mə-hä-rä'jə,* (*hist*) *n* a great Indian prince, *esp* a ruler of a state. — *n* **maharani** or **maharanee** (*-rä'nē*) the wife or widow of a maharaja; a woman with the rank of a maharaja in her own right. [Hindi, from Sans *mahat* great, and *rājan* king or *rānī* queen]

maharishi *mä-hä-rē'shi, n* a leading instructor in the Hindu faith. [Sans *mahat* great, and *rishi* sage]

mahatma *mə-hät'mä, -hat'mə, n* a religious sage; an adept; a wise and holy leader. [Sans *mahātman* high-souled]

Mahayana *mä-hə-yä'nə, n* the most widespread form of Buddhism, practised *esp* in China, Japan, Tibet and the Himalayas, that seeks enlightenment for all humanity, embraces many methods for attaining it, and recognizes many texts as scripture (cf **Hinayana**). — Also *adj*. — *n* **Mahaya'nist**. [Sans, literally great vehicle]

maha yoga *mä'hə yō'gə, n* a form of yoga practised with a master which incorporates all 8 classical yogas (also called **siddha yoga**). [Sans *mahat* great]

Mahdi *mä'dē, n* the great leader of the faithful Muslims, who is to appear in the last days; a title of various insurrectionary leaders, *esp* one who overthrew the Egyptian power in the Sudan in 1884–5. — Also **Meh'di**. — *n* **Mah'diism** or **Mah'dism**. — *n* **Mah'diist** or **Mah'dist**. [Ar *mahdīy*]

Mahican. See **Mohican**.

mahi-mahi *mä-hē-mä'hē, n* the dolphin-fish, *esp* its flesh prepared as food. [Hawaiian, from *mahi* strong]

mah-jong or **mah-jongg** *mä-jong', n* an old Chinese table game for four, played with small painted bricks or 'tiles'. [Chin, literally sparrows, perh in allusion to the chattering sound of the tiles during play]

mahlstick. See **maulstick**.

mahmal *mä'mäl, n* the empty litter sent to Mecca in the hadj.

mahoe *mä'hō-i, n* a small, bushy white-barked tree of New Zealand. [Maori]

mahogany *mə-hog'ə-ni, n* a tropical American tree (*Swietenia mahogoni*) of the family *Meliaceae*; its wood, valued for furniture-making; the colour of the wood, a dark reddish brown; a dining-table (*colloq*); gin and treacle (*obs slang* or *dialect*); brandy and water (*obs slang*). — Also *adj*. [Origin unknown]

Mahommedan and **Mahometan**. See under **Mohammedan**.

mahonia *mə-hō'ni-ə, n* a plant of the pinnate-leaved *Mahonia* genus (or section of *Berberis*) of the barberry family. [Named after Bernard *McMahon*, Irish-American gardener and botanist (died 1816)]

Mahoun *mə-hown, -hōōn* or **Mahound** *-hownd, hōōnd*, also *mä', n* Mohammed, imagined in the Middle Ages to be a pagan god (*archaic*); the devil (*Scot mə-hōōn'*).

mahout *mä-howt', n* the keeper and driver of an elephant. [Hindi *mahāut, mahāwat*]

Mahratta. See **Maratha**.

mahseer or **mahsir** *mä'sēr, n* a large freshwater fish (species *Barbus*) of Northern India. [Hindi *mahāsir*]

mahua or **mahwa** *mä'(h)wä, n* a kind of butter-tree (*Bassia*, or *Illipe, latifolia*) with edible flowers; an alcohol distilled from its flowers. — **mahua butter** a fat obtained from its seeds. — Also **mowa** or **mowra**. [Hindi *mahūā*]

mahzor or **machzor** *mahh-zör', mähh'zör, n* the Jewish prayer-book used for festivals and other special occasions: — *pl* **machzorim** or **mahzorim** (*-ēm'*). [Heb *mahzor* a cycle]

maid *mād, n* an unmarried woman, *esp* one who is young (*archaic* and *poetic*); a virgin (*archaic*); a spinster; a female servant; a young skate. — *vi* to work as a maidservant. — *n* **maid'hood**. — *adj* **maid'ish**. — *adj* **maid'less** without a maid. — **maid'-child** (*Shakesp*) a girl; **maid'servant** a female servant. — *adj* **maid'-pale** (*Shakesp*) pale, like a sick girl. — **maid of all work** or **maid'-of-all'-work** (*archaic*) a maid who does general housework; **maid of honour** see under **honour**; **old maid** a spinster; an extremely fussy or overly cautious person; a card game in which players match pairs of cards from a pack of 51, the loser being left with the unmatched card. [Short for **maiden**]

maidan *mī-dän', n* an open plain; an open space near a town, used as a sports ground or parade-ground in India, Pakistan, etc. [Urdu, from Pers *maidān*]

maiden *mād'n, n* a maid; a corn-maiden (*Scot*); a washing dolly; a clothes-horse; a horse that has never won a race; (*usu* with *cap*) a Scottish beheading machine similar to a guillotine (*hist*); a maiden over (*cricket*); a one-year old tree (*hortic*). — *adj* unmarried; virgin; female; relating to a virgin or young woman; consisting of maidens; unpolluted (*fig*); fresh; new; unused; in the original or initial state; grown from a seed; that has never been captured, climbed, trodden, penetrated, pruned, etc; (of a horse) that has never won a race; first. — *n* **maid'enhead** (*-hed*; ME sfx *-hēd(e) -hood*) virginity; the first attempt, experience, or use of anything (*obs*); the hymen. — *n* **maid'enhood** the state or time of being a maiden; maidenhead. — *adj* **maid'enish** (*derog*) like a maiden. — *adj* **maid'enlike**. — Also *adv*. — *n* **maid'enliness**. — *adj* **maid'enly** maiden-like; becoming a maiden; gentle; modest. — Also *adv*. — **maiden assize** (*law hist*) an assize at which no criminal cases were heard; **maiden aunt** an unmarried aunt; **maiden battle** a first contest; **maiden castle** a common (though largely unexplained) name for a prehistoric earthwork; a castle that has never been captured; **maiden century** (*cricket*) a batsman's or batswoman's first century; **maiden fortress** a fortress that has never been captured; **maid'enhair** a fern (*Adiantum*) with fine footstalks; extended to species of spleenwort (**maid'enhair-spleenwort**); **maid'enhair-tree** the ginkgo; **maiden herring** same as **maatjes**. — *adj* **maid'en-meek** (*literary*) meek as a maiden. — **maiden name** the surname of a married woman before marriage; **maiden over** (*cricket*) an over in which no runs are made; **maiden pink** a wild species of pink, *Dianthus deltoides*; **maiden speech** a person's first speech, *esp* that of an MP in Parliament; **maiden stakes** (in horse-racing) the prize in a race (**maiden race**) between horses that have not previously won a race. — *adj* **maid'en-tongued** (*Shakesp*) soft-spoken, like a girl. — **maiden voyage** the first voyage of a ship, etc; **maid'enweed** mayweed. — *adj* **maid'en-widowed** (*Shakesp*) widowed while still a virgin. [OE *mægden*]

maidism *mā'id-izm,* (*pathol*) *n* pellagra (attributed to a maize diet). [**maize**[1]]

maieutic *mī-, mā-ūt'ik, adj* (of the Socratic method of inquiry) bringing out latent thoughts and ideas. — *n sing* **maieut'ics** the Socratic method. [Gr *maieutikos*, from *maia* good woman, a midwife; Socrates, son of a midwife, called himself a midwife to men's thoughts]

maigre *mā'gər, meg'r', adj* (of food) containing no animal flesh and so able to be eaten on a fast-day; relating to a fast-day or to a fast. — *adv* without using animal flesh (*obs*). — *n* (also **meagre** *mē'gər*) a large Mediterranean food fish (*Sciaena aquila*); any of various fishes of the family *Sciaenidae*, noted for making a croaking or drumming sound. [Fr *maigre* lean, from L *macer*]

maik *māk, n*. Same as **mag**[1] or **make**[3].

maiko *mī'kō, n* an apprentice geisha: — *pl* **mai'ko** or **maik'os**. [Jap]

mail[1] *māl, n* defensive armour for the body, formed of overlapping or meshed steel rings; armour generally; the protective shell or scales of an animal. — *vt* to clothe in mail. — *adj* **mailed** covered in or protected by mail. — *adj* **mail'-clad** (*Scott*) wearing a coat of mail. — **mailed fist** (*fig*) physical or military force. [Fr *maille*, from L *macula* a spot or a mesh]

mail[2] *māl*, *n* a travelling bag (*obs*); a bag for carrying letters, parcels, etc; the contents of such a bag; post, the postal system; correspondence; a batch of letters, parcels, etc; the person or method of transport by which mail is conveyed. — *vt* to post; to send by post. — *adj* **mail'able** capable of being sent by mail. — **mail'bag** or (*esp NAm*) **mail'sack** a bag in which mail is carried; **mail'-boat** a boat that carries the public mail; **mail'box** a letter-box (*esp NAm*); a file for storing electronic mail (*comput*); **mail'-cart**, **-coach**, **-car**, **-carriage**, **-drag** or **-gig** a cart, etc formerly used to carry the public mail; a small hand-cart, with long handles, for the conveyance of children; **mail'-catcher** an apparatus for catching mail-bags thrown from a moving train; **mail drop** (*NAm*) a receptacle for mail; **mail'gram** (*US*) a message sent electronically to a post office and then delivered to the addressee by ordinary mail. — *vt* to send a mailgram to. — **mailing list** a list of, or computer file containing, the names and addresses of those to whom advertising material, information, etc, is to be posted; **mailing machine** any of various machines used in an office to seal, address, frank, etc, outgoing mail; **mail'man** or **mail'-carrier** (*NAm*) a postman; **mail'merge** (a computer program for) the producing of a series of letters addressed to individuals by merging a file of names with a file containing the text of the letter. — Also *vi.* — **mail order** an order for goods to be sent by post (*adj* **mail'-order**); **mail'-plane**, **mail'-train** or **mail'van** an aeroplane, train or van which carries the public mail; **mail'room** a room in an office, etc, for dealing with incoming and outgoing mail; **mail shot** an item of unsolicited, *usu* advertising, material sent by post. [OFr *male* a trunk, a mail, from OHGer *malha*, *malaha*, a sack]

mail[3] *māl*, (*Scot*; now chiefly *law*) *n* payment; rent. — *n* **mail'er** a person who pays rent, *esp* a tenant farmer; a cottar. — *n* **mail'ing** a rented farm; rent paid for this (*obs*). [Late OE *māl*, from ON *māl* speech, agreement; cf OE *mǣl*]

mail[4] or **maile** *māl*, (*obs*) *n* a halfpenny. [Anglo-Fr *mayle*, from assumed LL *metallea*; see **medal**]

mail[5] *māl*, (*Scot*) *n* a spot, *esp* one caused by iron oxide on cloth. — *vt* to spot or stain. [OE *māl*; see **mole**[2]]

mail[6] *māl*, *vt* to wrap up (*obs*); to confine (a bird) in a handkerchief, etc, to tame or silence it (*falconry*). [Ety doubtful, poss as for **mail**[2]]

maillot *mä'-yō*, *n* tights worn by a ballet-dancer, gymnast, etc; a one-piece close-fitting swimsuit; a jersey. [Fr, literally swaddling-clothes]

maim *mām*, *vt* to disable; to mutilate; to lame or cripple; to make defective. — *n* (*archaic*) serious bodily injury; an injury, a disability; the loss of any essential part. — *adj* (*obs*) maimed, crippled. — *adj* **maimed**. — *n* **maimedness** (*māmd'*, *mā'mid-nis*). — *n* **maiming**. [OFr *mahaing*]

main[1] *mān*, *n* strength (*esp* in the phrase *might and main*); the principal part; the mainland; the high sea; a great expanse (*Shakesp* and *Milton*); a principal pipe or conductor in a branching system distributing water, gas, electricity, etc; (in *pl*) the water, gas or electricity supply available through such a system; that which is essential; the most part; purpose (*obs*). — *adj* strong (*Milton*); sheer (as in *main force*); great; extensive; important; chief, principal; first in importance or extent; leading; general. — *adv* (*Scot* or *dialect*) exceedingly. — *adv* **main'ly** chiefly, principally; much (*obs* or *dialect*). — **main'boom** the spar that extends the foot of a fore-and-aft mainsail; **main'brace** the brace attached to the mainyard (see also **splice**); **main chance** see under **chance**; **main clause** (*gram*) same as **principal clause** (qv); **main course** the mainsail on square-rigged ships; the principal course of any meal; **main'-deck** the principal deck of a ship; **main'door** a door giving independent access to a house, distinguished from one opening into a common passage; a ground-floor house in a tenement building or villa-block, entered from the front by a door of its own (*Scot*); **main'frame** the central processing unit and storage unit of a computer; a large, powerful computer, often with many simultaneous users, as opposed to a minicomputer or microcomputer. — *adj* (of a computer) that is a mainframe. — **main'land** (*-lənd*, *-land*) the principal or larger land, as opposed to neighbouring islands; **main'lander**; **main line** a railway line between important centres; an important vein (*slang*). — *adj* **main'line**. — *vi* and *vt* (*slang*) to take (a narcotic) intravenously; to consume (something) voraciously or at speed. — **main'liner**; **main'lining**; **main'mast** (*-məst*, *-mäst*) the principal mast, usually second from the prow; **main memory** (*comput*) same as **main store**; **main purpose rule** (*law*) a rule presuming that an exemption clause in a contract, etc is not intended to defeat the main object of that contract; **main'sail** (*-sl*, *-sāl*) the principal sail, generally attached to the mainmast; **main sequence** (*astron*) the principal sequence of stars on the Hertzsprung-Russell diagram, running diagonally from upper left (high temperature, high luminosity) to lower right (low temperature, low luminosity) and containing about 90% of all known stars; **main'sheet** the sheet or rope attached to the lower corner of the mainsail; **main'spring** the spring that gives motion to any piece of machinery, *esp* that of a watch or a clock; principal motive, motivating influence (*fig*); **main'stay** a rope stretching forward and down from the top of the mainmast; chief support; **main store** the part (*comput*) of a computer's store (qv) holding data and programs immediately before, during, and immediately after processing or execution; **main stream** a river with tributaries; the chief direction or trend in any historical development, including that of an art. — *adj* **main'-stream** pertaining to the main stream (*lit* and *fig*); (of cigarette smoke) that which is drawn into a smoker's mouth or lungs; (of swing) coming in the line of development between early and modern (*jazz*); in accordance with what is normal or standard. — *vt* (*esp NAm*) to make mainstream; to integrate (handicapped children) into classes of able-bodied children (*educ*). — *adj* **Main Street** (also without *cap*; *US*) relating to the most mediocre or materialistic aspects of town or city life. — *n* **main'streeting** (*Can*) electioneering or canvassing of support by a political candidate in the main streets of town, etc; **main'top** a platform on the top of the lower mainmast; **maintop-gall'ant-mast** the mast above the maintopmast; **maintop'mast** the mast next above the lower mainmast; **maintop'sail** the sail above the mainsail, in square-rigged ships; **main'yard** the lower yard on the mainmast. — **in the main** for the most part; on the whole; **might and main** utmost strength; **Spanish Main** see under **Spanish**. [Partly OE *mægen* strength, partly ON *meginn* strong; influence of OFr *maine*, *magne*, (from L *magnus*) great, is questioned]

main[2] *mān*, (*obs*) *n* a banker's shovel for coins. [OFr *main*, from L *manus* hand]

main[3] *mān*, *n* in games of chance, a number (5 to 9) called before throwing the dice; a game of chance; a cockfighting match; a set of cocks engaged in a match; a match in some other sports, *esp* bowling (now *dialect*). [Perh same as **main**[2]]

main[4] *mān*, (*dialect*; *Shakesp*) *vt* to lame, maim.

mainor, **mainour** *mān'ər* or **manner** *man'ər*, (*archaic* or *hist*) *n* act or fact, *esp* of theft; that which is stolen. — **in** or **with the manner** in the act; in possession of the thing stolen. [Anglo-Fr *meinoure*, *mainoure*, *mainoevere*; see **manoeuvre**]

mainpernor. See under **mainprise**.

mainprise *mān'prīz*, (*law hist*) *n* suretyship, *esp* for the appearance of a prisoner. — *n* **mainpernor** (*-pûr'nər*) a person who gives mainprise. [Anglo-Fr *mainprise*, *mainpernour*, from *main* hand, and *prendre* to take]

mains *mānz*, (*Scot*) *n pl* a home farm. [**demesne** and **domain**]

maintain *mān-tān'*, *mən-*, *men-*, *vt* to observe or practise; to keep in existence or in any state; to preserve from capture, loss or deterioration; to uphold; to carry on; to keep up; to support; to make good; to support by argument; to affirm; to defend; to support in an action in which one is not oneself concerned (*law*). — *n* **maintainabil'ity**. — *adj* **maintain'able**. — *adj* **maintained'** financially supported, eg (of a school, etc) from public funds. — *n* **maintain'er**. — *n* **maintenance** (*mān'tən-əns*) the act of maintaining, supporting or defending; continuance; the means of support; defence, protection; (formerly illegal) outside interference in a lawsuit, etc in favour of one of the parties (*law*). — *vt* to keep in working order. — **main'tenance-man** a man keeping machines, etc in working order. — **cap of maintenance** (*hist*) a cap formerly worn by or carried before a person of high office or rank; **maintain capital intact** (*econ*) to make good that part of a company's or country's capital goods consumed in production. [Fr *maintenir*, from L *manū* (ablative) *tenēre* to hold in the hand]

maiolica. See **majolica**.

mair *mār*. Scots form of **more**.

maire *mer*, (*Fr*) *n* mayor.

maise *māz*. Same as **mease**[1].

maison de ville *me-zɔ̃ də vēl*, (*Fr*) *n* a town house or residence in town.

maisonnette or **maisonette** *māz-on-et'*, *mez-*, *n* a small house or flat. [Fr *maisonnette*]

maist. See ety for **most**.

maister *mās'tər*, (*obs* or *Scot*). Same as **master**. — *n* **mais'terdome** (*obs*). — *n* **mais'tring** (*obs*). — *n* **mais'try** (*obs*).

maître de ballet *metr' də bal-e*, *n* a person who trains dancers and takes rehearsals (formerly acting also as choreographer): — *fem* **maîtresse de ballet**. [Fr, ballet master, mistress]

maître d'hôtel *metr' dō-tel*, *n* a house-steward or major domo; the manager of a hotel; a head waiter. — Also (*colloq*) **maître d'** (*metr' dē*). — See also **à la maître d'hôtel**.

maize[1] *māz*, *n* a tall cereal grass (*Zea mays*) grown *esp* in America, producing large ears (corncobs) of yellow knernels which are eaten as a vegetable or dried and ground into meal (called also *Indian corn* or *mealies*); the yellow colour of maize kernels. — Also *adj*. — **water maize** *Victoria regia*. [Sp *maíz*, from Taino *mahís*]

maize[2] *māz*. Same as **mease**[1].

Maj *abbrev*: Major.

majesty *maj'is-ti*, *n* the greatness and glory of God; grandeur; dignity; elevation of manner or style; royal state; a title of monarchs (*His*, *Her* or *Your*, *Majesty*; *Their* or *Your Majesties*); a representation of God (sometimes Christ) enthroned; the canopy of a hearse. — *adj* **majestic** (*mə-jes'tik*) or **majes'tical** having or exhibiting majesty; stately; sublime. — *adv* **majes'tically** in a majestic manner. — *n* **majes'ticalness** or **majes'ticness** (*obs*) majesty. [Fr *majesté*, from L *mājestās*, *-ātis*, from *mājor*, *mājus*, compar of *magnus* great]

Majlis *mäj-lis'*, *n* the Iranian parliament; (also without *cap*) an assembly or council in various N African and Middle Eastern countries. — Also **Mejlis'**. [Pers *majlis*]

majolica *mə-jol'i-kə*, *-yol'* or **maiolica** *-yol'*, *n* tin-glazed, often highly decorated earthenware, produced *esp* in Italy in the 16c. — **majol'icaware**. [Ital *maiolica* from *Majorca*, from where it perh originated]

major *mā'jər*, *adj* greater, or great, in number, quantity, size, value or importance; (in boys' schools) senior; greater (than minor) by a semitone (*music*); involving a major third (see below; *music*). — *n* a person of full legal age (in UK, before 1970, 21 years; from 1970, 18 years); an officer in rank between a captain and lieutenant-colonel; by courtesy, a sergeant-major; anything that is major opposed to minor; (in *pl*) the major sports leagues (*US*); (a student taking) a main subject of study at a university or college (*NAm*, *Austr* and *NZ*); a kind of wig (*obs*). — *vi* to strut around with a self-important air (*Scott*); to specialize in a particular subject at college (with *in*; *NAm*, *Austr* and *NZ*); to specialize in a particular product, etc (with *in* or *on*). — *vt* to channel or concentrate (one's activities, efforts, etc) in a particular direction. — *n* **majorat** (*mä-zhō-rä*; *Fr*) primogeniture. — *n* **mājorette'** a member of a group of girls who march in parades, etc, wearing decorative, military-style uniforms, and *usu* twirling batons or playing instruments. — *n* **majorett'ing** the practice of performing as majorettes. — *n* **majority** (*mə-jor'i-ti*) pre-eminence; the greater number; the greater part, the bulk; the difference between the greater and the less number; full age (see **major** above); the office or rank of major. — Also *adj*. — *n* **mā'jorship**. — **major axis** (*math*) (in conic sections) the axis passing through the foci; **major-dō'mō** (Sp *mayor-domo*, from Med L *mājor domūs*) an official who has the general management in a large household; a general steward; **major-gen'eral** an officer in the army next in rank below a lieutenant-general; **major-gen'eralcy** or **major-gen'eralship** the office or rank of major-general; **major histocompatibility complex** (*immunol*) the collection of genes coding for the major histocompatibility antigens, which are involved in determining acceptance or rejection of transplanted organs (*abbrev* **MMC**); **majority carrier** (*electronics*) in a semiconductor, the type of carrier (electrons or holes) that carries most of the measured current; **majority rule** government by members, or by a body including members, of the largest ethnic group(s) in a country, as opposed to a political system which excludes them; **majority verdict** the verdict reached by the majority in a jury, as distinct from a unanimous verdict; **major key**, **mode** or **scale** (*music*) a key, mode or scale with its third a major third above the tonic; **major orders** in the RC Church, the higher degrees of holy orders, ie bishop, priest and deacon; **major premise** (*logic*) the premise in which the major term occurs; **major suit** (*bridge*) spades or hearts, valued more highly than diamonds or clubs; **major term** (*logic*) the term which is the predicate of the conclusion; **major third** (*music*) an interval of four semitones; **major tone** an interval of vibration ratio 8:9. — **go over to** or **join the majority** to die. [L *mājor*, compar of *magnus* great]

majoritaire *mä-zhor-ē-ter*, (*Fr*) *n* a member of a majority section of a political party, *esp* of a socialist one.

majority. See under **major**.

Major Mitchell *mā'jər mich'əl*, (*Austr*) *n* a cockatoo, *Caeatua leadbeateri*, with pink and white plumage. — *vi* (*facetious*) to follow a zig-zag route; to become lost. [Major Sir Thomas Mitchell (1792–1855), surveyor and explorer]

majuscule *mə-jus'kūl*, *maj'əs-kūl*, (*palaeog*) *n* a large letter whether capital or uncial. — Also *adj*. — *adj* **majus'cūlar**. [L (*littera*) *mājuscula* somewhat larger (letter)]

mak *mäk*, Scots form of **make**. — *n* **makar** see **maker** under **make**[1].

make[1] *māk*, *vt* to fashion, frame, construct, compose or form; to create; to bring into being; to produce; to conclude, contract; to bring about; to perform; to force; to cause; to result in; to cause to be; to convert or turn; to appoint; to render; to represent as doing or being; to reckon; to get as result or solution; to occasion; to bring into any state or condition; to establish; (in the navy) to promote; to prepare; to shut (as a door) (*Shakesp*); to shuffle (*cards*); to declare as trumps (*cards*); to obtain, gain or earn; to score; to constitute; to amount to; to count for; to turn out; to be capable of turning or developing into or serving as; to arrive in sight of; to reach, succeed in reaching; to accomplish, achieve; to attempt, offer or start; to be occupied with; to do; to cause or assure the success of; to persuade (*esp* a woman) to have sexual intercourse with one (*slang*); to have sexual intercourse with (*slang*). — *vi* to behave (as if), *esp* in order to deceive; to proceed; to tend, to result; to contribute; to flow; to versify (*archaic*); to be in condition for making; to matter (as *it maksna*, it does not matter; *Scot*): — *pr p* **māk'ing**; *pa t* and *pa p* **māde**. — *n* form or shape; structure, texture; build; formation; manufacture; brand; type; making; character or disposition; quantity made; establishment of an electric circuit or contact; trump declaration (*cards*). — *adj* **mak'able** or **make'able**. — *n* **māk'er** a person who makes; (with *cap*) the Creator; (*esp* in Scots form, **makar** *mak'*, *mäk'ər*) a poet (*archaic*); the declarer (*bridge*); a knave in cards (*obs*); a calker's tool. — *n* **māk'ing** the act of forming (often in combination, as in *bread-making*, *cabinet-making*, etc); structure; form; (in *pl*) gains; (in *pl*) materials or qualities from which something can be made; (in *pl*) loose tobacco and paper used to roll cigarettes (*slang*). — **make'-and-break'** the making and breaking of an electrical circuit; a device which causes this to happen. — **make'bate** (*archaic*) a mischief-maker. — *vi* **make'-believe** see **make believe** below. — *n* feigning (also **make'-belief**). — *adj* feigned. — *adj* **make'-do** makeshift. — *adj* **make-or-break** see **make or break** below. — *n* **make'over** a complete change in the style of a person's dress, appearance, etc, *esp* one following professional advice; a complete reorganization of a company under new management. — **make'-peace** (*Shakesp*) a peace-maker; **make'-ready** preparation of a letterpress sheet for printing, so as to obtain evenness of impression; **make'shift** a temporary expedient or substitute. — *adj* of the nature of or characterized by a temporary expedient. — **make'-up** the way anything is arranged, composed, or constituted, or the ingredients in its constitution; one's character, temperament, or mental qualities; cosmetics for self-beautification, worn *esp* by women, and by actors as an aid to impersonation; the effect produced thereby; the arrangement of composed types into columns or pages (*printing*); **make'-weight** that which is thrown into a scale to make up the weight; a person or thing of little value added to supply a deficiency. — **in the making** in the process of being formed, developed, etc, or of becoming; **make account of** see under **account**; **make a face** to grimace, contort the features; **make a figure** to be conspicuous; **make a fool of** see under **fool**; **make after** to follow or pursue; **make against** to militate or tell against; **make a (good) meal, dinner**, etc, to dine, etc (plentifully or heartily); **make allowances for** see under **allow**; **make a meal of** see under **meal**[1]; **make amends** to render compensation or satisfaction; **make an ass of oneself** to behave like a fool; **make a night** (or **day**) **of it** to extend an, *esp* enjoyable, activity through the whole night (or day); **make as if** or (*NAm*) **make like** or **as though** to act as if, to pretend that; **make at** to make a hostile movement against; **make away (with)** to put out of the way, get rid of, destroy, kill; **make believe** to pretend, feign; to play at believing; **make bold** see under **bold**; **make certain (of)** to find out; to put beyond doubt; to secure; **make do (with)** to manage (with the *usu* inferior or inadequate means available); **make down** to refashion so as to fit a smaller person; to turn down the sheets and blankets of (*Scot*); **make eyes at** see under **eye**; **make for** to set out for, seek to reach; to favour; **make free with** see under **free**; **make friends** to become friendly; to acquire friends; **make good, make light of, make little of, make love to, make merry** see under **good**, etc; **make head or tail of** to find any sense in; **make it** to reach an objective; to succeed in a purpose; to become a success (*colloq*); to have one's way sexually (with) (*slang*); **make much of** to treat with fondness, to cherish, to foster; to turn to great account; to find much sense in, succeed in understanding; **make no doubt** to have no doubt, to be confident; **make nothing of** to regard as being of little importance; to have no hesitation or difficulty in (doing); to be totally unable to understand; **make of** to construct from (as material); to understand by; to make much of, to pet (*obs* and *Scot*); to esteem (*obs*); **make off** to decamp; **make off with** to run away with; **make on** (*Shakesp*) to make much of; **make one's way** to proceed; to succeed; **make or break** or **make or mar** to be the crucial test that brings success or failure to (*adj* **make'-or-break'**); **make or meddle with** to have to do with, interfere with; **make out** to descry, to see; to discern; to decipher; to comprehend, understand; to prove; to seek to make it appear; to draw up; to achieve (*obs*); to fill up; to make do, get along somehow; to succeed; to engage in lovemaking (with) (*slang*); **make over** to remake or reconstruct; to make or suggest a complete change in a person's style of dress, appearance, etc; to transfer (*n* **make'over**); **make sail** to increase the quantity of sail; to set sail; **make someone's day** see under **day**; **make sure (of)** to ascertain; to put beyond doubt or risk; to secure; to feel certain; to betroth (*obs*); **make the best of** to turn to the best advantage; to take in the best spirit; **make the most of** to use to the best advantage; **make up** to fabricate; to feign; to collect; to put together; to parcel; to put into shape; to arrange; to settle (an argument); to become friends again (after a quarrel, etc); to constitute; to repair; to complete, supplement; to adjust one's appearance (as an actor for a part); to apply cosmetics to the face; to put type, etc into columns and pages; to set out and balance (accounts); to make good; to compensate; to decide (*Shakesp*); **make up one's mind** to come to a decision; **make up to** to make friendly, adulatory, or amorous approaches to; to compensate; **make way** see under **way**; **make with** (*colloq*; *orig NAm*) to start using, doing, etc (something), to bring on or into operation; **on the make** (*colloq*) bent on self-advancement or promotion, or on finding a sexual partner; **put the make on** (*slang*) make sexual advances to. [OE *macian*; Ger *machen*]

make[2] *māk*, *n*. Same as **mag**[1].

make[3] or (*Scot*) **maik** *māk* (*obs* or *dialect*) *n* a mate or consort; an equal. — *adj* **make'less** without a mate; matchless. [OE (*ge*)*mæcca*; see **match**]

makimono *mäk-i-mō'nō*, *n* a long, painted scroll, often with narrative text, designed to be unrolled from right to left: — *pl* **makimō'nos**. [Jap, from *maki* roll, scroll, and *mono* thing]

mako[1] *mä'kō*, *n* any of several sharks of the genus *Isurus*: — *pl* **ma'kos**. — Also **mako shark**. [Maori]

mako[2] *mä'kō* or **mako-mako** *mä'kō-mä'kō*, *n* a small, evergreen tree of New Zealand with red berries that turn purple as they ripen: — *pl* **ma'kos** or **ma'ko-ma'kos**. — Also called **wine-berry**. [Maori]

makunouchi *mak-ə-nōō'chi*, *n* the highest division in sumo wrestling; a top bout in this. [Jap]

MAL *abbrev*: Malaysia (IVR).

Mal (*Bible*) *abbrev*: (the Book of) Malachi.

mal *mal*, (*Fr*) *n* pain, sickness. — **mal de mer** (*də mer*) seasickness; **mal du pays** (*dü pā-ē*) homesickness, nostalgia; **mal du siècle** (*dü syekl'*) depression about the state of the world (used by Sainte-Beuve (1833) and current in the 20c). — **grand mal** see under **grand**; **petit mal** see under **petit**.

mal- *mal-*, *pfx* bad, badly. [Fr, from L *male* badly]

Malabar-rat *mal'ə-bär-rat'*, *n* the bandicoot rat. [*Malabar* in India]

Malacca-cane *məl-ak'ə-kān*, *n* a brown walking stick made from the stem of a rattan. [*Malacca*, a state in SW Malaysia, a centre of the trade]

malachite *mal'ə-kīt*, *n* a green mineral, basic copper carbonate. [Gr *malachē* mallow, as of the colour of a mallow leaf]

malacia *mal-ā'shi-ə*, (*med*) *n* pathological softening of tissue; abnormal appetite or food craving. [Gr *malakiā* softness]

malacology *mal-ə-kol'ə-ji*, *n* the study of molluscs. — *adj* **malacological** (*-kə-loj'*). — *n* **malacol'ogist**. [Gr *malakos* soft, and *logos* discourse]

malacophilous *mal-ə-kof'i-ləs*, (*bot*) *adj* pollinated by snails. — *n* **malacoph'ily** pollination by snails. [Gr *malakos* soft, and *phileein* to love]

Malacopterygii *mal-ə-kop-tər-ij'i-ī, n pl* a soft-finned suborder of bony fishes, including herrings and salmon. — *adj* and *n* **malacopteryg'ian**. [Gr *malakos* soft, and *pteryx, pterygos* a wing or fin]

Malacostraca *mal-ə-kos'trə-kə, n pl* the best-known class of crustaceans, including crabs, lobsters, shrimps, prawns, etc. — *adj* and *n* **malacos'tracan**. — *adj* **malacos'tracous**. [Gr *malakos* soft, and *ostrakon* a shell]

maladaptation *mal-ad-ap-tā'shən, n* faulty adaptation. — *adj* **maladap'ted**. — *adj* **maladap'tive**. [**mal-**]

maladdress *mal-ə-dres', n* awkwardness; clumsiness; tactlessness. [Fr *maladresse*]

maladjusted *mal-ə-just'id, adj* poorly or inadequately adjusted, *esp* to one's environment or circumstances; psychologically incapable of dealing with day-to-day situations. — *n* **maladjust'ment**. [**mal-**]

maladministration *mal-əd-min-is-trā'shən, n* bad management, *esp* of public affairs. — *vt* **maladmin'ister**. [**mal-**]

maladroit *mal'ə-droit, -droit', adj* not dexterous; unskilful; clumsy; tactless. — *adv* **maladroit'ly**. — *n* **maladroit'ness**. [Fr]

malady *mal'ə-di, n* illness; disease, whether of the body or the mind; a faulty condition. [Fr *maladie*, from *malade* sick, from L *male habitus* in ill condition, from *male* badly, and *habitus*, pa p of *habēre* to have or hold]

mala fide *mā'lə fī'dē, ma'lä fē'dā, (L) adv* in bad faith, treacherously.

Malaga *mal'ə-gə, n* a sweet dessert wine made from partially-dried grapes, from *Málaga*, in S Spain.

Malagasy *mal-ə-gas'i, adj* of or relating to Madagascar, its inhabitants, or their language. — *n* a native or inhabitant of Madagascar; the Austronesian language of Madagascar. — Also **Malagash'** (or *mal'*; *archaic*).

malagueña *mal-ə-gān'yə, n* a Spanish dance or folk tune resembling the fandango. [Sp, belonging to the city of Málaga]

malaguetta *mal-ə-get'ə, n* grains of Paradise (also **malaguetta pepper**). [Origin obscure]

malaise *mal-āz', n* uneasiness, discomfort; a feeling of debility or of impending sickness; a general air of depression or despondency. [Fr *malaise*]

malakatoone. Same as **melocoton**.

malamute or **malemute** *mäl'ə-mūt, n* (one of) a breed of powerful dogs with a double coat of hair, widely distributed in the Arctic regions and used *esp* for drawing sledges. — Also **Alaskan malamute** or **malemute**. [Inupiaq *malimiut*, Eskimo group in W Alaska]

malander, mallander or **mallender** *mal'ən-dər, n* an eruption of the skin behind a horse's knee (often in *pl*). [Fr *malandre*, from L *malandria* (sing or pl)]

malapert *mal'ə-pûrt, (archaic) adj* bold; forward; saucy; impudent. — *adv* **mal'apertly**. — *n* **mal'apertness**. [OFr, unskilful, from *mal* (L *malus*) bad, and *appert* for *espert* (L *expertus*; see **expert**) but understood in English as if from Fr *apert* open, outspoken, from L *apertus* open]

malapportionment *mal-ə-pōr'shən-mənt, (US) n* unequal or unfair apportioning of members to a legislative body. [**mal-**]

malappropriate *mal-ə-prō'pri-āt, vt* to misuse or misappropriate. — *n* **malappropriā'tion**. [**mal-**]

malapropism *mal'ə-prop-izm, n* the misapplication of words without mispronunciation, from Mrs *Malaprop* in Sheridan's play, *The Rivals*, who uses words *malapropos*.

malapropos *mal'a-prō-pō, mal-ə-prō-pō', adj* out of place; unsuitable; inapt, inappropriate. — *adv* inappropriately; untimely. [**mal-**]

malar *mā'lər, adj* of or relating to the cheek. — *n* the cheekbone. [L *māla* the cheek, from *mandere* to chew]

malaria *mə-lā'ri-ə, n* poisonous air rising from marshes, once believed to produce fever; miasma; the fever once attributed to bad air, actually due to a protozoan parasite transmitted by mosquitoes (*med*). — *adj* **malā'rial, malā'rian** or **malā'rious**. — *n* **malārio'logist**. — *n* **malārio'logy** the study of malaria. [Ital *mala aria*, from L *malus* bad, and *āēr, āeris* air]

malarkey or **malarky** *mə-lär'ki, (colloq; orig US) n* absurd talk; nonsense.

malassimilation *mal-ə-sim-i-lā'shən, n* imperfect assimilation or nutrition. [**mal-**]

malate. See under **malic**.

Malathion® *mal-ə-thī'on, n* a phosphorus-containing insecticide used chiefly in the house and garden. [From diethyl *male*ate]

malax *mal'aks* or **malaxate** *-aks-āt. vt* to soften by kneading, rubbing or mixing with a more liquid substance. — *n* **mal'axage**. — *n* **malaxā'tion** *specif* the action of a wasp, etc chewing prey before feeding on it; a kneading movement in massage. — *n* **mal'axātor** a kneading or grinding machine. [LL *malaxāre* to soften]

Malay *mə-lā'* or **Malayan** *mə-lā'ən, n* a member of a people inhabiting Malaysia, Singapore and Indonesia (formerly known as the Malay Archipelago); the Austronesian language of the Malays. — *adj* of the Malays, their language, or the countries inhabited by them. — *adj* **Malay'sian** (*-si-ən, -zhən* or *-shən*) relating to the Malay Archipelago or *esp* to Malaysia. — Also *n*. [Malay *malāyu*]

Malayalaam or **Malayam** *ma-lə-yä'ləm, n* the Dravidian language of Kerala in SW India. — Also *adj*.

malconformation *mal-kon-fōr-mā'shən, n* imperfect or disproportionate formation. [**mal-**]

malcontent *mal'kən-tent, adj* discontented or dissatisfied, *esp* in political matters. — *n* a discontented or disaffected person. — *adj* **malcontent'ed**. — *adv* **malcontent'edly**. — *n* **malcontent'edness**. [OFr *malcontent*]

mal del pinto. See under **pinta**[2].

mal de mer. See under **mal**.

maldistribution *mal-dis-tri-bū'shən, n* uneven, unfair or inefficient, distribution. [**mal-**]

male[1] *māl, (Spenser) n*. Same as **mail**[1].

male[2] *māl, adj* masculine; of or relating to the sex that begets (not bears) young, or produces relatively small gametes; staminate (*bot*); adapted to fit into a corresponding hollow part (*machinery*). — *n* a member of the male sex; apparently, a father (*Shakesp*). — **male chauvinist** or **male chauvinist pig** (*colloq*; *derog*) a man who believes in the superiority of men over women and behaves accordingly (*abbrev* **MCP**); **male'-fern** an elegant woodland fern formerly thought to be the male of the lady-fern; **male menopause** a critical period of change affecting late middle-aged men, often marked by decline in sexual power, loss of energy and decisiveness, etc; **male orchis** the early purple orchis (cf **Orchis**); **male order** (*archit*) the Doric order; **male rhymes** those in which stressed final syllables correspond; **male screw** see under **screw**. [OFr *male*, from L *masculus* male, from *mās* a male]

maleate. See under **malic**.

Malebolge *mä-lā-bol'jā, n* the eighth circle of Dante's Hell; a place characterized by filth or iniquity (*fig*). [Ital *male bolge* bad holes or pits, literally pockets]

malediction *mal-i-dik'shən, n* cursing; a calling down of evil, a curse. — *adj* **maledicent** (*-dī'sənt*) cursing. — *adj* **mal'edict** (*-dikt*; *archaic*) accursed. — *vt* and *vi* to curse. — *adj* **maledic'tive**. — *adj* **maledic'tory**. [L *maledīcere, -dictum*, from *male* ill, and *dīcere* to speak]

malefactor *mal'i-fak-tər, n* an evil-doer; a criminal. — *n* **malefac'tion** evil-doing; a crime, an offence (*Shakesp*). — *adj* (*rare*) **malefac'tory**. — *adj* **malefic** (*mə-lef'ik*) doing mischief; producing evil, baleful. — *adv* **malef'ically**. — *n* **mal'efice** (*-i-fis*; *archaic*) an evil deed; enchantment, sorcery. — *n* **maleficence** (*ef'i-səns*). — *adj* **malef'icent** or **maleficial** (*mal-i-fish'l*; *obs*) hurtful; wrong-doing. [L *malefacere* to do evil]

maleffect *mal-i-fekt', n* an adverse effect. [**mal-**]

maleic. See under **malic**.

malemute See **malamute**.

malengine *mal-en'jin*, (*Spenser*) *n* evil stratagem; deceit. [OFr *malengin*, from L *malus*, *-um* bad, and *ingenium* ingenuity]

malentendu *ma-lã-tã-dü*, (*Fr*) *n* a misunderstanding.

malevolent *mal-ev'ə-lənt*, *adj* wishing evil; ill disposed towards others; rejoicing in another's misfortune. — *n* **malev'olence**. — *adv* **malev'olently**. [L *malevolēns*, *-entis* ill disposed, wishing evil]

malfeasance *mal-fē'zəns*, *n* evil-doing, wrong-doing (*rare*); an illegal deed, *esp* by an official (*law*). — *adj* **malfea'sant**. [Fr *malfaisance*, from L *male* ill, and *facere* to do]

malformation *mal-för-mā'shən*, *n* (a) faulty structure; (a) deformity. — *adj* **malformed'**. **[mal-]**

malfunction *mal-fungk'shən*, *n* the act or fact of working imperfectly. — *vi* to work or function imperfectly. — *n* **malfunc'tioning**. **[mal-]**

malgrado *mal-grä'dō*, (*obs*) *prep* in spite of. [Ital]

malgre. Same as **maugre**.

malgré *mal-grā*, (*Fr*) *prep* in spite of. — **malgré lui, moi,** etc, in spite of his, my, etc efforts; willy-nilly; **malgré tout** (*too͞*) nevertheless, all things considered.

mali or **mallee** *mä'lē*, *n* a member of the gardener caste in India, etc. [Hindi *mālī*]

Malian *mä'li-ən*, *adj* of or relating to the Republic of *Mali* in W Africa. — *n* a native or citizen of Mali.

Malibu board *mal'i-boo͞ bōrd*, *n* a long, light surfing board equipped with fins. [*Malibu*, California]

malic *mā'lik*, *mal'ik*, *adj* obtained from apple juice, *esp* applied to an acid ($H_6C_4O_5$) found in unripe fruits. — *n* **ma'late** a salt or ester of malic acid. — *n* **maleate** (*mal'i-āt*) a salt or ester of maleic acid. — *adj* **maleic** (*mə-lē'ik*). — *n* **malonate** (*mal'ə-nāt*) a salt or ester of malonic acid. — **maleic acid** an acid, isomeric with fumaric acid, obtained from malic acid; **maleic hydrazide** a chemical used in retarding plant growth; **malonic acid** (*ma-lon'ik*) a white crystalline acid, $CH_2(COOH)_2$. [L *mālum* an apple; Gr *mēlon*]

malice *mal'is*, *n* ill-will; spite; disposition or intention to harm another or others; a playfully mischievous attitude of mind. — *vt* (*obs*) to have ill-will against; to wish to injure (*pa p* in *Spenser* **mal'ist**). — *adj* **malicious** (*mə-lish'əs*) bearing ill-will or spite; motivated by hatred or ill-will; mischievous. — *adv* **mali'ciously**. — *n* **mali'ciousness**. — **malice aforethought** (*law*) the predetermination to commit a crime *esp* against a person, ie serious injury or murder. [Fr, from L *malitia*, from *malus* bad]

malicho *mal'i-chō*, *-kō*, (*Shakesp*) *n* mischief. [Conjectured to represent Sp *malhecho* mischief]

malign *mə-līn'*, *adj* baleful; injurious; malignant. — *vt* to speak evil of, *esp* falsely and rancorously, to defame; to regard with malice or hatred (*obs*); to grudge (*obs*). — *n* **malign'er**. — *n* **malignity** (*mə-lig'ni-ti*) state or quality of being malign; a malicious act; great hatred, virulence; deadly quality. — *adv* **malign'ly**. — *n* **malign'ment**. [Fr *malin*, fem *maligne*, from L *malignus* for *maligenus* of evil disposition, from *malus* bad, and *gen-* root of *genus*]

malignant *mə-lig'nənt*, *adj* disposed to do harm; baleful; actuated by great hatred; Royalist or Cavalier (also with *cap*; *hist*); rebellious, disaffected (*obs*); tending to cause death, spreading or deteriorating rapidly, *esp* (of a tumor) cancerous (*pathol*). — *n* (*hist*; *usu* with *cap*) a Royalist or Cavalier. — *n* **malig'nance**. — *n* **malig'nancy**. — *adv* **malig'nantly**. [L *malignāns*, *-antis*, pr p of *malignāre* to act maliciously]

malik *mal'ik* or **melik** *mek'ik*, (*Ind*) *n* the head of a village; an owner; an employer. [Ar *mālik*]

Malines *mə-lēn'*. Same as **Mechlin**.

malinger *mə-ling'gər*, *vi* to feign sickness in order to avoid duty or work. — *n* **maling'erer**. — *n* **maling'ery** feigned sickness. [Fr *malingre* sickly]

malism *māl'izm*, *n* belief in the predominance of evil in the world. [L *malus* bad]

malison *mal'i-zn*, *-sn*, (*poetic*) *n* a curse (opposite *benison*). [OFr *maleison*; a doublet of **malediction**]

malist (*Spenser*). See under **malice**.

malkin *mö'kin*, *n* a dirty or lewd woman (*Shakesp*); a cat (*dialect*); a mop (*dialect*); a scarecrow (*dialect*); a hare (*Scot*). — Also **maw'kin**. [Dimin of *Matilda* or *Maud*]

mall *mal*, (*esp NAm*) *möl*, *n* a maul or heavy wooden hammer (*obs*); (a mallet used in) the old game of pall-mall (*hist*); a pall-mall alley (*hist*); (from a former alley of the kind in London) a level shaded walk; a public walk; a pedestrian shopping area or street, *esp* (*orig NAm*) an enclosed centre, often outside a town, with connected aisles of shops, restaurants, etc (*UK* also **shopping mall**). — *vt* to maul or beat. — **mall rat** (*US slang*) a person who spends much of their time in shopping malls. [See **maul** and **pall-mall**]

mallam *mal'əm*, *n* an African scribe, teacher or learned man. [Hausa]

mallander. See **malander**.

mallard *mal'ərd*, *n* a kind of wild duck common in the northern hemisphere, of which the male has a shiny green head. [OFr *mallart*, *malart*; origin obscure]

malleable *mal'i-ə-bəl*, *adj* able to be beaten, rolled, etc into a new shape (also *fig*). — *n* **malleabil'ity**. — *n* **mall'eableness**. [L *malleus* a hammer]

malleate *mal'i-āt*, *vt* to hammer; to beat thin. — *n* **malleā'tion** hammering; a hammer-mark. — *adj* **malleiform** (*mal'ē-i-förm*) hammer-shaped. — *n* **malleus** (*mal'i-əs*) any of the small bones of the middle ear in mammals. [Ety as for **malleable**]

mallecho. An editorial emendation of **malicho** (*Shakesp*).

mallee[1] *mal'ē*, *n* any of many small trees of the genus *Eucalyptus*, *esp Eucalyptus dumosa*; a mass of such trees (also **mallee scrub**); an arid area where mallee forms the predominant vegetation. — **mall'ee-bird, -fowl** or **-hen** an Australian mound-bird; **mallee gate** a makeshift gate. [Aboriginal]

mallee[2]. Same as **mali**.

malleiform. See under **malleate**.

mallemaroking *mal'i-mə-rō'king*, (*naut*; *rare*) *n* carousing of seamen in icebound ships. [Obs Du *mallemerok*, a romping woman, from *mal* foolish, and *marok*, from Fr *marotte* a favoured object]

mallemuck *mal'i-muk*, *n* the fulmar or similar bird. [Du *mallemok*, from *mal* foolish, and *mok* gull; Ger *Mallemuck*]

mallender. See **malander**.

malleolus *mə-lē'ə-ləs*, *n* a rounded bony projection on either side of the ankle. — *adj* **mallē'olar** (or *mal'i-*). [L *malleolus*, dimin of *malleus* hammer]

mallet *mal'it*, *n* a hammer with a large, *esp* wooden head; a soft-headed stick used to beat a gong, etc (*music*); a long-handled hammer for playing croquet or polo. [Fr *maillet*, dimin of *mail* a mall]

malleus. See under **malleate**.

malling jug *möl'ing jug*, *n* a type of tin-glazed jug produced in late 16c England. [From West *Malling* in Kent, where first found]

Mallophaga *mal-of'ə-gə*, *n pl* an order of wingless parasitic insects, bird-lice or biting-lice. — *adj* **malloph'agous**. [Gr *mallos* a flock of wool, and *phagein* to eat]

mallow *mal'ō*, *n* any plant of the genus *Malva*, from its emollient properties or its soft downy leaves; extended to other genera of *Malvaceae*; a mauve colour. [OE *m(e)alwe*, from L *malva*; Gr *malachē*, from *malassein* to soften]

malm *mäm*, *n* calcareous loam; earth of this kind, formerly used for making brick; an artificial mixture of clay and chalk. — Also **malm'stone**. [OE *m(e)alm* (*-stān*) a soft (stone)]

malmag *mal'mag*, *n* a nocturnal lemuroid monkey of the East Indies, the tarsier. [Philippine word]

malmsey *mäm'zi*, *n* a sort of grape; a strong, sweet wine, first made in Greece and exported from *Monembasia*. — Also **malvasia** (*mäl-vä-sē'ə*), **malvesie** (*mäl'və-zi*) or **malvoisie** (*mäl-voi'zi*). [LL *malmasia*; cf OFr *malvesie*, Fr *malvoisie*, Ital *malvasia*, Sp *malvasia*]

malnutrition *mal-nū-trish'ən*, *n* inadequate or faulty nutrition. **[mal-]**

malodour *mal-ō'dər*, *n* an unpleasant or offensive smell. — *adj* **malo'dorous**. — *n* **malo'dorousness**. [**mal-**]

malo-lactic *māl-ə-lak'tik*, *mal-*, *adj* concerning or involving the conversion of malic acid to lactic acid in the fermentation of wine.

malonate. See under **malic**.

malonic acid. See under **malic**.

Malpighia *mal-pig'i-ə*, *n* the Barbados cherry genus of tropical American trees, shrubs, and lianes, giving name to the family **Malpighiā'ceae** of the order *Geraniales*. — *adj* **Malpigh'ian** applied to several structures, *esp* in the kidney, investigated by Marcello *Malpighi* (1628–94), Italian anatomist.

malposition *mal-pə-zish'ən*, (chiefly *med*) *n* a wrong position, misplacement. [**mal-**]

malpractice *mal-prak'tis*, *n* an evil or improper practice; professional misconduct; treatment falling short of reasonable skill or care; the illegal attempt of a person in a position of trust to benefit at the expense of others. — *n* **malpractitioner** (*-tish'ən-ər*). [**mal-**]

malpresentation *mal-prez-ən-tā'shən*, *n* abnormal presentation in childbirth. [**mal-**]

mal soigné *mal swa-nyā*, (*Fr*) *adj* badly groomed, unkempt.

malstick. See **maulstick**.

malt *mölt*, *n* barley or other grain steeped in water, allowed to sprout, and dried in a kiln, used in brewing beer, etc; malt liquor, *esp* malt whisky; a malted milk drink (*US*). — *vt* to make into malt; to treat or combine with malt. — *vi* to become malt; to drink malt liquor (*facetious*). — *adj* containing or made with malt. — *n* **malt'ase** an enzyme that produces grape-sugar from maltose. — *adj* **malt'ed** containing or made with malt. — *n* **malt'ing** a building where malt is made. — *n* **malt'ose** a hard, white crystalline sugar, formed by the action of malt or diastase on starch. — *n* **malt'ster** a person who makes or deals in malt. — *adj* **malt'y**. — **malt'-dust** grain-sprouts produced and screened off in malt-making; **malted milk** (a drink made from) a powdered mixture of malted grains and dehydrated milk; **malt'-extract** a liquid extract obtained from malt and used as a flavouring in food; **malt'-floor** a perforated floor in the chamber of a malt-kiln, through which heat rises; **malt'-horse** a heavy horse of a kind formerly used by brewers; a dull, stupid person (*Shakesp*); **malt'-house**; **malting floor** a large store floor on which soaked grain is spread to germinate; **malt'-kiln**; **malt liquor** a liquor, such as beer or porter, formed from malt; **malt'-mill** a mill for grinding malt after drying in a kiln; **malt'man** a maltster; **malt tea** the liquid infusion of the mash in brewing; **malt vinegar** a strong-flavoured vinegar produced from malt liquor; **malt whisky** a whisky which is the product of one distillate of malted barley, etc, not a blend of several; **malt'worm** (*Shakesp*) a lover of malted liquors, a tippler. [OE *m(e)alt*; cf Ger *Malz*]

Malta *mol'*, *möl'tə*, *adj* of or relating to the island of Malta. — *adj* **Maltese** (*-tēz'*) of Malta, its people or their language. — *n* a native or inhabitant of Malta (*pl* **Maltese'**); the official language of Malta, Semitic with a strong Italian infusion. — **Malta fever** undulant fever, once common in Malta (see also **brucellosis**); **Maltese cross** the badge of the knights of Malta, a cross with four equal arms expanding from the centre, *usu* each with two points; (**maltese cross**) a mechanism providing intermittent frame-by-frame movement in a motion picture film projector (see *Geneva movement*); **Maltese dog** a very small spaniel with long silky hair. [L *Melita*, *from* Gr *Melitē*]

maltalent *mal'tal-ənt*, (*Spenser*) *n* ill-will. [Fr *mal* ill, and *talent* disposition; see **talent**[1]]

Maltese. See under **Malta**.

maltha *mal'thə*, *n* a thick mineral pitch; an ancient cement; mineral tar. [L, from Gr]

Malthusian *mal-thūz'i-ən*, *adj* relating to Thomas Robert *Malthus* (1766–1834), or to his teaching that the increase of population tends to outstrip that of the means of living. — *n* a disciple of Malthus. — *n* **Malthūs'ianism**.

maltreat *mal-trēt'*, *vt* to use roughly or unkindly. — *n* **maltreat'ment**. [Fr *maltraiter*, from L *male* ill, and *tractāre* to treat]

malva *mal'və*, *n* a plant of the mallow genus *Malva*, giving name to the family **Malvā'ceae**, including hollyhock, cotton, etc, related to the lime family. — *adj* **malvā'ceous**. [L; cf **mallow**]

malvasia. Same as **malmsey**.

malversation *mal-vər-sā'shən*, *n* dishonest or unethical conduct in office, such as bribery, extortion or embezzlement; corrupt administration (of funds). [Fr, from L *male* badly, and *versārī*, *-ātus* to occupy oneself]

malvesie or **malvoisie**. Same as **malmsey**.

mal vu *mal vü*, (*Fr*) *adj* looked upon with disapproval.

Mam *mam*, *n* (a member of) a S American Indian people of Guatemala; the Mayan language of this people. [Sp *mame*, from Amerindian]

mam *mam*, (*dialect*) *n* mother.

mama. See **mamma**[1].

mamba *mam'bə*, *n* a large, deadly African snake (*Dendraspis*), black or green. [Kaffir *im mamba* large snake]

mambo *mam'bō*, *n* a voodoo priestess; a Latin American dance or dance-tune of Haitian origin, resembling the rumba: — *pl* **mam'bos**. — *vi* to dance the mambo. [Am Sp, prob from Haitian]

mamee. See **mammee**.

mamelon *mam'ə-lən*, *n* a rounded hill or protuberance. [Fr, nipple]

mameluco *mam-e-lōō'kō*, *n* in Brazil, a person of mixed European and South American Indian parentage: — *pl* **mamelu'cos**. [Port; cf **Mameluke**]

Mameluke *mam'ə-lōōk*, (*hist*) *n* a member of a military force originally of Circassian slaves, forming the ruling class of Egypt from the mid 13c to the early 19c; a slave in a Muslim country, *esp* white. [Ar *mamlûk* a purchased slave, from *malaka* to possess]

mamilla or (*NAm*) **mammilla** *mam-il'ə*, *n* the nipple of the mammary gland; any nipple-shaped protuberance: — *pl* **mamill'ae** (*NAm -ē*). — *adj* **mam'illar** or **mam'illary** relating to the breast; nipple-shaped; studded with rounded projections. — *adj* **mam'illate** or **mam'illated** having mamillae; nipple-shaped. — *n* **mamillā'tion**. — *adj* **mamill'iform**. — *n* **mammillā'ria** a plant belonging to the *Mammillaria* genus of flowering cactus, with nipple-shaped tubercles in rows: — *pl* **mammilla'rias**. [L *mam(m)illa*, dimin of *mamma* breast]

mamma[1] or **mama** *mä-mä'* (*US mä'mə*), *n* mother (formerly considered genteel, now used chiefly by young children). — *n* **mammy** (*mam'i*) a child's word for mother; a Black nursemaid of White children (*US*). — **mamm'y-wagon** in West Africa, an open-sided bus. [Repetition of *ma*, a child's natural utterance]

mamma[2] *mam'ə*, *n* the milk gland; the breast: — *pl* **mamm'ae** (*-ē*). — *adj* **mamm'ary** of the nature of, or relating to, the mammae or breasts. — *adj* **mamm'ate** having breasts. — *n* **mammec'tomy** a mastectomy. — *n* **mamm'ifer** a mammal. — *adj* **mammif'erous** having mammae. — *adj* **mamm'iform** having the form of a breast. — *n* **mammilla** and **mammillaria** see under **mamilla**. — *adj* **mammogen'ic** (of hormones) promoting growth of the duct and alveolar systems of the milk gland. — *n* **mamm'ogram** or **mamm'ograph** an X-ray photograph of the breast. — *n* **mammog'raphy** radiological examination of the breast. — *n* **mamm'oplasty** plastic surgery to change the shape of the breasts, as by the use of silicone implants, etc. [L *mamma* breast]

mammal *mam'əl*, *n* a member of the **Mammalia** (*mə-mā'li-ə*), the class of animals that suckle their young. — *adj* **mammā'lian**. — *adj* **mammalif'erous** (*geol*) bearing remains of mammals. — *adj* **mammalog'ical**. — *n* **mammalogist** (*-al'ə-jist*). — *n* **mammal'ogy** the scientific study of mammals. [L *mammālis* of the breast, from *mamma* the breast]

mammary, **mammate** and **mammectomy**. See under **mamma²**.

mammee or **mamee** *mam-ē'*, *n* a fruit (also **mammee apple**) of the West Indies and surrounding regions, having a sweet taste and aromatic odour; the tree producing it (*Mammea americana*, family *Guttiferae*). — **mammee'-sapo'ta** the marmalade tree or its fruit. [Sp *mamey*, from Haitian]

mammer *mam'ər*, (*Shakesp*) *vi* to hesitate, to stand muttering and in doubt. [Prob imit]

mammet *mam'it*, **maumet**, **mawmet** *möm'it* or **mommet** *mom'it*, *n* an idol; a puppet, a figure dressed up (*Shakesp*). — *n* **mamm'etry**, **maum'etry** or **maw'metry** idolatry; idols collectively; Islam (*archaic*; *derog*). [**Mohammed**; cf **Mahoun** or **Mahound**]

mammifer and **mammiform**. See under **mamma²**.

mammilla. See **mamilla**.

mammock *mam'ək*, (*archaic* or *dialect*) *n* a broken or torn piece, a shred (also **mumm'ock**). — *vt* (*Shakesp*) to tear to pieces, to mangle. [Origin obscure]

mammogenic, **mammography**, etc. See under **mamma²**.

mammon *mam'ən*, *n* riches regarded as the root of evil; (with *cap*) the god of riches. — *adj* **mamm'onish** devoted to money-getting. — *n* **mamm'onism** devotion to gain. — *n* **mamm'onist** or **mamm'onite** a person devoted to riches; a worldling. — *adj* **mammonist'ic**. [LL *mam(m)ōna*, from Gr *mam(m)ōnās*, from Aramaic *māmōn* riches]

mammoplasty. See under **mamma²**.

mammoth *mam'əth*, *n* an extinct species of elephant of the Pleistocene age, with a thick, hairy coat and long upcurving tusks. — *adj* resembling the mammoth in size; gigantic. — **mamm'oth-tree** the sequoia. [Former Russ *mammot* (now *mamant* or *mamont*)]

mammy and **mammy-wagon**. See under **mamma¹**.

mamselle. See **mademoiselle**.

mamzer *mam'zər* or **momzer** *mom'zər*, *n* an illegitimate child, a child of an unrecognized marriage (*Judaism*); a detestable or untrustworthy person (often as a term of abuse; *US slang*): — *pl* **mam'zers** or **mom'zers**, **mam'zerim** or **mom'zerim**. [Yiddish, from Heb *mamzēr*]

Man. or **Manit**. *abbrev*: Manitoba.

man¹ *man*, *n* a human being; (*usu* with *cap*) mankind, the human genus (also in combination denoting a particular species of this); an adult human male; a male attendant or servant; a workman or male employee; a vassal; a follower; an uncommissioned soldier; a person possessing a distinctively manly character; a husband or male sexual partner; a piece used in playing chess, draughts, etc; a cairn or rock pillar; a hill with such a man; a ship, as in *man*-of-war; a word of familiar address; (*usu* in *pl*; with *cap*) in the Scottish Highlands, any of a group of men of strict religious belief, regarded as spiritual leaders in a parish (*hist*): — *pl* **men**. — *adj* and *combining form* male. — *vt* to provide with a man or men; to provide with a (human) worker, operator, etc; to strengthen or put manhood into; to accustom (a hawk) to being handled, *esp* by strangers (*falconry*): — *pr p* **mann'ing**; *pa t* and *pa p* **manned** (*mand*). — *n* **man'dom** (*rare*) humanity, man collectively. — *adj* **man'ful** having the good qualities of a man; manly; bold; courageous; vigorous; stout; noble-minded. — *adv* **man'fully**. — *n* **man'fulness**. — *n* **man'hood** the state of being a man; manly quality; human nature. — *n* **mankind'** the human race, the mass of human beings; (*man'kīnd*) human males collectively. — *adj* (*Shakesp*) man-like, viragoish. — *adj* **man'-like** having the appearance or qualities of a human being or of an adult human male. — *adv* in the manner of a man; in a way that might be expected of a man; manfully. — *n* **man'liness**. — *adj* **man'ly** befitting a man; brave; dignified; noble; relating to manhood; not childish or womanish. — *adj* **manned** (*mand*). — *adj* **mann'ish** (of a child or woman) resembling or behaving like an adult male (*usu derog*); masculine. — *n* **mann'ishness**. — **man-about-town'** a fashionable, sophisticated man. — *adj* **man-and-dog'** (of an enterprise, organization, etc) extremely small-scale, minimally-staffed. — **man-at-arms'** a soldier, *esp* mounted and heavily-armed; **man'-body** (*Scot*) a man; **man'-child** (*literary*) a male child; a boy: — *pl* **men'-children**; **man'-day** a day's work by one person: — *pl* **man'-days**; **man'-eater** a cannibal; a tiger or other animal that has acquired the habit of eating humans; a shark that eats human flesh; a woman given to acquiring and dispatching male lovers (*colloq*). — *adj* **man'-entered** (*Shakesp*) passed from boyhood into manhood. — **Man Friday** a factotum or servile attendant (from Robinson Crusoe's man). — *vt* **man'handle** to move by manpower; to handle or treat roughly (*orig slang*). — **man'hole** a hole large enough to admit a person, *esp* to a sewer, cable-duct, etc; **manhood suffrage** right to vote accorded to male citizens; **man'-hour** an hour's work by one person: — *pl* **man'-hours**; **man'hunt** an organized search for a person, *esp* one mounted by police, etc, for a criminal; **man-jack'** or **man jack** individual man (as *every man-jack*); **man-machine interface** (*comput*) the device or method by which a user communicates with a computer, eg a keyboard or mouse. — *adj* **man'-made** made by man; humanly made or originated; (of fibre, fabric, etc) artificial, synthetic. — **man-man'agement** the organization of the work of members of staff; **man-mill'iner** (*literary*) a male milliner; a man with frivolous interests or concerns (*archaic*; *derog*). — *adj* **man-mind'ed** having the mind or qualities of a man. — **man-of-war'** or **man-o'-war'** a warship; a soldier (*archaic* or *facetious*); (in full **man-of-war bird**) the frigate-bird; (see also **Portuguese man-of-war**): — *pl* **men-of-war'** or **men-o'-war'**; **man'-of-war's-man** a man who serves on board a warship; **man'-orchid** an orchid (*Aceras anthropophora*) whose flowers have a human-like shape; **man'pack** a package of supplies or equipment designed to be carried by one person; **man'power** the agency or energy of people in doing work; the rate at which a person can work; available resources in population or in able-bodied people; **Manpower Services Commission** the former name for the **Training Agency**; **man'-queller** (*Shakesp*) a man-killer, a murderer; **man'rider** or **manriding train** the formal name for a paddy (train) (qv). — *adj* **man'riding** used of equipment on oil rigs that is used by personnel and is built to a higher standard of safety than material-handling systems. — **man'-servant** a male servant: — *pl* **men'-servants**; **man'shift** the work done by one person in one shift or work period. — *adj* **man'-size** or **man'-sized** suitable for, or requiring, a man; very big (*colloq*). — **man'slaughter** the killing of a man; unlawful homicide without malice aforethought (*law*); **man'-slayer** a person who kills a man; **man'-stealer** a person who steals people, *esp* to make slaves of them; **man'trap** a trap for catching trespassers; any source of potential danger; **man'-watching** the study of body language; **man'-week** or **man'-year** a week's or year's work by one person: — *pl* **man'-weeks** or **man'-years**; **men'folk** or **men'folks** male people, *esp* a woman's male relatives; **mens'wear** clothing for men. — **as one man** all together; unanimously; **be one's own man** to be independent, not answerable to anyone else; **be someone's man** to be exactly the person someone is seeking for a particular purpose; **man alive** an exclamation of surprise; **man in the moon** a supposed likeness of a man's face seen on the surface of the moon; the fanciful character of children's rhymes, etc, derived from this; **man in the street** the ordinary, everyday man; Tom, Dick, or Harry; **man of business** (*esp Scot*) an agent or a lawyer; **man of God** a holy man; a clergyman; **man of his hands** a man of prowess; **man of law** a lawyer; **man of letters** a scholar; a writer; **man of sin** the devil; Antichrist; **man of skill** (*Scots law*) an expert witness; **man of straw** a person of no substance (*esp* financially); one nominally, but not really, responsible; a sham opponent or argument set up for the sake of disputation; **man of the match** the most outstanding player in a cricket, football, etc match (also *fig*); **man of the moment** the man (most capable of) dealing with the present situation; **man of the world** a man with experience of the pains and (*esp* sexual) pleasures of life; **man to man** one man to another as individuals in fight or talk; frank and confidential; **men in grey suits** unseen establishment figures holding the ultimate power in an organization, political party, etc; **men's movement** a movement begun in the US as a counterpart to the women's movement (qv), aiming to overturn the traditional male stereotype; **old man of the sea** see under **old**; **our man in ...** a company or government representative in, or journalist covering, a particular area; **to a man** without exception. [OE *mann*; Ger *Mann*, Du *man*]

man[2]. See **mun**[1].

mana *mä'nä*, (*anthropol*) *n* a supernatural power associated with people and things. [Maori]

manacle *man'ə-kl*, *n* a handcuff. — *vt* to handcuff; to shackle. [OFr *manicle*, from L *manicula*, dimin of *manica* sleeve, glove, handcuff, from *manus* hand]

manage *man'ij*, *vt* to train (a horse, etc) by exercise; to handle; to wield; to conduct; to control; to administer, be at the head of; to deal tactfully with; to husband, use sparingly (*archaic*); to contrive successfully; to have time for; to be able to cope with; to manipulate; to contrive; to bring about. — *vi* to conduct affairs; to get on, contrive to succeed. — *n* (*archaic*) (a) manège. — *n* **manageabil'ity** the quality of being manageable. — *adj* **man'ageable** that can be managed; governable. — *n* **man'ageableness**. — *adv* **man'ageably**. — *n* **man'agement** the art or act of managing; the manner of directing or of using anything; administration; skilful treatment; a body of managers. — *n* **man'ager** a person who manages; in an industrial firm or business, a person who deals with administration and with the design and marketing, etc of the product, as opposed to its actual construction; a person who organizes other people's activities; a person legally appointed to manage a business, property, etc as receiver; a party leader (*US*). — *n* **man'ageress** a female manager (not *usu* used in official titles). — *adj* **managē'rial** of or relating to a manager, or to management. — *n* **managē'rialism** the adoption of business methods and management structures in the running of public services, etc. — *adj* **managerialist**. — *n* **man'agership**. — *adj* **man'aging** handling; controlling; administering; contriving; domineering. — **managed fund** a unit-linked insurance or savings plan, etc, invested by professional managers; **management accountant** a cost-accountant producing information upon which managerial decisions are based; **management accounting** cost-accounting to facilitate the management of a business; **management buy-in** the purchase of a controlling share in a company by an outside management with support from banks, etc; **management buyout** the purchase, by its management, of the majority of the shares in a company, *esp* when an outside takeover is imminent; **management consultant** a specialist who advises firms on the most efficient procedures applicable to particular businesses or industries; **management consulting**; **management information system** (*comput*) a computerized system providing information for managerial decision-making; **managing director** a director in overall charge of an organization, often carrying out the decisions of a board of directors. [Ital *maneggio*, from L *manus* the hand]

manakin *man'ə-kin*, *n* a small passerine bird (family *Pipridae*) of tropical C and S America, related to the Cotinga family; (*erroneously*) a manikin. [See **manikin**]

mañana *man-yä'nə*, *män-yä'nä*, (*Sp*) *n* and *adv* tomorrow; (at) an unspecified time in the future.

manatee or **manati** *man-ə-tē'*, *n* a large aquatic herbivorous mammal (*Manatus* or *Trichechus*) of the warm parts of the Atlantic and the rivers of Brazil. [Sp *manatí*, from Carib *manatoui*; not connected with L *manus* hand]

mancala *man-kä'lə*, *n* any of several varieties of board game played in Africa and S Asia, using a board with rows of holes containing the pieces to be captured. [Ar *mangala*, from *nagala* to move]

mancando *mangk-an'dō*, (*music*) *adj* and *adv* fading away. [Ital, lacking]

manche *mänsh*, (*heraldry*) *n* a sleeve. [Fr]

Manchester *man'chis-tər*, *adj* belonging to or made in *Manchester*, or similar to goods made in Manchester, applied *esp* to cotton cloths. — **Manchester school** the followers of Bright and Cobden, advocates of free-trade and of individual freedom of action; **Manchester terrier** an English breed of small short-haired black-and-tan dog.

manchet *man'chit*, *n* the finest grade of wheat bread (*obs*); a round loaf or roll of this (*archaic* or *dialect*); a charge representing a loaf of manchet (*heraldry*). [Origin obscure]

manchineel *manch-i-nēl'*, *n* a tropical American tree (*Hippomane*) of the spurge family, with poisonous latex. [Sp *manzanilla*, dimin of *manzana* apple]

Manchu or **Manchoo** *man-chōō'*, *man'*, *n* a member of the Mongoloid race from which the NE Chinese region of Manchuria took its name, and which governed China from the 17c until 1912; the Ataic language of this people. — *adj* of or relating to the Manchus, their language, or to Manchuria. — *adj* **Manchur'ian**. [Manchu, pure]

mancipation *man-si-pā'shən*, (*Roman hist*) *n* a legal transfer by actual or symbolic sale. — *vt* **man'cipate**. — *adj* **man'cipatory** (*-pə-tə-ri*). [L *mancipātiō*, *-ōnis*, from *manus* hand, and *capere* to take]

manciple *man'si-pl*, *n* a steward; a purveyor, *esp* of a college or an inn of court. [OFr, from L *manceps*, *-cipis* a purchaser: see above]

Mancunian *man(g)-kūn'i-ən*, *adj* belonging to Manchester. — *n* a person born or living in Manchester. [Doubtful L *Mancunium* (*prob an error for Mamucium*), a Roman station in Manchester]

mancus *mang'kəs*, (*hist*) *n* an old English coin or its value, thirty pence: — *pl* **manc'uses**. [OE *mancus*]

-mancy *-man-si*, *-mən-si*, *combining form* divination (by a specified method). — **-mantic** *adj combining form* relating to (a specified form of) divination. [Gr *manteiā*]

mand (*Spenser*). Same as **manned**. See **man**[1].

Mandaean *man-dē'ən*, *n* and *adj* (a member) of an ancient S Babylonian sect, surviving in Iraq, their religion a corrupt Gnosticism, with many Jewish and Parsee elements (also called *Mendaites*, *Nasoraeans*, *Sabians*, or *Christians of St John*); (in, of, or relating to) the Aramaic dialect of their sacred books. — Also *adj*. [Mandaean *mandayyā* knowledge, gnosis]

mandala *mun'də-lə*, *n* in Buddhism and Hinduism, a pictorial symbol of the universe, *usu* a circle enclosing images of deities or geometric designs, often arranged in fours, used as an aid to religious meditation; in Jungian psychology, a symbol of the self, the wholeness or symmetry of the image corresponding to the degree of harmony in the self. [Sans *maṇḍala*]

mandamus *man-dā'məs*, (*law*) *n* a writ or command issued by a higher court to a lower: — *pl* **mandā'muses**. [L *mandāmus* we command]

mandarin *man'də-rin*, *-rēn*, *n* a member of any of nine ranks of officials under the Chinese Empire (*hist*); a statuette of a seated Chinese figure, often with a movable head (a *nodding mandarin*); (with *cap*) the most widely spoken form of Chinese, the official language of China; a high-ranking official or bureaucrat; a person of standing in the literary world, often one who tends to be reactionary or pedantic; (also **man'darine** or **mandarin orange**) a small kind of orange (of Chinese origin); its colour; a liqueur. — *adj* relating to a mandarin or mandarins; (of style or language) formal and ornate. — *n* **man'darinate** the rank or office of a mandarin; mandarins as a group. — **mandarin collar** or **neck** a high, narrow, stand-up collar the front ends of which do not quite meet; **mandarin duck** a crested Asiatic duck (*Aix galericulata*). [Port *mandarim*, from Malay (from Hindi) *mantrī* counsellor, from Sans *mantra* counsel]

mandate *man'dāt*, *n* a charge; a command from a superior official or judge to a subordinate, ordering him how to act, *esp* from the Pope to a legate, etc; legal authorization given to a person, eg a Member of Parliament to act on behalf of another; a rescript of the Pope; permission to govern according to declared policies, regarded as officially granted by an electorate to a particular political party or leader upon the decisive outcome of an election; the power conferred upon a state by the League of Nations in 1919 to govern a region elsewhere; (also with *cap*) any of the regions governed in this way (also **mandated territory**). — *vt* **mandate'** to assign by mandate; to invest with authority. — *n* **man'datary** or **man'datory** (*-də-tə-ri*) the holder of a mandate; a mandate. — *n* **mandā'tor** the giver of a mandate. — *adj* **man'datory** containing a mandate or command; of the nature of a mandate; bestowed by mandate; compulsory; allowing no option. [L *mandātum*, from *mandāre*, from *manus* hand, and *dare* give]

mandible *man'di-bl*, *n* a jaw or jawbone, *esp* the lower; either part of a bird's bill; an organ performing the functions of a jaw in the lower animals, such as one of the first pair of mouth appendages in insects or crustaceans. — *adj* **mandib'ular** relating to the jaw or jawbone. — *adj* **mandib'ulate** or **mandib'ulated**. [L *mandibula*, from *mandere* to chew]

mandilion. See **mandylion**.

Mandingo *man-ding'gō*, *n* an African people of the Niger valley; a member of this people; their language: — *pl* **Manding'o**, **Manding'oes** or **Manding'os**. — Also *adj*.

mandioc, **mandioca**, **mandiocca**. See **manioc**.

Man. Dir. *abbrev*: Managing Director.

mandir *mun'dər* or **mandira** *mun'dərä*, *n* a Hindu or Jain temple. [Hindi]

mandolin or **mandoline** *man'də-lin*, *-lēn*, *n* a round-backed instrument like a lute, sustained notes being played by repeated plucking; a kitchen utensil with a blade for slicing vegetables, etc. — *n* **mandō'la** or **mandō'ra** a large mandoline. [Ital *mandola*, *mandora*, dimin *mandolino*]

mandorla *man'dör-lə*, *n* an oval panel, or a work of art filling one; the vesica piscis. [Ital, almond]

mandrake *man'drāk*, *n* a poisonous plant (*Mandragora*) of the potato family, formerly thought to have magical powers because of the human-like shape of its forked root; extended to various other plants, such as white bryony. — Also (*Shakesp*) **mandragora** (*-drag'ə-rə*). [L *mandragora*, from Gr *mandragorās*]

mandrel or **mandril** *man'drəl*, *n* a bar of iron fitted to a turning-lathe on which articles to be turned are fixed; the axle of a circular saw. [Fr *mandrin*]

mandrill *man'dril*, *n* a large West African baboon with a red and blue muzzle and hindquarters. [Prob **man**[1] and **drill**[2]]

manducate *man'dū-kāt*, (*formal*) *vt* to chew or eat. — *adj* **man'ducable**. — *n* **manducā'tion**. — *adj* **man'ducatory** (*-kə-tə-ri*). [L *mandūcāre*, from *mandere* to chew]

mandylion or **mandilion** *man-dil'i-ən*, *n* a loose outer garment worn eg by soldiers over their armour (*hist*); (with *cap*) the name given to a cloth supposedly bearing the imprint of Christ's face, known in Orthodox Christianity as the Image of Edessa (modern Urfa in Turkey) from where it was taken to Constantinople in 944 and finally lost in the sack of 1204. [MFr *mandillon* cloak, and Late Gr *mandylion* cloth; cf ultimately L *mantel(l)um* napkin or cloak, and L *mantele*, *mantelium* napkin]

mane *mān*, *n* long hair on the back of the neck and neighbouring parts of a horse, lion, etc; a long bushy head of hair. — *adj* **maned**. — *adj* **mane'less**. — **mane'sheet** a covering for the upper part of a horse's head. [OE *manu*; ON *mön*; Ger *Mähne*]

-mane *-mān*, *combining form* an enthusiast or devotee (of a specified thing). [Gr *maniā*]

manège *man-ezh'*, *n* the managing of horses; the art of horsemanship or of training horses; the actions and paces learned by an individual horse; a riding-school. — *vt* to train (a horse). [Fr; cf **manage**]

maneh. Same as **mina**[1].

manes *mā'nēz*, (*Roman mythol*) *n pl* the spirits of the dead. [L *mānēs*]

manet *ma'net*, (*L*) as a stage direction, (he or she) remains on stage: — *pl* **manent**.

maneuver. US spelling of **manoeuvre**.

mang *mang*, (*archaic slang*) *vi* and *vt* to speak or talk (in). [Perh a corruption of **mag**[2]]

manga *mang'ga*, *n* a type of adult comic book popular in Japan. [Jap]

mangabeira *mang-ga-bā'rə*, *n* a Brazilian apocynaceous rubber tree (*Hancornia speciosa*). [Port, from Tupí *mangaba*]

mangabey *mang'gə-bā*, *n* the white-eyelid monkey, any species of the mainly West African genus *Cercocebus*, *esp* the sooty mangabey. [From a district in Madagascar, where, however, they are not found]

mangal *mang-gäl'*, *n* a brazier. [Turk]

mangalsutra *mang-gəl-soo'trə*, *n* a bead necklace worn by a married Hindu woman whose husband is living. [Sans]

manganese *mang-gə-nēz'*, *mang'*, *n* a hard brittle greyish-white metallic element (symbol **Mn**; atomic no 25); (*orig* and commercially) its dioxide (*black manganese*) or other ore. — *n* **mang'anate** a salt of manganic acid. — *adj* **manganic** (*-gan'ik*) of manganese of higher valency. — *adj* **manganif'erous** containing manganese. — *n* **Mang'anin**® an alloy of copper with manganese and some nickel. — *n* **mang'anite** a salt of manganous acid (*chem*); a grey ore, hydrated oxide of manganese (*mineralogy*). — *adj* **mang'anous** of manganese of lower valency. — **manganese bronze** a bronze or brass with a little manganese; **manganese spar** rhodochrosite; **manganese steel** a very hard, shock-resistant steel containing a higher than usual percentage of manganese; **manganic acid** a hypothetical acid existing only in solution. [Fr *manganèse*, from Ital *manganese*, from L *magnēsia*]

mange. See under **mangy**.

mangel-wurzel *mang'gl-wûr'zl* or **mangold-wurzel** *man'-gold-*, *n* a variety of beet cultivated as cattle food. — Also **mang'el** or **mang'old**. [Ger *Mangold* beet, and *Wurzel* root]

manger *mānj'ər*, *n* a trough from which horses and cattle take food. — **dog in the manger** see under **dog**[1]. [OFr *mangeoire*, from L *mandūcāre* to chew, eat]

mangetout *mãzh-too*, *n* a type of pea cooked and eaten together with its pod. — Also **mangetout pea** or **sugar pea**. [Fr, literally eat-all]

mangey. See **mangy**.

mangle[1] *mang'gl*, *vt* to hack, tear, or crush into a misshapen state; to mutilate or disfigure; to bungle (*fig*); to distort; to spoil. — *n* **mang'ler**. [Anglo-Fr *mangler*, *mahangler*, prob a frequentative of OFr *mahaigner* to maim, from *mahaing* a hurt]

mangle[2] *mang'gl*, *n* a rolling-press for smoothing linen; a similar (*usu* hand-turned) device with rollers for squeezing the water out of wet washing. — *vt* to smooth with a mangle, to calender; to squeeze the water out of with a mangle. — *n* **mang'ler**. [Du *mangel*, from Gr *manganon*; cf **mangonel**]

mango *mang'gō*, *n* a tropical, *orig* East Indian, tree (*Mangifera indica*) of the cashew-nut family; its yellowish-red fleshy fruit; a green musk-melon pickled: — *pl* **mang'oes**. — **wild mango** an African tree of the Simarubaceae with edible fruit, oil-giving seed, and termite-resistant wood. [Port *manga*, from Malay *manggā*, from Tamil *mān-kāy* mango-fruit]

mangold and **mangold-wurzel**. See **mangel-wurzel**.

mangonel *mang'gə-nel*, (*hist*) *n* a medieval war engine for throwing stones, etc. [OFr, from LL *mangonum*, from Gr *manganon*]

mangosteen *mang'gə-stēn*, *n* a tree, *Garcinia mangostana*, or its orange-shaped fruit, with thick, dark brown rind and juicy rose-coloured flesh. — Also **mang'ostan**. [Malay *mangustan*]

mangouste. See **mongoose**.

mangrove *mang'grōv*, *n* a tree, *esp* a species of Rhizophora, that grows in muddy swamps covered at high tide or on tropical coasts and estuary shores. [Origin obscure]

mangy, **mangey** *mānj'i* or **maungy** *mön'ji*, (*dialect*) *adj* scabby; affected with mange; shabby, seedy; mean, cowardly. — *n* **mange** (*mānj*; a back-formation) inflammation of the skin of animals caused by mites. — *n* **mang'iness**. [Fr *mangé* eaten, pa p of *manger*, from L *mandūcāre* to chew]

manhandle. See under **man**[1].

Manhattan *man-hat'ən*, *n* a cocktail consisting of vermouth, whisky, Angostura bitters, and curaçao or marashino. [*Manhattan*, New York]

manhole, **manhood** and **manhunt**. See under **man**[1].

mani *män'i*, *n* a stone prayer wall in a Tibetan Buddhist temple, *usu* carved with sacred images or texts. — Also **mani wall**. [Tibetan *máni*, from Sans *maṇi* precious stone]

mania *mā'ni-ə*, *n* a mental illness characterized by euphoria, excessively rapid speech and violent, destructive actions (*psychiatry*); the elated phase of manic-depressive psychosis (*psychiatry*); excessive or unreasonable desire; a craze. — *combining form* **-mānia** an abnormal and obsessive desire or inclination, or, more loosely, an extreme enthusiasm, for a specified thing. — *combining form* **-māniac** forming nouns and adjectives. — *n* **mā'niac** a person affected with (a) mania; a madman. — *adj* affected by or relating to (a) mania; raving mad. — *adj* **maniacal** (*mə-nī'ə-kl*). — *adv* **mani'acally**. — *adj* **manic** (*man'ik*) of or affected by mania. — *adv* **man'ically**. — **man'ic-depress'ive** a person suffering from manic-depressive psychosis. — Also *adj.* — **manic-depressive psychosis** a form of mental illness characterized by phases of depression and elation, either alone or alternately, with lucid intervals. [L, from Gr *maniā*]

Manichean or **Manichaean** *man-i-kē'ən*, *adj* relating to, following, or designating the beliefs of *Mani* or *Manichaeus*, a native of Ecbatana (c.216–c.276 AD), who taught that everything sprang from two chief principles, light and darkness, or good and evil. — *n* a believer in Manicheanism — also **Man'ichee**. — *n* **Maniche'anism**, **Man'icheism**, **Manichae'anism** or **Man'ichaeism** any belief in radical dualism.

manicure *man'i-kūr*, *n* the care of hands and nails; professional treatment for the hands and nails; a practitioner of this. — *vt* to apply manicure to. — *n* **man'icurist**. [L *manus* hand, and *cūra* care]

manifest *man'i-fest*, *adj* that may be easily seen by the eye or perceived by the mind; in Freudian psychoanalysis, applied to those parts of a dream remembered on waking (opposite of **latent**). — *vt* to make clear or easily seen; to put beyond doubt; to reveal or declare. — *n* the act of showing something publicly; (the form of) an apparition, ghost, etc; an open or public statement; a list or invoice of the cargo of a ship or aeroplane, used by customs officials and overseas agents; a list of passengers carried by an aeroplane. — *adj* **manifest'able** or **manifest'ible** that can be manifested or clearly shown. — *n* **manifestā'tion** act of disclosing what is dark or secret; that by which something is manifested; display; a mass-meeting, public procession or demonstration. — *adj* **manifest'ative**. — *adv* **man'ifestly** obviously, undoubtedly. — *n* **man'ifestness** the state of being manifest. [L *manifestus*, prob from *manus* the hand, and *festus* pa p of obs *fendere* to strike, to dash against (as in *offendere*)]

manifesto *man-i-fest'ō*, *n* a public written declaration of the intentions, opinions, or motives of a sovereign or of a leader, party, or body: — *pl* **manifest'os** or **manifest'oes**. — *vi* (*rare*) to issue a manifesto. [Ital; see **manifest**]

manifold *man'i-fōld*, *adj* various in kind or quality; many in number; having many features; performing several functions. — *n* a pipe with several lateral outlets to others, as in the exhaust system of the internal-combustion engine; an aggregate (*math*); a topological space or surface that is related in a particular way to Euclidean space (*math*); a carbon-copy; the manyplies (*dialect*; also in *pl*). — *vt* to multiply; to make simultaneous copies of. — *n* **man'ifolder**. — *adv* **man'ifoldly**. — *n* **man'ifoldness**. — **man'ifold-paper** thin paper for making copies; **man'ifold-writer** a copying apparatus. [**many**, and sfx **-fold**]

maniform *man'i-förm*, *adj* having the form of a hand. [L *manus* the hand, and *fōrma* a shape]

manihoc. See **manioc**.

Manihot *man'i-hot*, *n* a tropical American genus of the spurge family, including manioc. [**manioc**]

manikin or **mannikin** *man'i-kin*, *n* a dwarf; an anatomical model of a human body used for teaching purposes, as in art and medicine; a mannequin; a bird of the weaver-finch family found chiefly in S Asia and N Australia; (erroneously) a manakin. [Du *manneken*, a double dimin of *man*; Eng **man**[1]]

manila or **manilla** *mə-nil'ə*, *n* a cheroot or small cigar made in *Manila*; the fibre of the abaca plant; strong brownish paper *orig* made from abaca plant fibre. — **Manila** (or **Manilla**) **hemp** abaca plant fibre.

manilla *mə-nil'ə*, *n* a horseshoe-shaped ring used *esp* for ceremonial exchanges in parts of W Africa. [Sp, from LL *manilia* a bracelet, from L *manus* the hand, or L *monīlia* (pl of *monīle*) necklace, influenced by *manus*]

manille *mə-nil'*, *n* in the card games ombre and quadrille, the highest card but one. [Sp *malilla*]

manioc *man'i-ok*, *n* a plant of the Manihot genus, cassava; meal obtained from the root of this plant. — Also **man'dioc**, **mandio'ca**, **mandio'cca** and **man'ihoc**. [Tupí *mandioca*]

maniple *man'i-pl*, *n* a company of foot-soldiers in the Roman army (*hist*); (in the Western Christian Church) a clerical vestment used during the sacrament, a narrow strip worn on the left arm. — *adj* and *n* **manipular** (*mə-nip'ū-lər*). [L *manipulus*, from *manus* the hand, and *plēre* to fill]

maniplies. Same as **manyplies**.

manipular. See under **maniple** and **manipulate**.

manipulate *mə-nip'ū-lāt*, *vt* to work with the hands; to handle or manage; to give a false appearance to, change the character, etc, of; to turn to one's own purpose or advantage. — *adj* **manip'ulable** or **manip'ulatable** capable of being manipulated. — *adj* **manip'ular**, **manip'ulative** or **manip'ulatory** tending or attempting to manipulate. — *n* **manipulā'tion**. — *n* **manip'ulātor** a person who manipulates; a mechanical device for handling small, remote, or radioactive objects. — See also **master-slave manipulator** under **master**. [LL *manipulāre*, *-ātum*; see **maniple**]

Manis *mā'nis*, *n* the pangolin or scaly ant-eater. [Appar intended as sing of **manes**]

manitou *man'i-tōō*, *n* a spirit or sacred object among certain North American Indian tribes: — *pl* **man'itous**. — Also **manito** (*-tō*). [Algonquin]

manjack *man'jak*, *n* a W Indian boraginaceous tree (*Cordia macrophylla*); its fruit.

man-jack, **mankind**. See under **man**[1].

manky *mang'ki*, (*slang*; *orig Scot* and *dialect*) *adj* filthy, dirty, rotten. [Obs Scot *mank* defective, from OFr *manc*]

manly. See under **man**[1].

manna *man'ə*, *n* the food miraculously provided for the Israelites in the wilderness (*Bible*); delicious food for body or mind; anything advantageous happening to one as by divine intervention or fate; a sugary substance exuded from the **mann'a-ash** (*Fraxinus ornus*) or **mann'a-larch (Briançon manna)**, and other trees, from a species of tamarisk, from Alhagi, etc; edible fragments of the **mann'a-lichen** (*Lecanora*); float-grass seeds; honey-dew. — *adj* **mannif'erous**. — *n* **mann'ite** or **mann'itol** a sweet alcohol, $C_6H_8(OH)_6$, obtained from manna, from seaweeds of the genus Laminaria, etc. — *n* **mann'ose** a sugar ($C_6H_{12}O_6$) obtained by oxidizing mannitol. — **mann'a-croup** (*-kro͞op'*; Russ *krupa*) or **mann'a-groats** grains of manna-grass; **mann'a-dew** manna imagined to be solidified dew; **mann'a-grass** an aquatic grass (*Glyceria*) with edible seeds, float-grass. [Heb *mān hū* what is it?, or from *man* a gift]

mannequin *man'i-kin*, *n* a dummy figure, as used for display in shop windows, etc; a person, *usu* a woman, employed to wear and display clothes. [Fr, from Du; see **manikin**]

manner[1] *man'ər*, *n* the way in which anything is done; method; fashion; personal style of acting or bearing; custom; style of writing or of thought; sort (of; formerly often with omission of following *of*); style; (in *pl*) morals (*archaic*); (in *pl*) social conduct; (in *pl*) good behaviour. — *adj* **mann'ered** having manners (*esp* in combination, as *well-* or *ill-mannered*); affected with mannerism; artificial; stilted. — *n* **mann'erism** a constant sameness of manner; stiltedness; a marked peculiarity or trick of style or manner, *esp* in literary composition; manner or style becoming wearisome by its sameness; (*usu* with *cap*) a late 16c style of painting and architecture, *esp* in Italy, characterized by distortion of the human figure, bright harsh colours, etc. — *n* **mann'erist** a person inclined to mannerism; (*usu* with *cap*) an artist working in the style of Mannerism. — Also as *adj*. — *adj* **manneris'tic**. — *adv* **manneris'tically**. — *n* **mann'erliness**. — *adj* **mann'erly** showing good manners; well-behaved; not rude. — *adv* with good manners; civilly; respectfully; without rudeness. — **all manner of** all kinds of; **by no manner of means** under no circumstances; in no way whatever; **in a manner** in a certain way; **make one's manners** (*archaic*) to salute a person on meeting by a bow, curtsy, etc; **shark's manners** (*colloq*) rapacity; **to the manner born** accustomed to something (as if) from birth; naturally suited to a particular thing. [Fr *manière*, from *main*, from L *manus* the hand]

manner[2] *man'ər*, *n*. See **mainor**.

manniferous. See under **manna**.

mannikin. See **manikin**.

manning, mannish. See under **man**[1].

mannite, mannitol, mannose. See under **manna**.

mano *mä'nō*, *n* (in Mexico, the southwestern USA, etc) a stone roller for grinding maize or other grain by hand on a metate (qv): — *pl* **man'os**. [Sp, hand, from L *manus*]

manoao *mä'nō-ow*, *n* a shrub of the heath group: — *pl* **ma'noaos**. [Maori]

manoeuvre or (*NAm*) **maneuver** *ma-no͞o'vər*, *-nū'*, *n* a piece of skilful management; a stratagem; a skilful and clever movement in military or naval tactics; any movement skilfully or cleverly executed; (*usu* in *pl*) a large-scale battle-training exercise of armed forces. — *vi* and *vt* to perform a manoeuvre; to manage skilfully; to change the position of troops or ships; to effect or gain by manoeuvres. — *n* **manoeuvrabil'ity**. — *adj* **manoeu'vrable**. — *n* **manoeu'vrer**. — (*NAm*) **maneuverabil'ity**, etc. [Fr *manœuvre*, from L *manū* by hand, and *opera* work; cf **manure**]

manometer *man-om'i-tər*, *n* an instrument for measuring and comparing the pressure of fluids. — *adj* **manometric** (*man-ō-met'rik*) or **manomet'rical**. — *n* **manom'etry**. [Gr *manos* rare, thin, and *metron* measure]

ma non troppo *ma non trop'ō*, (*music*) *adv* but not too much. — See also **troppo**. [Ital]

manor *man'ər*, *n* the land belonging to a nobleman, or the part of this formerly reserved for his own use, including the manor-house; the district over which the court of the lord of the manor had authority (*hist*); a tract of land in N America for which a fee-farm rent was paid (*hist*); an area or base of operation, *esp* a police district (*slang*). — *adj* **manorial** (*ma-nö'ri-əl*) relating to or resembling a manor. — **man'or-house** or **man'or-seat** the house or seat belonging to a manor. [OFr *manoir*, from L *manēre*, *mānsum* to stay]

manqué *mā-kā*, (*Fr*) *adj* having had ambition or potential, but without it being fulfilled (placed after the noun, as in *poet manqué*).

manred *man'red*, (*obs*) *n* homage; a body of vassals. — Also (*Scot*) **man'rent**. [OE *mannrǣden*; **man**[1] and sfx *-rǣden*, expressing mode or state]

mansard-roof *man'särd-ro͞of*, *n* a roof having its angle divided to slope more steeply in the lower part than in the upper. — Also **man'sard**. [Employed by François *Mansard* or *Mansart* (1598–1666), French architect]

manse *mans*, *n* an ecclesiastical residence, *esp* that of a parish minister of the Church of Scotland. — **son of the manse** a minister's son. [LL *mansus*, *mansa* a dwelling, from *manēre*, *mānsum* to remain]

mansion *man'shən*, *n* abode, stay (*obs*); a resting-place on a journey (*obs*); a dwelling-place (*archaic*; often in *pl*); an apartment or separate lodging in a building (*obs*); a large house; a manor-house; a house (*astrol*); (in *pl*) a large block of flats. — *n* **man'sionary** (*Shakesp* **man'sonry**) residence; mansions. — **man'sion-house** a mansion, a large house. — **the Mansion House** the official residence of the Lord Mayor of London. [OFr, from L *mānsiō*, *-ōnis*, from *manēre*, *mānsum* to remain, to stay]

manslaughter. See under **man**[1].

mansonry. See under **mansion**.

mansuete *man'swēt*, (*archaic*) *adj* gentle; mild; tame. — *n* **man'suetude** (*-swi-tūd*). [L *mānsuētus*, from *manus* hand, and *suēscere* to accustom]

mansworn *man'swōrn*, *-swörn*, (*archaic*) *adj* perjured. [OE *mānswerian*, from *mān* evil, and *swerian* to swear]

manta *man'tə*, *n* a blanket; a cloak; a horse-cloth; a mantlet (*fortif*); (with *cap*) a type of gigantic fish with winglike fins and a whiplike tail; a giant ray or sea-vampire (also called **manta ray**). [Sp]

manteau or **manto** *man'tō*, (*hist*) *n* a woman's loose gown of the 17c–18c: — *pl* **man'teaus** (*-tōz*), **man'teaux** (*-tō*, *-tōz*), **man'toes** or **man'tos**. [Fr *manteau*, from L *mantellum*]

manteel *man-tēl'*, (*obs*) *n* a soldier's cloak; a woman's cape. [Fr *mantille*, from Sp *mantilla*]

mantel *man'tl*, *n* a manteltree; a mantelpiece; a mantelshelf. — *n* **man'telet** a mantlet. — **mantel clock** a clock designed to sit on a mantelpiece, often being wound and adjusted from the front; **man'telpiece** the ornamental structure over and in front of a fireplace; a mantelshelf; **man'telshelf** the ornamental shelf over a fireplace; **man'teltree** the lintel or arch of a fireplace. [**mantle**]

mantelet. See under **mantel** and **mantle**.

mantic *man'tik*, *adj* relating to divination; prophetic. — See also **-mancy**. [Gr *mantikos*, from *mantis* a prophet]

manticore *man'ti-kör* or **manticora** *-kö'rə*, *n* a fabulous animal with the body of a lion, tail of a scorpion, porcupine quills, and a human head. [L *manticora*, from Gr *mantichōrās*, a wrong reading for *martichorās*, from Persian *mardkhora* man-eater]

mantid. See under **mantis**.

mantilla *man-til'ə*, *n* a small cloak; a kind of veil covering the head and the shoulders. [Sp, dimin of *manta*]

mantis *man'tis*, *n* an insect of the genus (*Mantis*) of the cockroach family, which carry their large spiny forelegs in the attitude of prayer (also called **praying insect** or **praying mantis**). — *n* **man'tid** any member of the *Mantis* genus. — **mantis shrimp** a stomatopod crustacean with claws like those of the mantis. [Gr *mantis*, *-eōs* prophet]

mantissa *man-tis'ə*, *n* the fractional part of a logarithm (*math*); the significant digits of a floating point number (*comput*). [L, make-weight]

mantle *man'tl*, *n* a cloak or loose outer garment (*archaic*); a covering (*esp poetic*); the status, role, authority, etc of a person as assumed by or passed on to another (in allusion to Elijah, 1 Kings 19. 19 ff); a fold of the external skin of a mollusc or a brachiopod secreting the substance forming shell (*zool*); the back and folded wings of a bird; a scum on a liquid (*archaic*); a hood or network of fire-resistant material that becomes incandescent when exposed to a flame; the part of the earth immediately beneath the crust, constituting the greater part of the earth's bulk, and presumed to consist of solid heavy rock. — *vt* to cover (*esp poetic*); to obscure; to form a scum on (*archaic*); to suffuse with colour (*literary*); to disguise. — *vi* to spread or extend like a mantle; to develop a scum or crust (*archaic*); to froth or bubble; to be suffused with colour, to blush (*literary*); (of a hawk) to stretch the wings over the legs (*falconry*). — *n* **man'tlet** or **man'telet** a small cloak for women, worn *esp* in the 19c; a movable shield or screen (*fortif*). — *n* **man'tling** cloth suitable for mantles; the drapery of a coat-of-arms (*heraldry*). — **mantle rock** loose rock at the earth's surface. [Partly through OE *mentel*, partly through OFr *mantel* (Fr *manteau*), from L *mantel(l)um*]

manto. See **manteau**.

Mantoux test *man-tōō test*, (*med*) *n* a test for the existence of tuberculosis in humans by the injection of tuberculin into the skin. [From C *Mantoux* (1877–1956), French physician]

mantra *man'trə*, *n* a Vedic hymn (*Hinduism*); a sacred text used as an incantation; extended to music having a mystical effect; a word, phrase, etc, chanted or repeated inwardly in meditation (*Hinduism* and *Buddhism*). — Also **man'tram**. [Sans, instrument of thought]

mantrap. See under **man**[1].

mantua *man'tū-ə*, *n* a woman's loose outer gown, worn in the 17c–18c. — Also (*Scot*) **mant'y**. — **man'tua-maker** a dressmaker. [**manteau**, confused with *Mantua*, in Italy]

Mantuan *man'tū-ən*, *adj* of or relating to *Mantua* in Italy. — *n* a native or inhabitant of Mantua, *esp* Virgil. — Also the name of the Latin pastoral poet Baptista *Mantuanus* (1448–1516).

manty. See under **mantua**.

manual *man'ū-əl*, *adj* of the hand or hands; done, worked, or used by the hand(s), as opposed to automatic, computer operated, etc; working with the hands. — *n* drill in the use of weapons, etc (*military*); a handbook or handy compendium of a large subject or treatise; an instruction book for a piece of machinery, etc; an old office-book like the modern RC *Rituale*; an organ key or keyboard played by hand not foot; a primary feather. — *adv* **man'ually**. — **manual alphabet** sign language; **manual exercise** drill in handling arms (*military*). [L *manuālis*, from *manus* the hand]

manubrium *mā-nū'bri-əm*, *n* any handle-like structure; the presternum or anterior part of the breast-bone in mammals (*anatom*); the pendent oral part of a jellyfish, etc: — *pl* **manū'bria**. — *adj* **manū'brial**. [L *manūbrium* a handle]

manufacture *man-ū-fak'chər*, *vt* to make, *orig* by hand, now *usu* by machinery and on a large scale; to fabricate, concoct or invent; to produce unintelligently in quantity. — *vi* to be occupied in manufacture. — *n* the practice, act or process of manufacturing; anything manufactured. — *n* **manufact'ory** a factory or place where goods are manufactured. — *adj* **manufact'ural**. — *n* **manufact'urer** a factory worker (*obs*); a person or business engaged in manufacturing; a director or manager of a firm that manufactures goods; a person who makes, concocts or invents. — *adj* **manufact'uring** relating to or engaged in manufacture. [Fr, from L *manū* (ablative) by hand, and *factūra* a making, from *facere*, *factum* to make]

manuka *mä'nōō-kä*, *mə-nōō'kə*, *n* an Australian and New Zealand tree (*Leptospermum*) of the myrtle family, with hard, close-grained wood, and aromatic leaves formerly used as a substitute for tea. [Maori]

manul *mä'nōōl*, *n* a Central Asian wild cat. [Mongolian]

manumea *man-ə-mā'ə*, *n* a Samoan pigeon with a notched lower mandible. [Samoan]

manumit *man-ū-mit'*, *vt* to release from slavery; to set free: — *pr p* **manumitt'ing**; *pa t* and *pa p* **manumitt'ed**. — *n* **manumission** (*-mish'ən*). [L *manūmittere* or *manū mittere* or *ēmittere* to send from one's hand or control, from *manus* the hand, and *mittere*, *missum* to send]

manure *mən-ūr'*, formerly *man'ūr*, *vt* to hold or occupy (*obs*); to manage (*obs*); to cultivate (*obs*); to cover or enrich (soil) with any fertilizing substance. — *n* any substance, *esp* dung, added to soil to make it more fertile. — *n* **manūr'ance** (*archaic*) cultivation. — *n* **manūr'er**. — *adj* **manūr'ial**. — *n* **manūr'ing**. [Anglo-Fr *maynoverer* (Fr *manœuvrer*); see **manoeuvre**]

manus *mā'nəs*, *mä'nōōs*, *n* the hand or corresponding part of a vertebrate. [L]

manuscript *man'ū-skript*, *adj* written by hand or typed, not printed. — *n* a book or document written by hand before the invention of printing; copy for a printer, handwritten or typed; handwritten form. — *Abbrev* **MS**. [L *manū* (ablative) by hand, and *scrībere*, *scrīptum* to write]

Manx *mangks*, *n* the language of the Isle of *Man*, belonging to the Gadhelic branch of Celtic. — *adj* of or relating to the Isle of Man, its inhabitants or language. — **Manx cat** a breed of cat with only a rudimentary tail; **Manx'man**: — *fem* **Manx'woman**.

many *men'i*, *adj* (*compar* **more** *mōr*, *mör*; *superl* **most** *mōst*) consisting of a great number; numerous. — *n* and *pron* many people; a great number (*usu* with omission of *of*); company, retinue (*Spenser*; *perh* for **meinie**). — *adj* **man'y-coloured** having many colours. — *adj* **man'y-eyed** having many eyes. — *adj* **man'yfold** (compare **manifold**) many in number. — *adv* many times over. — *adj* **many-fold'ed** (*Spenser*) having many layers; having many folds. — *adj* **many-head'ed** having many heads; consisting of many. — **man'y-root** the ruellia plant, a member of the acanthus family. — *adj* **many-sid'ed** having many qualities or aspects; having wide interests or varied abilities. — **many-sid'edness**. — *adj* **many-tongued'**. — **many a** many (with singular noun and verb); **many-headed beast** or **monster** the people, the irrational mob (a translation of Horace's *belua multorum capitum*); **the many** the crowd, ordinary people in general. [OE *manig*]

manyatta or **manyata** *man-yat'ə*, *n* a small Masai settlement or encampment. [Masai]

manyplies *men'i-plīz*, *n sing* and *pl* the third stomach of a ruminant, the *omasum* or *psalterium*. — Also **man'iplies** and (*dialect*) **moniplies** or **monyplies** (*mon'*, *mun'*). [**many** and **ply**[1]]

manzanilla *man-zə-nil'ə*, *-nē'yə*, *n* a very dry, light sherry. [Sp; also meaning camomile; same root as **manchineel**]

manzanita *man-zə-nē'tə*, *n* a Californian species of bearberry. [Sp, dimin of *manzana* apple]

manzello *man-zel'ō*, *n* a musical instrument like the soprano saxophone: — *pl* **manzell'os**. [Origin uncertain]

Maoist *mow'ist*, *n* an adherent of the Chinese type of communism as expounded by *Mao* Tse-tung. — Also *adj*. — *n* **Mao'ism**. — **Mao'-jacket** or **Mao'-suit** a high-collared, *usu* cotton jacket or suit in the style of those worn by Mao Tse-tung and his followers, common dress in modern China.

Maori *mow'ri*, *mä'ō-ri*, *n* a member of the aboriginal people of New Zealand; the language of this people: — *pl* **Mao'ris**. — Also *adj*. — **Maori chief** a brightly-coloured fish of New Zealand; **Maoridom** the Maori world or culture; **Maori hen** the weka; **Maoriland** (*archaic*) New Zealand; **Maori side-step** (*Rugby football*) the action of running directly at, rather than swerving to avoid, an oncoming tackler; **Maoritanga** (*mow-ri-tän'gə*) Maori traditions and culture; the fact or state of being Maori. [Maori]

maormor *mär'mōr, -mör,* a wrong form of **mormaor**.

map *map, n* a representation in outline of the surface features of the earth, the moon, etc, or of part of it, *usu* on a plane surface; a similar plan of the stars in the sky; a representation, scheme or example of the layout or state of anything. — *vt* to make a map of; to place (the elements of a set) in one-to-one correspondence with the elements of another set (*math*): — *pr p* **mapp'ing**; *pa t* and *pa p* **mapped**. — *n* **mapp'er**. — *n* **mapp'ery** (*Shakesp*) *perh* working with or making maps, planning out. — *n* **mapp'ing** or **gene mapping** (*biol*) the determination of the positions and relative distances of genes on chromosomes by means of linkage (qv); **mapp'ist**. — **map'-measurer** an instrument for measuring distances on a map; **map'-mounter** a person who mounts maps, or backs them with cloth and fixes them on rollers, etc; **map'-pin** a pin with a coloured head used to mark points on a map; **map projection** see under **projection**; **map'-reading** the interpretation of what one sees on a geographical map. — *adv* **map'wise** in the manner of a map. — **map out** to plan, divide up, and apportion; to lay out a plan of; **off the map** out of existence; negligible; (of a location) remote from main thoroughfares, etc; **on the map** to be taken into account; **put on the map** to bring to public attention, to make well known. [L *mappa* a napkin, a painted cloth, orig Punic]

maple *mā'pl, n* any tree of the genus *Acer*, from the sap of some species of which sugar and syrup can be made; its timber. — *adj* of maple. — **maple candy** (*NAm*) a brittle confection made from maple sugar; **maple leaf** the emblem of Canada; (with *cap*) a one-ounce Canadian gold coin depicting a maple leaf on the reverse; **maple sugar**; **maple syrup**. [OE *mapul* maple]

mappemond *map'ə-mōnd, map-mōnd', n* a map of the world (*hist*); the world itself (*obs*). [LL *mappa mundī*]

mapstick. See **mopstick** under **mop**[1].

maquette *ma-ket', n* a small model of something to be made on a larger scale, *esp* a model in clay or wax of a piece of sculpture. [Fr]

maqui *mä'kē, n* a Chilean evergreen shrub (*Aristotelia maqui*, family *Elaeocarpaceae*) whose berry yields a medicinal wine. [Araucan]

maquiladora *mak-i-la-dö'rə, n* a factory or assembly plant owned by a US company in Mexico, operating under a free-trade agreement to allow duty-free export of finished products for sale in the US: — *pl* **maquilado'ras**. — Also *adj*. [Mex Sp, from Sp *maquillar* to make up]

maquillage *ma-kē-yäzh', n* (the art of using) cosmetics, make-up. [Fr]

maquis *mä'kē', n sing* and *n pl* a thicket formation of shrubs, as in Corsica and on Mediterranean shores (*bot*); (often with *cap*) French guerrilla resistance forces (1940–45), or a member of one. — *n* (often with *cap*) **maquisard** (*mä-kē-zär*) a member of the maquis. [Fr, from Ital *macchia*, from L *macula* mesh]

MAR *mär,* (*comput*) *abbrev*: memory address register.

Mar. *abbrev*: March.

mar *mär, vt* to interfere with (*obs*); to spoil; to impair; to injure; to damage; to disfigure: — *pr p* **marr'ing**; *pa t* and *pa p* **marred** (*Spenser* **mard**). — *n* **mar'dy** (*dialect*) a spoilt child; a timid or petulant cry-baby. — Also *adj* and *vt*. — **mar'plot** (*archaic*) someone who defeats or mars a plot by unwarranted interference. — *adj* and *vi* **mar'prelate** (to inveigh) after the manner of Martin *Marprelate*, the name assumed by the author of certain anti-episcopal tracts, 1588–9. — **mar'sport** (*archaic*) a spoilsport; **mar'text** (*rare*) an ignorant preacher. [OE *merran*]

mara *mə-rä', n* the so-called Patagonian hare or *Dolichotis*.

marabou *mar'ə-bōō* or **marabout** *-bōōt, n* an adjutant bird, *esp* an African species; its feathers; a plume or trimming of its feathers; a feather necklet; a very white raw silk. [Ety as for **marabout**[1]]

marabout[1] *mar'ə-bōōt, n* a Muslim hermit, *esp* in N Africa; a practitioner of the occult, a type of witch-doctor; a Muslim shrine. [Fr, from Ar *murābit* hermit]

marabout[2]. See **marabou**.

maraca *mə-rak'ə, n* a hand-held percussion instrument, *usu* one of a pair, consisting of a gourd or substitute filled with dried beans, beads, etc. [Carib]

marae *mə-rī', n* a Maori meeting-place, traditionally an open courtyard. [Maori]

maraging *mär'ā-jing,* (*metallurgy*) *n* a process by which a metal alloy is slowly cooled in the air, becoming very strong and resistant to corrosion. [From *mar*tensite and *aging*]

marah *mä'rä, n* bitterness; something bitter. [Heb]

maranatha *mar-ə-nä'thə*. See **anathema**.

Maranta *mə-ran'tə, n* the arrowroot genus of monocotyledons giving name to the family **Marantā'ceae**, related to the banana and ginger families. [After Bartolommeo *Maranta*, 16c Italian herbalist]

maraschino *mar-ə-skē'nō, -shē'nō, n* a liqueur distilled from a cherry grown in the Croatian region of Dalmatia: — *pl* **maraschi'nos**. — **maraschino cherry** a cherry preserved in real or imitation maraschino and used for decorating cocktails, cakes, etc. [Ital, from *marasca, amarasca* a sour cherry, from L *amārus* bitter]

marasmus *mə-raz'məs,* (*med*) *n* a wasting away of the body. — *adj* **maras'mic**. — *n* **Maras'mius** a common genus of toadstools, including the fairy-ring champignon, drying up in sunshine but recovering in damp. [Latinized, from Gr *marasmos*, from *marainein* to decay]

Maratha or **Mahratta** *mə-rät'ə, n* a member of a once dominant people of SW India. — *n* **Marathi** (*mə-rät'ē*) their Sanskritic language. [Hindi *marạtha*, from Sans *mahārāṣtra* great kingdom]

marathon *mar'ə-thon, -thən, n* (with *cap*) scene of the Greek victory over the Persians, 490 BC, about 22 miles from Athens; a marathon race; any long, severe test of endurance. — *adj* relating to marathon races or running; of great length in time, distance, etc; displaying powers of endurance and stamina. — *n* **mar'athoner**. — *adj* and *n* **Marathōn'ian**. — **marathon race** a long-distance foot-race (*usu* 26 miles 385 yards, 42·195 kilometres), commemorating the tradition that a Greek ran from Marathon to Athens with news of the victory; a long-distance race in other sports, eg swimming. [Gr *Marathōn*]

Marattia *mə-rat'i-ə, n* a genus of ferns giving name to the **Marattiā'ceae**, a tropical family of very large primitive eusporangiate ferns. [Named after G F *Maratti* (died 1777), Italian botanist]

maraud *mə-röd', vi* to wander in search of plunder. — *vt* to plunder or raid. — *n* (*archaic*) raiding; plundering. — *n* **maraud'er**. — *adj* **maraud'ing**. [Fr *maraud* rogue; origin obscure]

maravedi *mar-ə-vā'di,* (*hist*) *n* an obsolete Spanish copper coin of little value. [Sp *maravedí*, from Ar *Murābitīn* the dynasty of the Almoravides (11th and 12th centuries)]

marble *mär'bl, n* a hard, granular crystalline limestone taking a high polish and smooth finish; any rock of similar appearance taking a high polish; a slab, work of art, tombstone, tomb, or other object made of marble; a little hard ball (*orig* of marble) used in children's games; marbling; anything hard, cold, polished, white, or otherwise like marble (*fig*); (in *pl*) any of several games played with little (now *usu* glass) marbles; (in *pl*) one's wits or senses (*colloq*). — *adj* composed or made of marble; shining like marble; unyielding; hard; insensible; marbled. — *vt* to stain, vein or print to resemble marble. — *adj* **mar'bled** irregularly mottled and streaked like some kinds of marble; made from marble; furnished with marble. — *n* **mar'bler**. — *n* **mar'bling** a marbled appearance or colouring; the act of veining or painting in imitation of marble. — *adj* **mar'bly** like marble. — *adj* **marble-breast'ed** or **marble-heart'ed** (*literary*) hard-hearted, cruel, uncaring. — **marble cake** a sponge cake made by lightly mixing more than one shade of base mixture, having a marbled appearance when cut. — *adj* **marble-con'stant** (*literary*) constant or firm as marble, immovable. — **mar'ble-cutter** a person who hews marble; a machine for cutting marble; **mar'bled-white** a butterfly of the *Satyridae*. — *adj* **mar'ble-edged** (of a book) having the edges marbled. — **mar'ble-paper** paper coloured in imitation of variegated marble. — **Elgin marbles** a collection of marbles obtained chiefly from the Parthenon by Lord *Elgin* and purchased by the British Museum in 1816; **have** or **lose (all) one's marbles** have or lose one's wits (*colloq*). [OFr *marbre*, from L *marmor*; cf Gr *marmaros*, from *marmairein* to sparkle]

Marburg disease. See **green monkey disease** under **green**[1].

MARC *märk*, *abbrev*: *ma*chine *r*eadable *c*ataloguing, a standardized system used by libraries to produce bibliographic records that can be read by computer.

marc *märk*, *Fr mär*, *n* grapeskins and other refuse from wine-making; brandy made from this (also **marc brandy**); any fruit refuse, eg from the making of cooking oil. [Fr]

Marcan *mär'kən*, *adj* of the Evangelist St Mark or his gospel.

marcantant *mär'kən-tant*, (*Shakesp*) *n* a merchant. [Ital *mercatante*]

marcasite *mär'kə-sīt*, *n* sulphide of iron in orthorhombic crystals (in the gem trade it can be pyrite, polished steel, etc). [LL *marcasīta*, from Ar *marqashīt(h)ā*; origin unknown]

marcato *mär-kä'tō*, (*music*) *adj* marked; emphatic; strongly accented: — *superl* **marcatis'simo**. — Also *adv*. [Ital, from *marcare* to mark]

Marcel or **marcel** *mär-sel'*, *n* (in full **Marcel wave**) an artificial wave in hair, produced by styling with a hot iron, etc; a hairstyle with such waves — *vt* to style (hair) with marcel waves. — *adj* **marcelled'**. [*Marcel* Grateau (1852–1936), a French hairdresser]

marcella *mär-sel'ə*, *n* a type of cotton or linen fabric, in twill weave. [Anglicization of *Marseilles*]

marcescent *mär-ses'ənt*, *adj* (of a part of a plant) withering without falling off. — *adj* **marcesc'ible**. [L *marcēscēns*, *-entis*, pr p of *marcēscere*, from *marcēre* to fade]

Marcgravia *märk-grā'vi-ə*, *n* a tropical American genus of climbing epiphytic shrubs, with pitcher-like bracts developed as nectaries, visited by humming-birds, giving name to the family **Marcgraviā'ceae**, related to the tea family. [After Georg *Markgraf* (1610–44), German traveller]

March *märch*, *n* the third month of the year (in England until 1752 the year began on 25 March). — **March beer** a particularly strong beer traditionally brewed in March; **March hare** a hare gambolling in the breeding season, proverbially mad because of its antics. [L *Martius* (*mēnsis*) (the month) of Mars]

march[1] *märch*, *n* (*usu* in *pl*) a boundary; a border; a border district, *esp* in Scotland — used chiefly in *pl* **march'es**. — *vi* to have a common boundary. — *n* **march'er** an inhabitant or lord of a border district. — Also *adj*. — **march'-dyke** or **march'-dike** a boundary wall, *usu* of turf; **march'lands** a border area between countries; **march'man** a person living on or near a border; **march'-stone** a boundary stone; **march'-treason** (*history*) an offence against the laws of the marches, eg raiding the neighbouring country in time of peace. — **Lord marcher** (*hist*) a lord who had royal prerogative in, and jurisdiction over, lands in the marches; **riding the marches** the old ceremony of riding round the bounds of a town, etc. [Fr *marche*; of Gmc origin; cf **mark**[1], OE *mearc*]

march[2] *märch*, *vi* to walk in a markedly rhythmical military manner, or in a grave, stately or resolute manner; to advance steadily or irresistibly. — *vt* to cause to march; to force to go. — *n* a marching movement; an act of marching; the distance covered by marching, *esp* for a specified amount of time; regular advance; a piece of music written for marching to, or similar in character and rhythm, *usu* with a trio; a move made by a chess piece. — **marching orders** orders to march; dismissal from employment, etc (*colloq*); **marching regiment** one without permanent quarters; **march past** the march of a body of troops, etc in front of the person who reviews it. — **forced march** a march necessarily carried out at great speed; **on the march** marching; advancing; **rogue's march** music played in derision of a person expelled; **steal a march on** to gain an advantage over, *esp* in a sly or secret manner. [Fr *marcher* to walk, prob from L *marcus* a hammer]

marchantia *mär-kan'shi-ə*, *-ti-ə*, *n* a liverwort of the *Marchantia* genus, with a flat, lobed and branched thallus, growing in damp places, giving name to the family **Marchantiā'ceae**. [Named after Nicolas *Marchant* (died 1678), French botanist]

Märchen *mer'hhyən*, (*Ger*) *n* a story or fable, a folk-tale: — same form for *pl*.

marchesa *mär-kā'za*, *n* an Italian marchioness. — *n* **marchese** (*mär-kā'ze*) an Italian marquess. [Ital; cf **marchioness**]

marchioness *mär'shən-es*, *-is*, *n* the wife or widow of a marquis or marquess; a woman who holds a marquisate in her own right; a size of roofing slate 22 × 12in (55·88 × 30·48cm). [LL *marchiōnissa*, fem of *marchiō*, *-ōnis* a lord of the marches]

marchpane *märch'pān*, *n* until the 19c, same as **marzipan**. [Ital *marzapane*]

Marcionite *mär'shən-īt*, *n* a follower of *Marcion* of Sinope (died AD 165), who, partly under Gnostic influences, constructed an ethico-dualistic philosophy of religion. — Also *adj*. — *n* **Mar'cionist**. — *n* **Mar'cionītism**.

Marcobrunner *mär'kō-broo͞n-ər*, *n* a fine white German wine produced in Erbach, near Wiesbaden. [From the nearby *Markbrunnen* fountain]

Marconi® *mär-kō'ni*, *adj* relating to Guglielmo *Marconi* (1874–1937), or his system of wireless telegraphy. — *vt* and *vi* (without *cap*) to communicate by wireless telegraphy. — *n* **marcō'nigram** a message so transmitted. — *vt* and *vi* **marcō'nigraph**.

Marco Polo sheep *mär'kō pōl'ō shēp*, *n* a type of Asiatic wild sheep with large horns. [After the Venetian explorer (1254–1324)]

mard and **mardy**. See under **mar**.

Mardi Gras *mär-dē grä*, (*Fr*) *n* Shrove Tuesday celebrated with a carnival in many places, famously Rio de Janeiro.

mare[1] *mār*, *n* the female of the horse. — **mare's'-nest** a supposedly worthwhile discovery that turns out to have no real value; **mare's'-tail** a tall marsh plant of the genus *Hippuris*; also applied to the horsetail; (in *pl*) long straight strands of grey cirrus cloud. — **the grey mare is the better horse** the wife rules her husband, or is the more able partner. [OE *mere*, fem of *mearh* a horse; cognate with Ger *Mähre*, ON *merr*, and Welsh *march* a horse]

mare[2] *mār*, (*Shakesp*) *n* a folkloric evil spirit that terrifies or suffocates the sleeping person, the nightmare (qv).

mare[3] *mā'rē*, *ma're*, *-ri*, *n* any of various darkish level areas on either the Moon or Mars: — *pl* **maria** (*mā'ri-ə*, *ma'ri-a*). [L, sea]

mare clausum *mā'rē klö'səm*, *ma're klow'soo͞m*, (*L*) *n* a closed sea; a sea within the jurisdiction of one state. — **mare liberum** (*lib'ə-rəm*, *lē'be-roo͞m*) a sea open to free navigation by ships of any nation.

Marek's disease *mä'reks diz-ēz'*, *n* a viral cancerous disease causing paralysis in poultry. [After József Marek (1868–1952), Hungarian veterinary surgeon]

maremma *mär-em'ə*, *n* seaside marshland; an Italian sheepdog. [Ital, from L *maritima* seaside]

mareschal *mär'shl*, (*archaic*) *n*. Same as **marshal**.

Mareva injunction *mə-rē'və in-jung'kshən*, (*law*) *n* a court order freezing assets to prevent them being taken out of a country. [After the first company to be granted such an injunction]

marg. See **margarine**.

marg. *abbrev*: margin; marginal.

margarin *mär'gər-in, n* a mixture of palmitin and stearin once thought a compound; a glyceryl ester of margaric acid. — *n* **mar'garite** (*mär'gə-rīt*) a pearly-lustred mineral sometimes regarded as a lime-alumina mica. — *adj* **margaric** (*-gar'*) or **margarit'ic** pearl-like. — *adj* **margaritif'erous** pearl-bearing. — **margaric** or **margaritic acid** an acid intermediate between palmitic and stearic. [Gr *margarītēs* a pearl]

margarine *mär-jər-ēn', -gər-* (contraction **marg** *märg* or **marge** *märj*), *n* a butterlike substance made from vegetable oils and fats, etc. [Ety as for **margarite**]

margarita *mär-gə-rē'tə, n* a cocktail of tequila, lime or lemon juice, and orange-flavoured liqueur. [From the Sp name *Margarita*]

margarite *mär'ga-rīt, n* a pearly-lustred mineral, a mica formed from calcium and aluminium. — *adj* **margaric** (*-gar'ik*) or **margarit'ic** pearl-like. [Gr *margarītēs* a pearl]

margay *mär'gā, n* a spotted S American tiger-cat. [Fr (or Sp), from Tupí *mbaracaïa*]

marge[1] *märj, (poetic) n* margin, brink. [Fr, from L *margō, -inis*]

marge[2]. See **margarine**.

margin *mär'jin* or (*poetic* and *archaic*) **margent** *mär'jənt, n* an edge or border; (the width of) the blank edge on the page of a book or sheet of paper, or the rule (if any) separating it from the rest of the page; an amount (eg of time or money) allowed above what is strictly needed; a deposit to protect a broker against loss; difference between selling and buying price, profit. — *vt* to provide with a margin or margins; to write in the margin. — *adj* **mar'ginal** relating to a margin; in or on the margin; minor, subordinate or insignificant, not central, principal or mainstream; barely sufficient; not very relevant. — *n* anything in or on a margin, *esp* a marginal constituency. — *n pl* **marginā'lia** notes written in a margin. — *n* **mar'ginalism** an economic theory that the value of a product depends on its value to the final consumer. — *n* **mar'ginalist**. — *n* **marginal'ity**. — *vt* **mar'ginalize** or **-ise** to write notes in the margin of; to push to the edges of anything, *esp* of consciousness, society, etc in order to reduce effectiveness. — *adv* **mar'ginally**. — *adj* **mar'ginate** or **mar'ginated** (*bot* or *biol*) having a well-marked border. — *adj* **mar'gined**. — **marginal constituency, seat** or **ward** a constituency seat or ward held with a small majority and not providing a safe seat for any of the political parties; **marginal cost** or **revenue** (*econ*) the increase in a firm's total costs or revenue caused by producing one more unit of output; **marginal firm** one whose profits are equivalent to the normal expected returns from the capital invested in them; **marginal land** less fertile land which will be brought under cultivation only if economic conditions justify it; **marginal tax rate** (*finance*) the percentage of each pound of extra income paid in tax; **marginal-unit** (*econ*) the last unit to be added to, or the first removed from, any supply; **margin index** a form of thumb-index using coloured blocks rather than indentations in a book's margins. [L *margō, marginis*; cf **mark**[1] and **march**[1]]

margosa *mär-gō'sə, n* the tree that yields nim-oil. [Port *amargosa* (fem) bitter]

margrave *mär'grāv, n* a German nobleman of rank equivalent to an English marquess: — *fem* **margravine** (*mär'grə-vēn*). — *n* **mar'gravate** or **margrā'viate** the jurisdiction or position of a margrave. [MDu *markgrave* (Du *markgraaf*; Ger *Markgraf*), from *mark* a border, and *grave* (mod *graaf*) a count; cf Ger *Graf*, OE *gerēfa*, Eng **reeve**[1] and **sheriff**]

marguerite *mär-gə-rēt', n* the ox-eye daisy or other single chrysanthemum. [Fr, daisy, from Gr *margarītēs* pearl]

maria. See **mare**[3].

mariachi *mar-i-ä'chi, adj* designating a form of Mexican dance music played traditionally by strolling musicians. — *n* any of a group of musicians playing mariachi music: — *pl* **maria'chis**. [Mex Sp]

mariage blanc *ma-ri-azh blã, (Fr) n* an unconsummated marriage. [Fr, literally white marriage]

mariage de convenance *ma-rē-äzh də kɔ̃-və-nãs, (Fr)* same as **marriage of convenience** (see under **marriage**).

marialite *mā'ri-ə-līt, n* a variety of scapolite rich in sodium, chlorine, and silica, poor in calcium. [*Maria* Rose vom Rath, a mineralogist's wife]

Marian[1] *mā'ri-ən, adj* relating to the Virgin *Mary* or to Queen Mary (Tudor or Stuart). — *n* a devotee, follower, or defender of (either) Mary; an English Roman Catholic of Mary Tudor's time. — *n* **Mariol'atry** (Gr *latreiā* worship) (excessive) worship of the Virgin Mary, the veneration duly paid to her being properly hyperdulia (qv under **dulia**). — *n* **Mariol'ater** a person who practises Mariolatry. — *adj* **Mariol'atrous**. — *n* **Mariol'ogist**. — *n* **Mariol'ogy** the study of the nature of, and doctrines and traditions concerning, the Virgin Mary. — Also **Maryol'atry, Maryol'ogy**, etc. [L *Maria*]

Marian[2] *mar'i-ən, mā'ri-ən, adj* relating to the great Roman general Gaius *Marius* (died 86 BC).

mari complaisant *ma-rē kɔ̃-ple-zã, (Fr) n* a husband tolerant of his wife's infidelity. [Fr, literally obliging husband]

mariculture *mar'i-kul-chər, n* the cultivation of plants and animals of the sea in their own environment. [L *mare* sea]

marid *mar'id, mä-rēd', n* a jinn of the most powerful class. [Ar *mārid, marīd*, from *marada* to rebel]

Marie biscuit *mə-rē' bis'kit, n* a type of plain biscuit, *usu* thin with decorative indentations. [From the woman's name]

Marie-Jeanne *ma-rē-zhan', n* a bottle-size for wine, equivalent to three ordinary bottles (*usu* $2\frac{1}{4}$ litres).

marigold *mar'i-gōld, n* a composite plant (*Calendula*) or its orange-yellow flower; extended to other yellow flowers (see under **corn**[1], **marsh**). — **African** and **French marigold** Mexican composites (*Tagetes*). [From the Virgin *Mary*, and **gold**[2]]

marigraph *mar'i-gräf, n* an instrument for recording tide levels. — *n* **mar'igram** a record produced by this. [L *mare* sea, and Gr *graphein* to write]

marijuana or **marihuana** *ma-ri-wä'nə, -hhwä'nə, n* Indian hemp; its dried flowers and leaves smoked as an intoxicant. [Am Sp]

marimba *mə-rim'bə, n* an instrument resembling a xylophone, originally from Africa and now used *esp* in Latin American and jazz music (also **marim'baphone**). [African origin]

marine *mə-rēn', adj* of, in, near, concerned with or belonging to the sea; done or used at sea; inhabiting, found in or obtained from the sea. — *n* a soldier serving on board ship; a naval or mercantile shipping fleet; nautical service; naval affairs; a seascape. — *n* **marina** (*mə-rē'nə*) a berthing area for yachts, etc, prepared with every kind of facility for a sailing holiday. — *n* **mar'iner** (esp *literary*) a sailor. — **marine acid** hydrochloric acid; **marine boiler** a steamship boiler; **marine engine** a ship's engine; **marine glue** see under **glue**; **marine insurance** insurance of ships or cargoes; **marine soap** a coconut-oil soap, for washing with sea-water; **marine store** a place where old ships' materials are bought and sold; **marine stores** old ships' materials; supplies for ships; **marine trumpet** the tromba marina. — **tell that to the marines** (*colloq*) a phrase expressing disbelief and ridicule, from the sailor's contempt for the marine's ignorance of seamanship. [Fr, from L *marīnus*, from *mare* sea]

marinade *mar-i-nād', n* a liquor or pickle in which fish, meat, etc is steeped before cooking, to improve the flavour or tenderize; ingredients steeped in this way. — *vt* **mar'inade** or **mar'inate** to steep in a marinade. [Ety as for **marine**]

marinera *ma-ri-ner'a, n* a Peruvian folk-dance danced in pairs; the music for this. [Sp *marinero, -nera* marine]

marinière *ma-ri-ni-yer'*, *adj* (*esp* of mussels) cooked in white wine with onions and herbs. [Fr *à la marinière* in the manner of the bargeman's wife]

Marinist *mə-rē'nist*, *n* a follower or imitator of the Italian poet Giambattista *Marini* (1569–1625). — *n* **Marin'ism** the poetic style of Marini, characterized by strained conceits.

Mariolatry, **Mariology**, etc. See under **Marian**[1].

marionberry *mar'i-ən-ber-i*, *n* a hybrid fruit, a cross between a loganberry and a wild blackberry.

marionette *mar-i-ə-net'*, *n* a puppet with jointed limbs moved by strings. [Fr, dimin of the name *Marion*, itself a dimin of *Marie* Mary]

Mariotte's law. See **Boyle's law** under **law**[1].

mariposa *mar-i-pō'zə*, *n* any of various plants of the *Calochortus* genus, with white, yellow or blue tulip-like flowers, native to N America. — Also **mariposa lily** or **tulip**. [Sp, butterfly]

marischal. A Scots spelling of **marshal**.

marish *mar'ish*, (*obs*) *n* and *adj*. Same as **marsh**.

Marist *mar'ist*, *n* a member of an evangelical RC sect emphasizing teaching, preaching and foreign missions. — *adj* devoted to the service of the Virgin. [Fr *Mariste*]

maritage *mar'it-ij*, (*hist*) *n* the feudal superior's right to arrange the marriage of a vassal's heiress or heir, or to exact a fine in lieu of this; the fine exacted. [LL *marītāgium*]

marital *mar'i-təl*, *mə-rī'təl*, *adj* relating to a husband, or to a marriage; of the nature of a marriage. — *adv* **mar'itally** (or *mə-rī'*). [L *marītālis*, from *marītus* a husband]

maritime *mar'i-tīm*, *adj* relating to the sea; relating to seafaring or sea-trade; having a sea-coast; situated near the sea; living on the shore, littoral; having a navy and sea-trade; (of a climate) having little seasonal variation in temperature. [L *maritimus*, from *mare* sea]

marivaudage *mä-rē-vō-däzh*, *n* preciosity in literary style or expression. [Fr, from Pierre de *Marivaux* (1688–1763), French novelist and dramatist]

marjoram *mär'jə-rəm*, *n* an aromatic labiate plant (*Origanum*) used *esp* as a seasoning. [OFr *majorane*; origin doubtful]

mark[1] *märk*, *n* a boundary (*archaic*); a limit (*archaic*); a standard; a territory, *esp* a border territory (*archaic*); a tract of common land belonging to a village community (*hist*); a stone, post, etc, marking a boundary; an object indicating position or serving as a guide; an object to be aimed at, striven for, or attained, such as a butt, a goal, the jack at bowls, the pit of the stomach in boxing; a hawk's quarry (*obs*); a suitable victim (of trickery, theft, etc) (*slang*); that which exactly suits one (*slang*); a visible indication or sign; a symbol; a distinctive badge or device; a brand; a set, group, or class, marked with the same brand; a type, model, issue, etc (*usu* numbered, as in *mark* 1); a rubber stamp; a token; a substitute for a signature, eg an X; a distinguishing characteristic; an impression or trace; a discoloured spot, streak, smear, or other local (*usu* small) modification of appearance; note; distinction; noteworthiness; a point awarded for merit; a footprint; the impression of a Rugby football player's heel on the ground on making a fair catch; the starting-line in a race; a groove indicative of youth in a horse's incisor (as in *mark of mouth*); a tag on a lead-line indicating so many fathoms, feet, etc; the amount of departure (positive or negative), using equal intervals of time, from a space (a neutral or no-signal state) in accordance with a code (*telecomm*). — *vt* to make a mark on; to indicate; to record; to put marks on (a child's, student's, etc, written work) to show where it is correct or incorrect (also *vi*); to make emphatic, distinct, or prominent; to characterize in a specified, distinct way; to impress or stamp with a sign; to take note of; to regard; (in football, hockey, etc) to remain close to (one's opponent) in order to try and prevent him or her from obtaining or passing the ball (also *vi*). — *vi* to take particular notice. — *adj* **marked** having visible marks; indicated; noticeable; prominent; emphatic; watched and suspected; destined (with *for*); doomed. — *adv* **mark'edly** (*mär'kid-li*) noticeably. — *n* **mark'er** a person or tool that marks; something that marks a position, such as a stationary light or a flare; a person who marks the score at games, eg at billiards; a counter or other device for scoring; a bookmark; a marker pen (*US*); a recorder of attendances; a kind of school monitor; a memorial tablet (*US*); the soldier who forms the pivot round which a body of soldiers wheels when marching. — *n* **mark'ing** the act of making a mark or marks; (*esp* in *pl*) disposition or pattern of marks. — Also *adj*. — **mark'-down** see **mark down** below; **mark'er-beacon**, **mark'er-bomb** and **mark'er-flag**; **marker pen** a thick, *usu* fibre-tipped pen for writing on display boards, etc; **marking gauge** a carpenter's tool for scoring a line parallel to the edge of a piece of wood; **mark'ing-ink** indelible ink, used for marking clothes; **mark'ing-nut** the fruit of an East Indian tree (*Semecarpus*) of the cashew family, yielding a black juice used in marking clothes; **mark'man** one of the community owning a mark; a marksman; **marks'man** or **marks'woman** a person who is good at hitting a target; a person who shoots well; **marks'manship** skill as a marksman or markswoman; **mark/space ratio** (*telecomm*) the ratio of the time occupied by a mark to that occupied by the space between marks in a telecommunication channel or recording system using pulsed signals; **mark'-white** (*Spenser*) the centre of a target. — **a mark on** (*archaic slang*) (a person having) a preference for (a specified thing); **beside the mark** see under **beside**; **(God) bless** or **save the mark** (*archaic*) a phrase expressing ironical astonishment or scorn, from its use in archery; **make one's mark** to make a notable impression; to gain great influence; **mark down** to set down in writing; to label at a lower price or to lower the price of (*n* **mark'-down**); to note the position of; to destine for one's own; **mark off** to lay down the boundary lines of; to mark graduations on; to mark (on a list) as attended to or disposed of; **mark of the Beast** see under **beast**; **mark out** to lay out the plan or outlines of; to destine; **mark someone's card** to give someone the information he or she wants; to correct someone under a false impression, *esp* swiftly and with force, to put someone right; **mark time** to move the feet alternately in the same manner as in marching, but without moving forward; to merely keep things going without progressing; **mark up** to raise the price of. — *n* **mark'-up** a price increase; the difference between the wholesale and retail price of an item for sale. — **off the mark** off target; well away from the start in a race; **on your marks** (or **mark**) said before a race begins to prepare the runners for the starting command or signal; **pass the mark** to pass on the badge of demerit to the next offender (as formerly in some schools); **soft mark** (*colloq*) an easy dupe or victim; a person who is easy to cope with or manoeuvre; **up to the mark** satisfactory, up to standard; fit and well; **wide of the mark** (well) off target. [OE (Mercian) *merc* (WSax *mearc*) a boundary, a limit; Ger *Mark*, Gothic *marka*]

mark[2] *märk*, *n* a weight of 8 ounces for gold and silver (*obs*); its value in money at 20 pennies to an ounce = 13s 4d (*obs*); a coin of Germany (in 1924 officially named the Reichsmark; in 1948 the Deutsche mark or Deutschmark), of Finland (the *markka*, *pl markkaa*, *orig* equivalent to a franc), and formerly of various countries. [OE *marc*, of doubtful origin]

market *mär'kit*, *n* a periodic gathering of people for the purposes of buying and selling; a building, square or other public place used for such meetings; a shop (*orig US*); a region or type of clientele in which there is a demand for certain goods; buying and selling; opportunity for buying and selling; demand; the state of being on sale; bargain; sale; rate of sale; value. — *adj* relating to buying and selling; relating to a market or markets. — *vi* to deal at a market; to buy and sell. —

vt to put on the market, to sell: — *pr p* **mar'keting**; *pa t* and *pa p* **mar'keted**. — *adj* **mar'ketable** fit for the market; saleable. — *n* **marketabil'ity** or **mar'ketableness**. — *n* **marketeer'** a person who buys or sells, *esp* at a market; (*esp* with *cap*) a supporter of Britain's entry into the Common Market (see also **black-marketeer** under **black**). — *n* **mar'keter** a person who goes to, or buys or sells at, a market. — *n* **mar'keting** the business process of managing the flow of goods, services or processes from the producer to the user or customer, involving assessment of sales of the product, etc, and responsibility for its promotion, distribution and development. — *n* **marketiza'tion** (*econ*) conversion into or adoption of a market economy. — **mar'ket-bell** (*Shakesp*) a bell to give notice of the time of market; **market cross** a cross or similar structure set up where a market was formerly held; **mar'ket-day** the fixed day of the week on which a market is held in a particular town, etc; **market economy** an economy in which prices are determined by competition on the open market without government intervention; **market forces** the combined influences of supply and demand which determine the price and quantity of a product traded; **market-gar'den** a garden in which fruit and vegetables are grown for public sale; **market-gar'dener**; **market-gar'dening**; **mar'ket-hall** or **mar'ket-house** a building in which a market is held; **market leader** a company that sells more goods of a specified type than any other company; a brand of goods selling more than any other of its kind; **mar'ket maker** since the changes of 27 October 1986, a broker-dealer on the Stock Exchange; **mar'ket-making**; **mar'ket-man** or **mar'ket-woman** a person who sells, buys or works in a market; **market overt** (*law*) the sale of goods in open or public view; **mar'ketplace** the market-square of a town, etc; the world of commercial transactions; **market-price'** or **market-val'ue** the current price a commodity, etc will fetch at sale; **market profile** a description of the significant features, such as age and income, of members of a particular market; **market research** research to determine consumers' opinions about a product or service, by conducting interviews, analysing sales figures, etc; **market share** the percentage of the total market sales of a product attributable to a firm in a given period; **market square** the open space in a town where markets are or were formerly held; **mar'ket-town** a town having the privilege of holding a regular public market. — **go to market** (*Austr colloq*) to become very angry and violent; **in the market for** wanting to buy; **on the market** available for buying; on sale. [Late OE *market*, from ONFr *market* (Fr *marché*, Ital *mercato*), from L *mercātus* trade, a market, from *merx* merchandise]

markhor *mär'kör, n* a wild goat (*Capra falconeri*) of the mountains of Asia. [Pers *mārkhōr*]

markka *mär'kä, n* the standard monetary unit of Finland (100 *penni*): — *pl* **mar'kkaa** or **mar'kkas**. [Cf **mark**[2]]

Markov chain *mär'kof chān, n* a series of events, the probability of each of which depends on the probability of that immediately preceding it.

marksman and **markswoman**. See under **mark**[1].

marl[1] *märl, n* a calcareous clay often used as fertilizer; the ground (*poetic*). — *vt* to cover or fertilize with marl. — *adj* **mar'ly** like marl; containing large amounts of marl. — **marl'-pit** a pit where marl is dug; **marl'stone** (*geol*) a Middle Lias series of argillaceous limestones with ironstones, etc. [OFr *marle* (Fr *marne*), from LL *margila*, a dimin of L *marga* marl]

marl[2] *märl, vt* to bind with marline. [Du *marlen*, appar a frequentative of *marren* to bind]

marl[3] or **marle** *märl*, an *obs* form of **marvel**.

marl[4] *märl*, a dialect form of **marble**. — *adj* mottled. — *adj* **marled** marbled. — *n* **marl'ing**. — *adj* **marl'y** or **mirl'y** marbled.

marlin *mär'lin, n* a large oceanic fish of the genus *Makaira*, related to the swordfishes. [**marline-spike**]

marline *mär'lin, n* a small rope for winding round a larger one to keep it from wearing. — Also **mar'lin**. — **mar'line-spike** a spike for separating the strands of a rope in splicing (also **mar'linspike**). [Du *marling*, verbal noun from *marlen* (see **marl**[2]), or *marlijn*, from *marren* and *lijn* rope (cf **moor**[2] and **line**)]

marls. See **meril**.

marly. See **marl**[1] and **marl**[4].

marm. See **ma'am**.

marmalade *mär'mə-lād, n* a jam or preserve made from the pulp and sometimes rind of citrus fruit, *esp* oranges, originally of quinces. — *adj* (of a cat) having a coat marked with orange and brown streaks. — **marmalade tree** a tropical American sapotaceous tree (*Vitellaria*, or *Lucuma, mammosa*) cultivated for its fruit, the **marmalade plum**. [Fr *marmelade*, from Port *marmelada*, from *marmelo* a quince, from L *melimēlum*, from Gr *melimēlon* a sweet apple, from *meli* honey, and *mēlon* an apple]

marmarosis *mär-mə-rō'sis, n* conversion of limestone into marble. — *vt* **mar'marize** or **-ise**. [Gr *marmaros* crystalline rock, from *marmairein* to sparkle]

marmelize or **-ise** *mär'mə-līz*, (*jocular slang*) *vt* to thrash, defeat heavily, destroy, etc.

marmem alloy *mär'məm al'oi, n* an alloy which, under the influence of temperature changes, can be changed from one condition to another and back again. [*mar*tensite, *mem*ory, because the alloy 'remembers' its former condition]

Marmite® *mär'mīt, n* a spread for bread, etc made from yeast and vegetable extracts. [Ety as for **marmite**]

marmite *mär'mīt, mär-mēt', n* a lidded metal or earthenware cooking pot, *esp* for soup. [Fr, pot or kettle, from OFr, hypocrite (because of its contents being concealed)]

marmoreal *mär-mōr'i-əl, -mör', adj* of or like marble. [L *marmor* marble, from Gr *marmaros*; see **marmarosis**]

marmose *mär'mōs, n* a small South American opossum. [Fr, appar from *marmouset*; see **marmoset**]

marmoset *mär'mə-zet, n* a very small American monkey with a long hairy tail and furry tufts on its ears. [Fr *marmouset* grotesque figure]

marmot *mär'mət, n* a genus of stout burrowing rodents (*Marmota* or *Arctomys*), in N America called the woodchuck. [Ital *marmotto*, from Romansch *murmont*, from L *mūs, mūris*, mouse, and *mōns, montis* mountain]

marocain *mar'ə-kān, n* a dress material finished with a grain surface like morocco leather. [Fr *maroquin* morocco-leather; cf **maroquin**]

Maronian *ma-rō'ni-ən, adj* Virgilian. [Publius Vergilius *Marō* (*-ōnis*)]

Maronite *mar'ə-nīt, n* a member of a former Monothelite sect, now Uniats, living around Lebanon. [St *Marōn*, about AD 400, or John *Marōn*, a patriarch of the sect in the 7c]

maroon[1] *mə-rōōn', n* a brownish crimson; a detonating firework, *esp* one used as a distress signal. — *adj* of the colour maroon. [Fr *marron* a chestnut, from Ital *marrone* a chestnut]

maroon[2] *mə-rōōn', n* a fugitive slave, or a descendant of the same; a marooned person. — *vt* to put and leave ashore on a desolate island; to isolate uncomfortably (*lit* or *fig*). — *n* **maroon'er**. — *n* **maroon'ing**. [Fr *marron*, from Sp *cimarrón* wild]

maroquin *mar-ə-kēn', mar'ə-kin, mar'ə-kwin, n* goat-leather; morocco leather. [Fr; cf **marocain**]

maror *mä-rōr', -rör, n* a dish of bitter herbs (*esp* horseradish) eaten during the Jewish Passover, symbolizing the bitterness of the Egyptian oppression of the Israelites. [Heb]

marplot and **marprelate**. See under **mar**.

Marq *abbrev*: Marquis.

marque[1] *märk, n* reprisals (*obs*); a privateer. — **letter-of-marque'** or **letters-of-marque'** a privateer's licence to commit acts of hostility. [Fr]

marque[2] *märk*, *n* a brand or make, *esp* of car. [Fr]

marquee *mär-kē'*, *n* a large tent used for parties, exhibitions, etc. [From **marquise**, as if pl]

marquess *mär'kwis*, *n* in the UK, a title of nobility next below that of a duke: — *fem* **marchioness** (*mär'shən-es*, *-is*). — *n* **mar'quessate** the rank or position of a marquess. [Ety as for **marquis**]

marquetry or **marqueterie** *märk'i-tri*, *n* work, *esp* in furniture, inlaid with pieces of vari-coloured wood, ivory, metal, etc. [Fr *marqueterie*, from *marqueter* to inlay, from *marque* a mark]

marquis *mär'kwis*, *mar-kē'*, *n* a variant spelling of **marquess**, used *esp* by holders of pre-Union title; a title of nobility ranking next above a count in various European countries. — *n* **mar'quisate** the rank or position of a marquis. — *n* **marquise** (*mär-kēz'*) in various European countries, a marchioness; a style of parasol about 1850 (*hist*); an entrance canopy; a marquee; a ring set with gems arranged to form a pointed oval; a gem cut into the shape of a pointed oval; a chilled dessert halfway between a mousse and a parfait, often flavoured with chocolate. — *n* **mar'quisette** a woven clothing fabric, used also for curtains and mosquito nets. [OFr *marchis*, assimilated later to Fr *marquis*, from LL *marchēnsis* a prefect of the marches]

marram or **marrum** *mar'əm*, *n* a seaside grass (*Ammophila*, or *Psamma, arenaria*), frequently used to counter sand-erosion. [ON *marr* sea, *halmr* haulm, stem]

Marrano *mə-rä'nō*, *n* a medieval Spanish or Portuguese Jew converted to Christianity, *esp* one overtly practising Christianity to avoid persecution but secretly adhering to Judaism: — *pl* **Marra'nos**. [Sp, literally pig, the meat of which is forbidden to Jews]

marrels. See **meril**.

marriage *mar'ij*, *n* the ceremony, act or contract by which a man and woman become husband and wife; a similar ceremony, etc, between homosexuals; the union of a man and woman as husband and wife; a declaration of king and queen in bezique, etc; a close union (*fig*). — *adj* **marr'iageable** suitable for marriage. — *n* **marr'iageableness**. — **marr'iage-bed** the bed of a married couple; sexual intercourse within marriage (*euphem*); the rights and obligations of marriage; **marr'iage-bone** a merrythought; **marr'iage-broker** a person who, in certain cultures, arranges a marriage contract for a fee; **marriage bureau** an introduction agency for matching single people wishing to marry; a business agency designed to match entrepreneurs with potential investors (*fig*); **marr'iage-contract** a formal agreement to be married; an agreement concerning property rights between people about to marry; **marr'iage-favour** a knot or decoration worn at a marriage; **marriage guidance** help and advice given to people with marital problems; **marr'iage-licence** a licence to marry without proclamation of banns in a church; **marr'iage-lines** a certificate of marriage; **marriage of convenience** a marriage (or *fig*, a close business union, etc) for reasons of expediency rather than affection; **marriage partner** one's husband or wife; **marr'iage-portion** a dowry; **marr'iage-ring** a wedding ring; **marr'iage-settlement** an arrangement of property, etc before marriage, by which something is secured to the wife or her children if the husband dies. [OFr *mariage*; see **marry**[1]]

marrons glacés *ma-rɔ̃ gla-sā*, (*Fr*) *n pl* chestnuts poached in syrup and coated with a sugar glaze.

marrow[1] *mar'ō*, *n* the soft tissue in the hollow parts of the bones; pith or pulp of plants (*obs*); a vegetable marrow (see under **vegetable**); the essence or best part of anything; the inner meaning or purpose. — *adj* **marr'owish** of the nature of, or resembling, marrow. — *adj* **marr'owless** having no marrow. — *adj* **marr'owy** full of marrow; strong; forcible; pithy. — **marr'ow-bone** a bone containing marrow; (in *pl*) the knees or the bones of the knees; **marr'owfat** a rich kind of pea, called also **Dutch admiral pea**; **marr'ow-men** (*hist*) those who in the Church of Scotland supported the teaching of *The Marrow of Modern Divinity* (1645) after its republication in 1718; **marr'ow-squash** (*US*) vegetable marrow. — **spinal marrow** the spinal cord. [OE (Anglian) *merg*, *mærh* (W Sax *mearg*); Ger *Mark*]

marrow[2] *mar'ō*, (*N Eng*) *n* a mate; a companion; a match, equal, like; one of a pair. — *vi* to be a marrow. — *vt* to be a marrow to; to couple. — *adj* **marr'owless**. [Origin unknown]

marrowsky *mar-ow'ski*, *n* a spoonerism. — *vi* to utter a spoonerism. [Said to be from the name of a Polish count]

marrum. See **marram**.

marry[1] *mar'i*, *vt* to take for husband or wife; to give in marriage; to unite in matrimony; to unite, join, put together (sometimes with *up*; *fig*). — *vi* to take a husband or a wife: — *pr p* **marr'ying**; *pa t* and *pa p* **marr'ied**. — *adj* **marr'ied**. — *n* **marr'ier** a person who marries; the sort of person likely to take a husband or wife. — *n* and *adj* **marr'ying**. — **marry into** to become a member of (a family) by marriage; **marry off** to find a spouse for or succeed in marrying (eg one's son or daughter). [Fr *marier*, from L *marītāre* to marry, *marītus* a husband, from *mās*, *maris* a male]

marry[2] *mar'i*, (*archaic*) *interj* indeed! forsooth! — **marry come up** an exclamation of defiant protest. [By *Mary*]

Mars *märz*, *n* the Roman god of war; the planet next after the earth in terms of distance from the sun; iron (*alchemy*). [L *Mārs*, *Mārtis*]

Marsala *mär-sä'lə* (Ital *mär-sä'lä*), *n* a sweet, fortified wine from *Marsala* in Sicily.

Marseillaise *mär-sə-lāz'*, *-sā-ez'*, *n* the French national anthem, *orig* a revolutionary hymn composed by Rouget de Lisle in 1792, sung by the volunteers of *Marseilles* as they entered Paris, 30 July, and when they marched to the storming of the Tuileries.

marsh *märsh*, *n* a tract of wet land; a morass, swamp, or fen. — *adj* inhabiting or found in marshes. — *n* **marsh'iness**. — *adj* **marsh'y** of the nature of a marsh; covered with marshes. — **marsh-fe'ver** malaria; **marsh'-gas** methane; **marsh-harr'ier** a European harrier hawk frequenting marshes; **marsh hawk** a common N American hawk with a white patch on its rump (also **hen-harrier**); **marsh'land** marshy country; **marsh'lander** a person who inhabits marshland; **marsh'locks** a marsh-growing species of cinquefoil (*Potentilla* or *Comarum*; also **marsh-cinq'uefoil**); **marsh-mall'ow** a maritime marsh-growing plant (*Althaea officinalis*) very similar to the hollyhock; **marsh'mallow** a spongy, jellylike sweet, *orig* made from marsh-mallow root, now from sugar, egg white, gelatin, etc; an excessively soft, sweet or sentimental person or thing; **marsh'-man** an inhabitant of a marsh; **marsh marigold** the kingcup (*Caltha palustris*), a marsh plant of the buttercup family with flowers like big buttercups; **marsh'-robin** the chewink (qv); **marsh-sam'phire** a plant of the genus *Salicornia*, glasswort; **marsh tit** the grey tit (*Parus palustris*); **marsh warbler** a small brown and white Eurasian warbler with a pale stripe over the eyes; **marsh'wort** a small umbelliferous marsh plant related to celery. [OE *mersc*, *merisc*, orig adj; see **mere**[1]]

marshal *mär'shl*, *n* a farrier (*obs*); an officer in a royal household, *orig* the king's farrier, later having responsibility for military arrangements, the regulation of ceremonies, preservation of order, points of etiquette, etc; any official with similar functions; a law-court officer with responsibility for prisoners; a prison-keeper; (at Oxford University) a proctor's attendant or bulldog; the chief officer who regulated combats in the lists (*hist*); (in France and the French colonies) an officer of the highest military rank; a civil officer appointed to execute the process of the courts (*US*); the chief officer of a police or fire-brigade (*US*). — *vt* to arrange in order; to usher; to combine in or with one coat of arms. — *vi* to come together in order: — *pr p* **mar'shalling**; *pa t* and *pa p* **mar'shalled**. — *n* **mar'shalcy** the rank, office or department of a marshal; *esp* (in the form **Mar'shalsea**) till 1842 a prison in Southwark, under the marshal of the royal household. — *n* **mar'shaller**. — *n* **mar'shalling**. — *n* **mar'shalship**. — **marshalling yard** a place where railway wagons are sorted out and made up into trains. — **air-marshal**, etc see under **air**; **field marshal** see under **field**; **marshal of the Royal Air Force** an officer of supreme rank in the Royal Air Force, ranking with an admiral of the fleet or a field marshal. [OFr *mareschal* (Fr *maréchal*); from OHGer *marah* a horse, and *schalh* (Ger *Schalk*) a servant]

Marsilea *mär-sil'i-ə*, *n* a genus of aquatic leptosporangiate ferns, with four-lobed leaves and bean-like stalked sporocarps, giving name to a family **Marsileā'ceae**. — Also **Marsil'ia**. [Named after L F *Marsigli* (1658–1730), Italian naturalist]

Marsipobranchii *mär-sip-ō-brangk'i-ī*, *n pl* the *Cyclostomata* (qv). — *n* **mar'sipobranch**. — *adj* **marsipobranch'iate**. [Gr *marsipos* pouch, and *branchia* gills]

marsupium *mär-sū'pi-əm*, (*zool*) *n* a pouch. — *adj* **marsū'pial** relating to a pouch or to the *Marsupialia*; of the nature of a pouch; of the *Marsupialia*. — *n* a member of the *Marsupialia*. — *n pl* **Marsupiā'lia** an order of mammals co-extensive with the subclass *Metatheria*, animals whose young are born in a very imperfect state and are usually carried in a pouch by the female. [L *marsūpium*, from Gr *marsip(p)ion*, *marsyp(p)ion* a pouch]

mart[1] *märt*, *n* a place of trade, a market. — *vi* (*Shakesp*) to deal or trade. — *vt* (*Shakesp*) to sell or trade in. [Du *markt*, mart; cf **market**]

mart[2] *märt*, (*Scot* and *NEng*) *n* a cow or ox fattened, killed (*usu* about Martinmas), and salted for winter use. [Gaelic *mart* cow, ox]

martagon *mär'tə-gən*, *n* a purple Eurasian lily with petals curling backwards, the Turk's-cap lily. [Turk *martagān* a kind of turban]

martel *mär'təl*, (*hist*) *n* a medieval hammer-like weapon with a pointed head. — *vi* (*Spenser*) to hammer: — *pa t* **mar'telled**. [OFr *martel*]

martellato *mär-tel-lä'tō*, (*music*) *adj* played with a hammering touch, or with short quick detached strokes of the bow. — Also *adv*. [Ital, hammered]

martello *mär-tel'ō*, *n* (in full **martello tower**) a circular fort for coastal defence: — *pl* **martell'os**. [From Cape *Mortella* in Corsica, where one resisted for some time a British cannonade in 1794]

marten *mär'tən*, *n* an animal (eg the pine-marten) closely related to the weasel, or other species of *Mustela*. [Fr *martre*, from the Gmc root seen in Ger *Marder*, and OE *mearth* marten]

martenot. See **Ondes Martenot**.

martensite *mär'tin-zīt*, *n* a constituent of rapidly cooled steel consisting of a solid solution of carbon in iron and resulting from the decomposition of austenite at low temperatures. — *adj* **martensitic** (*-zit'ik*). [Named after Adolph *Martens* (died 1914), German metallurgist]

martial *mär'shl*, *adj* belonging or relating to Mars, the god of war, or to the planet Mars; of or relating to war, or to the armed forces; military; warlike. — *n* **mar'tialism**. — *n* **mar'tialist** (*rare*) a soldier. — *adv* **mar'tially**. — *n* **mar'tialness**. — **martial art** (*usu* in *pl*) any of various combative sports or methods of self-defence (*usu* of oriental origin) including karate and kung fu; **martial artist** a practitioner of martial arts; **martial law** the exercise of military power by a government, etc in time of emergency (war, riot, etc) with the temporary suspension of ordinary administration and policing. [Fr *martial*, from L *mārtiālis*, from *Mārs*]

Martian *mär'shən*, *adj* of Mars (god or planet); of war or battle (*Spenser*). — *n* (*science fiction*) an imagined inhabitant of Mars. [L *Mārtius*, from *Mārs*]

martin *mar'tin*, *n* a bird of the swallow genus (*Delichon* or *Chelidon*). — Also **mar'tinet** (*obs*). [The name *Martin*]

martinet[1] *mär-ti-net'*, *mär'*, *n* a system of drill drawn up by *Martinet*, a French general in the reign of Louis XIV (*obs*); a strict disciplinarian. — *n* **martinet'ism**.

martinet[2]. See under **martin**.

martingale *mär'tin-gāl*, *n* a strap passing between a horse's forelegs, fastened to the girth and to the bit, noseband or reins, to keep its head down; a short spar under the bowsprit (*naut*); (in gambling) the policy of doubling the stake on losing. [Fr, perh from a kind of breeches worn at *Martigues* in Provence]

Martini® *mär-tē'nē*, *n* a type of vermouth made by the firm of *Martini* and Rossi; (without *cap*) a cocktail of vermouth, gin, bitters, etc, *perh* named after its inventor.

Martini or **Martini-Henry** *mär-tē'nē -hen'ri*, *n* a 19c rifle with an action designed by Frederic *Martini* and barrel by H *Henry*, a gunsmith.

Martinmas *mär'tin-məs*, *n* the *mass* or feast of St *Martin*, 11 Nov, a quarter-day in Scotland. — Also (*obs*) **Mar'tlemas**.

martlet *märt'lit*, *n* the martin; a representation of a martin or swallow without feet, used as a bearing, a crest, or a mark of cadency for a fourth son (*heraldry*). [From Fr *martinet*, dimin of *martin* martin]

martyr *mär'tər*, *n* a person bearing witness to his or her religious beliefs by refusing to renounce them in death; a person who suffers for his or her beliefs; a person who suffers, or pretends to suffer, greatly from any cause, a victim. — *vt* to make a martyr of, *esp* by putting to death; to torture. — *n* **mar'tyrdom** the state of being a martyr; the sufferings or death of a martyr; torment generally. — *n* **martyrium** (*mär-tēr'i-əm*; (*L*)) same as **martyry**: — *pl* **martyria**. — *vt* **mar'tyrize** or **-ise** to offer as a sacrifice; to cause to suffer martyrdom; to martyr. — *adj* **martyrolog'ical**. — *n* **martyrol'ogist**. — *n* **martyrol'ogy** a history of martyrs; a discourse on martyrdom; an official list of martyrs. — *n* **mar'tyry** a shrine, chapel or monument erected in memory of a martyr. [OE, from L, from Gr, a witness]

marvel *mär'vl*, *n* a wonder; anything astonishing or wonderful; astonishment (*archaic*). — *vi* to wonder; to feel astonishment. — *vt* to wonder at (*obs*): — *pr p* **mar'velling**; *pa t* and *pa p* **mar'velled**. — *adj* **mar'vellous** astonishing; almost or altogether beyond belief; improbable, very good, extremely pleasing (*colloq*). — *adv* **mar'vellously**. — *n* **mar'vellousness**. — **marvel of Peru** (*pə-rōō'*) a showy garden flower (*Mirabilis jalapa*, family *Nyctaginaceae*) from Mexico, open and scented in the evening. [Fr *merveille*, from L *mīrābilis* wonderful, from *mīrārī* to wonder]

marver *mär'vər*, *n* a slab of marble, cast-iron, etc, on which molten glass is manually rolled during blowing. — *vt* and *vi* to roll (glass) on a marver. [Fr *marbre* marble]

Marxian *märks'i-ən*, *adj* of or relating to Karl *Marx* (1818–83) or his economic and political theories, the basis of modern communism. — *n* a follower of Marx, a Marxist. — *n* **Marx'ianism** Marxism. — *n* **Marx'ism**. — *n* and *adj* **Marx'ist**.

marxisant *märk-si-zã*, (*Fr*) *adj* of Marxist sympathies.

Mary *mār'i*, (*Austr derog slang*) *n* (also without *cap*) a woman, *esp* an Aboriginal woman. [Pidgin, from the woman's name]

marybud *mā'ri-bud*, *n* a marigold bud.

Mary Jane *mār'i jān*, (*NAm slang*) *n* marijuana. [assumed transl of **marijuana**]

Maryolatry, **Maryology**, etc. See under **Marian**[1].

marzipan *mär-zi-pan'*, *n* a sweet almond paste used in cakes and confectionery, formerly called **marchpane**. [Ger, from Ital *marzapane*]

Mas. See **Mass**.

mas *mas*, *n* a house or farm in the south of France. [Provençal]

mas. or **masc**. *abbrev*: masculine.

-mas *-məs*, *combining form* denoting a church festival or feast day, as in *Candlemas*, *Christmas*, *Martinmas*, etc. [Ety as for **mass**[2]]

masa *mas'ə*, *n* in Mexican cooking, a dough made from **masa harina**, ground, dried maize, used to make tamales, etc. [Sp, dough, from L *massa* a lump]

Masai *mä'sī*, *n* (a member of) an African people of the highlands of Kenya and Tanzania. — Also *adj*.

masc. See **mas**.

mascara *mas-kä'rə*, *n* colouring for the eyelashes, a cosmetic. [See ety for **mask**]

mascaron *mas'kə-ron*, (*archit*) *n* a grotesque face on a keystone, door-knocker, etc. [See ety for **mask**]

mascarpone *mas-kär-pō'nā*, *n* a soft Italian cream cheese. [Ital]

mascle *mas'kl*, *n* a lozenge-shaped, perforated bearing (*heraldry*); a lozenge-shaped plate for scale-armour. — *adj* **mas'cled**. — *adj* **mas'cūly**. [Appar OFr *mascle*, from LL *mascula*, from L *macula* mesh, influenced by OHGer *masca* mesh]

mascon *mas'kon*, *n* any of several mass concentrations of dense material, of uncertain origin, lying beneath the moon's surface. [*mass concentration*]

mascot *mas'kət*, *n* a talisman; a supposed bringer of good luck. [Fr *mascotte*]

masculine *mäs'*, *mas'kū-lin*, *-līn*, *adj* male (*rare*); characteristic of, peculiar to, or appropriate to, a man or the male sex; mannish; of the grammatical gender to which words denoting males belong. — *n* the male sex or nature; a male; a word of masculine gender. — *adv* **mas'culinely**. — *n* **mas'culineness**. — *n* **mas'culinist** an advocate of men's rights or privileges (coined in supposed imitation of *feminist*). — *n* **masculin'ity**. — *vt* **mas'culinize** or **-ise** to cause to develop a masculine character or appearance. — *vi* to develop such character or appearance. — **masculine ending** a stressed syllable at the end of a line (*prosody*); **masculine rhyme** a rhyme on a final stressed syllable; in French, one without a final mute *e*. [Fr, from L *masculīnus*, from *masculus* male, from *mās* a male]

masculy. See under **mascle**.

maser or **MASER** *māz'ər*, *n* a device used to amplify long-range radar and radio astronomy signals (very small when not amplified) while generating little unwanted noise within itself. — *vi* **mase** (a back-formation) to act as a maser by generating and amplifying microwaves. [*M*icrowave *a*mplification by *s*timulated *e*mission of *r*adiation]

MASH *mash*, (*US*) *n* *m*obile *a*rmy *s*urgical *h*ospital.

mash[1] *mash*, *n* in brewing and distilling, a mixture of crushed malt and hot water; a mixture, eg of bran with meal or turnips, beaten and stirred as a food for animals; any material beaten or crushed into a soft or pulpy state; mashed potatoes (*colloq*); a crushed condition; a muddle, hash, or bungle. — *vt* to make into a mash; to pound down or crush; to infuse (*dialect*). — *n* **mash'er**. — *n* **mash'ing**. — *adj* **mash'y** produced by mashing; of the nature of a mash. — **mash'man** a worker in a brewery or a distillery who helps to make the mash; **mash'-tub**, **mash'-tun**, **mash'-vat** or **mash'ing-tub** a vessel in which the mash is mixed in a brewery or distillery. [OE *masc(-wyrt)* mash(-wort)]

mash[2] *mash*, (*archaic slang*) *vt* to flirt with; to treat as a sweetheart, court. — *vi* to flirt. — *n* a person who mashes or is mashed; a masher; the action of mashing; an infatuation or crush. — *n* **mash'er** a man who dresses showily to attract attention, a dandy; a flirt. — **mashed on** in love with. [Ety doubtful]

mashallah *mä-shä'lä*, *interj* (among Muslims) what God will. [Ar *mā shā'llāh*]

mashie or **mashy** *mash'i*, *n* an iron golf club for lofting, a number five iron. — **mashie-nib'lick** a club between mashie and niblick, a number six iron. [Perh Fr *massue* club]

mashlam, **mashlin**, etc. See **maslin**.

mashua *mash'ū-ə*, *n* a tuber plant, *Tropaeslum tuberosum*, grown in the Andes.

masjid *mus'jid*, *n* a mosque. [Ar]

Mas-John. See **Mass**.

mask[1] *mäsk*, *n* a covering for the face, or the upper part of it, for concealment, disguise, protection, amusement or ceremonial purposes; a disingenuous or hypocritical expression or posture, a false face; a grotesque representation of a face worn in ancient or Japanese, etc drama, or used as an architectural ornament, etc; a fox's (or other animal) face or head; a mould of a face; a masque; a cosmetic face pack; a disguise, pretence, or concealment (*fig*); any means of screening or disguising; a screen to cover part of a light-sensitive surface (*photog*); a screen used to cover parts of a surface on to the exposed parts of which an integrated circuit is to be etched. — *vt* to cover the face of with a mask; to hide, cloak, screen or disguise; to coat (food) with a sauce, etc, before serving. — *vi* to masquerade; to be disguised in any way. — *adj* **masked** wearing a mask; concealed; personate (*bot*). — *n* **mask'er** a person who wears a mask; a masquerader; a device that produces a noise to mask a different auditory stimulus, used eg by tinnitus sufferers. — **masked ball** a ball at which the dancers wear masks. [Fr *masque*, from Sp *máscara* or Ital *maschera*, of doubtful origin, appar connected in some way with LL *mascus*, *masca* a ghost, and with Ar *maskharah* a jester, man in masquerade]

mask[2] *mäsk*, (*Scot*) *vt* to steep or infuse. — *vi* to be infusing. [See **mash**[1]]

maskalonge, **maskallonge**, **maskinonge** and **maskanonge**. See **muskellunge**.

maskirovka *mas-ki-rov'kə*, *n* the use or practice of deception as a military stratagem; camouflage. [Russ, camouflage, from *maska* disguise, mask]

maslin *mas'lin*, *n* a mixed grain, *esp* rye and wheat. — Also (*Scot*) **mash'lam**, **mash'lim**, **mash'lin**, **mash'loch** (*-lohh*) or **mash'lum**. [OFr *mesteillon*, from LL *mistiliō*, *-ōnis*, from L *mistus* mixed, from *miscēre* to mix]

masochism *maz'ə-kizm*, *n* pleasure, *esp* sexual pleasure, in being dominated or treated cruelly; morbid gratification in suffering pain, physical or mental. — *n* **mas'ochist**. — *adj* **masochist'ic**. [From the Austrian novelist Sacher-*Masoch* (1836–95), who described it]

mason *mā'sn*, *n* a person who cuts, prepares and lays stones; a builder in stone; a member of the society of freemasons. — *vt* to build or repair in stone, brick, etc. — *adj* **masonic** (*mə-son'ik*) relating to freemasonry. — *adj* **mā'sonried** constructed of masonry. — *n* **mā'sonry** the art, skill, or practice of a mason; the work of a mason; building-work in stone; freemasonry. — *adj* consisting of stone-work. — **mason bee** a small bee (*Osmia rufa*) which builds its nest in logs, old walls, etc; **mason's mark** a device carved on stones by a mason to identify his share in the work. — **master-mason** see under **master**. [OFr *masson* (Fr *maçon*), from LL *maciō*, *-ōnis*, prob Gmc; cf MHGer *mezzo* a mason, whence Ger *Steinmetz* a stone-mason; OHGer *meizan* to hew, whence Ger *Meissel* a chisel]

Mason-Dixon Line *mā'sn-dik'sn līn*, *n* the boundary between Pennsylvania and Maryland following a line surveyed between 1763 and 1767 by Charles *Mason* and Jeremiah *Dixon*, later thought of as separating the free Northern states from the slave states of the South.

mason jar *mā'sn jär*, (*US*) *n* (also with *cap*) an airtight glass jar for preserving food. [J L *Mason*, the patentee]

masoolah, **massoola** or **masula** *mä-sōō'lə*, (*hist*) *n* a tall, many-oared Indian surf-boat. [Origin obscure]

Masora or **Masorah** *mä-sō'rə*, *-sö'*, *n* a collection of critical notes on the text of the Old Testament. — Also **Masso'ra**, **Masso'rah** or **Maso'reth**. — *n* **Mas'orete** or **Mass'orete** (*-rēt*) a compiler of the Masora. — *adj* **Masoretic** or **Massoretic** (*-ret'ik*). [Heb *māsoreth*, mod *māsōrāh*]

masque *mäsk*, *n* a masked person; a company of maskers; a masquerade or masked ball; a form of courtly spectacle in vogue in the 16 and 17c, in which masked performers danced and acted, developing into a form of drama with scenery and music; a literary composition for the purpose; a mask (*obs*). — *n* **masqu'er** a masker. [Ety as for **mask**[1]]

masquerade *mäsk-ər-ād'*, *n* an assembly of people wearing masks, costumes, *esp* at a ball; disguise. — *vi* to wear a mask; to take part in a masquerade; to go in disguise; to pretend to be (with *as*). — *n* **masquerā'der**. [Fr *mascarade*; see **mask**[1]]

Mass, Mas *mäs*, **Mess** or **Mes** *mes*, (*obs*) *n* shortened form of **Master**. — **Mas'-John, Mass'-John, Mes'-John** or **Mess'-John** (*obs*) a contemptuous name for a Scottish parish minister.

Mass. *abbrev*: Massachusetts (US state).

mass[1] *mas*, *n* a lump of matter; matter, material (*obs*); a quantity; a collected or coherent body of matter; an unbroken expanse; the aggregate, total; the main body; the greater part; the principal part; the quantity of matter in any body, measured by its resistance to change of motion and the force of gravity exerted upon it; (in *pl*) the ordinary people, the people as a whole. — *adj* relating to a mass, or to large numbers or quantities, or to ordinary people as a whole. — *vt* to form into a mass; to bring together in masses. — *vi* to assemble or come together in a mass or masses. — *n* **mass'iness**. — *adj* **massive** (*mas'iv*) bulky; weighty; giving an impression of weight; not separated into parts or elements; without crystalline form; great in quantity; on a very large scale, or of great size or power (*fig*). — *adv* **mass'ively**. — *n* **mass'iveness**. — *adj* **mass'y** massive, made up of masses. — **mass defect** the difference between the sum of the masses of the neutrons and protons in a nucleus and the mass of the nucleus itself; **mass-energy equivalence** (*phys*) the fundamental principle that mass and energy are equivalent and interconvertible shown by the **mass-energy equation** $E = mc^2$; **mass market** the market for mass-produced goods. — *vt* **mass-mar'ket**. — **mass-mar'keting**; **mass media** and **mass medium** see under **medium**; **mass meeting** a large meeting for a public protest or discussion; **mass number** the atomic weight of an isotope, the number of nucleons in the nucleus; **mass observation** the study of the habits, opinions, etc of the general body of a community. — *vt* **mass-produce'** to produce in great quantity by a standardized process. — *adj* **mass-produced'**. — **mass production**; **mass radiography** the X-raying of large numbers of people by means of mobile units; **mass spectrograph** an instrument by means of which a positive ray spectrum can be obtained, the images due to particles of different masses being spaced according to the masses, so that the atomic weights of the particles can be deduced; **mass spectrometer** an instrument like the mass spectrograph but measuring not the masses of particles but the relative number of particles of each mass present; **mass spectrometry**. — **in mass** as a body; all together; **in the mass** in the aggregate; as a whole; indiscriminately; **law of mass action** (*chem*) the law stating that the rate of chemical change is proportional to the product of the concentrations of the reacting substances. [Fr *masse*, from L *massa* a lump, prob from Gr *māza* a barley cake, from *massein* to knead]

mass[2] (often with *cap*) *mas* or *mäs*, *n* the celebration of the Lord's Supper or Eucharist in RC and some Protestant churches; the religious service for it; a musical setting of certain parts of the RC liturgy; a church service (*Shakesp*). — **mass'-bell** a sacring bell; **mass'-book** the RC missal or service-book; **mass'priest** formerly, a RC secular priest, as distinct from one living under a rule; later, a priest retained in chantries, etc to say masses for the dead; a RC priest generally. [OE *mæsse*, from LL *missa*, from L *mittere* to send away, perh from the phrase at the close of service, *ite, missa est* (*ecclesia*) go, (the congregation) is dismissed]

massa *mas'ə*, (*esp Southern US*) *n* a corruption of **master**.

massacre *mas'ə-kər* (*Spenser* sometimes *-ak'*), *n* indiscriminate slaughter, *esp* with cruelty; carnage. — *vt* to kill with violence and cruelty; to slaughter. [Fr; origin doubtful]

massage *ma'säzh, mə-säzh'*, *n* a (system of) treatment for painful muscles, etc by stroking, pressing, tapping, kneading, friction, etc; manipulation, alteration of the appearance of something (*esp* data of any kind) to show it in a more favourable light. — *vt* to subject to massage; to present in a favourable light by devious means. — *n* **massa'gist** or **masseur** (*-sœr'*, *-sûr'*) a practitioner of massage: — *fem* **masseuse** (*-sœz'*). [Fr, from Gr *massein* to knead]

massaranduba *mas-ə-ran-dōō'bə*, *n* the Brazilian milk-tree (*Mimusops elata*). — Also **masseranduba** or **maceranduba**. [Port *maçaranduba*, from Tupí name]

massé *mas'ā*, *n* (in billiards, etc) a stroke made with the cue vertical or nearly so, so as to achieve a sharp swerve in the cue ball. [Fr]

masseter *mas-ē'tər*, *n* a muscle that raises the under jaw. [Gr *masētēr* (not *massētēr*) chewer, from *masaesthai* to chew]

masseur and **masseuse**. See under **massage**.

massicot *mas'i-kot*, *n* yellow lead monoxide. [Fr]

massif *ma-sēf'*, *mas'if*, *n* a central mountain mass; an orographic fault-block. [Fr]

massive, massy, etc. See under **mass**[1].

massoola. See **masoolah**.

Massora, Massorah and **Massorete**. See **Masora**.

massymore *mas-i-mōr'*, *-mör'*, (*Scott*) *n* a subterranean prison. [Perh Sp *mazmorra*; cf **mattamore**]

mast[1] *mäst*, *n* a long upright pole, *esp* one for carrying the sails of a ship. — *vt* to supply with a mast or masts. — *adj* **mast'ed**. — *adj* **mast'less**. — **mast'head** the top of a mast; the name of a newspaper or periodical in the typographical form in which it normally appears, or a similar block of information regularly used as a heading. — *vt* to raise to the masthead; to punish by sending to the masthead. — **mast'house** the place where masts are made or stored. — **before the mast** as a common sailor (ie with quarters in the forecastle, forward of the mast). [OE *mæst*; Ger *Mast*]

mast[2] *mäst*, *n* the fruit of the oak, beech, chestnut, and other forest trees, on which pigs feed; nuts, acorns. — *adj* **mast'ful**. — *adj* **mast'less**. — *adj* **mast'y** of the nature of mast; as if well fed on mast. — **mast cell** a cell in connective tissue thought to produce histamine and other agents controlling the release of acid in the stomach. — *adj* **mast'-fed**. [OE *mæst*; Ger *Mast*, whence *mästen* to feed]

MASTA *mas'tə*, *abbrev*: Medical Advisory Service for Travellers Abroad.

mastaba *mas'tə-bə*, *n* an ancient Egyptian tomb with sloping sides and a flat roof, having an outer chamber in which offerings were made, connecting with an inner one containing the image of the dead person, with a shaft descending to the actual grave. [Ar *mastabah* a bench]

mastectomy *mas-tek'tə-mi*, (*med*) *n* surgical removal of a breast. — **radical mastectomy** the surgical removal of a breast together with some pectoral muscles and lymph nodes of the armpit. [Gr *mastos* breast, and *ektomē* excision]

master *mäs'tər*, *n* a person (*esp* male) who commands or controls; a lord or owner; a leader or ruler; a teacher; an employer; the commander of a merchant ship; formerly, the navigator or sailing-master of a ship-of-war; a person eminently skilled in anything, *esp* art; a person who has complete knowledge of an art, science, etc; a workman who has set up on his own account, or is qualified to do so; (with *cap*) formerly prefixed to a name or designation as Mr is now, now only of a boy in this use; (*usu* with *cap*) a title of dignity or office, eg a degree conferred by universities, such as *Master of Arts*, etc, an official of the Supreme Court, the designation of the heir apparent to certain Scottish titles, or of his son, the head of certain university colleges, of a lodge of freemasons, etc; a husband (*dialect*); an original (film, record, etc) from which copies are made; a master-card. — *adj* chief; controlling; predominant; of a master; of the rank of a master; original. — *vt* to become master of; to overcome; to gain control over; to acquire a thorough knowledge of; to become skilful in; to rule as master; to temper, to season; to treat with lye (*tanning*). — *vi* (*archaic*; also *vt* with *it*) to act the master or be a schoolmaster. — *n* **mas'terate** the degree, title or rank of master. — *n* **mas'terdom** power of control; masterfulness. — *adj* **mas'terful** exercising the authority, skill or power of a master; imperious; masterly (*rare*). — *adv* **mas'terfully**. — *n* **mas'terfulness**. — *n* **mas'terhood**. — *n* **mas'tering** the action of the verb *master*; lye. — *adj* **mas'terless** without a master or owner; ungoverned; unsubdued; beyond control. — *n* **mas'terliness**. — *adj* **mas'terly** like a master; with the skill of a master; overbearing (*obs*). — *adv* with the skill of a master. — *n* **mas'tership** the condition, authority, status, office, or term of office of a master; rule or dominion; superiority. — *n* **mas'tery** the power or authority of a master; upper hand; control; supreme skill or knowledge. — **master-at-arms'** a ship's chief police officer; **master-build'er** a chief builder; a person who directs or employs others; **mas'ter-card** the card that commands a suit or is the highest of all those remaining to be played; **mas'ter-class** the dominant class in a society; a lesson, *esp* in music, given to talented students by a renowned expert; **mas'ter-clock** one that regulates other clocks electrically; **mas'ter-hand** the hand of a master; a person highly skilled; **mas'ter-joint** (*geol*) a joint of the most marked system of those by which a rock is intersected; **mas'ter-key** a key that opens many (different) locks, *esp* all the locks in a certain building; a clue able to guide one out of many difficulties (*fig*); **masterly inactivity** the position or part of a neutral or a Fabian combatant, carried out with diplomatic skill, so as to preserve a predominant influence without risking anything; **master-mar'iner** the captain of a merchant-vessel or fishing-vessel; **master-ma'son** a freemason who has attained the third degree; **mas'termind** a mind, or a person having a mind, of very great ability; the person conceiving or directing a project, *esp* a criminal enterprise. — *vt* to originate, think out, and direct. — **master page** a word-processing template which automatically inserts repeated elements in each page of a document; **master-pass'ion**; **mas'terpiece** a piece of work worthy of a master; one's greatest achievement. — Also **mas'terwork**; **master race** see **Herrenvolk**; **mas'tersinger** a Meistersinger (qv); **mas'terstroke** a stroke or performance worthy of a master; superior performance; an effective, well-timed act; **mas'ter-switch** a switch for controlling the effect of a number of other switches or contactors; **mas'ter-wheel** the wheel in a machine which imparts motion to other parts; **mas'terwort** a plant (*Peucedanum*, or *Imperatoria*, *ostruthium*) related to the parsnip, once used as a pot-herb and in medicine; applied also to *Astrantia*, etc. — **little masters** a 16–17c group of followers of the German painter and engraver Albrecht Dürer, notable for fine work on wood and copper; **master of ceremonies**, see under **ceremonies**; **master of the horse** the Roman *Magister Equitum*, an official appointed by the dictator to act next under himself; an equerry, *esp* a high official of the British court; **Master of the King's** or **Queen's Musick** an honorary title conferred by the British sovereign *usu* on a distinguished British composer; **Master of the Rolls** in England, the head of the civil division of the Court of Appeal, appointed by the Crown on the advice of the Prime Minister; **Master of the Temple** the preacher of the Temple Church in London; **master-slave manipulator** a manipulator, *esp* one used to handle, from behind a protective screen, radioactive material; **masters of the schools** at Oxford University, the conductors of the first examination (*Responsions*) for the degree of BA; **old masters** a term applied collectively to the great European painters, *esp* of the 16c and 17c; **passed master** one who has passed as a master; a qualified or accomplished master, a thorough proficient (also **pastmaster**). [Partly OE *mægester*, partly OFr *maistre* (Fr *maître*), both from L *magister*, from root of *magnus* great]

mastic or **mastich** *mas'tik*, *n* a pale yellow gum resin from certain Mediterranean trees, used for varnish or cement; a tree exuding mastic, *esp* the lentisk (*Pistachia lentiscus*, cashew-nut family); a bituminous or oily cement of various kinds. [Fr *mastic*, from LL *mastichum*, from Gr *mastichē*]

masticate *mas'ti-kāt*, *vt* to chew; to knead mechanically, as in rubber manufacture. — *adj* **mas'ticable** that may be chewed. — *n* **masticā'tion**. — *n* **mas'ticātor** a person who masticates; a tooth or jaw (*facetious*); a machine for grinding; a machine for kneading india-rubber. — *adj* **mas'ticatory** (*-kə-tə-ri*) chewing; adapted for chewing. — *n* a substance chewed to increase the saliva. [L *masticāre*, *-ātum*; cf Gr *mastax* jaw, *mastichaein* to grind the teeth]

masticot. Same as **massicot**.

mastiff *mas'tif*, *n* a thick-set, powerful breed of dog, often used as a watchdog. [OFr *mastin*, appar from L *mansuētus*, tame; perh confused with OFr *mestif* mongrel]

Mastigophora *mas-ti-gof'ə-rə*, (*zool*) *n pl* the flagellates in a wide sense. — *n* and *adj* **mastigoph'oran**. — *adj* **mastigophoric** (*-gə-for'ik*) or **mastigoph'orous** of the Mastigophora; whip-carrying. [Gr *mastīx*, *-īgos* whip, and *phoreein* to carry]

mastitis *mas-tī'tis*, *n* inflammation of the breast or udder. [Gr *mastos* breast, and **-itis**]

mastodon *mas'tə-don*, *n* an animal of the *Mastodon* genus of extinct mammals resembling elephants, so named from the teatlike prominences of the molar teeth of some species. — *adj* **mastodon'tic**. [Gr *mastos* breast, and *odous*, *odontos* a tooth]

mastodynia *mast-ō-dī'ni-ə*, (*med*) *n* pain in the breasts. [Gr *mastos* breast, and *odynē* pain]

mastoid *mas'toid*, *adj* like a nipple or a teat. — *n* a prominence on the temporal bone behind the ear (also **mastoid bone** or **process**); mastoiditis (*colloq*). — *adj* **mastoid'al**. — *n* **mastoidī'tis** inflammation of the air cells of the mastoid processes. [Gr *mastoeidēs* like a breast]

masturbate *mas'tər-bāt*, *vi* and *vt* to stimulate, *esp* by oneself, (the sexual organs) by manipulation, etc so as to produce orgasm. — *n* **masturbā'tion**. — *n* **mas'turbātor**. — *adj* **masturbat'ory**. [L *masturbārī*]

masty. See under **mast**[2].

masu *mä'soo*, *n* a Japanese salmon (*Oncorhynchus masou*). [Jap]

masula. See **masoolah**.

masurium *mə-soo'ri-əm*, *-sū'*, *n* a name proposed for element No. 43 when its discovery was prematurely claimed (see **technetium**). [*Masurenland*, in East Prussia, now in N Poland]

mat[1] *mat*, *n* a piece of fabric or material of any of various types and thicknesses, laid on the ground for any of various purposes, eg covering part of the floor, standing or lying on, wiping one's shoes on at a threshold, absorbing shock on landing or falling in gymnastics, wrestling, etc; a rug; a smaller piece of cloth, cork or other material for placing under a vase, dish, or other object to prevent damage to the surface it stands on; a sack of matting used to cover a chest of tea, coffee, etc; a certain weight held by such a sack; a closely interwoven or tangled mass, *esp* of hair or vegetation, or of brushwood protecting a riverbank; a web of rope-yarn. — *vt* to cover with mats; to interweave; to tangle closely. — *vi* to become tangled in a mass: — *pr p* **matt'ing**; *pa t* and *pa p* **matt'ed**. — *n* **matt'ing** mat-making; becoming matted; covering with mats; material used as mats. — **mat'grass** or **mat'weed** a small, tufted, rushlike moorland grass (*Nardus stricta*); marram. — **on the mat** on the carpet (*fig*). [OE *matt(e)*, *meatte*, from L *matta* a mat; perh of Punic origin]

mat[2], **matt** or **matte** *mat*, *adj* (of a surface) dull, lustreless or roughened to eliminate gloss. — *n* **mat** a dull uniform finish or surface; a border of dull gold or of white or colour round a picture; a punch for roughening a surface. — *vt* to produce a dull surface on; to frost (glass). [Fr *mat*; Ger *matt* dull; cf **checkmate**; **amate**[2], **mate**[2]]

mat. *abbrev*: matinée; matrix.

matachin *mat-ə-chēn'* or *-shēn'*, *n* a masked sword-dancer or sword-dance (*hist*); any of a group of Mexican Indian ritual dancers (*pl* **matachi'ni**, *fem* **matachi'na**). [Fr (obs) *matachin* and Sp *matachín*, perh from Ar *mutawajjihīn* masked]

matador *mat'ə-dör* or **matadore** *mat'ə-dōr*, *n* (*usu* **matador**) the man who kills the bull in bullfights; one of the three chief cards in the games ombre and quadrille; (*usu* **matadore**) a form of dominoes. — *n* **matadō'ra** a female matador. [Sp, from *matar* to kill, from L *mactāre* to kill, to honour by sacrifice, from *mactus* honoured]

matamata *ma-tə-mä'tə*, *n* a South American river-turtle. [Port, from Tupí *matamatá*]

match[1] *mach*, *n* a piece of inflammable material which easily takes or carries fire; a piece of treated cord, readily inflammable but slow-burning, for firing a gun, an explosive, etc; a short stick of wood or other material tipped with an easily ignited material. — **match'box** a box for holding matches; **match'-cord** (*obs*) a piece of rope used as a slow-match; **match'lock** the lock of a musket containing a match for firing it; a musket so fired; **match'-maker**; **match'stick** the wooden shaft of a match. — *adj* very thin, like a matchstick; (of figures in a drawing, etc) having limbs suggested by single lines. — **match'wood** touchwood; wood suitable for matches; splinters. [OFr *mesche* (Fr *mèche*); origin obscure]

match[2] *mach*, *n* that which tallies or exactly agrees with another thing; an equal; a person who can stand up to or get the better of someone else; a condition of exact agreement, compatibility or close resemblance, *esp* in colours; equality in contest; a compact (*obs*); a formal contest or game; a pairing; a marriage; a person to be gained in marriage. — *vi* to be exactly or nearly alike; to correspond; to form a union; to compete or encounter (*esp* on equal terms). — *vt* to be equal to; to be a counterpart to; to be compatible with, or exactly like, in colour, etc; to be able to compete with; to find an equal or counterpart to; to pit or set against another in contest or as equal; to treat as equal; to fit in with; to suit; to join in marriage; to make the impedances of (two circuits) equal, so as to produce maximum transfer of energy (*electronics*). — *adj* **match'able**. — *adj* **matched**. — *n* **match'er**. — *adj* **match'ing**. — *adj* **match'less** having no match or equal; superior to all; peerless; not matching (*Spenser*). — *adv* **match'lessly**. — *n* **match'lessness**. — **match'board** one of a number of boards with a tongue cut along one edge and a groove in the opposite edge, fitted one into the next to make a wall facing, etc; **match'boarding**; **matched sample** a group of people of the same age, sex, income, etc, as another group, used as a sample to test products; **match'-joint** the junction of matchboards; **match'-maker** a person who attempts to arrange marriages by bringing suitable partners together; a person who arranges boxing matches; **match'making**; **match'-play** scoring in golf according to holes won and lost rather than the number of strokes taken; **match point** the stage at which another point wins the match; the point that wins the match; a unit of scoring in bridge tournaments. — **to match** in accordance or co-ordination, *esp* in colour. [OE *gemæcca*; cf **make**[3]]

match-maker. See under **match**[1].

matchmaker. See under **match**[2].

mate[1] *māt*, *n* a companion; an equal; a fellow worker, occupant, etc (often in combination, as *workmate*, *flatmate*, etc); a friendly or ironic form of address; a husband or wife; an animal with which another is paired to produce young; one of a pair; a ship's officer under the captain or master; in the navy, formerly a rank to which a warrant-officer might be promoted; an assistant or deputy (as *plumber's mate*). — *vt* to be equal to, to rival (*archaic*); to marry; to cause (*esp* animals) to copulate; to couple; to fit. — *vi* to claim equality (*archaic*); to marry; (*esp* of animals) to copulate; to consort (*archaic*). — *adj* **mate'less** without a mate or companion. — *n* **mate'ship** (*esp Austr*) the bond between close friends. — *adj* **māt'y** or **mate'y** (*colloq*) friendly and familiar, *esp* in a studied or overdone manner. — *adv* **mā'tily**. — *n* **mā'tiness** or **mā'teyness**. — **mating type** (*bot*) a group of individuals within a species which cannot breed among themselves but which are able to breed with individuals of other such groups. [Prob MLGer *mate* or earlier Du *maet* (now *maat*); cf OE *gemetta* a messmate, and **meat**]

mate[2] *māt*, *adj* (*archaic*) checkmated; confounded; baffled; exhausted; daunted. — *vt* to checkmate; to subdue (*archaic*); to baffle (*archaic*); to confound (*archaic*). — *n* and *interj* checkmate. [OFr *mat* checkmated; see **checkmate**, and **mat**[2]]

mate[3] or **maté** *ma'tā*, *n* a S American species of holly (*Ilex paraguayensis*); an infusion of its leaves and green shoots, Paraguay tea. [Sp *mate*, from Quechua *mati* a gourd (in which it is made)]

matelassé *mat-lä-sā*, *adj* and *n* (a jacquard fabric) having a raised pattern as if quilted. — Also **matelasse** or **matellasse** (*mat-läs*). [Fr, from *matelas* a mattress]

matelot. See **matlo**.

matelote *mat'ə-lōt*, *n* a fish stew cooked in wine, onions, herbs, etc; a sort of hornpipe. [Fr, from *matelot* a sailor]

mater *mā'tər* or *mä'ter*, *n* mother (*slang*, *esp public school*); either of the two membranes of the brain, outer and inner, separated by the arachnoid, the *dura mater*, or *dura*, and *pia mater*, or *pia*. [L *māter*; cf Gr *mētēr*; **mother**]

materfamilias *mā'tər-fa-mil'i-as* or *mä'ter-*, *n* the mother of a family or household: — *pl* strictly **matresfamil'ias** (*-trās-*), sometimes **materfamil'iases**. [L *mater* a mother, and *familiās*, old genitive of *familia* a household]

material *mə-tē'ri-əl*, *adj* relating to matter; consisting of matter; being the substance of the thing (*Shakesp*); pithy, matterful (*Shakesp*); corporeal, not spiritual; bodily; physical; gross, lacking spirituality; relating to subject-matter; relevant; of serious importance, *esp* of legal importance; pertaining to matter as opposed to form (*philos*). — *n* that out of which anything is or may be made; a fabric; that which may be made use of for any purpose; a person who is suitable for a specified occupation, training, etc; (in *pl*) equipment, implements, etc needed for a task or activity. — *n* **matē'rialism** the doctrine that denies the independent existence of spirit, and maintains that there is but one substance, matter; the explanation of history as the working out of economic conditions; blindness to, or denial of, the spiritual; excessive devotion to bodily wants or financial success. — *n* **matē'rialist**. — Also *adj*. — *adj* **materialist'ic** or **materialist'ical**. — *adv* **materialist'ically**. — *n* **materializā'tion** or **-s-**. — *vt* **matē'rialize** or **-ise** to render material; to cause to assume bodily form; to reduce to or regard as matter; to render materialistic. — *vi* to take bodily form; to become actual; to take shape, develop; to turn up, put in an appearance, arrive (*colloq*). — *adv* **matē'rially** in material manner; in respect of matter or material conditions, or material cause; in a considerable or important degree. — *n* **matē'rialness** or **materiality** (*-al'i-ti*). — **material alteration** (*law*) a deliberate alteration (of date, amount, etc) to a bill of exchange; **material distinction** the distinction between individuals of the same species; **material evidence** evidence tending to prove or to disprove the matter under judgement; **material fact** any fact known to a potential insurant which might influence the provision of an insurance contract and which he or she is therefore obliged to disclose; **material fallacy** (*philos*) a fallacy in the matter or thought, rather than in the logical form. —

dialectical materialism Karl Marx's view of history as a conflict between two opposing forces, thesis and antithesis, which is resolved by the forming of a new force, synthesis, present conditions being due to a class struggle between the capitalists, whose aim is private profit, and the workers, who resist exploitation. [L *māteriālis*, from *māteria* matter]

materia medica *mə-tē'ri-ə med'i-kə, n* substances used in medicine; the science of their properties and use. [LL, medical material]

matériel *ma-tā-ri-el'* or *-ryel'*, *n* material; equipment; the baggage and munitions of an army. [Fr]

maternal *mə-tûr'nəl, adj* of a mother; motherly; on the mother's side; of the nature, or in the person, of a mother. — *adv* **mater'nally**. — *n* **mater'nity** the fact of being in the relation of mother; motherhood; motherliness; maternal nature; a maternity hospital or ward. — *adj* of or for women at or near the time of childbirth. — **maternal immunity** passive immunity acquired by the newborn baby or animal from its mother; **maternity leave** paid absence from work to which a pregnant woman is entitled immediately before and following her confinement; **maternity rights** the statutory rights of women employees relating to pregnancy, such as the right to maternity leave, to return to work after confinement, etc. [Fr *maternel* (Ital *maternale*) and *maternité*, from L *māternus*, from *māter* mother]

matey. See under **mate**[1].

matfelon *mat'fel-ən, n* the greater knapweed. [OFr *matefelon*; cf **mate**[2] and **felon**[2]]

matgrass. See under **mat**[1].

math[1] *math, (dialect) n* a mowing. [OE *mǣth*]

math[2]. See **mathematics** under **mathematic**.

math[3]. *abbrev*: mathematics.

mathematic *math-i-mat'ik* or **mathematical** *adj* relating to, or done by, mathematics; very accurate. — *adv* **mathemat'ically**. — *n* **mathematician** (*-mə-tish'ən*) a specialist or expert in mathematics. — *n* **mathemat'icism** the belief that everything can be described or explained ultimately in mathematical terms. — *n sing* or *n pl* **mathemat'ics** (*colloq* short form **maths**, or US **math**) the science of magnitude and number, the relations of figures and forms, and of quantities expressed as symbols. — *n* **mathematiza'tion** or **-s-**. — *vi* and *vt* **math'ematize** or **-ise** to explain, formulate or treat (something) in mathematical terms. — Also **mathemat'icize** or **-ise**. — *adj* **mathemat'icized** or **-s-**. — *adj* **math'ematized** or **-s-**. — **mathematical logic** same as **symbolic logic**. [Gr *mathēmatikē* (*epistēmē*, skill, knowledge) relating to learning, from *mathēma*, from root of *manthanein* to learn]

mathesis *mə-thē'sis* (*obs math'i-sis*), *n* mental discipline, *esp* mathematical. [Gr *mathēsis*]

maths. See **mathematics** under **mathematic**.

Mathurin *math'ū-rin* or **Mathurine** *-rēn, n* a Trinitarian canon. [Perh from their house near St *Mathurin's* chapel in Paris]

matico *mä-tē'kō, n* a Peruvian pepper shrub, used as a styptic: — *pl* **mati'cos**. [Sp dimin of *Mateo* Matthew]

Matilda *mə-til'də, (Austr) n* a swag. — **walk** or **waltz Matilda** to travel around carrying one's swag. [Woman's Christian name]

matily. See under **mate**[1].

matin *mat'in, n* morning (*Shakesp*); a morning song (*Milton*); (in *pl*, often *cap*) one of the seven canonical hours of the RC Church, usually sung between midnight and daybreak, or now by anticipation the afternoon or evening before; (in *pl*) the daily morning service of the Church of England. — *adj* of the morning; of matins. — *adj* **mat'inal**. [Fr *matines* (fem pl), from L *mātūtīnus* belonging to the morning, from *Mātūta* goddess of morning, prob related to *mātūrus* early]

matinée or **matinee** *mat'i-nā* or *mat(-ə)-nā', n* a performance of a play, concert, or showing of a film held in the daytime, *usu* the afternoon; a woman's dress for morning wear. — **matinée coat** or **jacket** a baby's coat or jacket made of wool or similar material; **matinée idol** a handsome actor or filmstar, popular *esp* among women. [Fr, a pre-dinner gathering or entertainment, from *matin* morning]

matiness. See under **mate**[1].

matjes. See **maatjes**.

matlo or **matlow** *mat'lō, (slang) n* a seaman, a sailor: — *pl* **mat'los** or **mat'lows** (*-lōz*). — Also **matelot** (*mat'lō*). [Fr *matelot*]

matooke or **matoke** *ma-tō'kā, n* in Uganda, plantain used as a staple food. [Bantu]

matrass *mat'rəs, n* a long-necked chemical flask; a hard-glass tube closed at one end. [Fr *matras*]

matriarch *mā'tri-ärk, n* the female head of a family, tribe or community; an elderly woman who dominates her family or associates; an elderly and much respected woman of great dignity. — *adj* **matriar'chal**. — *n* **matriar'chalism** a condition of society with matriarchal customs; the theory of such a society. — *n* **matriar'chate** the position of a matriarch; a matriarchal condition or community. — *n* **ma'triarchy** government by a mother or by mothers; an order of society in which descent is reckoned through the female line, or in which a woman is head of the family or the community. [Formed on the analogy of **patriarchy**, from L *māter* mother]

matric. See **matriculation** under **matriculate**.

matrice *mā'tris* or *mat'ris, n*. Same as **matrix**.

matrices. See **matrix**.

matricide *māt'* or *mat'ri-sīd, n* a murderer of his or her own mother; the murder of one's own mother. — *adj* **matricī'dal**. [L *mātricīda*, *mātricīdium*, from *māter* mother, and *caedere* to kill]

matriclinic, matriclinous, etc. See **matroclinic**.

matricula *mə-trik'ū-lə, n* a register of members, students, etc. — *adj* **matric'ular** relating to a register; contributed to the federal fund (as formerly by German states). [LL *mātrīcula* a register, dimin of L *mātrīx*]

matriculate *mə-trik'ū-lāt, vt* to admit to membership by entering one's name in a register, *esp* in a college or university. — *vi* to become a member of a college, university, etc, by being enrolled. — *n* a person admitted to membership in a society. — *n* **matriculā'tion** the act of matriculating; the state of being matriculated; an entrance examination (familiarly **matric'**). — *n* **matric'ulātor**. — *adj* **matriculā'tory**. [Ety as for **matricula**]

matrifocal *mat-ri-fō'kəl, (esp* in *anthropol) adj* centred on the mother; (of societies, families, etc) in which authority and responsibility rest with the mother. — *n* **matrifocal'ity**. [L *māter* a mother, and *focus* a hearth]

matrilineal *mat-ri-lin'i-əl* or **matrilinear** *-ər, adj* (of descent or kinship) reckoned through the mother or through females alone. — *adv* **matrilin'eally**. — *n* **mat'riliny** (or *-lī'ni*). [L *māter* a mother, and *līnea* a line]

matrilocal *mat-ri-lō'kl, adj* (of a form of marriage) in which the husband goes to live with the wife's group. [L *māter* mother, and *locālis*, from *locus* place]

matrimony *mat'ri-mən-i, n* the state of being married, wedlock; the marriage ceremony; a card game of chance in which one of the winning combinations is that of king and queen; the combination of king and queen in that and various other games. — *adj* **matrimonial** (*-mō'ni-əl*) relating to marriage. — *adv* **matrimo'nially**. [L *mātrimōnium*, from *māter*, *mātris* mother]

matrix *mā'triks* or *mat'riks, n* the womb (*obs*); the place in which anything is developed or formed; that in which anything is embedded, such as ground-mass, gangue, intercellular substance, cementing material; the bed on which a thing rests, such as the cutis under a nail, the hollow in a slab to receive a monumental brass; a mould, eg for casting printing type; a rectangular array of quantities or symbols (*math*); any rectangular arrangement of data in rows and columns; a table published by the Bank of England, giving recommended levels of Third World debt provision for individual institutions (*finance*): — *pl* **ma'trices** (*-tris-ēz* or *-iz*) or **ma'trixes**. — *Abbrev* **mat**. — *adj* **matric** (*māt'* or *mat'*) of, pertaining to, or having the properties of a matrix. — **matric potential** (*bot*) that component of the water potential of plants and soils that is due to the interaction of the water with colloids and to capillary forces; **matrix printer** a printer attached to a computer which prints characters as a series of dots by firing pins against an inked ribbon (also **dot matrix printer**). [L *mātrīx*, *-īcis* a breeding animal, later, the womb, from *māter* mother]

matroclinic *mat-rō-klin'ik* or **matroclinous** *-klī'nəs*, *adj* inherited from the mother; more like the mother than the father. — *n* **matroclī'ny**. — Also **matriclin'ic**, etc. [L *māter* (*or* Doric Gr *mātēr*) mother, and Gr *klīnein* to lean]

matron *mā'trən*, *n* a married woman; a *usu* married, and middle-aged to elderly, woman of dignified appearance and dependable personality; a woman in charge of domestic arrangements in a school or other institution; the senior nursing officer in charge of the nursing staff in a hospital; a prison wardress (*US*). — *n* **mā'tronage** or **mā'tronhood** the state of being a matron; a body of matrons. — *adj* **mā'tronal** matronly; motherly; grave. — *vt* **mā'tronize** or **-ise** to render matronly; to act as matron to; to chaperon. — *vi* to become a matron or matronly. — *adj* **mā'tronly** (of a woman) plump or portly with the onset of middle age, or dignified and imposing; belonging, or suitable, to a matron. — *n* **mā'tronship**. — *adj* **ma'tron-like**. — **matron of honour** see under **honour**. [Fr *matrone*, from L *mātrōna*, from *māter* mother]

matronymic. See **metronymic**.

matross *mə-tros'*, (*obs*) *n* a gunner's assistant in artillery. [Du *matroos*, appar from Fr *matelot* a sailor]

matryoshka *mat-ri-osh'kə*, *n* a hollow wooden doll containing a series of smaller dolls, fitting one within the other. — Also **matryoshka doll**. [Russ, dimin of *mat'* mother]

matsuri *mat-sōō'ri*, *n* a Shinto festival or public ceremony held at a shrine. [Jap]

Matt. (*Bible*) *abbrev*: (the Gospel according to St) Matthew.

matt. See **mat²**.

mattamore *mat-ə-mōr'*, *-mör'* or *mat'*, *n* a subterranean chamber. [Fr *matamore*, from Ar *matmūrah*]

matte¹ *mat*, *n* a product of the smelting of sulphide ores. — Also called *regulus* and *coarse metal*. [Fr]

matte² *mat*, *adj*. See **mat²**.

matte³ *mat*, (*cinematog*) *n* a kind of mask used to block out areas of the image, allowing a different image to be superimposed; an image produced in this way. [Fr]

matted. See under **mat¹**.

matter *mat'ər*, *n* that which occupies space, and with which we become acquainted by our bodily senses; that out of which anything is made, material; the subject or material of thought, speech, writing, dispute, etc; substance as distinct from form (*philos*); good sense (*Shakesp*); anything engaging the attention; whatever has physical existence, as distinct from mind (*philos*); an affair, thing, concern, subject or question; a thing or substance of the kind specified, such as *printed matter*, *vegetable matter*; cause or ground (eg *of concern*); a thing of consequence; something that is amiss, as in *what is the matter*?; that with which a court is concerned, something to be tried or proved; (with *neg*) importance, significance or consequence; an approximate amount, eg of money, as in *a matter of a few pounds*; material for work, type set up, copy, etc (*printing*); that which may be sent by post (*postal matter*); pus (*med*). — *vi* to be of importance, significance or consequence; to form or discharge pus (*med*). — *vt* (*obs*) to mind or concern oneself about. — *adj* **matt'erful** (*archaic*) full of matter, pithy. — *adj* **matt'erless** (now chiefly *dialect*). — *adj* **matt'ery** purulent; containing, discharging, or covered with pus. — *adj* **matter-of-fact'** adhering to literal, actual or pedestrian fact; not fanciful; prosaic. — **as a matter of fact** really; **for that matter** as for that; indeed; **matter of course** a thing occurring routinely, in natural time and order; **matter of form** a (mere) official procedure or conventional etiquette; **no matter** it does not matter; it makes no difference; **the matter (with)** (the thing that is) amiss (with). [OFr *matiere*, from L *māteria* matter]

Matthaean *math-ē'ən*, *adj* of the evangelist Matthew or his gospel. [*Matthew*]

mattie *mat'i*, (*Scot*) *n* a young herring with undeveloped roe. [Du *maatjes* (*haring*), from L Ger *mädeken* maiden]

matting. See under **mat¹**.

mattins. Same as **matins**, *pl* of **matin**.

mattock *mat'ək*, *n* a kind of pickaxe for loosening soil, with a cutting end instead of a point. [OE *mattuc*]

mattoid *mat'oid*, *n* a person on the borderline between sanity and insanity. [Ital *mattoide*, from matto mad]

mattress *mat'ris*, *n* a more or less resilient large, oblong pad for sleeping or lying on, *usu* forming part of a bed, composed of a strong cotton or linen outer case containing any of various types of stuffing, and sometimes also metal springs, or else made of a piece of foam rubber or plastic; a mass of brushwood, etc, used to form a foundation for roads, etc, or for the walls of embankments, etc. [OFr *materas* (Fr *matelas*), from Ar *matrah* a place where anything is thrown]

maturate *mat'ū'rāt*, *vt* to make mature; to cause to suppurate (*med*). — *vi* to become mature; to suppurate fully (*med*). — *n* **maturā'tion** a bringing or a coming to maturity; the process of suppurating fully; the final stage in the production of a germ-cell, at which the reducing division occurs. — *adj* **maturā'tional**. — *adj* **matur'ative** (or *mat'*) promoting ripening; causing suppuration. [L *matūrāre*, *-ātum*,to bring to ripeness or maturity]

mature *mə-tūr'* or US also *-tōōr'*, *adj* fully developed; having the mental, emotional and social development appropriate to an adult; perfected; ripe; well thought out; (of a bill, bond, or insurance policy) due for payment or conversion; in due time (*Milton*); suppurating. — *vt* to bring to ripeness, full development or perfection; to bring to a head; to cause to suppurate. — *vi* to come to or approach ripeness, full development, or perfection; to become due for payment or conversion (*finance*). — *adj* **matur'able** capable of being matured. — *adv* **mature'ly**. — *n* **mature'ness**. — *n* **matur'ity** ripeness; full development; the time of becoming due or convertable (*finance*). [L *mātūrus* ripe]

matutinal *mat-ū-tī'nl* or *mə-tū'ti-nl*, *adj* relating to the morning; happening early in the day. — Also **matutine** (*mat'ū-tīn*). [L *mātūtīnālis*, *mātūtīnus*; see **matin**]

matweed See under **mat¹**.

maty. See under **mate¹**.

matzo *mat'sə* or *-sō*, *n* unleavened bread, now *usu* in the form of large, square crackers, eaten during Passover, etc; a wafer or cracker of this: — *pl* (with verb *sing* or *pl*) **mat'zoth** (*-sōt* or *-sōth*) or **mat' zos**. — Also **mat'zoh**, **mat'za** or **mat'zah**: — *pl* **mat'zot**, **mat'zoth**, **mat'zas** or **mat'zahs**. — **matzo ball** a kind of dumpling made from ground matzo; **matzo meal** matzo ground into meal. [Yiddish *matse*; from Heb]

matzoon *mät-sōōn'* or **madzoon** *mäd-zōōn'*, *n* a food similar to yoghurt made from fermented milk. [Armenian *madzun*]

maud *möd*, *n* a Scottish shepherd's woollen plaid. [Origin unknown]

maudlin *möd'lin*, *adj* weeping (*archaic*); foolishly lachrymose, *esp* when in a fuddled, half-drunk state; weakly sentimental. — *n* **maud'linism** the tearful stage of drunkenness. [ME *Maudelein*, through OFr and L from Gr *Magdalēnē*, (woman) of Magdala, from the assumption that Mary Magdalene was the penitent woman of Luke 7. 38]

maugre or **maulgre** *mö'gər*, also *-gri* and *mö(l)-grē'*, (*archaic*) *prep* in spite of, notwithstanding; a curse upon (*Spenser*; with dative). — *adv* out of spite, motivated by ill-will. — *n* ill-will, spite (*obs*). — *vt* (*now Scot*) to show ill-will towards; to spite. [OFr *maugré*, *malgré* discontent, sorrow (Fr *malgré* in spite of), from L *male grātum*, from *male* badly, and *grātum* agreeable]

maul *möl*, *n* a war-club or mace (*obs*); a heavy wooden hammer or beetle, a mall; a loose scrum (*Rugby football*); in goal, a struggle for the ball when carried across the goal-line, but not yet touched down (*Rugby football*). — *vt* to beat with a maul or heavy stick; to handle roughly, batter or maltreat; to injure by pawing or clawing; to split with a maul (*US*). — *vi* to thrust forward in a close mass, *esp* in Rugby football. — *n pl* **maul'ers** (*slang*) hands. [Fr *mail*, from L *malleus* hammer]

maulgre. See **maugre**.

maulstick *möl'stik*, *n* a stick with a pad on the end, used by painters to steady the hand holding the brush. — Also **mahl'stick** or **mal'stick**. [Du *maalstok*, from *malen* to paint, and *stok* stick, assimilated to **stick**]

maulvi *möl'vi*, *n* a teacher of Islamic law, a learned man. [Urdu *mulvī*, from Ar *maulawiyy*]

maumet and **maumetry**. See **mammet** and **mammetry**.

maun *mön*, *män* or *mun*, (*Scot*) *vt* must. — **maunna** (*mön'ə* or *mun'ə*) must not. [See **mun**[1]]

maund[1] *mönd*, (*Shakesp*) *n* a basket. [OE *mand*]

maund[2] *mönd*, *n* a measure of weight in India and W Asia, its value varying in different places from about 25 to 85 pounds avoirdupois. [Hindi and Pers *man*]

maund[3] *mönd*, (*obs slang*) *vt* and *vi* to beg. — *n* **maund'er** a beggar. — *vi* to beg. [Poss Fr *mendier* to beg, from L *mendicāre*]

maunder[1] *mön'dər*, *vi* to grumble; to mutter; to talk in a rambling, inconclusive way, to drivel; to wander about or behave in a listless, aimless way. — *n* **maun'derer**. — *n* **maun'dering** drivelling talk. [Perh *maunder* (obs) to beg, from L *mendicāre* to beg]

maunder[2]. See **maund**[3].

maundy *mön'di*, *n* the religious ceremony of washing the feet of the poor, in commemoration of Christ's washing the disciples' feet (John 13), formerly practised by some monarchs. — **maundy money** the dole given away on **Maundy Thursday**, the day before Good Friday, by the royal almoner, *usu* a silver penny for each year of the sovereign's age, the small silver coins specially minted since 1662. [Fr *mandé*, from L *mandātum* command (John 13. 34)]

maungy. See **mangy**.

maunna. See **maun**.

Mauretania *mör-i-tān'yə*, *n* an ancient country in N Africa, corresponding to parts of present-day Algeria and Morocco. — *adj* **Mauretān'ian** of or relating to this country or its people. — *n* a native or inhabitant of Mauretania.

maurikigusari *mo-ri-ki-goō-sä'ri*, *n* a weapon consisting of a series of weights on a chain. [Jap]

Maurist *mö'rist*, *n* a member of the reformed Benedictine Congregation of St *Maur* settled from 1618 at the abbey of St *Maur*-sur-Loire, near Saumur, notable for its great scholarship. — Also *adj*.

Mauritius *mo-* or *mö-rish'əs*, *adj* of the island of *Mauritius* (named after Maurice (1567–1625), Prince of Orange). — **Mauritius hemp** the fibre of an amaryllidaceous plant, *Furcraea gigantea*.

Mauser *mow'zər*, *n* (any of) a series of German rifles, *esp* a magazine rifle of 1897. [Inventor's surname]

mausoleum *mö-so-lē'əm*, *n* a magnificent tomb or monument; a gloomy or spiritless place (*fig*). — *adj* **mausolē'an** relating to a mausoleum; grand, stately, imposing (*poetic*). [L *mausōlēum*, from Gr *Mausōleion*, the magnificent tomb of *Mausōlos* (died 353 BC), satrap of Caria, erected by his widow Artemisia at Halicarnassus]

mauther or **mawther** *mö'dhər*, (*dialect*, *esp E Anglia*) *n* a girl; a big awkward girl. — Also (*esp* vocatively) **mawr** or **mor**. [Origin obscure]

mauvais *mo-ve*, (*Fr*) *adj* bad, worthless: — *fem* **mauvaise** (*-vez*). — **mauvais goût** (*goō*) bad taste, lack of taste; **mauvaise honte** (*mo-vez ɔ̃t*) false modesty, bashfulness; **mauvais moment** (*mo-mã*) a bad, unpleasant moment (also **mauvais quart d'heure** (*kär dœr*) a brief but unpleasant experience, (literally) a bad quarter of an hour); **mauvais sujet** (*sü-zhā*) a worthless person; **mauvais ton** (*tɔ̃*) bad style, bad form.

mauve *mōv* or *möv*, *n* a purple aniline dye; its colour, that of mallow flowers, a light bluish purple. — *adj* of the colour of mauve. — *n* **mauv'in**, **mauv'line**, **mauve'lin** or **mauve'line** mauve dye. [Fr, from L *malva* mallow]

maven. Same as **mavin**.

maverick *mav'ər-ik*, (*orig US*) *n* a stray animal without an owner's brand, *esp* a calf; a person who does not conform, a determined individualist; anything dishonestly obtained; (with *cap*) a type of air-to-ground anti-tank missile, guided by a laser or TV camera. — *adj* that is, or is characteristic of, a maverick. — *vt* to seize without legal claim. [From Samuel *Maverick*, a Texas cattle-raiser]

mavin or **maven** *māv'in*, (*US slang*) *n* an expert, a pundit. [Yiddish, from Heb *mevin* understanding]

mavis *mā'vis*, *n* the song thrush (see **thrush**[1]). [Fr *mauvis*]

mavourneen *mə-voōr'nēn*, (*Ir*) *n* and *interj* my dear one. [Ir *mo mhurnín*]

maw[1] *mö*, *n* the stomach, *esp* (and now only) that of an animal; inclination, appetite (*Milton*); the craw of a bird (*obs*); the fourth stomach in ruminants; any other internal organ (now *rare*); the jaws or gullet of a voracious animal or (*facetious*) person; an insatiable gulf or ever-open mouth (*fig*). — *adj* **maw'bound** (of cattle) constipated by impaction of the rumen. — **maw'-worm** (now *rare*) a worm infesting the stomach or intestines. [OE *maga*; Ger *Magen*]

maw[2] *mö*, (chiefly *Scot*) *n* a seagull. [ON *mār*]

maw[3] *mö*, (*hist*) *n* an old card-game played with a pack of 36. [Origin unknown]

mawk *mök*, (now *dialect*) *n* a maggot. — *adj* **mawk'y** maggoty; mawkish. [ON *mathkr* maggot]

mawkish *mö'kish*, *adj* maggoty (*obs*); loathsome, disgusting; squeamish; insipid; sickly; weakly-sentimental, maudlin. — *adv* **mawk'ishly**. — *n* **mawk'ishness**. [Ety as for **mawk**]

mawkin. See **malkin**.

Mawlawi. See **Mevlevi**.

mawmet and **mawmetry**. See under **mammet**.

mawpus. See **mopus**[1].

mawr and **mawther**. See **mauther**.

mawseed *mö'sēd*, *n* poppy seed, *esp* as used for cagebird food. [Ger dialect *Mahsaat*, from *Mah* poppy, and *saat* seed]

max *maks*, (*obs*) *n* gin. [Origin obscure]

max. *abbrev*: maximum.

maxi *mak'si*, *adj* (*colloq*) or *combining form* signifying very, or extra, large or long, as in *maxi-coat*, *skirt* or *dress*, an ankle-length coat, skirt, etc. — *n* a maxi garment; a large size of racing yacht. — **max'i-single** a gramophone record longer than an ordinary single. [*maxi*mum]

maxilla *mak-sil'ə*, *n* a jawbone, *esp* the upper; (in arthropods) an appendage with masticatory function, just behind the mouth, modified in connection with feeding: — *pl* **maxill'ae** (*-ē*). — *adj* **maxill'ary** (or *maks'*) of or relating to a jaw or maxilla. — *n* a bone forming the posterior part of the upper jaw. — *n* **maxill'iped** (*-ped*) or **maxill'ipede** (*-pēd*) (in crustaceans) a jaw-foot, an appendage behind the mouth, adapted to help in passing food to the mouth. — *adj* **maxillofā'cial** (*esp* of surgery) of or relating to the jawbone and face. — *n* **maxill'ūla** (in crustaceans) a maxilla of the first pair: — *pl* **maxill'ūlae** (*-lē*). [L *maxilla* jawbone]

maxim *maks'im*, *n* a general principle, serving as a rule or guide; a pithy saying; a proverb. — *n* **max'imist** or **maxim-mong'er** a habitual maker of maxims. [Fr *maxime*, from L *maxima* (*sententia*, or some other word), greatest (opinion, etc), fem superl of *magnus* great]

Maxim *maks'im*, *n* short for **Max'im-gun**, an automatic machine-gun invented by Hiram *Maxim* (1840–1916).

maxima, **maximal** and **maximize**. See under **maximum**.

maxima cum laude *maks'i-ma kum lōd'ē* or *kŏŏm lowd'e*, (*L*) with distinction, with the greatest praise (of attainment of high standard in degree examinations).

maximal, etc. See under **maximum**.

maximin *mak'si-min*, *n* the highest value in a set of minimum values (*math*); in games theory, the strategy of making all decisions in such a way as to maximize the chances of incurring the minimal potential loss. [*maxi*mum and *min*imum]

maximum *maks'i-məm*, *adj* greatest. — *n* the greatest possible number, quantity, or degree; the highest point reached; the value of a variable when it ceases to increase and begins to decrease (*math*; opposite of *minimum*): — *pl* **max'ima**. — *adj* **max'imal** of the highest or maximum value. — *n* **max'imalist** a person who makes the fullest demands; a Bolshevik; one who demands the maximum programme. — *adv* **max'imally**. — *n* **maxima'phily** the study and collection of maximum cards (see below). — *vt* **max'imize** or **-ise** to raise to the highest degree. — *vi* to give greatest scope to a doctrine. — **maximum and minimum thermometer** a thermometer that shows the highest and lowest temperatures that have occurred since last adjustment; **maximum card** a picture postcard bearing a stamp depicting the same or a similar image and related postmark on the picture side; **maximum permissible concentration** (*radiol*) the recommended upper limit for the dose which may be received during a specified period by a person exposed to ionizing radiation (also **permissible dose**). [L, superl neuter of *magnus* great]

maxixe *mä-shē'shā*, *n* a Brazilian dance resembling the tango; the music for this. [Port]

maxwell *maks'wəl*, (*phys*) *n* the cgs unit of magnetic flux, equal to 10^{-8} weber. — **Maxwell's demon** (*phys* and *chem*) an imaginary creature who, by opening and closing a tiny door between two volumes of gas, suggests the possibility of concentrating slower molecules in one volume and faster in the other, thus breaking the second law of thermodynamics. [James Clerk-*Maxwell* (1831–79), Scottish physicist]

May *mā*, *n* now the fifth month of the year (see **March**); the early or gay part of life; (without *cap*) may blossom. — *vi* (also without *cap*) to gather may on Mayday; to participate in May sports. — *n* **may'ing** the observance of Mayday customs. — **may apple** an American plant, *Podophyllum*; the egg-shaped fruit of this; **may beetle** or **may bug** the cockchafer; **may'-bird** the whimbrel; the bobolink; **may bloom** or **may blossom** the hawthorn flower; **May day** the first day of May, given to sports and to socialist and labour demonstrations (see also **mayday**). — Also *adj*. — **May-dew'** the dew of May, *esp* that of the morning of the first day of May, said to whiten linen and beautify faces; **may'-duke** a variety of sour cherry; **May'fair** the West End of London, at one time scene of a fair in May; **may'flower** the hawthorn or other flower that blooms in May; **may'fly** a short-lived plectopterous insect (*Ephemera*) that appears in May; the caddis-fly; **May'-game** sport appropriate to Mayday; frolic generally; **May-la'dy** the queen of the May; **May laws** (*hist*) Prussian laws passed in three successive Mays (1873–75), restricting the power of the Church; **may'-lily** the lily of the valley; **May-lord'** a youth directing May-games; one enjoying transitory dignity; **May-meet'ings** meetings of various religious and philanthropic societies held in London in May; **May-morn'** or **-morn'ing** any morning in May, *esp* the first; youthful freshness as of May (*Shakesp*); **may'pole** a pole erected for dancing round on Mayday; **May queen** a young woman crowned with flowers as queen on Mayday; **May'time** the season of May; **may tree** the hawthorn. — **May-September** (or **May-December**) **marriage**, **romance**, etc a marriage, romance, etc between a young woman and a much older man. [OFr *Mai*, from L *Māius* (*mēnsis*), prob (month) sacred to *Māia*, mother of Mercury]

may[1] *mā*, *auxiliary v* expressing ability, possibility or contingency, permission or competence, probability, concession, purpose or result, a wish, or uncertainty (used with infinitive without *to*): — *infinitive* and *participles* obsolete; *2nd pers sing* (*archaic*) **mayst** or **may'est**; *3rd pers* **may**; *pa t* **might** (*mīt*) or (*obs* or *dialect*) **mought** (*mowt*) (also used instead of *may* to make a possibility more remote, a question more tentative, or to make requests or administer rebukes); *2nd pers sing* (*archaic*) **might'est** or **mightst**. — *adv* **may'hap** (or *-hap'*; *archaic*) perhaps. — **be that as it may** in spite of that; **may** (or **might**) **as well** used to make suggestions or to indicate frustration or despair; **may I add** or **it may be added** used to introduce an additional point; **may I ask** (*usu ironic*) used before or after a question; **that's as my be** that may be so. [OE *mæg*, pr t (old pa t) of *magan* to be able, pa t *mihte*; cognate with Gothic *magan*, Ger *mögen*]

may[2] *mā*, (*archaic* and *poetic*) *n* a maid. [Prob OE *mǣg* a kinswoman]

Maya *mä'yə*, *n* a S American Indian people of Central America and Southern Mexico who developed a remarkable pre-Columbian civilization; a member of this people (also **May'an**). — *adj* **Ma'ya** or **Ma'yan**. — *n* **Mayol'ogist**. — *n* **Mayol'ogy**.

maya *mä'yə*, *n* illusion; the world of phenomena (*philos*). [Sans *māyā*]

maybe *mā'bē*, *adv* perhaps, possibly. — *n* a possibility; a possible selection, appointee, etc. [*may be*, from **may**]

mayday *mā'dā*, *n* the international radiotelephonic distress signal for ships and aircraft. [Fr (infinitive) *m'aider*, pron *mā-dā*, help me]

Mayday. See under **May**.

mayest. See under **may**[1].

mayflower and **mayfly**. See under **May**.

mayhap. See under **may**[1].

mayhem *mā'hem* or *mā'əm*, *n* maiming; malicious damage (*legal* and *US*); (*erron*) havoc, chaos (*colloq*). [Ety as for **maim**]

Mayologist, etc. See under **Maya**.

mayonnaise *mā-ə-nāz'* or *mā'*, *n* a cold sauce consisting of a seasoned mixture of egg yolk, vegetable oil and lemon juice or vinegar; any cold dish of which it is an ingredient, such as *shrimp mayonnaise*. [Fr]

mayor *mā'ər* or *mār*, *n* the chief magistrate of a city or borough in England, Ireland, etc, whether man or woman; the head of a municipal corporation. — *adj* **may'oral**. — *n* **may'oralty** or **may'orship** the office of a mayor. — *n* **may'oress** a mayor's wife, or other woman who performs her social and ceremonial functions. — **Lord Mayor** the chief magistrate of certain English, Welsh, Irish and Australian cities and boroughs; **Mayor of the Palace** (*hist*) in Merovingian France, the king's major-domo or prime minister, the real ruler. [Fr *maire*, from L *mājor*, compar of *magnus* great]

maypole. See under **May**.

mayst. See **may**[1].

mayster *mās'ter*, **maysterdome**, etc. Spenserian forms of **master**, **masterdom**, etc.

mayweed *mā'wēd*, *n* stinking camomile (*Anthemis cotula*); corn feverfew (*Matricaria inodora*), a scentless mayweed; applied to various similar plants. [OE *mægtha*, mayweed, and **weed**[1]]

mazard or **mazzard** *maz'ərd*, *n* a head or skull (*Shakesp*); a wild European cherry. [Prob **mazer**]

mazarine[1] *maz-ə-rēn'*, *n* a rich blue colour; a blue gown or fabric. — Also *adj*. — *n* **mazarinade'** (*hist*) a satire or pamphlet against Cardinal *Mazarin* (1602–61). — **Mazarin** or **Mazarine Bible** the first printed Bible, printed by Gutenberg and Fust about 1450, of which the Cardinal had twenty-five copies; **mazarine hood** a hood of a form said to have been worn by the Duchesse de *Mazarin*.

mazarine[2] *maz-ə-rēn'*, *n* a 17c deep, *usu* metal, plate; a cooking and serving dish set inside a larger dish. — Also **mazarine dish** or **plate**. [Origin uncertain]

Mazdaism *maz'dä-izm* or **Mazdeism** *maz'dē-izm*, *n* the religion of the ancient Persians; Zoroastrianism. — *n* **Maz'daist** a Zoroastrian. — *adj* **Mazdē'an**. [See ety for **Ormuzd**]

maze[1] *māz*, *n* bewilderment (now *dialect*); a labyrinth; a set of intricate windings; any confusingly elaborate and complicated system, etc. — *vt* to bewilder; to confuse. — *adj* **maze'ful** (*Spenser*). — *n* **maze'ment**. — *adv* **mā'zily**. — *n* **mā'ziness**. — *adj* **mā'zy** winding or convoluted as a maze; confused, dizzy (*dialect*). [Prob from a lost OE word; the compound *āmasod* amazed, occurs]

maze[2] *māz*. See **mease**[1].

mazeltov or **mazel tov** *maz'əl-tōv*, *interj* a Jewish expression conveying congratulations or best wishes. [Yiddish, from Heb]

mazer *mā'zər*, *n* a hard wood, probably maple; a type of drinking-bowl made *esp* and *orig* of maple wood (*hist*). [OFr *masere*, of Gmc origin; cf OHGer *masar*, ON *mösurr*, a maple-tree]

mazhbi *maz'bi*, *n* a Sikh of low caste. [Hindi, from Ar *mazhab* religion or sect]

mazout. See **mazut**.

mazuma *mə-zo͞o'mə*, (*slang*) *n* money. [Yiddish]

mazurka *mə-zo͞or'kə* or *-zûr'*, *n* a lively Polish dance; the music for it, in triple time. [Pol, Masurian woman]

mazut or **mazout** *mə-zo͞ot'*, *n* petroleum residue after distillation. [Russ *mazat'* to daub or smear]

mazzard. See **mazard**.

MB *abbrev*: *Medicinae Baccalaureus* (*L*), Bachelor of Medicine; mark of the Beast.

Mb or **mb** *abbrev*: megabyte.

mb *abbrev*: millibar.

MBA *abbrev*: Master of Business Administration.

mbaqanga *m-bə-kang'gə*, (*SAfr*) *n* a type of Black African urban music, originating in Soweto. [Origin uncertain; perh related to Zulu *umbaqanga* porridge, mixture]

MBE *abbrev*: Member of (the Order of) the British Empire.

MBFR *abbrev*: Mutual Balanced Force Reduction.

MBI *abbrev*: management buy-in.

mbira *m-bē'rə*, *n* an African musical instrument played with the thumbs, consisting of several tuned metal strips attached at one end to a sound-board. [Shora]

MBO *abbrev*: management buyout.

MC *em-sē'*, *n* a master of ceremonies (see under **ceremony**).

MC *abbrev*: Member of Congress; Member of Council; Military Cross; Monaco (IVR).

Mc. See **Mac**[1].

MCA *abbrev*: monetary compensatory amounts.

MCC *abbrev*: Marylebone Cricket Club.

McCarthyism *mə-kär'thi-izm*, *n* the hunting down and removal from public employment of all suspected of Communism. — *adj* **McCar'thyite** of or relating to this kind of purge or any purge of dissident factions in a political party, etc. — *n* a practitioner or advocate of McCarthyism. [From Joseph *McCarthy* (1909–1957), US Senator]

McCoy: **the real McCoy**. See under **real**[1].

McGuffin. See **MacGuffin**.

McIntosh red *mak'in-tosh red*, *n* a red-skinned variety of eating apple. [John *McIntosh*, Canadian farmer (born 1777)]

McNaghten rules *mək-nö'tn ro͞olz*, (*Eng law*) *n pl* rules dating from Rex v *McNaghten* (1843), under which mental abnormality relieves from criminal responsibility only if the person was unaware of his or her actions or of committing a crime.

MCP *abbrev*: male chauvinist pig (qv under **male**[2]).

MCR *abbrev*: Middle Common Room.

Mc/s *abbrev*: megacycles per second.

MD *abbrev*: Managing Director; Maryland (US state; also **Md**); *Medicinae Doctor* (*L*), Doctor of Medicine; mentally deficient.

Md (*chem*) *symbol*: mendelevium.

Mdlle or **Mlle** *abbrev*: *Mademoiselle* (*Fr*), Miss.

Mdm. *abbrev*: **Madame**.

MDMA *abbrev*: *m*ethylene-*d*ioxy*m*eth*a*mphetamine (see **ecstasy**).

MDS *abbrev*: Master of Dental Surgery.

ME *abbrev*: Maine (US state; also **Me**); Methodist Episcopal; Middle East; Middle English; Mining or Mechanical Engineer; Most Excellent; myalgic encephalomyelitis (see under **myalgia**).

me[1] *mē* or *mi*, *pers pronoun* the form of **I** used for the objective (accusative and dative) case. — **me generation** the generation either of the 1970s, typically self-absorbed, or of the 1980s, typically greedy and materialistic. — See also **me-too**. [OE *mē*]

me[2]. An anglicized spelling of **mi**.

meacock *mē'kok*, (*Shakesp*) *adj* timorous, effeminate, cowardly. — *n* a milksop. [Origin unknown]

mea culpa *mē'ə kul'pə* or *mā'ä ko͝ol'pä*, (*L*) (by) my own fault, I am to blame (an acknowledgement of one's guilt or mistake).

mead[1] *mēd*, *n* an alcoholic drink made by fermenting honey and water, *usu* with the addition of spices, etc. [OE *meodu*; Ger *Met*, Welsh *medd*]

mead[2] *mēd*, (*poetic*) *n* a meadow [OE *mǣd*; see **meadow**]

meadow *med'ō*, *n* a tract of grassland, *esp* used for hay; a rich pasture-ground, *esp* beside a stream. — *adj* **mead'owy**. — **meadow-brown'** a butterfly of the *Satyridae*; **meadow foxtail** a perennial grass (*Alopecurus pratensis*), common in Europe and N Asia, and introduced into N America; **mead'ow-grass** any grass of the genus *Poa* (**floating meadow-grass** manna-grass, float-grass); **meadow lark** (*US*) a name for various species of birds of the genus *Sturnella* (family *Icteridae*); **meadow pipit** *Anthus pratensis*, a common brown and white European songbird; **mead'ow-rue** a genus (*Thalictrum*) of the buttercup family with rue-like leaves; **meadow saffron** *Colchicum autumnale* (also *autumn-crocus* or *naked lady*); **meadow-sax'ifrage** a saxifrage (*Saxifraga granulata*) that grows on banks and dry meadows; applied also to umbelliferous plants of the genera *Seseli* and *Silaus*. [OE *mǣd*, in oblique cases *mǣdwe*, from *māwan* to mow; Ger *Matte*]

meadowsweet *med'ō-swēt*, *n* the rosaceous plant queen-of-the-meadows (*Spiraea ulmaria*), a tall fragrant plant growing *esp* in watery meadows. [Earlier **mead-sweet**, which may be from **mead**[1] or from **mead**[2], as the obs **mead'wort** is in OE *meduwyrt*]

meagre *mē'gər*, *adj* having little flesh; lean, thin; poor in quality; lacking richness or fertility, barren; scanty, insubstantial, inadequate; without strength, weak; jejune, lacking fullness or imagination; maigre. — *n* the maigre. — *adv* **mea'grely**. — *n* **mea'greness**. [Fr *maigre*, from L *macer*, *macra*, *-rum* lean; cf Ger *mager*]

meal[1] *mēl*, *n* the food taken at one time; the act or occasion of taking food, such as a breakfast, dinner or supper. — *n* **meal'er** a person who takes meals at a boarding-house, lodging elsewhere. — **meals on wheels** a welfare service taking cooked, *usu* hot, meals to old people in need of such help; **meal ticket** a ticket that can be exchanged for a meal (*esp* at reduced price); a person or thing that one depends on for one's expenses or income (*colloq*); someone who can be depended upon; **meal'-tide** (*archaic*; *Scot* **meltith** *mel'tith*, a meal) mealtime; **meal'time** the time at which a meal is regularly taken. — **make a meal of** to consume as a meal; to enjoy to the full; to treat or perform in an unnecessarily laborious or meticulous way. [OE *mǣl* measure, time, portion of time; Du *maal*, Ger *Mahl*]

meal[2] *mēl*, *n* grain (now *usu* not wheat) or pulses ground to powder; in Scotland and Ireland, *specif* oatmeal; other material in powder form; a powdery surface-covering (chiefly *bot*). — *vt* to cover with meal; to add oatmeal to, *esp* to thicken (*Scot*); to grind into meal. — *vi* (chiefly *Scot*) to yield or be plentiful in meal. — *n*

meal'iness. — *adj* **meal'y** or (*Scot*) **meal'ie** like meal in texture, powdery, floury; containing oatmeal (*Scot*); covered with, or as if with, meal; having a powdery surface; speckled, flecked; whitish, pale. — **meal'-ark** (*Scot*) a large chest for holding oatmeal; **mealie pudding** (*Scot*) a white pudding; **meal'-man** or **meal'-monger** (*obs*) a dealer in meal; **Meal Monday** the second Monday in February, a St Andrews (and formerly, Edinburgh) University holiday, *orig* to allow the students to go home and replenish their stock of meal; **meal'-poke** (*Scot*) a bag for oatmeal, formerly *esp* one carried by a beggar; **meal'-tree** the wayfaring tree, from its mealy leaves and shoots; **meal'worm** the larva of a beetle (genus *Tenebrio*) frequently found in granaries and flour-stores; **mealy bug** a hothouse pest, a coccus insect with a white powdery appearance. — *adj* **meal'y-mouthed** (*-mowdhd*) smooth-tongued; over-squeamish, *esp* in choice of words. — **mealy-mouth'edness**. [OE *melu*, *melo*; Ger *Mehl*, Du *meel* meal]

meal[3] *mēl*, (*Shakesp*, in *pa p* **meal'd**) *vt* to stain or spot. [OE *mǣlan*]

mealie *mēl'i*, *n* (*esp SAfr*) an ear of maize; (*esp* in *pl*) maize. — Also **meal'y**. — **mealie meal** finely ground maize. [SAfr Du *milie* millet]

mean[1] *mēn*, *adj* low in rank or birth; base; sordid; low in worth or estimation; of little value or importance; poor, humble; low; inconsiderable; despicable; shabby; paltry; small-minded; ungenerous; stingy; malicious, bad-tempered; out of sorts, uncomfortable (*US*); skilful, excellent (*slang*). — *n* **mean'ie** or **mean'y** (*colloq*) an ungenerous, ungracious, small-minded, or malicious person. — *adv* **mean'ly**. — *n* **mean'ness**. — *adj* **mean'-born** (*archaic*). — *adj* **mean-spir'ited**. — **mean-spir'itedness**. [OE *geǣne*; Ger *gemein*; L *commūnis* common]

mean[2] *mēn*, *adj* intermediate; average; moderate (*obs*). — *n* that which is between or intermediate; an average amount or value; a middle state or position; an intermediate term in a progression; meantime (*Spenser*); a middle or intermediate part (*music*); an instrument or medium; a mediator or intercessor (*obs*). — *n sing* or *n pl* **means** that by whose instrumentality anything is caused or brought to pass; a way to an end; (*n pl*) pecuniary resources; (*n pl*) what is required for comfortable living. — *n* **mean'time** or **mean'while** the intervening time. — *adv* in the intervening time. — **mean free path** the average distance travelled by a molecule, atom, etc, between collisions; **mean lethal dose** (*radiol*) the single dose of whole body irradiation which will cause death, within a certain period, to 50% of those receiving it (*abbrev* **MLD**); **means test** the test of private resources, determining or limiting a claim to a concession or allowance. — *vt* **means'-test**. — **mean sun** an imaginary sun moving uniformly in the equator, its position giving **mean time** or **mean solar time** (coinciding with true sun time four times a year); **mean'-tone** (*music*) an interval of mean value between a major and a minor second, formerly used in a system of temperament. — **arithmetic** (or **arithmetical**) **mean** the sum of a number of quantities divided by their number; **by all means** certainly; **by any means** in any way; **by means** (*Spenser*) because; **by means of** with the help or use of; **by no means** certainly not; **geometric** (or **geometrical**) **mean** the *n*th root of the product of *n* quantities; **golden mean** the middle course between two extremes; a wise moderation; **harmonic mean** the reciprocal of the arithmetical mean of the reciprocals of two quantities; **in the mean** (*Spenser*) in the meantime; **quadratic mean** the square root of the arithmetical mean of the squares of the given quantities. [OFr *meien* (Fr *moyen*), from L *mediānus*, from *medius* middle]

mean[3] *mēn*, *vt* to have in mind as signification; to intend, to purpose; to destine, to design; to signify. — *vi* (with *well* or *ill*) to have good, or bad, intentions or disposition; (with *much*, *little*, etc) to be of much, little, etc importance (with *to*): — *pr p* **mean'ing**; *pa t* and *pa p* **meant** (*ment*). — *n* **mean'ing** that which is in the mind or thoughts; signification; the sense intended; purpose. — *adj* significant. — *adj* **mean'ingful** having a valid meaning; full of significance, expressive. — *adj* **mean'ingless** senseless; expressionless (*poetic*; *rare*); without significance, pointless, futile. — *adv* **mean'ingly** significantly, expressively; intentionally (*archaic*). [OE *mǣnan*; Ger *meinen* to think]

mean[4], **meane**, **mein** or **mene** *mēn*, (*Shakesp* and *Scot*) *vt* and *vi* to lament, to moan; to complain. [OE *mænan*; cf **moan**]

meander *mi-an'dər*, *n* a sinuosity or turning, *esp* of a river (*usu* in *pl*); a winding course; a maze (*obs*); an intricate fret pattern, *esp* the Greek key pattern (*art*); perplexity (*obs*). — *vi* to wind about in a circuitous course; to form an intricate pattern; to wander listlessly or randomly, to ramble (*perh* influenced by **maunder**). — *adj* **mean'dered** formed into or covered with mazy passages or patterns. — *adj* **mean'dering**, **mean'drian** (*obs*) or **mean'drous** winding, circuitous. [L *Maeander*, from Gr *Maiandros* a winding river in Asia Minor]

meane. See **mean**[4].

means. See **mean**[2].

meant *ment*, *pa t* and *pa p* of **mean**[3].

meany. See under **mean**[1].

meare *mēr*, Spenser's spelling of **mere**[2,3]. — **mear'd** (*Spenser*) *pa t* of **mere**[3].

mease[1] *mēz*, **maze**, **maize** or **maise** *māz*, (*dialect*) *n* a measure of five 'hundreds' of herrings, varying from 500 to 630. [OFr *meise* receptacle for herrings; ON *meiss* box, basket; OHGer *meisa*]

mease[2] *mēz*, (*Scot*) *vt* to assuage; to mitigate. [OFr *amesir*, from L *ad* to, and *mītis* mild]

measles *mē'zlz*, *n pl* (but *usu sing* in construction) an infectious fever accompanied by eruptions of small red spots on the skin; a disease of pigs and cattle, caused by larval tapeworms; a blister or a disease of trees (*obs*). — *n* **mea'sle** a tapeworm larva. — *vt* (*archaic*) to infect with measles. — *vi* (*archaic*) to contract measles. — *adj* **mea'sled** measly. — *n* **mea'sliness**. — *adj* **mea'sly** infected with measles, or with tapeworm larvae; spotty; paltry, miserable (*colloq*). — **German measles** rubella. [ME *maseles*; cf Du *mazelen* measles, OHG *masala* blister; Ger *Masern* measles]

measure *mezh'ər*, *n* the ascertainment of extent by comparison with a standard; a system of expressing the result of such ascertainment; the amount ascertained by comparison with a standard; that by which extent is ascertained or expressed; size; a standard or unit; a quantity by which another can be divided without remainder; an instrument for finding the extent of anything, *esp* a graduated rod or tape for length, or a vessel of known content for capacity; the quantity contained in a vessel of known capacity, formerly often a bushel; adequacy or due amount; some amount or degree, a portion; proportion; moderation; restraint; limit (*Milton*); extent; that which is meted out to one, treatment; a means to an end; an enactment or bill; rhythm; a unit of verse, one foot or two feet; metre; strict time; a bar of music; a strain; a dance, *esp* a slow and stately one; the width of a page or column, usually in *ems* (*printing*); (in *pl*) a series of beds or strata (*geol*). — *vt* to ascertain or show the dimensions or amount of (often with *out* or *up*); to mark out or lay off (often with *off* or *out*); to be a unit of measurement of; to mete out or distribute (with *out*); to proportion; to pit; to traverse; to sing or utter in measure (*Spenser*). — *vi* to be of the stated size; to take measurements. — *adj* **meas'urable** substantial enough, or not too large, to be measured or computed; moderate; in small quantity or extent. — *n* **meas'urableness**. — *adv* **meas'urably**. — *adj* **meas'ured** determined by measure; mensurable; rhythmical; with slow, heavy, steady rhythm; considered, calculated, deliberate; restrained. — *adv* **meas'uredly**. — *adj* **meas'ureless** boundless. — *n* **meas'urement** the act of measuring; the quantity found by measuring. — *n* **meas'urer**. — *n* and *adj* **meas'uring**. — **measured block**

(*printing*) a block of text of a fixed number of lines; **measurement goods** light goods carried for charges according to bulk, not weight; **measuring cup**, **jug** or **spoon** a cup, jug or spoon with graduations, or of a specific size, for measuring goods by volume; **meas'uring-rod** or **meas'uring-tape** a graduated rod or tape for making linear measurments; **meas'uring-wheel** a wheel with a perimeter of a standard length, used to make lateral measurements by recording the number of revolutions made as it is moved along the ground, etc; **measuring-worm'** a looper caterpillar. — **above**, **beyond** or (*archaic*) **out of all measure** to an exceedingly great degree; **be the** (or **a**) **measure of** to be the (or a) standard by which to judge the quality, etc of; **for good measure** as something extra or above the minimum necessary; **get** or **have someone's measure** to realize or know the nature of someone's character and abilities, *esp* having been previously deceived; **hard measures** harsh treatment; **in a** (or **some**) **measure** to some degree; **made to measure** see under **made**; **measure one's length** to fall or be thrown down at full length; **measure strength** to engage in a contest; **measure swords** to compare lengths of swords before a duel; to fight (*archaic*); **measure up** (often with *to*) to reach a certain, or a required, standard, to be adequate; **out of all measure** see **above measure** above; **short measure** less than the due and professed amount; **take measures** to adopt means to gain an end; **take someone's measure** to estimate someone's character and abilities; **tread a measure** to go through a dance; **within measurable distance of** getting dangerously close to (something *usu* calamitous); **within measure** moderately; **without measure** immoderately. [OFr *mesure*, from L *mēnsūra* a measure, from *mētīrī*, *mēnsum* to measure]

meat *mēt*, *n* anything eaten as food (*archaic*); a meal (*obs*); the edible part of anything, such as *lobster meat*, *crab meat*, etc; the flesh of animals used as food (sometimes beef, mutton, pork, veal, etc, as opposed to poultry or fish); game, etc, hunted for food; food for thought, substance, pith (*fig*); the centre of the blade of a cricket bat, etc. — *adv* **meat'ily**. — *n* **meat'iness**. — *adj* **meat'less** without food (*archaic*); not containing meat. — *adj* **meat'y** full of meat; full of useful content or substance; fleshy, brawny; fleshlike in taste or smell; pithy. — **meat'-axe** or (*NAm*) **meat'-ax** a cleaver; **meat'ball** a ball of minced meat; **meat'-eater** a person who eats meat; a carnivore; **meat'-fly** a blowfly; a flesh-fly; **meat'head** a stupid person (*US slang*); **meat jelly** jelly formed from the solidified juices of cooked meat; **meat loaf** a loaf-shaped mass of chopped or minced meat, cooked and usually eaten cold; **meat'man** a seller of butcher's meat; **meat market** a flesh-market; a place or occasion acting as a meeting-place for potential sexual partners (*slang*); **meat'-offering** a Jewish sacrificial offering of fine flour or first-fruits with oil and frankincense; **meat packing** (*US*) the slaughter and processing of animals, *esp* cattle, for sale as meat; **meat packer** (*US*); **meat paste** a spread made of ground meat; **meat pie** a pie containing meat, *esp* a small one for individual consumption; **meat plate** a large, *esp* oval, plate on which meat is served; **meat rack** a place where young male homosexual prostitutes gather (*slang*); **meat safe** a ventilated cupboard for storing meat; **meat'-salesman** a person who sells meat, *esp* to retail butchers; **meat'screen** a metal screen behind roasting meat, to throw back the fire's heat upon it; **meat-tea'** a high tea at which meat is eaten; **meat'-tub** a pickling-tub; **meat wagon** (*slang*, *esp US*) a police van for transporting prisoners; an ambulance; a hearse. — **meat and drink** (*fig*) a source of sustenance, invigoration or pleasure; **meat and potatoes** (*NAm slang*) the basic or essential parts of anything. [OE *mete*]

meath or **meathe** *mēdh*, *n* an *obs* form of **mead**[1].

meatus *mi-ā'təs*, (*anatom*) *n* an opening of a passage or canal: — *pl* **mea'tuses**. — *adj* **mea'tal**. [L *meātus* (pl *-ūs*), from *meāre* to go]

meawes. A Spenserian spelling of **mews** (pl of **mew**[1]).

meazel. See **mesel**.

mebos *mā'bos*, (*SAfr*) *n* salted or sugared dried apricots. [Perh from Jap *umeboshi* a kind of plum]

Mecca *mek'ə*, *n* the birthplace of Mohammed, a place of pilgrimage for Muslims; a place heavily visited by, or with a special attraction for, a particular person or group, eg St Andrews as a Mecca for golfers.

Meccano® *mi-kä'nō*, *n* (a set of) small metal plates, rods, nuts and bolts, etc with which models can be constructed.

mech. *abbrev*: mechanical; mechanics.

mechanic *mi-kan'ik*, *adj* mechanical. — *n* a person working at a manual trade, an artisan (*archaic*); a skilled worker, *esp* one specializing in making and repairing machinery; a person whose job is the repairing of motor vehicles; an air-mechanic; a term of contempt for a person of a low social class (*obs*); (also **card mechanic**) a card-sharper (*US* and *Austr slang*). — *adj* **mechan'ical** relating to machines or mechanics; relating to dynamics; dynamical; worked or done by machinery or by mechanism; acting or done by physical, not chemical, means; machinelike; of the nature of a machine or mechanism; without intelligence or conscious will; performed simply by force of habit; reflex; skilled in practical matters (*obs*); manual (*archaic*); having a manual trade (*archaic*); technical (*obs*); mechanistic (*philos*). — *n* (*Shakesp*) a manual worker, an artisan. — *adv* **mechan'ically**. — *n pl* **mechan'icals** the mechanical parts of anything (*colloq*). — *n* **mechanician** (*mek-ən-ish'ən*) a machine-maker; a person skilled in constructing machines and tools. — *n sing* **mechan'ics** dynamics, the science of the action of forces on bodies, including kinetics and statics; the art or science of machine-construction; the details of making or creating by manual or other process (also *n pl*); the system on which something works (also *n pl*). — *n pl* routine procedure or procedures. — *n* **mech'anism** a group of moving parts that interact to perform a function in a machine, etc; the arrangement and action by which a result is produced; a philosophy that regards the phenomena of life as explainable by mechanical forces; the means adopted unconsciously towards a subconscious end (*psychol*). — *n* **mech'anist** a mechanician; a believer in philosophical mechanism. — *adj* **mechanist'ic**. — *adv* **mechanist'ically**. — *n* **mechanizā'tion** or **-s-**. — *vt* **mech'anize** or **-ise** to make mechanical; to adapt to mechanical working; to provide with armoured armed vehicles. — *n* **mechanomorph'ism** the philosophy of mechanism; anthropomorphism applied to machines. — **mechanical drawing** instrument-aided drawing, eg of a machine, architectural construction, etc; **mechanical engineer**; **mechanical engineering** the branch of engineering concerned with the design and construction of machines or mechanical contrivances; **mechanical powers** the elementary forms or parts of machines, divided into three *primary* forms (the lever, inclined plane and pulley) and three *secondary* forms (the wheel-and-axle, the wedge and the screw); **mechanical tissue** any tissue that gives a plant the power to resist stresses; **mechanics' institute** (*hist*) an institution founded in England in 1823 to provide educational classes, libraries, etc, for its members (*orig* manual workers); **mechanized Sikh** a Sikh who shaves and crops his hair, and does not wear a turban; **mechanorecept'or** (*med*) a sense organ specialized to respond to mechanical stimuli such as pressure or deformation. [Gr *mēchanikos*, from *mēchanē* a contrivance]

mechatronics *mek-ə-tron'iks*, *n sing* the combined use or study of mechanical engineering and electronics in design and manufacture. — *adj* **mechatron'ic**. [*mech*anical and elec*tronics*]

Mechitharist. See **Mekhitarist**.

Mechlin *mek'* or *mehh'lin*, *n* (also **Mechlin lace**) a kind of bobbin lace produced at *Mechlin* or Malines, in

Belgium, in which the motifs are outlined with thick, glossy thread.

meconic *mi-kon'ik*, *adj* denoting an acid obtained from poppies. — *n* **meconate** (*mek'ən-āt* or *mēk'*) a salt of meconic acid. — *n* **mec'onin** a white, fusible, neutral substance ($C_{10}H_{10}O_4$) existing in opium. — *n* **mecō'nium** (L, poppy-juice) the first faeces of a newborn child, or of a newly emerged insect imago; opium. — *n* **meconops'is** (Gr *opsis* appearance) a plant of the *Meconopsis* genus of largely Asiatic poppies: — *pl* **meconops'ēs**. [Gr *mēkōn* the poppy]

Mecoptera *mē-kop'tə-rə*, *n pl* an order of insects linking the *Hymenoptera* with the *Trichoptera*; the scorpion-flies. [Gr *mēkos* length, and *pteron* wing]

Med *med*, *n* (*colloq*) the Mediterranean Sea, or the region surrounding it.

med. *abbrev*: medical; medicine; medieval; *medius*, *-dia*, *-dium* (*L*), middle.

medacca or **medaka** *mə-dä'kə*, *n* a small Japanese freshwater fish (*Oryzias latipes*), often kept in aquariums or ornamental ponds. [Jap *medaka*]

medaewart *med'ē-wärt*, (*Spenser*) *n* meadowsweet. [OE *meduwyrt*; see **meadowsweet**]

medal *med'l*, *n* a piece of metal *usu* in the form of a coin bearing some design or inscription, struck or cast *usu* in commemoration of an event or as a reward of merit. — *vt* to decorate with a medal: — *pr p* **med'alling** or (*NAm*) **med'aling**; *pa t* and *pa p* **med'alled** or (*NAm*) **med'aled**. — *n* **med'alet** a small medal, *esp* one bearing a representation of one or more saints, worn by Roman Catholics. — *adj* **medallic** (*mi-dal'ik*). — *n* **med'allist** or (*NAm*) **med'alist** a person with expert knowledge of medals, or a collector of medals; a designer or maker of medals; a person who has gained a medal, eg as a prize in sports, or for bravery. — **medal play** golf scored by strokes for the round, not by holes. [Fr *médaille*, from Ital *medaglia*; through LL from L *metallum* metal]

medallion *mi-dal'yən*, *n* a large medal; a bas-relief of a round (sometimes a square) form; a round ornament, panel, tablet, or design of similar form; a small, round or oval cut of meat, fish, etc. — *vt* (*rare*) to ornament or decorate with medallions; to make in the form of a medallion. [Fr *médaillon*]

Medau *mā'dow*, *n* a form of rhythmical exercise, mainly for women, using eg balls, hoops and clubs, developed by Hinrich *Medau* (1890–1974).

meddle *med'l*, *vt* and *vi* (*archaic*) to mix. — *vi* to concern oneself (with *with*; *archaic*); to engage in fight (*Shakesp*); to interfere unnecessarily and ill-advisedly (with *with* or *in*); to tamper (with *with*). — *n* **medd'ler**. — *adj* **medd'lesome** given to meddling. — *n* **medd'lesomeness**. — *n* and *adj* **medd'ling**. [OFr *medler*, a variant of *mesler* (Fr *mêler*), from LL *misculāre*, from L *miscēre* to mix]

Mede. See under **Median**.

medfly. See **Mediterranean fruit fly** under **mediterranean**.

media[1] *mē'di-ə*, *n* a voiced consonantal stop, or a letter representing it, *p*, *b* or *d* (*phonetics*); the middle coat of a blood-vessel layer in the wall of a blood vessel (*biol*); a middle primary vein of an insect's wing: — *pl* **mē'diae** (*-ē*). [L *media* (*littera*, *tunica* or *vena*) middle (letter, coat or vein), fem of *medius* middle]

media[2], **mediagenic**. See **medium**.

mediacy. See under **mediate**.

mediaeval. See **medieval**.

mediagenic. See under **medium**.

medial *mē'di-əl*, *adj* intermediate; (of a consonant) occurring between two vowels (*phonetics*); median; relating to a mean or average. — *n* (*phonetics*; *obs*) a media. — *adv* **me'dially**. [LL *mediālis*, from L *medius* middle]

Median *mē'di-ən*, (*hist*) *adj* of or relating to *Media*, an ancient kingdom north-west of Persia (corresponding to modern NW Iran), its people, or their Indo-European language (also *n*). — *n* **Mede** one of the people of Media, fused as a nation with the Persians about 500 BC. — *adj* **Me'dic**. — *n* **Mē'dism** the adoption of Persian interests, ie treachery to a Greek. — *vi* **Me'dize** or **-ise** to become Median, or like the Medians; to favour the Persians (called *Medes* by the Greeks). — *vt* to make Median. — **law of the Medes and Persians** a law that cannot be changed, 'which altereth not' (Dan 6. 12). [Gr *Mēdos* a Mede]

median *mē'di-ən*, *adj* in the middle, running through the middle; situated in the straight line or plane (*median line or plane*) that divides anything longitudinally into symmetrical halves. — *n* a straight line joining an angular point of a triangle with the middle point of the opposite side; a middle nervure of an insect's wing; in a series of values, the value middle in position (not *usu* in magnitude) (*statistics*); a median strip (*NAm*, *Austr* and *NZ*). — **median strip** (*NAm*, *Austr* and *NZ*) the central, often raised, strip separating opposing lanes of traffic on a motorway or dual carriageway. [L *mediānus*, from *medius* middle]

mediant *mē'di-ənt*, (*music*) *n* the third tone of a scale, about midway between tonic and dominant. [LL *mediāns*, *-antis*, pr p of *mediāre* to be in the middle]

mediastinum *mē-di-ə-stī'nəm*, (*anatom*) *n* a membranous septum, or a cavity, between two principal portions of an organ, *esp* the folds of the pleura and the space between the right and left lungs: — *pl* **mediastī'na**. — *adj* **mediastī'nal**. [Neuter of LL *mediastīnus* median (in classical L *mediastinus* is a drudge), from *medius* middle]

mediate *mē'di-it*, *adj* middle; intervening; indirect; related or acting through something intervening. — *vi* (*-āt*) to interpose between parties as a friend of each; to act as intermediary; to intercede; to be or act as a medium; to hold a mediate position. — *vt* to bring about, end, promote, obtain, or communicate by friendly intervention, or by intercession, or through an intermediary; to be the medium or intermediary of; to transmit, convey, pass on. — *n* **mē'diacy** mediateness. — *adv* **mē'diately**. — *n* **mē'diateness** the state of being mediate. — *n* **mediā'tion** the act of mediating or coming between; (an) intercession. — *adj* **mē'diative** (*-ə-tiv*). — *n* **mediatīzā'tion** or **-s-**. — *vt* **mē'diatize** or **-ise** to cause to act in a subordinate position or through an agent; to reduce from immediate to mediate vassal (of the empire) without loss of dignity; to annex, or to subordinate, as a smaller state to a larger neighbouring one. — *n* **mē'diātor** a person who mediates between parties in dispute: — *fem* (*archaic*) **mē'diātress** or **mediā'trix**: — *pl* **mediātrices** (*-trī'sēz*). — *adj* **mediatō'rial**. — *adv* **mediatō'rially**. — *n* **mē'diatorship**. — *adj* **mē'diatory**. [LL *mediāre*, *-ātum*, to be in the middle, from L *medius* middle]

Medibank *med'i-bank*, *n* (in Australia) a former government-run medical insurance scheme, now supplementary to **Medicare**. [*Medi*cal *bank*]

medic[1] *med'ik*, *adj* medical (*poetic*). — *n* a physician (*rare*); a medical student (*colloq*). — *n* **medicas'ter** (*archaic*) a quack. [L *medicus*]

medic[2]. See **medick**.

Medicaid *med'i-kād*, (also without *cap*) *n* (in the USA) a scheme providing assistance with medical expenses for people with low incomes. [*Medic*al *aid*]

medical *med'i-kl*, *adj* relating to the art of healing; relating to medicine as the art of the physician, as distinct from surgery. — *n* (*colloq*) a medical student; a medical examination to ascertain the state of a person's physical health. — *n* **medicaliza'tion** or **-s-**. — *vt* **med'icalize** or **-ise** to consider, describe or treat in medical terms. — *adv* **med'ically**. — **medical certificate** a certificate from a doctor stating that a person is, or has been, unfit for work, etc, or that a person has, or has not, passed a medical examination; **medical jurisprudence** forensic medicine; **medical officer** a doctor in charge of medical treatment, etc, in an armed service or other organization; **medical practitioner** a doctor or surgeon. — **Medical Officer of Health** (*abbrev* **MOH**) formerly, a public officer in charge of medical services in a town, etc. [LL *medicālis*, from L *medicus* a physician, from *medērī* to heal]

medicament *med-ik'ə-mənt* or *med'*, *n* a substance used in curative treatment, *esp* externally. — *vt* to treat with medicaments. — *adj* **medicamental** (*-ment'l*) or **medicament'ary**. — *adv* **medicament'ally**. [L *medicāmentum*, from *medicāre*]

Medicare *med'i-kār*, (also without *cap*) *n* (in the USA) a scheme providing medical insurance for people aged 65 and over, and for certain categories of disabled people; (in Australia) the system providing universal medical insurance. [*Medi*cal *care*]

medicaster. See under **medic**[1].

medicate *med'i-kāt*, *vt* to treat with medicine; to impregnate with anything medicinal; to drug, doctor, tamper with. — *adj* **med'icable** that may be healed. — *adj* **med'icated**. — *n* **medicā'tion** medical treatment; a medicine, drug, etc. — *adj* **med'icative**. [L *medicāre*, *-ātum* to heal, from *medicus*]

Medicean *med-i-sē'ən*, *adj* relating to the *Medici*, a distinguished Florentine family which attained to sovereign power in the 15c.

medicine *med'sin* or *-sn*, also (*esp US*) *med'i-sin* or *-sn*, *n* any substance used (*esp* internally) for the treatment or prevention of disease; a drug; the art or science of prevention, diagnosis, and cure (*esp* non-surgically) of disease; the practice or profession of a physician; remedial punishment; in primitive or tribal societies, a supernatural, *esp* curative, power; a thing possessing this, a charm; a physician (*Shakesp*). — *vt* to treat or cure by medicine. — *adj* **medicinable** (*med'sin-ə-bl*) having a healing power. — *adj* **medicinal** (*med-is'i-nl* or sometimes *med-i-sī'nl*; in *Shakesp*, etc, *med'si-nl*; *Milton* **med''cinal**) used in medicine; curative; relating to medicine; like medicine. — *adv* **medic'inally**. — *n* **mediciner** (*med'sin-ər* or *med-is'i-nər*; *archaic*) a physician. — **medicine ball** a heavy ball tossed and caught for exercise; **medicine bottle**; **medicine chest** a chest for keeping a selected set of medicines; **med'icine-dropper**; **med'icine man** or **woman** (in primitive or tribal societies) a person believed to heal by supernatural agency, a shaman. — **a dose** or **taste of one's own medicine** harsh or unpleasant treatment given, often in revenge, to someone used to giving such treatment to others. [L *medicīna*, from *medicus*]

medick or (*US*) **medic** *med'ik*, *n* any plant of the genus *Medicago* including lucerne, distinguished from clover by its spiral or sickle-shaped pods and short racemes. [L *mēdica*, from Gr *Mēdikē* (*poā*) Median (herb), ie lucerne]

medico *med'ik-ō*, (*slang*) *n* a medical practitioner or student: — *pl* **med'icos**. [Ital *medico*, or Sp *médico*, from L *medicus* a physician]

medico- *med'ik-ō-*, *combining form* relating to medicine or medical matters. — *adj* **medico-chirur'gical**, relating to both medicine and surgery. — *adj* **medico-le'gal** relating to the application of medicine to questions of law.

medieval or **mediaeval** *med-i-ē'vl* or (*US*) *mē-d(ē)-ē'vl*, *adj* of the Middle Ages. — *n* **medie'valism** or **mediae'valism** the spirit of the Middle Ages; devotion to medieval ideals; a practice, etc, revived or surviving from the Middle Ages. — *n* **medie'valist** or **mediae'valist** a person versed in the history, art, etc, of the Middle Ages; a devotee or follower of medieval practices. — *adv* **medie'vally** or **mediae'vally**. [L *medius* middle, and *aevum* age]

medina *mə-dē'nə*, *n* in North African cities, the ancient, native quarter. [Ar, town]

medio- *mē'di-ō-*, *combining form* denoting middle. [L *medius* middle]

mediocre *mē'di-ō-kər* or *-ō'kər*, *adj* middling or average in quality, performance, etc; rather inferior. — *n* **medioc'rity** (*-ok'*) the state of being mediocre; average or inferior quality, etc; a mediocre person. [Fr *médiocre*, from L *mediocris*, from *medius* middle]

Medism. See under **Median**.

meditate *med'i-tāt*, *vi* to consider thoughtfully (with *on* or *upon*); to engage in contemplation, *esp* religious. — *vt* to consider deeply, reflect upon; to turn over in the mind; to intend. — *adj* **med'itated**. — *n* **meditā'tion** the act of meditating; deep thought; serious continuous contemplation, *esp* on a religious or spiritual theme; a meditative discourse; a meditative treatment of a literary or musical theme. — *adj* **med'itātive**. — *adv* **med'itātively**. — *n* **med'itātiveness**. — **meditate the muse** (Latinism, after Milton) to give one's mind to composing poetry. [L *meditārī*, prob cognate with L *medērī* to heal]

mediterranean *med-i-tə-rā'ni-ən*, *adj* situated in the middle of earth or land; land-locked; (with *cap*) of the **Mediterranean Sea** and the area surrounding it (so called from being in the middle of the land of the Old World) or its shores; (of physical type) slight in build, and of dark complexion. — *n* (with *cap*) the Mediterranean Sea. — **Mediterranean fever** Malta or undulant fever; **Mediterranean fruit fly** a small black-and-white two-winged fly, *orig* native to Africa but now widely distributed, the larvae of which feed on ripening fruit (often shortened to **med'fly**); **Mediterranean race** a long-headed dark race of White people, of medium stature, inhabiting S Europe and N Africa. [L *mediterrāneus*, from *medius* middle, and *terra* earth]

medium *mē'di-əm*, *n* an intermediate or middle position or condition; the middle place or degree; a middle course; a mean (*obs*); (in *pl*, **mediums**) medium-dated securities; any intervening means, instrument or agency; instrumentality; a substance through which any effect is transmitted; that through which communication is maintained; (*pl* **media**) a channel (eg newspapers, radio, television) through which information, etc is transmitted to the public (also **mass medium**, *pl* **mass media**); (*pl usu* **media**) any material, eg magnetic disk, paper tape, on which data is recorded (*comput*); an enveloping substance or element in which a thing exists or lives; environment; the substance, eg oil or water, with which a pigment is mixed to make paint, the vehicle by which it is applied to a surface; a nutritive substance on which a culture (of bacteria, tissue, etc) may be fed; (*pl* **mediums**) in spiritualism, the person through whom spirits are said to communicate with the material world; (*pl* **mediums**) a person of supernormal sensibility: — *pl* **mē'dia** or **mē'diums**. — *adj* intermediate or moderate, coming midway between two opposing degrees or extremes; between fast and slow, long and short, etc; mean, average (*obs*); of a standard size of paper between demy and royal, now 18 in by 23 in. — *adj* **mediage'nic** able to communicate well or present a good image in the media, *esp* television. — *adj* **mediumis'tic** of or relating to spiritualistic mediums. — *adj* **me'dium-dated** (of securities) redeemable in five to fifteen year's time. — *adj* **me'dium-term** intermediate between short-term and long-term. — **medium waves** (*radio*) electromagnetic waves of between 200 and 1000 metres. — *adj* **me'dium-wave**. — **circulating medium** money passing from hand to hand, as coin, bank notes, etc. [L *medium*, neuter of *medius* middle]

medius *mē'di-əs*, *n* the middle finger. [L *medius* middle]

Medize. See under **Median**.

Medjidie *me-jēd'i-e*, *n* a Turkish order of knighthood founded by Sultan Abdu'l *Majīd*.

medlar *med'lər*, *n* a small tree (*Mespilus*, or *Pyrus*, *germanica*) related to the apple; its fruit. [OFr *medler*, *mesler*, from L *mespilum*, from Gr *mespilon*]

medle. An old spelling (*Shakesp* and *Spenser*) of **meddle**.

medley *med'li*, *n* a mingled and confused mass; a miscellany; a song or piece of music made up of bits from various sources; a cloth woven from yarn of different colours; a mêlée, a fight (*obs*). — **medley relay** a race in which each team member runs a different distance or (in swimming) uses a different stroke. [OFr *medler*, *mesler* to mix]

Médoc *mā-dok'*, *n* a French wine produced in the district of *Médoc*, department of Gironde.

medresseh. See **madrasa**.

medulla *me-dul'ə*, *n* the inner portion of an organ, hair, or tissue; bone-marrow; pith; a loose or spongy mass of hyphae: — *pl* **medull'ae** (-*ē*) or **medull'as**. — *adj* **medull'ar** or **medull'ary** consisting of, or resembling, marrow or pith. — *adj* **medull'ate** having medulla. — *adj* **med'ullated** provided with a medullary sheath. — **medulla oblongā'ta** (or -*ä'tə*) that part of the brain that tapers off into the spinal cord; **medullary ray** (*bot*) a band of cells (appearing as a ray in cross-section) cutting radially through wood and bast; **medullary sheath** a thin layer surrounding the pith (*bot*); a whitish fatty membrane covering an axis-cylinder (*anatom*). [L *medulla* marrow]

Medusa *me-dū'zə*, *n* one of the three Gorgons, whose head, with snakes for hair, turned beholders into stone, but was cut off by Perseus, and placed in Athena's aegis (*Gr mythol*); (without *cap*) a jellyfish; (without *cap*) an individual of the free-swimming sexual generation of jellyfishes and *Hydrozoa*: — *pl* **medū'sae** (-*zē*) or **medū'sas**. — *adj* **medū'san**. — *n* a medusa. — *adj* **medū'siform** like a jellyfish. — *adj* **medū'soid** like a medusa. — *n* a sexual hydrozoan that remains attached to the parent hydroid colony. [L *Medūsa*, from Gr *Medousa*, the Gorgon *Medusa* (literally, ruler)]

meed *mēd*, *n* wages (*archaic*); reward; what is bestowed for merit; measure, portion. [OE *mēd*; Ger *Miete*]

meek *mēk*, *adj* having a mild and gentle temper; submissive. — *vt* **meek'en** to render meek. — *vi* to become meek. — *adv* **meek'ly**. — *n* **meek'ness** the state or quality of being meek. [ON *mjūkr*; early mod Du *muik* soft]

meemie *mē'mi*, (*colloq*) *n* (in full **screaming meemie**) a hysterical person; (in *pl*) a fit of hysterics. [Origin unknown]

meer[1] *mēr*, an alternative spelling of **mere**[1,2,3]. — *adj* **meered** or **mered** (*Shakesp*) (possibly) set up as a *mere* or division, dividing; (according to some) sole, or entire.

meer[2]. See **mir**[2].

meerkat *mēr'kat*, *n* a monkey (*obs*); a South African carnivore (*Cynictis penicillata*), related to the ichneumon; the suricate; a ground-squirrel; a lemur. — Also **meer'cat**. [Du *meerkat* monkey, as if 'overseas cat', from *meer* sea, and *kat* cat, but perh really an Eastern word]

meerschaum *mēr'shəm*, *n* a fine light whitish clay, sepiolite — once supposed to be a petrified sea-scum; a tobacco-pipe made of it. [Ger, from *Meer* sea, and *Schaum* foam]

meet[1] *mēt*, (*archaic* or *formal*) *adj* fitting; qualified; even, quits (*Shakesp*). — *adv* fittingly (*Shakesp*). — *adv* **meet'ly**. — *n* **meet'ness**. [Prob from an OE (Anglian) form answering to WSax *gemǣte*, from *metan* to measure]

meet[2] *mēt*, *vt* to find or come across in passing (now *dialect*); to come face to face with; to come into the company of; to become acquainted with, be introduced to; to encounter in conflict or battle (*archaic*); to come into contact with, join; to encounter or experience as treatment or response; to match or oppose adequately, to refute, eg an argument; to be suitable to or satisfy, eg a demand or requirement; to be sufficient in payment for; (in *imperative*) as a request to receive or welcome a person on introduction; to cause to meet, bring into contact; to await the arrival of, keep an appointment with. — *vi* to come together from different points; to assemble; to come into contact; to have an encounter; to balance, come out correct: — *pa t* and *pa p* **met**. — *n* a meeting of participants in a fox-hunt; a gathering for a sports competition or race; a covert pre-arranged meeting between criminals, *esp* drug-dealers, or between police and an informant (*slang*); an intersection (*math*). — *n* **meet'ing** a coming face to face for friendly or hostile ends; an interview; an assembly; an organized assembly for the transaction of business; an assembly for religious worship, *esp* (in England) of Dissenters; a place of meeting; a junction. — **meet'ing-house** a house or building where people, *esp* Quakers, meet for public worship. — **give the** (or **a**) **meeting** (*archaic*) to appoint or come to a rendezvous, for a duel or other purpose; **meet halfway** to make concessions to, or come to a compromise with; **meet in with** or **wi'** (*Scot*) to meet with, come across; **meet the ear**, or **eye** to be readily apparent; **meet up (with)** to meet, by chance or arrangement; **meet with** to come to or upon, *esp* unexpectedly; to meet or come together with, *usu* for a purpose (*US*); to undergo, chance to experience; to obviate (as an objection) (*Bacon*); **well met** an old complimentary greeting. [OE *mētan* to meet, from *mōt*, *gemōt* a meeting]

mefloquine *mef'lō-kwin*, *n* an antimalarial drug.

meg. See **mag**[1].

mega *meg'ə*, (*slang*) *adj* enormous, huge; very good or great. — *adv* to a great extent, extremely. [From combining form **mega-**]

mega- *meg-ə-* (before a vowel **meg-**), **megal-** *meg-əl-* or **megalo-** *meg-ə-l-ō-*, *-o-* or *-ə-*, *combining form* meaning very big, unusually large, on a very large scale; in names of units, denoting a million. — **megamega-** *combining form* denoting a million million (same as **tera-**). — *n* **meg'abar**. — *n* **meg'abit**. — *n* **meg'abuck** (*NAm slang*) a million dollars; (in *pl*) very large sums of money. — *n* **meg'abyte** (loosely) a million bytes; 1 048 576 bytes. — *adj* **megacephalous** (*-sef'ə-ləs*; Gr *kephalē* head) large-headed. — *n pl* **Megacheiroptera** (*-kīr-op'tər-ə*) the fruit-bats. — *n* **megacity** (*meg'ə-sit-i*) a city of over a million inhabitants; a very large city. — *n* **meg'acurie**. — *n* **meg'acycle** a million cycles; a million cycles per second. — *n* **meg'adeath** death of a million people, a unit in estimating casualties in nuclear war. — *n* **meg'adose** a dose of drug, etc, far exceeding the normal amount taken. — *n* **meg'adyne**. — *n* **mega-far'ad**. — *n* **meg'afauna** (or *-fö'nə*) and **meg'aflora** (also *-flö'rə*) large animals and plants respectively, visible to the naked eye. — *n* **meg'afog** a fog-signal with megaphones pointing in several directions. — *n* **meg'a-gauss**. — *n* **meg'aherbivore** a herbivore weighing over 1 000kg, eg an elephant or rhinoceros. — *n* **meg'ahertz**. — *n* **meg'ajoule**. — *n* **meg'alith** (Gr *lithos* stone) a huge stone, as in prehistoric monuments (*archaeol*). — *adj* **megalith'ic** constructed with, or characterized by the use of, huge stones (*archaeol*). — *n* **megaloblast** an abnormally large nucleated red blood cell found in the bone-marrow of people suffering from a **megaloblastic anaemia** such as pernicious anaemia. — *n* **megalo-mā'nia** the delusion that one is great or powerful; (loosely) a lust for power; a passion for possessions on a grandiose scale. — *n* and *adj* **megalomā'niac**. — *adj* **megalomaniacal** (*-mə-nī'ə-kl*). — *n* **megalop'olis** a wide-spreading, thickly-populated urban area; an enormous city. — *n* and *adj* **megalopol'itan**. — *n* **meg'alosaur** or **megalosau'rus** (Gr *sauros* a lizard) a gigantic lizard-hipped Jurassic and Cretaceous dinosaur (*Megalosaurus*), carnivorous in habits. — *adj* **megalosau'rian**. — *n* **meg'anewton**. — *n* **meg'aparsec**. — *n* **meg'apode** (Gr *pous*, *podos* foot) a mound-bird. — *n* **meg'arad**. — *n* **meg'aron** (Gr *megaron*) the principal hall of an ancient Greek house. — *n* **meg'ascope** (Gr *skopeein* to view) an instrument for projecting an enlarged image. — *adj* **megascopic** (*-skop'ik*) enlarged; visible to the naked eye. — *n* **megasporangium** (*-spor-an'ji-əm*) a sporangium producing only megaspores: — *pl* **mega-sporan'gia**. — *n* **meg'aspore** the larger of two forms of spore; a spore giving rise to a female gametophyte. — *n* **megasporophyll** (*-spor'ə-fil*) a sporophyll that carries or subtends only megasporangia. — *n* **meg'astore** (*colloq*) a very large shop, *esp* any of the very large chain stores. — *n* **meg'astructure** a very large building or construction. — *n* **megatechnol'ogy** rapidly advancing high technology in eg microelectronics. — *n* **Megathē'rium** (Gr *thērion* wild beast) a genus of gigantic extinct S American ground-sloths. — *n* **meg'aton** (*-tun*) one million tons; a unit of explosive power equalling a million tons of TNT (**megaton bomb** a bomb of this force). — *n* **meg'atonnage** the total explosive capacity in megatons. — *n* **meg'avertebrate**. — *adj* **meg'avitamin** consisting of or relating to large doses of vitamins. — *n* **meg'avolt**. — *n* **meg'awatt** (**megawatt days per tonne** the unit of energy output from reactor fuel (day = 24 hours)). — *n* **meg'ohm** a million ohms. [Gr *megas*, fem *megalē*, neuter *mega* big]

Megaera *mə-jē'rə* or *me-gī'ra*, (*Gr mythol*) *n* one of the Furies. [L, from Gr *Megaira*]

megafarad, etc, **megalomania**, etc, **megasporophyll**. See under **mega-**.

megaphone *meg'ə-fōn*, *n* a funnel-shaped device for directing or magnifying sound, *esp* that of the voice. — *vt* and *vi* to communicate by megaphone. — *adj* **megaphon'ic**. — **megaphone diplomacy** diplomatic communication which is unsubtle or indirect, as when conducted through media announcements rather than direct approach. [**mega-**, and Gr *phōnē* voice]

megass or **megasse** *mə-gäs'*. Same as **bagasse**.

Megatherium ... to ... **megawatt**. See under **mega-**.

megillah *mə-gil'ə*, *n* a scroll containing a book of the Old Testament, *esp* the Book of Esther, to be read on certain feast days (*Judaism*); a lengthy or tedious account, a screed (*US slang*): — *pl* **megill'ahs** or **megill'oth** (*-lot*). [Hebr, roll, scroll]

megilp or **magilp** *mə-gilp'*, *n* a medium used in oil-painting, consisting of linseed-oil and mastic varnish or turpentine. [Origin unknown]

megohm. See under **mega-**.

megrim[1] *mē'grim*, *n* migraine (*obs*); vertigo, dizziness (also in *pl*; now *rare*); a whim, a caprice (*archaic* and *Scot*); (in *pl*) depression, doldrums (now *esp NAm*).

megrim[2] *mē'grim*, *n* the scaldfish.

Mehdi. See **Mahdi**.

Meiji *mā'ji*, *n* a period in Japanese history (1868–1912) following the overthrow of the shoguns, in which power was restored to the emperor. [Jap, literally enlightened rule]

mein. See **mean**[4].

meinie, **meiney**, **meiny** or (*Scot*) **menyie** *mā'ni*, *n* a retinue, a household (*Shakesp*); a herd (*obs*); a collection (*Scot*); a crowd, a rabble (*Scot*). [OFr *mesnie*, from L *mānsio -ōnis* a dwelling]

meint. See **ming**[1].

meiny. See **meinie**.

meiofauna *mī'ə-fö-nə* or *-fö'nə*, *n pl* animals less than 1mm and more than 0·1mm across. — *adj* **meiofau'nal**. [Gr *meion* less, and **fauna**]

meionite *mī'ən-īt*, *n* a scapolite with less sodium and silica than marialite. [Gr *meiōn* less, from the short vertical axis of its crystal]

meiosis *mī-ō'sis*, *n* understatement as a figure of speech, litotes (*rhetoric*); cell-division with reduction by pairing of the number of chromosomes towards the development of a reproductive cell (*biol*): — *pl* **meiō'ses**. — *adj* **meiotic** (*-ot'ik*). [Gr *meiōsis* diminution]

meishi *mā'shi*, *n* in Japan, a calling or business card. [Jap]

Meissen china, **porcelain** or **ware**. Same as **Dresden China**, etc.

Meissner effect *mīs'nər i-fekt'*, (*phys*) *n* an effect by which, by cooling a superconducting material below its critical temperature, its magnetic flux is expelled or excluded, depending on whether a magnetic field is applied before or after the cooling.

Meistersinger *mīs'tər-zing-ər* or *-sing-ər*, *n* any of the burgher poets and musicians of Germany in the 14–16c, the successors of the Minnesingers: — *pl* **Meistersinger** or **Meistersingers**. [Ger, master-singer]

meith *mēth*, (*Scot*) *n* a landmark; a boundary. [Prob ON *mith* a fishing-bank found by landmarks]

Mejlis. Same as **Majlis**.

me judice *mē jōō'di-sē* or *mā yōō'di-ke*, (*L*) I being judge, in my opinion.

Mekhitarist or **Mechitharist** *mehh-* or *mek-i-tär'ist*, *n* an Armenian Uniat monk of a congregation founded by *Mekhitar* (1676–1749) at Constantinople in 1701, since 1717 with headquarters near Venice. — Also *adj*.

mekometer *mə-kom'ə-tər*, *n* a device for accurate measurement of distances by means of a light beam. [Gr *mēkos* length]

mel *mel*, (*esp pharm*) *n* honey. [L]

mela *mē'lə*, *n* in the Indian subcontinent, a Hindu festival or fair. [Hindi, from Sans *melā* assembly]

melaconite *mel-ak'ən-īt*, *n* tenorite. [Gr *melās* black, and *konis* dust]

melamine *mel'ə-mēn*, *n* a white crystalline organic substance used in forming **melamine resins**, thermosetting plastics used as adhesives, coatings, etc. [Ger *Melamin*]

melampode *mel-am'pōd* or *mel'*, (*Spenser*) *n* the black hellebore. [Gr *melampodion*]

melanaemia *mel-ən-ē'mi-ə*, *n* the presence of melanin in the blood. [Gr *melās*, *-anos* black, and *haima* blood]

melancholy *mel'ən-kol-i* or *-kəl-i*, formerly *mel-ang'kol-i*, *n* black bile, considered one of the four chief bodily humours (*obs*); an excess of black bile, or the mental condition or temperament supposed to result from this (*obs*); surliness (*obs*); prolonged depression of spirits; dejection; melancholia; indulgence in thoughts of pleasing sadness; wistful pensiveness. — *adj* prone to, affected by, expressive of, or causing, melancholy; depressed; pensive; deplorable. — *n* **melanchō'lia** a mental state characterized by dejection and misery. — *n* **melanchō'liac** a sufferer from melancholia. — Also *adj*. — *adj* **melancholic** (*-kol'ik*) affected with, or caused by, melancholy or melancholia; dejected; mournful. — *n* a melancholiac. — *adj* **melanchō'lious**. [Gr *melancholiā*, *from melās*, *-anos* black, and *cholē* bile]

Melanesian *mel-ən-ēz'i-ən*, *-ēz'yən*, *-ēzh'ən* or *-ēzh'yən*, *adj* of or relating to *Melanesia*, a group of islands lying NE of Australia. — *n* a native or inhabitant of these islands; any of the languages spoken in Melanesia. — **Neo-Melanesian** see under **neo-**. [Gr *melās*, *-anos* black, and *nēsos* an island]

mélange or **melange** *mā-lãzh'*, *n* a mixture; a medley. [Fr]

melanin *mel'ə-nin*, *n* the dark pigment in skin, hair, etc. — *adj* **melanic** (*mi-lan'ik*) black or dark in pigmentation. — *n* **mel'anism** the biological condition of having dark skin, plumage, etc; more than normal development of dark colouring matter. — *adj* **melanist'ic**. — *n* **mel'anite** a black garnet. — *n* **melano** (*mi-lä'nō* or *mel'ə-nō*) an abnormally dark person or animal (formed on the analogy of *albino*): — *pl* **melanos**. — *n* **mel'anocyte** (*-sīt*, also *-lan'*) an epidermal cell that can produce melanin. — *n* **melanō'ma** any skin tumour consisting of melanin-pigmented cells; (also **malignant melanoma**) a malignant tumour consisting of melanin-pigmented cells, which usually develops from a mole and metastasizes rapidly: — *pl* **melanō'mata** or **melanō'mas**. — *n* **mel'anophore** (*-för*) a chromatophore containing melanin. — *n* **melanō'sis** a condition of skin or body characterized by abnormally large deposits of melanin; a discolouration caused by this. — *adj* **melanot'ic** or **mel'anous** dark-complexioned. — *n* **melanotrop'in** a hormone secreted by the pituitary gland which stimulates the production of melanin by melanocytes. — *n* **melanū'ria** the presence of a dark pigment in the urine. — *adj* **melanū'ric**. — *n* **melaphyre** (*mel'ə-fīr*; formed on analogy with *porphyry*) *orig* a dark porphyritic rock; applied very loosely to an altered basalt. [Gr *melās*, *-anos* black]

melanochroi *mel-ən-ok'rō-ī* or *-ō-krō'ī*, *n pl* one of the racial types proposed by T H Huxley (1825–95), having dark hair and white skin. — *adj* **melanochrō'ic** or **melanochroous** (*-ok'rō-əs*). [Gr *melās*, *-anos* black, and either *ōchros* pale, or *chroā* skin]

melanterite *mi-lan'tə-rīt*, *n* native copperas. [Gr *melantēriā* a black pigment]

Melastomaceae *mel-ə-stō-mā'si-ē* or *-māshiē*, *n pl* a tropical family of plants related to the myrtles, very abundant in South America, characterized by the leaf-veins diverging from the base and meeting at the tip, named from the Old World genus *Melastoma* (*mi-las'tō-mə*). — *adj* **melastomā'ceous**. [Gr *melās* black, and *stoma* mouth, from the staining effect of its fruit on the lips]

melatonin *mel-ə-tō'nin*, *n* a hormone secreted by the pineal gland during the hours of darkness that induces sleepiness and is thought to have useful application, eg in the treatment of jet lag. [Ety as for **melanin**, and sero*tonin*]

melba toast *mel'bə tōst*, *n* very thin crisp toast. — **melba sauce** a sauce for puddings, made from raspberries. — **peach Melba** see under **peach**. [Named after Dame Nellie *Melba* (1861–1931), Australian opera singer]

meld[1] *meld*, (*cards*) *vt* and *vi* to declare or show (a card or combination of cards) to claim a score. — *n* the act of melding; a card or combination of cards with which to meld. [OE *meldan*, or Ger *melden*]

meld[2] *meld*, (*orig US*) *vt* and *vi* to merge, blend, combine. — *n* a blending or merging. [Poss **melt** and **weld**]

melder *mel'dər*, (*Scot*) *n* the quantity of meal ground at one time. [ON *meldr*]

mêlée *mel'ā*, *n* a fight in which the combatants become intermingled; a confused, noisy conflict; an affray. [Fr, from *mêler* to mix; cf **meddle** and **mell**[1]]

Melia *mē'li-ə*, *n* a genus of trees including the nim or margosa, giving name to the family **Meliā'ceae** (mahogany, *Cedrela*, etc). — *adj* **meliā'ceous** (*-shəs*). [Gr *meliā* ash-tree (from a resemblance in leaves)]

Meliboean *mel-i-bē'ən*, *adj* in poetry, amoebaean. [From *Meliboeus*, in Virgil's first eclogue]

melic[1] *mel'ik*, *adj* to be sung; lyric; strophic. [Gr *melikos*, from *melos* song]

melic[2] *mel'ik*, *n* a grass (*Melica*) of the fescue family. — Also **mel'ic-grass**. [Origin obscure]

melicotton. See **melocoton**.

melik. See **malik**.

melilite *mel'i-līt*, *n* a tetragonal mineral, calcium aluminium magnesium silicate, often honey-yellow. [Gr *meli* honey, and *lithos* stone]

melilot *mel'i-lot*, *n* a genus (*Melilotus*) of clover-like plants with racemes of white or yellow flowers and a peculiar sweet odour. [Gr *melilōtos*, from *meli* honey, and *lōtos* lotus]

melinite *mel'in-īt*, *n* an explosive made from picric acid. [Fr *mélinite*, from Gr *mēlinos* quince yellow, from *mēlon* quince]

meliorate *mē'li-ə-rāt*, *vt* to make better. — *vi* to grow better, to improve. — *n* **meliorā'tion**. — *adj* **mē'liorātive** causing improvement; (of a word or sense) complimentary, favourable (opposite of *pejorative*). — *n* **mē'liorātor**. — *n* **mē'liorism** the doctrine that the world can be improved through human endeavour, as opposed to *optimism* and *pessimism*. — *n* **mē'liorist**. — *adj* **meliorist'ic**. — *n* **meliority** (*-or'i-ti*) betterness. [LL *meliōrāre*, *-ātum*, from L *melior* better]

meliphagous *mel-if'ə-gəs*, *adj esp* of birds, feeding upon honey. [Gr *meli* honey, and *phagein* (aorist) to eat]

melisma *mel-iz'mə*, *n* a song; a tune; a melodic embellishment: — *pl* **melis'mata** or **melis'mas**. — *adj* **melismatic** (*-mat'ik*) florid in melody, *esp* where one syllable is sung to a number of notes. [Gr *melisma*, *-matos* a song, tune]

mell[1] *mel*, (now *archaic*, *Scot* and *dialect*) *vt* and *vi* to mix, mingle. — *vi* (*usu* with *with*) to have to do, to associate; to have sexual intercourse (*obs*); to join in fight; to be concerned; to meddle. [OF *meller*; cf **meddle** and **medley**]

mell[2] *mel*, *n* a *Scots* and *N Eng* form of **mall** or **maul**.

mellay *mel'ā*, *n* another form of **mêlée**.

melliferous *mel-if'ə-rəs*, *adj* producing or forming honey. — *n* **mellificā'tion** honey-making. — *n* **mellif'luence** (L *fluere* to flow) a flow of sweetness; a smooth, sweet flow. — *adj* **mellif'luent** or **mellif'luous** flowing with honey or sweetness; (of sounds) sweetly smooth. — *adv* **mellif'luently** or **mellif'luously**. — *n* **mell'ite** honey-stone. — *adj* **mellit'ic**. — *adj* **melliv'orous** (L *vorāre* to devour) eating honey. [L *mel*, *mellis* honey]

mellow *mel'ō*, *adj* soft and ripe; well matured; soft to the touch, palate, ear, etc; genial; slightly, but genially, drunk. — *vt* to soften by ripeness or age; to mature. — *vi* to become soft; to be matured, ripened; to become gentler and more tolerant. — *adv* **mell'owly**. — *n* **mell'owness**. — *adj* **mell'owy** mellow. — **mell'ophone** a brass wind instrument resembling the French horn, but less rich in tone. — **mellow out** (*slang*) to become relaxed or calm (*esp* under the influence of drugs). [Prob OE *melu* meal, influenced by *mearu* soft, tender]

melocoton or **melocotoon** *mel-ō-kot-ōn'* or *-ōōn'*, (*obs*) *n* a large kind of peach. — Also **malakatoone'** or **melicott'on**. [Sp *melocotón*, from Ital *melocotogna* quince, peach, from LL *mēlum cotōneum*, from Gr *mēlon Kydōnion* Cydonian (Cretan) apple, quince]

melodeon or **melodion** *mi-lō'di-ən*, *n* a small reed-organ; a harmonium or type of accordion. [Ety as for **melody**]

melodica *mi-lod'i-kə*, *n* a small wind instrument with a mouthpiece at one end and a keyboard. [From *melod*eon and harmon*ica*]

melodrama *mel'ō-drä-mə* or *-drä'mə*, *n* a play with musical accompaniment to the action and spoken dialogue, with or without songs (*obs*); a kind of romantic and sensational drama, crude, sentimental, and conventional, involving poetic justice and happy endings; a film or play that is excessively sensational, emotional, etc. — Also (now *rare*) **mel'odrame** (*-dräm*). — *adj* **melodramat'ic** (*-drə-mat'ik*) of the nature of melodrama; overstrained; sensational. — *n* **melodramatist** (*-dram'ə-tist*) a writer of melodramas. — *vt* **melodram'atize** or **-ise** to make melodramatic. [Gr *melos* a song, and *drāma* action.

melody *mel'ə-di*, *n* an air or tune; music; an agreeable succession of single musical sounds, as distinguished from *harmony*. — *adj* **melodic** (*mi-lod'ik*). — *n sing* **melod'ics** the branch of music concerned with melody. — *adj* **melō'dious** full of melody; pleasant to listen to. — *adv* **melō'diously**. — *n* **melō'diousness**. — *n* **mel'odist**. — *vi* **mel'odize** or **-ise** to make music; to perform a melody. — *vt* to add a melody to; to make melodious. — **melodic minor** a minor scale with major sixth and seventh ascending and minor sixth and seventh descending. [Fr, through LL, from Gr *melōidiā*]

melomania *mel-ō-mā'ni-ə*, *n* a craze for music. — *n* **melomā'niac**. — *adj* **melomanic** (*-man'*). [Gr *melos* song, and *maniā* madness]

melon *mel'ən*, *n* any of several juicy, edible gourds; the plant bearing it; profits to be divided among stockholders, etc, *usu* in *cut the melon* (*NAm colloq*). — **mel'on-pear** a fruit, the pepino. [Fr, from L *mēlō*, *-ōnis*, from Gr *mēlon* an apple]

Melpomene *mel-pom'i-nē*, (*Gr mythol*) *n* the Muse of tragedy. [Gr *Melpomenē*, literally, songstress]

melt[1] *melt*, *vi* to change from a solid into a liquid state, *esp* by heat; to fuse; to dissolve; to stream with liquid; to lose distinct form; to blend; to shade off; to become imperceptible; to disperse, be dissipated, disappear (sometimes with *away*); to soften emotionally. — *vt* to cause to melt in any sense: — *pa t* **melt'ed** or *archaic* **mōlt**; *pa p* **melt'ed** or (*archaic*) **mōlt'en**, **ymōlt'en** or **ymōlt'**. — *n* the act of melting; the state of being melted; molten material; the quantity melted. — *n* and *adj* **melt'ing**. — *adv* **melt'ingly**. — *n* **melt'ingness**. — *adj* **mōlt'en** melted; made of melted metal. — *adv* **mōlt'enly**. — **melt'down** the process in which, due to a failure of the cooling system, the radioactive fuel in a nuclear reactor overheats, melts through its insulation, and is released into the environment; an unforeseen and disastrous failure, with possible wide-reaching effects, such as a crash on the stock-market; **melt'ing-point** the temperature at which a given solid begins to become liquid; **melt'ing-pot** a container for melting things in; a place characterized by the intermixing of several races or cultures; a state of dissolution preparatory to shaping anew (see also **in the melting pot** below);

melting temperature (*biol*) the temperature at which half the macromolecules in a solution are denatured, eg DNA dissociated into single strands; **melt'-water** water running off melting ice or snow. — **in the melting-pot** in the process of changing and forming something new; **molten salt reactor** one in which uranium is dissolved in a molten mixture of fluoride salts; **molten sea** see under **sea**. [OE *meltan* (intrans strong verb), and *mæltan*, *meltan* (causative weak verb, WSax *mieltan*); ON *melta* to digest, to malt, Gr *meldein*]

melt[2]. See **milt**.

meltith *mel'tith*, (*Scot*) *n* a meal; a cow's yield at one milking. [**meal-tide**]

melton *mel'tən*, *n* a strong cloth for overcoats. [*Melton* Mowbray, in Leicestershire]

Mem. *abbrev*: Member.

mem. *abbrev*: *memento* (*L*), remember; memorandum.

member *mem'bər*, *n* a distinct part of a whole, *esp* a limb of an animal; a clause (*gram*); a person who belongs to a society, club, political party, etc; a representative in a legislative body; an animal or plant that is part of a group. — *adj* **mem'bered** having limbs. — *n* **mem'bership** the state of being a member of or belonging to a society, etc; the members of a body, organization, etc regarded as a whole. — *adj* **mem'bral** relating to the limbs rather than the trunk. — **member of parliament** a member of the House of Commons (*abbrev* **MP**). [Fr *membre*, from L *membrum*]

membrane *mem'brān* or *-brin*, *n* a thin flexible solid sheet or film; a thin sheetlike structure, *usu* fibrous, connecting other structures or covering or lining a part or organ (*biol*); a skin of parchment. — *adj* **membranaceous** (*-brə-nā'shəs*), **membrān'eous** (*rare*) or **mem'branous** (*-brə-nəs*) like or of the nature of a membrane; thin, translucent, and papery (*bot*). — **membrane bone** one formed directly from connective tissue without passing through a stage of cartilage. [L *membrāna*, from *membrum*]

membrum virile *mem'brəm vir-ī'lē* or *-broŏm wir-ē'le*, (*L*) *n* the penis.

memento *mi-men'tō*, *n* something kept or given as a reminder; a fit of reverie (*obs*): — *pl* **memen'tos** or **-toes**. — **memento mori** (*mō'rī* or *mo'rē*) remember that you must die (*L*); anything (eg a skull) to remind one of mortality. [L, imperative of *meminisse* to remember]

Memnon *mem'non*, *n* an Ethiopian king who fought for the Trojans; a statue of Amenhotep, or Amenoph(is), III at Thebes in Egypt, thought by the Greeks to be of Memnon and to give out a musical sound at sunrise in salutation of his mother Eos (the Dawn). — *adj* **Memnōn'ian**. [Gr *Memnōn*]

memo *mem'ō*, *n* a contraction of **memorandum**: — *pl* **mem'os**.

memoir *mem'wär* or *-wör*, *n* (*usu* in *pl*) a written record set down as material for history or biography; a biographical sketch; a record of a study of some subject investigated by the writer; (in *pl*) the transactions of a society. — *n* **mem'oirism** the act or art of writing memoirs. — *n* **mem'oirist** a writer of memoirs. [Fr *mémoire*, from L *memoria* memory, from *memor* mindful]

memorabilia, **memorable**, etc. See under **memory**.

memorandum *mem-ə-ran'dəm*, *n* something to be remembered; a note to assist the memory; a brief note of some transaction (*law*); a summary of the state of a question (*diplomacy*): — *pl* **memoran'dums** or **memoran'da**. — *n* **memoran'dum-book** a book for keeping notes or memoranda. — **memorandum of association** a legal document required for registering a company under the Companies Act, stating the powers and objectives of the company with respect to the outside world. [L, a thing to be remembered, neuter gerundive of *memorāre* to remember]

memory *mem'ə-ri*, *n* the power of retaining and reproducing mental or sensory impressions; an impression so reproduced; a having or keeping in the mind; time within which past things can be remembered; commemoration; a religious service in commemoration; remembrance; of computers, a store (qv). — *n pl* **memorabil'ia** (from *L*) things worth remembering; noteworthy points; objects associated with a (*usu* famous) person or event, by which the memory of that person or event is kept alive. — *n* **memorabil'ity**. — *adj* **mem'orable** deserving to be remembered; remarkable; easily remembered. — *n* **mem'orableness**. — *adv* **mem'orably**. — *adj* **mem'orative** (*obs*) relating to memory; aiding the memory. — *adj* **memorial** (*ōr'* or *-ör'*) serving or intended to preserve the memory of anything; done in remembrance of a person, event, etc; relating to memory; remembered (*obs*). — *n* something which serves to keep in remembrance; a monument; a donation to charity in memory of someone who has died (*US*); a memorandum (*obs*); a written statement of facts; a record; memory (*obs*); (in *pl*) historical or biographical notices. — *n* **memor'ialist** a person who writes, signs or presents a memorial. — *vt* **memor'ialize** or **-ise** to present a memorial to; to commemorate; to petition by a memorial. — *adv* **memor'iter** (*L*) from memory; by heart. — *n* **memorīzā'tion** or **-s-**. — *vt* **mem'orize** or **-ise** to commit to memory; to cause to be remembered (*Shakesp*); to record, celebrate (*archaic*). — **Memorial Day** a day (Monday nearest 30 May) kept in honour of US servicemen killed in war (*orig* known as *Decoration Day* and kept, in most parts of the USA on 30 May, in honour of men killed in the US Civil War, 1861–65); **memoria technica** (*L*) artificial memory; a mnemonic device; **memory bank** (*comput*) a memory or store (qv); **memory card** (*comput*) an expansion card providing additional memory for a microcomputer. — *adj* **memory-res'ident** (*comput*) (of a program) able to be temporarily removed from and recalled to a screen while remaining in a computer's memory. — **memory trace** (*psychol*) a hypothetical change in the cells of the brain caused by the taking-in of information, etc. — **a memory like a sieve** see under **sieve**; **in living memory** within the memory of people still alive; **in memor'iam** to the memory of; in memory. [L *memoria* memory]

Memphian *mem'fi-ən*, *adj* relating to *Memphis*, an ancient capital of Egypt. — Also **Mem'phite** (*-fīt*) or **Memphitic** (*-fit'*).

mem-sahib *mem'-sä-ib*, *n* in colonial India, (a title of address for) a married European woman. [**ma'am** and **sahib**]

men, plural of **man**. — **menfolk**, **menfolks** and **menswear**. See under **man**.

menace *men'əs* or *-is*, *n* a threat or threatening; a show of an intention to do harm; a threatening danger. — *vt* to threaten. — *vi* to act in a threatening manner. — *n* **men'acer**. — *adj* **men'acing**. — *adv* **men'acingly**. [Fr, from L *mināciae* (pl) threats, from *minae* overhanging parts, threats]

menadione *men-ə-dī'ōn*, *n* vitamin K_3. [*me*thyl *na*phthoquinone, and *-dione*, sfx denoting a compound containing two carbonyl groups]

menage. *Obs* form of **manage**.

ménage *mā-näzh'*, *n* a household; the management of a house; a benefit society (*Scot*); an arrangement for selling on instalment (*Scot*). — **ménage à trois** (*a trwä*) a household composed of three people having sexual relations, *esp* a husband and wife and the lover of one of them. [Fr, from L *mānsiō* dwelling]

menagerie *mi-naj'ə-ri*, *n* a collection of wild animals in cages for exhibition; the place where these are kept; an unusual or outlandish assortment of people (*fig*). [Fr *ménagerie*, from *ménage* household]

menarche *mə-när'kē*, *n* the first menstruation. [Gr *mēn* month, and *archē* beginning]

mend *mend*, *vt* to remove a fault from; to repair; to make better; to correct; to improve; to improve upon; to supplement (*obs*). — *vi* to grow better; to reform. — *n* a repair; a repaired place, eg on a garment; an act of mending; (in *pl*) amends (*archaic*). — *n* **mend'er**. — *n* **mend'ing** the act of repairing; a repair; things requiring to be mended, *esp* clothes by sewing. — **mend one's pace** (*archaic*) to go quicker; **mend one's ways** to reform one's behaviour; **on the mend** improving, recovering. [Shortened from **amend**]

mendacious *men-dā'shəs, adj* lying; inclined to be untruthful. — *adv* **mendā'ciously**. — *n* **mendacity** (*-das'i-ti*) lying; a falsehood, a lie. [L *mendāx, -ācis*, connected with *mentīrī* to lie]

mendelevium *men-de-lē'* or *-lā'vi-əm, n* the element (symbol **Md**; atomic no 101) artificially produced in 1955 and named after the Russian D I *Mendeleev* (1834–1907), who developed the periodic table of elements.

Mendelian *men-dēl'i-ən, adj* pertaining to the Austrian-German, Gregor *Mendel* (1822–84), or his teaching on heredity by genes. — *n* a believer in Mendel's theory. — *n* **Men'delism** (*-də-lizm*).

mendicant *men'di-kənt, adj* begging; (of a friar) depending on alms. — *n* a beggar; a friar who depends on alms (*hist*). — *n* **men'dicancy** or **mendicity** (*-dis'i-ti*) the condition of being a beggar; the act of begging. [L *mendīcāns, -antis*, pr p of *mendīcāre* to beg, from *mendīcus* a beggar]

mene. See **mean**[4].

meneer *mən-ē'ər* or *mən-ēr', (SAfr) n* same as **mynheer**.

Menevian *men-ē'vi-ən, (geol) adj* and *n* Middle Cambrian. [LL *Menevia* St David's, in Dyfed, Wales]

meng and **menge**. See **ming**[1].

menhaden *men-hā'dn, n* an oily fish (*Brevoortia tyrannus*) of the herring family, found off the east coast of the United States. [From an Indian name]

menhir *men'hēr, n* a prehistoric megalith or standing stone. [Breton *men* stone, and *hir* long]

menial *mē'ni-əl, adj* of or pertaining to a train of servants or work of a humiliating or servile nature; servile. — *n* a domestic servant; someone performing servile work; a person of servile disposition. [Anglo-Fr *menial*; cf **meinie**]

Ménière's disease *mān-yerz'* or *-ē-erz' diz-ēz* or **syndrome** *sin'drōm, n* a disorder characterized by attacks of dizziness, buzzing noises in the ears, and progressive deafness, due to chronic disease of the labyrinth of the ear. [P *Ménière* (1799–1862), a French physician]

meninx *mē'ningks, n* any of three membranes that envelop the brain and spinal cord: — *pl* **meninges** (*men-in'jēz*). — *adj* **mening'eal**. — *n* **meningiō'ma** a tumour of the meninges of the brain and, more rarely, of the spinal cord. — *n* **meningitis** (*-jī'*) inflammation of the meninges. — *n* **meningocele** (*men-ing'gō-sēl*; Gr *kēlē* tumour) protrusion of the meninges through the skull. — *adj* **meningococc'al** (*men-ing-go-kok'l*) or **meningococcic** (*-kok'sik*) caused by a meningococcus. — *n* **meningococc'us** a coccus which causes epidemic cerebrospinal meningitis. [Gr *mēninx, -ingos* a membrane]

Menippean *men-ip-ē'ən, adj* relating to, or in imitation or emulation of, the Greek satirist *Menippos* (3c BC) of Gadara, *esp* humorously detailed or erudite.

meniscus *men-is'kəs, n* a crescent-shaped figure; a crescentic fibrous cartilage in a joint; a convexo-concave lens; a liquid surface curved by capillarity: — *pl* **menis'ci** (*-kī, -sī* or *-kē*) or **menis'cuses**. — *adj* **menis'coid** (*bot*) hourglass-shaped. — *n* **meniscec'tomy** (Gr *ektomē* cutting out) surgical removal of a meniscus cartilage. — **meniscus telescope** a telescope in which the spherical aberration of a concave spherical mirror is corrected by a meniscus lens. [Gr *mēniskos*, dimin of *mēnē* the moon]

menispermum *men-i-spûr'məm, n* any plant of the moonseed genus *Menispermum, esp Menispermum canadense*, giving name to a family **Menispermā'ceae** related to the buttercup family. — *adj* **menispermā'ceous**. [Gr *mēnē* moon, and *sperma* seed]

Mennonite *men'ən-īt, n* a member of a Protestant sect, originating in Holland and Switzerland and now found *esp* in the USA, believing in baptism on confession of faith, pacifism, etc. — Also *adj*. — *n* **Menn'onitism**. [From *Menno* Simons (died 1559), their chief founder]

menology *mē-nol'ə-ji, n* a register or calendar of Saints' days, *esp* of the Greek Church. [Late Gr *mēnologion*, from *mēn* month, and *logos* account]

Menominee or **Menomini** *mi-nom'i-nē, n* a member of a N American Indian people of Michigan and Wisconsin (*pl* **Menom'inee** or **Menom'inees**); the Algonquian language of this people; (without *cap*) a small whitefish found in the northern USA and Canada (also **menominee whitefish**). [Ojibwa]

meno mosso *mā'nō mos'sō, (music) adv* not so fast. [Ital]

menopause *men'ō-pöz, n* the ending of menstruation, change of life. — *adj* **menopaus'al** of, relating to or experiencing the menopause; suffering from strange moods or behaviour in middle age (*colloq*). — **male menopause** see under **male**[2]. [Gr *mēn* month, and *pausis* cessation]

menopome *men'ə-pōm, n* the hellbender, so-called from its persistent gill-aperture. [Gr *menein* to remain, and *pōma* lid]

menorah *mə-nō'rə* or *-nö'rə, n* (also with *cap*) a candelabrum with a varying number of branches, *usu* seven, used in Jewish religious ceremony. [Heb *menōrāh*]

menorrhagia *men-ə-rā'ji-ə, (med) n* excessive flow of blood during menstruation. [Gr *mēn* month, and *-rragia*, from *rhēgnynai* to break, burst]

menorrhoea or US **menorrhea** *men-ə-rē'ə, n* the normal flow of the menses. [Gr *mēn* month, and *rhoiā* flow]

Mensa *men'sə, n* one of the southern constellations, the Table; an international organization, founded in the UK in 1946, open to those with a high IQ rating. [L *mēnsa* table]

mensal[1] *men'səl, adj* monthly. — Also **men'sual**. [L *mensis* month]

mensal[2] *men'səl, adj* belonging to the table. [L *mēnsa* table]

mensch *mensh, (US slang) n* an honest, decent, morally-principled person. [Yiddish, a person]

mense *mens, (Scot) n* propriety; an ornament; credit. — *vt* to grace or set off (something). — *adj* **mense'ful** decorous; respectable; gracious; generous. — *adj* **mense'less** graceless, uncivil. [ON *mennska* humanity; cf OE *menniscu* humanity, *mennisc* human]

menses *men'sēz, n pl* the discharge of blood and other substances from the uterus during menstruation; the fact of menstruating, menstruation. [L *mēnsēs*, pl of *mēnsis* month]

mensh *mensh, (colloq)* short form of **mention**.

Menshevik *men'shə-vik, (hist) n* a moderate or minority socialist in revolutionary Russia, as opposed to *Bolshevik*. [Russ *menshye* smaller, and *(-v)ik*, agent suffix]

mens rea *menz rē'ə* or *mens rā'a, (law) n* a wrongful purpose; criminal intent; knowledge of the unlawfulness of an act. [New L, guilty mind]

mens sana in corpore sano *menz sä'nä in kör'pör-ā sä'nō, (L)* a healthy mind in a health body.

menstruum *men'strŏŏ-əm, n* a solvent, *esp* one used in the preparation of drugs (*orig* in *alchemy*): — *pl* **men'strua** or **men'struums** (**menstrua** also the menses). — *adj* **men'strual** monthly; relating to menstruation, or to the menses. — *vi* **men'struate** to discharge the menses, have a period. — *n* **menstruā'tion** the monthly discharge through the vagina of blood and other substances from the uterus in non-pregnant adult females. — *adj* **men'struous**. [L neuter of *mēnstruus* monthly, from *mēnsis*]

mensual. See **mensal**[1].

Mensur *men-sŏŏr', (Ger) n* a fencing contest between students at some universities, where it is fashionable to sport a duelling scar: — *pl* **Mensur'en**. [Ger, measurement (from the measured distance of the participants), from L *mēnsūra*]

mensurable *men'sh(y)ər-ə-bl* or *-sūr-, adj* measurable; having a fixed relative time-value for each note (*music*). — *n* **mensurabil'ity**. — *adj* **mens'ural** relating to measure; measurable (*music*). — *n* **mensurā'tion** the act or art of finding by measurement and calculation the length, area, volume, etc of bodies. — *adj* **men'surātive**. [L *mēnsūrāre* to measure]

menswear. See under **man**.

ment. See under **ming**[1].

mental[1]. See under **mentum**.

mental[2] *men'tl*, *adj* of or relating to the mind; done in the mind, *esp* in the mind alone, without outward expression; suffering from, provided for, or involved in the care of, disease or disturbance of the mind; mentally unbalanced (*slang*). — *n* **men'talism** the process of mental action; the theory that the physical world exists and is explicable only as an aspect of the mind, idealism (*philos*). — *n* **men'talist**. — *n* **mentality** (*-tal'i-ti*) mind; mental endowment; a type of mind; a way of thinking. — *adv* **men'tally**. — *n* **mentā'tion** mental activity. — *n* **menticide** (*men'ti-sīd*) the systematic reduction of a person's mind by psychological or other pressure to a point where views formerly repugnant will be accepted. — **mental age** the age in years, etc at which an average child would have reached the same stage of mental development as the individual under consideration; **mental cruelty** conduct in marriage, not involving physical cruelty or violence, that wounds feelings or personal dignity (in the USA, grounds for separation or divorce); **mental deficiency** mental retardation; **mental home** or **hospital**; **mental patient**; **mental retardation** retarded development of learning ability, whether arising from innate defect or from some other cause; **mental set** (*behav*) the tendency to consider new problems, etc, in the same way as old ones; a mindset. — **go mental** (*slang*) to become mentally unbalanced, go mad. [Fr, from L *mēns*, *mentis* the mind]

menthol *men'thol*, *n* a camphor obtained from oil of peppermint, used as a decongestant and local analgesic. — *adj* **men'tholated** containing menthol. [L *mentha* mint]

menticide. See under **mental**[2].

mention *men'shən*, *n* a brief notice; the occurrence or introduction of a name or reference. — *vt* to notice briefly; to remark; to name. — *adj* **men'tionable** fit to be mentioned; worth mentioning. — **honourable mention** an award of distinction not entitling to a prize; **not to mention** to say nothing of, a parenthetical rhetorical pretence of refraining from saying all one might say (and is about to say). [L *mentiō*, *-ōnis*]

mento *men'tō*, *n* a traditional Jamaican form of song or ballad, having a strong rhythm and often accompanying a dance: — *pl* **men'tōs**. [Origin unknown]

mentonnière *men-ton-i-er'*, (*hist*) *n* a piece of armour covering the chin and throat. [Fr, from *menton* chin, from L *mentum*]

mentor *ment'ər* or *-tör*, *n* a wise counsellor; a tutor; a trainer; a more senior or experienced colleague appointed to help and advise a junior employee (*business*). — *n* **mentee'** (*erron* formation) a person under the direction of a mentor, *esp* in business. — *adj* **mentorial** (*-tōr'* or *-tör'i-əl*). — *n* **men'toring**. — *n* **men'torship**. [Gr *Mentōr*, the tutor by whom (or Athena in his form) Telemachus, son of Odysseus, was guided]

mentum *men'təm*, (*anatom*) *n* the chin; the central part of the labium in insects. — *adj* **men'tal** of or relating to the chin. [L *mentum* the chin]

menu *men'ū*, *n* in a restaurant, etc, a list of dishes that may be ordered; the card listing these; a list of subjects, options (*fig*); *specif* a list of possible options or facilities displayed on a computer screen by software, and from which selection can be made via a keyboard or a mouse. — *adj* **men'u-driven** (of computer software) offering the user lists of options for movement through the system. [Fr, from L *minūtus* small]

menuisier *mə-nwē-zyā*, (*Fr*) *n* a joiner.

menyie. See **meinie**.

meo periculo *mē'ō pe-rik'ū-lō* or *mā'ō pe-rēk'ōō-lō*, (*L*) at my own risk.

meow *mi-ow'* or *myow*. Same as **miaow**.

MEP *abbrev*: Member of the European Parliament.

mepacrine *mep'ə-krēn*, *n* a bitter yellow powder derived from acridine dye compounds, formerly used against malaria (also **atabrin** or **atebrin**).

meperidine *me-per'i-dēn* or *-din*, *n* pethidine.

Mephistopheles *mef-is-tof'i-lēz*, *n* the devil in the *Faust* story. — Also **Mephistoph'ilis**, **Mephostoph'ilus**, etc: — *abbrev* **Mephis'tō**. — *adj* **Mephistophelē'an**, **Mephistophē'lian** or **Mephistophelic** (*-fel'*) cynical, scoffing, fiendish. [Ety unknown; prob influenced by Gr *mē* not, and *phōs*, *phōtos* light, or *philos* loving]

mephitis *me-fī'tis*, *n* a poisonous exhalation; a foul stink. — *adj* **mephitic** (*-fit'*) or **mephitical** (*me-fit'i-kl*). — *n* **meph'itism** (*-it-izm*) mephitic poisoning. [L *mephītis*]

meprobamate *mep-rō-bam'āt*, *n* a drug used as a muscle relaxant and as a sedative.

merc. See **mercenary**.

Mercalli scale *mər-kal'i skāl*, *n* a scale of intensity used to measure earthquake shocks, graded from 1 (very weak) to 12 (catastrophic). [From the inventor, Giuseppe *Mercalli* (1850–1914), Italian geologist]

mercantile *mûr'kən-tīl*, *adj* relating to merchants; having to do with trade; commercial; mercenary. — *n* **mer'cantilism**. — *n* **mer'cantilist**. — **mercantile agency** an agency supplying information about the financial status of companies and individuals; **mercantile law** the law relating to the dealings of merchants with each other; **mercantile marine** the ships and crews of any country employed in commerce; **mercantile system** an old economic strategy based on the theory that a nation's interests are best served by accumulating reserves of bullion, etc through the development of overseas trade and the restricting of imports, the impetus of much 17c and 18c colonization by European powers. [Fr, from Ital *mercantile*, from L *mercārī*; cf **merchant**]

mercaptan *mər-kap'tan*, *n* a substance analogous to an alcohol, with sulphur instead of oxygen. — *n* **mercap'tide** a compound in which a metal takes the place of a hydrogen atom of a mercaptan. [L *mercūrium captāns* laying hold of mercury, from the readiness with which it forms mercury mercaptide]

mercat *mer'kət*, (*Scot*) *n*. Same as **market** (*n*).

Mercator *mər-kā'tər* or *mer-kä'tōr*, *n* a Latin translation of the name of the Flemish-born German cartographer Gerhard Kremer (literally, shopkeeper, 1512–94). — **Mercator's projection** a representation of the surface of the globe in which the meridians are parallel straight lines, the parallels straight lines at right angles to these, their distances such that everywhere degrees of latitude and longitude have the same ratio to each other as on the globe itself.

mercenary *mûr'sin-ər-i*, *adj* hired for money; motivated by the hope of reward; too strongly influenced by desire of gain; sold or done for money. — *n* a person who is hired; a soldier hired into foreign service (*colloq* short form **merc** (*mûrk*)). — *adv* **mer'cenarily**. — *n* **mer'cenarism** the state of being a mercenary. [L *mercēnārius*, from *mercēs* hire]

mercer *mûr'sər*, *n* a dealer in textiles, *esp* expensive ones; a dealer in small wares. — *n* **mer'cery** the trade of a mercer; the goods of a mercer. [Fr *mercier*]

mercerize or **-ise** *mûr'sər-īz*, *vt* to treat (cotton fabric or thread) under tension with caustic soda, so as to cause swelling and increase the strength and dye absorbtion. — *n* **mercerīzā'tion** or **-s-**. — *n* **mer'cerizer** or **-s-**. [From John *Mercer* (1791–1866), the inventor of the process]

merchandise *mûr'chən-dīz*, *n* goods bought and sold for gain; trade (*Bible* and *Shakesp*); dealing. — *vt* **mer'chandize** or **-ise** to traffic in (*Shakesp*); to buy and sell; to plan the advertising or supplying of, or the selling campaign for (a product). — Also *vi* — *n* **mer'chandizer** or **-s-** a person who is responsible for supplying a product. — *n* **mer'chandizing** or **-s-** the selling of a product; the creation and selling of products, eg dolls and costumes, associated with a particular (*esp* children's) cinema film or television programme. [ME *marchandise*, from OFr]

merchant *mûr'chənt*, *n* a trader, *esp* wholesale; a shopkeeper (now *esp US*); a supercargo (*obs*); a merchantman; a person who specializes or indulges in a particular, *usu* undesirable, activity, eg *con merchant*, *speed merchant* (*slang*). — *adj* commercial. — *vi* to trade. — *vt* to trade in. — *adj* **mer'chantable** fit or ready for sale; marketable. — *n* **mer'chanting**. — *adj* and *adv* **mer'chantlike** (*Shakesp*) like a merchant. — *n* **mer'chantry** the business of a merchant; merchants collectively. — **merchant bank** see under **bank**[3]; **merchant bar** a bar of **merchant iron**, bar-iron made of repiled and rerolled wrought iron; **mer'chantman** a trading ship; a merchant (*Bible*): — *pl* **mer'chantmen**; **merchant navy** or **service** the mercantile marine; **merchant of death** arms manufacturers and dealers, *esp* those trading unscrupulously on the international market; **merchant prince** a merchant of great wealth, power, and consequence; **merchant ship** a ship that carries merchandise; **merchant tailor** a tailor who supplies the cloth for the clothes which he makes. — **speed merchant** see under **speed**. [Fr *marchand*]

merchet *mûr'chit*, (*hist*) *n* a fine paid to a lord for the marriage of a daughter. [Anglo-Fr *merchet*; see **market**]

merchild. See under **mermaid**.

mercury *mûr'kū-ri*, *n* a silvery metallic element (symbol **Hg**; atomic no 80) liquid at ordinary temperatures, also called *quicksilver*; the column of mercury in a thermometer or barometer; a plant (**dog's-mer'cury** *Mercurialis perennis*) of the spurge family; the plant Good-King-Henry; a preparation of mercury; a messenger; a common title for newspapers; mercurial character (*obs*); (with *cap*) the Roman god of merchandise, theft, and eloquence, messenger of the gods, identified with the Greek Hermes; (with *cap*) the planet nearest the sun. — *vt* **mer'curate** to mercurialize or treat with mercury; to convert into a compound with mercury. — *n* **mercurā'tion**. — *adj* **mercū'rial** containing mercury; of or like mercury; caused by mercury; (with *cap*) of or relating to Mercury the god or the planet; (sometimes with *cap*) having the qualities attributed to persons born under the planet, eloquent, etc; active, sprightly, often changing. — *n* a drug containing mercury; the plant mercury (*obs*); (sometimes with *cap*) a person born under the planet (*obs*). — *n* **mercū'rialism** a morbid condition due to mercury. — *n* **mercū'rialist** (*obs*) a believer in the medical use of mercury; a mercurial person. — *vt* **mercū'rialize** or **-ise** to treat with mercury or a drug containing mercury (*med*); to make mercurial. — *adv* **mercū'rially**. — *adj* **mercū'ric** containing bivalent mercury. — *vt* **mer'curize** or **-ise** same as **mercurate**. — *adj* **mer'curous** containing univalent mercury. — **mercury** (or **mercury tilt**) **switch** a quiet electric switch activated by the movement of mercury in a phial over the contacts; **mercury vapour light** or **lamp** a bright greenish-blue light, high in ultraviolet rays, produced by an electric discharge through mercury vapour. [L *Mercūrius*, prob from *merx*, *mercis* merchandise]

mercy *mûr'si*, *n* forbearance towards someone in one's power; a good thing regarded as derived from God; a happy chance (*colloq*); a forgiving disposition; clemency; compassion for the unfortunate. — *interj* an expression of thanks (now *obs*) or surprise (for *God have mercy*). — Also **mercy on us**. — *adj* **mer'ciable** (*Spenser*) merciful. — *adj* **mer'ciful** full of, or exercising, mercy. — *adv* **mer'cifully**. — *n* **mer'cifulness**. — *vt* **mer'cify** (*Spenser*, in *pa p* **mer'cifide**) to deal mercifully with, to pity. — *adj* **mer'ciless** without mercy; unfeeling; cruel. — *adv* **mer'cilessly**. — *n* **mer'cilessness**. — **mercy flight** an aircraft flight taking a seriously ill or injured person to hospital when other means of transport are impracticable or unavailable; **mercy killing** killing, *esp* painlessly, to prevent incurable suffering; **mer'cy-seat** the seat or place of mercy; the covering of the Jewish Ark of the Covenant; the throne of God. — **at the mercy of** wholly in the power of; **for mercy** (*obs*) or **for mercy's sake** an earnest conjuration in the form of an appeal to pity; **leave (a person) to someone's tender mercies** or **mercy** (*ironic*) to leave (a person) exposed to unpleasant treatment at someone's hands; **sisters of mercy** members of female religious communities who tend the sick, etc. [Fr *merci* grace, from L *mercēs*, *-ēdis*, the price paid, wages, later favour]

merdivorous *mûr-div'ə-rəs*, *adj* (of an insect) dung-eating. [L *merda* dung, and *vorāre* to devour]

mere[1] *mēr*, *n* a pool or lake. — Also (*obs*) **meer**. — **mere swine** (*obs*) a porpoise; a dolphin. [OE *mere* sea, lake, pool; Ger *Meer*, Du *meer*, L *mare* the sea]

mere[2] *mēr*, *adj* unmixed (*obs*); pure (*obs*); only what is said and nothing else, nothing more, nothing better; absolute (*obs*). — *adv* (*obs*) absolutely. — *adj* **mered** and **meered** see under **meer**[1]. — *adv* **mere'ly** purely (*obs*); entirely (*obs*); simply; only; without being more or better. [L *merus* unmixed]

mere[3] *mēr*, (*dialect*) *n* a boundary. — *vt* to bound; to mark off. — **meres'man** (*dialect*) a man appointed to ascertain boundaries; **mere'stone** (*dialect*) a boundary stone. [OE *gemǣre*]

mere[4] or **meri** *mer'i*, *n* a war-club. [Maori]

merel and **merell**. Same as **meril**.

merengue *mə-reng'gā*, *n* a Haitian or Dominican dance with a shuffling step. [Haitian *méringue* or Am Sp *merengue*]

meretricious *mer-i-trish'əs*, *adj* of the nature of or relating to prostitution; characteristic or worthy of a prostitute; flashy; gaudy. — *adv* **meretric'iously**. — *n* **meretric'iousness**. [L *meretrīx*, *-īcis* a prostitute, from *merēre* to earn]

merfolk. See under **mermaid**.

merganser *mûr-gan'sər*, *n* any bird of the genus *Mergus* (goosander, smew, etc). [L *mergus* a diving bird, and *ānser* a goose]

merge *mûrj*, *vt* to dip or plunge (*archaic*); to cause to be swallowed up or absorbed in something greater or superior; to cause to coalesce, combine, or amalgamate. — *vi* to be swallowed up, or lost; to coalesce; to lose identity in something else; to combine or amalgamate. — *n* **mer'gence**. — *n* **mer'ger** a sinking of an estate, title, etc, in one of larger extent or of higher value (*law*); the act of merging or combining, *esp* the combining of commercial companies into one. [L *mergere*, *mersum*]

meri. See **mere**[4].

mericarp *mer'i-kärp*, *n* a separating one-seeded part of a schizocarp, *esp* half of a cremocarp. [Gr *meros* a part, and *karpos* fruit]

meridian *mə-rid'i-ən*, *n* midday; a midday dram or nap (*Scot*); an imaginary great circle through the poles of the earth, the heavens, or any spherical body or figure, or its representation on a map; *specif*, that cutting the observer's horizon at the north and south points, which the sun crosses at local noon; (in Chinese medicine) any of several lines or pathways through the body along which life energy flows; culmination or highest point, as of success, splendour, power, etc. — *adj* of or at midday; on the meridian; pertaining to a meridian or the sun or other body on the meridian; at culmination or highest point. — *adj* **merid'ional** relating to the meridian; in the direction of a meridian; midday; culminating; southern; characteristic of the south. — *n* a southerner, *esp* in France. — *n* **meridional'ity**. — *adv* **merid'ionally**. — **meridian altitude** the arc of a meridian between a heavenly body and the horizon; **meridian circle** a telescope mounted to revolve in the plane of the meridian; **meridian passage** the transit or passage of a heavenly body across the observer's meridian. — **magnetic meridian** see under **magnet**; **prime** (or **first**) **meridian** the meridian from which longitudes are measured east or west, *specif* that through Greenwich. [L *merīdiānus*, *merīdiōnālis*, from *merīdiēs* (for *medīdiēs*) midday, from *medius* middle, and *diēs* day]

meril, merel or **merell** *mer'əl, n* a counter used in the game of merils; (in *pl*) a rustic game played by two people with counters on a figure marked on the ground, a board, etc, consisting of three squares, one within another, the object to get three counters in a row at the intersection of the lines joining the corners and the mid-points of the sides. — Also **marls, marr'els, mor'als, morr'is** or **mir'acles**. — **fivepenny morris** the game as played with five pieces each; **ninepenny morris** or **nine men's morris** with nine; the figure cut in the ground for the game (*Shakesp*). [OFr *merel* counter]

merimake *mer'i-māk*, (*Spenser*) *n* merrymaking; sport.

meringue *mə-rang'*, *n* a crisp, baked mixture of beaten egg whites and sugar, used as a pie topping or forming individual cakes or moulds; a small light cake or mould of this, *usu* filled. [Fr; origin unknown]

merino *mə-rē'nō*, *n* a sheep of a fine-woolled Spanish breed (also **merino sheep**); a free (ie non-convict) early immigrant in Australia, or descendant of such, *esp* in *pure merino* (*Austr*); a fine dress fabric, *orig* of merino wool; a fine woollen yarn, now mixed with cotton; knitted goods made of this; waste from fine worsted clothes: — *pl* **meri'nos**. — *adj* belonging to the merino sheep or its wool; made of merino. [Sp, a merino sheep, also a governor, from L *mājōrīnus* greater, also (LL) a head-man, from L *mājor* greater]

merism *mer'izm*, (*biol*) *n* repetition of parts. — *adj* **merist'ic**. [Gr *meros* part]

meristem *mer'is-tem*, *n* the formative tissue of plants, distinguished from the permanent tissues by the power its cells have of dividing and forming new cells. — *adj* **meristematic** (*-sti-mat'ik*). — **meristem culture** the aseptic culture on a suitable medium of excised shoot apical meristems (also **shoot tip culture**). [Gr *meristos* divisible, *merizein* to divide, from *meros* a part]

merit *mer'it, n* excellence that deserves honour or reward; worth; value; desert; that which one deserves, whether reward or punishment (*archaic*); (in *pl*, *esp* in *law*) the intrinsic right or wrong. — *vt* to earn; to have a right to claim as a reward; to deserve. — *vi* (*obs*) to acquire merit. — *n* **meritoc'racy** the class of people who are in prominent positions because of their ability, real or apparent; government by this class. — *n* **mer'itŏcrat**. — *adj* **meritŏcrat'ic**. — *adj* **meritorious** (*-tōr'* or *-tör'*) possessing merit or desert; deserving of reward, honour, or praise. — *adv* **meritor'iously**. — *n* **meritor'iousness**. — **order of merit** arrangement in which the best is placed first, the next best second, and so on; (*caps*) a strictly limited British order (*abbrev* **OM**), instituted in 1902, awarded for eminence in any field. [L *meritum*, from *merēre*, *-itum* to obtain as a lot, to deserve]

merk *merk*, *n* the old Scots mark or 13s 4d Scots, 13$\frac{1}{3}$d sterling. [**mark**[2]]

merkin *mûr'kin*, *n* a hairpiece for the pubic area. [Origin uncertain]

merle[1] or **merl** *mûrl*, (*archaic* or *literary Scot*) *n* the blackbird. [Fr, from L *merula*]

merle[2] *mûrl*, *adj* (of a dog, *usu* a collie) with bluish-grey fur flecked or streaked with black (also **blue merle**). — Also *n*. [Cf **marl**[4], **marly** and **mirly**]

merlin *mûr'lin*, *n* a species of small falcon, *Falco columbarius*. [Anglo-Fr *merilun*, from OFr *esmerillon*]

merling *mûr'ling*, (*obs*) *n* the whiting. [OFr *merlanke*, from L *merula* a sea-carp]

merlon *mûr'lən*, (*fortif*) *n* the part of a parapet between embrasures. [Fr *merlon*, from Ital *merlone*, from *merlo* battlement]

Merlot *mer-lō*, *n* a grape variety used to produce red wine, often blended as eg in claret; a light-bodied red wine produced solely from this grape. [Fr, literally small blackbird; cf **merle**[1]]

mermaid *mûr'mād*, *n* a fabulous creature with a woman's upper body and a fish's tail. — Also **mer'maid'en**. — **mer'child** and **mer'man** similar creatures with the upper body of a child and man respectively; **mer'folk** or **mer'people** such creatures collectively; **mermaid's glove** the largest kind of British sponge; **mermaid's purse** the egg-case of skate, etc. [OE *mere* lake, sea, and *mægden* maid]

meroblastic *mer-ō-blast'ik*, (*zool*) *adj* undergoing or involving cleavage in part of the ovum only, as where there is much yolk. — *adv* **meroblast'ically**. [Gr *meros* part, and *blastos* a shoot, bud]

merogenesis *mer-ō-jen'i-sis*, (*biol*) *n* segmentation. — *adj* **merogenetic** (*-ji-net'ik*). [Gr *meros* part, and *genesis* production]

merogony *mer-og'ə-ni*, *n* the production of an embryo from a fertilized fragment of an ovum without a nucleus. [Gr *meros* part, and *gonē* birth]

meroistic *mer-ō-ist'ik*, (*entomol*) *adj* (of an ovary) producing yolk-forming cells as well as ova. [Gr *meros* part, and *ōion* egg]

merome *mer'ōm*, *n* a merosome. [Gr *meros* part]

meronym *mer'ō-nim*, (*semantics*) *n* a word whose relation to another in meaning is that of part to whole, eg *whisker* in relation to *cat*. — *n* **meron'ymy**. [Gr *meros* part, and *onyma* name]

Merops *mer'ops*, *n* the bee-eater genus. — *n* **merop'idan** a bird of the bee-eater family (**Merop'idae**). [Gr *merops* bee-eater]

merosome *mer'ō-sōm*, *n* one of the serial segments of which a body is composed, such as the ring of a worm, a metamere, a somite. [Gr *meros* part, and *sōma* body]

Merovingian *mer-ō-vin'ji-ən*, *adj* pertaining to the first dynasty of Frankish kings in Gaul, founded by Clovis. — *n* a member of this family. [L *Merovingi*, from Merovaeus or *Merovech*, king of the Salian Franks (448–457), grandfather of Clovis]

merozoite *mer-ō-zō'īt*, (*zool*) *n* a young trophozoite resulting from the division of a schizont. [Gr *meros* part, and *zōion* animal]

merpeople. See under **mermaid**.

merry[1] *mer'i, adj* pleasant (*obs*); sportive; cheerful; noisily gay; causing laughter; enlivened by drink, tipsily cheerful; lively; used as an intensifier of *hell*, as in *play merry hell with*. — *adv* **merr'ily**. — *n* **merr'iment** gaiety with laughter and noise; mirth; hilarity. — *n* **merr'iness**. — **merry-an'drew** a quack's assistant (*hist*); a buffoon; a clown; **merry dancers** (*Scot*) the aurora borealis; **merry England** an idealistically jovial picture of life in England in the past, *esp* in Elizabethan times (as used *orig*, eg by Spenser, the phrase meant 'fair, pleasant England'); **merr'y-go-round** a revolving ring of wooden horses, etc for riding at a funfair; a roundabout; a whirl of activity, etc (*fig*); any activity inclined to circularity (*fig*); **merr'y-make** (*archaic*) a merrymaking. — *vi* to make merry. — **merr'ymaker**; **merr'ymaking** a merry entertainment; festivity, revelry; **merr'yman** (*obs*) a zany; a jester; **merry men** an outlaw's companions; followers, assistants (*facetious*); **merr'y-night** (*dialect*) a village festival or dance; **merr'ythought** a fowl's furcula or wishbone. — **make merry** to be festive; to indulge in lively enjoyment; to turn to ridicule (with *with* or *over*); **the merry monarch** Charles II. [OE *myr(i)ge*]

merry[2] *mer'i*, *n* a gean. [Fr *merise*]

mersalyl *mər-sal'il*, *n* a sodium salt ($C_{13}H_{16}NO_6HgNa$), used as a diuretic. [*mer*cury and *salicyl*]

merse *mûrs*, (*Scot*) *n* low flat marshland, *usu* by a river or estuary. [Scots form of **marsh**]

Mersey *mûr'zē* or *-zi*, *n* the river on which the city of Liverpool stands. — **Mersey beat** or **sound** popular music in the style of the Beatles and other Liverpool groups during the 1960s.

mersion *mûr'shən*, (*obs*) *n* dipping, *esp* in baptism. [L *mersiō*, *-ōnis*; cf **merge**]

Merulius *mə-rōō'li-əs*, *n* the dry rot fungus genus.

merum sal *mer'əm* or *mer'ŏŏm sal*, (*L*) pure salt, genuine Attic wit.

merveilleux *mer-ve-yø*, (*Fr*) *adj* marvellous: — *fem* **merveilleuse** (*mer-ve-yœz*). — *n* a fantastic extremist in fashion in France during the Republican government of 1795–99, a women aping classical modes.

merycism *mer'i-sizm*, *n* rumination, a disease symptom in man. [Gr *mērykismos*]

Mes. See **Mass**.

mesa *mā'sə*, *n* a flat-topped hill with steep sides, *esp* in the southwestern US. — **mesa transistor** (*electronics*) a transistor constructed by etching down the semiconductor wafer in steps so that the base and emitter regions appear as plateaux above the collector. [Sp, from L *mēnsa* table]

mesail *mes'āl* or **mezail** *mez-*, *n* a vizor, *esp* one made in two parts. [Fr *mézail*]

mesal. See **mesial**.

mésalliance *mā-zal-yãs*, (*Fr*) *n* an unsuitable marriage; marriage with someone of lower social rank.

mesaraic *mes-ə-rā'ik*, *adj* mesenteric. [Gr *mesaraikos*, from *mesos* middle, and *araiā* flank, belly]

mesarch *mes'ärk*, *adj* having the protoxylem surrounded by xylem formed later (*bot*); originating in a moderately moist habitat (*ecol*). — **mesarch succession** an ecological succession originating in a mesic habitat. [Gr *mesos* middle, and *archē* beginning]

mesaticephalic *mes-ə-ti-sef-al'ik* or **mesaticephalous** *-sef'ə-ləs*, (*med*) *adj* intermediate between dolichocephalic and brachycephalic. — *n* **mesaticeph'aly**. [Gr *mesatos* midmost, and *kephalē* head]

mescal *mes-kal'*, *n* the peyote cactus, genus *Lophophora*, found in Mexico and the southwestern USA, the dried tubercles (**mescal buttons**) of which are chewed or drunk in infusion as an intoxicant; an alcoholic spirit distilled from the fermented juice of the agave. — *n* **mescalin** (*mes'kəl-in*) the principal alkaloid ($C_{11}H_{17}NO_3$) in mescal, producing hallucinations and schizophrenia. — *n* **mescal'ism** the habitual use of mescal as an intoxicant; peyotism. [Sp *mescal*, *mezcal*, from Nahuatl *mexcalli*]

mesclun *mes'klōōn* or **mesclum** *mes'klōōm*, *n* a mixed green salad of young leaves and shoots, eg of rocket, of chicory, fennel, etc. [Fr, from Niçois *mesclumo* mixture]

mesdames and **Mesdemoiselles**. See **madam** and **mademoiselle**.

mese *mes'ē*, (*Gr music*) *n* the middle string of the lyre; its note; the keynote. [Gr *mesē* (*chordē*) middle (string)]

meseems. See under **seem**.

mesel or **meazel** *mēz'l*, (*obs*) *n* a leper; leprosy (*Shakesp*). — *adj* leprous. — *adj* **mes'eled**. [OFr *mesel*, from L *misellus*, dimin of *miser* wretched]

mesembrianthemum or conventionally **mesembryanthemum** *mi-zem-bri-an'thi-məm*, *n* any plant of a genus (*Mesembrianthemum*) of succulent plants (family *Aizoaceae*), mostly S African (also called Hottentot fig, ice-plant, Livingstone daisy). [Gr *mesēmbriā* midday, from *mesos* middle, *hēmerā* day, and *anthemon* a flower; some are open only about midday]

mesencephalon *mes-en-sef'ə-lon*, *n* the mid-brain. — *adj* **mesencephalic** (*-si-fal'ik*). [Gr *mesos* middle, and **encephalon**]

mesenchyme *mes'en-kīm*, (*zool*) *n* undifferentiated embryo cells, derived from mesoderm, which differentiate into connective tissue and muscle. [Gr *mesenchyma*, for Gr *enchyma* infusion]

mesentery *mes'ən-tər-i* or *mez'*, *n* a fold of the peritoneum, keeping the intestines in place (*anatom*); (in coelenterates) a vertical inward fold of the body wall (*zool*). — *adj* **mesenterial** (*-tē'ri-əl*) or **mesenteric** (*-ter'ik*). — *n* **mesenteron** (*-en'tər-on*) the mid-gut. [Gr *mesos* middle, and *enteron* intestines]

meseta *mə-sā'tə*, *n* a plateau, *specif* that of central Spain. [Sp, dimin of *mesa*; see **mesa**]

mesh *mesh*, *n* the opening between the threads of a net; the threads and knots surrounding such an opening; a network; a trap; the engagement of geared wheels, etc. — *vt* to catch in a net; to provide or make with meshes; to entwine; to co-ordinate or harmonize. — *vi* (of gear-teeth, etc) to become engaged; to work in conjunction, to harmonize (often with *with*); to become entangled. — *n* **mesh'ing**. — *adj* **mesh'y** formed like network. — **mesh'-work** a network, a web. [Perh MDu *maesche*; cf OE *max* net; Ger *Masche*]

meshuga, **meshugga** or **messhugge** *mi-shōō'gə*, (*slang*) *adj* mad; crazy. — *n* **meshu'gaas** or **mishe'gaas** (*-gäs*) madness, foolishness. — *n* **meshugg'enah** or **meshugg'eneh** a crazy person. [Yiddish, from Heb]

mesial *mē'zi-əl*, *adj* middle; facing towards the centre of the curve formed by the upper or lower teeth (*dentistry*); in or towards the median plane or line (also **mē'sal** or **mē'sian**). — *adv* **mē'sally** or **mē'sially**. [Gr *mesos* middle]

mesic[1]. See under **meson**.

mesic[2] *me'zik* or *mē'*, also *-sik*, *adj* relating to, or adapted to life with, a moderate supply of moisture. [Gr *mesos* middle]

Mes-John. See under **Mass**.

mesmerize or **-ise** *mez'mər-īz*, *vt* to hypnotize; to fascinate, dominate the will or fix the attention of. — *adj* **mesmeric** (*-mer'ik*) or **mesmer'ical**. — *n* **mes'merism** hypnotism as expounded, with some fanciful notions, from 1775 by Friedrich Anton or Franz *Mesmer*, a German physician (1734–1815); hypnotic influence. — *n* **mesmerīzā'tion** or **-s-**. — *n* **mes'merizer** or **-s-**, or **mes'merist**.

mesne *mēn*, (*law*) *adj* intermediate. [Law Fr *mesne* middle; cf **mean**[2]]

meso- *me-sō-* or *me-zō*, also *mē-*, *-so* or *zo*, or (before a vowel) **mes** *combining form* denoting middle. — *n* **Mesoamer'ica** Central America, between Northern Mexico and Panama. — *adj* **Mesoamer'ican** (also without *cap*). — *n* **mes'oblast** (Gr *blastos* shoot) the middle germinal layer. — *adj* **mesoblas'tic**. — *n* **mes'ocarp** (Gr *karpos* fruit) the middle layer of a pericarp. — *adj* **mesocephalic** (*-si-fal'ik*) or **-cephalous** (*-sef'ə-ləs*) having a medium skull, with a breadth of *approx* 75 to 80 per cent of its length. — *n* **mesoceph'alism** or **mesoceph'aly**. — *n* **mes'oderm** (Gr *derma* skin) the layer of embryonic cells between the ectoderm and the endoderm in a gastrula. — *n* **mesogloea** (*-glē'ə*; Gr *gloiā* glue) in coelenterates and sponges, a structureless gelatinous layer between ectoderm and endoderm. — *n* **mesohipp'us** one of the prehistoric group of three-toed ungulate mammals probably related to the modern horse. — *n* **mes'olite** (Gr *lithos* stone) a zeolite intermediate in composition between natrolite and scolecite. — *adj* **Mesolith'ic** intermediate between Palaeolithic and Neolithic. — *n* **mesom'erism** (*chem*) resonance; a type of tautomerism. — *n* **mes'omorph** (*-mörf*; Gr *morphē* form) a person of muscular bodily type, thought to correspond to a characteristically aggressive and extroverted personality type (see **ectomorph** and **endomorph**). — *adj* **mesomor'phic** or **mesomor'phous** relating to a mesomorph; relating to an intermediate state of matter between solid and liquid (*chem*). — *n* **mes'omorphy**. — *n* **mes'ophyll** (Gr *phyllon* leaf) the spongy tissue within a leaf. — *n* **mes'ophyte** (*-fīt*; Gr *phyton* plant) a plant intermediate between a xerophyte and a hydrophyte. — *adj* **mesophytic** (*-fit'ik*). — *n* **mes'oscaphe** (*-skāf*; Gr *skaphos* ship) a submersible observation chamber for use at less great depths than the bathyscaphe. — *n* **mes'osphere** the region of the earth's atmosphere above the stratosphere. — *adj* **mesothē'lial**. — *n* **mesothēliō'ma** (from **(epi)thelium** and **-oma**) a rare malignant tumour of the lining of the chest or abdomen, sometimes caused by blue asbestos dust. — *n* **mesothē'lium** the cell tissue that forms the lining of the chest and abdomen in vertebrates and lines the body cavity in vertebrate embryos. — *adj* **mesothoracic** (*-thö-* or *-thō-ras'ik*). — *n* **mesothor'ax** the middle one of the three segments of an insect's thorax. — *n pl* **Mesozō'a** (Gr *zōion* animal) minute animals once thought intermediate between Protozoa and Metazoa, *prob* Metazoa reduced by parasitism. — *adj* **Mesozō'ic** (Gr *zōē* life) of the

Secondary geological period, including the Triassic, Jurassic, and Cretaceous systems. [Gr *mesos* middle]

meson *mēz'on* or *mes'on*, *n* a short-lived subatomic particle of smaller mass than a proton (η-mesons, π-mesons (also called **pī'ons**), and κ-mesons, k-mesons (also called **kā'ons**); the muon, formerly classified as the μ-meson, is now known to be a lepton). — *adj* **mes'ic** or **meson'ic**. — *n* **mes'otron** (*obs*; after *electron*) formerly a meson, then a μ-meson. — **mesic** or **mesonic atom** a nucleus with an orbital meson. [Gr *meson* neuter of *mesos* middle]

mesonephric duct. Same as **Wolffian duct** under **Wolffian**.

mesophyll... to ... **Mesozoic**. See under **meso-**.

mesprise or **mesprize**. See **misprise**[1,2].

mesquin *mes-kɛ̃*, (*Fr*) *adj* mean, ungracious: — *fem* **mesquine** (*-kēn*). — *n* **mesquinerie** (*-kēn-ə-rē*) meanness.

mesquite or **mesquit** *mes-kēt'* or *mes'kēt*, *n* a leguminous tree or shrub (*Prosopis*) of N America, with nutritious pods; the wood of this used as fuel in barbecuing. [Mex Sp *mezquite*, from Nahuatl *mizquitl*]

mess[1] *mes*, *n* a dish of food, a course or meal (*archaic*); a set of usually four people served together at a banquet (*archaic*); a set of four (*Shakesp*); a number of people who take their meals together, *esp* in the armed forces; a place where such a group take their meals together; a cow's yield at one milking (*dialect*); a quantity of anything, *esp* of a specified food (*archaic* or *dialect NAm*); a take or haul of fish (*US*); a dish of soft, pulpy or sloppy food; liquid, pulpy or smeary dirt; excrement, *esp* of an animal (*colloq*); a mixture disagreeable to the sight or taste; a medley; (a person in a state of) disorder or confusion; embarrassment; a bungle. — *vt* to supply with a meal or food (*military*); to make a mess of (*usu* with *up*); to subject to a violent physical attack (with *up*) (*US colloq*); to muddle; to make dirty or messy. — *vi* to eat a meal, to dine (*archaic*); to eat at a common table; to belong to a mess; to make a mess; to play or trifle (with *with*); to meddle, involve oneself (with *with* or *in*) (*colloq*; *esp US*); to tangle or come into conflict (with *with*) (*colloq*; *esp US*). — *adv* **mess'ily**. — *n* **mess'iness**. — *adj* **mess'y** confused, untidy (also *fig*); involving, or causing, dirt or mess; bungling. — **mess deck** (*naut*) the crew's living-quarters on board ship; the crew's dining-hall (*US*); **mess'mate** a member of the same mess; a commensal; **mess'-room**; **mess'-tin** a soldier's utensil serving as plate, cup and cooking-vessel; **mess'-up** a mess, muddle, bungle or confusion. — **mess about** or **around** (*colloq*) to potter about; to behave in a foolish or annoying way; to meddle or interfere (with *with*); to treat badly or inconsiderately; to upset, put into a state of disorder or confusion; to have an adulterous or otherwise illicit sexual relationship (often with *with*); **mess of pottage** a material advantage accepted in exchange for something of higher worth, as by Esau (Gen 25. 29 ff); **mess or mell** (*Scot*) to associate, have to do; **mess up** (*colloq*; *esp US*) to make a mess of things, fail in some endeavour. [OFr *mes* (Fr *mets*) a dish, from L *mittere*, *missum* to send, in LL to place]

mess[2] *mes*, *n obs* form of **mass**[2].

Mess and **Mess-John**. See **Mass**.

message *mes'ij*, *n* any communication sent from one person to another; an errand; an official communication of a president, governor, etc, to a legislature or council; the teaching that a poet, sage, prophet, has to communicate to the world; an amount of digital information transmitted as a whole between a terminal and a computer, or between computers on a network (*comput*); (*usu* in *pl*) domestic shopping, a journey for the purpose, or the goods bought (*Scot*). — *vt* to send as a message; to transmit as by signalling. — *vi* (*Dickens*) to carry a message. — *n* **mess'aging** any form of electronic communication in which a message is sent directly to its destination, eg telex. — *n* **mess'enger** (*-ən-jər*) a person who brings a message; a person employed to carry messages and perform errands; a forerunner; a light scudding cloud preceding a storm; a small object sent along a line, as a paper up a kite string; the secretary-bird; a rope or chain connecting a cable with the capstan for heaving up the anchor; an officer who executes the summonses of the Court of Session, *usu* called a **mess'enger-at-arms** (*Scots law*). — **mess'age-boy** or **mess'age-girl** an errand boy or girl; **mess'age-stick** (*Austr*) a carved stick carried as identification by an Aboriginal messenger; **message switching** (*comput*) a communication system in which data is transmitted between computers on a network as a whole and not split into packets (see **packet switching** under **pack**[1]); **message unit** (*US*) a unit used in charging timed, eg long-distance, telephone calls; **messenger RNA** (*biochem*) a short-lived, transient form of RNA which serves to carry genetic information from the DNA of the genes to the ribosomes where the requisite proteins are made (*abbrev* **m-RNA**); **mess'enger-wire** a wire supporting an overhead cable. — **get the message** (*slang*) to understand; **king's** or **queen's messenger** an officer who carries official despatches. [Fr, from LL *missāticum*, from L *mittere*, *missum* to send]

messan *mes'ən*, (*Scot*) *n* a lapdog; a cur. [Perh Gaelic *measan*]

Messerschmitt *mes'ər-shmit*, *n* a German fighter aircraft used by the Luftwaffe in World War II, *esp* the ME-109. [Willy *Messerschmitt* (1898–1978), aircraft designer]

Messiah *mə-sī'ə*, *n* the expected deliverer of the Jews; by Christians, applied to Jesus; (also without *cap*) a hoped-for deliverer, saviour, or champion generally. — Also **Messī'as**. — *n* **Messī'ahship**. — *adj* **Messianic** (*mes-i-an'ik*) of or relating to a Messiah; (also without *cap*) inspired, or as though inspired, by a Messiah. — *n* **Messī'anism** belief in a Messiah. — *n* **Messī'anist**. [Gr *Messīās*, from Aramaic *m'shīhā*, Heb *māshīah* anointed, from *māshah* to anoint]

Messidor *mes-i-dör'*, *n* the tenth month of the French revolutionary calendar, roughly 19 June to 18 July. [Fr, from L *messis* harvest, and Gr *dōron* a gift]

Messier catalogue *mes-yā kat'ə-log*, (*astron*) *n* a listing of 108 galaxies, star clusters and nebulae compiled in 1770 and still widely used, designating objects M1, M2, etc. [Charles *Messier*, Fr astronomer, compiler of the list]

Messrs *mes'ərs*, *abbrev*: *Messieurs* (*Fr*), Sirs, Gentlemen; used as pl of **Mr**.

messuage *mes'wij*, (*law*) *n* a dwelling and offices with the adjoining lands appropriated to the household; a mansion-house and grounds. [Anglo-Fr; poss orig a misreading of *mesnage*; cf **ménage**]

mestee *mes-tē'* or **mustee** *mus-tē'*, *n* the offspring of a White person and a quadroon. — *n* **mestizo** (*mes-tē'zō*; Sp *-thō*) a person of mixed (*esp* Spanish and American Indian) parentage: — *pl* **mesti'zos**; *fem* **mesti'za**, *pl* **mesti'zas**. [Sp *mestizo*, from a LL derivative of L *mixtus* mixed]

mesto *mes'tō*, (*music*) *adj* sad. [Ital]

Met *met*. — **the Met** (*colloq*) Metropolitan Opera, New York; (London) Metropolitan police; Metropolitan Railway; the Met Office (see under **met**[2]).

met[1] *pa t* and *pa p* of **meet**[2].

met[2] *met*, *n* short form of **meteorology**. — **met'cast** a weather forecast; **met man** a weather forecaster; **Met Office** the Meteorological Office.

met. or **metaph**. *abbrev*: metaphor; metaphorical; metaphysics.

meta- *metə-* or (before a vowel) often **met-** *met-*, *combining form* signifying: among, with; after, later; often implies change, as in *metamorphose*; beyond, above, as in *metamathematics*. In *chem* **meta-** indicates (1) a derivative of, or an isomer or polymer of, the substance named, or (2) an acid or hydroxide derived from the **ortho-** form of the substance by loss of water molecules, or (3) a benzene substitution product in which the substituted atoms or groups are attached to two carbon atoms which are themselves separated by one carbon atom (in this sense commonly represented by **m**). — *adj* **metacarp'al** (also *n*). — *n* **metacarp'us** (Gr *karpos* wrist) the part of the hand (or its bones) between the wrist and the fingers, or the corresponding part of an animal, eg the foreleg of a horse between 'knee' and fetlock. — *n* **met'acentre** (Gr *kentron* point) the point of intersection of a vertical line through the centre of gravity of a body floating in equilibrium and that through the centre of gravity of the displaced liquid when the body is slightly displaced. — *adj* **metacen'tric**. — *n* **metachro'sis** (*-krō'sis*; Gr *chrōsis* colouring) ability to change colour in animals. — *n* **met'afiction** fiction which self-consciously comments on its status as fiction. — *adj* **metafic'tional**. — *n* **metagal'axy** the whole universe considered as a system of galaxies; any system of galaxies. — *adj* **metagalac'tic**. — *n* **metagen'esis** (Gr *genesis* generation; *biol*) alternation of generations. — *adj* **metagenet'ic**. — *adj* **metagnathous** (*met-ag'nə-thəs*; Gr *gnathos* jaw) (of birds) having crossed mandibles; (of insects) having biting jaws in the larvae, sucking in the adult state. — *n* **met'alanguage** a language or a system of symbols used to discuss another language or symbolic system. — *n* **metal'dehyde** a polymer of acetaldehyde. — *adj* **metalinguis'tic** of or relating to (a) metalanguage or to metalinguistics. — *adv* **metalinguis'tically**. — *n sing* **metalinguis'tics** the study of the relation between a language and other features of behaviour in a particular culture, of language structure in relation to meaning, of expression or gesture accompanying spoken language, etc. — *n sing* **metamathemat'ics** the logical analysis of formal mathematics, its concepts, terminology, use of symbols, etc. — *n* **met'amer** (Gr *meros* a part; *chem*) a compound metameric with another. — *n* **met'amere** (*-mēr*; *zool*) a segment, merosome, or somite. — *adj* **metamer'ic** (of chemical compounds) having the same molecular weight, but different structures and chemical properties; of or relating to a metamere or metameres. — *n* **metam'erism** a particular form of isomerism in which different groups are attached to the same central atom (*chem*); segmentation of the body along the primary axis, producing a series of homologous parts (*zool*). — *n* **met'aphase** the stage of mitosis at which the chromosomes form the equatorial plate. — *n* **metaphos'phate** a salt of metaphosphoric acid. — *adj* **metaphosphor'ic** applied to an acid (HPO_3) containing a molecule less of water than orthophosphoric acid. — *adj* **metapsychic** (*met-ə-sī'kik*) or **metapsych'ical** (from **psychic** on the analogy of **metaphysics**). — *n sing* **metapsych'ics** the study of psychic phenomena beyond the limits of ordinary or orthodox psychology; psychical research. — *adj* **metapsycholog'ical**. — *n* **metapsychol'ogy** theories and theorizing on psychological matters, such as the nature of the mind, which cannot be verified or falsified by experiment or reasoning. — *n* **metasequoi'a** a conifer (*Metasequoia glyptostrobodes*) discovered as a fossil and since found existing in China. — *n* **metasil'icate** (*-i-kāt*) a salt of metasilicic acid. — *adj* **metasilic'ic** (*-is'ik*) applied to an acid (H_2SiO_3) — *adj* **metasōmat'ic**. — *n* **metasōm'atism** (Gr *sōma, -atos* body; *geol*) metamorphism by chemical changes in minerals. — *n* **metastabil'ity** a state which appears to be chemically stable, often because of the slowness with which equilibrium is attained, eg that of a supersaturated solution; a metastable state. — *adj* **metastable** (*met'ə-stā-bl*) having metastability (**metastable state** an excited state, *esp* of an atom which has, however, insufficient energy to emit radiation). — *adj* **metatarsal** (*-tär'sl*) (also *n*). — *n* **metatar'sus** (Gr *tarsos* the flat of the foot) that part of the foot, or its bones, between the tarsus and the toes, or the corresponding part of an animal. — *n pl* **Metatheria** (*-thē'ri-ə*; Gr *thērion* a wild beast) the marsupials. — *adj* **metathoracic** (*-thö-ras'ik*). — *n* **metathorax** (*-thö'raks*) the third and last segment of an insect's thorax. — *n pl* **Metazoa** (*met-ə-zō'ə*; also without *cap*; Gr *zōion* animal) many-celled animals (opposed to single-celled *Protozoa*): — *sing* **metazō'on**. — *adj* and *n* **metazō'an**. — *adj* **metazō'ic**. — *adj* **metempiric** (*met-em-pir'ik*) or **metempir'ical** beyond the scope of experience; of or relating to metempiricism. — *n* **metempir'icism** (*-i-sizm*) the study of the existence of things beyond the scope of experience (also **metempirics** *n sing*). — *n* **metempir'icist**. [Gr *meta* among, with, beside, after]

metabasis *met-ab'ə-sis*, *n* a transition. — *adj* **metabatic** (*met-ə-bat'ik*). [Gr *metabasis*, from *meta* (see **meta-**), and *bainein* to go]

metabolism *met-ab'əl-izm*, *n* the sum total of the chemical changes in living organisms, *esp* with regard to their influence on the generation of energy, the processing of waste products, etc; these changes as they affect a specific substance in an organism; metamorphosis. — *n pl* **Metab'ola** in some classifications, insects that undergo metamorphosis. — *adj* **metabolic** (*-bol'ik*) relating to an organism's metabolism; exhibiting metamorphosis. — *n* **metab'olite** a product of metabolism. — *vt* and *vi* **metab'olize** or **-ise** to subject to, or be changed by, metabolism. [Gr *metabolē* change]

metacarpal, metacarpus, metacentre and **metacentric**. See under **meta-**.

metachronism *met-ak'ron-izm*, *n* (an example of) the error of dating an event too late (*opp* of *prochronism*). [Gr *metachronios, metachronos* anachronistic, out of date, from *meta* (see **meta-**), and *chronos* time]

metachrosis, metafiction, metafictional, metagalactic and **metagalaxy**. See under **meta-**.

metage *mēt'ij*, *n* official weighing of coal, grain, etc; the charge for such weighing. [**mete**[1]]

metagenesis, metagenetic and **metagnathous**. See under **meta-**.

metagrobolize or **-ise** *met-ə-grob'əl-īz* or **metagrabolize** or **-ise** *-grab'*, *vt* to mystify; to puzzle out. [Obs Fr *metagraboulizer* (Rabelais)]

métairie *mā-ter-ē'*, *n* a piece of land cultivated under the system of *métayage* (see under **métayer**). [Fr; see **métayer**]

metal *met'l*, *n* any of numerous opaque elementary substances, possessing a peculiar lustre, fusibility, conductivity for heat and electricity, readiness to form positive ions, for example, gold; an alloy; that which behaves chemically like a true metal; courage or spirit (now spelt **mettle**); intrinsic quality; the collective guns or fire-power of a warship (*obs*); or, or argent, as a tincture (*heraldry*); molten material for glass-making; country-rock (*mining*); broken stones used for macadamized roads or as ballast for railways; (in *pl*) the rails of a railroad. — *adj* made of metal. — *vt* to provide or cover with metal: — *prp* **met'alling** or (*NAm*) **met'aling**; *pa t* and *pa p* **met'alled** or (*NAm*) **met'aled**. — *adj* **met'alled** covered with metal, as a road. — *adj* **metallic** (*mi-tal'ik*) relating to, or like, metal; consisting of metal; (of a colour, etc) having the lustre characteristic of metals; (of a sound) like the sound produced by metal when struck. — *adv* **metall'ically**. — *n* **met'alliding** a high-temperature electrolytic technique for creating metal alloys on the surface of metals. — *adj* **metallif'erous** bearing or yielding metal. — *adj* **met'alline** of, like, consisting of, or mixed with, metal. — *n* **met'alling** road-metal, broken stones. — *n* **met'allist** or (*NAm*) **met'alist** a worker in metals. — *n* **metallīzā'tion** or **-s-**. — *vt* **met'allize** or **-ise** or (*NAm*) **met'alize** to make metallic; to deposit thin metal films on glass or plastic. — *adj* **metallogenet'ic** (*geol*) relating to metallogeny. — *adj* **metallogēn'ic** (or *-jen'*; *geol*) (of an element) occurring as an ore or a naturally occurring metal, as opposed to in rocks. — *adj* **metallogenetic** (*US*). — *n* **metallog'eny** (*geol*; from Fr, from Gr *genesis* origin) (the study of) the origin and distribution of mineral deposits, *esp* with regard to petrological, etc, features. — *n* **metallog'rapher**. — *adj* **metallograph'ic**. — *n* **metallog'raphy** the study of the structure and constitution of metals. — *n* **met'alloid** a non-metal; an element resembling a metal in some respects, such as selenium or tellurium. — *adj* **met'alloid** or **metalloid'al** relating to, or of the nature of, the metalloids. — *n*

metall'ophone an instrument like a xylophone with metal bars, the hammers being operated by hand or by means of a keyboard. — *adj* **met'ally** suggestive of metal. — **met'alwork**; **met'alworker**; **met'alworking**. [OFr, from L *metallum*, from Gr *metallon* a mine]

metalanguage and **metaldehyde**. See under **meta-**.

metalepsis *met-ə-lep'sis*, (*rhetoric*) *n* metonymy, *esp* of a double, complicated, or indirect kind. — *adj* **meta-lep'tic** or **metalep'tical**. [Gr *metalēpsis* substitution]

metalinguistics. See under **meta-**.

metall. or **metal**. *abbrev*: metallurgical; metallurgy.

metallic... to ... **metallophone**. See under **metal**.

metallurgy *met'əl-ûr-ji* or *met-al'ər-ji*, *n* art and science applied to metals, including extraction from ores, refining, alloying, shaping, treating, and the study of structure, constitution and properties. — *adj* **met-allur'gic** or **metallur'gical** relating to metallurgy. — *n* **met'allurgist** (or, now more *usu*, *-al'*). [Gr *metal-lourgeein* to mine, from *metallon* a mine, and *ergon* work]

metamathematics. See under **meta-**.

metamere and **metamerism**. See under **meta-**.

metamorphosis *met-ə-mör'fəs-is* or *-fōs'is*, *n* change of shape, transformation; the transformation of a human being to an animal, a stone, tree, etc (*folklore*); the marked change which some living beings undergo in the course of growth, as caterpillar to butterfly, tadpole to frog: — *pl* **metamor'phoses** (*-sēz* or *-fō'sēz*). — *adj* **metamor'phic** showing or relating to change of form; formed by alteration of existing rocks by heat, pressure, or other processes in the earth's crust (*geol*). — *n* **metamor'phism** transformation of rocks in the earth's crust (*contact metamorphism*, by contact with or neighbourhood of igneous material, or *regional meta-morphism*, owing to general conditions over a wide region). — *n* **metamor'phist** a person who believes that Christ's body merged into the Deity at the Ascension. — *vt* **metamor'phose** (*-fōz* or *-fōs*) to transform; to subject to metamorphism or metamorphosis; to de-velop in another form. — *vi* to undergo meta-morphosis. — **metamorphic technique** a form of therapy using massage on specific areas of the feet, hands, or head which are believed to relate to the body's prenatal experiences (also called **prenatal therapy**). [Gr *meta-morphōsis*, from *meta* (see **meta-**) and *morphē* form]

metanoia *met-ə-noi'ə*, *n* repentance; a fundamental change in character, way of life, etc; a spiritual conversion. [Gr *metanoia* a change of mind or heart, repentance]

metapelet *me-tä-pel'et*, *n* a woman acting as a foster mother to children on a kibbutz: — *pl* **metaplot'** (*me-tä-plōt'*). [Heb]

metaphase. See under **meta-**.

metaphor *met'ə-fər*, *n* a figure of speech by which a thing is spoken of as being that which it only resembles, as when a ferocious person is called a tiger. — *adj* **metaphoric** (*-for'ik*) or **metaphor'ical** — *adv* **meta-phor'ically**. — *n* **met'aphorist**. — **mixed metaphor** an expression in which two or more metaphors are incongruously joined, such as *to take arms against a sea of troubles*. [Gr *metaphorā*, from *meta* (see **meta-**) and *pherein* to carry]

metaphosphoric and **metaphosphate**. See under **meta-**.

metaphrase *met'ə-frāz*, *n* a turning of prose into verse, or verse into prose; a rendering in a different style or form; an altered wording; a word for word translation. — Also **metaphrasis** (*-af'rə-sis*). — *n* **met'aphrast** (*-frast*) a person who produces a metaphrase. — *adj* **metaphrast'ic**. [Gr *metaphrasis*, from *meta* (see **meta-**) and *phrasis* a speaking]

metaphysics *met-ə-fiz'iks*, *n sing* the branch of philosophy which investigates the first principles of nature and thought; ontology or the science of being; loosely and vaguely applied to anything abstruse, abstract, philo-sophical, subtle, transcendental, occult, supernatural or magical. — *n* **metaphys'ic** metaphysics; philosophi-cal groundwork. — *adj* metaphysical. — *adj* **meta-phys'ical** relating to metaphysics; abstract; beyond nature or the physical; supernatural; fanciful; addicted to far-fetched conceits (applied by Johnson to Donne, Cowley and others). — *adv* **metaphys'ically**. — *n* **metaphysician** (*-ish'ən*) a person skilled in metaphysics. [Originally applied to those writings of Aristotle which in the accepted order came after (Gr *meta*) those dealing with natural science (*ta physika*, from *physis* nature)]

metaplasia *met-ə-plā'si-ə*, *n* tissue transformation, such as of cartilage into bone. — *n* **metaplasis** (*-ap'lə-sis*) metaplasia; the period of maturity in the life-cycle. — *n* **met'aplasm** (*-plazm*) cell-contents other than pro-toplasm; a change in a word by addition, dropping or exchange of parts. — *adj* **metaplast'ic**. [Gr *metaplasis*, *metaplasmos*, a moulding afresh, from *meta* (see **meta-**) and *plassein* to form]

metapsychic, **metapsychical**, **metapsychics**, **metapsycho-logical**, **metapsychology**, **metasequoia**, **metasilicate**, **metasilicic**, **metasomatic**, **metasomatism**, **metastability** and **metastable**. See under **meta-**.

metastasis *met-as'tə-sis*, *n* removal from one place to another; transition; transformation; paramorphic change in rocks; metabolism (*rare*); transfer of disease from its original site to another part of the body (*pathol*); a secondary tumour distant from the original site of disease (*pathol*): — *pl* **metas'tasēs**. — *vi* **metas'tasize** or **-ise** (of a tumour, etc)to pass to another part of the body. — *adj* **metastatic** (*-stat'ik*). [Gr *metastasis* change of place, from *meta* (see **meta-**) and *stasis* a standing]

metatarsal, **metatarsus** and **Metatheria**. See under **meta-**.

metate *mə-tä'tē* or *-tä'tā*, *n* (in Mexico, the southwestern USA, etc) a stone with a concave surface, used in conjunction with a mano (qv) to grind maize or other grain. [Mex Sp, from Nahuatl *metlatl*]

metathesis *met-ath'ə-sis*, *n* transposition or exchange of places, *esp* between the sounds or letters of a word: — *pl* **metath'esēs**. — *vt* **metath'esize** or **-ise** to transpose (by metathesis). — *adj* **metathetic** (*met-ə-thet'ik*) or **metathet'ical**. [Gr, from *metatithenai* to transpose, from *meta* (see **meta-**) and *tithenai* to place]

metathoracic and **metathorax**. See under **meta-**.

métayer *mā-tā-yā'* or *mā'*, *n* a tenant farmer who gives a fixed proportion of the crops, rather than money, in payment for rent. — *n* **métayage** (*-yäzh'* or *mā'*) this system. [Fr, from LL *medietārius*, from L *medietās* half, from *medius* middle]

Metazoa, etc. See under **meta-**.

metcast. See under **met**[2].

mete[1] *mēt*, *vt* to measure; to apportion: — *pa t* **mēt'ed** or (*Spenser*) **mott**. — *n* measure. — **mete'stick**, **mete'wand** or **mete'yard** a measuring-rod. [OE *metan*; Ger *messen*]

mete[2] *mēt*, *n* a boundary or limit. [L *mēta* a goal or boundary]

metempiric, etc. See under **meta-**.

metempsychosis *met-emp-si-kō'sis*, *n* the passing of the soul after death into some other body: — *pl* **metem-psychō'sēs**. [Gr *metempsȳchōsis*, from *meta* (see **meta-**), *en* in, and *psȳchē* soul]

meteor *mē'tyər* or *mē'ti-ər*, *n orig*, any atmospheric phenomenon (now *rare*); a luminous appearance; one of numberless small bodies travelling through space, revealed to observation when they enter the earth's atmosphere as aerolites, fireballs or shooting stars; anything brilliant or dazzling but short-lived (*fig*). — *adj* **meteoric** (*mē-ti-or'ik*) above the earth's surface; atmospheric; influenced by weather; of or pertaining to meteors in any sense; of the nature of a meteor; transiently flashing like a meteor; remarkably rapid (*fig*). — *adv* **meteor'ically** in the manner of a meteor. — *n* **me'teorist** an expert on meteors. — *n* **me'teorite** a meteor that has fallen to earth as a lump of stone or metal. — *adj* **meteorit'ic**, **meteorit'ical** or **me'teorital** (*-īt-l*). — *n* **meteorit'icist**. — *n sing* **meteorit'ics** the science or study of meteors. — *n* **me'teorogram** a meteorograph record. — *n* **me'teorograph** an instrument by which several meteorological elements are recorded in combination. — *n* **me'teoroid** a meteor that has not reached the earth's atmosphere. — *n* **me'teorolite** (Gr *lithos* stone) a meteoric stone. — *adj* **meteorolog'ic** or **meteorolog'ical**. — *adv* **meteorolog'ically**. — *n* **meteorol'ogist**. — *n* **meteorol'ogy** the study of weather and climate. — *adj* **me'teorous** (or, *esp* in poetry, *mē-tē'ər-əs*) like a meteor, meteoric. — **meteor crater** a crater formed by the fall of a meteor; **meteoric iron** iron as found in meteorites; **meteoric stones** aerolites; **Meteorological Office** a government department issuing weather forecasts, etc; **meteorological satellite** a satellite used for weather observation and forecasting, carrying television cameras to transmit cloud formation changes and radiometers to measure terrestrial and solar radiation; **meteor** (or **meteoric**) **shower** or **storm** the profusion of meteors visible as the earth passes through a meteor swarm; **meteor streams** streams of dust revolving about the sun, whose intersection by the earth causes meteor showers; **meteor swarm** a number of meteoroids travelling on parallel courses. [Gr *ta meteōra* things on high, from *meta* and the root of *aeirein* to lift]

meteor. *abbrev*: meteorology.

meteorism *mē'tyər-izm* or *-ti-ər-*, (*med*) *n* excessive accumulation of gas in the intestines; tympanites. [Medical L *meteōrismus*, from Gr *meteōrismos* raising, or being raised, up, from *meteōrizein* to lift; cf **meteor**]

meter[1] *mē'tər*, *n* a measurer; an apparatus for measuring, *esp* the quantity of a fluid, or of electricity, used; a gauge or indicator; a parking meter. — *vt* to measure by a meter. — **meter maid** or **man** (*facetious*) a traffic warden. [**mete**[1]]

meter[2]. US spelling of **metre**[1,2].

-meter *-mi-tər* or *-mē-*, *combining form* denoting an instrument for measuring. — *adj combining form* **-metric** (*-met'rik*) or **-met'rical**. — *adv combining form* **-met'rically**. — *combining form* **-metry** (*-mi-tri*) signifying: measuring; the science of measuring. [Gr *metron* measure]

methadone *meth'ə-dōn*, (*pharm*) *n* a synthetic addictive drug similar to morphine, longer-acting than heroin. — Also **meth'adon** (*-don*). [di*methyl*amino-, *d*iphenyl and heptan*one*]

methamphetamine *meth-am-fet'ə-mēn* or **methylamphetamine** *mēth-il-*, (*pharm*) *n* a methyl derivative of amphetamine with rapid and long-lasting action, used as a stimulant to the central nervous system.

methanal *meth'ə-nal*, *n* formaldehyde.

methane *mē'thān* or *meth'ān*, *n* an odourless, colourless, inflammable gas (CH_4), the simplest hydrocarbon, produced by decomposition of vegetable matter in wet conditions (also called **marsh-gas**). — **methanom'eter** (*mining*) an instrument for detecting the presence of methane in mines. [**methyl**]

methanol *meth'ə-nol*, *n* methyl alcohol, wood spirit. [**methane**, and *-ol*, suffix from L *oleum* oil]

methaqualone *meth-ə-kwā'lōn*, *n* a hypnotic sedative drug ($C_{16}H_{14}N_2O$).

Methedrine® *meth'ə-drēn*, *n* a former proprietary name for an amphetamine, methylamphetamine hydrochloride, a soft drug, but used by drug addicts.

metheglin *meth-eg'lin*, *n* a Welsh fermented liquor made from honey. [Welsh *meddyglyn*, from *meddyg* medicinal (from L *medicus* physician), and *llyn* liquor]

methinks *mi-thingks'* (*archaic* or *jocular*) or (*obs*) **methink'eth** or **methink'** (*archaic* or *humorous*) *impersonal verb* it seems to me; I think: — *pa t* **methought** (*mi-thöt'*). [OE *mē thyncth* it seems to me; *thyncan* to seem, has been confused with *thencan* to think; cf Ger *dünken* to seem, *denken* to think]

methionine *meth-ī'o-nēn*, (*chem*) *n* an essential sulphur-bearing amino-acid.

method *meth'əd*, *n* the mode or rule used in carrying out a task or accomplishing an aim; orderly procedure; manner; orderly arrangement; methodicalness; classification; a system or rule; manner of performance; an instruction book systematically arranged (*archaic*). — *adj* **methodic** (*mi-thod'ik*) or **method'ical** carried out or arranged in a systematic and thoughtful way; disposed in a just and natural manner; observing method, inclined to be systematic; formal. — *adv* **method'ically**. — *n* **method'icalness**. — *n* **Meth'odism** (*Christian relig*) the principles and practice of the Methodists. — *n* **meth'odist** a person who observes method; (with *cap*) a follower of John and Charles Wesley, a name given first to a group of students at Oxford 'for the regularity of their lives as well as studies'; a member of the Methodist Church, a nonconformist denomination founded on John Wesley's doctrines. — *adj* **Methodist'ic** or **Methodist'ical** resembling the Methodists, *esp* as viewed by opponents; strict in religious matters. — *adv* **Methodist'ically**. — *vt* **meth'odize** or **-ise** to reduce to a system or method; to arrange in an orderly way. — *adj* **methodolog'ical**. — *n* **methodol'ogist**. — *n* **methodol'ogy** a system of methods and rules applicable to research or work in a given science or art; evaluation of subjects taught, and the principles and techniques of teaching them. — *n* **Meth'ody** a disrespectful nickname for a Methodist. — **method acting** acting as a personal living of a part, contrasted with mere technical performance (also called **the method**). [Gr *methodos*, from *meta* after, and *hodos* a way]

methomania *meth-ō-mā'ni-ə*, *n* an intermittent morbid craving for alcohol. [Gr *methē* strong drink, and *maniā* madness]

methotrexate *meth-ō-treks'āt*, *n* a drug ($C_{20}H_{22}N_8O_5$) used in cancer treatment and bone marrow transplantation.

methought. See **methinks**.

methoxamine hydrochloride *meth-oks'ə-mēn hī-drō-klör'īd*, *n* a drug used in slowing down the action of the heart.

meths *meths*, *n sing* short form of **methylated spirits**.

Methuselah *mi-thū'zə-lə* or *-thōō'*, *n* a patriarch said to have lived 969 years (Gen 5. 27); any very old person; a very large wine-bottle (holding about $6\frac{1}{2}$ quarts); as a bottle-size of champagne, the equivalent of eight ordinary bottles.

methyl *meth'il* or *mē'thīl*, (*chem*) *n* the radical (CH_3) of wood (or methyl) alcohol ($CH_3{\cdot}OH$). — *n* **methylamine** (*-a-mēn'*) an inflammable gas ($CH_3{\cdot}NH_2$), obtainable from herring brine (see also **dimethylamine** and **trimethylamine**). — *n* **methylamphetamine** see **methamphetamine**. — *vt* **meth'ylate** to mix or impregnate with methyl alcohol; to introduce the radical CH_3 into. — *n* a methyl alcohol derivative; a compound with a methyl group. — *n* **methylā'tion**. — *n* **methyldō'pa** an anti-hypertensive drug ($C_{10}H_{13}NO_4$). — *n* **meth'ylene** the hypothetical compound CH_2. — *adj* **methyl'ic**. — **methyl alcohol** see **methyl** above; **methylated spirit** or **spirits** alcohol made undrinkable (and therefore exempt from tax) with methyl alcohol, and *usu* other things, used as a fuel in lamps, etc; **methyl chloride** a refrigerant and local anaesthetic; **methyl group** (*chem*) the monovalent radical CH_3; **methyl-propyl ether** an inhalation anaesthetic; **methyltestos'terone** (*-ōn*) a synthetic androgen with similar actions and functions to those of testosterone; **methyl violet** an antiseptic dye used as a stain in microscopy and formerly used as a disinfectant, a mixture of the hydrochlorides of tetra-, penta-, and hexa-methylpararosaniline; crystal violet. [Gr *methu* wine, and *hȳlē* wood]

methysis *meth'i-sis*, (*pathol*; *rare*) *n* drunkenness. — *adj* **methys'tic** intoxicating. [New L, from Gr *methusis* drunkenness, from *methuein* to be drunk]

metic *met'ik*, (*hist*) *n* (in ancient Greece) a resident alien in a city, subject to a special tax. [Gr *metoikos*, from *meta* indicating change, and *oikos* a house]

metical *met'i-kəl*, *n* the monetary unit of Mozambique, equal to 100 centavos. [Port *metical*, from Ar *mithqāl* a measure of weight]

meticulous *me-tik'ū-ləs, adj* timid (*obs*); scrupulously careful; overcareful. — *adv* **metic'ulously**. — *n* **metic'ulousness**. [L *meticulōsus* frightened, from *metus* fear]

métier *mā'tyā, n* one's calling or business; that in which one is specially skilled. [Fr, from L *ministerium*]

metif *mā'tēf, n* (also with *cap*) the offspring of a White person and a quadroon. [Fr; cf **mestizo**]

Metis *mē'tis, n* a Greek personification of prudence. [Gr *mētis*]

Métis *mā-tēs', n* in Canada, a person of mixed White (*esp* French Canadian) and N American Indian parentage; (without *cap*) any person of mixed descent: — *pl* **Métis** (*-tēs'* or *-tēz'*); *fem* **Métisse'** (also without *cap*). [Fr; cf **mestizo**]

metol *mē'tol, n p*-methylaminophenol sulphate, the basis of a rapid developer for photographic negatives. [From *Metol*, a trademark]

Metonic *mi-ton'ik, adj* of or relating to the Athenian astronomer *Metōn* or his cycle (**Metonic cycle** beginning on 27th June, 432 BC) of 19 years after which the moon's phases recur on the same days of the year.

metonym *met'ə-nim, n* a word used in metonymy. — *adj* **metonym'ic** or **metonym'ical**. — *adv* **metonym'ically**. — *n* **metonymy** (*mi-ton'i-mi*) the use of the name of a single aspect of or adjunct to a thing as a way of referring to the whole thing itself, such as 'the ring' to mean 'boxing'. [Gr *metōnymiā*, from *meta*, indicating change, and *onyma* = *onoma* a name]

me-too *mē-too'*, *adj* imitative. — *n* a product resulting from me-tooism. — *n* **me-too'er** a person who imitates or adopts the policy or activity of another, for his or her own advantage. — *n* **me-too'ism** imitating the policy or activity which is proving successful for a rival. [Colloq interj *me too*]

metope[1] *met'o-pē* or *met'ōp*, (*archit*) *n* the slab, plain or sculptured, between the triglyphs of a Doric frieze. [Gr *metopē*, from *meta* and *opē* an opening for a beam-end]

metope[2] *met'ōp, n* the face, forehead or frontal surface generally. — *adj* **metopic** (*mit-op'ik*). — *n* **metopism** (*met'ə-pizm*) the condition of having a persistent metopic or frontal suture. — *n* **metoposcopy** (*met-ə-pos'kə-pi*; Gr *skopeein* to look) the study of character from the physiognomy. — *adj* **metoposcop'ic** or **metoposcop'ical**. — *n* **metopos'copist**. [Gr *metōpon* forehead, literally between the eyes, from *meta* and *ōps* eye]

metopon *met'ō-pon, n* a pain-relieving drug derived from opium but less habit-forming than morphine.

metopryl *met'ō-pril, n* an anaesthetic related to ether, but more powerful and having less disturbing after-effects.

metre[1] or (*US*) **meter** *mē'tər, n* the regulated succession of groups of syllables (long and short, stressed and unstressed) in which poetry is *usu* written; verse, or poetry generally; a scheme of versification, the character of a stanza as consisting of a given number of lines composed of feet of a given number, arrangement, and kind; musical time. — *vt* and *vi* to versify. — *adj* **metred** (*mē'tərd*) rhythmical. — *adj* **metric** (*met'rik*) or **met'rical** relating to metre; in metre; consisting of verses. — *adv* **met'rically**. — *n* **metrician** (*me-trish'ən*) a metricist. — *n* **met'ricist** (*-sist*) a person skilled in metres; someone who writes in metre. — *vt* **met'ricize** or **-ise** (*-sīz*) to analyse the metre of. — *n sing* **met'rics** the art or science of versification (also *n* **met'ric**). — *n* **metrificā'tion** metrical structure; the act of writing verse. — *n* **met'rifier** a versifier. — *n* **met'rist** a person skilled in the use of metre; a student of metre. — *n* **metromā'nia** a mania for writing verse. — **common metre** a quatrain in eights and sixes, of four and of three iambic feet alternately (also **service metre**, from its use in the metrical psalms, etc, and **ballad metre**, from its use in old ballads); **long metre** an octosyllabic quatrain, the four lines with four feet each; **short metre** the quatrain in sixes, with the third line octosyllabic. [OE *mēter* and OFr *metre*, both from L *metrum*, from Gr *metron* measurement, metre; and partly directly]

metre[2] or (*US*) **meter** *mē'tər, n* the fundamental unit of length in the metric system, *orig* intended to be one ten-millionth of the distance from pole to equator; later the distance between two marks on a platinum-iridium bar in Paris; defined more recently in terms of the wavelength in vacuo of the orange radiation of the krypton-86 atom; by British Act of Parliament (1963) 1 yard equals 0·9144 metre. — *adj* **metric** (*met'rik*) relating to the metre, or to the metric system. — *vt* and *vi* **met'ricate** to convert or change to the metric system. — *n* **metricā'tion**. — **metre-kilogram-second** or **metre-kilogramme-second** (*abbrev* **MKS**) **system** a system of scientific measurement having the metre, etc, as units of length, mass, time (with the addition of **ampere**, **MKSA**, forming the Giorgi system of units); **metric system** the SI or any decimal system of weights and measures; **metric ton** see under **tonne**. — **go metric** to metricate. [Fr *mètre*, from Gr *metron* measure]

metric[1] *met'rik, adj* quantitative. — *adj* **met'rical** pertaining to measurement. — *n sing* **met'rics** the theory of measurement. — *adj* **metrologic** (*-loj'ik*) or **metrolog'ical**. — *n* **metrol'ogist**. — *n* **metrol'ogy** the science of weights and measures, or of weighing and measuring. [Gr *metron* measure]

metric[2]. See under **metre**[1].

metric[3]. See under **metre**[2].

-metric and **-metrically**. See under **-meter**.

metricate. See under **metre**[2].

metri causa *met'rē kow'zə* or **metri gratia** *grä'ti-ä* or *grā'shi-ə*, (*L*) for the sake of the metre; for metrical harmony.

metrician, etc, **metrifier** and **metrist**. See under **metre**[1].

metro- *mētrō-, met-, mət-* or (before a vowel) **metr-** *combining form* signifying the uterus. — *n* **metritis** (*mə-trī'tis*) inflammation of the uterus. — *n* **metrorrhagia** (*mē-trō-rā'ji-ə* or *me-*; Gr *-rragia*, from *rhēgnynai* to break, burst) bleeding from the uterus between menstrual periods. [Gr *metra* womb]

métro *mā'trō, n* (often with *cap*) an urban railway system, running wholly or partly underground, *esp* and *orig* the Paris subway: — *pl* **mét'ros**. — Also **metro** or **Metro**. [Fr *métro*. Abbrev for *chemin de fer métropolitain* metropolitan railway]

metrology. See under **metric**[1].

metromania. See under **metre**[1].

metronome *met'rə-nōm, n* an instrument with an inverted pendulum that can be set to beat so many times a minute, the loud ticking giving the right speed of performance for a piece of music. — *adj* **metronomic** (*-nom'ik*). [Gr *metron* measure, and *nomos* law]

metronymic *met-rə-nim'ik, adj* derived from the name of one's mother or other female ancestor; indicating the mother; using such a system of naming. — *n* an appellation so derived (cf *patronymic*). — Also **matronym'ic** (*prob* from L *māter*, though Doric Greek is *mātēr*). [Gr *mētēr*, *-tros* mother, and *onyma* = *onoma* name]

metroplex *met'rō-pleks*, (*esp US*) *n* a large urban or metropolitan area, *esp* that formed by more than one city and the adjoining suburbs. [*metro*politan and com*plex*]

metropolis *mi-trop'ə-lis, n* the capital of a country, county, etc; the chief cathedral city of a country, such as Canterbury of England, or chief see of a province; the mother-city of an ancient Greek colony; the mother country or state of a colony; a chief centre, seat or focus; the main habitat of a particular species (*biol*): — *pl* **metrop'olises**. — *adj* **metropolitan** (*met-rə-pol'i-tən*) of a metropolis; of or comprising a city and its suburbs; of the mother-church. — *n* the bishop of a metropolis, presiding over the other bishops of a province, in the Eastern Orthodox churches, a person ranking between an archbishop and a patriarch, in the RC Church and the Church of England, an archbishop; an inhabitant of a metropolis. — *n* **metropol'itanate**. — *vt* **metropol'itanize** or **-ise** to make into or like a metropolis. — *adj* **metropolit'ical**. — **metropolitan county** or **district** a county or district in a heavily-populated industrial area of England, the district running more, and the county fewer, public services than other districts or counties. [Gr *mētropolis*, from *mētēr* mother, and *polis* city]

metrorrhagia. See under **metro-**.

metrostyle *met'rə-stīl*, *n* a device for regulating speed in a player-piano. [Gr *metron* measure, and *stȳlos* a pillar]

mettle *met'l*, *n* temperament; ardent temperament; spirit; sprightliness; courage. — *adj* (*Scot*) mettlesome. — *adj* **mett'led** or **mett'lesome** high-spirited; ardent. — *n* **mett'lesomeness**. — **put (someone) on his** or **her mettle** to rouse (a person) to put forth his or her best efforts. **[metal]**

meu *mū*, *n* the plant baldmoney or spignel. [L *mēum*, from Gr *mēon*]

meum et tuum *mē'əm et tū'əm* or *me'ōōm et tōō'ōōm*, (*L*) mine and thine.

meunière *mən-yer'* or *mø-nyer*, *adj* (of food, *esp* fish) lightly coated in flour and fried in butter, then served in butter, lemon juice and herbs, *esp* parsley. [Fr *à la meunière* in the manner of the miller's wife (from the coating of flour)]

meuse[1], **muse** or **mews** *mūs* or *mūz*, *n* a way of escape through a hedge, etc. — *vi* to pass through a meuse. [OFr *muce* a place for hiding things]

meuse[2]. See **mew**[3].

MeV *abbrev*: mega-electron-volt(s).

meve *mēv*, an *obs* form of **move** (*v*).

Mevlevi *mev-lə-vī'* or **Mawlawi** *mow-lä-wī'*, *n* (a member of) an order of Sufis *orig* from Turkey, practising frenzied ritual dancing as an aid to religious meditation (also called **whirling-dervish**): — *pl* **Mevlevīs'** or **Mawlawīs'**. [Turk *Mevlevi* or Pers *Mawlāwīya*, from *mawlānāa* literally our master, title given to a Sufi master]

mew[1] *mū*, *n* a gull. [OE *mǣw*; Du *meeuw*, ON *mār*, Ger *Möwe*]

mew[2] *mū*, *vi* (*esp* of a cat, kitten, or gull) to make a thin, high-pitched cry. — *n* this sound. — *interj* expressing derision (*obs*). [Imit]

mew[3] *mū*, *vt* to shed, moult or cast; to change, as the covering or dress; to confine, as in a cage. — *vi* to shed antlers or feathers; to moult. — *n* the process of moulting; a cage for hawks, *esp* while mewing; a coop; a place of confinement; a retreat; a hiding-place. — *n* **mews** or **meuse** (*mūz* or *mūs*; *orig pl* of **mew**, now commonly as *sing* with new *pl* **mews'es**) a street or yard of stabling (often converted into dwelling-houses or garages), so-called from the king's mews at Charing Cross when hawks were succeeded by horses. [OFr *muer*, from L *mūtāre* to change]

mewl *mūl*, *vi* to mew; to cry feebly, as a child. [Imit]

mews[1]. See **mew**[3].

mews[2]. See **meuse**[1].

MEX *abbrev*: Mexico (IVR).

Mex. *abbrev*: Mexican; Mexico.

Mexican *meks'i-kən*, *adj* of Mexico or its people. — *n* a native or citizen of Mexico; an Aztec; the Nahuatl language; a Mexican dollar; a coarse cotton cloth. — **Mexican hog** the peccary; **Mexican standoff** (*US colloq*) an impasse or stalemate; **Mexican tea** a kind of goosefoot, used as an anthelmintic; **Mexican wave** the wave-like action (popularized by the 1986 World Cup in Mexico) of different groups of spectators standing up and sitting down again in a progressive movement around a stadium. [Sp *Mexicano*, now *Mejicano*]

meynt. See **ming**[1].

MEZ *abbrev*: *mitteleuropäische Zeit* (*Ger*), Central European Time.

mezail. See **mesail**.

meze, **mezze** or **mézé** *mä'zā*, *n* a type of appetizer or hors d'oeuvre served in Greece, Turkey, Lebanon, etc, *esp* with an aperitif before dinner. [Turk *meze* a snack, an appetizer]

mezereon *me-zē'ri-ən*, *n* a European shrub (*Daphne mezereum*) whose flowers appear in early spring; its extremely acrid bark, or the bark of related species, used in medicine. — Also **mezē'reum** (*-əm*). [Ar and Pers *māzaryūn*]

mezuza or **mezuzah** *mə-zōōz'ə*, *n* a parchment scroll containing scriptural texts which is placed in a case and fixed to the doorpost by some Jewish families as a sign of their faith: — *pl* **mezu'zahs** or **mezuzoth** (*-zōō-zōt'*). [Heb, literally doorpost]

mezzanine *mez'ə-nēn*, *n* an entresol (*archit*; also **mezzanine floor**); a small low window in an attic, etc (*archit*; also **mezzanine window**); a room below the stage; the first balcony in a theatre, the circle (*NAm*). — Also *adj*. — **mezzanine finance** finance *usu* for the takeover of a large company, consisting of an unsecured, high-interest loan, sometimes with a share option for the lender. [Fr, from Ital *mezzanino*, from *mezzano*, from L *mediānus*, from *medius* middle]

mezza voce *met'sə vō'chā* or *med'zä*, (*music*) *adv* with medium volume or tone. — *adj* played or sung in this style. [Ital]

mezze. See **meze**.

mezzo *met'sō*, *n* a mezzo-soprano: — *pl* **mez'zos**.

mezzo-forte *met'sō-* or *med'zō-för'tā*, (*music*) *adv* rather loudly. — *adj* rather loud. [Ital]

Mezzogiorno *met-sō-jör'nō*, *n* southern Italy, including Sardinia and Sicily. [Ital, literally midday]

mezzo-piano *met'sō-* or *med'zō-pyä'nō*, also *-pē-ä'nō*, (*music*) *adv* rather softly. — *adj* rather soft. [Ital]

mezzo-relievo or **mezzo-rilievo** *met'sō-* or *med'zō-ril-yä'vō*, *n* a degree of sculptural relief halfway between high and low relief; a carving or sculpture in this form. [Ital]

mezzo-soprano *met'sō-* or *med'zō-sō-prä'nō*, *n* a voice between soprano and contralto; low soprano; a part for such a voice; a person possessing such a voice: — *pl* **mezzo-sopra'nos**. [Ital *mezzo* middle, and *soprano*]

mezzotint *met'sō-* or *med'zō-tint*, *n* a method of copperplate engraving giving an even gradation of tones by roughening a plate and removing the bur for lights; an impression from a plate so produced. — Also **mezzotinto** (*-tin'tō*): — *pl* **mezzotin'tos**. [Ital *mezzotinto*, from *mezzo* middle, half, and *tinto* tint, from L *tingere*, *tinctum* to dye]

MF *abbrev*: machine finished; medium frequency; Middle French; multi-frequency.

mf *abbrev*: mezzo-forte.

MFA *abbrev*: Multi-Fibre Arrangement.

mfd *abbrev*: manufactured.

MFH *abbrev*: Master of Foxhounds.

mfrs *abbrev*: manufacturers.

MFS *abbrev*: Marfan syndrome, a genetic disorder of connective tissue.

mft *abbrev*: *mistura* (for classical *L mixtura*) *fiat* let a mixture be made.

mfv *abbrev*: motor fleet vehicle.

MG *abbrev*: machine-gun; Morris Garages.

Mg (*chem*) *symbol*: magnesium.

mg *abbrev*: milligram(s).

mganga *m-gang'gə*, *n* in E Africa, a native doctor, a witch doctor. [Swahili]

MGB (*hist*) *abbrev*: *Ministerstvo Gosudarstvennoi Bezopasnosti* (*Russ*), the Ministry for State Security, the Soviet secret police from 1946 until replaced by the KGB in 1954.

Mgr *abbrev*: Manager; Monseigneur; Monsignor.

MHA *abbrev*: Member of the House of Assembly.

MHC *abbrev*: major histocompatibility complex.

MHD *abbrev*: magnetic hydrodynamic.

MHG *abbrev*: Middle High German.

mho *mō*, *n* formerly a unit of electric conductance, that of a body with a resistance of one ohm (now **siemens**): — *pl* **mhos**. **[ohm** spelt backwards]

mhorr *mör*, *n* a W African gazelle. [Ar]

MHR *abbrev*: Member of the House of Representatives.

MHz *abbrev*: megahertz.

MI *abbrev*: Michigan (US state; also **Mich**.); Military Intelligence. — **MI5** Security Services; **MI6** Secret

Intelligence Services (initials based on wartime Military Intelligence departments).

mi *mē*, *n* the third note of the scale in sol-fa notation. — Also anglicized in spelling as **me**. [See **Aretinian**]

MIA (*military*) *abbrev*: missing in action.

mia-mia *mī'ə-mī'ə*, *n* an Aboriginal dwelling hut. [Aboriginal]

miaow *mi-ow'* or *myow'*, *n* the characteristic cry of a cat. — *vi* to make this sound. — *interj* (*colloq*) said in response to a catty or spiteful remark.

miarolitic *mi-ə-rō-lit'ik*, (*geol*) *adj* having irregular cavities into which the constituent minerals of the rock project with perfectly terminated crystals. [Ital *miarolo*, local name of a granite]

miasma *mi-* or *mī-az'mə*, *n* foul vapours, eg from rotting matter; unwholesome air; any unwholesome atmosphere (*literally* and *fig*). — Also **mī'asm**: — *pl* **mias'mata, mias'mas** or **mī'asms**. — *adj* **mias'mal, miasmat'ic, mias'matous, mias'mic** or **mias'mous**. [Gr *miasma*, *-atos* pollution, from *miainein* to stain, pollute]

miaul *mi-öl'* or *mi-owl'*, *vi* to cry as a cat, to miaow. — *n* a miaow. [Fr *miauler*; imit]

Mic (*Bible*) *abbrev*: (the Book of) Micah.

mic. *abbrev*: mica.

mica *mī'kə*, *n* a rock-forming mineral (muscovite, biotite, lepidolite, etc) with perfect basal cleavage, the laminae flexible and elastic, and *usu* transparent, of various colours, used as an electric insulator and as a substitute for glass: — *pl* **mi'cas**. — *adj* **micaceous** (*-kā'shəs*). — *vt* **mi'cate** to furnish with mica. — **mi'ca-schist** or **mi'ca-slate** a metamorphic rock consisting of alternate folia of mica and quartz. [L *mīca* a crumb; use probably influenced by association with *micāre* to glitter]

Micawberish *mi-kö'bər-ish*, *adj* like Wilkins *Micawber* in Dickens's *David Copperfield*, jaunty and improvident, always 'waiting for something to turn up'. — *n* **Micaw'berism**.

mice *mīs*, plural of **mouse**.

micelle *mi-sel'* or **micella** *mī-sel'ə*, (*chem*) *n* a group of molecular chains, a structural unit found in colloids; a hypothetical unit of living matter. — *adj* **micell'ar**. [Dimin of L *mīca* crumb, grain]

Mich. *abbrev*: Michaelmas; Michigan (US state).

Michaelmas *mik'əl-məs*, *n* the festival of St *Michael*, 29 Sept, a quarter-day in England, Wales and Ireland. — **Michaelmas-dai'sy** a wild aster; any of several garden plants of the Aster genus with clusters of small purple, pink, blue, etc, flowers; **Michaelmas term** the autumn term at Oxford and Cambridge and some other universities, or at the Inns of Court. [**mass**[2]]

miche *mich*, (*dialect*) *vi* to mouch, skulk, slink; to loaf; to play truant. — *vt* to pilfer. — *n* **mich'er**. — *n* and *adj* **mich'ing**. [Poss same as **mooch**]

Michurinism *mē-choo'rin-ism*, *n* Lysenkoism. [I V *Michurin*, Russian horticulturalist]

mick *mik'*, **mickey** or **micky** *mik'i*, *n* an Irishman (rather *offensive slang*); a flask for alcohol (mainly *Can*); a wild young bull (*Austr*). — *adj* **mick'ey** (*US slang*) (of music, a band, etc) Mickey Mouse. — *n* **mickey, Mickey** or **Mickey Finn** (*slang*) a doped drink; that which is added to the drink, *usu* a stupefying drug or a strong laxative. — *vt* to drug someone's drink; to trick someone. — **Mickey Mouse** an animated cartoon character created by Walt Disney, 1928. — *adj* (*slang*) simple, easy, often derisively so; unimportant, insignificant; (of music, a band, etc) trite, corny. — **mick'ey-taking** (*slang*). — **take the mick, mickey, micky,** or (*rarely*) **mike** (or **a mike**), **out of** (*slang*; perhaps with different origin) to annoy; to make fun of. [*Michael*]

mickle *mik'l*, (*archaic*) *adj* much; great. — *n* a great quantity. — *adv* much. — *Scot* **muck'le**. — **many a little** (or **pickle**) **makes a mickle** (*often absurdly* **many a mickle makes a muckle**) every little helps. [OE *micel*, *mycel*]

micky. See **mick**.

Micmac *mik'mak*, *n* a N American Indian people of eastern Canada; a member of it; the Algonquian language of this people.

mico *mē'kō*, *n* a marmoset, *esp* the black-tailed: — *pl* **mi'cos**. [Port, from Carib *meku* monkey]

MICR *abbrev*: magnetic ink character recognition.

micra. See **micron**.

micro *mī'krō*, (*colloq*) *n* short for **microprocessor** or **microcomputer**: — *pl* **mi'cros**.

micro- *mī-krō-*, *mī-krə-*, or before a vowel sometimes **micr-**, *combining form* denoting (1) (a) abnormally, comparatively or extremely small; (b) using, or used in, or prepared for, microscopy; (c) dealing with minute quantities, objects or values; (d) dealing with a small area; (e) magnifying, amplifying; (f) reducing, or reduced, to minute size; (2) a millionth part, as in **mī'croampere** a millionth part of an ampere, **mi'crobar** one-millionth of a bar of pressure, **mī'crofarad, mī'crogram**, and many others. [Gr *mikros* little]

microanalysis *mī-krō-ə-nal'i-sis*, *n* chemical analysis of minute quantities. — *adj* **microanalyt'ical**. [**micro-** (1c)]

microanatomy *mī-krō-ə-nat'ə-mi*, *n* the study of the anatomical structures of microscopic tissues. [**micro-** (1c)]

microbalance *mī'krō-bal-əns*, *n* a balance for measuring very small weights. [**micro-** (1c)]

microbarograph *mī-krō-bar'ō-gräf*, *n* a barograph that records minute variations of atmospheric pressure. [**micro-** (1c)]

microbe *mī'krōb*, *n* a microscopic organism, *esp* a bacterium. — *adj* **micrō'bial, micrō'bian** or **micrō'bic**. — *n* **mīcrobiol'ogist**. — *n* **mīcrobiol'ogy** the biology of microscopic or ultramicroscopic organisms, such as bacteria, viruses or fungi. — *n pl* **mī'crobiota** the smallest soil organisms. — **microbiological mining** the use of natural or genetically-engineered bacteria to enhance or induce acid leaching of metals from ores (*bacterial leaching*); the use of bacteria to recover useful or toxic metals from natural drainage waters, mine drainage, or waste water from tips (*bacterial recovery*). — Also **bī'omining**. [Fr, from Gr *mikros* little, and *bios* life]

micro-brewery *mī-krō-broo'ə-ri*, *n* a small, independent brewery, *usu* supplying a single town or area. — *n* **mī'cro-brew**. [**micro-** (1a)]

microburst *mī'krō-bûrst*, *n* a sudden, violent downward rush of air *usu* associated with thunderstorms. [**micro-** (1d)]

microbus *mī'krō-bus*, *n* a minibus. [**micro-** (1a)]

microcapsule *mī'krō-kap-sūl*, *n* an extremely small, thin-walled capsule of plastic or wax, formed around liquid, powder, etc, which, when fractured, releases its contents to fulfil some purpose (such capsules have been used eg to make copying paper without carbon). — *n* **microencapsulā'tion**. [**micro-** (1a)]

microcar *mī'krō-kär*, *n* a very compact, small-engined car designed for use in large cities, *esp* in Japan. [**micro-** (1a)]

microcard *mī'krō-kärd*, *n* a card reproducing some 200 or more pages of a book in microscopic print for later reading by enlargement. [**micro-** (1f)]

microcassette *mī'krō-kə-set*, *n* a tiny cassette using very thin recording tape to give a similar recording time to standard cassettes. [**micro-** (1f)]

microcephalous *mī-krō-sef'ə-ləs*, *adj* abnormally small-headed. — Also **microcephalic** (*-si-fal'ik*). — *n* **microceph'al** an abnormally small-headed person. — *n* **microceph'aly** abnormal smallness of head. [Gr *mikros* little, and *kephalē* head]

Microcheiroptera or (*US*) **Microchiroptera** *mī-krō-kī-rop'tə-rə*, *n pl* bats other than fruit-bats (which are large); microbats. [**micro-** (1a) and **Chiroptera**]

microchemistry *mī-krō-kem'is-tri*, *n* chemistry dealing with very small quantities. [**micro-** (1c)]

microchip *mī'krō-chip*, *n* a chip (qv) of silicon, etc. [**micro-** (1f)]

Microchiroptera. See **Microcheiroptera**.

microcircuit *mī'krō-sûr-kit, n* an electronic circuit with components formed in one unit of semiconductor crystal. [**micro-** (1f)]

microcirculation *mī-krō-sûr-kū-lā'shən, n* the circulation of blood or lymph in the finest blood-vessels or capillaries of the circulatory and lymphatic systems. [**micro-** (1a)]

microclimate *mī'krō-klī-māt* or *-klī-mit, n* the climate of a small or very small area, *esp* if different from that of the surrounding area. — *n* **microclimatol'ogy** the study of a microclimate or microclimates. [**micro-** (1d)]

microcline *mī'krō-klīn, n* an anorthic potash-feldspar with its cleavage-angle differing very slightly from a right angle. [Gr *mikros* little, and *klīnein* to slant]

micrococcus *mī-krō-kok'əs, n* a rounded bacillus: — *pl* **micrococci** (*-kok'sī*). — *adj* **micrococc'al**. [**micro-** (1a) and Gr *kokkos* a grain]

microcode *mī'krō-kōd,* (*comput*) *n* a microinstruction or a sequence of microinstructions. [**micro-** (1c)]

microcomponent *mī-krō-kəm-pō'nənt, n* a minute component of eg a microcircuit. [**micro-** (1a)]

microcomputer *mī-krō-kəm-pū'ter, n* a tiny computer containing a microprocessor, often used as the control unit for some instrument, tool, etc, or as a personal computer; the microprocessor itself. — *n* **microcomput'ing**. [**micro-** (1f)]

microcopying *mī-krō-kop'i-ing, n* copying on microfilm. — *n* and *vt* **mī'crocopy**. [**micro-** (1f)]

microcosm *mī'krō-kozm, n* a little universe or world; an object, situation, etc contained within another and displaying all its characteristics on a smaller scale, a miniature version; man, who was regarded by ancient philosophers as a model or epitome of the universe. — *adj* **microcos'mic** or **microcos'mical** relating to the, or a, microcosm. — *n* **microcosmog'raphy**. — **microcosmic salt** sodium ammonium hydrogen phosphate, used as a blowpipe flux (*orig* obtained from human urine). — **in microcosm** on a small scale, as an exact copy or representative model of a larger group, etc. [Gr *mikros* small, and *kosmos* world]

microcrack *mī'krō-krak, n* a microscopic crack or fracture. — *vi* and *vt* to form, or cause to form, microcracks. — *n* **mī'crocracking**. [**micro-** (1a)]

microcrystalline *mī-krə-kris'təl-īn* or *-in, adj* having a crystalline structure visible only under the microscope. [**micro-** (1a)]

microcyte *mī'krə-sīt, n* a small red blood corpuscle. [**micro-** (1a), and Gr *kytos* a container (used as if = cell)]

microdetector *mī-krō-di-tekt'ər, n* an instrument for detecting minute amounts of changes. — *n* **microdetec'tion**. [**micro-** (1c)]

microdissection *mī-krō-di-sek'shən, n* dissection under the microscope. [**micro-** (1b)]

microdot *mī'krə-dot, n* a photograph of *usu* secret material reduced to the size of a large dot; a small pill containing concentrated LSD (*slang*). [**micro-** (1f)]

micro drive *mī'krō drīv, n* a device used on some microcomputers for writing and reading data to and from a continuous loop of tape held in a cartridge. [**micro-** (1f)]

microeconomics *mī-krō-ēk-ə-nom'iks* or *-ek-, n sing* that branch of economics dealing with individual households, firms, industries, commodities, etc. — *n pl* economic methods, principles, etc applicable to an individual firm, etc. — *adj* **microeconom'ic**. [**micro-** (1d)]

microelectronics *mī-krō-el-ik-tron'iks* or *-ē-lik-, n sing* the technology of electronic systems involving microminiaturization, microcircuits or other microelectronic devices. — *adj* **microelectron'ic**. [**micro-** (1f)]

microencapsulation. See under **microcapsule**.

microenvironment *mī-krō-en-vīr'ən-mənt,* (*ecol*) *n* the environment of small areas in contrast to large areas, with particular reference to the conditions experienced by individual organisms and their parts (eg leaves, etc). [**micro-** (1c)]

microevolution *mī-krō-ēv-ə-loo'shən* or *-ev-, n* evolutionary change taking place over a relatively short period within a species or subspecies as a result of the repeated selection of certain characteristics. [**micro-** (1c)]

microfauna *mī'krō-fö-nə* or *-fö'nə, n pl* extremely small animals, *usu* those invisible to the naked eye. [**micro-** (1a,b)]

microfelsitic *mī-krə-fel-sit'ik, adj* of the cryptocrystalline texture of a quartz-felsite groundmass. [**micro-** (1a)]

microfiche *mī'krə-fēsh, n* a sheet of microfilm suitable for filing: — *pl* **mī'crofiche** (*-fēsh*) or **mī'crofiches**. — **microfiche reader** an optical device which illuminates frames of microfiche and projects an enlarged image onto a screen to be read by the user. [**micro-** (1f), and Fr *fiche* slip of paper, etc]

microfilaria *mī-krō-fi-lā'ri-ə, n* the early larval stage of certain parasitic *Nematoda*. [**micro-** (1a)]

microfiling *mī'krō-fīl-ing, n* the process of microfilming the contents of a file. [**micro-** (1f)]

microfilm *mī'krə-film, n* a photographic film for preserving a microscopic record of a document, which can be enlarged in projection. — *vt* to record on microfilm. — **microfilm reader** an optical device which magnifies each page of microfilm and presents the image in an enlarged form on a screen to be read by the user. [**micro-** (1f)]

microfloppy *mī'krō-flop-i, n* a small (*usu* 3.5 in) magnetic floppy disk. [**micro-** (1f)]

microflora *mī-krō-flö-rə, n pl* extremely small plants, *usu* those invisible to the naked eye. [**micro-** (1a,b)]

microform *mī'krə-förm, n* any of the media of reproduction by microphotography, such as microfiche, microfilm, videotape, etc. [**micro-** (1f)]

microfossil *mī-krō-fos-l* or *-il, n* a fossil that may only be examined by means of a microscope. [**micro-** (1a,b)]

microgamete *mī-krə-gam'ēt* or *-ēt', n* the smaller, generally the male, gamete. [**micro-** (1a)]

microgram *mī'krə-gram, n* a micrograph, a photograph or drawing of an object under a microscope; a message typed and photographically reduced for sending by air, enlarged on receipt and printed on a card; the card concerned. [**micro-** (1f)]

microgranite *mī-krə-gran'it, n* a completely but minutely crystalline rock of the composition of granite. — *adj* **microgranit'ic**. [**micro-** (1a)]

micrograph *mī'krə-gräf, n* a pantograph instrument for minute writing or drawing; a minute picture; a drawing or photograph of a minute object as seen through a microscope. — *n* **micrographer** (*mī-krog'rə-fər*) a person who draws or describes microscopic objects. — *adj* **micrographic** (*mī-krə-graf'ik*) relating to micrography; minutely written or delineated; showing intergrowth of crystalline constituents on a microscopic scale (*geol*). — *n* **microg'raphy** study with the microscope; the description of microscopic objects. [**micro-** (1f) and Gr *graphein* to write]

microgravity *mī-krō-grav'i-ti, n* the state or condition of having little or no gravity. — Also *adj*. [**micro-** (1c)]

microgroove *mī'krə-groov, n* the fine groove of long-playing gramophone records. [**micro-** (1a)]

microhabitat *mī-krō-hab'i-tat* (*biol*) *n* a small area having environmental conditions differing from those of the surrounding area. [**micro-** (1d)]

microinjection *mī-krō-in-jek'shən, n* injection, eg into a single cell, performed under a microscope. — *vt* **microinject'**. [**micro-** (1a)]

microinstruction *mī'krō-in-struk-shən,* (*comput*) *n* a single, simple command encoding any of the individual steps, (eg add, compare) to be carried out by a computer. [**micro-** (1a)]

Microlepidoptera *mī-krō-lep-id-op'tər-ə, n pl* small moths of various kinds. [**micro-** (1a)]

microlight *mī'krə-līt, n* a very light, *usu* single-seat, aircraft having either fixed or flexible wings. — *adj* designating such an aircraft; very light in weight. — *n* **mī'crolighting**

the activity or sport of flying microlight aircraft. [**micro-** (1a)]

microlite *mī'krə-līt*, *n* a mineral composed of calcium, tantalum and oxygen, occurring in very small crystals; an incipient crystal, detected under the microscope by polarized light. — *n* **mī'crolith** a microlite; a very small stone implement of the Stone Age, *usu* used with a haft. — *adj* **microlith'ic**. — *adj* **microlitic** (*-lit'ik*). [**micro-** (1a) and Gr *lithos* a stone]

micrology *mī-krol'ə-ji*, *n* the study of microscopic objects; the study or discussion of trivialities. — *adj* **micrologic** (*-loj'*) or **microlog'ical**. — *adv* **microlog'ically**. — *n* **microl'ogist**. [Gr *mikros* little, and *logos* discourse]

micro-manipulation *mī-krō-mə-nip-ū-lā'shən*, *n* the technique of using delicate instruments, such as **micro-needles** and **micropipettes**, to work on cells, bacteria, etc, under high magnifications, or of working with extremely small quantities in microchemistry. [**micro-** (1b, c)]

micro-marketing *mī-krō-mär'kət-ing*, *n* marketing set in the context of individual business firms (cf **macro-marketing** under **macro-**). [**micro-** (1d)]

micromesh *mī'krō-mesh*, *adj* and *n* (having or made of) a very fine mesh, eg of hosiery. [**micro-** (1a)]

micro-meteorite *mī-krō-mē'tē-ə-rīt*, *n* a particle of meteoric dust too small to be consumed by friction in the atmosphere. [**micro-** (1a)]

micro-meteorology *mī-krō-mē-tē-ə-rol'ə-ji*, *n* the study of atmospheric conditions over a small area, and *usu* to a very limited height above the ground. [**micro-** (1d)]

micrometer *mī-krom'i-tər*, *n* an instrument, often attached to a microscope or telescope, for measuring very small distances or angles; (also **micrometer gauge** or **micrometer calliper** or **callipers**) an instrument which measures small widths, lengths, etc, to a high degree of accuracy. — *adj* **micrometric** (*mī-krə-met'rik*) or **micromet'rical**. — *n* **microm'etry** measuring with a micrometer. [**micro-** (1c)]

micrometer[2]. See **micrometre**.

micrometre or (*US*) **micrometer** *mī'krə-mē-tər*, *n* one millionth of a metre (denoted by μ). [**micro-** (2)]

micromicro- *mī-krō-mī-krō-* or before a vowel **micromicr-**, (*obs*; now **pico-**) *combining form* denoting a millionth of a millionth part, as in **micromicrocurie** (used in measuring the quantity of a radioactive substance present in stable material), **micromicrofarad**, etc. [**micro-** (2)]

micromillimetre *mī-krə-mil'i-mēt-ər*, *n* one millionth of a millimetre (*obs*; now **nan'omētre**); (*erroneously*) one thousandth of a millimetre. [**micro-** (2)]

micro-mini *mī'krō-min-i*, *adj* extremely small, micro-miniature. — *n* a very short miniskirt. [**micro-** (1a)]

microminiature *mī-krō-min'i-chər* or *-min'i-ə-chər*, *adj* made on an extremely small scale. — *n* **mīcro-miniaturizā'tion** or **-s-** reduction to extremely small size of scientific or technical equipment or any part of it. — *vt* **mīcromin'iaturize** or **-ise**. [**micro-** (1f)]

micron or **mikron** *mī'kron*, *n* a micrometre: — *pl* **mī'crons** or **mī'krons**, **mī'cra** or **mī'kra**. [Gr *mikron*, neuter of *mikros* little]

microneedle *mī'krō-nēd-l*, *n* a fine needle used in micro-manipulation (qv). [**micro-** (1b,c)]

Micronesian *mī-krə-nē'zhən*, *-zhyən*, *-zyən* or *-zi-ən*, *adj* of or relating to *Micronesia*, a group of small islands in the Pacific, north of New Guinea. — *n* a native or inhabitant of any of these islands. [Gr *mikros* little, and *nēsos* an island]

micronutrient *mī-krə-nū'tri-ənt*, *n* a nutritive substance required in minute quantities by a plant. — Also *adj*. [**micro-** (1a)]

micro-organism *mī-krō-ör'gən-izm*, *n* a microscopic (or ultramicroscopic) organism. [**micro-** (1a)]

micropalaeontology *mī-krō-pal-i-ion-tol'ə-ji*, *n* a branch of palaeontology dealing with microfossils. — *n* **micro-palaeontol'ogist**. [**micro-** (1a)]

micropegmatite *mī-krə-peg'mə-tīt*, *n* a micrographic intergrowth of quartz and feldspar. — *adj* **micropegmatitic** (*-tit'ik*). [**micro-** (1a)]

microphone *mī'krə-fōn*, *n* an instrument for intensifying sounds; a sensitive instrument (popularly contracted to **mike** *mīk*), similar to a telephone transmitter, for picking up sound waves to be broadcast or amplified and translating them, eg by means of a diaphragm and carbon granules, into a fluctuating electric current. — *adj* **microphonic** (*-fon'ik*). [Gr *mikros* small, and *phōnē* voice]

microphotograph *mī-krə-fōt'ə-gräf*, *n* strictly, a photograph reduced to microscopic size; loosely, a photomicrograph, or photograph of an object as magnified by the microscope. — *n* **microphotographer** (*-og'rə-fər*). — *adj* **microphotographic** (*-ə-graf'ik*). — *n* **micropho-tog'raphy**. [**micro-** (1f)]

microphyllous *mī-krō-fil'əs*, (*bot*) *adj* small-leaved. [Gr *mikros* little, and *phyllon* leaf]

microphysics *mī-krə-fiz'iks*, *n sing* physics dealing with subatomic particles. [**micro-** (1c)]

microphyte *mī'krō-fīt*, *n* a microscopic plant. — *adj* **microphyt'ic**. [**micro-** (1b)]

micropipette *mī-krō-pip-et'*, *n* a fine pipette used in micro-manipulation (qv). [**micro-** (1b,c)]

micropolis *mī-krop'ə-lis*, *n* a small city. [**micro-** (1a)]

micropore *mī'krō-pör*, *n* a very fine pore or opening in some material. — *n* **microporos'ity**. — *adj* **micro-por'ous**. — **microporous coatings** stains or clear coatings, intended for use on timbers, that allow a surface to breathe. [**micro-** (1a)]

microprint *mī'krō-print*, *n* a microphotograph of eg printed text, reproduced on paper, card, etc. — *adj* **mī'croprinted**. — *n* **mī'croprinting**. [**micro-** (1f)]

microprism *mī'krō-prizm*, *n* a tiny prism used as a focusing aid on a single-lens reflex camera, which produces a shimmering image until an object viewed through it is in focus. [**micro-** (1a)]

microprobe *mī'krō-prōb*, *n* a device that produces a very thin electron beam by means of which the chemical make-up of various compounds may be examined. [**micro-** (1b)]

microprocessor *mī-krō-prō'ses-ər*, *n* an integrated circuit on a silicon chip, or a number of these, acting as the central processing unit of a computer. — *n* **micro-prōcessing** [**micro-** (1f)]

micropropagation *mī-krō-pro-pə-gā'shən*, *n* propagation by growing new plants from single cells of the parent plant. [**micro-** (1c)]

micropsia *mī-krop'si-ə*, (*med*) *n* a condition of the eyes in which objects look smaller than usual. [Gr *mikros* little, and *opsis* appearance]

micropterous *mī-krop'tər-əs*, (*zool*) *adj* with reduced fins or hind-wings. [Gr *mikros* little, and *pteron* wing]

micropump *mī'krō-pump*, *n* a miniature pump surgically inserted under the skin to administer medication at regular intervals. [**micro-** (1a)]

micropyle *mī'krə-pīl*, *n* the orifice in the coats of the ovule leading to the apex of the nucellus, through which the pollen-tube commonly enters (*bot*); an opening by which a spermatozoon may enter an ovum (*zool*). — *adj* **micropy'lar**. [Gr *mikros* little, and *pylē* gate]

microscale *mī'krō-skāl*, *adj* extremely small-scale. [**micro-** (1a)]

microscope *mī'krə-skōp*, *n* an instrument for magnifying minute objects. — *adj* **microscopic** (*-skop'ik*) or **micro-scop'ical** relating to a microscope or to microscopy; magnifying; able to see minute objects; invisible or hardly visible without the aid of a microscope; minute. — *adv* **microscop'ically**. — *n* **microscopist** (*mī-kros'kop-ist* or *mī-krə-skō'pist*). — *n* **micros'copy**. — **acoustic microscope** one in which ultrasonic waves passed through the specimen are scanned by a laser beam; **come under the microscope** to be subjected to minute examination; **compound microscope** and **simple micro-scope** microscopes with respectively two lenses and a single lens; **electron**, **proton** and **ultraviolet microscope** one using a beam of electrons, protons, or ultraviolet rays respectively; **phase-contrast** (or **phase-difference**) **microscope** see under **phase**; **reflecting microscope** see under **reflect**. [Gr *mikros* little, and *skopeein* to look at]

microseism *mī'krə-sīzm*, *n* a slight earth-movement detectable only instrumentally. — *adj* **microseis'mic** or **microseis'mical**. — *n* **microseis'mograph** an instrument for recording microseisms and distant earthquakes. — *n* **microseismom'eter** an instrument for measuring microseisms. — *n* **microseismom'etry**. [Gr *mikros* little, and *seismos* earthquake]

microskirt. Same as **micro-mini** (n).

microsome *mī'krə-sōm*, *n* a minute granule or drop in cytoplasm. — *adj* **microsō'mal**. [Gr *mikros* little, and *sōma* body]

microspore *mī'krə-spör*, *n* the smaller of two forms of spore; a spore giving rise to a male gametophyte. — *n* **microsporangium** (*-spör-an'ji-əm*) a sporangium producing only microspores: — *pl* **microsporan'gia**. — *n* **microsporophyll** (*-spör'ə-fil*) a sporophyll that carries or subtends only microsporangia. [**micro-** (1a)]

microstructure *mī-krō-struk'chər* or *mī'*, *n* structure, *esp* of metals and alloys, as revealed by the microscope. [**micro-** (1a, b)]

microsurgery *mī-krō-sûr'jə-ri*, *n* surgery performed on cells or other very small plant or body structures, requiring the use of a microscope. — *n* **microsur'geon**. — *adj* **microsur'gical**. [**micro-** (1b)]

microswitch *mī'krō-switch*, *n* a minute electronic switch, activated by very slight movement or pressure. [**micro-** (1a)]

microtechnology *mī-krō-tek-nol'əj-i*, *n* microelectronic technology. [**micro-** (1f)]

microtome *mī'krə-tōm*, *n* an instrument for cutting thin sections of objects for microscopic examination. — *adj* **microtomic** (*-tom'ik*) or **microtom'ical**. — *n* **microtomist** (*-krot'ə-mist*). — *n* **microt'omy**. [Gr *mikros* little, and *tomē* a cut]

microtone *mī'krə-tōn*, (*music*) *n* an interval less than a semitone. — *adj* **microton'al**. — *n* **microtonal'ity**. [**micro-** (1a)]

microtubule *mī-krō-tū'būl*, *n* any of the relatively rigid structures in the cytoplasm of many plant and animal cells. — *adj* **microtū'būlar**. [**micro-** (1a)]

microtunneling *mī-krō-tun'əl-ing*, *n* a technique used in laying underground pipes, etc, in which miniature boring machines excavate the required channel without breaking or damaging the road surface. [**micro-** (1a)]

microwave *mī'krō-wāv*, *n* in radio communication, a wave having a very short wavelength; now *usu* a wave in the radiation spectrum between normal radio waves and infrared; a microwave oven. — Also *adj*. — *vt* to cook or defrost in a microwave oven. — *vi* to undergo microwaving. — *adj* **microwav'able** or **microwave'able** suitable for cooking, defrosting, or use in a microwave oven. — **microwave oven** an oven in which food is cooked or defrosted by the heat produced by microwaves passing through it; **microwave background** (*astron*) a background of microwave radiation, discovered in 1963, thought to be a relic of the Big Bang (also **cosmic background radiation**). [**micro-** (1a)]

microwire *mī'krō-wīr*, *n* a very strong, very fine filament of metal or other material. [**micro-** (1a)]

microwriter *mī-krō-rīt-ər*, *n* a hand-held five- or six-key device by means of which text can be generated on a printer or VDU. [**micro-** (1a)]

micrurgy *mī'krûr-ji*, *n* micro-manipulation. [**micro-** (1b, c) and Gr *-ourgos* (as in *metallourgos* working a mine), from *ergon* work]

Micrurus. See **Elaps**.

micturition *mik-tū-rish'ən*, (*med*) *n* the frequent desire to pass urine; the act of urinating. — *n* **mic'tion** (*obs*) voiding urine. — *vi* **mic'turate** (*irregularly formed*) to urinate. [L *micturīre*, *-ītum*, desiderative of *mingere*, *mi(n)ctum* to pass urine, *mi(n)ctiō*, *-ōnis* urination]

mid[1] *mid*, *adj* middle; situated between extremes; uttered with the tongue in a position between high and low (*phonetics*). — *n* the middle (*archaic* and *dialect*). — *adj* **midd'est** (*Spenser*) middle; middlemost. — *adj* **mid'most** middlemost. — *n* the very middle. — *adv* in the very middle. — *prep* in the very middle of. — *n* **midst** middle. — *adv* in the middle. — *prep* (also **'midst** as if for **amidst**) amidst (ME *middes*, from genitive of *mid*, with excrescent *t*, cf **whilst**; *perh* partly a *superl*). — **mid-age'** (*Shakesp*) middle age; **midair'** a region somewhat above the ground; the midst of a course through the air. — Also *adj*. — *adj* **mid-Atlan'tic** evincing both British and N American characteristics. — **mid'brain** the part of the brain derived from the second brain vesicle of the embryo; **mid'day** noon. — *adj* of, at, or relating to, noon. — **mid'field** the middle area of a football, etc pitch, not close to either team's goal; the players who operate in this area, acting as links between a team's defending and attacking players; **mid'fielder** a player in the midfield; **mid'-gut** (*biol*) that part of the alimentary canal formed from the original gastrula cavity and lined with endoderm; also, the small intestine; **mid'-heaven** the middle of the sky or of heaven; the meridian; **mid'-hour** the middle time; an intervening hour; **mid'iron** a heavy golf club used for long approach shots. — *adj* **mid'land** in the middle of, or surrounded by, land; distant from the coast; inland; *specif* (*esp* with *cap*) relating to or designating the central parts of England. — *n* the interior of a country; (in *pl*; *esp* with *cap*) the central parts of England. — **mid-leg'** the middle of the leg. — *adv* as high or deep as the middle of the leg. — **mid-Lent'** the middle of Lent; the fourth Sunday in Lent; **mid-life crisis** the feeling of panic, pointlessness, etc experienced at middle age by those who are concerned that they are no longer young; **midlitt'oral** that part of the seashore that lies between high and low neap tidemarks. — Also *adj*. — **mid-mor'ning**; **midnoon'** noon; **mid-o'cean** the middle of the ocean; **mid-ocean ridge** (*geol*) a major, largely submarine, mountain range where two plates are being pulled apart and new volcanic lithosphere is being created; **mid-off'** and **mid-on'** (*cricket*) a fielder on the *off* or *on* side respectively, nearly in line with the bowler; his or her position; **mid'-point** a point lying halfway between two other points (whether in time or space); a point lying at the centre of an area; **mid'rib** (*bot*) the rib along the middle of a leaf; **mid-sea'** the open sea; **mid-seas'on** (also *adj*). — *adj* **mid'ship** in the middle of a ship. — **mid'shipman** formerly, the title of a young officer (*orig* quartered *amidships*) entering the navy, later a junior ranking below a sub-lieutenant but above a naval cadet, now, since 1957, only a shore ranking used during training (shortened colloquially to **mid** or **midd'y**); **mid'shipmate** (*humorous*) a midshipman. — *adv* **mid'ships** amidships. — *adj* **mid'size** middle-sized, medium. — **mid-sky'** the middle of the sky; **midstream'** the middle of the stream. — *adv* in the middle of the stream. — **mid'summer** (also *-sum'*) the middle of the summer; the summer solstice, occurring about 21 June in the northern hemisphere; **Midsummer day** 24 June, a quarter-day in England, Wales and Ireland; **midsummer madness** temporary madness or erratic behaviour attributed to the hot sun of midsummer; **midsummer moon** the month during which midsummer occurs, associated with midsummer madness. — *adj* **mid-Victo'rian** of or characteristic of the middle part of Queen Victoria's reign (1837–1901). — *n* a person living in this period. — **mid'term** the middle of an academic term, term of office, etc; an examination held in the middle of an academic term (*US*). — *adj* relating to, or occurring at or around, the middle of term. — **mid'way** the middle of the way or distance (*obs*); a middle course (*archaic*); a central avenue in a fair or exhibition, or the sideshows, stalls, etc, set up there (*NAm*). — *adj* in the middle of the way or distance. — *adv* halfway. — *prep* halfway along or across. — **mid'-week** the middle of the week; (with *cap*) among Quakers, Wednesday (cf Ger *Mittwoch*). — *adj* in the middle of the week. — **Mid'west** Middle West. —

adj **Midwest'ern.** — **Midwest'erner**; **mid-wick'et** (*cricket*) a fielder on the on side, about midway between mid-on and square leg; his or her position; **mid-win'ter** the middle of winter; the winter solstice, occurring about 22 December in the northern hemisphere. — *adj* **mid'-year** in the middle of the (academic) year. [OE *midd*; cf Ger *Mitte*, L *medius*, Gr *mesos*]

mid[2]. Short for **midshipman** (see under **mid**[1]).

mid- *mid-*, *combining form* denoting the middle part of; of or in the middle of. [From **mid** (adj); not always hyphenated]

'mid or **mid**. Short form of **amid**.

MIDAS *mī'dəs*, *abbrev*: Missile Defence Alarm System.

Midas *mī'das*, (*Gr mythol*) *n* a king of Phrygia whose touch turned all to gold, and to whom Apollo gave ass's ears; a genus of marmosets. — **Midas's ear** a shell of the genus *Auricula*; **Midas touch** the ability to make money easily.

midbrain and **midday**. See under **mid**.

midden *mid'ən*, (*archaic*, *Scot* and *dialect*) *n* a dunghill; a refuse-heap or compost-heap; a mess, a clutter (*fig*); a kitchen-midden (*archaeol*). — **midd'en-cock** an ordinary, farmyard cock (as opposed to a gamecock); **midd'enstead** the site of a midden. [Scand, as Dan *mödding*, from *mög* dung; cf **muck**]

middle *mid'l*, *adj* equally distant (in measurement or in number of steps) from the extremes; avoiding extremes, done as a compromise; intermediate; intervening; of that voice which is intermediate between active and passive, reflexive or expressing an action in some way affecting the agent (*gram*); (with *cap*) (of languages) between Old and Modern (as *Middle English*, *Middle High German*, etc). — *vt* to place in the middle; to fold in the middle (*naut*); to hit (the ball) with the middle of the bat (*cricket*). — *n* the middle point, part or position; midst; the central portion, waist; the middle voice (*gram*); the middle term (*logic*); a middle article. — **middle-age'**. — *adj* **middle-aged'** (*-ājd'*) between youth and old age, variously reckoned to suit the reckoner. — **middle-age** (or **middle-aged**) **spread** a thickening of the body, *esp* the waist, attributable to the onset of middle-age; **Middle Ages** the time between the fall of the Western Roman empire and the Renaissance (5c–15c); **Middle America** the countries lying between the United States of America and Colombia, sometimes including the West Indies; the middle-class in the United States, *esp* the conservative elements of it. — *n* and *adj* **Middle-Amer'ican.** — **middle article** a newspaper article of literary or general rather than topical interest. — *adj* **midd'le-brack'et** in a midway grouping in a list. — **midd'lebreaker** (*US*) a lister. — *adj* **midd'lebrow** midway between highbrow and lowbrow. — Also *n*. — **middle C** the C in the middle of the piano keyboard; the first line below the treble or above the bass stave; **middle class** the section of society which comes between the aristocracy and the working-class. — *adj* **midd'le-class.** — **middle common room** (*abbrev* **MCR**) (in some universities) a common room for the use of post-graduate and mature students (cf **junior common room** under **junior**); **middle distance** (in a picture) the middle ground. — *adj* **midd'le-distance** (in athletics) of or denoting a race of 400, 800, or 1500 metres, or an athlete who takes part in such a race. — **middle ear** the part of the ear containing the malleus, incus and stapes; **midd'le-earth** the earth, considered as placed between the upper and lower regions; **Middle East** formerly, the countries from Iran to Burma (now Myanma); now generally used of an area including the Arabic-speaking countries around the eastern end of the Mediterranean Sea and in the Arabian Peninsula, sometimes along with Greece, Turkey, Cyprus, Iran and the greater part of N Africa. — *adj* **Middle-East'ern.** — **Middle-East'erner**; **middle eight** an eight-bar section occurring two-thirds of the way through a conventionally structured pop song and acting as a foil to the rest' of the piece; **Middle English** see under **English**; **middle game** the part of a chess game between the opening and the end game; **middle ground** the part of a picture between the foreground and background; a compromise position. — *adj* **midd'le-income** having, or relating to those who have, an average income which makes them neither rich nor poor. — **Middle Kingdom** China; the 11th and 12th dynasties in ancient Egypt (22c to 18c BC); **midd'leman** a person occupying a middle position; an intermediary, *esp* between producer and consumer; in Ireland, a person renting land in large tracts, and subletting it in smaller portions (*hist*); **middle management** the junior managerial executives and senior supervisory personnel in a firm. — *adj* **midd'lemost** nearest the middle. — **middle name** any name between a person's first name and surname; the notable quality or characteristic of a specified thing or person (*facetious*). — *adj* **middle-of-the-road'** midway between extremes; unexciting, mediocre. — **middle passage** (*hist*) the voyage across the Atlantic from Africa to the West Indies on board a slave-ship; **middle price** (of a stock market share) a price midway between the buying (offer) price and the selling (bid) price, as often shown in newspapers; **middle school** a school for children between the ages of about 9 to 13; in some secondary schools, an administrative unit *usu* comprising the third and fourth forms. — *adj* **midd'le-sized** of average size. — **Middle States** those states *orig* constituting the middle of the United States, ie New York, New Jersey, Pennsylvania and Delaware; **midd'le-stitching** monk's-seam; **middle term** (*logic*) that term of a syllogism which appears in both premises but not in the conclusion; **middle watch** that from midnight to 4 am; **midd'leweight** a weight category applied variously in boxing, wrestling and weightlifting; a sportsman of the specified weight for the category (eg in professional boxing above welterweight, **light'-middleweight** (maximum 70 kg/154 lb), **midd'leweight** (maximum 73 kg/160 lb), **su'per-middleweight** (maximum 77 kg/170 lb)); **Middle West** the region of the USA between the Appalachians and the Rockies, the Mississippi basin as far south as Kansas, Missouri, and the Ohio River. — *adj* **Middle Western.** — **Middle Westerner**; **midd'le-world** middle-earth. — **in the middle of** occupied with, engaged in (doing something); during; while. [OE *middel* (adj); Du *middel*, Ger *Mittel*; see **mid**[1]]

middling *mid'ling*, *adj* intermediate (*obs*); moderate (*colloq*); indifferent; mediocre; fairly good. — *adv* (*colloq*) fairly; fairly well. — *n* (*usu* in *pl*) goods of a middle quality, size or price; the coarser part of ground wheat; partially concentrated ore. [Orig Scots, from **mid**[1] and sfx **-ling**]

Middx *abbrev*: Middlesex.

middy[1] *mid'i*, *n* a colloquial short form of **midshipman**; (also **middy blouse**) a loose blouse worn, *esp* formerly, by women and *esp* children, having a collar with a broad flap at the back in the style of a sailor's uniform.

middy[2] *mid'i*, (*Austr colloq*) *n* a measure of beer, varying in amount from one place to another; the glass containing it. [Ety doubtful]

midfield, etc. See under **mid**.

Midgard *mid'gärd*, (*Scand mythol*) *n* the abode of men, middle-earth. [ON *mithgarthr* mid-yard]

midge *mij*, *n* a small gnat-like fly, *esp* of the family *Chironomidae*; a very small person. — *n* **midg'et** something very small of its kind; a very small person. [OE *mycg*, *mycge*; Ger *Mücke*]

Midi *mē-dē'*, *n* the south (of France). — *n* **midinette** (*-net'*) a young female worker, *esp* a shop assistant, in the Paris fashion or millinery business (apparently much seen in cafés at lunchtime). [Fr *midi*, midday; *midinette* is said to be from *midi* and *dînette* snack]

midi *mid'i*, *n* short for **midi-coat**, **midi-skirt**, etc, or **midi-system**.

midi- *mid'i-*, *combining form* denoting something of middle size, length, etc. — **mid'i-coat**, **mid'i-skirt**, etc a coat, skirt, etc, reaching to about mid-calf; **mid'i-system** a (*usu* one-piece) music system, resembling a medium-sized stack system, ie with CD, tape deck, etc, stacked vertically. [**mid**[1]; cf **mini-**]

midland, midmost, etc. See under **mid**[1].

midnight *mid'nīt, n* the middle of the night; twelve o'clock at night; pitch darkness (*fig*). — *adj* of or at midnight; dark as midnight. — *adj* and *adv* **mid'nightly** (occurring) every midnight. — **midnight blue** very dark, blackish blue; **midnight feast** a secret feast held during the night, *esp* by children; **midnight sun** the sun visible at midnight during summer in the polar regions. — **burn the midnight oil** see under **burn**[2]. [**mid-** and **night**]

mid-ocean ... to ... **midrib**. See under **mid**.

Midrash *mid'rash, n* the Hebrew exposition of the Old Testament, divided into *Haggada* and *Halachah*: — *pl* **Midrashim** (*mid-rä'shēm*) commentaries on individual books or sections of the Old Testament. [Heb, exposition]

midriff *mid'rif, n* the diaphragm, the division in the middle of the body between the abdomen and the thorax, or stomach and chest; (loosely) the area of the body, or of clothing, from below the breast down to the waist. [OE *midd* middle, and *hrif* belly]

midshipman and **midst**. See under **mid**[1].

midstream... to ... **mid-wicket**. See under **mid**[1].

midwife *mid'wīf, n* a woman, or occasionally a man, who assists women in childbirth: — *pl* **midwives** (*mid'wīvz*). — *vt* (also **mid'wive** *-wīv*) to assist in the birth of (a child) (also *fig*): — *pr p* **mid'wīfing** or **mid'wīving**; *pa t* and *pa p* **-wīfed** or **-wīved**. — *n* **mid'wifery** (*-wif-ə-ri, -wif-ri, -if-ri* or *-wīf'ri*) the art or practice of a midwife; assistance at childbirth; obstetrics. — **midwife toad** either of two species of small European toad (*Alytes obstetricians* and *Alytes cisternasi*), so called because the males bear the fertilized eggs on their backs until they hatch. [OE *mid* with (Ger *mit*, Gr *meta*), and *wīf* woman]

midwinter. See under **mid**[1].

mien *mēn, n* an air or look, manner, bearing (*literary*); a facial expression (*obs*). [Perh **demean**, influenced by Fr *mine*, of unknown origin]

mieve *mēv*, (*Spenser*) *vt*. Same as **move**.

miff *mif*, (*colloq*) *n* a slight feeling or fit of resentment; a minor quarrel, a tiff. — *vt* to put in a bad mood, annoy or offend. — *vi* to take offence; (of a plant) to wither away or fade (with *off*). — *adj* **miffed**. — *adv* **miff'ily**. — *n* **miff'iness**. — *adj* **miff'y** quick to take offence, touchy; (of a plant) liable to wither away or fade. — Also (*obs*) **mift'y**. [Cf Ger *muffen* to sulk]

MiG or **mig** *mig*, (*aeronautics*) *abbrev*: *Mi*koyan and *G*urevich (Soviet aircraft designers).

might[1] *mīt, pa t* of **may**[1]. — **mightst** and **mightest** see under **may**[1]. — **might'-have-been** a person who, or thing which, might have been, or might have come to something.

might[2] *mīt, n* power; ability; strength; energy or intensity of purpose or feeling. — *adj* **might'ful** (*Shakesp*) mighty; powerful. — *adv* **might'ily**. — *n* **might'iness** the state of being mighty; power; greatness; great amount; a title of dignity; excellency. — *adj* **might'y** having greater power; strong; valiant; very great; important; exhibiting might; wonderful. — *adv* (now *colloq*, *usu* with a tinge of irony except in *US*) very. — **might and main** utmost strength.

mignon *mē-nyɔ̃*, (*Fr*) *adj* small and dainty: — *fem* **mignonne** (*mē-nyon*).

mignonette *min-yə-net', n* any of various plants of the *Reseda* genus, including a fragrant garden annual with green flowers; a fine kind of lace. [Fr *mignonette*, fem dimin of *mignon* daintily small, a darling]

migraine (from 18c) *mē'grān* or *mī'* or **megrim** (from 14c) *mē'grim, n* a severe throbbing pain affecting only one half of the head or face and *usu* accompanied by nausea; a condition marked by recurring migraines; (for the following meanings, **megrim**) vertigo; (in *pl*) lowness of spirits; a caprice (*archaic*). — *n* **migraineur** (*-œr'*) a person who suffers migraines. — *adj* **mi'grainous**. [Fr *migraine*, from Gr *hēmikrāniā*, from *hēmi* half, and *krānion* skull]

migrate *mī-grāt', vi* to pass from one place to another; to change one's place of abode to another country, etc; to change habitat according to the season; to move (as parasites, phagocytes, etc) to another part of the body; to pass in a stream (as ions or particles). — *n* **mi'grant** a person or animal that migrates or is migrating. — Also *adj*. — **migrā'tion** a change of abode; a removal from one country or climate to another, *esp* in a large number; a number moving together in this way. — *n* **migrā'tionist** a person who emigrates; a person who explains facts by a theory of migration. — *n* **mi'grātor**. — *adj* **mi'gratory** (*-grə-tə-ri*) migrating, or accustomed to migration; wandering. — *n* **migrant worker** a person, *esp* an agricultural worker, who moves from place to place, or to another country, in search of work. [L *migrāre, -ātum*; cf *meāre* to go]

mihrab *mē-räb'* or *mēhh', n* a niche or slab in a mosque marking the direction of Mecca. [Ar *mihrāb*]

mikado *mi-kä'dō*, (*hist*) *n* a title given by foreigners to the Emperor of Japan: — *pl* **mika'dos**. [Jap, exalted gate]

mike[1] *mīk, n* a contraction of **microphone** or **microscope**.

mike[2]. Variant of **mick**.

mikron. See **micron**.

mil *mil, n* a unit (1/1000in) in measuring the diameter of wire; a proposed coin = £1/1000; (in Cyprus) a coin of this value; (in pharmacy) a millilitre; (in the building trade, etc) a millimetre; a unit of angular measurement, used *esp* with artillery, equal to 1/6400 of a circle or 0.05625°. [L *mīlle* a thousand]

mil. or **milit**. *abbrev*: military.

milady or **miladi** *mi-lād'i, n* a term of address used for an aristocratic or rich English lady, eg by household staff. [Fr modification of **my lady**]

milage. See under **mile**.

milch *milch* or *milsh, adj* giving milk. — **milch'-cow** a cow yielding milk or kept for milking; a ready source of gain or money (*fig*). [OE *milce* (found in the compound *thri-milce* May, when cows can be milked thrice a day); cf **milk**]

mild *mīld, adj* gentle in temper and disposition; not sharp or bitter; acting gently; gently and pleasantly affecting the senses; soft; calm. — *n* mild ale. — *vt* **mild'en** to make mild. — *vi* to become mild. — *adv* **mild'ly**. — *n* **mild'ness**. — **mild ale** formerly, new ale, without the taste that comes from keeping; now ale with less hop flavouring than pale ale. — *adj* **mild-spok'en** having a mild manner of speech. — **mild steel** steel containing very little carbon. — **put it mildly** to understate the case. [OE *milde* mild; cf Ger *mild*, ON *mildr*, gracious, etc]

mildew *mil'dū, n* honeydew (*obs*); a disease on plants, caused by the growth of minute fungi (*Erysiphe, Oidium*, etc); a similar appearance on other things or of another kind; a fungus causing the disease. — *vt* to taint with mildew. — *adj* **mil'dewy**. [OE *meledēaw, mildēaw*, from a lost word for honey, and *dēaw* dew; influenced by *melu* meal]

mile *mīl, n orig*, a Roman unit of length, 1000 (double) paces (*mīlle passūs* or *passuum*; about 1611 English yards); applied to various later units, now in Britain and the USA to one of 1760 yards or 5280 feet (1.61km.), the *statute mile*; a great distance or length (*colloq*). — *n* **mīl'age** or **mile'age** the total number of miles covered by a motor vehicle, etc; (also **milage** or **mileage allowance**) travelling allowance at so much a mile; miles travelled per gallon of fuel; use, benefit (*fig colloq*). — *n* **mī'ler** a runner of a mile race. — **mile'-castle** any of a series of small forts placed at mile intervals along a Roman wall; **mileom'eter** or **mīlom'eter** an instrument that records the number of miles that a vehicle, etc has travelled; **mile'-post** or **mile'stone** a post or stone marker showing distance in miles; a stage or reckoning-point; an important event, stage, etc (*fig*). — **geographical** or **nautical mile** one minute of latitude measured along the equator — 6082.66ft; in British practice, *Admiralty measured mile*, 6080ft (1.8532km); *international nautical mile* — official unit in the USA since 1954 — 6076.1033ft, or 1.852km; **Irish mile** (*obs*) 2240 yards; **Scots mile** (*obs*) about 1976 yards. [OE *mīl*, from L *mīlia*, pl of *mīlle* (*passuum*) a thousand (paces)]

miles gloriosus *mē'lāz glör-ē-ō'səs, mī'lēs, glōr-* or *-sōōs*, (*L*) *n* a vainglorous soldier, used as a stock character in Roman and later comedy: — *pl* **milites gloriosi** (*mē'lē-tāz glör-ē-ō'sē, mī'li-tēz, glōr-* or *-sī*). [From the eponymous hero of a play by Plautus]

Milesian[1] *mi-lē'zyən, -zhyən, -zhən* or *mī-*, *adj* of or relating to *Miletus*, an Ionian Greek city in Asia Minor. — *n* a native or citizen of Miletus. — **Milesian tales** witty voluptuous tales, from a lost book so called, by Aristides 'of Miletus' (2c BC). [Gr *Mīlēsios*, from *Mīlētos*]

Milesian[2] *mi-lē'shyən, -shən, -zhyən, -zhən* or *mī-*, *adj* of or relating to *Milesius* or *Miledh*, a mythical king of Spain, or his sons and their followers who seized Ireland; Irish. — *n* (*usu joc*) an Irishman.

milfoil *mil'foil*, *n* yarrow, or any other species of *Achillea*; extended to other plants with finely divided leaves, such as **water milfoil** (*Myriophyllum*, family *Haloragidaceae*). [OFr, from L *mīllefolium*, from *mīlle* a thousand, and *folium* a leaf]

miliary *mil'i-ər-i*, *adj* of or like millet-seed; characterized by small skin eruptions resembling millet-seed (*med*). — *n* **miliaria** (*mil-i-ā'ri-ə*; *med*) prickly-heat. [L *miliārius*, from *milium* millet]

Milice *mil-is*, (*Fr*) *n* the government militia in Vichy France. — *n* **Milicien** a member of this: — *pl* **Miliciens** (*mil-is-yẽ*). [Fr, militia]

milieu *mēl-yø'*, *n* environment, setting, medium, element: — *pl* **milieus'** or **milieux'** (*-yø*). [Fr, middle]

milit. *abbrev*: military.

militant *mil'it-ənt*, *adj* fighting; engaged in warfare; actively contending; combative; using violence; militaristic; strenuously active in support of a particular cause. — *n* a person who takes active part in a struggle; someone who seeks to advance a cause by violence; a strenuously active supporter of a particular cause; (with *cap*) a member of **Militant Tendency**, an extreme left-wing organization, formerly within the British Labour Party. — *n* **mil'itancy**. — *adv* **mil'itantly**. — *vi* **mil'itate** to serve as a soldier (*archaic*); to contend; to have weight, tell (*esp* with *against*); to fight for a cause. [Fr, from L *mīlitānt-* pr p stem of *mīlitāre*, *-ātum* serve as a soldier]

military *mil'i-tə-ri*, *adj* of or relating to soldiers, armies, or warfare; warlike. — *n* soldiery; the army; a soldier (*obs*). — *adj* **mil'itar** (*obs*) military. — *adv* **mil'itarily**. — *n* **mil'itarism** an excess of the military spirit; domination by an army, or military class or ideals; belief in the merits of such domination; a tendency to overvalue military power or to view things from the soldier's point of view. — *n* **mil'itarist** a soldier (*Shakesp*); a student of military science; a person imbued with militarism. — *adj* **militarist'ic**. — *n* **militarīzā'tion** or **-s-**. — *vt* **mil'itarize** or **-ise** to reduce or convert to a military model or method; to make militaristic; to subject to military domination. — **military academy** a training college for army officer cadets; **military band** a band of brasses, woodwinds, and percussion; **military cross** a decoration (*abbrev* **MC**) awarded since 1914 to army officers (below major) and warrant officers; **military honours** see under **honour**; **military medal** a medal awarded since 1916 to non-commissioned and warrant officers and serving men; **military police** a body of men and women functioning as a police force within the army; **military policeman** and **policewoman**. — **church militant** see under **church**. [Fr *militaire*, from L *mīlitāris* military, from *mīles*, *-itis*, a soldier]

militaria *mil-i-tā'ri-ə*, *n pl* weapons, uniforms, and other things connected with wars past and present. [**military**, and noun suffix *-ia*; or L, things military, neuter pl of *militāris* military]

militarize, etc. See under **military**.

militia *mi-lish'ə*, *n* a body of men enrolled and drilled as soldiers, but only liable to home service (transformed in 1908 into the Special Reserve; again called militia, 1921); the National Guard and its reserve (*US*); any military force made up of civilians, of varying size and standard of training, often hastily established in time of emergency; a general levy; a territorial force; troops of the second line. — **milit'iaman**. [L *mīlitia* military service or force, from *mīles*, *-itis* a soldier]

milk *milk*, *n* a white liquid secreted by female mammals for the nourishment of their young; a milklike juice or preparation; lactation. — *vt* to squeeze or draw milk from; to supply with milk; to extract money, venom, etc from; to extract; to manipulate or exploit, as if milking a cow. — *vi* to yield milk. — *adj* **milk'en** (*rare*) of or like milk. — *n* **milk'er** a person who milks cows, etc; a machine for milking cows; a cow that gives milk. — *adv* **milk'ily**. — *n* **milk'iness** cloudiness; mildness. — *n* **milk'ing** the act or art of milking (*lit* or *fig*); the amount of milk drawn at one time. — Also *adj*. — *adj* **milk'less**. — *adj* **milk'like**. — *adj* **milk'y** made of, full of, like, or yielding, milk; clouded; soft; gentle. — *adj* **milk-and-wa'ter** insipid; wishy-washy. — **milk'-bar** a shop selling milk, milk-shakes, etc for drinking on the premises; **milk cap** any fungus of the large and mainly inedible genus *Lactarius*, so called because of a milky fluid that it exudes when bruised; **milk chocolate** eating chocolate made from cocoa, cocoa-butter, sugar, and condensed or dried milk; **milk'-cow** a milch-cow; **milk-denti'tion** the first set of teeth; **milk'en-way** (*Bacon*) the Milky Way; **milk'-fever** a fever accompanying the secretion of milk shortly after childbirth; in cows, a condition that may occur (without fever) after calving, characterized by low sugar and calcium levels in the blood, paralysis and unconsciousness; **milk'fish** a large silvery fish (*Chanos chanos*) of the Pacific and Indian Oceans, widely used as food and often bred in fish-farms; a percoid fish (*Parascorpis typus*) of the coastal water of southern Africa; **milk'-float** a small, open-sided vehicle used to deliver milk on a milk round; **milk'-gland** a mammary gland; **milk glass** a *usu* white, but sometimes coloured, opaque glass; **milk gravy** (*NAm*) creamy gravy made with milk; **milk'-house** a place for keeping milk; **milking machine** a machine for milking cows; **milking-parlour** see under **parlour**; **milk'ing-stool** a stool on which the milker sits; **milk'ing-time**; **milk'-kinship** the bond arising from fostering; **milk'-leg** the painful swelling of a woman's leg due to thrombosis of the femoral veins after childbirth, white leg. — *adj* **milk-liv'ered** (*Shakesp*) white-livered, cowardly. — **milk'-loaf** a loaf of a sweetish kind of bread; **milk'maid** a woman or girl who milks cows, or works in a dairy; **milk'man** a man who sells or delivers milk; **milk'-molar** a grinding milk-tooth, shed and superseded by a premolar; **milk'-pan** a saucepan with a pouring lip on one or each side, used for heating milk, etc; **milk'-porridge** porridge made with milk instead of water; **milk-pudd'ing** rice, tapioca, etc, cooked with milk; **milk-punch'** a drink made of milk, rum or whisky, sugar, and nutmeg; **milk round** a milkman's normal morning route; the periodic recruitment of undergraduates by large companies; **milk'-run** a milkman's morning round; a routine flight (*US airforce slang*); any routine or uneventful journey or enterprise (*US slang*) **milk-shake'** a drink made from cold milk shaken up with a flavouring and sometimes ice cream; a stimulating drench containing sodium bicarbonate given to a racehorse before a race (*slang*); **milk sickness** trembles; the acute trembling, vomiting and weakness occurring in humans as a result of the consumption of meat or dairy products of cattle afflicted with trembles; **milk snake** *Lampropeltis doliata*, a non-venomous, N American snake of the Colubridae family, popularly believed to milk cattle; **milk'-sop** a piece of bread sopped or soaked in milk; a soft, unadventurous, effeminate man; **milk stout** stout sweetened with lactose; **milk'-sugar** lactose; **milk'-thistle** lady's thistle (*Silybum marianum*), with white-veined leaves; **milk'-tooth** one of the first or deciduous set of teeth; **milk train** a local, early morning train service; a slow train stopping at small, local stations; an early morning flight or patrol (*airforce slang*); **milk'-tree** a tree yielding a milklike nourishing juice, such as the cow-tree of Venezuela, or the massaranduba of Pará; **milk'-vetch** a plant of the genus *Astragalus*, cultivated as fodder and supposed to increase yield of milk; **milk'-walk** a milkman's round. — *adj* **milk'-warm** warm as new milk. — **milk'-weed** a plant of the genus *Asclepias*, from its milky juice (**milk-weed butterfly** the monarch butterfly). — *adj* **milk'-white**. — **milk'wood** any of various trees with latex; **milk'wort** a plant (producing *Polygala*) supposed by some to promote the production of milk in women (**sea'-milkwort** Glaux); **Milky Way** the Galaxy. — **milk and honey** abundance, plenty; luxury; **milk of human kindness** (*Shakesp*) compassionate nature; **milk of lime** or **milk of magnesia** a suspension of calcium hydroxide or magnesium hydroxide in water; **milk of sulphur** precipitated sulphur. [OE (Mercian) *milc* (WSax *meolc*) milk; Ger *Milch* milk; L *mulgēre*, Gr *amelgein*, to milk]

milko *mil'kō*, (*Austr colloq*) *n* a milkman. [From the cry 'Milk-Oh!']

mill[1] *mil*, *n* a machine for grinding by crushing between hard, rough surfaces, or for more or less similar operations; a building or factory where corn, wheat etc, is ground, or manufacture of some kind is carried on, such as spinning and weaving, paper-making, sawing of timber; a place or institution which mass-produces anything, *esp* in an impersonal or factory-like manner (*fig*); a snuffbox (also **mull**), *orig* one with grinding apparatus (*Scot*); a boxing match (*dated slang*). — *vt* to grind; to press, stamp, roll, cut into bars, full, furrow the edges of, or otherwise treat in a mill; to froth up; to beat severely with the fists (*dated slang*); to turn over in the mind, to mull (with *over*). — *vi* to move round in a curve; to practise the business of a miller; to box (*dated slang*); (often with *about* or *around*) (of a crowd) to move in an aimless and confused manner. — *adj* **milled** prepared by a grinding-mill or a coining-press; transversely grooved on the edge (as a coin or screw-head); treated by machinery, *esp* smoothed by calendering rollers in a paper-mill. — *n* **mill'er** a person who owns or works a mill. — *n* **mill'ing** the business of a miller; the act of passing anything through a mill; the act of fulling cloth; the process of turning and ridging the edge of a screw-head or coin; a gruelling; aimless and confused movement of a crowd. — *n* **milloc'racy** a governing class of mill-owners, or their rule. — *n* **mill'ocrat**. — **mill'board** stout pasteboard, used *esp* in binding books; **mill'dam** the dam of a millpond; a millpond; a millrace or tail-race (*Scot*); **miller's dog** same as **tope**[3]; **miller's-thumb'** the bull-head; **mill'-eye** the opening by which meal comes from a mill; **mill'-girl**; **mill'-hand** a worker in a mill; **mill'-head** (*mineral ext*) ore accepted for processing after removal of waste rock and detritus; **mill'-horse** a horse that turns a mill; **milling cutter** a hardened steel disc or cylinder with teeth on the periphery and faces, used in a milling machine for grooving, slotting, etc; **milling grade** (*mineral ext*) ore sufficiently rich, in eg metal, to repay the cost of processing; **milling machine** a machine-tool for shaping metal, with rotating cutters; **mill'-owner**; **mill'pond** a pond to hold water for driving a mill (proverbially smooth); the Atlantic Ocean (*facetious*); **mill'race** the current of water that turns a mill-wheel, or the channel in which it runs; **mill'rind** an iron support fitted across the hole in an upper millstone; **mill'run** a millrace; a test of the quality or mineral content of ore or rock by milling it; **mill'scale** scale formed on iron or steel during heating for forging; **mill-six'pence** (*Shakesp*) a milled sixpence; **mill'stone** either of the two stones used in a mill for grinding corn; a very heavy burden (*fig*); **millstone-grit'** a hard, gritty sandstone suitable for millstones; (with *cap*) a series of grits, sandstones, shales, underlying the British Coal Measures; **mill'-stream** the stream of water that turns a mill-wheel; **mill'tail** a tailrace; **mill'-tooth** a molar; **mill'-wheel** a waterwheel used for driving a mill; **mill'-work** the machinery of a mill; the planning and putting up of machinery in mills; **mill'wright** a wright or mechanic who builds and repairs mills. — *adj* **run-of-the-mill** see under **run**. — **gastric mill** in Malacostraca, a digestive organ, sometimes known as the stomach, provided with muscles and ossicles for the trituration of food; **go** or **put through the mill** to undergo or subject to probationary hardships, suffering or experience, or severe handling; **see through a millstone** to see far into or through difficult questions. [OE *myln*, from LL *molīna*, from L *mola* a mill, from *molere* to grind]

mill[2] *mil*, *n* the thousandth part of a US or Canadian dollar (not coined); a mil. [L *mīlle* a thousand]

mill[3] *mil*, (*slang*) *vt* and *vi* to rob; to steal.

mille *mēl*, (*Fr*) *n* thousand. — *n* **millefeuille** or **millefeuilles** (*mēl-fœy'*; Fr *feuille* leaf) a layered cake made with puff-pastry, cream etc; **millefleurs** (*mēl-flœr*; Fr *fleur* flower) a perfume prepared from many kinds of flowers; (also **mille fleurs**) a pattern of small, scattered flowers, used as a background in tapestry, on porcelain, etc.

millefiori *mēl-e-fē-ō'rē*, *n* an ornamental glass-making technique, in which variously coloured rods are fused together and cut into transverse sections, often for embedding in clear glass; glass produced in this way (also **millefiori glass**). [Ital, thousand flowers]

millenary *mil'in-ər-i* (also *-ēn'* or *-en'*), *n* a thousand; a thousand years; a thousandth anniversary; a signatory of the Millenary Petition (*hist*); a believer in the millennium. — *adj* consisting of a thousand, or a thousand years; relating to the millennium or to belief in it. — *adj* **millenā'rian** relating to the millennium. — *n* a believer in the millennium. — *n* **millenā'rianism**. — *n* **mill'enarism**. — **Millenary Petition** (*hist*) a petition of Puritan tendency, signed by nearly a thousand clergymen, presented to James VI and I on arrival in London in 1603. [L *mīllēnārius* of a thousand, from *mīlle* thousand]

millennium *mil-en'i-əm*, *n* a thousand years; a thousandth anniversary, millenary; the thousand years after the second coming of Christ; (*usu ironical*) a coming golden age: — *pl* **millenn'ia** or **millenn'iums**. — *adj* **millenn'ial**. — *n* **millenn'ialist** a believer in the millennium. — *n* **millenn'ianism**. — *n* **millenn'iarism**. [L *mīlle* a thousand, and *annus* a year]

millepede. See **millipede**.

millepore *mil'i-pōr* or *-pör*, *n* a hydrozoan coral with many pores or polyp-cells. [L *mīlle* a thousand, and *porus*, from Gr *poros* a passage]

miller. See under **mill**[1].

Millerian *mil-ēr'i-ən*, *adj* relating to W H *Miller* (1801–80), mineralogist, or to the crystallographic notation used by him, by which a plane is represented by indices (*Miller* or *crystal indices*) which are the reciprocals of its intercepts on the axes (expressed as fractions of the parameters). — *n* **mill'erite** native nickel sulphide, crystallizing in needles, named in his honour.

millesimal *mil-es'im-əl*, *adj* thousandth; consisting of thousandth parts. — *adv* **milles'imally**. [L *mīllēsimus*, from *mīlle* a thousand]

millet *mil'it*, *n* a food-grain (*Panicum miliaceum*); extended to other species and genera (*Setaria*, *Panicum*, etc). — **mill'et-grass** a tall, panicled woodland grass (*Milium effusum*); **mill'et-seed**. — *adj* of the size or appearance of seeds of millet; miliary. [Fr *millet*, from L *milium*]

milli- *mil'i-*, *combining form* in names of units, denoting a thousandth part. — *n* **mill'iampere**, **mill'iare** (*-är*), **mill'ibar**, **mill'ilitre**, etc, a thousandth part of an *ampere*, *are*, *bar*, *litre*, etc. — **millimicro-** (*obs*) *combining form* same as **nano-**. — **millimilli-** (*obs*) *combining form* same as **micro-**. [L *mīlle* a thousand]

Millian *mil'i-ən, n* a follower of the philosopher John Stuart *Mill* (1806–73). — Also *adj.*

milliard *mil'yärd, n* a thousand million. [Fr, from L *mīlle* a thousand]

milliary *mil'i-ər-i, adj* relating to a Roman mile. — *n* a Roman milestone. [L *mīliārius, -a, -um*]

millibar. See **bar**[2].

millième *mēl-yem', n* a coin representing one thousandth of the basic unit of currency, as in Egypt. — Also **millime** (*mē-lēm'*) in Tunisia. [Fr, from L *mīlle* a thousand]

millilitre *mil'i-lē-tər, n* a unit of volume, a thousandth of a litre (*abbrev* **ml**). [**milli-**]

millimetre *mil'i-mē-tər, n* a unit of length, a thousandth of a metre (*abbrev* **mm**). [**milli-**]

millimole *mil'i-mōl,* (*chem*) *n* a thousandth of a mole (*abbrev* **mmol**). [**milli-** and **mole**[1]]

milliner *mil'in-ər, n orig* a dealer in goods made in *Milan*, or 'fancy goods'; a person who makes or sells women's headgear, trimmings, etc. — *n* **mill'inery** the articles made or sold by milliners; the industry of making them. — **horse'-milliner** see under **horse**; **man-milliner** see under **man**. [*Milaner* a trader in Milan wares, *esp* silks and ribbons]

million *mil'yən, n* a thousand thousands (1 000 000); a very great number; a million pounds, dollars, etc; (in *pl*) the guppy. — Also *adj.* — *n* **millionaire** (*-ār'*) a person with resources worth a million pounds, dollars, etc (more or less): — *fem* **millionair'ess**. — *adj* **mill'ionary** relating to, or consisting of, millions. — *adj* and *adv* **mill'ionfold** (*usu* preceded by *a* or a numeral). — *adj* and *n* **mill'ionth** the ten hundred thousandth. — **the million** the mass of people generally, the multitude. [Fr, from LL *mīlliō, -ōnis,* from L *mīlle* a thousand]

millipede or **millepede** *mil'i-pēd, n* any myriapod of the class Chilognatha, vegetarian cylindrical animals with many joints, most of which bear two pairs of legs; a woodlouse (*rare*). — Also **mill'iped** or **mill'eped** (*-ped*). [L *mīllepeda* a woodlouse, from *mīlle* a thousand, and *pēs, pēdis* a foot]

millirem *mel'i-rem, n* a unit of radiation dosage, a thousandth of a rem. [**milli-**]

millisecond *mil'i-sek-ənd, n* a thousandth of a second (*abbrev* **ms**). [**milli-**]

millisievert *mil'i-sē-vert, n* a unit of radiation dosage, a thousandth of a sievert (*abbrev* **msv**). [**milli-**]

mill-mountain *mil'mownt'ən, n* purging flax (see under **flax**). [Origin unknown]

Mills bomb or **grenade** *milz bom* or *gri-nād',* a type of grenade, invented by Sir William *Mills* (1856–1932), used by the British forces in both World Wars.

milo *mī'lō, n* any of several drought-resistant varieties of sorghum, *orig* from Africa but introduced elsewhere, cultivated as a grain and fodder crop: — *pl* **mī'los**. — Also **milo maize**. [Sotho *maili*]

milometer. See **mileometer** under **mile**.

milord *mi-lörd'* or (*rare*) **milor**, *n* a term of address for an aristocratic or rich Englishman, eg by household staff. [Fr modification of **my lord**]

Milquetoast *milk'tōst, n* (also without *cap*) a very timid, unassertive person. [From the comic-strip character Caspar *Milquetoast* created by the American cartoonist H T Webster c.1952]

milreis *mil'rās, n* 1000 reis; a former Portuguese coin superseded by the escudo; a former Brazilian coin (now cruzeiro): — *pl* **mil'reis**. [Port, thousand reis]

milsey *mil'si,* (*Scot*) *n* a milk-strainer. [**milk**, and either **sye** or **sile**]

milt *milt* or **melt** *melt, n* the spleen (also, in Jewish cookery, **miltz** *milts*); the soft roe of male fishes. — *vt* (of fishes) to impregnate. — *n* **milt'er** a male fish, *esp* in the breeding season. [OE *milte,* Ger *Milz* spleen]

miltonia *mil-tō'ni-ə, n* a plant of the *Miltonia* genus of tropical American orchids with brightly-coloured flowers. [After Charles Fitzwilliam, Viscount *Milton* (1786–1857), English statesman and horticulturist]

Miltonic *mil-ton'ik, adj* relating to John *Milton* (1608–1674), English poet; relating to or in the characteristic style of his poetry. — *adj* and *n* **Miltonian** (*-tōn'i-ən*). — *n* **Mil'tonism** (*-tən-izm*). — **Miltonic sonnet** see under **sonnet**.

Miltown® *mil'town, n* meprobamate.

miltz. See **milt**.

Milvus *mil'vəs, n* the kite genus of birds of prey. — *adj* **mil'vine**. [L *milvus* a kite]

mim *mim,* (*Scot* and *dialect*) *adj* demure, prim. — *adj* **mim-mou'd'** (*-mōōd;* Scots form of **mouthed**). [Imit]

mimbar *mim'bär* or **minbar** *min', n* a mosque pulpit. [Ar *minbar*]

mime *mīm, n* (in ancient Greek and Roman theatre) a farcical play making great use of flamboyant gesture and facial expression; an actor in such a farce; a play without dialogue, relying solely on movement, expression, etc; an actor in such a play (also **mime artist**); acting without words; a mimic; a buffoon. — *vt* and *vi* to act as a mime; to move the mouth in time to recorded singing, giving the illusion of a live performance; to make the movements involved in the performing of a specific activity, eg as a clue in guessing-games; to mimic. — *n* **mīm'er**. — *n* **mimesis** (*mim-* or *mīm-ē'sis*) imitation or representation in art; the rhetorical use of a person's supposed or imaginable words; simulation of one disease by another (*med*); mimicry (*biol*). — *n* **mime'ster**. — *adj* **mimet'ic** or **mimet'ical** (*mim-* or *mīm-*) imitative; mimic; of, relating to or displaying mimicry, mimesis or miming. — *adv* **mimet'ically**. — *n* **mimetite** (*mim'i-* or *mīm'i-*) a mineral, lead arsenate and chloride (from its resemblance to pyromorphite). — *n* **mimic** (*mim'ik*) a mime-actor (*obs*); a person who imitates, *esp* someone who performs in ludicrous imitation of others' speech and gestures; an unsuccessful imitator or imitation; a plant or animal exemplifying mimicry. — *adj* miming (*obs*); imitative; mock or sham. — *vt* to imitate, *esp* in ridicule or so as to incur ridicule; to ape; to produce an imitation of; to resemble deceptively: — *pr p* **mim'-icking**; *pa t* and *pa p* **mim'icked**. — *adj* (*obs*) **mimical** (*mim'*). — *n* **mim'icker**. — *n* **mimicry** (*mim'*) an act of mimicking; the adoption by one species of the colour, habits, sound or structure of another species, either for camouflage or to deceive a third species into confusing them (*biol* and *zool*). — *n* **mīmog'rapher** a writer of mimes. — *n* **mīmog'raphy**. — *n* **Mīmus** the mockingbird genus. [Gr *mīmos* a mime, *mīmēsis* imitation, *mīmētēs* an imitator]

mimeograph *mim'i-ō-gräf, n* an apparatus on which handwritten or typescript sheets can be reproduced from a stencil; a copy so produced. — *vt* to produce a copy or copies of (something) in this way. [*Mimeograph,* formerly a trademark]

mimer... to .. **mimetite**. See under **mime**.

mimic[1] and **mimmick**. See under **minnick**.

mimic[2], **mimicker**, **mimographer**, **Mimus**, etc. See under **mime**.

miminy-piminy *mim'i-ni-pim'i-ni.* Same as **niminy-piminy**.

mimosa *mim-ō'zə, n* a plant of the sensitive plant genus *Mimosa, esp* that having clusters of yellow flowers; popularly extended to *Acacia* and other genera of the **Mimosā'ceae** (*mim-* or *mīm-*), a regular-flowered family of *Leguminosae*. — *adj* **mimosā'ceous** (*mim-* or *mīm-*). [Gr *mīmos* a mimic]

mimsy or **mimsey** *mim'zi,* (*orig dialect*) *adj* prim, demure; prudish. [**mim**; influenced by Lewis Carroll's invented word *mimsy*]

mimulus *mim'ū-ləs, n* a plant of the musk and monkey-flower genus *Mimulus* of the figwort family. [Gr *mīmos* a mime, with L dimin suffix *-ulus,* from the grinning corolla]

Min. *abbrev*: Minister; Ministry.

min. *abbrev*: minimum; minute(s).

mina[1] *mī'nə*, *n* a Greek weight, or sum of money, equivalent to 100 drachmas; a weight of money valued at fifty, or sometimes sixty, shekels (*Bible*): — *pl* **mī'nas** or **-nae** (*-ē*). — Also **maneh** (*mä'ne*) or **mna** (*mnä*). [L *mina*, from Gr *mnā*; cf Heb *māneh*]

mina[2]. See **myna**.

minacious *min-ā'shəs*, *adj* threatening. — *n* **minacity** (*-as'*). [L *mināx*, *-ācis*, from *minārī* to threaten]

Minamata disease *mi-nə-mä'tə diz-ēz'*, *n* a disease caused by eating fish contaminated by industrial waste containing mercury compounds, and characterized by a *usu* permanent condition involving impairment of speech and sight, muscular weakness, paralysis, etc, and sometimes coma or death. [From *Minamata*, a town in Japan where the disease was first recognized]

minar *min-är'*, *n* a tower. — *n* **min'aret** (or *-ret'*) a mosque tower, from which the call to prayer is given. [Ar *manār*, *manārat* lighthouse, from *nār* fire]

minatory *min'ə-tə-ri* or *mīn'*, *adj* threatening. [L *minārī*, *-ātus* to threaten]

minauderie *mēn-ō-də-rē'*, *n* a display of affectation. [Fr]

minbar. See **mimbar**.

mince *mins*, *vt* to cut into small pieces; to chop fine; to diminish, or suppress a part of, in speaking; to pronounce affectedly. — *vi* to walk with affected nicety; to speak affectedly: — *pr p* **minc'ing**; *pa t* and *pa p* **minced** (*minst*). — *n* minced meat; mincemeat. — *n* **minc'er** a person who minces; a machine for mincing meat, etc. — *adj* **minc'ing** not speaking frankly or openly; speaking or walking with affected nicety. — Also *n*. — *adv* **minc'ingly**. — **minced collops** see under **collop**; **mince'meat** meat chopped small; hence anything thoroughly broken or cut to pieces; a chopped, spiced mixture of dried fruit, peel, suet and other ingredients, *usu* steeped in brandy; **mince-pie'** a pie made with mincemeat, *esp* in the latter sense. — **make mincemeat of** to destroy utterly (*esp fig*); **mince matters** or **words** to speak of things with affected delicacy, or to soften an account unduly. [OFr *mincier*, *minchier*, from L *minūtus*; cf **minute**[1]]

minceur *mɛ̃-sœr*, (*Fr*) *adj* (of food or cooking) lean, low-fat.

mind *mīnd*, *n* memory; commemoration (*archaic* or *RC*); record, mention (*obs*); thought; judgement; opinion; purpose (*Shakesp* and *Milton*); inclination; attention; direction of the will; the state of thought and feeling; wits, right senses, sanity; consciousness; intellect; that which thinks, knows, feels, and wills; soul; personality; a thinking or directing person. — *vt* to remind (*archaic* and *Scot*); to bring to mind (*Spenser*); to remember (*Scot*); (*reflexive*) to remember (with *of*; *archaic*); to attend to; to tend, have care or oversight of; to be careful about; to beware of; to purpose (*Shakesp*); to have a mind to (*dialect*); to apply oneself to; to be troubled by, object to, dislike; to notice (*obs* or *dialect*). — *vi* to remember (with *of*; *dialect*); to attend; to care; to look out, take heed; to be troubled, object. — *interj* be careful, watch out. — *adj* **mind'ed** inclined; disposed. — *combining form* **-mind'ed** denoting having a mind of a specified kind or inclination. — *combining form* **-mind'edness** denoting inclination. — **mind'er** a person who minds a machine, child, etc; a child left to be minded (*archaic*); a short wooden stick used by a child to propel a hoop; a bodyguard, *orig* and *esp* of a criminal (*slang*); an aide or adviser employed by a public figure, *esp* to manage publicity (*slang*). — *adj* **mind'ful** bearing in mind; taking thought or care; attentive; observant; having memory (*archaic*); inclined (*obs*). — *adv* **mind'fully**. — *n* **mind'fulness**. — *n* **mind'ing** (*Scot*) a memory, something recalled; a *usu* small gift, to mark an occasion or in remembrance of the giver. — *adj* **mind'less** without mind; stupid; unmindful. — *adv* **mind'lessly**. — *n* **mind'lessness**. — *adj* **mind'-altering** (of a drug) causing violent changes of mood and behaviour. — **mind'-bender** a brain-teaser, a puzzle. — *adj* **mind'-bending** permanently inclining the mind towards certain beliefs, etc; forcing the mind to unwonted effort, teasing the brain. — *adj* **mind'-blowing** (of a drug) producing a state of ecstasy; (of an experience, etc) producing a similar state, exhilarating. — *adj* **mind-bod'y** relating to or designating the connection between the mind and the physical body. — *adj* **mind'-boggling** astonishing; incomprehensible. — **mind'-cure** or **mind'-healing** the cure or healing of mental or physical illness through the mind or by the supposed influence of another's mind; **mind'-curer** or **-healer**. — *adj* **mind'-expanding** (of a drug) causing heightened perception, psychedelic. — **mind'fuck** (*vulg slang*) an exhilarating experience; a sense or state of euphoria. — *adj* **mind'-numbing** (*colloq*) causing extreme boredom. — **mind'-reader** a thought reader, a psychic; **mind'-reading**; **mind'set** (a fixed) attitude or habit of mind; **mind's eye** visual imagination, mental view, contemplation; **mind-your-own-bus'iness** a Mediterranean plant (*Helxine soleirolii*) of the nettle family, having small, roundish leaves and producing tiny flowers (also called **baby's-tears**). — **absence of mind** inattention to what is going on owing to absorption of the mind in other things; **bear in mind** see under **bear**[1]; **blow one's** or **someone's mind** see under **blow**[3]; **break one's mind** (*obs*) to make known, confide or divulge one's thoughts; **cast one's mind back** to think about, try to recall past events, etc; **change one's mind** to come to a new resolution or opinion; **cross someone's mind** see under **cross**; **do you mind?** an interjection expressing annoyance or disagreement; (or **would you mind?**) do you object?; **have a good** or (*archaic*) **great mind** (**to**) to wish or to be inclined strongly (to); **have a mind of one's own** to be strong-willed and independent, unwilling to be persuaded or dissuaded by others; **have half a mind** (**to**) to be somewhat inclined (to); **if you don't mind** if you have no objection; **in two minds** wavering, undecided; **know one's own mind** to be sure of one's intentions and opinions; to be self-assured; **make up one's mind** to come to a decision; **mind one's p's and q's** to be watchfully accurate and punctilious; **mind out** (often with *for*) to beware (of), look out (for); **mind you** an expression used to introduce a qualification added to something already said; **mind your eye** (*slang*) look out; **mind your own business** this is not your concern; **month's mind** commemoration by masses one month after death or burial; strong desire or inclination; **never mind** do not concern yourself or be upset; it does not matter; you are not to be told; **of one** (or **a**, or **the same**) **mind** in accord, agreed; **of two minds** uncertain what to think or do; **on one's mind** in one's thoughts, *esp* as a cause of concern; **out of mind** forgotten; out of one's thoughts; **out of one's mind** mad; **piece of one's mind** see under **piece**; **presence of mind** a state of mental calmness in which all the powers of the mind are on the alert and ready for action; **put in mind** (**of**) to remind (of); **put out of one's mind** to think no more about, forget about; **set one's mind on** to be determined to have or attain; **set** or **put one's mind to** to focus one's attention on; **speak one's mind** to say plainly what one thinks; **take someone's mind off** to distract someone from; **time out of mind** from time immemorial; **to my**, etc **mind** to my, etc thinking, in my, etc opinion; to my, etc liking; **year's mind** a commemorative service on the anniversary of a death or burial. [OE *gemynd*, from *munan*, to think; Dan *minde* memorial, L *mēns* the mind]

Mindel *min'dl*, (*geol*) *n* the second glaciation in the Alpine region. — Also *adj*. — *adj* **Mindelian** (*-dē'li-ən*). [*Mindel*, a tributary of the Danube, in Bavaria]

Mindererus spirit *min-dər-ē'rəs*, *n* ammonium acetate solution, a diaphoretic. [Latinized name of the German physician R M *Minderer* (c.1570–1621)]

mine[1] *mīn*, *pronoun* genitive of **I**, used predicatively or absolutely, belonging to me; my people; that which belongs to me; (adjectivally, *esp* before a vowel or *h*, or after its noun) my (*archaic* and *poetic*). [OE *mīn*]

mine[2] *mīn*, *n* a place from which minerals, *esp* coal or precious metals, are dug (not *usu* a source of building-stone, and legally distinguished from a quarry by being artificially lighted); a cavity in the earth (*archaic*); a burrowing animal's gallery, such as an insect's in a leaf; an excavation dug under a position to give secret ingress, to subvert it, or to blow it up (*military*); an explosive charge placed in this; a submerged or floating charge of explosives in a metal case to destroy ships; a land-mine; a rich source (*fig*). — *vt* to excavate, tunnel, make passages in or under; to obtain by excavation; to exploit (a natural resource) without, or at a faster rate than, replenishing it; to work as a mine; to bring down or blow up by a mine; to cover (an area) with explosive mines; to lay explosive mines in or under. — *vi* to dig or work a mine or mines; to tunnel; to burrow; to lay mines; to proceed secretly or insidiously (*fig*). — *n* **mi'ner** a person who works in a mine; a soldier who lays mines; an insect or other animal that makes galleries in the earth, leaves, etc. — *n* and *adj* **min'ing**. — *adj* **min'y** relating to mines; like a mine. — **mine'-captain** the overseer of a mine; **mine'-detection**; **mine'-detector** an electromagnetic apparatus for detecting explosive mines; **mine'field** an area laid with explosive mines; an enterprise, etc containing many potential hazards or traps (*fig*); **mine'-hunter** a ship equipped for locating undersea mines; **mine'-layer** a ship for laying mines; **mine'-owner**; **miner's anaemia** ankylostomiasis; **miner's inch** the amount of water that will flow in twenty-four hours through an opening of one square inch at a pressure of six inches of water; **miner's lamp** a lamp carried by a miner, *usu* attached to a helmet or cap; **miner's phthisis** phthisis caused by breathing dusty air in mines; **miner's worm** the hookworm that causes ankylostomiasis; **mine'stone** ore, *esp* ironstone; **mine'-sweeper** a ship which drags the water to remove undersea mines; **mine'-thrower** (a *transl* of *Ger* **Minenwerfer** *mē'nən-ver-fər*, in soldiers' slang **minnie** *min'i*) a trench-mortar; **mine'-worker** a miner. [Fr *mine* (noun), *miner* (verb), of doubtful origin]

mine[3] *mīn*, (*Shakesp*, *Merry Wives of Windsor*, I. 3) *n perh* for **mind** (disposition), or **mien**.

mineola. See **minneola**.

mineral *min'ər-əl*, *n* any of various classes of inorganic substances, *esp* solid, naturally occurring and crystalline in form; a substance obtained by mining; ore; a substance neither animal nor vegetable; a mine (*Shakesp*); a poison (*Shakesp*); a mineral water (in a wide sense). — *adj* relating to minerals; having the nature of minerals; (*esp* of water) impregnated with minerals; of inorganic substance or nature. — *n* **min'eralist** a person with a specialist knowledge of minerals, a mineralogist. — *n* **mineralizā'tion** or **-s-**. — *vt* **min'eralize** or **-ise** to make into a mineral; to give the properties of a mineral to; to go looking for and examining minerals. — *n* **mineralīz'er** or **-s-** a person who, or that which, mineralizes; an element, eg sulphur, that combines with a metal to form an ore; a gas or vapour that promotes the crystallizing out of minerals from an igneous magma. — *adj* **mineralog'ical** pertaining to mineralogy. — *adv* **mineralog'ically**. — *n* **mineral'ogist** a person skilled or trained in mineralogy. — *vi* **mineralogize** or **-ise** (*-al'*) to collect or study minerals. — *n* **mineral'ogy** the science of minerals. — **mineral alkali** (*obs*) sodium carbonate; **mineral caoutchouc** elaterite; **mineral coal** coal in the ordinary sense, distinguished from charcoal; **mineral jelly** a soft yellow substance resembling soft soap, obtained from the less volatile residue of petroleum; **mineral kingdom** that department of nature which comprises substances that are neither animal nor vegetable; **mineral oil** any oil of mineral origin; **mineral pitch** natural asphalt; **mineral processing** the crushing and sizing of ore into waste and value by chemical, electrical, magnetic, physico-chemical methods and gravity; **mineral spring** or **well** a spring of mineral water; **mineral tallow** a soft yellowish natural hydrocarbon; **mineral tar** pissasphalt; **mineral water** spring water impregnated with minerals; an artificial imitation of this; an effervescent non-alcoholic beverage; **mineral wax** ozokerite; **mineral wool** a mass of fibres formed by blowing steam through molten slag. [Fr *minéral*, from *miner* to mine; cf **mine**[2]]

Minerva *min-ûr'və*, *n* the Roman goddess of wisdom, identified with the Greek Athena. — **Minerva Press** a London printing-house that issued sentimental novels about 1800. [L, prob from root of *mēns* the mind]

minestrone *min-i-strōn'i*, *n* a thick, mixed vegetable soup containing pasta or rice. [Ital]

minette *min-et'*, *n* an intrusive rock of orthoclase and biotite in a close-grained groundmass. [Fr]

minever. See **miniver**.

Ming *ming*, *n* a Chinese dynasty (1368–1643). — *adj* of the dynasty, its time, or *esp* its pottery and other art.

ming[1] *ming*, **meng** *meng* or **menge** *menj*, (*archaic*) *vt* and *vi* to mix; to unite, couple; to work up: — *pa t* and *pa p* **minged** or **menged** (older forms **meint**, **meynt** (*ment*, *mānt*), **ment**). [OE *mengan*; Ger *mengen*]

ming[2] *ming*, (*Scot*) *n* an unpleasant smell, a stink. — *adj* **ming'in** having an unpleasant smell, stinking. [Origin unknown]

minge *minj*, (*vulg slang*; *orig dialect*) the female genitalia; a woman, or women collectively, regarded as a sexual object or objects. [Romany]

mingle *ming'gl*, *vt* and *vi* to mix, blend, combine. — *n* a mixture; a medley. — *n* **ming'lement**. — *n* **ming'ler**. — *n* **ming'ling**. — *adv* **ming'lingly**. — **ming'le-mangle** a confused mixture, a jumble. — *adj* jumbled. — *vt* to confuse, jumble together. [Frequentative of **ming**]

mingy *min'ji*, (*colloq*) *adj* niggardly, stingy. — *n* **min'giness**. [Perh a portmanteau-word from **mangy** or **mean**[1] and **stingy**]

mini *min'i*, *n* short for **mini-car**, **mini-dress**, **mini-computer** or **miniskirt**; something small of its type. — *adj* (*colloq*) small, miniature.

mini- *min'i-*, *combining form* used to signify small (*abbrev* of **miniature**). — **mini'bike** a lightweight motorcycle, *esp* for use off the public road; **min'ibreak** a short holiday, eg a weekend or long weekend break; **min'ibudget** or **min'i-budget** a supplementary budget, produced *esp* in times of fiscal emergency; **mini-buff'et** a snack-bar on a train; **min'icab** a small motor vehicle licensed as a taxicab; **min'icabbing**; **min'icam** a portable, shoulder-held TV camera, as used in news reporting; **min'i-car**; **min'icomputer** a computer, which may have several terminals, lying in capability between a mainframe and a microcomputer; **min'idisk** a very compact magnetic disk storage medium for microcomputers; **min'i-dress** a dress with a hemline well above the knees; **min'i-floppy** a 5.25in floppy disk (*orig* distinguished from an 8in disk; cf **microfloppy**); **mini-lacrosse** see under **lacrosse**; **mini-mo'torway** one with two lanes; **min'ipill** a low-dose oral contraceptive containing no oestrogen; **mini-rocket launcher** a hand-gun firing tiny rockets; **min'irugby**, **min'ivolley**, etc a simplified version of rugby, volleyball, etc played with a reduced number of players on each side; **min'iseries** a short series of television programmes broadcast *usu* over consecutive days; **min'i-skis** short, slightly thick, skis for learners; **min'iskirt** a skirt whose hemline is well above the knees; **min'i-sub** or **mini-sub'marine** a small submarine used for underwater exploration, etc; **Min'itrack**® a system for tracking an earth satellite or a rocket by radio signals from it to a series of ground stations.

miniate. See under **minium**.

miniature *min'i-chər*, *min'i-ə-chər*, *min'yə-tūr* or *-tyər*, *n* rubrication (*obs*); manuscript illumination; a painting on a very small scale, on ivory, vellum, etc; the art of painting in this manner; a small or reduced copy, type or breed of anything; a small-scale version of anything; a chess problem with few pieces or moves. — *adj* on a small scale; minute; applied to cameras taking 35mm film. — *vt* to represent on a small scale. — *n* **min'iaturist** a person who paints or makes miniatures. — *n*

miniaturizā'tion or **-s-**. — *vt* **min'iaturize** or **-ise** to make very small; to make something on a small scale. — **in miniature** on a small or reduced scale. [Ital *miniatura*, from L *minium* red lead; meaning affected by association with L *minor*, *minimus*, etc, and their derivatives]

minibike... to ... **mini-buffet**. See under **mini-**.

minibus *min'i-bus*, *n* a light passenger horse-drawn vehicle (*obs*); a small motor bus. [L *minor* less, *minimus* least, and **omnibus**]

minicab... to ... **mini-dress**. See under **mini-**.

Minié ball or **bullet** *min'i-ā böl* or *bŏŏl'it*, *n* a cone-shaped bullet containing powder in its base, designed to expand when fired from a **Minié rifle**. [C E *Minié* (1814–79), French officer, the inventor]

minifloppy. See under **mini-**.

minify *min'i-fī*, *vt* to diminish, in appearance or reality. — *n* **minificā'tion**. [Ill-formed (after **magnify**) from L *minor* less]

minikin *min'i-kin*, *n* a little darling (*archaic* and *dialect*); a diminutive or undersized person or thing; a small sort of pin (now *dialect*); a thin length of gut used for the treble string of a lute (*obs*). — *adj* diminutive; dainty; affected; mincing. [Obs Du *minneken*, dimin of *minne* love; cf **minnesinger**]

minim *min'im*, *n* a least part; a note, formerly the shortest, equal to two crotchets (*music*); (in apothecaries' measure) one-sixtieth of a fluid drachm; (in apothecaries' weight) a grain; a short down-stroke in handwriting; a diminutive creature (*Milton*); a friar, sister, or lay member of any of three orders founded by St Francis of Paula (1416–1507), so called as if humbler than even the Friars Minor. — *adj* (*obs*) extremely minute. — **minim rest** a rest of the duration of a minim. [Ety as for **minimum**]

minimal *min'ə-məl*, *adj* of least, or least possible, size, amount or degree; of the nature of a minimum; negligible. — *n* **min'imalism**. — *n* **min'imalist** a Menshevik; a person advocating a policy of the least possible action, intervention, etc; a practitioner of minimal art. — Also *adj*. — **minimal art** art whose practitioners reject such traditional elements as composition and interrelationship between parts of the whole; **minimal invasive therapy** (*surg*) an operating procedure that does not necessitate stitching or scarring, eg gallstone removal by endoscopy and laser treatment. [Ety as for *minimum*]

minimax *min'i-maks*, (*math*) *n* (in game theory, eg *chess*) a strategy designed to minimize one's maximum possible loss; the theory (in a game for two players) that minimizing one's maximum loss equates with maximizing one's minimum gain. — *vt* to minimize the maximum possible extent of (one's loss). [*mini*mum and *max*imum]

miniment *min'i-mənt*, *n obs* form of **muniment**.

minimum *min'i-məm*, *n* the least quantity or degree, or the smallest possible; the lowest point or value reached; a value of a variable at which it ceases to diminish and begins to increase (*math*; *opp* of *maximum*): — *pl* **min'ima**. — *adj* smallest or lowest possible (obtained, recorded, etc). — *n* **min'imism** inclination to reduce a dogma to the least possible. — *n* **min'imist**. — *n* **minimizā'tion** or **-s-**. — *vt* **min'imize** or **-ise** to reduce to the smallest possible amount; to make as light or insignificant as possible; to estimate at the lowest possible; to lessen or diminish; to belittle. — *n* **min'imus** a being of the smallest size (*Shakesp*); in boys' schools, youngest of the surname. — **minimizing glass** a diminishing glass; **minimum lending rate** the minimum rate of interest (successor to the **bank-rate** (qv) and itself abolished in 1981) charged by the Bank of England to the discount market; **minimum wage** the lowest wage permitted by law or regulation for certain work; a fixed bottom limit to workers' wages in various industries. [L *minimus*, *-a*, *-um* smallest]

minion *min'yən*, *n* a darling, a favourite, *esp* of a prince; a flatterer; a servile dependant; an old type size, *approx* 7-point, between nonpareil and brevier, giving about $10\frac{1}{2}$ lines to the inch (*printing*). [Fr *mignon*, *mignonne*]

minipill and **minirugby**. See under **mini-**.

miniscule. An alternative, less acceptable, spelling of **minuscule**.

minish *min'ish*, (*archaic*) *vt* to make little or less; to diminish. [Fr *menuiser* to cut small (in carpentry, etc), from L *minūtia* smallness]

minister *min'is-tər*, *n* a servant (*archaic*); a person who administers or proffers anything, in service or kindness; a person who officiates at the altar; a member of the clergy (not now *usu*, as in *Prayer Bk*, of the Church of England); the head, or assistant to the head, of certain religious orders; a person transacting business for another, an agent; the responsible head of a department of state affairs; a diplomatic representative of a government in a foreign state, *esp* one ranking below an ambassador. — *vi* to give attentive service (to); to perform duties at a Christian service, to act as an ecclesiastical minister; to supply or do things needful; to conduce or contribute (to). — *vt* (*archaic*) to furnish, supply. — *adj* **ministē'rial** of or relating to a minister or ministry (in any sense); on the government side; administrative; executive; instrumental; conducive. — *adj* **ministē'rialist**. — *n* a supporter of the government in office. — *adv* **ministē'rially**. — *adj* **min'istering** attending and serving. — *n* **ministē'rium** the body of the ordained Lutheran ministers in a district: — *pl* **ministē'ria**. — *adj* **min'istrant** administering; attendant. — Also *n*. — *n* **ministrā'tion** the act of ministering or performing service; the office or service of a minister. — *adj* **min'istrative** (*-trə-tiv* or *-trā-tiv*) serving to aid or assist; ministering. — *n* **min'istress** a woman who ministers. — *n* **min'istry** the act of ministering; service; the office or duties of a minister; the clergy; the clerical profession; the body of ministers who manage the business of the country; a department of government, or the building it occupies; a term of office as minister. — **Minister of State** an additional, *usu* non-Cabinet, minister in (but ranking below the head of) a large government department; **Minister of the Crown** a government minister in the Cabinet; **Minister without Portfolio** a government minister, a member of the Cabinet having no specific department. [L *minister*, from *minor* less]

Minitel *mē-nē-tel*, *n* (in France) a public videotext system providing banking and mail order services, electronic messaging, etc.

Minitrack®. See under **mini-**.

minium *min'i-əm*, *n* vermilion; red lead; its colour. — *adj* **min'iate** of the colour of minium. — *vt* to paint with minium; to illuminate. — *n* **miniā'tion**. [L *minium* red-lead, also cinnabar]

miniver or **minever** *min'i-vər*, *n* white fur, *orig* a mixed or variegated fur; the ermine in winter coat. [OFr *menu* small, from L *minūtus*, and *vair* fur, from L *varius* particoloured]

minivet *min'i-vet*, *n* a brightly coloured shrike-like bird (*Pericrocotus* of several species) of India, etc. [Ety unknown]

minivolley. See under **mini-**.

mink *mingk*, *n* a small animal (of several species) of the weasel family; its fur; a coat or jacket made from its fur. [Perh from Swed *mänk*]

minke *mink'ə*, *n* the lesser rorqual. — Also **minke whale**. [From a Norwegian whaler, *Meincke*, who harpooned one by accident]

Minkstone *mink'stōn*, *n* a cast concrete with a very smooth finish.

Minn. *abbrev*: Minnesota (US state).

minneola or **mineola** *min-i-ō'lə*, *n* a variety of citrus fruit developed from a tangerine and a grapefruit and resembling an orange, grown in the USA and elsewhere. [Poss *Mineola* in Texas]

Minnesinger *min'i-sing-ər* or *-zing-ər*, *n* any of a 12c–13c school of German amatory lyric poets, often themselves noblemen, composing love-lyrics (**Minn'esang**) to be sung at aristocratic courts. [Ger *Minne* courtly love, and *Singer* singer]

minnick *min'ik*, **minnock** *-ək*, **mimic** or **mimmick** *mim'*, (*dialect*) *n* an affected person. — *vi* to be over-dainty in eating; to behave with affected primness. (In *Shakesp A Midsummer Night's Dream*, III. 2, by some amended to *mimic*).

minnie[1] *min'i*, (*Scot*; *hypocoristic*) *n* mother.

minnie[2]. See **mine-thrower** under **mine**[2].

minnock. See **minnick**.

minnow *min'ō*, *n* a very small freshwater fish (*Phoxinus phoxinus*) closely related to chub and dace; loosely extended to other small fish; a small, unimportant person or thing (*fig*). [Prob an OE form related to extant *myne*]

mino *mē'nō*, *n* a raincoat of hemp, etc: — *pl* **mi'nos**. [Jap]

Minoan *min-ō'ən* or *mīn-*, *adj* relating to or designating prehistoric Crete and its culture, from around 3000 BC to 1100 BC. — *n* a member of this culture, a prehistoric Cretan. [Gr *Mīnōs*, a legendary king of Crete]

minor *mī'nər*, *adj* lesser; inferior in importance, degree, bulk, etc; inconsiderable; lower; smaller (than major) by a semitone (*music*); in boys' schools, junior (placed after a surname); (with *cap*) Minorite. — *n* a person under the legal age of majority; the minor term, or minor premise (*logic*); (with *cap*) a Minorite or Minoress; anything that is minor opposed to major; a subsidiary subject studied at college or university (*NAm*); (in *pl*) the minor leagues in baseball, etc (*NAm*). — *vi* (*NAm*; with *in*) to study as a minor, subsidiary subject at college or university. — *n* **minoritaire** (*mē-nor-ē-ter*; *Fr*) a member of a minority section of a political (*esp* Socialist) party. — *adj* **Mī'norite** relating to or designating a Franciscan order observing the strict rule of St Francis. — *n* a member of such an order: — *fem* **Mī'noress**. — *n* **minority** (*min-* or *mīn-or'i-ti*) the condition or fact of being little or less; the state or time of being under age (also **mī'norship**); the smaller number; less than half; the party, social group, section of the population, etc of smaller numbers; the number by which it falls short of the other party (opposite of *majority*). — *adj* of the minority. — **minor axis** in conics, that perpendicular to the major axis; **minor canon** see under **canon**[2]; **minority carrier** (*electronics*) in a semiconductor, the type of carrier electrons or holes which carries the lesser degree of measured current; **minority group** a section of the population with a common interest, characteristic, etc which is not common to most people; **minor key, mode** or **scale** a key, mode or scale with its third a minor third above the tonic; **minor orders** the lower degrees of holy orders, ie porter, exorcist, lector and acolyte; **minor planet** a small planet, any one of many hundreds with orbits between those of Mars and Jupiter, an asteroid; **minor poet** a genuine but not great poet; **minor premise** (*logic*) that in which the minor term occurs; **minor prophets** the twelve from Hosea to Malachi in the Old Testament; **minor suit** (*bridge*) clubs or diamonds; **minor term** (*logic*) the term which is the subject of the conclusion; **minor third** (*music*) an interval of three semitones; **minor tone** an interval with a vibration ratio of 9/10. [L *minor* less; cf **minus**]

Minorca *min-ör'kə*, *n* a Mediterranean variety of laying poultry with glossy, *esp* black, plumage. [From the island of *Minorca* (Sp *Menorca*)]

Minoress, Minorite, minority, etc. See under **minor**.

Minotaur *min'* or *mīn'ə-tör*, (*mythol*) *n* the bull-headed monster in the Cretan Labyrinth, offspring of Pasiphae, wife of Minos. [Gr *Mīnōtauros*, from *Mīnōs* Minos, and *tauros* bull]

minshuku *min-shoo'koo*, *n* a Japanese guesthouse. [Jap]

minster *min'stər*, *n* a monastery (*obs*); an abbey church or priory church; often applied to a cathedral or other great church without any monastic connection. [OE *mynster*, from L *monastērium* a monastery]

minstrel *min'strəl*, *n orig* a professional entertainer; now *esp* a medieval musician, itinerant or attached to a noble household, who sang or recited his own or others' poems, accompanying himself on a stringed instrument; a poet, singer or musician (*poetic*); one of a troupe of entertainers, *orig* in 19c US, performing in blackface and playing banjos, etc. — *n* **min'strelsy** (*-si*) the art or occupation of a minstrel; music (*archaic*); a company or body of minstrels; a collection of minstrels' poems or songs. [OFr *menestrel*, from LL *ministeriālis*, from L *minister* attendant]

mint[1] *mint*, *n* a place where money is coined, *esp* officially; a source or place of fabrication (*fig*; *literary*); a vast sum of money. — *vt* to coin; to invent; to stamp. — *adj* in mint condition. — *n* **mint'age** coining; coinage; stamp; duty for coining. — *n* **mint'er**. — **mint condition** or **state** the condition of a new-minted coin; perfect condition, as if unused; **mint'-man** (*obs*) a person skilled in coining or coinage; **mint'-mark** a mark showing where a coin was minted; **mint'-master** a person supervising coinage at a mint; an inventor or coiner (*obs*). — *adj* **mint'-new** in mint condition. [OE *mynet* money, from L *monēta*; see **money**]

mint[2] *mint*, *n* any plant of the aromatic labiate genus *Mentha*, such as spearmint, peppermint or pennyroyal; any labiate (*US*); a sweet flavoured with mint or a synthetic substitute. — *adj* **mint'y**. — **mint-ju'lep** see under **julep**; **mint-sauce'** chopped spearmint or other mint mixed with vinegar and sugar, used *esp* as a sauce for roast lamb; money (with pun on **mint**[1]; *slang*). [OE *minte*, from L *mentha*, from Gr *minthē*, *mintha*]

mint[3] *mint*, (*Scot* and *dialect*) *vt* and *vi* (often with *at*) to purpose; to attempt; to aim a blow (at); to make a threatening movement (towards); to venture; to aspire (to); to hint. — *n* an attempt; aim; a threatening gesture; an incipient movement. [OE *myntan* to mean]

minuend *min'ū-end*, (*math*) *n* the number from which another is to be subtracted. [L *minuendus* (*numerus*), from *minuere* to lessen]

minuet *min-ū-et'*, *n* a slow, graceful dance in triple measure, invented in Poitou about the middle of the 17c and fashionable in 18c Europe; the music for, or as for, such a dance; the standard third movement in the classical sonata, symphony, etc. [Fr *menuet*, from *menu* small, from L *minūtus* small]

minus *mī'nəs*, *prep* diminished by (*math*); deficient in respect of, deprived of, without (*colloq*). — *adj* negative. — *n* a deficiency or subtraction; a negative quantity or term; the sign (also **minus sign**) of subtraction or negativity (−), opposite of *plus*. — **minus strain** (*bot*) one of two strains in heterothallism. [L *minus*, neuter of *minor* less]

minuscule *min'əs-kūl* or *-us'*, *n* a small, cursive script, originated by the monks in the 7–9c (*palaeog*; *opp* of **majuscule**); a manuscript written in it; a lower-case letter (*printing*). — *adj* written or printed in minuscule; very small; very unimportant. — *adj* **minus'cūlar**. [L (*littera*) *minuscula* smallish (letter)]

minute[1] *mīn-ūt'* or *min-ūt'*, *adj* extremely small; relating to the very small; exact, detailed. — *adv* **minute'ly**. — *n* **minute'ness**. [L *minūtus*, pa p of *minuere* to lessen]

minute[2] *min'it*, *n* the sixtieth part of an hour; the sixtieth part of an angular degree; an indefinitely small space of time; a particular moment; a brief jotting or note; (in *pl*) a brief summary of the proceedings of a meeting; a minute's walk, or the distance travelled in a minute. — *vt* to make a brief jotting or note of; to record in the minutes. — *adj* **minutely** (*min'it-li*; *Shakesp*) happening once a minute. — **min'ute-bell** a bell sounded every minute, in mourning; **min'ute-book** a book of minutes or short notes; **min'ute-drop** a drop falling at a minute's interval; **min'ute-glass** a sand-glass that runs for a minute; **min'ute-gun** a gun discharged every minute, as a signal of distress or mourning; **min'ute-hand** the hand that indicates the minutes on a clock or watch; **min'ute-jack** (*Shakesp*) a time-server, or a flighty, unstable person; **min'uteman** (often *cap*) a man ready to turn out at a minute's warning, *orig* a militiaman in the American War of Independence (*hist*); a member of an armed right-wing organization in the USA, formed to take prompt action against Communist activities; a three-stage intercontinental ballistic missile; **minute steak** a small, thin piece of steak which can be cooked quickly; **min'ute-watch** a watch that marks minutes; **min'ute-while** (*Shakesp*) a minute's time. — **up to the minute** right up to date. [Same word as **minute**[1]]

minutia *mi-nū'shi-ə*, *n* a minute particular or detail: — *usu* in *pl* **minū'tiae** (*-ē*). — *adj* **minū'tiose** (*-shi-ōs*). [L *minūtia* smallness]

minx *mingks*, *n* a pert young girl; a jade. [Poss from **minikin**; or LGer *minsk*, *minske* a wench or jade, cognate with Ger *Mensch* man, human being]

miny. See under **mine**[2].

minyan *min'yən* or *min-yan'*, (*Heb*) *n* the minimum number of people required by Jewish law to be present for a religious service to be held, ie ten male adults: — *pl* **minyanim** or **minyans**. [Heb, number]

Miocene *mī'ō-sēn*, (*geol*) *adj* of the Tertiary period preceding the Pliocene and having a smaller proportion of molluscan fossils of species now living. — *n* the Miocene system, period, or strata. [Gr *meiōn* smaller, and *kainos* recent]

miombo *mi-om'bō*, *n* an area of deciduous woodland occurring in parts of E Africa: — *pl* **miom'bos**. [Swahili]

miosis or **myosis** *mī-ō'sis*, abnormal contraction of the pupil of the eye. — *adj* **miot'ic**. — Also *n*. [Gr *mȳein* to close, blink]

MIPS or **mips** (*comput*) *abbrev*: millions of instructions per second.

MIR *abbrev*: mortgage interest relief.

mir[1] *mēr*, *n* a peasant farming commune in pre-Revolutionary Russia: — *pl* **mirs** or **mir'i**. [Russ, world]

mir[2] or **meer** *mēr*, *n* (also with *cap*) a Muslim ruler or commander, an ameer. [Hindi and Pers *mīr*, from Ar *amīr* ruler]

Mira *mī'rə*, *n* a variable star in the constellation Cetus. [L *mīra* (fem) wonderful]

mirabelle *mir'ə-bel*, *n* a European species of plum-tree; the small, yellow, firm-fleshed fruit of this; a colourless liqueur distilled from this fruit (also **mirabelle brandy**). [Fr]

mirabile dictu *mir-ä'bi-lā dik'too*, (*L*) wonderful to tell.

mirabile visu *mir-ä'bi-lā ve'soo*, (*L*) wonderful to see.

mirable *mīr'ə-bl*, *adj* (*Shakesp*) wonderful. — *n pl* **mirabi'lia** (*mir-* or *mīr-*; *rare*) wonders. — *n* **Mirabilis** (*mir-* or *mīr- ab'il-is*) the marvel of Peru genus; (without *cap*) short form of **aqua mirabilis** (*obs*). [L *mīrābilis* wonderful]

miracidium *mī'rə-sid-i-əm*, (*zool*) *n* the ciliated first-stage larva of a tremadote. [LL *miracidion*, from Gr *meirax* boy, girl]

miracle *mir'ə-kl*, *n* an event or act which breaks a law of nature, *esp* one attributed to a deity or supernatural force; a marvel, a wonder; a miracle play. — *adj* **miraculous** (*-ak'ū-ləs*) of the nature of a miracle; done by supernatural power; very wonderful or remarkable; able to perform miracles. — *adv* **mirac'ulously**. — *n* **mirac'ulousness**. — **miracle berry** or **fruit** a tasteless African red berry which becomes sweet-tasting when mixed with a sour substance; **mir'acle-monger** (*archaic*) a person who pretends to work miracles; **miracle play** a medieval religious drama based on the legends of the saints or of the Virgin Mary; a mystery play (qv); **miracle rice** a hybrid, high-yield rice developed for used in Asia, etc. [Fr, from L *mīrāculum*, from *mīrārī*, *-ātus* to wonder at]

miracles. See under **meril**.

mirador *mir-ə-dör'*, (*archit*) *n* a belvedere or watchtower. [Sp]

mirage *mi-räzh'*, *n* an optical illusion, appearing as a floating and shimmering image, like water, on the horizon, caused by the varying refractive index of surface layers of hot and cold air; something illusory (*fig*). [Fr *mirer* to look at, from L *mīrārī* to wonder at]

MIRAS *mī'ras*, *abbrev*: mortgage interest relief at source.

mirbane *mûr'bān*, *n* an apparently meaningless word, used in **essence** (or **oil**) **of mirbane**, a name for nitrobenzene as used in perfumery.

mire *mīr*, *n* deep mud; a marshy area, a bog; any problematical or ineluctable situation. — *vt* to plunge and fix in mire; to soil with mud; to swamp, bog down. — *vi* to sink in mud. — *n* **mir'iness**. — *adj* **mir'y** consisting of mire; covered with mire. — **mire'-drum** the bittern; **mire'-snipe** the common snipe. [ON *mȳrr* bog]

mirepoix *mēr-pwa'*, *n* sautéed, diced vegetables used for making sauces, or as as a base for braised meat or fish, etc. [Duc de Lévis-*Mirepoix*, 18c French general, whose cook is said to have created the dish]

mirific *mīr-if'ik* or **mirifical** *-if'ik-əl*, *adj* wonder-working; marvellous. — *adv* **mirif'ically**. [L *mīrificus*, from *mīrus* wonderful, and *facere* to do]

mirin *mir'in*, *n* a sweet rice wine used in Japanese cookery. [Jap]

miriti *mi-ri-tē'* or *mir'i-ti*, *n* any palm of the genus *Mauritia*. [Tupí]

mirk, etc. Same as **murk**, etc.

mirligoes *mûr'li-gōz*, (*Scot*) *n pl* dizziness.

mirliton *mûr'li-tən* or *mēr-lē-tɔ̃*, *n* a toy reed-pipe; a small almond tart made with puff-pastry. [Fr]

mirly. See under **marl**[4].

mirror *mir'ər*, *n* a surface, *orig* of polished metal, now *usu* of glass backed with metallic film, which reflects an image in front of it; such a surface set in a frame for mounting on a wall, holding in the hand, etc, *esp* to view oneself; any reflecting surface; a faithful representation of something (*fig*); a model or example, good or bad. — *vt* to reflect an image of in, or as if in, a mirror; to represent faithfully; to provide with a mirror or mirrors: — *pr p* **mirr'oring**; *pa p* **mirr'ored**. — *adj* and *adv* **mirr'orwise** with interchange of left and right sides. — **mirr'or-glass** a reflecting glass used, or as used, in a mirror; **mirror-im'age** an image with right and left reversed as in a mirror; **mirror machine** a fusion machine using the magnetic mirror principle to trap high-energy ions in a plasma; **mirror nuclides** pairs of nuclides, one containing the same number of protons as the other has neutrons; **mirror symmetry** the symmetry of an object and its reflected image; **mirr'or-writer** a person who writes mirrorwise; **mirr'or-writing** writing which is like ordinary writing as seen in a mirror, ie in reverse. [OFr *mireor*, *mirour*, from L *mīrārī*, *-ātus* to wonder at]

mirth *mûrth*, *n* merriness; pleasure; delight; noisy gaiety; jollity; laughter. — *adj* **mirth'ful** full of mirth; causing mirth; merry; jovial. — *adv* **mirth'fully**. — *n* **mirth'fulness**. — *adj* **mirth'less**. — *adv* **mirth'lessly**. — *n* **mirth'lessness**. [OE *myrgth*, from *myrige* merry]

MIRV *mûrv*, *n* a missile containing many thermonuclear warheads, able to attack separate targets; any of the warheads in such a missile. — *vt* **mirv** (*military slang*) to provide with such missiles or warheads. [*M*ultiple *I*ndependently Targeted *R*e-entry *V*ehicle]

miry. See under **mire**.

Mirza *mûr'zə* or *mēr'zə*, *n* as a Persian title (after a name), Prince; (before) official or learned man. [Pers *mirzā*, *mīrzā*]

MIS *abbrev*: Management Information System.

mis *mis*, (*Spenser*) *vi* to do amiss; to fail. [**miss**[1]]

mis- *mis-*, *pfx* denoting: wrongly, badly, as in *misbehave*, *mislead*, etc; wrong, bad, as in *misdeed*. [OE *mis-*; ON *mis-*, Gothic *missa-*, Ger *miss-*; cf **miss**[1]]

misacceptation *mis-ak-sep-tā'shən*, (*obs*) *n* misinterpretation. [**mis-**]

misadventure *mis-əd-ven'chər*, *n* bad luck; mishap; accidental killing. — *adj* **misadvent'ured** (*Shakesp*) unfortunate. — *n* **misadvent'urer**. — *adj* **misadvent'urous**. [ME, from OFr *mesaventure*]

misadvertence *mis-əd-vûrt'əns*, (*literary*) *n* inadvertence. [**mis-**]

misadvise *mis-əd-vīz'*, *vt* to advise badly or wrongly. — *adj* **misadvised'**. — *adv* **misadvī'sedly**. — *n* **misadvīs'edness**. [**mis-**]

misaim *mis-ām'*, *vt* to aim badly. [**mis-**]

misalign *mis-ə-līn'*, *vt* to align wrongly. [**mis-**]

misallege *mis-ə-lej'*, (*obs*) *vt* to allege wrongly. [**mis-**]

misalliance *mis-ə-lī'əns*, *n* an unsuitable alliance, *esp* in marriage. — *adj* **misallied'**. — *vt* **misally** (*mis-ə-lī'*): — *pr p* **misally'ing**; *pa t* and *pa p* **misallied'**. [Fr *mésalliance*]

misallot *mis-ə-lot'*, *vt* to allot wrongly. — *n* **misallot'ment**. [**mis-**]

misandry *mis'ən-dri*, *n* hatred of men. — *n* **mis'andrist**. — *adj* **mis'androus**. [Gr *misandria*, from *misandros* hating men]

misanthrope *mis'ən-thrōp*, *n* a hater of mankind, someone who distrusts everyone else. — Also **misanthropist** (*mis-an'throp-ist*). — *adj* **misanthropic** (*mis-ən-throp'ik*) or **misanthropical** hating or distrusting mankind. — *adv* **misanthrop'ically**. — *n* **misan'thropos** (*Shakesp*) a misanthrope. — *n* **misan'thropy** hatred or distrust of mankind. [Gr *mīsanthrōpos*, from *mīseein* to hate, and *anthrōpos* a man]

misapply *mis-ə-plī'*, *vt* to apply wrongly; to use for a wrong purpose. — *n* **misapplicā'tion** (*-ap-*). [**mis-**]

misappreciate *mis-ə-prē'shi-āt*, *vt* to fail to appreciate rightly or fully. — *n* **misappreciā'tion**. — *adj* **misappre'ciative**. [**mis-**]

misapprehend *mis-ap-ri-hend'*, *vt* to apprehend wrongly; to take or understand in a wrong sense. — *n* **misapprehen'sion**. — *adj* **misapprehen'sive**. — *adv* **misapprehen'sively** by or with misapprehension or mistake. — *n* **misapprehen'siveness**. [**mis-**]

misappropriate *mis-ə-prō'pri-āt*, *vt* to put to a wrong use; to take dishonestly for oneself. — *n* **misappropriā'tion**. [**mis-**]

misarrange *mis-ə-rānj'*, *vt* to arrange wrongly; to put in wrong order. — *n* **misarrange'ment**. [**mis-**]

misarray *mis-ə-rā'*, (*Scott*) *n* disarray. [**mis-**]

misassign *mis-ə-sīn'*, *vt* to assign wrongly. [**mis-**]

misaunter *mis-ön'tər*, (now *NEng dialect*) *n* a misadventure or mishap. [OFr *mesaventure*; cf **aunter**]

misavised *mis-ə-vīz'id*, (*Spenser*) *adj* ill-advised. [**mis-**]

misbecome *mis-bi-kum'*, (*archaic*) *vt* to be unbecoming or unsuitable to. — *adj* **misbecom'ing**. — *n* **misbecom'ingness**. [**mis-**]

misbegot *mis-bi-got'* or **misbegotten** *-got'n*, *adj* unlawfully begotten, illegitimate (*Shakesp*); monstrous. [**mis-** and *pa p* of **beget**]

misbehave *mis-bi-hāv'*, *vt* (*refl*) and *vi* to behave badly or improperly. — *adj* **misbehaved'** (*Shakesp*) badly behaved; ill-bred. — *n* **misbehav'iour**. [**mis-**]

misbelief *mis-bə-lēf'*, *n* belief in a false doctrine or notion. — *vt* **misbelieve** (*mis-bi-lēv'*) to believe wrongly or falsely. — *n* **misbeliev'er**. — *adj* **misbeliev'ing**. [**mis-**]

misbeseem *mis-bi-sēm'*, (*archaic*) *vt* to be unsuited or unsuitable to. [**mis-**]

misbestow *mis-bi-stō'*, *vt* to bestow improperly, or on the wrong person. — *n* **misbestow'al**. [**mis-**]

misborn *mis'börn* or *mis-börn'*, *adj* abortive (*obs*); deformed from birth (*obs*); born illegitimately and so of low social rank (*literary*). — *n* (*archaic*) **misbirth'** an abortion. [**mis-**]

misc. *abbrev*: miscellaneous.

miscalculate *mis-kal'kū-lāt*, *vt* and *vi* to calculate wrongly. — *n* **miscalculā'tion**. [**mis-**]

miscall *mis-köl'*, *vt* to call by a wrong name; (in games) to make a bad or inaccurate call; to call by a bad name, to abuse or revile verbally (*Spenser*; now mainly *Scot* and *dialect*; also **misca'**). [**mis-**]

miscanthus *mis-kan'thəs*, *n* any of several hardy, ornamental, perennial grasses (family *Gramineae*) of China and Japan.

miscarriage *mis-kar'ij*, *n* an act or instance of miscarrying; failure; failure to reach the intended result or destination; misconduct, a misdeed (*obs*); the act of giving birth spontaneously to a foetus too premature to survive, *usu* before the 28th week of pregnancy. — *vi* **miscarr'y** to be unsuccessful; to fail to attain the intended or complete effect; to give birth to an unviable foetus; to be born as an unviable foetus. — *vt* (*obs*) to lead astray. — **miscarriage of justice** failure of the courts to do justice. [**mis-**]

miscast *mis-käst'*, *vt* (*usu* in *passive*) to miscalculate (*obs*; also *vi*); to cast (an actor or actress) in an unsuitable role; to cast an unsuitable actor or actress in (a role, play, film, etc). [**mis-**]

miscegenation *mis-i-jin-ā'shən*, *n* mixing of race; interbreeding, intermarriage or sexual intercourse between different races. — *n* **miscegen** (*mis'i-jən*), **misc'egene** (*-jēn*) or **misc'egine** (*-jin* or *-jīn*) an individual of mixed race. — *vi* **misc'egenate** to practise miscegenation. — *vt* to produce by miscegenation. — *adj* (*rare*) of mixed race. — *n* **miscegenā'tionist**, **misc'egenātor** or **miscegenist** (*mis-ej'in-ist*) a person who favours or practises miscegenation. [L *miscēre* to mix, and *genus* race]

miscellaneous *mis-əl-ān'i-əs*, *adj* mixed or mingled; consisting of several kinds; (of a person) with a many-sided personality, multi-talented, etc (*literary*). — *adj* **miscellanarian** (*-ən-ā'ri-ən*; *obs*). — *n* a writer of miscellanies. — *adv* **miscellān'eously**. — *n* **miscellān'eousness**. — *n* **miscellanist** (*mis-el'ən-ist* or (*esp NAm*) *mis'əl*) a writer of miscellanies. — *n* **miscellany** (*mis-el'* or (*esp NAm*) *mis'əl-*) a mixture of various kinds; a collection of writings on different subjects or by different authors. — *n pl* **miscellā'nea** (*L neuter pl*) a miscellany. [L *miscellāneus*, from *miscēre* to mix]

mischallenge *mis-chal'ənj*, (*Spenser*) *n* an unjust challenge. [**mis-**]

mischance *mis-chäns'*, *n* bad luck; mishap. — *vi* to chance wrongly, happen unfortunately; to meet with bad luck. — *adj* **mischance'ful** (*archaic*). — *adj* **mischan'cy** (chiefly *Scot*) unlucky; dangerous. [ME, from OFr *meschance*]

mischanter *mis-chän'tər* or **mishanter** *mi-shän'*, (*Scot* and *NEng*) *n* an unlucky chance, misfortune. [**aunter**; perh influenced by obs *mischant*, *meschant*, from OFr *mescheant* (Fr *méchant*) unlucky, wicked]

mischarge *mis-chärj'*, *vt* to charge wrongly. — *n* a mistake in charging. [**mis-**]

mischief *mis'chif*, *n* an unfavourable consequence; evil; injury; damage, hurt; the troublesome fact; a source of harm; petty misdeeds or annoyance; pestering playfulness; a mischievous person; the devil (*colloq*). — Also *vt*. — *adj* **mischievous** (*mis'chiv-əs*; *Spenser usu* *-chēv'*) causing mischief; injurious; prone to mischief. — *adv* **mis'chievously**. — *n* **mis'chievousness**. — **mis'chief-maker** someone who stirs up trouble. — *n* and *adj* **mis'chief-making**. [OFr *meschef*, from *mes-* (from L *minus* less), and *chef* (from L *caput* the head)]

mischmetal *mish'met-l*, *n* an alloy of cerium with rare-earth metals and iron, used to produce the spark in cigarette and other lighters. [Ger *mischen* to mix, and **metal**]

miscible *mis'i-bl*, *adj* that may be mixed. — *n* **miscibil'ity**. [L *miscēre* to mix]

misclassify *mis-klas'i-fī*, *vt* to classify wrongly. — *n* **misclassificā'tion**. [**mis-**]

miscolour or (*NAm*) **miscolor** *mis-kul'ər*, *vt* to colour falsely; to give a wrong meaning to; to misrepresent. [**mis-**]

miscomprehend *mis-kom-pri-hend'*, *vt* to misunderstand. — *n* **miscomprehen'sion**. [**mis-**]

miscompute *mis-kəm-pūt'*, *vt* to compute or calculate wrongly. — *n* **miscomputā'tion** (*-kom-*) wrong computation; miscalculation. [**mis-**]

misconceit *mis-kən-sēt'*, (*Spenser*) *n* misconception. — *vt* to have a wrong conception of. [**mis-**]

misconceive *mis-kən-sēv'*, *vt* and *vi* to conceive wrongly; to mistake; to suspect (*obs*). — *n* **misconcep'tion**. [**mis-**]

misconduct *mis-kon'dukt*, *n* bad conduct; wrong management; adultery; improper behaviour, not necessarily morally reprehensible, such as would lead any reasonable employer to dismiss an employee (*legal*). — *vt* **misconduct** (*-kən-dukt'*). **[mis-]**

misconjecture *mis-kən-jek'chər, n* a wrong conjecture or guess. — *vt* and *vi* to guess or conjecture wrongly. **[mis-]**

misconster *mis-kon'stər, obs* form of **misconstrue**.

misconstruction *mis-kən-struk'shən, n* wrong construction, construing or interpretation; faulty construction. — *vt* **misconstruct'**. **[mis-]**

misconstrue *mis-kən-stroo'* or *-kon'stroo, vt* to construe or to interpret wrongly. **[mis-]**

miscontent *mis-kən-tent'*, (*archaic*) *n, adj*, and *vt* discontent. — *adj* **miscontent'ed**. — *n* **miscontent'ment**. **[mis-]**

miscopy *mis-kop'i, vt* to copy wrongly or imperfectly. — *n* an error in copying. **[mis-]**

miscorrect *mis-kə-rekt', vt* to alter or mark wrongly in would-be correction. — *n* **miscorrec'tion**. **[mis-]**

miscounsel *mis-kown'sl, vt* to advise wrongly. **[mis-]**

miscount *mis-kownt', vt* and *vi* to count wrongly, to miscalculate; to misjudge. — *n* a miscalculation. **[mis-]**

miscreant *mis'kri-ənt, n orig* a misbeliever, a heretic or infidel; a vile wretch, a detestable scoundrel. — *adj* unbelieving (*archaic*); depraved, scoundrelly, wicked. — *n* **mis'creance, mis'creancy** or **mis'creaunce** (*Spenser*) false religious belief. [OFr *mescreant*, from *mes-* (from L *minus* less), and L *crēdēns, -entis*, pr p of *crēdere* to believe]

miscreated *mis-krē-āt'-id* or (*poetic*) **miscreate** *mis-krē-āt', adj* created imperfectly or improperly; deformed. — *n* **miscreā'tion**. — *adj* **miscreā'tive** that creates imperfectly or improperly. — *n* **miscreā'tor**. **[mis-]**

miscreaunce. See under **miscreant**.

miscredit *mis-kred'it*, (*archaic*) *vt* to disbelieve. **[mis-]**

miscreed *mis-krēd'*, (*poetic*) *n* a false creed. **[mis-]**

miscue *mis-kū', n* a stroke spoiled by the slipping off of the cue (*billiards*, etc); a mistake; a wrong cue (in any sense). — *vt* to hit (a billiard ball) wrongly. — *vi* to make a faulty stroke (*billiards*, etc); to answer the wrong cue, or to miss one's cue (*theat*); to make a mistake. **[mis-**, or **miss[1]]**

misdate *mis-dāt', vt* to date wrongly. — *n* a wrong date. **[mis-]**

misdeal *mis-dēl', n* a wrong deal, as at cards. — *vt* and *vi* to deal wrongly; to divide improperly: — *pa t* and *pa p* **misdealt** (*-delt'*). **[mis-]**

misdeed *mis-dēd', n* a wrongdoing, a bad or wicked deed. [OE *misdǣd*]

misdeem *mis-dēm'*, (*archaic*) *vt* and *vi* to think badly (of); to judge wrongly; to have a mistaken opinion (of); to suspect: — *pa p* **misdeemed'** or (*Spenser*) **misdempt'**. — *adj* (*dialect*) **misdeem'ful**. — *adj* **misdeem'ing** misjudging; suspicious; deceiving (*Spenser*). — *n* misjudgement; suspicion. **[mis-]**

misdemean *mis-di-mēn', vt* (*refl*) and *vi* to misbehave. — *n* **misdemean'ant** a person guilty of petty crime or misconduct. — *n* **misdemean'our** or (*NAm*) **misdemean'or** bad conduct; a misdeed; (in UK formerly) a legal offence of less gravity than a felony. **[mis-** and **demean[1]]**

misdempt. See **misdeem**.

misdescribe *mis-dis-krīb', vt* to describe wrongly. — *n* **misdescrip'tion**. **[mis-]**

misdesert *mis-di-zûrt'*, (*Spenser*) *n* undeservedness. **[mis-]**

misdevotion *mis-di-vō'shən, n* misdirected devotion. **[mis-]**

misdiagnose *mis-dī'əg-nōz* or *-nōz', vt* to diagnose wrongly. — *n* **misdiagnō'sis**. **[mis-]**

misdial *mis-dī'əl* or *-dīl', vi* and *vt* to dial (a telephone number) incorrectly. **[mis-]**

misdid. See **misdo**.

misdiet *mis-dī'ət*, (*Spenser*) *n* improper feeding. **[mis-]**

misdight *mis-dīt'*, (*Spenser*) *adj* badly prepared or provided; in miserable circumstances. **[mis-]**

misdirect *mis-di-rekt'* or *-dī-, vt* to direct wrongly. — *n* **misdirec'tion**. **[mis-]**

misdo *mis-doo', vt* to do wrongly or badly; to injure (*obs*); to kill (*obs*). — *vi* to act wrongly or badly: — *pa t* **misdid'**; *pa p* **misdone'**; old *infinitive* (*Spenser*) **misdonne'**. — *n* **misdo'er**. — *n* **misdo'ing**. **[mis-]**

misdoubt *mis-dowt'*, (*archaic* and *dialect*) *vt* to have a doubt, suspicion, misgiving, or foreboding of or about; to suspect. — *n* suspicion; hesitation; misgiving. — *adj* (*Spencer*) **misdoubt'ful**. **[mis-]**

misdraw *mis-drö', vt* to draw or draft badly. — *n* **misdraw'ing**. **[mis-]**

misdread *mis-dred'*, (*Shakesp*) *n* dread of evil to come. **[mis-]**

mise *mēz* or *mīz, n* expenditure, outlay (*obs*); in Wales and the county palatine of Chester, a payment to a new king, prince, Lord of the Marches, or earl, to secure certain privileges (*hist*); the issue in a writ of right (*law*); the adjustment of a dispute by agreement (*hist*); a stake in gambling; the layout of cards. — **mise en place** (*mē zã plas*) the preparation, such as laying tables and setting out the required ingredients and utensils, carried out in a restaurant before a meal is served; **mise en scène** (*mē-zã-sen*) the act, result, or art, of setting a stage or film scene or arranging a pictorial representation; a style of direction in the cinema, the use of a relatively static camera with subjects in full shot, and very little cutting within a scene, often opposed to **montage**; setting, physical surroundings. [OFr *mise* placing or setting, from L *mittere, missum*]

misease *mis-ēz'*, (*archaic*) *n* distress; uneasiness. [OFr *mesaise*]

miseducation *mis-ed-ū-kā'shən, n* improper or damaging education. **[mis-]**

misemploy *mis-im-ploi', vt* to employ wrongly or badly; to misuse. — *n* **misemploy'ment**. **[mis-]**

misentreat *mis-in-trēt'*, (*obs*) *vt* to ill-treat. **[mis-** and **entreat** (to treat)**]**

misentry *mis-en'tri, n* a wrong entry. **[mis-]**

miser[1] *mī'zər, n* a wretch (*Spenser* and *Shakesp*); a person who lives miserably in order to hoard wealth; a tight-fisted or niggardly person. — *adj* like a miser. — *n* **mi'serliness**. — *adj* **mi'serly**. [L *miser* wretched]

miser[2] *mīz'ər, n* a well-boring instrument. [Origin doubtful]

miserable *miz'ə-rə-bl, adj* wretched; exceedingly unhappy; causing misery; extremely poor or mean; contemptible. — *n* a wretch; very weak tea (*rare*). — *n* **mis'erableness**. — *adv* **mis'erably**. [Fr, *misérable*, from L *miserābilis*, from *miser*]

misère *mē-zer'* or *miz-ār'*, (*cards*) *n* an undertaking to take no tricks. [Fr misery]

Miserere *miz-e-rē'ri* or *mis-e-rā're, n* the 50th Psalm of the Vulgate (51st in AV), from its first word (*RC*); a musical setting of this; (without *cap*) a misericord in a church stall. [L, 2nd pers sing imperative of *miserērī* to have mercy, to pity, from *miser* wretched]

misericord or **misericorde** *miz-er'i-körd* or *miz'ər-*, also *-körd', n* mercy, forgiveness, pity (*obs*); a relaxation of monastic rule; a room in a monastery where some relaxation of rule was allowed; a bracket on a turn-up seat in a choir-stall, allowing the user some support when standing, often intricately carved; a narrow-bladed dagger for killing a wounded enemy. [OFr *misericorde*, from L *misericordia*, from *misericors, -cordis* tender-hearted]

miserly. See under **miser[1]**.

misery *miz'ər-i, n* wretchedness; extreme pain; miserable conditions; misère (*cards*); avarice (*Shakesp*); a very unhappy experience; a doleful person (*colloq*). — **misery index** an estimate of the economic difficulty being experienced by a particular country, etc, *usu* calculated from the current rates of inflation and unemployment. [OFr, from L *miseria*]

misesteem *mis-es-tēm', n* disrespect. — *vt* to value wrongly. — *vt* **mises'timate** to estimate wrongly. **[mis-]**

misfaith *mis-fāth'*, (*archaic*) *n* distrust. [**mis-**]

misfall *mis-fök'*, (*obs*) *vt* to befall unluckily: — *pa t* **misfell'**; *pa p* **misfall'en** (*Spenser* **misfalne'**). [**mis-**]

misfare *mis-fār'*, (*Spenser*) *n* misfortune. — *vi* to fare badly. — *n* **misfar'ing** (*Spenser*) wrong-doing. [OE *misfaran*]

misfeasance *mis-fēz'əns*, (*law*) *n* the doing of a lawful act in a wrongful manner, as distinguished from *malfeasance*. — *n* **misfeas'or**. [OFr *mesfaisance*, from pfx *mes-* (from L *minus* less), and *faisance*, from *faire*, from L *facere* to do]

misfeature *mis-fē'chər*, *n* a bad or distorted feature, trait or aspect; deformity. — *adj* **misfeat'ured** having bad or distorted features, etc. — *adj* **misfeat'uring** distorting the features, disfiguring. [**mis-**]

misfeed *mis-fēd'*, *vt* to feed (eg a machine) incorrectly (with paper, materials, etc): — *pa t* and *pa p* **misfed'**. [**mis-**]

misfeign *mis-fān'*, (*Spencer*) *vi* to feign with bad intent. [**mis-**]

misfield *mis-fēld'*, (*cricket*) *vi* and *vt* to field badly or ineffectively. — *n* (*mis'-*) a mistake or failure in fielding. [**mis-**]

misfile *mis-fīl'*, *vt* to file (information) under the wrong headings, etc. [**mis-**]

misfire *mis-fīr'*, *vi* to fail to go off, explode or ignite, at all or at the right time; to fail to have the effect intended (*fig*). — *n* a failure to fire, or to achieve the desired effect. [**miss**[1], and **fire**]

misfit *mis'fit*, *n* a bad fit; a thing that fits badly; a person who cannot adjust to his or her social environment, job, etc. — *vt* and *vi* (*mis-fit'*) to fit badly. [**mis-**]

misform *mis-förm'*, *vt* to form or shape badly or improperly. — *n* **misformā'tion**. [**mis-**]

misfortune *mis-för'tūn*, *n* ill-fortune; an evil accident; calamity; an illegitimate child, or the having of one (*colloq*). — *adj* **misfor'tuned** (*archaic*) unfortunate. [**mis-**]

misgive *mis-giv'*, *vt* to suggest apprehensions to, fill with forebodings; to give erroneously. — *vi* to have apprehensive forebodings; to fail (*Scot*): — *pa t* **misgave'**; *pa p* **misgiv'en**. — *n* **misgiv'ing** mistrust; a feeling that all is not well. [**mis-**]

misgo *mis-gō'*, (*obs* or *dialect*) *vi* to go the wrong way or go astray: — *pa t* **miswent** (supplied from **miswend**); *pa p* **misgone** (*mis-gon'*; *obs*, now illiterally, **miswent'**). [**mis-**]

misgotten *mis-got'n*, (*Spenser*) *adj* ill-gotten; misbegotten. [**mis-**]

misgovern *mis-guv'ərn*, *vt* to govern badly or unjustly. — *n* **misgov'ernaunce** (*Spenser*) mismanagement. — *n* **misgov'ernment**. — *n* **misgov'ernor**. [**mis-**]

misgraft *mis-gräft'*, *vt* to graft unsuitably. — *adj* **misgraff** (*mis-gräf*; *Shakesp*) badly grafted or matched. [**mis-**]

misgrowth *mis-grōth'*, *n* an irregular growth; an excrescence; a sport of nature. [**mis-**]

misguggle *mis-gug'l* or **mishguggle** *mish-*, (*Scot*) *vt* to bungle, mar. [**mis-**]

misguide *mis-gīd'*, *vt* to guide wrongly; to lead into error; to ill-treat (*Scot*). — *n* (*obs*) misbehaviour. — *n* **misguid'ance**. — *adj* **misguid'ed** erring; misdirected; ill-judged. — *adv* **misguid'edly**. — *n* **misguid'er**. [**mis-**]

mishallowed *mis-hal'ōd*, (*archaic*) *adj* consecrated to evil. [**mis-**]

mishandle *mis-han'dl*, *vt* to handle wrongly or unskilfully; to maltreat. [**mis-**]

mishanter. Same as **mischanter**.

mishap *mis-hap'* or *mis'hap*, *n* bad luck; unlucky accident; misfortune. — *vi* (*obs*) to happen unfortunately. — *vi* **mishapp'en** (*Spenser*) to happen unfortunately. [**mis-**]

mishapt. A Spenserian form of **misshaped**.

mishear *mis-hēr'*, *vt* and *vi* to hear wrongly. [**mis-**]

mishegaas. See under **meshuga**.

mishguggle. See **misguggle**.

mishit *mis-hit'*, *vt* to hit (a ball) faultily. — *n* (*mis'hit*) a faulty hit. [**mis-**]

mishmash *mish'mash*, *n* a hotchpotch, medley. [Reduplication of **mash**[1]; cf Ger *Mischmasch*, from *mischen*, from L *miscere* to mix]

mishmee or **mishmi** *mish'mē*, *n* the bitter rootstock of an Assamese gold-thread plant (*Coptis teeta*), with tonic properties. [Said to be Assamese *mishmītīta*]

Mishnah or **Mishna** *mish'nä*, *n* the Jewish oral law, finally redacted AD 220 and forming the first section of the Talmud: — *pl* **Mishnayōth'**. — *adj* **Mishnā'ic** or **Mish'nic**. [Heb *mishnāh*, from *shānāh* to repeat, teach, learn]

misidentify *mis-ī-den'ti-fī*, *vt* to identify incorrectly. — *n* **misidentificā'tion**. [**mis-**]

misimprove *mis-im-prōōv'*, *vt* to turn to bad use; to make worse by would-be improvement. — *n* **misimprove'ment**. [**mis-**]

misinform *mis-in-förm'*, *vt* to inform or tell incorrectly or misleadingly. — *n* **misinform'ant**. — *n* **misinformā'tion**. — *n* **misinform'er**. [**mis-**]

misinstruct *mis-in-strukt'*, *vt* to instruct wrongly. — *n* **misinstruc'tion** wrong instruction. [**mis-**]

misintelligence *mis-in-tel'i-jəns*, *n* wrong or false information; misunderstanding; lack of intelligence. [**mis-**]

misintend *mis-in-tend'*, (*obs*) *vt* to intend or aim in malice. [**mis-**]

misinterpret *mis-in-tûr'prit*, *vt* to interpret wrongly; to explain wrongly. — *n* **misinterpretā'tion**. — *n* **misinter'preter**. [**mis-**]

misjoin *mis-join'*, *vt* to join improperly or unsuitably. — *n* **misjoin'der** (*law*) an incorrect union of parties or of causes of action in a suit. [**mis-**]

misjudge *mis-juj'*, *vt* and *vi* to judge wrongly. — *n* **misjudg'ement** or **misjudg'ment**. [**mis-**]

misken *mis-ken'*, (*Scot*) *vt* to be, or to appear, ignorant of; to fail or refuse to recognize. [**mis-**]

miskey *mis-kē'*, *vt* to key (data on a computer, etc keyboard) incorrectly: — *pa p* and *pa t* **miskey'ed**. [**mis-**]

misknow *mis-nō'*, *vt* to misapprehend, misunderstand. — *n* **misknowledge** (*mis-nol'ij*). [**mis-**]

mislay *mis-lā'*, *vt* to lay or place wrongly; to lay in a place not remembered; to lose: — *pa t* and *pa p* **mislaid'**. [**mis-** and **lay**[3]]

mislead *mis-lēd'*, *vt* to lead into error; to direct, inform or advise wrongly; to cause to go wrong: — *pa t* and *pa p* **misled'**. — *n* **mislead'er**. — *adj* **mislead'ing** deceptive. — *adv* **mislead'ingly**. [**mis-**]

misleared *mis-lērd'*, (*Scot* and *NEng dialect*) *adj* mistaught; unmannerly; ill-conditioned. [**mis-**, and **leared**, pa p of **lear**[1]]

misleeke *mis-lēk'*, (*Spenser*) *vi* for **mislike**.

misletoe. A former spelling of **mistletoe**.

mislight *mis-līt'*, (*poetic*) *vt* to lead astray by a light. [**mis-**]

mislike *mis-līk'*, (*archaic*) *vt* to dislike; to displease. — *vi* to disapprove. — *n* dislike; disapprobation. — *n* **mislīk'er**. — *n* **mislīk'ing**. [**mis-**]

mislippen *mis-lip'n*, (*Scot* and *NEng dialect*) *vt* to distrust; to suspect; to disappoint, deceive; to neglect, overlook. [**mis-**]

mislive *mis-liv'*, (*obs*) *vi* to live a bad life. [**mis-**]

misluck *mis-luk'*, (*esp Scot*) *n* bad luck, misfortune. — *vi* to meet with bad luck, to fail. [**mis-**]

mismake *mis-māk'*, (now *Scot*) *vt* to make or shape badly; to trouble or disturb: — *pa p* and *adj* **mismade'**. [**mis-**]

mismanage *mis-man'ij*, *vt* to conduct or manage badly, carelessly or wrongly. — *n* **misman'agement**. [**mis-**]

mismanners *mis-man'ərz*, (*obs*) *n pl* bad manners. [**mis-**]

mismarry *mis-mar'i*, *vt* and *vi* to marry unsuitably. — *n* **mismarri'age**. [**mis-**]

mismatch *mis-mach'*, *vt* to match unsuitably or badly. — *n* a bad match. — *n* **mismatch'ment**. [**mis-**]

mismate *mis-māt'*, *vt* and *vi* to mate unsuitably. — *adj* **mismat'ed**. [**mis-**]

mismeasure *mis-mezh'ər*, *vt* to measure wrongly. — *n* **mismeas'urement**. [**mis-**]

mismetre *mis-mēt'ər*, *vt* to spoil the metre of (a poem). **[mis-]**

misname *mis-nām'*, *vt* to call by an unsuitable or wrong name. **[mis-]**

misnomer *mis-nō'mər*, *n* a misnaming; a wrong or unsuitable name. — *vt* to misname. [OFr from *mes-* (from L *minus* less), and *nommer*, from L *nōmināre* to name]

miso *mē'sō*, *n* a paste, used for flavouring, prepared from soya beans and fermented in brine: — *pl* **mi'sos**. [Jap]

miso- *mis-ō-* or *mīs-ō-*, *combining form* signifying a hater of, hating. — *adj* **misocap'nic** (Gr *kapnos* smoke) hating smoke, *esp* that of tobacco. — *adj* **mis'oclere** (*-klēr*; Gr *kleros* clergy; *Fuller*) hating the clergy. — *n* **misogamist** (*-og'ə-mist*; Gr *gamos* marriage) a hater of marriage. — *n* **misog'amy**. — *n* **misogynist** (*-oj'i-nist* or *-og'*; Gr *gynē* a woman) a woman-hater. — *adj* **misogynist'ic**, **misogynist'ical** or **misog'ynous**. — *n* **misog'yny**. — *n* **misology** (*-ol'ə-ji*; Gr *logos* reason) hatred of reason, reasoning, or knowledge. — *n* **misol'ogist**. — *n* **misoneism** (*-nē'izm*; Gr *neos* new) hatred of novelty. — *n* **misonē'ist**. — *adj* **misonēist'ic**. [Gr *mīseein* to hate]

misobserve *mis-ob-zûrv'*, *vt* and *vi* to fail to observe; to observe incorrectly. — *n* **misobserv'ance**. **[mis-]**

misocapnic... to ... **misoneistic**. See under **miso-**.

misorder *mis-ör'dər*, *n* and *vt* disorder. **[mis-]**

misperceive *mis-pər-sēv'*, *vt* to perceive incorrectly, misunderstand. — *n* **mispercep'tion**. **[mis-]**

mispersuasion *mis-pər-swā'zhən*, (*rare*) *n* a wrong persuasion or notion; a false opinion. — *vt* **mispersuade'**. **[mis-]**

mispickel *mis'pik-əl*, *n* arsenical pyrites, a mineral composed of iron, arsenic, and sulphur. [Ger]

misplace *mis-plās'*, *vt* to put in a wrong place; to mislay; to set on, or attach to, a wrong or inapproproate object (*fig*); to indulge in in unsuitable circumstances (*fig*). — *n* **misplace'ment**. — **misplaced modifier** see **misrelated participle** under **misrelate**. **[mis-]**

misplay *mis-plā'*, *n* a wrong play, as in sport or games. — Also *vt* and *vi*. **[mis-]**

misplead *mis-plēd'*, *vt* and *vi* to plead wrongly. — *n* **misplead'ing** an error in pleading. **[mis-]**

misplease *mis-plēz'*, (*obs*) *vt* to displease. **[mis-]**

mispoint *mis-point'*, *vt* to punctuate wrongly. **[mis-]**

mispraise *mis-prāz'*, *vt* to praise wrongly; to reproach. **[mis-]**

misprint *mis-print'*, *vt* to print wrongly. — *vi* to make footprints in unusual positions. — *n* (*usu mis'print*) a mistake in printing. **[mis-]**

misprise[1] or **misprize** *mis-prīz'*, *vt* to scorn; to slight; to undervalue. — *n* (*Spenser* **mesprise**, **mesprize** or **misprize**) scorn; slighting; failure to value. [OFr *mespriser*, from pfx *mes-* (from L *minus* less), LL *pretiāre*, from L *pretium* price, value]

misprise[2] or **misprize** *mis-prīz'*, *vt* to mistake. — *n* (*Spenser* **mesprize**) error. — *adj* **misprised'** mistaken. [OFr *mespris*, pa p of *mesprendre* to commit an offence; cf **misprision**[1]]

misprision[1] *mis-prizh'ən*, *n* a mistake; the overlooking or deliberate concealing of the crime of another (*law*); any serious offence or failure of duty (*positive* or *negative*, according to whether it is maladministration or mere neglect). — **misprision of heresy**, **treason**, etc, knowledge of and failure to give information about heresy, treason, etc. [OFr *mes-* (from L *minus* less), and LL *prēnsiō*, *-ōnis*, from L *praehendere* to take]

misprision[2] *mis-prizh'ən*, (*archaic*) *n* failure to appreciate the true value, nature or extent of something. [**misprise**[1], after the model of **misprision**[1]]

mispronounce *mis-prə-nowns'*, *vt* to pronounce incorrectly. — *n* **mispronunciation** (*-nun-si-ā'shən*) wrong or improper pronunciation. **[mis-]**

misproportion *mis-prə-pōr'shən*, *n* lack of due proportion. — *adj* **mispropor'tioned**. **[mis-]**

misproud *mis-prowd'*, (*archaic*) *adj* unduly proud. **[mis-]**

mispunctuate *mis-pungk'tū-āt* or *-pungk'cho͞o-*, *vt* and *vi* to punctuate wrongly. — *n* **mispunctuā'tion**. **[mis-]**

misquote *mis-kwōt'*, *vt* to quote wrongly. — *n* **misquotā'tion**. **[mis-]**

misrate *mis-rāt'*, *vt* to value wrongly. **[mis-]**

misread *mis-rēd'*, *vt* to read wrongly; to misconstrue. — *n* **misread'ing**. **[mis-]**

misreckon *mis-rek'n*, *vt* and *vi* to reckon or compute wrongly, to miscalculate. — *n* **misreck'oning**. **[mis-]**

misregard *mis-ri-gärd'*, (*Spenser*) *n* inattention. **[mis-]**

misrelate *mis-ri-lāt'*, *vt* to relate incorrectly. — *n* **misrelā'tion**. — **misrelated participle** a participle which the grammatical structure of the sentence insists on attaching to a word it is not intended to qualify (eg *Lost in thought, the bus passed me without stopping*; also called **misplaced modifier**). **[mis-]**

misremember *mis-ri-mem'bər*, *vt* and *vi* to remember wrongly or imperfectly; to forget (*Scot* and *dialect*). **[mis-]**

misreport *mis-ri-pōrt'*, *vt* to report falsely, misleadingly or wrongly; to speak ill of (*Shakesp*). — *n* false reporting or report; bad repute (*obs*). **[mis-]**

misrepresent *mis-rep-ri-zent'*, *vt* to represent falsely; to give a misleading interpretation to the words or deeds of; to be an unrepresentative representative of. — *n* **misrepresentā'tion**. **[mis-]**

misroute *mis-ro͞ot'*, *vt* to route (eg a telephone call, traffic) wrongly. **[mis-]**

misrule *mis-ro͞ol'*, *n* disorder; bad or disorderly government. — *vt* and *vi* to govern badly. — **Lord of Misrule** a leader of Christmas revels; a promoter of anti-establishment or anti-traditionalist views or activities. **[mis-]**

Miss *mis*, *n* a title prefixed to the name of an unmarried (formerly, and now *dialect* and *US illiterate*, also a married) woman or girl (*orig* less respectful than *Mrs*); also prefixed to a representational title, *esp* in beauty contests, eg *Miss World*; (without the name) an eldest daughter, young lady of the house (*obs*); vocatively used alone in (*usu* mock) severity, or to address a waitress, female teacher, etc; (without *cap*) a schoolgirl, or a girl or woman with the faults attributed to schoolgirls; a person between a child and a woman, *esp* in reference to clothing size; a kept mistress (*obs*): — *pl* **miss'es** (either 'the Miss Hepburns' or 'the Misses Hepburn' may be said, the latter being more formal). — *n* **miss'hood**. — *adj* **miss'ish** schoolgirlish; having the faults attributed to schoolgirls, ie sentimental, insipid, namby-pamby, squeamish, silly, etc. — *n* **miss'ishness**. — *n* **miss'y** a (*usu* disparaging) form of address used to a little girl. — *adj* missish. — **Miss Nancy** (*colloq*) a very effeminate man. [Shortened form of **mistress**]

Miss. *abbrev*: Mississippi (US state).

miss[1] *mis*, *vt* (or *vi*, *archaic*, with *of*) to fail to hit, reach, find, meet, touch, catch, get, have, take advantage of, observe or see; to avoid (a specified danger); to fail (to do; *archaic*); to leave out, omit; to discover the absence of; to feel the loss or absence of; to think of (an absent person or thing) longingly, or (a former time) nostalgically; to do without (*Shakesp*). — *vi* to fail to hit or obtain; to fail; to go wrong (*obs*); to miss fire. — *n* the fact or condition or an act or occasion of missing; failure to hit the mark; loss; (the source of or reason for) a feeling of loss or absence; wrong-doing (*Shakesp*). — *adj* **miss'able**. — *adj* **miss'ing** not to be found; not in the expected place; lacking; of unascertained fate (*military*). — *adv* **miss'ingly** (*Shakesp*) with a sense of loss. — **missing link** a hypothetical extinct creature thought to be intermediate between man and the anthropoid apes; any one thing required to complete a series. — **give (something) a miss** to allow an opponent to score by intentionally missing (*billiards*); to leave out, omit or avoid something; **go missing** to disappear, *esp* unexpectedly and inexplicably; to be mislaid; **miss fire** to fail to go off or explode (cf **misfire**); **miss oneself** (*Scot*) to miss out on an enjoyable experience; **miss one's tip** (*slang*) to fail in one's plan or attempt; **miss out** to omit; (with *on*) to fail to experience or benefit (from); **miss stays** (*naut*) to fail in going about from one tack to another; **miss the bus** or **boat** (*colloq*) to lose one's opportunity; **near miss** see under **near**. [OE *missan*; Du *missen* to miss]

miss[2]. See **Miss**.

missa *mis'ə* or *-a*, (*L*) *n* (also with *cap*) the Mass (*RC*). — **missa** (or **Missa**) **solemnis** (*sol-em'nis*) high mass.

missal *mis'l*, (*RC*) *n* a book containing the complete service for mass throughout the year. [LL *missāle*, from *missa* mass]

missay *mis-sā'*, (*archaic*) *vt* and *vi* to say or speak amiss, wrongly, falsely, or in vain; to slander; to revile: — *pa t* and *pa p* **missaid** (*-sed'*). — *n* **missay'ing**. [**mis-**]

missee *mis-sē'*, *vt* and *vi* to see wrongly. [**mis-**]

misseem *mis-sēm'*, (*Spenser*) *vt* to be unbecoming to. — *adj* **misseem'ing** unbecoming. — *n* false appearance. [**mis-**]

missel *mis'l* or *miz'l*, *n* mistletoe (*obs*); the mistle-thrush. — **miss'el-bird** or **miss'el-thrush** a mistle-thrush. [OE *mistel*, *mistil* mistletoe]

missel-tree *mis'l-trē*, *n* a melastomaceous tree (*Bellucia aubletii*) of northern S America, with edible berries.

missend *mis-send'*, *vt* to send by mistake; to send to the wrong person or place: — *pa t* and *pa p* **missent'**. [**mis-**]

misset *mis-set'*, *vt* to set or place wrongly or unfitly; to put in a bad mood (*Scot*). [**mis-**]

misshape *mis-shāp'*, *vt* to shape badly or wrongly; to deform. — *n* deformity. — *adj* **misshap'en** or **mis-shaped'** (*Spenser* **mishapt**) badly-shaped, deformed. — *n* **misshap'enness**. [**mis-**]

missheathed *mis-shēdh'id*, (*Shakesp*) *adj* wrongly sheathed. [**mis-**]

missile *mis'īl* or (*NAm*) *mis'l*, *n* a weapon or object for throwing by hand or shooting from a bow, gun, or other instrument, *esp* a rocket-launched weapon, often nuclear. — *adj* capable of being thrown or projected; relating to a missile. — *n* **miss'ilery** or **missilry** (*-īl-ri* or *-l-ri*) missiles collectively; their design, manufacture and use. [L *missilis*, from *mittere*, *missum* to throw]

missing. See under **miss**[1].

mission *mish'ən*, *n* an act of sending, *esp* to perform some function; a flight with a specific purpose, such as a bombing raid or a task assigned to an astronaut or astronauts; the errand or purpose for which one is sent; that for which one has been or seems to have been sent into the world, vocation; a sending out of people on a political or diplomatic errand, for the spreading of a religion, etc; an organization that sends out missionaries; its activities; a station or establishment of missionaries; any particular field of missionary enterprise; the body of people sent on a mission; an embassy; a settlement for religious, charitable, medical, or philanthropic work in a district; a religious organization or district not fully developed as a parish; a series of special religious services conducted by a missioner. — *adj* of a mission or missions, *esp* characteristic of the old Spanish missions in California. — *vt* (*rare*) to commission. — *vt* and *vi* **miss'ionarize** or **-ise** to act as missionary (to, among, or in); to do missionary work. — *n* **miss'ionary** a person sent on a mission, *esp* religious. — *adj* relating to a mission or missions. — *n* **miss'ioner** a missionary; a person in charge of parochial missions. — *vt* and *vi* **miss'ionize** or **-ise** to do missionary work (upon, in, or among). — **mission architecture** the style of the old Spanish missions in California, etc; **missionary-bish'op** one having jurisdiction in an unconverted country, or in districts not yet formed into dioceses; **missionary position** in sexual intercourse, the face-to-face position with the male on top; **missionary selling** approaches made by manufacturers to develop goodwill with new contacts who are not the intended final purchasers of a particular product, and to increase sales; **Mission Indian** a member of any of the N American Indian tribes converted by early Spanish Catholic missionaries in California, etc. [L *missiō*, *-ōnis*, from *mittere* to send]

missis or **missus** *mis'is* or *-iz*, (*illiterate* or *colloq*) *n* lady of the house; wife; a term of address to a woman (*usu* by an unacquainted man). [**mistress**]

missive *mis'iv*, *adj* sent; missile (*obs*). — *n* that which is sent, as a letter; a messenger (*Shakesp*); a missile (*obs*); (in *pl*) letters sent between two parties in which one makes an offer and the other accepts it (*Scots law*). — **letter missive** a missive, *esp* from a sovereign or authority to a particular person or body, such as one giving *congé d'élire*. [LL *missīvus*, from L *mittere*, *missum* to send]

misspeak *mis-spēk'*, *vt* and *vi* to speak wrongly. [**mis-**]

misspell *mis-spel'*, *vt* and *vi* to spell wrongly: — *pa t* and *pa p* **misspelt'** or **misspelled'**. — *n* **misspell'ing** a wrong spelling. [**mis-**]

misspend *mis-spend'*, *vt* to spend badly; to waste or squander: — *pa t* and *pa p* **misspent'**. [**mis-**]

misstate *mis-stāt'*, *vt* to state wrongly or falsely. — *n* **misstate'ment**. [**mis-**]

misstep *mis-step'*, *vi* to make a false step; to make a mistake. — *n* a mistake in conduct, etc. [**mis-**]

missuit *mis-sōōt'* or *-sūt'*, *vt* to be unbecoming to. [**mis-**]

missummation *mis-sum-ā'shən*, *n* wrong addition. [**mis-**]

missus. See **missis**.

mist *mist*, *n* watery vapour seen in the atmosphere; cloud in contact with the ground; thin fog; rain in very fine drops; a fine spray of any liquid; a suspension of liquid in a gas; condensed vapour on a surface; a dimness or dim appearance; anything that dims or darkens the sight or the judgement. — *vt* to obscure or veil with, or as if with, mist; to apply a fine spray of water to (an indoor plant). — *vi* to become misty or veiled; to form a mist or vapour-cloud. — *n* **mist'er** a spray gun with a fine nozzle, used to apply moisture to the foliage of indoor plants. — *adj* **mist'ful** misty. — *adv* **mist'ily**. — *n* **mist'iness**. — *n* **mist'ing** mist; the action of the verb *mist*. — *adj* misty; hazy; dimming. — *adj* **mist'y** full of, covered with, obscured by, mist; like mist; dim; obscure; clouded; vague; not perspicuous; (of eyes) tearful. — **mist'-flower** a N American hemp-agrimony, with clusters of blue or violet flowers; **mist net** a net made of very fine threads used to trap birds. — *vt* **mist'-net** to trap in such a net. — **mist up** or **over** (of a surface) to become covered with condensed vapour; **Scotch mist** a thick wetting mist; a drizzle. [OE *mist* darkness, dimness; Icel *mistr*, Du *mist*]

mistake *mis-tāk'*, *vt* to understand wrongly; to take for another thing or person; to be wrong about; to think wrongly; to remove wrongfully (*obs*); (*appar*) to take or come upon to one's loss (*Spenser*); to believe wrongly to be (*Spenser*). — *vi* to err in opinion or judgement; to do amiss: — *pa t* **mistook'**; *pa p* **mistak'en** (also **mista'en'**). — *n* the act of taking or understanding something wrongly; something understood or taken wrongly; an error; (*mis'*) a faulty shot (*cinematography*). — *adj* **mistak'able**. — *adj* **mistak'en** understood wrongly; guilty of making a mistake; under a misapprehension; erroneous; incorrect; ill-judged. — *adv* **mistak'enly**. — *n* **mistak'enness**. — *n* **mistak'ing** (*Shakesp*) a mistake. — **mistaken identity** an error in identifying someone. — **and no mistake** (*colloq*) assuredly; **be mistaken** to make or have made a mistake; to be misunderstood; **mistake one's man** to think too lightly of the man one has to deal with; **mistake one's way** to take the wrong road. [ME *mistaken*, from ON *mistaka* to take wrongly, from *mis-* wrongly, and *taka* to take]

misteach *mis-tēch'*, *vt* to teach wrongly: — *pa t* and *pa p* **mistaught** (*mis-töt'*). [**mis-**]

mistell *mis-tel'*, *vt* to count, narrate or inform, wrongly: — *pa t* and *pa p* **mistold'**. [**mis-**]

mistemper *mis-tem'pər*, (*obs*) *n* and *vt* disorder. — *adj* **mistem'pered** tempered or mixed badly (*Shakesp*); mixed or prepared for an evil purpose (*Shakesp*). [**mis-**]

Mister *mis'tər, n* a title prefixed to a man's name, and to certain designations (as Mr Justice, Mr Speaker), written **Mr**; (without *cap*) sir (*colloq*). — *vt* **mis'ter** to address as 'mister'. [**master**]

mister[1] *mis'tər, n* craft, trade, profession (*obs*); manner, kind (*Spenser*; without *of* — what mister man, *orig* = man of what class, hence what kind of man); need, necessity (*Scot*). — *vi* (*Spenser*) to be necessary; to have need. — *vt* to need. — *n* **mis'tery** see **mystery**[2]. [OFr *mestier* (Fr *métier*) trade, from L *ministerium* service]

mister[2]. See under **mist**.

misterm *mis-tûrm', vt* to name wrongly or unsuitably. [**mis-**]

mistery. See **mystery**[2].

misthink *mis-thingk', vt* to think badly of (*Shakesp*); to think wrongly. — *vi* to have wicked or mistaken thoughts (*obs*): — *pa t* and *pa p* **misthought** (*mis-thöt'*). — *n* **misthought'** a wrong notion. [**mis-**]

mistico *mis'ti-kō, n* a small Mediterranean ship, between a xebec and a felucca in size: — *pl* **mis'ticos**. [Sp *místico*, prob from Ar]

mistigris *mis'ti-gris* or *-grē, n* a variation of poker in which a joker or blank card can be given any value; the card so used. [Fr *mistigri* knave of clubs]

mistime *mis-tīm', vt* to time wrongly. — *adj* **mistimed'** inopportune. [**mis-**]

mistitle *mis-tī'tl, vt* to call by a wrong or unsuitable title. [**mis-**]

mistle. Same as **mizzle**[1] or **missel**.

mistle-thrush *mis'l-thrush, n* a large European thrush fond of mistletoe berries. — Also **miss'el-thrush**. [See ety for **mistletoe**, and **thrush**]

mistletoe *mis'l-tō* or *miz', n* a hemiparasitic evergreen shrubby plant (*Viscum album*) with white, viscous berries, growing on the apple, apricot, etc (very rarely on the oak); extended to other species of its genus or family (*Loranthaceae*). [OE *misteltān*, from *mistel*, *mistil* mistletoe, and *tān* twig; see **missel**]

mistold *mis-tōld', pa t* of **mistell**.

mistook *mis-tŏŏk', pa t* of **mistake**.

mistral *mis'tral, n* a violent cold dry north-east wind in southern France. [Fr, from Provençal *mistral*, from L *magistrālis* masterful, *magister* master]

mistranslate *mis-trans-lāt', vt* and *vi* to translate incorrectly. — *n* **mistranslā'tion**. [**mis-**]

mistrayned *mis-trānd'*, (*Spenser*) *pa p* drawn away, misled. [**mis-**; see **train**[1]]

mistreading *mis-tred'ing*, (*Shakesp*) *n* a false step, misdeed. [**mis-**]

mistreat *mis-trēt', vt* to treat ill. — *n* **mistreat'ment**. [**mis-**]

mistress *mis'tris, n* (*fem* of **master**) a woman employer of servants or head of a house or family; a woman (or anything personified as a woman) having power of ownership; a woman teacher, *esp* in a school; a woman well skilled in anything; a woman loved and courted by a man (*archaic*); a woman involved in an established sexual relationship with a married man, sometimes supported by him financially; *vocatively* madam (*archaic* and *dialect*); the jack at bowls (*Shakesp*); (with *cap*) a title corresponding to the modern form **Mrs**, once prefixed to the name of any woman or girl (*archaic* or *dialect*). — *adj* (*literary*) principal; leading; ruling. — *vt* to make a mistress of, pay court to as a mistress; to address as mistress; to become or be mistress of or over; (with *it*) to play the mistress. — *adj* **mis'tressless**. — *adj* **mis'tressly**. — *n* **mis'tress-ship**. [OFr *maistresse* (Fr *maîtresse*), from LL *magistrissa*, fem from L *magister* master]

mistrial *mis-trī'əl, n* a trial void because of error; an inconclusive trial (*US*). [**mis-**]

mistrust *mis-trust', n* distrust. — *vt* to distrust; to suspect. — *vi* to be suspicious. — *adj* **mistrust'ful**. — *adv* **mistrust'fully**. — *n* **mistrust'fulness**. — *adv* **mistrust'ingly**. — *adj* **mistrust'less**. [**mis-**]

mistryst *mis-trīst'*, (*Scot*) *vt* to disappoint by not keeping an engagement. — *adj* **mistryst'ed** disturbed, put out. [**mis-**]

mistune *mis-tūn', vt* to tune wrongly or falsely; to put out of tune. [**mis-**]

misunderstand *mis-und-ər-stand', vt* to take in a wrong sense; to fail to appreciate the true nature, motives, etc of: — *pa t* and *pa p* **misunderstood'**. — *n* **misunderstand'ing** a mistake as to meaning; a slight disagreement. — *adj* **misunderstood'**. [**mis-**]

misuse *mis-ūs', n* improper use; application to a bad purpose; evil usage or behaviour (*Shakesp*). — *vt* **misuse** (*mis-ūz'*) to use for a wrong purpose or in a wrong way; to treat badly or wrongly; to speak badly of (*Shakesp*); to deceive (*Shakesp*): — *pa t* (*Spenser*) **misust** (*ūst'*). — *n* **misus'age** misconduct, evil practice (*Spenser*); bad or unfair treatment; wrong use. — *n* **misus'er**. [**mis-**]

misventure *mis-ven'chər, n* a misadventure. — *adj* **misvent'urous**. [**mis-**]

miswandred *mis-won'dərd*, (*Spenser*) *adj* strayed, gone astray. [**mis-**]

misween *mis-wēn'*, (*Spenser*) *vt* and *vi* to judge wrongly, have a wrong opinion of. [**mis-**]

miswend *mis-wend'*, (*Spenser*) *vi* to go astray or amiss; to come to grief, miscarry: — *pa t* and *pa p* **miswent'** (see **misgo**).

misword *mis-wûrd'*, *n* (*dialect*) an angry or harsh word. — *vt* to word incorrectly. — *n* **misword'ing**. [**mis-**]

misworship *mis-wûr'ship, vt* to worship wrongly. — *n* worship of a wrong object. [**mis-**]

miswrite *mis-rīt', vt* to write incorrectly. [**mis-**]

misyoke *mis-yōk', vt* to yoke or marry unsuitably. [**mis-**]

MIT *abbrev*: Massachusetts Institute of Technology.

mitch *mich*, (*dialect*) *vi* to play truant, *esp* from school. [Perh from OFr *muchier*, *mucier* to hide, lurk]

mite[1] *mīt, n* any of various tiny arachnids of the order *Acarida*, many of which carry disease, smaller than ticks and, unlike them, not always parasitic in habits. — *adj* **mīticīd'al**. — *n* **mīt'icide** (L *caedere* to kill) a poison or other agent that destroys mites. — *adj* **mīt'y** infested with mites. [OE *mīte*]

mite[2] *mīt, n orig* an old Flemish coin of very small value; used to translate the Gr *lepton* (Mark 12. 42) of which two make a *kodrantēs* or 'farthing' (*Bible*); a very small amount; a small contribution proportionate to one's means; a minute portion or fragment; a jot; a diminutive person; a small child. [MDu *mîte* (Du *mijt*); perh ult the same as **mite**[1]]

miter. See **mitre**[1,2].

mither. See **moider**.

Mithras *mith'ras* or **Mithra** *-rä, n* the ancient Persian god of light, whose worship became popular in the Roman Empire. — *n* **Mithraeum** (*-rē'əm*) a grotto or temple sacred to Mithras: — *pl* **Mithrae'a**. — *adj* **Mithrā'ic**. — *n* **Mithrā'icism** or **Mith'raism** (*-rä-izm*) belief in or worship of Mithras. — *n* **Mith'raist**. [L and Gr *Mithrās*, from OPers *Mithra*]

mithridate *mith'ri-dāt, n* an antidote to poison. — *adj* **mithridat'ic** or **mithradat'ic** antidotal; (with *cap*) relating to Mithridates (see below), *esp* to his wars against Rome (also **Mithradat'ic**). — *n* **mith'ridatism** (*-dāt-izm*) immunity to a poison acquired by taking gradually increased doses of it. — *vt* **mithrid'atize** or **-ise**. — **mithridate mustard** field penny-cress (*Thlaspi arvense*); **mithridate pepperwort** field cress (*Lepidium campestre*). [After *Mithridates*, king of Pontus (reigned *c*120–63 BC), who was said to have acquired immunity to poisons in this way]

MITI or **Miti** *abbrev*: Ministry of International Trade and Industry (Japan).

miticidal and **miticide**. See under **mite**[1].

mitigate *mit'i-gāt, vt* to mollify, appease; to make more easily borne; to lessen the severity, violence or evil of; to temper. — *adj* **mit'igable**. — *adj* **mit'igant** mitigating. — *n* **mitigā'tion**. — *n* and *adj* **mit'igātive**. — *n*

mit'igātor. — *adj* **mit'igātory**. [L *mītigāre*, *-ātum*, from *mītis* mild]

mitochondrion *mīt-* or *mit-ō-kon'dri-ən*, *n* an energy-producing body, threadlike to spherical in shape, present in cytoplasm: — *pl* **mitochon'dria**. — *adj* **mitochon'drial**. [Gr *mitos* thread, and *chondros* granule]

mitosis *mī-* or *mi-tō'sis*, *n* an elaborate process of cell-division involving the arrangement of chromosomes in definite figures; karyokinesis: — *pl* **mitō'ses** (*-sēz*). — *n* **mit'ogen** (Gr *gennaein* to engender) a substance that causes cells to divide. — *adj* **mitogenet'ic** or **mitogen'ic**. — *adj* **mitotic** (*-tot'ik*). — *adv* **mitot'ically**. — **mitotic index** the proportion in any tissue of dividing cells, *usu* expressed as per thousand cells. [Gr *mitos* fibre]

mitraille *mē'trī-y'*, *n* small shot or projectiles sent in a shower, *esp* from a mitrailleuse. — *n* **mitrailleur** (*-yœr'*) a machine-gunner; a mitrailleuse. — *n* **mitrailleuse** (*-yœz'*) a machine-gun (*orig* one having a number of barrels) that discharges a stream of small missiles. [Fr]

mitre[1] or (*NAm*) **miter** *mī'tər*, *n esp* in ancient Greece, a woman's headband; a belt or girdle (*Pope*, following *Homer*); an oriental hat or turban (*obs*); a high, pointed headdress, cleft crosswise on top and with two ribbons hanging from the back, worn by archbishops and bishops, and by some abbots in the Western Church; episcopal office or dignity (*fig*); a gasteropod of the genus *Mitra* or its conical shell (**mit're-shell**). — *vt* to adorn with a mitre. — *adj* **mī'tral** of or like a mitre; of the mitral valve. — *adj* **mit'riform** (*mīt'* or *mit'*) mitre-shaped. — **mitral valve** a mitre-shaped valve of the heart; **mi'tre-wort** bishop's cap. [Fr, from Gr *mitrā* fillet]

mitre[2] or (*NAm*) **miter** *mī'tər*, *n* a joint (also **mi'tre-joint**) in which each piece is cut at an angle of 45° to its side, giving a right angle between the pieces; sometimes applied to any joint where the plane of junction bisects the angle; an angle of 45°; a gusset, a tapered insertion (*needlework*). — *vt* to join with a mitre; to turn a corner in, by cutting out a triangular piece and joining (*needlework*). — *vi* to meet in a mitre. — **mitre fold** (in origami) a fold in which two corners are turned down at equal angles to meet each other in the centre; **mi'tre-wheel** a bevel-wheel having its face inclined 45° to its axis. [Prob same as **mitre**[1]]

mitt *mit*, *n* a mitten; a hand (*slang*); a padded leather glove worn by the catcher or first base player (*baseball*); a thick, roughly-shaped glove designed to absorb, protect, etc (as *bath mitt*, *oven mitt*, etc). [Abbrev of **mitten**]

Mittel-Europa or **Mitteleuropa** *mit-əl-yŏŏ-rō'pə*, *n* Central Europe. — *adj* and *n* **Mittel-Europē'an** or **Mittel-europē'an**. [Ger]

mitten *mit'n*, *n* a kind of glove with one, undivided section covering the fingers and one the thumb; a glove covering the hand and wrist, but only the base of the fingers and thumb; a boxing-glove (*slang*); dismissal (*slang*); (in *pl*) handcuffs (*slang*). — *adj* **mitt'ened** covered with a mitten or mittens. — **mitt'en-crab** a Chinese crab that can do damage to river banks. — **frozen mitten** (*slang*) a chilly reception, the cold shoulder; **get the mitten** (*slang*) to be dismissed, *esp* as a suitor. [OFr *mitaine*; origin obscure]

mittimus *mit'i-məs*, *n* a warrant granted for sending to prison a person charged with a crime (*law*); a writ by which a record is transferred out of one court to another (*law*); dismissal, discharge (*colloq*); a nick-name for a magistrate. [L, we send, from *mittere* to send]

Mitty: **Walter Mitty** *wöl'tər mit'i*, *n* an ordinary person who indulges in escapist daydreams of fame, power, etc; an intrepid daydreamer. [From the hero of a short story by James Thurber]

mity. See under **mite**[1].

mitzvah *mits'və* or *mits-vä'*, *n* a good deed: — *pl* **mitzvoth** (*-vōt'*) or **mitzvahs**. [Heb, (literally) commandment]

miurus *mī-ū'rəs*, *n* a hexameter with a short penultimate syllable. [Latinized from Gr *meiouros* curtailed, from *meiōn* less, and *ourā* a tail]

mix *miks*, *vt* to combine so that the parts of one thing, or the things of one sort, are diffused among those of another; to prepare or compound in such a way; to blend; to mingle; to join, combine; to piece together two lengths of film invisibly (*cinematog*); to combine and adjust (separate sound elements) for one recording (*music*, *broadcasting*, etc); to confound (*Milton*); to associate (*archaic*); to interbreed, cross; to involve. — *vi* to become, or to be capable of becoming, mixed; to be joined or combined; to associate; to have social intercourse. — *n* a mixing, mingling; a mixture, *esp* a standard mixture; a formula giving constituents and proportions; a jumble, a mess. — *adj* **mix'able**. — *adj* **mixed** (*mikst*) mingled; promiscuous; of or for both sexes; miscellaneous; confused; not select; combining characters of two or more kinds; between front and back (*phonetics*). — *adv* **mix'edly** (or *mikst'li*). — *n* **mix'edness** (or *mikst'*). — *n* **mix'er** a person who mixes; that by which or in which things are mixed; a person who is easily sociable in all sorts of company; a person who mixes drinks; a soft drink for adding to an alcoholic one; a troublemaker (*slang*); a device by means of which two or more input signals are combined to give a single output signal (*electronics*); a person who uses such a device (*colloq*). — *adj* **mixt** (same as **mixed**). — Also *pap* and *pat*. — *n* **mix'ter-max'ter**, **mix'tie-max'tie**, **mix'ty-max'ty** or **mix'y-max'y** (all *Scot*) a confused jumble. — *adj* and *adv* in a confused jumble. — *n* **mixtion** (*miks'chən*) a mixture of amber, mastic and asphaltum used as a mordant for gold-leaf; a mixture (*obs*). — *n* **mix'ture** (*-chər*) an act of mixing; the state of being mixed; the product of mixing; a product of mixing in which the ingredients retain their properties, as distinguished from a *compound* (*chem*); (in an organ) a compound-stop giving harmonics; a mixture of petrol vapour and air (*autos*). — *adj* **mix'y** mixed. — *adj* **mixed-abil'ity** of classes, etc accommodating members who differ in (*esp* academic) ability. — **mixed bag** any assortment of diverse people, things, characteristics, etc; **mixed blessing** something which has both advantages and disadvantages; **mixed bud** (*bot*) one containing young foliage leaves and also the rudiments of flowers or inflorescences; **mixed chalice** the chalice prepared for the eucharist, containing wine mixed with water; **mixed crystal** a crystal formed from two or more distinct compounds; **mixed doubles** a type of tennis match with a male and a female player as partners on each side; **mixed economy** a national economy of which parts are state-owned and other parts privately-owned; **mixed farming** farming of both crops and livestock; **mixed foursome** a golf match with a male and female player as partners on each side; **mixed grill** see under **grill**; **mixed language** one which contains elements (eg vocabulary, syntax) from two or more separate languages; **mixed marriage** one between people of different religions or races. — *adj* **mixed-mē'dia** (of a work in the arts) combining traditional forms, eg acting, dance, painting, and electronic media, eg tape recording. — **mixed metaphor** see under **metaphor**; **mixed number** one consisting of an integer and a fraction, eg $2\frac{1}{2}$; **mixed train** a railway train made up partly of passenger carriages and partly of goods wagons. — *adj* **mixed-up'** psychologically or socially confused, bewildered, and badly-adjusted. — **mix-in'** (*US*) a fight; **mixing valve** one which mixes hot and cold water (as in a **mixer tap**); **mix'-up** confusion; a confused jumble. — **mix it** (*slang*) to fight forcefully; to cause trouble. [L *miscēre*, *mixtus* to mix; exact relation to OE *miscian*, Ger *mischen*, uncertain]

mixen *miks'n*, *n* a dunghill. [OE *mixen*, from *mix*, *meox*, dung]

mixo- *miks-ō-*, *combining form* denoting mixed. — *adj* **mixobarbar'ic** part barbaric, part Greek. — *adj* **mixo-lyd'ian** (also with *cap*) in ancient Greek music, the same as **hyperdorian**; in old church music applied to an authentic mode extending from *g* to *g*, with *g* for its final. — *adj* **mixotroph'ic** (*biol*) combining different modes of nutrition. [Gr *mīxis* mixing, *misgein* to mix]

miz or **mizz** *miz*, (*colloq*) *n* and *adj* short form of **misery** or **miserable**.

mizmaze *miz'māz*, *n* a labyrinth; bewilderment. [**maze**[1]]

mizzen or **mizen** *miz'n*, *n* in a three-masted vessel, the hindmost of the fore-and-aft sails; the spanker or driver. — *adj* belonging to the mizzen; nearest the stern. — **mizz'en-course**; **mizz'en-mast**; **mizz'en-sail**. [Fr *misaine*, foresail, foremast, from Ital *mezzana* mizzen-sail, from LL *mediānus* middle, from L *medius* middle; the development of meaning is puzzling]

mizzle[1] *miz'l*, *vi* to rain in small drops. — *n* fine rain. — *n* **mizz'ling**. — *adj* **mizz'ly**. [Cf LGer *miseln* mist]

mizzle[2] *miz'l*, (*slang*) *vi* to decamp. [Origin obscure]

mizzle[3] *miz'l*, *vt* to confuse. [Origin obscure]

mizzonite *miz'ən-īt*, *n* a scapolite richer in sodium than meionite. [Gr *meizōn* greater, from its longer vertical axis]

MJ *abbrev*: megajoule(s).

MJI *abbrev*: Member of the Institute of Journalists.

Mjöllnir or **Mjölnir** *myœl'nir*, *n* Thor's terrible hammer. [ON]

MK *abbrev*: mark (of cars).

Mk *abbrev*: Mark (German currency); markka (Finnish currency).

MKS or **mks** *abbrev*: metre-kilogram-second (unit or system). — **MKSA** *abbrev*: metre-kilogram-second-ampere (unit or system).

ml *abbrev*: millilitre(s).

MLA *abbrev*: Member of the Legislative Assembly; Modern Language Association (*US*).

MLC *abbrev*: Meat and Livestock Commission; Member of the Legislative Council.

MLD *abbrev*: mean lethal dose (*radiol*); minimum lethal dose.

MLF *abbrev*: multilateral (nuclear) force.

MLitt *abbrev*: *Magister Litterarum* (*L*), Master of Letters, or of Literature.

Mlle *abbrev*: *Mademoiselle* (*Fr*), Miss: — *pl* **Mlles** *Mesdemoiselles*.

MLR *abbrev*: minimum lending rate.

MLRS *abbrev*: multiple launch rocket system.

MLSO *abbrev*: Medical Laboratory Scientific Officer.

MM *abbrev*: *Messieurs* (*Fr*), Gentlemen, Sirs; Military Medal.

mm *abbrev*: millimetre(s).

MMC *abbrev*: Monopolies and Mergers Commission.

Mme *abbrev*: *Madame* (*Fr*), Mrs: — *pl* **Mmes** Mesdames.

mmf *abbrev*: magnetomotive force.

MMI (*comput*) *abbrev*: man-machine interface.

mmol *abbrev*: millimole.

MMR *abbrev*: measles, mumps and rubella (vaccine).

MN *abbrev*: Merchant Navy; Minnesota (US state).

Mn (*chem*) *symbol*: manganese.

mna. See **mina**[1].

MND *abbrev*: motor neurone disease.

mneme *nē'mē*, (*psychol*) *n* a person's capacity for retaining the after-effects of a particular experience or stimulation. — *adj* **mnē'mic** relating to the mneme. — *n* **mne'mon** a hypothetical unit of memory. — **mnemonic** (*ni-mon'ik*) a device, eg a short verse, to help memory; (in *pl*, treated as *sing*) the art of assisting memory. — *adj* relating to the mneme. — *adj* **mnemon'ical**. — *n* **mnē'monist** a teacher or practitioner of mnemonics; someone from whose memory nothing is erased. — *n* **Mnemosyne** (*nē-mos'i-nē* or *-moz'*; *mythol*) the Greek Goddess of memory, mother of the Muses. — *adj* **mnemotechnic** (*nē-mō-tek'nik*) mnemonic. — *n pl* **mnemotech'nics** mnemonics. — *n* **mnemotech'nist**. [Gr *mnēmē* memory, *mnēmōn* mindful, and *Mnēmosynē* Mnemosyne]

MNR *abbrev*: marine nature reserve.

MO *abbrev*: Medical Officer; Missouri (US state; also **Mo.**); modus operandi; money order.

Mo (*chem*) *symbol*: molybdenum.

mo[1] *mō*, (*archaic*) *adv* and *adj* more. — Also **moe** (*obs*); (*Scot*) **mae** (*mā*) more (in number, not quantity). [OE *mā* (adv); cf **more**, **most**]

mo[2]. See **moment**.

mo[3]. *abbrev*: month.

-mo *-mō*, *sfx* the final syllable of certain Latin ordinal numbers, used in composition with English cardinal numbers to denote the number of leaves in a gathering of a book; see **twelvemo** and **sixteenmo** under **twelve** and **sixteen** respectively.

moa *mō'ə*, *n* a gigantic extinct bird (*Dinornis*) of New Zealand, resembling an ostrich. [Maori]

Moabite *mō'ə-bīt*, *n* one of the people of the ancient kingdom of *Moab*, east of the lower Jordan and the Dead Sea. — *adj* of or relating to Moab. — **Moabite stone** a basalt slab found (1868) at Dibon in Moab, with a long inscription in Hebrew-Phoenician letters, about the revolt of Mesha, king of Moab, against Israel (9c BC; 2 Kings 3).

moan *mōn*, *n* lamentation; a lament; a complaint; a grumble (*colloq*); a low murmur of pain; a sound like a murmur of pain. — *vt* to lament; to bemoan; to utter with moans; to condole with (*obs*). — *vi* to make or utter a moan; to grumble (*colloq*). — *n* **moan'er**. — *adj* **moan'ful** expressing sorrow; lamentable. — *adv* **moan'fully**. — **moaning minnie** a mortar used by German forces in World War II, producing a shrieking noise when fired (*war slang*); an air-raid siren (*war slang*); a person given to complaining (*colloq*). [Unrecorded OE *mān* (noun) answering to the verb *mǣnan*]

moat *mōt*, *n* a deep trench round a castle or fortified place, sometimes filled with water; a mote-hill. — *vt* to surround with a moat. — *adj* **moat'ed**. [OFr *mote* mound]

mob[1] *mob*, *n* the mobile or fickle common people; the vulgar; the rabble; a disorderly crowd; a riotous assembly; a gang; a large herd or flock (*Austr* and *NZ*). — *adj* of or relating to the mob or a mob. — *vt* to attack in a disorderly crowd; to crowd around, *esp* with vexatious curiosity or attentions; to drive by mob action. — *vt* and *vi* to form into a mob: — *pr p* **mobb'ing**; *pa t* and *pa p* **mobbed**. — *adj* **mobbed** crowded (*colloq*). — *n* **mobb'ing** (*behav*) a form of harassment directed at predators by potential prey. — *adj* **mobb'ish**. — *n* **mobile** (*mō'bi-li*; 17c) the mob. — *n* **moboc'racy** (*slang*) rule or ascendency exercised by the mob. — *n* **mob'ocrat**. — *adj* **mobocrat'ic**. — *n* **mobs'man** a member of a mob; a swell-mobsman (qv). — *n* **mob'ster** (*US*) gangster. — *adj* **mob-hand'ed** in large numbers; constituting a large group. — **mob'-law** lynch-law; the will of the mob. — **the mob** or **the Mob** (*US slang*) the Mafia; organized crime in general. [L *mōbile* (*vulgus*) fickle (multitude); from *movere* to move]

mob[2] *mob*, (*obs*) *n* a loose woman; a négligé dress; a mob-cap. — *vt* to muffle the head of. — *adj* **mobbed** in dishabille; muffled up. — **mob'-cap** a woman's indoor morning cap with puffy crown, a broad band, and frills (*hist*). — **mob it** (*obs*) to go unobtrusively to an unfashionable part of the theatre. [Perh *Mab*, for *Mabel*; but cf ODu *mop*; mod Du *mopmuts* a woman's nightcap]

mobble. See **moble**.

mobby or **mobbie** *mob'i*, *n* a frothy beverage made from a fermented liquid of boiled tree bark, added to sugar syrup (*W Indies*); fruit juice for brandy-making, or brandy made from it (*US archaic*). [Carib *mabi*]

mobile[1] *mō'bīl*, *-bēl* or *-bil*, *adj* movable; able to move about; easily or speedily moved; not fixed; changing rapidly; (of a liquid) characterized by great fluidity. — *n* (with *great*, *principal*, etc) translation of primum mobile (*obs*); a moving or movable body or part; an artistic structure, *orig* consisting of dangling forms, now sometimes having a base, in which movement is caused by air currents; short for **mobile phone**, **police**, **library**, etc. — *n* **mobile** (*mō-bi-li*) see **mob**[1]. — *n* **mobility** (*mō-bil'i-ti*) quality or power of being mobile; freedom or ease of movement; description of the drift of ions (including electrons and holes in semiconductors) under applied electric fields, additional to thermal agitation (*electronics*); the mob (*slang*). — *n* **mobilization** or **-s-** (*mō-* or *mo-bil-i-zā'shən* or *-ī-*). — *vt* **mō'bilize** or **-ise** to make movable, mobile, or readily available; to put in readiness for service in war; to call (eg troops) into active service. — *vi* to make armed forces ready for war; to undergo mobilization. — *n* **mo'bilizer** or **-s-**. — **mobile home** a caravan or other vehicle with sleeping, cooking, etc facilities; **mobile phone** a portable telephone operating by means of a cellular radio system; **mobile police** police patrolling in vehicles; **mobile shop**, **library**, etc a shop, library, etc set up in a motor vehicle and driven to customers' homes or neighbourhoods; **mobility allowance** money paid by the government to disabled people to compensate for their travel costs. [Fr, from L *mōbilis*, from *movēre* to move]

mobile[2]. See under **mob**[1].

Möbius strip *mœ'bē-əs strip*, (*math*) *n* the one-sided surface formed by joining together the two ends of a long rectangular strip, one end being twisted through 180 degrees before the join is made. [August F *Möbius* (1790–1868), German mathematician]

moble or **mobble** *mob'l*, (*obs*) *vt* to muffle, as in a mob. — *adj* **mob'led** (*Shakesp*) muffled; other suggestions are, richly endowed (cf Fr *meublé*), set in motion, violently agitated (L *mōbilis*), or that there is no meaning at all. [Frequentative of **mob**[2]]

mobocracy, **mobster**, etc. See under **mob**[1].

moccasin or **mocassin** *mok'ə-sin*, *n* a heelless N American Indian shoe of deerskin or other soft leather; a shoe or slipper more or less resembling it; a venomous N American pit-viper. — **mocc'asin-flower** a lady's-slipper orchid. [Algonquian]

moch *mohh*, (*Scot*) *n* misty and humid weather. — *adj* **moch'ie** or **moch'y** mouldy, damp; (of weather) humid and misty, muggy. — *n* **moch'iness**. [Origin uncertain; ult related to **muggy**]

Mocha *mok'ə* or *mō'kə*, *n* (also without *cap*) a fine coffee; *esp* a coffee, or coffee and chocolate, flavour; a deep brown colour; a soft leather used for gloves, made from sheepskin or goatskin. — **Mocha stone** a moss agate or similar stone. [Coffee and stone first brought from *Mocha*, on the Red Sea]

mochell (*Spenser*). Same as **muchel** (see under **much**).

mock *mok*, *vt* to deride; to scoff at derisively; to make fun of; to mimic in ridicule; to simulate; to defy, tantalize, disappoint, deceive, disparage, or make a fool of as if in mockery (*fig*). — *vi* to jeer; to scoff; to speak or behave insincerely or disparagingly. — *n* ridicule; a bringing into ridicule; a scoff; a mockery; a thing mocked; (*esp* in *pl*) a practice examination taken at school as a preparation for a public examination. — *adj* sham; false; resembling, or accepted as a substitute for, the true or real thing. — *adj* **mock'able** worthy of derision. — *n* **mock'age** (*obs*). — *n* **mock'er**. — *n* **mock'ery** derision; ridicule; a subject of ridicule; mimicry; imitation, *esp* a contemptible or insulting imitation; false show; insulting or ludicrous futility. — *n* and *adj* **mock'ing**. — *adv* **mock'ingly**. — *adj* **mock-hero'ic** in exaggerated imitation of the heroic style. — *n* a mock-heroic composition; (in *pl*) mock-heroic verses; (in *pl*) sham heroic utterances or behaviour. — *adj* **mock-hero'ical**. — *adv* **mock-hero'ically**. — **mock'ingbird** any of several American birds (genus *Mimus*) of the thrush family, that mimic other birds' songs and other sounds, *esp Mimus polyglottos* of the USA and Mexico; **mock'ing-thrush** a thrasher. — *adj* **mock-mod'est**. — **mock-mod'esty** sham modesty; **mock moon** a paraselene, or bright spot in the moon's halo, 22° to right or left of the moon, due to refraction from ice crystals floating vertically; **mock-or'ange** a tall shrub (*Philadelphus*, commonly called syringa) of the saxifrage family with strong-scented flowers; a kind of cherry-laurel (*US*); **mock-priv'et** a shrub (genus *Phillyrea*) related to privet; **mock sun** a parhelion or spot in the sun's halo; **mock turtle soup** an imitation of turtle soup, made of calf's head or veal; **mock'-up** a full-size dummy model; a rough layout of a printed text, package, etc showing size, colour, etc; a fabrication. — Also *adj*. — **mocks the pauses** (Shakesp, *Antony and Cleopatra* V.1) perhaps, throws away the opportunities given by the pauses; **put the mockers on** (*slang*) to put an end to, put paid to. [OFr *mocquer*; origin uncertain]

mockado *mok-ä'dō*, (*obs*) *n* a cloth of Flemish origin imitating velvet and *usu* of wool, popular in the 16–17c; trumpery: — *pl* **mocka'does**. [Prob Ital *mocaiardo* haircloth]

mockernut *mok'ər-nut*, *n* a kind of hickory nut (*Carya tomentosa*) with a kernel difficult to extract.

mocock *mō-kok'* or **mocuck** *mō-kuk'*, *n* a N American Indian birch-bark box or basket. [Orig Algonquian]

mocuddum. See **muqaddam**.

MOD *abbrev*: Ministry of Defence.

Mod[1] *mod*, *mōd* or *mōd*, *n* (also without *cap*) a Highland Gaelic literary and musical festival, held annually. [Gaelic *mòd*, from ON *mōt*; cf **moot**]

Mod[2] *mod*, *n* a member of a teenage faction, *orig* in the 1960s, distinguished by special dress (typically neat), etc, from their rivals, the Rockers.

mod. *abbrev*: moderate; modern.

mod con *mod kon*, *n* a *mod*ern *con*venience, any item of up-to-date plumbing, heating, etc.

mode *mōd*, *n* a way or manner of acting, doing, happening or existing; kind; form; manifestation; state of being (*philos*); a method of operation as provided by the software (*comput*); that which exists only as a quality of substance (*philos*); a mood (*gram*); character as necessary, contingent, possible or impossible (*logic*); a mood (*logic*); actual percentage of mineral composition (*petrology*); the value of greatest frequency (*statistics*); modality; fashion; that which is fashionable; fashionableness; a model of fashion (*obs*); alamode, or a garment made of it; openwork between the solid parts of lace; the method of dividing the octave according to the position of its steps and half-steps (*music*); in old music, the method of time-division of notes (*perfect* into three, *imperfect* into two, *major*, division of large into longs, *minor* of long into breves). — *adj* **modal** (*mōd'l*) relating to mode. — *n* a modal auxiliary. — *n* **mod'alism** the doctrine first set forth by Sabellius that the Father, the Son, and the Holy Spirit are not three distinct personalities but only three different modes of manifestation. — *n* **mod'alist** a person who holds this theory. — *adj* **modalist'ic**. — *n* **modality** (*mōd-al'i-ti*) fact or condition of being modal; mode; method, terms, style; any of the primary methods of sensation; classification of propositions as to whether true, false, necessary, possible or impossible (*logic*); the quality of being limited by a condition (*law*). — *adv* **mod'ally**. — *adj* **modish** (*mōd'ish*) fashionable; affectedly, foolishly or absurdly fashionable. — *adv* **mod'ishly**. — *n* **mod'ishness**. — *n* **mod'ist** a follower of the current fashion. — *n* **modiste** (*mō-dēst*; *Fr*) a professedly fashionable dressmaker or milliner. — **modal auxiliary** or **modal verb** in English, any of the verbs *can*, *could*, *may*, *might*, *will*, *would*, *shall*, *should*, *must* and *ought*, and sometimes *need*, *dare* and *used to*, which modify the sense of a main verb and express concepts such as politeness, certainty and obligation; **mode dispersion** (*telecomm*) in optical fibre communications, distortion of individual signals, caused by different modes of propagation of the light inside the fibre. — **Greek modes** consist each of two disjunct tetrachords with a whole tone (diazeuctic tone) between them, or two conjunct tetrachords with a whole tone above (where the prefix is *hyper-*) or below them (*hypo-*); **Gregorian**, **medieval** or **ecclesiastical modes** have the same names as Greek modes but do not correspond to them (see **authentic** and **plagal**; also **Aeolian**, **Locrian**, **Ionian**, **Dorian**, **Phrygian**, **Lydian**, **Mixolydian** and names under **hyper-** and **hypo-**); **major mode** (*music*) modern mode, consisting of two steps, a half-step, three steps, and a half-step; **minor mode** (*music*) a modern mode consisting of a step, a half-step, two steps, a half-step, and two steps. [L *modus*; partly through Fr *mode*]

model *mod'l*, *n* an architect's plan or design (*obs*); a preliminary solid representation, generally small, or in plastic material, to be followed in construction; something to be copied; a pattern; an imitation of something on a smaller scale; a person or thing closely resembling another; a person who poses for an artist, photographer, etc; a person who exhibits clothes for a shop by wearing them; a pattern or standard of excellence, often one to be copied or aspired to; an article of standard design or a copy of one; structural type; a medal (*obs*); a close covering or mould (*Shakesp*). — *adj* of the nature of a model; set up for imitation; completely suitable for imitation, exemplary. — *vt* to form after a model; to shape; to make a model or copy of; to form in some plastic material; (of a mannequin) to display (a garment) by wearing it. — *vi* to practise modelling: — *pr p* **mod'elling** or (*NAm*) **mod'eling**; *pa t* and *pa p* **mod'elled** or (*NAm*) **mod'eled**. — *n* **mod'eller** or (*NAm*) **mod'eler**. — *n* **mod'elling** or (*NAm*) **mod'eling** the act or art of making a model of something, a branch of sculpture; rendering of solid form; working as a model. — **Model T** a four-cylinder motor car designed and mass-produced by the Ford Motor Company in the USA in the early 20c. [OFr *modelle*, from Ital *modello*, dimin of *modo*, from L *modus* a measure]

modello *mə-del'ō*, (*Ital*) *n* an artist's detailed sketch or sculptural model for a larger work: — *pl* **modell'i** or **modell'os**. [Ital; cf **model**]

modem *mō'dəm* or *-dem*, (*comput*) *n* an electronic device which converts digital data from a computer into analogue signals that are transmissable to another computer over a telephone system. — *vt* to transmit or receive by means of a modem [*mo*dulator and *dem*odulator]

modena *mod'i-nə*, *n* a shade of crimson. [*Modena* in Italy]

moder *mō'dər*, *n* a layer of humus intermediate between mor and mull. [Ger, decay]

moderate *mod'ə-rāt*, *vt* to keep within measure or bounds; to regulate; to reduce in intensity; to make temperate or reasonable; to pacify; to preside as moderator over or at; to slow down (neutrons) in a nuclear reactor; to decide as an arbitrator (*obs*). — *vi* to become less violent or intense; to preside or act as a moderator. — *adj* (*-rit*) kept within measure or bounds; not excessive or extreme; temperate; of middle rate, average. — *n* a person whose views are far from extreme; a member of a faction in the Scottish Church in the 18c and early 19c, broad in matters of doctrine and discipline, opposed to Evangelicalism and popular rights. — *adv* **mod'erately**. — *n* **mod'erateness**. — *n* **moderā'tion** an act of moderating; the state of being moderated or moderate; freedom from excess; self-restraint; the process of slowing down neutrons in a nuclear reactor; (in *pl*) the first public examination for BA at Oxford (*colloq* **Mods** or **mods**). — *n* **mod'eratism** moderate opinions in religion or politics. — *n* **mod'erātor** a person who, or that which, moderates; a president, *esp* in Presbyterian church courts; formerly, an officer at Oxford and Cambridge who superintended degree examinations; either of two examiners presiding over Mathematical Tripos at Cambridge; a moderations examiner at Oxford; a person appointed to standardize the marking, etc of school public examinations; an oil-lamp with regulated flow of oil; material such as water, heavy water or graphite used to slow down neutrons in a nuclear reactor: — *fem* **mod'erātrix** (*obs*). — *n* **mod'erātorship**. — **moderate (in) a call** (of a presbytery) to act with the congregation in calling the minister it has chosen. [L *moderārī*, *-ātus*, from *modus* a measure]

moderato *mod-ə-rä'tō*, (*music*) *adj* and *adv* at a moderate speed. — *n* a movement or passage to be played at this speed. [Ital]

modern *mod'ərn*, *adj* of or characteristic of present or recent time; not ancient or medieval; (in education) mainly or wholly concerned with subjects other than Greek and Latin; of a style of type with contrasting thick and thin strokes, serifs at right-angles, curves thickened in the centre (*printing*); everyday, commonplace (*Shakesp*); (with *cap*) (of a language) of or near the form now spoken and written, distinguished from *Old* and *Middle*. — *n* a person living in modern times, *esp* distinguished from the ancient Greeks and Romans; a modernist; a modern printing type. — *n* **mod'ernism** modern usage, expression, or trait; modern spirit or character; a tendency to adjust Christian dogma to the results of science and criticism; (with *cap*) an early 20c movement in the arts characterized by the use of unconventional subject matter, experimental techniques, etc. — *n* **mod'ernist** an admirer of modern ideas, ways, literature, studies, etc; a person who favours modernism; (with *cap*) a practitioner of Modernism. — Also *adj*. — *adj* **modernis'tic**. — *n* **modern'ity**. — *n* **modernīzā'tion** or **-s-**. — *vt* **mod'ernize** or **-ise** to adapt to the present time, conditions, needs, language or spelling. — *vi* to adopt modern ways. — *n* **mod'ernizer** or **-s-**. — *adv* **mod'ernly**. — *n* **mod'ernness**. — **modern dance** a style of dance more expressive and less stylized than classical ballet; **modern jazz** a style of jazz which evolved in the early 1940s, characterized by greater rhythmic and harmonic complexity than previously. [LL *modernus*, from *modo* just now, orig ablative of *modus*]

modest *mod'ist*, *adj* restrained by a sense of propriety; unobtrusive; unpretentious; unassuming; diffident; decent; chaste; of thoughts or language, etc, pure and delicate; not excessive or extreme; moderate. — *adv* **mod'estly**. — *n* **mod'esty** the quality or fact of being modest; a veil-like covering for the part of a woman's breast revealed by the low neckline of a dress. [L *modestus*, from *modus* a measure]

modi. See **modus**.

modicum *mod'i-kəm*, *n* a small quantity; a small person (*obs*); (disrespectfully) a woman (*obs*): — *pl* **mod'icums**. [L neuter of *modicus* moderate, from *modus*]

modify *mod'i-fī*, *vt* to moderate; to determine the mode of (*philos*); to change the form or quality of; to alter slightly; to vary; to differentiate; (of a word or phrase) to limit or qualify the sense of (*gram*); to subject to an umlaut (*philol*); to assess, decree, or award (a payment) (*Scots law*): — *pr p* **mod'ifying**; *pa t* and *pa p* **mod'ified**. — *adj* **mod'ifiable**. — *n* **modification** (*-fi-kā'shən*) the act of modifying or state of being modified; the result of alteration or change; changed shape or condition; a change due to environment, lasting only as long as the operative conditions (*biol*). — *adj* **mod'ificātive** or **mod'ificātory** tending to modify; causing change of form or condition. — *adj* **mod'ified** (*-fīd*) altered by modification; homologous but developed in a different direction (*biol*). — *n* **mod'ifier** (*-fī-ər*) a person who modifies; a modifying agent; a diacritic indicating modification, *esp* an umlaut (*philol*). [Fr *modifier*, from L *modificāre*, *-ātum*, from *modus* a measure, and *facere* to make]

modillion *mod-il'yən*, (*archit*) *n* an ornamental bracket under a Corinthian or other cornice. [Ital *modiglione*, from L *modulus*, from *modus* a measure]

modiolus *mo-dī'ə-ləs*, *n* the axis of the cochlea of the ear; (with *cap*, also **Modī'ola**) the horse mussel genus. — *adj* **modī'olar**. [L *modiolus* nave of a wheel, water-wheel bucket, drinking-vessel, etc, dimin of *modus*]

modish, **modist** and **modiste**. See under **mode**.

modius *mō'di-əs* or *mod'i-ōōs*, *n* a Roman dry measure, about a peck; a cylindrical headdress of the gods: — *pl* **mō'dii** (*-ī*). [L *modius*]

modiwort. A Scots form of **mouldwarp**.

mods. See under **moderate**.

modulate *mod'ū-lāt*, *vt* to regulate, adjust; to inflect; to soften; to vary the pitch or frequency of; to impress characteristics of signal wave on (carrier wave) (*radio*); to vary the velocity of electrons in an electron beam. — *vi* to pass from one state to another; to pass from one key into another using a logical progression of chords that links the two keys (*music*). — *n* **modulabil'ity** the capability of being modulated. — *adj* **mod'ular** of or relating to mode or modulation, or to a module. — *n* **modular'ity**. — *adj* **mod'ularized** or **-ised** consisting of modules; produced in the form of modules; divided into modules. — *n* **modulā'tion**. — *n* **mod'ulātor** a person who, or that which, modulates; any device for effecting modulation (*radio*); a chart used in the tonic sol-fa notation on which modulations are shown. [L *modulārī, -ātus* to regulate; cf **module**]

module *mod'ūl*, *n* a small measure or quantity; a unit of size, used in standardized planning of buildings and design of components; a self-contained unit forming part of a spacecraft or other structure; a standard unit or part of machinery, etc in a system; a set course forming a unit in an educational scheme; an assembly within a geometrical framework of electronic units functioning as a system; a component part of a program, complete in itself and with its own function (*comput*); a measure, often the semidiameter of a column, for regulating proportions of other parts (*archit*); a model, image (*Shakesp*). — *adv* **mod'ulo** (*math*) with respect to a (specified) modulus. — *n* **mod'ulus** a constant multiplier or coefficient (*math*); a quantity used as a divisor to produce classes of quantities, each class distinguished by its members yielding the same remainders (*math*); the positive square root of the sum of the squares of the real and imaginary parts of a complex number (*math*); a quantity expressing the relation between a force and the effect produced: — *pl* **moduli** (*mod'ū-lī*). [L *modulus*, dimin of *modus* a measure]

modus *mō'dəs* or *mo'do͞os*, *n* manner, mode; the way in which anything works; a fixed payment instead of tithes: — *pl* **mō'dī**. — **modus operandi** (*op-ər-an'dī* or *-an'dē*) mode of operation, way of working; **modus vivendi** (*vi-ven'dī* or *-dē*; also *wē-wen'dē*) way of life or living; an arrangement or compromise by means of which those who differ may get on together for a time; such an arrangement between states or between a state and the Pope. [L *modus* manner]

moe *mō*. See **mo**[1] and **mow**[1].

moellon *mō'ə-lon*, *n* rubble in mason-work. [Fr]

Moeso-gothic *mē-sō-goth'ik*, *adj* relating to the *Goths* who settled in *Moesia* (corresponding to modern Bulgaria and Serbia) in the 4c and 5c. — *n* their language.

mofette *mō-fet'*, *n* an opening in the earth giving out carbon dioxide with some nitrogen and oxygen, the last stage of volcanic activity. [Fr, from Ital *mofeta*, perh L *mephītis* foul exhalation]

mofussil *mō-fus'l*, *n* (in India, Pakistan, etc) all areas outside the capital or great towns; rural as opposed to urban areas collectively. — *adj* provincial; rural. [Hindustani *mufassil*, from Ar *mufassal* distinct, separate, pa p of *fassala* to separate]

mog. See **moggy**.

Mogadon® *mog'ə-don*, *n* proprietary name for nitrazepam, a drug used to treat insomnia.

Mogen David. See **Magen David**.

moggan *mog'ən*, (*Scot*) *n* a footless stocking. [Origin unknown]

moggy, **moggie** *mog'i* or **mog** *mog*, *n* a cat (*slang*); a pet name for a cow, etc (*dialect*). [Perh *Maggie*]

Mogul *mō'gul mō-gul'*, *n* a Mongol or Mongolian, *esp* one of the followers of Baber, the conqueror of India (1483–1530) (also **Mughal**); a name applied to the best quality of playing-cards; (without *cap*) an influential person, a magnate. — *adj* relating to the Mogul Empire, architecture, etc. — **Great Mogul** the title formerly used by Europeans to refer to the Emperors of Delhi. [Pers *Mughul*, properly a Mongol]

mogul *mō'gəl*, *n* a mound of hard snow forming an obstacle on a ski-slope; (in *pl*) a skiing discipline or event that involves skiing down a run which includes moguls. — *adj* **moguled** (*mō'gəld*) (of a ski-run) having moguls. [Poss, from Norw dialect *muge* heap]

MOH *abbrev*: Medical Officer of Health.

mohair *mō'hār*, *n* the long, white, fine silken hair of the Angora goat; other hair as a substitute for it; cloth or yarn made from this, *usu* mixed with wool. [Ar *mukhayyar*; influenced by **hair**]

Mohammedan *mō-ham'i-dən*, **Mahommedan** *mə-hom'*, **Mahometan** *mə-hom'it-ən*, **Muhammadan** *mo͞o-ham'a-dən* or **Muhammedan** *-i-dən*, *adj* relating to Mohammed (formerly popularly rendered as Mahomet) or to his religion, Islam. — *n* a follower of Mohammed; a person who professes Islam, a Muslim. — *n* **Mohamm'edanism**, **Mohamm'edism**, etc, Islam, the religion of Mohammed, contained in the Koran. — *vt* and *vi* **Mohamm'edanize** or **-ise**, etc, to convert to, or conform to, Islam. — See also **Mahoun** and **mammet**. All of these terms are felt to be offensive by many Muslims, who prefer **Muslim**, **Islam**, **Islamic**, etc. [Ar *Muhammad*, the great prophet of Arabia (c.570–632); literally, praised]

Moharram *mō-hur'um*, **Muharram** or **Muharrem** *mo͞o-hur'um*, *n* the first month of the Muslim year; a great fast in commemoration of Hasan and Hosain (grandsons of Mohammed) during its first ten days; a public procession during the fast. [Ar *muharram* sacred]

Mohawk *mō'hök*, *n* a N American Indian of an Iroquois people of New York State; a Mohock; (often without *cap*) a skating movement consisting of a stroke on the edge of one skate followed by a stroke in the opposite direction on the same edge of the other skate. [From an Algonquian name]

mohel *mō'(h)el*, *moi'hel* or *-hel'*, also Heb *mö-hel'*, *n* an official Jewish circumciser. [Heb]

Mohican *mō-hē'kən* or **Mohegan** *-gən*, *n* a N American Indian of a people formerly living chiefly in the upper Hudson valley, or the Algonquian language spoken by them (also **Mahi'can**); a hairstyle in which the head is shaved except for a central strip from the nape to the brow, based on a Mohican style but now *esp* associated with punk fashion, in which the hair is spiked into a (*usu* brightly-coloured) crest. — Also *adj*. [Algonquian]

Moho, **Mohorovicic** or **Mohorovicician discontinuity** *mō'hō*, *mō-hō-rō'və-chich* or *mō-hō-rō'və-chich-i-ən dis-kon-ti-nū'i-ti*, *n* the boundary between the rocks of the earth's crust and the different rock of the mantle. [A *Mohorovičić*, (1857–1936), Croatian geologist, who deduced a difference of rock nature from the behaviour of earthquake shocks]

Mohock *mō'hok*, *n* one of a band of aristocratic ruffians of early 18c London. [**Mohawk**]

mohr. Same as **mhorr**.

Mohs scale *mōz skāl'*, *n* a scale of numbers from 1 to 10 (1 representing talc, 10 representing diamond) in terms of which the relative hardness of solids can be expressed. [F *Mohs* (1773–1839), German mineralogist]

mohur *mō'hər*, *n* a former Persian and Indian gold coin, in India equivalent to fifteen rupees. [Pers *mohr*]

moi *mwa*, *pers pronoun* me, often used *facetiously* in mock affectation, eg in the form of a question to express surprise at an allegation against one. [Fr]

moider *moi'dər*, **moither** *-dhər* or **mither** *mī'dhər*, (*dialect*) *vt* to confuse; to stupefy, overcome. — *vi* to work hard; to wander in thoughts or mind. [Dialect word; origin obscure]

moidore *moi'dōr* or *-dör*, *n* a disused gold coin of Portugal. [Port *moeda d'ouro*, literally money of gold, from L *monēta, dē, aurum*]

moiety *moi'ə-ti*, *n* half; either of two parts or divisions; a small share (*Shakesp*). [OFr *moite*, from L *medietās, -tātis* middle point, later half, from *medius* middle]

moil *moil*, (*archaic*) *vt* to wet; to bedaub; to defile. — *vi* (*dialect*) to toil; to drudge. — *n* (*dialect* and *archaic*) a spot; a defilement; labour; trouble; turmoil. — *n* **moil'er**. [OFr *moillier* (Fr *mouiller*) to wet, from L *mollis* soft]

moineau *moi'nō*, *n* a small flat bastion to protect a fortification while being erected. [Fr]

Moira or **Moera** *moi'ra*, *n* any of the three Fates, goddesses controlling Man's destiny (*Gr mythol*); fate, destiny: — *pl* **Moirai** or **Moerae** (*-rī*). [Gr *Moira*]

moire *mwär*, also *mwör*, *mōr* or *moir*, *n orig* watered mohair; now watered silk or other fabric with a watered appearance (also **moire antique**). — *adj* **moiré** (*mwär'ā* or *moi'ri*) watered. — *n* a watered appearance on a cloth or metal surface; sometimes for moire, the material. — **moiré effect** or **pattern** an optical effect, a shifting wavy pattern seen when two surfaces covered with regular lines are superimposed. [Fr, from English **mohair**]

moiser *moi'sər*, (*Yiddish*) *n* an informer.

moist *moist*, *adj* damp; humid; rainy; watery; (of eyes) tearful; juicy (*Shakesp*). — *vt* (*Shakesp*) to moisten. — *vt* **moisten** (*mois'n*) to make moist; to wet slightly. — *vt* **moist'ify** (*jocular*) to make moist. — *adv* **moist'ly**. — *n* **moist'ness**. — *n* **moist'ure** moistness; that which makes slightly wet; liquid, *esp* in small quantity. — *adj* **moist'ureless**. — *vt* **moist'urize** or **-ise** to add or restore moisture to. — *vi* to apply moisturizer. — *n* **moist'urizer** or **-s-** that which moisturizes, *esp* a cosmetic cream which restores moisture to the skin. [OFr *moiste* (Fr *moite*), perh from L *mustum* juice of grapes, new wine, perh L *mūcidus* mouldy]

moit. See **mote**².

moither. See **moider**.

mojo *mō'jō*, (*US slang*) *n* magic; a magic spell or charm: — *pl* **mo'jos** or **mo'joes**. [Prob W African in origin]

mokaddam. See **muqaddam**.

moke *mōk*, (*slang*) *n* a donkey; a worn-out or inferior horse (*Austr* and *NZ*); a variety performer on several instruments; a Black person (*US slang*; *offensive*). [Origin unknown]

moki *mō'ki*, *n* a New Zealand sea fish belonging either to the species *Latridopsis ciliaris* or *Chironemus spectabilis* (**red moki**); (formerly) the blue cod, *Parapercis colias*. [Maori]

moko *mō'kō*, *n* a system of tattooing practised by the Maoris; a Maori tattoo: — *pl* **mōkos**. [Maori]

mol. See under **mole**¹.

mola *mō'lə*, *n* a brightly-coloured appliqué or embroidered panel made by Cuna Indian women of Panama, used to decorate clothing: — *pl* **mo'las**. [Cuna]

molal. See under **mole**¹.

molar¹ *mō'lər*, *adj* used for grinding; designating or relating to a grinding tooth. — *n* a grinding tooth, or back tooth. [L *molāris*, from *mola* a millstone, from *molere* to grind]

molar² and **molarity**. See under **mole**¹.

Molasse *mō-läs'*, *n* a series of Oligocene or Miocene sandstones and sandy marls in Switzerland, France, and Germany. [Fr]

molasses *mo-las'iz*, *n sing* a thick, *usu* dark, treacle that is drained from sugar during refining. [Port *melaço* (Fr *mélasse*), from LL *mellāceum*, from *mel*, *mellis* honey]

mold. See **mould**¹·²·³ and **mole**².

moldwarp. Same as **mouldwarp**.

mole¹ *mōl*, (*chem*) *n* the amount of substance that contains as many (specified) entities (eg atoms, molecules, ions, photons) as there are atoms in 12 grams of carbon-12 (*abbrev* **mol** *mōl*); formerly defined as equal to gram-molecule. — *adj* **mol'al** of, relating to, or containing, a mole. — *n* **molal'ity** the concentration of a solution expressed as the number of moles of dissolved substance per thousand grams of solvent. — *adj* **mol'ar** of or relating to a mole; per mole; per unit amount of substance; of or relating to molecules; of or relating to mass or masses or to large masses (L *mōlēs* mass). — *n* **molar'ity** the concentration of a solution expressed as the number of moles of dissolved substance per litre of solution; **mole'-electronics** (also **molecular electronics**) the technique of growing solid-state crystals so as to form transistors, etc, for microminiaturization. [Ger, from *Molekül*, molecule; both words (Ger and Eng) ult from L *mōlēs* mass]

mole² *mōl*, *n* a spot, *esp* one caused by iron on linen (*obs* except in Scots form **mail** and in **iron-mould**); a small spot or raised mark on the skin, often pigmented and hairy. — Also (*Spenser*) **mōld**. [OE *māl*]

mole³ *mōl*, *n* a small insectivorous animal (genus *Talpa*) with very small eyes and soft fur, which burrows in the ground and casts up little heaps of loose earth; extended to related or similar animals; a person who works in darkness or underground; a spy who successfully infiltrates a rival organization, *esp* one not engaging in espionage until firmly established and trusted; a person with bad eyesight (*fig*); a boring machine which makes a tunnel, eg for a pipeline. — **mole'cast** a molehill; **mole'catcher** a person whose business it is to catch moles; **mole'-cricket** a burrowing insect (*Gryllotalpa*) of the cricket family, with forelegs like a mole's; **mole drainer** (*agric*) a pointed cylinder on the lower edge of a blade, which is drawn longitudinally through soil to form a drainage channel (**mole drain**). — *adj* **mole'-eyed** having eyes like those of a mole; seeing imperfectly. — **mole'hill** a little hill or heap of earth cast up by a mole; **mole'hunt**; **mole'hunter**; **mole plough** a mole drainer; **mole'rat** a name for several burrowing rodents (*Spalax*, *Bathyergus*, etc); **mole'skin** the skin or fur of a mole; a superior kind of fustian, double-twilled, cropped before dyeing; (in *pl*) clothes, *esp* trousers, made of this fustian; **mole'-spade** a small spade used by molecatchers. — **make a mountain out of a molehill** to magnify, overdramatize, etc a trifling matter; **mole out** to seek, or elicit, bit by bit, as if by burrowing. [ME *molle*, *mulle*; cf Du *mol*, LGer *mol*, *mul*; poss shortened from **mouldwarp**]

mole⁴ *mōl*, *n* a massive breakwater, causeway or masonry pier; an ancient Roman mausoleum. [Fr *môle*, from L *mōlēs* mass]

mole⁵ *mōl*, *n* an abnormal fleshy mass of tissue formed in the uterus; see also **hydatidiform mole** under **hydatid**. [L *mola* millstone]

mole⁶ *mō'li* or *-lā*, *n* in Mexican cooking, a sauce made mainly with chilli and chocolate, served with meat dishes. [Am Sp; see **guacamole**]

Molech. See **Moloch**.

molecule *mol'i-kūl* or *mōl'*, *n* the smallest particle of any substance that retains the properties of that substance, *usu* consisting of a limited group of atoms; a gram-molecule. — *adj* **molecular** (*mol-ek'ū-lər*). — *n* **molecularity** (*mol-ek-ū-lar'i-ti*). — *adv* **molec'ularly**. — **molecular biology** study of the molecules of the substances involved in the processes of life; **molecular electronics** see under **mole**¹; **molecular formula** a formula showing the number of atoms of each element in a molecule, eg benzene, C_6H_6; **molecular genetics** (*biol*) the study and manipulation of the molecular basis of heredity; **molecular pharmer** a researcher aiming to develop drugs, etc from the products of transgenic animals, eg from the milk of cows or sheep that carry a human gene; **molecular weight** a former term for relative molecular mass (qv). [Fr *molécule*, from L *mōlēs* mass]

molehill... to ... **moleskin**. See under **mole**³.

molendinar *mol-en'din-ər*, (*pedantically facetious*) *adj* relating to a mill or a miller. — *n* a molar tooth. — *adj* **molen'dinary** (*pedantically facetious*) relating to a mill. — *n* a mill. [LL *molendīnum* a mill, from L *molere* to grind]

molest *mə-* or *mō-lest'*, *vt* to vex; to interfere with in a troublesome or hostile way; to touch, interfere with or attack sexually; to annoy. — *n* annoyance. — *n* **molestā'tion** (*mo-* or *mō-*). — *n* **molest'er**. — *adj*

molest'ful. [Fr *molester*, from L *molestāre*, from *molestus* troublesome]

molimen *mō-lī'mən*, *n* a great effort, *esp* any physical effort made by the body in carrying out a natural function. — *adj* **moliminous** (*-lim'in-əs*). [L *mōlīmen*, from *mōlīrī* to toil, from *mōlēs* mass]

moline *mō'līn* or *-līn'*, (*heraldry*) *adj* like the rind of a millstone, applied to a cross with each arm ending in two outward curving branches. — *n* a moline cross. [L *mola* a mill]

molinet *mol'i-net*, *n* a stick used to whip drinking chocolate in the 18c. [Fr *moulinet*, dimin of *moulin* mill]

Molinism[1] *mol'in-izm*, *n* the doctrine of the 16c Spanish Jesuit Luis *Molina*, reconciling predestination and free will by God's foreknowledge, the efficacy of grace depending on the co-operation of the will. — *n* **Mol'inist**.

Molinism[2] *mol'in-izm*, *n* a form of religious quietism originated by the Spanish priest Miguel de *Molinos* (1627–96), striving towards the extinction of the will and a complete withdrawal from the senses. — *n* **Mol'inist**.

moll *mol*, *n* a gangster's girl-friend; a prostitute (*archaic*). [*Moll*, and old familiar form of *Mary*]

mollah and **molla**. See **mullah**.

mollie *mol'i*. Same as **mallemaroking**.

mollify *mol'i-fī*, *vt* to soften; to assuage; to cause to abate; to appease. — *vi* to become soft; to relax in severity or opposition. — *pr p* **moll'ifying**; *pa t* and *pa p* **moll'ified**. — *n* **mollification** (*-fi-kā'shən*). — *n* **moll'ifier**. [Fr *mollifier*, from L *mollificāre*, from *mollis* soft, and *facere* to make]

mollities *mol-ish'i-ēz*, (*archaic*) *n* softness, softening (*med*). — *adj* **mollitious** (*-ish'əs*) luxurious. [L *mollitiēs*, from *mollis* soft]

mollusc or (*NAm*) also **mollusk** *mol'əsk*, *n* an animal belonging to the large phylum of invertebrates, **Mollusca** (*-us'kə*), having no segments or limbs, and *usu* a mantle or fold of skin that secretes a shell (eg lamellibranchs, gasteropods, cephalopods, and some smaller groups); a lazy or sluggish person (*facetious*). — *adj* **mollus'can** (*NAm* also **mollus'kan**) or **mollus'cous** of or belonging to the Mollusca; like a mollusc. — *n* **mollus'cicide** (*-ki-sīd*) an agent for destroying molluscs, eg snails responsible for spread of disease. — *adj* **mollus'cicidal**. — *n* **mollus'coid** a member of a now abandoned division of invertebrates of the **Mollus-coid'ea**, Polyzoa and brachiopods. — *adj* of the Molluscoidea; like a mollusc. [L *molluscus* softish, from *mollis* soft]

Mollweide's projection *mol'vī-dəz prə-jek'shən*, *n* an equal-area representation of the surface of the globe in which the parallels of latitude are straight lines (closer together nearer the poles) and the meridians (apart from the central one) are curved, the curvature increasing toward the marginal meridians. [K *Mollweide* (died 1825), Ger mathematician and astronomer]

molly *mol'i*, *n* a milksop. — *n* **moll'ycoddle** an effeminate man. — *vt* to coddle. — **Molly Maguire** any member of an Irish society formed in 1843 to resist government evictions, who disguised themselves as women; a member of a Pennsylvanian secret society formed to resist oppressive conditions in the mines, and crushed in 1877. [*Molly*, dimin of *Mary*]

mollymawk *mol'i-mök* (*NZ colloq*). Same as **mallemuck**.

Moloch *mō'lok*, *n* a Semitic god to whom children were sacrificed (*Old Testament*; also **Mo'lech**); any cause to which dreadful sacrifice is made or destruction due; (without *cap*) an exceedingly spiny, harmless Australian lizard. — *vt* **mo'lochize** or **-ise** to sacrifice (as to Moloch). [Gr and L *Moloch*, from Heb *Mōlek*]

Molossian *mol-os'i-ən*, *adj* of *Molossia* or *Molossis* in the Epirus region of ancient Greece, famous in ancient times for its great mastiff dogs. — *n* **moloss'us** a metrical foot of three long syllables: — *pl* **moloss'ī**.

Molotov cocktail *mol'ə-tof kok'tāl*, *n* a crude form of hand-grenade consisting of a bottle containing an inflammable liquid, eg petrol, and a wick to be ignited just before the missile is thrown; a petrol bomb. [V M *Molotov* (1890–1986), Russian statesman]

molt[1]. See **moult**.

molt[2]. See **melt**[1].

molten *mōl'tən*, *adj* melted; made of melted metal. — *adv* **mōlt'enly**. — See also under **melt**. [Pa p of **melt**[1]]

molto *mol'tō*, (*music*) *adv* very; much. [Ital]

Molucca bean *mo-luk'ə bēn'*, *n* nicker nut or bonduc.

mol wt *abbrev*: molecular weight.

moly *mō'li*, *n* a magic herb given by Hermes to Odysseus as a counter-charm against the spells of Circe; a species of wild onion, *Allium moly*. [Gr *mōly*]

molybdenum *mol-ib'din-əm* (also *mol-ib-dē'nəm*), *n* a silvery-white metallic element (symbol **Mo**; atomic no 42). — *n* **molyb'date** a salt of molybdic acid. — *n* **molybdēn'ite** (or *-ib'dən-īt*) a mineral, molybdenum disulphide. — *n* **molybdenō'sis** a disease of cattle and sheep, characterized by chronic diarrhoea and emaciation, caused by an excess of molybdenum in the diet. — *adj* **molyb'dic**. — *n* **molybdō'sis** lead-poisoning. — *adj* **molyb'dous**. — **molybdic acid** H_2MoO_4. [Latinized neuter, from Gr *molybdaina* a lump of lead, a leadlike substance, from *molybdos* lead]

mom *mom*, (*US colloq*) *n* mother. — Also **momm'a** or **momm'y**. [See **mamma**[1]]

MOMA *mom'ə*, *abbrev*: Museum of Modern Art (New York).

mome[1] *mōm*, (*obs*) *n* a buffoon; a carper. [**Momus**]

mome[2] *mōm*, (*Spenser*) *n* a blockhead. [Origin obscure]

moment *mō'mənt*, *n* a point of time; a time so short that it may be considered as a point; a very short time (*slang abbrev* **mo**); a second; a precise instant; the present, or the right, instant; moving cause or motive (*Shakesp*); importance, consequence; an infinitesimal change in a varying quantity (*math*; *obs*); a stage or turning-point; an element or factor (as in *psychological moment*, rightly used); a measure of turning effect (the *moment of a force* about a point is the product of the force and the perpendicular on its line of action from the point). — *adj* **momentān'eous** momentary; instantaneous. — *adj* **mo'mentany** (*Shakesp*) momentary. — *adv* **mo'mentarily** for a moment; every moment; at any moment (*NAm*). — *n* **mo'mentariness**. — *adj* **mo'mentary** lasting for a moment; short-lived. — *adv* **mo'mently** every moment; for a moment. — *adj* occurring every moment; of a moment. — *adj* **momentous** (*-ment'*) of great consequence. — *adv* **moment'ously**. — *n* **moment'ousness**. — **moment of truth** the climax of a bullfight; a moment when, suddenly and dramatically, one is face to face with stark reality, often a testing moment (*fig*). [L *mōmentum*, for *movimentum*, from *movēre*, *mōtum* to move]

momentum *mō-men'təm*, *n* the quantity of motion in a body measured by the product of mass and velocity; force of motion gained in movement, impetus (*colloq*): — *pl* **moment'a**. [Ety as for **moment**]

MOMI *mō'mi*, *abbrev*: Museum of the Moving Image (London).

momma and **mommy**. See **mom**.

mommet. See **mammet**.

Momus *mō'məs*, (*Gr mythol*) *n* the god of ridicule. [Latinized from Gr *mōmos* blame, reproach, personified]

momzer. See **mamzer**.

Mon. *abbrev*: Monday; Monmouthshire (a former county, now mostly incorporated into modern Gwent).

mon *mon*, *n* a Japanese family badge or crest: — *pl* **mon**. [Jap]

mon-. See **mono-**.

mona *mō'nə*, *n* a W African monkey, *Cercopithecus mona*. [Ital, Sp, or Port *mona* monkey]

monachism *mon'ək-izm*, *n* monasticism. — *adj* **mon'achal**. — *adj* **mon'achist**. — *n* **Mon'achus** the monk-seal genus. [Gr *monachos* solitary, from *monos* single, alone]

monacid *mon-as'id* or **monoacid** *mon-ō-as'id, adj* having one replaceable hydrogen atom; capable of replacing one hydrogen atom of an acid. [**mono-**]

monact *mon'akt, (zool) adj* (of a sponge) having single-rayed spicules. — *adj* **monact'inal** (*-i-nəl* or *-ī'nəl*). — *adj* **monact'ine** (*-in*). [Gr *monos* single, alone, and *aktīs, -īnos* a ray]

monad *mon'ad, n* the number one, a unit (*hist*); an ultimate unit of being, material and psychical; a spirit; God; a hypothetical primitive living organism or unit of organic life; a flagellate of the genus *Monas* or other related genera; a univalent element, atom, or radical. — Also *adj*. — *adj* **monad'ic** or **monad'ical**. — *adj* **monad'iform** like a monad. — *n* **mon'adism** or **monadol'ogy** a theory or doctrine of monads, *esp* Leibniz's. — *n* **mon'as** a monad; (with *cap*) a genus of flagellates. [Gr *monas, -ados* a unit, from *monos* single, alone]

monadelphous *mon-ə-del'fəs, (bot) adj* (of stamens) united by the filaments in one bundle; (of a flower or plant) having all the stamens united in this way. — *n pl* **Monadel'phia** in Linnaeus's system, a class of plants with stamens united in one bundle. [Gr *monos* single, alone, and *adelphos* brother]

monadic ... to ... **monadology**. See under **monad**.

monadnock *mə-nad'nok, n* an isolated hill of hard rock that has resisted the erosion suffered by the land around it. [Mount *Monadnock*, New Hampshire, USA]

monadology. See under **monad**.

monal. See **monaul**.

monandrous *mon-an'drəs, adj* having or allowing one husband or male mate (at a time); having one stamen or one antheridium (*bot*). — *n pl* **Monan'dria** in Linnaeus's system, a class of plants with one stamen. — *n* **monan'dry** the condition or practice of being monandrous. [Gr *monos* single, alone, and *anēr, andros* a man, male]

monarch[1] *mon'ərk, n* a sole hereditary head of a state, whether titular or ruling; a large butterfly (*Danaus plexippus*) with orange and black wings. — *adj* **monarchal** (*-ärk'əl*), **monarch'ial, monarch'ic** or **monarch'ical**. — *n* **Monarch'ian** a Christian who denied the personal independent subsistence of Christ (*dynamic* when regarding the divinity of Christ as only a power (*dynamis*) communicated to him, *modalistic* when regarding Christ as the Father who had assumed flesh, a mere *modus* of the Godhead). — *n* **Monarch'ianism**. — *adj* **Monarchianis'tic**. — *n* **mon'archism** the principles of monarchy; love of monarchy. — *n* **mon'archist** an advocate of monarchy; a believer in monarchy; a Monarchian. — Also *adj*. — *adj* **monarchist'ic**. — *vt* **mon'archize** or **-ise** to rule over as a monarch; to convert into a monarchy. — *vi* (also *vt* with *it*) to play the monarch. — *n* **Monarch'o** (*Shakesp*) a foppish fantastic megalomaniac (from a crazy Italian seen around the court of Elizabeth I). — *n* **mon'archy** a kind of government of which there is a monarch; a state with monarchical government; the territory of a monarch. [Gr *monarchēs*, from *monos* single, alone, and *archein* to rule]

monarch[2] *mon'ärk, (bot) adj* having one xylem strand. [Gr *monos* single, alone, and *archē* origin]

monarda *mən-är'də, n* a plant of the *Monarda* genus of N American aromatic herbs of the mint (*Labiatae*) family. [N *Monardes* (died 1588), Spanish botanist]

monas. See **monad**.

monastery *mon'əs-tər-i* or *-tri, n* a house for a community of monks, or (sometimes) nuns. — *adj* **monastē'rial, monastic** (*-as'tik*) or **monas'tical** relating to monasteries, monks, or nuns; recluse; solitary. — *n* **monas'tic** a monk. — *adv* **monas'tically**. — *n* **monas'ticism** (*-sizm*) the monastic life or system of living. [Late Gr *monastērion*, from *monastēs* a monk, from *monos* single, alone]

Monastral blue® *mon-as'trəl bloo͞* and **Monastral green**® *grēn*, tradenames for certain phthalocyanine pigments.

monatomic *mon-ə-tom'ik, (chem) adj* consisting of one atom; having one replaceable atom or group; univalent. [**mono-**]

monaul or **monal** *mon'öl, n* a magnificent Himalayan pheasant (*Lophophorus*). [Nepali *munāl*]

monaural *mon-ö'rəl, adj* having or using only one ear; relating to one ear; (of a radio broadcast, etc) giving the effect of sound from a single direction, not stereophonic. [**mono-**]

monaxial *mon-aks'i-əl, adj* having only one axis. — *adj* **monax'on** monaxial. — *n* a monaxonic sponge or spicule. — *adj* **monaxon'ic**. — *n pl* **Monaxon'ida** an order of sponges with monaxon spicules only. [**mono-**]

monazite *mon'əz-īt, (mineralogy) n* a phosphate of cerium, lanthanum, neodymium, praseodymium, and *usu* thorium, a source of thorium itself. [Gr *monazein* to be solitary, on account of its rarity]

monchiquite *mon'shi-kīt, n* a fine-grained lamprophyric rock, composed of olivine and augite with little or no feldspar, in an analcite groundmass. [From the Serra de *Monchique*, in SW Portugal]

mondain *mɔ̃dɛ̃, adj* worldly, fashionable: — *fem* **mondaine** (*mɔ̃-den*). — *n* a person who lives in fashionable society. [Fr, from L *mundānus*, from *mundus* world]

Monday *mun'di* or *-dā, n* the second day of the week, the day following Sunday and the first day of the working week. — *adj* **Mon'dayish** having the Monday morning feeling (see below). — **Monday Club** a right-wing group of Conservatives formed in 1961, *orig* holding discussions over Monday lunch; **Monday morning feeling** the tiredness and disinclination to work felt at the prospect, after the weekend, of another week's work ahead. — **black Monday, Handsel Monday, Meal Monday, Plough Monday** see under **black**, etc. [OE *mōnandæg, mōnan*, genitive of *mōna* moon, and *dæg* day]

mondial *mon'di-əl, adj* of the whole world, worldwide. [Fr, from L *mundus* world]

mondo *mon'dō, (slang; orig US) adv* extremely, absolutely. [Ital, world, erroneously taken as an adverb in phrases such as *mondo bizarro*, etc]

monecious. Same as **monoecious**.

Monegasque *mon-ə-gask', n* a native or inhabitant of Monaco. — *adj* of or relating to Monaco or its inhabitants. [Fr *monégasque*, from Provençal *mounegasc*]

Monel metal® *mō-nel' met'l, n* a nickel-base alloy with high strength and resistance to corrosion.

moner *mōn'ər* or **moneron** *mon-ēr'on, n* the name given by German biologist Ernst Haeckel (1834–1919) to his hypothetical simplest protozoan, the organism on which his version of the evolution theory is based: — *pl* **monēr'a**. [Gr *monērēs* single]

monergism *mon'ər-jizm, (theol) n* the doctrine that regeneration is entirely the work of the Holy Spirit, the natural will being incapable of co-operation. [Gr *monos* single, alone, and *ergon* work]

monetary *mon'* or *mun'i-tər-i, adj* of or relating to money; consisting of money. — *n* **mon'etarism**. — *n* **mon'etarist** a person who advocates an economic policy based chiefly on the control of a country's money supply. — *n* **monetīzā'tion** or **-s-**. — *vt* **mon'etize** or **-ise** to give the character of money to, to coin as money. — **monetary unit** the principal unit of currency of a state. [L *monēta* (see **money**)]

moneth *munth* (*Spenser*). Same as **month**.

money *mun'i, n* coin, pieces of stamped metal used as a trading medium; any currency used in the same way; wealth: — *pl* **mon'eys** or **mon'ies** (*archaic* and *legal*) sums of money; money. — *adj* **mon'eyed** or **mon'ied** having money; materially rich, well off; consisting in money. — *n* **mon'eyer** a person who coins money legally (*archaic*); a capitalist (*obs*). — *adj* **mon'eyless** having no money. — **money'-bag** a bag for or of money; **mon'eybags** (*colloq*) a rich person; **money belt** a belt with a pocket in it for holding money; **mon'ey-bill** a bill introduced into parliament or congress for raising revenue or otherwise dealing with money. — *adj*

mon'ey-bound unable to move for lack of money. — **money'-box** a box for collecting or saving money, *usu* with a slit for insertion; **mon'ey-broker** a person who carries out transactions in money for others; **mon'ey-changer** a person who exchanges one currency for another; **money clip** a clip for holding (*esp* folded) bank notes together; **mon'ey-grubber** a sordid accumulator of wealth. — *n* and *adj* **mon'ey-grubbing**. — **mon'ey-lender** a professional lender of money at interest, *esp* an individual or small company arranging domestic loans at higher-than-commercial interest rates; **mon'ey-lending**; **mon'ey-maker** a person who acquires wealth; anything that brings profit; a person who earns money; **mon'ey-making** the act of gaining wealth. — *adj* lucrative, profitable. — **mon'eyman** a person employed or specializing in finance; **mon'ey-market** (the dealers in) the market for short-term loans for business, etc; **mon'ey-order** an order for money deposited at one post-office, and payable at another; **mon'ey-scrivener** (*old*) a person who does financial business for clients; **mon'ey-spider** a very small spider supposed to bring luck in money; **mon'ey-spinner** a money-spider; a successful speculator; any scheme that brings in much money; **money supply** the amount of money available to a country's economy; **mon'ey's-worth** something as good as money; full value; **mon'ey-taker** a person who receives payments of money, *esp* at an entrance-door; someone who can be bribed; **mon'eywort** a round-leaved loosestrife, creeping Jenny. — **for my** (or **our**) **money** if I (or we) were to choose, express an opinion, etc; **hard money** coin; **in the money** among the prize-winners (*racing*, etc); well-off; **make money** to acquire wealth; to make a profit; **money down** money paid on the spot; **money for jam, old rope**, etc, money obtained without effort; **money of account** a monetary unit (not represented by current coins) used in keeping accounts; **money talks** the wealthy have much influence; **on the money** (*US slang*) spot-on, exact, just right; **pots of money** a large amount of money; **put money into** to invest in; **put money on** to place a bet on; **put one's money where one's mouth is** to support one's stated opinion by betting money; to give practical (*esp* financial) rather than merely hypothetical support; **ready money** money paid for a thing at the time at which it is bought; money ready for immediate payment. [OFr *moneie* (Fr *monnaie*), from L *monēta* money, a mint, *Monēta* (the reminder) being a surname of Juno, in whose temple at Rome money was coined]

mong *mung*, (now *dialect*) *n* a mixture; a crowd. — **mong'corn** or **mung'corn** maslin. [OE *gemang*]

'mong and **'mongst** aphetic for **among** and **amongst**.

monger *mung'gər*, *n* (chiefly as a *combining form*) a dealer (except in a few instances, such as *ironmonger*), a person who trafficks in a petty, or discreditable way, or in unpleasant subjects, eg a *gossipmonger*. — *n* **mong'ering** or **mong'ery**. [OE *mangere*, from L *mangō*, *-ōnis* a furbisher, slave-dealer, from Gr *manganeuein* to use trickery]

Mongol *mong'gol*, *n* a member of Genghis Khan's clan, or of the various populations under him (*hist*); one of the people of Mongolia; their language; a member of a broad-headed, yellow-skinned, straight-haired, small-nosed human race, often with an epicanthic fold of skin (otherwise called *Tungus*); (often without *cap*) the old (no longer preferred, by some considered *offensive*) term for a person affected by Down's syndrome. — *adj* Mongolian. — *adj* **Mongolian** (*mong-gō'li-ən*) of Mongolia, the Mongols, or their language. — *n* the language of Mongolia. — *adj* **Mongolic** (*-gol'ik*) Mongolian; of Mongolian type; of the division of the Ural-Altaic languages to which Mongolian, Buriat, and Kalmuck belong. — *n* **Mong'olism** (often without *cap*) an old (no longer preferred) term for **Down's syndrome**. — *vt* **Mong'olize** or **-ise** to make Mongolian. — *adj* **Mong'oloid** of Mongolian race or type; (often without *cap*) affected with Down's syndrome (no longer preferred). — *n* a person of Mongolian race or type; (often without *cap*) an old term for a person affected by Down's syndrome (no longer preferred). — **Mongoloid eye** an eye with an epicanthic fold. [Said to be from Mongol *mong* brave]

mongoose *mong'* or *mung'gōōs*, *n* an Indian animal of the civet family, a great slayer of snakes and rats; any other species of the genus (*Herpestes*), including the ichneumon; a Madagascan lemur: — *pl* **mong'ooses**. — Also **mung'oose** or (*Fr*) **mangouste'**. [Marathi *mangūs*]

mongrel *mung'grəl*, *n* an animal, *esp* a dog, of a mixed breed (*usu* in contempt); a person, thing or word of mixed or indefinite origin or nature; that which is neither one thing nor another. — *adj* mixed in breed; ill-defined. — *n* **mong'relism**. — *vt* **mong'relize** or **-ise**. — *adj* **mong'relly**. [Prob from root of OE *mengan* to mix]

monial *mōn'i-əl*, *n* a mullion. [OFr, of unknown origin]

monicker or **moniker** *mon'i-kər*, (*slang*; *orig* tramps') *n* an alias, nickname or real name.

monied and **monies**. See under **money**.

monilia *mon-il'i-ə*, *n* a fungus of the *Monilia* genus, having conidia in branched chains. — *n* **moniliasis** (*-ī'ə-sis*) a disease of the mouth and digestive tract in birds, animals, and man (**thrush**[2]), caused by fungi of the genus *Monilia*. — *adj* **monil'iform** like a string of beads. [L *monīle* a necklace]

moniment *mon'i-mənt*. See **monument**.

moniplies *mun'* or *mon'i-plīz*. See **manyplies**.

monism *mon'izm*, *n* a philosophical theory that all being may ultimately be referred to one category; thus *idealism*, *pantheism* and *materialism* are monisms, as opposed to the dualism of matter and spirit. — *n* **mon'ist**. — *adj* **monist'ic** or **monist'ical** [Gr *monos* single, alone]

monition *mon-ish'ən*, *n* a reminding or admonishing; warning; notice; a summons to appear and answer (*law*). — *adj* **mon'itive** conveying admonition. — *n* **mon'itor** a person who admonishes; an adviser; a senior pupil who assists in school discipline, or any other pupil with a special responsibility; a back-board (*obs*); an apparatus for testing transmission in electrical communication; a person employed to supervise; a low iron-clad with revolving gun-turrets (from an American ship so named, the first of its kind, 1862); a genus (*Varanus*) of very large lizards of Africa, Asia, and Australia (from a belief that they give warning of the presence of a crocodile); a detector for radio-activity; an instrument used in a production process to keep a variable quantity within prescribed limits by transmitting a controlling signal; a screen in a television studio showing the picture being transmitted; the screen in any set of audio-visual equipment: — *fem* **mon'itress**. — *vt* to act as monitor to; to check (eg the body and clothing of people working with radioactive materials) for radioactivity; to track, or to control (an aeroplane, guided missile, etc); to watch, check, supervise. — *vi* (*radio*) to tap on to a communication circuit, *usu* in order to ascertain that the transmission is that desired; to listen to foreign broadcasts in order to obtain news, code messages, etc. — *adj* **monitorial** (*-ōr'* or *-ör'*) relating to a monitor. — *adv* **monito'rially**. — *n* **mon'itorship**. — *adj* **mon'itory** giving admonition or warning. [L *monēre*, *-itum* to remind]

monk *mungk*, *n* a hermit (*obs*); a man (other than a friar, but loosely often applied to a friar also) of a religious community living together under vows; a bullfinch; an inky blotch or overinked place in print; touchwood for firing mines (*obs*). — *n* **monk'ery** (*contemptuous*) monasticism; behaviour of monks; monks collectively. — *n* **monk'hood** the state or character of a monk. — *adj* **monk'ish** (*disparagingly*) relating to a monk; like a monk; monastic. — **monk'fish** the angel fish (shark); any of several types of angler fish; **monk's cloth** a type of heavy cotton cloth; **monk'-seal** a seal (*Monachus albiventer*) of the Black Sea, Mediterranean, and NW Africa, dark grey above, light underneath; **monks'hood**

wolfsbane, a poisonous ranunculaceous plant (*Aconitum*) with a large hoodlike posterior sepal; **monk's rhubarb** patience-dock; **monk's'-seam** (*naut*) a strong seam formed by overlapping two pieces and stitching on each side and down the middle (also *middle-stitching*). [OE *munuc*, from L *monachus*, from Gr *monachos*, from *monos* alone]

monkey *mungk'i*, *n* any mammal of the Primates except man and (*usu*) the anthropoid apes; an ape; a sheep (*Austr slang*); a term of contempt, or of playful endearment, for a mischievous or badly-behaved child or person; the falling weight of a pile-driver; a large hammer for driving bolts; 500 pounds, or dollars (*slang*); anger (*slang*); an oppressive burden or habit, *specif* a drug addiction (*US slang*); any of various kinds of container, *esp* for alcohol; a type of cannon (*obs*): — *pl* **monk'eys**. — *vi* (often with *around*) to meddle with anything, to fool. — *vt* to mimic, ape. — *adj* **monk'-eyish**. — *n* **monk'eyism** monkey-like behaviour. — **monk'ey-bag** a small money-bag, hung round the neck; **monk'ey-block** a small swivel-block, used to guide running rigging; **monk'ey-board** a foot-board behind a vehicle; a high-level platform on an oil-derrick; **monk'ey-boat** a narrow, half-decked river-boat; **monk'ey-bread** the baobab tree or its fruit; **monkey business** underhand dealings; mischievous behaviour; **monk'ey-engine** a pile-driving engine; **monk'ey-flower** a species of *Mimulus*; **monk'ey-gaff** (*naut*) a small gaff above the spanker gaff for the flag; **monk'ey-gland** ape's testicle, grafted experimentally on man (1920–30s) to effect rejuvenescence; **monk'ey-grass** a coarse fibre from the leaf-stalks of *Attalea funifera*, used for brooms, etc; **monk'ey-hammer** a drop-press with a ram, which is raised and let drop freely; **monk'ey-jacket** a short close-fitting jacket; **monk'ey-jar** a water-monkey; **monk'ey-nut** the peanut or ground-nut (*Arachis*); **monkey pod** the rain-tree; **monk'ey-pot** the round-lidded outer shell of the sapucaia nut; **monk'ey-pump** a straw let through a gimlet-hole for sucking alcohol from a cask; **monk'ey-puzzle** a coniferous tree (*Araucaria imbricata*) also called Chile pine, with close-set prickly leaves; **monk'ey-rail** a light rail above the quarter-rail on a ship; **monk'ey-rope** a forest creeper or liana; a rope round a sailor's waist for working in a dangerous place; **monk'ey-run** a favourite place of parade and striking up of acquaintance; **monk'ey-shine** (*US slang*) a monkeyish trick; **monk'ey-suit** (*slang*) a man's evening suit; **monk'ey-tail** a vertical scroll at the end of a hand-rail; **monk'ey-tricks** mischief, pranks; **monk'ey-wheel** a tackle-block over which a hoisting-rope runs; **monk'ey-wrench** a wrench with a movable jaw, an adjustable spanner. — **have a monkey on one's back** to be addicted to drugs (*US slang*); **have** or **get one's monkey up** (*slang*) to be angry; **make a monkey (out) of** to make a fool of; **not to give a monkey's** (*vulg slang*) not to care, or be interested, at all; **suck the monkey** (*slang*) to drink from a cask through an inserted tube; to drink rum, etc from a coconut. [Perh from MLGer *moneke*, connected with Sp and Port *mono* monkey]

monkfish and **monkshood**. See under **monk**.

Mon-Khmer *mōn-kmer'*, *adj* of a group of Austroasiatic languages that includes *Mon*, spoken in Pegu (Burma, now Myanma), and *Khmer* in Cambodia.

mono- *mon-ō-* or before a vowel **mon-** *mon-*, *combining form* denoting single. [Gr *monos* single, alone]

mono[1] *mon'ō*, (*colloq*) *n* a monaural gramophone record; monaural reproduction: — *pl* **mon'os**. — Also *adj*.

mono[2] *mon'ō*, (*colloq*) *n* short form of **infectious mononucleosis** (see under **infect**).

monoacid. Same as **monacid**.

monoamine *mon-ō-am'īn* or *-ēn*, *n* an amine containing only one amino-group. [**mono-**]

monobasic *mon-ō-bā'sik*, (*chem*) *adj* capable of reacting with one equivalent of an acid; (of an acid) having one replaceable hydrogen atom. [**mono-**]

monoblepsis *mon-ō-blep'sis*, *n* a condition in which vision is more distinct when one eye only is used. [Gr *monos* single, and *blepsis* sight]

monocardian *mon-ō-kär'di-ən*, *adj* having an undivided heart. [Gr *monos* single, alone, and *kardiā* heart]

monocarpellary *mon-ō-kär'pəl-ə-ri* or *-pel'*, (*bot*) *adj* of or with only one carpel. [**mono-**]

monocarpic *mon-ō-kärp'ik*, (*bot*) *adj* fruiting once only. — *n* **mon'ocarp** a monocarpic plant. — *adj* **monocarp'ous** monocarpic; having only one ovary; producing one fruit. [Gr *monos* single, alone, and *karpos* fruit]

monoceros *mo-nos'ər-os*, *n* a one-horned animal; the unicorn; *perh* the swordfish, or the narwhal (*Spenser*). — *adj* **monoc'erous**. [Gr *monokerōs*, from *monos* single, alone, and *keras* a horn]

monochasium *mon-ō-kā'zi-əm*, *n* a cymose inflorescence in which each axis in turn produces one branch: — *pl* **monocha'sia**. — *adj* **monocha'sial**. [Gr *monos* single, alone; apparently on the analogy of **dichasium**, as if that were from Gr *di-* twice, and *chasis* separation]

monochlamydeous *mon-ō-klə-mid'i-əs*, (*bot*) *adj* having a one-whorled perianth. — *npl* **Monochlamyd'eae** a division of the Archichlamydeae or choripetalae, usually with the perianth in one whorl. [**mono-**]

monochord *mon'ō-körd*, *n* an acoustic instrument with one string, sound-board and bridge, *esp* one with a movable bridge and a graduated sound-board for use in the analysis of sounds; a similar instrument with more than one string and bridge; a clavichord; a tromba marina. [**mono-**]

monochroic *mon-ō-krō'ik*, *adj* of one colour. [Gr *monochroos*, from *monos* single, alone, and *chrōs* colour]

monochromatic *mon-ō-krō-mat'ik*, *adj* of one colour or wavelength only; completely colour-blind; done in monochrome. — *n* **monochro'masy** complete colour-blindness. — *n* **monochro'mat** or **monochro'mate** a person who sees all colours as different shades of a single colour. — *n* **monochro'matism** monochromatic vision. — *n* **monochro'mator** a device capable of isolating and transmitting monochromatic or nearly monochromatic light. — *n* **mon'ochrome** representation in one colour; a picture in one colour; black and white; monochromy. — *adj* **monochro'mic**. — *n* **monochro'mist** a person who practises monochrome. — *adj* done, reproduced, etc in a single colour or hue; black and white. — *n* **mon'ochromy** the art of monochrome. [Gr *monochrōmatos*, from *monos* single, alone, and *chrōma*, *-atos* colour]

monocle *mon'ə-kl*, *n* a single eyeglass. — *adj* **mon'ocled** wearing a monocle. [Fr *monocle*, from Gr *monos* single, alone, and L *oculus* eye]

monocline *mon'ō-klīn*, (*geol*) *n* a fold in strata followed by resumption of the original direction. — *adj* **monoclīn'al**. [Gr *monos* single, alone, and *klīnein* to cause to slope]

monoclinic *mon'ō-klin-ik*, (*crystallog*) *adj* referable to three unequal axes, two intersecting each other obliquely and at right angles to the third. [Gr *monos* single, alone, and *klīnein* to incline]

monoclinous *mon'ō-klī-nəs* or *-klī'*, (*bot*) *adj* hermaphrodite. [Gr *monos* single, alone, and *klīnē* bed]

monoclonal *mon-ō-klō'nəl*, *adj* (of an antibody) derived from a single cell clone that can reproduce itself in vast quantities in the laboratory, having applications in the diagnosis and treatment of cancers, infections, etc. [**mono-**]

mono-compound *mon-ō-kom'pownd*, (*chem*) *n* a compound containing one atom or group of that which is indicated. [**mono-**]

monocoque *mon-ō-kok'* or *-kōk'*, *n* a fuselage or nacelle in which all, or nearly all, structural loads are carried by the skin (*aeronautics*); a motor vehicle structure in which body and chassis are a single unit, with all parts receiving stress (*autos*); the hull of a boat made in one piece (*naut*). [Fr, literally single shell]

monocotyledon *mon-ō-kot-i-lē'dən n* (often shortened to **monocot**) a plant of the **Monocotylē'dones** (*-ēz*) or **Monocot'ylae**, one of the two great divisions of angiosperms, the embryos with one cotyledon, leaves commonly parallel-veined, the parts of the flower *usu* in threes, the vascular bundles scattered and (with exceptions) without cambium. — *adj* **monocotylē'donous**. **[mono-]**

monocracy *mon-ok'rə-si*, *n* government by one person. — *n* **mon'ocrat** (*-ō-krat*). — *adj* **monocrat'ic**. [Gr *monos* single, alone, and *kratos* power]

monocrystal *mon'ō-kris-təl*, *n* a single crystal. — *adj* **monocrys'talline**. **[mono-]**

monocular *mon-ok'ū-lər*, *adj* one-eyed; of, for, or with, one eye. — Also **monoc'ulous**. [Gr *monos* single, alone, and L *oculus* an eye]

monoculture *mon'ō-kul-chər*, *n* the growing of one kind of crop only, or a large area over which it is grown. — *adj* **monocul'tural** of or relating to monoculture; of or relating to a single, shared culture (eg ethnic, social, religious). **[mono-]**

monocyclic *mon-ō-sīk'lik*, (*bot*) *adj* having one whorl or ring. **[mono-]**

monocyte *mon'ō-sīt*, (*anatom*) *n* a large phagocytic leucocyte with a single oval or kidney-shaped nucleus and clear cytoplasm. [Gr *monos* single, and *kytos* vessel]

monodactylous *mon-ō-dak'ti-ləs*, *adj* one-toed or one-fingered. [Gr *monos* single, alone, and *daktylos* finger, toe]

Monodelphia *mon-ō-del'fi-ə*, *n pl* one of the three primary divisions of mammals, the placental mammals or Eutheria. — *adj* **monodel'phian**, **monodel'phic** or **monodel'phous**. [Gr *monos* single, alone, and *delphys* womb]

monodic and **monodist**. See under **monody**.

Monodon *mon'ō-don*, *n* the narwhal. — *adj* **mon'odont** one-tusked; of the monodon. [Gr *monos* single, alone, and *odous*, *odontos* tooth, tusk]

monodrama *mon'ō-drä-mə*, *n* a dramatic piece for a single performer. — *adj* **monodramatic** (*-drə-mat'ik*). **[mono-]**

monody *mon'ə-di*, *n* (in Greek tragedy) a mournful ode or poem performed by a single mourner; any poem lamenting a death; a song for one voice; a composition in which one part or voice carries the melody, the others accompanying (*music*). — *adj* **monodic** (*-od'*) or **monod'ical**. — *n* **mon'odist** a person who writes monodies. [Gr *monōidiā*, from *monos* single, alone, and *ōidē* song]

monoecious *mon-ē'shəs*, (*biol*) *adj* hermaphrodite; having separate male and female flowers on the same plant. — *n pl* **Monoe'cia** in the Linnaean system, a class so characterized. — *n* **monoecism** (*-ē'sizm*). [Gr *monos* single, alone, and *oikos* a house]

monofil *mon'ō-fil*, *n* a single strand of synthetic fibre. — Also **monofil'ament**. [Gr *monos* single, alone, and L *fīlum* a thread]

monogamy *mon-og'ə-mi*, *n* the rule, custom or condition of marriage to one wife or husband at a time, or (now rarely) in life; the practice, custom or condition of having no more than one mate (*zool*) or, loosely, one sexual partner, at a time. — *adj* **monogamic** (*mon-ō-gam'ik*) or **monogamous** (*-og'əm-*). — *n* **monog'amist**. [Gr *monos* single, alone, and *gamos* marriage]

monogenesis *mon-ō-jen'i-sis*, *n* development of offspring from a parent like itself; asexual reproduction; community of origin. — *adj* **monogenet'ic**. — *adj* **monogen'ic** of or relating to monogenism; of or determined by a single gene. — *n* **monogenism** (*-oj'ən-izm*) the doctrine of the common descent of all living things, or of any particular group (*esp* mankind) from one ancestor or pair. — *n* **monog'enist**. — *adj* **monogenist'ic**. — *adj* **monog'enous**. — *n* **monog'eny** descent from one common ancestor or pair; asexual reproduction. **[mono-]**

monoglot *mon'ō-glot*, *n* a person who knows only one language. — Also *adj*. [Gr *monos* single, alone, and *glōtta* tongue]

monogony *mon-og'ən-i*, *n* asexual reproduction. [Gr *monos* single, alone, and *gonos* begetting]

monogram *mon'ə-gram*, *n* a figure consisting of several letters interwoven or written into one. — *adj* **monogrammatic** (*-grə-mat'ik*). [Gr *monos* single, alone, and *gramma*, *grammatos* a letter]

monograph *mon'ə-gräf*, *n* a treatise, book or paper written on one particular subject or any branch of it; a systematic account. — *vt* to write a monograph on. — *n* **monographer** (*mon-og'rə-fər*) or **monog'raphist** a writer of monographs. — *adj* **monographic** (*-graf'*) or **monograph'ical** relating to a monograph or a monogram; drawn in lines without colours. — *n* **monog'raphy** (*rare*) a monograph. [Gr *monos* single, alone, and *graphein* to write]

monogyny *mon-oj'i-ni* or *-og'*, *n* the custom, practice or condition of having only one wife; marriage with one wife; the habit of mating with one female. — *n pl* **Monogynia** (*mon-ō-jin'i-ə*) in various Linnaean classes of plants, an order having one style. — *adj* **monogyn'ian** (*bot*) belonging to the *Monogynia* order. — *adj* **monog'ynous** having one wife; practising monogyny; mating with one female; having one style; monogynian. [Gr *monos* single, alone, and *gynē* woman]

monohull *mon'ō-hul*, *n* a vessel with one hull, as opposed to a catamaran or trimaran. **[mono-]**

monohybrid *mon-ō-hī'brid*, *n* a cross between parents differing in one heritable character. **[mono-]**

monohydric *mon-ō-hī'drik*, *adj* containing one hydroxyl group. **[mono-]**

monolatry *mon-ol'ə-tri*, *n* the worship of one god without excluding belief in others. — *n* **monol'ater**. — *adj* **monol'atrous**. [Gr *monos* single, alone, and *latreiā* worship]

monolayer *mon'ō-lā-ər*, *n* a monomolecular layer. — **monolayer culture** (*biol*) a tissue culture technique in which thin sheets of cells are grown, on glass, in a nutrient medium. **[mono-]**

monolingual *mon-ō-ling'gwəl*, *adj* expressed in one language; speaking only one language. — *n* **monoling'ualism**. — *n* **monoling'uist**. [Gr *monos* single, and L *lingua* tongue]

monolith *mon'ō-lith*, *n* a single block of stone forming a pillar or column; anything resembling a monolith in uniformity, massiveness or intractability. — *adj* **monolith'ic** relating to or resembling a monolith; (of a state, an organization, etc) massive, and undifferentiated throughout; intractable for this reason. — **monolithic integrated circuit** see under **integrate**. [Gr *monos* single, alone, and *lithos* a stone]

monologue *mon'ə-log*, *n* a soliloquy or speech by one person, or a composition intended to be spoken by one person; a tedious, loud or opinionated speech that blocks conversation (*colloq*). — *adj* **monologic** (*-loj'*) or **monolog'ical**. — *n* **monol'ogist** a person who talks in or performs a monologue (also **mon'ologuist**). — *vi* **monologize** or **-ise** (*mon-ol'ə-jīz*) to indulge in this. — Also **monol'oguize** or **-ise** (*-gīz*). — *n* **monol'ogy** the habit of doing so. [Gr *monos* single, alone, and *logos* speech]

monomachy *mon-om'ə-ki*, *n* single combat; a duel. — Also **monomā'chia**. [Gr *monos* single, alone, and *machē* a fight]

monomania *mon-ō-mā'ni-ə*, *n* mental illness in which the mind is consumed by a single thought or idea; fanatical enthusiasm for a single subject or activity. — *n* **monomā'niac** a person affected with monomania. — *adj* **monomā'niac** or **monomaniacal** (*-mə-nī'ə-kl*). [Gr *monos* single, alone, and *maniā* madness]

monomark *mon'ō-märk*, *n* a particular combination of letters, figures, etc as a mark of identification. **[mono-]**

monomer *mon'* or *mōn'ə-mər*, (*chem*) *n* the simplest of any series of compounds having the same empirical formula (opposite of *polymer*). — *adj* **monomer'ic**. [Gr *monos* single, alone, and *meros* part]

monometallic *mon-ō-mi-tal'ik*, *adj* involving or using only one metal as a standard of currency. — *n* **monometallism** (*-met'əl-izm*). — *n* **monomet'allist**. **[mono-]**

monometer *mon-om'i-tər*, (*prosody*) *adj* consisting of one measure. — *n* a verse of one measure. [**mono-** and **meter**[1]]

monomial *mon-ō'mi-əl*, *n* an algebraic expression consisting of one term only; a name consisting of one word. — Also *adj*. [Ill-formed from Gr *monos* single, alone, and L *nōmen* name]

monomode *mon'ō-mōd*, *adj* designating a very fine optical fibre (less than 10 micrometres in diameter) used in telecommunications, in which the diameter of the inner core is comparable with the wavelength of light thus, as there is only one mode of light propagation, eliminating mode disperson. [**mono-**]

monomolecular *mon-ō-mol-ek'ū-lər*, *adj* (of a film or layer) one molecule in thickness. [**mono-**]

monomorphic *mon-ō-mör'fik*, (*biol*) *adj* existing in one form only. — *adj* **monomor'phous**. [Gr *monos* single, alone, and *morphē* form]

monomyarian *mon-ō-mī-ā'ri-ən*, *adj* having one adductor muscle. [Gr *monos* single, alone, and *mys*, *myos* muscle]

mononuclear *mon-ō-nū'kli-ər*, *adj* having a single nucleus; monocyclic. — *n* (*med*) **mononucleosis** (*mon-ō-nūk-li-ō'sis*) the presence in the blood of an abnormally large number of a type of leucocyte. — See also **infectious mononucleosis** under **infect**. [**mono-**]

monopetalous *mon-ō-pet'ə-ləs*, (*bot*) *adj* having petals united. [**mono-**]

monophagous *mon-of'ə-gəs*, *adj* feeding only on one kind of food. — *n* **monoph'agy** (*-ji*) feeding on one food; eating alone. [Gr *monos* single, alone, and *phagein* (aorist) to eat]

monophasic *mon-ō-fāz'ik*, *adj* (of electric current) single-phase (also called **mon'ophase**); having one period of rest and one of activity during the 24 hours (*biol*). [**mono-**]

monophobia *mon-ō-fō'bi-ə*, *n* morbid fear of being alone. — *adj* **monophō'bic**. — *n* a person affected by monophobia. [**mono-**]

monophonic *mon-ō-fon'ik*, *adj* homophonic; monaural (*opp* of *stereophonic*). — *n* **monoph'ony**. [Gr *monos* single, alone, and *phōnē* voice, sound]

monophthong *mon'of-thong*, *n* a simple vowel sound. — *adj* **monophthongal** (*-thong'gəl*). — *vt* **mon'ophthongize** or **-ise** (*-gīz*) to turn into a monophthong. [Gr *monophthongos*, from *monos* single, alone, and *phthongos* sound, vowel]

monophyletic *mon-ō-fi-let'ik* or *-fī-*, *adj* derived from a single stock or ancestral line. [Gr *monos* single, alone, and *phȳletikos* relating to a tribesman, from *phȳlē* tribe]

monophyodont *mon-ō-fī'ō-dont*, *adj* having only one set of teeth. — *n* an animal with only one set of teeth. [Gr *monophyēs* of simple nature, from *monos* single, and *odous*, *odontos* tooth]

Monophysite *mō-nof'i-zīt* or *-sīt*, (*Christian relig*) *n* a person who holds that Christ had only one nature, principally divine but with human form and attributes. — *adj* **Monophysitic** (*-sit'ik* or *-zit'ik*). — *n* **Monoph'ysitism**. — All words also without *cap*. [Gr *monos* single, alone, and *physis* nature]

monopitch *mon'ō-pich*, (*archit*) *adj* (of a roof) forming a single, uniform slope. [**mono-**]

Monoplacophora *mon-ō-plak-of'ə-rə*, *n pl* a very primitive limpet-like class of molluscs, believed, till the discovery (1952) of the living Neopilina off the W coast of Mexico, to have been extinct since early Silurian times. [Gr *monos* single, alone, *plax*, *plakos* plate, and *phoros* bearing, from the single piece of shell]

monoplane *mon'ə-plān*, *n* an aeroplane or glider with one set of planes or wings. [**mono-**]

monoplegia *mon-ō-plē'ji-ə*, (*med*) *n* paralysis limited to a single part of the body, or to one limb or muscle. [Gr *monos* single, alone, and *plēgē* stroke]

monopode *mon'ə-pōd*, now also **monopod** *mon'ə-pod*, *n* a one-footed person, *esp* a member of an imaginary race each having a single foot large enough to be used by its owner as a sunshade (Pliny, *Naturalis Historia*); a one-footed support, platform stand, etc, eg for a camera. — *adj* one-footed. — *adj* **monopo'dial** relating to or of the nature of a monopodium. — *adv* **monopo'dially**. — *n* **monopo'dium** (*bot*) a stem involved in **monopodial growth**, a pattern of growth in which a shoot continues to grow indefinitely and bears lateral shoots which behave similarly (cf **sympodial growth**). [L *monopodius*, *-um*, from Gr *monos* single, alone, and *pous*, *podos* foot]

monopole *mon'ō-pōl*, (*physics*) *n* (*usu* **magnetic monopole**) a particle, thought to exist, that has a single magnetic charge. [**mono-**]

monopoly *mon-op'ə-li*, *n* sole power, or privilege, of dealing in anything; exclusive command or possession; something of which one has such a sole power, privilege, command, or possession; (with *cap*; ®) a board-game for two or more players, their object being the acquisition of property. — *adj* **monopolis'tic**. — *vt* **monop'olize** or **-ise** to have a monopoly of; to keep to oneself; to engross. — *n* **monop'olizer**, **-s-** or **monop'olist**. — **Monopolies and Mergers Commission** a body set up by the government to investigate monopolies, etc, where a monopoly is defined as 25 per cent of the market; **Monopoly money** (*colloq*) large sums of money treated lightly as though of no real consequence or value, like the sham notes exchanged in Monopoly®. [L *monopōlium*, from Gr *monopōlion*, from *monos* single, alone, and *pōleein* to sell]

monoprionidian *mon-ō-prī-ə-nid'i-ən*, *adj* (of graptolites) serrated on one side. [Gr *monos* single, alone, and *priōn* a saw]

monopsony *mon-op'sə-ni*, *n* a situation where only one buyer exists for the product of several sellers, or where one of several buyers is large enough to exert undue influence over the price of a product. — *n* **monop'sonist**. — *adj* **monopsonis'tic**. [Gr *monos* single, alone, and *opsonia* a purchase, from *opsonein* to buy]

monopteros *mon-op'tər-os* or **monopteron** *-on*, *n* a circular Greek temple with one ring of columns. — *adj* **monop'teral**. [Gr *monos* single, alone, and *pteron* a wing]

monoptote *mon'op-tōt*, *n* a word with only one case form. [Gr *monoptōtos*, from *monos* single, alone, and *ptōtos* fallen; cf *ptōsis* case (see **case**[2])]

monopulse *mon'ō-puls*, *n* a type of radar system used in many gun-control and missile guidance systems, involving the transmission of a single pulse. [**mono-**]

monorail *mon'ō-rāl*, *n* a railway with carriages running astride of, or suspended from, one rail. — Also *adj*. [**mono-**]

monorchid *mon-ör'kid*, *adj* having only one testicle. — *n* **monorch'ism**. [Faultily formed from Gr *monorchis*, from *monos* single, alone, and *orchis*, *-eōs* testicle]

monorhine *mon'ō-rīn*, *adj* having one nostril. — Also **monorhin'al**. [Gr *monos* single, alone, and *rhīs*, *rhīnos* nose]

monorhyme *mon'ə-rīm*, *n* a series or tirade of lines all rhyming together. — Also *adj*. — *adj* **mon'orhymed**. [**mono-**]

monosaccharide *mon-ō-sak'ə-rīd*, *n* a simple sugar that cannot be hydrolyzed. [**mono-**]

monosepalous *mon-ō-sep'ə-ləs*, (*bot*) *adj* having the sepals all united. [**mono-**]

monosis. See **monosy**.

mono-ski *mon'ō-skē*, *n* a ski on which both feet are placed. — *vi* to use a mono-ski. — *n* **mon'o-skier**. [**mono-**]

monosodium glutamate *mon-ō-sō'di-əm gloo'tə-māt*, *n* a white crystalline salt which brings out the flavour of meat (*glutamate*, a salt of glutamic acid), widely used as an additive in the food industry (*abbrev* **MSG**).

monostich *mon'ə-stik*, *n* a poem of one line. — *adj* **monostichous** (*-os'tik-əs*) in one line; in one row. [Gr *monos* single, alone, and *stichos* row, line]

monostrophic *mon-ə-strof'ik*, (*prosody*) *adj* not divided into strophe, antistrophe, and epode; having the same strophic or stanzaic structure throughout. — *n pl*

monostroph'ics monostrophic verses. [Gr *monostrophikos*, from *monos* single, alone, and *strophē* a strophe]

monostyle *mon'ō-stīl*, (*archit*) *adj* consisting of a single shaft. — *adj* **monostyl'ar**. [Gr *monos* single, alone, and *stȳlos* a pillar]

monosy *mon'os-i*, (*biol*) *n* separation of parts normally fused. — Also **monō'sis**. [Gr *monōsis* solitariness, from *monos* single, alone]

monosyllable *mon-ə-sil'ə-bl*, *n* a word of one syllable. — *adj* **monosyllabic** (*-ab'ik*). — *n* **monosyll'abism**. **[mono-]**

monosymmetric *mon-ō-sim-et'rik* or **monosymmetrical** *-əl*, *adj* having only one plane of symmetry. **[mono-]**

monotelephone *mon-ō-tel'i-fōn*, *n* a telephone that transmits sounds of one pitch only. **[mono-]**

monothalamous *mon-ō-thal'ə-məs*, *adj* single-chambered; with only one cavity; (of fruit) formed from a single flower. — Also **monothalamic** (*-am'ik*). [Gr *monos* single, alone, and *thalamos* a chamber]

monothecal *mon-ō-thē'kl*, *adj* having only one theca. — Also **monothe'cous**. [Gr *monos* single, alone, and *thēkē* case]

monotheism *mon'ō-thē-izm*, *n* the belief in only one God. — *n* **mon'otheist**. — *adj* **monotheist'ic** or **monotheist'ical**. [Gr *monos* single, alone, and *theos* God]

Monotheletism *mon-ō-thel'i-tizm*, *n* the doctrine that Christ had only one will (opposed to *Ditheletism*). — Also **Monothelism** (*mon-oth'əl-izm*) or **Monothel'itism**. — *n* **Monoth'elēte** or **Monoth'elite**. — *adj* **Monothelet'ic** or **Monothelet'ical**. — All words also without *cap*. [Gr *monos* single, alone, and *thelētēs* a willer, from *thelein* to will]

monotint *mon'ə-tint*, *n* (a) drawing or painting in a single tint. **[mono-]**

monotocous *mon-ot'ə-kəs*, *adj* producing only one offspring at any one time; fruiting once only. [Gr *monos* single, alone, and *tokos* birth, offspring]

monotone *mon'ə-tōn*, *n* a single, unvaried tone or utterance; a succession of sounds having the same pitch; continued or extended sameness; sameness in colour. — *adj* in monotone; monotonic (*math*). — *vt* and *vi* to sing, declaim, speak or utter, in a monotone. — *adj* **monotonic** (*-ton'ik*) in monotone; (of a function or sequence) having the property of either never increasing or never decreasing (*math*). — *adj* **monotonous** (*mon-ot'ə-nəs*) uttered in one unvaried tone; marked by dull uniformity. — *adv* **monot'onously**. — *n* **monot'onousness**. — *n* **monot'ony** dull uniformity of tone or sound; absence of modulation in speaking or reading; tedious sameness or lack of variety (*fig*). [Gr *monos* single, alone, and *tonos* a tone]

monotreme *mon'ō-trēm*, *n* a member of the **Monotremata** (*mon-ō-trē'mə-tə*), the lowest order of *Mammalia*, having a single opening for the genital and digestive organs. — Also *adj*. — *adj* **monotre'matous**. [Gr *monos* single, alone, and *trēma*, *-atos* a hole]

monotroch *mon'ō-trok*, (*Scott*; *facetious*) *n* a wheelbarrow. [Gr *monos* single, alone, and *trochos* wheel]

Monotropa *mon-ot'rə-pə*, *n* a genus of plants related to wintergreen, including the bird's-nest and Indian pipe, nourished by a fungal mycorrhiza in humus. [Gr *monotropos* solitary, from *monos* single, alone, and *tropos* turn]

monotype *mon'ə-tīp*, *n* a sole type, a species forming a genus by itself (*biol*); a single print made from a picture painted on a metal or glass plate (*graphic art*); (with *cap*; ®) the name of a machine that casts and sets type, letter by letter (*printing*). — Also *adj*. — *adj* **monotypic** (*-tip'ik*). **[mono-]**

monovalent *mon-ō-vā'lənt* or *mon-ov'əl-ənt*, (*chem*) *adj* univalent. — *n* **monova'lence** or **monova'lency**. **[mono-]**

monoxide *mon-ok'sīd*, (*chem*) *n* an oxide with one oxygen atom in the molecule. **[mono-]**

monoxylon *mon-oks'i-lon*, *n* a canoe made from one log. — *adj* **monox'ylous**. [Gr, from *monos* single, alone, and *xylon* wood]

monozygotic *mon-ō-zī-got'ik*, (*biol*) *adj* developed from one zygote. — **monozygotic twins** twins developed from a single zygote, identical twins. **[mono-]**

Monroe doctrine *mən-rō' dok'trin*, *n* the principle of non-intervention of European powers in the affairs of independent countries in the American continents. — *n* **Monroeism** (*mən-rō'izm*) advocacy or support of this principle. — *n* **Monroe'ist** [President *Monroe*'s message to the US Congress, December 1823]

Monseigneur *mɔ̃-sen-yœr*, *n* my lord; a title in France given to a person of high birth or rank, *esp* to bishops, etc (written *abbrev* **Mgr**); (the title of) the Dauphin (*hist*): — *pl* **Messeigneurs** (*me-sen-yœr*). [Fr *mon seigneur* my lord, from L *meum seniōrem* (accusative) my elder]

Monsieur *mə-syø*, *n* sir; a title of courtesy in France = *Mr* in English (printed **M** or in full); the eldest brother of the king of France (*hist*); (without *cap*) a Frenchman generally, formerly *esp* one of high rank: — *pl* **Messieurs** (Fr *mes-yø*, written **MM**; Eng *mes'ərz*, written **Messrs**) or (of **monsieur**) **messieurs**. — **Monsieur de Paris** (*euphem*) the public executioner at the time of the French Revolution. — *n* (*archaic*) **moun'seer** (or *-sēr'*) used to represent illiterate or exaggeratedly anglicized pronunciation of **monsieur**. [Fr *mon sieur* my lord; cf **Monseigneur**]

Monsignor *mon-sēn'yər* (Ital *mon-sēn-yōr'*) or **Monsignore** *-yō'rā*, *n* a title conferred on prelates and on dignitaries of the papal household (*abbrev* **Monsig** or **Msgr**): — *pl* **Monsignors** (*-sēn'*) or **Monsigno'ri** (*-rē*). [Ital from Fr]

monsoon *mon-sōōn'*, *n* a seasonal wind of the Indian Ocean, the **wet monsoon** from the SW between April and October, and the **dry monsoon** from the NE the rest of the year; a similar wind elsewhere; in N and W India, the rains accompanying the SW monsoon; an extremely heavy fall of rain, a violent storm (*colloq*). — *adj* **monsoon'al**. — **break of the monsoon** the first onset of the monsoon rain. [Port *monção*, from Malay *mūsim*, from Ar *mausim* a time, a season]

mons pubis *monz pū'bis*, (*anatom*) *n* the mound of subcutaneous fatty tissue just above the genitals in humans: — *pl* **montes pubis** (*mon'tēz*). [L, hill of the pubis]

monster *mon'stər*, *n* anything deviating from the usual course of nature; a prodigy (*obs*); an extraordinary, grotesque or gigantic animal, as told of in fables and folklore; an abnormally formed animal or plant; anything gigantic or abnormally large; anything of abhorrent appearance or behaviour. — *adj* gigantic, abnormally large. — *n* **monstrosity** (*-stros'i-ti*; *obs* **monstruos'ity**) the state or fact of being monstrous; marked abnormality; an ugly or abnormally formed animal, plant, part or object; anything outrageously constructed. — *adj* **mon'strous** (*obs* **mon'struous**) deviating from the usual course of nature, unnatural; enormous, abnormally large; miraculous (*obs*); horrible, hideous; outrageous; preposterous. — *adv* (*archaic* and *US*) exceedingly. — *adv* **mon'strously**. — *n* **mon'strousness**. [Fr *monstre*, from L *mōnstrum* an evil omen, a monster, from *monēre*, *monitum* to warn]

monstera *mon-stē'rə*, *n* any plant of the *Monstera* genus of tropical American evergreen plants of the family *Araceae*, that have shining green perforated leaves and can be grown to a height of 20 feet as hothouse or indoor plants, *esp Monstera deliciosa* (having aerial roots) and *Monstera pertusa* (the 'Swiss cheese plant'). [New L, perh because the leaves were thought freakish]

monstrance *mon'strəns*, *n* the ornamental receptacle in which the consecrated host is exposed in RC churches for the adoration of the people. [OFr, from L *mōnstrāre* to show]

monstre sacré *mɔ̃-str' sak-rā*, *n* a person (*esp* in the world of theatre or cinema) whose appeal to the public is increased by his or her eccentricity. [Fr, sacred monster]

monstrosity, monstrous, etc. See under **monster**.

mons veneris *monz ven'ə-ris*, *n* the mons pubis on the female human body: — *pl* **montes veneris** (*mon'tēz*). [L, hill of Venus]

Mont. *abbrev*: Montana (US state); Montgomeryshire (former county, now part of Powys).

montage *mɔ̃-täzh'*, *n* (the act or process of making) a composite photograph; the setting-up, assemblage or superimposition of photographic or cinematic images; a picture made partly by sticking objects on the canvas; editing of a cinema film; a style of direction in the cinema, the use of frequent cutting and changes in camera position to actively create the action, as opposed to the **mise èn scene** style in which action is allowed to unfold before a relatively static camera; a cinematic scene in which an extended period of time is condensed into a few minutes of film time by presenting fragments of the events occurring in that period. — *vt* to make into, or set in, a montage. [Fr, from *monter* to mount]

Montagnard *mɔ̃-tä-nyär*, *n* a member of the Mountain or extreme democratic wing of the French Legislative Assembly (1 Oct 1791 to 21 Sept 1792), so called because sitting on the topmost benches. [Fr, mountain-dweller]

Montagu's harrier *mon'tə-gūz har'i-ər*, *n* a bird of prey (*Circus pygargus*) of the *Accipitridae* family, with long wings and tail, native to Europe. [After George *Montagu*, 18–19c British naturalist]

montane *mon'tān*, *adj* mountainous; mountain-dwelling. [L *montānus*, from *mōns*, *montis* a mountain]

Montanism *mon'tən-izm*, *n* a 2c heresy founded by the prophet and 'Paraclete' *Montānus* of Phrygia, an ascetic reaction in favour of the old discipline and severity. — *n* and *adj* **Mon'tanist**. — *adj* **Montanist'ic**.

montant *mont'ənt*, *n* a vertical member in panelling or framing; (in fencing) apparently an upward blow (also, as if *Sp*, **montant'o**; *Shakesp*). [Fr, from *monter* to rise]

montan wax *mon'tən waks*, (*chem*) *n* a bituminous wax extracted under high temperature and pressure from lignite, used in candles and some polishes. [L *montanus* of a mountain]

montaria *mont-ä-rē'ə*, *n* (in Brazil) a light canoe made of one log. [Port]

montbretia *mon-* or *mont-brēsh'yə*, *n* a plant of the *Montbretia* genus of S African iridaceous plants; a plant (*Crocosmia*) of the iris family bearing bright orange-coloured flowers; a plant of the genus *Tritonia*. [After a French botanist, Coquebert de *Montbret* (1780–1801)]

mont-de-piété *mɔ̃-də-pyā-tā* (*Fr*) or **monte di pietà** (*mon'tā dē pyā-tä'*; *Ital*) *n* a state pawnshop: — *pl* **monts-de-piété** (*mɔ̃-*) or **monti di pietà** (*mon'tē*). [Fund (literally mount) of pity or piety]

monte *mon'tā* or *-ti*, *n* a shrubby tract, a forest; a Spanish-American gambling card-game. — **three-card monte** a Mexican three-card trick. [Sp, mountain, scrub, cards remaining after a deal, from L *mōns*, *montis* a mountain]

Monte Carlo method *mon'ti kär'lō meth'əd*, (*math*) *n* a statistical procedure in which mathematical operations are performed on random numbers. [From the casino at *Monte Carlo* and the various numerical systems tried there to win at roulette]

monteith *mən-* or *mon-tēth'*, *n* a large 17 or 18c bowl, *usu* of silver, fluted and scalloped, for cooling punch-glasses (said to be named from 'a fantastical Scot' who wore his cloak so scalloped); a cotton handkerchief with white spots on a coloured background (from Glasgow manufacturers).

montelimar *mon-tel'i-mär* or *mɔ̃-tä-lē-mär*, *n* a type of nougat, *orig* made in *Montélimar*, SE France.

montem *mon'tem*, *n* a former custom of Eton boys to go every third Whit-Tuesday to a hillock on the Bath road and exact 'salt-money' from passers-by, for the university expenses of the senior scholar or school captain. [L *ad montem* to the hill]

Montenegrin *mon-ti-nē'grin*, *n* a native or inhabitant of the former Yugoslav republic of *Montenegro*. — Also *adj*.

montero *mon-tā'rō*, *n* a huntsman; a Spanish horseman's helmet-like cap with a flap (also **montero-cap'**): — *pl* **monte'ros**. [Sp *montero* a huntsman, from *monte*, from L *mōns*, *montis* a mountain]

Montessorian *mon-tes-ōr'i-ən* or *-ör'*, *adj* relating to Dr Maria *Montessori* or her method (c.1900) of nursery education, insisting on spontaneity and freedom from restraint.

Montezuma's revenge *mon-tə-zōōm'əz ri-venj'*, (*colloq*) *n* diarrhoea, *esp* caused by travelling in Mexico and/or eating Mexican food. [*Montezuma II*, a 15c Mexican ruler]

montgolfier *mon-gol'fi-ər* or *mont-*, *n* a hot-air balloon. [From the brothers *Montgolfier*, of Annonay, France, who sent up the first in 1783]

month *munth*, *n* one of the twelve conventional divisions of the year, or its length, a **calendar month**; such a length of time, loosely taken as four weeks or 30 days; the length of time taken by the moon to revolve once around the earth (29.53 days), a **lunar month**. — *n* **month'ling** (*archaic*) a month-old child. — *adj* **month'ly** performed in a month; done, recurring, or appearing once a month. — *n* a monthly publication; a monthly rose; (*pl*) the menses (*colloq*). — *adv* once a month; in every month. — **monthly nurse** a nurse attending a woman in the first month after childbirth; **monthly rose** a rose supposed to bloom every month; **month's mind** see under **mind**. — **anomalistic month** the interval between the moon's perigee passages = 27·5545 days; **a month of Sundays** see under **Sunday**; **sidereal** or **stellar month** the time in which the moon passes round the ecliptic to the same point among the stars = 27·3217 days; **solar month** one-twelfth of a solar year; **synodic month** the period of the moon's phases = 29·5306 days; **tropical** or **periodic month** the time from the moon's passing the equinox until it reaches it again = 27·3216 days. [OE *mōnath*, from *mōna* moon]

monticellite *mon-ti-sel'īt*, *n* an orthorhombic calcium magnesium silicate. [After the Italian mineralogist Teodoro *Monticelli* (1759–1845)]

monticle. See **monticule**.

monticolous *mon-tik'ə-ləs*, *adj* mountain-dwelling. [L *monticola* a mountain-dweller, from *mōns*, *montis* mountain, and *colere* to inhabit]

monticule *mon'-tik'ūl*, *n* a little elevation, hill, mound; a secondary volcanic cone. — Also **mon'ticle** or **monticulus**. — *adj* **montic'ulate** or **montic'ulous** having small projections. [L *monticulus*, dimin of *mōns* mountain]

Montilla *mon-tēl'ya*, *n* a sherry-like white wine produced in the region of *Montilla* in S Spain.

montmorillonite *mont-mə-ril'ə-nīt*, (*mineralogy*) *n* a hydrated silicate of aluminium, one of the important clay minerals and the chief constituent of bentonite and fuller's earth. [From *Montmorillon*, in France]

montre *mɔ̃tr'*, *n* the visible pipes of an organ, *usu* the open diapason. [Fr, sample, show]

monture *mon'tūr* or *mɔ̃-tür*, *n* a mounting, setting or frame. [Fr]

monument *mon'ū-mənt* (*obs* **mon'iment**), *n* anything that preserves the memory of a person or an event, such as a building, pillar, tomb, tablet, statue, etc; any structure, natural or artificial, considered as an object of beauty or of interest as a relic of the past; a historic document or record (sometimes confused with **muniment**); a stone, post, river, etc marking a boundary (*US*); a relic, indication or trace; a notable or enduring example; a warning token or admonition (*Spenser*); a prodigy (*Shakesp*). — *vt* to commemorate by or on a monument. — *adj* **monumental** (*-ment'əl*) of, relating to, or of the nature of a monument, tomb, memento or token; memorial; massive and lasting; vast; impressive; amazing; very large. — *adv* **monument'ally**. [L *monumentum*, *monimentum*, from *monēre* to remind]

mony *mun'i* or *mon'i*, a Scots form of **many**.

monyplies *mun'i-plīz*. See **manyplies**.

monzonite *mon'zən-īt*, *n* a coarse-grained intermediate igneous rock. — *adj* **monzonit'ic**. [Monte *Monzoni* in the Dolomite Mountains]

moo *mōō*, *vi* (of cattle) to low. — *n* a cow's low. — **moo'cow** (*hypocoristic*) a cow; **moo'-juice** (*facetious*) cow's milk. [Imit]

mooch or **mouch** *mōōch*, *vi* to play truant (*dialect*); to go blackberrying (*dialect*); to slouch about; to skulk; to loiter, wander (about); to sponge, cadge. — *vt* to pilfer; to beg, cadge (*orig US*). — *n* the act of mooching. — *n* **mooch'er** or **mouch'er**. [Perh OFr *muchier* to hide; cf **miche**]

mood[1] *mōōd*, *n* a form of the verb expressing the mode or manner of an action or of a state of being (*gram*); the form of the syllogism as determined by the quantity and quality of its three constituent propositions (*logic*); (in medieval music) mode in the sense of relative time value. [**mode**]

mood[2] *mōōd*, *n* temporary state of the emotions or of attitude; state of gloom or sullenness; anger, heat of temper (*obs*). — *adv* **mood'ily**. — *n* **mood'iness** sullenness. — *adj* **mood'y** indulging in moods; sullen; angry (*obs*); faked, pretended (*prison slang*). — *n* (*slang*) insidious, flattering talk; lies, deception. — *vt* (*slang*) to persuade by flattery and cajolery. — **mood'y-mad** (*Shakesp*) mad with anger. [OE *mōd* mind; cf Ger *Mut* courage]

Moog synthesizer® *mōōg sin'thi-sīz-ər*, *n* an electronic musical instrument with a keyboard, that can produce a wide range of sounds. [Developed by Robert *Moog*, an American engineer]

mooi *moi'*, (*SAfr*) *adj* fine, a general word of commendation. [Afrik, from Du]

mook *mōōk*, *n* a book produced in a magazine format, *esp* in Japan. [*m*agazine and b*ook*]

mooktar *mōōk'tär*, *n*. Same as **mukhtar**.

mool *mōōl*, a Scots and NEng form of **mould**[1].

moola or **moolah**[1] *mōō'lə*, (*slang*) *n* money. [Origin uncertain]

moolah[2]. See **mullah**.

mooli *mōō'li*, *n* a long white carrot-shaped root vegetable from E Africa, tasting similar to a radish. [Native word]

mooly. See **muley**.

Moon *mōōn*, *n* a system of printing for the blind, using large, embossed characters (**Moon type**) designed to be read from left to right and right to left in alternate rows. [British inventor William *Moon* (1818–94)]

moon *mōōn*, *n* (often with *cap*) the earth's natural satellite, illuminated to varying degrees by the sun depending on its position; its appearance to an observer on earth, in respect of its degree of illumination (*full moon*, *half moon*, etc); a natural satellite of any planet; a month (*literary*); anything in the shape of a moon or crescent; a crescent-shaped outwork (*fortif*). — *vt* to decorate with moons or crescents. — *vi* to wander about listlessly or gaze vacantly at anything (*usu* with *around* or *about*); to present one's bare buttocks to public view, *esp* through a vehicle window (*slang*, *esp US*). — *adj* **mooned** marked with the figure of a moon. — *n* **moon'er** a person who moons about. — *adj* **moon'ish** like the moon; variable; inconstant. — *adj* **moon'less** destitute of moonlight; (of a planet) having no moon. — *n* **moon'let** a small planetary satellite, whether natural or man-made. — *adj* **moon'y** of or relating to the moon; moon-like; crescent-shaped; bearing a crescent; round and shining; moonlit; inclined to moon, dreamy; fatuous; tipsy (*slang*). — *n* a noodle. — **moon'-ball** (*tennis*) a high arcing shot. — *vi* to hit such a shot. — **moon'beam** a beam of moonlight. — *adj* **moon'blind** affected with moon-eye; blinded by the moon; night-blind; dim-sighted, purblind (now *dialect*). — **moon boot** a bulky padded boot with a quilted fabric covering, for wearing in snow, reminiscent of an astronaut's boot; **moon'-bow** a rainbow cast by the moon; **moon'calf** a false conception or fleshy mass formed in the womb; a monster (*obs*); a deformed creature (*obs*); a dolt, fool; **moon daisy** the ox-eye daisy; **moon'eye** a disease affecting horses' eyes; a N American freshwater shad-like fish of the genus *Hiodon*, *esp Hiodon tergisus*. — *adj* **moon'-eyed** affected with mooneye, moon blind; round- or wide-eyed; drunk (*US slang*). — **moon'face** a full, round face. — *adj* **moon'-faced**. — **moon'-fish** the opah or other silvery disc-shaped fish; **moon flask** a type of Chinese porcelain vase with a wide, circular body and a short, narrow neck; **moon'-flower** the ox-eye daisy; a night-blooming plant of the *Convolvulaceae*, *Calonyction aculeatum*, or any of several related plants; **moon'-gate** a circular opening in a wall serving as a gateway, *esp* in Chinese architecture; **moon'-glade** the track of moonlight on water; **moon'-god** or **moon'-goddess** a god or goddess representing or associated with the moon; **moon'-knife** a leather-worker's crescent-shaped knife; **moon'light** the light of the moon, sunlight reflected from the moon's surface; smuggled alcoholic spirit. — *adj* lit by the moon; occurring in moonlight. — *vi* to work outside one's normal working hours, *esp* when the income from this is not declared for tax assessment. — **moon'lighter** a person who moonlights; in Ireland, a person who committed agrarian outrages by night about 1880, in protest against the introduction of the land-tenure system (*hist*); a moonshiner; **moonlight flit** or **flitting** a hasty removal by night, *esp* without paying due rent; **moon'lighting**. — *adj* **moon'lit** lit or illumined by the moon. — *adj* **moon'-loved** (*poetic*) loved by the moon. — **moon'-madness** (*archaic*) lunacy, once thought to be connected with the moon's changes; **moon'phase** the current phase of the moon, as indicated eg on a watch or calendar; **moon pool** (*oil industry*) the open shaft let through the hull of a deep-sea drilling vessel to accommodate the vertical pipe-line connected to the oil-well; **moon'quake** a tremor of the moon's surface. — *adj* (*Scott*) **moon'-raised** excited or maddened by the moon. — **moon'raker** a moon-sail; a Wiltshireman (from a Gotham story); **moon'raking** the following of crazy fancies; **moon'rise** the rising of the moon, or the time when this occurs; **moon'rock** rock from the moon's surface; a synthetic narcotic drug combining heroin and crack (*slang*); **moon'roof** a transparent roof section on a motor vehicle, *usu* opening or removable; **moon'sail** a small sail, sometimes carried above the sky-scraper; **moon'scape** the physical appearance of the surface of the moon, or a representation of it; a desolate landscape resembling this (*fig*); **moon'seed** a plant (*Menispermum*) with lunate seeds; **moon'set** the setting of the moon, or the time when this occurs; **moon'shine** moonlight; show without reality (*fig*); nonsense (*colloq*); a month (*Shakesp*); spirits illicitly distilled or smuggled. — *adj* lit by the moon; made of moonlight, bodiless (*fig*). — **moon'-shiner** a smuggler or illicit distiller of spirits. — *adj* **moon'shiny** lighted by the moon; visionary, unreal. — **moon'shot** an act, or the process, of launching an object or vehicle to orbit, or land on, the moon; **moon'stone** an opalescent orthoclase feldspar, *perh* sometimes selenite; **moon'strike** the act or process of landing a spacecraft on the surface of the moon. — *adj* **moon'-struck** (also **moon'-stricken**) mentally affected by the moon, lunatic, crazed. — **moon'walk** an astronaut's walk on the surface of the moon; a style of break-dancing. — Also *vi*. — **moon'wort** a eusporangiate fern (*Botrychium lunaria*) with lunate pinnae; any other plant of the genus; the plant honesty (from its silvery septum). — **eggs in moonshine** an old dish, fried eggs with onions and various flavourings; **over the moon** (*colloq*) delighted. [OE *mōna*; cf Ger *Mond*, L *mēnsis*, Gr *mēn*]

moong bean. Same as **mung bean**.

Moonie *mōōn'i, n* a colloquial (often *derog*) term for a member of the Unification Church, a sect founded in 1954 by Sun Myung *Moon*, a S Korean: — *pl* **Moon'ies**.

moonshee. See **munshi**.

moop. See **moup**.

Moor *mōōr, n* a Mauretanian; a member of the mixed Arab and Berber people of Morocco and the Barbary coast; one of the Arab and Berber conquerors and occupants of Spain from 711 to 1492; formerly in India, a Muslim; a Black person (*old*): — *fem* **Moor'ess**. — *n* **Moor'ery** a Moorish quarter. — *adj* **Moor'ish**. [Fr *More, Maure*, from L *Maurus*, doubtfully connected with Byzantine Gr *mauros*, black]

moor[1] *mōōr, n* a wide expanse of uncultivated ground, *esp* upland, often covered with heath, and having a poor, peaty soil; a heath; (*Scot*) **muir** (*mür, mār* or *mūr*). — *adj* **moor'ish** or **moor'y** resembling a moor; sterile; marshy; boggy. — **moor'-band** a hard ferruginous layer formed under moorland soil (also **moor'-band pan** or **moor'-pan**); **moor'buzzard** the marsh-harrier; **moor'cock** or **moor'fowl** red, or black, grouse; **moor'hen** the water-hen; a female moorfowl; **moor'ill** (*Scot*) a cattle disease of moorland districts, marked by haemoglobin in the urine; **moor'land** a tract of moor; moorish country. — *adj* of moorland. — **moor'log** a deposit of decayed woody material under a marsh, etc; **moor'man** an inhabitant of a in moor; **moor'-pout** or (*Scot*) **muir'-pout** (*-powt*), **moor'-poot** or (*Scot*) **muir'-poot** (*-pōōt*) a young grouse; **muir'burn** (*Scot*) the seasonal burning of heather, etc on moorland to promote new growth. [OE *mōr*]

moor[2] *mōōr, vt* to fasten by cable or anchor. — *vi* to make fast a ship, boat, etc; to be made fast. — *n* **moor'age** condition of being moored; act of mooring; a fee paid for mooring; a place for mooring. — *n* **moor'ing** act of mooring; that which serves to moor or confine a ship; (in *pl*) the place or condition of a ship so moored; anything providing security or stability. — **moor'ing-mast**. [Prob from an unrecorded OE word answering to MDu *mâren*]

moorva. See **murva**.

moose *mōōs, n* the American elk; a member of an American secret fraternity, the Loyal Order of Moose: — *pl* **moose**. — **moose'yard** an area where the moose tread down the snow and spend the winter. [Algonquian *mus, moos*]

moot *mōōt, n orig* a meeting; a deliberative or administrative assembly or court (*hist*); its meeting-place; discussion; a law student's discussion of a hypothetical case. — *vt* to argue, dispute; to propose for discussion. — *vi* to dispute, plead. — *adj* debatable. — *adj* **moot'able**. — *n* **moot'er**. — *n* **moot'ing**. — **moot case** a case for discussion; a case about which there may be difference of opinion; **moot'-court** a meeting for discussion of hypothetical cases; **moot'-hall** or **moot'-house** a town-hall or council chamber; a hall for moot-courts; **moot'-hill** a hill used for meetings on which the moot was held (often confused with **mote-hill**); **moot'man** a law student who argues in moots; **moot point** an undecided or disputed point. [OE (*ge*)*mōt* (n), *mōtian* (v), related to *mētan* to meet]

moove. An old spelling of **move**.

mop[1] *mop, n* a bunch of rags or lengths of yarn, or a piece of sponge on the end of a stick or pole, used for washing, removing dust, soaking up liquid, etc; any similar instrument, such as one for cleansing a wound, polishing, etc; a thick or bushy head of hair; an act of mopping; a hiring-fair (*prob* from the custom of carrying a badge of occupation; *dialect*). — *vt* to wipe, dab, soak up, or remove with, or as if with, a mop; to clear away or dispose of as residue: — *pr p* **mopp'ing**; *pa t* and *pa p* **mopped**. — *n* **mopp'er**. — *adj* **mopp'y** (*old slang*) drunk. — *n* **mop'sy** a dowdy; a slattern; a term of endearment (*obs*). — **mop'board** (*US*) skirting-board; **mop'head** (a person with) a shaggy unkempt head of hair. — *adj* **mop-head'ed** having a shaggy, unkempt head of hair. — **mop'stick** the handle of a mop; a hand-rail nearly circular in section; (also **map'stick**) a rod for raising a piano damper; **mop'-up** an action of mopping up. — **mops and brooms** half-drunk; out of sorts; **mop up** to clear away or clean up with a mop; to clear away, dispose of; to absorb (eg surplus credit); to capture or kill (enemy stragglers) after a victory, etc; **Mrs Mop** or **Mopp** a cleaner, charwoman. [Poss from OFr *mappe*, from L *mappa* a napkin; or poss from the name *Mabel*]

mop[2] *mop, n* a grimace. — *vi* to grimace. — Also (both *n* and *vi*) **mop and mow**. [Cf Du *moppen* to pout]

mopane or **mopani** *mo-pä'ni, n* a small S African tree of the *Leguminosae*, growing in areas of low rainfall, with rough bark and racemes of small green flowers. [Bantu]

mope *mōp, vi* to move aimlessly and listlessly; to be listless or depressed. — *vt* (*archaic*) to make spiritless or listless. — *n* a listless person; (*esp* in *pl*) moping. — *n* **mop'er**. — *adj* **mop'ey** or **mop'y**. — *adv* **mop'ingly**. — *adj* **mop'ish** dull; spiritless, listless. — *adv* **mop'ishly**. — *n* **mop'ishness**. — *n* **mop'us** (now *dialect*) a person who mopes. [Origin obscure]

moped *mō'ped, n* a lightweight motorcycle, *usu* with a two-stroke 50cc engine. [*mo*tor-assisted *ped*al cycle]

mopey. See under **mope**.

mopoke *mō'pōk, n* the owl *Ninox novaeseelandiae*, of Australia and New Zealand; the tawny frogmouth (to which the call is wrongly attributed; *Austr*); a dull-witted or boring person (*Austr slang*). — Also **mope'hawk** or **more'pork**. [Imit of the cry of the owl]

Mopp, Mrs. See under **mop**[1].

mopper, etc. See under **mop**[1].

moppet *mop'it, n* a rag-doll (*archaic*); a small woolly breed of dog (*rare*); a doll-like woman; (a term of endearment or contempt for) a little girl or child. [Dimin of **mop**]

mopus[1] *mop'əs* or **mawpus** *mö'pəs*, (*slang*) *n* a small coin.

mopus[2]. See under **mope**.

mopy. See under **mope**.

moquette *mō-ket', n* a carpet and soft furnishing material with a loose velvety pile, the back made of thick canvas, etc. [Fr]

MOR *abbrev*: middle-of-the road (music), *esp* in broadcasting.

Mor. *abbrev*: Morocco.

mor[1] *mör* or *mōr, n* a layer of humus formed by slow decomposition in acid conditions. — Cf **moder, mull**[6]. [Dan]

mor[2]. See **mauther**.

mora[1] *mō'rə* or *mö'-, n* delay, *esp* unjustifiable (*law*); the duration of a short syllable or half that of a long (*prosody*). [L, delay]

mora[2] or **morra** *mor'ə, n* the game of guessing how many fingers are held up. [Ital *mora*]

moraceous. See under **Morus**.

moraine *mo-rān', n* a ridgelike mass of earth, rock and stones at one time carried and finally deposited by a glacier; a garden imitation of this. — *adj* **morain'al** or **morain'ic**. [Fr]

moral *mor'əl, adj* of or relating to character or conduct considered as good or evil; ethical; adhering to or directed towards what is right; virtuous, *esp* in matters of sex; capable of knowing right and wrong; subject to moral law; having an effect on the mind or will; supported by evidence of reason or probability (opposed to *demonstrative*); (eg of a victory) real or effective, if not apparent; moralizing (*Shakesp*). — *n* (in *pl*) writings on ethics; the doctrine or practice of the duties of life; moral philosophy or ethics; principles and conduct, *esp* sexual; (in *sing*) the practical lesson that can be drawn from anything; an exposition of such lesson by way of conclusion; a symbol (*Shakesp*); (sometimes *mor-äl'*, after Ger *Moral* or Fr *morale*) morality; (*mor-äl'*, after Fr) confidence, morale (now *rare*); a certainty (*slang*, now *esp Austr*); an exact counterpart (*archaic slang*). — *vt* and *vi* (*archaic*) to moralize. — *n* **mor'alism** a moral maxim; moral counsel; morality as distinct from religion. — *n* **mor'alist** a person who teaches morals, or who practises moral duties; a moral as distinguished from a religious man; someone who takes pride in his or her morality. — *adj* **moralist'ic**. — *n* **morality** (*mor-al'i-ti*) the quality of being moral; that which renders an action right or wrong; the practice of moral duties apart from religion; virtue; the doctrine of actions as right or wrong; ethics; a medieval allegorical drama in which virtues and vices appear as characters (also **moral'ity-play**). — *n* **moralizā'tion** or **-s-** act of moralizing, explanation in a moral sense. — *vt* **mor'alize** or **-ise** to apply to a moral purpose; to explain in a moral sense; to make moral. — *vi* to speak or write on moral subjects; to make moral reflections or pronouncements, or speak in an admonitory tone about moral standards. — *n* **mor'alizer** or **-s-**. — *n* **mor'aller** (*Shakesp*) a moralist. — *adv* **mor'ally** in a moral manner; in respect of morals; to all intents and purposes, practically. — **moral agent** a person who acts under a knowledge of right and wrong; **moral certainty** a likelihood great enough to be acted on, although not capable of being certainly proved; **moral courage** the power to face disapprobation and ridicule; **moral defeat** a success so qualified as to count as a defeat, or to point towards defeat; **moral faculty** moral sense; **moral imagination** (*esp US*) in business ethics, the ability to create new solutions to ethical problems; **moral law** a law or rules for life and conduct, founded on what is right and wrong; the law of conscience; that part of the Old Testament which relates to moral principles, *esp* the ten commandments; **moral majority** the majority of a society that is presumed to favour a strict moral code; **moral philosophy** ethics; **Moral Rearmament** a movement succeeding the Oxford Group in 1938, advocating absolute private and public morality (*abbrev* **MRA**); **moral sense** that power of the mind which knows or judges actions to be right or wrong, and determines conduct accordingly; tropological interpretation of eg the Bible, seeking to establish some secondary meaning; **moral support** encouragement shown by approval rather than by active help; **moral theology** ethics treated with reference to a divine source; **moral victory** a defeat in appearance, but in some important sense a real victory. [L *mōrālis*, from *mōs*, *mōris* manner, custom, (esp in *pl*) morals]

morale *mor-äl'*, *n* morality (*archaic*); condition or degree of confidence, optimism, strength of purpose, etc, in a person or group. — **morale'-booster** a person, activity, etc which increases one's morale. [Fr, fem of *moral* moral; in later sense modification of **moral** to suggest Fr form and pron]

morality... to ... **moralizer**. See under **moral**.

morall (*Shakesp*, *Midsummer Night's Dream*) *n* emended by editors to **mural**, but possibly a misprint for **wall**.

moraller and **morally**. See under **moral**.

morals. Same as **merils**.

morass *mə-ras'*, *n* a tract of soft, wet ground; a marsh. — *adj* **morass'y**. — **morass ore** bog-iron ore. [Du *moeras*, from OFr *maresc*, influenced by Du *moer* moor]

morat *mō'rat* or *mö'*, *n* a drink made of honey and mulberry juice. [LL *mōrātum*, from *mōrum* mulberry]

moratorium *mor-ə-tō'ri-əm* or *-tö'*, *n* an emergency measure authorizing the suspension of payments of debts for a given time; the period thus declared; a temporary ban on, or decreed cessation of, any activity: — *pl* **morator'ia** or **morator'iums**. — *adj* **moratory** (*mor'ə-tə-ri*) delaying; deferring. [Neuter of LL *morātōrius*, adj from *mora* delay]

Moravian[1] *mo-rā'vi-ən*, *adj* of or relating to *Moravia*, part of Czechoslovakia, or to its inhabitants. — *n* one of the people of Moravia; a Czech dialect spoken in Moravia; a member of the *Unitas Fratrum* or *United Brethren*, a small body of Protestants of extraordinary missionary energy, founded in the 15c. — *n* **Morā'vianism**. [L *Moravia* Moravia, from *Morava* the river March]

Moravian[2] *mo-rā'vi-ən*, *adj* of the old province or the modern distict of Moray in NE Scotland. — *n* an inhabitant of Moray. [LL *Moravia*, from Gaelic *Muireibh* Moray]

moray, or (formerly) **murray**, **murrey** or **murry** *mō'rā*, *mō-rā'*, *mur'i* or *mur-ā'*, *n* any of several mainly tropical eels of the family *Muraenidae* (also **moray eel**). [Port *moreia*, from L *mūraena*, from Gr *(s)mȳraina*, fem of *(s)mȳros* eel]

morbid *mör'bid*, *adj* sickly; unwholesome; inclined to dwell on unwholesome or horrible thoughts; relating to, or of the nature of, disease (*med*). — *n* **morbid'ity** sickliness; unwholesomeness; ratio of incidence of an illness (*med*). — *adv* **mor'bidly**. — *n* **mor'bidness**. — **morbid anatomy** the science or study of diseased organs and tissues. [L *morbidus*, from *morbus* disease]

morbidezza *mör-bi-det'sə*, *n* the delicate or sensual rendering of flesh-tints in painting; delicacy, softness (*esp music*). [Ital]

morbiferous, etc. See under **morbus**.

morbilli *mör-bil'ī*, (*med*) *n pl* measles. — *adj* **morbill'iform**. — *n* **morbill'ivī'rus** a virus, different species of which are responsible for human measles, canine distemper, diseases specific to seals and goats, etc. — *adj* **morbill'ous**. [LL dimin of L *morbus* disease]

morbus *mör'bəs*, *n* disease (*L*; used in phrases). — *adj* **morbif'erous** disease-bringing. — *adj* **morbi'fic** disease-causing. — **morbus gallicus** literally, the French disease, ie syphilis. [L]

morceau *mör'sō*, *n* a morsel; a fragment; a piece of music; a short literary composition: — *pl* **mor'ceaux** (*-sō*). — **morceau de salon** (*də sä-lɔ̃*; *music*) a drawing-room piece. [Fr; see **morsel**]

mordacious *mör-dā'shəs*, *adj* given to biting; biting in quality (*lit* or *fig*). — *adv* **mordā'ciously**. — *n* **mordacity** (*-das'i-ti*). — *n* **mordancy** (*mör'dən-si*). — *adj* **mor'dant** biting; incisive; serving to fix dyes, paints or gold-leaf. — *n* a corroding substance; any substance that combines with and fixes a dyestuff in material that cannot be dyed direct; a substance used to cause paint or gold leaf to adhere to a surface. — *vt* to treat with a mordant. — *adv* **mor'dantly**. [L *mordēre* to bite]

mordent *mör'dənt*, (*music*) *n* a grace note in which the principal note is preceded in performance by itself and the note below (**lower mordent**) or itself and the note above (**upper** or **inverted mordent**); the character indicating it; sometimes extended to other graces. [Ger, from Ital *mordente*]

more[1] *mör*, *adj* (serving as *compar* of **many** and **much**) in greater number or quantity; greater in size or importance (now *rare*); additional; other besides. — *adv* to a greater degree; rather; again; longer; further; moreover. — *n* a greater thing; something further or in addition: — *superl* (*adj* and *adv*) **most** (*mōst*). — *adj* **mo'rish** or **more'ish** such that one wants more. — **any more** anything additional; further; **more and more** continually increasing; **more by token** (*dialect*) in proof of this, besides; **more or less** about; in round numbers; **no more** nothing in addition; never again; no longer in existence; dead. [OE *māra* greater; as an adv **more** has superseded **mo**[1]]

more[2] *mōr* or *mör*, *n* a root; a stump; a plant (*Spenser*). [OE *moru*, *more* carrot, parsnip; Ger *Möhre*]

more[3] *mōr'ē*, *mör'ē* or *mōr'e*, (*L*) *adj* in the manner. — **more majorum** (*mə-jōr'əm*, *-jör'əm* or *mä-yōr'ōōm*) after the manner of our or their ancestors. — **more suo** (*sū'* or *sōō'ō*) in his or her own way, in characteristic fashion.

moreen *mo-rēn'*, *n* a stout corded fabric, woollen, cotton, or both, often watered. [Poss connected with **moire**]

moreish. See under **more**[1].

morel[1] *mor-el'*, *n* any edible discomycete fungus of the genus *Morchella*. [Fr *morille*; cf OHGer *morhila* (Ger *Morchel*) a mushroom; **more**[2]]

morel[2] *mor-el'*, *n* a nightshade, *esp* black nightshade; (also *mor'əl*) a dark-coloured horse (*obs*). — *adj* blackish. [LL *morellus* blackish, perh from L *mōrum* a mulberry, perh Late Gr *mauros* black]

morel[3]. See **morello**.

morello *mə-rel'ō* or **morel** *mor-el'*, *mor'əl*, *n* a dark-red cherry, much used in cooking and for cherry brandy (also **morello cherry**): — *pl* **morell'os**. [Poss from Ital *morello* dark-coloured (see preceding); poss from Flem *marelle*, from Ital *amarella*, a dimin from L *amārus* bitter]

morendo *mo-ren'dō*, (*music*) *adj* and *adv* dying away, in speed and tone. [Ital, dying]

moreover *mör-ō'vər*, *adv* more over or beyond what has been said; further; besides; also. [**more**[1] and **over**]

morepork. See **mopoke**.

mores *mō'*, *mö'rēz* or *mō'rās*, *n pl* customs, manners. [L *mōs*, *mōris* custom]

Moresco *mor-es'kō*, *n* a Moorish dance or morris-dance (Ital *Moresca*); a Moor or Morisco: — *pl* **Mores'coes**. — *adj* Moorish. [Ital, Moorish]

Moresque *mor-esk'*, *adj* in the Moorish manner. — *n* an arabesque. [Fr, from Ital *Moresco*]

Moreton Bay *mör'tən bā*, *n* the first settlement in Queensland. — **Moreton Bay chestnut** an Australian papilionaceous tree (*Castanospermum australe*); its chestnut-like seed; **Moreton Bay fig** an Australian fig tree (*Ficus macrophilla*).

Morgan *mör'gən*, *n* any horse of an American breed developed in Vermont by Justin *Morgan* in the late 18c, light and sturdy for farm work, but also bred for trotting races.

morganatic *mör-gən-at'ik*, *adj* of or relating to a marriage between people of unequal rank (latterly only where one is of a reigning or mediatized house), the marriage being valid, the children legitimate, but unable to inherit the higher rank, the lower-born spouse not being granted the other's title. — *adv* **morganat'ically**. [LL *morganātica*, a gift from a bridegroom to his bride; cf Ger *Morgengabe*, OE *morgengifu* a morning gift]

morganite *mör'gə-nīt*, (*mineralogy*) *n* a pink or rose-coloured variety of beryl, obtained chiefly from California and Madagascar, used as a gemstone. [From J Pierpont *Morgan* (1837–1913), US financier]

morgay *mör'gā*, *n* the small spotted dogfish or bounce. [Cornish and Welsh *morgi*, from *mōr* sea, and *ci* dog]

morgen *mör'gən*, *n* a unit of land-measurement (in the Netherlands, S Africa, and parts of the USA, a little over two acres; formerly in Norway, Denmark and Prussia, about two-thirds of an acre). [Du and Ger; perh *morgen* morning, hence a morning's ploughing]

morgenstern *mör'gən-stûrn* or *-shtern*, *n* a morning-star (weapon). [Ger]

Morglay *mör'glā*, *n* Sir Bevis of Hampton's sword; hence, a sword. [Cf **claymore**]

morgue[1] *mörg*, *n* a place where dead bodies are laid out for identification, or kept prior to burial or cremation; a gloomy or depressing place (*fig*); a place, as in a newspaper office, where miscellaneous material for reference is kept. [Fr]

morgue[2] *mörg*, *n* haughtiness, arrogance. [Fr]

MORI *mor'i*, *abbrev*: Market and Opinion Research Institute.

moria *mö'ri-ə*, *n* folly. [Gr *mōriā*]

moribund *mor'i-bund*, *adj* about to die; in a stagnant or dying state. — *n* **moribund'ity**. [L *moribundus*, from *morī* to die]

moriche *mor-ē'chā*, *n* the miriti palm. [Carib]

morigeration *mö-rij-ə-rā'shən*, *n* deferential behaviour. — *adj* **morig'erate** or **morig'erous**. [L *mōrigerātiō*, *-ōnis*, from *mōs*, *mōris* custom, humour, and *gerere* to bear]

Moringa *mor-ing'gə*, *n* the horse-radish tree genus, constituting a family **Moringā'ceae**, apparently linking the poppies with the Leguminosae. [Perh Sinh *murungā*]

morion[1] or **morrion** *mör'i-ən*, *n* an open helmet, without visor or beaver. [Fr, prob from Sp *morrión*, from *morra* crown of the head]

morion[2] *mor'i-ən*, *n* black quartz. [Fr]

Morisco *mo-ris'kō*, *n* a Moor, *esp* a Christianized Moor in Spain after the fall of Granada in 1492; the Moorish language (*obs*); (without *cap*) a morris-dance or dancer; an arabesque: — *pl* **Moris'cos** or **Moris'coes**. — *adj* Moorish. — *n* and *adj* **Morisk'** (*obs*). [Sp, from *Moro* Moor, from L *Maurus*; cf **Moor**]

morish. See under **more**[1].

Morisonian *mor-i-sō'ni-ən*, *n* a member of the Evangelical Union, formed in 1843 by the Rev James *Morison* (1816–93), after his separation from the United Secession Church, incorporated with the Congregational Union of Scotland in 1896. — *n* **Morisō'nianism**.

morkin *mör'kin*, *n* an animal that has died by accident. — *n* **mor'ling** or **mort'ling** a sheep dead as a result of disease; its wool. [AngloFr *mortekine*, from L *morticīna* (fem adj) carrion, from *mors* death]

mormaor *mör-mā'ər*, (*hist*) *n* a high-ranking or chief steward. [Gaelic *mormaer*, now *mòrmhaor*, from *mòr* great, and *maor* steward]

Mormon *mör'mən*, *n* a member of a religious sect with headquarters since 1847 in Salt Lake City, Utah, polygamous till 1890, calling itself *The Church of Jesus Christ of Latter-day Saints*, founded in 1830 by Joseph Smith, whose *Book of Mormon* was given out as translated from the golden plates of *Mormon*, a prophet. — *n* **Mor'monism**. — *n* **Mor'monite**.

Mormops *mör'mops*, *n* a genus of repulsive-looking American leaf-nosed bats. [Gr *mormō* a bugbear, and *ōps* face]

morn *mörn*, (*poetic* and *dialect*) *n* the first part of the day; morning. — **the morn** (*Scot*) tomorrow; **the morn's morn** or **morning** (*Scot*) tomorrow morning; **the morn's nicht** (*Scot*) tomorrow night. [ME *morwen*, from OE *morgen*; Ger *Morgen*]

mornay *mör'nā* or **mornay sauce** *sös*, *n* a cream sauce with cheese flavouring. — *adj* (placed after the name of a food) served with this sauce. [Perh Philippe de *Mornay*, Fr Huguenot leader]

morne[1] *mörn*, *n* the blunt head of a jousting-lance. — *adj* **morné** (*mör-nā'*) (of a lion rampant) without teeth or claws. — *adj* **morned** (*heraldry*) blunted. [Fr *morner* (pa p *morné*) to blunt]

morne[2] *mörn*, (*archaic*) *adj* dismal, gloomy, sombre. [Fr]

morning *mörn'ing*, *n* the first part of the day, *usu* regarded as the period from dawn to noon or the midday-meal; the early part of anything; an early dram (chiefly *Scot*); a light meal before recognized breakfast (*dialect*). — *adj* of the morning; taking place or being in the morning. — *adv* **morn'ings** (*colloq* or *dialect*) in the morning. — **morning-after pill** a contraceptive pill taken within a specified time after intercourse; **morning coat** a cutaway coat worn as part of morning dress; **morning dress** dress, *esp* formal dress, worn in the early part of the day, as opposed to *evening-dress*; **morn'ing-gift** a gift made by the husband to the wife on the morning after marriage; **morning-glo'ry** a plant of the genus *Ipomoea* (*esp Ipomoea purpurea*) or *Convolvulus*, with showy flowers of various colours; a racehorse which runs faster in morning training than in the actual race (*slang*); **morn'ing-gown** a gown for wearing in the morning; **morn'ing-land** the east; **morn'ing-prayer** prayer in the morning; matins; **morn'ing-room** a sitting-room for use in the morning; **morning sickness** nausea and vomiting in the morning, common in the early stages of pregnancy; **morning star** a planet, *esp* Venus, when it rises before the sun; a precursor; a medieval weapon, a spiky ball attached directly or by a chain to a handle; **morn'ing-tide** the morning time; early part; **morning watch** the watch between 4 and 8am. — **the morning after** (*colloq*) the unpleasant after-effects of a night of excessive drinking, etc. [Contraction of ME *morwening*; cf **morn**]

Moro *mör'ō*, *n* a member of any of the tribes of Muslim Malays in the Philippine Islands: — *pl* **Moro** or **Moros**. [Sp, literally Moor, from L *Maurus*]

morocco *mə-rok'ō*, *n* a fine goatskin leather tanned with sumac, first brought from *Morocco* (also **morocco leather**); a sheepskin leather imitation of it; a very strong ale, anciently brewed in Westmorland: — *pl* **morocc'os**. — *adj* consisting of morocco. — **French morocco** an inferior kind of Levant morocco, with small grain; **Levant morocco** a fine quality of morocco, with large grain; **Persian morocco** a morocco finished on the grain side.

moron *mör'on*, *n* a somewhat feeble-minded person; a former category of mental retardation, describing a person with an IQ of 50–69, ie one who remains throughout life at the mental age of eight to twelve. — Also *adj*. — *adj* **moron'ic**. [Gr *mōros* foolish]

morose *mə-rōs'*, *adj* sour-tempered, *esp* when habitually so; gloomy, sullen; severe. — *adv* **morose'ly**. — *n* **morose'ness**. — *n* **morosity** (*-os'i-ti*; *obs*). [L *mōrōsus* peevish, from *mōs*, *mōris* manner]

morph[1] *morf*, (*zool*, etc) *n* a variant form of an animal, etc. [Gr *morphē* form]

morph[2]. See under **morphic**.

-morph *-mörf*, **morph-** *mörf-* or **morpho-** *mör'fō-*, *combining form* denoting (something) of a specified form, shape or structure. — **-morph'ic** *adj combining form*. — **-morph'ism** *n combining form*. [Gr *morphē* form]

morphallaxis, **morpheme**, etc. See under **morphic**.

Morpheus *mör'fūs*, *-fyəs* or *-fi-əs*, *n* the Greek god of dreams, son of Hypnos (sleep). — *adj* **morphē'an** (also *mör'*) or **morphet'ic** (irregularly formed). [Gr *Morpheus*, literally moulder, shaper, from *morphē* shape]

morphew *mör'fū*, *n* a skin eruption. [Ital *morfea*]

morphia. See **morphine**.

morphic *mör'fik*, *adj* relating to form, morphological. — *n* **morph** (*linguistics*; a back-formation from **morpheme**) the whole or a part of a spoken or written word corresponding to or representing one or more morphemes. — *n* **morphallax'is** regeneration in a changed form (*Gr allaxis* change). — *n* **morpheme** (*mör'fēm*) a simple linguistic unit that has meaning, and cannot be divided into smaller units. — *adj* **morphēm'ic**. — *n sing* **morphēm'ics** the study of morphemes. — *n* **morph'ing** (*cinematog*) the technique of using computer graphics to blend one cinema image into another, *esp* to transform or manipulate facial or bodily forms. — *n* **morphogenesis** (*-fə-jen'i-sis*) the origin and development of a part, organ or organism. — *adj* **morphogenet'ic**. — *n* **morphogeny** (*-foj'i-ni*) morphogenesis. — *n* **morphographer** (*-fog'rə-fər*). — *n* **morphog'raphy** descriptive morphology. — *n* **morphophōn'ēme** (either or any of) two or more phonemes which form variant morphs representing one morpheme (as in wi*f*e, wi*v*es). — *adj* **morphophonēm'ic**. — *n sing* **morphophonēm'ics**. — *n* **morphō'sis** morphogenesis. — *adj* **morphot'ic** relating to morphosis. — *adj* **morphotrop'ic**. — *n* **morphot'ropy** (*chem*) the effect on crystalline form of the addition or substitution of an element or radical. [Gr *morphē* form]

morphine *mör'fēn* or **morphia** *mör'fi-ə*, *n* the principal alkaloid in opium, a hypnotic drug used extensively for pain-relief. — *n* **mor'phinism** the effect of morphine on the system; the habit of taking morphine. — *n* **morphinomā'nia** habitual craving for morphine. — *n* **morphinomā'niac**. [Gr *Morpheus*, god of dreams]

morpho *mör'fō*, *n* a butterfly of the tropical American genus *Morpho*, of gigantic size and brilliant colouring, often bright blue: — *pl* **morph'os**. [Gr *Morphō*, a name of Aphrodite]

morpho-. See **morph-**.

morphogenesis, etc, **morphographer**, etc. See under **morphic**.

morphology *mör-fol'ə-ji*, *n* the science of form, *esp* that of the outer form, inner structure, and development of living organisms and their parts; the science of the external forms of rocks and land-features; the study of the forms of words. — *adj* **morpholog'ic** or **morpholog'ical**. — *n* **morphol'ogist**. [Gr *morphē* form, and *logos* word]

morphophoneme, etc. See under **morphic**.

morra. See **mora**[2].

morrhua *mor'ōō-ə*, *n* an old generic, now specific, name of the cod (*Gadus morrhua*). [LL *morua*]

morrice. An *obs* form of **morris**[1].

morrion. See **morion**[1].

morris[1], **morrice**. See **morris dance**.

morris[2]. See **meril** (for **nine men's morris**, etc).

Morris chair *mor'is chār*, *n* a kind of armchair with an adjustable, reclining back and removable cushions. [From William *Morris* (1834–96), English designer and architect]

morris dance *mor'is däns*, *n* a type of English folk-dance, *perh* of Moorish origin, which came to be associated with May games, with (latterly) Maid Marian, Robin Hood, the hobby-horse, and other characters, who had bells attached to their clothes; a tune for such a dance. — Also **morr'is** or **morr'ice**. — *vi* **morr'is** to perform by dancing. — **morr'is-dancer**; **morr'is-pike** (*Shakesp*) a Moorish pike. [**Moorish**]

Morrison shelter *mor'i-sən shel'tər*, *n* a kind of portable, steel air-raid shelter for indoor use, developed during World War II. [Herbert S *Morrison*, Secretary of State for Home Affairs and Home Security 1940–45, who officially recommended their use]

Morris-tube *mor'is-tūb*, *n* a small-bore rifle-barrel inserted in the breech of a larger, for short-range practice. [R *Morris* (died 1891), the inventor]

morro *mor'ō*, *n* a rounded hill or headland: — *pl* **morr'os**. [Sp]

morrow *mor'ō*, (*archaic* or *poetic*) *n* the day following the present; tomorrow; the next following day; the time immediately after any event. [ME *morwe* for *morwen*; cf **morn**]

morsal. See under **morsure**.

Morse *mörs*, *n* (a method of) signalling by a code in which each letter is represented by a combination of dashes and dots or long and short light-flashes, sound signals, etc, invented by Sam F B *Morse* (1791–1872). — Also *adj*.

morse[1] *mörs*, *n* the walrus. [Lappish *morsa*, or Finn *mursu*]

morse[2] *mörs*, *n* the fastening of a cope. [L *morsus* a bite, catch]

morsel *mör'səl*, *n* a bite or mouthful; a small piece of food; a choice piece of food, a dainty; a small piece of anything; a small person. — *vt* to divide into morsels; to apportion in small amounts. [OFr *morsel* (Fr *morceau*, Ital *morsello*), dimin from L *morsus*, from *mordēre*, *morsum* to bite]

morsing-horn *mör'sing-hörn*, *n* the small horn that used to hold the fine powder for priming. [Fr *amorcer* to prime (a gun)]

morsure *mörs'ūr*, *n* a bite. — *adj* **mors'al**. [L *morsus* bite]

mort[1] *mört*, *n* death (*obs*); a flourish sounded at the death of a buck, etc in hunting; a sheep that has died a natural death (cf **morling** or **mortling** under **morkin**); a dead body. — **mort'bell** a funeral bell; **mort'cloth** a pall; **mort'-head** a death's-head; **mort'-safe** a heavy grating used to guard a corpse against resurrectionists (*hist*); **mort'-stone** a wayside stone on which the bearers lay the bier for a rest. [Fr *mort* death, dead]

mort[2] *mört*, (*dialect*) *n* a great deal. [Origin obscure]

mort[3] *mört*, (*cant*) *n* a woman; a loose woman. [Origin obscure]

mort[4] *mört*, *n* a salmon, 3 years old. [Origin obscure]

mortal *mör'tl*, *adj* liable to death, certain to die at some future time; causing death; deadly; fatal; punishable with death; (of a sin) incurring the penalty of spiritual death, as opposed to *venial*; to the death; implacable; human; very great (*colloq*); tediously long (*colloq*); without exception (*colloq*); very drunk (*slang*). — *n* a human being. — *adv* (*dialect* or *colloq*) extremely; thoroughly. — *n* **mortality** (*-tal'i-ti*) the condition of being mortal; death; frequency or number of deaths, *esp* in proportion to population; the human race, nature or estate. — *vt* **mor'talize** or **-ise** to make mortal. — *adv* **mor'tally**. — *adj* **mor'tal-star'ing** (*Shakesp*) having a deadly look. — **bills of mortality** see under **bill**[3]. [L *mortālis*, from *morī* to die]

mortar *mör'tər*, *n* a vessel in which substances are pounded with a pestle; a short piece of artillery for throwing a heavy shell, a bomb, a lifeline, etc; a mixture of cement, sand and water with which bricks, etc are bonded. — *vt* to join or plaster with mortar; to bombard with a mortar. — **mor'tarboard** a square board, with a handle beneath, for holding mortar; a square-topped college cap. [OE *mortere*, from L *mortārium* a mortar, matter pounded]

mortgage *mör'gij*, *n* a conditional conveyance of, or lien upon, land or other property as security for the performance of some condition (*usu* the repayment of a loan to purchase the property itself), becoming void on the performance of the condition; the act of conveying, or the deed effecting it; a loan advanced by a building society, bank, etc, on the security of one's property; an individual (*usu* monthly) repayment of such a loan, or the amount repaid. — *vt* to pledge as security for a debt; to subject (a property) to a mortgage. — *n* **mortgagee'** a person to whom a mortgage is made or given; someone who gives or grants a mortgage. — *n* **mort'gagor** (*-jər*) a person who mortgages his or her property (also sometimes **mort'gager**). [OFr, from *mort* dead, and *gage* a pledge]

mortice. See **mortise**.

mortician *mör-tish'ən*, (*US*) *n* an undertaker. [L *mors*, *mortis* death]

mortiferous *mör-tif'ər-əs*, *adj* death-bringing; fatal. — *n* **mortif'erousness**. [L *mors*, *mortis* death, and *ferre* to bring]

mortify *mör'ti-fī*, *vt* to kill (*obs*); to destroy the vital functions of; to deaden; to subdue by severities and penance; to vex in a humiliating or embarrassing way; to dispose of by mortification (*Scots law*). — *vi* to lose vitality; to become gangrenous; to be subdued; to practise asceticism: — *pr p* **mor'tifying**; *pa t* and *pa p* **mor'tified**. — *adj* **mortif'ic** death-bringing; deadly. — *n* **mortification** (*mör-ti-fi-kā'shən*) the act of mortifying or state of being mortified; the death of part of the body; a subduing of the passions and appetites by a severe or strict manner of living; humiliation; chagrin; that which mortifies or vexes; a bequest to some charitable institution (*Scots law*). — *adj* **mor'tified**. — *n* **mor'tifier**. — *adj* and *n* **mor'tifying**. [Fr *mortifier*, from LL *mortificāre* to cause death to, from *mors*, *mortis* death, and *facere* to make]

mortise or **mortice** *mör'tis*, *n* a hole made in wood, stone, etc to receive a tenon; a recess cut into a printing-plate for the insertion of type, etc (*printing*). — *vt* to cut a mortise in; to join by a mortise and tenon. — *n* **mor'tiser** or **mor'ticer**. — **mor'tise-lock** or **mor'tice-lock** a lock whose mechanism is covered by being sunk into the edge of a door, etc. [Fr *mortaise*; ety unknown]

mortling. See under **morkin**.

mortmain *mört'mān*, (*law*; *hist*) *n* the legal status of property which is transferred inalienably to an ecclesiastical or other body, said to be a dead hand, ie one that can never part with it again. — **statutes of mortmain** acts of parliament restricting or forbidding the giving of property to religious houses. [Fr *morte* (fem) dead, and *main*, from L *manus* hand]

Morton's fork *mör'tənz förk'* or **crutch** *kruch*, *n* a casuistic device for trapping everyone alike, so-called from the practice of the 15c Archbishop of Canterbury and statesman John *Morton*, of exacting loans not only from the rich who could patently afford it, but also from the apparently poor, who were presumed to be saving money.

mortuary *mört'ū-ər-i*, *adj* connected with death or burial. — *n* a place for the temporary storage of dead bodies; a payment to the parish priest on the death of a parishioner or to a bishop or archdeacon on the death of a priest. [L *mortuārius*, from *mortuus* dead, and *morī* to die]

morula *mör'ū-lə*, *n* a solid spherical mass of cells resulting from the cleavage of an ovum; framboesia. — *adj* **mor'ular**. [L *mōrum* a mulberry]

Morus *mō'rəs*, *n* the mulberry genus, giving name to the family **Morā'ceae**, including fig, breadfruit and Ceará rubber. — *adj* **morā'ceous**. [L *mōrus* a mulberry tree; cf Gr *moreā*]

morwong *mör'wong* or *mō'wong*, *n* an Australasian food fish. [Aboriginal]

MOS *abbrev*: metal oxide semiconductor.

mos *abbrev*: months.

Mosaic *mō-zā'ik*, *adj* of or relating to *Moses*, the great Jewish lawgiver. — *n* **Mō'saism**. — **Mosaic Law** the law of the Jews given by Moses at Mount Sinai.

mosaic *mō-zā'ik*, *n* the fitting together in a design of small pieces of coloured marble, glass, etc; a piece of work of this kind; anything of similar appearance, or composed by the piecing together of different things; a leaf-mosaic; leaf-mosaic disease (or **mosaic disease**); a hybrid with the parental characters side by side and not blended. — *adj* relating to, or composed of, mosaic. — *adv* **mosā'ically**. — *n* **mosā'icism** (*-i-sizm*) the presence side by side of patches of tissue of unlike constitution. — *n* **mosā'icist** (*-i-sist*) a worker in mosaic. — **mosaic gold** an alloy of copper and zinc, ormolu; a stannic sulphide; **mosaic map** a composite photographic map made from aerial photographs. [Fr *mosaïque*, from LL *mosaicum*, *mūsaicum*, from *mūsa*, from Gr *mousa* a muse; cf LL *mūsaeum* or *mūsīvum* (*opus*) mosaic (work)]

Mosasauros *mō-sə-sö'rəs*, *n* a gigantic Cretaceous fossil pythonomorph reptile. [L *Mosa*, the Maas, near which the first was found, and Gr *sauros* a lizard]

mosbolletjie *mos-bol'ə-ki*, (*SAfr*) *n* a sweet bun made of dough leavened with grape must. [SAfr Du *most* must, and *bolletjie* bun, roll]

moschatel *mos-kə-tel'*, *n* a small plant (*Adoxa moschatellina*), constituting in itself the *Adoxaceae* (by some included in the honeysuckle family), with pale-green flowers and a supposed musky smell. [Fr *moscatelle*, from Ital *moschatella*, from *moscato* musk]

moschiferous *mos-kif'ər-əs*, *adj* producing musk. [LL *moschus*, from Gr *moschos* musk, and L *ferre* to bring]

mose *mōz*, *vi* only in *Shakesp*, *Taming of the Shrew*, III. 2. 51 — **mose in the chine** to have glanders. [Supposed to be for *mourn in the chine*, perh from Fr *morve d'eschine* glanders, running from the spine: the morbid matter of glanders was thought to come from the spine. Another suggestion is that *mose* is for *pose* catarrh, turned into a verb]

Moselle or **Mosel** *mō-zel'*, *n* a German white wine from the district of the river *Moselle* (Ger *Mosel*), with an aromatic flavour.

Moses basket *mō'zəz bäs'kit*, *n* a portable cot for babies. [Story of Moses in the bulrushes, from the Bible: Exod 2. 3]

mosey *mō'zi*, (*slang*) *vi* to move along slowly, saunter; to jog; to make off; to hurry. [Origin uncertain]

moshav *mō-shäv'*, *n* an agricultural settlement in Israel; (also **moshav ovdim** *ōv-dēm'*) a joint association of privately-owned farms, on which machinery and marketing are usually operated communally: — *pl* **moshavim** (*-shə-vēm'*) or **moshvei ovdim** (*mosh-vā'*). — **moshav shitufi** (*shi-too-fē'*) an Israeli agricultural association in which land and all resources are held in common, but the family unit is preserved, with its own house and garden: — *pl* **moshavim shitufim**. [Heb, dwelling]

moshing *mosh'ing*, (*slang*) *n* a style of energetic, sinuous dancing done in a crowded space to heavy metal or thrash music. [Origin uncertain; perh from *squash* and *mash*]

moskonfyt *mos-kon'fāt*, (*SAfr*) *n* a thick syrup made from grapes. [Afrik *mos* must, and *konfyt* jam]

Moslem *moz'lem* or *-ləm*, *n* and *adj*. Same as **Muslim**.

moslings *moz'lingz*, *n pl* the thin shavings taken off by the currier in dressing skins. [Perh *morsellings*, as if dimin of **morsel**]

mosque *mosk*, *n* a Muslim place of worship. [Fr *mosquée*, from Ital *moschea*, from Ar *masjid* (in N Africa pron *masgid*), from *sajada* (*sagada*) to pray]

mosquito *mos-kē'tō*, *n* loosely, any small biting or stinging insect; any of several long-legged insects of the family *Culicidae*, the females of which have their mouth-parts adapted for bloodsucking and can therefore transmit disease, including malaria: — *pl* **mosqui'toes** or **-os**. — **mosquito canopy**, **curtain** or **net** an arrangement of fine-meshed netting, *esp* over or round a bed, to keep out mosquitoes; **mosquito fish** the topminnow; **mosquito hawk** the nighthawk or goatsucker; **mosqui'to-weight** a light featherweight boxer. [Sp dimin of *mosca* a fly, from L *musca*]

moss *mos*, *n* a bog (now chiefly *Scots*); boggy ground or soil; any of the *Musci*, a class of *Bryophyta*, small plants with simply constructed leaves, and no woody material, attached by rhizoids, the zygote growing into a small spore-bearing capsule that grows parasitically on the parent plant; a mass of such plants; a mosslike growth, covering or excrescence; loosely extended to plants of similar appearance to true mosses; a moss-rose. — *vt* to cover with moss; to clear of moss. — *vi* to gather moss. — *n* **moss'iness**. — *adj* **moss'y** overgrown or abounding with moss; like moss; boggy. — **moss agate** chalcedony with moss-like inclusions of chlorite, manganese oxide, etc; **moss'back** (*NAm*) a person of antiquated views; **moss'bluiter** (*-blüt'ər* or *-blit'ər*; *Scot*) the bittern; **moss'-cheeper** (*Scot*) the titlark; **moss'-crop** (*Scot*) cotton-grass; **moss'-flow** (*Scot*) a watery bog; **moss green** a muted yellowy-green. — *adj* **moss'-grown** covered with moss. — **moss'-hag'** or **moss'-hagg'** (*Scot*) a pit or slough in a bog; **moss'land** wet, peaty land; **moss'-litter** a loose mass of lumps of peaty material; **moss'plant** a plant of moss; the sexual generation in the life-history of a moss, on which the asexual generation is parasitic; **moss'-rose** a variety of rose having a mosslike growth on and below the calyx; **moss stitch** a knitting stitch alternating plain and purl stitches along each row and in succeeding rows, producing a mosslike texture; **moss'-trooper** (*hist*) one of the freebooters that used to frequent the Border between Scotland and England in the 17c. — *n* and *adj* **moss'-trooping**. — **club moss** see under **club** and **lycopod**; **Iceland moss** see under **Iceland**. [OE *mōs* bog; Du *mos*, Ger *Moos* moss, bog]

Mossad *mos'ad*, *n* the Israeli state intelligence service (since 1951), established *orig* in 1937 as *Mossad le Alujeh Beth*, the Committee for Illegal Immigration, to oversee illegal Jewish immigration into Palestine.

Mössbauer effect *mœs'bow-ər if-ekt'*, (*nuc*) *n* a method of producing gamma rays with precise wavelengths, so that measurements can be made by gamma radiation. [Rudolf Ludwig *Mössbauer* (born 1929), German physicist]

mossbunker *mos'bung-kər*, *n* the menhaden, an oily fish of the herring family. [Du *mars-banker* the scad or horse-mackerel]

mossie[1] *mos'i* or **mozzie** *moz'i*, (*Austr* and *NZ colloq*) *n* short for **mosquito**.

mossie[2] *mos'i*, (*SAfr*) *n* (also **Cape sparrow**) a common S African sparrow, *Passer melanurus*, the male of which has a black head and curved white mark at the eye. [Afrik, from Du *mosje*, dimin of *mos* sparrow]

most *mōst*, *adj* (*superl* of **more**[1]) the majority of; in greatest quantity or number. — *adv* in the highest or greatest degree (used to form superlative of adjectives and adverbs); used as an intensifier; almost (*US dialect*; *perh* aphetic). — *n* the greatest number or quantity. — *adv* **most'ly** for the most part. — *adv* **most'what** (*Spenser*) for the most part, mostly. — **at most** or **at the most** at the maximum; **for the most part** chiefly; in the main; **make the most of** see under **make**[1]; **the mostest** (*facetious*) the most, the ultimate. [The Northumbrian form *māst* (*Scot* **maist**) may have occurred in OE beside the ordinary form *mǣst*; or the vowel may come from analogy with the comparative; cf Ger *meist*]

-most *-mōst*, *sfx* indicating superlative, eg *hindmost*, *farthermost*. [OE superl sfx *-mæst*, *-mest*]

MOT *em-ō-tē'*, *n* a compulsory annual check made by order of the *M*inistry *o*f *T*ransport on vehicles of more than a certain age. — Also **MOT test**. — *vt* to give an MOT to: — *pa t* and *pa p* **MOT'd**.

MOT *abbrev*: Ministry of Transport (now Transport Industries).

mot[1] *mot*, (*obs*) *n* a motto; a hunter's horn-call. [Fr, from L *muttum* a murmur]

mot[2] *mō*, (*Fr*) *n* a word; a pithy or witty saying. — **le mot juste** (*lə mō zhüst*) the word which fits the context exactly.

mot[3]. See **motte**[1].

mot[4]. See **mote**[1].

mote[1] *mōt*, (*archaic*) *vt* may; must: — 3rd *pers sing pr t* **mote**; *pa t* (*Spenser*) **mote** or **mot** (*mot*), in *pl* **mot'en** (but see also **must**[1]). — **so mote I thee** so may I prosper (see **thee**[2]). [OE *mōt* may, pa t *mōste*; confused with **mought**; Ger *muss* must]

mote[2] *mōt*, *n* a particle of dust; a speck; a seed or other foreign particle in wool or cotton (Yorkshire **moit**); a stain or blemish; anything very small. — *adj* **mōt'ed**, **mote'y** or (*Scot*) **motty** (*mot'i*) containing a mote or motes. — **mote spoon** a perforated spoon formerly used to remove tea leaves from a teacup or teapot spout, or for straining other liquids. [OE *mot*; Du *mot*]

mote[3]. See **motte**[2].

motel *mō-tel'*, *n* a hotel for motorists with rooms that are *usu* accessible from a parking area; a hotel with accommodation and servicing facilities for cars. — *n* **motel'ier** the owner or manager of a motel. [*mo*tor ho*tel*]

moten. See **mote**[1].

motet or **motett** *mō-tet'*, (*music*) *n* a polyphonic choral composition, *usu* unaccompanied, with a biblical or similar prose text; loosely, an anthem or church cantata. — *n* **motett'ist**. [Fr *motet*, dimin of *mot*; cf **mot**[2]]

motey. See under **mote**[2].

moth *moth*, *n* the cloth-eating larva of the clothes-moth; the imago of the same kind; any member of the *Heterocera*, a popular and unscientific division of the *Lepidoptera*, broadly distinguished from butterflies by having duller colouring, a thicker body, antennae not clubbed, wings not tilted over the back in rest, and by the habit of flying by night; that which eats away at anything gradually and silently; any of various kinds of insect vermin (*obs*); a fragile, frivolous creature, readily dazzled into destruction (*fig*); a light aeroplane: — *pl* **moths**. — *adj* **mothed** (*motht*) moth-eaten. — *adj* **moth'y** full of moths; moth-eaten. — **moth'ball** a ball of naphthalene, or a similar substance, for keeping away clothes-moths. — *vt* to lay up in mothballs; to spray with a plastic and lay up (a ship, etc); to lay aside temporarily, postpone work on, keep in readiness for eventual use. — *vt* **moth'-eat** (back formation) to prey upon, as a moth eats a garment. — *adj* **moth'-eaten** eaten or cut by the larvae of moths (also *fig*). — **moth'-flower** a flower pollinated by moths; **moth'-hunter** a goatsucker. — *adj* **moth'proof** (of clothes, etc) chemically rendered resistant to moths. — Also *vt*. — **(put) in mothballs** (to put) temporarily in abeyance. [OE *moththe*, *mohthe*; Ger *Motte*]

mother[1] *mudh'ər*, *n* a female parent; that which has produced or nurtured anything; the female head of a religious house or other establishment; a matron; a familiar term of address to, or prefix to the name of, an old woman; extended to a female ancestor, stepmother, mother-in-law or foster-mother; an apparatus for chicken-rearing; the womb (*obs*); hysteria (*obs*); short for motherfucker (*vulg slang*). — *adj* received by birth, as it were from one's mother; being a mother; acting the part of a mother; originating; used to generate others. — *vt* to give birth to; to acknowledge, adopt or treat as a son or daughter; to foster; to behave (too) protectively towards, as, or as if as, a mother; to attribute the maternity or authorship of (with *on* or *upon*); to find a mother for. — *n* **moth'erhood** the state of being a mother. — *n* **moth'ering** a rural English custom of visiting the mother church or one's parents on Mid-Lent Sunday (**Mothering Sunday**). — *adj* **moth'erless** without a mother. — *n* **moth'erliness**. — *adj* **moth'erly** relating to, or befitting, a mother; like a mother. — **mother'board** a printed circuit board that can be plugged into the back of a computer and into which can be slotted other boards so that the computer can operate various peripherals; **moth'er-cell** (*biol*) a cell that gives rise to others by division; **mother church** the church from which others have sprung; a principal church; **mother-cit'y** one from which another was founded as a colony; **mother coun'try** or **moth'erland** the country of one's birth; the home country of colonists, etc settled elsewhere; **moth'ercraft** knowledge and skill required for the care of a child; **mother fig'ure** an older woman who symbolizes for one the qualities and authority of one's mother; **moth'erfucker** (*vulg slang*, *esp US*) an extremely objectionable, unpleasant, etc person or thing; **Mother Hubbard** a woman's loose flowing gown, like that proper to the nursery heroine; **moth'er-in-law** the mother of one's husband or wife; a stepmother (*obs*): — *pl* **moth'ers-in-law**; **moth'er-in-law's tongue** a houseplant with sword-like leaves, *Sansevieria*; **motherland** see **mother country** above; **moth'er-liquor** or **moth'er-lye** mother-water; **mother lode** (*mining*) the main lode of any system. — *adj* **moth'er-na'ked** completely naked, as at birth. — **mother-of-mill'ions** ivy-leaved toadflax; **mother-of-pearl'** the nacreous internal layer of the shells in some molluscs (also *adj*); **moth'er-of-thousands** a perennial creeping plant with ivy-shaped leaves; **moth'er-right** (*archaic*) succession in the female line; matriarchy; **Mother's Day** a day for honouring mothers, as, in the USA, the second Sunday in May; also used for Mothering Sunday; **mother's help** a person employed to help a mother with domestic duties, *esp* the supervision of children; **mother ship** a ship having charge of torpedo-boats or small craft; a ship which provides a number of other, *usu* smaller, ships with services, supplies, etc; **moth'er's-mark** or **moth'er-spot** a birthmark; **mothers' meeting** a periodical meeting of mothers connected with a church; **mother's** (or **mothers'**) **ruin** (*slang*) gin; **mother superior** the head of a convent or any community of nuns; **mother-to-be'** a woman who is pregnant, *esp* with her first child; **mother tongue** native language; a language from which another has its origin; **moth'er-water** residual liquid, still containing certain chemical substances, left after others have been crystallized or precipitated from it; **mother wit** native wit; common sense; **moth'erwort** the labiate plant *Leonurus cardiaca*, or any of several related plants formerly used in the treatment of disorders of the uterus. — **be mother** (*facetious*) to pour the tea; **every mother's son** every man without exception; **fits of the mother** (*obs*) hysteria; **Mother Carey's chicken** or **goose** the storm petrel, or similar bird; **the mother and father** (or **father and mother**) (**of**) (*colloq*) the biggest, greatest (*usu fig*), as in *the mother and father of an argument* (or *all arguments*). [OE *mōdor*; Du *moeder*, ON *mōthir*, Ger *Mutter*, Ir and Gaelic *mathair*, L *māter*, Gr *mētēr*, Sans *mātr*]

mother[2] *mudh'ər*, *n* dregs; scum; a slimy mass of bacteria that oxidizes alcohol into acetic acid (in full, **mother of vinegar**). — *vi* to become mothery. — *adj* **moth'ery** like or containing mother. [Poss the same as **mother**[1]; or poss from Du *modder* mud; cf **mud**]

mothering and **motherly**. See under **mother**[1].

motif *mō-tēf'*, *n* a dominant or recurrent theme or subject in a musical, literary or other artistic work; a shape or design repeated in a pattern (*music*); an ornament added to a woman's garment, often symbolic; a design, symbol, etc on a manufactured article, whether decorative or identifying the manufacturer. [Fr *motif*; see **motive**]

motile *mō'tīl* or (*NAm*) *-til*, *adj* capable of moving spontaneously as a whole; characterized by motion; imagining most readily in terms of muscular action (*psychol*). — *n* (*psychol*) a person whose imagery naturally takes the form of feelings of action. — *n* **motility** (*-til'i-ti*). [L *mōtus* movement]

motion *mō'shən*, *n* the act, state or manner of changing place; a single movement; change of posture; power of moving or of being moved; agitation; a natural impulse; a working in the mind; a feeling, an emotion (*obs*); a prompting, an instigation (*obs*); a formal proposal put before a meeting; an application to a court, during a case before it, for an order or rule that something be done, *esp* something incidental to the progress of the cause rather than its issue (*law*); evacuation of the intestine; a piece of mechanism; progression of a part (*music*); a puppet show (*obs*); a puppet (*Shakesp*); (*usu* in *pl*) faeces. — *vt* to direct or indicate by a gesture; to move, propose; to make a movement indicating as one's intention (*obs*); to give motion to. — *vi* to offer a proposal. — *adj* **mō'tional**. — *n* **mō'tionist** (*Milton*) a person who is good at making suggestions or recommendations. — *adj* **mō'tionless** without motion. — **mō'tion-man** (*obs*) a puppeteer; **mō'tion picture** a cinema film; **motion sickness** same as **travel sickness**. — **angular motion** change of angle between a standard direction and a line joining the moving object and a fixed point; **go through the motions** to make a half-hearted attempt; to pretend; **laws of motion** Newton's three laws; (1) Every body continues in its state of rest, or of uniform motion in a straight line, except so far as it may be compelled by force to change that state; (2) Change of motion is proportional to force applied, and takes place in the direction of the straight line in which the force acts; (3) To every action there is always an equal and contrary reaction. [Fr *motion*, from L *mōtiō*, *-ōnis*, from *movēre*, *mōtum* to move]

motive *mō'tiv*, *adj* causing motion; having the power to cause motion; concerned with the initiation of action; moving (*obs*). — *n* an incitement of the will; a consideration or emotion that excites to action; a motif; a moving part of the body (*Shakesp*). — *vt* to motivate. — *vt* **mo'tivate** to provide with a motive; to induce; to give an incentive. — *n* **motivā'tion** motivating force, incentive. — *adj* **motivā'tional** relating to motivation. — *adv* **motivā'tionally**. — *n* **mo'tivator**. — *adj* **mo'tiveless**. — *n* **mo'tivelessness**. — *adj* **motiv'ic** of, having or concerning a musical motif. — *n* **motiv'ity** the power of moving or of producing motion. — **motivated art** art produced under the influence of hallucinogenic drugs; **motivation** or **motivational research** research into motivation, *esp* into consumer reaction, carried out scientifically; **motive power** the energy or source of the energy by which anything is operated. [LL *mōtīvus*, from L *movēre*, *mōtum* to move]

motley *mot'li*, *n* a cloth of mixed colours (*obs*); a variegated garment or outfit, *esp* that formerly worn by a jester; a patchwork (*obs*); a jester (*Shakesp*). — *adj* multicoloured; variegated; made of, or dressed in, motley; jester-like; made up of various elements or types, heterogeneous. — *adj* **mot'ley-mind'ed** (*Shakesp*) having heterogeneous and inconsistent thoughts or intentions. [Poss from OE *mot* a speck]

motmot *mot'mot*, *n* a tropical American bird (*Momotus* and related genera), related to rollers and kingfishers, that nibbles its tail-feathers into a racquet-shape. [Said to be Mexican name]

motocross *mō'tō-kros*, *n* a form of scrambling, motorcycle racing round a very rough circuit. [**motor**]

moto perpetuo *mō'tō per-pet'ōō-ō*, (*Ital*) *n* perpetual motion; a piece of music that goes swiftly without stop from beginning to end.

motor *mō'tər*, *n* a mover; that which gives motion; a machine whereby some source of energy is used to give motion or perform work, *esp* an internal-combustion engine or a machine for converting electrical into mechanical energy; a motor car; a muscle, or a nerve, concerned in bodily movement. — *adj* giving or transmitting motion; driven by a motor; of, for, with, or relating to, motor vehicles; concerned with the transmission of impulses; initiating bodily movement; relating to muscular movement or the sense of muscular movement. — *vt* and *vi* to convey, traverse or travel by a motor vehicle; to put on speed, to move fast (*colloq*). — *adj* **mo'torable** (of roads) able to be used by motor vehicles. — *adj* **moto'rial** motory. — *n* **mo'torist** a person who drives a motor car, *esp* for pleasure. — *n* **moto'rium** that part of the nervous system concerned in movement. — *n* **motorizā'tion** or **-s-**. — *vt* **mo'torize** or **-ise** to provide with, or adapt to the use of, a motor or motors; to interpret or imagine in terms of motor sensation. — *adj* **mo'tory** causing, conveying or imparting motion; motor. — **mo'tor-bandit** a robber who uses a motor car; **mo'tor-bicycle**, **-bike**, **-boat**, **-bus**, **-car**, **-coach**, **-cycle**, **-launch**, **-lorry** and **-ship** a bicycle, etc driven by a motor; **motorcade** (*mō'tər-kād*; after **cavalcade**) a procession of motor cars, *esp* ones carrying a head of state and his or her entourage; **motor caravan** a motor vehicle with living, sleeping, etc facilities, like a caravan; **mo'torcycling**; **mo'torcyclist**. — *adj* **mo'tor-driven** driven by a motor. — **motor generator** an electrical generator driven by an electric motor, whereby one voltage, frequency or number of phases, ie those of the motor, can be used to produce a different voltage, frequency or number of phases, ie those of the generator; **motor home** (*NAm*) a modern van-like vehicle of varying size fully equipped to be a travelling home, a motor caravan; **mo'tor-jet** a reciprocating engine with a fan for jet-propulsion; **mo'torman** a man who controls a motor, *esp* that of a tram-car or electric train; **mo'tormouth** a non-stop talker (*US slang*); **motor neurone** (*anatom*) a neurone conveying a voluntary or motor impulse; **motor neurone disease** a disease in which progressive damage to motor neurones leads to muscle weakness and degeneration; **motor-scoo'ter** a small motor-cycle, *usu* with an engine of under 225 cc; **motor-trac'tion** the conveyance of loads, including passengers, by motor vehicles; **motor-trac'tor** an internal-combustion engine for hauling loads, *esp* for drawing agricultural implements; **mo'torway** a trunk road for fast-moving motor vehicles, with separate carriageways for vehicles travelling in opposite directions, and limited access and exit points. — **motorway madness** (*colloq*) reckless driving in bad conditions on motorways, *esp* in fog. [L *mōtor*, from *movēre* to move]

motorail *mō'tō-rāl*, *n* a system of carrying cars and passengers by train on certain routes. [**motor**]

motorbike... to ... **motorway**. See under **motor**.

motoscafo *mō-tō-skä'fō*, (*Ital*) *n* a motorboat: — *pl* **motoscafi** (*-fē*).

Motown® *mō'town*, *n* a type of music that blends rhythm and blues and pop with gospel rhythms. [Motown Record Company in Detroit, Michigan (nicknamed *Motown*, for *motor town*), a major car-manufacturing centre]

motser *mot'sər* or **motza** *mot'zə*, (*Austr colloq*) *n* a large amount of money, *esp* the proceeds from a gambling win.

mott *mot*, (*Spenser*) *pa t* of **mete**[1].

motte[1], **mott** or **mot** *mot*, (SW *US*) *n* a clump of trees, *esp* on a prairie. [Mex Sp *mata*]

motte[2] *mot* or **mote** *mōt*, (*archaic*) *n* a mound, *esp* with a castle, a tumulus. — **mote'-hill**. — **motte and bailey** designating the type of castle commonly built by the Normans, with a keep built on a mound surrounded by a walled bailey. [OFr *mote* (Fr *motte*); often confused with **moot** or **moot-hill**]

mottle *mot'l*, *vt* to variegate blotchily. — *n* a blotched appearance, condition or surface; yarns of two colours folded together. — *adj* **mott'led**. — *n* **mott'ling**. — *adj* **mott'le-faced**. [Prob from **motley**]

motto *mot'ō*, *n* a short sentence or phrase adopted as representative of a person, family, etc, or accompanying a coat of arms; a passage prefixed to a book or chapter anticipating its subject; a scrap of verse or prose enclosed in a cracker or sweet wrapper: — *pl* **mott'oes** (*-ōz*). — *adj* **mott'ō'd** or **mott'oed**. [Ital, from L *muttum* a murmur]

motty. See under **mote**[2].

Motu *mō'too*, *n* a member of a group of aboriginal people of Papua New Guinea; their language, of the Malayo-Polynesian family: — *pl* **Motu** or **Motus**.

motu *mō'too*, *n* a small reef island in the S Pacific: — *pl* **motu** or **motus**. [Maori]

motuca *mō-too'kə* or **mutuca** *moo-too'kə*, *n* a large Brazilian biting fly of the family *Tabanidae*. [Tupí *mutuca* (Port *motuca*)]

motu proprio *mō'tū prō'pri-ō* or *mō'too pro'pri-ō*, (*L*) of his own accord without consultation.

motza. See **motser**.

MOU *abbrev*: memorandum of understanding.

mou' or **mou** *moo*, *n* a Scots form of **mouth**.

mouch, **moucher**, etc. Same as **mooch**, etc.

moucharaby *moo-shar'ə-bi*, *n* a balcony enclosed with lattice-work. [Fr, from Ar *mashrabiyyah*]

mouchard *moo-shär*, (*Fr*) *n* a police spy.

mouchoir *moo-shwär*, (*Fr*) *n* a pocket-handkerchief.

moudiewart, **moudiwart**, **moudiewort** and **moudiwort**. Scots forms of **mouldwarp**.

moue *moo*, (*Fr*) *n* a grimace of discontent, pout.

moufflon, **mouflon** or **muflon** *moof'lon*, *n* a wild sheep of the mountains of Corsica, etc; extended to large big-horned wild sheep of other kinds: — *pl* **moufflon**, etc or **moufflons**, etc. [Fr *mouflon*, from LL *mufrō*, *-ōnis*]

mought *mōt* or *mowt* (*Spenser möt*), (*obs* or *dialect*) *pa t* of **may**. See also **mote**[1].

mouillé *moo'yā*, (*phonetics*) *adj* (of *l* and *n*) sounded in a liquid manner, palatalized (as *gl* in 'seraglio', or *ñ* in 'señor'). [Fr. moistened]

moujik *moo-zhik'* or *moo'zhik*, *n*. Same as **muzhik**.

moulage *mool-äzh'*, *n* the making of moulds (*esp* of objects of interest in criminal investigation). [Fr, from MFr *mollage*, from OFr *mouler* to model, from *modle* a mould, from L *modulus* a measure]

mould[1] or (*NAm*) **mold** *mōld*, *n* loose soft earth; earth, considered as the material of which the body is formed or to which it returns; the earth of the grave; the ground, the land, the world (*obs* or *archaic*); (in *pl*) clods, *esp* in allusion to the grave (*Scot* **mouls** or **mools** *moolz*); soil rich in decayed matter. — *vt* to cover with soil. — *vi* (*obs*) to moulder. — *vi* **mould'er** to crumble to mould; to turn to dust; to waste away gradually. — *vt* to turn to dust. — *adj* **mould'y** like, or of the nature of, mould. — **mould'board** the curved plate in a plough which turns over the soil. [OE *molde*; Ger dialect *molt*, *molten*, Gothic *mulda*]

mould[2] or (*NAm*) **mold** *mōld*, *n* a woolly growth on bread, cheese, or other vegetable or animal matter; any one of various small fungi (such as *Mucor*, *Penicillium*, etc) of different classes, forming such growths. — *vi* to become mouldy. — *vt* to cause or allow to become mouldy. — *n* **mould'iness**. — *adj* **mould'y** overgrown with mould; like mould; stale; musty; miserable, lousy (*colloq derog*). [ME *mowle*; cf ON *mygla*]

mould[3] or (*NAm*) **mold** *mōld*, *n* a template; the matrix in which a cast is made; a formed surface from which an impression is taken; the foundation on which certain manufactured articles are built up; a thing formed in a mould, *esp* a jelly or blancmange; nature; a form, model or pattern; that which is or may be moulded; a set of mouldings (*archit*); a wire tray used to make paper by hand. — *vt* to knead; to mix (*obs*); to shape; to model; to form in a mould. — *adj* **mould'able**. — *n* **mould'er**. — *n* **mould'ing** the process of shaping, *esp* any soft substance; anything formed by or in a mould;

an ornamental edging or band projecting from a wall or other surface, such as a fillet, astragal or bead; a strip of wood that can be applied for the purpose. — **mould'-candle** a candle made in a mould, not dipped; **mould-fac'ing** a fine powder or wash applied to the face of a mould to ensure a smooth casting; **mould'ing-board** a baker's board for kneading dough; **mould'-loft** a room in which the several parts of a ship's hull are laid off to full size from the construction drawings. — *adj* **mould'-made** (of paper) made on a machine, but having a deckle-edge like that of handmade paper. [OFr *modle, molle* (Fr *moule*), from L *modulus* a measure]

mouldwarp *mōld'wörp*, (*archaic* and *dialect*) *n* a mole (the animal). — Also (*Scot*) **mowdiewart, mowdiwort** (*mow'-di-wûrt*), **moudiewart, moudiewort** (*mōō'di-wûrt*). [OE *molde* mould, earth, and *weorpan* to throw; cf OHGer *multwurf* (Ger *Maulwurf*), Dan *muldvarp*]

moulin *mōō'lē*, *n* a shaft in a glacier worn by water running down a crack. — *n* **moulinet** (*mōō-li-net'* or *mōō'*) a machine for bending a crossbow. — *n* **Moulinette®** (*mōō-li-net'*) or **Mouli®** (*mōō'li*) a hand-operated, rotary device for puréeing food. [Fr *moulin* mill, and dimin *moulinet*, from LL *molīnum*]

moult or (*NAm*) **molt** *mōlt*, *vi* to shed feathers or another covering; to be shed. — *vt* to shed. — *n* the act, process, condition or time of moulting. — *adj* **moult'en** (*Shakesp*) having moulted. — *n* **moult'ing**. [OE (*bi*)*mūtian* to exchange, from L *mūtāre*; the *l*, introduced in spelling on analogy with *fault*, etc, afterwards sounded]

mound[1] *mownd*, *n* a boundary-fence or hedge (*obs*); a bank of earth or stone raised as a protection; a hillock; a heap. — *vt* to enclose with a fence or an embankment (*obs*); to fortify with an embankment; to heap in a mound. — **mound'-bird** the megapode, a bird of the Australian family *Megapodidae*, gallinaceous birds that build large mounds as incubators; **Mound Builder** a member of any of the prehistoric N American Indian peoples who built great earthworks in the south-eastern United States; **mound'-builder** a mound-bird. [Origin obscure; OE *mund* means guardianship]

mound[2] *mownd*, (*esp heraldry*) *n* a sovereign's orb. [Fr *monde*, from L *mundus* the world]

mounseer *mown'sēr* or *-sēr'*, (*archaic*, *illiterate*, or *derisive*) *n* for *monsieur*, a Frenchman.

mount[1] *mownt*, *n* a mountain (*archaic* except as **Mount**, as prefix to a name); a small hill or mound, natural or artificial; a fleshy protuberance on the hand (*palmistry*). [OE *munt* and OFr *mont*, both from L *mōns, montis* mountain]

mount[2] *mownt*, *vi* to go up; to climb; to get up on horseback, a bicycle, etc; to extend upward; to extend backward in time; to rise in level or amount; to amount (*obs*). — *vt* to climb, ascend; to get up on; to cover or copulate with; to cause to rise, to lift, raise, erect; to place on anything high; to put on horseback, etc; to provide with an animal, bicycle, etc to ride on; to fix in a setting, on a support, stand or backing; to provide with accessories; to put in position and state of readiness for use or exhibition; to stage; to be armed with; to carry, wear, or put on; to put into operation, carry out. — *n* a rise; an act of mounting; manner of mounting; a step to mount by; a signal for mounting; an animal, bicycle, etc that is ridden; that upon which a thing is placed or in which it is set for fixing, strengthening, embellishing, *esp* the card surrounding a picture; the slide, cover-glass, etc used in mounting an object for the microscope. — *adj* **mount'ed** on horseback; equipped with horses; set on high; raised on steps, generally three, as a cross (*heraldry*); set up; set. — *combining form* **-moun'ted** set in or with a specified material, as *silver-mounted*. — *n* **mount'er**. — *n* **mount'ing**. — **mount'ing-block** a block or stone to enable one to mount a horse. — **have the mount** to ride (a particular horse) in a race; **mount guard** see under **guard**. [Fr *monter* to go up, from L *mōns, montis* mountain]

mountain *mownt'in*, *n* a high hill; a wine made from mountain grapes; (in Ireland) wild pasture land; a large quantity or excess, *esp* of agricultural, dairy, etc products bought up by an economic community to prevent a fall in prices; (with *cap*) the extreme party in the French Revolution (see **Montagnard**). — *adj* of a mountain; growing, dwelling, etc on or among mountains. — *adj* **mount'ained**. — *n* **mountaineer'** an inhabitant of a mountainous area; a climber of mountains; a member of the Mountain (*hist*). — *vi* to climb mountains. — *n* **mountaineer'ing** mountain climbing. — *adj* **mount'ainous** full of, or characterized by, mountains; large as a mountain; huge. — **mountain ash** the rowan-tree; **mountain beaver** the sewellel; **mountain bicycle** or **bike** a bicycle with a strong, heavy frame and wide tyres designed for use over rough terrain; **mountain biking**; **mountain blue** blue carbonate of copper; **mountain bramble** the cloudberry; **mountain cat** a catamount, a wild-cat; **mountain chain** a range of mountains forming a long line; **mountain cork** and **mountain leather** a matted mass of a fibrous amphibole, cork-like or leathery in texture respectively; **mountain devil** a moloch; **mountain dew** (*colloq*) whisky; **mountain flax** amianthus; **mount'ain-everlast'ing** the cat's-foot (*Antennaria dioica*), a small woolly composite plant of the hills and seashore; **mountain goat** a white goatlike animal of the Rocky Mountains (genus *Oreamnus*); any of various wild goats of mountainous regions; **mountain hare** a small species of hare, grey in summer, *usu* white in winter. — *adv* and *adj* **mount'ain-high** or **mount'ains-high** high as a mountain, overwhelmingly high. — **mountain laurel** an ericaceous shrub of N America (genus *Kalmia*); **Mountain Limestone** the lowest division of the Carboniferous division of Palaeozoic rock in England, the Carboniferous Limestone; **mountain lion** the puma or cougar; **mountain marrow** lithomarge; **mountain meal** bergmehl; **mountain railway** or (*NAm*) **mountain railroad** a light narrow-gauge railway for mountainous regions, *usu* a rack-railway; **mountain ringlet** *Erebia epiphron*, a rare alpine butterfly; **mountain sheep** the bighorn, a large wild sheep of the Rocky Mountains, with large horns; **mountain sickness** sickness brought on by breathing rarefied air; **mount'ainside** the slope of a mountain; **mountain soap** a greasy kind of halloysite; **Mountain Standard Time** (or **Mountain Time**) the time zone that includes the Rocky Mountains in the USA, and parts of Canada; **mountain tallow** hatchettite; **mountain tea** the American evergreen plant *Gaultheria procumbens* (also called **wintergreen**); **mount'ain-top**; **mountain wood** a fibrous wood-like asbestos. — **Old Man of the Mountain** a popular name for the chief of the *Hashsh āshīn* (see **assassin**). [OFr *montaigne*, from L *mōns, montis* mountain. In some compounds *mountain* is used like Ger *Berg*, as if = mine]

mountant *mownt'ənt*, *n* an adhesive paste for mounting photographs, etc; any substance in which specimens are suspended on a microscope slide. — *adj* (*Shakesp*) rising on high. [Fr *montant*, pr p of *monter* to mount]

mountebank *mown'ti-bangk*, *n* a quack seller of remedies, etc (*obs*); a buffoon; a charlatan. — *vt* to gain or bring about by mountebankery. — *vi* (or *vt* with *it*) to act as a mountebank. — *n* **moun'tebankery, moun'tebanking** or **moun'tebankism**. [Ital *montimbanco, montambanco*, from *montare* to mount, *in* on, and *banco* bench]

mountenance *mount'ən-əns* or **mountenaunce** *-äns*, (*Spenser*) *n* amount; distance. [Appar OFr *montance*, assimilated to **maintenance**; cf **mount**[2] and **mountant**]

Mounty or **Mountie** *mown'ti*, (*colloq*) *n* a member of the Royal Canadian *Mount*ed Police.

moup or **moop** *mōōp*, (*Scot*) *vt* to nibble, munch; to mumble. — *vi* to nibble or munch (with *at* or *on*); to consort or live (with *with*). [Origin obscure]

mourn *mörn* or (*rare*) *mōōrn*, *vi* to grieve for a death or other loss; to be sorrowful; to wear mourning; to murmur sorrowfully (*literary*). — *vt* to grieve for; to utter in a sorrowful manner (*poetic*). — *n* **mourn'er** a person who mourns a death, etc; a person who attends a funeral, *esp* a relative of the deceased; a person hired to lament or weep for the dead; a penitent at a revival meeting (*US*). — *adj* **mourn'ful** causing, suggesting, or expressing sorrow; feeling grief. — *adv* **mourn'fully**. — *n* **mourn'fulness**. — *n* **mourn'ing** the act of expressing grief; the dress of mourners, or other tokens of mourning (also *Scot* in *pl*); the period during which one is officially mourning a death. — *adj* grieving, lamenting; suitable for, or concerned with, mourning. — *adv* **mourn'ingly**. — **mourn'ing-band** a band of black material worn round the sleeve or (*hist*) the hat, to signify that one is in mourning; **mourn'ing-border** a black margin used on notepaper, etc, by those in mourning; a dirty edge on a fingernail (*colloq*); **mourn'ing-bride** the sweet scabious (*Scabiosa atropurpurea*), a Mediterranean plant with a dome-like flower-head; **mourn'ing-cloak** an undertaker's cloak, formerly worn at a funeral; a large butterfly, the Camberwell beauty (*US*); **mourn'ing-coach** a closed carriage formerly used for carrying mourners to a funeral; **mourn'ing-dove** a N American pigeon (*Zenaidura macroura*) with a plaintive-sounding cry; **mourn'ing-piece** a picture intended to be a memorial of the dead; **mourn'ing-ring** a ring worn in memory of a dead person; **mourn'ing-stuff** any lustreless black dress fabric, such as crape, cashmere, etc, for making mourning clothes. — **half-mourning** see under **half**; **in mourning** wearing black (in China, white) in token of mourning; (of a ship) painted blue; having black eyes (*slang*). [OE *murnan*; OHGer *mornēn* to grieve]

mournival *mör'ni-vəl*, *n* in the card-game gleek, a set of four aces, kings, etc. [Fr *mornifle*]

mousaka. Same as **moussaka**.

mouse *mows*, *n* any of several small rodents of the genus *Mus*, often found in houses and fields; extended to various voles and other animals more or less like the mouse, such as the *flitter*-mouse or *shrew*-mouse; a device, linked to a computer terminal by an electrical wire, which is moved by hand over a flat surface thereby causing the cursor to move correspondingly on screen (*comput*); a small lead weight used to balance sash windows; a term of endearment (*obs*); a muscle (*obs*); part of a hindleg of beef, next to the round (*dialect*; also **mouse'-buttock** or **mouse'piece**); a match for firing a cannon or mine (*obs*); a knot or knob to prevent slipping (*naut*; also **mous'ing**); a black eye, or discoloured swelling (*slang*); a timid, shy, colourless person: — *pl* **mice** (*mīs*). — *vi* (*mowz*) to hunt for mice or as if for mice; to prowl. — *vt* to treat or to tear as a cat does a mouse; to paw or handle amorously (*archaic*); to secure with a mouse (*naut*). — *n* **mouse'kin** (*archaic*) or **mous'ie** a young or little mouse. — *n* **mouser** (*mow'zer* or *mow'sər*) a cat good at catching mice; a prying person (*archaic*). — *n* **mousery** (*mows'ər-i*) a place where mice habitually gather. — *adj* **mousey** or **mousy** (*mows'i*) like a mouse in colour or smell; full of or infested with mice; noiseless, stealthy; (of hair) of a dull light-brown or greyish-brown colour; (of a person) shy or unassertive. — *n* and *adj* **mousing** (*mow'zing* or *mow'sing*). — *vt* **mousle** (*mowz'l*) to pull about roughly or disrespectfully. — **mouse'-colour** the grey colour of a mouse. — *adj* **mouse'-colour** or **mouse'-coloured**. — **mouse'-deer** a chevrotain. — *adj* **mouse'-dun** mouse-coloured. — **mouse'-ear** a name of several plants with soft leaves shaped like a mouse's ear, *esp* forget-me-not; **mouse-ear chickweed** any plant of the genus *Cerastium*, related to chickweed; **mouse-eared bat** a kind of bat, *Myotis myotis*, found chiefly in continental Europe and Western Asia; **mouse'-hole** a hole made or used by mice; a small hole or opening; **mouse'-hunt** (*Shakesp*) a mouser; **mouse'-milking** (*US slang*) the pursuit of any project requiring considerable time and money put into it, but yielding little profit; **mouse'-sight** myopia; **mouse'-tail** a small ranunculaceous plant (*Myosurus*) with a spike of seed-vessels very like the tail of a mouse; **mouse'-trap** a trap for mice; any cheese of indifferent quality; Cheddar cheese. [OE *mūs*, pl *mȳs*; Ger *Maus*, L *mūs*, Gr *mȳs* mouse, muscle]

mousmee or **mousmé** *mōō s'mā*, *n* a Japanese girl, *esp* a waitress. [Jap *musume*]

mousquetaire *mōōs-kə-ter'*, *n* a musketeer; a woman's cloak trimmed with ribbons, with large buttons, fashionable about 1855; a broad turnover linen collar worn a few years earlier. — **mousquetaire glove** a woman's glove, long-armed, loose at the top, and without a lengthwise slit. [Fr]

moussaka or **mousaka** *mōō-sä'kə*, *n* a Greek or Turkish dish consisting of alternate layers of minced lamb, aubergines and tomatoes, *usu* covered with béchamel sauce and cheese. [Mod Gr *mousakâs*, from Turk *musakka*]

mousse *mōōs*, *n* a light dish, either sweet or savoury, made with cream, eggs, flavouring etc, whisked separately and then folded together, *usu* eaten cold; a cosmetic preparation dispensed from an aerosol as a foam, used *esp* to style hair; a foamlike mixture of oil and sea water, produced by an oil spill and difficult to disperse (*oil industry*). [Fr, moss]

mousseline *mōōs-lēn'*, *n* fine French muslin; a very thin glassware; a claret glass made of it; a kind of mousse with whipped cream added; a dish made with mousseline sauce. — **mousseline-de-laine** (*-də-len'*) an all-wool muslin; **mousseline-de-soie** (*-də-swä'*) a silk muslin. — **mousseline sauce** a kind of sauce hollandaise made light by adding whipped cream or egg-white. [Fr]

moust. See **must**[5].

moustache *məs-*, *mus-* or *mōōs-täsh'* or (*US*) **mustache** (*məs-* or *mus'*), *n* the unshaved hair on a man's upper lip. — Also in *pl*. — *adj* **moustached'**. — *adj* **moustach'ial**. — **moustache'-cup** a cup with the top partly covered, formerly used to keep the moustache from getting wet. — **old moustache** an old soldier. — See also **mustachio**. [Fr *moustache*, from Ital *mostaccio*, from Doric Gr *mystax*, *-akos* the upper lip, moustache]

Mousterian *mōōs-tē'ri-ən*, *adj* of an early Palaeolithic culture between Acheulean and Aurignacian. [Le *Moustier*, a cave on the Vézère which has yielded implements of this age]

moutan *mōō'tan*, *n* a tree peony. [Chin]

mouter *mōōt'ər*, a Scots form of **multure**.

mouth *mowth*, *n* the opening in the head of an animal or human by which it eats and utters sound; any opening or entrance, eg of a bottle, river, cave, etc; a person thought of as a consumer of food; a speaker; a spokesman or spokewoman; cry, voice, utterance; a wry face, a grimace; backchat, insolence or boastful talk; the responsiveness of a horse to the bit: — *pl* **mouths** (*mowdhz*). — *vt* (*mowdh*) to utter or pronounce (*archaic*); to utter with exaggerated, affectedly pompous, or self-conscious action of the mouth; to form (words) silently by moving the lips; to declaim or spout; to take in the mouth; to feel, mumble or mangle with the mouth; to train to the bit. — *vi* to declaim, rant (also *vt* with *it*); to join mouths, to kiss (*Shakesp*); to grimace; (of a river, etc) to debouch. — *adj* **mouthable** (*mowdh'ə-bl*) lending itself to recitation or oratory. — *combining form* **-mouthed** (*mowdhd*) having a mouth of a specified type, as *wide-mouthed*. — *n* **mouther** (*mowdh'ər*) a person who mouths. — *n* **mouth'ful** (*mowth'fəl*) as much food, etc as fills the mouth; a small quantity of food or drink; a big word; a momentous utterance (*slang*); an outburst of strong language: — *pl* **mouth'fuls**. — *adj* **mouth'less**. — *adj* **mouthy** (*mowdh'i*) ranting; inclined to backchat, cheeky (*colloq*); affectedly over-emphatic. — **mouth-breather** (*mowth'-brēdhər*) a person who habitually breathes through the mouth; **mouth'-breeder** a cichlid fish that carries its young in its mouth for protection; **mouth'feel** the sensory perception of a particular food while chewed, etc in the mouth. — *adj* **mouth-filling** (*mowth'*) full-sounding. — **mouth'-friend** (*Shakesp*) a person who only professes friendship; **mouth'-harp** a mouth-organ; **mouth'-honour** (*Shakesp*) insincere civility. — *adj* **mouth'-made** (*Shakesp*) insincere. — **mouth music** music (*usu* accompanying dance) sung, not played on or accompanied by instrument(s); **mouth'-organ** a small musical instrument encasing metallic reeds, played by the mouth, a harmonicon or harmonica; Pan-pipes; **mouth'parts** any of the limblike parts adapted for feeding that surround the mouth of an arthropod; **mouth'piece** the piece of a musical instrument, tobacco-pipe, mask, etc held to or in the mouth; a cigarette-holder; a spokesman or spokeswoman. — *adj* **mouth-to-mouth'** designating a method of artificial respiration in which a person breathes air directly into the patient's mouth to inflate the lungs. — **mouth'wash** an antiseptic solution for cleansing the mouth and for gargling with; rubbish, nonsense (*colloq*). — *adj* **mouth'watering** causing the release of saliva in the mouth, highly appetizing (also *fig*). — **be all mouth** (*slang*) to be unable to support one's boastful talk with action; **by word of mouth** see under **word**; **down in the mouth** see under **down**[3]; **have a big mouth** (*colloq*) to (habitually) talk indiscreetly, loudly, or too much; **keep one's mouth shut** (*colloq*) not to divulge a secret, etc; **make a poor mouth** to profess poverty; **mouth off** (*slang, esp US*) to express one's opinions forcefully and loudly, sound off; to boast, brag; **shoot one's mouth off** (*slang*) to talk freely, inaccurately, tactlessly, etc; **shut** or **stop the mouth of** to silence. [OE *mūth*; Ger *Mund*, Du *mond*]

mouton *mōō'tən*, *n* a sheepskin which has been processed, sheared and dyed to resemble the fur of another animal. [Fr *mouton* a sheep]

mouvementé *mōōv-mā-tā*, (*Fr*) *adj* full of movement, lively.

move *mōōv*, *vt* to cause to change place or posture; to set in motion; to impel; to excite to action; to cause (the bowels) to be evacuated; to persuade; to instigate; to arouse; to provoke; to provoke to anger (*obs*; now *move to anger* or *move anger in*); to touch the feelings or sentiments of; to propose formally before those present at a meeting; to recommend. — *vi* to go from one place to another; to change place or posture; to walk, to carry oneself; to change residence; to make a motion as in an assembly; to bow or salute on meeting (*archaic*); to begin to act; to take action; to become active or exciting (*colloq*); to hurry up (*colloq*); to go about one's activities, live one's life, pass one's time; (in chess, draughts, etc) to transfer a piece in one's turn to another square: — *pr p* **mov'ing**; *pa t* and *pa p* **moved**. — *n* an act of moving; a beginning of movement; a proceeding or step, a manoeuvre; the changing of one's residence or business premises; play in turn, as at chess; (in chess, draughts, etc) one's turn to play; advantage depending on whose turn it is to play; the manner in which a chessman or other playing-piece is or can be moved. — *n* **movabil'ity** or **moveabil'ity**. — *adj* **movable** (*mōōv'ə-bl*) mobile; changeable; not fixed; other than heritable (*Scots law*). — Also (*esp law*) **move'able**. — *n* (*esp* in *pl*) a portable piece of furniture; a piece of movable or moveable property (*Scots law*). — *n* **mov'ableness** or **move'ableness**. — *adv* **mov'ably** or **move'ably**. — *adj* **move'less** motionless, immobile; immovable. — *adv* **move'lessly**. — *n* **move'lessness**. — *n* **move'ment** an act or manner of moving; change of position; an action or gesture; activity; impulse; motion of the mind, emotion; the moving parts in a mechanism, *esp* the wheelwork of a clock or watch; melodic progression; accentual character (*prosody*); tempo or pace; a main division of an extended musical composition, with its own more or less independent structure; the suggestion of motion conveyed by a work of art; a general tendency or current of thought, opinion, taste or action, whether organized and consciously propagated or a mere drift. — *n* **mov'er**. — *adj* **mov'ing** causing motion; changing position; affecting the feelings, sentiments or sympathies; pathetic. — *adv* **mov'ingly**. — **movable feast** a church feast, such as Easter, whose date varies from year to year; **movement chart** a chart plotting the movements of staff and documents within an office, intended to improve efficiency; **movement therapist** a specialist in **movement therapy**, a physical therapy for the mentally or physically disabled aimed at developing or improving voluntary body movements; **moving average** a sequence of values derived from an earlier sequence from which a mean was taken of each successive group of values with a constant number of members. — *adj* **mov'ing-coil** of, or relating to, electrical equipment that incorporates a coil of wire so placed within a magnetic field as either to vibrate when current is passed through it, or to generate a current when vibrated. — **moving map** a map used on board a ship or aircraft that adjusts to keep the position of the moving vessel always in correspondence with a fixed centre point on the map; **moving pavement** (in an airport, etc) a moving strip set into the floor that carries pedestrians along as though on a conveyor belt; **moving pictures** the cinema; cinema films in general; **moving staircase** an escalator. — **get a move on** to hurry up; to make progress; **know a move or two** to be sharp or streetwise; **make a move** to take a step, perform a manoeuvre; to prepare to depart; **make a move on** or **put the moves on** (*slang, esp US*) to make sexual advances to; **move heaven and earth** see under **heaven**; **move house** to move to a new place of residence; to move one's possessions to one's new home; **move in** to occupy new premises, etc; **move in on** (*colloq*) to advance towards, close in on; to take steps towards controlling or usurping; **move out** to vacate premises; **move over** or **up** to move so as to make room for someone, etc; **movers and shakers** (*esp US*) the people with power and influence; **on the move** changing or about to change one's place; travelling; progressing. [Anglo-Fr *mover*, OFr *movoir* (Fr *mouvoir*), from L *movēre* to move. The obsolete **meve, mieve** represent those forms in Fr with accented root-syllable, such as *meuvent* (3rd pers pl)]

movie *mōōvē*, (*colloq*) *n* a motion picture, a cinema film; a showing of such; (in *pl*, **movies**, *usu* with **the**) motion pictures in general, or the industry that produces them. — Also *adj*. — **mov'iegoer**; **mov'ieland** the world of film-making; **mov'ie-maker**. [*Mov*ing picture and suffix **-ie**]

Moviola® *mōō-vē-ō'lə*, *n* a brand of upright film-editing machine (also used generically) combining image and soundtrack facilities, largely superseded by the more flexible multi-track desk-type machine. [**movie** and **Pianola**]

mow[1] *mow*, also *mō*, *n* a wry face. — *vi* to make grimaces. — Also **moe** (*obs*). — **nae mows** (*nā mowz*; *Scot*) no laughing matter. [OFr *moue*, *moe* (Fr *moue*), or MDu *mouwe*, both meaning grimace]

mow[2] *mow* or *mō*, *n* a pile of hay, corn in sheaves, pease, etc, *esp* in a barn; a place in a barn for such a heap. — *vt* to heap in a mow: — *pr p* **mow'ing**; *pa t* and *pa p* **mowed** (*mowd*). — *vi* **mow'burn** to heat and ferment in the mow. — *adj* **mow'burnt**. [OE *mūga* heap; ON *mūgi* swath, crowd, mob]

mow[3] *mō*, *vt* to cut down, or cut the grass on, with a scythe or now *esp* a grass-cutting machine; to cut down in great numbers (also *fig*): — *pr p* **mow'ing**; *pa t* **mowed** (*mōd*); *pa p* **mowed** or **mown** (*mōn*). — *adj* **mowed** or **mown**. — *n* **mow'er** a person who mows grass, etc; a machine with revolving blades for mowing grass. — *n* **mow'ing** the act of cutting grass, etc; land from which grass is cut. — **mow'ing-machine**. [OE *māwan*; Ger *mähen*; L *metere* to reap]

MOW *abbrev*: Movement for the Ordination of Women.

mowa *mow'ə* or **mowra** *mow'rə*. Same as **mahua**.

mowdiwart, **mowdiewart**, **mowdiwort** and **mowdiewort**. Scots forms of **mouldwarp**.

mown. See under **mow**[3].

mowra. See **mowa**.

moxa *mok'sə*, *n* the leaf down of any of several wormwoods (*esp Artemisia moxa*), or sunflower pith, cotton-wool, or other material, *usu* formed into a cone or stick and burned as a counter-irritant or for cauterization in Oriental medicine. — *n* **moxibustion** (*-bust'yən*; modelled on *combustion*) cauterization by moxa; the burning of a herbal moxa as a counter-irritant. [Jap *mogusa*]

moxie *mok'si*, (*US slang*) *n* courage, daring; energy, vigour. [*Moxie*®, a soft drink]

moy *moi*, (*Shakesp*) *n* supposed by Pistol (misunderstanding a Frenchman's *moi* me) to be the name of a coin, or possibly a measure (Fr *muid*, from L *modius*) of corn.

moya *moi'ä*, *n* volcanic mud. [Prob Am Sp]

Moygashel® *moi'gə-shel*, *n* (also without *cap*) a type of linen manufactured in Northern Ireland. [Place name]

moyity (*Spenser*). Same as **moiety**.

moyle (*Spenser*). Same as **moil**.

moyl or **moyle** *moil*, (*obs*) *n* a mule. [OFr *mul*, *mule*]

moz or **mozz** *moz*, (*Austr slang*) *n* a curse or jinx. — *n* **mozz'le** luck, *esp* bad luck. [Heb *mazzāl* luck]

Mozarab *mō-zar'ab*, *n* a privileged Christian Spaniard under Moorish rule. — *adj* **Mozar'abic**. [Sp *Mozárabe*, from Ar *musta'rib* would-be Arab]

Mozartian or **Mozartean** *mō-tsär'ti-ən*, *adj* of or like (the style, etc of) Wolfgang Amadeus *Mozart* (1756–1791), Austrian composer.

moze *mōz*, (*textiles*) *vt* to gig, raise a nap on. [Origin obscure]

mozetta *mō-tset'ə*, *n* a short cape to which a hood may be attached, worn by popes, cardinals, bishops and abbots. — Also **mozzett'a**. [Ital, dimin from *mozzo* docked]

mozz. See **moz**.

mozzarella *mot-sə-rel'ə*, *n* a mild, white Italian cheese with a springy texture, *orig* (and still occasionally) made from buffalo's milk. [Ital]

mozzie. See **mossie**.

mozzle. See under **moz**.

MP *abbrev*: Member of Parliament; Metropolitan Police; Military Police; mounted police; Municipal Police (*US*).

mp *abbrev*: mezzo-piano; melting-point.

MPAA *abbrev*: Motion Picture Association of America.

mpg *abbrev*: miles per gallon.

mph *abbrev*: miles per hour.

MPharm *abbrev*: Master of Pharmacy.

MPhil *abbrev*: Master of Philosophy.

mpret *bret*, *n* a former title of the ruler of Albania. [Albanian, from L *imperātor* emperor]

MPS *abbrev*: Member of the Pharmaceutical Society; Member of the Philological Society.

MPV *abbrev*: multipurpose vehicle.

MR *abbrev*: Master of the Rolls; Mauritian rupee; motivation(al) research (investigative study of consumer reaction).

Mr *mis'tər*, *n* the normal form of title prefixed to a man's name, whether full name or surname only, or sometimes to an office held by a man: — *pl* sometimes **Messrs** (*mes'ərz*). — **Mr Right** (*colloq*) the ideal mate or marriage partner sought by a woman. [Abbrev of **Mister**]

MRA *abbrev*: Moral Rearmament.

MRC *abbrev*: Medical Research Council.

MRCA *abbrev*: multirole combat aircraft.

MRCGP *abbrev*: Member of the Royal College of General Practitioners.

MRCP *abbrev*: Member of the Royal College of Physicians.

MRE (*military*) *abbrev*: Meal(s) Ready to Eat.

MRG *abbbrev*: Minority Rights Group.

MRI *abbrev*: magnetic resonance imaging.

mridangam, **mridamgam**, *mri-däng'gəm*, **mridanga** *mri-däng'gə* or **mridang** *mri-däng'*, *n* a two-headed Indian drum, one of the heads being larger than the other. [Sans *mṛdaṃga*]

mRNA (*genetics*) *abbrev*: messenger RNA.

M-roof. See under **M**.

MRRP *abbrev*: manufacturer's recommended retail price.

Mrs *mis'iz*, *n* the normal form of title prefixed to a married woman's name, whether her full name with her own or her husband's given name, or her surname only. [Abbrev of **Mistress**]

MS *abbrev*: manuscript; Mauritius (IVR); Mississippi (US state); multiple sclerosis.

Ms *miz* or *məz*, *n* a title substituted for **Mrs** or **Miss** before the name of a woman, to avoid distinguishing between the married and the unmarried.

ms *abbrev*: manuscript; millisecond; (or **M/S**) months.

MSA *abbrev*: motorway service area.

MSc *abbrev*: Master of Science.

MSDOS or **MS-DOS** *em-es-dos'*, (*comput*) *abbrev*: Microsoft disk-operating system.

MSF *abbrev*: Manufacturing, Science and Finance (Union); Médecins sans Frontières; medium standard frequency.

MSG *abbrev*: monosodium glutamate.

Msgr *abrev*: Monsignor.

msl *abbrev*: mean sea-level.

MSS or **mss** *abbrev*: manuscripts.

MST *abbrev*: mountain standard time.

msv *abbrev*: millisievert(s).

MSW *abbrev*: magnetic surface wave (*radar*); Medical Social Worker.

MT *abbrev*: mean time; Mechanical Transport; Montana (US state).

Mt *abbrev*: metical (currency of Mozambique); Mount.

MTB *abbrev*: motor torpedo-boat.

MTBF (*aeronautics*) *abbrev*: mean time between failures.

MTD (*radar*) *abbrev*: moving target detector.

mth *abbrev*: month.

Mts *abbrev*: Mountains.

mu *mū*, *mōō* or *mü*, *n* the Greek letter M, μ, equivalent to M or m; as a numeral, $\mu' = 40$, $_{,}\mu = 40000$; used as a symbol for **micron** and **micro-** (2). — **mu-** (or **μ-**) **meson** a subatomic particle, classed formerly as the lightest type of meson, now as the heaviest type of lepton, having unit negative charge, now largely superseded by **muon** (qv). [Gr *mȳ*]

mucate and **mucedinous**. See under **mucus**.

much *much*, *adj* (*compar* **more**; *superl* **most**) a great quantity of; great (*obs*); many (*Shakesp*). — *adv* in a great degree; to a great extent; in nearly the same way; by far; (in old ironical use) like the modern slang 'not much', I don't think. — *n* a great deal; anything of importance or worth. — Also in unshortened form (*archaic*) **much'el** *adj*, *adv*, and *n* (*Spenser* **much'ell** or **moch'ell**; *Scot* and *NEng* **mick'le** or **muck'le**). — *adv* (*archaic* and *jocular*) **much'ly**. — *n* **much'ness** (*archaic*) greatness; magnitude. — **a bit much** too much to put up with, unreasonable; **as much as** or **much as** although, even though; **make much of** see under **make**[1]; **much about it** something like what it usually is; **much of a muchness** just about the same value or amount; **not much of a** a rather poor specimen of a; **not up to much** (*colloq*) not very good; **too much for** more than a match for; **too much of a good thing** more than can be tolerated. [ME *muche*, *muchel*, from OE *micel*, *mycel*]

mucic, **mucid**, **muciferous** and **mucigen**. See under **mucus**.

mucilage *mū'si-lij*, *n* a gluey mixture of carbohydrates in plants; any sticky substance; gum used as an adhesive. — *adj* **mucilaginous** (*-laj'*). — *n* **mucilag'inousness**. [LL *mucilago* mouldy juice, from *mucēre* to be mouldy]

mucin. See under **mucus**.

muck *muk*, *n* dung; manure; wet or clinging filth; anything contemptible or worthless; dirt, debris, rubble; gold (*poetic* and *archaic*); rubbishy reading matter; a mess. — *vt* to clear of muck (with *out*); to manure with muck; to make dirty (with *up*); to make a mess of, to bungle (with *up*; *n* **muck'-up**); to treat inconsiderately (with *about* or *around*). — *vi* (*usu* with *about* or *around*; *colloq*) to potter; to act the fool. — *n* **muck'er** a person who mucks; a money-grubber (*obs*); a mess; a mishap, disaster (*orig* a fall in the mire); a coarse, unrefined person; a best friend, mate, sidekick; a young townsman, not a student (*archaic US*). — *vt* to hoard (*obs*); to squander; to vitiate. — *vi* to come to grief; to make a muddle of anything. — *n* **muck'iness**. — *adj* **muck'y** nasty, filthy; of the nature of muck; like muck. — **muck'heap** a dunghill; **muck'-midden**; **muck'-rake** a rake for scraping filth. — *vi* to seek out and expose scandals or supposed scandals, whether for worthy or unworthy motives. — **muck'-raker**; **muck'-raking**. — *vi* **muck'spread** to spread manure. — **muck'spreader** an agricultural machine for spreading manure; **muck'sweat** (*Brit*) profuse sweat; **muck'-worm** a worm or grub that lives in muck; a person who acquires money by mean devices; a miser. — **Lady** or **Lord Muck** (*facetious*) a title or name applied to a woman or man assuming aristocratic airs; **make a muck of** (*colloq*) to make dirty; to bungle, mismanage; **muck in (with)** (*colloq*) to share with; to help, participate (in). [Prob Scand; cf ON *myki*, Dan *mög* dung]

muckender *muk'ən-dər*, (*obs*) *n* a handkerchief; a table-napkin. [Appar from some Languedocian dialect; cf Fr *mouchoir*, Sp *mocador*]

Mucker *mŏŏk'ər*, *n* a nickname for a member of a Königsberg sect (1835) of dualistic theosophists; (without *cap*; *muk'ər*) a fanatical reformer; a hypocrite. [Ger]

muckle *muk'l*, a Scottish form of **mickle**.

muckluck, **mukluk** or **mucluc** *muk'luk*, *n* an Eskimo sealskin boot. [Eskimo]

mucoid. See under **mucus**.

mucor *mū'kər*, *n* a mould of the *Mucor* genus of zygomycete fungi, including some of the commonest moulds, giving name to an order or family **Mūcorā'les** or **Mūcorin'eae**. [L, mould]

mucosa and **mucosity**. See under **mucus**.

mucous. See under **mucus**.

mucro *mū'krō*, (*biol*) *n* a short stiff sharp point forming an abrupt end: — *pl* **mūcrō'nes** (*-nēz*) or **mū'cros**. — *adj* **mu'cronate** (*-krən-āt*) or **mu'cronated** (*-id*). [L *mūcrō*, *-ōnis* a sharp point]

mucus *mū'kəs*, *n* the slimy fluid secreted by various membranes in the body, which it moistens and protects. — *n* **mu'cate** a salt of mucic acid. — *adj* **mucedinous** (*-sed'* or *-sēd'*) mouldy, mildewy. — *adj* **mu'cid** mouldy, musty. — *adj* **muciferous** (*-sif'*) secreting or conveying mucus. — *n* **mu'cigen** (*-si-jen*) a substance secreted by the cells of mucous membrane, converted into mucin. — *n* **mu'cin** (*mu'sin*) any one of a class of albuminous substances in mucus. — *adj* **mucoid** (*mū'koid*) like mucus. — *adj* **mucopū'rulent** of mucus and pus. — *n* **mucosa** (*mū-cō'sə*) a mucous membrane: — *pl* **mucō'sae** (*-sē*). — *adj* **mucosanguin'eous** consisting of mucus and blood. — *n* **mucos'ity**. — *adj* **mu'cous** like mucus; slimy; viscous; producing mucus. — *n* **mucoviscidō'sis** cystic fibrosis. — *adj* **mu'cūlent** like mucus. — **mucic acid** a colourless crystalline acid obtained from lactose; **mucous membrane** a lining of various tubular cavities of the body, eg the nose, with glands secreting mucus. [L *mūcus* nose mucus; cf *mungere* to wipe away]

mud *mud*, *n* wet soft earth; a mixture of earthy or clayey particles with water; a similar mixture with certain added chemicals used as a lubricant in drilling gas- or oil-wells; something worthless or contemptible; vilification, abuse, slander, thought of as sticking or clinging like mud. — *vt* to bury in mud; to clog with mud; to plaster with mud; to make dirty; to make turbid; to supply with mud. — *vi* to hide in the mud. — *n* **mudd'er** (*slang*) a racehorse that responds well to muddy conditions. — *adv* **mudd'ily**. — *n* **mudd'iness**. — *adj* **mudd'y** foul with mud; containing mud; covered with mud; of the nature of mud; like mud; mud-coloured; cloudy, murky; confused, befuddled; stupid. — *vt* and *vi* to make or become muddy: — *pr p* **mudd'ying**; *pa t* and *pa p* **mudd'ied**. — **mud'bath** a bath in mud, *esp* as a medical treatment; an outdoor event taking place in muddy conditions (*colloq*); **mud'-boat** a board or sled for conveyance over mud-flats or swamps; a boat for carrying away dredged mud; **mud'cat** (*US*) a name given to several species of catfish; **mud'-clerk** (*obs US*) an assistant purser; **mud'-cone** a cone formed by a mud volcano; **mud dauber** a wasp of the family *Sphecidae* that deposits its eggs in individual cells constructed of mud. — *adj* **muddy-head'ed** confused, muddled. — *adj* **muddy-mett'led** (*Shakesp*) spiritless. — **mud engineer** a person overseeing the use and supply of drilling mud on a gas- or oil-well; **mud'fish** a fish that burrows in mud, *esp* a lung-fish; **mud'flap** a flap fixed behind the wheels of a vehicle to prevent mud, etc, being thrown up behind; **mud'flat** a muddy stretch of land, *esp* near a river mouth, submerged at high water; **mud'guard** a curved hood fixed over a wheel to catch mud-splashes thrown up by it; **mud hen** any of a variety of water-birds, such as rails, coots or gallinules, that inhabit marshy places; **mud'-hole** a hole with mud in it; an opening for removing sediment from a boiler, etc; **mud'hook** (*slang*) an anchor; **mud'lark** a name for various birds that frequent mud; a person who searches the banks of tidal rivers for scrap metal, ropes, etc, to sell; a street urchin (*archaic slang*); a mudder (*Austr slang*). — *vi* to work or play in mud. — **mud lava** a stream of mud from a volcano; **mudlogg'er** a person who looks for traces of oil, gas, etc in mud excavated from a borehole; **mudlogg'ing**; **mud'-lump** a raised area of mud, often giving off gases, as in the Mississippi delta; **mud minnow** a small fish (*Umbra*) related to the pikes; **mud'pack** a cosmetic paste for cleansing the skin, containing fuller's earth; **mud pie** a small, moulded mass of mud made to play with by children; an insult or calumny hurled at someone; a rich dessert of chocolate and coffee mousse on a pastry base (*NAm*); **mud pump** a pump used in drilling deep holes (eg oil wells) that forces thixotropic mud to the bottom of the hole and flushes out rock chips; **mudpuppy** (*US*) the axolotl; an aquatic salamander (genus *Necturus*) of N America that retains certain larval features, including external gills; **mud'-scow** a flat mud-boat; **mud skipper** a goby found in Africa, Japan, etc, able to remain out of water and skip about on bare mud using its fins; **mud'slide** a slippage of a mass of mud down a hillside, etc; **mud'slinger**; **mud'slinging** vilification or malicious slander intended to discredit another; **mud'stone** an argillaceous rock not distinctly fissile; **mud turtle** a freshwater turtle of the genus *Kinosternon*, found in N and Central America; **mud volcano** a vent that emits gas and mud, often forming a conical mound; **mud'wort** a small mud-growing scrophulaceous plant (*Limosella aquatica*); **mud wrestling** competitive wrestling in an arena with a floor of wet mud. — **clear as mud** not at all clear; **his, her**, etc, **name is mud** he, she, etc, is very much out of favour; **mud in your eye** good health (used as a toast); **throw, fling** or **sling mud at** to insult, to slander. [Cf OLGer *mudde*, Du *modder*]

muddle *mud'l*, *vt* to make (eg water) muddy; to confuse; to mix up, fail to distinguish between (with *up*); to bungle; to mix, stir (drinks, etc; *US*). — *vi* to wallow, dabble, or grub in mud (*archaic*); to potter about; to blunder. — *n* confusion, mess; mental confusion, bewilderment. — *adj* **mudd'le-brained** mentally confused, muddled. — *n* **mudd'lehead** a blockhead. — *adj* **muddlehead'ed**. — *adv* **muddlehead'edly**. — *n* **muddle-head'edness**. — *n* **mudd'ler**. — **muddle away** to squander or fritter away confusedly; **muddle through** to get through difficulties blunderingly. [Frequentative of **mud**]

mudéjar *mŏŏ-dhā'hhar*, (*Sp*) *n* a Spanish Moor, *esp* one permitted to remain in Spain after the Christian reconquest: — *pl* **mudé'jares** (*-ās*). — *adj* of a style of architecture characteristic of the mudéjares. — Also with *cap*. [Ar *mudajjan* literally one allowed to remain]

mudge[1] *muj*, (*colloq* and *dialect*) *n* mud, sludge. [Perh from **mud** and **sludge**]

mudge[2] *muj*, (*colloq*) *vt* to blur, confuse. — *vi* to equivocate, prevaricate. — *n* **mud'ger**. [Orig used in *fudge and mudge*, poss from **muddle** and **fudge**[2]]

mudir *mōō-dēr'*, *n* a local governor. — *n* **mudir'ieh** or **mudir'ia** a mudir's province or office. [Ar *mudīr*]

mudra *mə-drä'*, *n* any of the symbolic hand gestures in Hindu religious ceremonies and classical Indian dance; a posture in which the body is held in yoga, an asana. [Sans, literally sign, token]

mueddin. See **muezzin**.

muenster. Same as **munster**.

muesli *mōō'zli* or *mü'zli*, *n* a dish of rolled oats, nuts, fruit, etc eaten *esp* as a breakfast cereal. — **muesli belt** (*humorous*) any area inhabited by (*usu* middle-class) health food addicts. [Swiss Ger]

muezzin *mōō-ez'in*, *n* the Muslim official who calls the faithful to prayer. — Also **muedd'in**. [Ar *mu'adhdhin*]

muff[1] *muf*, *n* a cylinder of fur or thick fabric for keeping the hands warm; a similar contrivance for keeping the feet, ears, etc warm; a mitt (*obs*); the female genitals (*vulg slang*). — *n* **muffettee'** (*obs*) a muffler; a woollen cuff. [Prob from Du *mof*; cf Ger *Muff* a muff]

muff[2] *muf*, (*colloq*) *n* a person who is awkward or unskilful, *esp* in sport; a duffer; a bungler, *esp* in sports; an unpractical person; a man lacking male vigour and heartiness (*derog*); someone who lacks savoir-faire; a failure, *esp* to hold a ball. — *vt* to perform awkwardly; to bungle; to miss. — *vi* to act clumsily, *esp* in letting a ball slip out of the hands. — *adj* **muff'ish**. [Poss **muff**[1]]

muffettee. See under **muff**[1].

muffin *muf'in*, *n* a soft, round, breadlike cake, eaten hot, with butter; a cup-shaped cake made with batter (*NAm*); a small plate; a man accompanying or chaperoning a young woman (*slang*); a poor ball-player. — *n* **muffineer'** a dish for keeping muffins hot; a castor for sprinkling salt or sugar on muffins. — **muff'in-bell** a bell rung by a muffin man; **muff'in-cap** a round flat cap for men; **muff'in-fight** or **-worry** (*colloq*) a tea-party; **muffin man** an itinerant muffin-seller; **muff'in-pan** (*NAm*) a baking tray with cup-shaped indentations for making muffins. [Origin unknown]

muffle[1] *muf'l*, *n* the thick naked upper lip and nose of an animal, eg a ruminant. [Fr *mufle*]

muffle[2] *muf'l*, *vt* to envelop, for warmth, concealment, stifling of sound, etc; to blindfold (*archaic*); to deaden or dull the sound of. — *n* a boxing-glove (*obs*); a means of muffling; a receptacle, oven, or compartment in which things can be heated in a furnace without contact with the fuel and its products; (a kiln containing) an inner chamber in which to fire painted porcelain, enamel, etc; a muffled state; a muffled sound. — *adj* **muff'led**. — *n* **muff'ler** a scarf for the throat; any means of muffling; someone who muffles; a silencer fitted to the exhaust of a motor vehicle (*NAm*). — **muffler shop** (*NAm*) a garage specializing in fitting and repairing mufflers. [Appar Fr *mouffle* mitten]

muflon. See **moufflon**.

MUFTI *abbrev*: Minimum Use of Force Tactical Intervention.

Mufti *muf'ti*, *n* an expounder of Muslim law: — *pl* **Muf'tis**. — *n* **Muf'tat** or **Muf'tiat** a religious judicial board in an Islamic state or republic. [Ar *muftī*, from *'aftā* to make a legal decision]

mufti *muf'ti*, *n* the civilian dress of someone who wears a uniform when on duty; plain clothes; a civilian. [Prob from **Mufti**]

mug[1] *mug*, *n* a cup with more or less vertical sides; its contents. — *n* **mug'ful** (*-fəl*): — *pl* **mug'fuls**. — *n* **mugg'er** a hawker of earthenware. — **mug'-house** (*obs*) an alehouse; **mug'-hunter** (*games*) a pot-hunter. [Poss Scand; cf Norw *mugga*, Swed *mugg*]

mug[2] *mug*, (*colloq*) *n* the face; the mouth. — *vi* (*theat*) to grimace. — **mug'shot** or **mug shot** (*colloq*) a photograph of a person's face, *esp* one taken for police records. [Poss from the grotesque face on a drinking-mug]

mug[3] *mug*, (*colloq*) *n* a simpleton; an easy dupe. — **a mug's game** something only fools would do. [Poss from **mug**[2]]

mug[4] *mug*, (*colloq*) *n* a sap or swot; an exam. — *vt* and *vi* (often with *up*) to study hard; to swot up. [Origin unknown]

mug[5] *mug*, *n* a woolly-faced sheep. — **mug'-ewe**, **mug'-lamb** and **mug'-sheep**.

mug[6] *mug*, (*slang*) *vt* and *vi* to attack from behind, seizing by the throat; to attack suddenly with the intention of robbing. — *n* **mugg'ee** the victim, or intended victim, of a mugger. — *n* **mugg'er**. — *n* **mugg'ing**. [Perh **mug**[2]]

mugearite *mōō-gēr'īt*, *n* a dark finely crystalline basic igneous rock composed mainly of oligoclase, orthoclase, and olivine, with iron oxides, developed at *Mugeary* in Skye.

mugger[1] *mug'ər*, *n* a broad-snouted Indian crocodile. [Hind *magar*]

mugger[2]. See under **mug**[1,6].

muggins *mug'inz*, *n* a children's card-game; a form of dominoes; a fool, sucker, *esp* used *facetiously* to refer to oneself as such. [Ety doubtful]

Muggletonian *mug-l-tō'ni-ən*, *n* a member of a sect founded by John Reeve and Lodowick *Muggleton* (1609–98), who claimed to be the two witnesses of Rev 11. 3–6.

muggy *mug'i*, *adj* foggy; (of weather) close and damp; (of straw, etc) wet or mouldy. — *n* **mugg'iness** dampness; a muggy condition. — *adj* **mugg'ish**. [Perh ON *mugga* mist]

Mughal. See **Mogul**.

mugwort *mug'wûrt*, *n* a common British wormwood. [OE *mucgwyrt*, literally midge-wort]

mugwump *mug'wump*, (*NAm*) *n* a N American Indian chief; a person of great importance, or one who thinks himself or herself to be so; someone who keeps politically aloof. — *n* **mug'wumpery**. [Algonquian *mugquomp* a great chief]

Muhammedan. See **Mohammedan**.

Muharram. See **Moharram**.

muid *mü-ē*, *n* an old French measure of capacity; a hogshead; a dry measure for corn, etc; (*SAfr*; *mā'id*) a sack of 3 bushels. [Fr, from L *modius*; cf Du *mud*]

muil. See **mule**[2].

muir, **muirburn**, etc. See under **moor**[1].

muist. See **must**[5].

mujahedin, **mujaheddin** or **mujahidin** *mōō'jə-həd-ēn'*, *n pl* Islamic fundamentalist freedom fighters. [Ar *mujāhidīn* fighters]

mujik. See **muzhik**.

mukhtar *mōōk'tär*, *n* an Indian lawyer; a chief local government official in Turkey. [Ar *mukhtār* chosen]

mukluk. See **muckluck**.

mulatto *mū-lat'ō*, *n* the offspring of a Black person and a person of European descent (also *adj*): — *pl* **mulatt'os** or **mulatt'oes**: — *fem* **mulatt'a** or **mulatt'ress**. [Sp *mulato*, dimin of *mulo* mule; Fr *mulâtre*]

mulberry *mul'bər-i*, *n* the edible blackberry-like fruit of any tree of the genus *Morus* (family *Moraceae*); the tree bearing it, with leaves on which silkworms feed; extended to various fruits or plants more or less similar superficially or really; the colour of the fruit, dark purple. — *adj* mulberry-coloured. — *adj* **mul'berry-faced** having a face blotched with purple. — **mul'berry-fig** the true sycamore (sycomore), a fig-tree with leaves like those of mulberry; **Mulberry harbour** a pre-constructed harbour (code name *Mulberry*) towed across the Channel for the 1944 landings in Normandy in World War II. [Prob OHGer *mulberi* (Mod Ger *Maulbeere*), from L *mōrum*; cf **Morus** and **berry**]

mulch *mulch* or **mulsh** *mulsh*, *n* loose material, strawy dung, etc, laid on the soil around plants, to protect roots, keep down weeds and retain moisture, sometimes with a nutritional function. — *vt* to cover with mulch. — *adj* soft. [Cf Ger dialect *molsch* soft, beginning to decay; OE *melsc*]

Mulciber *mul'si-bər*, *n* Vulcan, the Roman god of fire and metalworking. — *adj* **Mulcibē'rian**. [L]

mulct *mulkt, n* a fine; a penalty. — *vt* to fine; to swindle; to deprive (with *of*): — *pap* **mulct'ed** or **mulct**. [L *mulcta* a fine]

mule[1] *mūl, n* the offspring of a donkey (*esp* male) and a horse (*esp* female), widely used as a beast of burden; a hybrid; a cross between a canary and another finch; a cotton-spinning machine; an obstinate person; a coin with obverse and reverse designs struck from dies of two different issues; a person who smuggles drugs into a country for a dealer (*slang*). — *adj* hybrid. — *n* **muleteer** (*mūl-i-tēr'*) a mule-driver. — *adj* **mul'ish** like a mule; obstinate. — *adv* **mul'ishly**. — *n* **mul'ishness**. — **mule'-deer** a long-eared, black-tailed deer of N America. [OE *mūl*, from L *mūlus* was superseded by OFr; *mul* (masc; in Mod Fr the dimin *mulet* is used), *mule* (fem), from L *mūlus, mūla*]

mule[2] *mūl* or (*Scot*) **muil** *mül, n* a backless slipper. [Fr *mule*]

muley, mulley or **mooly** *mōōl'i* or *mūl'i, adj* hornless. — *n* a hornless cow; any cow. [Gaelic *maol* or Welsh *moel* bald]

mulga *mul'gə, n* any of several acacias, *esp Acacia aneura*, typically found in arid regions of Australia; (with *the*) the outback. — **mulga wire** (*Austr*) the bush telegraph. [Aboriginal]

muliebrity *mū-li-eb'ri-ti, n* womanhood. [L *muliebritās, -tātis*, from *mulier* a woman]

mull[1] *mul, n* a muddle. — *vt* to bungle. [Ety doubtful]

mull[2] *mul*, (*Scot*) *n* a promontory. [Prob Gaelic *maol* or ON *mūli* snout; cf Ger *Maul*]

mull[3] *mul*, (*Scot*) *n* a snuffbox. [See **mill**[1]]

mull[4] *mul, n* a soft muslin. — Also **mul'mul** or **mul'mull**. [Hindustani *malmal*]

mull[5] *mul, vi* and *vt* (often with *over*) to cogitate, ponder, turn over in the mind. [Origin obscure]

mull[6] *mul, vt* to crumble. — *n* a layer of humus formed by rapid decompostion, through the actions of a rich soil fauna, in near-neutral or alkaline conditions. — Cf **moder, mor**[1]. [Cf OE *myl* dust]

mull[7] *mul, vt* to warm, spice and sweeten (wine, ale, etc). — *adj* **mulled**. — *n* **mull'er**. [Origin obscure]

mull[8] *mul*, (*Shakesp*) *vt* to dull, stupefy. [Origin obscure; perh from the mulling of wine]

mullah, moolah, mollah or **molla** *mul'ə, mōōl'ə, mŏŏ'lə* or *mol'ə, n* a Muslim learned in theology and law; a Muslim schoolmaster or teacher; a title of respect for a person whose work lies in advising on or expounding the law, etc; a fanatical preacher of war on the infidel. [Pers, Turk and Hindi *mullā*, from Ar *maulā*]

mullarky. Same as **malarkey**.

mullein *mul'in, n* a tall, stiff, yellow-flowered woolly plant (*Verbascum*) of the *Scrophulariaceae*, popularly known as *hag-taper, Adam's flannel, Aaron's rod* or *shepherd's club*. [Anglo-Fr *moleine*]

muller *mul'ər, n* a flat heavy stone or iron pulverizing tool. [Perh OFr *moloir*, from *moldre* (Fr *moudre*) to grind]

mullet[1] *mul'it, n* a nearly cylindrical food fish of the family *Mullidae* (**red mullet**) or *Mugilidae* (**grey mullet**). [OFr *mulet*, dimin from L *mullus* red mullet]

mullet[2] *mul'it*, (*heraldry*) *n* a five-pointed star, the cadency mark of a son. [OFr *molette* rowel of a spur, from L *mola* a millstone]

mulley. See **muley**.

mulligan *mul'i-gən*, (*colloq*) *n* a stew made from various scraps of food (*US*); a second tee shot awarded after a poor initial shot (*golf*). [Perh from the surname]

mulligatawny *mul-i-gə-tö'ni, n* an East Indian curry-soup. [Tamil *milagu-tannīr* pepper-water]

mulligrubs *mul'i-grubz*, (*colloq*) *n pl* colic; sulkiness.

mullion *mul'yən*, (*archit*) *n* an upright division between the panes or casements of a window. — *adj* **mull'ioned**. [Poss by metathesis from older, synonymous *monial*, from OFr]

mullock *mul'ək*, (*Austr*) *n* rubbish, *esp* mining refuse. — **poke mullock at** to mock, ridicule. [From obs or dialect *mull* dust; cf OE *myl*]

mulloway *mul'ə-wā, n* a large Australian food-fish, *Sciaena antarctica*. [Origin unknown]

mulmul and **mulmull**. See **mull**[4].

mulse *muls*, (*obs*) *n* a drink of honey and wine or honey and water. [L *mulsum*, from *mulsus* mixed with honey]

mulsh. Same as **mulch**.

multi- *mul-ti-* , or sometimes before a vowel **mult-** *mult-*, *combining form* denoting much, many. — *adj* **multang'ular** having many angles. — *adj* **multan'imous** (L *animus* mind) having a many-sided mind. — *adj* **multartic'ulate** or **multiartic'ulate** many-jointed. — *adj* **multi-acc'ess** (*comput*) denoting a system which permits several operators working at different terminals to have access to its facilities at the same time. — *adj* **multi-auth'or** or **multi-auth'ored** denoting a text which has been written by several individuals. — *adj* **multicam'erate** (L *camera* chamber) having many chambers or cells. — *adj* **multicap'itate** (L *caput, -itis* head) many-headed. — *adj* **multicau'line** (L *caulis* stem) having many stems. — *adj* **multicell'ular** having or made up of many cells. — *adj* **multicen'tral** or **multicen'tric** having or proceeding from many centres. — *adj* **multichann'el** having or employing several communications channels. — *adj* **multicipital** (*mul-ti-sip'i-təl*; L *caput, -itis* head) having many heads, multicapitate. — *n* **multicolour** (*mul'ti-kul-ər*) diversity or plurality of colour. — *adj* many-coloured. — *adj* **mul'ticoloured**. — *adj* **multicos'tate** (L *costa* rib) many-ribbed. — *adj* **multicul'tural** (of a society) made up of many distinct cultural groups. — *n* **multicul'turalism** the policy of accommodating any number of distinct cultures within the one society without prejudice or discrimination. — *adj* **multicus'pid** having more than two cusps. — *n* a multicuspid tooth. — *adj* **multicus'pidate**. — *n* **mul'ticycle** (*obs*) a velocipede with more than three wheels; one intended to carry several people. — *adj* **multiden'tate** (L *dēns, dentis* tooth) many-toothed. — *adj* **multidentic'ūlate** having many denticulations or fine teeth. — *adj* **multidigitate** (*-dij'i-tāt*; L *digitus* finger) many-fingered. — *adj* **multidimen'sional** of more than three dimensions (*math*); having several aspects or dimensions. — *adj* **multidirec'tional** extending in a number of directions. — *adj* **multidisciplin'ary** involving a combination of several (academic) disciplines, methods, etc. — *adj* **multieth'nic** composed of or relating to more than one ethnic group. — *adj* **mul'tifaced** many-faced. — *adj* **multifac'eted** (of a gem) having many facets; having many aspects, characteristics, etc. — *adj* **multifactor'ial** involving or caused by many different factors. — *adj* **mul'tifid** or **multif'idous** cleft into many lobes. — *n* **mul'tifil** or **multifil'ament** a multiple strand of synthetic fibre. — *adj* **multifil'ament** composed of many filaments. — *adj* **multiflo'rous** many-flowered. — *adj* **mul'tifoil** having more than five foils or arcuate divisions. — *n* a multifoil ornament. — *adj* **multifō'liate** (L *folium* leaf) with many leaves. — *adj* **multifō'liolate** (*bot*) with many leaflets. — *adj* **mul'tiform** having many forms, polymorphic. — *n* that which is multiform. — *n* **multiform'ity**. — *adj* **mul'tigrade** of or relating to a motor oil with a viscosity such as to match the properties of several grades of motor oil. — *n* **multigrav'ida** (L *gravida* pregnant) a pregnant woman who has had one or more previous pregnancies: — *pl* **multigrav'idae** (*-dē*) or **multigrav'idas**. — *n* **mul'tigym** an apparatus incorporating weights and levers in a variety of arrangements, enabling one to exercise and tone up one set of muscles at a time. — *n* **mul'tihull** a sailing vessel with more than one hull. — *adj* **multiju'gate** or **multiju'gous** (L *jugum* yoke; *bot*) consisting of many pairs of leaflets. — *adj* **multilat'eral** (L *latus, lateris* side) many-sided; with several parties or participants. — *n* **multilat'eralism**. — *n* and *adj* **multilat'eralist** (a person) favouring multilateral action, *esp* in abandoning or reducing production of nuclear weapons. — *adj* **multilineal** (*-lin'*) or **multilin'ear** having many lines. — *adj* **multilingual** (*-ling'gwəl*; L *lingua* tongue) in many languages; speaking several languages; (of a country, state or society) in which several languages are spoken. — *n* **multilin'gualism** the ability to speak several languages. — *n* **multilin'guist** a person who is multilingual. — *adj* **multilō'bate** or **mul'tilobed** many-lobed. — *adj* **multilobular** (*-lob'ū-lər*) or **multilob'ulate** having many lobules. — *adj* **multilocular** (*-lok'ū-lər*) or **multiloc'ulate** many-chambered. — *n* **multil'oquence** much speaking. — *adj* **multil'oquent**. — *adj* **multil'oquous**. — *n* **multil'oquy**. — *n* **multimē'dia** the use of a combination of different media of communication (in eg entertainment or education); simultaneous presentation of several visual and/or sound entertainments. — Also *adj*. — *n* **multimillionaire'** a person who is a millionaire several times over. — *adj* **mul'timode** designating an optical fibre with a core diameter sufficiently larger than the wavelength of light to allow propagation of light energy in a large number of different modes. — *n* **multinat'ional** a large business company which operates in several countries. — *adj* of this type of company; multiracial (*SAfr*). — *adj* **multinō'mial** (*algebra*) consisting of more than two terms; relating to multinomials. — *n* a multinomial expression. — *adj* **multinom'inal** having many names. — *adj* **multinū'clear**, **multinū'cleate** or **multinū'cleated** having several nuclei. — *adj* **multinū'cleolate** having several nucleoli. — *n* **multi-own'ership** ownership of property on the principle of time-sharing (qv). — *n* **multipa'ra** (L *parĕre* to bring forth) a woman who has given birth for the second or subsequent time, or is about to do so, as distinct from a *primipara*. — *n* **multipar'ity** the condition of being a multipara; the condition of being multiparous. — *adj* **multip'arous** relating to a multipara; producing more than one at birth (*zool*); giving rise to several lateral axes (*bot*). — *adj* **multipar'tite** (L *partītus* divided) divided into many parts; much cut up into segments. — *n* **multipar'tyism** a political system based on the existence of more than one political party. — *n* **mul'tiped** (L *pēs*, *pedis* foot) a many-footed animal; a woodlouse (*obs*; also **multipede** *-pēd*). — *adj* **mul'tiphase** polyphase. — *n* **mul'tiplane** an aeroplane with more than two sets of supporting planes. — *n* **multi-ply** (*mul'ti-plī*) plywood of more than three thicknesses. — *adj* **multipō'lar** having several poles or axons. — *adj* **multip'otent** (L *potēns*, *-entis* powerful; *Shakesp*) having the power to do many things. — *n* **multipres'ence** the power of being in many places at once. — *adj* **multipres'ent**. — *n* **multipro'gramming** (*comput*) a technique of handling several programs simultaneously by interleaving their execution through time-sharing. — *adj* **multipur'pose**. — *adj* **multirā'cial** embracing, or consisting of, many races. — *n* **multirā'cialism** the policy of recognizing the rights of all in a multiracial society. — *adj* **multiram'ified** (L *rāmus* branch, and *facere* to make) having many branches. — *adj* **mul'tiscreen** designating a technique of cinema projection in which the screen is divided into several frames each showing separate images; (of a cinema) having more than one screen and auditorium. — *adj* **multisep'tate** (*biol*) having many septa. — *adj* **multisē'rial** or **multisē'riate** in many rows. — *n* **multiskill'ing** in technologically advanced industries, the training of employees in a variety of skills. — *adj* **multisonant** (*mul-tis'ən-ənt*; L *sonāns*, *-antis*, pr p of *sonāre* to sound) having many sounds; sounding much. — *adj* **multispī'ral** having many coils. — *adj* **mul'ti-stage** in a series of distinct parts; (of a rocket) consisting of a number of parts that fall off in series at predetermined places on its course. — *adj* **mul'tistorey** or (*esp NAm*) **mul'tistory** having a (large) number of levels of storeys. — *n* and *adj* **mul'tistrike** (designating) an ink ribbon for use on an electronic typewriter or printer which is struck by keys at different points vertically, often used to produce bold print. — *adj* **multisulc'ate** (L *sulcus* furrow) having many furrows. — *n* **multitask'ing** (*comput*) the action of running several processes or jobs simultaneously on a system. — *adj* of or relating to a system capable of doing this. — *adj* **mul'ti-track** (of a recording) made up of several different tracks blended together. — *adj* **multituber'culate** or **multituber'culated** (of eg teeth) having many tubercles. — *adj* **multiu'ser** (*comput*) of a computer, able to be used by several people at once. — *n* **multivā'lence** (or *-tiv'ə-*) or **multivā'lency** (or *-tiv'ə-*). — *adj* **multivā'lent** (or *-tiv'ə-*; *chem*) having a valency greater than one. — *adj* **multivār'iate** consisting of, or concerned with, many variables. — *adj* **multivār'ious** differing widely. — *n* **multiver'sity** a large university made of up several campuses. — *n* **multivibrā'tor** an electronic oscillating device using two transistors, the output of one providing the input of the other. — *adj* **multiv'ious** (L *via* way) going many ways. — *n* **multivit'amin** a pill containing several vitamins. — *adj* **multiv'ocal** (L *vōx vōcis* voice) having many meanings. — *n* a word of many meanings. — *adj* **multivoltine** (*-vol'tīn*; Ital *volta* turn, winding) of silkworm moths, having several annual broods. — *adj* **mul'ti-wall** made of three or more layers of special paper. — *adj* **multocular** (*mul-tok'ū-lər*; L *oculus* eye) having many eyes; (of a microscope) enabling several people to observe an object at once. — *adj* **multungulate** (*mul-tung'gū-lāt*; L *ungula* hoof) having the hoof divided into more than two parts. — *n* a multungulate mammal. [L *multus* much]

multangular ... to ... **multarticulate**. See under **multi-**.

multeity *mul-tē'i-ti*, *n* manifoldness, very great numerousness. [L *multus* much, many, and *-eity* as in *haecceity*]

multi-access ... to ... **multifactorial**. See under **multi-**.

multifarious *mul-ti-fā'ri-əs*, *adj* having great diversity; made up of many parts; manifold; in many rows or ranks (*bot*). — *adv* **multifā'riously**. — *n* **multifā'riousness** the state of being multifarious; multiplied variety; the fault of improperly joining in one bill distinct and independent matters, and thereby confounding them (*law*). [L *multifārius*; poss from *fārī* to speak]

multifid ... to ... **multiplane**. See under **multi-**.

multiple *mul'ti-pl*, *adj* consisting of many elements or components, *esp* of the same kind; manifold; compound; multiplied or repeated; allowing many messages to be sent over the same wire (*teleg*). — *n* a quantity which contains another quantity an exact number of times; an object for display, claimed to be art but designed for reproduction in numbers industrially. — *n* **mul'tiplet** an optical spectrum line having several components; a group of subatomic particles. — *adv* **multiply** (*mul'ti-pli*). — *adj* **multiple-choice'** (of an examination question) accompanied by several possible answers from which the correct answer is to be chosen. — **multiple cinema** a cinema which has been converted into two or more separate cinemas; **multiple fruit** a single fruit formed from several flowers in combination, such as a pineapple, fig or mulberry; **multiple personality** (*psychiatry*) a disorder in which the subject's personality fragments into a number of distinct personalities; **multiple sclerosis** a chronic progressive disease in which there is a patchy deterioration of the myelin forming a sheath for the nerve fibres, resulting in various forms of paralysis throughout the body; **multiple shop** or **store** any of a series of shops belonging to the same firm, often dispersed about the country; **multiple star** a group of stars so close as to seem one. — **common multiple** a number or quantity that can be divided by each of several others without a remainder; **least common multiple** the smallest number that forms a common multiple. [Fr, from LL *multiplus*, from root of L *plēre* to fill]

multiplepoinding *mul-ti-pl-pind'ing*, (*Scots law*) *n* a process by which a person who has funds claimed by more than one, in order not to have to pay more than once, brings them all into court so that one of them may establish his or her right.

multiplex *mul'ti-pleks*, *n* a multiple (*obs*); a system enabling two or more signals to be sent simultaneously on one communications channel (*telecomm*); a cinema divided up into several small cinemas, a multiple cinema. — *adj* multiple; of or designating a multiplex (*telecomm*). — *vt* to incorporate in a multiplex system (*telecomm*). — *n* **mul'tiplexer**. — *n* **mul'tiplexor** a device enabling a computer to transmit data to many terminals by switching quickly from one user's data to another's. [L *multiplex*, from *plicāre* to fold]

multiply[1] *mul'ti-plī*, *vt* to increase the number of; to accumulate; to magnify (*obs*); to reproduce; to obtain the product of (*math*). — *vi* to become more numerous; to be augmented; to reproduce; to perform the mathematical process of multiplication: — *pr p* **mul'tiplying**; *pa t* and *pa p* **mul'tiplied**. — *adj* **mul'tipliable** or **mul'tiplicable** (or *-plik'*). — *n* **mul'tiplicand** (or *-kand'*) a quantity to be multiplied by another (the multiplier). — *adj* **mul'tiplicate** (or *-tip'*) consisting of more than one; in many folds. — *n* the condition of being in many copies; any of these copies. — *n* **multiplicā'tion** the act of multiplying or increasing in number; increase of number of parts by branching (*bot*); the rule or operation by which quantities are multiplied. — *adj* **mult'iplicātive** (or *-plik'ə-tiv*) tending or having power to multiply; indicating how many times (*gram*). — *n* **mul'tiplicātor** (*math*) a multiplier. — *n* **multiplicity** (*-plis'i-ti*) the state of being manifold; a great number. — *n* **mul'tiplier** a person who multiplies; a quantity by which another is multiplied; a device or instrument for intensifying some effect (*phys*); a geared fishing-reel for drawing in the line quickly. — **multiplication constant** (*phys*) the ratio of the average number of neutrons produced by fission in one neutron lifetime to the total number of neutrons absorbed or leaking out in the same interval; **multiplication table** a tabular arrangement giving the products of pairs of numbers *usu* up to 12; **multiplying glass** (*obs*) a magnifying glass; a faceted glass for multiplying reflexions. — **multiply words** to say much; to be wordy. [Fr *multiplier*, from L *multiplicāre*, from *plicāre* to fold]

multiply[2] *mul'ti-pli*. See under **multiple**.

multi-ply ... to ... **multiramified**. See under **multi-**.

multiscience *mul-tish'əns*, *n* knowledge of many things. [LL adj *multiscius*, from L *scientia* knowledge]

multiseptate ... to ... **multituberculate**. See under **multi-**.

multitude *mul'ti-tūd*, *n* the state of being many; a great number or (*rare*) quantity; a crowd; the mob. — *adj* **multitud'inary** (*rare*). — *adj* **multitud'inous**. — *adv* **multitud'inously**. — *n* **multitud'inousness**. [L *multitūdō*, *-inis*, from *multus* much]

multiuser ... to ... **multocular**. See under **multi-**.

multum *mul'təm*, *n* an adulterant in brewing. [Prob neuter of L *multus* much]

multum in parvo *mul'təm* or *mōōl'tōōm in pär'vō*, also *-wō*, (*L*) much in little, a large amount in a small space.

multum non multa *mul'təm non mul'tə* or *nōn mōōl'ta*, (*L*) much, not many things.

multungulate. See under **multi-**.

multure *mul'tyər*, or (*Scot*) **mouter** *mōōt'ər*, *n* a fee, generally in kind, for grinding grain; the right to such a fee. — *vt* and *vi* to take multure (for). — *n* **mul'turer** or (*Scot*) **mou'terer** a person who receives multures; a miller; a person who pays multures. [OFr *molture*, *moulture*, from L *molitūra* a grinding]

mum[1] *mum*, *adj* silent. — *n* silence. — *interj* not a word. — *vi* (also **mumm**) to act in a mime; to act in a mummers' play; to masquerade: — *pr p* **mumm'ing**; *pa t* and *pa p* **mummed**. — *n* **mumm'er** an actor in a folk-play, *usu* at Christmas (*hist*); a masquerader; an actor (*facetious*). — *n* **mumm'ery** mumming; great show without reality; foolish ceremonial. — *n* **mumm'ing**. — *n* and *interj* **mum'-bud'get** (*obs*) mum. — *n* **mum'chance** a silent game with cards or dice (*obs*); a fool (*dialect*). — *adj* silent. — **mum's the word** complete silence or secrecy is demanded, or promised. [An inarticulate sound with closing of the lips; partly OFr *momer* to mum, *momeur* mummer; cf Du *mommen* to mask]

mum[2] *mum*, (*obs*) *n* a wheatmalt beer, sometimes with oat and bean meal. [Ger *Mumme*]

mum[3] *mum* or **mummy** *mum'i*, (*colloq*) *n* mother, used *esp* by a child to address or refer to its mother. — *adj* **mum'sy** (*colloq*) maternal; homely, comfy; old-fashioned. [Cf **mamma**[1]]

mum[4] *mum*. See **ma'am**.

mum[5] *mum*, (*esp NAm*) *n* a short form of **chrysanthemum**.

mumble *mum'bl*, *vt* and *vi* to say, utter or speak indistinctly, softly or perfunctorily; to mouth with the lips, or as if with toothless gums. — *n* **mum'blement** (*Carlyle*) mumbling speech. — *n* **mum'bler**. — *n* and *adj* **mum'bling**. — *adv* **mum'blingly**. — **mum'ble-news** (*Shakesp*) a tale-bearer. [Frequentative from **mum**[1]]

mumbo-jumbo *mum'bō-jum'bō*, *n* (with *cap*) a god or bugbear of W Africa; any object of foolish worship or fear; mummery, foolish ritual; baffling jargon, professional gobbledegook: — *pl* **mum'bo-jum'bos**. [Said to be from *Mama Dyanbo*, a Mandingo god]

mumchance, **mumm**, **mummer** and **mummery**. See under **mum**[1].

mummied and **mummify**. See under **mummy**[1].

mummock *mum'ək*. See **mammock**.

mummy[1] *mum'i*, *n* an embalmed or otherwise preserved dead body, *esp* as prepared for burial by the ancient Egyptians; the substance of such a body, formerly used medicinally; dead flesh; anything pounded to a formless mass; a bituminous drug or pigment. — *vt* to mummify: — *pr p* **mumm'ying**; *pa t* and *pa p* **mumm'ied**. — *n* **mumm'ia** mummy as a drug. — *n* **mummificā'tion**. — *adj* **mumm'iform**. — *vt* **mumm'ify** to make into a mummy: — *pr p* **mumm'ifying**; *pa t* and *pa p* **mumm'ified**. — **mumm'y-case**; **mumm'y-cloth** cloth for wrapping a mummy; a similar fabric used as a basis for embroidery; a fabric like crape with cotton or silk warp and woollen weft; **mumm'y-wheat** a variety of wheat alleged (incredibly) to descend from grains found in Egyptian mummy-cases. [OFr *mumie*, from LL *mumia*, from Ar and Pers *mūmiyā*, from Pers *mūm* wax]

mummy[2]. See under **mum**[3].

mump *mump*, *vt* to mumble or mutter (*dialect* and *Scot*); to mumble or munch (*dialect*); to obtain by, or visit for the purpose of, begging or sponging (*dialect*); to cheat (*obs*). — *vi* (*dialect* and *Scot*) to mumble; to sponge; to sulk; to grumble, complain (*Scot*); to mope; to grimace; to be silent (*archaic*); to play the beggar. — *n* **mump'er** a person who mumps; a beggar (*old slang*). — *adj* **mump'ish** having mumps; dull; sullen. — *adv* **mump'ishly**. — *n* **mump'ishness**. — **mump'ing-day** St Thomas's Day, 21 December, when the poor used to go around begging corn, money, etc. [Cf **mum**[1] and Du *mompen* to cheat]

mumps *mumps*, *n sing* a bout of gloomy silence (*old*); an acute infectious disease characterized by a painful swelling of the parotid gland. — *n pl* the swelling thus caused, protruding on either side of the face. [Suggesting the shape of the face when munching; cf **mump**]

mumpsimus *mump'si-məs*, *n* a view or opinion stubbornly held, even when shown to be misguided; a person holding such a view, or one adhering stubbornly to old ways. [An ignorant priest's blunder (in an old story) for L *sūmpsimus*, we have received, in the mass]

mumsy. See under **mum**[3].

mun[1] *mun*, (*dialect*) *vt* must — used in *pres* indicative only; 3*rd pers* **mun**. — Also **maun** or **man**. [ON *mon*, *mun*, or *man* (infinitive *monu*, *munu*), a preterite-present verb]

mun[2] *mun*, *n* a dialect form of **man**[1].

munch *munch* or *munsh*, *vt* and *vi* to chew with a steady, deliberate action of the jaws, and often with a crunching noise. — *n* **munch'er**. — **the munchies** (*slang*) an alcohol- or drug-induced craving for food. [Prob imit]

Munchausen or **Munchhausen** *mōōn'show-zən*, *n* an exaggerated, fantastical story, or its teller. — *adj* used to describe a syndrome in which a person feigns injury or illness in order to obtain hospital treatment. [Baron *Münchausen*, hero of a series of improbable adventure stories by R E Raspe (1737–94)]

munchkin *munch'kin*, *n* (*US slang*) a low-level employee, an underling. [Name of a fictional tiny people in L F Baum's *Wizard of Oz* (1900)]

Munda *mōōn'də*, *n* any member of a group of peoples of eastern India, or a speaker of their group of languages (also called **Kolarian**), a division of the Austroasiatic family of languages. — Also *adj*.

mundane *mun-dān'*, *adj* worldly; earthly; cosmic; ordinary, banal. — *adv* **mundane'ly**. — *n* **mundanity** (*-dan'i-ti*). [L *mundānus*, from *mundus* the world]

mundic *mun'dik*, *n* iron pyrites. [From Cornish]

mundify *mun'di-fī*, *vt* to cleanse, purify. — *n* **mundificā'tion**. — *adj* **mundif'icative**. [LL *mundificāre*, from L *mundus* clean, and *facere* to make]

mundungus *mun-dung'gəs*, (*archaic*) *n* a rank-smelling tobacco. [Sp *mondongo* black pudding]

mung bean *mōōng* or *mung bēn*, *n* a leguminous Asian plant, *Phaseolus aureus*, or its seeds, grown for forage and as a source of bean sprouts. [Hindi *mūng*]

mungcorn. See under **mong**.

mungo *mung'gō*, *n* the waste produced in a woollen-mill from hard spun or felted cloth, or from tearing up old clothes, used in making cheap cloth: — *pl* **mun'gos**. [Origin obscure]

mungoose. Same as **mongoose**.

Munich *mū'nik* or *-nihh*, *n* a buying off or appeasing by granting concessions. — *n* **Mu'nichism**. [From the pact signed at *Munich* (1938), in which Britain, France and Italy agreed to yield the Sudetenland of Czechoslovakia to Hitler]

municipal *mū-nis'i-pl*, *adj* relating to home affairs; relating to (the government of) a borough, town or city. — *n* **munic'ipalism** concern for the interests of one's municipality; belief in municipal control. — *n* **municipality** (*-pal'i-ti*) a self-governing town or district; its governing body; a district governed like a city; (in France and other European countries) an area representing the smallest administrative unit, governed jointly by a mayor and an elected council, a commune. — *n* **municipalizā'tion** or **-s-**. — *vt* **munic'ipalize** or **-ise** to make into a municipality; to bring under municipal control or ownership. — *adv* **munic'ipally**. [L *mūnicipālis*, from *mūniceps*, *-ipis*, an inhabitant of a *mūnicipium*, a free town, from *mūnia* official duties, and *capere* to take]

munificence *mū-nif'i-səns*, *n* magnificent liberality in giving; bountifulness. — *adj* **munif'icent**. — *adv* **munif'icently**. [L *mūnificentia*, from *mūnus* a present, and *-facere* to make]

munify *mū'ni-fī*, *vt* to fortify. — *n* **munifience** (*-nif'i-əns*; *Spenser*) defence, fortification. [Irregularly formed from L *mūnīre* to fortify, and *facere* to make]

muniment *mū'ni-mənt*, *n* (*usu* in *pl*) a means of defence; a record fortifying or making good a claim, *esp* a title deed to land; (in *pl*) furnishings, equipment, things provided. [L *mūnīmentum* fortification, later, title deed]

munition *mū-nish'ən*, *vt* to supply with munitions. — *n* (commonly in *pl*) fortification; defence; material used in war; weapons; military stores. — *vt* **munite'** (*Bacon*) to fortify, strengthen. — *n* **munitioneer'** or **munit'ion-worker** a worker engaged in making munitions: — *fem* (*obs colloq*) **munitionette'**. [L *mūnīre*, *-ītum* to fortify; *mūnīmentum* fortification, later, title-deeds, from *moenia* walls]

munnion *mun'yən*. Same as **mullion**.

Munro *mun-rō'*, *n* a designation *orig* of Scottish (now also English, Irish and Welsh) mountains over 3000 feet: — *pl* **Munros'**. — *n* **Munro'-bagger** a person whose aim is to climb every designated Munro. — *n* **Munro'-bagging**. [Orig list made by Sir H T *Munro* (1856–1919), Scottish mountaineer]

munshi or **moonshee** *mōōn'shē*, (*Ind*) *n* a secretary; an interpreter; a language teacher. [Hindi *munshī*, from Ar *munshi'*]

munster or **muenster** *mōōn'stər*, *n* a semi-soft, cow's milk cheese of *Munster* in NE France, often flavoured with caraway or aniseed.

munt. See **muntu**.

muntin *munt'in* or **munting** *munt'ing*, *n* the vertical framing piece between door panels. [**montant**]

muntjak or **muntjac** *munt'jak*, *n* a small S E Asian deer, the male of which has tusks and small antlers. [From the Malay name]

muntu *mōōnt'ōō*, (*SAfr slang*; *derog*) *n* a Black African. — Also **munt**. [Bantu *uMuntu* person]

Muntz metal *munts met'l*, *n* alpha-beta brass, 60% copper and 40% zinc. [G F *Muntz*, 19c English metallurgist]

muon *mū'on* or *mōō'*, (*phys*) *n* a lepton formerly classified as a **mu-** (or μ) **meson**. See **mu**. — *adj* **mūon'ic**. — *n* **muonium** (*mū-ōn'i-əm*) an isotope of hydrogen. — **muonic atom** (*mū-on'ik*) a hydrogen-like atom, formed by the slowing down of an energetic muon by ionization as it traverses matter.

muqaddam, **mokaddam** or **mocuddum** *mōō-kud'um* or *mō-*, *n* (in India, etc) a leader, a headman. [Ar]

muraena or **murena** *mū-rē'nə*, *n* a favourite food-fish of the Romans, a moray, of the genus **Muraena**, giving name to a family of eels, **Murae'nidae**. [L *mūraena*; see **moray**]

murage. See under **mure**.

mural *mū'rəl*, *adj* of, on, attached to, or of the nature of, a wall. — *n* a wall (in *Shakesp* only a conjectural emendation (*obs*); see **morall**); a mural decoration, *esp* a painting. — *n* **mur'alist** a person who paints or designs murals. — **mural circle** a large graduated circle, fixed to a wall, for measuring arcs of the meridian; **mural crown** an embattled crown given among the ancient Romans to the first soldier to mount the wall of a besieged city; **mural painting** a painting executed, *esp* in distemper colours, on the wall of a building. [L *mūrālis*, from *mūrus* a wall]

murder *mûr'dər*, *n* the act of putting a person to death intentionally and unlawfully; excessive or reprehensible slaughter that is not legally murder; torture, excessive toil or hardship (*hyperb*); a collective term for a number of crows. — *vt* to kill (*usu* a person) unlawfully with malice aforethought; to slaughter; to torture (*hyperb*); to beat, defeat utterly (*colloq*); to destroy (*colloq*); to spoil by performing badly (*colloq*); to consume voraciously (*colloq*). — Also (now only *dialect*) **murther** (*-dhər*). — *n* **murderee'** the victim, or intended victim, of a murderer. — *n* **mur'derer** (*obs* or *dialect* **mur'therer**) a person who murders, or is guilty of murder; a small cannon (also **mur'dering-piece** *obs*): — *fem* **mur'deress**. — *adj* **mur'derous**. — *adv* **mur'derously**. — **cry** or **scream blue murder** see under **blue**[1]; **get away with murder** to do as one pleases yet escape punishment or censure; **murder will out** murder cannot remain hidden; the truth will come to light. [OE *morthor*, from *morth* death; Ger *Mord*, Gothic *maurthr*; cf L *mors*, *mortis* death]

mure *mūr*, *n* a wall (*Shakesp*). — *vt* to wall in or up; to confine; to close. — *n* **mur'age** (*hist*) a tax for the building or upkeep of town-walls. — *adj* **mur'iform** (*bot*) with cells arranged like bricks in a wall. [Fr *mur* and L *mūrus* a wall]

murena. See **muraena**.

murex *mū'reks*, *n* a gasteropod mollusc of the *Murex* genus, yielding Tyrian purple dye: — *pl* **mu'rexes** or **mu'rices** (*-ri-sēz*). [L *mūrex*, *-icis*]

murgeon *mûr'jən*, (*Scot*) *n* a grimace. — *vt* and *vi* to mock with grimaces. [Origin obscure]

muriate *mūr'i-āt*, *n* (*archaic*) a chloride. — *adj* **mur'iāted** impregnated or combined with chlorine or a chloride. — *adj* **muriatic** (*-at'ik*) briny; hydrochloric (not in scientific use). [L *muria* brine]

muricate *mūr'i-kāt*, (*bot*) *adj* rough or warty with short sharp points. — Also **mur'icated**. [L *mūricātus*, from *mūrex*, *-icis* a murex, a sharp stone]

murices. See **murex**.

Muridae *mū'ri-dē*, *n pl* the mouse family. [L *mūs*, *mūris* a mouse]

murine *mūr'īn* or *-in, adj* mouselike; belonging to the mouse family or subfamily. — *n* a murine animal. — **murine typhus** a mild form of typhus endemic among rats and passed to humans by fleas. [L *mūrīnus*, from *mūs, mūris* mouse]

murk or **mirk** *mûrk*, also (*Scot*) *mirk, n* darkness (*lit* and *fig*). — *adj* dark; gloomy; obscure. — *adv* **murk'ily**. — *n* **murk'iness**. — *adj* **murk'ish**. — *adj* **murk'some**. — *adj* **murk'y** dark; obscure; gloomy. [OE *mirce* (n and adj), ON *myrkr*, Dan and Swed *mörk*; the forms with *i* are chiefly due to Spenser and Scottish influence]

murl *mûrl*, (*Scot*) *vt* and *vi* to crumble. — *adj* **murl'y**. [Origin obscure]

murlain, **murlan** or **murlin** *mûr'lən*, (*Scot*) *n* a round, narrow-mouthed basket. [Gaelic *mùrlan*]

murmur *mûr'mər, n* a low, indistinct sound, like that of running water; an abnormal rustling sound from the heart, lungs, etc; a muttered or subdued grumble or complaint; rumour (*Shakesp*). — *vi* to utter a murmur; to grumble. — *vt* to say or utter in a murmur. — *n* **murmurā'tion** murmuring; a doubtful word for a flock of starlings. — *n* **mur'murer**. — *n* and *adj* **mur'muring**. — *adv* **mur'muringly**. — *adj* **mur'murous**. — *adv* **mur'murously**. — **murmur vowel** (*phonetics*) a weak vowel, a schwa. [Fr *murmure*, from L *murmur*; cf Gr *mormȳrein* to surge]

murphy *mûr'fi*, (*colloq*) *n* a potato: — *pl* **mur'phies**. — **Murphy's game** a confidence trick whereby an envelope stuffed with paper is surreptitiously substituted for one full of money; **Murphy's law** that one of Sod's laws by which if something can go wrong, it will. [From the common Ir name *Murphy*]

murra or **murrha** *mur'ə, n* an unidentified precious material for vases, etc, first brought to Rome by Pompey (61 BC) from the East, conjectured to be agate. — *adj* **murrhine**, **murrine** (*mur'īn* or *-in*) or **myrrhine** (*mir'īn* or *-in*). [L *murra*; Gr *morria* (pl)]

murrain *mur'in* or *-ən, n* a pestilence (*obs*); now only a cattle-plague, *esp* foot-and-mouth disease. — *adj* affected with murrain; confounded. — *adv* confoundedly. — Also **murr'en** (*Shakesp* and *Milton*), **murr'ion** (*Shakesp*) or **murr'in** (*Spenser*). — *adj* **murr'ained**. [OFr *morine* pestilence, carcass]

murram *mur'əm, n* a tough, clayey gravel used as road metal in tropical Africa. [Native name]

murray. See **moray**.

murre *mûr, n* a guillemot; a razorbill. — *n* **murrelet** (*mûr'lit*) a name for various small birds related to the guillemot. [Origin obscure]

murren. See **murrain**.

murrey[1] *mur'i, n* and *adj* mulberry-colour, dark purplish red. [OFr *moré*, from L *mōrum* mulberry]

murrey[2]. See **moray**.

murrha, **murrhine** and **murrine**. See **murra**.

murrin and **murrion**. See **murrain**.

murry. Same as **moray**.

murther and **murtherer**. *Obs* or dialect forms of **murder** and **murderer**.

murva or **moorva** *mōōr'və, n* bowstring hemp. [Sans *mūrvā*]

mus. *abbrev*: music; musical; museum.

Musa *mū'zə, n* the banana genus, giving name to a family **Musā'ceae**, order **Musā'les**, of (mostly) gigantic tree-like herbs. — *adj* **musā'ceous**. [Latinized from Ar *mauz*]

Musak. See **Muzak**.

musang *mū-* or *mōō-sang', n* a paradoxure, or related animal. [Malay *mūsang*]

MusB *abbrev*: Bachelor of Music.

Musca *mus'kə, n* the house-fly genus; a small constellation in the south, between the Crux and the Chamaeleon. — *n* **muscatō'rium** (*Gr Ch*) a flabellum. — *adj* **muscid** (*mus'id*) of the house-fly family **Muscidae** (*mus'i-dē*). — *n* a member of the family. — **muscae volitantes** (*mus'ē vol-i-tan'tēz* or *mōōs'kī wo-li-tan'tās*; *L* fluttering flies) ocular spectra like floating black spots before the eyes. [L *musca* a fly]

muscadel. See **muscatel**.

Muscadet *mus'kə-dā* or *müs-kä-de, n* a variety of white grape grown *esp* in the lower Loire valley region of France; a typically light dry white wine made from this grape. [Fr; cf **muscatel**]

muscadin *müs-ka-dɛ̃*, (*hist*) *n* a Parisian fop or dandy; a middle-class moderate in the French Revolution. [Fr]

muscadine *mus'kə-dīn* or *-din*, (*archaic*) *n* muscatel (wine, grape or pear). [Perh Provençal *muscat*, fem *muscade*]

muscardine *mus'kär-din, -dēn* or *-dīn, n* a silkworm disease caused by a fungus (*Botrytis*). [Fr]

muscarine *mus'kər-in, n* an alkaloid poison found in certain fungi. — *adj* **muscarin'ic** of, like, or producing effects similar to muscarine. [L *muscarius*, from *musca* a fly]

muscat *mus'kat, n* muscatel wine; a musky variety of grape or its vine. [Provençal *muscat*]

muscatel *mus-kə-tel'* or *mus'* or **muscadel** *mus-kə-del'* or *mus', n* a rich spicy wine, of various kinds; a grape of musky smell or taste; the vine producing it; a raisin from the muscatel grape; a variety of pear. [OFr *muscatel, muscadel*, from Provençal *muscat* musky]

Muschelkalk *mōōsh'əl-kälk*, (*geol*) *n* the middle member of the Trias system in Germany, largely shelly limestone — not found in Britain. [Ger *Muschel* shell, and *Kalk* lime]

Musci *mus'ī, n pl* mosses, one of the two great divisions of the *Bryophyta*, the other being the *Hepaticae* or liverworts. — *n* **muscology** (*-kol'ə-ji*) bryology. — *adj* **mus'coid** (*-koid*) or **mus'cose** mosslike. [L *muscus* moss]

muscid. See under **Musca**.

muscle[1] *mus'l, n* a contractile structure by which bodily movement is effected; the tissue forming it; bodily strength; power, strength of other kinds (financial, political, etc) (*colloq*). — *vi* to force one's way, thrust. — *adj* **muscled** (*mus'ld*) having muscles. — *n* **musc'ling** delineation of muscles, as in a picture. — *adj* **musc'ly** muscular. — *adj* **muscular** (*mus'kū-lər*) relating to a muscle; consisting of muscles; having big or strong muscles; brawny; strong; vigorous. — *n* **muscularity** (*-lar'i-ti*). — *adv* **mus'cularly**. — *n* **musculā'tion** muscular action; musculature. — *n* **mus'culature** provision, disposition and system of muscles. — *adj* **mus'culous** (*obs*) muscular. — *adj* **musc'le-bound** having the muscles stiff and enlarged by over-exercise. — **musc'le-man** a man of extravagant physical development, *esp* one employed as an intimidator. — Also *fig*. — **musc'le-reading** interpretation of slight involuntary muscular movements; **muscle** or **muscular sense** kinaesthesis; **muscular Christianity** a vigorous combination of Christian living with devotion to athletic enjoyments, associated with Charles Kingsley (who repudiated the name); **muscular dystrophy** (*dis'trə-fi*) any of the forms of a hereditary disease in which muscles progressively deteriorate. — *adj* **musculo-skel'etal** relating to muscles and skeleton. — **muscle in** (*colloq*) to force one's way in (*lit* and *fig*); to grab a share. [Fr *muscle*, or directly from L *mūsculus*, dimin of *mūs* a mouse, muscle]

muscle[2]. See **mussel**.

muscology, **muscoid** and **muscose**. See under **Musci**.

muscone. Same as **muskone**.

muscovado *mus-kō-vä'dō, n* sugar in its unrefined state after evaporating the cane-juice and draining off the molasses: — *pl* **muscova'dos**. [Sp *mascabado*]

Muscovy *mus'kə-vi, n* an old Russian principality having Moscow as its capital (*hist*); extended to Russia in general (*archaic*). — *n* **Muscovian** (*-kō'vi-ən*; *obs*) a Muscovite. — *adj* Muscovite. — *n* **Mus'covite** a citizen of Moscow or, generally, a Russian. — *adj* of Muscovy (*hist*); Russian (*archaic*). — *n* **mus'covite** (*mineralogy*) common white mica, first obtained in Russia, a silicate of aluminium and potassium; the mica in the form of thin transparent plates, formerly used as a kind of glass (also **Muscovy glass**). — *adj* **Muscovitic** (*-vit'ik*). — **muscovy duck** see **musk duck** under **musk**. [*Moscovia*, Latinized from Russ *Moskva* Moscow]

muscular. See under **muscle**[1].

MusD *abbrev*: Doctor of Music.

Muse *mūz*, (*Gr mythol*) *n* any of the nine goddesses of the liberal arts, daughters of Zeus and Mnemosyne (**Calliope** of epic poetry; **Clio** of history; **Erato** of love poetry; **Euterpe** of music and lyric poetry; **Melpomene** of tragedy; **Polyhymnia** of sacred lyrics; **Terpsichore** of dancing; **Thalia** of comedy; **Urania** of astronomy); an inspiring goddess more vaguely imagined; poetic character; poetry or art; an inspired poet (*Milton*). [Fr, from L *Mūsa*, from Gr *Mousa*]

muse[1] *mūz*, *vi* to reflect in silence; to be mentally abstracted or absorbed in thought; to meditate or ponder (with *on*); to look or gaze in contemplation (with *on*). — *vt* to meditate on (*obs*); to wonder at (*Shakesp*); to say musingly. — *n* deep thought; contemplation; a state or fit of mental abstraction or absorption. — *adj* **mused** bemused, muzzy, fuddled. — *adj* **muse'ful** meditative. — *adv* **muse'fully**. — *n* **mus'er**. — *n* and *adj* **mus'ing**. — *adv* **mus'ingly**. [Fr *muser* to loiter, in OFr to muse; perh orig to hold the muzzle (OFr *muse*) in the air, as a dog that has lost the scent; perh influenced by **Muse**]

muse[2]. See **meuse**[1].

museologist and **museology**. See under **museum**.

muset. Same as **musit**.

musette *mū-zet'*, *n* an old type of French bagpipe; a simple pastoral melody or gavotte trio for, or in imitation of, the bagpipe; a small (*esp* army) knapsack (*US*). [Fr, dimin of *muse* a bagpipe]

museum *mū-zē'əm*, *n orig* a temple, home or resort of the Muses; a place of study; a resort of the learned; an institution or repository for the collection, exhibition and study of objects of artistic, scientific, historic or educational interest; an art gallery (*US*); a collection of curiosities: — *pl* **musē'ums**. — *n* **museol'ogist**. — *n* **museol'ogy** the study of museums and their organization. — **museum piece** a specimen so fine as to be suitable for exhibition in a museum, or (*facetiously*) so old-fashioned as to be unsuitable for anything else. [L *mūsēum*, from Gr *mouseion*; see **Muse**]

mush[1] *mush*, *n* meal, *esp* cornmeal, boiled in water or milk until thick; anything pulpy; sloppy sentimentality (*colloq*); rubbish; background noise from a wireless receiver; an umbrella (*slang*; see also **mushroom**). — *vt* to reduce to mush; to crush the spirit of, wear out (*dialect*). — *adv* **mush'ily**. — *n* **mush'iness**. — *adj* **mush'y**. — **mush'mouth** (*US slang*) a person who slurs or mumbles in speaking. — *adj* **mush'-mouthed** (*US slang*) speaking indistinctly or slurringly; tongue-tied. [Prob **mash**[1]]

mush[2] *mush*, (*Scot*) *vt* to notch or scallop the edges of. [Perh Fr *moucher* to trim]

mush[3] *mush*, (*NAm*) *vi* to travel on foot with dogs over snow. — *n* a journey of this kind. — *interj* and *imperative* a command to dogs to start moving or move faster. — *n* **mush'er**. [Prob Fr *marcher* to walk]

musha *mush'ə*, (*Ir*) *interj* expressing surprise. [Ir *maiseadh*]

mushroom *mush'ro͞om*, *n* an edible fungus of rapid growth with a stem and umbrella-shaped cap, *esp Agaricus*, or *Psalliota*, *campestris* or *field mushroom*; any edible fungus; any fungus of umbrella shape whether edible or not; any fungus; an object shaped like a mushroom eg a wooden one for use in darning; a hat with drooping brim; an umbrella (*slang*); a pinkish-brown colour, like that of the field mushroom; anything of rapid growth and decay (*fig*); someone who rises suddenly from a low condition (*fig*); an upstart. — *adj* of or like a mushroom in appearance, rapidity of growth, etc; of a pinkish-brown colour. — *vi* to expand like a mushroom cap; to gather mushrooms; to increase or spread with remarkable or disconcerting rapidity. — *n* **mush'roomer**. — **mush'room-anchor** an anchor with a mushroom-shaped head; **mushroom cloud** a mushroom-shaped cloud, *esp* one resulting from a nuclear explosion; **mushroom pink** a dusky brownish pink. [OFr *mousseron*, perh *mousse* moss, which may be of Germanic origin]

music *mū'zik*, *n* the art of expression in sound, in melody, and harmony, including both composition and execution; (the art of) instrumental performance, as distinct from singing; the science underlying it; a musical composition (*obs*); the performance of musical compositions; compositions collectively; a connected series of (pleasing) sounds; pleasing sound generally; melody or harmony; sound of a definite pitch, not mere noise; a band of musicians (*archaic*); musical instruments (*obs* or *dialect*); written or printed representation of tones, expression, etc, or of what is to be played or sung; sheets or books of parts or scores collectively; harmonious character; fun (*US*). — *adj* of or for music. — *vi* (*rare*) to perform music: — *pr p* **mu'sicking**. — *adj* **mu'sical** relating to, of, with, or producing, music; pleasing to the ear; of definite pitch (unlike mere noise); melodious; having skill in, or aptitude or taste for, music. — *n* a musical person, party or performance, *esp* a theatrical performance or film in which singing and *usu* dancing play an important part, a successor to musical comedy with a less frivolous plot. — *n* **musicale** (*mū-zi-käl'*; Fr *soirée musicale*) a social gathering with music, or the programme of music for it. — *n* **musicality** (*-al'i-ti*). — *adv* **mu'sically**. — *n* **mu'sicalness**. — *n* **musician** (*mū-zish'ən*) a person skilled in music; a performer or composer of music, *esp* professional. — *n* **musi'cianer** or **mu'sicker** (*obs* or *dialect*). — *adj* **musi'cianly** characteristic of, or becoming, a musician. — *n* **musi'cianship**. — *adj* **musicolog'ical**. — *n* **musicol'ogist**. — *n* **musicol'ogy** academic study of music in its historical, scientific and other aspects. — *n* **musicother'apy** the treatment of (*esp* mental) illness by means of music. — **musical box** a toy that plays tunes automatically, by means of projections from a revolving barrel twitching a comb; **musical chairs** the game of prancing round a diminishing row of chairs and securing one when the music stops; a series of interrelated shifts and changes involving a number of people (*facetious*); **musical comedy** a light dramatic entertainment with sentimental songs and situations held together by a minimum of plot; **musical director** the conductor of an orchestra in a theatre, etc; **musical flame** a flame that gives a musical tone when surrounded by an open tube; **musical glasses** see **harmonica**; **musical sand** sand of nearly uniform size of grain that gives out a definite note when walked on; **music box** a barrel-organ (*obs*); a musical box; a piano (*joc*); **music case** or **music folio** a case or portfolio for carrying sheet music; **music centre** a unit consisting of a record player, cassette-player and radio, with loudspeakers; **mu'sic-demy** a size of writing-paper, $20\frac{3}{4}$ in × $14\frac{3}{8}$ in; **music drama** a term used by Wagner to describe opera in which the musical, dramatic and visual elements are given equal emphasis; **music hall** *orig* and still sometimes a concert-hall, now *usu* a hall for variety entertainments; variety entertainment or vaudeville performed there, consisting of a series of turns by different artists, interspersed with interludes of song, dance, etc (also *adj*); **mu'sic-holder** a music-case; a clip, rack or desk for holding music during performance; **mu'sic-house** a concert-hall; a firm dealing in music or musical instruments; **music master**, **mistress** or **teacher** a teacher of music; **music paper** paper ruled for writing music; **music pen** a five-channelled pen for drawing the stave; **mu'sic-rack** a rack attached to a musical instrument for holding the player's music; **music roll** a case for carrying music rolled up; a roll of perforated paper for mechanical piano-playing; **music room** a room in which music is performed; a room beside the stage in which the musicians were stationed (*obs*); **mu'sic-seller** a dealer in printed music; **mu'sic-shell** a volute shell with markings like music; **music stand** a light adjustable desk for holding music during performance; **music stool** a piano stool; **music theatre** a form of musical composition given a partly-staged presentation, developed *esp* in the USA in the 1950s; **music therapist** a specialist in the use of **music therapy**, the controlled use of music in the treatment, education, etc of those with physical or mental disabilities or disorders. — **early music** medieval and Renaissance music (also sometimes extended to baroque); **face the music** see under **face**; **music of the spheres** see under **spheres**; **music to one's ears** anything that one is very glad to hear; **rough music** uproar; charivari. [Fr *musique*, from L *mūsica*, from Gr *mousikē* (*technē*) musical (art), from *Mousa* a Muse]

musimon *mūs'* or *mus'i-mon* or **musmon** *mus'mon*, *n* the moufflon. [L *mus(i)mō, -ōnis*]

musique concrète *mü-zēk kɔ̃-kret*, (*Fr*) *n* a kind of mid-20c music, made up of odds and ends of recorded sound variously handled.

musit *mū'zit*, (*Shakesp*) *n* a gap in a fence or thicket through which an animal passes. [**meuse**[1]]

musive *mū'siv*, (*obs*) *adj*. Same as **mosaic**.

musk *musk*, *n* a strong-smelling substance, used in perfumery, obtained chiefly from the male musk deer; a similar substance secreted by other animals, eg the civet; a synthetic reproduction of either substance, for used in perfumery; the odour of either substance, or of its synthetic substitute; the musk deer; a species of *Mimulus*, said once to have smelt of musk. — *adj* (used attributively with the names of many animals and plants) supposed to smell of musk. — *vt* to perfume with musk. — *adj* **musked** (*muskt*) smelling or tasting like musk. — *adv* **musk'ily**. — *n* **musk'iness**. — *n* **mus'kone** or **mus'cone** a macrocyclic ketone that gives musk its distinctive smell and is synthesized for use as an ingredient in perfumes. — *adj* **musk'y** having the odour of musk. — **musk'-bag, -cod, -pod, -pouch** or **-sac** a musk gland; **musk'-bag** or **musk'-ball** a bag or ball containing musk, as a perfuming sachet; **musk'-beetle** a longicorn beetle that smells of attar of roses; **musk'-cat** a musk-yielding animal, *usu* the musk deer, *prob* confused with the civet cat; a scented effeminate dandy; a courtesan; **musk'-cavy** the hog-rat; **musk deer** a hornless deer (*Moschus moschiferus*) of Asia, the chief source of musk; **musk duck** (also by confusion **muscovy duck**) a large musky-smelling S American duck (*Cairina moschata*); **musk gland** a skin pit in some animals producing musk; **musk'-mallow** a species of mallow with a faint odour of musk; **musk melon** any of various common varieties of melon, including the honeydew (the name *appar* transferred from a musky-scented kind); **musk orchid** a small musk-scented European orchid (*Herminium monorchis*); **musk ox** a long-haired ruminant (*Ovibos moschatus*) of northern Canada and Greenland, exhaling a strong musky smell; **musk pear** a fragrant variety of pear; **musk'-plant** a plant, *Mimulus moschatus*; **musk'-plum** a fragrant kind of plum; **musk'rat** the musquash; a musk-shrew; its skin; **musk rose** a fragrant species of rose, with white flowers; **musk'-sheep** the musk-ox; **musk'-shrew** the desman; a musky-smelling Indian shrew; **musk'-thistle** a thistle (*Carduus nutans*) with large drooping scented heads; **musk turtle** any of a group of small American turtles of the genus *Sternotherus*, *esp Sternotherus odoratus* which has a particularly musky smell. [Fr *musc*, from L *muscus*, Gr *moschos*, prob from Pers *mushk*, perh from Sans *muṣka* a testicle (for which the gland has been mistaken)]

muskeg *mus-keg'*, (*Can*) *n* a swamp, bog or marsh. [Cree Indian word]

muskellunge *mus'kə-lunj*, *n* a large N American freshwater fish (*Esox masquinongy*) of the pike family. — Also **maskallonge**, **maskalonge** (*mas'kə-lonj*), **maskinonge** or **maskanonge** (*mas'kə-nonj*). [Algonquian]

musket *mus'kit*, *n* a male sparrow-hawk; a military firearm, *esp* of a long-barrelled smooth-bore kind fired from the shoulder, a popular infantry weapon between the 16c and 18c. — *n* **musketeer'** a soldier armed with a musket. — *n* **musketoon'** or **musquetoon'** a short musket; a soldier armed with one. — *n* **mus'ketry** muskets collectively; practice with, or the art of using, small arms; fire of muskets; a body of troops armed with muskets. — *adj* **mus'ket-proof** capable of resisting the force of a musket-ball. — **mus'ket-rest** a forked support for the heavy 16c musket; **mus'ket-shot** shot for or from a musket; the discharge of a musket; the range of a musket. [OFr *mousquet*, musket, formerly a hawk, from Ital *moschetto*, perh from L *musca* a fly]

muskle. See **mussel**.

muskone, **muskrat** and **musky**. See under **musk**.

Muslim *muz'*, *mŏŏz'* or *mus'lim*, *n* a follower of the Islamic religion. — *adj* of, or belonging to, the followers of Islam. — *n* **Mus'limism**. — Also **Mos'lem** and **Mos'lemism**. [Ar *muslim*, pl *muslimīn*, from *salma* to submit (to God); cf **Mussulman** and **Islam**]

muslin *muz'lin*, *n* a fine soft plain-woven cotton fabric, of gauzy appearance; cotton cloth for shirts, etc (*US*); women collectively (*obs slang*; *derog*); sails, canvas (*naut slang*); a collector's name for several different moths. — *adj* made of muslin. — *adj* **mus'lined** clothed with muslin. — *n* **muslinet'** a coarse kind of muslin. — **mus'lin-kale** (*Scot*) thin broth made without meat. [Fr *mousseline*, from Ital *mussolino*, from Ital *Mussolo*, the town of Mosul in Mesopotamia]

musmon. See **musimon**.

muso *mū'zō*, (*slang*) *n* a musician, a music enthusiast (*esp Austr*); a pop musician who concentrates excessively on technical details (*derog*): — *pl* **mū'sos**. [**music**]

musquash *mus'kwosh*, *n* a large aquatic N American animal related to the voles, very destructive to dams and waterways (also **muskrat**); its fur. [Algonquian]

musquetoon. See under **musket**.

musrol *muz'rōl*, (*obs*) *n* the nose-band of a bridle. [Fr *muserolle*, from Ital *museruola*, from *muso* muzzle]

muss or **musse** *mus*, (now *NAm* and *dialect*) *n* a scramble (*Shakesp*); a disturbance, a row (*obs*); confusion, disorder; confused conflict (*archaic*); a mess. — *vt* and *vi* to disarrange; to mess (often with *up*). — *n* **muss'iness**. — *adj* **muss'y** disordered. [Perh different words; cf **mess**]

mussel *mus'l* (formerly also **muscle** *mus'l* or **muskle** *mus'kl*), *n* an edible marine lamellibranch shellfish of the family *Mytilidae* with a brownish-black elongated oval shell; a freshwater lamellibranch of the *Unionidae* with a slightly flatter shell; the shell of any of these; a mussel-plum. — *adj* **muss'elled** poisoned by eating infected mussels. — **muss'el-plum** a dark purple plum resembling a mussel-shell; **muss'el-scalp'** (*Scot* **muss'el-scaup**) a bed of mussels; **muss'el-shell**. [OE *mūs(c)le*; cf Ger *Muschel*, Fr *moule*; all from L *mūsculus*, dimin of *mūs* mouse]

mussitation *mus-i-tā'shən*, *n* low muttering; a speaking movement of the mouth but without sound. — *vt* **muss'itate** (*obs*) to mutter. [L *mussitāre*, frequentative of *mussāre* to mutter]

Mussulman or **Musulman** *mus'l-mən* or *-män'*, (*archaic*) *n* a Muslim: — *pl* **Muss'ulmans** (*erron* or *facetiously* **Muss'ulmen**): — *fem* (*erron* or *facetiously*) **Muss'ulwoman**. [Pers *musulmān*, from Ar *muslim*, *moslim* Muslim]

mussy. See under **muss**.

must[1] *must*, *auxiliary vb* (taking *infinitive* without *to*) used to express compulsion, necessity or obligation, with ellipsis of *vb* (as in *I must away*), resolute intention, likelihood or conviction, or inevitability; used only in the present (*orig* past) indicative: — *3rd pers sing* **must**; *pa t* **must** (often replaced by **had to**). — *n* an essential, a necessity; a thing that should not be missed or neglected. — Also *adj*. — **must needs** see under **need**. [Orig pa t of **mote**, from OE *mōste*, pa t of *mōt*; cf Ger *müssen*]

must[2] *must*, *n* new wine; unfermented, or only partially fermented, grape juice or other juice or pulp for fermentation; the process of fermentation. — *adj* **must'y**. [OE *must*, from L *mustum* (*vīnum*) new (wine)]

must[3] *must*, *n* a smell of dampness or staleness, mustiness; mould. [Appar a back formation from **musty**[2]]

must[4] or **musth** *must*, *n* a dangerous frenzy in some male animals, such as elephants. — *adj* in such a state. — *adj* **must'y** in a frenzy. [Pers and Hindi *mast* intoxicated]

must[5], **muist** or **moust** *müst* or *mōōst*, (*obs Scot*) *n* musk; hair-powder. — *vt* to powder. [OFr *must*, a form of *musc*; see **musk**]

mustache. The US spelling of **moustache**.

mustachio *mə-stä'shi-ō*, *n* (often in *pl*) a large, elegantly curling moustache: — *pl* **mustach'ios**. — *adj* **mustach'ioed**. [Sp *mostacho*, Ital *mostaccio*]

mustang *mus'tang*, *n* the feralized horse of the American prairies. [Sp *mestengo*, now *mesteño*, belonging to the *mesta* or graziers' union, combined with *mostrenco* homeless, stray]

mustard *mus'tərd*, *n* any of various species of the *Sinapis* section of plants of the genus *Brassica*, typically having yellow flowers and slender seed pods; their (powdered) seeds; a pungent condiment prepared from the seeds; the brownish-yellow colour of the condiment. — **mustard gas** the vapour from a poisonous blistering liquid, $CH_2Cl{\cdot}CH_2$, obtained from ethylene and sulphur chloride; **mus'tard-oil** a volatile oil obtained from black mustard seeds; **mustard plaster** a counter-irritant skin application made from black and white mustard flour, deprived of their fixed oil; **mus'tard-tree** a name given to a shrub *Salvadora persica* (family *Salvadoraceae*, *prob* related to *Oleaceae*) on the theory that it is the plant referred to in the New Testament, which others think is only black mustard grown tall, as it does in the Middle East. — **black mustard** *Brassica nigra*; **cut the mustard** (*colloq*) reach a required standard, make the grade; make a favourable impression on; **French mustard** the condiment prepared for the table by adding salt, sugar, vinegar, etc; **garlic-mustard** see under **garlic**; **hedge-mustard** see under **hedge**; **keen as mustard** (*colloq*) intensely enthusiastic; **mustard and cress** a salad of seedlings of white mustard and garden cress; **Sarepta mustard** *Brassica juncea*; **white mustard** *Brassica alba*; **wild mustard** charlock, a common cornfield weed with yellowy flowers. [OFr *mo(u)starde* (Fr *moutarde*), from L *mustum* **must**[2] (because the condiment was prepared with must)]

mustee. Same as **mestee**.

Mustela *mus-tē'lə*, *n* the marten genus, giving name to the family **Muste'lidae** (otters, badgers and weasels) and the subfamily **Mustelī'nae** (weasels and martens). — *adj* and *n* **mus'teline** (*-təl-īn*). [L *mustēla* weasel]

muster *mus'tər*, *n* a display, demonstration (*obs*); an example (*archaic*); a commercial sample; an assembly or gathering, *esp* of troops for inspection or duties; a gathering together, round-up; inspection; an assembly; a register; a round-up of livestock (*Austr* and *NZ*); (*perh orig* a misunderstanding) a company of peacocks. — *vt* and *vi* to show forth (*obs*); to assemble; to enroll; to number. — *vt* to summon up (often with *up*); to round up (livestock; *Austr* and *NZ*). — *vi* to pass muster. — *n* **must'erer** (*Austr* and *NZ*) a person who musters (livestock). — **mus'ter-book** (*Shakesp*) a book in which military forces or a ship's crew are registered; **mus'ter-file** (*Shakesp*) a muster-roll; **mus'ter-master** a person in charge of the muster-roll (*hist*); **mus'ter-roll** a register of the officers and men in each company, troop, regiment, ship's crew, etc; roll-call (*naut*). — **muster in** (*US*) to enroll, receive as recruits; **muster out** (*US*) to discharge from service; **pass muster** to bear examination, appear adequate. [OFr *mostre*, *moustre*, *monstre*, from L *mōnstrum*, from *monēre* to warn]

musth. See **must**[4].

musty[1]. See under **must**[2,4].

musty[2] *must'i*, *adj* mouldy; spoiled by damp; stale in smell or taste; deteriorated from disuse. — *adv* **mus'tily**. — *n* **mus'tiness**.

Musulman. Same as **Mussulman**.

mutable *mū'tə-bl*, *adj* that may be changed; subject to change; variable; inconstant, fickle. — *n* **mutabil'ity** or **mū'tableness**. — *adv* **mū'tably**. [L *mūtābilis* changeable]

mutagen *mū'tə-jən*, (*biol*) *n* a substance that produces mutations. — *n* **mutagen'esis** the origin or induction of a mutation. — *adj* **mutagen'ic** (*-jen'ik*). — *n* **mutagenic'ity** the condition of being mutagenic. — *vt* **mū'tagenize** or **-ise** to treat with mutagens. [*muta*tion and **-gen**]

mutandum *mū-tan'dəm*, (*biol*) *n* something to be altered: — *pl* **mutan'da**.

mutant *mū'tənt*, (*biol*) *adj* (of a gene, animal or organism) suffering, or resulting from, mutation; a form resulting from mutation. [L *mūtans*, *-antis*, pres p of *mūtāre* to change]

mutate *mū-tāt'*, *vt* and *vi* to cause or undergo mutation. — *n* **mutā'tion** change, *esp* biological or genetic; in German orthography, another name for the umlaut; (in Celtic languages) an alteration to the sound of an initial consonant caused by a preceding word; (in old music) a change of syllable for the same note in passing to another hexachord; a genetic change that can be transmitted to offspring as an inheritable divergence from ancestral type (*biol*). — *adj* **mutā'tional**. — *adv* **mutā'tionally**. — *n* **mutā'tionist** a believer in evolution by mutation. — *adj* **mu'tative** or **mu'tatory** changing; mutable. — *n* **mū'ton** the smallest element of a gene capable of giving rise to a new form by mutation. — **mutation mink** a much valued shade of mink produced by selective breeding; **mutation rate** the frequency, per gamete, of gene mutations in a given species per unit time (*esp* generation time); **mutation stop** an organ-stop whose tones differ from those the keys indicate by an interval other than a whole number of octaves. [L *mūtātio*, from *mūtāre*, *-ātum* to change, **mutate** being a back-formation from **mutation**]

mutatis mutandis *mū-tā'tis mū-tan'dis* or *mōō-tä'tēs mōō-tan'dēs*, (*L*) *adv* with necessary changes. — **mutato nomine** (*mū-tā'tō nom'i-nē* or *mōō-tä'tō nōm'i-ne*) the name being changed.

mutch *much*, (*Scot*) *n* a woman's close-fitting linen cap. [MDu *mutse*; Du *muts*, Ger *Mütze*]

mutchkin *much'kin*, (*hist*) *n* a Scottish liquid measure, three-quarters of an imperial pint, or a quarter of an old Scottish pint. [Obs Du *mudseken*]

mute[1] *mūt*, *adj* dumb; silent; refusing to plead (*law*); without vocal utterance, unspoken; unpronounced or faintly pronounced; pronounced by stoppage of the breath-passage, plosive (*phonetics*). — *n* a dumb person; a silent person; a person who refuses to plead (*law*); a hired funeral attendant; a dumb servant in an oriental household; an actor with no words to speak; a stop-consonant, a plosive (*phonetics*); a clip, pad, or other device for subduing the sound of a musical instrument. — *vt* to deaden or muffle the sound of (eg a musical instrument) with a mute; to silence. — *adj* **mut'ed** (of eg sound or colour) softened, not loud, harsh or bright. — *adv* **mute'ly**. — *n* **mute'ness**. — *n* **mut'ism** dumbness. — **mute button** a device on a telephone which when depressed allows the user to make comments inaudible to the person on the other end of the line; **mute swan** the common swan (*Cygnus olor*). — **mute of malice** (*law*) refusing to plead. [L *mūtus*]

mute[2] *mūt*, (now *dialect*) *vi* (of birds) to defecate. — *n* (*obs*) birds' faeces; an act of muting. [OFr *mutir*, *esmeutir*; prob Germanic; cf **smelt**]

mutessarif *mōō-təs-ä'rif*, *n* the head of a Turkish sanjak. — *n* **mutessa'rifat** his office or jurisdiction. [Turk *mutesarif*, from Ar *mutasarrif*]

muti *mōō'ti*, (*SAfr*) *n* traditional medicine, *esp* associated with witchcraft or witch doctors. [Zulu *umuthi* tree]

muticous *mūt'i-kəs*, (*bot*) *adj* awnless; spineless; pointless. [L *muticus* awnless]

mutilate *mū'ti-lāt*, *vt* to injure by cutting off a limb, to maim; to remove a material part of; to damage or spoil beyond recognition; to deform by slitting, boring, or removing a part. — *adj* mutilated. — *n* **mutilā'tion**. — *n* **mu'tilātor**. [L *mutilāre*, *-ātum*, from *mutilus* maimed]

mutiny *mū'ti-nē*, *n* insurrection against constituted authority, *esp* naval or military; revolt, tumult, strife. — *vi* to rise against authority, *esp* in military or naval service: — *pr p* **mu'tinying**; *pa t* and *pa p* **mu'tinied**. — *n* **mutine** (*mū'tin*) mutiny (*obs*); a mutineer, rebel (*Shakesp*). — *vi* (*Shakesp* and *Milton*) to mutiny, rebel. — *n* **mutineer'** a person who mutinies or takes part in a mutiny. — *vi* to mutiny. — *adj* **mu'tinous** ready or inclined to mutiny; rebellious, unsubmissive; of the nature of, or expressing, mutiny. — *adv* **mu'tinously**. — *n* **mu'tinousness**. — **Mutiny Act** an act regulating the government of the army, passed annually by the British parliament from 1689–1879, when it was superseded. [Fr *mutin* riotous, from L *movēre*, *mōtum* to move]

muton. See under **mutate**.

mutoscope *mū'tō-skōp*, *n* an early form of cinematograph. [L *mūtāre* to change, and Gr *skopeein* to look at]

mutt *mut*, (*slang*; *orig US*) *n* a blockhead; a dog, *esp* a mongrel. [Perh for **muttonhead**]

mutter *mut'ər*, *vi* to utter words in a low, indistinct voice; to murmur, *esp* in hostility, mutiny, or menace; to grumble; (of thunder) to rumble faintly. — *vt* to utter indistinctly. — *n* a murmuring (*Milton*); indistinct utterance; low rumbling; subdued grumbling. — *n* **mutterā'tion** (*Richardson*) complaining. — *n* **mutt'erer**. — *n* and *adj* **mutt'ering**. — *adv* **mutt'eringly**. [Prob imit, like dialect Ger *muttern*; L *muttīre*]

mutton *mut'n*, *n* a sheep (*obs* or *jocular*); sheep's flesh as food; women as food for lust, hence a prostitute (*obs slang*); an em (*printing*). — *adj* **mutt'ony**. — **mutton bird** an Australasian shearwater, *esp* the short-tailed, said by some to taste like mutton; **mutton chop** a piece of mutton cut from the rib. — *adj* (of whiskers) shaped like a mutton-chop, ie broad and rounded on the cheek, tapering to meet the hairline. — **mutton cloth** a plain-knitted cloth (*usu* cotton) of loose texture; **mutt'on-cut'let**. — *n pl* **mutt'on-dum'mies** (*slang*) white plimsolls. — **mutt'on-fist** a coarse, big hand; a printer's index-hand; **mutt'on-ham** a salted leg of mutton; **mutt'onhead** a heavy, stupid person. — *adj* **mutt'on-headed** stupid. — **mutt'on-su'et** the fat surrounding the kidneys and loins of sheep; **mutt'on-thumper** a clumsy bookbinder. — **mutton dressed as lamb** (*colloq*) an older woman who dresses or makes herself up in a style more suitable to a young one; **return to our muttons** (*colloq*) return to the subject of discussion (a playful translation of the judge's 'Revenons à nos moutons' in the old French farce of *Maître Pathelin*, in which the witnesses wander from the matter in dispute, some sheep). [OFr *moton* (Fr *mouton*) a sheep, from LL *multō*, *-ōnis*; perh of Celtic origin]

mutual *mū'tū-əl*, *adj* interchanged; reciprocal; given and received; common, joint, shared by two or more (*Shakesp*; now regarded by many as incorrect). — *n* **mu'tualism** symbiosis; the theory that mutual dependence is necessary for the welfare of the individual and society; practice based on this. — *n* **mutuality** (*-al'i-ti*). — *n* **mutualizā'tion** or **-s-**. — *vt* **mu'tualize** or **-ise** to put upon a mutual footing. — *adv* **mu'tually**. — **mutual admiration society** (*facetious*) a group of people or circle of friends lavish in their praise of each other; **mutual friend** (*Dickens*) a common friend; **mutual funds** (*US*) unit trusts; **mutual improvement society** a society whose members meet to hear lectures, read essays, hold debates, etc, in order to stimulate each other to improve in knowledge and in public speaking; **mutual inductance** (*electronics*) the generation of electromotile force in one system of conductors by a variation of current in another system linked to the first by magnetic flux; **mutual inductor** (*electronics*) a component consisting of two coils designed to have a definite mutual inductance; **mutual insurance** the system of a company in which the policy-holders are the shareholders; **mutual mistake** (*law*) the situation arising when parties to a contract are at cross-purposes as to its subject or terms; **mutual wall** a wall equally belonging to each of two houses. [Fr *mutuel*, from L *mūtuus*, from *mūtāre* to change]

mutuca. See **motuca**.

mutule *mūt'ūl*, *n* a kind of square, flat bracket, in Doric architecture, above each triglyph and each metope, with guttae. [L *mūtulus* a mutule, modillion]

mutuum *mū'tū-əm*, (*hist*) *n* a bailment consisting of a loan of goods for consumption, such as corn, coal, etc, to be returned in goods of the same amount. [L neuter of *mūtuus* lent]

mutuus consensus *mū'tū-əs kon-sen'səs* or *mōō'tōō-ōōs kōn-sān'sōōs*, (*L*) *n* mutual consent.

muu-muu *mōō'mōō*, *n* a simple loose dress worn chiefly in Hawaii. [Hawaiian *mu'u mu'u*]

mux *muks*, (*US* and *dialect*) *vt* to spoil, botch. — *n* a mess. [Origin obscure]

Muzak® *mū'zak*, *n* piped music (qv) as played in restaurants, shops, etc. — Also (*erron*) **Musak**. — *adj* **mū'zaky**.

muzhik, moujik or **mujik** *mōō-zhik'* or *mōō'zhik*, (*hist*) *n* a Russian peasant. [Russ *muzhik*]

muzzle *muz'l*, *n* the projecting jaws and nose of an animal; a strap or a cage for the mouth to prevent biting; the extreme end of a gun, etc. — *vt* to put a muzzle on; to keep from hurting; to gag or silence. — *vt* and *vi* (of an animal) to touch, thrust or investigate with the muzzle. — *n* **muzz'ler** a person who applies a muzzle; a blow on the mouth; a muzzle-loader; a direct headwind (*naut*). — **muzz'le-bag** a canvas bag fixed to the muzzle of a gun at sea, to keep out water; **muzz'le-load'er** a firearm loaded through the muzzle (opposed to *breech-loader*). — *adj* **muzz'le-load'ing**. — **muzz'le-veloc'ity** the velocity of a projectile the moment it leaves the muzzle of a gun. [OFr *musel* (Fr *museau*), from LL *mūsellum*, dimin of *mūsum* or *mūsus* beak]

muzzy *muz'i*, *adj* dazed, bewildered; tipsy; blurred; hazy. — *adv* **muzz'ily**. — *n* **muzz'iness**. [Origin unknown]

Mv *abbrev*: mendelevium (now **Md**).

mv *abbrev*: merchant vessel; motor vessel; muzzle velocity.

MVD *abbrev*: Ministervo Vrytrennikh Del, the Soviet Ministry of Internal Affairs from 1946–60.

MVDS *abbrev*: multipoint (or microwave) video distribution system.

MVO *abbrev*: Member of the (Royal) Victorian Order.

mvule *mvōō'le*, *n* a huge tropical African timber tree (*Chlorophora excelsa*) of the mulberry family.

MW *abbrev*: Malawi (IVR); medium wave; megawatt.

M-way. See under **M** (*abbrev*).

MWF *abbrev*: Medical Women's Federation.

MWGM (*Freemasonry*) *abbrev*: Most Worshipful (or worthy) Grand Master.

MX *abbrev*: missile experimental.

Mx *abbrev*: Middlesex.

mx *abbrev*: **maxwell** (unit measuring magnetic flux).

my *mī* (sometimes *mi*), *possessive adj* (in *attributive* use only) of or belonging to me; sometimes used in addressing others, eg formally, *my lord*, *my lady* or affectionately, patronizingly, etc, eg *my dear*, *my friend*; used in interjection, eg *my God!* — *interj* expressing surprise (*perh* for **my word** or **my God**). [**mine**[1], from OE *mīn* (genitive) of me]

Mya *mī'ə*, *n* a genus of lamellibranch molluscs, the gapers, including the American soft or long clam. [Gr *mȳs* or *myax* a mussel]

myal. See **myalism**.

myalgia *mī-al'ji-ə*, *n* pain in a muscle. — *adj* **myal'gic**. — **myalgic encephalomyelitis** (*en-sef-ə-lō-mī-ə-lī'tis*; Gr *encephalos* brain, and *myelos* spinal cord) a long-term post-viral syndrome with chronic fatigue and muscle pain on exercise (*abbrev* **ME**). [Gr *mȳs* muscle, and *algos* pain]

myalism *mī'əl-izm*, *n* a form of witchcraft of African origin, practised in the W Indies. — *adj* **my'al**. [Prob W African; cf Hausa *maye*]

myall[1] *mī'öl, n* an Australian aborigine living traditionally. — *adj* wild; unaccustomed to white society. [Aboriginal]

myall[2] *mī'öl, n* an Australian acacia of various species with hard, scented wood; the wood of such a tree. [Australian *maiāl*]

myasthenia *mī-əs-thē'ni-ə, n* muscular weakness or debility. — *adj* **myasthenic** (*-then'ik*). — **myasthenia gravis** (*grä'vis*) a chronic progressive disease in which the (*esp* facial) muscles become fatigued, with progressive muscular paralysis. [Gr *mys* muscle, and **asthenia**]

myc-. See **myco-**.

mycelium *mī-sē'li-əm, n* the white threadlike mass of filaments forming the vegetative part of a fungus: — *pl* **mycē'lia**. — *adj* **mycē'lial**. [Gr *mykēs* a mushroom]

Mycenaean *mī-sē-nē'ən, adj* of the ancient city state of *Mycēnae* (Gr *Mykēnai*) in Argolis, Agamemnon's kingdom, or its culture culminating in the Bronze Age.

Mycetes *mī-sē'tēz, n* the howler genus of S American monkeys. [Gr *mȳkētēs* bellower]

mycetes *mī-sē'tēz, n pl* fungi. — *combining form* **mycet-** or **myceto-** (*mī-sē-tō-, -o-*). — *n* **mycetol'ogy** mycology. — *n* **mycetō'ma** Madura foot, a disease of foot and leg in India, caused by a fungus. — *n pl* **Mycetozō'a** the *Myxomycetes* or slime-fungi (when classed as animals). — *n* and *adj* **mycetozō'an**. [Gr *mykēs, -ētos*, pl *mykētes* a mushroom]

myco- *mī-kō-*, or before a vowel **myc-** *mīk-*, *combining form* denoting: fungus; mushroom. — See also terms under **mycetes**. — *n* **mycobactē'rium** any of several Gram-positive parasitic or saprophytic bacteria, eg those causing leprosy and tuberculosis. — *n* **mycodomatium** (*-dō-mā'shyəm* or *-shi-əm*; Gr *domation* a chamber) a fungus-gall: — *pl* **mycodomā'tia**. — *adj* **mycologic** (*mī-kə-loj'ik*) or **mycolog'ical**. — *n* **mycologist** (*-kol'*). — *n* **mycol'ogy** the study of fungi. — *n* **mycophagist** (*mī-kof'ə-jist*; Gr *phagein* to eat) a toadstool-eater. — *n* **mycoph'agy**. — *n* **mycoplas'ma** (*-plaz'mə*) a member of the *Mycoplasma*, a genus of pathogenic agents apparently neither viruses nor true bacteria, including the cause of so-called 'virus' pneumonia: — *pl* **mycoplas'mas** or **mycoplas'mata**. — *n* **mycorrhiza** or **mycorhiza** (*mī-kō-rī'zə*; Gr *rhiza* root) a fungal mycelium investing or penetrating the underground parts of a higher plant and supplying it with material from humus instead of root-hairs. — *adj* **mycorrhī'zal** or **mycorhī'zal**. — *n* **mycosis** (*-kō'sis*) a disease due to growth of a fungus. — *adj* **mycotic** (*-kot'ik*). — *n* **mycotoxicosis** (*-tok-si-kō'sis*) poisoning caused by a mycotoxin. — *n* **mycotoxin** (*-tok'sin*) any poisonous substance produced by a fungus. — *adj* **mycotroph'ic** (*-trof'ik*; Gr *trophē* food) (of a plant) living in symbiosis with a fungus. [Gr *mykēs, -ētos*, pl *mykētes* a mushroom]

mydriasis *mi-drī'ə-sis, n* morbid dilatation of the pupil of the eye. — *adj* **mydriatic** (*mid-ri-at'ik*). — *n* a drug causing the pupil to dilate. [Gr *mydriāsis*]

myel- *mī-ə-l-* or **myelo-** *mī-ə-lō-, -lo-* or *-lə-*, *combining form* denoting bone marrow or the spinal chord. — *n* **my'elin** the substance forming the medullary sheath of nerve-fibres. — *n* **myelī'tis** inflammation of the spinal chord; inflammation of the bone marrow. — *n* **my'eloblast** an immature cell of bone marrow, found in the circulating blood only in diseased conditions. — *adj* **my'eloid** like, relating to, or of the nature of, marrow. — *n* **myeloma** (*-lō'mə*) a tumour of the bone marrow, or composed of cells normally present in bone marrow. — *n* **my'elon** the spinal cord. [Gr *myelos* marrow]

mygale *mig'ə-lē, n* an American bird-catching spider of the genus *Mygale*. [Gr *mȳgalē* a field-mouse, a shrew, from *mȳs* mouse, and *galeē* weasel]

myiasis *mī'i-ə-sis* or *mī-i-ā'sis, n* disease caused by presence of flies or their larvae. [Gr *myīa* fly]

mylodon *mī'lə-don, n* a sloth of the *Mylodon* genus of gigantic Pleistocene ground-sloths with a short, broad skull. — *adj* of or relating to this genus. — Also *n* and *adj* **my'lodont**. [Gr *mylē* a mill, and *odous, odontos* a tooth]

mylohyoid *mī-lō-hī'oid*, (*anatom*) *adj* relating to or near the jawbone and the hyoid bone. — *n* a muscle so placed. [Gr *mylē* a mill]

mylonite *mī'lən-īt, n* a hard, compact, often streaky granular rock produced by crushing. — *adj* **mylonitic** (*-it'ik*). — *n* **mylonītīzā'tion** or **-s-**. — *vt* **my'lonitize** or **-ise** to turn into mylonite. [Gr *mylōn* a mill]

myna, **mynah** or **mina** *mī'nə, n* any of various related sturnoid Asiatic birds of which the species *Gracula religiosa*, black with white spots on the wings, can be taught to imitate human speech. [Hindi *mainā*]

mynheer *mīn-hār'* or *mən-ār', n* my lord (*archaic*); Dutch for *Mr* or *sir*; a Dutchman or Afrikaaner. [Du *mijn* my, and *heer* lord]

myo- *mī'ō-* or *mī-o'-*, *combining form* denoting muscle. — *n* **my'oblast** a cell producing muscle-tissue. — *adj* **myoblast'ic**. — *adj* **myocar'dial** of or relating to the myocardium (**myocardial infarction** destruction of the myocardium due to interruption of blood supply to the area). — *n* **myocardiop'athy** any non-inflammatory disease of the myocardium. — *n* **myocardī'tis** inflammation of the myocardium. — *n* **myocar'dium** the muscular substance of the heart. — *adj* **myoelec'tric** of apparatus, etc which uses the small electric currents produced within the body which normally cause muscular contraction and relaxation. — *n* **myofī'bril** one of the elongated contractile cells that make up striated muscle. — *n* **my'ogen** an albumin, soluble in water, found in muscle. — *adj* **myogen'ic** (of contraction) arising spontaneously in a muscle, independent of nervous stimuli. — *n* **myoglō'bin** a protein that stores oxygen in muscle. — *n* **my'ogram** a myographic record. — *n* **my'ograph** an instrument for recording muscular contractions. — *adj* **myograph'ic** or **myograph'ical**. — *n* **myog'raphist**. — *n* **myog'raphy**. — *adj* **my'oid** like muscle. — *adj* **myolog'ical**. — *n* **myol'ogist**. — *n* **myol'ogy** the study of muscles. — *n* **myō'ma** a tumour composed of muscular tissue. — *n* **my'osin** a protein that contributes to the process of contraction in muscles. — *n* **myosī'tis** (irregularly formed) inflammation of a muscle. — *n* **myotonic dystrophy** a muscle-wasting disease that causes **myotonia**, or muscle-stiffness, as well as the usual symptoms of weakness and wasting. — *n* **my'otube** a cylindrical cell that develops from a myoblast, representing a stage in the development of muscle fibres. [Gr *mȳs, myos* muscle]

myomancy *mī'ō-man-si, n* divination from the movements of mice. — *adj* **myoman'tic**. [Gr *mȳs* a mouse, and *manteiā* divination]

myopia *mī-ō'pi-ə, n* short-sightedness. — *n* **my'ope** (*-ōp*) or **my'ops** (*-ops*) a short-sighted person. — *adj* **myopic** (*-op'*) short-sighted (also *fig*). — *n* a short-sighted person. [Gr *myōps* short-sighted, from *mȳein* to shut, and *ōps* the eye]

myosin. See under **myo-**.

myosis. See **miosis**.

myositis. See under **myo-**.

myosotis *mī-os-ō'tis* or **myosote** *mī'ə-sōt, n* a plant of the genus *Myosotis*, the forget-me-not genus of the borage family. [Gr *myosōtis* mouse-ear, from its furry leaves, from *mȳs, myos* a mouse, and *ous, ōtos* an ear]

myotube. See under **myo-**.

myrbane. Same as **mirbane**.

myria- *mir'i-ə-*, *combining form* denoting: ten thousand; a very large number. — See **myriad** and **myriapod**.

myriad *mir'i-əd, n* any immense number. — *adj* numberless. — *adj* and *n* (or *adv*) **myr'iadfold**. — *n* and *adj* **myr'iadth**. [Gr *mȳrias, -ados* ten thousand]

myriapod *mir'i-ə-pod, n* a member of the **Myriapoda** (*-ap'ə-də*), a class of crawling arthropods with many legs, such as the centipedes and millipedes. — Also **myr'iopod**, etc. [Gr *mȳriopous, -podos* many-footed, from *mȳrios* numberless, and *pous, podos* a foot]

Myrica *mi-rī'kə*, *n orig*, the tamarisk; the sweet-gale or bog-myrtle genus, of the family **Myricā'ceae**. [Gr *myrīkē* (*myrikē*) tamarisk]

myringa *mir-ing'gə*, (*anatom*) *n* the eardrum. — *n* **myringitis** (*-in-jī'tis*) inflammation of the eardrum. — *n* **myringoscope** (*-ing'gə-skōp*) an instrument for viewing the eardrum. — *n* **myringotomy** (*-ing-got'əm-i*) incision of the eardrum. [LL *miringa*, from Gr *mēninx* membrane]

myriorama *mir-i-ō-rä'mə*, *n* a picture composed of interchangeable parts that can be variously combined. [Gr *mȳrios* numberless, and *horāma* a view]

myrioscope *mir'i-ə-skōp*, *n* a variety of kaleidoscope. [Gr *mȳrios* numberless, and *skopeein* to view]

Myristica *mir-* or *mīr-is'ti-kə*, *n* the nutmeg genus of plants, giving name to the family **Myristicā'ceae**. — *adj* **myris'tic**. — *adj* **myristicivorous** (*-is-ti-siv'ə-rəs*) feeding upon nutmegs. — **myristic acid** a fatty acid ($C_{13}H_{27}$·COOH) obtained from nutmegs. [Gr *mȳrizein* to anoint]

myrmecoid *mûr'mik-oid*, *adj* antlike. [Gr *myrmēkoeidēs* like an ant]

myrmecology *mûr-mi-kol'ə-ji*, *n* the study of ants. — *adj* **myrmecolog'ic** or **myrmecolog'ical**. — *n* **myrmecol'ogist**. — *adj* **myrmecoph'agous** feeding on ants; of the ant-bear genus **Myrmecoph'aga**. — *n* **myr'mecophile**. — *adj* **myrmecoph'ilous** having a symbiotic relation with ants. — *n* **myrmecoph'ily**. [Gr *myrmēx*, *-ēkos* ant]

Myrmidon *mûr'mi-dən*, *n* one of a tribe of warriors who accompanied Achilles to Troy (*Gr mythol*); (without *cap*) a member of any ruffianly band under a daring leader; someone who carries out another's orders without fear or pity. — *adj* **myrmidō'nian**. — **myrmidons of the law** (*facetious*) policemen, bailiffs, etc. [Gr *Myrmidones* (pl)]

myrobalan *mī-rob'ə-lən*, or *mi-*, *n* the astringent fruit of certain Indian mountain species of the genus *Terminalia* (*Combretaceae*), used medicinally, and in ink, dyeing and tanning; the cherry-plum. — **emblic myrobalan** see under **emblic**. [Gr *mȳrobalanos* bito, from *myron* an unguent, and *balanos* an acorn]

myrrh *mûr*, *n* a bitter, aromatic, transparent gum, exuded from the bark of a tree of the genus *Commiphora*, used medicinally and in perfume and incense; sweet cicely. — *adj* **myrrh'ic**. — *n* **myrrh'ol** the volatile oil of myrrh. [OE *myrra*, from L *myrrha*, from Gr *myrrā*; of Semitic origin; cf Ar *murr*]

myrrhine. See under **murra**.

myrtle *mûr'tl*, *n* any of various evergreen shrubs of the genus *Myrtus*, with beautiful and fragrant leaves; extended to various other plants, some near related, others not, eg a kind of beech in Australia (see also under **bog, wax**). — **myr'tle-wax** wax from the candleberry. [OFr *myrtil*, dimin of *myrte*, from L *myrtus*, from Gr *myrtos*]

Myrtus *mûr'təs*, *n* the myrtle genus, giving name to the family **Myrtā'ceae**. — *adj* **myrtā'ceous**. [L, from Gr *myrtos*]

myself *mī-self'* or *mi-self'*, *pronoun* (used in apposition with *I* or *me*, for emphasis or clarification) in person; (used reflexively) me. [**me**[1] and **self**]

mysophobia *mī-sō-fō'bi-ə*, *n* morbid fear of contamination. [Gr *mysos* defilement, and *phobos* fear]

mystagogue *mis'tə-gog* or *-gōg*, *n* an initiator into religious mysteries. — Also **mystagō'gus**. — *adj* **mystagog'ic** (*-goj'* or *-gog'*) or **mystagog'ical**. — *n* **mys'tagogy** (*-goj-* or *-gog-*). [Gr *mystēs* an initiate, and *agōgos* a leader]

mystery[1] *mis'tər-i*, *n* a secret doctrine; (*usu* in *pl*) in ancient religious, etc rites, known only to the initiated, such as the *Eleusinian mysteries*; (in *pl*) the secrets of freemasonry, etc; a phenomenon, circumstance or happening that cannot be explained; someone or something inscrutable, an enigma; enigmatic quality; something obscure, abstruse or arcane; a tale of suspense that baffles and intrigues; a truth divinely imparted (*relig*); a sacrament (*relig*); (also **mystery play**) a play depicting the life of Christ; a shiftless, drifting girl (*slang*): — *pl* **mys'teries**. — *adj* **mystē'rious** containing mystery; having an air of mystery; obscure; secret; incomprehensible. — *adv* **mystē'riously**. — *n* **mystē'riousness**. — **mys'tery-man** a conjurer; a medicine man; **mys'tery-monger** a dealer in mysteries; **mystery ship** a Q-boat; **mystery tour** an excursion to a destination which remains secret until the journey's end. [L *mystērium*, from Gr *mystērion*, from *mystēs* an initiate, from *myeein* to initiate, from *mȳein* to close the eyes]

mystery[2] or **mistery** *mis'tər-i*, *n* office, service, duty (*obs*); craft, art, trade (*archaic*); skill (*Shakesp*); a trade guild (*hist*). [LL *misterium*, from L *ministerium*, from *minister* servant; confused with *mystērium* and prob with **maistry**, **mastery**]

mystic *mis'tik* or **mystical** *mis'ti-kəl*, *adj* relating to mystery, the mysteries, or mysticism; mysterious; sacredly obscure or secret; involving a sacred or a secret meaning hidden from the eyes of the ordinary person, only revealed to a spiritually enlightened mind; allegorical. — *n* **mys'tic** a person who seeks or attains direct communion with God or the divine in elevated religious feeling or ecstasy. — *adv* **mys'tically**. — *n* **mys'ticalness**. — *n* **mys'ticism** (*-sizm*) the habit or tendency of religious thought and feeling of those who seek direct communion with God or the divine; fogginess and unreality of thought (with suggestion of **mist**). — **mystic recitation** the recitation of parts of the Greek liturgy in an inaudible voice. [L *mysticus*, from Gr *mystikos*, from *mystēs* an initiate; cf **mystery**[1]]

mystify *mis'ti-fī*, *vt* to make mysterious, obscure, or secret; to involve in mystery; to bewilder; to puzzle; to hoax: — *pr p* **mys'tifying**; *pa t* and *pa p* **mys'tified**. — *n* **mystificā'tion**. — *n* **mys'tifier** someone who or that which mystifies; a hoaxer. — *adj* **mys'tifying** [Fr *mystifier*]

mystique *mis-tēk'* or *mēs-tēk*, *n* incommunicable spirit, gift or quality; the secret of an art as known to its inspired practitioners; a sense or aura of mystery, remoteness from the ordinary, and power or skill surrounding a person, activity, etc. [Fr]

myth *mith* or (*archaic*) *mīth*, *n* an ancient traditional story of gods or heroes, *esp* one offering an explanation of some fact or phenomenon; a story with a veiled meaning; mythical matter; a figment; a commonly-held belief that is untrue, or without foundation. — *adj* **myth'ic** or **myth'ical** relating to myths; fabulous; fictitious, untrue. — *adv* **myth'ically**. — *n* **myth'icism** (*-sizm*) theory that explains miraculous stories as myth. — *n* **myth'icist**. — *vt* **myth'icize** or **-ise** (*-i-siz*) to make the subject of myth; to explain as myth. — *n* **myth'icizer** or **-s-**. — *n* **myth'ism** mythicism. — *n* **myth'ist** a maker of myths; a mythicist. — *vt* **myth'ize** or **-ise** to mythicize. — *n* **mythogen'esis** the production or origination of myths. — *n* **mythog'rapher** a writer or narrator of myths. — *n* **mythog'raphy** representation of myths in art; collection or description of myths. — *n* **mythol'oger** or **mytholō'gian** a mythologist. — *adj* **mytholog'ic** or **mytholog'ical** relating to mythology, fabulous. — *adv* **mytholog'ically**. — *n* **mythol'ogist**. — *n* **mythol'ogization** or **-s-**. — *vt* **mythol'ogize** or **-ise** to interpret or explain the mythological character of; to turn into myth; to create myths. — *n* **mythol'ogizer** or **-s-**. — *n* **mythol'ogy** a body of myths; the scientific study of myths; symbolical meaning (*obs*). — *n* and *adj* **myth'omane** (a) mythomaniac. — *n* **mythomā'nia** (*psychiatry*) lying or exaggerating to an abnormal extent. — *n* and *adj* **mythomā'niac**. — *n* **mythopoe'ia** (*mith-ə-pē'ə*) the creation or formation of myths. — *adj* **mythopoeic** (*mith-ō-pē'ik*; Gr *poieein* to make) or **mythopoetic** (*-pō-et'ik*) myth-making. — *n* **mythopoe'ist** a myth-maker. — *n* **mythopō'et** a myth-maker; a writer of poems on mythical subjects. — *n* **mythus** (*mīth'əs*; *L*) or **mythos** (*mīth'os*; *Gr*) myth; mythology; theme, scheme of events; the characteristic or current attitudes of a culture or group, expressed symbolically (through poetry, art, drama, etc). — **mythical theory**

the theory of D F Strauss (1808–74) and his school, that the Gospels are mainly a collection of myths, developed during the first two centuries, from the imagination of the followers of Jesus. — **comparative mythology** the science that investigates myths and seeks to relate those of different peoples. [Gr *mȳthos* talk, story, myth]

Mytilus *mit'i-ləs*, *n* the common mussel genus, giving name to the family **Mytilidae** (*mī-til'i-dē*). — *adj* **mytil'iform**. — *adj* **myt'iloid**. [L *mȳtilus*, *mītulus*, *mūtulus*]

myxoedema or (*esp NAm*) **myxedema** *mik-sē-dē'mə*, *n* a diseased condition due to deficiency of thyroid secretion, characterized by loss of hair, increased thickness and dryness of the skin, increase in weight, slowing of mental processes, and diminution of metabolism. — *adj* **myxoede'matous** or (*esp NAm*) **myxede'matous**. — *adj* **myxoede'mic** or (*esp NAm*) **myxede'mic**. [Gr *myxa* mucus, and *oidēma* swelling]

myxoma *mik-sō'mə*, *n* a tumour of jellylike or mucous substance: — *pl* **myxō'mata**. — *n* **myxomatō'sis** a contagious virus disease of rabbits. — *adj* **myxō'matous**. [Gr *myxa* mucus]

myxomycete *mik-sō-mī-sēt'*, *n* any of the *Myxomycetes* class of very simple plants or slime-fungi, by some classed as animals (*Mycetozoa*), forming in the vegetative stage naked masses of protoplasm with many nuclei, creeping on wet soil, on rotten wood, etc. [Gr *myxa* mucus, and *mykētes*, pl of *mykēs* a mushroom]

Myxophyceae *mik-sō-fish'i-ē*, *n pl* the Cyanophyceae. [Gr *myxa* slime, and *phȳkos* seaweed]

myxovirus *mik'sō-vī-rəs*, *n* any of a group of related viruses causing influenza, mumps, etc. [Gr *myxa* mucus, and **virus**]

mzee *əm-zā*, *n* (E Africa) an old person. [Swahili]

MZM *abbrev*: metical (Mozambique currency).

mzungu *əm-zŏŏng'gŏŏ* *n* (in E Africa) a White person. [Swahili]

N

N or **n** *en*, *n* the fourteenth letter of the modern English alphabet, thirteenth of the Greek, representing a point nasal consonant sound, or before *g* or *k* a back nasal (as in *sing*, *sink*); anything having the shape of the letter; an indefinite number, *esp* in a series (*math*); as a medieval numeral, N = 90, and $\bar{N}$ = 90 000; a unit of measurement (**en**) = half an em (*printing*); an indefinite number, often (*colloq*) implicitly a large number. — *adj* **n^{th}** or **nth**. — *adj* **n'-type** (ie 'negative-type') of a semiconductor, having an excess of conduction electrons over mobile holes (see **hole**[1]). — **to the nth** (or **nth**) to any power; hence (*colloq*) to an unlimited degree.

N or **N.** *abbrev*: (also **kt**) knight; naira (Nigerian currency); navy; newton; ngultrum (Bhutanese currency); Norse; North or Northern; Norway (IVR); nuclear.

N (*chem*) *symbol*: nitrogen.

n or **n.** *abbrev*: name; nano-; neuter; new; nominative; noon; note; noun; number.

'n' a *colloq* shortening of **and**.

NA *abbrev*: Netherlands Antilles (IVR); North America.

Na (*chem*) *symbol*: sodium (formerly called **natrium**).

na *nä*, *adv* a Scottish form of **no**[1]; (*ni* or *nā*, enclitically; *Scot*) not.

n/a *abbrev*: not applicable.

NAACP *abbrev*: National Association for the Advancement of Colored People (*US*).

Naafi *nä'fi*, *n* an organization for providing canteens for servicemen and servicewomen; one of the canteens. — Also **NAAFI**. [From the initials of *N*avy, *A*rmy, and *A*ir *F*orce *I*nstitute(s)]

naam or **nam** *näm*, (*hist*; *law*) *n* distraint. [OE *nām*, related to *niman* to take]

naan. See **nan**.

naartje. See **nartjie**.

nab[1] *nab*, *vt* to seize, snatch; to arrest (*colloq*): — *pr p* **nabb'ing**; *pa t* and *pa p* **nabbed**. — *n* **nabb'er**. [Origin obscure; cf **nap**[4]]

nab[2] *nab*, *n* a hilltop; a promontory; a projection; the keeper of a door-lock. [ON *nabbr* or *nabbi*]

nab[3] *nab*, (*obs slang*) *n* the head; a hat.

Nabataean *nab-ə-tē'ən* or **Nabathaean** *-thē'*, *n* and *adj* (a member) of an ancient powerful Arab people who lived around Petra. [Gr *Nabat(h)aios*]

nabk *nabk* or *nubk*, *n* the Christ's-thorn. [Ar *nebq*]

nabla *nab'lə*, (*math*) *n* in Cartesian co-ordinates, the symbol ∇, an inverted delta, also called **del**, representing the vector operator $\mathbf{i}\partial/\partial x+\mathbf{j}\partial/\partial y+\mathbf{k}\partial/\partial z$. [Gr *nabla* nebel (qv), from the shape]

nabob *nā'bob*, *n* a nawab (*obs*); a European who has amassed a fortune in the East (*archaic*; used in Europe only); (in Europe) any person of great wealth, an important person. [Hindi *nawwāb*; see **nawab**]

nabs *nabz*, (*slang*) *n* a person, *esp* in such phrases as **his nabs**, himself. [Cf **nob**[2], **nib**[2]]

NAC *abbrev*: National Association for the Childless.

NACAB *abbrev*: National Association of Citizens' Advice Bureaux.

nacarat *nak'ə-rat*, *n* a bright orange-red; a fabric so coloured. [Fr]

nacelle *nä-sel'*, *n* a little boat (*obs*); the car of a balloon, airship, etc; a streamlined structure on an aircraft housing an engine, etc. [Fr, from LL *nāvicella*, from L *nāvis* ship]

nach. See **nautch**.

nache *nāch*, *n* the rump. [See **aitchbone**]

nacho *nach'ō*, *n* (*usu* in *pl*) a corn chip, *usu* topped with cheese or beans and flavoured with chilli, jalapeño peppers, etc. — *pl* **nach'os**. [Am Sp]

Nachschlag *nähh'shlähh*, (*music*) *n* a grace-note whose time is taken off the preceding note. [Ger, from *nach* after, and *Schlag* stroke]

nachtmaal *nähht'mäl*. Older form of **nagmaal**.

nacket *nak'it* or **nocket** *nok'it*, *n* a snack, light lunch. [Origin obscure]

NACODS *nā'kodz*, *abbrev*: National Association of Colliery Overmen, Deputies and Shotfirers.

nacre *nā'kər*, *n* mother-of-pearl or a shellfish yielding it. — *adj* **na'cred**. — *adj* **nā'creous** (also **nā'crous**). — *n* **nā'crite** a clay mineral, identical in composition to kaolinite but differing in optical characteristics and atomic structure. [Fr; prob of Eastern origin]

NACRO *nak'rō*, *abbrev*: National Association for the Care and Resettlement of Offenders.

nada *nä'də*, *n* nothing; nothingness. [Sp]

Na-Dene *nä-dēn'*, *nä-dā'ni* or *nä-dā-nā'*, *n* a group of N American Indian languages comprising Athabascan, Haida, Tlingit and Eyak.

nadir *nā'dēr*, *nad'ēr* or *-dər*, *n* the point of the heavens diametrically opposite to the zenith; the lowest point of anything, *esp* an emotional state. [Fr, from Ar *nadīr* (*nazīr*) opposite to]

nae *nā*, *adj* a Scots form of **no**[2]. — *adv* same as **no**[1], *esp* with a comparative. — **nae'body** nobody; **nae'thing** nothing.

naevus or *US* **nevus** *nē'vəs*, *n* a birthmark; a pigmented spot or an overgrowth of small blood-vessels in the skin: — *pl* **naevi** (*nē'vī*, *nī'vē*). — *obs* **naeve** (*nēv*; *pl* **naeves**). — *adj* **nae'void**. [L]

naff *naf*, (*slang*) *adj* inferior, worthless, *esp* in style or taste; vulgar, socially crass. — *n* an incompetent. — *adj* and *adv* **naff'ing** used as an offensive qualification. — *adv* **naff'ly**. — *n* **naff'ness**. — **naff all** nothing at all. — **naff off** an offensive injunction to go away. [Origin disputed; suggested derivations are: *naf*, back-slang for *fan(ny)* the female genitalia; *naff* navel or nothing; *naffy* (**Naafi**) generally contemptuous, specif 'shirking'; the phrase *not available for fucking or fornication*]

nag[1] *nag*, *n* a horse, *esp* a small one; a riding-horse, or an inferior horse (*colloq*); a jade (*Shakesp*). [ME *nagge*; origin obscure; cf MDu *negge*, *negghe* (mod Du *neg*, *negge*)]

nag[2] *nag*, *vt* or *vi* to find fault with, urge (to do something), cause pain to, or worry, constantly; (with *at*) to worry or annoy continually: — *pr p* **nagg'ing**; *pa t* and *pa p* **nagged**. — *n* **nag** or **nagg'er** a person, *esp* a woman, who persistently scolds or annoys another, *esp* a man. — *adj* **nagg'y**. [Cf Norw *nage* to grow, rankle, and Swed *nagga* to gnaw]

naga *nä'gə*, *n* a snake, *esp* the cobra (*Ind*); a divine snake (*Hindu mythol*). [Sans *nāga*]

nagana *nä-gä'nə*, *n* a disease of horses and cattle caused by a trypanosome transmitted by tsetse flies. — Also **ngana** (*əng-gä'nə*). [Zulu *nakane*]

nagapie *nahh'ə-pi*, (*SAfr*) *n* the bush-baby or nocturnal lemur. [Afrik, literally 'night-ape' (see **bush-baby**), from Du *nacht* night, and *aap* monkey]

nagari *nä'gə-rē*, *n* devanagari, the script in which Sanskrit, Hindi and other Indian languages are written; the group of alphabets to which devanagari belongs. [Sans *nāgarī* town-script, from *nāgaran* town (perh referring to a particular town); addition of *deva-* to form *devanagari* was a later development]

nagmaal *nähh'mäl, näk'*, (*SAfr*) *n* a Dutch Reformed Church Sacrament, the Lord's Supper. [Earlier *nachtmaal* night meal; from Du]

nagor *nā'gör*, *n* a W African antelope (*Redunca redunca*). [Fr, arbitrarily formed by Buffon from earlier *nanguer*]

Nah. *abbrev*: Nahum (*Old Testament*).

Nahal *na-häl'*, *n* an organization of young soldiers in Israel; (without *cap*) an agricultural settlement established and manned by such soldiers, *esp* in border areas. [Heb]

NAHT *abbrev*: National Association of Head Teachers.

Nahuatl *nä'wät-l*, *n* a member of a group of Indian peoples of S Mexico and Central America, including the Aztecs; the language of these peoples, Aztec. — Also *adj*.

NAI *abbrev*: non-accidental injury.

Naia. See **Naja**.

naiad *nī'ad* or *nā'əd*, *n* a river or spring nymph; the aquatic larva of the dragonfly, mayfly, stone-fly or damselfly: — *pl* **nai'adēs** or **nai'ads**. — *n* **Nai'as** a genus of water-plants, giving name to a family **Naiadā'ceae** related to or including the pondweeds. [Gr *nāias*, *-ados*, pl *-ades*, from *naein* to flow]

naiant *nā'ənt*, (*heraldry*) *adj* swimming horizontally. [Prob from an Anglo-Fr form of OFr *noiant*, pr p, from L *natāre* to swim]

naif or **naïf** *nä-ēf'*, *adj* naive.

naik *nä'ik*, *n* a lord or governor; a corporal of Indian infantry. [Urdu *nā'ik*, from Sans *nāyaka* leader]

nail *nāl*, *n* a horny plate at the end of a finger or toe, *usu* distinguished from a claw in being flattened; a claw; a small *usu* metal spike with a head, used for fastening wood, etc; a nail-shaped excrescence, *esp* one at the tip of a bird's bill; a measure of length (5.5cm or $2\frac{1}{4}$ inches). — *vt* to fix with a nail; to pin down or hold fast (also *fig*); to fasten, pierce (*rare* or *obs*), or stud (*rare*) with nails; to expose as a lie; to cause the downfall of (*colloq*); to catch or secure (*slang*). — *adj* **nailed** having nails; fastened with nails. — *n* **nail'er** a maker of nails. — *n* **nail'ery** a place where nails are made. — *n* **nail'ing** making nails; fastening with nails. — *adj* **nail'less**. — **nail'-bed** that portion of the true skin on which a fingernail or toenail rests; **nail'-biter**; **nail'-biting** chewing off the ends of one's fingernails. — *adj* (of an event or experience) which induces nail-biting (as a sign of anxiety, excitement or tension). — **nail'-bomb** an explosive device containing gelignite and packed with long nails; **nail'-brush** a brush for cleaning the nails; **nail'-file** a file for trimming fingernails or toenails; **nail gun** an implement used to put in nails; **nail'-head** the head of a nail; an ornament shaped like it. — *adj* **nail'-head'** or **nail'-head'ed** having a head suggesting that of a nail; having nail-head ornaments. — **nail'-head-spar'** calcite crystallized in a scalenohedron terminated by a rhombohedron; **nail'-hole** a hole made by or for a nail; a notch for opening a pocket-knife; **nail polish** nail varnish; **nail punch** or **set** a tool for punching the head of a nail below or flush with the surface; **nail'-rod** a strip of iron to be made into nails; iron in that form; strong coarse tobacco (*Austr*); a stick of liquorice; **nail'-scissors** small scissors designed *esp* for trimming the fingernails and toenails; **nail varnish** varnish for fingernails or toenails. — **a nail in one's** (or **the**) **coffin** any event, experience, etc which has the effect of shortening one's life; a contributory factor in the downfall of anything; **hard as nails** in excellent physical condition; physically or mentally tough; callous, unsympathetic, unsentimental; **hit the nail on the head** to touch the exact point; **nail a lie to the counter** to expose it and put it out of currency, from the old custom of shopkeepers with counterfeit coins; **nail down** to fasten (something) down with nails; to force (someone) to make a binding promise or to give his or her consent (*colloq*); to fix or establish (something) definitely; **nailed on** (of a horse) considered to be a near-certainty to win a race (*horse-racing slang*); **nail one's colours to the mast** see under **colour**; **nail up** to close or fasten with or as if with nails; **on the nail** on the spot, without delay, as payment. [OE *nægel*; Ger *Nagel*]

nain *nān*, (*Scot*) *adj* own. — *n* **nainsel'** or **nainsell'** own self; a Highlander (from the Highlander's formerly alleged habit of referring to himself or herself as *her nainsel'*). [**mine ain** my own]

nainsook *nān'so͝ok*, *n* a kind of muslin like jaconet. [Hindi *nainsukh*, from *nain* eye, and *sukh* pleasure]

Nair or **Nayar** *nī'ər*, *n* a people of Kerala who were formerly a noble and military caste of the Malabar coast and who practised a peculiar system of polyandry and matriliny.

naira *nī'rə*, *n* the standard unit of currency in Nigeria (100 *kobo*).

naissant *nās'ənt*, *adj* nascent; rising or coming forth (*heraldry*). [Fr, pr p of *naître*, from L *nāscī*, *nātus* to be born]

naive or **naïve** *nä-ēv'* or *nī-*, *adj* with natural or unaffected simplicity, *esp* in thought, manners or speech; artless; ingenuous; simplisitic. — *adv* **naive'ly** or **naïve'ly**. — *n* **naive'ness** or **naïve'ness**. — *n* **naiveté**, **naïveté** (*nä-ēv'i-tā*), **naivety** or **naïvety** (*nä-ēv'ti* or *nī-*) natural simplicity and unreservedness of thought, manner or speech; ingenuosity. — *adj* **naiv'ist**. — Also **naif** or **naïf**. — **naive painting** primitive painting. [Fr *naïf*, fem *naïve*, from L *nātīvus* native, from *nāscī*, *natus* to be born]

Naja *nā'jə* or *-yə*, *n* the cobra genus. — Also **Naia**. [Appar Linnaeus's misreading of **naga**, or of Sinh *naiā*, *nayā*]

naked *nā'kid*, *adj* without clothes; uncovered; bare; exposed; open to view; unconcealed; undisguised, blatant or flagrant; evident; unarmed; defenceless; unprovided; devoid (of); without ornament; without confirmation, supporting evidence, etc; simple; artless; without the usual covering; lacking some element (eg financial backing) necessary to complete or make valid a contract, etc (*commerce* and *finance*). — *adv* **na'kedly**. — *n* **na'kedness**. — **naked bed** (*obs*) a bed in which one is (*orig*) entirely naked, (later) without ordinary day clothes; **naked eye** the eye unassisted by any kind of optical instrument (eg a telescope); **naked lady** or **ladies** the meadow-saffron; the autumn crocus (also **naked boys**); **naked-light mine** (*min ext*) a non-fiery mine, where safety lamps are not required. [OE *nacod*; Ger *nackt*]

naker *nā'kər*, (*hist*) *n* one of a pair of small, medieval kettledrums. [OFr *nacre*, from Ar *naqāra*]

nala, **nalla** and **nallah**. Same as **nulla**.

NALGO *nal'gō*: National and Local Government Officers' Association.

naloxone *nal-ok'sōn*, *n* a potent drug ($C_{19}H_{21}NO_4$) used as an antidote for various narcotics, *esp* morphine. [*N-al*lylnor*oxy*morph*one*]

nam[1] *pa t* of **nim**.

nam[2]. See **naam**.

namaste *nä'məs-ti*, *n* (in India) a traditional form of greeting, a slight bow with the palms pressed together before the chest or face. — Also **namaskar** (*nä-məs-kär'*; Sans *kara* doing). [Sans *namas* obeisance, salutation, bow, and *te*, dative of *tuam* you]

namby-pamby *nam'bi-pam'bi*, *adj* lacking strength of character or (masculine) vigour, feeble; (of writing, etc) prettily or sentimentally childish. — *n* namby-pamby writing or talk; a namby-pamby person: — *pl* **nam'by-pam'bies**. — *adj* **nam'by-pam'bical**. — *n* **nam'by-pam'biness**. — *adj* **nam'by-pam'byish**. — *n* **nam'by-pam'byism**. [Nickname given by Carey or by Swift to *Ambrose* Philips (1674–1749), whose simple odes to children were despised by 18c Tories]

name *nām*, *n* that by which a person or a thing is known or called; a designation; reputation; fame; a celebrity; family or clan; seeming or pretension without reality; authority; behalf; assumed character (of); (often with *cap*) a person who, in return for a certain sum of money from a company, enterprise, undertaking, etc, agrees to guarantee payment of any losses made (*insurance* and *commerce*). — (as *adj*) famous, well-known (as in a *name brand* or *product*). — *vt* to give a name to; to mention the name of; to designate; to speak of or call by name; to state or specify; to utter (with cognate object); to mention for a post or office; to nominate; (of the Speaker) to mention (an MP) formally by name in the House of Commons as guilty of disorderly conduct; to make known the name of (someone implicated in a crime, an accomplice, etc) to the police, etc. — *adj* **nam'able** or **name'able** capable, or worthy, of being named. — *adj* **named**. — *adj* **name'less** without a name; anonymous; undistinguished; indescribable; unspeakable; illegitimate. — *adv* **name'lessly**. — *n* **name'lessness**. — *adj* **name'ly** (*Scot*) famous (for). — *adv* that is to say; by name; especially (*obs*). — *n* **nam'er**. — *n* **nam'ing**. — **name brand** a make of an article bearing a manufacturer's distinguishing name; **name'-calling** verbal abuse; **name'-child** a person called after one; **name'-day** the feast-day of the saint whose name one was given; the day when a ticket bearing the buyer's name, etc is given to the seller, ticket day (*stock exchange*); the day on which a name is bestowed; **name'-dropping** trying to impress others by casual mention of important or well-known persons as if they were one's friends; **name'-dropper**. — *vi* **name'-drop**. — **name'-part** the part that gives title to a play, title-role; **name'-plate** an attached plate bearing the name of occupant, owner, manufacturer, etc; a masthead (*journalism*; *US*); **name'sake** a person bearing the same name as another; **name'-son** a male name-child; **name'tape** a short piece of cloth tape attached to a garment, etc, marked with the owner's name. — *adj* **name'worthy** worth naming; distinguished. — **call names** to abuse verbally; **in name** fictitiously, as an empty title; **in all but name** in reality, essentially, although not formally or ostensibly; virtually; **in the name of** on behalf of; by the authority of; **name after** (or *NAm* **name for**) to give (a child) the same name as another person, in honour of that person; **name the day** to fix a day, *esp* for a marriage; **name names** to give specific names, *esp* so as to accuse or blame the people thus named; **no names, no pack-drill** (*colloq*) mention no names, then no-one gets into trouble; **proper name** a name given to a particular person, place or thing; **take a name in vain** to use a name lightly or profanely; **the name of the game** (*colloq*) the thing that is important or essential; the central trend or theme, what it's all about (*usu derog*); **to one's name** belonging to one; **you name it** this applies to whatever you mention, want, etc. [OE *nama*; Ger *Name*; L *nōmen*]

namma hole. Same as **gnamma hole**.

nan[1] or **naan** *nän*, *n* a type of slightly leavened bread, as baked in India and Pakistan, similar to pitta bread. [Hindi]

nan[2] and **nana**[1]. See **nanny**.

nana[2] *nä'nə*, (*orig Austr slang*) *n* an idiot, fool; the head, as in **off one's nana**. [Prob ba*nana*]

Nancy *nan'si*, (*derog slang*; also without *cap*) *n* an effeminate young man; a male homosexual: — *pl* **Nan'cies**. — Also **Nance, Nan'cy-boy** or **Miss Nan'cy** (also without *cap*). — Also *adj*. [From the girl's name]

Nancy-pretty *nan'si-prit'i*, *n* the plant *Saxifraga umbrosa*, London Pride. [Prob for **none so pretty**]

NAND *nand*, (*comput*) *n* a logic circuit that has two or more inputs and one output, the output signal being 1 if any of its inputs is 0, and 0 if all its inputs are 1. [*not and*]

Nandi bear *nan'di bār*, *n* a great fierce animal reputed to live in E Africa, perhaps the spotted hyena. [From the *Nandi* Forest, Kenya]

nandine *nan'din*, *n* a W African palm-civet. [Prob a native name]

N and Q *abbrev*: Notes and Queries.

nandu, **nandoo** or **nhandu** *nan'doo*, *n* the rhea, or S American ostrich. [Tupí *nandú*]

nanism *nān'* or *nan'izm*, *n* the condition of being dwarfed. — *n* **nanizā'tion** or **-s-** artificial dwarfing. [Gr *nānos*, *nannos* dwarf]

nankeen *nan'kēn* or *-kēn'*, *n* a buff-coloured cotton cloth first made at *Nanking* in China; a buff colour; (in *pl*) clothes, *esp* trousers, made of nankeen. — Also **nan'kin** (or *-kin'*).

nannoplankton. See under **nano-**.

nanny *nan'i*, *n* a she-goat (also **nann'y-goat**); a children's nurse, *esp* specially trained; a pet name for a grandmother: — *pl* **nann'ies**. — Also **nana** or **nanna** (*nän'ə*). — *adj* (*derog*; of institutions, the state, etc) protective to an intrusive extent. — *vt* to nurse; to overprotect; to supervise to the point of meddlesomeness: — *prp* **nann'ying**; *pat* and *pap* **nann'ied**. — *adj* **nann'yish** overprotective. [From the woman's name]

nannygai *nan'i-gī*, *n* a large edible marine fish, *Centroberyx affinis*, found off the SE coast of Australia. — Also **nann'yghai** or **nenn'igai**. [Aboriginal name]

nano- *nan-ō-* or *nān-ō-*, *combining form* denoting one thousand millionth, 10^{-9}, as in **nan'ogram, nan'ometre** and **nan'osecond**; of microscopic size, as in **nan'oplankton** or **nann'oplankton** very small forms of plankton. — *n* **nanotechnol'ogy** the manufacture of, and measuring, objects of tiny dimensions. [Gr *nānos* a dwarf]

Nansen passport *nan'sən päs'pört*, *n* a passport that the League of Nations issued after World War I to stateless people. [F *Nansen*, high commissioner for refugees with the League of Nations, 1920–22]

Nantz *nants*, (*archaic*) *n* brandy. [*Nantes* in France]

NAO *abbrev*: National Audit Office.

naos *nā'os*, *n* a temple; the inner cell of a temple. [Gr *nāos* temple]

nap[1] *nap*, *vi* to take a short or casual sleep: — *prp* **napp'ing**; *pap* **napped**. — *n* a short or casual sleep. — **catch someone napping** to detect someone in error that might have been avoided; to catch someone unprepared or off his or her guard. [OE *hnappian*]

nap[2] *nap*, *n* a woolly surface on cloth, now (distinguished from *pile*) such a surface raised by a finishing process, not made in the weaving; the woolly surface removed in the process; a cloth with such a surface; a downy covering or surface on anything; bedding or a bed-roll (*Austr colloq*). — *vt* to raise a nap on; to remove nap from: — *prp* **napp'ing**; *pat* and *pap* **napped**. — *adj* **nap'less** without nap, threadbare. — *n* **napp'iness**. — *adj* **napp'y** downy; shaggy. [ME *noppe*; appar from MDu or MLGer *noppe*]

nap[3] *nap*, *n* the card-game *Napoleon*; a call of five in that game; the winning of five tricks; a racing tip that professes to be a certainty, one that one may 'go nap' on. — *vt* to name (a particular horse) as certain to win: — *prp* **napp'ing**; *pat* and *pap* **napped**. — **go nap** to undertake to win all five tricks; to risk on a single attempt.

nap[4] *nap*, *vt* to seize; to steal. [Cf Swed *nappa*, Dan and Norw *nappe* to catch or snatch; relation to **nab**[1] uncertain]

Nap. *abbrev*: Napoleon.

napa or **nappa** *nap'ə*, *n* a soft leather made (*orig* at *Napa* in California) by a special tawing process, from sheepskin or goatskin.

napalm *nā'päm* or *na'*, *n* a petroleum jelly, highly inflammable, used in bombs and flame-throwers. — *vt* to attack or destroy with napalm bombs. [*na*phthenate *palm*itate]

nape *nāp*, *n* the back of the neck. [Origin uncertain]

Naperian. See **Napierian**.

napery *nāp'ə-ri*, (*archaic* or *Scot*) *n* household linen, *esp* for the table. [OFr *naperie*, from LL *napāria*, from *napa* a cloth, from L *mappa* a napkin]

naphtha *naf'thə* (sometimes *nap'tə*), *n* rock-oil; a vague name for the liquid inflammable distillates from coal-tar, wood, etc, *esp* the lighter and more volatile ones. — *n* **naph'thalene** an unpleasant-smelling hydrocarbon ($C_{10}H_8$) obtained by distillation of coal-tar, crystallizing in plates, used for killing moths, etc. — *adj*

naphthal'ic (*naf-thal'ik*) relating to or derived from naphthalene. — *vt* **naph'thalize** or **-ise** to treat with naphtha. — *n* **naph'thene** any of the cycloalkanes, many of which occur in petroleum. — *adj* **naphthe'nic**. — *n* **naph'thol** a hydroxyl derivative of naphthalene ($C_{10}H_7OH$), of two kinds. — *n* **naphthyl'amine** (or *-mēn'*) an amino-derivative of thalene ($C_{10}H_7NH_2$) of two kinds, used in dyeing. [Gr *naphtha*]

Napierian or **Naperian** *nā-pē'ri-ən*, *adj* relating to John *Napier* of Merchiston, Edinburgh (1550–1617), or to his system of logarithms; now applied to natural logarithms, logarithms to the base *e*, the limit of $(1+1/m)^m$ when *m* approaches infinity, Napier's own base being a quantity depending on e^{-1}. — **Napier's bones** (or **rods**) an invention of Napier's for multiplying and dividing mechanically by means of rods.

napiform *nā'pi-förm*, *adj* turnip-shaped. [L *nāpus* a turnip]

napkin *nap'kin*, *n* a small square of linen, paper, etc, used at table for wiping the mouth and hands, protecting clothing, etc; a baby's nappy; a handkerchief (*Scot* or *obs*). — **nap'kin-ring** a ring in which a table-napkin is rolled. [Dimin of Fr *nappe*, from L *mappa*]

Naples-yellow *nā'plz-yel'ō*, *n* a light-yellow pigment, lead antimoniate, *orig* an Italian secret.

NAPO *abbrev*: National Association of Probation Officers.

napoleon *nə-pōl'yən*, or *-i-ən*, *n* a twenty-franc gold coin issued by *Napoleon* I; a French modification of the game of euchre, each player receiving five cards and playing as an individual (commonly **nap**); a small, rich iced cake with layers of puff pastry filled with cream, custard or jam; (with *cap*) used generically in reference to *Napoleon* I, 1769–1821, Emperor of the French, to denote a person of paramount power and frightening ruthlessness. — *adj* **Napoleonic** (*-i-on'ik*) relating to *Napoleon* I or *Napoleon* III (1808–73). — *n* **Napol'eonism**. — *n* and *adj* **Napol'eonist**. — **napol'eonite** an orbicular diorite found in Corsica, Napoleon I's native island.

napoo *nä-po͞o'*, (*slang* of 1914 war) *adj* and *interj* no more; used up; good for nothing; dead. — *vt* to kill. [Fr *il n'y en a plus* there is no more]

nappa. See **napa**.

nappe *nap*, *n* a sheet of rock brought far forward by recumbent folding or thrusting (*geol*); a sheet (*math*); one of the two sheets on either side of the vertex forming a cone (*math*); a sheet of water flowing over a weir or similar structure. [Fr *nappe* tablecloth, from L *mappa*]

napper *nap'ər*, (*slang*) *n* the head.

nappy[1] *nap'i*, *n* a pad of disposable material or a folded square of towelling, muslin, etc placed between a baby's legs and kept in place by a fastening at the waist, for absorbing urine and faeces: — *pl* **napp'ies**. — **nappy rash** irritation of the skin on a baby's buttocks or genital area, *usu* caused by wet nappies. [A short form of **napkin**]

nappy[2] *nap'i*, *adj* (of liquor, *esp* beer) having a head, frothy; heady, strong; tipsy; (of a horse) nervous, jumpy, excitable. — *n* strong ale. [Perh from **nappy** shaggy; see under **nap**[2]]

napron *nā'prən*, *n* an earlier form (*Spenser*) of **apron**.

naras. See **narras**.

narc *närk* or **narco** *när'kō*, (*US slang*) *n* a narcotics agent: — *pl* **narcs** and **nar'cos**. [**narcotic**]

narceine or **narceen** *när'sēn*, a narcotic alkaloid in opium, $C_{23}H_{27}O_8N$. [Fr *narcéine*, from Gr *narkē* numbness]

narcissus *när-sis'əs*, *n* a plant of the daffodil genus *Narcissus*, of the Amaryllis family, *esp Narcissus poeticus* (the poet's narcissus): — *pl* **narciss'uses** or **narciss'ī**. — *n* **narciss'ism** sensual gratification found in one's own body, whether as a normal stage of development or a pathological condition. — *n* and *adj* **narciss'ist**. — *adj* **narcissis'tic**. [L, from Gr *Narkissos* a youth who pined away for love of his own image, and was transformed into the flower; the connection with *narkē* numbness (with reference to this plant's supposed effects on the body) seems to be fanciful]

narco. See **narc**.

narco- *när'kō-* or **narc-** *närk-*, *combining form* denoting using drugs; of or relating to the illicit production of drugs (as in *narco-terrorism*); numbness or torpor. — **nar'co-analysis** hypnoanalysis when narcotics are used in producing the hypnotic state; **nar'cocatharsis** narco-analysis; **nar'cohypnosis** the use of narcotics to produce hypnosis; **nar'cosyn'thesis** the bringing out of repressed emotions by narcotics so that they become freely accepted into the self; **nar'co-ther'apy** treatment of disturbed mental states by prolonged drug-induced sleep. [Gr *narkē* numbness or torpor]

narcolepsy *när'kō-lep-si*, (*pathol*) *n* a condition marked by short attacks of irresistible drowsiness. — *adj* **narcolep'tic**. [Gr *narkē* numbness, and *lēpsis* seizure]

narcosis *när-kō'sis*, drowsiness, unconsciousness or other effects to the central nervous system produced by a narcotic: — *pl* **narco'ses** (*-sēz*). [Gr *narkōsis*, from *narkē* numbness or torpor].

narcotic *när-kot'ik*, *adj* producing torpor, sleep, or deadness; affecting the central nervous system so as to produce dizziness, euphoria, loss of memory and of neuromuscular co-ordination, and eventually unconsciousness; of or relating to narcotic drugs, or the users of such drugs. — *n* anything having a narcotic effect, eg alcohol, an inert gas, or *esp* a drug. — *adv* **narcot'ically**. — *n* **nar'cotine** (*-kə-tēn*) one of the alkaloids in opium. — *n* **nar'cotism** the influence of narcotics. — **nar'cotist**. — *n* **narcotiza'tion** or **-s-**. — *vt* **nar'cotize** or **-ise** to subject to the influence of a narcotic. [Gr *narkōtikos*, from *narkē* numbness or torpor]

nard *närd*, *n* spikenard; a name for matweed (*Nardus stricta*); any of several aromatic plants formerly used in medicine. — *vt* to anoint with nard. [L *nardus*, from Gr *nardos*]

nardoo *när-do͞o'*, *n* an Australian cloverlike fern of the genus *Marsilea*; its spore-forming, multicellular body, ground into flour and used as a food by aboriginals. [Aboriginal]

nare *nār*, *n* (*archaic*) a nostril, *esp* a hawk's. — *n pl* **nār'ēs** (*L*; *anatom*) nostrils. — *adj* **nār'ial** or **nār'ine** (*-īn*) of or relating to the nostrils. — *n* **nār'icorn** a horny termination of a bird's nostril. [L *nāris*, pl *nārēs*, nostril]

narghile, **nargile** or **nargileh** *när'gil-i*, *n* a hookah. — Also **narghilly**, **narghily**, **nargilly**, **nargily**. [Pers *nārgīleh*, from *nārgīl* a coconut (from which it used to be made)]

narial, **naricorn** and **narine**. See under **nare**.

nark *närk*, (*slang*) *n* an informer; a police spy, as in *copper's nark*; a policeman; a person who curries favour, a pick-thank; an annoying, obstructive person, a spoilsport (*esp Austr* and *NZ*); a persistent fault-finder or complainer; an annoying, unpleasant or baffling circumstance; an expert. — *vi* to grumble. — *vt* and *vi* to watch; to spy; to annoy or irritate; to tease. — *adj* **narked** annoyed. — *adj* **nark'y** irritable. — **nark at** to fret with persistent criticism; **nark it**! stop it! [Romany *nāk* nose]

narks, the. See under **nitrogen narcosis**.

narquois *när-kwä*, (*Fr*) *adj* mocking, malicious.

narras or **naras** *nar'əs*, *n* edible melonlike fruit of a SW African long-rooted thorny cucurbitaceous shrub (*Acanthosicyos horrida*). [Hottentot *qnaras*]

narrate *nə-* or *na-rāt'*, *vt* to tell of (a series of events); to give a running commentary on (a film, etc). — *vi* to recount or relate events. — *adj* **narrāt'able**. — *n* **narrā'tion** the act of telling; that which is told; an orderly account of a series of events; the third part of a speech, comprising the exposition of the question (*rhetoric*). — *n* **narrative** (*nar'ə-tiv*) that which is narrated, a story; a written or spoken account of a series of events in the order in which they occur; that part of a literary work which relates events and action (as opposed to eg *dialogue*); the art, practice or technique of narration. — *adj* narrating; giving an account of any occurrence; inclined to narration;

telling a story. — *adv* **narr'atively**. — *n* **narrā'tor**. — *adj* **narr'atory** like narrative; consisting of narrative. [L *narrāre*, *-ātum*, prob from *gnārus* knowing]

narre *när*, (*Spenser*) *adv* an old comparative of **nigh**.

narrow[1] *nar'ō*, *adj* of little breadth; of small extent from side to side; closely confining; limited; contracted in mind or outlook; bigoted; not liberal; parsimonious (*colloq* or *dialect*); with little to spare; close; strict, precise; detailed, thorough; strict; keen; (of money) denoting the more liquid kinds (ie coins and notes), eg in hand, or readily withdrawn from a bank account, etc (*opp* of *broad*); (of a vowel) tense (*opp* of *broad*; *phonetics*); (of a phonetic transcription) with a different symbol for each phoneme and diacritical marks to show different varieties of these phonemes (*opp* of *broad*; *phonetics*); (of animal foodstuffs) relatively rich in protein as compared to fat and carbohydrate. — *n* a narrow part or place; (*usu* in *pl*) a narrow passage, channel or strait. — *adv* narrowly. — *vt* to make narrow; to contract or confine. — *vi* to become narrow; to reduce the number of stitches in knitting. — *n* **narr'owing** the act of making less in breadth; the state of being contracted; the part of anything which is made narrower. — Also *adj*. — *adv* **narr'owly**. — *n* **narr'owness**. — **narr'ow-boat** a canal-boat, *esp* one of 7 feet (2·1 metres) or less in width, and 72 feet (about 22 metres) in length. — *vt* **narr'owcast**. — **narr'owcasting** cable television; the production and distribution of material on video tapes, cassettes, etc; **narrow circumstances** poverty, pennilessness; **narrow escape** an escape only just managed. — *adj* **narr'ow-gauge'** (of a railway) less than 4 ft $8\frac{1}{2}$ inches (about 1·4 metres) in gauge. — **narrow gauge** a narrow-gauge railway. — *adj* **narr'ow-mind'ed** of a narrow or illiberal mind; bigoted, prejudiced. — *adv* **narr'ow-mind'edly**. — **narr'ow-mind'edness**; **narrow seas** the seas between Great Britain and the Continent and Great Britain and Ireland; **narrow squeak** a narrow escape. [OE *nearu*]

narrow[2]. See **nary**.

narthex *när'theks*, *n* a western portico or vestibule in an early Christian or Oriental church or basilica, to which women and catechumens were admitted; a vestibule between the church porch and the nave; (with *cap*) a former genus of umbelliferous plants, now included in the genus *Ferula*. [Gr *narthēx* giant fennel, a cane or stalk, a casket or a narthex]

nartjie (*orig* **naartje**) *när'chi*, (*Afrik*) *n* a small sweet orange like the mandarin. [Prob connected with **orange**]

narwhal *när'wəl*, *n* a kind of whale (*Monodon*) with one large projecting, spiral tusk (occasionally two tusks) in the male. [Dan *narhval*; ON *nąhvalr*, may be from *nār* corpse, and *hvalr* whale, from its pallid colour]

nary *nār'i*, (*NAm* and *dialect*) *adv* never, not. — **nary a** never a, not one. — Also **narrow a** (*nar'ō*). [A variant of *ne'er a* never a]

NAS *abbrev*: Noise Abatement Society; National Academy of Sciences (*US*).

nas *naz* or *näz*, (*obs*) for **ne has** (*Spenser*) has not, and **ne was** was not.

NASA *na'sə*, *abbrev*: National Aeronautics and Space Administration (in the US).

nasal *nā'zl*, *adj* of or relating to the nose; affected by, or sounded through, the nose. — *n* a sound uttered through the nose; a letter representing such a sound; a paired bone that forms the bridge of the nose; the nose-piece in a helmet. — *n* **Nasalis** (*naz-ā'lis*) the proboscis monkey genus. — *n* **nasality** (*nā-zal'i-ti*). — *n* **nasalization** or **-s-** (*nā-zə-lī-zā'shən*). — *vi* and *vt* **na'salize** or **-ise** to render (eg a sound) nasal. — *adv* **na'sally**. — *n* **nasion** (*nā'zi-on*) the median point of the nasofrontal suture. [L *nāsus* the nose]

nasard *naz'ərd*, *n* an organ mutation stop. [Fr]

nascent *nas'ənt* or *nās'ənt*, *adj* coming into being; beginning to develop; (of an atom or substance, *esp* hydrogen) at the moment of its formation and therefore with a higher reactivity than usual. — *n* **nasc'ence** (*rare*) or **nasc'ency**. [L *nāscēns*, *-entis*, pr p of *nāscī*, *nātus* to be born]

naseberry *nāz'bər-i* or *-ber'i*, *n* the sapodilla plum; the tree bearing it. — Also **neesberry** (*nēz'*) and **nisberry** (*niz'*). [Sp *néspera*, *níspero* medlar tree, from L *mespilus* medlar; cf **medlar**]

nashgab *nash'gab*, (*Scot*) *n* prattle; chatter; a pert chatterer. — Also **gab'nash**.

Nasik *nä'sik*, *n* a district of Bombay. — Also *adj*, *esp* of an elaborate form of magic square devised there.

nasion. See under **nasal**.

Naskhi. See **Neskhi**.

naso- *nā'zō-*, *combining form* denoting nose; of the nose (and something else). — *adj* **nasofront'al** pertaining to the nose and the frontal bone. — *adj* **nasolac'rymal** pertaining to the nose and tears, eg in reference to the duct that carries tears from the eye and the nose. — *n* **nasophar'ynx** that part of the pharynx above the soft palate. — *adj* **nasogas'tric** pertaining to the nose and stomach, such as a **nasogastric tube**, one which is passed into the stomach through the nose. [L *nāsus* nose]

nastalik or **nasta'liq** *nas-tə-lēk'*, *n* Persian cursive script, having long horizontal strokes and rounded characters. [Ar, from *naskhi* cursive script, and *talik* hanging]

nastic *näs'tik* or *nas'*, *adj* (of plant movements) not related to the direction of the stimulus. [Gr *nastos* close-pressed]

nasturtium *nas-tûr'shəm*, *n* (with *cap*) the water-cress genus of the Cruciferae family; (in popular use) the Indian cress (*Tropaeolum majus*), a garden climber, with bright orange, yellow or red flowers and edible leaves. [L *nāsus* nose, and *torquēre* to twist (from its pungency)]

nasty *näs'ti*, *adj* disgustingly foul; nauseous; filthy; obscene or indecent; (of eg a video) containing scenes which are either highly pornographic or extremely violent, or both; threatening; threatening danger; spiteful; ill-natured; difficult to deal with; awkward; unpleasant; (of eg a wound) sore; objectionable; good, lovely (*esp US slang*). — *n* (*colloq*) something or someone unpleasant or intractable; an obscene or sadistic film, as in *video nasty*. — *adv* **nas'tily**. — *n* **nas'tiness**. — **a nasty piece** (or **bit**) **of work** a person very objectionable in character and conduct. [Perh for earlier *nasky* (cf Swed dialect *naskug*, *nasket*); or perh connected with Du *nestig* dirty]

-nasty *-nas'ti*, *combining form* denoting nastic pressure or movement (in the direction specific in the first element) as in *epinasty* and *hyponasty*. [Gr *nastos* pressed close]

nasute *nā'zūt*, *-sūt*, or *-zūt'*, *-sūt'*, *adj* keen-scented; critically discriminating; beaked. — *n* a beaked soldier white ant. [L *nāsūtus*, from *nāsus* nose]

NAS/UWT *abbrev*: National Association of Schoolmasters/Union of Women Teachers.

Nat. *nat*, *abbrev*: National; Nationalist.

nat *nat*, (*colloq*; often with *cap*) *n* a nationalist.

nat. *abbrev*: national; native; natural; *natus* (*L*), born.

natal[1] *nā'tl*, *adj* of or connected with birth; native. — *adj* **natalitial** (*nat-* or *nāt-ə-lish'l*) pertaining to a birthday. — *n* **natality** (*nə-* or *nā-tal'i-ti*) birth; birth-rate. — **natal therapy** (in psychoanalysis) the treatment of rebirthing (qv). [L *nātālis*, from *nāscī*, *nātus* to be born]

natal[2]. See **nates**.

natale solum *na-tā'lē sō'ləm* or *nä-tä'le sol'ōōm*, (*L*) native soil.

natalitial, **natality**. See under **natal**[1].

natant *nāt'ənt*, (*formal*) *adj* floating; swimming. — *n* **natation** (*nat-* or *nāt-ā'shən*) swimming. — *adj* **nātato'rial** or **nā'tatory** pertaining to swimming; having the habit of swimming; adapted or used for swimming. — *n* **nātato'rium** (*US*) a swimming-pool: — *pl* **nātato'riums** or **nātato'ria**. [L *natāns*, *-antis*, pr p of *natāre*, frequentative of *nāre* to swim]

natch[1] *nach*, (*dialect*) *n* the rump. [See **aitchbone**]
natch[2] *nach*, (*slang*) *adv* of course, short for **naturally**.
natch[3]. See **nautch**.
nates *nā'tēz*, *n pl* the buttocks. — *adj* **nā'tal**. — *adj* **nā'tiform**. [L *natis*, pl *natēs*]
NATFHE *nat'fē*, *abbrev* National Association of Teachers in Further and Higher Education.
natheless and **nathelesse**. See **nathless**.
nathemore *nā-thə-mōr'* or *-mör'* or **nathemo** *-mō'*, (*Spenser*) *adv* not or never the more. [OE *nā thȳ mā* never the more (cf **nathless**)]
nat. hist. *nat hist*, *abbrev*: natural history.
nathless, natheless, nathelesse or **naythles** *nāth'*, *nath'*, *näth'*, *nādh'*, *nadh'*, *nädh'*(*ə*)*-les*, or (as *Spenser*) *-les'*, (*archaic*) *adv* and *prep* notwithstanding. [OE *nā* never, *thȳ* by that (instrumental case), and *lǣs* less]
natiform. See under **nates**.
nation[1] *nā'shən*, *n* a body of people marked off by common descent, language, culture, or historical tradition whether or not bound by the defined territorial limits of a state; the people of a state; an American Indian tribe or federation of tribes; a set of people, animals, etc; a great number; an old division of students in universities; (in *pl*) the heathens or Gentiles. — *adj* **national** (*nash'nəl* or *-ə-nəl*) pertaining to a nation or nations; belonging or peculiar to, characteristic of, or controlled by, a nation; public; general; attached to one's own country; nationalistic. — *n* a member or fellow-member of a nation; a national (as opposed to a *local*) newspaper; (with *cap*) the Grand National. — *n* **nat'ionalism**. — *n* **nat'ionalist** a person who favours or strives after the unity, independence, interests or domination of a nation; a member of a political party specially so called, eg the Irish Nationalist party who aimed at Home Rule; an advocate of nationalization. — Also *adj*. — *adj* **nationalist'ic**. — *adv* **nationalist'ically**. — *n* **nationality** (*-al'it-i*) membership of, or the fact or state of belonging to, a particular nation; nationhood; a national group (often one of several) forming a political state; a group or set having the character of a nation; national character. — *n* **nationalīzā'tion** or **-s-**. — *vt* **nat'ionalize** or **-ise** to make national; to make the property of the nation; to bring under national management; to naturalize; to make a nation of. — *adv* **nat'ionally**. — *n* **nationhood** (*nā'*) the state or fact of being a nation. — *adj* **nationless** (*nā'*) without nationality or nations. — *adj* **na'tionwide** covering the whole nation. — Also *adv*. — **national anthem** (or *rare* **air**) an official song or hymn of a nation, sung or played on ceremonial occasions; **National Assembly** an assembly of elected representatives, part of the legislature of various countries; the French legislative assembly from 1789 to 1791; **National Assistance** (formerly in Britain) a weekly allowance paid by the state to people on low incomes; **national bank** a commercial bank chartered by the Federal government and a member of the Federal Reserve System (*US*); **national call** (formerly **trunk call**) a long-distance telephone call within the country, not international; **national church** a church established by law in a country; **National Convention** a convention held every four years by a political party to choose its candidate for the forthcoming presidential elections (*US*); the sovereign assembly in France from 21 Sept 1792 to 26 Oct 1795; **National Curriculum** the curriculum taught in all schools in England and Wales from 1989, divided into core subjects (English, mathematics and science) and foundation subjects (technology and design, history, geography, music, art, physical education and a foreign language), with testing at regular intervals to assess each child's performance in comparison with nationally-set attainment targets, under the control of the **National Curriculum Council**; **national debt** money borrowed by the government of a country and not yet paid back; **National Front** (in Britain) an extreme right-wing political party with racist and fascist policies; **national grid** the grid (qv) of power-lines in, or of lines on maps of, Great Britain; **National Guard** a force which took part in the French Revolution, first formed in 1789; an organized military force in individual States, also subject to the call of the federal army (*US*); **National Health Service** in Britain, the system under which medical, dental, etc treatment is available free, or at a nominal charge, to all, paid for out of public taxation; **National Hunt** (also without *caps*) horse-racing over jumps, as opposed to *flat racing*; **national income** the total money earned (from wages, interest, rents, etc) by the residents of a nation; **national insurance** a system of compulsory insurance paid for by weekly contributions by employee and employer, and yielding benefits to the sick, retired, unemployed, etc; **national park** an area owned by or for the nation, set apart for the preservation and enjoyment of what is beautiful or interesting; **National Savings Bank** a department of the Post Office with which money may be deposited to accumulate interest; **national school** (in England, formerly) a school established by the **National Society** (established in 1811) to promote elementary education among poor people; **national service** compulsory service in the armed forces; **National Socialism** Nazism, the policies of the National Socialist Party; **National Socialist (German Workers') Party** an extreme nationalistic fascist party in Germany, led by Adolf Hitler, which ruled Germany from 1933 to 1945; **National Trust**, and **National Trust for Scotland** charitable bodies concerned with the preservation of historic monuments and buildings, and areas of natural beauty, in Great Britain and Northern Ireland. [L *nātiō*, *-ōnis*, from *nāscī*, *nātus* to be born]
nation[2] *nā'shən*, (*US dialect*) *n*, *adj*, *adv* and *interj* damnation.
native *nā'tiv*, *adj* belonging naturally; innate; inherent; natural; in a natural state; unsophisticated; occurring in a natural station; occurring naturally as a mineral (not manufactured), or naturally uncombined (as an element); belonging by birth; having a right by birth; born or originating in the place; being the place of birth or origin; belonging to the people originally or at the time of discovery inhabiting the country, *esp* when they are not regarded as fully civilized; connected by birth; born in slavery or bondage (*obs*); applied to Australian plants and animals which have been given the same name as a different plant or animal found elsewhere, eg the *native bear* (the koala); (of an oyster) raised in a (British) artificial bed. — *n* someone born in any place; someone born and for a long time resident in a place; someone born under a particular planet or sign; a member of a native race; a member of a non-white race, *esp* in a colonized country (*colloq derog*; no longer common); (in S Africa) a member of the black, Negroid race (now considered *offensive* and no longer in official use); a person of non-Aboriginal descent born in Australia; an indigenous species, variety, or breed, or an individual of it; a native oyster; a person born in slavery or bondage (*obs*). — *adv* **na'tively**. — *n* **na'tiveness**. — *n* **na'tivism** the belief that the mind possesses some ideas or forms of thought that are inborn and not derived from sensation; the tendency to favour the natives of a country in preference to immigrants. — *n* and *adj* **na'tivist**. — *adj* **nativis'tic**. — *n* **nativity** (*nə-tiv'i-ti*) the state or fact of being born; the time, place and manner of birth; nationality by birth; the fact or status of being native; (often with *cap*) the birth of Christ, hence the festival commemorating it, Christmas, or a picture representing it; a horoscope; slavery or bondage by birth (*obs*). — **Native American** an American Indian (also *adj*); **native bear** the koala. — *adj* **na'tive-born** born in the country; having a (specified) status by virtue of birth (*Scot*; *obs*). — **Native Canadian** a N American Indian of Canada (also *adj*); **native cat** a marsupial cat, a carnivorous, cat-sized white-spotted animal of the genus *Dasyurus*, with a pointed snout; **native com-**

panion see **brolga**; **native land** the land to which one belongs by birth; **native language** the language one acquires first, *usu* that of one's native land; **native rock** unquarried rock; **native speaker** someone who speaks the language in question as his or her native language. — **go native** see under **go**; **one's native heath** one's homeland, one's own locality. [L *nātīvus*, from *nāscī*, *nātus* to be born]

NATO or **Nato** *nā'tō*, *n* the *N*orth *A*tlantic *T*reaty *O*rganization (see under **north**).

natrium. See under **natron**.

natrolite *nāt'* or *nat'rə-līt*, *n* a common fibrous zeolite, hydrated sodium aluminium silicate. [**natron** and Gr *lithos* stone]

natron *nā'trən*, *n* a hydrated carbonate of sodium found on some lake borders. — *n* **na'trium** (*obs* or *chemists' Latin*) sodium. [Ar *natrūn*, from Gr *nitron*]

NATSOPA *nat-sō'pə*, *abbrev*: National Society of Operative Printers, Graphical and Media Personnel.

natter *nat'ər*, (*colloq*) *vi* to rattle on in talk, *esp* grumblingly; to chatter, talk much about little; to be peevish (*NEng dialect*). — Also *n*. — *n* **natt'erer**. — *adj* **natt'ered** or **natt'ery** peevish. [Origin obscure]

natterjack *nat'ər-jak*, *n* a European toad (*Bufo calamita*) with a yellow stripe down the back. [Origin unknown]

nattier blue *nat'i-ər bloo͞*, *n* a soft azure. [J M *Nattier* (died 1766), French painter]

NATTKE *nat'ki*, *abbrev*: National Association of Television, Theatrical and Kinematographic Employees (now **ETA**).

natty *nat'i*, (*colloq*) *adj* dapper; spruce; clever, ingenious, deft. — *adv* **natt'ily**. — *n* **natt'iness**. [Poss connected with **neat**[1]]

natura *nə-tūr'ə* or *na-too͞'ra*, (*L*) *n* nature. — **natura naturans** (*nat'ūr-əns* or *na-too͞'räns*) creative nature; **natura naturata** (*na-tūr-ā'tə* or *na-too͞-rä'ta*) created nature.

natural *nach'ərəl* or *nach'rəl*, *adj* relating to, produced by or according to nature, to the natural world or human nature; provided by or based on nature; not miraculous or supernatural; not the work of humans, not artificial; not interfered with by humans; inborn, innate, inherent; having the feelings that may be expected to come by nature, kindly; normal; happening in the usual course; spontaneous; not far-fetched; not acquired; without affectation; not fictitious; physical (*esp* as opposed to *spiritual* or *intellectual*); lifelike, like nature; based on an innate moral sense, innate reason or instinct rather than revelation; related by actual birth (not adoption, etc); hence (now *rare*) legitimate; (now *usu*) illegitimate; natural-born, or having the status of the natural-born; in a state of nature, unregenerate; (of classification) according to ancestral relationships (*biol*); according to the usual diatonic scale, not sharp or flat (*music*); (of a playing-card) not being a joker or a wild card; (of a sequence of cards) containing no wild cards. — *n* someone having a natural aptitude (for), or being an obvious choice (for); a thing assured by its very nature of success, a certainty; a tone that is neither sharp nor flat (*music*); a character cancelling a preceding sharp or flat (*music*); a white key in keyboard musical instruments; a buff colour; two cards making 21 dealt to a player as his or her first hand in pontoon; an idiot (*obs*). — *n* **nat'uralism** following of nature; a close following of nature without idealization (*esp* in art); the theory that this should be the aim of art and literature, *esp* the form of realism advocated or practised by Emile Zola; a world-view that rejects the supernatural and spiritual and explains the world in terms of natural influences and forces, and cause and effect; any religious or moral system based on this; the belief that natural religion is of itself sufficient; deism; any action based on natural desires and instincts. — *n* **nat'uralist** someone who studies nature, more particularly zoology and botany, *esp* zoology, and *esp* in the field; a dealer in live animals and articles of use and interest to students of nature, often a taxidermist; a believer in naturalism. — *adj* **naturalist'ic** relating to or in accordance with nature, natural history or naturalism. — *adv* **naturalist'ically**. — *n* **naturalīzā'tion** or **-s-**. — *vt* **nat'uralize** or **-ise** to grant the privileges of natural-born citizens to; to cause (an introduced species of plant, animal, etc) to adapt to a different climate or to different conditions of life; to adopt into the language; to admit among accepted institutions, usages, etc; to make natural or easy; to explain naturalistically. — *vi* to acquire citizenship in another country; to study natural history in the field; (of a plant, animal, etc) to adapt to a new environment. — *adv* **nat'urally** in a natural manner; by nature; according to nature or one's own nature; in a lifelike manner; normally; in the ordinary course; of course. — *n* **nat'uralness**. — **natural abundance** (*phys*) same as **abundance**; **natural background** the radiation due to natural radioactivity and to cosmic rays, enhanced by contamination and fall-out. — *adj* **nat'ural-born** native. — **natural childbirth** childbirth with as little medical intervention, *esp* as little anaesthesia, etc as possible, relying on the mother doing special breathing and relaxation exercises; **natural classification** see **natural system** below; **natural cycle IVF** IVF (qv) in which the woman is allowed to ovulate naturally rather than being given drugs to stimulate ovulation; **natural death** death owing to disease or old age, not violence or accident; **natural gas** gases issuing from the earth, whether from natural fissures or bored wells, applied particularly to the hydrocarbon gases associated with the production of petroleum and used as domestic or industrial fuel in place of town gas (see also **North Sea** gas); **natural historian**; **natural history** *orig* the description of all that is in nature, now used of the sciences that deal with the earth and its productions, ie botany, zoology and mineralogy, *esp* field zoology; **natural immunity** that level of immunity with which a person is born (cf **acquired immunity**); **natural killer cell** a naturally occurring lymphoid cell which attacks and destroys tumour cells and some virally infected cells; **natural language** a language which has evolved naturally (as opposed to *artificial language*); **natural law** a law of nature; the sense of right and wrong which arises from the constitution of the mind of man, as distinguished from the results of revelation or legislation; **natural logarithm** one to the base *e*; **natural magic** see under **magic**; **natural numbers** the whole numbers 1, 2, 3, and upwards, sometimes also including 0; **natural order** (in botany) a category now usually called a family; **natural philosopher**; **natural philosophy** the science of the physical properties of bodies; physics, or physics and dynamics; **natural radioactivity** radioactivity that is found in nature; **natural religion** see **natural theology** below; **natural resources** features, properties, etc of the land such as minerals, an abundance of water, timber, etc that occur naturally and can be exploited by man; **natural scale** a scale of music written without sharps or flats; **natural science** the science of nature, as distinguished from mental and moral science and from mathematics; **natural selection** evolution by the survival of the fittest with inheritance of their fitness by the next generation; **natural system** or **natural classification** a classification of plants and animals according to presumed relationship by descent, distinguished in botany from the artificial system of Linnaeus; **natural theology** or **natural religion** religion derived from reasoned facts, not revelation; **natural virtues** those virtues (*esp* justice, prudence, temperance and fortitude) of which people are capable; **natural wastage** (reduction of staff by) non-replacement of those who leave, eg through retirement; **natural year** see under **year**. [L *nātūrālis*, from *nātūra* nature]

nature *nā'chər*, *n* (often with *cap*) the power that creates and regulates the world; all the natural phenomena created by this power, including plants, animals, landscape, etc as distinct from people; the power of growth; the established order of things; the cosmos;

the external world, *esp* as untouched by man; the qualities of anything which make it what it is, governing its character and behaviour; essence; being; constitution; kind or order; naturalness; normal feeling; disposition or temperament; kindliness; conformity to truth or reality; inborn mind, character, instinct or disposition; vital power of man, animal (*obs*); the normal biological functions or needs of a body; course of life; nakedness; a primitive undomesticated condition or community; the countryside, *esp* when unspoilt or picturesque; the strength or substance of anything; that which an individual inherits, determining in parts its structure, character and behaviour, as distinguished from *nurture*, or what is learnt from experience, environment or training. — *adj* **na'tured** having a certain temper or disposition (*esp* in compounds, as in *good-natured*). — *adj* **na'turing** creative. — *n* **na'turism** communal nudity or nudity practised openly, sometimes in the belief that it encourages self-respect, respect for others and a feeling of being in harmony with nature; nature-worship. — *n* and *adj* **na'turist**. — *adj* **naturist'ic**. — *n* **nat'uropath** a person who who practises naturopathy. — *adj* **naturopath'ic**. — *n* **nāturop'athy** (also *nat-*) the promotion of health and natural healing by a system of diet, exercise, manipulation, care and hydrotherapy; the philosophy of the system. — **na'ture-cure** the practice of or treatment by naturopathy; **na'ture-god** a deity personifying some force of physical nature; **nature knowledge** see **nature study**; **na'ture-myth** a myth symbolizing natural phenomena; **na'ture-printing** printing from plates that have been impressed with some natural object; **nature reserve** an area of land specially managed and protected to preserve its flora and fauna; **nature strip** (*Austr*) a strip of grass, etc bordering a road or footpath or dividing two carriageways; **nature study** or **nature knowledge** a (school) discipline intended to cultivate the powers of seeing and enjoying nature by observation of natural objects, eg plants, animals etc; **nature trail** a path through the countryside, *usu* with signposts to draw attention to interesting natural features; **na'ture-worship** worship of the powers of nature; naturism. — **against nature** immoral or unnatural; **debt of nature** death; **ease** (or **relieve**) **nature** to evacuate the bowels; **from nature** (*painting* and *sculp*) using objects taken from nature as models; **in** (or **of**) **the nature of** of the same sort as, that amounts to. [Fr, from L *nātūra*, from *nāscī*, *nātus* to be born]

naturopath and **naturopathy**. See under **nature**.

naught *nöt*, *n* nothing (*archaic*); a nought (qv) (*esp NAm*); wickedness, evil (*obs*). — *adj* (*archaic*) good for nothing; worthless; bad; immoral; hurtful; foiled; ruined. — *adv* ill; not at all. — **be naught** (*obs*) keep out of the way; efface yourself; go to the devil; **bring to naught** (*archaic*) to frustrate, baffle; **come to naught** (*archaic*) to come to nothing, to fail; **set at naught** (*archaic*) to treat as of no account, to despise. — Also **nought**. [OE *nāht*, *nāwiht*, from *nā* never, and *wiht* whit]

naughty *nöt'i*, *adj* bad; badly-behaved; verging on the indecorous; titillating; now chiefly applied to children, or used playfully in feigned censure; worthless (*obs*); wicked (*Shakesp*). — *n* (*Austr* and *NZ colloq*) an act of sexual intercourse. — *adv* **naught'ily**. — *n* **naught'iness**. — **naughty nineties** (*joc*) the 1890s, renowned for gaiety and high living; **naughty pack** (*obs*) a person, *esp* a woman, of loose life, a 'bad lot'. [**naught**]

naumachy *nö'mə-ki* or **naumachia** *nö-mā'ki-ə*, *n* a mock sea-battle, performed as a spectacle among the ancient Romans; a place for this: — *pl* **nau'machies, naumā'chiae** (*-ki-ē*) or **naumā'chias**. [Gr *naumachiā*, from *naus* a ship, and *machē* a fight]

naunt *nänt*, (*archaic*) *n* aunt. [For **mine aunt**]

nauplius *nö'pli-əs*, *n* a larval form in many Crustacea, with one eye and three pairs of appendages: — *pl* **nau'plii** (*-pli-ī*). — *adj* **nau'pliiform** (*-plē-i-*). — *adj* **nau'plioid**. [L, a kind of shellfish, from Gr *Nauplios* a son of Poseidon, from *naus* a ship, and *pleein* to sail]

nausea *nö'si-ə*, *-shi-ə* or *-zhə*, *n* (*orig*) seasickness; a feeling of inclination to vomit; sickening disgust or loathing. — *adj* **nau'seant** producing nausea. — *n* a substance having this quality. — *vi* **nau'seate** to feel nausea or disgust. — *vt* to cause to feel sick; to loathe; to strike with disgust. — *adj* **nau'seāting** causing nausea or (*fig*) disgust. — *adv* **nau'seātingly**. — *adj* **nau'seātive** (*obs*) inclined to or causing nausea. — *adj* **nau'seous** (*-shəs*, *-shi-əs* or *-si-əs*) producing nausea; disgusting; loathsome. — *adv* **nau'seously**. — *n* **nau'seousness**. [L, from Gr *nausiā* seasickness, from *naus* a ship]

naut. *abbrev*: nautical.

nautch *nöch*, **nach** or **natch** *näch*, *n* (in India) a performance given by professional dancing women known as **nautch'-girls**. [Hindi *nāch* dance]

nautic. See **nautical**.

nautical *nöt'i-kəl*, *adj* of or relating to ships, to sailors, or to navigation. — Also **naut'ic** (*rare*). — *adv* **nau'tically**. — *n sing* **nau'tics** the science of navigation. — *n pl* water sports. — **Nautical Almanac** a periodical book of astronomical tables specially useful to sailors; **nautical mile** see under **mile**. [L *nauticus*, from Gr *nautikos*, from *nautēs* sailor, from *naus* a ship]

nautilus *nö-ti-ləs*, *n* a tetrabranchiate cephalopod of the genus *Nautilus* (*esp* **pearly nautilus**) of southern seas, with a chambered external shell; a Mediterranean dibranchiate cephalopod with a paperlike shell (**paper nautilus** or argonaut) wrongly believed by Aristotle to use its arms as sails: — *pl* **nau'tiluses** or **nau'tilī**. [L, from Gr *nautilos* a sailor, a paper nautilus, from *naus* ship]

NAV *abbrev*: net asset value.

nav. *abbrev*: naval; navigable; navigation; navigator.

Navaho. See **Navajo**.

navaid *nav'ād*, *n* any of the electronic devices designed to aid navigation in a ship or aircraft. [Formed from *nav*igational *aid*]

Navajo or **Navaho**, *nav'ə-hō*, *n* a N American Indian people of Utah, Arizona and New Mexico; a member of this people; their Athabascan language: — *pl* **Nav'ajos** or **Nav'ahos**. [Sp *Navajó*, name of a particular pueblo]

naval *nā'vl*, *adj* relating to warships or a navy; serving in a navy; nautical (*obs*). — *n* **nav'alism** the cult of naval supremacy or seapower. — **naval architect**; **naval architecture** the designing of ships; **Naval Brigade** a body of seamen organized to serve on land; **naval crown** (*hist*) a garland awarded to a Roman who had distinguished himself in a sea-fight; **naval officer** an officer in the navy; a custom-house officer of high rank (*US*). [L *nāvālis*, from *nāvis* a ship]

Navaratra *nav-ə-rä'trə* or **Navaratri** *-tri*, *n* a nine-day Hindu festival in honour of Durga. [Sans, period of nine nights, from *nava* nine, and *rātri* night]

navarch *nāv'ärk*, *n* an admiral in ancient Greece. — *n* **nav'archy** the office of navarch; a fleet. [Gr *nauarchos*, from *naus* ship, and *archē* rule]

navarho *nav'ə-rō*, *n* low-frequency, long-range radio navigation system for aircraft. [*nav*igation, *a*id, *rho* (ρ), a navigational symbol for distance]

navarin *nav'ə-rin* or *nav-a-rẽ*, *n* a stew of mutton or lamb, with turnip and other root vegetables. [Fr]

nave[1] *nāv*, *n* (*archit*) the middle or main body of a basilica, rising above the aisles; the main part of a church, generally west of the crossing, including or excluding its aisles. [L *nāvis* a ship]

nave[2] *nāv*, *n* the hub or central part of a wheel, through which the axle passes; the navel (*Shakesp*). [OE *nafu*; cf Du *naaf* and Ger *Nabe*]

navel *nā'vl*, *n* the umbilicus or depression in the centre of the abdomen; a central point; a nombril (*heraldry*). — **navel-gazing** (*colloq*) worthless, unproductive self-analysis, *esp* when direct action is required; **na'vel-or'ange** a variety of orange with a navel-like depression, and a smaller orange enclosed; **na'vel-string** the umbilical cord; **na'velwort** pennywort (Cotyledon). [OE *nafela*, dimin of *nafu* nave of a wheel]

navette *na-vet'*, *n* (in jewel-cutting) a pointed oval shape; a jewel cut in this shape. [Fr, shuttle, dimin of *nef* ship]

navew *nā'vū*, *n* a rape or coleseed with a carrot-shaped root; a wild Swedish turnip. [Fr *naveau*, dimin from L *nāpus*]

navicert *nav'* or *nāv'i-sûrt*, *n* a certificate detailing a ship's cargo, issued to a neutral ship in time of war. [*navi*gational *cert*ificate]

navicula *nav-ik'ū-lə*, *n* an incense-boat; a plant of the *Navicula* genus of diatoms. — *adj* **navic'ūlar** boat-shaped; relating to the navicular bone. — *n* the navicular bone. — **navicular bone** a boat-shaped bone on the thumb side of the wrist joint, the scaphoid bone; a corresponding bone in the ankle joint; **navicular disease** inflammation of the navicular bone in horses. [L *nāvicula*, dimin of *nāvis* a ship]

navigate *nav'i-gāt*, *vi* to conduct or manage a ship, aircraft, motor vehicle, etc, in sailing, flying or moving along; to find one's way and keep one's course, *esp* by water or air; to sail. — *vt* to direct the course of; to sail, fly, etc over, on or through. — *n* **navigability** (*-gə-bil'i-ti*). — *adj* **nav'igable** (of a river, channel, etc) deep enough and wide enough to be passed by ships, etc; dirigible. — *n* **nav'igableness**. — *adv* **nav'igably**. — *n* **navigā'tion** the act, science or art of conducting ships or aircraft, *esp* the finding of position and determination of course by astronomical observations and mathematical computations; travel or traffic by water or air (*esp NAm*); a voyage (*archaic*); shipping generally; a navigable route; a canal or artificial waterway. — *adj* **naviga'tional** relating to navigation. — *n* **nav'igator** a person who navigates or sails; a person who directs the course of a ship, etc; a person (*usu* co-driver) who describes the route to, and directs, the driver in a car rally or race; an explorer by sea; a navvy; an instrumental or other aid to navigation. — **navigational system** any system of obtaining bearings and/or ranges for navigational purposes by radio techniques; **navigation light** one of a set of lights shown by a ship or aircraft at night, indicating direction of travel. [L *nāvigāre*, *-ātum*, from *nāvis* a ship, and *agere* to drive]

Navstar. See **Global Positioning System** under **globe**.

navvy *nav'i*, (*colloq*) *n* a labourer, *orig* a labourer on a navigation or canal; a machine for digging out earth, etc (see **steam-navvy** under **steam**). — *vi* to work as a navvy, or like a navvy. — *vt* to excavate: — *pr p* **navv'ying**; *pa t* and *pa p* **navv'ied**. [**navigator**]

navy *nā'vi*, *n* (often with *cap*) the whole of a nation's ships-of-war, with the crews and supporting crews; (often with *cap*) the officers and men belonging to a nation's warships; navy blue; a fleet of ships (*archaic* or *poetic*). — *adj* of, used by or such as is supplied to the navy. — *n* and *adj* **navy blue** dark blue as in naval dress. — **navy list** a list of officers and ships of a navy; **navy yard** (*US*) a government dockyard. [OFr *navie*, from L *nāvis* a ship]

nawab *nə-wäb'* or *-wöb'*, (*hist*) *n* a deputy or viceroy in the Mogul empire; a Muslim prince or noble; an honorary title bestowed by the Indian government; a nabob (*rare*). [Hindi *nawwāb*, from Ar *nawwāb*, respectful pl of *nā'ib* deputy]

nay *nā*, (*archiac* or *dialect*) *adv* no (for former distinction between *nay* and *no* see **no**[1]; not only so, but; yet more; in point of fact. — *n* a denial; a vote against. — **nay'=say** a refusal. — *vt* to refuse; to deny, to contradict. — **nay'ward** (*Shakesp*) the negative side. [ME *nay*, *nai*, from ON *nei*; Dan *nei*; cognate with **no**[1]]

naya paisa. See under **paisa**.

Nayar. See **Nair**.

NAYPIC or **Naypic** *abbrev*: National Association of Young People in Care.

naythles. See **nathless**.

nayword *nā'wûrd*, *n* a catchword or watchword (*Shakesp*); a proverbial reproach, a byword (*Shakesp* **ayword**). [Origin obscure]

Nazarene *naz'ə-rēn*, *n* an inhabitant of *Nazareth*, in Galilee; (with **the**) Jesus Christ; a follower of Jesus of Nazareth, *orig* used of Christians in contempt; an early Jewish Christian; any of a group of German painters who, in the early 19c, tried to restore the quality of religious art. — Also **Nazarē'an** and **Naz'arite**.

Nazarite *naz'ə-rīt*, *n* a Jewish ascetic under a vow (see Num 6; also **Naz'irite**); a Nazarene. — *adj* **Nazaritic** (*-it'ik*). — *n* **Naz'aritism** (*-īt-izm*). [Heb *nāzar* to consecrate]

naze *nāz*, *n* a headland or cape. [OE *næs*; cf **ness**]

Nazi *nä'tsē*, *n* for *Ger National-sozialist* National Socialist, a member of the National Socialist German Workers' Party, founded in 1919 and achieving power in 1933 under the leadership of Adolf Hitler; a Hitlerite; any person with extreme racist and authoritarian opinions (*derog*). — Also *adj*. — *n* **Nazifica'tion**. — *vt* and *vi* **Naz'ify**. — *n* **Naz'ism** or **Naz'iism**. [Ger]

nazir *nä'zir*, *n* (formerly) an Indian court official who served summonses, etc; an official of various kinds. [Ar *nāzir* overseer]

Nazirite. See **Nazarite**.

NB *abbrev*: Nebraska (US state); New Brunswick (Can); North Britain or North British; *nota bene* (*L*), note well or take notice (also **nb**).

Nb (*chem*) *symbol*: niobium.

NBA *abbrev*: Net Book Agreement, an agreement within the book trade that net books may not be sold at less than the price fixed by the publisher.

NBC *abbrev*: National Broadcasting Company (US); nuclear, biological and chemical (warfare, weapons, etc). — **NBC suit** a suit that protects the wearer against the physical effects of nuclear, biological and chemical weapons.

NC *abbrev*: North Carolina (US state).

NCC *abbrev*: National Consumer Council; National Curriculum Council; Nature Conservancy Council.

NCCL *abbrev*: National Council for Civil Liberty.

NCO *abbrev*: non-commissioned officer.

NCT *abbrev*: National Childbirth Trust.

NCVQ *abbrev*: National Council for Vocational Qualifications.

ND or **N.Dak**. *abbrev*: North Dakota (US state).

Nd (*chem*) *symbol*: neodymium.

nd *abbrev*: no date, not dated.

Ndrangheta or **'Ndrangheta** *ən-dran-get'ə*, *n* a secret criminal organization in Calabria, controlling crime and other illegal activities. [Ital]

NE *abbrev*: Nebraska (US state; also **Nebr.**); New England; north-east.

Ne (*chem*) *symbol*: neon.

ne *nē* or *ni*, (*obs*) *adv* not. — *conj* nor. [OE *ne*]

né *nā*, *adj* (of a man) born, used in giving the original name of a titled man. — See also **née**. [Fr]

neafe or **neaffe** (*Shakesp*). See **nieve**.

neal *nēl*, *vt* and *vi* an aphetic form of **anneal**.

Neanderthal *ni-an'dər-täl*, *adj* of a Palaeolithic species of man whose remains were first found in 1857 in a cave in the *Neanderthal*, a valley between Düsseldorf and Elberfeld (1930, part of Wuppertal); primitive (*colloq*); extremely old-fashioned and reactionary (*colloq*). — Also **Nean'dertal**. — *n* **Nean'derthaler**, **Nean'dertaler**, **Nean'derthal** and **Nean'dertal** (also *fig*). — *adj* **Nean'-derthaloid**. — All words also without *cap*.

neanic *nē-an'ik*, (*zool*) *adj* relating to the adolescent period in the life-history of an individual. [Gr *neanikos* youthful]

neap *nēp*, *adj* (of tides) of smallest range, of least difference between high and low points. — *n* a neap tide, occurring after the first and third quarters of the moon. — *vi* to tend towards the neap. — *adj* **neaped** left aground between spring tides. [OE *nēp*, appar meaning helpless; *nēpflōd* neap tide]

Neapolitan *nē-ə-pol'i-tən*, *adj* of the city or the former kingdom of Naples. — *n* a native, citizen or inhabitant of Naples; (without *cap*) a small rectangular chocolate.

— **Neapolitan ice** ice-cream made in layers of different colours and flavours; **Neapolitan sixth** (*music*) a chord of the subdominant with its minor third and minor sixth; **Neapolitan violet** a scented double variety of sweet violet. [L *Neāpolitānus*, from Gr *Neāpolis* new town, from *neos*, *-ā*, *-on* new, and *polis* city]

near *nēr*, *adv* (*orig* as *compar* of **nigh**) nigher, more closely, to or at a shorter distance; (now as positive) to or at no great distance; close; closely; nearly; almost; narrowly; thriftily, parsimoniously (*archaic*): — *compar* **near'er**; *superl* **near'est**. — *prep* close to (**near'er** and **near'est** are also *preps*). — *adj* nigh; not far away in place or time; close in relationship, friendship, imitation, approximation or in any relation; close, narrow, so as barely to escape; (eg of a road) short, direct; stingy, parsimonious (*colloq*); (of horses, vehicles, roads, etc) left, left-hand: — *compar* **near'er**; *superl* **near'est**. — *vt* and *vi* to approach; to come nearer. — *adv* **near'ly** at or within a short distance; closely; intimately; scrutinizingly, parsimoniously; almost; approximately but rather less. — *n* **near'ness**. — **near beer** (in the USA) any of several beers containing $\frac{1}{2}$ per cent alcohol or less. — *adj* **near'-begaun** or **near'-gaun** (*Scot*) niggardly. — *adj* **near'-by** neighbouring. — *adv* (*usu* **near-by'**) close at hand. — *prep* (also **near by**) close to. — **near cut** (*old*) a short cut; **Near East** formerly an area including the Balkans and Turkey, and sometimes also the countries to the west of Iran; now synonymous with **Middle East** (qv); **near gale** a wind of force 7 on the Beaufort scale (force 8 being a *gale*). — *adj* **near'-hand** (*Scot*) near. — *adv* nearly. — *adj* **near'-legged** (*Shakesp*) (of horses) walking so that the legs interfere. — **near miss** (*lit* and *fig*) a miss that is almost a hit; **near point** the nearest point the eye can focus; **near'side** the side of a vehicle nearer to the kerb eg when it is being driven, in Britain the left side; the left side of a horse or other animal, or of a team of horses. — Also *adj*. — *adj* **near-sight'ed** short-sighted. — *adv* **near-sight'edly**. — *n* **near-sight'edness**. — **a near thing** a narrow escape; **near as a touch, as ninepence** or **as dammit** (*colloq*) very nearly. [OE *nēar*, comparative of *nēah* nigh (*adv*), and ON *nǣr*, comparative (but also used as positive) of *nā* nigh; cf Ger *näher*]

near- *nēr-*, *combining form* denoting almost, as in *adj* **near'-white** of a colour closely resembling white, and *n* **near'-silk'** artificial silk.

Nearctic *nē-ärk'tik*, *adj* of the New World part of the Holarctic region, including the part of N America to the north of the Tropic of Cancer, and Greenland. [Gr *neos* new, and *arktikos* northern, from *arktos* bear, the Great Bear]

neat[1] *nēt*, *adj* clean (*obs*); unmixed; undiluted; undiminished, net; clear, shining (*Spenser*); elegant; trim; tidy; finished, adroit; deft; well and concisely put; ingenious, effective, economical in effort or method; good, excellent (chiefly *NAm slang*). — *adv* neatly. — *vt* **neat'en** to make neat, tidy. — *adv* **neat'ly**. — *n* **neat'ness**. — *adj* **neat-hand'ed** dexterous. [Fr *net* clean, tidy, from L *nitidus* shining, bright, from *nitēre* to shine]

neat[2] *nēt*, (*archaic* or *dialect*) *n* an ox, cow, bull, etc: — *pl* **neat**. — **neat'-cattle**; **neat'-herd**; **neat'-house**; **neat's-foot oil** an oil obtained from the feet of oxen; **neat'-stall**; **neat's leather** leather made of the hides of neat. [OE *nēat* cattle, a beast, from *nēotan*, *nīotan* to use; cf Scot **nowt** from ON *naut*]

neath or **'neath** *nēth*, (*dialect* and *poetic*) *prep* beneath. [Aphetic for **aneath** or **beneath**]

NEB *abbrev*: National Enterprise Board; New English Bible.

Neb. *abbrev*: Nebraska (US state).

neb *neb*, (*Scot* and *N Eng dialect*) *n* a beak or bill; the mouth (*obs*); the nose; a nib; the sharp point of anything. — *vi* to bill. — *vt* to put a neb on. — *adj* **nebbed** (*nebd*) having a neb. [OE *nebb* beak, face; cognate with Du *neb* beak]

nebbich *neb'ihh*, **nebbish** or **nebish** *neb'ish*, *n* a colourless, insignificant, incompetent person, a perpetual victim. — Also **nebbishe** or **nebbisher** (*neb'ish-ər*). — Also *adj*. [Yiddish]

nebbuk, nebek and **nebeck** *neb'ək*. Same as **nabk**.

nebel *nē'bəl*, *n* a Hebrew instrument, apparently a harp. [Heb *nēbel*]

nebish. See **nebbich**.

neb-neb *neb'-neb*, *n* bablah pods. [Prob an African word]

Nebr. *abbrev*: Nebraska (US state).

nebris *neb'ris*, *n* a fawn-skin worn by Bacchus and his votaries. [Gr *nebris*]

nebuchadnezzar *neb-ū-kad-nez'ər*, *n* (also with *cap*) a large bottle, *esp* of champagne, the equivalent of 20 ordinary bottles. [*Nebuchadnezzar*, king of Babylon in 2 Kings 24–25, following the tradition of calling bottle-sizes after well-known Old Testament figures]

nebula *neb'ū-lə*, *n* a little cloudiness; a slight opacity of the cornea; a liquid for spraying; a faint, misty appearance in the heavens produced either by a group of stars too distant to be seen singly, or by diffused gaseous matter: — *pl* **neb'ulae** (*-lē*) or **neb'ulas**. — *adj* **neb'ular** relating to nebulae; like or of the nature of a nebula. — *adj* **neb'ulé** (*-lā*) or **neb'uly** (*heraldry*) wavy. — *n* **nebule** (*neb'ūl*) wavy moulding. — *n* **nebu'lium** an element formerly assumed in order to explain certain lines in the spectra of gaseous nebulae, lines now known to be due to states of oxygen, and also nitrogen, not possible under earthly conditions. — *n* **nebulīzā'tion** or **-s-**. — *vt* **neb'ulize** or **-ise** to reduce to spray. — *n* **nebulīz'er** or **-s-** a spraying apparatus, an atomizer. — *n* **nebulos'ity**. — *adj* **neb'ulous** hazy, vague, formless (*lit* and *fig*); cloudlike; like, of the nature of, or surrounded by a nebula. — *adv* **neb'ulously**. — *n* **neb'ulousness**. — **nebular hypothesis** the theory of Laplace that the solar system was formed by the contraction and breaking up of a rotating nebula. [L *nebula* mist; cf Gr *nephelē* cloud, mist]

NEC *abbrev*: National Executive Committee; National Exhibition Centre (Birmingham).

nécessaire *nā-ses-er*, (*Fr*) *n* a dressing-case, workbox.

necessary *nes'is-ə-ri*, *adj* that must be; that cannot be otherwise; unavoidable, inevitable; predestined; indispensable; (of a proposition) always true, and such that a denial leads to inevitable self-contradiction (*logic*); enforced (*archaic*); (of an agent) not free. — *n* that which cannot be left out or done without, eg food (used chiefly in *pl*); a toilet (*obs* or *dialect*); money (*colloq*). — *n* and *adj* **necessā'rian**. — *n* **necessā'rianism** see **necessitarianism** under **necessity**. — *adv* **nec'essarily** (or *nes-is-e'rə-li*) as a necessary consequence; inevitably; (loosely) for certain. — *n* **nec'essariness**. — **necessary house** or **place** (*obs* or *dialect*) a toilet; **necessary truths** such as cannot but be true. [L *necessārius*]

necessity *ni-ses'i-ti*, *n* a state or quality of being necessary; that which is necessary or unavoidable; unavoidable compulsion; compulsion as a law of nature, governing all human action; great need; poverty. — *n* and *adj* **necessitā'rian** or **necessā'rian**. — *n* **necessitā'rianism** or **necessā'rianism** the philosophical theory that human actions are determined by precursory circumstances and cannot be willed. — *vt* **necess'itate** to make necessary; to render unavoidable; to compel. — *n* **necessitā'tion**. — *adj* **necess'itied** (*Shakesp*) forced into a state of subjection or submissiveness as a result of poverty. — *adj* **necess'itous** in necessity; very poor; destitute. — *adv* **necess'itously**. — *n* **necess'itousness**. — **natural necessity** the condition of being necessary according to the laws of nature, **logical** or **mathematical** according to those of human intelligence, **moral** according to those of moral law; **of necessity** necessarily; **works of necessity** work so necessary as to be allowable on the Sabbath. [L *necessitās*, *-ātis*]

neck *nek*, *n* the part connecting head and trunk (often in allusion to the halter or the yoke; *fig*); the flesh of that part regarded as food; anything resembling that part; the part connecting the head and body of anything, eg a violin; the plain lower part of the capital of a column (*archit*); any narrow connecting part, eg an isthmus; anything narrow and throatlike, such as the upper part of a bottle; (in mosses and ferns) the upper tubular part of the archegonium (*bot*); a plug of igneous or fragmental rock filling a volcanic vent; a col; the part of a garment on or nearest the neck; the length of a horse's head and neck, used to measure its lead in a race; impudence, audacity (*slang*). — *vt* to strike, pull, or chop the neck of, *esp* so as to kill; to catch or fasten by the neck; to kiss amorously (*slang*); to make a neck on; to drink (*slang*). — *vi* (*slang*) to kiss amorously. — *n* **neck'atee** (*obs*) a neckerchief. — *adj* **necked** having a neck. — *n* **neck'ing** the neck of a column (*archit*); a moulding between the capital and shaft of a column, a gorgerin (*archit*); embracing, petting (*slang*). — *n* **neck'let** a simple form of necklace; a pendant strung for the neck; a small boa or fur for the neck. — **neck'band** the part of a shirt etc encircling the neck; a band worn on the neck; **neck'beef** the coarse flesh of the neck of cattle; inferior stuff; **neck'-bone** a cervical vertebra; **neck'cloth** a piece of folded cloth worn round the neck by men as a band or cravat, with the ends hanging down, often made of lace; **neck'erchief** an ornamental cloth, a kerchief for the neck; **neck'gear** apparel for the neck; **neck'-herr'ing** (*obs*) a heavy blow on the neck; **necking party** a petting party; **neck'lace** (*-lis* or *-ləs*) a lace, chain, or string of beads or precious stones worn around the neck; (in S Africa) the punishment of having a petrol-soaked tyre placed round the neck or shoulders and set alight, traditionally used by Blacks on Blacks thought to be government sympathizers (also called **neck'lacing**). — *vt* (in S Africa) to kill with a necklace. — **neck'line** the edge of a garment at the neck; **neck'-moulding** a moulding where the capital of a column joins the shaft; **neck'piece** a piece of cloth, etc forming, covering, or bordering a neck; **neck'-sweet'bread** the thymus gland of veal or lamb; **neck'tie** (*esp NAm*) a band of fabric tied round the neck under the collar and *usu* hanging down in front, a tie; a hangman's noose (*US slang*); **necktie party** (*US slang*) a lynching; **neck'verse** the test of ability to read for those who claimed benefit of clergy (qv under **clergy**), *usu* Psalm 51. 1, success giving the privilege of being branded on the hand instead of hanging; **neck'wear** clothing for the neck, such as ties or scarves; **neck'weed** hemp, source of the hangman's rope (*old slang*); a kind of speedwell, from its reputed medicinal virtue (*US*). — **get it in the neck** (*colloq*) to be severely dealt with or hard hit; **harden the neck** to grow more obstinate; **neck and crop** completely; bodily; in a heap; summarily and unceremoniously; **neck and neck** exactly equal; side by side; **neck of the woods** (*colloq*) a particular area, part of the country; **neck or nothing** risking everything; **save one's neck** to escape narrowly with one's life or reputation; **stick one's neck out** to put oneself at risk, expose oneself to trouble, danger, or contradiction; **talk through the back of one's neck** to talk wildly or absurdly wide of the truth; **tread on the neck of** to oppress or tyrannize over; **up to one's neck** deeply involved, *esp* in a troublesome situation. [OE *hnecca*; cf OHGer *hnac*, also OIr *cnocc* hill]

necro- *nek'rō-* or *-ro'*, *combining form* denoting dead or a dead body. — *n* **necrōbiō'sis** the natural degeneration and death of a cell in living tissue. — *adj* **necrobiot'ic**. — *n* **necrog'rapher** an obituary writer. — *n* **necrol'ater**. — *n* **necrol'atry** worship of, or morbid or sentimental reverence for, the dead or dead bodies. — *adj* **necrō-log'ic** or **necrōlog'ical**. — *n* **necrol'ogist**. — *n* **necrol'ogy** an obituary list. — *n* **nec'rōmancer** a sorcerer. — *n* **nec'rōmancy** the art of revealing future events by calling up and questioning the spirits of the dead; enchantment; sorcery. — *adj* **necrōman'tic** or **necrō-man'tical**. — *adv* **necrōman'tically**. — *adj* **necroph'-agous** feeding on carrion. — *n* **nec'rophile** (*-fīl*) someone who is morbidly attracted to, and *esp* has sexual intercourse with, corpses. — Also **nec'rophil** (*-fil*). — *n* **necrophilia** (*-fil'*) necrophilism. — *adj* **necro-philiac** (*-fil'iak*) or **necrophilic** (*-fil'ik*). — *n* **necroph'-ilism** or **necroph'ily** a morbid (*esp* sexual) attraction towards dead bodies. — *adj* **necroph'ilous**. — *n* **necrophōbe'**. — *n* **necrōphō'bia** a morbid horror of corpses. — *adj* **necrophō'bic**. — *adj* **necroph'orous** carrying away and burying dead bodies, as do burying beetles. — *n* **necrop'olis** a cemetery or burial site: — *pl* **necrop'olises** (*-lis-əz*) or **necrop'oleis** (*-līs*). — *n* **nec'-ropsy** (or *-rop'*) a post-mortem examination. — *adj* **necrōscop'ic** or **necrōscop'ical**. — *n* **necros'copy** a post-mortem examination, autopsy. — *n* **necrot'omy** dissection of a dead body; the surgical excision of necrosed bone from a living body. [Gr *nekros* dead body, dead]

necrosis *nek-rō'sis*, *n* death of part of the living body, *esp* of a concentrated area of cells owing to an interruption of the blood supply, etc, eg as a sympton of gangrene. — *vt* and *vi* **necrose** (*nek-rōs'*) to affect with or undergo necrosis. — *adj* **necrot'ic**. — *vt* and *vi* **nec'rōtize** or **-ise** to necrose. [Gr *nekros* dead body]

nectar *nek'tər*, *n* the name given by Homer, Hesiod, Pindar, etc to the beverage of the gods, giving life and beauty; the honey of the glands of plants; any delicious drink; anything very sweet or pleasant. — *adj* **nec-tā'real**, **nectā'rean**, **nectā'reous** or **nec'tarous** of or like nectar. — *adj* **nec'tared** imbued with nectar; mingled or filled with, or containing much, nectar. — *n* **nectā're-ousness**. — *adj* **nectā'rial** of the nature of a nectary. — *adj* **nectarif'erous** producing nectar. — *n* **nec'tarine** (*-ēn* or *-in*) (a tree bearing) a variety of peach with a smooth skin. — *adj* (*-in*) sweet as nectar. — *n* **nec'tary** (in plants) a glandular organ that secretes nectar. — **nec'tar-guide** a marking that guides insects to the nectary of a flower. [Gr *nektar*; ety dub]

nectocalyx *nek-tō-kā'liks*, *n* a hydrozoan swimming-bell: — *pl* **nectocā'lyces** (*-li-sēz*). [Gr *nēktos* swimming, and *kalyx* shell, flower-cup]

ned *ned*, (chiefly *Scot*; *slang*) *n* a young hooligan, a disruptive adolescent. [Poss the familiar form of *Edward*; see also **Ted**]

NEDC *abbrev*: National Economic Development Council. — Also (*colloq*) **Neddy** (*ned'i*).

neddy *ned'i*, *n* a donkey; a fool (*colloq*); a racehorse (*Austr slang*). [From *Edward*]

née *nā*, *adj* (of a woman) born, used in stating a woman's maiden name. — See also **né**. [Fr, fem pa p of *naître* to be born]

need *nēd*, *n* lack of something which one cannot well do without; necessity; a state that requires relief, such as extreme poverty or distress; lack of the means of living. — *vt* to have occasion for; to want; to require; (used before the infinitive with *to*, or in negative, interrogative, conditional, etc sentences without *to*) to require or be obliged (to do something); (used before a verbal noun) to require (to be dealt with in a particular way). — *vi* (*archaic*) to be necessary. — *n* **needcess'ity** a dialectal or illiterate combination of **need** and **necessity**. — *n* **need'er**. — *adj* **need'ful** full of need; having need; needy; necessary; requisite. — *adv* **need'fully**. — *n* **need'fulness**. — *adv* **need'ily**. — *n* **need'iness**. — *adj* **need'less** not needed; unnecessary; having no need (*Shakesp*). — *adv* **need'lessly**. — *n* **need'lessness**. — *adv* **need'ly** (*Shakesp*) necessarily. — *n* **need'ment** (*Spenser*) something needed. — *adv* **needs** of necessity; indispensably. — *adj* **need'y** very poor; necessary (*Shakesp*). — *n* **need'y-hood** (*Herrick*). — **need'-be** a necessity; **need'fire** fire produced by friction, to which a certain virtue is superstitiously attached; a beacon. — **had need** (*archaic*) ought to; **must needs** or **needs must** (often *ironic*) must inevitably; **the needful** ready money (*slang*); whatever is requisite, *usu* in *do the needful* (*colloq*). [OE *nēd*, *nīed*, *nȳd*; Du *nood*, OGer *Noth* (modern *Not*)]

needle *nēd'l*, *n* a small, sharp instrument with a hole for thread in the blunt end, for sewing; any similar slender, pointed instrument, as for knitting, etching, playing gramophone records, suturing, dissection, (hooked) for crochet; the suspended magnet of a compass or galvanometer; a pointer on a dial; the pointed end of a hypodermic syringe; a hypodermic injection (*colloq*); anything sharp and pointed; a pinnacle of rock; an obelisk; a long slender crystal; a strong beam passed through a wall as a temporary support; a long, narrow, stiff leaf; a feeling of irritation (*slang*); dislike, enmity (*slang*). — *adj* (of a contest) involving intense rivalry and acutely critical. — *vt* to sew; to pierce; to penetrate; to thread; to pass through; to underpin with needles; to irritate, goad, heckle; to add alcohol to (an already alcoholic drink) (*US slang*). — *vi* to pass out and in; to sew. — *n* **need'leful** as much thread as will serve conveniently for one threading of a needle. — *n* **need'ler** a needlemaker. — *adj* **need'ly** like needles. — **needle bank** a place where drug-users may exchange old hypodermic syringes for new ones, *usu* free of charge, to help prevent the spread of disease or infection; **need'le-bath** a shower-bath with very fine strong jets; **need'le-book** a needle-case in book form; **need'le-case** a case for holding needles; **need'lecord** a cotton material with closer ribs and flatter pile than corduroy; **need'le-craft** the art of needlework; lace made with a needle; embroidery on canvas, done with woollen yarns, used on chair covers, etc; **need'lefish** a pipefish; a garpike; **need'le-furze** the petty whin; **need'le-gun** a gun in which the cartridge is exploded by the impact of a spike; **needle paper** acid-free black paper used for wrapping needles; **need'lepoint** the point of a needle; a very sharp point; point-lace made with a needle; embroidery on canvas, done with woollen yarns, used on chair-covers, etc. — *adj* **need'le-point'ed** pointed like a needle, round in section; (eg of a fish-hook) without a barb. — **needle roller-bearing** a roller-bearing without a cage, in which long rollers of small diameter are used, located endwise by a lip on the inner or outer race. — *adj* **need'lestick** (of injuries) caused by medical staff pulling off a dirty or bloody hypodermic needle from a syringe and pricking their fingers with it by accident. — **needle time** the amount of time allowed to a radio channel for the broadcasting of recorded music; **need'le-tin** cassiterite in slender crystals; **needle valve** a cone-shaped valve, ending in a point, used to control the flow of a fluid; **need'lewoman** a woman who does needlework; a seamstress; **need'lework** work done with a needle; the business of a seamstress. — **get the needle** (*colloq*) to be irritated; **give the needle to** (*colloq*) to irritate; **look for a needle in a haystack** (or (*rare*) **bottle of hay**) to engage in a hopeless search [OE *nǣdl*; Ger *Nadel*; cognate with Ger *nähen* to sew; L *nēre* to spin]

neeld *nēld* or **neele** *nēl*, obsolete forms of **needle**.

neem, neemb and **neem tree**. See under **nim**[3].

neep *nēp*, (*Scot*) *n* a turnip. [OE *nǣp*, from L *nāpus*]

ne'er *nār*, *adv* contraction of **never**. — *adj* and *n* **ne'er'-do-well** (*Scot* **-weel**) good-for-nothing.

Ne'erday *nār'dā*, (chiefly *Scot*) *n* New Year's Day; (without *cap*) a gift on New Year's Day.

neesberry. Same as **naseberry**.

neeze or **neese** *nēz*, *vi* and *n* (to) sneeze. [Cf ON *hnjōsa*, and **sneeze**]

NEF *abbrev*: National Energy Foundation.

nef *nef*, *n* a church nave (*obs*); an ornamental stand or holder for a knife, fork, etc or for a table napkin, often in the shape of a ship. [Fr *nef* ship, nave, from L *nāvis*]

nefandous *ni-fan'dəs*, *adj* abominable. [L *nefandus* unspeakable, from *ne-* not, and *fandus* to be spoken, from *fārī* to speak]

nefarious *ni-fā'ri-əs*, *adj* extremely wicked; villainous. — *adv* **nefā'riously**. — *n* **nefā'riousness**. — *adj* **nefast** (*ni-fast'*) abominable. [L *nefārius*, *nefāstus*, from *nefās* wrong, crime, from *ne-* not, and *fās* divine law, prob from *fārī* to speak]

neg. *abbrev*: negative; negatively; negotiable.

negate *ni-gāt'*, *vt* to deny; to nullify; to imply the non-existence of; to make ineffective. — *n* **negation** (*-gā'shən*) the act of saying no; denial; a negative proposition (*logic*); something that is the opposite (of a positive quality, state, etc); a thing characterized by the absence of qualities. — *n* **negā'tionist** someone who merely denies, without offering any positive assertion. — *adj* **negative** (*neg'ə-tiv*) denying; expressing denial, refusal, or prohibition (*opp* of *affirmative*); denying the connection between a subject and a predicate (*logic*); lacking a positive quality; failing to affirm; opposite, contrary to, neutralizing, etc that which is regarded as positive; censorious (*US*); defeatist, pessimistic; obstructive, unconstructive; less than nothing (*math*); reckoned or measured in the opposite direction to that chosen as positive (*math*); at relatively lower potential (*elec*); of, having, or producing negative electricity (*elec*; see below); having dark for light and light for dark (*optics* and *photog*); in complementary colours (*optics* and *photog*); acid (*chem*); laevorotatory (*optics*); having the index of refraction for the extraordinary ray less than for the ordinary in double refraction (*optics*); in a direction away from the source of stimulus (*biol*). — *n* a word or statement by which something is denied; a word or grammatical form that expresses denial or opposition; a negative proposition or term; the right or act of saying no, or of refusing assent; the side of a question or the decision which denies what is affirmed; an image in which the lights and shades are reversed; a photographic plate bearing such an image; a quantity less than nothing (*math*); a negative quantity or quality. — *vt* to prove the contrary of; to reject by vote; to veto; to reject by veto; to deny; to neutralize. — *adv* **neg'atively**. — *n* **neg'ativeness**. — *n* **neg'ativism** a tendency to deny and criticize, without offering any positive assertions; a tendency to do the opposite of what one is asked to do. — *n* and *adj* **neg'ativist**. — *adj* **negativis'tic**. — *n* **negativ'ity** the fact of being negative. — *adj* **neg'atory** expressing denial. — *n* **negatron** (*neg'ə-tron*) a *negative* elec*tron*, as opposed to a *positron*. — **negative angle** one generated by a straight line moving clockwise; **negative electricity** electricity arising from the excess of electrons; **negative equity** the situation, caused by a fall in house prices, in which a person owns property that is worth less than the value of his or her mortgage; **negative feedback** the return of part of an output signal back to the input, as a way of increasing the quality of amplified sound; **negative income tax** see under **income**; **negative interest** money charged on or deducted from interest on bank deposits, etc; **negative pole** that pole of a magnet which turns to the south when the magnet swings freely; **negative proton** an antiproton; **negative reinforcement** (*behav*) in conditioning situations, a stimulus, *usu* aversive, that increases the probablity of escape or avoidance behaviour; **negative sign** the sign (−, read *minus*) of subtraction. [L *negāre*, *-ātum* to deny]

neglect *ni-glekt'*, *vt* to treat carelessly; to pass by without notice, to disregard; to omit by carelessness; to fail to give proper care and attention to. — *n* disregard; slight; lack of (proper) care or attention, negligence; omission; uncared-for state. — *adj* **neglect'able** (*rare*) negligible. — *n* **neglect'edness**. — *n* **neglect'er**. — *adj* **neglect'ful** careless; habitually neglecting or omitting to do things; slighting. — *adv* **neglect'fully**. — *n* **neglect'fulness**. — *adv* **neglect'ingly** carelessly; heedlessly. — *n* **neglection** (*-glek'shən*; *Shakesp*) negligence. — *adj* **neglect'ive** (now *rare*) neglectful. [L *neglegere*, *neglectum*, from *neg-* or *nec-* not, and *legere* to gather]

negligee *neg'li-jē*, *neg'li-zhā* or **negligée** *neg'li-zhā*, *n* a woman's loose decorative dressing-gown of flimsy material; a loose gown worn by women in the 18c; a necklace, *usu* of red coral. — Also **neg'ligé**. — *n* **négligé** (*nā'glē-zhā* or *ne'-*) casual or informal dress. — *adj* casually or informally dressed; carelessly or unceremoniously dressed; careless. [Fr, neglected]

negligence *neg'li-jəns*, *n* the fact or quality of being negligent; lack of proper care; habitual neglect; an act of carelessness or neglect (*archaic*), a slight; carelessness about dress, manner, etc; omission of duty, *esp* such care for the interests of others as the law may require. — *adj* **neg'ligent** neglecting; careless; inattentive, *esp* to duties or responsibilities; disregarding ceremony or fashion. — *adv* **neg'ligently**. — *n* **negligibil'ity**. — *adj* **neg'ligible** (sometimes **neg'ligeable**) such as may be ignored because very little or very unimportant. — *adv* **neg'ligibly**. [L *negligentia* for *neglegentia*, from *neglegere* to neglect]

négociant *nā-gō-sē-ã*, (*Fr*) *n* a merchant, *esp* a wine-merchant.

negotiate *ni-gō'shi-āt*, *vi* to confer for the purpose of mutual arrangement; to bargain; to traffic. — *vt* to arrange for by agreement; to manage; to transfer or exchange for value; to pass safely over, round, through, etc (eg a hazard); to cope with successfully (*colloq*). — *n* **negotiabil'ity**. — *adj* **nego'tiable** that can be negotiated; not fixed; (of bonds, etc) legally transferable. — *n* **nego'tiant** (*-shi-ənt*) a person, organization or state, etc involved in negotiations. — *n* **negotiā'tion**. — *n* **nego'tiātor**: — *fem* (*archaic*) **nego'tiatress** (*-shyə-*) or **negotiatrix** (*ni-gō'shyə-triks* or *ni-gō-shi-ā'triks*). [L *negōtiārī*, *-ātus*, from *negōtium* business, from *neg-* not, and *ōtium* leisure]

Negress. See under **Negro**.

Negrillo *ni-gril'ō*, *n* an African Negrito: — *pl* **Negrill'os**. [Sp, dimin of *negro* black]

Negrito *ni-grē'tō*, *n* a member of any of a number of pygmy negroid peoples of SE Asia and Africa: — *pl* **Negri'tos**. [Sp, dimin of *negro* black]

negritude or **négritude**. See under **Negro**.

Negro *nē'grō*, *n* (sometimes considered to be *derog* or *offensive*; formerly also without *cap*) a member of any of the dark-skinned peoples of Africa or a person racially descended from one of them: — *pl* **Ne'groes**. — *adj* of or relating to Negroes; black or darkly coloured (*zool*). — *n* **Ne'gress** (*usu* considered to be *offensive* or *derog*; formerly also without *cap*) a Negro woman or girl. — *n* **nē'gritude** translation of French **négritude** (apparently invented by the poet Aimé Césaire) the essential quality of the Negro genius. — Also **nigritude**. — *adj* **ne'groid** (also with *cap*) of Negro type; having physical characteristics associated with Negro races, eg full lips, broad nose, tightly curling hair, etc. — *n* a negroid person; someone who is a Negro in a broad sense only. — *adj* **negroid'al**. — *n* **ne'grōism** any peculiarity of speech among Negroes, *esp* in the southern US; devotion to the causes of the Black civil rights movement (*old-fashioned*; sometimes *derog*). — *n* **ne'grophil** or **ne'grophile** a person who has sympathy for the plight of Black people, *esp* one who actively supports the movement for greater political and social freedoms for oppressed Blacks. — *n* **negrophilism** (*ni-grof'*). — *n* and *adj* **negroph'ilist**. — *n* **ne'grophobe** someone who dislikes Negroes. — *n* **negropho'bia**. — **ne'gro-corn** (*W Indies*) durra; **ne'grohead** tobacco soaked in molasses and pressed into cakes, so called from its blackness; an inferior rubber; **Negro pepper** see under **pepper**. [Sp *negro*, from L *niger*, *nigra*, *nigrum* black]

Negus *nē'gəs*, (*hist*) *n* the king of Ethiopia. [Amharic]

negus *nē'gəs*, *n* a drink of port or sherry mixed with hot water, sweetened and spiced. [Said to be from Colonel *Negus*, its first maker, in Queen Anne's time]

Neh. (*Bible*) *abbrev*: (the Book of) Nehemiah.

neif. Same as **nieve**.

neigh *nā*, *vi* to utter the cry of a horse, or a similar cry. — *vt* to utter or say with such a cry. — *n* the cry of a horse. [OE *hnǣgan*]

neighbour or *NAm* **neighbor** *nā'bər*, *n* a person who lives near or next door to another; a person or thing that is near another; a fellow human being; one of a pair (*Scot*). — *adj* (*archaic* and *US*) neighbouring. — *vt* and *vi* to live or be near. — *vi* to associate with one's neighbours. — *n* **neigh'bourhood** or (*NAm*) **neigh'borhood** the state of being neighbours, kindly feeling; a set of neighbours; a district, locality, *esp* with reference to its inhabitants as a community; a district; a region lying near; a near position; nearness; all the points that surround a given point in a specified degree of closeness (*math*). — *adj* **neigh'bouring** or (*NAm*) **neigh'boring** being near; adjoining. — *adj* **neigh'bourless** or (*NAm*) **neigh'borless**. — *n* **neigh'bourliness** or (*NAm*) **neigh'borliness**. — *adj* **neigh'bourly** or (*NAm*) **neigh'borly** like or becoming a neighbour; friendly; social. — Also *adv*. — **neighbourhood law centre** see **law centre** under **law**; **neighbourhood watch** a scheme under which local householders agree to keep a general watch on each other's property and the local streets, to try to prevent crime. — *adj* **neigh'bour-stained** (*Shakesp*) stained with neighbours' blood. — **good neighbours** the fairies; **in the neighbourhood of** approximately, somewhere about. [OE *nēahgebūr*, from *nēah* near, and *gebūr* or *būr* a farmer]

neist *nēst*, a dialectal form of **nighest** (*obs*), **next**.

neither *nī'dhər* or *nē'dhər*, *adj* and *pronoun* not either, not one nor the other (of two); not any one (of more than two) (*archaic*; current usage of this sense is disputed). — *conj* not either; and not; nor yet. — *adv* not at all; in no case; either (usage disputed). [OE *nāther*, *nāwther*, abbrev of *nāhwæther*, from *nā* never, and *hwæther* whether; the vowel assimilated to **either**]

neive. Same as **nieve**.

nek *nek*, (*SAfr*) *n* a col. [Du, neck]

nekton *nek'ton*, *n* the assemblage of actively swimming organisms in a sea, lake, etc. [Gr *nēkton* (neuter), swimming]

nelis or **nelies** *nel'is*, *n* a winter pear: — *pl* **nel'is** or **nel'ies**. [Fr *nélis*]

nellie or **nelly** *nel'i*, *n*: **not on your nellie** or **nelly** (*slang*) not on any account. [Said to be from *not on your Nellie Duff*, rhyming with *puff*, meaning 'life']

nelly *nel'i*, *n* a large petrel. [Perh from the woman's name]

nelson *nel'sən*, *n* a wrestling hold in which the arms are passed under both the opponent's arms from behind, and the hands joined so that pressure can be exerted with the palms on the back of his or her neck. — Also **full nelson**. — **half nelson** this hold applied on one side only, ie with one arm under one of the opponent's arms; a disabling restraint (*fig*). [From the proper name]

nelumbium *ni-lum'bi-əm* or **nelumbo** *-bō*, *n* a plant of the *Nelumbium* genus of waterlilies including the Egyptian bean of Pythagoras, and the sacred lotus: — *pl* **nelum'biums** or **nelum'bos**. [Prob Tamil]

Nemathelminthes *nem-ə-thel-min'thēz*, *n pl* according to some, a phylum of worms with unsegmented, cylindrical bodies, including nematodes, Nematomorpha and Acanthocephala (divided by others into separate phyla). — *n sing* **nemathel'minth**. — *adj* **nemathelmin'thic**. [Gr *nēma*, *-atos* a thread, and *helmins*, *-minthos* worm]

nematic *nə-mat'ik*, (*chem*) *adj* being in or having a mesomorphic phase in which the atoms or molecules are arranged in parallel lines, but not in the parallel planes typical of a smectic substance. [Gr *nēma*, genitive *nēmatos* a thread]

nematocyst *nem'ət-ō-sist* or *nə-mat'*, *n* a stinging organ in jellyfishes, etc, a sac from which a stinging thread can be everted. — *adj* **nematocys'tic**. [Gr *nēma*, *-atos* a thread, and *kystis* a bladder]

nematode *nem'ə-tōd*, *n* a parasitic worm with an unsegmented, cylindrical body, a roundworm or threadworm. — Also *adj*. — *n pl* **Nematōd'a** or **Nematoid'ea** the class of nematodes. — *n* **nematodirī'asis** (Gr *-iāsis*, as in *psoriasis*, etc) a disease of young lambs caused by nematodirus larvae. — *n* **nematodī'rus** (Gr *deirē* neck) a worm of the *Nematodīrus* genus of parasitic nematode worms found in the intestines of mammals. — *adj* **nem'atoid**. — *n* **nematol'ogist**. — *n* **nematol'ogy** the study of nematodes. [Gr *nēma*, *-atos* thread, and *eidos* form]

Nematomorpha *nem-ət-ō-mör'fə*, *n pl* the hairworms. [Gr *nēma*, *-atos* thread, and *morphē* form]

nematophore *nem'ət-ō-fōr* or *-för*, *n* a mouthless type of hydrozoan polyp that engulfs food by pseudopodia. [Gr *nēma*, *-atos* thread, and *phoros*, carrying]

Nembutal® *nem'bū-təl*, *n* a proprietary name for sodium pentobarbitone, used as a sedative, hypnotic and antispasmodic.

nem. con. *abbrev*: *nemine contradicente* (qv).

nem. diss. *abbrev*: *nemine dissentiente* (qv).

Nemean *nem-ē'ən*, *nem'i-ən* or *nēm'i-ən*, *adj* of *Nemea* (Gr *Nemeā*), the valley of Argolis, famous for its games held in the second and fourth years of each Olympiad, and for the lion killed by Herakles.

Nemertinea *nem-ər-tin'i-ə*, *n pl* a phylum of wormlike animals, mostly marine, ciliated, often brightly coloured with a protrusile proboscis, the ribbonworm. — Also **Nemer'tea**. — *n* and *adj* **nemer'tean**, **nemer'tine** and **nemer'tian**. [Gr *Nēmertēs*, one of the nereids]

nemesia *nem-ē'zh(y)ə*, *-sh(y)ə* or *-si-ə*, *n* a plant of the S African genus *Nemesia* of the figwort family, including some brightly coloured garden flowers. [Gr *nemesion* a kind of catchfly]

Nemesis *nem'i-sis*, (*Gr mythol*) *n* the Greek goddess of retribution; (without *cap*) retributive justice; something that cannot be achieved; a rival or opponent who cannot be beaten: — *pl* **Nem'eses** (*-sēz*). [Gr *nemesis* retribution, from *nemein* to deal out or dispense]

nemine contradicente *nem'ə-nē kon-trə-di-sen'tē* or *nā'mi-ne kon-trä-dē-ken'te*, (*L*; often *abbrev* **nem. con.**) without opposition; no-one speaking in opposition; **nemine dissentiente** (*di-sen-shi-en'tē* or *-ti-en'te*; *L*; often *abbrev* **nem. diss.**) no-one dissenting.

nemn. See under **nempt**.

nemophila *nem-of'i-lə*, *n* a plant of the N American genus *Nemophila* (family *Hydrophyllaceae*), favourite garden annuals, *esp* one with blue, white-centred flowers. [Gr *nemos* a glade, wooded pasture, and *phileein* to love]

nemoral *nem'ə-rəl*, *adj* of a wood or grove. — *adj* **nem'orous** wooded. [L *nemus*, *-oris* a grove]

nempt *nemt*, (*Spenser*) named, called: — *pap* of the obsolete verb **nemn** to name. [OE *nemnan*]

nene *nā'nā*, *n* the Hawaiian goose, a rare bird of Hawaii, having grey-brown plumage, a black face and partially-webbed feet. [Hawaiian]

nenuphar *nen'ū-fär*, *n* a waterlily, *esp* the common white or yellow; (with *cap*) same as **Nuphar**. [LL *nenuphar*, from Ar and Pers *nīnūfar*, *nīlūfar*, from Sans *nīlotpala*, from *nīla* blue, and *utpala* lotus]

Neo *nē'ō* or *nā'ō*, *n* an artificial language launched by an Italian, Arturo Alfandari, in 1961.

neo- *nē-ō-*, *nē-ə-* or *nē-o-*, *combining form* denoting new, young, revived in a new form. — *adj* and *n* **Neo-Cath'olic** of, or a member of the school of, liberal Catholicism that followed Lamennais, Lacordaire and Montalembert about 1830; Anglo-Catholic with extreme leanings towards Rome. — *adj* and *n* **Neo-Chris'tian** of, or a believer in, a liberalized and rationalized Christianity. — *n* **Neo-Christian'ity**. — *adj* **neoclass'ic** or **neoclass'ical** belonging to a revival of the classical style, *esp* in art and architecture, *usu* in reference to one such major revival in the late 18c and early 19c. — *n* **neoclass'icism** (*-i-sizm*). — *n* **neo-class'icist**. — *n* **neocolōn'ialism** the quasi-colonialism practised by strong powers in dominating weaker, though politically independent, states by means of economic pressure. — *n* and *adj* **neocolō'nialist**. — *n* and *adj* **Neo-Darwin'ian** or **Neo-Dar'winist**. — *n* **Neo-Dar'winism** a later development of Darwinism, laying greater stress upon natural selection and denying the inheritance of acquired characteristics. — *n* **Neofascism** (*-fash'izm*) a movement attempting to reinstate the policies of fascism. — *n* and *adj* **Neofasc'ist**. — *n* **neogenesis** (*-jen'ə-sis*; *biol*, etc) regeneration of tissue. — *adj* **neogenetic** (*-et'ik*). — *n* and *adj* **Neo-Goth'ic** revived Gothic of the 19c. — *n* **neogrammā'rian** a philologist of the 19c German school that introduced scientific exactitude into the study of sound change. — *n* **Neohell'enism** the modern Hellenism inspired by the ancient; the devotion to ancient Greek ideals in literature and art, *esp* in the Italian Renaissance. — *n* **Neo-Impress'ionism** a style of painting which aimed at producing greater luminosity of colour by applying pure unmixed colours in small dots. — *n* and *adj* **Neo-Impress'ionist**. — *n* and *adj* **Neo-Kant'ian**. — *n* **Neo-Kant'ianism** the philosophy of *Kant* as taught by his successors. — *n* and *adj* **Neo-Lamarck'ian**. — *n* **Neo-Lamarck'ism** a modern adaptation of Lamarckism. — *n* and *adj* **Neo-Lat'in** Romance, ie Italian, Rhaeto-Romanic, French, Provençal, Spanish, Portuguese and Romanian. — *n* **Neo-Malthus'ianism** the doctrine of the necessity for birth-control to control population. — *n* **Neo-Melanē'sian** a creole language based on English, developed in Melanesia. — *n* **neo-Naz'i** a member or supporter of any of a number of modern movements espousing the principles of National Socialism or the like. — *n* **neo-Naz'ism**. — *n* and *adj* **neopā'gan**. — *n* **neopā'ganism** a revival of paganism, or its spirit. — *vt* and *vi* **neopā'ganize** or **-ise**. — *n* **Neo-Plas'ticism** (or **neoplasticism**) a style of abstract painting in which geometrical patterns are formed of patches of flat colour enclosed by intersecting vertical and horizontal lines. — *adj* **Neoplatonic** (*-plə-ton'ik*). — *n* **Neoplā'tonism** a combination of Platonism with Oriental elements, developed by Plotinus, Porphyry, Proclus, etc. — *n* and *adj* **Neoplā'tonist**. — *n* and *adj* **Neopythagorē'an**. — *n* **Neopythagorē'anism** a revived Pythagoreanism of Alexandria beginning in the first century BC. — *n* **neorē'alism** a modern form of realism in the arts and literature; *specif*, a cinematic movement, or a style of cinematography, originating in post-war Italy, characterized by socio-political content, and the use of mise-en-scène (qv) techniques and often non-professional actors to achieve a starkly realistic depiction of lower-class life. — *n* and *adj* **neorē'alist**. — *adj* **neorealist'ic**. — *n* **neotox'in** any harmful substance, eg in the environment, causing illness or allergy. — *adj* **Neotrop'ical** (*biol*) belonging to the tropics of the New World, tropical America. — *n* **neovī'talism** the theory or belief that complete causal explanation of vital phenomena cannot be reached without invoking some extra-material concept. — *n* and *adj* **neovī'talist**. [Gr *neos* new]

neoblast *nē'ə-bläst*, (*zool*) *n* (in many of the lower animals, such as *Annelida* (worms)) any of the large amoebid cells that play an important part in the phenomena of regeneration. [**neo-** and Gr *blastos* a shoot or bud]

Neo-Catholic. See under **neo-**.

Neoceratodus *nē-ə-ser-ə-tō'dəs*, *n* the name of the genus to which the barramunda belongs, now used in preference to *Ceratodus*. [**neo-** and **Ceratodus**]

Neo-Christian ... to ... **neo-colonialist**. See under **neo-**.

Neocomian *nē-ə-kō'mi-ən*, (*geol*) *n* Lower Cretaceous. [L *Neocōmium* Neuchâtel from Gr *kōme* a village]

Neo-Darwinism, etc. See under **neo-**.

neodymium *nē-ə-dim'i-əm*, (*chem*) *n* a silvery-grey toxic metallic element (symbol **Nd**; atomic no 60). [**neo-** and *didymium*, a once-supposed element found to consist of neodymium and praseodymium]

Neofascism, etc. See under **neo-**.

Neogaea *nē-ə-jē'ə*, (*biol*) *n* the Neotropical region. — *adj* **Neogae'an**. [**neo-** and Gr *gaia* the earth]

Neogene *nē-ə-jēn'*, (*geol*) *n* and *adj* Miocene and Pliocene. [Gr *neogenēs* new-born]

neogenesis... to ... **Neo-Latin**. See under **neo-**.

Neolithic *nē-ə-lith'ik*, *adj* of or relating to the later, more advanced, Stone Age. — *n* the Neolithic period. — *n* **ne'olith** a Neolithic artefact. [**neo-** and Gr *lithos* a stone]

neologism *nē-ol'ə-jizm* or **neology** *nē-ol'ə-ji*, *n* a new word, phrase or doctrine; a new use of an established word; the practice of coining or introducing neologisms; (*usu* **neology**) new doctrines, *esp* German rationalism (*theol*). — *n* **neolō'gian**. — *adj* **neologic** or **neological** (*-loj'-*). — *adv* **neolog'ically**. — *n* **neol'ogist**. — *adj* **neologis'tic** or **neologis'tical**. — *n* **neol'ogize** or **-ise** to introduce new words, coin neologisms. [**neo-** and Gr *logos* a word]

Neo-Malthusianism and **Neo-Melanesian**. See under **neo-**.

neomycin *nē-ə-mī'sin*, (*pharm*) *n* an antibiotic used to treat skin and eye infections. [**neo-**, Gr *mukēs* fungus, and sfx **-in**]

neon *nē'on*, *n* a gaseous element (symbol **Ne**; atomic no 10) found in the atmosphere by Sir William Ramsay (1852–1916). — Also as *adj*. — **neon lamp** or **light** an electric discharge lamp containing neon, giving a red glow, used eg for advertising signs; (loosely) one of a variety of tubular fluorescent lamps giving light of various colours; **neon lighting**. [Neuter of Gr *neos* new]

neonatal *nē-ə-nā'tl*, *adj* relating to the newly born. — *n* **nē'onate** a newly born child. — *adj* newly born. — *n* **neonatol'ogy** the care and treatment of the newly born. [New L *neonātus*, from Gr *neos* new, and L *nātus* born]

neo-Nazi, etc. See under **neo-**.

neonomianism *nē-ə-nō'mi-ə-nizm*, (*theol*) *n* the doctrine that the gospel is a new law and that faith has abrogated the old moral obedience. — *n* and *adj* **neonō'mian**. [**neo-** and Gr *nomos* law]

neopaganism, etc. See under **neo-**.

neophile *nē'ə-fīl*, *n* someone who loves novelty and new things; someone who is obsessive about keeping up to date with fasion, trends, etc. — *n* **neophil'ia**. — *n* **neophil'iac**. [**neo-** and **-phile**]

neophobia *nē-ə-fō'bi-ə*, a dread or hatred of novelty. — *n* **nē'ophobe**. — *adj* **neophō'bic**. [Gr *neos* new, and *phobos* fear]

neophyte *nē'ə-fīt*, *n* a new convert; a person newly baptized; a newly ordained priest; a novice in a religious order; a tiro or beginner. — *adj* **neophytic** (*-fit'ik*). [Gr *neophytos* newly planted, from *neos* new, and *phyein* to produce]

neopilina *nē-ō-pil-ī'nə*, *n* a mollusc of the genus *Neopilina* of Monoplacophora (qv). [**neo-** and *Pilina*, a Palaeolithic genus of similar appearance]

neoplasm *nē'ə-plazm*, (*pathol*) *n* a morbid new growth of tissue. — *adj* **neoplas'tic**. [**neo-** and Gr *plasma* something moulded]

Neo-Plasticism and **Neoplatonism**, etc. See under **neo-**.

neoprene *nē'ə-prēn*, *n* an oil-resisting and heat-resisting synthetic rubber made by polymerizing chloroprene. [**neo-** and **chlororprene**]

Neopythagoreanism and **neorealism**, etc. See under **neo-**.

neoteny *nē-ot'ə-ni* or **neoteinia** *nē-ō-tī'ni-ə*, (*biol*) *n* prolonged retention of larval or immature characteristics or features in the adult form. — *adj* **neotenic** (*nē-ō-ten'ik*). — *adj* **neot'enous**. [**neo-** and Gr *teinein* to stretch]

neoteric *nē-ō-ter'ik* or **neoterical** *-əl*, *adj* of recent origin, modern. — *n* a modern writer or philospher. — *adv* **neoter'ically**. — *n* **neot'erism** the introduction of new things, *esp* new words. — *n* **neot'erist**. — *vi* **neoterize** or **-ise** (*nē-ot'ə-rīz*). [Gr *neōterikos*, from *neōteros*, comparative of *neos* new]

Neotropical and **neovitalism**, etc. See under **neo-**.

Neozoic *nē-ō-zō'ik*, (*geol*) *adj* and *n* (relating to) the period between the Mesozoic and the present age. [**neo-** and Gr *zōikos* of animals]

nep *nep* or **nip** *nip*, (now *dialect*) *n* catmint. [L *nepeta*]

Nepalese *nep-ə-lēz'*, *adj* of Nepal or its people. — *n* a native or citizen of Nepal.

Nepali *ni-pö'lē*, *n* the official language of Nepal, belonging to the Indic branch of Indo-European languages; a native or citizen of Nepal: — *pl* **Nepal'i** or **Nepal'is**. — *adj* of Nepal, its people or its language.

nepenthe *ni-pen'thē*, *n* a drink or drug causing sorrow to be forgotten (*poetic*); the plant yielding it. — *adj* **nepen'thean**. — *n* **Nepen'thes** (*-thēz*) nepenthe; the pitcher-plant genus, constituting a family **Nepenthā'ceae** related to the family Sarracenia and the sundews. [Gr *nepenthēs*, *-es*, from pfx *nē-* not, and *penthos* grief]

neper *nā'pər* or *nē'*, *n* a unit for expressing the ratio of two currents, two voltages etc, the number of nepers being equal to the natural logarithm of the ratio. (Cf **decibel** and **bel**). [John *Napier*; see **Napierian**]

nepeta *nep'ə-tə*, *n* catmint. [L]

nephalism *nef'ə-lizm*, *n* total abstinence from alcoholic drinks. — *n* **neph'alist**. [Gr *nēphalios* sober; *nēphein* to be sober]

nepheline *nef'ə-lēn*, *n* a rock-forming mineral, silicate of sodium, potassium and aluminium, colourless, usually crystallizing in hexagonal prisms. — Also **neph'elite**. — *n* **neph'elinite** a basalt-like rock compound of nepheline and pyroxene, with no feldspar or olivine. — **neph'e-line-bas'alt** a basalt with nepheline instead of (or in addition to) feldspar. [Gr *nephelē* a cloud (from the clouding effect of acid on it)]

nephelometer *nef-ə-lom'i-tər*, *n* an instrument for measuring cloudiness, *esp* in liquids. — *adj* **nephelomet'ric**. — *n* **nephelom'etry**. [Gr *nephelē* cloud, and *metron* measure]

nephew *nev'ū* or *nef'ū*, *n* the son of one's brother or sister; extended to the same relation by marriage; a grandson or descendant (*obs*); a pope's or priest's son (*euphem*): — *fem* **niece**. [(O)Fr *neveu*, from L *nepōs*, *nepōtis* grandson; cf OE *nefa*, Ger *Neffe* nephew]

nepho- *nef-o-* or *-ō-*, *combining form* denoting cloud. — *n* **neph'ogram** a photograph of a cloud. — *n* **neph'ōgraph** (*-gräf*) an instrument for photographing clouds in order to determine their position. — *n* **nephology** (*nef-ol'ə-ji*) the study of clouds in meteorology. — *adj* **nephologic** (*-ə-loj'*) or **nepholog'ical**. — *n* **nephol'ogist**. — *n* **neph'ōscope** an apparatus which determines the direction and velocity of movement of clouds. [Gr *nephos* cloud]

nephro- *nef-ro-* or *-rō-* or **nephr-** *combining form* denoting kidney. — *n* **nephralgia** (*nef-ral'ji-ə*) or **nephral'gy** pain in the kidneys. — *n* **nephrec'tomy** surgical removal of a kidney. — *adj* **neph'ric**. — *n* **nephrid'ium** (in invertebrates and lower chordates) an organ serving the function of a kidney. — *n* **neph'rīte** the mineral jade, in the narrower sense, an old charm against kidney disease. — *n* **nephrit'ic** (*obs*) a medicine for the kidneys. — *adj* **nephrit'ic** or **nephrit'ical** relating to the kidneys, or nephritis, or jade. — *n* **nephrī'tis** inflammation of the kidneys. — *adj* **neph'roid** kidney-shaped. — *n* **nephrolepis** see separate entry. — *adj* **nephrolog'ical** (*-loj'*). — *n* **nephrol'ogist**. — *n* **nephrol'ogy** the science concerned with the structure, functions and diseases of the kidneys. — *n* **neph'ron** one of the filtering units of the kidney. — *n* **nephrop'athy** (Gr *pathos* suffering) disease of the kidneys. — *n* **neph'ropexy** (Gr *pēxis* fixing) fixation of a floating kidney. — *n* **nephroptō'sis** (Gr *ptōsis* fall) floating kidney. — *n* **nephrō'sis** a disease of the kidney characterized by non-inflammatory degeneration of the tubules. — *adj* **nephrot'ic**. — *n* **neph-rot'omy** incision into the kidney. [Gr *nephros* a kidney]

nephrolepis *nef-rə-lē'pis*, *n* any fern of the genus *Nephrolepis* with pinnate fronds and kidney-shaped indusia, some being grown as house plants. [Gr *nephros* a kidney, and *lepis* scale]

nepionic *nep'i-on-ik* or *nēp'i-on-ik*, (*biol*) *adj* relating to the embryonic period in the life-history of an individual. [Gr *nēpios* infant]

nepit. See **nit**[4].

ne plus ultra *nē plus ul'trə* or *nā plōōs ōōl'trä*, (*L*) nothing further; the uttermost point or extreme perfection of anything.

nepotism *nep'o-tizm*, *n* undue favoritism to one's relations and close friends, *orig* by a pope. — *adj* **nepotic** (*ni-pot'ik*) or **nepotis'tic**. — *n* **nep'otist**. [L *nepōs*, *nepōtis* a grandson]

Neptune *nep'tūn*, *n* the Roman sea-god, identified with the Greek Poseidon; a remote planet of the solar system, discovered in 1846. — *adj* **Neptū'nian** relating to Neptune or to the sea; formed by water (*geol*). — *n* an imagined inhabitant of Neptune; a Neptunist. — *n*

Nep'tūnist a believer in the origin of rocks generally as chemical precipitates from the sea (*opp* to *Plutonist* or *Vulcanist*). — *n* **neptū'nium** a radioactive metallic element (symbol **Np**; atomic no 93) named as next after uranium, as Neptune is next after Uranus. — **neptunium series** a series formed by the decay of artificial radio-elements, the first member being plutonium-241 and the last bismuth-209, neptunium-237 being the longest-lived. [L *Neptūnus*]

NERC *nûrk*, *abbrev*: Natural Environment Research Council.

nerd or **nurd** *nûrd*, (*slang*) *n* a clumsy, foolish, socially inept, feeble, unathletic, irritating or unprepossessing person. — *adj* **ner'dy**. [Origin unknown]

nereid *nē'rē-id*, *n* a sea-nymph, daughter of the sea-god *Nereus* (*Gr mythol*); a marine polychaete worm (genus *Nereis*, or related genus) superficially like a long myriapod; (with *cap*) the smaller of the two satellites of the planet Neptune, the other being Triton: — *pl* **ner'eids** or (in sea-nymph sense) **nereides** (*nē'rē-ə-dēz*). [Gr *nērēis* or *nēreis*, from *Nēreus*]

nerine *ni-rī'nē*, *n* any plant of the S African genus *Nerine*, related to the amaryllis, with scarlet or rose-coloured flowers, including the Guernsey lily. [L *nērinē* a nereid]

Nerita *ni-rī'tə*, *n* a round-shelled genus of gasteropods of warm seas. — *n* **nerite** (*nē'rīt*) a sea snail of the genus *Nerita* or its family **Nerit'idae**. — *adj* **neritic** (*nē-rit'ik*) belonging to the shallow waters near land. — *n* **Neritina** (*ner-it-ī'nə*) a brackish and freshwater genus related to *Nerita*. [Gr *nēreitēs*, *nēritēs* a sea snail (of various kinds)]

Nerium *nē'ri-əm*, *n* the oleander genus. [Latinized from Gr *nērion*]

nerk *nûrk*, (*slang*) *n* an irritating fool or idiot. [Poss **nerd** and **berk**]

nerka *nûr'kə*, *n* the sockeye salmon. [Origin unknown]

Nernst *närnst*, *adj* invented by or due to the German chemist and physicist Walter *Nernst* (1864–1941), applied *esp* to an electric lamp with a filament or rod of rare-earth oxides whose conductivity is greatly increased by heating.

nero-antico *nā-rō-an-tē'kō*, *n* a deep-black marble found in Roman ruins. [Ital, ancient black]

neroli *ner'ə-lē*, *n* an oil distilled from orange flowers. — Also **neroli oil**. [Said to be named from its discoverer, an Italian princess]

Neronian *nē-rō'ni-ən*, *adj* relating to *Nero*, Roman emperor from AD 54 to 68; excessively cruel and tyrannical. — *adj* **Neronic** (*-ron'ik*). [L *Nerō*, *-ōnis*]

nerve *nûrv*, *n* a cord consisting of bundles of fibres that conveys impulses of sensation or movement between the brain or other centre and some part of the body (*anatom*); self-possession; cool courage; impudent assurance, audacity (*colloq*); (in *pl*) nervousness, anxiety; (in *pl*) a disordered nervous system, *esp* when unable to deal successfully with emotional stress or tension; a sore or sensitive spot or point; a sinew (now chiefly *fig*); a bowstring (*poetic*); strength; a leaf-vein or rib (*bot*); a nervure in an insect's wing (*entomol*); a vault rib (*archit*). — *vt* to give strength, resolution, or courage to (oneself, etc). — *adj* **nerv'al** of the nerves. — *adj* **ner'vate** (of a leaf) having veins; nerved. — *n* **nervā'tion** or **nerv'ature** disposition of nerves, *esp* in leaves; venation. — *adj* **nerved** supplied with nerves. — *adj* **nerve'less** without nerves or nervures; without strength; inert; slack, flabby; unnerved; without nervousness, calm. — *adv* **nerve'lessly**. — *n* **nerve'lessness**. — *n* **nerve'let** a little nerve; a tendril. — *n* **nerv'er** someone who or something which nerves. — *adv* **nerv'ily**. — *adj* **nerv'ine** (*-ēn* or *-īn*) acting on the nerves; quieting nervous excitement. — *n* a drug that soothes nervous excitement. — *n* **nerv'iness**. — *adj* **nerv'ous** relating to the nerves; having the nerves easily excited or weak, agitated and apprehensive (often with *of*); caused by such a temperament or nervousness (such as *nervous energy*); in a jumpy state; shy; timid; having nerve; sinewy; strong, vigorous, showing strength and vigour. — *adv* **nerv'ously**. — *n* **nerv'ousness**. — *adj* **nerv'ūlar**. — *n* **nerv'ūle** a small branch of a nervure. — *n* **nervūrā'tion**. — *n* **nerv'ure** a leaf-vein; a chitinous strut or rib supporting and strengthening an insect's wing (*entomol*); a rib of a groined vault (*archit*). — *adj* **nerv'y** nervous; jumpily excited or excitable; calling for nerve or courage; cool; impudent or audacious (*NAm colloq*). — **nerve agent** a nerve gas or similar substance; **nerve block** local anaesthesia produced by injecting an anaesthetic into the nerve or nerves supplying that part of the body; **nerve cell** any cell forming part of the nervous system; a neuron; **nerve centre** an aggregation of nerve cells from which nerves branch out; (in an organization) the centre from which control is exercised (*fig*); **nerve end** or **ending** the free end of a nerve, generally with accessory parts forming an end-organ; **nerve fibre** an axon; **nerve gas** any of a number of gases, prepared for use in war, having a deadly effect on the nervous system, *esp* on nerves controlling respiration; **nerve** or **nervous impulse** the electrical impulse passing along a nerve fibre when it has been stimulated. — *adj* **nerve'-racking** or **nerve'-wracking** distressfully straining the nerves. — **nervous breakdown** a loose term indicating nervous debility following prolonged mental or physical fatigue; a euphemism for any mental illness; **nervous system** the brain, spinal cord and nerves collectively; **nervous wreck** (*colloq*) a very timid, anxious and jumpy person, *esp* when unable to deal successfully with stress or tension. — **bundle of nerves** (*colloq*) a very timid, anxious person; **get on one's nerves** to become oppressively irritating; **live on one's nerves** to be (constantly) in a tense or nervous state; to be of an excitable temperament; **lose one's nerve** to lose confidence in one's ability; to become suddenly afraid; **war of nerves** see under **war**[1]. [L *nervus* sinew; cf Gr *neuron*]

NES *abbrev*: National Eczema Society.

nescience *nesh'i-əns*, *nesh'əns*, *nes'i-əns* or *-yəns*, (*formal*) *n* lack of knowledge; ignorance. — *adj* **nesc'ient**. [L *nescientia*, from *nescīre* to be ignorant, from *ne-* not, and *scīre* to know]

nesh *nesh*, (*dialect*) *adj* soft, crumbly; tender; delicate in one's health; susceptible to cold; cowardly, afraid; lacking energy. — *n* **nesh'ness**. [OE *hnesce*]

Nesiot or **Nēsiōt** *nē'si-ōt*, (*anthropol*) *n* an Indonesian. [Gr *nēsiōtēs* an islander, from *nēsos* an island]

Neskhi, **Neski** *nes'ki* or **Naskhi** *nas'ki*, *n* Arabic cursive handwriting. [Ar *naskhī*]

ness *nes*, *n* a headland. [OE *næs*, *næss*]

-ness *-nəs*, *sfx* forming nouns from adjectives and participles denoting state or condition, or an example of this (such as *happiness*, *barrenness*, *kindness*). [OE *-nes*]

nest *nest*, *n* a structure prepared by animals for egg-laying, brooding and nursing, or as a shelter; a place of retreat, resort, residence, or lodgement; a den; a comfortable residence; a group of machine-guns in a position fortified or screened by sandbags or anything similar; a place where anything (*esp* anything undesirable) teems, prevails or is fostered; the occupants of a nest, eg a brood, a swarm, a gang etc; a set of things (eg boxes or tables) fitting one within another; a set of buildings, eg factories, divided into blocks and units; an accumulation; a tangled mass. — *vi* to build or occupy a nest; to go bird-nesting. — *vt* and *vi* to lodge or settle; to fit or place together or within another. — *vt* to group (words derived from the same root) together under one headword in a dictionary; to embed (a subroutine or block of data) within a larger one (*comput*). — *n* **nest'er** someone who builds a farm or homestead on land used for grazing cattle (*US hist*; *derog*); a nest-builder. *n* **nest'ful**. — *n* **nest'ing**. — *adj* **nest'like**. — **nest egg** an egg, real or sham, left or put in a nest to encourage laying; something laid up as the beginning of an accumulation; money saved; **nest'ing-box** a box set up for birds to nest in; **nest'ing-place**. —

feather one's nest see under **feather**. [OE *nest*; Ger *Nest*, L *nīdus*]

nestle *nes'l*, *vi* to lie or press close or snug as in a nest; to settle comfortably or half hidden; to nest (*archaic*). — *vt* to cherish, as a bird does her young; to push or thrust close; to provide a nesting-place for. — *n* **nestling** (*nes'ling* or *nest'*) a young bird in the nest; any young person or animal. — Also *adj*. [OE *nestlian*, from *nest* a nest]

Nestor *nes'tör* or *-tər*, *n* an old king of Pylos, a Greek hero at Troy remarkable for eloquence, wisdom and long life; an old counsellor; an old man; the kea parrot genus. [Gr *Nestor*]

Nestorian *nes-tō'ri-ən* or *-ö'*, *adj* relating to *Nestorius*, patriarch of Constantinople (428–31), or to his teaching, that the divinity and humanity of Christ were not united in a single self-conscious personality. — *n* a follower of Nestorius. — *n* **Nestō'rianism**.

net[1] *net*, *n* an open fabric, knotted into meshes; a piece, bag, screen or structure of such fabric used for catching fish, butterflies, etc, carrying parcels, stopping balls, dividing a tennis court, retaining hair or excluding pests; a network; machine-made lace of various kinds; a snare; a plan to trap or catch someone or something; a difficulty; a let (*lawn tennis*); (*usu* in *pl*) a practice pitch surrounded by nets (*cricket*); the shape of a three-dimensional figure when laid out flat (*math*). — *adj* of or like net or network. — *vt* to form into a net or network; to mark or cover with a net or network; to set with nets; to fish with nets; to form by knotting threads into meshes; to take with a net; (also *vi*) to put (eg a footbal) into a net to score; to capture; to send (eg a ball) into the net (*football, tennis* and *badminton*). — *vi* to form a net or network: — *pr p* **nett'ing**; *pa t* and *pa p* **nett'ed**. — *n* **net'ful** enough to fill a net. — *adj* **nett'ed** made into a net; reticulated; caught in a net; covered with a net. — *n* **nett'ing** the act or process of forming a net or network; a piece of network; any network of ropes or wire. — *adj* **nett'y** like a net. — **net'ball** a team game, played mainly by women, in which the ball is thrown into a net hung from a pole; **net cord** a string supporting a lawn tennis net; a shot in which the tennis-player strikes the net cord with the ball; **net'fish** any fish, like the herring, *usu* caught in nets (*opp* to *trawl-fish* and *line-fish*); **net'-fish'ery** a place for net-fishing; the business of net-fishing; **net'-fishing** fishing with nets; **net game** or **net'-play** (in tennis, etc) play near the net; **net'-player**; **net'-prac'tice** cricket practice within nets; **nett'ing-need'le** a kind of shuttle used in netting. — *adj* **net'-veined** (eg of a leaf or an insect's wing) having veins that branch and meet in a network. — *adj* **net'-winged** having net-veined wings. — **net'work** any structure in the form of a net; a system of lines, eg railway lines, resembling a net; a system of units, as eg buildings, agencies, groups of people, constituting a widely spread organization and having a common purpose; a group of people with a common interest, *esp* of those who meet socially, who share information, swap contacts, etc; an arrangement of electrical components; a system of stations connected for broadcasting the same programme (*radio* and *TV*); a system of computer terminals and other peripheral devices that can pass information to one another. — *vt* to broadcast on radio or TV stations throughout the country, as opposed to a single station covering only one region; to link (computer terminals and other peripheral devices) to enable them to operate interactively. — *vi* to form business or professional contacts with people met on a social basis. — *n* **net'worker** an employee who works from home on a personal computer linked to the computer network in his or her company's offices; a person who develops business and professional contacts through informal social meetings. — *n* **net'working**. — **dance in a net** to act in imagined concealment. [OE *net*, *nett*; Du *net*, Ger *Netz*]

net[2] or **nett** *net*, *adj* clear of all charges or deductions (*opp* to *gross*); (of weight) not including that of packaging; lowest, subject to no further deductions; (of eg a result) final or conclusive; clean (*obs*); bright (*obs*); unmixed, pure (*obs*); neat, trim (*rare*). — *vt* to gain or produce as clear profit: — *pr p* **nett'ing**; *pa t* and *pa p* **nett'ed**. — **net assets** the total value of the assets of a company minus current liabilities, used as an indication of the value of that company. — Also **net asset value**; **Net Book Agreement** see **NBA**; **net realizable value** the amount expected to be received from the sale of an asset after deducting all the expenses incurred in the sale. [**neat**[1]]

nete *nē'tē*, (*Gr music*) *n* the highest string or note of the lyre. [Gr *nētē* or *neatē* (*chordē*), literally, lowest (string)]

Neth. *abbrev*: Netherlands.

netheless *nedh'ə-les* or *nedh'les*, *adv* (*Spenser*) for **nathless**.

nether *nedh'ər*, *adj* lower. — *n pl* **neth'erlings** (*Dickens*) stockings. — *adj* **neth'ermore** (*rare*) lower. — *adj* **neth'ermost** lowest. — *adv* **neth'erward** or **neth'erwards** (*rare*) downwards. — **neth'erstock** (*hist*) a stocking; **neth'erworld** hell. — Also **nether regions**. [OE *neothera*, adj, from *nither*, adv, from the root *ni-* down; Ger *nieder* low]

Netherlander *nedh'ər-land-ər*, *n* an inhabitant of the *Netherlands* or Low Countries, now Holland, formerly also Belgium. — *adj* **Netherland'ic** or **Neth'erlandish** Dutch.

Nethinim *neth'in-im*, *n pl* the old Jewish temple servants. [Heb *nethīnīm*]

netsuke *net'skē*, *-skā* or *ne'tsōō-ke'*, *n* a small Japanese carved ornament, once used to fasten small objects (eg a purse or pouch for tobacco, medicines, etc) to a sash. [Jap *ne* root or bottom, and *tsuke*, from *tsukeru* to attach]

nett. See under **net**[2].

nettle[1] *net'l*, *n* any of various common weeds (genus *Urtica*) with stinging hairs; any of several similar plans, such as hemp-nettle. — *vt* to sting; to annoy. — *adj* **nett'lelike**. — *adj* **nett'lesome** irritable. — *adj* **nett'ly**. — **nett'le-cell** a nematocyst; **nett'le-cloth** cloth of nettle-fibre; thick japanned cotton; **nett'le-fish** a jellyfish; **nett'le-rash** urticaria, a rash of itchy red or white weals, *usu* the symptom of an allergy (also called *hives*); **nett'le-tree** a tree of the elm family (genus *Celtis*), with nettle-shaped leaves, edible drupes, and wood good for turning; a tropical and Australian tree (genus *Laportea*) of the nettle family, with virulently stinging leaves. — **dead-nettle** see under **dead**; **hemp-nettle** see under **hemp**. — **grasp the nettle** to set about an unpleasant task, duty, etc with firmness and resolution. [OE *netele*; Ger *Nessel*]

nettle[2]. Same as **knittle**.

netty, network, etc. See under **net**[1].

neuk *nük* or *nūk*, *n* a Scots form of **nook**.

neume or **neum** *nūm*, (*Med music*) *n* a succession of notes sung to one syllable; a sign giving a rough indication of rise or fall of pitch. [OFr, from Gr *pneuma* breath]

neur- *nūr-* or **neuro-** *nū'rō-*, *combining form* denoting a nerve cell, a nerve-fibre, nerve-tissue, or the nervous system (*esp* the brain and spinal cord); the nerves and some other system, as in *neurovascular* and *neuromuscular*; an area of research, etc associated with the nervous system, as in *neuroanatomist*, *neurobiologist* and *neurophysiology*. — *n* **neuralgia** (*nū-ral'jə* or *-jyə*; Gr *algos* pain) paroxysmal intermittent pain along the course of a nerve; pain of a purely nervous character. — *adj* **neural'gic**. — *n* **neuramin'idase** (*immunol*) an enzyme found on the surface of several viruses, which destroys the **neuraminic acid** on the surface of cells to which these viruses attach themselves, making the cells more likely to clump together. — *n* **neurasthenia** (*nū-rəs-thē'ni-ə*; Gr *astheneia* weakness) nervous debility. — *n* **neurasthē'niac** someone suffering from neurasthenia. — *adj* **neurasthenic** (*-then'ik* or *-thēn'ik*). — *n* a neurastheniac. — *n* **neurā'tion** nervation. — *n* **neurec'tomy** the surgical excision of part of a nerve. — *n* **neurilemm'a** or **neurolemm'a** (Gr *eilēma* covering) the external sheath of a nerve fibre. — *n* **neuril'ity** the essential character of nerve. — *n* **neur'ine** (*-ēn, -in* or *-īn*) a very poisonous ptomaine formed in putrefying flesh. — *n* **neur'ism** a supposed 'nerve-force' acting in evolution (cf **bathmism**). — *n* **neur'ite** an axon or dendrite. — *adj* **neuroanatom'ical**. — *n* **neuroanat'omist**. — *n* **neuroanat'omy** the study of the structure of the nervous system; the nerve structure of an organism. — *adj* **neurobiolog'ical**. — *n* **neurobiol'ogist**. — *n* **neurobiol'ogy** the branch of biology dealing with the anatomy and physiology of the nervous system. — *n* **neur'oblast** an embryonic nerve cell. — *n* **neuroblastō'ma** a malignant tumour composed of primitive nerve cells, starting either the adrenal gland or sympathetic nervous system, and most commonly affecting children: — *pl* **neuroblastō'mas** or **neuroblastō'mata** (*-mə-tə*). — *n* (*embryol*) a cavity in the embryonic nervous system which develops into the central canal of the spinal cord and ventricles in the brain. — *n* **neur'ochip** a microchip used in neural networks. — *n* **neur'ocomputer** a computer that uses neural networks to mimic the action of the human brain. — Also **neural computer**. — *n* **neurocomput'ing**. — *adj* **neuroen'docrine** relating to the nervous and endocrine systems, and to their interaction. — *n* **neuroendocrinol'ogy** the study of the interaction of the nervous and endocrine systems. — *n* **neuroethol'ogy** the description of features of animal behaviour in terms of the mechanisms of the nervous system. — *n* **neurofibril** (*-fī'bril*) one of a large number of fine fibres present in the cytoplasm of a nerve cell. — *adj* **neurofib'rillar** or **neurofibrill'ary**. — *n* **neurofibrō'ma** a fibroma of the peripheral nerves: — *pl* **neurofibrō'mas** or **neurofibrō'mata** (*-mə-tə*). — *n* **neurofibromatō'sis** a condition characterized by the formation of neurofibromas and areas of dark pigmentation on the skin. — *n* **neurogen'esis** the development and growth of nerves. — *adj* **neurogen'ic** caused or stimulated by the nervous system (*opp* to *myogenic*). — *n* **neurog'lia** (Gr *gliā* glue) the supporting tissue of the brain and spinal cord, etc. — *n* **neur'ogram** same as **engram**. — *n* **neurohor'mone** a hormone formed in the nervous system. — *n* **neurohypnol'ogy** or **neurypnol'ogy** old names for the science of hypnotism. — *n* **neurohypophy'sis** the posterior lobe of the pituitary gland (cf **adenohypophosis**): — *pl* **neurohypophy'ses** (*-sēz*). — *n* **neuroleptanalgē'sia** the administration of a tranquillizer and an analgesic at the same time to induce a sleeplike state eg for minor surgery. — *adj* **neuroleptanalgē'sic**. — *n* and *adj* **neurolep'tic** (a drug) able to reduce nervous tension. — *n* **neur'olinguist**. — *adj* **neurolinguis'tic**. — *n sing* **neurolinguis'tics** the branch of linguistics which deals with the processing and storage of language in the brain. — *adj* **neurolog'ical**. — *adv* **neurolog'ically**. — *n* **neurol'ogist**. — *n* **neurol'ogy** *orig* the study of the nervous system; that branch of medicine concerned with the diagnosis and treatment of diseases of the nervous system. — *n* **neurol'ysis** breaking down of nerve tissue, or exhaustion of a nerve. — *n* **neurō'ma** a tumour consisting of nerve tissue: — *pl* **neurō'mas** or **neurō'mata**. — *adj* **neuromuscular** relating to both nerves and muscles. — *n* **neur'opath** (*-path*; Gr *pathos* suffering) someone whose nervous system is diseased or in disorder. — *adj* **neuropath'ic** or **neuropath'ical**. — *n* **neuropathist** (*nūr-o-p'ə-thist*) a specialist in nervous diseases. — *n* **neuropathogen'esis** (the cause or origin of) the development of a disease or disorder of the nervous system. — *adj* **neuropatholog'ical**. — *n* **neuropathol'ogist**. — *n* **neuropathol'ogy** the pathology of the nervous system. — *n* **neurop'athy** nervous disease generally. — *n* **neuropep'tide** any of several peptides found in brain tissue, classifed as neurotransmitters and, in some cases, hormones. — *n* **neuropharmacol'ogist**. — *n* **neuropharmacol'ogy** the scientific study of the effects of drugs on the nervous system. — *adj* **neurophysiolog'ical**. — *n* **neurophysiol'ogist**. — *n* **neurophysiol'ogy** the physiology of the nervous system. — *n* **neur'opil** (*zool*; Gr *pilos* hair) (in vertebrates) a network of axons, dendrites and synopses within the central nervous system. — *n* **neur'oplasm** the protoplasm of a nerve cell. — *adj* **neuropsychiat'ric**. — *n* **neuropsychi'atrist**. — *n* **neuropsychi'atry** the branch of medicine dealing with diseases involving the mind and nervous system. — *adj* **neuropsychol'ogist**. — *n* **neuropsychol'ogy** the study of the relationship between the brain and nervous system and behaviour. — *n* **neuroradiol'ogy** the branch of radiology dealing with the diagnosis of diseases of the nervous system. — *n* **neur'oscience** any or all of the scientific disciplines studying the nervous system and/or the mind and mental behaviour. — *n* **neurosci'entist**. — *n* **neurosur'geon**. — *n* **neurosur'gery** surgery performed on the brain, spinal cord or other parts of the nervous system. — *adj* **neurosur'gical**. — *n* **neurot'omist**. — *n* **neurotomy** (*-ot'ə-mi*) the surgical cutting of a nerve. — *adj* **neurotox'ic**. — *n* **neurotoxic'ity** the degree to which a substance is poisonous to nerve tissue; the state caused by exposure to a neurotoxin. — *n* **neurotox'in** a substance poisonous to nerve tissue. — *n* **neurotransmitt'er** a chemical released from a nerve fibre by means of which an impulse passes to a muscle or another nerve. — *adj* **neurotroph'ic** of or relating to the nutrition of the nervous system, or to nutritional changes influenced by the nervous system. — *n* **neurot'rophy** nutrition of the nervous system; the influence of the nervous system on nutrition. — *adj* **neurotrop'ic** having a special affinity for or growing in nerve cells. — *adj* **neurovas'cular** relating to or affecting both nerves and blood vessels. — **neurypnology** see **neurohypnology** above. [Gr *neuron* a nerve]

neural *nū'rəl*, *adj* of or relating to the nerves or the central nervous system; dorsal, as opposed to *haemal*. — *adv* **neur'ally**. — **neural arch** the arch of a vertebra protecting the spinal cord; **neural computer** same as **neurocomputer** under **neur-**; **neural computing** computing using neurocomputers; **neural network** or **neural net** a computer system modelled on the human brain, which 'learns' by trial and error rather than being programmed; **neural plate** the part of the ectoderm of an embryo which develops into the neural tube; **neural tube** the channel formed by the closing of the edges of a fold in the ectoderm of an embryo, later developing into the spinal cord and cerebral hemispheres. [Gr *neuron* nerve]

neuralgia ... to ... **neurite**. See under **neur-**.

neuritis *nū-rī'tis*, *n* inflammation of a nerve or nerves, in some cases with defective functioning of the affected part. — *adj* **neuritic** (*-it'ik*) relating to, of the nature of or having neuritis. — *n* someone suffering from neuritis. [Gr *neuron* nerve, and **-itis**]

neuroanatomist ... to ... **neuromuscular**. See under **neur-**.

neuron *nū'ron* or **neurone** *nū'rōn*, *n* a cell with the specialized function of transmitting nerve impulses, a nerve cell. — *adj* **neurō'nal** or **neu'ronic**. [Gr *neuron* nerve]

neuropath ... to ... **neuropsychology**. See under **neur-**.

Neuroptera *nū-rop'tə-rə*, *n pl* a former order of insects, now placed in a superorder, **Neuropteroidea** (*nū-rop-tə-roi'di-ə*), the insects generally having four net-veined wings, including alder-flies, snake-flies, lacewings, etc. — *n* **neurop'teran** any insect of the order *Neuroptera*: — *pl* **neurop'terans** or **neurop'tera**. — *adj* **neurop'terous**. — *n* **neurop'terist** a student of the *Neuropteroidea*. [Gr *neuron* a nerve, *pteron* a wing, and *eidos* form]

neuroradiology and **neuroscience**, etc. See under **neur-**.

neurosis *nū-rō'sis*, *n orig* nervous activity distinguished from or associated with mental; functional derangement resulting from a disordered nervous system, *esp* without lesion of parts; mental disturbance characterized by a state of unconscious conflict, *usu* accompanied by anxiety and obsessional fears (also called *psychoneurosis*); loosely, obsession: — *pl* **neurōses** (*-sēz*). — *adj* **neurotic** (*-ot'ik*) of the nature of, characterized by or affected by neurosis; loosely, obsessive;

hypersensitive. — *n* a person suffering from neurosis; a drug used for treating nerve diseases (*archaic*). — *adv* **neurot'ically**. — *n* **neurot'icism** (*-i-sizm*). [Gr *neuron* nerve, and **-osis**]

neurosurgeon ... to ... **neurypnology**. See under **neur-**.

neuston *nū'ston*, *n* minute organisms that float or swim on the surface of water. [Gr, neuter of *neustos* swimming]

neut. *abbrev*: neuter; neutral.

neuter *nū'tər*, *adj* neither one thing nor another; neutral; neither masculine nor feminine (*gram*); neither active nor passive (*gram*); intransitive (*gram*); sexless; apparently sexless; sexually undeveloped; castrated; without an androecium or gynaeceum, or without a functional one (*bot*). — *n* a neutral; a neuter word, plant or animal; *esp* a worker bee, ant, etc; a castrated cat. — *vt* to castrate. [L *neuter* neither, from *ne* not, and *uter* either]

neutral *nū'trəl*, *adj* indifferent; taking no part on either side; not siding with either party; relating to neither party; not involved in a war or dispute; belonging to neither, *esp* of two adjoining countries; of no decided character; having no decided colour; indistinct in sound; with no noticeable smell; belonging to neither of two opposites, such as acid and alkaline or electrical positive and negative; not magnetized; (of a vowel) pronounced with the tongue in a relaxed, central position, as the vowel at the beginning of *around* (*phonetics*); neuter; (of eg a force or gear) without transmission of motion. — *n* a person or nation that takes no part in a contest, a war, etc; a citizen or ship belonging to a neutral state; an electric conductor ordinarily at zero potential; a position of gear in which no power is transmitted; a neuter. — *n* **neu'tralism** the policy of not entering into alliance with other nations or taking sides ideologically. — *n* **neu'tralist** someone who takes or favours a neutral position (also *adj*). — *adj* **neutralis'tic**. — *n* **neutrality** (*-tral'i-ti*) the fact or state of being neutral; those who are neutral. — *n* **neutralīzā'tion** or **-s-**. — *vt* **neu'tralize** or **-ise** to declare neutral, to grant neutrality to (eg a State); to make neutral chemically or electrically; to make inert; to make ineffective; to counteract; to nullify. — *vi* to become neutral or neutralized. — *n* **neu'tralizer** or **-s-**. — *adv* **neu'trally**. — **neutral axis** (*eng*) (in a beam subjected to bending) the line of zero stress; **neutral monism** the philosophical theory that mind and matter are made up of the same elements differently arranged, none of which can be classified as mental or physical; **neutral spirits** (*NAm*) non-flavoured alcohol of 190° proof or higher, used for blending with other alcoholic liquors; **neutral zone** the area between the attacking and defending zones in the middle of an ice-hockey rink; the area between the two scrimmage lines (*Am football*). [L *neutrālis*, from *neuter* neither]

neutron *nū'tron*, (*phys*) *n* an uncharged particle of about the same mass as the proton. — *n* **neutrett'o** a name suggested for a neutral meson; a type of neutrino: — *pl* **neutrett'os**. — *n* **neutrino** (*-trē'nō*) an uncharged particle with zero mass when at rest: — *pl* **neutri'nos**. — **neutron bomb** a type of nuclear bomb which destroys life by immediate intense radiation, without blast and heat effects to destroy buildings, etc; **neutron number** the number of neutrons in the nucleus of an atom; **neutron poison** non-fissile material which absorbs neutrons and is used for the control of nuclear reactors; **neutron radiography** radiography using a beam of neutrons; **neutron source** a source of neutrons, eg a nuclear reactor or a chemical or accelerator source; **neutron star** a supposed heavenly body of very small size and very great density, an almost burnt-out and collapsed star, whose existence, however, can only be inferred. [L *neuter* neither]

neutrophil *nū'trō-fil*, *adj* (of a cell, etc) stainable with a neutral dye. — *n* a neutrophil cell, etc; a leucocyte with granular cytoplasm and a lobular nucleus. [Ger, from L *neuter* (see **neuter**) and Gr *philos* (see **phil-** and **-phil**)]

Nev. *abbrev*: Nevada (US state).

névé *nā'vā*, *n* firn, the granular snow, not yet compacted into ice, lying on the surface at the upper end of a glacier; a field of granular snow. [Fr, from L *nix*, *nivis* snow]

nevel *nev'əl*, (*Scot*) *vt* to pound with the nieves or fists. [**nieve**]

never *nev'ər*, *adv* not ever; at no time; in no degree; not. — *interj* (*colloq*) surely not! — *adj* **nev'er-end'ing**. — *adj* **nev'er-fad'ing**. — *adj* **nev'er-fail'ing**. — *adv* **nev'ermore** at no future time. — *n* **nev'er-nev'er** the hire-purchase system (*colloq*); (sometimes with *cap*) a remote, thinly peopled or desolate area (also **never** (or **never-never**) **land** or **country**; sometimes with *caps*). — *n* **never-never land** (also with *caps*) an imaginary place, imaginary conditions, too fortunate ever to exist in reality. — *adv* **nevertheless'** notwithstanding; in spite of that. — *adv* **neverthemore'** (*obs*) none the more. — *n* **nev'er-was'** someone who never was of any account. — **never a** no; **never so** (*archaic*) ever so; **well I never!** or **I never did!** I never heard anything so surprising, shocking, etc. [OE *nǣfre*, from *ne* not, and *ǣfre* ever]

new *nū*, *adj* very recently made or produced; young; fresh; not much used; having lately become, happened or begun to be; recent, modern; (in place names) more recently founded and discovered than and named after, as in *New York* and *New Orleans*; not before seen or known; only lately discovered or experienced; other than the former or preceding, different; additional; strange, unaccustomed; lately begun; beginning afresh; renewed; reformed or regenerated; restored or resumed; (of crops) harvested early; not of an ancient family; fresh from anything; uncultivated or only recently cultivated. — *n* that which is new; newness. — *adv* (often joined by hyphen to an adj) newly; anew. — *vt* (*archaic*) to renew. — *vi* (*archaic*) to be renewed. — *adj* **new'ish** somewhat new; nearly new. — *adv* **new'-ishly**. — *n* **new'ishness**. — *adv* **new'ly** very lately; afresh; in a new or different way. — *n* **new'ness**. — **New Age** or **new age** a cultural trend that emerged in the late 1980s, concerned with the union of mind, body and spirit, expressed through popular interest in a variety of beliefs and disciplines, including mysticism, meditation, astrology and holistic medicine (also as *adj*); (also **New Age music**) a dreamy style of music of the late 1980s, *usu* using synthesizers. — Also *adj* **New-Age** or **new-age**. — **New Ageism** (also without *caps*) the New-Age movement; **New Ager** (also without *caps*) someone involved or interested in the New-Age movement; **new Australian** an immigrant to Australia; **new birth** renewal, *esp* spiritual; **new blood** (a person with) fresh talent; (a person exercising) a revitalizing influence. — *adj* **new'-blown** just come into bloom. — *adj* **new'born** newly born. — **new broom** (*fig*) see **new brooms sweep clean** under **broom**; **new chum** (*colloq*) a newly-arrived and inexperienced immigrant to Australia or New Zealand; a beginner, novice (*Austr slang*); **New Church** or **New Jerusalem Church** the Swedenborgian Church. — *adj* **new'come** recently arrived. — **new'comer** someone who has lately come; a beginner. — *adj* **new'-Commonwealth** of or belonging to members of the Commonwealth who have joined more recently than the *orig* self-governing dominions. — *vt* **new'-create** (*Shakesp*) to create anew. — **new critic** a practitioner of new criticism; **new criticism** literary criticism that concentrates on the text and rejects historical and biographical background information as unnecessary to an understanding of the work; **New Deal** Franklin D Roosevelt's policies for prosperity and social improvement in the United States, 1933–40; (without *caps*) any new arangements or conditions considered better than previous ones; **New Economic Policy** the Soviet economic programme from 1921–28, which allowed some private ownership of business; **New Englander** a native or citizen of any of the New England states (Connecticut, Maine, New Hampshire, Rhode Island, Vermont and Massachusetts); **New English Bible** a translation of the Bible and Apocrypha supervised by a commitee formed of representatives from all the major British Christian demoninations, first published in 1970. — *adj* **new'-fallen** newly fallen. — *adj* **newfangled** see separate entry. — *adj* **new'-fash'ioned** made in a new way or fashion; lately come into fashion. — *adj* **new'-fledged** having just got feathers. — *adj* **new'-found** newly discovered or devised. — **New Jersey tea** redroot; **New Jerusalem** the heavenly city; heaven; **New Jerusalem Church** see **New Church** above. — *adj* **new'-laid** newly laid. — **New Latin** the form of Latin in *esp* legal use since the Renaissance; **New Learning** the new studies of the Renaissance; **New Left** an extreme left-wing movement among students, etc, in the 1960s; **New Light** a member of a relatively more advanced or liberal religious school, applied *esp* to the party within the 18c Scottish Secession Church which adopted voluntaryist views of the relations of Church and State, also sometimes to the Socinianizing party in the Church of Scotland in the 18c, etc; **new look** a change in women's fashions (1947), notably to longer and fuller skirts; a radical modification in the appearance of something; **New Model Army** the Parliamentary army as remodelled by Cromwell in 1645; **New Red Sandstone** (*geol*) an old name for the Permian and Trias. — *n* and *adj* **new'ly-wed** (a person who is) recently married. — *adj* **new'-made** recently made. — **new man** a reformed character; a fitter, healthier man; (sometimes with *caps*) a man who is prepared to show his feelings and who has adopted modern ideas *esp* with regard to health, the environment and sharing family responsibilities. — *adj* **new'-marr'ied** newly married. — **new maths** a method of teaching mathematics which is more concerned with basic structures and concepts than numerical drills. — *vt* **new'-mod'el** to model or form anew. — **new moon** the moment when the moon is directly in line between the earth and sun, and therefore invisible; the time when the waxing moon becomes visible; the narrow waxing crescent itself. — *adj* **new'-mown** newly mown. — *adj* **new'-old'** old but renewed; having both new and old qualities at the same time. — **new penny** see under **penny**; **new poor** those who have come to think themselves poor by loss of advantages; **new rich** the recently enriched; parvenus; **New Right** a conservative movement which differs from the traditional Right in holding more staunchly right-wing or moralistic views, eg favouring the diminution or abolition of the welfare state and the restitution of capital punishment, and opposing abortion. — *adj* **new'-risen** having newly risen. — *adj* **new'-sad** (*Shakesp*) recently made sad. — **New'speak** a type of English described by George Orwell in his book *Nineteen Eighty-four* (1949), developed by reducing vocabulary to such a point, and forming new words of such ugliness and so little emotive value, that literature and even thought will be impossible; (also without *cap*) any type of language considered similar in style, etc (*esp derog*); **new star** a nova; **New Style** see **style**; **New Testament** the second part of the Christian Bible, consisting of writings about Christ and the Apostles after his death, and documents from the very first years of the Christian Church; **new town** a town planned and built by the government to aid housing conditions in nearby large cities, stimulate development, etc; **New Wave** a movement in French cinema in the late 1950s and 1960s which abandoned the linear narrative and experimented with untypical framing and fluid camera movements (also called **Nouvelle Vague**); a slightly later movement in jazz aiming at freedom from set patterns and styles; (also without *caps*) any similar new movement or grouping in the arts, media, music, etc. — Also *adj* **New-Wave** or **new-wave**. — **new woman** a name applied, *esp* by scoffers, in the late 19c to such women as actively sought freedom and equality with men; **New World** North, Central and South America; **New Year** the first few days of the year; **New Year's Day** the first day of the year; **New Year's Eve** the last day of the year, 31 December. — **of new** (*archaic*) anew; of late; **what's new?** (*colloq*) tell me your news; there's nothing new about that! [OE *nīwe*, *nēowe*; Ger *neu*, Ir *nuadh*, L *novus*, Gr *neos*]

Newcastle disease *nū'kä-səl diz-ēz'*, *n* an acute, highly contagious viral disease of chickens and other domestic and wild birds, first recorded at *Newcastle*-upon-Tyne in 1926 (also called **fowl-pest**).

newel *nū'əl*, *n* the upright column around which the steps of a circular staircase wind; an upright post at the end or corner of a stair handrail (also **newel post**). — *adj* **new'elled**. [OFr *noual* (Fr *noyau*) fruitstone, from LL *nucālis* nutlike, from L *nux*, *nucis* a nut]

newell *nū'əl*, (*Spenser*) *n* a new thing. [A combination of **novel** and **new**]

newfangled *nū-fang'gld*, earlier **newfangle** *-gl*, *adj* newly but superfluously devised; excessively or ostentatiously modern; unduly fond of new things. — *adv* **newfang'ledly**. — *n* **newfang'ledness** or **newfang'leness**. [ME *newefangel*, from *newe* (OE *nīwe*) new, and *fangel* ready to catch, from *fang-*, the stem of OE *fōn* to take]

Newfie *nū'fi*, (*colloq*, *esp Can*) a person born or living in Newfoundland (*nū'fənd-land*), in Canada.

Newfoundland *nū-fownd'lənd*, *adj* of *Newfoundland* (*nū'-fənd-land*). — *n* a very large, intelligent breed of dog from Newfoundland in Canada, *orig* and *esp* black, a strong swimmer.

Newgate *nū'gāt*, *n* a famous prison in London, *orig* housed in the *new gate* of the city, the latest building demolished in 1902–3. — **Newgate Calendar** a record of Newgate prisoners, with their crimes; **Newgate frill** or **Newgate fringe** a beard under the chin and jaw.

newmarket *nū-mär'kit* or *nū'*, *n* a card game in which the stakes go to those who succeed in playing out cards whose duplicates lie on the table; a close-fitting coat, *orig* a riding-coat, for men or women. [*Newmarket*, the racing town]

news *nūz*, *n* (*orig pl*) information on recent events and current affairs; a report of a recent event; (preceded by **the**) a presentation of news on the television or radio; tidings; newly received information; something one had not heard before; a subject, person, place, etc considered suitable material for newspaper readers or for radio and television bulletins; newspaper; newsprint. — *vt* to report. — *n* **news'iness**. — *adj* **news'less**. — *adj* **news'y** full of news or gossip. — *n* (*US*) a newsagent; a newsboy or newsgirl. — **news agency** an organization which collects material for newspapers, magazines, etc; **news'agent** a shop or show owner that sells newspapers; **news'boy** or **news'girl** a boy or girl who delivers or sells newspapers; **news'cast** a news broadcast or telecast; **news'caster** a person who presents newscasts or telecasts; a machine which gives a changing display of news headlines, etc; **news'casting**; **news conference** a press conference; **news'dealer** (*US*) a newsagent; **news fiction** see **faction**[2]; **newsflash** see under **flash**; **news'girl** see **newsboy** above; **news'hawk** or **news'hound** (*joc*) a reporter in search of news for eg a newspaper; **news'letter** a sheet of news supplied to members of a particular group or locality; *orig* a written or printed letter containing news sent by an agent to subscribers, the predecessor of the newspaper; **news magazine** or **news'magazine** a magazine, or radio or television broadcast, which discusses and comments on as well as reporting the news; **news'man** or **news'woman** a bringer, collector or writer of news; a seller of newspapers; **news'monger** a person who deals in news; a person who spends much time in hearing and telling news, a gossip; **news'paper** a collection of folded printed sheets of paper published periodically (*usu* daily or weekly) for circulating news, etc; the paper on which such a publication is printed; **news'-paperdom**; **news'paperism**; **news'paperman** or **news'-paper-woman** a journalist; **news'print** inexpensive paper for printing newspapers on; loosely, ink used for printing newspapers; **news'reader** a person who reads news on radio or television; **news'reel** a film showing, or a programme commenting on, news items; **news'**-

room a reading-room with newspapers, eg in a library; a room, etc, where news is made ready for a newspaper, newscast, etc; **news'-sheet** a printed sheet of news, *esp* an early form of newspaper; **news'-stand** a street stall for the sale of newspapers; **news'-theatre** a cinema showing chiefly newsreels; **news'trade** the business of newsagents; **news'-value** interest to the general public as news; **news'-vendor** a street seller of newspapers; **newswire** a teleprinter which transmits news stories as they occur and up-to-the minute stock market results, etc; **newswoman** see **newsman** above. — *adj* **news'worthy** sufficiently interesting to be told as news. — **news'worthiness**; **news'-writer** a reporter or writer of news. [Late ME *newes*; Fr *nouvelles*]

newt *nūt*, *n* a tailed amphibian (genus *Triturus*, *Molge* or *Triton*) of the salamander family, the word being formed with initial *n*, borrowed from the article **an**, and *ewt*, a form of archaic or dialect **evet** or **eft**[1]. [OE *efeta*, *efete*]

newton *nū'tən*, *n* the SI unit of force, equal to the force which, acting on a mass of one kilogramme, produces an acceleration of one metre per second per second. — *adj* **Newtonian** (*nū-tō'ni-ən*) relating to, according to, formed or discovered by, Sir Isaac *Newton* (1642–1727). — Also **Newtonic** (*-ton'ik*). — **Newtonian mechanics** the theory of mechanics dealing with the relationships between force and motion for large objects, based on Newton's laws of motion. — Also called **classical mechanics**; **Newtonian telescope** a form of reflecting telescope; **Newton's cradle** a sophisticated toy consisting of five metal balls hanging in a frame, caused to hit against one another at speeds which vary; **Newton's gravitational constant** see **gravitation** under **gravity**; **Newton's laws of motion** the three laws first stated by Newton (1687) describing the effect of force on the movement of a body; **Newton's rings** circular concentric interference fringes seen surrounding the point of contact of a convex lens and a plane surface.

next *nekst*, *adj* (*orig superl* of **nigh**) nearest in place, in kinship or other relation; nearest following (or preceding if explicitly stated) in time or order. — *adv* nearest; immediately after; on the first occasion that follows; in the following place. — *n* the next thing or person. — *prep* (*archaic* or *dialect*) nearest to. — *adv* **next'ly**. — *n* **next'ness** (*rare*). — **next best** next lowest in degree after the best; **next biggest**, **next dearest**, etc, next lowest (or highest, depending on context) in degree after the previous one mentioned. — *adj* **next'-door** dwelling in, occupying or belonging to the next house, shop, etc; at or in the next house; neighbouring. — *n* the people or household living next door. — *adv* **next-door'**. — **next friend** a person appointed or permitted by a court of law to act on behalf of a minor or other person under legal disability; **next Saturday**, etc, (on) the first Saturday, etc after the present day; (in Scotland often) (on) the Saturday, etc of next week. — **next door** at or in the next house (often with *to*); near, bordering on, very nearly (with *to*); **next of kin** see under **kin**[1]; **next to** adjacent to; almost; thoroughly acquainted with (*old US slang*); **next to nothing** almost nothing at all. [OE *nēhst* (*nīehst*), superlative of *nēh* (*nēah*) near; Ger *nächst*]

nexus *nek'səs*, *n* a bond; a linked group: — *pl* **nex'us**. [L *nexus*, pl *-ūs*, from *nectere* to bind]

NF *abbrev*: National Front; Norman French; Northern French.

NF or **Nfld.** *abbrev*: Newfoundland (Can province).

NF or **N/F** *abbrev*: no funds.

NFER *abbrev*: National Foundation for Educational Research.

NFS *abbrev*: National Fire Service; not for sale.

NFSC *abbrev*: National Federation of (Football) Supporters' Clubs.

NFSE *abbrev*: National Federation of Self-Employed.

NFT *abbrev*: National Film Theatre.

NFTS *abbrev*: National Film and Television School.

NFU *abbrev*: National Farmers' Union.

NFWI *abbrev*: National Federation of Women's Institutes.

NG *abbrev*: (in the US) National Guard.

ng *abbrev*: no good.

NGA *abbrev*: National Graphical Association.

ngaio *nī'ō*, *n* a New Zealand tree with white wood: — *pl* **ngai'os**. [Maori]

ngana. See under **nagana**.

NGC *abbrev*: New General Catalogue, a catalogue listing all the galaxies, clusters and nebulae known in 1888.

Ngoni. See under **Nguni**.

ngultrum *əng-gul'trəm*, *n* the standard monetary unit of Bhutan (100 *chetrun*).

Nguni *əng-gōō'ni*, *n* a group of Bantu-speaking peoples living in southern and eastern Africa, including the Zulu, Xhosa, Ndebele and Swazi; the languages spoken by these people: — *pl* **Nguni** or **Ngunis**. — Also **Ngoni** (*əng-gō'ni*).

ngwee *ng-gwē'*, *n* the hundredth part of a Zambian kwacha (qv), or a coin of this value: — *pl* **ngwee**. [Native word, bright]

NH *abbrev*: New Hampshire (US state).

NHBRC *abbrev*: National House-Builders' Registration Council (or Certificate).

NHI *abbrev*: National Health Insurance.

NHS *abbrev*: National Health Service.

NI *abbrev*: National Insurance; Northern Ireland.

Ni (*chem*) *symbol*: nickel.

niacin *nī'ə-sin*, *n* nicotinic acid.

niaiserie *nyez-ə-rē* or *nyez-rē*, (*Fr*) *n* simplicity, foolishness.

nib[1] *nib*, *n* something small and pointed; the writing point of a pen, *esp* a fountain pen; a bird's bill; a peak; a projecting point or spike; a timber carriage pole; a handle on a scythe's shaft (*dialect*); (in *pl*) crushed cocoa-beans; (in *pl*) included particles in varnish, wool, etc. — *vt* to provide with a nib; to point; to mend the nib of; to reduce to nibs: — *pa t* and *pa p* **nibbed**; *pr p* **nibb'ing** — *adj* **nibbed** having a nib; (eg of nuts) roughly crushed. [Ety as for **neb**]

nib[2] *nib*, (*slang*) *n* a person of the upper classes; a person of importance or appearance of importance. — **his nibs** or **her nibs** a mock title used for an important or self-important person, himself or herself; his or her mightiness. [Cf **nabs** and **nob**[2]]

nibble *nib'l*, *vt* to bite gently or by small bites; to eat a little at a time. — *vi* to bite gently; to show signs of cautious acceptance of or interest in eg an offer, or of gradual yielding, eg to temptation (with *at*); to find fault. — *n* the act of nibbling; a little bit; half a byte (also **nybble**; *comput*). — *n* **nibb'ler**. — *n* **nibb'ling**. — *adv* **nibb'lingly**. [Origin obscure; cf LGer *nibbelen*, Du *knibbelen*]

Nibelung *nē'bəl-ōōng*, *n* one of a supernatural race of dwarfs in Germanic mythology, guardians of a treasure wrested from them by Siegfried, the hero of the *Nibelungenlied*, an epic of c.1190–1210 (in the *Nibelungenlied*, the name *Nibelungen* is applied first to Siegfried's followers and subjects, and then to the Burgundians): — *pl* **Ni'belungen**. [Ger]

niblick *nib'lik*, *n* an old-fashioned golf club with a heavy head with wide face, used for lofting; now, a number eight or nine iron. [Origin uncertain]

NIC *abbrev*: Newly Industrialized Country; Nicaragua (IVR).

nicad *nī'kad*. Short form of *ni*ckel-*cad*mium, as applied to rechargeable batteries.

NICAM or **Nicam** *nī'kam*, *n* near-instantaneous companded audio multiplexing, a system by which digital stereo sound signals are transmitted along with the standard TV signal, to allow the viewer to receive sound of CD quality.

niccolite *nik'əl-īt*, *n* a hexagonal mineral, nickel arsenide, also called *kupfernickel*, copper-nickel. [See **nickel**]

nice *nīs*, *adj* agreeable, delightful, respectable, good in any way, satisfactory (often used as a vague commendation); (of a person) good-natured, friendly, kind;

bad, badly done, careless (*ironic*); forming or observing very small differences; calling for very fine discrimination; done with great care and exactness, accurate; delicate; dainty; fastidious; hard to please; over-particular; foolishly simple (*obs*); wanton (*Shakesp*); coy (*Milton*); critical, hazardous (*archaic*); easily injured (*obs*). — *adj* **nice'ish** or **nic'ish** somewhat nice. — *adv* **nice'ly**. — *n* **nice'ness** the quality of being nice. — *n* **nicety** (*nīs'i-ti*) critical subtlety; a matter of delicate discrimination or adjustment; the quality of being nice; degree of precision; fineness of perception or feeling; exactness of treatment; delicate management; a refinement (often in *pl*); fastidiousness; a delicacy; coyness (*Spenser* and *Shakesp*). — **nice and** (used almost adverbially) commendably, pleasantly; **to a nicety** with great exactness. [OFr *nice* foolish, simple, from L *nescius* ignorant, from *ne* not, and *scīre* to know]

Nicene *nī'sēn*, *adj* relating to the town of *Nicaea*, in Bithynia, Asia Minor, where an ecumenical council in AD 325 dealt with the theological controversy surrounding Arius of Alexandria, and where another in AD 787 condemned the Iconoclasts. — *n* and *adj* **Nicaean** (*nī-sē'ən*). — **Nicene Creed** the Christian creed based on the results of the first Nicene Council.

niche *nēsh* or *nich*, *n* a recess in a wall; a situation, place or condition appropriate for a person or thing; an area of habitat providing the conditions necessary for an organism or species to survive (*ecol*); the position or status of an organism or species within its community or ecosystem, dependent upon its behaviour and relationship with other organisms or species in that community (*ecol*); a small, specialized group identified as a market for a particular range of products or services (also as *adj*); a place in the market not subject to the normal pressures of competition (*commerce*). — *vt* to place in a niche; to ensconce (oneself). — *adj* **niched** placed in a niche. — **niche advertising** advertising aimed at a small, specialized group or market; niche marketing the marketing of a product aimed at a relatively small, specialized sector, or niche, of consumer society; [Fr, from Ital *nicchia* niche, of doubtful origin]

niche. See **nicker**[1].

Nichrome® *nī'krōm*, *n* trademark for a nickel-chromium alloy with high electrical resistance and ability to withstand high temperatures.

Nick *nik*, *n* the devil, *esp* **Old Nick**. — Also (*Scot*) **Nickie-ben'**. [Appar for *Nicholas*]

nick[1] *nik*, *n* a notch; a small cut; (*usu* preceded by **the**) a prison (*slang*); the line formed where floor and wall meet in a squash, etc court; a score for keeping an account (*archaic*); the precise moment of time; the precise point aimed at; (at the old dice game of hazard) a throw answering to a main; a hidden bottom in a beer tankard, the outer base being hollow (*obs*). — *vt* to notch; to cut (*usu* slightly); to snip; to cut off; to cut in notches (eg the hair of a fool; *Shakesp*); to catch (*slang*); to arrest (*slang*); to steal (*slang*); to rob; to make a cut in (a horse's tail muscle), so that the tail is carried higher; to defraud; to mark by cutting, carve out; to score, eg on a tally; to tally with (*obs*); to hit with precision; to hit off (*obs*); to catch in the nick of time; to cheat at hazard, to defeat by throwing a nick; at hazard, to throw the nick of. — *adj* (*colloq*) able to be stolen. — *vi* (of breeding animals) to mate well. — *n* **nick'er** someone who or something which nicks; any of a band of early 18c London rioters who made a practice of smashing windows by throwing copper coins at them. — **nick'stick** (*archaic*) a tally; **nick translation** a method of radioactively labelling a DNA molecule. — **in good nick** (*colloq*) in good health or condition; **in the nick of time** just in time; at the critical moment; **out of all nick** (*Shakesp*) out of all reckoning, exceedingly. [Poss connected with **nock** or **notch**]

nick[2] *nik*, (*archaic*) *vt* to deny (in the phrase *to nick with nay*). [Origin unknown; poss OE *ne ic* not I]

nickar. See **nicker**[3].

nickel *nik'l*, *n* an element (symbol **Ni**; atomic no 28), a white, magnetic, very malleable and ductile metal largely used in alloys; a five-cent piece (of copper and nickel; *NAm*). — *adj* of nickel. — *vt* to plate with nickel: — *pr p* **nick'elling** or *NAm* **nick'eling**; *pa t* and *pa p* **nick'elled** or *NAm* **nick'eled**. — *adj* **nick'elic** of trivalent nickel. — *adj* **nickelif'erous** containing nickel. — *n* **nick'eline** (*obs*) niccolite. — *vt* **nick'elize** or **-ise** to plate with nickel. — *adj* **nick'elous** of bivalent nickel. — *adj* **nickel-and-dime'** involving only a small amount of money; worth only a small amount of effort, concern, etc. — **nick'el-bloom** earthy annabergite; **nick'el-ochre** earthy annabergite; **nick'el-plat'ing** the plating of metals with nickel; **nick'el-sil'ver** an alloy of nickel, copper and zinc, German silver; **nickel-steel'** a steel containing some nickel. [Ger *Kupfer-nickel* niccolite, from *Kupfer* copper, and *Nickel* a mischievous sprite, goblin, because the ore looked like copper-ore but yielded no copper]

nickelodeon *nik-ə-lō'di-ən*, (*US*; *old*) *n* formerly, a cinema to which admission cost five cents; an old form of jukebox; a Pianola operated by inserting a five-cent coin. [**nickel** and **odeon**]

nicker[1] *nik'ər*, (chiefly *Scot* and *NEng*) *vi* to neigh; to snigger. — *n* a neigh; a snigger; a loud laugh. — Also **nicher** (*nihh'ər*).

nicker[2] *nik'ər*, (*archaic*) *n* a water-monster or water-demon. [OE *nicor*]

nicker[3] *nik'ər*, *n* a clay marble (also **knicker**); the round seed of a Caesalpinia (or Guilandina if this is considered a separate genus), used for playing marbles (also **nick'ar**). [Cf Du *knikker*, North Ger *Knicker*]

nicker[4] *nik'ər*, (*slang*) *n* a pound sterling.

nick-nack, etc. Same as **knick-knack**, etc.

nickname *nik'nām*, *n* a name given in contempt, or in jocular or fond familiarity. — *vt* to give a nickname to. [ME *neke-name*, for *eke-name*, an additional (descriptive) name, with *n* from the indefinite article; see **eke**[1] and **name**]

nickum *nik'əm*, (*Scot*) *n* a mischievous boy.

nickumpoop. See **nincompoop**.

nicky-tam *nik'i-tam'*, (*Scot*) *n* a piece of string, etc worn below the knee to keep the bottom of the trouser-leg lifted clear in dirty work or to exclude dust, etc.

nicol *nik'l*, *n* a crystal of calcium carbonate cut and cemented in such a way as to transmit only the extraordinary ray, used for polarizing light. — Also **Nicol** or **Nicol's prism**. [From William *Nicol* (c.1768–1851) of Edinburgh, its inventor]

nicompoop. See **nincompoop**.

nicotian *ni-kō'shyən* or *ni-kō'shən*, *adj* of tobacco. — *n* a tobacco smoker. — *n* **nicotiana** (*-shi-ä'nə* or *-ā'nə*) any plant of the tobacco genus *Nicotiana*, of the family *Solanaceae*. — *n pl* the literature of tobacco. — *n* **nicotinamide** (*-tin'*) a member of the vitamin B complex, deficiency of which can lead to the development of the disease pellagra. — *n* **nicotine** (*nik'ə-tēn*) a poisonous alkaloid ($C_{10}H_{14}N_2$) obtained from tobacco leaves. — *adj* **nic'otined**. — *adj* **nicotinic** (*-tin'ik*). — *n* **nic'otinism** a morbid state induced by excessive use of tobacco. — **nicotinic acid** a white crystalline substance, a member of the vitamin B complex, deficiency of which is connected with the development of the disease pellagra. [Jean *Nicot*, who sent tobacco to Catherine de Medici]

nicotine, etc. See under **nicotian**.

nicrosilal *nik-rō'sil-əl*, *n* a cast-iron alloy containing *ni*ckel, *chr*omium, and *sil*icon, used in high-temperature work.

nictate *nik'tāt*, *vi* to wink or blink. — Also **nic'titate**. — *n* **nictā'tion** or **nictitā'tion**. — **nictitating membrane** the third eyelid, developed in birds, reptiles and some mammals, a thin movable membrane that passes over the eye. [L *nictāre*, *-ātum* and its LL frequentative *nictitāre*, *-ātum* to wink]

nid *nid* or **nide** *nīd*, *n* a pheasant's nest or brood. [L *nīdus* nest]

nidal, **nidation**, etc. See under **nidus**.

niddering, **nidderling**, **nidering**, **niderling** and **niding**. See **nithing**.

niddle-noddle *nid'l-nod'l*, *adj* and *adv* with nodding head. — *vi* to noddle the head; to waggle. — *vt* and *vi* **nid'-nod'** to keep nodding. [**nod**]

nide. See **nid**.

nidget *nij'it*, (*archaic* or *illiterate*) *n* an idiot. [**idiot**, with *n* from the indefinite article]

nidicolous *nid-ik'ə-ləs*, *adj* (of young birds) staying for longer than average in the nest. [L *nīdus* a nest, and *colere* to inhabit]

nidificate. See **nidify**.

nidifugous *nid-if'ū-gəs*, *adj* (of young birds) leaving the nest soon after hatching. [L *nīdus* nest, and *fugere* to flee]

nidify *nid'i-fī*, *vi* to build a nest. — Also **nidificate** (*nid'i-fi-kāt*). — *n* **nidificā'tion**. [L *nīdus* nest, and *facere* to make]

nidor *nī'dör*, *n* a strong smell or fume, *esp* of animal substances cooking or burning. — *adv* **nī'dorous**. [L *nīdor*, *-ōris*]

nidus *nī'dəs*, *n* a nest or breeding-place; a place where anything is originated, harboured, developed or fostered; a place of lodgement or deposit; a point of infection; a nerve-centre: — *pl* **nī'dī**. — *adj* **nī'dal** relating to a nest or nidus. — *adj* **nīdament'al** nest-forming; (of glands) secreting material for the formation of a nest or of an egg-covering. — *n* **nīdament'um** an egg-capsule. — *n* **nīdā'tion** renewal of the lining of the uterus (*obs*); the process by which the blastocyst becomes attached to the wall of the uterus, implantation. — *n* **nidūlā'tion** (*nid-*) nest-building. [L *nīdus* a nest]

nie. An obsolete spelling of **nigh**.

niece *nēs*, *n* a brother's or sister's daughter; extended to a similar relation by marriage; *orig* a granddaughter, or any female descendant; euphemistically, a pope's or priest's daughter: — *masc* **nephew**. [OFr, from LL *neptia*, from L *neptis*]

nief. See **nieve**.

niello *ni-el'ō*, *n* a method of ornamenting metal by engraving, and filling up the lines with a black compound; a piece of work so produced; an impression taken from the engraved surface before filling up; the compound used in niello-work, sulphur with silver, lead or copper: — *pl* **niell'i** (*-ē*) or **niell'os**. — *vt* to decorate with niello: — *pr p* **niell'oing**; *pa t* and *pa p* **niell'oed**. — *adj* **niellāted** (*nē'*). — *n* **niell'ist**. [Ital *niello*, from LL *nigellum* a black enamel, from L *nigellus*, dimin of *niger* black]

Niersteiner *nēr'shtīn-ər* or *nēr'stīn-ər*, *n* a Rhine wine, named after *Nierstein*, near Mainz.

NIESR *abbrev*: National Institute of Economic and Social Research.

Nietzschean *nēch'i-ən*, *adj* of or relating to Friedrich *Nietzsche* (1844–1900) or his philosophy. — *n* a follower of Nietzsche. — *n* **Nietzsch'eanism**.

nieve, **neive** *nēv*, **neif** or **nief** (*Shakesp* **neafe** or **neaffe**) *nēf*, (*archaic* and *dialect*) *n* the fist. — *n* **nieve'ful** a closed handful. — **nie'vie-nick'-nack** or **nie'vie-nie'vie-nick'-nack** a Scottish children's pastime, a way of assigning by lot, by guessing which hand contains something, the holder repeating a rhyme. [ME *nefe*, from ON *hnefi*, *nefi*; cf Swed *näfve* fist]

nife *nī'fi*, *n* the earth's hypothetical core of nickel and iron. [Chemical symbols *Ni* (nickel) and *Fe* iron]

niff *nif*, (*slang*) *n* a stink. — *vi* to smell bad. — *adj* **niff'y**.

niffer *nif'ər*, (*Scot*) *vt* to barter. — *vi* to haggle. — *n* an exchange; the dice game hazard. [Poss **nieve**]

niffnaff *nif-naf'*, (*dialect*) *n* a trifle; a diminutive person. — *vi* to trifle. — *adj* **niff-naff'y** or **niff'y-naff'y** fastidious.

Niflheim *niv'l-hām*, (*Scand mythol*) *n* a region of mist, ruled over by Hel. [ON *Niflheimr*, from *nifl* mist, and *heimr* home]

nifty *nif'ti*, (*slang*) *adj* fine; spruce; sharp, neat; smart; quick; agile. — *adv* **nift'ily**. — *n* **nift'iness**.

NIG *abbrev*: Niger (IVR).

nigella *nī-jel'ə*, *n* any plant of the genus of ranunculaceous plants *Nigella*, with finely dissected leaves, and whitish, blue or yellow flowers, often almost concealed by their leafy involucres, one variety, *Nigella damascena*, being otherwise known as love-in-a-mist, devil-in-a-bush, and ragged lady. [Fem of L *nigellus* blackish, from *niger* black, from the plant's black seeds]

niger *nī'jər*, (*obs*) *n* a Negro. — **niger oil** an oil obtained from the black seeds (**ni'ger seeds**) of an E African composite plant, *Guizotia abyssinica*, also cultivated in India. [L *niger* black]

niggard *nig'ərd*, *n* a person who begrudges spending or giving away; a false bottom or side in a fire-grate. — *adj* mean, stingy. — *vt* and *vi* (*Shakesp*) to treat or behave as a niggard. — *n* **nigg'ardise** or **nigg'ardize** (*-īz*; *archaic*) niggardliness, meanness. — *n* **nigg'ardliness** meanness, stinginess. — *adj* **nigg'ardly** stingy. — *adv* stingily; grudgingly. [Origin obscure]

nigger *nig'ər*, *n* a Black person, or a member of any very dark-skinned race (*derog*, now *esp offensive*); a black insect larva of various kinds. — *adj* Black (*derog*, now *esp offensive*); blackish brown. — *vt* to exhaust by overcropping; to char; to blacken. — *n* (*derog*, now *esp offensive*) **nigg'erdom** Black people collectively. — *adj* (*derog*, now *esp offensive*) **nigg'erish**. — *n* (*derog*, now *esp offensive*) **nigg'erism** an idiom or expression (regarded as) characteristic of Black people; African blood. — *n* (*derog*, now *esp offensive*) **nigg'erling** a little Black person. — *adj* (*derog*, now *esp offensive*) **nigg'ery**. — **nigg'erhead** a nodule, boulder or boss of dark-coloured rock; an American river-mussel (genus *Quadrula*), a source of mother-of-pearl; negrohead tobacco; a tussock in a swamp (*US*). — **nigger in the woodpile** a hidden evil influence; **work like a nigger** to work extremely hard. [Fr *nègre*, from Sp *negro*; see **Negro**]

niggle *nig'l*, *vi* to trifle, potter; to busy oneself with petty criticism of detail; to move in a fidgety or ineffective way; to gnaw; to criticize in a petty way. — *vt* to worry, irritate or nag; to work, make or perform with excessive detail; to make a fool of. — *n* a minor criticism; small cramped handwriting. — *n* **nigg'ler**. — *n* **nigg'ling** fussiness, *esp* over minor detail; petty criticism. — *adj* over-elaborate; petty; fussy; cramped; (faintly but) persistently annoying. — *adv* **nigg'lingly**. — *adj* **nigg'ly**. [Cf Norw *nigle*]

nigh *nī*, *adj* (*obs*) near. — *adv* (*poetic*, *dialect* or *archaic*) nearly; near. — *prep* (*poetic*, *dialect* or *archaic*) near to. — *vt* and *vi* (*obs*) to approach, draw near; to touch. — *adv* and *prep* (*obs*) **nigh'-hand** near hand; almost, nearly. — *adv* **nigh'ly** (*obs*) almost; closely; sparingly (*Spenser*). — *n* (*obs*) **nigh'ness**. — **nigh on** almost, nearly. — Also **nigh-on** (as *adj*). [OE *nēah*, *nēh*; Du *na*, Ger *nahe*]

night *nīt*, *n* the end of the day, evening; (the period of) time from sunset to sunrise; the dark part of the 24-hour day; darkness; obscurity, ignorance, evil, affliction or sorrow (*fig*); death (*euphem*); the activity or experience of a night; a night set apart for some purpose, eg receiving visitors. — *adj* belonging to night; occurring or done in the night; working or on duty at night. — *adj* **night'ed** benighted; darkened, clouded (*Shakesp*). — **nightie** see **nighty** below. — *adj* **night'less** having no night. — *adj* and *adv* **night'long** lasting all night. — *adj* **night'ly** done or happening by night or every night; dark as night (*Shakesp*). — *adv* by night; every night. — *adv* **nights** (*orig genitive* of *n*; *colloq*) at or by night. — *adj* **night'ward** occurring towards night. — *n* (*colloq*) **night'y** or **night'ie** a nightgown. — **night air** the air at night; a peculiarly unwholesome gas, formerly imagined by some to circulate at night; **night'-ape** a bush-baby; **night'-attire** garments worn in bed; **night'-bell** a doorbell for use at night, *esp* at a hotel; **night'bird** a bird that flies or sings at night; a person who is active or about at night. — *adj* **night'-blind**. — *n* **night'-blindness** inability to see in a dim light, nyctalopia; **night'-brawler** a person who causes disturbances in the night; **night'cap** a cap worn at night in bed; a drink, *esp* an alcoholic or hot one, taken before going to bed; the last event of the day, *esp* the second of a pair of consecutive baseball games or the last horse race of the day (*esp NAm colloq*); **night'=cart** (*hist*) a cart used to remove the contents of outside lavatories before daylight; **night'-cellar** (*archaic*) a disreputable resort or tavern, open at night; **night'=chair** a night-stool; **night'-churr** the nightjar, so called from its cry; **night'class** a class at night school. — *n pl* **night'clothes** garments worn in bed. — **night'-cloud** stratus; **night'club** a club for drinking and entertainment, etc open between evening and morning; **night'-clubber**; **night'clubbing** dining, dancing, etc at a nightclub; **night'-crawl'er** a large earthworm which comes to the surface at night, used as bait for fishing; **night'-crow** (*Shakesp*) an undefined bird of ill omen that cries in the night; **night'-dog** (*Shakesp*) a dog that hunts in the night; **night'dress** clothes, *esp* a woman's or child's loose dresslike garment, for sleeping in; a nightgown; **night duty** work or duty done at night; **night'fall** the onset or beginning of the night; the close of the day; evening. — *adj* **night'faring** travelling by night. — **night fighter** a fighter plane equipped for interception at night; **night'fire** a fire burning in the night; a will-o'-the-wisp; **night'-fish'ery** a mode or place of fishing by night; **night'-flower** a flower that opens by night. — *adj* **night'-flow'ering**. — **night'-fly** a moth or fly that is active at night. — *adj* **night'-fly'ing** flying by night (also *n*). — **night'-foe** someone who attacks by night; **night'-foss'icker** (*Austr*) someone who rummages around at night for gold, etc in a mine or other working. — *adj* **night'-foun'dered** (*Milton*) lost in the night. — **night'-fowl** a night-bird; **night'gear** nightclothes; **night'-glass** a small hand-held telescope with concentrating lenses for use at night; **night'gown** a loose robe for sleeping in, for men or women; a dressing-gown (*obs*); **night'-hag** a witch supposed to be about at night; **night'hawk** an American nightjar, genus *Chordeiles*; a European nightjar; a nocturnal prowler; **night'-her'on** a heron of nocturnal habit, of various kinds; **night'-house** (*obs*) a tavern open during the night; **night'-hunter** someone who hunts, poaches or prowls about the streets for prey by night; **night'jar** any European nocturnal bird of the family *Caprimulgidae*, related to the swift family; **night'-latch** a door-lock worked by a key from outside and a knob from inside; **night letter** (*NAm*) a telegram sent overnight, and so at a cheaper rate; **night'life** activity in the form of entertainments at night; **night'-light** a lamp or candle that gives a subdued light all night; the faint light of the night; the light of phosphorescent sea-animals; **night'=line** a fishing-line set overnight; **night'-man** a night-watchman, night-worker or scavenger by night; **night'-mare** (OE *mære*, ME *mare* the nightmare incubus; cf OHGer *mara* incubus, ON *mara* nightmare) an unpleasant dream; a horrifying experience; a dream accompanied by pressure on the breast and a feeling of powerlessness to move or speak, personified as an incubus or evil spirit. — *adj* **night'marish** or (*rare*) **night'mary**. — *adv* **night'marishly**. — *n* **night'-marishness**; **night nurse** a nurse on duty during the night; **night out** a festive night away from home, work and responsibilities; a domestic, or other, servant's night off work; **night'-owl** an exclusively nocturnal owl; a person who sits up very late, or one who is habitually more active, alert, etc at night than during the day; **night'-pal'sy** (*archaic*) a numbness of the legs occurring on waking in the morning and passing off quickly; **night'piece** a picture or literary or musical description of a night-scene; a painting to be seen by artificial light; **night-por'ter** a porter in attendance during the night; **night'-rail** (*hist*) a loose wrap or dressing-jacket; **night'-rav'en** (*Shakesp*) a bird that cries at night, supposed to be of ill-omen; **night'-rest** the repose of the night; **night'rider** (*US*) a member of a secret band of *usu* White men who carried out lynchings, etc of Blacks and Black sympathizers, *esp* in the southern US after the Civil War; a member of the Ku-Klux Klan; **night'-robe** a nightgown; a dressing-gown; **night'-rule** (*Shakesp*) a revel at night; **night safe** a safe in the outside wall of a bank, in which customers can deposit money when the bank is closed; **night school** classes held at night for people who have left school, *esp* for those at work during the day; **night=sea'son** the night-time; **night shift** a gang or group of workers that takes its turn at night; the period for which it is on duty; a nightdress (*archaic*); **night'shirt** a shirt for sleeping in; **night'-shriek** a cry in the night; **night'-side** the dark, mysterious or gloomy side of anything; **night'-sight** power of vision by night; a sighting device on a camera, rifle, etc to enable it to be used at night; **night'-soil** the contents of outside lavatories, cesspools, etc generally carried away at night and sometimes used for fertilizer; **night'-spell** a charm against harm by night; **night'spot** (*colloq*) a nightclub; **night'stand** a bedside table; **night starvation** hunger pangs experienced in the middle of the night; **night'-steed** (*mythol*) one of the horses in the chariot of Night; **night'stick** (*NAm*) a truncheon; **night'-stool** a close-stool (qv under **close**[2]) for use in a bedroom; **night'-ta'per** a night-light burning slowly; **night terror** or *n pl* **night terrors** (*archaic*) the sudden starting from sleep in fright. — **night'-tide** night-time; a flood-tide in the night; **night'-time** the time when it is night. — *adj* **night'-tripp'ing** (*Shakesp*) tripping about in the night. — *adj* **night'-wak'ing** watching in the night. — **night'=walk** a walk in the night; **night'-walk'er** (*archaic*) a somnambulist; a person who walks about at night, *usu* for bad purposes, *esp* a prostitute. — *n* and *adj* **night'=wan'derer** someone who wanders about at night. — *adj* **night'-wan'dering**. — *adj* **night'-war'bling** singing in the night. — **night'-watch** a watch or guard at night; a person who is on guard at night; time of watch at night; **night'-watch'man** a person who is on watch at night, *esp* on industrial premises and building sites; a batsman, not a high scorer, put in to defend a wicket until the close of play (*cricket*); **night'wear** clothes worn at bedtime and while sleeping; **night'-work** work done at night; **night'-worker**. — **make a night of it** to spend the night, or a large part of it, in amusement or celebration; **night-night** (*colloq* or *childish*) goodnight; **of a night** or **of nights** in the course of a night; some time at night. [OE *niht*; Ger *Nacht*, L *nox*, Gr *nyx*]

nightingale[1] *nīt'ing-gāl*, *n* a small bird of the thrush family (genus *Luscinia*), celebrated for the rich love-song of the male, heard chiefly at night; a person with a beautiful singing voice. [OE *nihtegale*, from *niht* night, and *galan* to sing, Ger *Nachtigall*]

nightingale[2] *nīt'ing-gāl*, *n* a flannel scarf with sleeves, a garment formerly worn by hospital patients when sitting up in bed. [Florence *Nightingale* (1820–1910), Crimean hospital nurse]

nightjar ... to ... **night-season**. See under **night**.

nightshade *nīt'shād*, *n* a name given to various plants, *esp* of the *Solanaceae* family and chiefly poisonous or narcotic. — **black nightshade** a common plant of the nightshade family, *Solanum nigrum*, with poisonous leaves, white flowers and black berries; **deadly nightshade** the belladonna plant, all parts of which are poisonous; **enchanter's nightshade** see under **enchant**; **woody nightshade** bittersweet. [OE *nihtscada*, appar from *niht* night, and *scada* shade]

night shift ... to ... **nightworker**. See under **night**.

nig-nog[1] *nig'-nog*, (*slang*) *n* a fool; a raw recruit to the army or to a civilian service. [Origin uncertain]

nig-nog[2] *nig'-nog*, (*offensive slang*) *n* a person of a dark-skinned race. [Reduplicated form of **nigger**]

nigrescence *nī-* or *ni-gres'əns*, *n* blackness; dark colouring or pigmentation; blackening. — *adj* **nigresc'ent** growing black or dark; blackish. — *adj* **nigricant** (*nig'ri-kənt*) black; blackish. — *vt* **nig'rify** to blacken. — *n* **nig'ritude** blackness; see also under **Negro**. [L *niger* black]

Nigritian *ni-grish'ən*, *n* and *adj* (an inhabitant) of *Nigritia* or Sudan, *esp* Western Sudan, the original home of the Negro race in the narrow, technical sense. [L *niger* black]

nigritude. See under **Negro** and **nigrescence**.

nigromancy *nig'rō-man-si*, *n* an old form of **necromancy**, the black art. [From association with L *niger* black]

nigrosine *nig'rō-sēn* or *-ro-sin* or **nigrosin** *nig'rō-sin*, *n* a blackish coal-tar colour dye. [L *niger* black]

NIH *abbrev*: National Institutes of Health (*US*).

nihil *nī'hil*, *n* nothing. — *n* **ni'hilism** (*-hil-* or *-il-izm*) belief in nothing; denial of all reality, or of all objective truth (*philos*); extreme scepticism; nothingness; (sometimes with *cap*) in tsarist Russia, a terrorist movement aiming at the overturn of all the existing institutions of society in order to build it up anew on different principles; terrorism or anarchy; complete destructiveness. — *n* **ni'hilist**. — *adj* **nihilist'ic**. — *n* **nihility** (*-hil'*) nothingness; a mere nothing. [L *nihil* nothing]

nihil ad rem *nī'hil ad rem* or *ni-* (*L*) nothing to the point; **ni'hil obstat** (*ob'stat*; *RC*) nothing hinders, a book censor's form of permission to print.

nihonga *ni-hong'gə*, *n* a Japanese style of painting, using bright colours and traditional images. [Jap, Japanese painting]

-nik *-nik*, *combining form* denoting a person who does, practises, advocates, etc something, as in *beatnik*, *kibbutznik* or *peacenik*. [Russ sfx, influenced in meaning by Yiddish sfx denoting an agent]

nikau or **nikau palm** *ni'kow päm*, *n* a Maori name for the palm tree *Rhopalostylis sapida*, native to New Zealand.

Nike *nī'kē*, *n* the Greek goddess of victory. [Gr *nīkē* victory]

nikethamide *nik-eth'a-mīd*, *n* a drug used as a heart stimulant (also called **coramine**). [*nic*otinic acid, di-*ethyl*, and *amide*]

Nikkei index *nik'ā in'deks*, *n* the indicator of the relative prices of stocks and shares on the Tokyo stock exchange. [From the title of the newspaper publishing it]

niks-nie. See under **nix**[2].

nil *nil*, *n* nothing; zero. [L *nīl*, *nihil* nothing]

nil desperandum *nil des-per-an'dōōm*, (*L*) nothing is to be despaired of; never despair. [Horace, *Odes* I.vii.27]

Nile blue *nīl blōō*, *n* a very pale greenish blue colour.

Nile green *nīl grēn*, *n* a very pale green colour, thought of as the colour of the River *Nile*.

nilgai *nēl'* or *nil'gī*, **nilgau** or **nylghau** *-gow* or *-gö*, *n* a large Indian antelope, the male slaty-grey, the female tawny: — *pl* **nilgai**, **nilgais**, **nilgau**, **nilgaus**, **nylghau** or **nylghaus**. [Pers and Hindi *nīl* blue, and Hindi *gāī*, Pers *gāw* cow]

nill or **n'ill** *nil*, (*archaic*) *vt* will not; refuse: — *pa t* (*obs*) **nould**, **noulde** or **n'ould** (*nōōd*), also **nilled**. [OE *nylle*, from *ne* not, and *willan* to wish]

Nilometer *nī-lom'i-tər*, *n* a gauge for measuring the height of the river *Nile*. [Gr *neilometrion*]

Nilot *nīl'ot* or **Nilote** *-ōt*, *n* an inhabitant of the banks of the Upper Nile; a member of any of several peoples from E Africa and the Sudan; a Negro of the Upper Nile: — *pl* **Nilot**, **Nilots**, **Nilote** or **Nilot'es** (*-tēz*). — *adj* **Nilotic** (*-ot'ik*) of the Nile, the Nilots or the languages they speak. [Gr *Neilōtēs*]

nim[1] *nim*, *vt* to take (*obs*); to steal, pilfer (*archaic slang*): — *pa t* (*obs*) **nam** or (*archaic*) **nimmed**. — *n* **nimm'er**. [OE *niman* to take]

nim[2] *nim n* an old and widespread game, perhaps *orig* Chinese, in which two players take alternately from heaps or rows of objects (now *usu* matches). [Perh **nim**[1]]

nim[3] *nēm*, *n* an E Indian tree of the *Melia* genus, the fruit and seeds of which yield **nim'-oil**, an aromatic, medicinal oil. — Also **neem**, **neemb**, **neem tree** or **nimb**. [Hindi *nīm*]

nimbi. See **nimbus**.

nimble *nim'bl*, *adj* light and quick in motion, agile; active; swift. — *n* **nim'bleness** or (*Spenser*) **nim'blesse** quickness of motion either in body or mind. — *adv* **nim'bly**. — *adj* **nim'ble-fing'ered** skilful with the fingers; thievish. — *adj* **nimbl'e-foot'ed** swift of foot. — *adj* **nim'ble-witt'ed** quick-witted. [Appar OE *næmel*, *numol*, from *niman* to take; cf Ger *nehmen*]

nimbus *nim'bəs*, *n* a cloud or luminous mist encircling a god or goddess; a halo; a rain-cloud: — *pl* **nim'bī** or **nim'buses**. — *adj* **nimbed** (*nimd*). — *adj* **nim'bused**. — *n* **nimbostratus** (*-strā'* or *-stra'*) a low, dark-coloured layer of cloud, bringing rain: — *pl* **nimbostra'ti** (*-tī*). [L]

NIMBY or **Nimby** *nim'bi*, *n* (*slang*) a person who is willing to have something occur so long as it does not affect him or her or take place in his or her locality. — *n* **nimbyism**. [From '*n*ot *i*n *m*y *b*ack *y*ard']

nimiety *ni-mī'i-ti*, *n* (*rare*) excess. — *adj* **nimious** (*nim'i-əs*; *Scots law*) excessive. [L *nimis* too much]

niminy-piminy *nim'i-ni-pim'i-ni*, (*derog*) *adj* affectedly fine or delicate. — *n* affected delicacy. [Imit]

nimonic *ni-mon'ik*, *adj* of alloys used in high-temperature work, eg gas turbine blades, chiefly nickel, with chromium, titanium and aluminium. [*ni*ckel and *Mon*el metal]

Nimrod *nim'rod*, *n* any great hunter. [From the son of Cush in the Bible, Gen 10. 8–10]

nincompoop *ning'kəm-pōōp* or *nin'kəm-pōōp*, *n* a simpleton; an idiot, stupid person — earlier **nic'ompoop** and **nick'umpoop** — shortened to **nin'com**, **nin'cum** and also **poop**. [Origin unknown; probably not from L *nōn compos* (*mentis*) not in possession (of one's wits)]

nine *nīn*, *n* the cardinal number next above eight; a symbol representing it (9, ix, etc); a set of that number of things or people (such as a baseball team); a shoe or other article of size 9; a card with nine pips; a score of nine points, tricks, etc; the ninth hour after midday or midnight; the age of nine years; (with *cap* and *the*) the nine Muses. — *adj* nine in number; nine years old. — *adj* and *adv* **nine'fold** having nine parts, in nine divisions; nine times as much. — *adj* **ninth** (*nīnth*) last of nine; next after the eighth; equal to one of nine equal parts. — *n* a ninth part; a person or thing in ninth position; an octave and a second (*music*); a tone at that interval (*music*). — *adv* **nīnth'ly** in the ninth place, ninth in order. — **nine'-eyes** a lamprey (from its seven pairs of gill-pouches); a butterfish (from its spots). — *adj* **nine'-foot**, **nine'-inch**, **nine'-metre**, **nine'-mile**, etc measuring 9 feet, etc. — *adj* **nine'-hole** (of a golf course) having nine holes. — **nine'holes** a game in which a ball is to be bowled into nine holes in the ground or in a board; a difficulty, fix (*US*); **nine'pence** the value of nine pennies; a coin of that value; a high standard of niceness, nimbleness, etc. — *adj* **nine'penny** costing, offered at, or worth ninepence. — *n* a ninepence. — **nine'pin** a bottle-shaped pin set up with eight others for the game of **nine'pins** in which players bowl a ball at them (see **skittle**). — *n* and *adj* **nine'score** nine times twenty. — **nine worthies** see under **worth**[1]. — **nine days' wonder** see under **wonder**; **ninepenny marl**, **ninepenny morris** or **nine men's morris** see under **meril**; **nine points of the law** satisfying the majority of the legal requirements that could be raised in objection or contention, hence, virtually assured, legitimate, valid, etc; **to the nines** to perfection, fully, elaborately. [OE *nigon*; Du *negen*, L *novem*, Gr *ennea*, Sans *nava*]

nineteen *nīn-tēn'* or *nīn'tēn*, *n* and *adj* the total of nine and ten. — *n* and *adj* **nine'teenth** (or *-tēnth'*). — *adv* **nineteenth'ly**. — **nineteenth hole** (*joc*) a golf club-house, *esp* the bar or restaurant. — **nineteen to the dozen** (of speaking, done) in great quantity, not necessarily with equal quality. [OE *nigontēne* (*-tiene*); see **nine** and **ten**]

ninety *nīn'ti*, *n* and *adj* nine times ten. — *n pl* **nine'ties** the numbers ninety to ninety-nine; the years so numbered in a life or a century; a range of temperature from ninety to just less than one hundred degrees. — *adj* **nine'tieth** last of ninety; next after the eighty-ninth; equal to one of ninety equal parts. — *n* a ninetieth part; a person or thing in ninetieth position. — **naughty**

nineties see under **naughty**. [OE *nigontig* (*hund-nigontig*)]

ninja *nin'jə*, *n* (also with *cap*) one of a body of trained assassins and spies in feudal Japan, skilled in ninjitsu: — *pl* **nin'ja** or **nin'jas**. — *n* **ninjit'su** or **ninjut'su** a Japanese martial art, teaching stealth and camouflage. [Jap]

ninny *nin'i*, *n* a simpleton. — Also (*archaic* or *dialect*) **ninn'y-hammer**. [Poss from **innocent**, or poss from Ital *ninno* child, Sp *niño*]

ninon *nē'nɔ̃*, *n* a silk voile or other thin fabric. [Fr *Ninon*, a woman's name]

Nintendo® *nin-ten'dō*, *n* a video games console machine which allows computer games to be projected on to, and played using, a television screen. — *n* **Nintendinī̄tus** or **Nintendoī'tis** (*colloq*) obsessive playing of games on a Nintendo machine; severe muscle strain in the hands and wrists caused by excessive operating of the controls of a Nintendo machine. [The name of the manufacturer]

ninth. See under **nine**.

Niobe *nī'ō-bē*, (*Gr mythol*) *n* a daughter of Tantalus, turned into stone as she wept for her children, slain by Artemis and Apollo. — *adj* **Niobē'an**. [Gr *Niobē*]

niobium *nī-ō'bi-əm*, *n* a metallic element (symbol **Nb**; atomic no 41) discovered in the mineral tantalite and used in certain alloys (also, but not now officially, called **columbium**). — *n* **nī'obate** a salt of niobic acid. — *adj* **nio'bic** (**niobic acid** hydrated niobium pentoxide). — *n* **ni'obite** same as **columbite**. — *adj* **nīo'bous**. [**Niobe**, from the connection with tantalite]

Nip. See under **Nippoon**.

nip[1] *nip*, *n* a small quantity of spirits. — Also (*US*) **nipp'er**. — *vi* to take a nip: — *pr p* **nipp'ing**; *pa p* and *pa t* **nipped**. — *n* **nipp'erkin** (*archaic*) a small measure of alcoholic drink. [Origin obscure]

nip[2] *nip*, *vt* to pinch; to press between two surfaces; to remove or sever by pinching or biting (often with *off*); (eg of the cold or frost) to halt the growth or vigour of (eg vegetation); (*esp* of cold weather) to give a smarting or tingling feeling to; to concern closely and painfully (*obs*); to reprehend sharply (*obs*); to snatch (*esp US*); to steal (*colloq*); to arrest (*slang*). — *vi* to pinch; to smart; to go nimbly or quickly: — *pr p* **nipp'ing**; *pa t* and *pa p* **nipped** (*nipt*). — *n* an act or experience of nipping; the pinch of cold; a halt to the growth of vegetation caused eg by the cold or frost a nipping quality; pungency or bite (*Scot*); a sharp reprehension (*obs*); a more or less gradual thinning out of a stratum (*mineralogy*); a simple fastening of a rope by twisting it round the object; a part of a rope fastened in this way (*naut*); a small piece, such as might be nipped off; a cutpurse (*old slang*). — *n* **nipp'er** a person who or thing which nips; a chela or great claw, eg of a crab; a horse's incisor, *esp* of the middle four; a pickpocket or cutpurse (*slang*); a boy assistant to a costermonger, carter, etc; a little boy or (sometimes) girl (*colloq*); (in *pl*) small pincers; (in *pl*) any of various pincer-like tools; (in *pl*) handcuffs (*colloq*). — *vt* to seize (two ropes) together. — *adv* **nipp'ily**. — *n* **nipp'iness**. — *adv* **nipp'ingly**. — *adj* **nipp'y** pungent, biting; nimble, quick (*colloq*); niggardly; (*esp* of weather) very cold, frosty. — *n* (with *cap*; *old*) a waitress, *esp* one in a restaurant owned by J Lyons and Co Ltd (also **Nipp'ie**). — **nip'cheese** a stingy person (*slang*); a purser (*obs naut*). — **nip and tuck** (*US*) full speed; neck and neck; **nip in** to cut in; **nip in the bud** see under **bud**[1]. [Prob related to Du *nijpen* to pinch]

nip[3]. See **nep**.

nipa *nē'*, *nī'pə*, *n* (also with *cap*) a low-growing E Indian palm of brackish water (*Nipa fruticans*), with large feathery leaves used for thatching; an alcoholic drink made from it. [Malay *nīpah*]

nipperkin. See under **nip**[1].

nipperty-tipperty *nip'ər-ti-tip'ər-ti*, (*Scot*) *adj* finical; mincing; fiddle-faddle.

nipple *nip'l*, *n* the rounded projecting point of the breast, the outlet of the milk ducts in women and female animals; a teat; a small projection with an orifice, *esp* for regulating flow or lubricating machinery; any nipple-like protuberance. — *vt* to provide with a nipple. — **nipp'le-shield** a soft plastic shield worn over the nipple when breastfeeding by women whose nipples are particularly tender; **nipp'lewort** a tall composite weed (*Lapsana communis*) with small yellow heads, once valued as a cure for sore nipples. [A dimin of **neb** or **nib**[1]]

Nippon *nip-on'*, *n* the Japanese name for Japan. — *n* and *adj* **Nipponese'**. — *n* **Nip** (*offensive slang*) a Japanese person. [Jap *ni* sun, and *pon*, from *hon* origin]

nippy. See under **nip**[2].

nipter *nip'tər*, *n* the ecclesiastical ceremony of washing the feet, the same as *maundy*. [Gr *niptēr* a basin, from *niptein* to wash]

niramiai *ni-räm'i-ī*, (*sumo wrestling*) *n* a period (of minutes) spent stamping, thigh-slapping and glaring to intimidate an opponent before beginning to fight. [Jap]

NIRC *abbrev*: National Industrial Relations Court.

NIREX *nī'reks*, *abbrev*: Nuclear Industry Radioactive Waste Executive.

nirl *nirl*, (*Scot*) *n* a lump; a crumb; a stunted person. — *vt* to stunt; to shrink or shrivel; to pinch with cold. — *adj* **nirled** or **nirl'it**. — *adj* **nirl'y** or **nirl'ie** knotty; stumpy; stunted; niggardly. [Perh **knurl**; perh connected with Icel *nyrfill* niggard]

nirvana *nir-vä'nə*, *n* the cessation of individual existence, to which a Buddhist or Hindu aspires as the culmination of the meditative state; loosely, a blissful state. — Also **Nirvana**. [Sans *nirvāna* a blowing out]

nis[1], **n'is** or **nys** *nis* or *niz*, (*obs*) a contraction for **ne is**, is not.

nis[2] or **nisse** *nis*, (*Scand folklore*) *n* a brownie or friendly goblin: — *pl* **nisses**. [Dan and Swed *nisse*]

Nisan *nī'san* or *nē-sän'*, *n* the seventh civil, first ecclesiastical, month of the Jewish calendar (March to April), called Abib before the Captivity. [Heb *Nīsān*]

nisberry. Same as **naseberry**.

nisei *ne'sā'*, *n* an American or Canadian born of Japanese immigrant parents (cf **issei** and **sansei**). [Jap, second generation]

nisi *nī'sī*, (*law*) *adj* to take effect unless, after a time, some condition referred to is fulfilled. [The L conjunction *nisi* unless]

nisi prius *nī'sī prī'əs* or *ni'si pri'o͞os*, (*L*) unless previously, a name (from the first words of the writ) given to the jury sittings in civil cases.

nisse. Same as **nis**[2].

Nissen hut *nis'ən hut*, *n* a semi-cylindrical corrugated-iron hut designed by Colonel P N *Nissen* (1871–1930).

nisus *nī'səs*, *n* effort; striving; impulse. [L *nīsus*, pl *-ūs*]

nit[1] *nit*, *n* the egg of a louse or similar insect; a young louse; a term of contempt (*Shakesp*, etc). — *adj* **nitt'y** full of nits. — **nit'-grass** a rare grass (*Gastridium*) with nit-like flowers; **nit'-picker**; **nit'-picking** (*colloq*) petty criticism of minor details. — *vi* **nit'-pick**. [OE *hnitu*; Ger *Niss*]

nit[2] *nit*, (*colloq*) *n* a fool. [Poss from **nit**[1], or an abbrev of **nitwit**]

nit[3] *nit*, *n* a unit of luminance, one candela per square metre. [L *nitor* brightness]

nit[4] *nit*, (*comput*) *n* a unit of information (1·44 bits). — Also **nep'it**. [*N*apierian dig*it*]

nit[5] *nit* (*Austr colloq*): **keep nit** to keep watch.

nite *nīt*, (*colloq*) *n* and *adj* night. [A spelling of *night* reflecting its pronunciation]

niter. See **nitre**.

niterie or **nitery** *nīt'ə-ri*, (*colloq*) *n* a nightclub. [**night** and **-ery**]

nithing *nī'* or *ni'dhing*, (*hist*) *n* an infamous person; an abject coward; a traitor. — *adj* cowardly; dastardly; niggardly — wrongly **niddering**, **nidering**, **nidderling**, **niderling** (*nid'*) or **nī'ding**. [ON *nīthingr* (in OE as *nīthing*), from *nīth* contumely; Ger *Neiding*]

Nithsdale *niths'dāl*, *n* an 18c woman's riding-hood. [From the Countess of *Nithsdale*, who contrived her husband's escape from the Tower in her clothes in 1716]

nitid *nit'id*, (*poetic*) *adj* shining, bright; merry. [L *nitidus*, from *nitēre* to shine]

Nitinol *nit'in-ol*, *n* an alloy of nickel and titanium, in particular one which, when shaped and then heated to fix that shape, will after reshaping or deformation return to the original shape on reheating. [The chemical symbols *Ni* and *Ti*, and the initial letters of the US *N*aval *O*rdnance *L*aboratory in Maryland where the alloy was discovered]

niton *nī'ton*, *n* a former name for radon. [L *nitēre* to shine]

nitraniline. See under **nitro-**.

nitrate, **nitratine** and **nitration**. See under **nitre**.

nitrazepam *nī-trā'zi-pam*, *n* a hypnotic and tranquillizing drug taken for the relief of insomnia. [*Nitro-* and *-azepam* as in **diazepam**]

nitre or (*US*) **niter** *nī'tər*, *n* potassium nitrate or saltpetre (**cubic nitre** is sodium nitrate, or Chile saltpetre); sodium carbonate (*obs*); a supposed nitrous substance in the air, etc (*obs*). — *n* **ni'trate** a salt or ester of nitric acid; natural (potassium or sodium) or synthetic (calcium) nitrate, a fertilizer. — *vt* (*-trāt'*) to treat with nitric acid or a nitrate; to convert into a nitrate or nitro-compound. — *n* **nitratine** (*nī'trə-tin*) sodium nitrate as a mineral. — *n* **nitrā'tion**. — *adj* **ni'tric** of or containing nitrogen. — *n* **ni'tride** a compound of nitrogen with a metal. — *vt* to turn into a nitride; to harden the surface of by heating in ammonia gas. — *n* **ni'triding**. — *n* **nitrificā'tion** treatment with nitric acid; conversion into nitrates, *esp* by bacteria through the intermediate condition of nitrites. — *vt* and *vi* **ni'trify** to subject to or suffer nitrification: — *pr p* **ni'trifying**; *pa t* and *pa p* **ni'trified**. — *n* **ni'trile** (*-tril*, *-trēl* or *-trīl*) any of a group of organic cyanides (general formula R·C⋮N). — *n* **ni'trite** a salt or ester of nitrous acid. — *adj* **ni'trous** of, like, derived from or containing nitrogen. — *adj* **ni'try** (*obs*) applied to the air, as supposed to contain nitre (see above). — *n* **ni'tryl** nitroxyl (see under **nitro-**). — **nitric acid** HNO_3; **nitric anhydride** N_2O_5; **nitric oxide** NO; **nitrous acid** HNO_2; **nitrous anhydride** N_2O_3; **nitrous bacteria** one of the nitrobacteria (qv under **nitro-**); **nitrous oxide** laughing gas, N_2O. [Fr, from L *nitrum*, from Gr *nitron* sodium carbonate; prob of Eastern origin; cf Egyptian *ntr(j)*, Heb *nether*, Ar *nitrūn*]

Nitrian *nit'ri-ən*, *adj* belonging to *Nitriae* (Nitriai), a region of ancient Egypt west of the Nile delta, including the Natron lakes and a great conglomeration of hermit settlements. [Gr *nitriā* a soda pit, from *nitron* soda]

nitric, **nitride**, **nitriding**, **nitrify**, **nitrile** and **nitrite**. See under **nitre**.

nitro- *nī-trō-*, *combining form* indicating: of, made with or containing nitre, nitric acid or nitrogen; containing the group -NO_2. — *n* **nitro-an'iline** or **nitran'iline** any nitro-derivative of aniline. — *n pl* **ni'trobactē'ria** bacteria that convert ammonium compounds into nitrites, and *esp* those that convert nitrites into nitrates. — *n* **nitroben'zene** a yellow oily liquid ($C_6H_5NO_2$) obtained from benzene and nitric and concentrated sulphuric acid. — *n* **nitrocell'ulose** cellulose nitrate, used as an explosive, and in lacquers, glues, etc. — *n* **nitro-com'pound** or **nitro-deriv'ative** a compound in which one or more hydrogens of an aromatic or aliphatic compound are replaced by nitro-groups. — *n* **nitrocott'on** guncotton, an explosive made from cotton soaked in nitric and sulphuric acids. — *n* **nitroglyc'erine** a powerfully explosive compound produced by the action of nitric and sulphuric acids on glycerine. — *n* **ni'tro-group** the radical NO_2. — *n* **ni'trohydrochlor'ic acid** same as **aqua-regia**. — *n* **nitrom'eter** an apparatus for estimating nitrogen or some of its compounds. — *n* **nitromē'thane** a liquid (CH_3NO_2) obtained from methane and used as a solvent and as rocket-fuel. — *adj* **nitromet'ric**. — *n* **nitropar'affin** any of several compounds, derived from methane, in which a hydrogen atom is replaced by a nitro-group. — *adj* **nitro'philous** (of plants) growing in a place where there is a good supply of nitrogen. — *n* **nitrosamine** (*-sə-mēn'* or *-sa'mēn*) any of a class of neutral organic chemical compounds which cause cancer. — *n* **nitrosā'tion** conversion of ammonium salts into nitrites. — *n* **ni'tro-silk** an artificial silk in which fibres of cellulose nitrate are made and then turned into cellulose. — *adj* **nitrō'sō** of or containing a nitroso-group. — *n* **nitrō'sō-group** the group NO. — *adj* **ni'trosyl** nitroso. — *n* **nitro-tol'uene** a nitro-derivative of toluene. — *n* **nitrox'yl** the group NO_2. [Ety as for **nitre**]

nitrogen *nī'trə-jən*, *n* a gaseous element (symbol **N**; atomic no 7) forming nearly four-fifths of common air, a necessary constituent of every organized body, so called from its being an essential constituent of nitre. — *n* **nitrogenase** (*nī-troj'ə-nāz*) an enzyme complex that catalyses nitrogen in the nitrogen fixation process. — *n* **nitrogenizā'tion** or **-s-**. — *vt* **nitrogenize** or **-ise** (*-troj'*) to combine or supply with nitrogen. — *adj* **nitrog'enous** of or containing nitrogen. — **nitrogen cycle** the sum total of the transformations undergone by nitrogen and nitrogenous compounds in nature, circulating between the atmosphere, soil and living organisms, from free nitrogen back to free nitrogen; **nitrogen fixation** the bringing of free nitrogen into compounds with other elements, done naturally by means of bacteria in certain plants to make the nitrogen usable by those plants, or by man industrially, eg to make fertilizers; **nitrogen mustard** any of several compounds with a molecular structure resembling that of a mustard gas, used in cancer treatments; **nitrogen narcosis** the intoxicating and anaesthetic effect of too much nitrogen in the brain, experienced by divers at considerable depths (also called **rapture of the deep** or **rapture of the depths** and (*slang*) **the narks**). [Gr *nitron* sodium carbonate (but taken as if meaning nitre), and the root of *gennaein* to generate]

nitrosamine, **nitro-silk**, **nitroso**, **nitrotoluene** and **nitroxyl**. See under **nitro-**.

nitrous, **nitry** and **nitryl**. See under **nitre**.

nitty. See under **nit**[1].

nitty-gritty *nit'i-grit'i*, (*colloq*) *n* the basic or essential details, the fundamentals, *esp* in the phrase *get down to the nitty-gritty*. [Origin uncertain; perhaps from **grit**[1]]

nitwit *nit'wit*, (*slang*) *n* a blockhead, stupid person. — *adj* **nit'witted**. — *n* **nitwitt'edness**. — *n* **nitwitt'ery**. [Poss Ger dialect *nit* not, and **wit**]

nival *nī'vəl*, *adj* growing among snow. — *adj* **niveous** (*niv'i-əs*) snowy, white. — *n* **Nivôse** (*nē-vōz*) the 4th month of the French revolutionary calendar, the month of snow, from about 21 December to 19 January. [L *nix*, *nivis* snow]

nix[1] *niks*, (*Gmc mythol*) *n* a *usu* malignant or spiteful water-spirit: — *fem* **nix'ie** or **nix'y**. [Ger *Nix*, fem *Nixe*; cf **nicker**[2]]

nix[2] *niks*, (*slang*) *n* nothing; short for 'nothing doing, you'll get no support from me'; postal matter addressed wrongly (*old US*, *usu* in *pl*). — *vt* to veto, reject or cancel. — *n* **nix-nie** or **niks-nie** (*niks'nē*; *SAfr*) nothing at all. — **nix my dolly** (*obs slang*) never mind. [Colloq Ger and Du for Ger *nichts* nothing]

nix[3] *niks*, *interj* a cry to give warning of the approach of a person in authority, eg a policeman or teacher.

nizam *ni-zäm'* or *nī-zam'*, *n* (also with *cap*) formerly, the title of the prince of Hyderabad in India (to 1950); a Turkish soldier. [Hindi *nizām* regulator]

NJ *abbrev*: New Jersey (US state).

NK *abbrev*: natural killer (see **natural killer cell** under **natural**).

NL *abbrev*: Netherlands (IVR).

nl *abbrev*: *non licet* (*L*), it is not permitted; *non liquet* (*L*), it is not clear; *non lange* (*L*), not far.

NLRB *abbrev*: National Labor Relations Board (US).

NM or **N.Mex**. *abbrev*: New Mexico (US state).
n mile *abbrev*: (international) nautical mile.
NMR *abbrev*: Nuclear Magnetic Resonance.
NNE *abbrev*: north-north-east.
NNEB *abbrev*: Nursery Nurses' Examination Board.
NNI *abbrev*: Noise and Number Index.
NNW *abbrev*: north-north-west.
NO *abbrev*: natural order; New Orleans.
No (*chem*) *symbol*: nobelium.
no[1] *nō*, *adv* used as a sentence substitute to express a negative answer, refusal, disapproval, disbelief or to acknowledge a negative statement (formerly used *esp* in response to a question or statement containing a negative, in contradistinction to *nay*, used to express simple negation until superseded in this function by *no* in early 17c); not so; not; (with *compar*) in no degree, not at all. — *n* a denial; a refusal; a vote or voter for the negative: — *pl* **noes** or **nos**. — *n* **no'-no** (*colloq*) a failure, non-event; something which must not be done, said, etc; an impossibility, non-starter. — *pl* **no'-nos**, **no'-no's** or **no'-noes**. — **no can do** see under **can**; **no more** destroyed; dead; never again, not any longer; **not take no for an answer** to continue (with something) in spite of refusals; **the noes have it** no-votes or no-voters are in the majority. [OE *nā*, from *ne* not, and *ā* ever; cf **nay**]
no[2] *nō*, *adj* not any; not one; by no means properly called, certainly not, not at all. — *adj* **no-account'** (*US colloq*) worthless; insignificant. — **no'-ball** (*cricket*) a ball bowled in such a way that it is disallowed by the rules; **no-claims bonus** or **discount** a reduction in the price of an insurance policy because no claims have been made on it. — *adj* **no-fault'** (of insurance compensation payments) made without attachment to or admission of blame by any one person or party in particular. — **no-fines'** concrete from which the fine aggregate (ie sand) has been omitted. — *adj* **no'-frills** basic, not elaborate or fancy. — *adj* **no'-good** bad, worthless. — *n* a bad, worthless person. — **no-go area** see under **go**; **no-hope** and **no-hoper** see under **hope**[1]; **no'-man** someone ready to say 'no'; **no'-man's-land** a waste region to which no one has a recognized claim; neutral or disputed land, *esp* between entrenched hostile forces (also *fig*); **no'-meaning** lack of meaning; something said that is deficient in meaning. — *n* and *pronoun* **no one** or **no'-one** nobody. — *adj* **no-non'sense** sensible, tolerating no nonsense. — **no-score draw** (*football*) a match in which neither team manages to score; **no-show** a person who does not arrive for something he or she has booked, eg a restaurant table or a flight; an instance of such non-arrival; **no-side'** the end of a game at Rugby football. — *adj* **no-tech'** (*colloq*) not involving or using the most recent technology. — **no-trump'** or **no-trumps'** (*bridge*) a call for the playing of a hand without any trump suit. — *adj* **no-trump'**. — **no-trump'er** a no-trump call; a hand suitable for this; someone addicted to calling no-trumps. — *adv* **no'way**, **no'ways** or **no'wise** in no way, manner, or degree (see also below). — *adj* **no-win'** (of a situation) in which one is bound to lose or fail whatever one does. — **no doubt** surely; **no dice**, **no end** and **no go** see under **die**[2], **end** and **go**[1]; **no joke** not a trifling matter; **no one** no single; **no time** a very short time; **no way** (*colloq*) under no circumstances, absolutely not, an emphatic expression of disagreement or dissent. [OE *nān* none; see **none**]
no[3] *nō*, (*mod Scot*) *adv* not. [Perh from *nocht*; see **not**[1] and **nought**]
no[4], **nō** or **noh** *nō*, *n* (often with *cap*) the traditional Japanese style of drama developed out of a religious dance: — *pl* **no** or **noh**. — Also **nō'gaku** (*-gä-ko͞o*; Jap *gaku* music): — *pl* **no'gaku**. [Jap *nō*]
no. or **No.** *abbrev*: number.
n.o. (*cricket*) *abbrev*: not out.
Noachian *nō-ā'ki-ən*, *adj* of *Noah* or the time when he lived. — Also **Noachic** (*-ak'* or *-āk'*). — **Noah's ark** a child's toy in imitation of the Ark with its occupants (Genesis 6–9).
nob[1] *nob*, *n* the head (*colloq*); the knave of the suit turned up by the dealer in cribbage. — **one for his nob** a point scored for holding the nob in cribbage; a blow on the head. [Perhaps **knob**]
nob[2] *nob*, *n* a person of wealth or *esp* high social rank. — *adv* **nobb'ily**. — *n* **nobb'iness**. — *adj* **nobb'y** smart. [Origin obscure; cf **nabs** and **nib**[2]]
nobble *nob'l*, (*slang*) *vt* to injure or drug (a racehorse) to prevent it from winning; to get hold of, *esp* dishonestly; to win over, persuade or dissuade, eg by bribery or coercion; to swindle; to prevent from doing something; to seize or grab; to arrest. — *n* **nobb'ler** (*slang*) a person who nobbles; a finishing-stroke; a thimblerigger's assistant or accomplice; a dram of spirits. [Perh **nab**[1]]
nobbut *nob'ət*, (*dialect*) *adv* only. — *prep* except. — *conj* except that. [**no**[1,2] and **but**[1]]
Nobel prize *nō-bel' prīz'*, *n* any of the annual prizes for work in physics, chemistry, medicine or physiology, literature, the promotion of peace, and economics instituted by Alfred B *Nobel* (1833–96), Swedish discoverer of dynamite. — *n* **Nobel laureate** a (past) winner of the Nobel prize in any category.
nobelium *nō-bel'i-əm* or *-bēl'*, *n* the name given to a transuranic element (symbol **No**, atomic no 102) in 1957 when its production at the *Nobel* Institute, Stockholm, was claimed.
nobilesse. See under **noblesse**.
nobiliary. See under **nobility**.
nobility *nō-bil'i-ti*, *n* the quality of being noble; high rank; dignity; excellence; greatness of mind or character; noble descent; (with *the*) nobles as a body, the aristocracy, peerage. — *adj* **nobil'iary** of nobility. — *vt* **nobil'itate** to ennoble. — *n* **nobilitā'tion**. — **nobiliary particle** a preposition forming part of a title or certain names, eg Ger *von*, Fr *de*, Ital *di*. [Ety as for **noble**]
noble *nō'bl*, *adj* illustrious; high in social rank or character; of high birth; impressive; stately; generous; excellent, worthy. — *n* a person of high social title or rank; a peer; an obsolete gold coin worth approximately one-third of a pound sterling (33p or 6 shillings 8d) — *n* **no'bleness**. — *adv* **no'bly**. — **noble art** or **noble science** (with *the*) boxing; **noble gas** an inert gas; **no'bleman** a man who is noble or of high social rank; a peer: — *pl* **no'blemen**; *fem* **no'blewoman**: — *pl* **no'blewomen**. — **noble metal** one that does not readily tarnish on exposure to air, such as gold, silver, platinum (*opp* to *base metal*). — *adj* **no'ble-mind'ed**. — **no'ble-mind'edness**; **noble opal** precious opal, a translucent or semi-transparent bluish or yellowish white variety with brilliant play of colours; **noble rot** a mould which forms on over-ripe grapes and produces the characteristic richness of certain wines, eg Sauternes and Tokay; **noble savage** a romantic and idealized view of primitive man. — **most noble** an appellation formally prefixed to the title of a duke. [Fr *noble*, from L (*g*)*nōbilis*, from (*g*)*nōscere* to know]
noblesse *nō-bles'*, *n* nobility; nobleness; nobles collectively. — (*Spenser*) **no'blesse** or **no'bilesse**. — **noblesse oblige** (*ō-blēzh*) rank imposes obligations. [Fr]
nobody *nō'bə-di*, *pron* no person; no one. — *n* a person of no importance. — **nobody's business** (*slang*) a thing nobody could hope to deal with or nobody troubles about. — **like nobody's business** (*colloq*) very energetically or intensively. [**no**[2] and **body**]
NOC *abbrev*: National Olympic Committee.
nocake *nō'kāk*, *n* meal made of parched maize. [Algonquian; cf Narragansett *nokehick*]
nocent *nō'sənt*, (*rare*) *adj* hurtful; guilty. — *n* a person who is hurtful or guilty. — *adv* **nō'cently**. [L *nocēns*, *-entis*, pr p of *nocēre* to hurt]
nochel. See **notchel**.
nociceptive *nō-si-sep'tiv*, *adj* sensitive to pain; causing pain. [L *nocēre* to hurt, and re*ceptive*]
nock *nok*, *n* a notch, or a part carrying a notch, *esp* on an arrow or a bow; the forward upper end of a sail that sets with a boom. — *vt* to notch; to fit (an arrow) on the string of a bow. [Origin obscure, poss connected with Swed *nock* tip; appar not the same as **notch**]

nocket. See **nacket**.

noct- *nokt-* or **nocti-** *nok-ti-*, *combining form* denoting night. [L *nox*, *noct-*]

noctambulation *nok-tam-bū-lā'shən*, *n* sleep-walking. — *n* **noctam'bulism**. — *n* **noctam'bulist**. [L *nox*, *noctis* night, and *ambulāre*, *-ātum* to walk]

noctilio *nok-til'i-ō*, *n* any member of the S American genus *Noctilio*, the hare-lipped bat. [L *nox*, *noctis* night, and the ending of *vespertiliō* bat]

noctiluca *nok-ti-lōō'kə* or *-lū'*, *n* a member of the *Noctiluca* genus of phosphorescent marine flagellate infusorians, abundant around the British coasts: — *pl* **noctilu'cae** (*-sē*). [L *noctilūca* the moon, a lantern, from *nox*, *noctis* night, and *lūcēre* to shine]

noctilu'cent *nok-ti-lōō'sənt*, *adj* phosphorescent; glowing in the dark (*zool*); (of high-altitude dust- or ice-clouds) visible at night in latitudes greater than c.50°, where they reflect light from the sun below the horizon (*meteorol*). — Also **noctilu'cous** (*-kəs*). — *n* **nocti-lu'cence**. [L *nox*, *noctis* night, and *lūcēre* to shine]

noctivagant *nok-tiv'ə-gənt*, *adj* wandering in the night. — *n* **noctivagā'tion**. — *adj* **noctiv'agous**. [L *nox*, *noctis* night, and *vagārī* to wander]

Noctua *nok'tū-ə*, *n* a generic name sometimes used (without *cap*) as a general name for any member of the **Noctū'idae**, a large family (or group of families) of mostly nocturnal, strong-bodied moths, the owlet-moths. — *n* and *adj* **noc'tūid**. [L *noctua* an owl, from *nox*, *noctis* night]

noctuary *nok'tū-ə-ri*, *n* a record of the events or one's thoughts during the night. [L *nox*, *noctis* night, on the analogy of **diary**]

noctule *nok'tūl*, *n* the great bat, the largest British species. [Fr, from Ital *nottola*, from L *nox*, *noctis* night]

nocturn *nok'tûrn*, *n* (*RC*) any one of the three sections of the service of Matins; a daily portion of the psalter used at nocturns (*obs*). — *adj* **nocturn'al** belonging to night; happening, done, or active by night. — *n* an astronomical instrument for finding the time at night; a person, animal or spirit active by night. — *adv* **nocturn'ally**. — *n* **nocturne** (*nok'* or *-tûrn'*) a dreamy, romantic or pensive musical piece, generally for the piano, *esp* associated with the name of its inventor John Field (1782–1837) and Chopin, who developed it; a moonlight or night scene (*painting*). [L *nocturnus*, from *nox*, *noctis* night]

nocuous *nok'ū-əs*, (*rare*) *adj* hurtful, noxious. — *adv* **noc'uously**. — *n* **noc'uousness**. [L *nocuus*, from *nocēre* to hurt]

nod *nod*, *vi* to give a quick forward motion of the head, *esp* in assent, greeting or command; to let the head drop in weariness or dozing; to lean over as if about to fall; to bend or curve downward, or hang from a curved support; to dance, dip or bob up and down; to make a careless mistake through inattention. — *vt* to incline (the head); to move (the head) in assent, greeting or command; to signify or direct by a nod: — *pr p* **nodd'ing**; *pa t* and *pa p* **nodd'ed**. — *n* a quick bending forward of the head; a slight bow; a movement of the head as a gesture of assent, greeting or command; a nap. — *n* **nodd'er**. — *n* and *adj* **nodd'ing**. — *adv* **nodd'ingly**. — **nodding acquaintance** slight acquaintance; someone with whom one is only slightly acquainted; superficial, incomplete knowledge or understanding; **nodding donkey** (*colloq*; *esp US*) a type of pump for pumping oil from land-based oil-wells; **nodding duck** see under **duck**[3]. — **Land of Nod** sleep (in punning allusion to the biblical land, Gen 4. 16); **nod off** (*colloq*) to fall asleep; **nod through** in parliament, to allow to vote by proxy; to pass without discussion, a vote, etc; **on the nod** by general assent, ie without the formality of voting or without adequate scrutiny, etc; on credit (*slang*). [ME *nodde*, not known in OE]

nodal, etc. See under **node**.

nodded, **nodder** and **nodding**. See under **nod**.

noddle[1] *nod'l*, *n* the head (*slang*); the back of the head (*obs*); the nape of the neck (*dialect*). [Origin obscure]

noddle[2] *nod'l*, *vt* and *vi* to nod slightly; to keep nodding. [From **nod**]

noddy[1] *nod'i*, *n* a simpleton, a stupid person, a noodle; an oceanic bird (genus *Anous*) related to the terns, unaccustomed to man and therefore easily caught and so deemed stupid; an old game like cribbage; the knave in this and other games; an old form of cab with a door at the back. — **noddy suit** (*military slang*) an NBC suit. [Origin obscure; connection among meanings doubtful]

noddy[2] *nod'i*, *n* an inverted pendulum with a spring, used to test oscillation. [Perh from **nod**]

node *nōd*, *n* a knot; a knob or lump; a swelling; a place, often swollen, where a leaf is attached to a stem; a point of intersection of two great circles of the celestial sphere, *esp* the orbit of a planet or the moon and the ecliptic (*astron*); a point at which a curve cuts itself, and through which more than one tangent to the curve can be drawn (*geom*); a similar point on a surface, where there is more than one tangent-plane (*geom*); a point of minimum displacement in a system of stationary waves (*phys*); the point in an electrical network where two or more conductors are connected (*elec eng*); a point of intersection or junction in any branching system; a complication in a story (*fig*); a nodus. — *adj* **nō'dal** of or like a node or nodes. — *n* **nōdal'ity** knottedness; state of being nodal. — *vt* **nōd'alize** or **-ise** to make nodal. — *adv* **nō'dally**. — *adj* **nōd'āted** knotted. — *n* **nōdā'tion** knottiness; a knotty place. — *adj* **nodical** (*nōd'* or *nod'*) relating to the nodes of a celestial body; from a node round to the same node again. — *adj* **nodose** (*nōd-ōs'* or *nōd'ōs*) having nodes, knots or swellings; knotty. — *n* **nodosity** (*nō-dos'i-ti*) knottiness; a knotty swelling. — *adj* **nōd'ous** knotty. — *adj* **nodular** (*nod'ū-lər*) of or like a nodule; in the form of nodules; having nodules or little knots. — *adj* **nod'ulāted** having nodules. — *n* **nodūlā'tion**. — *n* **nod'ūle** a little rounded lump or swelling; a swelling on a root inhabited by symbiotic bacteria (*bot*); a nodus. — *adj* **nod'ūled**. — *adj* **nod'ūlose** or **nod'ūlous**. — *n* **nōd'us** (*L*) a knotty point, difficulty, complication; a knotlike mass of tissue or cells, swelling or knoblike protuberance (*anatom*); a swelling at the junction of nervures in an insect's wing: — *pl* **nōd'i** (*-ī*). [L *nōdus* knot; dimin *nōdulus*]

Noel or **Noël** *nō-el'*, *n* Christmas (also **Nowel** or **Nowell**; *obs* except in Christmas carols, on Christmas cards, etc); (without *cap*) a Christmas carol. [OFr (Fr *noël*; cf Sp *natal*, Ital *natale*), from L *natalis* belonging to a birthday]

noesis *nō-ē'sis*, *n* the activity of the intellect; purely intellectual apprehension or perception (*philos*). — *adj* **noemat'ical**. — *adv* **noemat'ically**. — *adj* **noetic** (*nō-et'ik*) of or relating to the mind or intellect; purely intellectual. [Gr *noēsis*, from *noeein* to perceive or think]

Noetian *nō-ē'shən*, *n* a Patripassian or follower of *Noëtus* of Smyrna (3c). — Also *adj*. — *n* **Noe'tianism**.

nog[1] *nog*, *n* egg-nog or a similar drink; Norwich strong ale (*obs*). — Also **nogg**. [Origin unknown]

nog[2] *nog*, *n* a stump or snag; a wooden peg, pin or cog; a brick-sized piece of wood inserted in a wall to receive nails. — *vt* to fix with nogs; to build with nogging: — *pr p* **nogg'ing**; *pa p* and *pa t* **nogged**. — *n* **nogg'ing** a brick or piece of rough timber filling between timbers in a partition or frame. [Origin unknown]

nogaku. See **no**[4].

nogg. See **nog**[1].

noggin *nog'in*, *n* a small mug or wooden cup; its contents, a measure of about a gill; a drink (of beer, spirits, etc) (*colloq*); the head (*colloq*). [Origin unknown; Ir *noigín*, Gaelic *noigean*, are believed to be from English]

nogging. See under **nog**[2].

noh. See **no**[4].

nohow *nō'how*, (*colloq*) *adv* not in any way, not at all; in no definable way. — *adj* (also **no'howish**) out of sorts.

noils *noilz*, *n pl* short pieces of wool or other fibre separated from the longer fibres eg by combing. — Also *n sing* **noil** the wool or other fibre so separated. [Origin unknown]

noint or **'noint**. An aphetic form of **anoint**.

noise (*Spenser* **noyes**) *noiz*, *n* sound of any kind; an unmusical sound; (an) over-loud or disturbing sound; din; (in *pl*) sounds made expressing sympathy, a reaction, feelings, etc without actual words; frequent or public talk; interference in the transference of heat, in an electrical current, etc; interference in a communication channel, as detected by hearing or (**visual noise**, eg snow on a television screen) sight; meaningless extra bits or words removed from data, or ignored, at the time of use (*comput*); rumour (*obs*); report (*Shakesp*); a band of musicians (*obs*). — *vt* (*literary*; *usu* with *about* or *abroad*) to spread by rumour or word of mouth. — *vi* to talk or call out loud (*rare*). — *adj* **noise'ful**. — *adj* **noise'less**. — *adv* **noise'lessly**. — *n* **noise'lessness**. — *adv* **nois'ily**. — *n* **nois'iness**. — *adj* **nois'y** making a loud noise or sound; accompanied by noise; clamorous; turbulent. — **noise abatement climb procedure** (*aeronautics*) the flying of a civil aircraft so that it climbs rapidly on take-off until reaching the built-up area, where it maintains a positive rate of climb until the area is overflown or it reaches 5000 ft; **noise control** (*acoustics*) reduction of unwanted noise by various methods, eg absorption or isolation; **noise'-maker** (*esp NAm*) a device for making a loud noise at a football match, festivity, etc, such as a clapper; **noise pollution** annoying or harmful (loud) noise. — **a big** or (*rare*) **a top noise** a person of great importance; **make a noise** to talk or complain a lot; **make a noise in the world** to achieve great notoriety; **noises off** (a stage direction indicating) sounds made off-stage to be heard by the audience. [Fr *noise* noise; perh from L *nausea* disgust, poss influenced by L *noxia*, in its (albeit disputed) meaning, disturbance or strife]

noisette[1] *nwa-zet'*, *n* a hybrid between China rose and musk-rose. [From Philippe *Noisette*, its first grower]

noisette[2] *nwa-zet'*, *n* a small piece of meat (*usu* lamb) cut off the bone and rolled; a nutlike or nut-flavoured sweet. — *adj* flavoured with or containing hazelnuts. [Fr, hazelnut]

noisome *noi'səm*, *adj* harmful to health; disgusting or offensive to sight or smell. — *adv* **noi'somely**. — *n* **noi'someness**. [**noy**]

noisy. See **noise**.

nole (*Shakesp*). See **noll**.

nolens volens *nō'lenz vō'lenz* or *nō'lāns vō'*, or *wō'lāns* (*L*; unwilling, willing) *adv* willy-nilly.

noli-me-tangere *nō-li-mē-tan'jə-ri*, (**noli me tangere** *nō-lē mā tang'ge-re*; from the Vulgate, John 20. 17) *n* a warning against touching; lupus, etc of the face (*archaic*); a species of balsam, *Impatiens noli-(me-) tangere*, that ejects its ripe seeds at a light touch; a work of art showing Christ appearing to Mary Magdelene after the Resurrection. — *adj* warning off. [L *nōlī* (imperative of *nōlle*) be unwilling, do not, *mē* me, and *tangere* to touch]

nolition *nō-lish'ən*, *n* unwillingness; absence of willingness; a will not to do. [L *nōlle* to be unwilling]

noll, **noul** or **nowl** (*Spenser* **noule**, *Shakesp* **nole**) *nōl*, *n* the top of the head. [OE *hnoll*]

nolle prosequi *no'le pros'ə-kwī*, (*L*; *law*) (an entry on a record to the effect that) the plaintiff or prosecutor will proceed no further with (part of) the suit.

nolo contendere *nō'lō kon-ten'də-ri*, (*L*) (literally) I do not wish to contend; a legal plea by which the accused does not admit guilt, but accepts conviction (eg when wishing to avoid lengthy legal proceedings), the charges being deniable if referred to in a separate case.

nolo episcopari *nō'lō e-pis-ko-pär'ī*, (*L*) (literally) I do not wish to be a bishop; refusal of responsible position.

nom *nɔ̃*, (*Fr*) *n* name. — **nom de guerre** (*də ger*) an assumed name; a pseudonym; **nom de plume** (see separate entry) is not French.

nom. or **nomin**. *abbrev*: nominal; nominative.

noma *nō'mə*, *n* a destructive ulceration of the cheek, *esp* that affecting hunger-weakened children. [L *nomē* ulcer, from Gr *nomē* ulcer, feeding, from *nemein* to feed, consume]

nomad or (*rare*) **nomade** *nōm'ad* or *-əd*, also *nom'*, *n* a member of a wandering pastoral community; a rover, wanderer. — Also *adj*. — **nomadic** (*nōm-* or *nom-ad'ik*). — *adv* **nomad'ically**. — *n* **nom'adism**. — *n* **nomadizā'tion** or **-s-**. — *vi* **nom'adize** or **-ise** to lead a nomadic or vagabond life. — *vt* to make nomadic, force into a nomadic life. — *adj* **nom'ady** living as or like a nomad. [Gr *nomas*, *nomados*, from *nemein* to drive to pasture]

nomarch and **nomarchy**. See under **nome**.

nombles *num'blz*. A variant of **numbles** (see under **umbles**).

nombril *nom'bril*, (*heraldry*) *n* a point a little below the centre of a shield. [Fr, navel]

nom de plume *nɔ̃ də plüm'* or *plōōm'*, also *nom*, *n* a pen-name, pseudonym. [Would-be Fr, from Fr *nom* name, *de* of, and *plume* pen]

nome *nōm*, *n* a province or department, *esp* in ancient Egypt or modern Greece. — *n* **nomarch** (*nom'ärk*) the governor of a nome. — *n* **nom'archy** a nome of modern Greece. — *n* **nom'os** (*Gr*) a nome: — *pl* **nomoi** (*nō'moi*). [Gr *nomos*]

nomen *nō'men*, (*L*) *n* a name, *esp* of the *gens* or clan, a Roman's second name, such as Gaius *Julius* Caesar: — *pl* **nō'mina**. — **nomen nudum** (*nū'dəm* or *nōō'dōōm*) in biology, a mere name published without a description.

nomenclator *nō'mən-klā-tər*, *n* a person who bestows names, or draws up a classified scheme of names; a person who announces a list of names of people, *esp* (*hist*) in canvassing for a Roman election; a book containing a list of words, a vocabulary (*obs*). — *adj* **no'menclātive**, **nomenclatorial** (*nō-men-klə-tō'ri-əl* or *-tö'*) or **nomenclā'tural**. — *n* **nomenclature** (or *nō-men'klə-chər* or *nō'mən-klā-chər*) a system of names; terminology; a list of names; a vocabulary (*obs*); an act or instance of naming, *esp* within a particular system; (now considered *loose*) a name. [L *nōmenclātor*, from *nōmen* a name, and *calāre* to call]

nomenklatura *no-men'klə-tū-rə*, (*usu derog*) *n* office-holders and managers in a communist regime (*esp* formerly in E Europe). [Russ]

nomic *nom'ik*, *adj* customary; (*esp* of spelling) conventional. [Gr *nomikos*, from *nomos* custom]

-nomic. See under **-nomy**.

nominal *nom'in-əl*, *adj* relating to or of the nature of a name or noun; of names; by name; only in name; so-called, but not in reality; inconsiderable, small, minor, in comparison with the real value, hardly more than a matter of form; nominalistic (*rare*); according to plan (*space flight*). — *n* (*gram*) a noun or phrase etc, standing as a noun. — *n* **nom'inalism** the doctrine that the objects to which general terms refer are related to one another only by the terms. — *n* and *adj* **nom'inalist**. — *adj* **nominalist'ic**. — *n* **nominaliza'tion** or **-s-**. — *vt* **nom'inalize** or **-ise** to form a noun (eg from a verb). — *adv* **nom'inally** in name only; by name; as a noun. — **nominal par** see under **par[1]**; **nominal value** same as **nominal par**. [L *nōminālis*, from *nōmen*, *-inis* a name]

nominate *nom'in-āt*, *vt* to propose formally for election; to appoint; to name; to mention by name; to designate. — *adj* (chiefly *Scots law*) nominated; elect. — *adj* **nom'inable** namable; fit to be named. — *adv* **nom'inately** by name. — *n* **nominā'tion** the act or power of nominating; state or privilege of being nominated; naming; (in horse breeding) the arranged mating of a mare with a stallion. — *adj* **nominatival** (*nom-in-ə-tī'vl* or *nom-nə-*). — *adv* **nominatī'vally**. — *adj* **nominative** (*nom'in-ə-tiv* or *nom'nə-tiv*) naming the subject (*gram*); (in the case) in which the subject is expressed (*gram*); (also *nom'in-ā-tiv*) nominated, appointed by nomination (not elected). — *n* the nominative case; a word in the nominative case. — *adv* **nom'inatively**. — *n* **nom'inātor** a person who nominates. — **nominative absolute** (*gram*) a nominative combined with a participle, but not connected with a finite verb or governed by any other word. [L *nōmināre*, *-ātum* to name, from *nōmen*]

nominee *nom-in-ē'*, *n* a person who is nominated by another; a person who acts on behalf of another person, *esp* to keep that person's identity hidden; a person on whose life an annuity or lease depends; a person in whose name stocks and shares, etc are registered, but who is not the actual owner of them; a person to whom the holder of a copyhold estate surrenders his or her interest (*obs*). [L *nōmināre*, *-ātum* to nominate, with *-ee* as if from Fr]

nomism *nōm'izm* or *nom'izm*, *n* religious legalism; the view that moral conduct consists in the observance of a law. — *adj* **nomist'ic** (*nom-*) based on law or on a sacred book. [Gr *nomisma* established custom, from *nomos* a law]

nomo- *nom-o-* or *nōm-o*, *combining form* denoting custom or law. [Gr *nomos* law]

nomocracy *nom-ok'rə-si* or *nōm-*, *n* government according to a code of laws. [Gr *nomos* law, and *kratos* power]

nomogeny *nom-* or *nōm-oj'ə-ni*, *n* the origination of life according to natural law, not miracle (*opp* to *thaumatogeny*). [Gr *nomos* law, and the root *gen-*, as in *genesis* origination]

nomography *nom-* or *nōm-og'rə-fi*, *n* the art of making nomograms. — *n* **nomog'rapher**. — *n* **nom'ogram** or **nom'ograph** a chart or diagram of scaled lines or curves used to help in mathematical calculations, comprising three scales in which a line joining values on two determines a third. — Also called **isopleth**. — *adj* **nomograph'ic** or **nomograph'ical**. — *adv* **nomograph'ically**. [Gr *nomos* law, and *graphein* to write]

nomology *nom-* or *nōm-ol'ə-ji*, *n* the science of law; the science of the laws of the mind; the science of the laws explaining or dealing with natural phenomena. — *adj* **nomological** (*-ə-loj'*). — *n* **nomol'ogist**. [Gr *nomos* law, and *logos* discourse]

nomos. See under **nome**.

nomothete *nom'ō-thēt* or (*Gr*) **nomothetes** (*nom-oth'i-tēz*), *n* a lawgiver; a legislator; (in ancient Athens) a member of a body charged with revision of the laws. — *adj* **nomothetic** (*-thet'ik*) or **nomothet'ical** giving laws, legislative; of or relating to the formulation of general or universal laws (*opp* to *idiographic*). [Gr *nomothetēs*, from *nomos* law, and the root *the-*, as in *tithenai* to set]

-nomy *-nə-mi*, *combining form* denoting a science or field of knowledge, or the discipline of the study of these. — *combining form* **-nom'ic** forming corresponding adjectives. [Gr *-nomia* administration, regulation]

non *non* or *nōn*, (*L*) not. — **non compos mentis** (*non kom'pos men'tis*) not of sound mind; **non licet** (*non lī'sit*) literally, it is not allowed; not permitted, unlawful (*law*); **non liquet** (*non lī'kwit*) literally, it is not clear; (of evidence, etc) unclear (*law*); **non multa, sed multum** (*non mo͝ol'tä, sed mo͝ol'to͞om*) not many but much; not great in number but great in signficance; **non obstante** (*ob-stan'tē* or *ob-stan'te*) not hindering; notwithstanding; **non placet** (*non plas'it*) literally, it does not please; a negative note.

non- *non*, *pfx* denoting not, absence of, reverse of (often when a form in *in-* or *un-* has a special meaning, or sometimes instead of *un-*); sometimes used of someone or something with pretensions, who or which is ludicrously unworthy of the name mentioned, eg **non'-hero** and **non'-event**; the words given below, or listed in the separate panel, include the most common words with *non-* but the prefix is living and many other words using it may be formed. — *n* **non-abil'ity** incapacity; inability. — *n* **non-accept'ance** lack of acceptance; refusal to accept. — *n* **non-ac'cess** (*law*) lack of opportunity for sexual intercourse. — *n* **non-accidental injury** (*social work*) an injury such as a bruise, burn or fracture, *esp* to a child, which was not caused by an accident but was deliberately inflicted by another (older) person. — *n* **non-admiss'ion** refusal of admission; failure to be admitted. — *n* **non-aggress'ion** abstention from aggression (also *adj*). — *adj* **non-aligned'** not aligned geometrically; not taking sides in international politics, *esp* not supporting either of the main international blocs, ie the former Warsaw Pact countries or the USA and the western European democracies. — *n* **non-align'ment**. — *n* **non-appear'ance** failure or neglect to appear, *esp* in a court of law. — *n* **non-atten'tion** inattention. — *adj* **non-attrib'utable** (of a press statement, etc) whose source is not able or permitted to be disclosed. — *adv* **non-attrib'utably**. — *n* **non-bearing wall** a wall bearing no load other than its own weight. — *n* **non-Chris'tian** a person who is not a Christian (also *adj*). — *adj* **non-chromosō'mal** not found on a chromosome; not involving chromosomes. — *n* **non'-claim** a failure to make claim within the time limited by law. — *adj* **non-class'ified** (of information) not classified secret. — *adj* **non-cog'nizable** (*law*) (of an offence) that cannot be judicially investigated. — *adj* **non-collē'giate** not belonging to a college or not having colleges (also *n*). — *n* **non-com'** (*colloq*) a non-commissioned officer. — *n* **non-com'batant** anyone connected with an army who is there for some purpose other than that of fighting, such as a surgeon or a chaplain; a civilian in time of war. — *adj* **non-comedogen'ic** (of cosmetics) not blocking the pores or causing spots or blackheads. — *adj* **non-commiss'ioned** not having a commission, as an officer in the army below the rank of commissioned officer or warrant officer. — *adj* **non-committ'al** not committing someone,

Some words with **non-** prefix.

non-abrā'sive *adj*.	**non-comply'ing** *adj*.	**non-marr'ying** *adj*.
non-absor'bent *adj*.	**non-conclu'sive** *adj*.	**non-mem'ber** *n*.
non-academ'ic *adj*.	**non-contā'gious** *adj*.	**non-nat'ural** *adj*.
non-access'ible *adj*.	**non-controver'sial** *adj*.	**non-obser'vance** *n*.
non-addic'tive *adj*.	**non-curr'ent** *adj*.	**non-operā'tional** *adj*.
non-admin'istrative *adj*.	**non-deliv'ery** *n*.	**non-pay'ment** *n*.
non-alcohol'ic *adj*.	**non-drink'er** *n*.	**non-poi'sonous** *adj*.
non-aller'gic *adj*.	**non-drī'ver** *n*.	**non-rā'cial** *adj*.
non-arri'val *n*.	**non-elect'** *adj*.	**non-read'er** *n*.
non-atten'dance *n*.	**non-elec'tion** *n*.	**non-scientif'ic** *n*.
non-automat'ic *adj* and *n*.	**non-essen'tial** *adj* and *n*.	**non-sex'ist** *adj*.
non-believ'er *n*.	**non-exis'tence** *n*.	**non-sol'uble** *adj*.
non-bellig'erency *n*.	**non-exis'tent** *adj*.	**non-swimm'er** *n*.
non-bellig'erent *adj* and *n*.	**non-flow'ering** *adj*.	**non-tech'nical** *adj*.
non-biolog'ical *adj*.	**non-func'tional** *adj*.	**non-tox'ic** *adj*.
non-break'able *adj*.	**non-fulfil'ment** *n*.	**non-vin'tage** *adj*.
non-clin'ical *adj*.	**non-harmon'ic** *adj*.	**non-vol'atile** *adj*.
non-commer'cial *adj*.	**non-invol'vement** *n*.	**non-vot'er** *n*.
non-complī'ance *n*.	**non-lin'ear** *adj*.	

or refraining from committing oneself, to any particular opinion or course of conduct; free from any declared preference or pledge; implying nothing, one way or the other, for or against. — *adv* **non-committ'ally**. — *n* a non-committal state or utterance. — *n* **non-commun'icant** a person who does not take communion on any particular occasion or in general, *esp* formerly according to the rites of the Church of England; a person who has not yet communicated. — *n* **non-commun'ion**. — *n* **non-compear'ance** (*Scots law*) failure to appear in a court of law. — *n* **non-compound'er** a person who does not compound or make composition; a Jacobite in favour of restoring James II unconditionally (*hist*). — *n* **non-con'** (*colloq*) a Nonconformist (also *adj*). — *n* **non-concurr'ence** refusal to concur. — *adj* **non-concurr'ent**. — *adj* **non-conduct'ing** not readily conducting, *esp* heat or electricity. — *n* **non-conduct'or** a substance or object that does not readily conduct heat or electricity. — *n* **non-conform'ance**. — *adj* **nonconform'ing** not conforming, *esp* to an established church. — *n* **nonconform'ist** a person who does not conform (*esp* a person who refused to conform or subscribe to the Act of Uniformity in 1662 making the Book of Common Prayer the only legal form of worship in England); *usu* applied in England (with *cap*) to a Protestant separated from the Church of England (also *adj*). — *n* **nonconform'ity** lack of conformity, *esp* to the established church. — *n* **non'-content** a person who is not content; (in the House of Lords) a person casting a negative vote. — *adj* **non-conten'tious** not subject to contention. — *adj* **non-contrib'utory** (of pensions) paid for entirely by the employer, with no contributions from the beneficiary; (of state benefit) not dependent on national insurance contributions paid by the beneficiary. — *n* **non-co-operā'tion** failure or refusal to co-operate, *esp* (in India before 1947) with the government. — *adj* **non-custō'dial** (of a legal sentence) not involving imprisonment. — *adj* **non-dai'ry** (of foods) containing no dairy produce. — *adj* **non-denominā'tional** not exclusively belonging to or according to the beliefs of any single denomination of the Christian church. — **nondescript** see separate entry. — *adj* **non-destruc'tive** having no destructive effect, *esp* of tests on products, substances or organisms. — **non-destructive testing** the testing of structures, metals, etc for flaws without impairing their quality. — *n* **nondisjunc'tion** (*biol*) the failure of paired chromosomes to separate during meiosis. — *adj* **non-divid'ing** (of a cell) not undergoing division. — *adj* **non-drip'** (of paint) thixotropic, of such a consistency that it does not drip when being applied. — *adj* **non-effect'ive** (*military*) having no effect; not efficient or serviceable; unfit or unavailable for service; relating to those who are unfit or unavailable. — *n* a member of a force who is unfit or unavailable for active service. — *adj* **non-effi'cient** not up to the standard required for service. — *n* a soldier who has not yet undergone the full number of drills. — *n* **non-e'go** (*metaphys*) the not-I, the object as opposed to the subject, whatever is not the conscious self. — *adj* **non-elec'tive** not chosen by election. — *adj* **non-elec'tric** (*obs*) conducting electricity. — *n* (*obs*) a conductor. — *n* **non-elec'trolyte** a substance, such as sugar, that gives a non-conducting solution. — *n* **non-en'try** (*Scots law*; *hist*) a vassal's heir's failure to renew investiture; a payment that was due to the superior on such failure. — *adj* **non-Euclid'ean** not according to Euclid's axioms and postulates. — *n* **non-event** see above at **non**. — *adj* **non-exec'utive** (of eg directors) not employed by a company full-time, but brought in for advisory purposes (also *n*). — *adj* **non-fat'** (of food) having had the fat removed. — **non-feasance** see separate entry. — *adj* **non-ferr'ous** containing no iron; not iron; relating to metals other than iron. — *adj* **non-fic'tion** (of a literary work) without any deliberately fictitious element, purely factual (**non-fiction novel** one whose material is entirely drawn from people and events in real life). — Also *n*. — *adj* **non-fic'tional**. — **non-flam film** acetate film. — *adj* **non-flamm'able** not easily set on fire; not flammable. — *adj* **non-for'feiting** (of a life insurance policy) not forfeited by reason of non-payment. — *n* **non-gre'mial** a non-resident member, *esp* of Cambridge University. — *adj* applied to the examinations now called *local*. — *n* **non-hero** see above at **non-**. — **non-homologous pairing** (*biol*) pairing between regions of non-homologous chromosomes, sometimes involving short stretches of similar, possibly repetitive, sequences. — *n* **non-interven'tion** a policy of systematic abstention from interference in the affairs of other nations. — *n* **non-intru'sion** (in Scottish Church history) the principle that a patron should not force an unacceptable minister on an unwilling congregation. — *n* and *adj* **non-intru'sionist**. — *adj* **non-invā'sive** (of medical treatment) not involving surgery or the insertion of instruments, etc into the patient. — *adj* **non-ion'ic** not forming ions. — *n pl* **non-ionic detergents** a series of detergents in which the molecules do not ionize in aqueous solution, unlike soap. — *adj* **non-i'ron** (of clothes or fabric) not needing ironing after washing. — *adj* **non-iss'uable** not capable of being issued; which one cannot dispute or take issue with. — *n* **non-join'der** (*law*) omission to join all the parties to an action or suit. — *adj* **non-judgemen'tal** or **non-judgmen'tal** relating to or having an open attitude without implicit judgement, *esp* moral. — *adv* **non-judgemen'tally** or **non-judgmen'tally**. — *adj* **nonjur'ing** not swearing allegiance. — *n* **nonjur'or** a person who refuses to swear allegiance, *esp* (with *cap*) a member of the clergy in England and Scotland who would not swear allegiance to William and Mary in 1689, holding themselves still bound by the oath they had taken to the deposed king, James II. — *adj* **non-lē'thal** (of eg aid to developing countries) not involving or including lethal or dangerous items, *esp* weapons. — *n* **non'-met'al** an element that is not a metal. — Also *adj*. — *adj* **non-metall'ic** not metallic; not of metal or like metal. — *adj* **non-mor'al** unconcerned with morality; involving no moral considerations. — *adj* **non-nat'ural** not natural; forced or strained. — *n* (*usu* in *pl*) in old medicine, anything not considered of the essence of man, but necessary to his wellbeing, such as air, food, sleep, rest, etc. — *adj* **non-negō'tiable** (of eg prices) not open to negotiation. — *adj* **non-net'** (of a book) without a price fixed by the publisher, but with one which is determined by each bookseller selling that book. — *adj* **non-nu'cleated** not nucleated. — *adj* **non-objec'tive** (*painting*) non-representational. — **nonpareil** see separate entry. — *adj* **nonpar'ous** not having given birth. — *adj* **non-partic'ipating** not taking part; (of shares, etc) not giving the holder the right to a share in profits. — *adj* **non-partisan'** (or *-pärt'*) not partisan; impartial. — *adj* **non-par'ty** independent of party politics. — *adj* **non-pathogen'ic** not causing disease. — *n* **non-perform'ance** neglect or failure to perform. — *adj* **non-persis'tent** (of eg insecticides and pesticides) decomposing rapidly after application and not lingering in the environment. — *n* **non'-per'son** a person previously of political, etc eminence, now out of favour; a complete nonentity. — *adj* **non-play'ing** (of eg the captain of a team) not taking an active part in the game(s). — **nonplus** see separate entry. — *adj* **nonpo'lar** without any permanent electric dipole moment. — *adj* **non-prior'ity** without privilege of priority. — *n* **non-produc'tion**. — *adj* **non-produc'tive** not producing the goods, results, etc required; not directly concerned in production. — *adj* **non-profess'ional** not professional or of a profession; not done in a professional capacity. — *n* **non-profi'cient** a person who has made no progress in the art or study in which he or she is engaged. — *adj* **non-prof'it-making** not organized or engaged in with the purpose of making a profit. — *n* **non-proliferā'tion** lack of proliferation, *esp* a limit imposed on the proliferation of (*usu* nuclear) weapons. — *adj* **non-provi'ded** (of an elementary school or education in England and Wales) maintained but not provided by the local education authority, and managed by a committee in which the trustees form the majority. — *adj* **non-quo'ta** not included in a quota. — *n* **non-regard'ance** (*Shakesp*) lack of due regard. — *adj* **non-representā'tional** (*painting*) not aiming at the realistic depiction of objects. — *n* **non-res'idence** the fact of not (permanently or for the moment) residing at a place, *esp* where one's official or social duties require one to reside or where one is entitled to reside. — *adj* and *n* **non-res'ident**. — *n* **non-resist'ance** the principle of not resisting violence by force, or of not resisting authority; passive submission. — *adj* **non-resist'ant** or **non-resist'ing**. — *adj* **non-restric'tive** (*gram*) used of a relative clause that does not restrict the people or things to which its antecedent may refer. — *adj* **non-return'able** (of a bottle, jar or other container) on which a returnable deposit has not been paid. — **non-return valve** a valve incorporating a device to prevent flow in one direction. — *adj* **non-rig'id** (of airships) having a balloon or gasbag with no internal framework to brace it, and no rigid keel. — *adj* **non-sched'uled** not according to a schedule; (of an airline) operating between specified points but not to a specific schedule of flights. — **nonsense** see separate entry. — *n* **non-se'quence** (*geol*) a break in the stratigraphical record, deduced generally on palaeontological evidence. — *adj* **non-skid'** or **non-slip'** (of a surface) designed to reduce chance of slipping to a minimum. — *n* **non-smo'ker** a person who does not smoke; a railway compartment in which smoking is forbidden. — *adj* **non-smok'ing**. — *adj* **non-soci'ety** not belonging to a society, *esp* not a member of a trade union; employing people who are not members of a trade union. — *adj* **non-spec'ialist** not devoting oneself to one particular subject, task, etc. — Also *n*. — *adj* **non-specif'ic** not specific; (of a disease) not caused by any specific, identifiable, agent. — **non-specific immunity** mechanisms that protect against non-microbial invasion of the body, including physical barriers (eg skin, mucous membranes) and enzyme inhibitors. — *adj* **non-stan'dard** not standard; (of language, vocabulary, etc) different to the usage of educated speakers, and (by some) not considered correct. — *n* **non-start'er** a horse which, though entered for a race, does not run; a person, idea, etc with no chance at all of success. — *adj* **non-stick'** (of eg a pan) treated so that food or other substance will not stick to it. — *adj* and *adv* **non-stop'** uninterrupted(ly); without any stop or halt. — **nonsuit** see separate entry. — *n* **non'-term** (*obs*) a vacation between terms; a time of inactivity. — *n* **non-thing'** something which does not exist; something trivial. — **non-U** see under **U**. — *adj* **non-u'nion** not attached to a trade union; not approved of by a union; employing, or produced by, non-union workers. — *n* **non-u'nionist**. — *n* **non-u'sager** (*hist*) a Nonjuror who rejected the usages. — *n* **non-u'ser** (*law*) omission to take advantage of a right. — *adj* **non-util'ity** not of the special kind made or sold for utility's sake. — *adj* **non-ver'bal** (of communication) not using or involving words, but using eg gesture instead. — *n* **non-vi'olence** (the ideal or practice of) refraining from violence on grounds of principle. — *adj* **non-vi'olent**. — **non-volatile memory** (*comput*) a type of memory that retains data even if the power is disconnected. — *adj* **non-vo'ting** not voting; (of shares, etc) not giving the holder the right to vote on company decisions. — *n* **non-white'** (a member of) a race other than the white race (also *adj*). [L *nōn* not]

nonage *non'ij* or *nōn'ij*, *n* legal infancy, minority; time of immaturity generally. — *adj* **non'aged**. [OFr *nonage*, from pfx *non-* (L *nōn*) and *age* age]

nonagenarian *nōn-* or *non-ə-ji-nā'ri-ən*, *n* a person who is ninety years old or between ninety and a hundred. — *adj* of that age. [L *nōnāgēnārius* relating to ninety, from *nōnāgintā* ninety]

nonagesimal *nōn-* or *non-ə-jes'i-məl*, *adj* ninetieth. — *n* the point of the ecliptic 90° from its intersection by the horizon. [L *nōnāgēsimus* ninetieth]

nonagon *non'ə-gon*, *n* a nine-sided geometrical figure. — *adj* **nonag'onal**. [L *nōnus* ninth, and Gr *gōniā* angle]

nonane *nōn'ān*, *n* a hydrocarbon (C_9H_{20}), ninth in the methane series. — **nonanoic acid** same as **pelargonic acid** (qv under **pelargonium**). [L *nōnus* ninth]

nonary *nōn'ə-ri*, *adj* (of a mathematical system) based on nine. [L *nōnārius*]

nonce[1] *nons*, *n* (almost confined to the phrase *for the nonce*, which in ME is sometimes a mere tag for rhyme's sake) the occasion; the moment, time being; the particular or express purpose (*Shakesp*). — *adj* (of a word or expression) occurring, adopted or coined for a particular occasion only. [From *for the nones*, ie *for then ones* for the once, *then* being the dative (OE *tham*) of **the** and *ones* the genitive (OE *ānes*) of **one** substituted for the dative]

nonce[2] *nons*, (*prison slang*) *n* a sexual offender, *esp* one who assaults children. [Ety uncertain]

nonchalance *non'shə-ləns*, *n* unconcern; coolness; indifference. — *adj* **non'chalant**. — *adv* **non'chalantly**. [Fr, from *non* not, and *chaloir* to matter, interest, from L *calēre* to be warm]

non-come *non-kum'* or *-kom'*, (*Shakesp*) *n* one of Dogberry's blundering words, *perh* a confusion of *nonplus* and *non compos mentis*.

non compos mentis. See under **non**[2].

nonconformist and **nonconformity**. See under **non**[1].

nondescript *non'di-skript*, *adj* not easily classified; not distinctive enough to be described, featureless (*derog*); neither one thing nor another; not described (*obs*). — *n* a featureless person or thing, or one not easily described. — *adv* **non'descriptly**. — *n* **non'descriptness**. [L *nōn* not, and *dēscrībere*, *-scrīptum* to describe]

none *nun*, *pron* (*pl* or *sing*) not one; no person or people; not the thing in question; not any; no portion or amount. — *adj* (separated from the noun; otherwise *archaic*; formerly *esp* before a vowel or *h*) no, not any. — *adv* in no degree; by no means; not at all. — **none'-so-prett'y** or **Nan'cy-prett'y** the hardy perennial plant London Pride (*Saxifraga umbrosa*). — *adj* **none'-spar'ing** (*Shakesp*) all-destroying. — *adv* **nonetheless'** (or **none the less**) nevertheless. — **none other** (often with *than*) no other person; **none the** (followed by *compar adj*) in no way, to no degree; **none too** (*colloq*) not very. [OE *nān*, from *ne* not, and *ān* one]

nonentity *non-en'ti-ti*, *n* a person or thing of no importance (*derog*); the state of not being; a thing which does not exist; [L *nōn* not, and *entitās* (see **entity**)]

Nones *nōnz*, *n pl* in the Roman calendar, the ninth day before the Ides (both days included), ie the 7th of March, May, July and October, and the 5th of the other months; (without *cap*) a church service originally held at the ninth hour, or three o'clock, afterwards earlier. [L *nōnae*, from *nōnus* ninth]

nonesuch or **nonsuch** *non'* or *nun'such*, *n* a unique, unparalleled or extraordinary thing (*archaic*); the plant black medick. [**none** and **such**]

nonet or (*rare*) **nonette** *nō-net'*, (*music*) *n* a composition for nine performers. — Also **nonet'to**: — *pl* **nonet'tos** or **nonet'ti** (*-tē*). [Ital *nonetto*]

non-feasance *non-fē'zəns*, (*law*) *n* omission of something which ought to be or have been done. [Pfx *non-* not, and OFr *faisance* doing, from *faire*, from L *facere* to do]

nong *nong*, (*Austr* and *NZ slang*) *n* a fool, idiot. [Origin uncertain]

nonillion *nō-nil'yən*, *n* a million raised to the ninth power, one followed by 54 zeros; one thousand raised to the tenth power, one followed by 30 zeros (*NAm*). — *adj* **nonill'ionth**. [L *nōnus* ninth, in imitation of **million** and **billion**]

nonjuring, etc. See under **non-**.

non licet, **non liquet** and **non multa, sed multum**. See under **non**.

nonny *non'i*, *n* a meaningless word in old ballad refrain, etc, *usu* 'hey, nonny', 'hey nonny nonny' or 'hey nonny no', once a cover for obscenity.

no-no. See under **no**[1].

non obstante. See under **non**[2].

nonpareil *non-pə-rel'* or *-rāl'*, also *non'*, *n* a person or thing without equal; a fine variety of apple; a kind of confectionery; an old type size, approximately, and still used synonymously for, six-point (*printing*). — *adj* unequalled; matchless. [Fr *non* not, and *pareil*, from a LL dimin of L *pār* equal]

non placet. See under **non**[2].

nonplus *nonplus'*, *vt* to perplex completely, make uncertain what to say or do: — *pr p* **nonpluss'ing** (or *US* **nonplus'ing**); *pa t* and *pa p* **nonplussed'** (or *US* **nonplused'**). — *n* a state in which no more can be done or said; great difficulty; perplexity. — *adj* **nonplussed'** (or *US* **nonplused'**). [L *nōn* not, and *plūs* more]

nonsense *non'səns*, *n* anything which makes no sense; language without meaning; absurdity, foolishness; trifling; humbug; trivial things; something which is manifestly false; an absurd, illogical or unintelligible statement or action. — Also *interj*. — *adj* **nonsensical** (*-sens'*) without sense; absurd; (of a word, syllable, etc) consisting of an arbitrary group of sounds and having no meaning. — *n* **nonsensicality** (*non-sens-i-kal'i-ti*), or **nonsens'icalness**. — *adv* **nonsens'ically**. — **nonsense verse** verse deliberately written to convey an absurd meaning, or without obvious meaning at all. — **no-nonsense** see under **no**[2]. [Pfx *non-* not, and **sense**]

non sequitur *non-sek'wi-tər*, *n* (the drawing of) a conclusion that does not follow logically from the foregoing premises; loosely, a remark, event or action that has no relation to what has gone before. — *abbrev* **non seq**. [L *nōn* not, and *sequitur* follows, 3rd singular present indicative of *sequi* to follow]

nonsuch. See **nonesuch**.

nonsuit *non'sūt* or *-sōōt*, (*law*) *n* (in England) the stopping of a suit by voluntary withdrawal of the plaintiff, or by the judge when the plaintiff has failed to make out cause of action or to bring evidence. — *vt* to subject (a plaintiff) to a nonsuit. [Anglo-Fr *no(u)nsute* does not pursue]

nonuple *non'ū-pl*, *adj* ninefold; having nine parts. — *n* **non'uplet** a group of nine, *esp* a group of nine notes played in the time of six or eight. [L *nōnus* ninth; *nonuplus*, not in L, formed on the analogy of *duplus*, *quadruplus*, etc]

noodle[1] *nōōd'l*, *n* a flat, *usu* string- or ribbon-shaped kind of pasta, *usu* made with eggs. [Ger *Nudel*]

noodle[2] *nōōd'l*, *n* a simpleton (*colloq*); a blockhead (*colloq*); the head (*slang*, *esp NAm*). — *n* (*colloq*) **nood'ledom**. [Cf **noddy**[1] and **noddle**]

noodle[3] *nōōd'l*, *vi* to improvise on a musical instrument in a casual or desultory way, *esp* in jazz. [Ety uncertain]

nook *nŏŏk*, *n* a corner; a narrow place formed by an angle; a recess; a secluded retreat. — *adj* **nook'y**. — *adj* **nook'-shotten** (*archaic*) shot out into nooks and corners. — **every nook and cranny** (*colloq*) everywhere. [ME *nok*, *noke*; prob Scand; Gaelic and Ir *niuc* is prob from the Northern form **neuk**]

nooky[1]. See under **nook**.

nooky[2] or **nookie** *nŏŏ'ki*, (*slang*) *n* sexual intercourse; a person, *usu* a woman, regarded as a sexual partner. [Ety uncertain]

noology *nō-ol'ə-ji*, *n* the science of the intellect. — *n* **nōogen'esis** evolution of mind. — *n* **nōom'etry** mind-measurement. — *n* **nō'osphere** (*Teilhard de Chardin*) the sphere of the mind, the collective memory and intelligence of the human race. — *n pl* **nōotrop'ics** another name for cognitive enhancers or smart drugs (qv). [Gr *noos* the mind, and *logos* discourse, *metron* measure, *sphaira* sphere, and *tropē* a turning]

noon *nōōn*, *n* the ninth hour of the day in Roman and ecclesiastical reckoning, three o'clock pm; afterwards (when the church service called *Nones* was shifted to midday) midday; middle; greatest height, the culminating point. — *adj* belonging to, or characteristic or typical of, midday; meridional. — *vi* to rest at noon. — *n* **noon'er** (*US colloq*) an activity undertaken during the lunch break; a brief, *esp* illicit, sexual encounter during the lunch break. — *n* **noon'ing** (*esp US dialect*) (an interval for) a meal or rest about noon; midday. — **noon'day** midday; the time of greatest prosperity (*fig*). — *adj* relating to midday; meridional. — **noon'tide** or **noon'time** (*literary*) the time of noon, midday. — *adj* relating to noon; meridional. [OE *nōn*, from L *nōna* (*hōra*) the ninth (hour)]

no-one. See under **no**[2].

noop *nōōp*, (*Scott*) *n* a knob, tip (of the elbow). [Cf **knop**]

noose *nōōs*, *n* a loop with running knot which draws tighter the more it is pulled, used for trapping or killing by hanging; a snare or bond generally, *esp* (*joc*) marriage. — *vt* to tie or catch in a noose; to make a noose in or of. — **put one's head in a noose** to put oneself into a dangerous or vulnerable situation. [Perh OFr *nous*, pl of *nou* (Fr *nœud*), from L *nōdus* knot]

NOP *abbrev*: National Opinion Poll or Polls.

nopal *nō'pəl* or *-päl*, *n* a Central American cactus of the genus *Nopalea*, used for rearing cochineal insects; broadly, the prickly pear (genus *Opuntia*). [Sp *nopal*, from Nahuatl *nopalli*]

nope *nōp*, (*slang*) *interj* an emphatic, *orig* N American form of **no**[1], pronounced with a snap of the mouth.

NOR *nör*, (*comput*) *n* a logic circuit that has two or more inputs and one output, the output signal being 1 if all its inputs are 0, and 0 if any of its inputs is 1. — Also *adj*. [*not or*]

NOR *abbrev*: nucleolar-organizing region.

Nor *abbrev*: Norman (also **Norm**); North; Norwegian; Norway.

nor[1] *nör*, *conj* and not; neither, used *esp* in introducing the second part of a negative proposition, correlative to *neither*. — **nor** ... **nor** ... (*archaic*) neither ... nor ...; **nor yet** and also not. [Appar from *nother*, a form of **neither**]

nor[2] *nör*, (*Scot* and *dialect*) *conj* than. [Origin obscure]

nor' *nör*, a short form of **north** (*esp* in combination).

noradrenalin *nör-ə-dren'ə-lin* or **noradrenaline** *-lin* or *-lēn*, *n* a neurotransmitter hormone related to adrenalin, produced by the adrenal glands. — Also (*esp US*) **norepinephrine** (*nör-ep-i-nef'rin* or *-rēn*).

Norbertine *nör'bərt-īn* or *-in*, *n* and *adj* Premonstratensian. [From *Norbert*, the founder (1119)]

Nordic *nör'dik*, *adj* of a tall, blond, dolichocephalic type of (generally Germanic) peoples in NW Europe (loosely used by Nazis); of or relating to Finland or Scandinavia. — Also *n*. — **Nordic skiing** competitive skiing involving cross-country and jumping events. [Fr *nord* north]

norepinephrine. See **noradrenalin**.

norethisterone *nör-ə-thist'ə-rōn*, *n* an oral progestogen.

Norfolk *nör'fək*, *adj* belonging to the English county of *Norfolk*. — **Norfolk capon** a red herring; **Norfolk dumpling** or **Norfolk turkey** a native or inhabitant of Norfolk; **Norfolk jacket** a loose pleated man's jacket with a waistband. — **Norfolk Island pine** a tall Araucaria of Norfolk Island (in the Pacific, named after the ducal family of *Norfolk*). [OE *northfolc* north folk]

nori *nö'ri* or *nō'ri*, *n* a seaweed of the genus *Porphyra* used as a foodstuff in Japan in the form of dried sheets (for wrapping sushi) or as a paste. [Jap]

noria *nō'ri-ə* or *nö'*, *n* an endless chain of buckets on a wheel for raising water from a stream into irrigation channels. [Sp *noria*, from Ar *nā'ūrah*]

norimon *nor'i-mon*, *n* a Japanese palanquin. [Jap *nori* to ride, and *mono* thing]

norite *nö'rīt*, *n* a type of rock, gabbro with a rhombic pyroxene. [**Norway**]

nork *nörk*, (*Austr slang*) *n* a woman's breast. [Perh from Norco Co-operative Ltd, NSW butter manufacturers]

norland or **norlan'** *nör'lənd* or *nör'lən*, (*Scot* and *poetic*) *n* the north country. — *adj* belonging to or coming from the north. [**north** and **land**[1]]

norm *nörm*, *n* a rule; a pattern; an authoritative standard; a type; the ordinary or most frequent value or state; an accepted standard of behaviour within a society; an average standard of achievement, work required, production, etc. — *n* **nor'ma** a rule; a standard; a square for measuring right angles. — *adj* **nor'mal** according to rule; not deviating from the standard; regular, typical, ordinary; well-adjusted mentally; functioning regularly; having an unbranched chain of carbon atoms (*chem*); (of a solution) having one gramme-equivalent of dissolved substance to a litre; perpendicular (*geom*). — *n* a normal or usual value, state, instance or specimen; a perpendicular. — *n* **nor'malcy** (*esp US*) normality, often of political, economic, etc conditions. — *n* **normal'ity**. — *n* **normalizā'tion** or **-s-** return to normality or the status quo. — *vt* **nor'malize** or **-ise** to make normal; to bring within or cause to conform to normal standards, limits, etc; to heat (steel) in order to refine the crystal structure and to relieve internal stress. — *vi* to become normal, regular. — *adv* **nor'mally** in a normal manner; usually, as a rule; typically. — *adj* **nor'mative** of or relating to a norm; establishing a standard; prescriptive. — *adv* **nor'matively**. — *n* **nor'mativeness**. — **normal distribution** (*statistics*) a frequency distribution represented by a symmetrical, bell-shaped curve; **normal school** in some countries, *esp* France and N Africa, a training-college for teachers; **normal solution** see **normal** above and also **standard solution**; **norm'-ref'erencing** (*education*) comparing a pupil's abilities with those of his or her peers. — *adj* **norm'-referenced**. [L *norma* a rule]

Norm *abbrev*. See under **Nor**.

norm. *abbrev*: normal.

Norma *nör'mə*, *n* the Rule, a small southern constellation. [L *norma* a rule]

normal, etc. See under **norm**.

Norman *nör'mən*, *n* a native or inhabitant of Normandy; a member of a Scandinavian people which settled in northern France about the beginning of the 10c, founded the Duchy of Normandy, and conquered England in 1066; Norman French; Norman architecture: — *pl* **Nor'mans**. — *adj* relating to the Normans or to Normandy. — *adj* **Normanesque**. — *n* **Nor'manism**. — *vt* and *vi* **Nor'manize** or **-ise** to make or become Norman in character. — **Norman architecture** a massive Romanesque style, prevalent in Normandy (10c–11c) and England (11c–12c), the churches with a semicircular apse and a great tower, deeply recessed doorways, small, round-headed windows and arches, and zigzag, billet, nail-head, and other characteristic ornaments; **Norman Conquest** the conquest of England by Duke William of Normandy (1066); **Norman cross** an elaborate memorial cross like a Gothic turret with pinnacles and with niches for figures; **Norman French** the dialect of French spoken by the Normans, (after 1066) used by some members of society in England, and in lawcourts. [OFr *Normanz*, *Normans*, nominative and accusative pl of *Normant* Northman, from Scand]

norman *nör'mən*, (*naut*) *n* a bar inserted in a windlass on which to fasten or veer a rope or cable.

normative, etc. See under **norm**.

Norn[1] *nörn*, (*Scand mythol*) *n* each of the three Fates, Urd, Verdande and Skuld. — Also (Latinized) **Norn'a**. [ON *norn*]

Norn[2] *nörn*, *n* the old Norse dialect of Orkney and Shetland. — Also *adj*. [ON *norrœna*]

Norroy *nor'oi*, (*heraldry*) *n* an English king-of-arms whose jurisdiction lies north of the Trent (since 1943, **Norroy and Ulster**). [OFr *nord* north, and *roy* king]

Norse *nörs*, *adj* Norwegian; ancient Scandinavian. — *n* the Norwegian language; the Germanic language of the ancient Scandinavians from which the modern Scandinavian languages are derived (also **Old Norse**). — *n* **Norse'man** a Scandinavian, a Viking. — **the Norse** the Norwegians or the Vikings. [Perhaps Du *noor(d)sch*; cf Icel *Norskr*; Norw *Norsk*]

norsel *nörs'l*, (*rare*) *n* a short piece of line for fastening fishing nets and hooks. — *vt* and *vi* (*obs*) to fit with or fit norsels. — *n* (*obs*) **nors'eller**. [OE *nostel*, *nostle*, *nosle* a fillet or band]

norteño *nör-tān'yō*, (*US*) *n* (used by Americans of Latin American origin, Mexicans, etc) a North American, *esp* one of European origin: — *pl* **norteñ'os**. — *fem* **norteñ'a**: — *pl* **norteñ'as**. [Am Sp, northerner]

north *nörth*, *adv* in the direction of that point of the horizon or that pole of the earth or heavens which at equinox is opposite the sun at noon in Europe or elsewhere on the same side of the equator, or towards the sun in the other hemisphere; in the slightly different direction (*magnetic north*) in which a magnetic needle points. — *n* the point of the horizon in that direction; the compass point corresponding to this; (often with *cap*) the region lying in that direction, eg the part of England lying north of the Humber, and the part of the USA lying north of Maryland and the Ohio river, *esp* those states north of the Mason-Dixon line during the civil war; the part placed relatively in that direction; the north wind (*poetic*); the industrialized nations; (*usu* with *cap*) the playing or position occupying the place designated 'north' on the table (*bridge*). — *adj* lying towards the north; forming the part, or that one of two, that is towards the north; blowing from the north; (of a pole of a magnet, *usu*) north-seeking. — *vi* (*archaic*) to turn or move towards the north. — *n* **norther** (*nörth'ər*) a wind or gale from the north, *esp* applied to a cold wind that blows in winter over Texas and the Gulf of Mexico. — *vi* (*nördh'ər*; *archaic*) to shift or veer to north. — *n* **north'erliness** (*-dh-*). — *adj* **north'erly** (*-dh-*) being toward the north; blowing from the north. — *adv* toward or from the north. — *n* a north wind. — *adj* **north'ermost** (*-dh-*; *obs*) northernmost. — *adj* **north'ern** (*-dh-*) relating to the north; being in the north or in the direction toward it; proceeding from the north. — *n* a native of the north. — *n* **north'erner** (*-dh-*) a native of or resident in the north, *esp* of the northern United States or the northern counties of England. — *n* **north'ernism** (*-dh-*) a northern idiom. — *vt* **north'ernize** or **-ise** (*-dh-*) to give a northern character to. — *adj* **north'ernmost** (*-dh-*) or **north'most** (*-th-*) most northerly. — *n* **north'ing** (*-th-*) motion, distance or tendency northward; the distance of a heavenly body from the equator northward; difference of latitude made by a ship in sailing; deviation towards the north. — *adj*, *adv*, and *n* **north'ward**, **nor'ward** or **norward** (*nörth'wərd*, *nör'wərd* or *nor'əd*). — *adj* and *adv* **north'wardly**. — *adv* **north'wards**. — *adj* **north'bound** bound for the north; travelling northwards. — *adj* **north'-country** belonging to the northern part of the country, *esp* of England. — **north-coun'tryman**. — *adj* and *adv* **north-east'** or **nor'-east'** (also *nörth'* or *nör'*) midway between north and east. — *n* the direction midway between north and east; the region lying in that direction; the wind blowing from that direction. — **north-east'er** or **nor'-east'er** a strong wind from the north-east. — *adj* and *adv* **north-east'erly** towards or from the north-east. — *adj* **north-east'ern** belonging to the north-east; being in the north-east, or in that direction. — *adj* and *adv* **north-east'ward** toward the north-east. — *n* the region to the north-east. — *adj* and *adv* **north-east'wardly**. — *adv* **north-east'wards**. — **northern fern** the hard fern (genus *Lomaria*); **northern hemisphere** (also with *caps*) that half of the globe which is north of the equator; **northern lights** the aurora borealis; **north'land** (also *adj*) land, or lands, of the north; **North'man** an ancient Scandinavian. — *n*, *adj* and *adv* **north-north-east'** and **north-north-west'** (in) a direction midway between north and north-east or north-west. — *adj* **north polar**. — **north pole** the end of the earth's axis in the Arctic regions; its projection on the celestial sphere; (*usu*) that pole of a magnet which when free points to the earth's north magnetic pole (logically the other end); **North Sea gas** natural gas obtained from deposits below the North Sea. — *adj* **north'-seeking** turning towards the earth's magnetic north pole. — **North Star** a star very near the north pole of the heavens, the Pole Star; **north water** the space of open sea left by the winter pack of ice moving southward. — *adj* and *adv* **north-west'** or **nor'-west'** (also *nörth'* or *nör'*) midway between north and west. — *n* the direction midway between north and west; the region lying in that direction; the wind blowing from that direction. — **north-west'er** or **nor'-west'er** a strong north-west wind (see also **nor'wester** below). — *adj* and *adv* **north-west'erly** toward or from the north-west. — *adj* **north'-west'ern** belonging to the north-west; being in the north-west or in that direction. — *adj, adv* and *n* **north-west'ward**. — *adj* and *adv* **north-west'wardly**. — *adv* **north-west'wards**. — **nor'wester** a sou'wester; a drink of some strong liquor (see also **north-wester** above). — **North Atlantic Treaty Organization** a political alliance linking the United States and Canada to a group of European States, established by the **North Atlantic Treaty**, 4 April 1949 (*abbrev* **Nato**); **north by east** (in, from or towards the direction which is) one point to the north of east on the compass; **north by west** (in, from or towards) one point to the north of west on the compass; **North-east Passage** a passage for ships along the north coasts of Europe and Asia to the Pacific, first made by Baron Nordenskjöld in 1878–79; **North-west Passage** a seaway from the Atlantic into the Pacific north of N America, first made (partly on the ice) by Sir Robert McClure, 1850–54. [OE *north*; cf Ger *Nord*]

Northants *nörth'antz, abbrev*: Northamptonshire.

Northumb. *nörth-um', abbrev*: Northumberland.

Northumbrian *nör-thum'bri-ən, n* a native of the modern *Northumberland*, or of the old kingdom of *Northumbria* (OE *Northhymbre, Northhymbraland*) which stretched from the Humber to the Forth, or of the modern region of Northumbria comprising Northumberland, Tyne and Wear, Co. Durham and Cleveland; the dialect of Old English spoken in Northumbria, later Northern English (including Scots). — *adj* of Northumberland or Northumbria.

Norueyses (*Spenser*). See under **Norway**.

norward, etc. Same as **northward**, etc.

Norway *nör'wā, adj* Norwegian. — *n* (*obs*) a Norwegian: — *pl* (*Spenser*) **Norueyses**. — **Norway haddock** the rose-fish or bergylt; **Norway lobster** see under **lobster**; **Norway pine** the red pine, *Pinus resinosa*; its wood; **Norway rat** the brown rat; **Norway spruce** the common European spruce *Picea excelsa* or *Picea abies*; its wood.

Norwegian *nör-wē'jən, adj* of Norway, its people or its language. — *n* a native or citizen of Norway; the language of Norway; a kind of fishing-boat used on the Great Lakes of America. — *adj* (*Shakesp*) **Norweyan** (*-wā'ən*) Norwegian. — **Norwegian oven** or **Norwegian nest** a haybox. [LL *Norvegia* Norway, from ON *Norvegr* (OE *Northweg*), from ON *northr* north, and *vegr* way]

nor'wester. See under **north**.

Nos or **nos** *abbrev*: numbers.

nose *nōz, n* the projecting part of the face used in breathing, smelling, and to some extent in speaking; the power of smelling; flair, a faculty for tracking out, detecting, or recognizing (*fig*); scent, aroma, *esp* the bouquet of wine; a projecting forepart of anything; a projection; a beak; a nozzle; the projecting edge of a step, a moulding or a mullion; the withered remains of the flower on a gooseberry, apple, etc, opposite the stalk; the connecting part of a pair of spectacles; an informer (*slang*). — *vt* and *vi* to proceed or cause to proceed gingerly, as if feeling with the nose. — *vt* to smell; to examine by smelling or as if by smelling; to track out, detect or recognize (often with *out*); to touch, press or rub with the nose; to thrust the nose into; to come or be face to face with (*archaic*); to oppose rudely face to face (*archaic*); to provide with a nose (*archaic*); to remove the nose from (a gooseberry, etc); to pronounce with a nasal sound. — *vi* to pry; to nuzzle; to move nose-first; to sniff (*archaic*); to taper away in a noselike form. — *adj* **nosed** having a nose (used *esp* in combination, as in *bottle-nosed, long-nosed*, etc). — *adj* **nose'less**. — *n* **nos'er** a blow on the nose; a bloody nose; a severe rebuff; a strong head-wind; a prying person. — *adj* **nos'ey** or **nos'y** long-nosed; large-nosed; prying; bad-smelling; fragrant; sensitive to smells; nasal in sound. — *n* a nickname for a person who pries. — *adv* **nos'ily**. — *n* **nos'iness** a tendency to pry. — *n* **nos'ing** the act of nosing; the projecting rounded edge of the step of a stair, sill, moulding, etc. — **nose'bag** a bag for food, hung on a horse's head; a picnicker's bag; food (*slang*); **nose'band** the part of a horse's bridle coming over the nose, attached to the cheek-straps; **nose'bleed** a bleeding from the nose; a name given to yarrow and various other plants (*obs* or *US*); **nose'bleeding**; **nose'-cone** the front, *usu* conical, part of a spacecraft, etc; **nose'dive** a headlong plunge. — *vi* to plunge nose-first; to drop or decline sharply (*fig*). — **nose'-flute** a flute blown by the nose; **nosegay** see separate entry; **nose heaviness** the state in which the forces acting upon an aircraft in flight are such that it tends to pitch downwards by the nose; **nose'-herb** (*Shakesp*) a herb valued for its smell; **nose job** (*colloq*) plastic surgery performed on the nose, *esp* to improve its shape or size; **nose'-leaf** a membranous appendage on some bats' snouts. — *adj* **nose'=led** led by the nose, ruled and fooled completely. — *n pl* **nose'-nippers** pince-nez. — **nose'-painting** reddening of the nose that often results from excessive drinking of alcohol; **nose'-piece** a nozzle; the end of a microscope tube carrying the objective; a nose-band; the part of a helmet formed to protect the nose; **nose'-rag** (*slang*) a handkerchief; **nose'-ring** an ornament worn in the septum of the nose or in either of its wings; a ring in the septum of the nose for controlling a bull, swine, etc; **nose'-wheel** the single wheel at the front of a vehicle, etc, *esp* an aircraft; **Nosey Parker** (*colloq*; also without *caps*) a prying person. — **by a nose** by a very short distance or small margin; **cut off one's nose to spite one's face** to injure or disadvantage oneself through an act of revenge or anger towards another; **follow one's nose** to go straight forward, or take the obvious or instinctive course; **get up someone's nose** (*colloq*) to annoy, irritate someone; **keep one's nose clean** (*colloq*) to keep out of trouble, ie not to behave badly or dishonestly; **lead by the nose** see under **lead**[1]; **look down one's nose at** to look at in a supercilious or condescending way; **make a long nose** see under **long**[3]; **nose out** to move forward slowly into traffic (in a vehicle); **nose to tail** (*esp* of vehicles in a queue) closely following one another; **nose to the grindstone** see under **grind**; **nose up** to direct or turn an aircraft nose upwards; **not see beyond** or **further than (the end of) one's nose** to see only what is immediately in front of one, ie not to see the long-term consequences of one's actions, etc; **on the nose** (in horse-race betting) to win only (not to come second or third); unsavoury, offensive (*Austr colloq*); **put someone's nose out of joint** see under **join**; **rub someone's nose in it** (*colloq*) to remind someone continually of something he or she has done wrong; **snap off someone's nose** to speak snappily; **through the nose** at a scandalously high price, exorbitantly; **thrust, poke** or **stick one's nose into** to meddle officiously with; **thumb one's nose** see under **thumb**; **turn up one's nose at** to refuse or receive contemptuously; **under one's (very) nose** in full view; close at hand; **with one's nose in the air** in a haughty, superior manner. [OE *nosu*; Ger *Nase*, L *nāsus*]

nosean *nōz'i-ən, n* a cubic mineral, aluminium sodium silicate and sulphate. — Also **nos'elite**. [Named after the German mineralogist K W *Nose* (died 1835)]

nosegay *nōz'gā, n* a bunch of fragrant flowers; a posy or bouquet. [**nose** (ie for the nose to smell) and **gay** (in obs sense of 'ornament')]

noselite. See under **nosean**.

nosey. See under **nose**.

nosh *nosh*, (*slang*) *vt* and *vi* to eat. — *vi* to nibble, eat between meals (*esp US*). — *n* food. — *n* **nosh'er**. — *n* **nosh'ery** (*colloq*) a café or restaurant. — **nosh'-up** (*slang*) a meal, *esp* a large one. [Yiddish]

no-show and **no-side**. See under **no**[2].

nosing. See under **nose**.

nosocomial *nos-ō-kō'mi-əl*, *adj* relating to a hospital. [Gr *nosokomeion* hospital, from *nosos* sickness, and *komein* to tend]

nosography *nos-og'rə-fi*, *n* the description of diseases. — *n* **nosog'rapher** — *adj* **nosographic** (*nos-ə-graf'ik*). [Gr *nosos* disease, and *graphein* to write]

nosology *nos-ol'ə-ji*, *n* the science of diseases; the branch of medicine which deals with the classification of diseases. — *adj* **nosological** (*-ə-loj'*). — *n* **nosol'ogist**. [Gr *nosos* disease, and *logos* discourse]

nosophobia *nos-ə-fō'bi-ə*, *n* morbid dread of contracting disease. [Gr *nosos* a disease, and *phobos* fear]

nostalgia *nos-tal'ji-ə*, *n* homesickness; the desire to return to some earlier time in one's life, or a fond remembrance of that time, *usu* tinged with sadness at its having passed. — *adj* **nostal'gic**. — *adv* **nostal'gically**. [Gr *nostos* a return, and *algos* pain]

nostalgie de la boue *nos-tal-zhē də la bōō*, (*Fr*) literally, nostalgia for mud, craving for a debased or depraved physical life without civilized refinements or fastidiousness.

nostoc *nos'tok*, *n* an alga of the *Nostoc* genus of blue-green algae, beaded filaments forming gelatinous colonies on damp earth, etc, once thought to be derived from stars. [Appar coined by Paracelsus]

nostology *nos-tol'ə-ji*, *n* the study of senility or the return to childish characteristics in old age. — *adj* **nostologic** (*-ə-loj'*) or **nostolog'ical**. [Gr *nostos* return, and *logos* discourse]

nostomania *nos-tō-mā'ni-ə*, *n* an abnormal desire to go back to familiar places. [Gr *nostos* return, and **mania**]

nostopathy *nos-top'ə-thi*, *n* an abnormal fear of going back to familiar places. [Gr *nostos* return, and *pathos* suffering]

nostos *nos'tos*, (*Gr*) *n* a poem describing a return or a return journey.

Nostradamus *nos-trə-dā'məs*, *n* a person who professes to foretell the future. — *adj* **nostradamic** (*-dam'ik*). [From the French astrologer (1503–1566)]

Nostratic *nos-tra'tik* *n* a hypothetical Eurasian language thought to be the common source of several major language families including the Indo-European and Semitic languages. — Also *adj*. [Ger *nostratisch*, from L *nostrās*, *-ātis* of our country]

nostril *nos'tril*, *n* either of the openings of the nose. [ME *nosethirl*, from OE *nosthyr(e)l*, from *nosu* nose, and *thyrel* opening; cf **drill**[1] and **thrill**]

nostrum *nos'trəm*, *n* any secret, quack or patent medicine; any favourite remedy or scheme. [L *nostrum* (neuter) our own, from *nōs* we]

nosy. See under **nose**.

NOT *not*, (*comput*) *n* a logic circuit that has one input and one output, the output signal being 1 if its input is 0, and 0 if its input is 1. [**not**[1]]

not[1] *not*, *adv* a word expressing denial, negation or refusal (used with verbs, and in place of a negative clause or predicate): — enclitic form **-n't**. — **not'-being** the state or fact of not existing; **not'-I** that which is not the conscious ego. — *adj* and *adv* **not-out'** (*cricket*) still in; at the end of the innings without having been put out. — **not at all** don't mention it; it's a pleasure; **not but what** (*archaic*) all the same, nevertheless; not that; **not on** (*colloq*) not possible; not morally, socially, etc acceptable; **not that** though it is not the case that. [Same as **naught** and **nought**]

not[2] or **nott** *not*, *adj* with close-cut hair; polled. — *adj* **not'head'ed**. — *adj* **not'-pat'ed** (*Shakesp*). [OE *hnot*]

nota bene *nō'tə ben'i*, *bēn'* or *no'tä ben'e*, (*L*) mark well, take notice (often *abbrev* **NB**).

notabilia. See under **notable**.

notable *nō'tə-bl*, *adj* worthy of being known or noted; remarkable; memorable; distinguished; noticeable; considerable; housewifely (*archaic*; sometimes with old pronunciation *not'*); capable, clever, industrious (*archaic*). — *n* a person or thing worthy of note, *esp* in *pl* for people of distinction and political importance in France in pre-Revolution times. — *n pl* **notabil'ia** (*L*) things worthy of notice; noteworthy sayings. — *n* **notabil'ity** the fact of being notable; a notable person or thing. — *n* **no'tableness**. — *adv* **no'tably**. [L *notābilis*, from *notāre* to mark]

notaeum *nō-tē'əm*, *n* the upper surface of a bird's trunk (as opposed to *gastraeum*). [Latinized from Gr *nōtaion* (neuter), adj, from *nōtos* or *nōton* the back]

notal. See under **note**[1] and **notum**.

notandum *nō-tan'dəm*, *n* something to be specially noted or observed: — *pl* **notan'da**. [L, gerundive of *notāre* to note]

notaphily *nō-taf'i-li*, *n* the collecting of bank-notes, cheques, etc as a hobby. — *adj* **notaph'ilic**. — *n* **notaph'ilism**. — *n* **notaph'ilist**. [**note**[1] and **phil-**]

notary *nō'tə-ri*, *n* an official authorized to certify deeds, contracts, copies of documents, affidavits, etc (generally **notary public**); anciently, a person who took notes or memoranda of others' acts. — *adj* **notā'rial**. — *adv* **notā'rially**. — *vt* **no'tarize** or **-ise** to attest to, authenticate (a document, etc) as a notary. — *n* **no'taryship**. — **apostolical notary** the official who dispatches the orders of the pope; **ecclesiastical notary** in the early church, a secretary who recorded the proceedings of councils, etc. [L *notārius*]

notation *nō-tā'shən*, *n* a system of specialized signs or symbols; the act of notating or writing down; annotation (*rare*). — *vt* **notate'** to write (music, etc) in notation. — *adj* **notā'tional**. [L *notātiō*, *-ōnis*, from *notāre*, *-ātum* to mark]

notch *noch*, *n* a nick; a V-shaped indentation; a narrow pass; a step or level (*colloq*). — *vt* to make a nick in; to cut (hair, etc) unevenly (*obs*); to form, fix or remove by nicking; to fit arrow to bowstring (also **nock**); to record by a notch; to score, achieve (often with *up*). — *adj* **notched** nicked. — *n* **notch'er**. — *n* **notch'ing** a method of joining timbers, by fitting into a groove or grooves. — *adj* **notch'y** having notches; (of a manual gearbox) not operating smoothly or easily. — **notch'back** a car whose rear does not slope continuously from the roof to the bumper, but juts out from the bottom of the rear window (also *adj*); **notch'-board** a board that receives the ends of the steps of a staircase. [Supposed to be from Fr *oche* (now *hoche*) with *n* from the indefinite article; not connected with **nock**]

notchel or **nochel** *noch'l*, *n* (*colloq*) notice that one will not be responsible for another's debts. — *vt* to repudiate the debts of (someone). [Origin unknown]

note[1] *nōt*, *n* a significant or distinguishing mark; a characteristic; that by which a person or thing is known; a significant tone or hint; a mark or sign calling attention; a written or printed symbol other than a letter; a stigma or mark of censure; an observation or remark; a comment attached to a text, explanatory, illustrative, critical, or recording textual variants; a brief written record, *esp* a jotting set down provisionally for use afterwards; an impression; a quality, hint or suggestion (of eg warning); a short statement or record; a bill or account (*obs*); a memorandum; a short informal letter; a formal, *esp* diplomatic paper or letter; a small size of paper used for writing; a mark representing a sound (**whole note**, a semibreve) (*music*); the sound or tone represented by the printed or written note; a key of a piano or other instrument; the song, cry or utterance of a bird or other animal; a tune (*obs*); music (*poetic*); a paper acknowledging a debt and promising payment, such a note of hand or promissory note and *esp* a bank-note; a voucher or receipt (*obs*); notice; attention; cognizance; distinction; reputation; eminence; importance; consequence; notability; intimation (*Shakesp*). — *vt* to make a note of; to notice; to pay close attention to; to indicate, show; to mark; to stigmatize (*obs*); to mention, to remark on; to record in writing or in musical notation; to add musical notation to; to set to music; to annotate; to denote. — *adj* **nōt'al**. — *adj* **nōt'ed** marked; well-known; celebrated; eminent; notorious. — *adv* **nōt'edly**. — *n* **nōt'edness**. — *adj* **note'less** not attracting notice; unmusical. — *n* **note'let** a short annotation or letter. — *n* a folded sheet of notepaper, *usu* with printed decoration, for short informal letters. — *n* **nōt'er** a person who notes or observes; a person who makes notes, an annotator. — **note'book** a book for keeping notes or memoranda; a portable laptop computer 210mm x 297mm in size; a billbook; **note'-case** a wallet for bank-notes; **note'-pad** a block of paper for writing notes; **note'paper** writing-paper intended for letters; **note row** (*music*) a tone row; **note'-shav'er** (*US*) a person who discounts bills at an exorbitant rate; a usurer. — *adv* **note'worthily**. — *n* **note'worthiness**. — *adj* **note'worthy** worthy of note or of notice. — **note a bill** to record, with a notary public, one's refusal as a merchant to accept a bill of exchange; **note of hand** a promissory note; **of note** well-known, distinguished; significant, worthy of attention; **strike the right** (or **a false**) **note** to act or speak appropriately (or inappropriately); **take note** to observe carefully or closely (often with *of*). [Fr, from L *nota* a mark]

note[2], **n'ote** or **no'te** *nōt*, (*Spenser*) *vt* wot not; (wrongly) could not. [OE *nāt*, for *ne wāt*; see **ne** and **wot**]

nothing *nuth'ing*, *n* no thing; the non-existent; absence of anything; zero number or quantity; the figure representing it, a nought; a thing or person of no significance or value; an empty or trivial utterance; a low condition; a trifle; no difficulty or trouble. — *adv* in no degree; not at all. — *n* **nothingā'rian** a person who has no particular belief, *esp* in religion. — *n* **nothingā'rianism**. — *n* **noth'ingism** nothingness; triviality. — *n* **noth'ingness** non-existence; the state of being nothing; worthlessness; insignificance; vacuity; a thing of no value. — **noth'ing-gift** (*Shakesp*) a gift of no value. — **be nothing to** not to be important to or concern (someone); not to be nearly as good as; **be nothing to do with** to be unconnected with; to be no concern of; **come to nothing** to have little or no result; to turn out a failure; **for nothing** for no good reason, in vain; free of charge; **have nothing on** (*slang*) to have no claim to superiority over; to have no information about (used *esp* by police of criminals); to have no engagement; to have no clothes on; **have nothing to do with** to avoid; to be unconnected with; to be no concern of; **like nothing on earth** (*colloq*) grotesque, frightful; **make nothing of** see under **make**; **next to nothing** almost nothing; **nothing but** only; **nothing doing** (*colloq*) an emphatic refusal; an expression of failure; **nothing for it but** no alternative but; **nothing if not** primarily, above all; at the very least; **nothing to it** or **nothing in it** having nothing in it worth while; easy; **nothing less than** or **nothing short of** at least; downright; **stop** or **stick at nothing** to be ruthless or unscrupulous; **sweet nothings** (*esp* whispered) words of affection and endearment; **to say nothing of** not to mention (see under **mention**); **think nothing of** to regard as easy or unremarkable; not to balk or scruple at; to have a low opinion of. [**no**[2] and **thing**]

Nothofagus *noth-ō-fā'gəs*, *n* a genus of timber-trees of the southern hemisphere, related to beech. [Gr *nothos* spurious, and L *fāgus* beech]

notice *nō'tis*, *n* intimation; announcement; a formal announcement made by one of the parties to a contract of his or her intention to terminate that contract; information, *esp* about a future event; warning; a writing, placard, board, etc conveying an intimation or warning; time allowed for preparation; cognizance; observation; heed; mention; a dramatic or artistic review; civility or respectful treatment; a notion (*obs*). — *vt* to mark or observe; to regard or attend to; to mention; to remark on, make observations about; to write or publish a notice of; to show sign of recognition of; to treat with civility. — *adj* **no'ticeable** that can be noticed, appreciable; worthy of notice; likely to be noticed. — *adv* **no'ticeably**. — **no'tice-board** a board for fixing notices on. — **at short notice** with notification only a little in advance; **give notice** to warn beforehand; to inform; to intimate, *esp* the termination of an agreement or (contract of) employment; **take notice** see under **take**. [Fr *notice*, from L *nōtitia*, from *nōscere*, *nōtum* to get to know]

notify *nō'ti-fī*, *vt* to make known; to declare; to give notice or information of: — *pr p* **no'tifying**; *pa t* and *pa p* **no'tified**. — *adj* **no'tifiable** that must be made known; (of diseases) that must be reported to public health authorities. — *n* **notification** (*-fi-kā'shən*) the act of notifying; the notice given; the paper containing the notice. — *n* **not'ifier**. [Fr *notifier*, from L *nōtificāre*, *-ātum*, from *nōtus* known, and *facere* to make]

notion *nō'shən*, *n* a concept in the mind of the various marks or qualities of an object; an idea; a vague impression or understanding; an opinion, *esp* one not very well founded; a caprice, whim or inclination; a liking or fancy; a mind (*Shakesp* and *Milton*); any small, useful article ingeniously devised or invented (*usu* in *pl*); (in *pl*) items of haberdashery, such as buttons, ribbon and thread (*NAm*). — *adj* **no'tional** of the nature of a notion; having a full meaning of its own, not merely contributing to the meaning of a phrase (*gram*); theoretical; hypothetical; ideal; fanciful; speculative, imaginary, unreal. — *n* **no'tionalist** a theorist. — *adv* **no'tionally** in notion or mental apprehension; in idea, not in reality. — *n* **no'tionist** a person who holds ungrounded opinions. [Fr, from L *nōtiō*, *-ōnis*, from *nōscere*, *nōtum* to get to know]

notitia *nō-tish'i-ə*, *n* a roll, list or register; a catalogue of public functionaries, with their districts; a list of episcopal sees. [L *nōtitia*; cf **notice**]

notochord *nō'tō-körd*, (*zool*) *n* a simple cellular rod, foreshadowing the spinal column, persisting throughout life in many lower vertebrates, such as the Amphioxus, etc. — *adj* **notochord'al**. [Gr *nōtos* back, and *chordē* a string]

Notodonta *nō-tō-dont'ə*, *n* a genus of moths whose larvae have toothlike humps, giving name to the family **Notodont'idae**. — *n* **notodont'id** a member of the family. [Gr *nōtos* back, and *odous*, *odontos* tooth]

Notogaea *nō-tō-jē'ə*, *n* a zoological realm including Australia, the islands north of it, New Zealand and Polynesia. — *adj* **Notogae'an** or **Notogae'ic**. [Gr *notos* south, and *gaia* land]

notonectal *nō-tō-nek'təl*, *adj* swimming on the back, as do certain insects; of the water-boatman genus (**Notonec'ta**) or family (**Notonec'tidae**) of hemipterous insects. [Gr *nōtos* back, and *nēktēs* a swimmer]

notorious *nō-tō'ri-əs* or *-tö'*, *adj* publicly known (now only in a bad sense); infamous. — *n* **notorī'ety** the state of being notorious; publicity; public exposure. — *adv* **noto'riously**. — *n* **noto'riousness**. [LL *nōtōrius*, from *nōtus* known]

notornis *no-tör'nis*, *n* a bird of the *Notornis* genus of flightless rails, long thought extinct, but found surviving in New Zealand in 1948. — See also **takahe**. [Gr *notos* south, and *ornis* a bird]

Notoryctes *nō-tō-rik'tēz*, *n* a blind burrowing marsupial of S Australia, the marsupial mole. [Gr *notos* south, and *oryktēs* digger]

Nototherium *nō-tō-thē'ri-əm*, *n* a genus of Tertiary Australian fossil marsupials related to the wombat. [Gr *notos* south, and *thērion* a wild beast]

Nototrema *nō-tō-trē'mə*, *n* the pouch-toad, a S American genus of tree frogs, with a brood-pouch on the female's back. [Gr *nōtos* the back, and *trēma* a hole]

notoungulate *nōt-ō-ung'ū-lāt* or **notungulate** *nōt-ung'ū-lāt*, *n* any one of an extinct group of herbivorous, hoofed mammals common in S America between the Palaeocene and Pleistocene eras. — Also *adj*. [Gr *nōtos* back, and L *ungulatus* hoofed]

notour *nō'tər*, (*Scot*; now only *legal*) *adj* well known, notorious. [LL *nōtōrius*]
Notre-Dame *not-r'-däm*, (*Fr*) *n* Our Lady.
no-trump. See under **no**[2].
nott. Same as **not**[2].
Notts. *notz*, *abbrev*: Nottinghamshire.
notum *nō'təm*, *n* the dorsal surface of the thorax in insects. — *adj* **nō'tal** of or relating to the back (of an insect). [Latinized from Gr *nōton* back]
notungulate. See **notoungulate**.
Notus *nō'təs*, *n* the south or south-west wind. [L *notus*, from Gr *notos*]
notwithstanding *not-with-stand'ing* or *-widh-*, *prep* in spite of. — *conj* in spite of the fact that, although. — *adv* nevertheless, however, yet. [Orig a participial phrase in nominative absolute, corresponding to L *non obstante*]
nougat *nōō'gä* or *nug'ət*, *n* a hard, chewy confection made of a sweet paste filled with chopped almonds, pistachio nuts, cherries, etc. [Fr (cf Sp *nogado* an almond-cake), from L *nux*, *nucis* a nut]
nought *nöt*, *n* not anything; nothing; the figure 0. — *adv* in no degree. — *adj* same as **naught**. — **noughts and crosses** a game in which one player tries to make three noughts, the other three crosses, in a row in the spaces of crossed parallel lines; **set at nought** to despise, disregard, flout. [Same as **naught**]
noul or (*Spenser*) **noule** *nōl*, *n*. Same as **noll**.
nould, noulde or **n'ould** (*Spenser*) *pa t* of **nill**.
noumenon *nōō'* or *now'mi-non*, *n* (in the philosophy of Kant) a thing in itself, an object regarded as having a status independent of its attributes; something whose existence is postulated but ultimately unknowable (eg God, the soul); a thing whose existence can be reasoned but never perceived: — *pl* **nou'mena**. — *adj* **nou'menal**. — *adv* **nou'menally**. [Gr *nooumenon* (contraction for *noeomenon*), neuter of pr p passive of *noeein* to think, from *noos* (*nous*) the mind]
noun *nown*, (*gram*) *n* a word used as the name of a person, animal, thing, place or quality, or a collection of these; formerly including the adjective. — *adj* **noun'al**. — *adj* **noun'y** having many nouns; having the nature or function of a noun. — **noun clause** or **noun phrase** a clause equivalent to a noun. [Anglo-Fr *noun* (OFr *non*; Fr *nom*), from L *nōmen*, *nōminis* a name]
nouns *nownz*, (*obs*) *n pl* used as a minced oath, in full *odds nouns*, for **God's wounds**.
noup *nōōp*, *nŏŏp*, (*obs Shetland*; *Scott*) *n* a crag; a steep headland. [ON *gnūpr*]
nourice *nur'is*, (*obs*) *n* a nurse. — **nour'ice-fee** payment for a nurse. [OFr *nurice*; see **nurse**[1]]
nourish *nur'ish*, *vt* to feed; to provide with food; to support; to encourage the growth of in any way; to allow to grow; to bring up; to cherish (*fig*); to educate; to suckle (*obs*). — *adj* **nour'ishable**. — *n* **nour'isher**. — *adj* **nour'ishing** providing nourishment or much nourishment. — *adv* **nour'ishingly**. — *n* **nour'ishment** the act of nourishing; the state of being nourished; that which nourishes; nutriment. [OFr *norir*, *nourir*, *-iss-* (Fr *nourrir*), from L *nūtrīre* to feed]
nouriture or **nourriture** *nur'i-chər*, *n* nourishment; food; bringing up, nurture (*obs*). [See **nurture**]
noursle *nûrs'l*, (*Spenser*) *vt* to bring up; to foster. — Also **nousle, nousell** or **nuzzle**[2]. [A form of **nuzzle** influenced by **nurse**]
nous *nows*, *n* intellect; talent; common sense (*slang*). [Gr *nous*, contracted from *noos*]
nousell and **nousle**. See **noursle**.
nousle. See **nuzzle**[1].
nout. See **nowt**[1].
nouveau *nōō-vō*, fem **nouvelle** *-vel*, (*Fr*) *adj* new. — *n* **nouvelle** a long short story. — **nouveau riche** (*rēsh*) a person (or persons collectively) with newly-acquired wealth, but without good taste or manners; an upstart: — *pl* **nouveaux riches** (*rēsh*). — Also *adj*. — **nouveau roman** (*rō-mã*) the anti-novel (qv); **nouvelle cuisine** see under **cuisine**; **Nouvelle Vague** (*väg*) a movement in French cinema (beginning just before 1960) in which traditional narrative techniques and regard to box-office appeal were abandoned in favour of a freer, simpler, understated style and sometimes a dogmatically political content (also called **New Wave**). — As *adj* applied to movements in other arts. — **art nouveau** see under **art**.
Nov. *nov*, *abbrev*: November.
nova *nō'və*, *n* a star that suddenly increases in brightness for a number of days or years: — *pl* **no'vae** (*-vē*) or **no'vas**. [L *nova* (*stella*) new (star); fem of *novus* new]
novaculite *nō-vak'ū-līt*, *n* a hone-stone, a very hard fine-grained siliceous rock, sometimes containing minute garnets. [L *novācula* razor]
novalia *nō-vā'li-ə*, (*Scots law*) *n pl* waste lands newly reclaimed. [L *novālia*]
Novatian *nō-vā'shən*, *adj* of or relating to the antipope *Novatianus* (AD 251), or his party or sect, who favoured severity against the lapsed. — *n* **Novā'tianism**. — *n* **Novā'tianist**.
novation *nō-vā'shən*, *n* the substitution of a new obligation for the one existing (*law*); innovation. [L *novātiō*, *-ōnis*, from *novus* new]
novel *nov'l* or *nuv'l*, *adj* new (*obs*); new and strange; of a new kind; felt to be new. — *n* a fictitious prose narrative or tale presenting a picture of real life, *esp* of the emotional crises in the life-history of the men and women portrayed; (with *the*) such writing as a literary genre; a new constitution or decree of Justinian or some other Roman emperor, supplementary to the Codex (often in *pl*); that which is new (earlier *no-vel'*; *obs*); a piece of news (*obs*). — *n* **nov'eldom** the world of fiction. — *n* **novelese** (*-ēz'*; *derog*) the hackneyed style typical of poor novels. — *n* **novelette'** a short novel, *esp* one that is feeble, trite and sentimental; Schumann's name for a short piano piece in free form. — *adj* **novelett'ish**. — *n* **novelett'ist**. — *adj* **nov'elish** savouring of a novel. — *n* **nov'elism** innovation, novelty (*obs*); favouring of innovation; novel-writing. — *n* **nov'elist** a novel-writer. an innovator (*obs*); a newsmonger or news-writer (*obs*). — *adj* **novelist'ic**. — *n* **novelizātion** or **-s-**. — *vt* **nov'elize** or **-ise** to make new or novel; to turn into a novel or novels. — *vi* to innovate; to write as a novelist. — *n* **nov'elizer** or **-s-**. — *n* **novella** (*-e'lə*) a short novel (*pl* **novelle** *-lā* or **novellas** *-əs*); (*-el'la*; *Ital*) a tale, short story (*pl* **novelle** *-lā*); (*-el'a*; *L*) a Roman Emperor's decree (*pl* **novellae** *-ē*). — *n* **nov'elty** newness; unusual appearance; anything new, strange or different from what was known or usual before; a small, *usu* cheap, manufactured article of unusual or gimmicky design: — *pl* **nov'elties**. [Partly through OFr *novelle* (Fr *nouvelle*), partly through Ital *novella*, partly direct, from L *novellus*, fem *novella*, from *novus* new]
November *nō-vem'bər*, *n* the eleventh month of the year, the ninth of the most ancient Roman year. [L *November*, from *novem* nine.
novena *nō-vē'nə*, (*RC*) *n* a devotion of prayers or services on nine successive days, to obtain a particular request, through the intercession of the Virgin or some saint. [L *novēnus* nine each, from *novem* nine]
novenary *nov'ə-nə-ri* or *-ē'nər-i*, *adj* relating to the number nine. — *n* a set of nine things. [L *novēnārius*, from *novem* nine]
novennial *nō-ven'yəl*, *adj* recurring every ninth year. [L *novennis*, from *novem* nine, and *annus* a year]
novercal *nō-vûr'kl*, *adj* pertaining to or befitting a step-mother. [L *novercālis*, from *noverca* a stepmother]
noverint *nōv'e-rint*, *n* a writ, beginning with the words *noverint universi*, let all men know. [L *nōverint*, 3rd person pl perfect subjunctive of *nōscere* to get to know]
Novial *nō'vi-əl* or *nō-vi-äl'*, *n* an artificial language devised by Otto Jespersen (1860–1943). [L *novus* new, and the initials of *i*nternational *a*uxiliary *l*anguage]
novice *nov'is*, *n* someone new in anything; a beginner; a new convert or church member; an inmate of a religious house who has not yet taken the vows; a competitor that has not yet won a recognized prize; a

racehorse that has not won a race in a season prior to the current season (*horse-racing*). — *n* **nov'icehood**. — *n* **nov'iceship**. — *n* **noviciate** or **novitiate** (*-ish'i-āt*) the state of being a novice, *esp* in a religious order; the period of being a novice, *esp* in a religious order; the novices' quarters in a religious house; a religious novice. [Fr, from L *novīcius*, from *novus* new]

novity *nov'i-ti*, (*obs*) *n* innovation; newness. [L *novitās*, *-ātis*, from *novus* new]

Novocaine® *nō'və-kān*, *n* a proprietary name for procaine (qv).

novocentenary *nō-vō-sen-tē'nər-i*, *n* a nine-hundredth anniversary. [L *novem* nine, and **centenary**]

novodamus *nō-vō-dā'məs*, (*Scots law*) *n* a charter or similar document containing a clause by which certain rights, privileges, etc are granted anew; the clause itself. [L (*de*) *novo damus* we grant anew]

novum *nō'vəm*, (*Shakesp*) *n* a dice game in which the chief throws were nine and five. [Poss L *novem* nine]

novus homo *nōv'əs hō'mō* or *nov'ōōs ho'mō*, (*L*) *n* a Roman magistrate whose ancestors had never held office; a new man.

now *now*, *adv* at the present time, or the time in question, or a very little before or after; immediately; in the present circumstances, as things are; nowadays; (in narrative) then; used meaninglessly or conversationally, or with the feeling of time lost or nearly lost, in remonstrance, admonition, warning, or taking up a new point. — *adj* present. — *n* the present time or the time in question. — *conj* (often followed by *that*) at this time when and because it is the fact; since at this time. — *interj* expressing admonition, warning or (when repeated) reassurance. — *n* **now'ness** the quality of constantly being in or taking place at the present moment; a lively and up-to-date quality. — **now'-casting** (*meteorol*) a system of rapid and very-short-range presenting of weather phenomena based on realtime processing of simultaneous observations from a network of remote sensing devices. — **as of now** from this time onward; **for now** until later; for the time being; just now; a moment ago; at this very moment; **now and then** or **now and again** sometimes; from time to time; **now ... now** at one time ... at another time; **now of late** (*archaic*) lately; **now then**! an interjection expressing admonition or rebuke; **the now** (*Scot*) at present; presently; very lately. [OE *nū*; Ger *nun*, L *nunc*, Gr *nȳn*]

nowadays *now'ə-dāz*, *adv* in these times. — Also *adj*. — *n* the present time. — (*Spenser*) **now a** (or **of**) **dayes**. [**now** and **days**, OE *dæges*, genitive of *dæg* day, to which the preposition **a** (OE *on*, which governed the dative) was later added]

noway and **noways**. See under **no**[2].

nowed *nowd*, (*heraldry*) *adj* knotted. [Fr *noué*]

Nowel and **Nowell**. See under **Noel**.

nowhere *nō'wār* or *nō'hwār*, *adv* in or to no place, not anywhere; out of the running. — *n* a non-existent place. — *adv* **no'whence** (*archaic*) from no place. — *adv* **no'whither** (*archaic*) to no place; in no direction. — **from** or **out of nowhere** suddenly and inexplicably; **get nowhere** to make no progress; **in the middle of nowhere** isolated, remote from towns or cities; **nowhere near** not nearly. [**no**[2], and **where**, **whence** or **whither**]

nowl *nōl*, (*Shakesp*) *n*. Same as **noll**.

nown *nōn*, (*obs*) *adj* own. [Orig by wrong division of **mine own**, **thine own**]

nowt[1] or **nout** *nowt*, (*Scot*) *n* cattle. — **nowt'-herd**. [ON *naut*; cognate with **neat**[2], OE *nēat*]

nowt[2] *nowt*, (*dialect* or *colloq*) *n* nothing. [**naught**]

nowy *nō'i* or *now'i*, (*heraldry*) *adj* having a convex curvature near the middle. [OFr *noé* (Fr *noué*), from L *nōdātus* knotted]

Nox *noks*, *n* (also without *cap*) nitrogen oxide, *esp* when regarded as emitted by cars, power stations etc, and as contributing towards pollution. — Also *n pl* **nox gases**. [*n*itrogen *ox*ide]

NO$_x$ *abbrev*: nitrogen oxide.

noxal *noks'l*, *adj* relating to wrongful injury by an object or animal belonging to another. [LL *noxālis*, from *noxa* hurt]

noxious *nok'shəs*, *adj* poisonous; unwholesome; harmful. — *adv* **nox'iously**. — *n* **nox'iousness**. [L *noxius*, from *noxa* hurt, from *nocēre* to hurt]

noy *noi*, *vt* (*Spenser*) to vex, hurt or annoy. — *n* (*obs* or *dialect*) vexation, hurt or trouble. — *n* **noy'ance** (*Spenser* and *Shakesp*) annoyance. — *n* **noyes** (*noiz*; *Spenser*) noise (see under **noise**). — *adj* **noy'ous** (*Spenser*) vexatious; grievous; injurious. — *adj* **noy'some** (*obs*) noisome; hurtful. [Aphetic forms of **annoy**, etc; see also **noisome**]

noyade *nwä-yäd'*, *n* execution by drowning, as carried out by the French revolutionist Carrier (1756–94) at Nantes, 1793–94. [Fr, from *noyer* to drown]

noyau *nwä-yō'*, *n* a liqueur made from brandy flavoured with bitter almonds or peach-kernels. [Fr, fruit-stone, from L *nucālis* nutlike, from *nux*, *nucis* a nut]

nozzer *noz'ər*, (*naval slang*) *n* a raw recruit. [Origin uncertain]

nozzle *noz'l*, *n* a little nose; the snout; a projection; an outlet tube, or spout; an open end of a tube; (in some turbines) specially shaped passages for expanding steam, creating kinetic energy of flow with a minimum loss; (in oil engines) openings, controlled by the injection valve, through which fuel is sprayed into the cylinder. [Dimin of **nose**]

NP *abbrev*: new paragraph (also **np**); New Providence (Bahamas); Notary Public.

Np (*chem*) *symbol*: neptunium.

np *abbrev*: *nisi prius* (*L*; qv); no place (of publication).

NPA *abbrev*: Newspaper Publishers' Assocation.

NPFA *abbrev*: National Playing Fields Association.

NPG *abbrev*: National Portrait Gallery.

NPL *abbrev*: National Physical Laboratory.

nr *abbrev*: near.

NRA *abbrev*: National Rifle Association; National Rivers Authority.

NRDC *abbrev*: National Research Development Corporation.

NRPB *abbrev*: National Radiological Protection Board.

NRV *abbrev*: net realizable value.

NS *abbrev*: new series (also **ns**); New Style; Nova Scotia (Can).

ns *abbrev*: nanosecond(s); non smoker (also **n/s**); not specified.

NSAID *abbrev*: non-steroidal anti-inflammatory drug.

NSB *abbrev*: National Savings Bank.

NSC *abbrev*: National Safety Council; National Security Council (*US*).

NSF *abbrev*: National Science Foundation; not sufficient funds (*finance*).

NSPCC *abbrev*: National Society for the Prevention of Cruelty to Children.

NSRA *abbrev*: National Small-bore Rifle Associaton.

NSU *abbrev*: non-specific urethritis.

NSW *abbrev*: New South Wales (*Austr*).

NT *abbrev*: National Theatre (now **RNT** Royal National Theatre); National Trust; New Testament; Northern Territory (*Austr*); no trumps (*cards*).

-n't. Shortened (enclitic) form of **not**[1].

NTA *abbrev*: National Training Award.

Nth *abbrev*: North.

nth. See under **N**.

ntp *abbrev*: normal temperature and pressure.

NTS *abbrev*: National Trust for Scotland.

NU *abbrev*: name unknown.

Nu. *abbrev*: ngultrum (Bhutanese currency).

nu *nū* or *nü*, *n* the thirteenth letter (N, ν) of the Greek alphabet, corresponding to N, n; as a numeral ν' = 50, $_{,}\nu$ = 50 000. [Gr *nȳ*]

NUAAW *abbrev*: National Union of Agricultural and Allied Workers.

nuance *nü-ãs*, *nwãs*, *nū-äns'*, *nū'əns* or *nū'ans*, *n* a delicate or subtle degree or shade of difference. — *vt* to give nuances to. — *adj* **nuanced**. [Fr, from L *nūbēs*, *nūbis* a cloud]

nub[1]. See **knub**.

nub[2] *nub*, *n* the point or gist; a small lump or chunk; a protuberance; a small bunch of fibres in yarn. — *adj* **nubb'ly** or **nubb'y**. — See also **knubb**. [Prob from **knub**]

nub[3] *nub*, (*obs slang*) *n* the gallows. — *vt* to hang. — **nubb'ing-cheat** the gallows; **nubb'ing-cove** a hangman. [Origin unknown]

nubbin *nub'in*, (*US*) *n* a small or underdeveloped ear of corn, fruit, etc. [Dimin of **nub**[1]]

nubble[1] See under **knub**.

nubble[2]. See **knubble**.

nubbly and **nubby**. See under **nub**[2].

nubecula *nū-bek'ū-lə*, *n* a cloudiness: — *pl* **nūbec'ulae** (*-lē*) the Magellanic Clouds. [L *nūbēcula*, dimin of *nūbēs* cloud]

nubia *nū'bi-ə*, *n* a fleecy head-wrap formerly worn by women. [L *nūbēs* a cloud]

nubiferous *nūbi'ə-rəs*, *adj* cloud-bringing. [L *nūbēs* a cloud, and *ferre* to bring]

nubiform *nūb'i-förm*, *adj* cloudlike. [L *nūbēs* a cloud]

nubigenous *nū-bij'i-nəs*, *adj* cloud-born. [L *nūbēs* a cloud, and *genus*, *generis* birth]

nubile *nū'bīl*, *-bil*, *adj* (*esp* of a woman) marriageable; sexually mature; sexually attractive. — *n* **nubility** (*-bil'i-ti*). [L *nūbilis*, from *nūbere* to veil oneself, hence to marry]

nubilous *nū'bi-ləs*, *adj* cloudy. [L *nūbilus*, from *nūbēs* a cloud]

nuc. *abbrev*: nuclear.

nucellus *nū-sel'əs*, *n* the mass of tissue within the integuments of a plant's ovule, containing the embryo-sac: — *pl* **nucell'i** (*-lī*). — *adj* **nucell'ar**. [A modern dimin from L *nux*, *nucis* a nut; L has dimin *nucella* a little nut]

nucha *nū'kə*, *n* the nape of the neck: — *pl* **nu'chae** (*-kē*). — *adj* **nū'chal**. [LL *nucha*, from Ar *nukhā'* spinal marrow]

nuciferous *nū-sif'ər-əs* (*bot*) *adj* nut-bearing. [L *nux*, *nucis* nut, and *ferre* to bear]

nucivorous *nū-siv'ə-rəs*, (*zool*) *adj* nut-eating. [L *nux*, *nucis* nut, and *vorāre* to devour]

nucleal *nū'kli-əl*, (*rare*) *adj* nuclear. [**nucleus**]

nuclear *nū'kli-ər*, *adj* of, or of the nature of, a nucleus; relating to the nucleus of an atom or the nuclei of atoms; relating to, derived from, or powered by the fission or fusion of atomic nuclei; possessing nuclear weapons. — *vt* **nu'clearize** or **-ise** to make nuclear; to supply or fit with nuclear weapons. — *n* **nuclearizā'tion** or **-s-**. — **nuclear binding energy** the binding energy that holds together the constituent nucleons of the nucleus of an atom; **nuclear charge** a positive charge arising in the atomic nucleus because of protons, equal in number to the atomic number; **nuclear chemistry** (*chem*) the study of reactions involving the transmutation of elements by spontaneous decay or particle bombardment; **nuclear disarmament** a country's act of giving up its nuclear weapons; **nuclear energy** a more exact term for **atomic energy**, energy released or absorbed during reactions taking place in atomic nuclei; **nuclear family** the basic family unit consisting of the mother and father with their children; **nuclear fission** spontaneous or induced splitting of an atomic nucleus; **nuclear-free zone** an area in which the transport, storage, manufacture and deployment of nuclear weapons, and the transport or disposal of nuclear waste, are officially prohibited; **nuclear fuel** material, such as uranium or plutonium, consumed to produce nuclear energy (also called **atomic fuel**); **nuclear fusion** the creation of a new nucleus by merging two lighter ones, with the release of energy; **nuclear magnetic resonance** resonance which can be produced in nuclei or most isotopes of the elements and which helps to identify the particular atoms involved; **nuclear medicine** diagnosis and treatment of disease using radiation detectors or radioactive materials; **nuclear physics** the science of forces and transformations within the nucleus of the atom; **nuclear power** power obtained from a controlled nuclear reaction. — *adj* **nuclear-powered**. — **nuclear reaction** a process in which an atomic nucleus interacts with another nucleus or particle, producing changes in energy and nuclear structure; **nuclear reactor** an assembly of fissile material with a moderator, in which a nuclear chain reaction is produced and maintained; the apparatus housing this; **nuclear sexing** testing a person's sex by examining cells from inside the cheek which, in females, have a material near the nucleus that can be stained blue; **nuclear threshold** the point in an armed conflict when nuclear weapons are resorted to; **nuclear warfare** warfare using nuclear weapons; **nuclear warhead**; **nuclear waste** radioactive waste; **nuclear weapon** a bomb, missile, etc deriving its destructive force from the energy released by a nuclear reaction; **nuclear winter** the period of lack of sunlight and resulting severe cold predicted by scientists as the aftermath of a nuclear war. [**nucleus**]

nuclease *nū'klē-āz*, *n* any of a number of enzymes inducing hydrolysis in nucleic acids. [**nucleus**]

nucleate *nū'kli-āt*, *vt* and *vi* to form into, or group around, a nucleus. — *vt* to act, in a process of formation, as a nucleus for (eg crystals). — *adj* **nu'cleate** or **nu'cleated** having a nucleus. — *n* **nucleā'tion** the action or process of nucleating; seeding clouds to control rainfall and fog formation. — *n* **nū'cleator**. [**nucleus**]

nucleide. See under **nuclide**.

nuclein *nū'kli-in*, *n* a colourless amorphous substance of varying composition, obtained from cell nuclei. [**nucleus**]

nucleo- *nū'kli-ō-* or *nū'kli-ə-*, *combining form* denoting nucleus; nucleic acid; nuclear. — *adj* **nucleophil'ic** of, relating to or involving electron contribution to covalent bonding. — *n* **nu'cleoplasm** the protoplasm in the nucleus of a cell. — *n* **nucleopro'tein** any of a group of compounds containing a protein molecule combined with a nuclein, important constituents of the nuclei of living cells. — *n* **nu'cleoside** a deoxyribase or ribose sugar molecule to which a purine or pyrimidine base is covalently bound. — *n* **nu'cleosome** a repeating unit of chromatin occurring along a strand of DNA. — *n* **nucleosyn'thesis** the process in which atomic nuclei bind together to form chemical elements (eg in stars). — *n* **nu'cleotide** a nucleoside with a phosphate group attached to the sugar, the individual components of a nucleic acid. [**nucleus**]

nucleolar, **nucleolate** and **nucleolated**. See under **nucleolus**.

nucleolus *nū'klē-ō'ləs*, *n* a body (sometimes two bodies) with a cell nucleus, indispensable to growth: — *pl* **nucleoli** (*nū-klē-ō'lī*). — Also **nu'cleole**. — *adj* **nu'cleolar**. — *adj* **nu'cleolate** or **nu'cleolated** having a nucleus or nucleolus; (of a spore) containing one or more conspicuous oil-drops. — **nucleolar-organizing region** the region of the chromosomal DNA that codes for ribosomal RNA. — *Abbrev* **NOR**. [**nucleus**]

nucleon *nū'kli-on*, *n* a general name for a neutron or a proton. — *n sing* **nucleon'ics** nuclear physics, *esp* its practical applications. [**nucleus**]

nucleophilic ... to ... **nucleotide**. See under **nucleo-**.

nucleus *nū'kli-əs*, *n* a central mass or kernel; that around which something may grow; a core of flint from which pieces have been flaked off; the densest part of a comet's head or a nebula; a nut kernel (*obs*); a nucellus (obs); a rounded body in the protoplasm of a cell, the centre of its life (*biol*); the massive part of an atom, distinguished from the outlying electrons (*phys*); a stable group of atoms to which other atoms may be attached so as to form series of compounds (*chem*): — *pl* **nuclei** (*nū'kli-ī*). — **nucleic acid** (*nū-klē'ik* or *-klā'-*) a general term for a natural polymer (which can be single- or double-stranded) in which bases (purines or pyrimidines) are attached to a sugar phosphate backbone. [L, from *nux*, *nucis* a nut]

nuclide *nū'klīd*, *n* a species of atom of any element distinguished by the number of neutrons and protons in its nucleus, and its energy state. — Sometimes also **nu'cleide**. **[nucleus]**

nucule *nūk'ūl*, *n* a nutlet. [L *nucula*, dimin of *nux*, *nucis* a nut]

NUCPS *abbrev*: National Union of Civil and Public Servants.

nude *nūd*, *adj* naked; bare; without clothes; showing or involving naked or almost naked figures; undraped; flesh-coloured; (of eg contracts and agreements) made without a consideration (*law*). — *n* a nude figure or figures; the condition of being naked; (with *the*) the representation of naked human figures as an art form; flesh-coloured fabric, used eg for stockings. — *n* **nudā'tion** the act of making bare. — *adv* **nude'ly**. — *n* **nude'ness**. — *adj* **nu'die** (*colloq*) (*esp* of films, shows, magazines, etc) naked or featuring nudity. — Also *n*. — *n* **nu'dism** the practice of going naked; (*esp US*) naturism. — *n* **nu'dist** a person who goes naked, or approves of going naked; (*esp US*) a naturist. — Also *adj*. — *n* **nu'dity** the state of being nude; a nude figure (*rare*): — *pl* **nu'dities** naked parts usually covered. [L *nūdus* naked]

nudge *nuj*, *n* a gentle poke or push, as with the elbow. — *vt* to poke or push gently, *esp* to draw someone's attention to something, or as a reminder or encouragement; to push slowly and gently. — *n* **nudg'er**. — **nudge, nudge** or **nudge, nudge, wink, wink** (*colloq*) a phrase appended in mock or would-be confidentiality, to an implication of disreputable practice, or to a sexual innuendo. — Also **nudge'-nudge'**. [Origin obscure; perh connected with Norw *nugge* to rub, or with **knock** or **knuckle**]

nudibranch *nū'di-brangk*, *n* a shell-less marine gasteropod, belonging to the **Nudibranchiā'ta**, with external, often branched gills on the back and the sides of the body. — Also *adj*. — *adj* **nudibranch'iate** of or belonging to members of the Nudibranchiata. — *n* a nudibranch. [Fr *nudibranche*, from L *nūdus* nude, and *branchia* gills]

nudicaudate *nū-di-kö'dāt*, *adj* (of eg rats) having a hairless tail. [L *nūdus* nude, and *cauda* tail]

nudicaul *nū'di-köl* or **nudicaulous** *nū-di-kö'ləs*, *adj* having a leafless stem. [L *nūdus* nude, and *caulis* stem]

nudism, **nudist** and **nudity**. See under **nude**.

nudnik *nŭd'nik*, (*slang*) *n* a tiring, dull or boring person. [Yiddish *nudyen* to bore, and **-nik**]

nuée ardente *nü-ā är-dãt*, *n* a cloud of hot gas, ash, etc from a volcano, spreading horizontally. [Fr, burning cloud]

nuff *nuf* and **nuffin** *nuf'in*. Slang or dialect forms of **enough** and **nothing**.

nugae *nū'gē*, *-jē* or *nōō'gī*, (*L*) *n pl* trifles.

nugatory *nū'gə-tə-ri*, *adj* trifling; worthless; inoperative; unavailing; futile. — *n* **nu'gatoriness**. [L *nūgātōrius*, from *nūgae* trifles, trumpery]

nuggar *nug'ər*, *n* a large boat used to carry cargo on the Nile. [Ar *nuqqār*]

nugget *nug'it*, *n* a lump, *esp* of gold; anything small but valuable (*fig*). — *adj* **nugg'ety** (*Austr*) stocky, thickset. [Origin unknown; there is a Swed dialect word *nug* a lump, block]

NUGMW *abbrev*: National Union of General and Municipal Workers.

NUI *abbrev*: National University of Ireland.

nuisance *nū'səns*, *n* something which annoys or hurts, *esp* if there is some legal remedy; that which is offensive to the senses; a person or thing that is troublesome or obtrusive in some way; hurt or injury (*obs*). — *n* **nui'sancer** (*rare*). — **nuisance value** the value or usefulness of someone's or something's capacity to cause problems when required. [Fr, from L *nocēre* to hurt]

NUJ *abbrev*: National Union of Journalists.

nuke *nūk*, (*slang*) *n* a nuclear weapon. — *vt* to attack using nuclear weapons; to reheat or cook in a microwave oven (*slang*). [Contraction of **nuclear**]

null[1] *nul*, *adj* of no legal force; void; invalid; having no significance; amounting to nothing, non-existent; (of a set) empty (*math*); quantitively, or amounting to, zero (*math*). — *n* something with no value or meaning, a cipher or nought (*obs*). — *vt* to annul, nullify; to wipe out (*obs*). — *n* **null'ity** the state of being null or void; something without legal force or validity; nothingness; lack of existence, force or efficacy. — *n* **null'ness**. — **decree of nullity** a decree that a marriage has never legally existed, eg because of a failure to publish the banns properly; **null and void** without legal force; not valid or binding. [L *nūllus* not any, from *nē* not, and *ūllus* any]

null[2] *nul*, *n* a knurl; a kink. — *vi* to kink. — *n* **null'ing** knurling. **[knurl]**

nulla, **nullah**, **nala** or **nallah** *nul'ə*, *n* a ravine; a watercourse; a stream or drain. [Hindi *nālā*]

nulla-nulla *nul'ə-nul'ə*, *n* an Australian Aborigine's club. — Also **null'a**. [Aboriginal]

nullifidian *nul-i-fid'i-ən*, *adj* having no faith, *esp* religious. — *n* a person who has no faith. [L *nūllus* none, and *fidēs* faith]

nullify *nul'i-fī*, *vt* to make null; to annul; to make void or of no force: — *pr p* **null'ifying**; *pa t* and *pa p* **null'ified**. — *n* **nullification** (*-fi-kā'shən*) a making void or of no effect, *esp* (*US*) of a contract by one of the parties, or of a law by one legislature which has been passed by another. — *n* **null'ifier** (*-fī-ər*). [Late L *nūllificāre*, from *nūllus* none, and *facere* to make]

nullipara *nul-ip'ə-rə*, *n* a woman who has never given birth to a child, *esp* if she is not a virgin. — *adj* **nullip'arous**. — *n* **nulliparity** (*-i-par'i-ti*). [L *nūllus* none, and *parere* to bring forth]

nullipore *nul'i-pōr* or *-pör*, *n* a coralline seaweed. [L *nūllus* none, and *porus* a passage, pore]

nulli secundus *nul'ī si-kund'əs* or *nōōl'ē se-kōōn'dōōs*, (*L*) second to none.

nullity and **nullness**. See under **null**[1].

NUM *abbrev*: National Union of Mineworkers.

Num. or **Numb.** (*Bible*) *abbrev*: (the Book of) Numbers.

numb *num*, *adj* having diminished power of sensation or motion; powerless to feel or act; stupefied; causing (*Shakesp*) or of the nature of (*Milton*) numbness. — *vt* to make numb; to deaden: — *pr p* **numbing** (*num'ing*); *pa t* and *pa p* **numbed** (*numd*). — *adv* **numb'ingly**. — *adv* **numb'ly**. — *n* **numb'ness**. — **numbskull** see **numskull**. [OE *numen*, pa p of *niman* to take]

numbat *num'bat*, *n* a small Australian marsupial (*Myrmecobius fasciatus*) which feeds on termites. [Aboriginal]

number *num'bər*, *n* that by which single things are counted or reckoned; quantity reckoned in units; a particular value or sum of single things or units; a representation in arithmetical symbols of such a value or sum; a full complement; a specified or recognized, and often exclusive set, class or group; the multitude (*obs*); some or many of the persons or things in question (often in *pl*); more than one; total quantity or amount; numerousness; (in *pl*) numerical superiority; numerability; a numeral or series of numerals indicating a thing's place in a series, or one assigned to it for reference, as in a catalogue; a label or other object bearing such an indication; a person or thing marked or designated in such a way; an item; an issue of a periodical or serial publication; a self-contained portion of an opera or other composition; arithmetical faculty; (in *pl*) rhythm, verses, music; the property in words of expressing singular, dual, trial, etc and plural (*gram*); a single item in a programme, *esp* of popular music and/or variety turns; an admired item of merchandise on show, *usu* of women's clothing (*colloq*); a person or thing thought of with affection or familiarity, *esp* a girl (*slang*); (with *cap*, in *pl*) the fourth book of the Old Testament, in which an account of a census is given. — *vt* to count; to count out in payment (*Milton*); to apportion; to have lived through; (also *vi*) to count as one of a group; (also *vi*) to mark with a number or assign a number to; (also *vi*) to amount to. — *n* **num'berer**. — *adj* **num'berless** without number; more than can be counted. — *adv* **num'berlessly**. — *n* **num'berlessness**. — **num'ber-cruncher** (*slang*) a computer designed to carry out large quantities of complex numerical calculations; a person who operates such a computer, or carries out such calculations in his or her head; **num'ber-crunching**; **number eight** (*Rugby football*) the forward whose position is at the back of the scrum; **number line** (*math*) an infinite straight line on which the points correspond to the set of real numbers; **number nine** (*military slang*) a purgative pill; **number one** chief, most important; the person or thing numbered one, the first in the numbered series; self, oneself (*slang*); the best-selling record at any particular time (*colloq*); lieutenant, first officer (under the rank of commander; *naut slang*); **number plate** the plaque on a motor vehicle showing its registration number; **numbers game**, **pool** or **racket** (*US*) an illegal form of gambling in which players bet on the appearance of a chosen sequence of numbers in the financial pages of a newspaper, etc; **numbers man** someone who runs a numbers game; **number system** (*math*) any set of elements which has two binary operations called addition and multiplication, each of which is commutative and associative, and which is such that multiplication is distributive with respect to addition; **number ten** (*colloq*) 10 Downing Street, official residence of the British Prime Minister; **number theory** the branch of mathematics studying integers and their properties; **number two** second-in-command. — **any number of** many; **beyond** or **without number** too many to be counted; **by numbers** (of a procedure, etc) performed in simple stages with foolproof guidance provided (as if) in the form of a sequence of numbered instructions or steps; **have** or **get someone's number** to size someone up; **his** (or **her**) **number is up** he (or she) is doomed, has not long to live; **in numbers** in large numbers; **number of the beast** see under **Apocalypse**; **number off** to call out numbers in sequence; **one's** (or **its**) **days are numbered** one's (or its) end is imminent. [Fr *nombre*, from L *numerus*]

numbles and **numble-pie**. See **umbles** and **humble-pie**.

numdah *num'dä*, *n* an embroidered felt rug made in India. [Cf **numnah**]

numen *nū'men*, *n* a presiding deity: — *pl* **nu'mina** (*-min-ə*). [L *numen*, *-inis* divinity]

numerable *nū'mər-ə-bl*, *adj* that may be numbered or counted. — *n* **numerabil'ity**. — *adv* **nu'merably**. [L *numerābilis*, from *numerus* number]

numeraire *nū'mə-rer* or (*Fr*) **numéraire** *nü-mā-rer*, *n* a standard for currency exchange rates, etc. [Fr; see ety for **numerary**]

numeral *nū'mə-rəl adj* relating to, consisting of, or expressing number. — *n* a figure, mark or group of figures used to express a number, such as 1, 2, I, V, α′, β′, etc; a word used to denote a number (*gram*); (in *pl*) a badge indicating regiment, year of curriculum, etc. — *adv* (*rare*) **nu'merally** according to number. [L *numerālis*, from *numerus* number]

numerary *nū'mə-rə-ri*, *adj* belonging to a certain number; contained within or counting as one of a body or a number (*opp* to *supernumerary*). [L *numerārius*, from *numerus* number]

numerate *nū'mə-rāt*, *vt* to read off as numbers (from figures); *orig* to enumerate, to number. — *adj* (*-ət*) having some understanding of mathematics and science; able to solve arithmetical problems; (see also **innumerate**). — Also *n*. — *n* **nu'meracy** the state of being numerate. — *n* **numerā'tion** the act of numbering; the art of reading figures and expressing the value in numbers; a system or method of numbering. — *n* **nu'merātor** a person who or thing which numbers; the upper number of a vulgar fraction, which expresses the number of fractional parts taken. [L *numerātus*, pa p of *numerāre* to number]

numeric *nū-mer'ik* or **numerical** *-kl*, *adj* belonging to, expressed in, or consisting in, a number or numbers; in number independently of sign (*math*); identical (*obs*; often with *same*). — *adv* **numer'ically**. — **numerical analysis** the study of methods of approximation and their accuracy, etc; **numerical control** automatic control of operation of machine tools by means of numerical data stored on magnetic or punched tape or on punched cards; **numerical forecasting** a method of weather forecasting based on a large number of observations at the earth's surface and throughout the atmosphere, and the calculation from these of the conditions which should follow in accordance wtih the known laws of physics; **numeric keypad** a numbered pad forming a separate section on a computer keyboard, for inputting data or occasionally commands. [L *numerus* number]

numerol'ogy *nū-mə-rol'ə-ji*, *n* the study of numbers as supposed to predict future events or influence people. — *adj* **numerolog'ical**. — *n* **numerol'ogist**. [L *numerus* number, and **-logy**]

numero uno *nū'me-rō ū'nō*, (*colloq*) *n* number one, the most important person or thing, often oneself. — Also *adj*. [Ital]

numerous *nū'mə-rəs*, *adj* great in number or quantity; many; consisting of or relating to a large number; rhythmical. — *n* **numeros'ity** numerousness; condition in respect of number; harmonious flow. — *adv* **nu'merously**. — *n* **nu'merousness**. [L *numerōsus*, from *numerus* number]

numerus clausus *nū'mə-rəs klö'zəs* or *nōō'me-rōōs klow'-sōōs*, *n* a quota restricting the number of students (*esp* those of a particular race or creed) entering an academic institution. [L, literally closed or restricted number]

numina. See under **numen**.

numinous *nū'min-əs*, *adj* pertaining to a divinity; suffused with, or arousing, deeply religious emotions, *esp* a sense of the presence of a divinity. — *n* a divinity or deity, a numen. — *n* **nu'minousness**. [L *nūmen*, *-inis* divinity]

numismatic *nū-miz-mat'ik*, *adj* relating to money, coins or medals. — *n sing* **numismat'ics** the study or collection of coins and medals. — Also **numismatol'ogy**. — *adv* **numismat'ically**. — *n* **numis'matist**. — *n* **numismatol'ogist**. [L *numisma*, from Gr *nomisma* current coin, from *nomizein* to use commonly, from *nomos* custom]

nummary *num'ə-ri*, *adj* relating to coins or money. — *adj* **numm'ūlar** coin-shaped. — *adj* **numm'ūlary** nummary. — *adj* **numm'ūlāted** coin-shaped. — *n* **nummūlā'tion** the arrangement of blood corpuscles in rouleaux. — *adj* **numm'ūline** coin-shaped; nummulitic. — *n* **numm'ūlite** a large coin-shaped fossil foraminifer, forming limestones. — *adj* **nummūlitic** (*-lit'ik*) relating to, composed of, or containing nummulites. [L *nummus* a coin]

numnah *num'nə*, *n* a felt, or now *usu* sheepskin, cloth or pad placed under a saddle to prevent chafing. [Hindi *namdā*]

numpty *num'ti* or *nump'ti*, (*Scot*; *derog*) *n* an idiot.

numskull or **numbskull** *num'skul*, *n* a blockhead. — *adj* **num'skulled**. [**numb** and **skull**]

nun[1] *nun*, *n* a female member of a religious order, *esp* one who has taken her final vows; a kind of pigeon with feathers on its head like a nun's hood; a blue tit; a male smew; a tussock moth (*Psiluria monacha*), a pest in pine forests. — *n* **nun'hood** the condition of a nun. — *n* **nunn'ery** a house for nuns, a convent; nunship: — *pl* **nunn'eries**. — *adj* **nunn'ish**. — *n* **nunn'ishness**. — *n* **nun'ship** the condition of a nun. — **nun's-fidd'le** an obsolete type of viol, a tromba marina; **nun's'-flesh** an ascetic temperament; **nun's'-veil'ing** a thin, soft, woollen dress-material. [OE *nunne*, from LL *nunna*, *nonna* a nun, an old maiden lady, *orig* mother; cf Gr *nannē* aunt, Sans *nanā* a child's word for mother]

nun[2] *nun*, (*obs*) *n* a spinning top. — **nun'-buoy** a buoy that tapers conically each way.

nunatak *nōō'na-tak*, *n* a point of rock appearing above the surface of land-ice: — *pl* **nu'nataks** or (*Swed*) **nu'nataker**. [Inuit]

nunc dimittis *nungk di-mit'is*, *n* (also with *caps*) the song of Simeon (from the Bible: Luke 2. 29–32) in the RC

Breviary and the Anglican evening service. [From the opening words, *nunc dīmittis* now lettest thou depart]

nunchaku *nun-cha'kōō*, *n* a weapon consisting of two short thick sticks joined by a length of chain, used in some martial arts. [Jap]

nuncheon *nun'shən*, *n* a light meal; a lunch. [ME *noneschenche* noon-drink, from OE *nōn* noon, and *scenc* drink; cf **noon** and **skink**]

nuncio *nun'shi-ō*, *n* an ambassador from the pope; a messenger; a person who brings tidings: — *pl* **nun'cios**. — *n* **nun'ciature** a papal nuncio's office or term of office. [Ital (now *nunzio*), from L *nūntius* a messenger, conjectured to be a contraction of *noventius*; cf *novus* new]

nuncle *nung'kl*, (*Shakesp*) *n* a contraction of **mine uncle**.

nuncupate *nung'kū-pāt*, *vt* to utter as a vow; to declare (a will) orally. — *n* **nuncūpā'tion**. — *adj* **nunc'ūpātive** (of a will) oral; designative. — *adj* **nunc'ūpatory** (*-pə-tə-ri*; *obs*) nuncupative; dedicatory. [L *nuncupāre* to call by name, prob from *nōmen* name, and *capere* to take]

nundine *nun'dīn* or *-din*, *n* the ancient Roman market-day, every eighth day (ninth by Roman reckoning, counting both days). — *adj* **nun'dinal** (*-din-*) relating to a fair or market. [L *nūndinae* market-day, from *novem* nine, and *diēs* a day]

nunnation *nun-ā'shən*, *n* the addition of a final *n* in the declension of nouns. [As if L *nunnātiō*, from Ar *nūn* the letter n]

nunnery. See under **nun**[1].

nuoc mam *nwok mäm*, *n* a spicy sauce made from raw fish. [Viet]

NUPE *nū'pē*, *abbrev*: National Union of Public Employees.

Nupe *nōō'pā*, *n* (a member of) a Negroid people living in W central Nigeria; the language spoken by this people: — *pl* **Nupe** or **Nupes**.

Nuphar *nū'fär*, *n* the yellow waterlily genus. [Pers *nūfar*, reduced form of *nīnūfar*; see **Nenuphar**]

nuptial *nup'shəl*, *adj* of or relating to marriage; relating to mating (*zool*). — *n* (*usu* in *pl*) marriage; wedding ceremony. — *n* **nuptiality** (*-shi-al'i-ti*) nuptial character or quality; marriage-rate; (in *pl*) wedding ceremonies and festivities. [L *nuptiālis*, from *nuptiae* marriage, from *nubere*, *nuptum* to marry]

NUR *abbrev*: National Union of Railwaymen.

nur and **nurr**. See **knur**.

nuraghe *nōō-rä'gā* or **nurhag** *nōō-räg'*, *n* a broch-like Sardinian round tower, probably of the Bronze Age: — *pl* **nuraghi** (*-gē*) or **nurhags**. — *adj* **nuragh'ic** relating to, found in, etc nuraghi. [Sardinian dialect]

nurd. See **nerd**.

nurdle *nûr'dl*, (*cricket*) *vi* to score runs by gently pushing or deflecting the ball with the bat rather than by hitting it hard.

nurl. See **knurl**.

Nurofen® *nū'rō-fen*, *n* a proprietary painkiller containing ibuprofen.

nurse[1] *nûrs*, *n* a woman who suckles a child, *esp* another person's child, a wet nurse (*archaic*); a person who tends a child; a person who has the care of the sick, feeble or injured, *esp* one who is trained for the purpose; a person given the task of supervising a new or incompetent employee (*rare*); a worker bee, ant, etc that tends the young; a budding form in tunicates; someone who or that which feeds, rears, tends, saves, fosters or develops anything, or preserves it in any desired condition; a shrub or tree that protects a young plant (*hortic*); the state of being nursed (in the phrases *at nurse* or *out to nurse*). — *vt* (also *vi*) to suckle (a baby); (also *vi*) to tend (eg an infant or a sick person); to bring up; to cherish; to manage or treat with care and economy; to play skilfully, manipulate carefully, or keep watchfully in touch with, in order to obtain or preserve the desired condition; to keep (the balls) together for a cannon or series of cannons (*billiards*); to hold, carry or cuddle (as a nurse does a child). — *adj* **nurse'like**. — *n* **nurse'ling** or **nurs'ling** that which is nursed or fostered; an infant that is being suckled. — *n* **nurs'er**. — *n* **nurs'ing** the profession or practice of caring for the sick, feeble or injured. — Also *adj*. — **nurse'-child** a child in the care of a nurse; a foster child; **nurse'maid** a woman employed to take care of children; a person who guides or cares for another. — *vt* to act as a nursemaid to. — *vt* and *vi* **nurse'-tend** to attend as a sick-nurse. — **nurse'-tender**; **nurse'-tending**; **nursing-bra** a bra for women who are breastfeeding, with cups which (partially) unfasten; **nur'sing-chair** a low chair without arms, used when feeding a baby; **nurs'ing-fa'ther** (*Bible*) a foster-father; **nursing home** a private hospital or residence providing care, eg to the elderly or infirm; **nursing officer** any of several grades of nurses having administrative duties. — **put (out) to nurse** to entrust to a nurse, *esp* a baby to a wetnurse, *usu* away from home; to put (an estate) under trustees. [OFr *norrice* (Fr *nourrice*), from L *nūtrīx*, *-īcis*, from *nūtrīre* to nourish]

nurse[2] *nûrs*, *n* a shark; a dogfish. — **nurse'hound** a European dogfish (*Scylliorhinus caniculus*); **nurse shark** any shark of the family *Orectolobidae*. [Earlier *nuss*, perh for (*an*) *huss*, *husk* a dogfish]

nursery *nûr'sə-ri*, *n* a room in a house set aside for children; a place providing residential or day-care for young children; a place for nursing; a place where young animals are reared, or where the growth of anything is promoted; a place where plants are reared for sale or transplanting; nursing (*Shakesp*); a race for two-year-old horses (also called **nursery stakes**); a nursery cannon (*billiards*). — *adj* relating to a nursery, or to early training. — **nursery cannon** (*billiards*) a cannon (*esp* one of a series) with the three balls close together and being moved as little as possible; **nurs'ery-gov'erness** a governess for children who still require a nurse's care; **nurs'erymaid** a woman employed in a nursery; a nursemaid; **nurs'eryman** a man who owns or works in a nursery for plants; **nursery nurse** a person trained in the care of young children, employed in a nursery; **nursery rhyme** a traditional rhyme known to children; **nursery school** a school for very young children (aged two to five). — *n pl* **nursery slopes** slopes set apart for novice skiers. [**nurse**[1]]

nursing. See under **nurse**[1].

nursle *nûrs'l*, a mistaken form of **nousle** or **nuzzle**[1].

nursling. See under **nurse**[1].

nurture *nûr'chər*, *n* upbringing; rearing; training; whatever is derived from the individual's experience, training, environment, distinguished from *nature*, or what is inherited; anything that nourishes, *esp* food. — *vt* to nourish; to bring up; to educate. — *adj* **nur'turable**. — *adj* **nur'tural**. — *adj* **nur'turant**. — *n* **nur'turer**. [OFr *noriture* (Fr *nourriture*), from LL *nūtritūra*, from L *nūtrīre* to nourish]

NUS *abbrev*: National Union of Seamen; National Union of Students.

NUT *abbrev*: National Union of Teachers.

nut *nut*, *n* popularly, any fruit with an edible seed in a hard shell; a hard dry indehiscent fruit formed from a syncarpous gynaeceum (*bot*); often the hazelnut, sometimes the walnut; the head (*slang*); a crazy person (also **nut'case**; *slang*); a person with an obsessive interest; a small, *usu* metal, hexagonal block with a hole in the middle, for screwing on the end of a bolt; a hard-headed person, one difficult to deal with, a tough; a young blood (*slang*; also **knut** *nut*); an en (*printing*); the ridge at the top of the fingerboard on a fiddle, etc (*music*); the mechanism for tightening or slackening a bow (*music*); a small lump of coal; a small, often ginger-flavoured biscuit or round cake; a coconut-shell drinking-cup; (in *pl*) a source of joy (*slang*); (in *pl*) the testicles (*slang*). — *vi* to look for and gather nuts. — *vt* to butt with the head (*slang*): — *pr p* **nutt'ing**; *pa t* and *pa p* **nutt'ed**. — *n* **nutā'rian** (*rare*) a person who thinks nuts are the best kind of food. — *n* **nut'let** a one-seeded portion of a fruit that divides as it matures, as in labiates; the stone of a drupe. — *adj* **nut'like**. — *adj*

nuts crazy (*slang*). — Also *interj* expressing defiance, contempt, disappointment, etc. — *n* **nutt'er** a crazy person (*slang*); a person who gathers nuts; nutbutter. — *n* **nutt'ery** an area of nut-trees; a mental hospital (*slang*). — *adv* **nutt'ily**. — *n* **nutt'iness**. — *n* **nutt'ing** the gathering of nuts. — *adj* **nutt'y** containing many nuts; having the flavour of nuts; mentally unhinged (*slang*); foolishly amorous (*slang*); — *adj* **nut'-brown** brown, like a ripe hazelnut. — **nut'butter** a butter-substitute or spread made from nuts; **nut'cracker** a bird (*Nucifraga*) of the crow family which feeds on nuts and pine seeds; (*usu* in *pl*) an instrument for cracking nuts. — *adj* like a pair of nutcrackers, eg toothless jaws. — **nutcracker man** a type of early human found in Tanzania in 1959, by some distinguished as a separate species *Zinjanthropus*; **nut cutlet** a cutlet-shaped portion of a moist vegetable and nut mixture; **nut'gall** a nutlike gall, produced by a gall wasp, chiefly on the oak; **nut'-grass** any of various American sedges, *esp* one with edible tuberous root; **nut'hatch** any of various birds of the family *Sittidae* that hack nuts and seek insects on the bark of trees like a creeper (also **nut'jobber** and **nut'pecker**); **nut'-hook** a stick with a hook for pulling down nut-bearing boughs; a bailiff; a thief who uses a hook; **nut'house** (*slang*) a mental hospital; a place where chaos and crazy behaviour reign; **nut'meal** meal made from nuts; **nut oil** an oil obtained from walnuts or other nuts; **nut pine** the stone-pine or other species with large edible seeds; **nut'shell** the hard covering of a nut; **nut'-tree** any tree bearing nuts, *esp* the hazel; **nut'-wee'vil** a weevil (*Balaninus*) whose larvae live on hazelnuts; **nut'wood** (the wood of) any nut-bearing tree, *esp* the walnut; **nut'-wrench** an instrument for turning nuts on screws. — **a (hard) nut to crack** a difficult problem; **be nuts on** or **about** (*slang*) to be very fond of; to be fanatically enthusiastic about; **do one's nut** (*slang*) to become extremely angry, to rage; **in a nutshell** in very small space; briefly, concisely; **not for nuts** (*colloq*) not very well, incompetently; **nuts and bolts** the basic facts, the essential, practical details; **off one's nut** (*slang*) mentally unhinged, crazy. [OE *hnutu*; ON *hnot*, Du *noot*, Ger *Nuss*]

nutant *nū'tənt*, *adj* nodding; drooping. — *vi* **nutate'** to nod; to droop; to perform a nutation. — *n* **nutā'tion** a nodding; a fluctuation in the precessional movement of the earth's pole about the pole of the ecliptic (*astron*); the sweeping out of a curve by the tip of a growing axis (*bot*); the periodic variation of the inclination of the axis of a spinning top (or gyroscope) to the vertical (*phys*). — *adj* **nutā'tional**. [L *nūtāre* to nod]

nutmeg *nut'meg*, *n* the aromatic kernel of an E Indian tree (*Myristica*), much used as a seasoning in cookery. — *vt* (*colloq*; *sport*) to pass or kick the ball through the legs of (an opposing player): — *pr p* **nut'megging**; *pa t and pa p* **nut'megged**. — *adj* **nut'megged**. — *adj* **nut'meggy**. [ME *notemuge*, from **nut** and inferred OFr *mugue* musk, from L *muscus* musk]

NU tone (*telecomm*) *abbrev*: number unobtainable tone.

nutria *nū'tri-ə*, *n* the coypu; its fur. [Sp *nutria* otter, from L *lutra*]

nutrient *nū'tri-ənt*, *n* any nourishing substance. — *adj* feeding; nourishing. — *n* **nu'triment** anything which nourishes; food. — *adj* **nutrimental** (*-ment'l*). — *n* **nutri'tion** the act or process of nourishing; food; the study of nutrients and the nutritional value of food. — *adj* **nutri'tional**. — *n* **nutri'tionist** an expert on foods and their nutritional values. — *adj* **nutri'tious** nourishing. — *adv* **nutri'tiously**. — *n* **nutri'tiousness**. — *adj* **nu'tritive** nourishing; of or concerned with nutrition. — *n* a nutritious food. — *adv* **nu'tritively**. [L *nūtrīre* to nourish]

nux vomica *nuks vom'ik-ə*, *n* an E Indian tree (*Strychnos nux-vomica*; family *Loganiaceae*) whose orange berries contain seeds which yield strychnine and other poisonous alkaloid substances; the seed itself; a drug, *esp* a heart stimulant, made from it. [L *nux* a nut, and *vomere* to vomit]

nuzzer *nuz'ər*, *n* a present to a superior. [Hindi *nazr* gift]

nuzzle[1] *nuz'l*, *vt* and *vi* to poke, press, burrow, root, rub, sniff, caress or investigate with the nose. — *vt* to thrust in (the nose or head). — *vi* to snuggle; to go with the nose toward the ground. — Also **nousle** (*nuz'l*) and (mistakenly) **nursle** (*nûr'sl*). [Frequentative verb from **nose**]

nuzzle[2] *nuz'l*, *vt* to train; to bring up; to foster. [Origin obscure; confused with **nurse**; see **noursle**]

NV *abbrev*: Nevada (US state); new version.

NVALA or **NVLA** *abbrev*: National Viewers' and Listeners' Association.

nvd *abbrev*: no value declared.

NVQ *abbrev*: National Vocational Qualification.

NW *abbrev*: north-west or north-western.

NWT *abbrev*: Northwest Territories (Can).

NY *abbrev*: New York (US city or state).

ny. An obsolete spelling of **nigh**.

nyaff *nyaf*, (*Scot*) *n* a small or worthless person or thing. — *vi* to yelp, yap; to talk frivolously or argue snappishly. [Perh imit of a small dog's bark]

nyala *ən-yä'lə* or *n-yä'lə*, *n* a large S African antelope: — *pl* **nyal'a** or **nyal'as**. [Bantu (*i*)*nyala*]

Nyanja *nyan'jə*, *n* (a member of) a Negroid people living around Lake Nyassa in Malawi; the Bantu language spoken by this people: — *pl* **Nyan'ja** or **Nyan'jas**.

nyanza *nyan'zə*, also *ni-* or *nī-an'zə*, *n* a lake (*esp* in African proper names). [Bantu]

nyas *nī'əs*, *n* an old form of **eyas** (qv).

NYC *abbrev*: New York City.

nychthemeron *nik-thē'mə-ron*, *n* a complete day of 24 hours, a night and a day. — *adj* **nychthē'meral**. [Gr *nychthēmeron*, from *nyx*, *nyktos* night, and *hēmerā* day]

Nyctaginaceae *nik-tə-jin-ā'si-ē*, *n pl* a family of mainly tropical American plants, including bougainvillea, and the marvel of Peru, related to the goosefoots and the pinks. — *adj* **nyctaginā'ceous**. [Gr *nyx*, *nyktos* night]

nyctalopia *nik-tə-lō'pi-ə*, *n* properly, night-blindness, abnormal difficulty in seeing in a faint light; by confusion sometimes, day-blindness. — *adj* **nyctalōp'ic**. — *n* **nyc'talops** (*-lops*) a person with nyctalopia: — *pl* **nyctalō'pes**. [Gr *nyktalōps* night-blind, day-blind, from *nyx*, *nyktos* night, *alaos* blind, and *ōps* eye, face]

nyctanthous *nik-tan'thəs*, (*bot*) *adj* flowering at night. [Gr *nyx*, *nyktos* night, and *anthos* flower]

nyctinasty *nik'ti-nas-ti*, (*bot*) *n* sleep-movement in plants (eg the closing of petals), the joint effect of changes in light and temperature. — *adj* **nyctinas'tic**. [Gr *nyx*, *nyktos* night, and *nastos* pressed]

nyctitropism *nik-tit'ro-pizm*, *n* the assumption by plants of certain positions at night, *esp* ones different to daytime positions. — *adj* **nyctitropic** (*-trop'*). [Gr *nyx*, *nyktos* night, and *tropos* turning]

nyctophobia *nik-tō-fō'bi-ə*, *n* morbid fear of the night or of darkness. [Gr *nyx*, *nyktos* night, and **phobia**]

nye[1]. An obsolete spelling of **nigh**.

nye[2] *nī*, *n* a variant of **nid** or **nide**.

nying (*obs*) *pr p* of **nie**, **ny** and **nye**[1].

nylghau. See **nilgai**.

nylon *nī'lən* or *-lon*, *n* any of numerous polymeric amides that can be formed into fibres, bristles or sheets; any material made from such filaments or fibres; a stocking made of such material. [Invented by the original manufacturers]

nymph *nimf*, *n* one of the divinities who lived in mountains, rivers, trees, etc (*mythol*); a young and beautiful maiden (often *ironic*); an insect pupa (*obs*); an immature form of some insects, such as the dragonfly and mayfly, similar to the adult but with wings and sex-organs undeveloped. — *n pl* **nymphae** (*-ē*; *anatom*) the labia minora. — *n* **Nymphaea** (*-ē'ə*) the white waterlily genus, giving name to a family of dicotyledons **Nymphaeā'ceae**, related to the buttercup family. — *adj* **nymphaeaceous** (*-i-ā'shəs*). — *n* **nymphae'um** a temple, sanctuary or grotto of the nymphs. — *adj* **nymph'al**. — *n* **nymph'alid** a butterfly of the family

Nymphal'idae, a brush-footed family with useless, reduced forelegs. — Also *adj*. — *adj* **nymphē'an**. — *n* **nymph'et** a young nymph; a sexually attractive and precocious young girl. — *adj* **nymph'ic** or **nymph'ical**. — *adj* **nymph'ish**. — *adj* **nymph'like**. — *adj* **nymph'ly**. — *n* (*colloq*) **nymph'o** a nymphomaniac: — *pl* **nym'phos**. — *n* **nymph'olepsy** a species of ecstasy or frenzy said to have seized those who had seen a nymph (*folklore*); a yearning for the unattainable. — *n* **nymph'olept** a person affected by nympholepsy. — *adj* **nympholept'ic**. — *n* **nymphomā'nia** morbid and uncontrollable sexual desire in women. — *n* and *adj* **nymphomā'niac**. — *adj* **nymphomaniacal** (*-mə-nī'ə-kəl*). [L *nympha*, from Gr *nymphē* a bride, a nymph]

Nynorsk *nü'nörsk*, *nü'* or *nē'*, *n* one of the two official written varieties of Norwegian (the other being Bokmål), based on W Norwegian dialects and Old Norse. [Norw, literally new Norwegian]

NYO *abbrev*: National Youth Orchestra.

nys *nis* or *niz*, (*Spenser*) is not. [**ne** and **is**]

nyssa *nis'ə*, *n* a tree of the genus *Nyssa* (family *Cornaceas*) of small American and Asiatic trees with overlapping petals. [New L, perh from Gr *meta* post]

nystagmus *nis-tag'məs*, *n* a spasmodic, involuntary lateral oscillatory movement of the eyes, found in miners, etc. — *adj* **nystag'mic** or **nystag'moid**. [Latinized from Gr *nystagmos*, from *nystazein* to nap]

nystatin *nis'tə-tin*, *n* an antifungal antibiotic, produced by a strain of the bacterium *Streptomyces noursei*, used in treating monilia and candida. [*New York State* (where it originated), and **-in**]

NZ *abbrev*: New Zealand (also IVR).

NZBC *abbrev*: New Zealand Broadcasting Corporation.

NZPA *abbrev*: New Zealand Press Association.

O

O[1] or **o** *ō*, *n* the fifteenth letter of the modern English alphabet, derived from Greek omicron, chief sounds in English being those in *note, not, for, work, son, do*; in telephone, etc, jargon, nought or nothing; anything round or nearly so; (*usu* in *pl*; *obs*) a spangle: — *pl* **Oes, Os, O's, oes** or **o's** (*ōz*). — As a medieval Roman numeral, **O** = 11, **Ō** = 11 000. — **O'-grade** or **Ordinary grade** in Scotland, (a pass in) a former examination generally taken at the end of the 4th year of secondary education. — Also *adj*. — **O'-level** or **Ordinary level** *esp* in England and Wales, (a pass in) a former examination generally taken at the end of the 5th year of secondary education. — Also *adj*.

O[2] or **oh** *ō*, *interj* used in addressing or apostrophizing, marking the occurrence of a thought, reception of information, or expressing wonder, admiration, disapprobation, surprise, protest, pain, or other emotion. The form O is chiefly used in verse (*O for, O that*). — **Fifteen O's** fifteen meditations on Christ's Passion, each beginning with O, composed by St Bridget; **O's of Advent** seven anthems each beginning with O, sung on the days before Christmas Eve.

O or **O.** *abbrev*: Ohio (US state); an ABO blood group.

O *ō*, (*chem*) *symbol*: oxygen.

O- *ō-*, (*chem*) *pfx* signifying ortho-.

O' *ō*, *pfx* in Irish patronymics, descendant of. [Ir *ó*, *ua*, from OIr *au* descendant]

o' or **o** *ō*, *ə*, a shortened form of **of** and **on**.

-o *-ō*, (*colloq*) *sfx* used to form diminutives and abbreviations, eg *wino, aggro*.

o/a *abbrev*: on account of.

oaf *ōf*, *n* a lout; an idiot; a dolt; a changeling (*obs*): — *pl* **oafs** or (rarely) **oaves** (*ōvz*). — *adj* **oaf'ish** loutish; clumsy; idiotic, doltish. [ON *ālfr* elf; cf **elf, ouphe**]

oak *ōk*, *n* a genus (*Quercus*) of trees of the beech family; their timber, much used for furniture, in building and in shipbuilding, etc; extended to various other trees, such as **poison-oak, she-oak** (qqv). — *adj* made of oak. — *adj* **oak'en** *esp old* or *poetic* made of oak. — *n* **oak'ling** a young oak. — *adj* **oak'y** like oak, firm; having many oaks. — **oak apple** a gall caused by an insect on an oak; **oak'-egg'er** an egger moth whose caterpillars feed on oak; **oak'enshaw** a little oak-wood; **oak'-fern** a fern (*Thelypteris dryopteris*) of the polypody family (translation of Gr *dryopteris*, a name *perh* given to ferns growing on oak-trees, transferred by Linnaeus to this species); **oak'-gall** a gall produced on the oak; **oak'leaf**; **oak'-leather** a fungus mycelium in the fissures of old oaks; **oak'-lump** the lichen lungwort; **oak'-mast** acorns collectively; **oak'-nut** a gall on the oak; **oak'-tree**; **oak wilt** a serious fungal disease of oak-trees, causing wilting and discoloration of foliage; **oak'-wood**. — **Oak-apple Day** 29 May, the anniversary of the Restoration in 1660, when country boys used to wear oak apples in commemoration of Charles II hiding in the branches of an oak (the Royal Oak) from Cromwell's troopers after the Battle of Worcester; **oak-leaf cluster** (*US*) a form of additional military decoration; **sport one's oak** (*university slang*, chiefly *Oxford* and *Cambridge*) to keep one's outer door shut when one does not want visitors; **The Oaks** a great English horse-race (founded 1779) for three-year-old fillies, so named from an estate near Epsom. [OE *āc*; ON *eik*, Ger *Eiche*]

oaker (*Spenser*). Same as **ochre.**

oakum *ō'kəm*, *n* old (*usu* tarred) ropes untwisted and teased out for caulking the seams of ships. [OE *ācumba* (*æcumbe*) from *ā-* away from, and the root of *cemban* to comb]

O & C *abbrev*: Oxford and Cambridge (Schools Examination Board).

O & M *abbrev*: organization and method(s).

OAP *abbrev*: old-age pensioner.

OAPEC *ō-ā'pek* *n* Organization of Arab Petroleum-Exporting Countries.

oar *ōr, ör*, *n* a light pole with a blade at one end for propelling a boat; a swimming organ; an oarsman or oarswoman; a stirring-pole. — *vt* to propel by or as if by rowing. — *vi* to row. — *n* **oar'age** oars collectively; rowing movement. — *adj* **oared** provided with oars. — *adj* **oar'less**. — *adj* **oar'y** having the form or use of oars. — **oar fish** a ribbon-fish (*Regalecus*). — *adj* **oar'-footed** having swimming feet. — **oar'-lap** a rabbit with its ears standing out at right angles to the head; **oar'-lock** (*rare*) a rowlock; **oars'man** or **oars'woman** a rower; a person skilled in rowing; **oars'manship** skill in rowing; **oar'weed** same as **oreweed** (see under **ore**[2]). — **lie** or **rest on one's oars** to abstain from rowing without removing the oars from the rowlocks; to rest, take things easily; to cease working; **put one's oar in** to interpose when not asked. [OE *ār*]

OAS *abbrev*: Organization of American States.

oas *abbrev*: on active service.

oasis *ō-ā'sis*, rarely *ō'ə-sis*, *n* a fertile spot or tract in a sandy desert; any place of rest or pleasure in the midst of toil and gloom; (with *cap*; ®) a block of light permeable material used to hold cut flowers, etc in a flower arrangement: — *pl* **oases** (*-sēz*). [Gr *oasis*, an Egyptian word; cf Coptic *ouahe*]

oast *ōst*, *n* a kiln to dry hops or malt. — *n* **oast house**. [OE *āst*]

oat *ōt* (more often in *pl* **oats** *ōts*), *n* a well-known genus (*Avena*) of grasses, *esp Avena sativa*, whose seeds are much used as food; its seeds; a musical pipe of oat-straw (*classical literature*); a shepherd's pipe (*literary* and *poetic*); pastoral song generally (*literary*). — *adj* **oat'en** consisting of an oat stem or straw; made of oatmeal. — *n* **oat'er** (*NAm colloq*) a Wild West film, a horse opera. — **oat'cake** a hard dry biscuit made with oatmeal; **oat'-grass** a grass of *Avena* or similar genus used more as fodder than for the seed; **oat'meal** meal made of oats. — *adj* of the pale variegated brown colour of oatmeal. — **feel one's oats** (*colloq*) to be frisky or (*esp NAm*) assertive; **get one's oats** (*slang*) to have sexual intercourse; **off one's oats** (*colloq*) without appetite, off one's food; **sow one's wild oats** to indulge in youthful dissipation or excesses; **wild oats** a wild species of oat (*Avena fatua*). [OE *āte*, pl *ātan*]

oath *ōth*, *n* a solemn appeal to a god or something holy or reverenced as witness or sanction of the truth of a statement; the form of words used; a more or less similar expression used lightly, exclamatorily, decoratively, or in imprecation; a swear-word; a curse: — *pl* **oaths** (*ōdhz*). — *adj* **oath'able** (*Shakesp*) capable of taking an oath. — **oath'-breaking** (*Shakesp*) perjury. — **on, under** or **upon oath** sworn to speak the truth; attested by oath; **take an oath** to pledge formally, have an oath administered to one. [OE *āth*; Ger *Eid*, ON *eithr*]

oats. See **oat**.

OAU *abbrev*: Organization of African Unity.

oaves. See oaf.

OB *abbrev*: old boy; outside broadcast.

ob *ob*, *n* an objection (in the phrase *ob and sol*, objection and solution). — **ob-and-soll'er** a disputant. [From the marginal note *ob* in old books of controversial divinity]

ob *abbrev*: obiit (*L*), died.

oba *ö'bä, ö'bə, n* in W Africa, a chief or ruler.

Obad (*Bible*) *abbrev*: (the Book of) Obadiah.

obang *ō'bang, n* an old Japanese oblong gold coin. [Jap *ōban*]

obbligato *ob-li-gä'tō, ob-bli-* or **obligato** *ob-li-*, (*music*) *n* a musical accompaniment of independent importance, *esp* that of a single instrument to a vocal piece: — *pl* **obbliga'tos**, **obbliga'ti** (*-tē*), **obliga'tos** or **obliga'ti**. — *adj* that cannot be done without, that must be used in performance. [Ital]

obcompressed *ob'kəm-prest*, (*bot*) *adj* flattened from front to back. [L pfx *ob-* towards; in New L, in the opposite direction, reversed]

obconic *ob-kon'ik* or **obcon'ical** *-əl*, (*bot*) *adj* conical and attached by the point. [L pfx *ob-*, as in **obcompressed**]

obcordate *ob-kör'dāt*, (*bot*) *adj* (of eg a leaf) inversely heart-shaped. [L pfx *ob-*, as in **obcompressed**]

obdiplostemonous *ob-dip-lō-stē'mən-əs*, (*bot*) *adj* having two whorls of stamens, the outer being situated opposite the petals. [L pfx *ob-*, as in **obcompressed**]

obdt *abbrev*: obedient.

obdurate *ob'dū-rət*, sometimes (eg *Shakesp* and *Milton*) *-dū'*, *adj* hardened in heart or in feelings; difficult to influence, *esp* in a moral sense; stubborn; hard. — *vt* and *vi* (*-rāt*; *rare*) to make or become obdurate. — *n* **ob'dūracy** (or *ob-dū'rə-si*) the state of being obdurate; invincible hardness of heart. — *adv* **ob'dūrately** (or *-dū'*). — *n* **ob'dūrateness** (or *-dū'*) or **obdūrā'tion**. — *vt* and *vi* **obdūre'** (*obs*) to obdurate. [L *obdūrāre*, *-ātum*, from *ob-* (intens) against, and *dūrāre* to harden, from *dūrus* hard]

OBE *abbrev*: (Officer of the) Order of the British Empire.

obeah. See **obi**[1].

obeche *ō-bē'chē, n* a large W African tree or its whitish wood. [Nigerian name]

obedience *ō-bē'dyəns, -di-əns, n* the act or practice of doing what one is told; the state of being obedient; willingness to obey commands; dutifulness; the collective body of people subject to any particular authority; a written instruction from the superior of an order to subordinate members; any official position under an abbot's jurisdiction; an obeisance (*archaic*). — *adj* **obē'dient** obeying; ready to obey. — *adj* **obediential** (*ō-bē-di-en'shl*) pertaining to or of the nature of obedience. — *n* **obēdientiary** (*-en'shə-ri*) someone subject to obedience; a person charged with an obedience in a monastery. — *adv* **obē'diently**. — **canonical obedience** the obedience, as regulated by the canons, of an ecclesiastic to another of higher rank; **passive obedience** unresisting and unquestioning obedience to authority, like that taught by some Anglican divines as due even to faithless and worthless monarchs. [L *obēdientia*; see **obey**]

obeisance *ō-bā'səns, n* a bow or act of reverence; an expression of respect; obedience (*obs*). — *adj* **obei'sant**. [Fr *obéissance*, from *obéir*, from L root, as **obey**]

obelisk *ob'ə-lisk, n* a tall, four-sided, tapering pillar, *usu* of one stone, topped with a pyramid; an obelus. — *adj* **obelisc'al** of, or of the nature of, an obelisk. — *adj* **obelisc'oid** of the form of an obelisk. — *adj* obeliscal. [Gr *obeliskos*, diminutive of *obelos* spit]

obelus *ob'i-ləs, n* a sign (— or ÷) used in ancient manuscripts to mark suspected, corrupt or spurious words and passages; a dagger-sign (†) used *esp* in referring to footnotes (**double obelus** ‡; *printing*): — *pl* **ob'eli** (*-lī*). — *n* **obelion** (*ō-bē'li-ən*) a point in the sagittal suture of the skull between the two parietal foramina. — *vt* **ob'elize** or **-ise** to mark with an obelus; to condemn as spurious, doubtful, corrupt, etc. [L *obelus*, from Gr *obelos* a spit]

Oberon *ō'bə-rən, ō'bə-ron, n* king of the fairies, husband of Titania. [OFr *Auberon*; prob Frankish]

obese *ō-bēs', adj* abnormally fat. — *n* **obese'ness** or **obesity** (*-bēs', -bes'*). [L *obēsus*, from *ob-* completely, and *edere*, *ēsum* to eat]

obey *ō-bā', vi* to render obedience; to do what one is told; to be governed or controlled. — *vt* to act as directed by; to comply with; to be controlled by. — *n* **obey'er**. [Fr *obéir*, from L *obēdīre*, from *oboedīre*, from *ob-* towards, and *audīre* to hear]

obfuscate *ob'fəs-kāt, ob-fus'kāt, vt* to darken; to obscure. — *adj* **ob'fuscated** (*colloq*) drunk. — *n* **obfuscā'tion**. — *adj* **obfuscā'tory**. [L *obfuscāre*, *-ātum*, from *ob-* intensive, and *fuscus* dark]

obi[1] *ō'bi* or **obeah** (*obs* **obia**) *ō'bi-ə, n* witchcraft and poisoning practised by Negroes of the W Indies, Guyana, etc; a fetish or charm. — *vt* to bewitch. — *n* **o'beahism**, **o'beism** or **o'biism**. — **o'bi-man**; **o'bi-woman**. [Of W African origin]

obi[2] *ō'bi, n* a broad sash worn with a kimono by the Japanese. [Jap *obi*, from *obiru* to wear]

obiit *ob'i-it, ō'bi-it*, (*L*) *pa t* died. — **obiit sine prole** (*sīn'ē prō'lē, sin'e prō'le*) died without issue.

obit *ob'it, ō'bit, n* an anniversary or other commemoration of a death; short form of **obituary**; date of death; funeral ceremonies; a religious office for a dead person; a death anniversary; death (*obs*). — *adj* **ob'ital** or **obit'ūal** pertaining to obits. [LL *obitus*, from *obīre*, *-ītum* to go to meet, travel over, die, from *ob* in the way of, and *īre* to go]

obiter *ob'i-tər, ō'bi-tər, ob'it-er*, (*L*) *adv* by the way, cursorily. — **obiter dictum** (*dik'təm, -tŏŏm*; often in *pl*) something said by the way, a cursory remark; a comment made by a judge which, though carrying weight, does not bear directly on the case in hand and therefore need not influence the decision (*legal*): — *pl* **obiter dicta** (*dik'tə, -ta*).

obituary *ə-bit'ū-ə-ri, adj* relating to or recording the death of a person or persons. — *n* an account of a deceased person; an announcement of someone's death; a collection of death-notices; in a newspaper often extended to include notices of births and marriages, etc; a register of deaths, *orig* in a monastery. — *n* **obit'ūarist** a writer of obituaries. [Med L *obituārius*, from *obitus*; see **obit**]

obj *abbrev*: object; objective.

object *ob'jikt, n* a material thing; that which is thought of or regarded as being outside, different from, or independent of, the mind (as opposed to *subject*); that upon which attention, interest, or some emotion is fixed; a thing observed; an oddity or deplorable spectacle; that towards which action or desire is directed, an end; a thing presented or capable of being presented to the senses (as opposed to *eject*); part of a sentence denoting that upon which the action of a transitive verb is directed, or standing in an analogous relation to a preposition (*gram*); interposition (*obs*); presentation to view or to the mind (*Shakesp*). — *vt* **object** (*əb-jekt', ob-*) to offer in opposition; to bring as an accusation; to put in front or in the way of anything or anybody (*archaic*); to present to sense or mind (*archaic*); to present, bring forward, or adduce (*archaic*); to impute (*obs*). — *vi* to be opposed, feel or express disapproval (with *to*, *against*); to refuse assent. — *adj* (*obs*) opposed, interposed or exposed. — *n* **objectificā'tion** (*-jekt-*). — *vt* **object'ify** to make objective. — *n* **objec'tion** the act of objecting; anything said or done in opposition; argument or reason against (with *to* or *against*); inclination to object, dislike, unwillingness. — *adj* **objec'tionable** capable of being objected to; requiring to be disapproved of; distasteful. — *adv* **objec'tionably**. — *vt* **object'ivate** to render objective. — *n* **objectivā'tion**. — *adj* **object'ive** (also *ob'*) relating to or constituting an object; of the nature of, or belonging to, that which is presented to consciousness (as opposed to *subjective*), exterior to the mind, self-existent, regarding or setting forth what is external, actual, practical, uncoloured by one's own sensations or emotions (*mod philos*); existing or considered only in relation to mind, subjective (*scholastic philos*; *obs*);

denoting the object (*gram*); in the relation of object to a verb or preposition (*gram*); objecting; (of lenses) nearest the object. — *n* (*-jekt'*) the case of the grammatical object; a word in that case (*gram*); an object-glass; the point to which the operations (*esp* of an army) are directed; a goal or aim. — *adv* **object'ively**. — *n* **object'iveness**. — *n* **object'ivism** a tendency to lay stress on what is objective; a theory that gives priority to the objective. — *n* **object'ivist**. — *adj* **objectivist'ic**. — *n* **objectiv'ity**. — *vt* **object'ivize** or **-ise** to objectify. — *adj* **ob'jectless** having no object; purposeless. — *n* **object'or**. — **ob'ject-ball** (*billiards*, etc) a ball that a player aims at striking with his own ball; **object code** (*comput*) the translated version of a program which has been assembled or compiled (cf **source code**); **ob'ject-finder** a device in microscopes for locating an object in the field before examination by a higher power; **ob'ject-glass** in an optical instrument, the lens or combination of lenses at the end next to the object; **objective test** a test or examination in which every question is set in such a way as to have only one right answer; **object language** a language that is being investigated or described by another language; **ob'ject-lesson** a lesson in which a material object is before the class; a warning or instructive experience; **object program** (*comput*) a program in machine language; **ob'ject-soul** a vital principle attributed by the primitive mind to inanimate objects. — **no object** *orig*, not considered of importance, not the thing aimed at, *esp* in *money no object*; not constituting an obstacle or problem, as in *distance*, *expense*, etc *no object*; **object of virtu** an article valued for its antiquity or as an example of craftsmanship, etc. [L *objectus*, pa p of *ob(j)icere*, or partly the noun *objectus*, *-ūs* (found in the ablative), or the frequentative verb *objectāre*, from *ob* in the way of, and *jacere* to throw]

objet *ob-zhā*, (*Fr*) *n* an object. — **objet d'art** (*där*) an article with artistic value; **objet de vertu** (*də ver-tü*) a Gallicized (by the English) version of object of virtu (qv); **objet trouvé** (*trōō-vā*) a natural or man-made object displayed as a work of art: — *pl* **objets** (*-zhā*) **d'art**, **de vertu** and **trouvés** (*-vā*).

objure *ob-jōōr'*, *vi* to swear. — *vt* to bind by oath; to charge or entreat solemnly. — *n* **objurā'tion** the act of binding by oath; a solemn charge. [L *objūrāre* to bind by oath, from *ob-* down, and *jūrāre* to swear]

objurgate *ob'jər-gāt*, or *-jûr'*, *vt* and *vi* to chide, scold. — *n* **objurgā'tion**. — *adj* **objur'gative** or **objur'gatory**. [L *objurgāre*, *-ātum* to rebuke, from *ob-* (intens), and *jurgāre* to chide]

obl *abbrev*: oblique; oblong.

oblanceolate *ob-län'si-ə-lāt*, (*bot*) *adj* (of eg a leaf) like a lance-head reversed, about three times as long as broad, tapering more gently towards base than apex. [Pfx *ob-*, as in **obcompressed**]

oblast *ob'läst*, *n* an administrative district in some republics of the former Soviet Union. [Russ]

oblate[1] *ob'lāt*, *ob-lāt'*, (*obs*) *adj* dedicated; offered up. — *n* a dedicated person, *esp* one dedicated to monastic life but not professed, or to a religious life. — *n* **oblā'tion** an act of offering; a sacrifice; anything offered in worship, *esp* a eucharistic offering; an offering generally. — *adj* **oblā'tional**. — *adj* **oblatory** (*ob'lə-tə-ri*). [L *oblātus* offered up, used as pa p of *offerre* to offer; see **offer**]

oblate[2] *ob'lāt*, *ob-lāt'*, *ō-blāt'*, *adj* flattened at opposite sides or poles, as a spheroid is, shaped like an orange (*opp* to *prolate*). — *n* **oblateness**. [On the analogy of **prolate**; L pfx *ob-* against, or (New L) in the opposite direction]

obligato. See **obbligato**.

oblige *ə-blīj'*, *ō-blīj'*, formerly *-blēj'*, *vt* to bind morally or legally; to constrain; to bind by some favour rendered, hence to do a favour to. — *vi* (*colloq*) to do something as a favour. — *n* **obligant** (*ob'li-gənt*; *Scots law*) someone who binds himself or herself to another to pay or to perform something. — *vt* **ob'ligate** (*-li-gāt* to bind by contract or duty; to bind by gratitude; to constrain (*US* and *archaic*). — *adj* (*bot*) by necessity, without option. — *n* **obligation** (*ob-li-gā'shən*) the act of obliging; a moral or legal bond, tie, or binding power; an action, promise or requirement of such a kind that failure to perform or fulfil it contravenes the law; the thing to which one is bound; a debt of gratitude; a favour; a bond containing a penalty in case of failure (*law*). — *adj* **obligā'tional**. — *adv* **obligatorily** (*o-blig'-ə-tər-i-li*, *ə-blig'*, *ob'lig-*). — *n* **oblig'atoriness** (or *ob'lig-*). — *adj* **oblig'atory** (or *ob'lig-*) binding; imposing duty; imposed as an obligation; obligate. — *n* **obligee** (*ob-li-jē'*) the person to whom another is bound by obligation (*law*); someone who is under an obligation for a favour. — *n* **oblige'ment** a favour conferred. — *adj* **oblīg'ing** prepared to confer favours; ready to do a good turn; courteous. — *adv* **oblīg'ingly**. — *n* **oblīg'ingness**. — *n* **obligor** (*ob'li-gör*; *law*) the person who binds himself or herself to another. — **obligate parasite** (*bot*) one that can grow only on its living host (cf **facultative parasite**). [Fr *obliger*, from L *obligāre*, *-ātum*, from *ob-* down, and *ligāre* to bind]

oblique *ō-blēk'*, *ə-blēk'*, *adj* slanting; neither perpendicular nor parallel; not at right angles; not parallel to an axis; not straightforward; indirect; underhand; not a right angle (*geom*); having the axis not perpendicular to the plane of the base; skew; asymmetrical about the midrib (*bot*); monoclinic (*crystallog*). — *n* an oblique line, figure, muscle, etc; an oblique movement or advance, *esp* one about 45° from the original direction. — *vi* to deviate from a direct line or from the perpendicular, to slant; to advance obliquely by facing half right or left and then advancing. — *vt* (*obs*) to turn aslant. — *n* **obliquation** (*ob-li-kwā'shən*; *obs*) obliqueness. — *adv* **oblique'ly**. — *n* **obliqueness** (*-blēk'*) or **obliquity** (*ob-lik'wi-ti*) the state of being oblique; a slanting direction; crookedness of outlook, thinking or conduct, or an instance of it; irregularity (*obs*). — *adj* **obliquid** (*ob-lik'wid*; *Spenser*) oblique. — *adj* **obliq'uitous**. — **oblique case** (*gram*) any case other than nominative and vocative; **oblique motion** (*music*) upward or downward motion of one part while another remains stationary; **oblique narration** or **speech** indirect speech (see **indirect**). — **obliquity of the ecliptic** (*astron*) the angle between the plane of the earth's orbit and that of the earth's equator. [L *oblīquus*, from *ob-* (intens), and the root of *līquis* slanting]

obliterate *ə-blit'ə-rāt*, *vt* to blot out, so as not to be readily or clearly readable; to efface; to close up and remove or destroy (a tubular part, etc; *med* and *biol*; also *vi*). — *adj* **oblit'erāted** effaced; without defined margins. — *n* **obliterā'tion**. — *adj* **oblit'erative**. — *n* **oblit'erator**. [L *oblitterāre*, *-ātum*, from *ob-* over, and *littera* (*lītera*) a letter]

oblivion *ə-bliv'i-ən*, *o-bliv'*, *n* forgetfulness; a state of having forgotten; amnesty, pardon or forgiveness, as in *act of oblivion* (*hist*); a state of being forgotten. — *adj* **obliv'ious** forgetful; apt to forget; raptly or absent-mindedly unaware (with *of* or *to*); causing, or associated with, forgetfulness (*poetic*); forgotten (*obs*). — *adv* **obliv'iously**. — *n* **obliv'iousness**. — *n* **obliviscence** (*ob-li-vis'əns*) forgetfulness; forgetting. — **act** or **bill of oblivion** (*hist*) an act or bill giving a general pardon for offences against the state. [L *oblīviō*, *-ōnis*, from the root of *oblīvīscī* to forget]

oblong *ob'long*, *adj* long in one direction; (of a rectangular shape or figure) not square, having adjacent sides unequal, *esp* considerably so; (of eg a leaf) nearly elliptical, with sides nearly parallel, ends blunted, two to four times as long as broad (*bot*). — *n* a rectangle with adjacent sides unequal; any oblong figure, whether angular or rounded. [L *oblongus*, from *ob-* (force obscure), and *longus* long]

Oblomovism *ob'lə-mov-izm*, *n* the inability to bring oneself to act, lazy inertia, from the character of *Oblomov*, the embodiment of physical and mental laziness, in the novel of the same name by the Russian author Ivan Goncharov (1859).

obloquy *ob'lə-kwi*, *n* reproachful language; censure; calumny, slander; disgrace. [L *obloquium*, from *ob* against, and *loquī* to speak]

obmutescent *ob-mū-tes'ənt*, *adj* speechless; persistently silent. — *n* **obmutesc'ence**. [L *obmūtescens*, *-entis*, pr p of *obmūtescere* to become dumb, from *ob-* (intens), and *mūtus* dumb]

obnoxious *ob-nok'shəs*, *əb-*, *adj* objectionable; offensive; noxious, hurtful (*erron*); exposed (*rare*); liable (to hurt, punishment, or censure; *obs*); subject to authority (*obs*). — *adv* **obnox'iously**. — *n* **obnox'iousness**. [L *obnoxius*, from *ob* exposed to, and *noxa* hurt]

obnubilation *ob-nū-bi-lā'shən*, (*literary*) *n* clouding; darkening. — *vt* (*obs*) **obnū'bilate**. [L *obnūbilāre* to cloud over, from L *ob-* over, and *nūbilus* cloudy]

obo *ō'bō*, *n* a vessel designed to carry oil and bulk ore, together or separately: — *pl* **o'bos**. [From *o*il *b*ulk *o*re]

oboe *ō'bō*, (*archaic*) *ō'boi*, *n* a double-reed treble woodwind instrument; an organ stop of similar tone; a person who plays the oboe, *esp* in an orchestra. — *n* **o'bōist** a player on the oboe. — **oboe d'amore** (*ō'bō dä-mō'rā*; Ital, oboe of love) an old oboe a minor third lower; **oboe di caccia** (*dē kat'cha*; of the chase) an obsolete alto or tenor oboe. [Ital *oboe*, from Fr *hautbois*; see **hautboy**]

obol *ob'əl*, *n* in ancient Greece, the sixth part of a drachma in weight or in money. — *adj* **ob'olary** (*Lamb*) extremely poor. — *n* **ob'olus** (*L*) an obol; in the Middle Ages applied to various small coins, such as the English halfpenny: — *pl* **ob'oli** (*-ī*). [Gr *obolos*]

obovate *ob-ō'vāt*, (*bot*) *adj* (of eg a leaf) egg-shaped in outline, with the narrow end next to the base. — *adv* **obō'vātely**. — *adj* **obō'void** (of a solid body, eg a fruit) egg-shaped, with the base as the narrower end. [Pfx *ob-*, as in **obcompressed**]

obreption *ob-rep'shən*, *n* surprising by stealth (*obs*); obtaining or seeking to obtain a gift, etc, by false statement, different both in sense and in etymology from *subreption* (*law*). — *adj* **obreptitious** (*-tish'əs*). [L *obreptiō*, *-ōnis*, from *ob* in the way of, and *rēpere* to creep]

obs *abbrev*: obscure; observation, as in **obs** (*obz*) **ward** (*med*); obsolete.

obscene *ob-sēn'*, *adj* offensive to the senses or the sensibility, disgusting, repellent; indecent, *esp* in a sexual sense; (less strongly) offending against an accepted standard of morals or taste; (of publications, etc) tending to deprave or corrupt (*law*); filthy, loathsome (*archaic*); ill-omened (*obs*). — *adv* **obscene'ly**. — *n* **obscene'ness** or **obscenity** (*-sen'* or *-sēn'*). [L *obscēnus*]

obscure *ob-skūr'*, *adj* dark; not distinct; not easily understood; not clear, legible, or perspicuous; unknown; hidden; inconspicuous; lowly; not famous; living or enveloped in darkness. — *n* darkness; an obscure place; indistinctness. — *vt* to darken; to make dim; to hide; to make less plain; to make doubtful. — *vi* (*obs*) to conceal oneself, hide; to darken. — *n* **ob'scūrant** (*-ant*, or *ob-skūr'ənt*) someone who tries hard to prevent enlightenment or reform. — *n* **obscūrant'ism** (or *-skūr'*) opposition to inquiry, reform or new knowledge. — *n* **obscūrant'ist** (or *-skūr'*) an obscurant. — *adj* of or relating to obscurantism. — *n* **obscūrā'tion** the act of obscuring or state of being obscured. — *adv* **obscūre'ly**. — *n* **obscūre'ment** (*rare*). — *n* **obscūre'ness**. — *n* **obscūr'er**. — *n* **obscūr'ity** the state or quality of being obscure; the state of being unknown or not famous; darkness; an obscure place, point or condition. [Fr *obscur*, from L *obscūrus*, from *ob-* over, and the root seen in L *scūtum* shield, Gr *skeuē* covering]

obsecrate *ob'si-krāt*, *vt* to beseech; to implore. — *n* **obsecrā'tion** supplication; one of the clauses in the Litany beginning with *by* (*Christian relig*). [L *obsecrāre*, *-ātum* to entreat; from *ob* before, and *sacrāre*, from *sacer* sacred]

obsequent *ob'si-kwənt*, *adj* (of a river) flowing in a contrary direction to the original slope of the land, parallel to the *consequent* and perpendicular to the *subsequent* streams. [L *ob* face to face with, and *sequēns*, *-entis*, pr p of *sequī* to follow]

obsequies *ob'si-kwiz*, *n pl* funeral rites and solemnities: — *sing* (*rare*) **ob'sequy** (*Milton* **obsequie**). — *adj* **obsequial** (*-sē'kwi-əl*) or **obsē'quious** (*Shakesp*); see also **obsequious**[1]). [LL *obsequiae*, a confusion of L *exsequiae* funeral rites, and *obsequium*; see **obsequious**[1]]

obsequious[1] *ob-sē'kwi-əs*, *adj* servilely ingratiating; fawning; *orig* compliant, obedient, dutiful. — *adv* **obsē'quiously**. — *n* **obsē'quiousness**. [L *obsequiōsus* compliant, from *obsequium* compliance, from *ob-* towards, and *sequī* to follow]

obsequious[2]. See under **obsequies**.

observe *əb-zûrv'*, *ob-*, *vt* to keep in view; to watch; to subject to systematic watching; to regard attentively; to watch critically and attentively in order to ascertain a fact; to ascertain by such watching; to notice; to pay attention to; to remark in words, to comment; to comply with; to act according to; to heed and to carry out in practice; to keep with ceremony; to celebrate; to keep (eg silence); to be deferential to or humour (*Shakesp*). — *vi* to take observations; to make remarks. — *n* (*Scot*) a remark. — *adj* **observ'able** discernible, perceptible; worthy of note; notable; to be observed. — *n* something that can be observed by the senses, with or without the help of instrument(s). — *n* **observ'ableness**. — *adv* **observ'ably**. — *n* **observ'ance** the keeping of a law, rule or custom, or due performance of a duty or ceremony; the keeping of a festival, etc with ceremony or according to custom; a custom observed or to be observed; a rule of religious life; an order or company accepting it (*esp* the Observants), or their house; a deferential act or treatment; watchful heed (*Shakesp*); now rarely, observation. — *n* **observ'ancy** observance; observation; a house of Observants. — *adj* **observ'ant** observing; having powers of observing and noting; taking notice; keeping an observance; carefully attentive. — *n* someone who complies strictly with a custom, etc; an obsequious attendant (*Shakesp*). — *n* **Observ'ant** or **Observ'antine** (*-ən-tin*, *-tēn*) a Franciscan friar of stricter rule. — *adv* **observ'antly**. — *n* **observā'tion** the act, or an act, of observing; the habit, practice, or faculty of seeing and noting; attention; the act of recognizing and noting phenomena as they occur in nature, as distinguished from *experiment*; a reading of an instrument; the result of such observing; watching; that which is observed; a remark; the fact of being observed; now rarely, observance. — *adj* **observā'tional** consisting of or containing observations or remarks; derived from observation, as distinguished from *experiment*. — *adv* **observā'tionally**. — *adj* **observ'ative** observant; observational. — *n* **ob'servātor** (now *rare* or *obs*) someone who observes in any sense; a remarker. — *n* **observ'atory** a building or station for making astronomical and physical observations; a viewpoint; a spying-place. — *n* **observ'er** a person who observes in any sense; a person whose function it is to take observations; formerly, an airman who accompanied a pilot to observe, now a flying officer (qv); a member of the Royal Observer Corps, a uniformed civilian organization affiliated to the Royal Air Force; someone deputed to watch proceedings. — *adj* **observ'ing** habitually taking notice; attentive. — *adv* **observ'ingly**. — **observation car** a railway carriage designed to allow passengers to view scenery; **observation post** a position (*esp* military) from which observations are made (and from which artillery fire is directed). [Fr *observer*, from L *observāre*, *-ātum*, from *ob* towards, and *servāre* to keep]

obsess *əb-ses'*, *ob-*, *vt* to occupy the thoughts of obstinately and persistently; to beset (*archaic*); to besiege (*obs*). — *n* **obsession** (*-sesh'ən*) a fixed idea; the morbid persistence of an idea in the mind, against one's will (*psychiatry*); persistent attack, *esp* of an evil spirit (*archaic*); the state of being molested in this way from outside, *opp* to *possession*, or control by an evil spirit from within (*archaic*); a siege (*obs*). — *adj* **obsess'ional**. — *adv* **obsessionally**. — *n* **obsess'ionist** someone who is obsessed by a fixed idea. — *adj* **obsess'ive** relating to or resulting from obsession; obsessing. — *adj* **obsessive-compul'sive** (*psychiatry*) denoting a form of neurosis in which the sufferer is driven to perform a particular act repeatedly. [L *obsidēre*, *obsessum* to besiege]

obsidian *ob-sid'i-ən*, *n* a vitreous acid volcanic rock resembling bottle-glass, a coarse green glass used in the making of bottles. [From *obsidiānus*, a false reading of L *obsiānus* (*lapis*), a stone found by one *Obsius* (wrongly *Obsidius*) in Ethiopia, according to Pliny]

obsidional *ob-sid'i-ən-əl*, *adj* pertaining to a siege. — Also **obsid'ionary**. [L *obsidiō*, *-ōnis* a siege; see **obsess**]

obsign *ob-sīn'*, or **obsignate** *ob-sig'nāt*, *vt* to seal or confirm. — *n* **obsignā'tion** (*-sig-*). — *adj* **obsig'natory**. [L *obsīgnāre* to seal up, from *ob-* over, and *sīgnāre* to mark, seal]

obsolescent *ob-sə-les'ənt*, *adj* going out of use or out of date; in course of disappearing or becoming useless; tending to become obsolete. — *vi* **obsolesce** (*-les'*) to be in the process of going out of use. — *n* **obsolesc'ence**. — *adj* **ob'solete** (*-lēt*) gone out of use; antiquated; no longer functional or fully developed. — *adv* **ob'soletely**. — *n* **ob'soleteness**. — *n* **obsolē'tion** (*rare*). — *n* **ob'solētism**. — **planned obsolescence** the deterioration or the going out of date of a product according to a prearranged plan, *usu* involving its replacement; the deliberate inclusion in a product, eg a car, of features which lead to deterioration or out-of-dateness before the end of its useful life, to ensure future sales. [L *obsolescere*, *obsolētum*, perh from pfx *ob* in opposition, *solēre* to be accustomed, to use (to), and inchoative sfx *-scere*]

obstacle *ob'stə-kl*, *n* anything that stands in the way of or hinders progress. — *adj* (*Shakesp*) stubborn. — **obstacle race** a race in which competitors have to get over, get through, or otherwise negotiate a variety of physical obstacles. [Fr, from L *obstāculum*, from *ob* in the way of, and *stāre* to stand]

obstetric *ob-stet'rik* or **obstetrical** *-əl*, *adj* pertaining to the care of women during pregnancy and childbirth. — *adv* **obstet'rically**. — *n* **obstetrician** (*ob-sti-trish'ən*) a man or woman skilled in practising, or qualified to practise, obstetrics. — *n sing* **obstet'rics** the science of midwifery. [L *obstetrīcius* (the *-īc-* confused with the suffix *-ic*), from *obstetrīx*, *-īcis* a midwife, from *ob* before, and *stāre* to stand]

obstinate *ob'sti-nit*, *adj* blindly or excessively firm; unyielding; stubborn; not easily subdued or remedied. — *n* **ob'stinacy** (*-nə-si*) or **ob'stinateness**. — *adv* **ob'stinately**. [L *obstināre*, *-ātum*, from *ob* in the way of, and *stanāre* (only in compounds), a form of *stāre* to stand]

obstipation *ob-sti-pā'shən*, (*pathol*) *n* severe constipation. [L *ob* against, and *stīpāre*, *-ātum* to press]

obstreperous *ob-strep'ə-rəs*, *adj* noisy; unruly; making a loud noise; clamorous. — *vt* **obstrep'erate** (*Sterne*). — *adv* **obstrep'erously**. — *n* **obstrep'erousness**. [L *obstreperus*, from *ob* before, against, and *strepere* to make a noise]

obstriction *ob-strik'shən*, (*obs*) *n* obligation. [L *obstringere*, *obstrictum* to bind up]

obstropalous *ob-strop'ə-ləs* and **obstropulous** *ob-strop'-ū-ləs*, illiterate forms of **obstreperous**.

obstruct *ob-strukt'*, *əb-*, *vt* to block up; to hinder from passing or progressing; to shut off; to hamper. — *vi* to be an obstruction; to practise obstruction. — *n* **obstruc'ter** (*rare*). — *n* **obstruc'tion** the act, or an act of obstructing; a state of being obstructed; that which hinders progress or action; an obstacle; the offence of obstructing another player (*sport*); opposition by delaying tactics, eg in a legislative assembly. — *adj* **obstruc'tional**. — *adv* **obstruc'tionally**. — *n* **obstruc'tionism**. — *n* **obstruc'tionist** someone, *esp* a politician in a legislative assembly, who practises obstruction. — Also *adj*. — *adj* **obstruct'ive** tending to obstruct; hindering. — *n* a hindrance; someone who hinders progress. — *adv* **obstruct'ively**. — *n* **obstruct'or**. — *adj* **obstruent** (*ob'stro͞o-ənt*) obstructing; blocking up. — *n* anything that obstructs, *esp* (*med*) in the passages of the body; an astringent drug (*med*); a stop or a fricative (*phonetics*). — **obstruction lights** (*aeronautics*) lights fixed to all structures near airports that constitute a danger to aircraft in flight. [L *obstruere*, *obstructum*, from *ob* in the way of, and *struere*, *structum* to pile up, build]

obtain *ob-tān'*, *əb-*, *vt* to get; to procure by effort; to gain; to reach (*archaic*); to hold or occupy (*obs*). — *vi* to be established; to continue in use; to hold good; to prevail or to succeed (*archaic*); to attain (*obs*). — *adj* **obtain'able**. — *n* **obtain'er**. — *n* **obtain'ment**. — *n* **obtention** (*-ten'shən*; *rare*) getting. [Fr *obtenir*, from L *obtinēre* to occupy, from *ob* against, and *tenēre* to hold]

obtect or **obtected** *ob-tekt'*, *-id*, (*entomol*) *adj* having wings and legs immovably pressed against the body in a hard chitinous case, as with many insect pupae. [L *obtegere*, *obtectum* to cover over, from *ob-* over, and *tegere* to cover]

obtemper *ob-tem'pər*, (*Scots law*) *vt* to yield obedience to. — Also *vi* (with *to* or *unto*). — Also **obtem'perate**. [L *obtemperāre*, *-ātum*, from *ob* before, and *temperāre* to restrain oneself]

obtend *ob-tend'*, (*obs*) *vt* to hold out in opposition; to put forward or allege. [L *obtendere* to stretch before, from *ob* in front of, and *tendere* to stretch]

obtention. See **obtain**.

obtest *ob-test'*, *vt* to call to witness; to adjure. — *vi* (with *against* or *with*) to protest. — *n* **obtestā'tion**. [L *obtestārī* to call as a witness, from *ob* before, and *testis* a witness]

obtrude *ob-tro͞od'*, *əb-*, *vt* to thrust forward or upon someone, unduly or in an unwelcome way. — *vi* to thrust oneself forward. — *n* **obtrud'er**. — *n* **obtrud'ing**. — *n* **obtrusion** (*-tro͞o'zhən*) an unwanted thrusting in, forward or upon. — *adj* **obtrusive** (*-tro͞o'siv*) unduly prominent, protruding or projecting; tending to thrust oneself in or forward. — *adv* **obtru'sively**. — *n* **obtru'siveness**. [L *obtrūdere*, from *ob* against, and *trūdere*, *trūsum* to thrust]

obtruncate *ob-trung'kāt*, *vt* to cut or lop off the head of. [L *obtruncāre*, *-ātum* to cut in pieces, mutilate, from *ob-* (intens) and *truncāre* to cut off]

obtrusion, obtrusive. See under **obtrude**.

obtund *ob-tund'*, (*rare*) *vt* to blunt or dull; to deaden. — *adj* **obtund'ent** dulling. — *n* an application to deaden irritation. [L *obtundere* to strike upon, from *ob* against, and *tundere* to thump]

obturate *ob'tū-rāt*, *vt* to stop up. — *n* **obturā'tion** stopping up; stopping of a hole to prevent the escape of gas (*gunnery*). — *n* **ob'turātor** a structure or device that closes a cavity; the structures closing a large opening in the hip-bone (*anatom*). [L *obtūrāre*, *-ātum* to stop up; etymology obscure]

obtuse *ob-tūs'*, *əb-*, *adj* blunt; not pointed; blunt or rounded at the tip (*bot*); greater than a right angle and less than 180° (*geom*); dull; dull-witted; insensitive. — *adv* **obtuse'ly**. — *n* **obtuse'ness**. — *n* **obtus'ity**. — *adj* **obtuse'-ang'led** or **-ang'ular** having an angle greater than a right angle and less than 180°. [L *obtūsus*, pa p of *obtundere*; cf **obtund**]

obumbrate *ob-um'brāt*, (*rare*) *vt* to overshadow. — *n* **obumbrā'tion**. [L *obumbrāre*, *-ātum*, from *ob* in the way of, and *umbra* shadow]

obvention *ob-ven'shən*, (*obs*) *n* any incidental occurrence or advantage, *esp* a fee. [L *obvenīre*, *-ventum* to come to meet, come by chance, from *ob* face to face with, and *venīre* to come]

obverse *ob'vûrs*, *ob-vûrs'*, *adj* turned towards one; complemental, constituting the opposite aspect of the same fact; having the base narrower than the apex (*bot*); obtained by obversion (*logic*). — *n* **obverse**

(*ob'vûrs*) the side of a coin containing the head or principal symbol, often confused with *reverse*; the face or side of anything normally presented to view; a counterpart or opposite aspect; a proposition obtained from another by obversion (*logic*). — *adv* **obverse'ly**. — *n* **obver'sion** the act of turning a thing toward one; a species of immediate inference where the contradictory of the original predicate is predicated of the original subject, the quality of the proposition being changed, eg to infer from *All A is B* that *No A is not B*; also called *permutation* and *equipollence* (*logic*). — *vt* **obvert'** to turn in the direction of, or face to face with, something: to infer the obverse of (*logic*). [L *obversus* turned against or towards, from *ob-* against, towards, and *vertere* to turn]

obviate *ob'vi-āt*, *vt* to prevent or dispose of in advance; to forestall; to meet on the way (*obs*). — *n* **obviā'tion**. [L *obviāre*, *-ātum*, from *ob* in the way of, and *viāre*, *viātum* to go, from *via* a way]

obvious *ob'vi-əs*, *adj* easily discovered or understood; clearly or plainly evident; not subtle; meeting one in the way (*obs*). — *adv* **ob'viously**. — *n* **ob'viousness**. [L *obvius*, from *ob via*; see **obviate**]

obvolute *ob'və-lūt*, *-lōōt*, or **obvoluted** *-id*, (*bot*) *adj* arranged so that each leaf of a pair is folded lengthwise, enclosing one half of the other. — *adj* **obvolvent** (*-vol'vənt*; *archaic*) enwrapping; curved downward or inward (*entomol*). [L *obvolūtus*, pa p, and *obvolvens*, *-entis*, pr p, of *obvolvere* to enwrap, from *ob* over, and *volvere*, *volūtum* to roll]

OC *abbrev*: Officer Commanding; Officer in Charge; (Officer of the) Order of Canada; original cover (*philat*).

oc *abbrev*: only child.

o/c *abbrev*: overcharge.

oca *ō'kə*, *n* a S American wood-sorrel with edible tubers. [Sp, from Quechua]

ocarina *ok-ə-rē'nə*, *n* a fluty-toned musical toy, *orig* of terracotta, egg-shaped, with a long mouthpiece. [Ital, dimin of *oca* a goose]

OCCAM or **occam** *ok'əm*, (*comput*) *n* a programming language.

Occamism or **Ockhamism** *ok'əm-izm*, *n* the doctrine of the nominalist schoolman, William of *Occam* or *Ockham* , who died about 1349. — *n* **Occ'amist** or **Ock'hamist**. — **Occam's** (or **Ockham's**) **razor** the principle that entities are not to be multiplied beyond necessity.

occamy *ok'ə-mi*, *n* a silvery alloy. [**alchemy**]

occasion *ə-kā'zhən*, *n* a case, instance or time of something happening; a suitable time, moment or opportunity; a special time or season; a chance of bringing about something desired; an opportunity; an event which, although not the cause, determines the time at which another happens; a reason, pretext or excuse; requirement; need; (*usu* in *pl*) business; a special ceremony, celebration or event; formerly, in Scotland, a communion service; doing, occasioning, matter of responsibility (*Shakesp*); events or course of events (*Shakesp*); (in *pl*) necessary bodily functions (*obs*). — *vt* to give occasion or rise to; to cause; to accustom (*obs*). — *adj* **occā'sional** happening or occurring infrequently, irregularly or now and then; produced on or for some special event or for special occasions; constituting the occasion; resulting from accident (*obs*). — *n* **occā'sionalism** the Cartesian explanation of the apparent interaction of mind and matter by the direct intervention of God on the occasion of certain changes occurring in one or the other. — *n* **occā'sionalist**. — *n* **occāsional'ity**. — *adv* **occā'sionally** on or for an occasion; now and then; casually (*obs*). — *n* **occā'sioner**. — **occasional cause** the event which in the Cartesian philosophy is only the occasion, not the true cause; that by which the efficient cause comes into operation; **occasional conformist** (*hist*) a Dissenter who qualified for office by conforming to the Church of England upon occasion; **occasional table** a small portable *esp* ornamental table. — **occasioned by** caused by; necessitated by; (which was) a consequence of (*obs*); **on occasion** from time to time; in case of need; as opportunity offers; **rise to the occasion** see under **rise**; **take occasion** to take advantage of an opportunity (to). [L *occāsiō*, *-ōnis* opportunity, from *ob*, in the way of, and *cadere*, *cāsum* to fall]

Occident or **occident** *ok'si-dənt*, *n* the quarter of the sky where the sun, stars and planets set; the west, *opp* to *Orient*. — *adj* **Occidental** or **occidental** (*-dent'l*) western; characteristic of the West (*esp* Europe, America, the Western United States); (of a gem) relatively less precious (because the best stones were presumed to come from the East). — *n* a westerner; a language invented by Edgar de Wahl (1922). — *n* **Occiden'talism** the culture and ways of Occidental peoples. — *n* **Occiden'talist** a student of Occidental languages; an Oriental who favours western ideas, customs, etc. — *vt* **occiden'talize** or **-ise** to cause to conform to western ideas or customs. — *adv* **occiden'tally**. — **occidental topaz** a semi-precious yellow quartz; **occidental turquoise** odontolite. [L *occidens*, *-entis* setting, pr p of *occidere*, from *ob* towards, down, and *cadere* to fall]

occiput *ok'si-put*, (*anatom*) *n* the back of the head or skull. — *adj* **occip'ital** pertaining to the back of the head. — *n* the occipital bone, the bone at the back of the skull. — *adv* **occip'itally**. [L *occiput*, from *ob* over, against, and *caput* head]

occlude *o-klōōd'*, *ə-*, *vt* to shut in or out; to cut or shut off; to stop or cover (a passage, cavity or opening); to bring together (the teeth or eyelids); (of eg a metal or other solid) to absorb or retain (eg a gas or liquid; *chem*). — *vi* (*dentistry*; of the teeth) to bite or close together. — *adj* **occlu'dent** causing or resulting in occlusion; occluding. — *n* that which occludes. — *n* **occlu'der** (*med*, *opthalmol*, etc) a device that occludes. — *adj* **occlu'sal** (*-səl*; *dentistry*) pertaining to the occlusion of teeth. — *n* **occlu'sion** (*-zhən*) a closing of an opening, passage or cavity; the act of occluding or absorbing; the bite or mode of meeting of the teeth (*dentistry*); the formation or condition of an occluded front (*meteorol*). — *adj* **occlu'sive** (*-siv*) serving to close; characterized by occlusion. — *n* (*phonetics*) a sound produced by closing the breath passage. — *n* **occlu'sor** (*anatom*) that which closes, *esp* a muscle for closing an opening. — **occluded front** (*meteorol*) an advancing cold front into which a mass of warm air has been driven obliquely, forming a bulge which narrows as the warm air is lifted up and the cold air flows in beneath. [L *occlūdere*, *-clūsum*, from *ob* in the way of, and *claudere* to shut]

occult *o-kult'*, *ok'ult*, *adj* hidden; secret; esoteric; unknown; beyond the range of sense or understanding; transcending the bounds of natural knowledge; mysterious; magical; supernatural; (of a line) faint or dotted or to be rubbed out later (*rare*); not discovered without test or experiment (*obs*). — *vt* **occult** (*o-kult'*) to hide or make disappear; to obscure, *esp* by occultation (*astron*). — *vi* to become temporarily invisible; (of a heavenly body) to be hidden by occultation (*astron*). — *n* **occultā'tion** a concealing, *esp* of one of the heavenly bodies by another; the state of being hidden. — *adj* **occult'ed**. — *adj* **occult'ing** (of a lighthouse, beacon, etc light) becoming temporarily invisible at regular intervals. — *n* **occ'ultism** the doctrine or study of things hidden or mysterious, theosophy, etc. — *n* **occ'ultist** someone who believes in occult things. — *adv* **occult'ly**. — *n* **occult'ness**. — **occult sciences** alchemy, astrology, magic, palmistry, etc. [L *occultus*, pa p of *occulere* to hide, from *ob-* over, and the root of *celāre* to hide]

occupance, etc, **occupation**, **etc**. See under **occupy**.

occupy *ok'ū-pī*, *vt* to take possession of; to capture; to hold; to keep possession of by being present in; to fill (a post, office); to take up (eg a space, time, etc); to tenant; to keep (often oneself) busy; to lay out in trade (*Bible*); to cohabit with (*obs*). — *vi* (*obs*) to hold possession; to trade; to cohabit: — *pr p* **occ'ūpying**; *pa t* and *pa p* **occ'ūpied**. — *n* **occ'ūpance** (*rare*) or **occ'**-

ūpancy the act or fact of occupying, or of taking or holding possession (*esp* of that which previously had no owner); possession; the time during which someone occupies a place or position. — *n* **occ'ūpant** someone who takes or has possession. — *vt* **occ'ūpāte** (*obs*) to occupy. — *adj* (*obs*) occupied. — *n* **occūpā'tion** the act of occupying; possession; the state of being employed or occupied; the time during which a country, etc, is occupied by enemy forces; that which occupies or takes up one's attention; one's habitual employment, profession, craft or trade. — *adj* occupational. — *adj* **occūpā'tional** connected with habitual occupation. — *adj* **occ'ūpātive** (*law*) held by tenure based on occupation. — *n* **occ'ūpier** (*-pī-ər*) a person who occupies; an occupant; someone who practises (*obs*); a dealer (*obs*). — **occupational ailment**, **disease** or **injury** a disease, injury, etc, to which workers engaged in a particular occupation are prone because of the conditions of that occupation; **occupational hazard** a danger to which workers in a particular occupation are exposed; **occupational pension** a pension paid by a person's employers, *usu* based on a personal pension scheme, as distinct from a state pension; **occupational therapy** the treatment of a disease (including a mental disease) or an injury by a regulated course of suitable work; **occupation level** in an archaeological site, any of several distinct layers of debris left by successive occupations, from which the site can be dated. — **army of occupation** troops stationed in the territory of a defeated enemy or subject country to keep order, to ensure compliance with the terms of a peace treaty, to prop up a weak or unpopular government, etc. [Fr *occuper*, from L *occupāre*, *-ātum*, from *ob* to, on, and *capere* to take; the *-y* is unexplained]

occur *o-kûr'*, *ə-*, *vi* (with *to*) to come into the mind of; to be or be found; to happen; (of festivals) to fall on the same day; to meet (*obs*): — *pr p* **occurr'ing**; *pa t* and *pa p* **occurred'**. — *n* **occurrence** (*-kur'*) the act or fact of occurring; anything that happens; an event, *esp* one unlooked for or unplanned. — *adj* **occurr'ent** occurring; happening; turning up; to be found; incidental. — *n* someone or something that meets or comes in contact (*obs*); an occurrence or an item of news (*archaic*). [L *occurrere*, from *ob* in the way of, and *currere* to run]

ocean *ō'shən*, *n* the vast expanse of salt water that covers the greater part of the surface of the globe; any one of its great divisions (Atlantic, Pacific, Indian, Arctic, Antarctic; also Southern (ie the belt of water round the earth between 40° and 66½° south) and German (ie the North Sea); any immense expanse or vast quantity (*fig*). — *adj* of or relating to the ocean generally. — *n* **oceanarium** (*ō-shən-ār'i-əm*) an enclosed part of the sea (also called **seaquarium**) or a large salt-water pond, in which dolphins, porpoises, etc, are kept and tamed. — *n* **oceanaut** (*ō'shə-nöt*) someone who lives for periods under the sea, in order to observe and explore. — *adj* **Oceanian** (*ō-shi-ä'ni-ən*) pertaining to *Oceania*, which includes Polynesia, Micronesia and Melanesia, with or without Australasia. — *adj* **oceanic** (*ō-shi-an'ik*) pertaining to the ocean; found or formed in the ocean or high seas, pelagic; wide like the ocean. — *n* **oceanid** (*ō-sē'ən-id*; *Gr mythol*) (with *cap*) a daughter of Oceanus; an ocean nymph: — *pl* **ocē'anids** or **oceanides** (*ō-sē-an'id-ēz*). — *n* **oceanographer** (*ō-shi-ən-og'rə-fər*, or *ō-shən-*, or *ō-si-ən-*). — *adj* **oceanographic** (*ō-shi-an-ə-graf'ik*, or *ō-shən-*, or *ō-si-an-*) or **oceanograph'ical**. — *n* **oceanog'raphy** the scientific study and description of the ocean. — *adj* **oceanolog'ical**. — *n* **oceanol'ogist**. — *n* **oceanol'ogy** oceanography. — **o'cean-bā'sin** the depression in which the waters of an ocean are contained. — *adj* **o'cean-going** sailing, or suitable for sailing, across the ocean. — **o'cean-grey'hound** a very fast steamer; **oceanic crust** that part of the Earth's crust that is normally characteristic of oceans, consisting of *approx* 5km water, 1km sediments and 5km basaltic rocks; **oceanic islands** islands far from the mainland; **ocean perch** a scorpion-fish, *Sebastes marinus*, also known as the *bergylt*, *redfish* or *rosefish*; **o'cean-stream'** (*Milton*) the river Oceanus (Okeanos), supposed to encircle the land of the world. [OFr *occean*, from L *Ōceanus*, from Gr *Ōkeanos*, the river, or its god]

ocellus *ō-sel'əs*, *n* a simple eye or eye-spot, distinguished from a compound eye, in insects and other lower animals; an eyelike or ringed spot of colour: — *pl* **ocell'ī**. — *adj* **ocell'ar** of, or of the nature of, an ocellus or ocelli. — *adj* **ocell'ate** (or *os'əl-āt*) or **oc'ellated** eyelike and ringed; having an eyelike spot or spots. — *n* **ocellation** (*os-ə-lā'shən*). [L *ocellus*, dimin of *oculus* an eye]

ocelot *o'si-lot* or *ō'*, *n* an American cat (*Felis pardalis*), like a small leopard; its fur. — *adj* **o'celoid** (*rare*). [Nahuatl *ocelotl* jaguar]

OCF *abbrev*: Officiating Chaplain to the Forces.

och *ohh*, *interj* expressing impatience, or contemptuous dismissal, pshaw, tut (*Scot*); in Ireland and part of Scotland, expressing regret.

oche *ok'i*, (*darts*) *n* the line, groove or ridge behind which a player must stand to throw. — Also **hockey** or **hockey line** [Ety uncertain; a connection with OE *oche* to lop (from OFr *ocher* to nick, cut a groove in), has been suggested; see also ety for **notch**]

ocher, **ocherous**, etc. See **ochre**.

ochidore *ok'i-dōr*, *-dör*, *n* Kingsley's name (not otherwise known) for a shore-crab.

ochlocracy *ok-lok'rə-si*, *n* mob-rule. — *n* **och'locrat** (*-lə-krat*). — *adj* **ochlocrat'ic** or **ochlocrat'ical**. — *adv* **ochlocrat'ically**. — *n* **ochlophobia** (*ok-lə-fō'bi-ə*; Gr *phobos* fear) fear of crowds. — *n* **ochlophō'biac**. — *adj* **ochlophō'bic**. [Gr *ochlokratiā*, from *ochlos* a crowd, and *kratos* power]

ochone. See **ohone**.

Ochotona *ok-ō-tō'nə*, (*zool*) *n* the pika genus. [Mongol *ochodona*]

ochre or *US* **ocher** *ō'kər*, *n* a native pigment composed of fine clay and an iron oxide (limonite in yellow ochre, haematite in red); a paint manufactured from it, used for colouring walls, etc; an earthy metallic oxide of various kinds; money, *esp* gold (*slang*). — *vt* to mark or colour with ochre. — *adj* **ochrā'ceous** or **ochreous** (*ō'kri-əs*), **o'chroid** or **o'chrous** (sometimes **o'cherous**) or **o'chry** (also **o'chrey** or **o'chery**) consisting of, containing or resembling ochre. — *adj* **ochroleu'cous** (Gr *leukos* white) yellowish white. [Fr *ocre*, from L *ōchra*, from Gr *ōchrā*, from *ōchros* pale yellow]

ochrea, etc. See **ocrea**.

ochrous, **ochry**, etc. See **ochre**.

ocker *ok'ər*, (*Austr colloq*; also with cap) *n* an oafish uncultured Australian. — *adj* boorish, uncultured; Australian. — *n* **ock'erism** or **Ock'erism** boorishness in Australians. [A form of *Oscar*, esp after a character in a television programme]

Ockhamism and **Ockham's razor**. See **Occamism**.

o'clock. See under **clock**.

ocotillo *ō-kō-tē'yō*, *n* a shrub, *Fouquieria splendens*, a native of Mexico and the south-western part of the United States, with spines and clusters of red flowers: — *pl* **ocotill'os**. [Am Sp, diminutive of *ocote*, a type of tree, from Nahuatl *ocotl*]

OCR (*comput*) *abbrev*: optical character recognition, reader or reading.

ocrea (commonly **ochrea**) *ok'ri-ə*, (*bot*) *n* a sheath formed of two stipules united round a stem: — *pl* **oc'reae** or **och'reae** (*-ē*). — *adj* **oc'reāte** or **och'reate**. [L *ocrea* a legging]

Oct *abbrev*: October.

oct *abbrev*: octavo.

oct- *okt-*, or **octa-** *ok-tə-*, *ok-ta'*, also **octo-** (qv) *combining form* denoting eight. — *n* **octachord** (*ok'tə-körd*; Gr *chordē* a gut string) an eight-stringed instrument; a diatonic series of eight tones. — *adj* **octachord'al**. — *n* **octagon** (*ok'tə-gon*; Gr *gōniā* an angle) a plane figure of eight sides and eight angles. — Also *adj*. — *adj* **octagonal** (*-ta'gən-əl*). — *adv* **octa'gonally**. — *n* **octa-**

hedron (*ok-tə-hē'drən*; Gr *hedrā* a base) a solid bounded by eight plane faces: — *pl* **octahē'drons** or **octahē'dra**. — *adj* **octahē'dral**. — *n* **octahē'drite** (*mineralogy*) anatase, crystallizing in square bipyramids. — *adj* **octamerous** (*ok-tam'*; Gr *meros* a part) having parts in eights. — *n* **octameter** (*ok-ta'mi-tər*; Gr *metron* a measure; *prosody*) a line of eight feet or measures. — *n pl* **Octan'dria** (Gr *anēr*, *andros* a man) a Linnaean class of plants with eight stamens. — *adj* **octan'drian**. — *adj* **octandrous** (*ok-tan'drəs*; *bot*) having eight stamens. — *adj* **octangular** (*ok-tang'gū-lər*) having eight angles. — *n* **octapody** (*ok-ta'pə-di*; Gr *pous*, *podos* foot; *prosody*) a line of eight feet. — *adj* **octapodic** (*ok-tə-pod'ik*). — *n* **octastich** (*ok'tə-stik*; Gr *stichos* row, line; *prosody*) a strophe of eight lines, also **octastichon** (*ok-ta'sti-kon*). — *adj* **octa'stichous** (*bot*) in eight rows. — *adj* **octastroph'ic** (Gr *strophē* strophe; *prosody*) consisting of eight strophes. — *adj* **octastyle** (*ok'tə-stīl*; Gr *stȳlos* a column; *archit*) having eight columns at the end. — *n* a building or portico so designed. — Also **oc'tostyle**. [Gr *okta-*, combining form of *oktō* eight]

octa. See **okta**.

octad *ok'tad*, *n* a set of eight things. — *adj* **octad'ic**. [Gr *oktas*, *-ados*]

octagon... to ... **octahedrite**. See under **oct-**.

octal *ok'təl*, *adj* pertaining to or based on the number eight. — *n* a numbering system using a base of eight. [Gr *oktō* eight]

octamerous... to ... **octandrous**. See under **oct-**.

octane *ok'tān*, *n* any of a group of eighteen isomeric hydrocarbons (C_8H_{18}), eighth in the methane series. — **octane number** or **rating** the percentage by volume of so-called iso-octane (see under **iso-**) in a mixture with normal heptane which has the same knocking characteristics as the motor fuel under test. [Gr *oktō* eight, and sfx *-ane*, as in meth*ane*]

octangular. See under **oct-**.

Octans *ok'tanz*, (*astron*) *n* a southern constellation containing the south celestial pole. [L *octāns* an eighth part]

octant *ok'tənt*, *n* an arc of one-eighth of the circumference of a circle; a sector of one-eighth of a circle; an angle-measuring instrument with such an arc; a division of space or of a solid figure or body divided into eight by three planes, *usu* at right angles; a position 45° distant from another position, *esp* of the moon from conjunction or opposition (*astron*). — *adj* **octantal** (*-tant'əl*). [L *octāns*, *-antis* an eighth]

octapla *ok'tə-plə*, *n sing* a book of eight (*esp* Biblical) parallel texts. [Gr *oktaplā* (contracted pl) eightfold]

octaploid *ok'tə-ploid*, *adj* eightfold; having eight times the basic number of chromosomes (*biol*). — *n* a cell, organism or form with eight sets of chromosomes. — *n* **oc'taploidy** the condition of being octaploid. — Also **oc'toploid**, etc. [Gr *oktaploos* eightfold, and *eidos* form]

octapody, **octapodic**. See under **oct-**.

octaroon. See **octoroon**.

octastich... to ... **octastyle**. See under **oct-**.

octave *ok'tiv*, *-tāv*, *n* a set of eight; the last day of eight beginning with a church festival; the eight days from a festival to its octave; an eighth, or an interval of twelve semitones (*music*); a note or sound an eighth above (or below) another (*music*); the range of notes or keys from any one to its octave (*music*); an organ stop sounding an octave higher than the keys indicate; a cask containing the eighth part of a pipe of wine; an eight-lined stanza; the first eight lines of a sonnet. — *adj* consisting of eight (*esp* lines); in octaves; sounding an octave higher (*music*). — *adj* **octāv'al** pertaining to an octave; based on the number eight. — **oc'tave-coupler** (*music*) a device in an organ whereby, when a key is struck, the note played is doubled; **oc'tave-flute'** the piccolo, an octave above the ordinary flute. — **great octave** (*music*) the bass octave, conventionally represented by capital letters, from C, on the second line below the bass stave, up; **law of octaves** the relationship which arranges the elements in order of atomic weight and in groups of eight, with recurring similarity of properties; **small octave** the tenor octave, from the second space in the bass. [Fr, from L *octāvus* eighth]

octavo *ok-tā'vō*, *adj* having eight leaves to the sheet; (conventionally) of a size so obtained, whether so folded or not. — *n* a book printed on sheets so folded; (conventionally) a book of such a size; contracted **8vo**, *usu* meaning demy octavo $8\frac{1}{2} \times 5\frac{1}{2}$ inches (146 × 228mm): — *pl* **octā'vōs**. [L *in octāvō* in the eighth, from *octāvus* eighth]

octennial *ok-ten'yəl*, *-i-əl*, *adj* happening every eighth year; lasting eight years. — *adv* **octenn'ially**. [L *octennium* eight years, from *annus* year]

octet, **octett** or **octette** *ok-tet'*, *n* a group of eight (lines of verse, electrons, musicians, etc); a composition for eight musicians. [On the analogy of **duet**, as Ital *ottetto*, Ger *Oktett*]

octillion *ok-til'yən*, *n* a million raised to the eighth power, expressed by a unit with forty-eight zeros; in US, one thousand raised to the ninth power, ie a unit with twenty-seven zeros. — *n* and *adj* **octill'ionth**. [Modelled on **million**, from L *octō* eight]

octingenary *oktin-jē'nə-ri*, or **octingentenary** *-jen-tē'nə-ri*, *n* an eight-hundredth anniversary. [L *octingēnārius* 800 each]

octo- *ok-tō-*,*-tə*, *-to'*, also **oct-** or **octa-** (qqv) *combining form* denoting eight. — *n* **octocentenary** (*ok-tō-sen-tēn'ə-ri*, *-sin-ten'* or *-sen'tin-*) an eight-hundredth anniversary. — *adj* **octofid** (*ok'tə-fid*; L *findere* to cleave; *bot*) cleft into eight segments. — *adj* **octogynous** (*ok-toj'i-nəs*; Gr *gynē* woman; *bot*) having eight pistils or styles. — *n pl* **Octogyn'ia** (*-jin'*; *bot*) in various Linnaean classes, an order with eight pistils. — *n* **octohe'dron** an octahedron. — *adj* **octopetalous** (*ok-tə-pet'ə-ləs*) having eight petals. — *adj* **octopod** (*ok'tə-pod*; Gr *pous*, *podos* foot) eight-footed or eight-armed. — *n* an octopus or other member of the **Octopoda** (*-to'*), an order of cephalopods with two gills. — *adj* **octo'podous**. — *adj* **octosepalous** (*ok-tə-sep'ə-ləs*; *bot*) having eight sepals. — *adj* **octo'stichous** octastichous. — *n* and *adj* **oc'tostyle** octastyle. — *adj* **octosyllabic** (*ok'tə-si-lab'ik*) consisting of eight syllables. — *n* a line of eight syllables. — *n* **octosyllable** (*-sil'ə-bl*) a word of eight syllables. [Gr *oktō*, and L *octō*]

October *ok-tō'bər*, *n* the tenth month, eighth in the most ancient Roman calendar; strong ale brewed in that month (*hist*). — *n* **Octo'brist** (*hist*) a member of a Russian moderate liberal party who made the tsar's manifesto of October 1905 their basis. [L *octōber*, from *octō* eight]

octocentenary. See under **octo-**.

octodecimo *ok-tō-des'i-mō*, *adj* having eighteen leaves to the sheet; contracted **18mo**, often read eighteenmo. — *n* a book with sheets so folded: — *pl* **octodec'imos**. [L *octōdecim* eighteen; cf **octavo**]

octofid. See under **octo-**.

octogenarian *ok-tō-ji-nā'ri-ən*, *n* someone who is eighty years old, or between eighty and ninety. — Also *adj*. — *adj* **octogenary** (*ok-tō-jē'nə-ri*, *ok-toj'i-nə-ri*). [L *octōgēnārius* pertaining to eighty]

octogynous. . . to . . . **octohedron**. See **octo-**.

octonary *ok'tə-nə-ri*, (*rare*) *adj* based on the number eight. — *n* a set of eight; an eight-line stanza. — *adj* **octonarian** (*ok-tə-nā'ri-ən*; *prosody*) having eight feet. — *n* a line of eight feet. — *n* **octonā'rius** an octonarian: — *pl* **octonā'riī**. [L *octōnārius*]

octonocular *ok-tō-nok'ū-lər*, *adj* having eight eyes. [L *octōnī* eight at a time, and *oculus* eye]

octoploid. Same as **octaploid**.

octopod, etc. See under **octo-**.

octopus *ok'tə-pəs*, formerly *ok-tō'*, *n* any eight-armed cephalopod of the genus *Octopus*; a person or organization with widespread influence (*fig*): — *pl* **oc'topuses**, (*archaic*) **octō'podēs** (or *-top'*; **oc'topī** is wrong). [Gr *octō eight, and pous* a foot]

octopush *ok'tə-po͝osh*, (*sport*) *n* a kind of underwater hockey, in which a lead puck, called a squid, is used in place of a ball and pushers in place of sticks. — *n* **oc'topusher**. [**octopus** and **push**]

octoroon or **octaroon** *ok-tə-ro͞on'*, *n* the offspring of a quadroon and a person of European descent; someone who has one-eighth Negro blood. [Modelled on **quadroon**, from L *octō* eight]

octosepalous. . . to . . . **octosyllable**. See under **octo-**.

octroi *ok'trwä* or *ok-trwa'*, *n* formerly, and still in some European countries, a commercial privilege, eg of exclusive trade; a toll or tax levied at the gates of a city on articles brought in; the place where, or officials to whom, it is paid; payment for passage of a car on a road. [Fr, from *octroyer* to grant, from some such LL form as *auctōrizāre* to authorize, from L *auctor* author]

OCTU *abbrev*: Officer Cadet Training unit.

octuor *ok'tū-ör*, *n* an octet. [L *octo* eight; modelled on *quattuor* four]

octuple *ok'tū-pl*, *adj* eightfold. — *vt* or *vi* to multiply by eight. — *n* **oc'tūplet** a group of eight notes to be played in the time of six (*music*); one of eight (children or animals) born at one birth. — *adj* **octūp'licate** eightfold; multiplied by eight. — Also *n*. [L *octuplus*; cf **duple**, **double**]

ocular *ok'ū-lər*, *adj* pertaining to the eye or to vision; formed in, addressed to, or known by, the eye; received by actual sight; eyelike. — *n* an eyepiece; an eye (*facetious*). — *n* **oc'ularist** (Fr *oculariste*) a person who makes artificial eyes. — *adv* **oc'ularly**. — *adj* **oc'ulate** or **oc'ulated** having eyes, or spots like eyes. — *n* **oc'ulist** a specialist in diseases and defects of the eye, an ophthalmologist. — *combining form* **oculo-** (*ok-ū-lō-*, *-lo'-*) meaning of or pertaining to the eye or eyes. — *adj* **oc'ulomō'tor** pertaining to or causing movements of the eye. — *n* **oculus** (*ok'ū-ləs*) a round window: — *pl* **oc'ulī**. [L *oculus* the eye]

OD *ō'dē'*, (*slang*) *n* an overdose (of drugs). — Also *vi*: — *pr p* **OD'ing**; *pa t* and *pa p* **OD'd**.

OD *abbrev*: Officer of the Day; Ordnance Datum or Data; (also **O/D**) overdraft or overdrawn.

od[1] *od* or *ōd*, *n* Reichenbach's arbitrary name for a force he supposed to manifest itself in light, magnetism, chemical action, hypnotism, etc. — *adj* **o'dic**. — *n* **o'dism** belief in od. — *n* **odyle** or **od'yl** (*od'il*, *ō'dil*; Gr *hȳlē* matter) od. — *n* **od'ylism**. — **od'-force** od.

od[2] or **odd** *od*, *n* and *interj* (*archaic*; also with *cap*) a form of **god**, used as a mild oath. — **od's-bobs'** God's body; **od's-bod'ikins** God's body; **od's-life'** God's life; **od's-nouns** (*-nownz'*) God's wounds; **od's-pit'ikins** (*Shakesp*) God's pity; **odzooks'** same as **gadzooks**. — These are often written without an apostrophe.

ODA *abbrev*: Overseas Development Administration.

oda *ō'də*, *n* a room in a harem. [Turk; cf **odalisque**]

odal, **odaller**. Same as **udal**, **udaller**.

odalisque, **odalisk** *ō'də-lisk*, or **odalique** *-lik*, *n* a female slave in a harem. [Fr, from Turk *ōdaliq*, from *ōdah* a chamber]

odd[1] *od*, *adj* unpaired; left over; additional; extra; not one of a complete set; not exactly divisible by two (*opp* to *even*); one in excess of half the number; left over after a round number has been taken; (used after the number) slightly over, as in *thirty odd*; with something additional in lower denominations or lower powers of ten; strange; queer; casual; out-of-the-way; standing apart; not matching (*Spenser*); at variance (*Shakesp*). — *adv* (*Shakesp*) oddly. — *n* one stroke more than one's opponent (*golf*); a stroke allowed in handicap (*golf*); one trick above book (*whist*). — *adj* **odd'ish**. — *n* **odd'ity** the state of being odd or singular; strangeness; a strange or odd person or thing. — *adj* **odd'-like** (*Scot*) odd; odd-looking. — *adv* **odd'ly**. — *n* **odd'ment** something remaining over; one of a broken set, often in *pl*). — *n* **odd'ness**. — *n pl* **odds** (*odz*, sometimes treated as *sing*) inequality; difference in favour of one against another; more than an even wager; the amount or proportion by which the bet of one exceeds that of another; the chances or probability; advantage; dispute; scraps; miscellaneous pieces, as in *odds and ends*. — **odd'ball** an eccentric person, nonconformist in some respect. — Also *adj* (of eg a thing, plan, circumstance). — **odd'-come-short** (*archaic*) a short remnant; (in *pl* **odd'-come-shorts**) odds and ends; **odd'-come-short'ly** (*archaic*) an early day, any time. — *adj* or *n* **odd-e'ven** (*Shakesp*; of the time about midnight) *appar* neither one thing nor another. — **Odd'fellow** a member of a secret benevolent society called the Independent Order of Oddfellows. — *adj* **odd'-job**. — **odd jobs** occasional pieces of work such as small house repairs; **odd-jobb'er** or **odd-job'man**; **odd legs** (*eng*) callipers with two hinged legs, one curved distally and placed against an edge and the other with a scribing point. — *adj* **odd'-look'ing**. — **odd lot** (*stock exchange*) a block of less than one hundred shares; **odd-lott'er** someone who deals in odd lots; **odd'-man** odd-jobman; an umpire; someone who has a casting vote; the singling out or elimination of one from a number for any purpose; **odds'man** (*Scot*) an umpire or arbiter. — *adj* **odds'-on'** (of a chance) better than even; in betting, a price which will result in a final return of less than double the original stake. — **at odds** at variance (with *with*); **long odds** or **short odds** see **long**[3] and **short**; **make no odds** to make no significant difference; **odd man out** or **odd one out** a person who is left out when numbers are made up; a person who, whether through personal inclination or rejection by others, gets set apart from the group to which he or she belongs, because of eg a difference of interests, behaviour, etc; **odds and ends** miscellaneous pieces, *perh orig* meaning points and ends; **odds and sods** (*colloq*) miscellaneous people, things, etc; **over the odds** (*colloq*) more than expected, normal, necessary, etc; **shout the odds** (*slang*) to talk too much or too loudly; **what's the odds?** what difference does it make? [ON *oddi* point, a triangle, odd number; cf ON *oddr*, OE *ord* point]

odd[2]. See **od**[2].

ode *ōd*, *n orig*, a poem intended to be sung; an elaborate lyric, often of some length, generally addressed to somebody or something. — *adj* **o'dic**. — *n* **o'dist** a writer of odes. [Fr *ode*, from Gr *ōidē*, contraction of *aoidē*, from *aeidein* to sing]

odea. See **odeon**.

ODECA *abbrev*: *Organisación de Estados Centro-americanos* (*Sp*), Organization of Central American States.

Odelsting or **Odelsthing** *ō'dəls-ting*, *n* the lower house of the Norwegian parliament. [Norw *odel* allodium, and *ting* (*thing*) court, parliament]

odeon *ō'di-ən*, *-dyən*, *-dē'-*, *n* in ancient Greece, a theatre for musical contests, etc; a concert-hall. — Also **ō'deum** a Roman odeon: — *pl* **ō'deums** or **ō'dea**. [Gr *ōideion*, L *ōdēum*]

odic[1]. See **od**[1].

odic[2]. See **ode**.

Odin *ō'din*, *n* the Scandinavian equivalent of the Germanic god Woden. — *n* **O'dinism** the ancient worship of Odin; a modern revival of this. — *n* **O'dinist**. [ON *Ōthenn*]

odism. See **od**[1].

odist. See **ode**.

odium *ō'di-əm*, *n* hatred; offensiveness; blame; reproach attaching to some act, etc (with *of*); the quality of provoking hate. — *adj* **o'dious** hateful; offensive; repulsive; causing hatred. — *adv* **o'diously**. — *n* **o'diousness**. [L *odium*]

odium theologicum *ōd'i-əm thē-ə-lo'ji-kəm*, *od'i-o͞om the-o-lo'gi-ko͞om*, (*L*) *n* the hatred of theologians for each other's errors (or each other).

odograph *od'ə-gräf*, *n* a device for plotting automatically a course travelled; an odometer; a pedometer. [Gr *hodos* a way, and *graphein* to write]

odometer *od-om'i-tər*, *n* an instrument attached to the wheel of a car, etc for measuring the distance travelled. — Also **hodom'eter**. — *n* **odom'etry** or **hodom'etry**. [Gr *hodos* a way, and *metron* a measure]

Odonata *ō-don-ā'tə*, (*zool*) *n pl* the dragonfly order. — *n* **odon'atist** or **odonatol'ogist** someone who studies, or is an expert on, dragonflies. — *n* **odonatol'ogy**. [Ionic Gr *odōn* a tooth]

odont- *od-ont-*, or **odonto-** *-tə-*, *-tō*, *-to'*, *combining form* denoting tooth. — *n* **odontalgia** (*-al'ji-ə*) or **odontal'gy** (*-al'ji*; Gr *algos* pain) toothache. — *adj* **odontal'gic**. — *adj* **odon'tic** dental. — *n* **odont'ist** (*facetious*) a dentist. — *n* **odont'oblast** (Gr *blastos* a shoot) a dentine-forming cell. — *n* **odon'tocete** (*-sēt*; Gr *kētos* whale) a toothed whale. — *adj* **odontogenic** (*-jen'ik*). — *n* **odontogeny** (*-oj'i-ni*) the origin and development of teeth. — *n* **odontogloss'um** (Gr *glōssa* tongue) a plant of the genus *Odontoglossum*, of tropical American orchids. — *n* **odont'ograph** an instrument for obtaining approximate curves for gear-teeth. — *n* **odontog'raphy** a description or history of teeth. — *adj* **odont'oid** toothlike (**odontoid peg** or **process** a projection from the second vertebra of the neck). — *n* **odont'olite** (Gr *lithos* stone) bone turquoise or occidental turquoise, a fossil bone or tooth coloured blue with phosphate of iron. — *adj* **odontolog'ic** or **odontolog'ical**. — *n* **odontol'ogist**. — *n* **odontol'ogy** the science of the teeth. — *n* **odontō'ma** a tumour arising in connection with the teeth: — *pl* **odontō'mas** or **odontō'mata**. — *adj* **odontō'matous** pertaining to odontoma. — *n* **odontopho'bia** (*psychol*) fear of teeth. — *adj* **odontophoral** (*-tof'ə-rəl*; Gr *-phoros* bearing) or **odontoph'oran**. — *n* **odon'tophore** (*-tə-fōr*, *-fôr*) the rasping apparatus in molluscs, ie the radula, its support, or the whole apparatus. — *adj* **odontoph'orous**. — *n* **Odontoph'orus** a genus of American quails. — *n pl* **odontornithes** (*-ör-nī'thēz*, or *-ör'ni-thēz*; Gr *ornis*, *ornīthos* bird) fossil birds with teeth (not a natural class). — *adj* **odontostom'atous** (Gr *stoma*, *-atos* mouth) having biting or toothed jaws. [Gr *odous*, *odontos* a tooth]

odour or (*US*) **odor** *ō'dər*, *n* smell; savour (*fig*); repute (*fig*). — *adj* **o'dorant**, **o'dorate** or **odorif'erous** emitting a (*usu* pleasant) smell. — *n* **o'dorant**. — *adv* **odorif'erously**. — *n* **odorif'erousness**. — *n* **odorim'etry** the measurement of the strength and persistence of odours, olfactometry (qv). — *adj* **odorous** (*ō'də-rəs*; sometimes formerly *ōd-ō'rəs*) emitting an odour or scent; sweet-smelling; fragrant; bad-smelling (*colloq*). — *adv* **o'dorously**. — *n* **o'dorousness**. — *adj* **o'doured**. — *adj* **o'dourless**. — **in bad odour** in bad repute or standing (with *with*); (similarly, but less commonly) **in good odour**; **the odour of sanctity** a fragrance after death alleged to be evidence of saintship; facetiously applied to the living who have denied themselves the sensual indulgence of washing; a sanctimonious manner. [Anglo-Fr *odour*, from L *odor*, *-ōris*]

odso *od'sō*, (*obs*) *interj* expressing surprise: — *pl* **od'sos**. [For **gadso**]

odyl, **odyle** and **odylism**. See under **od**[1].

Odyssey *od'i-si*, *n* a Greek epic poem, ascribed to Homer, describing the ten years' wanderings of *Odysseus* (Ulysses) on his way home from the Trojan war to Ithaca; (also without *cap*) a long wandering, or a tale of wandering. — *adj* **Odyssē'an**. [Gr *Odysseia*]

odzooks. See under **od**[2].

OE *abbrev*: Old English.

Oe *symbol*: oersted.

oe. Same as **oy**.

OECD *abbrev*: Organization for Economic Cooperation and Development.

oecist *ē'sist*, or **oikist** *oi'kist*, (*hist*) *n* the founder of a colony. [Gr *oikistēs*, from *oikos* a house]

oecology, etc, and **oecumenic**, **oecumenical**, etc. See **ecology**, **ecumenic**.

OED *abbrev*: Oxford English Dictionary.

oedema *ē-dē'mə*, *n* pathological accumulation of fluid in tissue spaces (*med*); dropsy; an unhealthy mass of swollen parenchyma (*bot*). — *adj* **oede'matose** or **oede'matous**. — Also **edē'ma**, etc. [Gr *oidēma*, *-atos* swelling]

Oedipus *ē'di-pəs*, (*Gr mythol*) *n* a king of Thebes who solved the Sphinx's riddle and unwittingly killed his father and married his mother. — *adj* **Oe'dipal**. — *adj* (*irreg*) **Oedipē'an**. — **Oedipus complex** (*psychol*) the attachment of a son to his mother with unconscious rivalry and hostility towards his father. [Gr *Oidipous*, literally Swell-foot]

OEEC *abbrev*: Organization for European Economic Cooperation (superseded by the OECD).

œil-de-bœuf *œ'ē-də-bœf*, *n* a little round window; an octagonal vestibule at the court of Versailles, hence one elsewhere: — *pl* **œils-de-bœuf** (*œ'ē-*). [Fr, ox-eye]

œillade *œ-yäd'*, formerly *äl'yad*, *il'yad*, *il'i-ad* (*Shakesp* **illiad** and **eliad**) *n* an ogle; a glance or wink (*Shakesp*). — Formerly also **eyliad** or **eyeliad** (*ī'li-ad*). [Fr *œillade*, from *œil* eye]

OEM *abbrev*: original equipment manufacturer.

oen- *ēn-*, or **oeno-** *-nə-*, *-nō-*, *-no'*, *combining form* wine. — Also **oin-** *oin-*, or **oino-**. — *adj* **oenan'thic** (Gr *anthos* flower) having or imparting the characteristic odour of wine. — *adj* **oenolog'ical**. — *n* **oenol'ogist**. — *n* **oenol'ogy** the science of wines. — *n* **oe'nomancy** divination from the appearance of wine poured out in libations. — *n* **oenomā'nia** dipsomania. — *n* **oen'omel** (Gr *meli* honey) wine mixed with honey. — *n* **oenom'eter** a hydrometer for measuring the alcoholic strength of wines. — *n* **oen'ophil** or **oenoph'ilist** a connoisseur of wine, also (now *usu*) **oen'ophile** (*-fīl*). — *n* **oenoph'ily** love of and knowledge of wines. [Gr *oinos* wine]

Oenothera *ē-nō-thē'rə*, sometimes *ē-noth'ə-rə*, *n* the evening-primrose genus of Onagraceae. [Gr *oinothēras*, perhap a wrong reading for *onothēras*, a plant whose roots smelt of wine, perh oleander]

o'er *ōr*, *ör*, (*Scot owr*; *poetic*, *archaic* or *Scot*) *prep* and *adv* shortened form of **over**. For compounds, see **over-**.

oerlikon *ûr'li-kon*, *n* (also with *cap*) an aircraft or anti-aircraft cannon of Swiss origin. [*Oerlikon*, near Zürich]

oersted *ûr'sted*, (*phys*) *n* the CGS unit of magnetic field strength. [After H C *Oersted* (1777–1851), Danish physicist]

Oes or **oes** *ōz*, a plural of **O** or **o** (see **O**[1]).

oesophagus or (*esp US*) **esophagus** *ē-sof'ə-gəs*, *n* the gullet: — *pl* **oesoph'agi** (*gī*). — *adj* **oesophageal** (*-fə-jē'əl*). — **peptic** or **reflux oesophagitis** heartburn. [Gr *oisophagos* gullet; origin unknown; possibly connected with *phagein* to eat]

oestrus *ēs'trəs*, *n* a gadfly or bot; a vehement stimulus or frenzy; (in the following meanings and words, also, *esp US*, **estrus** *es-*) heat or sexual impulse, *esp* in female mammals; oestrous cycle. — Also **oes'trum**. — *adj* **oes'tral**. — *n* **oestradī'ol** a natural oestrogen ($C_{18}H_{24}O_2$), also synthesized for use in cancer treatment and menstrual, etc disorders. — *n* **oestrogen** (*ēs'trə-jən*) any one of the female sex-hormones; a substance found in plants, or synthesized, that has similar effects. — *adj* **oestrogenic** (*-jen'*). — *adj* **oes'trous**. — **oestrous cycle** the series of physiological changes from the beginning of one period of oestrus to the beginning of the next. [L *oestrus*, from Gr *oistros*]

œuvre *œ-vr'*, (*Fr*) *n* work (of an artist, writer, etc): — *pl* **œuvres** (*œ-vr'*).

OF *abbrev*: Oddfellow; Old French.

of *ov*, *uv*, *əv*, *prep* from; from among; out from; belonging to; among; proceeding or derived from; made from, having for material; having or characterized by; in the manner that characterizes; with respect to; owing to; with; over; concerning; during; by; on; in; specified as; constituted by; short of, to (in giving the time, eg *quarter of five*; *US*); measuring; aged; owning. [OE *of*; Du *af*, Ger *ab*, L *ab*, Gr *apo*]

ofay *ō'fā*, *ō-fā'*, (*US Black derog slang*) *n* a white person. — Also *adj*. [Ety uncertain; possibly of African origin; *foe* in pig Latin also suggested, but unlikely]

off *of*, *adv* away; in or to a position that is not on something; in motion; out of continuity; out of connection, supply, activity, operation, or validity; to a finish, up; no longer available; in deterioration or diminution; into freedom. — *combining form* **-off** used to signify a knockout competitive event, *esp* one held to decide a draw, as in *jump-off, play-off, swim-off.* — *adj* most distant; on the opposite or farther side; on the side of a cricket-field; on the side opposite that on which the batsman stands (normally the bowler's left; *cricket*); (of a horse or vehicle) right; out of condition or form; not devoted to the particular or usual activity (eg *off-day*, *off-season*). — *prep* from; away from; removed from; opening out of; in or to a position or condition that is not on; disengaged from; disinclined to, not wanting; out to sea from; from a dish of; from a ball bowled by (*cricket*); with a handicap of (*golf*); not up to the usual standard of; not eating or drinking; not subject to or following. — *n* the offside. — *vt* to put off; to take off; to kill (*US slang*). — *vi* (or *vt* with *it*) to go off; to take off (with *with*; *colloq*). — *interj* away! depart! — *n* **off'ing** the region some distance offshore; a place or time some way off. — *adj* **off'ish** aloof in manner. — *adv* **off'-ward** or **off'-wards** off or away from, *esp* shore. — *adj* **off-air'** (of a recording, etc) received from a broadcast transmission; relating to, but not broadcast as part of, a radio or television programme. — *adj* **off-and-on'** occasional; intermittent. — *adj* **off'-beam** mistaken, wrongheaded, misguided. — *n* **off'beat** any of the *usu* unaccented beats in a musical bar. — *adj* away from standard; out of the usual; eccentric. — *adj* **off'-board** (*commerce*) of or relating to over-the-counter securities transactions. — **off'-break** (*cricket*) deviation of a ball on pitching, inwards from the offside; the spin given to a ball to cause such a deviation; a ball bowled so as to have such a deviation. — *adj* **off-Broad'way** (of US theatres) not on Broadway, the centre of commercial theatre in New York; of or relating to the kind of theatre productions often presented in theatres not on Broadway, ie experimental, non-commercial, etc (**off-off-Broad'way** of or relating to very low-cost, often highly experimental theatre, *usu* presented in cafés, etc, and often considered the US equivalent of British fringe theatre). — *adj* **off-cen'tre** not quite central. — **off'-chance** or **off chance** a remote chance (**on the off(-)chance** (with *that* or *of*) just in case, in the hope of (something happening). — *adj* **off-col'our** or **off-col'oured** (of eg a diamond) unsatisfactory in colour and so inferior; half-caste, not pure white; (**off-colour**) not completely healthy; (**off-colour**; of jokes, etc) smutty, blue (*colloq*). — **off'-come** a subterfuge (*Scot*); a pretext (*Scot*); the manner of coming off, issue or success; **off'-comer** (*colloq*) a person living in a place, *esp* a rural area, in which he or she was not born, an incomer; **off'cut** a small piece cut off or left over from a larger piece of some material (eg wood); **off'-cutter** (*cricket*) a fast bowler's delivery designed to move from off to leg, ie to move in towards a right-handed batsman (from a right-handed bowler); **off'-day** see **off** *adj* above; a day when one is not at one's best or most brilliant; **off'-drive** (*cricket*) a drive to the off side. — Also *vi* and *vt*. — *adj* **off'-duty** not on duty. — *n* and *adj* **off'-fore** of a horse, (relating to) the right fore-leg (*opp* to *near-fore*). — *adv* **offhand'** extempore; at once; without hesitating. — *adj* **off'hand** without study; impromptu; free and easy; ungraciously curt or summary. — *adj* **off'hand'ed**. — *adv* **offhand'edly**. — **offhand'edness**; **offhand grinding** (*eng*) grinding in which the tool, eg a grinding wheel, is held in the hand and worked freely. — *adj* **off'-job** outside normal work duties and conditions. — **off'-job** (or **off'-the-job**) **training** the part of a training course that a trainee follows away from the workplace at a college, etc, eg one day a week. — *adj* **off-key'** out of tune (*lit* and *fig*); conflicting, jarring, discordant. — **off'-li'cence** a licence to sell alcoholic liquors for consumption off the premises only; a shop having such a licence (*colloq*). — *adj* **off'-lim'its** prohibited, out of bounds. — *adj* **off'-line** (*comput*) not under the direct control of the central processing unit; not connected, switched off. — Also *adv*. — *vt* and *vi* **off'load** (*orig SAfr*) to unload; to get rid of (something unwanted) by passing to someone else (with *on to*). — *adj* **off-off-Broadway** see **off-Broadway** above. — *adj* **off'peak** not at the time of highest demand; relating to times of the day when television or radio audiences are smaller, advertising rates for these times being lower (*opp* to peak time, qv). — *adj* **off'-piste** of or relating to skiing on new snow-surfaces, not on established tracks or runs. — *adj* **off'-plan** pertaining to a home, etc bought before (completion of) building on the basis of plans seen, or to the buyer of such a property. — **off'print** a reprint of a single article from a periodical; **off'put** (*Scot*) the act of putting off (in any sense); **off'-putter**; **off'-putting** an act of putting off. — *adj* that puts off; disconcerting; causing disinclination or aversion. — **off-reck'oning** (*usu* in *pl*) a deduction; an account between army officers and governments concerning the men's clothes, etc (*obs*). — *adj* **off-road'** of or relating to paths, tracks etc, as opposed to roads; of or relating to vehicles, etc designed to operate away from roads. — *vt* and *vi* **off'saddle** to unsaddle. — **off-sales'** (*SAfr*) a shop where alcoholic drinks can be bought for consumption elsewhere. — **off'scouring** (*usu* in *pl*) matter scoured off; refuse; anything vile or despised; **off'scum** scum, refuse. — *n, adj* and *adv* **off'season** (of or at) a time (for eg a holiday) other than the most popular and busy. — **off'set** a thing set off against another as equivalent or compensation; a lateral shoot that strikes root and forms a new plant; a mountain spur; a side branch of anything; a sudden change of direction in a pipe; a reduction of thickness or the (*usu* sloping) ledge formed where part of a wall, buttress, bank, etc, is set back from the general face; a hillside terrace (*US*); a smudge on a newly printed sheet from another laid on it; offset printing; in surveying, a perpendicular from the main line to an outlying point. — *adj* set at an angle to the main alignment. — *vt* (*of-set'*, *of'set*) to set off against something as an equivalent or compensation. — *vi* to branch off; (*of'set*) to make an effort. — *adj* **offset'able** (or *of'-*). — **offset printing**, **offset lithography** or **offset-litho printing** a method of printing lithographs, etc, by first taking an impression from a plate on a rubber cylinder and then transferring the impression to paper or metal, etc, using oil-based ink. — *vt* **off-shake'** to shake off (*pa p Spenser* **off-shakt'**). — **off'shoot** a branch or derivative of anything. — *adv* **offshore'** and *adj* **off'shore** from the shore; at a distance from the shore; (placed or operating) abroad; sited or operating outside the restrictions of British law and tax. — **offshore purchase** a purchase by one country in another; **off'side** the far side; a horse's or vehicle's right, towards the middle of the road; (*cricket*) see **off** *adj*; (*football*, etc) the field between the ball and the opponents' goal. — *adj* and *adv* (**offside'**) on the offside; between the ball, or the last player who had it, and the opponents' goal; in American football, over the line of scrimmage or free-kick line when the ball is snapped. — **offsīd'er** a subordinate or side-kick (*Austr colloq*). — *adj* and *adv* **off-site'** (working, happening, etc) away from a working site, etc. — *n pl* **off'-sorts** wool set aside in sorting, or unsuitable for a given purpose. — **off'-spin** (*cricket*) (an) off-break; **off'-spinner** (*cricket*) a player who bowls off-breaks; **off'-spring** a child or children; progeny; issue; ancestry (*obs*); source (*obs*). — *adv* and *adj* **off-stage'** not on the stage as visible to the spectators. — *adj* and *adv* **off-stream'** of an industrial plant, etc, not in operation or production. — *adj* **off'-street** (of parking) in a car park. — **off'take** the act of taking off in any sense; a take-off; that which is taken off; a channel, passage, or pipe for removing a fluid. — *adj* **off-the-peg** see under **peg**. — *adj* **off-the-shelf** see under **shelf**. — *adj* **off'-white** not quite white, rather, yellowish or greyish white. — *n* a colour, paint, etc, which is off-white. — **a bit off** (*colloq*) (of behaviour, etc) unfair or unacceptable; **badly off** not well off, poor; **be off** to go away quickly (as a command, also **be off with you**); **break off** and **come off** see under **break**[1] and **come**; **from off** from a position on; **go off** and **go off with** see under **go**[1]; **ill off** poor or ill provided; **in the offing** in sight or at hand; expected, or likely to take place, shortly; **make off** and **make off with** see under **make**[1]; **off and on** occasionally, intermittently; **off beam** or **off the beam** see under **beam** or see **off-beam** above; **off duty** not on duty (*adj* **off'-duty**); **off one's oats, feed, head, rocker** or **trolley** see under **oat, feed**[1], **head, rock**[3] **and troll**[2]; **off the cuff** see under **cuff**[2]; **off the face** or **shoulder** (of a woman's hat, dress, etc) so as to reveal the face or shoulder; **off the peg** see under **peg**; **off the wall** (*orig US*) see under **wall**; **off with** take off at once; **put off, show off** or **take off** see under **put**[1], **show** and **take**; **tell off** to chide (*colloq*); to count; to assign, as for a special duty; **walk off** and **walk off with** see under **walk**; **well off** rich, well provided; fortunate. [Orig variant of **of**, distinguished from it by the 17c]

off *abbrev*: officer; official; officinal.

offal *of'l, n* waste or rejected parts, *esp* of a carcase; an edible part cut off in dressing a carcase, *esp* entrails, heart, liver, kidney, tongue, etc; anything worthless or unfit for use; refuse. [**off, fall**[1]]

offbeam... to ... **off-duty**. See under **off**.

offend *o-fend', ə-, vt* to displease; to make angry; to do harm to; to hurt the feelings of; to affront; to violate (a law); to cause to stumble or sin (*Bible*). — *vi* to sin; to break the law; to cause anger; to be made to stumble or sin (*Bible*). — *n* **offence'** (or *US* **offense**) any cause of anger or displeasure; an injury; a transgression, a breach of law; a crime; a sin; affront; assault; those players in a team who assume the attacking role (*sport*); the attacking team *esp* when in possession of the ball (*Am football*); attacking play, position or style (*sport*); a stumbling (*Bible*). — *adj* **offence'ful** (*Shakesp*) giving offence or displeasure; injurious. — *adj* **offence'less** (*Milton*) unoffending; innocent. — *adj* **offend'ed**. — *adv* **offen'dedly**. — *n* **offend'er**: — *fem* (*Shakesp*) **offend'ress**. — *adj* **offen'ding**. — *adj* **offens'ive** causing offence, displeasure or injury; used in attack (*sport, military*, etc); making the first attack. — *n* the act or course of action of the attacking party; the posture of an attacker; a great and sustained effort to achieve an end, as in *peace offensive*. — *adv* **offens'ively**. — *n* **offens'iveness**. — **give offence** to cause displeasure; **take offence** to feel displeasure, be offended. [L *offendere, offensum*, from *ob* against, and *fendere, fensum* to strike (found in compounds); cf **defend**]

Offer *of'ər abbrev*: Office of Electricity Regulation.

offer *of'ər, vt* to present, *esp* as an act of devotion, homage, charity, etc; to express willingness; to hold out for acceptance or rejection; to lay before someone; to present to the mind; to propose to give, pay, sell or perform; to attempt (violence, resistance, etc); to make a show of attempting, make as if; to give the enemy an opportunity for (battle). — *vi* to present itself; to be at hand; to incline or tend (*obs*); to make an offer, eg of marriage (*old*): — *pr p* **off'ering**; *pa t* and *pa p* **off'ered**. — *n* the act of offering; the state of being offered; the first advance; something which is offered; a proposal made; an attempt or essay; a knob on an antler. — *adj* **off'erable** that can be offered. — *n* **offeree'** the person to whom something is offered. — *n* **off'erer** or (*law*) **off'eror**. — *n* **off'ering** the act of making an offer; something which is offered; a gift; a church collection; a sacrifice; (in *pl*) in the Church of England, certain dues payable at Easter; that which is offered on an altar (*Bible*). — *n* **off'ertory** the act of offering; the thing offered; the verses or the anthem said or sung while the offerings of the congregation are being made; the money collected at a religious service; anciently, a linen or silken cloth used in various ceremonies connected with the administration of the eucharist. — **offer price** (*stock exchange*) the price an investor must pay for a share or unit. — **offer up** in eg joinery, to position on a trial basis, in order to test for size and suitability before fixing; **on offer** being offered for sale, consumption, etc; for sale as a special offer; **special offer** *esp* in a shop, the offering of something for sale, or that which is offered, *usu* for a short time, at a bargain price. [L *offerre*, from *ob* towards, and *ferre* to bring]

offhand, etc. See under **off**.

office *of'is, n* an act of kindness or attention; a service; (with *ill*, etc) a disservice; a function or duty; settled duty or employment; a position imposing certain duties or giving a right to exercise an employment; the possession of a post in the government; business; an act of worship; the order or form of a religious service, either public or private; that which a thing is designed or fitted to do; a place where business is carried on; a group of staff occupying such a place; a state department; the building in which it is housed; a doctor's consulting-room (*US*); a cockpit in an aeroplane (*slang*); a lavatory; a hint (*slang*): (in *pl*) the apartments of a house or the subsidiary buildings in which the domestic, etc, work is carried out. — *n* **off'icer** someone who holds an office; a person who performs some public duty; a person holding a commission in an army, navy or air force; someone who holds a similar post in any force or body organized on a similar plan; a policeman; an office-bearer in a society. — *vt* (of officers) to command or lead; to provide with officers. — *adj* **official** (*ə-fish'əl*) pertaining to an office; depending on the proper office or authority; done by authority; issued or authorized by a public authority or office; (of an explanation, etc) untrue but maintained in public, the truth being embarrassing or compromising; (of a drug) recognized in the pharmacopoeia (cf **officinal**). — *n* a person who holds an office; a subordinate public officer; the deputy of a bishop, etc. — *n* **offic'ialdom** officials as a body; the world of officials; officialism. — *n* **officialese'** stilted, wordy and stereotyped English alleged to be characteristic of official letters and documents. — *n* **offic'ialism** official position; excessive devotion to official routine and detail; the self-importance of a Jack-in-office. — *n* **officiality** (*ə-fish-i-al'i-ti*) or **officialty** (*ə-fish'əl-ti*; *rare*) the charge, office or jurisdiction of an official; the official headquarters of an ecclesiastical or other deliberative and governing body; officialism. — *adv* **officially** (*ə-fish'ə-li*). — *n* **officiant** (*ə-fish'i-ənt*) someone who officiates at a religious service, someone who administers a sacrament. — *vi* **offic'iate** to perform the duties of an office. — *n* **offic'iator**. — **off'ice-bearer** someone who holds office; someone who has an appointed duty to perform in connection with some company, society, church, etc; **off'ice-block** a large building in which an office or variety of offices is housed; **off'ice-book** a book of forms of church service; **off'ice-boy** and **off'ice-girl** a boy or girl employed to do minor jobs in an office; **off'ice-holder** someone who holds a government office; a civil servant, *usu* in administration (*US*); **office hours** the time during which an office is open for business, typically 9 am to 5 pm Monday to Friday; **off'ice-hunter** a self-seeking candidate for public employment; **office junior** an employee who carries out general office duties under the direction of an office supervisor; **off'ice-seeker** a candidate for office. — **last offices** rites for the dead; the preparation of a corpse for burial; **Office of Fair Trading** (*abbrev* **OFT**) a government agency set up in 1973 to protect traders and consumers against unfair trading practices; **officer of arms** (also with *caps*) any of the thirteen officers of the College of Arms (qv); **officer of the day** (*military*) the officer in charge of camp or unit security on any particular day; **official list** a list of the current prices of stocks and shares published daily by the London Stock Exchange; **official receiver** see under **receive**. [Fr, from L *officium* a favour, duty or service]

officinal *ə-fis'i-nəl, of-i-sī'nəl, adj* belonging to or used in a shop; used in medicine; recognized in the pharmacopoeia (*obs*; now **official**); sold by pharmacists. [LL *officīnālis*, from L *officīna* a workshop, later a monastic storeroom, from *opus* work, and *facere* to do]

officious *ə-fish'əs, adj* too forward in offering unwelcome or unwanted services; intermeddling; in diplomacy, informal, not official; obliging (*obs*); dutiful (*Shakesp*). — *adv* **offic'iously**. — *n* **offic'iousness**. [L *officiōsus*, from *officium*]

offing... to ... **offtake**. See under **off**.

Ofgas or **OFGAS** *of'gas, abbrev*: Office of Gas Supply.

oflag *of'läg, -lähh, n* a German prisoner-of-war camp for officers. [Ger, short for *Offizierslager* officers' camp]

OFM *abbrev*: *Ordo* (or *Ordinis*) *Fratrum Minorum* (*L*), (of) the Order of Minor Friars, the Franciscans.

OFT *abbrev*: Office of Fair Trading.

oft *oft* or *öft, adv* (now mainly *poetic* or as *combining form* as in *oft-repeated*) often. — *adv* **oft'times** (*poetic*) often. [OE *oft*; Ger *oft*, Gothic *ufta*]

Oftel or **OFTEL** *of'tel, abbrev*: Office of Telecommunications.

often *of'n, öf'n, of'ən, of'tən, adv* frequently; many times. — *adj* **oft'en** (*Bible*) frequent. — *n* **oft'enness** (*rare*) frequency. — *adv* **oft'entimes** (*archaic, literary* or *NAm*) many times; frequently. — **as often as not** in about half of the instances, quite frequently; **more often than not** in more than half the instances, frequently. [An extended form of **oft**].

Ofwat or **OFWAT** *of'wat, abbrev*: Office of Water Services.

ogam *og'əm* or **ogham** *og'əm, ō'əm, n* an ancient alphabet used in Celtic and Pictish inscriptions, its letters consisting of sets of parallel lines meeting or crossing a base line (the corner of the stone monument often serving as the base line); any of its twenty characters. — *adj* **ogam'ic** (or *og'*), **oghamic** (*ə-gam'ik, og'ə-mik, ō'ə-mik*) or **og'mic**. [OIr *ogam*, Mod Ir *ogham*]

ogdoad *og'dō-ad, n* a set of eight. [Gr *ogdoas, -ados*, from *oktō* eight]

ogee *ō'jē, ō-jē', n* a moulding S-shaped in section (*archit*); an S-shaped curve. — *adj* having S-shaped curves. — *adj* **ogee'd**. [Fr *ogive*; see **ogive**]

Ogen melon *ō'gen mel'ən, n* a kind of melon, small and green-skinned. [From the Israeli kibbutz where the variety was first developed]

oggin *og'in* (*naval slang*) *n* the sea. [Said to be from earlier *hogwash* the sea]

ogham and **oghamic**. See **ogam**.

ogive *ō'jīv, ō-jīv', (archit) n* a diagonal rib of a vault; a pointed arch or window; a graph representing cumulative frequency (*statistics*). — *adj* **ogī'val**. [Fr; origin doubtful, possibly from Ar *auj* summit]

ogle *ō'gl, vt* to eye impertinently or lecherously; to eye greedily. — *vi* to cast amorous glances; to stare impertinently. — *n* **o'gle**. — *n* **o'gler**. — *n* **o'gling**. [Cf LGer *oegeln*, frequentative of *oegen* to look at; Ger *äugeln* to leer, *Auge* eye]

ogmic. See under **ogam**.

Ogpu *og'pōō, og-pōō', n* the Russian secret police of 1922–34. [From the initials of *Obedinennoe Gosudarstvennoe Politicheskoe Upravlenie* Unified State Political Directorate]

ogre *ō'gər, fem* **ogress** *ō'gres, -grəs n* a man-eating monster or giant of fairy tales; an ugly, cruel or bad-tempered person, or one whose sternness inspires fear. — *adj* **o'greish** or **o'grish**. [Fr *ogre*, prob invented by Perrault]

Ogygian *ō-gij'i-ən, ō-jij'i-ən, adj* pertaining to the mythical Attic king *Ogygēs*; prehistoric, primeval; very old; of Calypso's island, *Ogygiā*. — **Ogygian deluge** a flood said to have occurred during the reign of Ogyges.

OH *abbrev*: Ohio (US state).

oh *ō, interj* denoting surprise, pain, sorrow, etc. [See **O**[2]]

OHG *abbrev*: Old High German.

ohm *ōm, n* the unit of electrical resistance in the SI and the MKSA systems, the resistance in a conductor in which a potential difference of one volt produces a current of one ampere; formerly defined as the resistance of a specified column of mercury under stated conditions. — *n* **ohm'age** electrical resistance measured in ohms. — *adj* **ohm'ic**. — *n* **ohmmeter** (*ōm'mēt-ər*) an instrument for measuring electrical resistance. — **Ohm's law** the law that strength of electric current is directly proportional to electromotive force and inversely to resistance. [Georg Simon *Ohm*, German electrician (1787–1854)]

OHMS *abbrev*: On Her (or His) Majesty's Service.

oho *ō-hō', interj* expressing triumphant surprise or gratification (*pl* **ohos'**).

-oholic and **-oholism**. See **-aholic**.

ohone or **ochone** *ō-hōn', -hhōn', (Ir* and *Highland Scot) interj* expressing lamentation. [Ir and Gaelic *ochoin*]

oi *oi, interj* used to attract attention, etc. [Imit]

-oid *-oid, n* and *adj combining form* denoting (something) which resembles or has the shape of, as in *anthropoid, asteroid, deltoid*. — *adj combining form* **-oidal**. [Gr *-oeidēs*, from *eidos* shape, form]

oidium *ō-id'i-əm, (bot) n* the conidial stage of the vine-mildew and other fungi: — *pl* **oid'ia** (*-ə*). [Gr *ōion* an egg, with dimin sfx *-idion* Latinized]

oik *oik, (colloq) n* a crass-witted, inferior person; a boor or lout; a cad; a chap, bloke (*slightly derog*). [Ety uncertain]

oikist. See **oecist**.

oil *oil, n* any greasy, *usu* flammable liquid derived from animals, plants, mineral deposits or by artificial means, and used as a lubricant, fuel, foodstuff, etc; the juice from the fruit of the olive tree; any similar liquid obtained from parts of other plants; (in *pl*) oil paints or oil painting; (in *pl*) oilskins; news, information, *esp* in *the good oil* (*Austr colloq*)). — *vt* to smear, lubricate or anoint with oil; to impregnate with oil; to turn (a solid fat) into oil. — *vi* to take oil aboard as fuel; (of a solid fat) to turn into oil; to move ingratiatingly, stealthily, slily or cravenly, as in *oil out*, to extricate oneself dishonourably (*colloq, esp old*). — *adj* **oiled** smeared, treated, lubricated or impregnated with oil; preserved in oil; tipsy (*esp* in *well-oiled*; *slang*). — *n* **oil'er** someone or something that oils; an oilcan; (in *pl*) oilskins; a ship driven by oil; a ship that carries oil, a tanker. — *n* **oil'ery** the commodities, business or establishment of an oilman. — *adv* **oil'ily**. — *n* **oil'iness**. — *adj* **oil'y** consisting of, containing or having the qualities of oil; greasy; unctuous. — **oil'-bath** a receptacle containing lubricating oil through which part of a machine passes; **oil'-beetle** a beetle (of the genus *Meloe*) that emits a yellowish oily liquid from its legs when disturbed; **oil'-belt** a belt of country yielding mineral oil; **oil'-bird** the guacharo; **oil'-burner** a ship that uses oil as fuel; a lamp-burner for use with oil; **oil'-cake** a cattle-food made of the residue of oil-seeds when most of the oil has been pressed out; **oil'can** a can for carrying oil or for applying lubricating oil; **oil'cloth** a canvas coated with linseed-oil paint; **oil'-colour** a colouring substance mixed with oil, an oil paint; **oil-control ring** (*autos*) same as **scraper ring**; **oil'-cup** a small cup-like container, *usu* attached to machinery, for holding and dispensing lubricating oil; **oil'-drum** a cylindrical metal barrel for oil; **oil'-engine** an internal-combustion engine burning vapour from oil; **oil'field** an area which produces mineral oil; **oil-filled cable** (*elec eng*) cable with a central duct filled with oil, eliminating gaseous voids and consequent ionization. — *adj* **oil'-fired** burning oil as fuel. — **oil'-gas** illuminating gas or heating gas made by destructive distillation of oil; **oil'-gauge** an instrument for indicating the level of lubricating oil in an engine, etc; **oil'-gland** the uropygial gland in birds, forming a secretion used in preening the feathers; **oil immersion** a technique, used to extend the resolving power of a light microscope, in which a thin film of oil is placed between a special oil-immersion objective lens and the specimen; **oil length** the ratio of drying oil to resin in eg a varnish (*adj* **long'-oil** having a high proportion, **short'-oil** a low proportion, of oil); **oil'man** a man who deals in oils; a man who owns an oil-well; a man involved in the operation of an oil-well, oil-rig, etc; **oil'-mill** a grinding-mill for expressing oil from seeds, etc; **oil'nut** the N American butter-nut, the buffalo-nut, or other oil-yielding nut; **oil paint** an oil-colour; **oil painting** a picture painted in oil-colours; the art of painting in oil-colours; **oil'-palm** a palm (*Elaeis guineensis*) whose fruit-pulp yields palm-oil; **oil'-pan** the sump in an internal-combustion engine; **oil'-paper** paper which has been oiled, eg to make it waterproof; **oil platform** a steel and/or concrete structure, either fixed or mobile, used in offshore drilling to support the rig and to keep stores, etc; **oil'-press** a machine for expressing oils from seeds or pulp. — *adj* **oil'-rich** having much oil. — **oil rig** the complete plant (machinery, structures, etc) required for oil-well drilling; (loosely) a mobile oil platform; **oil sand** sand or sandstone occurring naturally impregnated with petroleum; tar sand; **oil'-seed** any seed that yields oil; **oil-seed rape** a plant with vivid yellow flowers, yielding vegetable oil; **oil shale** a shale containing diffused hydrocarbons in a state suitable for distillation into mineral oils; **oil'-silk** a transparent silk fabric impregnated with oxidized oil; **oil'skin** cloth made waterproof by means of oil; a garment made of oilskin; **oil slick** a patch of oil forming a film on the surface of water or (rarely) a road, etc; **oil'stone** a whetstone used with oil; **oil string** same as **production string**; **oil'-tanker** a vessel constructed for carrying oil in bulk; **oil'-tree** any of several trees or shrubs from which oil is obtained, that mentioned in Isaiah 41.19 probably being the oleaster; **oil well** a boring made on land or the sea bed for extracting petroleum. — *adj* **long-oil** and **short-oil** see **oil length** above; **no oil painting** (*colloq facetious*) (facially) unattractive; **oil someone's palm** to bribe someone; **oil the wheels** to do something in order to make things go more smoothly, successfully, etc; **strike oil** to discover oil while boring for it; to find the way to success and riches. — See also **tall-oil**. [OFr *oile* (Fr *huile*), from L *oleum*, from Gr *elaion*, from *elaiā* olive-tree, olive]

OILC *abbrev*: Offshore Industry Liaison Committee.

oillet *oi'lit*, *n* an obsolete form of **eyelet**.

oink *oi'ngk*, *n* (the representation of) the noise made by a pig. — Also *interj*. — *vi* to make such a noise.

oino- *oi-nō-*, *-nə-*, *-no'*, *combining form* occurring as an occasional variant for **oeno-**.

ointment *oint'mənt*, *n* any greasy preparation for smoothing on to or rubbing into the skin for healing or cosmetic purposes; an unguent or lubricant; anything used in anointing. — *vt* **oint** (*Dryden*) to anoint. [Fr *oint*, pa p of *oindre*, from L *unguere* to anoint]

Oireachtas *er'ək-thəs*, *er'əhh-təs*, *n* the legislature of the Republic of Ireland (President, Seanad, and Dáil). [Ir, assembly]

OIRT *abbrev*: *Organisation Internationale de Radiodiffusion et Télévision* (*Fr*), International Organization of Radio and Television (in East Europe).

oiticica *oi-ti-sē'kə*, *n* any of several S American trees, *esp Licania rigida* and *Couepia grandiflora* (both rosaceous), whose nuts yield an oil used for quick-drying paints and varnishes. [Port, from Tupí *oity-cica*]

Ojibwa *ō-jib'wə*, *n* a member of a N American Indian people *orig* concentrated round Lakes Superior and Huron, also called Chippewa by Europeans; their language, of the Algonkian group: — *pl* **Ojib'wa** or **Ojib'was**. [Ojibwa, puckered, in reference to moccassin style]

ojime *ō'ji-mā*, *n* a carved bead through which pass the two cords attached to a Japanese inro or small container and which when slid down the cords serves to keep the inro closed. [Jap *o* string, and *shime* fastening]

OJOCS *ō'joks*, (*horse-racing*) *abbrev*: *o*vernight declaration of *jockeys*, a system introduced in 1992, whereby trainers must announce their jockeys by late afternoon on the day previous to the race.

OK or **okay** *ō-kā'*, (*colloq*) *adj* all correct; all right; satisfactory. — *adv* yes; all right, certainly. — *n* approval; sanction; endorsement: — *pl* **OKs**, **OK's** or **okays'**. — *vt* to mark or pass as right; to sanction: — *pr p* **OK''ing**, **OK'ing** or **okay'ing**; *pa t* and *pa p* **OK'd'**, **OKed'** or **okayed'**. [Various explanations of the letters have been given; evidence suggests that *OK* originated as an abbreviation of *oll korrekt*, a facetious misspelling of *all correct* current in the US in the 1830s, and was then used as a slogan by Van Buren's party in the 1840 US presidential election (Van Buren was born at Kinderhook, near Albany in New York and was known as *O*ld *K*inderhook)]

OK *abbrev*: Oklahoma (US state).

okapi *ō-kä'pē*, *n* an animal of Central Africa related to the giraffe: — *pl* **oka'pis**. [Native name]

okay. See **OK**.

oke[1] *ōk*, *n* a Turkish weight of about 1.3kg or $2\frac{4}{5}$ lb. [Turk *ōqah*, apparently through Gr from L *uncia* ounce]

oke[2] *ōk*, (*slang*) *adv* a clipped form of **OK**. — *adj* and *adv* **okey-dokey** (*ō-ki-dō'ki*) or **okey-doke** (*-dōk'*) (*slang*) OK.

okimono *ō-ki-mō'nō*, *ok-*, *n* a Japanese ornament or figurine. [Jap *oku* to put, and *mono* thing]

Okla. *abbrev*: Oklahoma (US state).

okra *ok'rə*, *ōk'rə*, *n* a tropical plant, *Hibiscus esculentus*, of the mallow family, with edible pods; the pods themselves; a dish prepared with the pods. — Also known as **gumbo** and **lady's fingers**. [From a W African name]

Okta or **octa** *ok'ta*, (*aeronautics* and *meteorol*) *n* a unit equal to one-eighth of the sky area, used in specifying cloud cover for airfield weather condition reports. [Gr *okta-* eight]

-ol *ol*, (*chem*) *sfx* signifying the presence of a hydroxyl group, used *esp* in the names of alcohols, as eg *phenol*, *ethanol*, *methanol*, *quinol*. [Alcoh*ol*]

Olbers' paradox *ol'bərz par'ə-doks*, (*astron*) *n* the apparent paradox, stated in 1826 and now explained by postulating a finite expanding universe, that the sky is dark at night although, as there are an infinite number of stars, it should be uniformly bright. [Heinrich *Olbers* (1758–1840), German astronomer and physicist, who first stated the paradox]

old *ōld*, *adj* advanced in years; having been long or relatively long in existence, use or possession; of a specified (or to-be-specified) age; of long standing; worn or worn out; out of date; superseded or abandoned; former; old-fashioned; antique; ancient; early; belonging to later life; belonging to former times; denoting anyone or anything with whom or with which one was formerly associated, such as *old school*, etc; (of a language) of the earliest or earliest known stage; long practised or experienced; having the characteristics of age; familiar, accustomed; in plenty, in excess, or wonderful (*esp* in *high old*; *colloq*); a general word of familiar or affectionate approbation or contempt (often *good old* or *little old*; *colloq*); reckoned according to Old Style (see **style**): — *compar* **old'er** or **eld'er** (qv); *superl* **old'est** or **eld'est** (qv under **elder**[2]). — *adv* (*Shakesp*) of old. — *n* an old person (*archaic* or, *esp* in *pl*, *mod colloq*); olden times, eld. — *vt* and *vi* **old'en** (*rare*) to age. — *adj* former, old, past (now *usu* only in phrases *in olden days/times*). — *n* **old'ie**, (rarely) **old'y** (*colloq*) an old person; a film, song, etc produced or popularized, etc a considerable time ago. — *adj* **old'ish** rather old. — *n* **old'ness**. — *n* **old'ster** a man getting old (*colloq*); a midshipman of four years' standing, a master's mate. — **old age** the later part of life; **old-age pension** a pension for someone who has reached old age, *esp* under a national system (first instituted in Britain in 1908; see also **retirement pension** under **retire**); **old-age pensioner**; **old bachelor** a rather elderly or confirmed bachelor; **Old Bailey** the Central Criminal Court in London; **Old Believer** (*hist*) in Russia, a dissenter from the Orthodox church, a Raskolnik; **Old Bill** a soldier with drooping moustache in World-War-I cartoons by Bruce Bairnsfather; the police (*slang*; sometimes with *the*); **old bird** an astute, experienced person; **old boy** one's father, husband, etc (*colloq*); an old or oldish man, *esp* one in authority, or one who has some air of youthfulness; a former pupil; an affectionately familiar term of address to a male of any age (*colloq*; also **old bean**, **old chap**, **old fellow**, **old man**, **old thing**); **Old-Boy network** (also without *caps*) the members of a society (*usu* upper-class), closely interconnected, who share information and secure advantages for each other; this form of association; **Old Catholic** a member of a body that broke away from the Roman Catholic Church on the question of papal infallibility; **old-clothes'man** someone who deals in cast-off garments; **Old Contemptibles** the British Expeditionary Force to France in 1914, from the then Kaiser's probably apocryphal reference to them as a *contemptible* little army; **old country** the mother-country; **old dear** (*slang*) an old lady; **Old Dominion** Virginia; **Old English** see **English**; the form of black-letter used by 16c English printers. — *adj* **old-estab'lished** long established. — *adj* **olde-worlde** (*ōldi-wûrld'i*; *colloq*) self-consciously imitative of the past or supposed past. — **old face** (*printing*) the early roman type such as Caslon used. — *adj* **old-fash'ioned** in the style of long ago; out of date; clinging to old things and old styles; with manners like those of a grown-up person (said of a child); (in **old-fashioned look**) quizzically disapproving or critical. — **old-fash'ionedness**. — **old fogey** or **old fogy** a dull old person, or someone with old-fashioned notions. — *adj* **old-fo'geyish** or **old-fo'gyish** like an old fogey. — **Old French** the French language till about 1400; **old gang** or **guard** the old and conservative element in a party, etc. — *adj* **old-gen'tlemanly** characteristic of an old gentleman. — **old girl** (*colloq*) an old or oldish woman, *esp* one with an air of youthfulness; a former pupil; an affectionately familiar form of address to a female of any age; **Old Glory** the US flag, the Stars and Stripes; **old gold** a dull gold colour like tarnished gold, used *esp* in textile fabrics; **old hand** an experienced performer; an old convict; **Old Harry**, **Old Nick**, **Old One**, **Old Poker**, or **Old Scratch** the devil. — *adj* **old-hat'** out-of-date. — **Old Hundred** or **Old Hundredth** a famous tune set in England about the middle of the 16c to Kethe's version of the 100th Psalm, marked 'Old Hundredth' in Tate and Brady (1696); **old lady** (*colloq*) one's mother or wife; **Old Light** (*Scot* **Auld Licht**) a member of a relatively less advanced religious school, applied *esp* to the party in the Scottish Secession Church who continued to hold unchanged the principle of connection between Church and State; **old maid** a spinster, *esp* one who is likely to remain a spinster; a woman, or often a man, of the character supposed to be common among spinsters, ie fussy, prim, conventional, over-cautious, methodical; a simple game played by passing and matching cards; also the player left with the odd card; **old-maid'hood** or **old-maid'ism**. — *adj* **old-maid'ish** like the conventional old maid, prim. — **old man** one's husband, father, or employer (*colloq*); the captain of a ship; a familiar, friendly or encouraging term of address; unregenerate human nature; an adult male kangaroo; a plant, the southernwood. — *adj* (*Austr colloq*; also with *hyphen*) of exceptional size, intensity, etc. — **old master** (often with *caps*) any great painter or painting of a period previous to the 19c (*esp* of the Renaissance); **old moon** the moon in its last waning quarter before its reappearance as a new moon; **Old Nick** see **Old Harry** above, and **Nick**; **Old Norse** see **Norse**; **Old Pretender** see under **pretend**; **old rose** a deep soft pink; **old salt** an experienced sailor; **old school** those whose ways, thoughts or attitudes are such as prevailed in the past (see also **old school tie** below). — Also *adj*. — **old soldier** an experienced person who knows how to make himself or herself comfortable, or how to turn things to his or her advantage; an empty bottle; **old song** a mere trifle, a very small price; **old squaw** or **old'squaw** (*US*) a kind of duck, the hareld; **old stager** an experienced person, an old hand; **old story** something one has heard before; something that happened long ago, or has happened often; **Old Style** see **style**; a typeface in imitation of old face (*printing*); **Old Testament** (*abbrev* **Old Test** and **OT**) see **testament**. — *adj* **old'-time** of or pertaining to times long gone by; of long standing; old-fashioned. — **old-tim'er** an experienced person, a veteran; someone who has been where he or she is for a long time; an old-fashioned person; (*esp* as a form of address; *US*) an old person; **Old Tom** (*archaic*) a kind of sweetened gin; **old wife** an old woman; someone who has the character ascribed to old women; a cap for curing a smoking chimney (*Scot*); a kind of duck, the hareld; a fish of various kinds, sea-bream, file-fish, alewife, menhaden, etc; **old woman** one's wife or mother (*colloq*); an old-womanish person. — *adj* **old-wom'anish** like an old woman, *esp* fussy; **old'-world** belonging to earlier times; old-fashioned and quaint; (with *cap*) of the Old World. — **Old World** the Eastern hemisphere. — **any old** see under **any**; **come the old soldier over someone** to impose on a person; **of old** long ago; in or of times long past; formerly; **old man of the sea** a person or burden that one cannot shake off, from the old man in the *Arabian Nights* who, having been carried across a stream by Sinbad the Sailor, refused to get down off his back; **old man's beard** a name for several plants including traveller's joy; **Old Red Sandstone** (*geol*) the lacustrine or continental equivalent of the (marine) Devonian, so called in contradistinction to the New Red Sandstone; **old school tie** a distinctive tie worn by old boys of a school; the emblem of (*esp* upper-class) loyalties shown by such people to each other; **the old sod** one's native country, *esp* used of Ireland, when also **the ould sod**. [OE *ald* (WSax *eald*); Du *oud*, Ger *alt*]

olden, etc, **oldster**. See under **old**.

olé *ō-lā'* (*Sp*) *interj* an exclamation of approval, support or encouragement, sometimes used in English as an expression of triumph. [Ar *wa-llāh* by God]

Olea *ō'li-ə*, *n* the olive genus, giving name to the family **Oleā'ceae**, including ash, privet and jasmine. — *adj* **oleā'ceous**. [L *olea* olive]

oleaginous *ō-li-aj'i-nəs*, *adj* oily; fawning or sycophantic (*facetious*). — *n* **oleag'inousness**. [L *oleāginus*, from *oleum* oil]

oleander *ō-li-an'dər*, *n* an evergreen shrub (*Nerium oleander*) of the Apocynaceae, with lance-shaped leathery leaves and beautiful red or white flowers, the rose-bay or rose-laurel. [LL *oleander*; derivation from *rhododendron*, influenced by *laurus* and *olea*, has been conjectured]

olearia *ō-li-ā'ri-ə*, *n* a plant of the *Olearia* genus of Australasian evergreen shrubs of the family Compositae, with white, yellow or mauve daisy-like flowers; a daisy-tree or bush (*colloq*). [After the German theologian and horticulturalist Johann Gottfried *Olearius* (1635–1711)]

oleaster *ō-li-as'tər*, *n* properly the true wild olive; extended to the so-called wild olive, *Elaeagnus*. [L *oleāster*, from *olea* an olive-tree, from Gr *elaiā*]

oleate *ō'li-āt*, *n* a salt of oleic acid. — *adj* **olefiant** (*ō-li-fī'ənt* or *ō-lē'fi-ənt*) oil-forming (in **olefiant gas** ethylene). — *n* **o'lefin** or **-fine** (*-fin*, *-fēn*) any hydrocarbon of the ethylene series. — *adj* **olē'ic** (or *ō'li-ik*) pertaining to or derived from oil (as in **oleic acid** $C_{18}H_{34}O_2$). — *adj* **oleif'erous** (of eg seeds) producing oil. — *n* **olein** (*ō'li-in*) a glycerine ester of oleic acid. — *n* **oleo** (*ō'li-ō*) short form of oleograph or oleomargarine; an oil-containing telescopic part of the landing-gear of an aircraft, acting as a shock-absorber on landing (also **oleo leg**): — *pl* **ō'leos**. — *n* **o'leograph** a print in oil-colours to imitate an oil painting. — *n* **oleog'raphy**. — *n* **oleomar'garine** margarine (*US*); a yellow fatty substance obtained from beef tallow and used in the manufacture of margarine, soap, etc. — *adj* **oleophil'ic** having affinity for oils; wetted by oil in preference to water. — *n* **oleum** (*ōl'i-əm*) a solution of sulphur trioxide in sulphuric acid (also **fuming sulphuric acid**). — **oleo leg** see **oleo** above; **oleo-res'in** a solution of a resin in an oil. [L *oleum* oil]

olecranon *ō-li-krā'non, ō-lek'rə-non,* (*anatom*) *n* a projection on the upper end of the ulna, at the elbow. — *adj* **olecrā'nal** (or *ō-lek'rə-nəl*). [Gr *ōlekrānon*, from *ōlenē* elbow, and *krānion* head]

olefin, oleic, olein, etc. See under **oleate**.

olent *ō'lənt, adj* having a smell. [L *olens, -entis*, pr p of *olēre* to smell]

Olenus *ō'le-nəs, n* a typically Upper Cambrian genus of trilobites. — *n* **Olenell'us** a similar Lower Cambrian genus. [Gr *Ōlenos*, who was turned to stone]

oleo. See under **oleate**.

oleraceous *ol-ə-rā'shəs, adj* of the nature of a pot-herb, for kitchen use. [L (*h*)*olerāceus*, from (*h*)*olus*, (*h*)*oleris* a pot-herb or vegetable]

oleum. See under **oleate**.

olfactory *ol-fak'tə-ri, adj* pertaining to, or used in, smelling. — *vt* **olfact'** (*facetious*) to smell. — *adj* **olfact'ible**. — *n* **olfac'tion**. — *adj* **olfac'tive**. — *n* **olfactol'ogist**. — *n* **olfactol'ogy** the scientific study of smells and the sense of smell. — *n* **olfactom'etry** the measurement of the sharpness of the sense of smell; the measurement of odours, odorimetry (qv). — *n sing* **olfactronics** (*-tron'iks*; modelled on elec*tronics*) the precise measurement, analysis and detection of odours by means of electronic instruments. [L *olfacere* to smell, from *olēre* to smell, and *facere* to make]

olibanum *ol-ib'ə-nəm, n* a gum-resin flowing from incisions in species of *Boswellia*, *esp* species in E Africa and Arabia, frankincense. [LL, prob from Gr *libanos* frankincense]

olid *ol'id, adj* rank-smelling. [L *olidus*, from *olēre* to smell]

olig- *ol-ig-*, or **oligo-** *ol-i-gō-, -gə-, -go'*, *combining form* denoting little, few. — *n* **oligaemia** (*ol-i-gē'mi-ə, -jē'mi-ə*) abnormal deficiency of blood. — *n* **ol'igarch** (*-ärk*; Gr *archē* rule) a member of an oligarchy. — *adj* **oligarch'al, oligarch'ic** or **oligarch'ical**. — *n* **ol'igarchy** (*-är-ki*) government by a small exclusive class; a state so governed; a small body of men who have the supreme power of a state in their hands. — *n* **oligist** (*ol'i-jist*; Fr *fer oligiste*, from *fer* iron, and Gr *oligistos*, superlative of *oligos* little; as containing less iron than magnetite; *mineralogy*) crystallized haematite. — *adj* **Oligocene** (*ol'i-gə-sēn*; Gr *kainos* new; as having few fossil molluscs of living species; *geol*) between Eocene and Miocene. — *n* the Oligocene system, period, or strata. — *n* **oligochaete** (*ol'i-gə-kēt*; Gr *chaitē* bristle) any worm of the **Oligochae'ta**, chaetopods in which the locomotor organs are reduced to bristles, eg earthworms, etc. — *adj* **oligochrome** (*ol'i-gə-krōm*; Gr *chrōma* colour) painted in few colours. — Also *n*. — *n* **oligoclase** (*ol'i-gə-klās, -klāz*; Gr *klāsis* cleavage, because thought to have a less perfect cleavage than albite; *mineralogy*) a soda-lime triclinic feldspar. — *n* **oligocythaemia** (*ol-i-gō-sī-thē'mi-ə*; Gr *kytos* a vessel, and *haima* blood) a deficiency of red cells in the blood. — *adj* **oligom'erous** (Gr *meros* a part) having few parts; having fewer members than the other whorls of a flower. — *n* **oligonū'cleotide** see **nucleic acid**. — *adj* **oligopolist'ic**. — *n* **oligopoly** (*ol-i-gop'ə-li*; Gr *pōleein* to sell) a situation in which there are few sellers of a particular product or service, and a small number of competitive firms control the market, *opp* to **oligopsony** (*ol-i-gop'sə-ni*; Gr *opsōnia* purchase of food) a situation in which a few large buyers purchase all or most of the output of a particular industry, each competitive buyer influencing the market. — *adj* **oligopsonist'ic**. — **oligosacch'arides** rare complex sugars thought to be associated with the spread of cancer cells, originating from breast cancer, round the body. — *adj* **oligotrophic** (*-trof'*; Gr *trophē* nourishment) (of a lake) having steep, rocky shores and scanty littoral vegetation, lacking in nutrients but rich in oxygen at all levels. — *n* **oliguria** (*o-li-gū'ri-ə*; Gr *ouron* urine; *med*) scantiness of urine secretion in proportion to liquid intake. [Gr *oligos* little, few]

olio *ō'li-ō, n* a savoury dish of different sorts of meat and vegetables; a mixture; a medley; a miscellany; a variety entertainment: — *pl* **o'lios**. [Sp *olla*, from L *ōlla* a pot; cf **olla**]

oliphant *ol'i-fənt, n* an obsolete form of **elephant**; an ancient ivory hunting-horn.

olitory *ol'i-tə-ri, adj* pertaining to kitchen vegetables. — *n* a kitchen-garden; a pot-herb. [L (*h*)*olitor* gardener, from (*h*)*olus*, (*h*)*oleris* a pot-herb or vegetable]

olive *ol'iv, n* a tree (*Olea europaea*) cultivated round the Mediterranean for its oily fruit; extended to many more or less similar trees; the small oval stoned fruit of the olive-tree, yellowish-green when unripe, ripening to a shiny black, with bitter-tasting flesh; a colour like the unripe olive; a person of olive-coloured complexion; an olive-shaped or oval object of various kinds; peace, of which the olive-leaf or branch was the emblem; a gasteropod mollusc (genus **Oliva**) of warm seas with an olive-shaped shell; a small rolled and stuffed piece of meat, as in *beef olive*. — *adj* of a yellowish-green colour like the olive. — *adj* **olivā'ceous** olive-coloured; olive-green. — *adj* **ol'ivary** olive-shaped. — *n* **olivenite** (*ō-liv'ə-nīt* or *ol'iv-*) a mineral, hydrated copper arsenate, often olive-coloured. — *n* **ol'ivet** an olive-shaped button; an oval mock-pearl used in trade with primitive peoples in Africa. — *n* **olivine** (*ol'iv-ēn*) an orthorhombic rock-forming mineral, silicate of iron and magnesium, often olive-green, often found, altered (qv), as serpentine. — **o'live-back** a N American forest thrush (*Hylocichla ustulata*); **olive branch** a symbol of peace; something which shows a desire for peace or reconciliation; a child (Psalm 128.3; *Prayer Bk*); **olive drab** the olive green of American military uniforms; **olive green** a dull dark yellowish green; **ol'ive-oil** oil pressed from the fruit of the olive; **ol'ive-shell** the shell of the mollusc Oliva; **ol'ive-yard** a piece of ground on which olives are grown; **ol'ivine-rock** dunite. [Fr, from L *olīva*]

Oliver[1] *ol'i-vər, n* the comrade-in-arms of Roland (qv).

Oliver[2]. See under **Bath**.

oliver *ol'i-vər, n* a forge-hammer worked by foot. [Origin unknown]

Oliverian *ol-i-vē'ri-ən, n* an adherent of the Protector, *Oliver* Cromwell (1599–1658).

Olivetan *ol-iv-ē'tən, n* one of an order of Benedictine monks founded in 1313, the original house being at Monte *Oliveto*, near Siena.

olla *ol'ə, ō'la, öl'yä, n* a jar or urn; an olio. — **olla-podrida** (*öl'yä-pö-drē'dä*; Sp, rotten pot) a Spanish mixed stew or hash of meat and vegetables; any incongruous mixture or miscellaneous collection. [L *ōlla* and Sp *olla* pot, and Sp *podrida*, from L *putrida* (*fem*) rotten]

ollav or **ollamh** *ol'äv, n* a learned man among the ancient Irish. [Ir *ollamh*]

olm *olm, ōlm, n* a blind, cave-dwelling, eel-like salamander of Europe (*Proteus anguinus*). [Ger]

-ology. The combining element is properly **-logy** (qv). — *n* **ology** (*ol'ə-ji*) a science whose name ends in -(*o*)*logy*; any science.

oloroso *ol-ə-rō'sō, -zō, ōl-, n* a golden-coloured medium-sweet sherry: — *pl* **oloro'sos**. [Sp, fragrant]

olpe *ol'pē, n* a Greek jug. [Gr *olpē*]

olykoek or **olycook** *ol'i-ko͝ok,* (*US*) *n* a kind of doughnut. [Du *oliekoek*, literally oil-cake]

Olympus *ə-lim'pəs, n* the name of several mountains, *esp* of one in Thessaly, in Greek mythology the abode of the greater Greek gods; heaven. — *n* **Olym'pia** a district in Elis, also the city of Pisa in it, where the Olympic games in honour of Olympian Zeus were celebrated. — *n* **Olym'piad** in ancient Greece, a period of four years, being the interval from one celebration of the Olympic games to another, used in reckoning time (the traditional date of the first games being 776 BC); in ancient Greece, a celebration of the Olympic games; a celebration of the modern Olympic games; (sometimes without *cap*) an international contest in bridge, chess, etc. — *n* **Olym'pian** a dweller on Olympus, any of the greater gods, *esp* Zeus (*Gr mythol*); a godlike person; a competitor in the Olympic games. — *adj* of Olympus; godlike; of Olympia (now *rare*). — *adj* **Olym'pic** of Olympia; of Olympus (now *rare*); of the Olympic games. — *n pl* **Olym'pics** the Olympic games, *esp* those of modern times; (sometimes without *cap*) an international contest in some mental exercise such as chess. — **Olympic games** in ancient Greece, the games celebrated every four years at Olympia; the quadrennial international athletic contests held at various centres since 1896; **Olympic torch** since 1936, a lighted torch brought from Olympia, Greece, to kindle the **Olympic flame**, which burns throughout the Olympic games. — **Winter Olympics** international contests in skiing, skating, and other winter sports, held in the same years as the modern Olympics. [Gr *Olympos*]

OM *abbrev*: Old Measurement; Order of Merit.

Om or **om** *ōm, om, n* a sacred syllable intoned as part of Hindu devotion and contemplation, symbolizing the Vedic scriptures, the three worlds (earth, atmosphere and air), and the Absolute. [Sanskrit]

-oma *-ō-mə, n combining form* denoting a tumour, abnormal growth, etc, as in *carcinoma, angioma, glioma*, etc: — *pl* **-ō'mas** or **-ō'mata**. [Gr ending of nouns formed from verbs with infinitive *-oun*]

omadhaun *om'ə-dön*, (*Ir*) *n* a fool. [Ir *amadan*]

omasum *ō-mā'səm, n* a ruminant's third stomach, the psalterium or manyplies: — *pl* **omā'sa**. — *adj* **omā'sal**. [L *omāsum* ox tripe; a Gallic word]

ombre *om'bər, -brā, um'bər, n* a game played with a pack of forty cards, *usu* by three persons, one against the others; the solo player. [Sp *hombre* a man, from L *homō, -inis*]

ombré *om'brā, adj* (of a fabric, etc) with colours or tones blending into each other to give a shaded or striped effect. [Fr, *pa p* of *ombrer* to shade]

ombrella. See under **umbrella**.

ombrometer *om-brom'i-tər, n* a rain-gauge. — *n* **om'brophil** (*-fil*) or **ombrophile** (*-fīl*) a plant tolerant of much rain. — *adj* **ombroph'ilous**. — *n* **om'brophobe** a plant intolerant of much rain. — *adj* **ombroph'obous**. [Gr *ombros* a rain-storm, and **-meter**, **-phil(e)** and **-phobe**]

ombú or **ombu** *om-boo'*, *n* a S American tree, a species of *Phytolacca*, that grows isolated in the pampas: — *pl* **ombús'** or **ombus'**. [Sp, from Guaraní *umbú*]

Ombudsman *om'boodz-man, -mən, n* (also without *cap*) *orig* in Sweden and Denmark a 'grievance man', an official who is appointed to investigate complaints against the Administration; in Britain officially 'Parliamentary Commissioner for Administration', a government official who investigates complaints against government departments; (often without *cap*) any official with a similar function: — *pl* **Om'budsmen**. [Swed, representative]

-ome *-ōm, n combining form* denoting a mass, as in *rhizome, biome*. [Gr *-ōma*]

omega *ō'mi-gə, US -mē', n* the last letter of the Greek alphabet, long o (*Ω, ω*); the conclusion; as a numeral ω' = 800, ͵ω = 800 000. [Late Gr *ō mega* great O (opposed to *omicron*); the earlier Gr name of the letter was *ō*]

omelet or **omelette** *om'lit, -let, n* a pancake made of eggs beaten up and fried in a pan (with or without cheese, herbs, ham, jam or other addition). [Fr *omelette*, earlier *amelette*, apparently by change of sfx and metathesis from *alemelle* (*l'alemelle* for *la lemelle*) a thin plate, from L *lāmella, lāmina* a thin plate]

omen *ō'mən, n* a sign of some future event, either good or evil; threatening or prognosticating character; an event prognosticated (*Shakesp*). — *vt* to portend. — *adj* **o'mened** affording or attended by omens, *esp* as *combining form*, as in *ill-omened*. [L *ōmen, -inis*]

omentum *ō-men'təm*, (*zool*) *n* a fold of peritoneum proceeding from one of the abdominal viscera to another: — *pl* **omen'ta**. — *adj* **omen'tal**. — **great omentum** the epiploon, a hanging flap of the peritoneum covering the intestines. [L *ōmentum*]

omer *ō'mər, n* a Hebrew dry measure containing about 2¼ litres, 1/10 epha. [Heb *'ōmer*]

omertà or **omerta** *om-er-ta', n* the Mafia code of honour requiring silence about criminal activities and stressing the disgrace of informing; a criminal conspiracy of silence. [Ital, dialect form of *umiltà* humility]

omicron *ō-mī'krən, ō'mi-, om'i-, n* the fifteenth letter of the Greek alphabet, short o (*O, o*); as a numeral *o'* = 70, ͵*o* = 70 000. [Late Gr *o mīcron* little O (opposed to *omega*); the earlier Greek name of the letter was *ou*]

ominous *om'i-nəs, adj* pertaining to, or containing, an omen; portending evil; inauspicious. — *adv* **om'inously**. — *n* **om'inousness**. [L *ōminōsus*, from *ōmen, -inis* an omen]

omit *ō-mit', ə-mit', vt* to leave out; to fail (to do something, etc); to fail to use, perform; to disregard (*Shakesp*); to leave off, let go (*Shakesp*): — *pr p* **omitt'ing**; *pa t* and *pa p* **omitt'ed**. — *adj* **omiss'ible** that may be omitted. — *n* **omission** (*-mish'n*) the act of omitting; a thing omitted. — *adj* **omiss'ive** omitting, of the nature of omission. — *n* **omiss'iveness**. — *n* **omitt'ance** (*Shakesp*) omission. — *n* **omitt'er**. [L *omittere, omissum*, from *ob-* in front, and *mittere, missum* to send]

omlah *om'lä, n* a staff of officials in India. [Ar *'umalā*]

ommateum *om-ə-tē'əm*, (*entomol*) *n* a compound eye: — *pl* **ommate'a**. — *n* **ommatid'ium** a simple element of a compound eye: — *pl* **ommatid'ia**. — *n* **ommatophore** (*-at'ə-fōr, -för*) an eye-stalk, as in snails. [Gr *omma, -atos* an eye]

omneity *om-nē'i-ti*, or **omniety** *om-nī'i-ti*, (*rare*) *n* allness, the condition of being all. [L *omnis* all]

omni- *om-ni-, combining form* denoting all. — *n pl* **omniana** (*-ä'nə, -ā'nə*) -ana (qv) about all sorts of things. — *n* **omnibenev'olence** universal benevolence. — *adj* **omnibenev'olent**. — *n* **omnicom'petence** competence in all matters. — *adj* **omnicom'petent**. — *adj* **omnidirec'tional** acting in all directions. — *adj* **omnifā'rious** of all kinds. — *adj* **omnif'erous** bearing or producing all kinds. — *adj* **omnif'ic** all-creating. — *adj* **om'niform** of, or capable of, every form. — *n* **omniform'ity**. — *vt* **om'nify** (*rare*) to make universal. — *adj* **omnigenous** (*-nij'i-nəs*) of all kinds. — *n* **omnipar'ity** general equality. — *adj* **omnip'arous** producing all things. — *adj* **omnipā'tient** enduring all things. — *n* **omnip'otence** or **omnip'otency** unlimited power. — *adj* **omnip'otent** all-powerful. — *adv* **omnip'otently**. — *n* **omnipres'ence** the quality of being present everywhere at the same time. — *adj* **omnipres'ent**. — *n* **omniscience** (*om-nis'i-əns, -nish'əns, -yəns*) knowledge of all things. — *adj* **omnisc'ient** all-knowing. — *adv* **omnisc'iently**. — *n* **om'nivore** an omnivorous person or animal. — *adj* **omniv'orous** all-devouring; feeding on both animal and vegetable food (*zool*). — *n* **omniv'ory** omnivorousness. [L *omnis* all]

omnibus *om'ni-bəs, n* a large road vehicle for carrying a considerable number of passengers of the general public, etc (now *usu* in shortened form **bus**); an omnibus box; an omnibus book; a waiter's or waitress's assistant: — *pl* **om'nibuses**. — *adj* widely comprehensive; of miscellaneous contents. — **omnibus book** a book containing reprints of several works or items, *usu* by a single author, or on a single subject, or of the same type; **omnibus box** a theatre box with room for a number of people; **omnibus clause** (eg *insurance*) one that covers many different cases; **omnibus edition** (*TV* and *radio*) a programme comprising or edited from all the preceding week's editions of a particular series; **omnibus train** one that stops at every station. [Literally, for all, dative pl of L *omnis*]

omnicompetence. . . **omnipotence**. . . **omniscience**. See under **omni-**.

omnium *om'ni-əm, n* a Stock Exchange term for the aggregate value of the different stocks in which a loan is funded. — **omnium-gath'erum** (*colloq*; *sham Latin*) a miscellaneous collection. [L, of all; genitive pl of *omnis* all]

omnivore, **omnivorous**, **omnivory**. See under **omni-**.

omohyoid *ō-mə-hī'oid*, (*anatom*) *adj* pertaining to shoulder-blade and hyoid. — *n* the muscle joining these. [Gr *ōmos* shoulder]

omophagia *ō-mə-fāj'yə*, *-i-ə*, *n* the eating of raw flesh, *esp* as a religious observance. — Also **omophagy** (*ō-mof'ə-ji*). — *adj* **omophagic** (*-faj'ik*) or **omophagous** (*-mof'ə-gəs*). [Gr *ōmophagiā*, from *ōmos* raw, and *phagein* to eat]

omophorion *ō-mə-fō'ri-on*, *-för'*, *n* an Eastern bishop's vestment like the pallium. [Gr *ōmophorion*, from *ōmos* shoulder, and *pherein* to carry]

omoplate *ō'mə-plāt*, *n* the shoulder-blade or scapula. — *n* **omoplatoscopy** (*-plə-tos'kə-pi*) divination by observing the cracks in a burning shoulder-blade. [Gr *ōmoplatē*, from *ōmos* shoulder, *platē* blade, and **-scopy**]

omphacite *om'fə-sīt*, (*mineralogy*) *n* a grass-green pyroxene. [Gr *omphax*, *-akos* an unripe grape]

omphalos *om'fə-los*, *n* the navel; a boss; a stone at Delphi believed to mark the centre of the world; a centre. — *adj* **omphalic** (*-fal'ik*). — *adj* **om'phaloid** navel-like. — *n* **om'phalomancy** divination of the number of future children from the knots in the navel-string. [Gr *omphalos* navel]

OMR (*comput*) *abbrev*: optical mark recognition.

omrah *om'rä*, *n* a Muslim lord. [Hindi *umrā*, orig pl of Ar *amīr*]

ON *abbrev*: Old Norse.

on *on*, *prep* in contact with the upper, supporting, outer or presented surface of; to a position in contact with such a surface of; in or to a position or state of being supported by; having for basis, principle or condition; subject to; in a condition or process of; towards or to; directed towards; in the direction of; against; applied to; with action applied to; with inclination towards; close to, beside; exactly or very nearly at; at the time, date or occasion of; very little short of; just after; concerning, about; with respect to; by (in oaths and adjurations); at the risk of; assigned to; in addition to; at the expense of, or to the disadvantage of (*colloq*); in (*obs*); (of gaining or taking) from (*Shakesp* and *Milton*): of (*obs* or *dialect*); (of marriage) to (*Scot*); (of waiting) for (*Scot*); against, as *one on one* (*US*). — *adv* in or into a position on something; towards something; in advance; on the way to being drunk (*slang*); forward; in continuance; in or into, or allowing connection, supply, activity, operation or validity; in progress; on the stage, the table, the fire, the programme, the menu, etc; not off. — *interj* forward! proceed! — *adj* on the side on which the batsman stands (normally the bowler's right) (*cricket*); in a condition expressed by the adverb *on*; agreed upon; acceptable (*colloq*); practicable, feasible (*colloq*); willing to participate in an activity, bet, etc. — *n* (*cricket*) the on side. — *vi* to go on (*colloq*); (with *with*) to put on (*colloq*). — *adj* **on-and-off'** off-and-on, intermittent, occasional. — *adj* **on'-board'** or **on'board** on, installed inside or carried aboard a vehicle or craft. — *n* **oncome** (*on'kum*, *-kəm*; *Scot*) a coming on; a sudden fall of rain or snow; the beginning of an attack by an insidious disease. — *n* **on'coming** an approach. — *adj* advancing; approaching. — **on'cost** overhead expenses (see also **oncosts**); an oncostman. — *adj* paid by time; causing oncost or oncosts. — **on'costman** a mine-worker paid by the day; **on'costs** all items of expenditure that cannot be allocated to a specific job; **on'ding** (*Scot*) onset, *esp* a sudden fall of rain or snow; **on'-drive** (*cricket*) a drive to the on side. — Also *vi* and *vt*. — **on'fall** an attack or onslaught, *esp* (*Scot*) of illness; a fall of rain or snow (*Scot*); **on'flow** a flowing on; an onward flow; **on'going** a going on; a course of conduct; an event; (in *pl*) proceedings or behaviour, *esp* misbehaviour. — *adj* (**on'-going**) currently in progress; continuing; which will not stop. — *adj* **on'-job'** combined with or in the course of normal work duties and conditions. — **on-job** (or **on-the-job**) **training** the part of a training course in which a trainee actually works on the job, *usu* at the workplace and under supervision. — *vt* **on'-lend** to lend (money which has already been borrowed from another company, etc). — **on'-licence** a licence to sell alcoholic liquors for consumption on the premises. — *adj* **on'-line** (*comput*) attached to, and under the direct control of, the central processing unit; obtained from or by means of on-line equipment; taking place as part of, or pertaining to, a continuous (*esp* production) process. — **on'looker** someone who is watching, a looker on, observer. — *adj* **on'looking**. — *adj* **on-off'** (of a switch, etc) which can be set to one of only two positions, either *on* or *off*. — **on'rush** a rushing onward; **on'set** a violent attack; an assault; a storming; the beginning or outset; **on'setter** (*archaic*) an assailant; **on'setting** incitement. — *adj* **onshore** (*on'shōr*, *-shör*) towards the land. — *adv* **on'shore**. — *adj* and *adv* **on'side** (*football*, etc) not offside. — *n* (*cricket*) see **on** *adj*. — *adj* and *adv* **on-site'** (working, happening, etc) on a site. — *adj* and *adv* **on'stage** on a part of the stage visible to the audience. — **onstead** (*on'sted*; *Scot*) a farmstead; a farmhouse with its offices; the offices alone. — *adj* and *adv* **on'-stream** of an industrial plant, etc, in or going into operation or production; passing through or along a pipe, system, etc (also *fig*). — *prep* **onto** see **on to** (below); to the whole of (*math*). — *adj* (*math*) describing a mapping of one set to a second set, involving every element of the latter. — *adj* **onward** (*on'wərd*) going on; advancing; advanced. — *adv* (also **on'wards**) towards a place or time in advance or in front; forward; in continuation of forward movement. — *adv* **on'wardly** (*rare*). — **on and off** off and on, intermittently, occasionally; **on and on (and on)** used in phrases containing the particle *on* to emphasize duration, distance, etc; **on stream** same as **on-stream**; **on to** to a place or position on (also **on'to**); forward to; aware of, cognizant of (*colloq*); **you're on!** (*colloq*) I agree to your proposal, terms etc. [OE *on*; Du *aan*; ON *ā*; Ger *an*; Gr *ana*]

on- *on-*, a dialect form of the prefix **un-**.

-on *ən* or *on*, *n combining form* indicating: (1) an elementary particle; (2) a quantum component or molecular unit.

onager *on'ə-jər*, *n* the wild ass of Central Asia; an ancient military engine for throwing great stones. [L, from Gr *onagros*, from *onos* an ass, and *agrios* wild]

Onagra *on'ə-grə*, (*bot*) *n* an old name for Oenothera, giving name to the family **Onagrā'ceae**. — *adj* **onagrā'ceous**. [Gr *onagrā*, the plant also known as *oinothēras*; see **Oenothera**]

onanism *ō'nən-izm*, *n* masturbation; coitus interruptus. — *n* **o'nanist**. — *adj* **onanist'ic**. [After the biblical *Onan*, son of Judah; see Gen 38.9]

ONC *abbrev*: Ordinary National Certificate (a qualification awarded by the Business and Technician Education Council).

once *wuns*, *adv* a single time; on one occasion; at a former time; at any time; at some time in the future (*rare*); firstly (*obs*): in short (*obs*). — *n* one time. — *adj* former. — *conj* when once; as soon as. — *n* **onc'er** a £1 note (*slang*); someone who goes to church once on Sunday (*eccles slang*). — *adj* **once-accent'ed** marked with one accent, applied to the octave beginning with middle C (*music*). — *adj* **once'-errand** see **errand**. — *adj* **once-for-all'** done, etc, once and for all. — *n* **once-o'ver** a single comprehensive survey; a quick (sometimes casual) examination. — **at once** without delay; alike; at the same time; **for once** on one occasion only; **once and again** more than once; now and then; **once** (or **once and**) **for all** once only and not again; **once in a way** or **while** occasionally; rarely; **once or twice** a few times; **once upon a time** at a certain time in the past, the usual formula for beginning a fairy tale. [OE *ānes*, orig genitive of *ān* one, used as adv]

onchocerciasis *ong-kō-sər-kī'ə-sis*, *n* a disease of man, also known as river blindness, common in tropical regions of America and Africa, caused by infestation by a filarial worm (*Onchocerca volvulus*), transmitted by various species of black fly, and characterized by subcutaneous nodules and very often blindness. [Gr *onkos* a hook, and *kerkos* a tail]

oncidium *on-sid'i-əm, n* an orchid of the tropical American genus *Oncidium*. [Gr *onkos* a hook]

onco- *ong-kō-, -kə-, -ko'*, *combining form* denoting tumour. — *n* **on'cogen** (*-kə-jen*) an agent causing oncogenesis. — *n* **on'cogene** (*-kə-jēn*) a gene, which may be carried by a virus, that affects the normal metabolism of a cell in such a way that it becomes cancerous; **oncogen'esis** the formation of cancerous tumours. — *n* **oncogenet'icist** someone who studies oncogenes. — *adj* **oncogenic** (*-kə-jen'*) of a virus, able to cause cancer, *esp* of one carrying an oncogene. — *n* **oncol'ogist**. — *n* **oncol'ogy** the study of tumours. — *n* **oncol'ysis** the destruction of tumours. — *adj* and *n* **oncolyt'ic**. — *n* **oncom'eter** an instrument for measuring variations in the bulk of bodily organs. — *n* **on'comouse** the name given to a strain of mouse, developed by Harvard University for research purposes, into which a human cancer gene has been introduced. — *n* **on'cornavirus** an oncogenic RNA virus. — *n* **oncot'omy** incision into a tumour. [Gr *onkos* bulk, mass or tumour]

oncome, oncoming. See under **on**.

Oncorhynchus *ong-kə-ringk'əs, n* a N Pacific genus of salmon. [Gr *onkos* hook, and *rhynchos* beak]

oncost, oncostman. See under **on**.

oncus. See **onkus**.

OND *abbrev*: Ordinary National Diploma (a qualification awarded by the Business and Technician Education Council).

ondatra *on-dat'rə, n* the musquash. [Huron Indian]

Ondes (or **ondes**) **Martenot** *ɔ̃d mär-tə-nō* or **ondes musicales** *mü-zi-kal* (*music*) *n pl* an electronic musical instrument, an early form of synthesizer, with a keyboard and thermionic valve oscillators. [Fr, Martenot waves (or musical waves), from its French inventor, Maurice *Martenot*]

ondine. Same as **undine**.

onding. See under **on**.

on-dit *ɔ̃-dē, n* rumour; hearsay: — *pl* **on-dits** (*-dē, -dēz*). [Fr]

one *wun, adj* single; of unit number; undivided; the same; a certain; a single but not specified; only; an emphatic word for *a*, as in *That is one big problem* (*slang*); first. — *n* the number unity; a symbol representing it; an individual thing or person, identified by implied reference to a known noun, as in *two red pens and a blue one*; a joke, as in *the one about* ... (*colloq*); a drink, as in *a quick one* (*colloq*); a thing bearing or distinguished by the number one. — *pronoun* somebody; anybody; I, me (*formal*). — *n* **one'ness** singleness; uniqueness; identity; unity; homogeneity or sameness. — *n* **oner, one-er** or **wunner** (*wun'ər*; all meanings *colloq* or *slang*) a person or thing unique or outstanding in any way; an expert; a single, uninterrupted action, process or operation (as in *in a oner*); a £1 note; a heavy blow; a big lie. — *pronoun* **oneself'** or **one's self** the emphatic and reflexive form of **one**. — **one-ac'ter** (*colloq*) a one-act play; **one-and-thir'ty** an old card-game like vingt-et-un, with the aim of making the pips add up to 31 and no more; **one-armed bandit** a fruit-machine (qv), a slot machine for gambling. — *adj* **one'-day** (of an event, etc) lasting for one day. — *adj* **one'-eyed** having only one eye. — *adj* **one'fold** simple, single-minded. — *adj* **one'-hand'ed** with, by or for one hand. — *adj* **one'-horse** drawn by a single horse; (of a place) poor, mean, lacking amenities. — **one-horse race** a race, competition, etc, in which one particular competitor or participant is certain to win. — *adj* **one'-ide'a'd** entirely possessed by one idea. — *adj* **one'-legg'ed**. — **one'-lin'er** (*colloq*) a short witty remark; a wisecrack, quip; a joke delivered in one sentence. — *adj* **one'-man** of, for or done by one man. — **one-man band** a musician who carries and plays many instruments simultaneously; (also **one-man show**) an organization, activity, etc, run very much by one person who refuses the help of others (*fig*); **one-man show** a show performed by one man; a one-man band (*fig*) or the person running it; **one-night'er** or **one-night stand** a performance or performances, or anything similar, given on one single evening in one place by one or more people who then travel on to another place; a sexual relationship lasting only one night (*colloq*). — *adj* **one'-off'** made, intended, done, etc for one occasion only. — Also *n*. — *adj* **one'-one'** one-to-one. — *adj* **one-on-one'** same as **one-to-one**. — **one-parent family** a family in which, due to death, divorce, etc, the children are looked after by only one parent. — *adj* **one'-piece** made in one piece. — *adj* **one'-shot** (intended to be) done, used, etc on only one occasion or for one particular purpose or project; one-off; not part of a serial. — Also *n*. — *adj* **one-sid'ed** limited to one side: partial; biased; developed on one side only; turned to one side. — *adv* **one-sid'edly**. — **one-sid'edness**; **one'-step** a dance of US origin danced to quick march time. — *vi* to dance a one-step. — *adj* **one'-stop** (of a store, etc) providing a variety of goods or services all at one source. — *adj* **one'-time** former, past. — *adj* **one'-to-one'** corresponding each one uniquely to one other; with one person meeting, opposing, playing, etc one other. — *adj* **one'-track** incapable of dealing with more than one idea or activity at a time; obsessed with one idea to the exclusion of others. — **one-two'** (*colloq*) a blow with one fist followed by a blow with the other (*boxing*, etc; also *fig*); a movement in which a player passes the ball to another player, then runs forward to receive it again from the other player (*football*); **one-up'manship** (*facetious*; *Stephen Potter*) the art of being one up, ie scoring or maintaining an advantage over someone. — *adj* **one'-way** proceeding, or permitting or set apart for traffic, in one direction only; not requiring reciprocal action, etc. — **one-way glass** or **mirror** a sheet of glass which can be looked through from one side but which appears from the other side to be a mirror; **one-world'er** someone who subscribes to one-worldism; **one-world'ism** a belief in the government of the world as a whole rather than as separate states and nations. — **a** (or **the**) **one** (*colloq*) a person special or remarkable in some way; **a one for** (*colloq*) an enthusiast for; **all one** just the same; not important; **at one** of one mind; reconciled (with *with*); **be made one** (*archaic*) to get married; **be one up on** to score an advantage over (another); **for one** as at least one, albeit possibly the only one, as in *I for one disagree*; **for one thing** as one reason for objection, there being potentially more; **in one** or **all in one** combined; as one unit, object, etc; **just one of those things** an unfortunate happening that must be accepted; **one and all** everyone without exception; **one another** see **another**; **one by one** singly in order; **one or two** a few. [OE *ān*; ON *einn*, Ger *ein*; L *ūnus*; Gr *oinē* ace]

oneiric or **oniric** *ō-nī'rik*, (*rare*) *adj* belonging to dreams. — *n* **oneirocrit'ic** an interpreter of dreams. — *adj* **oneirocrit'ical**. — *n* **oneirocrit'icism**. — *n* **oneirodynia** (*-ə-din'i-ə*) troubled sleep; nightmare. — *n* **oneirology** (*on-ī-rol'ə-ji*) the study of dreams. — *n* **oneir'omancer**. — *n* **oneir'omancy** divination by dreams. — *n* **oneiros'copist** an interpreter of dreams. — *n* **oneiros'copy**. [Gr *oneiros* a dream, and *kritikos* judging, *odynē* pain, **-logy**, **-mancy** and **-scopy**]

onely. A Spenserian spelling of **only**.

oner. See under **one**.

onerous *on'ə-rəs, ō'nə-rəs, adj* burdensome; oppressive. — *adv* **on'erously**. — *n* **on'erousness**. [L *onerōsus*, from *onus* a burden]

oneyre or **oneyer** *wun'yər*, (*Shakesp*) *n poss* meaning merely 'ones' in the phrase 'great oneyers' in 1 *Henry IV*. [*-yer* explained as the sfx in *lawyer*, etc]

onfall... to ... **ongoing**. See under **on**.

onion *un'yən, n* a pungent edible bulb of the lily family; the plant yielding it (*Allium cepa*); applied also to some related species; in World War I, a flaming rocket used against aircraft; the head (*slang*). — *vt* to apply an onion to; to produce by means of an onion. — *adj* **on'iony**. — **onion dome** a bulb-shaped dome having a sharp point, characteristic of Eastern Orthodox, *esp* Russian, church architecture. — *adj* **on'ion-eyed** (*Shakesp*) having the eyes full of tears. — **on'ion-skin** a very thin variety of paper. — **know one's onions** (*colloq*) to know one's subject or job well; **off one's onion** (*slang*) off one's head. [Fr *oignon*, from L *ūniō*, *-ōnis* union, a large pearl, an onion; see **union**[2] under **Unio**]

oniric, etc. See **oneiric**.

Oniscus *ə-nis'kəs*, *n* a genus of woodlice. — *adj* **onis'coid** of the family of Oniscus; like a woodlouse. [Gr *oniskos*, diminutive of *onos* an ass]

onkus or **oncus** *ong'kəs*, (*Austr colloq*) *adj* disordered; bad. [Ety unknown]

onliest. See under **only**.

onlooker, etc. See under **on**.

only *ōn'li*, *adj* single in number; without others of the kind; without others worth considering. — *adv* not more, other, or otherwise than; alone; merely; barely; just; pre-eminently (*obs*); singly (*rare*). — *conj* but; except that. — *prep* (*dialect*) except. — *adj* **onliest** (*ōn'li-əst*; *dialect*) only. — **if only** (as an expression of vain desire or regret) would that, I wish; if for no reason other than (to do something); **only too** very, extremely. [OE *ānlic* (adj), from *ān* one, and *-līc* like]

ono or **o.n.o.** *abbrev*: or near (or nearest) offer.

onocentaur *on-ə-sen'tör*, *n* a kind of centaur, half-man, half-ass. [Gr *onos* ass]

onomastic *on-ə-mas'tik*, *adj* pertaining to a name, *esp* pertaining to the signature to a paper written in another hand. — *adv* **onomas'tically**. — *n* **onomas'ticon** a dictionary of proper names. — *n sing* **onomas'tics** the study of the history of proper names. [Gr *onomastikos*, *-on*, from *onoma* a name]

onomatopoeia *on-ə-mat-ə-pē'ə*, *n* the formation of a word in imitation of the sound of the thing meant; a word so formed; the use of words whose sounds help to suggest the meaning (*rhetoric*). — Also **onomatopoesis** (*-pō-ē'sis*) or **onomatopoiesis** (*-poi-ē'sis*). — *adj* **onomatopoeic** (*-pē'ik*) or **onomatopoetic** (*-pō-et'ik*). [Gr *onomatopoiiā*, *-poiēsis*, from *onoma*, *-atos* a name, and *poieein* to make]

onrush... to ... **onside**. See under **on**.

onslaught *on'slöt*, *n* an attack or onset; assault. [Prob Du *aanslag* or Ger *Anschlag*, refashioned as Eng]

onst *wunst*, *adv* a dialect form of **once**.

onstead... to ... **onto**. See under **on**.

Ont. *abbrev*: Ontario (Canadian province).

ontogenesis *on-tə-jen'i-sis*, or **ontogeny** *on-toj'i-ni*, *n* the history of the individual development of an organized being, as distinguished from *phylogenesis*. — *adj* **ontogenet'ic** or **ontogen'ic**. — *adv* **ontogenet'ically** or **ontogen'ically**. [Gr *ōn*, *ontos*, pr p of *einai* to be, and **-genesis**, **-genetic**]

ontology *on-tol'ə-ji*, *n* the science that deals with the principles of pure being; that part of metaphysics which deals with the nature and essence of things. — *adj* **ontologic** (*-tə-loj'ik*) or **ontolog'ical**. — *adv* **ontolog'ically**. — *n* **ontol'ogist**. [Gr *ōn*, *ontos*, pr p of *einai* to be, and **-logy**]

onus *ō'nəs*, *n* burden; responsibility. — **onus probandi** (*ō'nəs prō-ban'dī*, *o'nŏŏs pro-ban'dē*; *legal*) the burden of proving. [L *onus*, *-eris* burden, weight]

onward, etc. See under **on**.

onymous *on'i-məs*, *adj* bearing the author's name. [**anonymous**]

onycha *on'i-kə*, *n* an ingredient in ancient Jewish incense; the nail-like operculum of a mollusc. — *n* **onych'ia** inflammation of the nail-bed. — *n* **on'ychite** onyx-marble. — *n* **onychī'tis** inflammation of the soft parts about the nail. — *n* **onych'ium** a pulvillus in insects. — *n* **onychocryptō'sis** ingrowing toenail. — *n* **on'ychomancy** divination by the fingernails. — *n* **onychophagist** (*-kof'ə-jist*) a nail-biter. — *n* **onychoph'agy**. — *n pl* **Onychoph'ora** (*zool*) Prototracheata, the class of primitive arthropods to which Peripatus belongs. [Ety as for **onyx**]

onyx *on'iks*, *n* an agate formed of alternate flat layers of chalcedony, white or yellow and black, brown or red, used for making cameos (*mineralogy*); onychite or onyx-marble; a fingernail-like opacity in the cornea of the eye. — **on'yx-mar'ble** a banded travertine or stalagmite, also called oriental alabaster. [Gr *onyx*, *onychos* nail, claw, onyx]

oo[1] or **oo'** *ōō*, *n* Scots forms of **wool**.

oo[2] *ōō*, *pronoun* a Scots form of **we**. — *possessive adj* **oor** our.

oo- *ō'ə-*, *ō-o'*, *combining form* denoting egg. — *n* **oocyte** (*ō'ə-sīt*; see **cyte**) an ovum before it matures and begins to divide. — *adj* **oog'amous**. — *n* **oogamy** (*ō-og'ə-mi*; see **-gamy**) union of unlike gametes. — *n* **oogenesis** (*ō-ə-jen'i-sis*; see **-genesis**) the genesis and development of the ovum. — Also **oogeny** (*ō-oj'i-ni*). — *adj* **oogenet'ic**. — *adj* **oogo'nial**. — *n* **oogonium** (*ō-ə-gō'ni-əm*; Gr *gonos*, offspring) the female reproductive organ in seaweeds and fungi: — *pl* **oogo'nia**. — *n* **oolite** (*ō'ə-līt*; Gr *lithos* a stone; *geol*) a kind of limestone composed of grains like the eggs or roe of a fish; (with *cap*) stratigraphically the upper part of the Jurassic in Britain, consisting largely of oolites. — *adj* **oolitic** (*ō-ə-lit'ik*). — *n* **ool'ogist**. — *n* **oology** (*ō-ol'ə-ji*; see **-logy**) the science or study of birds' eggs. — *n* **o'ophyte** (*ō'ə-fīt*; see **-phyte**) in ferns and mosses, the gametophyte. — *n* **oosphere** (*ō'ə-sfēr*; Gr *sphaira* sphere) an unfertilized ovum. — *n* **oospore** (*ō'ə-spōr*, *-spör*; Gr *sporos* seed) a zygote, *esp* a resting zygote. [Gr *ōion* egg]

o/o *abbrev*: offers over (a specified sum).

oobit. See under **woubit**.

oocyte. See under **oo-**.

oodles *ōō'dlz*, *n sing* or *n pl* abundance. — Also **ood'lins**. [Perh **huddle**]

oof *ōōf*, (*slang*) *n* money, *orig* **oof'tish**. [Yiddish, from Ger *auf* (*dem*) *Tische* on the table]

oogamous... to ... **oogonium**. See under **oo-**.

ooh *ōō*, *interj* expressing pleasure, surprise, etc. — Also *n* and *vi*. [Imit]

ooidal *ō-oi'dl*, *adj* egg-shaped. [Gr *ōioeidēs*, from *ōion* and *eidos* form]

oolakan *ōō'lə-kən*. Same as **eulachon**.

oolite... to ... **oology**. See under **oo-**.

oolong or **oulong** *ōō'long*, *n* a variety of black tea with the flavour of green. [Chin *wu-lung* black dragon]

oom *ōōm*, (*SAfr*) *n* uncle; used as term of respect for an elderly man. [Du]

oomiak or **oomiac**. Same as **umiak**.

oompah *ōōm'pä*, *n* a conventional representation of the deep sound made by a large brass musical instrument such as a tuba. — Also *vi* and *vt*.

oomph *ōōmf*, *ŏŏmf*, (*slang*), *n* vitality; enthusiasm; sex-appeal; personal magnetism. [Origin obscure]

oon *ōōn*, *n* a Scots form of **oven**.

oons *ōōnz*, (*archaic*) *interj* an oath, for God's *wounds*.

oont *ōōnt*, *n* in India, a camel. [Hindi *ūt*]

oop. See **oup**.

oophoron *ō-of'ə-ron*, *n* (*zool*) an ovary. — *vt* **oophorec'tomize** or **-ise**. — *n* **oophorec'tomy** (*surg*) removal of one or both ovaries, or of an ovarian tumour. — *n* **oophorī'tis** inflammation of the ovary. [Gr *ōiophoros*, *-on* egg-bearing]

oophyte. See under **oo-**.

oops *ōōps*, *interj* an exclamation drawing attention to or apologizing for, etc, a mistake.

oor. See **oo**[2].

oorial. Same as **urial**.

oorie. Same as **ourie**.

Oort cloud *ōōrt klowd*, *n* a cloud of frozen comet nuclei orbiting the solar system. [After the Dutch astronomer Jan Hendrik *Oort* (1900–92)]

oose *ōōs*, or **oosy** (both *Scot*). Same as **ooze**[2] and **oozy**.

oosphere, **oospore**. See under **oo-**.

ooze[1] *ōōz*, *n* gentle flow, as of water through sand or earth; slimy mud; a fine-grained, soft, deep-sea deposit, composed of shells and fragments of marine rhizopods, diatoms and other organisms; sap (*obs*); the liquor of a tan vat. — *vi* to flow gently; to percolate, as a liquid through pores or small openings; to leak. — *vt* to exude. — *adv* **ooz'ily**. — *n* **ooz'iness**. — *adj* **ooz'y** resembling ooze; slimy; oozing. [Partly OE *wōs* juice, partly OE *wāse* mud]

ooze[2] *ōōz*, (*Scot*) *n* fluff; nap. — *adj* **ooz'y**. [Prob pl of **oo**[1]]

OP *abbrev*: observation post (*military*) or point; opposite prompt (*theat*); *Ordinis* or *Ordo Praedicatorum* (*L*), (of) the order of Preachers, ie Dominicans.

Op or **op** *op*, *abbrev*: opera; operation; operator; opposite; optical (see **op art** below); opus.

op or **o/p** *abbrev*: out of print.

opacity, **opacous**. See under **opaque**.

opah *ō'pə*, *n* the kingfish (*Lampris*), a large sea-fish with laterally flattened body, constituting a family of uncertain affinities. [W African origin]

opal *ō'pl*, *n* amorphous silica with some water, *usu* milky white with fine play of colour, in some varieties precious and used as a gemstone; opal-glass; the colouring of opal. — *adj* of opal; like opal. — *adj* **o'paled**. — *n* **opalesc'ence** a milky iridescence. — *adj* **opalesc'ent**. — *adj* **o'paline** (*-ēn*, *-īn*) relating to, like or of opal. — *n* opal-glass; a photographic print fixed on plate-glass. — *adj* **o'palized** or **-s-** converted into opal; opalescent. — **o'pal-glass** white or opalescent glass. [L *opalus*; Gr *opallios*, perh from Sans *upala* gem]

opaque *ō-pāk'*, *adj* shady; dark; dull; that cannot be seen through; impervious to light or to radiation of some particular kind; obscure, hard to understand; impervious to sense; doltish. — *vt* to make opaque. — *n* **opacity** (*ō-pas'i-ti*) opaqueness. — *adj* **opacous** (*ō-pā'kəs*; *archaic*). — *adv* **opaque'ly**. — *n* **opaque'ness** the quality of being opaque; lack of transparency. [L *opācus*]

op art *op ärt*, *n* art using geometrical forms precisely executed and so arranged that movement of the observer's eye, or inability to focus, produces an illusion of movement in the painting. [*op*tical]

op cit *abbrev*: *opere citato* (*L*), in the work cited.

opcode *op'kōd*, *n* a code containing operation instructions for a microprocessor. [*op*eration, and **code**]

ope *ōp*, *adj* (*poetic*) *vt* and *vi* a short form of **open**.

OPEC *ō'pek*, *abbrev*: Organization of Petroleum-Exporting Countries.

opeidoscope *op-ī'də-skōp*, *n* an instrument for illustrating sound by means of light. [Gr *ōps* (*op-* in the oblique cases) voice, *eidos* form, and **-scope**]

open *ō'pn*, *adj* not shut; allowing passage out or in; exposing the interior; unobstructed; free; unenclosed; exposed; uncovered; liable; generally accessible; available; ready to receive or transact business with members of the public; willing to receive or accept, amenable (with *to*); public; free to be discussed; obvious; unconcealed; undisguised; unfolded, spread out or expanded; unrestricted; not restricted to any class of people, as in *open championship*; (of a town) without military defences; not finally decided, concluded, settled or assigned; not dense in distribution or texture; widely spaced; loose; much interrupted by spaces or holes; showing a visible space between (*naut*); clear; unfrozen; not frosty; not hazy; free from trees; frank; unreserved; unstopped (*music*); without use of valve, crook or key (*music*); (of an organ pipe) not closed at the top; (of a vowel sound) low, with wide aperture for the breath; (of a consonant) without stopping of the breath stream; (of a syllable) ending with a vowel. — *vt* to make open; to make as an opening; to make an opening in; to clear; to expose to view; to expound; to declare open; to begin. — *vi* to become open; to have an opening, aperture or passage; to serve as a passage; to begin to appear; to begin; to give tongue; to speak out. — *n* a clear space; public view; open market; a competition or sporting event open to all competitors; an opening. — *adj* **o'penable**. — *n* **o'pener**. — *n* **o'pening** the act of causing to be, or of becoming, open; an open place; an aperture; a gap; a street or road breaking the line of another; a beginning; a first stage; a preliminary statement of a case in court; the initial moves, or mode of beginning, in a game, etc; an event at which a new exhibition, shop, display, etc, is first opened to the public; the two pages exposed together when a book is opened; an opportunity for action; a vacancy. — Also *adj*. — *adv* **o'penly**. — *n* **o'penness**. — **open access** public access to the shelves of a library; **open adoption** adoption of a child with continued contact with the true parents; **open aestivation** (*bot*) aestivation without overlap or meeting of the edges of the perianth leaves. — *adj* **open-air'** outdoor. — *adj* **open-and-shut'** simple, obvious, easily decided. — *adj* **open-armed'** cordially welcoming. — **open book** anything that can be read or interpreted without difficulty; **open borstal** a borstal run on the same lines as an open prison (qv); **Open Brethren** that section of the Plymouth Brethren whose members are allowed to associate fully with non-members; **open bundle** (*bot*) a vascular bundle with cambium; **o'pen-cast** (*mining*) an open excavation in the land surface. — Also *adj* and *adv*. — *adj* **open-chain'** (*chem*) with atoms linked together like a chain with loose ends. — **open cheque** an uncrossed cheque which can be used to obtain cash on demand from a bank, etc; **open circuit** an electrical circuit broken so that current cannot pass; in television, the customary system in which the showing is for general, not restricted, viewing; **open court** a court proceeding in public; **open day** a day on which an institution (*esp* a school) is open to the public, *usu* with organized exhibitions or events; **open diapason** one of the chief foundation stops of an organ; **open door** free and equal opportunity of trading for all; unrestricted admission or immigration. — *adj* **open-door'**. — **open economy** one involved in overseas trade. — *adj* **open-end'** or **open-end'ed** not closely defined, general and adaptable to suit various contingencies; (of question, debate, etc) allowing free unguided answers or expressions of opinion; (of an investment trust) offering shares in unlimited numbers, redeemable on demand; (**open-end'ed**) without fixed limits. — *adj* **o'pen-eyed** astonished; fully aware of what is involved; watchful (*Shakesp*). — *adj* **o'pen-field** having the arable land in unenclosed strips held by different cultivators. — **open fire** an exposed fire on a domestic hearth. — *adj* **open-hand'ed** with an open hand; generous; liberal. — **open-hand'edness**; **open harmony** (*music*) chords not in close position. — *adj* **open-heart'ed** with an open heart; frank; generous. — **open-heart'edness**. — *adj* **o'pen-hearth** making use of, or having, a shallow hearth of reverberating type. — **open-heart surgery** surgery performed on a heart which has been stopped and opened up while blood circulation is maintained by a heart-lung machine; **open house** hospitality to all comers; **opening time** the time when bars, public houses, etc, can begin selling alcoholic drinks; **open learning** a system of learning based on individual study rather than formal classroom sessions, and using specially designed programmes of printed material, audio and video tapes, etc; **open letter** a letter addressed to one person but intended for public reading; **open market** a market in which buyers and sellers compete without restriction; **open marriage** a form of marriage which allows the partners social and sexual independence; **open mind** freedom from prejudice; readiness to receive and consider new ideas. — *adj* **open-mind'ed**. — **open-mind'edness**. — *adj* **open-mouthed'** gaping; expectant; greedy; clamorous; surprised, astonished. — **open note** (*music*) a note produced by an unstopped string, open pipe, or without a crook, etc; a printed or written note without a solid black head, a semibreve or minim (*US*); **open order** spaced-out formation for drill, etc. — *adj* **open-plan'** having few or no internal walls, partitions, etc. — **open-plan house** one whose rooms run from front to back with windows on both faces; **open prison** a prison without the usual close security, allowing prisoners considerably more freedom of movement than in conventional prisons; **open question** a matter undecided; a question formed so as to elicit a full response or an opinion rather than a yes or no answer; **open sandwich** one which has no bread, etc, on top; **open score** (*music*) one with a separate stave for each part; **open sea** unenclosed sea, clear of headlands; **open season** a time of the year when one may kill certain game or fish (also *fig*); **open secret** a matter known to many but not explicitly divulged; **open sesame** a spell or other means of making barriers fly open, from the story of Ali Baba and the Forty Thieves in the *Arabian Nights*; **open shop** a factory not confined to union labour; **open side** the part of the field between the scrum, etc, and the farther touch-line (*Rugby football*); **open sights** (*rifle-shooting*) in aiming, the eye unaided by the sights, *usu* in shooting at close range; **open skies** the open air; reciprocal freedom for aerial inspection of military establishments; unrestricted use of *esp* commercial airports and airways; **o'pen-stitch** (*Scot* **o'pen-steek**) a kind of open-work stitching; **open system** (*comput*) a network system complying with a set of international standards allowing general accessibility. — *adj* **o'pen-top** (*esp* of a vehicle) without a roof or having an open top; **open town** one without troops or military installations, and hence, according to international law, immune from attack of any kind; **open university** (also with *caps*) a British university (founded in 1971) having no fixed entry qualifications, whose teaching is carried out by correspondence and by radio and television, etc; **open verdict** a verdict in a coroner's court that death has occurred, without specifying the cause; a verdict that a crime has been committed, without specifying the criminal. — *n* and *adj* **o'pen-weave** (made of) a loosely woven fabric with visible spaces between the threads. — **o'penwork** any work showing openings through it, eg in embroidery. — *adj* open-cast. — **open fire** to begin to shoot; **open out** to make or become more widely open; to expand; to disclose; to unpack; to develop; to bring into view; to open the throttle, accelerate; **open up** to open thoroughly or more thoroughly; to lay open; to disclose; to make available for traffic, colonization, etc; to accelerate; to begin firing; to become more communicative; **with open arms** cordially. [OE *open*; cf Du *open*, ON *opinn*, Ger *offen*; prob related to **up**]

opepe *ō-pē'pē*, *n* a W African tree (*Sarcocephalus diderrichii*) yielding a hard yellowish wood used eg as a substitute for teak. [Yoruba]

opera[1] *op'ə-rə*, *n* musical drama; a company performing opera; an opera-house. — *adj* used in or for an opera. — *adj* **operatic** (*-at'ik*) pertaining to or resembling opera; (loosely) histrionic. — *adv* **operat'ically**. — **opera** (Fr **opéra** *o-pā-ra*) **bouffe** (*bōōf*) funny or farcical opera; **opera buffa** (*bōōf'ə*, *op'ā-ra bōōf'a*; Ital) comic opera, *esp* of the 18c, *opp* to *opera seria*; **opéra comique** (*kom-ēk*) (*Fr*) opera with some spoken dialogue, in the 18c having subjects less lofty than those of *grand opéra* (Eng grand opera), in the 19c having no restriction as to subject (either comic or tragic); **opera seria** (*sē'ri-ə*, *se'rya*; Ital) serious opera; **comic opera** opéra comique; opera of an amusing nature; an absurd emotional situation; **grand opera** opera without dialogue, *esp* if the subject is very dramatic or emotional; **light opera** a lively and tuneful opera; an operetta (qv); **soap opera** see **soap**. — See also **music-drama**, **musical**, **musical comedy**. — **op'era-cloak** an elegant cloak for evening wear, *esp* in the auditorium of a theatre; **op'era-dancer** a dancer in ballets introduced into operas; **op'era-glasses** or **o'pera-glass** small binoculars used by audiences in the theatre; **op'era-hat** a collapsible top hat; **opera house** a theatre for opera; **opera singer**. [Ital, from L *opera*; cf **operate**]

opera[2] *op'ə-rə*, *pl* of **opus**.

operate *op'ə-rāt*, *vi* to work; to exert strength; to produce any effect; to exert moral power; to be in activity, act, carry on business; to take effect upon the human system (*med*); to perform some surgical act upon the body with the hand or an instrument. — *vt* to effect, bring about or cause to occur; to work; to conduct, run or carry on. — *adj* **op'erable** capable of treatment by a surgical operation; able to be operated; practicable. — *n* **op'erand** something on which an operation is performed, eg a quantity in mathematics or, in computing, the values on which program instructions operate. — *adj* **op'erant** operative; active; effective. — *n* an operator. — *adj* **op'erāting**. — *n* **operā'tion** the act or process of operating; something which is done or carried out; agency; influence; a method of working; an action or series of movements; a surgical procedure. — *abbrev* **op** *esp* in military or surgical sense. — *adj* **operā'tional** relating to operations; ready for action. — *adj* **op'erative** having the power of operating or acting; exerting force; producing effects; efficacious. — *n* a worker in a factory; a labourer. — *adv* **op'eratively**. — *n* **op'erativeness**. — *n* **op'erātor** a person or thing that operates; someone responsible for the operation of a machine, instrument, or apparatus; someone employed to connect calls, etc, at a telephone exchange; someone who deals in stocks; the owner of a store, business, mine, etc (*US*); a symbol, signifying an operation to be performed (*math*); a crooked or calculating person, a shark (*colloq*, *esp US*); a sequence of DNA to which a repressor or an activator (a protein which increases the production of a gene product) can bind (*biol*). — **operant conditioning** (*psychol*) a learning procedure in which the subject's spontaneous response to a stimulus is reinforced if it is a desired response; **operating system** (*comput*) a software system which controls a computer's operational processes, same as **system software**; **operating table** the narrow table on which the patient lies during a surgical operation; **operating theatre** a room in a hospital, etc equipped for the performing of surgical operations; **operational** or **operations research** research to discover how a weapon, tactic or strategy can be altered to give better results; similar research to promote maximum efficiency in industrial spheres; **operative words** the words in a deed legally effecting the transaction (eg *devise and bequeath* in a will); (loosely; often in *sing*) the most significant word or words. [L *operārī*, *-ātus*, from *opera* work, effort, closely connected with *opus*, *operis* work]

operculum *ō-pûr'kū-ləm*, *n* a cover or lid (*bot*); the plate over the entrance of a shell (*zool*); the gill-cover of fishes; a coal-hole cover in a pavement: — *pl* **oper'cula**. — *adj* **oper'cular** belonging to the operculum. — *adj* **oper'culate** or **oper'culated** having an operculum. [L *operculum*, from *operīre* to cover]

opere citato *op'ə-rē sīt-ā'tō*, *op'er-e kit-ä'tō*, (*L*) in the work cited: — *abbrev* **op cit**.

operetta *op-ə-ret'ə*, *n* a short, light, often rather trivial, musical drama; often, *esp* formerly, light opera (see under **opera**[1]). — *n* **operett'ist** a composer of operettas. [Ital, dimin of *opera*]

operon *op'ə-ron*, (*biol*) *n* in bacteria, a set of functionally related genes that have a common promoter and are transcribed together. [*oper*ate and **-on** (2)]

operose *op'ə-rōs*, (*rare*) *adj* laborious; tedious. — *adv* **op'erosely**. — *n* **op'eroseness** or **operosity** (*-os'i-ti*). [L *operōsus*, from *opus*, *operis* work]

ophi- *of-i-*, or **ophio-** *of-i-ō-*, *of-i-ə-*, *of-i-o'*, *combining form* signifying snake. — *n* **ophical'cite** a marble containing green serpentine. — *n* **oph'icleide** (*-klīd*; Fr *ophicléide*, from Gr *kleis*, *kleidos* key) a keyed wind-instrument developed from the serpent, a bass or alto keybugle. — *n pl* **Ophid'ia** (Gr *ophidion*, dimin of *ophis*) the snakes as an order or suborder of reptiles. — *n* and *adj* **ophid'ian**. — *n* **ophidiā'rium** (*rare*) a snake-house. — *n* **Ophioglоss'um** (Gr *glōssa* tongue) the adder's-tongue genus, giving name to the **Ophioglossā'ceae**, a family of eusporangiate ferns. — *n* **ophiol'ater** a snake-worshipper. — *n* **ophiol'atry** (see **-latry**) snake-worship. — *adj* **ophiol'atrous**. — *n* **oph'iolite** serpentine (*obs*); a group of igneous rocks associated with deep-sea sediments; verd-antique. — *adj* **ophiolit'ic**. — *adj* **ophiolog'ic** or **ophiolog'ical**. — *n* **ophiol'ogist**. — *n* **ophiol'ogy** the study of snakes. — *n* **oph'iomorph** (see **-morph**) a caecilian amphibian. — *adj* **ophiomorph'ic** or **ophiomorph'ous** snakelike. — *adj* **ophioph'agous** (see **-phagous**) snake-eating. — *n* **ophioph'ilist** a snake-lover. — *n* **Oph'ism** the creed or religion of the Ophites. — *n* **oph'ite** a name given to various rocks mottled with green; at one time, serpentine-rock; later, a kind of diabase; (with *cap*) one of a Gnostic sect that reverenced snakes. — *adj* **ophitic** (*ə-fit'ik*) pertaining to ophite; having pyroxene crystals enclosing feldspar laths; (with *cap*) of the Ophites. — *n* **Oph'itism**. — *n* **Ophiuchus** (*-i-ōōk'əs, -ūk'*) the Serpent-Bearer, a constellation between Aquila and Libra on the celestial equator. — *n* **ophiura** (*-i-ōō'rə, -ū'rə*; Gr *ourā* tail) a member of the *Ophiura* genus of brittle-stars or sand-stars. — *n* and *adj* **ophiu'ran**. — *n* and *adj* **ophiu'rid**. — *n* and *adj* **ophiu'roid**. — *n pl* **Ophiu'ridae** and **Ophiuroid'ea** respectively a family and class of echinoderms like starfish with long, snaky, sharply differentiated arms, the brittle stars. [Gr *ophis* snake]

ophthalmo- *of-thal-mō-, -mə-, -mo'*, or before a vowel often **ophthalm-**, *combining form* denoting eye. — *n* **ophthal'mia** inflammation of the eye, *esp* of the conjunctiva. — *adj* **ophthal'mic** pertaining to the eye. — *n* **ophthal'mist** an ophthalmologist. — *n* **ophthalmī'tis** ophthalmia. — *adj* **ophthalmolog'ical**. — *n* **ophthalmol'ogist**. — *n* **ophthalmol'ogy** the science of the eye, its structure, functions and diseases. — *n* **ophthalmom'eter** an instrument for eye-measurements. — *n* **ophthalmom'etry**. — *n* **ophthalmophō'bia** the fear of being stared at. — *n* **ophthalmoplegia** (*-plē'jyə*; see **-plegia**) paralysis of one or more of the muscles of the eye. — *n* **ophthal'moscope** an instrument for examining the interior of the eye. — *adj* **ophthalmoscop'ic** or **ophthalmoscop'ical**. — *adv* **ophthalmoscop'ically**. — *n* **ophthalmos'copy** examination of the interior of the eye with the ophthalmoscope. — **ophthalmic optician** an optician qualified both to prescribe and to dispense spectacles, etc. [Gr *ophthalmos* eye]

opiate *ō'pi-āt, -ət*, *n* a drug containing opium or a substance with similar addictive or narcotic properties; something which dulls sensation, physical or mental. — *adj* inducing sleep. — *vt* (*ō'pi-āt*) to treat with opium; to dull. — *adj* **o'piated**. — Also **ō'pioid**. [**opium**]

opificer *ə-pif'i-sər*, (*obs*) *n* an artificer. [L *opifex, -icis*, from *opus* work, and *facere* to make]

opine *ō-pīn'*, *vt* to suppose; to form or express as an opinion. — *adj* **opi'nable** capable of being thought. [Fr *opiner*, from L *opīnārī* to think]

opinicus *ə-pin'i-kəs*, (*heraldry*) *n* a composite beast, part lion, part dragon, with features of other animals. [Origin unknown]

opinion *ə-pin'yən*, *n* what seems to one to be probably true; judgement; estimation; favourable estimation; self-confidence (*Shakesp*); arrogance (*Shakesp*); reputation (*Shakesp*). — *adj* **opin'ionāted**, **opin'ionātive** or **opin'ioned** unduly attached to and assertive of one's own opinions; stubborn. — *adv* **opin'ionately** (*obs*) and **opin'ionātively**. — *n* **opin'ionātiveness**. — *n* **opin'ionator** someone who holds or gives an opinion; an opinionated person. — Also (*rare*) **opin'ionist**. — **opinion poll** a test made of public opinion by questioning a representative sample of the population. — **a matter of opinion** a matter about which opinions differ. [L *opīniō, -ōnis*]

opisometer *op-i-som'i-tər*, *n* a map-measuring instrument with a wheel that traces a line on the map and then runs backward along a straight scale until the wheel reaches its original position on the screw that holds it. [Gr *opisō* backward, and **-meter**]

opioid. See under **opiate**.

opistho- *ə-pisth-ō-, -ə-, -o'*, or before a vowel **opisth-**, *combining form* signifying behind. — *n* and *adj* **opisthobranch** (*ə-pis'thə-brangk*; Gr *branchia* gills). — *n pl* **Opisthobranch'ia** an order of gasteropods having the gills behind the heart. — *adj* **opisthocoelian** (*-sē'li-ən*; Gr *koilos* hollow) hollow or concave behind, as eg a vertebra is. — Also **opisthocoe'lous**. — *n* **opisthodomos** (*op-is-thod'ə-mos*) a rear-chamber in a Greek temple. — *adj* **opisthogloss'al** (Gr *glōssa* tongue) having the tongue attached in front, free behind, as in frogs. — *adj* **opisthog'nathous** (see **-gnathous**) having receding jaws. — *n* **opis'thograph** a manuscript or slab inscribed on the back as well as the front. — *adj* **opisthograph'ic**. — *n* **opisthog'raphy**. — **opisthot'onos** (Gr, drawn backwards, from *teinein* to stretch, pull tight) extreme arching backwards of the spine and neck as a result of spasm of the muscles in that region. — *adj* **opisthoton'ic**. [Gr *opisthen* behind]

opium *ō'pi-əm*, *n* the dried narcotic juice of the white poppy; anything considered to have a stupefying or tranquillizing effect on people's minds, emotions, etc. — *n* **opiumism** (*pathol*) addiction to opium; the medical condition caused by the habitual use of opium. — **opium den** an establishment where opium can be smoked; **o'pium-eater** or **-smoker** a person who habitually takes opium. [L *opium*, from Gr *opion*, dimin from *opos* sap]

opobalsam *op-ə-böl'səm*, *n* balm of Gilead. [Gr *opobalsamon*, from *opos* juice, and *balsamon* balsam-tree]

opodeldoc *op-ə-del'dok*, *n* a name given by Paracelsus to various local medical applications; soap liniment. [Derivation unknown, apparently Gr *opos* juice]

opopanax *ə-pop'ə-naks*, *n* a gum-resin formerly used in medicine, obtained from the roots of a Persian (and S European) species of parsnip; a perfume obtained from the plant *Commiphora*. [Gr *opos* juice, and *panax* a panacea]

oporice *ə-por'i-sē*, *n* a former medicine prepared from quinces, pomegranates, etc. [Gr *opōrikē*, from *opōrā* late summer, summer fruits]

opossum *ə-pos'əm*, *n* any member of the American genus Didelphys, or family Didelphyidae, small marsupials, often pouchless, mainly arboreal, with prehensile tail; a phalanger (*Austr* and *NZ*); opossum-fur. — Also (*Austr* and *US*) **possum**, (formerly) **'possum**. [American Indian]

opotherapy *op-ə-ther'ə-pi*, *n* treatment by administration of extracts of animal organs, *esp* of ductless glands. [Gr *opos* juice, and **therapy**]

opp *abbrev*: oppose; opposed; opposite.

oppidan *op'i-dən*, *n* a townsman; in university towns, someone who is not a member of the university, or a student not resident in a college; at Eton (and formerly elsewhere) a schoolboy who is not a foundationer or colleger. — *adj* urban. [L *oppidānus*, from *oppidum* town]

oppignorate or **oppignerate** *o-pig'nə-rāt*, (*obs*) *vt* to pawn. — *n* **oppignorā'tion**. [L *oppīgnorāre, oppīgnerāre*, from *ob* against, and *pīgnus, -oris* or *-eris* a pledge]

oppilate *op'il-āt*, (*pathol*) *vt* to block up, stop up. — *n* **oppilā'tion**. — *adj* **opp'ilātive**. [L *oppīlāre, -ātum*, from *ob* in the way, and *pīlāre* to ram down]

oppo. See **opposite number** under **opposite**.

opponent *ə-pō'nənt*, *n* the person opposed to one in a contest, struggle, battle, etc; someone who opposes a course of action, belief, etc; an opponent muscle (*anatom*). — *adj* opposing; antagonistic (with *to*; formerly with *with*); placed opposite or in front; (of a muscle) opposing one part (eg a digit) to another (*anatom*). — *n* **oppo'nency**. [L *oppōnens, -entis*, pr p of *oppōnere*, from *ob* in the way of, and *pōnere* to place]

opportune *op'ər-tūn*, or *-tūn'* (*Shakesp op-ör'tūn*) *adj* occurring at a fitting time; conveniently presented; timely; convenient; suitable; opportunist. — *adv* **opportune'ly** (or *op'*). — *n* **opportune'ness** (or *op'*). — *n* **opportun'ism** (or *op'*) the practice of regulating actions by favourable opportunities rather than consistent principles. — *n* **opportun'ist** (or *op'*) someone (eg a politician) who waits for events before declaring his or her opinions, or shapes his or her conduct or policy to circumstances of the moment; a person without settled principles. — Also *adj*. — *adj* **opportunist'ic**. — *n* **opportun'ity** an occasion offering a possibility; advantageous conditions; (*esp* in *pl*) a chance, opening or prospect; opportuneness (*rare*); fitness (*obs*). — **opportunistic infection** an infection to which normal people are resistant but which occurs in those whose immune system has been compromised by illness; **opportunistic species** a species adapted to exploit temporary or local conditions; **opportunity cost** (*econ*) the cost of an investment (of money, resources, time, etc) in terms of its best alternative use. [Fr *opportun*, from L *opportūnus*, from *ob* before, and *portus*, *-ūs* a harbour]

oppose *ə-pōz'*, *vt* to place in front or in the way (with *to*); to place or apply face to face or front to front; to set in contrast or balance; to set in conflict; to place as an obstacle; to face; to resist; to contend with. — *vi* to make objection. — *n* **opposabil'ity**. — *adj* **oppos'able** that may be opposed; capable of being placed with the front surface opposite (with *to*; as eg a thumb to other fingers). — *adj* **oppo'sing**. — *adj* **oppose'less** (*Shakesp*) not to be opposed, irresistible. — *n* **oppos'er**. [Fr *opposer*, from L *ob* against, and Fr *poser* to place, from L *pausāre* to rest, stop; see **pose**[1]]

opposite *op'ə-zit*, *adj* placed, or being, face to face, or at two extremities of a line; facing on the other side; directly contrary; diametrically opposed; opposed; corresponding; (of leaves) in pairs at each node, with the stem between (*bot*); (of floral parts) on the same radius (*bot*). — *adv* in or to an opposite position or positions. — *prep* in a position facing, opposing, contrary to, etc; as a leading performer in the same film or play as (another leading performer). — *n* that which is opposed or contrary; an opponent; opposition (*Milton*). — *adv* **opp'ositely**. — *n* **opp'ositeness**. — *adj* **oppositive** (*-poz'*) characterized by opposing; adversative; inclined to oppose. — **opposite number** (*colloq*; *abbrev* **oppo** *op'ō*; *pl* **opp'os**) someone who has a corresponding place in another organization, set, etc, one's counterpart; a person who is allotted to one as partner, opponent, etc; one's cohabiting or marriage partner; one's mate. — **be opposite with** (*Shakesp*) to be perverse and contradictory in dealing with. [Fr, from L *oppositus*, from *ob* against, and *pōnere*, *positum* to place]

opposition *op-ə-zish'ən*, *n* the act of opposing or of setting opposite; the state of being opposed or placed opposite; opposed or opposite position; an opposite; contrast; contradistinction; resistance; a difference of quantity or quality between two propositions having the same subject and predicate (*logic*); a body of opposers; the parliamentary party that opposes the government or existing administration; the situation of a celestial body, as seen from the earth, when it is directly opposite to another, *esp* the sun (*astron*). — *adj* of the parliamentary opposition. — *adj* **opposi'tional**. — *n* **opposi'tionist** a member of the opposition. [L *oppositiō*, *-ōnis*, from L *oppōnere*, *oppositum* to place against or opposite]

oppress *ə-pres'*, *vt* to distress; to lie heavy upon; to treat with tyrannical cruelty or injustice; to load with heavy burdens, troubles, etc; to press against or upon; to crush (*obs*); to smother (*obs*); to overwhelm; to take by surprise (*obs*); to ravish (*obs*). — *n* **oppression** (*ə-presh'ən*) an act of oppressing; tyranny; a feeling of distress or of being weighed down; dullness of spirits; pressure (*Shakesp*). — *adj* **oppress'ive** tending to oppress; tyrannical; heavy; burdensome, troubling; overpowering. — *adv* **oppress'ively**. — *n* **oppress'iveness**. — *n* **oppress'or**. [Fr *oppresser*, from LL *oppressāre*, frequentative of L *opprimere*, *oppressum*, from *ob* against, and *premere* to press]

opprobrium *ə-prō'bri-əm*, *n* disgrace, reproach or imputation of shameful conduct; anything that brings such reproach; infamy. — *adj* **oppro'brious** reproachful, insulting or abusive; infamous, disgraceful (*archaic*). — *adv* **oppro'briously**. — *n* **oppro'briousness**. [L *opprobrium*, from *ob* against, and *probrum* reproach]

oppugn *ə-pūn'*, *vt* to attack, *esp* by argument; to oppose; to call in question. — *n* **oppugnancy** (*ə-pug'nən-si*; *Shakesp*) antagonism. — *adj* **oppug'nant** opposing; hostile. — *n* an opponent. — *n* **oppugner** (*o-pūn'ər*). [L *oppugnāre* to attack, from *ob* against, and *pugna* a fight]

Ops *abbrev*: Operations; Operations officer; Operations room.

OP's (*colloq*) *abbrev*: other people's.

opsimath *op'si-math*, *n* someone who learns late in life. — *n* **opsim'athy** learning obtained late in life. [Gr *opsimathēs*, from *opse* late, and *mathē* learning]

opsiometer *op-si-om'i-tər*, *n* an optometer. [Gr *opsis* sight, and **-meter**]

-opsis *-op'sis*, *combining form* denoting appearance of, or resemblance to, the thing specified, as in *meconopsis*; sight, as in *stereopsis*. [Gr *opsis* aspect, sight]

opsonium *op-sō'ni-əm*, *n* anything eaten with bread as a relish, *esp* fish. — *n* **opsomā'nia** any abnormal love for some special kind of food. — *n* **opsomā'niac**. — *adj* **opsonic** (*op-son'ik*) relating to opsonin. — *n* **op'sonin** a constituent of blood-serum which makes bacteria more readily consumed by phagocytes. [Latinized from Gr *opsōnion*, from *opson* cooked food, relish]

opt *opt*, *vi* where there is more than one possibility, to decide (to do), to choose or settle (with *for*); to make a choice, *esp* of nationality when territory is transferred. — *n* **opt'ant** a person who opts; someone who has exercised a power of choosing, *esp* his or her nationality. — *adj* **optative** (*opt'ə-tiv*, or *op-tā'tiv*) expressing a desire or wish; denoting a mood of verbs that expresses a wish (*gram*). — *n* (*gram*) a mood of verbs, eg in Greek, expressing a wish. — *adv* **op'tatively** (or *op-tā'*). — *n* **op'ter**. — **opt'-out** (*TV* and *radio*) a programme broadcast by a regional station which has temporarily opted out of the main network transmission. — **opt out** to choose not to take part (with *of*); (of a school or hospital) to leave local-authority control. [L *optāre*, *-ātum* to choose, wish]

opt *abbrev*: optative; optic; optical; *optime* (*L*), very well indeed; optimum; optional.

Optic® *op'tik*, *n* a device attached to an inverted bottle for measuring alcoholic liquid dispensed (also without *cap*).

optic *op'ti-k*, or **optical** *op'ti-kəl*, *adj* relating to sight, or to the eye, or to optics; (**optical**) constructed to help the sight; acting by means of light; amplifying radiation; visual. — *n* **op'tic** an eye (now mainly *facetious*); a lens, telescope, or microscope (*obs*). — *adv* **op'tically**. — *n* **optician** (*op-tish'ən*) a person who makes or sells optical instruments, *esp* spectacles (see also **ophthalmic optician**); formerly, a person skilled in optics. — *n sing* **op'tics** the science of light. — *adj* **optoacous'tic** relating to or combining both vision and hearing. — *adj* **optoelectron'ic** relating to optoelectronics; using both optical and electronic devices, etc. — *n sing* **optoelectron'ics** the study or use of devices involving the interaction of electronic and light signals, or the conversion of one to the other. — Also **optron'ics**. — *n* **optol'ogist** an optician. — *n* **optol'ogy**. — *n* **optom'eter** an instrument for testing vision. — *adj* **optomet'rical**. — *n* **optom'etrist** an ophthalmic optician; a person qualified to practise optometry. — *n* **optom'etry** the science of vision and eye-care; the science or procedure of examining the eyes and vision; the prescription and provision of spectacles, contact lenses, etc for the improvement of vision. — *n* **op'tophone** an instrument that translates printed characters into arbitrary sounds, and so enables the blind to read ordinary type. — **optical character reader** (*abbrev* **OCR**; *comput*) a light-sensitive device for inputting data directly to a computer by means of optical character recognition; **optical character recognition** (*abbrev* **OCR**; *comput*) the scanning, identification and encoding of printed characters by photoelectric means; **optical computing** the technique of controlling the computer by pulses of light instead of by electronic means; **optical-electronic device** (*phys*) an instrument used to locate weakly radiating sources by detecting their infrared emission; **optical fibre** a thin strand of glass through which light waves may be transmitted, used eg in some communications systems, fibre optics, etc; **optical maser** laser; **optical microscope** and **telescope** a microscope or telescope which operates by the direct perception of light from the object viewed, as opposed to an electron microscope or radio telescope; **optical spectrum** (*phys*) the visible radiation emitted from a source separated into its component frequencies; **optical splitter** (*telecomm*) a device for making direct connection between the customer and the exchange by splitting the signals, each of which then travels along its own fibre to its destination; **optic axis** the axis of the eye, a line through the middle of the pupil and the centre of the eye; in a doubly refracting crystal, a direction in which no double refraction occurs; **optic lobe** the part of the midbrain concerned with sight; **optic thalamus** (*anatom*) an older name for **thalamus**. [Gr *optikos* optic, from *optos* seen]

optimal, etc. See under **optimism**.

optimate *op'ti-māt*, *n* (*rare* in *sing*) a member of the aristocracy, *orig* in Rome: — *pl* (*L*) **optimā'tēs**. [L *optimās*, *-ātis*, from *optimus* best]

optime *op'ti-mi*, *n* (formerly) at Cambridge University, one of those in the second or third rank of mathematical honours (*senior* or *junior optime*), after the wranglers. [L *optimē* (adv) very well, best]

optimism *op'ti-mizm*, *n* a disposition to take a bright, hopeful view of things; hopefulness or confidence generally, *opp* to *pessimism*; a belief that everything is ordered for the best; Leibniz's doctrine that the world is the best of all possible worlds (*philos*); the teaching or belief that good in the end will triumph over evil. — *adj* **op'timal** optimum. — *n* **optimalizā'tion** or **-s-**. — *vt* **op'timalize** or **-ise** to bring to the most desirable or most efficient state. — *adv* **op'timally**. — *n* **op'timist** someone who maintains a hopeful, cheerful outlook; a supporter of the doctrine of optimism (*philos*). — *adj* **optimist'ic**. — *adv* **optimist'ically**. — *n* **optimizā'tion** or **-s-**. — *vi* **op'timize** or **-ise** to take the most hopeful view of anything. — *vt* to make the most or best of; to make as efficient as possible, *esp* by analysing and planning processes; to prepare or revise (a computer system or program) so as to achieve the greatest possible efficiency. [L *optimus* best]

optimum *op'ti-məm*, *n* that point at which any condition is most favourable: — *pl* **op'tima**. — *adj* (of conditions) best for the achievement of an aim or result; very best. [L, neuter of *optimus* best]

option *op'shən*, *n* an act of choosing; the power or right of choosing; a thing that may be chosen; an alternative for choice; a power (as of buying or selling at a fixed price) that may be exercised at will within a time-limit; a wish (*obs*). — *adj* **op'tional** left to choice; not compulsory; leaving to choice. — *adv* **op'tionally**. — **option clause** a clause in an insurance contract which gives the insurers an option to replace or reinstate the lost or damaged property as an alternative to paying its value. — **local option** and **soft option** see **local**, **soft**. — **keep** or **leave one's options open** to refrain from committing oneself (to a course of action, etc). [L *optiō*, *-ōnis*, from *optāre* to choose]

optoelectronic, **optologist**, **optometry**, **optophone**, etc. See under **optic**.

optronics. See **optoelectronics** under **optic**.

opulent *op'ū-lənt*, *adj* wealthy; loaded with wealth; luxuriant; over-enriched. — *n* **op'ulence** conspicuous wealth; luxury. — *adv* **op'ulently**. [L *opulentus*]

opulus *op'ū-ləs*, *n* in full *Viburnum opulus*, the guelder-rose. [L *opulus* a kind of maple]

opuntia *ō-pun'shi-ə*, *n* a plant of the prickly-pear genus (*Opuntia*) of the cactus family. [L *Opūntia* (*herba* plant) of *Opūs* (Gr *Opous*), a town of Locris where Pliny said it grew]

opus *ō'pəs*, *op'əs*, *op'o͞os*, *n* a work, *esp* a musical composition, *esp* one numbered in order of publication, eg *opus* 6 (abbreviated *op* 6); used in naming various styles of Roman masonry: — *pl* **o'puses** or **opera** (*op'ə-rə*). — **opus Dei** (*dā'ē*) the work of God; liturgical worship; in Benedictine monastic practice, the primary duty of prayer; (with *caps*) an international RC organization of lay people and priests; **opus latericium** (*la-tə-rish'i-əm*, *-ik'*, *-te-rik'i-o͞om*) a form of Greco-Roman brickwork; **opus musivum** (*mo͞o-sī'vəm*, *mū-*, *mo͞o-sē'wo͞om*) mosaic work; **opus operantis** (*op-ə-ran'tis*) the effect of a sacrament ascribed (as by Protestants) to the spiritual disposition of the recipient; **opus operatum** (*op-ə-rā'təm*, *op-e-rä'to͞om*) due celebration of a sacrament involving grace flowing from the sacramental act (the RC view); **opus reticulatum** (*ri-tik-yə-lā'təm*, *re-tik-o͞o-lä'to͞om*) reticulated work. [L *opus*, *-eris* work]

opuscule *o-pus'kūl*, (*rare*) *n* a little work. — Also **opuscle** (*ə-pus'l*) or **opus'culum** (*-pus'kū-ləm*): — *pl* **opus'cula**. [L dimin of *opus*]

OPW *abbrev*: Office of Public Works.

OR *ör*, (*comput*) *n* a logic circuit that has two or more inputs and one output, the output signal being 1 if any of its inputs is 1, and 0 if all of its inputs are 0. [**or**[1]]

OR *abbrev*: operational or operations research; (also **Or.**) Oregon (US state); other ranks (*military*).

or[1] *ör*, *conj* used to link alternatives and possibilities where there are two, and the last two where there are several (*no home*, *clothes or food*); to introduce the second alternative where the first is introduced by *whether*, *either*; to offer a synonym (*the mountain lion or cougar*); between numbers to indicate a vague amount (*five or six*); (often **or rather**) to introduce qualifications or doubts (*We shall know tomorrow - or shall we*?); to mean 'because in that case' (*He can't be back or he would have telephoned*). — **or else** alternatively; because otherwise, because if not; used absolutely as a threat (*Do it or else*!). [Contraction of ME *other*]

or[2] *ör*, (*archaic*) *conj* (or *adv*) and *prep* before (in time). — **or ever**, **or e'er**, or (by confusion) **or ere** (*poetic*) before ever, before even. [OE (Northumbrian) and ON *ār* early, with the sense of OE *ǣr* ere]

or[3] *ör*, (*heraldry*) *n* the tincture gold or yellow, indicated in engraving and chiselling by dots. [Fr, from L *aurum* gold]

-or *-ər*, agent *sfx* from L, corresponding to **-er** from OE. In most words one or other ending is standard but in some both endings occur (**-or** used *esp* in legal terms or in terms for a non-personal agent).

orach or **orache** *or'ich*, *n* an edible plant belonging to a genus (*Atriplex*) of the goosefoot family, sometimes used as spinach is. [OFr *arace* (Fr *arroche*), from L *atriplex*, from Gr *atraphaxys*]

oracle *or'ə-kl*, *n* a medium or agency of divine revelation; a response by or on behalf of a god; the place where such responses are given; the Jewish sanctuary; the word of God; a person with the reputation, or an air, of infallibility or great wisdom; an infallible indication; a wise, sententious or mysterious utterance; (with *cap*; ®) the former teletext (qv) service of the Independent Broadcasting Authority. — *vt* to utter as an oracle. — *vi* to speak as an oracle. — *adj* **oracular** (*ə-rak'ū-lər*) of the nature of an oracle; like an oracle; seeming to claim the authority of an oracle; delivering oracles; prophetic; equivocal; ambiguous; obscure. — Also **orac'ulous** (now *rare*). — *n* **oracularity** (*-lar'i-ti*), **orac'ularness** or **orac'ulousness**. — *adv* **orac'ularly** or **orac'ulously**. — **work the oracle** (*colloq*) to achieve the desired result by manipulation, intrigue, wire-pulling, favour, etc; to raise money. [L *ōrāculum*, from *ōrāre* to speak]

oracy. See under **oral**.

ora et labora *ö'ra*, *ō'rä et la-bö'ra*, *-bō'rä*, (*L*) pray and work.

oragious *ō-rā'jəs*, (*rare*) *adj* stormy. [Fr *orageux*]

oral *ō'rəl*, *ö'rəl*, *adj* relating to the mouth; near the mouth; uttered by the mouth; (eg of an examination) spoken, not written; (of a method of teaching and communicating with the deaf) using lip-reading and vocal expression rather than sign language; (eg of poetry) passed on by word of mouth, *esp* from generation to generation; (eg of medicine) taken through the mouth; pertaining to the infant stage of development when satisfaction is obtained by sucking. — *n* an oral examination. — *n* **o'racy** skill in self-expression and ability to communicate freely with others by word of mouth. — *n* **o'ralism** the use of or belief in the oral method of teaching and communicating with the deaf. — *n* **oral'ity** the state or quality of being oral; the preference for or tendency to choose the oral form of language. — *adv* **o'rally**. — **oral contraception** inhibition of the normal process of ovulation and conception by taking orally, and according to a prescribed course, any of a variety of hormone-containing pills; **oral contraceptive** a pill of this type; **oral history** (the study of) information on events, etc of the past, obtained by interviewing people who participated in them; **oral hygiene** and **oral hygienist** the same as, respectively, **dental hygiene** and **dental hygienist**; **oral rehydration therapy** the treatment of dehydration (caused by diarrhoea, etc) with drinks of a water, glucose and salt solution; **oral sex** sexual relations involving the use of the mouth to stimulate the genitals of one's partner. [L *ōs*, *ōris* the mouth]

orang. See under **orang-utan**.

Orange *or'inj*, *adj* relating to the family of the princes of *Orange*, a former principality in southern France from the 11c, passing by an heiress to the house of Nassau in 1531, the territory being ceded to France in 1713; favouring the cause of the Prince of Orange in Holland or in Great Britain and Ireland; of or favouring the Orangemen; extreme Protestant Irish Conservative. — *n* **Or'angism** or **Or'angeism**. — **Or'angeman** a member of a society revived and organized in Ireland in 1795 to uphold Protestant principles and supremacy.

orange *or'inj*, *n* a gold-coloured fruit (hesperidium, a specialized type of berry) with tough skin, within which are juicy segments; the tree (*Citrus* genus of family *Rutaceae*) on which it grows; extended to various unrelated but superficially similar fruits and plants; a colour between red and yellow. — *adj* pertaining to an orange; orange-coloured. — *n* **orangeade** (*or-in-jād'*) a drink made with orange juice. — *n* **or'angery** (*-ri*, *-ər-i*) a building for growing orange-trees in a cool climate. — *adj* **or'angey** (*-ji*) somewhat orange in colour, flavour, etc. — **or'ange-blossom** the white blossom of the orange-tree, often worn by brides; that of the mock-orange, similarly used. — *adj* **or'ange-coloured**. — **or'ange-flower** orange-blossom; **orange-flower water** a solution of oil of neroli; **or'ange-grass** a small American St John's-wort; **orange-lil'y** a garden lily with large orange flowers; **or'ange-peel** the rind of an orange, often candied; **or'ange-root** the plant golden-seal; **orange roughy** an edible fish *esp* of SW Pacific waters; **orange squash** a highly concentrated orange drink; **or'ange-squeezer** an instrument for squeezing out the juice of oranges; **or'ange-stick** a thin stick, *esp* of orange-wood, used in manicure and make-up. — *adj* and *n* **or'ange-taw'ny** (*Shakesp*) (of) a yellowish brown or tan colour. — **or'ange-tip** a European butterfly (*Anthocaris caedamines*) with an orange patch near the tip of the forewing; a similarly marked American species (*Euchloe genutia*); **or'ange-tree**; **or'ange-wife** (*Shakesp*) a woman who sells oranges; **or'ange-wood** the wood of the orange-tree. — **bitter**, **Seville**, or **sour orange** *Citrus aurantium* or its fruit, which is used to make marmalade; **sweet orange** *Citrus sinensis*, native of China and SE Asia, or any cultivated fruit derived from it. [Fr, ultimately from Ar *nāranj*; cf LL *arangia*, *aurantia*, *narancum*; Ital *arancia*, early *narancia*; Sp *naranja*; the loss of the *n* may be due to confusion with the indefinite article (*una*, *une*), the vowel changes to confusion with L *aurum*, Fr *or* gold]

orang-utan *ō-*, *ö-rang'-ōō-tan'*, *ō'*, *ö'rang-ōō'tan*, also **orang-outang** *ō-*, *ö-rang'-ōō-tang'*, *n* a reddish-brown, tree-dwelling anthropoid ape, found only in the forests of Sumatra and Borneo; erroneously, a chimpanzee. — Also **orang'**. [Malay *ōranghūtan* man of the woods (said not to be applied by the Malays to the ape), from *ōrang* man, and *hūtan* wood or wild]

orant *ō'rənt*, *ö'*, *n* a worshipping figure in ancient Greek and early Christian art. [L *ōrans*, *-antis*, pr p of *ōrāre* to pray]

ora pro nobis *ö'ra*, *ō'rä prō nō'bis*, *-bēs*, (*L*) pray for us.

orarian *ö-rā'ri-ən*, *ō-*, (*rare*) *adj* coastal. — *n* a coast-dweller. [L *ōrārius*, from *ōra* shore]

orarium[1] *ö-rā'ri-əm*, *ō-*, *n* a handkerchief (*antiq*); a stole (*obs*); a scarf attached to a bishops's staff. — *n* **ora'rion** a Greek Church deacon's stole. [L *ōrārium*, from *ōs*, *ōris* mouth]

orarium[2] *ö-rā'ri-əm*, *ō-*, *n* a book of private devotions. [L *ōrāre* to pray]

oration *ö-rā'shən*, *ō-*, *ə-*, *n* a formal speech; a harangue. — *vi* **orate'** (*esp facetious*) to harangue or hold forth. [L *ōrātiō*, *-ōnis*, from *ōrāre* to pray]

orator *or'ə-tər*, *n* a public speaker; an eloquent person; a spokesman (*obs*); a petitioner (*obs*): — *fem* **or'atress** or **oratrix** (*or-ā'triks*, or *or'ə-triks*). — *adj* **oratorial** (*or-ə-tō'ri-əl*, *-tö'*) of an orator, oratory, or an oratory. — *adj* **orato'rian** of an oratory. — *n* a priest of an oratory; (with *cap*) a member of an Oratory. — *adj* **oratorical** (*-tor'*) characteristic of an orator; addicted to oratory; rhetorical; relating to or savouring of oratory. — *adv* **orator'ically**. — *n* **or'atory** the art of the orator; rhetoric; rhetorical utterances or expression; a place for private prayer; a lectern for praying at; a place of public speaking (*obs*); (with *cap*) one of various congregations in the RC Church, *esp* the Fathers of the Oratory, established by St Philip Neri (1515–95); (with *cap*) a church of the Oratorians. [L *ōrātor*, *-ōris*, from *ōrāre* to pray]

oratorio *or-ə-tō'ri-ō*, *-tö'*, *n* a story, *usu* Biblical, set to music, with soloists, chorus, and full orchestra but without scenery, costumes or acting; the form of such a composition: — *pl* **orato'rios**. — *adj* **orato'rial**. [Ital *oratorio*, from L *ōrātōrium* an oratory, because they developed out of the singing at devotional meetings in church oratories]

orb[1] *örb*, *n* a circle; a sphere; anything spherical; a celestial body; an eyeball; the mound or globe of a monarch's regalia; the space within which the astrological influence of a planet operates; a sphere carrying a planet in its revolution; a cycle of time; an orbit; a world. — *vt* to surround (*archaic*); to form into an orb. — *adj* **orbed** in the form of an orb; circular. — *adj* **orbic'ular** approximately circular or spherical; round; having the component minerals crystallized in spheroidal aggregates (*petrology*). — *n* **orbiculā'ris** a muscle surrounding an opening: — *pl* **orbiculā'rēs**. — *adv* **orbic'ularly**. — *adj* **orb'y** (*rare*) orbed. [L *orbis* a circle]

orb[2] *örb*, (*obs*) *adj* bereaved, *esp* of children. — *n* (*archit*; *obs*) an obscure term generally understood to mean a blind window or blank panel. — *n* **orb'ity** (*obs*) bereavement, *esp* of children. [L *orbus* bereft]

Orbilius *ör-bil'i-əs*, *n* a flogging schoolmaster (from the Latin poet Horace's teacher).

orbis terrarum *ör'bis ter-ā'rəm*, *ter-ä'rōōm*, the circle of lands, the whole world. [L]

orbit *ör'bit*, *n* the path in which a celestial body moves round another (*astron*), or (*phys*) that in which an electron moves round the nucleus of an atom (also **or'bital**); a path in space round a celestial body; a regular course or beat, a sphere of action; (loosely) an orb; the hollow in which the eyeball rests (also (*anatom*) **or'bita**); the skin round a bird's eye (*zool*). — *vi* to move in or as though in orbit; to fly in a circle. — *vt* (of a spacecraft, moon or other satellite) to travel round (a body) by a circular or elliptical path; (of an aircraft) to circle (a given point); to put into orbit. — *adj* **or'bital**. — *n* (*phys*) an orbit (qv). — *n* **or'biter** a spacecraft or satellite which orbits the earth or another planet without landing on it. — **orbital engine** an axial two-stroke engine with curved pistons in a circular cylinder-block which rotates around a fixed shaft; **orbital road, motorway**, etc one which goes round the outside of a town. [L *orbita* a wheel-track, from *orbis* a ring or wheel]

orc *örk*, *n* a killer whale or orca; a fierce sea-monster (*mythol*); an ogre. — *n* **or'ca** a black-and-white toothed whale of the killer-whale genus *Orca*. [L *orca*]

Orcadian *ör-kā'di-ən*, *adj* of Orkney. — *n* an inhabitant or a native of Orkney. [L *Orcadēs*, from Gr *Orkades* Orkney (Islands)]

orcein. See **orcinol**.

orchard *ör'chərd*, *n* an enclosed garden of fruit-trees. — *n* **or'charding**. — *n* **or'chardist** or **or'chardman** someone who grows and sells orchard fruits. — **or'chard-grass** (*US*) cock's-foot grass; **or'chard-house** a glass-house for cultivating fruits without artificial heat. [OE *ort-geard*, prob from L *hortus* garden, and OE *geard*; see **yard**[2]. Some connect the first part with OE *wyrt*; see **wort**[1]]

orchat *ör'chət*, *n* an obsolete form of the word **orchard**. [Partly *dialect*, partly due to confusion with Gr *orchatos* a row of trees]

orchel, orchella. See **archil**.

orchestra *ör'kis-trə*, formerly *-kes'*, *n* a large company of musicians (strings, woodwind, brass, and percussion) playing together under a conductor; the part of a theatre or concert-room in which the instrumental musicians are placed; loosely applied to a small instrumental group, as in a restaurant; in the ancient Greek theatre, the place in front of the stage where the chorus danced. — *n* **orchē'sis** the art of dancing or rhythmical movement of the body, as in classical Greek dance. — *n* **orchesog'raphy** notation of dancing. — *adj* **orchestic** (*-kes'tik*) relating to dancing. — *n sing* **or-ches'tics** the art of dancing. — *adj* **orchestral** (*-kes'*) of or for an orchestra. — *n* **orches'tralist** an orchestral composer. — *vt* **or'chestrate** to compose or arrange (music) for performance by an orchestra; to organize so as to achieve the best or greatest overall effect (*fig*). — Also *vi*. — *n* **orchestrā'tion**. — *n* **or'chestrātor**. — *adj* **orches'tric** orchestic; orchestral. — *n* **orchestrina** (*-trē'nə'*) or **orches'trion** names given to various key-board or barrel-organ instruments designed to imitate an orchestra. — **orchestra stalls** front theatre seats, closest to the orchestra. [Gr *orchēstrā*, from *or-cheesthai* to dance]

orchid *ör'kid*, *n* any plant or flower of the **Orchidā'ceae** or **Orchid'eae**, a family of monocotyledons, including many tropical epiphytes, with highly specialized, often showy, flowers, the upper petal (or labellum; by twisting actually the lower) serving as a landing-place for insects, the one fertile stamen (or two) united with the gynaeceum as a column (qv), the pollen in masses. — *adj* **orchidā'ceous** or **orchid'eous**. — *n* **or'chidist** a fancier or grower of orchids. — *n* **orchidol'ogist**. — *n* **orchidol'ogy** knowledge of orchids. — *n* **orchidomā'nia** a craze for orchids. — *n* **orchidomā'niac**. — *n* **Or'chis** a genus of orchids, including several of the best-known British species; loosely applied to other genera; (without *cap*) a flower of any of these genera. — **or'chid-house** a place for growing orchids. [Gr *orchis*, *-ios* or *-eōs* a testicle (from the appearance of the root-tubers in Orchis and others); the *d* is a blunder, as if the genitive were *orchidos*]

orchil and **orchilla**. See **archil**.

orchitis *ör-kī'tis*, *n* inflammation of a testicle. — *adj* **orchitic** (*-kit'ik*). — *n* **orchidec'tomy** or **orchiec'tomy** (*-ki-ek'*) excision of one or both testicles. [Gr *orchis*, *-ios* or *-eōs* testicle]

orcinol *ör'sin-ol*, *n* a dihydric phenol obtained from archil and other lichens. — Also **or'cin** or **or'cine**. — *n* **orcein** (*ör'si-in*) a purple dyestuff got from orcinol. [See **archil**]

ord *örd*, (*obs*) *n* a point, eg of a weapon; a beginning. [OE *ord*; cf **odd**[1]]

ord *abbrev*: ordained; order; ordinary; ordnance.

ordain *ör-dān'*, *vt* to arrange; to establish; to decree; to destine; to order; to assign, set apart; to appoint; to set apart for an office; to invest with ministerial functions; to admit to holy orders. — *adj* **ordain'able**. — *n* **ordain'er**. — *n* **ordain'ment**. — *n* **ordinee'** a person who is being, or has just been, ordained. [OFr *ordener* (Fr *ordonner*), from L *ordināre*, *-ātum*, from *ordō*, *-inis* order]

ordeal *ör'dēl*, less justifiably *ör-dēl'* or *ör-dē'əl*, *n* any severe trial or distressing or trying experience; an ancient form of referring a disputed question to the judgement of God, by lot, fire, water, etc. — Latinized as **ordalium** (*ör-dā'li-əm*). — *adj* **ordā'lian**. — **ordeal bean** the Calabar-bean. [OE *ordēl*, *ordāl* (WSax would be *ordǣl*), from pfx *or-* out, and *dǣl* deal, share; cf Du *oordeel*, Ger *Urteil*]

order *ör'dər*, *n* arrangement; sequence; disposition; proper arrangement; proper condition; the condition of normal or proper functioning; a regular or suitable arrangement; a method; a system; tidiness; a restrained or undisturbed condition; a form of procedure or ceremony; the accepted mode of proceeding at a meeting; a practice; grade, degree, rank or position, *esp* in a hierarchy; the degree of a curve or equation; a command; a written instruction to pay money; a customer's instruction to supply goods or perform work; the goods supplied; a pass for admission or other privilege; a class of society; a body of persons of the same rank, profession, etc; a fraternity, *esp* religious or knightly; a body modelled on a knightly order, to which members are admitted as an honour; the insignia of such a body; a group above a family but below a class (*biol*); one of the different ways in which the column and its entablature with their various parts are moulded and related to each other (*archit*); one of the successively recessed arches of an archway; due action towards some end, *esp* in the old phrase 'to take order'; the position of a weapon with butt on ground, muzzle close to the right side; a portion or helping in a restaurant, etc (*US*); (in *pl*) the several degrees or grades of the Christian ministry. — *vt* to arrange; to set in order; to put in the position of order (*military*); to regulate; to command; to give an order for; to order to be (done, etc) (*US*); to conduct (*Shakesp*). — *vi* to give commands; to request the supply of something, *esp* food. — *interj* used in calling for order or to order. — *n* **or'derer**. — *n* **or'dering** arrangement; management; the act or ceremony of ordaining eg priests or deacons. — *adj* **or'derless** without order; disorderly. — *n* **or'derliness**. — *adj* **or'derly** in good order; regular; well regulated; of good behaviour; quiet; being on duty. — *adv* regularly; methodically. — *n* a non-commissioned officer who carries official messages for his superior officer, formerly the first sergeant of a company; a hospital attendant; a street cleaner. — **or'der-book** a book for entering the orders of customers, the special orders of a commanding officer, or the motions to be put to the House of Commons; the amount of orders received and awaiting completion; **order form** a printed form on which the details of a customer's order are written; **orderly bin** a street receptacle for refuse; **orderly officer** the officer on duty for the day; **orderly room** a room for regimental, company, etc, business; **order paper** a paper showing the order of business, *esp* in parliament. — **call to order** see **call**[1]; **full orders** the priesthood; **holy orders** an institution, in the Roman and Greek Churches a sacrament, by which a person is specially set apart for the service of religion; the rank of an ordained minister of religion; **in order** with the purpose (with *to* or *that*); in accordance with rules of procedure at meetings; appropriate, suitable, likely; (also **in good, working**, etc **order**) operating, or able to operate, well or correctly; in the correct, desired, etc order; **in** or **of the order of** more or less of the size, quantity or proportion stated; **in short order** (*US*) promptly; **minor orders** in the RC Church those of acolyte, exorcist, reader and doorkeeper, in the Eastern Churches, reader; **on order** having been ordered but not yet supplied; **order about** or **around** to give orders to in a domineering fashion; **order in council** an order by the sovereign with advice of the Privy Council; **order of battle** arrangement of troops or ships in preparation for a fight; **order of magnitude** the approximate size or number of something, *usu* measured in a scale from one value to ten times that value; (loosely) a rising scale in terms of size, quantity, etc; **order of the day** business set down for the day; a proclamation by a dictator or military commander; something necessary, normal, prevalent, particularly popular, etc at a given time; **out of order** not in order; (of actions, behaviour, etc, or of people as acting or behaving in some way) outside normally acceptable standards, excessive or uncontrolled (*colloq*); **sailing orders** written instructions given to the commander of a vessel before sailing; **sealed orders** instructions not to be opened until a specified time; **standing orders** see under **stand**; **take order** (*obs*) to take measures or steps; **take orders** to be ordained; **tall** or **large order** (*colloq*) an *esp* unreasonably large request or difficult assignment; **to order** according to, and in fulfilment of, an order. [Fr *ordre*, from L *ordō*, *-inis*]

ordinaire *ör'din-ār*, (*colloq*) *n* vin ordinaire; table wine. [Fr]

ordinal *or'din-əl*, *adj* indicating order of sequence; relating to an order. — *n* an ordinal numeral (eg *first*, *second*, *third*, etc, distinguished from *cardinal*); a book of rules (*obs*); a service-book; a book of forms of consecration and ordination. [LL *ordinālis*, from L *ordō*, *-inis* order]

ordinance *ör'din-əns*, *n* that which is ordained by authority, fate, etc; regulation; a bye-law (*US*); artistic arrangement; planning; a decree; a religious practice enjoined by authority, *esp* a sacrament; a social class or order (*Shakesp*); preparation (*obs*); equipment (*obs*); ordnance (*obs*). — *n* **or'dinand** a candidate for ordination. — *adj* **or'dinant** (*rare*) ordaining. — *n* a person who ordains. — *n* **or'dinate** a straight line parallel to an axis cutting off an abscissa; the *y*-coordinate in analytical geometry. — *vt* to ordain; to coordinate or order. — *adv* **ord'inately** in an ordered manner; restrainedly; with moderation. — *n* **ordinā'tion** the act of ordaining; admission to the Christian ministry by the laying on of hands of a bishop or a presbytery; established order. [L *ordināre*, *-ātum*, from *ordō* order]

ordinary *örd'i-nə-ri*, *örd'nə-ri*, *Scot* **ordinar** *örd'nər*, *adj* according to the common order or type; usual; of the usual kind; customary; plain; undistinguished; commonplace; (of a judge or jurisdiction) by virtue of office, not by deputation; (of a judge in Scotland) of the Outer House of the Court of Session (**Lord Ordinary**); plain-looking (*colloq*); of common rank. — *n* something settled or customary; the common run, mass or course; an ungeared bicycle with one large and one small wheel, a penny-farthing; one of a class of armorial charges, figures of simple or geometrical form, conventional in character (*heraldry*); a reference-book of heraldic charges; a judge acting in his own right by virtue of his office, eg an ecclesiastic such as a bishop or his deputy in ecclesiastical cases; a chaplain who attended those condemned to death, *esp* the chaplain of Newgate Prison (*hist*); a meal provided at a fixed charge; a place where such a meal is provided; the company partaking of it (*obs*); usual fare (*obs*). — *adv* **or'dinarily**. — *n* **or'dinariness**. — **Ordinary grade** and **level** see **O grade** and **O level** at **O**[1]; **ordinary seaman** a seaman ranking below an able seaman; **ordinary shares** shares in a company entitling the holder to the company's net profits as a dividend after preference shareholders have been paid (**preferred ordinary shares** have limited priority). — **in ordinary** in regular and customary attendance; **ordinary of the mass** the established sequence or fixed order for saying mass; **out of the ordinary** unusual. [L *ordinārius*, from *ordō*, *-inis* order]

ordinee. See under **ordain**.

ordnance *örd'nəns*, *n orig*, any arrangement, disposition, or equipment; munitions; great guns, artillery; a department concerned with supply and maintenance of artillery. — **Ordnance datum** the standard sea-level of the Ordnance Survey, now mean sea-level at Newlyn, Cornwall; **Ordnance Survey** the preparation of maps of Great Britain and Northern Ireland by the *Ordnance Survey* (*Department*) (until 1889 under the Board of Ordnance). [**ordinance**]

ordonnance *ör'də-nəns*, *n* co-ordination, *esp* the proper disposition of figures in a picture, parts of a building, etc. [Fr; cf **ordinance**]

Ordovician *ör-dō-vish'yən*, *-ən*, *adj* and *n* the geologist Charles Lapworth's word for Lower Silurian. [L *Ordovicēs*, a British tribe of North Wales]

ordure *örd'yər*, *n* dirt; dung; excrement; anything unclean (*fig*). — *adj* **or'durous**. [Fr, from OFr *ord* foul, from L *horridus* rough]

ore[1] *ōr*, *ör*, *n* a solid, naturally-occurring mineral aggregate, of economic interest, from which one or more valuable constituents may be recovered by treatment; precious metal (*poetic*). — **ore body** a mass or vein of ore. [OE *ār* brass, influenced by *ōra* unwrought metal; cf L *aes*, *aeris* bronze]

ore[2] *ör*, (*local*) *n* seaweed; tangle (*Laminaria*). — Also **ore'weed** or **oar'weed**. [OE *wār*]

ore[3] or **o're** *ōr*, *ör*, old spellings of **o'er** for **over**. — For compounds see **over-**. — **ore-wrought** or **ore-raught** (*Shakesp*) for **over-reached** in the sense of overtook; **ore-rested** (*Shakesp*) for **overwrested**.

öre *œ'rə*, *n* a coin and monetary unit in Sweden and (**øre**) Norway and Denmark: — *pl* **öre** and **øre**. See **krone**.

oread *ör'i-ad*, *ō'ri-ad*, (*mythol*) *n* a mountain nymph: — *pl* **o'reads** or **orē'adēs**. [L *oreās*, *-adis*, from Gr *oreias*, *oreiados*, from *oros* a mountain]

orectic. See under **orexis**.

Oreg. *abbrev*: Oregon (US state).

oregano *ö-ri-gä'nō* or (*US*) *ö-reg'ə-nō*, *n* the Mediterranean aromatic herb *Origanum vulgare* used in cooking; origanum: — *pl* **oreganos**. [Am Sp *orégano* wild marjoram, from L *orīganum*; see **origanum**]

oreide. See **oroide**.

oreography, etc. See **orography**.

oreology, etc. See **orology**.

Oreopithecus *ö-rē-ō-pi-thēk'əs*, *ō-*, or *-pith'ə-kəs*, *n* a hominid of which a complete skeleton was found in a Tuscan lignite mine. [Gr *oros* mountain, and *pithēkos* ape]

orepearch. See under **overperch**.

oreweed. See under **ore**[2].

ore-wrought. See under **ore**[3].

orexis *o-rek'sis*, *n* appetite. — *adj* **orec'tic**. [Gr *orexis*]

orf *örf*, *n* a viral infection of sheep, etc, communicable to man, characterized by the formation of vesicles and pustules on the skin and mucous membranes, *esp* on lips, nose and feet. [Dialect *hurf*; ON *hrūfa* scab]

orfe *örf*, *n* a golden-yellow semi-domesticated variety of id. [Ger *Orfe*, from Gr *orphōs* the great sea-perch]

organ *ör'gən*, *n* an instrument or means by which anything is done; a part of a body fitted for carrying on a natural or vital operation; a means of communicating information or opinions, eg a newspaper; a keyboard wind instrument consisting of a collection of pipes made to sound by means of compressed air; a system of pipes in such an organ, having an individual keyboard, a partial organ; a musical instrument in some way similar to a pipe-organ, including a pipeless organ; a barrel-organ; a region of the brain thought to be concerned with some mental or moral quality; a bump marking its position and development; a musical instrument in general (*obs*). — *n* **or'ganist** someone who plays an organ. — *n* **organis'trum** an early form of hurdy-gurdy. — *n* **organity** (*-gan'*) an organized whole. — *n* **or'ganon** (Gr; *philos*, etc) a method of investigation: — *pl* **or'gana**. — *n* **or'ganum** (L) an organon; in medieval music, a part in parallel motion to the canto fermo *usu* a fourth or fifth below or above: — *pl* **or'gana**. — **or'gan-bird** the Australian magpie or pied butcher-bird; **or'gan-builder** someone who constructs organs; **or'gan-gallery** a gallery in a church, etc, where an organ is placed; **or'gan-grinder** a person who plays a hand-organ by a crank; **or'gan-harmō'nium** a large harmonium; **or'gan-pipe** one of the sounding pipes of a pipe-organ; **organ-pipe coral** a coral, *Tubipora*, with tubes arranged like organ-pipes; **or'gan-point** a pedal-point; **or'gan-screen** an ornamented stone or wood screen in a church, etc, on which an organ is placed. — **organ of Corti** (*kör'ti*) the organ in the cochlea which contains the auditory receptors. [L *organum*, from Gr *organon* instrument, tool, from *ergon* work]

organdie *ör'gən-di*, *n* fine translucent plain-woven cotton dress material with a stiff finish; fine muslin; book-muslin. [Fr *organdi*]

organelle *ör-gə-nel'*, (*biol*) *n* a specialized part of a cell serving as an organ. [New L *organella*, dimin of L *organum* organ]

organic *ör-gan'ik adj* pertaining to, derived from, like or of the nature of an organ (in any sense); of an organism, organum or organization; organized; inherent in organization; structural; formed as if by organic process (*art*); of design, etc, based on or inspired by, natural forms (*art*); belonging to the etymological structure of a word (*philol*); instrumental; mechanical; containing or combined with carbon (*chem*); concerned with carbon compounds; (of crops, crop production, etc) produced without, or not involving, the use of fertilizers and pesticides not wholly of plant or animal origin; governed in its formation or development by inherent or natural factors rather than by a predetermined plan. — *adj* **organ'ical** (*obs*). — *adv* **organ'ically**. — *n* **organicism** (*ör-gan'i-sizm*) the conception of nature, life or society as an organism; the theory that all disease is due to an organic lesion. — *n* **organ'icist**. — **organic chemistry** the chemistry of carbon compounds; **organic disease** a disease accompanied by changes in the structures involved; **organic sensation** sensation from internal organs, eg hunger; **organic vein** (*obs*) the jugular vein. [Gr *organikos*, from *organon* instrument]

organism *ör'gə-nizm*, *n* organic structure, or that which has it; that which acts as a unified whole; a living animal or plant. — *adj* **organis'mal** or **organis'mic**. [**organize**]

organize or **-ise** *ör'gə-nīz*, *vt* to form into an organic whole; to co-ordinate and prepare for activity; to arrange; to obtain (*colloq*); to supply with organs. — *vi* to be active in organization; to become organic. — *n* **organīzabil'ity** or **-s-**. — *adj* **organīz'able** or **-s-**. — *n* **organīzā'tion** or **-s-** the act of organizing; the state of being organized; the manner in which anything is organized; an organized system, body or society; a political party machine (*US*); the singing of the organum. — *adj* **organīzā'tional** or **-s-**. — *adj* **or'ganized** or **-s-** having or consisting of parts acting in co-ordination; having the nature of a unified whole; organic. — *n* **or'ganīzer** or **-s-** someone or something that organizes; part of an embryo that influences the development of the rest; (also **or'ganizer-bag** or **-purse**, etc) a container with separate divisions, pockets, etc in which the contents can be arranged for ease and speed of access; (also **personal organizer**) a small ring-binder with divisions in which information, diary, personal notes, etc, can be kept to hand; a desktop, laptop or pocket electronic device for the same purpose. — **organization and methods** (*abbrev* **O and M**) the study and analysis of a company and its systems and procedures, in order to improve efficiency. [OFr *organiser*, from MedL *organizare*, from L *organum* organ]

organo- *ör-gə-nō-*, *-no'*, *combining form* denoting organ; (also *ör-gan'ō-*) organic, as in organometallic compounds in which carbon atoms are linked directly with metal atoms, such as *organolead*, *organotin*, or in similar compounds in which the inorganic element is non-metallic, such as *organophosphorus*; (of a chemical compound) containing an organic radical, such as *organochlorine*; any one of a group of compounds of chlorine and carbon used in pest control. — *n* **organogeny** (*ör-gə-noj'i-ni*) or **organogen'esis** the development of living organs. — *n* **organogram** (*-gan'*) a chart showing graded arrangement of personnel in an organization. — *n* **organog'raphy** a description of the organs of plants or animals. — *adj* **organolep'tic** (Gr root of *lambanein* to seize) affecting a bodily organ or sense; concerned with testing the effects of a substance on the senses, *esp* of taste and smell. — *adj* **organometall'ic** (*-gan-*) consisting of a metal and an organic radical; relating to compounds of this type. — *n* **organophos'phate** (*-gan-*) one of a group of chemical insecticides. — *n* **organother'apy** treatment of disease by administration of animal organs or extracts of them, *esp* of ductless gland extracts. [L *organum*; see **organ**]

organon, **organum**. See under **organ**.

organza *ör-gan'zə*, *n* a transparently thin material resembling organdie but made of silk or synthetic fibres. [Of uncertain origin]

organzine *ör'gən-zēn*, *n* a silk yarn of two or more threads put together with a slight twist. [Fr *organsin*, from Ital *organzino*, possibly from *Urgenj* Turkestan]

orgasm *ör'gazm*, *n* the culmination of sexual excitement; immoderate excitement; turgescence of any organ (*obs*). — *vi* to experience an orgasm. — *adj* **orgas'mic** or **orgas'tic**. [Gr *orgasmos* swelling]

orgeat *ör'ji-at*, *-zhat*, *or-zhä*, *n* a syrup or drink made from almonds, sugar, etc, formerly from barley. [Fr *orge*, from L *hordeum* barley]

orgia, **orgiast**, **orgic**. See under **orgy**.

orgillous. See **orgulous**.

orgone *ör'gōn*, *n* (also **orgone energy**) according to Wilhelm Reich, a vital force permeating the universe, which, concentrated in a specially made **orgone box**, could cure certain diseases. [*org*asm, and sfx *-one* indicating chemical derivative]

orgue *örg*, (*obs*) *n* a row of stakes let down like a portcullis; a weapon with several barrels in a row. [Fr, organ]

orgulous *ör'gū-ləs*, or **orgillous** *ör'gi-ləs*, (*Shakesp*) *adj* haughty. [OFr *orguillus*; cf Fr *orgueil*, Ital *orgoglio* pride; prob of Germanic origin]

orgy *ör'ji*, *n* a frantic unrestrained celebration; a riotous, licentious, or drunken revel; a bout of excessive or frenzied indulgence in some activity; (*usu* in *pl*) a secret rite, as in the worship of Bacchus; a religious or secret celebration in general (*obs*). — Also (properly *pl*) **or'gia**. — *n* **or'giast** someone who takes part in orgies. — *adj* **orgias'tic** or **or'gic** (*rare*). [Fr *orgies*, from L, from Gr *orgia* (pl)]

oribi *or'i-bi*, *n* a small S African antelope, the palebuck. [Afrik, appar from some native language]

orichalc *or'i-kalk*, (*Spenser* **oricalche**) *n* a gold-coloured alloy; brass. — *adj* **orichalceous** (*-kal'si-əs*). [Gr *oreichalkos*, from *oros* a mountain, and *chalkos* copper; sense influenced by association with L *aurum* gold]

oriel *ö'ri-əl*, *ō'*, *n* a small room or recess with a polygonal bay window, built out from a wall, resting on the ground or more *usu* supported on brackets or corbels; the window of an oriel (in full **oriel-win'dow**). — *adj* **o'rielled**. [OFr *oriol* porch, recess or gallery]

orient *ö'ri-ənt*, *ō'*, *adj* eastern (*usu poetic*); (of the sun, day, etc) rising (*archaic*); bright or pure in colour (*poetic*). — *n* the part where the sun rises; sunrise; purity of lustre in a pearl; an orient pearl; (with *cap*) the East; (with *cap*) the countries of the East. — *vt* **o'rient** (or *-ent'*) to set so as to face the east; to build (lengthwise) east and west; to place in a definite relation to the points of the compass or other fixed or known directions; to determine the position of, relatively to fixed or known directions; to acquaint (someone or oneself) with the present position relative to known points, or (*fig*) with the details of the situation. — *n* **o'riency** (*rare*) orient quality. — *adj* **oriental** or **Oriental** (*-ent'əl*) eastern; pertaining to, in, or from the east; orient. — *n* a native of the east; an Asiatic. — *n* **Orient'alism** an eastern expression, custom, etc; scholarship in eastern languages and/or cultures. — *n* **Orient'alist** an expert in eastern languages; an oriental. — *n* **orientality** (*-al'i-ti*). — *vt* and *vi* **orient'alize** or **-ise**. — *adv* **orient'ally**. — *vt* **o'rientāte** to orient. — *vi* to face the east; to be oriented. — *n* **orientā'tion** the act of orienting or orientating; the state of being oriented; determination or consciousness of relative direction; the assumption of definite direction in response to stimulus. — *n* **o'rientātor** an instrument for orientating. — *adj* **o'riented** (or *-ent'*) or **o'rientated** directed (with *towards*); often used in combination as second element of *adj*, as in *child-oriented households*; normally aware of the elements of one's situation, ie time, place, persons (*psychiatry*; also *fig*). — *n* **orienteer'** a person who takes part in orienteering. — *vi* to take part in orienteering. — *n* **orienteer'ing** the sport of making one's way quickly across difficult country with the help of map and compass. — **oriental alabaster** onyx-marble; **oriental amethyst**, **emerald** and **topaz** varieties of corundum resembling amethyst, emerald and topaz; **oriental ruby** the true ruby, a variety of corundum; **Oriental Region** Southern Asia and its islands from the Persian Gulf to Wallace's Line; **oriental turquoise** true turquoise; **orientation behaviour** the positioning of the body or of a behavioural sequence with respect to some aspect of the external environment; **orientation table** an indicator of tabular form for showing the direction of various objects, eg mountains. [L *oriens*, *-entis*, pr p of *orīrī* to rise]

orifice *or'i-fis*, *n* a mouth-like opening, *esp* small; an opening from the body or a body cavity. — *n* **or'ifex** (*Shakesp*) an orifice. — *adj* **orificial** (*-fish'əl*). [Fr, from L *ōrificium*, from *ōs*, *ōris* mouth, and *facere* to make]

oriflamme *or'i-flam*, *n* a little banner of red silk split into several points, carried on a gilt staff, the ancient royal standard of France. [Fr, from LL *auriflamma*, from L *aurum* gold, and *flamma* a flame]

orig *abbrev*: origin; original; originally.

origami *or-i-gä'mi*, *n* the *orig* Japanese art of folding paper so as to make bird forms, etc. [Jap, paper-folding, from *ori* folding, and *kami* paper]

origanum *o-rig'ə-nəm*, *n* any of various aromatic herbs of the marjoram genus (*Origanum*) of labiates, or of other genus, used in cookery. — *n* **or'igan** (*-gan*) or **origane** (*-gān*) marjoram, *esp* wild marjoram. — See also **oregano**. [L *orīganum*, from Gr *orīganon*]

Origenist *or'i-jən-ist*, *n* a follower of *Origen* (c.185–254 AD) in his allegorical method of scriptural interpretation or his theology, *esp* his heresies, ie the subordination though eternal generation of the Logos, pre-existence of all men, and universal restoration, even of the Devil. — *n* **Or'igenism**. — *adj* **Origenist'ic**.

origin *or'i-jin*, *n* the rising or first existence of anything; that from which anything first proceeds; the fixed starting-point or point from which measurement is made (*math*): the place of attachment from which a muscle, etc arises, as distinct from its *insertion* (*anatom*); source; derivation. — *adj* **orig'inal** pertaining to the origin or beginning; existing from or at the beginning; being such from the beginning; innate; standing as source in relation to something; not derived, copied, imitated or translated from anything else; originative; novel; originating or having the power to originate in oneself; creative; independent in invention; odd in character. — *n* an origin; that which is not itself, or of which something else is, a copy, imitation or translation; a real person, place, etc, serving as model for one in fiction; an inhabitant, member, etc, from the beginning; a person of marked individuality or oddity; (in *pl*; *Milton*) original elements. — *n* **original'ity**. — *adv* **orig'inally**. — *vt* **orig'inate** to give origin to; to bring into existence; to be the author, inventor or creator of. — *vi* to have origin; to begin; (of a train or bus) to start its journey (from a certain point). — *n* **originā'tion**. — *adj* **orig'inātive** having power to originate or bring into existence; originating. — *n* **orig'inātor**. — **original equipment manufacturer** (*comput*) a firm which makes basic computer hardware for other manufacturers to build their own products; **original sin** innate depravity and corruption believed to be transmitted to Adam's descendants because of his sin; **originating summons**, **application**, etc (*law*) one which originates legal proceedings. [L *orīgō*, *-inis*, from *orīrī* to rise]

orillion *o-ril'yən*, (*fortif*) *n* a semicircular projection at the shoulder of a bastion intended to cover the guns and defenders on the flank. [Fr *orillon*, from *oreille* an ear, from L *auricula*, dimin of *auris* ear]

O-ring *ō'ring*, *n* a toroidal ring, *usu* of circular cross-section, used eg as an air or oil seal. [From its shape]

oriole *ōr'i-ōl*, *ör'*, *n* a golden-yellow bird (*Oriolus galbula*, the **golden oriole** or **loriot**) with black wings, or other member of the genus or of the Old World family **Oriol'idae**, related to the crows; in America applied to birds of the *Icteridae* (see **Baltimore**). [OFr *oriol*, from L *aureolus* dimin of *aureus* golden, from *aurum* gold]

Orion *ə-rī'ən*, (*astron*) *n* a constellation containing seven very bright stars, three of which form **Orion's belt**. [*Ōriōn*, a giant hunter slain by Artemis]

orison *or'i-zən*, *n* a prayer. [OFr *orison* (Fr *oraison*), from L *ōrātiō*, *-ōnis*, from *ōrāre* to pray]

Oriya *ō-rē'yə*, *ö-*, *n* the language of Orissa in India, closely related to Bengali; a member of the people speaking it. — Also *adj*.

orle *örl*, (*heraldry*) *n* a border within a shield at a short distance from the edge; a number of small charges set as a border. [OFr, border, from a dimin formed from L *ōra* border]

orleans *ör'li-ənz*, *n* a fabric of cotton warp and worsted weft. — *n* **Or'leanist** a supporter of the family of the Duke of Orleans, brother of Louis XIV, as claimants to the throne of France. — Also *adj*. — *n* **Or'leanism**. [*Orléans*, a city in France]

Orlon® *ör'lon*, *n* a type of acrylic fibre or crease-resistant fabric made from it.

orlop *ör'lop*, *n* (also **orlop deck**) the lowest deck in a ship, a covering to the hold. [Du *overloop* covering]

Ormazd. See **Ormuzd**.

ormer *ör'mər*, *n* an ear-shaped shell, *esp* the edible *Haliotis tuberculata*, common in the Channel Islands, the ear-shell or sea-ear. [Channel Island Fr *ormer* (Fr *ormier*), from L *auris maris* sea-ear]

ormolu *ör'mə-lōō*, *n* an alloy of copper, zinc, and sometimes tin; gilt or bronzed metallic ware; gold-leaf prepared for gilding bronze, etc. [Fr *or*, from L *aurum* gold, and Fr *moulu*, pa p of *moudre* to grind, from L *molere* to grind]

Ormuzd or **Ormazd** *ör'muzd*, *n* a later form of the name **Ahura Mazda**, in early Zoroastrianism the creator and lord of the universe, later the good principle as opposed to *Ahriman*, the bad. [Pers *Ahura Mazdâ* the Wise Lord, or the Living God or Lord (*ahu* the living, life, or spirit, root *ah* to be), the Great Creator (*maz*, *dâ*)]

ornament *ör'nə-mənt*, *n* anything meant to add grace or beauty or to bring credit; a trinket such as a china figure, vase, etc, intended for display; additional beauty or decoration; a mark of honour; (*usu* in *pl*) articles used in the services of the church (*Prayer Bk*). — *vt* (*ör-nə-ment'*, *ör'nə-ment*) to adorn; to furnish with ornaments. — *adj* **ornament'al** serving to adorn; decorative, pleasantly striking in dress and general appearance. — *n* a plant grown for ornament or beauty. — *adv*

ornament'ally. — *n* **ornamentā'tion** the act or art of ornamenting; ornamental work. — *n* **ornament'er** or **ornament'ist**. [Fr *ornement*, from L *ornāmentum*, from *ornāre* to adorn]

ornate *ör-nāt'*, *ör'nāt*, *adj* decorated; much or elaborately ornamented. — *adv* **ornate'ly** (or *ör'*). — *n* **ornate'ness** (or *ör'*). [L *ornāre*, *-ātum* to adorn]

ornery *ör'nə-ri*, (*NAm dialect* or *colloq*) *adj* commonplace; inferior, poor, worthless; touchy, cantankerous; stubborn; mean, contemptible. [A variant of **ordinary**]

ornis *ör'nis*, *n* the birds collectively of a region, its avifauna. [Gr *ornis* bird]

ornithic *ör-nith'ik*, *adj* relating to birds. [Gr *ornithikos*, from *ornis*, *ornīthos* bird]

ornithichnite, **ornithischia**. See under **ornitho-**.

ornitho- *ör-ni-thō-*, *-thə-*, *-tho'*, or before a vowel **ornith-**, *combining form* signifying bird. — *n* **ornithichnite** (*ör-ni-thik'nīt*; Gr *ichnos* track) a fossil footprint of a bird. — *n pl* **Ornithischia** (*-this'ki-ə*; Gr *ischion* hip joint) the order of bird-hipped dinosaurs, herbivorous and often heavily armoured. — *n* and *adj* **ornithis'chian**. — *n pl* **Ornithodel'phia** (Gr *delphys* womb) the Prototheria or Monotremata, from the ornithic character of the urogenital organs. — *adj* **ornithodel'phian** (also *n*), **ornithodel'phic** or **ornithodel'phous**. — *n* **Ornithogaea** (*-nī-thə-jē'ə*; Gr *gaia* land) the New Zealand biological region; **ornithog'alum** (Gr *ornithogalon* star-of-Bethlehem) a plant of a large genus (*Ornithogalum*) of herbs of the family Liliaceae. — *adj* **ornitholog'ical**. — *adv* **ornitholog'ically**. — *n* **ornithol'ogist**. — *n* **ornithol'ogy** the study of birds. — *n* **ornithomancy** (*ör-nī'thō-man-si*, *ör'nith-ō-*; see **-mancy**) divination by means of birds, by observing their flight, etc. — *adj* **ornithoman'tic**. — *n* **ornithomorph** (*ör-nī'thō-mörf*, *ör'nith-ō-mörf*; see **-morph**) a figure or design in the form of a bird. — *adj* **ornithomorph'ic**. — *adj* **ornithoph'ilous** (see **-philous**) bird-pollinated. — *n* **ornithoph'ily**. — *n* **ornithophō'bia** fear of birds. — **or'nithopod** a member of the **Ornithop'oda**, a suborder of bipedal ornithischian dinosaurs. — *n* **ornithopter** (*-op'tər*; Gr *pteron* wing) a flying-machine with flapping wings. — *n* **ornithorhynchus** (*-ō-ring'kəs*; Gr *rhynchos* snout) the duckbill, of the *Ornithorhynchus* genus. — *n* **ornithosaur** (*ör-nī'thə-sör*; Gr *sauros* lizard) a pterodactyl. — *n* **ornithoscopy** (*-os'kə-pi*; see **-scopy**) augury by observation of birds. [Gr *ornis*, *ornīthos* a bird]

ornithoid *ör'ni-thoid*, *adj* bird-like. [Gr *ornis*, *ornīthos* bird, and *eidos* form]

ornithosis *ör-ni-thō'sis*, *n* the disease psittacosis. [Gr *ornis*, *ornīthos* bird, *and* **-osis**]

Orobanche *or-ō-bang'kē*, *n* the broomrape genus of dicotyledons, giving name to the family **Orobanchā'ceae**, root-parasites without green leaves. — *adj* **orobanchā'ceous**. [Gr *orobanchē* dodder, also broomrape, from *orobos* bitter vetch, and *anchein* to strangle]

orogenesis *or-ō-jen'i-sis*, *ōr-*, *ör-*, (*geol*) *n* mountain-building, the processes which take place during an orogeny. — *n* **or'ogen** an orogenic belt. — *adj* **orogenet'ic** or **orogen'ic**. — *n* **orogeny** (*or-oj'ə-ni*, *ōr-*, *ör-*) a period of mountain-building, during which rocks are severely folded, metamorphosed, and uplifted; orogenesis. — **orogenic belt** a *usu* elongated region of the earth's crust which has been subjected to an orogeny. [Gr *oros* mountain, and **-genesis**]

orography *o-rog'rə-fi*, or **oreography** *or-i-og'*, *n* the description of mountains. — *adj* **orograph'ic** or **oreograph'ic**, **orograph'ical** or **oreograph'ical**. [Gr *oros*, *oreos* mountain, and **-graphy**]

oroide *ō'rō-īd*, *ö'*, *n* an alloy of copper and zinc or tin, etc, imitating gold. — *n* **o'rēide** a similar or identical alloy. [Fr *or*, from L *aurum* gold, and Gr *eidos* form]

orology *o-rol'ə-ji*, or **oreology** *or-i-ol'*, *n* the scientific study of mountains. — *adj* **orolog'ical** or **oreolog'ical**. — *n* **orol'ogist** or **oreol'ogist**. [Gr *oros*, *-eos* mountain, and **-logy**]

oropesa *or-ō-pē'zə*, *-pā'sə*, *n* a fish-shaped float used in marine minesweeping to support the sweeping wire. [From the name of a trawler]

oropharynx *ō-rō-far'ingks*, *ö-*, *n* the part of the pharynx between the soft palate and the epiglottis. [L *ōs*, *ōris* a mouth, and **pharynx**]

ororotund, etc. See under **orotund**.

orotund *ö'rə-tund*, *ō'*, *o-*, *adj* (of a voice) full, round or sonorous; (of something said) pompous, grandiloquent. — Also **o'rorotund**. — *n* **orotund'ity** or **ororotund'ity**. [L *ōs*, *ōris* mouth, and *rotundus* round.

orphan *ör'fən*, *n* a child or animal deprived of father or mother, or (*usu*) both, through death; a machine etc, which has been phased out or superseded; a club-line (qv; *printing*). — Also *adj*. — *vt* to make an orphan. — *n* **or'phanage** a house for orphans; the state of being an orphan. — *n* **or'phanhood** or **or'phanism**. — **or'phan=asy'lum** (*archaic*). [Gr *orphanos*, related to L *orbus* bereaved]

orpharion *ör-fə-rī'ən*, *ör-fā'ri-ən*, *n* a large lute-like instrument with six to nine pairs of metal strings. — Also **orpheō'reon**. [*Orpheus* and *Arīōn*, mythical musicians]

Orpheus *ör'fūs*, *-fi-əs*, (*Gr mythol*) *n* a mythical Thracian musician and poet who could move inanimate objects by the music of his lyre, the founder or interpreter of the ancient mysteries. — *adj* **Orphē'an** pertaining to Orpheus; melodious. — *n* a musician; (in *pl*) a name adopted by some amateur musical societies. — *adj* **Or'phic** pertaining to the mysteries associated with Orpheus; esoteric. — *n* **Or'phism** the system taught in the Orphic mysteries; an early 20c style of abstract art using brilliant colour, also **Orphic Cubism**. — **Orpheus harmonica** the panharmonicon.

orphrey *ör'fri*, *n* gold or other rich embroidery, *esp* bordering an ecclesiastical vestment. [OFr *orfreis*, from L *auriphrygium* Phrygian gold]

orpiment *ör'pi-mənt*, *n* a yellow mineral, arsenic trisulphide, used as a pigment. [OFr, from L *auripigmentum*, from *aurum* gold, and *pigmentum* paint]

orpine or **orpin** *ör'pin*, *n* a purple-flowered, broad-leaved stonecrop. [Fr *orpin*]

Orpington *ör'ping-tən*, *n* a breed of poultry (white, black or buff). [*Orpington* in W Kent]

orra *or'a*, *-ə*, (*Scot*) *adj* odd; not matched; left over; occasional, casual; supernumerary; worthless. — **orra man** a farm-worker kept to do any odd job that may occur. [Origin unknown]

orrery *or'ər-i*, *n* a clockwork model of the solar system. [From Charles Boyle, fourth Earl of *Orrery* (1676–1731) for whom one was made]

orris[1] *or'is*, *n* the Florentine or other iris; its dried rootstock (**orr'is-root**) smelling of violets, used in perfumery. [Perh **iris**]

orris[2] *or'is*, *n* a kind of gold or silver lace used *esp* in the 18c; upholsterers' galloon and gimp. [Perh OFr *orfreis*; see **orphrey**]

orseille *ör-sāl'*, same as **archil** or **orchil**. — *adj* **orsellic** (*-sel'*). [Fr]

ORT *abbrev*: oral rehydration therapy (qv).

ort *ört*, (*dialect*) *n* (*usu* in *pl*) a fragment, *esp* one left from a meal. [Cf LGer *ort* refuse of fodder]

ortanique *ör'tə-nēk*, *n* a cross between the orange and the tangerine, or its fruit. [Portmanteau word: *or*ange, *tan*gerine, and un*ique*]

ORTF *abbrev*: Organisation de Radio et Television Française (*Fr*), the French Radio and Television Organization (until 1975).

orth-. See **ortho-**.

orthian *örth'i-ən*, (*music*) *adj* high-pitched. [Gr *orthios*]

orthicon *örth'i-kon*, *n* a television camera tube more sensitive than the earlier iconoscope; a further development is the **image orthicon**. [**ortho-** and *icono*scope]

ortho- *ör-thō-*, *-tho'*, or sometimes before a vowel **orth-**, *combining form* denoting straight; upright; perpendicular; right; genuine; derived from an acid anhydride by combination with the largest number of water molecules (distinguished from *meta-*; *chem*); having substituted atoms or groups attached to two adjacent carbon atoms of the benzene ring (distinguished from *meta-* and *para-*, in this sense commonly represented by *O-*; *chem*). — *n* and *adj* **or'tho** a contraction for **orthochromatic (plate)**: — *pl* **or'thos**. — *n* **orthoax'is** (*crystallog*) the orthodiagonal: — *pl* **orthoax'es** *-ak'sēz*. — *n* **orthobo'rate** a salt of **orthobo'ric acid** boric acid. — *n* **orthocaine** (*-kā'in*, *-kān*) a white crystalline substance used as a local anaesthetic. — *n* **or'thocentre** the point of intersection of the altitudes of a triangle. — *n* **Orthoceras** (*ör-thos'ə-ras*; Gr *keras*, horn) a genus of fossil cephalopods with straight shell. — *adj* **orthochromat'ic** (Gr *chrōma*, colour) correct in rendering the relation of colours, without the usual photographic modifications. — *n* **or'thoclase** (*-klās*, *-klāz*; Gr *klasis* fracture) common or potash feldspar, monoclinic, with cleavages at right angles. — *n* **or'tho-compound** (*chem*). — *n* **or'thocousins** children of two sisters or of two brothers. — *n* **orthodiag'onal** in a monoclinic crystal, that lateral axis which is perpendicular to the vertical axis. — *n* **orthodontia** (*-don'ti-ə*) or *n sing* **orthodont'ics** (Gr *odous*, *odontos* tooth) rectification of crookedness in the teeth. — *adj* **orthodont'ic**. — *n* **orthodont'ist**. — *adj* **or'thodox** (Gr *doxa* opinion) sound in doctrine; believing, or according to, the received or established doctrines or opinions, *esp* in religion; (with *cap*) of the Greek or Eastern Church (see **Eastern Church** under **east**). — *n* **or'thodoxy** the state or quality of being orthodox. — *adj* **orthodrom'ic** (Gr *dromos* a course or run; *geog*; *naut*) having great circles represented as straight lines. — *n* **orthod'romy** or *n sing* **orthodrom'ics** great-circle sailing, ie sailing by the most direct route. — *adj* **orthoepic** (*-ep'ik*; Gr *epos* a word) or **orthoep'ical**. — *n* **orthō'epist** (or *ör'thō-ep-ist*). — *n* **orthō'epy** (or *ör'thō-ep-i*) (the study of) correct pronunciation. — *n* **orthogen'esis** (see **-genesis**) the evolution of organisms systematically in definite directions and not accidentally in many directions; determinate variation. — *adj* **orthogenet'ic** relating to orthogenesis. — *adj* **orthogen'ic** orthogenetic; concerning the treatment of mentally and emotionally disturbed children. — *n sing* **orthogen'ics**. — *adj* **orthognath'ic** or **orthog'nathous** (Gr *gnathos* jaw) having a lower jaw that neither protrudes nor recedes. — *n* **orthog'nathism**. — *adj* **orthog'onal** (Gr *gōniā* angle) right-angled (**orthogonal projection** projection by lines perpendicular to the plane of projection). — *adv* **orthog'onally**. — *n* **or'thograph** a drawing in orthographic projection, *esp* of the elevation of a building. — *n* **orthog'rapher** a person skilled in orthography; a speller. — *adj* **orthograph'ic** or **orthograph'ical** pertaining or according to spelling; spelt correctly; in perspective projection, having the point of sight at infinity. — *adv* **orthograph'ically**. — *n* **orthog'raphist** an orthographer. — *n* **orthog'raphy** (Gr *orthographiā* spelling or elevation; see **-graphy**) the art or practice of spelling words correctly; spelling; orthographic projection; apparently for orthographer (*Shakesp*). — *adj* **orthopae'dic** or (*US*) **orthopē'dic**, also (*rare*) **orthopae'dical** or **orthopē'dical**. — *n sing* **orthopaedics** or (*US*) **orthopēdics** (*-pē'diks*; Gr *pais*, *paidos* a child) the art or process of curing deformities arising from (*orig* childhood) disease or injury of bones, also **or'thopaedy** or **or'thopēdy**, formerly **orthopedī'a** (or *-pēd'*). — *n* **orthopae'dist** or **orthopē'dist**. — *n* **orthophos'phate** an ordinary phosphate. — *adj* **orthophosphor'ic** phosphoric. — *n* **or'thophyre** (*-fīr*; *ortho*clase por*phyry*) a fine-grained syenitic rock with orthoclase crystals. — *adj* **orthophyric** (*-fir'ik*). — *n* **orthopin'akoid** in monoclinic crystals, a form consisting of two faces parallel to the orthodiagonal and the vertical axis. — *n* **orthopnoea** (*-thōpnē'ə*; Gr *orthopnoia*, from *pneein* to breathe) a condition in which one can only breathe when upright. — *n* **or'thopod** (*med slang*) an orthopaedic surgeon. — *n* **or'thopraxis** or **or'thopraxy** correct or orthodox practice *esp* in religion (see **praxis**). — *n* **or'thoprism** in monoclinic crystals, a form parallel to the orthodiagonal. — *n* **or'thopsychiatry** the branch of psychiatry concerned with prevention and correction of incipient mental illness. — *n pl* **Orthop'tera** (see **-ptera**) the cockroach order of insects with firm forewings serving as covers to the fan-wise folded hindwings. — *n* and *adj* **orthop'teran**. — *n* **orthop'terist** or **orthopterol'ogist** a student of the Orthoptera. — *n* **orthopterol'ogy**. — *n* **orthop'teron** (*pl* **orthop'tera**) any member of the Orthoptera. — *adj* **orthop'teroid**. — *adj* **orthop'terous** pertaining to the Orthoptera. — *adj* **orthop'tic** (Gr *optikos* optic) relating to normal vision. — *n sing* **orthop'tics** the treatment of defective eyesight by exercises and visual training. — *n* **orthop'tist**. — *adj* **orthorhom'bic** (Gr *rhombos* rhomb; *crystallog*) referable to three unequal axes at right angles to each other. — *adj* **orthoscop'ic** (Gr *skopeein* to look at) having or giving correct vision, true proportion, or a flat field of view. — *n* **orthosil'icate** a salt of **orthosilicic** (*-sil-is'ik*) **acid** H_4SiO_4. — *n* **orthō'sis** a device which supports, corrects deformities in, or improves the movement of, the movable parts of the body: — *pl* **orthō'ses**. — *adj* **orthostat'ic** (Gr *orthostatos*, from *statos* standing) standing erect; connected with the erect posture. — *adj* **orthos'tichous** (Gr *stichos* a row) arranged in vertical rows. — *n* **orthos'tichy** a straight row, eg of leaves vertically over one another on an axis. — *adj* **orthot'ic** of or relating to orthotics. — *n sing* **orthot'ics** the branch of medical science dealing with the rehabilitation of injured or weakened joints or muscles through artificial or mechanical support by orthoses. — *n* **or'thotist** someone skilled in orthotics. — *n* **orthotonē'sis** (Gr *tonos* accent; *linguistics*) accentuation of a proclitic or enclitic (*opp* to *enclisis*). — *adj* **orthoton'ic** taking an accent in certain positions but not in others, also **or'thotone**. — *adj* **orthotop'ic** (*med*; Gr *topos* place; of tissue, grafts, organ replacement, etc) done, put, occurring, etc at the normal place. — *adj* **orthotrop'ic** (Gr *tropos* a turn) manifesting orthotropism; (of a material, such as wood) having elastic properties varying in different planes. — *n* **orthot'ropism** growth in the direct line of stimulus, *esp* of gravity. — *n* **orthot'ropy** (of a material, such as wood) the state of being orthotropic. — *adj* **orthot'ropous** (of an ovule) straight, having the nucellus in direct continuation of the funicle. [Gr *orthos* straight, upright, right]

orthros *ör'thros*, *n* one of the Greek canonical hours, corresponding in the Eastern Orthodox Church to the Western lauds. [Gr *orthros* dawn]

ortolan *ör'tə-lən*, *n* a kind of bunting, common in Europe and eaten as a delicacy. [Fr, from Ital *ortolano*, from L *hortulānus* belonging to gardens, from *hortulus*, dimin of *hortus* a garden]

orval *ör'vəl*, (*obs*) *n* a plant of the sage genus, the clary. [Cf Fr *orvale*]

Orvieto *ör-vyā'tō*, *n* a white wine from *Orvieto* in Italy. — *n* **Orvietan** (*ör-vi-ē'tən*) a supposed antidote to poison ascribed to an Orvieto man.

Orwellian *ör-wel'i-ən*, *adj* relating to or in the style of the English writer George *Orwell* (1903–50); characteristic of the dehumanized authoritarian society described in his novel *1984*. — *n* a student of Orwell or his ideas.

oryctology *or-ik-tol'ə-ji*, (*obs*) *n* mineralogy; palaeontology. [Gr *oryktos* dug, quarried]

oryx *or'iks*, *n* an antelope of the African genus of antelopes (*Oryx*). [Gr *oryx*, *-ygos* a pick-axe or an oryx antelope]

Oryza *ō-rī'zə*, *ö-*, *n* a tropical genus of grasses, including rice. [Gr *oryza*]

OS *abbrev*: Old Style; Ordinary Seaman; outsize; Ordnance Survey.

Os (*chem*) *symbol*: osmium.

os *os*, (*anatom*) *n* a bone: — *pl* **ossa** (*os'ə*). [L]

OSA *abbrev*: *Ordinis* or *Ordo Sancti Augustini* (*L*), (of) the Order of St Augustine.

Osage *ō-sāj'*, *ō'sāj*, *n* an Indian of a tribe living in Oklahoma, etc. — Also *adj*. — **Osage orange** an ornamental tree (*Maclura*) of the mulberry family, often used for hedges, first found in the Osage country; its orange-like inedible fruit. [Osage *Wazhazhe*]

OSB *abbrev*: *Ordinis* or *Ordo Sancti Benedicti* (*L*), (of) the Order of St Benedict.

Oscan *os'kən*, *n* one of an ancient Italic people in southern Italy; their Indo-European language, generally considered to be related to Latin. — Also *adj*.

Oscar *os'kər*, *n* a gold-plated statuette awarded by the American Academy of Motion Picture Arts and Sciences to a film writer, actor, director, etc, for the year's best performance in his or her particular line; any similar award. [Name fortuitously given, possibly after an Academy employee's uncle]

oscheal *os'ki-əl*, (*med*) *adj* pertaining to the scrotum. [Gr *oscheon* scrotum]

oscillate *os'il-āt*, *vi* to swing to and fro like a pendulum; to vibrate; to radiate electromagnetic waves; to vary between certain limits; to fluctuate. — *vt* to cause to swing or vibrate. — *adj* **osc'illating**. — *n* **oscillā'tion**. — *adj* **osc'illātive** having a tendency to vibrate; vibratory. — *n* **osc'illātor** someone or something that oscillates; an apparatus for producing oscillations. — *adj* **oscillatory** (*os'il-ə-tə-ri*) swinging; moving as a pendulum does; vibratory. — *n* **oscill'ogram** a record made by an oscillograph. — *n* **oscill'ograph** an apparatus for producing a curve representing a number of electrical and mechanical phenomena which vary cyclically. — *n* **oscill'oscope** an instrument which shows on a fluorescent screen the variation with time of the instantaneous values and waveforms of electrical quantities, including voltages translated from sounds or movements. [L *ōscillāre*, *-ātum* to swing]

Oscines *os'i-nēz*, *n pl* the song-birds, forming the main body of the Passeriformes. — *adj* **osc'inine** or (faultily formed) **osc'ine**. [L *oscen*, *oscinis* a singing-bird]

oscitancy *os'i-tən-si*, *n* yawning; sleepiness; stupidity. — *adj* **osc'itant**. — *adv* **osc'itantly**. — *vi* **osc'itate** to yawn. — *n* **oscitā'tion** yawning; sleepiness. [L *ōscitāre* to yawn]

osculant *os'kū-lənt*, *adj* kissing; adhering closely; intermediate between two genera, species, etc, linking (*biol*). — *adj* **os'cular** pertaining to the mouth or osculum, or to kissing; osculating. — *vt* **os'culāte** to kiss; to have three or more coincident points in common with (*math*). — *vi* to be in close contact; to form a connecting link. — *n* **osculā'tion**. — *adj* **os'culatory** of or pertaining to kissing or osculation. — *n* a carved tablet kissed by the priest and (now rarely) by the people at mass. — *n* **os'cule** a little mouth; a small mouthlike aperture. — *n* **os'culum** an exhalant aperture in a sponge; a sucker on a tapeworm's head: — *pl* **os'cula**. — **osculating orbit** (*astron*) an ellipse whose elements represent the actual position and velocity of a comet at a given moment (*epoch of osculation*). [L *ōsculārī*, *-ātus* to kiss, from *ōsculum* a little mouth, a kiss, dimin of *ōs* mouth]

OSF *abbrev*: *Ordinis* or *Ordo Sancti Francisci* (*L*), (of) the Order of St Francis.

OSHA *abbrev*: Occupational Safety and Health Administration.

oshac *ō'shak*, *n* the ammoniac plant. [Ar *ushshaq*]

osier *ōzh'yər*, *-ər*, *ōz'i-ər*, *ōz'yər*, *n* any willow whose twigs are used in making baskets, *esp Salix viminalis*. — *adj* made of or like osiers. — *adj* **o'siered** covered or fringed with osiers; twisted like osiers. — *n* **o'siery** osier-work. — **o'sier-bed** a place where osiers grow. [Fr *osier* of unknown origin; there is a LL *ausāria* or *osāria* willow bed]

Osiris *ō-sī'ris*, *n* the greatest of Egyptian gods, son of Seb and Nut, or Heaven and Earth, husband of Isis, father of Horus. — *adj* **Osī'rian**. [Gr *Osīris*]

-osis *-ō'sis*, *n combining form* denoting (1) a condition or process; (2) a diseased condition. [L *-osis*, Gr *-ōsis*]

Osmanli *os-man'li*, *adj* of the dynasty of *Osmān*, who founded the Turkish empire in Asia, and reigned 1288–1326; of the Turkish empire; of the western branch of the Turks or their language. — *n* a member of the dynasty; a Turk of Turkey. [Cf **Ottoman**]

osmate. See under **osmium**.

osmeterium *oz-mē-tē'ri-əm*, or *os-*, *n* a forked process behind the head of certain caterpillars giving out a foul smell: — *pl* **osmetē'ria**. [Gr *osmē* smell, stink, and sfx *-tērion*, denoting instrument]

osmiate, **osmic**. See under **osmium**.

osmidrosis *oz-mi-drō'sis*, or *os-*, *n* the secretion of ill-smelling sweat. [Gr *osmē* smell, and *hidrōs* sweat]

osmium *oz'mi-əm*, *os'*, *n* a grey-coloured metal (*symbol* **Os**; atomic no 76) the heaviest substance known, whose tetroxide has a disagreeable smell. — *n* **os'mate** or **os'miate** a salt of the hypothetical osmic acid. — *adj* **os'mic** containing osmium in higher valency. — *adj* **os'mious** or **os'mous** containing osmium in lower valency. — *n* **osmirid'ium** iridosmine. — **osmic acid** strictly, a supposed acid H_2OsO_4; *usu* osmium tetroxide, an ill-smelling substance used as a stain for fats in microscope work. [Gr *osmē* smell]

osmosis *oz-mō'sis*, or *os-*, *n* diffusion of liquids through a semi-permeable membrane (*chem*); a gradual absorption or assimilation (*fig*). — Also **os'mose** (*archaic*). — *vi* and *vt* **osmose'** to undergo or cause to undergo osmosis. — *n* **osmom'eter** an apparatus for measuring osmotic pressure. — *n* **osmom'etry**. — *n* **osmoregulā'tion** the process by which animals regulate the amount of water in their bodies and the concentration of various solutes and ions in their body fluids. — *adj* **osmotic** (*-mot'ik*). — *adv* **osmot'ically**. — **osmotic pressure** the pressure exerted by a dissolved substance in virtue of the motion of its molecules, or a measure of this in terms of the pressure which must be applied to a solution in order just to prevent osmosis into the solution. [Gr *ōsmos* = *ōthismos* impulse, from *ōtheein* to push]

osmous. See under **osmium**.

osmund *oz'mənd*, or **osmunda** *oz-mun'də*, *n* a fern of the royal-fern genus *Osmunda*, giving name to a family **Osmundā'ceae**. [Origin unknown]

osnaburg *oz'nə-bûrg*, *n* a coarse linen, *orig* brought from *Osnabrück* in Germany; a coarse cotton. — Also *adj*.

osp *abbrev*: *obiit sine prole* (*L*), died without issue.

osprey *os'pri*, *-prā*, *n* a bird of prey (*Pandion haliaetus*) that feeds on fish; an egret or other plume used in millinery, not from the osprey. [Supposed to be from L *ossifraga*, misapplied; see **ossifrage**]

OSS (*US*) *abbrev*: Office of Strategic Services.

ossa. See **os**.

osseous *os'i-əs*, *adj* bony; composed of, or like, bone; of the nature or structure of bone. — *n* **ossā'rium** an ossuary. — *n* **ossein** (*os'i-in*) the organic basis of bone. — *n* **osselet** (*os'ə-let*, *os'let*) a hard substance growing on the inside of a horse's knee. — *n* **oss'icle** (*anatom*) a little bone or bone-like plate. — *adj* **ossic'ular**. — *adj* **ossif'erous** yielding or containing bones. — *adj* **ossif'ic** causing ossification. — *n* **ossificā'tion** the process or state of being changed into a bony substance. — *vt* **oss'ify** to make into bone or into a bone-like substance. — *vi* to become bone; to become rigid, hardened, inflexible or set into a conventional pattern: — *pr p* **oss'ifying**; *pa t* and *pa p* **oss'ified**. — *adj* **ossiv'orous** feeding on or consuming bones. [L *os*, *ossis* bone]

osseter *os-et'ər*, *n* a species of sturgeon. [Russ *osiotr*]

ossia *ō-sē'a*, (*Ital*) *conj* or (giving an alternative in music).

Ossian *os'i-ən*, *osh'*, *n* a legendary Gaelic poet whose poems James Macpherson professed to translate. — *adj* **Ossianesque** (*-esk'*) in the manner of Macpherson's Ossian. — *adj* **Ossianic** (*-an'ik*) relating to Ossian or to Macpherson's publications. [Gaelic *Oisin*]

ossicle, etc. See under **osseous**.

Ossie. A spelling variant of **Aussie**.

ossifrage *os'i-frāj*, *n* the lammergeier, a rare type of vulture; the osprey. — *n* **ossifraga** (*os-if'rə-gə*) the giant fulmar. [L *ossifraga*, probably the lammergeier, from *os*, *ossis* bone, and the root of *frangere* to break]

ossify, **ossivorous**, etc. See under **osseous**.

osso bucco *os'sō bŏŏk'kō*, *n* an Italian dish of (*usu* veal) knuckle cooked with the bone and stewed in wine, herbs, etc. [Ital, marrow-bone]

ossuary *os'ū-ə-ri*, *n* a place where bones are laid, eg a vault or charnel-house; an urn for bones. [L *ossuārium*, from *os* bone]

oste-. See **osteo-**.

ostensible *os-tens'i-bl*, *adj* seeming, or outwardly apparent; pretended or professed; that may be shown (*obs*). — *n* **ostensibil'ity**. — *adv* **ostens'ibly**. — *adj* **ostens'ive** of a clearly demonstrative nature (*logic*, etc); (of a definition) provided by pointing to examples of things to which the defined word or phrase properly applies; showing; deictic; ostensible. — *adv* **ostens'ively**. — *n* **osten'sory** (*RC*) a monstrance. — *n* **ostent'** appearance (*Shakesp*); portent (*rare*); ostentation (*rare*). — *n* **ostentā'tion** (*-tən-*) pretentious display intended to draw attention or admiration; boasting; the act of showing (*obs*). — *adj* **ostentā'tious** given to show; fond of self-display; showy. — *adv* **ostentā'tiously**. — *n* **ostentā'tiousness**. [L *ostendere*, *ostensum* (*ostentum*) to show, and its frequentative *ostentāre*, from pfx *obs-* in front, and *tendere* to stretch]

osteo- *os-ti-ō-*, *-ə-*, *-o'*, or **oste-** *os-ti-*, *combining form* signifying bone. — *adj* **osteal** (*os'ti-əl*) relating to, composed of, or resembling bone; sounding like bone on percussion. — *n* **osteitis** (*os-ti-ī'tis*) inflammation of a bone. — *n* **osteoarthrī'tis** a form of arthritis in which the cartilages of the joint and the bone adjacent are worn away. — *n* **osteoarthrō'sis** chronic non-inflammatory disease of the joints and the bone adjacent; osteoarthritis. — *n* **os'teoblast** (see **-blast**) a bone-forming cell. — *n* **osteoclasis** (*os-ti-ok'lə-sis*; Gr *klasis* fracture) fracture of a bone for correction of a deformity; absorption and destruction of bone tissue by osteoclasts. — *n* **os'teoclast** a surgical instrument for fracturing bone; a bone-destroying cell. — *n* **osteocoll'a** (Gr *kolla* glue) a calcareous incrustation on roots, etc, once thought able to unite broken bones. — *n* **os'teoderm** (Gr *derma* skin) a bony dermal plate. — *adj* **osteoderm'al**, **osteoderm'atous**, **osteoderm'ic** or **osteoderm'ous**. — *n* **os'teogen** a substance or layer from which bone is formed. — *n* **osteogen'esis** or **osteogeny** (*-oj'*) formation of bone (**osteogenesis imperfecta** the disease *brittle bones*, in which bones are abnormally liable to fracture). — *adj* **osteogenet'ic**, **osteogen'ic** or **osteog'enous**. — *n pl* **Osteoglossidae** (*-glos'i-dē*; Gr *glōssa* tongue) a family of bony fishes, including the arapaima. — *n* **osteog'raphy** the description of bones. — *adj* **ost'eoid** bone-like. — *n* **Osteol'epis** (Gr *lepis* scale) an Old Red Sandstone fossil fish with bone-like scales. — *adj* **osteolog'ical**. — *n* **osteol'ogist**. — *n* **osteol'ogy** the part of anatomy that deals with the study of bones and the skeleton. — *n* **osteō'ma** a tumour composed of bone or bone-like tissue. — *n* **osteomalacia** (*-mə-lā'shi-ə*; Gr *malakos* soft) softening of bones by absorption of their calcium salts, resulting from a deficiency of vitamin D. — *n* **osteomyelitis** (*-mī-ə-lī'tis*; Gr *myelos* marrow) inflammation of bone and bone-marrow. — *n* **os'teopath** (*-path*) or **osteop'athist** (*-ə-thist*) a practitioner of osteopathy. — *adj* **osteopathic** (*ost-i-ə-path'ik*). — *n* **osteop'athy** a system of healing or treatment consisting largely of manipulation of the bones, and massage. — *n* **osteopetrō'sis** a general name for a group of hereditary bone diseases, including *marble bone disease*, in which bone becomes abnormally dense. — **os'teophyte** (*-fīt*; see **-phyte**) an abnormal bony outgrowth. — *adj* **osteophytic** (*-fit'ik*). — *adj* **osteoplast'ic**. — *n* **os'teoplasty** plastic surgery of the bones, bone-grafting, etc. — *n* **osteoporō'sis** (root as **pore**[1]) development of a porous structure in bone due to loss of calcium, resulting in brittleness. — *n* **osteosarcoma** a malignant tumour derived from osteoblasts, composed of bone and sarcoma cells. — *n* **os'teotome** (Gr *tomos* cutting; *surg*) an instrument for cutting bones. — *n* **osteot'omy** the surgical cutting of a bone. [Gr *osteon* bone]

Ostiak. See **Ostyak**.

ostinato *os-tin-ä'tō*, (*music*) *n* a ground-bass: — *pl* **ostina'tos**. [Ital; ety as for **obstinate**]

ostium *os'ti-əm*, *n* a mouth-like opening (*anatom*); the mouth of a river (*obs*): — *pl* **os'tia**. — *adj* **os'tial**. — *n* **os'tiary** a doorkeeper (*eccles*); in the RC Church, a member of the lowest of the minor orders; a river-mouth (*obs*). — *adj* **os'tiate** having an ostium or ostia. — *n* **os'tiolate** having an opening. — *n* **os'tiole** a small opening. [L *ostium*]

OStJ *abbrev*: Officer of the Order of St John of Jerusalem.

ostler or (*obs* and *US*) **hostler** *os'lər*, (*US*) *hos'lər*, *n* a person who attends to horses at an inn: — *fem* **ost'leress**. [**hosteler**]

Ostmark *ōst'märk*, *n* (prior to unification) the standard monetary unit (100 pfennig) of the Democratic Republic of Germany (E Germany). [Ger, east mark]

Ostmen *ōst'men*, (*hist*) *n pl* the Danish settlers in Ireland. [ON *Austmenn* Eastmen]

-ostomy. The combining element is properly **-stomy** (qv).

Ostpolitik *ost'po-li-tēk*, *n* the W German policy, initiated in the 1960s, of establishing normal trade and diplomatic relations with the E European communist countries; any similar policy. [Ger, Eastern policy]

ostracize or **-ise** *os'trə-sīz*, *vt* to exclude from society or from one's social group; in ancient Greece, to banish by popular vote, the voters writing on potsherds the name of the person they wanted banished. — *n* **os'tracism** (*-sizm*) expulsion from society; banishment by ostracizing. [Gr *ostrakon* a shell, tile or potsherd]

ostracod *os'trə-kod*, *n* a member of the **Ostracō'da**, a class of minute crustacea with bivalve shells. — *adj* **ostracō'dan** or **ostracō'dous**. [New L, from Gr *ostrakōdēs* having a shell, from *ostrakon* shell]

ostracoderm *os'trə-kə-dûrm* *n* any member (such as *Cephalaspis*) of a group of Silurian and Old Red Sandstone fishes or fish-like animals, generally cased in bony armour with undeveloped lower jaw, with flippers but not ordinary paired fins. [Gr *ostrakon* shell, and *derma* skin]

ostrakon or **ostracon** *os'trə-kon*, *n* a potsherd or tile, *esp* one used in ostracism in Greece or for writing on in ancient Egypt: — *pl* **os'traka** or **os'traca**. — *adj* **ostracean** (*os-trā'shən*) or **ostrā'ceous** of the nature of an oyster. — *n* **Ostracion** (*os-trā'shi-on*) the coffer-fish genus. [Gr, shell]

Ostrea *os'tri-ə*, *n* the oyster genus. — *adj* **ostreā'ceous**. — *n* **ostreicul'ture** (*os-trē-i-*) oyster culture, the artificial breeding of oysters for sale. — *n* **ostrēicul'turist**. — *n* **os'treophage** (*-fāj*; see **-phage**) an oyster-eater. — *adj* **ostreophagous** (*os-tri-of'ə-gəs*) oyster-eating. — *n* **ostreoph'agy** (*-ə-ji*). [L *ostrea*, from Gr *ostreon* oyster]

ostreger *os'tri-jər*. A variant of **austringer**, a keeper of goshawks.

ostreophagous, etc. See under **Ostrea**.

ostrich *os'trich*, *-trij*, *n* the largest living bird (genus *Struthio*), found in Africa, flightless but remarkable for its speed in running, and prized for its feathers; a person who refuses to face, or who ignores, unpleasant facts, from the ostrich's habit of burying its head when chased, in the belief, supposedly, that it cannot be seen. — *n* **os'trichism** the habit or policy of ignoring or refusing to face unpleasant facts. — *adj* and *adv* **os'trich-like** (*usu* in reference to the supposed habit of hiding its head when in danger). — **os'trich-egg**; **os'trich-farm**; **os'trich-feather**. [OFr *ostruche* (Fr *autruche*), from L *avis* bird, and LL *struthiō*, from Gr *strouthiōn* an ostrich, and *strouthos* a bird]

Ostrogoth *os'trə-goth*, *n* an eastern Goth, a member of the Germanic people who established their power in Italy in 493, and were overthrown in 555. — *adj* **Os'trogothic**. [LL *Ostrogothī* eastern Goths]

Ostyak or **Ostiak** *os'ti-ak*, *n* a member of a Ugrian people of Siberia; their language. — Also *adj*.

OT *abbrev*: occupational therapy; Old Testament.
otalgia *ō-tal'ji-ə*, (*med*) *n* earache. — Also **otal'gy**. [Gr *ous*, *ōtos* ear, and *algē* pain]
otary *ō'tə-ri*, *n* any of the eared seals, including the sea-lions and fur seals, with well-developed external ears: — *pl* **o'taries**. — *adj* **o'tarine**. [Gr *ōtaros* large-eared, from *ous*, *ōtos* ear]
OTC *abbrev*: Officers' Training Corps; over-the-counter.
OTE *abbrev*: on-target earnings, the earnings of a salesman who achieves targeted sales; or the equivalent.
other *udh'ər*, *adj* second; alternate; different; different from or not the same as the one in question (often with *than*); not the same; remaining; additional; one of two; left (*prob*; *Spenser*). — *pronoun* (or *n*) other one; another; each other (*archaic* and *Scot*). — *adv* otherwise (with *than*). — *adj* **oth'erguess** see **othergates**. — *n* **oth'erness**. — *adv* **oth'erwhere** (*archaic* and *poetic*) elsewhere. — *adv* **oth'erwhile** or **oth'erwhiles** (*archaic* or *poetic*) at other times; sometimes. — *adv* **oth'erwise** in another way or manner; by other causes; in other respects; under other conditions. — *conj* else; under other conditions. — *adj* **oth'er-directed** (*sociol*) guided by standards set for one by external influences. — *n pl* **other ranks** members of the armed services not holding commissions. — **oth'erworld** a world other than, better than or beyond this. — Also *adj*. — *adj* **oth'erworld'ish**. — *n* **otherworld'liness**. — *adj* **otherworld'ly** concerned with the world to come, or with the world of the imagination, to the exclusion of practical interests. — **every other** each alternate; **in other words** this means; **or otherwise** or the opposite, as in *the efficiency or otherwise of the staff*; **other things being equal** associated circumstances being unchanged; **rather . . . than otherwise** rather than not; **someone, something, somewhere** etc **or other** an undefined person, thing, place, etc; **the other** (*vulg slang*) sexual relations; **the other day**, etc, on an unspecified day, etc, not long past. [OE *ōther*; cf Ger *ander*, L *alter*]
othergates *udh'ər-gāts*, (*obs*) *adv* in another way. — *adj* of another kind. — Also **oth'erguess** (in *Fielding*, *Goldsmith*, etc, **anotherguess**). — Also spelt as separate words, **other gates**, **other guess**. [**other**, and genitive of **gate**[2]]
otic *ō'tik*, (*med*) *adj* of or relating to the ear. — *n* **otī'tis** inflammation of the ear. — *combining form* **otō-** (or *ō-tə-*, *ō-tō'*) relating to the ear. — **o'tocyst** (*-sist*) an auditory or equilibristic vesicle. — *n* **o'tolith** (Gr *lithos* stone) a calcareous concretion in the ear of various animals, the movement of which helps the animal to maintain equilibrium; an ear-bone. — *n* **otol'ogist**. — *n* **otol'ogy** the branch of medicine concerned with the ear. — *n* **otorhinolaryngology** (*-rī-nō-lar-ing-gol'ə-ji*; Gr *rhīs*, *rhīnos* nose, and *larynx*, *-yngos* larynx) the branch of medicine dealing with the ear, nose and larynx and their diseases, often shortened to **otolaryngol'ogy**. — *n* **otorrhoea** (*ō-tə-rē'ə*; Gr *rhoiā* flow) a discharge from the ear. — *n* **otosclero'sis** formation of spongy bone in the capsule of the labyrinth of the ear. — *n* **o'toscope** an instrument for examining the ear. [Gr *ous*, *ōtos* ear]
otiose *ō'shi-ōs*, *ti-*, *adj* (of a word, expression, etc in a particular context) superfluous, redundant; unoccupied; indolent; functionless; futile. — *n* **otiosity** (*-os'i-ti*) or **o'tioseness** ease, idleness. [L *ōtiōsus*, from *ōtium* leisure]
otitis . . . otolaryngology . . . otology. See under **otic**.
-otomy *combining form* properly **-tomy** (qv).
otorhinolaryngology . . . otoscope. See under **otic**.
OTT (*colloq*) *abbrev*: over-the-top (qv).
ottar *ot'ər*. See **attar**.
ottava *öt-tä'vä*, *ō-tä'və*, *n* an octave. — *n* **ottavino** (*-vē'nō*) the piccolo: — *pl* **ottavin'os**. — **ottava rima** (*rē'mä*) an Italian stanza consisting of eight hendecasyllabic lines, rhyming *a b a b a b c c*. [Ital; cf **octave**]
otter *ot'ər*, *n* an aquatic fish-eating carnivore (*Lutra vulgaris*) of the weasel family with short smooth fur, a long slim body, and webbed feet; its brown short fur; a board travelling edge-up, manipulated on the principle of the kite, to carry the end of a fishing-line (or several hooked and baited lines) in a lake, or to keep open the mouth of a trawl (also **ott'er-board**); a device for severing the moorings of mines, a paravane. — *vt* or *vi* to fish with an otter-board. — **ott'er-hound** a large, rough-haired breed of dog formerly used in otter-hunting; **ott'er-hunting**; **ott'er-shrew** a large otter-like aquatic West African insectivore (*Potamogale velox*); **ott'er-trawl** a trawl with otter-boards; **ott'er-trawling**. [OE *otor*, related to **water**]
otto *ot'ō*. See under **attar**.
Ottoman *ot'ə-mən*, *adj* relating to the Turkish Empire or to the dynasty founded by *Othmān* or *Osmān*, or to his people, who overran the Near East and pushed into Europe in the 14c; Osmanli. — *n* a Turk of Turkey; (the following meanings without *cap*) a low, stuffed seat without a back, sometimes in the form of a chest; a cushioned seat for several people sitting with their backs to one another; a variety of corded silk. — *n* **Ott'amite** or **Ott'omite** a Turk.
ottrelite *ot'ri-līt*, *n* a mineral like chlorite but harder. — **ott'relite-slate** a clay slate with minute plates of ottrelite. [*Ottrez* in the Ardennes, and Gr *lithos* stone]
OU *abbrev*: the Open University; Oxford University.
ou or **ow** *ōō*, (*Scot*) *interj* expressing concession. — **ou ay** why yes; O yes.
ouabain or **wabain** *wä-bä'in*, *n* a poisonous alkaloid obtained from apocynaceous seeds and wood (*Strophanthus*, etc). [French spelling, from Somali *wabayo* a tree that yields it]
ouakari. See **uakari**.
oubit *ōō'bit*. See **woubit**.
oubliette *ōō-bli-et'*, *n* a dungeon with no opening except in the roof; a secret pit in the floor of a dungeon into which a victim could be precipitated. [Fr, from *oublier* to forget]
ouch[1] *owch*, (*archaic*) *n* a brooch; a clasped ornament; the socket of a precious stone. [OFr *nouche*]
ouch[2] *owch*, *interj* expressing pain. [Ger *autsch*]
oucht *ohht*, (*Scot*) *n* anything. [Cf **aught**]
Oudenarde *ōō'də-närd*, *n* a tapestry representing foliage, etc, once made at *Oudenarde* in Belgium.
OUDS *owdz*, *abbrev*: Oxford University Dramatic Society.
oughly. See **ouglie**.
ought[1] *öt*, *n* a variant of **aught**; also an illiterate corruption of **naught**. — *adv* (*Scot*) **oughtlings** (*ohh'linz*) at all.
ought[2] *öt*, *pa t* of **owe**; now *obs* or *dialect* except as an auxiliary verb, taking an infinitive with *to*, and *usu* with time expressed by the tense of the infinitive, expressing duty or obligation, rightness or suitability, or probability. — *n* **ought'ness** (*archaic*) rightness. [OE *āhte*, pa t of *āgan* to owe]
ouglie or **oughly**, old spellings of **ugly**. — *adj* **ough'ly-headed** (*Milton*).
Ouija® *wē'jə*, *n* a board with signs and letters of the alphabet on it, used with a planchette in attempts to receive messages from the dead. — Also without *cap*. [Fr *oui*, Ger *ja* yes]
ouistiti. A French spelling of **wistiti**.
ouk or **oulk** *ōōk*, *n* Scots form of **week**.
oulakan or **oulachon** *ōō'lə-kən*. See **eulachon**.
ould. Scots or Irish form of **old**.
oulong. Same as **oolong**.
ounce[1] *owns*, *n* the twelfth part of the (legally obsolete) pound troy = 480 grains; $\frac{1}{16}$ of a pound avoirdupois; a minute quantity. — **fluid ounce** the volume of an avoirdupois ounce of distilled water at 62° Fahrenheit, 0·0284 litre ($\frac{1}{20}$ pint); 0·0295 litre ($\frac{1}{16}$ US pint). [OFr *unce*, from L *uncia* the twelfth part; cf **inch**[1]]
ounce[2] *owns*, *n* formerly a lynx; now generally the snow leopard, a big cat of Asia with markings similar to a leopard's; the jaguar; the cheetah; sometimes vaguely any moderate-sized wild beast of the cat tribe. [Fr *once*, perh for *lonce* (as if *l'once*), from Gr *lynx*]

oundy *own'di*, (*obs*) *adj* wavy; undé (*heraldry*). [Fr *ondé*; cf **undate**]

OUP *abbrev*: Oxford University Press.

oup or **oop** *o͞op*, (*Scot*) *vt* to bind round with thread or cord; to join. [Appar **whip**]

ouphe or **ouph** *owf*, *o͞of*, (*Shakesp*) *n*. Same as **oaf**.

our *owr*, *possessive adj* or properly *pronoun* pertaining or belonging to us; when used predicatively or absolutely, **ours** (*owrz*), *dialect* **ourn** (*owrn*). — *pronoun* **ourselves'** (used *reflexively*) us; (used emphatically for clarification in apposition to **we** or **us**) personally; our normal or usual selves, as in *we can relax and be ourselves*: — *sing* **ourself'** used regally or, formerly, editorially. [OE *ūre*, genitive of *wē* we]

ourali *o͞o-rä'lē*. See **wourali**.

ourang-outang. Same as **orang-utan**.

ourari *o͞o-rä'rē*. See **wourali**.

ourebi. Same as **oribi**.

ourie, **oorie** or **owrie** *o͞o'ri*, (*Scot*) *adj* dingy; shabby; dreary; drooping; chill; inclined to shiver or shudder.

ouroboros *o͞o-rob'ə-ros* or *o͞o-rə-bor'əs*, (*mythol*) *n* a representation of a serpent with its tail in its mouth, symbolizing completion, totality, endlessness, etc. [Gr, literally 'tail-devouring', from *ourā* a tail, and *boraein* to eat]

ourology, **ouroscopy**, etc. Same as **urology**, etc.

ousel. See **ouzel**.

oust *owst*, *vt* to eject or expel. — *n* **oust'er** (*law*) ejection or dispossession. [Anglo-Fr *ouster* (OFr *oster*; Fr *ôter*) to remove; of obscure origin]

oustiti *o͞o-sti-tē'*, *n* a lock-opening tool, outsiders (qv under **outside**). [Fr, marmoset]

out (see also **out-**) *owt*, *adv* (shading into *adj* predicatively), not within; forth; to, towards, or at the exterior or a position away from the inside or inner part or from anything thought of as enclosing, hiding or obscuring; from among others; from the mass; beyond bounds; away from the original or normal position or state; at or towards the far end, or a remote position; seawards; not within, or away from, one's dwelling, work premises, etc; in or into the open air; in or into a state of exclusion or removal; not in office; not in use or fashion; debarred, not to be considered; no longer in the game; no longer in as a batsman, dismissed; not batting; out of the contest and unable to resume in time; in the condition of having won; away from the mark; at fault; in error; not in form or good condition; at a loss; in or into a disconcerted, perplexed or disturbed state; in or into an unconscious state; not in harmony or amity; in distribution; in or into the hands of others or the public; on loan; to or at an end; in an exhausted or extinguished state; completely; thoroughly; subjected to loss; in or to the field; in quest of or expressly aiming at something; in rebellion; on strike; in an exposed state; no longer in concealment or obscurity; in or into the state of having openly declared one's homosexuality; in or into the open; before the public; in or into society (*old*); on domestic service (*archaic*); in existence; at full length; in an expanded state; in bloom; in extension; loudly and clearly; forcibly; unreservedly. — *adj* external; outlying; remote; played away from home; outwards; not batting; exceeding the usual; in any condition expressed by the adverb *out*. — *n* a projection or outward bend (as in *outs and ins*); a way out, a way of escape; someone who is out; that which is outside; an omission in setting type (*printing*); a paying out, *esp* (in *pl*) rates and taxes, etc (*dialect*); an outing (*dialect*); a disadvantage, drawback (*US*); permission to go out (*US*). — *prep* forth from (*colloq* or *NAm*); outside of (now *rare*); without (*obs*). — *vt* to put out or throw out; to knock out; to make public the homosexuality of (a person in public life) without his or her permission (*colloq*); to make public any facts about (a person in public life) that he or she does not wish to be revealed (*colloq*). — *vi* to surface, be revealed, emerge publicly, as in *truth will out*; to go out (*colloq*); (with *with*) to bring out (*archaic* or *dialect*); (with *with*) to say suddenly or unexpectedly (*colloq*). — *interj* expressing peremptory dismissal; announcing that a player is out, the ball not in court, etc; indicating that one has come to the end of one's transmission (*radio*); alas (*archaic*); shame (*usu out upon*; *archaic*). — *adj* **out'ed** ejected. — *n* **out'ness** the state of being out; externality to the perceiving mind, objectiveness. — *adj* **at outs** (*US*) at odds; **from out** out from; **murder will out** see under **murder**; **out and about** able to go out, convalescent; active out of doors; **out and away** (*old*) by far; beyond competition. — *adj* **out'-and-out** thoroughgoing; thorough-paced; utter; absolute; unqualified. — *adv* **out-and-out'** finally and completely; definitely; unreservedly. — *n* **out-and-out'er** (*colloq*) any person or thing that is a complete or extreme type; a thoroughgoing partisan; a great lie. — **out at elbow** see **elbow**; **out for** abroad in quest of; aiming at obtaining or achieving; dismissed from batting with a score of; **out from under** out of a difficult situation; **out of** from within; from among; not in; not within; excluded from; from (a source, material, motive, condition, possession, language, etc); born of; beyond the bounds, range or scope of; deviating from, in disagreement with; away or distant from; without, destitute or denuded of; **out of character** see under **character**; **out of course** (*rare*) out of order; **out of date** or (as attributive *adj*) **out-of-date'** not abreast of the times; old-fashioned; obsolete; no longer valid; no longer current. — **out of doors** in or to the open air. — *adj* **out-of-doors'** or **out-of-door'** open-air, outdoor (see **out-**); outside of parliament. — *n* **out-of-doors'** the open air. — **out of it** excluded from participation; without a chance; **out of joint** see under **join**; **out of place** see under **place**; **out of pocket** see under **pocket**; **out of print** see under **print**; **out of sight** see under **sight**[1]; **out of sorts** see under **sort**; **out of temper** see under **temper**. — *adj* **out-of(-the)-bod'y** of or relating to an occurrence in which an individual has the experience of being outside his or her own body; **out of the question** see under **question**. — **out of the way** not in the way, not impeding or preventing progress. — *adj* **out-of-the-way'** uncommon, unusual; singular; secluded; remote. — **out of this world** see under **world**; **out of time** see under **time**; **out of work** see under **work**; **out on one's feet** as good as knocked out; done for, but with a semblance of carrying on. — *adv* and *prep* **out-o'ver** or **out-owre** (*owt-owr'*, *o͞ot-owr'*; *Scot*) out over; over. — **outs and ins** see **ins and outs** at **in**[1]; **out to** aiming, working resolutely, to; **out to out** in measurement from outside to outside; overall; **out upon** (*archaic*) shame on; **out with** let's do away with; not friendly with; see also **out** *vi* above; **out with it!** (*colloq*) say what you have to say, and be quick about it, spit it out. [OE *ūte*, *ūt*; Gothic *ut*, Ger *aus*, Sans *ud*]

Words formed with **out** *adv* are listed above, and those with **out-** *pfx* in the following entry or at the foot of the page; other *out-* words follow (p 1201).

Some words with **out-** prefix; see **out-** entry for numbered senses.

outbar' *vt* (1).	**outcompete'** *vt* (5).	**outeat'** *vt* (5).
outbox' *vt* (5).	**outcry'** *vt* (5), *vi* (2).	**outfight'** *vt* (5).
outbreathe' *vt* (2), *vi* (2).	**outdance'** *vt* (5).	**outflash'** *vt* (5), *vi* (2).
outburn' *vt* (5), *vi* (4).	**outdrink'** *vt* (5).	**outflow'** *vi* (2).
outburst' *vi* (1).	**outdrive'** *vt* (5).	

out- (see also **out**) *owt-*, *pfx* (1) outside, not within, outlying, eg *outhouse*, *outpatient*; (2) away from the inside or inner part (often *poetic*), eg *outspread*, *outpouring*, *outgoing*, *output*; (3) with prepositional force, meaning 'outside of', eg *outboard*, *outdoor*; (4) through, throughout, beyond, completely, eg *outwatch*, *outflank*, *outweary*; (5) indicating the fact of going beyond a norm, standard of comparison or limit, more than, more successfully than, farther than, longer than, etc, eg *outweigh*, *outmanoeuvre*, *outstep*, *outlast*, *out-Herod*. — *vt* **out-ask'** (*dialect*) to proclaim the banns of for the last time. — *n* **out'back** the parts of Australia remote from the cities, the bush country. — Also *adj* and *adv*. — *n* **out'backer**. — *vt* **outbal'ance** to outweigh. — *vt* **outbar'gain** to get the better of in a bargain. — *vt* **outbid'** to make a higher bid than. — *vt* **outblust'er** to exceed in blustering; to get the better of by bluster; to deprive (of) by bluster. — *adj* **out'board** (of an engine) designed to be attached to the outside of a ship or boat; towards or nearer the side of a ship or aircraft. — *adv* outside, or towards the outside of a ship or aircraft. — *adj* **out'bound** bound for a distant port, country, etc. — *n pl* **out'bounds** (*Spenser*) boundaries. — *vt* **outbrag'** to surpass in bragging or boasting; to excel in beauty or splendour (*Shakesp*). — *vt* **outbrave'** to excel in boldness or splendour (*Shakesp*); — *vt* to outface. — *n* **out'break** a breaking out of eg violence or illness; a disturbance. — *vi* **outbreak'** to burst forth. — *adj* **outbreath'd** (*-bretht'*; *Shakesp*) out of breath. — *adj* **out'bred** resulting from outbreeding. — *vi* and *vt* **outbreed'**. — *n* **outbreed'ing** breeding from parents not closely related; exogamy. — *n* **out'building** a building such as a barn, stable, etc separate from, but used in connection with, a dwelling-house or a main building; an outhouse. — *n* **out'burst** a bursting out; an eruption or explosion; a sudden violent expression of feeling. — *adv* **outby** or **outbye** (*owt-bī'*, *ōōt-bī'*; *Scot*) out of doors; a little way off; outwards; towards the shaft (*mining*). — *adj* **out'by** or **out'bye** outdoor; outlying. — *n* **out'cast** someone who has been cast out or rejected by society or home and family; anything rejected, eliminated or cast out; a quarrel (*Scot*). — *n* **out'caste** someone who is of no caste or has lost caste. — *vt* **outcaste'** to put out of caste. — *vt* **outclass'** to surpass so far as to seem in a different class, to be markedly better than. — *adj* **outclassed'**. — *n* **out'come** the issue; consequence; result. — *vt* **outcraft'y** (*Shakesp*) to exceed in craft. — *n* **out'crop** an exposed edge of rock or of a mineral vein at ground surface; a sudden emergence or occurrence. — *vi* (*-krop'*) to emerge from the ground in this way, to come to the surface. — *vt* **outcross'** to breed (individuals of different strains but the same breed); to outbreed. — *n* **out'cross**. — *n* **out'crossing**. — *n* **out'cry** a loud cry of protest, distress, etc; a confused noise; a public auction; public bargaining by a group. — *vt* **outdare'** to surpass in daring; to defy. — *vt* **outdate'** to put out of date. — *adj* **outdāt'ed** outmoded, old-fashioned, obsolete. — *vt* **outdis'tance** to leave far behind; to outstrip. — *vt* **outdo'** to surpass; to excel; to overcome. — *adj* **out'door** outside the door or the house; in or for the open air (**outdoor relief** (*hist*) help formerly given to a pauper not living in the workhouse). — *adv* **outdoors'** out of the house; in or into the open air; abroad (*archaic*). — *n* the world outside houses or other buildings, the open air. — *adj* **outdoor'sy** (*colloq*) of, characteristic of or suitable for or having a liking for the outdoors. — *vt* **outdure'** (*obs*) to outlast. — *vt* **outdwell'** (*Shakesp*) to stay beyond. — *n* **out'-dweller** someone who dwells elsewhere, *esp* one who owns land in a parish but lives outside it. — *n* **out'edge** the farthermost bound. — *vt* **outface'** to stare down; to confront boldly; to contradict (*obs*); to force by confronting (with *from*; *Shakesp*); to maintain boldly or impudently to the face of (that; *obs*). — *n* **outfall** (*owt'föl*) the outlet of a river, drain, etc; the amount that flows out; a sortie (*obs*); a quarrel (*dialect*). — *n* **out'field** arable land continually cropped without being manured, *opp* to *infield* (*Scot*); any open field at a distance from the farm-steading; any undefined district or sphere; at cricket and baseball, the outer part of the field; the players who occupy it. — *n* **out'fielder** one of such players. — *n* **out'fit** the act of fitting out for an enterprise; complete equipment; a set of (*esp* selected and matching) clothes; expenses for fitting out; a company travelling or working together for any purpose, formerly *esp* in charge of cattle (*US*); any set of persons, a gang (*colloq*); a business organization, etc (*colloq*). — *vt* to fit out, equip. — *vi* to get an outfit. — *n* **out'fitter** someone who makes or provides outfits; a person who deals in clothing, haberdashery, sporting equipment, etc. — *n* **out'fitting**. — *vt* **outflank'** to extend beyond or pass round the flank or side of; to circumvent. — *n* **out'fling** a sharp retort or gibe. — *n* **out'flow** a flowing out, a gush or outpouring. — *n* an outward current. — *n* **out'flush** a sudden glow. — *vt* **outfoot'** to outstrip; to outsail. — *vt* **outfox'** to get the better of by cunning; to outwit. — *vt* **outfrown'** to frown down. — *vt* **outgas'**. — *n* **outgass'ing** loss of, or removal of, occluded or adsorbed gas from a solid under vacuum conditions; also removal of gas from a liquid. — *n* **out'gate** (*Spenser* and *Northern*) an outlet; an exit. — *vt* **outgen'eral** to get the better of by generalship; to prove a better general than. — *n* **out'giving** a disbursement; an utterance; a declaration of policy. — *vt* **outglare'** to glare more than; to be more glaring than. — *vt* **outgo'** to outstrip; to surpass; to pass or live through; to overreach (*obs*). — *vi* to go out; to come to an end: — *pa t* **outwent'**; *pa p* **outgone'**. — *n* **out'go** (*pl* **out'goes**) that which goes out; expenditure, *opp* to *income*. — *n* **out'going** the act or state of going out; extreme limit; expenditure. — *adj* (of eg a tenant, office-bearer, etc) departing, leaving or retiring, *opp* to *incoming*; friendly, gregarious, extrovert. — *n pl* **out'-goings** expenditure. — *vt* **outgrow'** to surpass in growth; to grow out of, grow too big for; to eliminate or become free from in course of growth. — *n* **out'growth** that which grows out from anything; an excrescence; a product. — *n* **out'guard** a guard at a distance, or at the farthest distance, from the main body. — *vt* **outgun'** to defeat by means of superior weapons, forces, strength, etc. — *n* **out'-half** (*Rugby football*) a stand-off half. — *n* **out'haul** (*naut*) a rope for hauling out the clew of a sail (also **out'hauler**). — *vt* **out-Her'od** to outdo (the mystery-play character *Herod*) in violence (*Shakesp*, *Hamlet* III. 2. 14); to outdo, *esp* in what is bad. — *vt* **outhire'** (*Spenser* **outhyre**) to give out as if on hire. — **out'house** a building built near to or up against a main building. — *vt* **outjest'** to overcome by jesting (*Shakesp*); to excel in jesting. — *n* **out'jet** or **out'jut** a projection. — *n* and *adj* **outjett'ing** or **outjutt'ing**. — *vt* **outjock'ey** to outwit by trickery. — **out'land** (*usu* in *pl*) an outlying land or territory; a foreign land (*archaic* or *poetic*); land granted to tenants (*hist*). — *adj* outlying; foreign (*archaic*). — **out'lander** a foreigner; an uitlander. — *adj* **outland'ish** queer, bizarre; out-of-the-way; foreign

out'flowing *n*, *adj* (2).	**out'gush** *n* (2).	**outmatch'** *vt* (5).
outflush' *vi* (5).	**outgush'** *vi* (2).	**outpeep'** *vi* (2).
outfly' *vt* (5), *vi* (2).	**outhit'** *vt* (5).	**outpour'** *vt* (2), *vi* (2).
outgive' *vt* (5), *vi* (2).	**outjump'** *vt* (5).	**outpour'er** *n* (2).
out'goer *n* (2).	**outmarch'** *vt* (4), (5).	

(*archaic*). — *adv* **outland'ishly**. — **outland'ishness**. — *n* **out'lash** a sudden burst or stroke. — *vt* **outlast'** to last longer than. — *vt* **outlaunch'** (*Spenser* **outlaunce**) to launch forth. — *n* and *vt* **outlaw** see separate entry. — *n* **out'lay** an expenditure of money, resources, etc; that which is laid out. — *vt* **outlay'** to lay out in view; to expend; to surpass in laying. — *n* **out'leap** an act of leaping out; an excursion; an outburst. — *vt* **outleap'** to leap beyond or over; to surpass in leaping. — *vi* to leap out. — *vt* **outlearn'** to excel in learning; to get beyond the study of; to elicit (*Spenser*). — *n* **out'let** a vent or opening allowing the escape of something; a means of full or uninhibited expression; a market for a certain product, etc; a place where products or services are sold or distributed; a shop, etc selling a particular producer's products; an electrical power point (*US*). — *vt* **outlie'** to surpass in telling lies. — *vi* **outlie'** (*rare*) to lie in the open; to camp; to lie stretched out. — *vt* to lie beyond. — *n* **out'lier** a detached portion of anything lying some way off or out; an isolated remnant of rock surrounded by older rocks (*geol*); someone who lies in the open (*rare*); someone who lodges or lies apart from others or from a place with which he or she is connected; an outsider. — *n* **out'line** the outer line; the line by which any figure or object appears to be bounded; a line representing this in a drawing, etc; a sketch showing only the main lines; a general statement without details; a statement of the main principles; a setline in fishing. — *vt* to draw the exterior line of; to delineate or sketch. — *adj* **outlinear** (*owt-lin'i-ər*) like an outline. — *vt* **outlive** (*-liv'*) to live longer than; to survive; to live through; to live down. — *n* **out'lodging** a lodging beyond bounds. — *n* **out'look** a place for looking out from; a view or prospect; a prospect for the future; mental point of view; a vigilant watch. — *vt* **outlook'** (*Shakesp owt'*) to face courageously. — *vi* to look out. — *vt* **outlus'tre** (*Shakesp*) to outshine. — *adj* **out'lying** remote from the centre or main part; lying out or beyond; lodging apart; on the exterior or frontier; detached. — *vt* **outman'** to outdo in manliness; to outnumber in men. — *vt* **outmanoeu'vre** to surpass in or by manoeuvring. — *vt* **outman'tle** (*archaic* or *poetic*) to excel in dress or ornament. — *n* **out'marriage** marriage to a partner outside one's own group, religion, etc. — *vt* **outmeas'ure** to exceed in extent. — *vt* **outmode'** to put out of fashion. — *adj* **outmod'ed** outdated, old-fashioned or no longer current. — **outmost** see **outermost** under **outer**. — *vt* **outmove'** to move faster than; to get the better of by moving. — *vt* **outname'** to surpass in notoriety. — *vt* **outnight'** (*Shakesp*) to surpass in mentioning nights. — *vt* **outnum'ber** to exceed in numbers. — *vt* **outpace'** to walk faster than; to outstrip. — *vt* **out-par'amour** (*Shakesp*) to exceed in addiction to mistresses. — *n* **out'-parish** a parish associated with a town but beyond the boundary; an outlying parish. — *n* **out'part** (*obs*) a part remote from the centre. — *vt* **outpass'ion** to go beyond in passionateness. — *n* **out'-patient** a non-resident patient attending a hospital. — *vt* **outpeer'** (*Shakesp*) to surpass or excel. — *n* **out'-pension** a pension granted to someone who is not resident in an institution. — *vt* to grant an out-pension to. — **out'-pensioner** a non-resident pensioner. — *vt* **outperform'** to outdo or surpass in a specific field of activity. — *n* **out'placement** (*euphem*) dismissal from one's job, by sacking or redundancy. — *vt* **outplay'** to play better than, and so defeat. — *vt* **outpoint'** to score more points than. — *n* **out'port** a port out of or remote from the chief port; a port away from the town or customs area; a place of export. — *n* **out'-porter** a porter who carries luggage to and from, and not merely in, the place of employment. — *n* **out'post** a post or station beyond the main body of the army, etc; its occupants; a remote settlement or stronghold. — *n* **out'pouring** a pouring out; a passionate or fluent and voluble utterance. — *vt* **outpower'** to surpass in power. — *vt* **outpray'** to exceed in earnestness or length of prayer; to overcome in or by prayer. — *vt* **outprice'** to offer a better price, financial return, etc, than. — *vt* **outprize'** (*Shakesp*) to exceed in estimation. — *n* **out'put** quantity produced or turned out; data in either printed or coded form after processing by a computer; punched tape or print-out by which processed data leave a computer; a signal delivered by a telecommunications instrument or system. — *vt* (of a computer, etc) to send out, supply, produce (data, etc) as output. — *n pl* **out'quarters** quarters situated away from headquarters. — *vt* **outrank'** to rank above. — *vt* **outrate'** to offer a better rate of return than. — *vt* **outreach'** to reach or extend beyond; to overreach; to stretch forth. — *n* a reaching out; the extent or distance something can reach or stretch out; an organization's involvement in or contact with the surrounding community, *esp* that of a church for purposes of evangelism or that of community welfare organizations taking their services out to *esp* disadvantaged individuals and groups rather than expecting them to approach the welfare organizations. — *vt* **outred'** or **outredd'en** to surpass in redness. — *vt* **outreign'** to reign longer than; (*Spenser* **outraigne**) to reign to the end of. — *n* **outrelief'** outdoor relief. — *n* **out'ride** an unaccented syllable or syllables added to a foot, *esp* in sprung rhythm (*prosody*). — *vt* **outride'** to ride beyond; to ride faster than; to ride safely through (a storm). — *n* **out'rider** a person who rides beside a carriage as a guard; a rider sent ahead as a scout, or to ensure a clear passage. — *n* **out'rigger** a projecting spar for extending sails or any part of the rigging; a projecting device supported on a float, fixed to the side of a canoe, etc, to give stability; a projecting rowlock giving extra leverage to the oar; a boat having such rowlocks; a light racing-boat with projecting rowlocks; a projecting beam or framework attached to a building, ship or aircraft for any of various purposes; a projecting frame to support the controlling planes of an aeroplane; an extension from the splinter-bar of a carriage to take another horse. — *adj* **out'right** out-and-out; utter, thoroughgoing; unmitigated; downright; total, absolute; direct. — *adv* **outright'** totally, completely, without qualification; directly, without concealment or circumlocution; straight ahead; unreservedly; undisguisedly; at once and completely. — *n* **out'run** an outlying pasture or run. — *vt* **outrun'** to go beyond in running; to exceed; to get the better of or to escape by running (**outrun** or **overrun the constable** to run into debt; to live beyond one's means). — *n* **out'runner**. — *vt* **outsail'** to leave behind in sailing; to sail beyond. — *vt* **outscorn'** (*Shakesp*) to face out with scorn. — *vt* **outsell'** to be sold in larger quantities than; to fetch a higher price than; to exceed in value; to surpass in the number or amount of sales. — *n* **out'-sentry** a sentry placed at a distance. — *n* **out'set** a setting out; a beginning or start, *esp* in *at* or *from the outset*; an outward current. — *n* **out'setting**. — *n* **out'settlement** an outlying settlement. — *n* **out'shot** (*Scot*) a projection in a building or a recess made in the wall of a room. — *n* **out'sight** the power of seeing external things; (*owt'sīt*,

outrace' *vt* (5).	**out'rush** *n* (2).	**out'shoot** *n* (2).
outri'val *vt* (5).	**outsail'** *vt* (5).	**outsoar'** *vt* (5).
outroar' (*Shakesp*) *vt* (2).	**outscold'** (*Shakesp*) *vt* (5).	**outspeak'** *vt* (2), (5), *vi* (2).
outroot' *vt* (2).	**outshine'** *vi* (2), *vt* (5).	**outstare'** *vt* (5).
outrush' *vi* (2).	**outshoot'** *vt* (4), (5).	

o͞ot'sihht) outdoor possessions (*Scot*). — Also *adj*. — *vt* **outsit'** to sit beyond the time of; to sit longer than. — *adj* **out'size** over normal size, exceptionally large. — *n* an exceptionally large size; anything, *esp* a garment, of exceptionally large size. — *adj* **out'sized**. — *n pl* **out'skirts** (*usu* in *pl*) the outlying areas of a town, etc, suburbs; the fringes of a subject, etc. — *vt* **outsleep'** to sleep longer than; to sleep through; to sleep to or beyond the time of. — *vt* **outsmart'** (*colloq*; *orig US*) to show more cleverness or cunning than, to outwit. — *n* **out'sole** the outer sole of a boot or shoe which rests on the ground. — *vt* **outspend'** to spend more than or beyond the limits of. — *adj* **outspent'** thoroughly tired out. — *adj* **outspō'ken** speaking or spoken frankly, without circumlocution. — *n* **outspō'kenness**. — *vt* **outsport'** (*Shakesp*) to sport beyond the limits of. — *vt* and *vi* **outspread'** to spread out or over. — *adj* **out'spread** (or *owt-spred'*) spread out. — *n* an expanse. — *adj* **outspread'ing**. — *vi* **outspring'** (*literary*) to spring out. — *n* **out'spring** outcome. — *vt* **outstand'** to withstand; to stand or endure through or beyond (*archaic*). — *vi* to stand out or project; to stand out (to sea); to stand over or remain. — *adj* **outstand'ing** prominent; excellent, superior; unsettled; unpaid; still to be attended to or done. — *adv* **outstand'ingly**. — *vt* **outstare'** to stare down (*Shakesp*); to face the stare of boldly; to outdo in staring; to gaze at without being blinded. — *n* **out'station** a subsidiary branch or post, *esp* in an outlying area or remote from headquarters; a place far from the source of services, at which Australian aborigines live in a traditional manner; an outlying post on an Australian sheep station. — *vt* **outstay'** to stay beyond the limit of, as in *outstay one's welcome*; to stay longer than. — *vt* to endure longer than. — *vt* **outstep'** to step beyond, overstep. — *vt* **outstrain'** to stretch out. — *vt* **outstretch'** to stretch out; to reach forth; to spread out; to stretch to the end of; to stretch beyond. — *adj* **outstretched'** extended, proffered. — *vt* **outstrike** (*owt-strīk'*, or *owt'*) to outdo in striking. — *vt* **outstrip'** to outrun; to leave behind; to surpass; to outdo in denuding oneself. — *vt* **outsum'** to outnumber. — *vt* **outswear'** to exceed in swearing; to overcome by swearing. — *vt* **outsweet'en** to excel in sweetness. — *vt* **outswell'** to swell more than (*Shakesp*); to overflow. — *n* **out'swing** an outward swing or swerve. — *n* **out'swinger** a ball bowled to swerve from leg to off (*cricket*); a ball kicked to swerve away from the goal or from the centre of the pitch. — *vt* **outtake'** (*obs*) to take out; to except. — *n* **out'-take** (*cinema*) a sequence of film removed from the final edited version. — *prep* (*obs*) **outtake'** or (*obs*; *orig pap*) **outtak'en** except. — *vt* **outtell'** (*archaic* or *poetic*) to tell forth; to tell to the end; to tell or count beyond. — *vt* **outtongue'** (*Shakesp*) to speak louder than. — *vt* **outtop'** to reach higher than; to excel. — *n* **out'-tray** a shallow container for letters, etc, ready to be dispatched. — *n* **out'turn** the amount of anything turned out, produced or achieved, output. — *vt* **outven'om** (*Shakesp*) to exceed in poisonousness. — *vt* **outvill'ain** (*Shakesp*) to exceed in villainy. — *vt* **outvoice'** (*Shakesp*) to exceed in clamour or noise; to drown the voice of. — *vt* **outvote'** to defeat by a greater number of votes; to overrule by weight of opinion. — *n* **out'voter** a voter not resident in the constituency. — *n* **out'-wall** the outside wall of a building; external appearance (*Shakesp*). — *n* **out'wash** (*geol*) material borne by melted water from a glacier, found deposited beyond the terminal moraine. — *vt* **outwatch'** to watch longer than; to watch throughout the time of. — *vt* **outwear'** to wear out; to spend or live through; to outlive or outgrow; to outlast. — *vt* **outwea'ry** to tire out completely. — *vt* **outweed'** (*Spenser*) to root out. — *vt* **outweep'** to weep out or shed wholly; to surpass in weeping. — *vt* **outweigh'** to exceed in weight or importance. — *vt* and *vi* **outwell'** (*archaic* or *poetic*) to pour or well out. — *vt* **outwent'** see **outgo**. — *vi* **outwick'** in curling, to strike the outside of another stone and so send it within a circle. — *vt* **outwin'** (*Spenser*) to get out of. — *vt* **outwind** (*-wīnd'*; *obs*) to unwind, extricate. — *vt* **outwing'** to outstrip in flying; to fly beyond; to outflank. — *vt* **outwit'** to defeat by superior ingenuity; to surpass in wit or ingenuity: — *pr p* **outwitt'ing**; *pa t* and *pa p* **outwitt'ed**. — *prep* **outwith** (*owt'with*, *o͞ot'with*, *-with'*; *Scot*) outside of. — *adv* outwards. — *n* **out'work** (often in *pl*) a defence work that lies outside the principal wall or line of fortification; outdoor work, field work; work done away from the shop or factory, etc. — *vt* **outwork'** (*Shakesp*) to surpass in work; to work out or bring to an end; to finish: — *pa t* and *pa p* **outwrought'**. — *n* **out'worker**. — *adj* **outworn'** (or *owt'*) worn out; obsolete. — *vt* **outworth'** (*Shakesp*) to exceed in value. — *vt* **outwrest'** (*Spenser*) to extort.

outage *ow'tij*, *n* the amount of a commodity lost in transport and storage; the amount of fuel used on a flight; stoppage of a mechanism due to failure of power; a period during which electricity fails or is cut off; a period when a reactor is working at a low level (*nuc energy*). **[out]**

outdacious *owt-dā'shəs*, *adj* an illiterate perversion of **audacious**.

outer *ow'tər*, *adj* further out or without; external, *opp* to *inner*. — *n* the outermost ring on a target, or a shot striking it (*archery*); in an electrical distribution system either of the conductors whose potential is above or below the earth's; an unsheltered part of the spectator enclosure at a sportsground (*Austr* and *NZ*). — *adj* **out'ermost** or **out'most** (*-məst*, *-mōst*; OE *ūtemest*, superlative) most or furthest out; most remote from the centre; most distant. — **outer bar** the junior barristers who plead outside the bar in court, as opposed to Queen's (or King's) Counsel and others who plead within the bar; **outer dead-centre** the position of the crank of a reciprocating engine or pump when the piston is at its nearest to the crankshaft (also **bottom dead-centre**); **outer space** space beyond the earth's atmosphere; **out'erwear** or **outer garments** clothes such as jackets, suits, coats, etc worn over other clothes; clothes put on to go out of doors. — **on the outer** (*Austr* and *NZ*) excluded, out in the cold. [OE *ūterra*]

outfangthief *owt'fang-thēf*, (*hist*) *n* the right of judging and fining thieves pursued and brought back from outside one's own jurisdiction. [OE *ūtfangene-thēof*, from *ūt* out, the root of *fōn* to take, and *thēof* thief]

outher *ow'dhər*, *ō'dhər*, an old form, now *dialect*, of **either**.

outing *ow'ting*, *n* an outdoor excursion or airing; the act of making public another person's homosexuality or other personal information intended to be kept private; ejection; distance out. — **outing flannel** (*US*) a type of flannelette. **[out]**

outlaw *owt'lö*, *n* a person deprived of the protection of the law; (loosely) a bandit; an outcast; someone banished, exiled or on the run from the law; a wild, dangerous or unmanageable animal (*US*). — *vt* to place beyond the law; to deprive of the benefit of the law; to ban, make illegal, proscribe. — *n* **out'lawry** the act of putting a man out of the protection of the law; the state of being an outlaw. [OE *ūtlaga*, from ON *ūtlāgi*, from *ūt* out, and *lög* law]

outler *o͞ot'lər*, (*Burns*) *adj* not housed. — *n* a beast that is not housed; someone who is out of office. [Poss **outlier**]

outswim' *vt* (5).	**outtrav'el** *vt* (4), (5).	**outvie'** *vt* (5).
outtalk' *vt* (5).	**outval'ue** *vt* (5).	**outwalk'** *vt* (4), (5).
outthink' *vt* (5).		

outrage *owt'-rāj, -rij, n* gross or violent injury; an act of wanton mischief; an atrocious act; gross offence to moral feelings; great anger or indignation; violation; rape; excess, undue divergence from a mean (*Spenser*); violence beyond measure (*Shakesp*); clamour (*Spenser*). — *vt* to treat with excessive abuse; to shock grossly; to injure by violence, *esp* to violate, to ravish. — *adj* **outrageous** (*owt-rā'jəs*) iniquitous or disgraceful; shocking; monstrous; offensive or gross; furious; turbulent or violent; immoderate, wild or extravagant. — *adv* **outrā'geously**. — *n* **outrā'geousness**. [OFr *ultrage*, from *outre* beyond, from L *ultrā*; the word is not connected with **out** and **rage** but influenced by them]

outrance *ōō-trãs, n* the utmost extremity; the bitter end (**à outrance** to the bitter end of a combat, erroneously in Eng use, **à l'outrance**). [Fr, from *outre* beyond]

outré *ōō'trā, adj* beyond what is customary or proper; extravagant, fantastic. [Fr]

outrecuidance *ōōt-ər-kwē'dəns, ōōt-r'- kwē'dãs,* (*Scott*) *n* presumption or overweening. [Fr *outre* beyond, and OFr *cuider* to think or plume oneself, from L *cōgitāre*]

outremer *ōō-tr'-mer, n* the region beyond the sea; overseas. [Fr *outre* beyond, and *mer* sea]

outroop *owt'rōōp,* (*obs*) *n* an auction sale. — *n* **out'rooper** (*obs*) an auctioneer; the Common Crier of the City of London. [Du *uitroepen* to cry out, proclaim]

outrope *owt'rōp*, and **outroper** *owt'rōp-ər*. Same as **outroop** and **outrooper**.

outside *owt'sīd, owt-sīd', n* the outer side; the farthest limit; the outer part or surface; the exterior; an outside passenger (*archaic*); (in *pl*) the top and bottom quires of a ream of paper. — *adj* **out'side** on or from the outside; carried on the outside; exterior; superficial; external; extreme; (of a possibility) unlikely, remote; beyond the limit; not having membership; (of a criminal activity) carried out by a person or people not having contacts with someone near the victim; at a distance from a major centre of population (*Austr*); of a position nearer or near the edge of the field (*Rugby football*, etc). — *adv* **outside'** (sometimes *owt'*) on or to the outside; not within; out of prison. — *prep* **out'side** or **outside'** to or on the outside of; except for, apart from (*colloq*); in a position nearer the edge of the field than (*Rugby football*, etc). — *n* **outsi'der** a person who is not a member of a particular company, profession, etc, a stranger, a layman; a person not considered fit to associate with; a person who is not an inmate; a person who is not participating; a racehorse, competitor, team, etc not included among the favourites in the betting; a person whose place in a game, at work, etc, is on the outside; (in *pl*) a pair of nippers for turning a key in a keyhole from the outside. — **outside broadcast** a broadcast not made from within a studio; **out'side-car** an Irish jaunting-car in which the passengers sit back to back; **outside chance** a remote chance; **outside edge** see **edge**; **outside half** (*Rugby football*) a stand-off half; **outside left** and **right** in some games, forward players on the extreme left and right; **outside novel** the type of novel which deals with the author's thoughts and his or her relationship with the world. — **at the outside** at the most, etc; **get outside of** (*colloq*) to eat or drink; **outside in** same as **inside out**; **outside of** (*colloq, esp US*) in or to a position external to; apart from, except. [**out** and **side**[1]]

outspan *owt'span,* or *-span',* (*SAfr*) *vt* and *vi* to unyoke (oxen) or unharness (a horse) from a vehicle. — *n* (*owt'*) a stopping-place. [Du *uitspannen*]

outspeckle *ōōt-spek'l,* (*obs Scot*) *n* a laughing-stock, spectacle. [Perh connected with **kenspeckle**]

outward *ow'twərd, adj* toward the outside; on the outside; outer; external; exterior; appearing externally; apparent or seeming; formal; accidental or additional, not inherent; in a direction away from home or one's base; worldly, carnal (*theol*); dissolute (*dialect*). — *adv* outwards; away from port; to a foreign port; superficially. — *n* external appearance (*Shakesp*); the outside. — *adv* **out'wardly** in outward appearance, apparently, superficially; externally; in an outward manner. — *n* **out'wardness** externality; objectivity. — *adv* **out'wards** in an outward direction, out. — *adj* **outward-bound'** heading outward or to a foreign port. — *adj* **outward-sain'ted** (*literary*) appearing outwardly to be a saint. [**out** and **-ward**, **-wards**]

ouvert *ōō-ver, fem* **ouverte** *-vert,* (*Fr*) *adj* open.

ouvirandra *ōō-vi-ran'drə, n* the lattice-leaf of Madagascar. [From the Malagasy name]

ouvrage *ōō-vräzh,* (*Fr*) *n* work.

ouvrier *ōō-vrē-ā, fem* **ouvrière** *ōō-vrē-er,* (*Fr*) *n* a worker or operative.

ouzel or **ousel** *ōō'zl,* (*Shakesp* **woo'sel** or **woo'sell**), *n* a blackbird (*archaic*); apparently, a dark-complexioned person (*Shakesp*). — **ou'zel-cock**. — **ring ouzel** a blackish thrush with a broad white band on the throat; **water ouzel** the dipper. [OE *ōsle*; cognate with Ger *Amsel*]

ouzo *ōō'zō, n* an aniseed liqueur: — *pl* **ou'zos**. [Mod Gr]

ova. See **ovum**.

oval *ō'vəl, adj* strictly, egg-shaped, like an egg in the round or in section, rounded, longer than broad, broadest near one end; loosely, elliptical or ellipsoidal, or nearly so; rounded at both ends, about twice as long as broad, broadest in the middle (*bot*); pertaining to eggs (*obs*). — *n* an oval figure or thing, eg an oval field; a cricket or football ground (*Austr*). — *adv* **o'vally**. [L *ōvum* egg; *ōvālis* is modern Latin]

ovalbumin *ō-val'bū-min* or *ō-val-bū'min n* the albumin in egg whites. [L *ovum* egg, and **albumen**]

ovary *ō'və-ri, n* one of the two female reproductive glands; the part of the gynaeceum that contains the ovules (*bot*). — *adj* **ovā'rian** of or pertaining to the ovary. — *n* **ovā'riōle** one of the egg-tubes forming an insect's ovary. — *n* **ovāriot'omist**. — *n* **ovāriot'omy** (see **-tomy**; *surg*) the cutting of an ovary; the removal of ovaries because of a tumour. — *adj* **ovā'rious** (*rare*) consisting of eggs. — *n* **ovarī'tis** inflammation of the ovary, oophoritis. [New L *ōvārium*, from L *ōvum* egg]

ovate[1] *ov'āt, n* an Eisteddfodic graduate who is neither a bard nor a druid. [Welsh *ofydd* a philosopher or lord; fancifully identified with the unrelated Celtic word preserved in Gr as *ouāteis* (pl) Gaulish soothsayers]

ovate[2] *ō'vāt, adj* egg-shaped; shaped in outline like an egg, broadest below the middle (*bot*). [L *ōvātus* egg-shaped]

ovate[3]. See under **ovation**.

ovation *ō-vā'shən, n* an outburst of popular applause, an enthusiastic reception; in ancient Rome, a lesser triumph; rejoicing (*archaic*). — *vt* **ovate'** (facetious back-formation) to receive with an ovation. — *n* **ova'tor**. — **standing ovation** see under **stand**. [L *ovātiō, -ōnis*, from *ovāre* to exult]

oven *uv'n, n* an arched cavity or closed compartment for baking, heating or drying; a small furnace. — **o'ven-bird** a name for various birds that build domed or oven-shaped nests, *esp* the S American genus *Furnarius*; **oven glove** a type of thick reinforced glove worn when handling hot dishes. — *adj* **ov'en-ready** (of food) prepared beforehand so as to be ready for cooking in the oven immediately after purchase. — **ov'en-tit** a dialect name for various birds, including the willow-warbler; the oven-bird; **ov'enware** dishes, such as casseroles, that will stand the heat of an oven; **ov'enwood** brushwood. [OE *ofen*; Ger *Ofen*]

over *ō'vər, prep* above in place, rank, power, authority, contention, preference, value, quantity, number, etc; in excess of; above and from one side of to the other; down from or beyond the edge of; from side to side or end to end of; along; throughout the extent of; during; until after; across; on or to the other side of; on, on to, about, or across the surface of; in discussion, contemplation, study of or occupation with; concerning; on account of; recovered from the effects of; in a sunk, submerged, or buried state beyond the level of, as in *over head and ears*. — *adv* on the top; above; across; to or on the other side; from one person, party, condition, etc, to another; into a sleep; outwards so as to overhang or to fall from; down, away from an upright position; through, from beginning to end, *esp* in a cursory or exploratory way; throughout; into a reversed position; across the margin; again, in repetition; too much; in excess; left remaining; at an end. — *interj* indicating that the speaker now expects a reply (*radio*). — *adj* (*usu* as *pfx*) upper or superior; surplus; excessive. — *n* the series of balls (as *six-ball* or *eight-ball over*) or the play between changes in bowling from one end to the other (*cricket*); anything that is over; a surplus copy, etc; an excess, overplus. — *vt* to go, leap or vault over. — Also, only as *adv* and *prep*, **o'er** (*now usu poetic*), **ore** (*obs*), **o're** (*obs*), all pronounced *ōr* or *ör*, and in Scots **ower**, **owre** or **o'er**, pronounced *owr* or *ōr*. — *n* **overage** (*ō'və-rij*) surplus, excess (see also **over-age** under **over-**). — *adv* **o'verly** (*colloq*, *orig US*) excessively, too; casually (*Scot*); superciliously (*obs*). — *adj* casual (*Scot*); supercilious, superior (*obs*). — **o'ver-and-un'der** a double-barrelled gun having the barrels one on top of the other rather than side by side (also **under-and-o'ver**). — *adv* **overby'** a little way over, *esp* in Scots forms **owerby**, **o'erby** (*owr-bī'*). — *n* **over rate** (*cricket*) the rate at which overs are bowled. — *adj* **over-the-coun'ter** (of securities) etc, not listed on or traded through a stock exchange, but traded directly between buyers and sellers; (of drugs, etc) able to be bought or sold without prescription or licence. — *adj* **over-the-top'** excessive, extreme, too much. — **all over** at an end; everywhere; at his, her or its most characteristic (*colloq*); covered with, besmeared or bespattered with (*colloq*); **all over again** again from the beginning, anew; **be all over (someone)** to make a fuss of, fawn on (someone); **over again** all over again; **over against** opposite; **over and above** in addition to; besides; **over and out** an expression used to announce the end of one's transmission (*radio*); **over and over (again)** many times; repeatedly; **over head and ears** completely submerged; **over seas** to foreign lands; **over the hill** see under **hill**; **over the moon** see under **moon**; **over to you!** used to transfer the initiative in speaking, etc. [OE *ofer*; Ger *über*, L *super*, Gr *hyper*; cf **up**]

Words formed with **over** *prep* and *adv* are listed above, and those with **over-** *pfx* in the following entry or at the foot of the page; other *over-* words follow (p 1208).

over- *ō-vər*, *pfx* used with certain meanings of **over** *prep*, *adv*, or *adj*, as (1) above, across, across the surface; (2) beyond an understood limit; (3) down, away from the upright position; (4) upper or outer; (5) beyond what is usual or desirable; (6) completely; (7) (with *neg*) at all (as in *not over-generous*). — *vi* **overachieve'** to do better than predicted or expected. — *vt* and *vi* **overact'** to act or perform with exaggeration. — *adj* **over-age'** beyond the age limit specified for; too old (see also **overage** under **over**). — *adv* **overall'** or **over-all'** altogether; over the whole; everywhere (*Spenser*); above all (*obs*). — *adj* **o'verall** including everything; everything being reckoned; all-round. — *n* **o'verall** a protective loose coat worn over ordinary clothes for dirty work or (*archaic*) weather; (in *pl*) a one-piece protective work garment combining sleeved top and trousers, a boiler suit; dungarees (*US*); cavalryman's trousers. — *adj* **o'veralled**. — *vt* **overarch'** to arch over; to form an arch over. — *vi* to hang over like an arch. — *n* (*ō'*-) an overhead arch. — *adj* and *adv* **o'verarm** with the arm raised above the shoulder. — *vt* **overawe'** to daunt by arousing fear or reverence in. — *vt* **overbal'ance** to cause to lose balance; to exceed in weight, value or importance. — *vi* to lose balance, fall over. — *n* excess of weight or value. — *vt* **overbear'** to bear down, overpower; to overwhelm; to overrule (objections or an objector). — *vi* to be too productive. — *adj* **overbear'ing** inclined to domineer; haughty and dogmatic; imperious. — *adv* **overbear'ingly**. — *n* **overbear'ingness**. — *vt* **overbid'** to outbid; to make a bid that is greater than or counts above; to bid more than the value of. — Also *vi*. — *n* (*ō'*-) a higher bid; an unduly high bid. — *n* **overbidd'er**. — *n* **overbidd'ing**. — *n* **o'verbite** (*dentistry*) the (amount of) extension of the upper incisors beyond the lower when the mouth is closed. — *vi* **overblow'** to produce a harmonic instead of the fundamental tone, by increase of wind-pressure (*music*); to blow over, be past its violence; to blow with too much violence. — *vt* to blow away; to blow across; to overturn by blowing; to blow (an instrument) too strongly or deliberately so as to produce a harmonic (*music*); to cover with blossoms (*poetic* or *literary*). — *adj* **overblown'** blown over or past; burnt by an excessive blast, in the Bessemer steel process; inflated to excess; more than full-blown; excessive. — *adv* **overboard'** from on board, over the side of a ship or boat into the water (**go overboard about** or **for** (*slang*) to go to extremes of enthusiasm about or for; **throw overboard** to reject, jettison). — *vt* and *vi* **overbook'** to make more reservations than the number of places (in a plane, ship, hotel, etc) actually available. — *vi* **over-breathe'** (*med*) to hyperventilate. — *n* **over-breath'ing**. — *vt* **overbrow'** (*archaic* or *poetic*) to overhang like a brow; **overbuild'** to cover with buildings; to build above; to build in excess; to build too much upon or in. — *vt* **overbulk'** (*Shakesp*) to oppress by bulk, or to dwarf by greater bulk. — *vt* **overburd'en** *archaic* **overburth'en**) to burden too heavily. — *n* (*ō'vər*-) an excessive burden; rock that must be removed to expose a vein or seam (*mining*); alluvial soil, etc, overlying a bed of clay or other substance to be dug, mined or quarried. — *vt* **overburn'** to burn too much. — *vi* to be too zealous. — *adj* **overbus'y** too busy; officious. — *vt* to occupy (oneself) too much. — *vt* **overbuy'** to buy too much of; to buy for more expense than; to put (oneself) in the position of having bought too much; to buy too dear (*Shakesp*). — *vi* to buy too much: — *pa t* and *pa p* **overbought'**. — *vt* **overcall'** (*bridge*) to outbid; to bid above; to bid too high on; to rank as a higher bid than. — *n* (*ō'*-) a higher bid than the opponent's preceding one. — *vt* **overcan'opy** to cover as with a canopy: — *pa p* **overcan'opied** (*Shakesp* **over-cann'oped**). — *n* **overcapac'ity** the state of having more workers, machinery, factory space, etc than is needed to meet the existing demand for one's product. — *n* **overcapitalizā'tion** or **-s-**. — *vt* **overcap'italize** or **-ise** to fix the capital to be invested in, or the capital value of, too high. — *vt* **overcast'** to sew stitches over (a raw edge); to cover with stitches; to compute too high, overestimate; to recover, get over (*Scot*); to overthrow; to cast as a covering; to cast a covering over; to shade (*Spenser*). — *vi* to grow dull or cloudy. — *adj* clouded over. — *n* (*ō'*-) a cloudy covering. — *n* **overcast'ing**. —

Some words with **over-** prefix; see **over-** entry for numbered senses.

overabound' *vi* (5).	**overbeat'** *vt* (3), *vi* (3).	**overcare'ful** *adj* (5).
overabound'ing *adj* (5).	**o'verblanket** *n* (4).	**overcarr'y** *vt* (1, *obs*), (2), (5).
over-absorp'tion *n* (5).	**overboil'** *vt*, *vi* (2), (5).	**overcau'tious** *adj* (5).
overabun'dance *n* (5).	**overbold'** *adj* (5).	**overclad'** *adj* (1), (5).
overabun'dant *adj* (5).	**overbold'ly** *adv* (5).	**overcol'our** *vt* (1), (5).
overac'tive *adj* (5).	**overbound'** *vt* (1).	**over-con'fidence** *n* (5).
overactiv'ity *n* (5).	**o'verbridge** *n* (1).	**over-con'fident** *adj* (5).
over-anxi'ety *n* (5).	**overbridge'** *vt* (1).	**overcook'** *vt* (5).
over-anx'ious *adj* (5).	**overbrim'** *vi* (2).	**overcooked'** *adj* (5).
over-anx'iously *adv* (5).	**overbrimmed'** (*Scott*) *adj* (1).	**over-cool'** *vt* (5).

vt **overcatch'** (*obs* or *dialect*) to overtake (*pa p* **over-caught'**). — *vt* **overcharge'** to charge too much; to load to excess. — Also *vi*. — *n* **o'vercharge**. — *n* **o'vercheck** a large prominent check pattern combined with a smaller; a cloth with such a pattern; a check-rein. — *vt* **overcloud'** to cover over with clouds; to fill with gloom, sadness or anxiety. — Also *vi*. — *vt* **overcloy'** to surfeit. — *vt* **over-club'** (*golf*) to hit (a shot) too far through using a club with insufficient loft. — Also *vi*. — *n* **o'vercoat** an outdoor coat worn over one's indoor clothes, a topcoat. — *n* **o'vercoating** cloth for overcoats. — *vt* **overcome'** to get the better of; to conquer or subdue; to surmount; to come over; to cover, over-spread (*archaic*). — *vi* to be victorious. — *n* (*Scot*) **o'ercome** or **owrecome** (*owr'kum*) a crossing over; a surplus, excess; a fit or sudden access of illness; a refrain, byword or recurring theme. — *vt* **overcom'pen-sate** to allow too much in compensation of. — *vi* to go too far in trying to correct a fault that one (believes one) suffers from (with *for*; *psychol*). — *n* **overcompen-sā'tion**. — *adj* **overcompen'satory**. — *vt* **overcorrect'** to apply so great a correction to as to deviate in the opposite way; to correct beyond achromatism, so that the red rays come to a focus nearer the lens than the violet (*optics*). — *n* **overcorrec'tion**. — *vt* **overcount'** to outnumber; to reckon too high; to overreach. — *vt* **o'vercrop** to take too much out of by cultivation. — *vt* **overcrow'** (*archaic* or *literary*; *Spenser* **overcraw'**, *Shakesp* **orecrowe'**) to crow or triumph over. — *vt* **overcrowd'** to crowd too many people, animals, etc into. — *adj* **overcrow'ded**. — *n* **overcrow'ding**. — *adj* **overdat'ed** out of date. — *adj* **over-deter'mined** too firmly resolved (to); too resolute or stubborn; having more than the necessary determining data or factors. — *vt* **overdevel'op** to develop too far; to leave (a film) too long in the developer (*photog*). — Also *vi*. — *adj* **overdight** (*-dīt'*; *Spenser*) dight or covered over; over-spread. — *vt* **overdo'** to do too much (**overdo it** or **things** to tire oneself out); to overact; to exaggerate; to carry too far; to harass or to fatigue; to cook too much; to use too much of; to excel. — *n* **overdo'er**. — *adj* **overdone'**. — *n* **overdo'sage**. — *n* **o'verdose** an excessive dose of drugs, medicine, etc. — *vt* and *vi* **overdose'**. — *n* **o'verdraft** the overdrawing of a bank account; an arrangement with a bank allowing a customer to take more money from his or her account than is in it; the excess of the amount drawn over the sum against which it is drawn (see also **overdraught**). — *n* **o'verdraught** (*-dräft*), (*US*) **o'verdraft**, a current of air passing over, or coming from above, a fire in a furnace, kiln, etc. — *vt* **overdraw'** to exaggerate in drawing, etc; to exaggerate in telling, etc; to draw from (one's bank account) beyond one's credit. — *vt* and *vi* **overdress'** to dress too ostentatiously or elaborately. — *vt* **overdrive'** to work (someone, or oneself) too hard; to drive too hard; to outdrive. — *n* **o'verdrive** a gearing device which transmits to the driving shaft a speed greater than engine crankshaft speed; too long a shot in tennis, golf, etc. — *adj* **over-drowsed'** (*Wordsworth* **o'er-drows'ed**) overcome by drowsiness. — *adj* **overdue'** (or *ō'vər-*) behind time for arrival; still unpaid after the time it is due. — *adj* **overear'nest** too earnest; severe in manner (*Shakesp*). — *vt* **overeat'** (often with *oneself*; also *vi*) to eat too much; *perh* to nibble all over, *perh* to surfeit on (*Shakesp*). — *vt* **overexpose'** to give too much publicity to; to expose (a film) to too much light. — *n* **overexpo'sure**. — *adj* **over-ex'quisite** (*Milton*) excessively exact in imagining details. — *vt* **overeye'** (*obs*) to survey, look upon; to watch. — *n* **o'verfall** a rippling or race of water, *esp* caused by an uneven river- or sea-bed; a sudden increase of depth; a place or structure for overflow of surplus waters; a waterfall or cataract in a river. — *vt* **overfall'** to fall on or over; to assail. — *adv* **overfar'** too far; to too great an extent (*Shakesp*). — *adj* **overfin'ished** (of cattle and sheep) having too much finish (qv). — *n* **o'verflight** a flight above and over. — *vt* **o'verflour'ish** to cover with blossom, or with flourishes or ornament. — *vt* **overflow'** to flow over (a bank, rim, etc); to flow over the edge of; to flow over the surface of; to flood; to flow over and beyond; to cause to run over; (of eg people) to fill and then spread beyond (eg a room): — *pa t* **overflowed'**; *pa p* **over-flowed'**, formerly **overflown'**. — *vi* to flow over an edge or limit; to abound (with *with*). — *n* **o'verflow** a flowing over; that which flows over (**overflow meeting** a supplementary meeting of those unable to find room in the main meeting); an excess number or quantity; the error which arises when a computer calculates a number which is too large for it to store (*comput*); a pipe or channel for spare water, etc; an inundation; a superabundance. — *adj* **overflow'ing** flowing over; running over; overfull; overabounding (with *with*); exuberant. Also *n*. — *adv* **overflow'ingly**. — *adj* **overflush'** too flush. — *n* **o'verflush** superfluity. — *vt* **overfly'** to outsoar; to fly over. — *n* **o'verfold** a fold tilted over so that the dip on both sides of the axis is in the same direction. — *vt* **overfold'** to fold over; to thrust into an overfold. — *adj* **overfond'** too fond (with *of*); foolish to excess (*obs*). — *vt* **overfreight'** to overload: — *pa p*, *adj* **overfraught'**. — *n* **o'verfreight** an excessive load. — *vt* **overgall'** to blister or inflame all over, or greatly. — *vt* **overgang'** (*Scot* and *NEng*; *Scot* **o'ergang** *owr-gang'*) to dominate; to overspread; to exceed. — *n* **o'vergarment** a garment worn on top of others. — *vt* **overget'** to overtake (*obs*); to get over, recover from (*dialect* or *archaic*): to overcome, possess the mind of (*dialect* or *literary*). — *vt* **overgive'** (*Spenser*) to give over or up. — *vt* **overglaze'** to glaze over; to cover speciously. — *n* **o'verglaze** an additional glaze given to porcelain, etc. — *adj* applied to, or suitable for painting on, a glazed surface. — *vt* **overgloom'** (*poetic*) to cover with gloom; to scowl over. — *vt* **overgo'** (chiefly *dialect* or *archaic*) to exceed; to surpass; to overpower; to go over; to pass over, traverse; to spread over; to pass over, forbear to speak of. — *vi* to go over; to pass on: — *pa t* **overwent'**. — *n* **overgo'ing** passing over; crossing, traversing; transgression. — *vt* and *vi* **overgrain'** in painting, to grain over (a surface already grained). — *n* **overgrain'er** a brush for overgraining. — *vt* **overgrass'** to grass over, conceal with grass. — *vt* **overgreen'** to cover with green or verdure; to conceal (*Shakesp*). — *adj* and *adv* **overground'** above ground. — *vt* **overgrow'** to grow beyond; to grow more than; to grow too great for; to rise above; to cover with growth. — *vi* to grow beyond the normal or suitable size. — *adj* **overgrown** (*ō'vər-grōn*, or *-grōn'*) grown beyond the natural size; covered over with uncontrolled vegetation, weeds, etc. — *n* **o'vergrowth** excessive or abnormally great growth; excess or superfluity resulting from growth; that which

overcov'er *vt* (6).	**overem'phasis** *n* (5).	**overexpos'ure** *n* (5).
overcredu'lity *n* (5).	**overem'phasize** or **-ise** *vt* (5).	**overextend'** *vt* (5), *vi* (5).
overcred'ulous *adj* (5).	**overes'timate** *vt* (5), *n* (5).	**overfall'** *vi* (3).
overdar'ing *adj* (5).	**overestima'tion** *n* (5).	**overfamil'iar** *adj* (5).
overdevel'opment *n* (5).	**over-exact'** *adj* (5).	**overfamiliar'ity** *n* (5).
overdram'atize or **-ise** *vt* (5).	**overexcitabil'ity** *n* (5).	**overfed'** *pa t*, *pa p* (5).
o'verdress *n* (4).	**overexcit'able** *adj* (5).	**overfeed'** *vt* (5), *vi* (5).
overdust' *vt* (1).	**overexcite'** *vt* (5).	**overfill'** *vt* (5), *vi* (5).
overdye' *vt* (1), (5).	**overexert'** *vt* (5).	**overfine'** *adj* (5).
over-emo'tional *adj* (5).	**overexer'tion** *n* (5).	**overfine'ness** *n* (5).

grows over and covers anything; growth of a crystal around another (*crystallog*). — *vt* **overhaile'** or **overhale'** to draw over (*Spenser*); to overtake, overpower (*obs*); to examine (*obs*). — *n* **o'verhair** the long hair overlying the fur of many animals. — *adv* **o'verhand** with hand above the object; palm downwards; with hand or arm raised above the shoulders or (in swimming) coming out of the water over the head; from below (*mineralogy*); with stitches passing through in one direction and back round the edges (*needlework*). — *adj* done or performed overhand (**overhand knot** the simplest of all knots, tied by passing the end over the standing part and through the bight). — *vt* to sew overhand. — *adj* and *adv* **overhand'ed** with hand above; with too many hands. — *adj* **overhand'led** (*Shakesp*) handled or discussed too much. — *vt* **overhang'** to hang over; to project over; to impend over; to cover with hangings. — *vi* to hang over, lean out beyond the vertical. — *n* **o'verhang** a projecting part; degree of projection. — *vt* **overhaul'** to examine thoroughly and repair where necessary; to turn over for examination; to haul or draw over; to overtake or gain upon (*naut*). — *n* **o'verhaul** a hauling over; a thorough examination, *esp* with a view to repair. — *adv* **overhead'** above one's head; aloft; in the zenith; in complete submergence; taking one with another, in the lump, on the average apiece (*Scot*). — *adj* **o'verhead** above one's head; well above ground level; (of a projector) designed to sit on a speaker's desk and project transparencies on a screen behind him or her; all-round, general, average. — *n* (*usu* in *pl*; also **overhead costs** or **charges**) the general expenses of a business, such as heating and lighting of premises, etc, as distinct from the direct cost of producing an article. — *vt* **overhear'** to hear without being meant to hear, as an eavesdropper does; to hear by accident, as an unintentional or unnoticed listener does; to hear over again or in turn (*Shakesp*). — *vt* **overheat'** to heat to excess; to overstimulate (the economy) with the risk of increasing inflation (*econ*). — *vi* to become too hot; (of the economy) to become overstimulated. — *vt* and *vi* to make or become agitated. — *n* **o'verheat** too great heat. — *n* **overheat'ing**. — *vt* **overhent'** (*Spenser*) to overtake: — *pa t* and *pa p* **overhent'**. — *vt* **overhit'** to hit (a ball, etc) beyond the intended target (also *vi*); to go beyond (the right, fitting or intended level, point, etc). — *vt* **overhold'** (*Shakesp*) to overvalue. — *adj* **overhung'** overhanging; suspended from above; covered over with hangings or hanging vegetation, etc. — *vt* **overinform'** to give an excessive amount of information to; to animate too much. — *n* **overinsur'ance**. — *vt* **overinsure'** to insure for more than the real value. — *vt* **overiss'ue** to issue in excess (eg bank-notes or bills of exchange). — *n* **o'verissue** excessive issue. — *vt* **overjoy'** (*rare*) to fill with great joy; to transport with delight or gladness. — *n* **o'verjoy** (*rare*) joy to excess, transport. — *adj* **overjoyed'**. — *vt* **overjump'** to jump (too far) over; to jump farther than; to pass over. — *vt* **overkest'** (*Spenser*) for **overcast** (*pa t* and *pa p*). — *n* **o'verkill** something, eg power for destruction, in excess of what is necessary or desirable. — *n* **o'verking** a king holding sovereignty over inferior kings. — *adj* **o'verknee** reaching above the knee. — *vt* **overla'bour** (*archaic*) to labour excessively over; to be too exact or meticulous with; to overwork. — *vt* **overlade'** to overburden: — *pa p* **overla'den**. — **overlaid** *pa p* of **overlay**. — **overlain** *pa p* of **overlie**. — *adj* **o'verland** passing entirely or principally by land. — *adv* **overland'** (or *ō'*) by or over land. — *vt* and *vi* (*Austr*) to drive (cattle) across country; to journey across country, *esp* a long way. — *n* **o'verlander** (or *-land'*). — *vt* **overlap'** to extend over and beyond the edge of; to reach from beyond, across the edge, and partly rest on or cover; to coincide in part with; to ripple over (*poetic*). — *vi* (*Soccer*, *Rugby*, etc) to advance down the flank as an attacking manoeuvre. — *n* **o'verlap** an overlapping part or situation; a disposition of strata where the upper beds extend beyond the boundary of the lower beds of the same series (*geol*). — *vt* **overlard'** to smear over as with lard; to overload with fulsome expressions, eg of praise. — *vt* **overlaunch'** to join by long splices or scarfs (*shipbuilding*). — *vt* **overlay'** to cover by laying or spreading something over; to cover to excess, encumber; by confusion, to overlie; to put an overlay or overlays on (*printing*); to lay or place as a covering (*rare*); to span (*Milton*). — *pa t* and *pa p* **overlaid'**. — *n* **o'verlay** a covering; anything laid on or over to alter the appearance; a piece of paper pasted on the impression-surface of a printing-press, so as to increase the impression in a place where it is too faint; in artwork, a transparent sheet on which is drawn one element of the whole design, which is laid on top of another sheet or sheets to present the complete design; a large cravat (*Scot*; often **o'er'lay** or **owre'lay**). — *n* **overlay'ing** a superficial covering; something which overlays; plating. — *adv* **overleaf'** on the other side of the leaf of a book. — *vt* **overleap'** (*Scot* **owerloup'**) to leap over; to pass over without notice (**overleap oneself** to leap too far). — *n* **o'verleather** (*Shakesp*) the upper part of a shoe. — *vi* **overlend'** to lend too much. — *adj* **overlent'**. — *vt* **overlie'** to lie above or upon; to smother by lying on: — *pr p* **overly'ing**; *pa t* **overlay'**; *pa p* **overlain'**. — *n* **o'verlier** (or *-lī'*). — *vt* **overlive** (*-liv'*) to survive; to outlive; (*reflexive*) to outlast one's usefulness or time of vigour; (*reflexive*) to live too intensely, exhaust (oneself). — *vi* to survive; to live too long; to live too fast, or so as prematurely to exhaust oneself; to live on too high a standard of luxury. — *vt* **overload'** to load too heavily or fill too full. — *n* (*ō'*) an excessive load. — *vt* and *vi* **o'verlock** to oversew (a fabric edge, hem, seam, etc) with an interlocking stitch to prevent fraying. — *n* **o'verlocker** a person who or machine which does this. — *n* **o'verlocking** the process of doing this, or the stitching produced. — *vt* **overlook'** to look over; to see, or give a view of, from above; to view carefully; to oversee, superintend; to fail to notice or take into account; to allow (a misdemeanour, etc) to go unpunished; to slight; to bewitch by looking upon with the evil eye. — *n* **overlook'er**. — *n* **o'verlord** a supreme lord; a feudal superior; (with *cap*) the operational name for the Anglo-American invasion (1944) of Normandy in World War II. — *vt* **overlord'**. — *n* **o'verlordship**. — *adv* **overly** see under **over**. — *adj* **overly'ing** lying on the top. — *n* **o'verman** an overseer in mining, the man in charge of work below ground; Nietzsche's term for a superman. — *vt* **overman'** to supply (a ship) with too large a crew; to employ uneconomically large numbers of workers in (an industry, etc). — *n* **o'vermantel** an ornamental structure, often with a mirror, set on a mantel-shelf. — *vt*

overfish' *vt* (5).	**overfund'** *vt* (5).	**overhast'ily** *adv* (5).
overfond'ly *adv* (5).	**overfun'ding** *n* (5).	**overhast'iness** *n* (5).
overfond'ness *n* (5).	**overglance'** *vt* (1).	**overhast'y** *adj* (5).
overfor'ward *adj* (5).	**overgorge'** (*Shakesp*) *vt* (5).	**overhype'** *vt* (5).
overfor'wardness *n* (5).	**overgraze'** *vt* (5), *vi* (5).	**overinclined'** *adj* (5).
overfree' *adj* (5).	**overgrā'zing** *n* (5).	**overindulge'** *vt* (5).
overfree'dom *n* (5).	**o'vergreat** *adj* (5).	**overindul'gence** *n* (5).
overfree'ly *adv* (5).	**overgreed'y** *adj* (5).	**overindul'gent** *adj* (5).
overfull' *adj* (5).	**overhapp'y** *adj* (5).	**overinked'** *adj* (5).
overful(l)'ness *n* (5).	**overhaste'** *n* (5).	**overkeep'** *vt* (5).

overmast' (*naut*) to provide with too long or too heavy a mast or masts. — *vt* **overmas'ter** to gain or have the mastery of; to overpower; to dominate. — *vt* **overmatch'** (*esp US*) to be more than a match for; to match with a superior opponent; to defeat, overcome. — *n* **o'vermatch** someone who is more than a match; a match in which one player, etc, is superior; an overmatching. — *n* **o'vermatter** (*printing*) overset type matter, ie text that has been typeset but cannot be printed because of shortage of space. — *n* **overmeas'ure** (or *ō'*) something given over the proper measure. — *vt* (*-mezh'*) to measure above the true value. — *adj* **overmerr'y** extremely merry. — *vt* **overmount'** to rise above; to excel in mounting. — *vi* to mount too high. — *adj* and *adv* **o'vermuch** (or *-much'*) too much. — *vi* **overmul'tiply** to become too numerous. — *n* **overmultiplicā'tion**. — *vt* **overmult'itude** (*Milton*) to outnumber. — *vt* **overname'** (*Shakesp*) to repeat the names of. — *vt* **overnet'** to cover with a net; to overfish with nets. — *adj* **overnice'** too fastidious. — *adv* **overnice'ly**. — *n* **overnice'ness**. — *n* **o'vernight** (*Shakesp*; now chiefly *US*) the evening just past. — *adv* **overnight'** for the duration of the night, till the next morning during the night; in the course of the night; hence, extraordinarily quickly; on the evening of the day just past. — *adj* done or occurring or existing overnight; for the time from evening till next morning. — *n* **overnight bag** or **case** a small case for carrying the clothes, toilet articles, etc, needed for an overnight stay . — *n* **o'vernighter** a person stayling overnight; an overnight bag. — *vt* **overoff'ice** (*Shakesp* **o're-office**) *appar*, to lord it over by virtue of office, or perhaps to exercise one's office over. — *adv* **overpage'** overleaf. — *vt* **overpaint'** to put too much paint on; to depict with exaggeration. — *vt* **overpart'** in acting, to assign too difficult a part to. — *vt* **overpass'** to pass over; to pass by without notice; to exceed. — *vi* to pass over; to elapse. — *n* (*ō'-*) a road bridging another road or railway, canal, etc, a flyover. — *adj* **overpast'** over; at an end. — *vt* **overpay'** to pay too much; to be more than an ample reward for. — *n* **overpay'ment**. — *vi* **overped'al** to make excessive use of the sustaining pedal of a piano. — *vt* **overpeer'** (partly from **peer**[1], partly **peer**[2]; *Shakesp*) to peer over or down upon; to look down on; to tower over; to excel. — *vt* **overperch'** (*Shakesp* **orepearch'**) to fly up and perch on, fly over. — *vt* **overpersuade'** to persuade (someone) against his or her inclination. — *vt* **overpic'ture** to surpass pictorially; to cover with pictures. — *vt* **overpitch'** to bowl (the ball) so that its trajectory would bring it too close to the stumps (*cricket*); to pitch too far, or beyond the best distance. — *adj* **overpitched'** (of a roof) steeply pitched; (of a cricket ball) bowled so that it pitches too near the stumps. — *adj* **overplaced'** (*Spenser* **overplast**, *-pläst'*) placed above. — *vt* **overplay'** to overemphasize the importance or value of; to play better than (one's opponent); to try to gain more from (one's assets or advantages) than they can be expected to yield (**overplay one's hand** to overreach oneself in pressing one's advantage). — *vt* and *vi* to exaggerate (an emotion, acting rôle, etc); to hit the ball beyond (the green) (*golf*). — *n* **o'verplay**. — *n* **o'verplus** that which is more than enough; surplus. — *adj* surplus. — *vt* **overply'** to ply beyond what can be borne or sustained. — *vt* **overpoise'** to outweigh. — *n* **o'verpoise** a weight sufficient to weigh another down. — *vt* **overpost'** (*obs*) to hasten over quickly. — *vt* **overpow'er** to overcome or reduce to helplessness, by force; to subdue; to overwhelm; to make (an engine, etc) too powerful. — *adj* **overpow'ering** excessive in degree or amount; irresistible. — *adv* **overpow'eringly**. — *vt* **overpress'** to oppress; to burden too heavily; to press unduly; to put too much pressure on. — *n* **overpress'ure** excessive pressure, *esp* of work. — *vt* **overprice'** to ask too high a price for. — *adj* **overpriced'**. — *vt* **overprint'** to print too strongly or dark; to print too many copies of; to print over already printed matter (*esp* a postage stamp). — *n* **o'verprint** an offprint; something which is printed over an already printed surface, as on a postage stamp. — *vt* **overprize'** to value too highly; to surpass in value (*obs*). — *vt* and *vi* **overproduce'**. — *n* **overproduc'tion** excessive production; production in excess of the demand. — *adj* **overproof'** (or *ō'*) containing more alcohol than proof-spirit does. — *adj* **overqual'ified** having qualifications and skills in excess of those required for a particular job, etc. — *vt* **overrack'** to overstrain. — *vt* **overrake'** to sweep over. — *adj* **overrank'** too rank or luxurious. — *vt* **overrate'** to give too high a value to, think too highly of. — *n* **over rate** (*cricket*) see under **over**. — *vt* **overreach'** to reach or extend beyond; to overtake; to outwit or get the better of; (*reflexive*) to undo oneself by attempting too much, venturing too far, trying to be too clever, etc. — *vi* (of a horse) to strike the hindfoot against the forefoot: — *pa t* and *pa p* **overreached'**; *archaic* **overraught'**. — *n* **o'verreach** the act of over-reaching; the injury thereby done. — *vi* **overreact'** to react or respond with too much vehemence, or otherwise excessively. — *n* **overreac'tion**. — *vt* **overread** (*-rēd'*) to read over. — *adj* **overread** (*-red'*) having read too much. — *vt* and *vi* **overreck'on** to compute too highly. — *vt* **overred'** (*Shakesp*) to cover with a red colour. — *vt* **overren'** an archaic form of **overrun**. — *vt* **override'** to pass over; to overlap; to set aside; to be valid against; to be more important than, prevail over; to injure or exhaust by too much riding; to ride over; to trample down on horseback; to slide or mount on the top or back of; to outride, overtake (*obs*): — *pa t* **overrode'**; *pa p* **overridd'en**. — *n* **o'verride** an auxiliary (*esp* manual) control capable of temporarily prevailing over the operation of another (*esp* automatic) control. — *n* **o'verrider** an attachment on the bumper of a motor vehicle to prevent another bumper becoming interlocked with it. — *adj* **overrid'ing** dominant, stronger than anything else. — *vt* and *vi* **overruff'** (*cards*) to trump with a higher trump. — *n* **o'verruff** an act of overruffing. — *vt* **overrule'** to modify or to set aside by greater power; to prevail over the will of, against a previous decision of; to impose an overriding decision upon; to prevail over and set aside; to annul, declare invalid (*law*); to rule against; to disallow; to rule over (*obs*). — *vi* to prevail. — *n* **overrul'er**. — *n* **overrul'ing** (*law*) the process by which a precedent is overruled and superseded by a statute or a superior court. — *adj* dominating. — *vt* **overrun'** to spread over; to flow over; to grow over; to infest or swarm over; to infect widely; to spread over and take possession of; to run beyond; to exceed the limit of; to carry beyond a limit; to carry over into another line or page; to adjust the type of by overrunning (*printing*); to run over, across, through, all about; to run over, crush underfoot

overkind' *adj* (5).	**overpopulā'tion** *n* (5).	**overrash'ly** *adv* (5).
overkind'ness *n* (5).	**overpraise'** *vt* (5).	**overrash'ness** *n* (5).
overleav'en *vt* (5).	**overpraise'** (or **ō'**) *n* (5).	**overrate'** *vt* (2).
overlong' *adj* (5), *adv* (5).	**over-precise'** *adj* (5).	**o'verrate** *n* (2).
overloud' *adj* (5).	**overpreparā'tion** *n* (5).	**over-refine'** *vt* (5).
overlus'ty (*Shakesp*) *adj* (5).	**overprepare'** *vi* (5), *vt* (5).	**over-refine'ment** *n* (5).
overneat *adj* (5).	**overprepared'** *adj* (5).	**over-rev'** *vt* (5), *vi* (5).
overpaint' *vt* (1), (5).	**overprotec'tive** *adj* (5).	**overripe'** *adj* (5).
overpeo'ple *vt* (5).	**overproud'** *adj* (5).	**overri'pen** *vt*, *vi* (5).
overpop'ulate *vt* (5).	**overrash'** *adj* (5).	**overripe'ness** *n* (5).

or under wheel; to outdo in running (*rare*); to escape from by running faster (*dialect*); (*reflexive*) to injure or exhaust oneself by too much running. — *vi* to run over, overflow; to run beyond a limit; (of a vehicle engine) to slow down in response to a reverse torque transmitted through the gears from the wheels (**overrun the constable** see **outrun**): — *prp* **overrunn'ing**; *pa t* **overran'**; *pa p* **overrun'** — *n* **o'verrun** an act or occasion of overrunning; the extent of overrunning; an overrunning of type (*printing*); the overrunning of a vehicle engine (**overrun brake** a brake fitted to a trailer that prevents it from travelling faster than the towing vehicle when reducing speed or going downhill). — *n* **overrunn'er**. — *vi* **oversail'** (Fr *saillir* to project) to project. — *n* **o'versail** projection. — *vt* **overscore'** to score or draw lines across; to obliterate in this way. — *adj* **overscutched** (*-skucht'*, *-skuch'id*; *Scott*) worn out (after Shakesp, 2 *Henry IV* III. 2, where **overschutcht** is variously conjectured to mean overworn in service or whipped at the cart's tail). — *adj* **o'versea** or **o'verseas** across, beyond or from beyond the sea. — *adv* **overseas'** or (*rare*) **oversea'** in or to lands beyond the sea; abroad. — *n* **overseas'** foreign lands. — *vt* **oversee'** to superintend; to overlook, disregard; to see without being meant to see; to see or look over. — *adj* **overseen'** (*obs*) mistaken or ill-advised; drunk; versed (in). — *n* **o'verseer** (*-sēr*, *-sē-ər*) a person who oversees workmen, etc; a superintendent; formerly, an officer having care of the poor, and other duties; the manager of a plantation of slaves (*hist*); a critic or editor (*obs*). — *vt* and *vi* **oversell'** to sell more of than is available; to exaggerate the merits of; to sell for too high a price: — *adj* **oversold'**. — *vt* and *vi* **overset'** to upset; to disorder; to set more type or copy than there is space available for (*printing*); to oppress, press hard (*obs*). — *vt* **o'versew** (or *-sō'*) to sew (an edge or edges) overhand. — *vt* **overshade'** to throw a shade or shadow over; to darken. — *vt* **overshad'ow** to throw a shadow over; to cast into the shade by surpassing, to outshine; to darken; to shelter or protect. — *vt* **overshine'** (*Shakesp*) to shine over or upon, illumine; to outshine. — *n* **o'vershoe** a shoe, *esp* of waterproof material, worn over one's shoes to protect them. — *adv* **over-shoe'** or **over-shoes'** deep enough to cover the shoes. — *vt* **overshoot'** to shoot over or beyond (one's target); to pass beyond, exceed, fail to stop at (**overshoot oneself**, to venture too far, to overreach oneself); (of a train or aircraft) to fail to come to a halt at (a station) or on (a runway); to shoot, dart, or fly across overhead; to surpass in shooting; to injure or exhaust by too much shooting; to shoot with colour over the surface of. — Also *vi*: — *pa t* and *pa p* **overshot'**. — *n* **o'vershoot**. — *adj* **overshot'** shot over; too much shot over; surpassed; overdone; in error by overshooting the mark; drunk (*obs slang*). — *adj* **o'vershot** having the upper jaw protruding beyond the lower; (of a waterwheel) fed from above. — *vt* **overshow'er** to shower over. — *adj* **o'verside** acting or done over the side. — *adv* **overside'** over the side. — *prep* (*Spenser* **over side**) over the side of. — *n* **o'versight** a failure to notice; a mistake; an omission; supervision. — *vt* **oversize'** to cover with size. — *n* **o'versize** a large or larger size. — *adj* **o'versize** or **o'versized** (or *-sīzd'*) very large, or larger than normal. — *vt* **overskip'** to skip, leap or pass over; to overlook; to omit. — *n* **overslaugh** (*ō'vər-slö*; Du *overslaan* to miss or skip over; *military*) exemption from duty in turn when employed on something else; a sand-bar (*US*). — *vt* **overslaugh'** to remit or pass over by overslaugh; to pass over in favour of another (*US*); to hinder. — *vt* **oversleep'** to indulge (oneself) in sleeping too long; to sleep beyond. — *vi* to sleep too long. — *vt* **overslip'** to slip by; to escape the notice of; to slip unnoticed from; to let slip. — *vi* to slip by; to make a slip or error inadvertently. — *n* **o'verslip** (*obs*) an inadvertency; a close-fitting under-bodice. — *n* **o'versman** an overseer (*archaic*); an umpire (*Scot*). — *adj* **oversold** see **oversell**. — *n* **o'versoul** Emerson's term for the divine principle forming the spiritual unity of all being. — *vt* **oversow'** to sow after something has been already sown; to sow over. — *vt* **overspend'** to spend beyond (one's income, budget, etc); to exhaust or cripple (oneself) by spending. — *vi* to spend too much. — *n* an instance of overspending; the amount by which an allocated budget, etc, is overspent. — *adj* **overspent'** excessively fatigued. — *n* **o'verspill** something, or an amount, which is spilt over; a proportion of the population that leaves a district, displaced by changes in housing, etc; (in a public bar) beer, etc that overflows from a glass as it is being filled. — *n* **o'verspin** the spinning of a flying ball in the same direction as if it were rolling on the ground. — *vt* **overstaff'** to provide too many people as staff for. — *vt* **overstand'** (*archaic*) to out-stay. — *vt* **overstare'** (*Shakesp* **ore-stare'**) to outstare. — *vt* **overstate'** to state too strongly; to exaggerate. — *n* **overstate'ment**. — *vt* **overstay'** to stay beyond (a time limit). — *n* **overstay'er** an immigrant worker who stays beyond the time allowed by his or her work permit. — *vi* **o'versteer** (of a motor-car) to exaggerate the degree of turning applied by the steering-wheel. — *n* the tendency to do this. — *vt* **overstep'** to step beyond; to exceed; to transgress. — *n* **o'verstep** (*geol*) the transgression of an overlapping stratum over the edges of underlying unconformable strata. — *vt* **overstink'** to stink more than: — *pa t* **overstunk'**; *Shakesp* **orestunck'**. — *vt* and *vi* **overstrain'** to strain too much; to strain beyond the elastic limit. — *n* **o'verstrain** too great strain. — *adj* **overstrained'** strained to excess; exaggerated. — *vt* **overstretch'** to stretch to excess; to exaggerate. — *vt* **overstride'** to stride across; to stand astride of. — *vt* **overstrike'** to strike with a downward blow; to superimpose a new design on (a coin); to type on top of (a character already typed): — *pa t* **overstruck'**; *Spenser* **overstrooke'**. — *adj* **overstrung'** too highly strung; (of a piano) having two sets of strings crossing obliquely to save space. — *adj* **o'verstuffed** covered completely with well-stuffed upholstery. — *vt* **oversubscribe'** to subscribe for (eg shares) beyond the number offered. — *n* **oversubscrip'tion**. — *vt* **oversway'** (*rare*) to overrule; to bear down. — *vt* **overswear'** (*rare*) to swear anew. — *vt* and *vi* **overswell'** to overflow. — *vt* **overswim'** to swim across. — *vt* **overtake'** to draw level with and move past (something or someone travelling in the same direction); to catch up with; to manage to get done, put behind one; to catch; to come upon abruptly, as in *overtaken by darkness* or *disaster*; to take by surprise. — *adj* **overtā'ken** (*dialect*) fuddled. — *vt* **overtalk'** to talk over. — *vt* **overtask'** to impose too many tasks on; to impose too heavy a task on. — *vt* **overtax'** to tax excessively; to require too much of. — *vi* **overteem'** to teem, breed or produce in excess. — *vt* to exhaust or wear out by breeding. — *vt* **overthrow'** to throw over, overturn, upset; to ruin, subvert; to defeat utterly; to throw too far or too strongly. — *vi* (*obs*) to be overturned; to throw too far. — *n* **o'verthrow** the act of overthrowing or state of being overthrown; a ball missed at the wicket and returned from the field (*cricket*); a run scored in consequence. — *n* **overthrow'er**. — *n* **o'verthrust** (or **overthrust fault**; *geol*) a fault at a low angle from the horizontal in which the rocks on the upper side of the fault plane have moved

overroast' *vt* (5).	**oversim'plify** *vt* (5).	**overstain'** *vt* (1).
overscru'pulous *adj* (5).	**o'verskirt** *n* (4).	**overstock'** *vt* (5).
overscrup'ulousness *n* (5).	**o'versleeve** *n* (4).	**o'verstock** *n* (5).
oversexed' *adj* (5).	**overspec'ialize** or **-ise** *vi* (5).	**overstress'** *vt* (5).
o'vershirt *n* (4).	**overspecializā'tion** or **-s-** *n* (5).	**o'verstress** *n* (5).
oversimplificā'tion *n* (5).	**overspread'** *vt* (1).	**overstrew'** *vt* (1).

upwards in relation to the rocks on the lower side of the fault plane. — *vt* **overthwart'** (*obs*) to lie athwart; to cross. — *adj* opposite, transverse; contrary, perverse. — *adv* crosswise; opposite. — *prep* across, on the other side of. — *n* **o'vertime** time spent in working beyond the regular hours; work done in such time; pay for such work; in N America, same as **extra time** (*sport*). — *adj* and *adv* during, for or concerning such time. — *vt* (*ō-vər-tīm'*) to exceed the correct allowance of time for (a photographic exposure, etc). — *adj* and *adv* **overtime'ly** (*obs*) too early, untimely. — *n* **o'vertimer** a person who works overtime. — *n* **o'vertone** a harmonic or upper partial (*music*); (in *pl*) a subtle meaning, additional to the main meaning, conveyed by a word or statement; (in *pl*) an implicit quality, or constant association. — *vt* **overtop'** to rise over the top of; to be higher than; to surpass; to exceed. — *vi* to rise too high. — *vt* **overtow'er** to tower above. — *vi* to soar too high. — *vi* **over-trade'** to trade excessively or beyond capital; to buy in more than can be sold or paid for. — *vt* to involve in trade in such a way. — *n* **over-trad'ing**. — *vt* **overtrain'** to train so far as to do harm; to train too high. — *n* **o'vertrick** (*bridge*) a trick in excess of those contracted for. — *vt* **overtrip'** (*obs*) to trip nimbly over. — *vt* **overtrump'** to trump with a higher card than the trump already played. — *vt* **overturn'** to throw down or over; to upset; to subvert. — *n* **o'verturn** an overturning; a turnover. — *n* **overturn'er**. — *n* **overuse'** excessive use (**overuse syndrome** a condition of muscular strain found among musicians, formerly known as *musicians' cramp*). — *n* **overvaluā'tion**. — *n* **o'vervalue**. — *vt* **overval'ue** to set too high a value on. — *vt* **overveil'** to veil over or cover. — *n* **o'verview** a general survey; an inspection (*Shakesp*). — *n* **o'verwash** a washing over; material carried by glacier-streams over a frontal moraine (*geol*). — Also *adj*. — *vt* **overwatch'** to watch over; to watch through; to overcome with long watching. — *vt* **overwear'** to wear out; to outwear, outlive: — *pa t* **overwore'**; *pa p* **overworn'** (see below). — *vt* **overwear'y** to overcome with weariness, exhaust. — *adj* excessively weary. — *vt* **overweath'er** (*Shakesp*) to batter by violence of weather. — *vi* **overween'** (*archaic*) to expect too much; to be presumptuous or arrogant. — *vt* (*reflexive*) to think too highly of (oneself). — *adj* and *n* **overween'ing** (of a person) arrogant, conceited; (of pride) inflated, excessive, immoderate. — *vt* **overweigh'** to be heavier than; to outweigh; to weigh down. — *n* **o'verweight** weight beyond what is required or what is allowed; preponderance. — *adj* **overweight'** above the weight required; above the ideal or desired weight. — *vt* **overweight'** to weigh down; to put too heavy a burden on. — *adj* **over-weight'ed** not fairly balanced in presentation. — *pa t* **overwent'** see **overgo**. — *vt* **overwhelm'** to crush completely with something heavy or strong; to flow over; to bear down; to reduce to helplessness; to overpower; to affect overpoweringly; to defeat utterly, *usu* with superior numbers; to inundate or submerge, *esp* suddenly; to overhang (*obs*). — *n* and *adj* **overwhel'ming**. — *adv* **overwhel'mingly**. — *vt* **overwind** (*-wīnd'*) to wind too far: — *pa t* and *pa p* **overwound'**. — *vt* **overwing'** to fly over; to outflank (*obs*). — *vi* **overwin'ter** to pass the winter. — *vt* and *vi* to keep (animals, plants, etc) alive or to stay alive through the winter. — *adj* **overwise'** too wise; affectedly wise; wise in one's own estimation. — *adv* **overwise'ly**. — *n* **o'verword** or (*archaic*) **o'erword** (*ōr'*, *ör'*, *Scot owr'*; also **owre'word**) the refrain of a song; a habitual saying. — *vt* and *vi* **overwork'** to work too hard: — *pa t* and *pa p* **overworked'** or **overwrought'**. — *n* **o'verwork** additional work; (**overwork'**) excessive work. — *adj* **overworn'** (*-wōrn'*, *-wörn'*) worn out; subdued by toil; spoiled by use; threadbare; trite; exhausted of meaning or freshness by excessive use; out of date; spent or past. — *pa t* and *pa p* **overwound'** see **overwind**. — *vt* **overwrest'** to overstrain. — *vt* **overwrest'le** (*Spenser*) to overcome by wrestling. — *vt* **overwrite'** to write too much about; to write in a laboured manner; to cover over with writing or other writing; to superscribe; to exhaust by writing too much. — *vi* to write too much or in too contrived a manner. — *adj* **overwrought'** (see also **overwork**) worked too hard; too highly excited; in an over-emotional state; with highly strained nerves; worked or embellished all over; overdone, too elaborate. — *vt* **overyear'** (*obs*) to keep into a second or later year. — *adj* (*dialect*) kept from one year to the next. — *adv* (*dialect*) till next year.

overachieve ... to ... overswim. See under **over-**.

overt *ō'vûrt*, *ō-vûrt'*, *adj* open to view, not concealed; public; evident. — *adv* **overtly**. — **overt act** something obviously done in execution of a criminal intent. — **market overt** open or public market. [Fr *ouvert*, pa p of *ouvrir* to open]

overtake ... to ... overtrump. See under **over-**.

overture *o'vər-tūr*, *n* an instrumental prelude to an opera, oratorio, etc; a one-movement musical composition in similar style (sonata form); (*usu* in *pl*) an introductory proposition or opening move to negotiations, etc; an offer or proposal; an opening or opportunity; an opening or beginning; the method in the Presbyterian church of beginning legislation and maturing opinion by sending some proposition from the inferior courts to the General Assembly, and *vice versa*; also the proposal so sent; an opening up or disclosure (*Shakesp*); an open place (*Spenser*); an opening or aperture (*obs*). — *vt* to lay a proposal before; to put forward as an overture. [OFr *overture* (Fr *ouverture*) opening]

overturn ... to ... overyear. See under **over-**.

ovi- *ov-i-*, *ō-vi-*, or **ovo-** *-vō*, *-və-*, *combining form* denoting egg; ovum. — *n* **oviduct** (*ō'vi-dukt*; see **duct**; *zool*) the tube by which the egg escapes from the ovary. — *adj* **ovidū'cal** or **oviduc'tal**. — *adj* **oviferous** (*ō-vif'ə-rəs*; L *ferre* to bear) egg-carrying. — *adj* **oviform** (*ō'vi-förm*) egg-shaped. — *adj* **ovigerous** (*ōv-ij'ə-rəs*; L *gerere* to carry) egg-carrying. — *adj* **oviparous** (*ō-vip'ə-rəs*; L *parere* to bring forth) egg-laying. — *n* **ovipar'ity** (*-par'i-ti*). — *adv* **ovip'arously**. — *vi* **ovipos'it** to deposit eggs with an ovipositor. — *n* **oviposition** (*-pə-zish'ən*). — *n* **ovipositor** (*ō-vi-poz'i-tər*; L *positor*, from *pōnere* to place) an egg-laying organ in female insects and some female fishes. — *n* **ovisac** (*ōv'i-sak*; L *saccus*; see **sac**) a brood-pouch; an egg-capsule. — *n* **ovotest'is** (*pl* **ovotest'es** *-tēz*) an organ which produces both ova and spermatozoa. — *adj* **ovoviviparous** (*ō-vō-vi-vip'ə-rəs*, or *-vī-vip'*; L *vīvus* living, and *parere* to bring forth) (of certain reptiles and fishes) producing eggs which are hatched in the body of the parent. [L *ōvum* egg]

ovibos *ōv'i-bos*, *ov'i-bōs*, *n* the musk-ox. — *adj* **ovibō'vīne**. [L *ovis* sheep, and *bōs*, *bovis* ox]

ovicide *ō'vi-sīd*, (*facetious*) *n* sheep-killing. [L *ovis* sheep, and *caedere* to kill]

Ovidian *ō-vid'i-ən*, or *o-*, *adj* of, like or relating to the Latin poet *Ovid* (43 BC–AD 17).

oviform[1] *ov'i-förm*, *ō'vi-*, *adj* like a sheep; ovine. — *adj* **ovine** (*ō'vīn*) of or relating to sheep; sheep-like. [L *ovis* sheep, and **-form**]

oviform[2], **ovigerous**. See under **ovi-**.

ovine. See under **oviform**[1].

overstrong' *adj* (5).	**oversupply'** *vt* (5).	**overtrust'** *vi* (5).
overstud'y *vt* (5), *vi* (5).	**o'versupply** *n* (5).	**o'vertrust** *n* (5).
o'verstudy *n* (5).	**overte'dious** (*Shakesp*) *adj* (5).	**overuse'** *vt* (5).
overstuff' *vt* (5).	**overtire'** *vt* (5).	**overvi'olent** *adj* (5).
oversubt'le *adj* (5).	**overtoil'** *vt* (5).	**over-zeal'ous** *adj* (5).
oversubt'lety *n* (5).		

oviparous, ovipositor. See under **ovi-**.
ovist *ō'vist*, *n* a believer in the doctrine that the ovum contains all future generations in germ. [L *ōvum* egg]
ovo-. See under **ovi-**.
ovoid *ō'void*, *adj* (of a solid or plane figure) egg-shaped; egg-shaped and attached by the broad end (*bot*). — *n* an egg-shaped figure or body. — *adj* **ovoid'al** ovoid. [L *ōvum* egg, and **-oid**]
ovolo *ō'və-lō*, (*archit*) *n* a moulding with the rounded part composed of a quarter of a circle, or of an arc of an ellipse with the curve greatest at the top: — *pl* **ō'voli** (*-lē*). [Ital dimin, from L *ōvum* egg]
ovotestis, ovoviviparous. See under **ovi-**.
ovular. See under **ovule**.
ovulate *ov'ūl-āt*, *ōv'-*, *vi* to release ova from the ovary; to form ova. — *n* **ovulā'tion**. [From **ovule**]
ovule *ōv'ūl*, *ov'*, *n* in flowering plants, the body containing the egg cell, which on fertilization becomes the seed, consisting of the nucellus and its integuments with the embryo-sac (megaspore); an unfertilized ovum (*zool*). — **ov'ular** of or pertaining to an ovule. — *adj* **ōvulif'erous** carrying ovules. [Med L *ōvulum*, dimin of *ōvum* egg]
ovum *ō'vəm*, *n* an egg; the egg cell, or female gamete (*biol*): — *pl* **o'va**. [L *ōvum* egg]
ow[1]. Same as **ou**.
ow[2] *ow*, *interj* expressive of pain. [Spontaneous utterance]
owche *owch*, *n*. Same as **ouch**[1].
owe *ō*, *vt* to be indebted for; to be under an obligation to repay or render; to feel as a debt or as due; to have to thank; to bear (a person a grudge); to concede or be bound to concede as a handicap; to own (*obs* or *dialect*). — *vi* to be in debt: — *pa t* and *pa p* **owed**. — The old *pa t* **ought** and *pa p* **own**, now differently used, are given separately; see also **owing**. [OE *āgan* to own, possess, present indicative *āh*, preterite *āhte*, pa p *āgen*; ON *eiga*, OHGer *eigan* to possess]
owelty *ō'əl-ti*, (*law*) *n* equality. [Anglo-Fr *owelté*, from L *aequālitās*, *-ātis*]
Owenite *ō'in-īt*, *n* a disciple of Robert *Owen* (1771–1858), British social reformer, who proposed to establish society on a basis of socialistic co-operation; a follower of the ideas and leadership of David *Owen*, British politician and co-founder of the British Social Democratic Party (1981). — *adj* **Owenian** (*ō-ēn'i-ən*). — *n* **Ow'enism**. — *n* **Ow'enist**.
ower Scots form of **over**. For compounds see under **over-**.
owing *ō'ing*, *adj* due; to be paid; imputable. — **owing to** because of; in consequence of. [**owe**]
owl *owl*, *n* any member of the Strigiformes, nocturnal predacious birds with large broad heads, flat faces, large eyes surrounded by discs of feathers, short hooked beaks, silent flight, and howling or hooting cry; someone who sits up at night (also **night'-owl**); someone who sees badly or who avoids light; a solemn person; an owl-like breed of pigeon; a wiseacre; a dullard. — *vi* to behave like an owl. — *vt* (*hist*) to smuggle (*esp* wool or sheep from England to France). — *n* **owl'er** (*obs*) a smuggler (*esp* of wool or sheep). — *n* **owl'ery** a place inhabited or frequented by owls; owlishness (*Carlyle*). — *n* **owl'et** a young owl; an owl; a moth of the Noctuidae. — *adj* **owl'ish** like an owl; solemn, *esp* if also bespectacled; blinking; stupid; dull-looking. — *n* **owl'ishness**. — *adj* **owl'y** owlish. — *adj* **owl'-like**. — **owl'-car** (*old US*) a night tram-car. — *adj* **owl'-eyed** having blinking eyes like an owl. — **Owl'glass, Owle'-glass, Howle'glass** or **Owl'spiegle** *Tyll Eulenspiegel*, a mischievous clown hero of a folk-tale popular in Germany from the 16c or earlier; **owl'-light** (*poetic*) dusk, twilight; **owl'-moth** a gigantic S American moth of the Noctuidae; **owl'-parr'ot** the kakapo; **owl'-train** (*old US*) a night train. [OE *ūle*; Ger *Eule*, L *ulula*; imit]
own[1] *ōn*, *vt* to possess, have belonging to one; to acknowledge as one's own; to confess; to allow to be true; to admit, concede; to acknowledge, recognize; to claim as one's own (*obs*). — *vi* to confess (with *to*). — *n* **own'er** a possessor, proprietor; a captain of a warship (*slang*). — *adj* **own'erless**. — *n* **own'ership**. — **own'er-dri'ver** someone who drives his or her own car; **own'er-occupa'tion**. — *adj* **own'er-occ'upied**. — **own'er-occ'upier** a person who owns the house in which he or she lives; **owner's equity** the investment by an owner in his or her business. — **own up** to confess (often with *to*). [OE *āgnian*, from *āgen* one's own; cf **own**[2]]
own[2] *ōn*, *adj* and *pronoun* (preceded by *possessive adj* or *possessive case*) belonging to oneself and no-one else; often used with reflexive force (*my own, his own*, etc) serving instead of a genitive to *myself, himself*, etc; used with intensifying force (*her* (*very*) *own room*); used as an endearment (*my own* (*darling, dear*, etc)); used with a force similar to the emphatic *oneself*, etc (as in *he makes his own bed, his own worst enemy*). — *adj* **own-brand'** or **own-la'bel** (of a commodity) carrying the trademark or label of the store that sells it. — Also *n*. — **own goal** a goal scored by mistake against one's own team (*football*, etc); a move that turns out to the disadvantage of the party making it. — **come into one's own** to take possession of one's rights; to have one's talents or merits realized; **get one's own back** to retaliate, get even; **hold one's own** see under **hold**[1]; **of one's own** belonging to oneself and no-one else; **one's own** what belongs to oneself (as in *I may do what I like with my own*); **one's**, etc, **own man** or **woman** a free agent, not under another person's influence; **on one's own** on one's own account; on one's own initiative; by one's own efforts or resources; independently; set up in independence; alone, by oneself. [OE *āgen*, pa p of *āgan* to possess; cf **owe**]
owre[1] Scots form of **over**. For compounds see under **over-**.
owre[2] *owr*, (*Spenser*) *n*. Same as **ore**[1].
owrie. Same as **ourie**.
owsen *ow'sən*, *n pl* Scots form of **oxen** (see **ox**).
owt *owt*, (*dialect*) *n* anything. [Variant of **aught**]
ox *oks*, *n* a general name for the male or female of common domestic cattle (bull and cow), *esp* a castrated male of the species; extended to other animals of bovine type: — *pl* **ox'en** used for both male and female. — *n* **ox'er** *esp* in fox-hunting, an ox-fence; in show-jumping, an obstacle in the form of an ox-fence. — **ox'-ant'elope** any antelope of the hartebeest group; **ox'-bird** the dunlin; the ox-pecker; an African weaver-bird; applied also to various other birds; **ox'blood** a dark reddish-brown colour. — Also *adj*. — **ox'-bot** a warble-fly larva infesting cattle; **ox'-bow** (*-bō*) a collar for a yoked ox; a horseshoe-shaped bend in a river (forming an *ox-bow lake* when the neck is pierced and the bend cut off); **ox'-eye** a wild chrysanthemum, *Chrysanthemum leucanthemum*, with yellow disc and white ray (*ox-eye daisy*); sometimes (*yellow ox-eye*) the corn marigold; a name for various birds, *esp* the great titmouse; an elliptical dormer window. — *adj* **ox'-eyed** having large, ox-like eyes. — **ox'-fence** a fence for confining cattle; a hedge with a rail and in many cases also a ditch; **ox'gang, ox'gate** or **ox'land** (*obs*) a bovate or one-eighth of a carucate of ploughland, the share attributed to each ox in a team of eight (averaging about 13 acres); **ox'head** the head of an ox; a blockhead; **ox'-pecker** an African genus (*Buphaga*) of birds related to starlings, that eat the parasites on cattle (also **beefeater** or **ox-bird**); **ox'tail** the tail of an ox, *esp* as used for soup, stew, etc; **ox'-tongue** the tongue of an ox, used as food; a composite plant of the daisy family (*Picris echioides*) with yellow flowers and milky juice; **ox'-war'ble** a swelling on the back of an ox; the fly whose larva produces it. — **have the black ox tread on one's foot** to experience sorrow or misfortune. [OE *oxa*, pl *oxan*; Ger *Ochse*, Gothic *auhsa*, Sans *ukṣan*]
oxalis *ok'sə-lis*, *-sal'is*, *n* a plant of the wood-sorrel genus *Oxalis*, giving name to the family **Oxalidā'ceae**, closely related to the Geranium family. — *adj* **oxalic** (*-sal'ik*) applied to an acid ($C_2H_2O_4$) obtained from wood sorrel and other plants, used for cleaning metals and as a

bleaching agent. — *n* **ox'alate** a salt of oxalic acid. [Gr *oxalis*, from *oxys* sharp or acid]

oxazine *ok'sə-zēn*, *n* any of several isomeric compounds having the formula C_4H_5NO, with the nitrogen, oxygen and carbon atoms arranged in a ring. [**oxy-**[2], and **azine**]

Oxbridge *oks'brij*, *n* and *adj* (relating to) *O*xford and Cam*bridge* (universities), *esp* as typifying an upper-class-oriented kind of education, or as a road to unfair advantages, eg in obtaining jobs, or as the home of particular academic attitudes.

Oxfam *oks'fam*, *n* short form of Oxford Committee for Famine Relief.

Oxford *oks'fərd*, *adj* belonging to the city, county or university of Oxford; (without *cap*) a low-heeled laced shoe (also **Oxford shoe**); a light cotton or synthetic woven fabric (also (**Oxford cloth**) used for men's shirts. — *n* **Oxfordian** (*-förd'i-ən*; *geol*) a division of the Middle Jurassic. — Also *adj*. — **Oxford bags** very wide trousers; **Oxford blue** a dark blue (see also **blue**[1]); **Oxford clay** a dark blue or grey clay of the Oxfordian formation (*geol*); **Oxford English** a form of standard English in which certain tendencies are (sometimes affectedly) exaggerated, widely believed to be spoken at Oxford; **Oxford groups** informal circles of followers of Dr Frank Buchman, who exchanged religious experiences, and sought divine guidance individually (**the Oxford group** the name for his followers as a body from 1921–1938; see also **Moral Rearmament**); **Oxford movement** see **Tractarianism** under **tract**. [OE *Oxnaford* literally, oxen's ford]

oxide *ok'sīd*, *n* a compound of oxygen and some other element or radical. — *n* **ox'idant** a substance acting as an oxidizer. — *n* **ox'idase** any of a group of enzymes that promote oxidation in plant and animal cells. — *vt* **ox'idate** (*-id-āt*) to oxidize. — *n* **oxidā'tion** oxidizing; the process of forming an insulating layer of silicone dioxide on a silicone chip (*comput*). — *adj* **oxidīz'able** or **-s-**. — *vt* and *vi* **ox'idize** or **-ise** to combine with oxygen; to deprive (an atom or ion) of electrons; to make or become rusty; to put a protective oxide coating on (a metal surface). — *vi* to lose electrons. — *n* **oxidīz'er** or **-s-** an oxidizing agent. [Fr *oxide* (now *oxyde*), formed from *oxygène* oxygen]

oxime *ok'sēm*, (*chem*) *n* any of a number of compounds obtained by the action of hydroxylamine on aldehydes or ketones. [*O*xygen and *im*ide]

oximeter *ok-sim'i-tər*, *n* a photoelectric instrument for measuring oxygen saturation of the blood. [**oxi-**, older spelling of **oxy-**[2], and **-meter**]

oxlip *oks'lip*, *n orig* a hybrid between primrose and cowslip; now, a species of the genus Primula (*P. elatior*) like a large pale cowslip. — Also (*Shakesp*) **ox'slip**. [OE *oxanslyppe*, from *oxan*, genitive of *oxa* ox, and *slyppe* slime or a slimy dropping; cf **cowslip**]

Oxon *abbrev*: Oxfordshire; *Oxoniensis* (*L*), of Oxford.

Oxonian *ok-sō'ni-ən*, *adj* of or pertaining to Oxford or to its university. — *n* an inhabitant, native, student or graduate of Oxford; a kind of shoe (*hist*). [L *Oxonia* Oxford, from OE *Oxnaford*]

oxonium *ok-sō'ni-əm*, (*chem*) *n* a univalent basic radical, H_3O, in which oxygen is tetravalent, forming organic derivatives, **oxonium salts**. [*o*xygen and amm*onium*]

oxslip. See **oxlip**.

oxter *oks'tər*, (*Scot*) *n* the armpit. — *vt* to take under the arm; to support by taking the arm. [OE *oxta*]

oxy-[1] *ok-si-*, *combining form* denoting sharp; pointed; acid. [Gr *oxys*]

oxy-[2] *ok-si*, *combining form* denoting oxygen. — *adj* **ox'y=acet'ylene** involving, using or by means of, a mixture of oxygen and acetylene, *esp* in cutting or welding metals at high temperatures. — *n* **ox'y-a'cid**, **ox'y-com'pound**, **ox'y-salt**, etc, an acid, compound, salt, etc, containing oxygen; one in which an atom of hydrogen is replaced by a hydroxyl-group; **ox'y-bro'mide**, **-chlo'ride**, **-flu'or-ide**, **-hal'ide** or **-i'odide'** a compound of an element or radical with oxygen and a halogen (bromine, etc); **ox'yhaemoglo'bin** a loose compound of oxygen and haemoglobin. — *adj* **oxy-hy'drogen** involving or using a mixture of oxygen and hydrogen. — **oxy-calcium light** limelight. [Gr *oxys* sharp]

oxygen *ok'si-jən*, *n* a gas (atomic number 8; symbol **O**) without taste, colour or smell, forming part of the air, water, etc, and supporting life and combustion; something indispensable for existence. — *vt* **ox'ygenāte** (or *ok-sij'*) to oxidize; to impregnate or treat with oxygen. — *n* **oxygenā'tion**. — *n* **ox'ygenator** an apparatus performing functions of heart and lungs during an operation; something which supplies oxygen. — *vt* **ox'ygenize** or **-ise** to oxygenate. — *adj* **oxyg'enous**. — **oxygen debt** a depletion of the body's store of oxygen occurring during bursts of strenuous exercise, replaced after bodily activity returns to normal levels; **oxygen mask** a masklike breathing apparatus through which oxygen is supplied in rarefied atmospheres to mountaineers, aircraft passengers, etc; **oxygen tent** a tent-like enclosure in which there is a controllable flow of oxygen, erected round a patient to aid breathing. [Gr *oxys* sharp or acid, and the root of *gennaein* to generate, from the old belief that all acids contained oxygen]

oxymel *ok'si-mel*, *n* a mixture of vinegar and honey. [Gr *oxymeli*, from *oxys* sour, and *meli* honey]

oxymoron *ok-si-mō'ron*, *-mö'*, *n* a figure of speech by means of which contradictory terms are combined, so as to form an expressive phrase or epithet, such as *cruel kindness*, *falsely true*, etc. — *adj* **oxymoron'ic**. [Gr neuter of *oxymōros* literally, pointedly foolish, from *oxys* sharp, and *mōros* foolish]

oxyrhynchus *ok-si-ring'kəs*, *n* an Egyptian fish, sacred to the goddess Hathor, represented on coins and sculptures. [Gr *oxyrrynchos*, from *oxys* sharp, and *rhynchos* a snout]

oxytocin *ok-si-tō'sin*, *n* a pituitary hormone that stimulates uterine muscle contraction and milk production, also produced synthetically for use in accelerating labour. — *adj* and *n* **oxytō'cic** (a drug) stimulating uterine muscle contraction. [Gr *oxys* sharp, and *tokos* birth]

oxytone *ok'si-tōn*, *adj* having the acute accent on the last syllable (*Gr gram*); stressed on the final syllable. — *n* a word so accented. [Gr *oxys* sharp, and *tonos* tone]

oy, **oye** or **oe** *oi*, *ō-i*, *ō*, (*Scot*) *n* a grandchild. [Gaelic *ogha*, *odha*]

oyer *oi'ər*, *n* a hearing in a law-court, an assize. — **oyer and terminer** (*tûr'min-ər'*) a royal commission conferring power to hear and determine criminal causes (out of official use 1972). [Anglo-Fr *oyer* (Fr *ouïr*), from L *audīre* to hear]

oyez or **oyes** *ō-yes'*, *ō'yes*, *interj* the call of a public crier or officer of a law-court for attention before making a proclamation. — *n* (*oiz*; *Shakesp*) a proclamation. [OFr *oyez*, imperative of *oir* (Fr *ouïr*) to hear]

oyster *ois'tər*, *n* a bivalve shellfish (genus *Ostrea*) used as food; a secretive person (*colloq*); a source of advantage; the colour of an oyster, a pale greyish beige or pink. — *adj* of this colour. — **oys'ter-bank**, **-bed**, **-farm**, **-field** and **-park** a place where oysters breed or are bred; **oys'ter-catcher** a black and white wading bird, with red bill and feet, feeding on limpets and mussels (not oysters), also known as the sea pie; **oys'ter-fish'ery** the business of catching oysters; a place where oysters are caught or farmed; **oys'ter-knife** a knife for opening oysters; **oyster mushroom** an edible fungus (*Pleurotus ostreatus* or related species) found *esp* in clusters on dead wood; **oys'ter-patt'y** a small pie or pasty made from oysters; **oys'ter-plant** salsify, or a seaside boraginaceous plant (*Mertensia maritima*), both supposed to taste like oysters; **oys'ter-shell** the shell of an oyster; **oys'ter-tongs** a tool for gathering oysters; **oys'ter=wench**, **-wife** or **-woman** (all *obs*) a woman who sells oysters. — **the world is my** (*Shakesp* **world's mine**), **his**, etc, **oyster** the world lies before me, etc, ready to yield profit or success. [OFr *oistre* (Fr *huître*), from L *ostrea*, from Gr *ostreon* an oyster, from *osteon* a bone]

oystrige *oi'strij*, (*Spenser*) *n* for **ostrich**.

Oz *oz*, (*Austr slang*) *n* Australia. — Also *adj*.

oz or **oz**. *abbrev*: ounce: — *pl* **oz** or **ozs**. [15c Ital *ōz*, abbrev of *onza*]

Ozacling® *oz'ə-kling*, (*printing*) *n* transparent adhesive film from which printed material can be cut for application to illustrations, etc.

ozaena *ō-zē'nə*, *n* a fetid discharge from the nostrils. [Gr *ozaina* a fetid polypus of the nose, from *ozein* to smell]

Ozalid® *oz'ə-lid*, *n* a method of duplicating printed matter on to chemically treated paper; a reproduction made by this process.

ozeki *ō-zē'ki*, *n* a champion sumo wrestler. [Jap *ōzeki*]

ozokerite *ō-zō'kə-rīt*, *-kē'rīt*, or **ozocerite** *ō-zos'ə-rīt*, *ō-zō-sē'rīt*, *n* a waxy natural paraffin. [Gr *ozein* to smell, and *kēros* wax]

ozone *ō'zōn*, *n* an allotropic form (O_3) of oxygen present in the atmosphere, once regarded as health-giving, but toxic in concentrations such as may occur in industrial areas, having a pungent smell, formed when ultraviolet light or an electric spark acts on oxygen or air, and used in bleaching, sterilizing water, and purifying air; loosely, fresh bracing air; (see also **ozonosphere**). — *n* **ozonā'tion** ozonization. — *adj* **ozonif'erous** bringing or producing ozone. — *n* **ozonizā'tion** or **-s-**. — *vt* **ō'zonize** or **-ise** to turn into, charge with or treat with ozone. — *n* **ozoniz'er** or **-s-** an apparatus for turning oxygen into ozone. — *n* **ozon'osphere** or **ozone layer** a layer of the upper atmosphere where ozone is formed in quantity, protecting the earth from the sun's ultraviolet rays. — *adj* **ozone-friend'ly** (of certain aerosols, etc) not thought to be destructive of the ozone layer, being free of chlorofluorocarbons. [Gr *ozōn*, pr p of *ozein* to smell]

ozs. See **oz**.

P

P or **p** *pē*, *n* the sixteenth letter of the modern English alphabet, and of the Greek (see **pi**[1]), representing a voiceless labial stop. — **P-Celt** or **P-Kelt** see under **Celt**. — **mind one's p's and q's** see under **mind**.

P *abbrev* parking; Pastor; pedal (*music*); Portugal (IVR); Priest; Prince; pula (currency of Botswana). — *combining form* much used in designating Inland Revenue forms, eg **P45** the form given to an employee changing jobs, carrying a statement of earnings to date in the current tax year, and deductions made from those earnings by the employer.

P *symbol*: (in medieval Roman notation) 400 ($\bar{P}$ = 400 000); (on road signs etc) parking; pawn (*chess*); phosphorus (*chem*); power (*phys*); pressure (*phys*).

P *symbol*: power.

p *abbrev*: new pence; new penny; page: — *pl* **pp**; participle; peseta; peso; piano (*music*); pico-; positive. — *adj* **p'-type** (ie 'positive type' of a semiconductor) having an excess of mobile holes over conduction electrons.

p- (*chem*). See under **para-**[1].

PA *abbrev*: Panama (IVR); Pennsylvania (US state); personal appearance; personal assistant; Press Association; public address (system); publicity agent; Publishers Association.

Pa *symbol*: pascal; protactinium (*chem*).

pa[1] *pä*, *n* a childish or familiar word for father. [**papa**]

pa[2] or **pah** *pä*, *n* a Maori fort or settlement. [Maori]

Pa. *abbrev*: Pennsylvania (US state).

pa. *abbrev*: past.

p.a. or **pa** *abbrev*: per annum.

pa'anga *päng'gə*, *n* the standard unit of currency of Tonga, Tongan dollar (100 *seniti*). [Tongan, from a type of vine yielding disc-shaped seeds]

PABA *pa'bə*, *n* acronym for **para-aminobenzoic acid**.

pabouche *pə-bōōsh'*, *n* a slipper. [See **babouche**]

pabulum *pab'ū-ləm* or *-yə-*, *n* food of any kind, *esp* that of lower animals and of plants; provender; fuel; nourishment for the mind. — *adj* **pab'ūlar**. — *adj* **pab'ūlous**. [L *pābulum*, from *pāscere* to feed]

PABX *abbrev*: Private Automatic Branch Exchange.

PAC *abbrev*: Pan Africanist Congress.

paca *pä'kə*, *n* the so-called spotted cavy of South America, related to the agouti. [Sp and Port, from Tupí *paca*]

pacable *pāk'ə-bl* or *pak'*, (*archaic*) *adj* capable of being appeased; willing to forgive. — *n* **pacation** (*pə-kā'shən*). [L *pācāre* to appease, from *pāx*, *pācis* peace]

PACE *pās*, *abbrev*: Police and Criminal Evidence Act.

Pace *pās*, a dialect form of **Pasch**. — **pace egg** an Easter egg, one hard-boiled and dyed; **pace'-egging** begging for eggs, etc, at Easter; rolling pace eggs on the ground.

pace[1] *pās*, *n* a stride; a step; the space between the feet in walking, about 76 centimetres, or (among the Romans) the space between two successive positions of the same foot, *approx* 1·5 metres; gait; rate of walking, running, etc (of a person or animal); rate of speed in movement or work, often applied to fast living; a mode of stepping in horses in which the legs on the same side are lifted together; amble; a step of a stair, or the like; a pass or passage (*obs*). — *vt* to traverse with measured steps; to measure by steps (often with *out*); to train to perform paces; to set the pace for; to perform as a pace or paces. — *vi* to walk; to walk slowly and with measured tread; to amble. — *adj* **paced** having a certain pace or gait. — *n* **pac'er** a person who paces; a horse whose usual gait is a pace; a horse trained to pace in harness racing. — *adj* **pac'ey** or **pac'y** (*colloq*) fast; lively, smart. — **pace'-bowler** (*cricket*) a bowler who delivers the ball fast; **pace'-bowling**; **pace'maker** a person who sets the pace in a race (also *fig*); a small mass of muscle cells in the heart which control the heart-beat electrically; an electronic device (in later models, with radioactive core) used to correct weak or irregular heart rhythms; **pace'-setter** a pacemaker, except in anatomical and electronic senses. — **go the pace** to go at a great speed; to live a fast life; **keep** or **hold pace with** to go as fast as; to keep up with; **make** or **set the pace** to regulate the speed for others by example; **put someone through his** or **her paces** to set someone to show what he or she can do, to test someone; **show one's paces** to show what one can do; **stand**, **stay** or **stick the pace** to keep up with the pace or speed that has been set. [Fr *pas*, from L *passus* a step, from *pandere*, *passum* to stretch]

pace[2] *pā'sē*, *pä'kā* or *pä'chā*, *prep* with or by the leave of (expressing disagreement courteously). [L, ablative of *pāx* peace]

pacha, **pachalic**. See under **pasha**.

pachak. See under **putchock**.

pachinko *pə-ching'kō*, *n* a form of pin-ball popular in Japan. [Jap *pachin* (onomatopoeic) representing trigger sound]

pachisi *pä-chē'sē* or *-zē*, *n* an Indian game like backgammon or ludo. [Hindi *pacīsī* of twenty-five, from the highest throw]

pachy- *pak'i-*, *combining form* signifying thick. — *adj* **pachycarp'ous** (Gr *karpos* fruit) having a thick pericarp. — *adj* **pachydac'tyl** or **pachydac'tylous** (Gr *daktylos* digit) having thick digits. — *n* **pach'yderm** (Gr *derma* skin) strictly, any animal of the old classification Pachydermata, but *usu* an elephant, rhinoceros, or hippopotamus; an insensitive person. — *adj* **pachyderm'al**. — *npl* **Pachyderm'ata** in old classification, those ungulates that do not ruminate, ie elephant, horse, pig, etc. — *adj* **pachyder'matous** thick-skinned; of the pachyderms; insensitive. — *n* **pachyderm'ia** abnormal thickness of skin or mucous membrane. — *adj* **pachyderm'ic**. — *adj* **pachyderm'ous**. — *n* **pachym'eter** an instrument for measuring small thicknesses. [Gr *pachys* thick]

pacify *pas'i-fī*, *vt* to appease; to calm; to bring peace to. — *adj* **pac'ifiable**. — *adj* **pacif'ic** peacemaking; appeasing; inclining towards peace; peaceful; mild; tranquil; (with *cap*) of or pertaining to the ocean between Asia and America, so called by Magellan, the first European to sail on it, because he happened to cross it in peaceful weather conditions. — *n* (with *cap*) the Pacific Ocean. — *adj* **pacif'ical** pacific (rare except in **Letters pacifical**, letters recommending the bearer as one in peace and fellowship with the Church — also **Letters of peace** or **Letters Pacificae**). — *adv* **pacif'ically**. — *vt* **pacif'icāte** to give peace to. — *n* **pacificā'tion** peacemaking; conciliation; appeasement; a peace treaty. — *n* **pacif'icātor** a peacemaker. — *adj* **pacif'icatory** (*-ə-tə-ri*) tending to make peace. — *n* **pacif'icism** (*-sizm*) the beliefs and principles of pacificists. — *n* **pacif'icist** (*-sist*) a person who is opposed to war, or believes all war to be wrong. — *n* **pac'ifier** a person or thing that pacifies; a baby's dummy or teething-ring (*esp NAm*). — *n* **pac'ifism** and *n* **pac'ifist** popularly preferred forms of **pacificism** and **pacificist**. — **Pacific Rim** the coastal regions around the Pacific Ocean; the countries of these regions. [Partly through Fr *pacifier*, from L *pācificus* pacific, from *pācificāre*, from *pāx*, *pācis* peace, and *facere* to make]

pack[1] *pak*, *n* a bundle, *esp orig* one made to be carried on the back by a pedlar or pack-animal; a backpack, rucksack; a collection, stock, or store; a bundle of some particular kind or quantity (eg of wool c.109 kg (240 lb)); the quantity packed at a time or in a season; a complete set of playing-cards; a number of animals herding together or kept together for hunting; a shepherd's own sheep grazing along with his employer's as part payment (*Scot*); the forwards in a Rugby football team; a group of Cub Scouts in the Scout movement or of Brownies in the Guide movement; a worthless, disreputable or otherwise objectionable set of people; a gang, eg of thieves; a mass of pack-ice; a sheet for folding round the body to allay inflammation, fever, etc; the use or application of such a sheet; a built support for a mine-roof; packing material; a cosmetic paste; a number of photographic plates or films exposed together; the act of packing or condition of being packed; mode of packing; a person of worthless or bad character (*obs*); a compact package, *esp* of something for sale; a parachute folded in its fabric container; a group (of eg submarines) acting together. — *vt* to make into a bundled pack; to place compactly in a box, bag, or the like; to press together closely; to compress; to fill tightly or compactly; to fill with anything; to cram; to crowd; to envelop; to surround closely; to fill the spaces surrounding; to prepare (food) for preservation, transport and marketing; to send away, dismiss (*usu* with *off*); to form into a pack; to load with a pack; to carry in packs; to carry or wear (a gun) (*colloq*). — *vi* to form into a pack; to settle or be driven into a firm mass; to form a scrum; to be capable of being put into a compact shape; to put one's belongings together in boxes, bags, etc, eg for a journey (often with *up*); to travel with a pack; to take oneself off, to depart in haste (*usu* with *off*); to plot, intrigue, arrange privately (*Shakesp*). — *n* **pack'age** the act, manner or privilege of packing; a bundle, packet, or parcel; a case or other receptacle for packing goods in; a composite proposition, scheme, offer, etc in which various separate elements are all dealt with as essential parts of the whole (see also **package deal**); a computer program in general form, to which the user adds any data applicable in a particular case. — *vt* to put into a container or wrappings, or into a package. — *adj* **pack'aged** (*lit* and *fig*). — *n* **pack'ager** a specialist in the packaging of books, programs, etc. — *n* **pack'aging** anything used to package goods; the total presentation of a product for sale, ie its design, wrapping, etc; the designing and complete production of eg illustrated books, programmes for television, etc for sale to a publisher, broadcasting company, etc. — *n* **pack'er** a person who packs; someone who packs goods for sending out; an employer or employee in the business of preparing and preserving food; someone who transports goods by means of pack-animals (*US*); a machine or device for packing. — *n* **pack'et** a small package; a carton; a ship or vessel employed in carrying packets of letters, passengers, etc; a vessel plying regularly between one port and another (also **pack'et-boat**, **pack'et-ship**, etc); a large amount of money (*colloq*); a small group; a cluster of bacteria; used as equivalent to a quantum (*fig*); a serious injury (*slang*); a block of coded data (*comput*; see **packet-switching** below). — *vt* to parcel up. — *n* **pack'ing** the act of putting into packs or of tying up for carriage or storing; material for packing; anything used to fill an empty space or to make a joint watertight or airtight. — **package deal** a deal which embraces a number of matters and has to be accepted as a whole, the less favourable items along with the favourable; **package holiday** or **tour** one in which all major elements, *esp* travel and accommodation, are pre-arranged by a tour company, to whom the holidaymaker pays a single fee; **pack'-an'imal** an animal used to carry goods on its back; **pack'-cinch** (*-sinsh*) a wide girth for a pack-animal; **pack'-cloth** a cloth in which goods are enclosed; packsheet; **pack'-drill** a military punishment of marching about laden with full equipment; **pack'et-note** a size of notepaper c.14 × 23 cm (*orig* $5\frac{1}{2} \times 9$ in); **pack'et-switching** (*comput*) a system of communication in which packets of data are transmitted between computers of varying types and compatibility; **pack'-horse**, etc a horse, etc used to carry goods on its back; a drudge; **pack ice** a mass of large pieces of floating ice driven together by winds and currents; **pack'ing-box** a box or framework for packing goods in (also **pack'ing-case**); a stuffing box; **pack'ing-need'le** a strong needle for sewing up packages; **pack'ing-paper** a strong, thick kind of wrapping-paper; **pack'ing-press** a press for squeezing goods into a compact form for packing; **pack'ing-sheet** or **pack'sheet** coarse cloth for packing goods; **pack'-load** the load an animal can carry; **pack'man** a pedlar or a man who carries a pack; **pack'-mule** a mule used for carrying burdens; **pack'-rat** a kind of long-tailed rat, native to the western part of North America; **pack'-saddle** a saddle for pack-horses, pack-mules, etc; **packsheet** see **packing-sheet**; **pack'-staff** a staff for supporting a pedlar's pack when he or she rests (see also **pike**[1]); **pack'-thread** a coarse thread used to sew up packages; **pack'-train** a line of loaded pack-animals on the move; **pack'-twine** thin twine for tying up parcels; **pack'way** a narrow path fit for pack-horses. — **pack a punch** to be capable of giving a powerful blow; **pack it in** or **up** (*slang*) to stop or give up doing something; **pack up** (*slang*) to stop; to break down; **send someone packing** to dismiss someone summarily. [ME *packe*, *pakke*, appar from MFlem *pac* or Du or LGer *pak*]

pack[2] *pak*, (*obs*) *n* a secret or underhand arrangement. — *vi* to make such an arrangement (*Shakesp*). — *vt* (*esp* in *passive*) to bring into a plot as accomplice (*Shakesp*); to shuffle (cards) *esp* dishonestly (*obs*); to fill up (a jury or meeting) with people of a particular kind for one's own purposes. — **pack cards with** (*Shakesp*, etc) to make a dishonest arrangement with. [Prob **pact**]

pack[3] *pak*, (*Scot*) *adj* intimate, confidential. [Origin unknown]

package, **packer**, **packet**. See under **pack**[1].

packfong. An incorrect form of **paktong**.

paco *pä'kō*, *n* an alpaca: — *pl* **pa'cos**. [Sp, from Quechua *paco*]

pact *pakt*, *n* something which is agreed on; an agreement, *esp* informal or not legally enforceable. — *n* **pac'tion** (chiefly *Scot*) a pact. — *vt* to agree. — *adj* **pac'tional**. — **Warsaw Pact** see under **Warsaw Convention**. [L *pactum*, from *paciscere*, *pactum* to contract]

pacy. See under **pace**[1].

pactum *pak'təm* or *-tōōm*, (*L*) *n* a pact. — **pactum illicitum** (*i-lis'i-təm* or *i-lik'i-tōōm*) an illegal compact; **pactum nudum** (*nū'dəm* or *nōō'dōōm*) a pact in which a consideration is not given.

pad[1] *pad*, *n* a path (*dialect*); a thief on the high-road (usually **footpad**; *archaic*); (contraction of **pad'-horse**) a horse for riding on the road; an easy-paced horse (*archaic* or *dialect*). — *vi* to walk on foot; to trudge along; to walk with a quiet or dull-sounding tread; to rob on foot (*archaic*): — *pr p* **padd'ing**; *pa t* and *pa p* **padd'ed**. — **padd'ing-ken** (*thieves' slang*) a thieves' or tramps' lodging-house; **pad'-nag** (*archaic* or *dialect*) an ambling nag. — **pad the hoof** (*slang*) to walk, trudge; **stand pad** to beg by the roadside. [Du *pad* a path]

pad[2] *pad*, *n* anything stuffed with a soft material, to prevent friction, pressure, or injury, for inking or for filling out, shaping, etc; a block of absorbent material that holds ink to be used on a stamping device; a soft saddle; a cushion; a number of sheets of paper or other soft material fastened together in a block; a guard shaped to protect different parts of the body in various sports, eg a leg-guard for cricketers; the fleshy, thick-skinned undersurface of the foot of many animals, such as the fox; the foot of an animal, *esp* of one traditionally hunted for sport; its footprint; a water-lily leaf (*US*); (*usu* in *pl*) thick watered ribbon used for watch-guards; a rocket-launching platform; a bed, room, or home, *esp* one's own (*slang*); a device built into a road surface, operated by vehicles passing over it, controlling changes of traffic lights (**vehicle-actuated signals**) so as to give passage for a longer time to the greater stream of traffic. — *vt* to stuff, cover, or fill out with anything soft; to furnish with padding; to track by footprints; to impregnate, eg with a mordant: — *pr p* **padd'ing**; *pa t* and *pa p* **padd'ed**. — *n* **padd'er**. — *n* **padd'ing** stuffing; matter of less value introduced into a book or article in order to make it of the length desired; the process of mordanting a fabric. — **pad'-cloth** a cloth covering a horse's loins; **padded cell** a room with padded walls in a mental hospital; **pad'-el'ephant** a working elephant wearing a pad but no howdah; **pad'-saddle** a treeless, padded saddle; **pad'saw** a small saw-blade with a detachable handle, used for cutting curves and awkward angles (also **keyhole saw**); **pad'-tree** the wooden or metal frame to which harness-pads are attached. [Origin obscure; possibly connected with **pod**[1]]

pad[3]. Same as **ped**[1].

padang *pad'ang*, (*Malay*) *n* a field, *esp* a playing-field.

padauk or **padouk** *pä-dowk'*, *n* a Burmese timber tree of the red-sanders genus. [Burmese]

paddle[1] *pad'l*, *vi* to wade about or dabble in a liquid or semi-liquid; to walk unsteadily or with short steps; to play or toy with the fingers (*archaic*); to trifle (*obs*); to make (land) bare of grass by constant trampling, etc (*dialect*). — *vt* (*archaic*) to toy with or finger. — *n* **padd'ler** someone who paddles; (in *pl*) a protective garment worn by children when paddling. [Cf **pad**[1], and LGer *paddeln* to tramp about]

paddle[2] *pad'l*, **padle** *pä'dl* or *pä'* or **paidle** *pā'*, (*Scot*) *n* the lumpsucker. — Also **cock'-padd'le**, etc (*masc*), **hen'-padd'le**, etc (*fem*). [Origin unknown]

paddle[3] *pad'l*, *n* a small, long-handled spade; a short, broad, spoon-shaped oar, used for moving canoes; the blade of an oar; one of the boards of a paddle-wheel or water-wheel; a swimming animal's flipper; a paddle-shaped instrument for stirring, beating, etc; a small bat, as used in table-tennis (*US*). — *vi* to use a paddle or progress by use of paddles; to row gently; to swim about like a duck. — *vt* to propel by paddle; to strike or spank with a paddle or the like (*esp US*). — *n* **padd'ler**. — *n* **padd'ling** the act of paddling; a flock of wild duck on water. — **padd'le-board** one of the boards of a paddle-wheel; **padd'le-boat** a paddle-steamer; **padd'le-box** the covering of a paddle-wheel; **padd'le-shaft** the axle on which paddle-wheels turn; **padd'le-staff** a small spade or paddle; **padd'le-steam'er** a steamer propelled by paddle-wheels; **padd'le-wheel** a wheel-like framework with boards or paddles fitted across its edges, steam driven to strike water and propel a ship, or turned by a stream to drive a mill, etc; **padd'le-wood** the light, strong wood of a Guiana tree (*Aspidosperma*) of the dogbane family. — **paddle one's own canoe** to progress independently. [Origin obscure]

paddock[1]. See **puddock**.

paddock[2] *pad'ək*, *n* an enclosed field under pasture, *orig* near a house or stable; (in horse-racing) the enclosed area where horses are paraded and mounted before a race; (in motor-racing) an area near the pits where cars may be worked on before races; any enclosed field (*Austr* and *NZ*). [Appar from earlier *parrock*, from OE *pearroc* park]

Paddy *pad'i*, *n* a familiar, often derogatory name for an Irishman; (without *cap*) a rage (*colloq*); a paddy train (*mining slang*). — *n* **Padd'yism** a hibernicism. — **Paddy's lantern** the moon; **paddy train** (*mining slang*) an underground colliery train for transporting miners from one point to another, pulled by a diesel- or electrically-powered locomotive, or by a rope-haulage system (properly **man'rider** or **manriding train**); **paddy wagon** a black Maria; **padd'y-whack** (*slang*) an Irishman, *esp* a big one; a rage; a slap, smack, blow, spanking, beating.

paddy *pad'i*, *n* growing rice; rice in the husk. — **padd'y-bird** the Java sparrow or rice-bird; **padd'y-field** a rice field. [Malay *pādī* rice in the straw]

paddymelon. See **pademelon**.

padella *pa-del'ə*, *n* a shallow dish of fat with a wick used in illuminations. [Ital, a frying-pan, from L *patella*]

pademelon, **paddymelon** or **padymelon** *pad'i-mel-ən*, *n* any of several small wallabies. [Aboriginal]

paderero *pad-ə-rā'rō*. Same as **pederero**.

padishah *pä'di-shä*, *n* chief ruler; great king, a title of the Shah of Persia, and formerly of the Sultan of Turkey, the Great Mogul, or the (British) Emperor of India. [Pers *pad* master, and *shāh* king]

padle. See **paddle**[2].

padlock *pad'lok*, *n* a movable lock with a link turning on a hinge or pivot at one end, catching the bolt at the other. — Also *vt*. [Origin uncertain, possibly dialect Eng *pad* a basket, and **lock**[1]]

padma *pud'mə*, *n* the sacred lotus. [Sans]

padouk. Same as **padauk**.

padre *pä'drā*, *n* father, a title given to priests; an army chaplain; a parson. — *n* **padro'ne** (*-rō'ni*) a shipmaster (*archaic*); an innkeeper, café- or restaurant-owner; an employer, *esp* among Italian Americans; someone who jobs out hand-organs, or who gets children to beg for him (*obs*): — *pl* **padrō'ni** (*-nē*). [Port (also Sp and Ital) *padre*, Ital *padrone*, from L *pater* a father, *patrōnus* a patron]

Paduan *pad'ū-ən*, *adj* of *Padua* in NE Italy. — *n* a native of Padua; a counterfeit Roman bronze coin made at Padua in the 16th century; the pavan.

paduasoy *pad'ū-ə-soi* or *pä'də-soi*, *n* a corded silk used in the 18th century; a garment made of it. [Fr *pou-de-soie*, from *pou*, *pout*, *poult* (of unknown origin) *de soie* of silk; appar influenced by *Padua*]

padymelon. See **pademelon**.

Paean *pē'ən*, *n* the Homeric physician of the gods; later, an epithet of Apollo; (without *cap*) a lyric to Apollo or Artemis (or some other god); (without *cap*) a song of thanksgiving or triumph; (without *cap*) exultation. — Also **pē'an**. — *n* **pae'on** or **paeon'ic** (*prosody*) a foot of four syllables, any one long, three short. — *adj* **paeon'ic** (*-on'ik*). [L *Paeān*, *paeōn*, from Gr *Paiān*, *-ānos*, *paiōn*, *-ōnos*]

paed- or **ped-** *pēd-* or **paedo-** or **pedo-** *pē-dō-*, also sometimes **paid-** *pīd-* or **paido-** *pī-dō-*, *combining form* denoting child, boy. — *adj* **paedagog'ic** same as **pedagogic**. — *n* **paed'agogue** same as **pedagogue**. — *n* **paed'erast**, etc same as **pederast**, etc. — **paedeut'ic** or **paideut'ic** (also *n sing* **paedeutics** or **paideutics**) educational method or theory. — *adj* **paediat'ric** (Gr *īātrikos* medical) relating to the medical treatment of children. — *n* **paediatrician** (*-ə-trish'ən*). — *n sing* **paediat'rics** the treatment of children's diseases. — *n* **paedī'atrist**. — *n* **paedī'atry**. — *n* **paedobap'tism** infant baptism. — *n* **paedobap'tist**. — *adj* **paedodont'ic**. — *n sing* **paedodont'ics** the branch of dentistry concerned with care of children's teeth. — *n* **paedogen'esis** reproduction by an animal in the larval state. — *adj* **paedogenet'ic**. — *adj* **paedolog'ical**. — *n* **paedol'ogist**. — *n* **paedol'ogy** the study of the growth and development of children. — *adj* **paedomor'phic** of paedomorphism or paedomorphosis. — *n* **paedomorph'ism** (Gr *morphē* form) retention of juvenile characters in the mature stage. — *n* **paedomor'phosis** a phylogenetic change in which juvenile characteristics are retained in the adult. — *n* **paed'ophile** (*-fīl*) a person affected with paedophilia. — *n* **paedophilia** (*-fil'*) sexual desire whose object is children. — *adj* and *n* **paedophil'iac** or **paedophil'ic**. — *n* **paed'otribe** (*-trīb*; Gr *paidotribēs*) in ancient Greece, a gymnastic teacher. — *n* **paedot'rophy** (Gr *tropheiā* nursing) the art of rearing children. [Gr *pais*, *paidos* boy, child; *paideutēs* teacher]

paella *pī-el'ə* or *pä-el'ya*, *n* a stew containing saffron, chicken, rice, vegetables, seafood, etc. [Sp, from L *patella* pan]

paenula *pē'nū-lə*, *n* a Roman travelling cloak; a chasuble, *esp* in its older form. [L *paenula*]

paeon, **paeonic**. See **Paean**.
paeony. Same as **peony**.
pagan *pā'gən*, *n* a person following any (*esp* polytheistic) pre-Christian religion; a person who is not a Christian, Jew or Muslim, regarded as uncultured or unenlightened, a heathen; more recently, someone who has no religion; a person who sets a high value on sensual pleasures. — Also *adj*. — *adj* **pā'ganish** heathenish. — *n* **pā'ganism** — *vt* **pā'ganize** or **-ise** to render pagan or heathen; to convert to paganism. [L *pāgānus* rustic, peasant, also civilian (because the Christians reckoned themselves soldiers of Christ), from *pāgus* a district]
PAGE *abbrev*: polyacrylamide gel electrophoresis.
page[1] *pāj*, *n* a boy attendant; a boy employed as a messenger in hotels, clubs, etc; a messenger (boy or girl) in the US Congress, etc; a youth training for knighthood, receiving education and performing services at court or in a nobleman's household (*hist*); a contrivance for holding up a long skirt in walking (*hist*). — *vt* to attend as a page; to seek or summon by sending a page around, by repeatedly calling aloud for *esp* using a public address system, or by means of a pager. — *n* **page'hood** the condition of a page. — *n* **pā'ger** an electronic device, *esp* portable, which pages a person eg by means of a bleep, visual display, etc (cf **bleeper**). — **page'-boy** a page; (also **page-boy hairstyle**, **haircut**) a hairstyle in which the hair hangs smoothly to about jaw level and is curled under at the ends. [Fr *page*; of obscure origin]
page[2] *pāj*, *n* one side of a leaf of a book, etc (4 pages in a folio sheet, 8 in a quarto, 16 in an octavo, 24 in a duodecimo, 36 in an octodecimo); the type, illustrations, etc, arranged for printing one side of a leaf; a leaf of a book thought of as a single item; (in *pl*) writings, literature (*rhetoric*); an incident, episode, or whatever may be imagined as matter to fill a page; one of the blocks into which a computer memory can be divided for ease of reference. — *vt* to number the pages of; to make up into pages (*printing*). — *adj* **paginal** (*paj'*). — *vt* **paginăte** (*paj'*) to mark with consecutive numbers, to page. — *n* **paginā'tion** the act of paging a book; the figures and marks that indicate the numbers of pages. — *n* **pā'ging** the marking or numbering of the pages of a book. — **page description language** (*comput*) a language for specifying the compositon of a printed page; **page'-proof** a proof of a book, etc made up into pages. — *adj* **page-three'** shown on or appropriate for **page three**, the page on which, traditionally, certain popular newspapers print nude or semi-nude photographs of female models with well-developed figures. — **page'-turner** an exciting book, a thriller. [Fr, from L *pāgina* a page]
pageant *paj'ənt* or (*archaic*) *pāj'*, *n* a dramatic performance, scene, or part (*archaic*); a movable stage or carriage for acting on (*obs*); a stage machine (*obs*); a spectacle, *esp* a magnificent procession or parade; a series of tableaux or dramatic scenes connected with local history or other topical matter, performed either on a fixed spot or in procession; a piece of empty show; display. — *adj* of the nature of a puppet; specious. — *n* **page'antry** splendid display; pompous spectacle; a fleeting show. [Origin obscure; Anglo-L *pāgina* may be the classical word transferred from page to scene in a MS; or *pāgina* in the sense of slab may have come to mean boarding, framework]
paginal, **paginate**, etc. See under **page**[2].
pagle. See **paigle**.
pagoda *pə-gō'də* or **pagod** *pag'od*, and formerly also *pə-god'*, *n* an Eastern temple, *esp* in the form of a many-storeyed tapering tower, each storey with a projecting roof; an ornamental building in imitation of this; an idol, a demigod (*obs*); a former Indian coin, bearing the figure of a pagoda. — **pagoda sleeve** a funnel-shaped outer sleeve turned back to show lining and inner sleeve; **pago'da-tree** a name for various erect trees of pagoda-like form; a fabulous Indian tree that dropped pagodas (coins) when shaken. [Port *pagode*, from Pers *but-kadah* idol-house, or some other Eastern word]
pagri *pug'rē*, *n* a turban; a light scarf worn round the hat to keep off the sun. — Also **pugg'aree**, **pugg'ree** and **pugg'ery**. [Hindi *pagṛī*]
pagurian *pə-gū'ri-ən*, *n* and *adj* (a crustacean) of the hermit-crab genus, *Pagurus*. — Also **pagū'rid** (or *pag'*). [L *pagurus*, from Gr *pagouros* kind of crab]
pah[1] *pä*, *interj* an exclamation of disgust.
pah[2]. See under **pa**[2].
Pahari *pə-ha'ri*, *n* a group of Indo-European languages used in the region of the Himalayas, divided into **Eastern Pahari** (also called **Nepali**), **Central Pahari** and **Western Pahari** composed of many dialects.
Pahlavi. Same as **Pehlevi**.
pahoehoe *pə-hō'ē-hō-ē*, *n* a hardened lava with a smooth undulating shiny surface. [Hawaiian]
paid *pād*, *pa t* and *pa p* of **pay**[1]. — *adj* satisfied (*obs*); drunk (*Shakesp*); hired. — *adj* **paid-up'** paid in full; having fulfilled financial obligations. — **put paid to** to finish; to destroy chances of success in.
paid-. See **paed-**.
paideutic. See **paedeutic** under **paed-**.
paidle. See **paddle**[2].
paido-. See **paed-**.
paigle or **pagle** *pā'gl*, (*archaic* and *dialect*) *n* the cowslip, sometimes also the oxlip. [Origin unknown]
paik *pāk*, (*Scot*) *vt* to thump, drub. — *n* a blow; (in *pl*, with *his*, etc) a drubbing. [Origin unknown]
pail *pāl*, *n* an open cylindrical or conical container with a hooped handle, for holding or carrying liquids (also ice, coal, etc), a bucket; a pailful. — *n* **pail'ful** as much as fills a pail. [OE *pægel* a gill measure, appar combined with or influenced by OFr *paele* a pan, from L *patella* a pan, dimin of *patera*, from *patēre* to be open]
paillasse. Same as **palliasse**.
paillette *pal-yet'* or *pä-*, *n* a spangle. — *n* **paillon** (*pal'yən* or *pä-yɔ̃*) a piece of foil, to show through enamel, etc. [Fr]
Pain *pān*, *n* acronym for the advice charity Parents Against Injustice.
pain *pān*, *n* penalty; suffering; bodily suffering; (now only in *pl*) great care or trouble taken in doing anything; (in *pl*) the throes of childbirth; a tiresome or annoying person, task, etc (*colloq*). — *vt* to cause suffering to; to put to trouble (*archaic*; *esp reflexive*). — *adj* **pained** showing or expressing pain; suffering pain; distressed. — *adj* **pain'ful** full of pain; causing pain; requiring labour, pain, or care; laborious, painstaking (*archaic*); distressing, irksome; (of a performance, etc) embarrassingly or irritatingly bad (*colloq*). — *adv* **pain'fully**. — *n* **pain'fulness**. — *adj* **pain'less** without pain. — *adv* **pain'lessly**. — *n* **pain'lessness**. — **pain barrier** a level of extreme physical exertion beyond which resultant pain or discomfort begins to ease, *esp* in the phrase *go through the pain barrier*; **pain'-killer** anything that does away with pain, *esp* an analgesic; a nostrum claiming to end pain; **pains'taker** someone who takes pains or care; a careful worker. — *adj* **pains'taking** taking pains or care. — *n* careful diligence. — **be at pains (to)** or **take pains (to)** to put oneself to trouble, be assiduously careful (to); **for one's pains** as reward or result of trouble taken (*usu ironic*); **pain in the neck** (*fig*) a feeling of acute discomfort; an exasperating circumstance; a thoroughly tiresome person, task, etc; **under** or **on pain of** under liability to the penalty of. [Fr *peine*, from L *poena* satisfaction, from Gr *poinē* penalty]
painim *pā'nim*. See **paynim**.
paint *pānt*, *vt* to cover over with colouring matter; to represent in a coloured picture; to produce as a coloured picture; to apply with a brush; to apply anything to, with a brush; to describe or present as if by painting a picture (*fig*); to colour; to apply coloured cosmetics to; to adorn, diversify; to represent speciously or deceptively. — *vi* to practise painting; to use coloured cosmetics on the face; to tipple (*slang*). — *n* a

colouring substance spread or for spreading on a surface; a cake of such matter; coloured cosmetics. — *adj* **paint'able** suitable for painting. — *adj* **painted** covered with paint; ornamented with coloured figures; marked with bright colours; feigned. — *n* **paint'er** someone who paints; an artist in painting; a person whose occupation is painting; a house-decorator; a vivid describer. — *adj* **paint'erly** with the qualities of painting, as opposed to drawing, etc — ie with areas of colour, rather than line or drawn detail; as if painted. — *n* **paint'iness**. — *n* **paint'ing** the act or employment of laying on colours; the act of representing objects by colours; a painted picture; vivid description in words. — *n* **paint'ress** formerly, a woman artist who paints; a woman employed to paint pottery. — *n* **paint'ūre** (*Dryden*) the art of painting; a picture. — *adj* **paint'y** overloaded with paint, with the colours too glaringly used; smeared with paint; like paint, in smell, etc. — **paint'ball** (sometimes with *cap*) a type of war game where the ammunition used is paint fired from compressed-air guns; a paint-pellet as used in this; **paint'box** a box in which different paints (for picture-painting) are kept in compartments; **paint'-bridge** a platform used by theatrical scene-painters; **paint'brush** a brush for putting on paint; the painted cup (see below); **painted cloth** a hanging of cloth painted with figures, a substitute for tapestry, formerly common in taverns; **painted cup** a scrophulariaceous plant (*Castilleja*) with brightly coloured upper leaves; **painted grass** striped canary-grass, gardener's garters; **painted lady** the thistle-butterfly, orange-red spotted with white and black; a painted woman (*derog*); the painted cup; a parti-coloured pink, sweetpea, or gladiolus, etc; **painted snipe** a genus (*Rhynchaea*) of birds related to the snipes, the hen brightly coloured; **painted woman** (*derog*) a trollop; **painter's colic** lead colic; **paint'er-stain'er** a member of the London livery company of painters; **paint roller** a roller used in house-painting, etc instead of a brush. — *n sing* **paint'works** a paint-making factory. — **fresh as paint** very fresh and bright; **paint the lily** to attempt to beautify that which is already beautiful; **paint the town red** to enjoy a bout of unbridled revelry or celebration. [OFr *peint*, pa p of *peindre* to paint, from L *pingere* to paint]

painter[1] *pānt'ər*, (*naut*) *n* a rope for fastening a boat. — **cut the painter** to sever ties; **lazy painter** a small painter for use in fine weather only. [Origin obscure]

painter[2] *pānt'ər*, (*US*) *n* the cougar. **[panther]**

painter[3], **paintiness**, **painty**, etc. See under **paint**.

paiock, **paiocke**, **pajock** or **pajocke** *pā'ok* ? or *pā'jok* ?, *n* an obscure word in Shakespeare (*Hamlet* III.2) conjectured to mean peacock (possibly a misprint for *pacock*; possibly = *pea-jock*).

pair[1] *pār*, *n* two things equal, or suited to each other, or growing, grouped or used together; a set of two equal, matching or similar things forming one instrument, garment, etc, such as a pair of scissors, tongs, or trousers; the other of two matching things; a set of similar things generally; a pack (of cards; *obs*); a flight of stairs; a couple; husband and wife; two people engaged to or in love with each other; a male and a female animal mated together; two people or things associated together; a partner; two horses harnessed together; two cards of the same designation; (in *pl* with *sing v*) another name for **Pelmanism**; two voters on opposite sides who have an agreement to abstain from voting; either of such a pair; a duck in both innings (*cricket*); a boat rowed by two; (in *pl*) a contest, etc in which competitors take part in partnerships of two: — *pl* **pairs** or (*colloq*) **pair**. — *vt* to couple; to sort out in pairs. — *vi* to be joined in couples; to be a counterpart or counterparts; to mate; (of two opposing voters) to arrange to abstain, on a motion or for a period (also *vt*, usually *passive*). — *adj* **paired** arranged in pairs; set by twos of a similar kind; mated. — *n* **pair'ing**. — *adv* **pair'wise** in pairs. — **pair'-bond** a continuing and exclusive relationship between a male and female; **pair'-bonding**; **pair case** a double casing for a (pocket) watch, *usu* consisting of an inner plain casing for the movement and an outer decorative one; **paired reading** a teaching method in whch a child and an adult read together until the child is confident enough to read on alone. — *adj* **pair'-horse** (of a carriage) drawn by a pair of horses. — **pair'ing-time** the time when birds go together in pairs; **pair'-oar** a boat rowed by two. — Also *adj*. — **pair production** (*electronics*) the production of a positron and an electron when a gamma-ray photon passes into the electrical field of an atom; **pair-roy'al** three cards of the same denomination, *esp* in cribbage and in the *obs* post and pair; a throw of three dice all falling alike; a set of three (also **pairī'al** and **prī'al**). — **pair of colours** two flags carried by a regiment, one the national ensign, the other the flag of the regiment; hence, an ensigncy; **pair off** to arrange, set against each other, or set aside in pairs; to become associated in pairs. [Fr *paire* a couple, from L *paria*, neut pl of *pār*, afterwards regarded as a fem sing meaning equal]

pair[2] or **paire** *pār*, *v* (*obs*) aphetic forms of **appair**.

pairial. See **pair-royal** under **pair**[1].

pais *pā*, (*archaic*) *n* the people from whom a jury is drawn. [OFr]

paisa *pī'sä*, *n* in India and Pakistan, (a coin worth) one one-hundredth of a rupee (in India, for a time, described officially as **naya paisa** (*nə-yä'*) new paisa or pice: — *pl* **naye paise** (*-yā'* or *-sā*); in Bangladesh, (a coin worth) one one-hundredth of a taka.

paisano *pī-zä'nō*, *n* among people of Spanish or American descent in America, a person from the same area or town; hence, a friend: — *pl* **paisan'os**. [Sp, from Fr *paysan* peasant]

paisley *pāz'li*, *n* a woollen or other fabric with a pattern resembling Paisley pattern; an article made of this. — **paisley pattern** or **design** a type of pattern whose most characteristic feature is an ornamental device known as a 'cone' (rather like a tree cone), used in the **Paisley shawl**, a shawl made in *Paisley*, Scotland in the 19th century in the style of Kashmir shawls.

paitrick *pā'trik*, *n* a Scots form of **partridge**.

pajamas. See **pyjamas**.

pajock, **pajocke**. See **paiock**.

PAK *abbrev*: Pakistan (IVR).

Pak *abbrev*: Pakistan; Pakistani.

pakapoo *pak-ə-pōō'*, (*Austr* and *NZ*) *n* a Chinese version of lotto, in which betting tickets are filled up with Chinese characters. [Chinese]

pak-choi cabbage *päk'-choi kab'ij*, *n*. Same as **Chinese cabbage**.

pakeha *pä'kə-hä* or *pä'kē-hä*, (*NZ*) *n* a white man; a non-Polynesian citizen. [Maori]

pakfong. See **paktong**.

Pakhtu, **Pakhto**, **Pakhtun**, **Pakhtoon**. See **Pushtu**.

Pakistani *pä-kis-tän'i*, *n* a citizen of Pakistan; an immigrant from, or a person whose parents, etc are immigrants from, Pakistan. — Also *adj*. — *n* **Paki** (*pak'i*; *offensive British slang*) a Pakistani. — Also *adj*.

pakka *puk'ə*. Same as **pucka**.

pakora *pə-kö'rə*, *n* an Indian dish consisting of chopped vegetables, etc formed into balls, coated with batter and deep-fried. [Hindi]

paktong *pak'tong*, *n* nickel-silver. — Also (*erron*) **pack'-fong** or **pak'fong**. [Chin *pak* white, and *t'ung* copper]

PAL *pal*, *n* acronym for *phase alternation line*, the colour-television system most commonly used in Europe.

pal *pal*, (*colloq*) *n* a partner, mate; chum. — *vi* to associate as a pal: — *pr p* **pall'ing**; *pa t* and *pa p* **palled** (*pald*). — *adj* **pally** (*pal'i*). — *adj* **pal'sy** or **palsy-wal'sy** (*colloq*) over-friendly; ingratiatingly intimate. [Gypsy]

palabra *pa-lä'brä*, *n* a word; talk. — **pocas** (*pō'käs*) **palabras** few words. [Sp]

palace *pal'is*, *n* the house of a king or a queen; a very large and splendid house; a bishop's official residence; a large public building; a large and *usu* showy place of entertainment or refreshment. — **pal'ace-car** a sumptuously furnished railway-car; **palace guard** (one of) those responsible for the personal protection of a monarch; the group of intimates and advisers around a head of government, etc; **palace revolution** a revolution within the seat of authority. — **palace of culture** in Russia, a cultural and recreational centre; **palais de danse** (*pa-le də dãs*; *Fr*) a dance-hall. [Fr *palais*, from L *Palātium* the Roman emperor's residence on the *Palatine* Hill at Rome]

paladin *pal'ə-din*, (*hist*) *n* one of the twelve peers of Charlemagne's household; a knight-errant, or paragon of knighthood. [Fr, from Ital *paladino*, from L *palātīnus* belonging to the palace; cf **palatine**]

palae- or **palaeo-**, also (*NAm*) **pale-** or **paleo-**, *pal-i-* or *pal-i-ō-*, also *pāl-*, *combining form* meaning old; of or concerned with the very distant past. — *adj* **Palaearc'tic** of the Old World part of the Holarctic region. — *adj* **palaeanthrop'ic** or **palaeoanthrop'ic** (Gr *anthrōpos* man) of the earliest types of man. — *adj* **palaeanthropolog'ical** or **palaeoanthropolog'ical**. — *n* **palaeanthropol'ogist** or **palaeoanthropol'ogist**. — *n* **palaeanthropol'ogy** or **palaeoanthropol'ogy** the study of the earliest types of man. — *n* **Palaean'thropus** or **Palaeoan'thropus** (or *-thrō'*) an extinct genus of man, including the Neanderthal and Heidelberg races. — *adj* **palaeobiolog'ic** or **palaeobiolog'ical**. — *n* **palaebiol'ogist** or **palaeobiol'ogist**. — *n* **palaebiol'ogy** or **palaeobiol'ogy** the biological study of fossil plants and animals. — *adj* **palaeobotan'ic** or **palaeobotan'ical**. — *n* **palaeobot'anist**. — *n* **palaeobot'any** the study of fossil plants. — *adj* **Pal'aeocene** (*geol*) of or from the oldest epoch of the Tertiary period (also *n*). — *n* **palaeoclī'mate** the climate at any stage in the geological development of the earth. — *adj* **palaeoclimat'ic**. — *adj* **palaeoclimatolog'ic** or **palaeoclimatolog'ical**. — *n* **palaeoclimatol'ogist**. — *n* **palaeoclimatol'ogy**. — *adj* **palaeocrys'tic** (Gr *krystallos* ice) consisting of ancient ice. — *adj* **palaeoecolog'ic** or **palaeoecolog'ical**. — *n* **palaeoecol'ogist**. — *n* **palaeoecol'ogy** the (study of) the ecology of fossil animals and plants. — *n* **palaeoenvī'ronment** the environment in earlier ages. — *adj* **palaeoenvironment'al**. — *adj* **palaeoethnolog'ic** or **palaeoethnolog'ical**. — *n* **palaeoethnol'ogist**. — *n* **palaeoethnol'ogy** the science of early man. — *n* **palaeogaea** (*-jē'ə*; Gr *gaia* earth) the Old World as a biological region. — *n* and *adj* **Pal'aeogene** (*-jēn*; Gr *palai(o)genēs* born long ago) early Tertiary — Eocene and Oligocene. — *n* **palaeogeog'rapher**. — *adj* **palaeogeograph'ic** or **palaeogeograph'ical**. — *n* **palaeogeog'raphy** the study of the geography of geological periods. — *n* **palaeog'rapher** (Gr *graphein* to write) an expert in or student of palaeography. — *adj* **palaeograph'ic** or **palaeograph'ical**. — *n* **palaeog'raphist**. — *n* **palaeog'raphy** ancient modes of writing; the study of ancient modes of handwriting. — *adj* **palaeichthyolog'ic, palaeoichthyolog'ic, palaeicthyolog'ical** or **palaeoicthyolog'ical**. — *n* **palaeichthyol'ogist** or **palaeoicthyol'ogist**. — *n* **palaeichthyol'ogy** or **palaeoicthyol'ogy** the study of ancient varieties of fish. — *adj* **palaeolimnolog'ical**. — *n* **palaeolimnol'ogist**. — *n* **palaeolimnol'ogy** the scientific study of lakes of past ages. — *n* **pal'aeolith** (Gr *lithos* stone) a Palaeolithic artefact. — *adj* **Palaeolith'ic** of the earlier Stone Age. — *n* **palaeomag'netism** a study of the magnetism of ancient rocks and fossils, and of bricks, pottery, etc made in past ages. — *adj* **palaeontograph'ical**. — *n* **palaeontog'raphy** the description of fossil remains — descriptive palaeontology. — *adj* **palaeontolog'ical**. — *n* **palaeontol'ogist**. — *n* **palaeontol'ogy** (Gr *onta* neut pl of pr p of *einai* to be, and *logos* discourse) the study of fossils. — *adj* **palaeopatholog'ic** or **palaeopatholog'ical**. — *n* **palaeopathol'ogist**. — *n* **palaeopathol'ogy** the pathological study of the ancient remains of animals and humans. — *adj* **palaeopedolog'ical**. — *n* **palaeopedol'ogist**. — *n* **palaeopedol'ogy** the study of the soils of past geological ages. — *n* **palaeophȳtol'ogy** palaeobotany. — *n* **Palaeothē'rium** (Gr *thērion* a wild beast, from *thēr* animal, beast of prey) an odd-toed Eocene fossil ungulate with a tapir-like snout. — *n* **pal'aeotype** A J Ellis's phonetic adaptation of ordinary alphabetical type. — *adj* **palaeotypic** (*-tip'ik*). — *adj* **Palaeozo'ic** (Gr *zōē* life) of the division of the fossiliferous rocks, from Cambrian to Permian. — *adj* **palaeozoolog'ical**. — *n* **palaeozool'ogist**. — *n* **palaeozool'ogy** the study of fossil animals. [Gr *palaios* old]

palaestra *pal-ēs'trə* or *-es'*, (*antiq*) *n* a wrestling school; a gymnasium; wrestling; a training-ground. — *adj* **palaes'tral, palaes'tric** or **palaes'trical**. [L *palaestra*, from Gr *palaistrā*, from *palaiein* to wrestle]

palafitte *pal'ə-fit*, *n* a prehistoric lake dwelling. [Ital *palafitta*, from *palo* (from L *pālus*) a stake, and *fitto*, pa p of *figgere* (from L *figere*) to fix]

palagi *pə-la'ji*, *n* a Samoan word for a person from outside the Pacific Islands, *esp* a European.

palagonite *pal-ag'ə-nīt*, *n* an altered basic vitreous lava. — **palag'onite-tuff** a tuff composed of fragments of palagonite. [*Palagonia* in Sicily]

palais de danse. See under **palace**.

palama *pal'ə-mə*, *n* the webbing of a water-bird's foot: — *pl* **pal'amae** (*-mē*). — *adj* **pal'amate**. [Latinized from Gr *palamē* palm]

palamino. Same as **palomino**.

palampore or **palempore** *pal'əm-pōr* or *-pör*, *n* a flowered chintz bedcover common in the East. [From *Palampur*, N India, place of manufacture]

palanquin or **palankeen** *pal-ən-kēn'*, *n* a light litter for one passenger, a box borne on poles on men's shoulders. [Port *palanquim*; cf Hindi *palang* a bed, from Sans *palyaṅka* a bed]

palas *pal-äs'* or *-äsh'*, *n* the dhak tree. [Hindi *palās*]

palate *pal'it* or *-ət*, *n* the roof of the mouth, consisting of the *hard palate* in front and the *soft palate* behind; the prominent part of the lower lip that closes the tube of a personate corolla (*bot*); sense of taste; relish; mental liking; ability to appreciate the finer qualities of wine, etc (also *fig*). — *vt* to taste, to relish (*Shakesp*). — *adj* **pal'atable** pleasant to the taste; acceptable to the mind or feelings. — *n* **palatabil'ity**. — *n* **pal'atableness**. — *adv* **pal'atably**. — *adj* **pal'atal** pertaining to the palate; uttered by bringing the tongue to or near the hard palate (*phonetics*). — *n* a sound so produced. — *n* **palatalizā'tion** or **-s-**. — *vt* **pal'atalize** or **-ise** to make palatal. — *adj* **pal'atine** pertaining to the palate. — *n* a paired bone forming part of the roof of the mouth. — *adj* **pal'atō-alvē'olar** (or *-ōl'*; *phonetics*) produced by bringing the tongue to a position at or close to the hard palate and the roots of the upper teeth. — **cleft palate** a congenital defect of the palate, leaving a longitudinal fissure in the roof of the mouth. [L *palātum*]

palatial *pə-lā'shl*, *adj* of or like a palace, *esp* sumptuous and spacious. [See **palace**]

palatine[1] *pal'ə-tīn*, *adj* of the Palatine Hill or the palace of emperors there; of a palace; having royal privileges or jurisdiction; of a count or earl palatine (see below). — *n* an officer of the palace; a noble invested with royal privileges and jurisdiction; a subject of a palatinate; a fur tippet (from the Princess Palatine of 1676); (with *cap*) one of the seven hills of Rome. — *n* **palat'inate** (or *pa'lət-*) the office or rank of a palatine; the province of a palatine, *esp* an electorate of the ancient German Empire; (at Durham University) a light purple blazer. — *adj* (at Durham) light purple or lilac. — **count, earl,** etc, **palatine** a feudal lord with supreme judicial authority over a province; **county palatine** the province of such a lord. [L *palātīnus*; cf **palace**]

palatine[2]. See under **palate**.

palaver *pə-lä'vər*, *n* a conference, *esp orig* with African or other native tribespeople; a talk or discussion; idle copious talk; talk intended to deceive; a long, boring, complicated and seemingly pointless exercise; a fuss. — *vi* to hold a palaver; to chatter idly. — *vt* to flatter. — *n* **palav'erer**. [Port *palavra* word, from L *parabola* a parable, later a word, speech, from Gr *parabolē*; cf **parable, parabola**]

palay *pa-lā'*, *pä-lī'* or *-lā'*, *n* the ivory-tree, a small S Indian tree (*Wrightia*) of the dogbane family, with hard white wood. [Tamil]

palazzo *pə-lat'sō*, *n* an Italian palace, often one converted into a museum; a house built in this style: — *pl* **palazz'i** (*-at'sē*). [Ital from L *palātium*]

pale[1] *pāl*, *n* a stake of wood driven into the ground for fencing; any thing that encloses or fences in; a limit; the limit of what can be accepted as decent or tolerable (*fig*); an enclosure; a marked-off district; a broad stripe from top to bottom of a shield (*heraldry*). — *vt* to enclose with stakes; to fence; to encircle, crown (*Shakesp*). — *adv* **pale'wise** (*heraldry*) vertically, like a pale. — *n* **palificā'tion** (*pal-* or *pāl-*) the act of strengthening with stakes. — *adj* **pāl'iform**. — *n* **pāl'ing** the act of fencing; wood or stakes for fencing; a fence of stakes connected by horizontal pieces; an upright stake or board in a fence. — *adj* **pāl'y** (*heraldry*) divided by vertical lines. — **beyond the pale** intolerable; unacceptable; **English Pale** the district in Ireland within which only the English had power for centuries after the invasion in 1172; **Jewish Pale** the district of SW Russia in which only Jews were formerly allowed to live. [Fr *pal*, from L *pālus* a stake]

pale[2] *pāl*, *adj* whitish; (of a colour) not deep or vivid; not ruddy or fresh; wan; of a faint lustre, dim; lacking colour. — *vt* to make pale. — *vi* to turn pale. — *n* paleness. — *adv* **pale'ly**. — *n* **pale'ness**. — *adj* **pāl'ish** somewhat pale. — *adj* **pāl'y** (*archaic*) pale; palish. — **pale ale** a light-coloured bitter ale; **pale'buck** an antelope, the oribi. — *adj* **pale'-dead** (*Shakesp*) lustreless. — *adj* **pale'-eyed** (*Milton*) dim-eyed. — **pale'face** (attributed to American Indians) a white person. — *adj* **pale'-heart'ed** (*Shakesp*) dispirited. — *adj* **pale'=vis'aged** (*Shakesp*). [OFr *palle*, pale (Fr *pâle*), from L *pallidus* pale]

pale[3] *pāl*, (*dialect*) *n* a baker's peel; a cheese-scoop. — *vt* to test by inserting a cheese-pale. [L *pāla* spade]

pale[4]. See under **palea**.

pale-. See **palae-**.

palea *pā'li-ə*, (*bot*) *n* the membranous inner bract (*inferior palea*) or bracteole (*superior palea*) of an individual grass-flower, above the glumes; a scale on a fern-leaf or stem; a scale on the receptacle of some composite plants: — *pl* **pā'leae** (*-ē*). — *n* **pale** (*pāl*) a grass palea. — *adj* **paleā'ceous** chaffy. — *n* **palet** (*pāl'it*) a palea. [L *palea* chaff]

palely. See under **pale**[2].

palempore. See **palampore**.

paleness. See under **pale**[2].

paleo-, etc. See **palae-**.

Palestinian *pal-is-tin'i-ən*, *adj* pertaining to *Palestine* (Gr *Palaistīnē*). — *n* a native or inhabitant of Palestine; a member of a guerrilla movement or political body one of whose aims is to reclaim former Arab lands from Israel, to recreate a Palestinian Arab state. — **Palestine soup** artichoke soup, by a pun on *Jerusalem* (see **artichoke**). [Cf **Philistine**]

palestra. Same as **palaestra**.

palet. See **palea**.

paletot *pal'tō*, *n* a loose overcoat. [Fr]

palette *pal'it*, *n* a little board, *usu* with a thumb-hole, on which a painter mixes colours; the assortment or range of colours used by a particular artist or for any particular picture; a range or selection (*fig*); a plate against which one leans in working a drill; a small plate covering a joint in armour, *esp* at the armpit (*hist*). — **pal'ette-knife** a thin round-ended knife for mixing colours, cooking ingredients, etc. [Fr, from Ital *paletta*, from *pala* spade, from L *pāla* a spade]

palewise. See under **pale**[1].

palfrey *pöl'fri*, (*archaic* or *poetic*) *n* a saddle-horse, *esp* for a lady (in Spenser's *Faerie Queene* applied to Una's ass). — *n* **palfrenier** (*pal-frə-nēr'*) a groom. — *adj* **palfreyed** (*pöl'*) riding on or supplied with a palfrey. [OFr *palefrei*, from LL *paraverēdus*, prob from Gr *para* beside, LL *verēdus* a post-horse, appar a Celtic word; confused with L *frēnum* a bridle]

Pali *pä'lē*, *n* the sacred language of the Buddhists of India, etc, closely related to Sanskrit. [Sans *pāli* canon]

palification, paliform. See under **pale**[1].

palilalia *pal-i-lā'li-ə*, *n* a speech abnormality characterized by the increasingly rapid repetition of words or phrases. [Modern L, from Gr *palin* again, and *lalia* speech]

Palilia *pə-lil'i-ə*, *n pl* (or *sing*) the festival of Pales (L *Palēs*), Roman goddess of flocks, held on 21 April, traditional date of the founding of Rome.

palillogy *pal-il'ə-ji*, *n* a repetition of a word or phrase. [Gr *palillogiā*, from *palin* again, and *logos* word, speech]

palimony *pal'i-mən-i*, (*colloq*) *n* alimony or its equivalent demanded by one partner when the couple have been cohabiting without being married. [**pal** and **alimony**]

palimpsest *pal'imp-sest*, *n* a manuscript in which old writing has been rubbed out to make room for new; a monumental brass turned over for a new inscription. [Gr *palimpsēston*, from *palin* again, and *psāein* (contracted *psēn*) to rub]

palindrome *pal'in-drōm*, *n* a word, verse, or sentence that reads the same backward and forward. — *adj* **palindromic** (*-drom'* or *-drōm'*) or **palindrom'ical**. — *n* **pal'indromist** (or *pə-lin'*) an inventor of palindromes. [Gr *palindromos* running back, from *palin* back, and *dromos* a running]

paling. See under **pale**[1].

palingenesis *pal-in-jen'i-sis*, *n* a new birth; reincarnation; a second creation; regeneration; unmodified inheritance of ancestral characters; the re-formation of a rock by refusion: — *pl* **palingen'eses** (*-sēz*). — Also **palingenē'sia** or **palingen'esy**. — *n* **palingen'esist**. — *adj* **palingenet'ical**. — *adv* **palingenet'ically**. [Gr *palin* again, and *genesis* birth]

palinode *pal'i-nōd*, *n* a poem in which thoughts, feelings, etc expressed in an earlier poem are retracted; a recantation (*rare*). — Also (*obs*) **pal'inōdy**. [Gr *palinōidiā*, from *palin* back, and *ōidē* song]

palisade *pal-i-sād'*, *n* a fence of stakes; a stake so used (*military*). — *vt* to surround or defend with a palisade. — Also **palisā'do**: — *pl* **palisā'does**. — **palisade tissue** a tissue occurring in leaves, composed of cells placed closely together with their long axes perpendicular to the surface. [Fr *palissade* and Sp *palizada*, from L *pālus* a stake]

palisander *pal-i-san'dər*, *n* jacaranda or other rosewood. [Fr *palissandre*, from a name used in Guiana]

palish. See under **pale**[2].

palki or **palkee** *päl'kē*, *n* a palanquin. [Hindi *pālkī*]

pall[1] *pöl*, *n* a rich cloth (*archaic*); a covering of rich cloth; a corporal (*eccles*); a frontal; a chalice-cover; a cloth spread over a coffin or tomb; a cloak, mantle, outer garment (*esp eccles*); a pallium; a bearing representing a pallium (*heraldry*); a curtain, covering, or cloak, eg of smoke or darkness (*fig*). — *vt* to cover with, or as if with, a pall. — **pall'-bearer** one of the mourners at a funeral who used to hold up the corners of the pall; one of those carrying (or walking beside) a coffin at a funeral. [OE *pæll* a rich robe, from L *pallium*; see **pallium**]

pall[2] *pöl*, *vi* to lose strength (*obs*); to become vapid, insipid, or wearisome; to lose relish. — *vt* to daunt (*obs*); to weaken (*obs*); to pale (*obs*); to make vapid; to cloy. [Prob from **appal**]

palla *pal'ə*, *n* a Roman woman's mantle: — *pl* **pall'ae** (*-ē*). [L *palla*]

Palladian[1] *pə-lā'di-ən*, *adj* relating to *Pallas*, wisdom, or learning.

Palladian[2] *pə-lā'di-ən*, *adj* in the style of architecture introduced by Andrea *Palladio* (1518–80), modelled on Vitruvius. — *n* **Pallā'dianism**.

palladic, palladious. See under **palladium**.

Palladium *pə-lā'di-əm*, *n* a statue of *Pallas*, on whose preservation the safety of Troy depended; anything of similar virtue; a safeguard. [L, from Gr *palladion*, from *Pallas*, *Pallados* Pallas]

palladium *pə-lā'di-əm*, *n* a metallic element (symbol **Pd**; atomic no 46) resembling platinum, remarkable for its capacity for occluding hydrogen. — *adj* **palladic** (*-lad'*), **pallā'dious** or **palla'dous** containing palladium in smaller or greater proportion respectively. [Named by its discoverer Wollaston (in 1803 or 1804) after the newly discovered minor planet *Pallas*]

pallae. See under **palla**.

pallah *pal'ə*, *n* the impala. [Tswana *phala*]

Pallas *pal'as*, *n* the Greek goddess **Athēnē** (also **Pall'as Athē'nē**); a minor planet discovered by Olbers in 1802.

palled. See under **pal**.

pallescent *pə-les'ənt*, *adj* turning pale. — *n* **pallesc'ence**. [L *pallēscēns*, *-entis*, pr p of *pallēscere* to turn pale]

pallet[1] *pal'it*, *n* a palette; a flat wooden tool with a handle, such as that used for shaping pottery; a flat brush for spreading gold-leaf; a tool for lettering book-bindings; (in a timepiece) the surface or part on which the teeth of the escape wheel act to give impulse to the pendulum or balance; a disc of a chain-pump; a valve of an organ wind-chest, regulated from the keyboard; a board for carrying newly moulded bricks; a piece of wood built into a wall for the nailing on of joiner-work; a platform or tray for lifting and stacking goods, used with the fork-lift truck, and having a double base into which the fork can be thrust. — *adj* **pall'eted** carried on a pallet or pallets. — *n* **palletiza'tion** or **-s-** the adoption of pallets for moving goods; the packing of goods on pallets. — *vi* and *vt* **pall'etize** or **-ise**. — *n* **pall'etizer** or **-s-**. [**palette**]

pallet[2] *pal'it*, *n* a mattress, or couch, properly a mattress of straw; a small or poorly furnished bed. [Dialect Fr *paillet*, dimin of Fr *paille* straw, from L *palea* chaff]

pallia, **pallial**, **palliament**. See under **pallium**.

palliard *pal'yärd*, (*obs*) *n* a professional beggar, a vagabond; a rogue, libertine. [Fr *paillard*, from *paille* straw, from the vagabond's habit of sleeping on straw in barns, etc]

palliasse *pal-i-as'*, *pal-yas'* or *pal'*, *n* a straw mattress; an under-mattress. — Also **paillasse**. [Fr *paillasse*, from *paille* straw, from L *palea*]

palliate *pal'i-āt*, *vt* to cloak (*obs*); to disguise (*obs*); to excuse, extenuate; to soften by pleading something in favour; to mitigate; to alleviate. — *adj* see under **pallium**. — *n* **palliā'tion** the act of palliating. — *adj* **pall'iative** (*-ə-tiv*) serving to extenuate; mitigating; alleviating. — *n* something which lessens pain, etc, or gives temporary relief. — *adj* **pall'iatory**. [L *palliāre*, *-ātum* to cloak, from *pallium* a cloak]

pallid *pal'id*, *adj* pale, wan. — *n* **pallid'ity**. — *adv* **pall'idly**. — *n* **pall'idness**. [L *pallidus* pale]

palling. See under **pal**.

pallium *pal'i-əm*, *n* a large, square mantle, worn by learned Romans in imitation of the Greeks — the himation (*hist*); a white woollen vestment like a double Y, embroidered with crosses, worn by the Pope, and conferred by him upon archbishops; the mantle in molluscs, brachiopods, and birds (*zool*): — *pl* **pall'ia**. — *adj* (*zool*) **pall'ial**. — *n* **pall'iament** (*Shakesp*) a Roman consular candidate's robe. — *adj* **pall'iate** having a pallium. [L *pallium*]

pall-mall *pel'-mel'* or *pal'-mal'*, *n* an old game, in which a ball was driven through an iron ring with a mallet; an alley for the game (hence the street in London (*pal'-mal'*)). [Obs Fr *pale-maille*, from palmaille, from Ital *pallamaglio*, from *palla* ball (cf OHGer *pallâ*), and *maglio*, from L *malleus* a hammer; cf **ball**[1] and **pallone**]

pallone *päl-lō'nā*, *n* an Italian game in which a ball is struck with a gauntlet or armguard. [Ital, augmentative of *palla* ball]

pallor *pal'ər*, *n* paleness. [L *pallēre* to be pale]

pally. See under **pal**.

palm[1] *päm*, *n* the inner surface of the hand between wrist and fingers; the corresponding part of a forefoot, or of a glove; the sole of the foot (*rare*); a handsbreadth (7.5 or 10 cm — 3 or 4 inches); the length of the hand from wrist to fingertip; a sailmaker's instrument used instead of a thimble; a flat expansion, as of an antler, or the inner surface of an anchor fluke; an act of palming; an old game (also **palm'-play**) in which a ball was struck with the palm. — *vt* to touch or stroke with the palm; to hold in the palm; to take swiftly and unseen and conceal in the palm; to impose, pass off (*esp* with *off*, and *on* or *upon*); to bribe. — *adj* **palmar** (*pal'mər*) relating to the palm. — *adj* **palmate** (*pal'*) or **palmated** hand-shaped; having lobes radiating from one centre (*bot*); web-footed (*zool*). — *adv* **pal'mately**. — *adj* **palmatifid** (*pal-mat'i-fid* ; *bot*) shaped like the hand, with the divisions extending about halfway down. — *n* **palmā'tion** palmate formation; a palmate structure or one of its parts or divisions. — *adj* **palmatipart'ite** palmately divided rather more than halfway. — *adj* **palmatisect** (*pal-mat'i-sekt*) deeply cut in a palmate manner. — *adj* **palmed** (*pämd*) having a palm; held or concealed in the palm. — *n* **palm'ful** as much as the palm will hold. — *n* **palmiped** (*pal'mi-ped*) or **palmipede** (*-pēd*) a web-footed bird. — *adj* web-footed. — *n* **palmist** (*päm'ist*) someone who tells a person's fortune from the lines on his or her palm. — *n* **palm'istry**. — *n* **palmy** or **palmie** (*päm'i*; *Scot*) a stroke of the tawse on the palm. — **palm'-grease** or **palm'-oil** a bribe; **palm'top** a small hand-held portable computer (also *adj*). — **grease someone's palm** to bribe someone; **in the palm of one's hand** in one's power; at one's command. [L *palma*; cf Gr *palamē* and OE *folm*]

palm[2] *päm*, *n* any tree or shrub of the **Palmae** (*pal'mē*), a large tropical and sub-tropical family of monocotyledons, sometimes climbers but *usu* branchless trees with a crown of pinnate or fan-shaped leaves; a leaf of this tree carried as a token of rejoicing or of victory; emblematically, pre-eminence, the prize; a branch of willow or other substitute in symbolic or ceremonial use. — *adj* **palmaceous** (*pal-mā'shəs*) of the palm family. — *adj* **palmarian** (*pal-mā'ri-ən*) or **palmary** (*pal'mər-i*) worthy of the ceremonial palm; pre-eminent. — *n* **palmette** (*pal-met'* ; *Fr*) an ancient architectural ornament like a palm-leaf. — *n* **palmett'o** (*pal-*) a name for several kinds of palm, notably Sabal and the only European palm Chamaerops: — *pl* **palmettos** or **palmetoes**. — *n* **palmiet** (*pal-mēt'*) a South African aloe-like riverside plant of the rush family (*Prionum palmita*). — *n* **palmificā'tion** (*pal-*) artificial fertilization of dates by hanging a wild male flower-cluster on a cultivated female tree. — *n* **palmitate** (*pal'*) a salt of **palmit'ic acid**, a fatty acid ($C_{15}H_{31}$) obtained from palm-oil, etc. — *n* **palmitin** (*pal'*) a white fat abundant in palm-oil; a glycerine ester of palmitic acid. — *adj* **palm'y** bearing palms; flourishing; palmlike. — **pal'ma Christi** (*pal'mə kris'ti*) the castor-oil plant; **palm'-branch** a palm-leaf; **palm'-butt'er** palm-oil in a solid state; **palm'-cabb'age** the bud of the cabbage-palm; **palm'-cat'** or **palm'-civ'et** the paradoxure. — *adj* **palm'-court'** suitable to a **palm court**, a large, palm-tree-decorated room or conservatory in a hotel, etc, in which, traditionally, light music is played by a small orchestra, a **palm-court orchestra**. — **palm'-hon'ey** evaporated sap of the Chilean *coquito-palm*; **palm'-house** a glass house for palms and other tropical plants; **palmitic acid** see **palmitate** above; **palm'-ker'nel** the kernel of the oil-palm, yielding **palm-kernel oil**; **palm'-oil** an oil or fat obtained from the pulp of the fruit of palms, *esp* of the oil-palm; **palm'-su'gar** jaggery; **Palm Sunday** the Sunday before Easter, in commemoration of the strewing of palm-branches when Christ entered Jerusalem; **palm'-tree**; **palm-tree justice** justice without litigation and legal processes, from the old Arabic or Jewish idea of a wise man dispensing justice under a palm tree; **palm'-wine'** fermented palm sap. [OE *palm*, *palma*, *palme*, also directly from L *palma* palm-tree, from the shape of its leaves; see **palm**[1]]

palmar, **palmate**, etc. See under **palm**[1].

palmer *päm'ər*, *n* a pilgrim carrying a palm-leaf in token of having been in the Holy Land; a palmer-worm; a bristly artificial fly. — **palm'er-worm'** a hairy caterpillar of various kinds, *orig* one of wandering habits. [**palm**[2]]

Palmerin *pal'mər-in*, *n* a knightly champion. [From *Palmerin*, a Spanish (or Portuguese) romance hero found as a child among *palm*-trees]

palmette, **palmiet**, **palmitin**, etc. See under **palm**[2].

palmful. See under **palm**[1].

palmipede, **palmist**, etc. See under **palm**[1].

palmy. See under **palm**[1,2].

palmyra *pal-mī'rə*, *n* an African and Asiatic palm (*Borassus flabellifer*) yielding toddy, jaggery, and **palmy'ra-nuts**. — **palmy'ra-wood** properly, the wood of the palmyra palm; any palm timber. [Port *palmeira* palm-tree, confused with *Palmyra* in Syria]

palolo *pa-lō'lō*, *n* an edible sea-worm that burrows in coral-reefs, remarkable for its breeding swarms at a certain phase of the moon, the head remaining behind to regenerate: — *pl* **palo'los**. — Also **palolo worm**. [Samoan]

palomino *pal-ə-mē'nō*, *n* a horse of largely Arab blood, pale tan, yellow, or gold, with a white or silver mane and tail: — *pl* **palomin'os**. [Am Sp, from Sp, of a dove]

palooka *pə-lo͞o'kə*, (*US slang*) *n* a stupid or clumsy person, *esp* in sports. [Origin unknown]

palp[1] *palp*, *n* a jointed sense-organ attached in pairs to the mouth-parts of insects and crustaceans (also **pal'pus**: — *pl* **pal'pī**). — *adj* **pal'pal**. — *adj* **pal'pate** (*zool*) of, relating to or possessing a palp or palps. [LL *palpus* a feeler (L, a stroking), from L *palpāre* to stroke]

palp[2] *palp*, *vt* to feel, examine, or explore by touch; to speak fair (*obs*). — *n* **palpabil'ity**. — *adj* **palp'able** that can be touched or felt; perceptible; (of eg lies, etc) easily found out; obvious, gross. — *n* **palp'ableness**. — *adv* **palp'ably**. — *vt* **palp'āte** to examine by touching or pressing (*esp med*). — *n* **palpā'tion** the act of examining by means of touch. — *adj* **palp'able-gross'** (*Shakesp*). [L *palpāre*, *-ātum* to touch softly, stroke, caress, flatter]

palpal. See under **palp**[1].

palpate. See under **palp**[1,2].

palpebral *palp'i-brəl*, *adj* of or pertaining to the eyelid. [L *palpebra* the eyelid]

palpi. See under **palp**[1].

palpitate *pal'pi-tāt*, *vi* to throb; to beat rapidly; to pulsate; to quiver. — *vt* to cause to throb. — *adj* **pal'pitant** palpitating. — *n* **palpitā'tion** the act of palpitating; abnormal awareness of heart-beat. [L *palpitāre*, *-ātum*, frequentative of *palpāre*; cf **palp**[1,2]]

palpus. See under **palp**[1].

palsgrave *pölz'grāv*, *n* a count palatine: — *fem* **palsgravine** (*pölz'grə-vēn*). [Du *paltsgrave* (now *paltsgraaf*); cf Ger *Pfalzgraf*; see **palace** and **Graf**]

palstave *pöl'stāv* or **palstaff** *-stäf*, *n* a Bronze Age axe, the flanges of the head joined by a cross ridge to engage the ends of the prongs of the kneed shaft. [Du *paalstav*, from ON *pālstafr*]

palsy[1] *pöl'zi*, *n* loss of control or of feeling, more or less complete, in the muscles of the body, *esp* when this results in involuntary trembling; paralysis. — *vt* to affect with palsy; to deprive of action or energy; to paralyse. — *adj* **pal'sied**. [From **paralysis**]

palsy[2] or **palsy-walsy**. See under **pal**.

palter *pöl'tər*, *vi* to trifle in talk; to use trickery; to haggle; to equivocate. — *n* **pal'terer**. [Poss connected with **paltry**]

paltry *pöl'tri*, *adj* meagre, mean; of poor quality; trashy; worthless; not worth considering. — *adv* **pal'trily**. — *n* **pal'triness**. [Cf Dan *pialter* rags, LG *paltrig* ragged]

paludal *pal-ū'dl* or *-o͞o'*, also (*rare*) *pal'*, *adj* pertaining to marshes; marshy; malarial. — *adj* **palu'dic** of marshes. — *adj* **paludic'olous** (L *colere* to inhabit) marsh-dwelling; growing in marshes. — *adj* **palu'dinal**, **pal'udine** or **palu'dinous** of marshes; marshy. — *n* **pal'udism** malaria. — *adj* **pal'udose** or **pal'udous** of marshes; marshy; inhabiting marshes; malarial. — *n* **Pal'udrine**® a proprietary name for *proguanil hydrochloride*, a synthetic anti-malarial drug. — *adj* **palustral** (*-us'trəl*), **palus'trian** or **palus'trine** (*-trīn*) of marshes; inhabiting marshes. [L *palus*, *palūdis* a marsh; *palūster*, *-tris* marshy]

paludament *pə-lū'* or *-lo͞o'*, *-də-mənt*, *n* a Roman general's or high military officer's cloak. — Also **paludament'um**. [L *palūdāmentum*]

palustral, etc. See under **paludal**.

paly. See under **pale**[1,2].

palynology *pal-i-nol'ə-ji*, *n* the study of spores and pollen-grains. — *adj* **palynolog'ical**. — *n* **palynol'ogist**. [Gr *palȳnein* to sprinkle]

pam *pam*, *n* the knave of clubs, highest card in the game of loo; a game like nap, in which it is highest card. [Said to be from Fr *Pamphile*, from G *Pamphilos*, literally beloved of all]

pam *abbrev*: pamphlet.

pampa *pam'pə*, *n* (*usu* in *pl* **pampas** (*pam'pəz*) also used as *n sing* (*pam'pəs*) a vast treeless plain in southern S America. — *adj* **pam'pēan**. — *n* **pampero** (*pam-pā'rō*) a violent SW wind on and from the pampas: — *pl* **pampe'ros**. — **pampas grass** a tall, ornamental, reed-like grass (*Gynerium*, or *Cortaderia*) with large thick silvery panicles. [Sp, from Quechua *pampa*, *bamba* plain]

pampelmoose, **pampelmouse** *pam'pl-mo͞os*, *n*. See **pompelmoose**.

pamper *pam'pər*, *vt* to feed with fine food (*archaic*); to gratify to the full; to over-indulge. — *n* **pam'peredness**. — *n* **pam'perer**. [A frequentative from (obs) *pamp*, *pomp*; cf Ger dialect *pampen* to cram]

pampero. See under **pampa**.

pamphlet *pam'flit*, *n* a small book stitched but not bound; a separately published treatise, *usu* controversial, on some subject of the day; a small booklet of information. — *n* **pamphleteer'** a writer of (*esp* politically controversial or subversive) pamphlets. — *vi* to write pamphlets. — *n* and *adj* **pamphleteer'ing**. [Anglo-L *panfletus*, possibly from a Latin erotic poem *Pamphilus* (from Gr *Pamphilos* beloved of all) very popular in the Middle Ages]

PAMR *abbrev*: Public Access Mobile Radio.

Pamyat *pam'yət*, *n* a Russian anti-Semitic nationalist organization.

Pan *pan*, *n* the Greek god of pastures, flocks, and woods, worshipped in Arcadia, fond of music — with a goat's legs and feet, and sometimes horns and ears; later (from association with *pān* the whole) connected with pantheistic thought. — **Pan'-pipes** or **Pan's pipes** the syrinx, a musical instrument attributed to Pan, made of reeds of different lengths, fastened in a row. [Gr *Pān*]

pan[1] *pan*, *n* any broad, shallow container used in the home, in the arts or in industry; a saucepan; anything of similar shape, such as the upper part of the skull (*brain-pan*) or the patella (*knee-pan*); a lavatory bowl; a hollow in the ground, a basin, in which water collects in the rainy season, leaving a salt deposit on evaporation; a salt-pan; a salt-work; the part of a firelock that holds the priming; a hard layer (*hard-pan*) in or under the soil; a small ice-floe; a hollow metal drum as played in a steel band; a panful; the face (*slang*). — *vt* to wash in a goldminer's pan; to obtain by evaporating in a pan; to yield; to obtain; to cook and serve in a pan; to review or criticize harshly (*colloq*). — *vi* to wash earth for gold; to yield gold (*usu* with *out*); to result, turn out (with *out*); to come to an end, be exhausted (with *out*); to cake; to enlarge or embellish in speech: — *pr p* **pann'ing**; *pa t* and *pa p* **panned**. — *n* **pan'ful**: — *pl* **pan'fuls**. — *n* **pann'ikel** (*obs*) pannicle. — *n* **pann'ikin** a small metal cup; a little pan or saucer; enough to fill a cup. — *n* **pann'ing** washing for gold; the gold so obtained; harsh criticism (*colloq*). — **pan'cake** a thin flat round cake of eggs, flour, sugar, and milk, fried in a pan; pancake make-up; an aircraft descent made in an emergency with the wheels up and landing flat on the belly of the aircraft (also *adj*). — *vi* to descend or alight in such a way; (of a building) to collapse concertina-like. — *vt* to cause to make a pancake (descent or landing). — **pan drop** (*Scot*) a hard smooth peppermint sweet made in a revolving pan; **pan'handle** a strip of territory stretching out from the main body like the handle of a pan. — *vi* and *vt* (*US*) to beg (from someone) *esp* on the street. — **pan'handler**; **pan loaf** (*Scot*) a loaf baked in an individual tin, with a crust all round, rather than a **plain loaf** or **batch loaf**. — **flash in the pan** a mere flash in the pan of a flint-lock without discharge; a fitful show of beginning without accomplishing anything; a brief success; **pancake bell** a church bell rung on Shrove Tuesday, taken as the signal for pancake-making; **pancake ice** polar sea ice in thin flat slabs, found as winter draws near; **pancake make-up** cosmetic in cake form, moist, or moistened before application; **Pancake Tuesday** Shrove Tuesday. [OE *panne*; a word common to the West Germanic languages, possibly an early borrowing from L *patina*]

pan[2] *pän* or **pawn** *pön*, *n* betel leaf; betel. [Hindi *pān*]

pan[3] *pan*, *vt* to move (a cinema, video or still television camera) about (or as if pivoting about) an axis while taking a picture so as to follow a particular object or to produce a panoramic effect; (in broadcasting or recording) to cause (sound) to appear to move by electronic means. — Also *vi*: — *pr p* **pann'ing**; *pa t* and *pa p* **panned**. [**pan(orama)**]

pan- *pan-*, **pant-** *pant-*, or **panto-** *pan-tō-*, *combining form* meaning all. [Gr *pās, pāsa, pān*, genitive *pantos, pāsēs, pantos*]

panacea *pan-ə-sē'ə*, *n* a cure for all things; a healing plant, of varying description (*obs*; *Spenser* **panachaea**, *-kē'ə*). — *adj* **panacē'an**. [Gr *panakeia*, from *akos* cure]

panache *pa-näsh'* or *-nash'*, *n* a plume (*hist*); knightly splendour; swagger; grand manner, theatricality, sense of style. [Fr, from Ital *pennacchio*, from *penna* feather]

panada *pə-nä'də*, *n* a dish made by boiling bread to a pulp in water, and flavouring; a thick binding sauce of breadcrumbs or flour and seasoning. [Sp *pan* (L *pānis*) bread]

Panadol® *pan'ə-dol*, *n* a proprietary form of paracetamol.

panaesthesia or (*US*) **panesthesia** *pan-ēs-thē'zi-ə, -zyə* or *-es-*, *n* totality of perception; general awareness. — *n* **panaesthetism** (*-ēs'* or *-es'thi-tizm*). [Gr *aisthēsis* perception]

Pan-African *pan-af'ri-kən*, *adj* including or relating to all Africa, *esp* concerning policies of political unity among African states. — *n* **Pan-Af'ricanism**. [**pan-** and **African**]

Panagia. Same as **Panhagia**.

Pan Am *pan-am'*, *abbrev*: Pan-American (World Airways Incorporated).

Panama *pan-ə-mä'*, *n* a republic, town, and isthmus of Central America (also *adj*); (without *cap*) a panama hat. — *n* and *adj* **Panamanian** (*-mā'ni-ən*). — **panama hat** a lightweight hand-plaited men's hat made, not in Panama but in Ecuador, of plaited strips of the leaves of a South American cyclanthaceous plant (*Carludovica palmata*); an imitation version of this. [Sp *Panamá*]

Pan-American *pan-ə-mer'i-kən*, *adj* including all America or Americans, North and South — *n* **Pan-Amer'icanism**. [**pan-** and **American**]

Pan-Anglican *pan-ang'gli-kən*, *adj* representing or including all who hold the doctrines and polity of the Anglican Church. [**pan-** and **Anglican**]

Pan-Arab *pan-ar'əb*, or **Pan-Arabic** *-ar'əb-ik*, *adj* of or relating to the policy of political unity between all Arab states. — *n* **Pan-Ar'abism**. [**pan-** and **Arab**]

panaritium *pan-ə-rish'i-əm*, *n* a whitlow. [LL *panāricium* for *parōnychium*, from Gr *parōnychiā*, from *para* beside, and *onyx*, *-ychos* nail]

panarthritis *pan-är-thrī'tis*, *n* inflammation involving all the structures of a joint. [**pan-** and **arthritis**]

panary *pan'ə-ri*, *adj* of or pertaining to bread. — *n* a bread store. [L *pānārius*, from *pānis* bread]

panatella *pan-ə-tel'ə*, *n* a long, thin cigar. [Am Sp *panetela* a long, thin biscuit, from Ital, small loaf, from L *pānis* bread]

Panathenaea *pan-ath-i-nē'ə*, *n pl* the chief national festival of ancient Athens — the lesser held annually, the greater every fourth year. — *adj* **Panathenae'an**. — *adj* **Panathenā'ic**. [Gr *Panathēnaia*]

panax *pan'aks*, or *pān'*, *n* a tree or shrub of the genus *Polyscias*, related to, or included in, the genus *Panax*, of the Aralia family. [Gr *panax* a name for various healing plants; see **panacea**]

pancake. See under **pan**[1].

pance. See under **pansy**.

Panchatantra *pun-chä-tunt'rə*, *n* the oldest extant Sanskrit collection of beast-fables, in five books. [Sans, five books]

panchax *pan'chaks*, *n* any of several kinds of brightly coloured fish, genus *Aplocheilus*, native to Africa and SE Asia, often stocked in aquariums. [L, former generic name]

panchayat *pun-chä'yət*, *n* a village or town council. [Hindi *pañcāyat*, from Sans *pañca* five]

Panchen Lama *pän'chən lä'mə*, *n* a Tibetan religious leader second in importance to the Dalai Lama. [Chin *pan ch'an*]

pancheon or **panchion** *pan'shən*, *n* a coarse earthenware pan. [Appar connected with **pan**[1]; perh influenced by **puncheon**[2]]

panchromatic *pan-krō-mat'ik*, *adj* equally or suitably sensitive to all colours; rendering all colours in due intensity. — *n* **panchro'matism**. [Gr *chrōma*, *-atos* colour]

pancosmism *pan-koz'mizm*, (*philos*) *n* the theory that the material universe, within space and time, is all that exists. — *adj* **pancos'mic**. [**cosmism**]

pancratium *pan-krā'shi-əm*, *n* (in ancient Greece) a combination of boxing and wrestling. — *adj* **pancrā'tian**. — *n* **pancrā'tiast** (*-shi-ast*) a competitor or victor in the pancratium. — *adj* **pancratic** (*-krat'ik*) of the pancratium; excelling all round in athletics or accomplishments; (of a lens) adjustable to different degrees of magnification. — *n* **pan'cratist**. [Gr *pankration*, from *kratos* strength]

pancreas *pan(g)'kri-əs*, *n* a large gland discharging into the duodenum and containing islands of endocrine gland tissue. — *adj* **pancreat'ic**. — *n* **pan'creatin** the pancreatic juice; a medicinal substance to aid the digestion, prepared from extracts of the pancreas of certain animals. — *n* **pancreatec'tomy** surgical removal of all or part of the pancreas. — *n* **pancreatī'tis** inflammation of the pancreas. — **pancreatic juice** the alkaline secretion from the pancreas into the duodenum to aid the digestive process. [Gr *kreas*, *-atos* flesh]

pand *pand*, (*Scot*) *n* the valance of a bed. [Cf OFr *pandre* to hang]

panda *pan'də*, *n* a raccoon-like animal (*Ailurus fulgens*) of the Himalayas (also called the **common** or **lesser panda**); (also, more correctly, **giant panda**) a similar but much larger herbivorous bearlike animal (*Ailuropoda melanoleuca*) of Tibet and China, apparently linking the lesser panda with the bears. — **panda car** a police patrol car (formerly white with black markings). [Said to be its name in Nepal]

Pandaemonium. See **Pandemonium**.

Pandanus *pan-dā'nəs*, *n* the screw-pine, the typical genus of the **Pandanā'ceae**, a family of trees and bushes related to the bulrushes and bur-reeds. — *adj* **pandanā'ceous**. [Malay *pandan*]

pandar. See **pander**.

pandation *pan-dā'shən*, (*archaic*) *n* warping. [L *pandātiō*, *-ōnis*, from *pandāre*, *-ātum* to bend]

Pandean *pan-dē'ən*, *adj* of the god Pan; of Pan-pipes (qv at **Pan**). — **Pandean pipes** Pan-pipes. [Irregularly formed from *Pān*]

pandect *pan'dekt*, *n* a treatise covering the whole of any subject; (in *pl*; with *cap*) the digest of Roman law made by command of the Emperor Justinian in the 6c. — *n* **pandect'ist**. [L *pandecta*, from Gr *pandektēs*, from *pās*, *pān* all, and *dechesthai* to receive]

pandemic *pan-dem'ik*, *adj* affecting a whole people, epidemic over a wide area. — *n* a pandemic disease. — *n* **pandemia** (*-dē'mi-ə*) a widespread epidemic. — *adj* **pandē'mian** vulgar; sensual. [Gr *pandēmios*, from *dēmos* people]

Pandemonium or **Pandaemonium** *pan-di-mō'ni-əm*, *n* the capital of Hell in Milton's *Paradise Lost*; (without *cap*) any very disorderly or noisy place or assembly; (without *cap*) tumultuous uproar. — (the following also without *cap*) *adj* **Pandemō'niac**. — *adj* **Pandemonī'acal**. — *adj* **Pandemō'nian**. — *adj* **Pandemonic** (*-mon'ik*). [Gr *pās*, *pān* all, and *daimōn* a spirit]

pander *pan'dər*, *n* a person who procures for another the means of gratifying his or her base passions; a pimp. — *vt* to play the pander for. — *vi* to act as a pander; to minister to the passions; to indulge, gratify (with *to*). — *n* **pan'deress** a procuress. — *n* **pan'derism** the employment or practices of a pander. — *adj* **pan'derly** (*Shakesp*) acting as a pander. — *adj* **pan'derous**. — Also **pan'dar**, etc. [*Pandarus*, in the story of Troilus and Cressida as told by Boccaccio (*Filostrato*), Chaucer, and Shakespeare]

pandermite *pan-dûr'mīt*, *n* a hydrogen calcium borate found in great quantities at *Panderma* (Bandirma) on the Sea of Marmara.

pandiculation *pan-dik-ū-lā'shən*, *n* the act of stretching and yawning. [L *pandiculārī*, *-ātus* to stretch oneself]

Pandion *pan-dī'on*, *n* the osprey genus. [Gr *Pandīōn*, father of Procne and Philomela]

pandit. Same as **pundit**.

pandoor. See **pandour**.

P and O or **P & O** *abbrev*: Peninsular and Oriental (Steamship Navigation Company).

Pandora *pan-dō'rə* or *-dö'rə*, (*Gr mythol*) *n* the first woman, made for Zeus so that he might through her punish man for the theft by Prometheus of heavenly fire, given a box which she disobediently opened to release all the ills of human life. — **Pandora's box** any source of great and unexpected troubles. [Gr *pās*, *pān* all, and *dōron* a gift]

pandora *pan-dō'rə* or *-dö'rə* or **pandore** *pan-dōr'* or *-dör'*, *n* an ancient Eastern musical instrument like a long-necked lute with (commonly) three strings; a bandore. — *n* **pandū'ra** a pandora; a Neapolitan instrument like a mandoline with eight metal wires, played with a quill. — *adj* **pan'dūrate**, **pan'durated** or **pandū'riform** (*bot*) fiddle-shaped. [Gr *pandoura* a 3-stringed instrument, fancifully connected with *Pān*, but probably an Eastern word; cf **bandore** banjo, mandoline]

pandore *pan'dōr* or *-dör*, *n* an esteemed variety of oysters formerly caught at Prestonpans on the Firth of Forth. [Said to be from the *doors* of the salt-*pans* where they were found]

pandour *pan'dōōr*, *n* an 18th-century Croatian foot-soldier in the Austrian service; a robber. — Also **pan'door**. [Fr, from Serbo-Croat *pàndūr*, from LL *banderius* follower of a banner]

pandowdy *pan-dow'di*, (*US*) *n* a deep-pan apple pie or pudding richly spiced. [Origin unknown]

p and p or **p & p** *abbrev*: postage and packing.

pandura, **pandurate**, **panduriform**. See under **pandora**.

pandy[1] *pan'di*, (*colloq*) *n* a beating on the palm with a strap as a school punishment. — *vt* to slap. [L *pande* hold out, imperative of *pandere*]

pandy[2] *pan'di*, (*colloq*; *obs*) *n* an insurgent sepoy in the Indian Mutiny. [Said to be from *Pande*, a common surname]

pane[1] *pān*, *n* a piece of cloth (*obs*); a piece of cloth pieced together with others, or separated from others by slashing (*archaic*); a rectangular compartment; a panel; a slab of window glass; a flat side or face; a length of wall; the side of a quadrangle; a rectangular piece of ground; a large sheet of stamps issued by the Post Office; half such a sheet separated from the other half by a gutter; a page of a book of stamps. — *vt* to insert panes or panels in. — *adj* **paned** (*pānd*) made of panes or small squares; variegated. [Fr *pan*, from L *pannus* a cloth, a rag]

pane[2]. Same as **pean**[1] and **peen**.

panegoism *pan-eg'ō-izm*, *n* solipsism. [Gr *egō* I]

panegyric *pan-i-jir'ik* (or *US* sometimes *-jīr'*), *n* a eulogy, *esp* public and elaborate (on or upon); laudation. — *adj* **panegyr'ic** or **panegyr'ical**. — *adv* **panegyr'ically**. — *n* **panegyr'icon** (in the Greek Church) a collection of sermons for festivals. — *n* **pan'egyrist** (or *-jir'* or *-ej'ər-*). — *vt* **pan'egyrize** or **-ise** (or *-ej'ər-*) to write or pronounce a panegyric on; to praise highly. — *n* **pan'egyry** a great assembly; a religious festival. [Gr *panēgyrikos* fit for a national festival, from *pās*, *pān* all, and *agyris* (*agorā*) an assembly]

paneity *pa-nē'i-ti*, *n* the state of being bread. [L *pānis* bread]

panel *pan'l*, *n* a cloth under a saddle (*obs*); a crude form of saddle; a rectangular piece of any material; rectangular divisions on a page, *esp* for the illustrations in children's comics; a compartment; a bordered rectangular area; a thin flat piece sunk below the general surface of a door, shutter, wainscot, or the like, often with a raised border; a board with dials, switches, etc for monitoring or controlling the operation of an electrical or other apparatus; a compartment or hurdle of a fence; a strip of material inserted in a dress; a slip of parchment; such a slip containing a list of names, *esp* of jurors; a jury; prior to the introduction of the national health service, a list of doctors available to treat those who paid into a national health insurance scheme; such a doctor's list of patients; an accused person or persons (in *sing*; *Scots law*); a thin board on which a picture is painted; a large long photograph; a group of people chosen for some purpose, such as to judge a competition, serve on a brains trust, or be the guessers in radio and television guessing games (**panel games**); a representative group of consumers or shops who report on their habits of buying or using products or services over a period of time. — *vt* to furnish with a panel or panels; to put on trial (*Scots law*): — *pr p* **pan'elling**; *pa t* and *pa p* **pan'elled**. — *n* **pan'elling** panel-work. — *n* **pan'ellist** a member of a panel, *esp* in panel games. — **panel beating** the shaping of metal sheets for vehicle bodywork, etc; **panel beater**; **panel doctor** a doctor who was on the panel or had a panel; **panel heating** indoor heating diffused from floors, walls, or ceilings; **panel pin** a light, narrow-headed nail of small diameter used chiefly for fixing plywood or hardboard to supports; **panel saw** a fine saw for cutting very thin wood; **panel system** a system of office, etc design, in which partitions are used to create flexible work-areas within an open layout; **panel truck** (*US*) a delivery-van; **panel working** a method of working a coal-mine by dividing it into compartments. [OFr, from LL *pannellus*, from L *pannus* a cloth]

panentheism *pan-en-thē'izm* or *pan-en'-*, *n* the doctrine that the world is a part, though not the whole, of God's being. — *n* **panenthē'ist**. (or *pan-en'-*). [**pan-** and Gr *en* in, and *theos* God]

panettone *pan-e-tōn'ā*, *n* a kind of spiced cake, *usu* made with sultanas, traditionally eaten at Christmas in Italy: — *pl* **panettōn'i** (*-ē*). [Ital *panetto* a small loaf]

pan-European *pan-ū-rə-pē'ən*, *adj* of, concerning or relating to all European countries, or to the movement for political and/or economic union in Europe. [**pan-** and **European**]

panful. See under **pan**[1].

pang[1] *pang*, *n* a violent but *usu* brief pain; a painful emotion. — *vt* to inflict a pang on. — *adj* **pang'ing** (*Shakesp*) painful. — *adj* **pang'less**. [Poss **prong**; *pronge* and *prange* have been found]

pang[2] *pang*, (*Scot*) *vt* to stuff, cram. — *adj* stuffed, crammed, crowded; tight. — *adj* **pang'-full'** or **pang'-fu''** filled full. [Origin unknown]

panga *pang'gə*, *n* a broad, heavy African knife used as a tool and as a weapon.

Pangaea or **Pangea** *pan-jē'ə*, *n* the postulated super-continent that began to break up, forming the present continents of the earth. [**pan-** and Gr *gē* the earth]

pan-galactic *pan-gə-lak'tik*, *adj* of or pertaining to all the galaxies in the universe. [**pan-** and **galactic**]

pangamy *pan(g)'gə-mi*, *n* random mating. — *adj* **pangamic** (*pan-gam'ik*). [Gr *gamos* marriage]

pangenesis *pan-jen'i-sis*, *n* Darwin's theory that every cell of the body contributes gemmules to the germ-cells and so shares in the transmission of inherited characters. — *n* **pan'gen** or **pan'-gene** (*-jēn*) a hypothetical unit of living matter. — *adj* **pangenet'ic**. [Gr *genesis* production]

Pan-German *pan-jûr'mən*, *adj* pertaining to or including all Germans. — *n* **Pan-Ger'manism** a movement for a Greater Germany or union of all German peoples. [**pan-** and **German**]

Panglossian *pan-glos'i-ən*, or **Panglossic** *-ik*, *adj* taking an over-cheerful and optimistic view of the world as did Dr **Pan'gloss** in Voltaire's *Candide*.

pangolin *pang-gō'lin*, *n* the scaly ant-eater, an edentate mammal (Manis; order *Pholidota*) of Asia and Africa. [Malay *peng-gōling* roller, from its habit of rolling up]

pangrammatist *pan-gram'ə-tist*, *n* someone who contrives verses or sentences containing all the letters of the alphabet. — *n* **pan'gram** a sentence containing all the letters of the alphabet, eg *the quick brown fox jumps over the lazy dog*. [Gr *gramma, -atos* letter]

Panhagia or **Panagia** *pan-hā'gi-ə* or *pan-ha'gi-ə*, *adj* all-holy, an epithet of the Virgin in the Eastern Church; a cut loaf elevated in her honour; a medallion of the Virgin worn by bishops. [Gr *hagios* holy]

panhandle, **panhandler**. See under **pan**[1].

panharmonicon *pan-här-mon'i-kon*, *n* a mechanical musical instrument mimicking an orchestra.

panhellenic *pan-hel-ēn'ik*, or *-en'*, *adj* pertaining to all Greece; including all Greeks; (with *cap*) of or relating to Panhellenism. — *n* **panhellē'nion** or (*L*) **panhellē'nium** a council representing all the sections of the Greeks. — *n* **Panhell'enism** (*-ən-izm*) a movement or aspiration for the political union of all Greek (or former Greek) territories. — *n* **Panhell'enist**. — *adj* **Panhellenis'tic**. [Gr *Hellēnikos* Greek, from *Hellas* Greece]

panic[1] *pan'ik*, *n* frantic or sudden fright; contagious fear; great terror, often without any visible reason or foundation; a state of terror about investments, impelling investors to rush and sell what they possess. — *adj* relating or due to the god Pan; of the nature of a panic; inspired or caused by panic. — *vt* to throw into a panic. — *vi* to be struck by panic: — *pr p* **pan'icking**; *pa t* and *pa p* **pan'icked**. — *adj* **pan'icky** inclined to, affected by, resulting from, or of the nature of, panic. — **panic attack** (*behav*) an attack of intense terror and anxiety, lasting from several minutes to several hours; **pan'ic-bolt'** an easily moved bolt for emergency exits; **panic button** a button operating a distress or other emergency device or signal. — *vi* and *vt* **pan'ic-buy'** to buy up stocks of a commodity which threatens to be in short supply (often precipitating a greater shortage than might otherwise have occurred). — **pan'ic-buying**; **pan'ic-mong'er** someone who creates or fosters panics. — *adj* **pan'ic-strick'en** or **panic-struck** struck with panic or sudden fear. [Gr *pānikos* belonging to Pan; *pānikon* (*deima*) panic (fear), fear associated with the god Pan]

panic[2] *pan'ik*, *n* any grass of the genus Panicum (see below), or of various closely related genera (also **pan'ic-grass'**); the edible grain of some species. — Also **pan'ick** or **pann'ick**. — *n* **pan'icle** (*bot*) a raceme, or florescence in which the flowers occur on the main stalk, whose branches are themselves racemes; loosely, a lax irregular inflorescence. — *adj* **pan'icled**, **panic'ūlate** or **panic'ūlated** furnished with, arranged in, or like, panicles. — *adv* **panic'ūlately**. — *n* **Pan'icum** a large genus of grasses having the one- or two-flowered spikelets in spikes, racemes or panicles — including several of the millets. [L *pānicum* Italian millet]

panification *pan-i-fi-kā'shən*, *n* conversion into bread. [L *pānis* bread, and *facere* to make]

panim. A Miltonic spelling of **paynim**.

Panionic *pan-ī-on'ik*, *adj* of or including all Ionians. [**pan-** and **Ionic**]

panisk or **panisc** *pan'isk*, *n* an inferior god, attendant on Pan. [Gr *Pāniskos*, dimin of *Pān*]

panislam *pan-iz'läm*, *n* the whole Muslim world; panislamism. — *adj* **panislam'ic**. — *n* **panis'lamism** an aspiration or movement for the union of all Muslims. — *n* **panis'lamist**. [**pan-** and **Islam**]

Panjabi. Same as **Punjabi**.

panjandrum *pan-jan'drəm*, *n* an imaginary figure of great power and self-importance, a burlesque potentate, from the Grand Panjandrum in a string of nonsense made up by Samuel Foote, 18c English wit, actor and dramatist. — Also **panjan'darum**.

panleucopenia *pan-lū-kō-pē'ni-ə*, *n* a viral disease of cats marked by a deficiency of white blood cells and causing fever, diarrhoea, and dehydration. [**pan-** and **leucopenia**]

panlogism *pan'lə-jizm*, *n* the theory that the universe is an outward manifestation of the Logos. [**Logos**]

panmixia *pan-mik'si-ə*, (*biol*) *n* cessation of the influence of natural selection. — Also **panmix'is**. — *adj* **panmic'-tic** of, connected with or exhibiting panmixia. [Gr *mixis* mixing]

pannage *pan'ij*, (*archaic*) *n* food picked up by swine in the woods, mast; the right to pasture swine in a forest. [OFr *pasnage*, from LL *pastiōnāticum*, from *pascere*, *pastum* to feed]

panne *pan*, *n* a fabric resembling velvet, with a long nap. [Fr]

panned. See under **pan**[1,3].

pannelled *pan'ld*, *vt* (*pa t*). Conjectured to be a misprint for *spanielled*, ie followed or fawned on as by a spaniel (*Shakesp*, *Antony and Cleopatra* IV. 12).

pannick. See **panic**[2].

pannicle *pan'i-kl* or **panniculus** *pə-nik'ū-ləs*, *n* a thin, sheet-like investment. [L *panniculus*, dimin of *pannus* a cloth]

pannier[1] *pan'yər* or *pan'i-ər*, *n* a provision-basket; a basket carried on one's back; one of a pair of baskets slung over a pack-animal's back or over the rear wheel of a bicycle, motorcycle, etc; a sculptured basket (*archit*); a system of hoops formerly used for spreading out a woman's dress at the hips; the part spread out in this way; a piece of basket-work for protecting archers, or, when filled with gravel or sand, for forming and protecting dikes, embankments, etc; a covered basket of medicines and surgical instruments (*military*); hence (blunderingly) an ambulance (*military*). — *adj* **pann'-iered**. [Fr *panier*, from L *pānārium* a bread-basket, from *pānis* bread]

pannier[2] *pan'yər* or *-i-ər*, *n* a *colloq* name for a robed waiter in the Inns of Court. [Origin unknown]

pannikel. An *obs* form of **pannicle**.

pannikell *pan'i-kel*, (*Spenser*) *n* the skull. [**pannicle**]

pannikin. See under **pan**[1].

panning. See under **pan**[1,3].

pannose *pan'ōs*, (*bot*) *adj* like felt. [L *pannōsus*, from *pannus* cloth]

pannus *pan'əs*, (*pathol*) *n* a layer of new connective tissue that forms over the synovial membrane of joints in rheumatoid arthritis, or over the cornea in trachoma. [L *pannus* cloth]

panocha *pä-nō'chə*, *n* a Mexican coarse sugar. [Sp]

panoistic *pan-ō-is'tik*, (*entomol*) *adj* (of an ovary) producing ova only, not yolk-forming cells (opposite of *meroistic*). [Gr *ōion* an egg]

panomphaean *pan-om-fē'ən*, *adj* all-oracular, an epithet of Zeus; applied (after Rabelais) to the word 'drink' (which is celebrated by all nations). [Gr *omphē* a divine voice]

panophobia *pan-ō-fō'bi-ə*, *n* a form of melancholia marked by groundless fears; erroneously used for **pantophobia**. [Gr *Pān*, the god who inspired fears, and *phobos* fear]

panophthalmitis *pan-of-thal-mī'tis*, *n* inflammation of the whole eye. — Also **panophthal'mia**. [Gr *ophthalmos* eye]

panoply *pan'ə-pli*, *n* complete armour; a full suit of armour; a full or brilliant covering or array. — Also *fig*. — *adj* **pan'oplied** in panoply. [Gr *panopliā* full armour of a hoplite, from *pās*, *pān* all, and *hopla* (pl) arms]

panoptic *pan-op'tik*, *adj* all-embracing; viewing all aspects. — Also **panop'tical**. [Gr *panoptēs* all-seeing]

panopticon *pan-op'ti-kon*, *n* a prison in which all prisoners can be watched from one point; an exhibition room. [Gr *optikon* (neuter adj) for seeing]

panorama *pan-ə-rä'mə*, *n* a wide or complete view (*lit* and *fig*); a picture painted on the inside wall of a circular room, in such a way that all parts appear to be in perspective to a viewer at the centre; an extended picture unrolled bit by bit to give the impression of a sequence in time. — *adj* **panoramic** (*-ram'ik*). — **panorama head** a swivel device fitted to the head of a camera tripod to permit the sideways swinging motion of the camera when taking panning shots; **panoramic camera** one which takes very wide angle views, generally by rotation about an axis and by exposing a roll of film through a vertical slit; **panoramic sight** a gun sight that can be rotated, so enabling the user to fire in any direction. [Gr *horāma* a view, from *horaein* to see]

panpharmacon *pan-fär'mə-kon*, *n* a universal remedy. [Gr *pharmakon* a drug]

Pan-Presbyterian *pan-prez-bi-tē'ri-ən*, *adj* of, including, or representing all Presbyterians. [**pan-** and **Presbyterian** (see under **presbyter**)]

panpsychism *pan-sīk'izm*, *n* the theory that all nature has a psychic side. — *n* **panpsych'ist**. — *adj* **panpsychist'ic**. [**pan-** and **psychism** (see under **psyche**)]

pansexualism *pan-seks'ū-əl-izm*, *n* the view that all mental activity is derived from sexual instinct. — *adj* **pansex'ual**. — *n* **pansex'ualist**. [**pan-** and **sexualism** (see under **sex**)]

Pan-Slav *pan-släv'*, *adj* of, including, or representing, all Slavs. — *adj* **Pan-Slav'ic**. — *n* **Pan-Slav'ism** a movement for the union of all Slav peoples. — *n* **Pan-Slav'ist**. — *adj* **Pan-Slavon'ic**. [**pan-** and **Slav**]

pansophy *pan'sə-fi*, *n* universal knowledge. — *adj* **pansophic** (*-sof'ik*) or **pansoph'ical**. — *n* **pan'sophism**. — *n* **pan'sophist**. [Gr *sophiā* wisdom]

panspermatism *pan-spûr'mə-tizm*, **pansper'mism** *-mizm*, **pansper'my** *-mi* or **pansper'mia** *-mi-ə*, *n* the theory that life could be diffused through the universe by means of germs carried by meteorites or that life was brought to earth by this means. — *adj* **panspermat'ic**. — *n* **pansper'matist**. — *adj* **pansper'mic**. — *n* **pansper'mist**. [Gr *sperma*, *-atos* seed]

pansy *pan'zi*, *n* a name for various species of violet, *esp* the heart's-ease (*Viola tricolor*) and garden kinds derived from it, as well as other species with up-turned side petals and large leafy stipules; a soft bluish-purple; an effeminate or namby-pamby male (*derog slang*); a male homosexual (*derog slang*, often *offensive*). — Also (*obs*; *Spenser*, etc) **pance**, **paunce** or **pawnce** (*päns* or *pöns*). — *adj* bluish-purple; effeminate (*derog slang*). — *adj* **pan'sied**. [A fanciful use of Fr *pensée* thought, from *penser* to think, from L *pēnsāre* to weigh]

pant[1] *pant*, *vi* to gasp for breath; to run gasping; to throb; to wish ardently, to long, to yearn (with *for*); (of ship's hulls, etc) to bulge and shrink successively. — *vt* to gasp out (an utterance). — *n* a gasping breath; a throb. — *n* and *adj* **pant'ing**. — *adv* **pant'ingly**. [Appar related to OFr *pantoisier* to pant]

pant[2] *pänt*, (*Northern*) *n* a public fountain; a puddle by a midden. [Origin obscure]

pant-. See **pan-**.

pantable *pan'tə-bl*. Same as **pantofle**.

pantagamy *pan-tag'ə-mi*, *n* a word that ought to mean universal bachelorhood, applied with unconscious irony to the universal marriage of the Perfectionists, in which every man in the community is the husband of every woman. [Gr *gamos* marriage, and *agamiā* bachelorhood]

pantagraph. See **pantograph**.

Pantagruelism *pan-tə-grōō'əl-izm* or *-tag'rōō-*, *n* the theories and practice of *Pantagruel* as described by Rabelais (d 1553); burlesque ironical buffoonery as a cover for serious satire. — *adj* and *n* **Pantagruelian** (*-el'i-ən*). — *n* **Pantagruel'ion** a magic herb, hemp. — *n* **Pantagru'elist** (or *-tag'rōō-*).

pantaleon *pan-tal'i-on*, *n* a very large dulcimer invented about 1700 by *Pantaleon* Hebenstreit.

pantalets *pan-tə-lets'*, *n pl* long frilled drawers, worn by women and children in the first half of the 19c; a detachable ruffle for these, or one simulating these; extended to various trouser-like garments worn by women. — Also **pantalettes**. — *adj* **pantalett'ed**. [Dimin of **pantaloons**]

Pantaloon *pan-tə-lōōn'*, or *pan'*, *n* a character in Italian comedy, and afterwards in pantomime, a lean old man (*orig* a Venetian) more or less a dotard; (without *cap*; *Shakesp*) a feeble old man; (without *cap*; in *pl*) various kinds of trousers worn by or suggesting the stage pantaloon, such as the wide breeches of the Restoration, later combined breeches and stockings, later 18c trousers fastened below the calf or under the shoe, children's trousers resembling these, (*usu* **pants**) trousers generally or long woollen underpants. — *n* **pan'talon** a movement in a quadrille. — *adj* **pantalooned'**. — *n* **pantaloon'ery** buffoonery. [Fr *pantalon*, from Ital *pantalone*, from St *Pantaleone*, a favourite saint of the Venetians]

pantechnicon *pan-tek'ni-kon*, *n orig* a building in London intended for the sale of all kinds of artistic work, turned into a furniture-store; a furniture-van (in full **pantech'nicon-van'**); (loosely) a receptacle holding a large number of miscellaneous objects. [Gr *technē* art]

panter. See **pantler**.

pantheism *pan'thē-izm*, *n* the doctrine that nature and the physical universe are constituents of the essence of God, that they are part of what God is; the worship of all gods (*rare*); belief in many or all gods. — *n* **pan'thēist**. — *adj* **panthēist'ic** or **panthēist'ical**. — *n* **panthēol'ogist**. — *n* **panthēol'ogy** a synthesis of all religions and the knowledge of all gods. — *n* **Pantheon** (*pan'thi-on* or *pan-thē'on*) a temple of all the gods, *esp* the rotunda erected by Hadrian at Rome (on the site of Agrippa's of 27BC), now the church of Santa Maria Rotonda, a burial-place of great Italians; a building serving as a general burial-place or memorial of the great dead, as Sainte Geneviève at Paris; an 18c place of amusement in London (Oxford Street); all the gods collectively; a complete mythology. [Gr *theos* a god, and *pantheion* a Pantheon]

panthenol *pan'thin-ol*, *n* a vitamin of the B-complex, affecting the growth of hair.

pantheologist, etc, **Pantheon**. See under **pantheism**.

panther *pan'thər*, *n* a leopard, *esp* a large one or one in its black phase, formerly believed to be a different species; a puma (*NAm*): — *fem* **pan'theress**. — *adj* **pan'therine** (*-īn*). — *adj* **pan'therish**. — **Black Panther** a member of a militant black political movement dedicated to ending domination by whites. [Gr *panthēr*]

panti-, and **panties**. See under **pants**.

pantihose *pan'ti-hōz*, (*esp NAm*) *n pl* tights worn by women or children with ordinary dress, ie not theatrical, etc. [**panties** (see under **pants**), and **hose**]

pantile *pan'tīl*, *n* a roofing tile whose cross-section forms an ogee curve; a tile concave or convex in cross-section; a flat paving tile (*obs*). — *adj* (*obs slang*) dissenting, since chapels were often roofed with these. — *adj* **pan'tiled**. — *n* **pan'tiling**. [**pan**[1] and **tile**]

pantine *pan'tēn*, (*obs*) *n* a pasteboard jumping-jack, fashionable in the 18c. [Fr *pantine*, afterwards *pantin*]

pantisocracy *pant-is-ok'rə-si*, or *-īs-*, *n* a community (planned by Coleridge, Southey, and Lovell) in which all should have equal power. — *n* **pantis'ocrat**. — *adj* **pantisocrat'ic**. [Gr *pās*, *pantos* all, *isos* equal, and *krateein* to rule]

pantler *pant'lər*, (*Shakesp*) *n* the officer in a great family who had charge of the bread and other provisions. — Also **pant'er**. [Fr *panetier*, from L *pānis* bread]

panto. See under **pantomime**.

panto-. See **pan-**.

Pantocrator *pan-tok'rə-tər*, *n* the ruler of the universe, *esp* Christ enthroned, as in icons, etc. [Gr *kratos* power]

pantofle, **pantoffle** or **pantoufle** *pan'tof-l*, *-tof'l* or *-tōōf'l*, *n* a slipper; a high chopin (*hist*); an overshoe (*archaic*). — Also **pantable** (*pan'tə-bl*). — **on one's pantables** on one's dignity or high horse, lofty in manner. [Fr *pantoufle*]

pantograph *pan'tə-gräf*, *n* a jointed framework of rods, based on the geometry of a parallelogram, for copying drawings, plans, etc, on the same, or a different, scale; a similar framework for other purposes, such as for collecting a current from an overhead wire on electric locomotives, trams, etc. — *n* **pantographer** (*-tog'rə-fər*). — *adj* **pantographic** (*-tō-graf'ik*) or **pantograph'ical**. — *n* **pantog'raphy**. — Also (faulty) **pan'tagraph**, etc. — **laser pantography** a technique of tracing a circuit pattern on to a microchip by means of a laser beam. [Gr *graphein* to write]

pantomime *pan'tə-mīm*, *n* a Roman actor in mime (*hist*); a play or an entertainment in mime; a theatrical entertainment, *usu* about Christmas-time, developed out of this, no longer in mime, with showy scenery, topical allusions, songs and star attractions of the day, buffoonery and dancing, centred loosely on a nursery story, formerly ending with a transformation scene and a harlequinade; dumb show, mime; a situation of fuss, farce or confusion (*derog*). — *adj* of pantomime; pantomimic. — *n* and *adj* **pan'to** *colloq* form of **pantomime**: — *pl* **pan'tos**. — *adj* **pantomimic** (*-mim'ik*) or **pantomim'ical**. — *adv* **pantomim'ically**. — *n* **pan'tomīmist** an actor in or writer of pantomime. [L *pantomīmus*, from Gr *pantomīmos* imitator of all, from *pās*, *pantos* all, and *mīmos* an imitator]

panton *pan'tən*, (*Scot*) *n* a slipper. — **pan'ton-shoe'** a horse-shoe for curing a narrow and hoof-bound heel. [Appar connected with **pantofle**]

pantophagy *pan-tof'ə-ji*, *n* omnivorousness. — *n* **pantoph'agist**. — *adj* **pantoph'agous** (*-gəs*). [Gr *phagein* to eat]

pantophobia *pan-tə-fō'bi-ə*, *n* morbid fear of everything; (by confusion with **panophobia**) causeless fear. [Gr *pās*, *pantos* all, and *phobos* fear]

pantopragmatic *pan-tə-prag-mat'ik*, *adj* meddling in everybody's business. — *n* a universal busybody. — *n sing* **pantopragmat'ics** the science of universal benevolent interference. [From Peacock's imaginary society (*Gryll Grange*), from Gr *pās*, *pantos* all, and *pragmata* (pl) business]

pantoscope *pan'tə-skōp*, *n* a panoramic camera; a very wide-angled photographic lens. — *adj* **pantoscopic** (*-skop'ik*) giving a wide range of vision; bifocal. [Gr *skopeein* to look at]

pantothenic *pan-to-then'ik*, *adj* (literally) from all quarters; applied to an acid, a member of the vitamin B complex, so ubiquitous that the effects of its deficiency in man are not known. [Gr *pantothen* from everywhere]

pantoufle. See **pantofle**.

pantoum *pan-tōōm'*, properly **pantun** *pan-tōōn'*, *n* a repetitive verse-form *orig* Malay, quatrains rhyming *ab ab*, *bc bc*, etc, returning to rhyme *a* at the end. [Malay]

pantry *pan'tri*, *n* a small room or large walk-in cupboard where food is stored, a larder; a room in a large house where table linen is stored and cutlery, etc cleaned. — *n* **pan'trymaid**. — *n* **pan'tryman**. [Fr *paneterie*, from LL *pānitāria*, from L *pānis* bread]

pants *pants*, *n pl* knickers or underpants; trousers (*esp NAm*). — *n pl* **pant'ies** brief knickers for a girl or woman. — *combining form* **panti-** or **panty-** (*pan'ti-*). — **pants suit** or **pant suit** (*esp NAm*) a woman's suit of trousers and jacket. — **panty line** the outline of a person's underwear, sometimes visible beneath tight-fitting clothes; the limit on the upper thigh and *esp* the lower abdomen normally reached by a pair of briefs, the bikini line. — **(be caught) with one's pants down** (*colloq*) (to be caught) at an embarrassing and unsuitable moment, in a state of extreme unpreparedness; **(fly) by the seat of one's pants** (to get through a difficult or dangerous situation) by a combination of resourcefulness and sheer luck; **scare**, **bore**, etc **the pants off someone** (*slang*) to scare, bore, etc someone to a great degree. [**pantaloons**]

pantun. See **pantoum**.

panty. See under **pants**.

panty girdle *pan'ti gûr'dl*, *n* a woman's foundation garment consisting of panties made of elasticated material. — **pan'ty-waist** (*US*) an effeminate or cowardly man (from a child's garment of trousers and jacket buttoned together at the waist). [**panties**]

panzer *pant'sər* or *Eng pan'zər*, (*Ger*) *n* armour; a tank. — **panzer division** an armoured division.

paolo *pä'ō-lō*, *n* an obsolete papal silver coin: — *pl* **pa'oli** (*-lē*). [Ital *Paolo* Paul, ie Pope Paul V]

pap[1] *pap*, *n* soft food for infants, such as bread boiled with milk; mediocre, stultifying or worthless entertainment, writing, etc; mash; pulp. — *vt* to feed with pap. — *adj* **papp'y**. — **pap'-boat** a boat-shaped container for pap; **pap'-meat** soft food for infants; **pap'-spoon**. [Imit]

pap[2] *pap*, (*dialect*) *n* a nipple or breast; in place-names, a round conical hill. [Appar Scand]

pa p *abbrev*: past participle.

papa *pə-pä'* (or *esp US pä'pə*), *n* father (*old-fashioned pet name*, *jocular* or *genteel*); a pope (*pä'pä*; *obs*); a priest of the Eastern Orthodox Church (*pä'pä*). [Partly through Fr *papa*, partly directly from LL *pāpa*, Gr hypocoristic *papās*, *pappās* father]

papacy *pā'pə-si*, *n* the office of pope; a pope's tenure of office; papal government. [LL *pāpātia*, from *pāpa* pope]

papain *pə-pā'in*, *n* a digestive enzyme in the juice of papaw (Carica) fruits and leaves, used for tenderizing meat. [Sp *papaya* papaw]

papal *pā'pl*, *adj* of or pertaining to the pope or the papacy. — *adj* **pa'pable** likely to, or qualified to, become pope. — *n* **pa'palism** the papal system. — *n* **pa'palist** a supporter of the pope and of the papal system. — *vt* and *vi* **pa'palize** or **-ise** to render or become papal or papalist. — *adv* **pa'pally**. — **papal cross** a cross with three cross-bars; **Papal knighthood** a title of nobility conferred by the Pope; **Papal States** States of the Church (see under **state**). [LL *pāpālis*, from *pāpa* pope]

Papanicolaou smear *pap-ə-nik'o-low* (or *-nēk'*) *smēr* or **Papanicolaou test** (*test*) *n* a smear test for detecting cancer, *esp* of the womb, devised by George *Papanicolaou*, 20c US anatomist. — *abbrev* **Pap smear test** or **Pap test**.

papaprelatist *pā-pə-prel'ə-tist*, (*Scott*) *n* a supporter of popish prelates.

paparazzo *pa-pa-rat'sō*, *n* a photographer who specializes in spying on or harassing famous people in order to obtain photographs of them in unguarded moments, etc: — *pl* **paparazz'i** (*-sē*). [Ital]

Papaver *pə-pā'vər*, *n* the poppy genus, giving name to the family **Papaverā'ceae**. — *adj* **papaveraceous** (*pə-pav-* or *-pāv-ə-rā'shəs*) of the poppy family. — *n* **papaverine** (*pə-pav'ə-rēn*, *-rīn* or *-pāv'*) an alkaloid derived from poppy juice and used medicinally. — *adj* **papaverous** (*-pav'* or *-pāv'*) resembling or having the qualities of the poppy. [L *papāver* the poppy]

papaw[1]. See **papaya**.

papaw[2]. See **pawpaw**.

papaya *pə-pä'yə*, *n* the tree *Carica papaya*, or its large green-skinned edible fruit, native to South America but common in the tropics, the trunk, leaves, and fruit yielding papain, the leaves providing a powerful anthelmintic, an anti-worm preparation. — Also called **papaw**. [Sp *papayo* (tree), *papaya* (fruit) appar from Carib]

pape *pāp*, *n* a Scots form of **pope**[1]. — *adj* **pāp'ish** popish. — *n* (*dialect* and *illit*, by confusion with **papist**) a papist. — *n* **pāp'isher**.

paper *pā'pər*, *n* a material made in thin sheets as an aqueous deposit from linen rags, esparto, wood-pulp, or other form of cellulose, used for writing on, printing on, wrapping, and other purposes; extended to other materials of similar purpose or appearance, eg to papyrus, rice-paper, to the substance of which some wasps build their nests, to cardboard, and even to tinfoil ('silver paper'); a piece of paper; a written or printed document or instrument, note, receipt, bill, bond, deed, etc; (in *pl*) documents, *esp* for the purpose of personal identification, customs or passport controls, etc; a newspaper; an essay or literary contribution, *esp* one read before a society or submitted for a degree examination; a set of examination questions; free passes of admission to a theatre, etc, also the people so admitted; paper-money; stocks and shares (*stock exchange slang*); wallpaper; a wrapping of paper; a quantity of anything wrapped in or attached to a paper. — *adj* consisting or made of paper; papery; on paper. — *vt* to cover with paper; to fold in paper; to treat in any way by means of any type of paper, eg to sandpaper, etc; to paste end-papers and fly-leaves to. — *n* **pa'perer**. — *n* **pa'pering** the operation of covering with paper; the paper so used. — *adj* **pa'perless** using *esp* electronic means instead of paper for communication, recording, etc. — *adj* **pa'pery** like paper. — **pa'perback** a book with a flexible paper cover. — Also *adj*. — *vt* to publish in paperback form — **pa'per-birch'** an American birch with papery bark; **pa'perboard** a type of strong, thick cardboard; pasteboard; **pa'perbound** a paperback. — Also *adj*. — **pa'per-boy** or **-girl** a boy or girl who delivers newspapers; **pa'per-case** a box for writing materials, etc; **pa'per-chase** the game of hare and hounds, in which some runners (*hares*) set off across country strewing paper by which others (*hounds*) track them; **pa'per-cigar'** (*obs*) a cigarette; **pa'per-clip** a clip of bent wire or the like, for holding papers together; a letter-clip; **pa'per-cloth** a fabric prepared in the Pacific islands from the inner bark of the paper-mulberry; **pa'per-coal** a lignite that splits into thin layers; **pa'per-cred'it** credit given to a person on the strength of their providing proof of being owed money by a third party; **pa'per-cutter** a paper-knife; a guillotine; a machine for cutting paper in sheets, for trimming the edges of books, etc; **pa'per-day** (*law*) one of certain days in each term for hearing cases down in the paper or roll of business; **pa'per-enam'el** an enamel for cards and fine note-paper; **paper engineering** the technique of making pop-up books, etc. — *adj* **pa'per-faced** (*Shakesp*) having a thin face like a sheet of paper; faced with paper. — **pa'per-fastener** a button with two blades that can be forced through papers and bent back to hold the sheets together; **pa'per-feeder** an apparatus for delivering sheets of paper to a printing-press, etc; **pa'per-file** an appliance for filing papers; **pa'per-folder** a folder (2nd sense); **pa'per-gauge** a rule for measuring the type-face of matter to be printed, and the width of the margin; **pa'per-hanger** a professional hanger of wallpaper; a person who makes or deals in forged cheques (*US slang*). — *n pl* **pa'per-hangings** paper for covering walls. — **pa'per-knife** a thin, flat blade for cutting open the leaves of books, other folded papers or used as a letter-opener; **paper-mâch'é** papier-mâché; **pa'per-maker** a manufacturer of paper; **pa'per-making**; **pa'per-mar'bler** someone engaged in marbling paper; **pa'per-mill** a mill where paper is made; **paper money** banknotes, pieces of paper stamped or marked by government or by a bank, as representing a certain value of money, which pass from hand to hand instead of the coin itself; **pa'per-mul'berry** a tree (*Broussonetia papyrifera*) of eastern Asia and Polynesia, of the mulberry family, whose inner bark yields tapa cloth and paper-making material; **pa'per-mus'lin** a glazed muslin; **paper nautilus** the argonaut (see under **nautilus**); **pa'per-off'ice** an office where state-papers are kept; **paper profits** the appreciation in value of a bond, share, etc; **pa'per-pulp** pulpy material for making paper; **pa'per-reed** the papyrus; **pa'per-rul'er** a person who, or an instrument which, makes straight lines on paper; **pa'per-sail'or** an argonaut; **pa'per-stain'er** a person who prepares paper-hangings; a poor author, scribbler (*colloq derog*); **paper tape** (*comput*) a paper data-recording tape, which records information by means of punched holes; **paper tape punch** a machine that perforates paper tape; **paper tape reader** a device that senses and translates the holes punched in a paper tape into machine-processable form; **paper tiger** a person or organization that appears to be powerful but is in fact not; **pa'perware** items made of paper, eg books, manuals, packaging, etc; **pa'per-wash'ing** (*photog*) water in which prints have been washed; **pa'perweight** a small often decorative weight for keeping loose papers from being displaced; **pa'perwork** clerical work; the keeping of records as part of a job. — **on paper** planned, decreed, existing, etc in theory only; apparently, judging by statistics, but perhaps not in fact; **paper over** (**the cracks in**) to create the impression that there is or has been no dissent, error, or fault in (something doubtful); **paper the house** to fill a theatre by issuing free passes. [Anglo-Fr *papir*, OFr (Fr) *papier*, from L *papyrus*, from Gr *papȳros* papyrus]

papeterie *pap-ə-trē'*, *n* a stationery-case. [Fr, stationery, paper-trade]

Paphian *pā'fi-ən*, *adj* pertaining to *Paphos* in Cyprus, sacred to Aphrodite; lascivious. — *n* a native of Paphos; a votary of Aphrodite; a whore.

Papiamento *pap-i-ə-men'tō*, *n* a creole language derived from Spanish, spoken in the Dutch Antilles. [Sp *papia* talk]

papier collé *pä-pyā kol-ā*, *n* scraps of paper and odds and ends pasted out in (*usu* abstract) artistic composition. [Fr, glued paper]

papier-mâché *pap'yā-mä'shā*, *n* a material consisting of paper-pulp or of sheets of paper pasted together, often treated so as to resemble varnished or lacquered wood or plaster. — *adj* of papier-mâché. [Would-be French, from Fr *papier* (see **paper**) and *mâché* chewed, from L *masticātus*]

Papilio *pə-pil'i-ō*, *n* the swallow-tailed butterfly genus, giving name to the family **Papilionidae** (*-on'i-dē*), in which all six legs are fully developed in both sexes; (without *cap*) a butterfly of this genus: — *pl* **papil'ios**. — *adj* **papilionā'ceous** of butterflies; butterfly-like; of a form of corolla somewhat butterfly-like, with a large posterior petal (*vexillum*), two side petals or wings (*alae*), and two anterior petals forming a keel (*carina*); of the **Papilionā'ceae**, a family of Leguminosae characterized by such a corolla, including pea, bean, clover, gorse, laburnum, etc. [L *pāpiliō*, *-ōnis* butterfly]

papilla *pə-pil'ə*, *n* a small nipple-like protuberance; a minute elevation on the skin, *esp* of the finger-tips and upper surface of the tongue, in which a nerve ends; a protuberance at the base of a hair, feather, tooth, etc; a minute conical protuberance as on the surface of a petal: — *pl* **papill'ae** (*-ē*). — *adj* **papill'ar** or **papill'ary** like, of the nature of, or having, papillae. — *adj* **papill'ate**, **papillated** or **papillif'erous** (*pap-*) having papillae. — *adj* **papill'iform** in the form of a papilla. — *n* **papillī'tis** inflammation of the head of the optic nerve. — *n* **papillō'ma** a tumour formed by hypertrophy of a papilla or papillae, such as a wart, etc. — *adj* **papillōm'atous**. — *adj* **pap'illōse** full of papillae, warty. — Also **papill'ous**. — *adj* **papill'ūlate** finely papillose. — *n* **papill'ūle** a very small papilla. [L, dimin of *papula*]

papillon *pap-ē-yɔ̃*, *n* (a dog of) a breed of toy spaniel with erect ears. [Fr, butterfly]

papillose, **papillous**. See under **papilla**.

papillote *pap'il-ōt*, *n* a curl-paper for the hair; frilled paper used to decorate the bones of chops, etc (*cookery*); oiled or greased paper in which meat is cooked and served (*cookery*; also *pap-ē-yot'*). [Fr, appar from *papillon* butterfly, from L *pāpiliō*, *-ōnis*]

papillule, etc. See **papilla**.

papish, **papisher**. See under **pape**.

papist *pā'pist*, *n* a follower or advocate of the pope; a Roman Catholic (*derog*). — Also *adj*. — *n* **pā'pism** (often *derog*) popery. — *adj* **pāpist'ic** or **papist'ical** pertaining to popery, or to the Church of Rome, its doctrines, etc. — *adv* **pāpist'ically**. — *n* **pā'pistry** popery. [LL *pāpa* pope]

papoose *pə-poos'*, *n* a North American Indian baby or young child. — Also **pappoose'**. [Narraganset *papoos*]

papovavirus *pə-pō'və-vī'rəs*, *n* any of a group of DNA-containing oncogenic viruses. [Composite coinage, and **virus**]

pappadom. Same as **popadum**.

pappus *pap'əs*, *n* a ring or parachute of fine hair or down, representing the calyx limb, which grows above the seed and helps in wind-dissemination in composites and some other plants (*bot*); the downy beginnings of a beard. — *adj* **papp'ōse** (or *-ōs'*) or **papp'ous**. [L *pappus*, from Gr *pappos* a grandfather, down, a pappus]

pappy[1]. See under **pap**[1].

pappy[2] *pap'i*, (*US colloq*) *n* father. [**papa**]

paprika *pap'ri-kə* or *pa-prēk'ə*, *n* (a hot spice derived from) Hungarian red pepper, a species of Capsicum. [Hung]

Pap smear, **Pap test**. See under **Papanicolaou smear**.

Papuan *pap'ū-ən*, *adj* pertaining to *Papua* or New Guinea. — *n* a member of the black, dolichocephalic, frizzly-haired race inhabiting Papua, etc. [Malay *papuwa* frizzled]

papula *pap'ū-lə* or **papule** *pap'ūl*, *n* a pimple; a papilla: — *pl* **pap'ūlae** (*-lē*) or **pap'ules**. — *adj* **pap'ūlar**. — *n* **papūlā'tion** the development of papules. — *adj* **papūlif'erous**. — *adj* **pap'ūlose** or **pap'ūlous**. [L *papula* a pimple]

papyrus *pə-pī'rəs*, *n* the paper-reed (*Cyperus papyrus*, or related species), a tall plant of the sedge family, once common in Egypt; its pith cut in thin strips and pressed together as a writing material of ancient times; a manuscript on papyrus: — *pl* **papy'ri** (*-rī*). — *adj* **papyraceous** (*pap-i-rā'shəs*) like paper, papery. — *n* **papyrologist** (*pap-i-rol'ə-jist*). — *n* **papyrol'ogy** the study of ancient papyri. [L *papȳrus*, from Gr *papȳros*; probably Egyptian]

par[1] *pär*, *n* a state of equality; equal value; a norm or standard; the state or value of bills, shares, etc, when they sell at exactly the price marked on them — ie without *premium* or *discount*; equality of condition; the number of strokes that should be taken for a hole or a round by good play, two putts being allowed on each green (*golf*). — **par contest** (*bridge*) a competition in which points are awarded for the bidding of a prepared hand and for the playing of the hand in a directed contract; **par value** value at par. — **above par** at a premium, or at more than the nominal value; **at par** at exactly the nominal value; **below par** at a discount, or at less than the nominal value; out of sorts, not particularly good in health, spirits, etc; **nominal par** the value with which a bill or share is marked, or by which it is known; **no par value** with no stated nominal value; **on a par with** equal to; **par for the course** a normal, average result or (*colloq fig*) occurrence, state of affairs, etc; **par of exchange** the value of currency of one country expressed in that of another. [L *pār* equal]

par[2] *pär*, *n*. Same as **parr**.

par[3] *pär* or **para** *par'ə*, *n* colloquial short forms of **paragraph**.

par. *abbrev*: paragraph; parallel; parish.

para[1] *pär'ə*, *n* a small Turkish coin; the 40th part of a piastre; (in the states formerly constituting Yugoslavia) the 100th part of a dinar. [Turk *pārah*]

para[2] *par'ə*, *n* a colloquial short form of **paratrooper**.

para[3]. See **par**[3].

Pará *pä-rä'*, *n* a city, state, and estuary of Brazil. — **pará grass** piassava; **pará nut** Brazil nut; **pará rubber** rubber produced from the tree *Hevea brasiliensis*.

para-[1] *par'ə-*, *combining form* denoting beside; faulty; disordered; abnormal; false; a polymer of; a compound related to; closely resembling, or parallel to (as in *adj* and *n* **paramed'ic**, and *adj* **paramed'ical** (a person) helping doctors or supplementing medical work (see also under **para-**[2]); *adj* and *n* **paramilitary** (see separate entry); (in organic chemistry) having substituted atoms or groups attached to two opposite carbon atoms of the benzene ring — commonly represented by *p-* (as in a **pa'ra-compound** eg *p*-xylene). [Gr *para* beside]

para-[2] *par'ə-*, *pfx* denoting parachute. — *n* **par'abrake** a parachute used to help brake an aircraft when it has landed. — *n* **par'adoctor** a doctor who parachutes to patients in remote areas. — *n* **par'adrop** an air-drop. — *n* **par'afoil** a form of steerable parachute, consisting of air-filled nylon cells. — *n* **par'aglider** a glider with inflatable wings. — *n* **par'agliding** the sport of being towed through the air by plane while wearing a modified type of parachute, then being allowed to drift to the ground. — *n* **par'akiting** the sport of soaring suspended from a parachute which is being towed. — *n* **par'amedic** or **paramed'ico** (*pl* **-os**) a paradoctor (see also under **para-**[1]). — *adj* **par'amedic** or **paramed'ical**.

para-aminobenzoic acid *par-ə-a-mē'nō-ben-zō'ik as'id*, *n* a compound, $C_6H_4(NH_2)COOH$, found in most plants, but *esp* in yeast, and also in the liver, used in the production of dyes and pharmaceuticals.

para-aminosalicylic acid *par-ə-a-mē'nō-sal-i-sil'ik as'id*, *n* a drug used along with streptomycin in the treatment of tuberculosis: — *abbrev* **PAS**.

parabaptism *par-ə-bap'tizm*, *n* uncanonical baptism. [**para-**[1] and **baptism** (see under **baptise**)]

parabasis *pə-rab'ə-sis*, *n* (in clasical Greek comedy) a speech in which the chorus comes forward and addresses the audience. [Gr, a going aside, from *para-* beside, beyond, and *basis* a going]

parabema *par-ə-bē'mə*, *n* (in Byzantine architecture) either the chapel of the prothesis or the diaconicon, when walled off from the bema: — *pl* **parabe'mata**. — *adj* **parabemat'ic**. [Gr *para* beside, beyond, and *bēma* a step]

parabiosis *par-ə-bī-ō'sis*, *n* the physical union of two embryos or organisms, resulting in a functional connection, such as is the case with Siamese twins. — *adj* **parabio'tic**. — **parabiotic twins** Siamese twins. [Gr *para* beside, and *biōsis* manner of life]

parable *par'ə-bl*, *n* a comparison or similitude; a fable or story told to illustrate some doctrine or moral point; any such story told by Jesus Christ; a proverb (*archaic*); discourse (*archaic*). — *vt* to represent by a parable. [Gr *parabolē* a placing alongside, comparison, parabola, etc, from *para* beside, beyond, and *ballein* to throw]

parablepsis *par-ə-blep'sis*, *n* false vision; oversight. — Also **par'ablepsy**. — *adj* **parablep'tic**. [Gr, looking askance, from *para* beside, beyond, and *blepein* to see]

parabola *pə-rab'ə-lə*, *n* a curve, one of the conic sections, the intersection of a cone and a plane parallel to its side, or the locus of a point equidistant from a fixed point (the *focus*) and a fixed straight line (the *directrix*) — its equation with vertex as origin $y^2 = 4ax$; generalized to include any curve whose equation is $y^n = px^m$: — *pl* **parab'olas**. — *n* **parab'ole** (*-lē*; *rhetoric*) a comparison, simile, or metaphor. — *adj* **parabol'ic** (*par-ə-bol'ik*) or **parabol'ical** of or like a parable or a parabola or a parabole; expressed by a parable; belonging to, or of the form of, a parabola. — *adv* **parabol'ically**. — *n* **parab'olist**. — *vt* **parab'olize** or **-ise**

to set forth by parable; to treat as a parable; to shape like a parabola or paraboloid. — *n* **parab'oloid** a surface or solid generated by the rotation of a parabola about its axis. — *adj* **parab'oloid** or **paraboloid'al**. — **parabolic geometry** Euclidean geometry; **parabolic velocity** (*astron*) the velocity which a body at a given point would require to describe a parabola about the centre of attraction. [Ety as for **parable**]

parabolanus *par-ə-bō-lā'nəs*, *n* (in the early Eastern Church) a layman who tended the sick. [Gr *parabolos* venturesome, exposing oneself]

parabrake. See under **para-**[2].

Paracelsian *par-ə-sel'si-ən*, *adj* of or relating to the famous German Swiss philosopher and physician, *Paracelsus* (1493–1541), or resembling his theories or practice. The name was coined for himself by Theophrastus Bombastus von Hohenheim, and apparently implied a claim to be greater than Celsus.

paracentesis *par-ə-sen-tē'sis*, (*surg*) *n* tapping of a body cavity to remove fluid or gas, etc. [Gr *parakentēsis*, from *para* beside, beyond, and *kenteein* to pierce]

paracetamol *par-ə-sēt'ə-mol* or *-set'*, *n* a mild analgesic and antipyretic drug, often recommended instead of aspirin. [Gr *para* beside, beyond, and *acetam*ide]

parachronism *par-ak'rən-izm*, *n* an error in dating, *esp* when anything is represented as later than it really was. [Gr *para* beside, beyond, and *chronos* time]

parachute *par'ə-shōōt*, *n* a large fabric umbrella-like canopy, used where resistance to air is needed, *esp* one strapped to a person jumping from an aircraft, to give a slow descent, also one unfolded at the rear of an aircraft on landing, to assist braking (*colloq* short form **chute**); any structure serving a similar purpose, such as a pappus or a patagium. — *vi* to descend by parachute (also *fig*). — *vt* to take and drop by parachute (also *fig*). — *n* **par'achutist**. — **parachute troops**. [Fr *parachute*, from Ital *para*, imperative of *parare* to ward, from L *parāre* to prepare, and Fr *chute* fall]

paraclete *par'ə-klēt*, *n* an advocate or legal helper, or intercessor, pleader on behalf of another — applied (with *cap*) to the Holy Ghost (John 14.26). [Gr *paraklētos*, from *parakaleein* to call in, also to comfort, from *para* beside, beyond, and *kaleein* to call]

paracme *pər-ak'mē*, *n* the stage of decline or senescence after the culmination of development. [Gr *para* beside, beyond, and *akmē* a point]

paracrostic *par-ə-kros'tik*, *n* a poem whose initial letters reproduce its first verse. [**para-**[1] and **acrostic**]

paracusis *par-ə-kū'sis*, *n* disordered hearing. [Gr *para* beside, beyond, and *akousis* hearing]

paracyanogen *par-ə-sī-an'ə-jən*, *n* a polymer of cyanogen. [**para-**[1] and **cyanogen**]

parade *pə-rād'*, *n* show; display; ostentation; an assembling in order for exercise, inspection, etc; an area in which troops, etc assemble for this purpose; a procession; a public promenade; a row (of shops or houses); a parry (*fencing*). — *vt* to show off; to thrust to the attention of others; to lead about and expose to public attention; to traverse (a square, etc) in parade; to marshal in military order for inspection, etc. — *vi* to march up and down (as if) for show; to pass; to march, or drive, etc in procession or military order; to show off. — **parade'-ground** a square, etc, for the parading of troops. [Fr, from Sp *parada*, from *parar* to halt, from L *parāre*, *-ātum* to prepare]

paradiddle *par'ə-did-l*, *n* a drum roll in which the principal beats are struck by the left and right sticks in succession.

paradigm *par'ə-dīm*, *n* an example, exemplar; a set of the inflected forms of a word (*gram*); a basic theory, a conceptual framework within which scientific theories are constructed. — *adj* **paradigmatic** (*-dig-mat'ik*) or **paradigmat'ical**. — *adv* **paradigmat'ically**. [Fr *paradigme*, from Gr *paradeigma*, from *paradeiknynai* to exhibit side by side, from *para* beside, beyond, and *deiknynai* to show]

paradise *par'ə-dīs*, *n* a park or pleasure-ground *esp* in ancient Persia; a park in which foreign animals were kept; the garden of Eden; heaven; the place (intermediate or final) where the blessed dead go; any place or state of bliss; a parvis; a small private apartment (*archaic*). — *adj* **paradisaic** (*par-ə-dis-ā'ik*), **paradisa'ical**, **paradisal** (*-dī'səl*), **paradisean** (*-dis'i-ən*), **paradisiac** (*-dis'i-ak* or *-diz'i-ak*), **paradisiacal** (*-dis-ī'ə-kl*), **paradisial** (*-dis'* or *-diz'*), **paradisian** (*-dis'* or *-diz'*) or **paradisic** (*-dis'* or *-diz'*). — **par'adise-fish** a Chinese freshwater fish (*Macropodus*), often kept in aquaria for its beauty of form and colouring. — **bird of paradise** any bird of the family **Paradisē'idae**, inhabitants chiefly of New Guinea, closely related to the crows but of very beautiful plumage; **fool's paradise** see under **fool**[1]. [Gr *paradeisos* a park, from OPers *pairidaēza* park]

paradoctor. See under **para-**[2].

parador *par'ə-dör*, *n* any of several types of (*usu* country) dwellings, eg castles, convents, etc converted for use as tourist accommodation in Spain: — *pl* **paradores** (*-dör'ās*). [Sp]

parados *par'ə-dos*, *n* earthworks protecting against a rear attack. [Fr, from L *parāre* to prepare, and *dorsum* back]

paradox *par'ə-doks*, *n* something which is contrary to received, conventional opinion; something which is apparently absurd but is or may be really true; a self-contradictory statement; the state of being any of these. — *adj* **paradox'al**. — *n* **par'adoxer**. — *adj* **paradox'ical**. — *adv* **paradox'ically**. — *n* **paradox'icalness**. — *n* **Paradox'ides** (*-i-dēz*) a typically Middle Cambrian genus of trilobites, some very large (about two feet (60 cm) long). — *adj* **paradoxid'ian**. — *n* **par'adoxist**. — *n* **paradoxol'ogy** the utterance or maintaining of paradoxes. — *n* **par'adoxy** the quality of being paradoxical. — **paradoxical sleep** apparently deep sleep, with actual increased brain activity. [Gr *paradoxos*, *-on* contrary to opinion, from *para* beside, beyond, and *doxa* opinion]

paradoxure *par-ə-dok'sūr*, *n* a civet-like carnivore of southern Asia and Malaysia, the palm-cat of India. — *adj* **paradoxū'rine**. [Gr *paradoxos* paradoxical, from *para* beside, beyond, and *ourā* tail]

paradrop. See under **para-**[2].

paraenesis or **parenesis** *par-ēn'i-sis*, or *-en'*, *n* exhortation. — *adj* **paraenetic** (*-net'ik*) or **paraenet'ical**. [Gr *parainesis*, from *para*, beside, beyond, and *aineein* to commend]

paraesthesia or (*US*) **paresthesia** *par-ēs-thē'si-ə* or *-es-*, (*med*) *n* abnormal sensation in any part of the body. [Gr *para* beyond, and *aisthēsis* sensation]

paraffin *par'ə-fin*, *n orig* paraffin-wax, so named by its discoverer, Reichenbach, from its having little chemical affinity for other bodies; generalized to mean any saturated hydrocarbon of the methane series, gaseous, liquid, or solid, the general formula being C_nH_{2n+2}; paraffin-oil. — Also **par'affine**. — *vt* to treat with paraffin. — *adj* **paraffin'ic**, **par'affinoid** or **par'affiny**. — **par'affin-oil'** any of the mineral burning oils associated with the manufacture of paraffin, mixtures of liquid paraffin and other hydrocarbons; **par'affin-scale'** unrefined solid paraffin; **paraffin test** a test using paraffin to detect trace elements left on the skin of someone who has been in contact with explosives, etc; **par'affin-wax'** a white transparent crystalline substance produced by distillation of shale, coal, tar, wood, etc — a mixture of solid paraffins. — **liquid paraffin** a liquid form of petroleum jelly, used as a mild laxative. [L *parum* little, and *affīnis* having affinity]

paraffle or **parafle** *pə-rä'fl*, (*Scot*) *n* a pretentious display; a fuss. [Cf **paraph**]

parafoil. See under **para-**[2].

parage *par'ij*, *n* lineage (*obs*); high birth or rank; equality of birth or status, a state in which no homage or service is due (*feudal law*). [Fr]

paragenesis *par-ə-jen'i-sis*, or **paragenesia** *par-ə-jin-ē'zi-ə*, (*geol*) *n* the order in which minerals have developed in a given mass of rock; the development of minerals in such close contact that their formation is affected and they become a joined mass. — *adj* **paragenet'ic**. [**para-**[1] and **genesis**]

paraglider, paragliding. See under **para-**[2].

paraglossa *par-ə-glos'ə, n* either of two appendages of the ligula in insects: — *pl* **paragloss'ae** (-*ē*). — *adj* **paragloss'al**. — *adj* **paragloss'ate**. [Gr *para* beside, beyond, and *glōssa* tongue]

paragnathous *pər-ag'nə-thəs, adj* having equal mandibles. — *n* **parag'nathism**. [Gr *para* beside, beyond, and *gnathos* jaw]

paragnosis *par-ə-gnō'sis,* (*psychol*) *n* knowledge of matters not susceptible to investigation by traditional scientific methods. [Gr *para* beside, beyond, and *gnōsis* knowing]

paragoge *par-ə-gō'jē* or *-gē*, or **paragogue** *par'ə-gog, n* an addition to the end of a word, such as *t* in *against, amidst, amongst, whilst*, or *d* in *drownd* (mistakenly for *drown*). — *adj* **paragogic** (*-goj'ik* or *-gog'ik*) or **paragog'ical**. — **paragogic future** the cohortative tense in Hebrew, a lengthened form of the imperfect or future, *usu* confined to the first person, giving the sense of 'let me' or 'let us'. [Gr *paragōgē* a leading part, addition, from *para* beside, beyond, and *agein* to lead]

paragon *par'ə-gon* or *-gən, n* a model of perfection or supreme excellence; a match or equal (*archaic*); a mate (*Spenser*); a rival (*archaic*); (a) comparison (*Spenser*); emulation, competition (*Spenser*); a diamond of 600 carats or more; a black marble (*obs*); a camlet used in upholstery and dressmaking (*obs*); 20-point printing-type intermediate between great-primer and double-pica. — *vt* (*archaic* or *rare*) to compare; to match; to surpass (*Shakesp*); to hold up as a paragon (*Shakesp*). [OFr *paragon*, from Ital *paragone* touchstone; origin obscure]

paragonite *par'ə-gən-īt* or *pər-ag', n* a soda-mica, once mistaken for talc. [Gr *paragōn* misleading, from *para* beside, beyond, and *agein* to lead]

paragram *par'ə-gram, n* a play on words in which (*esp* initial) letters are changed. — *n* **paragramm'atist** a punster. [Gr (*skōmmata*) *para gramma* (jokes) by letter]

paragraph *par'ə-gräf, n* a sign (in ancient manuscripts a short horizontal line, in the Middle Ages ¶, now ⁋ or ¶) marking off a section of a book, etc; a distinct part of a discourse or writing marked by such a sign or now *usu* by indenting or extra space between lines; a short passage, or a collection of sentences, with unity of content or purpose; a musical passage forming a unit; a short separate item of news or comment in a newspaper. — *vt* to form into paragraphs; to write or publish paragraphs about. — *n* **par'agrapher** or **par'agraphist** a person who writes paragraphs, news items *esp* for newspapers. — *adj* **paragraphic** (*-graf'*) or **paragraph'ical**. — *adv* **paragraph'ically**. [Gr *paragraphos* written alongside, from *para* beside, beyond, and *graphein* to write]

paragraphia *par-ə-graf'i-ə, n* the writing of different words and letters to the ones intended, owing to disease or injury of the brain. — *adj* **paragraphic** (*-graf'ik*). [Gr *para* beside, beyond, and *graphein* to write]

Paraguay *par-ə-gwī'* or *-gwā', n* a country and river of South America. — **Paraguay tea** maté.

paraheliotropic *par-ə-hē-li-ō-trop'ik,* (*bot*) *adj* turning edgewise to the light. — *n* **paraheliotropism** (*-ot'rə-pizm*). [Gr *para* beside, beyond, and *hēlios* the sun, with *tropos* a turn, from *trepein* to turn]

parainfluenza virus *par-ə-in-floo-en'zə vī'rəs, n* any of a number of viruses causing influenza-like symptoms, *esp* in children.

parakeet or **parrakeet** *par'ə-kēt, n* a small long-tailed parrot of various kinds. — Also **paroquet, parroquet** (*-ket*), or **paraquito** (*pa-ra-kē'tō; pl* **paraqui'tos**). [Sp *periquito*, Ital *parrocchetto*, or OFr *paroquet* (Fr *perroquet*); the origin and relations of these have not been determined]

parakiting. See under **para-**[2].

paralalia *par-ə-la'* or *-lā'li-ə, n* a form of speech disturbance, particularly that in which a different sound or syllable is produced from the one intended. [Gr *para* beside, beyond, and *lalia* speech]

paralanguage *par-ə-lang'gwij, n* elements of communication other than words, ie tone of voice, gesture, facial expression, etc. — *adj* **paralinguist'ic**. — *n sing* **paralinguist'ics** the study of paralanguage. [**para-**[1], with **language** and **linguistic(s)**]

paraldehyde *par-al'di-hīd, n* a polymer, $(C_2H_4O)_3$, of acetaldehyde (acetic aldehyde), a liquid with a characteristic smell, used to induce sleep. [**para-**[1] and **aldehyde**]

paralegal *par-ə-lē'gl, adj* of, concerning or being a person who assists a professional lawyer. — Also *n* (*par'ə-lē-gl*). [**para-**[1] and **legal**]

paraleipsis *par-ə-līp'sis* or **paralipsis** *-lip'sis, n* a rhetorical figure by which one fixes attention on a subject by pretending to neglect it, as in 'I will not speak of his generosity', etc: — *pl* **paraleip'ses** or **paralip'ses**. — *n* **paraleipom'enon** or **paralipom'enon** a thing left out, added in supplement: — *pl* **paraleipom'ena** or **paralipom'ena** (*esp* in the Septuagint, etc) the Books of Chronicles. [Gr *paraleipsis, paraleipomenon* (neuter present particle passive), from *paraleipein* to leave aside, from *para* beside, beyond, and *leipein* to leave]

paralexia *par-ə-lek'si-ə, n* a defect in the power of seeing and interpreting written language, with meaningless transposition of words and syllables. [Gr *para* beside, beyond, and *lexis* a word]

paralinguistic, paralinguistics. See under **paralanguage**.

paralipsis, etc. See **paraleipsis**.

parallax *par'ə-laks, n* an apparent change in the position of an object caused by change of position in the observer; (in astronomy) the apparent change (measured angularly) in the position of a heavenly body when viewed from different points — when viewed from opposite points on the earth's surface this change is called the *daily* or *diurnal* or *geocentric parallax*, and when viewed from opposite points of the earth's orbit, the *annual* or *heliocentric parallax*. — *adj* **parallac'tic** or **parallac'tical**. — **parallactic motion** see **proper motion** (under **proper**). [Gr *parallaxis*, from *para* beside, beyond, and *allassein* to change, from *allos* another]

parallel *par'ə-lel, adj* (of lines, etc) extended in the same direction and equidistant in all parts; analogous, corresponding; alongside in time; exactly contemporary; having a constant interval (major and minor being reckoned alike; *music*). — *n* a parallel line; a line of latitude; an analogue, or like, or equal; an analogy; a tracing or statement of resemblances; a besieger's trench parallel to the outline of the place besieged; a printer's reference mark of two vertical lines; parallel arrangement. — *vt* to place so as to be parallel; to conform; to represent as parallel; to liken in detail; to find a parallel to; to match; to be or run parallel to. — *vi* to be or run parallel: — *pr p* **par'alleling**; *pa t* and *pa p* **par'alleled**. — *n* **par'alleling** a commercial practice whereby companies buy highly priced goods (eg perfume) in markets where prices are relatively low and sell them on in markets where prices are higher. — *n* **par'allelism** the state or fact of being parallel; resemblance in corresponding details; a balanced construction of a verse or sentence, where one part repeats the form or meaning of the other; comparison; development along parallel lines; the theory or belief (in full **psychophysical parallelism**) that mind and matter do not interact but correspond. — *n* **par'allelist** a person who draws a parallel or comparison; a believer in psychophysical parallelism. — *adj* **parallelis'tic**. — *vt* **par'allelize** or **-ise** to provide a parallel to. — *adv* **par'allelly**. — *adv* **par'allelwise**. — **parallel bars** a pair of fixed bars used in gymnastics; **parallel imports** imports brought into a country through other than official channels, thus circumventing regulations, etc; **parallel importer**; **parallel importing**; **parallel motion** a name given to any linkage by which circular motion may be changed into straight-line motion; **parallel processing** (*comput*) the processing of several elements of an item of information at the same time; **parallel ruler** or **rulers** rulers joined by two pivoted strips, for drawing parallel lines; **parallel slalom** a slalom race in which two competitors ski down parallel courses. — *adj* **par'allel-veined** (*bot*) having the main veins running side by side. — **in parallel** (of electrical apparatus) arranged in such a way that terminals of like polarity are connected together; (of electrical circuits) connected in such a way that any current flowing divides between them (cf **in series**); simultaneously (*fig*). [Gr *parallēlos*, as if *par' allēloin* beside each other]

parallelepiped *par-ə-lel-ep'i-ped* (or *-lel'ə-* or *-ə-pī'*), *n* a solid figure bounded by six parallelograms, opposite pairs being identical and parallel. — Also **parallelepip'edon** (*pl* **parallelepipeda**) and improperly **parallelopī'ped** or **parallelopī'pedon**. [Gr *parallēlepipedon*, from *parallēlos* and *epipedon* a plane surface, from *epi* on, and *pedon* ground]

parallelogram *par-ə-lel'ō-gram*, *n* a plane four-sided figure whose opposite sides are parallel. — *adj* **parallelogrammat'ic**, **parallelogrammat'ical**, **parallelogramm'ic** or **parallelogramm'ical**. — **parallelogram of forces** a figure in which the direction and amount of two component forces are represented by two sides of a parallelogram, those of their resultant by the diagonal. [Gr *parallēlogrammon*, from *grammē* a line]

paralogia *par-ə-loj'i-ə*, *n* impairment of reasoning power characterized by difficulty in expressing logical ideas in speech. — *n* **paral'ogism** false reasoning — also **paral'ogy**. — *vi* **paral'ogize** or **-ise** to reason falsely. [Gr *paralogismos*, from *para* beside, beyond, and *logismos*, from *logos* reason]

paralympics *pa-rə-lim'iks*, *n sing* an Olympic games for sportspeople with physical disabilities, running *para*llel to the able-bodied games. — *adj* **paralymp'ic**.

paralysis *pə-ral'i-sis*, *n* a loss of power of motion, or sensation, in any part of the body, palsy; deprivation of the power of action. — *vt* **paralyse** or (*US*) **paralyze** (*par'ə-līz*) to afflict with paralysis; to deprive of the power of action. — *n* **par'alyser** or (*US*) **par'alyzer**. — *adj* **paralytic** (*par-ə-lit'ik*) of or pertaining to paralysis; afflicted with or inclined to paralysis; helplessly drunk (*slang*). — *n* someone who is affected with paralysis. — *n* **paralysis time** (*nuc eng*) the time for which a radiation detector is rendered inoperative by an electronic switch in the control circuit. [Gr *paralysis* secret undoing, paralysis, from *lyein* to loosen]

paramaecium. See under **Paramecium**.

paramagnetic *par-ə-mag-net'ik*, *adj* magnetic in the ordinary sense (said of bodies that when freely suspended between the poles of a magnet place themselves parallel to the lines of force, as opposed to *diamagnetic*). — *n* **paramag'netism**. [**para-**[1] and **magnetic** (see under **magnet**)]

paramastoid *par-ə-mas'toid*, *adj* situated near the mastoid, paroccipital. — *n* a paramastoid process or projecting part. [**para-**[1] and **mastoid**]

paramatta or **parramatta** *par-ə-mat'ə*, *n* a fabric like that made from merino wool, made of worsted and cotton. [Appar from *Parramatta* in New South Wales]

Paramecium *par-ə-mē'si-əm* or *-mē'shi-əm*, *n* a genus of tiny animals including the slipper animalcule, a slipper-shaped infusorian; (without *cap*) an animal of the genus: — *pl* **paramē'cia**. — Often misspelled **paramoecium** or **paramaecium**. [Gr *paramēkēs* long-shaped, from *para* alongside, and *mēkos* length]

paramedic and **paramedical**. See under **para-**[1] and **para-**[2].

paramenstruum *par-ə-men'stro͞o-əm*, *n* the four days before and the four days after the onset of menstruation. [**para-**[1] and **menstruum**]

parament *par'ə-mənt*, (*obs*) *n* a rich decoration, hanging, or robe. [L *parāre* to prepare]

paramese *pa-ram'i-sē*, (*Gr music*) *n* the string or tone next above the mese. [Gr *paramesē*]

parameter *pə-ram'i-tər*, *n* a line or quantity which serves to determine a point, line, figure or quantity in a class of such things (*math*); a constant quantity in the equation of a curve; in conic sections, a third proportional to any diameter and its conjugate diameter; the latus rectum of a parabola; the intercept upon an axis of a crystal face chosen for purpose of reference (the *parametral plane*); a quantity to which an arbitrary value may be given as a convenience in expressing performance or for use in calculations (*elec*); a variable; a variable which is given a series of arbitrary values in order that a family of curves of two other related variables may be drawn; any constant in learning or growth curves that differs with differing conditions (*psychol*); a boundary or limit (*lit* and *fig*). — *adj* **param'etral** or **parametric** (*par-ə-met'rik*) or **paramet'rical**. [Gr *para* beside, beyond, and *metron* measure]

paramilitary *par-ə-mil'i-tər-i*, *adj* on military lines and intended to supplement the strictly military; organized as a military force, *esp* when engaged in active rebellion against the government, an occupying force, etc. — Also *n*. [**para-**[1] and **military**]

paramnesia *par-am-nē'zh(y)ə*, *n* a memory disorder in which words are remembered but not their proper meaning; the condition of believing that one remembers events and circumstances which have not previously occurred. [Gr *para* beside, beyond, and the root of *mimnēskein* to remind]

paramo *pä'rä-mō*, *n* a bare wind-swept elevated plain in South America: — *pl* **par'amos**. [Sp *páramo*]

paramoecium. See **Paramecium**.

paramorph *par'ə-mörf*, (*mineralogy*) *n* a pseudomorph formed by a change in molecular structure without change of chemical composition. — *adj* **paramorph'ic**. — *n* **paramorph'ism**. [Gr *para* beside, beyond, and *morphē* form]

paramount *par'ə-mownt*, *adj* superior to all others; supreme — *opp* of *paravail*. — *n* a paramount chief; a superior. — *n* **par'amouncy** or **par'amountcy**. — *adv* **par'amountly**. — **paramount chief** a supreme chief. [OFr *paramont*, *par* (L *per*) *à mont* (L *ad montem*); see **amount**]

paramour *par'ə-mo͞or*, *adv* (*obs*) by the way of love, as a lover, for love's sake, out of kindness. — *n* a lover of either sex, formerly in an innocent, now *usu* in the illicit, sense. [Fr *par amour* by or with love, from L *per amōrem*]

paramyxovirus *par-ə-mik'sō-vī-rəs*, *n* any of a group of single-stranded ribonucleic acid viruses which includes the mumps and measles viruses. [**para-**[1] and **myxovirus**]

Paraná *pa-ra-nä'*, *n* a river and state in Brazil. — **Paraná pine** the tree, *Araucaria brasiliana*, native to S Brazil, or its wood.

paranephros *par-ə-nef'ros*, *n* the suprarenal gland, near the kidney. — *adj* **paraneph'ric**. [Gr *para* beside, beyond, and *nephros* kidney]

paranete *par-a-nē'tē*, (*Gr music*) *n* the string or tone next below the nete. [Gr *paranētē*]

parang *pär'ang*, *n* a heavy Malay knife. [Malay]

paranitroaniline *par-ə-nī-trō-an'i-lēn*, *n* a nitro-derivative of aniline, used in dyeing. [**para-**[1] and **nitro-aniline** (see **nitro-**)]

paranoia *par-ə-noi'ə*, *n* a form of mental disorder characterized by constant delusions, *esp* of grandeur, pride, persecution; intense (*esp* irrational) fear or suspicion. — Also (rarely) **paranoea** (*-nē'ə*). — *adj* **paranoi'ac** (*-ak*) of paranoia. — *n* a victim of paranoia. — Also **paranoe'ic** or **paranoic** (*-no'ik*). — *adj* **par'anoid** or **paranoid'al** resembling paranoia. [Gr *paranoia*, from *para* beside, beyond, and *noos* mind]

paranormal *par-ə-nör'məl*, *adj* abnormal, *esp* psychologically; not explicable by the laws of nature or reason. — *n* that which is paranormal; (with **the**) paranormal occurrences or phenomena. [**para-**[1] and **normal**]

paranthelion *par-an-thē'li-on*, *n* a diffuse whitish image of the sun, having the same altitude, at an angular distance of 90° to 140°: — *pl* **paranthe'lia**. [Gr *para* beside, beyond, *anti* against, and *hēlios* the sun]

paranthropus *par-an'thrə-pəs*, *n* a hominid ape *usu* included in the species *Australopithecus robustus*. [**para-**[1] and Gr *anthrōpos* man]

paranym *par'ə-nim*, *n* a word whose meaning is altered to conceal an evasion or untruth, eg *liberation* used for *conquest*. [**para-**[1] and Gr *onyma*, *onoma* name]

paranymph *par'ə-nimf*, (*antiq*; *Milton*) *n* a friend who went with the bridegroom to fetch the bride, a groomsman or bridesmaid; someone who countenances and supports another. [Gr *paranymphos*, from *para* beside, beyond, and *nymphē* a bride]

paraparesis *pa-rə-pə-rē'sis*, (*med*) *n* weakness of muscles, *esp* in the legs, partial paralysis. — *adj* **paraparet'ic**. [**para-**[1] and **paresis**]

parapenting *par'ə-pent-ing* or *-pāt-ing*, *n* a cross between hang-gliding and parachuting, a sport in which the participant jumps from a high place wearing a modified type of parachute, which is then used as a hang-glider. [**para-**[2] and Fr *pent* slope]

parapet *par'ə-pit*, *n* a bank or wall to protect soldiers from the fire of an enemy in front; a low wall along the side of a bridge, edge of a roof, etc. — *adj* **par'apeted** having a parapet. [Ital *parapetto*, from pfx *para-* (see **parachute**) and Ital *petto*, from L *pectus* the breast]

paraph *par'af*, *n* a mark or flourish under one's signature. — *vt* to append a paraph to; to sign with initials. [Fr *paraphe*; cf **paragraph**]

paraphasia *par-ə-fā'zhyə* or *-zi-ə*, *n* a form of aphasia in which one word is substituted for another. — *adj* **paraphasic** (*-fā'zik* or *-sik*). [**para-**[1] and **aphasia**]

paraphernalia *par-ə-fər-nāl'yə* or *-i-ə*, *n pl* formerly, property other than dower that remained under a married woman's own control, *esp* articles of jewellery, dress and personal belongings; (the following all now *usu n sing*) ornaments of dress of any kind; trappings; equipment; miscellaneous accessories. [Late L *paraphernālia*, from *parapherna*, from Gr *para* beside, beyond, and *phernē* a dowry, from *pherein* to bring]

paraphilia *par-ə-fil'i-ə*, *n* sexual perversion. — *n* **paraphiliac** (*-fil'i-ak*) a person who indulges in abnormal sexual practices. — Also *adj*. [**para-**[1] and Gr *philia* fondness, liking for]

paraphimosis *par-ə-fī-mō'sis*, *n* strangulation of the glans penis by constriction of the prepuce. [**para-**[1] and **phimosis**]

paraphonia *par-ə-fō'ni-ə*, *n* (in Byzantine music) a melodic progression by fourths and fifths; a morbid change of voice; an alteration of the voice, as at puberty. — *adj* **paraphonic** (*-fon'ik*). [Gr *para* beside, beyond, and *phōnē* voice]

paraphrase *par'ə-frāz*, *n* (an) expression of the same thing in other words; an exercise in such expression; a verse rendering of a biblical passage for church singing, *esp* in the Church of Scotland. — *vt* to express in other words. — *vi* to make a paraphrase. — *n* **par'aphraser** or **par'aphrast** (*-frast*) a person who paraphrases. — *adj* **paraphrast'ic** or **paraphrast'ical**. — *adv* **paraphrast'ically**. [Gr *paraphrasis*, from *para* beside, beyond, and *phrasis* a speaking, from *phrazein* to speak]

paraphraxia *par-ə-fraks'i-ə* or **paraphraxis** *-fraks'is*, *n* inability to perform purposive movements properly. [**para-**[1] and Gr *phraxis* barricade]

paraphrenia *par-ə-frē'ni-ə*, *n* any mental disorder of the paranoid type. [**para-**[1] and Gr *phrēn* mind]

paraphysis *pə-raf'i-sis*, *n* a sterile filament among spore-bearing structures in lower plants: — *pl* **paraphyses** (*-sēz*). [Gr, a side-growth, from *para* beside, beyond, and *physis* growth]

parapineal *par-ə-pin'i-əl*, *adj* beside the pineal gland — applied to the pineal eye. [**para-**[1] and **pineal**]

paraplegia *par-ə-plē'jyə* or *-plē'jə*, *n* paralysis of the lower part of the body. — *adj* **paraplegic** (*-plēj'ik* or *-plej'ik*). — *n* a person suffering from paraplegia. [Ionic Gr *paraplēgiē* a stroke on the side, from *para* beside, beyond, and *plēgē* a blow]

parapodium *par-ə-pō'di-əm*, *n* one of the jointless lateral appendages of polychaete worms, etc; a swimming organ in some molluscs, a lateral expansion of the foot: — *pl* **parapō'dia**. — *adj* **parapō'dial**. [Gr *para* beside, beyond, and *pous*, *podos* a foot]

parapophysis *par-ə-pof'i-sis*, *n* a ventral transverse process of a vertebra: — *pl* **parapoph'yses** (*-sēz*). — *adj* **parapophysial** (*par-ap-ō-fiz'i-əl*). [**para-**[1] and **apophysis**]

parapsychism *par-ə-sī'kizm*, *n* panpsychistic parallelism. — *adj* **parapsy'chic** or **parapsy'chical**. — *adj* **parapsycholog'ical**. — *adv* **parapsycholog'ically**. — *n* **parapsychol'ogist**. — *n* **parapsychol'ogy** psychical research; the study of phenomena such as telepathy and clairvoyance which seem to suggest that the mind can gain knowledge by means other than the normal perceptual processes. — *n* **parapsychō'sis** an abnormal psychosis. [**para-**[1] and **psychism** (see under **psyche**)]

paraquadrate *par-ə-kwod'rāt*, (*anatom*) *n* the squamosal. [**para-**[1] and **quadrate**]

paraquat® *par'ə-kwot*, *n* a weed-killer very poisonous to human beings. [**para-**[1] and *quat*ernary, part of its formula]

paraquito *par-ə-kē'tō*. See **parakeet**.

para-red *par'ə-red'*, *n* an azo-dye for cottons, derived from paranitroaniline. [**para-**[1]]

pararhyme *par'ə-rīm*, *n* a form of rhyme in which the consonants, but not the vowel, of the last stressed syllable are identical in sound, as in *hair* and *hour*. [**para-**[1] and **rhyme**]

pararosaniline *par-ə-roz-an'i-lēn*, *n* a base entering into various dyestuffs, such as magenta. [**para-**[1] and **rosaniline**]

pararthria *par-är'thri-ə*, *n* disordered articulation of speech. [Gr *para* beside, beyond, and *arthron* a joint]

parasailing *par'ə-sā-ling*, *n* a sport similar to paragliding, the participant wearing water-skis and a modified type of parachute, and being towed into the air by a motorboat. [**para-**[2] and **sailing**]

parasang *par'ə-sang*, *n* an old Persian measure of length, reckoned at 30 stadia, or between 3 and 4 miles. [Gr *parasangēs*, from OPers (mod Pers *farsang*)]

parascending *par'ə-sen-ding*, *n* a sport similar to paragliding, the participant being towed into the wind behind a motor vehicle. — *n* **par'ascender**. [**para-**[2] and **ascending**]

parascenium *par-ə-sē'ni-əm*, *n* (in the Greek theatre) a wing, side-scene: — *pl* **parascē'nia**. [Gr *paraskēnion*, from *para* beside, beyond, and *skēnē* tent, stage]

parasceve *par'ə-sēv* or *par-ə-sē'vē*, *n* preparation (*obs*); the eve of the Jewish Sabbath, Friday, the day of preparation (*archaic*); Good Friday (*RC Church*). [LL *parascēvē*, from Gr *paraskeuē* preparation, from *para* beside, beyond, and *skeuē* equipment]

parascience *par'ə-sī-əns*, *n* the study of phenomena which cannot be investigated by rigorous traditional scientific method. [**para-**[1] and **science**]

paraselene *par-ə-se-lē'nē*, *n* a mock moon, a bright patch on a lunar halo: — *pl* **paraselē'nae** (*-nē*). [Gr *para* beside, beyond, and *selēnē* moon]

parasite *par'ə-sīt*, *n* a hanger-on or sycophant; a person who lives at the expense of society or of others and contributes nothing; an organism that lives in or on another living organism and derives subsistence from it without rendering it any service in return; in literary but not scientific use extended to an epiphyte. — *n* **parasitaemia** (*-ē'mi-ə*; Gr *haima* blood) the presence of parasites in the blood. — *adj* **parasitic** (*-sit'ik*) or **parasitical** of, of the nature of, caused by or like a parasite. — *adv* **parasit'ically**. — *n* **parasit'icalness**. — *n* **parasiticide** (*-sit'i-sīd*) that which destroys parasites. — *n* **par'asitism** (*-sīt-izm*) the act or practice of being a parasite. — *vt* **par'asitize** or **-ise** to be a parasite on (another organism); to infect or infest with parasites. — *adj* **par'asitoid** (*-sīt-*) parasitic in one phase of the life-history, thereafter independent. — Also *n*. — *n* **parasītol'ogist**. — *n* **parasītol'ogy**. — *n* **parasītō'sis** infestation with parasites. [Gr *parasītos*, from *para* beside, and *sītos* corn, bread, food]

parasol *par'ə-sol* or *-sol'*, *n* a sunshade, rather similar to an umbrella; an aeroplane with its wings overhead. — **parasol mushroom** a tall white edible mushroom (*Lepiota procera*) resembling a parasol. [Fr, from Ital *parasole*, from *para*, imper of *parare* to ward, from L *parāre* to prepare, and *sole*, from L *sōl*, *sōlis* the sun]

parasphenoid *par-ə-sfē'noid*, *adj* alongside the sphenoid bone. — *n* a bone of the skull, part of the cranial floor. [**para**[1] and **sphenoid** (see under **sphene**)]

parastatal *par-ə-stā'tl*, *adj* indirectly controlled by the state. [**para-**[1] and **statal** (see under **state**)]

parastichy *pər-as'ti-ki*, (*bot*) *n* a secondary spiral joining leaf-bases on an axis, visible where the leaves are crowded together, eg the scales of a pine-cone. [Gr *para* beside, beyond, and *stichos* a row]

parasuicide *par-ə-sū'i-sīd* or *-sōō'*, *n* a deliberate harmful act against one's own person (such as taking an overdose of drugs) which appears to be an attempt at suicide but which was probably not intended to be successful; a person who performs such an act. [**para-**[1] and **suicide**]

parasympathetic *par-ə-sim-pə-thet'ik*. See under **sympathy**.

parasynthesis *par-ə-sin'thi-sis*, *n* derivation of words from compounds, eg *come-at-able*, where *come* and *at* are first compounded and then the derivative suffix *-able* added. — *adj* **parasynthetic** (*-thet'ik*). — *n* **parasyn'theton** a word so formed: — *pl* **parasyn'theta**. [Gr]

parataxis *par-ə-tak'sis*, (*gram*) *n* the arrangement of clauses or propositions without connectives. — *adj* **paratac'tic** or **paratac'tical**. — *adv* **paratac'tically**. [Gr, from *para* beside, beyond, and *taxis* arrangement]

paratha *pə-rä'tə* or *-tä*, *n* a flat round cake of unleavened bread, traditionally eaten as an accompaniment to Indian food. [Hindi]

parathesis *pə-rath'i-sis*, *n* apposition (*gram*); the compounding of words without change, as (*L*) *rēspūblica* from *rēs* and *pūblica* (*philol*). [Gr, placing alongside]

parathyroid *par-ə-thī'roid*, (*anatom*) *adj* beside the thyroid. — *n* any of a number of small ductless glands apparently concerned with calcium metabolism. [**para-**[1] and **thyroid**]

paratonic *par-ə-ton'ik*, (*bot*) *adj* induced by external stimulus. [Gr *para* beside, beyond, and *tonos* a stretching]

paratroops *par'ə-trōōps*, *n pl* troops carried by air, to be dropped by parachute. — *n* **par'atrooper**. [**para-**[2] and **troop**]

paratyphoid *par-ə-tī'foid*, *n* a disease (of various types) resembling typhoid. — Also *adj*. [**para-**[1]]

paravail *par-ə-vāl'*, *adj* inferior; lowest (said of a feudal tenant); of least account — *opp* of *paramount*. [OFr *par aval* below, from L *per* through, *ad* to, and *vallem*, accusative of *vallis* valley]

paravane *par'ə-vān*, *n* a fish-shaped device, with fins or vanes, towed from the bow of a vessel, for deflecting mines along a wire and severing their moorings — sometimes called an 'otter'; an explosive device of similar design for attacking submerged submarines. [**para-**[1] and **vane**]

paravant or **paravaunt** *par-ə-vänt'* or *-vönt'*, (*Spenser*) *adv* in front, first, beforehand, pre-eminently. [OFr *paravant*, from *par* through, and *avant* before, from L *ab* from, and *ante* before]

par avion. See under **avion**.

parawalker *par'ə-wök-ər*, *n* a metal structure like an external skeleton worn by a paraplegic to enable him or her to walk. [**para-**[1] and **walker** (see under **walk**)]

Parazoa *par-ə-zō'ə*, *n pl* a division of the animal kingdom, the sponges, co-ordinate with *Protozoa* and *Metazoa* (also without *cap*). — *n* and *adj* **parazō'an**. — *n* **parazō'on** any member of the group Parazoa: — *pl* **parazō'a**. [Gr *para* beside, beyond, and *zōion* animal]

parboil *pär'boil*, *vt orig* to boil thoroughly; (*now* by confusion) to part-cook by boiling. [OFr *parboillir*, from LL *perbullīre* to boil thoroughly; influenced by confusion with **part**]

parbreak *pär'brāk*, (*archaic*) *n* an instance of vomiting. — *vt* and *vi* (*pär'* or *-brāk'*) to vomit: — *pa p* **parbreaked**. [ME *brake* to vomit; cf Du *braken*; the pfx may be Fr *par-*]

parbuckle *pär'buk-l*, *n* a purchase made by making fast a rope in the middle and passing the ends under and then over a heavy object, eg a barrel, to be rolled up or down a sloping surface; a sling made by passing both ends of a rope through its bight. — *vt* to hoist or lower by a parbuckle. [Earlier *parbunkel*, *parbuncle*; origin unknown]

Parca *pär'kə*, *n* a Fate, any one of the Roman goddesses Nona, Decuma, and Morta, identified with the Greek Moirai: — *pl* **Par'cae** (*-sē*). [L, prob connected with *parere* to produce, not *parcere* to spare]

parcel *pär'sl*, *n* a little part; a portion; a quantity; a group; a set; a pack (*depreciatively*); a lot; an item (*archaic*); a sum of money lost or won (*colloq*); a package, *esp* one wrapped in paper and tied with string; a continuous stretch of land. — *adv* (*archaic*) partly. — *adj* (*archaic*) in part. — *vt* to divide into portions (*esp* with *out*); to make up into parcels or a parcel (*esp* with *up*); possibly, to make up into a total, complete, round off, or to add up or detail, item by item (Shakesp, *Antony and Cleopatra*, V.2); to cover with tarred canvas (*naut*): — *pr p* **par'celling**; *pa t* and *pa p* **par'celled**. — *adv* **par'celwise** by parcels, piecemeal. — **par'cel-bawd** (*Shakesp*) someone partly a bawd; **parcel bomb** a bomb wrapped in a parcel and designed to detonate when unwrapped. — *adj* **par'cel-gilt'** partially gilded. — **parcel post** (also formerly **parcels post**) a Post Office service for parcels. [Fr *parcelle* (Ital *particella*), from L *particula*, dimin of *pars*, *partis* a part]

parcener *pär'sən-ər*, *n* a co-heir. — *n* **par'cenary** (*-ə-ri*) co-heirship. [Anglo-Fr *parcener*, from LL *partōnārius*, from *pars* part]

parch *pärch*, *vt* to make hot and very dry; to roast slightly; to scorch. — *vi* to be scorched; to become very dry. — *adj* **parched** very dry; very thirsty (*colloq*). — *adv* **parch'edly**. — *n* **parch'edness** (or *pärcht'*). [Origin unknown]

Parcheesi® *pär-chē'zi*, *n* a board game adapted from pachisi (also without *cap* and with one *e*).

parchment *pärch'mənt*, *n* the skin of a sheep, goat, or other animal prepared for writing on, etc; a piece of this material; a manuscript written on it; a thick, *esp* yellowish, fine quality writing paper resembling it; a parchment-like membrane or skin. — *adj* of parchment. — *vt* **parch'mentize** or **-ise** to make like parchment, *esp* by treating with sulphuric acid. — *adj* **parch'menty** like parchment. — **parchment paper** or **vegetable parchment** unsized paper made tough and transparent by dipping in sulphuric acid. — **virgin parchment** a fine kind of parchment made from the skins of new-born lambs or kids. [Fr *parchemin*, from L *pergamēna* (*charta*) Pergamene (paper), from Gr *Pergamos* Bergama, in Asia Minor]

parcimony. An archaic spelling of **parsimony**.

parclose *pär'klōz*, *n* a screen or railing in a church enclosing an altar or tomb, or separating a chapel or other portion from the main body of the church. [OFr pa p (fem) of *parclore*, from L *per* through, and *claudere*, *clausum* to close]

pard[1] *pärd*, *n* the leopard. — *n* **pard'al** (*-əl*), **pard'ale** (*-əl* or *-āl*; *Spenser*) or **pard'alis** a leopard; a small leopard once supposed a different species. — *adj* **pard'ed** spotted. — *n* **pard'ine** (*-īn*). [L *pardus* (masc), *pardalis* (fem), from Gr *pardos*, *pardalis*; prob of Eastern origin]

pard[2] *pärd* and **pard'ner** *-nər*, (*US*) *n* slang forms of **partner**.

pardi, **pardie**, **pardy**. See **perdie**.

pardon *pär'dn*, *vt* to forgive; to allow to go unpunished; to excuse; to tolerate; to grant in remission, refrain from exacting or taking; to grant remission of sentence to (even if the condemned has been found innocent). — *vi* to forgive; to grant pardon. — *n* forgiveness, either of an offender or of his or her offence; remission of a penalty or punishment; forbearance; a warrant declaring that a pardon has been granted; a papal indulgence; a festival at which indulgences are granted (*obs*). — *adj* **par'donable** that may be pardoned; excusable. — *n* **par'donableness**. — *adv* **par'donably**. — *n* **par'doner** a person who pardons; a licensed seller of papal indulgences (*hist*). — *n* and *adj* **par'doning**. — *adj* **par'donless** unpardonable. — **I beg your pardon**? or **pardon**? what did you say?; **pardon me** excuse me — used in apology and to soften a contradiction. [Fr *pardonner*, from LL *perdōnāre*, from L *per* through, away, and *dōnāre* to give]

pare *pār*, *vt* to cut or shave off the outer surface or edge of; to trim; to remove by slicing or shaving; to diminish by small amounts (often with *down*). — *n* **pār'er**. — *n* **par'ing** the act of trimming or cutting off; a piece which is pared off; the cutting off of the surface of grassland for cultivation. — **paring chisel** a long, thin chisel with bevelled edges. [Fr *parer*, from L *parāre* to prepare]

parecious. See **paroicous**.

paregoric *par-i-gor'ik*, *adj* soothing, lessening pain. — *n* a medicine that soothes pain, *esp* an alcoholic solution of opium, benzoic acid, camphor, and oil of anise. [Gr *parēgorikos*, from *parēgoreein* to exhort, comfort, from *para* beside, beyond, and *agorā* marketplace]

pareira *pə-rā'rə*, *n orig* a tropical menispermaceous climbing plant (*Cissampelos pareira*) or its root (now called **false pareira**); a South American plant of the same family (*Chondrodendron tomentosum*, **pareira brava** *brä'və*, ie wild); a tonic diuretic drug derived from the root of the latter. — **white pareira** (*Abuta rufescens*) another South American plant of the same family. [Port *parreira* wallclimber]

parella *pə-rel'ə*, *n* a crustaceous lichen (*Lecanora parella*) yielding archil; extended to others of similar use. — Also **parelle'**. [Fr *parelle*]

parencephalon *par-en-sef'ə-lon*, (*anatom*) *n* a cerebral hemisphere. [Gr *para* beside, beyond, and *enkephalon* brain]

parenchyma *pə-reng'ki-mə*, *n* the ordinary soft thin-walled tissue of plants, not differentiated into conducting or mechanical tissue; soft spongy indeterminate tissue in animals. — *adj* **parenchym'atous**. [Gr *para* beside, beyond, and *enchyma* infusion, inpouring]

parenesis. See **paraenesis**.

parent *pā'rənt*, *n* someone who begets or brings forth offspring; a father or a mother; a person who or thing which produces; that from which anything springs or branches; an author; a cause; (as a Gallicism) a relative. — *adj* (of an organization, etc) which has established a branch or branches over which it *usu* retains some control. — *vt* and *vi* to be or act as a parent (to). — *n* **pā'rentage** descent from parents; extraction; rank or character derived from one's parents or ancestors; the relation of parents to their children; the state or fact of being a parent; parents collectively, or *perh* parent (*Spenser*). — *adj* **parental** (*pə-rent'əl*). — *adv* **parent'ally**. — *n* **pā'renthood** the state of being a parent; the duty or feelings of a parent. — *n* **pā'renting** the upbringing of and care for a child. — *adj* **pā'rentless** without a parent. — **parent company** a company that holds the majority of the shares of another company or other companies; **par'ent-craft** the techniques of looking after babies and young children. [Fr *parent* kinsman, from L *parēns*, *-entis*, old pr p of *parere* to bring forth]

parenteral *par-en'tər-əl*, *adj* not intestinal; (said of the administration of a drug) not by way of the alimentary tract. — *adv* **paren'terally**. [Gr *para* beside, and **enteral**]

parenthesis *pə-ren'thi-sis*, *n* a word or passage of comment or explanation inserted in a sentence which is grammatically complete without it; a figure of speech consisting of the use of such insertion; a digression; an interval, space or interlude; (*usu* in *pl*) a round bracket () used to mark off a parenthesis: — *pl* **paren'theses** (*-sēz*). — *vi* **parenth'esize** or **-ise**. — *adj* **parenthetic** (*par-ən-thet'ik*) or **parenthet'ical** of the nature of a parenthesis; using or overusing parenthesis. — *adv* **parenthet'ically**. [Gr, from *para* beside, beyond, *en* in, and *thesis* a placing]

pareo. See **pareu**.

Pareoean *par-ē-ē'ən*, *adj* of a race inhabiting South China, Burma, etc, otherwise called Southern Mongoloid. — Also *n*. [Gr *para* beside, and *ēōs* dawn]

parergon *par-ûr'gon*, *n* a by-work, any work subsidiary to a person's principal employment: — *pl* **parer'ga**. [Gr, from *para* beside, beyond, and *ergon* work]

paresis *par'i-sis*, (*med*) *n* a diminished activity of function — a partial form of paralysis affecting muscle movements but not diminishing sensation. — *adj* **paretic** (*-et'ik*). — **general paresis** the manifestation of a syphilitic infection of long standing, consisting of progressive dementia and generalized paralysis. [Gr, from *parienai* to relax]

paresthesia. See **paraesthesia**.

pareu *pa-rā'o͞o* or **pareo** *pa-rā'ō*, *n* a wraparound skirt worn by men and women in Polynesia. [Tahitian]

par excellence *pär ek'se-lãs* or *ek'sə-ləns*, (*Fr*) *adv* as an example of excellence. — *adj* superior to all others of the same sort. [Fr, literally, by excellence]

parfait *pär-fe'* or *-fā*, *n* a kind of frozen dessert containing whipped cream, fruit and eggs. [Fr, literally, perfect]

parfleche *pär-flesh'*, *n* a dried skin, *usu* of buffalo; an article made of it. [Appar Canadian Fr]

pargana or **pergunnah** *pər-gun'ə* or *-ä*, *n* a division of an administrative disrict or zillah in India. [Hindi and Pers *parganah*]

pargasite *pär'gə-sīt*, *n* a green amphibole. [*Pargas* in Finland]

parget *pär'jit*, *vt* to plaster over; to cover with ornamental plasterwork; to decorate the surface of; to bedaub: — *pr p* **par'geting**; *pa t* and *pa p* **par'geted**. — *n* plaster spread over a surface; cow-dung plaster for chimney flues; ornamental work in plaster; surface decoration. — *vt* **parge** to plaster. — *n* **par'geter**. — *n* **par'geting**. — **parge'-work**. — The irregular forms **par'getting**, etc, are used by some. [Appar OFr *parjeter* to throw all over]

parhelion *pär-hēl'i-ən*, *n* a bright spot on the parhelic circle, the result of diffraction caused by the crystals in the atmosphere: — *pl* **parhē'lia**. — *adj* **parhelic** (*-hē'lik* or *-he'lik*) or **parheliacal** (*-hē-lī'ə-kl*). — **parhelic circle** a band of luminosity parallel to the horizon, the result of diffraction caused by ice crystals in the atmosphere. [Irregularly, from Gr *parēlion*, from *para* beside, beyond, and *hēlios* sun]

parhypate *pär-hip'ə-tē*, (*Gr music*) *n* the lowest note but one in a tetrachord, next above the hypate. [Gr *para* beside, beyond; see **hypate**]

pariah *pə-rī'ə*, *par'i-ə* or *pär'*, *n* a member of a caste in southern India lower than the four Brahminical castes; a person of low or no caste; a social outcast (*fig*); an ownerless half-wild dog of Eastern towns (in full **pariah dog**), a pye-dog. [Tamil *paraiyar*]

parial. Same as **pairial** (see **pair-royal** under **pair¹**).

Parian *pā'ri-ən*, *adj* of the island of *Paros* in the Aegean Sea. — *n* a native or inhabitant of Paros; a fine porcelain like marble. — **Parian marble** a fine white marble found in Paros.

parietal *pə-rī'i-tl*, (*anatom*) *adj* of a wall or walls; of, attached to, or having connection with the side, or the inside of the wall of a cavity, *esp* a plant ovary; pertaining to or near the parietal bone; residing, or relating to residence, within the walls of a college (*US*). — *n* either of the two bones (**parietal bones**) which form part of the sides and top of the skull, between the frontal and the occipital. — **parietal cells** cells in the stomach lining that produce hydrochloric acid. [L *parietālis*, from *pariēs*, *parietis* a wall]

pari-mutuel *par-ē-mü-tü-el*, (*Fr*) *n* a betting-machine which automatically pools stakes and distributes winnings — a totalizator; the tote, a system of betting in which the winners receive a proportion of the total money staked, less the management charge. [Fr, literally, mutual bet]

pari passu *pā'rī pas'ū* or *pa'rē pas'o͞o*, (*L*) with equal pace; together.

paripinnate *par-i-pin'it* or *-āt*, (*bot*) *adj* pinnate without a terminal leaflet. [L *pār* equal]

Paris *par'is*, *n* the capital of France. — *adj* of or originating in Paris. — *adj* **Parisian** (*pə-ri'zyən* or (*esp NAm*) *-zhyən* or *-zhən*) of or pertaining to Paris. — *n* a native or resident of Paris: — *Fr fem* **Parisienne** (*pa-rē-zē-en* or *-zyen*). — **Paris doll** (*obs*) a small figure dressed in the latest fashions, sent out by Paris modistes; **Paris green** copper arsenite and acetate, a pigment and insecticide. [L *Parīsiī* the Gallic tribe of the Paris district]

parischan, parishchane. See **parochin**.

parish *par'ish*, *n* a district having its own church, and its own minister or priest of the Established Church; a district assigned by a church to a minister or priest; a division of a county for administrative and local government purposes (not now in Scotland); (in Louisiana) a county; the people of a parish; a congregation or a denomination (*US*). — *adj* belonging or relating to a parish; employed or supported by the parish; for the use of the parish. — *n* **par'ishen** see **parochin**. — *n* **parishioner** (*pə-rish'ə-nər*) a person who belongs to or is connected with a parish; a member of a parish church. — **parish church** the church of the establishment for a parish; **parish clerk** the clerk or recording officer of a parish; the person who leads the responses in the service of the Church of England; **parish council** a body elected to manage the affairs of a parish; **parish councillor**; **parish minister** or **priest** the minister or priest who has charge of a parish; **parish pump** the symbol of petty local interests; parochialism. — Also *adj*. — **parish register** a book in which the baptisms, marriages, and burials in a parish are recorded; **parish top** a spinning-top formerly kept for the amusement of the parish. — **on the parish** (*hist*) in receipt of poor-relief, ie food, shelter, etc provided by the parish. [Anglo-Fr *paroche* (Fr *paroisse*), from L *parochia*, from Gr *paroikiā* an ecclesiastical district, from *para* beside, and *oikos* a dwelling; altered by confusion with Gr *parochos* a purveyor]

parison *par'i-sən*, *n* a lump of glass before it is moulded into its final shape. [Fr *paraison*, from *parer* to prepare, from L *parāre*]

parisyllabic *par-i-si-lab'ik*, *adj* (of a noun or verb) having the same number of syllables in (almost) all inflected forms. [L *pār* equal]

paritor *par'i-tər*, (*Shakesp*) *n* aphetic for **apparitor**.

parity[1] *par'i-ti*, *n* equality in status; parallelism; equivalence; a standard equivalence in currency; equality of price or value in different markets (*commerce*); (of two or more numbers) the property of being (both or all) odd or even (*math*). — **parity check** (*comput*) the addition of a redundant bit to a word to make the total number of 1's even or odd in order to detect simple bit errors; **parity law** a law that a symmetry obtains in the natural world with no distinction between right and left, long held as basic, but shown in 1957 not to apply in the field of nuclear physics. [Fr *parité*, from L *paritās*, from *pār* equal]

parity[2] *par'i-ti*, *n* the condition or fact of having borne children. [L *parere* to bring forth]

park *pärk*, *n* an enclosed piece of land in which animals are kept for hunting purposes; a tract of land surrounding a mansion, kept as a pleasure-ground, constituting a private estate; hence (with *cap*) often part of the name of a house, street, or district; (an area containing) a group of buildings housing related enterprises, eg a *science park*; a piece of land in a town for public recreation; a football, etc pitch (*colloq*); a piece of country kept in its natural condition as a nature-reserve or for public recreation; a paddock, grass field (*Scot*); a field (*Ireland*); a level valley among mountains (*US*); a place occupied by artillery, wagons, etc (*military*); a piece of ground where motor-cars or other vehicles may be left untended; an enclosed basin for oyster-culture. — *vt* to enclose in a park; to make a park of; to bring (eg artillery) together in a body; to place and leave (a vehicle) in a parking-place or elsewhere; to deposit and leave, put (*colloq*); to register (securities) under some other name in order to hide their true ownership (*stock exchange slang*). — *vi* to leave a vehicle in a car park, parking-place, or elsewhere. — *n* **park'er** a park-keeper (*obs*); a person who parks a vehicle. — *n* **park'ie** *colloq* form of **park-keeper**. — *n* **park'ing** the action of the verb park; a turf strip, sometimes with trees, along the middle of a street (*US*). — *adj* **park'ish**. — *adj* **park'like**. — *adj* **park'ly**. — *adv* **park'ward** or **park'wards**. — *adj* **park-and-ride'** (of a transport system) designed to encourage the maximum use of public transport within a city, etc by providing bus and train links from large car parks on the outskirts. — Also *n*. — **parking lot** (*NAm*) a car park; **parking meter** a coin-operated meter that charges for motor car parking-time; **park'ing-place** a place where one may temporarily stop and leave a vehicle; **park'ing-ticket** a notice of a fine, or summons to appear in court, for a parking offence; **park'-keeper** a person employed to patrol a public park, keep order, etc; **park'land** or **park'lands** parklike grassland dotted with trees; **park'-off'icer** a park-keeper; **park'way** a broad road adorned with turf and trees, often connecting the parks of a town. [OFr *parc*, of Gmc origin; cf OE *pearruc pearroc*]

parka *pärk'ə*, *n orig* a fur shirt or coat with a hood, now a similar garment made of a wind-proof material worn for outdoor pursuits. — Also **parkee** or **parki** (*pärk'ē*). [Aleutian word]

parkie. See under park.

parkin *pär'kin*, or **perkin** *pûr'kin*, (*Northern*) *n* a biscuit or gingerbread made with oatmeal and treacle. [Ety unknown]

Parkinson's disease *pär'kin-sənz diz-ēz'*, *n* shaking palsy, a disease characterized by rigidity of muscles, tremor of hands, etc, studied by James *Parkinson* (1755–1824). — Also **Par'kinsonism**.

Parkinson's law *pär'kin-sənz lö*, (*facetious*) *n* any one of the laws propounded by C Northcote *Parkinson*, *esp* the law that in officialdom work expands so as to fill the time available for its completion.

parkish. See under **park**.

parkleaves *pärk'lēvz*, *n* a woodland shrub with yellow flowers, once considered a panacea; tutsan. [Appar **park** and **leaf**]

parky *pär'ki*, (*colloq*) *adj* chilly. [Origin unknown]

parlance *pär'ləns*, *n* speaking (*archaic*); conversation (*archaic*); a manner of speaking; an idiom. [Ety as for **parle**]

parlando *pär-län'dō*, (*music*) *adj* and *adv* in declamatory style; recitative. [Ital, speaking; cf **parle**]

parlay *pär'lā*, *vt* to bet (*orig* stake plus winnings), or lay out (*orig* investment plus earnings), in a later venture; to succeed in converting (an asset) into something more valuable; to exploit (a talent, characteristic, etc) to achieve personal success or fame. — Also *n*. [Fr *paroli*; from Neapolitan]

parle *pärl*, (*archaic*) *vi* to talk; to confer; to parley. — *n* talk; speech; parleying. [Fr *parler* to speak, LL *parlāre*, from *parabolare*, from Gr *parabolē* a parable, a word]

parley[1] *pär'li*, *vi* to speak with another; to confer; to hold discussions with an enemy. — *n* talk; a conference with an enemy; a conference. — *n* **parleyvoo'** (Fr *parlez-*

vous? do you speak?; *slang*) French; a Frenchman. — *vi* to speak French. [Ety as for **parle**]

parley[2]. See under **parliament**.

parliament *pär'lə-mənt*, *n* a meeting for deliberation; an assemblage of the political representatives of a nation, often forming the supreme legislative body; (in France until the Revolution) one of certain superior and final courts of judicature, in which also the edicts of the king were registered before becoming law; gingerbread in the form of rectangular biscuits (also **par'liament-cake** or (*Scot*) **par'ley** or **par'ly**); a little-used term for a group of owls. — *n* **parliamentā'rian** an adherent of Parliament in opposition to Charles I; a person who is skilled in the ways of parliament. — *adj* (*hist*) on the side of parliament during the Civil War. — *n* **parliamenta'rianism** or **parliament'arism** the principles of parliamentary government; the parliamentary system. — *adv* **parliamentarily** (*-ment'ər-i-li*). — *adj* **parliament'ary** pertaining to parliament; enacted, enjoined, or done by parliament; according to the rules and practices of legislative bodies; (of language) civil, decorous; (in the Civil War) for Parliament against the Royalists. — *n* **parliamenting** (*-ment'ing*) acting as a member of parliament; debating. — **parliamentary agent** a person employed by private individuals or societies for drafting bills or managing business to be brought before parliament; **parliamentary burgh** see under **burgh**; **parliamentary train** a railway train which, by act of parliament (1844), ran daily with sufficient accommodation for passengers at a penny a mile; **par'liament-heel** a slight careening of a ship; **par'liament-hinge'** a hinge allowing a door to be laid back along the wall; **par'liament-house** a building where parliament sits or has sat; **par'liament-man'** a member of parliament; a parliamentarian. — **act of parliament** a statute that has passed through both the House of Commons and the House of Lords, and received the formal royal assent; **(Act of) Parliament clock** a type of wall clock (*usu* of mahogany, and with a large uncovered dial found *esp* in public houses) which became popular around 1797 in response to an act of parliament imposing a tax on all clocks and watches; **Parliamentary Commissioner for Administration** see **Ombudsman**. [Fr *parlement*, from *parler* to speak]

parlour or (*esp NAm*) **parlor** *pär'lər*, *n* a room where conversation is allowed in a monastery or nunnery; a private room for conversation or conference in a public building, office, etc; a more or less private room in an inn or public house; a simple unpretentious drawing-room or dining-room, or a smaller room of similar kind; a family sitting-room or living-room (*old-fashioned*); a shop fitted out like a room, or a room attached to a shop, *esp* for personal services to customers, or one providing a particular service or selling specified goods, such as a beauty parlour or an ice-cream parlour (*orig US*). — *adj* used in or suitable for a parlour. — **par'lour-board'er** a pupil at a boarding-school who enjoys particular privileges; **par'lour-car** or **par'lor-car** (*US*) a luxuriously fitted railway saloon carriage; **parlour game** an (*esp* informal) indoor game; **par'lour-maid** a maid-servant who waits at table; **parlour pink** a rather tepid Socialist; **parlour tricks** minor social accomplishments; performances intended to impress. — **beauty parlour** and **funeral parlour** see under **beauty** and **funeral**; **milking parlour** a special room or building in which cows are milked. [Anglo-Fr *parlur* (Fr *parloir*) from *parler* to speak]

parlous *pär'ləs*, *adj* perilous. — *adv* (*archaic* and *facetious*) extremely. [A form of **perilous** (see under **peril**)]

parly. See under **parliament**.

parmacitie *pär-məs-it'i*, *n Shakesp* for **spermaceti**.

Parmesan *pär-mi-zan'* or *pär'mi-zan*, *adj* pertaining to *Parma* in N Italy. — *n* Parmesan cheese, a hard dry cheese made from skimmed milk mixed with rennet and saffron, used grated as a garnish on pasta dishes and soups. — **Parma violet** Neapolitan violet.

Parnassus *pär-nas'əs*, *n* a mountain in Greece, sacred to Apollo and the Muses; a collection of poems. — *adj* **Parnass'ian** of Parnassus; of the Muses; of a school of French poetry supposed to believe in art for art's sake (from the collections published as *le Parnasse contemporain*, 1866–76). — *n* a poet; a member of the Parnassian school. — *n* **Parnass'ianism**. — **grass of Parnassus** a white-flowered plant of wet moors (*Parnassia palustris*), of the saxifrage family.

Parnellism *pär'nəl-izm*, *n* the principles and policy of Charles Stewart *Parnell* (1846–91) who sought to promote Home Rule for Ireland. — *n* **Par'nellite** a follower of Parnell. — Also *adj*.

paroccipital *par-ok-sip'i-tl*, (*anatom*) *adj* near the occiput. [**para-**[1] and **occiput**]

parochial *pə-rō'ki-əl*, *adj* of or relating to a parish; (of sentiments, tastes, etc) restricted or confined within narrow limits; denominational (*US*). — *n* **parō'chialism** a system of local government which makes the parish the unit; provincialism, narrowness of view. — *n* **parōchiality** (*-al'*). — *vt* **parō'chialize** or **-ise** to make parochial; to form into parishes. — *vi* to do parish work. — *adv* **parō'chially**. — **parochial board** (formerly, in Scotland) a board charged with poor-relief. [L *parochiālis*, from *parochia*; see **parish**]

parochin, **parochine**, **parischan**, **parischane** or **parishen** *pä'rish-in*, (*Scot*) *n* a parish.

parody *par'ə-di*, *n* a burlesque or satirical imitation; an imitation so poor as to seem a deliberate mockery of the original. — *vt* to make a parody of: — *pr p* **par'odying**; *pa t* and *pa p* **par'odied**. — *adj* **parod'ic** or **parod'ical**. — *n* **par'odist**. — *adj* **parodist'ic**. [Gr *parōidiā*, from *para* beside, and *ōidē* an ode]

paroemia *pə-rē'mi-ə*, *n* a proverb, adage. — *adj* **paroe'miac**. — *n* (*Gr prosody*) the anapaestic dimeter catalectic. — *adj* **paroe'mial**. — *n* **paroemiog'rapher** a writer or collector of proverbs. — *n* **paroemiog'raphy**. — *n* **paroemiol'ogy** the study of proverbs. [Gr *paroimiā*, a proverb, from *paroimos* by the road, from *oimos* road]

paroicous *pə-roi'kəs*, (*bot*) *adj* (of certain mosses) having the male and female reproductive organs beside or near each other. — Also **parecious** or **paroecious** (*pə-rē'shəs*). [Gr *paroikos* dwelling beside, from *para* beside, and *oikos* a dwelling]

parol. See **parole**.

parole *pə-rōl'*, *n* conditional release of a prisoner; the condition of having given one's word of honour, or privilege of having it accepted; word of honour (*esp* by a prisoner of war, to fulfil certain conditions; *military*); officers' daily password in a camp or garrison (*military*); word of mouth; (*usu pa-rol'*) language as manifested in the speech of individuals, as opposed to *langue* (*linguistics*). — *adj* pertaining to parole; (*usu* **parol**, *usu par'*) given by word of mouth, as opposed to *documentary*, as in *parol evidence*. — *vt* **parole'** to put on parole; to release on parole. — *vi* to give parole. — *n* **parolee'** a prisoner who has been conditionally released. [Fr *parole* word, from L *parabola* a parable, saying, from Gr; see **parable**]

paronomasia *par-on-o-mā'syə*, *-zyə* or *-zh(y)ə*, *n* a play on words — also **paronom'asy** (*-ə-si* or *-ə-zi*). — *adj* **paronomastic** (*-mas'tik*) or **paronomas'tical** (*-əl*). — *n* **paronym** (*par'o-nim*) a word from the same root or having the same sound as another. — *adj* **paron'ymous**. — *n* **paron'ymy**. [Gr *para* beside, and *onoma*, *onyma* name]

paronychia *par-o-nik'i-ə*, *n* a whitlow (*med*); (with *cap*) the whitlow-wort genus of plants. — *adj* **paronych'ial**. [Gr *para* beside, and *onyx*, *onychos* nail]

paronymous, **paronymy**. See under **paronomasia**.

paroquet. See **parakeet**.

parotid *pə-rot'id* or *-rōt'*, *adj* near the ear. — *n* the parotid gland, a salivary gland in front of the ear — also **parō'tis**. — *adj* **parot'ic** near or adjacent to the ear. — *n* **parotidī'tis** or **parotī'tis** inflammation of the parotid gland, as in mumps. [Gr *parōtis*, *-idos*, from *para* beside, and *ous*, *ōtos* ear]

parousia *pə-rōō'zi-ə* or *-row'zi-ə*, (*theol*) *n* the second coming of Christ. [Gr *parousiā* presence, arrival]

paroxysm *par'oks-izm*, *n* a fit of acute pain; a sudden recurrence of symptoms; a fit of passion, laughter, coughing, etc; any sudden violent action. — *adj* **paroxys'mal**. [Gr *paroxysmos*, from *para* beyond, and *oxys* sharp]

paroxytone *par-ok'si-tōn*, *adj* (in ancient Greek) having the acute accent on the last syllable but one; having a heavy stress on the penultimate syllable. — *n* a word so accented. [Gr *paroxytonos*, from *para* beside, *oxys* acute, and *tonos* tone]

parp *pärp*, (*colloq*) *vt* to sound (a car horn), to toot or blast (a car horn or trumpet, etc). — Also *vi*. — *n* a toot or blast of a horn, etc. [Imit]

parpen *pär'pən*, *n* a stone passing through a wall from face to face; a wall of such stones; a partition; a bridge parapet. — Also **par'pane**, **par'pend**, **par'pent**, **par'-point**, **per'pend** and **per'pent**. — **par'pen-stone**; **par'pen-wall**. [OFr *parpain*]

parquet *pär'kā* or *pär'kē*, *n* a floor-covering of wooden blocks fitted in a pattern; the stalls of a theatre (*US*; **parquet circle** that part of the auditorium behind these). — *adj* of parquetry. — *vt* to cover or floor with parquetry: — *pa p* **par'queted** or **parquett'ed**. — *n* **par'quetry** (*-ki-tri*) flooring in parquet. [Fr *parquet*, dimin of *parc* an enclosure]

parr *pär*, *n* a young salmon up to two years of age, before it becomes a smolt; the young of several other kinds of fish. [Ety unknown]

parrakeet. See **parakeet**.

parral. See **parrel**.

parramatta. See **paramatta**.

parrel or **parral** *par'əl*, *n* a band by which a yard is fastened to a mast. — **parrel truck** a wooden ball strung on a parrel. [Cf OFr *parail* rigging]

parrhesia *pa-rē'syə* or *-zyə*, *n* boldness of speech. [Gr *parrēsiā*, from *para* beside, beyond, and *rhēsis* speech]

parricide *par'i-sīd*, *n* the murder of a parent or near relative, or the murder of anyone to whom reverence is considered to be due; a person who commits such a crime. — *adj* **parricīd'al**. [Fr, from L *parricīdium*, *pāricīdium* (the offence), *parricīda*, *pāricīda* (the offender), from *caedere* to slay; the connection with *pater*, father, is apparently fanciful]

parritch *pär'ich* or *par'ich*, *n* a Scots form of **porridge**.

parrock *par'ək*, (*dialect*) *n* a small field or enclosure, *esp* one used for lambs; a paddock. — *vt* to confine in a parrock. [OE *pearroc*]

parroquet. See **parakeet**.

parrot *par'ət*, *n* one of a family of tropical and subtropical birds with brilliant plumage, a hooked bill, and zygodactyl feet, good imitators of human speech; an uncritical repeater of the words of others. — *vt* to repeat by rote; to teach to repeat by rote. — *vi* to talk like a parrot (also *vt* with *it*): — *pa p* **parr'oted**. — *n* **parr'oter**. — *n* **parr'otry** unintelligent imitation. — *adj* **parr'oty** like a parrot or parrot-coal. — **parr'ot-beak**, **parr'ot-bill** or **parr'ot-jaw** the New Zealand glory-pea, from the form of its flowers; **parr'ot-coal** (*Scot*) cannel coal (possibly from chattering as it burns); **parr'ot-cry'** a catch-phrase senselessly repeated from mouth to mouth; **parr'ot-disease'** psittacosis. — *adv* **parr'ot-fashion** by rote. — **parr'ot-fish** a name applied to various fishes, *esp* of the wrasse family and the related *Scaridae*, from their colours or their powerful jaws; **parrot mouth** a congenital malformation of the jaw that occurs in horses and other grazing animals preventing normal feeding; **parr'ot-wrasse'** a parrot-fish, *esp* a Mediterranean species (*Scarus cretensis*) prized by the ancients. [Possibly Fr *Perrot*, dimin of *Pierre* Peter]

parry *par'i*, *vt* to ward or keep off; to turn aside, block or evade; to avert: — *pr p* **parr'ying**; *pa t* and *pa p* **parr'ied**. — *n* a turning aside of a blow or a thrust or of an attack of any kind, eg an argument or a jibe. [Perh from Fr *parez*, imper of *parer* from L *parāre* to prepare, in LL to keep off]

parse *pärz*, also *pärs*, (*gram*) *vt* to describe (a word) fully from point of view of classification, inflexion, and syntax; to analyse (a sentence). — *n* **pars'er**. — *n* **pars'ing** describing a word from the point of view of classification, etc; analysis of a sentence; the breaking down of a string of characters, eg a program statement, into its component parts (*comput*). [L *pars* (*ōrātiōnis*), a part (of speech)]

parsec *pär'sek* or *pär-sek'*, *n* the distance (about 19 billion miles) at which half the major axis of the earth's orbit subtends an angle of one second, a unit for measurement of distances of stars. [*par*allax and *sec*ond]

Parsee or **Parsi** *pär'sē* or *-sē'*, *n* a descendant of the Zoroastrians who emigrated from Persia to India in the 8c; a Persian dialect dominant during the time of the Sassanidae. — Also *adj*. — *n* **Par'seeism**, **Par'siism** (or *-sē'*) or **Par'sism** the religion of the Parsees. [Pers *Pārsī*, from *Pārs* Persia]

parsimony *pär'si-mən-i*, *n* sparingness or reluctance in the spending of money; praiseworthy economy in the use of means to achieve an end; avoidance of excess; frugality; niggardliness. — *adj* **parsimonious** (*-mō'ni-əs*). — *adv* **parsimō'niously**. — *n* **parsimō'niousness**. — **law of parsimony** the principle of Occam's razor (see under **Occamism**). [L *parsimōnia*, from *parcere*, *parsus* to spare]

parser, **parsing**. See under **parse**.

parsley *pärs'li*, *n* a bright green umbelliferous herb (*Carum petroselinum*) with finely divided, strongly scented leaves, used in cookery. — **parsley fern** a fern (*Cryptogramma crispa*) with bright green crisped leaves similar in appearance to parsley. [OE *petersilie*, modified by Fr *persil*, both from L *petroselīnum*, from Gr *petroselīnon*, from *petros* a rock, and *selīnon* parsley]

parsley-piert *pärs'li-pērt* or **parsley-pert** *-pûrt*, *n* a dwarf species of lady's-mantle (*Aphanes arvensis*), a weed of dry waste ground. [Prob Fr *perce-pierre*, literally pierce-stone]

parsnip or (*old*) **parsnep** *pärs'nip*, *n* an umbelliferous plant (*Pastinaca sativa* or *Peucedanum sativum*) or its edible carrot-like root. [L *pastināca*, from *pastinum* a dibble; prob affected by **neep**]

parson *pär'sn*, *n* the priest or incumbent of a parish; a rector; any minister of religion; a person who is licensed to preach. — *n* **par'sonage** the residence of a parson; *orig* the house, lands, tithes, etc, set apart for the support of the minister of a parish; tithes (*Scott*). — *adj* **parsonic** (*-son'ik*) or **parson'ical**. — *adj* **par'sonish**. — **par'son-bird** the tui; **parson's nose** the piece of flesh at the tail-end of a (cooked) fowl (also **pope's nose**). [OFr *persone*, from L *persōna* a person, prob in legal sense, or a mouthpiece]

part *pärt*, *n* something less than the whole; a portion; that which along with others makes up, has made up, or may at some time make up, a whole; a constituent; a component; a member or organ; an equal quantity; an equal or nearly equal division, constituent, etc, as in eg *three parts oil to one part vinegar*; share; region; direction, hand, or side; participation; concern; interest; a role or duty; a side or party; a character taken by an actor in a play; the words and actions of a character in a play or in real life; a voice or instrument in orchestral, etc music; that which is performed by such a voice or instrument; a copy of the music for it; a constituent melody or succession of notes or harmony; a section of a work in literature (see also **partwork** below), or in music; a separately published portion or number (see also **partwork** below); an inflected form of a verb; the place where the hair is parted, a parting (*NAm*); a quantity which taken a certain number of times (when unspecified, less than the whole) will equal a larger quantity; (in *pl*) intellectual qualities, talents, or conduct. — *adj* in part; partial. — *adv* in part; partly. — *vt* to divide; to separate; to break; to put or keep apart; to set in different directions; to distribute; to share; to leave, quit, depart (*Shakesp*). — *vi* to become divided or separated; to separate; to go different ways; to depart; to come or burst apart; to relinquish (with *with*); to share (*Bible*). — *adj* **part'ed** divided; separated; departed; assigned a part; endowed with parts or abilities (*Shakesp*); (of a leaf) deeply cleft (*bot*). — *n* **part'er**. — *n* **partibil'ity**. — *adj* **part'ible** that may or must be parted or divided up (*esp* of inherited property); separable. — *n* **part'ing** the action of the verb to part; a place of separation or division; a dividing line; a line of skin showing between sections of hair brushed in opposite directions on the head; leave-taking. — *adj* separating; dividing; departing; leave-taking; of or at leave-taking. — *adv* **part'ly** in part; in some degree. — **part-exchange'** a transaction in which an article is handed over as part of the payment for another article. — Also *adj* and *adv*. — **part'ing-cup'** a two-handled drinking-cup; **part'-off** (*W Indies*) a screen used to divide a room into two separate areas; **part'-own'er** a joint owner; **part'-pay'ment** payment in part; **part'-singing**; **part'-song** a melody with parts in harmony, *usu* unaccompanied. — *adj* and *adv* **part'-time'** (done) for part of the usual working time only. — *vi* to work part-time. — **part'-tim'er**; **part'work** one of a series of publications (*esp* magazines) issued at regular intervals, eventually forming a complete course or book; **part'-writing** composition of music in parts. — **for my part** as far as concerns me; **for the most part** commonly; mostly; **in bad** or **ill part** unfavourably; **in good part** favourably; without taking offence; **in great part** to a great extent; **in part** partly; so far as part is concerned; not wholly but to some extent; **on the part of** so far as concerns; as done or performed by; in the actions of; on the side of; **part and parcel** essentially a part; **part brass rags** (*sea slang*) to quarrel; **part company** to separate; **parting of the ways** a point at which a fateful decision must be made; **part of speech** one of the various classes of words; **part way** some way, not all the way, approaching but not reaching, as eg *go part way towards an objective*; **take part in** to share or to assist in; **take part with** to take the side of; **take someone's part** to support or side with someone (in an argument, etc). [OE and Fr *part*, from L *pars*, *partis*]

partake *pär-* or *pər-tāk'*, *vi* to take or have a part or share (*usu* with *of* or *in*); to take some, *esp* of food or drink; to have something of the nature or properties (of); to make common cause (*Shakesp*). — *vt* to have a part in; to share; to have a share in the knowledge of; to give a share of (*Shakesp*); to inform (*Spenser*): — *pr p* **partā'king**; *pa t* **partook'**; *pa p* **partā'ken**. — *n* **partā'ker**. — *n* **partā'king**. [Back-formation from **partaker**, from **part** and **taker**]

partan *pär'tn*, (*Scot*) *n* any edible crab. [Gaelic]

parted, parter. See under **part**.

parterre *pär-ter'*, *n* a formal arrangement of flower-beds; the pit of a theatre, *esp* the part under the galleries. [Fr, from L *per* along, and *terra* the ground]

parthenocarpy *pär-then-ō-kär'pi*, (*bot*) *n* the production of a fruit without a preliminary act of fertilization. — *adj* **parthenocar'pic**. [Gr *parthenos* a virgin, and *karpos* a fruit]

parthenogenesis *pär-thi-nō-jen'i-sis*, *n* reproduction by means of an unfertilized ovum. — *adj* **parthenogenetic** (*-ji-net'ik*). [Gr *parthenos* a virgin, and *genesis* production]

Parthenon *pär'thi-non*, *n* the temple of Athēnē *Parthenos*, on the Acropolis at Athens. [Gr *Parthenōn*, from *parthenos* a virgin]

Parthian *pär'thi-ən*, *adj* of *Parthia* in ancient Persia. — *n* a native of Parthia. — **a Parthian shot** a parting shot, from the Parthian habit of turning round in the saddle to discharge an arrow at a pursuer.

parti *par-tē'*, (*Fr*) *n* a group of people; a decision; a marriageable person considered as a match or catch. — **parti pris** (*prē'*) bias, preconceived opinion.

partial *pär'shl*, *adj* relating to a part only; not total or entire; inclined to favour one person or party; having a preference or fondness (with *to*); of partiality (*Shakesp*); component; subordinate (*bot*). — *n* (*acoustics*) a partial tone, one of the single-frequency tones which go together to form a sound actually heard. — *n* **par'tialism**. — *n* **par'tialist** someone who is biased; someone who sees or knows only part; a particularist (*theol*). — *n* **partiality** (*-shi-al'i-ti*). — *vt* **par'tialize** or **-ise** (*Shakesp*) to bias. — *adv* **par'tially**. — **partial derivative** (*math*) a derivative obtained by letting only one of several independent variables vary; **partial fraction** one of a number of simple fractions whose sum is a complex fraction; **partial pressure** the pressure exerted by any component in a mixture of gases. — **partial out** (*statistics*) to eliminate (a factor) so as to assess other factors when they are independent of its influence. [Fr, from LL *partiālis*, from L *pars* a part]

partibility, partible. See under **part**.

particeps criminis *pär'ti-seps kri'mi-nis* or *par'ti-keps krē'mi-nis*, (*L*) *n* someone who, though not present, helps in any way with the commission of a crime or who after the deed aids those who did it.

participate *pär-tis'i-pāt*, *vi* to have a share, or take part (in); to have some of the qualities (of). — *vt* to receive a part or share of (*archaic*). — *adj* **partic'ipable** capable of being participated in or shared. — *adj* **partic'ipant** participating; sharing. — *n* a person, group, etc taking part. — *adv* **partic'ipantly**. — *adj* **partic'ipating** (of insurance) entitling policy-holders to a share of the company's additional profits. — *n* **participā'tion** the act of participating (as in the phrase **worker participation** the involvement of employees at all levels in the policy-making decisions of a company, etc). — *adj* **partic'ipātive** capable of participating; participable. — *n* **partic'ipator** someone who participates; a person who has a share in the capital or income of a company. — *adj* **partic'ipatory** participable. [L *participāre*, *-ātum*, from *pars*, *partis*, part and *capere* to take]

participle *pär'ti-sip-l*, (*gram*) *n* a non-finite form of a verb used to form compound tenses (eg *broken* in the phrase *had broken*) and as an adjective (eg *burning* in the phrase *the burning bush*) — **present participle** and **past** or **perfect participle** referring respectively to an action roughly contemporaneous or past; the present participle is active, the past usually passive. — *adj* **particip'ial**. — *adv* **particip'ially**. [OFr (Fr *participe*), from L *participium*, from *pars*, *partis* a part, and *capere* to take]

particle *pär'ti-kl*, *n* a little part; a very small portion; a clause of a document; a minute piece of anything, eg dust; a little hard piece; a material point (*mech*); a smallest amount; a short, *usu* indeclinable word, such as a preposition, a conjunction or an interjection; a prefix or suffix; a crumb of consecrated bread or a portion used in the communion of the laity (*RC*). — *adj* **partic'ulate** having the form of, or relating to, particles. — *n* a particulate substance. — **particle accelerator** a device by means of which the speed of atomic particles may be greatly accelerated; **particle physics** the study of fundamental particles and of fundamental interactions (also called **high-energy physics**); **particle size** (*geol*) the general dimensions, eg average diameter or volume, of grains in a rock or sediment. [L *particula*, dimin of *pars*, *partis* a part]

parti-coated, parti-coloured. See under **party**.

particular *pər-tik'ū-lər*, *adj* relating to a part; predicating of part of the class denoted by the subject (*logic*); pertaining to a single person or thing; individual; special; worthy of special attention; detailed; markedly and discriminatingly or intimately attentive towards a person (*obs*); noteworthy; definite; concerned with or marking things single or distinct; minutely attentive and careful; fastidious in taste; particularist. — *n* a distinct or minute part; a single point; a single instance; a detail; an item; personal relation (*Shakesp*); a favourite (*colloq*); a favourite drink (*esp London particular*, a Madeira wine for the London market; hence, from its colour, a London fog; *colloq*). — *n* **partic'ularism** attention to one's own interest or party;

a minute description; the doctrine that salvation is offered only to particular individuals, the elect, and not to the race (*theol*); attention to the interest of a federal state before that of the confederation; the policy of allowing much freedom in this way. — *n* and *adj* **partic'ularist**. — *adj* **particularist'ic**. — *n* **particularity** (*-lar'i-ti*) the quality of being particular; minuteness of detail; a single instance or case; a detail; peculiarity; marked attention to a person (*obs*). — *n* **particulariza'tion** or **-s-**. — *vt* **partic'ularize** or **-ise** to render particular; to mention the particulars of; to enumerate in detail; to mention as a particular or particulars. — *vi* to mention or attend to minute details. — *adv* **partic'ularly** in a particular manner; individually; severally; in detail; in the manner of a particular proposition; intimately; notably; in a very high degree. — *n* **partic'ularness**. — **in particular** especially; in detail; severally, individually (*obs*). [Ety as for **particle**]

partie carrée *par-tē kar-ā*, (*Fr*) *n* a party consisting of two men and two women.

partim *pär'tim*, (*L*) *adv* in part.

parting. See under **part**.

partisan[1] or **partizan** *pär-ti-zan'* or *pär'ti-zan*, *n* an adherent, *esp* a blind or unreasoning adherent, of a party or a faction; a light irregular soldier who scours the country and forays; (in World War II) an irregular resister within the enemy occupation lines. — Also *adj*. — *n* **par'tisanship** (or *-zan'*). [Fr *partisan*, from a dialect form of Ital *partigiano*, from *parte* (L *pars*, *partis*) part]

partisan[2] *pär'ti-zan*, *n* a halberd-like weapon with twin axe-blades or spikes, common in the Middle Ages; a man armed with one. [Fr *partizane* (now *pertuisane*), from Ital *partesana*, of doubtful origin]

partita *pär-tē'tə*, (*music*) *n* (*esp* 18c) a suite; a set of variations. [Ital]

partite *pär'tīt*, *adj* divided; (*esp* of plant leaves) cut nearly to the base. — *n* **partition** (*-tish'ən*) the act of dividing; the division of a country into politically autonomous states; the state of being divided; a separate part; that which divides; a wall between rooms; a barrier, septum or dissepiment (*bot*); a score (*music*). — *vt* to divide into shares; to divide into parts by walls, septa, or anything similar. — *n* **parti'tioner** a person who partitions property. — *n* **parti'tionist** a person who favours the partition of a country. — *n* **parti'tionment**. — *adj* **par'titive** parting; dividing; distributive; indicating that a part is meant (*gram*). — *n* a partitive word (eg *some*, *most*). — *adv* **par'titively**. — **partition coefficient** (*chem*) the ratio of the equilibrium concentrations of a substance dissolved in two immiscible solvents (also called **distribution coefficient**); **parti'tion-wall'** an internal wall. [L *partītus*, pa p of *partīrī* or *partīre* to divide, from *pars* part]

Partitur *pär-ti-tōōr'* (*Ger*) or **partitura** *pär-ti-tōōr'a*, (*Ital*) *n* a score in music. [L *partītus*; cf **partite**]

partizan. See under **partisan**[1].

Partlet *pärt'lit*, *n* a proper name for a hen, from Chaucer's *Pertelote* in the Nun's Priest's Tale; sometimes applied to a woman. [OFr *Pertelote*, a woman's name]

partlet *pärt'lit*, (*obs*) *n orig* a collar or ruff; a woman's covering for the upper breast, neck and shoulders, often finished with a ruff or frill; a kind of shirt. [Appar OFr *patelette* a band]

partly. See under **part**.

partner *pärt'nər*, *n* a sharer; an associate; a person engaged with another or others in business; a person who plays on the same side with another in a game; a person who dances or goes to a formal dinner with another; a husband or wife; either member of a couple living together in a sexual relationship; an associate in commensalism or symbiosis (*bot*); (in *pl*; *naut*) a wooden framework round a hole in the deck, supporting a mast, etc. — *vt* to join as a partner (*Shakesp*); to be the partner of. — *n* **part'nership** the state of being a partner; a contract between individuals engaged in any business. [Prob a form of **parcener**]

parton *pär'ton*, (*phys*) *n* a hypothetical particle thought to be a constituent of nucleons. [**part** and *-on*, formed on the analogy of **neutron**, **proton**, etc]

partook *pär-tōōk'*, *pa t* of **partake**.

partridge *pär'trij*, *n* any member of a genus (*Perdix*) of game-birds of the pheasant family; extended to many other birds, *esp* (in North America) the Virginian quail and the ruffed grouse, and (in South America) the tinamou: — *pl* **par'tridge** or **par'tridges**. — **par'tridge-berry** a North American trailing plant of the madder family (*Mitchella repens*) or its fruit; applied also to the checker-berry; **par'tridge-wood'** a hard variegated tropical American wood (*Andira*) of the Papilionaceae, used by American cabinet-makers; oak or other wood speckled owing to attack by a fungus. [Fr *perdrix*, from L *perdīx*, from Gr *perdīx*]

parture *pärt'yər*, (*Spenser*) *n* departure. [Prob **part**]

parturient *pär-tū'ri-ənt*, *adj* of or related to childbirth; giving or about to give birth; bringing or about to bring about anything new. — *n* **partūri'tion** the act of giving birth. [L *parturīre*, desiderative from *parere* to bring forth]

party *par'ti*, *n* a part (*obs*); a side in a battle, game, lawsuit, or other contest; a body of people united in favour of a political or other cause; the spirit of faction; a small body of people associated together in any occupation or amusement; a detachment (*military*); a company; a social gathering, *esp* one serving as a celebration; a game (*obs*); a person concerned in any affair, as in *third party*; a person who enters into a contract, eg of marriage; a possible match in marriage; a person (*colloq*). — *adj* pertaining to a party; parted or divided (*heraldry*). — *vi* (*colloq*) to attend, hold or take part in parties or similar entertainments; to have a good time. — *n* **par'tyism** devotion to a (particular political) party. — *adj* **par'ti-coat'ed** or **par'ty-coat'ed** having on a coat of various colours. — *adj* **par'ti-col'oured** or **par'ty-col'oured** variegated. — **par'ty-call'** a social call on one's host or hostess after a party; **par'ty-cap'ital** advantage or credit to one's party derived from some contingency; **par'ty-gov'ernment** government by the prevailing political party; **par'ty-ju'ry** a jury half of natives and half of aliens; **party line** a telephone exchange line shared by two or more subscribers; a boundary between properties; the policy rigidly laid down by the political party leaders; **party machine** see under **machine**; **party man** a faithful member of a political party; **party plan selling** same as **party selling**; **party politics** politics viewed from a party standpoint, or arranged to suit the views or interests of a party; **par'ty-pooper** someone who spoils the enjoyment of others at a party or social occasion by their lack of enthusiasm, or by their inability or unwillingness to participate; **party sales**; **party selling** the selling of products by agents earning commission in the homes of customers who invite friends and neighbours as to a social gathering. — *adj* **par'ty-size** (of an item of food, etc) smaller than the usual size, intended to be used as a snack at parties. — **party spirit** the unreasonable spirit of a party-man; a festive atmosphere. — *adj* **par'ty-spir'ited**. — **par'ty-ver'dict** a joint verdict; **party wall** a wall between two adjoining properties or houses. — **the party's over** a favourable, enjoyable, carefree, etc situation has ended. [Fr *partie*, fem (and also *parti*, masc), pa p of *partir*, from L *partīre*, *partīrī* to divide, from *pars* a part]

parulis *pə-rōō'lis*, (*med*) *n* a gumboil. [Gr *para* beside, and *oulon* the gum]

parure *pa-rür'*, *n* a set of ornaments, etc. [Fr]

parvanimity *pär-və-nim'i-ti*, *n* smallness of mind. [L *parvus* little, and *animus* mind]

parvenu *pär'və-nü* or *-nū*, *n* an upstart; someone newly risen into wealth, notice, or power, *esp* if vulgar or exhibiting an inferiority complex. — Also *adj*. [Fr pa p of *parvenir*, from L *pervenīre* to arrive]

parvis *pär′vis* or **parvise** *pär′vēs*, *n* an enclosed space, or sometimes a portico, at the front of a church; a room over a church porch (*erron*). [OFr *parevis*; same root as **paradise**]

parvovirus or **Parvo virus** *pär′vō-vī-rəs*, *n* any of a group of viruses which contain DNA and which are the causes of various animal (including canine) diseases. [L *parvus* little, and **virus**]

PAS. See **para-aminosalicylic acid**.

pas *pä*, (*Fr*) *n* a step or dance *esp* in ballet; action; precedence: — *pl* **pas** (*pä*). — **pas d'armes** (*därm*) a joust, a tilt or a tourney; **pas de bourrée** (*də bōō-rā*) a ballet movement in which one foot is swiftly placed behind or in front of the other; **pas de chat** (*də sha*) a ballet leap in which each foot is raised in turn to the opposite knee; **pas de deux**, **trois**, **quatre**, etc (*də dø*, *trwä*, *kä-tr'*) a ballet sequence involving two, three, four, or more dancers; **pas redoublé** (*rə-dōōb-lā*) a quickstep; **pas seul** (*sœl*) a dance for one person, a solo dance. — **have the pas of someone** to take precedence over someone. [Fr, from L *passus*; cf **pace**]

PASCAL *pas-kal′*, *n* a high-level computer programming language.

pascal *pas′kal*, *n* a unit of pressure, the newton per square metre, a supplementary SI unit. — **Pascal's triangle** a group of numbers arranged to form a triangle in which each number is the sum of the two numbers to its right and left in the line above. [Blaise *Pascal*, French philosopher and scientist]

Pasch *pask* or (*dialect*) **Pace** *pās*, *n* the Passover; Easter (*archaic*). — *adj* **pasch′al**. — **pasch′al-can′dle** a large candle blessed and placed on the altar on the day before Easter; **pasch′al-flow′er** same as **pasque-flower**; **paschal (full) moon** the first full moon on or after the spring equinox, Easter being reckoned in the Roman Catholic church as the first Sunday after the paschal moon; **pasch′al-lamb** the lamb slain and eaten at the Passover; **pasch′-egg** or (*dialect*) **pace′-egg** an Easter-egg. — **Pasch of the Cross** Good Friday. [L *pascha*, from Gr *pascha*, from Heb *pesach* the Passover, from *pāsach* to pass over]

pascual *pas′kū-əl*, *adj* growing on land used for grazing. [L *pascuum* pasture]

pasear *pä-sā-är′*, (*US slang* and *dialect*) *vi* to take a walk. — *n* a walk. — *n* **paseo** (*pä-sā′ō*) a walk; a street or promenade. [Sp]

pash[1] *pash*, (*Shakesp*) *vt* to strike, to dash, to crush. — *vi* to dash. — *n* a blow. [Perh imit]

pash[2] *pash*, (*Shakesp*) *n* the head. [Origin unknown]

pash[3] *pash*, *n* a slang contraction of **passion**.

pasha *pa′shə* or *pä-shä′*, *n* a Turkish title (abolished 1934) given to governors and high military and naval officers. — Also **pacha**. — *n* **pash′alik** or **pach′alic** (or *pä-shä′lik*) the jurisdiction of a pasha. [Turk *paşa*; cf **bashaw**]

pashm *push′əm*, *n* the fine underfleece of the goats of Northern India, used for making rugs, shawls, etc. — Also **pashim** (*push′ēm*) or **pashmina** (*push-mē′nə*). [Pers, wool]

Pashto, **Pashtu**, **Pashtun**. See **Pushtu**.

pasigraphy *pə-sig′rə-fi*, *n* a system of ideographic writing. — *adj* **pasigraphic** (*pas-i-graf′ik*) or **pasigraph′ical**. [Gr *pāsi* (dative pl) to or for all, and *graphein* to write]

paso doble *pä′sō dō′blā*, (*Sp*) *n* a march *usu* played at bullfights; a two-step; the music for this dance.

Pasok *pas′ok*, *abbrev*: Panhellenic Socialist Movement.

paspalum *pas′pä-ləm*, *n* any plant of an American and tropical genus (*Paspalum*) of pasture grasses, a common example being pampas-grass. [Gr *paspalos* millet]

paspy *päs′pi*. Same as **passepied**.

pasque-flower *päsk′flowr*, *n* a species of anemone (*Anemone pulsatilla*) with bell-shaped purple flowers; extended to some other species. [Fr *passefleur*, appar from *passer* to surpass, modified after **Pasch**, as flowering about Easter]

Pasquil *pas′kwil* or **Pasquin** *pas′kwin*, *n* the nickname (*perh* after somebody who lived near) of an ancient statue dug up in Rome in 1501, to which it became customary to attach lampoons and satires; an imaginary lampooner or satirist; a lampoon or satire. — *vt* and *vi* to lampoon or satirize. — *n* **pas′quilant**, **pas′quiler** or **pasquinā′der** a lampooner. — *n* **pasquināde′** a lampoon. — *vt* to lampoon. [Ital *Pasquino*, *Pasquillo*]

pass *päs*, *vi* to proceed; to go or be transferred from one place to another; to transfer the ball to another player (*football*, etc); to make one's way; to reach, extend, or have a course; to undergo change from one state to another; to be transmitted, communicated or transacted; to change ownership; to change; to shade off (*obs*); to be astir; to circulate; to be accepted or reputed or known; to go by; to go unheeded or neglected; to elapse, to go away; to disappear, come to an end, fade out; to die; to move over, through or onwards; to go or get through an obstacle, difficulty, test, ordeal, examination, etc; to get through an examination without honours; to be approved; to meet with acceptance; to be sanctioned; to be made law; to be talented; to come through; to be voided; to happen; to sit or serve (upon a jury); to adjudicate; to be pronounced; to care, reck (with *of* or *for*; *obs*); to surpass or beat everything (*obs*); to exceed bounds; to perform a pass (see noun below); to abstain from making a call or declaration (*cards*). — *vt* to go or get by, over, beyond, through, etc; to undergo, experience; to undergo successfully; to spend (time); to omit; to disregard; to exceed; to surpass; to cause or allow to pass; to transfer, transmit; to transfer (the ball) to another player (*football*, etc); to hand; to utter, pronounce; to circulate; to pledge (as one's word); to emit, discharge; to perform a pass with or upon; to perform as a pass; to esteem (*obs*): — *pa t* and *pa p* **passed** (*päst*) or rarely **past**. — *n* a way by which one may pass or cross; a narrow passage, *esp* through or over a range of mountains or other difficult region; a narrow defile; an act of passing; the passing of an examination, *esp* to do so without honours at degree level; currency (*obs*); reputation (*Shakesp*); event, issue, fulfilment, consummation; a state or condition (as in *pretty* or *sad pass*); a predicament, critical position; a passport; a written permission to go somewhere or do something, authorization, a permit; permission to be in a certain area (*SAfr*); a free ticket; a ticket or similar document paid for or received as a concession, allowing free or cheaper use of a facility, eg a **bus pass**; a thrust (*fencing*); transference of the ball to another team-member (*football*, etc); transference in a juggling trick; an amorous advance (*colloq*); a movement of the hand over anything, eg by a magician or mesmerist; perhaps trick, perhaps conduct (*Shakesp*, *Measure for Measure* V. 1. 375). — *adj* **pass′able** that may be passed, travelled over, or navigated; that may bear inspection; that may be accepted or allowed to pass; tolerable. — *n* **pass′ableness**. — *adv* **pass′ably**. — *n* **pass′er**. — *n* **passimeter** (*pas-im′i-tər*) an automatic ticket-issuing machine. — *adj* **passing** (*päs′ing*) going by, through, or away; transient, fleeting; happening now; incidental; casual; surpassing (*archaic*). — *adv* (*archaic*) exceedingly; very. — *n* the action of the verb to pass; a place of passing; a coming to an end; death; gold or silver thread with a silk core. — *adj* **pass′less** having no pass; impassable. — **pass-back′** an act of passing (a ball, etc) to a member of one's own team nearer one's own goal; **pass band** (*radio*) a frequency band in which there is negligible attenuation; **pass′-book** a book that passes between a trader and a customer, in which credit purchases are entered; a bank-book; a booklet containing permission to be in a certain area, and other documents (*SAfr*); **pass′-check** a passout ticket; **pass degree** a university or college degree without honours; **passed pawn** (*chess*) a pawn having no opposing pawn before it on its own or an adjacent file; **pass′er-by** someone who passes by or near: — *pl* **pass'ers-by**; **pass'ing-bell** a bell tolled immediately after a death, *orig* to invite prayers for the soul passing into eternity; **pass'ing-note** (*music*) a note inserted to allow a smooth passage between other notes, but itself forming no essential part of the harmony; a note forming an unprepared discord in an unaccented place in the measure (also (*NAm*) **passing tone**); **passing shot** (*tennis*) a shot hit past and beyond the reach of an opponent; **pass'key** a key enabling one to enter a house; a key for opening several locks. — *n pl* **pass laws** (*SAfr*) laws restricting the movements of blacks. — **pass'man** (*archaic*) a person who gains a degree without honours; a prisoner who is permitted to leave his cell in order to carry out certain duties (*slang*). — *n* and *adj* **pass'out** (a ticket, etc) entitling someone who goes out to return. — **pass'word** (*orig military*) a secret word by which a friend may pass or enter (a camp, etc); a set of characters which a user inputs to a computer to gain access (*comput*). — **bring to pass** to bring about, cause to happen; **come to pass** to happen (apparently *orig* a noun in these expressions); **in passing** while doing, talking about, etc something else; **make a pass at** to aim a short blow at, especially ineffectually (*colloq*); to make an amorous advance to (*colloq*); **pass as** or **for** to be mistaken for or accepted as; **pass away** to come to an end, go off; to die; to elapse; **pass by** to move, go beyond or past; to ignore or overlook; **pass off** to impose fraudulently, to palm off; to take its course satisfactorily; to disappear gradually; **pass on** to go forward; to proceed; to die; to transmit, hand on; **pass on** or **upon** to give judgement or sentence upon; to practise artfully, or impose, upon; to palm off; **pass out** to distribute; to die; to faint, become unconscious or dead drunk (*slang*); to go off; to complete military, etc training; **pass over** to overlook, to ignore; to die; **pass the time of day** to exchange any ordinary greeting of civility; **pass through** to undergo, experience; **pass up** to renounce, to have nothing to do with; to neglect (an opportunity). [Fr *pas* step, and *passer* to pass, from L *passus* a step]

pass. *abbrev*: passive.

passacaglia *pas-a-käl'ya*, (*music*) *n* a slow solemn old Spanish dance-form, slower than the chaconne, in triple time, usually on a ground bass. [Italianized from Sp *pasacalle*, from *pasar* to pass, and *calle* street, appar because often played in the streets]

passade *pä-säd'*, *n* the motion of a horse to and fro over the same ground in dressage exercises. — *n* **passado** (*pä-sä'dō*; *obs*; *fencing*) a thrust with one foot advanced: — *pl* **passa'does** or **passa'dos**. [Fr *passade*, Sp *pasada*, from L *passus* step]

passage[1] *pas'ij*, *n* a means or way of passing; an alley; a corridor or lobby; a navigable channel or route; a crossing-place, ford, ferry, bridge, or mountain-pass; an act of passing; transit; a crossing; migration; transition; lapse, course; transmission; evacuation of the bowels; the passing of a bill; a journey (now only by water or air, or *fig*); right of conveyance; possibility of passing; that which passes; traffic (*Shakesp*); an occurrence, incident, episode; transaction, interchange of communication or intercourse, dealings together; a continuous but indefinite portion of a book, piece of music, etc, of moderate length; a run, figure, or phrase in music; a stage in the maintenance or controlled development of micro-organisms under analysis, in which they are introduced into the host or culture, allowed to multiply, and extracted (*biol*); an old dicing game, the object to throw doublets above (passing) ten, with three dice. — *vi* to make or perform a passage. — *vt* (*biol*) to submit (a micro-organism) to a passage. — **pass'age-boat** a boat plying regularly for passengers. — *n pl* **passage beds** (*geol*) transitional strata. — **passage grave** a burial chamber situated below ground and connected to the surface by a passage; **pass'age-money** fare; **pass'ageway** a way of access; a corridor; an alley. — **bird of passage** a migratory bird; a transient visitor (*fig*); **passage of arms** any armed struggle; an encounter, *esp* in words; **work one's passage** to earn one's passage at sea by unpaid labour on board (also *fig*). [Fr *passage*, from L *passus* step]

passage[2] *pas-äzh'* or *pas'ij*, (*dressage*) *n* a slow sideways walk; a rhythmical trot with diagonal pairs of legs lifted high. — *vi* to move at a passage. — *vt* to cause (a horse) to move at a passage. [Fr *passager*, from *passéger*, from Ital *passeggiare* to walk, from L *passus* step]

passament. See under **passement**.

passamezzo. See under **passy-measure**.

passant *pas'ənt*, (*heraldry*) *adj* walking towards the dexter side, with dexter fore-paw raised. [Fr]

passé, *fem* **passée**, *pa-sā*, (*Fr*) *adj* past one's best, faded; out of date, or nearly so; no longer fashionable.

passemeasure. See under **passy-measure**.

passement or **passment** *pas'mənt* or **passament** *-ə-mənt*, *n* a decorative trimming of beads, braid, etc. — *vt* to adorn with passement. — *n* **passementerie** (*päs-mā-tə-rē*) passement. [Fr]

passenger *pas'in-jər*, *n* someone who passes (*obs*); someone who travels in a private or public conveyance (as opposed to someone who drives or operates the vehicle, etc); someone carried along by others' efforts (*fig*). — *adj* of or for passengers. — **pass'enger-mile'** one mile travelled by one passenger, as a measure of volume of traffic; **pass'enger-pigeon** an extinct North American pigeon that flew in vast numbers in search of food. [OFr *passagier* (Fr *passager*), with inserted *n*, as in *messenger* or *nightingale*]

passe-partout *päs-pär-tōō'*, *n* a means of passing anywhere; a master-key; a card or something similar cut as a mount for a picture; a kind of simple picture-frame, *usu* of pasteboard, the picture being fixed by strips pasted over the edges; adhesive tape or paper used in this way. [Fr, a master-key, from *passer* to pass, *par* over, and *tout* all]

passepied *päs-pyā*, *n* a dance of Breton origin like a slightly quicker minuet, popular in 17c and 18c. [Fr, literally, pass-foot]

passer. See under **pass**[1].

Passeres *pas'ə-rēz*, *n pl* an old order of birds (also called Insessores) comprising more than half of all the birds. — *n pl* **Passerifor'mēs** the huge order of perching birds (sparrow-like in form) including amongst others all British songsters. — *adj* and *n* **pass'erine** (*-īn*). [L *passer* a sparrow]

passible *pas'i-bl*, *adj* susceptible to or capable of suffering, or of feeling. — *n* **passibil'ity**. — *n* **pass'ibleness**. — *adv* **pass'ibly**. [L *passibilis*, from *patī*, *passus* to suffer]

passiflora *pas-i-flō'rə* or *-flö'rə*, *n* any plant of the passion-flower genus, family **Passiflorā'ceae**. [L *passiō* passion, and *flōs*, *flōris* flower]

passim *pas'im*, (*L*) *adv* everywhere; throughout (*esp* a cited piece of writing); dispersedly.

passimeter, **passing**. See under **pass**[1].

passion *pash'n*, *n* (*usu* with *cap*) the sufferings (*esp* on the Cross) and death of Christ; martyrdom; suffering; a painful bodily ailment (such as *iliac passion*); the fact, condition, or manner of being acted upon; passivity (*philos*); a passive quality; strong feeling or agitation of mind, *esp* rage, often sorrow; a fit of such feeling, *esp* rage; an expression or outburst of such feeling; ardent love; sexual desire; an enthusiastic interest or direction of the mind; the object of such a feeling. — *vt* to imbue with passion. — *vi* to exhibit passion. — *adj* **pass'ional** of or relating to the sufferings of a Christian martyr. — *n* **pass'ional** or **pass'ionary** a book of the sufferings of saints and martyrs. — *adj* **pass'ionate** moved by passion; showing strong and warm feeling; easily moved to passion; intense, fervid; compassionate (*Shakesp*); moving to compassion (*Spenser*). — *vt* to express with passion; to imbue with passion, to impassion. — *adv* **pass'ionately**. — *n* **pass'ionateness**. — *adj* **pass'ioned** moved by passion; expressing passion; expressed with passion. — *n* **Pass'ionist** a member of a Roman Catholic congregation devoted to the commemoration of the Passion of Christ by missions, etc. — *adj* **pass'ionless** free from or lacking passion, *esp* sexual desire; not easily excited to anger. — **pass'ion-flower** any flower or plant of the genus *Passiflora*, consisting mostly of climbers of tropical and warm temperate America, from a fancied resemblance of parts of the flower to the crown of thorns, nails, and other emblems of Christ's Passion; the plant itself; **passion fruit** any edible passion-flower fruit, *esp* the granadilla; **Pass'ion-mū'sic** music to which words describing the sufferings and death of Christ are set; **Passion play** a religious drama representing the sufferings and death of Christ; **Passion Sunday** the fifth Sunday in Lent; **Pass'iontide** the two weeks preceding Easter; **Passion week** Holy week; the week before Holy week. [OFr *passiun* and L *passiō*, *-ōnis*, from *patī*, *passus* to suffer]

passive *pas'iv*, *adj* suffering (*obs*); acted upon, not acting; inert; lethargic; not reacting; not actively resisting; bearing no interest (*finance*); under a liability (*Scots law*); in or of which the subject is the person or thing that sustains, rather than performs, the action of the verb (*gram*). — *n* the passive voice (*gram*); a passive verb (*gram*); a passive person. — *vt* **pass'ivate** (*eng*) to give (a metal) greater resistance to corrosion by coating the surface with eg oxides or phosphates. — *adv* **pass'ively**. — *n* **pass'iveness**. — *n* **pass'ivism** passive resistance. — *n* **pass'ivist** a passive resister. — *n* **passiv'ity**. — **passive immunity** the short-term immunity acquired either artificially, through the administration of antibodies, or naturally, as in the very young who receive antibodies through the placenta or in colostrum; **passive obedience** absolute submission to the ruling power; obedience to the 'divine right of kings'; **passive resistance** deliberate refusal (on principle) to do what law or regulation orders, and submission to the consequent penalties; **passive resister**; **passive smoking** the involuntary inhalation of tobacco smoke that has been produced by others. [L *passīvus*, from *patī*, *passus* to suffer]

passless ... to ... **passman**. See under **pass**.

passment. See **passement**.

passout. See under **pass**[1].

Passover *päs'ō-vər*, *n* an annual feast of the Jews, to commemorate the exodus of the Israelites from captivity in Egypt, so named from the destroying angel passing over the houses of the Israelites when he slew the first-born of the Egyptians. — *adj* pertaining to the Passover.

passport *päs'pōrt* or *-pört*, *n* authorization to leave a port either to put to sea or to proceed inland; a permit for entering a country; that which gives privilege of entry to anything (*fig*). [Fr *passeport*; cf **pass**[1] and **port**[4]]

passus *pas'us*, *n* a section of a poem of story, a canto or fit. [L *passus*, plural *-ūs*, a step]

password. See under **pass**[1].

passy-measure or **passemeasure** *pas'i-mezh'ər*, *n* an old dance, a pavan in quicker time, called also **passamezzo** (*pas-sa-met'sō*; *pl* **-zōs**) or **passy measures pavan** (in *Shakesp appar* misprinted *panin*). [Ital *passemezzo*]

past *päst*, *adj* bygone; elapsed; ended; in time already passed; expressing action or being in time that has passed, preterite (*gram*); just before the present; past one's best; having served a term of office. — *n* time that has passed; things that have already happened; (one's) early life or bygone career, *esp* if marked by tragedy or scandal; the past tense; a verb or verbal form in the past tense. — *prep* after; after the time of; beyond, in place, position, etc; beyond the possibility of. — *adv* by; laid aside in store, for later use (*Scot*). — *vt* and *vi* an unusual *pa p* of **pass**[1]. — **past master** someone who has held the office of master (eg among freemasons); hence, someone thoroughly proficient (see also **passed master** under **master**); **past participle** see under **participle**. — **I**, etc **would not put it past him**, etc (*colloq*) I, etc regard him, etc as (*esp* morally) capable of (some action disapproved of); **past it** (*colloq*) or **past one's best** having decreased strength, ability, etc due to advancing age; **past praying for** beyond hope of redemption or recovery. [An old pa p of **pass**]

pasta *päs'tə* or *pas'tə*, *n* flour dough in fresh, processed (eg spaghetti, macaroni, shell shapes), and/or cooked form. [Ital, paste]

pastance *pas'təns*, (*archaic*) *n* a pastime. [Appar Fr *passe-temps* pastime]

paste *pāst*, *n* any soft plastic mass; dough for piecrust, etc; a doughy sweet; a smooth preparation of food suitable for spreading on bread; a glue whose main ingredients are flour and water; any of various adhesives, eg one for hanging wallpaper; material for making pottery; the basis of a person's character (*fig*); a fine kind of glass for making artificial gems. — *adj* of paste. — *vt* to fasten or cover with paste; to thrash (*slang*); to defeat utterly (*slang*). — *n* **pāst'er** someone who pastes; a slip of gummed paper. — *n* **pāst'iness**. — *n* **pāst'ing** (*slang*) a beating; a thorough defeat. — *adj* **pāst'y** like paste in texture; (of a complexion) pale and unhealthy looking. — **paste'board** a stiff board made of sheets of paper pasted together; a visiting-card, playing-card, or ticket (*slang*). — *adj* of pasteboard; sham; trumpery. — **paste'-down** the outer leaf of an endpaper that is pasted down on the inside cover of a book; formerly, a paper used to line the inside cover of a book; **paste'-eel'** a nematoid worm found in paste; **paste'-grain** an imitation of morocco leather, used in binding books and in making fancy goods; **paste'-up** a draft of a printed page consisting of text, artwork, photographs, etc pasted on to a sheet, for photographing or as a plan for a printing plate; a collage. — *adj* **past'y-faced'** having a pale and dull complexion. [OFr *paste* (Fr *pâte*), from LL *pasta*, from Gr *pasta* barley porridge (neuter pl of *pastos* sprinkled, salted), from *passein* to sprinkle]

pastel *pas'təl* or *-tel*, *n* a chalk-like crayon made from powdered pigments bound together with gum; a drawing made with pastels; the process or art of drawing with pastels; woad. — *adj* in pastel; (of colour) soft, quiet. — *n* **pastellist** (*pas'* or *-tel'*). [Fr *pastel*, from Ital *pastello*, from L *pasta* paste]

paster. See under **paste**.

pastern *pas'tərn*, *n* any rope, strap, etc used to tie up a horse by the leg, a hobble (*obs*); the part of a horse's foot from the fetlock to the hoof, where the shackle is fastened. [OFr *pasturon* (Fr *paturon*), from OFr *pasture* pasture, a tether for a horse; cf **pester**]

Pasteurian *pas-tûr'i-ən*, *adj* relating to Louis *Pasteur* (1822–95), French chemist and bacteriologist, or his methods. — *n* **Pasteurell'a** a genus of bacteria which cause various serious infectious diseases, including plague; (without *cap*) a bacterium of this genus: — *pl* **Pasteurellas** or **Pasteurellae** (*-ē*). — *n* **Pasteurellō'sis** a disease caused by organisms of the genus *Pasteurella*: — *pl* **Pasteurellō'sēs**. — *n* **pas'teurism** Pasteur's method of inoculation with the attenuated virus of certain diseases, *esp* hydrophobia. — *n* **pasteurīzā'tion** or **-s-** sterilization of milk, etc, by heating. — *vt* **pas'teurize** or **-ise**. — *n* **pas'teurizer** or **-s-** an apparatus for sterilizing milk, etc.

pastiche *pas-tēsh'*, *n* a jumble; a pot-pourri; a composition (in literature, music, or painting) made up of bits of other works or imitations of another's style. — Also **pasticcio** (*pas-tit'chō*; *pl* **pasticci** *-chē*). — *n* **pasticheur** (*-ē-shœr'*) someone who makes pastiches. [Fr (from Ital) and Ital, from Ital *pasta*, paste; see **paste**]

pasties *past'iz*, *n pl* decorative nipple covers of a kind worn by striptease artists, etc.

pastil *pas'til*, *n*. Same as **pastel** or **pastille**.

pastille *pas'til* or *pas-tēl'*, *n* a small cone of charcoal and aromatic substances, burned as incense, or for fumigation or fragrance; a small (often medicated) sweet; a paper tube containing a firework which causes a small wheel to rotate; the same as **pastel** (*art*). [Fr, from L *pāstillus* a little loaf]

pastime *päs'tīm*, *n* that which serves to pass away the time; a hobby or recreation. [**pass** and **time**]

pastiness, pasting. See under **paste**.

pastis *pas-tēs'*, *n* an alcoholic drink flavoured with aniseed. [Fr]

pastor *päs'tər*, *n* a person who has care of a flock or of a congregation; a shepherd; a member of the clergy; in the Catholic Apostolic Church, a minister of the lowest grade; the rose-coloured starling (*Pastor roseus*), from its following sheep for the sake of parasites. — *adj* **pas'toral** relating to, depicting or evoking rural life, the countryside, etc, *esp orig* shepherds or shepherd life; of the nature of pastureland; of or pertaining to the pastor of a church and his or her obligations to the congregation; addressed to the clergy of a diocese by their bishop. — *n* a poem, play, romance, opera, piece of music, or picture depicting the life of (*usu* idealized or conventionalized) shepherds, or rural life in general; such writing as a genre; a pastoral letter; a book on the care of souls; a pastoral staff. — *n* **pastorale** (*päs-to-rä'lā*; *Ital*) a pastoral composition in music; a pastoral, rustic, or idyllic opera or cantata. — *n* **pas'toralism** pastoral character, fashion, cult or mode of writing. — *n* **pas'toralist**. — *adv* **pas'torally**. — *n* **pas'torate** the office of a pastor; a pastor's tenure of office; a body of pastors. — *adj* **pas'torly** suitable for a pastor. — *n* **pas'torship**. — **pastoral address** or **letter** an address or a letter by a pastor to his people, or by a bishop to his clergy; **pastoral charge** position of a pastor; the church, etc, over which a pastor is placed; an address to a newly ordained minister. — *n pl* **pastoral epistles** those in the Bible to Timothy and Titus. — **pastoral staff** a crosier, a tall staff forming part of a bishop's insignia, headed like a shepherd's crook; **pastoral theology** that part of theology which deals with the duties of pastors in relation to the care of souls. [L *pāstor*, from *pāscere*, *pāstum* to feed]

pastourelle *päs-tōō-rel'*, *n* a medieval poetic genre, *esp* Provençal and French, a dialogue between a knight and a shepherdess; a movement in a quadrille. [Fr, little shepherdess]

pastrami *pəs-trä'mi*, *n* a smoked, highly seasoned (*esp* shoulder) cut of beef. [Yiddish, from Romanian *pastramă*, from *a păstra* to serve]

pastry *pās'tri*, *n* articles made of paste or dough collectively; crust of pies, tarts, etc; a small cake; a place where pastry is made (*Shakesp*); the art or practice of making pastry (*obs*). — **pas'trycook** a maker or seller of pastry. [**paste**]

pasture *päs'chər*, *n* feeding (*archaic*); food (*Spenser*); grazing; growing grass for grazing; grazing land; a grazing ground, piece of grazing land. — *vi* to graze. — *vt* to put to graze; to graze on. — *adj* **past'urable** fit for pasture. — *n* **past'urage** the business of feeding or grazing cattle; pasture-land; grass for feeding; right of pasture. — *adj* **past'ural** of pasture. — *adj* **past'ureless**. — **past'ure-land** land suitable for pasture. [OFr *pasture* (Fr *pâture*), from L *pāstūra*, from *pāscere*, *pāstum* to feed]

pasty[1] *pās'ti*, *adj*. See under **paste**.

pasty[2] *pas'ti* or *päs'ti*, *n* a (*usu* individual) meat and vegetable pie with an all-round crust, typically a pastry round folded in two around the filling, with the join crimped. [OFr *pastée*, from L *pasta*; see **paste**]

PAT *abbrev*: planned activities time (*teaching*); Professional Association of Teachers.

Pat *pat*, *n* a nickname for an Irishman. [**Patrick**]

pat[1] *pat*, *n* a gentle stroke with a flat surface, such as the palm of the hand; such a stroke as a caress or mark of approbation; a sound as of such a stroke; a small lump, *esp* of butter, such as might be moulded by patting. — *vt* to strike (now only to strike gently) with the palm of the hand or other flat surface; to shape by patting. — *vi* to tap; to make the sound of pats, eg with the feet: — *pr p* **patt'ing**; *pa t* and *pa p* **patt'ed**. — *adv* and *adj* hitting the mark precisely; at the right time or place; exactly to the purpose; with or ready for fluent or glib repetition; (of a hand in poker) not likely to be improved by drawing (*US*). — *adv* **pat'ly** (*rare*) fitly, conveniently; glibly, fluently. — *n* **pat'ness**. — **pat'ball** rounders; gentle hitting in other games. — **off pat** exactly memorized; pat; **pat on the back** a mark of encouragement or approbation; **stand pat** (in poker) to decide to play one's hand as it is; to refuse to change. [Prob imit]

pat[2]. See **pit**[3].

pat[3] *pat*, (*Scot*) *n* a pot. — **pat'-lid'**.

pat. *abbrev*: patent; patented.

pa t *abbrev*: past tense.

pataca *pə-tä'kə*, *n* the basic unit of currency in the Portuguese colonies of Macao and Timor (100 *avos*); a coin of one pataca in value. [Port]

patagium *pat-ə-jī'əm*, *n* a bat's wing-membrane; the parachute of a flying-squirrel, etc; the fold of integument between the upper arm and the forearm of a bird; a paired scale on a moth's pronotum: — *pl* **patagi'a**. — *adj* **patagial** (*pə-tā'ji-əl*). [L *patagīum*, from Gr *patageion* an edging]

Patagonian *pat-ə-gō'ni-ən*, *n* a member of the native population of Patagonia; a giant. — *adj* of Patagonia; gigantic. [Sp *patagón*, big foot — the tallness of the Patagonians was grossly exaggerated by travellers]

patamar *pat'ə-mär*, *n* a vessel, on the Bombay coast, with an arched keel and a great stem and stern rake. [Port, from Konkani *pātamāri*]

pataphysics or **'pataphysics** *pat'ə-fiz-iks*, *n* 'the science of imaginary solutions' invented by the French dramatist Alfred Jarry (1873–1907), writer of symbolic farce, from which is descended the theatre of the absurd.

Patarin or **Patarine** *pat'ər-in* or *-ēn*, (*hist*) *n orig* an adherent of a popular party in Milan opposed to marriage of priests (11c); later a nickname for Manichaeans, Cathari, and other heretics. [Said to be from *Pattaria* a district in Milan]

Patavinity *pat-ə-vin'i-ti*, *n* the diction of the people of Padua, *esp* Livy; the use of dialect; provincialism generally. [L *patavīnitās*, from *Patavium* Padua]

patball. See under **pat**[1].

patch[1] *pach*, *n* a piece put on or to be put on to mend a defect; a dressing, *esp* a plaster for a cut or sore; a pad for an injured eye; a piece of ground or plot of land; an area or district, etc regularly visited, patrolled or traded in, etc; an overlay to obtain a stronger impression (*printing*); a small piece of black silk, etc, stuck by ladies on the face, to bring out the complexion by contrast, or as a political party badge — common in the 17c and 18c; an imitation beauty spot; a smallish area differing in colour or otherwise from its surroundings; a period of time; a scrap or fragment; a scrap pieced together with others; a group of instructions added to a computer program to correct a mistake (*comput*). — *vt* to mend with a patch; to put a patch on; to apply as a patch; to join in patchwork; to mend or construct hastily, clumsily, or temporarily (commonly with *up*); to resolve (an argument), settle (differences), sometimes only temporarily (*usu* with *up*); to construct as a patchwork; to mark with patches; to connect (a telephone call) using a patchboard (with *through*), to put through. — *adj* **patch'able**. — *adj* **patched**. — *n* **patch'er**. — *adv* **patch'ily**. — *n* and *adj* **patch'ing**. — *adj* **patch'y** covered with patches; diversified in patches; inharmonious, incongruous, irregular. — **patch'board** (*telecomm*, etc) a panel with multiple electric terminals into which wires may be plugged to form a variety of electric circuits; **patch'-box** a fancy box for holding the patches worn on the face, generally having a mirror inside the lid; **patch'-pocket** a simple pocket consisting of a piece of material sewn on all but one side on to the outside of a garment; **patch test** a test for allergy in which allergenic substances are applied to areas of skin which are later examined for signs of irritation; **patch-up'** a provisional repairing; **patch'work** needlework formed of patches or pieces sewed together; an incongruous combination; work patched up or clumsily executed; a surface diversified in patches; **patch'-work quilt** a bedcover which may or may not be quilted, one side of which is made up of patchwork. — **hit** or **strike a bad patch** to experience a difficult time, to encounter unfavourable conditions, etc; **not a patch on** not fit to be compared with. [ME *pacche*; origin unknown; poss connected with **piece**]

patch[2] *pach*, *n* a fool or jester (*archaic*); a stupid person (*dialect*); a bad-tempered or peevish person (*dialect*). — *n* **patch'ery** (*Shakesp*) knavery. — **patch'cocke** or **patch'ocke** (*Spenser*) perhaps a clown (reading and meaning doubtful; cf **paiock**). [Perh from **patch**[1], from the patched coat; nickname of Cardinal Wolsey's fool, Sexton; perh Ital *pazzo* fool]

patchouli or **patchouly** *pach'ōō-lē*, also *pə-chōō'lē*, *n* a labiate shrub (*Pogostemon patchouly*) of SE Asia; a perfume derived from its dried branches. [Tamil *pacculi*]

patchwork, **patchy**. See under **patch**[1].

pate *pāt*, *n* the crown of the head, *esp* when bald; the head; intelligence (*fig*). — *adj* **pāt'ed** having a pate. [Origin unknown]

pâté *pät'ā* or *pat'ā*, *n orig* a pie or pastry; now *usu* a paste made of blended meat, herbs, etc. — **pâté de foie gras** (*də fwä grä*) *orig* a pasty of fattened goose liver; now *usu* a paste made from the liver. [Fr]

patella *pə-tel'ə*, *n* a little pan (*antiq*); the knee-cap (*anatom*); a saucer-like apothecium (*bot*); (with *cap*) the limpet genus: — *pl* **patell'as** or **patell'ae** (-*ē*). — *adj* **patell'ar** of the knee-cap. — *adj* **patell'ate** (or *pat'*) saucer-shaped; limpet-shaped — *n* **patellec'tomy** the surgical removal of the patella. — *adj* **patell'iform** patellate. — **patellar reflex** the knee-jerk. [L, dimin of *patina* a pan]

paten *pat'ən*, *n* a plate; a communion plate; a chalice-cover; a metal disc. [OFr *patene*, from L *patena*, *patina* a plate, from Gr *patanē*]

patent *pā'tənt* or (*esp* in *letters-patent* and *Patent Office*, and *US*) *pat'ənt*, *adj* lying open; conspicuous, obvious, evident; generally accessible; protected by a patent; spreading (*bot*); expanding; ingenious (*colloq*). — *n* an official document, open, and bearing a government seal, conferring an exclusive right or privilege, such as a title of nobility, or *esp* the sole right for a term of years to the proceeds of an invention; something invented and protected by a patent; a privilege; a certificate. — *vt* to secure a patent for. — *n* **pā'tency** openness; obviousness. — *adj* **pā'tentable**. — *n* **pātentee'** someone who holds a patent, or to whom a patent is granted. — *adv* **pā'tently** openly, obviously. — *n* **pā'tentor** a person, body, authority, etc that grants a patent. — **patent agent** someone who obtains patents on behalf of inventors; **patent leather** finely varnished leather; **patent log** a device for recording the speed of a vessel, consisting of a submerged rotator attached by line to a dial on the ship's rail; **patent medicine** (strictly) a medicine protected by a patent; (loosely) any proprietary medicine, *esp* one liable to stamp duty, since made by secret process or for some other reason; **Patent Office** an office for the granting of patents for inventions; **patent outside** or **inside** a newspaper printed on the outside or inside only, sold to a publisher who fills the other side with his own material, such as local news, etc; **pā'tent-right** the exclusive right reserved by letters-patent (qv). — *n pl* **pā'tent-rolls** the register of letters-patent (qv) issued in England. — **patent still** a still performing several operations at once, and producing a purer spirit than a pot-still. — **nothing patent** (*slang*) not very good. [L *patēns*, *-entis*, pr p of *patēre* to lie open]

pater *pā'tər*, (*slang*, *usu facetious*) *n* father. [L *pater*]

patera *pat'ə-rə*, *n* a round flat dish holding the wine used by the Romans in ritual sacrifices; a round flat ornament in bas-relief in friezes, etc, often applied loosely to rosettes and other flat ornaments (*archit*): — *pl* **pat'erae** (-*rē*). [L, from *patēre* to lie open]

patercove *pat'ər-kōv*, *n* Same as **patrico**.

paterero *pat-ə-rā'rō*, *n*. Same as **pederero**: — *pl* **patere'ros** or **patere'roes** (-*rōz*).

paterfamilias *pā-tər-fə-mil'i-as* or *pat'ər-*, *n* the father or other male head of a family or household; any man regarded as exerting a paternal influence on others (often *facetious*): — *pl* strictly **patresfamil'ias** (-*trās*-), sometimes **paterfamil'iases**. [L *pater* a father, and *familiās*, old genitive of *familia* a household]

paternal *pə-tûr'n(ə)l*, *adj* of a father; on the father's side; derived or inherited from the father; fatherly; showing the disposition or manner of a father. — *n* **pater'nalism** a system or tendency in which well-meaning supervision and/or regulation, etc is apt to become unwelcome interference. — *adj* **paternalis'tic**. — *adv* **pater'nally**. — *n* **pater'nity** the state or fact of being a father; fatherhood; the relation of a father to his children; origin on the father's side; origination or authorship. — **paternity leave** leave of absence from work granted to a husband so that he can be with his wife and assist her during and after childbirth. [L *pater* (Gr *patēr*) a father]

paternoster *pat-ər-nos'tər* or *pāt'*, *n* (with *cap*) the Lord's Prayer; a muttered formula or spell; a harangue; a large bead in a rosary, at which, in telling, the Lord's Prayer is repeated; a rosary; anything strung like a rosary, *esp* a fishing-line with hooks at intervals; an ornament shaped like beads, used in astragals, etc (*archit*); a lift for goods or passengers, consisting of a series of cars moving on a continuous belt, the floors remaining horizontal at the top and bottom of travel. [L *Pater noster* 'Our Father', the first words of the Lord's Prayer]

pater patriae *pā'tər pā'tri-ē* or *pa'ter pa'tri-ī*, (*L*) *n* the father of his country.

Paterson's curse *pa'tər-sənz kûrs*, (*Austr*) *n* any of various naturalized *orig* European herbs regarded as harmful to livestock. [Ety doubtful]

pâte-sur-pâte *pät'-sür-pät'*, *n* a type of decoration used on pottery, in which layers of slip are applied to a low relief. [Fr, paste-upon-paste]

path *päth*, *n* a way trodden out by the feet; a footpath; a way for pedestrians; a course, route or line along which anything moves; a course of action or conduct: — *pl* **paths** (*pädhz*). — *vi* (*Shakesp*) to go. — *adj* **path'less** without a path; untrodden. — **path'finder** a person who explores the route, a pioneer; a radar device used as an aircraft navigational aid; a radar device for guiding missiles into a target area; **path'way** a path; (in neurology) the route of a sensory impression to the brain, or of a motor impulse from the brain to the musculature; the sequence of reactions by which one substance is metabolically converted to another (*bio-chem*). [OE *pæth*; Ger *Pfad*]

path. or **pathol.** *abbrev*: pathological; pathology.

-path *-path*, *n combining form* a sufferer from a particular disorder, as in *psychopath*; a therapist for a particular disorder, as in *osteopath*. — *combining form* **path'o-** denoting disease or disorder, as in *pathology*. — *n combining form* **-pathy** mental or emotional sensitivity or receptiveness; disease, disorder; therapy for a particular disorder. — *adj combining form* **-pathet'ic** or **-path'ic**. — *n combining form* **-pathist** denoting a therapist for a particular disorder. — *n* **pathogen** (*path'ō-jen*) an organism or substance that causes disease. — *n* **pathogen'esis** or **pathogeny** (*pə-thoj'ə-ni*) (mode of) production or development of disease. — *adj* **pathogenetic** (*path-ō-ji-net'ik*) or **pathogenic** (*-jen'ik*) producing disease. — *n* **pathogenicity** (*-is'i-ti*) the quality of producing or the ability to produce disease. — *adj* **pathog'enous** same as **pathogenetic** above. — *adj* **pathognomon'ic** (*-og-nō-*; Gr *gnōmōn* judge, index) indicative of a particular disease. — *n* **pathog'nomy**. — *n* **pathog'raphy** a description of or article on a disease; abnormality. — *adj* **patholog'ic**. — *adj* **patholog'ical** relating to pathology; relating to or caused by disease; (loosely) habitual or compulsive. — *adv* **patholog'ically**. — *n* **pathol'ogist** a person skilled in pathology, *usu* having as a duty the performing of post-mortems. — *n* **pathol'ogy** the study of diseases or abnormalities or, more particularly, of the changes in tissues or organs that are associated with disease; a deviation from the normal, healthy state. — *n* **pathopho'bia** (Gr *phobos* fear) morbid fear of disease. [Ety as for **pathos**]

Pathan *pə-tan'* or *put-än'*, *n* an Afghan proper; a person of Afghan race settled in India. — Also *adj*. [Afghan *Pakhtun*]

pathetic, etc. See under **pathos**.

-pathetic. See under **-path**.

pathic. See under **pathos**.

-pathic. See under **-path**.

-pathist. See under **-path**.

patho- See under **-path**.

pathos *pā'thos*, *n* the quality that arouses pity. — *adj* **pathetic** (*pə-thet'ik*) relating to or affecting the passions or their expressions (*obs*); affecting the emotions of pity, grief or sorrow; touching; sadly inadequate; contemptible, derisory (*colloq*); applied to the superior oblique muscle, which turns the eyeball downwards, and to the trochlear nerve connecting with it (*anatom*). — See also **-pathetic** under **-path**. — *n* that which is pathetic; the style or manner designed to excite emotion; (in *pl*) attempts at pathetic expression. — *adj* **pathet'ical**. — *adv* **pathet'ically**. — *adj* **pathic** (*path'ik*) passive (and see also **-pathic** under **-path**). — *n* a passive subject; a catamite. — **pathetic fallacy** (in literature, etc) the transference of human emotions to inanimate objects. [Gr *pathos* experience, feeling, pathos]

pathway. See under **path**.

-pathy. See under **-path**.

patible *pat'i-bl*, *adj* capable of suffering or being acted on; passible. [L *patibilis*, from *patī* to suffer]

patibulary *pə-tib'ū-lə-ri*, *adj* of or pertaining to a gibbet or gallows. [L *patibulum* a gibbet]

patience *pā'shəns*, *n* the quality of being able calmly to endure suffering, toil, delay, vexation, or any similar condition; sufferance; a card-game of various kinds, generally for one person, the object being to fit the cards, as they turn up, into some scheme; a species of the dock plant (also **pa'tience-dock'**; *Rumex patientia*) used like spinach, or other species of dock; also applied to bistort. — *adj* **pā'tient** sustaining pain, delay, etc, calmly and without complaint; not easily provoked; persevering in long-continued or intricate work; expecting with calmness; long-suffering; enduring; susceptible (of an interpretation). — *n* someone who bears or suffers (*obs*); a person under medical or surgical treatment; a doctor's client. — *vt* (*Shakesp*) to make patient. — *adv* **pā'tiently**. [Fr, from L *patientia*, from *patī* to bear]

patin. *Obs* form of **paten**.

patina *pat'i-nə*, *n* a shallow Roman pan; a eucharistic paten; a film of basic copper carbonate that forms on exposed surfaces of copper or bronze; a similar film of oxide, etc, on other metals; a film or surface appearance that develops on other substances (wood, flint, etc) on long exposure or burial; a sheen acquired from constant handling or contact (also *fig*). — *adj* **pat'i-nāted**. — *n* **patinā'tion**. — *adj* **pat'ined**. [L *patina* a dish]

patine. *Obs* form of **paten**.

patio *pa'ti-ō* or *-tyō*, *n* a courtyard; a paved area *usu* adjoining a house, where outdoor meals can be served, etc: — *pl* **pat'ios**. [Sp, a courtyard]

pâtisserie or **patisserie** *pa-tēs'ə-rē*, *n* a shop which sells fancy cakes, etc; such cakes. [Fr]

pat-lid. See under **pat**³.

patly. See under **pat**¹.

Patna rice *pat'nə rīs*, *n* a long-grained rice, *orig* grown at *Patna* in India, served with savoury dishes.

patness. See under **pat**¹.

Pat Off *abbrev*: Patent Office.

patois *pat'wä*, *n* spoken regional dialect; (loosely) jargon: — *pl* **patois** (*-wäz*). [Fr; origin disputed, some suggesting corruption of *patrois*, from LL *patriensis* a local inhabitant]

patonce *pə-tons'*, (*heraldry*) *adj* (of a cross) having four arms expanding in curves from the centre, with floriated ends. [Origin unknown]

patres conscripti *pät'*, *pat'rēz* or *-rās kon-skrip'tī* or *-tē*, (L) the conscript fathers, those enrolled as Roman senators.

patresfamilias. See **paterfamilias**.

patria potestas *pā'* or *pa'tria po-tes'täs*, (*L*) *n* the authority of a Roman father over his children.

patrial *pā'* or *pa'tri-əl*, *adj* pertaining to one's native land; (of a word) denoting a native or inhabitant of the place from whose name the word was formed; pertaining to the legal right to enter and stay in the UK, or to one who has this right. — *n* a patrial word; a citizen of the UK, a British colony or the British Commonwealth, who for certain reasons (eg because a parent was born in the UK) has a legal right to enter and stay in the UK. — *n* **pa'trialism**. — *n* **patrial'ity** the condition of being a patrial. — *n* **patrializā'tion** or **-s-**. — *vt* **pa'trialize** or **-ise**. [Obs Fr, from L *patria* fatherland]

patriarch *pā'tri-ärk*, *n* a man who governs his family by paternal right, a male head of a family; one of the early heads of families from Adam downwards to Abraham, Jacob, and his sons (*Old Testament*); a bishop ranking above primates and metropolitans; the head of certain Eastern Churches; a father or founder; a venerable old man; an oldest inhabitant; an old leader of any group; the most imposing and greatest of its kind. — *adj* **patriarch'al** belonging or subject to a patriarch; like a patriarch; of the nature of a patriarch. — *n* **patri-arch'alism** the condition of tribal government by a patriarch. — *n* **pa'triarchate** the province, dignity, office, term or residence of a church patriarch; patriarchy. — *n* **pa'triarchism** government by a patriarch. — *n* **pa'triarchy** a community of related families under the authority of a patriarch; the patriarchal system. — **patriarchal cross** a cross with two horizontal bars. [Gr *patriarchēs*, from *patriā* family, from *patēr* father, and *archē* rule]

patriation *pā-tri-ā'shən*, *n* the transferring of responsibility for the Canadian constitution (as enshrined in the British North America Act of 1867) from the British parliament to the Canadian parliament. — *vt* **pāt'riate**. [L *patria* fatherland]

Patrician. See under **patrick**.

patrician *pə-trish'ən*, *n* a member or descendant by blood or adoption of one of the original families of citizens forming the Roman people (*opp* of *plebeian*); a nobleman of a new order nominated by the emperor in the later Roman Empire; an imperial Roman provincial administrator in Italy or Africa; a hereditary noble; an aristocrat. — Also *adj*. — *adj* **patri'cianly**. — *n* **patriciate** (*pə-trish'i-āt*) the position of a patrician; the patrician order. [L *patricius*, from *pater*, *patris* a father]

patricide *pat'ri-sīd*, *n* the murder of one's own father; a person who murders his or her father. — *adj* **patricī'dal**. [Doubtful L *patricīda*, as if from *pater*, *patris* father, and *caedere* to kill; prob an error for *parricīda*; see **parricide**]

patrick *pat'rik*, *n* a 17c Irish halfpenny. — *adj* **Patrician** (*pə-trish'ən*) of St Patrick. — **St Patrick's cabbage** a saxifrage, London pride; **St Patrick's cross** a red saltire on a white background, representing Ireland. [St *Patrick* (L *Patrīcius*), 5c christianizer of Ireland]

patriclinic, **patriclinous**, etc. See under **patroclinic**.

patrico *pat'ri-kō*, (*slang*) *n* a hedge-priest: — *pl* **pat'ricoes**. — Also **pat'ercove**. [First part unexplained; see **cove**²]

patrifocal *pat'ri-fō-kəl*, (*anthropol*, etc) *adj* centred on the father; (of societies, families, etc) in which authority and responsibility rest with the father. — *n* **patrifo-cal'ity**. [L *pater*, *patris* father, and *focus* a hearth]

patrilineal *pat-ri-lin'i-əl* or **patrilinear** *-ər*, *adj* traced through the father or through males alone. — *n* **patrilineage** (*-lin'i-ij*). — *adv* **patrilin'eally**. — *n* **pat'ri-**

liny patrilineal descent. [L *pater*, *patris* father, and *līnea* line]

patrilocal *pat-ri-lō'kl*, *adj* (of a form of marriage) in which the wife goes to live with the husband's group. [L *pater*, *patris* father, and *locālis*, from *locus* place]

patrimony *pat'ri-mən-i*, *n* an inheritance from a father or from ancestors; a church estate or revenue. — *adj* **patrimonial** (*-mō'ni-əl*). — *adv* **patrimō'nially**. [L *patrimōnium* a paternal estate, from *pater*, *patris* a father]

patriot *pā'tri-ət* or *pat'ri-ət*, *n* a person who truly, though sometimes unquestioningly, loves and serves his or her country. — *adj* devoted to one's country. — *adj* **patriotic** (*pat-ri-ot'ik* or *pāt-*) devoted to one's country; like a patriot; motivated by a love of one's country; for the public good (*rare*). — *adv* **patriot'ically**. — *n* **pā'triotism** (or *pat'*). [Gr *patriōtēs* fellow-countryman, from *patrios*, from *patēr* a father]

Patripassian *pat-ri-pas'i-ən*, *n* a member of one of the earliest classes of anti-Trinitarian sectaries (2c), who denied the distinction of three persons in one God, maintaining that God the Father suffered along with, or in the person of, God the Son. — Also *adj*. — *n* **Patripass'ianism**. [L *pater*, *patris* father, and *patī*, *passus* to suffer]

patristic *pə-tris'tik* or **patristical** *-əl*, *adj* pertaining to the fathers of the Christian Church. — *n* **patris'ticism** (*-sizm*) the mode of thought, etc, of the fathers. — *n sing* **patris'tics** the knowledge of the fathers as a subject of study — sometimes **patrol'ogy**. — **patristic similarity** (*bot*) similarity due to common ancestry. [Gr *patēr*, *pat(e)ros* a father]

patroclinic *pat-rō-klin'ik* or **patroclinous** *-klī'nəs*, *adj* inherited from the father; more like the father than the mother. — *n* **patroclī'ny**. — Also **patriclinic**, **patriclinous**, etc. [Gr *patēr*, *pat(e)ros*, L *pater*, *patris* father, and *klinein* to lean]

patrol *pə-trōl'*, *vi* to move systematically round or go the rounds of an area, for the purpose of watching, repressing, protecting, inspecting, etc; (of a police officer) to be on duty on a beat. — *vt* to keep (an area) under surveillance by patrolling; to perambulate: — *pr p* **patrōll'ing**; *pa t* and *pa p* **patrōlled'**. — *n* the act or service of patrolling; perambulation; a person or group of people patrolling an area; a body of aircraft, ships, etc having patrolling duties; a small detachment of soldiers, etc sent on reconnaissance or to make an attack, etc; one of the units of eight or so Scouts or Guides forming a troop. — *n* **patroll'er**. — **patrol car** that used by police to patrol an area; **patrol'man** or *fem* **patrol'woman** a police officer on duty on a beat (*NAm*); a police officer without rank (*NAm*); (or **patrol**) a person on patrol to help motorists in difficulties; **patrol'-wagon** (*NAm*) a prison-van. [OFr *patrouiller* to patrol, orig to paddle in the mud]

patrology. See under **patristic**.

patron *pā'trən*, *n* (in ancient Rome) the former master of a freed slave, retaining certain rights; a Roman patrician who gave legal aid and other protection to his client in return for services; (formerly) a person who accepted a dedication and gave the author a present; a protector; a person, group or organization, etc which gives support, encouragement and often financial aid; a (regular) customer; a habitual attender; an upholder; a proprietor of a restaurant, etc; someone who has the right to appoint to any office, *esp* to a living in the church (*Ch of Eng*); a guardian saint; a captain of a Mediterranean vessel; a slave-owner; a pattern (*obs*): — *fem* **pā'troness** or (of a restaurant, etc) **patronne** (Fr; *pa-tron*). — *n* **patronage** (*pat'*) support given by a patron; protection (*Spenser*); guardianship of saints; the right of bestowing offices, privileges, or church benefices (*Ch of Eng*); habitual commercial dealings. — *vt* (*Shakesp*) to countenance. — *adj* **patronal** (*pa-*, *pə-trō'nl*, *pāt'* or *pat'rən-l*). — *vt* **patronize** or **-ise** (*pat'* or *pāt'*) to act as a patron toward; to give encouragement to; to assume the condescending air of a patron toward; to give one's custom to or to frequent habitually. — *n* **pat'ronizer** or **-s-**. — *adj* **pat'ronizing** or **-s-**. — *adv* **pat'ronizingly** or **-s-**. — *adj* **pā'tronless**. — **patron saint** a saint regarded as the protector of a particular group, nation, etc. [L *patrōnus*, from *pater*, *patris* a father]

patronymic *pat-rə-nim'ik*, *adj* derived from the name of a father or an ancestor. — *n* a name so derived. [Gr *patrōnymikos*, from *patēr* a father, and *onyma* (*onoma*) a name]

patroon *pə-troōn'*, *n* a captain of a ship; a coxswain of a longboat; a holder of a grant of land under the old Dutch government of New York or New Jersey. — *n* **patroon'ship**. [Fr *patron*, Sp *patrón*, and Du *patroon*; cf **patron**]

patsy *pat'si*, (*slang*, *esp NAm*) *n* an easy victim, a sucker; a scapegoat, fall guy. [Ety uncertain; perh from Ital *pazzo* fool or Yiddish *Putz* fool, simpleton]

patte *pat* or *pät*, *n* a narrow band keeping a belt or sash in its place. [Fr]

patté or **pattée** *pa-tā'* or *pat'i*, (*heraldry*) *adj* (of a cross) spreading towards the ends, or having the ends expanded in three clawlike divisions. [Fr, pawed]

patted. See under **pat**[1].

patten[1] *pat'n*, *n* a wooden shoe, a clog (*hist*); a wooden sole mounted on an iron ring to raise the shoe above the mud (*hist*); the base of a pillar (*archit*). — *vi* (*obs*) to go on pattens. — *adj* **patt'ened** with pattens. [OFr *patin* clog (now skate), perhaps from *patte* paw]

patten[2]. An old form (*Shakesp*) of **paten**.

patter[1] *pat'ər*, *vi* to pat or strike often, as hailstones do; to make the sound of a succession of light pats; to run with short quick steps. — *n* the sound of pattering. [Frequentative of **pat**]

patter[2] *pat'ər*, *vi* to repeat the Lord's Prayer (*obs*); to gabble prayers (*obs*); to talk or sing rapidly and glibly; to talk in this way, *esp* on the stage, as accompaniment to action or for comic effect. — *vt* to repeat hurriedly, to gabble. — *n* glib talk, chatter, *esp* the insincere speech of salesmen, etc; the jargon of a particular class or group, etc. — *n* **patt'erer** a street seller relying heavily on patter. — **patt'er-song** a comic song in which a great many words are sung or spoken very rapidly. — **patter flash** to talk the jargon of thieves. [**paternoster**]

pattern *pat'ərn*, *n* a person or thing to be copied; a model; a design or guide with help of which something is to be made (eg a set of dressmaker's paper templates); a model of an object to be cast, from which a mould is prepared; a sample; a typical example; a decorative design; a particular disposition of forms and colours; a design or figure repeated indefinitely; the distribution of shot on a target. — *vt* to make or be a pattern for (*Shakesp*); to match, parallel (*Shakesp*); to take as a pattern; to fashion after a pattern; to make a pattern on. — **patt'ern-maker** a person who makes the patterns for moulders in foundry-work; **pattern race** a horse-race open to all comers in a particular category, eg of a certain age or weight, *usu* contested by top-class horses, the object being to find the best; **patt'ern-shop** the place in which patterns for a factory are prepared; **patt'ern-wheel** the count-wheel in a clock. [Fr *patron*, patron, pattern; cf **patron**]

patting. See under **pat**[1].

pattle *pat'* or *pät'l* or **pettle** *pet'l*, (*Scot*) *n* a small long-handled spade for cleaning a plough. [Origin obscure; cf **paddle**[3]]

patty *pat'i*, *n* a little pie; a small flat cake of minced beef or other food. — **patt'y-pan** a pan for baking patties. [Fr *pâté*; cf **pasty**]

patulous *pat'ū-ləs*, (*esp bot*) *adj* spreading. — *n* **pat'ulin** a drug derived from the mould *Penicillium patulum*. [L *patulus*, from *patēre* to lie open]

patzer *pats'ər*, (*slang*) *n* a poor chess player. [Ger *patzen* to bungle, make a mess of]

paua *pä'wə* or *pow'ə*, *n* the New Zealand name for the abalone; its shell used as an ornament or decoration. — Also **paw'a**. [Maori]

pauciloquent *pö-sil'ə-kwənt*, *adj* of few words, speaking little. [L *paucus* little, and *loquī* to speak]

paucity *pö'sit-i*, *n* fewness; smallness of quantity; insufficiency, dearth. [L *paucitās*, *-ātis*, from *paucus* few]

paughty *pöhh'ti*, (*Scot*) *adj* haughty. [Origin unknown]

paul[1]. Same as **pawl**.

paul[2] *pöl*, *n* a paolo, qv.

pauldron *pöl'drən* or **pouldron** *pōl'*, *n* a separable shoulder-plate in armour. [OFr *espalleron*, from *espalle* the shoulder]

Paulian *pöl'i-ən* or **Paulianist** *pöl'i-ən-ist*, *n* a follower of Paul of Samosata, a 3c Monarchian Unitarian of Antioch. — Also *adj*.

Paulician *pöl-ish'ən*, *n* a member of a 7c sect in Armenia and later in Thrace, with Marcionite and Adoptianist affinities (*perh* from Paul of Samosata, or the apostle, or one of their founders). — Also *adj*.

Pauli exclusion principle. Same as **exclusion principle**.

Pauline *pöl'īn*, *adj* of the apostle Paul. — *n* a member of any religious order named after him; a scholar of St Paul's School, London. — *adj* **Paulinian** (*-in'i-ən*) Pauline. — *n* **Paul'inism** the teaching or theology of Paul. — *n* **Paul'inist**. — *adj* **Paulinist'ic**. [L *Paulus*, *Paullus*, a Roman cognomen, meaning 'little']

Paul Jones *pöl jōnz*, *n* a dance in the course of which each man takes a number of partners in succession — *perh* from the Scottish-American seaman Paul Jones (1747–92), who excelled in the capture of prizes.

paulo-post-future *pö'lō-pōst-fū'chər*, *adj* and *n* future perfect (*gram*); future immediately after the present. [L *paulō* a little, *post* after, and *futūrum* future]

paulownia *pöl-ō'ni-ə*, *n* any tree of the Chinese and Japanese genus *Paulownia*, of the figwort family, with showy flowers. [Named after the Russian princess Anna *Pavlovna*]

Paul Pry *pöl prī*, *n* a person who pries into other people's business — from a character in John Poole's play (1825) so named.

Paul's-man *pöls'man*, *n* formerly, a lounger in the middle aisle of St Paul's, London.

paunce. See **pansy**.

paunch *pönch* or *pönsh*, *n* the belly; a protuberant belly; the first and largest stomach of a ruminant; a rope mat to prevent chafing (*naut*). — *vt* to eviscerate. — *adj* **paunch'y** big-bellied. [OFr *panche* (Fr *panse*), from L *pantex*, *panticis*]

pauper *pö'pər*, *n* a destitute person; a person not required to pay costs in a law suit; a person supported by charity or by some public provision (*hist*): — *fem* **pau'peress**. — *n* **pau'perism** the state of being a pauper. — *n* **pauperizā'tion** or **-s-**. — *vt* **pau'perize** or **-ise** to reduce to pauperism; to accustom to expect or depend on outside support. [L, poor]

pause[1] *pöz*, *n* intermission; a temporary stop; a short break; cessation caused by doubt; hesitation; a mark for suspending the voice (*prosody*); a continuance of a note or rest beyond its time, or a mark indicating this (*music*). — *vi* (*Shakesp vt reflexive*) to make a pause. — *vt* to cause to stop. — *adj* **paus'al**. — *adj* **pause'ful**. — *adv* **pause'fully**. — *adj* **pause'less**. — *adv* **pause'lessly**. — *n* **paus'er**. — *n* and *adj* **paus'ing**. — *adv* **paus'ingly**. — **give pause** to cause to hesitate. [Fr, from L *pausa*, from Gr *pausis*, from *pauein* to cause to cease]

pause[2] *pöz*, (*dialect*) *vt* to kick. [Origin unknown]

pavage. See under **pave**.

pavane *pav-än'* or **pavan** *pav'ən*, *n* a slow formal dance of Spanish origin, popular in Europe in the 16c and 17c; music for it, in 4-4 time. — Also **pav'en** or **pav'in**. [Fr *pavane*, or Sp or Ital *pavana*, prob from L *pāvō*, *-ōnis* peacock]

pave *pāv*, *vt* to cover with slabs or other close-set pieces, so as to form a level surface for walking on; to cover with anything close-set; to be such a covering for. — *n* (*US*) pavement. — *n* **pā'vage** a charge, or right to levy a charge, for paving streets. — *adj* **paved**. — *n* **pave'ment** a paved surface, or that with which it is paved; a footway by the side of a street (sometimes even when unpaved); a paved road or its surface (*NAm*); a floor-like surface; an underlying bed, *esp* of fireclay under coal. — *vt* to pave; to be a pavement for. — *adj* **pā'ven** paved. — *n* and *adj* **pā'ving**. — *n* **pā'viour** a person who lays paving stones; a machine for tamping down paving stones; a paving-stone. — Also **pā'ver** or (*NAm*) **pā'vior**. — **pavement artist** a person who seeks a living by drawing coloured pictures on the pavement; **pavement epithelium** epithelium in the form of a layer of flat cells; **pavement light** a window of glass blocks in the pavement to light a cellar; **pa'ving-stone** a slab of stone or concrete used in a pavement, etc. — **on the pavement** homeless; **pave the way for** to prepare the way for; to make easier; to help to bring on. [Fr *paver*, prob a back-formation from *pavement*, from L *pavīmentum*, from *pavīre* to beat hard; cognate with Gr *paiein* to beat]

pavé *pa-vā*, (*Fr*) *n* pavement; a setting of jewellery with the stones close together, covering the metal.

pavement, paven[1]. See under **pave**.

paven[2]. See **pavane**.

paver. See under **pave**.

pavid *pav'id*, *adj* timid. [L *pavidus* afraid, from *pavēre* to be frightened]

pavilion *pə-vil'yən*, *n* a tent, *esp* a large or luxurious one; a tent-like covering; a canopy (*obs*); a light building at a sports ground for players and spectators of a game; an ornamental or showy building (often turreted or domed) for pleasure purposes; a projecting section of a building, *usu* highly decorated and with a tent-like roof; a hospital block; an exhibition building; (in gem-cutting) the under-surface of a brilliant, opposite to the crown; the bell of a horn; the outer ear; a flag or ensign (*obs*). — *vt* to provide with pavilions; to cover, eg with a tent. — **pavil'ion-roof** a tent-like roof. — **Chinese pavilion** a set of bells hanging from a frame on a pole. [Fr *pavillon*, from L *pāpiliō*, *-ōnis* a butterfly, a tent]

pavin. See **pavane**.

paving. See under **pave**.

pavior, paviour. See under **pave**.

pavis or **pavise** *pav'is*, *n* a shield for the whole body. [OFr *pavais*, from Ital *pavese*, prob from *Pavia* in Italy]

pavlova *pav-lō'və*, *n* a type of sweet dish consisting of a meringue base topped with whipped cream and fruit (also with *cap*). [Named in honour of the Russian ballerina Anna *Pavlova*]

Pavlovian *pav-lō'vi-ən*, (*psychol* and *physiol*) *adj* relating to the work of the Russian physiologist, Ivan *Pavlov*, on conditioned reflexes; (of reactions, responses, etc) automatic, unthinking.

Pavo *pā'vō*, *n* the peacock genus; a southern constellation. — *n* **pavonazzo** (*pa-və-nat'sō*) a brightly coloured marble. — *n* **pavone** (*pə-vōn'*; *Spenser*) a peacock. — *adj* **pavō'nian** or **pavonine** (*pav'ən-īn*). [L *pāvō*, *-ōnis* peacock]

paw[1] *pö*, *n* a clawed foot; a hand, or handwriting (*facetious* or *derog*). — *vi* to draw the forefoot along the ground; to strike the ground with the forefoot; to strike out with the paw; to feel about or over anything, *esp* offensively. — *vt* to scrape, feel, handle, or strike with the forefoot or hand; to handle indecently, coarsely, or clumsily. [OFr *poe*, *powe*, prob Gmc; cf Du *poot*, Ger *Pfote*]

paw[2] *pö*, (*obs*) *interj* pah. — *adj* (also **paw'paw**) foul; obscene.

pawa. See **paua**.

pawaw. See **powwow**.

pawk *pök*, (*Scot*) *n* a trick. — *adv* **pawk'ily**. — *n* **pawk'iness**. — *adj* **pawk'y** drily or slyly humorous. [Origin unknown]

pawl *pöl*, *n* a catch engaging with the teeth of a ratchet wheel to prevent backward movement. [Origin obscure; poss connected with Du or Fr *pal*, L *pālus* stake]

pawn[1] *pön*, *n* something deposited as security for repayment or performance; the state of being pledged (as *in* or *at pawn*). — *vt* to give as security for repayment of borrowed money, *esp* to a pawnbroker; to pledge or stake. — *n* **pawnee'** a person who takes anything in pawn. — *n* **pawn'er** a person who gives a pawn or pledge as security for money borrowed. — **pawn'broker** a broker who lends money on pawns; **pawn'broking**; **pawn'shop** a shop of a pawnbroker; **pawn'ticket** a ticket marked with the name of the article, the amount advanced, etc, delivered to the pawner of anything. [OFr *pan*; cf Du *pand*; connection with L *pannus*, cloth, very doubtful]

pawn[2] *pön*, *n* a small chess piece of lowest rank and range; a humble tool or lightly valued agent (*fig*); an easily manipulated person. [OFr *paon* a foot-soldier, from LL *pedō*, *-ōnis*, from L *pēs*, *pedis* the foot]

pawn[3] *pön*, *n* a gallery or covered walk. [Cf Du *pand*]

pawn[4], **pown** or **powin** *pown*, (chiefly *Scot*) *n* a peacock. [OFr *poun*, Fr *paon*, from L *pāvō*, *-ōnis*]

pawn[5]. See **pan**[2].

pawnce. See **pansy**.

Pawnee *pö'nē* or *-nē'*, *n* a member of a tribe of N American Indians, *orig* from Nebraska, etc, afterwards settling in Oklahoma; their language. — Also *adj*.

pawnee[1] *pö'nē*. See under **brandy**.

pawnee[2], **pawner**, **pawnshop**, etc. See under **pawn**[1].

pawpaw[1] *pö'pö* or **pawpaw** *pə-pö'*, *n* a tree (*Asimina triloba*) of the custard-apple family, or its fruit, native to the USA; the papaya. [Prob variant of **papaya**]

pawpaw[2]. See under **paw**[2].

PAX *abbrev*: Private Automatic Exchange.

pax[1] *paks*, *n* the kiss of peace; an osculatory. — *interj* (*colloq*) (let's call a) truce. — **pax'-board** or **pax'-brede** (ie board) an osculatory. [L *pāx* peace]

pax[2] *paks*, (*L*) *n* peace. — **pax vobiscum** (*vo-bis'kəm*, *vō-*, or *wō-bēs'kŏŏm*) peace be with you.

paxiuba *päsh-ē-ōō'bə*, *n* a Brazilian palm (*Iriartea exorrhiza*) with stilt-roots. [Port, from Tupí]

paxwax *paks'waks*, *n* the strong tendon in an animal's neck. [Originally *fax-wax*, from OE (Anglian) *fæx* (WSax *feax*) hair, and *weaxan* to grow]

pay[1] *pā*, *vt* to satisfy, gratify (*obs*); to give what is due (in satisfaction of a debt, in exchange, in compensation or in remuneration, etc) to (the person, etc to whom it is owed); to give (money, etc) in satisfaction of a debt, in exchange, compensation, remuneration, etc; to settle or discharge (a claim, bill, debt, etc); to hand over money, etc, for; (of a sum of money, etc) to be or yield satisfactory remuneration or compensation for, or enough to discharge; to yield (a certain sum, profit, etc); to be profitable to, to benefit; to render, confer (attention, heed, court, a visit, etc); to thrash (*Shakesp* and *dialect*); (of a rope) to allow or cause to run out (*naut*). — *vi* to hand over money or other equivalent, or compensation, etc (with *for*); to afford to make payment, or constitute an equivalent or means of making payment (with *for*); to be worth one's trouble; to be profitable; to suffer or be punished (with *for*); to be the subject of payment: — *pr p* **pay'ing**; *pa t* and *pa p* **paid**, or in the nautical sense **payed** (*pād*). — *n* satisfaction (*obs*); money given for service; salary, wages; receipt of wages, etc, service for wages, etc, hire or paid employment (*esp* for an evil purpose); payment or time of payment; remunerative yield of mineral. — *adj* **paid** see separate article. — *adj* **pay'able** that may or should be paid; due; profitable. — *n* **payee'** someone to whom money is paid. — *n* **pay'er**. — *n* and *adj* **pay'ing**. — *n* **pay'ment** the act of paying; the discharge of a debt by money or its equivalent in value; that which is paid; recompense; reward; punishment. — **pay-as-you-earn'** a method of income-tax collection in which the tax is paid by deduction from earnings before they are received (*abbrev* **PAYE**); **payback** see **pay back** below; **pay bed** a bed, *specif* in a National Health Service hospital, available to a patient who pays for its use (**private pay bed** one available to a patient who pays for its use and for his or her own treatment; cf **amenity bed**); **pay'-bill** or **pay'-sheet** a statement of money to be paid to workmen, etc; **pay'-box** or **pay'-desk** a box or desk at which a customer pays; **pay'-day** a regular day for payment, eg of wages; **pay'-dirt** or **pay-grav'el** gravel or sand containing enough gold to be worth working (**pay-dirt** also *fig*); **pay'fone** same as **payphone**; **paying guest** (*euphem*) a lodger; **pay'-list** or **pay'-roll** a list of people entitled to receive pay, with the amounts due to each; (**payroll**) the money for paying wages; **pay'-load** that part of the cargo of an aeroplane or other conveyance for which revenue is obtained; the part of a rocket's equipment that is to fulfil the purpose of the rocket, such as a warhead, or apparatus for obtaining information; **pay'master** the master who pays; the official in an organization, government, etc who pays out money; **Paymaster General** the minister at the head of a department of the Treasury that makes payments on behalf of government departments; in the navy, an officer in charge of the bureau dealing with payments, clothing, etc (*US*); formerly also a similar officer in the army (*US*); **pay'ment card** a credit card; **pay'-off** (time of) payment — reward or punishment; outcome; a particularly useful or desirable result; dénouement; **pay'-office** the place where payments are made; **pay-out** see **pay out** below; **pay'-packet** an envelope containing a person's wages; wages; **pay'phone** a coin- or card-operated public telephone; **payroll** see **pay-list** above; **payroll giving** contributions to charity which are deducted from one's wages and paid by one's employer directly to the charity concerned; **pay'slip** a note to a worker (giving an analysis) of the sum paid in wages; **pay'-station** (*US*) a telephone call-box. — **in the pay of** receiving payment in return for services, used *esp* in a sinister sense; **pay back** to pay in return (a debt); to give tit for tat (*n* **pay'back**); **pay cash** to pay for something at the time of the transaction, ie not using credit terms; **pay down** to pay (eg a first instalment) in cash on the spot; **pay for** to make amends for; to suffer for; to bear the expense of; **pay in** to contribute to a fund; to deposit money in a bank account; **pay off** to pay in full and discharge (a debt); to take revenge upon; to requite; to fall away to leeward (*naut*); to yield good results, justify itself (see also **pay-off** above); **pay one's** (or **its**) **way** to have or bring enough to pay expenses; to compensate adequately for initial outlay; **pay out** to release (a rope, etc) gradually, to feed or run out; to disburse (*n* **pay'out**); to punish deservedly; **pay round** to turn the ship's head; **pay the piper** see under **pipe**[1]; **pay through the nose** to pay more than the fair price, to pay dearly; **pay up** to pay in full; to pay arrears; to accept the necessity and pay; to pay on demand. [Fr *payer*, from L *pācāre* to appease; cf *pāx* peace]

pay[2] *pā*, (*naut*) *vt* to smear (a wooden boat) with tar, etc as waterproofing: — *pa t* and *pa p* **payed**. [OFr *peier*, from L *picāre* to pitch]

PAYE. See **pay-as-you-earn** under **pay**[1].

paynim *pā'nim*, (*obs*) *n* heathendom; a heathen; a non-Christian, *esp* a Muslim. — Also *adj*. — Also **pai'nim** or **pā'nim** (*Milton*). — *n* **pay'nimry** heathendom. [OFr *paienisme* paganism, from L *pāgānismus*, from *pāgānus* a pagan]

pay-off, **pay-office**. See under **pay**[1].

payola *pā-ō'lə*, *n* a secret payment or bribe to secure a favour, *esp* the promotion of a commercial product by a disc-jockey; the practice of making or receiving payments of this kind. [Facetiously coined from **pay**[1] and Victr*ola*, a make of gramophone, or pian*ola*]

pay-out ... to ... **pay-roll**. See under **pay**[1].

pays *pā-ē*, (*Fr*) *n* country. — **les Pays Bas** (*lā pā-ē bä*) the Low Countries, the Netherlands.

paysage *pā-ē-zäzh'*, *n* a landscape, a landscape painting (*obs* for a time then reborrowed). — *n* **paysagist** (*pā'zə-jist*) a landscape-painter. [Fr]

paysd *pāzd*, (*Spenser*) for **peised** (see **peise**) or **poised** (see **poise**[1]).

payslip, pay-station. See under **pay**[1].

pazazz or **pazzazz**. See **pizzazz**.

PB *abbrev*: Pharmacopoeia Britannica; Plymouth Brethren.

Pb (*chem*) *symbol*: lead.

pbuh *abbrev*: peace be upon him (always used by Muslims when mentioning the name of Mohammed).

PBX (*telecomm*) *abbrev*: private branch exchange, a private telephone switching apparatus which routes calls between extensions and the public telephone network, and internally between extensions.

PC *abbrev*: personal computer; Police Constable; Political Correctness; Politically Correct; Privy Councillor.

pc *abbrev*: per cent; personal computer; postcard.

PCAS *abbrev*: Polytechnics Central Admissions System.

PCB *abbrev*: polychlorinated biphenyl, any of several compounds with various industrial applications, regarded as environmental pollutants.

PCC *abbrev*: parochial church council; Press Complaints Commission.

pce *abbrev*: piece.

PCM *abbrev*: pulse code modulation.

pcm *abbrev*: per calender month.

PCN *abbrev*: personal communications network, a network for mobile telephone users.

PCP *abbrev*: pentachlorophenol, a water-insoluble fungicide widely regarded as an environmental pollutant; ®phencyclidine, a depressant drug taken illegally as a hallucinogen (also called (*colloq*) **angel dust**); Pneumocystis carinii pneumonia, a major cause of death among Aids patients.

PCR *abbrev*: politically correct retailing; polymerase chain reaction.

PCS *abbrev*: Principal Clerk of Session.

pct (*esp NAm*) *abbrev*: percent.

pd abbrev: paid.

pd (*chem*) *symbol*: palladium.

PDI *abbrev*: pre-delivery inspection.

pdq *abbrev*: (*colloq*) pretty damn quick, hence as soon as possible.

PDSA *abbrev*: People's Dispensary for Sick Animals.

PE *abbrev*: Peru (IVR); physical education; Protestant Episcopal.

p/e *abbrev*: price-earnings ratio.

pea[1] *pē*, *n* the nutritious seed of the papilionaceous climbing plants *Pisum sativum* (garden pea) and *Pisum arvense* (field pea); the plant itself (also **pea'-plant**); extended to various similar seeds and plants (*esp* of the genus Lathyrus) and to various rounded objects, eg roe of salmon and some other fish, very small pieces of coal or small rounded stones: — *pl* **peas**. — **pea'berry** a small round coffee seed, growing singly; **peacod** see under **pease**[1]; **pea'-crab** a little round crab (*Pinnotheres*) that lives symbiotically in lamellibranch shells; **pea gravel**. — *n* and *adj* **pea'-green** (or *-grēn'*) yellowish-green, like the colour of soup made from split peas; bright green like fresh peas. — **pea'-iron** limonite in little round nodules; **pea'pod** the seed case of a pea; **pea'-ri'fle** a rifle throwing a very small bullet; **peas'cod** see **peasecod** under **pease**[1]; **pea shingle**; **pea'shooter** a small tube for blowing peas through, used as a toy weapon; **pea-soup, pea-souper, pea-soupy** see **pease-soup** under **pease**[1]. — **pea'-stone** pisolite; **pea-straw** see **pease-straw** under **pease**[1]; **pea'-trainer** an erection for pea-plants to climb on; **pea-vin'er** a machine that picks, washes and grades peas. — **Egyptian pea** the chick-pea; **split peas** peas stripped of their membranous covering, dried and halved; **Sturt's desert pea** see under **desert**. [Singular formed from **pease**[1] which was mistaken for a plural]

pea[2] *pē*, *n* an *obs* term for a **pea'fowl**, a male or female peacock. — **pea'-chick** a young peafowl; **pea'-hen** the female of the peacock. [OE *pēa* (*pāwa*), from L *pāvō*]

peace *pēs*, *n* a state of quiet; freedom from disturbance; freedom from war; cessation of war; a treaty that ends a war; freedom from contention; ease of mind or conscience; tranquillity; quiet; stillness; silence. — *vi* (*Shakesp*) to be silent — passing in the *imperative* into *interj* silence; be silent; hist. — *adj* **peace'able** disposed to peace; peaceful. — *n* **peace'ableness**. — *adv* **peace'ably**. — *adj* **peace'ful** enjoying peace; tending towards or favouring peace; inclined to peace; belonging to time of peace; consistent with peace; tranquil; calm; serene. — *adv* **peace'fully**. — *n* **peace'fulness**. — *adj* **peace'less**. — *n* **peace'lessness**. — *n* **peace'nik** a pacifist, *esp* in a derogatory sense. — **peace'-breaker** a person who breaks or disturbs the peace; **Peace Corps** (in the USA) a government agency that sends volunteers to developing countries to help with agricultural, technological and educational schemes; **peace dividend** money left over from a government's defence budget as a result of negotiated arms reduction policies, available for peaceable (*esp* social) use; the fact of having such surplus money; **peace drug** or **pill** (*colloq*) a hallucinogen (PCP); **peace establishment** the reduced military strength maintained in time of peace; **peace'-keeper**. — *adj* **peace'-keeping** (**peace-keeping force** a military force sent into an area with the task of preventing fighting between opposing factions). — **peace'maker** a person who makes or produces peace; a person who reconciles enemies; a revolver (*old facetious*); **peace'making**; **peace'-monger** a peacemaker from the point of view of those who think him or her a sentimental busybody; **peace'-off'ering** (among the Jews) a thank-offering to God; a gift offered towards reconciliation, propitiation, or deprecation; **peace'-off'icer** an officer whose duty it is to preserve the peace; a police-officer. — *adj* **peace'-part'ed** (*Shakesp*) dismissed from the world in peace. — **peace'-par'ty** a political party advocating the making or the preservation of peace; **peace pill** see **peace drug** above; **peace'-pipe** the calumet; **peace'time** time when there is no war. — *adj* of peacetime. — **peace'-warrant** a warrant of arrest issued by a Justice of the Peace. — **at peace** in a state of peace; not at war; **breach of the peace** see under **breach**; **hold one's peace** to remain silent; **in peace** in enjoyment of peace; **keep the peace** to refrain from disturbing the public peace; to refrain from, or to prevent, contention; **kiss of peace** see under **kiss**; **letter of peace** see **pacifical** under **pacify**; **make one's peace with** to reconcile or to be reconciled with; **make peace** to end a war; **peace of God** the protection from acts of private warfare formerly offered by the Church to consecrated persons and places, and on Sundays and holy days; **swear the peace** to take oath before a magistrate that a certain person ought to be put under bond to keep the peace; **the king's** or **queen's peace** see under **king**. [OFr *pais* (Fr *paix*) from L *pāx*, *pācis* peace]

peach[1] *pēch*, *vt* (*Shakesp*) to accuse, inform against, betray. — *vi* (with *on*) to betray one's accomplice; to become an informer. — *n* **peach'er**. [Aphetic form of **appeach**]

peach[2] *pēch*, *n* a sweet, juicy, velvety-skinned stone-fruit; the tree (*Prunus*, or *Amygdalus*, *persica*) bearing it, closely related to the almond; extended to other fruits and fruit-trees, such as the quandong; peach-brandy (*US*); anything regarded as a very choice example of its kind, *esp* a girl (*slang*; *US* also **peacherino** *-ə-rē'nō*; *pl* **-nos**); a yellow slightly tinged with red. — *adj* of the peach; of the colour of a peach. — *adj* **peach'y** coloured or tasting somewhat of peach; very good, excellent (*slang*). — **peach'-bloom'** the powdery bloom on a peach; a similar appearance on the face, on pottery, etc; a peach flower (also **peach'-bloss'om**); its pinkish colour; a moth with wings so coloured (*Thyatira batis*). — Also *adj*. — **peach'-blow** a pinkish glaze on porcelain, *esp* Chinese porcelain. — Also *adj*. — **peach'-brand'y** a spirit distilled from the fermented juice of the peach. — *adj* **peach'-coloured** of the colour of a ripe peach (yellowish, tinged with red) or of peach-blossom (pink). — **peach Melba** a dish named in honour of the Australian soprano Dame Nellie *Melba*, consisting of peach halves served with ice-cream and *usu* a raspberry sauce; **peach'-palm** the pupunha, a South American palm (*Bactris* or *Guilielma*) with an edible fruit like a peach in appearance; **peach'-stone**; **peach'-tree**; **peach'-water** a flavouring extract from peach-leaves; **peach'-wood** the wood of the peach-tree; Nicaragua wood (Caesalpinia); **peach'-yell'ows** a virus disease that turns peach-leaves yellow and kills the tree. [OFr *pesche* (Fr *pêche*, Ital *persica*, *pesca*), from L *Persicum* (*mālum*) the Persian (apple); its native country is unknown]

pea-chick. See under **pea**[2].

pea-coat. Same as **pea-jacket**.

peacock *pē'kok*, *n* a genus (Pavo) of large birds of the pheasant kind, consisting of the common peacock (*Pavo cristatus*) and the Javan (*Pavo muticus*), noted for their showy plumage, *esp*, in the former, the deep iridescent greenish blue in the neck and tail-coverts; the male of either species; a vain person; peacock-blue (also *adj*); a peacock butterfly. — *vt* to make like a peacock; to pick the best parts out of (*Austr*). — *vi* to strut about or behave like a peacock; to acquire the choicest pieces of land (ie near water) (*Austr*). — *n* **peacock'ery** vain ostentation. — *adj* **pea'cockish**. — *adj* **pea'cock-like**. — *adj* **pea'cocky**. — **pea'cock-blue'** the deep greenish blue of the peacock's neck. — Also *adj*. — **peacock butterfly** a butterfly (*Inachis io*) with wingspots like those of the peacock's train; **pea'cock-copp'er** copper-pyrites, from the colours of its tarnish; **pea'cock-fish** a variegated Mediterranean wrasse; **pea'-cock-flower** a name for various species of Poinciana (flamboyant tree, Barbados pride); **pea'cock-ore'** bornite; copper-pyrites; **pea'cock-pheas'ant** an Asiatic genus (*Polyplectron*) related to the peacocks and Argus pheasants; **pea'cock-stone** a jeweller's name for the cartilaginous ligament of some molluscs; **pea'cock-throne'** the throne of the kings of Delhi, carried off to Persia in 1739. [**pea**[2] and **cock**]

pea-crab. See under **pea**[1].

peafowl. See under **pea**[2].

peag *pēg* or **peak** *pēk*, *n* North American Indian shell-money. [Massachusetts *piak*]

pea-hen. See under **pea**[2].

pea-jacket *pē'-jak'it*, *n* a sailor's coarse thick overcoat. — Also **pea'-coat**. [Du *pîe* (now *pij*) coat of coarse stuff, and **jacket** or **coat**]

peak[1] *pēk*, *n* a point; the pointed end or highest point of anything; the top of a mountain, *esp* when sharp; a summit; the highest point of a curve, etc on a graph; any point or period of maximum activity, intensity, performance, skill, etc; a sharp projection; the projecting front of a cap or (formerly) of a widow's hood; a projecting point of hair on the forehead; a pointed beard; the upper outer corner of a sail extended by a gaff or yard (*naut*); the upper end of a gaff (*naut*). — *adj* maximum; of a maximum. — *vi* to rise in a peak; to reach the height of one's powers, popularity, etc; (of prices, etc) to reach a highest point or level (sometimes with *out*). — *vt* (*naut*) to tilt up. — *adj* **peaked** having a peak or peaks. — *adj* **peak'y** having a peak or peaks; like a peak. — **peak'-load** the maximum instantaneous demand of electricity, or load on a power-station. — **off-peak** at, of or relating to a regular period of relatively low customer demand, eg for electricity or rail travel; **peak (viewing** or **listening) hours** or **time** the period in the day when the maximum number of people are watching television (approximately 5.00 pm–10.00 pm) or listening to the radio. [Found from the 16th century (*peked* in the 15th); appar connected with **pike**[1]]

peak[2] *pēk*, *vi* to sneak or slink about (*Shakesp*); to mope (*obs*); to droop, to look thin or sickly. — *adj* **peaked**, **peak'ing** or **peak'y** having a pinched or sickly look, sharp-featured. [Origin unknown]

peak[3]. See **peag**.

peal[1] *pēl*, *n* a loud sound; a number of loud sounds one after another; a set of bells tuned to each other; a chime or carillon; the changes rung upon a set of bells. — *vi* to resound in peals; to appeal (*Spenser*). — *vt* to give forth in peals; to assail with din (*Milton*). [Appar aphetic for **appeal**]

peal[2] or **peel** *pēl*, (*dialect*) *n* a grilse; a young sea-trout. [Origin unknown]

pean[1] *pēn*, *n* a heraldic fur, differing from ermine only in the ground being sable and the spots or. [Perhaps OFr *pene*, *panne*]

pean[2]. Same as **paean** (*US*).

pean[3]. Same as **peen**.

peanut *pē'nut*, *n* the monkey-nut or groundnut (*Arachis*); (in *pl*) something very trifling or insignificant, *esp* a paltry sum of money, chickenfeed (*colloq*). — **peanut butter** a paste made from ground roasted peanuts; **peanut oil** oil expressed from peanuts. [**pea**[1] and **nut**]

pear *pār*, *n* a fruit, a pome tapering towards the stalk and bulged at the end; the tree (*Pyrus communis*) of the apple genus which bears it; extended to various fruits (such as **alligator-pear**, **anchovy-pear**, **prickly-pear**, etc); (in gem-cutting) a pear-shaped brilliant. — **pear'-drop** a pear-shaped pendant; a sweet shaped and flavoured like a pear; **pear'monger** a seller of pears; **pear'-push** or **pear'-switch** an electric push-button in a hanging pear-shaped bob. — *adj* **pear'-shaped** tapering towards one end and bulged at the other; in the shape of a pear; (of a vocal quality) mellow, resonant, non-nasal. — **pear'-tree**. — **go pear-shaped** (*colloq*) to put on weight around the hips, waist or bottom; to go awry or out of kilter. [OE *pere*, *peru*, from LL *pira*, from L *pirum* (wrongly *pyrum*) pear]

pearce and **peare**. Spenserian spellings of **pierce** and **peer**.

pearl[1] *pûrl*, *n* a typically round, milky-white concretion of nacre formed in certain species of oyster and other shellfish, around a foreign body or otherwise, prized as a gem; nacre, mother of pearl; a paragon or prized example; a lustrous globule; a granule; a tubercle of an antler burr; cataract of the eye; a five-point type (about 15 lines to the inch) (*printing*). — *adj* made of or like pearl; granulated; (of an electric light bulb) made from frosted, rather than clear, glass as a precaution against glare. — *vt* to set or adorn with pearls or pearly drops; to make pearly; to make into small round grains. — *vi* to take a rounded form; to become like pearls; to fish for pearls. — *adj* **pearled**. — *n* **pearl'er** a pearl-fisher or a pearl-fisher's boat. — *n* **pearl'iness**. — *n* and *adj* **pearl'ing**. — *adj* **pearl'ized** or **-ised** treated so as to give a pearly or lustrous surface. — *adj* **pearl'y** like pearl, nacreous; rich in pearls. — *n* (in *pl*) pearl-buttons; (in *pl*) costermongers' clothes covered with pearl-buttons; a costermonger, or a member of his family, wearing such clothes: — *pl* **pearl'ies**. — **pearl'-ash'** partly purified potassium carbonate; **pearl'-bar'ley** see under **barley**[1]; **pearl'-butt'on** a mother-of-pearl button; **pearl disease** bovine tuberculosis; **pearl'-div'er** someone who dives for pearls; **pearl'-essence** a silvery preparation from fish scales used in making artificial pearls; **pearl'-eye** cataract. — *adj* **pearl'-eyed**. — **pearl'-fisher** someone who fishes for pearls; **pearl'-fishery**; **pearl'-fishing**; **pearl'-gray'** or **pearl'-grey'** a pale grey. — Also *adj*. — **pearl'-mill'et** the bulrush millet or spiked millet (*Pennisetum typhoideum*), a grain much grown in India; **pearl'-muss'el** a freshwater mussel (*Unio margaritifera*) that yields pearls; **pearl'-oys'ter** any oyster that produces pearls, *esp Avicula* (or *Meleagrina*) *margaritifera*; **pearl'-pow'der** a cosmetic of basic bismuth nitrate or of bismuth oxychloride; **pearl'-sā'go** sago in round granules; **pearl'-shell** mother-of-pearl; a pearly or pearl-bearing shell; **pearl'-sheller**; **pearl'-shelling**; **pearl'-spar** a pearly-lustred pale dolomite; **pearl'-stone** perlite; **pearl'-tapiō'ca** tapioca granulated and graded according to its size; a potato-starch imitation; **pearl'-white** material made from fish-scales, used in making artificial pearls; basic nitrate of bismuth, used in medicine and as a cosmetic; bismuth trichloride, used as a pigment; lithopone; calcium sulphate; **pearl'wort** a member of a genus (*Sagina*) of small plants related to chickweed; **pearly gates** (from the Bible; Rev 21) entrance to heaven; **pearly king** a costermonger whose costume is considered the most splendidly decorated with pearl-buttons: — *fem* **pearly queen**; **pearly nautilus** see under **nautilus.** — **cultured pearl** a true pearl formed by artificial means, eg by planting a piece of mother-of-pearl wrapped in oyster epidermis in the body of an oyster; **false, imitation** or **simulated pearl** an imitation pearl, eg a glass bulb coated with pearl essence. [Fr *perle*, prob from dimin of L *perna* leg, leg-of-mutton-shaped; cf Ital dialect *perna* pearl, Ital *pernocchia* pearl-oyster]

pearl[2] *pûrl*, *n* a small loop on the edge of lace, ribbon, etc; (in knitting) purl. — *vt* to purl. — *n* **pearl'ing** or **pearl'in** (*Scot*) lace of silk or of thread; (in *pl*) edgings of such lace or clothes trimmed with it. — **pearl'-edge** an edging of small loops. [Cf **purl**[3]]

Pearl Harbour *pûrl här'bər*, *n* (*fig*) a sudden and devastating attack. — *vt* (*rare*) to mount a surprise attack of great force. [*Pearl Harbor*, US naval base near Honolulu, attacked by the Japanese air force on 7 December 1941]

pearlies. See under **pearl**[1].

pearlin. See under **pearl**[2].

pearlite *pûr'līt*, *n* a constituent of steel composed of alternate plates of ferrite and cementite. — *adj* **pearlit'ic**. [**pearl**[1]]

pearly. See under **pearl**[1].

pearmain *pār'mān*, *n* a variety of apple. [Appar OFr *parmain, permain*]

pearst. Spenserian spelling of **pierced** (see under **pierce**).

peart *pērt*, (*dialect*) *adj* lively; saucy; in good health and spirits. — Also (*obs*) **piert**. — *adv* **peart'ly**. [**pert**]

peasant *pez'ənt*, *n* a member of a lowly class of small-holders (*hist*); a person who works on the land; a person who lives in the country, a rustic (*colloq*); an ignorant or uncultured person (*derog*). — *adj* of or relating to peasants, rustic, rural; rude. — *n* **peas'antry** peasants as a class; the condition or quality of a peasant. — *adj* **peas'anty** in the style of a peasant. — **peasant proprietor** a peasant who owns and works his own farm; **Peasants' Revolt** Wat Tyler's rising of 1381; **Peasants' War** a popular insurrection in Germany, in 1525. [OFr *paisant* (Fr *paysan*), from *pays*, from assumed L *pāgēnsis*, from *pāgus* a district]

pease[1] *pēz*, *n* (*archaic*) a pea or pea-plant (*pl* **pease**; *old pl* **peason** *pēz'ən*), now almost wholly superseded by the new singular **pea** and plural **peas** (see **pea**[1]) except in a collective sense. — **pease'-bann'ock** a bannock made of pease-meal; **pease'-blossom**; **pease'-brose'** brose made of pease-meal; **pease'cod, peas'cod** or **pea'cod** the pod of the pea. — *adj* **pease'cod-bell'ied** (of a doublet) peaked downwards in front. — **pease'cod-cuirass'** a cuirass shaped like the peasecod-bellied doublet; **pease'-meal, pease'-porr'idge** or **pease'-pudd'ing** meal, porridge, or pudding made from pease; **pease'-soup** or **pea'-soup** soup made from pease; a thick yellow heavy-smelling fog (also **pea'-soup'er**). — *adj* **pea'-soup'y**. — **pease'-straw** or **pea'-straw** the stems and leaves of the pea-plant after the peas have been picked. [ME *pēse*, pl *pēsen*, from OE *pise*, pl *pisan*, from LL *pisa*, L *pisum*, from Gr *pison* or *pisos*]

pease[2]. See **peise**.

peaseweep *pēz'wēp*. See **peewit**.

peason. The old *pl* of **pease**[1] (qv).

peat[1] *pēt*, *n* a shaped block dug from a bog and dried or to be dried for fuel; the generally brown or nearly black altered vegetable matter (chiefly bog-moss) found in bogs, from which such blocks are cut. — *n* **peat'ary**, **peat'ery**, **pēt'ary**, **peat'-bank**, **peat'-bed**, **peat'-bog**, **peat'-land**, **peat'-moor** or **peat'-moss** a region, bog, moor, etc, covered with peat; a place from which peat is dug. — *adj* **peat'y** like, of the nature of, abounding in, or composed of peat; smoky in flavour, like whiskies distilled using water from areas rich in peat, or in the production of which peat has been used as a fuel. — **peat'-caster** a person who digs peats and throws them on the bank to dry; **peat'-casting**; **peat'-creel** a basket for carrying peats; **peat'-hag** or **peat'-hagg** a hag in a peat-bog (see **hag**[3]); **peat'-hole**; **peat'man** a carter or seller of peats; **peat'-reek'** the smoke of peat, believed by some to add a special flavour to whisky; highland whisky; **peat'-reek'er** ornamental apparatus for producing the smell of peat-smoke; **peat'-smoke'**; **peat'-spade** a spade having a side wing at right angles for cutting peat in rectangular blocks; **peat'-stack'** a stack of peats, drying or stored. [From the 13c in SE Scotland in Anglo-Latin as *peta* a peat; possibly of British origin; cf **piece**]

peat[2] *pēt*, (*obs*) *n* an endearment applied to a woman, girl, friend or favourite; an advocate favoured by a judge (*Scot*). — *n* **peat'ship** (*Scott*). [Origin obscure]

peau de soie *pō-də-swä'*, *n* a type of smooth silk or rayon fabric. [Fr, literally skin of silk]

peavey or **peavy** *pē'vi*, (*US*) *n* a lumberman's spiked and hooked lever. [Joseph *Peavey*, its inventor]

peaze. See **peise**.

peba *pē'bə*, *n* a South American armadillo. [Tupí]

pebble *peb'l*, *n* a small roundish stone, *esp* worn down by water; transparent and colourless rock-crystal; a lens made of it; a semi-precious agate; a grained appearance on leather, as if pressed by pebbles; a large size of gunpowder. — *adj* of pebble. — *vt* to stone or pelt; to cover with pebbles; to impart pebble to (leather). — *adj* **pebb'led**. — *n* **pebb'ling**. — *adj* **pebb'ly** full of pebbles. — **pebble-bed reactor** (*nuc eng*) a reactor with a cylindrical core into which spherical fuel pellets are inserted; **pebb'ledash** a method of coating exterior walls with small pebbles set into the mortar; this coating. — *vt* to treat or coat with pebbledash. — **pebb'le-glasses** (often *facetious*) spectacles with very thick lenses; **pebb'le-pow'der** gunpowder in large cubical grains; **pebb'le-stone** a pebble; **pebb'le-ware** a fine pottery of mixed coloured clays. [OE *papol(-stān)*, a pebble(-stone)]

pébrine *pā-brēn'*, *n* a destructive protozoan disease of silkworms. [Fr]

PEC *abbrev*: photoelectric cell. — Also *n* **pec** (*pek*).

pec *pek*, *n colloq* short form for a pectoral muscle (*usu* in *pl*).

pecan *pi-kan'*, *n* a North American hickory (also **pecan'-tree**); its edible smooth-shelled nut (also **pecan'-nut'**). [N Amer Indian name; cf Cree *pakan*]

peccable *pek'ə-bl*, *adj* liable to sin. — *n* **peccabil'ity**. — *n* **pecc'ancy** sinfulness; transgression. — *adj* **pecc'ant** sinning; offending; morbid, diseased or disease-producing (*med*). — *adv* **pecc'antly**. [L *peccāre*, *-ātum* to sin]

peccadillo *pek-ə-dil'ō*, *n* a trifling fault, a small misdemeanour: — *pl* **peccadill'os** or **peccadill'oes**. [Sp *pecadillo*, dimin of *pecado*, from L *peccātum* a sin]

peccancy, **peccant**, etc. See under **peccable**.

peccary *pek'ə-ri*, *n* either of two species of pig-like South American animals. [Carib *pakira*]

peccavi *pek-ä'vē*, *n* an admission of guilt or sin: — *pl* **pecca'vis**. [L *peccavi* I have sinned]

pech or **pegh** *pehh*, (*Scot*) *vi* to pant. — *n* a pant. [Imit]

Pecht or **Peght** *pehht*, (*Scot*) *n* a Pict. [OE (Anglian) *Pehtas* (WSax *Peohtas*) Picts]

peck[1] *pek*, *n* formerly, a measure of capacity for dry goods, 2 gallons, or one quarter of a bushel; a measuring vessel holding this quantity; an indefinitely great amount (eg *a peck of troubles*). [ME *pekke*, *pek*, from OFr *pek* generally a horse's feed of oats; origin unknown]

peck[2] *pek*, *vt* to strike or pick up with the point of the beak or other sharp instrument; to make (a hole, etc), render or cause to be (damaged, pierced, etc) by a quick movement of the beak, etc; to eat sparingly or with affectation of daintiness, or (*slang*) to eat in general; to kiss in a quick or cursory manner or movement. — *vi* to strike or feed with the beak or in a similar manner; to eat daintily or sparingly (with *at*); to nit-pick or quibble (with *at*); to nag or criticize (with *at*). — *n* an act of pecking; a hole made by pecking; a quick or cursory kiss; food (*slang*). — *n* **peck'er** that which pecks; a woodpecker; a kind of hoe; a part with an up-and-down movement in a telegraph instrument; spirit, resolve, humour (as if *orig* beak, nose, as in *keep your pecker up*; *slang*); a penis (*slang, orig US*). — *n* **peck'ing**. — *adj* **peck'ish** somewhat hungry (*colloq*); irritable (*US slang*). — *n* **peck'ishness**. — **peck'erwood** (*US*) a woodpecker; **pecking order** or **peck order** a social order among poultry (or other birds) according to which any bird may peck a less important bird but must submit to being pecked by a more important one; order of prestige or power in a human social group; order of importance or prevalence. [Appar a form of **pick**[1]]

peck[3] *pek*, *vt* (or *Shakesp* **pecke**) to pitch; to jerk. — *vi* to incline; to stumble, *esp* of a horse by failing to put the foot down flat. — *n* **peck'ing** stone-throwing. [A form of **pitch**[2], cf **pick**[2]]

Pecksniffian *pek-snif'i-ən, adj* like, or of, the hypocrite *Pecksniff* in Dickens's novel *Martin Chuzzlewit*.

Pecora *pek'ə-rə, n pl* the Cotylophora, or ruminants other than camels and chevrotains. [L pl of *pecus, -oris* cattle]

pecten *pek'tən, n* a comb-like structure of various kinds, eg in a bird's or reptile's eye; the pubic bone; a tactile organ in scorpions; a member of the scallop genus (*Pecten*) of molluscs, with a ribbed shell: — *pl* **pec'tines** (*-tin-ēz*). — *adj* **pectinaceous** (*-ā'shəs*) like the scallops. — *adj* **pec'tinal** of a comb; comb-like; having bones like the teeth of a comb. — *adj* **pec'tinate** or **pec'tinated** toothed like a comb; having narrow parallel segments or lobes; like the teeth of a comb. — *adv* **pec'tinately**. — *n* **pectinā'tion** the state of being pectinated; a comb-like structure. — *adj* **pectin'eal** of the pubic bone; comb-like. — *adj* **pec'tinibranchiate** (*-brangk-i-āt*) having comb-like gills. [L *pecten, -inis* a comb]

pectic *pek'tik, adj* of, relating to, or derived from pectin. — *n* **pec'tin** a mixture of carbohydrates found in the cell-walls of fruits, used for the setting of jams and jellies. — *n* **pectīzā'tion** or **-s-**. — *vt* and *vi* **pec'tize** or **-ise** to congeal. — *n* **pec'tōse** a pectin-yielding substance contained in the fleshy pulp of unripe fruit. — **pectic acid** an insoluble substance (of several varieties) formed by hydrolysis of pectins. [Gr *pēktikos* congealing, from *pēgnynai* to fix]

pectinaceous, pectinal, pectinate, etc, **pectination, pectineal, pectines**, etc. See under **pecten**.

pectisation, pectise, pectization, pectize. See under **pectic**.

pectolite *pek'tə-līt, n* a zeolite-like monoclinic acid, calcium sodium silicate. [Gr *pēktos* congealed, and *lithos* stone]

pectoral *pek'tə-rəl, adj* of, for, on, or near the breast or chest; coming from the heart or inner feeling (*fig*). — *n* armour for the breast of a person or a horse; an ornament worn on the breast, *esp* the breastplate worn by the ancient Jewish high-priest, and the square of gold, embroidery, etc, formerly worn on the breast over the chasuble by bishops during mass; a chest-protector; a medicine for the chest; a pectoral cross; a pectoral fin; either of the two muscles (*pectoralis major* and *pectoralis minor*) situated on either side of the top half of the chest and responsible for certain arm and shoulder movements (*colloq* short form **pec**). — *adv* **pec'torally**. — *n* **pectoril'oquy** (L *loquī* to talk) the sound of a patient's voice heard through the stethoscope when applied to the chest in certain morbid conditions of the lungs. — **pectoral cross** a gold cross worn on the breast by bishops, etc; **pectoral fins** the anterior paired fins of fishes; **pectoral girdle** the shoulder-girdle, consisting of shoulder-blade and collar-bone (and coracoid in vertebrates other than mammals); **pectoral theology** the theology of those who make much of experience and emotion as guides to a knowledge of divine truth. [L *pectorālis*, from *pectus, pectoris* the breast]

pectose. See under **pectic**.

peculate *pek'ū-lāt, vt* and *vi* to appropriate dishonestly for one's own use, pilfer, embezzle. — *n* **peculā'tion**. — *n* **pec'ulātor**. [L *pecūlārī, -ātus*, from *pecūlium* private property, related to *pecūnia* money]

peculiar *pi-kū'lyər, adj* own; of one's own; belonging exclusively (to); privately owned; appropriated; preserved; characteristic; special (to); very particular; odd, strange; having eccentric or individual variations in relation to the general or predicted pattern, as in *peculiar motion* or *velocity* (*astron*); (of a star) having a variable magnetic field. — *n* private property or right (*obs*); a parish or church exempt from the jurisdiction of the ordinary or bishop in whose diocese it is placed; anything exempt from ordinary jurisdiction; (*usu* with *cap*) one of the Peculiar People (see below); a type of unusual kind that has to be specially cast (*printing*). — *n* **peculiarity** (*-li-ar'i-ti*) the quality of being peculiar or singular; that which is found in one and in no other; something which distinguishes anything from others; individuality; oddity. — *vt* **pecu'liarize** or **-ise** to set apart. — *adv* **pecu'liarly**. — *n* **pecu'lium** private property, *esp* that given by a father to a son, etc. — **peculiar motion** see **proper motion** under **proper**; **Peculiar People** the Jews, as God's chosen people (New Eng Bible 'special possession', Deuteronomy 26.18, 'a people marked out as his own', Titus 2.14); an Evangelical denomination, founded in 1838, believing in the divine inspiration of the Holy Scriptures, and practising believers' baptism, Holy Communion, and Divine healing. [L *pecūlium* private property]

pecuniary *pi-kū'nyə-ri* or *-ni-ə-ri, adj* relating to money; consisting of money. — *adv* **pecu'niarily**. — *adj* **pecu'nious** (*rare*) rich. [L *pecūnia* money, from the root that appears in L *pecudēs* (pl) cattle, and **fee**]

ped[1] *ped*, (*dialect*) *n* a pannier or hamper. — Also **pad**. [Origin unknown]

ped[2] *ped, n* short for **pedestrian**.

ped[3] *ped, n* a naturally-formed unit or mass of soil, such as a crumb, block or aggregate. [Gr *pedon* ground]

ped-[1]. See **paed-**.

ped-[2]. See **pedi-**.

-ped *-ped* or **-pede** *-pēd, combining form* denoting foot. — *adj combining form* **-pedal** (*-ped'l*). [L *pēs, pedis* foot]

pedagogue *ped'ə-gog, n* a teacher; a pedant. — *vt* to teach. — *adj* **pedagogic** (*-gog'* or *-goj'*) or **pedagog'ical**. — *adv* **pedagog'ically**. — *n sing* **pedagog'ics** (*-gog'* or *-goj'*) the science and principles of teaching. — *n* **ped'agogism** (*-gizm* or *-jizm*) or **ped'agoguism** the spirit or system of pedagogy; teaching. — *n* **ped'agoguery** (*-gog-ə-ri*) a school; schoolmastering; pedagoguishness. — *adj* **ped'agoguish** like a pedagogue. — *n* **ped'agoguishness**. — *n* **ped'agogy** (*-gog-i* or *-goj-i*) the science of teaching; instruction; training. [Partly through Fr and L from Gr *paidagōgos* a slave who led a boy to school, from *pais, paidos* boy, and *agōgos* leader, from *agein* to lead]

pedal *ped'l* (in *zool* also *pē'dl*), *adj* of the foot; of the feet of perpendiculars (*geom*); of, with, or pertaining to, a pedal or pedals. — *n* (*ped'l*) a lever pressed by the foot; the lower and thicker part of a piece of straw; a plait made of these; a pedal-point; a pedal-organ; a pedal-board. — *vi* to use a pedal or pedals; to advance by use of the pedals. — *vt* to drive or operate by using the pedals: — *pr p* **ped'alling** (or in US **ped'aling**); *pa t* and *pa p* **ped'alled** (or in US **ped'aled**). — *n* **pedalier** (*-ēr'*) a pedal-board attached to a piano for the bass strings. — *n* **ped'aller** a person who uses pedals. — *n* **ped'alling**. — *n* **pedalo** (*ped'ə-lō*) a small pedal-propelled boat used (*esp* on lakes) for pleasure: — *pl* **ped'aloes** or **ped'alos**. — **ped'al-ac'tion** the apparatus worked by the pedals of a musical instrument; **ped'al-board** or **ped'al-clavier'** the keyboards or pedals of an organ or other instrument; **ped'al-bone** a horse's coffin-bone; **pedal cycle**; **ped'al-organ** the division of an organ played by means of pedals; **ped'al-point** organ point, a tone or tones (*usu* tonic and dominant) sustained normally in the bass, while other parts move independently; **ped'al-pushers** formerly, women's knee-length breeches, gathered below the knee; now, any (*esp* tight-fitting) women's trousers reaching just below the knee; **pedal**

steel guitar an electric steel guitar on a fixed stand and fitted with foot pedals for adjusting pitch, creating glissando effects, etc. [L *pedālis*, from *pēs*, *pedis* foot]

-pedal. See under **-ped**.

Pedaliaceae *pi-dā-li-ā'si-ē*, *n pl* a family of tubifloral dicotyledons related to the bignonias. [Gr *pēdalion* a rudder, from the keeled fruit]

pedalier, **pedaller**, **pedalo**, etc. See under **pedal**.

pedant *ped'nt*, *n* a schoolmaster (*Shakesp*); an over-educated person who parades his or her knowledge; a person who values academic learning too highly; a person fond of making over-fine distinctions, or one insisting on strict adherence to or interpretations of rules, etc. — *adj* **pedantic** (*pid-ant'ik*) or **pedant'ical** schoolmasterly; of the character or in the manner of a pedant. — *adv* **pedant'ically**. — *n* **pedant'icism** (*-i-sizm*) a pedant's expression. — *vt* **pedant'icize** or **-ise** (*-i-sīz*) to make pedantic, give pedantic form to. — *n* **ped'antism** pedantry; pedanticism. — *vi* **ped'antize** or **-ise** to play the pedant. — *vt* to turn into a pedant. — *n* **pedantoc'racy** government by pedants. — *n* **pedant'ocrat**. — *adj* **pedantocrat'ic**. — *n* **ped'antry** the character or manner of a pedant; a pedantic expression; unduly rigorous formality. [Ital *pedante* (perh through Fr *pédant*); connection with **pedagogue** not clear]

pedate *ped'āt*, *adj* footed; foot-like; palmately lobed with the outer lobes deeply cut, or ternately branching with the outer branches forked (*bot*). — *adv* **ped'ately**. — *adj* **pedatifid** (*pi-dat'i-fid*) divided in a pedate manner, but having the divisions connected at the base. [L *pedātus* footed, from *pēs*, *pedis* foot]

pedder *ped'ər* or **pether** *pedh'ər*, (now *Scot*) *n* a pedlar. — **pedd'er-coffe** (*prob -kōv*; *Scott* after *David Lyndsay*; see **cove**[2]). [Appar from **ped**[1]]

peddle *ped'l*, *vi* to go from place to place or house to house selling (small goods); to trifle. — *vt* to sell or offer as or like a pedlar; to deal in or sell (drugs) illegally, *usu* in small quantities; to promote (ideas, etc) enthusiastically and persistently. — *n* (*esp US*) **pedd'ler**. — *adj* **pedd'ling** unimportant. — *n* the trade or tricks of a pedlar. [Appar partly a back-formation from **pedlar**, partly from **piddle**]

-pede. See **-ped**.

pederasty *ped'ə-rast-i*, sexual relations, *specif* anal intercourse, between a man and a boy. — *n* **ped'erast** a man who practises pederasty. — *adj* **pederast'ic**. [Gr *pais* boy, and *erastēs* lover]

pedererо *ped-ə-rā'rō*, *n* an old gun for discharging stones, pieces of iron, etc, also for firing salutes. — Also **padere'ro**, **patere'ro**, **pedre'ro**, etc: — *pl* **pedere'roes** or **pedere'ros**, etc. [Sp *pedrero*, from L *petra* stone, from Gr *petrā*]

pedesis *ped-ē'sis*, *n* Brownian movement. — *adj* **pedetic** (*pi-det'ik*). [Gr *pēdēsis* jumping]

pedestal *ped'is-tl*, *n* the support of a column, statue, vase, etc; the fixed casting which holds the brasses in which a shaft turns, called also *axle-guard* or *pillow-block*. — *vt* to place on a pedestal. — *adj* **ped'estalled**. — **pedestal desk** a desk for which sets of drawers act as the side supports for the writing surface. — **put** or **set on a pedestal** to regard as worthy of a worshipping admiration, *esp* to attribute an unnatural degree of moral or sexual purity to. [Fr *piédestal*, from Ital *piedistallo*, for *piè di stallo* foot of a stall, from *piè* foot (L *pēs*, *pedis*), *di* of (L *dē*), and *stallo* stall (see **stall**).

pedestrian *pi-des'tri-ən*, *adj* on foot; of or related to walking; not mounted on Pegasus, hence prosaic, uninspired; flat or commonplace. — *n* a walker, someone travelling on foot; someone who practises feats of walking or running (*rare*). — *n* **pedes'trianism** walking, *esp* as an exercise or athletic performance; pedestrian quality (*fig*). — *n* **pedestrianizā'tion** or **-s-**. — *vi* **pedes'trianize** or **-ise** to walk. — *vt* to convert (a street) to use by pedestrians only. — **pedestrian crossing** a part of a roadway (often controlled by traffic lights) marked for the use of pedestrians who wish to cross, and on which they have right of way; **pedestrian precinct** see under **precinct**. [L *pedester*, *-tris*, from *pēs*, *pedis*]

pedetentous *ped-i-ten'təs*, *adj* proceeding slowly. [L *pedentim*, *-temptim*, from *pēs*, *pedis* foot, and *temptāre*, *-ātum* to make trial of]

pedetic. See under **pedesis**.

pedi- *ped'i-* or **ped-** *ped-*, *combining form* denoting foot. [L *pēs*, *pedis* foot]

pediatrics. *NAm* spelling of **paediatrics** (see under **paed-**).

pedicab *ped'i-kab*, *n* a light vehicle consisting of a tricycle with the addition of a seat, *usu* behind, covered by a half hood, for a passenger or passengers. [L *pēs*, *pedis* the foot, and **cab**]

pedicel *ped'i-sel*, (*biol*) *n* the stalk of a single flower in an inflorescence; the stalk of a sedentary animal; the stalk of an animal organ, eg a crab's eye. — *n* **pedicellā'ria** a stalked (or sessile) bladed snapping forceps on the surface of a starfish or sea-urchin: — *pl* **pedicellā'riae**. — *adj* **ped'icellate** (or *-dis'* or *-sel'*) provided with a pedicel. [Botanists' dimin of L *pēs*, *pedis* the foot]

pedicle *ped'i-kl*, *n* a short stalk or pedicel (*bot*); a narrow stalk-like structure or short bony process (*zool*); in deer, a bony protrusion of the skull from which an antler grows. — *adj* **ped'icled**. — *adj* **pedic'ūlate** stalked; belonging to the **Pediculā'tī**, the angler-fish order, whose pectoral fins have a wrist-like articulation. — *adj* **pedic'ulated**. [L *pediculus* a little foot, from *pēs*, *pedis* foot]

Pediculus *pi-dik'ū-ləs*, *n* the louse genus; (without *cap*) a louse: — *pl* **pedic'ulī**. — *adj* **pedic'ular** of lice; lousy. — *n* **Pediculā'ris** the lousewort genus. — *n* **pediculā'tion** or **pediculō'sis** lousiness. — *adj* **pedic'ulous** lousy. [L *pēdiculus*, dimin of *pēdis* a louse]

pedicure *ped'i-kūr*, *n* the treatment of corns, bunions and other minor ailments of the feet; a person who treats the feet. — *vt* to apply foot-treatment to. — *n* **ped'icurist**. [L *pēs*, *pedis* foot, and *cūra* care]

pedigree *ped'i-grē*, *n* a line of ancestors; a scheme or record of ancestry; lineage; genealogy; distinguished and ancient lineage; derivation, descent; succession, series, set. — *adj* of known descent, pure-bred, and of good stock. — *adj* **ped'igreed** having a pedigree. [Appar Fr *pied de grue* crane's-foot, from the arrow-head figure in a stemma]

pediment *ped'i-mənt*, (*archit*) *n* a triangular structure crowning the front of a Greek building, less steeply sloped than a gable; a similar structure in later architecture, whether triangular or any other shape, over a portico, door, window or niche. — *adj* **pedimental** (*-ment'l*). — *adj* **ped'imented** furnished with a pediment; like a pediment. [Earlier *periment*, prob for **pyramid**]

pedipalp *ped'i-palp*, *n* the second paired appendage in Arachnida (also **pedipalp'us**; *pl*-**palp'ī**); a whip-scorpion. — *n pl* **Pedipalp'i** (*-ī*) or **Pedipalp'ida** the whip-scorpions, an order of Arachnida with large pedipalps. [L *pēs*, *pedis* foot, and *palpus* stroking, in LL a feeler]

pedlar *ped'lər*, *n* a person who goes about with a small stock or selection of goods for sale (technically, someone who carries the goods personally, eg in a pack, disinguished from a *hawker*, who has a horse and cart, etc); a person who peddles. — *n* **ped'lary** the wares or occupation of a pedlar. [Prob from **pedder**, with inserted *l*, as in **tinkler** from **tinker**]

pedo-. See **paed-**.

pedology[1] *ped-ol'ə-ji*, *n* the study of soils. — *adj* **pedological** (*-ə-loj'*). — *n* **pedol'ogist**. [Gr *pedon* ground, and *logos* discourse]

pedology[2]. *NAm* spelling of **paedology** (see under **paed-**).

pedometer *pid-om'i-tər*, *n* an instrument for counting paces and so approximately measuring distance walked. [L *pēs*, *pedis* foot, and Gr *metron* measure]

pedrail *ped'rāl*, *n* a tractor with foot-like pieces on the circumference of its wheels; one of the pieces. [L *pēs*, *pedis* foot, and **rail**]

pedrero *ped-rā'rō*. See **pederero**.

pedro. See **sancho-pedro**.

peduncle *pi-dung'kl*, *n* the stalk of an inflorescence or of a solitary flower; the stalk by which a sedentary animal (such as a barnacle) is attached to a substratum (such as a rock) (*zool*); any stalklike part in a body (*zool*); a narrow stalklike connecting part (eg between the thorax and abdomen of insects); a tract of white fibres in the brain; a narrow process of tissue linking a tumour to normal tissue. — *adj* **pedun'cular**. — *adj* **pedun'culate** or **pedun'culated**. [Botanists' L *pedunculus*, from L *pēs*, *pedis* the foot]

pee[1] *pē*, *n* the sixteenth letter of the alphabet (P, p).

pee[2] *pē*, (*colloq*) *vi* to urinate. — Also *n*. [For **piss**]

peece. An obsolete spelling of **piece**.

peek *pēk*, *n* a sly look, a peep. — *vi* to peep. — *n* **peek'abo'** or **peek'aboo'** a child's peeping game. [Origin obscure]

peel[1] *pēl*, *vt* to pill, pillage, plunder (*obs*); to strip off the skin, bark, or other covering from; to strip (eg skin or other covering layer) off. — *vi* to come off like skin; to lose or shed the skin; to undress (*colloq*). — *n* rind, *esp* that of oranges, lemons, etc, in the natural state or candied. — *adj* **peeled** pillaged; bald; tonsured; stripped of skin, rind, or bark. — *n* **peel'er** a person who peels; a plunderer; a plant that impoverishes the soil; an instrument or machine for peeling or decorticating. — *n* **peel'ing** the act of stripping; a piece, strip, or shred stripped off; the removing of the layers of a paper overlay, to get a lighter impression (*printing*). — **peel-and-eat'** (*Scot*) potatoes served in their jackets. — Also *adj*. — **pack and** (or **or**) **peel** to have dealings (with; *Scott*); **peel off** to leave a flying formation by a particular manoeuvre (*aeronautics*); (of a ship) to veer away from a convoy; (of a person or group of persons) to veer off, separate from the mass. [OE *pilian*, from L *pilāre* to deprive of hair, from *pilus* a hair; perh influenced by Fr *peler* to skin; cf **pill**[2]]

peel[2] or **pele** *pēl*, *n* a stake (*obs*); a palisaded enclosure (*hist*); a peel-house. — **peel'-house** or **peel'-tower** (also **pele'-house** or **pele'-tower**; also with *cap*) *orig* a fortified dwelling-house, *usu* entered by ladder to the first floor, with a vaulted ground floor for cattle, common on the English/Scottish Borders (*hist*); now a loosely used term. [Anglo-Fr *pel*, from L *pālus* stake]

peel[3] *pēl*, *n* a shovel, *esp* a baker's wooden shovel; an instrument for hanging up paper to dry; the blade of an oar (*US*; *archaic*). [OFr *pele*, from L *pāla* a spade]

peel[4] *pēl*, (*croquet*) *vt* to cause (another player's ball) to go through the next hoop. [After British croquet player Walter *Peel* (fl. 1868)]

peel[5]. Same as **peal**[2].

peeler[1] *pēl'ər*, *n* a policeman, from Sir Robert *Peel* who established the Irish police (1812–18) and improved the force in Britain (1828–30). — *n* **Peel'ite** a follower of Peel in the reform of the Corn-laws in 1846.

peeler[2]. See under **peel**[1].

peelgarlic. See **pilgarlick**.

peel-house, peel-tower. See under **peel**[2].

peelie-wally *pē'li-wal'i*, (*Scot*) *adj* pale, ill-looking, off-colour. [Thought to be reduplicated form of Scot *peelie* thin, emaciated; perhaps a connection with **wally**[1], in allusion to the paleness of china, or of dentures]

peeling. See under **peel**[1].

peen, pean, pein, pene *pēn* or **pane** *pān*, *n* the end of a hammer head opposite the hammering face. — *vt* to strike or work (metal) with a peen; to fix (eg a rivet) by hammering into place (*usu* with *in* or *over*). [Origin uncertain; cf Norw *pen*, Ger *Pinne*, Fr *panne*]

peenge *pēnj* or *pēnzh*, (*Scot*) *vi* to whine like a peevish child. [Perh based on **whinge**]

peeoy, pioy or **pioye** *pē-ō'i*, (*Scot*) *n* a home-made firework, a cone of damp gunpowder.

peep[1] *pēp*, *vi* to cheep like a chicken. — *n* a high feeble sound. — *n* **peep'er** a young bird; a tree-frog (*US*). — **not a peep** (*colloq*) no noise, not a sound. [Imit; cf **pipe**[1], L *pīpāre*, Fr *pépier*, Ger *piepen*, *piepsen* to cheep, Gr *pīpos* a young bird]

peep[2] *pēp*, *vi* to look through a narrow opening; to look out from concealment; to look slyly, surreptitiously, or cautiously; to be just showing; to begin to appear. — *vt* to cause to project slightly from concealment; to direct as if to view. — *n* a sly or cautious look; a beginning to appear; a speck of light or flame; a glimpse; a slit; an eye (*slang*). — *n* **peep'er** someone who peeps; a prying person; the eye (*slang*); any of various types of glass or lens (*slang*). — **peep'-hole** a hole through which one may look without being seen; **peeping Tom** a man who furtively spies on other people, *esp* one who peeps in at windows; a voyeur; **peep'-show** a small entertainment, film or series of pictures, *esp* of erotic or pornographic nature, viewed through a small hole, *usu* fitted with a magnifying glass; **peep'-sight** a back-sight with a small hole. — *adj* **peep'-through** capable of being seen through. — **peep'-toe** a shoe cut away so as to show the toe. — Also *adj*. — **Peep-o'-day Boys** an Ulster Protestant society (1780–95) opposed to the Catholic *Defenders*; **peep of day** the first appearance of light in the morning. [Origin obscure]

peep[3] or **peepe** *pēp*, (*Shakesp*) *n* earlier forms of **pip**[3].

peeper. See under **peep**[1,2].

peepul. See **pipal**.

peer[1] *pēr*, *n* an equal; a fellow; an antagonist (*Spenser*); a nobleman of the rank of baron upward; generally, a nobleman; a member of the House of Lords; one of Charlemagne's paladins; a member of any similar body: — *fem* **peer'ess**. — *vt* to equal; to confer a peerage on (*colloq*). — *vi* to rank as equal. — *adj* pertaining to a peer group. — *n* **peer'age** the rank or dignity of a peer; the body of peers; a book of the genealogy, etc, of the different peers. — *adj* **peer'less** unequalled; matchless. — *adv* **peer'lessly**. — *n* **peer'lessness**. — **peer group** a group of people equal in age, rank, merit, etc; **peer pressure** compulsion towards doing or obtaining the same things as others in one's peer group. — **House of Peers** the House of Lords; **life peer** or **peeress** a person invested with a non-hereditary peerage, entitling them to the title of baron or baroness and a seat in the House of Lords; **spiritual peer** a bishop or archbishop qualified to sit in the House of Lords, as opposed to a **temporal peer** any other member. [OFr (Fr *pair*), from L *pār*, *paris* equal]

peer[2] *pēr*, *vi* to look narrowly or closely; to look with strain, or with half-closed eyes; to peep; to appear. — *vt* (*obs*) to protrude. — *adj* **peer'y** inclined to peer; prying; sly. [Origin unknown; perh partly ME *piren* (cf LGer *pīren*), influenced by *pere* aphetic form of **appear**, partly from *pere* itself]

peerage, peeress. See under **peer**[1].

peerie[1] or **peery** *pēr'i*, (*Scot*) *n* a pear- or cone-shaped wooden peg-top. [Appar **pear**, pronounced *pēr* in Scots]

peerie[2] *pēr'i*, (*Orkney* and *Shetland*) *adj* small. [Origin uncertain]

peerless, etc. See under **peer**[1].

peery. See under **peerie**[1].

peesweep *pēz'wēp*. See **peewit**.

peetweet *pēt'wēt*, (*US*) *n* the spotted sandpiper. [Imit]

peeve, peeved. See under **peevish**.

peever *pē'vər*, (*Scot*) *n* a tile, slab, tin-lid, etc used in playing hop-scotch. — *n sing* **peev'ers** hop-scotch.

peevish *pēv'ish*, *adj* foolish (*obs*); vexatious (*obs*); perverse (*Shakesp*); wayward; irritable; fretful, complaining. — *vt* **peeve** (back-formation) to irritate. — *vi* to be fretful; to show fretfulness. — *n* a fretful mood; a grievance or grouse. — *adj* **peeved** (*colloq*) annoyed. — *adv* **peev'ishly**. — *n* **peev'ishness**. [Origin unknown]

peewee. See **peewit**.

peewit or **pewit** *pē'wit*, also *pū'it*, *n* the lapwing; its cry. — Also (*Scot*) **pees'weep, pease'weep** and **pee'wee**. [Imit]

peg *peg*, *n* a pin (*esp* of wood); a fixture for hanging a hat or coat on; a pin for tuning a string (*music*); a small stake for securing tent-ropes, or marking a position, boundary claim, etc; a pin for scoring, as in cribbage; a pin in a cup to show how far down one may drink;

hence a drink measure, *esp* of brandy and soda; a degree or step; a set level applied to eg an exchange rate or a price (*econ*); a wooden or other pin used in shoemaking; a turtle harpoon; a clothes-peg; a cricket stump; a piton; a peg-top; a wooden leg (*colloq*); a leg (*colloq*); a poke or thrust (*dialect* or *slang*); a theme (*fig*). — *vt* to fasten, mark, score, furnish, pierce, or strike with a peg or pegs; to insert or fix like a peg; to pin down; to score (as at cribbage); to keep from falling or rising by buying or selling at a fixed price (*Stock exchange*); to hold (prices, pensions, etc) at a fixed level, or directly related to the cost of living; to stabilize; to drive (a coach, etc) (*obs slang*); to throw or target. — *vi* (*usu* with *away*) to keep on working assiduously; to make one's way vigorously: — *pr p* **pegg'ing**; *pa t* and *pa p* **pegged**. — *adj* **pegged**. — *n* **pegg'ing**. — **peg'board** a board having holes into which pegs are placed, used for playing and scoring in games or for display or storage purposes; **peg'-box** part of the head of a musical instrument in which the pegs are inserted; **peg'-leg** (*colloq*) a simple wooden leg; a man with a wooden leg; **peg'-tank'ard** a drinking-vessel having each one's share marked off by a knob; **peg'-top** a spinning top with a metal point, spun by winding a string round it and suddenly throwing it; (in *pl*) trousers narrowing at the ankles. — *adj* shaped like a top. — **a peg too low** tipsy; depressed; **off the peg** of a garment, (bought) ready to wear from an already-existing stock; of an item, (bought) ready to use, not purpose-built; not adjusted to suit the circumstances, etc (*fig*; *adj* **off'-the-peg'**); **peg away** to work on assiduously; **peg back** (in sport, *esp* racing) to gain an advantage over an opponent; **peg down** to restrict (someone) to an admission, following a certain course of action; **peg out** (in croquet) to finish by driving the ball against the peg; (in cribbage) to win by pegging the last hole before show of hands; to mark off with pegs; to become exhausted, be ruined, or die (*slang*); **round peg in a square hole** or **square peg in a round hole** a person who is unsuited to the particular position he or she occupies; **take down a peg (or two)** to bring down, deflate, humiliate or humble. [Cf LGer *pigge*, Du dialect *peg*, Dan *pig*]

Pegasus *peg'ə-səs*, *n* the winged horse that sprang from Medusa's blood, by later writers associated with the Muses (*Gr mythol*); hence, an embodiment of the power that raises a poet's imagination above the earth; (without *cap*) a member of a genus (*Pegasus*) of small fishes superficially like sea-horses, of the coasts of Asia and Australia, with large, wing-like, pectoral fins; one of the constellations in the northern sky. — *adj* **Pegasē'an**. [L *Pēgasus*, from Gr *Pēgasos*]

peggy *peg'i*, *n* a small warbler of various kinds, eg the whitethroat; a washerwoman's dolly; a size of roofing slate 25·4 × 35·6 cm (10 × 14 inches). [Hypocoristic from *Margaret*]

pegh. See **pech**.

Peght. See **Pecht**.

pegmatite *peg'mə-tīt*, *n* graphic granite, a granite with markings like Hebrew characters; a very coarsely crystallized granite, as in dykes and veins (*geol*); any very coarse-grained igneous rock occurring in this manner. — *adj* **pegmatitic** (*-tit'ik*). [Gr *pēgma* a bond, framework, from the root of *pēgnynai* to fasten]

Pehlevi *pā'le-vē* or **Pahlavi** *pä'lä-vē*, *n* an ancient West Iranian idiom of the Sassanide period (3rd–7th century AD), largely mixed with Semitic words; the characters used in writing it. — Also *adj*. [Pers *Pahlavi* Parthian]

PEI *abbrev*: Prince Edward Island.

peignoir *pen'wär*, *n* a woman's dressing-gown, *esp* a fine lightweight one (*orig* one worn when combing the hair); (loosely) a morning-gown. [Fr, from *peigner*, from L *pectināre* to comb]

pein. See **peen**.

peinct *pānt*. An obsolete spelling of **painting**.

peine forte et dure *pen fort ā dür*, (*Fr*; *hist*) *n* literally, strong and severe punishment, a kind of judicial torture involving pressing with weights.

peirastic *pī-ras'tik*, *adj* experimental; tentative. — *adv* **peiras'tically**. [Gr *peirastikos*, from *peira* a trial]

peise, **peize**, **pease**, **peaze** or **peyse** *pāz* or *pēz*, (*obs*) *n* weight; a weight; a balance; a blow (*Spenser*). — *vt* to balance (*Spenser*, *Shakesp*); to poise (*Spenser*); to put weights on, weigh down (*Shakesp*). — *vi* (*Spenser*) to press or settle downwards. [OFr *peis* weight, *peser* to weigh; cf **poise**[1]]

peishwa, **peishwah**. See **peshwa**.

pejorate *pē'jər-āt* or *pi'*, *vt* to make worse. — *n* **pejorā'tion** a making or becoming worse; deterioration. — *adj* **pejor'ative** (or *pē'*) derogatory, disparaging, depreciating. — *n* a derogatory word or suffix. — *adv* **pejor'atively** (or *pē'*). [L *pējor* worse]

pekan *pek'ən*, *n* the wood-shock, a large North American marten with dark brown fur. [Can Fr *pékan*, from Algonquin *pékanē*]

Pekingese or **Pekinese** *pē-kin-ēz'* or *pē-king-*, *adj* of *Peking* (now *usu* Beijing), China. — *n* a native or inhabitant of Peking; *esp* formerly, the chief dialect of Mandarin; a dwarf pug-dog of a breed brought from Peking (also *colloq* short form **peke**). — **Pekin** or **Pekin duck** a large white breed of duck, bred *esp* for food; **Peking man** a type of fossil man first found (1929) SW of Peking, related to Java man.

pekoe *pēk'ō* or *pek'ō*, *n* a scented black tea. [Chin *pek-ho* white down]

pela *pā'lä*, *n* white wax from a scale-insect. [Chin *peh-la* white wax]

pelage *pel'ij*, *n* an animal's coat of hair or wool. [Fr]

Pelagian *pi-lā'ji-ən*, *n* a follower of *Pelagius*, a 5c British monk, who denied original sin. — Also *adj*. — *n* **Pelā'gianism**.

pelagic *pi-laj'ik*, *adj* oceanic; of, inhabiting, or carried out in, the deep or open sea; living in the surface waters or middle depths of the sea; (of sediments) deposited under deep-water conditions. — *adj* **pelagian** (*pi-lā'ji-ən*) pelagic. — *n* a pelagic animal. [Gr *pelagos* sea]

pelargonium *pel-ər-gō'ni-əm*, *n* any plant of a vast genus (*Pelargonium*) of the Geraniaceae family of plants, having clusters of red, pink or white flowers, often cultivated under the name of geranium. — **pelargonic acid** an oily fatty acid, obtained *esp* from the leaves of plants of the Pelargonium genus — also called **nonanoic acid**. [Gr *pelargos* stork, the beaked capsules resembling a stork's head]

Pelasgic *pe-las'jik*, *adj* pertaining to the *Pelasgians* or *Pelasgi*, prehistoric inhabitants of Greece, of unknown origin. — Also **Pelas'gian**. — **Pelasgian architecture** cyclopean architecture.

Pele *pā'lā*, *n* the Hawaiian volcano goddess. — **Pele's hair** volcanic glass drawn out into threads as it flies through the air.

pele[1]. See **peel**[2].

pele[2]. A Spenserian spelling of **peal**[1].

Pelecypoda *pel-e-sip'ə-də*, *n pl* the Lamellibranchs. [Gr *pelekys* axe, and *pous*, *podos* foot]

pelerine *pel'ə-rin* or *-rēn*, *n* a woman's tippet or cape, *esp* one with long pointed ends coming down in front. [Fr *pèlerine* tippet, pilgrim (fem); see **pilgrim**]

pelf *pelf*, (*derog*) *n* riches (in a bad sense); money. [OFr *pelfre* booty; cf **pilfer**]

pelham *pel'əm*, (often with *cap*) *n* on a horse's bridle, a type of bit, a combination of the curb and snaffle designs. [Perh the name *Pelham*]

pelican *pel'i-kən*, *n* a large tropical and subtropical waterfowl with an enormous pouched bill, fabled in the Middle Ages to wound its breast and feed its young with its blood; an alembic with beaks that lead back to the body, used for continuous distillation; a dentist's beaked instrument (*hist*); an old species of ordnance, or its shot. — **pel'ican-fish** a deep-sea fish (Eurypharynx) with an enormous mouth and comparatively small body; **pel'ican-flower** the goose-flower, an Aristolochia with a gigantic flower; **pel'ican's-foot'** a marine gasteropod mollusc (*Aporrhais pes-pelicani*); its shell, which has a lip like a webbed foot. — **pelican in her piety** (*heraldry*) a pelican with wings indorsed, feeding her young with her blood. [LL *pelicānus*, from Gr *pelekan*, *-ānos* pelican; cf *pelekās*, *-āntos* a woodpecker, and *pelekys* an axe]

pelican crossing *pel'i-kən kros'ing*, *n* a pedestrian-operated street crossing, having a set of lights including an amber flashing light which indicates that motorists may proceed only if the crossing is clear. [Adapted from *pe*destrian *li*ght *con*trolled *crossing*]

pelisse *pe-lēs'*, (*hist*) *n orig* a fur-lined or fur garment, *esp* a military cloak; a lady's long mantle; a young child's overcoat. [Fr, from LL *pellicea* (*vestis*), from L *pellis* a skin]

pelite *pē'līt*, *n* any rock derived from clay or mud. — *adj* **pēlitic** (*-lit'ik*). — *n* **pē'loid** any naturally produced medium used in medical practice as a cataplasm. — *n* **pēlol'ogy**. — *n* **pēlother'apy** treatment by mud baths and the like. [Gr *pēlos* clay, mud]

pell *pel*, (*obs*) *n* a skin or hide; a roll of parchment. [OFr *pel* (Fr *peau*), from L *pellis* a skin or hide]

pellach, **pellack**. See **pellock**.

pellagra *pel-ag'rə* or *-āg'rə*, *n* a chronic disease marked by shrivelled skin, wasted body, mental illness and paralysis, caused by a dietary deficiency of certain vitamin-B_2 elements. — *n* **pellag'rin** someone afflicted with pellagra. — *adj* **pellag'rous** connected with, like, or afflicted with pellagra. [Gr *pella* skin, and *agrā* seizure; or Ital *pelle agra* rough skin]

pellet *pel'it*, *n* a little ball; a small rounded boss; a small rounded mass of compressed iron ore, waste material, etc; a small pill; a ball of shot, *esp* a flat-ended ball for use in air-rifles, etc; a mass of undigested refuse thrown up by a hawk or owl. — *vt* to form into pellets (*Shakesp*); to form (eg seeds for easier planting) into a pellet by surrounding with an inert substance which breaks down with moisture; to hit, pelt or bombard with pellets. — *vt* **pell'etify**, **pell'etize** or **-ise** to form (*esp* solid waste material, iron ore, etc) into pellets. — *n* **pelletīzā'tion** or **-s-**. [OFr *pelote*, from L *pila* a ball]

pellicle *pel'i-kl*, *n* a thin skin or film; a film or scum on liquid. — *adj* **pellic'ūlar**. [L *pellicula*, dimin of *pellis* skin]

pellitory[1] *pel'i-tə-ri*, *n* a plant (*Parietaria officinalis*) of the nettle family, growing on old walls (called *pellitory of the wall*), or other member of the genus. — cf **pellitory**[2]. [L (*herba*) *parietāria*, from *parietārius*, from *pariēs*, *parietis* a wall]

pellitory[2] *pel'i-tə-ri*, *n* a N African and S European plant (*Anacyclus pyrethrum*), known as *pellitory of Spain*, related to camomile; extended to various similar plants, such as yarrow and feverfew. — cf **pellitory**[1]. [ME *peletre*, from L *pyrethrum*, from Gr *pyrethron* pellitory of Spain; see **Pyrethrum**]

pell-mell *pel'-mel'*, *adv* confusedly; headlong; helter-skelter; vehemently. — *adj* confusedly mingled; indiscriminate; headlong. — *n* disorder; confused mingling; a hand-to-hand fight. [OFr *pesle-mesle* (Fr *pêle-mêle*), *-mesle* being from OFr *mesler* (Fr *mêler*) to mix, meddle, from LL *misculāre*, from L *miscēre*; and *pesle* a rhyming addition, perh influenced by Fr *pelle* shovel]

pellock or **pellack** *pel'ək* or **pellach** *pel'əhh*, (*Scot*) *n* a porpoise. [Origin unknown]

pellucid *pe-lū'sid* or *-lōō'sid*, *adj* perfectly clear; transparent. — *n* **pellucid'ity**. — *adv* **pellu'cidly**. — *n* **pellu'cidness**. [L *pellūcidus*, from *per* through, and *lūcidus* clear, from *lūcēre* to shine]

pelma *pel'mə*, *n* the sole of the foot. — *adj* **pelmatic** (*-mat'ik*). — *n pl* **Pelmatozō'a** a division of the Echinodermata, typically stalked, including crinoids and the fossil blastoids and cystoids. [Gr *pelma*, *-atos* sole, stalk]

Pelmanism *pel'mən-izm*, *n* a system of mind training to improve the memory; (*usu* without *cap*) a card game in which the cards are spread out face down and must be turned up in matching pairs. [The *Pelman* Institute, founded 1898, which devised the system]

pelmet *pel'mit*, *n* a fringe, valance, or other device hiding a curtain rod. [Perh Fr *palmette*]

peloid, **pelology**. See under **pelite**.

Pelopid *pel'ō-pid*, (*Gr mythol*) *n* a descendant of *Pelops*, son of Tantalus, and grandfather of Agamemnon and Menelaus.

Peloponnesian *pel-ō-pə-nē'sh(y)ən*, *-zh(y)ən* or *-zyən*, *adj* of the *Peloponnesus* or Peloponnese, the southern peninsula of Greece. — *n* a native of the Peloponnese. — **Peloponnesian War** a war between Athens and Sparta, 431–404 BC. [Gr *Peloponnēsos* Peloponnese, from *Pelops* (see **Pelopid**), and *nēsos* an island]

peloria *pi-lō'ri-ə* or *-lö'ri-ə*, *n* regularity in a normally irregular flower. — Also **pelorism** (*pel'ər-izm*) or **pel'ory**. — *adj* **peloric** (*pi-lor'ik*), **pel'orized** or **-ised**. [Gr *pelōr* a monster]

pelorus *pel-ōr'əs* or *-ör'*, *n* a kind of compass from which bearings can be taken. [Perh *Pelorus* Hannibal's pilot]

pelory. See **peloria**.

pelota *pel-ō'tə*, *n* any of various related games of Basque origin, popular in Spain, S France and Latin America, in which two players hurl a ball against a marked wall using a basket-like racket strapped to the wrist. [Sp *pelota* ball]

pelotherapy. See under **pelite**.

pelt[1] *pelt*, *n* a raw animal hide with the fur still on; a hawk's prey when killed, *esp* when torn. — *n* **pelt'ry** the skins of animals with the fur on them; furs. — **pelt'monger** a dealer in skins. [Appar a back-formation from *peltry*, from OFr *pelleterie*, from L *pellis* a skin]

pelt[2] *pelt*, *vt* to hurl, or fire, in a persistent or rapid stream; to assail (formerly with repeated blows, now *usu*) with a torrent of missiles or blows, or of words, reproaches, pamphlets, etc; to drive by showers of missiles, etc; to shower. — *vi* to shower blows or missiles; (of rain or hail, etc) to beat vigorously (sometimes with *down*); to speak angrily; to speed. — *n* a blow; a pelting; a downpour, eg of rain; a storm of rage; a rapid pace. — *n* **pelt'er** someone who or that which pelts; a shower of missiles; a sharp storm of rain, of anger, etc. — *vi* to go full pelt; to pelt (*dialect*). — *n* and *adj* **pelt'ing**. — **full pelt** or **at full pelt** at full speed. [Origin obscure]

pelta *pel'tə*, (*antiq*) *n* a small light shield or buckler. — *n* **peltast** (*pelt'ast*) a light-armed Greek soldier with a pelta. — *adj* **pelt'ate** (*bot*) having the stalk attached not to the edge but near the middle of the under-surface. [L, from Gr *peltē*]

Peltier effect *pel'ti-ā i-fekt'*, (*phys*) *n* the generation or absorption of heat at a junction, within an electric circuit, of two metals. [From Jean *Peltier*, 19c French physicist]

pelting[1] *pel'ting*, (*Shakesp*) *adj* paltry, contemptible. — *adv* **pelt'ingly**. [Appar connected with **paltry**]

pelting[2]. See under **pelt**[2].

peltmonger. See under **pelt**[1].

Pelton-wheel *pel'tn-(h)wēl'*, *n* a water-wheel with specially shaped cups around the circumference into which one or more jets of water are aimed at high speed, invented by Lester Allen *Pelton*, American engineer (1829–1908).

peltry. See under **pelt**[1].

pelvis *pel'vis*, (*anatom*) *n* the bony cavity at the lower end of the trunk, of which the part above the plane through the promontory of the sacrum and the pubic symphysis is the *false pelvis*, the part below the *true pelvis*; the bony frame enclosing it; the cavity of the kidney; the basal part of a crinoid cup: — *pl* **pel'vises** or **pel'ves** (*-vēz*). — *adj* **pel'vic**. — *adj* **pel'viform** basin-shaped. — *n* **pelvim'eter** an instrument for measuring the pelvis. — *n* **pelvim'etry**. — **pelvic fin** a fish's paired fin homologous with a mammal's hindleg; **pelvic girdle** or **arch** the posterior limb-girdle of vertebrates, with which the hind-limbs articulate, consisting of the haunch-bones (ilium, pubis and ischium united), which articulate with the sacrum; **pelvic inflammatory disease** a damaging inflammatory condition affecting a woman's pelvic organs, *esp* the Fallopian tubes, caused by a bacterial infection. [L *pelvis* a basin]

pembroke *pem'bro͝ok, n* (in full **pembroke table**) a small four-legged table with hinged flaps. [Appar from *Pembroke*, in Wales]

pemmican or **pemican** *pem'i-kən, n* a North American Indian preparation of lean meat, dried, pounded, and mixed with fat and other ingredients; a highly condensed, nutritious preparation of dried ingredients, used *esp* as emergency rations; highly condensed information or reading-matter (*fig*). [Cree *pimekan*]

pemoline *pem'ə-lēn, n* a white crystalline powder, $C_2H_8N_2O_2$, used as a stimulant of the central nervous system, *esp* in the treatment of fatigue, depression and memory loss.

pemphigus *pem'fi-gəs, n* a diseased condition of the skin with watery vesicles. — *adj* **pem'phigoid**. — *adj* **pem'phigous**. [False Latin, from Gr *pemphix, -īgos* blister]

PEN *pen, abbrev*: (the International Association of) Poets, Playwrights, Editors, Essayists and Novelists.

Pen *abbrev*: Peninsula.

pen[1] *pen, n* a small enclosure, *esp* for animals; a cattle farm (*Caribbean*); an estate or plantation (*Caribbean*); animals kept in, and enough to fill, a pen; a dam or weir; a covered dock, eg for servicing submarines. — *vt* to put or keep in a pen; to confine; to dam: — *pr p* **penn'ing**; *pa t* and *pa p* **penned** or **pent**. — **pen'fold** a fold for penning cattle or sheep; a pound. — **submarine pen** a dock for a submarine, *esp* if protected from attack from above by a deep covering of concrete. [OE *penn* pen]

pen[2] *pen, n* a large feather; a flight-feather; a quill; a cuttle-bone; an instrument used for writing (with ink or otherwise), formerly made of a quill, but now of other materials; a nib; a nib with a holder; writing; literary style; an author. — *vt* to write, to commit to paper: — *pr p* **penn'ing**; *pa t* and *pa p* **penned**. — *n* **pen'ful** as much ink as a pen can take at a dip; as much as the reservoir of a fountain-pen can hold; what can be written with one dip of ink. — *adj* **penned** written; quilled. — *n* **penn'er** (*archaic*) a case for carrying pens. — **pen'-and-ink'** writing materials; a pen drawing. — *adj* writing; written; (of a drawing) executed with pen and ink. — **pen'-case** a receptacle for a pen or pens; **pen'craft** penmanship; the art of composition; **pen'-driver** a clerk; **pen'-feather** a quill feather; a pin-feather (*dialect*). — *adj* **pen'-feathered**. — **pen'-friend** or **pen'-pal** an otherwise unknown person (*usu* abroad) with whom one corresponds; **pen'-gun** (*Scot*) a popgun made of a quill; **pen'holder** a rod on which a nib may be fixed; **pen'knife** *orig* a knife for making or mending pens; a small pocket-knife; **pen'light** a small pen-shaped electric torch (**penlight battery** a long, thin battery, as used in a penlight); **pen'man** a person skilled in handwriting; a writer or author: — *fem* **pen'woman**; **pen'manship**; **pen name** a writer's assumed name; **pen'-nib** a nib for a pen; **pen'-pusher** (*colloq*) a clerk who does boring, routine writing; **pen'-wiper** a piece of cloth, leather, etc, for wiping ink from pens. — **talk like a pen-gun** to chatter volubly. [OFr *penne*, from L *penna* a feather]

pen[3]. Slang short form of **penitentiary** (qv under **penitent**).

pen[4] *pen, n* a female swan. [Origin unknown]

penal *pē'nl, adj* pertaining to, liable to, imposing, constituting, or used for, punishment; constituting a penalty; very severe. — *n* **pēnalīzā'tion** or **-s-**. — *vt* **pē'nalize** or **-ise** to make (something) punishable; to impose a penalty or disadvantage on (eg someone guilty of an offence or lapse). — *adv* **pē'nally**. — **penal code** a codified system of law relating to crime and punishment; **penal laws** laws imposing penalties, *esp* (*hist*) in matters of religion; **penal servitude** hard labour in a prison under different conditions from ordinary imprisonment, substituted in 1853 for transportation, then abolished 1948; **penal settlement** a settlement peopled by convicts. [L *poenālis*, from *poena*, from Gr *poinē* punishment]

penalty *pen'l-ti, n* punishment; suffering or loss imposed for breach of a law; a fine or loss agreed upon in case of non-fulfilment of some undertaking; a fine; a disadvantage imposed upon a competitor for breach of a rule of the game, for failing to attain what is aimed at, as a handicap, or for any other reason arising out of the rules; a kick, shot or stroke awarded or imposed as a result of a breach of the rules; a loss or suffering brought upon one by one's own actions or condition; a score for an opponent's failure to complete a contract or for the bidder's success when the call is doubled (*bridge*). — **penalty area** or **box** (in association football) the area or box in front of the goal in which a foul by the defending team may result in a penalty kick being awarded against them; **penalty bench** or **box** (in ice-hockey) an area or box beside the rink in which a player must stay for his or her allotted penalty period; **penalty corner** (in hockey) a free stroke taken on the goal line; **penalty goal** one scored by a penalty kick or shot; **penalty kick** a free kick, or the privilege granted to a player to kick the ball as he or she pleases, because of some breach of the rules by the opposing side; **penalty line** the boundary of the penalty area; **penalty shot**; **penalty spot** (in association football and men's hockey) a spot marked in front of the goal from which a penalty kick or shot is taken. — **death penalty** punishment by putting to death; **under** (or **on**) **penalty of** with liability in case of infraction to the penalty of. [LL *poenālitās*; see ety for **penal**]

penance *pen'əns, n* repentance (*obs*); an act of humiliation or punishment, either undertaken voluntarily or imposed by a priest to express or show evidence of sorrow for sin; the sacrament by which absolution is conveyed (involving contrition, confession, and satisfaction) (*RC* and *Orthodox Church*); expiation; punishment (*Milton*); hardship. — *vt* to impose penance on. [OFr; cf **penitence**]

Penang-lawyer *pi-nang'-lö'yər, n* a walking stick made from the stem of a prickly dwarf palm (*Licuala acutifida*); misapplied to a Malacca cane. [*Penang*, its place of origin, and **lawyer**, or poss from Malay *pinang līyar* wild areca, or *pinang láyor* fire-dried areca]

penannular *pen-an'ū-lər* or *pēn-, adj* in the form of an almost complete ring. [L *paene* almost, and *annulāris* annular]

penates *pe-nā'tēz* or *pe-nä'tās, n pl* the household gods of a Roman family. [L *penātēs*, prob from the root found in *penus* provisions, storeroom, *penes* in the house of, and *penetrāre* to penetrate]

pence *pens, n* a plural of **penny**; a new penny (*colloq*).

pencel. See **pensil**.

penchant *pã'shã, n* a liking or inclination (with *for*); decided taste; bias. [Fr, pr p of *pencher* to incline, from assumed LL *pendicāre*, from L *pendēre* to hang]

pencil *pen'sl, n* a writing or drawing instrument that leaves a streak of graphite, chalk, slate, or other solid matter, *esp* (*lead-pencil*) one of graphite enclosed in wood and sharpened as required; a small stick of various materials shaped like a lead-pencil, for medical, cosmetic, or other purpose; a fine paint-brush; a small tuft of hairs; the art of painting or drawing; a system of straight lines meeting in a point (*geom*); a set of rays of light diverging from or converging to a point (*optics*); a narrow beam of light (*phys*); something long, fine and narrow in shape. — *vt* to paint, draw, write, or mark with a pencil; (with *in*) to enter provisionally, eg in a diary; to note (something) allowing for or expecting later alteration (*fig*); to apply a pencil to: — *pr p* **pen'cilling**; *pa t* and *pa p* **pen'cilled**. — *adj* **pen'cilled** painted, drawn, written or marked with a pencil; marked as if with a pencil; showing fine concentric streaking; having pencils of rays; radiated; tufted. — *n* **pen'ciller**. — *n* **pen'cilling** the art or act of painting, writing, sketching, or marking with a pencil; marks made with a pencil; fine lines on flowers or feathers; a sketch; the marking of joints in brickwork with white painting. — **pen'cil-case** a case for pencils; metal case used to hold a movable piece of blacklead or the like, used as a pencil; **pen'cil-ce'dar** juniper of various kinds suitable for lead-pencils; **pen'cil-com'pass** a compass having a pencil on one of its legs; **pen'cil-lead** graphite for pencils; a stick of it for a metal pencil-case; **pen'cil-ore** radiating botryoidal graphite; **pen'cil-sharpener** an instrument for sharpening lead-pencils, etc, by rotation against a blade or blades; **pen'cil-sketch**; **pencil skirt** a straight, close-fitting skirt; **pen'cil-stone** a pyrophyllite used for making slate-pencils. [OFr *pincel* (Fr *pinceau*), from L *pēnicillum* a painter's brush, dimin of *pēnis* a tail]

pencraft. See under **pen**[2].

pend[1] *pend*, (*Scot*) *n* a vaulted passage; a vaulted entrance to a passageway. [L *pendēre* to hang]

pend[2] *pend*, *vi* to hang, as in a balance, to impend. — *adj* **pend'ing** hanging; impending; remaining undecided; not fully dealt with or completed. — *prep* during; until, awaiting. [Fr *pendre* or L *pendēre* to hang; sometimes aphetic for **append** or for **depend**]

pend[3]. An old spelling of **penned**, from **pen**[1] or **pen**[2].

pendant or sometimes **pendent** *pen'dənt*, *n* anything hanging, *esp* for ornament; a hanging ornament *esp* one worn on a chain, etc around the neck; the hanging (*esp* decorated) end of a waist-belt; an earring; a lamp hanging from the roof; an ornament of wood or of stone hanging downwards from a roof; a pennant (*naut*); a pendant-post (see below); anything attached to another thing of the same kind, an appendix; a companion picture, poem, etc. — *n* **pen'dency** a state or quality of being pendent; droop. — *adj* **pen'dent** (or sometimes **pen'dant**) hanging; dangling; drooping; overhanging; not yet decided; grammatically incomplete, left in suspense. — *n* **pendentive** (*-dent'*; *archit*) one of four spherical triangles formed by a dome springing from a square base; part of a groined vault resting on one pier. — *adv* **pen'dently**. — *n* **pen'dicle** a pendant; a dependency or appendage; a thing attached to something else, such as a privilege to a post, or a small piece of land to a rented property. — *n* **pen'dicler** the tenant of a pendicle. — **pen'dant-post'** a post placed against a wall, *usu* resting on a corbel or capital, with a tie-beam or hammer-beam fixed to its upper end. [Fr *pendant*, pr p of *pendre* to hang, from L *pendēns*, *-entis*, pr p of *pendēre* to hang]

pendente lite *pen-den'tē lī'tē* or *pen-den'te li'te*, (*L*) *adv* during the process of litigation.

pendicle. See under **pendant**.

pendragon *pen-drag'ən*, *n* an ancient British supreme chief. — *n* **pendrag'onship**. [Welsh *pen* head, and *dragon* a dragon, dragon-standard]

pendulum *pen'dū-ləm*, *n* theoretically, a heavy material point suspended by a weightless thread, free to swing without friction (*simple pendulum*); any weight so hung from a fixed point as to swing freely (*compound pendulum*); the swinging weight which regulates the movement of a clock; anything that swings, passes or is free to swing or be passed to and fro; anything that undergoes obvious and regular shifts or reversals in direction, attitude, opinion, etc: — *pl* **pen'dulums**. — *adj* **pen'dular** relating to a pendulum. — *vi* **pen'dulate** to swing, vibrate. — *adj* **pen'duline** building a pendulous nest. — *n* **pendulos'ity**. — *adj* **pen'dulous** hanging loosely; swinging freely; drooping; dangling; overhanging; suspended from the top; floating in air or space. — *adv* **pen'dulously**. — *n* **pen'dulousness**. — **pendulum arbitration** (*business*) a process used to settle disputes, in which the arbitrator chooses one complete final offer, no adjustment of terms being allowed. — **compensation pendulum** a pendulum so constructed that its rod is not much altered in length by changes of temperature. [Neuter of L *pendulus* hanging, from *pendēre* to hang]

pene. See **peen**.

Peneian *pē-nē'ən*, *adj* relating to the river *Pēnēus* in the famous Vale of Tempe in Thessaly. [Gr *Pēnēios*, now Salambria]

penelopize or **-ise** *pi-nel'ə-pīz*, *vi* to act like *Penelope*, the wife of Ulysses, who in his long absence, undid her day's weaving work at night, to create work as an excuse with which to deter suitors. [Gr *Pēnelopē*]

peneplain *pē'ni-plān* or *-plān'*, *n* a land surface so worn down by denudation as to be almost a plain. — Also **pe'neplane**. [L *paene* almost, and **plain**[2]]

penes. See **penis**.

penetrate *pen'i-trāt*, *vt* to thrust or force a way into the inside of; to pierce into or through; to insert the penis into the vagina of; to force entry within a country's borders or through an enemy's front line (*military*); to gain access into and influence within (a country, organization, market, etc) for political, financial, etc, purposes; to permeate; to reach the mind or feelings of; to pierce with the eye or understanding, see into or through whether with the eye or intellect (*fig*); to understand. — *vi* to reach the inside; to be understood (*colloq*). — *n* **penetrability** (*-trə-bil'i-ti*). — *adj* **pen'etrable**. — *n* **pen'etrableness**. — *adv* **pen'etrably** so as to be penetrated. — *n pl* **penetrā'lia** (*pl* of L *penetral* or *penetrāle*) the inmost parts of a building; the most holy place in a temple; innermost mysteries. — *adj* **penetrā'lian**. — *n* **pen'etrance** (*genetics*) the frequency, expressed as a percentage, with which a gene exhibits an effect. — *n* **pen'etrancy**. — *adj* **pen'etrant** penetrating. — *n* (*chem*) a substance which increases the penetration of a liquid into porous material or between contiguous surfaces, by lowering its surface tension. — *adj* **pen'etrāting** piercing; having keen and deep insight; sharp; keen; discerning. — *adv* **pen'etrātingly**. — *n* **penetrā'tion** the act or power of penetrating or entering; acuteness; discernment; the space-penetrating power of a telescope; the sexual act of inserting the penis into the vagina; the process and practices of espionage or infiltration within an organization, country, etc. — *adj* **pen'etrātive** tending or able to penetrate; piercing; having keen and deep insight; reaching and affecting the mind. — *adv* **pen'etrātively**. — *n* **pen'etrātiveness**. — *n* **pen'etrātor**. — **penetration agent** a person employed to penentrate and obtain information within an organization, country, etc. [L *penetrāre*, *-ātum*, from *penes* in the house, possession, or power of; formed on the model of *intrāre* to enter, from *intus* within; cf **penates**]

penfold. See under **pen**[1], and cf **pinfold**.

penful. See under **pen**[2].

penguin[1] *peng'gwin* or *pen'*, *n* any bird of the order *Sphenisciformes*, flightless sea birds of the Southern Hemisphere with modified flipper-like wings used for swimming, and black or bluish plumage except for the mainly white breast; a former name for the great auk; a training aeroplane that cannot fly (*slang*): a member of the Women's Royal Air Force, 'flappers who did not fly' (*old slang*). — Also **pin'guin**. — *n* **pen'guinery** or **pen'guinry** a penguin rookery or breeding-place. [According to some, Welsh *pen* head, and *gwyn* white, or the corresponding Breton words, though the great auk had a black head with two white patches: conjectures are *pin-wing*, and L *pinguis* fat]

penguin[2]. Same as **pinguin**[2].

penholder. See under **pen**[2].

peni. Spenserian spelling of **penny**.

penial. See under **penis**.

penicillate *pen-i-sil'it*, *-āt*, or *pen'*, *adj* tufted; forming a tuft; brush-shaped. — *adj* **penicill'iform** paint-brush-shaped. — *n* **penicill'in** a group of substances that stop the growth of bacteria, extracted from moulds, *esp* from *Penicillium notatum*, of the genus of fungi, **Penicill'ium** (**Ascomycetes**; see under **ascus**), which includes also the mould of jam, cheese, etc (*Penicillium glaucum*). — *n* **penicill'inase** an enzyme, produced by certain bacteria, that inactivates the effect of some penicillins. [L *pēnicillus* paintbrush, dimin of *pēnis* tail]

penie. Spenserian spelling of **penny**.
penile. See under **penis**.
penillion. See **pennill**.
peninsula *pen-in'sū-lə*, *n* a strip of land jutting out into water, a near-island. — *adj* **penin'sular**. — *n* **peninsular'ity**. — *vt* **penin'sulate** to form into a peninsula. — **peninsular unit** (in estate agent, etc parlance) a kitchen unit projecting into the room, a breakfast bar; **Peninsular War** the war in Spain and Portugal carried on by Great Britain against Napoleon's marshals (1808–14). — **the Peninsula** Spain and Portugal. [L *paenīnsula*, from *paene* almost, and *īnsula* an island]
penis *pē'nis*, *n* the external male organ used for copulation, and also (in mammals) for the excretion of urine: — *pl* **pē'nises** or **pē'nes** (*-nēz*). — *adj* **pē'nial** or **pē'nile**. — **penis envy** (*psychol*) the Freudian concept of a woman's subconscious wish for male characteristics. [L *pēnis*, orig a tail]
penistone *pen'i-stən*, *n* a cloth, a coarse frieze, formerly made at *Penistone* in Yorkshire.
penitent *pen'i-tənt*, *adj* suffering pain or sorrow for past sin and feeling a desire to reform; contrite; repentant; expressing sorrow for sin; undergoing penance; appropriate to penance. — *n* a person who repents of his or her sin; someone who has confessed sin, and is undergoing penance; a member of one of various orders devoted to penitential exercises and work among criminals, etc (*RC*). — *n* **pen'itence**. — *n* **pen'itency** (*rare*). — *adj* **penitential** (*-ten'shl*) of the nature of, pertaining to or expressive of penitence. — *n* a book of rules relating to penance; a penitent; (in *pl*) the behaviour or garb of a penitent; black clothes (*colloq*). — *adv* **peniten'tially**. — *adj* **penitentiary** (*-ten'shə-ri*) relating to penance; penitential; penal and reformatory. — *n* a penitent; an officer who deals with cases of penitence and penance; a RC office (under the *Grand Penitentiary*) at Rome dealing with cases of penance, dispensations, etc; a book for guidance in imposing penances; a place for the performance of penance (*obs*); an asylum for prostitutes (*archaic*); a reformatory prison or house of correction; a prison (*US*). — *adv* **pen'itently**. — **penitent form** a seat for penitents at an evangelistic meeting; **penitential garment** a rough garment worn for penance; **penitential psalms** seven psalms suitable for singing by penitents — the 6th, 32nd, 38th, 51st, 102nd, 130th, 143rd. [L *paenitēns*, *-entis*, pr p of *paenitēre* to cause to repent, to repent]
penk. Same as **pink**^{7}.
penknife, **penlight**, **penman**, etc. See under **pen**^{2}.
Penn. *abbrev*: Pennsylvania (US state).
penna *pen'ə*, *n* (*ornithol*) a feather, *esp* one of the large feathers of the wings or tail: — *pl* **penn'ae** (*-ē*). — *adj* **pennaceous** (*-ā'shəs*) featherlike. — *adj* **penn'ate** pinnate; winged, feathered, or like a wing in shape. — *n* **penne** (*pen*; *Spenser*) a pen; a pinion. — *adj* **penned** feathered; quilled; winged. — *adj* **penn'iform** feather-shaped. [L *penna* feather]
pennal *pen'əl* or *pen-äl'*, *n* formerly, a name for a freshman at a German university. — *n* **penn'alism** a system of fagging once in vogue at German universities. [Ger *Pennal*, from L *pennāle* pen-case]
pennant^1 *pen'ənt* or (*naut*) *pen'ən*, *n* a line dangling from the masthead, etc, with a block for tackle, etc (*naut*); a long narrow flag; a signalling or identifying flag; a pennon; a flag awarded for victory in a game, championship, etc (*esp* in baseball) (*US*). — **broad pennant** a long swallow-tailed flag flown by a commodore. [A combination of **pendant** and **pennon**]
pennant^2 *pen'ənt*, *n* and *adj* literally brook-head, a Welsh place name. — **pennant flag** a Welsh or West Country stone used for paving (also **pennant grit**, **rock** or **stone**). [Welsh *pen* head, and *nant* brook]
pennate. See under **penna**.
pennatula *pen-at'ū-lə*, *n* a member of the typical genus (*Pennatula*) of sea-pens: — *pl* **pennat'ūlae** (*-ē*) or **pennat'ūlas**. — *adj* **pennatulā'ceous**. [Fem of L *pennātulus* winged, from *penna* feather]
penne (*Spenser*). See under **penna**.
penneeck or **penneech** *pen-ēk'*, (*Scott*) *n* an old card game with a new trump for every trick.
penner. See under **pen**^{2}.
pennied, **pennies**. See under **penny**.
penniform. See under **penna**.
penniless. See under **penny**.
pennill *pen'il* or in Welsh *pen'ihl*, *n* literally, a verse or stanza: — *pl* **penill'ion**. — **penill'ion-singing** a form of Welsh verse-singing in which the singer improvises an independent melody and verse arrangement against an accompaniment (*usu* on the harp) consisting of a traditional Welsh melody repeated; a modern, modified form of penillion-singing involving one or more singers and allowing advance preparation. [Welsh]
pennine *pen'īn*, *n* a mineral of the chlorite group found in the *Pennine* Alps (between Switzerland and Italy), a hydrous silicate of aluminium, magnesium, and ironic. — Also **penn'inite** (*-in-īt*).
Pennisetum *pen-i-sē'təm*, (*bot*) *n* a genus, mainly African, of grasses with bristles around the spikelets, including bulrush millet or pearl millet. [L *penna* feather, and *saeta* bristle]
pennon *pen'ən*, *n* a medieval knight-bachelor's ensign; a flag or streamer attached to a lance; a flag; a long narrow flag or streamer; a pinion or wing (*Milton*). — *n* **penn'oncelle**, **pen'oncelle**, **penn'oncel** or **pen'oncel** a small flag like a pennon. — *adj* **penn'oned** bearing a pennon. [OFr *penon* streamer, arrow-feather, prob from L *penna* feather]
penn'orth. See **pennyworth** under **penny**.
penny *pen'i*, *n* a coin, *orig* silver, later copper, then bronze from 1860, worth 1/12 of a shilling, or 1/240 of a pound, now (also **new penny**) equal to a hundredth part of £1; its value; applied to various more or less similar coins; a cent (*US colloq*); a small sum; money in general; a denarius (*New Testament*); pound, in *four-penny*, *sixpenny*, *tenpenny nails*, being of four, six, ten *pound* weight to the thousand: — *pl* **pennies** *pen'iz* (as material objects) or **pence** *pens* (as units of value). — *adj* sold for a penny; costing a penny. — *adj* **penn'ied** possessed of a penny. — *adj* **penn'iless** without a penny; without money; poor. — *n* **penn'ilessness**. — *n* and *vi* **penny-a-line'**. — **penny-a-lin'er** a hack writer of the worst, or worst-paid, kind; **penny-a-lin'erism** a hack writer's expression; **penny arcade** an amusement arcade with slot machines *orig* operated by a penny; **penn'y-bank** a savings-bank that takes pennies; **penny black** the first adhesive postage stamp, issued by Britain, 1840; **penn'y-bun** or **penn'y-bun mushroom** a cep, *Boletus edulis*; **penn'ycress** a cruciferous plant of the genus *Thlaspi*, with round flat pods; **penn'y-dog'** the tope or miller's dog, a kind of shark; **penny dreadful** see under **dread**; **penn'y-far'thing** a penny and a farthing; an 'ordinary', an old-fashioned bicycle with a big wheel at the front and a little one at the back; **penn'y-fee** wages in money; (without *hyphen*) a small wage (*Scot*); **penny gaff** (*slang*) a low-class theatre. — *adj* **penny'-in-the-slot'** worked by putting a penny in a slot. — **penn'yland** (*hist*) land valued at a penny a year; **penny loafer** (*orig US*) a style of casual shoe with a slot into which a coin could be placed; **penny mail** (*Scot*) rent in money, not in kind; a small sum paid to a feudal lord; **penn'y-piece** a penny; **penn'y-pig** (*Scot*) a money-box, properly of earthenware (pig). — *vi* **penn'y-pinch'**. — *adj* **penn'y-pinch'ing** miserly, too concerned with saving money. — *adj* **penn'y-plain'** plain, straightforward, unpretentious (from 19c children's paper cut-out figures for toy theatres, costing one penny if plain, twopence if coloured; hence, **penny-plain, twopence-coloured** used of any two basically similar articles, one having a more attractive appearance). — **penn'y-post'** a means of, or organization for, carrying a letter for a penny; **penn'y-rent'** rent in money; income; **penny share** or **stock** (*stock exchange*) a share or stock trading

for less than £1 or $1, *usu* bought very speculatively; **penn'y-stone** or **-stane** (*Scot*) a round flat stone used as a quoit; **penn'ystone-cast'** a stone's throw for such a stone; **penn'y-wedd'ing** a wedding at which the guests each contribute a small sum towards the entertainment, etc, the surplus being presented as a gift to the bride and bridegroom; **penn'yweight** a unit equal to twenty-four grains of troy weight (the weight of a silver penny); **penn'y-whist'le** a tin whistle or flageolet; **penn'y-wis'dom** prudence in petty matters. — *adj* **penn'y-wise** careful at saving small sums, *esp* when careless in the saving of larger ones (**pound foolish**); niggardly on occasions when generosity is needed or expected. — **penn'y-wort** a name given to various plants with round leaves, *esp Hydrocotyle* (an umbelliferous marsh-plant) and navelwort (Cotyledon); **penn'yworth** a penny's worth of anything; the amount that can be got for a penny; a good bargain (also **penn'orth** *pen'ərth*; *colloq*). — **a penny for your thoughts** (*colloq*) what are you thinking (so deeply) about?; **a pretty penny** a considerable sum of money; **in penny numbers** a very few, or a very little, at a time; **not a penny the worse** none the worse; **pennies from heaven** money obtained without effort and unexpectedly; **Peter's pence** Rome-scot, a tax or tribute of a silver penny paid to the Pope — in England perhaps from the time of Offa of Mercia, in Ireland from Henry II, abolished under Henry VIII; a similar tax elsewhere; a voluntary contribution to the Pope in modern times; **spend a penny** see under **spend**; **the penny drops** now I (etc) understand; **turn an honest penny** to earn some money honestly; **two a penny** in abundant supply and of little value. [OE *penig*, oldest form *pending*; cf Ger *Pfennig*; Du *penning*; ON *penningr*]

pennyroyal *pen-i-roi'əl*, *n* a species of mint (*Mentha pulegium*) once valued in medicine; a related plant, *Hedeoma pulegioides* (*US*). [ME *puliol real*, from Anglo-Fr *puliol real*, from L *pūleium*, *pūlegium* pennyroyal, and *regālis*, *-e* royal]

pennyweight, **pennyworth**. See under **penny**.

pennywinkle. Same as **periwinkle**².

penology or **poenology** *pē-nol'ə-ji*, *n* the study of punishment in its relation to crime; the management of prisons. — *adj* **penological** (*-nə-loj'*). — *n* **penologist** (*-nol'ə-jist*). [Gr *poinē* punishment, and *logos* discourse]

penoncel, **penoncelle**. See under **pennon**.

pensée *pã-sā*, (*Fr*) *n* thought.

pensel. See **pensil**.

pensieroso *pen-sye-rō'sō*, (*Ital*) *adj* melancholy; thoughtful.

pensil, **pensel** or **pencel** *pen'sl*, *n* a small pennon. [Anglo-Fr *pencel*, dimin of *penon* pennon]

pensile *pen'sīl* or *-sil*, *adj* hanging; suspended; overhanging; (of birds) building a hanging nest. — *n* **pen'sileness** or **pensility** (*-sil'i-ti*). [L *pēnsilis*, from *pendēre* to hang]

pension *pen'shən*, *n* a Government allowance of money to a person who has retired, has been disabled, has reached old age, been widowed, orphaned, etc; an allowance paid by an employer to a retired employee; a periodical payment, as tribute, wages, etc (*obs*); an allowance of money as a bribe for future services, as a mark of favour, or in reward of one's own or another's merit; (now pronounced as *Fr*, *pã-syɔ̃*) a continental boarding-house; board. — *vt* to grant a pension to. — *adj* **pen'sionable** entitled, or entitling, to a pension. — *adj* **pen'sionary** receiving a pension; of the nature of a pension. — *n* a person who receives a pension; someone whose services are available to anyone paying the price, a hireling; the syndic or legal adviser of a Dutch town (*hist*). — *n* **pen'sioner** a person who receives a pension; a dependent; a gentleman-at-arms (*obs*); someone who pays out of his or her own income for commons, chambers, etc, at Cambridge University, the equivalent of an Oxford *commoner*; a boarder, *esp* in a religious house (*obs*). — **Grand Pensionary** (*hist*) the president of the States-general of Holland; **pension off** to dismiss, or allow to retire, with a pension; to dismiss or discard as no longer of value. [Fr, from L *pēnsiō*, *-ōnis*, from *pendere*, *pēnsum* to weigh, pay]

pensionnat *pã-syo-na*, (*Fr*) *n* a boarding-school.

pensive *pen'siv*, *adj* meditative; expressing thoughtfulness with sadness. — *adj* **pen'siv'd** (*Shakesp*) made pensive. — *adv* **pen'sively**. — *n* **pen'siveness**. [Fr *pensif*, *-ive*, from *penser* to think, from L *pēnsāre* to weigh, from *pendere* to weigh]

penstemon or **pentstemon** *pen-stē'mən* or *pent-*, *n* a plant of a mainly N American showy-flowered genus (*Penstemon* or *Pentstemon*) of Scrophulariaceae, with a sterile fifth stamen. [Gr *pente* five, and *stēmōn* warp, as if stamen]

penstock *pen'stok*, *n* a sluice; (in a hydroelectric or other plant) a valve-controlled water conduit. [**pen**¹ and **stock**¹]

pensum *pen'səm*, *n* a task; a school imposition (*US*). [L *pēnsum*]

Pent *abbrev*: Pentecost.

pent¹ *pa t* and *pa p* of **pen**¹, to shut up. — *adj* **pent'-up'** held in; repressed.

pent² *pent*, *n* a penthouse; a sloping or overhanging covering. — **pent'roof** a roof that slopes one way only. [From **penthouse**, appar influenced by Fr *pente* slope]

pent- *pent-* or **penta-** *pen-tə-*, *combining form* denoting five. [Gr *pente* five]

pentachlorophenol *pen-tə-klor-ə-fē'nöl*, *n* a widely used fungicidal and bactericidal compound, used *esp* as a wood preservative.

pentachord *pen'tə-körd*, (*music*) *n* a musical instrument with five strings; a diatonic series of five notes. [**penta-** and Gr *chordē* string]

pentacle *pent'ə-kl*, *n* a pentagram or similar figure (sometimes a hexagram) or amulet used as a defence against demons. [LL *pentaculum*, appar from Gr *pente*; according to some, OFr *pentacol*, from *pendre* to hang, *à* on, and *col* the neck]

Pentacrinus *pen-tak'rin-əs*, *n* a genus of fossil crinoids, in the form of a feathery five-rayed star on a long pentagonal stalk. — *adj* **pentac'rinoid** like or related to Pentacrinus. — *n* a young form of some crinoids that resembles Pentacrinus. [**penta-** and Gr *krinon* lily]

pentact *pent'akt*, *adj* five-rayed. — *n* a five-rayed sponge spicule. — *adj* **pentactinal** (*-ak'tin-əl* or *-ak-tī'nəl*). [**pent-** and Gr *aktīs*, *aktīnos* ray]

pentacyclic *pen-tə-sī'klik*, *adj* having five whorls. [**penta-** and Gr *kyklos* wheel]

pentad *pent'ad*, *n* a set of five things; a period of five years or five days; an atom, element or radical with a combining power of five. — Also *adj*. — *adj* **pentad'ic**. [Gr *pentas*, *-ados*]

pentadactyl or **pentadactyle** *pen-ta-dak'til*, *adj* having five digits. — *n* a person with five fingers and five toes. — *adj* **pentadactyl'ic** or **pentadac'tylous**. — *n* **pentadac'tylism**. — *n* **pentadac'tyly**. [**penta-** and Gr *daktylos* finger, toe]

pentadelphous *pen-tə-del'fəs*, *adj* having five bundles of stamens; united in five bundles. [**pent-** and Gr *adelphos* brother]

pentagon *pen'tə-gon*, *n* a rectilineal plane figure having five angles and five sides (*geom*); a fort with five bastions; (with *cap*) the headquarters of the US armed forces at Washington (from the shape of the building). — *adj* **pentagonal** (*pen-tag'ən-əl*). — *adv* **pentag'onally**. [Gr *pentagōnon*, from *pente* five, and *gōnia* angle]

pentagram *pen'tə-gram*, *n* a stellate pentagon or five-pointed star; such a figure used as a symbol in magic, mysticism, etc. [Gr *pentagrammon*, from *pente* five, and *gramma* a letter]

pentagraph a wrong form of **pantograph**.

Pentagynia *pen-tə-jin'i-ə*, (*obs*) *n pl* a Linnaean order of plants (in various classes) with five pistils. — *adj* **pentagyn'ian** or **pentagynous** (*-aj'*). [**penta-** and Gr *gynē* a woman, in the sense of female]

pentahedron *pen-tə-hē'dron, n* a five-faced solid figure: — *pl* **pentahē'drons** or **pentahē'dra**. — *adj* **pentahē'dral**. [**penta**- and Gr *hedrā a seat*]

pentalogy *pen-tal'əji, n* a pentad, *esp* of published works; a series of five related books. [**penta**-and -**logy**]

pentalpha *pen-tal'fə, n* a pentacle. [**pent**- and Gr *alpha* the letter alpha]

Pentameron *pen-tam'ər-ən, n* a famous collection of folk-tales in Neapolitan dialect by Giambattista Basile (d 1632) supposed to be told during five days. [Ital *Pentamerone*, from Gr *pente* five, and *hēmerā* day]

pentamerism *pen-tam'ər-izm, n* the condition of being pentamerous. — *adj* **pentam'erous** having five parts or members; having parts in fives. — *n* **pentam'ery**. [**penta**- and Gr *meros* a part]

pentameter *pen-tam'ə-tər, n* a line of verse of five measures or feet. — Also *adj*. — **elegiac pentameter** a verse of two penthemimers, the first admitting spondees instead of dactyls, the second dactyls only; **iambic pentameter** a somewhat unsuitable name for the line used in the English heroic couplet and blank verse. [Gr *pentametros*, from *pente* five, and *metron* a measure]

pentamidine *pen-tam'i-dēn, (pharm) n* a drug first used to combat tropical diseases such as sleeping-sickness, later found effective against a form of pneumonia common in AIDS patients. [*pen*tane, *amid*e and chem sfx -*ine*]

Pentandria *pen-tan'driə, (obs) n pl* in Linnaeus's classification, a class of plants with five stamens. — *adj* **pentan'drian** or **pentan'drous**. [**pent**- and Gr *anēr, andros* a man, male]

pentane *pent'ān, (chem) n* a hydrocarbon (C_5H_{12}), fifth member of the methane series. [**penta**-]

pentangle *pen'tang-gl, n* a pentacle; a pentagon. — *adj* **pentang'ular**. [**pent**- and **angle**[1]]

pentaploid *pent'ə-ploid, adj* fivefold; having five times the haploid number of chromosomes (*biol*). — *n* a cell, organism, or form with five sets of chromosomes. — *n* **pent'aploidy** the condition of having five sets of chromosomes. [Gr *pentaploos* fivefold, and *eidos* form]

pentapody *pen-tap'ə-di, n* a measure of five feet. — *adj* **pentapodic** (*pent-ə-pod'ik*). [**penta** and Gr *pous, podos* a foot]

pentapolis *pen-tap'ol-is, n* a group of five cities, *esp* those of Cyrenaica — Cyrene, Berenice, Arsinoe, Ptolemais, and Apollonia. — *adj* **pentapolitan** (*pent-ə-pol'i-tən*). [**penta**- and Gr *polis* a city]

pentaprism *pent'ə-prizm, (photog) n* a five-sided prism that corrects lateral inversion by turning light through an angle of 90°, used on reflex cameras to allow eye-level viewing. [**penta**- and **prism**]

pentarch[1] *pent'ärk*, (of roots) having five vascular strands. [**pent**- and Gr *archē* beginning]

pentarch[2] *pent'ark, n* a ruler or governor in a pentarchy. — *n* **pentarchy** (*pent'ärk-i*) government by five persons; a group of five kings, rulers, states, or governments. [**pent**- and Gr *archē* rule]

pentastich *pent'ə-stik, n* a group of five lines of verse: — *pl* **pentastichs** (*-stiks*). — *adj* **pentastichous** (*pen-tas'ti-kəs*) five-ranked. [**pent**- and Gr *stichos* row, line]

pentastyle *pen'tə-stil, adj* having five columns in front. — *n* a building or portico with five columns. [**penta**- and Gr *stȳlos* a pillar]

pentasyllabic *pen-tə-si-lab'ik, adj* five-syllabled. [**penta**- and **syllabic** (see under **syllable**)]

Pentateuch *pen-tə-tūk, n* the first five books of the Old Testament. — *adj* **pentateuch'al**. [Gr *pentateuchos* five volumed, from *penta* and *teuchos* a tool, (later) a book]

pentathlete *pen-tath'lēt, n* a competitor in the pentathlon.

pentathlon *pen-tath'lon, n* a sporting contest made up of five exercises — wrestling, disc-throwing, spear-throwing, leaping, and running; a five-event contest at the modern Olympic games from 1906–24; a five-event Olympic games contest for women; (**modern pentathlon**) an Olympic games contest consisting of swimming, cross-country riding and running, fencing and revolver-shooting — also (Latin) **pentath'lum**. [Gr *pentathlon*, from *pente* five, and *athlon* contest]

pentatomic *pent-ə-tom'ik, (chem) adj* having five atoms, *esp* five atoms of replaceable hydrogen; pentavalent. [**pent**- and Gr *atomos* atom]

pentatonic *pent-ə-ton'ik, (music) adj* consisting of five tones or notes — applied *esp* to a scale, a major scale with the fourth and seventh omitted. [**penta**- and Gr *tonos* tone]

pentavalent *pen-tə-vā'lənt* or *pen-tav'ə-lənt, (chem) adj* having a valency of five. [**penta**- and -**valent**]

pentazocine *pen-tā'zə-sēn, n* a pain-killing drug believed to be non-addictive.

penteconter *pen-ti-kon'tər, n* an ancient Greek ship with fifty oars. [Gr *pentēkontērēs*, from *pentēkonta* fifty]

Pentecost *pent'i-kost, n* a Jewish festival held on the fiftieth day after the Passover (also called the **Feast of Weeks**, and **Shabuoth** or **Shavuot**); the Christian festival of Whitsuntide, seven weeks after Easter. — *adj* **Pentecost'al** of or relating to Pentecost; of or relating to any of several fundamentalist Christian groups placing great emphasis on the spiritual powers of the Holy Spirit. — *n* a Pentecostalist; (in *pl*) offerings formerly made to the parish priest at Whitsuntide. — *n* **Pentecost'alist** a member of a Pentecostal church. [Gr *pentēkostē* (*hēmerā*), fiftieth (day)]

Pentel® *pen'tel, n* (also without *cap*) a type of disposable felt-tip or ballpoint pen.

Pentelic *pen-tel'ik* or **Pentelican** *pen-tel'ik-ən, adj* of Mount *Pentelicus* near Athens, famous for the marble found there.

pentene. See **pentylene**.

penteteric *pen-ti-ter'ik, adj* occurring every fourth (or by the old mode of reckoning, fifth) year. [Gr *pentetērikos*, from *etos* a year]

penthemimer *pen-thi-mim'ər, (prosody) n* a metrical group of $2\frac{1}{2}$ feet. — *adj* **penthemim'eral**. [Gr *pente* five, *hēmi*-half, and *meros* a part]

penthia *pen'thi-ə, n* (according to Spenser) another name for the unidentified plant Astrophel.

penthouse *pent'hows, n orig* a separate room or dwelling on a roof; now *usu* a flat on the top floor, or roof, of a (*usu* tall) building, *esp* a luxury flat; a shed or lean-to projecting from or adjoining a main building; (in real tennis) a roofed corridor surrounding the court; a protection from the weather over a door or a window; anything of similar form, eg an eyebrow: — *pl* **pent'houses** (*-how-ziz*). — *vt* to provide or cover with, or as if with, a penthouse. [For **pentice**, from Fr *appentis*, from LL *appendicium* an appendage]

pentice or **pentise** *pen'tis*. Same as **penthouse**.

pentimento *pen-ti-men'tō, (art) n* the revealing of a (part of a) painting beneath another painted over it at a later time; such a part or painting revealed: — *pl* **pentimen'ti** (*-tē*). [Ital, from *pentirsi* to repent]

pentlandite *pent'lənd-īt, n* a native sulphide of iron and nickel. [Joseph Barclay *Pentland* (1797–1873), traveller in South America]

pentobarbitone *pen-tə-bär'bit-ōn* or *US* **pentobarbital** *-bär'bi-tal, (pharmacol) n* a barbiturate drug, $C_{11}H_{17}N_2O_3$, with hypnotic, sedative, and anticonvulsant effects.

pentode *pent'ōd, (electronics) n* a thermionic tube with five electrodes. [Gr *pente* five, and *hodos* way]

pentomic *pen-tom'ik, adj* (of an army division) formed into five units, *esp* when using atomic weapons. [Gr *pente* five, and **atomic**]

pentose *pent'ōs, (chem) n* a sugar (of various kinds) with five oxygen atoms. — *n* **pent'osan** (*-san*) or **pent'osane** (*-sān*) a carbohydrate that yields pentose on hydrolysis. [Gr *pente* five]

Pentothal® *pen'tō-thal, n* a registered trademark for thiopentone sodium (in *NAm* thiopental sodium), an intravenous anaesthetic, a sodium thiobarbiturate compound. — Also **Pentothal sodium**.

pentoxide *pent-ok'sīd*, (*chem*) *n* a compound having 5 atoms of oxygen combined with another element or radical. [Gr *pente* five, and **oxide**]

pentroof. See under **pent**[2].

Pentstemon. See under **Penstemon**.

pent-up. See under **pent**[1].

pentylene *pent'i-lēn*, (*chem*) *n* amylene, an unsaturated hydrocarbon (C_5H_{10}) of the olefine series (in several isomers). — Also **pent'ene**. [Gr *pente* five, and *hȳlē* matter]

penuche, **penuchi**. Same as **panocha**.

penuchle. See **pinochle**.

penult *pi-nult'* or *pē'nult* or **penult'ima** *-imə*, *n* the last but one syllable. — *adj* **penult'imate** last but one. — *n* the penult; the last but one. [L *paenultima* (*syllaba*, etc), from *paene* almost, and *ultimus* last]

penumbra *pen-um'brə*, *n* a partial or lighter shadow round the perfect or darker shadow of an eclipse; the less dark border of a sun-spot or any similar spot; the part of a picture where the light and shade blend into each other. — *adj* **penum'bral**. — *adj* **penum'brous**. [L *paene* almost, and *umbra* shade]

penury *pen'ū-ri*, *n* want, lack; great poverty. — *adj* **penū'rious** lacking (*obs*); scanty (*obs*); niggardly; miserly. — *adv* **penū'riously**. — *n* **penū'riousness**. [L *pēnūria*]

peon *pē'on*, *n* a day-labourer, *esp* formerly in Spanish-speaking America, one working off a debt by bondage; in India (*pūn*), a foot-soldier (*hist*), a policeman (*hist*), or a messenger; in SE Asia, a minor office worker. — *n* **pē'onage** or **pē'onism** agricultural servitude of the above kind. [Sp *peón* and Port *peão*, from LL *pedō*, *-ōnis* a foot-soldier, from L *pēs*, *pedis* a foot]

peony or **paeony** *pē'ə-ni*, *n* any plant of the genus *Paeonia*, of the buttercup family, perennial and deciduous shrubs having large showy crimson, pink, yellow or white globular flowers; its flower. — Also *obs* forms **pī'oney** and **pī'ony**. [OE *peonie* and OFr (Northern) *pione* (Fr *pivoine*), from L *paeōnia*, from Gr *paiōniā*, from *Paiōn*, *Paiān* physician of the gods (see **Paean**) from its use in medicine]

people *pē'pl*, *n* (in the following senses, used as a *sing* with a *pl* **peoples** (often **people** in the Bible)) a set of persons; a nation; a community; a body of persons held together by a common origin, speech, culture, political union, or by a common leadership, headship, etc; transferred to a set of animals as if forming a nation; (in the following senses, used as a *pl*) the mass of the nation; general population; populace; the citizens; voters; subjects; followers; retainers; employees; servants; attendants; congregation; close relatives; members of one's household; parents; ancestors and descendants; inhabitants of a place; transferred to animal inhabitants; the persons associated with any business; laity; (approaching a *pronoun*) they, one, folks. — Often used in combination to denote belonging or relating to the people, general populace (as in *people-power*, *people-oriented*, etc). — *vt* to stock with people or inhabitants; to inhabit; to occupy as if inhabiting. — **people mover** a car, carriage, etc, used to transport people at airports, etc, usually running on a fixed rail or track; **people's democracy** a form of government in which the proletariat, represented by the Communist Party, holds power — seen ideologically as a transitional state on the way to full socialism; **people's front** same as **popular front** (qv under **popular**); **People's Party** see **populist** under **popular**; **People's Republic** a name adopted by some socialist or communist states. [OFr *poeple*, from L *populus*]

PEP *pep*, *abbrev*: personal equity plan; political and economic planning.

pep *pep*, (*colloq*) *n* vigour, go, spirit, life. — *vt* to put pep into (*usu* with *up*). — *adj* **pep'ful**. — *adj* **pepp'y**. — **pep pill** a pill containing a stimulant drug; **pep talk** a strongly-worded talk designed to arouse enthusiasm for a cause or course of action. [**pepper**]

peperino *pep-ə-rē'nō*, *n* a dark tuff with many crystals and rock-fragments, found in the Alban Hills. [Ital *peperino*, from L *piper* pepper]

peperomia *pep-ər-ō'mi-ə*, *n* any of a large genus (*Peperomia*) of subtropical herbaceous plants of the family *Piperaceae*, many grown as house plants for their ornamental foliage. [Gr *peperi* pepper, and *homoios* like, similar]

peperoni. See **pepperoni**.

pepful. See under **pep**.

pepino *pə-pē'nō*, *n* a purple-striped pale yellow fruit with sweet flesh, oval (often elongated) in shape; the spiny-leaved S American plant (*Solanum muricatum*) that bears this fruit. — Also called **mel'on-pear**. [Sp, cucumber.]

peplos *pep'los* or **peplus** *pep'ləs*, *n* a draped outer robe worn *usu* by women in ancient Greece. — *n* **pep'lum** a peplos; an overskirt supposed to be like the peplos; hence, a short skirt-like section attached to the waist-line of a dress, blouse or jacket. [Gr *peplos*]

pepo *pē'pō*, *n* the type of fruit found in the melon and cucumber family, a large many-seeded berry formed from an inferior ovary, *usu* with hard epicarp: — *pl* **pē'pos**. [L *pepō*, *-onis*, from Gr (*sikyos*) *pepōn* (a melon eaten) ripe, distinguished from a cucumber eaten unripe]

pepper *pep'ər*, *n* a pungent aromatic condiment consisting of the dried berries of the pepper plant, whole or ground (*black pepper*), or with the outer parts removed (*white pepper*); any plant of the genus *Piper*, *esp Piper nigrum*, or of the family *Piperaceae*; a plant of the solanaceous genus *Capsicum* or one of its pods (*red*, *yellow* or *green pepper*; also called **sweet pepper**); cayenne (also **cayenne pepper**); extended to various similar condiments and the plants producing them. — *vt* to sprinkle or flavour with pepper; to sprinkle; to pelt with shot, etc; to pelt thoroughly; to do for. — *vi* to pelt; to shower liberally; to discharge shot, etc, in showers. — *n* **pepp'erer** a grocer (*obs*); someone who or that which peppers. — *n* **pepp'eriness**. — *n* **pepp'ering**. — *adj* **pepp'ery** having the taste or qualities of pepper; pungent; hot, choleric, irritable. — *adj* **pepper-and-salt'** mingled black and white; (of hair) flecked or streaked with grey. — **pepp'er-box** a pepper-pot; a turret or other object of similar shape; **pepp'er-cake** a kind of spiced cake or gingerbread; **pepp'er-caster** or **-castor** a pepper-pot; **pepp'ercorn** the dried berry of the pepper plant; something of little value. — *adj* like a peppercorn (eg the small tight knots in which certain African peoples traditionally wear their hair); trivial, nominal, as in *peppercorn rent*. — *adj* **pepp'ercorny**. — **pepp'er-gin'gerbread** (*Shakesp*) hot-spiced gingerbread; **pepp'er-grass** any cress of the genus *Lepidium*; pillwort (*Pilularia*); **pepp'ermill** a small handmill in which peppercorns are ground; **pepp'ermint** an aromatic and pungent species of mint (*Mentha piperita*); the essence distilled from it; a sweet flavoured with it; **peppermint cream** a sweet creamy peppermint-flavoured substance; a sweet made of this; **pepp'ermint-drop** a peppermint-flavoured, *usu* hard, sweet; **pepp'er-pot** a pot or bottle with a perforated top for sprinkling pepper; a West Indian dish of cassareep, flesh or dried fish, and vegetables, *esp* green okra and chillies; **pepper tree** an evergreen tree of the genus *Schinus*, chiefly native to tropical America, often grown for its ornamental appearance; **pepp'erwort** a cress of the genus *Lepidium*, *esp dittander* (*L latifolium*). — **Jamaica pepper** allspice; **long pepper** the fruit of *Piper longum*; **Negro pepper** the produce of Xylopia (familiar Anonaceae), also called **Ethiopian pepper**. [OE *pipor*, from L *piper*, from Gr *peperi*, from Sans *pippali*]

pepperoni or **peperoni** *pep-ə-rō'ni* *n* a hard, spicy beef and pork sausage. [Ital *peperoni*, pl of *peperone* chilli, pepper, from L *piper* pepper]

Pepper's ghost *pep'ərz gōst*, *n* a phantom produced on the stage by a sheet of glass reflecting an actor on an understage. [John H *Pepper* (1821–1900), improver and exhibitor of H Dircks's invention]

peppy. See under **pep**.

pepsin or **pepsine** *pep'sin*, *n* any of a group of digestive enzymes in the gastric juice of vertebrates, which breaks down proteins under acidic conditions; a preparation containing pepsin from a pig's or other stomach (*med*). — *vt* **pep'sinate** to treat with pepsin; to mix or combine with pepsin. — *n* **pep'sinogen** a zymogen found in granular form in the mucous membrane of the stomach mucosa which converts into pepsin in a slightly acid medium. — *adj* **pep'tic** relating to or promoting digestion; having a good digestion; of or relating to pepsin or the digestive juices. — *n* **pepticity** (*-tis'i-ti*) eupepsy. — *n pl* **pep'tics** (*jocular*) the digestive organs. — *n* **pep'tidase** an enzyme which breaks down peptides into their constituent amino acids. — *n* **pep'tide** any of a number of substances formed from amino-acids in which the amino-group of one is joined to the carboxyl group of another. — *n* **peptīzā'tion** or **-s-**. — *vt* **pept'ize** or **-ise** to bring into colloidal solution; to form into a sol from a gel. — *n* **pep'tōne** a product of the action of enzymes on proteins, used eg as a bacteriological culture medium. — *n* **peptonīzā'tion** or **-s-**. — *vt* **pep'tonize** or **-ise** to convert into peptones. — **peptic ulcer** an ulcer of the stomach, duodenum, etc. [Gr *pepsis* digestion, from *peptein* to digest]

Pepysian *pēp'si-ən*, *adj* pertaining to Samuel *Pepys* (1633–1703), his inimitable diary, or the collections he bequeathed to Magdalene College, Cambridge.

per[1] *pûr* or *pər*, *prep* for each or a; (chiefly commercial) by; in the manner or direction of (*heraldry*). — **as per usual** (*colloq*) as usual. [L and OFr *per*]

per[2] *pûr* or *per*, (*L*) through, by means of, according to (also **as per**). — **per annum**, **diem** or **mensem** (*an'əm* or *-ōōm*, *dī'əm* or *dē'em*, or *men'səm* or *men'sem*) yearly, daily or monthly); **per ardua ad astra** (*är'dū-ə ad as'trə* or *är'dōō-ä ad as'trä*) by steep and toilsome ways to the stars — Air Force motto; **per capita** (*kap'i-tə* or *kap'i-tä*) or **per caput** (*kap'ōōt*) (counting) by heads; for each person; all sharing alike; **per contra** (*kon'trə* or *kon'trä*) on the contrary; as a contrast; **per fas et nefas** (*fas et nē'fas* or *fäs et ne'fäs*) through right and wrong; **per impossibile** (*im-po-si'bi-lē* or *im-po-si'bi-le*) by an impossibility; if it were so, which it is not; **per incuriam** (*in-kū'ri-am* or *in-kōō'ri-am*; *legal*) through lack of care, a phrase designating a court decision that is mistaken and therefore not binding as a precedent; **per minas** (*mī'* or *mē'näs*; *legal*) by means of threats, by menaces; **per procurationem** (*prok-ū-rā-shi-ō'nem* or *prō-kōō-rä-ti-ō'nem*) by the agency of another, by proxy; **per saltum** (*sal'təm* or *sal'tōōm*) at a single leap; all at once; **per se** (*sē* or *sā*) by himself, etc; essentially; in itself; **per stirpes** (*stûr'pēz* or *stir'pās*) (of an inheritance) bequeathed in blocks to families who subdivide it equally among the members, rather than directly to individuals themselves (per capita).

per. *abbrev*: period; person.

per- *pûr-* or *pər-*, *combining form* denoting: (1) the highest degree of combination with oxygen or other element or radical (*chem*); (2) in words from Latin, through, beyond, or thoroughly, or indicating destruction.

peracute *pûr-ə-kūt'*, *adj* very sharp or violent. [L *peracūtus*, from *per-* thoroughly, and *acūtus* sharp]

peradventure *pûr-əd-ven'chər*, *adv* by adventure; by chance; perhaps. — *n* (*obs*) uncertainty; question. [OFr *per* (or *par*) *aventure* by chance]

peraeon, **peraeopod**. See **pereion**.

perai *pē-rī'*. See **piranha**.

perambulate *pər-am'bū-lāt*, *vt* to walk through, about, around, up and down, or over; to pass through for the purpose of surveying; to establish the boundary of (eg a parish) by ceremonially walking round it, to beat the bounds of; to patrol; to wheel in a pram. — *vi* to walk about. — *n* **perambulā'tion** the act of perambulating; a survey or inspection by travelling through; beating the bounds; the district within which a person has the right of inspection. — *n* **peram'bulātor** a person who perambulates; a wheel for measuring distances on roads; a light hand-pushed carriage for a baby or young child (now *usu* **pram**). — *adj* **peram'bulatory**. [L *perambulāre*, *-ātum*, from *per* through, and *ambulāre* to walk]

per an. *abbrev*: per annum (see **per**[2]).

Perca. See **perch**[1].

percale *per-käl'* or *pər-kāl'*, *n* a closely woven French cambric. — *n* **percaline** (*pûr-kə-lēn'* or *pûr'-*) a glossy cotton cloth. [Fr; cf Pers *purgālah* rag]

percase *pər-kās'*, (*obs*) *adv* perchance; perhaps. [L *per* through, by, and *casus* a chance, a fall]

perce *pûrs*, (*Spenser*) same as **pierce**. — Also (*infin*) **percen**. — *adj* (*Spenser*) **perce'able** pierceable. — *adj* **perce'ant** (*Keats*) piercing.

perceive *pər-sēv'*, *vt* to become or be aware of through the senses; to get knowledge of by the mind; to see, see clearly; to understand; to discern; to view subjectively; to believe, suppose; to see partially, or be mistaken in (what one sees). — *adj* **perceiv'able**. — *adv* **perceiv'ably** perceptibly. — *n* **perceiv'er**. — *n* and *adj* **perceiv'ing**. — **perceived noise decibel** a unit used to measure the amount of annoyance caused to people by noise. [OFr *percever*, from L *percipere*, *perceptum*, from pfx *per-* thoroughly, and *capere* to take]

per cent (sometimes written or printed with a point after it as if an abbreviation for *per centum*, but pronounced as a complete word, *pər-sent'*) in the hundred; for each hundred or hundred pounds. — *n* a percentage; (in *pl*, in combination) securities yielding a specified percentage (eg *three-percents*). — *n* **percent'age** rate per hundred; an allowance of so much for every hundred; a proportional part; commission (*colloq*); profit, advantage (*colloq*). — *adj* **percent'al** or **percen'tile**. — *n* **percen'tile** the value below which falls a specified percentage (eg 25, 50 or 75) of a large number of statistical units (eg scores in an examination); percentile rank. — **percentile rank** grading according to percentile group. — **play the percentages** (in sport, gambling, etc) to play, operate or proceed by means of unspectacular safe shots, moves, etc as opposed to spectacular but risky ones which may not succeed, on the assumption that this is more likely to lead to success in the long run. [L *per centum*]

percept *pûr'sept*, *n* an object perceived by the senses; the mental result of perceiving. — *n* **perceptibil'ity**. — *adj* **percep'tible** that can be perceived; that may be known by the senses; discernible. — *adv* **percep'tibly**. — *n* **percep'tion** the act or power of perceiving; discernment; apprehension of any modification of consciousness; the combining of sensations into a recognition of an object; direct recognition; a percept; reception of a stimulus (*bot*). — *adj* **percep'tional**. — *adj* **percep'tive** able or quick to perceive; discerning; active or instrumental in perceiving. — *n* **percep'tiveness**. — *n* **perceptiv'ity**. — *adj* **percep'tūal** of the nature of, or relating to, perception. [L *percipere*, *perceptum*; see **perceive**]

perch[1] *pûrch*, *n* a spiny-finned freshwater fish of the genus **Perca** (*pûr'kə*); extended to various similar or related fishes. — *n pl* **Percidae** (*pûr'si-dē*) the perch family. — *adj* **per'ciform**, **per'cine** (*-sīn*) or **per'coid** (*-koid*). [L *perca* (partly through Fr *perche*), from Gr *perkē* a perch, perh connected with *perknos* dusky]

perch[2] *pûrch*, *n* a pole (*obs* or *dialect* except in special uses); a rod for a bird to alight, sit, or roost on; anything serving that purpose for a bird, a person, or anything else; a high seat; a pole serving as a navigation mark; a pole joining the fore and hind gear of some vehicles; a bar or frame for stretching cloth for examination; a bar for fixing leather for softening treatment; a peg or bar for hanging things on (*obs*); a rod or pole, a measure of $5\frac{1}{2}$ yards (5·03 metres) or (*square perch*) $30\frac{1}{4}$ square yards (25·3 sq metres); a measure of stonework, $24\frac{3}{4}$ or 25 cubic feet (0·7 cu metres). — *vi* to alight, sit or roost on a perch; to be set on high; to be balanced on a high or narrow footing; to settle. — *vt* to place, as on a perch; to stretch, examine, or treat on a perch. — *adj* **perch'ed** (*Milton*) having perches. — *n* **perch'er** a bird with feet adapted for perching. — *adj* **perch'ery** (of eggs) laid by hens kept in a modified deep litter system, where provision is made for the birds to roost as they would in the wild on branches, etc. — *n* **perch'ing** examination of cloth on a perch; a process of leather-softening. — *adj* with feet adapted for perching; insessorial. — **perched block** a block of rock carried by a glacier and left perched high up, often in an unstable position, when the ice recedes; **perching birds** the Passeriformes. [Fr *perche*, from L *pertica* a rod]

perchance *pər-chäns'*, *adv* by chance; as it may happen; perhaps. [Anglo-Fr *par chance*]

perched, percher, perchery. See under **perch**[2].

percheron *per'shə-rɔ̃* or *pûr'shə-ron*, *n* a draught-horse of a breed originating in La *Perche* in Southern Normandy. — Also *adj*. [Fr]

perchloric *pər-klō-rik* or *-klö'rik*, (*chem*) *adj* containing more oxygen than chloric acid — applied to an oily explosive acid, $HClO_4$. — *n* **perchlō'rate** a salt of perchloric acid. [**per-** (1)]

perchloroethylene *pər-klör-ō-eth'i-lēn*, *n* a liquid used as a solvent in dry-cleaning.

Percidae, perciform, percine. See under **perch**[1].

percipient *pər-sip'i-ənt*, *adj* perceiving; having the faculty of perception; observant, perceptive. — *n* a person who perceives or can perceive; someone who receives impressions telepathically or by other means outside the range of the senses. — *n* **percip'ience** or (*rare*) **percip'iency**. [L *percipiēns*, *-entis*, pr p of *percipere*; cf **perceive, percept**]

percoct *pər-kokt'*, *adj* well-cooked; overdone; hackneyed. [L *percoctus*, from *percoquere* to cook thoroughly]

percoid *pûr'koid*. See under **perch**[1].

percolate *pûr'kə-lāt*, *vt* and *vi* to pass through pores, small openings, etc; to filter; to make (coffee) in a percolator. — *n* a filtered liquid. — *n* **percolation** (*pûr-kō-lā'shən*). — *n* **per'colātor** an apparatus for percolating; a coffee pot inside which boiling water is made to pass repeatedly over coffee grounds laid on a filter. [L *percōlāre*, *-ātum*, from *per* through, and *cōlāre* to strain]

percolin *pûr'kə-lin*, *n* a small bird, a cross between a partridge and a quail.

percurrent *pər-kur'ənt*, *adj* running through the whole length. — *adj* **percursory** (*-kūr'*) cursory. [L *percurrere* to run through, *percursor* one who runs through]

percuss *pər-kus'*, *vt* to strike so as to shake; to strike or tap sharply; to tap for the purposes of diagnosis. — *adj* **percuss'ant** (*heraldry*) bent round and striking the side (eg of a lion's tail) — also **percussed'**. — *n* **percussion** (*-kush'ən*) striking; impact; tapping directly or indirectly upon the body to find the condition of an organ by the sound (*med*); massage by tapping; the striking or sounding of a discord, etc, as distinguished from preparation and resolution (*music*); collectively, instruments played by striking — drum, cymbals, triangle, etc (*music*); a device for making an organ-pipe sound promptly by striking the reed (*music*). — *adj* **percus-s'ional**. — *n* **percuss'ionist** a musician who plays percussion instruments. — *adj* **percussive** (*-kus'*). — *adv* **percuss'ively**. — *n* **percuss'or** a percussion hammer. — *adj* **percutient** (*-kū'shyent*) striking or having the power to strike. — *n* that which strikes or has the power to strike. — **percuss'ion-bull'et** a bullet that explodes on striking; **percuss'ion-cap** a metal case containing a substance which explodes when struck, formerly used for firing rifles, etc (see also **cap**); a small paper case of the same type, used to make children's toy guns sound realistic (*usu* **cap**); **percuss'ion-fuse** a fuse in a projectile that acts on striking; **percuss'ion-hamm'er** a small hammer for percussion in diagnosis; **percuss'ion-lock** a gun lock in which a hammer strikes a percussion-cap; **percuss'ion-pow'der** powder that explodes on being struck, fulminating powder. — **bulb of percussion** see under **bulb**. [L *percussiō*, *-ōnis*, from *percutere*, *percussum*, from pfx *per-* thoroughly, and *quatere* to shake]

percutaneous *pər-kū-tā'ni-əs*, *adj* done or applied through the skin. — *adv* **percutā'neously**. [**per-** (2), and L *cutis* the skin]

percutient. See under **percuss**.

perdendo *per-den'dō*, (*music*) *adj* and *adv* slowing and softening at the same time. — Also **perden'dosi** (*-sē*). [Ital]

perdie or **perdy** *pər-dē'*, sometimes *pûr'dē*, (*Spenser*, *Shakesp*) *adv* assuredly. — Also **pardi'**, **pardie'** or **pardy'**. [OFr *par dé* by God]

perdition *pər-dish'ən*, *n* loss (*archaic*); ruin (*archaic*); utter loss or ruin (*archaic*); everlasting misery after death, damnation (*Christian relig*); hell (*Christian relig*). — *adj* **perdi'tionable**. [L *perditiō*, *-ōnis*, from *perdere*, *perditum*, from pfx *per-* entirely, and *dare* to give, give up]

perdu or **perdue** *pər-dū'*, *adj* lost to view; concealed; in a post of extreme danger (*obs*); on a forlorn hope or on a desperate enterprise (*obs*); reckless. — *n* an outlying sentinel (*Shakesp*); someone lying in concealment or ambush; a person on a forlorn hope (*obs*). — **lie perdu** or **perdue** (*military*) to lie in ambush, concealed and on the watch. [Fr, pa p of *perdre* to lose, from L *perdere* to destroy; see **perdition**]

perduellion *pər-dū-el'yən*, (*archaic*) *n* treason. [L *perduelliō*, *-ōnis*]

perdurable *pər-dūr'ə-bl* (*rare*; *Shakesp pûr'*), *adj* very durable, long continued; everlasting. — *n* **perdūrabil'ity**. — *adv* **perdūr'ably** (*Shakesp pûr'*) very durably; everlastingly. — *n* **perdūr'ance**. — *n* **perdūrā'tion**. — *vi* **perdūre'** to endure. [L *perdūrāre*, from *per* through, and *dūrāre* to last]

perdy. See **perdie**.

père *per*, (*Fr*) *n* father. — **Père David's** (*dā'vidz*, *dā'vēdz* or *-vēdz'*) **deer** a breed of large grey deer discovered in China by Father A *David*, 19th-century French missionary, and now surviving only in captivity.

peregal *per'i-gl*, (*obs*) *adj* fully equal. — *n* an equal. [OFr *paregal*, from L pfx *per-* thoroughly, and *aequālis* equal]

peregrine *per'i-grin*, *adj* foreign (*archaic*); outlandish (*archaic*); making a pilgrimage or journey (*archaic*); applied to a species of falcon (*Falco peregrinus*), so named because taken not from the (inaccessible) nest (as an eyas is) but captured in flight. — *n* a foreign resident (*archaic*); a pilgrim or traveller in a foreign land (*archaic*); a peregrine falcon. — *vi* **per'egrinate** to travel about; to live in a foreign country; to go on a pilgrimage. — *vt* to traverse. — *adj* foreign-looking. — *n* **peregrinā'tion** travelling about; wandering; pilgrimage; a complete and systematic course or round; a sojourn abroad. — *n* **per'egrinātor** someone who travels about. — *adj* **per'egrinatory** of or pertaining to a peregrinator; wandering. — *n* **peregrin'ity** foreignness; outlandishness. [L *peregrīnus* foreign, from *peregre* abroad, from *per* through, and *ager* field]

pereion *pə-rī'on* or *-rē'*, *n* the thorax in Crustacea: — *pl* **perei'a**. — *n* **perei'opod** a crustacean's thoracic walking-leg. — Also in corrected forms **peraeon** and **peraeopod** (*-rē'*). [Faultily formed from Gr *peraioein* to transport, to carry across]

pereira *pə-re'rə* or **pereira bark** (*bärk*), *n* a Brazilian apocynaceous tree, the bark of which is used medicinally; the bark itself. [From Jonathan *Pereira*, 19th-century English pharmacologist]

peremptory *pər-em'* or *pər-emp'tə-ri*, or *per'əm-* or *per'-əmp'tə-ri*, *adj* precluding debate or dispute (*Roman law*); final; admitting no refusal or denial; definitely fixed (*law*); utter (*obs*); dogmatic; imperious; arrogantly commanding. — *adv* **peremp'torily** (or *per'*). — *n* **peremp'toriness** (or *per'*). [L *peremptōrius*, from *perimere*, *peremptum* to destroy, prevent, from pfx *per-* entirely, and *emere* to take, to buy]

perennial *pər-en'yəl*, *adj* lasting through the year; perpetual; never failing; growing constantly; lasting more than two years (*bot*); (of insects) living more than one year. — *n* a plant that lives more than two years. — *vi* **perenn'ate** to live perennially; to survive from season to season, *esp* through a period of inactivity. — *n* **perennā'tion** (*per-*). — *n* **perennial'ity** the quality of being perennial — also **perenn'ity** (*archaic*). — *adv* **perenn'ially**. [L *perennis*, from *per* through, and *annus* a year]

perennibranchiate *pər-en-i-brang'ki-it* or *-āt*, *adj* retaining the gills throughout life. — *adj* and *n* **perenn'ibranch** (*-brangk*). [L *perennis* lasting through the years, and *branchiae* gills]

perennity. See under **perennial**.

perestroika *per-i-stroy'kə*, (*Russ*) *n* reconstruction or restructuring, *specif* the restructuring of political and economic systems carried out in the former Soviet Union in the 1980s. [Russ]

perf. *abbrev*: perfect.

perfay *pər-fā'*, (*archaic*) *interj* by my faith. [OFr *par fei*]

perfect *pûr'fekt* or *-fikt*, *adj* done thoroughly or completely; completed; mature; complete; having all organs in a functional condition; having androecium and gynaeceum in the same flower (*bot*); completely skilled or versed; thoroughly known or acquired; exact; exactly conforming to definition or theory; without flaw, blemish or fault; having every moral excellence; sheer, utter; absolute; completely contented (*Shakesp*); denoting completed action (*gram*); certain, convinced (*Shakesp*); of the simpler kind of consonance (*music*); triple (*old music*; applied to time). — *n* the perfect tense; a verb in the perfect tense. — *vt* **perfect** (*pər-fekt'* or *pûr'*) to make perfect; to finish; to teach fully, to make fully skilled in anything; to print the second side of (a sheet of paper). — *n* **perfectā'tion** (*rare*). — *n* **perfect'er** (or *pûr'*). — *n pl* **perfect'i** (*-ī*) a body of Catharists in the 12th and 13th centuries, living very strict lives. — *n* **perfectibil'ian** a believer in the perfectibility of mankind. — *n* **perfect'ibilism** the belief that man is capable of becoming perfect or of progressing indefinitely towards perfection. — *n* **perfect'ibilist**. — *n* **perfectibil'ity** capability of becoming perfect; perfectibilism. — *adj* **perfect'ible** capable of becoming or being made perfect. — *n* **perfec'tion** the state of being perfect; a quality in perfect degree; the highest state or degree; an embodiment of the perfect; loosely, a degree of excellence approaching the perfect. — *vt* **perfec'tionate** to bring to perfection. — *n* **perfec'tionism**. — *n* **perfec'tionist** a person who claims to be perfect; a person who aims at or calls for nothing short of perfection; someone who holds some doctrine concerning perfection; someone who thinks that moral perfection can be attained in this life; (with *cap*) one of the Bible Communists or Free-lovers, a small American sect founded by J H Noyes (1811–86), which settled at Oneida in 1848, holding that the gospel if accepted secures freedom from sin. — *adj* **perfectionist'ic** seeking to attain perfection; being a perfectionist. — *adj* **perfect'ive** tending to make perfect; (of a verb aspect) denoting completed action (*gram*). — *adv* **perfect'ively**. — *adv* **per'fectly**. — *n* **per'fectness** the state or quality of being perfect; completeness. — *n* **perfect'o** (*Sp*, perfect; *pl* **perfect'os**) a large tapering cigar. — *n* **perfect'or** someone who perfects; a machine for printing both sides at once. — **perfect binding** an unsewn bookbinding in which the backs of the gathered sections are sheared off and the leaves held in place by glue; **perfect cadence** (*music*) one passing from the chord of the dominant to that of the tonic; **perfect competition** (*econ*) free competition for the sale of a commodity; **perfect fifth** (*music*) the interval between two sounds whose vibration frequencies are as 2 to 3; **perfect fluid** an ideal fluid, incompressible, of uniform density, and offering no resistance to distorting forces; **perfect fourth** (*music*) the interval between sounds whose vibration frequencies are as 3 to 4; **perfect gas** same as **ideal gas**; **perfect insect** the imago or completely developed form of an insect; **perfect interval** (*music*) the fourth, fifth, or octave; **perfect metals** noble metals; **perfect number** (*math*) a number equal to the sum of its factors (including unity), as $6 = 1 + 2 + 3$, $28 = 1 + 2 + 4 + 7 + 14$; **perfect pitch** (*music*) the pitch of a note as determined by the number of vibrations per second; the ability to identify or remember a note accurately; a term often used for **absolute pitch** (see under **absolute**); **perfect tense** a tense signifying action completed in the past (eg *I have said*) or at the time spoken of (**past perfect** or **pluperfect** eg *I had said*; **future perfect** eg *I shall have left by then*); **perfect year** see **year**. — **to perfection** perfectly. [ME *parfit*, from OFr *parfit*; assimilated to L *perfectus*, pa p of *perficere*, from pfx *per-* thoroughly, and *facere* to do]

perfecta *pər-fek'tə*, (*orig US*) *n* a form of bet in which the punter has to select, and place in the correct order, the two horses or dogs, etc which will come first and second in a race. [Am Sp (*quiniela*) *perfecta* perfect (quiniela); cf **quinella** and **trifecta**]

perfervid *pər-fûr'vid*, (*poetic*) *adj* very fervid; ardent; eager. — *n* **perfervidity** (*pûr-fər-vid'i-ti*). — *n* **perfer'vidness**. — *n* **perfer'vour** or **perfer'vor**. [L *perfervidus*, from *prae* before, and *fervidus* fervid]

perfet *pûr'fet*, *adj* an older form (used by Milton) of **perfect**.

perficient *pər-fish'ənt*, *adj* effectual; actually achieving a result. [L *perficiēns*, *-entis*, pr p of *perficere* to complete, from pfx *per-* thoroughly, and *facere* to do, make]

perfidious *pər-fid'i-əs*, *adj* faithless; unfaithful, deceitful, treacherous. — *adv* **perfid'iously**. — *n* **perfid'iousness**. — *n* **perfidy** (*pûr'fid-i*). [L *perfidiōsus*, from *perfidia* faithlessness, from pfx *per-*, implying destruction, and *fidēs* faith]

perfluor- or **perfluoro-** *pər-flōōr-* or *pər-floor'ō-*, *combining form* denoting (in a chemical compound) substitution of most or all of the hydrogen by fluorine. — *n* **perfluorocar'bon** an organic compound in which much of the hydrogen has been replaced by fluorine; any binary compound of carbon and fluorine, similar to a hydrocarbon. [**per**(1), **fluorine** and **carbon**]

perfoliate *pər-fō'li-āt*, (*bot*) *adj* (of a leaf) having the base joined around the stem, so as to appear pierced by the stem (*orig* said of the stem passing through the leaf, or of the plant). — *n* **perfoliā'tion**. [**per-** (2), and L *folium* a leaf]

perforans *pûr'fər-ans*, (*anatom*) *n* the long flexor muscle of the toes, or the deep flexor muscle of the fingers, whose tendons pass through those of the perforatus. — *n* **perforatus** (*pûr-fər-ā'tes*) the short flexor of the toes or the superficial flexor of the fingers. [Ety as for **perforate**]

perforate *pûr'fə-rāt*, *vt* to bore through or into; to pierce or to make a hole through; to make a series of small holes in (paper, etc) to facilitate tearing; to penetrate; to pass through by a hole. — *adj* pierced by a hole or holes; having an aperture; dotted with pellucid dots (*bot*); pierced by rows of small holes for easy separation (eg of a sheet of postage-stamps) (more usually **per'forated**). — *adj* **per'forable**. — *adj* **per'forant** perforating. — *n* **perforation** (*pûr-fə-rā'shən*) the act of making a hole; the formation of a hole or aperture; the condition of being perforated; a hole through or into anything; a series, or one of a series, of small holes, as for ease in tearing paper. — *adj* **per'forātive** having the power to pierce. — *n* **per'forātor** someone who bores; a boring instrument or organ. [L *perforāre*, *-ātum*, from *per* through, and *forāre* to bore]

perforce *pər-fōrs'* or *-förs'*, *adv* by force; of necessity. [OFr *par force*]

perform *pər-förm'*, *vt* to do; to carry out duly; to act in fulfilment of; to carry into effect; to fulfil; to bring about; to render; to execute; to go through duly; to act; to play in due form. — *vi* to do what is to be done; to execute a function; to act, behave; to act a part; to play, sing or dance; to do feats, tricks, or other acts for an audience; to lose one's temper (*Austr colloq*). — *adj*

perform'able capable of being performed; practicable. — *n* **perform'ance** the act of performing; a carrying out of something; something done; a piece of work; manner or success in working; execution, *esp* as an exhibition or entertainment; an act or action; the power or capability of a machine (*esp* a motor vehicle) to perform; an instance of awkward, aggressive, embarrassing, etc, behaviour (*colloq*). — *adj* **perform'a-tive** of a statement or verb that itself constitutes the action described, eg *I confess my ignorance*. — *n* such a statement (opposite of **constative**). — *n* **perform'er** a person who performs; someone who does or fulfils what is required; an executant; someone who takes part in a performance or performances; an entertainer. — *adj* **perfor'ming** that performs; trained to perform tricks. — *n* performance. — **performance art** a theatrical presentation in which several art forms, such as acting, music and photography, are combined; **performance test** (*psychol*) a test, *usu* to assess a person's intelligence, done by observing his or her ability to manipulate eg blocks of different colours or shapes; **performing arts** those for which an audience is usually present, eg drama, ballet, etc; **performing right** the right to give a public performance of a piece of music, a play, etc. [Anglo-Fr *parfourmer*, appar an altered form of *parfourner*, from OFr *parfournir*, from *par*, from L *per* through, and *fournir* to furnish]

perfume *pûr'fūm*, formerly and still sometimes *pər-fūm'*, *n* fragrance; sweet-smelling smoke or fumes from burning; a fragrant substance (*usu* a liquid) applied to the body to give a pleasant smell; any substance made or used for the sake of its pleasant smell. — *vt* **perfume** (*pər-fūm'* or *pûr'fūm*) to scent. — *adj* **per'fumed** (or *pər-fūmd'*). — *adj* **per'fumeless** (or *-fūm'*). — *n* **perfū'mer** a person who fumigates; a maker or seller of perfumes. — *n* **perfū'mery** perfumes in general; the art of preparing perfumes; the shop or place in a shop where perfumes are sold. — *adj* **per'fūmy**. [Fr *parfum*, from L *per* through, and *fūmus* smoke]

perfunctory *pər-fungk'tə-ri*, *adj* done merely as a duty to be got through; done for form's sake, or in mere routine; acting without zeal or interest; merely formal; hasty and superficial. — *adv* **perfunc'torily**. — *n* **perfunc'toriness**. [L *perfunctōrius*, from *perfunctus*, pa p of *perfungī* to execute, from pfx *per-* thoroughly, and *fungī* to do]

perfuse *pər-fūz'*, *vt* to pour or diffuse through or over; to pass (a liquid) through an organ or tissue. — *n* **perfusate** (*-fūz'āt*) that which is perfused. — *n* **perfusion** (*-fū'zhən*) the pouring on or diffusion through anything; treatment by continous blood transfusion (*med*). — *n* **perfu'sionist** the member of a surgical team administering this. — *adj* **perfusive** (*-fū'siv*). [L *perfūsus* poured over, from *per* through, and *fundere*, *fūsus* to pour]

pergameneous *pûr-gə-mē'ni-əs*, *adj* parchment-like. — *adj* **pergamentaceous** (*-mən-tā'shəs*) parchment-like. [L *pergamēna*; see **parchment**]

pergola *pûr'gə-lə*, *n* a framework for climbing plants, more open than a trellis, and *usu* passing overhead to form a canopied wall. [Ital, from L *pergula* a shed]

pergunnah. See **pargana**.

perh *abbrev*: perhaps.

perhaps *pər-haps'*, *adv* it may be; possibly; as it may happen. [From the pl of **hap**[1], after the model of **peradventure**, **percase**, and **perchance**]

peri *pē'ri*, *n* (in Persian mythology) a beautiful but malevolent being with supernatural powers; a beautiful fairy. [Pers *parī* or *perī* a fairy]

peri- *per'i-* or *pə-ri'-*, *combining form* denoting (1) around; (2) (*esp* in *astron*) near. [Gr *peri* around]

periagua *per-i-ä'gwə*. See **piragua**.

periaktos *per-i-ak'tos*, *n* (in the ancient Greek theatre) a tall revolving prism at the side of the stage, projecting a variety of backdrops. [Gr, revolving]

perianth *per'i-anth*, (*bot*) *n* the calyx and corolla together, *esp* when not clearly distinguishable. — Also *adj*. [**peri-** (1), and Gr *anthos* flower]

periapt *per'i-apt*, (*Shakesp*) *n* an amulet. [Gr *periapton* something hung round, from *peri* around, and *haptein* to fasten]

periastron *per-i-as'tron*, (*astron*) *n* that stage in the orbit of a comet, a component of a binary star, etc when it is closest to the star around which it revolves. [**peri-** (2), and Gr *astron* star]

periblast *per'i-blast*, (*biol*) *n* the outer layer of protoplasm surrounding the nucleus of a cell or ovum; cytoplasm. [**peri-** (1), and Gr *blastos* a sprout]

periblem *per'i-blem*, (*bot*) *n* the layer of primary meristem from which the cortex is formed, covering the plerome. [Gr *periblēma* garment, mantle, from *peri* around, and *ballein* to throw]

peribolos *per-ib'o-los*, *n* a precinct; its enclosing wall: — *pl* **perib'oloi**. — Also (Latinized) **perib'olus**: — *pl* **perib'olī**. [Gr, from *peri* around, and *ballein* to throw]

pericardium *per-i-kär'di-əm*, (*anatom*) *n* the sac round the heart. — *adj* **pericar'diac**, **pericar'dial** or **pericar'dian**. — *n* **pericardī'tis** inflammation of the pericardium. [Latinized from Gr *perikardion*, from *peri* around, and *kardiā* heart]

pericarp *per'i-kärp*, (*bot*) *n* the wall of a fruit, derived from that of the ovary. — *adj* **pericar'pial**. [Gr *perikarpion*, from *peri* around, and *karpos* fruit]

pericentral *per-i-sen'trəl*, *adj* surrounding a centre or central body. — *adj* **pericen'tric**. [**peri-** (1), and Gr *kentron* point, centre]

perichaetium *per-i-kē'shyəm*, (*bot*) *n* a sheath or cluster of leaves around the archegonia (or the antheridia) in mosses and liverworts. — *adj* **perichae'tial** (*-shl*). [**peri-** (1), and Gr *chaitē* flowing hair]

perichondrium *per-i-kon'dri-əm*, (*anatom*) *n* the fibrous membrane covering a cartilage. — *adj* **perichon'drial**. [**peri-** (1), and Gr *chondros* cartilage]

perichoresis *per-i-kor-ē'sis*, (*theol*) *n* circumincession. [Gr, rotation, from *perichorein* to rotate, from *peri* around, and *chorein* to make room]

perichylous *per-i-kī'ləs*, (*bot*) *adj* having water-storing tissue outside the green tissue. [**peri-** (1), and Gr *chȳlos* juice]

periclase *per'i-klāz* or *-klās*, (*chem*) *n* magnesium oxide occurring naturally in isometric crystals. [Gr pfx *peri-* very, and *klasis* fracture (from its perfect cleavage)]

Periclean *per-i-klē'ən*, *adj* of *Pericles* (d 429 BC) or the golden age of art and letters at Athens.

periclinal *per-i-klī'nəl*, *adj* sloping downwards in all directions from a point (*geol*); parallel to the outer surface (*bot*). — *n* **per'icline** a variety of albite feldspar of oblique appearance. [Gr *periklinēs* sloping on all sides, from *peri* around and *klīnein* to slope]

periclitate *pər-ik'li-tāt*, (*archaic*) *vt* to endanger. [L *perīclitārī*, *-ātus*]

pericon *per-i-kōn'*, *n* an Argentinian folk-dance performed by couples dancing in a ring: — *pl* **pericones** (*-kō'nāz*). [Am Sp]

pericope *pər-ik'o-pē*, *n* an extract or passage, *esp* one selected for reading in church. [Gr *perikopē*, from *peri* around, and *koptein* to cut]

pericranium *per-i-krā'ni-əm*, *n* the membrane that surrounds the cranium; (loosely) the skull or brain. — *adj* **pericrā'nial**. — *n* **per'icrāny** (*obs*) pericranium. [Latinized from Gr *perikrānion*, from *peri* around, and *krānion* skull]

periculous *pər-ik'ū-ləs*, (*obs*) *adj* dangerous. [L *perīculum* danger]

pericycle *per'i-sī-kl*, (*bot*) *n* the outermost layer or layers of the central cylinder. — *adj* **pericy'clic**. [Gr *perikyklos* all round, from *peri* around, and *kyklos* a circle]

pericynthion *per-i-sin'thi-ən*, *n*. Same as **perilune**. [**peri-** (2), and *Cynthia*, a name of the goddess of the moon]

periderm *per'i-dûrm*, *n* the horny cuticular covering of a hydroid colony; the cork-cambium with the cork and other tissues derived from it, forming a protective outer covering in plants. — *adj* **periderm'al**. [**peri-** (1) and Gr *derma* skin]

peridesmium *per-i-des'mi-əm*, (*anatom*) *n* the areolar tissue round a ligament. [**peri-** (1) and Gr *desmos* a band]

peridial. See under **peridium**.

peridinian *per-i-din'i-ən*, *n* a dinoflagellate. — *n* **Peridin'ium** a genus of dinoflagellates; (without *cap*) a member of the genus: — *pl* **peridin'iums** or **peridin'ia**. [Gr *peridinein* to whirl around]

peridium *pər-id'i-əm*, *n* the outer coat of a fungus fruit-body. — *adj* **perid'ial**. [Latinized from Gr *pēridion*, dimin of *pērā* a wallet]

peridot *per'i-dot* or **peridote** *-dōt*, *n* olivine; a green olivine used in jewellery. — *adj* **peridot'ic**. — *n* **peridotite** (*-dō'tīt*) a coarse-grained igneous rock mainly composed of olivine, *usu* with other ferro-magnesian minerals but little or no feldspar. [Fr *péridot*; origin unknown]

peridrome *per'i-drōm*, *n* the space between the cell and surrounding pillars in an ancient temple. [Gr *peridromos* running round, from *peri* around, and *dromos* a run]

periegesis *per-i-ē-jē'sis*, *n* a description in the manner of a tour; a progress or journey through. [Gr *periēgēsis*, from *peri* around, and *hēgeesthai* to lead]

perigastric *per-i-gas'trik*, (*physiol*) *adj* surrounding the alimentary canal. — *n* **perigastrī'tis** inflammation of the outer surface of the stomach. [**peri-** (1) and Gr *gastēr* belly]

perigee *per'i-jē*, (*astron*) *n* the point of the moon's, or any artificial satellite's, orbit at which it is nearest the earth (opposite of *apogee*). — *adj* **perigē'al** or **perigē'an**. [Gr *perigeion* neuter of *perigeios* round or near the earth, from *peri* and *gē* earth]

perigenesis *per-i-jen'i-sis*, *n* reproduction (according to Haeckel's theory) by transmission not only of chemical material but of vibrations of plastidules. [**peri-** (1) and Gr *genesis* generation]

periglacial *per-i-glā'si-əl*, *-glās'yəl* or *-glā'shəl*, *adj* bordering a glacier; of, like or pertaining to a region bordering a glacier. [**peri-** (1) and L *glaciālis* icy, from *glaciēs* ice]

perigon *per'i-gən*, *n* an angle of 360° — also called a **round angle**. [**peri-** (1) and Gr *gōniā* angle]

perigone *per'i-gōn*, (*bot*) *n* an undifferentiated perianth; a covering of the seed in sedges. — *adj* **perigō'nial**. — *n* **perigō'nium** a cluster of leaves round moss antheridia. [**peri-** (1) and Gr *gonē* generative organ]

Perigordian *per-i-gör'di-ən*, *adj* pertaining to the Palaeolithic epoch to which the Lascaux Cave paintings and other examples of primitive art belong. [*Périgord* region in SW France]

perigynous *pər-ij'i-nəs*, (*bot*) *adj* having the receptacle developed as a disc or open cup, with sepals, petals, and stamens borne on its margin, the carpels not embedded in it; (of sepals, petals, or stamens) inserted on the receptacle in such a way, distinguished from *epigynous* and *hypogynous*. — *n* **perig'yny**. [**peri-** (1) and Gr *gynē* woman (used for female)]

perihelion *per-i-hē'li-ən*, *n* the point of the orbit of a planet or a comet at which it is nearest to the sun (opposite of *aphelion*); culmination (*fig*). — Also *adj*. [**peri-** (2) and Gr *hēlios* the sun]

perihepatic *per-i-hi-pat'ik*, *adj* (*physiol*) surrounding the liver. — *n* **perihepatitis** (*-hep-ə-tī'tis*; *med*) inflammation of the peritoneum covering the liver. [**peri-** (1) and Gr *hēpar*, *hēpatos* liver]

perikaryon *per-i-kar'i-on*, *n* that part of a nerve cell which contains the nucleus: — *pl* **perikar'ya**. [**peri-** (1) and Gr *karyon* kernel]

peril *per'il*, *n* danger. — *vt* to expose to danger: — *pr p* **per'illing**; *pa t* and *pa p* **per'illed**. — *adj* **per'ilous** dangerous. — *adv* **per'ilously**. — *n* **per'ilousness**. [Fr *péril*, from L *perīculum*]

perilune *per'i-lūn* or *-lo͞on*, *n* the point in a spacecraft's orbit round the moon where it is closest to it — also **pericynthion**. [**peri-** (2) and Fr *lune*, from L *luna* moon]

perilymph *per'i-limf*, *n* the fluid surrounding the membranous labyrinth of the ear. [**peri-** (1) and **lymph**]

perimeter *pər-im'i-tər*, *n* the circuit or boundary of any plane figure, or the sum of all its sides (*geom*); an instrument for measuring the field of vision (*ophthalmol*); the boundary of a camp or fortified position; the outer edge of any area. — *adj* **perimetric** (*per-i-met'rik*), **perim'etral** or **perimet'rical**. — *n* **perim'etry**. [Gr *perimetros*, from *peri* around, and *metron* measure]

perimorph *per'i-mörf*, *n* one mineral enclosing another. — *adj* **perimorph'ic**. — *adj* **perimorph'ous**. [**peri-** (1) and Gr *morphē* form]

perimysium *per-i-miz'i-əm*, (*anatom*) *n* the connective tissue which surrounds and binds together muscle fibres. [**peri-** (1) and *-mysium*, from Gr *mus* muscle]

perinaeum. See **perineum**.

perinatal *per-i-nā'tl*, *adj* pertaining to the period between the seventh month of pregnancy and the first week of the baby's life. [**peri-** (1) and **natal**[1]]

perinephrium *per-i-nef'ri-əm*, *n* the fatty tissue surrounding the kidney. — *adj* **perineph'ric**. — *n* **perinephrī'tis** (*med*) inflammation of the perinephrium. [**peri-** (1) and Gr *nephros* kidney]

perineum or **perinaeum** *per-i-nē'əm*, (*physiol*) *n* the lower part of the body between the genital organs and the anus. — *adj* **perine'al**. [Latinized from Gr *perinaion*]

perineurium *per-i-nū'ri-əm*, (*physiol*) *n* the sheath of connective tissue surrounding a bundle of nerve fibres. — *adj* **perineu'ral**. — *n* (*med*) **perineurī'tis** inflammation of the perineurium. [**peri-** (1) and Gr *neuron* nerve]

period *pē'ri-əd*, *n* the time in which anything runs its course; an interval of time at the end of which events recur in the same order; the time required for a complete oscillation — reciprocal of the frequency; the time of a complete revolution of a heavenly body about its primary; the difference between two successive values of a variable for which a function has the same value (*math*); the recurring part of a circulating decimal (*math*); a set of figures (*usu* three) in a large number marked off eg by commas; a series of chemical elements represented in a horizontal row of the periodic table; a stretch of time; a long stretch, an age; one of the main divisions of geological time; a stage or phase in history, in a person's life and development, in a disease, or in any course of events; a time; a division of the school day, the time of one lesson; the end of a course; a recurring time; the menstrual discharge or the time when it occurs; an end (*rare*); a goal (*archaic*); a complete sentence, *esp* one of elaborate construction; a division analogous to a sentence (*music*); (in *pl*) rounded rolling rhetoric; a mark (.) at the end of a sentence, a full stop (the word is inserted at the end of a sentence to emphasize the finality of the statement); a rhythmical division in Greek verse. — *adj* (of eg architecture, furniture or a play) characteristic, representative, imitative of, belonging to or dealing with a past period. — *vt* (*Shakesp*) to put an end to. — *adj* **periodic** (*pēr-i-od'ik*) relating to a period or periods; of revolution in an orbit; having a period; recurring regularly in the same order; (loosely) occurring from time to time; characterized by or constructed in periods; pertaining to periodicals (*rare*). — *adj* **period'ical** periodic; published in numbers at more or less regular intervals; of, for, or in such publications. — *n* a magazine or other publication that appears at stated intervals (not *usu* including newspapers). — *n* **period'icalist** a person who writes in a periodical. — *adv* **period'ically** at regular intervals; in a periodic manner; in a periodical publication; (loosely) from time to time. — *n* **periodicity** (*-dis'*) the fact or character of being periodic; frequency. — *n* **periodīzā'tion** or **-īsā'tion** division into periods. — **periodic function** (*math*) one whose values recur in a cycle as the variable increases; **periodic law** that the properties of atoms are periodic functions of their atomic numbers; **periodic sentence** a sentence constructed in such a way that it is not until the final clause that the requirements of sense and grammar are met; **periodic system** the classification of chemical elements according to the periodic law; **periodic table** a table of chemical elements in order of atomic number arranged in horizontal series and vertical groups, showing how similar properties recur at regular intervals; **periodic wind** a wind which blows at or for a certain period, eg a trade-wind, a monsoon, a land-breeze, a sea-breeze; **period of grace** a specific time allowed to both parties to a contract to fulfil any obligations arising from that contract; **period piece** an object belonging to a past age *esp* with charm or value; a person ludicrously behind the times; a play, novel, etc, set in a past time. — **the period** the current age, or age in question. [Fr *période*, from L *periodus*, from Gr *periodos*, from *peri* around, and *hodos* a way]

periodate *pər-ī'ō-dāt*, *n* a salt or ester of periodic acid. — **periodic acid** (*per-ī-od'ik*) an acid (H_5IO_6) containing more oxygen than iodic acid. [**per-** (1) and **iodine**]

periodontal *per-i-ō-dont'əl*, *adj* (pertaining to tissues or regions) round about a tooth. — *n* **periodon'tia** (*-shi-ə*), **periodon'tics** (*n sing*) or **periodontol'ogy** the branch of dentistry concerned with periodontal diseases. — *n* **periodon'tist**. — *n* **periodontī'tis** the inflammation of the tissues surrounding the teeth. [**peri-** (1) and *odous*, *odontos* tooth]

perionychium *per-i-o-nik'i-əm*, (*anatom*) *n* the skin surrounding a fingernail or toenail. [**peri-** (1) and Gr *onux* a nail]

Periophthalmus *per-i-of-thal'məs*, *n* a genus of fishes, related to gobies, with protruding mobile eyes and pectoral fins used as legs. [Latinized from Gr *peri* around, and *ophthalmos* eye]

periosteum *per-i-os'ti-əm*, *n* a tough fibrous membrane covering the surface of bones. — Also **per'iost**. — *adj* **perios'teal**. — *adj* **periostit'ic**. — *n* **periostī'tis** inflammation of the periosteum. [Gr *periosteon* (neuter adj), from *peri* around, and *osteon* a bone]

periostracum *per-i-os'trə-kəm*, *n* the horny outer layer of a mollusc's shell. [Latinized from Gr *peri* around, and *ostrakon* shell]

periotic *per-i-ō'tik* or *-ot'ik*, *adj* around the inner ear. — *n* a periotic bone. [**peri-** (1) and Gr *ous*, *ōtos* the ear]

peripatetic *per-i-pə-tet'ik*, *adj* walking about; itinerant (eg of a teacher who is employed to teach at more than one establishment, travelling from one to another); Aristotelian. — *n* a pedestrian; an itinerant; an Aristotelian. — *adj* **peripatet'ical**. — *n* **peripatet'icism** (*-i-sizm*) the philosophy of Aristotle. [Gr *peripatētikos*, from *peripatos* a walk, from *peri* around, and *pateein* to walk; Aristotle is said to have taught in the walks of the Lyceum at Athens]

Peripatus *pər-ip'ə-təs*, *n* a genus of arthropods of the Onychophora, showing affinities with worms; (without *cap*) a member of the genus. [Gr *peripatos* a walking about; cf **peripatetic**]

peripeteia or **peripetia** *per-i-pe-tī'ə*, *n* a sudden change of fortune, *esp* in drama. — Also **perip'ety**. — *adj* **peripetei'an** or **peripeti'an**. [Gr *peripeteia*, from *peri* around, and *pet-* the root of *piptein* to fall]

periphery *pər-if'ə-ri*, *n* a line or surface acting as a boundary; the outside of anything; a surrounding region. — *adj* **periph'eral** of or relating to a periphery; not of primary importance, incidental, minor. — *n* a peripheral unit. — *n* **peripheral'ity**. — *adj* **peripheric** (*per-i-fer'ik*) or **peripher'ical** (*archaic*). — **peripheral unit** or **devices** (in a computer system) the input (eg card reader), output (eg magnetic tape), and storage devices, which are connected to or controlled by the central processing unit; **periphery camera** same as **all-round camera**. [Gr *periphereia*, from *peri* around, and *pherein* to carry]

periphonic *per-i-fon'ik*, *adj* of or pertaining to a sound system with many speakers. [**peri-** (1) and Gr *phōnē* voice]

periphrasis *pər-if'rə-sis*, *n* circumlocution; round-about expression: — *pl* **periph'rases** (*-sēz*). — *n* **periphrase** (*per'i-frāz*) periphrasis: — *pl* **periphrās'es**. — *vt* to say with circumlocution. — *vi* to use circumlocution. — *adj* **periphrastic** (*per-i-fras'tik*) or **periphras'tical** using periphrasis; using at least two words instead of a single inflected form, *esp* of a verb tense involving an auxiliary. — *adv* **periphras'tically**. [Gr *periphrasis*, from *peri* around, and *phrasis* speech]

periphyton *pər-if'i-ton* or *per-i-fī'ton*, *n* aquatic organisms which are attached to, or cling to, stems and leaves of rooted plants, rocks, etc. [**peri-** (1) and Gr *phutos*, from *phutein* to grow]

periplast *per'i-pläst*, (*zool*) *n* intercellular substance; the ectoplasm of flagellates; a cuticle covering the ectoplasm. [**peri-** (1), and Gr *plastos* moulded]

periplus *per'i-plus*, *n* a circumnavigation; a narrative of a coasting voyage. [Gr *periploos*, contraction *-plous*, from *peri* around, and *ploos*, *plous* a voyage]

periproct *per'i-prokt*, (*zool*) *n* the region around the anus, *esp* in a sea-urchin. [**peri-** (1) and Gr *prōktos* anus]

peripteral *pər-ip'tə-rəl*, (*archit*) *adj* having one row of columns all round. — *n* **perip'tery** a peripteral building; the turbulent air immediately adjacent to a flying or falling object. [Gr *peripteros*, from *peri* around, and *pteron* a wing]

perique *pə-rēk'*, *n* a strongly-flavoured tobacco from Louisiana. [Perh *Périque*, nickname of a grower]

perisarc *per'i-särk*, (*zool*) *n* (in some Hydrozoans) the chitinous layer covering the polyps, etc. [**peri-** (1) and Gr *sarx*, *sarkos* flesh]

periscian *pər-ish'i-ən*, *n* a person living inside the polar circle, whose shadow moves round in a complete circle on those days on which the sun does not set. — Also *adj*. [**peri-** (1) and Gr *skiā* a shadow]

periscope *per'i-skōp*, *n* a device (eg a tube with mirrors) by which an observer can look at something which is not in the direct line of sight (eg over the heads of a crowd or out of a submarine, etc). — *adj* **periscopic** (*-skop'ik*). [Gr *periskopeein* to look around]

periselenium *per-i-si-lē'ni-əm*, (*astron*) *n* (in an elliptical orbit about the moon) that point which is closest to the moon. [**peri-** (2) and Gr *selēnē* moon]

perish *per'ish*, *vi* to pass away completely; to waste away; to decay; to lose life; to be destroyed; to be ruined or lost. — *vt* to destroy; to ruin; to cause to decay; to distress with cold, hunger, etc. — *n* **perishabil'ity**. — *adj* **per'ishable** that may perish; subject to speedy decay. — *n* that which is perishable; (in *pl*) food or other stuff liable to rapid deterioration. — *n* **per'ishableness**. — *adv* **per'ishably**. — *adj* **per'ished** distressed by cold, hunger, etc (*colloq* or *dialect*); (of materials such as rubber) weakened or injured by age or exposure. — *n* **per'isher** (*slang*) a reprehensible and annoying person. — *adj* **per'ishing** (*colloq* or *dialect*) freezing cold; vaguely used as a pejorative. — Also *adv*. — *adv* **per'ishingly**. — **do a perish** (*Austr colloq*) almost to die of lack of food or drink. [OFr *perir*, pr p *perissant*, from L *perire*, *peritum* to perish, from pfx *per-*, *and īre* to go]

perisperm *per'i-spûrm*, (*bot*) *n* nutritive tissue in a seed derived from the nucellus. — *adj* **perisper'mal**. — *adj* **perisper'mic**. [**peri-** (1) and Gr *sperma* seed]

perispomenon *per-i-spō'mən-on*, *adj* having a circumflex accent on the last syllable. — *n* a word carrying such an accent. [Gr, drawn round, circumflexed, from *peri* around, and *spaein* to pull, pluck]

perissodactyl *pər-is-ō-dak'til*, (*zool*) *adj* having an odd number of toes. — *n* an animal of the **Perissodac'tyla**, a division of ungulates with an odd number of toes, including the horse, tapir, rhinoceros, and some extinct species (distinguished from the *Artiodactyla*). — *adj* **perissodac'tylate**. — *adj* **perissodactyl'ic**. — *adj* **perissodac'tylous**. [Gr *perissos* odd, and *daktylos* a finger, toe]

perissology *per-is-ol'ə-ji*, *n* verbiage; pleonasm. [Gr *perissologiā*, from *perissos* excessive, and *logos* speech]

perissosyllabic *pər-is-ō-sil-ab'ik*, *adj* having an additional syllable. [Gr *perissosyllabos*, from *perissos* excessive, and *syllabē* syllable]

peristalith *pər-is'tə-lith*, *n* a stone circle. [Irregularly formed from Gr *peri* around, *histanai* to set up, and *lithos* a stone]

peristaltic *per-i-stal'tik*, *adj* forcing onward by waves of contraction, as the alimentary canal and other organs do their contents. — *n* **peristal'sis**. — *adv* **peristal'tically**. [Gr *peristaltikos*, from *peristellein* to wrap round, from *peri* around, and *stellein* to place]

peristerite *pər-is'tər-īt*, *n* an albite feldspar with a pigeon-like play of colour. [Gr *peristerā* pigeon]

peristeronic *pər-is-tər-on'ik*, *adj* of pigeons; pigeon-fancying. [Gr *peristerōn*, *-ōnos* pigeon-house]

peristome *per'i-stōm*, *n* the area, or a structure, surrounding a mouth; the fringe of teeth around the mouth of a moss-capsule; the margin of a gasteropod shell. — *adj* **peristōm'al**. — *adj* **peristomat'ic**. — *adj* **peristōm'ial**. [**peri-** (1), and Gr *stoma*, *-atos* mouth]

peristrephic *per-i-stref'ik*, *adj* moving round, revolving, rotatory. [Irregularly, from Gr *peristrephein* to whirl, from *peri* around, and *strephein* to turn]

peristyle *per'i-stīl*, (*archit*) *n* a range of columns round a building or round a square; a court, square, etc, with columns all round. — *adj* **peristy'lar**. [L *peristȳl(i)um*, from Gr *peristȳlon*, from *peri* around, and *stȳlos* a column]

peritectic *per-i-tek'tik*, *adj* in the state between solid and liquid; melting. [**peri-** (1) and Gr *tektikos* able to melt]

perithecium *per-i-thē'si-əm* or *-shi-əm*, *n* a flask-shaped fruit-body in fungi: — *pl* **perithe'cia**. — *adj* **perithe'cial**. [**peri-** (1) and Gr *thēkē* case]

peritoneum or **peritonaeum** *per-i-tən-ē'əm*, (*zool*) *n* a serous membrane enclosing the viscera in the abdominal and pelvic cavities. — *adj* **peritonē'al** or **peritonae'al**. — *n* **peritonēos'copy** (*med*) the visual examination of the peritoneal cavities by means of an endoscope inserted through an incision in the abdomen. — *adj* **peritonitic** (*-it'ik*) of peritonitis; suffering from peritonitis. — *n* **peritonī'tis** (*med*) inflammation of the peritoneum. [Gr *peritonaion*, from *peri* around, and *teinein* to stretch]

peritrich *per-it'rik*, *n* a bacterium bearing a ring of cilia around the body: — *pl* **perit'richa** (*-kə*). — *adj* **perit'richous** of or pertaining to peritricha; bearing a ring of cilia around the body. [**peri-** (2) and Gr *thrix*, *trichos* hair]

peritus *pe-rē'tŏŏs*, *n* a theological expert acting as a consultant within the Roman Catholic Church: — *pl* **periti** (*-tē*). [LL, from L, skilled]

perityphlitis *per-i-tif-lī'tis*, *n* inflammation of some part near the caecum or blind-gut. [**peri-** (1) and Gr *typhlos* blind]

perivitelline *per-i-vi-tel'ēn*, (*biol*) *adj* surrounding the yolk of an egg. [**peri-** (1) and **vitelline**]

periwig *per'i-wig*, (*hist*) *n* a wig. — *vt* to dress with, or as if with, a wig: — *pr p* **per'iwigging**; *pa t* and *pa p* **per'iwigged**. — *adj* **per'iwig-pā'ted** wearing a periwig. [Earlier *perwyke*, *perwig*, *perywig*, etc, from Fr *perruque*; see **peruke** and **wig**[1]]

periwinkle[1] *per'i-wingk-l*, *n* a creeping evergreen plant, growing in woods (*Vinca minor* and *Vinca major*; family **Apocynaceae**); the light blue colour of some of its flowers. — *adj* of this colour. [ME *peruenke*, from OE *peruince*, from L *pervinca*]

periwinkle[2] *per'i-wingk-l*, *n* an edible gasteropod with a spiral shell (*Littorina littorea*) abundant between tide-marks, or any other member of the genus; extended to other kinds. — Also **pennywinkle**. [OE (pl) *pinewinclan* (or perh *winewinclan*), from *wincle* a whelk]

perjink *pər-jingk'*, (*Scot*) *adj* prim; finical. — Also **perjink'ety**. — *n* **perjink'ity** a nicety. [Origin unknown]

perjure *pûr'jər*, *vt* to lie under oath to tell the truth, to forswear oneself (*refl*); to cause to swear falsely. — *vi* to swear falsely. — *n* (*Shakesp*) a perjured person. — *adj* **per'jured** having sworn falsely; (eg of an oath) being sworn falsely. — *n* **per'jurer**. — *adj* **perjurious** (*-jōō'ri-əs*) or **per'jurous** (*archaic*) guilty of or involving perjury. — *n* **per'jury** false swearing; the breaking of an oath; the crime committed by someone who, when giving evidence on oath or affirmation as a witness in a court of justice, gives evidence which he or she knows to be false (*law*). [OFr *parjurer*, from L *perjūrāre*, from *per-* negative prefix, and *jūrāre* to swear]

perk[1] *pûrk*, (*v* and *adj* now *archaic*) *vi* to bear oneself with self-confidence or self-assertion; to cock up; to stick out; to thrust forward (also *vt* with *it*); to move with pert briskness; to sit upright; to cock or toss or hold up the head; to dress smartly, dress up. — *adj* brisk; self-confident in manner. — *adv* **perk'ily**. — *n* **perk'iness**. — *adj* **perk'y** self-assertive; cocky; pert; in good spirits. — **perk up** to recover spirits or energy, *esp* in sickness; to jerk up, cock up; to decorate so as to look newer, more interesting, etc, to smarten up. [Origin uncertain]

perk[2] *pûrk*, a Northern and East Anglian form of **perch**[2].

perk[3] *pûrk*, (*colloq*) *n*. Short for **perquisite**.

perk[4] *pûrk*, *vt* and *n*. Short for **percolate** or **percolator** (referring to coffee).

perkin. See **parkin**.

perky. See under **perk**[1].

perlite *pûrl'īt*, *n* any acid volcanic glass with a perlitic structure; pearlite. — *adj* **perlitic** (*-it'ik*) showing little concentric spheroidal or spiral cracks between rectilineal ones. [Fr *perle*, Ger *Perle* pearl]

perlocution *pûr-lə-kū'shən*, (*philos*) *n* the effect (eg frightening, comforting, persuading) produced when a particular word is uttered, regarded as an act (cf **illocution**). — *adj* **perlocū'tionary**. [**per-** (2) and **locution**]

perlous *pûr'ləs*, (*Spenser*) *adj*. Same as **perilous** (see under **peril**).

perlustrate *pər-lus'trāt*, (*archaic*) *vt* to traverse and inspect. — *n* **perlustrā'tion**. [L *perlustrāre*, *-ātum*]

perm[1] *pûrm*, (*colloq*) *n* short form of **permutation**. — *vt* to permute; to arrange a forecast according to some defined system of combination or permutation. [**permutation**]

perm[2] *pûrm*, (*colloq*) *n* short form of **permanent wave**. — *vt* (*colloq*) to impart a permanent wave to (hair). [**permanent**]

permaculture *pûr'mə-kul'tūr*, *n* a system of natural agriculture, requiring generous mulching, no artificial fertilizers, use of natural resources, and only minimal weeding. [*perma*nent agri*culture*]

permafrost *pûr'mə-frost*, *n* permanently frozen subsoil. [*perma*nent *frost*]

permalloy *pûrm'a-loi*, *n* any of various alloys of iron and nickel, often containing other elements, eg copper, molybdenum, chromium, which has high magnetic permeability. [*perm*eable *alloy*]

permanent *pûr'mə-nənt*, *adj* remaining, or intended to remain, indefinitely, not expected to change or vary, not temporary. — *n* **per'manence** the fact or state of being permanent. — *n* **per'manency** permanence; a thing that is permanent. — *adv* **per'manently**. — **permanent magnet** see under **magnet**; **permanent press** a process by which clothes can be made to retain pleats, trouser-creases, etc; **permanent set** (*engineering*) the distortion or extension of a structure, etc, which remains after the elastic limit has been exceeded by stress, load, etc; **permanent teeth** the adult teeth, which come after the milk-teeth lost in childhood; **permanent wave** a long-lasting artificial wave or curl in hair induced by chemical treatment, now usually contracted as **perm**; **permanent way** the finished road of a railway. [L *permanēns*, *-entis*, pr p of *permanēre*, from *per* through, and *manēre* to continue]

permanganic *pûr-mang-gan'ik*, *adj* applied to an acid ($HMnO_4$) and its anhydride (Mn_2O_7) containing more oxygen than manganic acid and anhydride. — *n* **permanganate** (*pər-mang'gə-nāt*) a salt of permanganic acid, *esp* **potassium permanganate** ($KMnO_4$) which is used as an oxidizing and bleaching agent and as a disinfectant. [**per-** (1) and **manganese**]

permeate *pûr'mi-āt*, *vt* to pass through the pores of; to penetrate and fill the pores of; to pervade; to saturate. — *vi* to diffuse. — *n* **permeabil'ity**. — *adj* **per'meable**. —

adv **per'meably**. — *n* **permeam'eter** an instrument for measuring permeability, *esp* of magnetizing force and flux. — *n* **per'meance** the act of permeating; the reciprocal of the reluctance of a magnetic circuit. — *n* **per'mease** any enzyme which acts to assist the entry of certain sugars into cells. — *n* **permeā'tion**. — *adj* **per'meative** having the power to permeate. — **permeability coefficient** (*geol*) a measure of the ability of a rock or soil to allow fluids to pass through it. — **magnetic permeability** the ratio of flux density to magnetizing force. [L *permeāre*, from *per* through, and *meāre* to pass.

permethrin *pər-mē'thrin, n* a garden pesticide, used against whitefly, etc.

Permian *pûr'mi-ən,* (*geol*) *n* the uppermost Palaeozoic system. — *adj* of that system. — *n* and *adj* **Permo-Carbonif'erous** Upper Carboniferous and Lower Permian. [*Perm*, in Russia, where it is widely developed]

per mil or **per mill** *abbrev*: *per mille* (*L*), by the thousand, or in each thousand.

permis de séjour *per-mē də sā-zhōōr,* (*Fr*) *n* permission to reside in a foreign country, given by the police of that country; the permit issued.

permissible, etc. See under **permit**.

permit *pər-mit', vt* to allow; (*refl*) to indulge (in) (*archaic*); to leave, refer, submit (to) (*obs*). — *vi* to allow: — *pr p* **permitt'ing**; *pa t* and *pa p* **permitt'ed**. — *n* (*pûr'*) permission, *esp* in writing; an official document giving authorization; a licence. — *n* **permissibil'ity**. — *adj* **permiss'ible** that may be permitted; allowable. — *adv* **permiss'ibly**. — *n* **permission** (*-mish'ən*) an act of permitting; authorization, leave. — *adj* **permiss'ive** granting permission or liberty; permitted, optional; lenient, indulgent; allowing much freedom in social conduct *esp* concerning sexual matters (as in **the permissive society**, in which the people of most (*esp* western) countries are said to have lived since the sexually and socially liberating 1960s). — *adv* **permiss'ively**. — *n* **permiss'iveness**. — *n* **permitt'ance** (*rare*) permission. — *n* **permitt'er**. — *n* **permittiv'ity** (*absolute permittivity*) the ratio of the electric displacement in a medium to the electric field intensity producing it; (*relative permittivity*) the ratio of the electric displacement in a medium to that which would be produced in free space by the same field. — **permissible dose** (*radiol*) same as **maximum permissible concentration**; **permissive temperature** (*biol*) the temperature at which a temperature-sensitive mutant will grow (cf **restrictive temperature**). [L *permittere*, *-missum* to let pass through, from *per* through, and *mittere* to send]

Permo-. See under **Permian**.

permutate *pûr'mū-tāt* or **permute** *pər-mūt', vt* to interchange, transmute, change the order of; to subject to permutation. — *n* **permūtabil'ity**. — *adj* **permūt'able** interchangeable. — *n* **permutā'tion** barter (*obs*); transmutation; the arrangement of a set of things in every possible order (*math*); any one possible order of arrangement of a given number of things taken from a given number; immediate inference by obversion (*logic*); (*esp* in football pools) a forecast of a specified number of results from a larger number of matches based on some defined system of combination or permutation (often shortened to **perm**); any such system. [L *permūtāre* to change thoroughly, from pfx *per-*, and *mūtāre* to change]

pern *pûrn, n* a honey-buzzard (*Pernis*). [French zoologist Georges Cuvier's mistake for Gr *pternis* a kind of hawk]

pernancy *pûr'nən-si,* (*law*) *n* receiving. [Anglo-Fr *pernance* (OFr *prenance*)]

Pernettya *pər-net'i-ə, n* a genus (family *Ericaceae*) of evergreen shrubs with bright berries. [A J *Pernetty*, explorer]

pernicious[1] *pər-nish'əs, adj* destructive; highly injurious; malevolent. — *adv* **perni'ciously**. — *n* **perni'ciousness**. — **pernicious anaemia** see under **anaemia**. [L *perniciōsus*, from pfx *per-*, and *nex*, *necis* death by violence]

pernicious[2] *pər-nish'əs,* (*Milton*) *adj* swift, ready, prompt. [L *pernīx*, *-īcis* nimble]

pernickety *pər-nik'i-ti, adj* finical; (of a task) exacting minute care. — *n* **pernick'etiness**. [Scots; origin unknown]

pernoctate *pûr'nok-tāt, vi* (*usu facetious*) to pass or spend the night. — *n* **pernocta'tion** *n* passing the night; a watch, vigil. [**per-** (2) and L *nox*, *noctis* night]

Pernod® *per'nō, n* an alcoholic drink made in France, flavoured with aniseed, *usu* mixed with water and drunk as an apéritif.

perone *per'o-nē, n* the fibula. — *adj* **peronē'al**. — *n* **peronē'us** one of several fibular muscles. [Gr *peronē*]

Peronism *pe'ron-izm* or *pə-rō'nizm, n* the political beliefs of Juan *Peron* (1895–1974), former president of Argentina. — *n* **Peronis'mo** (*Sp*) Peronism. — *n* **Peronist**. — *n* **Peronist'a** (*Sp*).

peroration *per-ə-rā'shən, -ō-* or *-ö-, n* the conclusion of a speech, a summing up; a rhetorical performance. — *vi* **per'orate** to make a peroration; to harangue (*colloq*). [L *perōrātiō*, *-ōnis*, from *per* through, and *ōrāre* to speak, from *ōs*, *ōris* the mouth]

perovskia *pə-rov'ski-ə, n* a genus of hardy deciduous shrubs of the Labiatae family, grown for their aromatic grey-green foliage and blue flowers.

perovskite *pə-rov'skīt, n* a mineral form of calcium titanate ($CaTiO_3$), yellow, brown or almost black in colour, having some rare-earth elements, which is used in certain high-temperature ceramic superconductors. [Named after Russian statesman Count Lev Alekseevich *Perovski* (1792–1856)]

peroxide *pər-oks'īd, n* an oxide with the highest proportion of oxygen; one that yields hydrogen peroxide on treatment with an acid; the bleach hydrogen peroxide, H_2O_2 (*colloq*). — *vt* to treat or bleach with hydrogen peroxide. — *n* **perox'idāse** an enzyme, found in many plants, bacteria and leucocytes, which acts as a catalyst in the oxidation of various substances by peroxides. — *n* **peroxidā'tion**. — *vt* and *vi* **perox'idize** or **-ise**. [**per-** (1) and **oxide**]

perpend[1] *pər-pend', vt* to weigh in the mind, to consider carefully. [L *perpendere*, from pfx *per-*, and *pendere* to weigh]

perpend[2] *pûr'pənd*. Same as **parpen**.

perpendicular *pûr-pən-dik'ū-lər, adj* erect; vertical; upright; in the direction of gravity or at right angles to the plane of the horizon; at right angles (to a given line or surface; *geom*); in the Perpendicular style of architecture. — *n* an instrument for determining the vertical line; a straight line or plane perpendicular to another line or surface; verticality or erectness; (in a ship) a vertical line from each end of the water-line; a meal or entertainment at which the guests do not sit (*slang*). — *n* **perpendicularity** (*-lar'i-ti*) the state of being perpendicular. — *adv* **perpendic'ularly**. — **Perpendicular style** a late English style of Gothic architecture (late 14c to mid-16c) marked by vertical window-tracery, the depressed or four-centre arch, fan-tracery vaulting, and panelled walls. [L *perpendiculāris*, from *perpendiculum* a plumb-line, from pfx *per-*, and *pendēre* to hang]

perpent *pûr'pənt*. Same as **parpen**.

perpetrate *pûr'pi-trāt, vt* to commit or execute (*esp* an offence, a poem, or a pun). — *adj* **per'petrable**. — *n* **perpetrā'tion**. — *n* **per'petrātor**. [L *perpetrāre*, *-ātum*, from pfx *per-*, and *patrāre* to achieve]

perpetual *pər-pet'ū-əl, adj* never ceasing; everlasting; not temporary; incessant; (of a sports trophy, etc) awarded every year; continuously blooming; perennial. — *adv* perpetually. — *n* a perennial; a continuously blooming hybrid rose. — *n* **perpet'ualism**. — *n* **perpet'ualist** a person who advocates the perpetual continuation of anything. — *n* **perpetuality** (*-al'i-ti*). — *adv* **perpet'ually**. — **perpetual calendar** a calendar by means of which it may be ascertained on which day of the week any given day has fallen or will fall; one which may be used for any year, or for more than a year; **perpetual check**

(*chess*) a situation in which one player's king is continually placed in check by the other player who may thereby claim a draw; **perpetual curate** formerly in the Church of England, an incumbent of a parish who had no endowment of tithes — since 1868 called vicar; **perpetual motion** a hypothetical machine, or motion of such a machine, that should do work indefinitely without an external source of energy; **perpetual-mo'tionist** a believer in the possibility of perpetual motion; **perpetual screw** an endless screw. [L *perpetuālis*, from *perpetuus* continuous]

perpetuate *pər-pet'ū-āt*, *vt* to cause to last for ever or for a very long time; to preserve from extinction or oblivion; to pass on, to cause to continue to be believed, known, etc. — *adj* (*archaic*) perpetuated. — *adj* **perpet'ūable**. — *n* **perpet'ūance** perpetuation. — *n* **perpetūā'tion** continuation or preservation for ever, or for a very long time; preservation from extinction or oblivion. — *n* **perpet'ūātor**. [L *perpetuāre*, *-ātum*, from *perpetuus* perpetual]

perpetuity *pûr-pi-tū'i-ti*, *n* the state of being perpetual; endless time; duration for an indefinite period; something lasting for ever; the sum paid for a perpetual annuity; the annuity itself; an arrangement whereby property is tied up, or rendered inalienable, for all time or for a very long time. [L *perpetuitās*, *-ātis*, from *perpetuus* perpetual]

perpetuum mobile *pər-pet'ū-əm mō'bil-i* or *per-pet'ŏŏ-ŏŏm mō-bil-e*, (*L*) *n* perpetual motion.

perplex *pər-pleks'*, *vt* to embarrass or puzzle with difficulties or intricacies; to bewilder; to tease with suspense or doubt; to complicate; to interweave; to tangle. — *n* (*obs*) a difficulty. — *adv* **perplex'edly**. — *n* **perplex'edness**. — *adj* **perplex'ing**. — *adv* **perplex'ingly**. — *n* **perplex'ity** the state of being perplexed; confusion of mind arising from doubt, etc; embarrassment; doubt; intricacy; tangle. [L *perplexus* entangled, from pfx *per-*, and *plexus* involved, pa p of *plectere*]

per pro *abbrev*: *per procurationem* (*L*) (see under **per**[2]).

perquisite *pûr'kwi-zit*, *n* (often *colloq* shortened to **perk**) property acquired otherwise than by inheritance (*law*; *obs*); an incidental benefit from one's employment; a casual profit; anything left over that a servant or other has by custom a right to keep; a tip expected on some occasions; emoluments; something regarded as falling to one by right. — *n* **perquisition** (*-zish'ən*) a strict search; diligent inquiry. — *n* **perquis'itor** the first purchaser of an estate. [L *perquīsītum*, from *perquīrere* to seek diligently, from pfx *per-*, and *quaerere* to ask]

perradius *pər-rā'di-əs*, *n* any one of the primary radii of a coelenterate: — *pl* **perradii** (*-ī*). — *adj* **perra'dial**. [**per-** (2) and **radius**]

Perrier® *per'i-ā*, *n* a sparkling mineral water from a spring of that name in Southern France; (loosely) any sparkling mineral water. — Also **Perrier water**.

perrier *per'i-ər*, (*obs*) *n* a machine or gun firing stones. [OFr]

perron *per'ən* or *per-ɔ̃'*, *n* a raised platform or terrace at an entrance door; an external flight of steps leading up to it. [Fr, from L *petra* stone]

perruque, **perruquier**. See **peruke**.

perry *per'i*, *n* fermented pear juice. [OFr *peré*, from LL *pēra* (L *pirum*) pear]

Pers *abbrev*: Persian.

pers *abbrev*: person; personal.

persant or **persaunt** (*Spenser*). Same as **perceant** (see under **perce**).

perscrutation *pûr-skrŏŏ-tā'shən*, *n* a thorough search. [**per-** (2) and L *scrūtārī* to search carefully]

perse[1] *pûrs*, *adj* dark blue or bluish-grey. — *n* such a colour; a cloth of such colour. [OFr *pers*]

perse[2] *pûrs*, a Spenserian form of **pierce**: — *pa p* and *pa t* **perst**.

persecute *pûr'si-kūt*, *vt* to harass, afflict, hunt down, or put to death, *esp* for religious or political opinions. — *n* **persecū'tion**. — *adj* **per'secūtive**. — *n* **per'secūtor**. — *adj* **per'secūtory**. — **persecution complex** (*psychiatry*) a morbid fear that one is being plotted against by other people. [L *persequī*, *persecūtus*, from pfx *per-*, and *sequī* to follow]

Perseid. See under **Perseus**.

perseity *pər-sē'i-ti*, *n* an independent existence. [L *per sē* in itself]

perseline *pûr'si-lēn*, *n* a Spenserian form of **purslane**.

Perseus *pûr'sūs* or *-si-əs*, *n* a fabled Greek hero who slew the Gorgon Medusa, and rescued Andromeda from a sea-monster (*Gr mythol*); a constellation in the northern sky. — *n* **Per'seid** (*-si-id*) a meteor of a swarm whose radiant is in the constellation Perseus. [Gr *Perseus*]

persevere *pûr-si-vēr'*, formerly (*Shakesp*) *pər-sev'ər*, *vi* to continue (*obs*); to continue steadfastly; to keep on striving. — *n* **persevē'rance** (formerly *pər-sev'ər-əns*) the act or state of persevering; continued application to anything which one has begun; persistence despite setbacks. — *adj* **persev'erant** steadfast. — *vi* **persev'erate** to recur or tend to recur (*psychiatry*); to repeat the same actions or thoughts. — *n* **perseveration** (*pûr-sev-ər-ā'shən*) meaningless repetition of an action, utterance, thought, etc; the tendency to experience difficulty in leaving one activity for another. — *n* **persev'erātor**. — *adj* **persevē'ring**. — *adv* **persevē'ringly**. — **perseverance of saints** the Calvinistic doctrine that those who are effectually called by God cannot fall away so as to be finally lost. [Fr *persévérer*, from L *persevērāre*, from *persevērus* very strict, from pfx *per-*, and *sevērus* strict]

Persian *pûr'shən*, *-shyən*, *-zhən* or *zhyən*, *adj* of, from, or relating to *Persia* (now Iran), its inhabitants, or language. — *n* a native or citizen of Persia; the language of Persia; a male figure serving as a column (*archit*); a Persian cat. — *vt* and *vi* **Per'sianize** or **-ise**. — *adj* **Persic** (*pûr'sik*) Persian. — *n* the Persian language. — *vt* and *vi* **Per'sicize** or **-ise** (*-sīz*) to turn Persian; to assimilate to what is Persian. — *n* **Per'sism** a Persian idiom. — *n* **Per'sist** a person who has a scholarly knowledge of Persian language, culture, history, etc. — **Persian berry** a name given to the fruit of several buckthorns; **Persian blinds** persiennes; **Persian carpet** a rich, soft carpet of the kind woven in Persia; **Persian cat** a kind of cat with long, silky hair and a bushy tail; **Persian Gulf** the Arabian Gulf, the arm of the Arabian Sea which separates Iran (to the N) from (to the S) Saudi Arabia and the Arab States; **Persian lamb** a lamb of the Karakul or Bukhara breed; its black, curly fur used to make coats, hats, etc; **Persian powder** an insect-powder made from Pyrethrum; **Persian wheel** a large undershot wheel for raising water.

persicaria *pûr-si-kā'ri-ə*, (*bot*) *n* a species of knotgrass with black-blotched leaves; extended to other species of Polygonum, by some made a separate genus. [LL *persicāria* peach-tree, from the similarity in leaves]

persico or **persicot** *pûr'si-kō*, *n* a cordial flavoured with kernels of peaches and apricots. [Fr *persico* (now *persicot*), from Ital *persico*, from L *persicum* a peach]

persienne *per-si-en'*, *n* an Eastern cambric or muslin with a coloured printed pattern; (in *pl*) Persian blinds, outside shutters of thin movable slats in a frame. [Fr, Persian (fem)]

persiflage *pûr-si-fläzh'* or *pûr'*, *n* banter; flippancy. — *n* **persifleur** (*-flûr'*) a banterer. [Fr, from *persifler* to banter, from L *per* through, and Fr *siffler*, from L *sībilāre* to whistle, to hiss]

persimmon *pər-sim'ən*, *n* a tree of the American or African genus *Diospyros*; its plum-like fruit. [From an Am Indian word]

Persism, **Persist**. See under **Persian**.

persist *pər-sist'*, *vi* to continue steadfastly or obstinately, *esp* against opposition (often with *in*); to persevere; to insist; to continue to be, to remain (*Milton*); to continue to exist; to remain in the mind after the external cause is removed. — *vt* to assert or repeat insistently. — *n* **persis'tence** or **persis'tency** the quality of being persistent; perseverance; obstinacy; duration, *esp* of an effect after the stimulus has been removed. — *adj* **persis'tent** persisting; pushing on, *esp* against opposition; tenacious; fixed; constant or constantly repeated; remaining after the usual time of falling off, withering, or disappearing (*zool*; *bot*); continuing to grow beyond the usual time. — Also *n.* — *adv* **persis'tently**. — *adv* **persis'tingly**. — *adj* **persis'tive** (*Shakesp*) persistent. — **persistent cruelty** (*law*; in matrimonial proceedings) behaviour likely to cause danger to the life or health of a spouse. — **persistent vegetative state** (*med*) an irreversible condition induced by lack of oxygen, in which the organism is still alive, but is incapable of any thought processes and any voluntary physical action (*abbrev* **PVS**). [L *persistere*, from *per*, and *sistere* to cause to stand, to stand, from *stāre* to stand]

person *pûr'sn*, *n* a living soul or self-conscious being; a character represented, as on the stage; a capacity in which one is acting; a personality; a human being, sometimes used contemptuously or patronizingly; an individual of a compound or colonial animal; the outward appearance, etc of a human being; bodily form; human figure (often including clothes); bodily presence or action; a personage (*obs*); a human being (*natural person*), or a corporation (*artificial person*) regarded as having rights and duties under the law; a hypostasis of the Godhead (*theol*); a form of inflexion or use of a word as it, or its subject, relates to the person, persons, thing, or things speaking (*first person*), spoken to (*second person*), or spoken about (*third person*) (*gram*): — *pl* in the sense of an individual human being, *usu* **people** (*pē'pl*) qv; in formal, technical, etc use **per'sons**. — *combining form* **-person** (*-pûr-sn*) used instead of **-man** to avoid illegal or unnecessary discrimination on grounds of sex, eg *barperson, chairperson, postperson.* — *adj* **per'sonable** of good appearance, attractive; easy to get on with, likeable. — *n* **per'sonableness**. — *n* **per'sonage** bodily frame or appearance; a person, *esp* an important or august one; a character in a play or story; recognized or imagined character or personality (*Spenser*, etc). — *n* **per'sonhood**. — *vt* **per'sonize** or **-ise** to personify. — **Person Friday** a Man or Girl Friday (see **man** and **girl**); **per'sonpower** manpower, applying to either sex. — *adj* **per'son-to-per'son** (of a telephone call) personal; involving meeting or contact. — Also *adv.* — **in person** in actual bodily presence; by one's own act, not by an agent or representative; **on** or **about one's person** with one, worn or carried about one's body. [L *persōna* an actor's mask]

persona[1] *pər-sō'nə*, *n* Jung's term for a person's system of adaptation to, or manner assumed when dealing with, the world — the outermost part of the consciousness, the expression of the personality, masking one's inner thoughts and feelings, etc; social facade or public image; a Roman actor's mask; a character in fiction, *esp* drama; a speaker in a poem: — *pl* **perso'nae** (*-nē* or *-nī*) or **perso'nas**. [Ety as for **person**]

persona[2] *pər-sōn'ə* or *-a*, (*L*) *n* person. — **persona grata** (*grā'*, *grä'tə* or *-a*) a person who is acceptable, liked, or favoured, *esp* one who is diplomatically acceptable to a foreign government (also used as *adj*); **persona muta** (*mū'tə* or *mōō'ta*) a character in an opera who neither speaks nor sings; **persona non grata** opposite of **persona grata**. — **dramatis personae** see under **drama**; **in propria persona** (*LL*; *in prō'pri-ə* or *pro'pri-a*) in person.

personable, personage. See under **person**.

personal *pûr'sən-l*, *adj* of the nature of a person; of or relating to a person or personality; relating, referring, or pointing to a particular person or persons; aiming offensively at a particular person or persons; belonging or peculiar to a person; own; one's own; of private concern; relating to private concerns; bodily; in bodily presence; (of a telephone call) made to a particular person; by one's own action; indicating person (*gram*); tailored to the needs of a particular person; done in person; opposed to *real*, originally not recoverable by a *real action* (for the restitution of the specific thing), but such as compensation might be claimed for (*English law*); hence (now) passing at death not to the heir (as real property) but to the executor. — *n pl* **personalia** (*-ā'li-ə*) notes, anecdotes, or particulars relating to persons. — *n* **per'sonalism** the character of being personal; a theory or doctrine that attributes personality, or spiritual freedom and responsibility, as distinct from mere individuality, to human beings, *esp* that enunciated by Emmanuel Mounier in 1936. — *n* **per'sonalist** someone who writes personal notes; a believer in, or follower of, personalism. — *adj* **personalis'tic**. — *n* **personalizā'tion** or **-s-**. — *vt* **per'sonalize** or **-ise** to apply to, or take as referring to, a definite person; to tailor to or cater for the desires of a particular person; to mark with a person's name, initials, monogram, etc; to give a mark or character to (something) so that it is identifiable as belonging to a certain person (*colloq*); to personify. — *adv* **per'sonally** in a personal or direct manner; in person; individually; for my part (*colloq*). — *n* **per'sonalty** (*law*) personal estate, all the property which, when a person dies, goes to the executor or administrator, as distinguished from the realty, which goes to the heir-at-law. — **personal chair** a university chair created for the period of tenure of a particular person; **personal column** a newpaper column containing personal messages, advertisements, etc; **personal communications network** see **PCN**; **personal computer** a single-user microcomputer; **personal dosimeter** a sensitive tubular electroscope, charged by a generator and discharged by ionizing radiation, used by workers in areas of potential radiation hazard; **personal effects** those belongings worn or carried about one's person; private or intimate possessions; **personal equation** see under **equal**; **personal estate** or **property** property other than land or buildings (opposite to *real*) passing at death to one's executor, not to one's heir at law; **personal exception** (*Scots law*) a ground of objection which applies to an individual and prevents him from doing something which, but for his conduct or situation, he might do; **personal identification number** see **PIN**; **personal identity** the continued sameness of the individual person, through all changes, as testified by consciousness; **personal organizer** see under **organize**; **personal pronoun** (*gram*) a pronoun which stands for a definite person or thing; **personal property** see **personal estate** above; **personal remark** a remark, *esp* derogatory, made to, referring to, or aimed at a particular person or persons; **personal rights** rights which belong to a person as a living, rational being; **personal security** a pledge given by a person, as distinguished from the delivery of some object of value as security; **personal service** delivery of a message or an order into a person's hands, as distinguished from delivery in any other indirect way; attention or service of the proprietor of a concern, rather than one of his employees or assistants; **personal stereo** a small lightweight cassette-player designed to be carried around (eg in one's pocket or attached to one's belt) and listened to through earphones; **personal transaction** something done by a person's own effort, not through the agency of another. [L *persōna* an actor's mask, perh from Etruscan *phersu* masked figures, commonly associated (in spite of difference of quantity) with *personāre*, *-ātum*, from *per* and *sonāre* to sound; cf **parson**]

personality *pər-sən-al'i-ti*, *n* the fact or state of being a person or of being personal; existence as a person; individuality; distinctive or well-marked character; a person *esp* a remarkable one; a celebrity; direct reference to, or an utterance aimed at, a particular person or persons, *esp* of a derogatory nature, a personal remark; personalty (*law*; *rare*); the integrated organization of all the psychological, intellectual, emotional, and physical characteristics of an individual, especially as they are presented to other people (*psychol*); the sum of such characteristics which make a person attractive socially. — **personality cult** excessive adulation of the individual, *esp* someone in public life; **personality disorder** (*psychiatry*) any of various types of mental illness in which a person tends to behave in ways which are harmful to her or himself or to others. **[person]**

personalize, etc, **personally**, **personalty**. See under **personal**.

personate *pûr'sən-āt*, *vt* to assume the likeness or character of; to play the part of; to mimic; to pass oneself off as, to impersonate, *esp* with criminal intent; to represent in the form of a person; to symbolize. — *adj* feigned (*archaic*); mask-like; (of a lipped corolla) closed by an upward bulge of the lower lip (*bot*). — *adj* **per'sonāted** feigned. — *n* **per'sonāting**. — *n* **personā'tion**. — *adj* **per'sonātive** dramatic; presenting or presented through persons. — *n* **per'sonātor**. **[person]**

personhood. See under **person**.

personify *pər-son'i-fī*, *vt* to represent as a person; to ascribe personality to; to be the embodiment of; to personate (*rare*): — *pr p* **person'ifying**; *pa t* and *pa p* **person'ified**. — *n* **personificā'tion**. — *n* **person'ifier**. [L *persōna* a person, and *facere* to make: see **persona**[2]]

personize. See under **person**.

personnel *pûr-sən-el'*, *n* the persons employed in any service; (loosely) people in general; an office or department that deals with employees' appointments, records and welfare, etc. — **personnel carrier** a military vehicle, often armoured, for carrying troops; **personnel monitoring** monitoring for radioactive contamination of any part of an individual or their clothing. [Fr, personal]

perspective *pər-spek'tiv*, or formerly *pûr'*, *n* optics (*obs*); a telescope, microscope, or other optical instrument (also **perspective glass**; *obs*); the art or science of drawing objects on a surface, so as to give the picture the same appearance to the eye as the objects themselves; appearance, or representation of appearance, of objects in space, with effect of distance, solidity, etc; correct proportion in all the parts; a picture in perspective; a picture or model that seems confused except when viewed in the right direction, or in some other way gives a fantastic effect (*Shakesp*); a peep-show (*obs*); a vista; a prospect of the future; inspection (*obs*); a way of regarding facts and their relative importance; point of view. — *adj* optical (*obs*); pertaining or according to perspective. — *adj* **perspectī'val**. — *adv* **perspec'tively**. — *n* **perspec'tivism** the theory that things can only be known from an individual point of view at a particular time (*philos*); the use of subjective points of view in literature and art. — *n* **perspec'tivist** an artist whose work emphasises the effects of perspective; someone who studies the rules of perspective. — **perspective plane** the surface on which the picture of the objects to be represented in perspective is drawn. — **in** (or **out of**) **perspective** according to (or against) the laws of perspective; in correct (or incorrect) proportion; in (or not in) prospect (*obs*). [L (*ars*) *perspectīva* perspective (art), from *perspicere*, *perspectum*, from *per*, and *specere* to look]

Perspex® *pûr'speks*, *n* a proprietary thermoplastic resin of exceptional transparency and freedom from colour, used for windscreens, etc.

perspicacious *pûr-spi-kā'shəs*, *adj* clear-sighted (*archaic*); clear-minded, astute, perceptive, discerning. — *adv* **perspicā'ciously**. — *n* **perspicacity** (*-kas'i-ti*). [L *perspicāx*, *-ācis*; see **perspective**]

perspicuous *pər-spik'ū-əs*, *adj* expressed or expressing clearly; lucid. — *n* **perspicū'ity**. — *adv* **perspic'ūously**. — *n* **perspic'ūousness**. [L *perspicuus*; see **perspicacious**, **perspective**]

perspire *pər-spīr'*, *vi* to exude; to sweat. — *vt* to exhale. — *adj* **perspīr'able** capable of being perspired or of perspiring. — *vi* **perspirate** (*pûr'spir-āt*; *rare*) to sweat. — *n* **perspiration** (*-spir-ā'shən*) the act of perspiring; sweat. — *adj* **perspīr'atory**. [L *perspīrāre*, *-ātum*, from *per* through, and *spīrāre* to breathe]

perst. See **perse**[2].

perstringe *pər-strinj'*, (*obs*) *vt* to constrain; to touch on; to dull; to censure. [L *perstringere*, from pfx *per-* thoroughly, and *stringere* to bind]

persuade *pər-swād'*, *vt* to induce by reasoning, advice, etc; to bring to any particular opinion; to cause to believe; to convince; to seek to induce (*obs*); to urge (*Shakesp*). — *vi* to plead (*obs*); to prevail (*obs*); to use persuasive methods. — Also **perswade'** (*obs*). — *adj* **persuād'able**. — *n* **persuād'er** someone who or that which persuades; a gun (*slang*); a device used to fit metal type into a chase (*printing*). — *n* **persuasibility** (*-swās-i-bil'i-ti*). — *adj* **persuās'ible** capable of being persuaded. — *n* **persuasion** (*-swā'zhən*) the act, process, method, art, or power of persuading; an inducement; the state of being persuaded; settled opinion; a creed; a party adhering to a creed; a kind (*facetious*). — *adj* **persuasive** (*-swās'*) having the power to persuade; influencing the mind or passions. — *n* that which persuades or wins over. — *adv* **persuā'sively**. — *n* **persuā'siveness**. — *adj* **persuā-s'ory** persuasive. [L *persuādēre*, *-suāsum*, from pfx *per-*, and *suādēre* to advise]

persue[1] *pûrs'ū*, (*Spenser*) *n* a track of blood. [Fr *percée* act of piercing, confused with **pursue**]

persue[2]. An obsolete spelling of **pursue**.

persulphate *pər-sul'fāt*, *n* that sulphate of a metal which contains the relatively greater quantity of oxygen or of the acid radical; a salt of **persulphuric** (*-fū'rik*) **acid** ($H_2S_2O_8$). **[per-** (1) and **sulphate]**

perswade. Obsolete spelling of **persuade**.

PERT (*business*) *abbrev*: programme evaluation and review technique.

pert *pûrt*, *adj* open (*obs*); unconcealed; brisk; perky (*Shakesp*); jaunty; flourishing; adroit (*obs*); forward; saucy; impertinent; presumingly free in speech; objectionable (*obs*). — *n* an impudent person. — *adv* **pert'ly**. — *n* **pert'ness**. [Aphetic for **apert**; see also **peart]**

pertain *pər-* or *pûr-tān'*, *vi* to belong; to relate (with *to*). — *n* **per'tinence** or **per'tinency** (*pûr'*) the state of being pertinent; an appurtenance (*obs*). — *adj* **per'tinent** pertaining or related; to the point; fitted for the matter on hand; fitting or appropriate; suitable; apposite. — *n* (chiefly *Scot*) a minor property forming part of a heritable estate. — *adv* **per'tinently**. [OFr *partenir*, from L *pertinēre*, from pfx *per-*, and *tenēre* to hold]

pertake. An old spelling (*Spenser*, *Shakesp*) of **partake**.

perthite *pûrth'īt*, (*geol*) *n* a parallel intergrowth of orthoclase and albite. — *adj* **perthitic** (*-it'ik*). [*Perth*, Ontario, where it was found]

pertinacious *pûr-ti-nā'shəs*, *adj* thoroughly tenacious; holding obstinately to an opinion or a purpose; obstinate; unyielding. — *adv* **pertinā'ciously**. — *n* **pertinā'ciousness** or **pertinacity** (*-nas'i-ti*) the quality of being pertinacious or unyielding; obstinacy; resoluteness. [L *pertināx*, *-ācis* holding fast, from pfx *per-*, and *tenāx* tenacious, from *tenēre* to hold]

pertinence, **pertinent**, etc. See under **pertain**.

perttaunt like an obscure phrase in Shakespeare (*Love's Labour's Lost*, V. 2.), possibly meaning like a *pair taunt* or *purtaunt'*, a double pair-royal. **[pair**[1], and Fr *tant* so much, ie counting as much again as a pair-royal in post and pair]

perturb *pər-tûrb'*, *vt* to disturb greatly; to agitate — also **per'turbate** (*pûr'tər-bāt*). — *adj* **pertur'bable**. — *n* **pertur'bance** perturbation. — *n* **pertur'bant** anything that perturbs. — *adj* perturbing. — *n* **perturbā'tion** the act of perturbing or state of being perturbed; disquiet of mind; irregularity; the disturbance produced in the simple elliptic motion of one heavenly body around another by the action of a third body, or by the non-sphericity of the principal body (*astron*); a perturbing agent. — *adj* **perturbā'tional**. — *adj* **pertur'bative**. — *n* **per'turbātor**. — *adj* and *n* **pertur'batory**. — *adj* **perturbed'**. — *adv* **pertur'bedly**. — *n* **pertur'ber**. — **perturbation theory** (*phys*) a mathematical method of determining the effect of small local changes on the behaviour of a system. [L *perturbāre, -ātum*, from pfx *per-*, and *turbāre* to disturb, from *turba* a crowd]

pertuse *pər-tūs'*, *adj* punched; pierced; slit. — Also **pertūs'ate** (or *pûr'*) or **pertused** (*-tūst'*). — *n* **pertusion** (*-tū'zhən*). [L *pertundere, -tūsum*, from *per* through, and *tundere* to strike]

pertussis *pər-tus'is*, (*med*) *n* whooping-cough. — *adj* **pertuss'al**. [**per-** (2) and L *tussis* cough]

Peru *pə-rōō'*, *n* a country of S America. — *adj* **Peru'vian** of Peru. — *n* a native or inhabitant of Peru. — **Peruvian bark** cinchona bark. — **balsam of Peru** or **Peru balsam** a fragrant acrid black viscid liquid, containing esters of benzoic and cinnamic acids, obtained from a tropical American papilionaceous tree, *Myroxylon pereirae*; **marvel of Peru** see under **marvel**. [Sp *Perú*]

peruke *pər-ōōk'*, formerly *per'*, *n* a wig. — Also (*Fr*) **perruque** (*per-ük*). — *adj* **peruk'ed** wearing a peruke. — *n* **perru'quier** (*-ōōk'yər*, or *-ük-yā*) a wigmaker. [Fr *perruque*, from Ital *parrucca* (Sp *peluca*); connection with L *pilus* hair, very doubtful]

peruse *pər-ōōz'*, *vt orig* to use up, wear out; to pass in scrutiny, one by one or piece by piece (*Shakesp*); to examine in detail; to revise; to read attentively or critically; (loosely) to read. — *n* **perus'al** the act of perusing; careful examination; scrutiny; study; reading. — *n* **perus'er**. [L pfx *per-* thoroughly, and *ūtī, ūsus* to use]

Peruvian. See under **Peru**.

perv *pûrv*, (*colloq*) *n* a (sexual) pervert; an act of perving (*Austr*); someone who pervs (*Austr*). — *vi* to behave as a perv; (with *at* or *on*) to look at lustfully or for sexual pleasure (*Austr*). — Also **perve**. — Also *adj*. [**pervert** qv under **perverse**]

pervade *pər-vād'*, *vt* to pass through (*rare*); to diffuse or extend through the whole of, to permeate. — *n* **pervasion** (*-vā'zhən*). — *adj* **pervasive** (*-vā'siv*) tending to pervade, or having the power to pervade. — *adv* **perva'sively**. — *n* **perva'siveness**. [L *pervādere*, from *per* through, and *vādere* to go]

perverse *pər-vûrs'*, *adj* turned aside from right or truth; obstinately determined when in the wrong; capricious and unreasonable in opposition; wrong-headed, stubborn; wayward; deliberately wicked; against the evidence or judge's direction on point of law (*legal*); adverse (*Milton*). — *adv* **perverse'ly**. — *n* **perverse'ness**. — *n* **perversion** (*-vûr'shən*) the act or process of perverting; the condition of being perverted; the product of the process of perverting; a diverting from the true object; a turning from what is right or true; a distortion; a misapplication; a pathological deviation of sexual instinct; the formation of a mirror-image (*math*); the mirror-image itself. — *n* **pervers'ity** the state or quality of being perverse. — *adj* **pervers'ive** tending to pervert. — *vt* **pervert'** to cause to turn away from the right course; to misconstrue, to interpret wrongly; to corrupt; to cause to turn from truth or virtue; to divert, turn (*Shakesp*); to form a mirror-image of (*math*). — *vi* to go wrong, or away from the right course. — *n* **pervert** (*pûr'vûrt*) a person who has abandoned the doctrine assumed to be true; someone whose sexual instinct is perverted. — *n* **pervert'er**. — *adj* **pervert'ible**. [Partly through Fr, from L *pervertere, perversum*, from pfx *per-* wrongly, and *vertere* to turn]

perviate. See under **pervious**.

pervicacious *pûr-vi-kā'shəs*, *adj* very obstinate. — *n* **pervicā'ciousness**, **pervicacity** (*-kas'i-ti*) or **pervicacy** (*pûr'vi-kə-si*; *obs*). [L *pervicāx, -ācis*, from pfx *per-*, and *vincere* to prevail]

pervious *pûr'vi-əs*, *adj* permeable; passable; penetrable; open (to new ideas, persuasion, etc). — *vt* **per'viate** to make a way through. — *adv* **per'viously**. — *n* **per'viousness**. [L *pervius*, from *per* through, and *via* a way]

Pes *abbrev*: peseta (Spanish currency).

Pesach or **Pesah** *pā'sahh*, *n* the festival of Passover. [Heb]

pesade *pə-zäd*, *-sād'* or *-zād'*, *n* a dressage manoeuvre in which a horse rears up on its hindlegs without forward movement. [Fr; from Ital]

pesant, **pesaunt**. Old spellings of **peasant**.

pesante *pes-an'tā*, (*music*) *adj* heavy; weighty. — Also *adv*. [Ital]

peseta *pe-sā'ta* or *-ə*, *n* the Spanish standard monetary unit (100 *céntimos*). [Sp, dimin of *pesa* weight]

pesewa *pə-sōō'a*, *-sā'wa* or *-ə*, *n* a Ghanaian unit of currency: — *pl* **pesewa** or **pesewas**. — See **cedi**.

Peshito or **Peshitto** *pe-shē(t)'tō* or **Peshitta** *-tə*, *n* a Syriac translation of the Bible. — Also *adj*. [Syriac *p'shī(t)tô, -tâ* the simple]

peshwa *pāsh'wa*, *n* the chief minister of the Mahrattas, later the real sovereign. — Also **peish'wa** or **peish'wah**. [Pers *pēshwā* chief]

pesky *pes'ki*, (*colloq*) *adj* annoying, troublesome (used as a pejorative). — *adv* **pes'kily**. [Perh **pest**]

peso *pā'sō*, *n* a Spanish five-peseta piece; a Mexican dollar; in S and Central America and the Philippines, a coin of various values, eg 100 centavos: — *pl* **pe'sos**. [Sp, from L *pēnsum* weight]

pessary *pes'ə-ri*, *n* a surgical plug worn in the vagina to support the womb; a suppository inserted into the vagina. [Fr *pessaire*, from LL *pessārium*, from Gr *pessos* a pebble, pessary]

pessima. See under **pessimum**.

pessimism *pes'i-mizm*, *n* the doctrine that the world is bad rather than good (*philos*); a tendency to look on the dark side of things; a depressing view of life; (loosely) despondency, hopelessness; the worst state (*obs*). — *n* **pess'imist** a person who believes that everything is tending to the worst; a person who looks too much on the dark side of things (opposite of *optimist*). — *adj* **pessimis'tic** or **pessimis'tical**. — *adv* **pessimis'tically**. [L *pessimus* worst]

pessimum *pes'i-məm*, *n* that point at which any condition is least favourable: — *pl* **pess'ima**. — *adj* (of conditions) worst, least favourable. — Also **pess'imal**. [L, neuter of *pessimus* worst]

pest *pest*, *n* any deadly epidemic disease; plague (now *rare*;) anything destructive; any insect, fungus, etc that destroys cultivated plants; a troublesome person or thing. — *adj* **pest'ful** pestilential. — *adj* **pestici'dal** pertaining to a pesticide. — *n* **pesticide** (*pes'ti-sīd*) a substance for killing pests. — *adj* **pestif'erous** bringing plague or pestilence; pestilential; noxious; pestilent; annoying; plague-stricken. — *adv* **pestif'erously**. — *n* **pest'ilence** any deadly epidemic disease; bubonic plague; any morally harmful influence. — *adj* **pest'ilent** deadly; producing pestilence; hurtful to health and life; pernicious; mischievous; vexatious. — *adj* **pestilential** (*-len'shl*) of the nature of pestilence; producing or infested with pestilence; destructive; baneful; detestable; pestering. — *adv* **pestilen'tially**. — *adv* **pest'ilently**. — *adj* **pestolog'ical**. — *n* **pestol'ogist**. — *n* **pestol'ogy** the study of agricultural pests and methods of combating them. — **pest'house** (*hist*) a hospital for patients suffering from plague or any other infectious or contagious disease. — *adj* **pest'ilence-stricken**. [Fr *peste* and *pestilence*, from L *pestis, pestilentia*]

Pestalozzian, *pes-ta-lot'si-ən*, *adj* pertaining to Johann Heinrich *Pestalozzi* (1746-1827) or his programme of educational reform. — *n* a follower of Pestalozzi.

pester *pes'tər*, *vt* to clog (*obs*); to huddle (*Milton*); to infest (*archaic*); to annoy persistently. — *n* an annoyance. — *n* **pes'terer**. — *adv* **pes'teringly**. — *n* **pes'terment**. — *adj* **pest'erous**. [Appar from OFr *empestrer* (Fr *empêtrer*), to entangle, from L *in* in, and LL *pāstōrium* a foot-shackle, from L *pāstus*, pa p of *pāscere* to feed; cf **pastern**; influenced by **pest**]

pesticide, **pestiferous**, **pestilence**, etc. See under **pest**.

pestle *pes'l*, also *pest'l*, *n* an instrument for pounding or grinding, *esp* a small club-like kitchen utensil used in conjunction wth a small bowl or mortar; a leg of an animal, *esp* as food (now *dialect*). — *vt* to pound. — *vi* to use a pestle. [OFr *pestel*, from L *pistillum* a pounder, from *pīnsere, pistum* to pound]

pesto *pes'tō, n* an Italian sauce made chiefly of basil and cheese, with nuts and olive oil, originating in Liguria. [Ital]

pestology. See under **pest**.

PET *abbrev*: polyethylene terephthalate; positron emission tomography (brain scanner; *med*).

Pet (*Bible*) *abbrev*: (the Letters of) Peter.

pet[1] *pet, n* a tame animal kept for companionship or amusement; an indulged favourite; used as an endearment. — *adj* kept as a pet; for or of pet animals; indulged; cherished; favourite. — *vt* to treat as a pet; to fondle; to pamper; to indulge. — *vi* (*colloq*) to indulge in amorous caressing: — *pr p* **pett'ing**; *pa t* and *pa p* **pett'ed**. — *adj* **pett'ed**. — *n* **pett'er**. — *n* **pett'ing**. — **pet aversion** or **hate** a chief object of dislike; **pet'-day** (*Scot*) a day of sunshine in the middle of bad weather; **pet name** a name used in familiar affection. — *vi* **pet'-sit** to look after a pet in its owner's absence. — **pet'-sitter**; — **petting party** (*colloq*) a gathering for the purpose of amorous caressing as an organized sport. [Origin unknown; not from Gaelic]

pet[2] *pet, n* a slighted and offended feeling; a slight or childish fit of aggrieved or resentful sulkiness; the sulks, huff. — *vi* to be peevish, to sulk. — *adj* **pett'ed** in a pet; apt to be in a pet. — *adv* **pett'edly**. — *n* **pett'edness**. — *adj* **pett'ish** peevish; sulky; inclined to sulk; of the nature of or expressive of sulkiness. — *adv* **pett'ishly**. — *n* **pett'ishness**. [Origin unknown]

PETA (*US*) *abbrev*: People for the Ethical Treatment of Animals.

peta- *pe'tə-, combining form* denoting one thousand million million, 10^{15}, as in *petajoule* and *petametre*. [Origin uncertain; prob Gr **penta-**]

petal *pet'l, n* one of the *usu* brightly coloured leaflike parts of a flower, a corolla leaf. — *adj* **petalif'erous** or **pet'alous** having petals. — *adj* **pet'aline** (*-īn*) of or like a petal. — *n* **pet'alism** a method of ostracism practised in ancient Syracuse, the name being written on an olive-leaf. — *adj* **pet'alled** having petals; also used as *combining form*, as in *white-petalled*. — *n* **pet'alōdy** (Gr *eidos* form) transformation, *esp* of stamens, into petals. — *adj* **pet'aloid** having the appearance of a petal. — *n* **petalomā'nia** abnormal increase in number of petals. — *adj* **petalous** see **petaliferous** above. [Gr *petalon* a leaf]

pétanque *pā-tāk', n* the name in S France for the game, of Provençal origin, in which steel bowls are rolled or hurled towards a wooden marker ball, in other regions called **boules**.

petar. See **petard**.

petara *pi-tä'rə, n* a travelling box or basket for clothes. — Also **pita'ra** or **pita'rah**. [Hindi *pitārāh, petārāh*]

petard *pe-tär* or *-tärd', n* a case containing an explosive, used for blowing in doors, etc (*Shakesp* **petar'**); a moving firework. — **hoist with his own petard** see under **hoist**. [OFr, from *péter* to crack or explode, from L *pēdere* to break wind]

petary *pē'tər-i, n* a peat-bog. [Medieval L *petāria*, from root of **peat**[1]]

petasus *pet'ə-səs, n* a low broad hat worn by the Greeks in antiquity; either the broad petasus that Hermes is represented as wearing in early Greek art or, by association, the winged hat he wears in later art. [Latinised from Gr *petasos*]

petaurist *pe-tö'rist, n* a flying phalanger. — *adj* **petaur'ine**. [Gr *petauristēs* an acrobat]

petchary *pech'ə-ri, n* the grey king-bird. [Imit]

petcock *pet'kok, n* a small tap or valve for draining condensed steam from steam-engine cylinders, or for testing the water-level in a boiler. [Poss obs *pet* to fart, or **petty**, and *cock* a tap]

petechia *pe-tē'ki-ə, (med) n* a small red or purple spot on the skin, the result of a ruptured blood vessel: — *pl* **pete'chiae** (*-ē*). — *adj* **petech'ial**. [Latinized from Ital *petecchia*]

peter[1] *pē'tər, vi* to dwindle away to nothing, be dissipated or exhausted (with *out*). [Origin unknown; orig US mining slang]

peter[2] *pē'tər, n* the Blue Peter (flag); a call for trumps (*whist*); a high card followed by a low card, so played as a signal to one's partner (*bridge*). — *vi* to signal that one has a short suit (*whist*); to play a high card followed by a low card (*bridge*). — **pe'ter-boat** a kind of fishing-boat; a dredger's boat that goes equally well forward or astern; **pe'ter-man** a fisherman (in allusion to the apostle); **Peter-see-me'** a Spanish wine (from a grape introduced by Pedro *Ximenes*); **Peter's pence** see under **penny**; **Peter's projection** (*cartog*) an equal area map, one that shows accurately the relative sizes of continents, oceans, etc.

peter[3] *pē'tər, (slang) n* a safe; a prison cell; a till (*Austr*); the witness box (*Austr*). — **pe'terman** a safe-blower.

Peterloo *pē-tər-lōō', n* a popular term for the incident at St Peter's Fields, Manchester, in 1819, in which a peaceable demonstration for reform was charged by cavalry, leaving 11 dead and 400 to 500 injured. [St *Peter*'s Fields and Water*loo*]

peter-boat, peter-man. See under **peter**[2].

peterman. See under **peter**[3].

Peter Pan *pētər pan, n* a character in J M Barrie's play of that name (1904), hence the type of person who never grows up, *esp* a youthful or immature man. — **Peter Pan collar** a flat collar with rounded ends.

Peter principle *pē'tər prin'si-pl, (facetious) n* the theory that members of an organization, etc, are generally promoted to posts one stage above their level of competence. [Advanced by Laurence Peter and Raymond Hull in their book, *The Peter Principle* (1969)]

petersham *pē'tər-shəm, n* a heavy corded ribbon used for belts, hat-bands, etc; a heavy greatcoat designed by Lord *Petersham*; rough-napped cloth, generally dark blue, of which it was made. [Lord *Petersham*, a 19th-century English army officer]

pether. See **pedder**.

pethidine *peth'ə-dēn, n* a synthetic analgesic and hypnotic, acting like morphine, much used in childbirth. — Also called **meperidine** (*mə-per'i-dēn* or *-din*). [Perh mixture of *piperidine* and *ethyl*]

pétillant *pā-tē-yã, (Fr) adj* (of wine) slightly sparkling.

petiole *pet'i-ōl, n* a leaf-stalk (*bot*); a stalk-like structure, *esp* that of the abdomen in wasps, etc (*zool*). — *adj* **pet'iolar** of, or of the nature of, a petiole. — *adj* **pet'iolāte, pet'iolāted** or **pet'ioled** stalked. — *n* **pet'iolule** (*-ol-ūl; bot*) the stalk of a leaflet in a compound leaf. [L *petiolus* a little foot, a petiole]

petit formerly *pet'it*, now *pet'i, pə-tē'* or as Fr *pə-tē, adj* a form of **petty** (qv), in sense of insignificant, *obs* except in legal and other French phrases: — *adj* **petite** (*pə-tēt'*) applied to a woman, small-made (with a suggestion of neatness); a variant spelling of **petit**, applied to either sex (*obs*). — In phrases, the earlier borrowings tend to be the more highly anglicized. — **petit battement** (*bat-mâ ; ballet*) a light tapping or beating with the foot; **petit bourgeois** (*bōōr-zhwä*) a member of the lower middle class; **petite bourgeoisie** (*bōōr-zhwä-zē*) the lower middle class; **petit déjeuner** (*dā-zhœ-nā*) breakfast; **petit four** (*fōr, för* or *fōōr*) a small very fancy biscuit; **petit grain** (*grã*) dried unripe bitter oranges, or an oil distilled from them or their leaves and twigs; **petit jury** (*legal*) a jury of twelve people, in Britain now the only form of jury (also **petty jury**; see also **grand jury** under **grand**[1]); **petit maître** (*me-tr'*) a fop; **petit mal** (*mal*) a mild form of epilepsy without convulsions; **petit pain** (*pɛ̃*) a breadroll; **petit point** (*point* or *pwɛ̃*) tapestry work using small stitches diagonal to the canvas threads; **petits pois** (*pə-tē pwä*) small green peas. [Fr *petit, petite*]

petition *pə-tish'ən, n* a supplication; a prayer; a formal request to an authority; a written supplication signed by a number of people; a written application to a court of law; the thing asked for; a parliamentary bill (*obs*); an axiom or postulate (*obs*). — *vt* to address a petition to; to ask for. — *adj* **peti'tionary**. — *n* **peti'tioner**

someone who petitions; (with *cap*) one of the party that petitioned Charles II in 1680 to summon Parliament— opposed to *Abhorrer* (*hist*). — *n* **petit'ioning**. — *n* **peti'tionist**. — *adj* **petitory** (*pet'i-tə-ri*) petitioning. — **Petition of Right** a parliamentary declaration, in the form of a petition of the rights of the people, assented to by Charles I in 1628. [L *petītiō, -ōnis*, from *petere* to ask]

petitio principii *pe-tish'i-ō prin-sip'i-ī* or *pe-tē'ti-ō prēn-kip'i-ē*, (*logic*) *n* a begging of the question. [L]

petitory. See under **petition**.

Petrarchan *pe-trär'kən* or **Petrarchian** *-ki-ən*, *adj* pertaining to or in the style of the Italian poet Francesco *Petrarca* or *Petrarch* (1304–74). — *n* a follower or imitator of Petrarch. — *adj* **Petrarch'al**. — *n* **Petrarch'i-anism**. — *n* **Petrarch'ianist**. — *n* **Petrarchism** (*pe'trärk-izm*, or *pe-trärk'izm*). — *n* **Pe'trarchist** (or *-trärk'*). — *vi* **Petrarchize** or **-ise** (*pe'trärk-īz* or *-trärk'*) to write in Petrarch's manner, to imitate Petrarch. — The older pronunciation of Petrarch, *pē'trärk*, gives alternative pronunciations for the above words. — **Petrarchan** (or **Petrarchian**) **sonnet** see under **sonnet**.

petrary *pet'rə-ri*, *n* a contrivance for hurling stones. [LL *petrāria*, from L *petra*, from Gr *petrā* rock]

petre *pē'tər*, (*colloq*) *n* short form of **saltpetre**.

petrel *pet'rəl*, *n* any bird of the genus *Procellaria* related to the albatrosses and fulmars, *esp* one of the **storm** (popularly **stormy**) **petrel** species or Mother Carey's chickens, dusky sea-birds, rarely landing except to lay their eggs, and including the smallest web-footed bird known. [L *Petrus* Peter, from the fact that it appears to walk on the water; see Matthew 14.29]

Petri (or **petri**) **dish** *pē'tri*, *pā'tri* or *pet'ri dish*, *n* a shallow glass dish with an overlapping cover used for cultures of bacteria. — Also **Petri plate**. [R J *Petri*, German bacteriologist]

petrify *pet'ri-fī*, *vt* to turn into stone; to fossilize by molecular replacement, preserving minute structure (*geol*); (loosely) to encrust with stony matter; to make hard like a stone; to fix in amazement, fear, horror, etc. — *vi* to become stone, or hard like stone: — *prp* **pet'rifying**; *pat* and *pap* **pet'rified**. — *n* **petrifac'tion** turning or being turned into stone; a petrified object; a fossil. — *adj* **petrifac'tive** or **petrif'ic** petrifying. — *n* **petrificā'tion** petrifaction. [L *petra*, from Gr *petrā* rock, and L *facere*, *factum* to make]

Petrine *pē'trīn*, *adj* pertaining to or written by the Apostle *Peter*. — *n* **Pē'trinism** (*-trin-izm*) the Tübingen theory of F C Baur (1792–1860) and his school, of a doctrinal trend in primitive Christianity towards Judaism, ascribed to Peter and his party in opposition to *Paulinism*. [L *Petrinus*, from Petrus, Gr *Petros* Peter]

petrissage *pā-trēs-äzh'*, *n* massage by longitudinal rubbing and lateral squeezing. [Fr, from *pétrir* to knead]

petro-[1] *pet'rō-*, *combining form* signifying petroleum. — *n* and *adj* **petrōchem'ical** (of or relating to) any chemical obtained from petroleum. — *n* **petrōchem'istry**. — *n* **pet'rocurr'ency**, **pet'romoney**, **pet'rodollars** and **pet'ro-pounds** currency, etc, acquired by the oil-producing countries as profit from the sale of their oil to the consumer countries. [*petro*leum]

petro-[2] *pet-rō-* or *pi-tro'-*, *combining form* signifying rock. — *n* **pet'rodrome** (Gr *dromos* a running) an African elephant shrew of the genus **Petrodromus**. — *n* **petro-gen'esis** (the study of) the origin, formation, etc, of rocks. — *adj* **petrogenet'ic**. — *n* **pet'rōglyph** (Gr *glyphein* to carve) a rock-carving, *esp* prehistoric. — *adj* **petrōglyph'ic**. — *n* **pet'rōglyphy**. — *n* **pet'rōgram** (Gr *gramma* a drawing) a picture on stone. — *n* **petrog'rapher**. — *adj* **petrograph'ic** or **petrograph'ical**. — *adv* **petrograph'ically**. — *n* **petrog'raphy** (Gr *graphein* to write) the systematic description and classification of rocks. — *adj* **petrolog'ical**. — *adv* **petro-log'ically**. — *n* **petrol'ogist**. — *n* **petrol'ogy** (Gr *logos* discourse) the science of the origin, chemical and mineral composition and structure, and alteration of rocks. — *adj* **petrōphys'ical**. — *n* **petrōphys'icist**. — *n sing* **petrōphys'ics** (Gr *physikos* natural) that branch of physics pertaining to the physical properties of rocks. — **petrographic province** (*geol*) a region characterized by a group of genetically related rocks. [Gr *petrā* rock]

petrol *pet'rol* or *-rəl*, *n* formerly, petroleum; now a mixture of light volatile hydrocarbons obtained by the fractional distillation or cracking of petroleum, used as a fuel in motor-cars, aeroplanes, etc (US **gasoline**); petrol blue. — *vt* to supply with petrol: — *prp* **pet'rolling**; *pat* and *pap* **pet'rolled**. — *n* **pet'rolage** treatment with petrol to stamp out mosquitoes. — *n* **petrolatum** (*-ā'təm*) petroleum jelly. — *adj* **petroleous** (*pi-trō'li-əs*) containing or rich in petroleum. — *n* **petroleum** (*pi-trō'li-əm*) a (*usu* liquid) mineral oil containing a mixture of hydrocarbons obtained from oil wells, and used to make petrol, paraffin, lubricating oil, fuel oil, etc. — *n* **pétroleur** (*pā-trol-œr*) and *fem* **pétroleuse** (*-øz*) (*Fr*) a rioter who uses petroleum, as in the Paris uprising of 1871. — *adj* **petrolic** (*pi-trol'ik*) of petrol or petroleum. — *adj* **petrolif'erous** (*pet-*) yielding petroleum. — **petrol blue** a vibrant blue colour; **petrol bomb** a petrol-filled Molotov cocktail or similar small explosive device; **petroleum coke** almost pure carbon, the final by-product of the distillation of crude oil, used in refining, electrodes, as a fuel, etc; **petroleum ether** a volatile mixture of hydrocarbons distilled from petroleum and used as a solvent; **petroleum jelly** soft paraffin (*paraffinum molle*), a mixture of petroleum hydrocarbons used in emollients, as a lubricant, etc (see also **liquid paraffin** under **paraffin**); **petrol lighter** a cigarette-lighter in which the striking of a spark ignites a petrol-soaked wick; **petrol pump** a machine from which measured amounts of petrol are dispensed for use in motor vehicles; **petrol station** a garage which sells petrol, a filling station. [L *petra* rock, and *oleum* oil]

petrology. See under **petro-**[2].

petronel *pet'rə-nel*, *n* a short large calibre rifle carried by mounted soldiers in the 16th and 17th centuries. [Fr *petrinal*, from L *pectus*, *pectoris* the chest, whence fired, or L *petra* stone, ie gun-flint]

petronella *pet-rən-el'ə*, *n* a Scottish country-dance.

petrous *pet'rəs*, *adj* stony; petrosal. — *adj* **petrosal** (*pi-trōs'əl*) relating to the stony part of the temporal bone around the inner ear. — Also *n*. [L *petrōsus*, from *petra*, from Gr *petrā* rock]

pe-tsai cabbage *pā-tsī' kab'ij*. Same as **Chinese cabbage**.

petted, etc. See under **pet**[1,2].

Petter engine *pet'ər en'jin*, *n* a kind of oil-engine. [Makers' name]

petter. See under **pet**[1].

pettichaps or **petty-chaps** *pet'i-chaps*, *n* the garden or other warbler. [N of England; appar **petty** and **chap**[3]]

petticoat *pet'i-kōt*, *n* a skirt, *esp* an under-skirt, or a garment of which it forms part; any garment or drapery of similar form; *orig* a short or small coat; a woman (*colloq*); any bell-shaped structure. — *adj* (*usu facetious*) feminine; female; of women. — *adj* **pett'i-coated**. — **pett'icoat-breeches** loose short breeches worn by men in the 17th century; **petticoat government** domination by women; **pett'icoat-tails'** small *usu* triangular cakes of shortbread. [**petty** and **coat**[1]]

pettifogger *pet'i-fog-ər*, *n* a lawyer who deals, often deceptively and quibblingly, with trivial cases. — *vi* **pett'ifog** to play the pettifogger. — *n* **pett'ifoggery**. — *n* and *adj* **pett'ifogging** paltry, trivial, cavilling (behaviour). [**petty** and MLGer *voger* a person who does things]

petting. See under **pet**[1].

pettish, etc. See under **pet**[2].

pettitoes *pet'i-tōz*, *n pl* pig's feet as food (formerly *appar* also other parts and of other animals); human feet (*Shakesp*). [Origin obscure, but early associated with **petty** and **toe**]

pettle[1] *pet'l*, (*Scot*) *vt* to indulge, pet. [Frequentative of **pet**[1]]

pettle[2] *pet'l*. Same as **pattle**.

petty *pet'i, adj* small; of little or less importance; minor; trifling; lower in rank, power, etc; inconsiderable, insignificant; contemptible; small-minded. — *n* a junior schoolboy. — *adv* **pett'ily**. — *n* **pett'iness**. — **Petty Bag** a former office of the Court of Chancery; a clerk of that office; **petty bourgeois** and **bourgeoisie** variants of **petit bourgeois** and **petite bourgeoisie** (qv under **petit**); **petty cash** miscellaneous small sums of money received or paid; a sum of money kept for minor expenses which *usu* do not need to be referred to a higher authority; **petty-chaps** see **pettichaps**; **petty jury** see **petit jury** under **petit**; **petty larceny** see under **larceny**; **petty officer** a naval officer ranking with a non-commissioned officer in the army; **Petty Sessions** a court in which magistrates try trivial cases and refer others to a higher court; **petty whin** a low spiny papilionaceous shrub (*Genista anglica*) like a small whin. [Fr *petit*]

petulant *pet'ū-lənt, adj orig* wanton, lascivious; showing peevish impatience, irritation, or caprice; forward, impudent in manner. — *n* **pet'ulance** or **pet'ulancy**. — *adv* **pet'ulantly**. [L *petulāns, -antis*, from assumed *petulāre*, dimin of *petere* to seek]

Petunia *pē-tū'nyə* or *-ni-ə, n* a South American genus of ornamental plants closely related to tobacco; (without *cap*) a plant of this genus. [Tupí *petun* tobacco]

petuntse *pe-tōōnt'si, n* a feldspathic rock used in making Chinese porcelain. — Also **petuntze**. [Chin *pai-tun-tse* little white brick]

pew *pū, n* an enclosed compartment or fixed bench in a church; formerly a place for a preacher or reader; a box or stall in another building; a seat (*slang*). — **pew'-chair** an additional seat hinged to the end of a pew; **pew'-fellow** an occupant of the same pew; hence, a companion; **pew'-holder** a person who rents a pew; **pew'-opener** an attendant who showed people to pews; **pew'-rent** rent paid for the use of a pew. [OFr *puie* raised place, balcony, from L *podia*, pl of *podium*, from Gr *podion*, dimin of *pous, podos* foot]

pewit *pē'wit* or *pū'it*. Same as **peewit**.

pewter *pū'tər, n* formerly an alloy of three to nine parts of tin and one of lead; now tin with a little copper, antimony, and/or bismuth; a container made of pewter, *esp* a beer-tankard; the bluish-grey colour of pewter; prize-money (*slang*). — *adj* made of pewter. — *n* **pew'terer** someone who works in pewter. — **pew'ter-mill** a lapidary's pewter polishing-wheel for amethyst, agate, etc. [OFr *peutre*; cf Ital *peltro*, LGer *spialter*, Eng **spelter**]

peyote *pā-yō'tā, n* a Mexican intoxicant made from cactus tops — also called **mescal**. — *n* **peyō'tism** the taking of peyote, *esp* as part of a religious ceremony; a N American Indian religion in which peyote is taken sacramentally, a form of Christianity. — *n* **peyō'tist**. [Nahuatl *peyotl*]

peyse. See **peise**.

pezant. An old spelling of **peasant**.

Peziza *pe-zī'zə, n* a genus of discomycete fungi with cup-like apothecia. — *adj* **pezi'zoid**. [Gr *pezis* a puff-ball]

PF *abbrev*: Patriotic Front; Procurator Fiscal.

Pf *abbrev*: pfennig (German currency).

pf *abbrev*: (*music*) pianoforte.

PFA *abbrev*: Professional Footballers' Association.

pfennig *pfen'ig* or *-ihh, n* a German coin, the hundredth part of a mark. — Also (*obs*) **pfenn'ing**.

PFLP *abbrev*: Popular Front for the Liberation of Palestine.

PG *abbrev*: Parental Guidance (a certificate denoting a film in which some scenes may be unsuitable for young children); paying guest.

Pg *abbrev*: Portugal; Portuguese.

PGA *abbrev*: Professional Golfers' Association.

PGM *abbrev*: Past Grand Master.

pH *pē-āch'* or **pH value** (*val'ū*), *n* a number used to express degrees of acidity or alkalinity in solutions — formerly the logarithm to base 10 of the reciprocal of the concentration of hydrogen ions — now related by formula to a standard solution of potassium hydrogen phthalate, which has value 4 at 15°C.

PHAB *fab, abbrev*: Physically Handicapped and Able Bodied.

Phacelia *fə-sē'li-ə*, (*bot*) *n* a chiefly American genus of annuals of the *Hydrophyllaceae* family; (without *cap*) any plant of the genus.

phacoid *fak'* or *fāk'oid* or **phacoidal** *fə-koi'dl, adj* lentil-shaped; lens-shaped. — *n* **phacolite** (*fak'ə-līt*) a zeolite often lenticular in shape. — *n* **phac'olith** a small lenticular igneous intrusion, shaped by folding in an anticline. [Gr *phakos* a lentil, *eidos* form, and *lithos* stone]

Phaedra complex *fēd'rə kom'pleks*, (*psychol*) *n* the difficult relationship which can arise between a new step-parent and the (*usu* teenage) son or daughter of the original marriage. [Greek story of *Phaedra* who fell in love with her stepson and committed suicide after being repulsed by him]

phaeic *fē'ik, adj* dusky. — *n* **phae'ism** duskiness, incomplete melanism (in butterflies). [Gr *phaios* dusky]

phaelonion. See **phelonion**.

phaen- *fēn-* or **phaeno-** *fē-no-*. Same as **phen-** or **pheno-** (qv).

phaenogam *fē'nō-gam, n* a spermatophyte or phanerogam. — *n pl* **Phaenogamae** (*fē-nog'ə-mē*). — *adj* **phaenogamic** (*-nō-gam'ik*) or **phaenogamous** (*-nog'ə-məs*). — Also **phe'nogam**, etc. [Gr *phainein* to show, and *gamos* marriage]

phaenology, **phaenomenon**, **phaenotype**. Same as **phenology**, **phenomenon**, **phenotype**.

phaeo- *fē-ō-*, *combining form* denoting dusky, as in **phaeomelanin** (*fē-ō-mel'ə-nin*), a reddish-brown pigment in animals, including birds. [Gr *phaios* dusky]

Phaeophyceae *fē-ō-fish'i-ē, n pl* the brown seaweeds, one of the main divisions of algae, in which the chlorophyll is masked by a brown pigment. [Gr *phaios* dusky, and *phȳkos* seaweed]

Phaethon *fā'i-thon, n* the son of Helios, the Greek sun-god, who came to grief in driving his father's chariot (*Gr mythol*); the tropic-bird genus (as seeking to keep to the sun's course). — *adj* **Phaethon'tic**. [Gr *Phaethōn, -ontos*, literally, shining; cf *phaos, phōs* light]

phaeton *fā'i-tən* or *fā'tən, n* an open four-wheeled carriage for one or two horses. [From **Phaethon**]

phag- *fag* or **phago-** *fag-ō-*, *combining form* denoting 'feeding' or 'eating', as in **phagocyte** (qv). — *combining form* **-phaga** (*-fag-ə*) denoting (in zoological names) 'eaters'. — *combining form* **-phage** (*-fāj* or *-fäzh*) denoting eater or destroyer. — *combining form* **-phagous** (*-fəg-əs*) denoting feeding on. — *combining form* **-phagus** (*-fəg-əs*) denoting one feeding in a particular way, or on a particular thing. — *combining form* **-phagy** (*-fə-ji*) denoting eating of a specified nature. [Gr *phagein* to eat]

phage. Short for **bacteriophage**.

phagedaena or **phagedena** *faj-* or *fag-i-dē'nə*, (*med*) *n* hospital gangrene, rapidly spreading destructive ulceration, once common in hospitals. — *adj* **phagedae'nic** or **phagedē'nic**. [Gr *phagedaina*, from *phagein* to eat]

phagocyte *fag'ō-sīt, n* a white blood-corpuscle that engulfs bacteria and other harmful particles. — *adj* **phagocytic** (*-sit'*) or **phagocyt'ical**. — *n* **phag'ocytism** (*-sīt-*) the nature or function of a phagocyte. — *vt* **phag'ocytose** (*-sīt-ōs*) to subject to phagocytic action. — *n* **phagocytō'sis** destruction by phagocytes. [Gr *phagein* to eat, and *kytos* a vessel]

phagophobia *fag-ō-fō'bi-ə, n* fear of or aversion to eating. [**phago-** and **phobia**.]

-phagous, **-phagus**, **-phagy**. See under **phag-**.

Phalaenopsis *fal'i-nop-sis*, (*bot*) *n* a genus of evergreen epiphytic orchids.

phalange, etc. See under **phalanx**.

phalanger *fal-an'jər*, *n* any one of a group of small arboreal Australasian marsupials, an opossum. [Gr *phalangion* spider's web, from their webbed toes]

phalanstery *fal'ən-stə-ri*, *n* the set of buildings occupied by a phalange in the ideal social system of Fourier (1772–1837), a vast structure set in a square league of cultivated land. — *adj* **phalansterian** (*-stē'ri-ən*). — *n* **phalanstē'rianism** or **phal'ansterism**. — *n* **phal'ansterist**. [Fr *phalanstère*, formed from Gr *phalanx* on the model of *monastère* monastery]

phalanx *fal'angks* or *fāl'angks*, *n* a solid formation of ancient Greek heavy-armed infantry; a solid formation of soldiers; a solid body of supporters or partisans; a solid body of people generally; a Fourierist community; a bone of a digit; the part of a finger or toe corresponding to it; a joint of an insect's leg; a bundle of stamens: — *pl* **phal'anxes** or (*biol*) **phalanges** (*fal-an'jēz*). — *adj* **phalangal** (*fal-ang'gl*) phalangeal. — *n* **phalange** (*fal'anj*) a phalanx (in biological senses); (also *fal-âzh*) a socialistic community in Fourier's scheme, consisting of 1800 people living in a phalanstery; the Falange, Primo de Rivera's Spanish fascist party; the Christian right-wing group in Lebanon, modelled on the Spanish Falange: — *pl* **phal'anges**. — *adj* **phalan'geal**. — *n* **phalangid** (*fal-an'jid*) a long-legged arachnid, a harvester spider. — *n* **phalan'gist** a Spanish falangist; a member of the Lebanese phalange. [Gr *phalanx*, *-angos* a roller, phalanx, phalange, spider]

phalarope *fal'ə-rōp*, *n* a wading bird (*Phalaropus*) with feet like those of a coot. [Gr *phalaris* a coot, and *pous* a foot]

phallus *fal'əs*, *n* the penis; the symbol of generation in primitive religion; (with *cap*) the stinkhorn genus of fungi: — *pl* **phall'ī** or **phall'uses**. — *adj* **phall'ic**. — *n* **phall'icism** (*-sizm*) or **phall'ism** worship of the generative power of nature. — *n* **phall'in** and **phalloid'in** two of the poisons occurring in the fungus *Amanita phalloides*. — *adj* **phallocen'tric** centred on the phallus; dominated by or expressive of male attitudes. — *n* **phallocentric'ity**. — *n* **phall'ocrat** a person who supports or assumes the existence of a male-dominated society; a man who argues for his superiority over women because of his masculinity. — Also *adj*. — *adj* **phallocrat'ic**. — *adj* **phall'oid** like a phallus in shape. [L, from Gr *phallos*]

Phanariot *fa-nar'i-ot*, *n* one of the Greeks inhabiting the *Fanar* quarter of Constantinople; one of a class of Greek officials, in Turkish history mostly diplomats, administrators and bankers, also hospodars of Wallachia and Moldavia. — *adj* **Phanar'iot**. — Also **Fanariot**. [Gr *phānarion* lighthouse, from that on the Golden Horn]

phanerogam *fan'ər-ō-gam*, (*biol*; *old*) *n* a spermatophyte. — *n pl* **Phanerogamae** (*-og'ə-mē*) or **Phanerogamia** (*-ō-gam'i-ə*) a division of plants comprising all spermatophytes. — *adj* **phanerogam'ic**. — *adj* **phanerog'amous**. [Gr *phaneros* visible, and *gamos* marriage]

phanerophyte *fan'ə-rə-fīt* or *fə-ner'ə-fīt*, (*biol*) *n* a tree or shrub with the perennating buds borne more than 25 cm above soil level. [Gr *phaneros* visible, and *phyton* plant]

Phanerozoic *fan-ər-ə-zō'ik*, (*geol*) *adj* denoting the geological period of time from the Cambrian period to the present. — Also *n*. [Gr *phaneros* visible, and *zōion* an animal]

phang. An old spelling (*Shakesp*) of **fang**.

phansigar *pän'sē-gär* or *fän'-*, *n* formerly in India, a thug. [Hindi *phasī* a noose, and Pers agent suffix *-gār*]

phantasiast. See under **phantasy**.

phantasm *fan'tazm*, *n* a vision; an illusion; an airy or insubstantial figure, an apparition, a spectre; a counterfeit; an impostor (*obs*). — Also **phantas'ma**: — *pl* **phan'tasms** or **phantas'mata**. — *n* **phan'tasim** or **phan'tasime** (*Shakesp*) a fantastic person. — *adj* **phantas'mal**. — *adj* **phantasmā'lian** (*rare*). — *n* **phantasmal'ity**. — *adv* **phantas'mally**. — *adj* **phantas'mic** or **phantas'mical**. — *adj* **phantasmogenet'ic** producing or causing phantasms. — *adv* **phantasmogenet'ically**. [Gr *phantasma*, from *phantazein* to make visible, from *phainein* to bring to light, from *phaein* to shine]

phantasmagoria *fan-taz-mə-gō'ri-ə* or *-gö'*, *n* a fantastic dreamlike series of illusive images or of real forms. — *adj* **phantasmago'rial** pertaining to or resembling a phantasmagoria. — *adj* **phantasmagor'ic** or **phantasmagor'ical**. [A name given to a show of optical illusions in 1802, from Fr *phantasmagorie*, from Gr *phantasma* an appearance, and perh *agorā* an assembly]

phantasy, **phantastic**, **phantastry**. Same as **fantasy**, etc. — *n* **phantā'siast** one of those Docetae who believed Christ's body to have been a mere phantom (see under **Docetism**).

phantom *fan'təm* (*Spenser* **phantosme** *fan-tōm'*), *n* a deceitful appearance; an immaterial form, a spectre; a visionary experience, such as a dream; an unreal vision or appearance, an illusion. — *adj* illusory; unreal, non-existent; spectral; imaginary; ghostly-looking; transparent and hardly visible. — *adj* (all *archaic*) **phantomat'ic**, **phan'tomish** or **phan'tomy** relating to a phantom. — **phantom circuit** (as in telecommunications) an additional circuit which does not in fact exist, the extra performance being obtained by suitable arrangements of real circuits; **phantom limb** the sensation experienced by an amputee of the amputated limb still being attached to the body; **phantom material** (*radiol*) material producing absorption and backscatter of radiation similar to human tissue, hence used to study radiation doses, etc (also called **tissue equivalent material**); **phantom pain** a sensation of pain in a phantom limb; **phantom pregnancy** false pregnancy (qv). [OFr *fantosme*, from Gr *phantasma*]

phar or **pharm** *abbrev*: pharmaceutical; pharmacopoeia; pharmacy.

Pharaoh *fā'rō*, *n* a title of the kings of ancient Egypt; faro (*obs*). — *adj* **pharaonic** (*fā-rā-on'ik*). — **Pharaoh** (or **Pharaoh's**) **ant** a tiny yellow-brown tropical ant which has spread through many countries and infests heated buildings, eg hospitals, restaurants, blocks of flats; **Pharaoh's serpent** the coiled ash of burning mercuric thiocyanate, a type of indoor firework; **Pharaonic circumcision** the ancient practice of female circumcision by the removal of the clitoris and labia majora and minora. [L and Gr *pharaō*, from Heb *par'ōh*, from Egyptian *pr-'o* great house]

phare *fār*, *n* a lighthouse. [Fr; see **pharos**]

Pharisee *far'i-sē*, *n* a member of an ancient Jewish sect, a lay democratic party among the Jews, whose legalistic interpretation of the Mosaic law led to an obsessive concern with the mass of rules covering the details of everyday life; anyone more careful of the outward forms than of the spirit of religion, a formalist; a very self-righteous or hypocritical person. — *adj* **pharisā'ic** or **pharisā'ical** pertaining to or like the Pharisees; hypocritical. — *adv* **pharisā'ically**. — *n* **pharisā'icalness**. — *n* **phar'isāism** (also **phar'iseeism**). [OE *pharisēus*, from LL *pharisaeus*, from Gr *pharisaios*, from Heb *pārūsh* separated]

pharm. See **phar**.

pharmaceutic *fär-mə-sū'tik* (or *-kū'tik*) or **pharmaceu'tical** *-əl*, *adj* pertaining to the knowledge or art of preparing medicines. — *n* **pharmaceu'tical** a chemical used in medicine. — *adv* **pharmaceu'tically**. — *n sing* **pharmaceu'tics** the science of preparing medicines. — *n* **pharmaceu'tist**. [Gr *pharmakeutikos*]

pharmacognosy, **pharmacokinetic**, etc, **pharmacology**, etc. See under **pharmacy**.

pharmacopoeia *fär-mə-kə-pē'* or *-pe'yə*, *n* a book or list of drugs with directions for their preparation; a collection of drugs. — *adj* **pharmacopoe'ial**. — *adj* **pharmacopoe'ian**. [Gr *pharmakopoiiā*, from *pharmakon* a drug, and *poieein* to make]

pharmacy *fär'mə-si*, *n* the art, practice or science of collecting, preparing, preserving, and dispensing medicines; a druggist's shop; a dispensary. — *n* **phar'macist** (*-sist*) a druggist, a person skilled in pharmacy;

someone legally qualified to sell drugs and poisons. — *n sing* **pharmacodynam'ics** the science of the action of drugs on the body. — *n* **pharmacog'nosist**. — *adj* **pharmacognos'tic**. — *n* **pharmacog'nosy** the study of drugs of plant and animal origin. — *adj* **pharmacokinet'ic**. — *n* **pharmacokinet'icist**. — *n sing* **pharmacokinet'ics** the study of the way the body deals with drugs. — *n* **pharmacol'ogist**. — *n* **pharmacol'ogy** the science of drugs. — *n* **pharmacop'olist** (Gr *pōleein* to sell) a dealer in drugs. [Gr *pharmakeiā* use of drugs, *pharmakon* a drug]

pharos *fā'ros*, *n* a lighthouse or beacon. [From the famous lighthouse on the island of *Pharos* in the Bay of Alexandria]

pharynx *far'ingks*, (*anatom*) *n* the cleft or cavity forming the upper part of the gullet, lying behind the nose, mouth, and larynx: — *pl* **phar'ynges** (*-in-jēz*) or **phar'ynxes**. — *adj* **pharyngal** (*fa-ring'gl*) or **pharyngeal** (*fa-rin'ji-əl* or *-jē'əl*). — *adj* **pharyngitic** (*far-in-jit'ik*) pertaining to pharyngitis. — *n* **pharyngitis** (*far-in-jī'tis*) inflammation of the mucous membrane of the pharynx. — *n* **pharyngol'ogy** the study of the pharynx and its diseases. — *n* **pharyngoscope** (*fa-ring'gə-skōp*) an instrument for inspecting the pharynx. — *n* **pharyngoscopy** (*far-ing-gos'kə-pi*). — *n* **pharyngot'omy** the operation of making an incision into the pharynx. [Gr *pharynx*, *-ygos*, later *-yngos*]

phase[1] *fāz*, *n* a stage in growth or development (*lit* and *fig*); the aspect or appearance of anything at any stage; the stage of advancement in a periodic change, measured from some standard point; the appearance at a given time of the illuminated surface exhibited by the moon or a planet — also **phasis** (*fā'sis*); the sum of all those portions of a material system which are identical in chemical composition and physical state (*chem*); a morph (*zool*); one of the circuits in an electrical system in which there are two or more alternating currents out of phase with each other by equal amounts (*elec*): — *pl* **phases** (*fā'ziz* or *-sēz*). — *vt* to do by phases or stages. — *adj* **phased** adjusted to be in the same phase at the same time; by stages. — *adj* **phase'less** unchanging. — *adj* **phā'sic** (or *-sik*). — **phase-contrast** (or **phase-difference**) **microscope** one in which the clear detail is obtained by means of a device that alters the speed of some of the rays of light, the resulting high-contrast image making staining unnecessary. — **in** (or **out of**) **phase** in the same phase together (or in different phases); **phase in** (or **out**) to begin (or cease) gradually to use or make, etc; **primary phase** crude technical raw material. [Gr *phasis* from *phaein* to shine]

phase[2]. See **feeze**.

phaseolin *fə-sē'ə-lin*, *n* a protein found in kidney-beans used to increase the protein content and nutritional value of other crops. [L *phaseolus* a kidney-bean]

phasic, **phasis**[1]. See under **phase**[1].

phasis[2]. See under **phatic**.

Phasma *faz'mə*, *n* the spectre-insect (stick-insect and leaf-insect) genus. — *n* **phas'mid** a member of the **Phas'midae** or **Phasmat'idae**, the family to which the genus Phasma belongs, or of the (sub)order **Phasmatō'dea**. [Gr *phasma* a spectre]

phatic *fat'ik*, *adj* using speech for social reasons, to communicate feelings rather than ideas. — *n* **phasis** (*fā'sis*). [Gr *phasis* utterance]

PHB *abbrev*: polyhydroxybutyrate.

PhD *abbrev*: *Philosophiae Doctor* (*L*), Doctor of Philosophy.

pheasant *fez'nt*, *n* a richly-coloured, long-tailed (in the male form), gallinaceous bird (*Phasianus colchicus*), a half-wild game-bird in Britain; extended to others of the same or related genus (such as *golden*, *silver*, *Argus*, or *Amherst's* pheasant) and to other birds; the tufted grouse (*US*); a francolin (*SAfr*); the lyre-bird (*Austr*); also the coucal (*swamp pheasant*); the flesh of any of these birds as food: — *pl* **pheasant** or **pheasants**. — *n* **pheas'antry** an enclosure for rearing pheasants. — **pheas'ant's-eye** a ranunculaceous plant (Adonis) with deep-red dark-centred flowers; a fragrant form of Narcissus, of the division *Narcissus Poeticus*, that has pure white petals and a small coloured cup with a red rim. [Anglo-Fr *fesant*, from L *phāsiānus*, from Gr *phāsiānos* (*ornis*) (bird) from the river Phasis, in Colchis (ancient Asia)]

pheazar *fē'zər*, (*Shakesp*) *n perh* one who feezes, *perh* for **vizier**.

pheer, **pheere**. Same as **fere**[1].

pheeze, **pheese**. Same as **feeze**.

phellem *fel'əm*, (*bot*) *n* cork. — *n* **phell'oderm** (Gr *derma* skin) a layer of secondary cortex formed by the phellogen on its inner side. — *n* **phellogen** (*fel'ō-jen*) a layer of meristem that forms cork on the outside, otherwise known as cork-cambium. — *adj* **phellogenetic** (*-ji-net'ik*). — *adj* **phell'oid** cork-like and formed like cork, but not (or very slightly) suberized. — *n* **phelloplas'tic** a model in cork. — *n sing* **phelloplas'tics** the making of models in cork. [Gr *phellos* cork]

phelonion or **phaelonion** *fi-lō'ni-on*, *n* an Eastern vestment like a chasuble. [Late Gr *phailonion*, *phelonion*, dimin of *phailonēs*, *phelonēs*, for *phainolēs*, from L *paenula* a cloak]

phen- *fēn-* or **pheno-** *fēn-ō-*, *combining form* denoting: showing; visible; related to benzene (see **phene**). [Gr *phainein* to show]

phenacetin *fin-as'i-tin*, *n* an antipyretic drug, $C_{10}H_{13}NO_2$. [**acetic** and **phene**]

phenacite *fen'ə-sīt* or **phenakite** *-kīt*, *n* a mineral, beryllium silicate, sometimes deceptively like quartz. — *n* **phen'akism** deceit. — *n* **phenakist'oscope** an instrument in which figures on a disc seen successively through a slit give the impression of motion. [Gr *phenax* and *phenākistēs* a deceiver, and *skopeein* to look at]

phenate. See under **phene**.

phencyclidine *fen-sī'kli-dēn*, *n* an analgesic and anaesthetic drug, $C_{17}H_{25}N{\cdot}HCl$, also used as a hallucinogen. [*phen-*, *cyclo-*, and piper*idine*]

phene *fēn*, *n* an old name for benzene. — *n* **phēn'ate** a phenolate. — *adj* **phēn'ic** (or *fen'*) of benzene or of phenyl. [Gr *phainein* to show, because obtained in the manufacture of illuminating gas]

phenetics *fi-net'iks*, (*biol*) *n sing* a system of classification of organisms based on observable similarities and differences irrespective of whether or not the organisms are related. — *adj* **phenet'ic** [*pheno*type and gen*etics*]

phengite *fen'jīt*, *n* a transparent stone used in ancient times for windows, *prob* selenite; sometimes applied to kinds of mica. — Also **phengites** (*fen-jī'tēz*). [Gr *phengītēs*, from *phengos* light]

phengophobia *fen-gō-fō'bi-ə*, *n* fear of or aversion to daylight, photophobia. [Gr *phainein* to show, and **phobia**]

phenic. See under **phene**.

Phenician. Same as **Phoenician**.

pheno-. See **phen-**.

phenobarbitone *fē-nō-bär'bi-tōn*, *n* a sedative and hypnotic drug.

phenocryst *fē'nō-krist*, *n* a larger crystal in a porphyritic rock. [Gr *phainein* to show, and **crystal**]

phenogam, etc. See **phaenogam**.

phenol *fē'nol*, *n* carbolic acid, a weak acid, C_6H_5OH, produced as hygroscopic needles from coal-tar, a powerful disinfectant; extended to the class of aromatic compounds with one or more hydroxyl groups directly attached to the benzene nucleus, weak acids with reactions of alcohols. — *n* **phēn'olate** a salt of a phenol. — *adj* **phenol'ic**. — *n* **phenolphthalein** (*fē-nol-fthal'i-in* or *-thal'*) a substance ($C_{20}H_{14}O_4$) derived from phenol and phthalic anhydride, brilliant red in alkalis, colourless in acids, used as an indicator. — **phenolic resins** a group of plastics made from a phenol and an aldehyde. [See **phene**; *-ol* from **alcohol**]

phenology or **phaenology** *fē-nol'ə-ji*, *n* the study of organisms as affected by climate, *esp* dates of seasonal phenomena, such as opening of flowers or arrival of migrants. — *adj* **phenological** (*-ə-loj'*). — *n* **phenol'ogist**. [Gr *phainein* to show, and *logos* discourse]

phenolphthalein. See under **phenol**.

phenom *fē-nom'*, (*slang*) *n* someone or something phenomenally good.

phenomenon or now rarely **phaenomenon** *fi-nom'i-nən* or *-non*, *n* anything directly apprehended by the senses or one of them; an event that may be observed; the appearance which anything makes to our consciousness, as distinguished from what it is in itself (*philos*); a feature of life, social existence, etc; (loosely) a remarkable or unusual person, thing, or appearance, a prodigy: — *pl* **phenom'ena** (sometimes used *erron* for *n sing*). — *adj* **phenom'enal** pertaining to a phenomenon; of the nature of a phenomenon; very or unexpectedly large, good, etc (*colloq*). — **phenomenalise** see **phenomenalize**. — *n* **phenom'enalism** the philosophical doctrine that phenomena are the only realities, or that knowledge can only comprehend phenomena — also called *externalism* (*philos*). — *n* **phenom'enalist**. — *adj* **phenomenalist'ic**. — *n* **phenomenality** (*-al'i-ti*) the character of being phenomenal. — *vt* **phenom'enalize** or **-ise** to represent as a phenomenon. — *adv* **phenom'enally**. — *n* **phenom'enism** phenomenalism. — *n* **phenom'enist**. — *vt* **phenom'enize** or **-ise** to bring into the world of experience. — *adj* **phenomenolog'ical**. — *n* **phenomenol'ogist**. — *n* **phenomenol'ogy** the science of or a description of phenomena; the philosophy of Edmund Husserl (1859–1938), opposed to positivism, and concerned with describing personal experiences without seeking to arrive at metaphysical explanations of them. [Gr *phainomenon*, pl *-a*, neuter pr p passive of *phainein* to show]

phenothiazine *fē-nō-thī'ə-zēn* or *fenō-*, *n* a toxic, heterocyclic compound, $C_{12}H_9NS$, used as a veterinary anthelmintic; any of a number of derivatives of this, used as tranquillizers. [**pheno-**, **thio-**, **azo-** and *-ine*]

phenotype *fēn'ō-tīp*, *n* the observable characteristics of an organism produced by the interaction of genes and environment; a group of individuals having the same characteristics of this kind. — *vt* to categorize by phenotype. — *adj* **phenotypic** or **phenotypical** (*-tip'*). [Gr *phainein* to show, and **type**]

phenyl *fē'nil*, *n* an organic radical, C_6H_5, found in benzene, phenol, etc. — *n* **phenylal'anin** or **phenylal'anine** an essential amino-acid present in most proteins. — *n* **phenylbutazone** (*-būt'ə-zōn*) an analgesic and antipyretic used in the treatment of rheumatic disorders and also, illegally, in horse-doping. — *adj* **phenyl'ic**. — *n* **phenylketonuria** (*-kē-tō-nū'ri-ə*) an inherited metabolic disorder in infants in which there is an inability to break down phenylalanine, later resulting in mental defect, unless a phenylalanine-free diet is given. — *n* **phenylketonū'ric** a person who suffers from phenylketonuria. — Also *adj*. [**phene**, and Gr *hȳlē* material]

pheon *fē'on*, (*heraldry*) *n* the barbed head of a dart or arrow, *esp* as a heraldic bearing. [Ety dubious]

Pherecratic *fer-e-krat'ik*, or **Pherecrataean** *-krə-tē'ən*, *adj* of the Greek poet *Pherecratēs*. — *n* a metre used by him, spondee, dactyl, spondee, with variations.

pheromone *fer'ə-mōn*, *n* a chemical substance secreted by an animal which influences the behaviour of others of its species, eg that secreted by the queen bee. [Gr *pherein* to bear, and **hormone**]

phese. See **feeze**.

phew *fū*, *interj* an exclamation of relief, astonishment, petty vexation, unexpected difficulty, impatience, contempt, etc. [A half-formed whistle]

phi *fī* or *fē*, *n* the twenty-first letter (*Φ*, *ϕ*) of the Greek alphabet, *orig* as aspirated *p* (as in *upheave*), now pronounced as *f* and transliterated *ph*; as a Greek numeral $\phi' = 500$, $,\phi = 500000$. [Gr *phei*]

phial *fī'əl*, *n* a container for liquids, *esp* now a small bottle, *usu* for medicine. — *vt* to put or keep in a phial: — *pr p* **phi'alling**; *pa t* and *pa p* **phi'alled**. — *adj* **phi'aliform** saucer-shaped. [L *phiala*, from Gr *phialē* a broad shallow bowl]

Phi Beta Kappa *fī* (or *fē*) *bē*'(or *bā'*)*tə kap'ə*, *n* the oldest of the American college societies. [Gr *Φ.B.K.*, the initial letters of its motto, from *Philosophiā biou kybernētēs* Philosophy is the guide of life]

Phil *abbrev*: Philadelphia (US state); (the Letter to the) Philippians (*Bible*); philological; philology; philosophical; philosophy.

phil- *fil-* or **philo-** *fil-ō-*, *combining form* denoting: loving; lover. — *sfx* **-phil** (*-fil*) or **-phile** (*-fīl*) lover of; loving. — *sfx* **-philia** or **-phily** love of. — *sfx* **-philic** (also, as *n sfx* lover of) or **-philous** loving. — *sfx* **-philus** (in zoological names) lover of (*usu* a specified food). [Gr *philos* friend, from *phileein* to love]

philabeg. See **filibeg**.

Philadelphian *fil-ə-del'fi-ən*, *adj* of the Pergamene city of Philadelphia or Philadelpheia (Ala-shehr); of Philadelphia, Pennsylvania, USA; of a mystic sect emphasizing brotherly love, founded in London in 1652 under the influence of Boehme. — *n* a native or inhabitant of Philadelphia; a member of the Philadelphian sect. — **Philadelphia chromosome** an abnormal small chromosome found in patients suffering from a certain form of leukaemia; **Philadelphia lawyer** a very able, shrewd, or sharp lawyer. [**phil-**, and Gr *adelphos* a brother, *adelphē* a sister]

Philadelphus *fil-ə-del'fəs*, *n* a genus of tall deciduous shrubs with showy flowers (family **Philadelphā'ceae**); (without *cap*) any shrub of this genus, *esp* the mock-orange. [New L, from Gr *philadelphon* loving one's brother]

philamot. See **filemot**.

philander *fil-an'dər*, *n* (with *cap*) a proper name for a lover in Greek literature; a lover; a man who seeks the company of women, or who follows women around; a male flirt; a philandering. — *vi* to womanize; to flirt or have casual affairs with women; to make love. — *n* **philan'derer** a man who enjoys and often has a reputation for philandering. [Gr *philandros* fond of men or of a husband, from *anēr*, *andros* a man, husband; misapplied as if meaning a loving man]

philanthropy *fil-an'thrə-pi*, *n* love of mankind *esp* as shown by contributing (money, time, etc) to general welfare. — *n* **philanthrope** (*fil'ən-thrōp*) or *usu* **philan'thropist** someone who tries to benefit mankind. — *adj* **philanthropic** (*-throp'ik*) or **philanthrop'ical** doing good to others, benevolent. — *adv* **philanthrop'ically**. [**phil-** and Gr *anthrōpos* a man]

philately *fil-at'i-li*, *n* the study and collection of postage and revenue stamps, related labels, etc; stamp-collecting. — *adj* **philatelic** (*fil-ə-tel'ik*). — *n* **philat'elist**. [Fr *philatélie*, invented in 1864, from Gr *atelēs* tax-free, from *a-* (privative) and *telos* tax]

-phile. See under **phil-**.

Philem (*Bible*) *abbrev*: (the Letter to) Philemon.

philharmonic *fil-är-mon'ik*, also *-här-* or *-ər-*, *adj* fond of music. — **philharmonic pitch** a musical pitch slightly higher than French pitch (439 vibrations a second for A). [**phil-**, and Gr *harmoniā* harmony]

philhellenic *fil-hel-ēn'ik* or *-en'ik*, *adj* loving or having an enthusuiasm for Greece, *esp* Greek culture; favouring the Greeks. — *n* **philhellene** (*-hel'ēn*) or **philhellenist** (*-hel'in-ist*) a supporter of Greece, *esp* in 1821–32. — *n* **philhell'enism**. [**phil-**, and Gr *Hellēn* a Greek]

philhorse or **pilhorse** *fil'hörs* or *pil'hörs*, (*Shakesp*) *n*. Same as **fill-horse** or **thill-horse**. [See under **fill**[2] and **thill**[1]]

-philia. See under **phil-**.

philibeg. Same as **filibeg**.

-philic. See under **phil-**.

Philippian *fil-ip'i-ən*, *n* a native of *Philippi* in Macedonia. — Also *adj*.

Philippic *fil-ip'ik*, *n* one of the three orations of Demosthenes against Philip of Macedon; (without *cap*) any discourse full of invective. — *vi* **Phil'ippize** or **-ise** to side with Philip; to utter an oracle inspired by Philip, or by bribery of the prevailing power. [Gr *philippikos*, *philippizein*, from *Philippos* Philip]

philippina, **philippine**. Same as **philopoena**.

Philistine *fil'is-tīn* (or *US fil-is'tīn*), *n* in ancient times one of the inhabitants of south-west Palestine, enemies of the Israelites; a name applied by German students to anyone not connected with the university (also **Phili-s'ter**; *Ger*); (also without *cap*) a person of material outlook, *usu* indifferent or hostile to culture; (without *cap*) an enemy (*slang*); (without *cap*) a bailiff (*slang*). — *adj* **Philistē'an**, **Philis'tian** (both *Milton*) or **Phil'istine**. — *adj* **phil'istine** (of a person) material in outlook, uncultured. — *n* **Phil'istinism** (sometimes without *cap*). — *vt* **Phil'istinize** or **-ise** (*-tin-*). [Gr *Philistīnos*, *Palaistīnos*, from Heb *P'lishtīm*]

phillabeg, **phillibeg**. Same as **filibeg**.

phillipsite *fil'ips-īt*, (*mineralogy*) *n* a zeolite, hydrated silicate of potassium, calcium, and aluminium, often cross-shaped by twinning. [J W *Phillips*, mineralogist]

phillumeny *fil-ōō'mən-i*, *n* the collecting of matchbox labels. — *n* **phillu'menist**. [L *lūmen*, *-inis* light]

Phillyrea *fil-ir'i-ə*, *n* the mock privet genus, Mediterranean shrubs related to olive and privet. [Gr *philyreā*]

philo-. See under **phil-**.

Philodendron *fil-ō-den'dron*, *n* a genus of tropical American climbing plants; (without *cap*) a plant of this genus. [Gr *philodendros* fond of trees]

philogyny *fil-oj'i-ni*, *n* love of women. — *n* **philog'ynist**. — *adj* **philog'ynous**. [Gr *philogyniā*, from gynē a woman]

philology *fil-ol'ə-ji*, *n* the science of language, *esp* of its historical development, historical linguistics; the study of ancient literary and non-literary texts; the study of culture through ancient texts; *orig* the knowledge which enabled men to study and explain the languages of Greece and Rome. — *n* **philol'oger**, **philologian** (*-ə-lō'*), **philol'ogist** or **phil'ologue** (*-log*) a person who studies or has knowledge of philology. — *adj* **philologic** (*-ə-loj'ik*) or **philolog'ical**. — *adv* **philolog'ically**. — **comparative philology** the study of languages by comparing their history, forms, and relationships with each other. [Gr *philologiā*, from **phil-** (qv) and *logos* word]

philomath *fil'ə-math*, *n* a lover of learning. — *adj* **philomath'ic** or **philomath'ical**. — *n* **philomathy** (*-om'ə-thi*) love of learning. [Gr *philomathēs* fond of learning, from *math-*, root of *manthanein* to learn]

Philomel *fil'ō-mel* or **Philomela** *-mē'lə*, *n* the nightingale personified in Greek mythology. — Also (*obs*) **Phil'o-mene** (*-mēn*). [Gr *Philomēla*, daughter of Pandion, changed into a nightingale or swallow]

philomot *fil'ə-mot*, (*Addison*) *n*. Same as **filemot**.

philopena, **philopoena** or **philippina** *fil-ip-ē'nə* or **philippine** *fil'ip-ēn*, *n* a game in which each of two people eats a twin kernel of a nut, and one pays a forfeit to the other on certain conditions; the nut itself; the gift made as a forfeit. [Appar from the Ger formula of claiming the gift, *Guten Morgen*, *Vielliebchen*, Good morning, well-beloved, confused with Gr *philos* friend, *poinē* penalty, and with Ger *Philippchen* little]

philoprogenitive *fil-ō-prō-jen'i-tiv*, *adj* having or relating to instinctive love of offspring; inclined to produce offspring. — *n* **philoprogen'itiveness**. [**philo-**, and L *progeniēs* progeny]

philosopher *fi-los'ə-fər*, *n* a lover of wisdom; a person who studies or is versed in or devoted to philosophy; formerly, a student of natural science or of the occult; now mainly a metaphysician; someone who acts calmly and rationally in changing or trying situations. — *n* **philosophas'ter** (see **-aster**) a superficial philosopher; someone who poses as a philosopher. — *n* **phil'osophe** (*-sof*, *-zof* or *-zof'*) a philosopher; a thinker of the type of the French Encyclopaedists. — *n* **philos'opheress** or **philos'ophess** (both *rare*). — *adj* **philosophic** (*-sof'* or *-zof'*) or *usu* **philosoph'ical** pertaining or according to philosophy; skilled in or given to philosophy; befitting a philosopher; adopting or ready to adopt a rational approach, *esp* calmly uncomplaining in defeat or difficulty. — *adv* **philosoph'ically**. — *n* **philos'ophism** would-be philosophy. — *n* **philos'ophist**. — *adj* **philosophist'ic** or **philosophist'ical**. — *vi* **philos'ophize** or **-ise** to reason like a philosopher; to form philosophical theories. — *vt* to explain philosophically. — *n* **philos'ophizer** or **-s-** a would-be philosopher. — *n* **philos'ophy** *orig* the pursuit of wisdom and knowledge; investigation or contemplation of the nature of being; knowledge of the causes and laws of all things; the principles underlying any sphere of knowledge; reasoning; a particular philosophical system; calmness of temper, stoicism. — **philosopher's stone** an imaginary stone or mineral compound, long sought after by alchemists as a means of transforming other metals into gold; **philosophical pitch** a pitch used in acoustical calculations based on 512 vibrations for treble C. — **moral** and **natural philosophy** see under **moral** and **natural**. [Gr *philosophos*, from *sophiā* wisdom]

-philous. See under **phil-**.

philoxenia *fil-ok-sē'ni-ə*, *n* hospitality. [Gr, from *xenos* guest, stranger]

philtre or **philter** *fil'tər*, *n* a drink (or rarely a spell) to excite love. [Fr *philtre*, from L *philtrum*, from Gr *philtron*, from *phileein* to love, and *-tron*, agent-suffix]

philus, **-phily**. See under **phil-**.

phimosis *fī-mō'sis*, (*med*) *n* narrowness or constriction of the foreskin, which prevents it from being drawn back over the glans penis. [Gr *phīmōsis* muzzling, from *phīmos* a muzzle]

phinnock. Same as **finnock**.

phisnomy *fiz'nə-mi*, *n* an old form of **physiognomy**, in the sense of the face.

phiz *fiz* or **phizog** *fiz-og'*, (*slang*) *n* the face. [**physiognomy**]

phlebitis *fli-bī'tis*, *n* inflammation of a vein. — *n* **phlebolite** (*fleb'ə-līt*; Gr *lithos* stone) a calcareous concretion found in a vein. — *n* **phlebot'omist** a blood-letter; a technician trained to take blood for testing. — *vt* **phlebot'omize** or **-ise** (Gr *tomē* a cut) to bleed; to perform phlebotomy on (a patient). — *n* **phlebot'omy** blood-letting; surgical incision into a vein. [Gr *phleps*, *phlebos* a vein]

Phlegethontic *fleg-i-thon'tik*, *adj* of or like the *Phlegethon*, a fiery river of Hades. [Gr *phlegethōn*, *-ontos*, pr p of *phlegethein*, from *phlegein* to burn]

phlegm *flem*, *n* the thick, slimy matter secreted in the throat, and discharged by coughing, regarded in old physiology as one (cold and moist) of the four humours or bodily fluids; the temperament supposed to be due to the predominance of this humour, sluggish indifference; calmness; one of the principles of old chemistry, a watery distilled liquid. — Following words pronounced *fleg-* unless indicated otherwise. — *adj* **phlegmagogic** (*-goj'ik* or *-gog'ik*). — *n* **phleg'magogue** (*-gog*) a medicine expelling phlegm. — *n* **phlegmā'sia** inflammation, *esp Phlegmasia alba dolens* white-leg. — *adj* **phlegmat'ic** or **phlegmat'ical** generating, or having a great deal of, phlegm; of a calm, unemotional, unexcitable disposition. — *adv* **phlegmat'ically**. — *n* **phleg'mon** purulent inflammation. — *adj* **phlegmon'ic**, **phleg'monoid** or **phleg'monous**. — *adj* **phlegmy** (*flem'i*). [By later return to Greek spelling, from ME *fleem*, *fleme*, *flemme*, from OFr *flemme*, *fleume*, from L *phlegma*, from Gr *phlegma*, *-atos* flame, inflammation, phlegm (regarded as produced by heat), *phlegmasiā*, *phlegmonē* inflammation, from *phlegein* to burn]

Phleum *flē'əm*, *n* a small genus of grasses, timothy-grass. [Gr *phleōs* plume-grass]

phloem *flō'əm*, (*bot*) *n* a type of tissue in plants responsible for the circulation of elaborated food substances. [Gr *phloos* bark]

phlogiston *flo-jis'ton*, *-gis'ton* or *-tən*, *n* an imaginary element, believed in the 18th century to separate from every combustible body in burning. — *adj* **phlogis'tic** of, like, or containing phlogiston (*chem*); combustible (*archaic*); inflammatory (*med*); fiery. — *vt* **phlogis'ticate** to combine with phlogiston. [Gr neuter of verbal adj *phlogistos* burnt, inflammable, from *phlogizein* to set on fire]

phlogopite *flog'ə-pīt*, *n* a magnesia mica, yellow or brown in colour. [Gr *phlogōpos* fiery-looking, from *phlox* flame, and *ōps* face]

Phlomis *flō'mis*, *n* a genus of labiate herbs and shrubs with whorls of white, yellow or purple flowers and wrinkled, often woolly, leaves; (without *cap*) a plant of this genus. [Gr *phlomis* mullein]

Phlox *floks*, *n* a Siberian and American genus of Polemoniaceae, well-known garden plants; (without *cap*) a plant of this genus, with clusters of white, red or bluish-purple flowers: — *pl* **phlox** or **phlox'es**. [Gr *phlox* flame, wallflower, from *phlegein* to burn]

phlyctaena or **phlyctena** *flik-tē'nə*, (*med*) *n* a small blister or vesicle: — *pl* **phlyctae'nae** or **phlycte'nae** (*-nē*). [Gr *phlyktaina* a blister, from *phlyein* to swell]

pho. Same as **foh**.

phobia *fō'bi-ə* or (*rare*) **phobism** *fō'bizm*, *n* a fear, aversion or hatred, *esp* a morbid and irrational one. — **-phobe** *combining form* denoting someone who has a (specified) phobia. — **-phobia** *combining form* denoting a fear or hatred of (a specified object, condition, etc). — *adj* **phō'bic** like or pertaining to a phobia; suffering from a (specified) phobia. — *n* someone afflicted with a phobia. — *n* **phō'bist**. [Gr *phobos* fear]

Phoca *fō'kə*, *n* the common seal genus; (without *cap*) a seal; (without *cap*) a scaly sea-monster (*Spenser*): — *pl* **pho'cas** or **pho'cae** (*-sē*). — *n pl* **Phocidae** (*fō'si-dē*) the true seals, with backward-turned hind-flippers and no external ear. — *adj* **pho'cine** (*fō'sīn*) relating to seals; seal-like. [L *phōca*, from Gr *phōkē* a seal]

Phocaena *fō-sē'nə*, *n* the porpoise genus. [Gr *phōkaina*]

phocomelia *fō-kō-mēl'i-ə -mel'* or *-yə*, *n* the condition of having one or more limbs like a seal's flippers, shortened and close to the body. [Gr *phōkē* seal, and *melos* limb]

phoebe *fē'bi*, *n* a N American flycatcher of the genus *Sayornis*. [Imit]

Phoebus *fē'bəs*, *n* Apollo, the Greek sun-god (*Gr mythol*); the sun. — *n* **Phoebe** (*fē'bē*) Apollo's sister Artemis, the moon-goddess (*Gr mythol*); the moon. — *adj* **Phoebe'an**. [Latinized, from Gr *Phoibos*, *Phoibē*; *phoibos*, *-ē* bright, *phaein* to shine]

Phoenician *fi-nish'ən* or *-yən*, *adj* of ancient *Phoenicia*, on the coast of Syria, its people, colonies (including Carthage), language, and arts. — *n* one of the people of Phoenicia; their Semitic language. [Gr *Phoinix*, *-īkos*]

phoenix *fē'niks*, *n* a legendary Arabian bird, worshipped in ancient Egypt, the only individual of its kind, that burned itself every 500 years or so and rose rejuvenated from its ashes; hence anything that rises from its own or its predecessor's ashes; a paragon; a southern constellation. — *n* **phoen'ixism** (*stock exchange*) the practice of forming, *usu* with the same directors, workforce, premises, etc of a bankrupted company, a new company that is therefore able to continue the same trading debt-free. [OE *fenix*, later assimilated to L *phoenīx*, from Gr *phoinix*]

phoh. Same as **foh**.

Pholas *fō'ləs*, *n* the piddock genus of rock-boring molluscs; (without *cap*) a mollusc of this genus: — *pl* **pholades** (*fō'lə-dēz*). [Gr *phōlas*, *-ados*, (adj) lurking in a hole, (n) the date-shell]

pholidosis *fol-id-ō'sis*, (*zool*) *n* arrangement of scales, as in fishes and reptiles. [Gr *pholis*, *-idos* scale]

phon *fon*, *n* (*acoustics*) a unit of loudness, the number of phons of a particular sound being equal to the number of decibels of a pure tone (with a frequency of 1 000 hertz) judged, or proved by measurement, to be of the same loudness. — *combining form* **phon-** (*fōn-*) sound, voice. — *adj* **phonal** (*fōn'l*) vocal. — *n* **phonasthenia** (*fō-nas-thē'ni-ə*; Gr *astheneia* weakness) weakness of voice; difficulty in speaking. — *n* **phonautograph** (*fōn-ö'tə-gräf*) an instrument for recording sound vibrations. — *adj* **phonautographic** (*-graf'ik*). — *adv* **phonautograph'ically**. — *n* **phonmeter** (*fon'mē-tər*) or **phonometer** (*fə-nom'i-tər*; Gr *metron* measure) an apparatus for estimating loudness levels in phons. — *n* **pho'non** (*physics*) a quantum of thermal energy in a crystal lattice made to vibrate by sound waves or heat. [From Gr *phōnē* sound]

phon. *abbrev*: phonetics.

phonate *fo-nāt'*, *vi* to utter vocal sound or sounds. — *n* **phōnā'tion** production of vocal sound. — *adj* **phōn'atory** (or *fō-nā'tər-i*). [From Gr *phōnē* sound]

phonautograph, etc. See under **phon**[1].

phone[1] *fōn*, (*phonetics*) *n* a single elementary speech sound. [Gr *phōnē* sound]

phone[2] or **'phone** *fon*, *n* short for **telephone**. — *vt* and *vi* to telephone. — *n* **phō'ner** a person who telephones. — **phone call**; **phone'card** a card, bought from newsagents, tobacconists, post offices, etc, which can be used instead of cash to pay for phone calls from appropriate telephone kiosks. — Also *adj*. — **phone freak** (or **phreak**) (*slang*) a person who misuses the phone by telephoning obscene messages to strangers, or trying to make free calls, etc; **phone freaking** (or **phreaking**); **phone'-in** a radio or television programme in which phone calls are invited from listeners or viewers and are broadcast live, with discussion by an expert or panel, etc, in the studio; **phoner-in'**.

-phone *-fōn*, *adj* and *noun combining form* used to signify speaking, or someone who speaks (a given language), as in *Francophone*. [Gr *phōnē* voice, sound]

phoneme *fōn'ēm*, (*linguistics*) *n* the smallest significant unit of sound in a language; any of the speech sounds in a language that serve to make one word different from another. — *adj* **phonemat'ic** phonemic. — *adv* **phonemat'ically**. — *adj* **phonemic** (*-nēm'* or *-nem'*). — *adv* **phonēm'ically**. — *n* **phonēm'icist**. — *n* **phonemicizā'tion** or **-s-**. — *vt* **phonēm'icize** or **-ise** to analyse into phonemes; to treat as a phoneme. — *n sing* **phonēm'ics** the science or study of the phonemes of a language; the phonemes of a language and the patterns and structures in which they occur. [Gr *phōnēma* an utterance, sound made]

phonendoscope *fon-en'də-skōp*, *n* a device which amplifies small sounds (*esp* in the human body). [**phon-** and Gr *endō* within, and *skopeein* to view]

phoner, etc. See under **phone**[2].

phonet. *abbrev*: phonetics.

phonetic *fə-net'ik*, *adj* of, concerning, according to, or representing the sounds of spoken language. — Also **phonet'ical**. — *adv* **phonet'ically** according to pronunciation. — *n* **phonetician** (*fō-ni-tish'ən*) someone who is expert in phonetics. — *n* **phonet'icism** phonetic character or representation. — *n* **phonet'icist** someone who advocates phonetic spelling. — *n* **phoneticiza'tion** or **-s-** or **phonetiza'tion** or **-s-**. — *vt* **phonet'icize** or **-ise** or **phōn'etize** or **-ise** to make phonetic; to represent phonetically. — *n sing* **phonet'ics** that branch of linguistic science that deals with pronunciation and speech production. — *n pl* phonetic representations. — *n* **pho'netism** phonetic writing. — *n* **pho'netist** a phonetician; an advocate or user of phonetic spelling. — **phonetic alphabet** a list of symbols used in phonetic transcriptions; a system (used in voice communications) in which letters of the alphabet are identified by means of code words; **phonetic spelling** the writing of a language by means of a separate symbol for every sound; an unconventional spelling system adopted as a guide to pronunciation. [Gr *phōnētikos* relating to speech]

phoney or (*esp US*) **phony** *fō'ni*, (*colloq*) *adj* counterfeit, fake; unreal. — *n* someone insincere, a fraud; something not genuine, a fake. — *vt* to fake, counterfeit, achieve by faking. — *n* **phon'eyness** or (*esp US*) **phon'iness**. [Origin uncertain; perh from Ir *fáinne* a ring, from the old practice of tricking people into buying gilt rings which they believed to be genuine gold]

phonic *fon'ik* or *fōn'ik*, *adj* relating to sounds, *esp* vocal sound; voiced. — *adv* **phon'ically** (or *fō'nik-*). — *n sing* **phon'ics** (or *fōn'iks*) the science of sound, or of spoken sounds; the phonic method. — **phonic ear**® a type of radio microphone system, for the benefit of the deaf, in which the teacher wears a transmitter and the student wears a receiver, either with a built-in or an individual hearing aid; **phonic method** a method of teaching reading through the phonetic value of letters or groups of letters. [Gr *phōnikos* relating to speech]

phoniness. See under **phoney**.

Phonmeter. See under **phon**[1].

phono- *fō-nō*, *fō-no* or *fō-nə*, *combining form* denoting voice or sound. — *adj* **phonocamptic** (*fō-nə-kamp'tik*; Gr *kamptein* to bend; *archaic*) reflecting sound, echoing; relating to echoes. — *n sing* **phonocamp'tics** the acoustics of echoes. — *n* **phō'nofiddle** a one-stringed musical instrument which sounds through a metal amplifying horn. — *n* **phonogram** (*fō'nə-gram*) a character representing a sound; a phonographic record. — *n* **phonograph** (*fō'nə-gräf*; Gr *graphein* to write) a character used in writing, etc to represent a sound; Edison's instrument for recording sounds on a cylinder and reproducing them; the ordinary word for any gramophone (*US old*). — *n* **phonographer** (*fō-nog'rə-fər*) or **phonog'raphist** a writer of phonographic shorthand. — *adj* **phonographic** (*fō-nə-graf'ik*) phonetic; of phonography; of or by means of the phonograph. — *adv* **phonograph'ically**. — *n* **phonog'raphy** (*fō-nog'rə-fi*) the art of representing each spoken sound by a distinct character; Pitman's phonetic shorthand; the use of the phonograph. — *adj* **phonolog'ical**. — *n* **phonol'ogist**. — *n* **phonology** (*fō-nol'ə-ji*; Gr *logos* discourse) phonetics; now generally (the study of) the system of sounds in a language, and sometimes the history of their changes. — *n* **phonopho'bia** a morbid fear of noise, or of speaking aloud. — *n* **phonophore** (*fō'nə-fōr* or *-för*) or **phonopore** (*fō'nō-pōr* or *-pör*; Gr *phoros* carrying, *poros* passage) a sound-conducting apparatus, of various kinds; a device for telephoning and telegraphing simultaneously by the same wire. — *n sing* **phonotac'tics** (Gr *tassein* to arrange) (the study of) the order or arrangement of sounds and groups of sounds in a particular language. — *n* **phonotype** (*fō'nə-tīp*; Gr *typos* impression) phonetic type. — *vt* to print phonetically. — *adj* **phonotyp'ic** (*-tip'ik*) or **phonotyp'ical**. — *n* **phō'notypist** (or *-tīp'ist*). — *n* **phō'notypy** (*-tīp-i*). [Gr *phōnē* sound, voice]

phonog. *abbrev*: phonography.

phonogram ... to ... **phonography**. See under **phono-**.

phonolite *fō'nə-līt*, *n* clinkstone, a fine-grained intermediate igneous rock that rings when struck by a hammer, composed of nepheline (or leucite), sanidine, and other minerals. — *adj* **phonolitic** (*-lit'ik*). [Gr *phōnē* and *lithos* a stone]

phonology, etc. See under **phono-**.

phonometer, **phonon**. See under **phon**.

phonophobia ... to ... **phonotypy**. See under **phono-**.

phony. See under **phoney**.

phooey *fōō'i*, *interj* an exclamation of contempt, scorn, disbelief, etc. [Perh connected with **phew**, or a similar exclamation, or perh from Yiddish *fooy*, Ger *pfui*]

-phore or **-phor** *-för*, *combining form* used to denote 'carrier', as in *semaphore* and *chromatophore*. — *n combining form* **-phoresis** (*fə-rē'sis*) denoting a transmission, migration, as in *electrophoresis*. — *adj combining form* **-phorous**. [Gr *phoros* bearing, from *pherein*]

phorminx *för'mingks*, (*music*) *n* a kind of cithara: — *pl* **phormin'ges** (*-jēz*). [Gr]

Phormium *för'mi-əm*, *n* a New Zealand genus of the lily family, New Zealand flax or flax-lily; (without *cap*) a plant of this genus. [Latinized, from Gr *phormion* mat, faggot, kind of sage]

phosgene *fos'jēn*, *n* a poisonous gas, carbonyl chloride ($COCl_2$), prepared from carbon monoxide and chlorine in sunlight. [Gr *phōs* light, and the root of *gignesthai* to be produced]

phosphate, etc, **phosphatide**, **phosphaturia**. See under **phosphorus**.

phosphene *fos'fēn*, *n* light seen when the eyeball is pressed; a luminous pattern seen when the brain is stimulated electrically. [Gr *phōs* light, and *phainein* to show]

phosphide, **phosphine**, **phosphite**. See under **phosphorus**.

Phosphorus *fos'fər-əs* or **Phosphor** *fos'fər*, *n* the morning-star. [L *phōsphorus*, from Gr *phōsphoros* light-bearer, from *phōs* light, and *phoros* bearing, from *pherein* to bear]

phosphorus *fos'fə-rəs*, *n* a non-metallic element (symbol **P**; atomic no 15), a waxy, poisonous, and inflammable substance giving out light in the dark. — *n* **phosphate** (*fos'fāt*) a salt of phosphoric acid. — *vt* to treat or coat with a phosphate as a means of preventing corrosion. — *adj* **phosphatic** (*fos-fat'ik*) of the nature of or containing a phosphate. — *n* **phos'phatide** a phospholipid. — *vt* **phos'phatize** or **-ise** to phosphate. — *n* **phosphaturia** (*fos-fat-ū'ri-ə*) excess of phosphates in the urine. — *n* **phos'phide** (*-fīd*) a compound of phosphorus and another element. — *n* **phos'phine** (*-fēn* or *-fīn*) phosphuretted hydrogen gas (PH_3); extended to substances analogous to amines with phosphorus instead of nitrogen. — *n* **phos'phite** a salt of phosphorous acid. — *n* **phospholip'id** a lipid which contains a phosphate group and *usu* also a nitrogenous group, a component of cell membranes. — *n* **phosphōn'ium** the radical PH_4, analogous to ammonium. — *n* **phosphopro'tein** any of a number of compounds formed by a protein with a substance containing phosphorus, other than a nucleic acid or lecithin. — *n* **phos'phor** phosphorus; a phosphorescent or fluorescent substance generally. — *vt* **phos'phorate** to combine or impregnate with phosphorus; to make phosphorescent. — *vi* **phosphoresce'** to shine in the dark like phosphorus. — *n* **phosphoresc'ence**. — *adj* **phosphoresc'ent**. — *n* **phos'phoret** (or *-et*; *obs*) a phosphide. — *adj* **phos'phoretted** (or *-et'*) see **phosphuretted** below. — *adj* **phosphoric** (*fos-for'ik*) of or like phosphorus; phosphorescent; containing phosphorus in higher valency (*chem*) (**phosphoric acid** any of the following acids — orthophosphoric, H_3PO_4, metaphosphoric, HPO_3, pyrophosphoric, H_4P_2O; **phosphoric anhydride** P_2O_5). — *vt* **phos'phorise** see **phosphorize** below. — *n* **phos'phorism** (*obs*) phosphorescence; poisoning by phosphorus. — *n* **phos'phorite** (*mineralogy*) impure massive apatite. — *vt* **phos'phorize** or **-ise** to combine or impregnate with phosphorus; to make phosphorescent. — *adj* **phos'phorous** phosphorescent; containing phosphorus in lower valency (*chem*) (**phosphorous acid** H_3PO_3; **phosphorous anhydride** P_2O_3). — *n* **phosphor'ylase** an enzyme playing a part in phosphorylation. — *vt* **phosphor'ylate**. — *n* **phosphorylā'tion** the act or process of converting a sugar into a compound of phosphorus and of splitting the latter to yield energy for vital processes. — *n* **phosphuret** (*fos'fūr-et* or *-et'*; *obs*) a phosphide. — *adj* **phos'phuretted** (or *-et'*) combined with phosphorus (**phosphuretted** or **phosphoretted hydrogen** phosphine). — **phos'phor-bronze'** an alloy of copper, tin and phosphorus; **phossy jaw** necrosis of the jawbone with fatty degeneration of the kidney, common among matchmakers when yellow phosphorus was used. [L *phōsphorus*, from Gr *phōsphoros* light-bearer, from *phōs* light, and *phoros* bearing, from *pherein* to bear]

phot *fot* or *fōt*, *n* the CGS unit of illumination, 1 lumen per square centimetre. [Gr *phōs*, *phōtos* light]

phot. *abbrev*: photographic; photography.

phot- See **photo-**.

photic *fō'tik*, *adj* of light; light-giving; sensitive to light; accessible to light (as eg the uppermost layer of sea). — *n sing* **phōt'ics** optics. [Gr *phōs*, *phōtos* light]

Photinia *fō-tin'iə*, *n* a genus of evergreen or deciduous trees and shrubs of the *Rosaceae* family, grown for their foliage, and the deciduous varieties for autumn colour and the fruits which succeed their small white flowers; (without *cap*) a plant of the genus.

photism *fō'tizm*, *n* a hallucinatory vision of light; a visual sensation that results from the experience of hearing, feeling, tasting, smelling or thinking something. [Gr *phōs*, *photos* light]

photo *fō'to*, *n* short form of **photograph**: — *pl* **phōtos**. — As *combining form* see **photo-**[2].

photo-[1] *fō-tō-*, *fō-to'* or *fō-tə-* or **phot-** *combining form* signifying light. — *adj* **photoac'tive** affected physically or chemically by light or other radiation. — **photo'-ageing** ageing (*esp* of the skin) caused by exposure to ultraviolet light. — *n* **photobiol'ogist**. — *n* **photobiol'ogy** a branch of biology dealing with the effects of light and other forms of radiant energy on organisms. — *n* **photocatal'ysis** the promotion, acceleration or retardation of a chemical reaction by light. — *adj* **photocatalyt'ic**. — *n* **pho'tocell** a photoelectric cell. — *adj* **photochem'ical**. — *n* **photochem'ist**. — *n* **photochem'istry** the part of chemistry dealing with changes brought about by light, or other radiation, and with the production of radiation by chemical change. — *adj* **photochromic** (*-krōm'ik*) changing colour, and hence changing the amount of light transmitted when the incident light increases, or decreases. — *n* a photochromic material. — *n sing* **photochrom'ics** the science and technology of photochromic materials. — *n pl* photochromic materials. — *n* **photochrom'ism**. — *n* **pho'tochromy** a former process of colour photography. — *adj* **photoconduct'ing** or **photoconduc'tive** relating to, or showing, photoconductivity. — *n* **photoconductiv'ity** the property of varying conductivity under the influence of light. — *adj* **photodegra'dable** (of plastic) that will decompose after exposure to certain forms of light. — *n* **photodi'ode** a two-electrode semiconductor device, used as an optical sensor. — *n* **photodissociā'tion** (*chem*) dissociation produced by the absorption of radiant energy. — *adj* **photoelas'tic** relating to or exhibiting photoelasticity. — *n* **photoelastic'ity** the property of certain solids of exhibiting optical changes due to compression or other stresses. — *n* **photoelectric'ity** electricity or a change of electric condition, produced by light or other electromagnetic radiation. — *adj* **photoelec'tric** relating to photoelectricity, to photoelectrons, or to electric light (**photoelectric cell** any device in which incidence of light of suitable frequency causes an alteration in electrical state, *esp* by photo-emission, eg in order to activate a switch, etc). — *n* **photoelec'trode** an electrode which is activated by light. — *n* **photoelec'tron** an electron ejected from a body by the incidence of ultra-violet rays or X-rays upon it. — *n sing* **photoelectron'ics** the science dealing with the interactions of electricity and electromagnetic radiations, *esp* those that involve free electrons. — *n* **photo-emiss'ion** the emission of electrons from the surface of a body on which light falls. — *n* **photofiss'ion** nuclear fission induced by gamma rays. — *n* **pho'toflood** or **photoflood lamp** an incandescent tungsten lamp in which excess voltage produces very strong light, but reduces the life of the lamp. — *n* **photogen** (*fō'tə-jən*; see **-gen**) a light-producing organ in animals; a light paraffin oil (also **photogene**). — *n* **pho'togene** (*-jēn*) an after-image; a sensitive emulsion; a photograph (*obs*). — *adj* **photogenic** (*-jen'* or *-jēn'*) producing light; produced by light; see also **photogenic** under **photo-**[2]. — *n* **photokinesis** (*-ki-nē'sis* or *-kī-*; Gr *kīnēsis* movement) movement occurring in response to variations in light intensity. — *vi* **photoluminesce'** to produce photoluminescence. — *n* **photoluminesc'ence** luminescence produced by exposure to visible light or infrared or ultraviolet radiation. — *adj* **photoluminesc'ent**. — *vt* **pho'tolyse** to cause photolysis in. — *vi* to undergo photolysis. — *n* **photolysis** (*fō-tol'i-sis*; see **-lysis**) decomposition or dissociation under the influence of radiation (*chem*); the grouping of chloroplasts in relation to illumination (*bot*). — *adj* **photolytic** (*fō-tə-lit'ik*). — *n* **photom'eter** an instrument for measuring luminous intensity, *usu* by comparing two sources of light. — *adj* **photomet'ric**. — *n* **photom'etry** (the branch of physics dealing with) the measurement of luminous intensity. — *n* **photomul'tiplier** a photocell with a series of dynodes which amplify the emission current. — *adj* **photonas'tic** (*-nas-tik*). — *n* **pho'tonasty** (Gr *nastos* close-pressed; *biol*) a response in plants, etc to a change of intensity of light without regard to the direction of the light source. — *n* **photope'riod** the period during every 24 hours when an organism is exposed to daylight. — *adj* **photoperiod'ic**. — *n* **photoperiodic'ity**. — *n* **photope'riodism** the physiological and behavioural reactions of organisms to changes in the length of the daylight period. — *adj* **pho'tophil** (see **-phil**) light-loving; turning towards the light. — *n* an organism that seeks the light. — *adj* **photophil'ic**. — *adj* **photophilous** (*-tof'*). — *n* **photoph'ily**. — *n* **photopho'bia** (see **-phobia**) a fear of or aversion to light. — *n* and *adj* **phō'tophobe**. — *adj* **photophobic** (*-fōb'ik*). — *n* **pho'tophone** (Gr *phōnē* voice) an apparatus which transmits a sound signal, *usu* a voice, in the form of a modulated light signal, to a distant photoelectric cell, where it is reconverted to sound. — *adj* **photophonic** (*-fon'ik*). — *n* **photophony** (*-tof'ə-ni*). — *n* **pho'tophore** (*-fōr* or *-för*; see **-phore**; *zool*) a luminiferous organ. — *n* **photophoresis** (*-fə-rē'sis*; see **-phoresis**) migration of suspended particles under the influence of light. — *n* **photōp'ia** vision in bright light, the eye's adjustment to daylight. — *adj* **photop'ic**. — *n* **photopolarim'eter** a telescopic instrument for photographing planets and other distant objects and measuring the polarization of light from them. — *n* **photopsia** (*fō-top'si-ə*) or **photopsy** (*-top'si*; Gr *opsis* appearance) the appearance of flashes of light, owing to irritation of the retina. — *n* **photorecep'tor** a nerve-ending receiving light stimuli. — *adj* **photorefract'ive** of a material whose refractive index changes in response to light. — *adj* **photoresist'** (of an organic material) that polymerizes on exposure to ultraviolet light and in that form resists attack by acids and solvents. — Also *n*. — *adj* **photosens'itive** affected by light, visible or invisible. — *n* **photosensitiv'ity**. — *vt* **photosens'itize** or **-ise** to make photosensitive by chemical or other means. — *n* **photosens'itizer** or **-s-**. — *n* **pho'tosphere** the luminous envelope of the sun's globe, the source of light. — *adj* **photospheric** (*-sfer'ik*). — *n* **photosynthesis** (*-sin'thi-sis*; *bot*) the building up of complex compounds by the chlorophyll apparatus of plants by means of the energy of light. — *adj* **photosynthet'ic**. — *adj* **phototac'tic**. — *n* **phototax'is** (Gr *taxis* arrangement; *biol*) locomotory response or reaction of an organism or cell to the stimulus of light. — *n* **phototeleg'raphy** telegraphy by means of light (see also under **photo-**[2]).— *adj* **phototherapeut'ic**. — *n* **phototherapy** (*-ther'ə-pi*) or **phototherapeutics** (*n sing*; *-pū'tiks*; Gr *therapeuein* to tend) the treatment of disease by light. — *n* **phototrope** (*-trōp*) a substance exhibiting phototropism. — *adj* **phototropic** (*-trop'ik*). — *n* **phototropism** (*fōt-ot'rəp-izm*; see **-trope**) orientation in response to the stimulus of light (*bot*); reversible colour change on exposure to light (*chem*). — *n* **photot'ropy** change of colour due to wavelength of incident light. — *adj* **photovoltaic** (*-vol-tā'ik*) producing an electromotive force across the junction between dissimilar materials when the junction is exposed to light or ultraviolet radiation, eg in a **photovoltaic cell**. — *n sing* **photovolta'ics** the science and technology of photovoltaic devices and substances. [Gr *phōs*, *phōtos* light]

photo-[2] *fō-tō-*, *fō-to'* or *fō-tə-*, *combining form* denoting: photographic; made by, or by the aid of, photographic means; representing **photo** (qv) short form of **photograph**, or **photographic** or **photographical** (see under **photography**). — *n* **photo call** an arranged opportunity for press photographers to take publicity photographs of eg a celebrity. — *n* **pho'tocomposition** (*printing*) filmsetting, the setting of copy by projecting images of letters successively on a sensitive material from which printing plates are made. — *adj* **photocop'iable**. — *n* **pho'tocopier** a machine which makes photocopies. — *n* **pho'tocopy** a photographic reproduction of written matter, etc. — *vt* to make a photocopy of. — *n* **pho'tocopying** — *n* **pho'to-engraving** or **pho'to-etching** any process of engraving by aid of photography, *esp* from relief plates. — *n* **photo-fin'ish** a race finish in which a special type of photography is used to show the winner, etc; a neck-and-neck finish to any contest. — *n* **Pho'tofit**® (also without *cap*) a method of making identification pictures using photographs of facial elements, an alternative to identikit (qv). — *adj* **photogen'ic** (*-jen'ik*, *-jē'nik*) photographic (*obs*); having the quality of photographing well, appearing attractive in photographs; (loosely) attractive, striking. — *n* **photog'eny** (*-toj'i-ni*; *obs*) photography. — *n* **photogeol'ogy** the study of geology by means of aerial photographs. — *n* **photoglyph** (*-glif*; Gr *glyphē* carving) a photographic engraving; a photogravure. — *adj* **photoglyph'ic**. — *n* **photog'lyphy**. — *n* **pho'togram** a photograph; a type of picture produced by placing an object on or near photographic paper which is then exposed to light. — *adj* **photogrammet'ric**. — *n* **photogramm'etrist**. — *n* **photogramm'etry** (*image technol*) the use of photographic records for precise measurement of distances or dimensions, eg aerial photography for surveying. — *n* **photogravure** (*fō-tō-grə-vūr'*; Fr *gravure* engraving) a method of photo-engraving in which the design etched on the metal surface is intaglio, not relief; a picture produced by this method. — *n* **photojour'nalism** journalism in which written material is subordinate to photographs. — *n* **photojour'nalist**. — *n* and *vt* **photolith'ograph**. — *n* **photolithog'rapher**. — *adj* **photolithograph'ic**. — *n* **photolithog'raphy** a process of lithographic printing from a photographically produced plate. — *n* **photomac'rograph** a photograph of an object that is unmagnified or only slightly magnified. — *adj* **photomacrograph'ic**. — *n* **photomacrog'raphy**. — *adj* **pho'to-mechan'ical** pertaining to mechanical printing from a photographically prepared plate. — *adv* **pho'to-mechan'ically**. — *n* **photomicrograph** (*fō-tō-mī'krə-gräf*; see **micro-** and **-graph**) an enlarged photograph of a microscopic object taken through a microscope. — *n* **photomicrographer** (*-krog'rə-fər*). — *adj* **photomicrographic** (*-krə-graf'ik*). — *n* **photomicrog'raphy**. — *n* **photomon'tage** (*-täzh*) (the art of compiling) a picture made by cutting up photographs, etc, and arranging the parts so as to convey, without explicitly showing, a definite meaning. — *n* **photo opportunity** an opportunity for press photographers to get good or interesting pictures of a celebrity, either arranged by the celebrity (*esp* for publicity purposes) or arising more or less by chance during some event the celebrity is participating in. — *n* **pho'to-process** any process by which a matrix for printing is got by photographic means. — *n* **photore'alism** (*art*) an *esp* detailed, precise painting style (suggestive of and often worked from a photograph), giving an effect of (often exaggerated) realism. — *adj* **photorealis'tic**. — *n* **pho'to-relief** a plate or image in relief got by photographic means. — *n* **pho'tosetting** photocomposition. — *n* **Photostat**® (*fō'tō-stat*; see **-stat**) a photographic apparatus for making facsimiles of manuscripts, drawings, etc, directly; a facsimile so made. — *vt* and *vi* to photograph by Photostat: — *pr p* **Pho'tostatting**; *pa t* and *pa p* **Pho'tostatted**. — *n* **phototelegraph** (*fō'tō-tel'i-gräf*) an instrument for transmitting drawings, photographs, etc, by telegraphy. — *n* **phototeleg'raphy** (see also under **photo-**[1]. — *n* **phototype** (*fō'tō-tīp*; Gr *typos* impression) a printing block on which the material is produced photographically; a print made from such a block; the process of making such a block. — *vt* to reproduce by phototype. — *n* **phototype'setting** the production of type images on a photographic medium by optical means and often using a computer connected to a device which enables publication with high-quality print. — *adj* **phototypic** (*-tip'ik*). — *n* **phototypy** (*fō'tō-tī-pi* or *fō-tot'i-pi*). — *n* **photoxylography** (*fō-tō-zī-log'rə-fi*; see **xylo-** and **-graph**) wood-engraving after a photographic impression on a woodblock. — *n* **photozincography** (*fō-tō-zing-kog'rə-fi*) the process of engraving on zinc by taking an impression by photography and etching with acids. — *n* **photozinc'ograph** a picture so produced. [**photograph** (see under **photography**)]

photography *fə-tog'rə-fi*, *n* the art or process of producing permanent and visible images by the action of light, or other radiant energy, on chemically prepared surfaces. — *n* **photograph** (*fō'tə-gräf*) an image so produced. — *vt* to make a picture of by means of photography. — *vi* to take photographs; to be capable of being photographed. — *n* **photog'rapher**. — *adj* **photographic** (*-graf'ik*) or **photograph'ical**. — *adv* **photograph'ically**. — *n* **photog'raphist** (*rare*). [Gr *phōs*, *phōtos* light, and *graphein* to draw]

photon *fō'ton*, *n* a quantum of light or other electromagnetic radiation. — *n sing* **photon'ics** the study of the applications of photons, eg in communication technology. [Gr *phōs*, *phōtos* light, with *-on* after **electron**]

phr *abbrev*: phrase.

phrase *frāz*, *n* a manner of expression in language; an expression; a group of words (sometimes as in *Shakesp* a single word) generally not forming a clause but felt as expressing a single idea or constituting a single element in the sentence; a pithy expression; a catchword; an empty or high-sounding expression; fussy talk about one's feelings (*Scot*); a short group of notes felt to form a unit (*music*) — *vt* to express in words; to style; to flatter or wheedle (*Scot*); to mark, bring out, or give effect to the phrases of (*music*). — *adj* **phrās'al** consisting of, or of the nature of, a phrase. — *adj* **phrase'less** incapable of being described. — *n* **phraseogram** (*frā'zi-ə-gram*) a single sign, written without lifting the pen, for a whole phrase (*esp* in shorthand). — *n* **phra'seograph** a phrase that is so written. — *adj* **phraseolog'ic** or **phraseolog'ical**. — *adv* **phraseolog'ically**. — *n* **phraseol'ogist** a maker or collector of phrases. — *n* **phraseol'ogy** style or manner of expression or arrangement of phrases; peculiarities of diction; a collection of phrases in a language. — *n* **phra'ser** a mere maker or repeater of empty phrases. — *n* **phra'sing** the wording of a speech or passage; the grouping and accentuation of the sounds in performing a melody (*music*). — *adj* using phrases, *esp* (*Scot*) airing one's views or feelings or making flowery speeches. — *adj* **phra'sy** inclined to use wordy phrases. — **phrasal verb** a phrase, consisting of a verb and an adverb or preposition, or both, having the function of a verb, eg *blow over*, *sift through*, *put up with*; **phrase book** a book containing or explaining phrases of a language; **phrase'man**, **phrase'maker** **phrase'monger** a user or maker of wordy or fine-sounding phrases. — **turn of phrase** an expression; one's manner of expression. [Gr *phrasis*, from *phrazein* to speak]

phratry *frā'tri*, *n* a social division of a people, often exogamous. [Gr *phrātriā*; cf L *frāter*, Eng **brother**]

phreatic *frē-at'ik*, *adj* pertaining to underground water supplying, or probably able to supply, wells or springs, or to the soil or rocks containing it, or to wells; (of underground gases, etc) present in or causing volcanic eruptions. — *n* **phreat'ophyte** a deep-rooted plant drawing its water from the water table or just above it. — *adj* **phreatophyt'ic**. [Gr *phrear* well, and *phreātia* cistern]

phrenesiac *fri-nē'zi-ak*, (*Scott*) *adj* hypochondriac. [Ety as for **phrenesis**]

phrenesis *fri-nē'sis*, *n* phrenitis; delirium; frenzy. — For *adj* and *n* **phrenetic**, *adj* **phrenetical**, and *adv* **phrenetically**, see **frenetic**. — *n* **phren'ism** a supposed 'mind-force' described by E D Cope as active in nature and evolution. — *adj* **phrenit'ic** of or affected with phrenitis. — *n* **phrenī'tis** inflammation of the brain; brain-fever. [Gr *phrēn*, *phrenos* midriff (supposed seat of passions, mind and will)]

phrenic *fren'ik*, *adj* of or near the midriff; mental (*obs*). [Fr *phrénique*, from Gr *phrēn*, *phrenos* midriff]

phrenism, **phrenitic**, **phrenitis**. See under **phrenesis**.

phrenology *fri-nol'ə-ji*, a would-be science of mental faculties supposed to be located in various parts of the skull and investigable by feeling the bumps on the outside of the head. — *adj* **phrenologic** (*fren-ə-loj'ik*) or **phrenolog'ical**. — *adv* **phrenolog'ically**. — *n* **phrenol'ogist**. — *vt* **phrenol'ogize** or **-ise** to examine phrenologically. [Gr *phrēn, phrenos* midriff (supposed seat of passions, mind, will) and **-logy**]

phrensical, **phrensy**, **phrentick**. Old forms of **frenzical**, **frenzy**, **frantic** (or **phrenetic**, qv under **frenetic**).

phrontistery *fron'tis-tə-ri*, *n* a thinking-place. [Gr *phrontistērion*, from *phrontistēs* a thinker, from *phroneein* to think; applied by Aristophanes to the school of Socrates]

Phrygian *frij'i-ən*, *adj* pertaining to *Phrygia* in Asia Minor, or to its people. — *n* a native of Phrygia; a Montanist; the language of the ancient Phrygians. — **Phrygian cap** an ancient type of conical cap with the top turned forward, which in the French Revolution came to symbolize liberty; **Phrygian mode** (in ancient Greek music) a mode of two tetrachords with a semitone in the middle of each and a whole tone between the tetrachords (eg: *d e f g*; *a b c d*; but reckoned downwards by the Greeks); (in old Church music) an authentic mode extending from *e* to *e*, with *e* as its final.

phthalic *thal'ik* or *fthal'ik*, (*chem*) *adj* applied to three acids, $C_6H_4(COOH)_2$, and an anhydride, derived from naphthalene. — *n* **phthal'ate** a salt or ester of phthalic acid. — *n* **phthal'ein** (*-i-in*) any one of a very important class of dye-yielding materials formed by the union of phenols with phthalic anhydride. — *n* **phthal'in** a colourless crystalline compound obtained by reducing a phthalein. — *n* **phthalocy'anin** or **phthalocy'anine** any of a group of green and blue organic colouring matters of great fastness and brilliance. [**naphthalene**]

phthiriasis *thī-rī'ə-sis* or *fthī-rī'ə-sis*, *n* infestation with lice. [Gr *phtheiriāsis*, from *phtheir* a louse]

phthisis *thī'sis*, also *fthī'* or *tī'*, (*med*; *old*) *n* wasting disease; tuberculosis, *esp* of the lungs. — *n* **phthisic** (*tiz'ik*, sometimes *thī'sik*, *fthī'sik* or *tī'sik*) phthisis; vaguely, a lung or throat disease. — *adj* **phthis'ical** or **phthis'icky**. [Gr *phthisis*, from *phthi(n)ein* to waste away]

phut *fut*, *n* a dull sound *esp* of collapse, deflation, etc. — Also *adv* as in **go phut** to break, become unserviceable; to come to nothing. — *vi* to make, go, or land with a phut or phuts. [Hindi *phatnā* to split]

pH value. See **pH**.

phyco- *fī-kō-*, *combining form* denoting seaweed. — *n* **phycocyan** (*sī-ən*) or **phycocyanin** (*-ə-nin*; Gr *kyanos* dark blue) a blue pigment found in algae. — *n* **phycoerythrin** (*-e-rith'rin*; Gr *erythros* red) a red pigment found in algae. — *adj* **phycolog'ical**. — *n* **phycologist** (*-kol'ə-jist*). — *n* **phycol'ogy** the study of algae. — *n pl* **Phycomycetes** (*-mī-sē'tēz*; Gr *mykētes*, pl of *mykēs* a fungus) a class of fungi showing affinities with the green seaweeds. — *n* **phycomy'cete** a fungus of this class. — *n* **phycophaein** (*-fē'in*; Gr *phaios* grey) a brown pigment found in seaweeds. — *n* **phycoxan'thin** (Gr *xanthos* yellow) a yellow pigment found in diatoms, brown seaweeds, etc. [Gr *phȳkos* seaweed]

phyla. See **phylum**.

phylactery *fi-lak'tə-ri*, *n* a charm or amulet; (among the Jews) a slip of parchment inscribed with certain passages of Scripture, worn in a box on the left arm or forehead; a reminder; ostentatious display of religious forms; a case for relics; (in medieval art) a scroll at the mouth of a figure in a picture bearing the words he or she is supposed to speak. — *adj* **phylacteric** (*-ter'ik*) or **phylacter'ical**. [Gr *phylaktērion*, from *phylax* a guard]

phyle *fī'lē*, *n* a tribe or division of the people of a state in ancient Greece, at first on a kinship, later on a local, basis. — *n* **phylarch** (*fī'lärk*) the chief officer of a tribe; (in Athens) the commander of the cavalry of a tribe. — *n* **phy'larchy** the office of phylarch. [Gr *phȳlē*]

phyletic *fī-let'ik*, (*biol*) *adj* pertaining to a phylum; according to presumed evolutionary descent. [Gr *phȳletikos*, from *phȳlē*]

phyllary *fil'ə-ri*, (*bot*) *n* an involucral bract. [Gr *phyllarion*, dimin of *phyllon* leaf]

phyllite *fil'īt*, *n* a rock intermediate between clay-slate and mica-schist. [Gr *phyllon* a leaf]

phyllo. See **filo**.

phylloclade *fil'ō-klād*, (*bot*) *n* a flattened branch with the form and functions of a leaf. [Gr *phyllon* leaf, and *klados* shoot]

phyllode *fil'ōd*, (*bot*) *n* a petiole with the appearance and function of a leaf-blade. — *n* **phyll'ody** (*-ō-di*) transformation of flower parts into leaves. — *adj* **phyll'oid** leaf-like. [Gr *phyllon* leaf, and *eidos* form]

phyllomania *fil-ō-mā'ni-ə*, (*bot*) *n* excessive production of leaves, at the expense of flower or fruit production. [Gr *phyllon* leaf, and *maniā* madness]

phyllome *fil'ōm*, (*bot*) *n* any leaf or homologue of a leaf. [Gr *phyllōma* foliage]

phyllophagous *fi-lof'ə-gəs*, *adj* leaf-eating. [Gr *phyllon* leaf, and *phagein* to eat]

phyllopod *fil'ə-pod*, *n* a crustacean of the order **Phyllopoda** (*-op'ə-də*), entomostracans with foliaceous legs. [Gr *phyllon* leaf, and *pous, podos* foot]

phylloquinone *fil-ō-kwin'ōn* or *-ōn'*, *n* vitamin K_1, one of the fat-soluble vitamin K group, essential for normal blood coagulation. [Gr *phyllon* leaf, and **quinone**]

phyllotaxis *fil-ō-tak'sis*, (*bot*) *n* the disposition of leaves on the stem. — Also **phyll'otaxy**. — *adj* **phyllotact'ic** or **phyllotact'ical**. [Gr *phyllon* a leaf, and *taxis* arrangement]

Phyllotria. See **Elodea**.

phylloxera *fil-ok-sē'rə*, *n* an insect of the *Phylloxera* genus of insects, similar to greenfly, very destructive to vines. [Gr *phyllon* a leaf, and *xēros* dry]

phylogeny *fī-loj'i-ni*, *n* evolutionary pedigree or genealogical history — also **phylogenesis** (*fī-lō-jen'i-sis*). — *adj* **phylogenet'ic**. — *adv* **phylogenet'ically**. [Gr *phȳlon* race, and *genesis* origin]

phylum *fī'ləm*, *n* a main division of the animal or the vegetable kingdom: — *pl* **phy'la**. [New L, from Gr *phȳlon* race]

phys *abbrev*: physician; physics; physiology.

physalia *fī-sā'li-ə*, *n* a member of the *Physalia* genus of large oceanic colonial hydrozoans with a floating bladder, including the Portuguese man-of-war. — *n* (*bot*) **physalis** (*fis'* or *fīs'ə-lis*) a member of the Cape gooseberry genus *Physalis*, of Solanaceae, with persistent bladdery calyx. [Gr *phȳsallis* a bladder, from *phȳsaein* to blow]

physeter *fi-sē'tər*, *n* a sperm whale (*old*); a spouting whale (*obs*). [Gr *phȳsētēr* a blower, a whale, from *phȳsaein* to blow]

physharmonica *fis-här-mon'i-kə*, *n* an early form of harmonium. [Gr *phȳsa* bellows, and **harmonica**]

physic *fiz'ik*, *n orig* natural philosophy, physics (*obs*): the science, art, or practice of medicine (*obs*); a medicine (*rare*); anything healing or wholesome (*fig*). — *adj* (*obs*) physical, natural; medicinal. — *vt* (*obs*) to give medicine to; to heal: — *pr p* **phys'icking**; *pa t* and *pa p* **phys'icked**. — *adj* **phys'ical** pertaining to the world of matter and energy, or its study, natural philosophy; material; materialistic (*obs*); bodily; requiring bodily effort; involving bodily contact; medical (*rare*); medicinal (*obs*); wholesome (*Shakesp*). — *n* a physical examination of the body, eg to ascertain fitness. — *n* **phys'icalism** the theory that all phenomena are explicable in spatiotemporal terms and that all statements are either analytic or reducible to empirically verifiable assertions. — *n* **phys'icalist**. — *n* **physical'ity** physical quality; preoccupation with the bodily. — *adv* **phys'ically**. — *n* **physician** (*fi-zish'n*) a doctor; someone legally qualified to practise medicine; someone skilled in the use of physic or the art of healing; someone who makes use of medicines and treatment, distinguished from a surgeon who practices manual operations; a healer or healing influence (*fig*). — *n* **physi'ciancy** the post or office of physician. — *n* **physi'cianer** (*rare*) a physician. — *n* **physic'ianship**. — *n* **phys'icism** (*-sizm*) belief in the material or physical as opposed to the spiritual. — *n* **phys'icist** (*-sist*) an expert in or student of physics; a student of nature (*obs*); someone who believes the phenomena of life are purely physical. — *adj* **phys'icky** like medicine. — *adj* **physicochem'ical** relating to or involving both physics and chemistry; pertaining to physical chemistry (see below). — *n sing* **phys'ics** *orig* natural science in general; now, the science of the properties (other than chemical) of matter and energy, and the forces and interrelationships between them. — **physical astronomy** the study of the physical condition and chemical composition of the heavenly bodies; **physical chemistry** the study of the dependence of physical properties on chemical composition, and of the physical changes accompanying chemical reactions; **physical force** force applied outwardly to the body, as distinguished from persuasion, etc; **physical geography** the study of the earth's natural features, eg its mountain chains and ocean currents, etc; **physical jerks** (*colloq*) bodily exercises; **physic garden** *orig* a garden of medicinal plants; a botanic garden; **physic nut** the purgative seed of the tropical American tree *Jatropha curcas*, of the spurge family. [Gr *physikos* natural, from *physis* nature]

physi- *fiz-i-* or **physio-** *fiz-i-ō*, *-ə-*, *-o'*, *combining form* signifying nature. [Gr *physis* nature]

physio *fiz'i-ō*, (*colloq*) *n* a physiotherapist: — *pl* **phys'ios**.

physiocracy *fiz-i-ok'rə-si*, *n* government, according to François Quesnay (1694–1774) and his followers, by a natural order inherent in society, land and its products being the only true source of wealth, direct taxation of land being the only proper source of revenue. — *n* **phys'iocrat** (*-ō-krat*) someone who maintains these opinions. — *adj* **physiocrat'ic**. [**physio-** and **-cracy**]

physiognomy *fiz-i-on'ə-mi* or *-og'nə-mi*, *n* the art of judging character from appearance, *esp* from the face; the face as an index of the mind; the face (*colloq*); the general appearance of anything; character, aspect. — *adj* **physiognomic** (*-nom'ik*) or **physiognom'ical**. — *adv* **physiognom'ically**. — *n* **physiogn'omist**. [Gr *physiognōmiā*, a shortened form of *physiognōmoniā*, from *physis* nature, and *gnōmōn*, *-onos* an interpreter]

physiography *fiz-i-og'rə-fi*, *n* description of nature, descriptive science; physical geography. — *n* **physiog'rapher**. — *adj* **physiographic** (*-ō-graf'ik*) or **physiograph'ical**. [**physio-** and **-graphy**]

physiolatry *fiz-i-ol'ə-tri*, *n* nature-worship. — *n* **physiol'ater** a nature-worshipper. [**physio-** and **-latry**]

physiologus *fi-zi-ol'ə-gəs*, *n* a work containing descriptions of animals, a bestiary. [Gr *physiologos* a natural philosopher]

physiology *fiz-i-ol'ə-ji*, *n* the science of the processes of life in animals and plants. — *adj* **physiologic** (*-ə-loj'ik*) or **physiolog'ical**. — *adv* **physiolog'ically**. — *n* **physiol'ogist**. [**physio-** and **-logy**]

physiotherapy *fiz-i-ō-ther'ə-pi*, *n* treatment of disease by remedies such as massage, fresh air, physical exercise, etc, rather than by drugs. — Also *n sing* **physiotherapeutics** (*-pū'tiks*). — *adj* **physiotherapeut'ic**. — *n* **physiother'apist**. [**physio-** and Gr *therapeiā* treatment]

physique *fi-zēk'*, *n* bodily type, build, or constitution. [Fr]

physitheism *fiz'i-thē-ism*, *n* the ascription of physical form and attributes to deity; deification of the powers of nature. — *adj* **physitheis'tic**. [**physi-** and Gr *theos* god]

phyt- *fīt-* or **phyto-** *fī-tō-*, *-tə-* or *-to'*, *combining form* denoting plant. — *combining form* **-phyte** used to indicate a plant belonging to a particular habitat, or of a particular type. — *adj combining form* **-phytic** (*-fit-ik*). — *n* **phytoalex'in** (Gr *alexein* to ward off) any substance produced by a plant as a defence against disease. — *n* **phytobenthos** (*-ben'thos*; Gr *benthos* depth) plants living at the bottom of water collectively. — *n* **phytochem'ical** a chemical derived from a plant. — *adj* of chemicals in plants. — *n* **phy'tochrome** a plant pigment which absorbs red or infra-red rays and acts as an enzyme controlling growth, flowering, germination, etc. — *n* **phytogen'esis** or **phytogeny** (*-toj'i-ni*) evolution of plants. — *adj* **phytogenet'ic** or **phytogenet'ical** relating to phytogenesis. — *adj* **phytogenic** (*-jen'ik*) of vegetable origin. — *n* **phytogeog'rapher**. — *adj* **phytogeograph'ic**. — *n* **phytogeog'raphy** the geography of plant distribution. — *n* **phytog'rapher** a descriptive botanist. — *adj* **phytograph'ic**. — *n* **phytog'raphy** descriptive botany. — *n* **phytohor'mone** a plant hormone, regulating growth, etc. — *n* **Phytolacc'a** the pokeweed genus, giving name to the family **Phytolaccā'ceae**, related to the pinks and the goosefoots. — *adj* **phytolog'ical**. — *n* **phytol'ogist** a botanist. — *n* **phytol'ogy** botany. — *n* **phy'ton** the smallest part of a plant that when cut off may grow into a new plant. — *n* **phytonadione** (*fī-tō-nə-dī'ōn*) phylloquinone, vitamin K_1. — *adj* **phytopatholog'ical**. — *n* **phytopathol'ogist**. — *n* **phytopathology** (Gr *pathos* suffering) the study of plant diseases. — *adj* **phytophagic** (*-faj'ik*) or **phytophagous** (*-tof'ə-gəs*; Gr *phagein* to eat) plant-eating. — *n* **phytoplank'ton** (Gr *plankton* (neuter) wandering) vegetable plankton. — *n* **phyto'sis** the presence of vegetable parasites or disease caused by them. — *n* **phytosterol** (*-tos'tə-rol*; formed on the model of *cholesterol*) a substance very like cholesterol obtained from plants. — *n* **phytot'omist**. — *n* **phytotomy** (*-tot'ə-mi*; see **-tomy**) plant anatomy. — *adj* **phytotox'ic** poisonous to plants; pertaining to a phytotoxin. — *n* **phytotoxic'ity** harmfulness to plants. — *n* **phytotox'in** a toxin produced by a plant. — *n* **phytotron** (*fī'tō-tron*) an apparatus that produces climates artificially for the study of plant growth. [Gr *phyton* plant]

PI *abbrev*: Phillippines (IVR); Private Investigator.

pi[1] *pī* or *pē*, *n* the sixteenth letter (*Π*, *π*) of the Greek alphabet, corresponding to the Roman P; as a numeral *π'* stands for 80, *͵π* for 80 000; a symbol for the ratio of the circumference of a circle to the diameter, approx 3·14159 (*math*). — **pi-** (or *π*-) **meson** the source of the nuclear force holding protons and neutrons together (*phys*). — Also called **pion**. [Gr *pei*, *pī*]

pi[2] (*printing*). Same as **pie**[3].

pi[3] *pī*, (*colloq*) *adj* obtrusively religious, sanctimonious. — *n* a pious or sanctimonious person or talk. — **pi'-jaw** sermonizing; an admonition. [Short form of **pious**]

PIA *abbrev*: Pakistan International Airlines.

pia[1] *pē'ə*, *n* a tropical monocotyledonous plant (*Tacca*; family *Taccaceae*) with a rhizome yielding E India or Madagascar arrowroot. [Polynesian name]

pia[2] *pī'ə* or *pē'a*, (*L*) *fem adj* pious. — **pia desideria** (*dez-i-dēr'i-ə* or *dā-sēd-er'i-a*) pious regrets; **pia fraus** (*frōz* or *frows*) pious fraud.

piacevole *pyə-chā'vo-lā*, (*music*) *adj* pleasant, playful. [Ital]

piacular *pī-ak'ū-lər*, *adj* expiatory; requiring expiation; atrociously bad. — *n* **piacularity** (*-lar'i-ti*). [L *piāculum* sacrifice, from *piāre* to expiate, from *pius* pious]

piaffe *pi-af'* or *pyaf*, (*dressage*) *vi* to perform a piaffer. — *n* **piaff'er** a movement on the spot in which the horse's feet are lifted in the same succession as a trot, but more slowly. — Also called **Spanish walk**. [Fr *piaffer*]

pia mater *pī'ə mā'tər*, (*anatom*) *n* the vascular membrane surrounding the brain and spinal cord; the brain (*Shakesp*). [L *pia māter* tender mother, a medieval translation of Ar *umm raqīqah* thin mother]

pianoforte *pya'nō-fōr-ti*, *pē-a'*, *pyä'* or *pē-ä'*, *n* now generally shortened to **piano** (*pya'nō*, *pē-a'*, or *-ä'*), a large musical instrument, a shaped wooden case on legs, with a keyboard at which the player sits, the keys working small hammers to sound tautened wires inside: — *pl* **pia'nofortes** and **pian'os**. — *n* **pianette** (*pē-ə-net'*) a small upright piano. — *n* **pianino** (*pya-nē'nō* or *pē-ə-nē'nō*) *orig* an upright piano; a small upright piano: — *pl* **piani'nos**. — *n* **pi'anism** the technique of playing the pianoforte. — *adj* and *adv* **pianissimo** (*pya-nēs'si-mō* or *pē-ə-nis'i-mō*) very soft. — *n* **pianist** (*pē'ə-nist* or *pyan'ist*; also *pē-an'ist*) a person who plays the pianoforte, *esp* expertly (also (*Fr*) **pianiste** (*pē-a-nēst'*) sometimes used as *fem*). — *adj* **pianist'ic** of or relating to pianism or a pianist. — *adv* **pianist'ically**. — *adj* and *adv* **piano** (*pyä'nō* or *pē-ä'nō*) soft, softly. — *n* a pianoforte (see above); a soft passage. — *n* **Pianola**® (*pya-nō'lə* or *pē-ə-*) a mechanical, playerless piano with keys operated by air pressure, the sequence determined by the pattern of perforations in a removable paper roll (a **piano roll**). — *n* **piano'list**. — **pia'no-accord'ion** a sophisticated type of accordion with a keyboard like that of a piano; **pia'no-or'gan** a piano like a barrel-organ, played by mechanical means; **pian'o-play'er** a pianist; a mechanical contrivance for playing the piano; **piano roll** see at **Pianola**® above; **pian'o-school** a school where piano-playing is taught; a method or book of instruction for the piano; **pian'o-stool** a stool for a pianist, *usu* adjustable in height, and often hollow for storing sheet music; **pian'o-wire** wire used for piano strings, and for deep-sea soundings, etc. — **player piano** a Pianola. [Ital, from *piano* soft, from L *plānus* level, and *forte* loud, from L *fortis* strong]

piano nobile *pyä'nō nō'bi-lā*, (*archit*) *n* the main floor of a large house or villa, *usu* on the first floor. [Ital, noble storey]

piarist *pī'ə-rist*, *n* a member of a religious congregation for the education of the poor, founded in Rome in 1597 by Joseph Calasanza. [L *patrēs scholārum piārum* fathers of pious schools]

piassava *pē-əs-ä'və* or **piassaba** *-bə*, *n* a coarse stiff fibre used for making brooms, etc, obtained from Brazilian palms, *Attalea* (coquilla) and *Leopoldinia* (chiqui-chiqui); the tree yielding it. [Port from Tupí]

piastre *pi-as'tər*, *n* a unit of currency in current or former use in several N African and Middle Eastern countries, equal to 1/100 of a (Sudanese, Egyptian, Syrian, etc) pound; a coin of this value; a piece of eight. [Fr, from Ital *piastra* a leaf of metal; see **plaster**]

piazza *pē-ät'sə*, also *pē-ad'zə* or *pē-az'ə*, *n* a place or square surrounded by buildings; (erroneously) a walk under a roof supported by pillars; a veranda (*US*). — *adj* **piazz'ian**. [Ital, from L *platea*, from Gr *plateia* a street (fem of *platys* broad)]

pibroch *pē'brohh*, *n* the classical music of the bagpipe, free in rhythm and consisting of theme and variations. [Gaelic *piobaireachd* pipe-music, from *piobair* a piper, from *piob*, from Eng **pipe**[1]]

pic *pik*, (*colloq*) *n* a picture: — *pl* **pics** or **pix**.

Pica *pī'kə*, *n* the magpie genus; (without *cap*) an unnatural craving for unsuitable food (*med*). [L *pīca* magpie]

pica[1] *pī'kə*, (*printing*) *n* an old type size, approximately, and still used synonymously for, 12-point, giving about 6 lines to the inch, much used in typewriters; a size of type giving ten characters or spaces to the inch. — **small pica** 11-point. [Possibly used for printing *pies*; see **pie**[2]]

pica[2]. See under **Pica**.

picador *pik-ə-dōr'* or *-dör'*, now *usu pik'*, *n* a mounted bullfighter with a lance. [Sp, from *pica* a pike]

picamar *pik'ə-mär*, *n* a bitter oily liquid obtained from tar. [L *pix*, *picis* pitch, and *amārus* bitter]

picaresque. See under **picaroon**.

picarian *pik-ā'ri-ən*, *adj* belonging to an obsolete order (**Pica'riae** *-ē*) of birds *incl* the woodpeckers. — *n* any member of the order. [L *pīcus* woodpecker]

picaroon *pik-ə-rōōn'*, *n* a person who lives by his or her wits; a cheat; a pirate. — *adj* **picaresque** (*-resk'*). — **picaresque novels** the tales of Spanish rogue and vagabond life, much in vogue in the 17c; novels of similar type. [Sp *picarón*, augmentative of *pícaro* rogue]

picayune *pik-ə-ūn'*, *n* a small coin worth $6\frac{1}{4}$ cents, current in the USA before 1857; a five-cent piece, or other small coin; anything of little or no value (*US colloq*). — *adj* (*US colloq*) petty. — *adj* **picayun'ish**. [Provençal *picaioun* an old Piedmontese copper coin]

piccadill *pik'ə-dil*, **piccadell** *-del*, **piccadillo** *-dil'ō* (*pl* **picca-dill'oes**), or **piccadilly** *-i*, also **pick-**, (*obs*) *n* a cut or vandyked edging, *esp* to a woman's collar; a wide high collar of the early 17c; a stiff support for a collar or ruff; (in the form **piccadilly**) a man's standing-up collar with the points turned over, first worn about 1870. [Cf Sp *picadillo* a kind of hash, or *pica* spear, hence wire support for a ruff]

piccalilli *pik-ə-lil'i*, *n* a pickle of various vegetable substances with mustard and spices. [Ety uncertain]

piccaninny or **pickaninny** *pik-ə-nin'i*, (now *offensive*) *n* a little child, *esp* a Black child; an Aborigine child (*Austr*). — *adj* very little. — *n* **picc'anin** (*SAfr*) a piccaninny. [Orig W Indian, from Port *pequenino*, dimin of *pequeno* little, or possibly Sp *pequeño niño* little child]

piccies. See under **piccy**.

piccolo *pik'ə-lō*, *n* a small flute, an octave higher than the ordinary flute; an organ stop of similar tone: — *pl* **picc'olos**. [Ital, little]

piccy *pik'i*, (*colloq*) *n* a picture, *esp* a photograph: — *pl* **picc'ies**.

pice *pīs*, *n* a (former) small Indian coin, $\frac{1}{4}$ anna: — *pl* **pice**. — **new pice** 1/100 rupee, a paisa (qv). [Hind *paisā*]

Picea *pis'i-ə* or *pīs'i-ə*, *n* the spruce genus of conifers. [L *picea* pitch-pine, from *pix* pitch]

piceous *pis'i-əs*, *adj* like pitch; inflammable; black; reddish black. — *n* **picene** (*pī'sēn*) a hydrocarbon ($C_{22}H_{14}$) derived from tar. [L *piceus*, from *pix* pitch]

pichiciago *pich-i-si-ä'gō*, or *-ā'gō*, *n* a small burrowing S American armadillo: — *pl* **pichicia'gos**. [Am Indian]

pichurim *pich'ōō-rim*, *n* a S American tree (*Nectandra puchury*) of the laurel family; its aromatic kernel (also **pichurim bean**). [Port *pichurim*, from Tupí *puchury*]

picine. See under **Picus**.

pick[1] *pik*, *n* a tool for breaking ground, rock, etc, with a head pointed at one end or both, and a handle of varying length fitted to the middle; a pointed hammer; an instrument of various kinds for picking; an act, opportunity, or right of choice; a portion picked; the best or choicest; dirt on a printing type; a diamond in cards, also a spade (*Northern dialect*). — *vt* to break up, dress or remove with a pick; to make with a pick or by plucking; to poke or pluck at, as with a sharp instrument or the nails; to clear, remove, or gather by single small movements; to detach, extract, or take separately and lift or remove; to pluck; to pull apart; to cull; to choose; to select, *esp* one by one or bit by bit; to peck, bite, or nibble; to eat in small quantities or delicately; to open (eg a lock) by a sharp instrument or other unapproved means; to rifle by stealth; to seek and find a pretext for (eg a quarrel). — *vi* to use a pick; to eat in small or delicate mouthfuls; to pilfer. — *adj* **picked** (*pikt*) selected, hence the choicest or best; (of flowers or fruit) plucked; exquisite, refined, punctilious (*Shakesp*); having spines or prickles, sharp-pointed. — *n* **pick'edness**. — *n* **pick'er** a person who picks or gathers up; a tool or machine for picking; someone who removes defects from and finishes electrotype plates; a pilferer. — *n* **pick'ery** (*Scots law*) pilfering. — *n* **pick'ing** the action of the verb to pick; the quantity picked; that which is left to be picked; dabbing in stoneworking; the final finishing of woven fabrics by removing burs, etc; removing defects from electrotype plates; (in *pl*) odd gains or perquisites. — *adj* **pick'y** (*colloq*) fussy or choosy, *esp* excessively so; able to pick out or pick over dexterously. — **pick'-cheese** the blue or the great titmouse; the fruit of the mallow; **picker-up'**; **pick'lock** an instrument for picking or opening locks; a person who picks locks; **pick'-me-up** a stimulating drink; a medicinal tonic. — *n* and *adj* **pick'-'n'-mix'** (an assortment of loose sweets) chosen by the individual customer from a range of types available at a self-service counter; (a discriminatory selection) chosen to suit one's individual taste or needs (*fig*). — **pick'-pocket** someone who picks or steals from other people's pockets; **pick'-purse** someone who steals the purse or from the purse of another; **pick'-thank** someone who seeks to ingratiate himself or herself by officious favours, or by tale-bearing; **pick'-tooth** a toothpick; **pick'-up** an act of picking up; reception; a stop to collect something or someone; a recovery; something picked up; accelerating power; a device for picking up an electric current; (also **pick-up head**) a transducer, activated by a sapphire or diamond stylus following the groove on a gramophone record, which transforms the mechanical into electrical impulses; a light motor vehicle with the front of a saloon car and the rear in the form of a small truck; a man's chance, informal acquaintance with a woman, or vice versa *usu* implying a sexual relationship; the woman, or man in such a relationship; a game, or a team, for which the captains pick their players alternately from a single group or squad. — *adj* for picking up; picked up. — **pick-your-own'** a method of selling fruit or vegetables by which private customers pick the produce they wish to buy at the place where it is grown; produce sold in this way. — *adj* sold or operating by this system. — **pick a hole in someone's coat** to find fault with someone; **pick at** to find fault with; to nibble food without enthusiasm; to poke at and detach pieces from, using the fingernails, etc; **pick holes in** to find fault with; **pick oakum** to make oakum by untwisting old ropes; **pick off** to kill selectively, or one by one, by shooting with great accuracy, *usu* from a distance; to detach and remove; **pick on** to single out, *esp* for anything unpleasant; to nag at; to carp at; **pick one's way** to choose carefully where to put one's feet, as (or as if) on dirty or dangerous ground; **pick out** to make out, distinguish; to pluck out; to select from a number; to mark with spots of colour, etc; **pick over** to go over and select; **pick someone's brains** to make use of another's brains or ideas for one's own ends; **pick to pieces** to pull apart; to criticize adversely in detail; **pick up** to lift from the ground or floor; to improve gradually; to gain strength bit by bit; to take into a vehicle, or into one's company; to scrape acquaintance informally with, *esp* of a man with a woman; to acquire by chance; to gain; to come upon, make out, distinguish (eg a signal, a track, a comet, etc); **pick up the pieces** to restore (*esp* emotional) matters to their former equilibrium after they have been brought to disarray or collapse. [Ety obscure; cf **peck**[2], **pike**[1]]

pick[2] *pik*, a Northern form of **pitch**[1]; also of **pitch**[2] *esp vi* to throw the shuttle across the loom, and *n* a throw of the shuttle, or a weft thread; also a form of **pique**[1]. — **pick'-and-pick'** (*weaving*) a term indicating alternate picks of yarns of two different colours or kinds.

pickaback *pik'ə-bak* or *now usu* **piggyback** *pig'i-bak*, *adv* (carried) on the back and shoulders of someone like a pack; on something, or as an addition to something. — *adj* on the back like a pack; of or for a piggyback; (of a vehicle or plane) conveyed on top of another; of or relating to a surgical procedure which leaves the patient's own heart functioning along with a transplanted heart (*med*). — *n* a ride on someone's back. — Also **pick'back** or **pick'apack**. — **pickaback** (or **piggyback**) **plant** a popular name for the perennial plant *Tolmiea menziesii*, which produces plantlets at the base of the leaf. [Connection with **pick**[2] (pitch), **pack**[1] and **back**[1] obscure]

pickadill, pickadel, pickadillo, pickadilly. See **piccadill**.

pickaninny. See **piccaninny**.

pickaxe *pik'aks*, *n* a picking tool, with a point at one end of the head and a cutting blade at the other, used in digging. [ME *pikois*, from OFr *picois* a mattock, *piquer* to pierce, *pic* a pick]

pickeer *pi-kēr'*, *vi* to forage (*obs*); to skirmish; to scout; to flirt (*obs*). — *n* **pickeer'er**. [Ety uncertain]

pickelhaube *pik-l-how'bə* or *pik'*, *n* a German spiked helmet. [Ger]

pickerel *pik'ər-əl*, *n* a young pike; a pike, *esp* of smaller species (*US*). — **pick'erel-weed** pondweed; Pontederia (*US*). [**pike**[1]]

pickery. See under **pick**[1].

picket *pik'it*, *n* a pointed stake or peg driven into the ground, eg for fortification, tethering, military punishment or surveying; a surveyor's mark; a small outpost, patrol, or body of men set apart for some special duty; picket-duty; a person or group stationed to watch and dissuade those who go to work during a strike; the old military punishment of standing on one foot on a pointed stake. — *vt* to tether to a stake; to strengthen or surround with pickets; to peg down; to subject to the picket; to post as a picket; to deal with as a picket or by means of pickets; to place pickets at or near. — *vi* to act as picket: — *pr p* **pick'eting**; *pa t* and *pa p* **pick'eted**. — Also **piqu'et** or **picqu'et**. — *n* **pick'eter** a person who pickets in a labour dispute. — **pick'et-duty**; **pick'et-fence** (*US*) a fence made of pales; **pick'et-guard** a guard kept in readiness in case of alarm; **pick'et-line** a line of people acting as pickets in a labour dispute. — **picket out** (in a labour dispute) to close or bring to a standstill by picketing. [Fr *piquet*, dimin of *pic* a pickaxe]

pickle[1] *pik'l*, *n* a liquid, *esp* brine or vinegar, in which food is preserved; an article of food preserved in such liquid; (in *pl*) preserved onions, cucumber, gherkins, etc, as a condiment; acid or other liquid used for cleansing or other treatment as part of a manufacturing process; a tricky situation, predicament or muddle (*colloq*); a troublesome child (*colloq*). — *vt* to preserve with salt or vinegar, etc; to rub with salt or salt and vinegar, as an old naval punishment; to clean or treat with acid or other chemical. — *adj* **pick'led** treated with a pickle; drunk (*slang*). — *n* **pick'ler** someone who pickles; a container for pickling; an article suitable, or grown, for pickling. — **pick'le-herring** a pickled herring; a merry-andrew, a clown (*obs*). — **have a rod in pickle** to have a punishment ready. [ME *pekille*, *pykyl*, *pekkyll*, *pykulle*; cf Du *pekel*; Ger *Pökel*]

pickle[2] *pik'l*, or **puckle** *puk'l*, (*Scot*) *n* a small quantity; a grain of corn. [Origin unknown]

pickle[3] *pik'l*, *vt* and *vi* to peck; to pick; to eat sparingly; to pilfer. [Dimin or frequentative of **pick**[1]]

pickmaw *pik'mö*, (*Scot*) *n* the black-headed gull. [Perh **pick**[2] (pitch), and **maw**[2]]

Pickwickian *pik-wik'i-ən*, *adj* relating to or resembling Mr *Pickwick*, the hero of Dickens's *Pickwick Papers*. — *n* a member of the Pickwick Club. — **in a Pickwickian sense** in a recondite or merely imaginary sense, a phrase by which a member of the Pickwick Club explained away unparliamentary language.

picky. See under **pick**[1].

picnic *pik'nik*, *n orig* a fashionable social entertainment, towards which each person contributed a share of the food; an open-air meal taken by a number of people on a country excursion; an undertaking that is mere child's play (often *ironically*). — *adj* of or for a picnic; picnicking. — *vi* to have a picnic — *pr p* **pic'nicking**; *pa t* and *pa p* **pic'nicked**. — *n* **pic'nicker**. — *adj* **pic'nicky**. [Fr *pique-nique*]

pico- *pē-kō-* or *pī-kō-*, *combining form* denoting a millionth of a millionth part, a million millionth, as in **picocurie, picosecond**, etc. [Sp *pico* a small quantity]

picornavirus *pi-kör'nə-vī-rəs*, *n* any of a group of viruses including the enteroviruses and rhinoviruses. [**pico-**, **RNA**, and **virus**]

picot *pē'kō*, *n* a loop in an ornamental edging; a raised knot in embroidery. — *vt* to ornament with picots. — *adj* **picoté** (*pē-ko-tā*). [Fr *picot* point, prick]

picotee *pik-ə-tē'*, *n* a variety of carnation, *orig* speckled, now edged with a different colour. [Fr *picoté*, prickled]

picotite *pik'ə-tīt*, (*mineralogy*) *n* a dark spinel containing iron, magnesium, and chromium. [From *Picot*, Baron de la Pérouse, who described it]

picquet. See **picket**.

picra *pik'rə*, *n* short for **hiera-picra**. — *n* **pic'rate** a highly explosive salt of picric acid. — *adj* **pic'ric** (**picric acid** $C_6H_2(NO_2)_3.OH$ trinitrophenol, used as a yellow dye-stuff and as the basis of high explosives). — *n* (*mineralogy*) **pic'rite** a coarse-grained igneous rock composed mainly of olivine with ferromagnesian minerals and usually some plagioclase. — *n* **picrocar'mine**

a stain for microscope work made from carmine, ammonia, water and picric acid. — *n* **picrotox'in** a bitter poisonous principle in the seeds of *Cocculus indicus*. [Gr *pikros* bitter]

Pict *pikt*, *n* one of an ancient people of obscure origins who lived in Britain, *esp* NE Scotland; (in Scottish folklore) one of a dwarfish race of underground dwellers, to whom (with the Romans, the Druids and Cromwell) ancient monuments are generally attributed; Steele's term for a painted woman. — *adj* **Pict'ish**. — *n* the language of the Picts, of uncertain affiliations and origins. — **Picts' house** an earth-house (qv). [L *Pictī* Picts; possibly the same as *pictī*, *pa p* of *pingere* to paint; cf **Pecht**]

pictarnie *pik-tär'ni*, (*Scott*) *n* a tern. [Origin unknown]

pictograph *pik'tə-gräf*, *n* a picture used as a symbol in picture-writing. — *n* **pic'togram** a pictograph; a graphic representation. — *adj* **pictographic** (*-graf'ik*). — *adv* **pictograph'ically**. — *n* **pictography** (*pik-tog'rə-fi*) picture-writing. [L *pictus* painted, and Gr *graphein* to write, or *gramma* a letter, figure]

pictorial *pik-tō'ri-əl* or *-tö'*, *adj* of a painter (*obs*); of or relating to painting or drawing; of, by means of, like, or of the nature of a picture or pictures; vivid. — *n* a periodical in which pictures are prominent. — *adv* **picto'rially**. — *adj* **pictorical** (*-tor'i-kl*; *rare*). — *adv* **pictor'ically** (*rare*) in the manner of a painter. [L *pictor*, *-ōris* painter, from *pingere*, *pictum* to paint]

picture *pik'chər*, *n* the art or act of painting; an imitative representation of an object on a surface; a photograph; a portrait; a tableau; a visible or visual image; a mental image; (an image on) a television screen; a person exactly like another as in *He's the picture of his father*; an impressive or attractive sight, like a painting, or worthy of being painted; a visible embodiment; a vivid verbal description; a cinema film; (in *pl*) a cinema show, or the building in which it is given. — *vt* to depict or represent in a picture; to form a likeness of in the mind; to describe vividly in words. — *adj* **pic'tural** relating to, illustrated by, or consisting of pictures. — *n* (*Spenser*) a picture. — **pic'ture-book** a book of pictures; **pic'ture-card** (*cards*) a court card, a card bearing the representation of a king, queen or knave (jack); **pic'ture-cord** cord for hanging pictures; **pic'ture-frame** a frame for surrounding a picture; **pic'ture-gallery** a gallery, hall, or building where pictures are exhibited; **pic'ture-goer** a frequent visitor to the cinema; **pic'ture-hat** a lady's wide-brimmed hat, such as those that appear in portraits by Gainsborough; **pic'ture-house** or **pic'ture-palace** a building for cinema shows; **Pic'turephone®** a device which allows speakers on the telephone to see each other; **pic'ture-play** a story told in motion pictures; **picture postcard** a postcard bearing a picture, traditionally a local view. — *adj* (**pic'ture-postcard**) like a postcard in traditional or idealized prettiness. — **picture ratio** see **aspect ratio**; **pic'ture-restorer** a person who cleans and tries to restore old pictures; **pic'ture-rod**, **pic'ture-rail** or **pic'ture-moulding** a rod or moulding on a wall from which pictures may be hung; **pic'ture-window** a *usu* large window designed to act as a frame to an attractive view; **pic'ture-wire** wire for hanging pictures; **pic'ture-writing** the use of pictures to express ideas or relate events. — **get the picture** (*colloq*) to understand the situation; **in the picture** having a share of attention; adequately briefed; **put me**, etc **in the picture** give me, etc all the relevant information. [L *pictūra*, from *pingere*, *pictum* to paint]

picturesque *pik-chə-resk'*, *adj* like a picture; such as would make a striking picture, implying some measure of beauty together with quaintness or immediate effectiveness; (of language) vivid and colourful, or (*facetious*) vulgar; having taste or feeling for the picturesque. — *adv* **picturesque'ly**. — *n* **picturesque'ness**. [Ital *pittoresco*, from *pittura* a picture, from L *pictūra*]

picul *pik'ul*, *n* a Chinese weight, about 60 kg. [Malay *pikul* a man's load]

Picus *pī'kəs*, *n* an ancient Italian god, a son of Saturn, turned into a woodpecker by Circe; the woodpecker genus. — *adj* **pī'cine** (*-sīn*). [L *Pīcus*]

PID (*med*) *abbrev*: pelvic inflammatory disease.

piddle *pid'l*, *vi* to deal in trifles; (*esp* with *about*) to trifle, mess about; to eat with little relish; to urinate (*colloq*). — *n* (*colloq*) urine; an act of urination. — *n* **pidd'ler** a trifler. — *adj* **pidd'ling** trifling, paltry. [Origin obscure]

piddock *pid'ək*, *n* the pholas. [Origin unknown]

pidgin *pij'in*, *n* a Chinese corruption of **business** (also **pidg'eon** or **pig'eon**); affair, concern (*colloq*; also **pidg'eon** or **pig'eon**); any combination and distortion of two languages as a means of communication. — *n* **pidginīzā'tion** or **-s-**. — **pidgin English** a jargon, mainly English in vocabulary with Chinese arrangement, used in communication between Chinese and foreigners; any lingua franca consisting of English and another language.

pi-dog. See **pye-dog**.

pie[1] *pī*, *n* a magpie; a chatterer. [Fr, from L *pīca*]

pie[2] or **pye** *pī*, *n* a book of rules for determining the Church office for the day. — **by cock and pie** (*Shakesp*) an altered oath, *appar* by God and the pie. [LL *pīca*, poss the same as L *pīca* magpie (from the black and white appearance of the page)]

pie[3], **pye** or **pi** *pī*, *n* type confusedly mixed (*printing*); a mixed state; confusion. — *vt* to reduce to pie: — *pr p* **pie'ing** or **pye'ing**; *pa t* and *pa p* **pied**. [Origin obscure; perh connected with **pie**[4], or **pie**[2]]

pie[4] *pī*, *n* a quantity of meat, fruit, or other food baked within or under a crust of prepared pastry; an easy thing (*slang*); a welcome luxury, prize, or spoil (*colloq*). — **pie chart**, **pie diagram** or **pie graph** a circle divided into sections by radii so as to show relative numbers or quantities; **pie'-counter** a counter at which pies are sold; the source of patronage, bribes, spoils of office (*US*; *archaic*); **pie'crust** the pastry covering or enclosing a pie; **piecrust table** a Chippendale table with a carved raised edge; **pie'dish** a deep dish in which pies are made. — *adj* **pie'-eyed** (*colloq*) drunk. — **pie'man** someone who sells pies, *esp* in the street; **pie'-plant** (*US dialect*) rhubarb; **pie'-shop**. — **a finger in the pie** see under **finger**; **Périgord pie** a pie of partridge flavoured with truffles (*Périgord*, France, now contained in the departments of Dordogne and Lot-et-Garonne); **pie in the sky** some improbable future good promised without guarantee (from early 20c song). [Origin unknown; possibly from **pie**[1], as a miscellaneous collector; the Gaelic *pighe* is from English]

pie[5] *pī*, *n* a small Indian coin, withdrawn after 1957, equal to 1/3 of a pice, or 1/12 of an anna. [Marathi *pā'ī* a fourth]

piebald *pī'böld*, *adj* black and white in patches; loosely, of other colours in patches; motley; heterogeneous. — *n* a piebald horse or other animal. — Also **pyebald**. [**pie**[1] and **bald**]

piece *pēs*, *n* a part or portion of anything, *esp* detached; a separate lump, mass or body of any material, considered as an object (in Scots without *of* following); a distance; a span of time; a single article; a definite quantity, eg of cloth or paper; a literary, dramatic, musical, or artistic composition; a work executed in graffiti; a production, a specimen of work; an example; an exemplification or embodiment; a sandwich or a little bread, buttered or not, *esp* as a lunch (*Scot*); a gun; a portion (*obs*); a wine-cup (*obs*); a coin; a man in chess, draughts, or other game (in chess sometimes excluding pawns and the king); a person, now *usu* (disrespectfully) a woman. — *vt* to enlarge by adding a piece; to patch; to combine. — *vi* to have a between-meal snack (*US slang*); to create a piece in graffiti (*slang*). — **-piece** *combining form* consisting of a given number of separate parts, pieces, members, etc, as in *three-piece suite*. — *adj* **piece'less** not made of pieces. — *adv* **piece'meal** (**meal**[1] in sense of 'measure') in pieces: to pieces; bit by bit. — *adj* done bit by bit; fragmentary. — *n* a small piece; bit by bit proceeding. — *vt* to dismember. — *vt* **piec'en** (*dialect*) to join (*esp* broken threads in spinning). — *n* **piec'ener** or **piec'er** a person who is employed in a spinning-factory to join broken threads. — **piece'-goods** textile fabrics made in standard lengths; **piece'-rate** a fixed rate paid according to the amount of work done; **piece'-work** work paid for by the piece or quantity, not by time. — **all to pieces** or **to pieces** into a state of disintegration or collapse; through and through, thoroughly (*US*); **a piece** each; **a piece of** an instance of; a bit of, something of; **a piece of cake** see under **cake**; **piece of eight** see under **eight**; **a piece of one's mind** a frank outspoken reprimand; **go to pieces** to break up entirely (*lit* and *fig*); to lose completely the ability to cope with the situation; **in pieces** in, or to, a broken-up state; **of a piece** as if of the same piece, the same in nature; homogeneous, uniform; in keeping, consistent (with *with*); **piece of goods** (*dialect*; *derog*) a woman; **piece of work** a task; a fuss, ado; a person (*usu* with **nasty**, etc); **piece out** to eke out; **piece together** to put together bit by bit; **piece up** to patch up; *perh* to incorporate in one's own share (*Shakesp*); **the piece** (*Scot*) apiece; **to pieces** see **all to pieces** above. [OFr *piece*, from LL *pecia*, *petium* a fragment, a piece of land (thought to be of Celtic (Brythonic) origin); cf **patch**[1], **peat**[2], **petty**, and *Pit-* in place names]

pièce *pyes*, (*Fr*) *n* a piece, item; (a barrel of) about 220 litres (of wine). — **pièce de résistance** (*də rā-zē-stās*) the substantial course at dinner, the joint; the best item; **pièce d'occasion** (*do-ka-zyɔ̃*) something (*usu* a literary or musical work) composed, prepared, or used for a special occasion.

piecen, **piecener**, **piecer**, **piecemeal**. See under **piece**.

pied[1] *pīd*, *adj* variegated like a magpie; of various colours. — *n* **pied'ness**. [**pie**[1]]

pied[2]. See **pie**[3].

pied-à-terre *pyā-da-ter*, (*Fr*) *n* a dwelling kept for temporary, secondary, or occasional lodging: — *pl* **pieds-à-terre**.

piedmont *pēd'mənt*, (*US*) *n* a mountain-foot region. — Also *adj*. — *n* **pied'montite** a dark red mineral, a hydrous silicate of calcium, aluminium, manganese and iron. [*Piedmont* in Italy, literally mountain-foot]

pied noir *pyā nwär*, (*Fr*) *n* a North African (*esp* Algerian) person of French descent: — *pl* **pieds noirs**.

piel'd *pēld*, (*Shakesp*) *adj* tonsured. [See **peel**[1]]

Piemontese *pē-mont-ēz'*, *n* a breed of cattle *orig* from N Italy, bred for beef with a low fat content.

piend *pēnd*, *n* a salient angle. [Origin unknown]

piepowder *pī'pow-dər*, (*obs*) *n* a wayfarer, itinerant. — **Court of Piepowder** or **Piepowders** an ancient court held in fairs and markets to administer justice in a rough-and-ready way to all comers — also **Court of Dusty Feet**. [OFr *piedpoudreux*, from *pied* (L *pēs*, *pedis*) foot, and *poudre* (L *pulvis*) dust]

pier *pēr*, *n* a mass of stone, ironwork, or woodwork projecting into the sea or other water, as a breakwater, landing-stage, or promenade; a jetty or a wharf; the mass of stonework between the openings in the wall of a building; the support of an arch, bridge, etc; a masonry support for a telescope or the like; a buttress; a gate pillar. — *n* **pier'age** a toll paid for using a pier. — **pier'-glass** *orig* a mirror hung between windows; a tall mirror; **pier'-head** the seaward end of a pier; **pier'-table** a table fitted for the space between windows. [ME *pēr*, LL *pēra*; origin doubtful]

pierce *pērs*, *vt* to thrust or make a hole through; to enter, or force a way into; to touch or move deeply; to penetrate; to perforate; to make by perforating or penetrating. — *vi* to penetrate. — *n* a perforation; a stab; a prick. — *adj* **pierce'able** capable of being pierced. — *adj* **pier'ced** perforated; penetrated. — *n* **pierc'er** someone who or that which pierces; any sharp instrument used for piercing; a sting; a keen eye (*archaic*). — *adj* **pierc'ing** penetrating; very acute; keen, sharp. — *adv* **pierc'ingly**. — *n* **pierc'ingness**. [OFr *percer*; of doubtful origin]

Pierian *pī-ē'ri-ən*, *adj* of *Pieria* in Thessaly, the country of the Muses; of the Muses. — *n* **pierid** (*pī'ə-rid*) any butterfly of the Pieridae family. — *n pl* **Pierides** (*pī-er'i-dēz*) the nine Muses: — *sing* **Pī'eris**. — *n* **Pī'eris** the cabbage butterfly genus, typical of the family **Pier'idae** (*-dē*); a genus of American and Asiatic shrubs, of the family *Ericaceae*. — *adj* **pieridine** (*pī-er'i-dīn*) of the Pieridae. [Gr *Pīeriā*]

Pierrot *pē'ə-rō* or *pyer-ō*, *n* a white-faced clown with loose long-sleeved garb; (without *cap*) formerly, a member of a group of entertainers in similar dress at seaside resorts, etc; an 18c women's low-cut basque, with sleeves. — *n* **pierrette** (*pē-ə-ret'*) a female performer in a pierrot group. [Fr, dimin of *Pierre* Peter]

pierst. (*Spenser*) short form of **pierced** (*pa t* and *pa p*).

piert. Same as **peart**; see also **parsley-piert**.

piet. Same as **pyot**.

pietà *pyā-tä'*, (*art*) *n* a representation of the Virgin with the dead Christ across her knees. [Ital, from L *pietās*, *-ātis* pity]

pietism, **pietist**, etc. See under **piety**.

pietra dura *pyā'trə do͞o'rə*, *n* inlaid mosaic work with hard stones, such as jasper, agate, etc, or, strictly, with one type of stone only: — *pl* **pietre dure** (*pyā'tre do͞o're*) used as *n sing* for this type of (*usu* relief) mosaic work done with a variety of semi-precious stones. [Ital, hard stone]

piety *pī'i-ti*, *n* pity (*obs*); the quality of being pious; dutifulness; devoutness; sense of duty towards parents, benefactors, etc; dutiful conduct. — *n* **pī'etism**. — *n* **pī'etist** someone marked by strong devotional feeling; a name first applied to a sect of German religious reformers of deep devotional feeling (end of 17c). — *adj* **pietist'ic** or **pietist'ical**. [OFr *piete*, from L *pietās*, *-ātis*]

piezo- *pī'i-zō-* or *pī-ē'zō-*, or *-zo'*, *combining form* denoting pressure. — *adj* **piezo** short for **piezoelectric**. — *n* **piezochem'istry** the chemistry of substances under high pressure. — *adj* **piezoelec'tric**. — *n* **piezoelectri'city** electricity developed in certain crystals by mechanical strain, and the effect of an electric field in producing expansion and contraction along different axes. — *adj* **piezomagnet'ic**. — *n* **piezomag'netism** magnetism developed in a similar way to piezoelectricity, using a magnetic instead of an electric field. — *n* **piezometer** (*-om'i-tər*) an instrument for measuring pressure or compressibility. [Gr *piezein* to press]

piffero *pif'ə-rō*, *n* a fife; an Italian bagpipe; a crude oboe: — *pl* **piff'eros**. — *n* **pifferaro** (*-ä'rō*) a piffero-player: — *pl* **pifferari** (*-rē*). [Ital, from OHGer *pfīfari* piper]

piffle *pif'l*, (*colloq*) *n* nonsense; worthless talk. — *vi* to trifle; to act ineffectually. — *adj* **piff'ling** trivial, petty. — *n* **piff'ler**. [Origin unknown]

pig[1] *pig*, *n* any mammal of the family *Suidae*, omnivorous ungulates with thick, bristly skin, *esp* the domesticated *Sus scrofa*, a farm animal bred as food for humans; its flesh as food, *esp* that of the young animal; someone who is like the popular image of a pig, dirty, greedy, gluttonous, or cantankerous (also used mildly in reproach); an oblong mass of unforged metal, as first extracted from the ore; the mould into which it is run, *esp* one of the branches, the main channel being the *sow*; a device that is propelled through a pipeline or duct by pneumatic, hydraulic or gas pressure, for clearing, cleaning, tracking or scanning purposes, etc (*tech*; *min ext* same as **go-devil**); a feast (*slang*); a policeman (*slang*; *derog*); a segment of an orange (*slang*); something very difficult (*slang*). — *vi* to give birth to pigs; to live, herd, huddle, sleep, or feed like pigs; to eat greedily (*slang*): — *pr p* **pigg'ing**; *pa t* and *pa p* **pigged**. — *n* **pigg'ery** a place where pigs are kept; piggishness. — *n* **pigg'ing** (*tech*) operating a pig (qv) or running a pig along a pipeline. — *adj* (*slang*) expressing aversion, of something troublesome, unpleasant or difficult. — *adj* **pigg'ish** like a pig; greedy; dirty; cantankerous; mean. — *adv* **pigg'ishly**. — *n* **pigg'ishness**. — **pigg'ie**, **pigg'y**, **pig'let** or **pig'ling** a little pig. —

n pl **pigg'ies** a child's word for toes. — *adj* **pigg'y** like a pig. — **pig'-bed** a pig's sleeping place; a mould of sand in which a pig of iron is cast; **pig'boat** (*US naval slang*) a submarine; **pig'-deer** the babiroussa. — *adj* **pig'-eyed** having small, pinkish, dull eyes with heavy lids. — *adj* **pig'-faced**. — **pig'feed** food for pigs; **pig'-fish** (*US*) a name for various kinds of grunt (*Haemulon*, etc); in Australia, a name for various wrasses; **piggyback** see under **pickaback**; **pigg'y-bank** see under **pig**[2]. — *adj* **pighead'ed** having a pig-like head; stupidly obstinate. — *adv* **pighead'edly**. — **pighead'edness**; **pig'-herd**. — *adj* **pig'-ig'norant** (*colloq*; *derog*) very ignorant. — **pig'-in-the-midd'le** or **pigg'y-in-the-midd'le** a children's game in which a person standing between two or more others tries to intercept a ball, etc, passing back and forth between them; a person caught between opposing viewpoints, strategies, etc (*fig*); **pig'-iron** iron in pigs or rough bars. — *vi* **pig'-jump** (*Austr*; of a horse) to jump from all four legs without bringing them together. — **pig Latin** a secret language or jargon made up by children, *esp* one in which an initial consonant is transposed to the end of the word, followed by *-ay*, so that eg *pig* becomes *igpay*; **pig'-lead** lead in pigs; **pig'-lily** (*SAfr*) the lily of the Nile; **pig-man** a man responsible for or expert in looking after pigs; **pig'meat** bacon, ham or pork; **pig'nut** the earth-nut (*Conopodium*); **pig'pen** a pigsty; **pig'-rat** the bandicoot rat; **pig'sconce** a pigheaded person; a blockhead; **pig'skin** the skin of a pig prepared as a strong leather; a saddle (*slang*); a football (*NAm slang*); **pig'-sticker**; **pig'-sticking** boar-hunting with spears; **pig'sty** a pen for keeping pigs; a very dirty or untidy place (*colloq*); **pig's'-wash** or **pig'wash** swill; **pig's whisper** a low whisper (*dialect*); a very short space of time; **pig swill** or **pig'swill** kitchen, etc, waste fed to pigs; **pig'tail** the tail of a pig; the hair of the head plaited behind or at the side; a short length of rope or cable; a roll of twisted tobacco; **pig'weed** goosefoot, amaranth, cow-parsnip, or other plant eaten by pigs; **pig'-woman** a woman who roasted pigs at fairs. — **a pig in a poke** see under **poke**[1]; **make a pig of oneself** (*colloq*) to overindulge in food or drink; **make a pig's ear of (something)** (*colloq*) to make a mess of something, to do something badly or clumsily; **pig it** (*colloq*) to live in squalid or dirty surroundings; **pig out** to overeat, go on a binge; **pigs might fly** (*colloq*; as an expression of scepticism) that is highly unlikely; **when pigs fly** (*colloq*) never. [ME *pigge*; cf Du *bigge big*]

pig[2] *pig*, (*Scot*) *n* an earthenware crock, hot-water bottle, or other vessel; earthenware; a potsherd. — **pigg'y-bank** a money box made of pottery, shaped like a pig through false association with **pig**[1]; a child's money box, whether or not pig-shaped; **pig'-man** or **-woman** a dealer in earthenware articles. — **pigs and whistles** wrack and ruin. [Origin unknown]

pigeon[1] *pij'ən* or *-in*, *n orig* a young dove; a dove; any bird of the dove family; extended to various other birds (eg the *Cape pigeon*); a girl (*obs*); someone who is fleeced (*slang*); short for **stool pigeon** (see under **stool**). — *vt* to gull or hoax. — *n* **pig'eonry** a place for keeping pigeons. — **pig'eon-berry** (*US*) pokeweed or its fruit. — *adj* **pig'eon-breast'ed** or **-chested** having a narrow chest with the breast-bone projecting. — **pig'eon-chest**; **pig'eon-fancier** someone who keeps and breeds pigeons for racing or exhibiting; **pig'eon-fancying**; **pig'eon-flier** or **-flyer** someone who sends out homing pigeons; **pig'eon-flying**. — *adj* **pig'eon-heart'ed** timid. — **pig'eonhole** a niche for a pigeon's nest; a hole of similar appearance; a compartment for storing and classifying papers, for leaving letters, etc; a compartment of the mind or memory; (in *pl*) the stocks; (in *pl*) an old outdoor game like bagatelle. — *vt* to furnish with or make into pigeonholes; to put into a pigeonhole; to classify methodically, or too rigidly; to lay aside and delay action on, or treat with neglect. — **pig'eonholer**; **pig'eon-house** a dovecot. — *adj* **pig'eon-liv'ered** mild. — **pig'eon-pair** boy and girl twins or a boy and girl as sole children in a family; **pig'eon-pea** dal; **pig'eon-post** transmission of letters by pigeons; **pig'eon's-blood** a dark red colour, ruby; **pigeon's milk** partly digested food regurgitated by pigeons to feed their young; an imaginary liquid for which children are sent, eg on 1 April. — *adj* **pig'eon-toed** having the toes more or less turned inward; (of birds) having all toes at one level. — **pig'eon-wing** a caper or leap in dancing. — **clay pigeon** see under **clay**. [OFr *pijon*, from L *pīpiō*, *-ōnis*, from *pīpīre* to cheep]

pigeon[2]. Same as **pidgin**.

piggin *pig'in*, *n* a small pail or bowl constructed of staves and hoops, like a barrel, one stave usually prolonged as a handle; a vessel of various other kinds. [Poss from **pig**[2]; the Celtic words seem to be from English]

pigging, **piggish**, **piggy**, etc. See under **pig**[1].

piggyback. See **pickaback**.

pight *pīt*, an old *pa t* and *pa p* (*Spenser*) of **pitch**[2], pitched, set; also a false archaism for the present tense. — *adj* well-knit (*Spenser*); resolved (*Shakesp*).

pightle *pī'tl*, *n* a small enclosure; a croft. [Ety dubious]

pigmean. See under **pygmy**.

pigment *pig'mənt*, *n* paint or dye; any substance used for colouring; that which gives colour to animal and vegetable tissues; piment (*Scott*). — *adj* **pigmental** (*-men'tl*) or **pig'mentary**. — *n* **pigmentā'tion** coloration or discoloration by pigments in the tissues. — *adj* **pig'mented**. [L *pīgmentum*, from *pingere* to paint]

pigmy. Same as **pygmy**.

pignorate or **pignerate** *pig'nər-āt*, (*archaic*) *vt* to give or take in pledge or pawn. — *n* **pignorā'tion**. [L *pignus*, *-eris* or *-oris* a pledge]

pigsney, **pigsny** or **pigsnie** *pigz'ni*, *n* a term of endearment (sometimes contempt), *esp* to a woman (*archaic* or *dialect*); an eye (playfully; *obs*). [**pig's eye**, with prosthetic *n* (from *an eye*, *mine eye*)]

pi-jaw. See **pi**[3].

pika *pī'kə*, *n* the tailless hare (Ochotona), a small mammal of the order Rodentia or, in some classifications, Lagomorpha, found in mountain regions. [Tungus *piika*]

pike[1] *pīk*, *n* a sharp point; a weapon with a long shaft and a sharp head like a spear, formerly used by foot-soldiers; a spiked staff; a sharp-pointed hill or summit; a voracious freshwater fish (*Esox lucius*) with a pointed snout; extended to various other fishes; a pick (*dialect*). — *vt* to kill or pierce with a pike; to pick (*dialect*). — *adj* **piked** (*pīkt* or *pīk'id*) spiked; ending in a point. — *n* **pīk'er** someone who picks (*dialect*); a pilferer (*dialect*); a person who bets, gambles, speculates, or does anything else in a very small way; a shirker or mean character (*slang*). — **pike'-head** the head of a pike or spear; **pike'man** a man armed with a pike; someone who wields a pick; **pike'-perch** a percoid fish with pike-like jaws; **pike'staff** the staff or shaft of a pike; a staff with a pike at the end. — **plain as a pikestaff** (*orig* **packstaff**) perfectly plain or clear. [OE *pīc* pick, spike; but also partly from Fr *pic* with the same meaning, and *pique* the weapon, and prob partly from Scand]

pike[2] *pīk*, *vi* (*old colloq*) to speed. — *vt* (*obs*) to betake (oneself) quickly. [Perh orig *get oneself a pikestaff* (a pilgrim's spiked staff); perh Fr *piquer* to spur]

pike[3] *pīk*, *n* a turnpike; a toll; a main road (*US*). — *n* **pī'ker** a tramp. — **pike'-keeper** or **pike'man** a man in charge of a turnpike. [Short for **turnpike**]

pike[4] *pīk*, (*diving* and *gymnastics*) *n* (also **piked position**) a posture in which the body is bent sharply at the hips with legs kept straight at the knees and toes pointed. — *vi* to adopt this position. — *adj* **piked**. [Origin uncertain]

pikelet *pīk'lit*, *n* a kind of tea-cake, or crumpet, or muffin (*dialect*); a drop-scone (*Austr* and *NZ*). [Welsh *bara pyglyd* pitchy bread]

pikul. Same as **picul**.

pila. See under **pilum**.

pilaff. See under **pilau**.

pilaster *pi-las'tər*, *n* a square column, partly built into and partly projecting from a wall. — *adj* **pilas'tered**. [Fr *pilastre*, from Ital *pilastro*, from L *pīla* a pillar]

pilau *pi-low'*, *n* a highly spiced Eastern dish of rice with a fowl or other meat, or fish, boiled together or separately. — Also **pillau'**, **pilaw'**, **pilaff'** (or *pil'*), or **pilow'**. — Also *adj*. [Pers *pilāw*, Turk *pilāw*, *pilāf*]

pilch *pilch*, (*archaic*) *n* an outer garment, *orig* a fur cloak, later a coarse leather or woollen cloak; a rug for a saddle; a light saddle; a flannel cloth for wrapping a child. — *n* **pilch'er** a scabbard (*Shakesp*). [OE *pyl(e)ce*, from LL *pellicea*, from L *pellis* skin]

pilchard *pil'chərd*, *n* a European sea fish like the herring, but smaller, thicker, and rounder, common off Cornwall. — Earlier (*Shakesp*) **pil'cher**. [Origin unknown; poss Scand (cf Norw *pilk* artificial bait); Ir *pilseir* is prob from English]

pilcorn *pil'körn*, *n* the naked oat, a variety in which the glume does not adhere to the grain. [For **pilled corn** (see **pill**[2])]

pilcrow *pil'krō*, *n* a paragraph-mark. [Origin obscure]

pile[1] *pīl*, *n* a set of things fitted or resting one over another, or in a more or less regular figure; a heap of combustibles for cremating a dead body, or for the burnt-offering, or for burning to death; a set of weights fitting one within another; a stack of arms; a heap of shot; a set of wrought-iron bars placed together for welding and rolling into one; a series of alternate plates of two metals for generating an electric current; a set of coins placed vertically one upon another; a great amount of money, a fortune (*slang*); a large amount or supply (*colloq*); a tall building; a nuclear reactor, *orig* the graphite blocks forming the moderator for the reactor (*obs*); the under iron for striking coins (*obs*); the reverse of a coin (*obs*). — *vt* to lay in a pile or heap; to collect in a mass; to heap up or load in a heap or heaps; to accumulate; to weld and roll (several iron bars) into one. — *vi* to come into piles; to accumulate; to go in crowds; to get in or out (with *in* or *out*; *colloq*). — *n* **pī'ler**. — **pile'-cap** the top of a nuclear reactor; see also under **pile**[2]; **pile'-up** a large-scale collision, *esp* of motor vehicles. — **pile arms** to prop three muskets, *orig* with fixed bayonets, so that the butts remain firm, the muzzles close together pointing obliquely — also *stack arms*; **pile it on** (*colloq*) to overdo or exaggerate something; **pile on** (or **up**) **the agony** (*colloq*) to affect or exaggerate distress, pain, etc, eg in order to win sympathy; to add cruelly to another's pain, grief, etc; **pile up** to run ashore; to form a disorderly mass or heap; to become involved in a pile-up (qv); to accumulate. [Fr, from L *pīla* a pillar]

pile[2] *pīl*, *n* an arrow-head; a Roman javelin; a large stake or cylinder driven into the earth to support foundations; an inverted pyramidal figure (*heraldry*). — *vt* to drive piles into; to support with or build on piles. — *n* **pī'ling**. — **pile'-cap** (*civ eng*) a reinforced concrete block cast around a set of piles to create a unified support; see also under **pile**[1]; **pile'-driver** a mechanical contrivance for driving in piles; (in games) a very heavy stroke, kick, etc; **pile'-dwelling** a dwelling built on piles, *esp* a lake-dwelling; **pile shoe** the iron or steel point fitted to the foot of a pile to give it strength to pierce the earth and so assist driving; **pile'work** work or foundations made of piles; **pile'-worm** a ship-worm. [OE *pīl*, from L *pīlum* a javelin]

pile[3] *pīl*, *n* a covering of hair, *esp* soft, fine, or short hair; down; human body-hair; a single hair; the raised or fluffy surface of a fabric, carpet, etc; (as distinguished from *nap*) the raised surface of a fabric made not in finishing but in weaving, either by leaving loops (which may be cut) or by weaving two cloths face to face and cutting them apart. — *adj* **pī'leous** (*rare*) relating to or consisting of hair. — *adj* **pīlif'erous** bearing hairs; ending in a hair-like point. — *adj* **pīl'iform** hair-like. [L *pilus* a hair]

pile[4] *pīl*, *n* (*usu* in *pl*) a haemorrhoid. — *n* **pile'wort** the lesser celandine (*Ranunculus ficaria*), once thought a remedy for piles. [L *pila* a ball]

pilea, **pileate**, **pileated**, **pilei**. See under **pileum**.

pileorhiza *pī-li-ō-rī'zə*, (*bot*) *n* a root-cap. [L *pīleus* or *pīleum* (see **pileum**), Gr *rhiza* root]

pileous. See under **pile**[3].

piler. See under **pile**[1].

pileum *pī'li-əm*, *n* the top of a bird's head: — *pl* **pil'ea**. — *adj* **pi'leate** or **pi'leated** cap-shaped; capped; crested. — *n* **pi'leus** a Roman felt cap; the expanded cap of a mushroom or toadstool, or other fungus: — *pl* **pilei** (*pī'li-ī*). [L *pīleum*, *pīleus*, for *pilleum*, *pilleus* a felt cap; cf Gr *pīlos* felt, a felt cap]

pilfer *pil'fər*, *vi* and *vt* to steal in small quantities. — *n* **pil'ferage**, **pil'fering** or (*old*) **pil'fery** petty theft. — *n* **pil'ferer**. — *adv* **pil'feringly**. [Prob connected with **pelf**]

pilgarlick or **peelgarlic** *pil-*, *pēl-gär'lik*, *n* a baldpate (*obs*); a poor wretch; in whimsical self-pity, oneself. — *adj* **pilgar'licky**. [**pill**[2] or **peel**[1], and **garlic**, because like a pilled or peeled head of garlic]

pilgrim *pil'grim*, *n* a wanderer, wayfarer (*archaic* and *poetic*); a person who travels *esp* a distance to visit a holy place; allegorically or spiritually, a person journeying through life as a stranger in this world; a Pilgrim Father; an original settler; a newcomer. — *adj* of or pertaining to a pilgrim; like a pilgrim; consisting of pilgrims. — *n* **pil'grimage** the journeying of a pilgrim; a journey to a shrine or other holy place, or to a place venerated for its associations; the journey of life; a lifetime. — *adj* visited by pilgrims. — *vi* to go on a pilgrimage; to wander. — *n* **pil'grimager** (*contemptuously*) a person who goes on a pilgrimage. — *n* **pil'grimer** someone who goes on a pilgrimage. — *vi* (or *vt* with *it*) **pil'grimize** or **-ise** to play the pilgrim. — **pil'grim-bott'le** a flat bottle with ears at the neck for a cord; **Pilgrim Fathers** the Puritans who sailed for America in the *Mayflower*, and founded Plymouth, Massachusetts, in 1620; **pilgrim's shell** a scallop shell (called a cockle) used as a sign that one had visited the shrine of St James of Compostela; **pilgrim's sign** a badge, often a leaden brooch, obtained at the shrine and worn on the hat by a pilgrim. [Assumed OFr *pelegrin* (Fr *pèlerin*), from L *peregrīnus* foreigner, stranger; see **peregrine**]

pilhorse *pil'hörs*. See under **philhorse**.

pili[1] *pē-lē'*, *n* the nut (also **pili'-nut'**) of trees of the burseraceous genus *Canarium*. [Tagálog]

pili[2]. See **pilus**.

piliferous, **piliform**. See under **pile**[3].

piling. See under **pile**[2].

Pilipino *pil-i-pē'nō* *n* the official language of the Philippines, based on Tagálog. [Pilipino, from Sp *Filipino* Philippine]

pill[1] *pil*, *n* a little ball, flattened sphere or disc, etc of medicine for swallowing (see also **the pill** below); a ball, eg a cannon-ball, tennis-ball, or (in *pl*) billiards (*facetious*); anything disagreeable that must be accepted; a tiresome person; a doctor (*slang*; also in *pl*); (in *pl*) little balls that form on the surface of fabric during use, through rubbing, etc. — *vt* to dose with pills; to form into pills; to blackball (*slang*). — *vi* (of fabric) to (have a tendency to) develop pills on the surface. — *n* **pill'ing**. — **pill'-box** a box for holding pills; a kind of one-horse carriage (*archaic*); a small blockhouse (*military slang*); a small round brimless hat; **pill'-bug** a wood-louse that rolls itself into a ball; **pill'head** or **pill'-popper** (*slang*) a regular, *usu* addicted, taker of sedative and/or stimulant pills, eg barbiturates and amphetamines; **pill'worm** a millipede that curls up; **pill'wort** a water-fern (*Pilularia*) found at lake-margins, with pill-like sporocarps. — **the pill** any of various contraceptive pills (see **oral contraception**); **on the pill** taking contraceptive pills regularly. [L *pila*, perh through OFr *pile*, or from a syncopated form of the dimin *pilula*]

pill[2] *pil*, *vt* and *vi* to plunder (*archaic*); to peel (*dialect*); to make or become hairless (*obs*). — *n* (*Spenser*) a husk or integument. — *n* **pill'age** the act of plundering; plunder. — *vt* and *vi* to plunder. — *n* **pill'ager**. [OE *pylian* and OFr *peler*, both from L *pilāre* to deprive of hair; cf **peel**]

pillar *pil'ər*, *n* a detached support, not necessarily cylindrical or of classical proportions (*archit*); a structure of similar form erected as a monument, ornament, object of worship, etc; a tall upright rock; a mass of coal or rock left in a mine to support the roof; anything in the form of a column; a supporting post; the post supporting a bicycle saddle; (in a car) a vertical column of bodywork, eg the door pillar separating the front and rear doors; a cylinder holding the plates of a watch or clock in position; a pillarbox; someone who, or anything that, sustains. — *n* **pill'arist** or **pill'ar-saint** an ascetic living on the top of a pillar, a stylite. — **pillar box** a short hollow pillar for posting letters in (**pillar-box red** the traditional bright red colour of British pillar boxes); **pill'ar-root** a supporting root descending from a branch. — **from pillar to post** from one state of difficulty to another; hither and thither; **Pillars of Islam** the five major Islamic duties — the statement of faith, prayer, fasting, almsgiving, and pilgrimage to Mecca. [OFr *piler* (Fr *pilier*), from LL *pīlāre*, from L *pīla* a pillar]

pillau. See under **pilau**.

pillicock *pil'i-kok*, *n* the penis (allusively in *Shakesp*); a term of endearment to a boy. [Cf Norw dialect *pill*]

pillion *pil'yən*, *n* a pad or light saddle for a woman; a cushion behind a horseman for a second rider (*usu* a woman) or for a bag; the passenger-seat of a motorcycle, or a baggage-carrier, usable as an extra seat. — *adv* on a pillion. — *vt* to seat on or provide with a pillion. — *n* **pill'ionist** or **pill'ion-rider** someone who rides pillion. — **pill'ion-seat**. [Prob Ir *pillín*, Gaelic *pillin*, *pillean*, a pad, a pack-saddle, from *peall* a skin or mat, from L *pellis* skin]

pilliwinks *pil'i-wingks*, *n pl* an instrument of torture for crushing the fingers. [Origin unknown]

pillock *pil'ək*, (*slang*) *n* a stupid or foolish person. [**pillicock** and dialect forms *pillick*, *pilluck*]

pillory *pil'ə-ri*, *n* (*hist*) a wooden frame, supported by an upright pillar or post, with holes through which the head and hands were put as a punishment, abolished in England in 1837. — *vt* to set in the pillory (*hist*); to hold up to ridicule: — *pr p* **pill'orying**; *pa t* and *pa p* **pill'oried**. — Also **pill'orize** or **-ise**. [OFr *pilori*; Provençal *espilori*; of uncertain origin]

pillow *pil'ō*, *n* a cushion for a sleeper's head; any object used for the purpose; a cushion for lace-making; a support for part of a structure; something resembling a pillow in shape or feel. — *vt* to lay or rest for support; to serve as pillow for; to provide or prop with pillows. — *vi* (*archaic*) to rest the head. — *adj* **pill'owed** supported by or provided with a pillow. — *adj* **pill'owy** like a pillow; round and swelling; soft. — **pill'ow-bere** (*archaic*) or **pill'ow-beer** (*archaic*) a pillowcase; **pillow-block** see under **pedestal**; **pill'owcase** or **pill'owslip** a cover for a pillow; **pill'ow-cup** a last cup before going to bed; **pill'ow-fight**; **pill'ow-fighting** the game of thumping one another with pillows; **pill'ow-lace** lace worked with bobbins on a padded cushion; **pill'ow-lava** lava showing pillow-structure; **pill'ow-structure** (in lavas) separation into pillow-shaped blocks; **pillow talk** talk between lovers in bed. [OE *pyle*, also *pylu*, from L *pulvīnus*]

pill-popper, **pillworm**, **pillwort**. See under **pill**[1].

pilniewinks. See under **pinnywinkle**.

Pilocarpus *pī-lō-kär'pəs*, *n* a genus of S American rutaceous shrubs, including jaborandi. — *n* **pilocar'pin** or **pilocar'pine** (*-pēn*) an alkaloid ($C_{11}H_{16}O_2N_2$) obtained from jaborandi leaves. [Gr *pīlos* felt, a felt cap, and *karpos* fruit]

pilose *pī'lōs*, *adj* hairy; having scattered soft or moderately stiff hairs. — *n* **pilosity** (*-los'i-ti*). — *adj* **pī'lous** hairy. [L *pilōsus*, from *pilus* hair]

pilot *pī'lət*, *n* a steersman (*archaic*); a person who conducts ships in and out of a harbour, along a dangerous coast, etc; a person who actually operates the controls of an aircraft, hovercraft, spacecraft, etc; someone who is qualified to act as pilot; a guide; a cowcatcher (*US*); a pilot film or broadcast. — *adj* pertaining to pilot(s); acting as guide or control; trial (of eg a model on a smaller scale) serving to test the qualities or future possibilities of a machine, plant, etc, or (of a film or broadcast) to test public reaction so as to assess the probable popularity of a proposed radio or television series. — *vt* to act as pilot to. — *n* **pī'lotage** piloting; a pilot's fee. — *adj* **pī'lotless** without a pilot; (of an automatic aeroplane) not requiring a pilot. — **pi'lot-balloon'** a small balloon sent up to find how the wind blows; **pi'lot-boat** a boat used by pilots on duty; **pilot burner**, **jet** or **light** (see also below) a small gas-burner kept alight to light another; **pilot cloth** a coarse, stout cloth for overcoats; **pilot engine** a locomotive sent before a train to clear its way, as a pilot; **pi'lot-fish** a carangoid fish that accompanies ships and sharks; **pi'lot-flag** or **-jack** the flag hoisted at the fore by a vessel needing a pilot; **pi'lot-house** a shelter for steering-gear and pilot (also called **wheel-house**); **pi'lot-jacket** a pea-jacket; **pilot lamp** or **light** a small electric light to show when current is on, or for some other purpose; **pi'lotman** a railway employee assigned to guide trains across a section of single-track line; **pilot officer** (in the Air Force) an officer ranking with an army second-lieutenant; **pi'lot-plant** prototype machinery set up to begin a new process; **pilot project** or **scheme** a scheme serving as a guide on a small scale to a full-scale scheme; **pi'lot-whale** any of several types of whale of the *Globicephala* genus, family *Delphinidae*. [Fr *pilote*, from Ital *pilota*, appar for earlier *pedota*, which may be from Gr *pēdon* oar, in pl, rudder]

pilotis *pi-lot'ē* or *pi-lo-tēz'*, (*archit*) *n pl* a series of slender columns or stilts used on the ground floor of a building to raise the main floor to first-floor level, and leaving open space below (eg for car-parking). [Fr *pillars* stilts.]

pilous. See under **pilose**.

pilow. See under **pilau**.

Pils *pils* or *pilz*, *n* a lager beer similar to Pilsener.

Pilsener or **Pilsner** *pilz'* or *pils'nər*, *n* (also without *cap*) a light-coloured, flavoursome variety of lager, *orig* brewed in *Pilsen*, Czechoslovakia.

Piltdown man *pilt'down man'*, *n* a once-supposed very early form of man represented by parts of a skull found at *Piltdown*, Sussex (1912), the skull being exposed as a fake in 1953 (see also **Eoanthropus**).

pilule *pil'ūl*, *n* a little pill. — Also **pil'ula**. — *adj* **pil'ular**. [L *pilula*, dimin of *pila* ball]

pilum *pī'ləm*, *n* the heavy javelin used by Roman foot-soldiers: — *pl* **pī'la**. [L *pīlum*]

pilus *pī'ləs*, *n* a hair: — *pl* **pī'lī**. [L *pilus*]

piment *pi-ment'*, (*obs*) *n* spiced sweetened wine. — Also (*Scott*) **pigment** (*pig'mənt*). — *n* **pimento** (*pi-ment'ō*) formerly, Cayenne pepper; now allspice or Jamaica pepper, the dried unripe fruits of a W Indian tree (*Pimenta officinalis*) of the myrtle family; the tree itself; its wood: — *pl* **pimen'tos**. — *n* **pimiento** (*pi-mē-en'tō*) the sweet, red, yellow or green pepper, capsicum: — *pl* **pimien'tos**. [OFr *piment*, Sp *pimiento*, from L *pīgmentum* paint]

pimp *pimp*, *n* a man who lives with, and sometimes solicits for, a prostitute and lives off her earnings, or one who solicits for a prostitute or brothel and is paid for his services; a person who procures gratifications for the lust of others, a pander. — *vi* to act or live as a pimp; to pander. [Origin obscure, perh related to Fr *pimpant* well-dressed, smart, from OFr *pimper* to dress smartly]

pimpernel *pim'pər-nel*, *n* burnet (*obs*); burnet saxifrage (Pimpinella) (*obs*); now, the poor man's weather glass (*Anagallis arvensis*), a plant of the primrose family, with scarlet (or blue, etc) flowers. — *n* **Pimpinell'a** the anise and burnet saxifrage genus of umbelliferous plants. — **bastard pimpernel** a small plant (*Centunculus minimus*) related to the scarlet pimpernel; **bog pimpernel** *Anagallis tenella*; **water pimpernel** a water plant of the primrose family, brookweed; **yellow pimpernel** the wood loosestrife (*Lysimachia nemorum*). [OFr *pimpernelle*, mod Fr *pimprenelle*, and Ital *pimpinella* burnet; origin doubtful]

Pimpinella. See under **pimpernel**.

pimping *pimp'ing*, *adj* petty; puny; paltry; sickly. [Origin obscure]

pimple *pim'pl*, *n* a pustule; a small swelling, protuberance, or hill. — *adj* **pim'pled** or **pim'ply** having pimples. [Origin uncertain]

PIN *abbrev*: personal identification number, a multi-digit number for use with a debit card and computerized cash-dispenser to authorize access to information, withdrawal of cash, etc.

pin *pin*, *n* a piece of wood or of metal used for fastening things together; a peg or nail; a sharp-pointed piece of wire with a rounded head for fastening clothes, etc; an ornamental elaboration of this; a cylindrical part inserted into something, such as the stem of a key, or part of a lock that a hollow-stemmed key fits; the projecting part of a dovetail joint; a peg aimed at in quoits; a peg in the centre of an archery target; the rod of a golf flag; a skittle or ninepin; a chess piece (*obs*); a tuning peg in a stringed instrument; a measuring peg in a drinking-cup; a degree, stage, pitch; a leg (*colloq*); a peak; the projecting bone of the hip; a hard spot or excrescence; a cask of $4\frac{1}{2}$ gallons; short for clothes-pin, rolling-pin, tirling-pin, etc; an act of pinning or state of being pinned; anything of little value. — *vt* to fasten with a pin; to fix, to fasten, to enclose, to hold down (*fig*); to make a small hole in; to insert chips of stone between the stones of; to cause an opponent's piece to be unable to move without checking its own king (*chess*): — *pr p* **pinn'ing**; *pa t* and *pa p* **pinned**. — *n* **pinn'er** someone who pins; a pin-maker; a pinafore; a head-dress with lappets flying loose; one of these lappets. — *n* **pinn'ing** a fastening; a chip of stone, etc, inserted in a joint of masonry. — **pin'ball** a form of bagatelle; a scoring game, played on a slot-machine, in which a ball runs down a sloping board set with pins or other targets; **pin'-butt'ock** (*Shakesp*) a sharp, pointed buttock; **pin'case** (*obs*); **pin curl** a lock of hair made to curl by winding it around one's finger, etc, and securing it with a hairpin; **pin'-cushion** a small pad for holding pins; **pin'down** a discredited technique for controlling and disciplining disruptive children, *esp* teenagers, in residential care, involving solitary confinement and removal of clothing other than nightwear or underwear, and sometimes physical punishment and mental harassment. — Also *adj*. — **pin'-dust** brass filings, a product of pin-making. — *adj* **pin'-eyed** (bot) long-styled, with the stigma like a pinhead in the throat of the corolla (*esp* of a *Primula*). — **pin'-feather** a young, unexpanded feather. — *adj* **pin'-feathered**. — *adj* **pin'-fire** (of a firearm) discharged by a pin driven into the fulminate. — **pin'fish** a spiny fish of various kinds; **pin'head** the head of a pin; a stupid person (*slang*); **pin'hole** a hole for or made by a pin, or such as a pin might make; **pinhole camera**; **pinhole photography** the taking of photographs by the use of a pinhole instead of a lens; **pin'hooker** (*slang*) a speculator who buys up foals hoping to make a profit on them when selling them as yearlings for racing; **pin'-leg** (*Scot*) a wooden leg; **pin'-maker**; **pin'-making**; **pin'-man** a seller of pins; a matchstick drawing, in which the limbs and body are represented by single lines; **pin'-money** *orig* money allotted by a man to his wife or female dependants for private expenses; extra money earned by a man or woman to spend on incidental or luxury items; a trifling amount of money; **pin'point** the point of a pin; anything very sharp or minute. — *vt* to place or define very exactly. — **pin'-prick** the prick of a pin; a petty irritation, or something done to irritate; **pin'-stripe** a very narrow stripe in cloth; cloth with such stripes; a garment made of such cloth, *esp* a suit (*colloq*). — *adj* **pin'-striped** (of fabric or garments) having pin-stripes; (of a person) wearing a pin-striped suit (*colloq*). — **pin'table** a pinball machine; **pin'tail** a type of duck, *Anas acuta*, with a pointed tail; a sand-grouse. — *adj* **pin'tailed** having a long, narrow tail. — **pin tuck** a very narrow ornamental tuck. — *adj* **pin'-up** (of a person) such as might have their portrait pinned up on a wall for admiration. — *n* a person of such a kind; a portrait or photograph so pinned up for admiration. — **pin'-wheel** a wheel with pins at right angles to its plane, to lift the hammer of a striking clock; a paper toy windmill; a revolving firework. — **a merry pin** (*archaic*) a merry mood; **on pins and needles** in agitated expectancy; **pin and web** (*Shakesp*) a disease of the eye, *appar* cataract, characterized by a small excrescence like a pin-head, and a film (also **web and pin**); **pin it on** or **pin it on to (someone)** to blame it on (someone), prove (someone) responsible for something; **pin one's faith** or **hopes on** to count, rely or bank solely on; **pin on one's sleeve** (*obs*) to make entirely dependent on oneself, or at one's disposal; **pins and needles** a tingling feeling in one's arm, hand, leg or foot, due to impeded circulation (see also **on pins and needles** above); **pin someone down** to get someone to commit himself or herself (to), to make someone express a definite opinion. [OE *pinn*, prob from L *pinna* a feather, a pinnacle]

piña *pē'nyə*, *n* the pineapple (*obs*); a fine cloth of pineapple leaf fibre (also **pi'ña-cloth**). [Sp, pine cone, pineapple]

piña colada *pē'nyə kə-lä'də*, *pē'nya kō-lä'dha*, or **pina colada** *pē'nə kə-lä'də*, *n* a drink made from pineapple juice, rum and coconut. [Sp, strained pineapple]

pinacoid. See under **pinakoid**.

pinacotheca *pin-ə-kō-thē'kə*, *n* a picture-gallery. — Also **pinakoth'ek** (Ger, from Gr). [Latinized from Gr *pinakothēkē*, from *pinax*, *-akos* a tablet, picture, and *thēkē* repository]

pinafore *pin'ə-fōr* or *-för*, *n* a loose protective or decorative garment worn, formerly *esp* by a child, over a dress; a pinafore dress. — *adj* **pin'afored**. — **pinafore dress** or **skirt** a dress without sleeves or collar or a skirt with a bib, designed to be worn over a blouse or sweater. [**pin** and **afore**]

pinakoid or **pinacoid** *pin'ə-koid*, *n* a crystal face, or a crystallographic form consisting of a pair of faces, parallel to two axes. — *adj* **pinakoid'al** or **pinacoid'al**. [Gr *pinax*, *-akos*, slab, and *eidos* form]

pinaster *pī-* or *pi-nas'tər*, *n* the cluster-pine. [L *pīnāster*, from pīnus pine]

piñata *pin-yä'tə* or *pin-ya'ta*, *n* a hollow pottery or papier-mâché figure filled with sweets, gifts, etc and hung from a ceiling, to be smashed by blindfolded people with sticks at a Christmas or other party in Latin American countries. [Sp, literally, pot]

pince-nez *pēs'-nā*, *n* a pair of eye-glasses without side-pieces, having a springed clip to hold them firmly on the nose: — *pl* **pince'-nez** (*-nāz* or *-nā*). — *adj* **pince'-nezed** (*-nād*). [Fr, pinch nose]

pincer *pin'sər*, *n* a grasping claw or forceps-like organ; (in *pl*) a gripping tool with jaws and handles on a pivot, used for drawing out nails, squeezing, etc; (in *pl*) a twofold advance that threatens to isolate part of an enemy's force (*fig*). — *vt* to pinch with pincers. — **pin'cer-movement**. [OFr *pincer* to pinch]

pinch *pinch* or *pinsh*, *vt* to compress a small part of between fingers and thumb or between any two surfaces, to nip; to squeeze; to crush; to nip off; to bite (*obs*); to bring or render by squeezing or nipping; (of eg cold or hunger) to affect painfully or injuriously; to cause to show the effects of such pain or injury; to harass; to hamper; to restrict; to stint, be miserly or frugal with; to find fault with (*obs*); to steal (*slang*); to arrest (*slang*); to over-urge (*horse-racing*); to move along with a lever. — *vi* to nip or squeeze; to be painfully tight; to encroach; to carp; to live sparingly; to narrow, taper off (*mining*). — *n* an act or experience of pinching; a critical time of difficulty or hardship; an emergency; a pleat (*obs*); an upward curl of a hat-brim (*obs*); a place of narrowing, folding, difficulty, or steepness; a quantity taken up between the finger and thumb; hence, any small quantity; an iron bar used as a lever. — *adj* **pinched** having the appearance of being tightly squeezed; hard pressed by want or cold; (of the face, or general appearance) haggard with cold, tiredness, hunger, etc; narrowed; straightened. — *n* **pinch'er** someone who or something which pinches; (in *pl*) pincers (*dialect*). — *n* and *adj* **pinch'ing**. — *adv* **pinch'ingly**. — **pinch'cock** a clamp that stops the flow of liquid by pinching a tube; **pinch'commons** a niggard with food; **pinch effect** (*nuc eng*) in a plasma carrying a large current, the constriction arising from the interaction of the current with its own magnetic field; **pinch'fist**, **pinch'gut** or **pinch'penny** a niggard. — *vi* **pinch'-hit** (*baseball*) to bat in place of another in an emergency (also *fig*). — **pinch'-hitter**; **pinch'point** a constricted, awkward or congested point, eg in the traffic system. — **at a pinch** in a case of necessity or emergency; **feel the pinch** (*colloq*) to be in financial difficulties, to find life, work, etc difficult because of lack of money; **know where the shoe pinches** to know by direct experience what the trouble or difficulty is; **take with a pinch of salt** see under **salt**[1]. [OFr *pincier*; prob Gmc]

pinchbeck *pinch'* or *pinsh'bek*, *n* a yellow alloy of copper with much less zinc than ordinary brass, simulating gold, invented by Christopher *Pinchbeck* (c 1670–1732), watchmaker. — *adj* sham; in bad taste.

pindari or **pindaree** *pin-dä'rē*, *n* a mercenary freebooter troublesome in India till 1817. [Hind *pindārī*]

Pindaric *pin-dar'ik*, *adj* after the manner or supposed manner of the Greek lyric poet *Pindar*. — *n* a Pindaric ode; an irregular ode, according to the 17c conception of Pindar. — **Pin'darism** the manner or supposed manner of Pindar; 'intoxication of style' (*Matthew Arnold*). — *n* **Pin'darist**. — *vt* and *vi* **Pin'darize** or **Pin'darise** (*də-rīz*). [Gr *pindarikos*, from *Pindaros*]

pinder *pin'dər*, *n* someone who impounds cattle. — Also **pinn'er**. [OE *pyndan* to shut up, from *pund*; cf **poind**, **pound**[2]]

pine[1] *pīn*, *n* any tree of the north temperate coniferous genus *Pinus*, with pairs or bundles of needle-leaves on short shoots and scale-leaves only on long shoots, represented in Britain by the **Scots pine** (*Pinus sylvestris*; often called *Scots fir*); extended to various more or less nearly related trees and to some plants only superficially similar; the timber of the pine; a pineapple plant or its fruit. — *adj* of pines or pinewood. — *n* **pī'nery** a pine-house; a pine-forest. — *adj* **pī'ny** (wrongly **pī'ney**) of, like, or abounding in pine trees. — **pine'apple** a pine cone (*obs*); a large S American multiple fruit shaped like a pine cone; the bromeliaceous plant (*Ananas*) bearing it; a finial shaped like a pine cone or a pineapple; a bomb (*slang*); a hand grenade (*slang*); **pineapple weed** the rayless mayweed (*Matricaria suaveolens*), from its smell; **pine'-barren** a level sandy tract growing pine trees; **pine-beau'ty** and **pine-car'pet** kinds of moths whose larvae feed on pine trees; **pine'-beet'le** any beetle that attacks pine trees, *esp* the **pine'-chāfer** (*Hylurgus piniperda*) which bores up through the leader; **pine cone** the cone or strobilus of a pine tree; **pine'-finch** an American finch like the goldfinch; a large grosbeak of pine-forests; **pine'-house** a house in which pineapples are grown; **pine kernel** the edible seed of a pine tree of various species; **pine marten** a British species of marten, *Mustela martes*, now rare, dark brown, with yellowish throat, and partly arboreal in habit; **pine needle** the acicular leaf of the pine tree; **pine tar** a dark, oily substance obtained from pine wood, used in paints, etc, and medicines; **pine tree**; **pinewood** a wood of pine trees; pine timber; **pine'-wool** a fibrous substance prepared from the leaves of the pine. — **pine-tree money** a silver money coined at Boston in the 17c bearing the figure of a pine tree. [OE *pīn*, from L *pīnus*]

pine[2] *pīn*, *vi* to waste away, *esp* under pain or mental distress; to languish with longing; to long; to repine. — *vt* to torment (*obs*); to consume, cause to wear away; to starve; to grieve for (*Milton*). — *n* punishment, torture (*obs*); suffering (*archaic*); want, starvation (*Spenser*). [OE *pīnian* to torment, from L *poena* punishment]

pineal *pin'i-əl* or *pīn'i-əl adj* shaped like a pine-cone; connected with the pineal body. — *n* **pinealec'tomy** surgical removal of the pineal body. — **pineal body** or **gland** a small organ at the end of an upgrowth from the optic thalami of the brain, that releases melatonin into the bloodstream; **pineal eye** a vestigial third eye in front of the pineal body, best developed in a New Zealand repitle, the tuatara. [L *pīnea* a pine-cone, from *pīnus* pine]

pineapple, **pinery**, **piney**. See **pine**[1].

pinetum *pī-nē'təm*, *n* a plantation of pine trees; a collection of pine trees for botanical or ornamental purposes: — *pl* **pine'ta**. [L *pīnētum* pine grove, from *pīnus* pine]

pinfold *pin'fōld*, *n* a pound or enclosure for cattle. — *vt* to impound. [OE *pundfald*, affected by *pyndan*; see **pound**[2], **fold**[2], and **pinder**]

ping *ping*, *n* a sharp ringing or whistling sound, eg of a bullet. — *vi* to make such a sound. — *vt* to cause to make such a sound. — *n* **ping'er** an acoustic transmitter for the study of ocean currents; (**Pinger**®) a domestic clockwork device set to give a warning signal at a chosen time; any of various devices sending out an acoustic signal for directional, timing, etc purposes. — **Ping'-Pong'**® a trademark for table tennis. — *adj* (without *cap*) moving backwards and forwards, to and fro (*fig*). [Imit]

pingle *ping'gl*, *ping'l*, (*Scot* and *dialect*) *vi* to strive; to struggle with difficulties, exert oneself strongly; to work ineffectually; to trifle or dally, *esp* with food. — *vt* to contend strongly with; to harass, worry; to eat with feeble appetite. — *n* a strenuous contest or exertion. — *n* **ping'ler**. — *adj* **ping'ling**. [Cf Swed *pyngla* to be busy in small matters, to work in a trifling way]

pingo *ping'gō*, *n* a large cone-shaped mound having a core of ice formed by the upward expansion of freezing water surrounded by permafrost: — *pl* **ping'os** or **ping'oes**. [Eskimo]

Ping-Pong. See under **ping**.

pinguid *ping'gwid*, *adj* fat. — *vt* and *vi* **ping'uefy** (*-gwi-fī*) to fatten; to make or become greasy. — *n* **Pinguic'ula** the butterwort genus. — *n* **pinguid'ity** or **ping'uitude** fatness. [L *pinguis*, fat]

pinguin[1]. Same as **penguin**[1].

pinguin[2] *ping'gwin*, *n* a West Indian plant, *Bromelia pinguin*; its fruit. — Also **peng'uin**. [Perh L *pinguis* fat; confused with **penguin**[1]]

pinhead, **pinhole**, etc. See under **pin**.

pinion[1] *pin'yən*, *n* a wing; the last joint of a wing; a flight feather, *esp* the outermost. — *vt* to cut a pinion of; to confine the wings of; to confine by holding or binding the arms. [OFr *pignon*, from L *pinna* (*penna*) wing]

pinion[2] *pin'yən*, *n* a small wheel with teeth or 'leaves', a small cog. [Fr *pignon* pinion, in OFr battlement, from L *pinna* pinnacle]

pinite *pin'īt* or *pīn'*, *n* a greyish-green or brown hydrous silicate of aluminium and potassium, *usu* amorphous. [Ger *Pinit*, from the *Pini* mine in Saxony]

pink[1] *pingk*, *n* a small sailing ship, *usu* with a narrow stern. — Also **pink'ie** or **pink'y**. [MDu *pin(c)ke*; Ger *Pinke*]

pink[2] *pingk*, *vt* to stab or pierce, *esp* with a sword or rapier; to decorate by cutting small holes or scallops; to make a serrated edge on. — *n* a stab; an eyelet. — *adj* **pinked** pierced or worked with small holes; with the edge serrated. — **pink'ing-īron** (*archaic*) a tool for pinking or scalloping; **pink'ing-shears** scissors with serrated cutting edges. [Cf LGer *pinken*, to peck]

pink[3] *pingk*, *n* any plant or flower of the caryophyllaceous genus *Dianthus*, including carnation and sweet william; extended to some other plants, such as **sea pink** (thrift), **Carolina pink** (see **Carolina**, and **pinkroot** below), **Indian pink** (see **pinkroot** below); the colour of a wild pink, a light red; a scarlet hunting-coat or its colour; the person wearing it; a person who is something of a socialist but hardly a red (also **pink'ō**: — *pl* **pink'os** or **pink'oes**; *colloq*); the fine flower of excellence; the most perfect condition; the highest point, the extreme; an exquisite (*obs*). — *adj* of the colour pink; slightly socialistic; slightly pornographic, somewhat blue (*cinema*, etc). — *vt* and *vi* to make or become pink. — *n* **pink'iness**. — *n* **pink'ing** the reddening of gemstones by heat. — *adj* **pink'ish** somewhat pink. — *n* **pink'ishness**. — *n* **pink'ness**. — *adj* **pink'y** slightly pink. — **pink elephants** see under **elephant**; **pink'-eye** acute contagious conjunctivitis; an acute contagious infection in horses due to a filterable virus, the eye sometimes becoming somewhat red; a red discoloration in salt fish, etc. — *adj* **pink'-eyed** having pink eyes (see also under **pink**[5]). — **pink gin** gin with angostura bitters; **pink'root** Indian pink, Carolina pink, or other species of Spigelia; its root, a vermifuge. — **in the pink** in perfect health or condition; **pink of perfection** the acme of perfection. [Ety doubtful]

pink[4] *pingk*, *n* a yellow lake (**lake**[1], qv). — **Dutch pink** a yellow lake obtained from quercitron bark; blood (*slang*). [Prob different word from **pink**[3]]

pink[5] *pingk*, *vi* to wink; to blink; to peer; to peep. — *adj* (*Shakesp*) blinking. — *adj* **pink'-eyed** having small or half-shut eyes (see also under **pink**[3]). — *adj* **pink'y** winking. [Du *pinken* to wink]

pink[6] *pingk*, *adj* (*Shakesp*) small. — *n* (*Scot*) anything small, such as a peep of light. — *adj* **pink'ie** or **pink'y** (*Scot*) small. — *n* (*Scot*, *US*) the little finger. [Du *pink* the little finger]

pink[7] *pingk* or **penk** *pengk*, *n* a minnow; a samlet. [Cf Ger dialect *Pinke*]

pink[8] *pingk*, *n* a tinkling sound; a chaffinch's call; a chaffinch; a type of sea bird (*obs*). — *vi* (of an engine) to detonate or knock. — *n* (in an engine) a characteristic metallic knocking noise caused by detonation. [Imit]

Pinkerton *ping'kər-tən*, *n* a private detective. — Also without *cap*. [Allan *Pinkerton*, 1819–84, American detective]

pinkie. See under **pink**[1,6].

pinko. See under **pink**[3].

Pinkster *pingk'stər*, (*archaic US*) *n* Whitsuntide. — Also **Pinxter**. [Du *pinkster*(*en*), *MDu pinxter*, ultimately, from Gr *pentēkostē* pentecost]

pinky. See under **pink**[1,3,5,6].

Pinna *pin'ə*, *n* a genus of molluscs related to the mussels, with triangular shells. [Gr]

pinna *pin'ə*, (*biol*) *n* a leaflet of a pinnate leaf, or any similar expansion; a wing, fin, feather, or similar expansion; the outer ear, *esp* the upper part: — *pl* **pinn'ae** (-*ē*). — *adj* **pinn'ate** or **pinn'ated** shaped like a feather; having a row of leaflets on each side of the rachis, or other expansions arranged in similar manner; (*usu* **pennate**) having wings, fins, or wing-like tufts. — *adv* **pinn'ately**. — *adj* **pinnatifid** (*pin-at'i-fid*) (of leaves) pinnately cut roughly halfway down. — *adj* **pinnatipart'ite** (of leaves) pinnately cut rather more than halfway. — *adj* **pinnat'iped** (of birds) with lobate feet. — *adj* **pinnat'isect** (of leaves) pinnately cut nearly to the midrib. — *n* **pinn'iped** (-*i-ped*) or **pinn'ipede** (-*pēd*; see **-ped**) a member of the **Pinnipē'dia**, or paddle-footed Carnivora, ie seals, sea-lions, and walruses. — *adj* **pinn'ūlate** or **pinn'ulated**. — *n* **pinn'ūle** a lobe of a leaflet of a pinnate leaf; a branchlet of a crinoid arm. — Also **pinn'ūla**. [L *pinna* a feather, dimin *pinnula*]

pinnace *pin'is* or -*əs*, *n* a small vessel with oars and sails; a boat with eight oars; a warship's tender boat; loosely, a small boat; a whore (*fig*; *obs*). [Fr *pinasse*]

pinnacle *pin'ə-kl*, *n* a slender turret or spiry structure in architecture; a high pointed rock or mountain like a spire; the highest point. — *vt* to be the pinnacle of; to set on a pinnacle; to raise as a pinnacle; to provide with pinnacles. — *adj* **pinn'acled**. [Fr *pinacle*, from LL *pinnāculum*, dimin from L *pinna* a feather]

pinnae, **pinnate**, etc, **pinnatifid**... to ... **pinnatisect**. See under **pinna**.

pinner *pin'ər*. See under **pin** and **pinder**.

pinnet *pin'it*, *n* a pinnacle (*Scott*); a streamer (*Scot*). [Perh **pennant**, associated with L *pinna* pinnacle]

pinnie or **pinny** *pin'i*, *n* short for **pinafore**, *esp* applied to an apron or overall worn by a woman or child.

pinniewinkle. See **pinnywinkle**.

pinniped, **pinnipede**, **Pinnipedia**. See under **pinna**.

pinnock *pin'ək*, (*dialect*) *n* the hedge-sparrow; the blue tit. [ME *pynnuc*]

pinnoed *pin'ōd*, (*Spenser*) *pa p* pinioned. [Perh a misprint]

pinnula, **pinnulate**, **pinnule**, etc. See under **pinna**.

pinny. See **pinnie**.

pinnywinkle, **pinniewinkle**, *pin'i-wingk-l*, and **pilniewinks** *pil'ni-wingks*, mistaken forms of **pilliwinks**.

pinochle, **pinocle** or **penuchle** *pēn'uk-l*, *n* a game like bezique; (in this game) a declaration of queen of spades and knave of diamonds. [Origin unknown]

pinocytosis *pī-nō-sī-tō'sis*, (*immunol*) *n* ingestion by cells of vesicles containing fluid from the environment. [From Gr *pinein* to drink, and **-cyt-** and **-osis**(2)]

pinole *pē-nō'lā*, *n* parched Indian corn or other seeds ground and eaten with milk; a mixture of vanilla and aromatic substances in chocolate. [Sp from Aztec *pinolli*]

piñon *pin'yon* or *pēn'yōn*, (*US*) *n* an edible pine seed; the tree bearing it. [Sp]

Pinot *pē'nō*, (also without *cap*) *n* a variety of both black and white grape; a wine made from the Pinot grape, eg *Pinot Noir*. [Fr *pin* pine, from the similarity of the grape bunch to a pine-cone in shape]

pinpoint. See under **pin**.

pinscher. See **Doberman pinscher**.

pint *pīnt*, *n* a measure of capacity equal to half a quart or 4 gills, in imperial measure (liquid or dry), about 0·568 litre or 20 fluid ounces, in US measure (liquid) 0·473 litre or 16 US fluid ounces, (dry) 0·551 litre; a pint of beer (*colloq*). — *n* **pint'a** (*pīn'tə*; *colloq*) a pint of milk; generally, a drink. — **pint'-pot** a pot for holding a pint, *esp* a pewter pot for beer; a seller or drinker of beer. — *adj* **pint'-size** or **-sized** (*colloq*) very small, *usu* of a person. — **pint'-stoup** a vessel for holding a Scots pint (about 3 imperial pints). [Fr *pinte*; origin uncertain]

pinta[1]. See under **pint**.

pinta[2] *pin'tə*, *n* a contagious skin disease occurring in the tropics, characterized by loss of skin pigmentation, also called **mal del pinto** (*mal del pin'tō*; *Sp*, disease of the spotted person). [Sp, from LL *pinctus*, from L *pictus* painted]

pintable. See under **pin**.

pintado *pin-tä'dō*, *n* a kind of petrel, the Cape pigeon; the guinea fowl; chintz (*obs*): — *pl* **pinta'dos**. [Port, painted]

pintail. See under **pin**.

Pinteresque *pin-tə-resk'*, *adj* in the style of the characters, situations, etc, of the plays of Harold *Pinter*, 20c English dramatist, marked *esp* by halting dialogue, uncertainty of identity, and air of menace.

pintle *pin'tl*, *n* the penis (*archaic* or *dialect*); a bolt or pin, *esp* one on which something turns; the plunger or needle of the injection valve of an oil engine, opened by oil pressure on an annular face, and closed by a spring. [OE *pintel*]

pinto *pin'tō*, (*US*) *adj* mottled; piebald. — *n* a piebald horse: — *pl* **pin'tos**. — **pinto bean** a kind of bean resembling a kidney bean, mottled in colour. [Sp, painted]

pinxit *pingk'sit*, (*L*) (he or she) painted (this). — *abbrev* **pinx**.

Pinxter. See under **Pinkster**.

piny[1]. See **pine**[1].

piny[2] *pī'ni*, (*obs* or *dialect*) *n* same as **peony**.

Pinyin *pin'yin'*, *n* an alphabetic system (using Roman letters) for the transcription of Chinese, *esp* Mandarin. [Chin, phonetic, alphabetic (transcription)]

piolet *pyo-lā'* or *pyō-lā'*, *n* an ice-axe; an early form of ski stick. [Fr, from Piedmontese dialect *piola*]

pion *pī'on*, *n* a *pi*-meson (see **pi**[1] and **meson**). — *adj* **pīon'ic**.

pioned *pī'ə-nid*, (*Shakesp*) *adj perh* trenched, excavated (cf **pioneer**); *perh* overgrown with wild orchises, said to be called **pionies** (peonies) at Stratford.

pioneer *pī-ə-nēr'*, *n* someone who is among the first in new fields of enterprise, exploration, colonization, research, etc; a military artisan, employed in peacetime in painting and repairing barracks, and such work, in war in preparing the way for an army, and minor engineering works, such as trenching; an excavator; a labourer. — *adj* (of a species) characteristically among the first to establish itself on the bared ground (*bot*). — *vt* to act as pioneer to; to prepare as a pioneer. — *n* **pī'oner** or **py'oner** (*Shakesp*) a military pioneer; an excavator. — *n* **pī'oning** (*Spenser* **py'onings**) pioneer work; trenching. — **pioneer species** (*bot*) a species which tends to be among the first to occupy bare ground. [OFr *peonier* (Fr *pionnier*), from *pion* a foot-soldier, from LL *pedō*, *pedōnis*, from L *pēs*, *pedis* a foot; cf **pawn**[2] and **peon**]

pioney and **piony** *pī'ə-ni*, *n* obsolete forms of **peony**.

pioted. See under **pyot**.

piou-piou *pū-pū*, *n* a French private soldier. [Fr slang; perh *pion*; see **peon**]

pious *pī'əs*, *adj* dutiful; showing, having, or resulting from piety; professing to be religious. — *adv* **pi'ously**. — **pious fraud** a deception practised with a good end in view; a religious humbug (*colloq*); **pious opinion** a belief widely held but not made a matter of faith. [L *pius*]

pioy, **pioye**. Same as **peeoy**.

pip[1] *pip*, *n* roup in poultry, etc; an ailment or distemper vaguely imagined; syphilis (*slang*); spleen, hump, disgust, offence (*colloq*). — *vt* to affect with the pip. — **give someone the pip** (*colloq*) to annoy or offend someone. [Appar from MDu *pippe*, from LL *pipīta*, from L *pītuīta* rheum]

pip[2] *pip*, *n* a pippin (*obs*); a small hard seed or fruitlet in a fleshy fruit. — *adj* **pip'less**. — *adj* **pipp'y**. [Appar from **pippin**]

pip[3] *pip*, earlier **peep** or **peepe** (*Shakesp*) *pēp*, *n* a spot on dice, cards or dominoes; a star as a mark of rank (*colloq*); a speck; (on a radar screen) indication, eg spot of light, of the presence of an object; a single blossom or corolla in a cluster (*bot*). — **a pip** (or **peepe**) **out** two-and-thirty, one in excess of the total of pips aimed at in the old card-game of one-and-thirty, hence, having overshot one's mark; tipsy. [Ety uncertain]

pip[4] *pip*, *n* a short, high-pitched signal analogous in sound to the word 'pip', *esp* as used in radio signals, the speaking clock, payphones, etc. — **the pips** (*colloq*) the six pips broadcast by the BBC, made up of five short (counting down from 55 to 59 seconds) and one long (marking the start of the new minute and hour).

pip[5] *pip*, (*slang*) *vt* to blackball; to pluck, plough, reject, or fail in an examination; to foil, thwart, get the better of; to hit with a bullet, etc; to wound; to kill; to defeat. — *vi* to die (*esp* with *out*; *archaic*): — *pr p* **pipp'ing**; *pa t* and *pa p* **pipped**. — **pipped at the post** defeated at the point when success seemed certain, or at the last moment. [Perh from **pip**[2]]

pip[6] *pip*, *vi* to chirp, as a young bird does. [Cf **peep**[1]]

pipa *pē'pə*, *n* a toad of the *Pipa* genus of S American toads, the female being noted for carrying her developing young on her back, the Surinam toad. [Surinam dialect]

pipage. See under **pipe**[1].

pipal, **pipul** or **peepul** *pē'pul* or *-pəl*, *n* the bo tree. [Hindi *pīpul*]

pipe[1] *pīp*, *n* a metal or plastic tube for the conveyance of water, gas, etc; any tube, or tubular part or thing, natural or artificial; a musical wind instrument, or part of an instrument, consisting of or including a tube; any of an organ's upright metal tubes; (in *pl*) a bagpipe; the note of a bird; a voice, *esp* a high voice; (*usu* in *pl*) the windpipe; any of various hollow organs in an animal body; a pipe-like volcanic vent, a cylindrical mass of ore, etc; an entrance to a decoy; a tube with a bowl at one end for smoking; a fill of tobacco; the smoking of a fill of tobacco; a stick of eg pipeclay for curling hair or a wig (*Sterne*); a boatswain's whistle. — *vi* to play a musical pipe; to whistle (as the wind or a boatswain does); to speak or sing, *esp* in a high voice; to peep or sing, as a bird does; to weep; to become pipy. — *vt* to play on a pipe; to lead or call by means of a pipe; (with *in*) to accompany or call ceremonially in with pipe music; to render, or cause to be, by playing a pipe; to propagate by piping (*hortic*); to force (icing, cream, etc) out through a nozzle in a thin strip as decoration; to ornament with piping; to supply with pipes; to convey by pipe; to transmit (television, radio signals) by electricity or along a wire. — *n* **pīp'age** conveyance or distribution by pipe. — *adj* **piped** (*pīpt*) tubular or fistulous; transported by means of a pipe; transmitted simultaneously to many outlets from a central control location by means of an audio system, telephone or electricity line, etc. — *n* **pipe'ful** enough to fill a pipe: — *pl* **pipe'fuls**. — *adj* **pipe'less**. — *adj* **pipe'like**. — *n* **pīp'er** a player on a pipe, *esp* a bagpipe; a broken-winded horse; a young pigeon or other bird; a kind of gurnard; a pipe-smoker; a decoy dog; a kind of caddis-worm. — *adj* **pīp'ing** playing a pipe; sounding like a pipe; producing a shrill sound, whistling; thin and high-pitched; characterized by pipe-playing (as opposed to martial music, as in the phrase *the piping times of peace*); hissing hot; very hot. — *n* the action of the verb pipe in any sense; pipe-playing; a system of pipes; tubing; small cord used as trimming for clothes; strings and twists of icing ornamenting a cake; a slip or cutting from a joint of a stem (*hortic*); the action of hydraulicking. — *adj* **pīp'y** pipelike; having pipes; piping. — **pipe'-case** a case for a tobacco-pipe; **pipe'clay** a fine white, nearly pure, kaolin, free from iron, used for making tobacco-pipes and fine earthenware, and for whitening military belts, etc. — *vt* to whiten with pipeclay. — **pipe-cleaner** a length of wire with tufts of fabric twisted into it, used to clean pipe-stems; **piped music** continuous background music played in a restaurant, etc, or piped from a central studio to other buildings; **pipe dream** a futile and unreal hope or fancy such as one has when relaxing while smoking a pipe (*orig* an opium-smoker's fantasy); **pipe'-dreamer**; **pipe'fish** a fish (of several species) of the sea-horse family, a long thin fish covered with hard plates, the jaws forming a long tube; **pipe fitting** any of the wide variety of pipe connecting-pieces used to make turns, junctions, and reductions in piping systems; **pipe'-key** a key with a hollow barrel; **pipe'-layer** someone who lays pipes for water, gas, etc; a political wire-puller (*old US slang*); **pipe'-laying**; **pipeless organ** a musical instrument, played like an organ, in which sounds, built up from whatever harmonics may be chosen, are produced by a loudspeaker; **pipe'-light** or **-lighter** a spill for lighting a pipe; **pipe'line** a long continuous line of piping to carry water from a reservoir, oil from an oilfield, etc; a line of piping to carry solid materials; any continuous line of communication, or supply, or of progress and development (*fig*); see also **in the pipeline** below. — *adj* (of a processor, program, etc) carrying out two or more instructions simultaneously by performing processes in one sequence (*comput*). — **pipe'lining**; **pipe major** the chief of a band of bagpipers; **Pipe Office** (*hist*) an office in the Court of Exchequer in which the Clerk of the

Pipe made out the Pipe Roll; **pipe'-opener** (*colloq*) a walk or spell of exercise in the fresh air; a practice-game or trial run; **pipe organ** a musical organ with pipes; **pipe'-rack** a rack for storing tobacco-pipes; **Pipe Roll** (*hist*) the Great Roll of the Exchequer, containing yearly accounts of sheriffs, etc (possibly from its pipelike form); **pipe'-stem** the tube of a tobacco-pipe; **pipe'stone** a red argillaceous stone used by N American Indians for making tobacco-pipes; **pipe'-stopp'le** or **-stapp'le** (*Scot*) a tobacco-pipe stem; anything very thin and brittle-looking; **pipe'-track** the course of a pipe across country; **pipe'-tree** (*obs*) mock orange (*white pipe-tree*); the lilac (*blue pipe-tree*); **pipe'work** a vein of ore in the form of a pipe; piping or pipes collectively, eg in an organ; **pipe'wort** a rare rush-like water plant (*Eriocaulon septangulare*) of Ireland and the Hebrides, the only European representative of its family, Eriocaulaceae; **pipe'-wrench** a wrench that grips a pipe when turned one way; **piping crow** an Australian bird (*Gymnorhina*) called a magpie, really related to the shrikes; **piping hare** a pika. — **boatswain's pipe** see **boatswain's whistle** under **whistle**; **drunk as a piper** very drunk; **in the pipeline** waiting to be considered or dealt with; in preparation; **pay the piper** to bear the expense (and so **call the tune** have control); to have to pay heavily; **pipe and tabor** a small recorder, fingered by the left hand, and a small drum beaten with the right, formerly in use in rustic jollities; **pipe down** to dismiss (a ship's company) from muster (the final order of the day); to subside into silence; to stop talking or be quiet (*colloq*); **pipe of peace** see **calumet**; **pipe one's eye, tune one's pipes** to weep; **pipe up** (*colloq*) to interject, say something; to begin to speak; **piping hot** (of food, *usu* when served) very hot, literally so hot as to make a hissing or sizzling noise; **put that in your pipe and smoke it!** (*colloq*; of some unwelcome home truth, etc) there! how do you like that? [OE *pīpe*, from L *pīpāre* to cheep; cf Du *pijp*, Ger *Pfeife*]

pipe[2] *pīp*, *n* a cask or butt (of wine), of two hogsheads, varying according to the wine, ordinarily about 105 gallons in Britain, 126 US gallons; a Portuguese wooden cask or *pipa*, used for storage and as a measure of (*esp* port) wine, holding 500 litres (formerly 429 litres); the measure of a pipe. — **pipe'-wine** (*Shakesp*) wine from the cask, not bottled. [OFr *pipe* cask, tube; cf **pipe**[1]]

pip emma *pip em'ə*, (*mil slang*) *adv* post meridiem, in the afternoon (cf **ack emma**). [Formerly signallers' names for the letters PM]

Piper *pip'ər*, *n* the pepper genus, giving name to a family **Piperā'ceae** of dicotyledons. — *adj* **piperaceous** (*-ā'shəs*). — *n* **piper'azine** (*piper*id*ine* and **az-** nitrogen) a crystalline nitrogen compound used in medicine, insecticides and anti-corrosion substances. — *adj* **piperic** (*pip-er'ik*) applied to an acid ($C_{12}H_{10}O_4$) obtained from piperine. — *n* **piper'idine** a liquid base ($C_5H_{11}N$) with a peppery odour, obtained from piperine. — *n* **pip'erine** an alkaloid ($C_{17}H_{19}O_3N$) found in pepper. — *n* **pip'eronal** (or *pi-per'*) a phenolic aldehyde of very pleasant odour, used as a perfume and in flavourings, etc — also called **heliotropin**. [L *piper* pepper]

piper. See under **pipe**[1].

pipette *pi-pet'*, *n* a tube for transferring and measuring fluids. — *vt* to transfer or measure, using a pipette. [Fr, dimin of *pipe* pipe]

pipi[1] *pē'pē*, *n* a Brazilian Caesalpinia; its pods used in tanning. [Tupí *pipai*]

pipi[2] *pi'pē*, *n* any of various edible shellfishes of Australasia. [Mauri]

piping. See under **pipe**[1].

pipistrelle *pip-is-trel'*, *n* a small reddish-brown bat, the commonest British bat. [Fr, from Ital *pipistrello*, a form of *vespertilio*, from L *vespertiliō* bat, from *vesper* evening]

pipit *pip'it*, *n* any member of a lark-like genus (*Anthus*) of birds related to wagtails. [Prob imit]

pipkin *pip'kin*, *n* a small pot, now only of earthenware; a piggin (*US dialect*). [Poss a dimin of **pipe**[2]]

pipped. See under **pip**[5].

pippin *pip'in*, *n* a fruit pip (*obs*); an apple of various varieties; something or someone especially nice, attractive, good, etc (*old slang*). [OFr *pepin*]

pipping. See under **pip**[5].

pippy. See **pip**[2].

pipsqueak *pip'skwēk*, (*slang*) *n* something or someone insignificant or contemptible; a German shell of the 1st World War; a two-stroke motor-cycle. [**pip**[4] and **squeak**]

pipul. Same as **pipal**.

pipy. See under **pipe**[1].

piquant *pē'kənt* or *-änt*, *adj* stinging; pleasantly pungent; appetizing; stimulating, provocative. — *n* **piq'uancy**. — *adv* **piq'uantly**. [Fr, pr p of *piquer* to prick]

pique[1] *pēk*, *n* animosity or ill-feeling; offence taken; a feeling of anger or vexation caused by wounded pride; resentment of a slight; dudgeon; point or punctilio (*obs*). — *vt* to wound the pride of; to nettle; to arouse, stir, provoke; (*reflexive*) to pride (oneself; with *on*, *upon*, or (*Boswell*) *at*). [Fr *pique* a pike, pique, *piquer* to prick; cf **pike**[2], **prick**]

pique[2] *pēk*, *n* (in piquet) the scoring of 30 points in one hand before the other side scores at all. — *vt* to score a pique against. — *vi* to score a pique. [Fr *pic*; see **piquet**[2]]

pique[3] *pēk*, (*Browning*) *n* for **peak**[1].

piqué *pē'kā*, *n* a stiff corded cotton fabric; inlaid work of gold or silver in point or strip (sometimes with mother-of-pearl) on tortoiseshell or ivory. — Also *adj*. — **piqué work** inlaying in piqué; needlework with a raised design made by stitching. [Fr, pa p of *piquer* to prick]

piquet[1]. Same as **picket**.

piquet[2] *pi-ket'*, *-kā'*, *n* a game for two with 32 cards, with scoring for declarations and tricks. [Fr; origin unknown]

Pir *pēr*, (also without *cap*) *n* a Muslim title of honour given to a holy man or religious leader. [Pers *pīr* old man, chief]

piracy. See under **pirate**.

piragua *pi-ra'gwə* or *-rä'*, *n* a S American dugout canoe, or a craft with a single trunk as foundation, often a schooner-rigged barge. — Also **peria'gua**, or (*Fr*) **pirogue** (*pi-rōg'*). [Sp *piragua*, from Carib *piraqua*]

pirai. See **piranha**.

Pirandellian *pir-an-del'i-ən*, *adj* pertaining to, or in the style of, the writings of the Italian dramatist and novelist Luigi *Pirandello* (1867–1936).

piranha *pi-rän'ə*, **piraña** *pē-rän'yə*, **piraya** *pē-rä'yə*, **perai** *pe-rī'*, or **pirai** *pē-*, *n* a ferocious S American river-fish (*Serrasalmo* or *Pygocentrus*) of the Characinidae. [Port from Tupí *piranya*, *piraya*]

pirarucu *pē-rä-rōō-kōō'*, *n* the arapaima.

pirate *pī'rət* or *-rit*, *n* a person who, without authority, attempts to capture ships at sea; a robber or marauder operating at sea; a pirates' ship; a person who publishes a work without the authority of the owner of the copyright, or otherwise makes use of or takes over another person's work without legal sanction; a private bus, or its driver, plying on the recognized route of others; someone who, in ordinary life, shows the predatory spirit of the sea rovers; a person who runs an unlicensed radio station. — *adj* operating illegally; (loosely) operating, produced, sold, etc, separately from and in defiance of the official system. — *vt* to rob as a pirate; to publish or reproduce without permission of the copyright owner, or otherwise usurp (someone else's work or ideas); to use, tap, operate, produce, etc (something) illegally. — *n* **piracy** (*pī'rə-si* or (*rare*) *pi'*) the crime of a pirate; robbery on the high seas; unauthorized publication or reproduction; infringement of copyright. — *adj* **piratic** (*pī-rat'ik*) or **pirat'ical** pertaining to a pirate; practising piracy. — *adv* **pirat'ically**. [L *pīrāta*, from Gr *peirātēs*, from *peiraein* to attempt]

piraya. See **piranha**.

piri-piri[1] *pir'ē-pir'ē* or *pēr'ē-pēr'ē*, *n* a sauce made with red peppers. — Also *adj*. [Ety uncertain; perh from Swahili *pilipili* pepper]

piri-piri[2] *pir'ē-pir'ē* or *pēr'ē-pēr'ē*, *n* a New Zealand weed with prickly burrs (*Acaenae sanguisorbae*) used medicinally and as a tea. [Maori]

pirl. See **purl**[1].

pirlicue or **purlicue** *pir'* or *pûr'li-kū*, (*Scot*) *n* a peroration; a résumé in conclusion. — *vt* and *vi* to summarize in conclusion. [Origin uncertain]

pirn *pûrn* or (*Scot*) *pirn*, *n* a reel, bobbin, or spool. — **wind someone a bonny pirn** to set a fine problem for someone, involve someone in difficulties. [Origin unknown]

pirnie *pir'ni*, (*Scot*) *adj* unevenly wrought; striped. — *n* (*Scot*) a striped woollen nightcap. — *adj* **pirn'it** (*Scot*) interwoven with different colours; striped. [Appar connected with **pirn**]

pirogue *pi-rōg'*. See **piragua**.

pirouette *pir-ōō-et'*, *n* (in dancing) a spin performed on the tip or point of the toe or on the ball of the foot. — *vi* to spin round thus. — *n* **pirouett'er**. [Fr]

pirozhki *pē-rozh'kē* or **piroshki** *pē-rosh'kē*, *n pl* small triangular pastries with meat, fish or vegetable fillings. [Russ, little pies]

pis aller *pē-zal-ā* or *pēz a'lā*, (*Fr*) the last or worst shift, a makeshift.

Pisces *pīs'ēz*, *pis'ēz*, *pis'kēz* or *pisk'ās*, *n pl* the class of fishes (*zool*); the Fishes, the twelfth sign of the zodiac, or the constellation that formerly coincided with it (*astron*); a person born between 20 February and 21 March under this sign. — *n* **piscary** (*pisk'ə-ri*) the right of fishing; a fishing pond. — *n* **piscā'tor** an angler: — *fem* **piscā'trix**. — *adj* **piscatorial** (*pis-kə-tō'ri-əl* or *-tö'*) or **piscatory** (*pis'kə-tə-ri*) relating to fishing or fishermen; fishing. — *combining form* **pisci-** (*pis-i*) denoting fish. — *adj* **piscicolous** (*pis-ik'ə-ləs*) parasitic in or on fishes. — *adj* **piscicul'tural**. — *n* **pis'ciculture** the rearing of fish by artificial methods. — *n* **piscicul'turist**. — *n* **piscifau'na** the assemblage of fishes in a region, formation, etc. — *adj* **pis'ciform** having the form of a fish. — *adj* **piscine** (*pis'īn*) of fishes; of the nature of a fish. — *adj* **pisciv'orous** fish-eating, living on fishes. [L *piscis* a fish; pl *piscēs*; *piscātor* fisher]

piscina *pis-ē'nə* or *pis-ī'nə*, *n* a fish-pond; a swimming-pool (as in Roman baths); a basin and drain in old churches, *usu* in a niche south of an altar, into which water used in washing the sacred vessels was emptied: — *pl* **pisci'nas**, or **pisci'nae**. — Also **piscine** (*pis'ēn* or *-ēn'*). [L *piscīna*, from *piscis* fish]

piscine[1], **piscivorous**. See under **Pisces**.

piscine[2]. See **piscina**.

pisé *pē'zā*, *n* rammed earth or clay for walls or floors. — Also *adj*. [Fr]

pish *pish*, (*old-fashioned*) *interj* expression of impatience or contempt. — *n* an utterance of the exclamation. — *vt* to pooh-pooh. [Imit]

pishogue *pi-shōg'*, (*Ir*) *n* sorcery. [Ir *piseog*]

pisiform *pī'si-förm* or *piz'i-förm*, *adj* pea-shaped. — *n* a pea-shaped bone of the carpus. [L *pisum* pea, and *fōrma* shape]

pisky. See **pixie**.

pismire *pis'mīr*, (*archaic*) or *dialect*) *n* an ant or emmet. [**piss**, from the strong smell of the ant-hill, and ME *mire* (doubtful OE *mīre*) ant]

pisolite *pī'sə-līt* or *piz'ə-līt*, (*geol*) *n* a coarse oolite. — *adj* **pisolitic** (*-lit'ik*). [Gr *pisos* pease, and *lithos* stone]

piss *pis*, (*vulgar*) *vi* to urinate. — *vt* to discharge as urine; to urinate on. — *n* urine. — *adj* **pissed** (*slang*) extremely drunk; annoyed, pissed off (*NAm*). — **piss'-a-bed** (*dialect*) the dandelion; **piss artist** (*slang*) someone who drinks heavily; a person who is all talk, a foolish show-off; **piss'head** (*slang*) a heavy drinker, a habitual drunkard; **piss'-pot** (*archaic*) a chamberpot; **piss-up** (*vulgar slang*) a drinking bout. — **a piece of piss** (*vulgar slang*) an easy thing to do, a piece of cake; **piss about** or **around** (*slang*) to behave in a foolish or time-wasting way; **pissed off** (*slang*) annoyed; fed up; **piss off** (*interj*; *vulg*) go away; **piss (someone) off** (*slang*) to annoy or upset (someone); **take the piss (out of)** (*slang*) to mock, tease (*n* **piss'-taker**. — *n* **piss'-taking**). [Fr *pisser*]

pissasphalt *pis'as-falt*, *n* a semi-liquid bitumen. [Gr *pissa* pitch, and *asphaltos* asphalt]

pissoir *pē-swär*, *n* a public urinal. [Fr]

pistachio *pis-ta'chi-ō*, *-shi-ō*, or *-chyō*, or *pis-tä'*, or *pis-tā'*, *n* the almond-flavoured yellowish-green fruit-kernel of a small western Asiatic tree (*Pistacia vera*) of the same genus of the cashew family as the mastic tree; flavouring obtained from these nuts; light green colour: — *pl* **pista'chios**. — Also *adj*. [Sp *pistacho* and Ital *pistacchio*, from LL *pistāquium*, from Gr *pistakion*, from Pers *pistah*]

pistareen *pis-tə-rēn'*, *n* an old Spanish two-real piece formerly used in the US. [Prob **peseta**]

piste *pēst*, *n* a beaten track, *esp* a ski trail in the snow; a strip of ground used for some sporting activity, eg fencing. [Fr]

pistil *pis'til*, (*bot*) *n* the ovary of a flower, with its style and stigma. — *adj* **pis'tillary**. — *adj* **pis'tillate** having a pistil but no (functional) stamens, female. — *n* **pis'tillode** an abortive pistil. [L *pistillum* a pestle]

pistol *pis'tl*, *n* a small hand gun, held in one hand when fired. — *vt* to shoot with a pistol: — *pr p* **pis'tolling**; *pa t* and *pa p* **pis'tolled**. — *n* **pistoleer'** (*obs*) someone who carries or uses a pistol. — **pistol grip** a handle (*usu* with a trigger mechanism) for a camera, etc, shaped like the butt of a pistol; **pistol shot**. — *vt* **pis'tol-whip** to hit (someone) with a pistol. — **hold a pistol to someone's head** (*fig*) to use threats to force someone to do what one wants. [Through Fr and Ger from Czech]

pistole *pis-tōl'*, (*hist*) *n* any of numerous old gold coins of varying value, eg a Spanish coin of the 17c worth about 17 contemporary English shillings, or a Scots 12-pound piece of William III worth one contemporary English pound. — *n* **pis'tolet** (*hist*) a pistol; a pistole; a gold coin of various kinds, of an average worth of 6s in the 16c. [OFr *pistole*, earlier *pistolet*]

pistoleer, **pistolling**, etc, **pistol-whip**. See under **pistol**.

piston *pis'tən*, *n* a cylindrical piece moving to and fro in a hollow cylinder, as in engines and pumps; a valve mechanism for altering the effective length of the tube in brass and musical instruments; a push-key for combining a number of organ stops. — **piston ring** a split ring fitted in a circumferential groove around a piston rim forming a spring-loaded seal against the cylinder wall; **piston rod** the rod to which the piston is fixed, and which moves up and down with it. [Fr, from Ital *pistone*, from *pestare* to pound, from L *pinsere*, *pistum*]

pit[1] *pit*, *n* a hole in the earth; a mine shaft; a mine, *esp* a coalmine; a place from where minerals are dug; a prison, *esp* a castle prison entered from above (*archaic*); a cavity in the ground or in a floor for any purpose, such as the reception of ashes or the inspection of the underside of motor cars, etc; a place beside the track where cars in a race can be refuelled and repaired; a hole for storing root-crops; a covered heap of potatoes, etc; a grave, *esp* one for many bodies; hell, or its lowest depths; a hole used as a trap for wild animals; an enclosure in which animals are kept in captivity (*esp* bears); an enclosure for cockfights or the like; *orig* the ground floor of a theatre, or its occupants, or the part of the ground floor behind the stalls, now *usu* the area in front of the stage reserved for the orchestra in a theatre (also **orchestra pit**); a bed (*slang*); a very dirty or untidy place (*slang*); part of a corn-exchange floor assigned to some particular business, now *esp* a securities or commodities trading floor (*US*); a noisy card game mimicking a US corn exchange; any hollow or depression, eg the *pit of the stomach* below the breastbone; an indentation left by smallpox; a minute depression in a surface; a hollow made by a raindrop; a thin place in a cell-wall, affording communication with another cell (*bot*). — *vt* to mark with little hollows;

to lay in a pit; to set (eg cocks in a cockpit); to match (with *against*). — *vi* to become marked with pits; to retain an impression for a time after pressing (*med*): — *pr p* **pitt'ing**; *pa t* and *pa p* **pitt'ed**. — *adj* **pitt'ed** marked with small pits. — *n* **pitt'ing**. — *n* **pitt'ite** (*old*) someone who frequents the pit of a theatre. — **pit brow** (*coalmining*) the top of a shaft; **pit bull** or **pit bull terrier** a large breed of bull terrier developed *orig* for dog-fighting; **pit'-coal** coal in the ordinary sense, not *charcoal*; **pit'-dwelling** a primitive home made by roofing over a pit; **pit'fall** a lightly covered hole as a trap; a hidden danger or unsuspected difficulty (*fig*); **pit'head** (*coalmining*) the ground at the mouth of a pit, and the machinery, etc, on it; **pit'man** a man who works in a coal pit or a sawpit, *esp* at sinking, repair, and inspection of shafts and at pumping in a mine; a rod connecting a rotary with a reciprocating part (*US*); **pit-pony** a pony employed for haulage in a coalmine; **pit'prop** a (*usu* timber) support in the workings of a coal mine; **pit'-saw** a saw used in a sawpit; **pit'-saw'yer** a bottom-sawyer; **pit stop** a stop a racing-car makes during a motor race when it goes into the pits for repairs; **pit'-village** a group of miners' houses near a pit; a cluster of pit-dwellings; **pit viper** any member of an American group of snakes, including the rattle-snake, able to detect prey in the dark by means of a pit sensitive to body heat between eye and nose. — **pit and gallows** a feudal baron's right to drown female and hang male felons; **the pits** (*slang*) the absolute worst place, conditions, thing, person, etc possible. [OE *pytt*, from L *puteus* a well]

pit[2] *pit*, (*esp NAm*) *n* a fruit-stone. — *vt* to remove the stone from: — *pr p* **pitt'ing**; *pa t* and *pa p* **pitt'ed**. [Appar Du *pit*]

pit[3] *pit*, (*Scot*) *vt* to put: — *pa t* **pat** (*pät*); *pa p* **putten** (*put'n*) or **pitt'en**. [See **put**[1]]

pita[1] *pē'tə*, *n* the fibre of various species of Bromelia, Agave, etc. — Also **pi'ta-flax** or **-hemp**. [Sp, from Quechua *pita* fine thread]

pita[2]. See **pitta**.

Pitaka *pit'ə-kə*, *n* any one of the three divisions of the Buddhist canon. [Sans, basket]

pitapat *pit'ə-pat*, **pitty-pat** *pit'i-pat* or **pit-pat** *pit'pat'*, *adv* with a pattering or tapping noise; with a palpitating sensation. — *adj* fluttering; pattering. — *n* a light, quick step; a succession of light taps; a pattering noise; a palpitating sensation. — *vi* to step or tread quickly; to patter or tap lightly; to palpitate: — *pr p* **pit-a-patt'ing**; *pa t* and *pa p* **pit-a-patt'ed**. [Imit]

pitara or **pitarah**. See **petara**.

pitch[1] *pich*, *n* the black shining residue of distillation of tar, etc; extended to various bituminous and resinous substances, such as *Burgundy pitch*; resin from certain pine trees. — *vt* to smear, cover, or caulk with pitch. — *n* **pitch'iness**. — *adj* **pitch'y** like or characteristic of pitch; smeared with pitch; full of pitch; black. — *adj* **pitch'-black** black as pitch. — *adj* **pitch-dark'** utterly dark. — **pitch'pine** a name for several American pines that yield pitch and timber (*Pinus palustris*, *Pinus rigida*, etc); **pitch'stone** a volcanic glass of resinous lustre, *usu* acid; **pitch'-tree** a tree yielding pitch, turpentine, or resin, *esp* silver fir, spruce, kauri pine, Amboina pine. [OE *pic*, from L *pix*, *picis*]

pitch[2] *pich*, *vt* to thrust or fix in the ground; to set up; to establish; to set or plant firmly; to set in position; to lay out for sale; to set, cover, stud, or face; to pave (a road) with stones set on end or on edge; to make a foundation of stones for; to set in array (*obs*); to pit in opposition; to determine or fix (*obs*); to establish the slope of; to set in a key, to give this or that musical pitch, emotional tone, or degree of moral exaltation, etc, to; to fling, throw, or toss, *esp* in such a manner as to fall flat or in a definite position; to loft so as not to roll much on falling (*golf*); to bowl (the ball) so as to strike the ground (at a particular spot) (*cricket*); to deliver to the batsman by an overhand or underhand throw (*baseball*). — *vi* to settle; to alight; to fix the choice (on); to encamp; to plunge forward; to oscillate about a transverse axis (*aeronautics*); (of a ship) to plunge and lift alternately at bow and stern; to slope down; to descend or fall away abruptly; to interlock: — *pa t* and *pa p* **pitched**, or *obs* **pight** (qv). — *n* the act or manner of pitching; a throw or cast; degree, *esp* of elevation or depression; highest point (*fig*; literal meaning is *archaic*); height; a descent; slope or degree of slope; ground between the wickets (*cricket*); a place set apart for playing or practising a game; the point where a ball alights; a station taken by a street trader, etc; a salesman's particular line of persuasive talk; the degree of acuteness of a sound that makes it a high or low, etc, note, or the standard degree of acuteness assigned to a particular note (*music*); degree of intensity; distance between successive points or things, such as the centres of teeth in a wheel or a saw, characters in type or the threads of a screw; (of a propeller) the angle between the chord of the blade and the plane of rotation; the distance a propeller would advance in one revolution. — *n* **pitch'er** a person who pitches; a paving-stone or sett; a baseball player who delivers the ball to the batsman; one who pitches a stall; a cutting or stake intended to take root. — *n* **pitch'ing** the action of the verb to pitch; a facing of stone; a foundation of stone for a road surface; a cobblestone surface of a road. — **pitch-and-toss'** a game in which coins are thrown at a mark, the player who throws nearest having the right of tossing all, and keeping those that come down heads up; **pitch circle** in a toothed wheel, an imaginary circle along which the tooth pitch is measured and which would put the wheel in contact with another that meshed with it; **pitched battle** a deliberate battle on chosen ground between duly arranged sides; a violent confrontation generally; **pitched roof** a roof having two surfaces sloping down-wards from a central ridge. — *adj* **pitch'ed-roofed** or **pitch'-roofed**. — **pitch'-farthing** chuck-farthing; **pitch'-fork** a fork for tossing hay, etc; a tuning-fork. — *vt* to lift with a pitchfork; to throw suddenly into a position or situation. — **pitching tool** a blunt-edged chisel, used to knock off superfluous stone; **pitch'man** (also **pitch'-person**; *fem* **pitch'woman**) a street or market trader (*NAm*); an advertising man, *esp* in the media; someone who delivers a strong sales pitch; **pitch'pipe** a small pipe to pitch the voice or to tune strings, etc with; **pitch'-wheel** a toothed wheel which operates with another of the same design. — **pitch and pay** (*Shakesp*) to pay ready money; **pitch and putt** (a game played on) a golf course with short holes, needing only a pitch from tee to green; **pitch in** (*colloq*) to set to work briskly; to join in, cooperate; **pitch into** to assail vigorously; to throw oneself into (work, a task, etc); **pitch on** or **upon** to let one's choice fall on or upon. [14c; ety uncertain]

pitchblende *n* a black mineral composed of uranium oxides, a source of uranium and radium. [Ger *Pechblende*, **pitch**[1] and **blende**]

pitcher[1] *pich'ər*, *n* a vessel, *usu* of earthenware, for holding or pouring liquids; a cylindrical tinned milk-can (*Scot*); a jug or ewer (*US*); a modified leaf or part of a leaf in the form of a pitcher, serving to catch insects. — *n* **pitch'erful**. — **pitch'er-plant** an insectivorous plant with pitchers, *esp* Nepenthes, also Sarracenia, Darling-tonia, etc. — **(little) pitchers have (long) ears** children tell tales; there may be listeners. [OFr *picher*, from LL *picārium* a goblet, from Gr *bīkos*, a wine-vessel]

pitcher[2]. See under **pitch**[2].

pitch-pole *pich'pōl*, *n* a somersault (*obs*); a type of harrow (*rare*). — *vi* to go head over heels; to somersault; to flip over lengthways; (of a boat) to turn stern over bow. — Also **pitch'-poll**. [**pitch**[2] and **poll**[1]]

pitchy. See under **pitch**[1].

piteous *pit'i-əs*, *adj* compassionate (*archaic*); paltry (*Milton*); arousing or deserving pity. — *adv* **pit'eously**. — *n* **pit'eousness**. [OFr *pitos*, *piteus*; cf **pity**]

pitfall. See under **pit**[1].

pith *pith*, *n* the soft tissue within the ring of vascular bundles in the stems of dicotyledonous plants; similar material elsewhere, as the white inner skin of an orange; the soft spongy interior of a feather; spinal marrow; the innermost, central or most important part; condensed substance, essence; mettle; vigour; substance, weight, significance; importance. — *vt* to remove the pith of; to sever, pierce, or destroy the marrow or central nervous system of; to kill (animals) in this way. — *adj* **pith'ful**. — *adv* **pith'ily**. — *n* **pith'iness**. — *adj* **pith'less**. — *adj* **pith'like**. — *adj* **pith'y** full of pith; forcible; strong; energetic; sententious and masterful. — **pith'ball** a pellet of pith; **pith hat** or **helmet** a sun helmet made of sola pith; **pith'-tree** a tropical African papilionaceous tree (*Herminiera elaphroxylon*) whose very pithlike wood is used for floats, canoes, etc. [OE *pitha*; Du *pit*, kernel]

pithead. See under **pit**[1].

Pithecanthropus *pith-ə-kan'thrə-pəs* or *pith-i-kan-thrō'pəs*, *n* a fossil hominid discovered by Dr Eugene Dubois in Java in 1891–92, a former genus of primitive man, now included in the genus Homo. [Gr *pithēkos* ape, and *anthrōpos* man]

pithecoid *pith-ē'koid*, *adj* ape-like. [Gr *pithēkos* ape, and *eidos* form]

pithos *pith'os*, *n* a large Greek storage jar. [Gr]

pithy. See under **pith**.

pitiable, etc, **pitied**, **pitier**, **pitiful**, **pitiless**, etc. See under **pity**.

pitman. See under **pit**[1].

pit-mirk *pit-mûrk'*, (*Scot*) *adj* pitch-dark.

piton *pē'ton*, or Fr *pē-tɔ̃*, *n* an iron peg or stanchion to which a rope may be attached, used in mountaineering. [Fr]

Pitot tube *pē'tō tūb*, *n* a tube with openings at one end and one side, placed in a stream of liquid, an airstream, etc, to measure the velocity and pressure of flow, or speed of an aircraft, etc. [From its originator, Henri *Pitot*, 18c French physicist]

pit-pat. See under **pitapat**.

Pitta *pit'ə*, *n* a genus of birds, the so-called ant-thrushes of the Old World; (without *cap*) a bird of this genus. [Telugu *pitta*]

pitta or **pita** *pit'ə*, *n* (also **pitta bread** or **pita bread**) a type of slightly leavened bread, originating in the Middle East, *usu* made in the form of flat hollow ovals; one of these ovals. [Mod Gr, a cake]

pittance *pit'əns*, *n* a special additional allowance of food or drink in a religious house, or a bequest to provide it; a dole; a very small portion or quantity; a miserable wage. [OFr *pitance*, from L *pietās* pity]

pitted. See under **pit**[1,2].

pitten. See under **pit**[3].

pitter *pit'ər*, *vi* to make a sound like a grasshopper. — *adv* **pitt'er-patt'er** (*-pat'ər*) with light pattering sound. — *vi* to make or move with such a sound. — *n* such a sound. [Imit]

pittie-ward *pit'i-wərd*, (*Shakesp*) *n poss*, little park (*The Merry Wives of Windsor* III, 1, 5).

Pittite *pit'īt*, *n* a follower of William *Pitt* (1759–1806), British statesman. — Also *adj*. — *n* **Pitt'ism**.

pittite. See under **pit**[1].

pittosporum *pi-tos'pə-rəm*, *n* an evergreen shrub native to Australasia and parts of Africa and Asia, with leathery leaves and purple, white or greenish-yellow flowers (also called *parchment bark*). [Mod L, from Gr *pitta* pitch, and *sporos* seed]

pitty-pat. See **pitapat**.

pituita *pit-ū-ī'tə* or **pituite** *pit'ū-īt*, (*archaic*) *n* phlegm, mucus. [L *pītuīta*]

pituitary *pi-tū'i-tə-ri*, *adj* of or relating to the pituitary gland; of or relating to pituita — phlegm or mucus (*archaic*). — *n* **pitū'itrin** a hormone produced by the pituitary gland. — **pituitary gland** or **body** a ductless endocrine gland at the base of the brain affecting growth, once thought to produce mucus. [L *pītuīta* phlegm]

pituri *pit'ər-i*, *n* an Australian solanaceous shrub, *Duboisia hopwoodii*; the narcotic obtained from its leaves. [Aboriginal]

pity *pit'i*, *n* a feeling of sorrow for the sufferings and misfortunes of others, compassion; a cause or source of such a feeling; an unfortunate chance; a matter for regret. — *vt* to feel pity for; to feel grief at; to cause pity in (*obs*): — *pr p* **pit'ying**; *pa t* and *pa p* **pit'ied**. — *adj* **pit'iable** to be pitied; miserable, contemptible. — *n* **pit'iableness**. — *adv* **pit'iably**. — *n* **pit'ier**. — *adj* **pit'iful** feeling pity; compassionate; exciting pity; sad, wretched; despicable. — *adv* **pit'iful** (*Shakesp*) or **pit'ifully**. — *n* **pit'ifulness**. — *adj* **pit'iless** without pity; merciless, cruel. — *adv* **pit'ilessly**. — *n* **pit'ilessness**. — *adv* **pit'yingly**. — **it pitieth me, you, them**, etc (*Prayer Bk*) it causes pity in me, you, them, etc. [OFr *pite* (Fr *pitié*, Ital *pietà*), from L *pietās*, *pietātis*, from *pius* pious]

pityriasis *pit-i-rī'i-sis*, *n* (*med*) any of several skin diseases marked by the formation and flaking away of branny scales, *esp pityriasis versicolor*. — *adj* **pit'yroid** (*archaic*) bran-like. — *n* **pityrospor'um** a yeast-like fungus which can cause *pityriasis versicolor*. [Gr *pityron* bran]

più *pyoo͞* or *pē'oo͞*, (*Ital*; *music*); *adv* more. — **più mosso** (*mō'sō* or *mo'so*) quicker.

pium *pi-oo͞m'*, *n* a small but very troublesome Brazilian biting fly. [Tupí]

piupiu *pē'oo͞-pē-oo͞*, *n* a skirt, traditionally made from strips of flax, worn by Maori men and women for dances, celebrations and ceremonial occasions. [Maori]

pivot *piv'ət*, *n* a pin or shaft on which anything turns; a soldier upon whom, or position on which, a body wheels; a centre-half in football, or a similarly placed player in other games; a person or thing on whom or which anything depends or turns; the action of turning the body using one foot as a pivot. — *adj* of the nature of a pivot; cardinal; serving as a pivot. — *vt* to mount on a pivot. — *vi* to turn on or as if on a pivot. — *adj* **piv'otal** of, containing, or acting like a pivot; crucially important. — *adv* **piv'otally**. — *adj* **piv'oted**. — *n* **piv'oter** someone who makes and fits pivots; a golfer who turns his body. — *n* **piv'oting** the pivot-work in machines. — **pivot bridge** a swing-bridge moving on a vertical pivot in the middle; **piv'ot-man** a man on whom a body of soldiers turns; a man of cardinal importance in industry, etc. [Fr *pivot*, perh related to Ital *piva* pipe, peg, pin]

pix[1] *piks*, *n*. Same as **pyx**.

pix[2] *piks*, (*colloq*) *n pl* pictures, *usu* in the sense of photographs: — *sing* **pic**.

pixel *pik'səl*, (*comput*, *image technol*) *n* the smallest element with controllable colour and brightness in a video display, or in computer graphics. [**pix**[2] and *el*ement]

pixie or **pixy** *pik'si*, or (*dialect*; SW England) **pisky** *pis'ki*, *n* a small fairy. — *adj* **pixie hood** a child's pointed hood, *usu* tied under the chin. — *adj* **pix'y-led** bewildered. — **pix'y-ring** a fairy-ring; **pix'y-stool** a toadstool or mushroom. [Origin obscure; cf Swed *pysk*, *pyske* a small fairy]

pixilated or **pix'illated** *pik'si-lā-tid* (*esp US*) *adj* bemused, bewildered; slightly crazy; intoxicated — *n* **pixilā'tion** or **pixillā'tion** (see also separate entry). [*Pix*ie and poss tit*illated*]

pixilation or **pixillation** *pik-si-lā'shən*, *n* a technique for making human figures and animals appear to be animated artificially, eg by the use of stop-frame camera methods, *usu* to create a whimsical effect (*cinema*, *theatre*, *TV*); from *pixil*ated and anim*ation*); a video effect in which a picture is broken down into a comparatively small number of square elements (*image technol*; associated with **pixel**); see also under **pixilated**.

pixy. See **pixie**.

pizazz. See **pizzazz**.

pize *pīz*, *n* a term of imprecation, pox, pest. [Origin uncertain]

pizza *pēt'sə*, *n* a flat *usu* round slab of dough topped with tomato sauce, cheese and various chopped vegetables and/or meats, and baked. — *adj* **pizzaiola** (*pēt-sī-ō'-lə*) having a rich sauce made with tomatoes. — *n* **pizzeria** (*pēt-sə-rē'ə*) a bakery or restaurant where pizzas are sold and/or made. [Ital]

pizzazz, **pizazz**, **pazzazz**, or **pazazz** *pə-zaz'*, (*colloq*) *n* a combination of flamboyance, panache and vigour, in behaviour, display or performance. [Onomatopoeic coinage by Diana Vreeland, US fashion editor (*c* 1903–89)]

pizzicato *pit-si-kä'tō*, (*music*) *adj* played by plucking the string (not *arco* or *col arco*, with the bow). — *adv* by plucking. — *n* a tone so produced; a passage so played; the manner of playing by plucking: — *pl* **pizzica'tos**. [Ital, twitched, from *pizzicare* to twitch]

pizzle *piz'l*, *n* a penis; that of a bull used as an instrument of punishment, in flogging. [LGer *pesel* or Flem *pezel*]

Pk *abbrev*: Park (in place and street names).

PL *abbrev*: Poet Laureate; Poland (IVR); Public Library.

Pl *abbrev*: Place (in street names, etc).

pl *abbrev*: plural.

PLA *abbrev*: Port of London Authority.

placable *plak'* or *plāk'ə-bl*, *adj* that may be appeased; easily appeased; relenting; willing to forgive, forgiving. — *n* **placabil'ity**. — *n* **plac'ableness**. — *adv* **plac'ably**. [L *plācābilis*, from *plācāre* to appease]

placard *plak'ärd*, *n* an official permit or proclamation with a thin seal (*obs*); a written or printed notice stuck on a wall or otherwise publicly displayed; a notice written or printed on wood, cardboard or other stiff material, and carried, hung, etc, in a public place; a placcat or placket (*obs*). — *vt* (sometimes *plə-kärd'*) to publish or notify by placard; to post or set up as a placard; to put placards on or in. [OFr *plackart*, *placard*, etc, from *plaquier* to lay flat, plaster, from MFlem *placken* to plaster]

placate *plə-kāt'*, *plā-kāt'*, *vt* to conciliate. — *n* **placā'tion** propitiation. — *adj* **placatory** (*plak'* or *plāk'ə-tə-ri*, *plə-kā'*) conciliatory. [L *plācāre*, to appease, related to *placēre*]

placcat or **placcate**. See **placket**.

place *plās*, *n* a portion of space; a portion of the earth's surface, or any surface; a position in space, or on the earth's surface, or in any system, order, or arrangement; a building, room, piece of ground, etc, assigned to some purpose (eg *place of business*, *entertainment*, *worship*); a particular locality; a town, village, etc; a dwelling or home; a mansion with its grounds; a battlefield (*obs*); a fortress, fortified town (*obs*); an open space in a town, a market-place or square; (with cap) used in street names *esp* for a row or group of houses, a short street or a circus; a seat or accommodation in a theatre, train, at table, etc; space occupied; room; the position held by anybody, employment, office, a situation, *esp* under government or in domestic service; due or proper position or dignity; that which is incumbent on one; precedence; position in a series; high rank; position attained in a competition or assigned by criticism; position among the first three in a race; stead; pitch reached by a bird of prey (*obs* except in **pride of place**, qv under **pride**); (in reading-matter, narrative, conversation, etc) the point which the reader or speaker has reached when he stops or is interrupted; a topic, matter of discourse (*obs*); a passage in a book (*obs*). — *vt* to put in any place; to assign to a place; to find a place, home, job, publisher, etc, for; to find a buyer for (*usu* a large quantity of stocks or shares; *commerce*); to propose, lay or put (with *before*); to induct; to appoint; to identify; to invest; to arrange (a loan, bet, etc); to put (trust, etc, in); to state the finishing positions of (the competitors, *esp* the first three) in a race or competition; to ascribe (with *to*; *archaic*). — *vi* (*esp US*) to finish a race or competition (in a specified position); to finish a race in second (if otherwise unspecified) position (*horse-racing*). — *adj* **placed** set in place or in a place; having a place; among the first three in a race; inducted to a position or office. — *adj* **place'less** without place or office. — *n* **place'ment** placing or setting; assigning to places; assigning to a job; a job so assigned. — *n* **plac'er**. — *n* **plac'ing** position, *esp* a finishing position in a race or competition; the process of finding an intermediary buyer for large numbers of (*usu* newly issued) shares, etc (*commerce*). — **place card** a card placed before each setting on the table at a banquet, formal dinner, etc, with the name of the person who is to sit there; **place'-hunter** (*archaic*) someone who covets and strives after a public post; **place kick** (in football) a kick made when the ball has been placed on the ground for that purpose; **place'-kicker**; **place'man** someone who has a place or office under a government, *esp* if gained by selfishness or ambition: — *pl* **place'-men**; **place mat** a table mat set at a person's place setting; **place'-monger** someone who traffics in appointments to places; **place name** a geographical proper name; **place setting** each person's set of crockery, cutlery and glassware as used at a dining table. — **all over the place** scattered; in a muddle or mess, confused, disorganized (*colloq*); **fall into place** to be resolved; **give place (to)** to make room (for); to be superseded (by); **go places** see under **go**; **have place** to have existence; **in place** in position; opportune; **in place of** instead of; **in the first place** firstly, originally; **know one's place** to show proper subservience; **lose one's place** to falter in following a text, etc, not know what point has been reached; **lose the place** (*colloq*) to flounder, be at a loss, be all at sea; to lose one's temper; **out of place** out of due position; inappropriate, unseasonable; **put** or **keep someone in his** or **her place** to humble someone who is arrogant, presumptuous, etc, or keep him or her in subservience; **take one's place** to assume one's rightful position; **take place** to come to pass, to occur; to take precedence; **take someone's place** to act as substitute for, or successor to, someone; **take the place of** to be a substitute for. [Partly OE (Northumbrian) *plæce* market-place, but mainly Fr *place*, both from L *platea*, from Gr *plateia* (*hodos*) broad (street)]

placebo *plə-sē'bō*, *n* vespers for the dead (*RC*); a medicine given to humour or gratify a patient rather than to exercise any physically curative effect; a pharmacologically inactive substance administered as a drug either in the treatment of psychological illness or in the course of drug trials; a sycophant (*obs*): — *pl* **placē'bos**. [From the first words of the first antiphon of the office of vespers, *Placēbō Dominō* I shall please the Lord]

placenta *plə-sen'tə*, *n* the structure that unites the unborn mammal to the womb of its mother and establishes a nutritive connection between them (*zool*); the part of the carpel that bears the ovules (*bot*); any mass of tissue bearing sporangia or spores: — *pl* **placen'tae** (*-tē*) or **placen'tas**. — *adj* **placen'tal**. — *n* a placental mammal. — *n pl* **Placentalia** (*plas-ən-tā'li-ə*) Eutheria, the subclass of placental mammals. — *n* **placentā'tion** the arrangement and mode of attachment of placentae or of placenta and fetus. — *adj* **placent'iform** cake-shaped. — *n* **placentol'ogy** the scientific study of placentae. [L *placenta* a flat cake, from Gr *plakoeis* (contraction of *plakous*) from *plax*, *plakos* anything flat]

placer[1] *plas'ər* or *plās'ər*, *n* a superficial deposit from which gold or other mineral can be washed. — **plac'er-gold**. [Sp *placer* sandbank, from *plaza* place]

placer[2]. See under **place**.

placet[1] *plā'set* or *pla'ket*, *n* a vote of assent in a governing body; permission given, *esp* by a sovereign, to publish and carry out an ecclesiastical order, such as a papal bull or edict. [L *placet* it pleases, 3rd pers sing pres indicative of *placēre* to please]

placet[2]. A wrong form of **placit**, qv under **placitum**.

placid *plas'id*, *adj* displaying calmness of nature, not easily disturbed or angered. — *n* **placid'ity** or **plac'idness**. — *adv* **plac'idly**. [L *placidus*, from *placēre* to please]

placing. see under **place**.

placitum *plas'i-təm* or *plak'i-to͝om*, *n* a decision of a court or an assembly; a plea or pleading: — *pl* **plac'ita**. — Also **plac'it** (and wrongly **plac'et**). — *adj* **plac'itory** relating to pleas or pleading. [L pa p neuter of *placēre* to please]

plack *plak*, *n* an old Scottish copper coin worth a third part of an English penny of the same period. — *adj* **plack'less**. [Prob Flem *placke*, an old Flemish coin, *orig* a flat disc]

placket *plak'it*, *n* (in armour) a breastplate or backplate, or a leather doublet with strips of steel (also *obs* **placc'ate**); an apron (*archaic*); a petticoat (*archaic*); the wearer of a petticoat, a woman (*archaic*); an opening in a skirt, shirt, etc for a pocket, or at the fastening; a piece of material sewn behind this; a pocket, *esp* in a skirt. — *Shakesp* also **placc'at**. — **plack'et-hole** (*archaic*) a slit in a skirt. [Origin obscure; perh a variant of **placard**, breastplate]

placoderm *plak'ə-dûrm*, *adj* (of fossil fishes) covered with bony plates. — *n* a fish so covered. [Gr *plax*, *plakos* anything flat, and *derma* skin]

placoid *plak'oid*, *adj* (of scales) plate-like; (of fish, eg sharks) having placoid scales, irregular plates of hard bone, not imbricated. [Gr *plax*, *plakos* anything flat and broad, and *eidos* form]

plafond *pla-fɔ̃*, *n* a ceiling, *esp* decorated; a soffit; an earlier version of contract bridge. [Fr, ceiling, score above the line in bridge, from *plat* flat, and *fond* bottom]

plagal *plā'gl*, (*music*) *adj* of a Gregorian mode, having the final in the middle of the compass instead of at the bottom (opposite of *authentic*). — **plagal cadence** one in which the subdominant chord precedes the tonic. [Gr *plagios*, sidewise, from *plagos* a side]

plage *pläzh*, *n* a fashionable beach; a bright, highly disturbed area in the chromosphere, *usu* presaging, or associated with, a sunspot. [Fr]

plagiary *plā'ji-ə-ri*, *n* (*archaic*) someone who steals the thoughts or writings of others and presents them as his or her own; the crime of plagiarism. — *adj* (*obs*) practising, or obtained by, literary theft. — *n* **pla'giarism** the act or practice of plagiarizing. — *n* **pla'giarist** a person who plagiarizes. — *vt* and *vi* **pla'giarize** or **-ise** to steal from (the writings or ideas of another). [L *plagiārius*, a kidnapper, plagiary, from *plaga* a net]

plagio- *plāji-ō-*, *-ə-*, *-o'* *combining form* meaning oblique. [Gr *plagios* oblique]

plagiocephaly *plā-ji-ō-sef'ə-li*, (*med*) *n* a twisted condition of the head, the front of the skull being larger on one side, the back larger on the other.

plagioclase *plā'ji-ō-klās*, *-klāz*, or *plaj'*, *n* a feldspar whose cleavages are not at right angles, eg albite, anorthite, or any mixture of them. [Gr *plagios* oblique, and *klasis* a fracture]

plagiostome *plā'ji-ō-stōm*, *n* any fish families of the **Plagiostomata** (*-stō'mə-tə*) or **Plagiostomi** (*-os'tə-mī*), the cross-mouthed fishes, sharks and rays, whose mouth is a transverse slit on the underside of the head. — *adj* **plagiostom'atous** or **plagios'tomous**. [Gr *plagios* crosswise, and *stoma*, *-atos* mouth]

plagiotropism *plā-ji-ot'rə-pizm*, *n* orienting at an angle to the direction of stimulus. — *adj* **plagiotropic** (*-ō-trop'ik*). — *adv* **plagiotrop'ically**. — *adj* **plagiotropous** (*-ot'rə-pəs*). [Gr *plagios* crosswise, and *tropos* a turning]

plagium *plā'ji-əm*, *n* the crime of kidnapping. [L *plagium*, from *plaga* a net]

plague *plāg*, *n* a deadly epidemic or pestilence, *esp* a fever caused by a bacillus (*Bacillus pestis*) transmitted by rat-fleas from rats to man, characterized by buboes, or swellings of the lymphatic glands, by carbuncles and petechiae; murrain; a sudden abnormal infestation, such as *a plague of greenfly*; any troublesome thing or person; a nuisance or vexation (*colloq*); a blow or wound (*obs*); an affliction regarded as a sign of divine displeasure. — *vt* to infest with disease (*rare*); to pester or annoy. — *adj* **plague'some** (*colloq*) troublesome, annoying. — *adv* **pla'guily** confoundedly. — *adj* **plaguy** (*archaic*) or **plaguey** (*plā'gi*) of, or of the nature of, plague; vexatious; troublesome; confounded. — *adv* (*Shakesp*) confoundedly. — **plague'-pit** a common grave for plague victims; **plague'-sore** an ulcer due to plague; **plague'-spot** a spot on the skin indicating plague; a place where disease is constantly present; an evil place. — *adj* **plague'-stricken**. — **a plague on** may a curse rest on; **avoid like the plague** (*colloq*) to keep well away from, shun absolutely; **what the** (or *Shakesp* **a**) **plague** what the devil. [OFr *plague*, from L *plāga* a blow; cf Gr *plēgē*]

plaice *plās*, *n* a flatfish of the family Pleuronectidae (*Pleuronectes platessa*), brown with orange spots, used as food; any of several related fish (*NAm*). — **plaice'-mouth** a mouth placed awry. — *adj* wry-mouthed. [OFr *plaïs* (Fr *plie*), from LL *platessa* a flatfish, perh from Gr *platys* flat]

plaid *plād*, *plad*, *n* a long piece of woollen cloth, worn over the shoulder, *usu* in tartan as part of Highland dress, or checked as formerly worn by Lowland shepherds; cloth for it, tartan; a plaidman. — *adj* like a plaid in pattern or colours. — *adj* **plaid'ed** wearing a plaid; made of plaid cloth. — *n* **plaid'ing** a strong woollen twilled fabric. — **plaid'man** a Highlander; **plaid'-neuk** (*-nük*) a pocket at the end of a plaid. [Perh Gaelic *plaide* a blanket; but that may be from the Scots word]

Plaid Cymru *plīd kum'ri*, (*Welsh*) *n* the Welsh Nationalist party. [*Plaid* party; *Cymru* Wales]

plain[1] *plān*, (*archaic*), *vt* and *vi* to complain; to lament. — *n* a complaint. — *n* **plain'ant** a person who complains; a plaintiff. — *adj* **plain'ful**. — *n* **plain'ing** (*Shakesp*) complaint. [OFr *plaigner* (Fr *plaindre*), from L *plangere* to beat the breast, lament]

plain[2] *plān*, *adj* flat; level; even; unobstructed; without obscurity; clear; obvious; simple; downright, utter; not ornate; unembellished; unvariegated; uncoloured; unruled; without pattern, striation, markings, etc; without gloss; uncurled; not twilled; (in knitting) denoting a straightforward stitch with the wool passed round the front of the needle (opposite of *purl*); not elaborate; without addition; not highly seasoned; deficient in beauty; ugly (*euphem*); without subtlety; candid; outspoken; straightforward; undistinguished; ordinary; other than a court card; other than trumps. — *n* an extent of level land; the open country, *esp* as a field of battle or as a setting for pastoral or romantic literature (*poetic*). — *adv* clearly; distinctly. — *vt* (*Shakesp*) to make plain. — *adj* **plain'ish**. — *adv* **plain'ly**. — *n* **plain'ness**. — **plain'chant** plainsong; **plain chocolate** dark chocolate, made with some sugar added but without milk. — *adj* **plain'clothes** wearing ordinary clothes, not uniform (eg of a policeman on detective work). — **plain cook** someone competent in plain cookery. — *vi* **plain'-cook** to practise plain cookery. — **plain cookery** the cooking of ordinary simple traditional dishes. — *vt* and *vi* **plain'-darn** to darn with the ordinary cross pattern. — **plain dealer** a person who is candid and outspoken. — *n* **plain dealing**. — *adj* **plain'-dealing**. — *adj* **plain'-heart'ed** having a plain or honest heart; sincere. — **plain'-heart'edness**; **plain Jane** (*colloq derog*) a plain, dowdy girl. — *adj* **plain'-Jane** ordinary, unremarkable; plain, *esp* of a garment — **plain language** straightforward, understandable language; **plain sailing** sailing in open, unrestricted waters (*naut*); an easy, straightforward task, affair, etc (*fig*); see also **plane sailing** under **plane**[2]; **plains'man** a dweller in a plain, *esp* in N America: — *pl* **plain'smen**; **plain'song** unmeasured, unaccompanied music sung in unison in ecclesiastical modes from early times, and still in use in RC and some Anglican churches; a simple melody; that to which a descant can be added. — *adj* (*Shakesp*) singing a simple theme. — **plain speaking** straightforwardness or bluntness of speech. — *adj* **plain'-spoken** plain, rough, and sincere; frank, candid, *esp* if rather blunt. — **plain'stanes** (*Scot*) flagstones, pavement (also **plain'stones**); **plain'work** plain needlework, as distinguished from embroidery. — **plain as a pikestaff** see under **pike**[1]. [Fr, from L *plānus* plain]

plainant, plainful, plaining. See under **plain**[1].

Plains *plānz*, (also without *cap*; *esp US*) *adj* of or from the Great Plains of N America and Canada. — **Plains Indian** a member of any of the N American Indian tribes *orig* inhabiting the Great Plains.

plaint *plānt*, *n* lamentation (*literary*); complaint (*archaic*); a mournful song; a statement of grievance, *esp* the exhibiting of an action in writing by a complainant in a court of law. — *adj* **plaint'ful** (*archaic*) complaining. — *adj* **plaint'less**. [OFr *pleinte* (Fr *plainte*), from L *plangere, planctum* to beat the breast, lament]

plaintiff *plān'tif*, (*Eng law*) *n* a person who commences a suit against another (opposite of *defendant*). — Also *adj* (*Spenser*). [OFr *plaintif* (masc adj) complaining]

plaintive *plān'tiv*, *adj* mournful; querulous. — *adv* **plain'-tively**. — *n* **plain'tiveness**. [OFr *plaintif, plaintive*, from L *plangere*; see **plaintiff** and **plaint**]

plaister *plās'tər*, (*obs* or *Scot*) *n* a form of **plaster**.

plait *plat* or *plāt* or (now *rare*) *plēt*, *n* a braid in which strands are passed over one another in turn; material so braided; a braided tress (in these senses sometimes spelt **plat**); a pleat (*rare*; in this sense pronounced *plēt*). — *vt* to braid or intertwine (*usu plat*); to pleat (now *rare*; *usu plēt*). — *adj* **plait'ed**. — *n* **plait'er**. — *n* **plait'ing**. [OFr *pleit, ploit* (Fr *pli*), from L *plicāre, -itum, -ātum* to fold]

plan *plan*, *n* a figure or representation of anything projected on a plane or flat surface, *esp* that of a building or floor, as disposed on the ground; a large-scale detailed map of a small area; a scheme for accomplishing a purpose; an intended method; a scheme drawn up beforehand; a scheme of arrangement; (in the Methodist churches) a quarterly programme of services with preachers for each church in the circuit. — *vt* to make a plan of; to design; to lay plans for; to devise; to purpose. — *vi* to make plans: — *pr p* **plann'ing**; *pa t* and *pa p* **planned**. — *adj* **plan'less**. — *adj* **planned** intended; in accordance with, or achieved by, a careful plan made beforehand. — *n* **plann'er** a person who plans, *esp* the development of a town, etc; a calendar showing the whole year, etc, at a glance, used for forward planning. — **planned economy** one in which the government decides levels of production, prices and wages, etc; **planned obsolescence** see under **obsolescent**; **planning permission** permission from a local authority to erect or convert a building or to change the use to which a building or piece of land is put; **plan-position indicator** (*radar*) an apparatus in which the position of reflecting objects is shown on the screen of a cathode-ray tube, as if on a plan (*abbrev* **PPI**). [Fr, from L *plānus* flat]

planar, planation. See under **plane**[2].

planarian *plə-nā'ri-ən*, *adj* and *n* turbellarian (see **Turbellaria**). [Mod L *Planāria*, genus name, from *plānārius* on level ground (taken as if meaning flat), from *plānus* flat]

planch *plansh*, *n* a plank (*obs*); a floor (*dialect*); a slab. — *vt* (*obs*) to floor; to board. — *adj* **planch'ed** (*Shakesp*) boarded. — *n* **planchet** (*plan'shit*) a blank metal disc to be stamped as a coin. — *n* **planchette** (*plā-shet* or *plan-shet'*) a board mounted on two castors and a pencil-point, used as a medium for automatic writing and supposed spirit-messages. [Fr *planche*, from L *planca*]

Planck's constant *plangks kon'stənt*, *n* the constant (*h*), in the expression for the quantum of energy, equal to $6{\cdot}626 \times 10^{-34}$ Js (joule seconds); **Planck's law** the basis of quantum theory, that the energy of electromagnetic waves is confined in indivisible packets or quanta. [Max Karl Ernst Ludwig *Planck*, 1858–1947, German physicist]

plane[1] *plān*, *n* any tree of the genus *Platanus*, *esp* the oriental plane (*Platanus orientalis*) and the N American plane or buttonwood (*Platanus occidentalis*), trees with palmatifid leaves shedding their bark in thin slabs; in Scotland, the great maple (*Acer pseudoplatanus*). — **plane'-tree**. [Fr *plane*, from L *platanus*; see **platane**]

plane[2] *plān*, *n* a surface of which it is true that, if any two points on the surface be taken, the straight line joining them will lie entirely on the surface (*geom*); any flat or level material surface; one of the thin horizontal structures used as wings and tail to sustain or control aeroplanes in flight; short for aeroplane or airplane (also **'plane**); an act of planing or soaring; in mines, a main road for the transport of coal or other mineral; any grade of life or of development or level of thought or existence. — *adj* having the character of a plane; pertaining to, lying in, or confined to a plane; level; smooth. — *vt* to make plane or smooth (see also **plane**[3]). — *vi* to travel by aeroplane; to soar; to volplane; (of a boat) to skim across the surface of the water. — *adj* **planar** (*plān'ər*) relating to a plane; lying in a single plane, flat. — *n* **planation** (*plə-nā'shən*) making level. — *n* **planer** (*plān'ər*) someone who levels or makes plane; a smoothing instrument (see also **plane**[3]); a wooden block beaten with a mallet to level a forme of type (*printing*). — **planar diode** one with plane parallel electrodes; **plane chart** a chart used in plane sailing, the lines of longitude and latitude being projected on to a plane surface, so being represented parallel. — *adj* **plane'-polarized** or **-ised** (of light) consisting of vibrations in one plane only. — **plane sailing** the calculation of a ship's place in its course as if the earth were flat instead of spherical; see also **plain sailing** under **plain**[2]; **plane'-table** an instrument used in field-mapping, with a sighting-telescope for observing objects, whose angles may be noted on a paper on the table of the instrument; an inclined table on which ore is dressed. — *vt* to survey with a plane-table. — **planing bottom** (*aerodynamics*) the part of the under surface of a flying-boat hull that provides hydrodynamic lift. [L *plānum* a flat surface, neuter of *plānus* flat; cf **plain**[2] and **plane**[3]]

plane[3] *plān*, *n* a carpenter's tool for producing a smooth surface by paring off shavings; any similar smoothing or paring tool or machine. — *vt* to smooth or remove with a plane (see also **plane**[2]). — *n* **plā'ner** someone who uses a plane; a tool or machine for planing. — **plā'ning-machine** a machine for planing wood or metals. [Fr *plane*, from LL *plāna*, from *plānāre* to smooth]

planer. See under **plane**[2,3].

planet *plan'it*, *n* any of the celestial bodies (including the earth, but other than a comet or meteor) that revolve about the sun reflecting the sun's light and generating no heat or light of their own, these being Mercury, Venus, Earth, Mars, Jupiter, Saturn, Uranus, Neptune and Pluto; a satellite of a planet (*secondary planet*); an astrological influence vaguely conceived; (in old astronomy) a heavenly body whose place among the fixed stars is not fixed (including sun and moon). — *n* **planetā'rium** a machine showing the motions and orbits of the planets, often by the projecting of their images on to a (domed) ceiling; a hall or building containing such a machine: — *pl* **planetā'ria**. — *adj* **plan'etary** relating to the planets or a planet, or this planet; consisting of or produced by planets; under the influence of a planet (*astrol*); erratic; revolving in an orbit. — *n* **planetes'imal** in one theory of the origin of the solar system, any of many very small units absorbed into the planets as these formed. — *adj* **planetic** (*plən-et'ik*) or **planet'ical**. — *n* **plan'etoid** a minor planet; an artificial body put into orbit. — *adj* **planetoi'dal**. — *n* **planetol'ogist**. — *n* **planetol'ogy** the science of the planets. — **planetary nebula** a ring-shaped nebula around a star, consisting of a shell of gas, illuminated by the star's short-wave radiation. — *adj* **plan'et-strick'en** or **plan'et-struck** (*astrol*) affected by the influence of the planets, *esp* adversely; blasted. —

inferior planets those within the earth's orbit (Mercury and Venus); **minor planets** the numerous group of asteroids between the orbits of Mars and Jupiter; **superior planets** those outside the earth's orbit. [Fr *planète*, from Gr *planētēs* wanderer, from *planaein* to make to wander]

plangent *plan'jənt, adj* resounding, resonant; noisy, loud, ringing, clangorous; resounding mournfully. — *n* **plan'gency**. — *adv* **plan'gently**. [L *plangēns, -entis,* pr p of *plangere* to beat]

plani- *plan-i-, combining form* signifying plane (see **plane**[2]). — *n* **planigraph** (*plan'i-gräf*) an instrument for reducing or enlarging drawings. — *n* **planimeter** (*plə-nim'i-tər*) an instrument for measuring the area of a plane figure. — *adj* **planimetric** (*plān-* or *plan-i-met'rik*) or **planimet'rical**. — *n* **planim'etry** the mensuration of plane surfaces. — *n* **planisphere** (*plan'is-fēr*) a sphere projected on a plane; a map of the celestial sphere, which can be adjusted so as to show the area visible at any time. — *adj* **planispher'ic**. [L *plānus* flat]

planish *plan'ish, vt* to polish (metal, etc); to flatten. — *n* **plan'isher** a person who or tool that planishes. [Obs Fr *planir, -issant,* from *plan* flat]

planisphere, etc. See under **plani-**.

plank *plangk, n* a long piece of timber, thicker and *usu* narrower than a board; a special board on which fish, etc, is cooked and served (*NAm*); one of the principles or aims that form the platform or programme of a political party, etc. — *vt* to cover with planks; to pay down or table (with *down*); to cook on a plank (*US*); to put down with a thump or plump (often with *down*; *Scot* or *dialect*) — *n* **plank'ing** the act of laying planks; a series of planks; work made up of planks. — **plank'-bed** a prison bed of wood without a mattress. — **walk the plank** to suffer the former maritime punishment of being forced to walk off the end of a plank projecting over the ship's side. [L *planca* a board]

plankton *plangk'tən, n* the drifting organisms in oceans, lakes or rivers. — *adj* **planktonic** (*-ton'ik*). [Neuter of Gr *planktos, -ē, -on* wandering]

planned, planner, planning. See under **plan**.

plano- *plān'ō-* or *plan'ō-, combining form* signifying plane (see **plane**[2]). — *adj* **plano-concave** (*plā'nō-kon'kāv*) plane on one side and concave on the other. — *adj* **plano-conical** (*plā'nō-kon'i-kəl*) plane on one side and conical on the other. — *adj* **plano-convex** (*plā'nō-kon'veks*) plane on one side and convex on the other. — *n* **planometer** (*plə-nom'ə-tər*) a flat device used as a gauge for flat surfaces. — *n* **Planor'bis** a genus of pond-snails with flat spiral shells. [L *plānus* flat]

planoblast *plan'ō-bläst, n* a free-swimming medusa. — *n* **planogam'ete** a motile gamete. [Gr *planos* wandering]

plano-concave ... to ... **Planorbis**. See under **plano-**.

plant *plänt, n* a vegetable organism, or part of one, ready for planting or lately planted; a slip, cutting, or scion; an offshoot; a young person; a sapling; a cudgel; any member of the vegetable kingdom, *esp* (popularly) one of the smaller kinds; growth; amount planted; the sole of the foot; mode of planting oneself, stand; something deposited beforehand for a purpose; equipment, machinery, apparatus, for an industrial activity; a factory; the buildings, equipment, etc of eg a school, university or other institution; a bedded oyster (*US*); a thief's hoard (*slang*); a spy, detective, picket or cordon of detectives, or police trap (*slang*); an object, etc deployed so as to incriminate someone unjustly; a deceptive trick, put-up job (*slang*); a shot in which one pockets, or tries to pocket, a red ball by causing it to be propelled by another red ball which has been struck by the cue ball or by some other red ball (*snooker*). — *vt* to put into the ground for growth; to introduce; to insert; to fix; to place firmly; to set in position; to station, post; to found; to settle; to locate; to place or deliver (eg a blow or a dart); to leave in the lurch; to bury (*slang*); to hide (*slang*); to deploy (stolen goods, etc) in such a way as to incriminate someone; to interpose (a question or comment) as a snare or stumbling block; to place as a spy, etc (*slang*); to instil or implant; to furnish with plants; to colonize; to stock; to furnish or provide (with things disposed around); to salt (a mine) (*slang*). — *vi* to plant trees, colonists, etc. — *adj* **plant'able**. — *n* **plant'age** (*Shakesp*) plants in general. — *n* **plantā'tion** a place planted, *esp* with trees; formerly a colony; an estate used for growing cotton, rubber, tea, sugar, or other product of warm countries; a large estate (*Southern US*); the act or process of introduction; the act of planting (*Milton*). — *n* **plant'er** a person who plants or introduces; the owner or manager of a plantation; a pioneer colonist; a settler; an instrument for planting; an ornamental pot or other container for plants. — *n* **plant'ing** the act of setting in the ground for growth; the art of forming plantations of trees; a plantation (*Scot*). — *adj* **plant'less**. — *n* **plant'let** or **plant'ling** a little plant. — *n* **plantoc'racy** a ruling class of plantation owners and managers; government by plantation owners and managers. — *n* **plant'ule** a plant embryo. — **plant'-associa'tion** or **plant'-forma'tion** an assemblage of plants growing together under similar conditions, as in a salt-marsh or a pine-wood; **plantation song** a style of song sung by the black workers on American plantations; **plant hormone** see **growth substance**; **plant'-house** a structure for growing plants of warmer climates; **plant'ie-cruive** (*-krōōv*; *Orkney* and *Shetland*) a kitchen garden, an enclosure for cabbage. — *adj* **plant'-like**. — **plant'-lore** folklore of plants; **plant'-louse** an aphis or greenfly: — *pl* **plant'-lice**. — **plant'-pot** a pot for growing a plant in; **plants'man** or **plants'woman** a person who has great knowledge of and experience in gardening. — **plant out** to transplant to open ground, from pot or frame; to dispose at intervals in planting. [OE *plante* (n), from L *planta* shoot, slip, cutting, and OE *plantian* (verb)]

planta *plan'tə, -ta,* (*anatom*) *n* (also **planta pedis** *ped'is*) the sole of the foot. — *adj* **plan'tar** of or relating to the sole of the foot. — *adj* **plan'tigrade** (*zool*; L *-gradus* walking) walking fully on the soles of the feet. — *n* an animal that walks on the soles of the feet. [L]

plantage. See under **plant**.

plantain[1] *plan'tin, -tān, n* any roadside plant of genus **Plantā'gō** (eg waybread or ribgrass; family **Plantaginā'ceae**) that presses its leaves flat on the ground and has greenish flowers on a slim stem. — *adj* **plantaginaceous** (*plan-taj-i-nā'shəs*). — **plantain lily** a plant of the *Hosta* genus with white, blue or lilac flowers. [L *plantāgō, -inis,* from *planta* the sole of the foot]

plantain[2] *plan'tin, -tān, n* a musaceous plant; its fruit, a coarse green-skinned banana used as a staple food in tropical countries; (in India) a banana. — **plan'tain-eater** an African bird (*Musophaga*) of the family *Musophagidae*, a touraco. [Origin doubtful]

plantain[3] *plan'tin, -tān,* (*obs*) *n* a platane or plane-tree. [Obs Fr *plantain*, from L *platanus*]

plantar. See under **planta**.

plantation. See under **plant**.

plantigrade. See under **planta**.

Plantin *plan'tin, n* the name of a family of typefaces based on 16c Flemish types. [Christophe *Plantin* (1514–89), Antwerp printer]

planting, etc ... to ... **plantule**. See under **plant**.

planula *plan'ū-lə, n* a free-swimming two-layered, often flattened larva of coelenterates, etc: — *pl* **plan'ulae** (*-lē*). — *adj* **plan'ular**. — *adj* **plan'uliform**. — *adj* **plan'uloid**. [Dimin of L *plānus* flat]

planuria *plan-ū'ri-ə, n* the discharge of urine through an abnormal passage. — Also **plan'ury**. [Gr *planos* wandering, and *ouron* urine]

planxty *plangks'ti, n* an Irish dance or dance-tune, like a jig but slower. [Origin unknown; not native Irish]

plap *plap, n* a flatter sound than a plop. — *vi* to make, or move with, such a sound. [Imit]

plaque *pläk* or *plak, n* a plate, tablet, or slab hung on, applied to or inserted in a surface as an ornament, memorial, etc; a tablet worn as a badge of honour; a patch, such as a diseased area (*med*); a film composed of saliva and bacteria that forms on teeth (*dentistry*); an area in a bacterial or tissue culture where the cells have been destroyed by infection with a virus. — *n* **plaquette'** a small plaque. [Fr; cf **plack**]

plash[1] *plash*, *vt* to interweave (branches and twigs) by partly cutting through, bending and twining, so as to form a hedge, etc; to bend down; to break down; to make, mend, or treat (a hedge) by cutting, bending, and interweaving stems and branches. — *n* a plashed branch; a plashed place. — *n* **plash'ing**. [OFr *plassier*, from L *plectere* to twist; cf **pleach**]

plash[2] *plash* or (*Spenser*) **plesh** *plesh*, *n* a shallow pool; a puddle. — *n* **plash'et** a puddle. — *adj* **plash'y**. [OE *plæsc*]

plash[3] *plash*, *n* a dash of water; a splashing sound; a sudden downpour (*esp Scot*). — *vi* to dabble in water; to splash. — *vt* to splash. — *adj* **plash'y**. [Cf MLGer *plaschen*, early Mod Du *plasschen*; perh connected with **plash**[2]]

plasm *plazm*, *n* a mould or matrix (*obs*); a formative substance, protoplasm, used as a combining form as in *cytoplasm*, *germ plasm*; plasma. — *n* **plas'ma** plasm; a bright green chalcedony (*geol*); protoplasm; the liquid part of blood, lymph, or milk; a very hot ionized gas, having approximately equal numbers of positive ions and of electrons, highly conducting (*phys*). — *n* **plasmapherē'sis** the process of taking only the plasma from a blood donor, the blood cells being separated from the plasma by a centrifuge and returned to the donor. — *adj* **plasmat'ic**, **plasmat'ical** or **plas'mic** of or occurring in plasma; protoplasmic. — *n* **plas'mid** a circular piece of DNA which can exist and reproduce autonomously in the cytoplasm of cells. — *n* **plas'min** fibrinolysin, an enzyme that breaks down the fibrous protein (fibrin) in blood clots. — *n* **plasmin'ogen** (*-ə-jən*) the substance in blood plasma from which plasmin is formed. — *n* **plasmodesm** (*plaz'mō-dezm*; Gr *desmos* bond) a thread of protoplasm connecting cells: — *pl* **plasmodesma'ta**. — *adj* **plasmo'dial**. — *n* **plasmo'dium** a naked mass of protoplasm with many nuclei, as in myxomycetes; a parasitic sporozoan of the genus *Plasmodium* which causes malaria: — *pl* **plasmo'dia**. — *n* **plasmog'amy** fusion of cytoplasm only. — *n* **plasmolysis** (*-mol'i-sis*; see **-lysis**) removal of water from a cell by osmosis, with resultant shrinking. — *adj* **plasmolytic** (*-mō-lit'ik*). — *vt* **plas'molyze** or **plas'molyse** (*-līz*). — *n* **plasmosō'ma** (*pl* **plasmosō'mata**) or **plas'mosome** (see **-some**) a nucleolus. [Gr *plasma*, *-atos* a thing moulded, from *plassein* to mould]

plast or **plaste** *plăst*, (*Spenser*) *pa t* and *pa p* of **place**.

-plast *plast*, *combining form* denoting a particle of living matter or an organized living cell. [Gr *plastos* formed]

plaster *pläs'tər*, *n* a fabric coated with an adhesive substance for local application as a remedy, or with a pad for the protection of a cut, etc; (*esp* formerly) a curative substance spread on linen and applied locally; a pasty composition that sets hard, *esp* a mixture of slaked lime, sand, and sometimes hair, used for coating walls, etc; plaster of Paris; calcium sulphate, gypsum. — *adj* made of plaster. — *vt* to apply plaster, or a plaster, or a plaster cast to; to treat with plaster; to bedaub; to smear; to cover excessively, injudiciously, or meretriciously; to stick (with *on* or *over*); to reduce to plaster or a sticky mass; to damage by a heavy attack; to smooth (hair) down; to smooth (with *over*); to treat with gypsum; to attach with plaster. — *vi* (with *over*) to smooth plaster over (cracks, etc). — *adj* **plas'tered** daubed, treated, etc, with plaster; shattered; intoxicated (*slang*). — *n* **plas'terer** a person who plasters, or someone who works in plaster. — *n* **plas'teriness**. — *n* **plas'tering**. — *adj* **plas'tery** like plaster. — **plas'terboard** a slab of hardened plaster faced on both sides with paper or thin board, used to form or line interior walls; **plaster cast** a copy obtained by pouring a mixture of plaster of Paris and water into a mould formed from the object; an immobilizing and protective covering of plaster of Paris for a broken limb, etc; **plaster saint** a virtuous person; someone who pretends hypocritically to be virtuous; **plas'terstone** gypsum; **plas'terwork**. — **plaster of Paris** gypsum (*orig* found near *Paris*) partially dehydrated by heat, which dries into a hard substance when mixed with water. [OE *plaster* (in medical sense) and OFr *plastre* (builder's plaster) both from LL *plastrum*, from L *emplastrum*, from Gr *emplastron* for *emplaston*, from *en* on, and *plassein* to mould, apply as a plaster]

plastic *plas'tik* or *pläs'tik*, *adj* having the power to take on different forms, mouldable; shaping, formative; of or relating to moulding or modelling; modifiable; capable of permanent reshaping without giving way; capable of or relating to metabolism and growth; made of plastic; unattractively synthetic or artificial. — *combining form* denoting growing, forming, as in *neoplastic*. — *n* a mouldable substance, *esp* now any of a large number of polymeric substances, most of them synthetic, mouldable at some stage under heat or pressure (see **thermoplastic**, **thermosetting**), used to make domestic articles and on many engineering products; a modeller or sculptor (*obs*); the art of modelling or of sculpture; short for **plastic money** (*colloq*). — *n sing* **plas'tics** the scientific study, or industrial production, of plastic materials; plastic surgery; the art of modelling or sculpture. — *adj* dealing with plastic materials (as in *the plastics industry*). — *n* **plasticity** (*-tis'i-ti*) the state or quality of being plastic; the quality in a picture of appearing to be three-dimensional. — *vt* and *vi* **plas'ticize** or **-ise** (*-ti-sīz*) to make or become plastic. — *n* **plasticiz'er** or **-s-** a substance that induces plasticity. — **plastic art** the art or any of the arts of shaping in three dimensions, such as ceramics, sculpture, modelling; art which is, or appears to be, three-dimensional; **plastic bag** a bag made of polythene, etc in any of various sizes and qualities, *esp* one with handles used as a carrier; **plastic bomb** a bomb made with a certain explosive chemical that can be moulded; **plastic bullet** a four-inch cylinder of PVC fired for the purpose of riot control; **plastic clay** clay from which earthenware and bricks are made; **plastic explosive** an adhesive explosive material of jelly-like consistency; **plastic force** the force or power of growth in animals and plants; **plastic money** (*colloq*) credit cards, bankers cards; **plastic operation** a surgical operation which restores a lost part, or repairs a deformed or disfigured part, of the body; **plastic surgeon**; **plastic surgery** the branch of surgery concerned with plastic operations. [Gr *plastikos* from *plassein*, to mould]

Plasticene® a kind of modelling material that remains soft and can be reworked, used *esp* by children.

plastid *plas'tid* or *pläs'tid*, *n* a living cell (*obs*); a differentiated granule in protoplasm. — *n* **plast'idule** Haeckel's hypothetical unit of living protoplasm. [Gr *plastis*, *-idos* modeller (fem)]

plastilina *pläs-ti-lē'nə*, *n* a mixture of clay with oil, zinc oxide, wax, and sulphur for modelling. [Ital]

plastique *plas-tēk'*, *n* graceful poses and movements in dancing. [Fr, from Gr *plastikos* (see **plastic**)]

plastisol *plas'ti-sol*, *n* a suspension of powdered resin in liquid plasticizer, convertible by heat into a solid plastic and used in castings and linings. [**plastic** and **sol**[2]]

plastogamy *plast-og'ə-mi*, *n* plasmogamy. [Gr *plastos* moulded, and *gamos* marriage]

plastron *plas'tron*, *n* a steel breastplate worn under the hauberk (*hist*); a fencer's wadded breast-shield; the ventral section of the shell of a tortoise or turtle, or other animal; the front of a dress shirt; a separate ornamental front part of a woman's bodice. — *adj* **plas'tral**. [Fr *plastron*, from Ital *piastrone*, from *piastra* breastplate; cf **piastre**, **plaster**]

-plasty *-plas'ti*, *combining form* signifying plastic surgery involving a bodily part, tissue or a specified process, as in *rhinoplasty*. [Gr *-plastia*; cf **-plast**]

plat[1]. See **plait**.

plat[2] *plat*, *n* a plot of ground (*archaic*); a diagram or a plan (*obs* or *US*); a scheme (*obs*). — *vt* (now *US*) to make a plan of, plot out. [**plot**[1], influenced by **plat**[3]]

plat[3] *plat*, *n* a flat thing (*obs*); a flat surface, part, or side (*obs*); a mould-board (*dialect*); a flat place or region (*esp US*). [Appar Fr *plat*]

platane or **platan** *plat'ən*, *n* a plane tree, any tree of the genus **Plat'anus**, giving name to the family **Platanā'ceae**, related to the witch-hazel family. — *adj* **platanā'ceous**. [L *platanus*, from Gr *platanos*, from *platys* broad]

platanna *plə-tan'ə*, *n* (also **platanna frog**) an African frog, *Xenopus laevis*, used in research, and formerly used in tests for pregnancy. [Afrikaans, from *plat-hander* flat-handed]

platband *plat'band*, *n* a fascia or flat moulding projecting less than its own breadth; a lintel or flat arch; an edging of turf or flowers. [Fr *platebande* flat band]

plat du jour *pla dü zhōōr*, *n* a dish on a restaurant menu specially recommended that day. [Fr]

plate *plāt*, *n* a sheet, slab, or lamina of metal or other hard material, *usu* flat or flattish; metal in the form of sheets; a broad piece of armour; a scute or separate portion of an animal's shell; a broad thin piece of a structure or mechanism; a plate-like section of the earth's crust, involved in plate tectonics (see below); a piece of metal, wood, etc, bearing or to bear an inscription to be affixed to anything; an engraved piece of metal for printing from; an impression printed from it, an engraving; an illustration in a book, *esp* a whole-page one separately printed and inserted; a mould from type, etc, for printing from, as an electrotype or stereotype; part of a denture fitting the mouth and carrying the teeth; the whole denture; a device worn in the mouth by some children in order to straighten the teeth; a film-coated sheet of glass or other material to photograph on; a plate-rail (see below); a horizontal supporting timber in building; a five-sided white slab at the home base (*baseball*); a light racing horseshoe; a thermionic valve anode (*orig* flat); precious metal, *esp* silver (*hist*; Sp *plata* silver); a silver coin (*Shakesp*); wrought gold or silver; household utensils in gold or silver; table utensils generally; plated ware such as **Sheffield plate** a silver-plated copper ware; a cup or other prize for a race or other contest; a race or contest for such a prize; a shallow dish of any of various sizes according to purpose, eg *dessert plate*, *dinner plate*, *side plate*; a plateful; a portion served on a plate; a church collection; (in *pl*) the feet (*slang*; *orig* rhyming slang for *plates of meat*). — *vt* to overlay with metal; to armour with metal; to cover with a thin film of another metal; to make a printing plate of. — *adj* **plā'ted** covered with plates of metal; covered with a coating of another metal, *esp* gold or silver; armoured with hard scales or bone (*zool*). — *n* **plate'ful** as much as a plate will hold. — *n* **plate'let** a minute particle in blood, concerned in clotting. — *n* **plā'ter** a person who or something which plates; a moderate horse entered for a minor, *esp* a selling, race. — *n* **plā'ting**. — *adj* **plā'ty** plate-like; separating into plates. — **plate'-armour** protective armour of metal plates; **plate'-basket** a basket for forks, spoons, etc; **plate'-fleet** (*hist*) ships that carried American silver to Spain; **plate glass** a fine kind of glass used for mirrors and shop-windows, *orig* poured in a molten state on an iron plate. — *adj* (**plate'-glass**) made with or consisting of plate glass; (of a building) having large plate glass windows, appearing to be built entirely of plate glass; (hence) used of any very modern building or institution, *esp* British universities founded in the mid 20c. — **plate'-layer** a person who lays, fixes, and attends to the rails of a railway; **plate'-leather** a chamois leather for rubbing gold and silver. — *adj* **plate'-like**. — **plate'man** a man who has the care of silver-plate in a hotel, club, etc; **plate'mark** a hallmark; **plate'-powder** a polishing powder for silver; **plate'-print'ing** the process of printing from engraved plates; **plate'-proof** a proof taken from a plate; **plate rack** a frame for holding plates, etc, when not in use or when draining after washing; **plate rail** on early railways, a flat rail with an outer flange; **plate'-room** a room where silver-plated goods or printing plates are kept; **plate'-ship** (*hist*) a ship bringing silver to Spain from America; **plate tectonics** (*geol*) the interrelating movements of the rigid plates or sections that make up the earth's crust, riding on the semi-molten rock of the interior; the science or study of these movements; the study of the crust in terms of this theory; **plate'-warmer** an apparatus for warming dinner plates or keeping them warm. — **half'-plate** (in photography) a size of plate measuring $4\frac{3}{4}$ by $6\frac{1}{2}$ inches ($4\frac{1}{4}$ by $5\frac{1}{2}$ in the US; **quar'ter-plate** a plate size $3\frac{1}{4}$ by $4\frac{1}{4}$ inches; **whole'-plate** a plate size $6\frac{1}{2}$ by $8\frac{1}{2}$ inches); **hand** or **give (someone something) on a plate** (*fig*) to cause or allow (someone) to achieve or obtain (something) without the least effort; **on one's plate** (*fig*) in front of one, waiting to be dealt with. [OFr *plate*, fem (and for the dish *plat*, masc), flat, from Gr *platys* broad]

plateasm *plat'i-azm*, *n* pronunciation with a wide mouth-opening, as in Doric Greek. [Gr *plateiasmos*, from *platys* broad]

plateau *pla'tō* or *pla-tō'*, *n* a large level tract of elevated land, a tableland; an ornamented tray, plate, or plaque; a lady's flat-topped hat; a temporary stable state reached in the course of upward progress; the part of a curve representing this: — *pl* **plateaux** (*-tōz*) or **plateaus**. — *vi* to reach a level, even out (sometimes with *out*). [Fr, from OFr *platel*, dimin of *plat*]

platen *plat'n*, *n* the work-table of a machine-tool; a flat part that in some printing-presses pushes the paper against the forme; the roller of a typewriter. [Fr *platine*, from *plat* flat]

plateresque *plat-ə-resk'*, (*archit*) *adj* applied to a style resembling silversmith's work. [Sp *plateresco*, from *platero* silversmith, from *plata* silver]

platform *plat'förm*, *n* a raised floor for speakers, musicians, etc; a raised pavement alongside the track in a railway station giving access to trains; a position prepared for mounting a gun; any raised level surface; a terrace; a flooring; a plateau; a deck for a temporary or special purpose; a floating installation *usu* moored to the sea bed, for drilling for oil, marine research, etc; flooring outside an inner entrance to some buses, trams, or sometimes railway carriages; a site; a platform shoe or boot; the thick heavy sole of such a shoe or boot; a basis; the publicly declared principles and intentions of a political party, taken as forming the basis of its policies; any situation giving one access to an audience, that one can exploit as an opportunity for promoting one's views; the people occupying the platform at a meeting, etc; public speaking or discussion (*fig*); a medium for discussion; a scheme of church government or of administrative policy; a scheme, device, plan of action (*Shakesp*); a ground-plan (*obs*); a plane figure or surface (*obs*). — *adj* on, relating to, admitting to, etc, a platform; (of shoes, boots, etc) having a very thick sole (a **platform sole**), giving extra height. — *vt* to provide with a platform; to sketch, plan; to place on, or as if on, a platform. — *vi* (*rare*) to speak or appear on a platform. [Fr *plateforme*, literally flat form]

platforming *plat'förm-ing*, *n* a process for reforming low-grade petrol into high-grade, using a platinum catalyst. [**plat(inum)** and **form**]

plating. See under **plate**.

platinum *plat'in-əm*, *n* a noble metal (symbol **Pt**; atomic no 78), a steel-grey element, very valuable, malleable and ductile, very heavy and hard to fuse (older name **plat'ina**). — *adj* made of platinum. — *adj* **platinic** (*plə-tin'ik*) of platinum, *esp* tetravalent. — *adj* **platinif'erous** platinum-bearing. — *vt* **plat'inize** or **-ise** to coat with platinum. — *n* **plat'inoid** one of the metals with which platinum is always found associated — *palladium*, *iridium*, etc; an alloy of copper, zinc, nickel, and tungsten resembling platinum. — *n* **plat'inotype**

(also with *cap*) an obsolete method of photography by reducing a compound of platinum; a photograph so produced. — *adj* **plat'inous** of bivalent platinum. — **platinum black** platinum in the form of a velvety black powder. — *adj* **platinum-blond'** (of hair) silvery blond. — **platinum blonde** a woman with hair of this colour; **platinum disc** a framed copy in platinum of an LP record that has sold over 300 000 copies (1 million in the US), awarded to the recording artist(s) by the record company; **platinum lamp** an electric lamp with a platinum filament. — **go platinum** (*colloq*) (of a recording or an artist) to sell in quantities sufficient to merit a platinum disc. [Sp *platina*, from *plata* silver]

platitude *plat'i-tūd*, *n* flatness; a dull commonplace or truism; an empty remark made as if it were important. — *n* **platitudinā'rian** someone who indulges in platitudes. — *vi* **plat'itudinize** or **-ise**. — *adj* **platitud'inous**. [Fr, from *plat* flat]

Platonic *plə-ton'ik*, *adj* of or relating to Plato, the Greek philosopher (about 427–347 BC), or to his philosophy; (often without *cap*; of love) between soul and soul, *orig* between male friends, without sensual desire (a Renaissance interpretation of Plato's theory); relating to or experiencing platonic love. — *n* a Platonist; a platonic lover; (*usu* in *pl*) platonic love. — *adj* **Platon'ical** (now *rare*). — *adv* **platon'ically**. — *n* **Platon'icism** the doctrine, practice, or profession of platonic love; Platonism (*obs*). — *n* **Plā'tonism** the philosophy of Plato; Platonicism. — *n* **Plā'tonist** a follower of Plato. — *vt* **Platonize** or **-ise** (*plā'tən-īz*) to render Platonic. — *vi* to follow Plato. — **Platonic solid** any of the five regular polyhedrons (tetrahedron, hexahedron, octahedron, dodecahedron, and icosahedron); **Platonic year** see under **year**. [Gr *platōnikos*, from *Platōn*, *-ōnos* Plato]

platoon *plə-tōōn'*, *n orig* a small body of soldiers in a hollow square formation, or such a body firing together; a subdivision of a company (*military*); a squad; a group of people acting together; a volley (*archaic*). [Fr *peloton* ball, knot of men, from L *pila* ball]

Platt-Deutsch *plät'-doich*, *n* and *adj* Low German. [Ger]

platted and **platting**. Same as **plaited** and **plaiting** (see under **plait**).

platteland *plä'tə-länt*, (*SAfr*) *n* rural districts. [Afrik]

platter *plat'ər*, *n* a large flat plate or dish; a gramophone record (*slang*, *esp US*). [Anglo-Fr *plater*, from *plat* a plate]

platy. See under **plate**.

platy- *plat'i-*, *combining form* signifying flat or broad. [Gr *platys*, broad]

platycephalous *plat-i-sef'ə-ləs*, *adj* having the vault of the skull flattened. — Also **platycephalic** (*-si-fal'ik*). [**platy-** and **-cephalous**]

Platyhelminthes *plat-i-hel-min'thēz*, *n pl* the flatworms, a phylum including planarians, tapeworms, and flukes. [**platy-** and Gr *helmins*, *-inthos* intestinal worm]

platypus *plat'i-pəs* or *-pōōs*, *n* an aquatic burrowing and egg-laying Australian monotreme (genus *Ornithorhynchus*), one of the primitive forms of mammals, with broadly webbed feet and duck-like bill: — *pl* **plat'ypuses**. [**platy-** and Gr *pous*, *podos* a foot]

platyrrhine *plat'i-rīn* or **platyrrhinian** *plat-i-rin'i-ən*, *adj* broad-nosed; belonging to the division of the monkeys found in S America, which have widely spaced nostrils. — *n* a New World monkey; a broad-nosed person. [Gr *platyrrīs*, *-īnos*, from *rhīs*, *rhīnos* nose]

platysma *plat-iz'mə*, *n* a broad sheet of muscle in the neck. [Gr *platysma* a flat piece]

plaudit *plö'dit*, *n* (now *usu* in *pl*) an act of applause; praise bestowed, enthusiastic approval. — *adj* **plaud'itory**. [Shortened from L *plaudite* applaud, an actor's call for applause at the end of a play, plural imperative of *plaudere*, *plausum* to clap the hands]

plaudite *plö'dit-i* or *plow'dit-e*, (*L*) *imperative* applaud; clap your hands.

plausible *plö'zi-bl*, *adj* that may be applauded (*obs*); acceptable (*obs*); likely, reasonable, seemingly true; seemingly worthy of approval or praise; fair-showing; specious; smooth-tongued and ingratiating. — *n* **plausibil'ity** or **plaus'ibleness**. — *adv* **plaus'ibly** in a plausible manner; with applause, by acclamation (*Shakesp*); commendably, pleasantly (*obs*). — *adj* **plausive** (*plö'ziv*) plausible (*Shakesp*); pleasing (*Shakesp*); applauding. [L *plaudere* to clap the hands]

plaustral *plös'trəl*, *adj* (*facetious*) of a wagon. [L *plaustrum* a wagon]

play *plā*, *vi* to operate (*obs*); to move about irregularly, lightly, or freely; to have some freedom of movement; to flicker, flutter, shimmer, pass through rapid alternations; to appear faintly and fleetingly (*usu* with *round*); to move in, discharge, or direct a succession, stream, or shower (eg of water, light, waves, or missiles); to engage in pleasurable activity; to perform acts not part of the immediate business of life but in mimicry or rehearsal or in display; to amuse oneself; to sport; to make sport; to trifle; to behave without seriousness; to behave amorously or sexually; to take part in a game; (with *for*) to compete on the side of; to proceed with the game, perform one's part in turn; to deliver a ball, etc, in the course of a game; to contend with weapons (*archaic*); to wield a weapon; to gamble; to have a holiday (*Shakesp*; also *Scot*); to be off work (*N Eng*); to perform on a musical instrument; to produce or emit music; (of music) to come forth; to act a part; to co-operate (*colloq*). — *vt* to perform; to ply, wield; to cause or allow to play; to set in opposition, pit; to send, let off, or discharge in succession or in a stream or shower; to give a limited freedom of movement to; hence, to manage; to allow (a fish) to tire itself by its struggles to get away; to engage in (a game or recreative mimicry); to oppose (in a game, sport, etc); to proceed through (a game, part of a game — eg a stroke, trick — or an aggregate of games — eg a rubber, set); to stake or risk in play; to gamble on (*colloq*); to bring into operation in a game, as by striking (a ball), by throwing (a card) on the table, by moving (a chess piece); to compete against in a game or sport; to compete on the side of (with *for*); to act (eg comedy or a named play); to act the part of, in a play or in real life; to act or perform in (eg a circuit of theatres or halls or a town, etc); to pretend in fun; to perform music on; to perform (a tune, etc) on a musical instrument; to cause (a radio, stereo system, etc) to emit sound; to lead, bring, send, render, or cause to be by playing; (*reflexive*) to amuse (oneself; *obs* and *Scot*); (*reflexive*) to waste time, fool around (*colloq*): — *pr p* **play'ing**; *pa t* and *pa p* **played**. — *n* activity; operation; action of wielding; light fluctuating movement or change; some freedom of movement, as opposed to absolute tightness or tautness; scope; recreative activity; display of animals in courtship; amusement; fun; dalliance; a game (*Shakesp*); the playing of a game; manner of playing; procedure or policy in a game; holiday (*Shakesp* and *Scot*); a fair or festival (*dialect*); being off work (*N Eng*); gambling; a drama or dramatic performance; manner of dealing, as in *fair play* (*fig*). — *adj* **play'able** capable (by nature or by the rules of the game) of being played, or of being played on. — *n* **play'er** a person who plays; a person participating in or skilled at *esp* a game or sport; an actor; a trifler; an instrumental performer; a mechanism for playing a musical instrument; an apparatus for playing records, etc, as in *record-player*, *cassette-player*; (in N Ireland) a terrorist, *esp* one who is young and unknown; anyone who has an interest in and who plays a part in, eg formulating a policy, taking a decision, etc (*colloq*). — *adj* **play'ful** full of fun, frolicsome, frisky; high-spirited, humorous. — *adv* **play'fully**. — *n* **play'fulness**. — *n* **play'let** a short play. — *adj* **play'some** playful. — *vi* **play'-act**. — **play'-acting** performance of plays; pretence; **play'-actor** or **play'-actress** professional actor or actress (*usu derog*); **play'back** the act of reproducing a recording of sound or visual material, *esp* immediately after it is made; a device for doing this (see also **play back** below); **play'bill** a bill announcing a play; **play'book** a printed play or book of plays; **play'-box** (*old*) a box for toys and other valued possessions, *esp* in a boarding-school; **play'boy** a boy-actor (*archaic*); a light-hearted irresponsible person, *esp* rich, leisured and pleasure-seeking: — *fem* (*rare*) **play'girl**; **play'bus®** a bus equipped with facilities for children's play, driven to districts where no adequate playgroup facilities are available; **play'-day** a holiday; **play'-debt** a debt incurred in gambling. — *adj* **played'-out** exhausted; used up; no longer good for anything. — **play'er-pian'o** a mechanical piano, a Pianola® (qv under **pianoforte**); **play'fellow** a playmate; **playgirl** see **playboy** above; **play'-gōer** someone who habitually attends the theatre; **play'-gōing**; **play'ground** an outdoor area for playing in, *esp* one connected with a school; a holiday region; **play'group** an informal, sometimes voluntarily run group having morning or afternoon sessions attended by preschool children sometimes with their mothers or fathers, for creative and co-operative play; **play'house** a theatre; a child's toy house, *usu* big enough for a child to enter; **play'ing-card** one of a pack (*usu* of fifty-two cards, divided into four suits) used in playing games; **play'ing-field** a grass-covered space set apart, marked out, and kept in order for games (**a level** or **flat playing-field** (*colloq*) fair competition); **play'-leader** a person trained to supervise and organize children's play in a playground, etc; **play'-list** those recordings selected to be broadcast regularly by a radio station; **play'-mare** (*Scot*) a hobby-horse, as in the old morris-dance; **play'mate** a companion in play, *esp* child's play; **play'-off** a game to decide a tie; a game between the winners of other competitions; see also **play off** below; **play'pen** an enclosure within which a young child may safely play; **play'room** a room for children to play in; **play'school** a nursery school or playgroup; **play'-spell** a time allowed for play; **play'suit** a set of clothes for a child or woman, *usu* shorts and a top, for sunbathing, relaxing, etc; **play'thing** a toy; a person or thing treated as a toy; **play'time** a time for play; (in schools) a set period for playing, *usu* out of doors; **play'-way** the educational use of play; **play'world** an imaginary world feigned in play; **play'wright** or **play'-writer** a dramatist. — **bring, call** or **come into play** to bring, call or come into exercise, operation or use; **hold in play** (or *archaic* **hold play**) to keep occupied, *esp* to gain time or detain; **in** (or **out of**) **play** (of a ball, etc) in (or not in) a position to be played; **make a play for** (*colloq*) to try to get; to attempt to seduce; **make great play with** or **of** to make a lot of; to treat or talk of as very important; **make play** to keep things going, push on with the game; **play about** to behave irresponsibly, not seriously; **play along** (with *with*) to co-operate or agree with someone, *usu* temporarily; **play a part** (with *in*) to be instrumental in, help in doing something; to act a theatrical role; **play around** to play about; to have amorous affairs with men or women other than one's spouse; **play at** to engage in the game of; to make a pretence of; to practise without seriousness; **play back** to play (a sound or video recording) that has just been made; **play ball** (*colloq*) to co-operate; **play by ear** see under **ear** (see also **play it by ear** below); **play down** to treat (something) as not very important or probable, *esp* less so than it is; **play fair** (sometimes with *with*) to act honestly; **play false** (sometimes with *with*; *archaic*) to act dishonestly towards or betray someone; **play fast and loose** to act in a shifty, inconsistent, and reckless fashion; **play fine** (in billiards) to strike the object-ball near the edge (as opposed to **play full**, to strike it nearer the middle than the edge); **play for safety** to play safe; **play for time** to delay action or decision in the hope or belief that conditions will become more favourable later; **play hard to get** to make a show of unwillingness to co-operate with a view to strengthening one's position; **play havoc** or **hell with** to upset, disorganize; to damage; **play into the hands of** to act so as to give, *usu* unintentionally, an advantage to; **play it** (*colloq*; *usu* followed by an *adj*) to behave in or manage a particular situation in a stated way, as in *play it cool*; **play it by ear** to improvise a plan of action to meet the situation as it develops (see also **play by ear** under **ear**); **play it** (or **one's cards**) **close to the** (or **one's**) **chest** to be secretive about one's actions or intentions in a particular matter; **play off** to manipulate so as to counteract; to set (one person against another); to play from the tee (*golf*); to have as a handicap (*golf*); to toss off (*Shakesp*); to bring off (eg a hoax); **play on** to strike the ball on to one's own wicket (*cricket*); (also **play upon**) to direct one's efforts to the exciting of, work upon (feelings, emotions, etc); **play on** or **upon words** a pun or other manipulation of words depending on their sound; **play out** to play to the end; to wear out, to exhaust; **play safe** to take no risks; **play the field** (*colloq*) to spread one's interests, affections or efforts over a wide range of subjects, people, activities, etc, rather than concentrating on any single one; **play the game** to act strictly honourably; **play up** to strike up, begin the music; to redouble one's efforts, play more vigorously; to show up well in a crisis or emergency; to give (*esp* undue) prominence to, or to boost; to fool; to function faultily (*colloq*); to behave unco-operatively (*colloq*); (of an impaired part of the body) to give one trouble or pain (*colloq*); **play upon** see **play on** above; **play up to** to act so as to afford opportunities to (another actor); to flatter; **play with** to play in the company of, or as partner or opponent to; to dally with; to stimulate (the genitals of), to masturbate (oneself or someone else). [OE *pleg(i)an*, verb, *plega*, noun]

playa *plä'yə*, *n* a basin which becomes a shallow lake after heavy rainfall and dries out again in hot weather. [Sp]

plaza *plä'zə*, *n* a public square or open, *usu* paved, area in a city or town. [Sp]

PLC or **plc** *abbrev*: public limited company.

plea *plē*, *n* a lawsuit (*Scots law* and *hist*); a pleading; a prisoner's or defendant's answer to a charge or claim; a claim (*Shakesp*); an excuse; a pretext; an urgent entreaty. — *vt* and *vi* to dispute in a law-court. — *n* **plea bargain** and *vi* **plea'-bargain**. — *n* **plea'-bargaining** the (*esp US*) legal practice of arranging more lenient treatment by the court in exchange for the accused's admitting to the crime, turning State's evidence, etc. [OFr *plai*, *plaid*, *plait*, from LL *placitum* a decision, from L *placēre*, *-itum* to please]

pleach *plēch*, *vt* to intertwine the branches of (eg a hedge); to fold (the arms; *Shakesp*); to plash. [From form of OFr *pless(i)er*, from L *plectere*; see **plash**[1]]

plead *plēd*, *vi* to carry on a plea or lawsuit; to argue in support of a cause against another; to put forward an allegation or answer in court; to implore, make an entreaty (with *with*). — *vt* to maintain by argument; to allege in pleading; to put forward as a plea; to offer in excuse; to sue for (*archaic* and *Scot*): — *pa t*, *pa p* **plead'ed** also (*Spenser*, *Scot*, *US*, and *dialect*) **pled**. — *adj* **plead'able** capable of being pleaded. — *n* **plead'er** a person who pleads; an advocate. — *adj* **plead'ing** imploring. — *n* the act of putting forward or conducting a plea; (in *pl*) the statements of the two parties in a lawsuit; entreaty. — *adv* **plead'ingly**. — **pleading diet** (in Scots law) a preliminary appearance in court of the accused person before a trial, at which the accused indicates whether he or she will plead guilty or not guilty, and lodges any special pleas, eg of insanity, etc. — **plead guilty** (or **not guilty**) to state that one is guilty (or innocent) of a crime with which one is charged; **special pleading** unfair or one-sided argument aiming rather at victory than at truth. [OFr *plaidier*; cf **plea**]

pleasance *plez'əns*, (*archaic* and *poetic*) *n* pleasure; enjoyment; pleasantness; complaisance, pleasant behaviour (*obs*); that which gives pleasure; a pleasure-ground or specialized part of a garden. [OFr *plaisance*, from *plaisant*, pr p of *plaisir*; cf **pleasant**]

pleasant *plez'ənt*, *adj* pleasing; agreeable; inoffensive; affable; good-humoured; cheerful; merry (*obs*); tipsy (*facetious*). — *adv* **pleas'antly**. — *n* **pleas'antness**. — *n* **pleas'antry** an agreeable remark made for the sake of politeness; pleasantness, enjoyment (*obs*); jocularity; a facetious utterance or trick: — *pl* **pleas'antries**. [OFr *plaisant*, pr p of *plaisir* to please]

please *plēz*, *vt* to give pleasure to; to delight; to satisfy; to be the will or choice of (to do something). — *vi* to give pleasure; to like, think fit, choose (*orig* impersonal with dative, eg *it pleases* (*to*) *me*; later *me pleases*; then *I please*). — *interj* used in making polite requests, or in politely accepting an offer, etc, as in *yes, please*. — *adj* **pleased** (*plēzd*) grateful; delighted; willing, or inclined (to do something). — *n* **pleas'er**. — *adj* and *n* **pleas'ing**. — *adv* **pleas'ingly**. — *n* **pleas'ingness**. — *n* **pleaseman** (*plēz'man* or *-mən*; *Shakesp*) an officious fellow, a pick-thank. — **if you please** if you like; a polite formula of request or acceptance (*old*); forsooth (*ironic*); certainly (*ironic*); **may it please you** or **so please you** deferential or polite formulas of address or request; **please**, also (now *rare*) **please to** a polite formula equivalent to **if you please**, now felt as imperative, perhaps *orig* from the older **please it you** or **please it** (sometimes printed **pleaseth** in *Shakesp*) or **please you** may it please you; **pleased as Punch** delighted; **please yourself** do as you like. [OFr *plaisir* (Fr *plaire*), from L *placēre* to please]

pleasure *plezh'ər*, *n* agreeable emotions; gratification of the senses or of the mind; sensuality; dissipation; a source of gratification; what the will prefers; purpose; command. — *vt* (*archaic*) to give pleasure to. — vi (*archaic*; with *in*) to take pleasure in. — *adj* **pleasurable** (*plezh'ə-rə-bl*) able to give pleasure; delightful; gratifying; pleasure-seeking (*obs*). — *n* **pleas'urableness**. — *adv* **pleas'urably**. — *adj* **pleas'ureful**. — *adj* **pleas'ureless**. — *n* **pleas'urer** a pleasure-seeker. — **pleasure boat** a boat used for pleasure or amusement. — *adj* **pleas'ure-giving**. — **pleasure ground** ground laid out in an ornamental manner for pleasure and recreation; **pleasure house** a house to which one retires for recreation or pleasure; **pleasure-pain principle** the principle that dominates the instincts, directing one's behaviour towards seeking pleasure and avoiding pain; **pleas'ure-seeker** someone who seeks pleasure; a holiday-maker; **pleas'ure-seeking**; **pleasure trip** an excursion for pleasure. — **at pleasure** when, if or as one pleases. [ME and OFr *plesir*]

pleat *plēt*, *n* any of several types of fold sewn or pressed into cloth; a plait (qv) or braid (*obs* or *dialect*). — *vt* to make pleats in; to plait or intertwine (*obs* or *dialect*). — *adj* **pleat'ed**. — *n* **pleat'er**. [From **plait**]

pleb *pleb*, (*colloq*) *n* a person of unpolished manners or vulgar tastes, a plebian, a boor. — *adj* **plebb'y**. — *n* **plebifica'tion**. — *vt* **pleb'ity** to make plebeian or vulgar. [**plebeian**]

plebeian *pli-bē'ən* (*Shakesp* also **plebean** *pleb'i-ən*), *adj* of the Roman plebs (see separate entry); of the common people; low-born; undistinguished; vulgar-looking; vulgar, lacking taste or refinement. — *n* a member of the plebs (qv) of ancient Rome; a commoner; a member of a despised social class; a boor, a vulgarian. — *n* **plebei'anism**. — *vt* **plebei'anize** or **-ise**. [L *plēbēius*, from *plēbs*, *plēbis*]

plebiscite *pleb'i-sit* or *-sīt*, *n* a law enacted by the plebs assembled in the *Concilia tributa* (*Roman hist*); a direct vote of the whole nation or of the people of a district on a special point; an ascertainment of general opinion on any matter. — *adj* **plebisc'itary**. [Partly through Fr *plébiscite*, from L *plēbiscītum*, from *plēbs* plebs, and *scītum* decree, from *scīscere* to vote for]

plebs *plebz*, *n* one of the two divisions of the Roman people, *orig* the less privileged politically. — See also **pleb** and **plebeian**. [L *plēbs*, *plēbis*]

Plecoptera *ple-kop'tər-ə*, *n pl* the stonefly order of insects, with hind-wings folded fanwise. — *adj* **plecop'terous**. [Gr *plekein* plait, and *pteron* wing]

Plectognathi *plek-tog'nə-thī*, (*zool*) *n pl* an order of bony fishes including file-fishes, globe-fishes, coffer-fishes and sun-fishes. — *adj* **plectognathic** (*-tə-gnath'ik*) or **plectog'nathous** (*-nə-thəs*). [Gr *plektos* plaited, and *gnathos* a jaw]

Plectoptera *plek-top'tə-rə*, *n pl* the mayfly order of insects, otherwise known as *Ephemeroptera*.— *adj* **plectop'terous**. [Gr *plektos* twisted, and *pteron* a wing]

plectrum *plek'trəm*, *n* the quill or other device for plucking the strings of the ancient Greek lyre or other musical instrument; a pointed device held in the fingers or on the thumb, with which the strings of eg a guitar are struck. — Also **plec'tre** (*-tər*) or **plec'tron**: — *pl* **plec'tra**, **plec'trums**, **plec'tres** or **plec'trons**. [L *plēctrum*, from Gr *plēktron*, from *plēssein* to strike]

pled *pled*. See **plead**.

pledge *plej*, *n* something given as a security; a gage; a token or sign of assurance; a child, as a token of love or binding obligation; someone who becomes surety for another (*obs*); a hostage (*obs*); a solemn promise; a friendly sentiment expressed by drinking; a state of being given, or held, as a security. — *vt* to give as security; to bind by solemn promise; to vow; to give assurance of; to drink a toast in response to; to drink at the invitation of another; to drink to the health of. — *adj* **pledge'able**. — *n* **pledgee'** the person to whom a thing is pledged. — *n* **pledger**, **pledgeor** or **pledgor** (*plej'ər*). — **take** or **sign the pledge** to give a written promise to abstain from intoxicating liquor. [OFr *plege* (Fr *pleige*), from LL *plevium*, *plivium*, prob Gmc]

pledget *plej'it*, *n* a wad of lint, cotton, etc, used as dressing for a wound or sore; an oakum string used in caulking. [Origin unknown]

pledgor. See under **pledge**.

-plegia *-plē-ji-ə*, *combining form* denoting paralysis, as in *paraplegia*, *quadriplegia*. — *adj* and *n combining form* **-plēgic**. [Gr *plēgē* stroke, from *plēssein* to strike]

Pleiad *plī'ad*, *n* any one of the seven daughters of Atlas and Pleione, changed into stars after his death (one 'lost' or invisible) (*Gr mythol*); a brilliant group of seven, *esp* seven Alexandrian tragic poets or a group of 16c French poets (*usu* as in Fr, **Pléiade** *plā-ē-äd*) comprising Ronsard, Du Bellay, Baïf, Daurat, and others variously selected. — **Plei'ads** or **Pleiades** (*plī'ə-dēz*) a group of six stars visible to the naked eye and a multitude of telescopic stars in the shoulder of the constellation Taurus. [Gr *pleias*, *plēias*, *-ados*, pl *-ades*]

plein-air *plen'-er'*, *adj* open-air; attaching importance to painting in the open air. — *n* **plein-air'ist** a plein-air painter. [Fr *en plein air* in the open air]

pleio- or **plio-** *plī-ō-*, *-ə-*, *-o'*, or **pleo-** *plē-ō-*, *-ə-*, *-o'*, *combining form* signifying more. [Gr *pleiōn* or *pleōn*, compar of *polys* many, much]

Pleiocene *plī-ō-sēn*, *adj* and *n*. Same as **Pliocene**.

pleiochasium *plī-ō-kā'zi-əm*, *n* a cymose inflorescence in which each branch bears more than two lateral branches. [Gr *chasis* separation; but cf **monochasium**]

pleiomerous *plī-om'ər-əs*, *adj* having more than the normal number of parts. — *n* **pleiom'ery** the condition of having more than the normal number. [Gr *meros* part]

pleiotropic *plī-ō-trop'ik*, *adj* (of a gene) having an effect simultaneously on more than one character in the offspring. — *n* **pleiot'ropism**. [Gr *tropos* turn]

Pleistocene *plīs'tə-sēn*, *adj* of the geological period following the Pliocene, having the greatest proportion of fossil molluscs of living species. — *n* the Pleistocene system, period, or strata. [Gr *pleistos* most (numerous), and *kainos* recent, from the proportion of living species of molluscs]

plenary *plē'nə-ri*, *adj* full; entire; complete; absolute; unqualified; passing through all its stages (as opposed to *summary*; *law*); having full powers; (of an assembly, session, etc) to be attended by all members or delegates. — *adv* **plē'narily**. — *n* **plē'narty** the state of a benefice when occupied. — **plenary indulgence** in the RC Church, full or complete remission of temporal penalties to a repentant sinner; **plenary inspiration** inspiration which excludes all mixture of error; **plenary powers** full powers to carry out some business or negotiations. [LL *plēnārius*, from L *plēnus* full, from *plēre* to fill]

plenilune *plen', plēn'i-lōōn* or *-lūn*, *n* the full moon; time of full moon. — *adj* **plenilu'nar**. [L *plēnilūnium*, from *plēnus* full, and *lūna* moon]

plenipotence *pli-nip'ə-təns*, or **plenipotency** *pli-nip'ə-tən-si*, *n* complete power. — *adj* **plenip'otent** having full power. — *adj* **plenipotential** (*plen-i-pə-ten'shəl*). — *adj* **plenipoten'tiary** (*-shə-ri* or *-shyə-ri*) having or conferring full powers; (of authority or power) absolute. — *n* a person invested with full powers, *esp* a special ambassador or envoy to some foreign court. — Archaic colloquial short form **plen'ipo**: — *pl* **plen'ipos** or **plen'ipoes**. [L *plēnus* full, and *potentia* power]

plenish *plen'ish*, (*archaic* or *Scot*) *vt* to supply, stock; to provide (eg a house or farm) with necessary furniture, implements, stock, etc. — *n* **plen'ishing** (*Scot*) furniture. [OFr *plenir*, *-iss-*, from L *plēnus* full]

plenist. See under **plenum**.

plenitude *plen'i-tūd*, *n* fullness; completeness; plentifulness; repletion. — *adj* **plenitud'inous**. [L *plēnitūdō*, *-inis*, from *plēnus* full]

pleno jure *plē'nō jōōr'ē* or *plā'nō yōōr'e*, (*L*) *adv* with full authority.

plentitude an error for **plenitude**.

plenty *plen'ti*, *n* a full supply; all that can be needed; an abundance; a substantial number or amount. — *adj* plentiful (*Shakesp*); in abundance. — *adv* (*colloq*) abundantly. — *adj* **plenteous** (*plen'tyəs*; *literary*) fully sufficient; abundant; fruitful; well provided; rich; producing or giving plentifully. — *adv* **plen'teously**. — *n* **plen'teousness**. — *adj* **plen'tiful** copious; abundant; yielding abundance. — *adv* **plen'tifully**. — *n* **plen'tifulness**. — **horn of plenty** see **cornucopia**; **in plenty** abundant, as in *food in plenty*. [OFr *plente*, from L *plēnitās*, *-ātis*, from *plēnus* full]

plenum *plē'nəm*, *n* a space completely filled with matter, as opposed to *vacuum*; (also **plenum chamber**) a sealed chamber containing pressurized air (*aeronautics*, etc); a full assembly. — *n* **plē'nist** someone who believes all space to be a plenum. — **plenum system** or **plenum ventilation** (*archit*) an air-conditioning system in which the air propelled into a building is maintained at a higher pressure than that of the atmosphere. [L *plēnum* (*spatium*) full (space)]

pleo-. See **pleio-**.

pleochroism *plē-ok'rō-izm*, *n* the property in some crystals of transmitting different colours in different directions. — *adj* **pleochroic** (*plē-ō-krō'ik*). [Gr *chroā* colour]

pleomorphic *plē-ō-mör'fik*, *adj* occurring in several different forms, polymorphic; changing form several different times during its life cycle (*biol*). — Also **pleomor'phous**. — *n* **pleomor'phism** or **plē'omorphy**.

pleon *plē'ən*, *n* the abdomen of a crustacean, bearing the swimming legs. — *n* **ple'opod** a swimming leg. [Gr *pleōn* swimming, pr p of *pleein*]

pleonasm *plē'ə-nazm*, *n* redundancy, *esp* of words; a redundant expression. — *n* **plē'onast** someone who is given to pleonasm. — *n* **ple'onaste** (Fr *pléonaste*) a dark green to black magnesia-iron spinel (from its multitude of faces). — *adj* **pleonas'tic** or **pleonas'tical**. — *adv* **pleonas'tically**. [Gr *pleonasmos*, from *pleōn* more]

pleonexia *plē-ə-nek'si-ə*, *n* greed, avarice. — *adj* **pleonec'tic**. [Gr]

pleopod. See under **pleon**.

pleroma *pli-rō'mə*, *n* fullness; abundance; (in Gnosticism) the divine being, including all aeons (qv) which emanate from it. — *adj* **pleromatic** (*-mat'ik*). [Gr *plērōma*, from *plērēs* full]

plerome *plē'rōm*, (*bot*) *n* the central part of the apical meristem, the part of the primary tissue from which growth takes place. [Gr *plērōma* filling]

plerophory *pli-rof'ə-ri*, *n* full conviction. — Also **plerophō'ria**. [Gr *plērophoriā*]

plesh *plesh*, (*Spenser*) *n* a plash, a pool. [**plash**[2]]

plesiosaur *plē'si-ə-sör*, *n* a great Mesozoic fossil Sauropterygian reptile (genus *Plesiosaurus* or related genus) with a long neck, short tail, and four flippers. — *adj* **plesiosaur'ian**. [Gr *plēsios* near, and *sauros* lizard]

plessimeter, **plessor**, etc. See under **plexor**.

plethora *pleth'ə-rə*, sometimes *pli-thō'rə* or *-thö'*, *n* excessive fullness of blood; over-fullness or excess in any way; loosely, a large amount. — *adj* **plethoric** (*pli-thor'ik*; sometimes *pleth'ə-rik*) or **plethor'ical**. — *adv* **plethor'ically**. [Gr *plēthōrā* fullness, from *pleos* full]

plethysmograph *ple-thiz'mə-gräf*, (*med*) *n* an apparatus for measuring variations in the size of parts of the body, eg when varying amounts of blood flow through them. [Gr *plēthysmos* enlargement, and *graphein* to write]

pleugh *plōō* or *plōōhh*, *n* Scots form of **plough**. — Also **pleuch**.

pleura *plōō'rə*, *n* a delicate serous membrane that covers the lung and lines the cavity of the chest; a side-piece, *esp* a pleuron (see below): — *pl* **pleu'rae** (*-rē*). — *adj* **pleu'ral**. — *n* **pleurapoph'ysis** a lateral process of a vertebra, with the morphological character of a rib; a rib: — *pl* **pleurapoph'yses**. — *n* **pleurisy** (*plōō'ri-si*) inflammation of the pleura. — *adj* **pleurit'ic** or **pleurit'ical** of, affected with, or causing pleurisy. — *n* (**pleuritic**) a sufferer from pleurisy. — *n* **pleurī'tis** pleurisy. — *adj* and *n* **pleur'odont** (an animal, *esp* a reptile) with teeth attached to the inside of the jawbone, rather than rooted in it. — *n* **pleurodynia** (*plōō-rō-din'i-ə*; Gr *odynē*, pain) neuralgia of the muscles between the ribs. — *n* **pleu'ron** the side-wall of a somite, *esp* of an insect's thorax: — *pl* **pleu'ra**. — *n* **pleuropneumo'nia** pleurisy complicated with pneumonia; a contagious disease of cattle, caused by a filterable virus, characterized by pleurisy and pneumonia. — *n* **pleurot'omy** (*med*) incision into the pleura. — **pleu'risy-root** an American asclepias plant (*Asclepias tuberosa*) reputed as a diaphoretic and expectorant. [Gr *pleurā* and *pleuron* rib, side]

Pleuronectes *plōō-rə-nek'tēz*, *n* the plaice genus, giving name to the family **Pleuronec'tidae**. [Gr *pleurā* side, and *nēktēs* a swimmer]

plexiform. See under **plexus**.

plexiglass (® in *US*, with *cap*) *plek'si-gläs*, *n* a type of light, transparent thermoplastic. [*pl*astic *flex*ible *glass*]

plexor *pleks'ər* or **plessor** *ples'ər*, (*med*) *n* a percussion hammer. — *n* **plexim'eter** or **plessim'eter** a small plate to receive the tap in examination by percussion. — *adj* **pleximet'ric** or **plessimet'ric**. — *n* **plexim'etry** or **plessim'etry**. [Gr *plēxis* a stroke, *plēssein* to strike]

plexus *pleks'əs*, *n* a complex network of nerves, ganglia, blood vessels and lymphatic vessels anywhere in the body, such as the *solar plexus* behind the stomach, serving the viscera; any involved network: — *pl* **plex'uses** or **plex'us** (L *plexūs*). — *adj* **plex'iform** in the form of a network; complex. — *n* **plex'ure** an interweaving. [L *plexus*, *-ūs* a weaving]

pliable *plī'ə-bl*, *adj* easily bent or folded; flexible; adaptable; easily persuaded; yielding to influence. — *n* **plīabil'ity**. — *n* **plī'ableness**. — *adv* **plī'ably**. [From Fr *plier* to fold]

pliant *plī'ənt*, *adj* bending easily; flexible; tractable; easily influenced; *perh* suitable, *perh* of compliant mood (*Shakesp*). — *n* **plī'ancy**. — *adv* **plī'antly**. — *n* **plī'antness**. [Pr p of Fr *plier* to bend]

plica *plī'kə*, *n* a fold; plica Polonica: — *pl* **pli'cae** (*-sē*). — *adj* **plī'cal**. — *adj* **plī'cate** (or *pli-kāt'*) or **plī'cāted** (or *pli-kā'ted*) folded fanwise, pleated. — *vt* **plī'cate** (also *pli-kāt'*) to pleat. — *adv* **plicately**. — *n* **plīcā'tion** or **plicature** (*plik'*) the act of folding; the state of being folded; a fold. — **plica Polonica** a matted condition of the hair, with an adhesive secretion, a parasitic fungus, and vermin, formerly prevalent in Poland. [L *plica* a fold]

plié *plē'ā*, *n* a movement in ballet, in which the knees are bent while the body remains upright. [Fr, bent]

plied, **plier**, **plies**. See under **ply**[1,2].

pliers *plī'ərz*, *n pl* a tool like a pair of pincers, with serrated jaws for gripping small objects, and for bending and cutting wire. [From **ply**[1]]

plight[1] *plīt*, *n* risk (*obs*); pledge (*archaic*); engagement (*archaic*); promise (*archaic*). — *vt* to pledge: — *pa p* **plight'ed**, also **plight**. — *n* **plight'er**. — *adj* **plight'ful** grievous. — **plight one's troth** to pledge oneself in marriage. [OE *pliht* risk; *plēon* to risk; cf Du *plicht*, Ger *Pflicht* an obligation]

plight[2] *plīt*, *n* a difficult or dangerous situation, an alarming predicament; a fold (*Spenser*); a plait, or mode of plaiting (*archaic*); condition, trim (*archaic*); good condition (*archaic*); mood (*archaic*); array (*Spenser*). — *vt* (*obs*) to plait, weave, fold, enfold: — *pa p* **plight'ed**, also (*Spenser*) **plight**. — *adj* **plight'ed** plaited; involved (*Shakesp*). [Assimilated in spelling to **plight**[1], but derived from OFr *plite*, from L *plicāre*, *plĭcitum*; see **plait**]

plim *plim*, (*dialect*) *vt* and *vi* to swell. [Perh connected with **plump**[2]]

plimsoll or **plimsole** *plim'səl*, *-sol* or *-sōl*, *n* a rubber-soled canvas shoe (the line where the sole joined the upper having been supposed to resemble the Plimsoll line). — **Plimsoll line** or **mark** (*-səl* or *-sol*) a ship's load-line, or set of load-lines for different waters and conditions, required by the Merchant Shipping Act (1876) passed at the instance of Samuel *Plimsoll* (1824–98).

pling *pling*, (*comput slang*) *n* an exclamation mark.

plink *plingk*, *n* a short, relatively high-pitched, sound, as of the string of a musical instrument being plucked. — Also *vt* and *vi*. [Imit]

plinth *plinth*, *n* the square block under the base of a column; a block serving as a pedestal; a flat-faced projecting band at the bottom of a wall; any similar projecting base, eg in furniture. [L *plinthus*, Gr *plinthos* a brick, squared stone, plinth]

plio-. See **pleio-**.

Pliocene *plī'ō-sēn*, (*geol*) *adj* of an epoch of the Tertiary period following the Miocene epoch, and having a greater proportion of molluscan species now living. — *n* the Pliocene system, epoch, or strata. [Gr *pleiōn* greater, more numerous, and *kainos* recent]

Pliohippus *plī-ō-hip'əs*, *n* a Miocene and Pliocene genus of fossil horses. [Gr *hippos* horse]

pliosaur *plī'ə-sör*, *n* a fossil marine reptile similar to the plesiosaur, with a shorter neck, larger head, and more powerful jaws. [Gr *pleōn* more, and *saurus* lizard]

pliskie *plis'ki*, (*Scot*) *n* condition or plight; a mischievous trick. [Origin unknown]

plissé *plē-sā*, (*Fr*) *adj* (of a fabric) chemically treated to produce a shirred or puckered effect.

PLO *abbrev*: Palestine Liberation Organization.

ploat. See **plot**[2].

plod[1] *plod*, *vi* to walk heavily and laboriously; to study or work on steadily and laboriously. — *vt* to traverse or make (one's way) by slow and heavy walking: — *pr p* **plodd'ing**; *pa t* and *pa p* **plodd'ed**. — *n* a heavy walk; a thud. — *n* **plodd'er** a person who keeps on plodding; a dull, heavy, laborious person; someone who gets on more by sheer toil than by inspiration. — *adj* and *n* **plodd'ing**. — *adv* **plodd'ingly**. [Prob imit]

plod[2] *plod*, (*obs*) *vt* to plot. [**plot**[1], by confusion with foregoing]

-ploid *-ploid*, (*biol*) *adj combining form* indicating the possession of a certain number of chromosome sets, as in *haploid*, *diploid*, *triploid*, etc. — *n combining form* **-ploid'y**. — *n* **ploid'y** the number of chromosome sets in a cell; the condition of having a certain number of chromosome sets. [From the termination *-ploos* -fold, in Gr *haploos* onefold, *diploos* twofold, etc, and **-oid**]

plong, **plonge** and **plongd**. Spenserian spellings of **plunge** and **plunged**.

plonk[1] *plongk*, *vt* to put down, etc, so as to make a hollow or metallic sound, or heavily, or emphatically. — *vi* to plump down, plonk oneself. — *n* a plonking movement or the sound made by it. — *adv* with a plonk, as in *it landed plonk on the desk*. — Also *interj*. — *n* **plonk'er** a large marble (also **plunk'er**); anything large, *esp* a smacking kiss (*colloq*); a stupid person, a clot, an idiot (*slang*); a penis (*vulg slang*). — *adj* **plonk'ing** (*colloq*) enormous (sometimes *adverbially* or *intens* with *great*); relating to the practice of plonking. — *n* the practice of uttering jejune or pedestrian remarks in a deliberate and portentous tone. — *adj* **plonk'y** relating to or in the style of such a practice. [Imit]

plonk[2] *plongk*, *n* (*orig Austr slang*) wine, *esp* of poor quality. [Ety doubtful; prob from Fr *blanc* white, from *vin blanc* white wine]

plook, **plookie**. See **plouk**.

plop *plop*, *n* the sound of a small object falling vertically into water; the sound of the movement of small bodies of water; the sound of a cork coming out of a bottle, or of a bursting bubble. — *adv* with a plop; plump. — *vi* to make the sound of a plop; to drop or plump into water; (*slightly vulg colloq*) to defecate. — *vt* to let drop with a plop: — *pr p* **plopp'ing**; *pa t* and *pa p* **plopped**. [Imit]

plosive *plō'siv* or *-ziv*, (*phonetics*) *adj* and *n* (a consonantal sound) accompanied by plosion. — *n* **plo'sion** (*phonetics*) the release of breath after stoppage in articulating certain consonantal sounds.

plot[1] *plot*, *n* a small piece of ground; a spot or small area on any surface (*obs*); a ground plan of a building, plan of a field, etc; the story or scheme of connected events running through a play, novel, etc; a secret scheme, *usu* made in combination with others, to bring about something, often illegal or evil, a conspiracy; a stratagem or secret contrivance. — *vt* to lay out in plots, dispose; to make a plan of; to create the plot of (a play, etc); to represent on or by a graph; to conspire or lay plans for. — *vi* to conspire: — *pr p* **plott'ing**; *pa t* and *pa p* **plott'ed**. — *adj* **plot'ful**. — *adj* **plot'less**. — *n* **plott'er**. — *n* and *adj* **plott'ing**. — *adv* **plott'ingly**. — *adj* **plot'-proof** safe from any danger by plots. — **plott'ing-paper** paper ruled in squares for graph-drawing. [OE *plot* a patch of ground; influenced by (or partly from) Fr *complot* a conspiracy; cf **plat**[2]]

plot[2] *plot* or *plōt*, or **ploat** *plōt*, (*Northern*) *vt* to dip or steep in very hot water; to burn, scald, scorch; to scald and pluck; to pluck, strip of feathers, hair, etc; to fleece (*fig*); to remove fluff, etc, from (a garment) (*not Scot*). — *n* **plott'ie** or **plott'y** a spiced hot drink, such as mulled wine. [Cf MDu and Flem *ploten* to pluck, but other roots may be involved]

plotter[1] *plot'ər*. Same as **plouter**.

plotter[2], **plotting**. See under **plot**[1].

plottie, **plotty**. See under **plot**[2].

plough or (*US* or *archaic*) **plow**, *plow*, *n* an instrument for turning up the soil in ridges and furrows; a joiner's plane for making grooves; agriculture (*fig*); a plough-team; ploughed land; (with *cap*) the grouping formed by the seven brightest stars of the constellation of the Great Bear. — *vt* to turn up with the plough; to make furrows or ridges in; to make with a plough; to put into or render with a plough (also *fig*); to tear, force, or cut a way through; to furrow; to wrinkle; to reject in an examination (*university slang*); to fail in (a subject) (*university slang*). — *vi* to work with a plough; (with *through* or *into*) to crash, force one's way, move, drive, etc, violently or uncontrollably (through or into; see also **plough (one's way) through** below); to fail (*slang*). — *adj* **plough'able**. — *n* **plough'er**. — *n* **plough'ing**. — *adv* and *adj* **plough'wise** as in ploughing. — **plough'boy** a boy who drives or guides horses in ploughing; **plough'gate** (*Scot hist*) an undetermined or variable unit of land, by later writers taken as about 50 English acres, but earlier much more; a quantity of land of the extent of 100 Scots acres; **plough'-iron** the coulter, share, or other iron part of a plough; **plough'-jogger** (*facetious*) a ploughman; **plough'land** land suitable for tillage; as much land as could be tilled with one plough (with a proportionate amount of pasture), a carucate or eight oxgangs (*hist*); **plough'man** a man who ploughs: — *pl* **plough'men**; **ploughman's lunch** a cold meal of bread, cheese, cold meat, pickle, etc; **ploughman's spikenard** see under **spikenard**; **Plough Monday** an old ploughmen's festival, the Monday after Twelfth Day, supposed to mark the resumption of work after the holidays; **plough'share** (OE *scear* ploughshare, from *scieran* to shear, cut) the detachable part of a plough that cuts the under surface of the sod from the ground; a bird's pygostyle (also **ploughshare bone**); **plough'-staff** a tool for clearing a plough of earth, etc; **plough'-stilt** a plough-handle; **plough'-tail** the end of a plough where the handles are; farm-labour (*fig*); **plough'-team** the team of horses, oxen, etc (*usu* two), that pulls a simple plough; **plough'-tree** a plough-handle; **plough'wright** someone who makes and mends ploughs. — **plough a lonely furrow** to be separated from one's former friends and associates and go one's own way; **plough back** (*fig*) to reinvest (profits of a business) in that business; **plough in** to cover with earth by ploughing; **plough (one's way) through** to work, read, eat, etc, steadily but slowly and laboriously through; **plough the sands** to work in vain or to no purpose; **put one's hand to the plough** to begin an undertaking. [Late OE *plōh, plōg* a ploughland; cf ON *plōgr*]

plouk or **plook** *plōōk*, (*Scot*) *n* a small lump or knob; a pimple, spot. — *adj* **plouk'ie** or **plook'ie**. [Gaelic *pluc*]

plouter or **plowter** *plow'tər*, (*Scot*) *vi* to dabble in liquid; to potter. — *n* a paddling or dabbling. — Also **plott'er**. [Prob imit]

plover *pluv'ər*, *n* a general name for birds of the family (*Charadriidae*) to which the lapwing and dotterel belong; extended to some related birds; a dupe (*old slang*); a prostitute (*old slang*). — *adj* **plov'ery** abounding in plovers. — **plover's egg** a lapwing's egg, or substitute. [Fr *pluvier*, from L *pluvia* rain; possibly from their restlessness before rain; cf Ger *Regenpfeifer* literally rain-piper]

plow *plow* (chiefly American). Same as **plough**.

plowter. See **plouter**.

ploy *ploi*, *n* an employment, doings, affair, frolic, escapade, or engagement for amusement; a method or procedure used to achieve a particular result; a manoeuvre in a game, conversation, etc. [Prob **employ**]

PLP *abbrev*: Parliamentary Labour Party.

PLR *abbrev*: public lending right (see under **public**).

plu *abbrev*: plural.

pluck *pluk*, *vt* to pull off, out, or away; to pull forcibly; to snatch away; to rescue; (with *down*) to bring down, humble (*archaic*); to pull; to tug; to sound (a musical string) by pulling sharply with the nails or a plectrum, to pick; to twitch; to strip, *esp* of feathers; to despoil, rob, fleece; to fail, refuse a pass to, in an examination — from the custom of *plucking* (a piece of silk at the back of) *the proctor's gown*, in protest (*old slang*); to swindle (*slang*). — *vi* to make a pulling or snatching movement (with *at*). — *n* a single act of plucking; the heart, liver, and lungs of an animal; hence, heart, courage, spirit. — *adj* **plucked** subjected to plucking; having pluck. — *n* **pluck'er**. — *adv* **pluck'ily**. — *n* **pluck'iness**. — *adj* **pluck'y** having courageous spirit and pertinacity. — **pluck off** (*Shakesp*) to abate, come down the scale; **pluck up** to pull out by the roots; to summon up (*esp* courage); to gather strength or spirit. [OE *pluccian*; related to Du *plukken*, Ger *pflücken*]

pluff *pluf*, (*Scot* or *dialect*) *n* a puff; a mild explosion; a shot; a powder-puff. — *vt* to puff; to shoot. — *vi* to go off with a puff; (eg of a cake) to rise. — *adj* **pluff'y** puffed up; fluffy. [Imit]

plug *plug*, *n* any peg or bung stopping, or for stopping, a hole, *esp* one preventing the escape of water from a sink; a stopper; a mechanism releasing the flow of water in a lavatory; filling for a tooth; volcanic rock stopping a vent; a device with metal pins for inserting into a socket to make an electrical connection; a piece of wood inserted in a wall to take nails; a fire-plug; a spark plug; a plug-hat (*slang*); a blow or punch; a compressed cake of tobacco; a piece of it cut for chewing; a worn-out horse; a book that will not sell; a piece of favourable publicity, *esp* one incorporated in other material (*colloq*); anything worn-out or useless; an instance of dogged plodding. — *vt* to stop with a plug or as a plug; to insert a plug in; to insert as a plug; to shoot (*slang*); to punch with the fist (*slang*); to force into familiarity by persistent repetition, *esp* for advertising purposes (*slang*); to din into the ears of the public. — *vi* (*slang*) to go on doggedly (often with *away*): — *pr p* **plugg'ing**; *pa t* and *pa p* **plugged**. — *n* **plugg'er** someone who plugs in any sense; that which plugs, *esp* a dentist's instrument. — *n* **plugg'ing** the act of stopping with a plug, or punching (*slang*), or promoting (*slang*); material of which a plug is made. — **plug'-hat** (*US*) a top hat; **plug-ug'ly** (*US*) a street ruffian; a thug, tough. — *adj* (*colloq*) extremely ugly. — **plug in** to connect (an electrical apparatus, etc) with the electricity supply by inserting a plug into a socket (*adj* **plug'-in**); **pull the plug on** (*colloq*) to end, put a stop to. [Appar Du *plug* a bung, a peg; cf Swed *plugg* a peg, Ger *Pflock*]

plum *plum*, *n* an oval drupe or stone-fruit with juicy, sweet-tasting yellowish flesh and typically a purple skin when ripe, or the tree producing it (*Prunus domestica* or related species) of the rose family; extended to various fruits and trees more or less similar (eg *sapodilla plum*, *coco-plum*, *date-plum*); a raisin as a substitute for the true plum; plum-colour; a sugar-plum; a big stone embedded in concrete; something choice that may be extracted (sometimes in reminiscence of Jack Horner) or attained to, such as one of the best passages in a book, one of the prizes of a career, or a government office as a reward of services, etc; (formerly) a sum of £100 000; its possessor. — *adj* plum-colour; choice, cushy. — *adj* **plumm'y** full of plums; plum-like; desirable, profitable; (of voice) overly rich and resonant, or, loosely, affectedly drawling, *esp* as thought characteristic of upper-class speech; (of a person) with a plummy voice, loosely, upper-class. — **plum'-bloss'om**; **plum'-cake** a cake containing raisins, currants, etc. — *n* and *adj* **plum'-colour** deep reddish-purple. — **plum'cot** Luther Burbank's hybrid between *plum* and *apricot*; **plumdamas** (*-dä'məs*; *Scot*) a damson; **plum-duff'** a boiled flour-pudding made with raisins; **plum'-porr'idge** an antiquated dish, of porridge with plums, raisins, etc; **plum-pudd'ing'** an English national dish made of flour and suet, with raisins, currants, and various spices; **plum'-stone**; **plum'-tree**. [OE *plūme*, from L *prūnum*; cf Gr *prou(m)non*]

plumage *plōōm'ij*, *n* a natural covering of feathers; feathers collectively. — *adj* **plum'aged**. [Fr, from *plume*, from L *plūma* a feather, down]

plumassier, **plumate**. See under **plume**.

plumb *plum*, *n* a heavy mass, as of lead, hung on a string to show a vertical line, or for some other purpose; verticality; a sounding lead, a plummet. — *adj* vertical; (of the wicket in cricket) level, true; unquestionably in a leg-before-wicket position (*cricket slang*); sheer, thorough-going, out-and-out. — *adv* vertically; precisely; utterly (*esp US*, now *archaic* or *dialect*). — *vt* to test by a plumb line; to make vertical; to sound as by a plumb line; to pierce the depth of, fathom, by eye or understanding; to weight with lead; to seal with lead; to supply or fit (a building, etc) with plumbing; to connect (eg a bath, washing-machine, etc) with the plumbing system, ready for use (*usu* with *in*). — *vi* to hang vertically; to work as a plumber. — *n* **plumbate** (*plum'bāt*) a salt of plumbic acid. — *adj* **plumbeous** (*plum'bi-əs*) leaden; lead-coloured; lead-glazed. — *n* **plumber** (*plum'ər*) *orig* a worker in lead; now someone who installs and mends pipes, cisterns, and other fittings for the supply of water and gas and for household drainage. — *n* **plumb'ery** plumber-work; a plumber's workshop. — *adj* **plumbic** (*plum'bik*) due to lead; of quadrivalent lead. — *adj* **plumbiferous** (*-bif'*) yielding or containing lead. — *n* **plumbing** (*plum'ing*) the operation of making plumb; the craft of working in lead; the work of a plumber; the system of pipes in a building for gas, water and drainage; (the design, style, working, etc, of) lavatories (*euphem*); the urinary system or tract (*facetious*). — *n* **plum'bism** (*-bizm*) lead poisoning. — *n* **plumbisol'vency** or, erroneously, **plumbosol'vency**. — *adj* **plumbisol'vent** or **plumbosol'vent** able to dissolve lead. — *n* **plum'bite** (*-bīt*) a salt of the weak acid lead hydroxide. — *adj* **plumb'less** incapable of being sounded. — *adj* **plumbous** (*plum'bəs*) of bivalent lead. — *n* **plumbum** (*plum'bəm*; *obs*) lead. — **plumb bob** a weight at the end of a plumb line; **plumb'er-work** the work of a plumber; **plumbic acid** an acid of which lead dioxide is the anhydride; **plumb line** a line to which a bob is attached to show the vertical line; a vertical line; a plummet; **plumb rule** a board with plumb line and bob, for testing the verticality of walls, etc. [Fr *plomb* and its source L *plumbum* lead]

plumbago[1] *plum-bā'gō*, *n* (with *cap*) a Mediterranean and tropical genus of ornamental plants (some cultivated) giving name to the **Plumbaginaceae** (*-baj-i-nā'si-ē*), a family of salt-steppe and seaside plants including sea pink and sea lavender, related to the primrose family; any plant of this genus: — *pl* **plumbā'gos**. — *adj* **plumbaginaceous** (*-baj-i-nā'shəs*). [L *plumbāgō*, Pliny's translation of the Greek name *molybdaina* lead, lead ore, the plant *Plumbago* (from its blue flowers)]

plumbago[2] *plum-bā'gō*, *n* graphite: — *pl* **plumbā'gos**. — *adj* **plumbaginous** (*-baj'i-nəs*). [L *plumbāgō*, *-inis*, from *plumbum* lead]

plumbate, **plumbeous**, **plumber**, etc. See under **plumb**.

plumber-block. Same as **plummer-block**.

plumbic, **plumbiferous**, **plumbing**, **plumbum**, etc. See under **plumb**.

plumcot, **plumdamas**. See under **plum**.

plume *plōōm*, *n* a feather, *esp* a large showy one; the vane of a feather; a bunch or tuft of feathers; a feather, or anything similar, used as an ornament, symbol, crest, etc; a feather as a token of honour; the plumule of a seed; any feathery structure (*obs*); anything resembling a feather, such as a thin wisp of rising smoke, etc — *vt* to preen; (*reflexive*) to pride (oneself; with *on* or *upon*); to adorn with plumes; to set as a plume (*Milton*); to strip of feathers. — *n* **plumassier** (*plōō-mä-sēr'*) a worker in feathers: a feather-seller. — *adj* **plu'mate**, **plu'mose** or **plu'mous** feathered; feathery; plume-like. — *adj* **plumed** feathered; adorned with a plume; plucked (*obs*). — *adj* **plume'less**. — *n* **plume'let** a plumule; a little tuft. — *n* **plu'mery** plumes collectively. — *adj* **plumigerous** (*-ij'ə-rəs*) plumaged. — *adj* **plu'miped** having feathered feet. — *n* **plu'mist** a feather-dresser. — *adj* **plu'my** covered or adorned with down or plume; like a plume. — **plume'-bird** a long-tailed bird of paradise; **plume'-grass** a tall grass (*Erianthus*) related to sugar-cane, with great silky panicles, grown for ornament; **plume'-moth** any moth of the families Pterophoridae and Orneodidae, with deeply cleft wings. — *adj* **plume'-pluckt** (*Shakesp*) stripped of plumes, humbled. — **plume poppy** the popular name for any plant of the genus *Macleaya*, hardy, very tall flowering perennials of the *Papaveraceae*. [OFr, from L *plūma* a small soft feather]

plummer-block *plum'ər-blok*, *n* a metal frame or case for holding the end of a revolving shaft. [Origin unknown]

plummet *plum'it*, *n* a leaden or other weight, *esp* on a plumb line, sounding-line, or fishing line; a plumb rule. — *vt* to fathom, sound. — *vi* to plunge headlong. [OFr *plomet*, dimin of *plomb* lead; see **plumb**]

plummy. See under **plum**.

plump[1] *plump*, *vi* to fall or drop into liquid, *esp* vertically, passively, resoundingly, without much disturbance; to flop down; to rain suddenly and heavily (*esp Scot*); to come suddenly or with a burst; to give all one's votes without distribution; to choose or opt decisively or abruptly (with *for*). — *vt* to plunge or souse; to fling down or let fall flat or heavily; to blurt; to strike or shoot (*slang*). — *n* the sound or act of plumping; a sudden heavy fall of rain (*esp Scot*); a blow (*slang*). — *adj* and *adv* with a plump; in a direct line; downright; in plain language; without hesitation, reserve, or qualification. — *n* **plump'er** a plump, fall or blow; an undistributed vote that could have been divided; someone who gives all his or her votes to one candidate or option; a downright lie (*slang*); anything very big of its kind, a whopper (*slang*). — *adv* **plump'ly**. [LGer *plumpen* or Du *plompen*, to plump into water; prob influenced by **plumb** and **plump**[2]]

plump[2] *plump*, *adj* somewhat fat and rounded; chubby; well filled out, full; (of a cheque) large, generous (*colloq*). — *vt* and *vi* to make or grow plump; to swell or round. — *vi* (*rare*) **plump'en**. — *n* **plump'er** a pad kept in the mouth to round the cheeks, used by actors. — *adj* **plump'ish**. — *adv* **plump'ly**. — *n* **plump'ness**. — *adj* **plump'y** or **plump'ie** (*Shakesp*) plump. [Appar the same word as Du *plomp* blunt, LGer *plump*]

plump[3] *plump*, (*archaic* or *dialect*) *n* a cluster; a clump (of trees, spearmen, waterfowl, etc). [Origin unknown]

plumula *plōōm'ū-lə*, *n* a plumule: — *pl* **plum'ulae** (*-lē*). — *adj* **plumulā'ceous** or **plum'ular**. — *n* **Plumulā'ria** a genus of Hydrozoa forming feathery colonies. — *n* and *adj* **plumulā'rian**. — *adj* **plum'ulate** downy. — *n* **plum'ule** a little feather or plume; a down feather; the embryo shoot in a seed; a scent-giving scale on the forewing of some male butterflies. — *adj* **plum'ulose**. [L *plūmula*, dimin of *plūma* a feather, down feather]

plumy. See under **plume**.

plunder *plun'dər*, *vt* to carry off the goods or possessions of by force, to pillage; to carry off as booty; to carry off booty from. — *vi* to pillage, carry off plunder. — *n* pillage; booty; personal or household goods (*US*). — *n* **plun'derage** the stealing of goods on board ship. — *n* **plun'derer**. — *adj* **plun'derous**. [Ger *plündern* to pillage, from *Plunder* household stuff, now trash]

plunge *plunj*, *vt* to put or thrust suddenly under the surface of a liquid, or into the midst of, the thick of, or the substance of anything; to immerse. — *vi* to fling oneself or rush impetuously, *esp* into water, downhill, or into danger or discourse; to turn suddenly and steeply downward; to fire down on an enemy from a height; to gamble or squander recklessly; (of a ship) to pitch; to pitch suddenly forward and throw up the hindlegs. — *n* an act of plunging. — *n* **plung'er** a person who plunges; part of a mechanism with a plunging movement, such as the solid piston of a force-pump; a suction instrument for cleaning blockages in pipes; a cavalryman (*obs military slang*); a reckless gambler or squanderer. — *adj* and *n* **plung'ing**. — **plunge bath** a bath large enough to immerse the whole body; **plunge-cut milling** (*eng*) milling without transverse movement of the workpiece relative to the cutter; **plunging fold** (*geol*) a fold whose axis is not horizontal; **plunging neckline** a low-cut neckline in a woman's dress, blouse, etc. — **take the plunge** to commit oneself definitely after hesitation. [OFr *plonger*, from L *plumbum* lead]

plunk *plungk*, *vt* to twang; to pluck the strings of (a banjo, etc); to plonk. — *vi* to plump. — Also *n*, *adv*, and *interj*. — *n* **plunk'er** a large marble (also **plonk'er**). [Imit]

plup *abbrev*: pluperfect.

pluperfect *plōō-pûr'fikt*, (*gram*) *adj* denoting action that took place before the past actions being described, eg *had entered*, *had been crying*. — *n* the pluperfect tense; a pluperfect verb or form. [L *plūs quam perfectum* (*tempus*) more than perfect (tense)]

plur *abbrev*: plural.

plural *plōōr'l*, *adj* numbering more than one; more than onefold; expressing more than one, or, where dual is recognized, more than two (*gram*). — *n* (*gram*) the plural number; a plural word form. — *n* **plur'alism** plurality; the holding by one person of more than one office at once, *esp* ecclesiastical livings; a system allowing this; a philosophy that recognizes more than one principle of being (opposite of *monism*) or more than two (opposite of *monism* and *dualism*); a (condition of) society in which different ethnic, etc, groups preserve their own customs, or hold equal power. — *n* **plur'alist** someone who holds more than one office at one time; a believer in pluralism. — Also *adj*. — *adj* **pluralist'ic**. — *n* **plurality** (*-al'i-ti*) the state or fact of being plural; numerousness; a plural number; the greater number, more than half; a majority over any other, distinguished from *majority*, which is used for an absolute majority or majority over all others combined (*US*); the holding of more than one benefice at one time; a living held by a pluralist. — *n* **pluralīzā'tion** or **-s-**. — *vt* **plur'alize** or **-ise** to make plural. — *vi* to hold two or more benefices or offices simultaneously. — *adv* **plu'rally**. — **plural society** one in which pluralism is found; **plural vote** the power of voting in more than one constituency, or more than once in one. [L *plūrālis*, from *plūs*, *plūris* more]

pluri- *plo͞or'i-*, *combining form* denoting: several; *usu* more than two. — *adj* **plurilit'eral** (*Heb gram*) containing more letters than three. — *adj* **pluriloc'ular** multilocular. — *n* **plurip'ara** a multipara. — *n* **pluri-pres'ence** presence in more places than one at the same time. — *adj* **plurise'rial** or **plurise'riate** (*-ri-ət*) in several rows. [L *plūs*, *plūris* more]

plurisie *plo͞or'i-si*, (*Shakesp*) *n* superabundance. [L *plūs*, *plūris* more; confused with **pleurisy** (qv under **pleura**)]

plus *plus*, (*math* and *colloq*) *prep* with the addition of. — *adj* positive; additional; having an adverse handicap (*games*); used postpositively to mean rather more than, as in 200 *plus*, of a grade higher than, as in *alpha plus* or (*colloq*) unusually great, as in *success plus*. — *conj* (*colloq*) and also, in addition. — *n* an addition; a surplus; a positive quality or term; an advantage (*colloq*); the sign (also **plus sign**) of addition or positivity (+), opposite of *minus* (-): — *pl* **plus'es** or **pluss'es**. — *vt* and *vi* to increase (in value): — *pr p* **plus'ing** or **pluss'ing**; *pa t* and *pa p* **plused** or **plussed** — **plus'age** or **pluss'age** an extra amount. — **plus strain** (*bot*) one of the two strains in heterothallism. — **plus or minus** (used in approximating) with the addition or subtraction of, with an error range of (so many). [L *plūs* more]

plus-fours *plus'-fōrz'* or *-förz'*, *n pl* baggy knickerbockers or a knickerbocker suit. [**plus four**; from the four additional inches of cloth required to create the overhang at the knee]

plush *plush*, *n* a fabric with a longer and more open pile than velvet; (in *pl*) footman's breeches. — *adj* of plush; (also **plush'y**) luxurious, *orig* pretentiously so (*colloq*). [Fr *pluche* for *peluche*, from L *pīla* hair; cf **pile**³]

plus-twos *plus-to͞oz*, *n pl* a shorter and less baggy version of plus-fours.

pluteus *plo͞o'ti-əs*, *n* a sea-urchin or brittle-star larva, shaped like a many-legged easel. — *adj* **plu'teal**. [L *pluteus* a shed, boarding, desk]

Pluto *plo͞ot'ō*, *n* the Greek god of the underworld (*Gr mythol*); a planet beyond Neptune, discovered in 1930. — *n* **plu'ton** (*geol*) a mass of rock which has solidified below the earth's surface. — *adj* **Pluto'nian** of Pluto; of the underworld. — *adj* **Plutonic** (*-ton'ik*) of Pluto; (also without *cap*) hypogene, deep-seated, relating to or formed under conditions of subterranean heat (*geol*); Plutonist. — *n* **Plutonism** (*plo͞o'tən-izm*). — *n* and *adj* **Plu'tonist** (*hist of geol*) Vulcanist. — *n* **plutō'nium** the element (symbol **Pu**; atomic no 94), named as next after neptunium (93; the planet Pluto being beyond Neptune) having many isotopes, the fissile isotope ^{239}Pu being particularly important in the production of nuclear power. [L *Plūtō*, *-ōnis*, from Gr *Ploutōn*, *-ōnos* Pluto]

pluto- *plo͞o-tō-*, *-tə*, *-to'*, *combining form* denoting wealth. — *n* **plutocracy** (*plo͞o-tok'rə-si*) government by the wealthy; a ruling body or class of rich men. — *n* **plutocrat** (*plo͞o'tə-krat*) someone who is powerful because of his or her wealth. — *adj* **plutocrat'ic**. — *n* **pluto-democ'racy** a wealth-dominated democracy. — *n* **plutol'atry** (see **-latry**) worship of wealth. — *n* **plutol'o-gist**. — *n* **pluton'omist**. — *n* **plutol'ogy** or **pluton'omy** political economy. [Gr *ploutos* wealth]

pluvial *plo͞o'vi-əl*, *adj* of or by rain; rainy. — *n* (from *Med L pluviāle* a rain-cloak) a cope or ceremonial mantle (*hist*); a period of prolonged rainfall (*geol*). — *n* **pluviom'eter** a rain-gauge. — *adj* **pluviomet'ric** or **pluviomet'rical**. — *n* **Pluviôse** (*plü-vē-ōz*; Fr) the fifth month of the French Revolutionary calendar, the rainy month, about 20 January to 18 February. — *adj* **plu'viose** or **plu'vious** rainy. — **pluvius insurance** insurance cover taken out eg by the organizer of a fête against loss of takings due to rain. [L *pluvia*, rain]

ply¹ *plī*, *n* a fold; a layer or thickness; a layer of hard rock or of hard or soft rocks in alternation (*mineralogy*); a bend; a bend or set; a strand; condition, *esp* good condition (*Scot*): — *pl* **plies**. — *vt* and *vi* to bend or fold: — *pr p* **ply'ing**; *pa t* and *pa p* **plied**; *3rd pers sing* **plies**. — *n* **pli'er** someone who plies. — **ply'wood** boarding made of thin layers of wood glued together, the grain of each at right angles to that of the next. [(O)Fr *pli* a fold, *plier* to fold, from L *plicāre*]

ply² *plī*, *vt* to work at steadily; to use or wield diligently or vigorously; to keep supplying or assailing (with); to importune; to row or sail over habitually. — *vi* to work steadily; to make regular journeys over a route; to be in attendance for hire; to beat against the wind; to make one's way, direct one's course: — *pr p* **ply'ing**; *pa t* and *pa p* **plied**; *3rd pers sing* **plies**. — *n* **pli'er** someone who plies; a trader (*obs*); a tout (*obs*). [Aphetic, from **apply**]

Plymouth *plim'əth*, *n* a port in Devon; a port named after it in Massachusetts, with the supposed landing-place of the Pilgrims (Plymouth Rock). — *n* **Plym'outhism**. — *n* **Plym'outhist**, **Plym'outhite** or **Plymouth Brother** one of the **Plymouth Brethren**, a religious sect, founded in Dublin c.1825, out of a reaction against High Church principles and against a dead formalism associated with unevangelical doctrine (its first congregation was established at Plymouth in 1831); **Plymouth Rock** an American breed of poultry; a nickname for a Plymouth Brother.

plywood. See under **ply**¹.

PM *abbrev*: Past Master; Postmaster; (or **pm**) *post meridiem* (*L*), after noon; (or **pm**) *post mortem* (*L*), after death; Prime Minister; Provost-Marshal.

Pm (*chem*) *symbol*: promethium.

pm *abbrev*: premium; see also under **PM**.

PMBX (*telecomm*) *abbrev*: private manual branch exchange.

PMG *abbrev*: Paymaster-General; Postmaster-General.

PMO *abbrev*: Principal Medical Officer.

Pmr *abbrev*: Paymaster.

PMRAFNS *abbrev*: Princess Mary's Royal Air Force Nursing Service.

PMS *abbrev*: premenstrual syndrome.

PMT *abbrev*: photomechanical transfer; premenstrual tension.

pn *abbrev*: promissory note.

PNdB *abbrev*: perceived noise decibel.

pneum-. See under **pneumo-**.

pneuma *nū'mə*, *n* breath; spirit, soul; a neume. — *n* **pneumathode** (*nū'mə-thōd*; Gr *hodos*, a way) a respiratory opening in plants. — *adj* **pneumatic** (*-mat'ik*) relating to air or gases; containing or inflated with air; (of a woman's figure) full, generously proportioned, *esp* referring to a large bust (*slang*); worked or driven by compressed air; containing compressed air; with air-cavities (*zool*); spiritual. — *adj* **pneumat'ical** (*rare*). — *adv* **pneumatically**. — *n* **pneumaticity** (*nū-mə-tis'i-ti*) the condition of having air-spaces. — *n sing* **pneumat'ics** the science of the mechanical properties of gases, pneumatology (also **pneumodȳnam'ics**). — *combining form* **pneumato-** (*nu-mə-tō-*, *-tə*, *-to'*) denoting breath or air (see also **pneumo-**). — *adj* **pneumatolog'ical**. — *n* **pneumatol'ogist**. — *n* **pneumat-ol'ogy** the theory of the existence of spirits or spiritual beings; psychology (*archaic*); the doctrine of the Holy

Spirit (*theol*); pneumatics (*archaic*). — *n* **pneumatol'ysis** (see **-lysis**) the destructive action of the hot vapours of magma on igneous rock. — *adj* **pneumatolyt'ic**. — *n* **pneumatom'eter** an instrument for measuring the quantity of air breathed or the force of breathing. — *n* **pneu'matophore** (or *-mat'*) an upward-growing respiratory root in swamp plants. — **pneumatic trough** a vessel with a perforated shelf, for filling gas-jars over a liquid. [Gr *pneuma*, *-atos* breath, from *pneein* to breathe]

pneumo- *nū-mō-*, *-mə-*, **pneum-** *nūm-*, **pneumon-** *nū-mon-*, *-mən-*, or **pneumono-** *nū-mə-nō-*, *-nə-*, *combining form* denoting: lung; (**pneumo-**, as a reduced form of **pneumato-**) air or breath. — *n* **pneumococc'us** a bacterium in the respiratory tract which is a causative agent of pneumonia. — *n* **pneumoconiosis** (*nū-mō-kō-ni-ō'sis*; Gr *konia* dust), **pneumokonio'sis** or **pneumonokonio'sis** any of various diseases caused by habitually inhaling mineral or metallic dust, as in coalmining. — *n* **pneumoconiot'ic** a person suffering from pneumoconiosis. — *n sing* **pneumodynamics** same as **pneumatics** (qv under **pnuema**). — *adj* **pneumogas'tric** (Gr *gastēr* belly) pertaining to the lungs and stomach. — *n* the vagus. — *n* **pneumonec'tomy** surgical removal of lung tissue. — *n* **pneumō'nia** inflammation of the lung. — *adj* **pneumonic** (*-mon'*) pertaining to the lungs. — *n* a medicine for lung diseases. — *n* **pneumonī'tis** pneumonia. — *n* **pneu'mono-ultramicroscopicsil'icovolcanoconio'sis** a form of pneumoconiosis caused by very fine silicate or quartz dust. — *n* **pneumotho'rax** (*med*) the existence, or introduction of, air between the lung and chest-wall; lung collapse resulting from the escape of air from the lung into the chest cavity, a potential hazard of working in compressed air, eg deep-sea diving. — **pneumocystis carinii pneumonia** (*med*) a potentially fatal infection which can affect people whose immune system is damaged by disease (eg AIDS) or drugs; **pneumonia blouse** (*facetious*) a low-necked blouse, once an object of disapproval. [Gr *pneumōn*, *-onos* lung, from *pneein* to breathe]

PNG *abbrev*: Papua New Guinea (also IVR).

Pnyx *pniks* or *niks*, *n* the meeting-place of the ancient Athenian assembly. [Gr *pnyx*, genitive *pyknos*, perh cognate with *pyknos* crowded]

PO *abbrev*: Petty Officer; Pilot Officer; Postal Order; Post Office.

Po (*chem*) *symbol*: polonium.

po[1] *pō*, (*colloq*) *n* a shortening of **chamberpot**: — *pl* **pos**. [**pot**, prob from a euphem French pronunciation]

po[2] *pō* (*colloq*) *adj* a shortening of **po-faced**.

po *abbrev*: postal order.

po. *abbrev*: pole.

POA *abbrev*: Prison Officers' Association.

poa *pō'ə*, *n* any plant of the meadow-grass genus *Poa*. — *adj* **pōā'ceous**. [Gr *poā* grass]

poach[1] *pōch*, *vt* to cook slowly in simmering liquid. — *n* **poach'er** someone who poaches eggs; a container with hollows for poaching eggs in. — **poached-egg flower** Romneya; an annual, *Limnanthes douglasii*, with yellow and white flowers. [Appar Fr *pocher* to pocket, from *poche*, pouch, the white forming a pocket around the yolk]

poach[2] *pōch*, *vi* to intrude on another person's land in order to pursue or kill game, or on another person's fishing to catch fish; to encroach on another's rights, profits, area of influence, etc, or on a partner's place or part in a game; to seek an unfair advantage; (*Shakesp*, **potche**) to thrust; to trample in mud; to become trampled and muddy. — *vt* to take illegally on another's ground or in another's fishing; to seek or take game or fish illegally on; to take in unfair encroachment; to poke or thrust (*dialect*); to stir up (*dialect*); to trample into holes and mud. — *n* **poach'er**. — *n* **poach'iness**. — *n* **poach'ing**. — *adj* **poach'y** spongy and sodden. [A form of **poke**[3] or from OFr *pocher* to poke]

poaka *pō-ä'kə*, (*Maori*) *n* a NZ bird, one of the stilts.

poake. A Shakespearian spelling of **poke**[1].

pocas palabras *pō'käs pal-äb'räs*, (*Sp*) *n* few words.

po'chaise. See **pochay**.

pochard *pō'chərd*, *poch'ərd*, **pockard** *pok'ərd*, or **poker** *pōk'ər*, *n* a red-headed diving-duck (*Nyroca* or *Aythya ferina*), *esp* the male, the female being the dun-bird. [Origin obscure]

pochay *pō'shā* and **po'chaise** *-shāz*. See **post-chaise** (under **post**[2]).

pochette *po-shet'*, *n* a small bag, *esp* one carried by women; a pocket notecase or wallet. [Fr, dimin of *poche* pocket]

pochoir *posh'wär*, *n* a form of colour stencilling, by hand, on to a printed illustration. [Fr, stencil]

pock[1] *pok*, *n* a small elevation of the skin containing pus, as in smallpox. — *adj* **pocked**. — *adj* **pock'y** marked with pustules; infected with pox; confounded, damned (*obs colloq*). — **pock'mark** or **pock'pit** the mark, pit, or scar left by a pock; similar pitting or scarring of any surface. — *adj* **pock'marked**. — *adj* **pock'pitted**. [OE *poc* a pustule; Ger *Pocke*, Du *pok*; see **pox**]

pock[2] *pok*, *n* a Scots form of **poke**[1]. — **pockman'tie** or **pockmank'y** corrupt forms of **portmanteau**, influenced by **pock**; **pock-pudding** (*pok'-pud'n*) a bag-pudding; a Scottish contemptuous name for a mere Englishman.

pockard. See **pochard**.

pocket *pok'it*, *n* a little pouch or bag, *esp* one fitted in or attached to a garment or a billiard-table or the cover of a book; a cavity; a rock cavity filled with ore, veinstone, etc; a portion of the atmosphere differing in pressure or other condition from its surroundings; a small isolated area or patch, as of military resistance, unemployment, etc; the innermost compartment of a pound-net; one's personal stock of money; a bag of wool, etc, containing about ½ sack. — *adj* for the pocket; of a small size. — *vt* to put in one's pocket or a pocket; to receive and keep for oneself, to accept (a cash prize payment, etc); to appropriate; to take stealthily; to conceal; to enclose; to hem in; to play into a pocket (*billiards*, etc). — *vi* to form a pocket: — *pr p* **pock'eting**; *pa t* and *pa p* **pock'eted**. — *n* **pock'etful** as much as a pocket will hold: — *pl* **pock'etfuls**. — *adj* **pock'etless**. — **pocket battleship** a small battleship, built to specifications limited by treaty, etc; **pock'et-book** a notebook; a wallet for papers or money carried in the pocket; a small book for the pocket; a handbag (*US*); **pocket borough** see under **borough**; **pock'et-comb** a hair-comb small enough for carrying in the pocket; **pock'et-glass** a small looking-glass for carrying in the pocket; **pocket gopher** any American burrowing rodent of the family Geomyidae, with outward-opening cheek-pouches; **pock'et-handk'erchief** a handkerchief for carrying in the pocket; **pock'et-hole** the opening in a garment giving access to a pocket; **pocket knife** a knife with one or more blades folding into the handle, for carrying in the pocket; **pocket money** money carried for occasional expenses; an allowance, *esp* to a child; **pocket mouse** a small rodent of the genus *Perognathus*, native to the N American desert; **pock'etphone**; **pock'et-picking** the act or practice of picking other people's pockets; **pock'et-piece** a coin carried to bring luck; **pock'et-pis'tol** a pistol for carrying in the pocket; a small travelling flask for liquor. — *adj* **pock'et-sized** small enough for the pocket. — **in one's pocket** under one's control or influence; very close to one; **in** (or **out of**) **pocket** with or without money; the richer or the poorer by a transaction (*adj* **out'-of-pock'et** of expenses, etc, paid in cash); **line one's pockets** to make or take money dishonestly from business entrusted to one; **pick a person's pocket** to steal from his or her pocket; **pocket an insult, affront**, etc to submit to or put up with it without protest; **pocket one's pride** to humble oneself to accept a situation. [Anglo-Fr *pokete* (Fr *pochette*, dimin of *poche* pocket)]

pockmanky, pockmantie. See under **pock**[2].

pocky, etc. See under **pock**[1].

poco *pō'kō*, (*Ital*) *adj* little. — *adj* **pococuran'te** (*-kōō-ran'tā* or *-kū-ran'ti*; Ital *curante*, *pr p* of *curare* to care) uninterested; indifferent; nonchalant. — *n* a habitually uninterested person. — *n* **pococurant'ism** (*-kū-rant'izm*) or **pococuranteism** (*-kū-rant'i-ism*). — *n* **pococurant'ist**. — **poco a poco** little by little.

poculiform *pok'ū-li-förm*, *adj* cup-shaped. [L *pōculum* cup]

pod[1] *pod*, *n* the fruit, or its shell, in peas, beans, and other leguminous plants, the legume; sometimes extended to the siliqua; a silk cocoon; a musk-bag; a paunch; a groove along an auger or bit; the socket into which a bit, etc, fits; a protective housing for (external) engineering equipment, eg aircraft engines, nuclear reactor, space or submarine instruments, or for weapons carried externally, eg on an aircraft; a decompression compartment. — *vt* to shell or hull. — *vi* to form pods; to fill as pods: — *pr p* **podd'ing**; *pa t* and *pa p* **podd'ed**. — *adj* **podd'y** corpulent. — *n* (*Austr colloq*) a young animal, *esp* a calf or lamb. [Origin uncertain]

pod[2] *pod*, *n* a school, *esp* of whales or seals; sometimes applied to groups of other animals, fish and birds. [Origin unknown]

pod[3] *pod*, (*colloq*; *photog*) a short form of **tripod**, **monopod**, etc.

pod *abbrev*: pay on delivery.

pod- *pod-*, *combining form*. See **podo-**.

-pod *-pod* or **-pode** *-pōd*, *combining form* denoting foot. [Gr *pous*, *podos* foot]

podagra *po-dag'rə*, *pod'ə-grə*, (*med*) *n* gout, properly in the feet. — *adj* **podag'ral** (or *pod'*), **podag'ric**, **podag'rical** or **podag'rous** (or *pod'*) gouty. [Gr *podagrā*, from *pous*, *podos* foot, and *agrā* a catching]

poddy. See under **pod**[1].

-pode. See **-pod**.

podestà *pod-est-tä'*, (*hist*) *n* a governor, chief magistrate, or judge in an Italian town. [Ital *podestà*, from L *potestās*, *-ātis* power]

podex *pō'deks*, *n* the rump; the anal region. [L *pōdex*]

podge *poj* or **pudge** *puj*, *n* a squat, fat and flabby person or thing. — *n* **podg'iness** or **pudg'iness**. — *adj* **podg'y** or **pudg'y**. [Origin obscure]

podiatrist, **podiatry**. See under **podo-**.

podium *pō'di-əm*, *n* a continuous pedestal, a stylobate (*archit*); a platform, dais; a foot or hand (*anatom*); a tube-foot: — *pl* **pō'dia**. — *adj* **pō'dial**. [Latinized from Gr *podion*, dimin of *pous*, *podos* foot]

podley *pod'li*, (*Scot*) *n* a young coalfish. [**pollack**]

podo- *pod-ō-*, *-ə-*, *-o'*, or *pōd-*, or **pod-** *pod-* or *pōd-*, *combining form* denoting foot. — *adj* **pō'dal** or **pōdal'ic** of the feet. — *n* **podargus** (*pə-där'gəs*; Gr *podargos* swift-footed) a bird of the frogmouth genus *Podargus*. — *n* **podi'atrist**. — *n* **podiatry** (*pod-ī'ə-tri*; Gr *iātros*, *iātros* physician) treatment of disorders of the foot. — *n* **podite** (*pod'īt*) a walking leg of a crustacean. — *n* **podocarp** (*pō-dō-kärp*; Gr *karpos* fruit) a yew tree of the eastern and southern genus *Podocarpus*. — *n* **podoconio'sis** (*med*) endemic elephantiasis of the lower legs. — *n* **Podogona** (*-og'ə-nə*; Gr *gonos* reproductive organ) the Ricinulei (qv). — *n* **podol'ogist**. — *n* **podol'ogy** the scientific study of the feet. — *adj* **podophthalmus** (*-of-thal'məs*; Gr *ophthalmos* eye) having eyes on stalks, as do many higher crustaceans. — *n* **Podophyllum** (*-ō-fil'əm*, *-of'i-ləm*; Gr *phyllon* leaf) a genus of the barberry family. — *n* **podophyll'in** a cathartic resin obtained from its rhizome. — *n* **Podostemon** (*-ō-stē'-mən*; Gr *stēmōn* warp, as if stamen, from the stalk on which the stamens stand) the typical genus of a family of dicotyledons, **Podostemaceae** (*-mā'si-ē*), growing in tropical waterfalls, the vegetative parts more like a thallus than an ordinary flowering plant. — *n* **Podura** (*-dū'rə*; Gr *ourā tail*) a genus of springtails. [Gr *pous*, *podos* foot]

Podsnappery *pod-snap'ər-i*, *n* British Philistinism as exemplified in Mr *Podsnap* in Dickens's novel *Our Mutual Friend*.

podsol or **podzol** *pod-zol'* or *pod'-*, *n* any of a group of soils characterized by a greyish-white leached and infertile topsoil and a brown subsoil, typical of regions with a subpolar climate. — *adj* **podsol'ic**. [Russ, from *pod* under, and *zola* ash]

Podunk *pō'dungk* (*US*), *n* an imaginary, typical, dull, outdated country town. [From either of two villages, near Worcester, Mass., or Hartford, Connecticut]

Podura. See under **podo-**.

poe-bird or **poy-bird** *pō'i-bûrd*, (*obs*) *n* the New Zealand parson-bird or tui. [Captain Cook's name, from Tahitian *poe* pearl beads, taken by him to mean earrings, on account of the side-tufts of the bird's neck]

poem *pō'im* or *-əm*, *n* a composition in verse; a composition of high beauty of thought or language and artistic form, typically, but not necessarily, in verse; anything supremely harmonious and satisfying. — *adj* **poemat'ic**. [Fr *poème*, from L *poēma*, from Gr *poiēma*, from *poieein* to make]

poenology. Same as **penology**.

poesy *pō'i-zi*, *n* poetry collectively or in the abstract; a poem (*obs*); a motto or posy (*obs*). — *vi* (*Keats*) to utter poetry. [Fr *poésie*, from L *poēsis*, from Gr *poiēsis*, from *poieein* to make]

poet *pō'it* or *-ət*, *n* the author of a poem or (formerly) of any work of literary art; a verse-writer; someone skilled in making poetry; someone with a poetical imagination: — *fem* **pō'etess**. — *n* **pōetas'ter** (see **-aster**) a petty poet; a writer of contemptible verses. — *n* **pōetas'tering**. — *n* **pōetas'tery** or **pōetas'try**. — *adj* **poetic** (*pō-et'ik*) or **poet'ical** of the nature or having the character of poetry; pertaining or suitable to a poet or to poetry; expressed in poetry; in the language of poetry; imaginative. — *n* a writer of poetry (*obs*); poetics (qv below). — *n sing* **poet'ics** the branch of criticism that relates to poetry. — *adv* **pōet'ically**. — *n* **poet'icism** a word or phrase that is typically, *usu* tritely, poetic. — *vt* and *vi* **poet'icize** or **-ise** to make poetic; to write poetry about; to write, speak, or treat, poetically. — *n* **pōet'icule** a petty poet. — *vi* **pō'etize** or **-ise** to write as a poet. — *vt* to make poetical; to record or celebrate in poetry. — *n* **pō'etresse** (*Spenser*) a poetess. — *n* **pō'etry** the art of the poet; the essential quality of a poem; poetical composition or writings collectively (rarely in *pl*); poetical quality. — *n* **pō'etship**. — **poetic justice** ideal or fitting apportioning of reward and punishment; **poetic licence** an allowable departure from strict fact, rule or logic for the sake of effect, as frequently occurs in poetry; **poet laureate** formerly, a person who received a degree in grammar (ie poetry and rhetoric) at the English universities; now, (with cap) the poet appointed to a lifetime post in the Royal household, required to compose poems for state occasions, etc. — **poetry in motion** exceedingly beautiful, harmonious, rhythmical, etc, movement. [Fr *poète*, from L *poēta*, from Gr *poiētēs*, from *poieein* to make]

POEU *abbrev*: Post Office Engineering Union.

po-faced *pō'fāst*, (*colloq*) *adj* stupidly solemn and narrow-minded; stolid, humourless. — Also shortened to **po**. [Perh *pot-faced* or *poor-faced*]

poffle *pof'l*, (*Scot*) *n* a pendicle. [Origin obscure]

pogge *pog*, *n* the armed bullhead (*Agonus cataphractus*), a bony-plated fish. [Origin unknown]

pogo *pō'gō*, *vi* to jump up and down on the spot to music, a popular punk form of dancing of the 1970s: — *pr p* **po'going**. — Also *n*. — *n* **pogo dance** and *vi* **po'go-dance**. [**pogo stick**, from the movement]

pogo effect *pō'gō i-fekt'* (*space flight*) *n* unstable, longitudinal oscillations induced in a launch system, mainly due to fuel-sloshing (qv) and engine vibration. [Poss **pogo stick**, from the movement]

pogonotomy *pō-gō-not'ə-mi*, *n* shaving. [Gr *pōgōn*, *pōgōnos* beard, and *tomē* a cutting]

pogo stick *pō'gō stik*, *n* a child's toy consisting of a stick with a handle and footholds, mounted on a strong spring, on which to stand and bounce along. [*Pogo*, a trademark]

pogrom *pog'rəm* or *pog-rom'*, *n* an organized massacre, *orig* (late 19c) *esp* of Russian Jews. [Russ, destruction, devastation]

poh *pō*, *interj* expressing impatient contempt. [Cf **pooh**]

pohutukawa *pə-hōō-tə-ka'wə*, *n* the New Zealand Christmas tree which bears red blooms at Christmas time, *Metrosideros tomentosa*, of the family *Myrtaceae*. [Maori]

poi *pō'ē*, *n* a Hawaiian dish, a paste of fermented taro root. [Hawaiian]

poignado or **poinado** *poi-nä'dō*, *n* obsolete forms of **poniard**: — *pl* **poi(g)na'does**.

poignant *poin'yənt*, *-ənt*, *adj* stinging, pricking; sharp; acutely painful; penetrating; pungent; piquant; touching, moving, exciting pathos. — *n* **poign'ancy**. — *adv* **poign'antly**. [OFr *poignant*, pr p of *poindre*, from L *pungere* to sting]

poikilitic *poi-ki-lit'ik*, *adj* mottled; having small crystals of one mineral irregularly scattered in larger crystals of another (*petrology*). — *n* **poi'kilocyte** (*-ō-sīt*) an irregular red blood corpuscle. — *n* **poi'kilotherm** a cold-blooded animal. — *adj* **poikilotherm'al** or **poikilotherm'ic** having a variable blood-temperature, 'cold-blooded'. — *n* **poikilotherm'y** (or *poi'-*) cold-bloodedness. [Gr *poikilos* variegated]

poilu *pwa-lü*, (*Fr*) *n* a French private solider (nickname; meaning 'hairy').

poinado. See **poignado**.

poinciana *poin-si-ä'nə*, *n* a tree of the tropical genus *Poinciana* of the Caesalpiniaceae . [After De *Poinci*, a French W Indian governor]

poind *pēnd* or *pind*, (*Scot*) *vt* to distrain; to impound. — *n* **poind'er**. — *n* **poind'ing**. [OE *pyndan* to impound; cf **pound**[2]]

poinsettia *poin-set'i-ə*, *n* a spurge, *Euphorbia pulcherrima*, with petal-like bracts, *usu* scarlet, and small yellow flowers, *orig* from Mexico and Central America. [From Joel Roberts *Poinsett* (1779–1851), American Minister to Mexico]

point[1] *point*, *n* a dot; a small mark used in Semitic alphabets to indicate a vowel, to differentiate a consonant, or for other purpose; a dot separating the integral and fractional parts of a decimal; a mark of punctuation; that which has position but no magnitude (*geom*); a whit (as in *no point*; *Shakesp*); a place or station, considered in relation to position only; a place or division in a scale, course, or cycle (as in *boiling point*, *dead point*); a moment of time, without duration; a precise moment; a state; a juncture; a critical moment; the verge; a culmination; a conclusion; resolution (*obs*); condition, case, plight (as in *in good point*; *obs*); any one of nine fixed positions on a shield (*heraldry*); the entry, or the first notes, of a subject, eg in a fugue (formerly marked by a dot; *obs*); a short strain or phrase of music, a call on an instrument, *esp* military, as in a *point of war* (*archaic*); a unit in scoring, judging, or measurement; a unit used in quoting changes of prices of stocks and securities; a feature or character taken into account in judging; a distinctive mark or characteristic; a unit of measurement of type, approximately $\frac{1}{72}$ inch; one of thirty-two divisions of the compass (**points of the compass**) or the angle between two successive divisions ($\frac{1}{8}$ of a right angle); a unit in rationing by coupon; (in piquet) the strongest suit held and called, or the score for holding it; a particular; a heading, clause, or item; a position forming a main element in the structure of an argument or discourse; a matter in debate, under attention, or to be taken into account; that which is relevant; that upon which one insists or takes a stand; the precise matter; the essential matter; that without which a story, joke, etc, is meaningless or ineffective; a clearly defined aim, object, or reason; a particular imparted as a hint; lace made with a needle (also **point'-lace**); loosely, lace; a piece of point-lace (*obs*); a sharp end; a tip, or free end; a thing, part, or mark with a sharp end; a piercing weapon or tool; an etching-needle; the sharp end of a sword; (in *pl*) sword-fighting; a tine; a spike; a tapering piece in electrical apparatus, such as the end of a lightning-conductor; a cape or headland; the tip of the chin (*boxing*); a horse's or other animal's extremity; a tagged lace formerly used for fastening clothes; a nib; a movable rail by means of which trains are transferred from one track to another; a tapering division of a backgammon board; a fielder, or his position, on the offside straight out from and near the batsman (as if at the point of the bat; *cricket*); a defence position (*lacrosse*); the leading party of an advanced guard; a position at the head of a herd; a socket for making a connection with electric wiring; pointedness; pungency; sting; the act or position of pointing; the vertical rising of a hawk, indicating the position of the prey; a feat (*obs*); pointe; $\frac{1}{100}$ part of a carat. — *adj* (*phonetics*) articulated with the tip of the tongue. — *vt* to insert points in; to mark with points; to mark off in groups of syllables for singing; to sharpen; to give point to; to prick in or turn over with the point of a spade; to show the position or direction of or draw attention to (now *usu* with *out*); to place in a certain direction, direct (with *at*); to indicate; to insert white hairs in (a fur); to rake out old mortar from, and insert new mortar in, the joints of; to ration by points. — *vi* to have or take a position in a direction (with *at*, *to*, *toward*, etc); to indicate a direction or position by extending a finger, a stick, etc; of dogs, to indicate the position of game by an attitude; to hint; to aim. — *adj* **point'ed** having a sharp point; sharp; Gothic (*archit*); keen; telling; epigrammatic; precise; explicit; aimed at particular persons; (of a remark) having a marked personal application. — *adv* **point'edly**. — *n* **point'edness**. — *n* **point'er** someone who points, in any sense; a rod for pointing to a blackboard, map, screen, etc; an index-hand; a hint, tip, suggestion, indication; a tool for clearing out old mortar from joints; a breed of dogs that point on discovering game; a horse ridden in point-to-point races (*horse-racing*); (in *pl*) two stars of the Great Bear nearly in a straight line with the Pole Star. — *n* **point'ing**. — *adj* **point'less**. — *adv* **point'lessly**. — *n* **point'lessness**. — *adj* **point'y** having points, or pointed in shape. — **point after** (*Am football*) a goal kick taken after a touch down is scored; **point'-duty** the duty of a policeman stationed at a particular point to regulate traffic; **point'ing-stock** a thing to be pointed at, a laughing-stock; **point'-lace** (see *n* above). — *n* **point of sale** (in retailing) the place where a sale is made (*abbrev* **POS**). — *adj* **point'-of-sale'** of, relating to, or occurring at the place where a sale is made. — **point-of-sale terminal** an electronic terminal used at retail outlets (eg supermarket check-outs) which records, and processes *esp* for stock-control purposes, sales-transaction information (*abbrev* **POS** or **POST**); **point set** (*math*) an aggregate; **points'man** someone on point-duty; someone in charge of rail points; **point'-source** a source of radiation that is, or is considered as, a mathematical point. — *adj* **point'-to-point'** from one fixed point to another; across country. — *n* a cross-country race, a steeplechase; **point-to-poin'ter** a horse ridden in a point-to-point. — **at a point**, **at point** or **points** or **at all points** (*Shakesp*, etc) in readiness; resolved; completely; in all respects; **at the point of** on the verge of; **cardinal point** see under **cardinal**; **carry one's point** to gain what one contends for; **dead point** see under **dead**; **from point to point** from one detail to another (*obs*); **give points to** to give odds to; to give an advantageous hint on any subject; **in point** apposite; **in point of** in the matter of; **in point of fact** as a matter of fact; **make a point of** to treat as essential, make a special object of; **not to put too fine a point on it** to speak bluntly; **on the point of** close upon; very near; **point for point** exactly in all particulars; **point of honour** see under **honour**; **point of no return** that point on a flight from which one can only go on, for lack of fuel to return (also *fig*); **point of order** a question raised during a formal meeting or debate, eg in Parliament, whether proceedings are according to the rules; **point of view** the position from which one looks at anything, literally or figuratively; **point of the compass** see *n* above; **point out** to point to, show, bring someone's attention to; **point up** to emphasize; **potatoes and point** a feigned Irish dish, potatoes alone, with a herring, etc, to point at; **put upon points** to ration by points; **score points off someone** to advance at the expense of another; to outwit, get the better of someone in an argument or repartee; **stand upon points** to be punctilious; **stretch** (or **strain**) **a point** to go further (*esp* in concession) than strict rule allows; **to the point** apposite; **to point** (*Spenser*, *Shakesp*) to the smallest detail; **up to a point** partly, not wholly. [Partly Fr *point* point, dot, stitch, lace, partly Fr *pointe*, sharp point, pungency, respectively from L *punctum* and LL *puncta*, from L *pungere*, *punctum* to prick]

point[2] *point*, *vt* to appoint, determine, fix. [Aphetic for **appoint**]

point-blank *point'-blangk'*, *adj* aimed directly at the mark without allowing for the downward curve of the trajectory; permitting such an aim, ie at very close range; direct; straightforward; blunt. — *adv* with point-blank aim; directly; bluntly; flat. — *n* a point-blank shot or range; reach (of jurisdiction) (*Shakesp*). [Appar from **point** (verb) and **blank** (of the target)]

point d'appui *pwẽ da-pwē*, *n* (*Fr*) a point of support, a prop or fulcrum.

point-device or **point-devise** *point'-di-vīs'*, *n* (*obs*) the point of perfection (in the phrase *at point device*). — *adj* (*archaic*) fastidiously exact, *esp* in dress. — *adv* with exactitude; down to the smallest detail. [Literally to the point arranged, or arranged to the point, from OFr *devis* devised]

pointe *pwẽt*, (*Fr*; *ballet*) *n* the extreme tip of the toe, or the position of standing on it.

pointel *poin'tl*, *n* a sharp instrument, *esp* a style; a pistil (*obs*). [OFr]

pointillism *pwan'til-izm*, or **pointillisme** *pwẽ-tē-yēzm*, *n* (in painting) the use of separate dots of pure colour instead of mixed pigments. — *adj* **pointillé** (*pwẽ-tē-yā*) ornamented with a pattern of dots made by a pointed tool. — *n* and *adj* **poin'tillist** or **pointilliste** (*-tē-yēst*). [Fr *pointillisme* from *pointille*, dimin of *point* point]

poise[1] *poiz*, *vt* to weigh (*obs*); to hold so as to get some notion of the weight; to carry or hold in equilibrium; to ponder, weigh in the mind (*rare*); to weight, weigh down (*obs*); to make stable, ballast (*obs*); to balance; to counterbalance (*obs*). — *vi* to hang in suspense; to hover. — *n* weight (*obs*); balance; equilibrium; a weight, eg of a clock (*obs*); bias; momentum (*Spenser*); impact (*Shakesp*); carriage or balance of body; dignity and assurance of manner; suspense. — *adj* **poised** having or showing poise or composure; balanced. — *n* **pois'er**. [OFr *poiser* (Fr *peser*), from L *pēnsāre*, frequentative of *pendere* to weigh, and OFr *pois*, from L *pēnsum* weight]

poise[2] *pwäz*, *n* a CGS unit of viscosity (not an SI unit). [J L M *Poise*uille (1799–1869), French physician]

poison *poi'zn*, *n* any substance which, taken into or formed in the body, destroys life or impairs health; any malignant influence; a substance that inhibits the activity of a catalyst (*chem*); a material that absorbs neutrons and so interferes with the working of a nuclear reactor. — *vt* to administer poison to; to injure or kill with poison; to put poison on or in; to taint; to mar; to embitter; to corrupt. — *adj* poisonous. — *adj* **poi'sonable**. — *n* **poi'soner**. — *adj* **poi'sonous** having the quality or effect of poison; noxious; offensive (*colloq*). — *adv* **poi'sonously**. — *n* **poi'sonousness**. — **poi'son-fang** one of two large tubular teeth in the upper jaw of venomous snakes, through which poison passes from glands at their roots when the animal bites; **poi'son-gas** any injurious gas used in warfare; **poi'son-gland** a gland that secretes poison; **poi'son-ivy**, **poi'son-oak** or **poi'son-sumac** or **-sumach** names for various N American sumacs with ulcerating juice; **poi'son-nut** nux vomica; **poison pen** a writer of malicious anonymous letters; **poison pill** (*colloq*) any of various actions, such as merger, takeover or recapitalization, taken by a company to prevent or deter a threatened takeover bid; a clause or clauses in a company's articles of association put into effect by an unwanted takeover bid, and making such a takeover less attractive. — **what's your poison**? (*colloq*) what would you like to drink? [OFr *puison* poison, from L *pōtiō*, *-ōnis* a draught, from *pōtāre* to drink; cf **potion**]

poisson *pwa-sɔ̃*, (*Fr*) *n* a fish. — **poisson d'avril** (*dav-rēl*) an April fool.

Poisson's distribution *pwä-sɔ̃z dis-tri-bū'shən*, (*statistics*) *n* a distribution that, as a limiting form of binomial distribution, is characterized by a small probability of a specific event occurring during observations over a continuous interval (eg of time or distance). — *n* **Poisson's ratio** (*phys*) one of the elastic constants of a material, defined as the ratio of the lateral contraction per unit breadth to the longitudinal extension per unit length when a piece of material is stretched. [After S Denis *Poisson* (1781–1840), French mathematician]

poitrel *poi'trəl*, *n* armour for a horse's breast. [OFr *poitral*, from L *pectorāle* a breastplate, from *pectus*, *-oris* the breast]

pokal *pō-käl'*, *n* an ornamental drinking-vessel. [Ger, from Ital *boccale*, from Gr *baukalis* a vessel for cooling wine, etc]

poke[1] *pōk*, *n* (now chiefly *dialect*; also *Scot* **pock**[2]) a bag; a pouch; a pokeful; a pocket. — *n* **poke'ful** as much as a poke will hold. — **a pig in a poke** a thing bought unseen, or a commitment made to something unknown or unknowable. [ME *poke*; affinities uncertain]

poke[2] *pōk*, *n* a projecting brim or front of a bonnet; a poke-bonnet. — *adj* **poked**. — **poke'-bonnet** a bonnet with a projecting front formerly worn by women. [Perh from **poke**[1], or from **poke**[3]]

poke[3] *pōk*, *vt* to thrust or push the end of anything against or into; to prod or jab; to cause to protrude; to thrust forward or endways; to make, put, render, or achieve by thrusting or groping; to stir up, incite; to dress with a poking-stick (*obs*); (of a man) to have sexual intercourse with (*slang*); to change (a number) in the memory of a computer; to seclude or confine in a poky place (*colloq*). — *vi* to thrust, make thrusts; to protrude; to feel about, grope; to bat gently and cautiously (*cricket*); to potter; to stoop; to pry about; to live a dull or secluded life. — *n* an act of poking. — *n* **pō'ker** someone who pokes; a rod for poking or stirring a fire; an instrument for doing poker-work; a stiff person; a mace or mace-bearer (*facetious*); a poking-stick. — *adj* **po'ker** or **pō'kerish** like a poker; stiff. — *adv* **pō'kerishly**. — *n* **pokey**, **pokes** see **poky** below. — *adj* **pō'king** pottering; petty; confined; stuffy; shabby. — *adj* **pō'ky** or **pō'key** poking, confined; slow, lacking energy or speed (*colloq*); powerful (*colloq*). — *n* (*NAm*) jail: — *pl* **pō'kies** or **pō'keys**. — **pō'ker-work** work done by burning a design into wood with a heated point; **pō'king-stick** a small rod formerly used for adjusting the pleats of ruffs. — **better than a poke in the eye (with a burnt** or **sharp stick)** (*colloq*) an expression of pleasure, *esp* qualified (*Austr*); generally, referring to something only moderately desirable; **by the holy poker**; a facetious oath of unknown meaning, perhaps belonging to **poker**[1] below; **poke fun at** to banter, taunt; **poke one's head** to stoop, hold the head forward; **poke one's nose** to pry; **red-hot poker** Kniphofia or Tritoma. [ME *pōken*; appar of LGer origin]

poke[4] *pōk*, *n* a name for various American species of *Phytolacca* (also **poke'weed** and **poke'berry**); American or white hellebore (**Indian poke**). [Of Amer Ind origin]

poker[1] *pō'kər*, *n* a bugbear. — *adj* **pō'kerish** causing terror; uncanny. — **Old Poker** see **old Harry** under **old**. [Cf Dan *pokker*, Swed *pocker*]

poker[2] *pō'kər*, *n* a round game at cards, first played in America about 1835. — **poker face** an inscrutable face, useful to a poker-player; its possessor. — *adj* **po'ker-faced**. [Ety uncertain; poss from German or French]

poker[3]. See **pochard**.
poker[4] etc. See under **poke**[3].
pokerish. See under **poker**[3].
pokeweed. See under **poke**[4].
pokey, etc, **pokies**, **poking**, etc, **poky**. See under **poke**[3].
POL (*military*) *abbrev*: petrol, oil and lubricants.
Polabian *pō-lā'bi-ən, n* a member of a former W Slavonic people occupying the basin of the lower Elbe; their extinct language. — Also *adj*. [Slav *po* beside, and *Labe* the Elbe]
polacca *po-lak'ə, n* a three-masted Mediterranean vessel, with fore and main masts each in one piece (also **polacre** *po-lä'kər*); a polonaise, or composition in the manner of a polonaise. [Ital *polacca, polacra* Polish (fem); Fr *polacre*: application to the vessel not explained]
Polack *pōl'ak*, (*slang*; *usu derog*) *n* a Pole. — *adj* Polish. [Pol *Polak*; Ger *Polack*]
Poland *pō'lənd, adj* of Poland, Polish. — *n* **Po'lander** (*obs*) a Pole.
polar *pō'lər, adj* of, or pertaining to, a pole (see **pole**[1]) or poles; belonging to the neighbourhood of a pole; referred to a pole; of the nature of, or analogous to, a pole; axial; having polarity; directly opposed. — *n* (*geom*) the locus of the harmonic conjugate of a fixed point or pole with respect to the points in which a transversal through it cuts a circle or other conic. — *n* **polarim'eter** an instrument for measuring the rotation of the plane of polarization of light, or the amount of polarization of light. — *adj* **polarimetric** (*pō-lə-ri-met'rik*). — *n* **polarimetry** (*pō-lə-rim'i-tri*). — *n* **Polaris** (*pō-lä'ris*) the Pole Star. — *n* **polariscope** (*pō-lar'i-skōp*) an instrument for showing phenomena of polarized light. — *n* **polarity** (*pō-lar'i-ti*) the state of having two opposite poles; the condition of having properties different or opposite in opposite directions or at opposite ends; the tendency to develop differently in different directions along an axis, as a plant towards base and apex, some animals towards head and tail; particular relation to this or that pole or opposed property rather than the other; directedness (*fig*); **polarization** or **-s-** (*pō-lə-rī-zā'shən*) an act of polarizing; the state of being polarized; development of poles; loosely, polarity; the effect of deposition of products of electrolysis upon electrodes, resulting in an opposing electromotive force; the restriction (according to the wave theory) of the vibrations of light to one plane; opposedness or doubleness of aspect or tendency. — *vt* **polarize** or **-ise** (*pō'lə-rīz*) to subject to polarization; to give polarity to; to develop new qualities or meanings in (*fig*); to split into opposing camps (also *vi*). — *vi* to acquire polarity. — *adj* **po'larized** or **-s-**. — *n* **po'larīzer** or **-s-** a device for polarizing light. — *n* **polarog'raphy** a technique for determining the concentration and nature of the ions in a solution by an electrolytic process in which the current through the cell is measured as a function of the applied voltage. — *adj* **Po'laroid**® a trademark applied to photographic equipment, light-polarizing materials, etc. — *n* **po'laron** (*electronics*) a free electron trapped by polarization charges on surrounding molecules. — **polar axis** (*astron*) that diameter of a sphere which passes through the poles; in an equatorial telescope, the axis, parallel to the earth's axis, about which the whole instrument revolves in order to keep a celestial object in the field; **polar bear** a large white bear found in the Arctic regions; **polar body** (*biol*) one of two small cells detached from the ovum during the maturation divisions; **polar circle** the Arctic or the Antarctic Circle; **polar co-ordinates** (*math*) co-ordinates defining a point by means of a radius vector and the angle which it makes with a fixed line through the origin; **polar distance** angular distance from the pole; **polar equation** (*math*) an equation in terms of polar co-ordinates; **polar forces** forces that act in pairs and in different directions, as in magnetism; **polar lights** the aurora borealis or australis; **polar wandering** movement of the magnetic poles and of the poles of the earth's rotation through geological time. [L *polāris*, from *polus*; see **pole**[1]]
polder *pōl'dər, n* a piece of low-lying reclaimed land; the first stage in its reclamation. — Also *vt*. [Du]
Pole *pōl, n* a native or citizen of Poland; a Polish-speaking inhabitant of Poland.
pole[1] *pōl, n* the end of an axis, *esp* of the earth, the celestial sphere, or any rotating sphere; either of the two points on a great or small circle on a sphere, in which its axis cuts the surface of the sphere; the point on a crystal face where the normal from the origin cuts the sphere of projection; the end of an elongated body; a differentiated end; either of the two points of a body in which the attractive or repulsive energy is concentrated, as in a magnet; an electric terminal or electrode; a fixed point (*geom*); a point from which a pencil of rays radiates; a fixed point defining a polar; an opposite extreme (*fig*); the heavens (*poetic*, after Greek use). — **Pole Star** Polaris, a star near the N pole of the heavens; a guide or director. — **poles apart** or **asunder** widely separated, very different. [L *polus*, from Gr *polos* pivot, axis, firmament]
pole[2] *pōl, n* a long rounded shaft, rod, or post, *usu* of wood; a small tree; a single shaft to which a pair of horses may be yoked; a measuring rod of definite length; hence a measure of length, $5\frac{1}{2}$ yards of area, $30\frac{1}{4}$ square yards; the position next to the inner boundary-fence in a racecourse or on a racing circuit, etc (now *usu* **pole position**); the tail of certain animals. — *vt* to propel, push, strike, or stir with a pole; to provide or support with poles. — *vi* to use a pole. — *n* **pō'ler** (*Austr*) one of a pair of bullocks harnessed to the pole; a shirker. — *n* **pō'ling** supplying, propelling, or stirring with a pole or poles; poles collectively. — *adj* **pole'-clipt** (*Shakesp*) hedged in with poles. — **pole position** the most advantageous position in any competition or race, etc (see also above); **pole vault** an athletic event in which the competitor uses a pole to achieve great height in jumping over a cross-bar. — *vi* **pole'-vault**. — **pole'-vaulter**. — **pole on** (*Austr slang*) to impose on; **under bare poles** with all sails furled; **up the pole** (*slang*) in a predicament; drunk; crazed; in favour (*military*). [OE *pāl* (Ger *Pfahl*), from L *pālus* a stake]
pole-axe or **pole-ax** *pōl'aks, n* a battle-axe, *orig* short-handled; a long-handled axe or halbert; a sailor's short-handled axe for cutting away rigging; a butcher's axe with a hammer-faced back. — *vt* to strike or fell with or as if with a pole-axe (also *fig*). [Orig *pollax*, from **poll** head, and **axe**, confused with **pole**[2]]
polecat *pōl'kat, n* a large relative of the weasel, which emits a stink, called also *fitchet* and *foumart* (*Mustela putorius*); a prostitute (*Shakesp*); a skunk (*US*). — **pole'cat-ferret** the hybrid offspring of the ferret and polecat. [ME *polcat*; poss Fr *poule* hen, and **cat**[1]] •
Pol Econ *abbrev*: Political Economy.
polemarch *pol'i-märk, n* a title of several officials in ancient Greek states, *orig* a military commander. [Gr *polemarchos*, from *polemos* war, and *archē* rule]
polemic *po-lem'ik, adj* given to disputing; controversial. — *n* a controversialist; a controversy; a controversial writing or argument. — *adj* **polem'ical**. — *adv* **polem'ically**. — *n* **polem'icist** or **pol'emist** someone who writes polemics or engages in controversy. — *n sing* **polem'ics** the practice or art of controversy. — *vt* **pol'emize** or **-ise**. [Gr *polemikos*, from *polemos* war]
polemonium *pol-i-mō'ni-əm, n* a plant of the Jacob's ladder genus *Polemonium*, giving name to the **Polemoniā'ceae**, the phlox family. — *adj* **polemoniā'ceous**. [Gr *polemōnion* St John's wort, or other plant]
polenta *po-len'tə, n* an Italian porridge made of maize, barley, chestnut, or other meal. [Ital, from L *polenta* peeled barley]
poley *pō'li*, (*Austr*) *adj* (of cattle) hornless. — Also *n*. [**poll**[1]]
poleyn *pō'lān, n* a piece of armour protecting the knee. [ME, from OFr *polain*]

polianite *pō'li-ən-īt*, *n* a steel-grey mineral, manganese dioxide. [Gr *poliainesthai* to grow grey, from *polios* hoary]

Polianthes *pol-i-an'thēz*, *n* the tuberose genus of the amaryllid family. [Gr *polios* hoary, and *anthos* a flower]

police *pə-lēs'*, *n* a body of men and women employed to maintain order, etc; its members collectively; the system of regulations for the preservation of order and enforcement of law (*archaic*); the internal government of a state (*archaic*). — *adj* of the police. — *vt* to control as police; to provide with police; to guard or to put or keep in order. — **police burgh** see under **burgh**; **police'-con'stable** a policeman or policewoman of ordinary rank; **police'-court** a former name for a borough court; **police dog** a dog trained to help the police; **police force** a country's full complement of police; the body of police serving any individual area; **police inspector** a superior officer of police who has charge of a department, next in rank to a superintendent; **police'-judge** or **police'-mag'istrate** a judge or magistrate who formerly presided in a police-court; **police'man** a man who is a member of a police force; **police'-manure'** (*Scot*) street sweepings used as manure; **police office** or **police station** the headquarters of the police of a district, used also as a temporary place of confinement; **police officer** a member of a police force, *esp* a constable; **police state** a country in which secret police are employed to detect and stamp out any opposition to the government in power; **police trap** a strategic means whereby the police keep motor traffic under scrutiny and detect offenders against the law; a concealed and concerted timing arrangement to enforce a speed limit; **police'woman** a woman who is a member of a police force. [Fr, from L *polītīa*, from Gr *polīteiā*, from *polītēs* a citizen, from *polis* a city]

policy[1] *pol'i-si*, *n* a constitution (*obs*); the art of government; statecraft; a course of action, *esp* one based on some declared or respected principle; a system of administration guided more by interest than by principle; dexterity of management; prudence; cunning; in Scotland (sometimes in *pl*), the pleasure-grounds around a mansion. [OFr *policie* (Fr *police*), from L *polītīa*, from Gr *polīteiā* (see **police**); in Scots perh influenced by L *polītus* embellished]

policy[2] *pol'i-si*, *n* a document containing a contract of insurance; a kind of gambling by betting on the numbers to be drawn in a lottery (*US*). — **pol'icy-holder** a person who holds a contract of insurance; **pol'icy-shop** a place where the game of policy is played. [Fr *police* policy, appar from LL *apodissa* a receipt, from Gr *apodeixis* proof]

polio *pō'li-ō*, *n* short form of **poliomyelitis**; a person who has or has had polio, *esp* someone paralysed by it (*rare*): — *pl* **po'lios**.

poliomyelitis *pōl-i-ō-mī-ə-lī'tis* or *pol-*, (*med*) *n* a viral infection, one form of which attacks the muscle-controlling nerves of the brain and spinal cord and causes paralysis, formerly called infantile paralysis. [Gr *polios* grey, and *myelos* marrow, and **-itis**]

poliorcetic *pol-i-ər-set'ik*, *adj* of or pertaining to the beleaguerment of towns or fortresses. — *n sing* **poliorcet'ics** siegecraft. [Gr *poliorkētikos*, from *poliorkein* to besiege, from *polis* city, and *erkos* an enclosure]

Polish *pō'lish*, *adj* of Poland, its people, or its language. — *n* the Slavonic language of the Poles.

polish *pol'ish*, *vt* to make smooth and glossy by rubbing; to bring to a finished state; to impart culture and refinement to. — *vi* to take a polish. — *n* an act of polishing; gloss; refinement of manners; a substance applied to produce a polish. — *adj* **pol'ishable**. — *adj* **pol'ished** cultured, refined; accomplished; (of rice) with the husk removed. — *n* **pol'isher**. — *n pl* **pol'ishings** particles removed by polishing. — *n* **pol'ishment**. — **pol'ishing-paste**; **pol'ishing-powder**; **pol'ishing-slate** a diatomaceous slaty stone used for polishing glass, marble, and metals. — **polish off** (*colloq*) to finish off; to dispose of finally; **polish up** or **polish up on** to work at or study in order to improve. [OFr *polir*, *polissant*, from L *polīre* to polish]

Politburo or **Politbureau** *po-lit'bū-rō* or *pol'*, *n* in the former Communist countries, the policy-making committee, effectively the most powerful organ of the Communist Party's executive (in the Soviet Union from 1952 to 1966, the name then being replaced by *Presidium*). [Russ *politicheskoe* political, and *byuro* bureau]

polite *po-līt'*, *adj* refined, cultivated; having courteous manners; glossy, polished (*obs*). — *adv* **polite'ly**. — *n* **polite'ness**. — *n* **politesse** (*pol-ē-tes'*; *Fr*) superficial politeness. — **polite literature** belles-lettres, ie poetry, essays, standard novels, etc, as distinguished from scientific treatises and the like. [L *polītus*, pa p of *polīre* to polish]

politic *pol'i-tik*, *adj* in accordance with good policy; acting or proceeding from motives of policy; prudent; discreet; astutely contriving or intriguing; political (*rare*); constitutional (*obs*). — *adj* **polit'ical** pertaining to policy or government; pertaining to parties differing in their views of government; interested or involved in politics; politic (*obs*). — *adv* **polit'ically**. — *n* **politicas'ter** (*Milton*; see also **-aster**) a petty politician. — *n* **politician** (*-tish'ən*) someone versed in the science of government; someone engaged in political life or statesmanship; someone interested in party politics; a politic person; someone who makes a profession or a game of politics; an intriguer (*US*; *obs*). — *adj* (*Milton*) politic. — *n* **politicīzā'tion** or **-s-**. — *vt* **polit'icize** or **-ise** (*-i-sīz*) to make political. — *vi* to play the politician; to discuss politics. — *n* **pol'iticking** engaging in political activity, such as seeking votes. — *vi* **pol'itick**. — *n* **pol'iticker**. — *adv* **pol'iticly**. — *combining form* **polit'ico-** (*-kō-*) used to form nouns or adjectives, denoting politics or political, as in *politico-economic*, *politico-industrial*. — *adj* **polit'ico-econom'ic** of political economy; of politics and economics. — *n* **pol'itics** (*sing*) the art or science of government; (as *sing*) the management of a political party; (as *sing* or *pl*) political affairs or opinions; (as *pl*) manoeuvring and intriguing; (as *pl*) policy-making, as opposed to administration; (as *pl*) the civil rather than the military aspects of government. — *n* **politique** (*pol-ē-tēk*; *Fr*) in French history, one of a moderate party between Huguenots and Catholics; a religious indifferentist; a temporizer. — **political animal** in the original Aristotelian sense, a social animal, one which lives in communities; someone who is enthusiastic about or involved in politics; someone who enjoys politicking; **political correctness** (*adj* phrase **politically correct**; *orig US*) the avoidance of expressions or actions that may be understood to exclude or denigrate groups or minorities traditionally perceived as disadvantaged by eg race, sex, disability, class, political alignment or sexual inclination; the use of recommended alternative expressions intended to be non-discriminatory; **political economy** the science of the production, distribution, and consumption of wealth; **political geography** that part of geography which deals with the division of the earth for purposes of government, eg states, colonies, counties, and the work of man, such as towns, canals, etc; **political prisoner** someone imprisoned for his or her political beliefs, activities, etc; **political science** the science or study of government, its principles, aims, methods, etc; **political status** the status of a political prisoner; **political verse** Byzantine and modern Greek accentual verse, *esp* iambic verse of fifteen syllables. [Gr *polītikos*, from *polītēs* a citizen]

politico *pō-lit'i-kō*, (*colloq*) *n* a politician, or a person who is interested in politics (*usu derog*): — *pl* **polit'icos** or **polit'icoes**. [Ital or Sp]

politico-, *combining form*. See under **politic**.

politique. See under **politic**.

polity *pol'i-ti, n* political organization; form of political organization, constitution; a body of people organized under a system of government. [Gr *polīteiā*]

polka *pōl'kə* or *pol'kə, n* a Bohemian dance or a tune for it, in 2-4 time with accent on the third quaver, invented about 1830; applied to various things fashionable at the same time, *esp* a woman's jacket. — *vi* **polk** to dance a polka. — **pol'ka-dot** a pattern of dots. [Perh Czech *půlka* half-step; or from Pol *polka* a Polish woman]

Poll or **poll** *pol, n* a parrot. — **poll'-parrot**. — *vt* and *vi* to parrot. [*Poll*, a common name for a parrot; cf **Polly**]

poll[1] *pōl, n* the head; the hair of the head; the head and shoulders of a ling, a type of cod (*obs*); the blunt end of the head of a hammer, miner's pick, etc; a head as a unit in numbering, an individual; a number of individuals (*Shakesp*); a register, *esp* of voters; a voting; an aggregate of votes; the taking of a vote; a taking of public opinion by means of questioning (also **opinion poll**); a polled animal. — *adj* polled; cut evenly (as in **deed poll**, opposite of *indenture*). — *vt* to cut the hair, horns, top (of a tree), or edge (of a deed) from; to tax excessively, practise extortion upon (*archaic*); to receive or take the votes of; to receive, take, or cast (a vote); to receive (a stated number of votes); to question (someone) in a poll. — *vi* to practise extortion (*archaic*); to vote. — *adj* **polled** shorn; pollarded; deprived of horns; hornless. — *n* **poll'er**. — *n* **poll'ing** the action of the verb; a technique by which each of several terminals connected to the same central computer is periodically interrogated in turn by the computer to determine whether it has a message to transmit (*comput*). — *n* **poll'ster** someone who carries out, or who puts his or her faith in, a public opinion poll. — **poll'-axe** a pole-axe (qv); **poll'ing-booth** the place, *esp* the partially enclosed cubicle, where a voter records his or her vote; **poll'-money** or **poll'-tax** a tax of so much a head, ie on each person alike; **poll tax** (also with *caps*; *colloq*) the community charge. — **at the head of the poll** having the greatest number of votes at an election. [Cf obs Du and LGer *polle* top of the head]

poll[2] *pol*, (*Cambridge*) *n* the mass of students who do not seek or obtain honours; a pass degree. — **poll'-degree'**; **poll'man**. [Said to be from Gr *hoi polloi* the many]

pollack *pol'ək, n* a common fish of the cod family, with a long narrow jaw and no barbel; extended to the coalfish. — Also **poll'ock**. [Ety obscure; connection with Gaelic *pollag* doubtful]

pollan *pol'ən, n* an Irish whitefish, *esp* that (*Coregonus pollan*) found in Lough Neagh, Northern Ireland. [Perh Ir *poll* lake; cf **powan**]

pollard *pol'ərd, n* a tree having the whole crown cut off, leaving it to send out new branches from the top of the stem; a hornless animal of horned kind; fine bran; flour or meal containing it; a base foreign coin bearing a head (*obs*). — *adj* pollarded; awnless; bald. — *vt* to make a pollard of. [**poll**[1]]

poll-axe. Same as **pole-axe**.

pollen *pol'ən, n* the fertilizing powder formed in the anthers of flowers. — *vt* to cover or fertilize with pollen. — *n* **polleno'sis** hay fever. — *vt* **poll'inate** to convey pollen to. — *n* **pollinā'tion**. — *n* **poll'inātor**. — *adj* **pollin'ic** of or pertaining to pollen. — *adj* **pollinif'erous** bearing or producing pollen. — *n* **pollin'ium** an agglutinated mass of pollen-grains: — *pl* **pollin'ia**. — **pollen analysis** use of pollen grains in peat bogs, etc, as a means of determining past vegetation and climates or the age of fossil remains; **poll'en-basket** a hollow in a bee's hindleg in which pollen is carried; **pollen count** the amount of pollen in the atmosphere, estimated from deposits on slides exposed to the air; **poll'en-grain** a grain of pollen, the microspore in flowering plants; **poll'en-sac** a cavity in an anther in which pollen is formed, the microsporangium of flowering plants; **poll'en-tube** an outgrowth from a pollen-grain by which the gametes are conveyed to the ovule. [L *pollen, -inis* fine flour]

pollent *pol'ənt, adj* strong. [L *pollēns, -entis*, pr p of *pollēre* to be strong]

pollex *pol'eks, n* the thumb, or its analogue in animals: — *pl* **pollices** (*pol'i-sēz*). — *adj* **poll'ical**. [L *pollex, -icis*]

pollice verso *pol'i-sē vûr'sō, pol'i-ke ver'* or *wer'sō*, (*L*) with the thumb turned up or outwards (now often assumed, *prob* wrongly, to mean downwards), the signal made by the spectators for the death of a Roman gladiator.

pollicie or **pollicy** (*Spenser*). Same as **policy**[1].

pollicitation *pol-is-i-tā'shən, n* a promise; a promise which has not yet been accepted. [L *pollicitātiō, -ōnis*]

pollination, etc, **pollinic**, etc. See under **pollen**.

polliwig, polliwog. See under **pollywog**.

pollman. See under **poll**[2].

pollock. Same as **pollack**.

pollster, poll-tax, etc. See **poll**[1].

pollusion *po-lōō'zhən, -lū'*, (*Shakesp*) *n* Goodman Dull's blunder for **allusion** in *Love's Labour's Lost* IV. 2. 46.

pollute *po-lōōt'* or *-lūt', vt* to make dirty physically; to contaminate, make (any feature of the environment) offensive or harmful to human, animal, or plant life; to make unclean morally; to defile ceremonially, profane. — *adj* defiled. — *n* **pollu'tant** something that pollutes. — *adj* **pollu'ted**. — *adv* **pollu'tedly**. — *n* **pollu'tedness**. — *n* **pollu'ter**. — *n* **pollution** (*po-lōō'shən* or *-lū'*). — *adj* **pollu'tive** causing pollution. [L *polluere, pollūtus*, from *pol-*, a form of *prō* or *per*, and *luere* to wash]

Pollux *pol'uks, n* the twin brother of Castor (*mythol*); a star in the constellation of the Twins. [L for Gr *Polydeukēs*]

Polly *pol'i, n* a form of the name **Molly**; a parrot. [Cf **Poll**]

polly *pol'i*, (*old colloq*) *n* Apollinaris (qv) water.

pollyanna *pol-i-an'ə, n* someone whose naive optimism may verge on the insufferable (also with *cap*). — *adj* **pollyann'aish** or **pollyann'ish**. — *n* **pollyann'aism** a pollyannaish observation. [From *Pollyanna*, fictional creation of Eleanor Hodgman Porter (1868–1920)]

pollywog or **polliwog** *pol'i-wog*, or **pollywig** or **polliwig** *-wig, n* a tadpole. — Also **porwigg'le**. [ME *pollwyggle*, from **poll**[1] and **wiggle**]

polo[1] *pō'lō, n* a game like hockey played on horseback using long-handled mallets (**polo sticks**) and a ball, of Oriental origin; a similar aquatic (*water polo*), bicycle (*bicycle polo*), or skating (*rink polo*) game; a jersey with a polo neck: — *pl* **pō'los**. — *n* **po'loist**. — **polo neck** a pullover collar fitting the neck closely and doubling over, as *orig* in the jersey worn by polo-players; a jersey with such a collar; **polo shirt** a short-sleeved open-necked casual shirt, typically of a knitted cotton fabric, sometimes extended to a similar long-sleeved shirt. [Balti (Tibetan dialect in Kashmir) *polo* polo ball; Tibetan *pulu*]

polo[2] *pō'lō, n* a Spanish gypsy dance: — *pl* **pō'los**. [Sp, an Andalusian popular song]

poloidal *po-loi'dəl, adj* of eg a magnetic field, generated by an electric current flowing in a ring. [*pol*ar and tor*oidal*]

polonaise *pol-ə-nāz', n* a woman's bodice and skirt in one piece, showing an underskirt; a similar child's garment once worn in Scotland; a Polish national dance or promenade of slow movement in 3-4 time; a musical form in the same rhythm. [Fr, Polish (fem)]

Polonia *pol-ō'ni-ə, n* the medieval Latin name for Poland. — *adj* and *n* **Polo'nian**. — *n* **po'lonism** a Polish idiom or characteristic. — *n* **polonium** (*pol-ō'ni-əm*) a radioactive element (symbol **Po**; atomic no 84) discovered by Mme Curie (a Pole). — *n* **Polonization** or **-s-** (*pō-lən-ī-zā'shən*). — *vt* and *vi* **po'lonize** or **-ise** to make or become Polish. — *n* **polo'ny** or **polo'nie** (*Scot*) a child's polonaise.

polony[1] *po-lō'ni, n* a dry sausage of partly cooked meat. [Prob *Bologna*, in Italy; perh *Polonia*]

polony[2]. See under **Polonia**.

polt *pōlt*, *n* a hard blow (now *dialect*); a club (*obs*). — *vt* (*dialect*) to beat. — **polt'foot** a club-foot. — *adj* club-footed. — *adj* **polt'-footed**. [Origin obscure]

poltergeist *pōl'* or *pol'tər-gīst*, *n* a mysterious invisible force asserted to throw or move things about; a noisy ghost. [Ger *poltern* to make a racket, and *Geist* ghost]

poltroon *pol-trōōn'* (*Shakesp* **poul'troone**) *n* a despicable coward. — Also *adj* . — *n* **poltroon'ery** lack of spirit. [Fr *poltron*, from Ital *poltrone*, from *poltro* lazy]

poluphloisboiotatotic, **poluphloisboiotic**. See **polyphloisbic** under **poly-**.

polverine *pol'vər-ēn*, (*obs*) *n* glass-makers' potash. [Ital *polverino*, from L *pulvis*, *pulveris* dust]

poly *pol'i*, (*colloq*) *n* a polytechnic: — *pl* **pol'ys**.

poly- *pol-i-*, *combining form* denoting: many; several; much; a polymer, such as *polyethylene* (see below); affecting more than one part (*med*). — *adj* **polyacid** (*-as'id*) having several replaceable hydrogen atoms; capable of replacing several hydrogen atoms of an acid. — *n* **polyacrylamide** (*-ə-kril'ə-mīd*) the highly cross-linked polymer of acrylamide (**polyacrylamide gel electrophoresis** a technique for separating nucleic acids or proteins on the basis of charge, shape and/or size — *abbrev* **PAGE**). — *adj* **pol'yact** (Gr *aktīs*, *-īnos* ray), **polyactī'nal** (or *-akt'in-əl*) or **polyact'ine** (of a marine animal) having many rays or tentacles. — *n pl* **Polyadel'phia** (Gr *adelphos* brother) in Linnaeus's system, a class of plants with three or more bundles of stamens. — *adj* **polyadel'phous** (of stamens) united in several bundles; having the stamens so united. — *n* **polyam'ide** a polymeric amide, such as nylon. — *n pl* **Polyan'dria** (Gr *anēr*, *andros* man, male) in Linnaeus's system, a class of plants with many stamens inserted in the receptacle. — *adj* **polyan'drous** having or allowing several husbands or male mates (at a time); having a large and indefinite number of stamens or of antheridia (*bot*). — *n* **pol'yandry** (or *-an'*) the condition or practice of being polyandrous; the social usage of some peoples in certain stages of civilization in which a woman normally has several husbands. — *n* **polyan'thus** (Gr *anthos* flower) a many-flowered supposed hybrid between cowslip and primrose; also applied to certain hybrid roses: — *pl* **polyan'thuses**. — *adj* **pol'yarch** (*-ärk*; Gr *archē* origin) having many xylem strands. — *n* **pol'yarchy** (*-ärk-i*; Gr *archein* to rule) government by many persons. — *adj* **polyatom'ic** (*chem*) having many atoms, or replaceable atoms or groups; multivalent. — *adj* **polyax'ial** (L *axis*) or **polyax'on** (Gr *axōn* axis) having many axes or several axis cylinders. — *n* a monaxonic sponge spicule. — *adj* **polyaxon'ic**. — *adj* **polybās'ic** capable of reacting with several equivalents of an acid; (of acids) having several replaceable hydrogen atoms. — *n* **polycar'bonate** any of a range of strong thermoplastics. — *adj* **polycarp'ic** (Gr *karpos* fruit) fruiting many times, or year after year. — *adj* **polycarp'ous** polycarpic; having an apocarpous gynaeceum. — *adj* **polycent'ric** multicentric. — *n pl* **Polychaeta** (*-kē'tə*; Gr *chaitē* bristle) a class of marine chaetopods with numerous bristles. — *n* **pol'ychaete** (*-kēt*) any worm of the Polychaeta. — *adj* **polychlor'inated** (**polychlorinated biphenyl** see **PCB**). — *n* **polychlor'oprene** neoprene. — *n* **pol'ychrest** (*-krest*; Gr *polychrēstos* from *chrēstos* useful) a thing, *esp* a medicine, useful in several ways. — *adj* **polychroic** (*-krō'ik*) pleochroic. — *n* **pol'ychroism**. — *adj* **pol'ychrome** (*-krōm*; Gr *chrōma* colour) many-coloured. — *n* a work of art (*esp* a statue) in several colours; varied colouring. — *adj* **polychromat'ic** or **polychrom'ic**. — *n* **pol'ychromy** the art of decorating in many colours. — *n* **pol'yclinic** a general clinic or hospital. — *adj* **polycon'ic** pertaining to or composed of many cones. — *adj* and *n* **pol'ycotton** (of) a fabric made from polyester and cotton. — *adj* **polycotyle'donous** (*bot*) with more than two cotyledons. — *adj* **polycrot'ic** (Gr *krotos* a beat) (of the pulse) having several beats to each heart-beat. — *n* **polyc'rotism**. — *n* **pol'ycrystal** an object composed of several or many variously orientated crystals. — *adj* **polycrys'talline**. — *n* **pol'yculture** the simultaneous production of several different crops and types of livestock in one region. — *adj* **polycyclic** (*-sī'klik*; Gr *kyklos* wheel) having many circles, rings, whorls, turns, or circuits; containing more than one ring of atoms in the molecule. — *n* **polycythaemia** (*-sī-thē'mi-ə*; **-cyt-** cell, and *haima* blood) an excess of red blood corpuscles. — *adj* **polydac'tyl** having more than the normal number of fingers or toes. — Also *n*. — *n* **polydac'tylism** or **polydac'tyly**. — *adj* **polydac'tylous**. — *n* **polyde'monism** or **polydae'monism** the belief in and worship of numerous supernatural powers. — *n* **polydip'sia** (Gr *dipsa* thirst) excessive thirst. — *adj* **polyem'bryonate**. — *adj* **polyembryonic** (*-on'ik*). — *n* **polyembryony** (*-em'bri-ən-i*) formation of more than one embryo from one ovule or from one fertilized ovum. — *n* **polyes'ter** any of a range of polymerized esters, some thermoplastic, some thermosetting. — *n* **polyeth'ylene** or **pol'ythene** a generic name for certain thermoplastics, polymers of ethylene manufactured in a range of qualities from light and rigid to thin and flexible, and used to make a variety of products *incl* domestic utensils, storage bags, carrier bags, etc. — *n* **polygala** (*pol-ig'ə-lə*; Gr *polygalon* milkwort, *gala* milk) any plant of the milkwort genus *Polygala*, giving name to the family **Polygalā'ceae**. — *adj* **polygalaceous** (*-lā'shəs*). — *n pl* **Polygamia** (*pol-i-gā'mi-ə*; Gr *gamos* marriage) in Linnaeus's classification, a class having male, female, and hermaphrodite flowers. — *n* **pol'ygam** a plant of this class. — *adj* **polygamic** (*-gam'ik*). — *n* **polygamist** (*pol-ig'*). — *adj* **polyg'amous**. — *adv* **polyg'amously**. — *n* **polygamy** (*pol-ig'ə-mi*) the rule, custom, or condition of marriage to more than one person at a time, or (now rarely) in life; sometimes used for polygyny; mating with more than one in the same breeding season (*zool*); occurrence of male, female, and hermaphrodite flowers on the same or on different plants (*bot*). — *n* **pol'ygene** (*-jēn*) any of a group of genes that control a single continuous character (eg height). — *n* **polygen'esis** multiple origin, *esp* of mankind. — *adj* **polygenet'ic** of polygenesis; springing from several sources; (of dyes) giving different colours with different mordants. — *adj* **polygen'ic** polygenetic; forming more than one compound with a univalent element. — *n* **polyg'enism** belief in multiple origin, *esp* of mankind. — *n* **polyg'enist**. — *adj* **polyg'enous** of multiple origin or composition. — *n* **polyg'eny** polygenesis. — *adj* **pol'yglot** (Gr *polyglōttos*, from *glōtta*, tongue) in, of, speaking, or writing, many languages. — *n* someone who speaks or writes many languages; a collection of versions in different languages of the same work, *esp* a Bible. — Also **pol'yglott**. — *adj* **polyglott'al**, **polyglott'ic**, **polyglott'ous**. — *n* **pol'ygon** (*-gon* or *-gən*; Gr *polygōnon*, from *gōniā* angle) a plane figure bounded by straight lines, *esp* more than four; an object in the form of a polygon, *esp* in the building of earthworks and fortifications. — *adj* **polyg'onal** (**polygonal numbers** figurate numbers). — *adv* **polyg'onally**. — *n* **polygon'atum** (Gr *polygonaton*, from *gony*, *-atos* knee) the Solomon's seal genus *Polygonatum*, of the lily family. — *n* **polyg'onum** (Gr *polygonon*) any plant of the knot-grass genus *Polygonum*, with swollen joints and sheathing stipules, of the dock family **Polygonā'ceae**. — *adj* **polygonā'ceous**. — *n* **polyg'ony** (*Spenser*) the plant bistort. — *n* **pol'ygraph** a copying, multiplying, or tracing apparatus; a copy; an instrument which measures very small changes in body temperature, pulse rate, respiration, etc, and which is often used as a lie-detector. — *adj* **polygraph'ic**. — *n* **polygraphy** (*po-lig'rə-fi*) voluminous writing; the use of the polygraph as a lie-detector. — *n pl* **Polygynia** (*-jin'*; Gr *gynē* woman, female) in various Linnaean classes of plants, an order with more than twelve styles. — *adj* **polygyn'ian** of the Polygynia. — *adj* **polygynous** (*-lij'* or *-lig'i-nəs*) having several wives; mating with several females; having several styles; polygynian. — *n* **polygyny**

(*-lij'* or *-lig'*) the custom, practice, or condition of having a plurality of wives or styles; the habit of mating with more than one female. — *n* **polyhalite** (*-hal'īt*; Gr *hals* salt) a triclinic mineral, sulphate of magnesium, potassium, and calcium. — *adj* **polyhed'ral**. — *adj* **polyhedric** (*-hēd'* or *-hed'*). — *n* **polyhē'dron** (or *-hed'*; *Gr hedrā* seat) a solid figure or body bounded by plane faces (*esp* more than six): — *pl* **polyhed'rons** or **polyhed'ra**. — *n* **polyhis'tor** (Gr *polyistōr*, from *historeein* to inquire, learn) a person of great and varied learning. — *n* **polyhistorian** (*-tō'ri-ən* or *-tö'*). — *adj* **polyhistoric** (*-tor'ik*). — *n* **polyhis'tory** (*-tə-ri*). — *n* **polyhy'brid** a cross between parents differing in several heritable characters. — *adj* **polyhy'dric** having several hydroxyl groups, polyhydroxy. — *adj* **polyhydrox'y** (*chem*) (of a compound) containing two or more hydroxyl groups per molecule. — *n* **polyhydroxybu'tyrate** a natural polymer which can be used to manufacture fully biodegradable plastic (*abbrev* **PHB**). — *n* **Polyhymnia** (*pol-i-him'ni-ə*) or **Polymnia** (*pol-im'ni-ə*; Gr *hymnos* hymn, ode) the muse of the sublime lyric. — *n* **polyī'soprene** a rubber-like polymer of isoprene. — *n* **polylemm'a** (*logic*; Gr *lēmma* an assumption) a form of argument in which the maintainer of a certain proposition is committed to accept one of several propositions all of which contradict his or her original contention. — *n* **polymas'tia**, **polymast'ism** or **pol'ymasty** (Gr *mastos* breast) the presence of supernumerary breasts or nipples. — *adj* **polymas'tic**. — *n* **pol'ymath** (Gr *polymathēs*, from the root of *manthanein* to learn) a person whose knowledge covers a wide variety of subjects. — *adj* **polymath'ic**. — *n* **polym'athy** much and varied learning. — *n* **pol'ymer** (Gr *meros* part; *chem*) any naturally occurring or synthetic substance with large molecules made up of a repetitive series of smaller units, *esp* one of those of higher molecular weight as produced by polymerization. — *n* **polymerase** (*pol'i-mər-ās*) an enzyme present in cell nuclei which promotes the polymerization of DNA (**polymerase chain reaction** a powerful technique for amplifying DNA sequences without using genetic manipulation methods which need biological vectors — *abbrev* **PCR**). — *adj* **polymeric** (*-mer'ik*) of, in a relation of, or manifesting polymerism. — *n* **polym'eride** a polymer. — *n* **polym'erism**. — *n* **polymerīzā'tion** or **-s-**. — *vt* **polym'erize** or **-ise** to combine to form a more complex molecule having the same empirical formula as the simpler ones combined; to cause to form a polymer; to make polymerous. — *vi* to change into a polymer. — *adj* **polym'erous** having many parts; having many parts in a whorl (*bot*). — *n* **polym'ery** the condition of being polymerous. — *n* **Polymnia** see **Polyhymnia** above. — *n* **pol'ymorph** (Gr *polymorphos* many-formed, from *morphē* form) any one of several forms in which the same thing may occur; an organism occurring in several forms; a substance crystallizing in several systems. — *adj* **polymorph'ic**. — *n* **polymorph'ism**. — *adj* **polymorph'ous**. — *n* **polymyositis** (*-mī-ō-sī'tis*; see **myo-**) inflammation of several muscles at the same time. — *adj* **Polynē'sian** (Gr *nēsos* an island) of *Polynesia*, one of the three groups into which the Pacific islands are divided, its prevailing race of light-brown-skinned people, or their languages (a division of the Austronesian). — *n* a native of Polynesia; a member of the light-brown-skinned race of Polynesia. — *n* **polyneuritis** (*-nūr-ī'tis*) simultaneous inflammation of several nerves. — *adj* and *n* **polynō'mial** (*math*) (an expression) consisting of a sum of terms each containing a constant and one or more variables raised to a power. — *n* **polynō'mialism**. — *n* **polynucleotide** (*pol-i-nū'kli-ə-tīd*) a compound (eg nucleic acid) that is made up of a number of nucleotides. — *n* **polyō'ma** a small DNA virus which causes tumours in mice. — *n* **polyomino** (*pol-i-om'in-ō*; on the false analogy of *domino*) a flat, many-sided shape made up of a number of identical squares placed edge to edge: — *pl* **polyom'inos**. — *n* **polyonym** (*pol'i-ō-nim*; Gr *onyma*, a form of *onoma* name) a name consisting of several words. — *adj* **polyonym'ic** (of a name) of more than two words. — *adj* **polyon'ymous** having many names. — *n* **polyon'ymy** multiplicity of names for the same thing. — *n* **polypep'tide** a peptide in which many amino-acids are linked to form a chain. — *adj* **polypet'alous** with free petals. — *n* **polyphagia** (*-fā'ji-ə*; Gr *phagein* to eat) bulimia; the habit in animals, *esp* certain insects, of eating many different kinds of food. — *adj* **polyphagous** (*po-lif'ə-gəs*) (of an animal) eating many different kinds of food; given to eating excessive amounts of food, *esp* as the result of a pathological condition. — *n* **polyph'agy** (*-ji*) the character of being polyphagous. — *n* **polyphar'macy** the (*esp* indiscriminate and excessive) use of many different drugs in treating a disease. — *adj* **pol'yphase** having several alternating electric currents of equal frequency with uniformly spaced phase differences. — *adj* **polyphasic** (*-fāz'ik*) going through several phases of activity followed by rest in any twenty-four hours. — *adj* **Polyphē'mian** or **Polyphē'mic**. — *n* **Polyphē'mus** (*Gr mythol*) the Cyclops blinded by Odysseus. — *adj* **polyphiloprogenitive** (*pol-i-fil-ō-prō-jen'i-tiv*) (of imagination or inventiveness) very fertile. — *adj* **polyphloisbic** (*pol-i-flois'bik*; Gr *polyphloisbos*, from *phloisbos* din), **poluphloisboiotic** (*pol-ōō-flois-boi-ot'ik*), or **polyphloesboean** (*pol-i-flēs-bē'ən*, the *oi* and *oe* from the genitive ending in Homer's phrase *polyphloisboio thalassēs*, of the much-roaring sea) loud-roaring. — *adj* **poluphloisboiotatot'ic** (*Thackeray*; as if from a Gr superlative in *-otatos*). — *n* **pol'yphon** (*-fon*) or **pol'yphone** (*-fōn*; Gr *phōnē* a voice) a lute-like musical instrument; a musical box playing tunes from perforated metal discs; (**pol'yphone**) a letter or symbol having more than one phonetic value, able to be pronounced or sounded in more than one way (*phonetics*). — *adj* **polyphonic** (*-fon'ik*) many-voiced; of polyphones; of polyphony. — *n* **pol'yphonist** a contrapuntist. — *n* **polyph'ony** composition of music in parts each with an independent melody of its own. — *adj* **polyphyletic** (*-fi-let'ik* or *-fī-*; Gr *phyletikos* pertaining to a tribesman, from *phylē* a tribe) of multiple origin; descended by convergent lines from several ancestral groups. — *adj* **polyphyllous** (*-fil'əs*; Gr *phyllon* leaf) (*bot*) having the perianth leaves free. — *adj* **polyphȳ'odont** having more than two successive dentitions. — *n pl* **Polyplacoph'ora** (Gr *plax*, *plakos* a plate, slab) an order of molluscs, *incl* eg the chitons, bilaterally symmetrical, with a shell composed of eight transverse dorsal plates. — *adj* **pol'yploid** (on the analogy of *haploid* and *diploid*) having more than twice the normal haploid number of chromosomes. — *n* **pol'yploidy** the polyploid condition. — *n* **pol'ypod** an animal with many feet; a polypody. — *n* **Polypodium** (*-pō'di-əm*; Gr *podion*, dimin of *pous* a foot) the typical genus of **Polypodiā'ceae**, the family with stalked sporangia and vertical annulus to which most ferns belong, so named from the many-footed appearance of the rhizome. — *n* **pol'ypody** any fern of the genus Polypodium, *esp Polypodium vulgare*. — *n* **Polyporus** (*po-lip'ə-rəs*; Gr *poros* a pore) a large genus of pore fungi (qv), often forming hoof-like and bracket-like growths on trees. — *n* **polyprop'ylene** a polymer of propylene, similar in properties to polyethylene. — *n* **polyprō'todont** (Gr *prōtos*, first, and *odous*, *odontos* tooth) any member of the **Polyprotodont'ia**, the sub-order of marsupials, including opossums, dasyures, etc, with many small incisors. — *n* **Polyp'terus** (Gr *pteron* a fin) an African genus of Crossopterygian river fishes, with the dorsal fin represented by detached rays. — *n* **polyptych** (*pol'ip-tik*; Gr *ptychos* a fold) a picture, altarpiece, etc, consisting of four or more panels hinged or folding together. — *n* **pol'yrhythm** the simultaneous combination of different rhythms in a piece of music. — *adj* **polyrhyth'mic**. — *n* **polysaccharide** (*-sak'ə-rīd*) a carbohydrate of a class including starch and insulin, etc, that hydrolyzes into more than one simple sugar.

— *n* **polyse'mant** (-*sē'*) or **pol'yseme** (-*sēm*) (*linguistics*) a word with more than one meaning. — *n* **pol'ysemy** (*linguistics*). — *adj* **polysep'alous** (*bot*) having the sepals separate from each other. — *n* **polysilox'ane** any of a number of polymers which are the basis of silicone chemistry. — *n* **pol'ysome** a group of ribosomes linked by a molecule of ribonucleic acid and functioning as a unit in the synthesis of proteins. — *n* **pol'ysomy** a condition in which one or more extra chromosomes, *esp* sex chromosomes, are present in the cells of the body. — *n* **Polys'tichum** (-*kəm*; Gr *stichos* a row) a genus of shield-ferns also known by the name Aspidium. — *adj* **polysty'lar** or **pol'ystyle** (Gr *stȳlos* column) having many columns. — *n* **polysty'rene** a polymer of styrene resistant to moisture and to chemicals, with many commercial and industrial applications. — *adj* **polysyllab'ic** or **polysyllab'ical**. — *adv* **polysyllab'ically**. — *n* **polysyllab'icism** or **polysyll'abism**. — *n* **polysyll'able** a word of many, or of more than three, syllables. — *n* **polysyll'ogism** a series of syllogisms, the conclusion of one serving as the premiss for the next. — *n* **polysyndeton** (-*sin'di-tən*; Gr *syndeton* a conjunction; *rhetoric*) figurative repetition of connectives or conjunctions. — *n* **polysyn'thesis**. — *adj* **polysynthet'ic** or **polysynthet'ical** made up of many separate elements; built up of a number of small crystals in parallel growth (*crystallog*); combining many simple words of a sentence in one, as in the native languages of America, also called *incorporating* (*philol*). — *adv* **polysynthet'ically**. — *n* **polysynthet'icism** (-*i-sizm*) or **polysyn'thetism** the character of being polysynthetic. — *adj* **polytechnic** (-*tek'nik*; Gr *technikos*, from *technē* art) of many arts or technical subjects. — *n* a college where such subjects are taught up to and including degree level, traditionally offering a wide variety of vocational courses on a full- or part-time basis. — *adj* **polytech'nical**. — *adj* **pol'ytene** (-*tēn*; L *taenia* band) (of abnormally large chromosomes) composed of many reduplicated strands. — *n* **polytetrafluoreth'ylene** or **polytetrafluoroeth'ylene** a plastic with non-adhesive surface properties. — *adj* **polythal'amous** (Gr *thalamos* a chamber) having several cells or chambers. — *n* **pol'ytheism** (-*thē-izm*; Gr *theos* a god) the doctrine of a plurality of gods. — *n* **pol'ytheist**. — *adj* **polytheist'ic** or **polytheist'ical**. — *adv* **polytheist'ically**. — *n* **pol'ythene** see **polyethylene** above. — *adj* **polytocous** (*pol-it'ə-kəs*; Gr *tokos* birth) producing many or several at a birth or in a clutch. — *adj* **polyto'nal**. — *n* **polytonal'ity** use at the same time of two or more musical keys. — *n* **Polytrichum** (*po-lit'ri-kəm*; Gr *thrix*, *trichos* hair) a genus of tall hairy-capped mosses. — *n* **pol'ytunnel** plastic sheeting stretched over rows of plants as protection from weather, etc. — *adj* **polytypic** (-*tip'ik*) having many types and representatives. — *adj* **polyunsat'urated** (*chem*) containing more than one carbon-carbon double bond in the molecule (**polyunsaturated fats** or **oils** glycerides of polyunsaturated fatty acids, containing no cholesterol). — *n* **polyurethane** (-*ū'rə-thān*) any of a range of resins, both thermoplastic and thermosetting, used in the production of foamed materials, coatings, etc. — *n* **polyuria** (-*ū'ri-ə*; *med*) excessive secretion of urine. — *adj* **polyvalent** (*po-li-vā'lənt* or *pol-iv'ə-lənt*) multivalent. — *n* **polyvī'nyl** a vinyl polymer. — Also *adj*. — **polyvinyl acetate** a colourless resin used in paints, adhesives, and as a coating for porous surfaces; **polyvinyl chloride** a vinyl plastic used as a rubber substitute for coating electric wires, cables, etc, and as a dress and furnishing fabric (*abbrev* **PVC**). — *n* **pol'ywater** a supposed form of water, said to be a polymer, with properties different from those of ordinary water. — *n pl* **Polyzō'a** (Gr *zōion* an animal) a phylum of aquatic animals, almost all colonial, with a cup-shaped body, U-shaped food-canal, and a wreath of tentacles about the mouth: — *sing* **polyzo'on**. — *n* and *adj* **polyzo'an**. — *adj* **polyzoarial** (-*ā'ri-əl*). — *n* **polyzoā'rium** or **polyzō'ary** a polyzoan colony, or its supporting skeleton. — *adj* **polyzō'ic** having many zooids; pertaining to the Polyzoa. — *adj* **polyzo'nal** (Gr *zōnē* belt) composed of many zones or belts. — *adj* **polyzō'oid** like or of the nature of a polyzoon. [Gr *polys*, *poleia*, *poly* much]

polyacid... to ... **polyaxonic**. See under **poly-**.

poly bag *pol'i bag*, (*colloq*) *n* a polythene bag, a plastic bag.

polybasic... to ... **polyneuritis**. See under **poly-**.

polynia *pol-in'i-ə* or **polynya** -*in'yə*, *n* open water amid sea ice, *esp* in Arctic waters. [Russ *polyn'ya*]

polynomial... to ... **polyonymy**. See under **poly-**.

polyp or (*obs*) **polype** *pol'ip*, *n* an octopus or cuttlefish (*obs*); later extended to other animals with many arms or tentacles, *esp* coelenterates and Polyzoa; an individual of a colonial animal; a pedunculated tumour growing from mucous membrane (*pathol*): — *pl* **pol'yps** or **pol'ypes** (*pol'ips*). — *n* **pol'ypary** the common supporting structure of a colony of polyps. — *n* **pol'ypide** or **pol'ypite** a polyp of a colonial animal. — *n* **polyp'idom** (Gr *domos* house) a polypary. — *adj* **pol'ypine**. — *adj* **pol'ypoid** (*med*) like a polypus. — *n* **polypō'sis** the presence or development of polyps. — *adj* **pol'ypous** of the nature of a polyp. — *n* **polypus** (*pol'i-pəs*; Gr *polypous*, adapted into L as 2nd declension) a pedunculated tumour growing from the mucous membrane: — *pl* **po'lypī**. [L *polypus*, from Gr *polypous*, *-podos*, from *pous* foot]

polypeptide... to ... **polyrhythmic**. See under **poly-**.

polysaccharide... to ... **polyzooid**. See under **poly-**.

Pom. See under **pom**[2].

pom[1] *pom*, (*colloq*) *n* a Pomeranian dog.

pom[2] or **Pom** *pom*, (*Austr* and *NZ colloq*) *n* and *adj* short for **pommy** (qv).

pomace *pum'is*, *n* crushed apples for cider-making, or the residue after pressing; anything crushed to pulp, *esp* after oil has been expressed. — **pom'ace-fly** a fruit-fly (Drosophila). [Appar LL *pōmācium* cider, from L *pōmum* apple, etc]

pomaceous. See under **pome**.

pomade *pom-äd'*, *n* ointment for the hair, Latinized as **pomā'tum**. — *vt* to anoint with pomade, put pomade on. [Fr *pommade*, from Ital *pomada*, *pomata* lip-salve, from L *pōmum* an apple]

Pomak *pō-mäk'*, *n* a Bulgarian Muslim.

pomander *pom-* or *pōm-an'dər*, *n* a ball of perfumes, or a perforated globe or box in which this or a similarly perfumed preparation is kept or carried. [OFr *pomme d'ambre* apple of amber]

pomato *pom-ä'tō*, *-ā'tō*, *n* a tomato grafted on a potato: — *pl* **poma'toes**. [Portmanteau word]

pomatum. See under **pomade**.

pombe *pom'be*, *n* any of various Central and East African alcoholic drinks. [Swahili]

pome *pōm*, *n* an apple (*rare*); any of the fruits of the apple family, eg apple, pear or quince, the enlarged fleshy receptacle enclosing a core formed from the carpels (*bot*); a king's globe or orb; a priest's hand-warming ball of hot water. — *adj* **pomaceous** (-*ā'shəs*) relating to, consisting of, or resembling apples; of the apple family or the apple section of the rose family. — *n* **pome'roy** or **pomroy** (*pom'* or *pum'roi*) an old variety of apple. — *n* **pom'iculture** fruit-growing; pomology. — *adj* **pomif'erous** bearing apples, pomes, or fruit generally. — *adj* **pomolog'ical**. — *n* **pomol'ogist**. — *n* **pomol'ogy** the study of fruit-growing. — **pome'-cit'ron** the citron; **pome'-water** or **pom'water** (*Shakesp*) a sweet juicy apple. [L *pōmum* a fruit, an apple]

pomegranate *pom'i-gran-it*, *pom'ə-* or *pom'gran-it*, formerly *pum-gran'it*, *pom-*, *n* an Oriental fruit much cultivated in warm countries, with a thick leathery rind and numerous seeds with pulpy edible seed-coats; the tree (*Punica granatum*; family *Punicaceae*) bearing it. [OFr *pome grenate*, from L *pōmum* an apple, and *grānātum* having many grains]

pomelo *pum'*, or *pom'il-ō*, *n* the grapefruit-like fruit of a tropical tree grown in Eastern countries; the tree that bears it; a grapefruit (*NAm*); a similar pear-shaped fruit or the tree that bears it, also called **shaddock**: — *pl* **pom'elos**. [Ety uncertain]

Pomeranian *pom-i-rā'ni-ən, adj* of *Pomerania*. — *n* a native of Pomerania; a spitz or Pomeranian dog, a cross from the Eskimo dog, with a sharp-pointed face and an abundant white, creamy, or black coat.

pomeroy. See under **pome**.

Pomfret a spelling representing the older pronunciation (*pum'frit*) of **Pontefract** (now *pon'ti-frakt*), *n* a town in Yorkshire. — **pomfret** (*pum'* or *pom'*), **pomfret cake** or **Pontefract cake** a round flat liquorice sweet made there. [Anglo-Fr *Pontfret*, from L *pōns, pontis* bridge, and *fractus* broken]

pomfret *pom'frit, n* any of several fishes, including an East Indian fish valued as food. [Earlier *pamflet*, from Fr *pample*, from Port *pampo*]

pomiculture, **pomiferous**. See under **pome**.

pommel *pum'l, n* a knob (*obs*); a ball-shaped finial; a knob on a sword-hilt; the high part of a saddle-bow; a heavy-headed ramming tool; either of two handles on top of a gymnastics horse. — *vt* (*usu* spelt **pummel**, qv). — *adj* **pomm'elled** having a pommel, in heraldry also **pommelé** (*pom'ə-li*) or **pomm'etty**. [OFr *pomel* (Fr *pommeau*), from L *pōmum* an apple]

pommy *pom'i*, (*Austr* and *NZ colloq*, often *derog*) *n* an immigrant from the British Isles; a British (*esp* English) person in general. — Also *adj*. — Often shortened to **pom**. [Origin obscure; perh from **pomegranate**, alluding to the colour of the immigrants' cheeks, or rhyming slang for *jimmygrant*, immigrant, or from the abbrev POME (Prisoner of Mother England) stamped on the shirts of early convict-settlers]

pomoerium *pō-mē'ri-əm, n* an open space around a town, within and beyond the walls. [L *pōmoerium*, appar for *postmoerium*, from *post* and *moiros*, old form of *mūrus* wall]

pomologist, etc. See under **pome**.

Pomona *pō-mō'nə, n* the Roman goddess of fruits. [L *Pōmōna*, from *pōmum* fruit, apple]

pomp *pomp, n* a procession; great show or display; ceremony; ostentation; vanity or self-importance; consequential bearing. — *n* **pomposity** (*-os'i-ti*) solemn affectation of dignity; a ridiculously pompous action, expression, or person. — *adj* **pomp'ous** stately (*archaic*); self-important. — *adv* **pomp'ously**. — *n* **pomp'ousness**. [Fr *pompe*, from L *pompa*, from Gr *pompē* a sending, escort, procession, from *pempein* to send]

pompadour *pom'pə-dōōr, n* a fashion of dressing women's hair by rolling it back from the forehead over a cushion (*hist*); a corsage with a low square neck (*hist*); a pattern for silk, with pink, blue, and gold leaves and flowers; a pink colour. — *adj* in or pertaining to the style of hairdressing or dress described above, associated with Mme de Pompadour's time. [Marquise de *Pompadour* (1721–64)]

pompano *pomp'ə-nō, n* a general name for carangoid fishes (family *Carangidae*), *esp* edible American fishes of the genus *Trachynotus*: — *pl* **pomp'ano** or **pomp'anos**. [Sp *pámpano* a fish of another family]

Pompeian *pom-pē'ən, adj* pertaining to *Pompeii*, a city buried by an eruption of Mount Vesuvius in AD 79, excavated since 1755. — **Pompei'an-red'** a red colour like that on the walls of Pompeian houses.

pompelmoose *pom'pəl-mōōs, n* the shaddock, *esp* the grapefruit. — Also **pam'pelmoose**, **pam'pelmouse**, **pom'pelmous**, **pom'pelmouse**, **pum'ple-nose**, **pom'pelo** (*pl* **pom'pelos**), or **pom'elo**. [Du *pompelmoes*; origin obscure]

Pompey *pom'pi*, (*slang*) *n* Portsmouth.

pompey *pom'pi*, (*Dickens*) *vt* to pamper (qv).

pompholyx *pom'fə-liks, n* a vesicular eruption or eczema chiefly on the palms and soles (*med*); impure zinc oxide. — *adj* **pomphol'ygous**. [Gr *pompholyx, -ygos* bubble, slag, from *pomphos* a blister]

pompier *pom'pi-ər*, or *pɔ̃-pyā, adj* (of art) conventional, traditional, uninspired. [Fr *pompier* fireman, from an alleged resemblance of mythological heroes in rigidly traditional art]

pompier-ladder *pom'pi-ər-lad'ər*, or *pɔ̃-pyā-, n* a fireman's ladder, a pole with cross-bars and hook. [Fr *pompier* fireman, from *pompe* pump]

pompion *pump'i-ən*. See under **pumpkin**.

pompom[1] *pom'pom*, (*colloq*) *n* a machine-gun; a *usu* multi-barrelled anti-aircraft gun. [Imit]

pompom[2] *pom'pom*, **pompon** *pom'pon*, or (*obs*) **pompoon** *pom-pōōn', n* a jewelled hair ornament on a pin (*obs*); a fluffy or woolly ball, tuft, or tassel worn on a shoe, hat, etc. [Fr *pompon*]

pomposity, **pompous**. See under **pomp**.

pomroy, **pomwater**. See under **pome**.

'pon *pon*, aphetic for **upon**.

ponce *pons*, (*slang*) *n* a man who lives on the immoral earnings of a prostitute; a pimp; an obnoxious person; an effeminate, posturing man. — *vi* to act as or like a pimp. — *adj* **pon'cy** or **pon'cey**. — **ponce about** or **around** to fool about; to act the ponce or in a showy manner. [Ety uncertain]

ponceau[1] *pɔ̃-sō', n* and *adj* poppy colour. — *n* a red dye: — *pl* **ponceaux** (*-sōz'*). [Fr]

ponceau[2] *pɔ̃-sō', n* a small bridge or culvert. [Fr]

poncho *pon'chō, n* a South American cloak, a blanket with a hole for the head; a cyclist's waterproof cape of similar design; any similar garment: — *pl* **pon'chos**. [Sp from Araucanian]

pond *pond, n* a small *usu* artificial lake; the stretch of water between locks in a canal; (also with *cap*) the Atlantic (*facetious*). — *vt* to make into a pond. — *vi* to collect into a pond. — *n* **pond'age** the capacity of a pond. — **pond'-life** animal life in ponds; **pond lily** a waterlily; **pond'-master** the man in charge of a swimming-pond; **pond snail** a pond-dwelling snail, *esp Limnaea*; **pond'weed** any plant of the genus Potamogeton (**Canadian pondweed** Anacharis). [ME *ponde*; cf **pound**[2]]

ponder *pon'dər, vt* to weigh (*obs*); to weigh in the mind; to think over; to consider. — *vi* to think (often with *on* and *over*). — *n* **ponderabil'ity**. — *adj* **pon'derable** able to be weighed or measured; having sensible weight; appreciable. — *adj* **pon'deral** pertaining to weight; ascertained by weight. — *n* **pon'derance** or **pon'derancy** weight. — *vt* and *vi* (*literary*) **pon'derate** to weigh; to ponder. — *n* (*literary*) **ponderā'tion** weighing or weighing up. — *n* **pon'derer**. — *adv* **pon'deringly**. — *n* **pon'derment**. — *n* **ponderosity** (*-os'i-ti*). — *adj* **pon'derous** heavy; weighty; massive; unwieldy; lumbering; (of a speech, etc) solemnly laboured. — *adv* **pon'derously**. — *n* **pon'derousness**. [L *ponderāre*, and *pondus, ponderis* a weight]

pondok *pon'dok* or **pondokkie** *pon-dok'i*, (*SAfr*) *n* a crude dwelling, a hut, shack, etc. [Hottentot *pondok* a hut, or perh Malay *pondók* a leaf shelter]

pone[1] *pōn*, (*US*) *n* maize bread; a maize loaf or cake. [Algonquian *pone*]

pone[2] *pō'ni* or *pōn*, (*cards*) *n* the player to the right of the dealer, who cuts the cards; sometimes the player to the left. [L *pōne*, imperative of *ponere* to place]

ponent *pō'nənt*, (*Milton*) *adj* western. [Ital *ponente*, setting (of the sun), from L *pōnēns, -entis*, pr p of *pōnere* to put]

ponerology *pon-ə-rol'ə-ji*, (*theol*) *n* the doctrine of wickedness. [Gr *ponēros* bad, and *logos* discourse]

poney. See **pony**.

pong[1] *pong*, (*theat slang*) *vi* to make impromptu additions to one's part in order to extend it, to gag.

pong[2] *pong*, (*colloq*) *vi* to smell bad. — *n* a bad smell. — *adj* **pong'y**. [Prob Romany *pan* to stink]

ponga or **punga** *pong'ə, n* a tall tree fern of New Zealand (*Cyathea dealbata*), with large thick leaves. [Maori]

pongee *pun-* or *pon-jē', n* a soft unbleached silk, made from cocoons of a wild silkworm; a fine cotton. [Perh Chin *pun-chī* own loom]

pongo *pong'gō, n* an anthropoid ape, *orig* probably the gorilla, but transferred to the orang-utan; a monkey; a soldier (*services slang*); an Englishman (*Austr colloq*): — *pl* **pong'os** or (*Austr*) **pong'oes**. — *adj* and *n* **pon'gid** (*-jid*). [Congo *mpongi*]

pongy. See under **pong**[2].

poniard *pon'yərd*, *n* a small dagger. — *vt* to stab with a poniard. [Fr *poignard*, from *poing*, from L *pugnus* fist]

ponk *ponk*, *vi* and *n* a rare variant of **pong**[2].

pons *ponz*, (*anatom*) *n* a connecting part, *esp* the *pons Varolii*, a mass of fibres joining the hemispheres of the brain: — *pl* **pon'tēs**. — *adj* **pon'tal**, **pon'tic** or **pon'tile** relating to the pons of the brain. [L *pōns*, *pontis* a bridge]

pons asinorum *ponz as-i-nōr'əm*, *-nör'* or *pōns as-i-nōr'o͞om*, (*L*) *n* the asses' bridge (see under **ass**[1]); any severe test of a beginner.

pont *pont*, *n* in S Africa, a small ferry boat guided across narrow stretches of water by a rope or cable. [OE *punt* shallow boat]

pontage *pont'ij*, *n* a toll paid on bridges; a tax for repairing bridges. [LL *pontāgium*, from L *pōns*, *pontis* a bridge]

pontal. See under **pons**.

Pontederia *pont-e-dē'ri-ə*, (*bot*) *n* an American genus of monocotyledonous water- or bog-plants, called pickerel-weed, giving name to a family **Pontederiā'ceae**. [After Giulio *Pontedera* (1688–1757), Italian botanist]

Pontefract. See under **Pomfret** (former spelling).

pontes. See **pons**.

pontianac or **pontianak** *pont-i-ä'nak*, *n* the naturally occurring rubber-like substance, jelutong. [*Pontianak*, in Borneo]

Pontic *pon'tik*, *adj* of the ancient kingdom and Roman province of *Pontus*, or of the *Pontus* Euxinus or Black Sea. [Gr *Pontikos*, from *pontos* sea]

pontic. See under **pons**.

ponticello *pon-ti-chel'ō*, *n* the bridge of a stringed instrument: — *pl* **ponticell'os**. [Ital, dimin of *ponte* bridge, from L *pōns*, *pontis*]

pontie. See **punty**.

pontifex *pon'ti-feks*, *n* (in ancient Rome) a member of a college of priests that had control of matters of religion, their chief being *Pontifex Maximus*; a pontiff; a bridge-builder: — *pl* **pontifices** (*-tif'i-sēz* or *-kās*). — *n* **pon'tiff** a pontifex; a high priest; a bishop, *esp* the pope or *sovereign pontiff* (*RC*); an oracular person. — *adj* **pontif'ic** or **pontif'ical** of or belonging to a pontiff; splendid; pompously dogmatic. — *n* **pontif'ical** an office-book for bishops. — *n* **pontifical'ity**. — *adv* **pontif'ically**. — *n pl* **pontif'icals** the formal clothes of a priest, bishop, or pope. — *n* **pontif'icate** (*-kət*) the dignity of a pontiff or high-priest; the office and dignity or reign of a pope. — *vi* (*-kāt*) to perform the duties of a pontiff; to behave, *esp* to speak, in a pompous, self-important way. — *n* **pon'tifice** (*-fis*; *Milton*) bridge-work, a bridge. — *vi* **pon'tify** to play the pontiff. — **pontifical mass** mass celebrated by a bishop while wearing his full vestments. [L *pontifex*, *pontificis* (partly through Fr *pontife*), which was supposed to be from *pōns*, *pontis* a bridge, and *facere* to make, but is possibly from an Oscan and Umbrian word *puntis* propitiatory offering]

pontil, **pontile**[1]. See under **punty**.

pontile[2]. See under **pons**.

Pont-l'Évêque *pɔ̃-lā-vek*, (*Fr*) *n* a soft Cheddar cheese originating in *Pont-l'Évêque* in NW France.

pontlevis *pont-lev'is*, *pɔ̃-lə-vē*, *n* a drawbridge. [Fr]

pontoon[1] *pon-to͞on'*, *n* a flat-bottomed boat, a ferryboat, barge, or lighter; such a boat, or a float, used to support a bridge; a bridge of boats; a low vessel carrying plant, materials, and men for work at sea or on rivers; the floating gate of a dock; a boat-like float of a seaplane; a float. — Also **ponton** (*pon'tən* or *pon-to͞on'*). — *vt* to cross by pontoon. — *n* **pontoneer'**, **pontonier'**, **pontonnier'** or **pontoon'er** a builder of pontoon-bridges. — **pontoon bridge** a platform or roadway supported upon pontoons. [Fr *ponton*, from L *pontō*, *-ōnis* a punt, pontoon, from *pōns* a bridge]

pontoon[2] *pon-to͞on'*, *n* a card game of chance, or the winning score of 21 points which is its object. [**vingt-et-un** (qv)]

ponty. See **punty**.

pony, formerly also **poney**, *pō'ni*, *n* any of several breeds of small horse, *usu* one less than 14·2 hands high; 25 (*slang*); a translation, crib or key (*US slang*); a small glass, *esp* of beer. — *vt* and *vi* (*old slang*) to pay or settle (with *up*); to prepare or translate by help of a crib. — **pony carriage**; **pony engine** a shunting engine; **pony express** (in the US) a former method of long-distance postal delivery employing relays of horses and riders; **ponyskin** the skin of a foal, *esp* from the Kirghiz Steppes, used as a fur; **po'nytail** a hair style in which the hair is gathered together at the back and hangs down like a pony's tail; **po'ny-trekking** cross-country pony-riding in groups as a pastime. — **Jerusalem pony** an ass. [Scots **powny**, **powney**, **pownie**, prob from OFr *poulenet*, dimin of *poulain*, from LL *pullānus* a foal, from L *pullus* a young animal]

poo *po͞o*, (*slang*) *n* and *vi* same as **poop**[5]. — **in the poo** (*Austr*) in an awkward situation.

pooch *po͞och*, (*colloq*, *esp NAm*) *n* a dog, *esp* a mongrel.

pood *po͞od*, *n* a Russian weight, c. 36 lb avoirdupois. [Russ *pud*]

poodle *po͞od'l*, *n* a breed of domestic dog of various sizes, which has curly hair (often clipped to a standard pattern); a lackey. — **pood'le-dog** a poodle; an assiduous follower; **pood'le-faker** (*Anglo-Ind slang*) a (*usu* young) man who sought the company of women, a ladies' man. [Ger *Pudel*; LGer *pudeln* to paddle, splash]

poof *po͞of*, formerly **pouf**, **pouffe** *po͞of* or *po͝of*, or **puff** *puf*, (*slang*) *n* a male homosexual. — Also **poof'tah**, **poof'ter** or **poufter** (*-tə* or *-tər*). — *adj* **poof'y** effeminate. [Fr *pouffe* puff]

poogye or **poogyee** *po͞o'gē*, *n* an Indian nose-flute. [Hindi *pūgī*]

pooh *po͞o* or *po͝o*, *interj* an exclamation of disdain, dismissal, or disgust (eg at an offensive smell). — *vt* **pooh-pooh'**, **poo-poo'** to make light of; to ridicule, dismiss contemptuously. [Imit]

Pooh-Bah *po͞o'-bä'*, *n* a person who holds many offices simultaneously; a person who affects superiority. [Character in Gilbert and Sullivan's *The Mikado*]

pooja or **poojah**. Same as **puja**.

pook or **pouk** *po͞ok*, (*Scot*) *vt* to pluck; to pinch: — *pa t* and *pa p* **pook'it** or **pouk'it**. [Origin unknown]

pooka *po͞o'kə*, *n* (in Irish folklore) a malevolent goblin or spirit, sometimes assuming an animal form, said to haunt bogs and marshes. [Ir *púca*]

pool[1] *po͞ol*, *n* a small body of still water; a temporary or casual collection of water or other liquid; a puddle; a deep part of a stream; an underground accumulation (in the pores of sedimentary rock) of petroleum or gas; a swimming-pool. — *n* and *adj* **pool'side**. [OE *pōl*; Du *poel*, Ger *Pfuhl*; relation to Ir and Gaelic *poll*, and Welsh *pwll* undetermined]

pool[2] *po͞ol*, *n* the stakes in certain games; the collective stakes of a number of people who combine in a betting arrangement; an organized arrangement for betting in this way; a group of people combining in this way; a game, or a set of players, at quadrille, etc; a game or contest of various kinds in which the winner receives the pool; any of various games played on a billiard-table, each player trying to pocket a number of (*esp* coloured and numbered) balls; a common stock or fund; a combination of interest; a combine; an arrangement for eliminating competition; a group of people who may be called upon as required, eg, a group of typists; (in *pl*) football pools, betting by post on the results of a number of football games. — *vt* to put into a common fund or stock. — *vi* to form a pool. — **scoop the pool** (*colloq*; *gambling*) to win a substantial amount of money from collective stakes. [Fr *poule* a hen, also stakes (poss through an intermediate sense of plunder), but associated in English with **pool**[1]]

poon *pōōn, n* an Indian tree, *Calophyllum inophyllum*, or other species of the genus (family *Guttiferae*). — **poon'-oil** an oil expressed from its seeds; **poon'-wood**. [Sinh *pūna*]

poonac *pōō'nak, n* coconut oil-cake. [Sinh *punakku*]

poontang *pōōn'tang,* (*US slang*) *n* sexual intercourse. [Fr *putain* a prostitute]

poop[1] *pōōp, n* the after part of a ship, the part towards the stern; a high deck at the stern. — *vt* (of a wave) to break over the stern of; to ship (waves) over the stern. — *adj* **pooped** having a poop. [Fr *poupe*, from L *puppis* the poop]

poop[2] or **poupe** *pōōp,* (*obs*) *vt* to befool; to cozen; to undo; to do for: — *pa p* in *Shakesp* **poupt**. [Cf Du *poep* clown]

poop[3] *pōōp, n* short for **nincompoop**.

poop[4] *pōōp,* (*slang, esp NAm*) *vt* to make out of breath; to exhaust. — *vi* to become winded or exhausted; (often with *out*) to cease. [Orig unknown]

poop[5] *pōōp,* (*slang*) *n* faeces; defecation. — *vi* to defecate. — **poop scoop** or **poop'er-scooper** an implement for lifting and removing faeces (*esp* one used by dog-owners to remove faeces deposited by their pets on pavements, in parks, etc).

poo-poo. See under **pooh**.

poor *pōōr, adj* possessing little or nothing; without means (*esp* financial) of subsistence; needy; deficient; lacking; unproductive; scanty; mere; inferior; inadequate, shameful; sorry; spiritless; in a sorry condition; (in modest or ironical self-depreciation) humble; unfortunate, to be pitied (*esp* of the dead). — *adj* **poor'ish**. — *adv* **poor'ly** in a poor manner; badly; inadequately; in a small way; meanly. — *adj* unwell. — *n* **poor'ness**. — **poor'-box** a money-box for gifts for the poor; **Poor Clare** see under **Clare**; **poor'house** (or *Scot* **poor's'-house, puir's'-house, -hoose**) a house established at the public expense for sheltering the poor, a workhouse (*hist*); **poor-John'** (*Shakesp*) salt hake; **poor law** (often in *pl*) the law or laws relating to the support of the poor. — *adj* **poor'-law**. — *vi* **poor'-mouth** to claim poverty. — *vt* to malign. — **poor rate** (*hist*) a rate or tax for the support of the poor; **poor relation** any person or thing similar but inferior or subordinate to another; **poor'-relief** money, food, etc for the poor; **poor's'-box** a poor-box. — *adj* **poor'-spir'ited** lacking in spirit. — **poor'-spir'itedness**; **poor's'-roll** (*Scots law*) the list of poor litigants allowed to sue *in formā pauperis*; **poor white** (*usu derog*) a member of a class of poor, improvident, and incompetent white people in the Southern States of the US, S Africa and elsewhere, often called by the Blacks *poor white trash*. — **poor man of mutton** (*Scot*) cold mutton broiled, *esp* the shoulder; **poor man's weather glass** the pimpernel, reputed to close its flowers before rain. [OFr *poure, povre* (Fr *pauvre*), from L *pauper* poor]

poor-oot. See **poor-out** under **pour**.

poort *pōrt* or *pōōrt,* (*SAfr*) *n* a mountain pass. [Du, from L *porta* gate]

poortith *pōōr'tith,* (*Scot*) *n* poverty. [OFr *pouerteit, poverteit*, from L *paupertās, -ātis*]

poorwill *pōōr'wil, n* a NW American nightjar (*Phalaenoptilus*), smaller than the whippoorwill. [From its note]

poot. See **pout**[3].

Pooter *pōō'tər, n* a petit bourgeois, conventional and unimaginative. — *n* **Poo'terism**. [Charles *Pooter* in *Diary of a Nobody*, by G and W Grossmith]

pooter *pōō'tər, n* an entomological collecting bottle into which small arthropods are introduced by suction. [Ety obscure]

poove *pōōv,* (*slang*) *n* same as **poof** (qv). — *n* **poo'very**. — *adj* **poo'vy**.

pop[1] *pop, n* a mild explosive sound, like that of drawing a cork; a shot; a pistol (*slang*); ginger beer, champagne or other effervescing drink (*slang*); pawn, or an act of pawning (*slang*). — *vi* to make a pop; to shoot; to burst with a pop; (of eyes) to protrude; to come, go, slip, or pass suddenly, unexpectedly or unobtrusively; to pitch or alight; to propose marriage (*slang*). — *vt* to cause to make a pop or to burst with a pop; to shoot; to thrust or put suddenly or quickly; to pawn (*slang*); to swallow in pill form or inject (a drug) (*drug-taking slang*): — *pr p* **popp'ing**; *pa t* and *pa p* **popped**. — *adv* with a pop; suddenly. — *n* **popp'er** someone who pops; anything that makes a pop; a press-stud; a utensil for popping corn; (in *pl*) amyl nitrate or butyl nitrate inhaled from a crushed capsule (*drug-taking slang*). — *n* **popp'it** or **popp'et** one of *usu* a number of beads each having a small protrusion on one side and a hole on the other, by means of which they can be linked together. — **pop'corn** maize burst open and swelled by heating; a kind of maize suitable for this; **pop'-eye** a prominent or protruding eye. — *adj* **pop'-eyed** having prominent or protruding eyes; open-eyed, agog (as from interest, excitement, etc). — **pop'-fastener** a press-stud; **pop'-gun** a tube for shooting pellets by compressed air; a contemptible gun; **pop'over** a thin hollow cake or pudding made from batter; **popp'ing-crease** see under **crease**; **pop'-shop** (*slang*) a pawnshop. — *adj* **pop'-up** (of appliances, books, etc) having mechanisms or pages that rise or move quickly upwards. — **pop'-visit** a visit at an odd time, a casual visit; **pop'-weed** bladderwort. — **pop off** (*colloq*) to make off; to die; to fall asleep; **pop one's clogs** (*slang*) to die; **pop the question** (*colloq*) to make an offer of marriage. [Imit]

pop[2] *pop,* (*colloq*) *adj* popular. — *n* currently popular music (also **pop music**), *esp* the type characterized by a strong rhythmic element and the use of electrical amplification. — *adj* **popp'ish** or **popp'y** of or like pop music. — **pop art** art drawing deliberately on commonplace material of modern urbanized life; **pop artist**; **pop concert** a concert at which pop music is played; **pop festival**; **pop group** a (*usu* small) group of musicians who play pop music; **pop record**; **pop singer**; **pop song**. — **top of the pops** (*old-fashioned*) (of a recording) currently (among) the most popular in terms of sales; currently very much in favour (*fig*).

pop[3]. See under **poppa, poppet**[1]**, poppycock**.

pop. *abbrev*: popular; popularly; population.

popadum or **poppadum** *pop'ə-dəm, n* a thin circle or strip of dough fried in oil, etc until crisp. — Also in several variant spellings. [Tamil, Malayalam, *poppatam*]

pope[1] *pōp, n* (often *cap*) the bishop of Rome, head of the RC Church; formerly applied also to the patriarch of Alexandria and other bishops; any spiritual head; a person wielding, assuming, or thought to assume authority like that of the pope; a parish priest in the Greek Orthodox Church; the head of the Coptic Church. — *n* **pope'dom** the office, dignity, or jurisdiction of the pope; a pope's tenure of office. — *n* **pope'hood** or **pope'ship** the condition of being pope. — *n* **pope'ling** a little pope. — *n* **po'pery** a hostile term for Roman Catholicism or whatever seems to savour of it. — *adj* **po'pish** (*hostile*) relating to the pope or to popery. — *adv* **po'pishly**. — **Pope Joan** a mythical female pope; an old card-game like newmarket; **pope's eye** the gland surrounded with fat in the middle of the thigh of an ox or a sheep; a cut of steak (also called **popeseye steak**); **pope's head** a long-handled brush; **pope's knights** Roman Catholic priests, formerly called Sir; **pope's nose** the parson's nose (qv). — **Black Pope** see under **black**. [OE *pāpa*, from LL *pāpa*, from Gr *pappas* (late Gr *papās*), hypocoristic for father]

pope[2] *pōp, n* the ruff, a European freshwater fish.

poperin. See **poppering**.

popery, popeship. See under **pope**[1].

Popian *pōp'i-ən, adj* pertaining to Alexander *Pope* (1688–1744), the poet.

popinjay *pop'in-jā, n* a parrot; a figure of a parrot set up to be shot at (*hist*); a conceited person; a fop or coxcomb. [OFr *papegai*; cf LL *papagallus*; Late Gr *papagallos* (also *papagas*), a parrot; prob Eastern; influenced by **jay**]

popish, etc. See under **pope**[1].

popjoy *pop'joi*, *vi* to amuse oneself. [Poss connected with **popinjay**]

poplar *pop'lər*, *n* a genus (*Populus*) of rapidly growing trees of the willow family, including aspen, white poplar, black poplar (with its variety Lombardy poplar), cottonwood, etc; widespread in northern temperate regions; the tulip-tree, tulip-poplar (*US*). — **trembling poplar** the aspen. [OFr *poplier*, from L *pōpulus* poplar-tree]

poplin *pop'lin*, *n* a corded fabric with a silk warp and worsted weft; an imitation in cotton or other material. — *n* **poplinette'** an imitation poplin. [Perh Fr *popeline*, from Ital *papalina* papal, from the papal town of Avignon, where it was made]

popliteal *pop-lit'i-əl*, or often *pop-lit-ē'əl*, *adj* of the back of the knee. — Also **poplit'ic**. [L *poples*, *-itis*]

poppa *pop'ə*, (*colloq esp NAm*) *n* papa. — Short form **pop** or **pops**.

poppadum. See **popadum**.

popped, **popper**[1]. See under **pop**[1].

popper[2] *pop'ər*, (*US*) a corn-popper (see under **corn**).

Popperian *pop-ē'ri-ən*, *adj* of or relating to the theories, teachings, etc of the British philosopher Sir Karl *Popper* (b 1902). — *n* a student or supporter of Popper's philosophy.

poppering *pop'ər-ing* or **poperin** *-in*, *n* a variety of pear. — Also **poppering pear** (*Shakesp* **pop'rin**). [*Poperinghe* in Belgium]

poppet[1] *pop'it*, *n* a puppet (*obs*); a doll (*obs*); a darling (short form **pop**); a timber support used in launching a ship; a lathe-head; a valve that lifts bodily (also **popp'et-valve**). [An earlier form of **puppet**]

poppet[2]. See under **pop**[1].

poppied. See under **poppy**[1].

popping. See under **pop**[1].

poppish. See under **pop**[2].

poppit. See under **pop**[1].

popple *pop'l*, *vi* to flow tumblingly; to heave choppily; to bob up and down; to make the sound of rippling or bubbling, or of repeated shots. — *n* a poppling movement or sound. — *adj* **popp'ly**. [Imit; or a frequentative of **pop**[1]]

poppy[1] *pop'i*, *n* a cornfield plant (of several species) or its large scarlet flowers; any other species of the genus *Papaver*, such as the opium poppy, or of the related genera *Glaucium* (**horned poppy**; see under **horn**) or Meconopsis (see **Welsh poppy** below), etc; also extended to various unrelated plants. — *adj* **popp'ied** covered or filled with poppies; soporific; affected by opium. — **Poppy Day** *orig* Armistice Day (qv), later the Saturday nearest Armistice Day, or (later) Remembrance Sunday (qv), when artificial poppies are sold for war charity; **popp'y-head** a capsule of the poppy; a finial in wood, *esp* at a pew end; **popp'y-oil** a fixed oil from the seeds of the opium poppy; **poppy seed**; **popp'y water** a soporific drink made from poppies. — **blue poppy** a blue Meconopsis of the northern temperate zone; **Flanders poppy** an emblem, from World War 1, of the fallen British soldiers; **Welsh poppy** *Meconopsis cambrica*, which has pale-yellow flowers. [OE *popig*, from L *papāver* poppy]

poppy[2]. See under **pop**[2].

poppycock *pop'i-kok*, (*slang*) *n* balderdash. — Short form **pop**. [Du *pappekak*, literally soft dung]

poprin. See **poppering**.

pops. See under **poppa**.

Popsicle® *pop'sikl*, (*NAm*) *n* an ice lolly.

pops. See under **poppa**.

popsy *pop'si*, (*old-fashioned*) *n* term of endearment for a girl or young woman (also **pop'sy-wop'sy**); an attractive young woman (*colloq*). [Prob dimin abbrev of **poppet**]

populace *pop'ū-ləs*, *n* the common people; those not distinguished by rank, education, office, etc. [Fr, from Ital *popolazzo*, from L *populus* people]

popular *pop'ū-lər*, *adj* of the people; pleasing to, enjoying the favour of or prevailing among the people; liked by one's associates; suited to the understanding or the means of ordinary people; seeking the favour of the common people (*obs*); democratic; plebeian (*obs*); vulgar (*obs*). — *n* something popular, such as a popular or moderate-priced concert, (tabloid) newspaper, etc (short form **pop**; cf **pop**[2]). — *n* **popularity** (*-lar'i-ti*) the fact or state of being popular; seeking to gain favour with the people. — *n* **popularīzā'tion** or **-s-**. — *vt* **pop'ularize** or **-ise** to make popular; to democratize; to present in a manner suited to ordinary people; to spread among the people. — *n* **pop'ularīzer** or **-s-**. — *adv* **pop'ularly**. — *vt* **pop'ulate** to people; to supply with inhabitants; to devastate (*obs*). — *vi* to multiply by propagation. — *adj* (*-lət*, *-lāt*; *obs*) inhabited, peopled. — *n* **populā'tion** the act of populating; the number of inhabitants; the number of inhabitants of a particular class; the plants or animals in a given area; a group of persons, objects or items considered statistically. — *n* **pop'ulism**. — *n* **pop'ulist** (in the US) a member of the People's Party, founded in 1891, advocating public ownership of public services, graduated income tax, etc, or of a similar party elsewhere (*hist*); someone who believes in the right and ability of the common people to play a major part in governing themselves; a supporter, wooer or student of the common people. — *adj* (of a political or social programme, cause, etc) appealing to the mass of the people. — *adj* **pop'ulous** full of people; numerously inhabited; numerous (*Shakesp*); popular (*rare*). — *adv* **pop'ulously**. — *n* **pop'ulousness**. — **popular front** an alliance of the more progressive or left-wing political parties in the state; **population explosion** see under **explode**; **population inversion** (*phys*) the reversal of the normal ratio of populations of two different energy states, ie, that normally fewer and fewer atoms occupy states of successively higher energies. [L *populus* the people]

poral. See under **pore**[1].

porbeagle *pör'bē-gl*, *n* a N Atlantic and Mediterranean shark of the genus *Lamna*. [From Cornish dialect; origin unknown]

porcelain *pōrs'lin*, *pörs'* or *-lən*, *n* a fine earthenware, white, thin, transparent or semi-transparent, first made in China; objects made of this, china. — *adj* of porcelain. — *n* **porcell'anite** a jasper-like shale highly indurated by contact metamorphism. — *vt* **porcell'anize** or **-ise** or **porc'elainize** or **-ise** to bake into porcelain or porcellanite. — *adj* **porcell'anous** (or *pōr'*, *pör'*) like porcelain — also **porcellā'neous**, **porc'elainous** or **porcelai'neous**. — **porcelain cement** cement for mending china; **porcelain clay** kaolin. [OFr *porcelaine*, from Ital *porcellana* cowrie]

porch *pōrch* or *pörch*, *n* a building forming an enclosure or protection for a doorway; a portico or colonnade; a veranda (*US*); the Stoic school of philosophy, from the Painted Porch in the Agora of Athens where Zeno taught. [OFr *porche*, from L *porticus*, from *porta* a gate]

porcine *pör'sīn*, *adj* of pigs; swinish. [L *porcīnus*, from *porcus* a swine]

porcpisce *pör'pis*, (*Spenser*) *n* Same as **porpoise**.

porcupine *pör'kū-pīn*, *n* a large spiny rodent of various kinds. — **por'cupine-grass** a coarse, hard, spiny, tussocky grass (*Triodia*) that covers vast areas in Australia, commonly called spinifex; **por'cupine-wood** the wood of the coconut palm, from its spine-like markings. [OFr *porc espin*, from L *porcus* a pig, and *spīna* a spine]

pore[1] *pōr* or *pör*, *n* a minute passage or interstice, *esp* the opening of a sweat-gland. — *adj* **por'al** of or pertaining to pores. — *n* **por'iness**. — *adj* **poromer'ic** (of eg synthetic leather) permeable to water vapour. — *n* **poroscope** (*pōr'*, or *pör'ə-skōp*) an instrument for investigating porosity or for examining pores or fingerprints. — *adj* **poroscopic** (*-skop'ik*). — *n* **poroscopy** (*-os'kə-pi*). — *adj* **porose'** (*-ōs*, or *pōr'*, *pör'*). — *n* **porosity** (*-os'i-ti*) the quality or state of being porous; the ratio of the volume of pores to the total volume (of eg a rock); a thing or part that is porous. — *adj* **por'ous** having many pores; permeable by fluids, etc. — *n* **por'ousness**. — *adj* **por'y**. — **pore fungus** any fungus having the spore-bearing surface within small pores or tubes; **porous alloys** alloys obtained by taking the constituents in powder form and pressing them together; **porous plaster** a plaster for the body, with holes to prevent wrinkling. [Fr, from L *porus*, from Gr *poros* a passage]

pore[2] *pōr* or *pör*, *vi* to gaze with close and steady attention (*usu* with *over*, *on* or *upon*); to ponder. — *n* **por'er**. [Origin obscure]

porge *pōrj* or *pörj*, *vt* in Jewish ritual, to cleanse (a slaughtered animal) ceremonially by removing the forbidden fat, sinews, etc. [Ladino (Jewish Spanish) *porgar* (Sp *purgar*), from L *pūrgāre* to purge]

porgy or **porgie** *pör'gi*, *n* a name given to many fishes, chiefly American species of sea-bream. [Partly Sp and Port *pargo*, appar from L *pargus*, a kind of fish; partly from Am Ind names]

Porifera *por-if'ə-rə*, *n pl* a phylum of animals, the sponges. — *n* **por'ifer** a member of the Porifera. — *adj* **porif'eral** or **porif'eran** of the Porifera. — *adj* **porif'erous** having pores. [L *porus* a pore, and *ferre* to bear]

poriness. See under **pore**[1].

porism *pōr'izm* or *pör'izm*, *n* in ancient Greek geometry, a corollary; also a kind of proposition intermediate between a problem and a theorem, according to some a proposition affirming the possibility of finding such conditions as will render a certain problem capable of innumerable solutions. — *adj* **porismat'ic** (*pör-*) or **porismat'ical**. — *adj* **poris'tic** or **poris'tical**. [Gr *porisma* a corollary, porism, from *poros* a way]

pork *pōrk* or *pörk*, *n* a pig (*obs*); pig's flesh as food; government money to be used for a pork barrel (*US*). — *n* **pork'er** a young pig; a pig fed to be slaughtered and used for pork. — *n* **pork'ling** a young pig. — *adj* **pork'y** pig-like; fat. — **pork barrel** (*US slang*) (a bill or policy promoting spending of Federal or state money on) projects undertaken because of their appeal to the electorate rather than their meeting a real need; the money itself; **pork'-butch'er** someone who kills pigs or sells pork; **pork-chop'** a slice from a pig's rib; **pork-pie'** a pie made of minced pork. — **pork-pie hat** a hat with a low flat circular crown, shaped somewhat like a pie. [Fr *porc*, from L *porcus* a hog]

porky[1] *pör'ki*, (*colloq*) *n* a lie: — *pl* **por'kies**. [rhyming slang *pork pie* lie]

porky[2]. See under **pork**.

Porlock *pör'lok*, *n* the name of a town in Somerset. — *n* **por'locking** irksome intrusion or interruption. — **a person from Porlock** someone who intrudes, someone who interrupts at an awkward moment. [From the visitor who disastrously interrupted Coleridge as he wrote his dream-inspired poem *Kubla Khan*]

porn- *pörn-* or **porno-** *pör-nō*, *-ə-*, *-o'*, *combining form* denoting obscene or obscenity. — *n* and *adj* **porn** or **por'no** colloquial shortenings of **pornography** and **pornographic**. — *n* **pornocracy** (*pör-nok'rə-si*; see **-cracy**) the influence of courtesans *esp* over the papal court in the earlier half of the 10c. — *n* **pornography** (*pör-nog'rə-fi*; see **-graphy**) books, magazines, films, etc dealing with or depicting sexual acts, in a more or less explicit way, intended to arouse sexual excitement; description or portrayal of prostitutes and prostitution. — *n* **pornog'rapher**. — *adj* **pornographic** (*pör-nə-graf'-ik*). — *adv* **pornograph'ically**. — *n* **por'nōmag** a pornographic periodical. — *n* **pornotō'pia** (by facetious analogy with *Utopia*) the perfect setting for the antics described in pornography. — *adj* **pornotō'pian**. — **porn shop** a shop selling pornographic literature, etc; **porn squad** the branch of the police force that enforces the law as regards obscene publications. [Gr *pornē* a prostitute]

porogamy *pör-* or *pōr-og'ə-mi*, (*bot*) *n* the entry of the pollen-tube through the micropyle (opposite of *chalazogamy*). — *adj* **porogamic** (*-ō-gam'ik*). [Gr *poros* a pore, and **-gamy**]

poromeric, **poroscope**, etc, **porose** etc. See under **pore**[1].

porosis *pō-rō'sis* or *pö-*, (*med*) *n* formation of callus, the knitting together of broken bones: — *pl* **poro'ses**. [Gr *pōrōsis*, from *pōros* callus]

porosity, **porous**, etc. See under **pore**[1].

porpentine *pör'pən-tīn*, (*Shakesp*) *n*. Same as **porcupine**.

porpess, **porpesse**. See under **porpoise**.

Porphyra *pör'fir-ə*, *n* a genus of seaweeds, with flat translucent red or purple fronds, also called purple laver. [Gr *porphyrā* purple (dye)]

porphyria *pör-fi'ri-ə*, *n* (*pathol*) any of various disorders of metabolism resulting in the excretion of an excessive quantity of porphyrins in the urine, some types characterized by skin photosensitivity. — *n* **por'phyrin** (*-fi-rin*) any of a large group of red or purple crystalline pigments present in plant and animal tissues. [Gr *porphyrā* purple (dye)]

porphyrio *pör-fir'i-ō*, *n* any bird of the purple-coot genus *Porphyrio*: — *pl* **porphyr'ios**. [Gr *porphyriōn* purple coot]

porphyrogenite *pör-fir-oj'ən-īt*, *n* a Byzantine emperor's son born in the purple or porphyry room assigned to empresses; hence, a prince born after his father's accession; a person born into the nobility, or a position of high rank. — *n* **porphyrogenitism** (*-ō-jen'it-izm*) the Byzantine principle of the first son born after his father's accession succeeding to the throne. — *n* **porphyrogen'iture**. [L *porphyrogenitus* for Gr *porphyrogennētos*, from *porphyros* purple, and *gennētos* born]

porphyry *pör'fi-ri*, *n* a very hard, variegated rock of a purple and white colour, used in sculpture (*porfido rosso antico*); (loosely) an igneous rock with large crystals in a fine-grained groundmass (*geol*). — *n* **por'phyrite** an old-fashioned name for an altered andesite or fine-grained diorite; porphyry. — *adj* **porphyritic** (*-it'ik*) like, or of the nature of, porphyry; having large crystals scattered among small or in a fine-grained or glassy groundmass. — *adj* **por'phyrous** purple. [Gr *porphyrītēs*, from *porphyros* purple]

porpoise *pör'pəs*, *n* a short-snouted genus (Phocaena) of the dolphin family, 1·2 to 2·5 metres (4 to 8 feet) long, gregarious in habits, yielding an oil and leather; extended to similar forms, *esp* (loosely) the dolphin. — Formerly also **por'pess** or **por'pesse** (*obs*), or **porc'pisce** (*Spenser*). — *vi* to move like a porpoise. [OFr *porpeis*, from L *porcus* a pig, and *piscis* a fish]

porporate *pör'pə-rət*, (*Browning*) *adj* clad in purple. [Ital *porporato*, from L *purpurātus*]

porraceous *por-ā'shəs*, *adj* leek-green. [L *porrāceus*, from *porrum* a leek]

porrect *por-ekt'*, *vt* to stretch forth; to present, hold out for acceptance. — *adj* extended forward. — *n* **porrec'tion**. [L *porrigere*, *porrectum* to stretch out]

porrenger. See **porringer**.

porridge *por'ij*, *n* a kind of food *usu* made by slowly stirring oatmeal or rolled oats in boiling water or milk (in Scotland traditionally treated as a *pl*); pottage (*obs*); jail, or a jail sentence, *esp* in the phrase **do porridge**, to serve a jail sentence (*slang*). — **porr'idge-stick** a stick for stirring porridge. [**pottage** perh altered by influence of obs or dialect *porray* vegetable soup, from L *porrum* leek]

porrigo *por-ī'gō*, *n* scalp disease of various kinds: — *pl* **porri'gos**. — *adj* **porriginous** (*-ij'*). [L *porrīgō*, *-inis* dandruff]

porringer or **porrenger** *por'in-jər*, *n* a small dish for soup, porridge, etc; a headdress shaped like such a dish (*Shakesp*). [Earlier *poddinger*, related to *pottinger*; *see* **porridge**, **pottage**; for inserted *n* cf **passenger**, **messenger**]

port[1] *pōrt* or *pört*, (*naut*) *n* the larboard or left side of a ship. — *adj* left. — *vt* and *vi* to turn left. — **port the helm** in former helm orders, to turn the tiller to port, or the upper part of the wheel to starboard, and so the rudder, and the ship, to starboard; since 1933 **port** means turn the ship to port. [Ety doubtful]

port[2] *pōrt* or *pört*, *n* an instrumental tune; a bagpipe composition. — **port a beul** (*bē'əl*) mouth music. [Gaelic]

port[3] *pōrt* or *pört*, *n* bearing; demeanour; carriage of the body, deportment; imposing bearing; style of living; a retinue (*obs*); the position of a ported weapon. — *vt* to carry or convey (*obs*); to hold in a slanting direction upward across the body (*mil*). — *n* **portabil'ity**. — *adj* **port'able** easily or conveniently carried or moved about; endurable (*Shakesp*); (of a computer program) easily adapted for use on a wide range of computers. — *n* a portable article. — *n* **port'age** an act of carrying; carriage; the price of carriage; a space, track, or journey, over which goods and boats have to be carried or dragged overland; a sailor's private venture in a voyage (*Shakesp*). — *n* **port'ance** (*Spenser*; *Shakesp*) carriage, bearing. — *adj* **port'ate** (*heraldry*) in a position as if being carried. — *adj* **port'atile** portable. — *adj* **port'ative** easily carried. — *n* (*hist*) a portable organ (often *pair of portatives*). — **port-cray'on** (or **porte-**) (Fr *porte-crayon*) a handle for holding a crayon; **porte-bonheur** (*port'-bon-œr'*; *Fr*) a charm carried for luck; **porte'-monnaie'** (*-mon-e'*; *Fr*) a purse or pocket-book; **port'-fire** a slow-match or match-cord. [Fr *port*, *porter*, from L *portāre* to carry]

port[4] *pōrt* or *pört*, *n* a harbour; a town with a harbour. — **port admiral** the admiral commanding at a naval port. — *n pl* **port charges** harbour dues. — **port of call** a port where vessels can call for stores or repairs; **port of entry** a port where merchandise is allowed by law entry to and exit from a country. [OE *port*, from L *portus*, *-ūs* related to *porta* a gate]

port[5] *pōrt* or *pört*, *n* a gate or gateway (*obs*); a town gate, or its former position (now chiefly *Scot*); an opening in the side of a ship; a porthole or its cover; a passage-way for a ball or curling-stone; an outlet or inlet for a fluid; any socket on a data-processor by means of which electronic information can pass to and from peripheral units (*comput*); part of a horse's bit curved for the tongue. — *n* **portabil'ity** (*comput*) the ability of programs to be used on different types of computers. — *n* **port'age** (*Shakesp*) an opening. [Fr *porte* (perh also OE *port*), from L *porta* gate]

port[6] *pōrt* or *pört*, *n* (also **port wine**) a fortified wine (dark-red or tawny, sometimes white) of the Douro valley, shipped from *Oporto*, Portugal. — *adj* **port'y** of the nature, taste or colour of port. — **port-wine stain** or **mark** a deep red, slightly raised (often extensive) birthmark. — **port-wi'ny** porty.

port[7] *pōrt* or *pört*, (*hist*) *n* a town with market privileges; a borough. — **port'man** (*hist*) a burgess, *esp* one chosen to administer town affairs; **port'reeve** (OE *portgerēfa*; *hist*) a mayor or principal magistrate. [Connection with **port**[4] and **port**[5] obscure]

port[8] *pōrt* or *pört*, (*Austr colloq*) *n* a bag, a suitcase. [Abbrev of **portmanteau**]

porta *pōr'* or *pör'tə*, (*zool*) *n* a gate-like structure, *esp* the transverse fissure of the liver. — *adj* **por'tal**. — **portal system** the portal vein with its tributaries, etc; **portal vein** the vein that conveys to the liver the venous blood from intestines, spleen, and stomach. [L *porta* gate]

portability. See **port**[3] and **port**[5].

portable. See under **port**[3].

portage. See under **port**[3,5].

portague. See under **Portuguese**.

Portakabin® *pōr'* or *pör'tə-kab-in*, *n* a small *portable* building for use as a temporary office, etc.

portal[1] *pōrt'* or *pört'əl*, *n* a gate or doorway, *esp* a great or magnificent one; any entrance; the arch over a gate (*archit*); the lesser of two gates. [OFr *portal*, from LL *portāle*, from L *porta* a gate]

portal[2]. See under **porta**.

Portaloo® *pōr'* or *pör'tə-lōō*, *n* a *portable* lavatory. [**loo**[1]]

portamento *pōr-ta-men'tō*, (*music*) *n* a continuous glide from one tone to another; sometimes applied to an execution between staccato and legato: — *pl* **portamen'ti** (*-tē*). — Also *adj* and *adv*. [Ital]

portance. See under **port**[3].

portas. See **portesse**.

portate, portatile, portative, port-crayon. See under **port**[3].

portcullis *pōrt-* or *pört-kul'is*, *n* a grating that can be let down to close a gateway of a castle, fortress, etc; a lattice (*heraldry*); one of the pursuivants of the English College of Heralds; an Elizabethan silver halfpenny with a portcullis on the reverse. — *vt* to obstruct, as with a portcullis. [OFr *porte coleïce* sliding gate]

port de bras *por-də-bra*, (*Fr*) *n* the practice or technique of arm movements in ballet; a balletic figure illustrating this technique.

Porte *pōrt* or *pört*, (*hist*) *n* the Turkish imperial government, so called from the Sublime Porte or High Gate, the chief office of the Ottoman government at Constantinople. [Fr *porte*, from L *porta* gate]

porte-bonheur, etc. See under **port**[3].

porte-cochère *port-ko-sher'*, *n* a house entrance admitting a carriage. [Fr *porte*, from L *porta* gate, and Fr *cochère*, fem adj from *coche* coach]

portend *pōr-* or *pör-tend'*, *vt* to betoken; to warn of as something to come; to presage. — *n* **portent** (*pōr'* or *pör'tent*) that which portends or foreshows; the quality of being portentous, ominousness; an evil omen; a prodigy, a marvel. — *adj* **portentous** (*-tent'*) ominous; prodigious, extraordinary; impressive or solemn; pompous, self-important. — *adv* **portent'ously**. — *n* **portent'ousness**. [L *portendere*, *portentum*, from *por-*, equivalent to *prō* or *per*, and *tendere* to stretch]

porteous. See under **portesse**.

porter[1] *pōrt'* or *pört'ər*, *n* a door-keeper or gate-keeper; a caretaker in a college, university, etc, or in a block of flats; a person at the door or entrance to an office block, factory, etc who greets visitors, takes messages, allows or monitors entrance, etc; someone who waits at the door to receive messages: — *fem* **port'eress** or **port'ress**. — *n* **port'erage** the office or duty of a porter. — **porter's lodge** a house or an apartment near a gate for the use of the porter. [OFr *portier*, from LL *portārius*, from L *porta* a gate]

porter[2] *pōrt'* or *pört'ər*, *n* a person employed at a railway station, hotel, market, etc to carry passengers' luggage, parcels, etc; a dark-brown malt liquor, *prob* from its popularity with London porters. — *n* **port'erage** carriage; the charge made by a porter for carrying goods. — *adv* **port'erly** like a porter. — *adj* (*obs*) of a porter; coarse. — **porter'-house** a house where porter is sold; a chop-house; **port'erhouse** or **por'terhouse-steak** a choice cut of beefsteak next to the sirloin. [OFr *porteour* (Fr *porteur*), from L *portātor*, *-ōris*, from *portāre* to carry]

portesse *pōrt'*, *pört'əs* or *-es*, (*hist*) *n* a portable breviary. — Also **port'ess**, **port'as**, **port'hors**, **port'house**, **port'ous**, **port'hos** or **porteous** (*pōr'* or *pör'tyəs*). — **porteous roll** (*Scots law*) a list of persons to be tried. [OFr *portehors* (LL *porteforium*), from L *portāre* to carry, and *forīs* out of doors]

portfolio *pōrt-* or *pört-fō'li-ō*, *n* a case or pair of boards for holding loose papers, drawings, etc; a collection of such papers, eg drawings or photographs put together as examples of a student's work; a list of securities held; the office of a cabinet minister with responsibility for a government department; the area of responsibility of such a minister: — *pl* **portfo'lios**. [Ital *portafogli(o)*, from L *portāre* to carry, and *folium* a leaf]

porthole *pōrt'* or *pört'hōl*, *n* a hole or opening in a ship's side for light and air, or (formerly) for pointing a gun through. [**port**[5] and **hole**]

porthors, porthos, porthouse. See under **portesse**.

portico *pōr'* or *pör'ti-kō*, *n* a range of columns along the front or side of a building (*archit*); a colonnade; the Painted Porch (*philos*; see **porch** and **stoic**): — *pl* **por'ticos** or **por'ticoes**. — *adj* **por'ticoed** provided with a portico. [Ital, from L *porticus*, a porch]

portière *por-tyer'*, *n* a curtain hung over the door or doorway of a room; a portress, concierge. [Fr]

portigue. See under **Portuguese**.

portion *pōr'* or *pör'shən*, *n* a part; an allotted part; an amount of food served to one person; destiny; the part of an estate descending to an heir; a dowry. — *vt* to divide into portions; to allot as a share; to provide with a portion. — *adj* **por'tioned**. — *n* **por'tioner** (*Scots law*) the holder of a small feu *orig* part of a greater; a portionist of a benefice (**heir'-por'tioner** see under **heir**). — *n* **por'tionist** a postmaster of Merton College; one of two or more incumbents sharing a benefice. — *adj* **por'tionless** having no portion, dowry, or property. [OFr, from L *portiō*, *-ōnis*]

Portland *pōrt'* or *pört'lənd*, *adj* belonging to or associated with the Isle of *Portland*, a peninsula of Dorset. — *n* **Portlandian** (*-land'i-ən*) a group of sands and limestones, the middle group of the Upper or Portland Oolite. — Also *adj*. — **Portland arrowroot** or **Portland sago** a farina prepared in the Isle of Portland from wake-robin tubers; **Portland cement** a cement made by burning a mixture of clay and chalk of the colour of Portland stone; **Portland sheep** a breed of small, black-faced sheep found in the Isle of Portland; **Portland stone** an oolitic building-stone which is quarried in the Isle of Portland.

portland. See under **portlast**.

portlast *pōrt'* or *pört'ləst*, (*obs naut*) *n* probably the gunwale. — Also **portoise** (*-tiz*) and wrongly **port'land**. — **yards down a portlast** with yards down on or near the deck. [Origin unknown]

portly *pōrt'* or *pört'li*, *adj* having a dignified bearing or mien (*archaic*); corpulent, stout. — *n* **port'liness**. [**port**[3]]

portman. See under **port**[7].

portmanteau *pōrt-* or *pört-man'tō*, *n* a large travelling-bag that folds back flat from the middle; a rack for hanging clothes (*rare*); Lewis Carroll's term for a blend, a word into which are packed the sense (and sound) of two words, eg *slithy* for *lithe* and *slimy* also **portmanteau word**: — *pl* **portman'teaus** or **portman'teaux** (*-tōz*). — Also (both *obs*) **portman'tle** or **portman'tūa**. — *adj* combining or covering two or more things of the same kind. [Fr, from *porter* to carry, and *manteau* a cloak]

portoise. See under **portlast**.

portolano *pör-tə-lä'nō*, *n* in the Middle Ages, a navigation manual giving sailing directions and illustrated with charts showing ports, coastal features, etc: — *pl* **portola'nos** or **portola'ni** (*-nē*). — Also **portolan**, **portulan** or **portulan chart** (*por'tə-lən* or *-tū-*). [Ital, navigation manual, harbour-master]

portous. See under **portesse**.

portrait *pōr'* or *pör'trit*, *n* a painting, photograph or other likeness of a real person; a vivid description in words; portraiture (*rare*). — *adj* (of something rectangular in format) having the shorter sides at the top and bottom (opposite of *landscape*; *printing*). — *vt* (*obs*) to portray. — *n* **por'traitist** or **por'trait-painter**. — *n* **por'traiture** a likeness; the art or act of making portraits; a collection of portraits; verbal description. — *vt* **portray** (*pōr-* or *pör-trā'*) to paint or draw the likeness of; to describe in words; to adorn with portraiture or representations (*obs*). — *n* **portray'al** the act of portraying; a representation. — *n* **portray'er**. — **por'trait-bust**; **por'trait-gallery**; **por'trait-painting**. [OFr *po(u)rtrait*, *po(u)rtraire*, from L *prōtrahere*, *-tractum*; see **protract**]

portray, **portrayal**. See under **portrait**.

portreeve. See under **port**[7].

portress. See under **porter**[1].

Port Salut *pör sa-lü'*, *n* a mild cheese *orig* made at the Trappist monastery Le *Port* du *Salut* in Bayonne, France.

Portugaise *pōr-* or *pör-tū-gāz'*, *adj* Portuguese; in a Portuguese style. — **à la Portugaise** cooked with tomato or having a prevalent flavour of tomato; with a tomato-based sauce, often with onion, garlic and herbs. [Fr]

Portuguese *pōr-*, *pör-tū-gēz'*, or *pōr'* or *pör'*, *adj* of *Portugal*, its people, and its language. — *n* a native or citizen of Portugal; the language of Portugal: — *pl* **Portuguese** (from which the vulgar *sing* **Portuguee'** or **-gee'**). — *n* **portague** or **portigue** (*pōrt'* or *pört'ə-gū*) an old Portuguese gold coin of the 16c and 17c, worth about £4. — **Portuguese man-of-war** any of several hydrozoans of the genus Physalia, having tentacles able to give a painful, sometimes deadly, sting.

portulaca *pōr-* or *pör-tū-lā'kə*, *n* any plant of the purslane genus *Portulaca*, giving name to the family **Portulacā'ceae**, mostly succulent herbs of dry places, related to the *Caryophyllaceae*. [L *portulāca* purslane]

porty. See under **port**[6].

porwiggle. See under **pollywog**.

pory. See under **pore**[1].

POS. See **point of sale** under **point**[1].

pos[1] *poz*, (*slang*) *adj* short for **positive**.

pos[2]. See under **po**[1].

pos. *abbrev*: position; positive.

posada *pō-sä'də*, *n* a Spanish inn, or one in a Spanish-speaking country. [Sp, from *posar* to lodge]

posaune *pō-zow'nə*, *n* the trombone. [Ger]

pose[1] *pōz*, *n* an attitude; an assumed attitude; an affectation of a mental attitude; (in dominoes) the right to begin the game; a secret hoard (*Scot*). — *vi* to assume or maintain a pose; to attitudinize. — *vt* to put in a suitable attitude; to posit; to assert; to claim; to put forward, propound. — *adj* **pose'able**. — *n* **pos'er** a person who poses *esp* (*colloq*) someone who dresses or behaves, etc, so as to be noticed. — *n* **poseur** (*pōz-œr'*; *Fr*) an attitudinizer; person who adopts poses and affects opinions, etc, in order to impress others: — *fem* **poseuse** (*-œz'*). — *adj* **pos'ey** or (*rare*) **posy** (*derog*) affected, adopting poses for effect. [Fr *poser* to place, from LL *pausāre* to cease, from L *pausa* pause, from Gr *pausis*; between Fr *poser* and L *pōnere*, *positum*, there has been confusion, which has influenced the derivatives of both words]

pose[2] *pōz*, *vt* (*archaic*) to puzzle; to perplex by questions; to bring to a standstill. — *n* **pos'er** someone who or something which poses; a difficult question. — *n* and *adj* **pos'ing**. — *adv* **pos'ingly**. [Aphetic, for **oppose**, or **appose**, confused with it]

posé *pō-zā'*, (*heraldry*) *adj* standing still. [Fr, pa p of *poser*; see **pose**[1]]

Poseidon *pos-ī'don* or *-dōn*, (*Gr mythol*) *n* the Greek sea-god, identified with Neptune by the Romans. — *adj* **Poseidōn'ian**. [Gr *Poseidōn*, *-ōnos*]

poser. See under **pose**[1,2].

poseur, **poseuse**. See under **pose**[1].

posh[1] *posh*, (*obs slang*) *n* money, *esp* a small amount, a halfpenny; a dandy. [Appar from Romany *posh* half]

posh[2] *posh*, (*colloq*) *adj* smart, stylish, top-class; expensive, and therefore of the wealthy classes; superb. — *adv* in a way associated with the upper clases, as *talk posh*. — *vt* and *vi* (*usu* with *up*) to trim up, to polish. — *adv* **posh'ly**. — *n* **posh'ness**. [Popularly supposed to be from '*p*ort *o*utward *s*tarboard *h*ome', the most desirable position of cabins when sailing to and from the East before the days of air-conditioning, but no evidence has been found to support this; poss linked with **posh**[1]]

poshteen. See under **posteen**.

posigrade *poz'i-grād*, (*aeronautics* and *astronautics*) *adj* having or producing positive thrust; of or pertaining to a posigrade rocket. — **posigrade rocket** a small propellant rocket that is fired to give forward acceleration when required, *esp* on a multi-stage rocket when jettisoning a redundant stage. [*Posi*tive in contrast to retro*grade*]

posit *poz'it*, *vt* to set in place, dispose; to postulate, assume as true, definitely or for argument's sake: — *pr p* **pos'iting**; *pa t* and *pa p* **pos'ited**. [L *pōnere*, *positum* to lay down]

position *poz-ish'ən*, *n* situation; place occupied; attitude, disposition, arrangement; state of affairs; a proposition or thesis; the ground taken in argument or in a dispute; a principle laid down; place in society; high standing; a post or appointment; occurrence in an open or closed syllable; situation of the left hand in playing the violin, etc (*music*); method of finding the value of an unknown quantity by assuming one or more values; the commitment of a dealer in commodities, currencies or securities (*stock exchange*). — *adj* of or defining position. — *vt* to set in place; to determine the position of, locate. — *adj* **posi'tional**. — *adj* **posi'tioned** placed. — **position ratio** a ratio determining the position of a point in a range or of a ray in a pencil — that of the distances from two fixed points in the range, or of the sines of the angular distances from two fixed rays. [Fr, from L *positiō, -ōnis*, from *pōnere, positum* to place]

positive *poz'i-tiv, adj* definitely, formally or explicitly laid down; express; beyond possibility of doubt; absolute; expressing a quality simply without comparison (*gram*); downright, out-and-out; fully convinced; over-confident in opinion; matter-of-fact; concrete; material; actual; characterized by the presence of some quality, not merely absence of its opposite; affirmative; feeling or expressing agreement to or approval of something; having a good or constructive attitude; having qualities worthy of approval; (of a bacteriological test) confirming the presence of the suspected organism, etc; greater than zero, or conventionally regarded as greater than zero, indicating such a quantity (*math*); in the direction of increase, actual or conventional; in a direction towards the source of stimulus (*biol*); having the lights and shades not reversed (*photog* and *optics*); having a relatively high potential (*elec*); of, having or producing, positive electricity (see below); dextrorotatory (*optics*); having a greater index of refraction for the extraordinary than for the ordinary ray in double refraction; basic (*chem*). — *n* that which is positive; reality; a positive quantity; a positive quality; the positive degree, or an adjective or adverb in it; an image in which lights and shades or colours, or both, are unchanged; a photographic plate with the lights and shades of the original; a positive organ (see below). — *adv* **pos'itively**. — *n* **pos'itiveness** the state or quality of being positive; certainty; confidence. — *n* **pos'itivism** actual or absolute knowledge; certainty; assurance; positive philosophy (see below). — *n* **pos'itivist** a believer in positivism. — *adj* **positivist'ic**. — *n* **positiv'ity**. — **positive action** same as **affirmative action**; **positive angle** one generated by a straight line moving anti-clockwise; **positive discrimination** see under **discriminate**; **positive electricity** electricity developed, eg in glass by rubbing with silk, arising from deficiency of electrons; **positive organ** a small supplementary church organ, *orig* portable and placed upon a stand; **positive philosophy** the philosophical system originated by Auguste Comte (1798–1857), its foundation being the doctrine that man can have no knowledge of anything but phenomena, and that the knowledge of phenomena is relative, not absolute; also 20c developments of this (**logical positivism**) much concerned with determining whether or not statements are meaningful; **positive pole** (of a magnet) that end (or pole) which turns to the north when the magnet swings freely; **positive rays** canal-rays, a stream of positively electrified particles towards the cathode of a vacuum-tube (**positive-ray analysis** the detection of gases, and determination of their molecular weights, by measuring the parabolas produced on a photographic plate by positive rays deflected in two directions at right angles to each other by a magnetic and an electric field); **positive reinforcement** (*behav*) the following of a response by a positive event or stimulus, thus increasing the likelihood of the response being repeated; **positive sign** the sign (read *plus*) of addition; **positive vetting** a method of screening individuals to ensure their suitability for highly responsible positions. [L *positīvus* fixed by agreement, from *pōnere, positum* to place]

positron *poz'i-tron*, (*phys*) *n* a particle differing from the electron in having a positive charge; a *pos*itive elec*tron*. — Also **pos'iton**. — *n* **positronium** (*-trōn'i-əm*) a positron and an electron bound together as a short-lived unit, similar to a hydrogen atom. — **positron emission tomography** (or **PET**) **scanner** a device that uses gamma rays to monitor brain activity, by following the movement of a radioactive tracer substance injected into the bloodstream.

posnet *pos'nit, n* a small cooking-pot with feet and a handle. [OFr *pocenet*]

posology *pos-ol'ə-ji, n* the science of quantity; the science of dosage. — *adj* **posological** (*-ə-loj'i-kl*). [Gr *posos* how much, and *logos* a word, discourse]

poss[1] *adj* a colloquial shortening of **possible**.

poss[2] *pos*, (*dialect*) *vt* to agitate (clothes) in washing them, with a stick, etc. — *n* (*archaic*) **poss'er** or **poss'-stick** a wooden stick, *usu* with a perforated metal plate on the bottom, for possing clothes in a wash-tub. [Perh imit modification of Fr *pousser* to push, from L *pulsāre* to beat]

posse *pos'i, n* power; possibility; a force or body (of constables); any group temporarily established for some purpose. — **in posse** (*law*) in potentiality; possibly; **posse comitatus** (*kom-i-tā'təs* or *-tä'tōōs*) force of the county, men called out by the sheriff to aid in enforcing the law. [L *posse* to be able, and *comitātūs* of the county]

possess *poz-es', vt* to inhabit, occupy (*obs*); to have or hold as owner, or as if owner; to have as a quality; to seize; to obtain; to attain (*Spenser*); to maintain; to control; to be master of; to occupy and dominate the mind of; to put in possession (with *of*, formerly with *in*); to inform, acquaint; to imbue; to impress with the notion or feeling; to prepossess (*obs*). — **possess'able**. — *adj* **possessed'** in possession; self-possessed; dominated by a spirit that has entered one, or some other irresistible influence. — *n* **possession** (*poz-esh'ən*) the act, state or fact of possessing or being possessed; a thing possessed; a subject foreign territory. — *adj* **possess'ional** pertaining to possession. — *adj* **possess'ionary**. — *adj* **possess'ionate** (*formal*) holding or allowed to hold possessions (opposite of *mendicant*). — *n* a possessionate monk. — *adj* **possess'ioned**. — *adj* **possess'ive** pertaining to or denoting possession; unwilling to share what one has with others; reluctant to allow another person to be independent of oneself, too inclined to dominate; genitive (*gram*). — *n* (*gram*) a possessive adjective or pronoun; the possessive case or a word in it. — *adv* **possess'ively**. — *n* **possess'iveness** extreme attachment to one's possessions; desire to dominate another emotionally. — *n* **possess'or**. — *n* **possess'orship**. — *adj* **possess'ory**. — **what possesses him?, her?**, etc what malign influence causes him, her, etc, to act so foolishly?, what has come over him or her?; **writ of possession** (*law*) a process directing a sheriff to put a person in possession of property recovered in ejectment. [OFr *possesser*, from L *possidēre, possessum*]

posset *pos'it, n* a drink, milk curdled with eg wine, ale or vinegar, formerly used as a remedy for colds, etc; a small amount of milk, etc, regurgitated by a baby after a feed. — *vt* (*Shakesp*) to curdle. — *vi* to make a posset; (of a baby) to regurgitate a little milk, etc, after feeding (*dialect*). — **posset cup** a large cup or covered bowl for posset. [ME *poschot, possot*; origin unknown]

possible *pos'i-bl, adj* capable of existing or happening; not contrary to the nature of things; that could be true, conceivable, contingent; capable of being done or managed, achievable, practicable; such as one may tolerate, accept or get on with; potential, capable of development. — *n* a possibility; something or someone that is potentially selectable; the highest possible score in shooting; one's best (*Gallicism*); (in *pl*) necessaries (*slang*). — *n* **poss'ibilism** the policy of confining efforts to what is immediately possible or practicable. — *n* **poss'ibilist**. — *n* **possibil'ity** the state of being possible; a candidate, etc capable of winning, being successful, etc; that which is possible; a contingency; (in *pl*) potential, promise for the future. — *adv* **poss'ibly** perhaps; by any possible means, within the limits of possibility; conceivably, with reason. [L *possibilis*, from *posse* to be able]

possie or **pozzy** *poz'i*, (*Austr colloq*) *n* a position. [Shortened forms of **position**]

Possum® or **possum** *pos'əm*, *n* any of a range of electronic services by means of which severely disabled people can perform tasks, eg operate household equipment or a word-processor. [*p*atient-*o*perated *s*elector *m*echanism]

possum[1] (formerly also **'possum**) *pos'əm*, *n* in America, an aphetic form of **opossum** (*colloq*); applied also to the Australasian phalanger. — *vi* (*Austr* and *US*) to play possum. — **play possum** to feign death, sleep, illness or ignorance; to dissemble; **stir the possum** (*Austr*) to liven things up.

possum[2]. See **Possum**®.

POST. See **point-of-sale terminal** under **point**[1].

post[1] *pōst*, *n* a stout, stiff stake or pillar of timber or other material, *usu* fixed in an upright position; an upright member of a frame, a vertical timber supporting a horizontal one (often in compounds, as in *doorpost*, *goalpost*); an upright pole marking the beginning or end of a race track, a starting-post or winning-post; the pin of a lock; the shaft of an earring, the part that passes through the hole in the earlobe; a solid thickish stratum (*geol*); a pillar of coal left in a mine as a support; a tavern doorpost, on which a score was chalked (*Shakesp*). — *vt* to stick up on a post, hence on a board, door, wall, hoarding, etc; to announce, advertise or denounce by placard; to announce the name of in a published list; to placard as having failed in an examination, or failed to be classed; to announce (a ship) as overdue; to affix a bill or notice to. — **post hole** (*archaeol*) a hole sunk in the ground to take a fence post, roof support, etc; **post mill** a windmill pivoted on a post. — **between you and me and the (bed-, lamp-, gate-**, etc) **post** in confidence; **first past the post** having reached the winning-post first, having won the race (see also **first-past-the-post** under **first**); **from pillar to post** see under **pillar**; **sheriff's post** (*hist*) a post at a sheriff's door (see under **sheriff**). [OE *post*, from L *postis* a doorpost, from *pōnere* to place]

post[2] *pōst*, *n* an officially established system for the conveyance and delivery of mail; letters and parcels delivered by this system, mail; a collection or delivery of mail; a post office, or post-office letter-box; a messenger carrying letters by stages or otherwise (*hist*); a public letter-carrier (*hist*); a postman (*obs* or *dialect*); a mail-coach (*hist*); a packet-boat (*obs*); a posthorse (*Shakesp*); a fixed place or stage on a road, for forwarding letters and change of horses (*hist*); a name often given to a newspaper; haste (*Shakesp*); a size of writing-paper, double that of common notepaper (*orig* with watermark, a post horn). — *vt* to put into a letter-box, or hand over at a post office, for conveyance and delivery; to enter in a ledger, or (with *up*) update (a ledger), or transfer to another book or account (*book-keeping*); to supply with news or the latest information; to shift or transfer (eg blame) to another (with *over* or *off*; *Shakesp*). — *vi* to travel with posthorses or with speed; to move up and down in the saddle, in time with the horse's movements. — *adv* with posthorses; with speed. — *n* **post'er** someone who travels post (*Shakesp*); a posthorse (*hist*); the person who posts a letter; see also **poster**[1]. — *n* **post'ie** (*Scot* and *Austr colloq*) a postman. — *n* and *adj* **post'ing**. — **post'bag** a mail-bag; a term used collectively for letters received; **post'box** a letter-box; **post boy** (*hist*) a boy who rides posthorses or who carries letters; a postilion; **post'bus** a small bus used for delivering mail and for conveying passengers, *esp* in rural areas; **post'card** a card for writing messages on, often with a picture on one side, designed for sending through the post without an envelope; such a card not issued by the post office, as distinct from a postal card (qv under **postal**) (*US*). — *vt* to send a postcard to. — **post chaise** (popularly **po''chay**, **po'chay** and **po''chaise**) (*hist*) a carriage, *usu* four-wheeled, for two or four passengers, with a postilion, used in travelling with posthorses. — *vi* **post-chaise'** to travel by post chaise. — **post'code** a code, often a combination of letters and numbers, specific to a particular section of housing, added to addresses to ease the task of sorting mail for delivery. — *vt* to provide with or affix a postcode. — **post day** the day on which the post or mail arrives or departs. — *adj* and *adv* **post-free'** without charge for postage; with postage prepaid. — **posthaste'** (from the old direction on letters, *haste, post, haste*) haste in travelling like that of a post. — *adj* speedy; immediate. — *adv* with utmost haste or speed. — **post horn** a postman's horn; a long straight brass horn blown by a coach guard; **post'horse** a horse kept for posting; **post'house** an inn, *orig* where horses were kept for posting; a post office; **post letter** a letter in the custody of the post office; **post'man** a man who delivers mail; a post or courier (*hist*); **postman's knock** a party game in which players take turns to pretend to deliver a letter, and get a kiss from the 'recipient'; **post'mark** the mark stamped upon a letter at a post office defacing the postage stamp or showing the date and place of despatch or of arrival; **post'master** a person in charge of a local post office; someone who supplies posthorses (*hist*); a portionist or scholar on the foundation of Merton College, Oxford; **postmaster general** the minister at the head of a country's postal services; (with *caps*) this post in the UK, abolished in 1969; **post'mastership**; **post'mistress** a woman in charge of a local post office; **post office** an office for receiving and transmitting letters by post, and other business; (with *caps*) a government department or national authority in charge of the conveyance of letters, etc in various countries (**Post Office Saving's Bank** the older name of the National Savings Bank); **post-office box** one of a series of private numbered boxes or locations in a post office, where mail is kept until called for by the addressee. — *adj* **post'-paid'** having the postage prepaid. — **post'person** a postman or postwoman; **post'rider** (*hist*) the rider of a posthorse; **post road** (*hist*) a road with stations for posthorses; **post time** the time for the despatch or for the delivery of letters; **post town** and **post village** a town or village with a post office; **post'woman** a woman who delivers mail. — **general post** a game in which the players change places simultaneously; **keep posted** (*colloq*) to supply with the latest news. [Fr *poste*, from Ital *posta*, from L *posita*, from *pōnere*, *positum* to place]

post[3] *pōst*, *n* an appointment; office, position or job; a fixed place or station, *esp* a place to which a soldier or body of soldiers is assigned for duty; a body of soldiers so stationed; (generally) one's place of duty, one's station; full rank as naval captain (see **post captain** below); a settlement or trading establishment, *esp* in a remote area; a bugle call (*first* or *last post*) summoning soldiers to their quarters at night, or (*last post*) blown at funerals. — *vt* to station somewhere on duty; to transfer (personnel, a military unit) to a new location; to appoint to a post; to send or appoint (to a ship) as full captain. — **post captain** (formerly) a full captain distinguished from a commander (called a captain by courtesy). [Ital *posto*, from L *positum*, from *ponere* to place]

post[4] *pōst*, *n* a stake in a game; a good or winning hand as in the old card game of **post and pair**, in which players vied on the goodness of their hand, a pair-royal (qv) being best. — *vt* to stake. [**post**[3], or Ital *posta* a stake]

Words beginning with the prefix **post-** are listed in the following entry or in the separate panel.

post- *pōst-*, *pfx* meaning (1) after, as in *post-classical*, *post-primary*, *post-Reformation*, *postwar*, etc; (2)

behind, as in *post-nasal*, *post-ocular* (*esp anatom*). — *adj* **post-bell'um** after the war. — *n* **postcava** (-*kā'və*; *anatom*) the inferior vena cava, the vein carrying blood from the lower limbs and abdomen. — *n* **post-commun'ion** the part of the eucharistic office after the act of communion. — *adj* succeeding communion. — *vt* **postdate'** to date after the real time; to mark with a date (eg for payment) later than the time of signing. — *adj* **post-dilu'vial** after the Flood; after the diluvial period (*obs geol*). — *n* and *adj* **post-dilu'vian**. — *adj* **post-doc'toral** pertaining to academic work carried out after obtaining a doctorate (*colloq abbrev* **post-doc'**; also *n*). — *n* **post-ech'o** (*audio*) the unwanted effect of a faint repetition heard just after the actual sound on a tape recording, caused by the transfer of material between surfaces of the wound tape (see also **pre-echo**): — *pl* **post-ech'oes**. — *n* **post'-entry** an additional entry of merchandise at a custom-house; a subsequent insertion or entry (*bookkeeping*); a late entry in a race. — *adj* **post-exil'ian** or **post-exil'ic** after the time of the Babylonian captivity of the Jews. — *n* **post-existence** existence in a subsequent life. — *n* **post'face** something added by way of a concluding note at the end of a written work (opposite of *preface*; *rare*). — *n* **post'fix** a suffix. — *vt* **postfix'** to add at the end; to suffix. — **post-forming sheet** (*plastics*) a laminated sheet suitable for drawing and forming to shape when heated. — *adj* **post-glā'cial** occurring or formed after a glacial period. — *n* a postglacial period or deposit of material. — *n* **postgrad'uate** a student studying or researching for an advanced qualification after obtaining a first university degree. — *adj* relating to such students or their work. — *adj* **post-hypnot'ic** (**post-hypnotic suggestion** a suggestion made to a hypnotized subject, who does not act upon it until some time after emerging from the hypnotic trance). — *n* **Post-Impress'ionism** (also without *caps*) a movement in painting succeeding Impressionism, at the end of the 19c, van Gogh, Gauguin, Matisse and Cézanne being some of the exponents and its aim being subjective interpretation of things, as distinct from the objective representation typical of Impressionism. — *n* and *adj* **Post-Impress'ionist**. — *adj* **postindus'trial** (of a society, economy, etc) no longer dependent on heavy industry. — *adj* **post-lin'gual** subsequent to the acquisition of language (**post-lingually deafened** having lost one's hearing, as distinct from being deaf since birth; see also **pre-lingual**). — *n* **post'lude** (*music*) a concluding movement or voluntary (opposite of *prelude*). — *adj* **postmerid'ian** belonging to the afternoon or evening, the time of day after the sun has crossed the meridian. — *n* **post-millenā'rian** a believer in post-millennialism. — *adj* **post-millenn'ial**. — *n* **post-millenn'ialism** the doctrine that the Second Advent will follow the millennium. — *n* **post-millenn'ialist**. — *adj* **post-mod'ern**. — *n* **post-mod'ernism** a style (in any of the arts) following upon, and showing movement away from or reaction against, a style, theory, etc termed 'modernist'; returning to traditional materials and an earlier, *esp* classical, style, *esp* in reaction eg to international modern (qv under **international**; *archit*). — *adj* and *n* **post-mod'ernist**. — *adj* **post-mor'tem** (L *mortem*, accusative of *mors*, *mortis* death) after death (as *adv phrase*, **post mortem**). — *n* a post-mortem examination, an autopsy; an after-the-event discussion, *esp* of what went wrong, held after a game or other contest. — *adj* **postna'tal** relating to or typical of the period after birth. — *n pl* **postnā'tī** (or -*nä'tē*) those born after the event (understood as being) referred to (see also **antenati**). — *adj* **post-Ni'cene** after the Nicene council. — *n* **post-nup'tial** after marriage. — *n* **post-obit** (-*ob'it* or -*ōb'it*; L *obitum*, accusative of *obitus* death) taking effect after someone's death. — *n* a borrower's bond securing payment on the death of someone from whom he or she has expectations. — *adj* **post-op'erative** relating to the period just after a surgical operation. — *adj* **postpar'tum** or **post-par'tum** after childbirth. — *vt* **postpose'** (*gram*) to place after in the syntax of a sentence, etc. — *n* **postposi'tion** the position of a word after another that it modifies, to which it is syntactically related; such a word; placing or position after. — *adj* **postposi'tional**. — *adv* **post-posi'tionally**. — *adj* **postpos'itive** (*gram*) used in postposition. — *adv* **postpos'itively**. — *adj* **postpran'dial** (L *prandium* a repast) after-dinner. — *n* **post-produc'tion** (*cinematog*, *TV*) the work of editing and dubbing a film that follows the shooting of it. — *n* **postscē'nium** the part of the stage behind the scenery. — *n* **post'script** (L *postscrīptum* something written after, *pa p* of *postscrībere* to write after) a part added to a letter after the signature (*usu* introduced by the initials **PS**); a supplement added to the completed text of a book, etc; a talk following a news broadcast, etc; a comment or information provided additionally; (**PostScript®**) a page-description language by means of which commands are given to the printer or other output device in terms of graphics (as opposed to dot-using codes), facilitating the reproduction of unusual or non-standard features, widely used in desktop publishing (*comput*). — *n* **post-struc'turalism** a revision of the structuralist (qv) view of literature, holding that language has no objectively identifiable or absolute meaning, and that therefore texts allow of any number of interpretations. — *n* and *adj* **post-struc'turalist**. — *n* **post-synchronizā'tion** or **-s-** (*cinematog*) the process of recording and adding a soundtrack to a film after it has been shot (*colloq short forms* **post-synch'** and **post-synch'ing**). — *vt* **post-synch'ronize** or **-ise**. — *vt* **post-ten'sion** to stretch the reinforcing wires or rods in (pre-stressed concrete) after the concrete is set. — *adj* **post-ten'sioned**. — *adj* **Post-Ter'tiary** later than Tertiary, ie Pleistocene and Recent. — Also *n*. — *adj* **post-traumat'ic** (**post-traumatic stress disorder** the mental stress that can follow a traumatic experience, characterized by flashbacks, nightmares, anxiety, etc). — *adj* **post-vin'tage** (**post-vintage thoroughbred** see under **thorough**). — *adj* **post-vi'ral** (**post-viral syndrome** a condition, following a viral infection, characterized by periodic fatigue, diminished concentration, depression, dizziness, etc; see also **myalgic encephalomyelitis** under **myalgia**). — *adj* **post-vocal'ic** (*phonetics*) after a vowel. — *adj* **postwar'** (**post-war credit** a portion of income tax credited to an individual for repayment after World War II). [L *post* after, behind]

postage *pōs'tij*, *n* money charged or paid (*esp* in advance in the form of a stamp) for conveyance by post; travel with posthorses (*obs*). — **postage meter** (*esp NAm*) a franking-machine; **postage stamp** a small adhesive label, or a printed or embossed stamp, showing that a postal charge of the specified amount has been paid; an area of astonishing smallness (*facetious*). [**post**[2]]

postal *pōs'təl*, *adj* of, by or relating to, the mail service. — *n* (*US*; in full **postal card**) a postcard issued by the post office with a printed stamp. — *adv* **pos'tally**. — **postal ballot** the submission of votes by post; **postal card** (*US*) see **postal** above; **postal code** a postcode (qv under

Some words with **post-** prefix; see **post-** entry for numbered senses.

postclass'ical *adj* (1).	**postmen'strual** *adj* (1).	**posto'ral** *adj* (2).
postco'ital *adj* (1).	**postna'sal** *adj* (2).	**post-pri'mary** *adj* (1).
postconsonan'tal *adj* (1).	**postoc'ular** *adj* (2).	**post-Reform'ation** *adj* (1).
postmenopau'sal *adj* (1).		

post[2]); **postage meter** (*NAm*) a postal meter (qv under **postage**); **postal note** (*Austr* and *NZ*) a postal order; **postal order** an order issued by the postmaster authorizing the holder to receive at a post office payment of the sum printed on it; **postal tube** a cylinder for sending rolled-up papers by post; **postal union** an association of the chief countries of the world for international postal purposes; **postal vote** a vote submitted by post rather than placed directly into a ballot-box. [**post**[2]]

post chaise, **postcode**. See under **post**[2].

posteen *pos-tēn'*, *n* an Afghan greatcoat, generally of sheepskin with the fleece on. — Also (*erron*) **poshteen'**. [Pers *postī* leather]

poster[1] *pōs'tər*, *n* a large printed bill, notice, advertisement or placard for displaying on a wall, etc. — *vt* to stick bills or posters on; to advertise or publish by posters. — *n* **posterizā'tion** (*image technol*) a video effect in which the picture is produced in a limited number of flat tones and colours. — **poster colours** or **paints** matt watercolours for designing posters and other reproduction work; **poster session** a presentation of information or a short paper, *esp* at a conference, by means of wall-mounted posters and illustrations, the presenter being available to explain, discuss or elaborate on the material. [**post**[1]]

poster[2]. See under **post**[2].

poste restante *pōst res-tãt'*, *n* a department of a post office where letters are kept till called for. [Fr, remaining post]

posterior *pos-tē'ri-ər*, *adj* coming after; later; positioned behind or at the back; on the side next to the axis (*bot*). — *n* (*usu* in *pl*) one's descendants; posterity; (formerly in *pl*) one's rear parts, the buttocks (*colloq facetious*); (in *pl*) latter part (*Shakesp*; *facetious*). — *n* **posterior'ity** — *adv* **postē'riorly**. [L *posterior*, compar of *posterus*, following, later, coming after, from *post* after]

posterity *po-ster'i-ti*, *n* those coming after; succeeding generations; all one's descendants. [L *posteritās*, *-ātis* the future, future generations, from *posterus* next, following, later]

postern *post'ərn* or *pō'*, *n* a back door or gate; a small private door; a sallyport (qv under **sally**[1]). — *adj* (of a door, gate, etc) back; private. [OFr *posterne*, *posterle*, from L *posterula*, a dimin from *posterus* coming after]

postface, **postfix**, **post-glacial**, **post-graduate**. See under **post-**.

posthaste, **posthorse**, **posthouse**. See under **post**[2].

posthumous *post'ū-məs*, *adj* after death; (of a child) born after the father's death; (of a literary or musical composition) published after the author's or composer's death. — *adv* **post'humously**. [L *posthumus*, *postumus*, superl of *posterus* coming after, from *post* after; the *h* inserted from false association with *humāre* to bury]

postiche *pos-tēsh'*, *adj* superfluously and inappropriately superadded to a finished work; counterfeit or false. — *n* a superfluous and inappropriate addition; a hairpiece, a wig. [Fr, from Ital *appositizio* artificial, false, from LL (unattested) *appositicius* superadded, from L *appositus*; see **apposite**]

posticous *pos-tī'kəs*, (*bot*) *adj* posterior; outward, extrorse. [L *postīcus* hinder, from *post* after]

postie. See under **post**[2].

postil *pos'til*, *n* a marginal note, *esp* in the Bible; a commentary; a homily; a book of homilies. — *vt* and *vi* to gloss. — *vt* and *vi* **pos'tillate**. — *n* **postillā'tion**. — *n* **pos'tillātor** or **pos'tiller**. [OFr *postille* (Ital *postilla*), from LL *postilla*, possibly from L *post illa* (*verba*) after those (words)]

postilion or **postillion** *postil'yən* or *pō*, (*hist*) *n* a post boy; someone who guides posthorses, or horses pulling any sort of carriage, riding on one of them. [Fr *postillon*, from Ital *postiglione*, from *posta* post]

postillate, etc. See under **postil**.

postliminary *pōst-lim'i-nə-ri*, *adj* subsequent; sometimes erroneously used for **postliminiary** (see **postliminy**). [Constructed on the analogy of **preliminary**; see **postliminous**]

postliminous *pōst-lim'i-nəs*, *adj* being by way of a supplement or appendix, postliminary. — Also (*erron*) **poslimin'ious**. [L *post* after, and *līmen* threshold]

postliminy *pōst-lim'i-ni*, *n* the right of returned exiles, prisoners, etc, to resume their former status; the right by which persons or things taken in war are restored to their former status. — *adj* **postlimin'iary** or **postlimin'ious**. [L *postlīminium*, literally return behind the threshold, from *post* behind, and *līmen*, *-inis* threshold]

postlude. See under **post-**.

postman, **postmark**, **postmaster**. See **post**[2].

post-meridian. See under **post-**.

post meridiem *pōst mə-rid'-əm* or *me-rē'di-em*, (*L*) after noon (*abbrev* **PM**).

postnatal, **postpartum**. See under **post-**.

postpone *pōst-pōn'*, *pəs-pōn'*, *vt* to put off to a future time; to defer; to delay; to subordinate (*obs*); to postpose (*gram*). — *n* **postpone'ment** or (*rare*) **postpō'nence**. — *n* **postpō'ner**. [L *postpōnere*, from *post* after, and *pōnere* to put]

postpose, etc, **postprandial**, **postscenium**, **postscript**. See under **post-**.

postulancy, **postulant**. See under **postulate**.

postulate *pos'tū-lāt*, *vt* to claim; to take for granted, assume; to assume as a possible or legitimate operation without preliminary construction (*geom*); to nominate, subject to sanction of ecclesiastical authority. — *vi* to make demands. — *n* (*pos'tū-lət*) that which is postulated; a stipulation; an assumption; a fundamental principle; a position assumed as self-evident; an operation whose possibility is assumed (*geom*); an axiom (*geom*); a necessary condition; a person nominated to a benefice by the king, pending the pope's consent (*Scot hist*). — *n* **pos'tulancy** the state or period of being a postulant. — *n* **pos'tulant** a petitioner; a candidate, *esp* for holy orders or admission to a religious community. — *n* **postulā'tion**. — *adj* **postulā'tional**. — *adv* **postulā'tionally**. — *n* **pos'tulator** (*eccles*; *RC*) the presenter of a case for beatification or canonization. — *adj* **pos'tulatory** supplicatory; assuming or assumed as a postulate. [L *postulāre*, *-ātum* to demand, from *poscere* to ask urgently]

postulatum *pos-tū-lā'təm* or *pos-tōō-lä'tōōm*, (*L*) *n* something postulated, a postulate. [Neuter pa p of *postulāre*, *-aātum* to demand]

posture *pos'chər*, *n* the way one holds one's body in standing, sitting or walking; carriage, bearing; a particular position or attitude of the body; a pose or attitude adopted for effect; the relative disposition of parts of any object; a mental attitude adopted towards a particular issue, etc; a state of affairs. — *vi* to assume a posture; to pose; to attitudinize. — *vt* to place in a particular pose. — *adj* **pos'tural**. — *n* **pos'turer** and **pos'turist** someone who attitudinizes; an acrobat. — **pos'ture-maker** and **pos'ture-master** a teacher or exponent of artificial postures of the body (*hist*); an acrobat or contortionist (*obs*). [Fr, from L *positūra*, from *pōnere*, *positum* to place]

posy[1] *pō'zi*, *n* a little bunch of flowers; a motto or sentiment, eg engraved inside a ring (*archaic*). [Alteration of **poesy**]

posy[2]. See **posey** under **pose**[1].

pot[1] *pot*, *n* any of various *usu* deep and round domestic containers used as cooking utensils, or for preservation and storage; the contents or capacity of such a container; a chamberpot (qv); a flowerpot or plantpot (qqv); a teapot (qv); earthenware, or a handmade earthenware vessel; a vessel of fireclay used to contain the glass during melting (*glass*); a trophy, *esp* a cup (*colloq*); a pocket, or a stroke in which the object ball enters a pocket (*billiards*); (*usu* in *pl*) a large sum of money (*colloq*); a large stake or bet (*colloq*); a heavily backed horse; an important person (*usu big pot*; *slang*); a pot-belly (*colloq*); a pot shot (*colloq*); a simple helmet (*hist*); a wicker trap for lobsters, etc, a lobster pot; a size of paper (also **pott**) about 12 by 15 inches (30.5 by 38 cm; so called from its original watermark). — *adj* made of clay or earthenware. — *vt* to put into pots, for preserving, etc; to cook in a pot; to plant in a pot; to manufacture (pottery); to drain molasses from (sugar) during the refining process; to shoot (a creature) for the pot (ie as a meal), by a pot shot, or generally to bag, win, secure; to pocket (a billiard ball); to epitomize or summarize, *esp* simplistically; to sit (a baby) on a chamberpot. — *vi* to make pottery, *esp* by hand; to take a pot shot (with *at*); to tipple (*Shakesp*): — *pr p* **pott'ing**; *pa t* and *pa p* **pott'ed**. — **pot'ful** as much as a pot will hold: — *pl* **pot'fuls**. — *adj* **pott'ed** cooked or preserved in a pot; condensed, concentrated; abridged; (of music, etc) recorded for reproduction, canned (*colloq*). — **pot' ale** refuse from a grain distillery; **pot bank** a pottery; **pot barley** barley whose outer husk has been removed by millstones. — *adj* **pot'-bellied**. — **pot-bell'y** (*colloq*) a protuberant belly; a person who has a protuberant belly; wood- or coal-burning stove of bulbous design (*NAm*); **pot'-boiler** a work in art or literature produced merely with regard to saleability, to secure the necessaries of life; a producer of such works; a pebble heated up and used for boiling water (*archaeol*); **pot'-boiling**. — *adj* **pot'-bound** (of a pot plant) having its roots cramped by too small a pot, without room for growth. — **pot'boy** a serving boy in a public house; **pot companion** a comrade in drinking; **pot furnace** (*glass*) a furnace, which may be variously fired, in which a number of pots are set; **pot'gun** a mortar; a pop-gun; **pot'-hanger** a device for hanging a pot or a pothook on; **pot hat** a bowler hat; formerly, a top hat; **pot'-head** a stupid person; **pot herb** a vegetable, *esp* one used for flavouring, eg parsley; **pot'hole** a hole worn in rock in a stream bed by eddying detritus; a deep hole eroded in limestone, a pot (see **pot⁴**); a hole worn in a road surface. — *vi* and *vt* to explore (limestone potholes). — **pot'holer**; **pot'holing**; **pot'hook** a hook for hanging a pot over a fire; a hooked stroke in writing; **pot'house** (*old*) an alehouse; **pot'-hunter** someone who hunts to get food; someone who shoots merely for the sake of a bag; someone who competes merely for the sake of prizes; **pot'-hunting**; **pot'-lid** the cover of a pot; (*Scot* **pat'-lid**) a curling-stone played exactly on the tee; **pot liquor** a thin broth in which meat has been boiled; **pot luck** (in the expression **take pot luck**) what may happen to be in the pot and so be available to make a meal, *esp* for the unexpected arrival; whatever happens to be available; **pot'man** a pot companion; a pot boy; **pot metal** an alloy of copper and lead; scraps of old iron pots, etc; **pot plant** a plant grown in a pot; **pot roast** a dish of braised meat, *esp* with added vegetables. — *vt* (**pot'-roast**) to braise. — **pot'sherd** (*-shûrd*; *esp archaeol*) a fragment of pottery (also **pot'shard**, (*Spenser*) **pot'share**); **pot'shop** a small public house; **pot shot** a shot within easy range; a casual or random shot; a shot taken at a bird or animal with a view to one's next meal. — *adj* **pot'-sick** (of a plant) sickly from growing in a pot. — **pot stick** a stick for stirring what is being cooked in a pot; **pot still** a still in which heat is applied directly to the pot containing the wash (as opposed to a *patent still*). — *adj* (**pot'-still**) made in a pot still. — **pot'stone** impure talc or steatite, a massive finely felted aggregate of talc, *usu* with mica and chlorite, from which cooking pots were fashioned in earlier times; **potting shed** a garden shed in which plants are grown in pots before being planted out in beds. — *adj* **pot-val'iant** or **pot-val'orous** full of drink-inspired courage. — **pot valour**; **pot'-walloper** see separate entry for **pot-waller**. — **big pot** (*colloq*) an important person; **go to pot** to go to ruin; to go to pieces (*orig* to supply the cooking-pot, not the melting-pot); **keep the pot boiling** or **a-boiling** to procure the necessaries of life; to keep things going briskly without stopping; **pot of gold** the object of fairytale quests, traditionally to be dug up where the rainbow ends; any vainly sought source of weatlh, etc; **pot on** to transfer (a plant) into a larger pot; **pot up** to put (a plant) into a pot; **put someone's pot on** (*Austr colloq*) to inform on someone, give someone away; to undo or finish someone; **the pot calling the kettle black** castigation of another's faults by someone with the same short-comings. [Late OE *pott*; cf Ger *Pott*; Swed *potta*; Dan *potte*; Fr *pot*; origin unknown]

pot² *pot*, (*colloq*) *n* the drug cannabis in any of its forms, *incl* marijuana and hashish. — **pot'-head** a habitual taker of cannabis. [Perh a shortening of Mexican Sp *potiguaya*]

pot³ *pot*, *n* short form of **potentiometer**.

pot⁴ *pot*, (*dialect*) *n* a deep hole eg in limestone country, a pothole. [Perh same as **pot¹**, or from a Scandinavian source]

potable *pō'tə-bl*, *adj* fit to drink. — *n* (*rare*) a beverage. [L *pōtābilis*, from *pōtāre* to drink]

potage *po'täzh*, *n* thick soup. [Fr]

potager *pot'ə-jər* or *pot'ə-zhā*, *n* a vegetable garden or kitchen garden laid out in a decorative way, often incorporating flowers. [Fr, from **potage**]

potamic *pə-tam'ik*, *adj* of or relating to rivers. — *adj* **potamolog'ical**. — *n* **potamol'ogist**. — *n* **potamol'ogy** the scientific study of rivers. [Gr *potamos* a river]

potamogeton *pot-ə-mō-jē'ton* or *-gē'ton*, *n* a plant of the pondweed genus, *Potamogeton*, of water plants, with floating and submerged leaves, giving name to a family of monocotyledons, **Potamogetonā'ceae**. [Gr *potamogeitōn* pondweed, from *potamos* river, and *geitōn* neighbour]

potash *pot'ash*, *n* (also, earlier, **pot'-ash** and **potass** *pə-tas'*, *pot'as*) a powerful alkali, potassium carbonate, *orig* obtained in a crude state by lixiviating wood *ash* and evaporating the solution in *pots*; (in *pl*, *usu* **pot ashes** or **pot'-ashes**) the original name for the alkali in its crude form; potassium hydroxide (*caustic potash*); sometimes the monoxide or (vaguely) some other compound of potassium; potash water. — *adj* containing or rich in potassium. — *vt* to treat with potash. — **potash alum** alum (qv); **potash water** or **potass water** an aerated water containing potassium bicarbonate. [Eng **pot** and **ash**, or the corresponding Du *pot-asschen* (modern *potas*)]

potass. See under **potash**.

potassa *pə-tas'ə*, (*chem*; now *rare*) *n* potash; potassium monoxide or potassium hydroxide; formerly used for potassium in compound names, eg *carbonate of potassa*. [New L, from **potass**; see **potash**]

potassium *pə-tas'i-əm*, *n* an element (symbol **K**, for *kalium*; atomic no 19) a silvery alkali metal discovered by Davy in 1807 in potash, occurring naturally in compounds. — *adj* **potass'ic**. — **potassium-argon dating** estimation of the date or prehistoric mineral formation from the proportion of potassium-40 to argon-40, the latter having developed from the former by radioactive decay and being trapped in the rock; **potassium carbonate** a white deliquescent substance used in manufacturing glass and soap (see also **potash**); **potassium chlorate** a soluble crystalline substance that is a powerful oxidizing agent and is used in manufacturing explosives, fireworks and matches; **potassium chloride** a crystalline substance used as a fertilizer and in photographic processing; **potassium cyanide** a poisonous soluble solid used *esp* in extracting gold and silver from their ores; **potassium hydroxide** a white deliquescent substance used in manufacturing liquid soaps, shampoos and detergents, caustic potash; **potassium iodide** a crystalline solid used in photography, also added to table salt to prevent iodine deficiency; **potassium nitrate** a crystalline oxidizing agent used as a meat preservative, fertilizer and in explosives; **potassium permanganate** a purple crystalline oxidizing agent used as a disinfectant and in analytical chemistry; **potassium sorbate** a substance used as an antifungal food perservative; **potassium sulphate** a soluble substance used in glass-making and as a fertilizer. [**potass** or **potassa**]

potation *pə-tā'shən, n* the activity of drinking; a draught; liquor. [L *pōtātiō, -ōnis*, from *pōtāre, -ātum* to drink]

potato *pə-tā'tō, n orig* the sweet potato, plant or tuber (see under **sweet**); now *usu* a S American plant, *Solanum tuberosum*, widely grown in temperate regions, or its tuber; someone who sits or lies about by the hour in vegetable-like inertia, as in *couch potato, beach potato* (*slang*): — *pl* **potā'toes**. — **potato apple** the small berry-like fruit of the potato plant; **potato blight** a destructive disease of the potato caused by the parasitic fungus *Phytophthora infestans*; **potato-bogle** (*Scot*) a scarecrow; **potato chips** (*usu* simply **chips**) long thinly sliced pieces of potato fried in fat; potato crisps (*US* and elsewhere); **potato crisps** (*usu* simply **crisps**) very thin crisp fried slices of potato, widely produced commercially; **potato disease** or **rot** any of several bacterial or fungal diseases of potatoes; **potato finger** (*Shakesp*) a fat finger; **potato pit** a clamp of potatoes; **potato race** any of various types of race involving the picking up, carrying or passing on of potatoes; a stopping-and-starting style of sprinting race; **potato ring** an 18c Irish ceramic or metal (*esp* silver) ring for standing a bowl on; **potato spirit** alcohol made from potatoes; **potato trap** (*slang*) the mouth. — **hot potato** (*slang*) a controversial issue; a tricky problem or assignment that one would prefer not to touch; **small potatoes** (*US*) anything of no great worth; **the potato** or **the clean potato** (*colloq*) the right thing. [Sp *patata*, from Haitian *batata* sweet potato]

potatory *pə-tā'tə-ri*, (*rare*) *adj* relating to (excessive) drinking. [L *pōtātōrius*, from *pōtāre, -ātum* to drink]

pot-au-feu *pot-ō-fø*, (*Fr*) *n* a large earthenware cooking-pot or casserole; a stew, *esp* with boiled beef and vegetables, traditionally cooked in such a pot in France: — *pl* same as *sing*.

potch or **potche** *poch, pōch*. A variant of **poach**[2] in sense of thrust or trample. — *n* **potch'er** (*paper-making*) a machine for breaking and bleaching pulp.

pote *pōt, vt* and *vi* to poke, thrust, *esp* with the foot (*obs* except *dialect*); to crimp with a poting-stick (*obs*). — **po'ting-stick** (*obs*) a poking-stick for ruffs, etc. [OE *potian* to thrust]

poteen or **potheen** *po-tyēn', -chēn'* or *-tēn', n* Irish whiskey illicitly distilled. [Ir *poitín*, dimin of *pota* pot, from Eng **pot** or Fr *pot*]

potence[1]. See under **potent**[1].

potence[2] *pō'təns, n* a gibbet (*obs*); a gibbet-shaped structure; (in watchmaking) a bracket for supporting the lower pivot; a revolving ladder in a dovecot; a right-angled military formation. [Med L *potentia* a crutch]

potencé *pō'tən-sā*, (*heraldry*) *adj* (of a cross) having limbs that terminate in a crossbar. — *n* a figure in the shape of T. [Fr, from **potence**[1]]

potency. See under **potent**[1].

potent[1] *pō'tənt, adj* powerful; mighty; strongly influential; cogent; (of a male) capable of erection, sexual intercourse, or ejaculation. — *n* a prince or potentate (*Shakesp*). — *n* **pō'tency** or (more rarely) **pō'tence** the quality of being potent; power; potentiality; strength or effectiveness, eg of a drug; in a male, the ability to have sexual intercourse; (**potency**) a wielder of power, a potentate; (**potency**; of a point with respect to a circle) the rectangle between the segments into which a chord of the circle is divided at the point (*geom*). — *vt* **pō'tentize** or **-ise** to make potent. — *adv* **pō'tently**. [L *potens, -entis*, pr p of *posse* to be able]

potent[2] *pō'tent*, (*obs*) *n* a crutch with a crosspiece fitting under the arm; a support. — *adj* (*heraldry*) (of a cross) having limbs terminating in crossbars, potencé. [Fr *potence* a crutch, support]

potentate *pō'tən-tāt, n* a powerful ruler; a monarch. [L *potentātus* power, a ruler, from *potens*; see **potent**[1]]

potential *pə-ten'shl, adj* powerful, efficacious; latent; possible or likely, though as yet not tested or actual; expressing power, possibility, liberty, or obligation (*gram*). — *n* the range of capabilities that a person or thing has; powers or resources not yet developed or made use of; anything that may be possible; a possibility; the potential or subjunctive mood, or a verb in it (*gram*); the work done in bringing a unit of mass, electricity, etc from infinity to a point in a field of force, expressed as a function of that point (*phys*). — *n* **potential'ity** — *adv* **poten'tially**. — **potential barrier** (*phys*) a place in a field of force where the potential is high and the passage of particles impeded; **potential difference** (*phys*) a difference in the electrical states existing at two points, which causes a current to tend to flow between them; **potential energy** (*phys*) the power of doing work, possessed by a body in virtue of its position; **potential well** (*phys*) an area of low potential in a field of force. [L *potentiālis*, from *potentia* power]

potentiary *pə-ten'shi-ə-ri*, (*Thackeray*) *n* a person invested with power or influence. [From **plenipotentiary**]

potentiate *pə-ten'shi-āt, vt* to give power to; to make (drugs or chemicals) more potent or effective by using them in combination; to stimulate or boost the activity of (*biochem, physiol*). — *adj* **poten'tiated**. — *n* **potentia'tion**. [L *potentia* power]

potentilla *pō-tən-til'ə, n* a plant of the genus *Potentilla* of the rose family, including silverweed and barren strawberry, differing from Fragaria (strawberry) in having a dry receptacle. [LL, dimin of L *potēns* powerful, from its once esteemed medicinal virtues]

potentiometer *pə-ten-shi-om'i-tər, n* (short form **pot**) an instrument for measuring difference of electric potential; a rheostat. — *adj* **potentiōmet'ric**. [L *potentia* and **-meter**]

pothecary *poth'i-kə-ri, n* an aphetic form of **apothecary**. — Also **pot'icary**.

potheen. See **poteen**.

pother *podh'ər* (formerly *pudh'ər*) or **pudder** *pud'ər, n* a choking smoke or dust; fuss; commotion; turmoil. — *vt* to fluster or perplex. — *vi* to make a pother. — *adj* **poth'ery**. [Origin unknown; appar not connected with **powder**]

pothole, pothook, pothouse. See under **pot**[1].

poticary. See **pothecary**.

potiche *po-tēsh', n* an Oriental vase rounded or polygonal in shape, narrowing at the neck. — *n* **potichomania** (*-shə-mā'ni-ə*) a craze for imitating Oriental porcelain by lining glass vessels with paper designs, etc. [Fr *potiche, potichomanie*]

potin *pot-ɛ̃', n* an old alloy of copper, zinc, lead and tin. [Fr]

potion *pō'shən, n* a draught of liquid medicine, poison or some magic elixir. [Fr, from L *pōtiō, -ōnis*, from *pōtāre* to drink]

potlatch *pot'lach, n* in NW USA, an Indian winter festival, the occasion for emulation in extravagant gift-giving and, in one tribe, even property-destruction; any feast or gift (*colloq*). — Also **pot'lach**. [Chinook, from Nootka *patlatsch* a gift]

potometer *pə-tom'ə-tər, n* an instrument for measuring the rate at which a plant takes in water. [Gr *poton* drink]

potoo *pō-tō', n* any of several birds of the genus *Nyctibius* of tropical America, related to the nightjar, short-legged and large-eyed, with a small downward-curving beak and protective grey, white and buff colouring. [Imit of its cry]

potoroo *pō-tə-ro͞o'* or *pot-, n* a small marsupial related to the kangaroo, the rat-kangaroo. [Aboriginal]

potpourri *pō-po͞o'ri, pō',* or *-rē', n orig* a mixed stew, olla-podrida; a fragrant mixture of dried petals, leaves, spices, etc used to scent a room, etc; a selection of tunes strung together, a medley; a literary production composed of unconnected parts; a hotch-potch or miscellany. [Fr *pot* pot, *pourri* rotten (pa p of *pourrir*, from L *putrēre* to rot) translating Sp *olla podrida*]

potsherd. See under **pot**[1].

potstone. See under **pot**[1].

pott. A variant spelling of **pot**[1], *esp* as a paper size.

pottage *pot'ij, n* vegetables boiled with or without meat (*archaic*); a thick soup; soup; oatmeal porridge (*obs*).

[Fr *potage* food cooked in a pot, later, soup, from *pot* jug, pot]

potter[1] *pot'ər*, *n* a maker of pottery. — *n* **pott'ery** articles of baked clay collectively, *esp* earthenware vessels; a place where such goods are commercially manufactured; the work or art of the potter. — *adj* made of clay or earthenware. — **potter's wheel** (a device incorporating) a horizontally revolving dish on which to shape clay vessels such as bowls, plates, jugs, etc. [**pot**]

potter[2] *pot'ər*, *vi* to busy oneself in a desultory way with trifling tasks; to progress in an unhurried manner, to dawdle (with *along*, etc). — *n* pottering; diffuse talk. — *n* **pott'erer**. — *n* and *adj* **pott'ering**. — *adv* **pott'eringly**. [Frequentative of **pote**]

pottery. See under **potter**[1].

pottingar *pot'in-gər*, (*obs Scot*) *n* a form of **apothecary**.

pottinger *pot'in-jər*, *n* a maker of *pottage*; a small bowl, a porringer. [Earlier *pottager*; for inserted *n* cf **messenger**, **passenger**, etc]

pottle *pot'l*, *n* half a gallon, or thereabouts (*archaic*); a pot containing this amount (*archaic*); a punnet or small, *esp* conical, basket for strawberries. — *adj* **pott'le-bodied** having a body shaped like a pottle. — *adj* **pott'le-deep** to the bottom of the pottle-pot. — **pott'le-pot** (*Shakesp*) a half-gallon pot or drinking-vessel. [OFr *potel*, dimin of *pot* pot]

potto *pot'ō*, *n* a member of a W African genus (*Perodicticus*) of lemurs; also applied to the kinkajou: — *pl* **pott'os**. [Said to be a W African name]

Pott's disease *pots diz-ēz'*, (*pathol*) *n* a weakening disease of the spine caused by tuberculous infection, often causing curvature of the back. — **Pott's fracture** a fracture of the lower end of the fibula *usu* wth dislocation of the ankle, sometimes with a fracture also of the malleolus of the tibia. [Named after Sir Percival(l) *Pott* (1714–88), English surgeon, who first described them]

potty[1] *pot'i*, (*colloq*) *adj* crazy, dotty; (with *about*) madly keen on; trifling, petty. — *n* **pott'iness**. [Origin obscure]

potty[2] *pot'i*, (*hypocoristic* or *facetious*) *n* a chamberpot, *esp* one designed for children too young to use a full-size toilet. — **pott'y-chair** a child's chair fitted with a potty; **pott'y-training** the process of teaching a young child to use a potty. [Dimin of **pot**[1]]

pot-waller *pot'-wŏl-ər*, *n* in certain English boroughs, before the Reform Bill of 1832, someone who satisfied the test as a voter by boiling his pot on his own fireplace within the borough, sometimes in the open air before witnesses to establish a bogus claim. — Variously altered popularly to **pot'-wabbler**, **-wobbler**, **-walloner**, **-wall'oper**. — *adj* **pot'-wall'oping**. [**pot** and OE *w(e)allan* to boil]

pouch *powch* (*Scot pōōch*), *n* a pocket, purse or bag; in marsupials such as the kangaroos, a pocket of skin on the belly, in which the young are carried till weaned; a fleshy fold in the cheek of hamsters and other rodents, for storing undigested food; a puffy bulge under the eye. — *vt* to pocket; to form into a pouch; to tip. — *vi* to form a pouch; to be like a pouch. — *adj* **pouched** having a pouch. — *n* **pouch'ful**: — *pl* **pouch'fuls**. — *adj* **pouch'y** baggy. — **pouched mouse** a small marsupial, *Phascologale*; an American jumping rodent (*Dipodomys*) with cheek pouches opening outwards; **pouched rat** a pocket gopher. [ONFr *pouche* (OFr *poche*); cf **poke**[1]]

pouder and **poudre**. Obsolete spellings of **powder**.

pouf[1] or **pouffe**, *pōōf*, *n* a puffed or bouffant type of hairstyle fashionable in the 18c; a pad worn in the hair by 18c women to help shape such a hairstyle; in dressmaking, material gathered up into a bunch; a soft ottoman; a large firmly stuffed drum-shaped or cube-shaped hassock for use as a low seat. — *vt* to give a puffed shape to (clothing or hair). — *adj* **poufed** or **pouffed**. [Fr *pouf*]

pouf[2] and **pouffe**. Less common spellings of **poof**.

pouftah and **poufter**. Other spellings of **pooftah** and **poofter**.

Poujadist *pōō-zhäd'ist*, *n* a follower of the French politician Pierre *Poujade* (b 1920), antiparliamentarian champion of the small man and of tax reduction. — *n* **Poujad'ism**. [Fr *Poujadiste*]

pouk and **poukit**. See under **pook**.

pouke. See **puck**[1].

poulaine *pōō-lān'*, *n* a long, pointed shoe-toe. [OFr (*à la*) *Poulaine* (in the fashion of) Poland]

poulard *pōō-lärd'*, *n* a fattened or spayed hen. [Fr *poularde*, from *poule* hen]

poulder and **pouldre**. Obsolete spellings of **powder**.

pouldron *pōl'drən*. See **pauldron**.

poule *pōōl*, *n* a hen, *esp* a chicken for boiling; a promiscuous young woman; (*slang*, *esp US*; **poule de luxe** (*də lüx*; *pl* **poules** (*pōōl*) **de luxe**) a prostitute; a movement in a quadrille. [Fr]

poulp or **poulpe** *pōōlp*, *n* the octopus. [Fr *poulpe*, from L *pōlypus*, from Doric Gr *pōlypos* = *polypous*; see **polyp**]

poult *pōlt*, *n* a chicken; the young of the common domestic fowl or other farmyard or game bird. [Fr *poulet*, dimin of *poule* hen; see **pullet**]

poulterer *pōl'tə-rər* and (*archaic*) **poul'ter** *n* a dealer in dead fowls and game. — **poulters' measure** a rhymed couplet in which the first line has 12, the second 14, syllables — from the varying number of eggs formerly sold by poulterers as a dozen. [ME *poulter*, from OFr *pouletier*, from *poulet*; see **poult**]

poultfoot. Same as **poltfoot** (qv under **polt**).

poultice *pōl'tis*, *n* a hot semi-liquid mixture spread on a bandage and applied to the skin to reduce inflammation, formerly used as a treatment for boils. — *vt* to put a poultice on. [L *pultēs*, *pl* of *puls*, *pultis* (Gr *poltos*) porridge]

poultroone. See **poltroon**.

poultry *pōl'tri*, *n* domestic or farmyard fowls collectively; the meat of such fowls. — **poult'ry-farm** and **poultry yard** a farm or yard where poultry are bred or confined. [OFr *pouleterie*, from *pouletier* poulterer]

pounce[1] *powns*, *vi* to spring or swoop suddenly in an attempt to attack or seize (with *on*, *upon*); to seize or fix upon eagerly (with *on*, *upon*); to dart. — *vt* to seize with the claws; to emboss by blows on the other side (*hist*; *perh* from a different source); to puncture or pink (*obs*); to ornament with small holes (*hist*). — *n* an act of pouncing on one's prey, victim, etc; the claw or talon of a hawk or other bird of prey, *esp* the innermost, or any but the hind claw; a punch or thrust (now *dialect*); a puncture (*obs*). — *adj* **pounced** equipped with claws. [ME; orig sense was talon; perh derived in some way from L *punctiō*, *-ōnis*, from *pungere*, *punctum* to prick; cf **puncheon**[1]]

pounce[2] *powns*, *n* sandarach, cuttle-bone, or other fine powder formerly used for preparing a writing surface or absorbing ink; coloured powder shaken through perforations to mark a pattern on a surface beneath. — *vt* to prepare with pounce; to trace, transfer or mark with pounce; to powder or sprinkle (*obs*). — **pounce bag** or **pounce box** a perforated bag or box for sprinkling pounce; **pounce pot** a container for pounce for preparing writing surfaces, etc. [Fr *ponce* pumice, from L *pūmex*, *pūmicis*]

pouncet-box *pown'sit-boks*, *n* a pomander (*Shakesp*; also shortened to **poun'cet**); sometimes used for **pounce-box** (qv under **pounce**[2]). [Prob for *pounced-box*, ie perforated box; see **pounce**[2]]

pounching (*Spenser*). Same as **punching** (see under **punch**[3]).

pound[1] *pownd*, *n* a unit of weight of varying value, long used in western and central Europe, more or less answering to the Roman *libra* and represented by its symbol *lb*; in avoirdupois weight, 16 ounces avoirdupois, 7000 grains, or 0·45359237 kg; formerly, in troy weight, 12 ounces troy, 5760 grains, or about 373·242 grams; a pound weight (*Shakesp*); the balance (*Spenser*); a unit of money, *orig* the value of a pound weight of silver; the standard unit of currency in the

UK, formerly 20 shillings, now 100 (new) pence (the pound sterling, written £, for *libra*); the *pound scots* (*hist*; at the time of the Union with England in 1707 worth 1s. 8d.); the unit of currency in some former British dependencies and certain other countries, including Ireland, Cyprus, Malta, Sudan, Egypt, Syria, Lebanon, and (formerly) Australia, New Zealand and Jamaica: — *pl* formerly **pound**, now **pounds** (except *colloq* and in compounds and certain phrases). — *vt* (*slang*) to bet on as almost a certainty. — *n* **pound'age** a charge or tax made on each pound sterling or weight; a commission, or a share in profits, of so much a pound; bodyweight, *esp* if excessive. — *n* **pound'al** (*phys*) the foot-pound-second unit of force, ie that required to give acceleration of one foot per second per second to a one-pound mass. — *n* **pound'er** a specimen weighing a pound; (in *combining form* **-pounder**) something weighing or carrying so many pounds, a field gun designed to fire shot weighing so many pounds, or person who has, receives or pays, so many pounds sterling. — **pound cake** a sweet rich cake containing a pound, or equal proportions, of each chief ingredient; **pound day** a day on which gifts of one pound weight of various goods are invited for charity. — *adj* **pound-fool'ish** neglecting the care of large sums in attending to little ones (ie being *penny-wise*). — **pound force** the gravitational force of 1lb weight and mass; a unit of such force (*abbrev* **lbf**); **pound sign** the sign £, representing the pound sterling; **pound weight** as much as weighs a pound; a weight of one pound used in weighing. — **pound of flesh** strict exaction of one's due in fulfilment of a bargain, etc, to the point of making the other party suffer beyond what is reasonable (from *Shakesp, Merchant of Venice*). [OE *pund*, from L (*libra*) *pondō* (pound) by weight, *pondō* by weight, from *pendere* to weigh]

pound[2] *pownd*, *n* an enclosure in which to keep stray animals, distrained goods or vehicles removed by the police, etc; any confined place; a pond (now *Scot* and *dialect*); a level part of a canal between two locks; the last compartment of a pound net. — *vt* to put in a pound; to enclose, confine. — *n* **pound'age** a charge for pounding stray cattle. — **pound'-keeper** or **pound'-master**; **pound net** an arrangement of nets for trapping fish. [OE *pund* (in compounds) enclosure]

pound[3] *pownd*, *vt* to beat into fine pieces or to a pulp; to grind to a powder, eg with a pestle; to beat or thump with the fists, etc, to batter; to keep treading (the streets, pavements, etc); to bruise; to lay on, shower (*Spenser*). — *vi* (of the heart) to thump; (of feet, hooves, etc) to strike the ground resoundingly; to run with heavy steps; to struggle on. — *n* the act or sound of pounding. — *n* **pound'er**. [OE *pūnian* to beat; *-d* excrescent, as in **sound**[3], **bound**[4]]

poundage. See under **pound**[1,2].

poundal. See under **pound**[1].

poupe *pōōp* and **poupt** *pōōpt* (*Shakesp*; *pa p*). See **poop**[2].

pour *pōr* or *pör*, *vt* to cause or allow to flow in a stream; to send forth or emit in a stream; to serve (tea, wine, etc) by pouring; to recount (one's story) or rehearse (one's woes) volubly (with *forth*, *out*); to send downstream (*Spenser*); to spread out (*obs*); to drain (eg cooked potatoes; *Scot*). — *vi* to stream; to rain heavily; to emanate or proceed in profusion; to pour out tea, coffee, etc; (of a container, eg a teapot) to allow liquid contents to run out duly. — *n* a pouring; an amount poured at a time. — *adj* **pour'able** that can be poured. — *n* **pour'er**. — *n* **pourie** (*pōōr'i*; *Scot*) a container with a spout; a cream jug; an oilcan. — *n* and *adj* **pour'ing**. — **pour'-out** or **poor'-oot** (*Scot*) the scattering of coins to children as the bride and bridegroom depart after a wedding. — **it never rains but it pours** when things, *esp* troublesome things, start happening, they happen all at once; **pouring wet** raining hard; **pour oil on troubled waters** see under **water**. [ME *pouren*; origin obscure]

pourboire *pōōr-bwär'*, *n* a gratuity, a tip. [Fr, from *pour* for, and *boire* to drink]

pourie. See under **pour**.

pourparler *pōōr-pär'lā*, *n* (*usu* in *pl*) an informal preliminary conference. [Fr]

pourpoint *pōōr'point*, *n* a medieval quilted doublet. [Fr]

poursew or **poursue**, **poursuit** or **poursuitt**. Spenserian for **pursue** and **pursuit**.

pourtray An archaic spelling of **portray**: — *pa p* in *Spenser* **pour'trahed** (3 syllables), **pourtrayd**, **purtraid**, **purtrayd**. — *n* **pour'traict**. An obsolete spelling of **portrait**.

pousowdie. See **powsowdy**.

pousse *pōōs*, (*Spenser*) *n* pease. [**pulse**[2]]

pousse-café *pōōs-ka-fā*, *n* a cordial, liqueur, or combination of several in layers, served after coffee. [Fr, push-coffee]

poussette *pōōs-et'*, *n* a figure in country dancing in which couples hold both hands and move up or down the set, changing places with the next couple. — *vi* to perform a poussette. [Fr, dimin of *pousse* push]

poussin *pōō-sɛ̃'*, *n* a chicken reared for eating at four to six weeks old; a small whole poussin, served as an individual portion, roasted, or split and fried or grilled. [Fr]

pout[1] *powt*, *vi* to push out the lips the lower lip or both lips in an expression either sulky or sexually alluring; to protrude. — *vt* to cause (*esp* the lips) to protrude. — *n* a pouting expression, or act of pouting; a protruding condition. — *n* **pout'er** someone who pouts; a variety of pigeon that can puff out its crop. — *n* **pout'ing**. — *adv* **pout'ingly**. — *adj* **pout'y** inclined to pout, sulky. [ME *powte*, of doubtful origin]

pout[2] *powt*, *n* a fish of the cod family, the bib (also **whiting pout**). — *n* **pout'ing** the whiting pout. — **eel'pout** see under **eel**; **horn pout** or **horned pout** an American catfish (*Amiurus*). [OE (*ǣle-*) *pūte* (eel)pout, perh connected with **pout**[1] with reference to the fish's inflatable membrane on the head]

pout[3] or **poot** *pōōt*, *n* a Scots form of **poult**. — *vi* to shoot at young partridges or young grouse.

pouther *pōō'dhər*. A Scots form of **powder**.

pout net *powt net*, (*Scot*) *n* a fishing net of conical shape with a semicircular mouth, its flat edge being dragged or pushed along the stream bed [Origin uncertain]

poverty *pov'ər-ti*, *n* the state of being poor; need, want of necessities; a lack or deficiency; meagreness or inadequacy; a band of pipers (*obs*). — *adj* **pov'erty-stricken** suffering from poverty. — **poverty line** the dividing line between incomes that are sufficient, and incomes that are insufficient, to purchase life's necessities; **poverty trap** a state of poverty from which there is no escape, any increase in income resulting in a diminution or withdrawal of low-income government benefits. [OFr *poverte* (Fr *pauvreté*), from L *paupertās*, *-ātis*, from *pauper* poor]

POW *abbrev*: prisoner of war.

pow[1] *pow*, (*Scot*) *n* a head, a poll; a head of hair. [**poll**[1]]

pow[2] *pow*, (*Scot*) *n* a slow-moving stream, generally found in carse lands; a small creek at the mouth of a river or in an estuary, affording a landing-place for boats, *esp* on the Forth. [Scot *poll*]

pow[3] *pow*, (*colloq*, *esp US*) *interj* imitative of impact, etc.

powan *pow'ən*, *pō'ən*, *n* a species of whitefish (*Coregonus*) found in Loch Lomond and Loch Eck. [Scots form of **pollan**]

powder *pow'dər*, *n* any solid in the form of fine dust-like particles; (also **face powder**) a cosmetic in this form patted on to the skin to give it a soft smooth appearance; hair powder (qv under **hair**); gunpowder; dust (*obs*); powder snow (*skiing*); a dose of medicine in powder form. — *vt* to reduce to powder, to pulverize; to sprinkle, daub or cover with powder; to sprinkle with salt or spices in preserving, to salt (*obs* or *dialect*); to sprinkle. — *vi* to crumble into powder; to use powder for the hair or face. — *adj* **pow'dered** reduced to powder eg (of food) through dehydration and crushing; sprinkled, daubed or dusted with powder; salted. — *adj* **pow'dery** of the nature of powder; covered with powder; dusty; friable. — **powder blue** a pale blue colour, *orig* produced from powdered smalt (qv); **powder box** a box for face powder, hair powder, etc; **powder burn** a minor burn caused to skin in proximity to a gunpowder explosion; **powder compact** see **compact**[1]; **powder closet** or **pow'dering-clos'et** (*hist*) a small room in which hair was powdered; **powder down** a kind of down on some birds that readily disintegrates in powder; **powdered sugar** (*NAm*) very fine sugar produced by grinding granulated sugar; **powder flask** or **powder horn** a flask (*orig* a horn) for carrying gunpowder; **pow'dering-gown** a loose dressing-gown worn while the hair was being powdered; **pow'dering-tub** a vessel in which meat is salted; a tub used in the treatment of venereal disease by sweating (*obs*); **powder keg** a small barrel for gunpowder; a potentially explosive situation; **powder magazine** a place where gunpowder is stored; **powder metallurgy** the science and art of preparing metals for use by reducing them, as a stage in the process, to powder form; **powder mill** a mill in which gunpowder is made; **powder monkey** a boy carrying powder from the magazine to the gunners on a ship-of-war (*hist*); generally, someone who carries out blasting operations; **powder puff** a pad of velvety or fluffy material for dusting powder on to the skin; an effeminate male homosexual (*slang*); **powder room** a ship's powder magazine; a room for powdering the hair (also **pow'dering-room**); a ladies' cloakroom or toilet (*euphem*); **pow'der-skiing** (the art of) skiing in powder snow such as that encountered off piste; **powder snow** freshly fallen loose thick dry snow; **powdery mildew** a plant disease affecting eg roses, caused by a parasitic fungus (family *Erysiphaceae*), whose spores appear as a powdery white covering on leaves and stems; any of the fungi that cause this disease. — **keep one's powder dry** to preserve one's energies so as to be able to act when the moment comes, play a waiting game; to observe all practical precautions. [OFr *poudre*, from L *pulvis, pulveris* dust]

Powellism *pow'əl-izm*, *n* the views on immigration and on various economic issues expressed by J Enoch *Powell*, politician and scholar (b 1912). — *n* and *adj* **Pow'ellite**.

powellite *pow'əl-it*, *n* a mineral, calcium molybdate. [After John Wesley *Powell* (1834–1902), American geologist, etc]

powellize or **-ise** *pow'əl-īz*, *vt* to season and preserve (timber) by boiling in a saccharine solution. [W *Powell*, the inventor of the process]

power *pow'ər* or *powr*, *n* the skill, physical ability, opportunity or authority to do something; strength or energy; force or effectiveness; an individual faculty or skill; capacity for producing an effect; the moving force of anything; control or influence exercised over others; right to command, authority; political control; rule; governing office; permission to act; a paper giving authority to act; potentiality; a person or group wielding authority or strong influence; that in which such authority or influence resides; a state influential in international affairs; (a state having) military strength of a specified kind; an armed force (*archaic*); (often in *pl*) a spiritual agent; a being of the sixth order of the celestial hierarchy (*Med relig*); a great deal or great many (now *dialect* or *colloq*); a mark of subjection (*Bible*; 1 Cor 11.10; New Eng Bible 'a sign of authority'); the sound value of a letter; the rate at which a system absorbs energy from, or passes energy into, another system, *esp* the rate of doing mechanical work, measured in watts or other unit of work done per unit of time (*mech, physics*, etc); any of the forms of energy, or any of these as the driving force of a machine, etc; mechanical or electrical energy as distinct from manual effort; an instrument serving as a means of applying energy (see **mechanical powers** under **mechanic**); the product of a number of equal factors (as in 12 *to the power of* 4, *or* $12^4 = 12 \times 12 \times 12 \times 12$, generalized to include negative and fractional numbers (*math*); the specified number of such factors, the index or exponent; the potency (qv) of a point with respect to a circle (*geom*); magnifying strength, or a lens possessing it (*optics*). — *adj* concerned with power; (of eg a tool) worked, or assisted in working, by mechanical or electrical power; motor-driven; involving a high degree of physical strength and skill (*esp sport*, as in *power tennis*). — *vt* to equip with mechanical or electrical power. — *vi* and *vt* (*slang*) to move or propel with great force, energy or speed. — *adj* **pow'ered** (often as *combining form*) equipped with mechanical, etc power, as in *nuclear-powered*. — *adj* **pow'erful** having great power; mighty; forcible; efficacious; intense; impressive, noticeable; (of a smell) strong and *usu* disagreeable; great in quantity (*colloq*). — *adv* (*colloq*) exceedingly. — *adv* **pow'erfully**. — *n* **pow'erfulness**. — *adj* **pow'erless** without power, deprived of power; weak; impotent; helpless. — *adv* **pow'erlessly**. — *n* **pow'erlessness**. — **pow'er-amplifier** or (*colloq*) **pow'er-amp** (*electronics*) the stage or element in an amplifer that regulates power output (also **power unit**). — *adj* **pow'er-assisted** helped by or using mechanical power. — **power block** a politically important and powerful group or body; **pow'erboat** a boat propelled by a motor, a motorboat; **power breakfast, lunch** or **tea** (*colloq*) a high-level business discussion held over breakfast, lunch or tea; **power cut** an interruption of, or diminution in, the electrical supply in a particular area; **power dive** a *usu* steep dive by an aeroplane, made faster by using the engine(s). — Also *vi* and *vt* (**pow'er-dive**). — **pow'er-diving**. — *adj* **pow'er-dressed**. — **power dressing** the wearing, by businesswomen, of smart suits tailored on austerely masculine lines so as to give an impression of confident efficiency and having a daunting effect on colleagues, contacts, etc. — *adj* **pow'er-driven** worked by (*esp* mechanical or electrical) power. — **power drill, lathe, loom** or **press** a drill, lathe, loom or press worked by electricity or other form of power such as water or steam; **power factor** (*elec eng*) the ratio of the total power dissipated in an electric circuit to the total equivalent volt-amperes applied to that circuit; **pow'erhouse** a place where power is generated, a power station; a remarkably forceful or energetic person (*colloq*); **pow'erlifting** the sport of weightlifting; **power line** a cable or conductor supplying mains electricity, *esp* an overhead one supported on poles or pylons; **power pack** a device for adjusting an electric current to the voltages required by a particular piece of electronic equipment; **power plant** an industrial plant for generating power; the assemblage of parts generating motive power in a motor car, aeroplane, etc; **pow'er-play** strong, attacking play designed to put pressure on the defence, with players and action concentrated in one small area (*team sport*); similarly concentrated pressure applied as a tactic in eg military, political or business encounters; **power point** a wall socket at which an electrical appliance may be connected to the mains; formerly, a 15-amp socket as distinct from a 5-amp one; **power politics** international politics in which the course taken by states depends upon their knowledge that they can back their decisions with force or other coercive action; **power series** (*math*) an infinite series of the form a_nx^n, or $a_0+a_1x^1+a_2x^2+a_3x^3$ ..., ie whose terms are ascending integral powers of a variable multiplied by constants; **power set** (*math*) a set comprising all the subsets of a given set; **power-sharing** joint responsibility for shaping and executing policy held by all parties within an organization, etc; **power station** an electricity generating station; **power steering** a steering system in a vehicle in which the rotating force exerted on the steering wheel is supplemented by engine power; **power structure** the distribution and application of power within an organization or community; **pow'ertrain** (*eng*) (in a motor vehicle) the drive-transmitting sequence represented by the engine, transmission, and parts connecting gearbox to wheel; **power unit** a power-amplifier (qv above). — **in someone's power** at someone's mercy; within the limits of what someone can do; **in power** in office; in potentiality (*Spenser*); **power of attorney** see under **attorney**; **the powers that be** the existing ruling authorities (*Bible*; Rom 13.1). [OFr *poer* (Fr *pouvoir*), from LL *potēre* (for L *posse*) to be able]

powin, pown. See **pawn**[4].

pownd. Spenserian spelling of **pound**[3].

powney, pownie, powny *pow'ni*. See etymology of **pony**.

powre. Spenserian spelling of **pour**.

powsowdy or **pousowdie** *pow-sow'di*, (*Scot*) *n* any mixture of heterogeneous kinds of food. — [Origin uncertain]

powter *pow'tər*, (*Scot*) *vi* to poke; to rummage. — *vt* to poke; to get by groping. [Origin obscure]

powwaw *pow-wö'*, (*Shakesp*) *interj* pooh.

powwow *pow'wow* or **pawaw** *pä-wö'*, *n* a conference, *orig* one between or with American Indians; amongst American Indians, a rite, often with feasting; an American Indian shaman, a magician or medicine man. — *vi* (*pow-wow'*) to hold a powwow; to confer. [Algonquian *powwaw*, *powah* a priest, literally a dreamer]

pox *poks*, (*usu* as *combining form*) any of several virus diseases causing a rash of pustules (as in *chickenpox*, *cowpox*); smallpox (*archaic*); syphilis (*colloq*; also formerly, *great pox*, *French pox*, *Spanish pox*); sheep-pox. — *vt* (*obs*) to infect with pox, ie, *usu*, syphilis. — *adj* **pox'y** suffering from pox; spotty; dirty, diseased, rotten (*slang*); applied in irritation to anything unpleasant or troublesome (*slang*). — **pox'virus** any one of a group of DNA-containing animal viruses, including those which cause smallpox, cowpox, myxomatosis and certain fibromata. — **a pox on** (or **of**), **a pox take**, etc (*archaic*) a plague on, curse (so-and-so, such-and-such), used as an imprecation. [*Pl* of **pock** pustule]

poy-bird. See **poe-bird**.

poynant *poin'ənt*, (*Spenser*, etc) *adj*. Same as **poignant**.

poynt, poyse, poyson. Old spellings of **point, poise, poison**.

poz or **pozz** *poz*, *adj* an old slang shortening of **positive**.

pozzolana *pot-sə-lä'nə* or **pozzuolana** *-swə-*, *n* a volcanic dust first found at *Pozzuoli*, near Naples, which forms with mortar a cement that will set in air or water. — *adj* **pozzola'nic**.

pozzy. See **possie**.

PP *abbrev*: parish priest; past president; present pupil.

pp *abbrev*: pages; *per procurationem* (*L*), by proxy (also *per pro* (*L*), for and on behalf of); pianissimo (*music*); past participle.

PPA *abbrev*: Pre-school Playgroups Association.

PPC *abbrev*: *pour prendre congé* (*Fr*), to take leave; prospective parliamentary candidate.

ppc *abbrev*: picture postcard.

PPE *abbrev*: Philosophy, Politics and Economics, as a university school or course of study.

PPI *abbrev* Plan Position Indicator.

ppm *abbrev*: parts per million.

PPP *abbrev*: Private Patients' Plan.

PPS *abbrev*: Parliamentary Private Secretary; *post post-scriptum* (*L*), an additional postscript.

PQ *abbrev*: Province of Quebec (Canada).

PR *abbrev*: prize ring; proportional representation; public relations; Puerto Rico.

Pr. *abbrev*: priest; Prince; Provençal.

Pr (*chem*) *symbol*: praseodymium.

pr *abbrev*: pair; per; *per rectum* (*L*; *med*), through the rectum.

pr. *abbrev*: present; price.

praam. Same as **pram**[2].

prabble *prab'l*, (*Shakesp*) *n* a spelling representing the Welsh pronunciation of **brabble**.

practic (also spelt **practick** or **practique**) *prak'tik*, (*archaic*) *adj* relating to, or of the nature of, practice or action; practising; in practice; skilled (*Spenser*); cunning (*Spenser*). — *n* practice as opposed to theory; (*esp* in *pl*) practices, doings; practical experience; legal usage or case law (*esp Scots law*); a practical man. [*Obs Fr practique*, from L *practicus*, from Gr *praktikos* relating to action, from *prassein* to do]

practicable *prak'ti-kə-bl*, *adj* capable of being done, carried out or accomplished, feasible; capable of being used or followed, usable; (of a road, etc) passable; (of a stage window, light switch, etc) functioning, practical (qv). — *n* **practicabil'ity** or **prac'ticableness**. — *adv* **prac'ticably**. [Fr *practicable* and L *practicāre*, from *practicus*; see **practic**]

practical *prak'ti-kl*, *adj* in, relating to, concerned with, well adapted to, or inclining to look to, actual practice, actual conditions, results, or utility; efficient in action; (potentially) effective in use; (of clothes, equipment, etc) plain, sensible or suitably tough for everyday use; workable; being such in effect if not in name; virtual; trained by experience, not professionally; practising, actually engaged in a specified profession (*a practical farmer*); (of a piece of stage equipment, *esp* electric lights, etc) capable of being operated on stage (*theat*). — *n* a practical examination or lesson, eg in a scientific subject; (*usu* in *pl*) a practical man (*old*). — *n* **prac'ticalism** devotion to what is practical. — *n* **prac'ticalist**. — *n* **practical'ity** practicalness; a practical matter, a practical feature or aspect of an affair. — *adv* **prac'tically** for all practical purposes, virtually; very nearly, as good as; in a practical way; by a practical method. — *n* **prac'ticalness**. — **practical arts** those that are materially useful, eg dressmaking, carpentry; **practical joke** a trick played on someone, as distinct from a joke told; **practical politics** proposals or measures that may be carried out at once or in the near future; **practical reason** or **reasoning** (*philos*) reasoning that governs decisions to act or is employed in weighing up relative advantages or merits of various courses; **practical units** an *obs* system of electrical units, in which the ohm, ampere and volt were defined by physical magnitudes. [An expansion of **practic** *adj* (qv)]

practice *prak'tis*, *n* the process of carrying something out, actual doing; action, performance; habitual action, a habit; a custom; a way of proceeding, generally; a normal method of legal procedure; repeated performance as a means of acquiring skill, eg in playing a musical instrument; form so acquired; the exercise of a profession; a professional person's business, as a field of activity or a property; negotiation (*archaic*); scheming, plotting or trickery; the process of working upon someone's feelings; a compendious way of multiplying quantities involving several units, by means of aliquot parts (*arith*). [From **practise** (verb) with spelling by analogy with *advice*, *device*]

practician *prak-tish'ən*, (*old*) *n* a practiser or practitioner; a practical man. [Obs Fr *practicien*, from L *practica*, Gr *praktikē* a skill]

practicum *prak'-ti-kəm*, (*NAm*) *n* a course of practical work undertaken to supplement academic studies. [Neuter of L *practicus* practical; cf Ger *Praktikum* a course of practical work]

practise *prak'tis*, formerly *-tīz'*, (*NAm*) **practice** *vt* to carry out in practice (eg what one preaches); to go in for, or make a habit of; to exercise (eg self-control); to live one's life in accordance with (a religion); to work at or follow (a profession, eg medicine or law); to exercise oneself in (an art, etc), on (a musical instrument) or in the performance of (a musical piece, song, speech, etc) in order to acquire or maintain skill; to train by practice, to drill; to frequent (*obs*); to work (some evil) against someone (with *on*, *upon*); to effect (*obs*); to contrive by some means (*Milton*); to plot (*Shakesp*); to attempt or proceed (to do something; *obs*). — *vi* to follow a profession, eg medicine or law, to be in practice; to exercise oneself in any art, eg instrumental music; to act habitually (*obs*); to scheme, plot or intrigue (with *against*; *obs*) to tamper with (with *upon*, *on*); to have dealings (with *with*; *obs*); to work upon (someone's feelings) unscrupulously (with *on*, *upon*) (*old*). — *n* **practisant** (*obs*) a fellow conspirator. — *adj* **prac'tised** skilled through practice. — *n* **prac'tiser**. —

adj **prac'tising** actually engaged in a specified profession; actively following, and holding faithfully to, a particular religion, etc. [Med L *practizāre*, altered from *practicāre*, from L *practica*; see **practician**]

practitioner *prak-tish'ə-nər*, *n* someone who is in practice, *esp* in medicine; someone who practises or goes in for something specified. [Formed irregularly from **practician**]

practive *prak'tiv*, (*obs*) *adj* practical, active, concerned with practice. [Modelled on *active*]

practolol *prak'tə-lol*, *n* a drug formerly used to treat cardiac arrhythmia, but suspected of causing side effects including eye damage.

prad *prad*, (*slang*) *n* a horse. [Du *paard*, from LL *paraverēdus*; see **palfrey**]

prae-. See **pre-**.

praecava. See **precava**.

praecoces *prē-kō'sēs* or *prī-kō'kāz*, *n pl* (*ornithol*; *old*) birds whose young are hatched with a covering of down and can leave the nest at once to seek food (as opposed to *altrices*). — *adj* **praecocial** or (*NAm*) **precocial** (*prē-kō'shl* or *-shyəl*) of or relating to the praecoces; premature, forward. [L *pl* of *praecox*, *-cocis*; see **precocious**]

praedial or **predial** *prē'di-əl*, *adj* relating to, connected with, or derived from, the land; landed; rural; agrarian; attached to the land or a farm. — *n* a praedial slave. [LL *praediālis*, from *praedium* an estate]

praefect. See **prefect**.

praeludium *prē-lū'di-əm* or *prī-lōō'di-ōōm*, (*L*) *n* a prelude: — *pl* **praelu'dia**. [L *prae* before, and *ludere* to play]

praemunire *prē-mū-nī'ri* or *prī-mōō-nē're*, *n* a writ issued under statutes of Richard II, summoning a person accused of suing in a foreign court for matters cognizable by the law of England, used *esp* against papal claims, and later extended to various offences; an offence that could be so dealt with; the penalty for such an offence; a predicament or scrape (*usu humorous*). [From the words of the writ, *praemūnīre faciās* cause to warn, or see that thou warn, the word *praemūnīre*, properly to fortify in front, defend, being confused with *praemonēre* to forewarn]

praenomen *prē-nō'mən* or *prī-nō'men*, *n* the name prefixed to the family name in ancient Rome, as, eg, *Gaius* in Gaius Julius Caesar; the generic name of a plant or animal (*rare*): — *pl* **praeno'mens** or **praenomina** (*-nō'mi-nə*). [L, from *prae* before, in front of, and *nōmen* name]

praepostor, **prepostor** *prē-pos'tər* or **prepositor** *-poz'itər*, *n* the name used for a prefect in some English public schools. [L *praepositus*, pa p of *praepōnere*, from *prae* in front, and *pōnere* to put]

Praeraphaelite. See **Pre-Raphaelite**.

Praesepe *prī-sē'pi*, *n* a cluster of stars in the constellation Cancer.

praeses. See **preses**.

praesidium. See **presidium**.

praeter-. See **preter-**.

praetor *prē'tər* or *-tör*, or *prī'tor*, or (*esp NAm*) **pretor** *prē'tər*, *n* a magistrate of ancient Rome next in rank to the consuls. — *adj* **praeto'rial**. — *adj* **praetorian** (*-tō'* or *tö'*). — *n* a former praetor or man of equivalent rank; a member of the emperor's bodyguard. — *n* **praeto'rium** a general's tent; a governor's residence; a court or headquarters. — *n* **prae'torship**. — **praetorian gate** the gate of a Roman camp in front of the general's tent, and nearest to the enemy; **praetorian guard** the bodyguard of the Roman Emperor. [L *praetor*, for *praeitor*, from *prae* in front of, before, and *īre*, *itum* to go]

pragmatic *prag-mat'ik*, *adj* concerned with what is practicable, expedient and convenient, or with practical consequences, rather than with theories and ideals; matter-of-fact, realistic; seeing historical events purely in terms of their practical lessons; relating to, or of the nature of, pragmatism (*philos*); relating to affairs of state; meddlesome, opinionated, pragmatical. — *n* a busybody (*old*); an opinionated person (*old*); an edict (*hist*); a man of business (*obs*). — *adj* **pragmat'ical** interfering with the affairs of others, officious, meddlesome; self-important; opinionated, dogmatic; active (*obs*); practical, matter-of-fact, pragmatic (*obs*). — *n* **pragmatical'ity**. — *adv* **pragmat'ically**. — *n* **pragmat'icalness**. — *n sing* **pragmat'ics** the study of inherent practical usage, and social and behavioural aspects, of language; a study of linguistic sign systems and their use. — **pragmatic sanction** a special decree issued by a sovereign, such as that of the Emperor Charles VI, settling his dominions upon Maria Theresa. [Gr *pragmatikos*, from *prāgma*, *-matos* deed; see **pragmatism**]

pragmatism *prag'mə-tizm*, *n* pragmatic quality, realism, matter-of-factness; concern for the practicable rather than for theories and ideals; a humanistic philosophy, or philosophic method, that makes practical consequences the test of truth (*philos*); a treatment of history in terms of cause and effect and practical lessons (*old*). — *n* **prag'matist** a pragmatic person; someone who advocates the practicable rather than the ideal course; a believer in philosophical or historical pragmatism. — *n* **pragmatiza'tion** or **-s-**. — *vt* **prag'matize** or **-ise** to interpret or represent as real; to rationalize (a myth). — *n* **prag'matizer** or **-s-**. [Gr *prāgma*, *-matos* deed, from *prāssein* to do]

prahu. See as **prau**.

Prairial *pre-ri-äl'* or *pre-ryäl'*, *n* the ninth month of the French revolutionary calendar, the month of meadows, about 20 May to 18 June. [Fr, from *prairie* meadow]

prairie *prā'ri*, *n* a treeless plain, flat or rolling, naturally grass-covered. — *adj* **prai'ried**. — **prairie chick'en**, **fowl**, **grouse** or **hen** an American genus (*Cupidonia* or *Tympanuchus*) of grouse; the sharp-tailed grouse (*Pedioecetes*) of the western USA; **prairie dog** a gregarious burrowing and barking N American marmot (*Cynomys*); **prairie-oyster** (*US*) a raw egg with condiments; **prairie schooner** an emigrants' long covered wagon; **prairie turnip** breadroot; **prairie value** the value of land in its natural state before it has been improved by man; **prairie wolf** the coyote. [Fr, from LL *prātaria*, from L *prātum* a meadow]

praise *prāz*, *vt* to express admiration or approval of; to commend; to extol; to glorify or worship (one's god) with hymns, thanksgiving, etc; to assign a value to, appraise (*Shakesp*). — *n* the expression of admiration or approval; commendation; glorification, worship; the musical part of worship; praise-deserving merit (*old*); (in ejaculatory expressions) substitued for God (*obs Scot colloq*). — *adj* **praise'ful**. — *adj* **praise'less**. — *n* **prais'er**. — *n* and *adj* **prais'ing**. — *adv* **prais'ingly**. — *adv* **praise'worthily**. — *n* **praise'worthiness**. — *adj* **praise'worthy** worthy of praise; commendable. — **sing the praises of** to commend enthusiastically. [OFr *preiser*, from LL *preciāre* for L *pretiāre* to prize, from *pretium* price]

praiseach *prash'ahh*, *n* a kind of oatmeal porridge, often with vegetables; a mess, a jumble of small pieces; wild mustard (*Brassica arvensis*). [Ir, from L *brassica* cabbage]

Prakrit *prä'krit*, *n* a name for (any of) the Indo-Aryan dialects contemporary with Sanskrit, or for (any of) the later languages derived from them. — *adj* **Prakrit'ic**. [Sans *prākṛta* the natural, from *prakṛti* nature]

praline *prä'lēn*, *n* an almond or nut kernel with a brown coating of sugar, or a similar confection made with crushed nuts. — Also **prawlin** (*prö'lin*). [Fr *praline*, from Marshal Duplessis-*Praslin*, whose cook invented it]

Pralltriller *präl'tril-ər*, (*music*) *n* an upper or inverted mordent, a grace in which the principal note is preceded in performance by itself and the note above. [Ger]

pram[1] *pram*, *n* a small wheeled carriage for a baby, pushed by a person on foot; a milkman's hand cart. [Shortening of **perambulator**]

pram[2] or **praam** *präm*, *n* a flat-bottomed Dutch or Baltic lighter; a fishing vessel, lighter or tender of the Dutch and Baltic coasts, generally flat-bottomed with a squared-off prow; a barge fitted as a floating battery. [Du *praam*, of Slavic origin]

prana *prä'nə*, *n* the breath of life; in Hindu religion, *esp* yoga (qv), breath as the essential life force. — *n* **pranaya'ma** (*yoga*) controlled breathing. [Sans]

prance *präns*, *vi* (of a horse) to bound from the hind legs; to caper or dance along; to move with an exaggeratedly springing gait; to swagger, to parade ostentatiously; to ride a prancing horse. — *vt* to cause to prance. — *n* an act of prancing; a prancing gait; swagger. — *n* **pranc'er**. — *adj* and *n* **pranc'ing**. — *adv* **pranc'ingly**. [ME *praunce*; related to Dan *pransk* spirited (of a horse)]

pranck, prancke. See **prank**[3].

prandial *pran'di-əl*, (*esp facetious*) *adj* relating to dinner. [L *prandium* a morning or midday meal]

prang *prang*, (*orig airmen's slang*) *n* a vehicle crash; a bombing-attack. — *vt* to crash or smash (a vehicle or aircraft); to crash into (eg another car); to bomb (a target) or bomb (a place) heavily; to shoot down (an aircraft). [Prob imit]

prank[1] *prangk*, *n* a trick; a practical joke; a frolic; a malicious or mischievous trick; an evil deed (*obs*). — *vi* to play pranks. — *adj* **prank'ful, prank'ish, prank'some** and **prank'y**. — *n* **prank'ster** someone given to playing pranks, a practical joker. [Origin uncertain]

prank[2] *prangk*, (*archaic*) *vt* to dress or adorn showily; to bespangle or cover in colourful profusion; to place in a setting, like a jewel. — *vi* (also *vt* with *it*) to make an ostentatious show. — *n* and *adj* **prank'ing**. — *adv* **prank'ingly**. [Related to Du *pronken*, Ger *prunken* to show off; cf **prink**]

prank[3], **pranck** or **prancke** *prangk*, (*obs*) *vt* to pleat or fold; to set in order. [Origin uncertain]

prank[4] *prangk*, (*rare*) *n* prancing, capering. — *vi* (and *vt* with *it*) to prance. — *vi* **prank'le** to prance lightly. [Poss connected with **prance**]

prase *prāz*, *n* a leek-green quartz. [Gr *prason* leek]

praseodymium *prā-zi-ə-dim'i-əm*, *n* an element (symbol **Pr**; atomic no 59), a metal with green salts, isolated, along with neodynium, from the once-supposed element didymium. [Gr *prasios* leek-green, from *prason* leek, and **didymium**]

prat[1] or **pratt** *prat*, (*slang*) *n* the buttocks. — *vt* (*Shakesp* punningly) to beat on the buttocks. — *n* **prat'fall** (*US slang*) a fall landing on the prat; a humiliating blunder or ignominous failure. — Also *vi*. [Origin uncertain]

prat[2] *prat*, (*abusive slang*) *n* a fool, an ineffectual person. [Poss a use of **prat**[1]]

prate *prāt*, *vi* to talk foolishly or sententiously; to talk boastfully or insolently; to tattle; to be loquacious. — *vt* to utter in a prating manner; to blab. — *n* foolish or superfluous talk. — *n* **pra'ter**. — *n* and *adj* **pra'ting**. — *adv* **pra'tingly**. [Cf LGer *praten*, Dan *prate*, Du *praaten*]

pratie or **praty** *prā'ti*, *n* an Anglo-Irish form of **potato**.

pratincole *prat'ing-kōl*, *n* a bird related to the plovers, with swallow-like wings and tail. [L *prātum* meadow, and *incola* an inhabitant]

pratique *pra-tēk'* or *prat'ik*, *n* permission given to a ship to trade or deal in a port after quarantine or on showing a clean bill of health. [Fr, intercourse, from L *practica* practice, from Gr *prāssein* to do]

pratt. See **prat**[1].

prattle *prat'l*, *vi* to talk idly and volubly, to chatter inconsequentially; (of a young child) to utter baby talk. — *vt* to utter in a prattling way. — *n* empty talk. — *n* **pratt'lement** prattle. — *n* **pratt'ler** someone who prattles; a little child (*old*). — **pratt'lebox** a prattler. [Dimin and frequentative of **prate**]

praty. See **pratie**.

prau *prä'o͞o* or *prow*, **prahu** *prä'o͞o* or *prä'ho͞o* or **proa** *prō'ə*, *n* a Malay sailing-boat or rowing-boat, *esp* a fast sailing-vessel with both ends alike, and a flat side with an outrigger kept to leeward. [Malay *prāū*]

praunce. Spenser's form of **prance**.

pravity *prav'i-ti*, (*rare*) *n* wickedness. [L *prāvitās*, *-ātis*]

prawle *pröl*, *n* Shakespeare's Welsh form of **brawl**.

prawlin. See **praline**.

prawn *prön*, *n* a small edible shrimp-like crustacean (*Palaemon serratus* or any related species). — *vi* to fish for prawns. — **prawn cocktail** a dish of prawns with salad, mayonnaise, etc, served as an appetizer or starter; **prawn cracker** a light, deep-fried prawn-flavoured crisp traditionally eaten as an accompaniment to Chinese, etc food. — **come the raw prawn** (*Austr slang*) to make an attempt to deceive. [ME *prayne*, *prane*; origin unknown]

praxinoscope *prak'sin-ə-skōp*, *n* an optical toy creating the illusion of motion by reflection of a sequence of pictures in a rotating box. [Irregularly formed from Gr *prāxis* doing, and **-scope**]

praxis *prak'sis*, *n* the practice or practical side of an art or science, as distinct from its theoretical side; customary or accepted practice; (an example or a collection of examples serving to provide) a practical exercise. [Gr *prāxis*, from *prāssein* to do]

Praxitelean *prak-si-tə-lē'ən*, *adj* of, relating to, reminiscent of or in the style of *Praxiteles*, Greek sculptor (fl. c. 350 BC).

pray *prā*, *vi* to express one's desires to, or commune with, a god or some spiritual power (with *to*); to intercede with one's god on behalf of another person, etc (with *for*); to ask earnestly (often with *for*). — *vt* to ask earnestly and reverently, in the course of worship; to hope earnestly or fervently; to supplicate; to beg or entreat; to say (a prayer); to render, get, put, or cause to be, by praying (*rare*): — *pr p* **pray'ing**; *pa t* and *pa p* **prayed**. — *interj* (often *ironic*) I ask you, may I ask. — *n* **prayer** (*prā'ər*) someone who prays. — *n* and *adj* **pray'ing**. — *adv* **prayingly**. — **praying insect** or **mantis** see **mantis**. — **pray against** in Parliament, to address a prayer to the Crown for the annulment of (an order or obligation); **pray in aid** (*law*; *Shakesp*) to call in, or call for, help. [OFr *priere*, from MedL *precāria*, from L *precārius* obtained by prayer, from *prex*, *precis* prayer]

prayer[1] *prār* or *prā'ər* *n* the act of praying; entreaty; an address to a god or spiritual power in the form of a petition or offer of praise, penitence, etc; generally, the act of communing with one's god; the wish put forward or the words used; the thing prayed for; a form used or intended for use in praying; public worship; (in *pl*) (a time set aside for) worship in a family, school, etc; a petition to a public body, eg a legislature; in Parliament, a motion addressed to the Crown asking for the annulment of an order or regulation. — *adj* **pray'erful** given to prayer, expressing one's earnest desires through prayer; in a spirit or mental attitude of prayer. — *adv* **prayer'fully**. — *n* **prayer'fulness**. — *adj* **prayer'less** without or not using prayer. — *adv* **prayer'lessly**. — *n* **prayer'lessness**. — **prayer bead** one of the beads on a rosary; a jequirity bean; **prayer book** a book containing prayers or forms of devotion, *esp* the Book of Common Prayer of the Church of England; **prayer flag** in Tibetan Buddhism, a flag on which a prayer is inscribed; **prayer mat** same as **prayer rug**; **prayer meeting** a shorter and simpler form of public religious service, in which laymen often take part; **pray'er-monger** someone who prays mechanically; **prayer rug** a small carpet on which a Muslim kneels at prayer; **prayer wheel** a drum wrapped with strips of paper inscribed with prayers deemed by Buddhists of Tibet to be proffered when the drum is turned. [OFr *preier* (Fr *prier*) to pray, from L *precārī*, from *prex*, *precis* a prayer]

prayer[2]. See under **pray**.

Words beginning with the prefix **pre-** are listed in the following entries and in the separate panels.

pre- (as living prefix) *prē-*, or **prae-** (*L* spelling, more common formerly) *prē-* or *prī-*, *pfx* (1) before in time, beforehand, in advance, as in *prehistoric*, *pre-war*, *prewarn*; (2) in front, in front of, the anterior part of, as in *predentate, premandibular, presternum* (*esp anatom*); (3) surpassingly, to the highest degree, as in *pre-eminent, pre-potent*. — *prep* (without hyphen; *colloq*) before, prior to. [L *prae*, in front of, before]

preace *prēs* (*Spenser*). Same as **press**[1].

preach *prēch, vi* to deliver a sermon; to discourse earnestly; to give advice in a sententious, tedious, obtrusive or offensive manner. — *vt* to set forth or expound in religious discourses; to deliver (a sermon); to proclaim or teach publicly; to advise, advocate, recommend or inculcate; to render or put by preaching. — *n* (*colloq*) a sermon. — *n* **preach'er** someone who discourses publicly on religious matters; a minister or clergyman; an assiduous inculcator or advocate. — *n* **preach'ership**. — *vi* **preach'ify** (*colloq*) to preach, *esp* tediously; to sermonize or moralize; to give advice wearisomely. — *adv* **preach'ily**. — *n* **preach'iness**. — *n* and *adj* **preach'ing**. — *n* **preach'ment** a sermon (*derog*); a sermon-like discourse; sermonizing. — *adj* **preach'y** given to tedious moralizing; savouring of preaching. — **preaching-cross** a cross in an open place at which monks, etc, preached; **preaching friar** a Dominican; **preach'ing-house** a Methodist church. — **preach down** or **up** respectively, to decry or extol; **preaching with a view** preaching as a candidate in a vacant pastoral charge; **the Preacher** the authors or spokesman of the Book of Ecclesiastes in the Old Testament; the book itself. [Fr *prêcher*, from L *praedicāre, -ātum* to proclaim]

pre-Adamite *prē-ad'ə-mīt, n* someone who lived, or a descendant of those who lived, or a believer in the existence of a human race, before *Adam*. — Also *adj*. — *adj* **pre-adamic** (*-ə-dam'ik*) or **pre-adam'ical** existing before Adam. — *adj* **pre-adamit'ic** or **pre-adamit'ical**. [**pre-** (1)]

preadaptation *prē-ad-ap-tā'shən*, (*biol*) *n* the possession by organisms of features apparently functionless in their present environment that will have a function in aiding survival in a future one. — *adj* **preadap'ted**. — *adj* **preadap'tive**. [**pre-** (1)]

preadmonish *prē-əd-mon'ish, vt* to forewarn. — *n* **preadmoni'tion**. [**pre-** (1)]

preamble *prē-am'bl, n* a preface; an introduction, *esp* that of an Act of Parliament, giving its reasons and purpose; (*Milton* **praeamble**) a prelude. — Also *vt* and *vi*. — *adj* **pream'būlary** or **pream'būlatory**. — *vi* **pream'būlate** to go first (*obs*); to make a preamble. [Fr *préambule*, from L *prae* in front of, and *ambulāre* to go]

preamplifier *prē-amp'li-fī-ər, n* (often shortened to **pre'amp**) an electronic device that boosts and clarifies the signal from eg a radio, record-player, microphone, etc before it reaches the main amplifier. [**pre-** (1)]

prease or **preasse** (*Spenser*). Same as **press**[1].

preaudience *prē-ö'di-əns, n* the right to be heard before another; precedence at the bar among lawyers. [**pre-** (1)]

Preb. *abbrev*: Prebend; Prebendary.

prebend *preb'ənd, n* the share of the revenues of a cathedral or collegiate church allowed to a clergyman who officiates in it at stated times. — *adj* **prebendal** (*pri-ben'dl*; **prebendal stall** the cathedral stall, or the benefice, of a prebendary). — *n* **preb'endary** a resident clergyman who enjoys a prebend, a canon; the honorary holder of a disendowed prebendal stall. [LL *praebenda* an allowance, from L *praebēre* to allow, grant]

prebiotic *prē-bī-ot'ik, adj* relating to the time before the appearance of living things. [**pre-** (1)]

preborn *prē-börn', adj* being carried in the womb, unborn [**pre-** (1)]

Pre-Cambrian *prē-kam'bri-ən*, (*geol*) *adj* and *n* (of or relating to) the earliest geological era; Archaean. [**pre-** (1)]

pre-cancel *prē-kan'səl, vt* to cancel (a postage stamp), eg by applying a postmark before use. — Also *n*. [**pre-** (1)]

pre-cancerous *prē-kan'sə-rəs, adj* (of tissue) showing structural alterations recognized as associated with the subsequent development of cancer. [**pre-** (1)]

precarious *pri-kā'ri-əs, adj* depending on chance; insecure; uncertain; dangerous, risky; depending upon the will of another; supplicating (*obs*). — *adv* **precā'riously**. — *n* **precā'riousness**. [L *precārius*, from *precārī* to pray]

precast *prē-käst', adj* (of concrete blocks, etc), cast before being put in position. [**pre-** (1)]

precative *prek'ə-tiv, adj* supplicating; expressing entreaty (*gram*). [L *precātīvus*, from *precārī* to pray]

precatory *prek'ə-tə-ri, adj* of the nature of, or expressing, a wish, request or recommendation. [L *precātōrius*, from *precārī* to pray]

precaution *pri-kö'shən, n* a measure taken beforehand to ensure a satisfactory result, to prevent an undesirable one, or to steer clear of danger; due circumspection or foresight; (in *pl*) the using of contraceptives (*colloq*). — *vt* (*obs*) to forewarn. — *adj* **precau'tional, precau'tionary** or **precau'tious**. [**pre-** (1)]

precava or **praecave** *prē-kā'və*, (*anatom*) *n* the superior vena cava, the vein carrying blood from the head, arms and thorax. [**pre-** (2)]

precede *pri-sēd', vt* to go before in position, time, rank or importance; to cause to be preceded, to preface or introduce. — *vi* to be before in time or place. — *n* **precedence** (*pres'i-dəns* or *prē'si-dəns*, also *pri-sē'dəns*) the act of going before in time; the right of going before; priority; the fact of being before in rank; the place of honour; the foremost place in ceremony (also **precedency** *pres'i-dən-si, prē'si-* or *pri-sē'dən-si*). — *n* **precedent** (*pres'i-dənt* or *prē'si-dənt*) a previous incident, legal case, etc that is parallel to one under consideration; the measures taken or judgement given in such a case, serving as a basis for a decision in the present one; that which precedes; the original of a copy (*Shakesp*); a token (*Shakesp*); a model (*obs*). — *adj* (*pri-sē'dənt*) preceding. — *adj* **precedented** (*pres'*, *prē'si-*) having a precedent; warranted by an example. — *adj* **precedential** (*pres-i-den'shl*) of the nature of a precedent. — *adv* **pre'cedently**. — *adj* **precē'ding** going before in time, rank, etc; antecedent; previous; foregoing; immediately before. — **take precedence over** or **of** to precede in ceremonial order. [Fr *précéder*, from L *praecēdere, -cēssum*, from *prae* before, and *cēdere* to go]

preceese *pri-sēz'*. A Scots form of **precise**.

precentor *pri-sen'tər*, or *prē* (*Scot pri-zen'tər*), (*eccles*) *n* the leader of the singing of a church choir or con-

Some words with **pre-** prefix; see **pre-** entry for numbered senses.

preacquaint' *vt* (1).
preacquaint'ance *n* (1).
preadoles'cence *n* (1).
preadoles'cent *adj* (1).
preannounce' *vt* (1).
preappoint' *vt* (1).
prearrange' *vt* (1).
prearrange'ment *n* (1).
preassur'ance *n* (1).
pre-buy' *vi* and *vt* (1).
prechris'tian or pre-Chris'tian *adj* (1).
preclass'ical *adj* (1).
preco'ital *adj* (1).
precolo'nial *adj* (1).
pre-Colum'bian *adj* (1).
precompose' *vt* (1).
precondemn' *vt* (1).
pre-con'quest *n* (1).
preconsonan'tal *adj* (1).
preconstruct' *vt* (1).
preconstruc'tion *n* (1).
preconsume' *vt* (1).
precool' *vt* (1).
precopula'tory *adj* (1).
precut' *vt* and *adj* (**pre'cut**) (1).
predawn' *n* (1).
predefine' *vt* (1).
predefini'tion *n* (1).
predesign' *vt* (1).

gregation; in some English cathedrals, a member of the chapter who deputes this duty to a succentor: — *fem* **precen'tress** or **precen'trix**. — *n* **precen'torship**. [LL *praecentor*, *-ōris*, from L *prae* before, and *canere* to sing]

precepit *pres'i-pit*, (*Shakesp*) *n* a precipice.

precept *prē'sept*, *n* a rule of action; an instruction in moral conduct, a principle, maxim or commandment; a practical instruction in a technique; a written order, writ or warrant from a magistrate or other authority to a subordinate official eg to convene a court or jury, hold an election etc (*law*); a document granting possession or bestowing a privilege (*Scot*); an order to levy money under a local rating or taxation system; a command or mandate (*old*). — *adj* **preceptial** (*pri-sep'shl*; *Shakesp*) consisting of precepts. — *adj* **precep'tive** containing or giving precepts; directing in moral conduct; didactic. — *n* **precep'tor** someone who delivers precepts; a teacher; an instructor; a tutor (*US*); the head of a school; the head of a preceptory of Knights Templars: — *fem* **precep'tress**. — *adj* **precepto'rial** (*prē-*). — *adj* **precep'tory** (*pri-*) giving precepts. — *n* a community of Knights Templars (occasionally extended to a commandery of the Hospitallers); its estate or buildings. [L *praeceptum*, neuter pa p of *praecipere* to take beforehand, from *prae* before, and *capere* to take]

precession *pri-sesh'ən*, *n* the fact or act of preceding; a progression or going forward (*erron* for **procession**; *obs*); the precession of the equinoxes (see below) or the analogous phenomenon in spinning tops and the like, whereby the wobble of the spinning object causes its axis of rotation to become cone-shaped. — *vi* **precess** (*-ses'*; a back-formation from **precession**; of a spinning-top, etc) to wobble. — *adj* **precess'ional**. — **precession of the equinoxes** a slow westward motion of the equinoctial points along the ecliptic, caused by the greater attraction of the sun and moon on the excess of matter at the equator, such that the times at which the sun crosses the equator come at shorter intervals than they would otherwise do. [LL *praecessiō*, *-ōnis*, from *praecēdere*; see **precede**]

précieuse *prā-syœz'*, *n* a woman affecting a fastidious over-refinement. [Fr, from the literary women of 17c France who were extremely fastidious in their use of language]

precinct *prē'singkt*, *n* a space, *esp* an enclosed one, around a building (eg a cathedral, college, etc) or other object (also in *pl*); a district or division within certain boundaries; a district of jurisdiction or authority; a division for police or electoral purposes (*US*); (in *pl*) environs. — **pedestrian precinct** a traffic-free area of a town, *esp* a shopping centre; **shopping precinct** a shopping centre, *esp* if traffic-free. [LL *praecinctum*, neuter pa p of *praecingere*, from *prae* around, in front of, and *cingere* to gird]

precious *presh'əs*, *adj* of great price or worth; cherished; very highly esteemed; (with a *possessive*) grand, fine, much-vaunted (*ironic*, as in *sick of hearing about his precious children*); egregious (*ironic*); too consciously refined, fastidious or dainty. — *adv* extremely, confoundedly, as in *precious little*, *few*, etc (*colloq*); preciously (*Shakesp*). — *n* used as a term of endearment. — *n* **preciosity** (*presh-i-os'i-ti* or *pres-*) fastidious over-refinement. — *adv* **prec'iously**. — *n* **prec'iousness**. — **precious metals** gold, silver, platinum (also, rarely, mercury or others of high price); **precious stone** a stone of value and beauty, *esp* with regard to its use in jewellery or ornamentation, a gem. [OFr *precios* (Fr *précieux*), from L *pretiōsus*, from *pretium* price]

precipice *pres'i-pis*, *n* a high vertical or nearly vertical cliff or rock face; a perilous state of affairs; a headlong fall (*obs*). — *adj* **prec'ipiced**. [L *praecipitium* a headlong fall, a precipice, from *praeceps*, *praecipitis* headlong, steep]

precipitant *pri-sip'i-tənt*, *adj* falling headlong; rushing downwards or onwards at too great a velocity; impulsively hasty, precipitate. — *n* (*chem*) a substance tht causes the formation of a precipitate, a precipitating agent. — *n* **precip'itance** or **precip'itancy** the quality of being precipitate; a headlong fall; headlong haste or rashness; an impulsively hasty action. — *adv* **precip'itantly**. [L *praecipitans*, pr p of *praecipitāre* to throw headlong]

precipitate *pri-sip'itāt*, *vt* to hurl headlong; to force into hasty action; to pitch (oneself) over-enthusiastically into action, etc; to bring on suddenly or prematurely; to cause to come out of solution or suspension and settle as a solid deposit (*chem*); to cause (moisture, water vapour) to condense and fall as rain, hail, snow, etc (*meteorol*). — *vi* to come out of solution or suspension and settle as a solid deposit (*chem*); (of moisture, water vapour) to condense and fall as rain, hail, snow, etc (*meteorol*); to rush in haste; to fall headlong (*Shakesp*). — *adj* (*pri-sip'i-tət*) falling, hurled or rushing headlong; sudden and hasty; without deliberation; rash. — *n* (*-tət*) a substance separated from solution or suspension, *usu* falling and settling at the bottom as a solid deposit; moisture deposited as rain, hail, snow, etc (*meteorol*). — *adv* **precip'itately**. — *n* **precipitā'tion** the act of precipitating; a headlong fall or rush; a sheer drop (*Shakesp*); impulsive action; great hurry; rash haste; impulsiveness; rain, hail, snow and sometimes also dew (*meteorol*); the amount of rainfall, etc; the separation of suspended matter, the formation or sinking of a precipitate, or the precipitate itself (*chem*). — *adj* **precip'itātive**. — *n* **precip'itātor** someone who precipitates; a precipitating agent; an apparatus or tank for precipitation. [L *praecipitāre*, *-ātum* to throw or cast headlong, from *praeceps*, *-ipitis* headlong, steep, from *prae* in front, and *caput*, *-itis* head]

precipitin *pri-sip'i-tin*, (*med*) *n* an antibody which in contact with an antigen produces a precipitate. — *n* **precipitinogen** (*-tin'ə-jen*) a soluble antigen that stimulates the formation of a precipitin. — *adj* **precipitinogen'ic**. [Formed from **precipitate**]

precipitous *prə-sip'i-təs*, *adj* like a precipice; sheer; precipitate (*rare*). — *adv* **precip'itously**. — *n* **precip'itousness**. [Obs Fr *précipiteux*, from L *praeceps* headlong, steep; see **precipitate**]

précis *prā'sē*, *n* an abstract, a summary: — *pl* **précis** (*-sēz*). — *vt* to make a précis of: — *pr p* **précising** (*prā'sē-ing*); *pa t* and *pa p* **précised** (*prā'sēd*). [Fr]

precise *pri-sīs'*, *adj* definite; exact; accurate; free from vagueness; very, identical; scrupulously exact; over-

Some words with **pre-** prefix; see **pre-** entry for numbered senses.

predevel'op *vt*, *vi* (1).	**prenego'tiate** *vi*, *vt* (1).	**pre-posi'tion** *vt* (2).
predevel'opment *n* (1).	**prenegotia'tion** *n* (1).	**prepro'grammed** *adj* (1).
predoom' *vt* (1).	**preno'tify** *vt* (1).	**prerecord'** *vt* (1).
pre-employ' *vt* (1).	**prenu'bile** *adj* (1).	**prerecord'ed** *adj* (1).
pre-engage' *vt* (1).	**prenup'tial** *adj* (1).	**pre-Reforma'tion** *adj* (1).
pre-engage'ment *n* (1).	**preoc'ular** *adj* (2).	**pretest'** *vt* (1).
pre'flight *adj* (1).	**preopera'tional** *adj* (1).	**pre-war'**, **pre'-war** *adj*, *adv* (1).
preheat *vt* (1).	**preop'erative** *adj* (1).	**prewarm'** *vt* (1).
pre-let' *vt* (1).	**preo'ral** *adj* (2).	**prewarn'** *vt* (1).
premix' *vt* (1).	**preor'der** *vt* (1).	

exact; prim; formal; scrupulous in observing the rules of religion (*old*); puritanical (*hist*). — *adv* **precise'ly** in a precise manner; exactly; (as a rejoinder) quite, I agree entirely. — *n* **precise'ness**. — *n* **precisian** (*pri-sizh'ən*) an over-precise person; a formalist; a Puritan (*hist*; *derog*). — *n* **preci'sianism**. — *n* **preci'sianist** a precisian. — *n* **preci'sion** the quality of being precise; exactness; minute accuracy; mental separation or abstraction of ideas, etc (partly associated with **prescission**; *Berkeley*); reliability, reproducibility or repeatability (*statistics*, etc); a precise definition (*obs*). — *adj* operating, or carried out, with minute accuracy. — *n* **precis'ionist** someone who insists on precision; a purist. — *adj* **precisive** (*pri-sī'siv*) dividing off, separating or abstracting mentally; relating to precision. [Fr *précis*, *précise* from L *praecīsus*, pa p of *praecīdere*, from *prae* around, and *caedere* to cut]

preclinical *prē-klin'i-kəl*, (*med*) *adj* taking place before, or without yet having gained, practical clinical experience with patients; of, relating to or occurring during the stage before the symptoms of a disease are recognizable; (of a drug) not yet having undergone clinical testing. [**pre-** (1)]

preclude *pri-klōōd'*, *vt* to rule out, eliminate or make impossible; to hinder by anticipation, counteract in advance, obviate; to prevent (with *from*); to shut out beforehand; to close beforehand. — *n* **preclusion** (*pri-klōō'zhən*). — *adj* **preclusive** (*-klōō'siv*) tending to preclude; hindering beforehand. — *adv* **preclu'sively**. [L *praeclūdere*, *-clūsum*, from *claudere* to shut]

precocial. See under **praecoces**.

precocious *pri-kō'shəs*, *adj* early in developing or reaching some stage of development; (of a child) strikingly advanced or mature in mental development, speech, social behaviour, etc, sometimes irksomely so; (of a talent or aptitude) abundantly apparent at an early stage; (of plants) flowering or fruiting, or (of fruit) ripening, early; flowering before leaves appear; (of birds) praecocial (qv). — *adv* **precō'ciously**. — *n* **precō'ciousness** or **precocity** (*pri-kos'i-ti*) the state or quality of being precocious; early, if not over-early, development or maturity of mind. [L *praecox*, *-ocis*, from *prae* before, and *coquere* to cook, ripen]

precognition *prē-kog-nish'ən*, *n* foreknowledge; a preliminary examination of witnesses as to whether there is ground for prosecution (*Scots law*); evidence so obtained; a formally prepared statement of evidence, etc, submitted in advance to an inquiry or court, *usu* read out by the submitter at the inquiry (*Scots law*). — *adj* **precog'nitive** (*pri-*). — *vt* **precognosce** (*prē-kog-nos'*) to take a precognition of. [L *praecognitio*, *-ōnis* foreknowledge, and *praecognoscere* to know beforehand]

precognize *prē'kəg-nīz*, *vt* to know beforehand. — *adj* **precog'nizant** having foreknowledge. [**pre-** (1)]

preconceive *prē-kən-sēv'*, *vt* to conceive or form a notion of before having actual knowledge. — *n* **preconceit'** (*obs*) a preconceived notion. — *n* **preconcep'tion** the act of preconceiving; an opinion formed in advance, without actual knowledge. [**pre-** (1)]

preconcert *prē-kən-sûrt'*, *vt* to settle beforehand. — *n* **preconcert** (*-kon'*) a previous arrangement. — *adv* **preconcert'edly**. — *n* **preconcert'edness**. [**pre-** (1)]

precondition *prē-kən-dish'ən*, *n* a condition that must be satisfied beforehand, a prerequisite. — *vt* to prepare beforehand. [**pre-** (1)]

preconize or **-ise** *prē'kə-nīz*, *vt* to proclaim; to summon publicly; (of the pope) to proclaim and ratify the election of as bishop. — *n* **preconization** or **-s-** (*prē-k-ənī-zā'shən* or *-kon-i-*). [L *praecō*, *-ōnis* a crier, a herald]

preconscious *prē-kon'shəs*, *adj* (of memories, ideas, etc) currently absent from, but which can be readily recalled to, the conscious mind (*psychol*); having occurred, existed, etc) before consciousness, or the conscious self, developed. — *n* **precon'sciousness**. [**pre-** (1)]

precontract *prē-kən-trakt'*, *vt* to contract beforehand; to betroth previously. — *n* **precontract** (*-kon'*) a previous contract or betrothal. [**pre-** (1)]

precook *prē-kōōk'*, *vt* to cook partially or completely beforehand. [**pre-** (1)]

precordial or **praecordial** *prē-kör'di-əl*, *adj* in front of the heart. [**pre-** (2), and L *cor*, *cordis* heart]

precritical *prē-krit'i-kl*, *adj* preceding a crisis or critical phase; prior to the development of the critical faculties. [**pre-** (1)]

precurrer *prē-kur'ər*, (*Shakesp*) *n* a forerunner. [L *praecurrere* to go before]

precurse *pri-kûrs'*, (*Shakesp*) *n* a prognostication, foretoken. [L *praecursus* a forerunning]

precursor *prē-kûr'sər*, *n* something that exists or goes in advance of another; an indication of the approach of an event; a forerunner, herald or harbinger; a predecessor; a substance from which the one in question is derived or manufactured (*chem*). — *adj* **precur'sory** or **precur'sive**. [L *praecurrere*, *-cursum* to run or go before, precede]

predacious or (*irreg*) **predaceous** *pri-dā'shəs*, *adj* living by prey; predatory. — *n* **predā'ciousness** or **predac'ity**. [Formed from **predatory**]

predate[1] *prē-dāt'*, *vt* to date before the true date; to antedate; to be earlier than. [**pre-** (1)]

predate[2] *pri-dāt'*, *vt* to eat, prey upon. — *vi* to hurt prey. — *n* **preda'tion** plundering, depredation; the killing and consuming of other animals for survival, the activity of preying. — *adj* **pred'ative**. [L *praedātio*, *-ōnis* from *praedāri*, *-ātus*, **predate** being a back-formation from **predation**; see **predator**]

predator *pred'ə-tər*, *n* an animal that preys on another; a predatory person, state or other body. — *adv* **pred'atorily**. — *n* **pred'atoriness**. — *adj* **pred'atory** (of creatures) killing and feeding on others; (of people, states, etc) plundering or exploiting those that are weaker; relating to or characterized by plundering or preying; destructive, deleterious (*obs*). [L *praedātor*, from *praedāri*, *-ātus* to plunder, from *praeda* booty]

predecease *prē-di-sēs'*, *vt* to die before (another person, or, unusually, an event). — Also *n* (*rare*). — *adj* **predeceased'** deceased at an earlier time. [**pre-** (1)]

predecessor *prē'di-ses'ər* or US *pred'*, *n* the person who preceded one in one's job or position; the previous version, model, etc of a particular thing, product, etc; (with reference to a day, week, etc) the one preceding the one in question; an ancestor. [L *praedēcessor*, from *prae* before, and *dēcessor* a retiring officer, from *dē* away, and *cēdere* to go, depart]

predella *pri-del'ə*, *n* the platform or uppermost step on which an altar stands; a board behind an altar, a retable; a painting or sculpture on the face of either of these; a painting in a compartment along the bottom of an altarpiece or other picture. [Ital, prob, from OHGer *pret* board]

predentate *prē-den'tāt*, *adj* having teeth in the forepart of the jaw only. [**pre-** (2)]

predesignate *prē-dez'ig-nāt* or *-des'*, *vt* to specify beforehand. — *adj* designated in advance; having the quantification of the predicate distinctly expressed (*logic*; *Sir W Hamilton*). — *n* **predesignā'tion**. — *adj* **predes'ignatory**. [**pre-** (1)]

predestine *prē-des'tin* or *pri-*, *vt* to destine or decree beforehand; to foreordain. — *adj* **predestinā'rian** believing in or relating to the doctrine of predestination. — *n* someone who holds the doctrine of predestination. — *n* **predestinā'rianism**. — *vt* **predes'tināte** to determine beforehand; to preordain by an unchangeable purpose. — *adj* (*-it*) foreordained; fated. — *n* **predestinā'tion** the act of predestinating or fact of being predestined; the doctrine that whatever is to happen has been unalterably fixed by God from the beginning of time, *esp* with regard to which souls are to be saved and which damned (*theol*); fixed fate. — *adj* **predes'tinative**. — *n* **predes'tinātor** someone who predestinates or foreordains; a predestinarian (*obs*). — *n* **predes'tiny** irrevocably fixed fate. [**pre-** (1)]

predetermine *prē-di-tûr'min*, *vt* to determine or settle beforehand. — *adj* **predeter'minable**. — *n* **predetermin'ate** (*nət*) determined beforehand. — *n* **predeterminā'tion**. — *n* **predeter'minism** determinism. [**pre-** (1)]

predevote *prē-di-vōt'*, *adj* foreordained. [**pre-** (1)]

predial. See **praedial**.

predicable *pred'i-kə-bl*, *adj* capable of being predicated or affirmed of something; attributable. — *n* anything that can be predicated of another, or *esp* of many others; one of the five attributes, ie genus, species, difference, property and accident (*logic*). — *n* **predicabil'ity**. [L *praedicabilis*, from *praedicāre* to proclaim, and *-abilis* able]

predicament *pri-dik'ə-mənt*, *n* an difficult position, a plight or dilemma; a situation or set of circumstances generally; one of the classes or categories which include all predicables (*logic*). — *adj* **predicamental** (*-ment'l*). [LL *praedicāmentum* something predicated or asserted]

predicant *pred'i-kənt*, *adj* preaching; predicating. — *n* a preacher; a preaching friar or Dominican; another spelling of predikant; an affirmer of anything. [L *praedicāns*, *-antis*, pr p of *praedicāre* to proclaim; see **predicate**]

predicate *pred'i-kāt*, *vt* to affirm or assert; to state as a property or attribute of the subject of a proposition (*logic*); to imply, entail the existence of; to make (an expression) the predicate of a proposition; to base on certain grounds (with *on*, *upon*; *US*); to preach (*rare*); sometimes erroneously for **predict**. — *n* (*-kət*) that which is predicated of the subject of a proposition, or the second term of a proposition, affirmed or denied by means of the copula (*logic*); the word or words in a sentence by which something is said about the subject (*gram*). — *n* **predicā'tion**. — *adj* **predicative** (*pri-dik'ə-tiv* or *pred'i-kā-tiv*) (*of an adjective*) contained within, *esp* normally, the predicate of a sentence (*gram*); expressing predication or affirmation; affirming or asserting. — *adv* **predicatively**. — *adj* **pred'icatory** affirmative. — **predicate calculus** see under **calculus**. [L *praedicāre*, *-ātum* to proclaim, from *prae* forth, and *dicāre* (orig) to proclaim]

predict *pri-dikt'*, *vt* to foretell, *esp* on the basis of present knowledge. — *adj* **predic'table** capable of being predicted; easily foreseen, only to be expected; boringly consistent, lacking the capacity to surprise; unoriginal, trite. — *n* **predictabil'ity** or **predic'tableness**. — *adv* **predic'tably**. — *n* **prediction** (*-shən*) the act or art of predicting; something foretold. — *adj* **predic'tive** foretelling, anticipating; prophetic. — *adv* **predic'tively**. — *n* **predic'tor** someone or something that predicts (also **predic'ter**); an anti-aircraft range-finding and radar device. [L *praedictus*, pa p of *praedīcere*, from *dīcere* to say]

predigest *prē-dī-jest'* or *-di-*, *vt* to break down (food) by means that simulate the digestive process, to make it more easily digestible; to present (literature, complex subject matter, etc) in a simplified form, or simplistically, to make it more comprehensible. — *n* **predigestion** (*-jest'yən*) preliminary digestion; hasty digestion (*obs*). [Pfx **pre-** (1)]

predikant *prā-di-känt'* or **predicant** *pred'i-kant*, *n* a Dutch Reformed preacher, *esp* in South Africa. [Du, from L *praedicāns*, *-antis*; see **predicant, preach**]

predilection *prē-di-lek'shən* or *pred-i-*, *n* a favourable predisposition; a special liking or preference. — *adj* (*rare*) **predilect'** or **predilec'ted** chosen in preference; favoured. [L *praedīligere* to prefer, from *prae* above others, and *dīligere*, *dīlectum* to love]

predispose *prē-dis-pōz'*, (often with *to*, *towards*) *vt* to dispose or incline (someone) beforehand (eg to react in a certain way); to render favourable or conducive to something; to render (someone) liable or susceptible (eg to an illness; also without direct object). — *adj* **predispō'sing**. — *n* **predisposition** (*-pə-zish'ən*). — *adj* **predisposi'tional**. [**pre-** (1)]

prednisone *pred'ni-zōn* or *-sōn*, *n* a drug similar to cortisone, used eg as an anti-inflammatory agent. [Perh from *pre*gnant, *di*ene and cort*isone*]

predominate *pri-dom'i-nāt*, *vi* to be dominant; to prevail; to be most prominent or noticeable; to be most numerous or abounding; to be superior in strength or authority; to have a commanding position. — *vt* to prevail over (*Shakesp*). — *n* **predom'inance** or **predom'inancy**. — *adj* **predom'inant** preponderating; prevailing; most numerous or prominent; ruling; having superior power; ascendant; commanding in position or effect. — *adv* **predom'inantly**. — *adj* **predom'inate** (*-nət*; *rare*) predominant. — *n* **predominā'tion**. [**pre-** (3)]

Pre-Dravidian *prē-drə-vid'i-ən*, *adj* belonging or relating to a dark, woolly-haired, broad-nosed race of people, including Sakai, Veddas and Australian aborigines. — Also *n*. [**pre-** (1)]

predy, of unknown pronunciation, (*obs naut*) *adj* cleared for action. — *vt* to make ready. [Origin uncertain; poss from make the shi*p ready*]

pree *prē*, (*Scot*) *vt* to make a trial of, *esp* by tasting or by kissing. [**prieve** (see under **prief**)]

pre-echo *prē-ek'ō*, *n* the unwanted effect of a faint sound anticipating the actual sound on a tape recording, caused by the transfer of material between surfaces of the wound tape (*audio*; see also **post-echo** under **post-**); a foretaste: — *pl* **pre-ech'oes**. [**pre-**(1)]

pre-eclampsia *prē-i-klamp'si-ə*, (*med*) *n* a toxic condition occurring in late pregnancy, with eclamptic symptoms, eg high blood pressure, excessive weight gain, proteins in the urine, oedema, and sometimes severe headaches and visual disturbances. [**pre-** (1), and see **eclampsia**]

pre-elect *prē-i-lekt'*, *vt* to choose beforehand. — *n* **pre-elec'tion** election in anticipation; preference (*obs*). — *adj* before election. [**pre-** (1)]

pre-embryo *preē-em'bri-ō*, (*biol*) *n* the name used for the formation that will become the human embryo, in the first fourteen days after fertilization: — *pl* **pre-em'bryos**. — *adj* **pre-embryon'ic**. [**pre-** (1)]

preemie, **premie** or **premy** *prē'mē*, (*US slang*) *n* short for *prem*ature baby.

pre-eminent *prē-em'i-nənt*, *adj* supreme among the eminent; more important or influential than others; surpassing others in good or bad qualities; outstanding; extreme. — *n* **prē-em'inence**. — *adv* **prē-em'inently**. [**pre-** (3)]

pre-emphasis *prē-em'fə-sis* (*telecomm*) *n* the process of increasing the strength of some frequency components of a signal to assist them to override noise or other distortion in the system. [**pre-** (1)]

pre-empt *prē-emt'* or *-empt'*, *vt* to secure as first comer; to secure by pre-emption; to take possession of, to appropriate; to forestall or thwart (a person or plan); to supplant or replace (a television programme, etc). — *vi* (*bridge*) to make a pre-emptive bid. — *adj* **prē-empt'ible**. — *n* **pre-emp'tion** the act or right of purchasing before others are offered the chance to do so; (also **pre-emption right**) the right of a citizen to purchase a certain amount of public land if certain conditions are fulfilled (*US*); a piece of land so obtained; a belligerent's right to seize neutral contraband at a fixed price; seizure; the act of attacking first to forestall hostile action. — *adj* **prē-empt'ive** having the effect of pre-empting; (of an attack or strike) effectively destroying the enemy's weapons before they can be used (*military*). — *n* **prē-empt'or**. — **prē-emptive bid** (*bridge*) an unusually high bid intended to deter others from bidding. [L *prae* before, and *emptiō*, *-ōnis* a buying, from *emere* to buy, **pre-empt** being a back-formation from **pre-emption**]

preen[1] *prēn*, *vt* (of a bird) to clean and arrange (the feathers), or to clean and arrange the feathers of (a part of the body); to groom (oneself) *esp* with evident vanity; to plume, pride or congratulate (oneself) (with *on*). — Also *vi*. — **preen gland** a bird's uropygial gland, which secretes oil used in preening the feathers. [Appar **prune²** assimilated to **preen²**]

preen² *prēn*, (*Scot*) *n* a pin. — *vt* to pin. [OE *prēon* pin, brooch]

pre-establish *prē-is-tab'lish*, *vt* to establish beforehand. — **pre-established harmony** see under **harmonic**. [**pre-** (1)]

preeve *prēv*, *n* and *vt*. An obsolete form of **proof** and **prove**.

pre-exilic *prē-eg-zil'ik*, *adj* before the exile, used of Old Testament writings prior to the Jewish exile (c. 586–538 BC). — Also **pre-exil'ian**. [**pre-** (1)]

pre-exist *prē-ig-zist'*, *vi* to exist beforehand, *esp* in a former life. — *vt* to exist before. — *n* **prē-exist'ence** previous existence, *esp* of the soul before the generation of the body with which it is united in this world, or of Christ before his incarnation (*theol*). — *adj* **prē-exist'ent**. [**pre-** (1)]

pref. *abbrev*: preface.

prefab *prē'fab*, (*colloq*) *n* a prefabricated building, *esp* a house.

prefabricate *prē-fab'ri-kāt*, *vt* to make standardized parts of beforehand, for assembling later. — *adj* **prefab'ricated** composed of such parts. — *n* **prefabricā'tion**. — *n* **prefab'ricātor**. [**pre-** (1)]

preface *pref'is*, *n* something said by way of introduction or preliminary explanation; a statement, *usu* explanatory, placed at the beginning of a book, not regarded as forming (like the introduction) part of the composition; the ascription of glory, etc, in the liturgy of consecration of the eucharist (*eccles*); anything preliminary, introductory or immediately antecedent (with *to*). — *vt* to precede or serve to introduce; to open or introduce; to provide with a preface; to say by way of preface (*obs* or *rare*); to front, place or be in front of (*rare*). — *vi* (*old*) to make preliminary remarks. — *adj* **prefacial** (*pri-fā'shl*; *rare*). — *adj* **prefatorial** (*pref-ə-tō'ri-əl* or *-tö'*) serving as a preface or introduction. — *adv* **prefato'rially** or **prefatorily** (*pref'ə-tə-ri-li*). — *adj* **pref'atory** of or pertaining to a preface; serving as a preface or introduction; introductory. [Fr *préface*, from LL *prēfātia* for L *praefātiō*, from *prae* before, and *fārī*, *fātus* to speak]

prefade *prē-fād'*, *vt* deliberately to give (newly manufactured jeans, cloth, etc) a faded appearance by some artificial process; to adjust (sound) to a suitable level before fading in (*audio*). [**pre-** (1)]

prefard *pri-fārd'*. A Spenserian form of **preferred**.

prefatorial, etc. See under **preface**.

prefect or (*esp hist RC* and *old*) **praefect** *prē'fekt*, *n* a name given to any of various officials placed in authority over others; a commander or magistrate (*Roman hist*); a school pupil with some measure of authority over others, *esp* in the form of minor disciplinary powers; the administrative head of a department in France, of a province in Italy, or of any similar administrative district elsewhere; a senior teacher at a Jesuit school, or (also **prefect apostolic**) a church official in charge of a missionary district (*RC*). — *adj* **prefectorial** (*prē-fek-tō'ri-əl* or *-tö'*). — *n* **prē'fectship**. — *adj* **prefect'ural**. — *n* **prē'fecture** the office, term of office, or district of a prefect; in Japan, any of 46 administrative districts headed by a governor; the house or office occupied by a prefect. — **prefect of police** the head of the Paris police. [OFr *prefect* (Fr *préfet*) and L *praefectus*, pa p of *praeficere*, from *prae* above, superior to, and *facere* to make]

prefer *pri-fûr'*, *vt* to hold in higher estimation; to like better (with *to*, or *rather than*; not with *than* alone); to choose or select rather or sooner than others; to advance or promote over the head of colleagues; to submit (a charge or accusation) to a court of law for consideration (*law*); to give priority to (particular creditors); to put forward, offer or present, for acceptance, etc (*archaic*); to set in front (*obs*): — *pr p* **preferring** (*pri-fûr'ing*); *pa t* and *pa p* **preferred** (*pri-fûrd'*). — *n* **preferabil'ity** (*pref-*). — *adj* **pref'erable** (*obs* **preferrable** *pri-fûr'*) to be preferred; more desirable; having priority. — *adv* **pref'erably** from choice; as is better or more desirable. — *n* **pref'erence** the choice, favouring, liking of one rather than another, estimation of one above another (*in preference to* rather than); the state of being preferred; that which is preferred; priority (**preference** (also **preferential**) **shares** or **stock** shares or stock on which dividends must be paid before those on other kinds); an advantage given to one over another; a card game resembling auction bridge. — *adj* **preferential** (*pref-ə-ren'shl*) having, giving, or allowing, a preference; discriminating in favour of someone or something (**preferential tariff** or **duties** a lower tariff or duties imposed on imports from some (eg developing) countries than on those from others; (of a ballot or voting) requiring the voter to put candidates in order of preference; see also **preference shares** above. — *n* **preferen'tialism**. — *n* **preferen'tialist** someone who favours a preferential tariff. — *adv* **preferen'tially**. — *n* **prefer'ment** advancement; promotion; a superior appointment or position, *esp* in the Church, enhancing one's social and financial status; the act of preferring. — *n* **preferr'er**. [Fr *préférer*, from L *praeferre*, from *prae* before, and *ferre* to bear]

prefigure *prē-fig'ər*, *vt* to imagine beforehand; to foreshadow or be a foretoken of. — *adj* **prefig'urate** (*-ū-rət*) prefigured. — *vt* to prefigure. — *n* **prefigūrā'tion**. — *adj* **prefig'ūrative**. — *n* **prefig'urement** (*-ər-mənt*). [**pre-** (1)]

prefix *prē-fiks'* or *prē'fiks*, *vt* to put before, or at the beginning; to add as a prefix; to fix beforehand. — *n* **pre'fix** an affix added at the beginning of a word; a title placed before a name, eg *Mr*, *Sir*. — *n* **prefixion** (*-fik'shən*). — *n* **prefix'ture**. [L *praefīgere*, *-fīxum*, from *prae* in front, and *fīgere* to fix]

prefloration *prē-flō-rā'shən* or *-flö-*, (*bot*) *n* the manner in which the petals and sepals are folded in the flower bud, aestivation. [**pre-** (1), and L *flōs*, *flōris* flower]

prefoliation *prē-fō-li-ā'shən*, (*bot*) *n* the manner in which the leaf is folded within the leaf bud, vernation. [**pre-** (1), and L *folium* leaf]

preform *pre-förm'*, *vt* to form beforehand (*Shakesp*); to determine the shape of beforehand. — *n* **prēformā'tion**. — *n* **prēformā'tionism**. — *n* **prēformā'tionist** a believer in the now exploded theory that the plant or animal (and therefore all its descendants) was already preformed in the germ (the ovum, according to the ovists, the sperm, according to the animalculists) and had only to be unfolded without formation of any new parts. — *adj* **prēfor'mative**. [**pre-** (1)]

prefrontal *prē-front'l* or *-frunt'l*, (*anatom*) *adj* in front of, or in the forepart of, the frontal bone, lobe, scale, etc; belonging or relating to such a part. — *n* a bone or scale so situated. [**pre-** (1)]

prefulgent *prē-ful'jənt*, *adj* extremely bright. [**pre-** (3)]

preggers *preg'ərz*, (*colloq*, *esp upper-class*) *adj* pregnant.

pre-glacial *prē-glā'shl*, *adj* earlier than the glacial period. [**pre-** (1)]

pregnable *preg'nə-bl*, *adj* capable of being taken by assault or force; vulnerable. [Fr *prenable*, from *prendre* to take; see **impregnable**]

pregnant¹ *preg'nənt*, *adj* (of a woman or female animal) carrying a child or young in the womb; impregnated; fertilized (*obs*); heavily laden, swelling (*obs*); fertile, teeming, fruitful (*obs*); (of the mind or wit) inventive, productive; productive of results, momentous, significant for the future; loaded (eg with significance, menace, etc); full of meaning, significance or implications; pithy, witty, to the point (eg *Shakesp*); full of promise (*obs*); receptive, disposed, ready, apt, ready to act (*Shakesp*); conveying a compressed meaning beyond what the grammatical construction can strictly carry (*gram*). — *n* **preg'nancy** or (*obs*) **preg'nance**. — *adv* **preg'nantly**. [L *praegnāns*, *-antis*, from earlier *praegnās*, *-ātis*, thought to be from *prae* before, and the root of *gnāscī* to be born]

pregnant² *preg'nent*, (*archaic*) *adj* (of evidence, proof, reasons, arguments) weighty, cogent, convincing, obvious or clear. [OFr *preignant*, pr p of *preindre*, from L *premere* to press]

pregustation *prē-gus-tā'shən*, *n* a foretaste. [**pre-** (1)]

prehallux *prē-hal'uks*, (*zool*) *n* a rudimentary innermost toe. [**pre-** (2)]

preheminence. An obsolete spelling of **pre-eminence**.

prehend *pri-hend'*, *vt* to seize or grasp (*rare*); to apprehend without conscious perception (*philos*). — *adj* **prehen'sible** (*rare*) capable of being grasped or apprehended. — *adj* **prehen'sile** (*-sīl*; *zool*) capable of grasping. — *n* **prehensility** (*prē-hen-sil'i-ti*). — *n* **prehension** (*pri-hen'shən*) the action of grasping (*zool*); intellectual or (*philos*) unconscious apprehension. — *adj* **prehensive** prehensile, relating to grasping (*zool*); relating to (unconscious) apprehension. — *n* **prehen'sor** someone or something that grasps or seizes. — *adj* **prehen'sory** or **prehenso'rial** prehensile (*zool*). [L *praehendere*, *-hēnsum* to seize]

prehistoric *prē-his-tor'ik* or **prehistorical** *prē-his-tor'i-kəl*, *adj* belonging or relating to a time before extant historical records; antiquated, completely out of date (*colloq*); primitive (*colloq*). — *n* **prēhistō'rian**. — *adv* **prēhistor'ically**. — *n* **prēhis'tory**. [**pre-** (1)]

prehnite *prā'nīt*, (*mineralogy*) *n* a zeolite-like mineral, an acid calcium aluminium silicate, *usu* a pale green. [Named after Colonel van *Prehn*, who brought it from S Africa in the 18c]

prehuman *prē-hū'mən*, *adj* at a stage of development before full humanity has been developed; earlier than the appearance of man. [**pre-** (1)]

preif or **preife** *prēf*. Obsolete forms of **proof**.

pre-ignition *prē-ig-nish'ən*, *n* the premature ignition of the explosive mixture of fuel and air in an internal-combustion engine. [**pre-** (1)]

prejink *pri-jingk'*. Same as **perjink**.

prejudge *prē-juj'*, *vt* to judge or decide upon before hearing the whole case, or all sides, etc; to condemn unheard. — *n* **prejudge'ment** or **prejudg'ment**. [Fr *préjuger*, from L *praeiudicāre*; see **prejudicate**]

prejudicate *pri-jōō'di-kāt*, (*obs*) *vt* to spoil, prejudice; to influence or bias, to prejudice; to judge beforehand. — *vi* to act in a prejudicial manner; to form an opinion beforehand. — *adj* (*-kət*) (of an opinion) preconceived; (of a person) biased; settled in advance (*rare*). — *adj* **preju'dicant** (*-kənt*) prejudging. — *n* **prejudicā'tion**. — *adj* **prejud'icātive**. [L *praejūdicāre*, *-ātum*, from *prae* before, and *judicāre* to judge]

prejudice *prej'ōō-dis*, *n* a judgement or opinion formed prematurely or without due consideration of relevant issues; prepossession or bias in favour of or against anything; unthinking hostility; injury or harm; disadvantage; a prejudgement (*obs*); (*Spenser* **prejudize**) prognostication. — *vt* to fill with prejudice; to prepossess or bias in favour or against something; to injure, harm or endanger; to prejudge, *esp* unfavourably (*obs*). — *adj* **prej'udiced** having prejudice; biased. — *adj* **prejudicial** (*-dish'l*) injurious; detrimental; prejudiced (*obs*). — *adv* **prejudic'ially**. — **without prejudice** a phrase used to require an understanding that nothing said at this stage is to detract from one's rights, to damage claims arising from future developments, or to constitute an admission of liability. [Fr *préjudice* injury, wrong, and L *praejūdicium* a previous judgement, harm, injury, from *prae* before, and *jūdicium* judgement]

pre-judicial *prē-jōō-dish'l*, (*law*) *adj* relating to matters to be decided before a case comes to court. [L *praejūdicium* a preliminary enquiry]

prelacy. See **prelate**.

prelapsarian *prē-lap-sā'ri-ən*, *adj* belonging or relating to the time before the Fall, Man's first lapse in sin. [**pre-** (1), and L *lāpsus* a fall]

prelate *prel'it*, *n* an ecclesiastic of high rank; an abbot or prior or the superior of a religious order; a clergyman; a chief priest (*obs*): — *fem* **prel'atess**. — *n* **prelacy** (*prel'ə-si*) the office or authority of a prelate; the order of bishops or the bishops collectively; church government by prelates; episcopacy. — *n* **prel'ateship**. — *adj* **prelatial** (*pri-lā'shəl*) of a prelate. — *adj* **prelatic** (*pri-lat'ik*) or **prelat'ical** relating to prelates or prelacy; episcopal or episcopalian (*derog*). — *adv* **prelat'ically**. — *n* **prelā'tion** preferment; promotion; eminence. — *adj* **prel'atish** (*Milton*). — *n* **prel'atism** (*usu derog*) episcopacy or episcopalianism; domination by prelates. — *n* **prel'atist** an upholder of prelacy. — *vt* and *vi* **prel'atize** or **-ise** to make or to become prelatical. — *n* **prel'ature** (*Milton*). — *n* **prel'aty** prelacy. [Fr *prélat*, from L *praelātus*, from *prae* before, and *lātus* borne]

prelect *pri-lekt'*, *vi* to lecture. — *n* **prelec'tion**. — *n* **prelec'tor** a public reader or lecturer. [L *praelegere*, *-lectum*, from *prae* in front, and *legere* to read]

prelibation *prē-lī-bā'shən*, *n* a foretaste; an offering of first-fruits. [L *praelībātiō*, *-ōnis*, from *prae* before, and *lībāre* to taste]

prelim *prē'lim* or *pri-lim'*, (*colloq*; often in *pl*) *n* a preliminary or entrance examination; (in *pl*) the preliminary matter, ie titles, preface, contents list, introduction, of a printed book (*printing*).

preliminary *pri-lim'i-nə-ri*, *adj* introductory; preparatory; preceding or preparing for the main matter. — *n* an introductory or preparatory measure, activity, statement, etc (often in *pl*, **prelim'inaries**); a preliminary or entrance examination. — *adv* **prelim'inarily**. [L *prae* before, and *līmen*, *-inis* threshold]

prelingual *prē-ling'gwəl*, *adj* before the use of language. — **prelingually deaf** deaf since before the acquisition of language, ie from birth (see also **post-lingual** under **post-**). [**pre-** (1)]

prelude *prel'ūd*, *n* an event that precedes and prepares the ground for one more momentous; anything done, said, performed, etc by way of an introduction or preliminary; a preliminary strain, passage or flourish, often improvised (*music*); an introduction to or first movement of a suite, or a movement preceding a fugue (*music*); an overture (*music*); an introductory voluntary (*music*); a short independent composition with a recurring motif, *esp* for the piano; a poetical composition of introductory nature or function. — *vt* (*prel'ūd* or *esp* formerly *pri-lūd'* or *-lōōd'*) to precede as a prelude, serve as prelude to; to introduce with a prelude; to perform as a prelude. — *vi* to provide a prelude; to perform a prelude; to serve as a prelude. — *adj* **preludial** and **preludious** (*pri-lōō'* or *-lū'*; *rare*). — *adj* **prelusive** (*-lōō'siv*, *lū'*) of the nature of a prelude; introductory. — *adv* **prelu'sively** and **prelu'sorily**. — *adj* **prelu'sory** (*-sə-ri*) introductory. [Fr *prélude*, from LL *praelūdium*, from L *lūdere* to play]

preludio *pre-lōō'di-ō*, (*Ital*) *n* a prelude: — *pl* **prelu'di** (*-dē*).

premandibular *prē-man-dib'ū-lər*, (*anatom*) *adj* in front of the lower jaw. — *n* a bone so placed in fishes, etc. [**pre-** (2)]

premarital *prē-mar'i-təl*, *adj* before marriage. [**pre-** (1)]

premature *prem'ə-tūr*, *prē'mə-* or *-tūr'*, *adj* occurring before the usual or expected time; unduly early; over-hasty; (of a human baby) born less than 37 weeks after conception, or (sometimes) having a birth weight of between $2\frac{1}{2}$ and $5\frac{1}{2}$ pounds irrespective of length of gestation; ripe before the due time. — *adv* **prematurely**. — *n* **prematureness**. — *n* **prematur'ity**. [L *praemātūrus*, from *prae* in advance, and *mātūrus* ripe]

premaxilla *prē-mak-sil'ə*, (*anatom*) *n* a bone in front of the maxilla: — *pl* **premaxill'ae** (*-ē*). — *adj* **premaxill'ary** (or *-mak'*). — *n* the premaxilla. [**pre-** (2)]

premed *prē-med'* (*colloq*) *adj* premedical. — *n* premedication; (also **premed'ic**) a premedical student; premedical studies.

premedical *prē-med'i-kl*, *adj* of or relating to a course of study undertaken in preparation for professional medical training. [**pre-** (1)]

premedicate *prē-med'i-kāt*, *vt* to administer premedication to. — *n* **premedicā'tion** drugs given to sedate and prepare a patient, *esp* for the administration of a general anaesthetic prior to surgery, etc. [**pre-** (1)]

premeditate *prē-med'i-tāt*, *vt* to plan or think out beforehand; to meditate upon beforehand. — *vi* to deliberate beforehand. — *adj* **premed'itated**. — *adv* **premed'itātedly**. — *n* **premeditā'tion**. — *adj* **premed'itātive**. [L *praemeditārī*, *-ātus*, from *prae* before, and *meditārī* to meditate]

premenstrual *prē-men'stro͞o-əl*, *adj* preceding menstruation. — **premenstrual tension** or **syndrome** a condition characterized by a variety of symptoms, eg depression, nervous tension, headaches and pain in the breasts, caused by hormonal changes preceding menstruation (*abbrev* **PMT** or **PMS**). [**pre-** (1)]

premia. See **premium**.

premie. See **preemie**.

premier *prem'i-ər*, *-yər*, also *prēm'i-ər*, or (formerly) *pri-mēr'*, or (in French context) *prə-myā*, *adj* prime or first; chief; leading, principal (as in *premier danseur* the principal male dancer of a ballet company, etc); most ancient, created earliest (as in *premier earl*) (*heraldry*, *etc*). — *n* a person of chief rank or office; a prime minister or head of government; the Secretary of State (*obs*; *US*). — *n* **première** (*prəm-yer'* or *prem'yər*) the first performance of a play or showing of a film (also **premiere**); the principal female dancer of a ballet company, a prima ballerina (also **première danseuse** *dā-søz*); a leading lady in a theatrical company. — *vt* (also **premiere**, **premier**) to give a first showing or performance of. — Also *vi*. — *n* **prem'iership** the office of prime minister; in Australia, a competition between sporting clubs, or victory in this. [Fr *premier* (fem *première*), from L *prīmārius* of the first rank, from *prīmus* first]

premier cru *prə-myā krü*, (*Fr*) *n* the best of the grands crus (qv under **grand**[2]).

premillenarian *prē-mil-ə-nā'ri-ən*, *n* a believer in the premillennial coming of Christ. — Also *adj*. — *n* **premillena'rianism**. [**pre-** (1)]

premillennial *prē-mil-en'yəl*, *adj* before the millennium. — *n* **premillenn'ialism** premillenarianism. — *n* **premillenn'ialist**. [**pre-** (1)]

premise *prem'is*, *n* a proposition stated or assumed for the sake of argument, *esp* one of the two propositions in a syllogism from which the conclusion is drawn (*logic*; also **prem'iss**); (*usu* in *pl*) the matter set forth at the beginning of a deed (*law*); (in *pl*) the beginning of a deed setting forth its subject-matter (*law*); (in *pl*) the aforesaid (property; *law*); hence, a building and its adjuncts, *esp* a public house or place of business; a presupposition (also **prem'iss**); a condition stipulated beforehand (*Shakesp*); (in *pl*) antecedent happenings or circumstances (*Shakesp*). — *vt* **premise** (*pri-mīz'* or *prem'is*) to mention or state first, or by way of introduction; to prefix; to state or assume as a premise; to perform or administer as a preliminary (*med*). — *adj* **premī'sed** (*Shakesp*) sent before due time. [Fr *prémisse* from L (*sententia*, etc) *praemissa* (a sentence, etc) put before, from *prae* before, and *mittere*, *missum* to send]

premium *prē'mi-əm*, *n* a sum regularly payable for insurance; an admission fee paid by someone entering an apprenticeship or profession; a sum added to a fixed wage, rate, etc, a bonus; excess over original price or par (opposite of *discount*); anything offered as an incentive to buy; a reward, prize or bounty: — *pl* **pre'miums** or (*rare*) **pre'mia**. — *adj* of highest quality, and so costly. — **Premium Bond** or **Premium Savings Bond** a Government bond, the holder of which gains no interest, but is eligible for a money prize allotted by a draw held at stated intervals. — **at a premium** in great demand; above par; **put a premium on** to attach particular value to, to esteem highly. [L *praemium* prize, reward, from *prae* above, and *emere* to buy]

premolar *prē-mō'lər*, (*anatom*) *adj* in front of the true molar teeth. — *n* a tooth between the canine and molars (called molar or milk-molar in the milk dentition). [**pre-** (2)]

premonish *prē-mon'ish*, (*rare*) *vt* to admonish or warn beforehand. — *n* **premon'ishment**. [**pre-** (1); modelled on **admonish**]

premonition *prē-mə-nish'ən* or *prem-* *n* a feeling that something is going to happen before it actually does, a presentiment or intuition; a forewarning. — *adj* **premon'itive** or **premon'itory** conveying a warning or premonition. — *n* **premon'itor** someone or something that gives warning beforehand. — *adv* **premon'itorily**. [L *praemonēre* to give prior warning to, from *prae* before, and *monēre* to warn]

Premonstratensian *pri-mon-strə-ten'shən*, *-shyən* or *si-ən*, *adj* of an order of canons regular, the Norbertines or White Canons, founded by St Norbert in 1119 at *Prémontré* near Laon, or of a corresponding order of nuns. — *n* a member of the order. — Also (*n* and *adj*) **Premon'strant**. [L *prātum mōnstrātum* the meadow pointed out, or (*locus*) *praemōnstrātus* (the place) foreshown (in a vision), ie *Prémontré*]

premorse *pri-mörs'*, *adj* ending abruptly, as if bitten off. [L *praemorsus* bitten in front, from *prae* in front, and *mordēre*, *morsum* to bite]

premosaic *prē-mō-zā'ik*, *adj* before the time of *Moses*. [**pre-** (1) and **Mosaic**]

premotion *prē-mō'shən*, *n* an (*esp* divine) impulse determining the will. [**pre-** (1)]

premove *prē-mo͞ov'*, *vt* to incite or prompt to action. — *n* **premove'ment**. [**pre-** (1)]

premy. See **preemie**.

prenasal *prē-nā'zl*, (*anatom*) *adj* in front of the nose. — *n* a bone at the tip of the nose, as in pigs. [**pre-** (2)]

prenatal *prē-nā'tl*, *adj* before birth. — **prenatal therapy** see **metamorphic technique** under **metamorphosis**. [**pre-** (1)]

prenominate *pri-nom'i-nāt*, *vt* to name or state beforehand. — *adj* (*-nət* or *-nāt*) forenamed. [**pre-** (1)]

prenotion *prē-nō'shən*, *n* a preconception. [**pre-** (1)]

prent *prent*, (*Scot*). Same as **print**.

prentice or **'prentice** *pren'tis*. Aphetic for **apprentice**. — *n* **pren'ticeship** or **'pren'ticeship**.

prenzie *appar adj* in *Shakesp* (*Measure for Measure*, III.1. 92 and 95) variously explained as representing primsie, princely, Fr *prenez garde*, or connected with **prone**[2] (a homily), or a misprint.

preoccupy *prē-ok'ū-pī*, *vt* to engross or fill the mind of (someone) or dominate (someone's attention, thoughts, mind, etc) to the exclusion of other concerns; to prejudice, bias (*obs*); to occupy, fill or (*obs*) wear beforehand or before others. — *n* **prēocc'upancy** the circumstance of occupying before others; the condition of being preoccupied. — *n* **prēocc'upant** a prior occupant. — *vt* **prēocc'upate** (*obs*) to preoccupy; to anticipate. — *n* **prēoccupā'tion** absorption, engrossment; abstraction, pensiveness; an enthusiasm, chief interest or obsession; prejudice (*obs*); the act or fact of occupying beforehand or before others. — *adj* **prēocc'upied** lost in thought, abstracted; having one's attention wholly taken up, engrossed (with *with*); already occupied; (of a genus or species name) not available for adoption because it has already been applied to another group. [**pre-** (1)]

preoption *prē-op'shən*, *n* (the right of) first choice. [**pre-** (1)]

preordain *prē-ör-dān'*, *vt* to ordain, appoint or determine beforehand. — *n* **preordain'ment**. — *n* **preor'dinance** a rule previously established; that which is ordained beforehand. — *n* **preordinā'tion** the act of preordaining. [**pre-** (1)]

prep *prep*, (*colloq*) *n* a preparatory school (also **prep school**); a pupil in a preparatory school; a preparatory race, ie a minor one that tests a horse's capabilities before the major one (*horse-racing*); preparation, homework (*school slang*). — *vt* (*orig NAm*; *med*) to prepare (a patient) for an operation, etc: — *pr p* **prepp'ing**; *pa t* and *pa p* **prepped**.

prep. *abbrev*: preparation.

prepack *prēpak'*, *vt* to pack (eg food) before offering for sale. — *adj* **prēpacked'**. [**pre-** (1)]

prepaid. See **prepay**.

preparation, **preparative**, **preparator**. See under **prepare**.

preparatory *pri-par'ə-tə-ri, adj* introductory, preliminary, antecedent; serving to prepare; attending a preparatory school or undergoing preparatory instruction. — *adv* preparatorily, previous or prior (with *to*). — *adv* **prepar'atorily**. — **preparatory school** a *usu* private school that prepares pupils for public school or other higher school; a private school that prepares young people for college (*NAm*). [LL *praeparātōrius*, from *parāre* to prepare]

prepare *pri-pār'*, *vt* to make or get ready; to equip or fit out; to bring into a suitable state for some purpose; to put into the necessary frame of mind, to brace mentally (for, or to do, something); to adapt, adjust, acclimatize in readiness (for, or to do, something); to train, eg for an examination; to learn, eg for examination purposes; to make a preliminary study of (work prescribed for a class); to provide, supply (*archaic*); to bring into a required state by subjecting to some technical process; to make, produce, mix or compound (eg a chemical) by some process; to cook and dress for serving (food, a meal); to think out beforehand (eg a plan, strategy); to draw up (a document, report, etc); to anticipate or lead up to (eg a discord by use of the dissonant note as a consonance in the preceding chord; *music*). — *vi* to make oneself ready; to make preparations; to be under preparation (*esp archaic*). — *n* preparation (*Shakesp*). — *n* **preparation** (*prep-ə-rā'shən*) the act or process of preparing; a preliminary measure or arrangement; the process or course of being prepared; the preliminary study of prescribed classwork, homework; readiness; something that has been prepared or made up, eg a medicine, ointment, application, etc; an anatomical or other specimen prepared for study or preservation; the day before the Sabbath or other Jewish feast-day; devotional exercises, prayers, etc preparing for or introducing an office, eg Holy Communion; the previous introduction, as an integral part of a chord, of a note continued into a succeeding dissonance (*music*). — *adj* **preparative** (*pri-par'ə-tiv*) serving to prepare; preliminary. — *n* something done, performed, administered, etc, to prepare the way; a preparation. — *adv* **prepar'atively**. — *n* **prepar'ator** (*esp technical; old*) someone who prepares medicines, scientific specimens, etc. — *adj* **prepared** (*pri-pārd'*) made ready, fit or suitable; already treated or processed, ready mixed or ready made; ready, willing, or not disinclined (to do something). — *adv* **preparedly** (*-rid-li*). — *n* **prepāredness** (*-rid-nəs*). — *n* **prepā'rer**. [Fr *préparer*, from L *praeparāre*, from *prae* before, and *parāre* to make ready]

prepay *prē'pā'*, *vt* to pay before or in advance: — *pa t* and *pa p* **prēpaid'**. — *adj* **prepay'able**. — *n* **prepay'ment**. [**pre-** (1)]

prepense *pri-pens'*, *adj* (*esp law*) premeditated; intentional, chiefly in the phrase 'malice prepense', ie malice aforethought or intentional. — *vt* (*Spenser*) to consider. — *adv* **prepense'ly**. — *adj* **prepens'ive** (*Fielding*). [OFr *purpense*]

prepollence *pri-pol'əns, n* predominance. — *n* **prepoll'ency**. — *adj* **prepoll'ent**. [LL *praepollentia*, from *prae* beyond, above, and *pollēre* to be strong]

prepollex *prē-pol'əks*, (*zool*) *n* (in some animals) a rudimentary innermost finger. [**pre-** (2)]

preponderate[1] *pri-pon'də-rāt, vi* to prevail or exceed in number, quantity, importance, influence, or force (with *over*); to weigh more; to turn the balance. — *vt* (*obs*) to outweigh. — *n* **prepon'derance** or **prepon'derancy**. — *adj* **prepon'derant**. — *adv* **prepon'derantly** or **prepon'derātingly**. [L *praeponderāre, -ātum*, from *prae* above, beyond, and *ponderāre, -ātum* to weigh, from *pondus* a weight]

preponderate[2] *pri-pon'də-rāt*, (*Fielding*) *vt* and *vi* to ponder beforehand. [**pre-** (1)]

prepone *prē-pōn'*, *vt* to reschedule for an earlier time or date, to advance or bring forward. [**pre-** (1), on the model of **postpone**]

prepose *prē-pōz'*, (*gram*, etc) *vt* to place or prefix (a word, etc) before another. [L *praepōnere, -positum* to place in front]

preposition[1] *prep-ə-zish'ən*, (*gram*) *n* a word placed *usu* before a pronoun, noun or its equivalent to express position, movement, circumstance, etc relative to or affecting it; a prefix (*obs*). — *adj* **preposi'tional**. — *adv* **preposi'tionally**. [L *praepositiō, -ōnis*, from *praepōnere, -positum*, from *prae* before, and *pōnere* to place]

preposition[2] *prē-pə-zish'ən*, (*esp gram*) *n* position in front. [**pre-** (2)]

prepositive *pri-poz'i-tiv*, (*gram*) *adj* placed before or prefixed to another word. — *adv* **prepos'itively**. [LL *praepositīus*, from *praepōnere, -positum* to place in front]

prepositor. See **praepostor**.

prepossess *prē-pə-zes'*, *vt* to bias or prejudice, *esp* favourably, to impress; to preoccupy; to fill (eg the mind) beforehand with some opinion or feeling; to possess or take beforehand (*obs* or *law*). — *adj* **prepossessed'** biased, prejudiced. — *adj* **prepossess'ing** tending to prepossess; making a favourable impression; attractive, pleasing. — *adv* **prepossess'ingly**. — *n* **prepossession** (*-zesh'ən*) bias, *usu* favourable; preoccupation; previous possession. [**pre-** (1)]

preposter. See **praepostor**.

preposterous *pri-pos'tə-rəs, adj* utterly absurd; contrary to the order of nature or reason; literally inverted, having or putting the last first (*rare*). — *adv* **prepos'terously**. — *n* **prepos'terousness**. [L *praeposterus* reversed, from *prae* before, and *posterus* after]

prepotent *prē-pō'tənt, adj* powerful in a very high degree; prevailing over others or another in taking effect; (of a parent) having a stronger fertilizing influence and therefore the ability to transmit to offspring more hereditary characteristics than the other parent (*biol*); taking precedence in effect. — *n* **prepo'tence** or **prepo'tency**. [**pre-** (3)]

preppy *prep'i*, (*orig NAm colloq*) *adj* vaguely denoting the style and looks of those who (might wish to seem to) have attended a preparatory school (qv), ie expensively fashionable in a neatly groomed, respectably conservative way. — *n* a present or former pupil of a preparatory school, or someone cultivating the appearance of one. — *adv* **prepp'ily**. — *n* **preppi'ness**. [**prep school**]

pre-print *prē'-print*, *n* part of a publication printed in advance. [**pre-** (1)]

prepuberty *prē-pū-bər-ti*, *n* the period of childhood before, *esp* immediately before, puberty. — *adj* **prepu'bertal**. [**pre-** (1)]

prepubescent *prē-pū-bes'ənt, adj* prepubertal. [**pre-** (1)]

prepuce *prē'pūs*, (*anatom*) *n* the loose skin of the penis, the foreskin; a similar fold of skin over the clitoris. — *adj* **preputial** (*pri-pū'shyəl* or *-shəl*). [L *praepūtium*]

prepunctual *prē-pungk'tū-əl, adj* more than punctual; coming before time. [**pre-** (3)]

pre-qualify *prē-kwol'i-fī, vi* to qualify beforehand (eg for a short list). — *n* **pre-qualificā'tion**. [**pre-** (1)]

prequel *prē'kwəl*, (*colloq*) *n* a film or book produced as a follow-up to one that has proved a success, based on the same leading characters but showing what happened before the start of the original story. [**pre-** (1) and **sequel**]

Pre-Raphaelite or (as spelt by D G Rossetti) **Praeraphaelite** *prē-raf'ā-ə-līt, n* someone who seeks to return to the spirit and manner of painters before the time of *Raphael* (1483–1520); a member of a group (the Pre-Raphaelite Brotherhood, or 'PRB', 1848) of painters and others (D G Rossetti, W Holman Hunt, J E Millais, etc) who practised or advocated a truthful, almost rigid, adherence to natural forms and effects. — Also *adj*. — *n* **Pre-Raph'aelism** or **Pre-Raph'aelitism**. — *adj* **Pre-Raphaelis'tic** or **Pre-Raphaelitis'tic**. — *adj* **Pre-Raphaeli'tish**. [**pre-** (1), *Raphael*, and sfx **-ite**]

prerelease *prē-ri-lēs'*, *n* the release of a motion-picture film before its official date of release; the exhibition of a film so released. — Also *adj*. [**pre-** (1)]

prerequisite *prē-rek'wi-zit*, *n* a condition or requirement that must previously be satisfied. — *adj* required as a condition of something else. [**pre-** (1)]

prerogative *pri-rog'ə-tiv*, *n* a privilege that is exclusive to a person, group, etc; a right arising out of one's rank, position or office; a faculty peculiar to the nature of any being, eg a human being; the right of voting first (*rare*). — *adj* arising out of or held by prerogative; voting first. — *adj* **prerog'atived** (*Shakesp*) having a prerogative. — *adv* **prerog'atively**. — **Prerogative Court** formerly, a court having jurisdiction over testamentary matters. — **royal prerogative** the discretionary rights which a sovereign has by virtue of office, varying from country to country. [L *praerogātīvus* asked first for his vote, from *prae* before others, and *rogāre*, *-ātum* to ask]

prerosion *prē-rō'zhən*, *n* corrosion of a crystal by a solvent forming new faces (*prerosion faces*) on the corners and edges. [L *praerōdere*, *-rōsum* to gnaw at the tip, from *prae* in front, and *rōdere* to gnaw]

prerupt *prē-rupt'*, *adj* broken off; abrupt. [L *praeruptus*, from *prae* in front, and *rumpere* to break]

Pres. *abbrev*: President.

pres. *abbrev*: present.

presa *prā'sä*, *-sə* or *-zä*, *n* a symbol (·X·, ·S· or :S:) used to indicate the points at which successive voice or instrumental parts enter a round, canon, etc: — *pl* **pre'se** (*-sā* or *-zā*). [Ital, an act of taking up]

presage *pri-sāj'*, *vt* to portend; to forebode; to warn of as something to come; to forecast; to have a presentiment of; to point out, reveal (*Spenser*). — *vi* to have or utter a foreboding. — *n* (*pres'ij*, formerly also *pri-sāj'*) an indication of the future; a prognostic; an omen; a foreboding; a presentiment. — *adj* **presage'ful**. — *n* **presage'ment** (*obs*). — *n* **presa'ger**. [L *praesāgium* a foreboding, from *prae* before, and *sāgus* prophetic]

presanctify *prē-sangk'ti-fī*, *vt* to consecrate beforehand. — *n* **presanctificā'tion**. [**pre-** (1)]

presbycousis or **presbycusis** *pres-bi-koo'sis*, or **presbyacousis** or **presbyacusis** *-ə-koo'sis*, (*med*) *n* progressive loss of hearing with advancing old age. [Gr *presbys* old, and *akousis* hearing]

presbyopia *prez-bi-ō'pi-ə*, *n* difficulty in accommodating the eye to near vision, long-sightedness, a defect increasing with age (also **pres'byopy**). — *n* **pres'byope** someone suffering from presbyopia. — *adj* **presbyopic** (*-op'ik*). [Gr *presbys* old, and *ōps*, *ōpos* the eye]

presbyte *prez'bīt*, *n* in strict etymological sense, an old man, but used for a presbyopic person. — *adj* **presbyt'ic** (*-bit'*). — *n* **pres'bytism**. [Gr *presbȳtēs* an old man]

presbyter *prez'bi-tər*, *n* (in the Presbyterian Church) an elder; (in Episcopal churches) a minister or priest ranking between a bishop and a deacon; a member of a presbytery; a presbyterian (*obs*). — *adj* **presbyt'eral** of a presbyter or presbyters. — *n* **presbyt'erate** (*-rət*) the office of presbyter; a body of presbyters; the order of presbyters. — *adj* **presbyterial** (*-tē'ri-əl*) of a presbytery; of church government by elders. — *adv* **presbytē'rially**. — *n* **pres'bytership**. — *n* **pres'bytery** a church court ranking next above the kirk session, consisting of the ministers and one ruling elder from each church within a certain district; the district so represented; the presbyterian system; part of a church reserved for the officiating priests, the eastern extremity; a priest's house (*RC*). [Gr *presbyteros*, comparative of *presbys* old]

Presbyterian *pres-bi-tē'ri-ən*, *adj* of or belonging to any Protestant Church with a system of government by elders or presbyters developed as a result of the Reformation led by Calvin in Geneva and by John Knox in Scotland; (also without *cap*) of, relating to or maintaining this form of church government. — *n* a member of such a church; (also without *cap*) an upholder of the Presbyterian system. — *n* **Presbytē'rianism** (also without *cap*) the form of church government by presbyters. — *vt* and *vi* (also without *cap*) **Presbytē'rianize** or **-ise** to make or become Presbyterian; to move towards Presbyterianism. — **Reformed Presbyterian Church** the Cameronians (qv); **United Presbyterian Church** a religious body formed by the union of the Secession and Relief Churches in 1847, included in the United Free Church from 1900, and (except a minority) in the Church of Scotland from 1929. [Eccles L *presbytērium* presbytery]

preschool *prē'skool'* or *prē'skool*, *adj* before school; not yet at school. — *n* a nursery school or kindergarten. — *n* **prē'schooler** a preschool child. [**pre-** (1)]

prescience *pres'i-əns*, *presh'*, *-əns*, *-yəns* or *prē'*, *n* foreknowledge; foresight. — *adj* **pre'scient**. — *adv* **pre'sciently**. [L *praesciēns*, *-entis*, pr p of *praescīre*, from *prae* before, and *scīre* to know]

prescientific *prē-sī-ən-tif'ik*, *adj* of or relating to the time before the scientific age, before knowledge was systematized. [**pre-** (1)]

prescind *pri-sind'*, *vt* to cut off, cut short, separate; to abstract. — *vi* to withdraw one's attention (*usu* with *from*). — *adj* **prescind'ent**. — *n* **prescission** (*pri-sish'-ən*). [L *praescindere* to cut off in front]

prescious *pre'shyəs* or *prē'*, *adj* prescient. [L *praescius*, from *praescīre*; cf **prescience**]

prescission. See under **prescind**.

prescribe *pri-skrīb'*, *vt* to lay down as a rule or direction; to give as an order; to enjoin (*archaic*); to give instructions for the preparation and dispensing of (a medicine, etc) or for (a certain procedure, diet, etc), as a remedy (*med*); to limit, confine, set bounds to (*obs*); to claim as a prescriptive right (*law*; *obs*). — *vi* to lay down rules; to give or make out a prescription (*med*); to make a claim on account of long possession (with *to*, *for*; *law*); to become unenforceable or invalid through time, to lapse (*law*). — *n* **prescrib'er**. — *n* **prescript** (*prē'skript*; formerly *-skript'*; *archaic*) an ordinance or rule; a remedy or treatment prescribed. — *adj* (*prē'* or *-skript'*; *rare*) prescribed. — *n* **prescriptibil'ity** (*pri-*). — *adj* **prescrip'tible** (*law*; *rare*) subject to prescription; invalidated by lapse of time. — *n* **prescrip'tion** the act of prescribing or directing; a written direction for the preparation or dispensing of a medicine (**by** or **on prescription** (obtainable) on presentation of a doctor's prescription); the medicine itself; a formula or recipe; enjoyment, possession, use, etc from time immemorial or for a period of time fixed by law by which a legal right or title is acquired (*law*; also **positive prescription**); any claim based on long use, or an established custom taken as authoritative; limitation of time within which action may be taken (*law*; also **negative prescription**). — *adj* **prescrip'tive** prescribing, laying down rules; pronouncing on right and wrong usage (*linguistics*); (of a right, etc) consisting in, or acquired by, custom or long-continued use; customary. — *adv* **prescrip'tively**. — *n* **prescrip'tiveness**. — *n* **prescrip'tivism** (recommendation of) the practice of laying down rules, *esp* on correct and incorrect usage in language; the contention that moral pronouncements have prescriptive force in the manner of imperatives, and no truth value (*philos*). — *n* **prescrip'tivist**. [L *praescrībere*, *-scrīptum* to write before, lay down in advance, object to, from *prae* before, in front, and *scrībere* to write]

prescutum *prē-skūt'əm*, *n* a tergal plate in front of the scutum of insects (*entomol*). [**pre-** (1)]

prese. See **presa**.

preselect *prē-si-lekt'*, *vt* to select beforehand. — *n* **preselec'tion**. — *n* **preselec'tor** a component of a radio receiver, improving reception. [**pre-** (1)]

pre-sell *prē-sel'*, *vt* to sell (something) before it has been produced. [**pre-** (1)]

presence *prez'əns*, *n* the state or circumstance of being present (opposite of *absence*); one's attendance at an event, etc; someone's company or immediate neighbourhood; the place where a great personage is; a presence-chamber (*obs*); an assembly, *esp* of great persons (*obs*); the physical impression created by one's person; imposing, commanding or authoritative physical bearing; military or political representation or influence; a being felt to be present, *esp* in a supernatural way. — **presence chamber** the room in which a great personage receives company. — **in the presence of** in front of, or in the near vicinity of (someone); **presence of mind** the power of keeping one's wits about one; coolness and readiness in emergency, danger or surprise; **real presence** (*theol*) the true and substantial presence, according to the belief of Roman Catholics, Eastern Orthodox, etc, of the body and blood of Christ in the eucharist. [OFr, from L *praesentia*; see **present**[1]]

pre-senile *prē-sē'nīl*, (*med*) *adj* belonging to or typical of the period of life preceding, *esp* just preceding, old age. — **pre-senile dementia** a condition similar to senile dementia that has its onset in middle age. [**pre-** (1)]

presension. See under **presentient**.

present[1] *prez'ənt*, *adj* being here or in the place in question (opposite of *absent*); ready at hand; found or existing in the thing in question; now under view or consideration; now existing, not past or future; denoting a verb tense used to express an action happening or condition existing just now, or for making general statements (*gram*); (of a verb or participle) in or of the present tense (*gram*); immediate; (with *to*) having a place in, entering into (the thoughts, mind, etc; *old*); (of a person, the mind, etc) attentive to the matter in hand, not absent or abstracted (*obs*). — *n* the present time; the present tense; a verb in the present tense; the present business or occasion; the present document or (in *pl*) writings (*law*, etc). — *adv* **pres'ently** at present, now (*obs* or *Scot* and *NAm*); before long, in a while; directly, immediately; necessarily, inevitably, ipso facto (*old*); for the time being (*obs*); at once (*obs*). — *n* **pres'entness**. — *adj* **pres'ent-day** belonging to or found in the present time, contemporary. — **at present** at the present time, now; **for the present** as far as concerns the present time, for the moment; now, for the time being. [OFr, from L *praesēns*, *-sentis* present]

present[2] *prez'ənt*, *n* a gift; a percentage of the prize money given to a winning jockey (*horse-racing*). [OFr *present*, orig presence, hence gift (from the phrase *mettre en present à*, to put into the presence of, hence to offer as a gift to)]

present[3] *pri-zent'*, *vt* to give, make a gift of (something to someone) or furnish (someone with something *esp* as a gift) *esp* formally or ceremonially; to deliver, convey or hand over; to introduce (one person to another, *esp* more distinguished, person); to introduce (someone) at court; to betake (oneself) to an appointed place to await instructions, interviews, etc; to bring (an actor or other performer) before the public, on stage, etc; to stage (a play), show (a film), etc; to introduce or compère (a television or radio show); to exhibit to view; to have as a characteristic; to pose or set (a problem, etc) or burden (someone with a problem, etc); to offer for consideration or acceptance (ideas, proposals, etc); to offer (a sight or other perceptual data) to the senses; to set out (written work, etc) in any manner; (of an idea, opportunity, etc) to suggest or offer (itself); to hand over (a cheque) for acceptance or (a bill) for payment; to assemble arguments for, and expound (a case); to depict, portray or represent; to bring before God's presence for dedication (*Bible*); to appoint (a clergyman to a benefice); to nominate (a scholar, etc to a foundation); to put forward (a candidate for examination, the award of a degree, etc); to bring (an offence, etc) to the notice of the authorities (*old*); to charge or bring up for trial (*old*); to symbolize (*archaic*); to represent the character of, act, impersonate (*archaic*); to apply; to offer the greetings of, 'remember' (someone to someone) (*obs*); to point, direct, aim, turn in some direction; to put on (eg a cheerful face) in public; to hold (a weapon) in the aiming position or vertically in front of the body in salute to a superior (**present arms** to hold (one's weapon) in the vertical saluting position; *military*). — *vi* (of the baby's head, shoulder or buttocks) to be in the position for emerging first (*obstetrics*); (of a patient) to report to a doctor (with certain signs and symptoms; *med*); (of chances, opportunities, etc) to offer, be available (*rare*); to make presentation to a living (*eccles*). — *n* the position of a weapon in presenting arms or in aiming (**at present** in the presenting-arms position). — *n* **presentabil'ity**. — *adj* **present'able** capable of being presented; fit to be presented; fit to be seen; passable. — *adv* **present'ably**. — *ns* **present'ableness**. — *n* **presentation** (*prez-ən-tā'shən*) the act of presenting; the manner in which something is presented, laid out, explained or advertised; the expounding or unfolding of eg a case, argument, etc; the right of presenting; that which is presented; something performed for an audience, a play, show or other entertainment; an illustrated talk presenting information eg to a business audience; immediate cognition (*psychol*); representation; the position of a baby in the womb just before birth, ie whether head or buttocks downwards (*obstetrics*). — *adj* that has been presented; of or for presentation. — *adj* **presentā'tional**. — *n* **presentā'tionism** (*psychol*) the doctrine of immediate cognition of objects. — *n* **presentā'tionist**. — *adj* **presentative** (*pri-zent'ə-tiv*) subject to the right of presentation (*eccles*); presenting an idea to the mind, (*esp* one that is not imitative); pertaining to immediate cognition (*psychol*). — *n* **presentee** (*prez-ən-tē'*) someone who is presented to a benefice. — *n* **presenter** (*pri-zent'ər*). — *adj* **present'ive** (*linguistics*) presenting a conception to the mind, not a mere relation. — *n* **present'iveness**. — *n* **present'ment** the act of presenting; a statement; a jury's statement to a court of matters within its knowledge; a representation; an image, delineation, picture; a theatrical representation or performance; a presentation to consciousness (*psychol*, *metaphys*). [OFr *presenter*, from L *praesentāre*, from *praesēns* present (in place or time)]

presential *pri-zen'shl*, (*rare*) *adj* relating to presence; having or implying actual presence; present; as if present; having presence of mind, alert; formed from the present tense (*gram*). — *n* **presentiality** (*-shi-al'i-ti*). — *adv* **presen'tially**. [Med L *praesentiālis*, from *praesentia* presence]

presentient *prē-sen'shyənt*, *-shənt* or *shi-ənt*, *adj* having a presentiment. — *n* **prēsen'sion**. [**pre-** (1)]

presentiment *pri-zen'ti-mənt* or *-sen'*, *n* a premonition or foreboding, *esp* of evil. — *adj* **presentimental** (*-men'tl*). [**pre-** (1)]

presentive, presentment. See under **present**[3].

preserve *pri-zûrv'*, *vt* to keep safe from harm or loss; to keep safe from danger or death, to keep alive; to keep in existence; to retain; to maintain, keep up; to keep sound; to keep from or guard against decay; to freeze, dry, pickle, season, boil in sugar or otherwise treat (food) for keeping; to guard (game, or land, rivers, etc) against shooting or fishing by unauthorized persons. — *vi* to preserve game, fish, ground, or water, etc. — *n* a jam, pickle or other preserved form of fruit or vegetables; an area of land or stretch of water where game or fish are reared for private shooting or fishing; an area of work or activity regarded as restricted to certain people and forbidden to outsiders; (in *pl*) spectacles or goggles to protect the eyes from dust or strong light (*old*). — *n* **preservabil'ity**. — *adj* **preserv'able**. — *n* **preservā'tion** (*prez-*) the process of preserving or of being preserved; repair. — *n* **preservā'tionist** someone who is interested in preserving traditional and historic things. — *adj* **preserv'ative** serving to preserve. — *n* a preserving agent, eg a chemical added to food; a safeguard; a prophylactic medicine, etc. — *adj* and *n* **preserv'atory**. — *n* **preserv'er**. — **preservation order** a legally binding directive ordering the preservation of a building deemed to be historically important; **preserv'ing-pan** a large pan *usu* with a hooped handle and a lip, in which jams, etc are made. — **well preserved** (*colloq*; of a person) not showing the signs of ageing one would expect in a person of such an age. [Fr *préserver*, from L *prae* before, and *servāre* to keep]

preses or **praeses** *prē'siz*, (chiefly *Scot*) *n* a president or chairman: — *pl* **prē'ses** or **prae'ses** (*-sēz*). [L *praeses, -idis*, from *praesidēre*; see **preside**]

preset *prē-set'*, *vt* to adjust (a piece of electronic equipment, etc) so that it will operate at the required time; to set initially or preliminarily: — *pr p* **presett'ing**; *pa t* and *pa p* **preset'**. — *n* (*prē'*) a device or control that presets. [**pre-** (1)]

pre-shrink *prē-shringk'*, *vt* to shrink (cloth) before it is made up into garments, etc. [**pre-** (1)]

preside *pri-zīd'*, *vi* to act as chairman, be in the chair; to be at the head of the table (at a meal); to be in charge or in a position of superintendance (with *over*); to be the guardian or tutelary god of a place (with *over*); to dominate (a place, scene, etc) like a presence (with *over*); to be at the organ or piano, *orig* as a kind of conductor. — *vt* (*rare*) to be at the head of, to control. — **presiding officer** a person in charge of a polling-place. [Fr *présider*, from L *praesidēre*, from *prae* above others, and *sedēre* to sit]

president[1] *prez'idənt*, *n* the elected head of a republic; the head of a board, council, or department of government; someone who is chosen to preside over the meetings of a society, conference, etc; in the European Community, a member state that assumes a role analogous to this for a six-month period; the title of the head of certain colleges, universities and other institutions; the chairman of a company, a bank governor, or head of an organization generally (*esp US*); a colonial or state governor (*hist*). — *adj* (*Milton*) presiding, superintending. — *n* **pres'idency** the office of a president, or his or her dignity, term of office, jurisdiction or official place of residence; each of three main divisions of India (*hist*); a Mormon governing council. — *n* **pres'identess** (*old*) a female president or the wife of a president. — *adj* **presidential** (*-den'shl*) of a president or presidency; presiding, superintending. — *n* **pres'identship**. — **Lord President** the presiding judge of the Court of Session; **Lord President of the Council** a member of the House of Lords who presides over the privy council. [Fr *président*, from L *praesidēns, -ēntis*, pr p of *praesidēre*; see **preside**]

president[2] (*Spenser, Shakesp, Milton*) for **precedent**.

presidial *pri-sid'i-əl*, *adj* relating to a garrison, a presidio or a president; provincial (*Fr hist*). [Fr *présidial*, from LL *praesidiālis*, from *praeses, -idis* governor, and *praesidium* garrison]

presid'iary *pri-sid-i-ə-ri*, *adj* garrisoning, serving as a garrison; of a garrison. [L *praesidiārius*, from *praesidium* garrison]

presidio *pri-sid'i-ō* or *pre-sē'dhyō*, *n* (in areas of Spanish control or settlement) a military post; a penal settlement: — *pl* **presid'ios**. [Sp, from L *praesidium* garrison]

presidium *pri-sid'i-əm*, *n* a standing committee in the former Soviet system (also **praesidium**): — *pl* **presidiums** or **presidia**. [L *praesidium* a garrison, from *praesidēre* to preside]

presignify *prē-sig'ni-fī*, *vt* to intimate beforehand. — *n* **prēsignificā'tion**. [**pre-** (1)]

press[1] *pres*, also (all *obs*) **preace**, **prease** and **preasse** *prēs*, *vt* to exert a pushing force upon; to squeeze; to compress; to clasp; to thrust (something into or against something else); to squeeze out, express (eg juice from fruit); to iron (clothes); to produce (a gramophone record) from a mould by a compressing process; to raise to the shoulders and then raise above the head (*weightlifting*); to flatten and dry (flowers, set) or otherwise shape and condense by the application of weight or other squeezing force; to imprint, stamp, print (*obs*); to put to death by application of heavy weights (*hist*); (of troubles, etc) to bear heavily on, oppress; to harass; to beset; to urge strongly or insistently; to importune; to insist on; to invite with persistent warmth; to offer urgently or abundantly (with *upon*); to present (eg a point) with earnestness, to impress on one's hearers; to lay stress upon; to hurry on with great speed, to expedite; to bring (charges) officially against someone (*law*); to throng, crowd (*archaic*). — *vi* to exert pressure or to push with force (with *on, against*, etc); to crowd; to thrust oneself forward with violence (*archaic*); to be urgent in application, entreaty, or effort (with *for*); to strive (*obs*); to strive or strain too hard, to hit too forcefully, to the loss of ease and effectiveness (*golf* and *tennis*). — *n* an act of pressing; pressure; an apparatus or machine for flattening, compressing or otherwise forcing into shape, or for extracting juice, etc, or for punching solid articles from soft metal, clay, etc; a printing-machine, a printing-press; (the practice or process of) printing; a printing organization; often extended to a publishing house; printing activities; newspapers and periodicals collectively; the journalistic profession; (with *cap*) a common name for a newspaper; (favourable or unfavourable) reception by newspapers and periodicals generally; a crowd, throng; the action of crowding or thronging; the thick of a fight; stress (*archaic*); urgency, hurry (*archaic*); a lift to shoulder level, then above the head (*weightlifting*); a cupboard or shelved closet or recess; a bookcase. — *adj* **pressed** under pressure, in a hurry; (with *for*) short of (time or money; *colloq*). — *n* **press'er**. — *n* **press'ful**. — *n* **press'ing** an article or articles, *esp* gramophone records, made from the same mould or press. — *adj* urgent; importunate; crowding. — *adv* **press'ingly**. — *n* **pression** (*presh'ən*; *rare*) pressure; impress. — **press agent** an agent who arranges for newspaper advertising and publicity, *esp* for an actor or theatre; **press association** an association of newspapers formed to act as a news agency for the members of the association, each supplying local news, etc to the association; (with *caps*) a British news agency formed as a press association in 1868; **press bed** a bed enclosed in a cupboard, or folding up into it; **press book** a book printed at a private press; **press box** a structure or area set aside for the use of reporters at sports, shows, etc; **press button** a push-button. — Also *adj* (**press'-button**). — **press conference** a meeting of a public personage with the press for making an announcement or to answer questions; **Press Council** in the UK, a body set up in 1953 to monitor and uphold standards in journalism; **press cutting** a paragraph or article cut out of a newspaper or magazine; **pressed day** the third day of a three days' visit; **pressed glass** glass given shape and pattern by pressure in a mould; **press fastener** a press stud; **press'fat** (*Bible*) the vat for collecting the liquor from an olive or wine press; **press gallery** a reporters' gallery at a sports stadium, theatre, etc; **press'man** an operator of a printing-press; (and **press'woman**) a journalist or reporter; **press'mark** a mark on a book to show its location in a library; **press office** the department of an organization, government ministry, etc, responsible for releasing information concerning its activities to the press; **press officer**; **press proof** the last proof before printing; **press release** an official statement or report supplied to the press; **pressroom** the room in which printing-presses are housed and operated; a room for the use of journalists; **press stud** a clothes-fastener consisting of complementary halves that interlock when pressed together; **press'-up** a gymnastic exercise performed face down, raising and lowering the body on the arms while keeping the trunk and legs rigid; **press'work** the operation of a printing-press; printed matter; journalistic work. — **at press** or **in the press** in course of printing; about to be published; **be hard pressed** to be at a loss (to manage something), be in a jam; **go to press** to begin to print or to be printed; **liberty** or **freedom of the press** the right of publishing material without submitting it to a government authority for permission; **press ahead, forward** or **on** to continue, *esp* energetically, often in spite of difficulties or opposition; **press flesh** (or **the flesh**) (*orig US*; of politicians, etc) to go about shaking hands with people, *esp* potential supporters (*n* **flesh'-pressing**); **press of canvas** or **sail** as much sail as can be carried; **press the button** to put machinery into operation; to start things moving, *esp* in a momentous or irreversible way; **the press** printed matter generally, *esp* newspapers; journalists as a class. [Fr *presser*, from L *pressāre*, frequentative of *premere*, *pressum* to press]

press[2] *pres*, *vt* to carry off and force into service, *esp* in the navy (*hist*); to requisition, commandeer; to turn to use in an unsuitable or provisional way. — *n* recruitment by force into service, impressment; authority for impressing. — **press gang** a gang or body of sailors under an officer, empowered to impress men into the navy. — Also *vt* (**press'-gang**) to force into service in the army or navy; to dragoon into participation in any enterprise (*colloq*). — **press money** earnest-money (qv under **earnest**[2]). [**prest**[2]]

pressie. See **prezzie**.

pression. See under **press**[1].

pressor *pres'ər*, (*physiol*) *adj* causing an increase in blood pressure. [LL, something or someone that presses, from *premere*, *pressum* to press]

pressure *presh'ər*, *n* the action of pressing or squeezing; the state of being pressed; impression, stamp (*Shakesp*); constraining force or influence; coercion, forceful persuasion; the need to perform a great deal at speed; tension, strain or stress; (*usu* in *pl*) a cause of anxiety; urgency; a strong demand; the force produced by pressing; a force exerted on a surface *specif* by a gas or liquid, measured as so much weight upon a unit of area; difference of electrical potential. — *vt* to apply pressure to; to subject to pressure; to force by pressure, to pressurize, coerce (with *into*). — *n* **pressurizā'tion** or **-s-**. — *vt* **press'urize** or **-ise** to adjust the pressure within (an enclosed compartment such as an aircraft cabin) so that nearly normal atmospheric pressure is constantly maintained; to subject to pressure; to force by pressure (into doing something), to coerce. — **pressure altitude** (*aeronautics*) the apparent altitude of the local ambient pressure related to the international standard atmosphere; **pressure cabin** a pressurized cabin in an aircraft. — *vt* **press'ure-cook** to cook in a pressure cooker. — **pressure cooker** a thick-walled pan with an airtight lid, in which food is cooked at speed by steam under high pressure; **pressure gradient** (*meteorol*) the rate of change of the atmospheric pressure horizontally in a certain direction on the earth's surface as shown by isobars on a weather chart; **pressure group** a number of people who join together to influence public opinion and government policy on some issue; **pressure helmet** an airman's helmet for use with a pressure suit; **pressure point** any of various points on the body on which pressure may be exerted to relieve pain, control bleeding, etc; **pressure ridge** a ridge formed by lateral pressure in floating ice in polar waters; **pressure suit** an automatically inflating suit worn by aircraft crew against pressure-cabin failure at very high altitudes; **pressure-tube reactor** a nuclear reactor in which the fuel elements are contained in many separate tubes rather than in a single pressure vessel; **pressure vessel** a nuclear containment vessel, *usu* of thick steel or prestressed concrete, capable of withstanding high pressure; **pressure waistcoat** a waistcoat worn by aircraft crew through which oxygen passes under pressure to the lungs to aid breathing at high altitudes; **pressurized water reactor** a nuclear reactor using water-cooling at a pressure such that the boiling point of the water is above the highest temperature reached. — See also **boiling-water reactor**, **light-water reactor**. [L *pressura*, from *premere* to press]

prest[1] *prest*, (*Spenser*, *Shakesp*) *adj* ready. [OFr *prest*, from L *praestō* at hand]

prest[2] *prest*, (*obs*) *vt* to lend; to pay in advance; to engage by paying earnest money; to enlist; to impress for service. — *n* a loan; payment in advance; enlistment money. — *n* **prestā'tion** payment or service required by custom or promise. [OFr *prester*, from L *praestāre* to offer, discharge]

Prestel® *pres'tel*, *n* the viewdata (qv) system of British Telecom.

Prester John *pres'tər jon*, *n* the mythical medieval Christian priest-king of a vast empire conceived, during the crusades, to be in Central Asia, but according to a later tradition in Ethiopia. [OFr *prestre* (Fr *prêtre*) priest]

presternum *prē-stûr'nəm*, (*anatom*) *n* the anterior part of the sternum. [**pre-** (2)]

prestidigitation *pres-ti-dij-i-tā'shən*, *n* sleight of hand. — *n* **prestidig'itātor** a conjurer. [Fr *prestidigitateur*, from *preste* nimble, and L *digitus* finger]

prestige *pres-tēzh'*, *n orig* a conjuring trick or illusion (*obs*); hence, charm, magic, glamour (qv); hence, a name or reputation to conjure with, standing or ascendancy in people's minds owing to associations, station, success, etc. — *adj* consisting in, or for the sake of, prestige; considered to have or give prestige; superior in quality, style, etc. — *adj* **prestigious** (*-tij'əs*) having prestige, esteemed; lending or conferring prestige; deceitful, juggling, using legerdemain (*obs*). [Fr, from L *praestigium* delusion, from *praestringere* to dazzle, blind; see also **prestriction**]

prestigiator *pres-tij'i-ā-tər*, *n* a conjurer. [L *praestigium* delusion; see **prestige**]

presto *pres'tō*, (*music*) *adj* very quick. — *n* a presto movement or passage: — *pl* **pres'tos**. — *adv* quickly, quicker than *allegro*. — *adv* or *interj* (also more *usu* **hey presto** as in conjuring tricks) at once. — *adv*, *n* and *adj* (*superl*) **prestis'simo**: — *pl* **prestis'simos**. [Ital, from L *praestō* at hand]

pre-stressed *prē-strest'*, *adj* (of concrete) strengthened with stretched wires or rods rather than large steel bars as in reinforced concrete. [**pre-** (1)]

prestriction *pri-strik'shən*, (*obs*, *rare*) *n* blindness; blindfolding. [L *praestrictiō*, *-ōnis*, from *praestringere* to draw tight, bind, restrain, blind]

pre-stun *prē-stun'*, *vt* to stun (cattle) before slaughter, to lessen suffering. [**pre-** (1)]

presume *pri-zūm'* or *-zōōm'*, *vt* to suppose (something to be the case) though one has no proof; to take for granted; to assume provisionally; to be so bold as (to do something) *esp* without the proper right or knowledge, to make bold, dare or venture. — *vi* to venture beyond what one has ground for; to act forwardly or without proper right, to take liberties; (with *on*, *upon*) to rely or count on, *esp* without justification, or to take unfair advantage of (eg someone's good nature). — *adj* **presūm'able** that may be presumed or supposed to be true. — *adv* **presūm'ably** as one may reasonably suppose or expect, doubtless. — *n* **presūm'er**. — *adj* **presūm'ing** venturing without permission; unreasonably or impertinently bold. — *conj* (often with *that*) making the presumption that. — *adv* **presūm'ingly**. — *n* **presumption** (*-zum'shən* or *-zump'shən*) the act of presuming; supposition; strong probability; that which is taken for granted; an assumption or belief based on facts or probable evidence; confidence grounded on something not proved; a ground or reason for presuming; conduct going beyond proper limits, impertinent overboldness; a presumption of fact or presumption of law (*law*). — *adj* **presumptive** (*-zump'tiv* or *-zum'tiv*) grounded on probable evidence; giving grounds for presuming (see **heir** for **heir-presumptive**); presuming (*obs*); used of embryonic tissue which will in the normal course of development be differentiated into a particular organ or tissue (*biol*). — *adv* **presump'tively**. — *adj* **presumptuous** (*-zump'tū-əs* or *-zum'*) tending to presume, impertinently bold. — *adv* **presump'tuously**. — *n* **presump'tuousness**. — **presumption of fact** (*law*) an assumption of a fact from known facts; **presumption of law** (*law*) an assumption made failing proof to the contrary; an inference established as a rule of law, not contradictable by evidence. [L *praesūmere*, *-sūmptum*, from *prae* before, and *sūmere* to take, from *sub* under, and *emere* to buy]

presuppose *prē-sə-pōz'*, *vt* to assume or take for granted; to involve as a necessary antecedent, imply. — *n* **presupposition** (*prē-sup-ə-zish'ən*) the act of assuming or presupposing; something taken for granted beforehand, an assumption. [**pre-** (1)]

presurmise *prē-sər-mīz'*, (*Shakesp*) *n* a surmise previously formed. [**pre-** (1)]

pret. *abbrev*: preterite

prêt-à-porter *pre-ta-por-tā*, (*Fr*) *n* and *adj* ready-to-wear (garments).

pre-tax *prē-taks'*, *adj* before the deduction of tax. [**pre-** (1)]

pre-teen *prē-tēn'*, *n* (*usu* in *pl*) a child who is not yet, *esp* not quite yet, a teenager. — Also *adj*. [**pre-** (1)]

pretence or *NAm* **pretense** *pri-tens'*, *n* an act of pretending; make-believe; an act put on deliberately to mislead, a sham, a false show; a claim, *esp* an unjustified one (eg to expertise in something); an assertion, by implication false; a misleading declaration of intention (as in *under false pretences*); show or semblance; a trivial pretext; pretentiousness, show, affectation or ostentation; an aim, purpose or thing aimed at (*obs*). — *adj* **pretence'less** without a pretext. [Anglo-Fr *pretense*, from Med L *praetēnsus* for L *praetentus*, pa p of *praetendere* to pretend]

pretend *pri-tend'*, *vt* to make believe; to feign or affect (to be or do something); to imply, assert or claim falsely; to claim to feel, profess falsely (eg friendship); to venture, attempt, undertake or be so bold as (to do something); to stretch forth, or in front (*Spenser*); to offer (*obs*); to purpose (*obs*); to indicate (*obs*). — *vi* to feign; to make believe; to make claim (to eg expertise in something); to aspire (with *to*; *archaic*); to be a suitor (with *to*; *archaic*); to reach or go forward (*obs*). — *adj* (*colloq* or *hypocoristic*) imaginary, make-believe. — *n* **preten'dant** (or **-ent**) a claimant; a suitor; a pretender. — *adj* **preten'ded**. — *adv* **preten'dedly**. — *n* **preten'der** a claimant, *esp* to a throne; a candidate; a suitor (*obs*); someone who pretends. — *n* **preten'dership**. — *adv* **preten'dingly**. — **Old Pretender** and **Young Pretender** respectively the son and grandson of James II and VII as claimants to the British throne. [L *praetendere* to stretch forward, hold in front, allege, from *prae* before, and *tendere, tentum, tēnsum* to stretch]

pretension *pri-ten'shən*, *n* foolish vanity or pretence, self-importance or affectation, pretentiousness; a claim, by implication an unjustified one; an aspiration, eg to marriage; a pretext. [Med L *praetensio, -onis*, from L *praetendere*; see **pretend**]

pre-tension *prē-ten'shən*, *vt* to stretch (the reinforcing wires or rods in pre-stressed concrete) before the concrete is cast. — *adj* **pre-ten'sioned**. [Pfx **pre-** (1)]

pretentious *pri-ten'shəs*, *adj* pompous, self-important or foolishly grandiose; phoney or affected; showy, ostentatious; (of a claim) false (*rare*). — *adv* **preten'tiously**. — *n* **preten'tiousness**. [Formerly *pretensious*, from L *pretensio*; see **pretension**]

preter- or (*esp* in obsolete words) **praeter-** *prē'tər-*, *pfx* signifying beyond, as in *adj* **preterhu'man** more than human. [L *praeter*]

preterite or **preterit** *pret'ə-rit*, *adj* denoting a verb tense used to express past action (*gram*); past, belonging to the past. — *n* (*gram*) this tense of verbs, the past tense (also **preterite tense**); a word in this tense; a form of this tense. — *n* **pret'erist** someone who holds the prophecies of the Apocalypse already fulfilled (*theol*). — *n* **pret'eriteness**. — *n* **preterition** (*prē-tə-rish'ən*) the act of passing over; omission of mention in a will; paraleipsis (*rhetoric*); the doctrine that God passes over the non-elect in electing to eternal life. — *adj* **preteritive** (*pri-ter'i-tiv*) used only in the preterite (*gram*). — *adj* **preter'ito-pres'ent**, **-presen'tial** or **pret'erite-pres'ent** (*gram*) used of verbs that have an original preterite still preterite in form but present in meaning such as the modal or modal auxiliary verbs. — *n* a verb of this type. [L *praeteritus*, pa p of *praeterīre* to go past, from *praeter* beyond, and *īre*, *itum* to go]

preterm *prē'tûrm'*, *adj* born prematurely. [**pre-** (1)]

pretermit *prē-tər-mit'*, (*rare*) *vt* to pass by; to omit; to leave undone; to desist from for a time: — *pr p* **prētermitt'ing**; *pa t* and *pa p* **prētermitt'ed**. — *n* **pretermission** (*-mish'ən*). [L *praetermittere, -missum*, from *mittere* to send]

preternatural *prē-tər-nach'ə-rəl*, *adj* out of the ordinary course of nature; abnormal; supernatural. — *n* **preternat'uralism** preternatural character or event; belief in the preternatural. — *adv* **preternat'urally**. — *n* **preternat'uralness**. [**preter-**]

preterperfect *prē-tər-pûr'fikt*, (*old gram*) *n* perfect. — *adj* **preterpluper'fect** pluperfect (*gram*); beyond the more than perfect (*facetious*). [**preter-**]

pretext *prē'tekst*, *n* an ostensible motive or reason, put forward as an excuse or to conceal the true one. [L *praetextus, -ūs* pretext, outward show, and *praetextum* pretext, from *prae* in front, and *texere* to weave]

pretty *prit'i*, *adj* (*usu* of women and girls) facially attractive, *esp* in a feminine way; attractively small, neat, dainty or graceful; charming to look at, decorative; (of music, sound, etc) delicately melodious; superficially attractive or insipidly charming only, lacking striking beauty or distinction; tricky, clever; ingenious; grand, fine (*esp ironic*); commendable; neat; stalwart (*archaic* or *Scot*); considerable, substantial. — *n* a pretty thing or person; a knick-knack; the fairway of a golf course; the fluted part of a glass: — *pl* **prett'ies**. — *adv* fairly; rather; very, extremely; prettily (*colloq* or *dialect*). — *vt* (with *up*) to prettify. — *n* **prettificā'tion**. — *vt* **prett'ify** to make pretty in an excessively ornamental or over-dainty way. — *adv* **prett'ily** in a pretty manner; pleasingly; elegantly; neatly. — *n* **prett'iness** the quality of being pretty; an instance of the quality; a prettyism. — *adj* **prett'yish** somewhat pretty. — *n* **prett'yism** trivial daintiness of style or an instance of it. — *n* **pretty-prett'iness**. — *n* **pretty-prett'y** (*colloq*) a knick-knack: — *pl* **pretty-prett'ies**. — *adj* insipidly pretty, over-pretty or over-dainty. — *adj* **prett'y-spoken** speaking or spoken prettily. — **a pretty penny** a good large sum; **only pretty Fanny's way** (*T Parnell*) only what must be expected and accepted of the person; **pretty much** more or less; **pretty nearly** almost; **pretty well** almost, more or less; **sitting pretty** enjoying one's advantageous position; happily unaffected by problems besetting others. [OE *prættig* tricky, from *prætt* trickery; the origin of the word is uncertain]

pretzel *pret'səl*, *n* a crisp salted biscuit made in rope shape and twisted into a kind of loose knot. [Ger]

preux chevalier *proō shə-val-yā*, (*Fr*) *n* a valiant knight.

prevail *pri-vāl'*, *vi* to be victorious (with *over*, *against*); to win through; to have the upper hand, have the edge; to urge successfully, to persuade (with *on*, *upon*); to be usual or most usual; to predominate; to hold good, be in use, be customary; to gain strength (*obs*). — *vt* (*obs*) to avail; to persuade. — *adj* **prevail'ing** very general or common; most common or frequent; predominant; currently popular; powerful, effective; controlling. — *adv* **prevail'ingly**. — *n* **prevail'ment** (*Shakesp*) the power of overcoming. — **prevailing wind** the wind that blows most frequently in any particular region. [L *praevalēre* to be superior or stronger, from *prae* above, beyond, and *valēre* to be strong]

prevalent *prev'ə-lənt*, *adj* prevailing; widespread; common, frequent; widely practised or accepted; powerful; victorious (*obs*). — *n* **prev'alence** or **prev'alency**. — *adv* **prev'alently**. [L *praevalēns, -ēntis*, pr p of *praevalēre*; see **prevail**]

prevaricate *pri-var'i-kāt*, *vi* to avoid stating the truth or coming directly to the point; to quibble; to deviate (*obs*); to shift about from side to side (*obs*); to undertake an enterprise with the object of wrecking it (*obs*); to betray a client by collusion with his or her opponent (*law*). — *vt* (*obs*) to pervert, transgress. — *n*

prevaricā'tion. — *n* **prevar'icātor** someone who prevaricates; formerly in Cambridge University, a satirical orator at Commencement. [L *praevāricārī*, *-ātus* to walk straddlingly or crookedly, to act collusively, from *prae* above, beyond, and *vāricus* straddling, from *vārus* bent]

preve. See **prove**.

prevene (*pri-vēn'*, *vt* to precede (*rare*); to anticipate (*obs*). — *n* **prevenancy** (*prev'ən-ən-si*; *rare*) courteous anticipation of others' wishes. — *n* **prevē'nience**. — *adj* **prevē'nient** antecedent, preceding, anticipatory; predisposing; preventive (*obs*). [L *praevenīre* to precede; see **prevent**]

prevent *pri-vent'*, *vt* to stop (someone from doing something, or something from happening), to hinder; to stop the occurrence of, to make impossible, to avert; to thwart; to anticipate, forestall (*obs*); to balk (someone of his or her purpose), to debar or preclude (*obs*); to precede (*obs*): to be, go, or act earlier than (*obs*); to go faster than (*obs*); to satisfy in advance (*obs*); to meet or provide for in advance (*obs*). — *n* **preventabil'ity**. — *adj* **preven'table** or **preven'tible**. — *n* **preven'ter** someone or something that prevents or hinders; a supplementary rope or part (*naut*). — *n* **preven'tion** the action of preventing; avoidance or preclusion of something by care and forethought; an anticipation or premonition (*obs*); an obstruction (*obs*). — *adj* **preven'tive** or (by irregular formation) **preven'tative** tending to prevent or hinder; prophylactic; concerned with the prevention of smuggling (*hist*). — *n* that which prevents; a prophylactic. — *adv* **preven'tively**. — *n* **preven'tiveness**. — **preventive detention** prolonged imprisonment, with corrective training, for persistent or dangerous offenders of 30 or over for periods of from 5 to 14 years. [L *praevenīre*, *-ventum* to come before, to anticipate, from *prae* before, and *venīre* to come]

preverb *prē'vûrb*, (*linguistics*) *n* a particle or prefix which precedes a verb or verb-root. — *adj* **prever'bal** occurring or standing before a verb; relating to the period of babyhood before the development of speech. [**pre-** (1)]

pre-vernal *prē-vûr'nl*, (*bot*) *adj* flowering before spring; coming early into flower or leaf. [**pre-** (1)]

preview or US **prevue** *prē'vū*, *n* a showing or viewing of a film, exhibition, etc, before it is open to the public; a public performance of a play before it offciallly opens; an advance showing to the public of excerpts from a film, a trailer (*NAm*); a hint or foretaste. — *vt* (*prē'vū*) to give or attend a preview of (an exhibition, play, etc); (*prē-vū'*) to look at beforehand (*rare*); to foresee. — *vi* (of an exhibition, play, etc) to be previewed. [**pre-** (1)]

previous *prē'vi-əs*, *adj* occurring before, earlier; already arranged, prior; former; premature, over-hasty (*facetious*). — *n* (*police colloq*) previous convictions. — *adv* (with *to*) prior to, before. — *adv* **prē'viously**. — *n* **prē'viousness**. — **previous examination** the little go at Cambridge (qv under **go**[1]); **previous question** (in the House of Commons) a motion to end the present debate before a vote is taken; (in the House of Lords and US assemblies) a motion to vote without delay on the matter being debated; (in public meetings) a motion to pass on to the next business. [L *praevius* leading the way, from *prae* before, and *via* a way]

previse *prē-vīz'*, *vt* (*rare*, *literary*) to foresee; to forewarn. — *n* **prevision** (*-vizh'ən*) foresight; foreknowledge. — *vt* to endow with prevision. — *adj* **previsional** (*-vizh'ə-nəl*). [L *praevidēre*, *-vīsum*, from *prae* before, and *vidēre* to see]

pre-wash *prē'-wosh*, *n* a preliminary wash before the main wash, *esp* in a washing-machine; a setting for this on an automatic washing-machine. — Also *vt*. [**pre-** (1)]

prewyn. A Shakespearian form of **prune**[3].

prex *prex*, (*US college slang*) *n* the president of a college (also **prex'y**).

prey *prā*, *n* the creature or creatures that a predatory beast hunts and kills as food; a victim or victims; a sufferer from (depression, fears, etc) (with *to*); booty, plunder (*archaic*, *rare*); that which is preserved from loss in battle, eg one's own life (*Bible*); depredation (*rare*); the act of seizing (*Spenser*, *Shakesp*). — *vi* (with *on* or *upon*) to hunt and kill (another creature) as food, to attack as prey; to bully, exploit or terrorize as victims; to distress or afflict; to make depredations on; to take plunder from. — *vt* (*Spenser*) to plunder. — *adj* **prey'ful** (*Shakesp*) bent upon prey. — **beast** or **bird of prey** one that devours other animals, *esp* higher animals, applied *usu* to the Carnivora and Falconiformes. [OFr *preie* (Fr *proie*), from L *praeda* booty]

prezzie or **pressie** *prez'i*, (*colloq*) *n* a present or gift.

prial *prī'əl*. Same as **pair-royal** (qv under **pair**[1]).

Priapus *prī-ā'pəs*, *n* an ancient deity personifying male generative power, guardian of gardens, later regarded as the chief god of lasciviousness and sensuality. — *adj* **Priapean** (*prī-ə-pē'ən*). — *adj* **Priapic** (*-ap'ik*) of or relating to Priapus; (without *cap*) of, relating to, exhibiting, etc a phallus; (without *cap*) overly concerned or preoccupied with virility and male sexuality. — *n* **prī'apism** persistent erection of the penis (*pathol*); licentiousness, lewdness. [Latinized from Gr *Priāpos*]

pribble *prib'l*, *n* a modification of **prabble**, *usu* found with it in *pribble and prabble*. — Also **pribb'le-prabb'le**.

price *prīs* (also *Spenser* **prise** *prīs* or *prīz*) *n* the amount, *usu* in money, for which a thing is sold or offered; that which one forgoes or suffers for the sake of or in gaining something; money offered for the capture or killing of anybody; (the size of) the sum, etc, by which one can be bribed; betting odds; preciousness, worth, value (*archaic*); (also **prize**) valuation (*Spenser*, *Shakesp*). — *vt* to fix, state, or mark the price of; to ascertain the price of (*colloq*); to pay the price of (*Spenser*); to prize, value (*Shakesp*). — *adj* **priced** having a price assigned; valued at such-and-such a price. — *adj* **price'less** beyond price; invaluable; supremely and delectably absurd. — *adv* **price'lessly**. — *n* **price'lessness**. — *n* **pri'cer**. — *adj* **pri'cey** or **pri'cy** (*colloq*) expensive: — *compar* **pri'cier**; *superl* **pri'ciest**. — *n* **pri'ciness**. — **Price Code** a set of regulations used by the British government between 1973 and 1979 to control prices, as a measure against inflation; **Price Commission** a body set up by the British government in 1973 (abolished in 1979) to control prices, as a measure against inflation; **price control** the fixing by a government of maximum, or sometimes minimum, prices chargeable for goods or services; **price current** (often in *pl*, **prices current**) a list of prevailing prices at any time; a list of prices paid for any class of goods, etc; **price'-cutting** lowering of prices to secure custom; **price-earnings ratio** the ratio of the market price of a common stock share to its earnings; **price'-fixing** the establishing of the price of a commodity, etc by agreement between suppliers or by government price control, rather than by the operation of a free market; **price index** an index number which relates current prices to those of a base period or base date, the latter *usu* being assigned the value of 100; **price level** the average of many prices of commodities; **price list** a list of prices of goods offered for sale; **price ring** a group of manufacturers who co-operate for the purpose of raising or maintaining the price of a commodity above the level that would be established by a free market, a cartel; **price tag** a tag or label showing price; the cost of something, typically a project or undertaking; **price war** a form of commercial competition in which firms competing in the same market successively lower their prices in order to secure a larger share of that market. — **above** or **beyond price** so valuable that no price can or would be enough; **at a price** at a somewhat high price; **in great price** (*archaic*) in high estimation; **of price** (*archaic*) of great value; **price of money** the rate of discount in lending or borrowing capital; **price oneself out of the market** to charge more than customers or clients are willing to pay; **price on someone's head** a reward for someone's capture or slaughter; **what price ...?** what about (this or that) now?, what are the chances of (this or that) happening now?, so much for (this or that); what do you think of?; **without price** beyond price, priceless; without anything to pay. [OFr *pris* (Fr *prix*), from L *pretium* price; cf **praise**, **prize**[3]]

prick *prik*, *vt* to pierce slightly with a fine point; to cause slight pain by doing this; (of eg the conscience) to cause pangs to; to pierce (a hole); to urge with, or as if with, a spur or goad; to incite; (*usu* with *up*; of an animal) to erect, cock, stick up (its ears); to insert (eg seedlings) in small holes (*usu* with *in*, *out*, etc); to indicate with a prick or dot, to tick off, hence to select; to trace (eg a pattern) with pricks; to write out in musical notation (*obs*); to pin (*obs*); to deck out (*obs*); to pick, poke or pluck out with a point (*obs*); to stick all over or stud (with something; *obs*); to pierce the skin of (a suspected witch) to find insensitive spots (*hist*). — *vi* to pierce, make punctures; to have a sensation of pricking, to smart; (of the conscience) to cause one pangs; (of wine) to begin to turn sour; (of an animal's ears; with *up*) to stand erect; to ride with spurs, or quickly (*archaic*); to detect witches by the pricking method (*hist*). — *n* the act, feeling, or stimulus of piercing or puncturing; a puncture; a mark or wound made by puncturing; a penis (*vulg*); a term of abuse for a person one dislikes or thinks a fool (*vulg*); a hare's footprint; anything sharp and piercing, such as a thorn, spine, goad (*obs* or *archaic*); a note in written music (*obs*); a graduation on a dial (*Shakesp*); a dot (*obs*); a point of space or time (*obs*); an hour-point on a clock (*Shakesp*); a point, peak, acme (*Spenser*); the centre of an archery target (*obs*); a mark or target (*obs*). — *n* **prick'er** a piercing instrument; a witch-finder; a light horseman; a priming wire. — *n* and *adj* **prick'ing**. — *adj* **prick'-eared** having erect or noticeable ears. — **prick'-louse** or **prick'-the-louse** (*Scot*) a tailor; **prick'-me-dain'ty** (*Scot*) an affected person. — *adj* over-precise. — **prick'-song** (*Shakesp*) written music; descant; **prick spur** a spur with one point; **prick-the-gar'ter** fast-and-loose; **prick'wood** the spindle-tree; the dogwood. — **kick against the pricks** to react futilely against discipline or authority, to the extent of injuring oneself (*Bible*, Acts 9.5); **prick up one's ears** to begin to listen intently. [OE *prica* point; cf Du *prik*]

pricket *prik'it*, *n* a fallow deer buck in his second year, with straight unbranched antlers; a spike serving as a candlestick; a candlestick with such a spike. [**prick**]

prickle *prik'l*, *n* a sharp point growing from the epidermis of a plant or from the skin of an animal; a little prick. — *vt* and *vi* to prick slightly. — *vi* to have a prickly feeling. — *n* **prick'liness**. — *n* and *adj* **prick'ling**. — *adj* **prick'ly** full of or covered with prickles; tingling as if prickled; easily annoyed, irritable, thin-skinned. — **prick'le-back** the stickle-back; **prickly ash** the tooth-ache-tree (Xanthoxylum); **prickly heat** a skin disease, inflammation of the sweat glands with intense irritation; **prickly pear** a cactaceous genus (Opuntia) with clusters of prickles; its pear-shaped fruit. [OE *pricel*]

pride *prīd*, *n* the state or feeling of being proud; excessive self-esteem; haughtiness; a proper sense of what is becoming to oneself and scorn of what is unworthy; self-respect, personal dignity; a feeling of pleasure or satisfaction on account of something worthily done by oneself or someone connected with one, one's family, possessions, etc; something of which one is proud; splendour; magnificence; beauty displayed; ostentation; exuberance; prime, flower; high spirit, mettle; a peacock's attitude of display; sexual excitement in a female animal (*Shakesp*); a company of lions; used in plant names, eg *pride of India*, *London pride*. — *vt* to congratulate or pique (oneself) (with *on*); to make proud (*obs*). — *adj* **pride'ful**. — *adv* **pride'fully**. — *n* **pride'fulness**. — *adj* **pride'less**. — **pride of place** the distinction of a position of special prominence or chief importance; the culmination of an eagle's or hawk's flight (see **place**); **take (a) pride in** to be proud of; to be conscientious about maintaining high standards in (one's work, etc). [OE *prȳde*, *prȳte*, from *prūd*, *prūt* proud]

pridian *prid'i-ən*, *adj* of or relating to yesterday. [L *prīdiānus*, from *prīdiē* the previous day, from *prius* before, and *diēs* day]

pried. See **pry**.

prie-dieu *prē'dyø'*, *n* a praying-desk or chair for praying on. [Fr, pray-God]

prief or **priefe** *prēf*, (*Spenser* or *Scot*) *n* proof. — *vt* **prieve** to prove; to test. [See ety of **proof**, **prove**]

prier, **pries**. See under **pry**.

priest *prēst*, *n* (in the Roman Catholic and Orthodox churches) an ordained minister; (in the Anglican church) a minister ranking between a deacon and a bishop; an official conductor of religious rites; a mediator between a god and worshippers; a club or mallet for killing fish. — *vt* to ordain as priest. — *vi* to act as priest. — *n* **pries'tess** a female priest in non-Christian religions. — *n* **priest'craft** priestly policy directed to worldly ends. — *n* **priest'hood** the office or character of a priest; the priestly order. — *n* **priest'liness**. — *n* **priest'ling** a contemptible priest. — *adj* **priest'ly** belonging to, characteristic of or befitting a priest or priests. — *n* **priest'ship**. — **priest'-king** a king with priestly functions. — *adj* **priest'-like**. — *adj* **priest'-rid** or **-ridden** dominated by priests. — **priest's** or **priest hole** a secret room providing a hiding-place for a Roman Catholic priest in time of persecution or repression (*hist*). [OE *prēost*, from L *presbyter*, from Gr *presbyteros* an elder]

prieve. See under **prief**.

prig[1] *prig*, *n* a precisian, a puritan; a person of precise morals without a sense of proportion; a sanctimonious person, certain of his or her blamelessness and critical of others' failings; a coxcomb (*obs*). — *n* **prigg'ery**. — *adj* **prigg'ish**. — *adv* **prigg'ishly**. — *n* **prigg'ishness**. — *n* **prigg'ism**. [Origin uncertain]

prig[2] *prig*, (*Scot*) *vi* to entreat; to importune; to haggle: — *pr p* **prigg'ing**; *pa t* and *pa p* **prigged**. — **prig down** to seek to beat down (a price or the seller). [Origin uncertain]

prig[3] *prig*, *n* a tinker (*obs cant*); a thief (*slang*; *Shakesp*). — *vt* to filch: — *pr p* **prigg'ing**; *pa t* and *pa p* **prigged**. — *n* **prigg'er** a thief. — *n* **prigg'ing**. — *n* **prigg'ism**. [Origin uncertain]

prill *pril*, *vt* to turn into pellet form, eg by melting and letting the drops solidify in falling. — *n* a pellet, or pelleted material, formed by prilling. [Cornish mining term, of uncertain origin]

prim[1] *prim*, *adj* rigidly punctilious and precise; stiffly formal; over-demure; prudishly disapproving. — *vt* to deck or dress with great nicety; to set (the face) or purse (the lips, mouth) in a prim expression. — *vi* to look prim; to prim the mouth: — *pr p* **primm'ing**; *pa t* and *pa p* **primmed**. — *adv* **prim'ly**. — *n* **prim'ness**. [Late 17c cant]

prim[2] *prim*, *n* (*med colloq*) a primigravida, as in **elderly prim** one of 25 and over.

prima *prē'mə* or *-ma*, (*Ital*) *adj* first. — **prima ballerina** (*bal-ə-rēn'ə* or *ba-le-rē'na*, or **prima ballerina assoluta** (*as-so-lōō'ta* or *-tə*) the leading ballerina (Ital *assoluta* without rival): — *pl* **prima ballerinas** or **prime** (*-mā*) **ballerine** (*-nā*) **assolute** (*-tā*); **prima donna** or **prima donna assoluta** (*don'ə* or *don'na*) the leading female singer in an opera company (without rival); (**prima donna**) a person, *esp* a woman, who is temperamental, over-sensitive and hard to please: — *pl* **prima donnas** or **prime donne** (*-nā*) (**assolute**). [Ital, feminine of *primo* first, from L *prīmus*]

primacy *prī'mə-si*, *n* the (condition of being in) the position or place that is first in rank or importance; the office or dignity of a primate.

primaeval. See **primeval**.

prima facie *prī'mə fā'shē*, *-shi-ē*, *prē'mä*, *fak'i-ā*, (*L*) on the first view; at first sight; (of evidence) sufficient to support the bringing of a charge (*law*); (of a case) supported by prima facie evidence (*law*).

primage *prīm'ij*, *n* a payment, in addition to freight, made by shippers for loading, *orig* a gratuity to captain and crew, afterwards made to owners. [Anglo-L *prīmāgium*]

primal, *prī'məl*, *adj* first; primitive; original; chief, fundamental. — *n* **primal'ity**. — *adv* **pri'mally**. — **primal therapy** or **primal scream therapy** rebirthing (qv) therapy, during which patients are encouraged to scream as they re-experience the agonies of birth and frustrations of infancy. [Med L *prīmālis*, from L *prīmus* first]

primary *prī'mə-ri*, *adj* first; original; of the first order (eg in a system of successive branchings); first-formed; primitive; chief; elementary; fundamental; first-hand, direct; belonging to the first stages of education, elementary; (of a feather) growing on the manus (*ornithol*); relating to primaries (*US*); (with *cap*) Palaeozoic (but *orig* applied to rocks supposed to be older than any fossiliferous strata; *geol*). — *n* that which is highest in rank or importance, a planet in relation to its satellites; a primary coil; a primary feather; a primary school; a substance obtained directly, by extraction and purification, from natural, or crude technical, raw material (cf *intermediate*); a meeting of the voters of a political party in an electoral division to nominate candidates, or to elect delegates to a nominating convention representing a larger area (*US politics*); an election (also **primary election**) by local members of a party of candidates to be nominated for election, or of delegates to nominate them (*US politics*). — *adv* **prī'marily**. — *n* **prī'mariness**. — **primary assembly** in US politics, a primary; **primary battery** or **cell** a battery or cell producing an electric current by irreversible chemical action; **primary coil** one carrying an inducing current; **primary colours** those from which all others can be derived by mixing, that is (for light) the three spectral colours red, green and blue, which, mixed equally, produce white light, or (for pigments) cyan, magenta and yellow, which, mixed equally produce black (*printing*), or (in general use) red, yellow and blue; also, all the colours of the spectrum, red, orange, yellow, green, blue, indigo, and violet; **primary meristem** any of the three meristematic tissues in the developing plant embryo, from which epidermis, ground tissue and vascular bundles arise; **primary planet** a planet distinguished from a satellite; **primary production** (*ecol*) see under **production**; **primary school** a school providing primary education, *usu* for children between 5 and 11; **primary stress** (*linguistics*) the main stress in a word, the stress that falls on the most heavily accented syllable. [L *prīmārius*, from *prīmus* first]

primate *prī'māt* or *-mit*, *n* a bishop or archbishop to whose see was formerly annexed the dignity of vicar of the holy see (*RC Church*); an archbishop over a province (*Ch of Eng*); a member of the order **Primates** (*prī-mā'tēz*) the highest order of mammals, including lemurs, monkeys, anthropoid apes and humans (*zool*). — *adj* **primā'tal**. — *n* **pri'mateship**. — *adj* **primā'tial** (*-shl*) and **primatic** (*-mat'ik*) or **primat'ical**. — *n* **primatol'ogist**. — *n* **primatol'ogy** the study of the Primates. [LL *prīmās*, *-ātis*, from L *prīmus* first]

prime[1] *prīm*, *adj* first in order of time, rank or importance; primary; chief; main; of the highest quality; (of broadcasting time) commanding the highest audience figures; original; in sexual excitement (*Shakesp*); (of a number other than one) divisible by no whole number except unity and itself (*arith*); (of two or more numbers) relatively prime (see below) (with *to*; *arith*). — *n* the first of the lesser hours of the Roman breviary; the time of this office, about six in the morning, or sometimes sunrise; the time from the beginning of the artificial day to terce (about nine); the beginning; the spring; the world's youth; the new moon, or its first appearance (*obs*); the best part; the height of perfection; full health and strength; a prime number; a first subdivision or symbol marking it (′) (*math*, etc); a fundamental tone; an old card-game, probably the same as primero; the first guard against sword thrusts, also the first and simplest thrust (*fencing*). — *adv* **prime'ly**. — *n* **prime'ness**. — *adj* **prī'my** (*Shakesp*) in one's prime, blooming. — **prime cost** see under **cost**[1]; **prime rate** or **prime lending rate** the lowest rate of interest charged by a bank at any given time, *usu* available only to large concerns with high credit ratings, forming the base figure on which other rates are calculated; **prime meridian** a meridian chosen to represent 0°, *esp* that passing through Greenwich, from which other lines of longitude are calculated; **prime minister** the chief minister of state; **prime mover** in medieval astronomy, the primum mobile; a natural source of energy; a machine that transforms energy from such a source into motive power; the main cause or instigator of an action, project, etc; **prime number** a number, other than one, divisible only by itself or unity; **prime time** (*radio* and *television*) the peak period for viewing and listening during the day, having the highest rates (*adj* **prime'-time**); **prime vertical** a great celestial circle passing through the east and west points of the horizon, and cutting the meridian at right angles at the zenith. — **prime of life** the period of one's life following youth, during which one is at one's most active, productive and successful; **relatively prime** (*arith*) having no common integral factor but unity. [L *prīmus* first; partly through OE *prīm*, from L *prīma* (*hōra*) first (hour)]

prime[2] *prīm*, *vt* to charge, fill; to supply (a gun, firearm, bomb, etc) with powder or other means of igniting the charge; to lay a train of powder to; to bring into activity or working order by a preliminary charge (eg people by giving them liquor, a pump by pouring in water, an internal-combustion engine by injecting gas or oil); to coach or cram beforehand with information or instructions; to apply a primer to, preparatory to painting; to make up with cosmetics (*obs*). — *vi* to prime a gun; (of a boiler) to send water with the steam into the cylinder; (of the tides) to recur at progressively shorter intervals. — *n* **prī'mer** someone or something that primes; a priming-wire; a detonator; a preparatory first coat of paint, etc; the particular type of paint used for this. — *n* **prī'ming** the progressive shortening of the interval between tides as spring tide approaches; a detonating charge that fires a propellant charge; a tube for priming an internal-combustion engine; a priming-wire; a preparatory coat of paint. — **prī'ming-iron** or **-wire** a wire passed through the touch-hole of a cannon to clear it and pierce the cartridge; **prī'ming-powder** detonating powder; a train of powder. [Ety obscure]

primer *prī'mər* or *prim'ər* or **primmer** *prim'er*, *n* a small prayer book or book of hours for lay people, used also for teaching reading; a first reading-book; an elementary introduction to any subject; (*prim'ər*) printing type of two obsolete sizes, **long primer** (*approx* 10-point) and **great primer** (*approx* 18-point). [L *prīmārius* primary]

primero *pri-mā'rō*, *n* an old card-game. [Sp *primera*]

primeur *prē-mœr*, (*Fr*) *n* novelty; early fruit.

primeval or **primaeval** *prī-mē'vl*, *adj* belonging to the earth's beginnings; primitive; instinctive. — *adv* **prime'vally** or **primae'vally**. [L *prīmaevus*, from *prīmus* first, and *aevum* an age]

primigenial *prī-mi-jē'ni-əl*, *adj* first or earliest formed or produced; original; primal. — Also, erroneously, **primoge'nial**. [L *prīmigenius*, from *prīmus* first, and *genus* kind]

primigravida *prī-mi-grav'i-də*, (*obstetrics*) *n* a woman pregnant for the first time: — *pl* **primigrav'idae** (*-dē*) or **primigrav'idas**. — See also **prim**[2]. [New L, from *primus* first, and feminine adj *gravida* pregnant]

primine *prī'min*, (*bot*) *n* the outer (or rarely the inner or first formed) coat of an ovule. [L *prīmus* first]

primipara *prī-mip'ə-rə*, (*obstetrics*) *n* a woman who has given birth for the first time only, or is about to do so:

— *pl* **primip'arae** (*-rē*) or **primip'aras**. — *n* **primipar'ity**. — *adj* **primip'arous**. [New L feminine, from L *primus* first, and *parere* to bear, bring forth]

primitiae *prī-mish'i-ē*, *n pl* first-fruits (*relig*); the first year's revenue of a benefice (also **primi'tias** (*Spenser*)). — *adj* **primitial** (*-mish'l*) of or relating to first-fruits; (loosely) primeval, original. [L *prīmitiae*, from *prīmus* first]

primitive *prim'i-tiv*, *adj* belonging to earliest times or the earlier stages of development; original; ancient; antiquated, old-fashioned; simple, rough, crude or rudimentary; not derivative (*philol*); fundamental; first formed, of early origin (*biol*); of the earliest formation (*old geol*); (of a culture or society) not advanced, lacking a written language and having only simple technical skills; simple, naive or unsophisticated in style and approach (*art*). — *n* that from which other things are derived; a root word; (with *cap*) a Primitive Methodist; a painter or picture of pre-Renaissance date or manner; a 19c and 20c school of painting, characterized by simplicity or naivety of approach to subject and technique. — *adv* **prim'itively**. — *n* **prim'itiveness**. — *n* **prim'itivism** approbation of primitive ways, primitive Christianity, primitive art, etc; Primitive Methodism. — *n* **prim'itivist**. — **Primitive Methodism**. — **Primitive Methodist** a member of a religious body (Primitive Methodist Connection) founded in 1810, united with the Wesleyan Methodists and United Methodists in 1932; **primitive streak** in developing mammals, birds and reptiles, a thickening of the upper layer of the blastoderm along the axis of the future embryo. [L *prīmitīvus*, an extension of *prīmus* first]

primo[1] *prē'mō*, (*Ital*) *adj* first. — *n* (*music*) the first or principal part in a duet or trio: — *pl* **pri'mos**. [L *prīmus* first]

primo[2] *prī'mo* or *prē'mō*, *adv* in the first place. [L, ablative of *prīmus* first]

primogenial. See **primigenial**.

primogenit *prī-mō-jen'it*, (*obs*) *adj* and *n* first-born. — *adj* **primogen'ital**, **primogen'itary** and **primogen'itive**. — *n* **primogen'itive** (*Shakesp*) primogeniture. — *n* **primogen'itor** an earliest ancestor; a forefather; the founding ancestor of a people: — *fem* **primogen'itrix**. — *n* **primogen'iture** the circumstance of being first-born; the principle or right of inheritance of the first-born child or (**male primogeniture**) son. — **primogen'itureship** (*rare*). [L *prīmōgenitus*, from *prīmō* first (adv), and *genitus* born, or *genitor* begetter]

primordial *prī-mör'di-əl*, *adj* existing from the beginning, *esp* of the world; original; rudimentary; earliest formed. — *n* the first principle or element. — *n* **primor'dialism**. — *n* **primordiality** (*-al'i-ti*). — *adv* **primor'dially**. — *n* **primor'dium** the primitive source; the first discernible rudiment. — **primordial soup** (*biol*) a solution of organic compounds believed to have composed the earth's lakes and oceans, from which cellular life developed. [L *prīmordium*, from *prīmus* first, and *ordīrī* to begin]

primp *primp*, *vi* to dress in a fussy or affected manner; to preen, titivate. — *vt* to tidy, smarten or titivate (oneself or one's hair, outfit, etc). [Connected with **prim**]

primrose *prim'rōz*, *n* a plant (*Primula vulgaris*) or its pale yellow flower, common in spring in woods and meadows; extended to other plants of the genus Primula; formerly used for some other (and brighter) flower, also the daisy and (*US*) a kind of wild rose; a conventionalized flower, sometimes four-petalled (*heraldry*); the pale yellow colour of a primrose; the choicest (*Spenser*). — *adj* pale yellow, like a primrose. — *vi* to gather primroses. — *adj* **prim'rosed**. — *adj* **prim'rosy**. — **Primrose League** an association for Conservative propaganda formed in 1883 in memory of Lord Beaconsfield, named from his supposed favourite flower; **primrose path** or **way** (from *Shakesp*, *Hamlet* and *Macbeth*) the life of pleasure; **primrose peerless** the two-flowered daffodil. — **evening primrose** see under **evening**. [OFr *primerose*, as if from L *prīma rosa*; perhaps really through ME and OFr *primerole*, from LL *prīmula*, from *prīmus* first]

primsie *prim'zi*, (*Scot*) *adj* prim, demure. [**prim**]

primula *prim'ū-lə*, *n* a plant of the *Primula* genus of flowers including the primrose, cowslip, oxlip, etc, from which is named the dicotyledonous family **Primulā'ceae**, including pimpernel, water violet, cyclamen, etc. — *adj* **primulā'ceous**. — *n* **prim'uline** (*-lēn*) a yellow coal-tar dye. [LL, little first one or firstling, from L *prīmus* first]

primum mobile *prī'məm mō'bi-lē*, *mob'i-lē*, or *prē'mŏŏm mō'bi-le*, *n* in medieval astronomy, the outermost of the revolving spheres of the universe, carrying the others round in 24 hours; any great source of motion. [L]

primus *prī'məs*, *adj esp* formerly in boys' public schools, appended to the surname of the oldest or most senior of several boys with the same surname. — *n* (for *primus episcopus* first bishop) a presiding bishop in the Scottish Episcopal Church, without metropolitan authority. — **primus inter pares** (*prī'məs in'tər pār'ēz* or *prē'mŏŏs in'ter pär'ās*) first among equals. — Also, modernly, *fem* **prima** (*-mə* or *-ma*) **inter pares**. [L, first]

Primus® *prī'məs*, *n* (also **primus stove**) a portable cooking stove burning vaporized oil.

primy. See under **prime**[1].

prin. *abbrev*: principal.

prince *prins*, *n* the son of a sovereign; a non-reigning male member of a royal or imperial family; a sovereign of a small territory; a title of nobility, as eg formerly in Germany (*Fürst*); a ruler, leader or chief (*obs*); a sovereign, a king or queen (*archaic*); anybody or anything that is first in merit or demerit, the most outstanding or notorious representative of a class, as in *the prince of gamblers*. — *vt* (with *it*) to play the prince. — *n* **prince'dom** a principality; the estate, jurisdiction, sovereignty or rank of a prince. — *n* **prince'hood** the rank or quality of a prince. — *n* **prince'kin** a little or young prince. — *n* **prince'let** or **prince'ling** a petty prince. — *adj* **prince'like** like, characteristic of or befitting a prince. — *n* **prince'liness**. — *adj* **prince'ly** of or belonging to a prince or princess; of the rank of prince; princelike; befitting a prince; magnificent; sumptuous; lavish. — Also *adv*. — *adj* **prin'cified** ridiculously dignified. — **prince-bish'op** a bishop ranking as prince or having the power of prince of his diocese; **Prince Charming** the prince in the tale of Cinderella, symbolizing the romantic ideal of a handsome husband; **prince consort** a prince who is husband of a reigning queen; **prince-impe'rial** the eldest son of an emperor; **prince's feather** a tall showy Amaranthus with spikes of rose-coloured flowers; London pride; any of various other plants; **prince's metal** a gold-like alloy of copper and zinc, with more zinc than in brass, Prince Rupert being credited with its invention. — **prince of darkness** or **prince of this world** Satan; **Prince of Peace** Christ; the Messiah; **Prince of Wales** since 1301, a title *usu* conferred on the eldest son of the English, and later British, sovereign; **Prince Rupert's drops** see under **drop**. [Fr, from L *princeps*, from *prīmus* first, and *capere* to take]

princess *prin'ses* or *prinses'*, *n* the wife or daughter of a prince; the daughter of a sovereign, or a non-reigning female member of a royal or imperial family; a title of nobility in some countries; an affectionate form of address to a woman or girl; a woman who is pre-eminent in her field or class; a desirable but remote or unattainable woman; a size of roofing slate, 24 × 14in (610 × 356mm). — *adj* (also **princesse** *Fr*; *prin'* or *-ses'*) denoting a close-fitting style of dress with a flared skirt, composed of vertical panels extending from shoulder to hem (**princess dress** a dress in this style; **princess line** this style). — *adv* **prin'cessly** like a princess. — **princess royal** a title which may be conferred on the eldest daughter of a sovereign. [OFr *princesse*, feminine of *prince*]

principal *prin'si-pl*, *adj* highest in rank or importance; chief, main; constituting a capital sum or principal (*finance*). — *n* the head of a college or university, or sometimes of a school; someone who takes a leading part; a leading actor or performer in a play, show, etc; the person who commits a crime, or someone who aids and abets him or her in doing it (*law*); a person for whom another becomes surety (*law*); a person who, being *sui juris*, employs someone else to do an act which he or she is competent himself to do (*law*); someone who fights a duel; the sum of money on which interest is paid; a main beam, rafter, girder or timber; a roof-truss; the structural framework of a roof; an organ stop like the open diapason but an octave higher (*music*). — *n* **principality** (*-pal'i-ti*) the status, dignity or power of a prince; the condition of being a prince; the territory of a prince or one that he derives his title from; (in *pl*) one of the nine orders of angels in the Celestial hierarchy (*Med theol*). — *adv* **prin'cipally**. — *n* **prin'cipalness**. — *n* **prin'cipalship**. — **principal boy** (*theat*) the role of the young male hero in pantomime, *usu* played by a woman; **principal clause** a clause which could function as an independent sentence, a main clause (*gram*); **principal parts** (*gram*) those forms of a verb from which all other forms may be deduced, eg, in English, the infinitive, the past tense and the past participle. — **the Principality** Wales. [L *principālis*, from *princeps*, *-ipis* chief]

principate *prin'si-pāt*, *n* princehood; principality; the Roman empire in its earlier form in which something of republican theory survived. [L *principātus*, from the emperor's title *princeps* (*cīvitātis*) chief (of the city or state)]

principium *prin-sip'i-əm* or *pring-kip'i-ōōm*, *n* a beginning; a first principle or element; the general's quarters in a Roman camp: — *pl* **princip'ia**. — *adj* **princip'ial** elementary. [L *principium*]

principle *prin'si-pl*, *n* a source, root, origin; a fundamental or primary cause; a beginning (*obs*); essential nature; a theoretical basis or assumption from which to argue, etc; an instinct or natural tendency (as in *the pleasure-pain principle*), or a faculty of the mind; a source of action; a scientific law, *esp* as explaining a natural phenomenon or the way a machine works; a fundamental truth on which others are founded or from which they spring; a law or doctrine from which others are derived; a general rule that guides one's (moral) conduct; consistent regulation of behaviour according to moral law; the morality or moral aspect of eg a policy or course of action; a norm of procedure (as in *the principle of first come first served*); a component (*obs*); a constituent of a substance that gives it its distinctive character (*chem*); motive power or the source of it (*Milton*). — *vt* (*obs*) to ground in principles; to impress a doctrine on. — *adj* **prin'cipled** holding certain principles; having, or behaving in accordance with, good principles; invoking or founded on a principle. — **first principles** fundamental principles, not deduced from others; **in principle** so far as general character or theory is concerned without respect to details or particular application; broadly or basically; in theory; **on principle** on grounds of (moral) principle; for the sake of obeying or asserting a particular principle of morality or wisdom; **principle of contradiction** the logical principle that a thing cannot both be and not be; **principle of equivalence** a statement of the theory of relativity, shown by an observer being unable to distinguish whether the laboratory is in a uniform gravitational field or in an accelerated frame of reference; **principle of least time** a statement that the path of a ray, eg of light, from one point to another will be that taking the least time (see also **Fermat's principle of least time**); **principle of relativity** a universal law of nature stating that the laws of mechanics are not affected by a uniform rectilinear motion of the system of co-ordinates to which they are referred (see also **relativity** under **relate**); **principle of the excluded middle** (*logic*) the principle that a thing must be either one thing or its contradictory; **principle of sufficient reason** see under **reason**. [L *principium* beginning, from *princeps*]

princox *pring'koks* or *prin'*, (*Shakesp*) *n* a conceited fellow; a coxcomb; a jocular, grotesque or ironical endearment. — Also **prin'cock** (*-kok*). [Origin obscure]

prink *pringk*, *vt* to titivate, groom or smarten (*usu* oneself; sometimes with *up*). — *vi* to preen oneself. — **prink about** to behave archly or flirtatiously. [Appar connected with **prank**[2]]

print *print*, *n* an impression; a mould or stamp; a moulded pat of butter; exactitude of plaiting, crimping, or setting (a ruff, hair, etc) (*archaic*); exactitude (*archaic*); printed state; printed characters or lettering; an edition; a printed copy; a printed picture; an engraving; a newspaper; a positive photograph made from a negative (or negative from positive); a printed cloth, *esp* calico stamped with figures; a plaster-cast in low relief (*archit*); a fingerprint. — *adj* printed (*obs*); of printed cotton. — *vt* to impress (characters, etc) on paper, etc, by means of types, plates or blocks; to reproduce (text or pictures) by such means; to cause to be so reproduced; to publish (a book, article, etc); to press (something) into a yielding surface, so as to leave an indented mark; to impress (a surface); to mark (a figure, design, etc) in or on a surface by pressure; to stamp a pattern on or transfer it to (eg a textile); to produce as a positive picture from a negative, or as a negative from a positive (*photog*); to write in separated, as opposed to joined-up, characters, in the manner of typography; to express in writing (*Shakesp*); to designate in print (*Milton*); to fix or impress (a scene, etc) indelibly (on the memory, etc). — *vi* to practise the art of printing; to publish a book; to yield an impression or (*photog*) a positive, etc; to write in separated characters, in typographic style. — *adj* **print'able** capable of being printed; fit to print. — *n* **print'er** someone or something that prints; someone who is employed in printing books, etc; any of a variety of devices for printing eg telegraph messages, photographs, the output from a computer, etc; a cotton cloth made for printing. — *n* **print'ing** the act, art or business of the printer; the whole number of copies printed at one time, an impression. — *adj* **print'less** receiving or leaving no impression. — **printed circuit** a wiring circuit, free of loose wiring, formed by printing the design of the wiring on copper foil bonded to a flat base and etching away the unprinted foil; **printed circuit board** the combined circuit and supporting base; **printer's devil** see under **devil**; **printer's ink** printing-ink; **printer's mark** an engraved device used by printers as a trademark; **printer's pie** a jumble of indiscriminately mixed type (*printing*); any confused jumble; **print'head** or **print'ing-head** the part or unit in a printer that does the work of reproducing characters on paper; **print'ing-house** a building where printing is carried on; a printing-office; **print'ing-ink** ink used in printing, a *usu* thickish mixture of pigment (such as carbon black) with oil and sometimes varnish; **print'ing-machine** a printing-press worked by power; **print'ing-office** an establishment where books, etc are printed; **printing paper** a paper suitable for printing purposes; **print'ing-press** a machine by which impressions are taken in ink upon paper from types, plates, etc; **print'-out** the printed information or output from a computer, etc; **print run** the number of copies of a book, newspaper, etc, printed at a time; **print'-seller** a seller of prints or engravings; **print shop** a print-seller's shop; **print'-through** the degree to which matter printed on one side of paper, etc is visible from the other side (*printing*); in magnetic tape recordings, the transfer of a recording from one layer to another when the tape is wound on a spool (*comput*, *video*, etc); **print'works** an establishment where cloth is printed. — **in print** (of a text, etc) existing in printed form; (of a book) printed and still available from a publisher; (of hair or a ruff, etc) in exact order, formally set, crimped, pleated or plaited (*obs*); **out of print** no longer in print; no longer available from a publisher; **print out** to print; to produce a print-out of. [ME *print*, *prente*, etc, from OFr *preinte*, *priente*, from *preindre*, *priembre*, from L *premere* to press]

prion[1] *prī'on*, *n* any petrel of the genus *Pachyptila*, blue-grey above and white below, feeding on the plankton of the southern oceans. [Gr *priōn* a saw]

prion[2] *prī'ōn*, (*pathol*) *n* a transmittable or inheritable mutant or 'rogue' protein, postulated as the cause of certain diseases of the brain and nervous system in animals and humans, including BSE and scrapie (qqv). [Coined from **protein**]

prior[1] *prī'ər*, *adj* previous, earlier; (of an engagement) already arranged for the time in question; more important, pressing or urgent. — *adv* (with *to*) before; up to the time of, until. [L *prior*, *-ōris* former, previous, superior]

prior[2] *prī'ər*, *n* the deputy of the abbot in an abbey (*claustral prior*); the head of a priory of monks (*conventual prior*) or of a house of canons regular or of friars; in Italy, formerly, a magistrate. — *n* **prī'orāte** the rank or term of office of a prior or prioress; a priory or the community it comprises. — *n* **pri'oress** an abbess's deputy; the head of a priory of nuns. — *n* **prī'orship** the office or tenure of office of a prior. — *n* **prī'ory** a convent of monks or nuns subject to an abbey. — **grand priory** a province of the Knights of St John, under a **grand prior**. [L *prior*, *-ōris*, a superior or principal, from the adj (see **prior**[1])]

priority *prī-or'i-ti*, *n* the state of being first in time, place, or rank; preference; the privilege of preferential treatment; something that ought to be considered or dealt with in the earliest stage of proceedings. — *adj* having, entitling to, or allowed to those who have, priority. — *n* **prioritiza'tion** or **-s-**. — *vt* and *vi* **prior'itize** or **-ise** to arrange, deal with, etc in order of priority, importance or urgency; to accord priority or urgent status to. — **get one's priorities right** to give things appropriate attention in appropriate order. [Med L *priōritās*, from *prior* former, previous, earlier, superior]

prisage *prī'zij*, *n* the former right of the English kings to two tuns of wine from every ship importing twenty tuns or more. [OFr *prise* taking]

Priscianist *prish'ə-nist* or *-yə-nist*, *n* a grammarian. — **break Priscian's head** to breach the rules of grammar. [*Priscianus*, Latin grammarian (*fl.* c.500 AD)]

prise[1] or **prize** *prīz*, *vt* to force (*esp* up, out or open) with a lever; to draw (eg information) laboriously (out of someone). — *n* (a tool giving) purchase or leverage. [Fr *prise* hold, grip, a capture; see **prize**[2]]

prise[2]. See **price**, and **prize**[1,2,3].

priser. Obsolete form of **prizer**; see under **prize**[1,3].

prism *prizm*, *n* a solid whose ends are similar, equal and parallel polygons, and whose sides are parallelograms (*geom*); an object of that shape, *esp* a triangular prism of glass or the like for resolving light into separate colours; a crystal form of three or more faces parallel to an axis (*crystallog*); (loosely) prismatic colours or spectrum. — *adj* **prismat'ic** or **prismat'ical** resembling, belonging to or using a prism; built up of prisms (*crystallog*); (of colours or light) (as though) produced by means of a prism, hence clear and brilliant. — *adv* **prismat'ically**. — *n* **pris'moid** (*geom*) a figure like a prism, but with similar unequal ends. — *adj* **pris'moidal**. — *adj* **pris'my** prismatic in colour. — **prismatic colours** the seven colours into which a ray of white light is refracted by a prism, that is red, orange, yellow, green, blue, indigo and violet; **prismatic compass** a surveying instrument which by means of a prism enables the compass reading to be taken as the object is sighted; **prismatic powder** pebble-powder. — **triangular**, **quadrilateral**, etc, **prism** a prism whose ends are triangles, quadrilaterals, etc. [Gr *prīsma*, *-atos* a piece sawn off, sawdust, a prism, from *prīein* to saw]

prison *priz'n*, *n* a public building for the confinement of convicted criminals and accused persons waiting to be tried, a jail; any place of confinement or situation of intolerable restriction; custody, imprisonment. — *vt* (*poetic*) to shut in prison; to enclose; to restrain. — *n* **pris'oner** someone under arrest or confined in prison; a captive, *esp* in war; anyone kept under restraint against his or her will. — *n* **pris'onment** (*Shakesp*) imprisonment, confinement. — *adj* **pris'onous** (*Dickens*). — **prison bars** the bars of a prison window, door, etc; whatever confines or restrains; (as *n sing*) prisoners' base; **pris'on-breaker** someone who escapes from prison; **pris'on-breaking**; **prison camp** an enclosed guarded camp where prisoners of war or political prisoners are kept; **prison crop** hair cut very short; **prison door**; **prisoners'** (or **prisoner's**) **base** a game in which those caught are held as prisoners (*appar* for *prison bars*); **prison house** a prison or prison building; **prison officer** the official title of a warder (still so called unofficially) in prison; **prison ship**; **prison van** a closed vehicle for transporting prisoners; **prison visitor** someone who visits prisoners in jail as a voluntary service; **prison yard**. — **prisoner of conscience** see under **conscience**; **prisoner of war** a person captured during a war, *esp* a member of the armed forces, but also including militia, irregular troops and, under certain conditions, civilians; **take prisoner** to capture and hold as a prisoner. [OFr *prisun*, from L *prensiō*, *-ōnis*, for *praehensiō* seizure, from *praehendere*, *-hensum* to seize]

prissy *pris'i*, *adj* insipidly prim, prudish or fussy; effeminate. [Probably **prim** and **sissy**]

pristane *pris'tān*, (*chem*) a saturated hydrocarbon oil found in the livers of some marine creatures, eg sharks. [Coined from Gr *pristis* sawfish, shark]

pristine *pris'tēn* or *-tīn*, *adj* original; former; belonging to the earliest time; pure, unspoilt, unchanged; fresh, clean, unused or untouched. [L *pristinus* former, early; cf *priscus* ancient]

prithee or **prythee** *pridh'ē* or *-i*, (*archaic*) *interj* (used in expressing requests, desires, etc) pray, please. [Contracted form of *I pray thee*]

prittle-prattle *prit'l-prat'l*, *n* empty talk. [Reduplication of **prattle**]

privacy *priv'ə-si* or *prī'və-si*, *n* seclusion; (one's right to) freedom from intrusion by the public; avoidance of notice, publicity or display; secrecy, concealment; a place of retreat or retirement (*rare*); a private matter (*rare*). [**private**]

privado *pri-vä'dō*, (*obs*) *n* a private friend, *esp* of a prince: — *pl* **priva'dos** or **priva'does**. [Sp, from L *prīvātus* private]

privat-dozent or **-docent** *prē-vät'-dō-tsent'*, *n* in German universities, a recognized teacher who is not a member of the salaried staff. [Ger, from L *prīvātus* private, and *docens*, *-entis* teaching, from *docēre* to teach]

private *prī'vət*, *adj* (of a person or individual) not in public office; (of a member of parliament) not holding government office; (of a soldier) not an officer or non-commissioned officer; peculiar to oneself, personal, individual; own; relating to personal affairs; set apart or divorced from matters of state; in an unofficial capacity; belonging to or concerning an individual person or company; (of industries, etc) owned and run by private individuals, not by the state; not coming under the state system of education, health care, social welfare, etc; paid for or paying individually by fee; independent; not open to or available for the use of the general public; not made known generally; confidential; retired from observation, secluded; of reserved personality, shunning publicity; alone (*old*); privy (*obs*). — *n* privacy; a private person (*Shakesp*, *Milton*); (in *pl*) private parts; a private soldier; a secret message (*Shakesp*). — *adv* **prī'vately**. — *n* **prī'vateness** (*rare*). — *n* **privatizā'tion** or **-s-**. — *vt* **prī'vatize** or **-ise** to transfer from ownership by the state into private ownership; to denationalize. — *n* **pri'vatizer** or **-s-**. — **private act** or **bill** one that deals with the concerns of private persons; **private company** a company with restrictions on the number of shareholders, whose shares may not be offered to the general public; **private detective** see **detective** under **detect**; **private enterprise** an economic system in which individual private firms operate and compete freely; **private eye** (*colloq*) a private detective; **private hotel** a term of uncertain meaning, popularly understood to imply that the proprietors do not commit themselves to receiving chance travellers; **private house** the dwelling-house of a private individual, as contrasted with a shop, office or public building; **private income** private means; **private investigator** (*esp NAm*) a private detective; **private judgement** freedom to judge for oneself, eg (*relig*) untrammelled by the interpretation of the church; **private law** that part of law which deals with the rights and duties of persons as individuals in relation to each other; **private life** personal, social and family relationships and activities, *esp* of someone much in the public eye; **private means** income from investments, etc as opposed to salary or fees for work done; **private member's bill** a bill introduced and sponsored by a private member in parliament; **private parts** (*euphem*) the external sexual or excretory organs; **private patient** in the UK, a patient whose treatment is not being paid for by the National Health Service; **private pay bed** see **pay bed** under **pay**; **private practice** in the UK, medical practice that does not come under the National Health Service; **private press** a printing concern run by a private individual for recreation rather than profit-making; **private school** a school run independently by an individual or a group, *esp* for profit; **private secretary** a secretary who looks after the personal and confidential affairs of a business person, etc; an aide to a government minister or senior official; **private sector** the part of a country's economy owned, operated, etc, by private individuals and firms (as opposed to *public sector*); **private treaty** a method of selling property in which the selling price is negotiated directly by the buyer and seller; **private view** a preview of an art exhibition, etc held for specially invited guests, before it is opened to the general public; **private wrong** an injury done to an individual in his or her private capacity. — **in private** not in public; away from public view; secretly. [L *prīvātus*, pa p of *prīvāre* to deprive, to separate]

privateer *prī-və-tēr'*, *n* a private vessel commissioned to seize and plunder an enemy's ships in wartime; the commander or one of the crew of a privateer. — *vi* to cruise in a privateer. — *n* **privateer'ing**. — **privateers'man** a crew member on a privateer. [**private**]

privation *prī-vā'shən*, *n* the state of being deprived of something, *esp* of what is necessary for comfort; the absence of a quality (*logic*). [L *prīvātio*, *-ōnis*, from *prīvāre* to deprive]

privative *priv'ə-tiv*, *adj* causing privation; consisting in the absence or removal of something; (of an affix, etc) expressing absence or negation (*gram*). — *n* that which is privative or depends on the absence of something else; a term denoting the absence of a quality (*logic*); a privative affix or word (*gram*). — *adv* **priv'atively**. [L *prīvātīvus*, from *prīvāre* to deprive]

privet *priv'it*, *n* a half-evergreen European shrub (*Ligustrum vulgare*) of the olive family, used for hedges; applied to other members of the genus. [Origin uncertain]

privilege *priv'i-lij*, *n* an advantage, right or favour granted to or enjoyed by an individual, or a select few; freedom from burdens borne by others; advantages and power enjoyed by people of wealth and high social class; a happy advantage; (an opportunity that one interprets as) a special pleasure or honour, as in *a privilege to meet you*; a prerogative; a franchise, monopoly or patent granted to an individual or company; an option to purchase or sell securities (*US stock exchange*); a sacred and vital civil right; advantage yielded in a struggle (*Shakesp*); right of sanctuary (*Shakesp*). — *vt* (*usu* in *passive*) to grant a privilege to; to exempt (with *from*); to authorize or license. — *adj* **priv'ileged** enjoying a privilege or privileges; enjoying the advantages of wealth and class. — **breach of privilege** any interference with or slight done to the rights or privileges of a legislative body; **privilege of parliament** or **parliamentary privilege** special rights or privileges enjoyed by members of parliament, such as freedom of speech (not subject to slander laws), and freedom from arrest except on a criminal charge; **question of privilege** any question arising out of the rights of an assembly or of its members; **writ of privilege** an order for the release of a privileged person from custody. [Fr *privilège*, from L *prīvilēgium*, from *prīvus* private, and *lēx*, *lēgis* a law]

privy *priv'i*, *adj* private; of or belonging to a particular person, own, personal; for private uses; secret; (of a place, etc) appropriate to withdrawal or retirement; (with *to*) sharing the knowledge of (something secret), apprised of, party to; familiar, intimate (*obs*). — *n* a person having an interest in an action, contract, conveyance, etc (*law*); a lavatory, *esp* in its own shed or outhouse (*old*). — *adv* **priv'ily** (*literary*) privately; secretly. — *n* **priv'ity** privacy (*archaic*); secrecy (*archaic*); something kept private or secret (*obs*); innermost thoughts or private counsels (*obs*); knowledge, shared with another, of something private or confidential; knowledge implying concurrence; any legally recognized relation between different interests. — **privy chamber** a private apartment in a royal residence; **privy council** *orig* the private council of a sovereign, advising in the administration of government; (with *caps*) now in the UK, a committee of advisors to the sovereign whose membership consists of all present and past members of the Cabinet and other eminent people, its functions being mainly formal or performed by committees, etc; (with *caps*) in certain countries of the British Commonwealth, a body of advisers to the governor-general, including eg cabinet ministers of the country concerned; **privy councillor** or **counsellor** (also with *caps*); **privy purse** (also with *caps*) an allowance for the private or personal use of the sovereign; **privy seal** see under **seal**[1]. — **gentlemen of the privy chamber** officials in the royal household in attendance at court; **Lord Privy Seal** see under **seal**[1]. [Fr *privé*, from L *prīvātus* private]

prix fixe *prē fēks*, (*Fr*) *n* fixed price.

prize[1] (*Spenser*, *Shakesp* **prise**) *prīz*, *n* a reward or symbol of success offered or won in competition by contest or chance, or granted in recognition of excellence; anything well worth striving for; a highly valued acquisition; privilege or advantage (*Shakesp*); esteem (*Spenser*); valuation, appraisal (*Shakesp*). — *adj* awarded, worthy of, or constituting a prize; treasured; (ironically) perfect, great (as in *a prize fool*). — *vt* to value; to value highly; to set a price on (*obs*); (*Spenser* **pryse**) to pay for. — *adj* **pri'zable** valuable. — *adj* **prized** valued highly; treasured. — *n* **pri'zer** (*rare*) an appraiser. — **prize list** a list of winners; **prize'man** or **prize'woman** a winner of a prize, *esp* an academic prize; **prize'-winner**. [A differentiated form of **price** and **praise**, from OFr *pris* (n), and *prisier* (vb), from L *pretium* price]

prize[2] (*Spenser*, *Shakesp* **prise**) *prīz*, *n* that which is taken by force, or in war, *esp* a ship; seizure (*obs*). — *vt* to make a prize of. — **prize court** a court for judging regarding prizes made on the high seas; **prize crew** a crew put aboard a prize to bring her to port; **prize money** share of the money or proceeds from any prizes taken from an enemy. [Fr *prise* capture, thing captured, from L *praehensa*, feminine pa p of *praehendere* to seize]

prize[3] (*Spenser* **prise**) *prīz*, *n* an athletic contest (*obs*); a match (*old*). — *n* **pri'zer** a contestant in a prize or match. — **prize'fight** a public boxing-match fought for money, *esp* in the 18c and 19c; **prize'fighter** *orig* someone who fights in a prize; a professional boxer; **prize'fighting**; **prize ring** a ring for prizefighting; the practice itself. — **play one's** (or **a**) **prize** to engage in a match; to sustain one's part. [Possibly from **prize**[1]]

prize[4]. See **prise**[1].

prn *abbrev*: *pro re nata* (*L*), as the need arises.

PRO *abbrev*: Public Record Office; public relations officer.

pro[1] *prō*, (*L*) *prep* for. — **pro aris et focis** (*ār'ēz et fō'sēz* or *är'ēs et fō'kēs*) for altars and firesides; for the sake of one's religion and one's home; **pro bono publico** (*bo'nō pub'li-kō* or *bō'nō pŏŏ'bli-kō*) for the public good; **pro forma** (*för'mə* or *fōr'mä*) as a matter of form. — *adj* **pro-for'ma** (of an account, etc) made out to show the market price of specified goods; with goods being paid for before dispatch. — *n* a pro-forma invoice; loosely, an official form or record for completion. — Also **profor'ma**. — **pro hac vice** (*hak vī'sē, wē'ke* or *vē'ke*) for this turn or occasion; **pro indiviso** (*in-di-vī'sō, -zō, in-dē-wē'sō, -vē'*) as undivided; applied in law to rights which two or more persons hold in common (*law*); **pro memoria** (*mə-mōr'ē-ə* or *-mör'*, *me-mō'ri-ä*) for a memorial; **pro patria** (*pā'tri-ə* or *pä'tri-ä*) for one's country; **pro rata** (*rā'tə* or *rä'tä*) in proportion; **pro re nata** (*rē nā'tə* or *rā nä'tä*) for a special emergency, as the need arises or circumstances dictate; **pro tanto** (*tan'tō*) for so much; **pro tempore** (*tem'pə-rē* or *tem'po-re*) for the time being.

pro[2] *prō*, *n* (*colloq*) a contraction of **professional** (golfer, cricketer, actor, etc), of **probationary** (nurse), and of **prostitute**: — *pl* **pros** (*prōz*). — *adj* of or relating to a pro or pros. — *adj* **pro'-am'** (of eg a golf tournament) involving both professionals and amateurs. — Also *n*. — *adj* **pro-celeb'rity** (of eg a golf tournament) involving professionals and celebrities such as film stars.

pro[3] *prō*, *adv* in favour. — *prep* in favour of. — *n* someone who favours or votes for some proposal; a reason or argument in favour: — *pl* **pros** (*prōz*). — *adv* **pro and con** (L *prō et contrā*) for and against. — *vt* and *vi* to consider or discuss for and against: — *pr p* **pro'ing and conn'ing** or **pro-and-conn'ing**; *pa p* **pro'd and conned, con'd** or **pro-and-conned'**. — **pros and cons** reasons or arguments for and against. [L *prō* for]

pro-[1] *prō-*, (*Gr*) *combining form* denoting before (in time or place); earlier than; in front of; the front part of; primitive; rudimentary. [Gr prep *pro* before; cf L *prō*, Eng **for, fore**]

pro-[2] *prō-*, (*L*) *combining form* (1) occurring as an etymological element with the senses before (in place or time), forward, forth, publicly; as a living prefix (2) denoting instead of, in place of, acting on behalf of, as in *pro-chancellor* (qv); (3) denoting tending to cause; (4) denoting in favour of, supporting, backing, as in *pro-American, pro-European, pro-privatization, pro-conservation*. — *adj* **pro-choice'** (denoting the lobby) upholding or supporting the right of a woman to have an abortion. — *adj* **pro-life'** (denoting the lobby) opposing abortion, euthanasia and experimentation on human embryos. — *n* **pro-li'fer**. — *n* **pro-marketeer'** a person in favour of Britan's entry into, or continued membership of, the European Single Market. [L prep *prō*, earlier *prōd*, in combination sometimes *pro-*; cf **pro-**[1]]

proa *prō'ə*. See **prau**.

proactive *prō-ak'tiv*, *adj* tending actively to instigate changes in anticipation of future developments, as opposed to merely reacting to events as they occur; ready to take the initiative, acting without being prompted by others; (of a prior mental experience) tending to affect, interfere with or inhibit a subsequent, *esp* learning, process (*psychol*). [**pro-**[1]]

proairesis *prō-ā'ri-sis*, or *-ī'ri-sis*, *n* the act of choosing. [Gr, choosing]

pro-am. See under **pro**[2].

prob *prob*, (*colloq*) *n* a problem.

prob. *abbrev*: probable.

probable *prob'ə-bl*, *adj* having more evidence for than against; giving ground for belief, likely to be correct; likely to happen; likely to have happened, likely to be the case; plausible; capable of being proved (*rare*). — *n* a probable opinion; a person or thing likely to be selected; a candidate with a good chance of success; something that is a likelihood. — *n* **probabil'iorism** the doctrine that in case of doubt one is constrained to choose the more probable opinion. — *n* **probabil'iorist**. — *n* **prob'abilism** the doctrine that in a disputed or doubtful case of law one should follow the opinion supported by a recognized Doctor of the Church (*RC theol*); the theoretical premise that knowledge, scientific rules, etc cannot be absolute but can suffice to represent probability (*philos*). — *n* **prob'abilist**. — *adj* **probabilis'tic**. — *n* **probabil'ity** the quality of being probable, likelihood; the appearance of truth; that which is probable; the chance or likelihood of something happening; a measure of the likelihood of something occurring, expressed as a ratio of positive cases to total potential cases: — *pl* **probabil'ities**. — *adv* **prob'ably**. — **probable error** a quantity assumed as the value of an error, such that the chances of the real error being greater are equal to those of its being less; **probable evidence** evidence not conclusive, but carrying some degree of force. — **in all probability** quite probably. [Fr, from L *probābilis*, from *probāre*, *-ātum* to prove]

proball *prō'bl*, (*Shakesp*) *adj* supposed to mean plausible. [Apparently a contracted form of **probable**]

proband *prō'band*, *n* a person with some distinctive characteristic (*esp* a physical or mental disorder) who serves as the starting-point for a genetic study of the transmission of this feature through his or her descendants. [L *probandus*, gerundive of *probāre* to test]

probang *prō'bang*, (*med*) *n* a slender flexible rod, tipped with a sponge or button, for passing down the throat and into the oesophagus, in order to apply medication or remove an obstruction. [Called *provang* by its inventor, the Welsh judge, Walter Rumsey (1584–1660); origin uncertain; probably influenced by **probe**]

probate *prō'bāt* or *-bit*, *n* the proof before a competent court that a written paper purporting to be the will of a person who has died is indeed his or her lawful act; the official copy of a will, with the certificate of its having been proved. — *adj* relating to the establishment of wills and testaments. — *vt* (*NAm*) to establish the validity of (a will) by probate; to place a probate on; to place a probation sentence on. — *adj* **probative** (*prō'bə-tiv*) testing; affording proof. — *adj* **prō'batory** testing. — **Probate Court** a court created in 1858 to exercise jurisdiction in matters touching the succession to personal estate in England; **probate duty** (*hist*) a tax on property passing by will. [L *probāre*, *-ātum* to test, prove]

probation *prō-bā'shən* or *prə-*, *n* testing; proof; a preliminary time or condition appointed to allow suitability or unsuitability (eg of a new employee) to appear; noviciate; suspension of sentence, allowing liberty under supervision on condition of good behaviour (*esp* to young, or first, offenders); time of trial; moral trial. — *adj* **probā'tional** relating to, serving purpose of, probation or trial. — *adj* **probā'tionary** probational; on probation. — *n* a probationer. — *n* **probā'tioner** someone who is on probation or trial; an offender under probation; a novice; someone licensed to preach, but not ordained to a pastorate (*esp Scot*). — *n* **probā'tionership**. — **probation officer** a person appointed to advise and supervise offenders under probation. [L *probātio*, *-ōnis*, from *probāre* to test]

probe *prōb*, *n* an instrument for exploring a wound, locating a bullet, etc; an act of probing; an exploratory bore; a prod; an investigation; any of various instruments of investigation in space research (eg a multi-stage rocket), electronics, etc; a pipelike device attached to an aircraft for making connection with a tanker aeroplane so as to refuel in flight; a device used in docking two space modules; a radioactive or otherwise labelled fragment of DNA or RNA used to find and identify nucleic acid sequences by hybridizing with them. — *vt* to examine with or as if with a probe; to examine searchingly. — *vt* and *vi* to pierce. — *adj* **pro'beable**. — *n* **pro'ber** someone or something that probes. — **probe scissors** scissors used to open wounds, one blade having a button at the end. [L *proba* proof, later examination, from *probāre* to prove]

probit *prō'bit*, (*statistics*) *n* a unit for measuring probability in relation to an average frequency distribution. [*Prob*ability un*it*]

probity *prō'bi-ti* or *prob'*, *n* uprightness; moral integrity; honesty. [L *probitās*, -ātis, from *probus* good, honest]

problem *prob'ləm*, *n* a matter difficult to settle or solve; a source of perplexity; a question or puzzle propounded for solution; the question how to win in so many moves beginning with a hypothetical situation (*chess*); a proposition in which something is required to be constructed, not merely proved as in a theorem (*geom*). — *adj* presenting, posing or constituting a problem; difficult to deal with, intractable. — *adj* **problemat'ic** or **problemat'ical** of the nature of a problem; questionable; doubtful; (of a proposition) stating what is possible but not necessarily the case (*logic*). — *adv* **problemat'ically**. — *n pl* **problemat'ics** matters that are problematic or that raise questions. — *n* **prob'lemist** a person who composes or solves chess, etc problems. — **problem child** one whose character presents an exceptionally difficult problem to parents, teachers, etc; **problem novel** or **play** one presenting or expounding a social or moral problem; **problem page** a page or section in a magazine devoted to dealing with readers' personal problems; **problem-solving behaviour** the use of various strategies to overcome difficulties in attaining a goal. [Gr *problēma*, *-atos*, from *pro* before, in front, and *ballein* to throw]

proboscis *prō-bos'is* or *prə-*, also *-bosk'* or *-bōs'* *n* a trunk or long snout; a trunk-like process such as the suctorial mouth-parts of some insects; a nose (*facetious*): — *pl* **probosc'ises** or **probosc'ides** (*-i-dēz*). — *n pl* **Proboscid'ea** the elephant order of mammals. — *adj* and *n* **proboscid'ean** or **proboscid'ian**. — **proboscis monkey** a very long-nosed monkey (*Nasalis larvatus*). [L, from Gr *proboskis* a trunk, from *pro* expressing motive, and *boskein* to feed]

probouleutic *prō-bōō-lū'tik*, *adj* for preliminary deliberation. [Gr *probouleusis* preliminary deliberation]

procacity *prə-kas'i-ti*, *n* petulance. — *adj* **procacious** (*-kā'shəs*). [L *procācitās*, *-ātis*, from *procāx* forward, insolent, shameless, from *procāre* to demand]

procaine *prō'kān*, *n* a crystalline substance used as a local anaesthetic. [**pro-**[2] (2) and **cocaine**]

procaryon, etc. See **prokaryon**.

procathedral *prō-kə-thē'drəl*, *n* a church used temporarily as a cathedral. [Pfx **pro-**[2] (2)]

proceed *prō-sēd'* or *prə-*, *vi* to go on; to continue; to advance; to pass on; to begin and go on; to act according to a method; to go from point to point; to advance to a higher degree (as in *proceed MA*) or more developed state; to prosper; to come forth; to result; to be descended; to take measures or action; to take legal action; to prosecute; to go on, be transacted, happen (*Shakesp*). — *vt* to say in continuation. — *n* **prō'ceed** (*usu* in *pl*) outcome; money got from anything. — *adj* **procedural** (*-sēd'yə-rəl*). — *n* **procē'dure** a mode of proceeding; a method of conducting business, *esp* in a law case or a meeting; a course of action; a step taken or an act performed. — *n* **proceed'er**. — *n* **proceed'ing** the action of moving forward; progress; advancement; a course of conduct; *perh* an advantage (*Shakesp*); a step; an operation; a transaction; (in *pl*) a record of the transactions of a society. [Fr *procéder*, from L *prōcēdere*, from *prō* before, and *cēdere*, *cessum* to go]

proceleusmatic *pros-e-lūs-mat'ik*, *adj* inciting, encouraging. — *n* a foot of four short syllables (*ancient prosody*). [Gr *prokeleusmatikos*, from *pro* before, and *keleuein* to urge, order]

Procellaria *pros-e-lā'ri-ə*, *n* the petrel genus. — *adj* **procella'rian**. [L *procella* a storm]

procephalic *prō-si-fal'ik*, *adj* of the forepart of the head. [Gr *pro* before, and *kephalē* head]

procerebrum *prō-ser'i-brəm*, *n* the fore-brain; the prosencephalon. — *adj* **procer'ebral**. [L *prō* before, and *cerebrum* brain]

procerity *prō-ser'i-ti*, *n* tallness. [L *prōcēritās*, *-ātis*, from *prōcērus* tall]

process[1] *prō'ses* or (*esp NAm*) *pros'* (*Milton prō-ses'*), *n* a state of being in progress or being carried on; course; a narrative (*Shakesp*); a series of actions or events; a sequence of operations or changes undergone; a photo-process (*printing*); a writ by which a person or matter is brought into court (*law*); an action, suit, or the proceedings in it as a whole; progression; proceeding; an edict (*Shakesp*); a projection or projecting part, *esp* on a bone (*biol*, *anatom*). — *vt* to serve a summons on; to sue or prosecute; to subject to a special process; to produce or print photo-mechanically; to prepare (eg agricultural produce) for marketing by some special process, eg canning or bottling; to arrange (documents, etc) systematically; to examine and analyse; to test the suitability of (a person) for some purpose; (of a computer) to perform operations of adding, subtracting, etc, or other operations on (data supplied); to subject (data) to such operations. — *adj* **prō'cessed** produced by a special process, eg synthetically, photo-mechanically, etc; subjected to a certain process. — *n* **prō'cessor** something or someone that processes; a device which processes data (*comput*); a central processing unit (*comput*). — *adj* **process'ual** governed by or related to an established process; having a direct function (*NAm*). — **process block** a photo-mechanically made block for printing a picture; **process control** direct automatic control of a physical industrial process by computer; **pro'cess-server** a sheriff's officer. — **data=processing** the handling and processing of information by computers; **in the process** (or **in process) of** in the course of (doing something, being made, etc). [Fr *procès*, from L *prōcessus*, *-ūs* advance; cf **proceed**]

process[2]. See under **procession**.

procession *prō-sesh'ən* or *prə-*, *n* the act of proceeding; a file or train of people, vehicles, boats, etc moving forward together by way of ceremony, display, demonstration, etc; the movement of such a train; a litany sung in procession (*Christian church*). — *vi* (*rare*) to go in procession. — *vt* (*rare*) to go through or around in procession; to celebrate by a procession. — *vi* **process** (*prō-ses'*; back-formation) to go in procession. — *adj* **process'ional**. — *n* (*Christianity*) a book of litanies, hymns, etc for processions; a hymn sung in procession. — *n* **process'ionalist**. — *adj* **process'ionary**. — *n* **process'ioner** (*US*) a county officer who determines boundaries. — *n* **process'ioning** going in procession; perambulation of boundaries (*US*). — **processionary moth** a European moth (*Cnethocampa processionea*) whose caterpillars go out seeking food in great processions. — **Procession of the Holy Ghost** (*Christian theol*) the emanation of the Holy Spirit from the Father (*single procession*), or from the Father and Son (*double procession*). [L *prōcessiō*, *-ōnis*; cf **proceed**]

processor, **processual**. See under **process**[1].

procès-verbal *pro-se-ver-bäl*, (*Fr*) *n* a written statement or report: — *pl* **-verbaux** (*ver-bō*).

prochain or **prochein ami** or **amy** *pro-shen a-mē*, (*law*) *n* next friend (qv). [OFr]

pro-chancellor *prō-chän'sə-lər*, *n* in certain British universities, the deputy to the vice-chancellor (qv). [**pro-**[2] **(2)**]

prochronism *prō'krə-nizm*, *n* a dating of an event before the right time (*opp* of *metachronism*). [Gr *pro* before, and *chronos* time]

procidence *prōs'i-dəns* or *pros'*, (*med*) *n* prolapse. — *adj* **pro'cident**. [L *prōcidentia*, from *prō* forward, and *cadere* to fall]

procinct *prō-singkt'*, (*Milton*) *n* preparedness. [L *prōcinctus*, *-ūs*, from *prō* beforehand, and *cingere*, *cinctum* to gird]

proclaim *prō-klām'* or *prə-*, *vt* to cry aloud; to publish abroad; to announce officially; to denounce; to announce the accession of; to place under restrictions by proclamation. — *n* a proclamation; a proclaiming. — *n* **proclaim'ant**. — *n* **proclaim'er**. — *n* **proclamation** (*prok-lə-mā'shən*) the act of proclaiming; that which is proclaimed; an official notice given to the public; a proscription. — *adj* **proclamatory** (*-klam'ə-tə-ri*). [Fr *proclamer*, from L *prōclāmāre, proclāmāre*, from *prō* out, and *clāmāre* to cry]

proclitic *prō-klit'ik*, (*linguistics*) *adj* (of a word) transferring its stress to the following word, or lacking stress and forming a phonological unit with the following word. — *n* a proclitic word. — *n* **pro'clisis** (or *prok'*) pronunciation of a word as a proclitic. [A 19c coinage on the analogy of **enclitic**, from Gr *pro* forward, and *klīnein* to lean]

proclivity *prō-kliv'i-ti* or *prə-*, *n* inclination; propensity. — *adj* **proclive** (*-klīv'*; *archaic*) inclined; prone; headlong. [L *prōclīvis*, from *prō* forward, and *clīvus* a slope]

procoelous *prō-sē'ləs*, *adj* cupped in front. [Gr *pro* before, and *koilos* hollow]

proconsul *prō-kon'sl*, *n* a Roman magistrate with almost consular authority outside the city, *orig* one whose consulate had expired, often the governor of a province (*hist*); sometimes applied to a governor of a colony or dominion; a member of the genus *Proconsul* of prehistoric African anthropoid apes. — *adj* **procon'sular** (*-sū-lər*). — *n* **procon'sulate** (*-sū-lit* or *-lāt*). — *n* **procon'sulship** the office, or term of office, of a proconsul. [L *prōconsul*]

procrastinate *prō-kras'ti-nāt*, *vi* to defer action; to put off what should be done immediately. — *vt* (*rare*) to put off till some future time, to defer. — *n* **procrastinā'tion** the act or habit of putting off, dilatoriness. — *adj* **procras'tinative**, **procras'tināting** or **procras'tinatory**. — *n* **procras'tinativeness**. — *n* **procras'tinātor**. [L *procrāstināre*, *-ātum*, from *prō* onward, and *crāstinus* of tomorrow, from *crās* tomorrow]

procreate *prō'kri-āt*, *vt* to engender; to beget; to generate. — *vi* to produce offspring. — *n* **prō'creant** (*-kri-ənt*) a generator. — *adj* generating; connected with or useful in reproduction. — *n* **prōcreā'tion**. — *adj* **prōcreā'tional**. — *adj* **prō'creātive** having the power to procreate; generative; productive. — *n* **prō'creātiveness**. — *n* **prō'creātor** a parent. [L *prōcreāre*, *-ātum*, from *prō* forth, and *creāre* to produce]

Procrustean *prō-krus'ti-ən*, *adj* violently making conformable to a standard from *Procrustes* (Gr *Prokroustēs*) a legendary Greek robber, who stretched or cut his captives' legs to make them fit a bed (hence **Procrustean bed**) [Gr *prokrouein* to lengthen out]

procrypsis *prō-krip'sis*, (*biol*) *n* protective coloration. — *adj* **procryp'tic**. — *adv* **procryp'tically**. [Gr *pro* before, and *krypsis* hiding, from *kryptein* to hide]

proctal *prok'tl*, *adj* anal or rectal. [Gr *prōktos* anus]

procto- *prok-tə-*, *-tō-* or *-to'* or (before a vowel) **proct-**, *combining form* denoting rectum or anus. — *n* **proctalgia** (*-al'ji-ə*; see **-algia**) neuralgic pain in the rectum. — *n* **proctī'tis** inflammation of the rectum. — *adj* **proctodae'al** (*-tō-dē'əl* or *-tə-*). — *n* **proctodae'um** (Gr *hodaios* on the way) the posterior part of the alimentary canal, formed embryonically by invagination of the ectoderm. — *n* **proctol'ogist**. — *n* **proctol'ogy** the medical study and treatment of the rectum. — **proc'toscope** an instrument for examining the rectum. — *n* **proctos'copy**. [Gr *prōktos* anus]

proctor *prok'tər*, *n* an official in English universities whose functions include enforcement of university regulations; an examination supervisor or invigilator at a university (*US*); a procurator or manager for another; an attorney in the ecclesiastical courts; a representative of the clergy in Convocation. — *n* **proc'torage**. — *adj* **procto'rial** (*-tōr'* or *-tör'i-əl*). — *adv* **procto'rially**. — *vt* **proc'torize** or **-ise** to exercise the power of a proctor against. — *n* **proc'torship**. — **king's** or **queen's proctor** an official who intervenes in divorce cases in England if collusion or fraud is suspected. [**procurator**]

procumbent *prō-kum'bənt*, *adj* lying or leaning forward; prone; prostrate; growing along the ground (*bot*). [L *prōcumbens*, *-entis*, pr p of *prōcumbere*, from *prō* forward, and *cumbere* to lie down]

procurator *prok'ū-rā-tər*, *n* a financial agent in a Roman imperial province, sometimes administrator of part of it (*hist*); someone who manages affairs for another; someone authorized to act for another; an agent in a law court. — *adj* **procuratorial** (*-rə-tō'ri-əl* or *-tör'*). — *n* **proc'uratorship**. — *n* **proc'uratory** (*-rə-tər-i*) authorization to act for another. — **procurator fiscal** see under **fisc**. [L *prōcūrātor*, *-ōris*; see **procure**]

procure *prō-kūr'* or *prə-*, *vt* to contrive to obtain or bring about; to encompass (eg someone's downfall, etc); to obtain (prostitutes) for clients; to induce (*obs*); to induce to come, bring (*Shakesp*); to urge earnestly (*Spenser*). — *vi* to pander, pimp. — *adj* **procur'able** available, obtainable. — *n* **procuracy** (*prok'ū-rə-si*) the office of a procurator. — *n* **procurā'tion** the management of another's affairs; the instrument giving authority for this; a sum paid by incumbents to the bishop or archdeacon on visitations; the process of procuring. — *n* **procure'ment** the act of procuring. — *n* **procur'er** someone who procures; a pander. — *n* **procur'ess** a female procurer, a bawd. [Fr *procurer*, from L *prōcūrāre* to manage, from *prō* for, and *cūrāre*, *-ātum* to care for]

procureur *pro-kü-rœr*, (*Fr*) *n* a procurator. — **procureur général** (*zhān-ā-ral*) in France, the public prosecutor-in-chief.

Procyon *prō'si-ən*, *n* a first-magnitude star in the constellation of the Lesser Dog; the raccoon genus, giving name to the family **Procyon'idae** (raccoons, coatis, etc). [Gr *Prokyōn* the star Procyon, rising before the Dogstar, from *pro* before, and *kyōn* a dog]

Prod *prod*, (*offensive slang*) *n* (*esp* in Ireland) a Protestant.

prod *prod*, *vt* to prick; to poke, eg with a fingertip or the end of a stick: — *pr p* **prodd'ing**; *pa t* and *pa p* **prodd'ed**. — *n* an act of prodding; a sharp instrument such as a goad, awl or skewer. [Origin uncertain; OE *prodbor* seems to mean auger]

prodigal *prod'i-gl*, *adj* wasteful of one's means; squandering; lavish. — *n* a waster; a spendthrift; a wanderer returned (also **prodigal son**). — *adv* (*Shakesp*) prodigally. — *n* **prodigality** (*-gal'i-ti*) the state or quality of being prodigal; extravagance; profusion; great liberality. — *vt* **prod'igalize** or **-ise** to spend lavishly, to waste. — *adv* **prod'igally**. [Obs Fr, from L *prōdigus*, from *prōdigere* to squander, from pfx *prōd-* (early form of *prō-*) away, forth, and *agere* to drive]

prodigy *prod'i-ji*, *n* a portent (*archaic*); any person or thing that causes great wonder; a wonder; a monster; a child of precocious genius or virtuosity. — *n* **prodigios'ity**. — *adj* **prodig'ious** astonishing; more than usually large in size or degree; monstrous; of the nature of a prodigy (*archaic*). — *adv* **prodig'iously**. — *n* **prodig'iousness**. [L *prōdigium* a prophetic sign, from pfx *prōd-* (earlier form of *prō-*) in advance, and prob the root of *adagium* (see **adage**)]

proditor *prod'i-tər*, *n* a traitor. — *adj* **prodito'rious** (*-tör'i-əs* or *-tōr'*) or **prod'itory**. [L *prōditor*, *-ōris*, from *prōdere*, *-itum* to betray, from *prō* forth, and *dare* to give]

prodnose *prod'nōz*, (*slang*) *n* a prying, meddlesome person; a detective. — *vi* (*rare*) to pry. [**prod** and **nose**]

prodrome *prod'rōm*, *n* an introductory treatise; a premonitory event; a sign of approaching disease. — Also **prod'romus** (*prod'rə-məs*; *pl* **prod'romī**). — *adj* **prod'romal** and **prodrom'ic**. [Latinized from Gr *prodromos* forerunner, from *pro* before, and *dromos* a run]

produce *prə-dūs'*, *vt* to bring into being; to bring forth; to yield; to bring about; to make; to put (a play, show, etc) on the stage; to prepare (a programme) for broadcasting on radio or television; to prepare for exhibition to the public; to bring forward or out; to extend. — *vi* to yield; to create value. — *n* **produce** (*prod'ūs*) that which is produced; product; proceeds; crops; yield, *esp* of fields and gardens. — *n* **produce'ment** (*Milton*) product. — *n* **produc'er** someone who produces commodities; someone who produces a play, show, programme, etc; someone who exercises general control over, but does not actually make, a cinema film (cf **director**); a furnace in which a mixed combustible gas is produced by passing air and steam through incandescent coke. — *n* **producibil'ity**. — *adj* **produc'ible** capable of being produced; capable of being generated or made; capable of being exhibited. — *n* **product** (*prod'əkt* or *-ukt*) a thing produced; a result; a work; offspring; a quantity obtained by multiplying (*math*); a substance obtained from another by chemical change (*chem*). — *n* **productibil'ity** (*prə-dukt-*) the capability of being produced. — *adj* **pro-duct'ile** capable of being drawn out in length. — *n* **produc'tion** the act of producing or process of being produced; that which is produced; fruit; product; a work, *esp* of art; the staging of a play, show, etc; the staged performance itself; a bringing out; change in biomass expressed on an area basis, *primary production* being by green plants, *secondary production* by heterotrophic organisms (*ecol*); the creation of values (*pol econ*); extension; a document produced in court (*Scots law*). — *adj* **produc'tional**. — *adj* **produc'tive** having the power to produce; generative; that produces (with *of*); producing richly; fertile; efficient. — *adv* **produc'tively**. — *n* **produc'tiveness**. — *n* **productiv'ity** (*prod-* or *prōd-*) the rate or efficiency of work, *esp* in industrial production. — **producer gas** gas made in a producer, chiefly a mixture of hydrogen and carbon monoxide diluted with nitrogen; **producer** (or **producers'**) **goods** goods, such as raw materials and tools, used in the production of consumer(s') goods; **production car**, **vehicle**, etc one made in the routine course of production, as distinct from one made for a special purpose such as testing; **production line** an assembly line (qv); **production platform** an oil platform (qv); **production string** the smallest casing in an oil well, reaching from the producing zone to the well head — also **oil string**; **productivity deal** an agreement whereby employees receive increased wages or salaries if they agree to improve their efficiency and increase their output; **product life cycle** the four stages of marketing a product, ie introduction, growth, maturity and decline; **product placement** a disguised form of advertising whereby a particular product is included noticeably in a shot in a feature film, etc. — **make a production of** (or **out of**) (*colloq*) to make an unnecessary fuss or commotion about (something). [L *prōdūcere*, *-ductum*, from *prō* forward, and *dūcere* to lead]

proem *prō'em*, *n* an introduction; a prelude; a preface. — *adj* **proemial** (*prō-ē'mi-əl*). [Fr *proème*, from L *pro-oemium*, from Gr *prooimion*, from *pro* before, and *oimē* a song, *oimos* a way]

proembryo *prō-em'bri-ō*, (*bot*) *n* a group of cells formed in the dividing zygote, from which part the embryo arises: — *pl* **proem'bryos**. [**pro-**[1]]

proenzyme *prō-en'zīm*, *n* an enzyme in an inactive form which can be activated, often by another enzyme. [**pro-**[1]]

Prof. *abbrev*: professor.

prof *prof*, *n* a familiar contraction of **professor**.

proface *prō-fās'*, (*Shakesp*) *interj* may it profit you, a phrase of welcome. [OFr *prou* profit, and *fasse*, 3rd pers sing present subjunctive of *faire* to do]

profane *prō-fān'* or *prə-*, *adj* not sacred; secular; showing contempt of sacred things; (of language) irreverent or blasphemous; uninitiated; unhallowed; ritually unclean or forbidden. — *vt* to treat (something holy) with contempt or insult; to desecrate; to violate; to put to an unworthy use. — *n* **profanation** (*prof-ə-nā'shən*). — *adj* **profanatory** (*prō-fan'ə-tər-i*). — *adv* **profane'ly**. — *n* **profane'ness**. — *n* **profān'er**. — *n* **profanity** (*-fan'*) irreverence; that which is profane; profane language or conduct; a blasphemy or oath. [L *profānus* outside the temple, not sacred, unholy, from *prō* before, and *fānum* a temple]

profectitious *prō-fek-tish'əs*, *adj* derived from a parent or ancestor. [LL *profectīcius*, from L *proficīscī*, *profectus* to proceed]

profess *prə-fes'* or *prō-*, *vt* to make open declaration of; to declare in strong terms; to claim, often insincerely, to have a feeling of; to pretend to; to claim to be expert in; to be professor of; to receive into a religious order by profession (*RC*). — *vi* to enter publicly into a religious order; to pretend friendship (*Shakesp*); to be a professor. — *adj* **professed'** openly declared; avowed; alleged; acknowledged; having made a profession (of a religious belief, etc). — *adv* **profess'edly**. — *adj* **pro-fess'ing** avowed; pretending, soi-disant. — *n* **profession** (*-fesh'ən*) the act of professing; an open declaration; an avowal; a declaration of religious belief made upon entering a religious order; a pretence. — *n* **professor** (*prə-fes'ər*) someone who professes; someone who openly declares belief in certain doctrines; a university or college teacher of the highest grade, *esp* the head of a department (used as a title prefixed to the name); in N America, a university or college teacher of any grade (prefixed to the name), rising from *assistant professor*, *associate professor* to full *professor* — see also **associate professor**; a title assumed by charlatans, quacks, dancing-masters, etc: — *fem* (*rare*) **profess'oress**. — *n* **profess'orate** professoriate. — *adj* **professorial** (*prof-es-ō'ri-əl* or *prof-es-ö'ri-əl*). — *adv* **professo'rially**. — *n* **professo'riate** the office or chair of a professor; his or her period of office; a body of professors. — *n* **profess'orship**. [L *professus*, pa p of *profitērī*, from *prō* publicly, and *fatērī* to confess]

profession[1] *prə-fesh'ən*, *n* a non-manual occupation requiring some degree of learning or training; a calling, habitual employment; the collective body of people engaged in any profession. — *adj* **profess'ional** of, belonging to or relating to a profession; engaged in a profession or in the profession in question; competing for money prizes or against those who sometimes do so; undertaken as a means of subsistence, as opposed to *amateur*; showing the skill, artistry, demeanour or standard of conduct appropriate in a member of a profession or of a particular profession; (of a foul, etc) deliberate, intended (to prevent the opposition from scoring) (*euphem*; *sport*). — *n* someone who makes his or her living by an art that is also practised at an amateur level; someone who engages in sport for livelihood or gain or against those who do so (with various rules of interpretation for each sport) (opposite of *amateur*); a member of a profession; a person following a career; (in full, *professional examination*) any one of the successive examinations towards a degree in medicine (in Scottish universities). — *n* **profess'ionalism** the status of professional; the competence or the correct demeanour of those who are highly trained and disciplined; the outlook, aim, or restriction of the mere professional; the predominance of professionals in sport. — *n* **professionalizā'tion** or **-s-**. — *vt* **profess'ionalize** or **-ise** to give a professional character to; to give over to professionals. — *adv* **profess'ionally**. [L *professiō*, *-ōnis* from *professus*; see **profess**]

profession[2]. See under **profess**.

proffer *prof'ər*, *vt* to offer for acceptance, to tender or present; to offer to undertake: — *pr p* **proff'ering**; *pa t* and *pa p* **proff'ered**. — *n* an offer or tender; the act of proffering; an incipient act. — *n* **proff'erer**. [Anglo-Fr *proffrir*, from L *prō* forward, and *offerre*; see **offer**]

proficient *prə-fish'ənt* or *prō-fish'ənt*, *adj* competent; well-skilled; thoroughly qualified. — *n* a person who is making progress in learning (*Shakesp*); an adept; an expert. — *n* **profi'cience** (now *rare* or *obs*) or **pro-fi'ciency**. — *adv* **profi'ciently**. [L *prōficiens*, *-entis*, pr p of *prōficere* to make progress]

profile *prō'fīl* (formerly also *-fēl* and *prō'fil*), *n* an outline; a head or portrait in a side view; the outline of any object without foreshortening (*art*); a drawing of a vertical section of country, an engineering work, etc; a graph; a short biographical sketch, eg in a newspaper or magazine; an outline of the characteristic features (of eg a particular type of person); an outline of the course of an operation; one's manner, attitude or behaviour considered with regard to the extent to which it attracts attention to oneself and one's activities or reveals one's feelings, intentions, etc, or the extent of one's involvement, etc (as in *low*, *high*, etc *profile*); a public image, *esp* one created and controlled by design. — *vt* to draw in profile; to make an outline of; to show in profile; to give a profile to; to shape the outline of; to write or give a profile of. — *n* **prō'filer**. — *n* **prō'filist** someone who draws profiles. [Ital *profilo*, from L *prō* before, and *fīlum* a thread]

profit *prof'it*, *n* gain; the gain resulting from the use of capital; the excess of selling price over first cost; advantage; an increase in good or value; benefit; improvement. — *vt* to benefit or be of advantage to. — *vi* to gain advantage; to receive profit; to make progress, to improve (*Shakesp*); to be of advantage. — *n* **profitabil'ity**. — *adj* **prof'itable** yielding or bringing profit or gain; lucrative; productive. — *n* **prof'itable-ness**. — *adv* **prof'itably**. — *n* **profiteer'** (*derog*) a person who takes advantage of an emergency to make exorbitant profits. — *vi* to act as a profiteer. — *n* **profiteer'ing**. — *n* **prof'iter**. — *n* **prof'iting**. — *adj* **prof'itless** without profit. — *adv* **prof'itlessly**. — *adj* **prof'it-orientated** whose chief aim is profit. — **prof'it-sharing** a voluntary agreement under which an employee receives a share, fixed beforehand, of the profits of a business; **prof'it-taker**; **prof'it-taking** the selling-off of shares, commodities, etc, in order to profit from a rise in the purchase price. [Fr, from L *prōfectus* progress, from *prōficere*, *prōfectum* to make progress]

profiterole *prə-fit'ə-rōl*, *n* a small puff of choux pastry, *usu* filled with cream and covered with a chocolate sauce. [Fr; dimin of *profit* profit]

profligate *prof'li-git* or *prof'li-gāt*, *adj* overthrown, defeated (*obs*); debauched, having given oneself over to vice; dissolute; prodigal, rashly extravagant. — *n* a person leading a profligate life; someone who is recklessly extravagant or wasteful. — *n* **prof'ligacy** (*-gə-si*) the state or quality of being profligate; a life devoted to vice; abundance, profusion. — *adv* **prof'li-gately**. [L *prōflīgātus*, pa p of *prōflīgāre*, from *prō* forward, and *flīgere* to dash]

profluent *prō'flōō-ənt*, (*Milton*) *adj* flowing out or onwards. — *n* **pro'fluence**. [L *prō* forth, and *fluere* to flow]

Pr. of Man. (*Bible*) *abbrev*: (the Apocryphal Book of the) Prayer of Manasses.

proforma or **pro-forma**. See under **pro**[1].

profound *prə-fownd'* or *prō-fownd'*, *adj* deep; deep-seated; far below the surface; intense; abstruse; intellectually deep; penetrating deeply into knowledge. — *n* (*poetic*) the sea or ocean; an abyss or great depth. — *adv* **profound'ly**. — *n* **profound'ness** or **profundity** (*-fund'*) the state or quality of being profound; the depth of a place, of one's knowledge, etc; something which is profound. [Fr *profond*, from L *profundus*, from *prō* forward, and *fundus* bottom]

profulgent *prə-ful'jənt* or *prō-ful'jənt*, *adj* shining out, radiant. [L *prō* forth, and *fulgens*, *-entis*, pr p of *fulgēre* to shine]

profuse *prə-fūs'* or *prō-fūs'*, *adj* excessively liberal; lavish; extravagant; overabundant. — *adv* **profuse'ly**. — *n* **profuse'ness**. — *n* **profuser** (*-fūz'ər*; *Herrick*) a prodigal or spendthrift. — *n* **profusion** (*-fū'zhən*) the state of being profuse; extravagance; prodigality. [L *prōfūsus*, pa p of *prōfundere*, from *prō* forth, and *fundere* to pour]

prog[1] *prog*, *vt* (*obs* or *dialect*) to pierce; to prick; to poke. — *vi* (*obs* or *dialect*) to poke about for anything; to forage for food; to beg. — *n* a pointed instrument (now *esp dialect*); a thrust (*dialect*); provisions, *esp* for a journey (*colloq*). [Origin unknown; perh several distinct words]

prog[2] *prog*, (*university slang*) *n* a proctor. — *vt* to proctorize. — *n* **progg'ins** a proctor.

prog[3] *prog*, (*colloq*) *n* a radio or television *prog*ramme.

progenitor *prō-jen'i-tər*, *n* a forefather; an ancestor; a parent; the founder of a family: — *fem* **progen'itress** or **progen'itrix**. — Also *fig*. — *adj* **progenito'rial** (*-tōr'i-əl* or *-tör'i-əl*). — *n* **progen'itorship**. — *n* **progen'iture** an act or instance of begetting. — *n* **progeny** (*proj'ə-ni*) offspring; descendants; race; lineage (*Shakesp*). — Also *fig*. [L *prōgenitor* and *prōgeniēs*, from *prōgignere*, from *prō* before, and *gignere*, *genitum* to beget]

progeria *prō-jer'i-ə*, *n* a rare disease causing premature ageing in children. [Gr *pro* before, and *gēras* old age]

progesterone *prō-jes'tər-ōn*, *n* a female sex hormone that prepares the uterus for the fertilized ovum and maintains pregnancy. — *n* **proges'tin** (**pro-**[1], *ges*tation, and *-in*) any hormone concerned with changes before pregnancy, *esp* **proges'togen** any of a range of hormones of the progesterone type (several synthetic progestogens are used in oral contraceptives). [*pro-gestin*, *ster*ol, and *-one*]

proggins. See under **prog**[2].

proglottis *prō-glot'is*, *n* a detachable tapeworm segment: — *pl* **proglott'idēs**. [Gr *pro* before, and *glōttis*, *-idos* a pipe mouthpiece]

prognathous *prog'nə-thəs*, also *prog-nā'thəs* or *prōg-nā'thəs*, (*zool*) *adj* with a projecting jaw. — Also **prognathic** (*prog-nath'ik* or *prōg-nath'ik*). — *n* **prog'na-thism** (or *-nath'izm* or *-nāth'izm*). [Gr *pro* forward, and *gnathos* a jaw]

Progne *prog'nē*, *n* a personification of the swallow, or sometimes of the nightingale (*poetic*); an American genus of swallows. [Philomela's sister, L *Procnē* (or *Prognē*, from Gr *Proknē*) transformed into a swallow, or a nightingale]

prognosis *prog-nō'sis*, *n* a forecasting or forecast, *esp* of the course of a disease: — *pl* **prognō̄s'es** (*-ēz*). — *n* **prognostic** (*prog-nost'ik* or *prəg-nost'ik*) a foretelling, forecast or prediction; an indication of something to come, an omen; a symptom on which prognosis can be based (*med*). — *adj* indicating what is to happen by signs or symptoms; of prognosis. — *vt* **prognos'ticāte** to foretell; to indicate the coming of. — *n* **prog-nosticā'tion**. — *adj* **prognos'ticātive**. — *n* **prognos'ticātor** a predictor or foreteller; a person who predicts coming events, future weather conditions, etc (*obs*). [Gr *prognōsis*, from *pro* before, and *gignōskein* to know]

prograde *prō'grād*, *adj* (of metamorphism) from a lower to a higher metamorphic level, or caused by a rise in temperature or pressure (*geol*); (of movement or rotation) in a forward direction, ie in the same direction as that of adjacent bodies (*astron*). — *vi* (*geog*; of a coastline, etc) to advance seawards because of a build-up of sediment. — *n* **progradā'tion**. [**pro-**[2] (1) and contrast with retro*grade*]

programme or (*esp NAm*, and *comput*) **program** *prō'gram*, *n* a public notice (*obs Scot*); a paper, booklet, or the like, giving an outline of proceedings arranged for an entertainment, conference, course of study, etc, with relevant details; the items of such proceedings collectively; a plan of things to be done; a TV or radio presentation produced for broadcast singly or as one of a series; the sequence of actions to be performed by a computer in dealing with data of a certain kind; a sequence of encoded instructions to a computer to fulfil a task or series of actions; a course of instruction (by book or teaching machine) in which subject-matter is broken down into a logical sequence of short items of information, and a student can check immediately the suitability of his or her responses; a curriculum or course of study (*esp US*). — *vt* to provide with, enter in, etc a programme; to prepare a program for (a computer, etc); to create a certain pattern of thought, reaction, etc in the mind of (*fig*). — *n* **programmabil'ity** (*comput*). — *adj* **programm'able** (*comput*) capable of being programmed to perform a task, calculation, etc automatically. — *n* a programmable calculator. — *adj* **programmatic** (*-grə-mat'ik*) of a programme; of, or of the nature of, programme music. — *adj* **pro'grammed**. — *n* **pro'grammer** a person who programs a computer; (also **programme picture**) a B-movie, a low-budget cinema film produced to accompany the main picture of a cinema show. — *n* **pro'gramming**. — **programmed learning** learning by programme (see **programme** above); **programme music** music that is intended to depict a scene or tell a story; **programme picture** see **programmer**; **programming language** a system of codes, symbols, rules, etc designed for communicating information to, on or by a computer; **Programming Language 1** (*abbrev* **PL/1**) a computer programming language which combines the best qualities of commercial- and scientific-oriented languages; **program**, or **programme, trader**; **program**, or **programme, trading** the automatic buying or selling of securities, etc by computer when the price reaches pre-set limits. — **programme evaluation and review technique** a method of planning, monitoring and reviewing the progress, costs, etc of a complex project. [Gr *programma* proclamation, from *pro* forth, and *gramma* a letter]

progress *prō'gres*, sometimes (*esp US*) *pro'*, *n* a forward movement; an advance; a continuation; an advance to something better or higher in development; a gain in proficiency; a course; movement from place to place; a procession; an official or state journey made by a dignitary, noble or other person of high rank; a circuit. — *vi* **progress'** (formerly, as eg *Shakesp*, *prō'*) to go forward; to make progress; to go on, continue; to go on a state or official journey; to go. — *vt* to traverse (*obs*); to cause (*esp* building or manufacturing work) to proceed steadily. — *n* **progression** (*prə-gresh'ən* or *prō-gresh'ən*) motion onward; the act or state of moving onward; progress; movement by successive stages; a regular succession of chords (*music*); movements of the parts in harmony (*music*); a change from term to term according to some law (*math*); a series of terms so related (see **arithmetic**, **geometry**, **harmony**). — *adj* **progress'ional**. — *adj* **progress'ionary**. — *n* **progress'ionism** sympathy with or advocacy of progress; belief that social or other evolution is towards higher or better things. — *n* **progress'ionist** a believer in progressionism; a progressive; a person who favours progress or reform. — Also *adj*. — *n* **progress'ism** (or *prō'* or *pro'*) progressionism. — *n* **progress'ist** (or *prō'* or *pro'*) a person who advocates a progressive policy; a progressionist. — *adj* **progress'ive** moving forward; making progress; modern, *esp* displaying or applying liberal or enlightened views or practices; of the nature of progress; advancing by successive stages; (of a disease, condition, etc) increasing steadily in severity or extent; (in games, eg **progressive whist**) played by several sets of players, some of whom move from one table to the next after each hand according to the rules of the game; (of a dance) involving moving on to a new partner at some point in the sequence of movements; advancing towards better and better or higher and higher; in favour of social and political progress or reform; (*usu* with *cap*) applied to a political party with progressive policies; (of taxation) in which the rate increases as the amount to be taxed increases. — *n* someone who favours progress or reform; (*usu* with *cap*) a member of a party with 'progressive' in its title. — *adv* **progress'ively**. — *n* **progress'iveness**. — *n* **progress'ivism**. — *n* **progress'ivist**. — **in progress** going on; in course of happening or being produced. [OFr *progresse* (now *progrès*), from L *prōgressus*, from *prō* forward, and *gradī*, *gressus* to step]

progymnasium *prō-jim-nā'zi-əm* or (*Ger*) *prō-gim-nä'zi-ŏŏm*, *n* in Germany, a gymnasium (qv) for pupils up to age 16 only, at which university entrance qualifications are not obtainable. [Ger]

prohibit *prə-hib'it* or *prō-hib'it*, *vt* to forbid; to prevent. — *n* **prohib'iter** or **prohib'itor**. — *n* **prohibition** (*prō-hi-bi'shən* or *prō-i-bi'shən*) the act of prohibiting, forbidding or interdicting; an interdict; the forbidding by law of the manufacture and sale of alcoholic drinks; (*usu* with *cap*) the period (1920–33) when the manufacture and sale of alcoholic drinks was prohibited in the USA. — *adj* **prohibi'tionary**. — *n* **prohibi'tionism**. — *n* **prohibi'tionist** a person who favours prohibition, *esp* of the manufacture and sale of alcoholic drinks. — *adj* **prohibitive** (*-hib'*) tending to make impossible or preclude. — *adv* **prohib'itively**. — *n* **prohib'itiveness**. — *adj* **prohib'itory** that prohibits or forbids; forbidding. [L *prohibēre*, *prohibitum*, from *prō* before, and *habēre* to have]

proign *proin*. An obsolete form of **prune**[2].

proin or **proine** *proin*. Obsolete forms of **prune**[1,2,3].

project *proj'ekt* or *prō'jekt* *n* a notion (*Shakesp*); speculative imagination (*obs*); a projection; a scheme of something to be done; a proposal for an undertaking; an undertaking; an exercise *usu* involving study and/or experimentation followed by the construction of something and/or the preparation of a report (*educ*). — *vt* **project** (*prə-jekt'* or *prō-jekt'*) to throw out or forward; to speak or sing in such a way as to aim (the voice) at the rear of the auditorium, etc (*theat*, etc); to throw, kick or propel; to cause to jut out or stretch out; to scheme, plan or devise; to set out, to set before the mind (*Shakesp*); to cast (eg a light, a shadow or an image) on a surface or into space; to throw an image of; to show outlined against a background; to predict or expect on the basis of past results or present trends; to derive a new figure from, so that each point on the new figure corresponds to a point of the original figure according to some rule, *esp* by a system of parallel, converging or diverging rays through the original points meeting a surface (*geom*); to externalize; to make objective. — *vi* to jut out; to throw projecting powder on a metal which is to be transmuted (*alchemy*). — *adj* **projec'tile** caused by projection; impelling; capable of being thrown or thrust out or forward. — *n* **projectile** (*prō-jek'tīl* or *prə-jek'tīl*; also, less commonly, *proj'ik-tīl*; *US -til*) a body projected by force; a missile, *esp* one discharged by a gun. — *n* and *adj* **projec'ting**. — *n* **projec'tion** (*-shən*) an act or method of projecting; the fact or state of being projected; planning; something which is projected; an instance of jutting out; something which juts out; the standing out of a figure; a figure obtained by projecting another (*geom*); a method of representing geographical detail on a plane, or the representation so obtained (also **map projection**); a projected image; the reading of one's own emotions and experiences into a particular situation (*psychol*); a person's unconscious attributing to other people of certain attitudes towards himself or herself, *usu* as a defence against his or her own guilt, inferiority, etc (*psychol*); the throwing in of powdered philosopher's stone (projecting powder) to effect transmutation, hence transmutation itself in general (*alchemy*). — *adj* **projec'tional**. — *n* **projec'tionist** someone who projects or makes projections, *esp* in map-making; an operator of a film-projector; an operator of certain television equipment. — *adj* **projec'tive** projecting; of projection; derivable by projection (*geom*); unchanged by projection (*geom*). — *n* **projectivity** (*proj-ək-tiv'i-ti*). — *n* **projectiza'tion** or **-s-** the direction of aid to developing countries towards a specific project, without regard to wider issues or needs. — *n* **project'ment** (*rare*) design or plan. — *n* **projec'tor** someone who plans some enterprise; a promoter of speculative schemes for money-making; an apparatus for projecting, *esp* an image or a beam of light; a straight line joining a point with its projection (*geom*). — *n* **projec'ture** a jutting out. — **projecting powder** or **powder of projection** (*alchemy*) the philosopher's stone in powder form; **projection television** optical presentation of a TV picture on a separate open screen; **projective geometry** a branch of geometry dealing with **projective properties**, ie those properties of figures which remain unchanged when the figures are projected. [L *prōjicere, prōjectum*, from *prō* forth, and *jacere* to throw]

projet de loi *pro-zhā də lwa*, (*Fr*) *n* a legislative bill.

prokaryon *prō-kar'i-ən*, (*biol*) *n* the nucleus of a blue-green alga, bacterium, etc, with no membrane separating the DNA-containing area from the rest of the cell (cf *eukaryon*). — *n* **prokar'yote** (*-ōt*) or **prokar'yot** (*-ət*) a cell or organism with such a nucleus or nuclei. — Also *adj*. — *adj* **prokaryot'ic**. — Also **procar'yon**, etc. [**pro-**[1], and Gr *karyon* a kernel]

proke *prōk*, (*dialect*) *vt* and *vi* to poke. — *n* **prōk'er** a poker. [Origin obscure]

prolactin *prō-lak'tin*, *n* a hormone produced by the pituitary gland, which stimulates lactation and also acts as a contraceptive.

prolamine *prō'lə-mēn* or **prolamin** *prō'lə-min*, *n* one of a group of alcohol-soluble proteins.

prolapse *prō-laps'* or *prō'laps*, (*med*) *n* a falling down or out of place (*usu* of an organ, *esp* the womb). — Also **prolap'sus**. — *vi* **prolapse'** to slip out of place [L *prōlābī, prōlapsus* to slip forward, from *prō* forward, and *lābī* to slip]

prolate *prō'lāt* or (*rarely*) *prō-lāt'*, *adj* (of eg a spheroid) drawn out along the polar diameter (*opp* of *oblate*); widespread. — *vt* **prolate'** (*obs*) to lengthen out in utterance. — *adv* **prolately**. — *n* **prolateness**. — *n* **prolation** (*prō-lā'shən*) utterance; the time-ratio of a semibreve to a minim (three minims to a semibreve in *great* or *perfect prolation*, two in *lesser* or *imperfect prolation*) (*medieval music*). — *adj* **prolative** (*prō-lā'tiv* or *prō'lə-tiv*; *gram*) completing the predicate. [L *prōlātus* produced, from *prō* forward, and *lātus*, used as pa p of *ferre* to carry]

prole[1] *prōl*, (*colloq*) *n* and *adj* proletarian.

prole[2], **proler**. Obsolete forms of **prowl** and **prowler**.

proleg *prō'leg*, (*zool*) *n* an insect larva's abdominal leg, distinguished from a thoracic or 'true' leg. [**pro-**[2] (2) and **leg**]

prolegomena *prō-leg-om'in-ə*, *n pl* (sometimes used as *n sing*) an introduction, *esp* to a treatise; an introductory study: — *sing* **prolegom'enon**. — *adj* **prolegom'enary** or **prolegom'enous**. [Gr *prolegomenon*, pl *-a*, neuter of pr p passive of *prolegein*, from *pro* before, and *legein* to say]

prolepsis *prō-lep'sis*, or *prō-lēp'sis*, *n* anticipation; the rhetorical figure of anticipation, ie the use of a word not literally applicable till a later time; a figure of speech by which objections are anticipated and answered: — *pl* **prolep'sēs**. — *adj* **prolep'tic** or **prolep'tical**. — *adv* **prolep'tically**. [Gr *prolēpsis*, from *pro* before, and *lambanein* to take]

proletarian *prō-li-tā'ri-ən*, *adj* of the poorest labouring class; of the proletariat; having little or no property. — *n* a member of the poorest class; a member of the proletariat; a plant without reserves of food (*bot*). — *n* **proletā'rianism** the condition of the poorest classes. — *n* **proletarianizā'tion** or -s-. — *vt* **proletā'rianize** or **-ise**. — *n* **proletā'riat** or (*esp* formerly) **proletā'riate** the poorest labouring class; the wage-earning class, *esp* those without capital. — *n* and *adj* **pro'letary** (*-ər-i*) proletarian. [L *prōlētārius* (in ancient Rome) a citizen of the sixth and lowest class, who served the state not with his property but with his offspring (*prōlēs*)]

prolicide *prō'li-sīd*, *n* the killing of offspring; the killing off of the human race. — *adj* **prolicī'dal**. [L *prōlēs* offspring, and *caedere* to kill]

pro-life, pro-lifer. See under **pro-**[2].

proliferate *prō-lif'ə-rāt*, *vi* to grow by multiplication of parts (cells, buds, shoots, etc) (*biol*); to reproduce by proliferation (*biol*); to reproduce abundantly (*biol*); to greatly increase in numbers rapidly. — *vt* to produce by multiplication of parts; to cause to grow or increase rapidly. — *n* **proliferā'tion** growth and extension by multiplication of cells (*biol*); production of vegetative shoots from a reproductive structure (*biol*); repeated production of new parts (*biol*); production of shoots that may become new plants (*biol*); production of abnormal or supernumerary parts (*biol*); a structure formed by proliferating (*biol*); a great and rapid increase in numbers; the spread of nuclear weapons capability to countries not already possessing such weapons. — *adj* **prolif'erative** or **prolif'erous**. — *adv* **prolif'erously**. [L *prōlēs* offspring, and *ferre* to bear]

prolific *prə-lif'ik* or *prō-lif'ik*, *adj* reproductive; fertilizing; fertile; producing many offspring; (of an author, artist, etc) producing many works; fruitful; abundant. — *n* **prolif'icacy** (*-ə-si*). — *adj* **prolif'ical** (*rare* or *obs*). — *adv* **prolif'ically**. — *n* **prolificā'tion** the production of young; development of a shoot by continued growth of a flower (*bot*). — *n* **prolificity** (*-is'i-ti*). — *n* **prolif'icness**. [L *prōlēs* offspring, and *facere* to make]

proline *prō'lēn* or *prō'-lin*, *n* an amino-acid commonly occurring in proteins. [Ger *Prolin*, contracted from *Pyrrolidin* pyrroline]

prolix *prō'liks* or *prō-liks'*, *adj* long and wordy; long-winded; dwelling too long on particulars; long (*obs* or *rare*). — *adj* **prolixious** (*prō-lik'shəs*; *Shakesp*) dilatory, tiresome or superfluous. — *n* **prolix'ity**. — *adv* **prolixly**. — *n* **prolixness**. [L *prōlixus*, from *prō* forward, and *līquī* to flow]

proll *prōl*, **proller** *prōl'ər*. Obsolete forms of **prowl** and **prowler**.

prolocutor *prō-lok'ū-tər*, *n* a spokesman; a chairman, *esp* of the lower house of Convocation: — *fem* **prōloc'utrix**. — *n* **prolocu'tion** (*prō-* or *pro-*) an introductory speech or saying. — *n* **prōloc'utorship**. [L *prōlocūtor*, from *prōloquī*, *-locūtus* to speak out, from *loquī* to speak]

prologue *prō'log*, *n* in a classical Greek play, the part before the entry of the chorus; an introduction to a poem, etc; a speech before a play; the speaker of a prologue; an introductory event or action. — *vt* to introduce; to preface. — *vi* **pro'logize** or **-ise** (*-gīz* or *-jīz*) to speak a prologue. — Also **pro'loguize** or **-ize**. [Fr, from L *prologus*, from Gr *prologos*, from *pro* before, and *logos* speech]

prolong *prə-long'* or *prō-long'*, *vt* to lengthen out; to postpone (*Spenser* and *Shakesp*). — *vi* to lengthen out. — *adj* **prolongable** (*prō-long'ə-bl*). — *vt* **prolongate** (*prō'long-gāt*) to lengthen. — *n* **prolongation** (*-long-gā'shən*) a lengthening out; a piece added in continuation; a continuation. — *n* **prolonger** (*-long'ər*). [L *prōlongāre*, from *prō* forward, and *longus* long]

prolonge *prō-lonj'* or *prō-lɔ̃zh*, (*military*) *n* a rope for a gun-carriage. [Fr]

prolusion *prō-lōō'zhən* or *prō-lū'zhən*, *n* a preliminary performance, activity or display; an essay preparatory to a more solid treatise. — *adj* **prolu'sory** (*-sə-ri*). [L *prōlūsiō*, *-ōnis*, from *prō* before, and *lūdere*, *lūsum* to play]

PROM *prom*, (*comput*) *abbrev*: programmable read-only memory.

prom *prom*, *n* a contraction of **promenade**; a promenade concert; a school or college dance (*NAm*). — **the Proms** a series of promenade concerts held annually in London.

promachos *prom'ə-kos* or *prom'a-hhos*, *n* a champion or defender; a tutelary god. [Gr]

pro-marketeer See **pro-**[2].

promenade *prom-i-näd'* or *prom'* (also, *esp US*, *prom-i-nād'*), *n* a walk, ride or drive, for pleasure, show or gentle exercise; (also *-nād*) a processional sequence in a dance; a school or college dance, a prom (*NAm*); a place where people walk to and fro; a paved terrace on a sea front; an esplanade. — *vi* to walk, ride or drive about; (also *-nād*) to make a promenade in dancing. — *vt* to lead about and exhibit; to walk, ride or drive about or through. — *n* **promenader** someone who promenades; (*-näd'ər*) a member of the standing portion of the audience at a promenade concert. — **promenade concert** one in which part of the audience stands throughout and can move about; **promenade deck** a deck on which passengers may walk about. [Fr, from *promener* to lead about (*se promener* to take a walk), from L *prōmināre* to drive forwards, from *prō* forward, and *mināre* to push, *minārī* to threaten]

prometal *prō'met-l*, *n* a kind of cast-iron highly resistant to heat.

promethazine *prō-meth'ə-zēn*, *n* a drug used, generally in the form of its hydrochloride, as an antihistamine, to counteract travel sickness, and as a pre-operative sedative. [**propyl**, **methyl**, **azo-** and **-ine**[1]]

Promethean *prō-mē'thi-ən* or *-thyən*, *adj* pertaining to *Prometheus* (*prō-mēthūs*) who, according to Greek myth, stole fire from heaven, for which Zeus chained him to a rock to be tortured by a vulture; daringly innovative. — *n* (*hist*) a glass tube containing sulphuric acid and an inflammable mixture brought together by pressing, an early kind of match. — *n* **promē'thium** (formerly **promē'theum**) a radioactive lanthanide element (symbol **Pm**; atomic no 61). [Gr *Promētheus*]

prominent *prom'i-nənt*, *adj* standing out; projecting; most easily seen; catching the eye or attention; in the public eye. — *n* **prom'inence** the state or quality of being prominent; a prominent point or thing; a projection. — *n* **prom'inency** a prominence. — *adv* **prom'inently**. — **solar prominence** a reddish cloud of incandescent gas shooting out from the sun, visible during a total eclipse. [L *prōminens*, *-entis*, pr p of *prōminēre* to jut forth, from *prō* forth, and *minae* projections, threats]

promiscuous *prō-mis'kū-əs*, *adj* confusedly or indiscriminately mixed; collected together without order; indiscriminate (now *usu* referring to someone indulging in indiscriminate sexual intercourse); haphazard; belonging to a mixed set; far from choice (*old slang*); casual, accidental (*colloq*). — *n* **promiscū'ity** (*prom-*) mixture without order or distinction; promiscuous sexual intercourse. — *adv* **promis'cuously**. [L *prōmiscuus*, from *prō* (intensive), and *miscēre* to mix]

promise *prom'is*, *n* an undertaking to do or keep from doing something; expectation, or that which raises expectation; a ground for hope of future excellence; fulfilment of what is promised (*rare*). — *vt* to undertake by promise to do, give, etc; to betroth; to encourage to expect; to give reason to expect; to assure; to undertake to bestow. — *vi* to make a promise or promises; to give rise to or reason for hopes or expectations; to act as sponsor (*rare*). — *n* **promisee'** the person to whom a promise is made. — *adj* **prom'iseful**. — *adj* **prom'iseless**. — *n* **prom'iser**. — *adj* **prom'ising** giving grounds for hope or expectation; likely to turn out well. — *adv* **prom'isingly**. — *n* **prom'isor** (*law*) the person making a promise. — *adj* **promiss'ive** (*prə-*) conveying a promise; of the nature of a promise. — *n* **promiss'or** (*Roman law*) the maker of a promise. — *adv* **prom'issorily**. — *adj* **prom'issory** containing a promise of some undertaking to be fulfilled. — **prom'ise-breach** (*Shakesp*) the breaking of a promise; **prom'ise-breaker** (*Shakesp*). — *adj* **prom'ise-crammed** (*Shakesp*) fed to repletion with empty promises. — **prom'ise-keeping** (*Shakesp*); **promised land** the land promised by God to Abraham and his descendants, Canaan; heaven; **promissory note** a written promise to pay a sum of money on some future day or on demand. — **be promised** to have a previous engagement (*Shakesp*); to be betrothed (to another); **breach of promise** see under **breach**; **the Promise** the assurance of God to Abraham that his descendants would become the chosen people. [L *prōmissum* neuter pa p of *promittere* to send forward, from *prō* forward, and *mittere* to send]

prommer *prom'ər*, (*colloq*) *n* a (regular) attender of promenade concerts, *esp* a promenader.

promo *prō'mō*, (*colloq*) *n* a short form of **promotion**, *esp* in the sense of a promotional video recording: — *pl* **pro'mos**. — Also *adj*.

promontory *prom'ən-tər-i* or *-tri*, *n* a headland or high cape; a projection, ridge or eminence (*anatom*). — *adj* standing out like a promontory. [LL *prōmontōrium* (L *prōmunturium*), assimilated to *mōns* mountain]

promote *prə-mōt'* or *prō-mōt'*, *vt* to help forward (*obs* or *dialect*); to further; to further the progress of; to raise to a higher grade; to raise (a pawn) to the rank of queen (*chess*); to move (*esp* a football team) to a higher division of a league (*sport*); to take steps for the passage or formation of; to set in motion (eg the office of a judge in a criminal suit) (*eccles law*); to encourage the sales of by advertising. — *n* **promotabil'ity**. — *adj* **promō'table** able to be promoted or suitable for promotion. — *n* **promō'ter** a person who promotes; a person who takes part in the setting-up of companies; the organizer of a sporting event, *esp* a boxing match; a professional informer (*obs*); a DNA region in front of the coding sequence of a gene, involved in the initiation of transcription (*biol*); a substance that increases the efficiency of a catalyst (*chem*); a substance that encourages the formation or growth of tumour cells (*med*). — *n* **promō'tion** (*-shən*) the act of promoting; advancement in rank or in honour; encouragement; preferment; a venture, *esp* in show business; advertising in general, or an effort to publicize and increase the sales of a particular product. — *adj* **promo'tional**. — *adj* **promō'tive**. — *n* **promō'tor** a person who presents candidates for graduation in Scottish universities. — **be on one's promotion** to have the right to or hope of promotion; to be on good behaviour with a view to promotion. [L *prōmovēre*, *-mōtum*, from *prō* forward, and *movēre* to move]

prompt *prompt* or *promt*, *adj* ready in action; performed at once; paid or due at once; ready for delivery; readily inclined (*Shakesp*). — *adv* promptly, punctually, to the minute. — *vt* to incite; to instigate; to move to action; to supply forgotten words to, *esp* in a theatrical performance; to help with words or facts when at a loss; to suggest to the mind. — *n* a time limit for payment (*commerce*); an act of prompting; words provided by the prompter; a question, statement or fixed sequence of characters which appears on a computer screen, showing that the operator may proceed, or choose from set options. — *n* **prompt'er** someone who prompts, *esp* actors. — *n* **prompt'ing**. — *n* **prompt'itude** promptness; readiness; quickness of decision and action. — *adv* **prompt'ly**. — *n* **prompt'ness**. — *n* **prompt'uary** a repository; a reference book of facts. — *n* **prompt'ure** (*Shakesp*) a suggestion; instigation. — **prompt'-book** or **prompt'=copy** a copy of a play for the prompter's use; **prompt'=box** a box for the prompter in a theatre; **prompt neutron** one released in a primary nuclear fission process with practically zero delay; **prompt'-note** (*commerce*) a reminder note of the time-limit for a payment; **prompt side** the side of the stage where the prompter is, *usu* to the actor's left in Britain, to the right in the USA. [L *promptus*, from *prōmere* to bring forward]

promulgate *prom'əl-gāt* (*US prə-mul'gāt*), *vt* to proclaim or announce publicly; to make widely known; to put (eg a law) into effect by proclamation (also, *archaic*, **promulge** *prō-mulj'*). — *n* **promulgā'tion**. — *n* **prom'ulgātor**. [L *prōmulgāre*, *-ātum*]

promuscis *prō-mus'is*, (*entomol*) *n* a proboscis, *esp* of Hemiptera. — *adj* **promusc'idate** (*entomol*) like or having a promuscis. [L *promuscis*, *-idis*, an altered form of *proboscis*]

promycelium *prō-mī-sē'li-əm*, (*bot*) *n* a short germ-tube put out by some fungal spores, producing spores of different types. [**pro-**[1]]

pronaos *prō-nā'os*, *n* the vestibule in front of a temple: — *pl* **prona'oi**. [Gr *pronāos*, from *pro* before, and *nāos* a temple]

prone[1] *prōn*, *adj* with the face, ventral surface or palm of the hand downward; prostrate; directed downward; (loosely) lying or laid flat; descending steeply; disposed, inclined, naturally tending; willing; ready, eager (*Shakesp*); in *Measure for Measure* I.2, of uncertain meaning — perhaps passive, or with downcast eyes, or fervent (*Shakesp*). — **-prone** *combining form* liable to suffer a specified thing, as in *accident-prone*. — *vt* **prōn'ate** (*physiol*) to turn (the foot) sole inwards; to turn (the hand) palm downward or backward with radius and ulna crossed (*opp* of *supinate*). — Also *vi* (of a hand or foot). — *n* **prōnā'tion** (*physiol*) the act of pronating. — *n* **prōnā'tor** (*physiol*) the muscle of the forearm that pronates the hand. — *adv* **prone'ly**. — *n* **prone'ness**. [L *prōnus* bent forward]

prone[2] *prōn*, (*obs*) *n* a place in a church where intimations are given out; hence, a homily. — *n* **proneur** (*prō-nœr'*) a flatterer. [Fr *prône*]

pronephros *prō-nef'ros*, (*zool*) *n* in vertebrates, the anterior portion of the kidney, functional in the embryo but functionless and often absent in the adult. — *adj* **proneph'ric**. [**pro-**[1] and Gr *nephros* kidney]

prong *prong*, *n* a fork of any kind (now chiefly *dialect*); a tine, tooth or spike of a fork or forked object; a tine, spur or projection, eg on an antler; a fork of a stream or inlet (*US*). — *vt* to stab with a prong; to furnish with prongs. — *adj* **pronged** having prongs. — **prong'buck** the pronghorn (properly the male); **prong'-hoe** a hoe with prongs; **prong'horn** an American antelope-like ruminant (*Antilocapra americana*), the only representative of the family *Antilocapridae*, with deciduous horns pronged in front. — *adj* **prong'-horned**. [ME *prange*; origin obscure]

pronk *prongk*, *vi* (of a springbok, etc) to leap in the the air with arched back; to strut or show off (*SAfr*). [Afrik, to show off, strut or prance]

pronominal. See under **pronoun**.

pronotum *prō-nō'təm*, *n* the back of an insect's prothorax: — *pl* **pronō'ta**. — *adj* **pronō'tal**. [**pro-**[1], and Gr *nōton* back]

pronoun *prō'nown*, *n* a word used instead of a noun, noun phrase, etc already known or understood from the context, or (eg *it*) as a dummy subject or object with little or no meaning. — *adj* **pronominal** (*prə-nom'in-əl* or *prō-nom'in-əl*) belonging to, or of the nature of, a pronoun. — *adv* **pronom'inally**. [**pro-**[2]]

pronounce *prə-nowns'* or *prō-nowns'*, *vt* to proclaim; to utter formally or rhetorically; to declare; to utter; to articulate. — *vi* to pass judgement; to articulate one's words. — *n* (*Milton*) pronouncement. — *adj* **pronounce'able** capable of being pronounced. — *adj* **pronounced'** marked with emphasis; marked, very noticeable. — *adv* **pronoun'cedly** (*-səd-li*). — *n* **pronounce'ment** a confident or authoritative assertion or declaration; the act of pronouncing. — *n* **pronoun'cer**. — *n* and *adj* **pronoun'cing**. — *n* **pronunciation** (*prō-nun-si-ā'shən*) a way of pronouncing; articulation. [Fr *prononcer*, from L *prōnūntiāre*, from *prō* forth, and *nūntiāre* to announce, from *nūntius* a messenger]

pronto *pron'tō*, (*slang*) *adv* promptly, quickly. [Sp, from L *prōmptus* at hand]

Prontosil® *pron'tō-sil*, (now *rare*) *n* a trademark for some of the sulphonamide drugs.

pronucleus *pro-nū'kli-əs*, (*biol*) *n* the nucleus of a germ-cell after it has fully matured and before fertilization. — *adj* **pronū'clear**. [**pro-**[1]]

pronunciamento *prō-nun-si-ə-men'tō*, *n* a manifesto; a formal proclamation: — *pl* **pronunciamen'tos** or **pronunciamen'toes**. [Sp]

pronunciation. See under **pronounce**.

pronuncio *prō-nun'shi-ō*, *n* a papal ambassador of lower diplomatic status than a nuncio: — *pl* **pronun'cios**. [**pro-**[2] (2)]

proo or **pruh** *prōō*, (*Scot*) *interj* a call to a cow to come near, or to a horse to stop.

prooemium *prō-ē'mi-əm*, *n* same as **proem**. — Also **prooe'mion**.

pro-oestrus *prō-ēs'trəs*, (*zool*) *n* in mammals, the coming-on of heat in the oestrus cycle. [**pro-**[1]]

proof *prōōf*, *n* something which proves or establishes the truth of anything; the fact, act or process of proving or showing to be true; demonstration; evidence that convinces the mind and goes toward determining the decision of a court; an instrument of evidence in documentary form (*law*); the taking of evidence by a judge upon an issue framed in pleading (*Scots law*); a trial before a judge without a jury (*Scots law*); a checking operation (*arith*); a test; experience (*obs*); issue, outcome or upshot (*obs*); testing, *esp* of guns; ability to stand a test; invulnerability; impenetrability; armour of proof (see below); a standard strength of spirit (alcohol and water of relative density 12/13 at 51°F, ie 49.28 per cent of alcohol by weight); an impression taken for correction (*printing*); an early impression of an engraving; a coin, intended for display, etc rather than circulation, struck from polished dies on polished blanks (also **proof coin**); the first print from a negative (*photog*): — *pl* **proofs**. — *adj* impervious; invulnerable; of standard strength (of alcohol). — *vt* to make impervious, *esp* to water; to take a proof of; to test. — *adj* and *verb combining form* **-proof** denoting (to make) able to withstand or resist, as in *waterproof*, *childproof*, *weatherproof*, etc. — *n* **proof'ing** the process of making waterproof, gasproof, etc; material used for this purpose. — *adj* **proof'less** lacking proof or evidence. — **proof'-charge** a charge used to test the strength of a gun. — *vt* **proof'-correct** (*printing*) to correct in proof. — **proof'-correcting** or **proof correction**; **proof'-house** a building fitted out for proving firearms; **proof'-mark** a mark stamped on a gun to show that it has stood the test; **proof'-puller** (*printing*) a person who pulls proofs. — *vt* and *vi* **proof'read** to read and correct (printed matter) in proof. — **proof'reader** a person who reads printed proofs to look for and correct errors; **proof'reading**; **proof'-sheet** an impression taken on a slip of paper for correction before the final printing; **proof spirit** a standard mixture of alcohol and water; **proof text** a passage of the Bible adduced in proof of a doctrine. — **armour of proof** (*hist*) armour that has been tested, or can be confidently relied on; **artist's proof** a first impression from an engraved plate or block; **burden of proof** see under **burden**[1]; **over**, or **under**, **proof** containing in 100 volumes enough alcohol for so many volumes more, or less, than 100; **proof before letters** a proof taken before the title is engraved on the plate. [OFr *prove* (Fr *preuve*); see the ety for **prove** for an explanation of the vowel in *obs* or *Scot* forms **preeve**, **prief(e)**]

prootic *prō-ot'ik*, (*anatom*) *adj* in front of the ear. — *n* an anterior bone of the auditory capsule. [**pro-**[1], and Gr *ous*, *ōtos* ear]

PROP *prop*, *abbrev*: Preservation of the Rights of Prisoners.

prop[1] *prop*, *n* a rigid support; a supplementary support; a stay; a strut; a timber supporting a mine roof; a supporter or upholder; a leg (*slang*); a boxer's extended arm (*slang*); either of the two forwards at the ends of the front row of the scrum (also **prop forward**; *Rugby football*); an act of propping in a horse (*horse-racing*, *orig Austr*). — *vt* to hold up by means of something placed under or against (often with *up*); to support or to sustain (often with *up*); to keep (a failing enterprise, etc) going (often with *up*); to hit straight or knock down (*slang*). — *vi* (*horse-racing*, *orig Austr*) (of a horse) to stop suddenly: — *pr p* **propp'ing**; *pa t* and *pa p* **propped**. — *n* **propp'ant** (*min ext*) a material, eg sand, used to keep open fissures in an oil-bearing sediment. — See also **fracking**. — **prop forward** see above; **prop'-root** a root growing down from a trunk or branch, serving to prop up a tree. [ME *proppe*; cf Du *proppe* vine-prop, support]

prop[2] *prop*, (*slang*) *n* a tie-pin; a brooch. [Du *prop*]

prop[3] *prop*, *n* a *colloq* or *slang* short form of: propeller; (theatrical) property; (geometrical) proposition. — *n pl* **props** stage properties. — *n sing* a person in charge of theatrical properties. — **prop-jet** see separate entry; **prop shaft** see **propeller shaft**.

prop. *abbrev*: proper; properly; property; proposition.

propaedeutic *prō-pē-dū'tik*, *n* (often in *pl*) a preliminary study. — *adj* **propaedeut'ic** or **propaedeut'ical**. [Gr *propaideuein* to teach beforehand, from *pro* before, and *paideuein* to teach]

propaganda *prop-ə-gan'də, n* the organized spreading of doctrine, true or false information, opinions, etc, *esp* to bring about change or reform; an association or scheme for doing this; the information, etc spread; (with *cap*) a Roman Catholic committee, founded in 1622, responsible for foreign missions and the training of missionaries. — *n* **propagan'dism** the practice of propagating tenets or principles; zeal in spreading one's opinions; proselytism. — *n* and *adj* **propagan'dist**. — *adj* **propagandis'tic**. — *vt* and *vi* **propagan'dize** or **-ise**. — **propaganda machine** all the means employed in the process of spreading propaganda; the process itself. [L *congregatio de propaganda fide*, congregation for propagating the faith, the full title of the Propaganda]

propagate *prop'ə-gāt, vt* to increase by natural process; to multiply; to pass on; to transmit; to spread from one to another; to increase (*obs*). — *vi* to multiply; to breed. — *adj* **prop'agable**. — *n* **propagā'tion**. — *adj* **prop'agātive**. — *n* **prop'agātor** someone or something that propagates; a heated, covered box in which plants may be grown from seed or cuttings. — *vt* **propage** (*prō-pāj'*; *Congreve*) to beget or propagate. — *n* **prop'agule** or **prōpag'ulum** a small plant outgrowth, eg a bud or a spore, which becomes detached from the parent and grows into a new plant (*bot*); any part of an organism from which a new individual can be produced (*biol*); the minimum population of a species from which a new colony can be produced (*ecol*). [L *prōpāgāre, -ātum*, connected with *prōpāgō* a layer]

propale *prō-pāl'*, (*obs Scot*) *vt* to disclose. — *vi* (*Scott*) to make a display. [LL *prōpalāre*, from *prōpalam* openly, from *prō* forth, and *palam* openly]

propane *prō'pān, n* a hydrocarbon gas (C_3H_8), the third member of the methane series. — *n* **propanol** (*prō'pə-nol*) propyl alcohol. — **propanō'ic acid** same as **propionic acid**. [**propionic**]

proparoxytone *prō-par-ok'si-tōn, adj* (in ancient Greek) having the acute accent on the third last syllable; having heavy stress on the third last syllable. — *n* a word accented or stressed in this way. [Gr *proparoxytonos*; see **paroxytone**]

propel *prə-pel'* or *prō-pel'*, *vt* to drive forward: — *pr p* **propell'ing**; *pa t* and *pa p* **propelled'**. — *n* **propell'ant** something which propels; an explosive for propelling projectiles; the fuel used to propel a rocket, etc; the gas in an aerosol spray. — *adj* **propell'ent** driving. — *n* a driving agent; a motive. — *n* **propell'er** someone who, or something which, propels; a driving mechanism; a shaft with spiral blades (*screw-propeller*) for driving a ship, aeroplane, etc; a steamer with a screw-propeller; a helical device for blowing air (*air-propeller, propeller fan*); an artificial bait which spins (*angling*). — *n* **propel'ment** propulsion; a propelling mechanism. — **propell'er-blade**; **propeller shaft** the shaft of a propeller; the driving shaft between the gearbox and the rear axle in a motor vehicle (also **prop shaft**); **propelling pencil** a pencil with a replaceable lead held in a casing that can be turned to push the lead forward as it is worn down. [L *prōpellere*, from *prō* forward, and *pellere* to drive]

propend *prə-pend'* or *prō-pend'*, (*Shakesp*) *vi* to incline. — *adj* **propend'ent** inclining or inclined (*obs*). — *adj* **propense** (*-pens'*; *obs*) inclined; sometimes used in the sense of *prepense*, deliberate, premeditated. — *adv* **propense'ly**. — *n* **propense'ness**, **propen'sion** (*Shakesp*) or (now *usu*) **propens'ity** inclination of mind; favourable inclination; a tendency to good or evil; disposition; a tendency to move in a certain direction. — *adj* **propen'sive** inclined (*obs*). [L *prōpendēre, -pensum* to hang forward]

propene. See **propylene**.

propense, **propensity**, etc. See under **propend**.

proper *prop'ər, adj* own; appropriate; peculiar; confined to one; in natural colouring (*heraldry*); strict; strictly applicable; strictly so-called (*usu* after *n*); thorough, out-and-out (now *colloq* or *slang*); actual, real; befitting; decorous, seemly; conforming strictly to convention; goodly; belonging to only one; comely; used only on a particular day or festival (*liturgical*). — *n* (*liturgical*) a service, psalm, etc set apart for a particular day or occasion. — *adv* (*colloq*) very, exceedingly. — *adv* **prop'erly** in a proper manner; strictly; entirely, extremely (*colloq*). — *n* **prop'erness**. — **proper chant** (*obs*) the key of C major. — *adj* **proper-false'** (*Shakesp*) handsome and deceitful. — **proper fraction** a fraction that has a numerator of a lower value than the denominator; **proper motion** a star's apparent motion relative to the celestial sphere, due partly to its own movement (**peculiar motion**), and partly to that of the solar system (**parallactic motion**); **proper noun** or **proper name** the name of a particular person, animal, thing, place, etc, in English *usu* written with an initial capital letter (*opp* of *common noun*). [Fr *propre*, from L *proprius* own]

properdin *prō-pûr'din, n* a natural immunizing substance varyingly present in the blood, possibly with a bearing on resistance to malignant disease. [L *prō* for, and *perdere* to destroy]

properispomenon *prō-per-i-spom'ə-non, n* (in ancient Greek) a word with the circumflex accent on the penultimate syllable. — Also *adj*. [Gr *properispōmenon*, neuter pr p passive of *properispaein* to put a circumflex on the penultimate syllable (see **perispomenon**)]

property *prop'ər-ti, n* that which is proper to any person or thing; a quality that is always present; a characteristic; an essential detail (*Shakesp*); any quality; propriety, fitness (*obs*); that which is one's own; the condition of being one's own; a piece of land owned by somebody; right of possessing, employing, etc; ownership; an asset, something which brings profit or income (see also **hot property** under **hot**[1]); an article required on the stage (often shortened to **prop**); a mere tool or cat's-paw (*obs*); individuality, personal identity (*Shakesp*). — *vt* (*Shakesp*) to treat as a property; to appropriate. — *adj* of the nature of a stage property. — *adj* **prop'ertied** imbued with properties (*Shakesp*); possessing property. — **property band** any of the various ranges of house values, on the basis of which sums payable under the Council Tax are calculable; **property man**, **master**, **mistress**, etc the person who has charge of stage properties; **property qualification** a qualification (eg for office or voting) depending on possession of a certain amount of property; **property room** the room in which stage properties are kept; **property tax** a tax levied on property, at the rate of so much per cent on its value. [OFr *properte*; see **propriety**]

prophage *prō'fāj*, (*biol*) *n* a phage genome which replicates in synchrony with its host, into whose genome it is often integrated. [**pro-**[1]]

prophase *prō'fāz*, (*biol*) *n* a preliminary stage of mitosis, preceding the formation of the equatorial plate; the first stage of meiosis. [**pro-**[1]]

prophecy *prof'i-si, n* inspired or prophetic utterance; prediction; public interpretation of Scripture, or preaching (*obs*). [OFr *prophecie*, from L *prophētīa*, from Gr *prophēteia*, from *prophētēs* prophet]

prophesy *prof'i-sī, vi* to utter prophecies; to speak prophetically; to expound the Scriptures (*obs*); to preach (*obs*); to foretell the future. — *vt* to foretell: — *pa t* and *pa p* **proph'esied**. — *n* **proph'esier**. — *n* **proph'esying**. [A variant of **prophecy**]

prophet *prof'it, n* someone who speaks on behalf of a deity; someone who proclaims a divine message; an inspired teacher, preacher or poet; someone who speaks on behalf of a group, movement or doctrine; a minister of the second order of the Catholic Apostolic Church; a foreteller, whether claiming to be inspired or not; a tipster (*slang*): — *fem* **proph'etess**. — *n* **proph'et-hood**. — *adj* **prophetic** (*prə-fet'ik*) or **prophet'ical**. — *adv* **prophet'ically**. — *n* **prophet'icism** prophetic quality. — *n* **proph'etism** the actions of a prophet or prophets. — *n* **proph'etship**. — **prophet's thumbmarks** (*horse-racing*) indentations in a horse's skin. — **former**

prophets the Old Testament books of Joshua, Judges, Samuel and Kings; **latter prophets** the prophets properly so called; **major prophets** the prophets whose books come before that of Hosea, ie Isaiah, Jeremiah and Ezekiel, as opposed to the **minor prophets**, the prophets from Hosea to Malachi; **prophet of doom** a person who continually predicts unfortunate events, disasters, etc; **school of the prophets** a school among the ancient Jews for training young men as teachers of the people; **the Prophet** Mohammed; **the prophets** one of the three divisions into which the Jews divide their Scriptures, consisting of the *former* and the *latter* prophets (see above). [Fr *prophète*, from L *prophēta*, from Gr *prophētēs*, from *pro* for, and *phanai* to speak]

prophylactic *pro-fi-lak'tik*, *adj* guarding against disease. — *n* something that prevents disease; a condom (*usu US*). — *n* **prophylax'is** preventive treatment against diseases, etc. [Gr *prophylaktikos*, from *pro* before, and *phylax*, a guard; *prophylaxis* is not a Greek word]

prophyll *prō'fil*, (*bot*) *n* a bracteole. [**pro-**[1], and Gr *phyllon* leaf]

propine *prə-pīn'*, (*archaic*, chiefly *Scot*) *vt* to pledge in drinking; to present or offer. — *n* a tip; a gift. [L *propīnāre*, from Gr *propīnein* to drink first, from *pro* before, and *pīnein* to drink]

propinquity *prə-ping'kwi-ti*, *n* nearness. [L *propinquitās*, *-ātis*, from *propinquus* near, from *prope* near]

propionic acid *prō-pi-on'ik as'id*, *n* one of the fatty acids, C_2H_5·COOH; the first of the series that yields derivatives of a fatty character. — *n* **prō'pionate** any ester or salt of propionic acid. [**pro-**[1], and Gr *pīōn* fat]

propitiate *prə-pish'i-āt*, *vt* to render favourable; to appease. — *adj* **propi'tiable**. — *n* **propitiā'tion** the act of propitiating; atonement; atoning sacrifice. — *adj* **propi'tiātive**. — *n* **propi'tiātor**. — *adv* **propi'tiatorily** (*-shi-ə-tər-i-li*). — *adj* **propi'tiatory** propitiating; expiatory. — *n* the Jewish mercy-seat, the covering over the Ark of the Covenant; a propitiation (*archaic*). — *adj* **propitious** (*-pish'əs*) favourable; disposed to be gracious; of good omen. — *adv* **propi'tiously**. — *n* **propi'tiousness**. [L *propitiāre*, *-ātum* to make favourable, from *propitius* well-disposed]

prop-jet *prop'-jet*, (*aeronautics*) *adj* and *n* (a jet aeroplane) having a turbine-driven propeller. [**prop**(eller) and **jet**]

propodeon *prō-pod'i-on*, (*entomol*) *n* in some Hymenoptera, the first abdominal segment, fused with the thorax and so in front of the waist — sometimes, and incorrectly, Latinized as **propod'eum**. [**pro-**[1], and Gr *podeōn* a wineskin neck]

propolis *prop'ə-lis*, *n* bee-glue, a brown sticky resinous substance gathered by bees from trees and used by them as cement and varnish. [Gr]

propone *prə-pōn'*, *vt* (now *Scot*) to put forward, propose, propound; to put before a court of law. — *adj* **propōn'ent** bringing forward, proposing; bringing an action. — *n* a propounder or proposer; a favourer or advocate. [L *prōpōnere*, from *prō* forward, and *pōnere* to place]

proportion *prə-pōr'shən* or *prə-pör'shən*, *n* the relation of one thing to another in magnitude; appropriate relationship of parts to each other as regards size, quantity, etc; due relation; relation of rhythm or of harmony (*music*); adjustment in due ratio (*Shakesp*); ratio; the identity or equality of ratios (*math*); the rule of three, the method of finding the value of a quantity that stands in the same ratio to a given quantity as two other quantities stand in relation to each other (*math*); equal or just share; relative share, portion, inheritance, contribution, quota or fortune; a part or portion (*colloq*); (in *pl*) dimensions; form, figure (*obs*). — *vt* to adjust or fashion in due proportion; to regulate the proportions of; to be in due proportion to (*Shakesp*); to divide proportionally. — *adj* **propor'tionable** that may be proportioned; having a due or definite relation. — *n* **propor'tionableness**. — *adv* **propor'tionably**. — *adj* **propor'tional** relating to proportion; in proportion; having the same or a constant ratio (*math*); proportionate, in suitable proportion. — *n* (*math*) a number or quantity in a proportion. — *n* **proportional'ity** the state of being proportional; the weighing-up of good against evil (eg evil means of achieving good ends) or of the relative evilness of proposed actions, eg in consideration of the concept of a just war (*ethics*). — *adv* **propor'tionally**. — *adj* **propor'tionate** in fit or correct proportion; proportional. — *vt* to adjust in proportion. — *adv* **propor'tionately**. — *n* **propor'tionateness**. — *adj* **propor'tioned**. — *n* **propor'tioning** adjustment of proportions. — *adj* **propor'tionless** badly proportioned. — *n* **propor'tionment**. — **proportional representation** any of various systems which give or are intended to give parties in an elected body a representation as nearly as possible proportional to their voting strength. — **in proportion** (often with *to*) in a (given) ratio; having a correct or harmonious relation (with something); to a degree or extent which seems appropriate to the importance, etc of the matter in hand; **out of (all) proportion** not in proportion. [L *prōportiō*, *-ōnis*, from *prō* in comparison with, and *portiō* part, share]

propose *prə-pōz'*, *vt* to put forward or exhibit (*obs*); to bring to one's own or another person's attention; to propound; to face (*Shakesp*); to imagine or suppose (*Shakesp*); to offer for consideration or acceptance; to formulate as something to be exacted (*Shakesp*); to proffer; to offer; to suggest or put to someone as something to be done; to purpose or intend; to move formally; to nominate; to invite one's companions, etc to drink (a toast); to enunciate. — *vi* to form or put forward an intention or design; to offer, *esp* marriage; to converse (*Shakesp*). — *n* a proposal (*obs*); talk, discourse (*Shakesp*). — *adj* **propōs'able**. — *n* **propōs'al** an act of proposing; an offer, *esp* of marriage; a tender (*US*); anything proposed; a plan. — *n* **propōs'er**. [Fr *proposer*, from pfx *pro-*, *and poser* to place; see **pose**[1]]

proposition *prop-ə-zish'ən*, *n* an act of propounding or (more rarely) proposing; the thing propounded or proposed; an offer (*Shakesp*); a question propounded (*Shakesp*); a statement of a judgement; a form of statement in which a predicate is affirmed or denied of a subject (*logic*); a premise, *esp* a major premise (*logic*); a statement of a problem or theorem for (or with) solution or demonstration (*math*); enunciation of a subject in a fugue (*music*); a possibility, suggestion, course of action, etc, to be considered; any situation, thing or person considered as something to cope with, eg an enterprise, job, opponent, etc (*slang*, *orig US*); an invitation to sexual intercourse (*colloq*). — *vt* to make a proposition to (someone), *esp* to solicit (a woman) for sexual relations. — *adj* **proposi'tional**. — **propositional calculus** see under **calculus**. [L *prōpositiō*, *-ōnis*, from *prō* before; see **position**]

propound *prə-pownd'*, *vt* to offer for consideration; to set forth as an aim or reward; to purpose (*Spenser*); to produce for probate (*law*). — *n* **propound'er**. [**propone**]

proppant. See under **prop**[1].

propraetor *prō-prē'tər*, *prō-prē'tör* or *prō-prī'tor*, *n* a magistrate of ancient Rome, who, after acting as praetor in Rome, was appointed to the government of a province. — *adj* **propraetorial** (*-tō'ri-əl* or *-tö'ri-əl*) or **propraeto'rian**. [L *prōpraetor*, from *prō praetōre* for the praetor]

propranolol *prop-ran'ə-lol*, *n* a compound, $C_{16}H_{21}NO_2$, used in the form of its hydrochloride as a beta-blocker (qv) *esp* in the treatment of cardiac arrhythmia, angina and hypertension; (with *cap*) propranolol hydrochloride. [**propyl** and **propanol**]

proprietor *prō-prī'ə-tər*, *n* an owner: — *fem* **proprī'etress** or (imitation Latin) **proprī'etrix**. — *n* **proprī'etary** an owner; a body of owners; ownership; a proprietary or patented drug (*med*); a business secretly owned by or controlled by the CIA and used to provide cover for its agents and activities (*US*). — *adj* of the nature of property; legally made only by a person or body of persons having special rights, *esp* a patent or trademark; pertaining to or belonging to the legal owner; (of a company, etc) privately owned and run; owning property. — *adj* **proprīetorial** (*-tō'ri-əl* or *-tö'ri-əl*). — *adv* **proprīeto'rially**. — *n* **proprī'etorship**. [LL *proprietārius*, from *proprius* own; **proprietor** has been formed irregularly; it is not a Latin word]

propriety *prō-prī'ə-ti*, *n* ownership (*obs*); rightness, eg in the use of words; appropriateness; seemliness; decency; conformity with good manners; conformity with convention in language and conduct; a character, quality or property (*obs*); particular nature, individuality (*Shakesp*). [Fr *propriété*, from L *proprietās*, *-ātis*, from *proprius* own]

proprioceptive *prō-pri-ō-sep'tiv*, (*biol*) *adj* of, pertaining to, or made active by, stimuli arising from movement in the tissues. — *n* **propriocep'tor** a sensory nerve-ending receptive of such stimuli. — **proprioceptive sense** the sense of muscular position. [L *proprius* own, after **receptive**]

proproctor *prō-prok'tər*, *n* a proctor's substitute or assistant. [**pro-**[2] **(2)**]

proptosis *prop-tō'sis*, (*pathol*) *n* forward displacement, *esp* of the eye. [Gr *proptōsis*, from *pro* forward, and *ptōsis* fall]

propugnation *prō-pug-nā'shən*, (*Shakesp*) *n* defence. [L *prō* for, and *pugnāre* to fight]

propulsion *prə-pul'shən*, *n* the act of causing something to move forward; a force which causes forward movement. — *adj* **propul'sive**. — *n* **propul'sor** something which propels or provides propulsion. — *adj* **propul'sory**. [L *prōpellere*, *prōpulsum* to push forward; see **propel**]

propyl *prō'pil*, *n* the alcohol radical C_3H_7. — *n* **pro'pylamine** an amine of propyl. — *n* **pro'pylene** or **pro'pene** a gaseous hydrocarbon (C_3H_6). — *adj* **propyl'ic**. — **propyl alcohol** propanol, an aliphatic alcohol, C_3H_7OH. [**propionic**, and Gr *hȳlē* matter]

propylaeum *prop-i-lē'əm* or **propylon** *prop'i-lon*, *n* a gateway of architectural importance, leading into a temple, etc: — *pl* **propylae'a** or **prop'yla**. — *n* **prop'ylite** (*geol*) an andesite altered by solfataric action, *orig* applied to andesites of the beginning (or gateway) of the Tertiary period. — *n* **propylītīzā'tion** or **-s-**. — *vt* **prop'ylitize** or **-ise**. [Gr *propylaion* (used in pl, *-a*) and *propylon*, from *pro* before, and *pylē* a gate]

pro rata. See under **pro**[1].

prorate *prō-rāt'* or *prō'rāt*, (mainly *US*) *vt* to distribute proportionately. — *adj* **prorāt'able**. — *n* **prorā'tion**. [**pro rata**]

prore *prōr* or *prör*, (*poetic*) *n* a prow; a ship. [Obs Fr, from L *prōra* prow, from Gr *prōira*]

prorector *prō-rek'tər*, *n* a university or college rector's substitute or assistant. [**pro-**[2] **(2)**]

prorogue *prə-rōg'* or *prō-rōg'*, *vt* to prolong (*obs*); to postpone (*Shakesp*); *perh* to keep from exertion (*Shakesp*); to discontinue the meetings of for a time without dissolving. — *vt* **prō'rogāte** to prorogue; to extend by agreement, in order to make a particular action competent (*Scots law*). — *n* **prōrogā'tion**. [L *prōrogāre*, *-ātum*, from *prō* forward, and *rogāre* to ask]

prosaic *prō-zā'ik* or **prosaical** *prō-zā'ik-əl*, *adj* like prose; unpoetical; matter-of-fact; commonplace; dull; in or relating to prose (*rare*). — *adv* **prosā'ically**. — *n* **prosā'icalness**. — *n* **prosā'icism** (*-i-sizm*) prosaism. — *n* **prosā'icness** the quality of being prosaic. — *n* **prō'sāism** a prose idiom; a prosaic phrase; prosaic character. — *n* **prō'sāist** a writer of prose; a commonplace person. — *n* **prosateur** see under **prose**. [L *prosa* prose]

prosauropod *prō-sör'ə-pod*, *n* a reptile-like dinosaur of the division *Prosauropoda* which lived in the Triassic period. — Also *adj*.

proscenium *prō-sē'ni-əm*, *n* the front part of the stage; the curtain and its framework, *esp* the arch that frames the more traditional type of stage (**proscenium arch**). [L, from Gr *proskēnion*, from *pro* before, and *skēnē* stage]

prosciutto *pro-shōō'tō*, *n* finely cured uncooked ham, often smoked: — *pl* **prosciut'ti** or **prosciutt'os**. [Ital, literally 'pre-dried']

proscribe *prō-skrīb'*, *vt* to put on the list of those who may be put to death; to outlaw; to ostracize; to prohibit; to denounce. — *n* **prōscrib'er**. — *n* **prō'script** a person who is proscribed. — *n* **prōscrip'tion**. — *adj* **prōscrip'tive**. — *adv* **prōscrip'tively**. [L *prōscribere*, from *prō-* before, publicly, and *scrībere*, *scrīptum* to write]

prose *prōz*, *n* ordinary spoken and written language with words in direct straightforward arrangement without metrical structure; all writings not in verse; a passage of prose for translation from or, *usu*, into a foreign language, as an exercise; a composition in prose (*obs*, except as an exercise in Latin or Greek); a narrative (*obs*); a piece of dull, tedious speaking or writing; a familiar, gossipy, talk (*colloq*; *esp* formerly); (something having) prosaic character; a prosy talker. — *adj* of or in prose; not poetical; plain; dull. — *vi* to write prose; to speak or write tediously. — *vt* to compose in prose; to turn into prose. — *n* **prosateur** (*prō-za-tœr*; Fr) a prose-writer. — *n* **prō'ser**. — *vt* **prō'sify** to make (something) prosaic; to turn (something) into prose. — *vi* to write prose. — *adv* **prō'sily**. — *n* **prō'siness**. — *n* **prō'sing** speaking or writing in a dull or prosy way. — *adj* **prō'sy** dull, tedious, humdrum; addicted to prosing. — **prose'-man** (*Pope*) or **prose'man** a writer of prose; **prose poem** a prose work or passage having some of the characteristics of poetry; **prose'-writer**. [Fr, from L *prōsa*, from *prorsus* straightforward, from *prō* forward, and *vertere*, *versum* to turn]

prosector *prō-sekt'ər*, *n* a person who dissects bodies to illustrate anatomical lectures; the official anatomist of a zoological society. — *adj* **prosecto'rial** (*-ōr'i-əl* or *-ör'i-əl*). — *n* **prosec'torship**. [LL *prōsector*, from *prōsecāre*, *-sectum* to cut up, from *prō-* away, and *secāre* to cut]

prosecute *pros'i-kūt*, *vt* to carry on with, persevere with or pursue, in order to reach or accomplish; to engage in or practise; to follow up; to pursue or chase (*obs*); to pursue by law; to bring before a court. — *vi* to carry on a legal prosecution. — *adj* **pros'ecūtable**. — *n* **prosecū'tion** the act of prosecuting in any sense; the prosecuting party in legal proceedings. — *n* **pros'ecūtor** someone who prosecutes or pursues any plan or business; someone who carries on a civil or criminal suit. — *adj* **prosecutorial** (*pros-i-kū-tō'ri-el* or *-tö'ri-əl*). — *n* **pros'ecūtrix** (New L) a female prosecutor: — *pl* **pros'ecūtrixes** or **prosecutrices** (*pros-i-kū-trī'sēz* or *pros-i-kū'tri-sēz*). — **director of public prosecutions** or **public prosecutor** a person appointed to conduct criminal prosecutions in the public interest (in the USA, **prosecuting attorney** or **district attorney**). [L *prōsequī*, *-secūtus*, from *prō* onwards, and *sequī* to follow]

proselyte *pros'i-līt*, *n* someone who has changed from one religion or opinion to another; a convert, *esp* from paganism to Judaism. — *vt* and *vi* (*US*) to proselytize. — *n* **pros'elytism** being, becoming, or making a convert; conversion. — *vt* **pros'elytize** or **-ise** to convert. — *vi* to make proselytes. — *n* **pros'elytizer** or **-s-**. — **proselyte of the gate** (*hist*) a heathen allowed to live in Palestine on making certain concessions to Judaism. [Gr *prosēlytos* a newcomer, resident foreigner, from *pros* to, and the stem *elyth-* used to form aorist for *erchesthai* to go]

prosencephalon *pros-en-sef'ə-lon*, (*zool*) *n* the forebrain, comprising the cerebral hemispheres and olfactory processes. — *adj* **prosencephalic** (*-si-fal'ik*). [Gr *pros* to, used as if equivalent to *pro* before, and *enkephalon* brain, from *en* in, and *kephalē* head]

prosenchyma *pros-eng'ki-mə*, (*bot*) *n* a plant-tissue of long cells with pointed ends, conducting or supporting tissue. — *adj* **prosenchymatous** (*-kim'ə-təs*). [Gr *pros* to, and *enchyma* an infusion, pouring in]

proseuche *pros-ū'kē* or **proseucha** *pros-ū'kə*, *n* a place of prayer, an oratory: — *pl* **proseu'chae** (*-kē*). [Gr *proseuchē* prayer, place of prayer, from *pros* to, and *euchē* prayer]

prosify. See under **prose**.

prosilient *prō-sil'i-ənt, adj* outstanding. — *n* **prosil'iency**. [L *prōsiliens, -entis*, pr p of *prōsilīre* to leap forward, from *prō-* forward, and *salīre* to leap]

prosimian *prō-sim'i-ən, n* a primate of the suborder **Prosimii**, eg the lemur, loris and tarsier. — Also *adj*. [**pro-**[1], and L *simia* ape]

prosing. See under **prose**.

prosit *prō'sit, interj* good luck to you, a salutation in drinking healths. [L *prōsit*, 3rd pers sing present subjunctive of L *prōdesse* to be of use, from *prō(d)-* for, and *esse* to be]

proslambanomenos *pros-lam-ban-om'e-nos*, (*ancient Gr music*) *n* an additional note at the bottom of the scale. [Gr pr p passive of *proslambanein* to take in addition, from pfx *pros-*, and *lambanein* to take]

proso *prō'sō* or **proso millet** (*mil'it*), *n* a name for one of the main varieties of millet, *Panicum miliaceum*, grown *esp* in Russia and China. [Russ]

prosody *pros'ə-di, n* the study of versification. — *adj* **prosodial** (*pros-ō'di-əl* or *prəs-ō'di-əl*), **prosodic** (*-od'ik*) or **prosod'ical**. — *n* **prosō'dian** or **pros'odist** someone skilled in prosody. — *adv* **prosod'ically**. [L *prosōdia*, Gr *prosōidiā*, from *pros* to, and *ōidē* a song]

prosopagnosia *pros-ō-pag-nō'si-ə*, (*psychiatry*) *n* inability to recognize faces of persons well-known to the sufferer. [LL *prosopagnosia*, from Gr *prosōpon* face, *a-* without, and *gnōsis* knowledge]

prosopography *pros-ō-pog'rə-fi, n* a biographical sketch, a description of a person's appearance, character, life, etc; the compiling or study of such material. — *adj* **prosopograph'ical**. [Gr *prosōpon* face, person, and *graphein* to write]

prosopon *pros-ō-pon'*, (*theol*) *n* the outer appearance, personification or embodiment of one of the persons of the Trinity. — *n* **prosopopoeia** or **prosopopeia** (*pros-ō-pō-pē'ə*) personification. — *adj* **prosopopoe'ial** or **prosopope'ial**. [Gr *prosōpopoiiā*, from *prosōpon* face, person, and *poieein* to make]

prospect *pros'pekt, n* outlook; direction of facing; a lookout or viewpoint (*Milton*); a wide view; view, sight, field of view; a scene; a pictorial representation; a position for being observed (*Shakesp*); a survey or mental view; outlook on the probable future; expectation; chance of success; a wide street (also with *cap*; also *Russ* **Prospekt** *prəs-pyekt'*); a prospect-glass (*obs*); a probable customer (*esp US*); a place thought likely to yield a valuable mineral (*mining*); a sample, or a test, or the yield of a test of a sample from such a place; a probable source of profit. — *vi* **prospect** (*prəs-pekt'*) to look around (*obs*); (*prəs-pekt'*; *US pros'pekt*) to make a search, *esp* for chances of mining; to promise or yield results to the prospector. — *vt* (*-pekt'*) to face or view (*obs*); (*-pekt'* or *pros'pekt*) to explore, search, survey or test for profitable minerals. — *n* **prospect'ing** (*US pros'*) searching a district for minerals with a view to further operations. — *n* **prospec'tion** looking to the future; foresight. — *adj* **prospec'tive** probable or expected future; looking forward; yielding distant views; looking to the future. — *n* prospect. — *adv* **prospec'tively**. — *n* **prospec'tiveness**. — *n* **prospec'tor** (*US pros'*) someone who prospects for minerals. — *n* **prospec'tus** the outline of any plan submitted for public approval, particularly of a literary work or of a joint-stock concern; an account of the organization of a school, etc: — *pl* **prospec'tuses**. — **pros'pect-glass** (*obs* or *dialect*) a telescope or field glass; **prospec'tive-glass** (*obs*) a prospect-glass; a scrying crystal for seeing future or faraway events. [L *prōspectus*, from *prōspicere, prōspectum*, from *prō-* forward, and *specere* to look]

prosper *pros'pər, vi* to thrive; to get on; to experience favourable circumstances; to flourish; to turn out well. — *vt* to cause to prosper. — *n* **prosperity** (*-per'i-ti*) the state of being prosperous; success; good fortune. — *adj* **pros'perous** thriving; affluent; successful. — *adv* **pros'perously**. — *n* **pros'perousness**. [L *prosperus* favourable]

prostacyclin *pros-tə-sī'klin, n* a prostaglandin which dilates blood vessels and inhibits blood clotting. [**prosta-** as for **prostaglandin**, and **cyclic**]

prostaglandin *pros-tə-gland'in, n* any of a group of chemical substances secreted by various parts of the body into the bloodstream and found to have a wide range of effects on the body processes, eg on muscle contraction. [*prosta*te *gland*, a major source of these]

prostanthera *pros-tan-thē'rə, n* any bush of the Australian labiate genus *Prostanthera*, with strongly scented leaves and red or white flowers. [Gr *prostithenai* to add, and L *anthera* anther]

prostate *pros'tāt, n* a gland in males at the neck of the bladder, which releases a liquid that forms part of semen. — Also **prostate gland**. — *n* **prostatec'tomy** (*pros-tə-*) surgical removal of (part of) the prostate gland. — *adj* **prostatic** (*pros-tat'ik*). — *n* **pros'tatism** (*-tət-izm*) an illness or disorder associated with enlargement of the prostate. — *n* **prostatī'tis** inflammation of the prostate gland. [Gr *prostatēs*, someone who stands in front, the prostate, from *pro* before, and *sta* the root of *histanai* to set up]

prosthesis *pros'thə-sis* (*esp linguistics*) or *pros-thē'sis* (*esp med*), *n* prothesis, the addition of a sound or syllable to the beginning of a word, eg for ease of pronunciation (*linguistics*); the fitting of artificial parts to the body (*med*); such an artificial part: — *pl* **prostheses** (*-sēz*). — *adj* **prosthetic** (*-thet'ik*) relating to prosthesis; pertaining to a group or radical of different nature, such as a non-protein part of a protein molecule (*chem*). — *n* an artificial part of the body. — *n sing* **prosthet'ics** the surgery or dentistry involved in supplying artificial parts to the body. — *n* **pros'thetist**. [Gr *prosthesis*, adj *prosthetikos*, from *pros* to, and *thesis* putting]

prosthodontia *pros-thō-don'shi-ə*, (*dentistry*) *n* provision of false teeth. — Also *n sing* **prosthodon'tics**. — *n* **prosthodon'tist**. [Gr *prosthesis* addition, from *pros* to, *thesis* putting, and *odous, odontos* tooth]

prostitute *pros'ti-tūt, vt* to devote to, or offer or sell for, an unworthy, evil or immoral use; to hire out for sexual intercourse; to degrade by publicity or commonness; to devote or offer as a religious act (*obs*). — *adj* openly devoted to lewdness; given over (to evil); shamefully or ignobly mercenary; hackneyed, debased by commonness (*obs*). — *n* a person (*usu* a woman or a homosexual man) who accepts money in return for sexual intercourse; someone who offers their skills, efforts or reputation for unworthy ends. — *n* **prostitū'tion** the act or practice of prostituting; devotion to unworthy or shameful purposes. — *n* **pros'titūtor**. [L *prōstituere, -ūtum* to set up for sale, from *prō* before, and *statuere* to place]

prostomium *prō-stō'mi-əm*, (*zool*) *n* the part of a worm's head in front of the mouth. — *adj* **prostō'mial**. [Gr *pro* before, and *stoma* mouth]

prostrate *pros'trāt, adj* prone; lying or bent with one's face on the ground; (loosely) lying at length, with the body stretched out; procumbent, trailing (*bot*); lying at someone's mercy; reduced to helplessness; completely exhausted. — *vt* **prostrate'** (or *pros'*) to throw forwards on the ground; to lay flat; to overthrow; to reduce to impotence or exhaustion; to bend in humble reverence (*reflexive*). — *n* **prostrā'tion**. [L *prōstrātus*, pa p of *prōsternere*, from *prō* forwards, and *sternere* to spread]

prostyle *prō'stīl*, (*Gr archit*) *n* a front portico without antae; a building with such a portico and no other. — *adj* having a prostyle. [Gr *prostȳlon*, from *pro* before, and *stȳlos* a column]

prosy. See under **prose**.

prosyllogism *prō-sil'ə-jizm*, (*logic*) *n* a syllogism whose conclusion becomes the major premise of another. [Gr *pro* before, and *syllogismos* syllogism]

Prot. *abbrev*: Protestant.

prot-. See **proto-**.

protactinium *prōt-ak-tin'i-əm*, *n* a radioactive element (atomic no 91; symbol **Pa**) that yields actinium on disintegration. [Gr *prōtos* first, and **actinium**]

protagonist *prō-tag'ən-ist*, *n orig* the chief actor, character or combatant; now often applied to any (or in *pl*, all) of the main personages or participants in a story or event; (loosely) a champion or advocate. [Gr *prōtos* first, and *agōnistēs* a combatant or actor]

protamine *prō'tə-mēn*, *n* any of the simplest proteins, found *esp* in the sperm of certain fish. [**proto-** and **amine**]

protandry *prōt-an'dri*, *n* in a hermaphrodite organism, the maturation and loss of the male elements before the female elements develop (*zool*); in a flower, opening of the anthers before the stigmas can receive pollen, so preventing self-pollination (*bot*): — *opp* of *protogyny*. — *adj* **protan'drous**. [Gr *prōtos* first, and *anēr*, *andros* man, male]

protanomaly *prō-tə-nom'ə-li*, (*med*) *n* a form of colour blindness in which there is a decreased response to red. — *adj* **protanom'alous**. [Gr *protos* first (red being the first primary colour), and *anomalos* abnormal]

protanopia *prō-tən-op'i-ə*, (*med*) *n* a form of colour blindness in which red and green are confused because the retina does not respond to red. — *n* **prō'tanope** a sufferer from protanopia. — *adj* **prōtanop'ic** colour-blind to red. [Gr *protos* first (red being the first primary colour), and *ops* eye]

pro tanto. See under **pro**[1].

protasis *prot'ə-sis*, *n* the conditional clause of a conditional sentence (*opp* of *apodosis*); the first part of a dramatic composition (*opp* of *epitasis*). — *pl* **prot'asēs**. — *adj* **protatic** (*prə-tat'ik*). [Gr *protasis* proposition, premise, protasis, from *pro* before, and *tasis* a stretching]

protea *prō'ti-ə*, *n* a plant of the large S African genus *Protea* of shrubs or small trees, of the mainly Australian family **Proteā'ceae**, with big cone-shaped heads of flowers. — *adj* **proteā'ceous**. [**Proteus**, from the varied character of the family]

Protean and **protean**. See under **Proteus**.

protease. See under **protein**.

protect *prə-tekt'* or *prō-tekt'*, *vt* to shield from danger, injury, change, capture or loss; to defend; to strengthen; to seek to foster by import duties; to act as regent for (*Shakesp*); to screen off (eg machinery) for safety. — *adj* **protect'ed**. — *adj* **protect'ing**. — *adv* **protect'ingly**. — *n* **protec'tion** the act of protecting; the state of being protected; defence; that which protects; a guard; a pass or other document guaranteeing against molestation or interference; a fostering of home produce and manufactures by import duties; patronage; concubinage; control of another country's foreign relations, and sometimes internal affairs, without annexation. — *n* **protec'tionism**. — *n* **protec'tionist** someone who favours the protection of trade by duties on imports. — Also *adj*. — *adj* **protec'tive** affording protection; intended to protect; defensive; sheltering. — *n* that which protects; a condom (*esp US*). — *adv* **protec'tively**. — *n* **protec'tiveness**. — *n* **protec'tor** someone who protects from injury or oppression; a protective device; a means of protection; a guard; a guardian; a regent; (*usu* with *cap*) the head of the state during the Commonwealth (*Lord Protector*; *hist*): — *fem* **protec'tress** or **protec'trix**. — *adj* **protec'toral** of a protector or a regent. — *n* **protec'torāte** the position, office, term of office or government of a protector; (with *cap*) the Commonwealth period (*hist*); guardianship; authority over a vassal state; the relation assumed by a state over a territory which it administers without annexation and without admitting the inhabitants to citizenship. — *adj* **protectorial** (*prō-tek-tōr'i-əl* or *-tör'i-əl*). — *adj* **protec'torless**. — *n* **protec'torship**. — *n* **protec'tory** an institution for destitute or delinquent children. — **protected state** a state under the protection of another state but less subject to the control of that state than a protectorate; **protection money** money extorted from shopkeepers, businessmen, etc, as a bribe for leaving their property, business, etc, unharmed; **protective coloration** similarity of animals' colour to that of their natural surroundings, which helps to prevent them from being seen by their enemies; **protective custody** detention of a person ostensibly for his or her personal safety but often in fact from doubt as to his or her possible actions eg as an enemy of the state; **protective tariff** an import tax designed to protect the home markets rather than raise revenue. — **cathodic protection** see under **cathode**. [L *prōtegere*, *-tectum*, from *prō-* in front, and *tegere* to cover]

protégé *prō'tə-zhā*, or *pro'tə-zhā*, *n* someone under the protection or patronage of another person; a pupil; a ward: — *fem* **pro'tégée** (*-zhā*). [Fr, from pa p of *protéger* to protect, from L *prōtegere*]

proteiform. See under **Proteus**.

protein *prō'tēn* or *prō'tē-in*, *n* any member of a group of complex nitrogenous substances that are an important constituent of the bodies of plants and animals — compounds of carbon, hydrogen, oxygen, nitrogen, *usu* sulphur, often phosphorus, etc, their molecules consisting of one or several polypeptide chains, each of which is a linear polymer of several hundred amino acids. — *n* **protease** (*prō'tē-ās* or *-āz*) any enzyme that splits up proteins. — *n* **proteid** (*prō'tē-id*; *archaic*) a former name for protein. — *adj* **proteinaceous** (*prō-tēn-ā'shəs*), **proteinic** (*prō-tēn'ik*) and **protein'ous**. — *adj* **proteoclastic** (*-klas'tik*) same as **proteolytic**. — *n* **proteoglycan** (*-glī'kan*) a fibrous macromolecular protein found in cartilage. — *vt* **pro'teolyse** (*-ō-līz*). — *n* **proteolysis** (*-ol'i-sis*) splitting of proteins by enzymes. — *adj* **proteolytic** (*-ō-lit'ik*). — *n* **prō'teōse** any of a number of substances formed from proteins by proteolysis. — **protein structure** the three-dimensional structure of a protein resulting from the sequence of amino acids in the polypeptide chain, the binding of non-protein moieties, and the association with other protein subunits. [Gr *prōteios* primary, from *prōtos* first]

pro tem *prō'tem'*, short for **pro tempore** (*L*), for the time being.

protend *prō-tend'*, (*archaic*) *vt* to stretch forth; to hold out. — *n* **protense'** (*Spenser*) extension in time. — *n* **proten'sion** duration. — *n* **proten'sity**. — *adj* **proten'sive**. [L *prōtendere*, *-tentus* (*-tēnsus*), from *prō-* forward, and *tendere* to stretch]

proteolysis, etc. See under **protein**.

proterandry *prot-ər-an'dri*, or *prōt-ər-an'dri*, (*bot* and *zool*) *n* protandry. — *adj* **proteran'drous**. [Gr *proteros* earlier, and *anēr*, *andros* man, male]

proterogyny *prot-ər-oj'i-ni* or *prōt-ər-oj'i-ni*, also *-og'*, (*bot* and *zool*) *n* protogyny. — *adj* **proterog'ynous**. [Gr *proteros* earlier, and *gynē* woman, female]

Proterozoic *prot-ər-ō-zō'ik*, or *prōt-ər-ō-zō'ik*, *n* and (*geol*) *adj orig*, Lower Palaeozoic (Cambrian to Silurian); Pre-Cambrian; Upper Pre-Cambrian. [Gr *proteros* earlier, and *zōē* life]

protervity *prō-tûr'vi-ti*, *n* peevishness; perversity; wantonness. [L *prōtervus* or *protervus*]

protest *prə-test'* or *prō-test'*, *vi* to express or record dissent or objection; to make a solemn affirmation, profession or avowal. — *vt* to make a solemn declaration of; to declare; to declare the non-acceptance or non-payment of (a bill of exchange); to proclaim (*Shakesp*); to vow (*Shakesp*); to call to witness (*Milton*); to make a protest against. — *n* **prō'test** an affirmation or avowal; a declaration of objection or dissent; the noting by a notary-public of an unpaid or unaccepted bill; a written declaration, *usu* by the master of a ship, stating the circumstances attending loss or injury of ship or cargo, etc. — *adj* expressing, or used to express, dissent or objection. — *n* **Protestant** (*prot'is-tənt*) one of those who, in 1529, protested against an edict of Charles V and the Diet of Spires denouncing the Reformation; a member or adherent, or someone who shares the beliefs, of one of those churches founded by the Reformers (formerly by some confined to Anglicans or Lutherans, now disavowed by some Anglicans), or of any of the churches which have developed or separated from them; (without *cap*) an avowed lover (*Herrick*); (without *cap*; sometimes *prō-tes'tənt*) someone who protests. — *adj* **Protestant** (*prot'is-tənt*) of, or pertaining to, Protestants, or more *usu*, Protestantism; (without *cap*; *prot'is-tənt* or *prō-tes'tənt*) protesting. — *n* **Prot'estantism** the Protestant form or forms of religion; the Protestant denominations; the state of being a Protestant. — *vt* **Prot'estantize** or **-ise**. — *n* **protestation** (*prot'is-*, *prō-tes-tā'shən*) an avowal or solemn declaration; a declaration in pleading (*law*); a protest (*rare*). — *n* **protest'er** or **protest'or** someone who protests, *esp* (*Scot hist*) a Remonstrant or opponent of the Resolutioners. — *adv* **protest'ingly**. — **Protestant work ethic** an attitude to life stressing the virtue of hard work over enjoyment, popularly associated with the Protestant denominations. — **under protest** unwillingly, having made a protest. [Fr *protester*, from L *prōtestārī*, *-ātus* to bear witness in public, from *prō* before, and *testārī*, from *testis* a witness]

proteus *prō'tūs* or *prō'-ti-əs*, *n* the olm, a member of a European genus (*Proteus*) of blind, cave-dwelling tailed amphibians; a member of a genus (*Proteus*) of rodlike bacteria found in the intestines and in decaying organic matter: — *pl* **pro'teuses**. — *adj* **Protean** or **protean** (*prō-tē'ən* or *prō'ti-ən*) readily assuming different shapes; variable; inconstant. — *adj* **proteiform** (*prō-tē'i-fōrm*). [Gr *Prōteus*, an ancient Greek sea-god who assumed many shapes to evade having to foretell the future]

Protevangelium *prōt-ev-an-jel'i-əm*, *n* God's warning to the serpent (Gen 3.15) that there would be enmity between its offspring and Eve's and that her offspring would crush the serpent's head — seen as the earliest announcement of the gospel; a gospel attributed to James the Less; an inferred source of the canonical gospels. [Gr *prōtos* first, and L *evangelium*, from Gr *euangelion* gospel]

prothalamion *prō-thə-lā'mi-on*, *n* a poem celebrating a coming marriage: — *pl* **prothalā'mia**. — Also **prothalā'mium** (*pl* **-mia**). [Appar coined by Spenser from Gr *pro* before, and *thalamos* a bride-chamber]

prothallus *prō-thal'əs* or **prothallium** *prō-thali-əm*, *n* the gametophyte or sexual generation in ferns and related plants, a small plate of tissue derived from a spore and bearing antheridia and archegonia; the homologous stage in gymnosperms: — *pl* **prothall'ī** and **prothall'ia**. — *adj* **prothall'ial**, **prothall'ic** and **prothall'oid**. [Gr *pro* before, and *thallos* a young shoot]

prothesis *proth'i-sis*, *n* in the Greek Church, the preliminary oblation of the eucharistic elements before the liturgy; the table used for this; the chapel or northern apse where the table stands; the development of an extra initial sound at the beginning of a word (*linguistics*). — *adj* **prothetic** (*prə-thet'ik* or *prō-thet'ik*). [Gr *prothesis*, from *pro* before, and the root of *tithenai* to place]

prothonotary *prō-thon'ət-ə-ri* or *prō-thō-nō'tə-ri*, or **protonotary** *prō-ton'ət-ə-ri* or *prō-tō-nō'tə-ri*, *n* a chief notary or clerk; a chief secretary of the chancery at Rome; a chief clerk or registrar of a court. — *adj* **prothonotā'rial** or **protonotā'rial**. — *n* **prothonotā'riat** or **protonotā'riat** the college constituted by the twelve apostolical prothonotaries (bishops and senior members of the curia) in Rome. [LL *prōt(h)onotārius*, from Gr *prōtos* first, and L *notārius* a clerk]

prothorax *prō-thō'raks* or *prō-thö'raks*, (*entomol*) *n* the anterior segment of the thorax of insects: — *pl* **prothor'axes** or **prothor'aces** (*-ə-sēz*). — *adj* **prothoracic** (*-ras'ik*). [**pro-**[1]]

prothrombin *prō-throm'bin*, *n* a proteinlike substance present in blood plasma. [**pro-**[1] and **thrombin**]

prothyl and **prothyle**. See **protyle**.

Protista *prō-tis'tə*, (*biol*) *n pl* a large group of unicellular organisms on the borderline between plants and animals; a proposed term for a biological kingdom including Protozoa and Protophyta. — *n* **prō'tist** any member of the Protista. — *adj* **protist'ic**. — *n* **protistol'ogist**. — *n* **protistol'ogy**. [Gr *prōtistos* very first, from *prōtos* first]

protium *prō'ti-əm* or *-shi-əm*, *n* ordinary hydrogen of atomic weight 1, as distinguished from deuterium and tritium. [Gr *prōtos* first]

Proto® *prō'tō*, *SAfr n* the name of a type of breathing apparatus used in mine rescues. — **Proto** (or **proto**) **team** a team of people trained to deal with underground rescues, etc.

proto- *prō'tō-* or, before a vowel, **prot-** *prōt-*, *combining form* denoting first; first of a series; first-formed; primitive; ancestral; a (specified) protolanguage (*linguistics*). [Gr *prōtos* first]

protoactinium *prō-tō-ak-tin'i-əm*, (*chem*) *n* a former variant of **protactinium**.

protoavis *prō-tō-ā'vis*, *n* a member of the genus *Protoavis* of the Triassic period, with a dinosaur-like tail and hind legs but certain anatomical features characteristic of modern birds. [**proto-** and L *avis* bird]

Protochordata *prō-tō-körd-ā'tə*, (*zool*) *n pl* a division of the Chordata comprising the Cephalochordata, Hemichordata and Urochordata (ie all members of the Chordata except the vertebrates), marine animals distinguished by the absence of a cranium, of a vertebral column and of specialized anterior sense organs. — *n* and *adj* **prōtōchord'ate**. [**proto-** and **Chordata**]

Protococcus *prō-tō-kok'əs*, *n* a former genus of rounded unicellular algae, one of which (renamed *Pleurococcus vulgaris*) forms a green film common on trees, etc. — *adj* **protococc'al**. — *n pl* **Protococcales** (*-ā'lēz*) the order of green algae to which *Pleurococcus vulgaris* belongs. [**proto-**, and Gr *kokkos* a berry]

protocol *prō'tō-kol*, *n* an original note or minute, or the draft of a record, contract or transaction; a draft treaty; an official or formal account or record; a factual record of observations, eg in scientific experiments (chiefly *US*); a record of transfer of lands (*US*); an official formula; a body of diplomatic etiquette; the regulations, customs, etiquette, etc to be observed by any group or on any occasion; a set of rules governing the transmission of data between two computers which cannot communicate directly. — *vi* to issue or form protocols. — *vt* to make a protocol of: — *pr p* **pro'tocolling**; *pa t* and *pa p* **pro'tocolled**. — Also **prō'tocolize** or **-ise**. — *adj* **prōtocol'ic**. — *n* **prō'tocolist** a registrar or clerk. [Fr *protocole*, from LL *prōtocollum*, from Late Gr *prōtokollon*, a glued-on descriptive first leaf of a manuscript, from Gr *prōtos* first, and *kolla* glue]

protogalaxy *prō-tō-gal'ək-si*, *n* a large cloud of gas thought to be slowly condensing into stars, an early stage in the formation of a galaxy. [**proto-**]

protogine *prō'tō-jin* or *prō'tō-jēn*, *n* a gneissose granite with sericite, found in the Alps. [Gr *prōtos* first, and *gīnesthai* to come into being (as once thought to be the first-formed granite)]

protogyny *prōt-oj'i-ni* or *prōt-og'i-ni*, *n* in a hermaphrodite organism, ripening of the female germ-cells before the male (*zool*); in a flower, ripening of the stigmas before the stamens (*bot*): — *opp* of *protandry*. — *adj* **protog'ynous**. [**proto-**, and Gr *gynē* woman, female]

proto-historic *prō-tō-his-tor'ik*, *adj* belonging to the earliest age of history, just after the prehistoric and before the development of written records, etc. — *n* **proto-his'tory**. [**proto-**]

protohuman *prō-tō-hū'mən*, *n* a prehistoric primate, a supposed ancestor of modern man. — Also *adj*. [**proto-**]

protolanguage *prō'tō-lang-gwij*, *n* a hypothetical language (eg *Proto-Germanic*, *Proto-Indo-European*) regarded as the ancestor of other recorded or existing languages, and reconstructed by comparing these. [**proto-**]

protolithic *prō-tō-lith'ik*, *adj* of or pertaining to the earliest Stone Age. [**proto-**, and Gr *lithos* stone]

protomartyr *prō'tō-mär-tər*, *n* the first martyr in any cause, *esp* St Stephen. [Late Gr *prōtomartyr*]

protomorphic *prō-tō-mörf'ik*, *adj* primordial; primitive. [**proto-**]

proton *prō'ton*, (*phys*) *n* an elementary particle of positive charge and unit atomic mass, the atom of the lightest isotope of hydrogen without its electron. — *adj* **protonic** (*prō-ton'ik*). — **proton beam** a beam of protons produced by a proton accelerator; **proton synchrotron** see **accelerator** under **accelerate**. [Gr, neuter of *prōtos* first]

protonema *prō-tə-nē'mə*, (*bot*) *n* a branched filament produced by germination of a moss spore, giving rise to moss plants from buds: — *pl* **protonē'mata**. — *adj* **protonē'mal** or **protonematal** (*prō-tō-nem'ə-təl*). [**proto-**, and Gr *nēma* thread]

protonotary. Same as **prothonotary**.

protopathic *prō-tə-path'ik*, (*physiol*) *adj* of or relating to a certain type of nerve which is only affected by the coarser stimuli, eg pain; of or relating to this kind of reaction. — *n* **protop'athy**. [**proto-** and **pathic**]

Protophyta *prōt-of'i-tə*, (*biol*) *n pl* a group of unicellular plants. — *n* **protophyte** (*prō'tə-fīt*) a member of the Protophyta. — *adj* **protophytic** (*prō-tō-fit'ik*). [**proto-**, and Gr *phyton* a plant]

protoplasm *prō'tə-plazm*, *n* living matter, the physical basis of life. — *adj* **protoplasm'ic**, **protoplas'mal** and **protoplasmat'ic**. — *n* **prō'toplast** the person who, or thing which, was first formed; an original; the first parent; the living part of a plant cell excluding the cell wall, or isolated from the cell wall by some means such as the action of enzymes (*biol*). — *adj* **protoplas'tic**. [**proto-**, and Gr *plasma* form, from *plassein* to form]

protore *prōt'ōr* or *prōt'ör*, or **proto-ore** *prō'tō-ōr* or *-ör*, (*geol* and *min ext*) *n* metalliferous material prior to the formation of ore by enrichment. [**proto-**]

protospatharius *prō-tə-spä-thā'ri-əs*, (*hist*) *n* the captain of the guards at Byzantium. — Also (*Fr*) **protospathaire** (*prō-tōspä-tār'* or *-spä-thār'*) or **protospataire'**. [Gr *prōtos* first, and *spathārios* a guardsman, from *spathē* a blade]

protostar *prō'tō-stär*, *n* a condensing mass of gas, a supposed early stage in the formation of a star. [**proto-**]

protostele *prō'tə-stēl* or *prō'tə-stēl-i*, (*bot*) *n* a stele in which the vascular tissue forms a solid core, with centrally-placed xylem surrounded by phloem. [**proto-**]

Prototheria *prō-tə-thē'ri-ə*, (*zool*) *n pl* the monotremes. — *adj* **protothē'rian**. [**proto-**, and Gr *thēr* wild beast]

Prototracheata *prō-tə-trak-i-ā'tə*, (*zool*) *n pl* a class of primitive tracheate arthropods including the genus *Peripatus*. [**proto-**; see **trachea**]

prototrophic *prō-tō-trof'ik*, (*biol*) *adj* of bacteria, feeding only on inorganic matter. [**proto-**, and Gr *trophē* food]

prototype *prō'tə-tīp*, *n* the first or original type or model from which anything is copied; an exemplar; a pattern; an ancestral form. — *vt* to make, or use, a prototype of. — *adj* **pro'totypal** and **prototypical** (*-tip'i-kl*). [Fr, from Gr *prōtos* first, and *typos* a type]

protoxide *prō-tok'sīd* (*chem*) *n* that oxide of a series which has the smallest number of oxygen atoms. [**proto-**]

protoxylem *prō-tə-zī'ləm*, (*bot*) *n* the first part of the xylem to be formed. [**proto-**]

Protozoa *prō-tō-zō'ə*, *n pl* the lowest and simplest of animals, unicellular forms or colonies multiplying by fission. — *n* **protozō'an** or **protozō'on** a member of the Protozoa: — *pl* **proto-zō'ans** and **proto-zō'a**. — *adj* **protozō'al** or **protozō'an**. — *adj* **protozō'ic** pertaining to the Protozoa; containing remains of the earliest life on Earth (variously applied) (*obs geol*). — *adj* **protozoolog'ical** (*-zō-ə-loj'i-kl*). — *n* **protozool'ogist**. — *n* **protozool'ogy**. [**proto-**, and Gr *zōion* an animal]

protract *prō-trakt'*, *vt* to draw out or lengthen in time; to prolong; to put off in time, to postpone (*obs*); to lengthen out; to protrude; to draw to scale. — *adj* **protrac'ted** drawn out in time; prolonged; postponed (*obs*); lengthened out; drawn to scale. — *adv* **protrac'tedly**. — *adj* **protrac'tile** (*-tīl*, *US -til*) or **protrac'tible** able to be thrust out. — *n* **protrac'tion** (*-shən*) the act of protracting or prolonging; the delaying of the termination of something; the plotting or laying down of the dimensions of anything on paper; a plan drawn to scale. — *adj* **protrac'tive** drawing out in time; prolonging; delaying. — *n* **protrac'tor** someone who, or something which, protracts; an instrument for measuring or drawing angles on paper; a muscle whose contraction draws a part of the body forward or away from the body (*anatom*). [L *prōtrahere*, *-tractum*, from *prō* forth, and *trahere* to draw]

protreptic *prō-trep'tik*, *adj* exhorting or encouraging; didactic. — *n* an exhortation. — *adj* **protrep'tical**. [Gr *protreptikos*, from *pro* forward, and *trepein* to turn, direct]

protrude *prō-trōōd'*, *vt* to thrust or push out or forward; to obtrude. — *vi* to stick out or project. — *adj* **protrud'able**, **protrusible** (*-trōōs'i-bl*) or **protru'sile** (*-sīl*, *US -sil*) able to be protruded. — *adj* **protru'dent** protruding, prominent. — *n* **protru'sion** (*-zhən*) the act of protruding; the state of being protruded; something which protrudes. — *adj* **protru'sive** thrusting or impelling forward; protruding. — *adv* **protru'sively**. — *n* **protru'siveness**. [L *prōtrūdere*, *-trūsum*, from *prō* forward, and *trūdere* to thrust]

protuberance *prō-tūb'ər-əns*, *n* a bulging out; a swelling. — *adj* **protū'berant**. — *adv* **protū'berantly**. — *vi* **protū'berate** to bulge out. — *n* **protūberā'tion**. [L *prōtūberāre*, *-ātum*, from *prō* forward, and *tūber* a swelling]

protyle *prō'tīl*, *n* a name proposed by Sir William Crookes in 1886 for a hypothetical primitive substance from which the chemical elements were thought to have possibly been formed. — Also **prothyle**, **prothyl** or **protyl** (*-til*). [Gr *prōtos* first (though Crookes himself gave Gr *pro* before, as the etymon), and *hȳlē* matter]

proud *prowd*, *adj* having excessive self-esteem; arrogant; haughty; having a proper sense of self-respect; exultantly aware of the credit due to or reflected on oneself; having a glowing feeling of gratification (because of; with *of*); giving reason for pride or boasting; manifesting pride; having an appearance of pride, vigour, boldness and freedom; stately; high-spirited, fearless, untamable; swelling; sexually excited (*esp* of some female animals); of eg a nail-head, projecting or standing out from a plane surface. — *adj* **proud'ful** (*esp dialect*) proud. — *adj* **proud'ish** somewhat proud. — *adv* **proud'ly**. — *n* **proud'ness** (*rare*) pride. — **proud flesh** a growth or excrescence of flesh in a wound, excessive granulation tissue. — *adj* **proud-heart'ed** (*Shakesp*) having a proud spirit; **proud-mind'ed** (*Shakesp*) proud in mind; **proud'-pied** (*Shakesp*) gorgeously variegated; **proud-stom'ached** (*archaic*) haughty, arrogant. — **do someone proud** (*colloq*) to provide lavish entertainment for someone; to honour someone, give someone cause for pride. [OE *prūd*, *prūt* proud; perh from a LL word connected with L *prōdesse* to be of advantage]

proul and **prouler**. Earlier forms of **prowl** and **prowler**.

Proustian *prōōs'ti-ən*, *adj* pertaining to Marcel *Proust* (1871–1922), French novelist, or to his novels or his style. — *n* an admirer of Proust.

proustite *prōōs'tīt*, *n* a red silver ore, sulphide of arsenic and silver, also known as *ruby silver ore*. [J L *Proust* (1754–1826), French chemist, who distinguished it from pyrargyrite]

Prov. *abbrev*: (the Book of) Proverbs (*Bible*); Provincial; Provost.

provand or **provend** *prov'ənd*, or **proviant** *prov'i-ənt*, *n* an allowance of food; provender (*Shakesp*); provisions; fodder. — *adj* **prov'ant** (*obs*) issued to soldiers, hence inferior. [MLGer *provande*, Du *provande* or *proviand*, Ger *Proviant*, appar from LL *provenda* for L *praebenda*, from *praebēre* to allow]

prove *prōōv*, *vt* to experience or suffer; to test; to test the genuineness of; to ascertain; to establish or ascertain as truth by argument or otherwise; to demonstrate; to check by the opposite operation (eg division by multiplication) (*arith*); to obtain probate of (a will) (*law*); to cause or allow (dough) to rise. — *vi* to try or test, *esp* by tasting; to turn out; to be shown afterwards; to become (*archaic*); to turn out well (*obs*); (of dough) to rise: — *pa p* **proved**. — Also (*obs*) **preve**, with *pa p* **prov'en** surviving as the usual pa p form in the US (pronounced *prōōv'n*) and becoming commoner in Britain (pronounced *prōōv'n* or *prōv'n*); and retained *specif* for *Scots law* (pronounced *prōv'n*) in **not proven**, a verdict declaring that guilt has been neither proved nor disproved. — *adj* **prove'able** or **prov'able**. — *adv* **prove'ably** or **prov'ably**. — *n* **prov'er**. — *n* **prov'ing**. — *adj* testing, as in **proving ground** a place for testing scientifically (also *fig*) and **proving flight** a test flight. — **prove oneself** to do something which shows one's ability, courage, loyalty, etc; **the exception proves the rule** generally held to mean that the finding or making of an exception proves that the rule holds good for all cases that aren't exceptions, but held by some to mean that the exception tests the rule, thereby proving its general validity. [OFr *prover* (Fr *prouver*) from L *probāre*, from *probus* excellent; perh partly from OE *prōfian* to assume to be, from L *probāre*. Fr formerly had two forms of the verb (*preuver* and *prouver*), using respectively the vowels developed from the original L *o* in stressed and unstressed positions, and ME also has two forms, giving **preeve**, **prieve**, etc, whence Scot **pree**, as well as **prove**]

provection *prō-vek'shən*, (*linguistics*) *n* the transferring of a letter from the end of one word to the beginning of the next, eg *a newt* from *an ewt*. [LL *provectio*, from L *pro-* forth, and *vehere*, *vectum* to carry]

proveditor *prō-ved'i-tər*, **proveditore** *prō-ved-i-tō're* or *prō-ved-i-tö're*, and **provedor**, **provedore** or **providor** *prov-i-dōr'* or *prov-i-dör'*, *n* a high official, governor, inspector or commissioner, *esp* in the Republic of Venice (*hist*); a purveyor. [Ital *provveditore* (formerly *proveditore*), Port *provedor*, Sp *proveedor*]

proven. See **prove**.

provenance *prov'i-nəns*, *n* source, *esp* of a work of art. [Fr, from L *prō-* forth, and *venīre* to come]

Provençal *prov-ã-säl'*, *adj* of or pertaining to *Provence*, in France, or to its inhabitants or language. — *n* a native of Provence; the language of Provence, *langue d'oc*. — *adj* **Provençale** (*prov-ã-säl'*) in cooking, prepared with oil and garlic and *usu* tomatoes. [L *prōvinciālis*, from *prōvincia* province]

Provence-rose *pro-vãs'-rōz*, *n* the cabbage rose, *Rosa centifolia*, *orig* cultivated in Provence.

provend. See **provand**.

provender *prov'in-dər* or *prov'ən-dər*, *n* food; dry food for animals, such as hay or corn, *esp* a mixture of meal and cut straw or hay. — *vt* and *vi* to feed. [OFr *provendre* for *provende*, from LL *provenda*; see **provand**]

provenience *prō-vē'ni-əns*, (chiefly *US*) *n* provenance. [L *prōvenīre*; see **provenance**]

proventriculus *prō-ven-trik'ū-ləs*, (*zool*) *n* in birds, the anterior thin-walled part of the stomach, containing the gastric glands; in insects and crustaceans, the muscular thick-walled chamber of the gut. [**pro-**[1], and L *ventriculus*, dimin of *venter* belly]

proverb *prov'ərb*, *n* a short familiar saying expressing a supposed truth or moral lesson; a byword; a saying that requires explanation (*obs*, eg *Bible*); (in *pl* with *cap*) a book of maxims in the Old Testament; a dramatic composition in which a proverb gives a name and character to the plot. — *vt* to speak of proverbially; to make a byword of; to provide with a proverb. — *adj* **prover'bial** (*prə-vûr'bi-əl*) like or of the nature of a proverb; expressed or mentioned in a proverb; notorious. — *n* **prover'bialism** a saying in the form of, or like, a proverb. — *n* **prover'bialist**. — *vi* **prover'bialize** or **-ise** to speak in proverbs. — *adv* **prover'bially**. [Fr *proverbe*, from L *prōverbium*, from *prō-* publicly, and *verbum* a word]

proviant. See **provand**.

provide *prə-vīd'* or *prō-vīd'*, *vt* to make ready beforehand (*obs*); to prepare for future use (*obs*); to supply; to afford or yield; to appoint or give a right to a benefice, *esp* before it is actually vacant; to stipulate. — *vi* to make provision, to procure supplies, means or whatever may be desirable or necessary; to take measures (for or against). — *adj* **provī'dable**. — *pa p* or *conj* **provi'ded**, *pres p* or *conj* **provī'ding** (often with *that*) on condition; on these terms; with the understanding. — *n* **provī'der**. — **provided school** formerly, in England and Wales, a school maintained by, and under the management of, the local authority. [L *prōvidēre*, from *prō* before, and *vidēre* to see]

providence *prov'i-dəns*, *n* foresight; prudent management and thrift; timely preparation; the foresight and benevolent care of God (*theol*); God, considered in this relation (*usu* with *cap*; *theol*); an instance of God's arranging or intervening in something for his purpose (*theol*); an occurrence attributed to God's ordering or intervention (*theol*); a disaster (*US*). — *adj* **prov'ident** seeing beforehand, and providing for the future; prudent; thrifty; frugal. — *adj* **providential** (*prov-i-den'shl*) affected by, or proceeding from, divine providence; provident (*rare*). — *adv* **providen'tially**. — *adv* **prov'idently**. — **provident society** same as **friendly society**. [L *prōvidens*, *-entis*, pr p of *prōvidēre*, from *prō* before, and *vidēre* to see]

providor. See **proveditor**.

province *prov'ins*, *n* a portion of an empire or a state marked off for purposes of government or in some way historically distinct; the district over which an archbishop has jurisdiction; a territorial division of the Jesuits, Templars and other religious orders; a faunal or floral area (*biol*); a region; a field of duty, activity or knowledge; a department; (in *pl*) all parts of the country except the capital (*esp theat* and *journalism*). — *adj* **provincial** (*prə-vin'shl*) relating to a province; belonging to a province or the provinces; local; showing the habits and manners of a person from a province or country district; unpolished, unsophisticated; narrow-minded. — *n* an inhabitant of a province or country district; an unpolished or unsophisticated person; the superintendent of the heads of the religious houses in a province (*RC*). — *n* **provin'cialism** a manner, mode of speech or turn of thought peculiar to a province or a country district; a local expression; the state or quality of being provincial; the ignorance and narrowness of interests shown by someone who gives his or her attention entirely to local affairs. — *n* **provin'cialist**. — **provinciality** (*prə-vin-shi-al'i-ti*). — *vt* **provin'cialize** or **-ise** to make provincial. — *adv* **provin'cially**. [Fr, from L *prōvincia* an official charge, hence a province]

provincial rose *prə-vin'shl rōz*, *n* a rose, a variety of *Rosa gallica*, cultivated at *Provins* (*pro-vɛ̃s*) in Seine-et-Marne, France (also **province rose** and **Provins rose**); a shoe rosette (*Shakesp*).

provine *prə-vīn'*, *vt* and *vi* to propagate by layering. [Fr *provigner*, from OFr *provain*, from L *prōpāgō*, *-inis* a slip, layer]

provirus *prō-vī'rəs*, (*med*) *n* the form of a virus when it is integrated into the DNA of a host cell. — *adj* **provī'ral**. [**pro-**[2] (2)]

provision *prə-vizh'ən*, *n* the act of providing; something that is provided or prepared; measures taken beforehand; a clause in a law or a deed; a stipulation; a rule for guidance; an appointment by the pope to a benefice not yet vacant; preparation; previous agreement; a store or stock; (*usu* in *pl*) a store of food; (in *pl*) food. — *vt* to supply with provisions or food. — *adj* **provi'sional** provided for the occasion; to meet necessity; (of eg an arrangement) adopted on the understanding that it may be changed later; containing a provision. — *adj* and *n* **Provi'sional** (a member) of the

Provisional IRA (Irish Republican Army), the militant group which in 1969 split from the main body of the IRA (which was thereafter known as the Official IRA) (*colloq* shortening **Prō'vō**: — *pl* **Pro'vos**). — *adv* **provi'sionally**. — *adj* **provi'sionary** (*rare*) provisional. — **provisional judgement** a judgement given as far as the available evidence admits, but subject to correction when more light is shed on the matter; **provisional order** an order granted by a secretary of state, which, when confirmed by the legislature, has the force of an act of parliament; **provisional remedy** a means of detaining in safety a person or property until a decision is made on some point in which they are concerned; **provision merchant** a general dealer in articles of food. [Fr, from L *prōvīsiō*, *-ōnis*, from *prōvidēre*; see **provide**]

proviso *prə-vī'zō* or *prō-vī'zō*, *n* a provision or condition in a deed or other writing; the clause containing it; any condition: — *pl* **provī'sos** or **provī'soes**. — *adv* **provī'sorily** (*-zə-ri-li*). — *adj* **provī'sory** containing a proviso or condition; conditional; making provision for the time; temporary. [From the L law phrase *prōvīsō quod* it being provided that]

provisor *prə-vī'zər* or *prō-vī'zər*, (*obs* or *hist*) *n* someone who provides; a purveyor; a person to whom the pope has granted the right to the next vacancy in a benefice. — **Statute of Provisors** an act of the English parliament passed in 1351 to prevent the pope from exercising the power of creating provisors. [L *prōvīsor*, *-ōris* provider]

provitamin *prō-vit'ə-min* or *prō-vīt'ə-min*, (*physiol*) *n* a substance which is not a vitamin but which is readily transformed into a vitamin within an organism. [L *prō* before, and **vitamin**]

Provo. See **Provisional** under **provision**.

provocable, etc. See under **provoke**.

provoke *prə-vōk'*, *vt* to call up or evoke (feelings, desires, etc); to summon (*archaic*); to call out or challenge (*obs*); to excite or call into action, to stimulate; to incite or bring about; to excite with anger or sexual desire; to annoy or exasperate. — *vi* (*Dryden*) to appeal. — *adj* **provocable** (*prov'ək-ə-bl* or *prə-vōk'ə-bl*; *esp* formerly) provokable. — *n* **prov'ocant**. — *n* **provocateur** (*pro-vo-ka-tœr*; Fr) someone who stirs up unrest and dissatisfaction for political ends (see also **agent provocateur**). — *n* **provocā'tion** the act of provoking; something that provokes; any cause of anger. — *adj* **provocative** (*-vok'ə-tiv*) tending, or intended, to provoke or excite. — *n* anything that provokes. — *adv* **provoc'atively**. — *n* **provoc'ativeness**. — *n* **prov'ocātor**. — *adj* **provoc'atory**. — *adj* **provōk'able**. — *n* **provoke'ment** (*Spenser*). — *n* **provōk'er**. — *adj* **provōk'ing** irritating; stimulating. — *adv* **provōk'ingly**. [L *prōvocāre*, *-ātum*, from *prō-* forth, and *vocāre* to call]

provost *prov'əst*, *n* the dignitary presiding over a cathedral or collegiate church; in certain colleges, the head; in Scotland, the chief magistrate of a burgh, corresponding to a mayor in England; an officer who arrests and keeps in custody (*Shakesp*). — *adj* (*prə-vō'*, *US prō'vō*) pertaining to military police, as in **provost officer**. — *n* **prov'ostry** the position or authority of a provost. — *n* **prov'ostship** the position of a provost. — **provost-mar'shal** (*prə-vō'-*, US *prō'vō-*) (in the army and air force) the head of military police, an officer with special powers for enforcing discipline and securing prisoners until trial; (in the navy) the officer (master-at-arms) having charge of prisoners; **provost-ser'geant** (*prə-vō'-*, *US prō'vō-*) a sergeant of military police. — **Lord Provost** the chief magistrate of Edinburgh, Glasgow, Perth, Aberdeen or Dundee; **Lady Provost** the wife (or other female relative, etc) of a Lord Provost, *esp* when supporting him in certain of his official duties. [OE *profast* (*prafost*), OFr *provost* (Fr *prévôt*), from LL *prōpositus*, from *prō-* for *prae* at the head, and *positus* set]

prow[1] *prow*, formerly sometimes *prō*, *n* the front part of a ship; the nose of an aeroplane; a projecting front part; a ship (*poetic*). [Fr *proue*, or Port, Sp or Genoese *proa*, from L *prōra*, from Gr *prōira*]

prow[2]. See under **prowess**.

prowess *prow'is* or *prow'es*, *n* bravery; valour; daring; accomplishment. — *adj* **prow** (*prow*; *archaic*) valiant. — *adj* **prow'essed**. [OFr *prou* (Fr *preux*); connected with L *prōd-* in *prōdesse* to be useful]

prowl *prowl*, formerly *prōl*, *vi* to keep moving about, restlessly as if in search of something or stealthily (as if) in search of prey or plunder. — *n* the act of prowling. — *n* **prowl'er**. — *n* and *adj* **prowl'ing**. — *adv* **prowl'ingly**. — **prowl car** (chiefly *US*) a police patrol car. — **on the prowl** occupied in prowling. [ME *prollen*; origin unknown]

prox. *abbrev*: proximo (qv).

prox. acc. *abbrev*: proxime accessit (qv).

proximate *proks'i-mit* or *proks'i-māt*, *adj* nearest or next; without anything between, eg a cause and its effect; near and immediate. — *adj* **prox'imal** (*biol*) at the near, inner or attached end (opposite of *distal*). — *adv* **prox'imally**. — *adv* **prox'imately**. — *n* **proximā'tion** and **proxim'ity** immediate nearness in time, place, relationship, etc. — **proximate cause** a cause which immediately precedes the effect; **proximate object** (*philos*) an object or thing which must exist, or otherwise it would be logically impossible to have cognition of it; **proximity fuse** a device for causing a missile to explode when it comes near the target. [L *proximus* next, superl of *prope* near]

proxime accessit *proks'i-mā ak-ses'it* or *a-kes'it*, *n* the person next in order of merit to the winner: — *pl* **proxime accessits**. [L, he or she came closest]

proximo *proks'i-mō*, (*old commerce*) *adv* next month. [L *proximo* (*mense*) next (month)]

proxy *prok'si*, *n* the agency of someone who acts for another; someone who acts or votes for another; the writing by which he or she is authorized to do so; a substitute. — *adj* **proxy-wedd'ed** (*Tennyson*) wedded by proxy. [**procuracy**]

proyn or **proyne** *proin*. Obsolete forms of **prune**[1,2,3].

prozymite *proz'i-mīt*, *n* a person who uses leavened bread in the eucharist (as opposed to an *azymite*). [Gr *prozȳmia* ferments]

PRS *abbrev*: Performing Rights Society.

PRT *abbrev*: petroleum revenue tax.

Pru *proo͞*, (*colloq*) *abbrev*: Prudential Assurance Company.

Pruce *proo͞s*, (*obs*) *n* Prussia. — *adj* Prussian. [Anglo-Fr *Prus*, *Pruz*, etc]

prude *proo͞d*, *n* a person of priggish or affected modesty; someone who has or pretends to have extreme propriety. — Also *adj* (*rare*). — *n* **pru'dery** the manners, opinions, etc of a prude. — *adj* **pru'dish**. — *adv* **pru'dishly**. — *n* **pru'dishness**. [OFr *prode*, fem of *prou*, *prod* excellent; cf **prow**[2], **proud**]

prudent *proo͞'dənt*, *adj* cautious and wise in conduct; discreet; characterized by, behaving with, showing, having or dictated by forethought. — *n* **pru'dence** the quality of being prudent; wisdom applied to practice; attention to self-interest; caution. — *adj* **prudential** (*proo͞-den'shl*) having regard to considerations of prudence; relating to prudence; prudent; concerned with administration (*US*). — *n* (generally in *pl*) a matter or consideration of prudence; a prudent maxim. — *n* **pruden'tialism** a system based on prudence alone. — *n* **pruden'tialist**. — *n* **prudentiality** (*proo͞-den-shi-al'i-ti*). — *adv* **pruden'tially**. — *adv* **pru'dently**. [L *prūdēns*, *prūdentis*, contraction of *prōvidēns*, pr p of *prōvidēre* to foresee]

prudery. See under **prude**.

prud'homme *prü-dom'*, *n* a discreet man (*obs*); a skilled workman (*obs*); in France, a member of a board for settling labour disputes. [OFr *prud* or *prod* (nominative *pros*) good, and *homme* man]

prudish, etc. See under **prude**.

pruh. See **proo**.

pruina *proo-ī'nə*, (*bot*) *n* a powdery bloom or waxy secretion. — *adj* **pruinose** (*proo'i-nōs*) covered with pruina; having a frosted look. [L *pruīna* hoar-frost]

pruine. A Shakespearian spelling of **prune**[3].

prune[1] *proon*, *vt* to trim by lopping off superfluous parts; to remove anything superfluous from (*fig*); to remove by pruning. — Formerly also **proin**, **proine**, **proyn** and **proyne**. — *n* **pru'ner**. — *n* **pru'ning** the act of pruning or trimming. — **pru'ning-bill** or **prun'ing-hook** a hooked bill for pruning with; **pru'ning-knife** a large knife with a slightly hooked point for pruning; **prun'ing-saw** a saw with a *usu* tapering straight or curved blade, often attached or attachable to a long handle, for pruning trees, etc. — *n pl* **pru'ning-shears** shears for pruning shrubs, etc. [OFr *proignier*; origin unknown]

prune[2] *proon*, (*archaic*) *vt* to preen. — Formerly also **proin**, **proine**, **proyn**, **proyne** and **proign**. [Origin obscure]

prune[3] *proon*, *n* a plum (*obs*); a dried plum; a plum suitable for drying (*US*); the dark purple colour of prune juice; a dud pilot (*airmen's slang*); a despised or silly person (*colloq*). — Formerly also **pruine**, **prewyn** (*Shakesp*), **proin**, **proine**, **proyn** and **proyne**. — *adj* of the colour of prune juice. — **prunes and prisms** part of a formula for setting the lips into a pleasing shape, 'serviceable in the formation of a demeanour' (Dickens, *Little Dorrit*); hence, (often **prisms**), a somewhat prim manner of speaking, or any trivial and superficial refinement. [Fr, from L *prūna*, pl of *prūnum* (taken for a *n sing*); cf Gr *prou(m)non* plum]

prunella[1] *proo-nel'ə*, *n* sore throat; quinsy; (with *cap*; also **Brunella**) the self-heal genus of labiate plants, once reputed to cure prunella. [Latinized from Ger *Bräune* quinsy (from the brownness of the tongue), or LL *brūnus*, from general Germanic *brūn* brown]

prunella[2] *proo-nel'ə*, *n* a strong silk or woollen material, formerly used for academic and clerical gowns and women's shoes — also **prunelle'** and **prunell'o** (*pl* **prunell'os**). — *adj* made of prunella. [Appar Fr *prunelle* sloe, dimin of *prune* plum]

prunella[3] *proo-nel'ə*, *n* a bird of the genus *Prunella* (formerly *Accentor*), the hedge-sparrow or other accentor. [L *prunum* a plum]

prunello[1] *proo-nel'ō*, *n* a little prune; a kind of dried plum: — *pl* **prunell'os**. [Obs Ital *prunella*, dimin of *pruna* (now *prugna*) plum]

prunello[2]. See **prunella**[2].

prunt *prunt*, *n* a moulded glass ornament attached to a glass object such as a vase; a tool for making it. — *adj* **prunt'ed**. [Origin uncertain]

prunus *proo'nəs*, *n* a tree or shrub belonging to the genus *Prunus*, including the plum, apricot, peach, cherry, almond and sloe. [L, plum tree]

prurient *proo'ri-ənt*, *adj* itching; having an unhealthy interest in sexual matters; arousing such interest; causing itching (*bot, rare*). — *n* **pru'rience** or **pru'riency**. — *adv* **pru'riently**. [L *prūriens*, *-entis*, pr p of *prūrīre* to itch]

prurigo *proo-rī'gō*, (*med*) *n* an eruption on the skin, causing great itching: — *pl* **prurī'gos**. — *adj* **pruriginous** (*-rij'i-nəs*). [L *prūrīgō*, *-inis*, from *prūrīre* to itch]

pruritis *proo-rī'təs*, (*med*) *n* itching. — *adj* **pruritic** (*-rit'ik*). [L *prūrītus*, from *prūrīre* to itch]

prusik sling *prus'ik sling*, or **prusik** (*mountaineering*) *n* (also *cap*) a type of rope sling attached to a climbing rope, which grips firmly when carrying weight but when unweighted can be moved up the rope. — *vi* and *vt* to climb or raise (oneself) up by means of two such slings: — *pr p* **pru'siking**; *pa t* and *pa p* **prus'iked**. — **prusik knot** (also *cap*) the type of knot by which a prusik sling is attached to a rope. [Karl *Prusik*, Austrian climber]

Prussian *prush'ən*, *adj* of or pertaining to *Prussia*, a former state of N Central Europe, now in Germany. — *n* an inhabitant, native or citizen of Prussia. — *n* **Pruss'ianism** the spirit of Prussian nationality; arrogant militarism. — *vt* and *vi* **Pruss'ianize** or **-ise** to make or become Prussian. — *n* **Pruss'ianizer** or **-s-**. — *n* **prussiate** (*prus'* or *prush'i-āt*; *chem*) a cyanide; a ferricyanide; a ferrocyanide. — *adj* **pruss'ic** (also sometimes *proos'ik*) pertaining to Prussian blue. — *n* **Prussificā'tion**. — *vt* **Pruss'ify** to Prussianize, assimilate to Prussian ways, etc. — **Prussian** (or **prussian**) **blue** ferric ferrocyanide, a colour pigment, discovered in Berlin; the very dark blue colour of this; **prussic acid** hydrocyanic acid, a deadly poison, first obtained from Prussian blue. — **Old Prussian** the extinct Baltic language of the former inhabitants of East and West Prussia.

pry[1] *prī*, *vi* to peer or peep into something that is private (also *fig*); to examine things with impertinent curiosity: — *pr p* **prying**; *pa t* and *pa p* **pried**; *3rd pers sing pr t* **pries**. — *n* an act of prying (*rare*); someone who pries (cf *Paul Pry*, in John Poole's (1792–1879) comedy of that name). — *n* **prī'er** (also **pry'er**) someone who pries. — *n* and *adj* **pry'ing**. — *adv* **pry'ingly**. — **pry out** to investigate or find out by prying. [ME *prien*; origin unknown]

pry[2] *prī*, *vt* a form of **prize**[1].

prys and **pryse**. Old spellings of **price** and **prize**[3].

pryse *prīz*, (*Scott*) *n* a horn-blast at the taking or killing of a deer. [OFr *pris* taken; cf **prize**[2]]

prytaneum *prit-an-ē'əm*, (*antiq*) *n* the town hall of an ancient Greek city: — *pl* **prytanē'a**. [Latinized from Gr *prytaneion*, from *prytanis* a presiding magistrate]

pr'ythee or **prythee** *pridh'ē*. Same as **prithee**.

Przewalski's horse *prə-zhi-val'skiz hörs*, *n* a wild horse discovered in Central Asia by Nikolai *Przewalski* (1839–88), Russian explorer. — Various other spellings exist.

PS *abbrev*: *Pferdestärke* (*Ger*), horsepower (now *esp* metric horsepower); Pharmaceutical Society; Philological Society; Police Sergeant; postscript; private secretary; prompt side (*theat*).

Ps. *abbrev*: Psalm or Psalms (also **Psa.**); (the Book of) Psalms (*Bible*).

PSA *abbrev*: pleasant Sunday afternoon; Property Services Agency; Public Services Authority.

psaligraphy *sa-lig'rə-fi*, *n* the art of paper-cutting to make pictures. [Gr *psalis* shears, and *graphein* to write]

psalm *säm*, *n* a devotional song or hymn, *esp* one of those included in the Old Testament **Book of Psalms**. — *n* **psalmist** (*säm'ist*) a composer of psalms, *esp* (with *cap*) David. — *adj* **psalmodic** (*sal-mod'ik*) or **psalmod'ical** pertaining to psalmody. — *n* **psalmodist** (*sal'mə-dist* or *säm'ə-dist*) a singer of psalms. — *vi* **psalmodize** or **-ise** (*sal'mə-dīz* or *säm'*) to practise psalmody. — *n* **psalmody** (*sal'* or *säm'*; Gr *psalmōidiā* singing to the harp) the singing of psalms, *esp* in public worship; psalms collectively. — **psalm'-book** a book containing psalms for purposes of worship; **psalm'-tune**. [OE *psalm*, *psealm*, from LL *psalmus*, from Gr *psalmos*, music of or to a stringed instrument, from *psallein* to pluck]

Psalter *söl'tər*, *n* the **Book of Psalms**, *esp* when printed separately from the rest of the Bible; (without *cap*) a book of psalms. — *adj* **psalterian** (*söl-tē'ri-ən*) pertaining to a psalter; like a psaltery. — *n* **psal'tery** an ancient and medieval stringed instrument like the zither, played by plucking; (with *cap*; *rare*) the Psalter. — *n* **psal'tress** a woman who plays the psaltery. [OE *saltere*, from L *psaltērium*, from Gr *psaltērion* a psaltery]

psalterium *söl-tē'ri-əm*, (*animal physiol*) *n* the third division of a ruminant's stomach, the omasum or manyplies: — *pl* **psaltē'ria**. [From the appearance of its lamellae, like a stringed instrument; see **psaltery**]

psammite *sam'īt*, (*rare geol*) *n* any rock composed of sand-grains. — *adj* **psammitic** (*sam-it'ik*). — *n* **psamm'ophil** or **psamm'ophile** a sand-loving plant. — *adj* **psammoph'ilous**. — *n* **psamm'ophyte** (*sam'-ō-fīt*; *biol*) a plant that grows only on sand. — *adj* **psammophytic** (*sam-ō-fit'ik*). [Gr *psammos* sand]

p's and q's *pēz ən(d) kūz'*, *n pl* correct social manners and behaviour, *esp* in the phrase **to mind one's p's and q's**. [Various explanations have been given; among these are the supposed admonition to children learning to write not to confuse the letters *p* and *q*, and an alteration of *p(l)ease* and *(than)k you's*]

PSBR (*econ*) *abbrev*: Public Sector Borrowing Requirement.

psc (*military*) *abbrev*: passed staff college.

pschent *ps'hhent*, *pskent* or *skent*, (*antiq*) *n* the crown of the Egyptian pharaohs. [Gr, from Egyp]

PSDR (*econ*) *abbrev*: Public Sector Debt Repayment.

psellism *sel'izm* or *psel'izm*, *n* a defect in articulation — also **psellis'mus**. [Gr *psellismos*, from *psellos* stammering]

psephism *sē'fizm* or *psē'fizm*, (*antiq*) *n* a decree of the Athenian assembly (from their voting with pebbles). — *n* **pse'phite** (*geol*) a rock composed of pebbles, a conglomerate. — *adj* **psephit'ic**. — *n* **psēphol'ogy** the sociological and statistical study of election results and trends — also **psephoanal'ysis**. — *adj* **psepholog'ical**. — *n* **psephol'ogist**. [Gr *psēphos* a pebble]

pseud *sūd* or *sōōd*, (*colloq*) *n* a pretentious person, *esp* intellectually. — *adj* (also **pseud'o**) false, sham; pretentious. — *n* **pseud'ery** (*colloq*) falseness; pretentiousness. — *adj* **pseud'ish** false, spurious; pretentious. [**pseud-**]

pseud. *abbrev*: pseudonym.

pseud- *sūd-*, or **pseudo-** *sū'dō-*, or (*NAm*) *sōōd-* and *sōō'dō-*, *combining form* sham, false, spurious; deceptively resembling; isomerous with or closely related to (*chem*); temporary, provisional. — *n* **pseudaesthē'sia** imaginary feeling, eg in an amputated limb. — *n* **pseudax'is** (*bot*) a sympodium. — *n pl* **pseudepig'rapha** books ascribed to Old Testament characters, but not judged genuine by scholars. — *adj* **pseudepigraph'ic**, **pseudepigraph'ical** or **pseudepig'raphous**. — *n* **pseudepig'raphy** the ascription to books of false names of authors. — *n* **pseudimā'go** (*entomol*) a subimago. — *n* **pseu'doacid** a compound which is not an acid but which is isomeric with and transformable into an acid. — *adj* **pseudo-archā'ic** sham antique; artificially archaistic; clumsily and inaccurately imitative of the old, eg in style. — *n* **pseudo-ar'chāism**. — *n* **pseu'dobulb** (*bot*) a swollen stem internode in some orchids. — *n* **pseu'docarp** (*bot*) a fruit formed from other parts in addition to the gynaeceum. — *n* **pseudo-Christian'ity**. — *n* **pseudoclass'icism**. — *n* **pseu'docode** (*comput*) instructions written in symbolic language which must be translated into an acceptable program language before they can be executed. — *n* **pseudocyesis** (*-sī-ē'sis*; *psychol*; Gr *kyēsis*, from *kyein* to be pregnant) a psychosomatic condition marked by many of the symptoms of pregnancy. — **pseudoephedrine** (*-ef'i-drēn* or *-i-fed'rin*; *chem*) a naturally occurring isomer of ephedrine, used in the form of its hydrochloride as a bronchodilator. — *n* **pseudofolliculī'tis** (*med*) a chronic disorder, *esp* of the neck, of men who shave, in which the tips of the shaved hairs cause the formation of papules. — *adj* and *n* **pseudo-Goth'ic** sham or would-be Gothic. — *n* **pseu'dograph** a writing falsely ascribed. — *n* **pseudog'raphy** unsatisfactory spelling. — *n* **pseudohermaph'roditism** (*anatom*) a congenital condition in which a man has external genitalia resembling those of a woman, and vice versa. — *n* **pseudologia** (*-lō'ji-ə*; *med*; Gr, falsehood) lying in speech or writing. — *n* **pseudologia fantastica** pathological lying, a psychiatric disorder in which the sufferer has an uncontrollable tendency to tell lies and create fantastic stories. — *n* **pseud'ologue** a liar; a person suffering from pseudologia fantastica. — *n* **pseudol'ogy** the art or science of lying. — *n* **pseu'domartyr** a false martyr. — *n* **pseu'domembrane** a false membrane. — *n* **pseudomō'nad** (or, *esp US*, *-dom'-*), or **pseudomō'nas** (*bacteriol*) a member of the genus *Pseudomonas* of schizomycetes, comprising short rod-shaped bacteria which are found in soil and in water: — *pl* **pseudomō'nads** (or *-dom'-*) or **pseudomō'nadēs**. — *n* **pseu'domorph** (*geol*) a portion of a mineral showing the outward form of another which it has replaced by molecular substitution or otherwise. — *adj* **pseudomor'phic** or **pseudomor'phous**. — *n* **pseudomor'phism**. — *n* **pseu'donym** a fictitious name assumed, eg by an author. — *n* **pseudonym'ity**. — *adj* **pseudon'ymous**. — *adv* **pseudon'ymously**. — *n* **pseu'dopod** a psychic projection from a medium (*spiritualism*); a foot-like process of the body wall, not a true leg but serving as one, as eg in caterpillars (*entomol*); a pseudopodium. — *n* **pseudopō'dium** (*biol*) a process protruding from the cell of a protozoan, etc, used for movement or feeding: — *pl* **pseudopō'dia**. — *adj* **pseudoran'dom** (*comput*) referring to a set of numbers generated by a computer and therefore not entirely random, but sufficiently so for most purposes. — *n* **pseu'doscope** a kind of stereoscope that interchanges convex and concave in appearance. — *n* **pseudoscor'pion** any member of the order **Pseudoscorpionid'ea** of arachnids, tiny carnivorous creatures resembling tailless scorpions, found under stones, bark, leaves, etc. — *n* **pseudosolu'tion** (*chem*) a colloidal suspension. — *n* **pseudosymm'etry** (*crystallog*) a deceptively close approach by a crystal to a higher degree of symmetry, eg when the axes of a tetragonal crystal are so close to being equal that on casual inspection the crystal appears to be cubic (**pseudocub'ic symmetry**) or when a crystal that is not quite hexagonal appears to be so (**pseudohexag'onal symmetry**). [Gr *pseudēs* false]

PSGB *abbrev*: Pharmaceutical Society of Great Britain.

pshaw *pshö*, *shö* or *pshə*, *interj* expressing contempt or impatience. — *vi* to say 'pshaw'. — *vt* to say 'pshaw' at. [Spontaneous expression]

psi *psī*, *psē*, *sī* or *sē*, *n* the twenty-third letter (Ψ, ψ) of the Greek alphabet, equivalent to *ps*; as a Greek numeral $\psi' = 700$, $\psi = 700\,000$. — *n* **psī'on** a psi particle. — *adj* **psion'ic**. — *n sing* **psion'ics** the use of the paranormal in the treatment of illness, etc. — **psi particle** an elementary particle with a very long life, formed by an electron-positron collision; **psi phenomena** the phenomena of parapsychology. [Gr *psei*]

psi *abbrev*: pounds per square inch.

psilanthropism *sī-lan'thrə-pizm* or *psī-lan'thrə-pizm*, *n* the doctrine that Christ was a mere man. — *adj* **psilanthropic** (*-throp'ik*). — *n* **psilan'thropist**. — *n* **psilan'thropy**. [Gr *psīlos* bare, and *anthrōpos* man]

psilocin *sī'lō-sin*, *n* a hallucinogenic drug found, like psilocybin, in the Mexican mushroom *Psilocybe mexicana* and other mushrooms. [**psilocybin**]

psilocybin *sī-lō-sī'bin*, *n* a hallucinogenic drug, obtained from the Mexican mushroom *Psilocybe mexicana* and other mushrooms. [Gr *psīlos* bare, and *kybē* head]

psilomelane *sī-lom'ə-lān* or *sī-lō-mel'ān*, or *psī-*, *n* (*geol*) an oxide of manganese, *usu* with barium, etc, occurring in smooth black botryoidal masses. [Gr *psīlos* bare, and *melās*, *-anos* black]

Psilophyton *sī-lō-fī'ton* or *psī-lō-fī'ton*, *n* (*palaeontol*) a very simple Devonian fossil pteridophyte, from which is named the order **Psilophytales** (*-fī-tā'lēz*), early landplants. [Gr *psīlos* bare, and *phyton* plant]

psilosis *sī-lō'sis* or *psī-lō'sis*, *n* loss of hair (*pathol*); sprue (from the loss of epithelium) (*obs pathol*); deaspiration (*Gr gram*). — *adj* **psilot'ic** relating to psilosis. [Gr *psīlōsis*, from *psīlos* bare]

Psilotum *sī-lō'təm* or *psī-lō'təm*, *n* (*bot*) a genus of rootless pteridophytes from which is named the order **Psilotā'ceae**. [Gr *psīlōton* the name of some plant, from *psīlos* bare (because of the almost leafless stem)]

psion, etc. See under **psi**.

PSIS *abbrev*: Permanent Secretaries Committee on the Intelligence Services.

Psittacus *sit'ə-kəs* or *psit'ə-kəs*, *n* the grey-parrot genus. — *adj* **psitt'acine** (*-sīn*) of or like parrots. — *n* **psittacosis** (*-kō'sis*) a contagious viral disease of birds such as parrots and parakeets and also chickens, ducks, pigeons, communicable to humans, with symptoms of fever, headache, nausea, etc. [Gr *psittakos* parrot]

PSL (*econ*) *abbrev*: private sector liquidity, one measure of the money supply.

psoas *sō'əs* or *psō'əs*, *n* a muscle of the loins and pelvis (*anatom*); the tenderloin. [Gr (pl) *psoai*, the accusative *psoās* being mistaken for a nominative singular]

psocid *sō'sid*, *sō'kid*, *psō'sid* or *psō'kid*, *n* any member of the family **Psocidae** or of the order Psocoptera (to which the Psocidae belong), tiny winged or wingless insects, eg booklice, barklice, etc, which feed on decaying animal or vegetable matter, fungi, lichens, etc. [From *Psocus*, a genus included in the family and order, from Gr *psōchein* to grind up]

Psocoptera *sō-kop'tər-ə* or *psō-kop'tər-ə*, *n pl* the Corrodentia, an order of insects consisting of the booklice, barklice, etc. [*Psocus* a genus included in the order, and Gr *pteron* wing]

psora *sō'rə*, *sō'rə*, *psō'rə* or *psō'rə*, (*obs med*) *n* scabies, itch. — *n* **psorī'asis** a skin disease in which red scaly papules and patches appear. — *adj* **psoriat'ic**. — *adj* **pso'ric**. — **psoriatic arthropathy** or **psoriatic arthritis** (*med*) any of various forms of arthitis occurring in people suffering from psoriasis. [Gr *psōrā*, *psōriāsis* itch]

psoralen *sō'rə-len* or *sō'rə-len*, (*chem* and *med*) *n* any of a number of naturally occurring chemicals, found eg in parsnips, celery and parsley, which make the skin more sensitive to ultraviolet light and which are used in the treatment of acne and psoriasis, and in some suntan lotions, but which because of their sensitizing effect are carcinogenic. [From *Psoralea*, a genus of leguminous plants which contain psoralens]

pst or **psst** *pst*, *interj* used to attract someone's attention quietly or surreptitiously. [Imit]

PST *abbrev*: Pacific Standard Time.

PSV *abbrev*: public service vehicle.

PSW *abbrev*: psychiatric social worker.

psych or **psyche** *sīk*, (*slang*) *vt* to subject to psychoanalysis; to work out (a problem, the intentions of another person, etc) psychologically (often with *out*); to defeat or intimidate by psychological means (sometimes with *out*); to get (oneself or another person) psychologically prepared for some challenge, ordeal, etc (*usu* with *up*); to stimulate (*usu* with *up*). — *n* **psych'-up** (*slang*) the act of psyching oneself or someone else up. [**Psychological**, **psychoanalysis**, etc]

psychagogue. See under **psycho-**.

psyche[1] *sī'kē*, *n* the soul, spirit or mind; the principle of mental and emotional life, conscious and unconscious; a butterfly (*obs*); a cheval-glass; (with *cap*) the personification of the soul, depicted as a young woman with butterfly wings, the beloved of Eros (*Gr mythol*); (with *cap*) a genus of bombycid moths (the females wingless, sometimes legless); (with *cap*) one of the minor planets. — *n* **psychoph'ily** (*bot*) pollination by butterflies. [Gr *psȳchē* soul, butterfly, *Psȳche* Psyche]

psyche[2]. See **psych**.

psychedelic, **psychiatrist**, **psychic**, etc. See under **psycho-**.

psycho *sī'kō* (*colloq*) *n* a psychopath. — *pl* **psy'chōs**. — *adj* psychopathic.

psycho- *sī-kō*, *-kə-*, *-ko'*, or **psych-** *sīk-*, *combining form* soul or spirit; mind, mental; psychological. — *n* **psych'agogue** (*-ə-gog*; Gr *agōgos* guide) the conductor of souls to the underworld (a title of Hermes); someone who calls up spirits; someone who guides the mind; a means of restoring consciousness. — *n* **psychasthenia** (*sī-kəs-thē'ni-ə* or *-thə-nī'ə*; Gr *astheneia* weakness; *obs*) a severe functional mental disorder, characterized by fixed ideas, ruminative states and hypochondriacal conditions. — *n* **psychedelia** (*sī-kə-dē'li-ə*) or (more correctly but less commonly) **psychodēl'ia** the production of, or the culture associated with, psychedelic experiences. — *n pl* (objects, etc associated with) psychedelic experiences. — *adj* **psychedel'ic** or (more correctly but less commonly) **psychodel'ic** (or *-dē'lik*; Gr *dēlos* visible, clear) pertaining to a state of relaxation and pleasure, with heightened perception and increased mental powers generally; pertaining to drugs which cause, or are believed to cause, the taker to enter such a state; pertaining to visual effects and/or sound effects whose action on the mind is a little like that of psychedelic drugs; dazzling in pattern. — *n* **psychī'ater** (Gr *iātros* physician; *archaic*) a psychiatrist. — *adj* **psychiat'ric** or **psychiat'rical**. — *n* **psychī'atrist** a person who is medically qualified to treat diseases of the mind. — *n* **psychī'atry**. — *adj* **psy'chic** or **psy'chical** pertaining to the psyche, soul or mind; spiritual; spiritualistic; beyond, or apparently beyond, the physical; sensitive to, in touch with, or apparently having powers or capabilities derived from, something that has not yet been explained physically, eg apparently prescient or telepathic. — For compound nouns formed with **psychic** and **psychical**, see below **psychotropic**. — *n* **psy'chic** that which is of the mind or psyche; a spiritualistic medium. — *adv* **psy'chically**. — *n* **psy'chicism** psychical research. — *n* **psy'chicist**. — *n sing* **psy'chics** the science of psychology; psychical research. — *n* **psy'chism** the doctrine of a universal soul. — *n* **psy'chist** a psychologist (*obs*); a person interested in psychical research (also **psy'chicist**); a player who makes psychic bids (*bridge*). — *adj* **psychoac'tive** of a drug, affecting the brain and influencing behaviour, heightening sensitivity, etc (also **psychotrop'ic**). — *vt* **psychoan'alyse** or (*US*) **-yze** to subject to psychoanalysis. — *n* **psychoanal'ysis** a method of investigation and psychotherapy whereby nervous diseases or mental ailments are traced to forgotten hidden concepts in the patient's mind and treated by bringing these to light. — *n* **psychoan'alyst** someone who practises psychoanalysis. — *adjs* **psychoanalyt'ic** or **psychoanalyt'ical**. — *n* **psych'obabble** excessive or needless use of psychologists' jargon; needless, meaningless or mindless use of jargon generally, eg by those involved in some of the modern spiritual and therapeutic movements or organizations. — *adj* **psychobiograph'ical**. — *n* **psychobiog'raphy** a biography concerned mainly with the psychological development of its subject. — *adj* **psychobiolog'ical**. — *n* **psychobiol'ogist**. — *n* **psychobiol'ogy** the study of the relationship between the functions of the body and the mind. — *n* **psychochem'ical** a psychoactive chemical. — Also *adj*. — *n* a substance with psychoactive effect, *esp* a chemical intended as a weapon of war, *specif* a psychogas. — *n* **psychochem'istry** the treatment of mental illness by drugs. — *n* **psychodelia** and *adj* **psychodelic** see **psychedelia** and **psychedelic** above. — *n* **psychodram'a** a method of treatment of mental disorders in which the patient is led to objectify and understand his or her difficulty by spontaneously acting it out. — *adj* **psychodramat'ic**. — *adj* **psychodynam'ic** pertaining to mental and emotional forces, their source in past experience, and their effects. — *n sing* **psychodynam'ics** the study of psychodynamic forces, etc. — *n pl* psychodynamic forces. — *n* **psy'chogas** a gas which makes a person's performance deteriorate very seriously without his or her being aware of it. — *n* **psychogen'esis** (the study of) the origin or development of the mind (also **psychogenet'ics**); origination in the mind. — *adj* **psychogenet'ic** or **psychogenet'ical**. — *adj* **psychogen'ic** originating in the mind or in a mental condition. — *adj* **psychogeriat'ric**. — *n* **psychogeriatric'ian**. — *n sing* **psychogeriat'rics** the study of the psychological problems of old age. — *n* **psychog'ony** the origin or development of the mind or soul. — *n* **psych'ogram** writing supposedly produced by a spirit or under the influence of a spirit. — *n* **psych'ograph** an instrument by which a psychogram is obtained. — *adj* **psychograph'ic** or **psychograph'ical**. — *n sing* **psychograph'ics** the quantitive study of personalities and attitudes, used as a tool in marketing. — *n* **psychog'raphy** writing supposedly produced by or under the influence of a spirit; psychological biography or delineation. — *n* **psychohistor'ian**. — *adj* **psychohistor'ical**. — *n* **psychohis'tory** history studied from a psychological point of view. — *n* **psy'choid** the hypothetical regulative principle directing the behaviour of an organism. — *n* **psychokinē'sis** movement by psychic agency. — *adj* **psychokinet'ic**. — *n* **psycho-**

ling'uist. — *adj* **psycholinguis'tic**. — *n sing* **psycholinguis'tics** the study of language development, language in relation to the mind, language in thought, etc. — *adj* **psycholog'ic** or **psycholog'ical**. — For compound nouns formed with **psychological**, see below **psychotropic**. — *adv* **psycholog'ically**. — *n* **psychol'ogism** a doctrine depending on psychological conceptions; the view that all natural and social sciences should be based on psychology. — *n* **psychol'ogist** a person who has studied and is qualified in psychology. — *vi* **psychol'ogize** or **ise**. — *n* **psychol'ogy** the science of the mind; the study of mind and behaviour; attitudes, etc characteristic of an individual, type, etc, or animating specific conduct; subtle or cunning behaviour or actions, using (or supposedly using) a knowledge of a person's mind in order to achieve one's own ends. — *n* **psychom'eter** someone who has the occult power of psychometry; an instrument for measuring reaction times, etc. — *adj* **psychomet'ric** or **psychomet'rical**. — *n* **psychometrician** (*-trish'ən*) or **psychom'etrist**. — *n sing* **psychomet'rics** the branch of psychology dealing with measurable factors. — *n* **psychom'etry** psychometrics; the occult power of divining properties of things by mere contact. — *adj* **psychomō'tor** pertaining to such mental action as induces muscular contraction. — *n* **psychoneuroimmunol'ogy** the study of the effects of mental states and other psychological factors in the body's immune system. — *n* **psychoneurō'sis** mental disease without any apparent anatomical lesion; a functional disorder of the mind in someone who is legally sane and shows insight into his or her condition: — *pl* **psychoneurō'sēs**. — *n* and *adj* **psychoneurot'ic**. — *adj* **psychonom'ic**. — *n sing* **psychonom'ics** the study of the individual mind in relation to its environment. — *n* **psychopannychism** (*-pan'ik-izm*; Gr *pannychos* all night long, from *pās* all, and *nychios* nightly) (belief in) the sleep of the soul from death to resurrection. — *n* **psychopann'ychist** someone who holds this belief. — *n* **psy'chopath** (*-path*) someone who shows a pathological degree of specific emotional instability without specific mental disorder; someone suffering from a behavioural disorder resulting in inability to form personal relationships and in indifference to or ignorance of his or her obligations to society, often manifested by antisocial behaviour such as acts of violence, sexual perversion, etc. — *adj* **psychopath'ic** pertaining to psychopathy or the behaviour or condition of a psychopath. — *n* a psychopath. — *n* **psychop'athist** or **psychopathol'ogist**. — *n* **psychopathol'ogy** the branch of psychology that deals with the abnormal workings of the mind; an abnormal psychological condition. — *n* **psychop'athy** any disorder of mental functions, insanity. — *n* **psychopharmacol'ogist**. — *n* **psychopharmacol'ogy** the study of the effects of drugs on the mind. — *n* **psychophily** see under **psyche**[1]. — *adj* **psychophys'ical** (see also **psychophysical parallelism** under **parallel**). — *n* **psychophys'icist**. — *n sing* **psychophys'ics** the study of the relation between mental and physical processes. — *n* **psychophysiol'ogy** experimental or physiological psychology. — *n* **psy'chopomp** (Gr *pompos* guide) a conductor of souls to the other world. — *n* **psychoprophylax'is** a method of training for childbirth aimed at enabling women to manage and control the pain of labour. — *adj* **psychosex'ual** of or relating to the psychological aspects of sex, eg sexual fantasies. — *n* **psychō'sis** mental condition; a serious mental disorder characterized by eg illusions, delusions, hallucinations, mental confusion and a lack of insight on the part of the patient into his or her condition: — *pl* **psychō'sēs**. — *adj* **psychosō'cial** of or relating to matters both psychological and social. — *adj* **psychosomat'ic** (Gr *sōma* body) of mind and body as a unit; concerned with or denoting physical diseases having a psychological origin. — *n sing* **psychosomat'ics** the study of psychosomatic conditions. — *adj* **psychosomimet'ic** of a drug, producing symptoms like those of mental illness; referring to (eg drug-induced) changes in behaviour and personality resembling those due to psychosis. — *n* **psychosur'gery** brain surgery in the treatment of cases of mental disorder. — *n* **psychosyn'thesis** the combining of the various individual elements of the mind or personality into an integrated whole by psychoanalysis or other mode of psychotherapy; *specif*, a form of psychotherapy created by Italian psychiatrist Roberto Assagioli (died 1974) emphasizing the importance of the individual's free will and employing techniques such as meditation adopted from eastern religions. — *n sing* **psychotech'nics** the use of psychological theory in politics, economics, etc. — *n sing* **psychotherapeut'ics** or *n* **psychother'apy** treatment of mental illness by hypnosis, psychoanalysis and similar psychological means. — *n* **psychother'apist**. — *adj* **psychot'ic** pertaining to psychosis. — *n* a person suffering from a psychosis. — *n* **psychot'icism**. — *adj* **psychotomimet'ic** psychosomimetic. — *adj* **psychotox'ic** harmful to the mind or personality. — *adj* **psychotrop'ic** same as **psychoactive**. — *n* a psychotropic drug. — **psychical research** investigation of phenomena apparently implying a connection with another world; **psychic bid** (*bridge*) bid of a suit in which one is not strong to deceive an opponent, or for some other reason; **psychic determinism** the Freudian theory that mental processes are always determined by motivations, conscious or unconscious; **psychic force** a power not physical or mechanical, supposed to cause certain so-called spiritualistic phenomena; **psychological block** an inability to think about, remember, etc a particular subject, event, etc for psychological reasons; **psychological moment** strictly speaking, the psychological element or factor (Ger *Moment*); misunderstood by a French translator from German and applied to the moment of time when the mind could best be worked on; hence now often the very moment, the nick of time; **psychological operation** one carried out in **psychological warfare**, the use of propaganda to influence enemy opinion or morale (contracted to **psyop** (*sī'op*) and **psywar** (*sī'wör*)); **psychophysical parallelism** see **parallelism** under **parallel**. [Gr *psȳchē* soul, butterfly]

psychrometer *sī-krom'i-tər*, *n orig* a thermometer; now, a wet-and-dry-bulb hygrometer. — *adj* **psychrometric** (*sī-krō-met'rik*) or **psychromet'rical**. — *n* **psychrom'etry**. [Gr *psȳchros* cold, and *metron* a measure]

psychrophilic *sī-krō-fil'ik*, (*bot*) *adj* growing best at low temperatures. [Gr *psȳchros* cold, and *phileein* to love]

psylla *sil'ə n* an insect of the genus *Psylla*; (also **psyll'id**) an insect of the homopterous family **Psyllidae** (*-dē*) (which includes the genus *Psylla*), sap-sucking plant pests also known as jumping plant lice. — **psyllid yellows** a disease of potato plants caused by psyllids, in which the leaves turn yellow and curl up. [Gr *psylla* a flea]

psyop and **psywar**. See **psychological operation** and **warfare** under **psycho-**.

PT *abbrev*: personal trainer, or training; physical therapy; physical training; postal telegraph; pupil teacher; purchase tax (*hist*).

Pt (*chem*) *symbol*: platinum.

pt *abbrev*: past; past tense; pint or pints; point; post-town.

PTA *abbrev*: Parent-Teacher Association.

pta *abbrev*: peseta.

ptarmic *tär'mik* or *ptär'mik*, *n* a substance that causes sneezing. [Gr *ptarmos* a sneeze]

ptarmigan *tär'mi-gən*, *n* a mountain-dwelling species of grouse (Lagopus mutus), which turns white in winter, known outside the British Isles as the rock ptarmigan; extended to other species of *Lagopus*, such as the willow grouse, but not to *Lagopus scoticus*, the red grouse. [Gaelic *tàrmachan*; the initial *pt-* derives from an incorrect assumed connection with Gr *ptarmos* — see **ptarmic**]

PTE *abbrev*: Passenger Transport Executive.

Pte *abbrev*: Private (*military* and *commerce*).

pter-, **-ptera** etc. See **ptero-**.

pteranodon *ter-an'ə-don* or *pter-an'ə-don*, *n* a toothless flying reptile of the Cretaceous period with a horn-like crest. [Gr *pteron* wing, *an-* without, and *odous*, *odontos* tooth]

Pterichthys *tər-ik'this* or *pter-ik'this*, *n* a genus of Old Red Sandstone fish-like creatures with wing-like appendages. [Gr *pteron* a wing, and *ichthys* a fish]

pteridology. See under **Pteris**.

pteridophyte *ter'id-ō-fīt* or *pter'id-ō-fīt*, (*bot*) *n* a vascular cryptogam or a member of the **Pteridophyta** (*-of'i-tə*), one of the main divisions of the vegetable kingdom including ferns, lycopods and horsetails. [Gr *pteris*, *-idos* a fern, and *phyton* a plant]

pteridosperm *ter'id-ō-spûrm* or *pter'id-ō-spûrm*, *n* a fossil plant of a group resembling ferns, but having seeds. [Gr *pteris*, *-idos* fern, and *sperma* seed]

pterin *ter'in* or *pter'in* *n* any of a group of substances occurring as pigments in butterfly wings, important in biochemistry. — **pteroic acid** (*ter-ō'ik* or *pter-ō'ik*) the original folic acid found in spinach; **pteroylglutamic acid** (*ter'ō-il-gloo-tam'ik* or *pter-'ō*) the simplest folic acid, effective in correcting the anaemia in pernicious anaemia but inneffective against the concomitant neurological complications. [Gr *pteron* a wing]

pterion *ter'i-on*, *tē'ri-on*, *pter'i-on* or *ptē'ri-on*, *n* in craniometry, the suture where the frontal, squamosal and parietal bones meet the wing of the sphenoid: — *pl* **pter'ia**. [Gr dimin of *pteron* wing]

Pteris *ter'is*, *tē'ris*, *pter'is* or *ptē'ris*, *n* a genus of ferns with spore-clusters continuous along the pinnule margin, *usu* taken to include bracken, which some separate as **Pterid'ium**. — *n* **pteridol'ogist**. — *n* **pteridol'ogy** the study of ferns. — *n* **pteridomā'nia** a passion for ferns. — *n* **pteridoph'ilist** a fern-lover. [Gr *pteris*, *-idos* or *-eōs* male-fern, from *pteron* a feather]

ptero- *ter-ō-*, *pter-ō-*, *-ə-*, *-o'*, or **pter-** *ter-*, *pter-*, *combining form* denoting feather, wing. — **-ptera** *combining form* (*zool*) used to denote organisms having a specified type or number of wings or wing-like parts. — *adj combining form* **-pteran** or **-pterous**. [Gr *pteron* wing]

pterodactyl or (*rare*) **pterodactyle** *ter-ə-dak'til* or *pter-ə-dak'til*, *n* a fossil (Jurassic and Cretaceous) flying reptile with large and bird-like skull, long jaws, and a flying-membrane attached to the long fourth digit of the forelimb. [Gr *pteron* wing, and *daktylos* finger]

pteroic acid. See under **pterin**.

pteropod *ter'ə-pod* or *pter'ə-pod*, *n* any member of the **Pteropoda** (*-op'ə-də*), a group of gasteropods that swim by means of wing-like expansions of the foot. — **pteropod ooze** a deep-sea deposit composed largely of pteropod shells. [Gr *pteron* wing, and *pous*, *podos* foot]

pterosaur *ter'ə-sör* or *pter'ə-sör* *n* a member of the **Pterosaur'ia**, an extinct order of flying reptiles, including the pterodactyls. — *n* and *adj* **pterosaur'ian**. [Gr *pteron* wing, and *sauros* lizard]

-pterous. See under **ptero-**.

pteroylglutamic acid. See under **pterin**.

pterygium *ter-ij'i-əm* or *pter-ij'i-əm*, *n* a vertebrate limb (*zool*); a wing-like growth (*biol*); a wing-shaped area of thickened conjunctiva which spreads over part of the cornea and sometimes over the eyeball (*med*): — *pl* **pteryg'ia**. — *adj* **pteryg'ial**. — *n* a bone in a fin. [Latinized from Gr *pterygion*, dimin of *pteryx*, *-ygos* wing]

pterygoid *ter'i-goid* or *pter'i-goid*, *adj* (*anatom*) wing-like; of or near the pterygoid. — *n* (in full, **pterygoid bone**, **plate** or **process**) in various vertebrates, a paired bone of the upper jaw behind the palatines, known in human anatomy as the pterygoid plates of the sphenoid bone. [Gr *pteryx*, *-ygos* wing]

Pterygotus *ter-i-gō'təs* or *pter-i-gō'təs*, *n* a genus of eurypterids, so named because of their broad swimming paddles. [Latinized from Gr *pterygōtos* winged]

pteryla *ter'i-lə* or *pter'i-lə*, (*zool*) *n* a tract of skin bearing contour feathers in birds: — *pl* **pter'ylae** (*-lē*). — *adj* **pterylograph'ic** or **pteryograph'ical**. — *adv* **pterylograph'ically**. — *n* **pterylog'raphy** a description of pterylae. — *n* **pterylō'sis** arrangement of pterylae. [Gr *pteron* feather, and *hȳlē* forest]

PTFE (*chem*) *abbrev*: polytetrafluoroethylene.

ptilosis *til-ō'sis*, *n* plumage or mode of feathering. [Gr *ptilōsis*, from *ptilon* a down feather]

ptisan *tiz'n* or *tiz-an'*, *n* a medicinal drink made from barley; a decoction. — Also **tisane**. [Gr *ptisanē* peeled barley, barley-gruel, from *ptissein* to winnow]

PTO *abbrev*: please turn over; Public Telecommunications Operator.

ptochocracy *tō-kok'rə-si* or *ptō-kok'rə-si*, *n* the rule of beggars or paupers, wholesale pauperization. [Gr *ptōchos* a beggar, and **-cracy**]

Ptolemaic *tol-i-mā'ik*, *adj* pertaining to the *Ptolemies*, Greek kings of Egypt (from Alexander the Great's general to Cleopatra's son), or to *Ptolemy* the astronomer (*fl* AD 150) — also **Ptolemaean** (*-mē'ən*). — *n* **Ptolemā'ist** a believer in the **Ptolemaic system**, Ptolemy's form of the ancient Greek planetary theory, according to which the heavenly bodies revolve about the earth in motions compounded of eccentric circles and epicycles.

ptomaine *tō'mān*, *tō-mān'*, also (now *rare*) *tō'mā-īn*, *tō'mā-ēn* or *tō'mā-in*, (*chem*) *n* a loosely used name for amino-compounds, some poisonous, formed from putrefying animal tissues, eg putrescine, cadaverine, neurine and choline. — **ptomaine poisoning** (*obs med* or loosely) food poisoning, formerly thought to be caused by ptomaines, few of which, it is now known, are poisonous if eaten. [Ital *ptomaina*, from Gr *ptōma* a corpse]

ptosis *tō'sis* or *ptō'sis*, (*med*), *n* downward displacement; drooping of the upper eyelid: — *pl* **ptō'ses** (*-sēz*). [Gr *ptōsis*, from *piptein* to fall]

PTSD (*med*) *abbrev*: post-traumatic stress disorder.

PTT *abbrev*: Post, Telegraph and Telephone/Telecommunications, designating the statutory body which exists in some countries with responsibility for the operation and regulaton of all public services; (formerly) Postes, Télégraphes et Téléphones (*Fr*); (now) Postes, Télécommunications et Télédiffusion (*Fr*).

Pty or **pty**. *abbrev*: proprietary.

ptyalin *tī'ə-lin* or *ptī'ə-lin*, *n* a ferment in saliva that turns starch into sugar. — *adj* **ptyalagogic** (*-ə-goj'ik* or *-gog'ik*). — *n* **ptyalagogue** (*-al'ə-gog*; *med*) a sialagogue. — *n* **pty'alism** (*med*) excessive flow of saliva. — *vt* **pty'alize** or **-ise** to induce ptyalism in. [Gr *ptyalon* spittle, from *ptyein* to spit]

ptyxis *tiks'is* or *ptiks'is*, (*bot*) *n* the folding of each individual leaf in the bud, distinguished from *vernation*, the arrangement of the whole. [Gr *ptyxis*]

PU *abbrev*: pick-up.

Pu (*chem*) *symbol*: plutonium.

pu (*horse-racing*) *abbrev*: pulled up.

pub *pub*, (*colloq*) *n* a public house. — **pub'-crawl** a progression from pub to pub, stopping for one or more drinks in each. — Also *vi* (*usu* **go pubbing**) to participate in such a progression.

Pub.Doc. *abbrev*: public document.

puberty *pū'bər-ti*, *n* the beginning of sexual maturity. — *adj* **pū'beral** or **pū'bertal**. — *adj* **pūberulent** (*-ber'ū-lənt*) or **pūber'ūlous** feebly or minutely pubescent. — *n* **pū'bes** (*-bēz*; *anatom*) the lower part of the hypogastric region; the hair which grows there at puberty. — *n* **pūbescence** (*-es'əns*) puberty; a soft downy covering, *esp* in plants, of adpressed hairs (*bot*). — *adj* **pūbes'cent**. — *adj* **pū'bic** of the pubes or the pubis. — *n* **pūbis** (for L *os pūbis* bone of the pubes; *anatom*) a bone of the pelvis which in humans forms the anterior portion of the *os innominatum*: — *pl* **pū'bises** (**pū'bēs** is not possible, as *pubis* is a genitive singular, not a nominative singular). — *combining form* **pū'biō-** (wrongly **pū'bo-**). [L *pūber* and *pūbēs*, *-eris* grown-up, downy, and *pūbēs*, *-is* grown-up youth, the pubes]

public *pub'lik*, *adj* of or belonging to the people; pertaining to a community or a nation; general; common to, shared in by, or open to, all; generally known; in open view, unconcealed, not private; engaged in, or concerning, the affairs of the community; employed by the government, a local authority, etc; devoted or directed to the general good (now *rare* except in *public spirit*; cf **public-spirited** below); international; open to members of a university as a whole, not confined to a college; of a public house; (of eg housing) owned by a local authority, etc, not private. — *n* the people, the state, the nation (*obs*); the general body of mankind; the people, in any vague or indefinite sense or grouping; a part of the community regarded from a particular viewpoint, eg as an audience or a target for advertising; public view, a public place, society, or the open, as in *in public*; a public house, a tavern (*archaic*). — *n* **pub'lican** the keeper of an inn or public house; a tax-farmer (*Roman hist*); a tax-collector (*Roman hist*). — *n* **publicā'tion** the act of publishing or making public; a proclamation; the act of sending out (a book, etc) for sale; something that is published, a book. — *n* **pub'licist** (*-sist*) someone who publicizes something; an advertising agent; someone who writes on or is skilled in public law, or on current political topics (*rare*). — *n* **publicity** (*pub-lis'i-ti*) publicness, the state of being open to everyone's observation or knowledge; notoriety; acclaim; the process of making something known to the general public; advertising. — *vt* **pub'licize** or **-ise** (*-sīz*) to give publicity to; to make known to the general public, to advertise. — *adv* **pub'licly**. — *n* **pub'licness** (*rare*). — **public art** works of art put on display for the general public in public places as opposed to museums, etc; the provision of such works of art; **public bar** a bar, *usu* less well furnished than a lounge bar, and *usu* serving drinks at lower prices; **public bill** or **act** a parliamentary bill or act of legislation affecting the general public; **public company** a company whose shares can be purchased on the stock exchange by members of the public; **public convenience** see **convenience** under **convenient**; **public corporation** one owned by the government and run on business principles, being for the most part self-governing; **public defender** (*US*) a defence lawyer engaged at public expense to represent those unable to pay legal fees; **public document** any document, such as a statistical report or register, which is made public and which can be consulted by members of the public; **public domain** the status of a published work which is not, or is no longer, subject to copyright. — *adj* (**public-domain'**; *comput*) available to the general public free of charge. — **public enemy** someone whose behaviour is considered to be a menace to a community in general; **public expenditure** spending by government, local authorities, etc; **public funds** government-funded debt; **public health** the maintenance of the health of a community, eg by sanitation, hygienic food preparation, etc, and the measures to achieve this; **public holiday** a general holiday; **public house** a house open to the public (*obs*); a building chiefly used for selling alcoholic liquors to be consumed on the premises; an inn or tavern; **public image** see under **image**; **public inquiry** an investigation held in public into various aspects (eg safety, environmental effect) of eg a proposed engineering or building project. — *adj* **public-key'** (*comput*) of a system of cryptography in which encoding of messages to a particular recipient is done using a public (communal) key, and decoding is by a different key known only to the recipient. — **public lands** lands belonging to a government, *esp* such as are open to sale, grant, etc; **public law** the law governing relations between public authorities, such as the state, and the individual; sometimes used for international law which, however, may be either public or private; **public lecture** a lecture open to the general public; **public nuisance** an illegal act harming the general community rather than an individual (*law*); an annoying, irritating person (*colloq*); **public opinion** the opinion of the general public on matters which affect the whole community; **public orator** an officer of English universities who is the voice of the Senate on all public occasions; **public ownership** ownership by the state, eg of nationalized industry; **public prosecutor** an official whose function is to prosecute people charged with offences; **public relations** the relations between a person, organization, etc and the public; the business of setting up and maintaining favourable relations; a department of government, an industrial firm, etc, dealing with this. — Also *adj* (**public-rela'tions**). — **public school** a school under the control of a publicly elected body and publicly funded; an endowed grammar school providing a liberal education for those who can afford it, Eton, Harrow, Rugby, Winchester, Westminster, Shrewsbury, Charterhouse, St Paul's, Merchant Taylors', etc. — *adj* **pub'lic-school**. — **public sector** government-financed industry, social service, etc; **public servant** a person employed by the government; **public speaking** the making of formal speeches to a large audience; the art of making such speeches; **public spending** spending by the government. — *adj*. **public-spir'ited** having feelings actuated by regard to the public interest; with a regard to the public interest. — *adv* **public-spir'itedly**. — **public transport** buses, trains, etc for the use of the general public; **public trustee** (also with *caps*) an official who is appointed to act as a trustee or executor where required; **public utility** a service or supply provided in a town etc, for the public, as gas, electricity, water or transport; a company providing such a service, and *usu* having a monopoly (*US*); (in *pl*) public utility shares; **public woman** (*obs*) a prostitute; **public works** building, etc operations funded by the state. — **go public** to become a public company; **in public** openly, publicly; **public address system** a system that enables (large) groups of people to be addressed clearly, consisting of microphones, amplifiers and loudspeakers; **public health inspector** see **environmental health officer**; **public lending right** an author's right to payment when his or her books are borrowed from public libraries; **public opinion poll** a taking of public opinion based on the answers of scientifically selected elements in the community to questioning. [L *pūblicus*, from *pop(u)lus* the people]

publican, **publication**, **publicity**, etc. See under **public**.

publish *pub'lish*, *vt* to make public; to divulge; to announce; to proclaim; to issue to the public; to produce and offer for sale (*orig* any article, now books, newspapers, etc); to put into circulation; (*esp* in *passive*) to publish the work of (an author). — *vi* (of an author) to have one's work published; to publish a book, newspaper, material, etc. — *adj* **pub'lishable**. — *n* **pub'lisher** someone who makes something public; someone who publishes books; someone who attends to the issuing and distributing of a newspaper; a newspaper proprietor (*US*). — *n* **pub'lishment** publication (*rare*); publication of banns (*US archaic*). [Fr *publier*, from L *pūblicāre*, with *-ish* on the model of other verbs]

Puccinia *puk-sin'i-ə*, *n* a genus of rust-fungi, including the wheat-rust, parasitic in alternate generations on barberry and wheat or other grass. — *adj* **pucciniā'ceous**. [Named after Tomaso *Puccini* (died 1735), Italian anatomist]

puccoon *puk-ōōn'*, *n* bloodroot; extended to species of gromwell and other American plants yielding pigments. [Algonquian name]

puce *pūs*, *n* and *adj* brownish-purple or deep purplish-pink. [Fr *puce*, from L *pūlex*, *-icis* a flea]

pucelle *pū-sel'*, (*obs*) *n* a maid or virgin, *esp* (with *cap*) the Maid of Orleans, Jeanne d'Arc (1412–31); a slut (also **puzzle**). — *n* **pū'celage** (*obs*) virginity. [Fr, from LL *pūlicella*; origin doubtful]

puck[1] *puk* or **pouke** *pōōk*, *n* a goblin or mischievous sprite; (with *cap*) Robin Goodfellow, a merry fairy in eg

Shakespeare's *Midsummer Night's Dream*, etc (**Puck-hairy** in Ben Jonson's *Sad Shepherd*). — *adj* **puck'ish** impish; full of mischief. [OE *pūca*; cf ON *pūki*, Ir *puca*, Welsh *pwca*]

puck[2] *puk*, *n* a hard thick rubber disc used instead of a ball in ice-hockey. [Origin unknown]

pucka. See **pukka**.

pucker *puk'ər*, *vt* to wrinkle; to make gathers in (*needlework*). — Also *vi*. — *n* a corrugation or wrinkle; a group of wrinkles, *esp* irregular ones; agitation, confusion (*colloq*). — *adj* **puck'ery** astringent; tending to wrinkle. — **pucker up** (*slang*) to set one's lips into a position ready for kissing. [Cf **poke**[1]]

puckfist *puk'fist* or *-fīst*, *n* a puffball fungus; a braggart (*archaic*); a niggardly person (*obs*). [Appar **puck**[1] and the root of OE *fisting* breaking of wind]

puckish. See under **puck**[1].

puckle. See **pickle**[2].

pud[1] *pud*, (*colloq*) *n* a paw, fist or hand — also **pudd'y**. [Cf **pad**[2], or Du *poot* paw]

pud[2] *po͝od*. Same as **pood**.

pud[3] *po͝od*, (*colloq*) *n* pudding.

pudden, **puddening**, etc. See **pudding**.

pudder *pud'ər*. Same as **pother**.

pudding *po͝od'ing*, *n* the dessert course of a meal; meat, fruit, etc cooked in a casing of suet dough; a soft kind of cooked dish, *usu* farinaceous, commonly with sugar, milk, eggs, etc; a skin or gut filled with seasoned minced meat and other materials (such as blood or oatmeal), a kind of sausage; stuffing for a cooked carcase (*Shakesp*); (*usu* in *pl*) entrails (*archaic*); a pad of rope, etc used as a fender on the bow of a boat or elsewhere (also **pudd'ening**); material gain (*archaic*); a fat, dull or heavy-witted person (*colloq*). — Also (now *colloq* or *dialect*) **pudden** (*po͝od'n* or *pud'n*). — *adj* **pudd'ingy** (*-ing-i*). — **pudd'ing-bag** a bag for cooking a pudding in; a piece of good fortune. — *adj* **pudd'ing-faced** having a fat, round, smooth face. — *adj* **pudd'ing-head'ed** (*colloq*) stupid. — **pudd'ing-pie** a suet-dough pudding with meat baked in it; any of various kinds of pastry; **pudd'ing-pipe** the long pulpy pod of the purging cassia tree; **pudd'ing-plate** a shallow bowl-like plate, *usu* smaller than a soup-plate; **pudd'ing-sleeve** a large loose sleeve gathered in near the wrist; **pudd'ing-stone** (*geol*) conglomerate; **pudd'ing-time** (*obs*) dinner-time; the right moment. — **in the pudding club** (*slang*) pregnant. [ME *poding*; origin unknown; relation to LGer *pudde-wurst* black pudding, and to Fr *boudin* black pudding, is obscure]

puddle *pud'l*, *n* a small muddy pool; a non-porous mixture of clay and sand; a muddle (*colloq*); a muddler (*colloq*). — *vt* to make muddy; to work into puddle, to stir and knead; to cover with puddle; to make watertight by means of clay; to convert from pig-iron into wrought-iron. — *vi* to make a puddle or puddles, to cause a puddle or puddles to form; to mess about, *esp* in puddles or mud; to stir up a muddy mess. — *n* **pudd'ler**. — *n* **pudd'ling**. — *adj* **pudd'ly** full of puddles. [Appar dimin of OE *pudd* ditch]

puddock *pud'ək*, or **paddock** *pad'ək*, (*archaic* and *Scot*) *n* a toad or frog. — **padd'ock-stool** a toadstool. [Dimin from late OE *pade*, *padde* toad; ON *padda*]

puddy. See under **pud**[1].

pudency *pū'dəns-i*, *n* (*Shakesp*) shamefacedness, modesty. — *adj* **pudendal** (*-den'dəl*) pertaining to the pudenda. — *n* **puden'dous** (*obs*) shameful. — *n* **puden'dum** and *n pl* **puden'da** the external genital organs, *esp* female. — *adj* **pu'dent** (*rare*) modest. — *adj* **pu'dibund** shamefaced; prudish. — *n* **pudibund'ity**. — *adj* **pu'dic** modest (*obs*); pudendal. — *n* **pudicity** (*-dis'i-ti*; *rare*) modesty. — *n* **pu'dor** (*obs*) sense of shame. [L *pudēre* to make (or be) ashamed; *pudendum* something to be ashamed of; *pudīcus* chaste; *pudibundus* shamefaced]

pudge, **pudgy**. Same as **podge**, **podgy**.

pudsy or **pudsey** *pud'zi*. Same as **pudgy** or **podgy**.

pudu *po͞o'do͞o*, *n* a small S American deer, about 30 cm (1 ft) high, with spiky antlers. [Am Sp, from a S American Indian language)]

pueblo *pweb'lō*, *n* a town or settlement (in Spanish-speaking countries); a communal habitation of the Indians of New Mexico, etc; (with *cap*) an Indian of the pueblos: — *pl* **pueb'los**. [Sp, town, from L *populus* a people]

puer *pūr*, *n* and *vt*. Same as **pure** (in tanning).

puerile *pū'ər-īl* or *US -il*, *adj* pertaining to children (*rare*); childish; trifling; silly. — *n* **puerilism** (*pū'ər-il-izm*; *psychol*) reversion to a childlike state of mind. — *n* **pūerility** (*-il'i-ti*) the quality of being puerile; something that is puerile; a childish expression; an instance of childishness or foolish triviality. [L *puerīlis*, from *puer* a child]

puerperal *pū-ûr'pər-əl*, (*med*) *adj* relating to childbirth. — *adv* **pūer'perally**. — *n* **pūerpē'rium** (*med*) the time from onset of labour to return of the womb to its normal state. — **puerperal fever** (*med*) *orig* any fever occurring in connection with childbirth; now confined to endometritis or septicaemia caused by the introduction of bacteria into the genital tract; **puerperal psychosis** (or *archaic* **mania**; *med*) a mental illness sometimes occurring after childbirth. [L *puerpera* a woman in labour, from *puer* a child, and *parere* to bear]

puff *puf*, *vi* to blow in whiffs; to breathe out vehemently or pantingly; to snort scornfully (*obs*); to emit puffs; to issue in puffs; to make the sound of a puff; to go with puffs; to swell up (*esp* with *up*). — *vt* to drive with a puff; to blow; to emit in puffs; to play (eg a wind instrument) or smoke (eg a pipe) with puffs; to inflate or swell (*esp* with *up*); to elate unduly; to extol, *esp* in disingenuous advertisement; to put out of breath. — *n* a sudden, forcible breath, blast or emission; a gust or whiff; a cloud or quantity of vapour, dust, air etc, emitted at one time; a sound of puffing; a downy pad for powdering (eg one's face); anything light and porous, or swollen and light; a biscuit or cake of puff-pastry or the like; a part of a fabric gathered up so as to be left full in the middle (*needlework*); a quilted bedcover; ostentation; praise intended as, or serving as, advertisement; a homosexual (*slang*; see **poof**). — *adj* **puffed** distended; inflated; (of eg a sleeve) gathered up into rounded ridges; out of breath. — *n* **puff'er** someone who puffs; a steam-engine; a steamboat, *esp* in Scotland a small cargo-carrying boat used in coastal waters; someone employed to bid at an auction to incite others and so run up prices; a wheel-lock pistol; a pufferfish. — *n* **puff'ery** advertisement disguised as honest praise; puffs collectively. — *adv* **puff'ily**. — *n* **puff'iness**. — *n* **puff'ing**. — *adv* **puff'ingly**. — *adj* **puff'y** puffed out with air or any soft matter; swollen, engorged; bombastic; coming in puffs; puffing; short-winded. — **puff'-adder** a thick, venomous African snake (*Bitis arietans* or related species) that distends its body when irritated; **puff'ball** a gasteromycete fungus (*Lycoperdon*, etc) with ball-shaped fructification filled when ripe with a powdery mass of spores; a tight-waisted full skirt gathered in at the hem to an underskirt, so as to be shaped like a ball; any similar short or long ball-shaped skirt; **puff'bird** any bird of a Central and S American family related to the barbets, with the habit of puffing out the head-feathers; **puff'-box** a box for powder for the face or body and a puff; **puffer fish** a globefish; **puff pastry** or US **puff paste** pastry composed of thin flaky layers; **puff'-puff** (*esp* formerly) a child's word for a railway engine or train. — **puffed out** quite out of breath; inflated, distended, expanded; **puffed up** swollen; inflated with pride, presumption, or the like. [OE *pyffan*, or a related form; cf Ger *puffen*, etc]

puffin *puf'in*, *n* any of various sea-birds (*esp* of the genus *Fratercula*) of the auk family, with brightly coloured parrot-like beaks, *esp* (in Britain) *Fratercula arctica*. [Origin obscure; a connection with **puff** is conjectured]

puftaloon *puf-tə-lōōn'*, (*Austr*) *n* a type of fried cake, *usu* eaten hot with jam, honey or sugar. — Also **pufftaloon'as**, **puftaloon'ies**, etc. [Origin unknown]

pug[1] *pug*, *n* a goblin or sprite (*obs*; in Ben Jonson, **Pug**, an inferior devil); a term of endearment (*obs*); a prostitute (*obs*); a senior servant (*archaic slang*); a monkey (*obs* or *dialect*); a fox (*archaic*); a pug-dog; a pug-nose; a pug-moth; a pug-engine. — *adj* **pugg'ish** or **pugg'y** like a monkey or a pug-dog; snub-nosed. — *n* **pugg'y** a term of endearment (*obs*); a monkey (*Scot*; also **pugg'ie**); a fox (*archaic*). — **pug'-dog** a small short-haired dog with a wrinkled face, upturned nose, and short curled tail; **pug'-engine** a shunting engine. — *adj* **pug'-faced** monkey-faced. — **pug'-moth** a name for the smaller moths of the geometrid family *Larentidae*; **pug'-nose** a short, thick nose with the tip turned up. — *adj* **pug'-nosed**. [A connection with **puck**[1] is conjectured]

pug[2] *pug*, *n* clay, ground and worked with water. — *vt* to beat; to grind with water and make plastic; to pack with pugging. — *n* **pugg'ing** beating or punching; the working of clay for making bricks, in a pug-mill; clay, sawdust, plaster, etc, put between floors to deaden sound. — **pug'-mill** a machine for mixing and tempering clay. [Origin unknown]

pug[3] *pug*, (*Anglo-Ind*) *n* an animal's footprint. — *vt* to track. [Hindustani *pag*]

pug[4]. See **pugil**[2].

pug[5]. See under **pugging**[1].

puggaree, **puggery**. Same as **pagri**.

pugging[1] *pug'ing*, (*Shakesp*) *adj* thieving. — *vt* and *vi* **pug** (*dialect*) to tug. [Origin unknown]

pugging[2]. See under **pug**[2].

puggled *pug'ld*, (*Scot*) *adj* mentally or physically exhausted. — *vt* **pugg'le**. [Perh Eng dialect *puggled* very drunk, or an alteration of Eng *buggered*]

puggree. See **pagri**.

puggy. See under **pug**[1].

pugh. An old spelling of **pooh**.

pugil[1] *pū'jil*, *n orig* a small handful; now, as much as the thumb and two fingers can lift, a pinch. [L *pugillus*]

pugil[2] *pū'jil*, *n* (*obs*) a boxer. — *n* **pu'gilism** the art or practice of boxing; prize-fighting. — *n* **pu'gilist** (*abbrev* **pug** *pug*; *slang*). — *adj* **pugilist'ic** or **pugilist'ical**. — *adv* **pugilist'ically**. [L *pugil* a boxer]

pugnacious *pug-nā'shəs*, *adj* given to fighting; combative; quarrelsome. — *adv* **pugnā'ciously**. — *n* **pugnā'ciousness** or **pugnacity** (*-nas'i-ti*) inclination to fight; fondness for fighting; quarrelsomeness. [L *pugnāx*, *-ācis*, from *pugnāre* to fight]

Pugwash conference *pug'wosh kon'fər-əns*, *n* any of a series of conferences held at intervals by scientists from many countries to discuss the dangers and difficulties into which the world is running. [Name of the village in Nova Scotia where the first conference was held in 1957]

puh. A Shakespearian spelling of **pooh**.

puir *pür* or *pār*, (*Scot*) *adj* poor.

puisne (*Shakesp* **puisny**) *pū'ni*, *adj* an *obs* form of **puny**, surviving as applied to certain judges, meaning junior; petty, insignificant (*Shakesp*). — *n* a puisne judge. [OFr, from *puis*, from L *posteā* after, and *né*, from L *nātus* born]

puissant or **puissaunt** *pū'is-ənt*, *pwis'ənt* or (*poetic*) *pū-is'ənt*, (*archaic*) *adj* powerful. — *n* **puissance** (*pū'is-əns*, *-öns'*, *-äns' pwis'əns*, etc; also **puissaunce**) power (*archaic*); (*usu pwēs'äs* or *pwēs'-äns*) (a showjumping competition with very high jumps showing) the power of a horse. — *adv* **puissantly** (*-ənt-li*). [Fr *puissant*, appar formed as a pr p from a vulgar L substitute for L *potēns*, *-entis*; see **potent**]

puja *pōō'jə*, (*Hinduism*) *n* (an act of) worship; reverential observance; a festival. [Sans *pūjā* worship]

puke[1] *pūk*, *vt* and *vi* (*slang*) to vomit. — *vt* (*archaic*) to cause to vomit. — *n* vomit (*slang*); an emetic (*archaic*); a despicable person (*slang*). — *n* **pū'ker** (*archaic*) an emetic. [Poss connected with Flem *spukken* and Ger *spucken*]

puke[2] *pūk*, (*obs*) *n* a fine woollen cloth; a colour between russet or purple and black. — *adj* made of puke (*Shakesp*); of the colour puke. [MDu *puuc* the best woollen cloth]

pukeko *puk'ə-kō*, *n* a New Zealand wading bird with bright plumage; — *pl* **puk'ekos**. [Maori]

pukka, **pucka** or **pakka** *puk'ə*, (*esp Anglo-Ind*) *adj* thoroughly good; thorough; complete; solidly built; settled; durable; permanent; full-weight; straightforward; genuine; sure. — **pukka sahib** a gentleman. [Hindustani *pakkā* cooked, ripe]

puku *pōō'kōō*, *n* an antelope (*Adenota*, or *Kobus*, *vardoni*) found in southern central Africa, *esp* in swampy areas and near rivers. [Zulu *mpuku*]

pula *pōō'lä*, *n* the standard unit of currency in Botswana (100 *thebes*). [Tswana, rain]

pulchritude *pul'kri-tūd*, (*formal*) *n* beauty. — *adj* **pulchritud'inous**. [L *pulchritūdō*, *-inis*, from *pulcher* beautiful]

puldron (*obs*). Same as **pauldron**.

pule *pūl*, *vt* and *vi* to pipe; to whimper or whine. — *n* **pū'ler**. — *n* and *adj* **pū'ling**. — *adv* **pū'lingly**. — *adj* **pū'ly** whining; sickly. [Imit; cf Fr *piauler*]

Pulex *pū'leks*, *n* the flea genus, giving name to the family **Pulicidae** (*-lis'i-dē*). — *n* **pū'licide** (*-sīd*; L *caedere* to kill) a poison or other agent which destroys fleas. [L *pūlex*, *-icis*]

Pulitzer prize *pōō'lit-sər* or *pū'lit-sər prīz*, *n* any of various annual prizes for American literature, journalism and music. [J *Pulitzer* (1847–1911), US newspaper publisher who instituted the prizes]

pulka *pul'kə*, *n* a Laplander's boat-shaped sledge. — Also **pulk** or **pulk'ha**. [Finnish *pulkka*, Lappish *pulkke*, *bulkke*]

pull *pōōl*, *vt* to pluck; to remove by plucking; to extract; to pick by hand; to strip, to deprive of feathers, hair, etc; to draw or drag; to move, or try or tend to move, towards oneself or in the direction so thought of; to make, or cause to be, by pulling; to row; to transport by rowing; to move in a particular direction when driving (*usu* with *out*, *over*, etc); to stretch; to hold back (eg a blow in boxing, or a racehorse to prevent its winning; see also **pull up** below); to take as an impression or proof, *orig* by pulling the bar of a handpress (*printing*); to hit to the left (to the right for a lefthanded player) (*cricket*, *golf*); to bring down; to take a drink of; to draw or fire (a weapon); to snatch or steal (*slang*); to arrest (*slang*); to raid (*slang*); to seduce (*esp* a woman; *slang*; see also **pull a bird** below); to attract (eg a crowd; *slang*); to withdraw. — *vi* to give a pull; to perform the action of pulling anything; to tear or pluck; to drag or draw; to strain at the bit; to exert oneself; to go with a pulling movement; to move in a particular direction, *esp* when in a motor vehicle (*usu* with *away*, *out*, *over*, etc); to row; to suck; to succeed in an attempt at seduction (*slang*; see also **pull a bird** below); to strike the ball to the left (or to the right if left-handed) (*cricket*, *golf*). — *n* an act, bout or spell of pulling; a pulling force; a row; a stiff ascent; a draught of liquor; a proof, a single impression (*printing*); advantage; influence; an apparatus for pulling; the quantity pulled at one time; resistance; a shot that travels too far to the left (or to the right for a lefthanded player) (*golf*). — *n* **pull'er**. — **pull'-back** a hindrance; a drawback; a retreat or withdrawal; a device formerly used for making a skirt hang close and straight in front (see also **pull back** below). — *adj* **pull'-down** able or intended to be pulled down in some way or by some means; (of a computer menu) able to be accessed by means of the cursor or a key, and displayed over the material already on screen. — **pull'-in** a stopping-place (also *adj*); a transport café (see also **pull in** below). — *adj* **pull'-on** (of eg clothes) requiring only to be pulled on, without fastening. — *n* a pull-on garment of any kind. — *adj* **pull'-out** denoting a section of a magazine, etc, that can be removed and kept separately (see also **pull out** below). — **pull'over** a jersey, jumper, or other body garment put on over the head; **pull'-tab** a ring pull, a tongue of metal with a ring attached to it, which pulls to open a beer, etc can; in eg illustrations, *esp* in children's books, a piece of paper or card attached to a part of an illustration, which can be pulled to make (that part of) the illustration move or alter in some way; **pull'-through** a cord with a rag for cleaning a rifle barrel; **pull'-up** an act of pulling up; a sudden stoppage; a suitable place (*esp* for lorry-drivers, etc) for pulling up; an exercise in which one hangs from a bar by the hands, and pulls oneself up so that one's chin is level with the bar. — **pull a bird** (*slang*) to succeed in forming a (sexual) relationship with a girl; **pull about** to distort; to treat roughly; **pull a face** to grimace; **pull a fast one on** (*slang*) to take advantage of by a trick; **pull ahead** to move into the lead; **pull apart or pull to pieces** to cause to break into pieces by pulling; to criticize harshly; **pull away** to move into the lead; to withdraw; **pull back** to retreat or withdraw (see also **pull'-back** above); **pull caps** (*archaic*) to scuffle; **pull devil, pull baker** (in an argument, competition, etc) do your best, both sides; **pull down** to take down or apart; to demolish; to bring down; to reduce in health or vigour; to cause to come down into some position by pulling or by some other means (see also **pull-down** above); **pull for** to row for; to support; **pull in** to draw in; to make tighter; to draw a motor vehicle into the side of the road, or drive into the car-park of a café, etc, and halt (see also **pull'-in** above); to arrest; to earn; of a train, to arrive at a station; **pull off** to carry through successfully; **pull oneself together** to regain one's self-control; to collect oneself, preparing to think or to act; **pull one's punches** see under **punch**[3]; **pull one's weight** to give full effect to one's weight in rowing; to do one's full share of work, co-operate wholeheartedly; **pull out** to draw out; to drive a motor vehicle away from the side of the road or out of a line of traffic; of a train, to leave a station; to abandon a place or situation which has become too difficult to cope with (*colloq*; *n* **pull'-out**; see also above); **pull over** to draw over to the side of the road, either to stop or to allow other vehicles to pass; **pull rank** see under **rank**; **pull round** to bring, or come, back to good health or condition or to consciousness; **pull someone's leg** see under **leg**; **pull the long bow** to lie or boast inordinately; **pull the rug from under (someone)** see under **rug**[1]; **pull through** to bring or get to the end of something difficult or dangerous with some success (see also **pull'-through** above); **pull together** to co-operate; **pull up** to pull out of the ground; to tighten the reins; to bring to a stop; to halt; (of a horse) to be brought to a halt by the jockey or (*reflexive*) to stop of its own volition (*horse-racing*); to take to task; to gain ground; to arrest; **pull up stakes** to prepare to leave a place. [OE *pullian* to pluck or draw]

pullet *pŏŏl'it*, *n* a young hen, *esp* from first laying to first moult. — **pull'et-sperm** (*orig* the chalaza, once believed to be the male element in the egg; *Shakesp*, *derog*) eggs. [Fr *poulette*, dimin of *poule* a hen, from LL *pulla* a hen, fem of L *pullus*, a young animal]

pulley *pŏŏl'i*, *n* a wheel turning about an axis, and carrying a rope, chain or band on its rim, used for raising weights, changing direction of pull, transmission of power, etc; a block; a combination of pulleys or blocks: — *pl* **pull'eys**. [ME *poley*, *puly*, from OFr *polie*, from LL *polegia*, supposed to be from a dimin of Gr *polos* axle]

Pullman *pŏŏl'mən* or **Pullman car** *kär*, *n* a luxuriously furnished railway saloon or sleeping-car, first made by George M *Pullman* (1831–97) in America.

pullorum disease *pə-lōr'em diz-ēz* or *pə-lör'əm*, (*vet*) *n* a serious, often fatal, disease of young poultry caused by the bacterium *Salmonella pullorum* (formerly *Bacterium pullorum*). [L *pullorum*, genitive pl of *pullus* chicken]

pullulate *pul'ū-lāt*, *vi* to sprout; to sprout or breed abundantly; to teem; to increase rapidly. — *n* **pullulā'tion**. [L *pullulāre*, *-ātum*, from *pullulus* a young animal, sprout, from *pullus*]

pulmo *pul'mō*, *pŏŏl'mō*, (*med*) *n* a lung: — *pl* **pulmo'nes** (*-nēz*). — *n* **pul'mobranch** (*-brangk*; *zool*) a lung-book (qv). — *adj* **pulmobranch'iate**. — *n* **Pulmonaria** (*-mə-nā'ri-ə*) the lungwort genus of the borage family. — *adj* **pul'monary** (*-mən-ər-i*) of the lungs or respiratory cavity; leading to or from the lungs; of the nature of lungs; having lungs; diseased or weak in the lungs. — *n pl* **Pulmonā'ta** an air-breathing order or subclass of Gasteropoda, including many land and freshwater snails. — *n* **pul'monate** (*zool*) a member of the Pulmonata. — *adj* having lungs, lung-sacs, lung-books or similar organs. — *adj* **pulmonic** (*-mon'ik*) of the lungs. — *n* (*obs*) a sufferer from, or medication for, lung disease. — *n* **Pul'motor®** an apparatus for forcing air and/or oxygen into, and air out of, the lungs. [L *pulmō*, *-ōnis* lung]

pulp *pulp*, *n* any soft fleshy part of an animal, eg the tissue in the cavity of a tooth; the soft part of plants, *esp* of fruits; any soft structureless mass; the soft mass obtained from the breaking and grinding of rags, wood, etc before it is hardened into paper; crushed ore; nonsense; sentimentality; a cheap magazine printed on wood-pulp paper, or of a trashy and sentimental or sensational character (also **pulp magazine**); fiction of the type published in such a magazine; a film, etc of such a type. — *vt* to reduce to pulp; to make pulpy; to deprive of pulp. — *vi* to become pulp or like pulp. — *n* **pulp'er** a machine for reducing various materials to pulp. — *vt* **pulp'ify**. — *adv* **pulp'ily**. — *n* **pulp'iness**. — *adj* **pulp'ous**. — *adj* **pulp'y**. — **pulp'board** a coarse cardboard made *usu* from a single layer of pulp; **pulp'-cavity** the hollow of a tooth which contains pulp; **pulp'-engine** a machine for making pulp for paper; **pulp'mill** a machine or factory for pulping wood, roots or other material; **pulp novel**; **pulp novelist**; **pulp'stone** a grindstone for pulping wood; **pulp'wood** wood suitable for paper-making; a board of compressed wood-pulp and adhesive. [L *pulpa* flesh, pulp]

pulpit *pŏŏl'pit*, *n* a raised structure for preaching from; an auctioneer's desk or the like; preachers or preaching collectively; a position one can exploit as a means of promulgating one's views; a platform (*obs*); a safety railing at the bow or stern of a yacht. — *adj* belonging to the pulpit. — *adj* **pul'pited**. — *n* **pulpiteer'** or **pul'piter** someone who speaks from a pulpit, a preacher. — *n* **pul'pitry** sermonizing. — *n* **pul'pitum** (*archit*) a rood-loft. [L *pulpitum* a stage]

pulpitum. See under **pulpit**.

pulpous, **pulpy**, etc. See under **pulp**.

pulque *pŏŏl'kā* or *pŏŏl'kē*, *n* a fermented drink made in Mexico from agave sap. [Am Sp]

pulsar. See under **pulsate**.

pulsate *pul'sāt* or *pul-sāt'*, *vi* to beat, throb; to vibrate; to change repeatedly in force or intensity; to thrill with life or emotion. — *n* **pul'sar** (*-sär*; for 'pulsating star', but see also **pulsating star** below) any of a number of interstellar sources of regularly pulsed radiation, first discovered in 1967, and thought to be rotating neutron stars. — *n* **pulsatance** (*pul'sə-təns* or *pul-sā'təns*; *phys*) the angular frequency of a periodic motion, frequency multiplied by 2π. — *adj* **pul'satile** (*-sə-tīl* or *US -til*) capable of pulsating; pulsatory; rhythmical; played by percussion (*music*). — *n* **Pulsatill'a** pasque-flower (because it is beaten by the wind). — *n* **pulsā'tion** a beating or throbbing; a motion of the heart or pulse; any measured beat; vibration. — *adj* **pulsative** (*pul'sə-tiv* or *-sāt'iv*). — *n* **pulsā'tor** (or *pul'sə-tər*) a machine, or part of a machine, that pulsates or imparts pulsation, eg for separating diamonds from earth, for regulating the rhythmical suction of a milking machine, or for pumping. — *adj* **pulsatory** (*pul'sə-tə-ri* or *-sā'tə-ri*) beating or throbbing. — **pulsating current** an electric current that changes periodically in intensity but not direction; **pulsating star** a type of variable star of regularly fluctuating brightness, the fluctuations being caused by the expansion and contraction of the star. [L *pulsāre*, *-ātum* to beat, frequentative of *pellere*, *pulsum* to drive]

pulse[1] *puls*, *n* a beating or throbbing; a measured beat or throb; a vibration; a single variation, beat or impulse; a signal of very short duration (*radio*); the beating of the heart and the arteries; a thrill (*fig*). — *vi* (of eg the heart) to beat; to throb; to pulsate. — *vt* to drive by pulsation; to produce, or cause to be emitted, in the form of pulses. — *adj* **pulsed**. — *adj* **pulse'less**. — *n* **pulse'lessness**. — *n* **puls'idge** (*Shakesp*; used by Mistress Quickly in 2 *Henry IV* II. 4. 25) pulse. — *adj* **pulsif'ic** producing a single pulse. — *n* **pulsim'eter** an instrument for measuring the strength or quickness of the pulse. — *n* **pulsom'eter** a pulsimeter; a pump that draws in water by condensation of steam in two chambers alternately. — **pulse code modulation** a system of transmission in which the audio signals are sampled periodically, coded in digital form, and transmitted (*abbrev* **PCM**); **pulse'jet** or **puls'ojet** in jet propulsion, an intermittent jet; **pulse'-rate** the number of beats of a pulse per minute; **pulse'-wave** the expansion of the artery, moving from point to point, like a wave, as each beat of the heart sends the blood to the extremities. — **feel someone's pulse** to test or measure someone's heartbeat by feeling for the pulse eg at the neck or wrist; to explore a person's feelings or inclinations in a tentative way; **keep one's finger on the pulse** to keep in touch with current events, ideas, opinions, etc. [L *pulsus*, from *pellere*, *pulsum*; partly OFr *pouls*, *pous*, remodelled on Latin]

pulse[2] *puls*, *n sing* or *n pl* the seeds of leguminous plants as food collectively, beans, peas, lentils, etc; (any of) the plants yielding them. — *adj* **pultā'ceous** macerated and softened. [L *puls*, *pultis* porridge; cf Gr *poltos* and **poultice**]

pulsidge, **pulsojet**, etc. See under **pulse**[1].

pultaceous. See under **pulse**[2].

pultrusion *pōōl-trōō'zhən*, *n* a process for producing reinforced plastic products in which strands of the reinforcing material are surrounded with liquid resin and then pulled through a *usu* heated die to shape and cure the resin. [**pull** and **extrusion**]

pultun, **pultan**, **pulton** or **pultoon** *pul'tun*, *pul'tən*, *pul'tōōn*, *n* an Indian infantry regiment. [Hindustani *pultan*, from **battalion**]

pulture. See **puture**.

pulu *pōō'lōō*, *n* a silky fibre from the Hawaiian tree-fern leaf-bases. [Hawaiian]

pulv. (*pharm*) *abbrev*: *pulvis* (*L*), powder.

pulver *pul'vər*, *vt* (*obs*) to reduce to powder. — *adj* **pul'verable** (*rare*). — *n* **pulverā'tion** (*rare*) pulverization. — *n* **pul'verine** barilla ash. — *adj* **pul'verīzable** or -s- (or *-īz'ə-bl*). — *n* **pulverīzā'tion** or -s-. — *vt* **pul'verize** or **-ize** to reduce to dust or fine powder; to defeat thoroughly, to destroy, to thrash (*fig*). — *vi* to turn into dust or powder. — *n* **pul'verīzer** or -s- someone who pulverizes; a machine for pulverizing or for spraying. — *adj* **pul'verous** dusty or powdery. — *n* **pulverulence** (*-ver'ū-ləns*). — *adj* **pulver'ūlent** consisting of fine powder; powdery; dusty-looking; readily crumbling. — **Pulver Wednesday** or **pulvering day** (*obs*) Ash Wednesday. [L *pulvis*, *pulveris* powder]

pulvil *pul'vil*, (*obs* or *hist*) *n* perfumed powder; extended to snuff and other powders. — Also **pulvil'io**, **pulvill'io** (*pl* **pulvill'ios**, *pulvill'ios*) and **pulville'**. — *vt* **pul'vil** to powder or scent with pulvil: — *pr p* **pul'villing**; *pa t* and *pa p* **pul'villed**. — *adj* **pul'vilized** or -s-. [Ital *polviglio*, from *polve* powder, from L *pulvis*]

pulvillar, etc. See under **pulvinus**.

pulvinus *pul-vī'nəs*, (*bot*) *n* a cushion-like swelling, *esp* one at the base of a leaf or leaflet, by whose changes of turgidity movements are effected: — *pl* **pulvi'ni** (*-nī*). — *adj* **pulvill'ar** of a pulvillus; cushion-like. — *adj* **pulvill'iform**. — *n* **pulvill'us** a little cushion or pad (*esp obs med*); a pad between the claws of an insect's foot (*entomol*): — *pl* **pulvill'i** (*-ī*). — *adj* **pulvinar** (*-vī'nər*, *-när*) cushion-like; of a pulvinus (*bot*). — *n* a Roman cushioned seat (*hist*); a small pillow or pad (*obs med*); a knob on the optic thalamus (*anatom*). — *adj* **pul'vinate** (*-vin-āt*) or **pul'vinated** (*esp biol*) cushion-like; pillowy; bulging. — *n* **pul'vinule** (*bot*) the pulvinus of a leaflet. [L *pulvīnus* cushion, pillow; dimin *pulvillus*]

pulwar *pul'wär*, *n* a light keelless boat used on the Ganges. [Hindustani *palwār*]

puly. See under **pule**.

pulza-oil *pōōl'zə-oil*, *n* an oil obtained from physic-nut seeds. [Origin unknown]

puma *pū'mə*, *n* the cougar (*Felis concolor*), a large reddish-brown American cat, also called **mountain lion**: — *pl* **pu'mas**. [Am Sp, from Quechua]

pumelo *pum'i-lō*. Same as **pomelo**.

pumice *pum'is* or (*esp Scot*) *pū'mis*, *n* an acid glassy lava so full of gas cavities that it floats in water; a frothy portion of any lava; a piece of such lava used for smoothing or cleaning. — *vt* to smooth or clean with pumice-stone — also **pumicate** (*pū'mi-kāt*; *rare*). — *adj* **pumiceous** (*-mish'əs*). — **pum'ie-stone**. [OE *pumic-* (*-stān*), pumice(-stone); reintroduced, from OFr *pomis*; both from L *pūmex*, *-icis*]

pumie or **pumy** *pum'i*, (*Spenser*) *n* a pebble or stone. — Also **pumie stone**, **pumy stone**. [**pumice-stone**]

pummel *pum'l*, *n* a less usual spelling of **pommel**. — *vt* to beat, pound or thump, *esp* with the fists: — *pr p* **pumm'elling**; *pa t* and *pa p* **pumm'elled**. [**pommel**]

pump[1] *pump*, *n* a machine for raising and moving fluids (*orig esp* bilge-water in ships), or for compressing, rarefying, or transferring gases; a stroke of a pump; an act of pumping. — *vt* to raise, force, compress, exhaust, empty, remove or inflate with a pump; to discharge by persistent effort; to move in the manner of a pump; to shake (someone's hand) vigorously up and down, as though working a pump-handle; to subject to, or elicit by, persistent questioning; to pump water on (*obs*); to put out of breath (*esp* in *passive*; often with *out*; *colloq*). — *vi* to work a pump; to work like a pump; (of mercury in a barometer) to rise and fall suddenly; to spurt; to propel or increase the speed of a sailing-boat by rapidly pulling the sails in and out (*naut*). — *n* **pump'er**. — *adj* **pump'-action** denoting a repeating rifle or shotgun whose chamber is fed by a pump-like movement. — **pumped storage** in a hydroelectric system, the use of electricity at times of low demand to pump water up to a high storage reservoir, to be used to generate electricity at times of high demand; **pump gun** a pump-action gun; **pump'-handle** the lever that works a pump; **pump'-head** or **pump'hood** a frame covering the upper wheel of a chain-pump, serving to guide the water into the discharge-spout; **pump'-priming** starting a pump working efficiently by introducing fluid to drive out the air; investing money in order to stimulate commerce, local support, etc; **pump'-room** the room at a mineral spring in which the waters are drunk; **pump'-water** water from a pump; **pump'-well** a well from which water is obtained by pumping; the compartment in which a pump works. — **pump iron** (*colloq*) to exercise with weights, to develop one's muscles. [Ety uncertain]

pump[2] *pump*, *n* a light shoe without a fastening, worn *esp* for dancing. — *adj* **pumped** wearing pumps. [Origin unknown]

pumpernickel *pōōmp'ər-nik-l* or *pump'ər-nik-l*, *n* a coarse dark rye bread. [Ger; orig a term of abuse ('Smelly Nick' or 'Farty Nick'), possibly then applied to the bread because of its gas-creating effect on the digestive system]

pumpkin *pump'kin* or *pum'kin*, *US* often *pung'kin*, *n* a plant (*Cucurbita pepo*) of the gourd family, or its fruit. — Also (*obs*) **pomp'ion**, **pump'ion**. [OFr *pompon*, from L *pepō*, from Gr *pepōn* ripe; see **pepo**]

pumple-nose. See **pompelmoose**.

pumy. See **pumie**.

pun[1] *pun*, *vt* to pound (*Shakesp*); to ram; to consolidate by ramming: — *pr p* **punn'ing**; *pa t* and *pa p* **punned**. — *n* **punn'er** a tool for punning, a ram. [See **pound**[3]]

pun[2] *pun*, *vi* to play on words alike or nearly alike in sound but different in meaning: — *pr p* **punn'ing**; *pa t* and *pa p* **punned**. — *n* a play on words. — *n* and *adj* **punn'ing**. — *adv* **punn'ingly**. — *n* **pun'ster** a person who makes puns. [A late-17c word; origin unknown; Ital *puntiglio* a fine point, has been conjectured (see **punctilio**), as has a connection with **pun**[1]]

puna *po͞on'ə*, *n* a bleak tableland in the Andes; a cold wind there; mountain sickness. [Am Sp, from Quechua]

punalua *po͞o-nə-lo͞o'ə*, (*anthropol*) *n* a system of group marriage, sisters (by blood or tribal reckoning) having their husbands in common, or brothers their wives, or both. — *adj* **punalu'an**. [Hawaiian]

punce[1]. See **punch**[3].

punce[2] or **poonce** *po͞ons*, (*Austr slang*) *n* an effeminate man. [Variant of **ponce**]

Punch *punch* or *punsh*, *n* a hook-nosed hunchback, chief character in the puppet-show 'Punch and Judy'; the name of a humorous illustrated weekly magazine, published 1841–1992. [Shortened from **Punchinello**]

punch[1] *punch* or *punsh*, *adj* (*dialect*) short and thick. — *n* a thick-set short man (*obs*); a short-legged draught-horse, chestnut in colour, *orig* bred in Suffolk (also **Suffolk punch**). — *adj* **punch'y**. [Poss shortened from **puncheon**[2], or from **Punchinello**, or a variant of **bunch**]

punch[2] *punch* or *punsh*, (*obs*) *po͞onsh*, *n* a drink traditionally of spirits, water, sugar, lemon juice, and spice (but now with many variations). — **punch'-bowl** a large bowl for making punch in; a large bowl-shaped hollow in the ground; **punch'-ladle** a ladle for filling glasses from a punch-bowl. [Traditionally thought to be from Hindi *pāc*, five, from Sans *pañca* (from the supposed five original ingredients), but there are difficulties with this, as the original pronunciation seems to have been *po͞onsh*, which would not be a reflex of *pāc*, and there could be anything from three to six ingredients; a connection with **puncheon**[2] has also been suggested]

punch[3] *punch* or *punsh*, *vt* to prod; to poke; to drive (cattle; *US* and *Austr*); to strike with the fist; to thump; to kick (*dialect*; also **punce** *puns*); to stamp, pierce, perforate, indent, by a forward, downward, etc movement of a tool or part of a machine; to make, obtain or remove by such a movement (often with *out*); to press in vigorously (a key or button), or the key or button of; to record by pressing a key. — *vi* to perform an act of punching; to clock (*in* or *out*). — *n* a vigorous blow, or attempted blow, with the fist; striking power; effective forcefulness; a tool or machine for punching; a die; a prop for a mine-roof. — *n* **punch'er** someone who punches; an instrument for punching; a cow-puncher or cattle drover (*US*); the driver of a team (*Austr*). — *adj* **punch'y** vigorous, powerful; punch-drunk (*colloq*). — **punch'-bag** or (*US*) **punch'ing-bag** a large stuffed bag used for boxing practice; **punch'-ball** a suspended ball used for boxing practice; **punch'-card** or **punched card** a card with perforations representing data, used in the operation of computers. — *adj* **punch'-drunk** having a form of cerebral concussion from past blows in boxing, with results resembling drunkenness; dazed (*colloq abbrev* **punch'y**). — **punched tape** (*comput*) same as **paper tape**; **punch line** the last line or conclusion of a joke, in which the point lies; the last part of a story, giving it meaning or an unexpected twist; **punch'-prop** a short piece of wood used as a prop (*mining*); **punch'-up** a fight with fists. — **pull one's punches** to hold back one's blows; to be deliberately less hard-hitting in one's criticism than one might be. [**pounce**[1]; or from **puncheon**[1]; possibly in some senses for **punish**]

puncheon[1] *pun'chn* or *pun'shn*, *n* a dagger (*obs*); a tool for piercing or for stamping; a short supporting post; a split trunk with one face smoothed for flooring, etc. [OFr *poinson*, from L *pungere*, *punctum* to prick]

puncheon[2] *pun'chn* or *pun'shn*, *n* a cask; a liquid measure of from 70 to 120 gallons (*obs* or *hist*). [OFr *poinson* a cask; origin obscure]

Punchinello *punch-i-nel'ō* or *punsh-i-nel'ō*, *n* a hook-nosed character in an Italian puppet-show; a buffoon, any grotesque personage: — *pl* **Punchinell'os** or **Punchinell'oes**. [Ital *Pulcinella* a Neapolitan buffoon, of doubtful origin]

punchy. See under **punch**[1,3].

punctate *pungk'tāt* or **punctated** *pungk'tāt-id*, (*biol* or *pathol*) *adj* dotted; pitted. — *n* **punctā'tion**. — *n* **punctā'tor** someone who marks something with dots, *esp* applied to the Massoretes, who invented the Hebrew vowel-points. [L *punctum* a point, puncture, from *pungere*, *punctum* to prick]

punctilio *pungk-til'i-ō* or *pungk-til'-yō*, *n* a point in behaviour or ceremony requiring, or only observed by those having, fine or over-fine sensibilities with regard to etiquette; a point about which one is scrupulous; nicety or exact observance of etiquette: — *pl* **punctil'ios**. — *adj* **punctil'ious** scrupulous and exact; attentive to etiquette and punctilios. — *adv* **punctil'iously**. — *n* **punctil'iousness**. [Ital *puntiglio* and Sp *puntillo*, dimins of *punto*, from L *punctum* a point]

puncto *pungk'tō*, **puncto banco**. See **punto**.

punctual *pungk'tū-əl*, *adj* exact in keeping time and appointments; done at the exact time; up to time; of the nature of a point; pertaining to a point or points (*math*); of punctuation; precise, exact (*obs*); punctilious; pertaining to a point in time (*linguistics*). — *n* **punc'tualist** (*obs*; *rare*) an authority on or observer of punctilios. — *n* **punctuality** (*-al'i-ti*). — *adv* **punc'tually**. [LL *punctuālis*, from *punctum* a point]

punctuate *pungk'tū-āt*, *vt* to mark with points; to mark off (a piece of writing) with full stops, commas, question marks, etc; to intersperse; to emphasize. — *n* **punctuā'tion** the act or art of dividing sentences by points or marks; in the theory of punctuated equilibrium, any of the bursts of rapid change interspersed among the long periods of stability (*biol*). — *n* **punctuā'tionist** a believer in punctuated equilibrium. — *adj* **punc'tuātive**. — *n* **punc'tuātor**. — **punctuated equilibrium** or **equilibria** (*biol*) (a theory which states that evolution happens in) short bursts of major change punctuated by long periods of stability. [LL *punctuāre*, *-ātum* to prick, from L *punctum* (see **punctum**)]

punctum *pungk'təm*, (*anatom*) *n* a point or dot; a minute aperture: — *pl* **punc'ta**. — *adj* **punc'tūlate** or **punc'tūlated** minutely dotted or pitted. — *n* **punctūlā'tion**. — *n* **punc'tūle** a minute dot, pit or aperture. — **punctum caecum** (*pungk'təm sē'kəm* or *po͞ongk'to͞om kī'ko͞om*; L, blind spot; *anatom*) the point of the retina from which the optic nerve fibres radiate. [L *punctum*, from *pungere*, *punctum* to prick]

puncture *pungk'chər*, *n* an act of pricking; a small hole made with a sharp point; perforation of a pneumatic tyre, a flat tyre. — *vt* to make a puncture in; to deflate (someone's pride, self-confidence, etc). — *vi* to get a puncture. — *n* **puncturā'tion**. — *adj* **punc'tured** perforated; pierced; marked with little holes; consisting of little holes. — **punc'turer**. [L *punctūra*, from *pungere* to prick]

pundigrion *pun-dig'ri-on*, (*obs*) *n* a pun. [Origin unknown; Ital *puntiglio* is only a conjecture]

pundit *pun'dit*, *n* any learned person; an authority, now *usu* someone who considers himself or herself an authority; (also **pan'dit**) a Hindu learned in Sanskrit and in Hindu culture, philosophy and law. — *n* **pun'ditry**. [Hindi *paṇḍit*, from Sans *paṇḍita*]

pundonor *po͞on-dō-nōr'* or *po͞on-dō-nör'*, *n* a point of honour: — *pl* **pundonor'es** (*-ās*). [Sp, from *punto de honor*]

punga. See **ponga**.

pungent *pun'jənt*, *adj* sharp; ending in a hard sharp point (*bot*); pricking or acrid in taste or smell; keenly touching the mind; painful; sarcastic. — *n* **pun'gency** (*Crabbe*, **pun'gence**). — *adv* **pun'gently**. [L *pungens*, *-entis*, pr p of *pungere* to prick]

Punic *pū'nik, adj* of ancient Carthage; Carthaginian; faithless, treacherous, deceitful (as the Romans alleged the Carthaginians to be); purple (*obs*). — *n* the Semitic language of ancient Carthage. — *n* **Pu'nica** the pomegranate genus, constituting the family **Punicā'ceae** (*si-ē*; related to the myrtle and loosestrife families). — *adj* **punicā'ceous**. — **Punic apple** (*obs*) the pomegranate; **Punic faith** treachery. [L *Pūnicus*, from *Poenī* the Carthaginians]

Punica fides *pū'ni-kə fī'dēz* or *pōō'ni-kä fi'dās*, (*L*) Punic faith (see above).

punily. See **puny**.

punish *pun'ish, vt* to cause (someone) to suffer for an offence; to cause someone to suffer for (an offence); to handle, treat or beat severely (*colloq*); to consume a large quantity of (*colloq*). — *vi* to inflict punishment. — *n* **punishabil'ity**. — *adj* **pun'ishable**. — *n* **pun'isher**. — *adj* **pun'ishing** causing suffering or retribution; severe, testing (*colloq*). — *adv* **pun'ishingly**. — *n* **pun'ishment** the act or method of punishing; a penalty imposed for an offence; in conditioning, the weakening of a response which is followed by an aversive or noxious stimulus, or by the withdrawal of a pleasant one (cf **negative reinforcement**); severe handling (*colloq*). [Fr *punir, punissant*, from L *pūnīre* to punish, from *poena* penalty]

punitive *pū'ni-tiv, adj* concerned with, inflicting, or intended to inflict, punishment. — *n* **punition** (*-nish'ən*; *obs*) punishment. — *adj* **pu'nitory** punitive. — **punitive damages** see **exemplary damages**. [L *pūnīre* to punish]

Punjabi, also (less commonly) **Panjabi** and (formerly) **Punjabee** or **Punjaubee** *pun-jä'bē, -jö', n* a native or inhabitant of the *Punjab* in India and Pakistan; the language of the Punjab. — *adj* of the Punjab. [Hindi *Pañjābī*]

punk[1] *pungk, n* a prostitute (*obs*); anything or anyone worthless; nonsense; a foolish person; a homosexual, often a boy (*slang*); a follower of punk rock, often recognizable by the use of cheap utility articles, eg razor blades, plastic rubbish bags, safety-pins, as clothes or decoration. — *adj* rotten; worthless; miserable. — *n* **punk'iness**. — **punk poetry** poetry inspired by punk rock; **punk rock** a style of popular music of the late 1970s, fast and aggressive, with violent, often obscene lyrics expressing anti-establishment and anarchic views, also called **new wave**. [Origin unknown; poss from **punk**[2]]

punk[2] *pungk, n* touchwood; tinder; amadou, a preparation made from fungi to be used as tinder. [Poss **spunk**; or poss of Am Ind origin]

punka or **punkah** *pung'kə*, (*Ind*) *n* a fan; palm-leaf fan; a large mechanical fan for cooling a room. [Hindi *pākhā* a fan]

punner, punning, punster. See under **pun**[1,2].

punnet *pun'it, n* a small shallow chip-basket for fruit such as strawberries. [Origin unknown]

punt[1] *punt, n* a flat-bottomed boat with square ends, *esp* one propelled by means of a long pole pushed against the bottom of a river, etc. — *vt* to propel by pushing a pole against the bottom; to transport by punt. — *vi* to go in a punt; to go shooting in a punt; to propel a punt or boat with a pole. — *n* **punt'er**. — **punt'-fishing** fishing from a punt; **punt'-gun** a heavy large-bore gun used for shooting water fowl from a punt; **punt'-pole** a pole for propelling a punt; **punts'man** a sportsman who uses a punt. [OE *punt*, from L *pontō, -ōnis* punt, pontoon; cf **pontoon**[1]]

punt[2] *punt, vi* to stake against the bank (*gambling*); to back a horse (*horse-racing*). — *n* **punt'er** someone who punts, a professional gambler; a customer or client (*colloq*); an ordinary person (*colloq*, sometimes *derog*). [Fr *ponter*]

punt[3] *punt, n* the act of kicking a dropped football before it touches the ground; *specif*, in American football, such a kick into the opposing team's territory at the fourth down when it seems unlikely that the team in possession of the ball will gain the required ten yards' advance in four downs; the depression in the bottom of a glass container, a kick. — *vt* to kick in this manner or for this reason; to knock. — *n* **punt'er**. [Origin obscure]

punt[4] *pōōnt, n* the Irish pound.

puntee. See **punty**.

punto *pun'tō*, also **puncto** *pungk'tō*, (*obs*) *n* a moment; a point or punctilio; a pass or thrust in fencing: — *pl* **pun'tos** or **punc'tos**. — **punto banco** (Ital *banco* bank) or **puncto banco** a gambling game similar to baccarat; **punto dritt'o** (Ital *dritto* direct; *obs fencing*) a direct or straight hit; **punto river'so** or (*Shakesp*) **rever'so** (Ital *riverso* reversed; *obs fencing*) a back-handed stroke. [Sp and Ital *punto*, from L *punctum* a point]

punty, puntee, pontie or **ponty** *pun'ti*, **pontil** or **pontile** *pon'til, n* an iron rod used in holding and manipulating glassware during the process of making. [Prob Fr *pontil*, appar from Ital *pontello, puntello*, dimin of *punto* point]

puny *pū'ni, adj* puisne (*obs*); inexperienced (*Shakesp*); stunted; feeble: — *compar* **pū'nier**; *superl* **pū'niest**. — *adv* **pū'nily**. — *n* **pū'niness**. [**puisne**]

pup *pup, n* a short form of **puppy**. — *vt* and *vi* to give birth to a pup or pups: — *pr p* **pupp'ing**; *pa t* and *pa p* **pupped**. — **pup'fish** either of two varieties of tiny fish of the family Cyprinidae, native to the warmer waters of the western US; **pup tent** a small tent, easily carried. — **buy a pup** to be swindled; **in pup** of a bitch, pregnant; **sell a pup** to inveigle someone into a specious bad bargain; to swindle.

pupa *pū'pə, n* an insect in the *usu* passive stage between larva and imago (*entomol*); an intermediate stage of development in some other invertebrates (*biol*): — *pl* **pupae** (*pū'pē*) or **pū'pas**. — *adj* **pū'pal** of a pupa. — *adj* **pūpā'rial**. — *n* **pūpā'rium** the last larval skin separated but retained as a hard protective covering for the pupa; sometimes, the covering and the pupa: — *pl* **pūpā'ria**. — *vi* **pū'pate** to become a pupa. — *n* **pūpā'tion**. — *adj* **pūpigerous** (*-pij'ə-rəs*) having a puparium. — *adj* **pūpip'arous** having pupae developed within the body of the mother, giving birth to offspring already at the pupal stage. — **pu'pa-case** a puparium. [L *pūpa* a girl, a doll]

pupil[1] *pū'pl* or *pū'-pil, n* someone who is being taught, a student or schoolchild; any of the students or schoolchildren that, as a teacher, one is instructing or has instructed, as in *one of her pupils*; a boy up to the age of 14, or a girl up to 12 (*Roman* and *Scots law*); a ward (*law*). — *adj* under age. — *n* **pu'pillage** or **pu'pilage** the state of being a pupil or student; the time during which one is a pupil or student (in *Shakesp*, etc, sometimes taken as two words, **pupil age**). — *adj* **pu'pillar** or **pu'pilar** pupillary. — *n* **pupillar'ity** the state or time of being legally a pupil. — *adj* **pu'pillary** pertaining to a pupil or ward, or someone under academic discipline. — *n* **pu'pilship**. — **pupil teacher** a pupil who does some teaching *esp* as part of his or her training for later entry into the profession. [Fr *pupille*, from L *pūpillus, pūpilla*, dimins of *pūpus* boy, *pūpa* girl]

pupil[2] *pū'pl* or *pū'-pil, n* the round opening in the eye through which the light passes; a central spot, *esp* within a spot. — *n* **pupilabil'ity** an intentionally unintelligible word in Sterne's *Tristram Shandy*. — *adj* **pu'pillar, pu'pilar, pu'pillary** or **pu'pilary**. — *adj* **pu'pillate** (*zool*) having a central spot of another colour. [L *pūpilla* pupil of the eye, *orig* the same as **pupil**[1], from the small image to be seen in the eye]

pupiparous. See under **pupa**.

puppet *pup'it, n* a doll or image moved by strings, wires, rods or the hand; a marionette; a person, state, etc under the control of another. — *adj* behaving like a puppet; controlled by others. — *n* **puppeteer'** a person who manipulates puppets. — *n* **pupp'etry** play of, or with, puppets; puppets collectively; puppet-like action; puppet-shows; anything like or associated with puppets; puppets' dress (*obs*). — **pupp'et-play** a drama performed by puppets; **pupp'et-show** an exhibition of puppets; a puppet-play; **pupp'et-valve** same as **poppet-valve**. [Earlier **poppet**; cf OFr *poupette*, dimin from L *pūpa*]

puppodum *pup'ə-dəm*. Same as **popadum**.

puppy *pup'i*, *n* a young dog, a whelp; a lapdog or toy dog (*obs*); a young seal; a young rat; a conceited young man; a puppet (*dialect*). — *vt* and *vi* to pup. — *n* **pupp'ydom**. — *n* **pupp'yhood**. — *adj* **pupp'yish**. — *n* **pupp'yism** conceit in men. — **pupp'y-dog**; **pupp'y-fat** temporary fatness in childhood or adolescence. — *adj* **pupp'y-headed** (*Shakesp*) having the mind of a puppy. — **puppy love** same as **calf-love**; **pupp'y-walker** a person who brings up a puppy until it is ready for training as a working dog; an experienced policeman who introduces a new recruit to his or her beat (*slang*). [Appar Fr *poupée* a doll or puppet, from L *pūpa*]

pupunha *po͞o-po͞on'yə*, *n* the peach-palm; its fruit. [Port, from Tupí]

pur[1]. See **purr**.

pur[2] *pûr*, (*obs*) *n* the knave in the game of post and pair.

pur[3] *pür*, (*Fr*) *adj* pure. — **pur sang** (*sã*) pure blood; thoroughbred; total.

Purana *po͞o-rä'nə*, *n* any one of a class of sacred books of Hindu mythology, cosmology, etc, written in Sanskrit. — *adj* **Puranic** (*-rän'ik*). [Sans *purāṇa*, from *purā* of old]

Purbeck *pûr'bek*, *adj* of the Isle (really a peninsula) of *Purbeck*, in Dorset. — *n* and *adj* **Purbeck'ian** (*geol*) Jurassic of the uppermost stage. — **Purbeck marble** or **stone** a freshwater shelly limestone quarried in the Isle of Purbeck.

purblind *pûr'blīnd*, *adj* nearly blind; *orig* apparently wholly blind; dim-sighted, *esp* spiritually. — *adv* **pur'blindly**. — *n* **pur'blindness**. [**pure** (or perh OFr intensifying pfx *pur-*), and **blind**]

purchase *pûr'chəs*, *vt* to buy; to obtain by effort, risking danger, etc; to seek to bring about (*obs*); to bring about (*obs*); to acquire; to get in any way other than by inheritance (*law*); to be amends for (with *out*) (*Shakesp*); to raise or move by a mechanical power. — *vi* to strive (*Shakesp*); to make purchases; to accumulate possessions (*obs*). — *n* the act of purchasing; seizure (*obs*); that which is purchased; acquisition; prize, booty (*archaic*); whatever one can do for oneself by expedients (*obs*); annual rent; a bargain (*obs*); a price (*obs*); any mechanical advantage in raising or moving bodies or apparatus; an advantageous hold, or means of exerting force advantageously. — *adj* **pur'chasable**. — *n* **pur'chaser**. — **purchase money** the money paid, or to be paid, for anything; **purchase system** the system by which, before 1871, commissions in the British army could be bought; **purchase tax** formerly, a British form of sales-tax levied on specified goods and at differential rates. — **not worth a day's, etc, purchase** not likely to last a day, etc; **so many years' purchase** the value or price of a house, estate, etc, equal to the amount of so many years' rent or income. [OFr *porchacier* to seek eagerly, pursue, from *pur* (L *prō*) for, and *chacier* to chase]

purdah *pûr'də*, *n esp* formerly, in Hindu and Muslim communities, the seclusion of women from the sight of strangers, by means of a screen or curtain in the home or by a veil worn in public; the screen, curtain, etc used for this; seclusion generally (*fig*). — *adj* **pur'dahed** (of a woman) secluded, in purdah. — **purdah bus, carriage,** etc one for women only, in which the occupants are screened by shutters or blinds. [Urdu and Pers *pardah* curtain]

Purdey® *pûr'di*, *n* a gun manufactured by the firm of James *Purdey* and Sons Ltd. — *adj* denoting such guns, gun-mechanisms, etc.

purdonium *pûr-dō'ni-əm*, *n* a kind of coal-scuttle introduced by a Mr *Purdon*.

pure *pūr*, *adj* clean; unsoiled; unmixed; not adulterated; free from guilt or defilement; chaste; free from bad taste, bad grammar, bad manners, insincerity, barbarism, etc; modest; mere; that and that only; utter, sheer; free (from any stated characteristics); of a study, confined to that which belongs directly to it; non-empirical, involving an exercise of the mind alone, without involving the results of experimentation; excellent, fine (*obs*); homozygous, breeding true (*biol*); unconditional (*law*); free from ritual uncleanness. — *n* purity; dog's faeces or any similar substance used by tanners (*hist*; also **puer**). — *adv* purely; utterly, completely (*colloq*); without mixture. — *vt* to cleanse or refine; to treat with pure (also **puer**). — *adv* **pure'ly** chastely; unmixedly; unconditionally; wholly, entirely; wonderfully, very much (*dialect*). — *n* **pure'ness**. — *n* **purism** see separate entry. — *n* **purity** see separate entry. — *adj* **pure'-blood, pure-blood'ed** and **pure'-bred** of unmixed race. — **pure culture** (*bot*) a culture containing a pure stock of one species of micro-organism; **pure mathematics** mathematics treated without application to observed facts of nature or to practical life; **pure reason** reason alone, without involvement of emotion, etc; in Kant, the power of grasping a priori forms of knowledge (*philos*); **pure science** science considered apart from practical applications. [Fr *pur*, from L *pūrus* pure]

purée or **puree** *pū'rā*, *n* food material reduced to pulp eg by being processed in a liquidizer; a soup without solid pieces. — *vt* to make a purée of. [Fr]

Purex *pūr'eks*, *n* a process for recovering plutonium and uranium from spent uranium fuel by using tributyl phosphate as a solvent. [*pur*ification and *ex*traction]

purfle *pûr'fl*, *vt* to ornament the edge of, eg with embroidery or inlay. — *n* a decorated border; a profile (*obs*). — *n* **pur'fling** a purfle, *esp* around the edges of a violin. [OFr *pourfiler*, from L *prō* before, and *fīlum* a thread]

purfled *pûr'fld*, (*Scot*) *adj* short-winded. — *adj* **pur'fly** (*Carlyle*).

purge *pûrj*, *vt* to purify; to remove impurities from; to clear of undesirable elements or persons; to remove as an impurity; to clarify; to clear from accusation; to expiate; to empty (the bowels); to make (someone) evacuate the bowels; to atone for or wipe out (*esp* a contempt of court; *law*). — *vi* to become pure by clarifying; to empty the bowels; to empty the bowels frequently; to take a purgative. — *n* the act of purging; an expulsion or massacre of people regarded as untrustworthy or otherwise undesirable; a purgative. — *n* **purgation** (*-gā'shən*) a purging; a clearing away of impurities; the act of clearing from suspicion or imputation of guilt (*law*); a cleansing. — *adj* **purgative** (*pûrg'ə-tiv*) cleansing; having the power of emptying the intestines. — *n* a medicine that empties the intestines. — *adv* **pur'gatively**. — *adj* **purgato'rial** or **purgato'rian** pertaining to purgatory. — *adj* **pur'gatory** purging or cleansing; expiatory. — *n* a place or state in which souls are after death purified from venial sins (*RC*); any kind or state of suffering for a time; intense discomfort (*colloq*); a ravine (*US*); a swamp (*US*). — *n* **purger** (*pûrj'ər*). — *n* and *adj* **purging** (*pûrj'*). — **purging buckthorn, purging cassia, purging flax** see under **buckthorn, cassia, flax**. [Fr *purger*, from L *pūrgāre*, *-ātum*, from earlier *pūrigāre*, from *pūrus* pure]

puri or **poori** *po͞o'ri*, *n* a small cake of unleavened Indian bread, deep-fried and served hot; a small round cake filled with a spicy vegetable mixture and deep-fried. [Hindi]

purify *pū'ri-fī*, *vt* to make pure; to cleanse from a foreign or harmful matter; to free from guilt, from ritual uncleanness, or from improprieties or barbarisms in language. — *vi* to become pure: — *pr p* **pu'rifying**; *pa t* and *pa p* **pu'rified**. — *n* **purificā'tion**. — *adj* **pu'rificātive**. — *n* **pu'rificātor** a cloth used during the celebration of Holy Communion to wipe the vessels and the hands and lips of the celebrant. — *adj* **pu'rificātory** serving to purify or cleanse. — *n* **pu'rifier**. — **Purification of the Blessed Virgin Mary** a feast observed in the RC Church on 2 February, in commemoration of the purification of the Virgin Mary according to the Jewish ceremonial (Lev 12. 1–4) forty days after the birth of Christ. [Fr *purifier*, from L *pūrificāre*, from *pūrus* pure, and *facere* to make]

purim *pū'rim* or *po͞or-ēm'*, (*Judaism*) *n* the Feast of Lots held about 1 March, in which the Jews commemorate their deliverance from the plot of Haman, as related in the Book of Esther (see *esp* 3. 7). [Heb *pūrīm* (singular *pūr*), lots; origin unknown]

purine *pūr'in* or *pūr'ēn*, or **purin** *pū'rin*, *n* a white crystalline substance $C_5H_4N_4$, which with oxygen forms uric acid ($C_5H_4N_4O_3$) and is the nucleus of many other derivatives; any of a number of these derivatives, cyclic di-ureides, such as adenine and guanine, *esp* one which is part of the nucleotide chains of DNA and RNA. [Contracted from L *pūrum ūricum* (*acidum*) pure uric (acid)]

purism *pūr'izm*, *n* fastidious, *esp* over-fastidious, insistence on purity (*esp* of language in vocabulary or idiom). — *n* and *adj* **pūr'ist**. — *adj* **pūris'tic** or **pūris'tical**. — *adv* **pūris'tically**. [L *pūrus* pure]

Puritan *pūr'i-tən*, *n* a person who in the time of Elizabeth and the Stuarts wished to carry the reformation of the Church of England further by purifying it of ceremony; an opponent of the Church of England on account of its retention of much of the ritual and belief of the Roman Catholics; an opponent of the Royalists in the 17c; (the following meanings also without *cap*) a person of similar views to, or in sympathy with, those of the historical Puritans; a person strictly moral in conduct; slightingly, someone professing a too-strict morality; an advocate of purity in any sense. — *adj* (also without *cap*) pertaining to the Puritans. — *adj* **pūritanic** (*-tan'ik*) or **puritan'ical** (*usu derog*). — *adv* **pūritan'ically**. — *n* **pūr'itanism**. — *vt* and *vi* **pūr'itanize** or **-ise**. [L *pūrus* pure]

purity *pūr'i-ti*, *n* the condition of being pure; freedom from mixture of any kind, or from sin, defilement or ritual uncleanness; chastity; sincerity; freedom from foreign or improper idioms or words. [L *pūritās*, *-ātis*, from *pūrus* pure]

purl[1] *pûrl*, *vi* to flow with a murmuring sound; to flow in eddies; to curl or swirl. — *n* a trickling brook (*obs*); a movement or murmuring eg of a stream among stones; an eddy or ripple (also **pirl**). — *n* and *adj* **purl'ing**. [Cf Norw *purla* to babble, Swed dialect *porla* to purl, ripple]

purl[2] *pûrl*, (except for first sense, *colloq*) *vi* to spin round; to capsize; to go head over heels; to fall headlong or heavily. — *vt* to throw headlong. — *n* a heavy or headlong fall; an upset. — *n* **purl'er** a headlong or heavy fall or throw, *esp* in the phrases *go* or *come a purler*. [Connected with **purl**[3]]

purl[3] *pûrl*, *vt* to embroider or edge with gold or silver thread; to fringe (eg lace) with a wavy edging. — *vt* and *vi* to knit with a purl stitch. — *n* twisted gold or silver wire; a loop or twist, *esp* on an edge (also **pearl**); a succession of such loops, or a lace or braid having them; a fold, pleat or frilling; knitting with a purl stitch. — *adj* (also **pearl**) denoting an inverted stitch made with the wool passed behind the needle (*knitting*; *opp* of *plain*). [Origin uncertain; perhaps from different words; cf **pearl**[2]]

purl[4] *pûrl*, *n* formerly, ale with wormwood; ale warmed and spiced. [Origin unknown]

purler[1] *pûrl'ər*, (*orig* and *esp Austr*) *n* something extremely good.

purler[2]. See **purl**[2].

purlicue. Same as **pirlicue**.

purlieu *pûr'lū*, *n* (frequently in *pl*) a person's usual haunts; (in *pl*) borders or outskirts; *orig* a tract of land regarded as part of a (*esp* royal) forest, later excluded but still subject to certain forest laws, eg regarding hunting. [Anglo-Fr *puralee* land by perambulation, from OFr *pur* (= L *prō*) for, and *allee*, going; infl by Fr *lieu* place]

purlin or **purline** *pûr'lin*, (*building*) *n* a piece of timber stretching across the principal rafters to support the common or subsidiary rafters. [Origin obscure]

purloin *pər-loin'* or *pûr'loin*, *vt* and *vi* to filch, steal. — *n* **purloin'er**. [Anglo-Fr *purloigner* to remove to a distance, from *pur-* (L *prō*) for, and *loin* (L *longē*) far]

purpie or **purpy** *pur'pi*, (*obs Scot*) *n perh* purslane, *perh* brooklime. — **water purpie** brooklime. [Perh OFr *porpié*, from LL *pullī pēs* colt's foot, purslane; perh from **purple**, from the colour of the brooklime's flower]

purple *pûr'pl*, *n* a mixture of blue and red; crimson (*hist*); the Tyrian crimson dye, obtained in ancient times from various shellfish (Murex, Purpura, Buccinum, etc) (*hist*); any shellfish from which the dye is obtained; a crimson cloth or garment worn in ancient times by kings and emperors (*hist*); the rank, power or position of king or emperor; the red robe of a cardinal; the cardinalate (from the red hat and robes); (with **the**) bishops; a purple pigment; a purple-red pigment in the rods of the mammalian eye and in parts of other eyes (*biol*; **visual purple**); a purple flower (see **long-purples**); (in *pl*) purpura; (in *pl*) swine-fever; (in *pl*) ear-cockle (see under **ear**[1]). — *adj* of the colour purple; blood-red, bloody (*hist*); of writing, fine or over-ornate. — *vt* to make purple. — *vi* to become purple. — *adj* **pur'plish** or **pur'ply** somewhat purple. — **purple airway** a reserved course for a royal flight. — *adj* **pur'ple-born** porphyrogenite. — *adj* **pur'ple-coloured**. — **purple emperor** one of the largest of British butterflies and one of the most richly coloured (*Apatura iris*); **purple finch** an American finch, the male of which has a red head and breast; **purple fish** a shellfish yielding purple dye; **purple heart** the purple-coloured wood of species of *Copaifera* (of the family *Caesalpiniaceae*) (also **purple wood**); a mauve heart-shaped tablet of a stimulant drug of the amphetamine type; (with *caps*) a US decoration for wounds received on active service. — *adj* **pur'ple-hued**. — *adj* **pur'ple-in-grain** dyed fast in purple. — **purple patch** a passage of fine, or (often) over-ornate, writing. — **born in the purple** born in the purple chamber of the Byzantine empresses (*hist*; see **Porphyrogenite**); hence, of exalted birth; **purple of Cassius** a red or purple pigment discovered by Andreas Cassius (c.1683), made from stannous, stannic and gold chlorides in solution. [OE (Northumbrian) *purpl(e)* purple (*adj*), from *purpur* purple (*n*), from L *purpura*, from Gr *porphyrā* purple fish]

purport *pûr-pōrt'*, *pûr-pört'*, *pûr'pərt*, *pûr'pōrt*, *pûr'pört*, *n* the meaning conveyed; substance, gist, tenor; outward appearance or guise, as conveying an impression (*Spenser*); purpose (*rare*). — *vt* **purport'** (also *pûr'*) (of a document, etc) to give out as its meaning; to convey to the mind; to seem, claim or profess (to mean, be, etc); to mean or intend (rare). — *adv* **purport'edly**. — *adj* **pur'portless**. [OFr, from *pur* (Fr *pour*), from L *prō* for, and *porter*, from L *portāre* to carry]

purpose *pûr'pəs*, *n* an idea or aim kept in the mind as the goal towards which one's efforts are directed; the power of seeking the goal desired; the act or fact of purposing; a desired goal; a useful function; a definite intention; the intention of going (*Shakesp*); purport (*Shakesp*); conversation, conversational speech (*Spenser*); (in *pl*; *obs*) a sort of conversational game involving questions and answers. — *vt* to intend. — *vi* (*Spenser*) to converse or talk. — *adj* **pur'posed** intentional; intended; set on a purpose; purposeful. — *adj* **pur'poseful** directed towards a purpose; motivated by a sense of purpose. — *adv* **pur'posefully**. — *n* **pur'posefulness**. — *adj* **pur'poseless** without purpose; aimless; having no purpose in mind. — *adv* **pur'poselessly**. — *n* **pur'poselessness**. — *adj* **pur'pose-like** (*Scot*) efficient-looking; purposeful. — *adv* **pur'posely** intentionally. — *adj* **pur'posive** directed towards an end; showing intention or resolution, purposeful. — *n* **pur'posiveness**. — *adj* **purpose-built'** specially made or designed to meet particular requirements. — **on purpose** (also *obs* **of purpose** and *old* **of set purpose**) intentionally; **to good** (or **some**) **purpose** with good effect; **to the purpose** to the point, relevant to the matter in question. [OFr *pourpos*, *propos*, from L *prōpositum* a thing intended, from *prō* forward, and *pōnere*, *positum* to place; cf **propose**]

purpresture *pûr-pres'chər*, *n* encroachment on public property. [OFr *purpresture*, from *pur* (L *prō*), for, and *prendre*, from L *praehendere* to take]

Purpura *pûr'pū-rə*, *n* a genus of marine gasteropods yielding a purple dye; (without *cap*) purples, an eruption of small purple spots, caused by extravasation of blood (*med*). — *n* and *adj* **pur'pure** (*obs* except *heraldry*) purple. — *adj* **purpū'real** (*poetic*) purple. — *adj* **purpū'ric** (*med*) relating to purpura. — *n* **pur'purin** a purple colouring-matter obtained from madder. [L *purpura*, from Gr *porphyrā* purple fish]

purpy. See **purpie**.

purr or (*obs*) **pur** *pûr*, *vi* (of a cat) to utter a soft, low, vibrating sound when contented; (of a vehicle engine or other machinery) to make a sound similar to this; (of a person) to express pleasure or gratification. — *vt* to express by purring; to say or utter in a tone vibrating with satisfaction. — *n* an act or the sound of purring. — *n* and *adj* **purr'ing**. — *adv* **purr'ingly**. [Imit]

purse *pûrs*, *n* a small bag for carrying money; a sum of money in a purse; a sum given as a present or offered as a prize; funds; formerly, a live coal flying out of the fire, regarded as a good omen; a woman's handbag (*US*); a purse-like receptacle or cavity (*obs med* or *biol*). — *vt* to put into a purse or one's own purse, to pocket; to contract (one's lips) into a rounded, puckered shape, *esp* in order to express displeasure, etc; to contract or draw into folds or wrinkles. — *vi* to pucker; to steal purses (*obs*). — *n* **purse'ful** as much as a purse can hold; enough to fill a purse. — *n* **purs'er** formerly, a naval paymaster; an officer in charge of cabins, stewards, etc. — *n* **purs'ership**. — **purse'-bearer** a person who has charge of another person's money; a treasurer; a person who carries in a bag the Great Seal for the Lord Chancellor, or the royal commission for the Lord High Commissioner; **purse'-net** a bag-shaped net that closes by a drawstring at the neck; **purse'-pride**. — *adj* **purse'-proud** proud of one's wealth; insolent from wealth. — **purse'-seine** a seine-net that can be drawn into the shape of a bag; **purse'-seiner** a fishing-vessel equipped with such nets; **purse'-sharing** the sharing-out of an individual fee or prize between all members of the recipient's firm or team; **purse'-snatcher**; **purse'-snatching**; **purse'-strings** the strings fastening a purse (*usu fig*); **purse'-taking** robbing. — **privy purse** an allowance for a sovereign's private expenses; **public purse** the nation's finances. [OE *purs*, appar from LL *bursa*, from Gr *byrsa* a hide]

pursew. Spenser's usual spelling of **pursue**.

purslane *pûrs'lin*, *n* a pot-herb and salad herb (*Portulaca oleracea*) of the family Portulacaceae; any member of the genus or the family. — Also **purslain**. — **sea purslane** a fleshy seaside sandwort (*Arenaria*, or *Honckenya*, *peploides*); any of various species of orach; **water purslane** a small-flowered prostrate lythraceous plant of wet places (*Lythrum portula*). [OFr *porcelaine*, from L *porcilāca*, *portulāca*; see **Portulaca**]

pursue *pər-sū'* or *pər-sōō'*, *vt* to harass or persecute, to persist in opposing or seeking to injure; to prosecute or sue (*Scots law*); to follow in order to overtake and capture or kill; to chase; to hunt; to follow with haste; to follow up; to follow the course of; to be engaged in; to carry on; to seek to obtain or attain; to proceed in accordance with; to proceed with. — *vi* to follow; to go on or continue; to act as a prosecutor at law. — *adj* **pursu'able**. — *n* **pursu'al** or (more often) **pursu'ance** pursuit; the act of carrying out or following (eg *in pursuance of this policy*). — *adj* **pursu'ant** pursuing; in pursuance (with *to*; approaching an *adv*). — *adv* **pursu'antly**. — *n* **pursu'er** someone who pursues; a plaintiff (*Scots law*). — *n* and *adj* **pursu'ing**. — *adv* **pursu'ingly**. [Anglo-Fr *pursuer*, *pursiwer*, from popular L forms *prosequere* or *-īre or persequere* or *-īre*, for L *prōsequī* and *persequī*, from *prō-* and *per-* (the prefixes being confused), and *sequī* to follow]

pursuit *pər-sūt'* or *pər-sōōt'*, *n* the act of pursuing; endeavour to attain; occupation; employment; that which is pursued; a cycle race in which two riders start at opposite sides of a track and try to overtake each other. — **pursuit plane** a type of military aeroplane used in pursuing enemy aeroplanes. [Anglo-Fr *purseute*, from the same root as **pursue**]

pursuivant *pûr'si-vənt*, *-swi-vənt*, *n* an attendant or follower; a state messenger with power to execute warrants; an officer ranking below a herald. [Fr *poursuivant*, pr p of *poursuivre* to pursue]

pursy[1] *pûrs'i*, *adj* puffy; fat; short-winded. — *n* **purs'iness**. [OFr *poulsif* broken-winded, from *poulser* (Fr *pousser*), from L *pulsāre* to drive]

pursy[2] *pûrs'i*, *adj* pursed up; puckered. [**purse**]

purtenance *pûr'tən-əns*, (*obs*) *n* something which pertains or belongs; the guts, *esp* of an animal. [Earlier form of **pertinence**]

purty *pûr'ti*, (*dialect*, *esp US*) *adj* pretty.

purtraid, **purtrayd**. See **pourtray**.

purulent *pū'rū-lənt* or *pū'rōō-lənt*, *adj* consisting of, of the nature of, forming, full of, characterized by, or like pus. — *n* **pū'rulence** or **pū'rulency**. — *adv* **pū'rulently**. [L *pūrulentus*, from *pūs*, *pūris* pus]

purvey *pûr-vā'*, *vt* to provide or furnish; to supply. — *vi* to provide meals or provisions as one's business. — *n* **purvey'ance** the act of purveying; preparation in advance (*Spenser*); furnishings, equipment (*Spenser*); a procuring of provisions; that which is supplied; the former royal prerogative of procuring provisions for the court at a fixed price, requisitioning horses, etc (*hist*). — *n* **purvey'or** someone whose business is to provide food or meals; an official who formerly exacted provisions for the use of the royal household. [Anglo-Fr *purveier*, from L *prōvidēre*; see **provide**]

purview *pûr'vū*, *n* the body or enacting part of a statute distinguished from the preamble; enactment; scope; range; field of activity or view; competence. [Anglo-Fr *purveu*, provided, pa p of *purveier*; see **purvey**]

pus *pus*, *n* a thick yellowish fluid formed by suppuration, consisting of serum, white blood cells, bacteria and debris of tissue. [L *pūs*, *pūris*; cf Gr *pyon*]

puschkinia *pōōsh-kin'i-ə*, *n* any plant of the genus *Puschkinia*, spring-flowering bulbous plants native to western Asia with bell-shaped flowers, including *Puschkinia scilloides*, the striped squill. [A Mussin-*Puschkin* (died 1805), Russ scientist]

Puseyism *pū'zi-izm*, *n* Tractarianism, the High Church and Catholic principles of Dr E B *Pusey* (1800–1882) and other Oxford divines, as set out in the 'Tracts for the Times' (1833–41). — *adj* **Pūseyist'ic** or **Pūseyist'ical**. — *n* **Pū'seyite**.

push[1] *pōōsh*, *vt* to thrust or press against; to drive by pressure; to press or drive forward; to urge; to press hard; (of a plant) to produce (fruit, shoots, roots, etc); to advance or carry to a further point; to promote, or seek to promote, vigorously and persistently; to make efforts to promote the sale of; to effect by thrusting forward; to peddle (drugs); to come near, be approaching (an age or number). — *vi* to make a thrust; to butt (*obs*); to exert pressure; to make an effort; to press forward; to make one's way by exertion; to reach out; to be urgent and persistent; to play a push-stroke. — *n* a thrust; an impulse; pressure; a help to advancement; enterprising or aggressive pertinacity; an effort; an onset; an offensive; a push-stroke; a gang of roughs (*Austr*); a group of people sharing an interest or background (*Austr*); a company; dismissal or rejection (*colloq*). — *adj* **pushed** (*colloq*) in a hurry; short of money. — *n* **push'er** someone who pushes; a machine, or part of a machine that pushes; a propeller placed behind the wing of an aircraft; an aeroplane propelled by such a propeller; a child's table implement, or a finger of bread, used for pushing food on to a fork or spoon; the stick used to propel the puck in the game of octopush; a self-assertive person; someone who assiduously seeks social advancement; a drug peddler. — *adj* **push'ful** energetically or aggressively enterprising. — *adv* **push'fully**. — *n* **push'fulness**. — *adj* **push'ing** pressing forward eg in business; enterprising; self-assertive. — *adv* **push'ingly**. — *n* **push'iness**. — *adj* **push'y** aggressive; self-assertive, *esp* obtrusively so. — **push'-ball** a game in which an enormous ball is pushed; **push'-bike** (also, *esp* formerly **push'-bicycle** or **push'-cycle**) a bicycle driven by pedals; **push'-button** a knob, eg on a doorbell or a vending machine, which when pressed causes the bell, vending machine, etc to operate. — *adj* operated by, or using, a push-button or push-buttons. — **push-button civilization** one in which the ordinary unskilled person has the benefits of technology at the pressing of a button; **push-button war** one carried on by guided missiles, released by push-button; **push'-cart** (*US*) a street vendor's barrow; **push'-chair** a lightweight wheeled folding chair for conveying a baby or child; **push'-off** the act of pushing a boat off from the shore, etc, or, in swimming, of pushing oneself off the end of the pool in turning; a send-off; **push'-out** the act of pushing (someone or something) out, eg of pushing an opponent out of the ring in some forms of wrestling; **push'-over** an easy thing; a person or side easily overcome; a person easily persuaded or won over; **pushover try** (*Rugby football*) one in which the attacking side in a scrum pushes the defenders back until the ball crosses the goal line; **push'-pin** a children's game in which pins are pushed one across another (*Shakesp*); a large-headed drawing-pin, used *esp* to mark points on maps (*US*). — *adj* **push'-pull** denoting any piece of apparatus in which two electrical or electronic devices act in opposition to each other, used eg of an amplifier in which two thermionic valves so acting serve to reduce distortion. — **push-pull train** one which can be pulled or pushed by the same locomotive; **push'rod** in an internal combustion engine, a metal rod that opens, and sometimes closes, the valves. — *vt* **push'-start** to start (a motor-car) by pushing it while it is in gear. — *n* the act of starting a car in this way. — **push'-stroke** a push instead of an ordinary hit or stroke at a ball; in billiards, etc, an illegal stroke in which the cue is still in contact, or comes into contact again with the cue-ball when the cue-ball touches the object-ball; **push'-tug** a tug for pushing, rather than pulling, barges; **push'-up** a press-up (see under **press**[1]). — **at a push** when circumstances urgently require; if really necessary; **give** (or **get**) **the push** to dismiss or reject, or be dismissed or rejected; **push along** (*colloq*) to leave, to go on one's way; **push around** to bully; **push for** to make strenuous efforts to achieve; **push off** of a rower or a boat, to leave the bank, shore, etc; to depart (*colloq*); **push one's fortune** to busy oneself in seeking a fortune; **push one's luck** see under **luck**; **push out** (of person, boat) to row or be rowed out towards open water; **push the boat out** see under **boat**; **push the bottle** to take one's liquor and pass the bottle round; **push through** to compel acceptance of; **push up the daisies** (*colloq*) to be dead and buried. [Fr *pousser*, from L *pulsāre*, frequentative of *pellere*, *pulsum* to beat]

push[2] *pŏŏsh*, (*Shakesp*) *interj* pish. — *n* an exclamation of 'push'. [**pish**]

Pushtu, **Pashtu**, **Pushtoo** *push'tōō*, **Pushto**, **Pashto** *-tō*, **Pakhtu** *puhh'tōō*, or **Pakhto** *-tō*, *n* an official language of Afghanistan also spoken in parts of Pakistan; a native speaker of this, a Pathan. — *adj* of or pertaining to this language or people. — *n* **Push'tun**, **Pash'tun**, **Pakh'tun** or **Pakh'toon**, etc a member of a Pushtu-speaking tribe in Pakistan and Afghanistan; in *pl* the tribe. — Also *adj*. [Afghan *Pashtō*, *Pakhtō*]

pusillanimous *pū-si-lan'i-məs*, *adj* lacking firmness or determination; mean-spirited; cowardly. — *n* **pusillanim'ity**. — *adv* **pusillan'imously**. [L *pusillanimis*, from *pusillus* very little, and *animus* mind]

pusle. An *obs* spelling of **puzzle**[1,2].

puss[1] *pŏŏs*, *n* a familiar name for a cat; (in hunting or coursing) a hare; a playfully pejorative name for a child or a girl; a puss-moth. — *n* **puss'y** a dimin of **puss** (also **puss'y-cat**); anything soft and furry; a willow-catkin; the female pudenda (*slang*); sexual intercourse (*slang*); a woman considered as a sexual object (*slang derog*). — **puss'-gentleman** (*obs*) a dandy; **puss'-moth** a thick-bodied hairy notodontid moth (*Dicranura*, or *Cerura*, *vinula*) whose caterpillar feeds on willow or poplar leaves; **puss'yfoot** a prohibitionist (from *Pussyfoot*, nickname of William E Johnson (1862–1945), US revenue officer noted for his stealthy ways and his prohibitionist campaigns). — *vi* to go stealthily; to act timidly, cautiously or non-committally. — **puss'y-footer**; **pussy-will'ow** a common American willow, *Salix discolor* or other species with silky spring catkins. — **puss in the corner** a children's game in which the places are continually being changed, while the player who is out tries to secure one of the places while it is empty. [Cf Du *poes* puss; Ir and Gaelic *pus*, a cat; **pussy** in the sexual sense perh from a different word, cf ON *pussa* the female genitalia]

puss[2] *pŏŏs*, *n* (*slang*) the face. [Ir *pus* a mouth]

pussel *pus'l* or *puz'l*, (*Shakesp*) *n* a slut. [**pucelle**]

pusser *pus'ər*, (*UK* and *Austr naval slang*) *adj* regulation, smart, genuine, official, formal, etc. — *n* a supply officer — the possessive form **pusser's** is used in many compounds eg **pusser's dagger** a seaman's knife, and often with a *derog* sense, eg **pusser's sneer** and **pusser's logic** a false economy. [**purser**]

pussy. See under **puss**[1].

pustule *pus'tūl*, *n* a pimple containing pus; a pimple-like or warty spot or lump. — *adj* **pus'tulant** causing pustulation. — Also *n*. — *adj* **pus'tular** or **pus'tulous**. — *vt* and *vi* **pus'tulate**. — *n* **pustulā'tion**. [L *pustula*]

put[1] *pŏŏt*, *vt* to place, or cause to be, in such and such a position, state, predicament, relation, etc; to set; to place, lay or deposit; to apply; to append or affix; to connect; to add; to commit; to assign; to start (someone *on* eg a diet, a study or a track); to push or thrust; to cast, throw or hurl (*esp* by a thrusting movement of the hand from the shoulder); to drive; to impel; to convey or transport; to force or constrain; to incite; to subject; to reduce; to convert; to render; to express; to assert; to propound; to submit to a vote; to impose; to impute; to call on, oblige, stake, venture or invest; to repose (eg trust, confidence). — *vi* to thrust (*archaic* or *Northern*); to proceed, make one's way (*naut*); to set out, *esp* hurriedly; to flow (*US*): — *pr p* **putting** (*pŏŏt'ing*); *pa t* and *pa p* **put**. — *n* a push or thrust; a throw, *esp* of a heavy object from the shoulder; on the stock exchange, an option of selling within a certain time certain securities or commodities, at a stipulated price (also **put option**). — *n* **putter** (*pŏŏt'ər*) someone who puts; someone who pushes or hauls trams in a coal-mine (*hist*). — *n* **putt'ing** putting the shot (qv in phrases). — **put'-and-take** a gambling game played with a top on which are marked instructions to give to or take from a bank or pool of objects; **put'-down** a snub; an action intended to assert one's superiority; **put'-in** (*Rugby football*) the act of throwing the ball into a set scrum; **put'-off** an excuse or evasion; a postponement; **put'-on** a hoax; **put option** see **put** *n* above; **putt'er-on** (*Shakesp*) an instigator; **putt'er-out** (*obs*) someone who deposited money on going abroad, on condition of receiving a larger sum on his return, if he ever returned; **put-through** a transaction in which a broker arranges the buying and the selling of shares; **putt'ing-stone** a heavy stone used in putting the shot. — *adj* **put-up'** arranged beforehand in a false but deceptively plausible way. — **put about** to publish or circulate; to change the course of (*esp* a ship) or to change course; to distress (*Scot*); **put across** to carry out successfully, to bring off; to perform so as to carry the audience with one; **put an end**, or **a stop**, **to** to cause to discontinue; **put away** to renounce; to divorce; to kill (*esp* an old or ill animal);

to stow away, pack up or set aside; to put into the proper or desirable place; to imprison; to admit to a mental hospital (*colloq*); to eat (*colloq*); **put back** to push backward; to delay; to repulse; to turn and sail back for port (*naut*); to reduce one's finances (*colloq*); **put by** to set aside; to parry; to store up; **put case** see under **case**[2]; **put down** to crush or quell; to kill (*esp* an old or ill animal); to snub or humiliate; to degrade; to snub, silence or confute (*Shakesp*); to enter, write down on paper; to reckon; to attribute; to give up (*rare*); to surpass or outshine; to preserve, put in pickle (*dialect*); of an aeroplane, to land (often with *at*); to pay (a deposit); to put (a baby) to bed (*colloq*); to drop (a catch) (*cricket*); **put for** to make an attempt to gain; **put forth** to extend; to propose; to publish; to exert; to display; to lend at interest; to set out from port; to produce or extrude; **put forward** to propose; to advance; **put in** to introduce; to insert; to lodge, deposit or hand in; to make a claim or application (*for*); to enter; to enter a harbour; to interpose; to perform towards completing a total; to spend, pass or fill up (time) with some occupation; to appoint; **put in an appearance** see under **appear**; **put in mind** to remind; **put it across someone** to defeat someone by ingenuity; **put it on** to pretend (to be ill, etc); **put it past someone** (*usu* with *not*) to judge it inconsistent with someone's character; **put the make on** see under **make**; **put off** to lay aside; to take off (*archaic*); to lay aside the character of; to palm off; to dismiss (*archaic*); to turn (someone) aside from what he or she wants or intends with evasions, excuses or unsatisfying substitutes; to divert, turn aside from a purpose; to postpone; to idle away, spend in vain; to disconcert; to cause aversion or disinclination in; to push from shore; **put on** to clothe oneself or someone else with; to assume (a character or quality), *esp* deceptively; to mislead or deceive; to superimpose; to impose; to affix, attach, apply; to add (eg weight, charges, etc); to stake or wager; to move forward; to move faster (*obs*); to set to work; to set in operation; to incite; to turn on the supply of; to score; to stage. — as *pa p*, clad (as in *well put on* or *well putten on*, *Scot*), respectably dressed. — **put on to** to make aware of; to connect with by telephone; **put out** to expel; to dismiss from a game and innings; to send out; to stretch out; to extinguish; to place (money) at interest; to expand; to publish; to disconcert; to inconvenience; to offend; to dislocate; to exert; to produce; to place with others or at a distance; to go out to sea, leave port; to remove bodily or blind (an eye); to render unconscious (*slang*); of a woman, to be willing to grant sexual favours (*US slang*); **put over** to refer (*Shakesp*); to carry through successfully; to impress an audience, spectators, the public, favourably with; to impose, pass off; **put through** to bring to an end; to accomplish; to put in telephonic communication; to cause to undergo or suffer; to process (*comput*); **putting the shot**, **stone** or **weight** the act or sport of hurling a heavy stone or weight from the hand by a sudden thrust from the shoulder (see also **putt**[1]); **put to** to apply; to add to; to connect with; to harness; to shut; to set to; **put to death** see under **death**; **put to it** to press hard; to distress; **put to rights** see under **rights**; **put to sea** to begin a voyage; **put to the sword** see under **sword**; **put two and two together** to draw a conclusion from various facts; **put up** to accommodate with lodging; to take lodgings; to nominate or stand for election; to offer for sale; to present (eg a good game, a fight, or a defence, a prayer); to parcel up; to supply and pack (an order, a picnic, etc); to stow away, put aside; to sheathe; to settle beforehand; to compound; to endure tamely (*obs*); to start (a hare) from cover; **put-up job** a dishonest scheme prearranged *usu* by several people; **put upon** to take undue advantage of; to impose on; **put up to** to incite to; to make conversant with, to supply with useful information or tips about; **put up with** to endure; **stay put** to remain passively in the position assigned. [Late OE *putian* (found in the verbal noun *putung* instigation); there were also *potian* and *pȳtan*, which may account for some of the dialect forms; cf Dan *putte*, Swed *putta*]

put[2] *put*. See **putt**[1,2,3].

putamen *pū-tā'mən*, *n* a fruit-stone (*bot*); the membrane within an egg-shell (*zool*); the lateral part of the lenticular nucleus of the cerebrum (*anatom*): — *pl* **putamina** (*-tăm'in-ə*). [L *putāmen* clippings, waste, from *putāre* to prune]

putative *pū'tə-tiv*, *adj* supposed; reputed; commonly supposed to be. — **putative marriage** a marriage supposed invalid by canon law, but entered into in good faith by at least one of the parties. [L *putātīvus*, from *putāre*, *-ātum* to suppose]

putcher *po͝och'ər*, *puch'ər*, or **putcheon** *po͝och'ən* or *puch'ən*, *n* a conical wicker or wire trap for catching salmon. [Origin unknown]

putchock, **putchuk** or **pachak** *puch-uk'*, *n* costus-root (see **Costus**). [Hindustani *pachak*; origin obscure]

puteal *pū'ti-əl*, *n* a wall round the top of a well. [L *puteal*, *-ālis*, from *puteus* a well]

puteli *put'e-lē*, *n* a flat-bottomed boat used on the Ganges. [Hindi *paṭelī*]

putid *pū'tid*, *adj* rotten; foul. [L *pūtidus*]

putlog *put'log* or **putlock** *put'lok*, *n* a cross-piece in a scaffolding, the inner end resting in a hole left in the wall. [Origin obscure; **putlock** seems to be the older form]

putois *pü-twä'*, *n* a brush of polecat's hair, or of some substitute for it, for painting pottery. [Fr]

put-put *put'-put*, *put-put'*, *po͞ot'-po͞ot* or *po͞ot-po͞ot'*, *n* the noise of a small motor. — *vi* to make such a noise: — *pr p* **put-putting**; *pa t* and *pa p* **put-putted**. [Imit]

putrefy *pū'tri-fī*, *vt* to cause to rot; to corrupt. — *vi* to rot: — *pr p* **pu'trefying**; *pa t* and *pa p* **pu'trefied**. — *adj* **putrefacient** (*-fā'shənt*) causing putrefaction. — *n* **putrefaction** (*-fak'shən*) rotting. — *adj* **putrefac'tive**. — *adj* **putrefī'able**. — *n* **putrescence** (*-tres'əns*) incipient rottenness. — *adj* **putresc'ent**. — *adj* **putresc'ible**. — *n* **putresc'ine** (*-ēn* or *-in*) a substance, $H_2N(CH_2)_4NH_2$, formed during the putrefaction of flesh. — *adj* **pu'trid** rotten; wretchedly bad (*slang*). — *n* **putrid'ity** or **pu'tridness**. — *adv* **pu'tridly**. — **putrid fever** (*obs med*) typhus. [L *putrefacere*, *putrescere*, and *putridus*, from *puter*, *putris* rotten]

putsch *po͝och*, *n* a sudden revolutionary outbreak; a coup d'état. — *n* **putsch'ist** a person who takes part in a putsch. [Swiss Ger dialect]

putt[1] *put*, *vt* to hurl (a shot, stone or weight) in the sport of putting the shot; (*Scot*; also **put** *put* or *po͞ot*; see under **put**[1]); to strike in making a putt (*golf*; also *archaic* **put** *put*). — *vi* to make a putt or putts (*golf*): — *vt* and *vi* (in combination with a number) to take a given number of putts to put the ball in the hole, as in *he four-putted (at) the last hole* (*golf*): — *pr p* **putt'ing**; *pa p* and *pa t* **putted**. — *n* a throw (*Scot*; also **put** *put* or *po͞ot*; see **put**[1]); a delicate stroke such as is made with a putter on, or sometimes near, a putting-green, with the object of rolling the ball, if possible, into the hole (*golf*). — *n* **putt'er** someone who putts or can putt; a short stiff golf-club with an upright striking-face, used in putting. — *n* **putt'ing** the exercise of hurling a heavy weight (*Scot*; also **putting the shot**; see under **put**[1]); the act or art of making a putt (*golf*); a game played with putters and golf-balls on a small course with several holes. — **putt'ing-cleek** a putter of cleek design, the blade long and narrow, running straight from the shaft; **putt'ing-green** the turf, made firm and smooth for putting, round each of the holes of a golf-course; according to the rules, everything within 20 yards of the hole, hazards excluded; a small golf-course with several holes for practice or for putting as an informal game; **putt'ing-stone** see under **put**[1]. — **putt out** to complete a hole in a round of golf by putting the ball into the hole. [A Scottish form of **put**[1]]

putt[2] or **put** *put*, *n* an old card-game like nap. [Perh **put**[1]]

putt[3] or **put** *put*, (*archaic*) *n* a greenhorn; a bumpkin. [17c slang; origin unknown]
puttee, *put'ē*, or **puttie** *put'i*, *n* a cloth strip wound round the leg from ankle to knee as a legging. [Hindi *paṭṭī*]
putten. See **pit**[3].
putter[1] *put'ər*. The *orig* US form of **potter**[2].
putter[2]. See under **put**[1].
putter[3]. See under **putt**[1].
puttie. See **puttee**.
puttier. See **putty**.
putto *po͝ot'ō*, *n* a plump, naked, very young boy, often winged, in Renaissance or Baroque art: — *pl* **putti** (*po͝ot'ē*). [Ital]
puttock *put'ək*, *n* a kite (*Shakesp*); a buzzard; a kite-like person. [ME *puttok*, perh connected with OE *pyttel* kite]
putty *put'i*, *n* a fine cement of slaked lime and water (*plasterers' putty*); a cement of whiting and linseed oil (*glaziers'* or *painters' putty*); *orig* putty-powder (*polishers'* or *jewellers' putty*); a yellowish grey colour; a weak-willed, easily manipulated person (*fig*). — *vt* to fix, coat or fill with putty: — *pr p* **putt'ying**; *pa t* and *pa p* **putt'ied**. — *n* **putt'ier** a glazier. — *adj* **putt'y-coloured**. — *adj* **putt'y-faced** having a putty-coloured face. — **putt'y-knife** a blunt, flexible tool for laying on putty; **putt'y-powder** stannic oxide (often with lead oxide) used for polishing glass. [Fr *potée* potful, putty-powder, from *pot*]
puture *pū'tyər* or **pulture** *pul'tyər*, (*hist*) *n* the claim of foresters, etc to food for man, horse and dog within the bounds of a forest. [Anglo-Fr *puture*, and ONFr *pulture*, from LL *pu(l)tūra*, appar from L *puls*, *pultis* porridge]
putz *po͝ots*, *n* (*US*) in Pennsylvanian Dutch homes, a representation of the Nativity traditionally placed under a Christmas tree: — *pl* **putz'es**. [Ger *putzen* to decorate]
puy *pwē*, *n* a small volcanic cone, eg in Auvergne. [Fr, hill, from L *podium* a height; cf **pew**, **podium**]
puzel, **puzzel**. Same as **pucelle**, **pussel**.
puzzle[1] *puz'l*, *vt* to perplex; to bewilder; to cause difficulty in solving or understanding to; to set a problem that causes difficulty to; to entangle, complicate; to solve by systematic or assiduous thinking (with *out*). — *vi* to be bewildered; to work hard at solving something; to search about. — *n* bewilderment; perplexity; anything that puzzles; a problem; a riddle or a toy designed to test skill or ingenuity. — *n* **puzz'ledom** (*rare*) bewilderment. — *n* **puzz'lement** the state of being puzzled. — *n* **puzz'ler**. — *adj* **puzz'ling** posing; perplexing. — *adv* **puzz'lingly**. — **puzz'le-head** someone who is puzzle-headed. — *adj* **puzz'le-headed** having one's head full of confused notions. — **puzz'le-headedness**; **puzz'le-monkey** a monkey-puzzle; **puzz'le-peg** a piece of wood fastened under a dog's jaw so as to keep the dog's nose off the ground; **puzzle-prize book** a book containing a puzzle, the successful solver of which is rewarded with a prize. [Origin obscure]
puzzle[2]. See **pucelle**.
puzzolana *po͝ot-sō-lä'nə*, *n*. Same as **pozzolana**.
PVA *abbrev*: polyvinyl acetate (see under **poly-**).
PVC *abbrev*: polyvinyl chloride (see under **poly-**).
PVFS *abbrev*: post-viral fatigue syndrome (see under **post-**).
PVS *abbrev*: persistent or permanent vegetative state, an *esp* post-traumatic brain-damaged state in which the subject, though able to breathe, remains unconscious and must be artificially fed.
Pvt. (*military*) *abbrev*: Private.
PW *abbrev*: Policewoman.
pw *abbrev*: per week.
PWA (*US*) *abbrev*: person with Aids.
PWD *abbrev*: Public Works Department.
PWR *abbrev*: pressurized water reactor.
pwt *abbrev*: pennyweight.
PX *pē eks*, *n* a shop selling goods for US servicemen and their families overseas. [Abbrev of **post** and **exchange**]
pxt *abbrev*: *pinxit* (*L*), painted (this).
PY *abbrev*: Paraguay (IVR).
pyaemia *pī-ē'mi-ə*, (*med*) *n* infection of the blood with bacteria from a septic focus, with abscesses in different parts of the body. — Also **pye'mia**. — *adj* **pyae'mic**. [Gr *pyon* pus, and *haima* blood]
pyat. See **pyot**.
pycnic. Same as **pyknic**.
pycnidium *pik-nid'i-əm*, (*bot*) *n* in some fungi a receptacle like a perithecium, containing hyphae which produce conidia. — *n* **pycnid'iospore** a conidium produced in a pycnidium. [Gr *pyknos* thick, dense, and dimin sfx *-idion*, Latinized to *-idium*]
pycnite *pik'nīt*, (*geol*) *n* a columnar variety of topaz. [Gr *pyknos* dense]
pycno- or **pykno-** *pik-nō-*, *pik-nə-* or *pik-no'-*, *combining form* dense, close. — *n* **pycnoconid'ium** (*bot*) a pycnidiospore. — *n* **pycnodysostosis** or **pyknodysostosis** (*-dis-os-tō'sis*; *med*; Gr *dys* abnormal, *osteon* bone, and *-osis* diseased state) a rare inherited bone disease characterized by short stature and fragility and thickening of the bones. — *n* **pycnog'onid** a member of the **Pycnogon'ida** (Gr *gony* knee) the sea-spiders, a class of marine arthropods with more leg than body. — *adj* **pycnog'onoid**. — *n* **pycnom'eter** or **pyknom'eter** an instrument for determining specific gravities. — *n* **pyc'non** in ancient Greek music, that part of the tetrachord (chromatic or enharmonic) where the smallest intervals fall; in medieval music, a semitone. — *n* **pycnōs'is** (*biol*) the shrinkage of the stainable material of a nucleus into a deeply staining knot, *usu* a feature of cell degeneration. — *n* **pyc'nospore** (*bot*) a pycnidiospore. — *adj* **pycnostyle** (Gr *stȳlos* column; *archit*) (of ancient Greek temples and buildings of a similar style) with close-set columns, $1\frac{1}{2}$ diameters apart. — *n* a pycnostyle building. [Gr *pyknos* dense]
pye[1]. See **pie**[2].
pye[2]. See **pie**[3].
pyebald. See **piebald**.
pye-dog *pī'-dog*, *n* (in Asia) an ownerless or pariah dog. — Also **pi'-dog** or **pie'-dog**. [Hindustani *pāhī* outsider]
pyeing. See **pie**[3].
pyelitis *pī-ə-lī'tis*, (*med*) *n* inflammation of the pelvis of the kidney. — *adj* **pyelitic** (*-lit'ik*). — *n* **py'elogram** an X-ray picture of the renal pelvis, the kidney and the ureter. — *n* **pyelography** (*-log'rə-fi*). — *n* **pyelonephritis** (*-nef-rī'tis*) inflammation of the kidney and the renal pelvis. — *adj* **pyelonephritic** (*-rit'ik*). [Gr *pyelos* a trough]
pyemia. See **pyaemia**.
pyengadu *pyeng-gä-do͞o'*, *n* the ironwood (*Xylia* of the family *Mimosaceae*) of Burma, etc. [Burmese *pyeng-kadō*]
pyet. See **pyot**.
pygal *pī'gəl*, (*zool*) *adj* belonging to the rump or posteriors of an animal. — *n* the posterior median plate of a chelonian carapace. [Gr *pȳgē* rump]
pygarg *pī'gärg*, (*archaic*, eg in the Authorized Version) *n* possibly the addax antelope — translated as 'white-rumped deer' in the New English Bible, and as 'ibex' in the New International Version. [Gr *pȳgē* rump, and *argos* white]
pygidium *pī-gid'i-əm* or *pī-jid'i-əm*, (*zool*) *n* in insects, the tergum of the last abdominal somite; the tail-shield of a trilobite. — *adj* **pygid'ial**. [Latinized from Gr *pȳgidion*, dimin of *pȳgē* rump]
pygmy or **pigmy** *pig'mi*, *n* a member of any of the dwarf human races — Negritos, Negrillos and others; a dwarf; any person, animal or thing relatively diminutive or in some way insignificant; a person of low moral, etc stature; an anthropoid ape (*obs*); one of the ancient diminutive people who lived in underground houses, etc in whom some scholars see the historical origins of the fairies and elves of folklore; an elf; *orig* a member of a race of dwarfs said by Homer and other ancient writers to have lived in N Africa and to have fought and been destroyed by cranes (*mythol*). — *adj*

dwarfish; (*esp* of a breed or species) diminutive; of the pygmies. — *adj* **pygmaean** or **pigmaean**, **pygmean** or **pigmean** (*pig-mē'ən*). — *adj* **pyg'moid** or **pig'moid**. [Gr *pygmaios* measuring a *pygmē* (13½ inches, the distance from elbow to knuckles)]

pygostyle *pī'gō-stīl*, (*zool*) *n* the bone of a bird's tail. [Gr *pȳgē* rump, and *stȳlos* a column]

pyjamas *pi-jä'məz*, formerly also *pī-jä'məz*, or (*US*) **pajamas** *pə-jä'məz*, *n pl* light loose-fitting trousers and a jacket or top, worn *esp* for sleeping in; loose trousers tied round the waist, worn in the East. — *adj* **pyja'ma'd** or **pyja'maed** wearing pyjamas. — **pyjama cricket** (*Austr*) cricket played under floodlights and in coloured clothing; **pyjama jacket**; **pyjama trousers**. [Pers and Hindustani *pāējāmah*, from *pāē* leg, and *jāmah* clothing]

pyknic *pik'nik*, *adj* (of a human racial type) characterized by short squat stature, small hands and feet, relatively short limbs, domed abdomen, short neck, and round face. [Gr *pyknos* thick]

pykno-, **pyknodysostosis**, **pyknometer**. See **pycno-**.

pyknosome *pik'nə-sōm*, *n*. Same as **amplosome**.

pylon *pī'lon*, *n* a structure for supporting power-cables; a guiding mark at an aerodrome; an external structure on an aeroplane for attaching an engine, etc; a gateway, gate-tower, gatehouse or building through which an entrance passes, *esp* the gateway of an Egyptian temple (*archit*); an artificial leg (*med*): — *pl* **py'lons**. [Gr *pylōn*, *-ōnos*, from *pylē* a gate]

pylorus *pī-lō'rəs*, *pī-lö'rəs*, *pi-lō'rəs* or *pi-lö'rəs*, (*anatom*) *n* the opening from the stomach to the intestines. — *adj* **pylor'ic** (*-lor'*). [L, from Gr *pylōros* a gate-keeper, the pylorus, from *pylē* an entrance, and *ōrā* care; cf *ouros* a guardian]

pyne. Same as **pine**[2].

pyogenic *pī-ə-jen'ik*, (*med*) *adj* pus-forming. — *n* **pyogen'esis**. — *adj* **py'oid** purulent. — *n* **pyorrhoea** (*-rē'ə*; Gr *rhoiā* flow) discharge of pus; now, suppuration in the sockets of teeth. — *adj* **pyorrhoe'al** or **pyorrhoe'ic**. [Gr *pyon* pus]

pyoner, **pyonings**. See under **pioneer**.

pyorrhoea. See **pyogenic**.

pyot, **pyat**, **pyet** or **piet** *pī'ət*, (*Scot*) *n* a magpie. — *adj* pied. — *adj* **pi'oted**. [**pie**[1]]

pyracanth *pī'rə-kanth* or **pyracantha** *pī-rə-kan'thə*, *n* a thorny evergreen shrub of the genus *Pyracantha*, related to the hawthorn. [Gr *pyrakantha*, from *pȳr* fire, and *akanthos* thorn]

pyral. See under **pyre**.

pyralis *pir'ə-lis*, *n* an insect once supposed to live or breed in fire (*obs*); (with *cap*) a genus of moths, giving name to a heterogeneous family, the **Pyralidae** (*pir-al'i-dē*). — *n* and *adj* **pyr'alid** (a member) of this family. [Gr *pyralis*, from *pȳr* fire]

pyramid *pir'ə-mid*, *n* a solid figure on a triangular, square, or polygonal base, with triangular sides meeting in a point; any object or structure of that or a similar form, *esp* a huge ancient Egyptian monument; a crystal form of three or more faces each cutting three axes (*crystallog*); (in *pl*) a game played on a billiard-table in which the balls are arranged in pyramid shape: — *pl* **pyr'amids**, also (*obs*) **pyramides** (*pir-am'i-dēz*) and (*poetic*) **pyram'ids** and **pyram'ides** (3 syllables). — *vi* (chiefly *US*) to increase one's holdings, profits, etc during a boom period by using paper profits for further purchases. — *adj* **pyram'idal**, **pyramid'ic** or **pyramid'ical** having the form of a pyramid. — *adv* **pyram'idally** or **pyramid'ically**. — *n* **pyramid'ion** the small pyramidal apex of an obelisk. — *n* **pyram'idist** or **pyramidol'ogist** someone who studies the Egyptian pyramids. — *n* **pyramidol'ogy**. — *n* **pyr'amis** (*Shakesp*, etc) a pyramid: — *pl* **pyram'ides** (*-i-dēz*) or **pyr'amises**. — *n* **pyram'idon** an organ-stop with pipes like inverted pyramids. — **pyramid selling** a method of distributing goods by selling batches to agents who then sell batches at increased prices to sub-agents, and so on. — **pyramid of numbers** the relative decrease in numbers at each stage of a food chain, characteristic of animal communities. [Gr *pyramis*, *-idos*]

pyrargyrite *pīr-är'jir-īt* or *pir-är'jir-īt*, *n* ruby-silver ore, sulphide of silver and antimony. [Gr *pȳr* fire, and *argyros* silver]

pyre *pīr*, *n* a pile of combustible material for burning a dead body. — *adj* **pyr'al**. [L *pyra*, from Gr *pyrā*, from *pȳr* fire]

Pyrenaean. See **Pyrenean**.

pyrene[1] *pī'rēn*, (*bot*) *n* a fruit-stone. — *n* **pyrē'nocarp** (Gr *karpos* fruit) a perithecium. — *n* **pyrē'noid** a small round albuminous body concerned in starch-formation, found in the chloroplasts of some algae, etc. — *n pl* **Pyrēnomycē'tēs** (Gr *mykēs* fungus) a group of Ascomycetes whose characteristic fructification is the perithecium. — *adj* **pyrēnomycē'tous**. [Gr *pȳrēn*, *-ēnos* fruit-stone]

pyrene[2] *pī'rēn*, *n* a hydrocarbon ($C_{16}H_{10}$) obtained by dry distillation of coal. [Gr *pȳr* fire]

Pyrenean or (*obs*) **Pyrenaean** *pir-ə-nē'ən*, *adj* of the *Pyrenees*, the mountains between France and Spain. — *n* a native of the Pyrenees; (in *pl*) the Pyrenees (*obs*). — *n* **pyrenē'ite** a black garnet. — **Pyrenean mountain dog** a large dog with a dense white coat, bred in the Pyrenees to guard flocks. [L *Pȳrēnaeus*, from Gr *Pȳrēnaios*]

pyrenoid, etc. See under **pyrene**[1].

Pyrethrum *pī-rēth'rəm*, (*esp US*) *pī-reth'rəm*, (*rare*) *pir-eth'rəm*, *n* a former genus of composite plants, including feverfew, now considered as belonging to the genus *Chrysanthemum*; (without *cap*) a name still applied to various garden flowers, *esp* varieties of *Chrysanthemum coccineum*; (without *cap*) insect-powder made from the flower-heads of various species of pyrethrum; (without *cap*) in pharmacy, the root of pellitory of Spain (see **pellitory**[2]). — *n* **pyrēth'rin** (or, *esp US*, *-reth'*) either of two insecticidal oily esters prepared from pyrethrum flowers. — *n* **pyrēth'roid** (or, *esp US*, *-reth'*) any of various synthetic compounds related to the pyrethrins, and sharing their insecticidal properties. [L, from Gr *pyrethron* pellitory of Spain]

pyretic *pī-ret'ik* or *pir-et'ik*, *adj* of, of the nature of, for the cure of, fever. — *n* **pyretol'ogy** the study of fevers. — *n* **pyretother'apy** treatment by inducing a high body temperature. [Gr *pyretikos* feverish, from *pyretos* fever, from *pȳr* fire]

Pyrex® *pī'reks*, *n* a type of glassware containing oxide of boron and so resistant to heat. [An arbitrary coinage, from **pie**[4]; appar nothing whatever to do with Gr *pȳr* fire]

pyrexia *pī-rek'si-ə*, (*med*) *n* fever. — *adj* **pyrex'ical** and **pyrex'ic**. [Gr *pyrexis*, from *pyressein* to be feverish, from *pȳr* fire]

pyrheliometer *pir-hē-li-om'i-tər* or *pīr-hē-li-om'i-tər*, *n* an instrument for measuring the heating effect of the sun's rays. — *adj* **pyrheliometric** (*-ō-met'rik*). [Gr *pȳr* fire, *hēlios* sun, and *metron* measure]

pyridine *pir'i-dēn* or *pir'i-din* *n* a strong-smelling, colourless, strongly basic liquid, C_5H_5N, obtained in the distillation of bone-oil, coal-tar, etc. — *n* **pyridox'in** or **pyridoxine** a pyridine derivative, a member of the vitamin B complex. — *n* **pyrim'idine** a six-membered heterocyclic compound containing two nitrogen atoms in the 1, 3 positions, eg cytosine, thymine and uracil, important bases found in DNA and RNA. [Gr *pȳr* fire]

pyriform *pir'i-fōrm*, *adj* pear-shaped. [L *pyrum*, misspelling of *pirum* a pear, and *fōrma* form]

pyrimethamine *pi-ri-meth'ə-mēn* or *pī-ri-meth'ə-mēn*, *n* a powerful anti-malaria drug. [Gr *pȳr* fire, *methyl*, and **amine**]

pyrimidine. See under **pyridine**.

pyrites *pīr-ī'tēz* or *pir-ī'tēz*, *n* a brassy yellow mineral, iron disulphide, crystallizing in the cubic system, occurring in octahedra, pyritohedra, etc (also called **pyrite** *pī'rīt*, and **iron pyrī'tēs**); extended to a large class of mineral sulphides and arsenides. — *adj* **pyritic** (*pir-*

it'ik or *pīr-it'ik*) or **pyrit'ical**. — *adj* **pyritif'erous**. — *vt* **pyr'itize** or **-ise** to convert into, or replace by, pyrites. — *adj* **pyritohē'dral**. — *n* **pyritohē'dron** a pentagonal dodecahedron: — *pl* **pyritohē'dra**. — *adj* **pyr'itous**. — **arsenical pyrites** mispickel; **cockscomb pyrites** or **spear pyrites** a twinned form of marcasite; **copper pyrites** sulphide of copper and iron, chalcopyrite, a mineral very similar to iron pyrites; **magnetic pyrites** pyrrhotite. [Gr *pyrītēs* striking fire, from *pȳr* fire]

pyrithiamine *pi-ri-thī'ə-mēn* or *pi-ri-thī'ə-mēn*, *n* an anti-vitamin causing thiamine (vitamin B_1) deficiency. [Gr *pȳr* fire, and **thiamine**]

pyro *pī'rō*, (*photog*) *n* a short form of **pyrogallol**.

pyro- *pī'rō-*, *combining form* denoting: fire, heat, fever; obtained by heating or as if by heating, or by removing (theoretically) a molecule of water, as in **pyro-acet'ic**, **pyrophosphor'ic**, **pyrosulphu'ric**, **pyrotartar'ic**, etc **acid**, related in this way to acetic, phosphoric, etc, acid, and in the derivative salts **pyrophos'phate**, **pyrotar'trate** etc (*chem*). — *n* **pyroballogy** (*-bal'ə-ji*; *Sterne*; Gr *ballein* to throw, and **-logy**) the science of artillery. — *adj* **pyrochem'ical** relating to, producing, or produced by, chemical changes at high temperatures. — *adj* **pyro-clas'tic** (*geol*; Gr *klastos*, broken) (of rocks) formed of fragments thrown out by volcanic action. — *n pl* **pyroclas'tics** ash and other debris ejected by a volcano (also **py'roclast** *n*). — *adj* **pyro-elec'tric** (*phys*) becoming positively and negatively electrified at opposite poles on heating or cooling; of pyro-electricity. — *n* **pyro-electric'ity** the property of being pyro-electric; the study of the phenomena shown by pyro-electric crystals. — *n* **pyrogallol** (*-gal'ol*) a phenol obtained by heating *gallic* acid, used in photographic developing (also called **pyrogall'ic acid**). — *n* **py'rogen** (*-jen*; see **-gen**; *med*) a substance causing heat or fever. — *adj* **pyrogenic** (*pī-rō-jen'ik*), **pyrogenetic** (*-jin-et'ik*), and **pyrogenous** (*-roj'ə-nəs*) produced by, or producing, heat or fever. — **pyrognostic** (*pī-rog-nos'tik*; *mineralogy*; see **-gnostic**) pertaining to the testing of minerals by flame. — *npl* **pyrognos'tics** the properties of a mineral revealed by such testing. — *n* **pyrography** (*pī-rog'rə-fi*; see **-graphy**) poker-work. — *n* **pyrogravure** (*-grə-vūr'*; Fr *gravure* engraving) pyrography. — *n* **pyrokinesis** (*-kī-nē'sis* or *-ki-nē'sis*; Gr *kīnēsis* movement), the ability to start fires by thought alone. — *n* **pyrolater** (*pī-rol'ə-tər*) a fire-worshipper. — *n* **pyrol'atry** (see **-latry**) fire-worship. — *adj* **pyroligneous** (*-lig'ni-əs*; *chem*; L *ligneus*, from *lignum* wood) obtained by distillation of wood (**pyroligneous acid** wood-vinegar, a mixture of acetic acid, methyl alcohol, etc; **pyroligneous alcohol** wood-spirit, methyl alcohol). — *n* **pyrolusite** (*-lū'sīt* or *-lōō'sīt*; *geol*; Gr *lousis* washing, from its use in decolorizing molten glass) *n* naturally-occurring manganese dioxide. — *vt* **py'rolyse** or (*US*) **py'rolyze** to decompose by pyrolysis. — *n* **pyrolysis** (*pi-rol'i-sis*; see **-lysis**) decomposition of a substance by heat. — *adj* **pyrolytic** (*-lit'ik*). — *n* **pyromancy** (*-man-si*; see **-mancy**) divination by fire. — *n* **pyromā'nia** an obsessive urge to set light to things. — *n* and *adj* **pyromā'niac**. — *adj* **pyromaniacal** (*-mə-nī'ə-kl*). — *adj* **pyroman'tic** pertaining to pyromancy. — *n* **pyromeride** (*pī-rom'ər-īd*; *geol*; Gr *meros* part, as if meaning only partly fusible) a nodular rhyolite. — *n* **pyrometer** (*pī-rom'i-tər*; see **-meter**) an instrument for measuring high temperatures. — *adj* **pyrometric** (*pī-rō-met'rik*) and **pyromet'rical** (**pyrometric cones** same as **Seger cones**). — *n* **pyrom'etry**. — *n* **pyromorphite** (*-mör'fīt*; Gr *morphē* form) an ore (chloride and phosphate) of lead, so called because the globule formed by heating a small quantity of ore crystallizes on cooling. — *n* **pyrophobia** (*-fō'bi-ə*; see **-phobia**) an irrational fear of fire. — *n* and *adj* **pyrophō'bic**. — *n* **pyrophone** (*-fōn*; Gr *phōnē* sound) an organ producing interference-tones by pairs of flames in tubes, invented by Eugène Kastner (1852–82). — *n* **pyrophorus** (*pī-rof'ə-rəs*; Gr *pyrophoros* fire-carrier) a substance that takes fire on exposure to air (*chem*); (with *cap*) a genus of tropical American fireflies, elaterid beetles. — *adj* **pyrophoric** (*-rō-for'ik*) and **pyroph'orous**. — **pyrophosphate** and **pyrophosphoric** see **pyro-** above. — *n* **pyropho'tograph** a burnt-in photograph, eg on glass or porcelain. — *adj* **pyrophotograph'ic**. — *n* **pyrophotog'raphy**. — *n* **pyrophyllite** (*-fil'īt*; Gr *phyllon* leaf) a clay mineral that separates into layers on heating with a blowpipe. — *n* **pyroscope** (*-skōp*; see **-scope**) an instrument for measuring the intensity of radiant heat. — *n* **pyrosis** (*pī-rō'sis*; Gr *pyrōsis*) water brash. — *n* **Pyrosoma** (*-sō'mə*; Gr *sōma* body) a genus of compound tunicates, with brilliant phosphorescence. — *n* **py'rosome**. — *n* **pyrostat** (*-stat*) a type of thermostat for use at high temperatures. — *adj* **pyrostat'ic**. — **pyrosulphate**, **pyrosulphuric**, **pyrotartaric**, etc see **pyro-** above. — *adj* **pyrotech'nic** or **pyrotech'nical**. — *adv* **pyrotech'nically**. — *n* **pyrotechnician** (*-nish'ən*) a person who makes fireworks or puts on firework displays. — *n sing* **pyrotechnics** (*-tek'niks*; Gr *technikos* skilled, from *technē* art) the art of making fireworks; (also *n pl*) a display (or the displaying) of fireworks; (also *n pl*) showy display in talk, music, etc; (also *n pl*) a display of temper. — *n* **pyrotech'nist** a pyrotechnician; a person given to pyrotechnics. — *n* **py'rotechny** pyrotechnics. — *n* **pyroxene** (*pī'rok-sēn*; Gr *xenos* stranger, because the 18c Fr mineralogist Haüy thought that pyroxene crystals in lava had been caught up accidentally) a general name for a group of minerals distinguished from amphiboles by a cleavage angle of about 87°, metasilicates of calcium, magnesium, aluminium and other metals, *usu* green or black, very common in igneous rocks — augite, diopside, enstatite, etc. — *adj* **pyroxenic** (*-sen'ik*). — *n* **pyrox'enite** (*-ən-īt* or *-ēn'īt*) a rock compound essentially of pyroxene. — *n* **pyroxyle** (*-rok'sil*) same as **pyroxylin**. — *adj* **pyroxylic** (*-sil'ik*; *obs*) pyroligneous. — *n* **pyroxylin** or **pyroxyline** (*-rok'si-lin*; Gr *xylon* wood) any of the nitrocelluloses. [Gr *pȳr* fire]

pyroballogy.. to ... **pyrokinesis**. See under **pyro-**.

Pyrola *pir'ə-lə*, *n* the wintergreen genus, giving name to the family **Pyrolā'ceae**, related to the heaths. [Dimin of *pyrus*, a misspelling of L *pirus* a pear-tree]

pyrolater... to ... **pyromorphite**. See under **pyro-**.

pyrope *pī'rōp*, *n* a fiery red gemstone (also *poetic* **pyrō'pus**); a red magnesia-alumina garnet, used in jewellery (*mineralogy*). [Gr *pyrōpos* fiery-eyed, from *pȳr* fire, and *ōps*, *ōpos* eye, face]

pyrophobia... to ... **pyroxyline**. See under **pyro-**.

pyrrhic *pir'ik*, *n* an ancient Greek war-dance; a foot of two short syllables (*prosody*). — *adj* pertaining to the dance or to the foot. — *n* **pyrrhicist** (*pir'i-sist*; *hist*) a pyrrhic dancer. [Gr *pyrrichē* (*orchēsis*) pyrrhic dance, said to be from *Pyrrichos*, the inventor]

Pyrrhic *pir'ik*, *adj* of or pertaining to *Pyrrhus*, king of Epirus (318–272 BC). — **Pyrrhic victory** a victory gained at too great a cost, in allusion to Pyrrhus's exclamation after his defeat of the Romans at Heraclea on the Siris (280), 'Another such victory and we are lost'.

Pyrrhonism *pir'ən-izm*, *n* the complete scepticism of *Pyrrhō* (Gr *Pyrrōn*) of Elis (3c BC). — *adj* and *n* **Pyrrhonian** (*pir-ō'ni-ən*). — *adj* **Pyrrhonic** (*-on'ik*). — *n* **Pyrrh'onist**.

pyrrhotite *pir'ō-tīt*, *n* magnetic pyrites, an iron sulphide, often containing nickel. — Also **pyrrh'otine** (*-tēn*). [Gr *pyrrotēs* redness, from *pȳr* fire]

pyrrhous *pir'əs*, *adj* reddish. [Gr *pyrros* flame-coloured, from *pȳr* fire]

pyrrole *pi'rōl*, (*chem*) *n* a colourless toxic liquid found in many naturally-occurring compounds, eg porphyrins and chlorophyll. — *n* **pyrrolidine** (*pi-rol'i-dēn*) a colourless strongly alkaline base, C_4H_9N, both occurring naturally and produced from pyrrole. [Gr *pyrros* flame-coloured, and L *oleum* oil]

Pyrus *pī'rəs*, *n* the pear and apple genus of the rose family. [Misspelling of L *pirus* pear-tree]

pyruvate *pī-rōō'vāt*, (*chem*) *n* a salt or ester of pyruvic acid. — **pyruvic acid** (*-rōō'vik*) an organic acid, an intermediate in the metabolism of proteins and carbohydrates. [Gr *pȳr* fire, and L *ūva* grape]

Pythagorean *pī-thag-ər-ē'ən* or *pi-thag-ər-ē'ən, adj* pertaining to the Greek philosopher *Pythagoras* of Samos (6c BC), or to his philosophy; transformed, as if by transmigration of the soul (a doctrine taught by Pythagoras); vegetarian; of a diatonic scale perfected by Pythagoras, with its intervals based on mathematical ratios (*music*). — *n* a follower of Pythagoras. — *n* **Pythagorē'anism** or **Pythag'orism** the doctrines of Pythagoras. — **Pythagorean letter** or **Samian letter** the Greek letter *Y* which was, for Pythagoras, a symbol of the parting of the ways for vice and virtue; **Pythagorean theorem** or **theorem of Pythagoras** the theorem that the square on the hypotenuse of a right-angled triangle is equal to the sum of the squares on the other two sides.

Pythia *pith'i-ə,* (*hist*) *n* the priestess who delivered the oracles of Pythian Apollo at Delphi. — *adj* **Pyth'ian** of Delphi, the oracle there, the priestess, or the games held nearby. — *n* a native or inhabitant of Delphi; the priestess of Apollo there; Apollo. — *adj* **Pyth'ic** Pythian; ecstatic. — **Pythian games** one of the four national festivals of ancient Greece, in honour of Apollo, held every four years at Delphi; **Pythian verse** (*prosody*) the dactylic hexameter. [Gr *Pȳthō*, the former name of Delphi; see **python**]

pythium *pith'i-əm, n* a fungus of the genus *Pythium*, a cause of damping-off of seedlings. [Gr *pȳthein* to cause to rot]

pythogenic *pī-thō-jen'ik, adj* produced by filth. [Gr *pȳthein* to rot, and **-genic**]

python *pī'thən, n* a large snake that crushes its victims, *esp* and properly, one of the Old World genus *Python*, related to the boas; (with *cap*) the great snake killed by Apollo at Pȳthō (Delphi), the name coming, according to legend, from *pȳthein* to rot, because it rotted (*Gr mythol*); a familiar or possessing spirit; someone possessed by a spirit; someone who utters oracles. — *n* **Py'thoness** the priestess of the oracle of Apollo at Delphi; (without *cap*) a witch. — *adj* **pythonic** (*-thon'ik*). — *n* and *adj* **python'omorph** (*-ō-mörf*; see **-morph**) (a member) of the **Pythonomorp'ha**, in some classifications an extinct suborder of *Squamata*, large marine reptiles of the Cretaceous period, with long, scaly bodies and paddle-shaped limbs.

Pythonesque *pī-thən-esk', adj* (of humour) bizarre and surreal, as in the BBC television comedy programme *Monty Python's Flying Circus*.

pyuria *pī-ū'ri-ə,* (*med*) *n* the presence of pus in the urine. [Gr *pyon* pus, and *ouron* urine]

pyx *piks, n* a box; a vessel in which the host is kept after consecration, now *usu* that in which it is carried to the sick (*RC*); a box at the Mint in which sample coins are kept for testing. — *vt* to test the weight and fineness of eg the coins deposited in the pyx. — *n* **pyxid'ium** (*bot*) a capsule that opens by a transverse circular split: — *pl* **pyxid'ia**. — *n* **pyx'is** a little box or casket for jewels, drugs, toilet materials, etc: — *pl* **pyx'ides** (*-id-ēz*). — **trial of the pyx** trial by weight and assay of gold and silver coins by a jury of goldsmiths; the periodic official testing of sterling coinage. [L *pyxis* a box, from Gr *pyxis, -idos*, and dimin *pyxidion*, from *pyxos* box-tree]

pzazz. Same as **pizzazz**.

Q

Q or **q** *kū*, *n* the seventeenth letter of the modern English alphabet, derived from the abandoned Greek letter koppa (qv), and representing in English the same sound as k; in English normally followed by *u* (*qu* being pronounced *kw*, or in words from or modelled on French, Spanish, etc sometimes *k*), but sometimes without following *u* in transliteration of the related Semitic letter qōph (pronounced *kōf*) as in *qadi* (more *usu cadi* or *kadi*); Old English used the spelling *cw* instead of *qu*, and medieval Scots had the spelling *quh* for the sound *hw* (*Eng* spelling *wh*). — **Q-Celt**, **Q-Kelt**, etc see under **Celt**. [L *cū*]

Q *kū*, (*US*) *n* trichosanthin, a drug used in the treatment of AIDS. — Also **compound Q**. [Perh because it is an extract from a Chinese *cu*cumber root]

Q or **Q**. *abbrev*: quality; Quebec (also **Que**.); queen (*cards* and *chess*); Queensland (also **Qld**); query; question; quetzal (Guatemalan currency); a measure of the efficiency of an electrical component as a ratio between stored energy and energy loss (also **Q factor**). — **Q'-boat** or **Q'-ship** a merchant vessel manned by Navy personnel and with concealed guns, used to deceive and destroy submarines; **Q'-fever** an acute disease characterized by fever and muscular pains, transmitted by the rickettsia *Coxiella burnetii*; **Q'-sort** a psychological test designed to discover subjects' personality types by having them rank traits in the order most appropriate to their own personalities; **Q'-train** a special train carrying railway police and with closed-circuit TV, used to deal with railway vandals and trespassers (named after **Q-boat** above).

Q *symbol*: as a medieval numeral, 500; a unit of heat energy equal to 10^{18} British thermal units (*US*). — **Q̄** as a medieval numeral, 500 000.

Q symbol: electric charge (*phys*); quality or quality-value.

Q_{10} (*biol*). See **temperature coefficient**.

q or **q**. *abbrev*: quart; quarter; query; quintal.

QA *abbrev*: quality assurance.

qa-, **qe-**, **qi-**, **qo-**, **qu-**. Arabic and Hebrew words spelt this way are in most cases given at **k-** or **c-**.

qabalah. See **cabbala**.

Qaddish, **qadi**, **qaimaqam**, **qalamdan**. Same as **Kaddish**, **cadi**, **kaimakam**, **kalamdan**.

Qajar *ka-jär'*, *n* the dynasty that united and ruled Iran from 1779 to 1925. — *adj* of the dynasty, its time, *esp* its art, porcelain, etc.

qalamdan. Same as **kalamdan**.

QALY *abbrev*: quality-adjusted life year, a cost-benefit unit used to assess different surgical operations and medical treatments in terms of the length and quality of life they produce, measured against their cost.

qanat *kä-nät'*, *n* an underground tunnel for carrying irrigation water. [Ar *qanāt* pipe]

Q & A *abbrev*: question and answer.

QANTAS *kwon'təs*, *abbrev*: Queensland and Northern Territory Aerial Service (the Australian international airline).

QARANC *abbrev*: Queen Alexandra's Royal Army Nursing Corps.

QARNNS *abbrev*: Queen Alexandra's Royal Naval Nursing Service.

qasida *ka-sē'də*, *n* a formal Arabic poem of praise or mourning. [Ar]

qat. See **kat**[1].

QB *abbrev*: Queen's Bench.

QC *abbrev*: Queen's College; Queen's Counsel.

QCD *abbrev*: quantum chromodynamics.

QE2 *abbrev*: Queen Elizabeth the Second (the liner).

QED *abbrev*: quantum electrodynamics; *quod erat demonstrandum* (*L*), which was to be demonstrated (or proved; also **q.e.d.**).

QEF *abbrev*: *quod erat faciendum* (*L*), which was to be done.

QEH *abbrev*: Queen Elizabeth Hall (on London's South Bank).

QEI *abbrev*: *quod erat inveniendum* (*L*), which was to be found.

qi, **chi** or **ch'i** *chē*, (*Chin med*) *n* an individual person's life-force, the free flow of which within the body is believed to ensure physical and spiritual health. — *n* **qigong** or **qi gong** (*chē-gōōng*; Chin *gong* skill, exercise) a system of meditational exercises for promoting physical and spiritual health by deep breathing. [Chin *qì* breath, energy]

qibla. Same as **kiblah**.

qid *abbrev*: (in prescriptions) *quater in die* (*L*), four times a day.

qigong. See under **qi**.

qinghaosu *ching-how-sōō'*, *n* a crystalline compound extracted from the artemisia plant, used *esp* to treat malaria (also called **artemisinin**). [Chin, from *qing hao* artemisia]

qintar *kin-tär'*, *n* an Albanian unit of currency equal to one hundredth of a lek. [Albanian]

qiviut *kiv'i-ət*, *n* the wool of the undercoat of the arctic musk-ox. [Imit]

QL (*comput*) *abbrev*: query language.

ql *abbrev*: (in prescriptions) *quantum libet* (*L*), as much as you please; quintal.

Qld *abbrev*: Queensland (Australian state).

QM *abbrev*: Quartermaster.

QMG *abbrev*: Quartermaster-General.

QMS *abbrev*: Quartermaster-Sergeant.

qoph. Same as **koph**.

Qoran. Same as **Koran**.

QPM *abbrev*: Queen's Police Medal.

QPR *abbrev*: Queen's Park Rangers (Football Club).

qq *abbrev*: quartos.

qqv or **qq.v.** *abbrev*: *quae vide* (*L*), which (*pl*) see (*sing* **qv**).

qr *abbrev*: quarter.

qs *abbrev*: (in prescriptions) *quantum sufficit* (*L*), a sufficient quantity.

QSM *abbrev*: Queen's Service Medal (*NZ*).

QSO *abbrev*: quasi-stellar object (quasar); Queen's Service Order (*NZ*).

QT. See **quiet**.

qt *abbrev*: quantity; quart.

q.t. See **quiet**.

qto *abbrev*: quarto.

QTS *abbrev*: Qualified Teacher Status.

qty *abbrev*: quantity.

Qu. *abbrev*: Queen; question.

qu. or **quar.** *abbrev*: quart; quarter; quarterly.

qua *kwā* or *kwä*, *adv* in the capacity of. [L *quā*, adverbial ablative fem of *quī* who]

Quaalude® *kwā'lōōd* or *-lūd*, also *kwä'*, (*US*) *n* proprietary name for the drug methaqualone.

quack[1] *kwak*, *n* the cry of a duck. — *vi* to utter (a sound like) a quack. — *n* **quack'er**. — *vi* **quack'le** (*dialect*) to quack. [Imit]

quack[2] *kwak*, *n* someone who claims, and practises under the pretence of having, knowledge and skill (*esp* in medicine) that he or she does not possess; a doctor (*slang*); a charlatan. — Also *adj*. — *vi* to behave like a quack. — *vt* to advertise, sell or treat in the manner of a quack. — *n* **quack'ery** the pretensions or practice of a quack, *esp* in medicine. — **quack'salver** (*archaic*) a quack. — *adj* (*obs*) **quack'salving**. [Du *quacksalver* (now *kwakzalver*) perh someone who quacks about their salves (remedies)]

quad[1] *kwod*, *n* short form of **Quaalude**® (*US*; *colloq*), **quadrangle**, **quadraphonics**, **quadraphony**, **quadrat**, **quadrillion** (ie 10^{15}), **quadruped** (ie horse), **quadruplet**. — *adj* short form of **quadraphonic**, **quadruple**. — *vt* to fill with quadrats.

quad[2] or **Quad** *kwod*, *n* a small, powerful four-wheel drive vehicle, used eg in military, agricultural and sporting activities. [**quadruple**]

quad[3]. Same as **quod**[2].

quadr-. See **quadri-**.

quadragenarian *kwod-rə-ji-nā'ri-ən*, *n* a person who is forty years old, or between forty and fifty. — Also *adj*. [L *quadrāgēnārius*, from *quadrāgēnī* forty each]

Quadragesima *kwod-rə-jes'i-mə*, *n* the first Sunday in Lent; the forty days of Lent (*obs*). — *adj* **quadrages'imal** of Lent; lasting forty days. [L *quadrāgēsimus*, *-a*, *-um* fortieth, from *quadrāgintā* forty, from *quattuor* four]

quadrangle *kwod-rang'gl* or *kwod'*, *n* a plane figure with four angles (and therefore four sides); an object or space of that form; a court or open space, *usu* rectangular, enclosed by a building (such as a college); a block of buildings containing a quadrangle. — *adj* **quadrang'ular** (*-gū-lər*). — *adv* **quadrang'ularly**. — **complete quadrangle** a figure composed of four points joined by six straight lines or sides. [Fr, from L *quadrangulum*, from *quattuor* four, and *angulus* an angle]

quadrans *kwod'ranz* or *kwad'räns*, (*antiq*) *n* a Roman copper coin, the fourth part of an as: — *pl* **quadran'tēs**. [L]

quadrant *kwod'rənt*, *n* the fourth part of a circle or its circumference, a sector or an arc of 90° (also *adj*); an area, object or street of that form; an instrument with an arc of 90° for taking altitudes; one of the four segments or areas into which something is divided. — *adj* **quadrantal** (*-rant'l*). [L *quadrans*, *-antis* a fourth part, from *quattuor* four]

quadraphonics or **quadrophonics** *kwod-rə-fon'iks* or *-ro-*, *n sing* a system of sound transmission using a minimum of four speakers fed by four, or sometimes three, separate channels. — Also **quadrophony** (*-rof'*) or **quadraph'ony**. — *adj* **quadraphon'ic** or **quadrophon'ic**.

quadraplegia, **-plegic**. Erroneous forms of **quadriplegia**, **-plegic**.

quadrat *kwod'rət*, *n* (*printing*) a piece of type-metal less high than the letters, used in spacing between words and filling out blank lines (commonly called a **quad**), distinguished as *en* (▮), *em* (■), *two-em* (■ ■), and *three-em* (■ ■ ■); a small area (*usu* one square metre) of ground marked off for the detailed investigation of animal and plant life (*ecol*). — *adj* **quad'rate** (*-rāt* or *-rit*) square; rectangular; squarish; squared; square, as a power or root (*obs math*); complete (*obs*); conformable (*obs*). — *n* a square or quadrate figure or object; the quadrate bone, suspending the lower jaw in vertebrates other than mammals; quartile (*obs astron*) — *vt* and *vi* to square; to conform — *adj* **quadratic** (*-rat'ik*) of or like a quadrate; involving the square but no higher power, as a *quadratic equation* (*algebra*); tetragonal (*crystallog*). — *n* a quadratic equation; (in *pl*) the branch of algebra dealing with quadratic equations. — *adj* **quadrat'ical**. — *n* **quadrā'trix** a curve by which a curved figure (such as a circle) may be squared. — *n* **quad'rature** (*-rə-chər*) squaring; the finding of a square with an area equal to a given figure (*math*); an angular distance of 90°; the position of a heavenly body at such an angular distance from another body, or the time of its being there; a phase angle of 90° within a cycle (*electronics*); squareness (*obs*); a square space (*Milton*). — *n* **quadrā'tus** the name of several quadrangular muscles. — **B quadrā'tum** quadrate B (see under **B**); **quadrature of the circle** see under **square**. [L *quadrātus*, pa p of *quadrāre* to square, from *quattuor* four]

quadratura *kwod-rə-tōōr'ə*, (*art*) *n* a work having a trompe l'œil effect, eg a wall or ceiling painted with arches, colonnades, etc in strong perspective: — *pl* **quadratur'e** (*-re*). [Ital]

quadrella *kwod-rel'ə*, (*Austr*) *n* a group of four (*esp* the last four) horse races at a meeting, for which the punter selects the four winners. [L *quadr-* four, and *-ella*, dimin suffix]

quadrennium *kwod-ren'i-əm* or **quadriennium**, etc *-ri-en'*, *n* (a period of) four years: — *pl* **quadrenn'ia**. — *adj* **quadrenn'ial** lasting four years; once in four years. — *n* a quadrennial event. — *adv* **quadrenn'ially**. — The forms **quadrienn'ium**, etc are etymologically correct but now less usual. [**quadri-** and L *annus* year]

quadri- *kwod-ri-* or sometimes before a vowel **quadr-** *kwod-r*, *combining form* denoting: four; square. — *adj* **quad'ric** (*math*) of the second degree. — *n* a curve, etc of the second degree. — *adj* **quadricentennial** (*kwod-ri-sen-ten'i-əl*; modelled on **centennial**) lasting four hundred years; once in four hundred years. — *n* a four-hundredth anniversary. — *n* **quadricone** (*kwod'ri-kōn*) a quadric cone, or cone having a conic as base. — *adj* **quadriennial**, etc see **quadrennium**. — *adj* **quadrifarious** (*kwod-ri-fā'ri-əs*; L *quadrifārius*, *poss* from *fāri* to speak) fourfold; in four rows. — *adj* **quadrifid** (*kwod'ri-fid*; L, from the root of *findere* to cleave; *bot*) cleft in four. — *adj* **quadrifoliate** (*kwod-ri-fō'li-āt*; L *folium* a leaf) four-leaved. — *adj* **quadriform** (*kwod'ri-fōrm*; L *fōrma* form) fourfold; having four forms or aspects. — *n* **quadriga** (*kwod-rī'gə* or *kwad-rē'ga*; L, a later singular from *quadrīgae* a team of four, for *quadrijugae*, from *jugum* yoke) in Greek and Roman times a two-wheeled chariot drawn by four horses abreast: — *pl* **quadrī'gae** (*-jē* or *-gī*). — *adj* **quadrigeminal** (*kwod-ri-jem'i-nl*; L *geminī* twins) having four similar parts. — Also **quadrigem'inate** and **quadrigem'inous**. — *adj* and *n* **quadrilateral** see separate entry. — *adj* **quadrilingual** (*-ling'gwəl*; L *lingua* tongue) using four languages. — *adj* **quadriliteral** (*kwod-ri-lit'ər-əl*; L *lītera* a letter) consisting of four letters. — *n* a word or a root of four letters. — *n* **quadrillion**, etc see separate entry. — *adj* **quadrilocular** (*kwod-ri-lok'ū-lər*; L *loculus*, *dimin* of *locus* place) having four compartments. — *n* **quadringenary** (*kwod-rin-jē'nər-i*; L *quadringēnārius* of four hundred each) a four-hundredth anniversary or its celebration. — *adj* **quadrinomial** (*kwod-ri-nō'mi-əl*; modelled on **binomial**; *algebra*) consisting of four terms. — *n* an expression of four terms. — **quadripartite**, **quadriplegia**, etc see separate entries. — *n* **quadrireme** (*kwod'ri-rēm*; L *rēmus* an oar) an ancient ship with four sets of oars. — *vt* **quad'risect** to divide into four, *usu* equal, parts. — *n* **quadrisection** (*kwod-ri-sek'shən*; L *sectiō*, *-onis* cutting) division into four equal parts. — *adj* **quadrisyllab'ic**. — *n* **quadrisyllable** (*kwod-ri-sil'ə-bl*) a tetrasyllable. — *n* **quadriv'alence** (or *-vā'*). — *adj* **quadrivalent** (*kwod-riv'ə-lənt* or *-vā'lənt*) having a valency of four. — *n* the structure formed by the pairing of four homologous chromosomes during meiosis in tetraploid organisms. — *n* **quadrivium** (*kwod-riv'i-əm*; *L*, the place where four roads meet, from *via* a way) in medieval education, the four branches of mathematics (arithmetic, geometry, astronomy, music). — *adj* **quadriv'ial**. [L *quadri-*, from *quattuor* four]

quadriceps *kwod'ri-seps*, (*anatom*) *n* the large thigh muscle that extends the leg. — *adj* **quadricipital** (*-sip'i-tl*). [Modelled on **biceps** with **quadri-** as prefix]

quadrilateral *kwod-ri-lat'ər-l*, *adj* four-sided. — *n* a plane figure bounded by four straight lines (*geom*); a group of four fortresses, *esp* Mantua, Verona, Peschiera and Legnaga. — **complete quadrilateral** a figure consisting of four straight lines intersecting in six points or vertices. [**quadri-** and L *latus*, *lateris* side]

quadriliteral . . . **quadrivium**. See under **quadri-**.

quadrille[1] *kwə-dril'* or *kə-*, *n* a square dance for four couples or more, in five movements; music for such a dance; one of four groups of horsemen (*obs*). — *vi* to dance quadrilles. — *n* **quadrill'er**. [Fr, from Sp *cuadrilla* a troop, appar from *cuadra*, from L *quadra* a square]

quadrille[2] *kwə-dril'* or *kə-*, *n* a four-handed game with 40 cards, similar to ombre. — *vi* to play quadrille. [Fr, perh from Sp *cuatrillo* the game of quadrille, or *cuartillo* fourth part]

quadrillion *kwod-* or *kwəd-ril'yən*, *n* in UK, France and Germany, a million raised to the fourth power, written as 10^{24}, or one and 24 zeros; in N America and increasingly in UK, a thousand to the fifth power, written as 10^{15}, or one and 15 zeros. — *n* and *adj* **quadrill'ionth**. [Modelled on **million**, with **quadri-** as prefix]

quadripartite *kwod-ri-pär'tīt*, *adj* in four parts; having four participants; (of eg a leaf) deeply cleft into four parts (*bot*); (of eg a vault) divided into four compartments (*archit*). — *n* **quadriparti'tion**. [**quadri-** and L *partīrī, -ītum* to divide]

quadriplegia *kwod-ri-plēj'(i)ə* or *-plēj'yə*, (*med*) *n* paralysis of both arms and both legs. — *n* and *adj* **quadripleg'ic**. [**quadri-** and Gr *plēgē* a blow]

quadripole *kwod'-ri-pōl*, (*electron*) *n* a network with two input and two output terminals. [Fr *quadripôle*, from **quadri-** and **pole**[1]]

quadroon *kwod-rōōn'*, *n* a person of one-quarter Negro descent; extended to refer to any person or animal of similarly mixed ancestry. — Also **quarteroon'**. [Sp *cuarterón*, from *cuarto* a fourth]

quadrophonic(s), **quadrophony**. See **quadraphonics**.

quadru- *kwod-rōō-*, a variant of **quadri-**. — *adj* **quadrumanous** (*kwod-rōō'mən-əs*; L *manus* a hand) belonging to the **Quadru'mana**, a former name for the primates other than man, which have all four feet with an opposable digit. — *n* **quadru'man** (*-man*) or **quadrumane** (*-mān*). — *n* **quadrumvir** (*kwod-rum'vər*; L *vir* a man) a member of a **quadrum'virate**, a group of four men acting together in some capacity.

quadruped *kwod'rōō-ped*, *n* a four-footed animal, *usu* a mammal, *esp* a horse. — *adj* four-footed. — *adj* **quadrupedal** (*-rōō'pi-dəl*). [**quadru-**, and L *pēs, pedis* a foot]

quadruple *kwod'rōō-pl* or (*esp Scot*) *-rōō'*, *adj* fourfold; having four parts, members or divisions. — *n* four times as much; a coin worth four pistoles (*hist*). — *vt* to increase fourfold, multiply by four; to equal four times. — *vi* to become four times as much. — *n* **quad'ruplet** (or *-rōō'*) any combination of four things; one of four (children or animals) born at one birth (*colloq*; *usu abbrev* **quad**); a group of four notes performed in the time of three (*music*); a cycle for four riders. — *adv* **quad'ruply** (*-pli* or *-rōō'pli*) in a fourfold manner. — **Quadruple Alliance** a league formed in 1718 by Britain, France, Austria and Holland against Spain; **quadruple time** (*music*) a time with four beats to the bar. [Fr, from L *quadruplus*, from the root of *plēre* to fill]

quadruplex *kwod'rōō-pleks*, *adj* fourfold; (of a Morse telegraphic system) capable of sending four messages at once, two each way, over one wire. — *n* an instrument of this kind; a videotape recording and reproduction system using four rotating heads to produce transverse tracks on magnetic tape. — *vt* to make quadruplex. — *adj* **quadru'plicate** fourfold. — *n* one of four corresponding things; fourfoldness. — *vt* to make fourfold. — *n* **quadruplicā'tion**. — *n* **quadruplicity** (*-plis'i-ti*). — *n* **quad'ruply** (*-plī*; *Scots law*) a reply to a triply. [L *quadruplex, -icis* fourfold, from *plicāre, -ātum* to fold]

quaere *kwē'rē* or *kwī're*, *v imperative* inquire (suggesting doubt, or desirability of investigation). — *n* a query, question. — See also **query**. — *v impers* **quaeritur** (*kwē-rī'tər* or *kwī'ri-tōōr*) the question is asked. — *n* **quaesitum** (*kwē-sī'təm* or *kwī-sē'tōōm*) something sought for; the true value. [L *quaerere, quaesītum* to inquire]

quaestionary *kwēs'tyən-ə-ri*, (*Scott*) *n* a pardoner. [Med L *questiōnārius*]

quaestor *kwēs'tör, -tər* or *kwīs'tor*, *n* an ancient Roman magistrate, in early times an investigator, prosecutor or judge in murder cases, later a treasurer with various other functions; in the Middle Ages (*usu* **ques'tor**) a church official who granted indulgences, a pardoner; a treasurer. — *adj* **quaestorial** (*-tō'ri-əl* or *-tö'*). — *n* **quaes'torship**. — *adj* **quaes'tūary** money-making; gain-seeking. — *n* a gain-seeker; a pardoner. [L *quaestor, -ōris*, from *quaerere, quaesītum* to seek]

quae vide. See **quod**[1].

quaff[1] *kwäf* or *kwof*, *vt* to drink or drain in large draughts. — *vi* to drink deeply or eagerly. — *n* a draught. — *n* **quaff'er**. [Origin obscure]

quaff[2] *kwäf*. An *obs* variant of **quaich**.

quag *kwag* or *kwog*, *n* a boggy place, *esp* one that moves or quivers underfoot. — *n* **quagg'iness**. — *adj* **quagg'y**. [Cf **quake**]

quagga *kwag'ə*, *n* an extinct S African wild ass (*Equus quagga*), less fully striped than the zebras, to which it was related. [Perh Hottentot *quacha*]

quagmire *kwag'mīr* or *kwog'*, *n* wet, boggy ground that yields, moves or quivers under the feet; a difficult, problematic situation. — *vt* to entangle, as in a quagmire. — *adj* **quag'miry**. [Appar **quag** and **mire**]

quahog *kwö'hog* or *kwə-hog'* or **quahaug** *-hög* or *-hög'*, *n* an edible clam (*Venus mercenaria*) of the N American Atlantic coast, also known as round clam; another variety of clam, *Cyprina islandica*, also known as *black quahog*. — Also **cohog**. [Narraganset Ind *poquauhock*]

quaich or **quaigh** *kwāhh*, (*Scot*) *n* a shallow drinking-cup, *orig* of staves and hoops, now *usu* of silver or pewter. [Gaelic *cuach* a cup]

Quai d'Orsay *kā dör-sā*, *n* the French Foreign Office. [Name of a quay on the Seine where it is situated]

quail[1] *kwāl*, *vi* to flinch; to fail in spirit; to slacken (*Shakesp*); to languish, decline (*archaic*). — *vt* (*obs*) to subdue; to daunt. — *n* **quail'ing** (*Shakesp*). [ME *quayle*; origin obscure]

quail[2] *kwāl*, *n* a genus (*Coturnix*) of small birds of the partridge family; in N America extended to various small game-birds, such as the California quail (*Lophortyx*) and the bobwhite; a whore (*Shakesp*). — **quail'-pipe** a whistle for luring quails into a net (also **quail'-call**); the throat (*obs*). [OFr *quaille*; prob Gmc]

quaint *kwānt*, *adj* pleasantly odd; whimsical; charmingly old-fashioned; skilful, *esp* in use of language (*Shakesp*); cunning (*obs*); ingenious (*obs*); fine (*Spenser* and *Milton*); affectedly fanciful or elaborate (*obs*); affectedly fastidious or prim (*Spenser*). — *adv* **quaint'ly**. — *n* **quaint'ness**. [OFr *cointe*, from L *cognitus* known; perh confused with *comptus* neat]

quair. *Obs* variant of **quire**[1].

quake *kwāk*, *vi* to quiver or vibrate; to tremble, *esp* with cold or fear. — *vt* to cause to tremble (*Shakesp*); to cause to vibrate. — *n* a tremor; an earthquake; a shudder. — *n* **quā'ker**. — *n* **quā'kiness**. — *n* **quā'king**. — *adv* **quā'kingly**. — *adj* **quā'ky** shaky. — **quaking ash** the aspen; **quā'king-grass** a moorland grass of the genus *Briza*, with pendulous, panicled, tremulous spikelets. [OE *cwacian*; perh related to *quick*]

Quaker *kwā'kər*, *n* one of the Religious Society of Friends, founded by George Fox (1624–91); a dummy cannon (also called **Quaker gun**). — *adj* of Quakers; of Philadelphia ('the Quaker city', because founded by William Penn, Quaker) (*US*). — *n* **Quā'kerdom**. — *n* **Quā'keress**. — *adj* **Quā'kerish** or **Quā'kerly** like a Quaker. — *n* **Quā'kerism**. — **Quā'ker-bird** the sooty albatross; **Quā'ker-buttons** the round seeds of nux vomica; **Quā'ker-colour** drab. [Nickname (not adopted by themselves, and earlier applied to another sect) given them by Justice Bennet at Derby, because Fox told them to *quake* at the word of the Lord]

quale *kwā'li* or *kwä'li* or *-lā*, (*logic*) *n* a quality or property of something: — *pl* **qua'lia** (*-li-ə*). [L, neuter of adj *qualis* of what kind]

qualify *kwol'i-fī*, *vt* to ascribe a quality to; to characterize; to add a quality to the connotation of (a word) (*gram*); to render capable or suitable; to provide with legal power; to limit by modifications; to moderate, mitigate; to appease; to abate, reduce the strength of; to vary; to prove, confirm (*Scots law*). — *vi* to take the necessary steps to fit oneself for a certain position, activity or practice; to fulfil a requirement; to have the necessary qualities or qualifications; to be eligible (for a final round, etc) after successfully completing one or more qualifying rounds: — *pr p* **qual'ifying**; *pa p* and *pa t* **qual'ified**. — *adj* **qual'ifiable** (*-fī-ə-bl*). — *n* **qualification** (*-fi-kā'shən*) qualifying; distinctive quality; modification; restriction; that which qualifies; a quality that fits a person for a task, etc; a necessary condition; an accomplishment (*obs*); the attaching of quality to, or the distinction of affirmative and negative in, a term (*logic*). — *adj* and *n* **qual'ificātive**. — *n* **qual'ificātor** (*RC*) a person who examines and prepares ecclesiastical causes for trial. — *adj* **qual'ificātory**. — *adj* **qual'ified** (*-fīd*) fitted, competent, having the necessary qualification; modified; limited. — *adv* **qual'ifiedly** (*-fīd-li*). — *n* **qual'ifier** (*-fī-ər*). — *n* and *adj* **qual'ifying**. — **qualification test** the evaluation of an article to be used in space flight to verify that it functions correctly under the conditions occurring during flight; **qualifying round** a preliminary round in a competition, to limit the number of competitors. — **qualified majority voting** a system of majority voting, without veto, used in the EC Council of Ministers, in which each vote is weighted according to the size of the country; **Qualified Teacher Status** accredited status (awarded by the Department of Education and Science) required by any school teacher wishing to teach in England and Wales. [Fr *qualifier* or LL *quālificāre*, from L *quālis* of what sort, and *facere* to make]

qualis ab incepto *kwā'lis ab in-sep'tō* or *kwä'lis ab in-kep'tō*, (*L*) as from the beginning.

quality *kwol'i-ti*, *n* that which makes a thing what it is; nature; character; kind; property; attribute; social status; high social status; persons of the upper class collectively; grade of goodness; excellence; profession, *esp* (*Shakesp*) the actor's profession; manner (*Shakesp*); skill, accomplishment; timbre, that characteristic of a sound that depends on the overtones present, distinguished from loudness and pitch (*acoustics*); the character of a vowel that depends on the position of the mouth and tongue when it is uttered (*phonetics*); the character of a proposition as affirmative or negative (*logic*); approximate penetrating power (*radiography*); (*usu* in *pl*) a quality newspaper. — *adj* of a high grade of excellence; (of newspapers, etc) of a high standard of journalism. — *adj* **qual'itātive** relating to, or concerned with, quality (*esp* opposed to *quantitative*). — *adv* **qual'itātively**. — *adj* **qual'itied** endowed with a quality or qualities. — **qualitative analysis** (*chem*) identification of the constituents of a sample without regard to their relative amounts (cf **quantitative analysis** under **quantity**); **quality control** the inspection, testing, etc of samples of a product, *esp* at various stages of production, to ensure maintenance of high standards; **quality time** time during which one is not distracted but devotes one's full attention to one's companion, child, etc. — **quality of life** non-material standard of living measured by environmental and cultural amenities, etc; **total quality** a work ethos according to which continuous efforts are made to perform all aspects of one's work better (also *adj*). [OFr *qualité*, from L *quālitās*, *-tātis*, from *quālis* of what kind]

qualm *kwäm* or *kwöm*, *n* a sudden feeling of faintness or sickness; a sickly feeling; an uneasiness, eg of conscience; a misgiving. — *adj* **qualm'ing**. — *adj* **qualm'ish**. — *adv* **qualm'ishly**. — *n* **qualm'ishness**. — *adj* **qualm'less**. — *adj* **qualm'y**. [Perh OE *cwealm* death, murder, torment, pain]

quamash. See **camass**.

quandang. See **quandong**.

quandary *kwon'də-ri* or (formerly) *kwon-dā'ri*, *n* a state of perplexity; a dilemma; a hard plight (*obs*). [Origin obscure]

quand même *kã mem*, (*Fr*) nevertheless, whatever the consequences may be.

quandong *kwan'* or *kwon'dong*, *n* a small Australian tree (*Santalum acuminatum*) of the sandalwood family; its edible drupe (*native peach*) or edible kernel (**quan'dong-nut**); an Australian tree (*Elaeocarpus grandis*) (**silver**, **blue** or **brush quandong**); a disreputable person, *esp* a sponge, parasite (*Austr colloq*) . — Also **quan'dang** or **quan'tong**. [Aboriginal]

quango *kwang'gō*, *n* a board funded by, and with members appointed by, central government, to supervise or develop activity in areas of public interest: — *pl* **quan'gos**. [*qu*asi-*a*utonomous *n*on-*g*overnmental (sometimes *n*ational *g*overnment) *o*rganization]

quannet *kwon'it*, *n* a flat file used like a plane. [Origin unknown]

quant *kwant*, *n* a punting or jumping pole, with a flat end. — *vt* to punt. [Cf **kent**[1]; poss connected with L *contus*, Gr *kontos*]

quanta, **quantal**. See **quantum**.

quantic *kwon'tik*, (*math*) *n* a rational integral homogeneous function of two or more variables. — *adj* **quan'tical**. [L *quantus* how great]

quantify *kwon'ti-fī*, *vt* to fix or express the quantity of; to express as a quantity; to qualify (a term in a proposition) by stating the quantity (*logic*). — *adj* **quan'tifiable**. — *n* **quantification** (*-fi-kā'shən*). — *n* **quan'tifier**. — **quantification of the predicate** (*logic*) the attachment of a sign of quantity to the predicate. [L *quantus* how great, and *facere* to make]

quantise. See under **quantum**.

quantity *kwon'ti-ti*, *n* the amount of anything; bulk; size; a sum; a determinate amount; an amount, portion; a considerable amount or large portion; a fragment, scrap (*Shakesp*); length or shortness of duration of a sound or syllable (*acoustics*); extension (*logic*); the character of a proposition as universal or particular; anything which can be increased, divided or measured; proportion (*Shakesp*). — *adj* **quan'titātive** or **quan'titive** relating to, or concerned with, quantity (*esp* opposed to *qualitative*). — *adv* **quan'titātively** or **quan'titively**. — **quantitative analysis** (*chem*) identification of the relative amounts of substances making up a sample (cf **qualitative analysis**); **quantity discount** (*commerce*) a reduction in the unit price of goods when large quantities are purchased; **quantity surveyor** a person who estimates quantities required, obtains materials, evaluates work done, etc for construction work. — **unknown quantity** a quantity whose mathematical value is not known; a factor, person or thing whose importance or influence cannot be foreseen (*fig*). [OFr *quantité*, from L *quantitās*, *-tātis*, from *quantus* how much]

quantivalence *kwon-tiv'ə-ləns* or *-ti-vā'ləns*, *n* valency. — *adj* **quantiv'alent** (or *-vā'*). [L *quantus* how much, and *valēns*, *-entis*, pr p of *valēre* to be worth]

quantize. See **quantum**.

quantometer or (*US* formerly) **Quantometer**® *kwon-tom'i-tər*, *n* an instrument that shows by spectrographical analysis the percentages of the various elements present in a metallic sample. [L *quantus* how much, and **meter**[1]]

quantong. See **quandong**.

quantum *kwon'təm*, *n* quantity; amount (*esp law*); a naturally fixed minimum amount of some entity which is such that all other amounts of that entity occurring in physical processes in nature are integral multiples of it (*phys*): — *pl* **quan'ta**. — *adj* (loosely) sudden, spectacularly different. — *adj* **quan'tal** of, or pertaining to, a quantum (*phys*); having one of only two possible states or values. — *n* **quantizā'tion** or **-s-**. — *vt* **quan'tize** or **-ise** to express in terms of quanta or in accordance with the quantum theory. — **quantum chromodynamics**

a theory of strong interactions (qv) between elementary particles, including the interaction that binds protons and neutrons to form a nucleus; **quantum efficiency** in a photocell or in photosynthesis, the number of electrons released per photon of incident radiation of specified wavelength (also **quantum yield**); **quantum electrodynamics** a relativistic quantum theory of electromagnetic interactions; **quantum field theory** the overall theory of fundamental particles and their interactions; **quantum jump** or **leap** the sudden transition of an electron, atom, etc from one energy state to another; a sudden spectacular advance, *esp* one which dramatically skips over intermediate stages of understanding or development; **quantum mechanics** a branch of mechanics based on the quantum theory, used in predicting the behaviour of elementary particles; **quantum number** any of a set of integers or half-integers which together describe the state of a particle or system of particles; the **principal quantum number**, for instance, specifies the shell an electron occupies; **quantum theory** Planck's theory of the emission and absorption of energy not continuously but in finite quanta; **quantum yield** see **quantum efficiency**. [L *quantum*, neuter of *quantus* how much]

quantum meruit *kwon'təm mer'ū-it* or *kwan'tŏŏm mer'ŏŏ-it*, (*law*) a fair reward for services rendered where there is no agreed rate of payment, literally (*L*) as much as he or she has earned.

quantum sufficit *kwon'təm suf'is-it* or *kwan'tŏŏm sŏŏ'fik-it*, (*L*) a sufficient quantity.

Quapaw *kwö'pö*, *n* (a member of) a N American Indian people, *orig* from Arkansas, most of whom moved to Oklahoma in the 19c (*pl* **Qua'paws** or **Qua'paw**); the Siouan language of this people. [*Quapaw*, literally people going with the current]

quaquaversal *kwā-kwə-vûr'sl* or *kwä-kwä-*, *adj* dipping outward in all directions from a centre (*geol*); facing or bending all ways. — *adv* **quaquaver'sally**. [L *quāquā* whithersoever, and *vertere*, *versum* to turn]

quarantine[1] *kwor'ən-tēn*, *n* a time (*orig* for a ship forty days) of compulsory isolation or detention to prevent spread of contagion or infection; isolation or detention for such a purpose; the place where the time is spent; any period of enforced isolation; a period of forty days (*obs law*). — *vt* to subject to quarantine. — **quarantine flag** a yellow flag displayed by a ship in quarantine, with a black spot if there is contagious disease on board. [Ital *quarantina*, from *quaranta* forty, from L *quadrāgintā*]

quarantine[2]. See **quarrender**.

quare *kwār*, *adj* dialect variant of **queer**.

quare impedit *kwā'rē im'pə-dit* or *kwä'rā im-ped'it*, (*law*) *n* a writ issued in cases of disputed presentation to a benefice, requiring the defendant to state his or her reasons for hindering the presentation. [L, why does he (or she) hinder?]

quarenden, **quarender**. See **quarrender**.

quark[1] *kwörk* or *kwärk*, (*phys*) *n* a fundamental subatomic particle (currently seen as any of six types: *bottom*, *top*, *up*, *down*, *charmed* and *strange*), not yet observed directly, but suggested as the units out of which all other subatomic particles are formed. [From word coined by James Joyce in *Finnegans Wake*]

quark[2] *kwärk* or *kwörk*, *n* a low-fat, soft cheese made from skim-milk. [Late MHGer *twarc*, *quarc*, or *zwarc*]

quarrel[1] *kwor'əl*, *n* ground of complaint or action; a cause that is fought for; an unfriendly contention or dispute; a breach of friendship; a complaint, charge (*obs*); an objection (*obs*); action at law (*obs*); quarrelsomeness (*Shakesp*); a quarreller (*Shakesp*). — *vi* (often with *with*) to cavil, find fault; to dispute violently; to fall out; to disagree violently. — *vt* to call in question (*obs*); to object to (*obs*); to chide (now *Scot*); to bring or render by quarrelling (*obs*): — *pr p* **quarr'elling**; *pa t* and *pa p* **quarr'elled**. — *n* **quarr'eller**. — *n* and *adj* **quarr'elling**. — *adj* **quarr'ellous** (*Shakesp*) quarrelsome. — *adj* **quarr'elsome** disposed to quarrel. — *adv* **quarr'elsomely**. — *n* **quarr'elsomeness**. — **quarrel with one's bread and butter** to act in a way prejudicial to one's means of subsistence; **take up a quarrel** (*Shakesp*) to settle a dispute. [OFr *querele*, from L *querēla*, from *querī*, *questus* to complain]

quarrel[2] *kwor'əl*, *n* a square-headed arrow as for a crossbow (*Spenser* **quar'le**); a diamond pane of glass; a square tile. — **quarr'el-pane**. [OFr *quarrel* (Fr *carreau*), from LL *quadrellus*, from *quadrus* a square]

quarrender, **quarender** *kwor'ən-dər*, **quarantine** *-ən-tin*, **quarenden** *-dən* or **quarrington** *-ing-tən*, (*SW England*) *n* a kind of early red apple. [Perh cf Fr *quarantain*, appar applied to quick-growing peas and maize]

quarry[1] *kwor'i*, *n* an open excavation for building-stone, slate, etc; any source of building-stone, etc; a great mass of stone or rock (*obs*); a source from which information can be extracted (*fig*). — *vt* to dig from, or as from, a quarry; to cut into or cut away; to extract (information) from a source: — *pr p* **quarr'ying**; *pa t* and *pa p* **quarr'ied**. — *adj* **quarr'iable**. — *n* **quarr'ier** a quarryman. — **quarr'yman** a man who works in a quarry; **quarr'ymaster** the owner of a quarry; **quarr'y-sap** or **quarr'y-water** the water in the pores of unquarried or newly quarried stone. [LL *quareia*, for *quadrāria*, from L *quadrāre* to square]

quarry[2] *kwor'i*, *n* a hunted animal; a bird flown at by a hawk; prey; a victim; a hunter's heap of dead game; a deer's entrails given to the hounds (*obs*); a hawk's reward for a kill (*obs*); a heap of corpses (*Shakesp*); in *Macbeth* I. 2 *perh* slaughter, spoil, but variant reading is **quarrel**. [OFr *cuiree*, *curee*, said to be from *cuir*, from L *corium* a hide]

quarry[3] *kwor'i*, *n* a quarrel of glass; a square paving-tile or slab. — **quarry tile** a square unglazed floor tile. [A form of **quarrel**[2]; or perh from OFr *quarré*, from L *quadrātus* squared]

quart[1] *kwört*, *n* the fourth part of a gallon, or two pints (in UK, 1.14 litre, in US, 0.946 litre in liquid measure, 1.1 litres in dry measure); a vessel containing two pints; as much as will fill it; a quarter, region (*Spenser*); a fourth (*music hist*). — *n* **quartā'tion** the mixing of gold with three parts of silver as a stage towards purification. — **quart'-pot**. [Fr *quart*, *-e*, from L *quārtus*, *-a*, *-um* fourth, from *quattuor* four]

quart[2] or **quarte** *kärt*, *n* a sequence of four cards in piquet, etc; the fourth of eight parrying or attacking positions in fencing (also **carte**). — **quart and tierce** practice between fencers. [Fr *quarte*, from Ital and L *quarta* fourth]

quartan *kwör'tən*, *adj* (of a fever) occurring every third (by inclusive reckoning fourth) day. — *n* quartan malaria. [L *quārtānus* of the fourth]

quarte. See **quart**[2].

quarter *kwör'tər*, *n* a fourth part; a 25-cent piece, 25 cents, quarter of a dollar; the fourth part of an hour, of the year, of the moon's period (or the moon's position at the end of it), of the world, etc; one of the four periods of play into which certain games are divided; the fourth part of a cwt = 28 (or in US 25) lb avoirdupois; 8 bushels (*perh orig* a fourth of a ton of corn); a quarter of a pound, 4oz (*colloq*; also **quarter-pound**); a cardinal point, or any point, of the compass; the region about any point of the compass; a region generally; a town district inhabited by a particular class; an unspecified person or group regarded as a source of information, support, etc; a part of an army, camp, etc (*Shakesp*); (*usu* in *pl*) lodging, *esp* for soldiers; an assigned station or position; terms, relations, treatment, *esp* favourable (*Shakesp*); mercy granted to an antagonist (*perh* from sending to quarters); the part of a ship's side abaft the beam; a limb with adjacent parts of the trunk, *esp* (*hist*) of the dismembered body of an executed person, or of an animal carcass; a haunch of a live animal; each of the two pieces on a boot or shoe from the centre of the heel to the vamp; each side of a horse's hoof; one of the four parts of a quartered shield (*heraldry*); an ordinary occupying one-fourth of the field (*heraldry*); a quartering (*heraldry*). — *vt* to divide into four equal or nearly equal parts; to dismember (the body of a traitor, etc) (*hist*); to divide into parts or compartments; to station, lodge or put in quarters; to bear, place or divide quarterly (*heraldry*); (*esp* of dogs) to range for game, to search thoroughly. — *vi* to be stationed; to lodge; (of a dog) to range for game; to drive a carriage or cart with the wheels between the ruts, or the horse(s) astride a rut; to drive to the side of the road, or from side to side; (of the wind) to blow on to a ship's quarter. — *combining form* **quar'ter-** (denoting adjectivally) one-fourth part (of); (denoting adverbially) to the extent of one-fourth. — *n* **quar'terage** a quarterly payment; quarters, lodging. — *adj* **quar'tered**. — *adj* **quar'tering** (of a ship) sailing nearly before the wind; (of a wind) striking on the quarter of a ship. — *n* assignment of quarters; a series of small upright posts for forming partitions, lathed and plastered only, or boarded also (*archit*); the division of a coat by horizontal and vertical lines (*heraldry*); one of the divisions so formed; the marshalling of coats in these divisions, indicating family alliances; any one of the coats so marshalled. — *adj* **quar'terly** relating to a quarter, *esp* of a year; recurring, or published, once a quarter; divided into or marshalled in quarters (*heraldry*). — *adv* once a quarter; in quarters or quarterings (*heraldry*). — *n* a quarterly periodical. — **quart'erback** (*Am football*) the player between the forwards and the half-backs, who directs the attacking play of the team; **quar'ter-blood** a person of one-quarter American Indian descent. — *adj* **quar'ter-bound** having leather or cloth on the spine only, not the corners. — **quar'ter-boy** or **quar'ter-jack** an automaton that strikes the quarter-hours. — *adj* **quar'ter-bred** (of horses, cattle, etc) having only one-fourth pure blood. — **quar'ter-day** the day on each of the year's quarters on which rent or interest is paid; **quar'terdeck** the part of the deck of a ship abaft the mainmast, used by cabin passengers and by superior officers (and saluted on warships); **quar'ter-decker** (*navy slang*) a stickler for naval etiquette; **quar'ter-evil** or **quarter-ill** black-quarter; **quar'ter-fi'nal** the round before the semi-final in a knockout competition; **quar'ter-gallery** a projecting balcony on a ship's quarter; **quar'ter-guard** a guard of a battalion in camp; **quar'ter-gunner** (*US*) a naval petty-officer, under the gunner, a gunner's mate; **quar'ter-horse** (*US*) a horse that can run a quarter of a mile or so at great speed; **quarter hour** a period of fifteen minutes; a point marking such a period on a clock, etc. — *adv* **quarter-hour'ly**. — **quar'ter-jack** see **quarter-boy**; a quartermaster (*slang*); **quar'terlight** a small triangular window in a car for ventilation; **quar'termaster** an officer who finds quarters for soldiers, and attends to supplies; a petty officer who attends to the helm, signals, etc (*naut*): — *fem* **quar'termistress** (or **quartermaster**); **quartermaster-gen'eral** a staff-officer who deals with transport, marches, quarters, fuel, clothing, etc; **quartermaster-ser'geant** a non-commissioned officer who assists the quartermaster; **quarter-mil'er** an athlete whose speciality is the quarter-mile race; **quar'ter-note** a crotchet (*NAm*); a quarter-tone; **quar'ter-plate** see under **plate**; **quar'ter-rail** a rail stretching from a ship's gangway to its stern. — *adj* **quar'ter-repeating** (of a repeating watch or clock) that strikes the quarter hours. — **quar'ter-road** a road divided into four strips by ruts and horse-track; **quar'ter-round** a moulding whose section is about a quadrant, an ovolo. — *vt* **quar'ter-saw** to saw (timber) from quartered logs, so that the face of the planks is at an angle of at least 45° to the growth rings: — *pa t* and *pa p* **quar'ter-sawed** or **quar'ter-sawn**. — **quar'ter-seal** the seal kept by the director of the Chancery of Scotland, known also as 'the testimonial of the Great Seal'; **quarter section** (*NAm*) an area of land half a mile square, 160 acres; **quar'ter-sessions** a court formerly held quarterly by justices of the peace (superseded in England and Wales in 1972 by crown courts); **quar'terstaff** a long wooden pole with an iron tip, an old weapon of defence; the use of this weapon; **quar'ter-tone** half a semitone; **quar'ter-wind** a wind blowing on a ship's quarter. — **(a) quarter after** or **past** fifteen minutes after (a specified hour); **(a) quarter to** fifteen minutes before the hour; **at close quarters** in very near proximity; hand-to-hand; **keep a quarter** or **a bad quarter** (*obs*) to make a disturbance; **keep good quarter** (*Shakesp*) to keep good watch or good order. [OFr *quarter*, from L *quārtārius* a fourth part, from *quārtus* fourth]

quartern *kwör'tən* or *kwör'tərn*, *n* a quarter, *esp* of various measures, such as a peck, a stone, a pound (weight), a pint or a hundred. — **quar'tern-loaf** a four-pound loaf, made from a quarter of a stone of flour. [Anglo-Fr *quartrun*, OFr *quarteron*, from *quart(e)* fourth part]

quarteroon. See under **quadroon**.

quartet, **quartette** or **quartett** *kwör-tet'*, *n* a set of four; a composition for four voices or instruments; a set of performers or instruments for such compositions. — Also (*Ital*) **quartet'to** (*kwär-tet'tō*; *pl* **quartet'ti** *-tē*). [Ital *quartetto*, dimin of *quarto*, from L *quārtus* fourth]

quartic *kwör'tik*, (*math*) *adj* of the fourth degree. — *n* a function, curve or surface of the fourth degree. [L *quārtus* fourth]

quartier *kär-tē-ā*, (*Fr*) *n* a specified district in a French town or city. — **quartier latin** (*la-tẽ*) the 'Latin quarter' of Paris, on the left bank of the Seine, *orig* inhabited by writers, artists and students.

quartile *kwör'tīl*, *n* an aspect of planets when their longitudes differ by 90° (*astrol*); in frequency-distribution, a value such that a fourth, a half, or three-quarters of the numbers under consideration fall below it. — Also *adj*. — **quartile deviation** (*statistics*) the distance between the values below which the lowest fourth and above which the highest fourth fall. [L *quārtus* fourth]

quarto *kwör'tō*, *adj* (of paper) having the sheet folded into four leaves or eight pages (often written **4to**); (*demy quarto* $8\frac{3}{4} \times 11\frac{1}{4}$in; *medium quarto* $9 \times 11\frac{1}{2}$in; *royal quarto* $10 \times 12\frac{1}{2}$in). — *n* a book consisting of sheets so folded, or of such a size: — *pl* **quar'tos**. — **small quarto** a square octavo; a book having eight leaves to a sheet but the shape of a quarto. [L (*in*) *quārtō* (in) one-fourth]

quartodeciman *kwör-tō-des'i-mən*, *n* an early Christian who celebrated Easter on the 14th of Nisan (the Jewish Passover) without regard to the day of the week. — Also *adj*. [LL *quartodecimānus*, from L *quārtus decimus* fourteenth]

quartz *kwörts*, *n* the commonest rock-forming mineral, composed of silica, occurring in hexagonal crystals (clear and colourless when pure) or crypto-crystalline. — *adj* made or composed of or with quartz. — *adj* **quartzif'erous** quartz-bearing. — *n* **quartz'ite** a metamorphosed sandstone with the grains welded together. — *adj* **quartzitic** (*-it'ik*) of or like quartzite. — *adj* **quartz'ose** of, like or rich in quartz. — *adj* **quartz'y**. — **quartz crystal** a disc or rod cut in certain directions from a piece of piezoelectric quartz and ground so that it vibrates naturally at a particular frequency; **quartz-crystal clock** or **watch** one in which a quartz crystal, energized by a microcircuit, does the work of the pendulum or hairspring of the traditional clock or watch; **quartz glass** fused quartz resistant to high temperatures and transparent to ultraviolet radiation; **quartz lamp**, **quartz-halogen lamp** or **quartz-iodine lamp** a compact source of light used for high-intensity flooding of large areas, in car (fog-)lamps, cine-projectors, etc; **quartz'-mill** a mill or machine for crushing gold-bearing quartz; **quartz-por'phyry** an igneous rock with crystals of quartz and feldspar in a compact or finely crystalline ground-mass of the same; **quartz'-rock** quartzite; **quartz'-schist** a schistose quartzite with mica. [Ger *Quarz*, from MHGer *quarz*, from WSlav *kwardy* hard]

quasar *kwā'sär*, *-zär* or *-sər*, *n* a (starlike) point source of radiation (radio waves, etc) outside our galaxy, *usu* with a very large red shift, forming the most distant and most luminous class of bodies so far discovered. [*quasi*-stell*ar* object]

quash *kwosh*, *vt* to crush; to subdue or extinguish suddenly and completely; to annul, reject as invalid. [OFr *quasser* (Fr *casser*), from L *quassāre*, frequentative of *quatere* to shake]

Quashee or **Quashie** *kwosh'i*, *n* a W African Negro personal name; (without *cap*) a Black, *esp* in the W Indies; a stupid or unsophisticated Black (*W Indies*). [Twi name given to a person born on Sunday]

quasi *kwā'sī* or *kwä'zē*, *adv* as if, as it were. — *combining form* **quasi-** denoting: in a certain manner, sense or degree; in appearance only, as in **quasi-historical** and **quasi-stellar**. — **quasi-contract** (*law*) a concept which allows a plaintiff to recover money from a defendant if non-payment would confer an unjust benefit on the latter. [L]

Quasimodo *kwas-i-mō'dō*, *n* the first Sunday after Easter, Low Sunday. [From the first words of the introit for the day, 1 Pet 2. 2: L *quasi modo geniti infantes*, as newborn babes]

quassia *kwosh'ə* or *kwosh'yə*, *n* a S American tree (*Quassia amara*; family Simarubaceae), whose bitter wood and bark are used as a tonic; now generally a W Indian tree of the same family (*Picraena excelsa*). [Named by Linnaeus after a Black slave, *Quassi*, who discovered its value against fever]

quat *kwot*, *n* a pimple (now *dialect*); an insignificant person (*Shakesp*). [Origin unknown]

quatch. See **quich**.

quatch-buttock *kwoch'-but-ək*, (*Shakesp*) *n appar* a flat or squat buttock.

quatercentenary *kwot-* or *kwat-ər-sen-tēn'ər-i*, also *-sin-*, *-ten'ər-i* or *-sen'tin-*, *n* a 400th anniversary, or its celebration. [L *quater* four times, and **centenary**]

quaternary *kwo-tûr'nər-i*, *adj* consisting of four; by fours; in fours; of the fourth order; based on four; with four variables; (with *cap*) Post-Tertiary (*geol*). — *n* the number four; a set of four; (with *cap*) the Post-Tertiary era or group of strata (Pleistocene and Recent) (*geol*). — *adj* **quater'nate** in sets of four. — *n* **quater'nion** a set or group of four; the operation of changing one vector into another, or the quotient of two vectors, depending on four geometrical elements and expressible by an algebraical quadrinomial (*math*); (in *pl*) a calculus concerned with this, invented by Sir William Rowan Hamilton (1805–65). — *adj* **quater'nion'd** (*Milton*) divided into groups of four. — *n* **quater'nionist** a student of quaternions. — *n* **quatern'ity** fourfoldness; a set of four; a fourfold godhead. [L *quaternī* four by four]

quatorze *kə-törz'*, *n* (in piquet) the four aces, kings, queens, knaves or tens, which count as 14 points. — *n* **quatorzain** (*kat'ər-zān* or *kät-ör'zān*) a stanza or poem of fourteen lines. — **Quatorze Juillet** (*ka-torz zhōō-yā*) or **the Quatorze** 14 July, Bastille Day, a French national holiday. [Fr *quatorze*, *quatorzaine*]

quatrain *kwot'rān*, *n* a stanza of four lines, *usu* rhyming alternately. [Fr]

quatrefoil *kat'ər-foil* or *kat'rə-foil*, *n* a four-petalled flower or leaf of four leaflets; an openwork design or ornament divided by cusps into four lobes (*archit*). — Also **quat'refeuille** (*-fœ-ē* or *-fīl*). [OFr *quatre* four, and *foil* (Fr *feuille*) leaf]

quattrocento *kwät-rō-chen'tō*, *n* the 15c in reference to Italian art and literature. — *n* **quattrocent'ism**. — *n* **quattrocen'tist**. [Ital, four (for fourteen) hundred]

quaver *kwā'vər*, *vi* to tremble, quiver; to speak or sing with tremulous uncertainty; to trill. — *vt* to say or sing tremulously. — *n* a trembling, *esp* of the voice; half a crotchet (*music*). — *n* **quā'verer**. — *n* and *adj* **quā'vering**. — *adv* **quā'veringly**. — *adj* **quā'very**. [Frequentative from obs or dialect *quave*, early ME *cwavien* to shake; related to **quake**, **quiver**[1]]

quay *kē*, *n* a landing-place; a wharf for the loading or unloading of vessels. — *n* **quay'age** provision of quays; space for, or system of, quays; payment for use of a quay. — *n* and *adj* **quay'side**. — Earlier forms **kay** (*kā*) and **key**. [OFr *kay*, *cay*, perh Celtic; partly assimilated to Mod Fr spelling *quai*]

quayd *kwād*, (*Spenser*) *adj* or *pa p* daunted. [Perh for **quelled**]

Que. *abbrev*: Quebec (also **Q**).

queach *kwēch*, (*obs*) *n* a thicket. — *adj* **queach'y** or **queech'y** forming a thicket; boggy; sickly. [Origin obscure]

quean *kwēn*, *n* a saucy girl (*archaic*); a woman of worthless character (*archaic*); a girl (*Scot*). — In NE Scotland **queyn** or **quine** (*kwīn*), *dimin* **queyn'ie** or **quin'ie**, the ordinary words for a girl. [OE *cwene* woman; cf **queen** (OE *cwēn*)]

queasy or **queazy** *kwē'zi*, *adj* uneasy; causing nausea; nauseated, squeamish, feeling as if about to vomit; (of the mind or conscience) fastidious, scrupulous; (of circumstances) unsettled (*obs*); hazardous (*obs*). — *adv* **quea'sily**. — *n* **quea'siness**. [Poss OFr *coisier* to hurt, or ON *kveisa* a boil]

Quebecker or **Quebecer** *kwi-bek'ər*, *n* an inhabitant of *Quebec*, in Canada. — *n* **Québecois** (*kā-bek-wa*; *Fr*) an inhabitant of Quebec, *esp* a French-speaking one. — Also *adj*.

quebracho *kā-brä'chō*, *n* the name of several S American trees yielding very hard wood, eg *white quebracho* Aspidosperma (family Apocynaceae), and *red quebracho* Schinopsis (family Anacardiaceae); their wood or bark: — *pl* **quebra'chos**. [Sp, from *quebrar* to break, and *hacha* axe]

Quechua *kech'wə* or **Quichua** *kēch'wə*, *n* a Peruvian Indian of the race that was dominant in the Inca empire; the language of the Quechua. — Also *adj*. — *adj* **Quech'uan** or **Quich'uan**. — Also *n*. [Sp *Quechua*, *Quichua*]

queechy. See **queach**.

queen *kwēn*, *n* a female monarch; the wife of a king; a presiding goddess; a woman or (*fig*) anything that is pre-eminent in excellence, beauty, etc; a sexually functional female social insect; an adult female cat; a male homosexual, *esp* if effeminate (*slang*); a playing-card bearing the picture of a queen, in value next below a king; (in chess) a piece that can be moved any distance in any straight line; a size of roofing-slate, 3 feet by 2. — *vt* to make a queen of; to make (a pawn) into a queen when it reaches the far side of the chessboard; to rule over as queen; to supply with a queen; (with *it*) to behave like a queen, to lord it. — *n* **queen'craft** skill or policy on the part of a queen. — *n* **queen'dom** queenhood; the realm of a queen. — *n* **queen'hood** the state of being a queen. — *n* **queen'ie** a Solway scallop. — *n* **queen'ing** a variety of apple. — *n* **queen'ite** a queen's partisan. — *adj* **queen'less**. — *n* **queen'let** a petty queen. — *adj* **queen'-like** like a queen. — *n* **queen'liness**. — *adj* **queen'ly** becoming or suitable to a queen; like a queen. — *adv* in the manner of a queen. — *n* **queen'ship** the state, condition or dignity of a queen. — *adj* **queen'y** camp, effeminate. — **Queen Anne** the simplified Renaissance architectural style of the early 18c, or an imitation of it; the furniture style of the early 18c, incorporating greater attention to comfort, the use of walnut, and cabriole legs; **queen bee** a fertile female bee; a woman who dominates, or is the centre of attention among, her associates; a woman in an important business position; **queen bee substance** or **queen substance** a pheromone secreted by a queen bee which attracts drones and keeps workers infertile; **queen'-cake** a small, soft, sweet cake with currants; **queen-con'sort** the wife of a reigning king; **queen-dow'ager** a king's widow; **queen'-fish** a Californian blue and silver fish, *Seriphus politus* (also known as *drum-fish*); a tropical food and game fish of the *Carangidae*; **queen mother** a queen-dowager who is mother of the reigning king or queen; a queen or queen bee that is a mother; **queen-of-the-mead'ow** or **-mead'ows** meadow-sweet; **queen'-post** one of two upright posts in a trussed roof, resting on the tie-beam and supporting the principal rafter; **queen-re'gent** a queen who reigns as regent; **queen-reg'nant** a queen reigning as monarch; **queen's'-arm** a musket. — **Queen's Bench** (or **King's Bench** in a king's reign) a division of the High Court of Justice; **queen's bounty** see under **bounty**; **Queen's Counsel** (or **King's Counsel** in a king's reign) an honorary rank of barristers and advocates; a barrister or advocate of this rank; **Queen's English** see **King's English**; **queen's evidence** (or **king's evidence** in a king's reign) evidence given for the Crown by a criminal against his or her accomplice(s) (**turn queen's evidence** to give such evidence); **Queen's Guide** (or **King's Guide** in a king's reign) the rank awarded to a (Girl) Guide upon reaching the highest level of proficiency and in recognition of service to the community; a Guide of this rank. — *adj* **queen'-size** (of furnishings, etc, *esp* beds and bedding) larger than standard size, but smaller than the largest size. — **Queen's Proctor** see **King's Proctor** under **king**; **queen's pudding** queen of puddings (see below); **Queen's Regulations** (or **King's Regulations** in a king's reign) the regulations governing the British Armed Forces; **Queen's Scout** (or **King's Scout** in a king's reign) a Scout who has reached the highest level of proficiency, etc; **Queen's Speech** (or **King's Speech** in a king's reign) the sovereign's address to parliament at its annual opening ceremony, describing proposed government legislation; **queen'-stitch** an embroidery pattern of square within square; **Queen's tobacco pipe** a kiln at London Docks for burning contraband goods (till 1891); **queen substance** see **queen bee substance** above; **Queen's ware** cream-coloured Wedgwood ware; **queen's yellow** basic mercuric sulphate. — **Queen Anne's Bounty** a fund for augmenting poor livings of the Church of England, formed (1703) out of first-fruits and tenths; **Queen Anne's dead** that is old news; **Queen of Heaven** Ashtoreth; Juno; the Virgin Mary (*RC*); **queen of puddings** a pudding made with egg, breadcrumbs, fruit or jam, etc, topped with meringue; **Queen of the May** a May queen. [OE *cwēn*; Gothic *qēns*; ON *kvæn*, *kvān*; Gr *gynē*; cf **quean**]

queene-apple *kwēn'-ap-l*, (*Spenser*) *n appar* a quince. [See **quince**]

Queensberry Rules *kwēnz'bər-i ro͞olz*, *n pl* rules applied to boxing, *orig* drawn up in 1867 and named after the Marquess of *Queensberry*, who took a keen interest in sport; (loosely) standards of proper behaviour in any fight, physical or verbal.

Queensland *kwēnz'lənd*, *n* a state in NE Australia. — *n* **Queens'lander** an inhabitant or native of Queensland. — **Queensland nut** the macadamia nut.

queer *kwēr*, *adj* odd, singular, quaint; open to suspicion; counterfeit; slightly mad, eccentric; vaguely unwell, faint or giddy; homosexual (*derog slang*). — *vt* (*slang*) to spoil; to put (someone) in a difficult position, or in another's bad books; to ridicule; to cheat. — *n* (*derog slang*) a male homosexual. — *n* **queer'dom** (*derog slang*) the state of being homosexual; homosexuals collectively. — *adj* **queer'ish**. — *n* **queer'ity** oddity. — *adv* **queer'ly**. — *n* **queer'ness**. — **queer'-basher**; **queer'-bashing** (*slang*) the practice of making gratuitous verbal or physical attacks on homosexuals; **Queer Street** debt or other difficulties; the imaginary place where debtors, etc live. — **queer someone's pitch** to spoil someone's chances; **queer the pitch** (*showmen's slang*) to make the place of performance unavailable; **shove the queer** (*slang*) to pass bad money. [Perh Ger *quer* across; cf **thwart**]

queest *kwēst*. Same as **cushat**. — Also **quest**, **quoist** and **quist**.

queez-maddam *kwēz'-mad'əm*, (*Scott*) *n* a French jargonelle pear. [Fr *cuisse-madame*]

queint[1] *kwānt*, (*Spenser*) *adj*. Same as **quaint**.

queint[2] *kwānt*, (*obs*) *pa p* of **quench**.

quelch *kwelsh* or *kweltsh*, *vi* and *vt* to squelch. [Imit]

Quelea *kwē'li-ə*, *n* a bird of the *Quelea* genus of African weaver birds, very destructive to crops, *esp Q. quelea*. [From African name]

quell *kwel*, *vt* to extinguish; to crush; to subdue; to disconcert, to abash (*Spenser*); to kill (*obs*). — *vi* to die, perish (*Spenser*); to subside, abate (*Spenser*). — *n* slaying (*Shakesp*); power of quelling (*Keats*). — *n* **quell'er**. [OE *cwellan* to kill, causal of *cwelan* to die; cf **quail** (verb)]

quelque chose *kel-kə shōz*, (*Fr*) *n* something unspecified; an unimportant thing.

queme *kwēm*, (*Spenser*) *vt* to please, suit, fit. [OE *cwēman*; Ger *bequem* fit]

quena *kā'nə*, *n* a type of bamboo flute from the Andes, held vertically for playing. [Am Sp, from Quechua]

quench *kwensh* or *kwentsh*, *vt* to put out (a fire, etc); to put out the flame, light or sight of, or the desire for; to stop (a discharge of electrically charged particles); to reduce luminescence in (excited particles) (*phys*); to cool with liquid; to slake; to damp down; to put an end to; to put to silence; to destroy; to extinguish hope, etc in (*obs*). — *vi* to be extinguished; to die down; to lose zeal; to subside in passion, grow cold (*Shakesp*). — *adj* **quench'able**. — *n* **quench'er** a person who or thing that quenches; a draught or drink; something introduced into a luminescent material to reduce the duration of phosphorescence (*nuc*). — *n* and *adj* **quench'ing**. — *adj* **quench'less** not to be extinguished. — *adv* **quench'lessly**. — **quenched spark** an oscillatory spark discharge extinguished after the first few oscillations. [OE *cwencan*, found only in the compound *ācwencan* to quench, causative of *cwincan* (*ācwincan*); cf OFris *kwinka* to go out]

quenelle *kə-nel'*, *n* a poached forcemeat dumpling of chicken, veal or fish. [Fr]

quep *interj* erroneously for **gup**[1].

Quercus *kwûr'kəs*, *n* the oak genus of the beech family. — *n* **quercetum** (*kwûr-sē'təm*) a collection of oak-trees. — *n* **quer'citron** (*-si-trən*) a N American oak, the dyer's oak or yellow-barked oak; its inner bark, yielding a yellow crystalline pigment **quercetin** (*-sə-tin*) or **flavin**. [L *quercus* oak]

querimony *kwer'i-mən-i*, *n* complaint. — *adj* **querimonious** (*-mō'ni-əs*). — *adv* **querimō'niously**. [L *querimōnia*, from *querī* to complain]

querist. See **query**.

quern *kwûrn*, *n* a stone mill for grinding corn, worked by hand. — **quern'stone**. [OE *cweorn*; ON *kvern*, Gothic (*asilu-*)*qaírnus* (ass-)mill]

querpo. See **en cuerpo**.

quersprung *kver'shpro͝ong*, (*skiing*) *n* a jump-turn at right angles. [Ger]

querulous *kwer'ū-ləs*, *-o͞o-* or *-ə-ləs*, *adj* complaining; peevish. — *adv* **quer'ulously**. — *n* **quer'ulousness**. [LL *querulōsus*, from *querī* to complain]

query or formerly often **quaere** *kwē'ri*, *n* an inquiry; a doubt; a question mark (?). — *vt* to inquire into; to question; to doubt; to mark with a query. — *vi* to question: — *pa t* and *pa p* **que'ried**. — *n* **que'rist** an inquirer. — *n* and *adj* **que'rying**. — *adv* **que'ryingly**. — **query language** (*comput*) any of various formalized sets of commands used to search and retrieve information in a database. [L *quaere*, imperative of *quaerere*, *quaesītum* to inquire]

quesadilla *kes-ə-dē'yə*, (*Mex cookery*) *n* a tortilla filled with cheese, chillis, etc, folded and fried or grilled. [Mex Sp, dimin of *queseda*, from *quese* cheese]

quest[1] *kwest*, *n* the act of seeking; search; pursuit; an adventure, expedition or undertaking with the purpose of achieving or finding some definite object; the object sought for; a searching party; a jury of inquest; inquiry, investigation; the collection of alms or donations (*RC*); a searching for game by dogs, or their baying or barking on finding it. — *vi* to go in search; to go begging; (of dogs) to search for game; (of dogs) to bark, yelp. — *vt* to go in quest of or after. — *n* **quest'ant** (*Shakesp*), **quest'er** or **quest'rist** (*Shakesp*) a person who goes on a quest. — *n* and *adj* **quest'ing**. — *adv*

quest'ingly. [OFr *queste* (Fr *quête*), from L (*rēs*) *quaesīta* (a thing) sought, from *quaerere*, *quaesītum* to seek]

quest[2]. See **queest**.

question *kwes'chən*, *n* an inquiry; an interrogation; the putting of a problem; a demand for an answer; an interrogative sentence or other form of words in which an inquiry is put; a unit task in an examination; a problem; a subject of doubt or controversy; discussion, conversation (*Shakesp*); a subject of discussion, *esp* the particular point actually before a group of people or deliberative body; subjection to examination; examination by torture (*hist*); objection, demur; doubt; the measure to be voted upon; (vaguely) a relevant matter. — *vt* to put questions to; to call to account; to examine by questions; to inquire; to inquire concerning; to throw doubt upon, regard as doubtful; to challenge, take exception to. — *vi* to ask questions; to inquire; to discuss, converse (*Shakesp*). — *n* **questionabil'ity**. — *adj* **quest'ionable** that may be questioned; doubtful, uncertain; open to suspicion; possibly dishonest, improper, immoral, etc; such as questions may be put to, not unwilling to be conversed with (*Shakesp*). — *n* **quest'ionableness**. — *adv* **quest'ionably**. — *adj* **quest'ionary** asking questions (*rare*); in the form of questions. — *n* an asker of questions (*obs*); a questionnaire; a quaestionary (*Scott*). — *n* **questionee'** someone who is questioned. — *n* **quest'ioner**. — *n* and *adj* **quest'ioning**. — *adv* **quest'ioningly**. — *n* **quest'ionist** a questioner, a doubter; an undergraduate in his last term before proceeding to a degree (*obs Cambridge* and *Harvard*). — *adj* **quest'ionless** unquestioning; beyond question or doubt. — *adv* (now *rare*) certainly. — **ques'tion-begging** begging the question (see under **beg**[2]). — Also *adj*. — **ques'tion-mark** a point of interrogation (?); a query or unresolved doubt; **ques'tion-master** someone who presides over a quiz, discussion programme or meeting, and puts the questions to the participants; **question tag** a tag question; **question time** (in parliament) a period during each day when members can put questions to ministers. — **at question** questionable, open to question; **in question** under consideration; in dispute, open to question; **make question** to demur; **out of question** without any doubt; **out of the question** not to be thought of; **question of fact** (*Eng law*) that part of the issue which is decided by the jury; **question of law** that part decided by the judge. [OFr, from L *quaestiō*, *-ōnis*, from *quaerere*, *quaesītum* to ask]

questionnaire *kwes-chən-ār'* or *kes-tē-on-er'*, *n* a prepared set of written questions, for purposes of statistical compilation or comparison of the information gathered; a series of questions. [Fr, from *questionner* to question, and *-aire* -ary]

questor. See **quaestor**.

questrist. See **quest**[1].

quetch. See **quich**.

quethe. See **quoth**.

quetsch *kwech* or *kvech*, *n* a variety of plum, or brandy distilled from it. [Ger dialect *quetsch(e)* wild plum]

quetzal *ket-säl'*, *ket'* or *kwet'səl*, *n* a golden-green Central American bird (the *resplendent trogon*) with very long tail-feathers; the Guatemalan currency unit, or dollar (100 centavos; *pl* **quetzales** *-sä'-les*). [Nahuatl *quetzalli*]

queue *kū*, *n* a line of people, etc awaiting their turn for service or attention; a set of data processing tasks waiting in a buffer to be processed in **FIFO** order (*comput*); a data storage system of this kind (*comput*); a braid of hair hanging down the back of the head, a pigtail; the tail of a beast (*heraldry*). — *vt* to place or arrange in a queue. — *vi* to form, or take one's place in, a queue (often with *up*). — *adj* **queued** (*kūd*) tailed; in a queue. — *n* **queu'ing** or **queue'ing**. — *vi* and *vt* **queue'-jump**. — **queue'-jumping** going ahead of one's turn in a queue, waiting list, etc (*lit* and *fig*). [Fr, from L *cauda* a tail]

quey *kwā*, (*Scot*) *n* a heifer; a young cow that has not yet had a calf. [ON *kvīga*; Dan *kvie*]

queyn, queynie. See **quean**.

quh- *hw-*, *obs* Scots spelling for *wh-*. [OE *hw-*]

quia timet *kwē'ə tim'et*, (*law*) of or denoting an (action to obtain an) injunction to prevent a possible future harmful act. [L, because he or she fears]

quibble *kwib'l*, *n* an evasive turning away from the point in question to something irrelevant, merely verbal, trivial or insignificant; a petty complaint or observation; a pun, play on words. — *vi* to raise petty or irrelevant objections; to argue over unimportant details; to pun or evade the issue by punning. — *n* **quibb'ler**. — *n* **quib'lin** (*obs*) a quibble. — *n* and *adj* **quibb'ling**. — *adv* **quibb'lingly**. [Perh dimin of obs *quib* quibble, which may be from L *quibus*, dative or ablative pl of *quī* who, a word frequent in legal use; or a variant of **quip**]

quich *kwich*, (*Spenser*) *vi* to stir, to move. — Also (*obs* or *dialect*) **quatch**, **quetch** or **quitch**. [OE *cweccan* to shake, causative of *cwacian* to quake]

quiche *kēsh*, *n* a flan of plain pastry filled with a cooked egg mixture *usu* containing cheese, onion or other vegetables, ham, etc. [Fr, from Ger dialect *küchen*, dimin of *Kuchen* cake]

Quichua. See **Quechua**.

quick[1] *kwik*, *adj* swift; speedy; brief; nimble; ready; sensitive; readily responsive; prompt to act; ready-witted; prompt to perceive or learn; hasty; living, alive (*archaic*, *Bible*, *liturgical*, etc); pregnant (*archaic*); (of a hedge) composed of living plants; (of a fire, etc) burning briskly; (of an oven) hot; (of sand, etc) mobile, shifting; sharp (*fig*). — *adv* (*colloq*) without delay; rapidly; soon. — *n* the sensitive parts of the body surface, *esp* under the nails; the tenderest or deepest feelings; the innermost or vital part; the living flesh (*archaic*); the living (*archaic*); a living thing (*Spenser*); a living plant, *esp* hawthorn in a hedge (also collectively); the life (*archaic*). — *vt* **quick'en** to accelerate; to impart energy or liveliness to; to invigorate; to stimulate; to give life to; to revive. — *vi* to move faster; to become alive or lively; to revive; to be stimulated; (of a pregnant woman) to reach the stage in pregnancy when the movement of the baby can be felt. — *n* **quick'ener**. — *n* and *adj* **quick'ening**. — *n* **quick'ie** (*colloq*) something that takes, or is to be done in, a short time; an alcoholic drink to be rapidly consumed; a brief or hurried act of sexual intercourse. — Also *adj*. — *adv* **quick'ly**. — *n* **quick'ness**. — *adj* **quick-an'swered** (*Shakesp*) quick at answering. — **quick assets** readily realizable assets. — *adj* **quick'-born** (*archaic*) born alive. — *adj* **quick'-change** quick in making a change, *esp* (of a performer) in appearance (**quick-change artist** such a performer; a person who changes rapidly or frequently in mood or opinion). — *adj* **quick'-conçeiving** (*Shakesp*) quick at understanding. — *adj* **quick'-eyed** having a keen eye. — **quick fire** rapid and continuous gunfire. — *adj* **quick'-fire** (of questions, etc) following in rapid succession; (also **quick'-firing**) designed to allow a quick succession of shots. — **quick'-firer**. — *adj* **quick'-fix** expedient and temporary as a solution. — **quick'-freeze** very rapid freezing of food so that its natural qualities are unimpaired. — Also *vt* and *vi*. — *adj* **quick'-frozen**. — **quick'-hedge** a hedge of living plants; **quick'lime** unslaked lime, calcium oxide. — *adj* **quick'-lunch** (of a café, etc) that serves quickly-eaten lunches with prompt service. — **quick march** (*military*) a march at a fast pace. — *interj* the command to start such a march. — **quick'-match** cotton thread impregnated with an inflammable mixture; **quick'sand** a loose watery sand which swallows up anyone who walks on it, or objects placed on it; anything similarly treacherous. — *adj* **quick'-sandy**. — *adj* **quick'-scented** or **quick'-scenting** having a keen scent. — *adj* **quick'-selling**. — *adj* **quick'set** formed of living plants set into place. — *n* a living plant, slip or cutting, *esp* of hawthorn, or a series of them, set to grow for a hedge;

a quickset hedge. — *adj* **quick-sight'ed** having quick sight or discernment. — **quick-sight'edness**; **quick'silver** mercury. — *adj* of mercury; quick-moving; mercurial. — *vt* to overlay or to treat with quicksilver or amalgam. — *adj* **quick'silvered**. — **quick'silvering** the mercury on the back of a mirror. — *adj* **quick'silverish** or **quick'-silvery**. — **quick'step** a march step or tune in fast time; a fast foxtrot. — *vi* to dance a quickstep. — *adv* **quick'sticks** or **quick'-stick** (*colloq*) without delay. — *adj* **quick-tem'pered** irascible. — **quick'thorn** hawthorn; **quick time** (*military*) a rate of about 120 steps per minute in marching; **quick trick** (*bridge*) a card that should win a trick in the first or second round of the suit; **quick'-water** a solution of nitrate of mercury. — *adj* **quick-witt'ed** able to think quickly and effectively. — **quick-witt'edness**. — **a quick one** a quick drink; a quickie; **quick on the draw** swift to draw a gun from its holster; prompt in response or action. [OE *cwic*; ON *kvikr* living]

quick[2] *kwik*, *n* couch grass or its rootstocks. — Also **quick'en** or **quick grass**. [Scot and NEng form of **quitch**[1]]

quicken[1] *kwik'ən*, (*Scot* and *NEng*) *n* the rowan. — Also **quick'beam** (*Eng*), **quick'en-tree**, **wick'en** or **wick'y**. [OE *cwicbēam*, *cwictrēow* aspen]

quicken[2]. See **quick**[1,2].

quid[1] *kwid*, (*slang*) *n* a pound sterling (£); (formerly) a guinea: — *pl* **quid**; or in sense of ready money (*obs slang*) **quids**. — **not the full quid** (*Austr colloq*) simple-minded, dopey; **quids in** (*slang*) in a very favourable or profitable situation. [Origin obscure]

quid[2] *kwid*, *n* something chewed or kept in the mouth, *esp* a piece of tobacco. [**cud**]

quid[3] *kwid*, *n* that which a thing is, substance. [L, what]

quidam *kwī'dam* or *kwē'dam*, *n* somebody; a certain person: — *pl* **quidams**. [L *quīdam*]

quiddany *kwid'ə-ni*, *n* a jelly or thick syrup made from quince-juice and sugar. [L *cotōnea* quince, from *cydōnia*; see **quince**]

quiddity *kwid'i-ti*, *n* the inherent nature or essence of anything; any trifling nicety; a quibble. — Also (*archaic*) **quidd'it**. — *adj* **quidd'itātive**. [Med L *quidditās*, *-tātis*]

quiddle *kwid'l*, (*dialect*) *vi* to trifle. — *n* a fastidious person. — *n* **quidd'ler**.

quidnunc *kwid'nungk*, *n* an inquisitive, gossiping person. [L *quid nunc*? what now?]

quid pro quo *kwid prō kwō*, (*L*) something given or taken as equivalent to another, often as retaliation or in return for a previous favour; the action or fact of giving or receiving thus. [Literally, something for something]

quiesce *kwi-* or *kwī-es'*, *vi* to quiet down; (of consonants in Hebrew) to become silent. — *vt* (*comput*) to stop the operations of, make inactive. — *n* **quiesc'ence** or **quiesc'ency** rest; inactivity; (in Hebrew) a consonant's becoming silent. — *adj* **quiesc'ent** resting; (of a letter) not sounded; inactive, without input to activate it (*comput*); still. — *adv* **quiesc'ently**. [L *quiēscere* to rest]

quiet *kwī'ət*, *adj* at rest; calm; undisturbed; free from disturbing noise; without loudness, gaudiness, ostentation, formality or obtrusiveness of any kind; still; without bustle or restlessness; without much activity; peaceful; gentle; inoffensive. — *n* freedom from noise or disturbance; calm; stillness; rest; peace. — *vt* and *vi* to quieten. — *vt* and *vi* **quī'eten** to make or become quiet. — *n* and *adj* **quī'etening**. — *n* **quī'eter**. — *n* and *adj* **quī'eting**. — *n* **quī'etism** mental tranquillity; the doctrine that religious perfection on earth consists in passive and uninterrupted contemplation of the Deity. — *n* **quī'etist**. — *adj* **quīetist'ic**. — *n* and *adj* **quī'etive** sedative. — *adv* **quī'etly**. — *n* **quī'etness**. — *adj* **quī'etsome** (*Spenser*) undisturbed. — *n* **quī'etude** quietness. — **on the quiet** (*colloq*; or *slang* **on the QT** or **q.t.**) clandestinely, secretly; unobtrusively. [L *quiētus* quiet, calm]

quietus *kwī-ē'təs* or *kwi-ā'tōōs*, *n* discharge from life; extinction, death; silencing, quashing or elimination; discharge from office; an acquittance on payment of money due. [L *quiētus est* he is at rest or quiet]

quiff *kwif*, *n* a tuft of hair brushed up and back away from the forehead, or (formerly) a lock of hair oiled and brushed down over the forehead; a prostitute (*slang*); a male (*esp* effeminate) homosexual (*slang*). [Poss **coif**]

quight. See **quit, quite**[2].

qui-hi or **qui-hye** *kwī'-hī'*, *n* a prosperous Anglo-Indian, *esp* in Bengal, during British colonial rule. [Hindi *koī hai*, the call for a servant, Is anyone there?, from *koī* anyone, and *hai* is]

quill[1] *kwil*, *n* the hollow basal part of a feather; a large feather; a porcupine's spine; a goose or other feather used as a pen; a pen generally, or by metonymy, the writer's profession; something made from a quill feather, such as a toothpick, an angler's float or a plectrum; a weaver's bobbin (*orig* made of reed or other material); a hollow non-rotating shaft (also **quill drive**; *eng*); a reed, hollow stalk or internode, etc (*obs*); a small tube (*obs*); a musical pipe made from a hollow stem; hence throat, or *perh* voice (*Shakesp*); a roll of curled bark, eg of cinnamon; a cylindrical fold (*obs*). — *vt* to goffer, crimp; to wind on a bobbin. — *adj* **quilled** provided with, or formed into quills; tubular. — *n* **quill'ing** a ribbon or strip gathered into flutings. — **quill'-driver** (*derog*) a clerk (now *services slang*); an assiduous writer; **quill'-driving**; **quill'-feather** a large stiff wing or tail feather; **quill'man** a clerk; **quill'-nib** a quill-pen shortened for use with a holder; **quill'-pen** a quill used as a pen. — *adj* using or suggestive of old-fashioned, slow and protracted methods or style (in office or literary work). — **quill'wort** any plant of the genus Isoetes (from the quill-like leaves). [Origin obscure; cf LGer *quiele*, Ger *Kiel*]

quill[2] *kwil*, (*Shakesp*) *n* a combination (in the phrase **in the quill** in a body, in concert). [Fr *cueille* a gathering]

quillai *ki-lī'*, *n* the soap-bark tree. — *n* **Quillaja** or **Quillaia** (*ki-lī'ə* or *-lē'ə*) a genus of S American rosaceous trees whose bark has soaplike properties; a quillai. [Am Sp]

quillet *kwil'it*, *n* a subtlety in argument; a quibble. [Perh L *quidlibet* what you will]

quillon *kē-yɔ̃*, *n* either arm of the cross guard of a sword-handle. [Fr]

quilt *kwilt*, *n* a bed-cover consisting of padding between two outer layers of cloth stitched through all three layers into compartments or channels; any material or piece of material so treated; a duvet, continental quilt; a patchwork quilt; a thick coverlet; a thick covering placed over beehive frames; the inner part of a cricket or hockey ball. — *vt* to pad, cover or line with a quilt; to form into a quilt; to stitch in; to seam like a quilt; to cover with interlaced cord; to thrash. — *adj* **quilt'ed**. — *n* **quilt'er** a person or machine that makes quilting. — *n* **quilt'ing** the act of making a quilt or quilted material; something which is quilted; cloth for making quilts; cloth with a pattern like a quilt; a covering of rope-yarn; a thrashing with a rope's end. — **quilt'ing-bee** or **-party** a gathering of women to help someone in making a quilt, combined with social amusement; **quilt'ing-cotton** cotton wadding; **quilt'ing-frame** an adjustable frame for holding a fabric for quilting. [OFr *cuilte* (Fr *couette*), from L *culcita* a cushion]

quim *kwim*, (*vulg slang*) *n* the female genitalia. [Origin uncertain; a relationship with **coomb**, **cwm** has been suggested]

quin. See **quintuplet**.

quina, **kina** or **china** *kē'nə*, *n* cinchona bark; any tree yielding it; quinine. — Also **quinaquina**, **kinakina**, **chinachina** (*kē-nä-kē'nə*) or **quinquina** (*kin-* or *king-kē'nə*, also *kwing-kwī'nə*). — *adj* **quinic** (*kwin'ik*). — **quinic acid** an acid obtained from cinchona bark. [Sp *quina*, *quinaquina*, from Quechua *kina*, *kina-kina*, *kinkina* bark]

quinacrine *kwin'ə-krēn*, (*pharm*) *n* another name for **mepacrine**. [*quin*ine and *acrid*ine]

quinary *kwī'nər-i, adj* fivefold; by or in fives; of the fifth order; based on five; with five variables. — *n* a set of five. — *adj* **qui'nate** (*bot*) consisting of five leaflets. [L *quīnī* five by five]

quince *kwins, n* a golden, round or pear-shaped, fragrant, acid fruit, used *esp* for jellies, marmalade, etc; the tree or shrub (*Cydonia oblonga*), related to pear and apple, that bears it; extended to the closely related *Japanese quince* (see **japonica**) and to the unrelated *Bengal quince*, the bael-fruit. [Orig pl of *quine*, from OFr *coin* (Fr *coing*), from L *cotōneum*, from Gr *kydōnion*, from *Kydōniā* a town in Crete]

quincentenary *kwin-sen-tēn'ər-i, -sin-ten'ər-i* or *-sen'tin-ər-i, n* and *adj* a five-hundredth anniversary or its celebration. — *adj* and *n* **quincentennial** (*-ten'i-əl*). [Irregularly formed from L *quinque* five, and **centenary**]

quinche *kwinsh* (*Spenser*), *vi* to stir, move. [Ety uncertain]

quincunx *kwin'kungks, n* an arrangement of five things at the corners and centre of a square (eg as seen on cards and dice), or of a great number of things (*esp* trees) spaced in the same way; an aspect of 150° between two heavenly bodies (*astrol*). — *adj* **quincuncial** (*-kun'shl*) of or in a quincunx; (of aestivation) having two leaves overlapping at each edge, two underlapping at each edge, and one overlapping and underlapping (*bot*). — *adv* **quincun'cially**. [L *quīncunx*, from *quīnque* five, and *uncia* a twelfth part]

quine. See **quean**.

quinella *kwi-nel'ə*, (*orig US*, now *esp Austr*) *n* a form of bet in which the punter has to select the two horses (or dogs, etc) which will come in first and second but not give their order of placing. [Am Sp *quiniela*]

quingentenary *kwin-jen-tē'nər-i, -ten'ər-i* or *-jen'tən-ər-i, n* a quincentenary. — Also *adj*. [L *quīngentī* five hundred]

quinic. See **quina**.

quinie. See **quean**.

quinine *kwin-ēn', kwin'ēn* or (*NAm*) *kwī'nīn, n* a colourless, odourless, very bitter alkaloid ($C_{20}H_{24}O \cdot 3H_2O$), obtained from cinchona bark, or one of its salts, used as an antipyretic and analgesic, formerly widely used to treat malaria. — *n* **quin'idine** (*-i-dēn*) a crystalline alkaloid drug, isomeric with quinine, used to treat irregularities in the heart rhythm. — **quinine water** a beverage made by flavouring water with quinine, lemon, etc. [See **quina**]

quink-goose *kwingk'-gōōs, n* the brent-goose.

quinnat *kwin'ət, n* the king-salmon. [From an Am Ind name]

quinoa *kē'nō-ə, n* a S American goosefoot, with seeds used as rice, and leaves used as spinach. [Sp *quínoa*, from Quechua *kinua*]

quinol *kwin'ol, n* a reducing agent and photographic developer, $C_6H_4(OH)_2$, obtained by reduction of quinone, hydroquinone. — *n* **quinoid** (*kwin'oid*) a quinonoid substance. — *adj* **quinoid'al**. — *n* **quin'oline** (*-ə-lēn*) a pungent, colourless, oily liquid (C_9H_7N), first obtained from quinine and used eg as a food preservative. — *n* **quin'olone** any of a group of antibiotics *esp* effective against infections of the urinary and respiratory tracts resistant to conventional antibiotics. — *n* **quinone** (*kwin'ōn* or *kwin-ōn'*) a golden-yellow crystalline compound ($C_6H_4O_2$) *usu* prepared by oxidizing aniline; a reddish or colourless isomer of this; a general name for a benzene derivative in which two oxygen atoms replace two hydrogen. — Also **kinone** (*kē'nōn*). — *adj* **quinonoid** (*kwin-ōn'oid* or *kwin'ən-oid*) like a quinone. [**quina**]

quinqu- *kwin-kw* or **quinque-** *kwin-kwi-*, *combining form* denoting five. — *n* **quinquagenarian** (*kwin-kwə-ji-nā'ri-ən*; L *quīnquāgēnārius*, from *quīnquāgēnī* fifty each) a person who is fifty years old, or between fifty and fifty-nine. — Also *adj*. — *adj* **quinquecostate** (*kwin-kwi-kos'tāt*; L *costa* rib) five-ribbed. — *adj* **quinquefarious** (*kwin-kwi-fā'ri-əs*; L *-fārius, poss* from *fārī* to speak) fivefold; in five rows. — *adj* **quinquefoliate** (*kwin-kwi-fō'li-āt*; L *folium* leaf) with five leaflets. — *n* **quinquenn'iad** quinquennium. — *n* **quinquennium** (*kwin-kwen'i-əm*; L *annus* year) a period of five years: — *pl* **quinquenn'ia**. — *adj* **quinquenn'ial** occurring once in five years; lasting five years. — *n* a fifth anniversary or its celebration. — *adv* **quinquenn'ially**. — *n* **quinquereme** (*kwin'kwi-rēm*; L *rēmus* an oar) an ancient ship with five banks of oars. — *n* **quinquev'alence** (or *-vā'*). — *adj* **quinquevalent** or **quinquivalent** (*kwin-kwev'ə-lənt* or *-kwi-vā'*) having a valency of five. [L *quīnque* five]

Quinquagesima *kwin-kwə-jes'i-mə, n* (also **Quinquagesima Sunday**) the Sunday before Lent begins, *appar* as being fifty days before Easter Sunday (by inclusive reckoning). — *adj* **quinquages'imal** of the number fifty; of fifty days. [L *quīnquāgēsimus, -a, -um* fiftieth; cf **Quadragesima, Sexagesima, Septuagesima**]

quinque-, quinquennium, etc. See **quinqu-**.

quinquina. See **quina**.

quinquivalent. See under **quinqu-**.

quinsy *kwin'zi, n* suppurative tonsillitis, acute inflammation of the tonsil with the formation of pus around it. — *adj* **quin'sied** suffering from quinsy. — **quin'sy-berry** the blackcurrant; **quins'y-wort** squinancy-wort. [LL *quinancia*, from Gr *kynanchē*; see **cynanche**]

quint[1] *kwint, n* an organ-stop a fifth above the foundation stops; a fifth (*music*); the E string of a violin; a five-stringed tenor viol (also **quinte**); (*kint*; *old-fashioned kent*) a sequence of five cards in piquet, *esp* **quint major** ace to ten, and **quint minor** knave to seven. [Fr *quinte*, from L *quīntus, -a, -um* fifth]

quint[2]. See **quintuplet**.

quint- *kwint-*, *combining form* denoting fifth. [L *quīntus* fifth]

quinta *kin'tə, n* a country house in Spain or Portugal. [Sp and Port]

quintain *kwin'tin* or *-tən*, (*hist*) *n* a post for tilting at, often with a turning cross-piece to strike the unskilful tilter; the sport of tilting at such a post. [OFr *quintaine*, thought to be from L *quīntāna via* the road adjoining the fifth maniple in a camp]

quintal *kwin'tl, n* 100 kilograms; (formerly) a hundredweight. [Fr and Sp *quintal*, from Ar *qintār*, from L *centum* a hundred]

quintan *kwin'tən, adj* (of a chill or fever) occurring every fourth (or by inclusive reckoning fifth) day. [L *quintānus* of the fifth]

quinte[1] *kēt*, (*fencing*) *n* the fifth of eight parrying or attacking positions. [Fr]

quinte[2]. See **quint**[1].

quintessence *kwin-tes'əns* or *kwin'*, *n* the pure concentrated essence of anything; the most essential part, form or embodiment of anything; *orig* a fifth entity, in addition to the four elements. — *adj* **quintessential** (*-ti-sen'shl*). — *vt* **quintessen'tialize** or **-ise**. — *adv* **quintessen'tially**. [Fr, from L *quīnta essentia* fifth essence]

quintet, quintette or **quintett** *kwin-tet'*, *n* a composition for five voices or instruments; a set of performers or instruments for such compositions; a group of five people or things. — Also (*Ital*) **quintet'to** (*kwēn-tet'tō*): — *pl* **quintet'ti** (*-tē*). [Ital *quintetto*, dimin of *quinto*, from L *quīntus* fifth]

quintic *kwin'tik*, (*math*) *adj* of the fifth degree.

quintile *kwin'tīl, n* any of four values which divide the items of a frequency distribution into five groups; any of the five groups so formed; an aspect of 72° between two heavenly bodies (*astrol*). [L *quīntus* fifth]

quintillion *kwin-til'yən, n* a million raised to the fifth power, written as 10^{30}, or one and thirty zeros; in N America, a thousand to the sixth power, written as 10^{18}, or one and eighteen zeros. — *n* and *adj* **quintill'ionth**. [Modelled on **million**, with **quint-** as prefix]

quintroon *kwin-trōōn'*, (*rare*) *n* the offspring of a person of European descent and an octoroon; a person who is fifth (inclusive) in descent from a Negro. [Sp *quinterón*, from L *quīntus* fifth]

quintuple *kwin'tū-pl* or *kwin-tū'pl, adj* fivefold; having five parts, members or divisions. — *n* five times as much. — *vt* and *vi* to multiply by five. — *n* **quin'tūplet** (also *-tū'*) a set of five things; a group of five notes played in the time of four; one of five (children or animals) born at one birth (*colloq abbrev* **quin** or (*NAm*) **quint**). [L *quīntus* fifth, on the model of **quadruple**]

quintuplicate *kwin-tū'pli-kāt, adj* fivefold. — *n* one of five corresponding things; fivefoldness. — *vt* to make fivefold. — *n* **quintuplicā'tion**. [L *quīntuplex, -icis*, from *quīntus* fifth, and *plicāre* to fold]

quinze *kwinz, n* a card game, like vingt-et-un, the object being to score as close to fifteen as possible without going above it. [Fr, fifteen]

quip *kwip, n* a short, clever remark; a gibe; a quibble; a fanciful jest or action; a knick-knack (*archaic*). — *vi* to utter a quip or quips. — *vt* (*obs*) to assail with quips. — *adj* **quipp'ish**. — *n* **quip'ster** a person given to making clever remarks. [Perh from obs *quippy*, which may be from L *quippe* forsooth]

quipu *kē'pōō, n* a mnemonic device consisting of various colours of knotted cords, used by the ancient Peruvians. — Also **quip'o** (*pl* **quip'os**). [Quechua *quipu* knot]

quire[1] *kwīr*, (*printing*) *n* the twentieth part of a ream, 24 sheets of paper (now often 25) of the same size and quality; (formerly) four sheets of paper or parchment folded together to make eight leaves; a (quire-filling) book or poem (*obs*; also **quair** *kwār*). — *vt* to fold in quires. [OFr *quaier* (Fr *cahier*), prob from LL *quaternum* a set of four sheets, from L *quattuor* four]

quire[2] *kwīr, n obs* spelling of **choir**. — *n* (*obs*) **quirister** (*kwir'*) chorister.

Quirinus *kwi-rī'nəs* or *kwi-rē'nōōs, n* an Italic god of war, etc, afterwards identified with the deified Romulus (*ancient Rome*). — *n* **Quirinal** (*kwir'in-əl*) one of the hills of Rome; the Italian government, as opposed to the Vatican (from the palace on the hill). — *n pl* **Quirinalia** (*kwir-i-nā'li-ə*; *ancient Rome*) a festival held in honour of Quirinus, on 17 February. [L *Quirīnus*]

quirister. See **quire**[2].

Quirites *kwi-rī'tēz* or *kwi-rē'tās, n pl* the citizens of ancient Rome in their civil capacity. [L *Quirītēs*, orig the Samnite people of *Cures* (united with the Romans)]

quirk *kwûrk, n* a trick or peculiarity of action, style or behaviour; a sudden turn, twist, jerk or flourish; an acute sharp-edged groove alongside a moulding (*archit*); an artful evasion; a quibble; a quip; a trick, knack, way (*Shakesp*). — *vi* to quip; to move jerkily. — *vt* to provide with a quirk. — *adv* **quirk'ily**. — *n* **quirk'iness**. — *adj* **quirk'ish**. — *adj* **quirk'y**. [Origin unknown]

quirt *kwûrt, n* a Spanish-American braided hide riding-whip. — *vt* (*US*) to strike with a quirt. [Mex Sp *cuarta*]

quisling *kwiz'ling, n* a person who aids the enemy; a native puppet prime minister set up by an occupying foreign power. [Vidkun *Quisling*, who played that part in Norway during German occupation (1940–45)]

quist *kwist*. See **queest**.

quit *kwit* or (*archaic*) **quite** (*Spenser* **quight** or **quyte**) *kwīt*, *vt* to depart from; to cease to occupy; (with *of*) to rid (oneself); to let go; to leave off, cease (*esp NAm*); to behave, acquit (oneself; *archaic*); to absolve, release from obligation; to clear off, discharge (a debt, etc); to repay, requite (*obs*); to free, rid (*obs*); to clear of blame, etc, acquit (*obs*). — *vi* to leave off, cease (*esp NAm*); to depart: — *pr p* **quitt'ing** (*archaic* **quīt'ing**); *pa t* and *pa p* **quitt'ed** or **quit** (*archaic* **quīt'ed**). — *adj* **quit** set free; clear, rid; quits; released from obligation. — *adj* **quits** even; neither owing nor owed. — *n* **quitt'al** (*Shakesp*) requital. — *n* **quitt'ance** a release; a discharge from debt; a receipt; requital. — *vt* (*obs*) to repay. — *n* **quitt'er** a shirker; a person who gives up easily. — **quit'claim** (*law*) a deed of release, as of relinquishment of a claim or portion of mining ground. — *vt* to relinquish claim or title to; to release, discharge. — **quit'-rent** a (*usu* nominal) rent in money or kind in lieu of services. — **call it quits** or **cry quits** (or formerly **quittance**) to declare oneself even with another, and so satisfied; **double or quits** see under **double**; **quit scores** to balance accounts. [OFr *quiter* (Fr *quitter*), from LL *quiētāre* to pay, from L *quiētāre* to make quiet, from *quiētus* quiet]

qui tam *kwī tam* or *kwē tam, n* a legal action by an informer partly on his or her own behalf, partly on the state's. [From the first words, L *quī tam* who as much (for the king as for himself)]

quitch[1] *kwich, n* couch grass. — Also **quitch grass**. [OE *cwice*; cf **couch grass, quick**[2]]

quitch[2]. See **quich**.

quite[1]. See **quit**.

quite[2] (*Spenser* **quight**) *kwīt, adv* completely, wholly, entirely; really, actually; somewhat, fairly; exactly, indeed, yes (*colloq*; often **quite so**). — **quite a** (*colloq*) (with *adj* and *n*) a very; (with *n* alone) an outstanding or exceptional; **quite something** (*colloq*) something remarkable or excellent. [**quit**]

quittance. See **quit**.

quitter[1] or **quittor** *kwit'ər, n* pus (*obs* except *Jamaica*); (**quittor**) a fistulous sore on a horse's hoof (*vet*). [Poss OFr *quiture* cooking, from L *coctūra*]

quitter[2]. See **quit**.

quiver[1] *kwiv'ər, vi* to shake with slight and tremulous motion; to tremble; to shiver. — *vt* (of a bird) to cause (the wings) to move rapidly. — *n* **quiv'er** or **quiv'ering**. — *adv* **quiv'eringly**. — *adj* **quiv'erish**. — *adj* **quiv'ery**. [Prob imit, perh connected with **quiver**[3]]

quiver[2] *kwiv'ər, n* a case for arrows. — *adj* **quiv'ered** provided with a quiver; kept in a quiver. — *n* **quiv'erful** (*fig*) a large family (Psalm 27. 5). [OFr *cuivre*; prob Gmc in origin; cf OHGer *kohhar* (Ger *Kocher*), OE *cocer*]

quiver[3] *kwiv'ər*, (*Shakesp*) *adj* nimble, active. [ME *cwiver*, from OE *cwifer*, found in the adverbial form *cwiferlice* zealously]

qui vive *kē vēv*: **on the qui vive** on the alert; lively and ready for action. [From the French sentry's challenge, literally (long) live who?, ie whom do you support?, from *qui* who, and *vive*, 3rd pers sing present subjunctive of *vivre* to live, from L *vīvere*]

quixotic *kwik-sot'ik, adj* like Don *Quixote*, the knight in the romance of Cervantes (1547–1616), extravagantly romantic in ideals or chivalrous in action; (of ideals, actions) absurdly generous and unselfish. — *adv* **quixot'ically**. — *n* **quix'otism**. — *n* **quix'otry**.

quiz *kwiz, n* a set of questions (designed for amusement or entertainment), such as a test on general knowledge or on a special subject; a TV or radio programme, or organized event, in which contestants are asked a prepared set of questions; an interrogation; an oral test (*NAm*); the remaining noun senses are *obs*: an odd-looking person or (*Jane Austen*) thing; a monocle, often with a handle; a piece of banter or quiet mockery; a mocking look; a hoax; a person who practises any of these; a bandalore (qv): — *pl* **quizz'es**. — *vt* to question, interrogate; to test (a class, etc) orally (*NAm*); to poke fun at; to eye, *esp* with an air of mockery. — *vi* to poke fun: — *pr p* **quizz'ing**; *pa t* and *pa p* **quizzed**. — *n* **quizz'er**. — *n* **quizz'ery**. — *adj* **quizz'ical** mocking, questioning; amusing, comical. — *n* **quizzical'ity**. — *adv* **quizz'ically**. — *n* **quizzificā'tion** quizzing. — *vt* **quizz'ify** to cause to look odd (*obs*). — *n* **quizz'iness** (*rare*) oddness. — *n* **quizz'ing**. — **quiz'master** question-master; **quiz show** a TV or radio quiz; **quizz'ing-glass** a monocle. [Origin obscure]

quo' *kə, ko, kō* or *kwō, vt* a Scots form of **quoth**. — **quod** an obsolete form of **quoth**, used *esp* at the end of a poem, followed by the poet's name.

quoad *kwō'ad*: **quoad hoc** (*hōk* or *hok*) as far as this; **quoad omnia** (*om'ni-ə* or *-a*) in respect of all things; **quoad sacra** (*sā'krə* or *sa'kra*; *Scot*) as far as concerns sacred matters (applied to a parish created and functioning for ecclesiastical purposes only). [L, so far as, from *quō* whither, and *ad* to]

quod[1] *kwod*: **quod erat demonstrandum** (*er'at dem-ən-stran'dəm* or *dăm-ōn-stran'doŏm*) which was to be proved or demonstrated (often *abbrev* **QED**); **quod erat faciendum** (*fā-shē-en'dəm* or *fa-ki-en'doŏm*) which was to be done (also *abbrev* **QEF**); **quod** (*pl* **quae** *kwē*, *kwī*) **vide** (*vī'dē*, *vi'* or *wi'de*) which see. [L, neuter of *quī* who]

quod[2] *kwod*, (*slang*) *n* prison. — *vt* to imprison. [Origin unknown]

quod[3]. See **quo'**.

quodlibet *kwod'li-bet*, *n* a philosophical argument or disputation, *esp* as an exercise; a humorous medley of tunes. — *n* **quodlibetā'rian** a person who engages in quodlibets. — *adj* **quodlibet'ic** or **quodlibet'ical**. [L, what you please, from *quod* what, and *libet* it pleases]

quodlin *kwod'lin*. An obsolete form of **codlin**.

quoif *koif*. Same as **coif**.

quoin *koin*, *n* a salient angle, *esp* of a building; a cornerstone, *esp* a dressed cornerstone; a keystone; a voussoir; a wedge, *esp* for locking type in a chase, or for raising a gun. — *vt* to wedge; to secure or raise by wedging. [See **coin**]

quoist *kwoist*. See **queest**.

quoit *koit* or *kwoit*, *n* a heavy flat ring for throwing so as to encircle a hob or pin; a dolmen cover; a dolmen; (in *pl*, treated as *sing*) the game played with quoits. — *vi* to play at quoits. — *vt* to throw like a quoit. — *n* **quoit'er**. [Origin obscure]

quo jure? *kwō joŏ'rē* or *yoŏ're*, (*L*) by what right?

quokka *kwok'ə*, *n* a small tailed wallaby (*Setonix brachyurus*) found in SW Australia. [Aboriginal]

quoll *kwol*, *n* a small Australian marsupial, the native cat (*Dasyurus macrurus*). [Aboriginal]

quondam *kwon'dam*, *adj* former. [L, formerly]

quonk *kwongk*, (*colloq*) *n* any accidental noise made too close to a microphone and thus disrupting a radio or television programme. — *vi* to make such a noise. [Imit]

Quonset hut® *kwon'set hut*, *n* the US equivalent of the Nissen hut.

quooke *kwoŏk*, (*Spenser*) *pa t* of **quake**.

quop *kwop*, (*obs* or *dialect*) *vi* to throb. [ME *quappe*; imit]

Quorn® *kwörn*, *n* a vegetable protein composed of minute filaments, derived from a type of microscopic plant, used as a low-calorie, cholesterol-free meat substitute that absorbs flavours in cooking. [Coined by the marketing company]

quorum *kwō'* or *kwö'rəm*, *n* a minimum number of persons necessary for transaction of business in any body; *orig* a number of specially named justices of the peace who had to be present before any business could be done (*obs*); (loosely) the whole body of justices (*obs*). — *adj* **quo'rate** having or being (at least) a quorum. [L *quōrum* of whom, from the wording of the commission, of whom we will that you, so-and-so, be one (two, etc)]

quot. *abbrev*: quotation.

quota *kwō'tə*, *n* a proportional share, a part assigned; a regulated quantity of goods allowed by a government to be manufactured, exported, imported, etc; a regulated number of immigrants allowed into a country per year, students allowed to enrol for a course, fish allowed to be caught, etc: — *pl* **quo'tas**. — **quota immigrant** an immigrant (to the USA) admitted as one of the yearly quota allowed to his or her country of origin, as opposed to a **non-quota immigrant** (eg as child or wife of a resident citizen); **quota quickie** a quickly-produced, low-budget, poor-quality film made in Britain (but *usu* US-financed) in the 1920s and 30s to exploit a government measure requiring UK cinemas to show a set quota of British-made films; **quota sample** a proportional sample of people in a specific category or categories of the population defined in terms of age, sex, social class, etc; **quota sampling** the use of quota samples to obtain data, as for opinion polls and marketing purposes; **quota system** the imposition of specified quotas by a government or other agency. [L *quota* (*pars*) the how-manieth (part), from *quotus* of what number, from *quot* how many]

quote *kwōt*, or formerly *kōt* (*Shakesp* **coat**, **coate** or **cote**), *vt* to cite as evidence, authority, illustration or example; to give the actual words of; *orig* to divide into chapters, verses, etc, number the chapters of, or mark with references (*obs*); to give the current price of, *esp* to state the market price of (shares, etc) on the Stock Exchange list; to enclose within quotation-marks; to examine, scrutinize (*Shakesp*); to record, note, set down, mention, in writing or mentally (*obs*); to set down in the prompter's book as due to be called (*theat*). — *vi* to give the actual words, used as *interj* to indicate that what follows immediately is a quotation. — *n* (*colloq*) a quotation; a quotation-mark. — *adj* **quō'table** lending itself, herself or himself to quotation; fit to quote. — *n* **quō'tableness** or **quōtabil'ity**. — *adv* **quō'tably**. — *n* **quōtā'tion** the act of quoting; something that is quoted; a short passage of music, written or played, extracted from a longer piece; a statement of price and terms submitted to a prospective purchaser (*commerce*); the current price of shares, etc on the Stock Exchange list; registration of a company, etc with the Stock Exchange so that shares may be listed; a quadrat for filling blanks in type (*orig* those between marginal references). — *adj* **quōtā'tious** given to quoting. — *adj* **quō'tative** quotatious; indicating or consisting of a quotation. — Also *n*. — *n* **quō'ter**. — *adj* **quōte'worthy**. — **quōtā'tion-mark** either of the marks (*printing* and *colloq* **quotes**) used to note the beginning and end of a quotation (see also **inverted commas** under **comma**); **quoted company** one whose shares are quoted on the Stock Exchange. [LL *quotāre* to divide into chapters and verses, from L *quotus* of what number, from *quot* how many]

quoth *kwōth*, (*archaic*) *vt* (1st and 3rd *pers sing*, *pa t*, of the otherwise *obs* verb **quethe**) said (followed by its subject). — *interj* **quō'tha** forsooth, indeed (*literally* quoth he; see **a**, *pronoun*). [OE *cwæth*, preterite of *cwethan* to say; cf **bequeath**]

quotidian *kwo-tid'i-ən*, *adj* daily; (of a fever, etc) recurring daily; (of any activity of a living creature or a living part) that follows a regular recurrent pattern; everyday, commonplace. — *n* a fever or chill that recurs daily. [L *quotīdiānus*, from *quotīdiē* daily, from *quot* how many, and *diēs* day]

quotient *kwō'shənt*, (*math*) *n* the number of times one quantity is contained in another; a ratio, *usu* multiplied by 100, used in giving a numerical value to ability, etc (see **achievement quotient** and **intelligence quotient**). [L *quotiens*, *quotiēs*, how often, from *quot* how many (with *t* from false appearance of being a participle)]

quotition *kwō-tish'ən*, *n* a division regarded as repeated subtraction or measuring. [From L *quot*]

quotum *kwō'təm*, *n* quota. [L, neuter of *quotus*; see **quota**]

quo vadis? *kwō vä'dis*, (*L*) where are you going?, the words used by Peter to Christ (John 16.5; Vulgate version) and, in tradition, by Christ later appearing to Peter as he fled from Rome.

quo warranto *kwō wo-ran'tō*, (*law*) *n* a writ calling upon a person to show by what warrant he or she holds (or claims) a franchise or office. [L *quō warrantō* by what warrant]

Quran, **Qur'an** *koŏ-rän'*. See **Koran**.

quyte. See **quit**.

qv or **q.v.** *abbrev*: *quantum vis* (*L*), as much as you wish; *quod vide* (*L*), which see (*pl* **qqv** or **qq.v.**).

qwerty or **QWERTY** *kwûr'ti*, *n* the standard arrangement of keys on an English-language typewriter keyboard; a keyboard having its keys laid out as on a standard typewriter (also **qwerty keyboard**). — *adj* of or having such a keyboard. [From the letters at the top left-hand side of the keyboard]

qy *abbrev*: query.

R

R or **r** *är*, *n* the eighteenth letter in the modern English alphabet (sometimes called the 'dog letter', from the trilling of the tip of the tongue in its pronunciation in rhotic accents); as a medieval numeral, R = 80; $\bar{R}$ = 80 000. — **R months** the time when oysters are in season (from the spelling of the names of the months from September to April); **the three R's** reading, writing and arithmetic. [L *er*]

R or **R.** *abbrev*: rand (*SAfr* currency); Réaumur's thermometric scale (also **Réau**); Rector; *rex* (*L*) King, or *regina* (*L*) Queen; River; Russia (IVR; provisional); Röntgen unit; ruble(s); rupee(s). — **R18** *symbol*: (a certificate) designating a film for restricted distribution only, in venues (or from premises) to which no one under eighteen may be admitted.

R *symbol*: electric resistance.

® *symbol*: registered trademark.

r or **r.** *abbrev*: radius; *recipe* (*L*) take; right; run(s).

RA *abbrev*: Rear Admiral; Republic of Argentina (IVR); rheumatoid arthritis; Royal Academician; Royal Academy; Royal Artillery.

Ra *rä* or **Re** *rā*, *n* the ancient Egyptian sun-god.

Ra (*chem*) *symbol*: radium.

RAAF *abbrev*: Royal Australian Air Force.

rabanna *rə-ban'ə*, *n* a Madagascan raffia fabric. [Malagasy]

rabat or **rabatte** *rə-bat'*, (*geom*) *vt* to rotate into coincidence with another plane. — *n* **rabatt'ing**. — *n* **rabat'ment** or **rabatte'ment**. [Fr *rabattre* to lower]

rabato *rə-bä'tō*. Same as **rebato**. — *n* **rabatine** (*rab'ə-tēn*; *Scott*) a low collar.

Rabb. *abbrev*: Rabbinical.

rabbet *rab'it*, *n* a groove cut to receive an edge. — *vt* to groove; to join by a rabbet: — *pr p* **rabb'eting**; *pa t* and *pa p* **rabb'eted**. — **rabb'eting-machine'**; **rabb'eting-plane**; **rabbet'ing-saw**; **rabb'et-joint**. [Fr *rabat*, from *rabattre* to beat back]

rabbi (with *cap* when prefixed, as in *Chief Rabbi*) *rab'ī*, *n* a Jewish expounder or doctor of the law (also **rabbin** *rab'in*; *archaic*); the leader of a Jewish synagogue: — *pl* **rabb'is** or **rabb'ins**. — *n* **rabb'inate** the post or tenure of office of a rabbi; a body or gathering of rabbis. — *adj* **rabbin'ic** or **rabbin'ical** relating to the rabbis or to their opinions, learning and language. — *n* **Rabbin'ic** the late Hebrew language. — *adv* **rabbin'ically**. — *n* **rabb'inism** the doctrine or teaching of the rabbis; a rabbinical peculiarity of expression; the late Jewish belief which regarded the oral and written laws as being of equal value. — *n* **rabb'inist** or **rabb'inite** a person who adheres to the Talmud and traditions of the rabbis. — *n* **rabboni** (*rab-ō'ni* or *-nī*) my great master. [Heb *rabbi* my great one, from *rabh* great master]

rabbit¹ *rab'it*, *n* a small burrowing animal of any of several genera of the family *Leporidae*, related to the hare; its flesh (as food); its fur; a persistent but incurably inferior player at lawn tennis or other game; a timid person; an unimportant, insignificant person; same as **go-devil** (*min ext*); (in *pl*; also **white rabbits**) spoken before anything else on the first day of the month, to invoke good luck. — *vi* to hunt rabbits; to talk at length and in a rambling fashion (*colloq*; often with *on*; *orig* rhyming slang *rabbit and pork*, talk). — *n* **rabb'iter** a person who hunts rabbits. — *n* **rabb'itry** a place where rabbits are kept; the practice of playing as a rabbit in games. — *adj* **rabb'ity**. — **rabb'itfish** the king of the herrings (*Chimaera*) or other fish thought to resemble a rabbit; **rabb'it-hole** a rabbit's burrow; **rabbit hutch** a box for housing rabbits; **rabbit punch** a blow on the back of the neck; **rabb'it-squirrel** a viscacha of the genus *Lagidium*, found in the mountainous parts of western S America; **rabb'it-sucker** (*Shakesp*) a sucking rabbit; **rabb'it-warren** see under **warren**. — **Welsh rabbit** see **rarebit** under **rare¹**; **white rabbits** see under **rabbit** above. [ME *rabet*; poss from ONFr]

rabbit² *rab'it*, *vt* to confound (often in *od rabbit*, *d'rabbit*, or *drabbit*, for *God rabbit*). [Perh a facetious substitution for **rat¹**]

rabble¹ *rab'l*, *n* a disorderly gathering or crowd; a mob; (with *the*) the lowest class of people; a confused stream of words. — *adj* of or like a rabble. — *vt* and *vi* to gabble. — *vt* to mob. — *n* **rabb'lement** a rabble; tumult. — *n* **rabb'ling** *esp* (*Scot hist*) the mobbing and ousting of the Episcopal 'curates' at the Revolution. — *vi* **rabb'le-rouse**. — **rabb'le-rouser** a person who stirs up the common people to discontent and violence *esp* by inflammatory speeches, a demagogue; **rabb'le-rousing**; **rabble rout** (*obs*) the mob, rabble. [Cf Du *rabbelen* to gabble, LGer *rabbeln*]

rabble² *rab'l*, *n* a device for stirring molten iron, etc in a furnace. — *vt* to stir with a rabble. — *n* **rabb'ler**. [Fr *râble*, from L *rutābulum* a poker]

rabboni. See under **rabbi**.

Rabelaisian *rab-ə-lā'zi-ən*, *n* a follower, admirer or student of François *Rabelais* (died 1553 or 1554). — *adj* of or like Rabelais; extravagantly humorous; robustly outspoken; coarsely indecent. — *n* **Rabelais'ianism**.

rabi *rub'ē*, *n* the spring grain harvest in India, Pakistan, etc. [Ar *rabī'* spring]

rabid *rab'id*, *adj* raging; fanatical (*fig*); affected with rabies. — *adj* **rab'ic** of rabies. — *adv* **rab'idly**. — *n* **rabid'ity** or **rab'idness**. — *n* **rabies** (*rā'bēz*, *-bi-ēz* or *ra'*) the disease called hydrophobia (fear of water being a symptom), caused by a virus transmitted by the bite of an infected animal. [L *rabidus* (adj), *rabiēs* (n), from *rabere* to rave]

RAC *abbrev*: Royal Armoured Corps; Royal Automobile Club.

raca *rä'kə*, (*Bible*) *adj* worthless. [Chaldee *rēkā* (a term of reproach)]

racahout or **raccahout** *rak'ə-hōōt*, *n* acorn meal. [Fr, from Ar *rāqaut*]

raccoon or **racoon** *rə-kōōn'*, *n* a smallish American animal (*Procyon lotor*, or other species) with black-striped tail and face, related to the bears; its fur. — **raccoon'-berry** a member of the *Podophyllum*; **raccoon'-dog** a raccoon-like wild dog (*Nyctereutes*) of E Asia. [Algonquian]

race¹ *rās*, *n* the descendants of a common ancestor, *esp* those who inherit a common set of characteristics; such a set of descendants, narrower than a species; a breed; a stud or herd (*obs*); ancestry, lineage, stock; the condition of belonging by descent to a particular group; inherited disposition; a class or group, defined otherwise than by descent; a sex (*obs*); peculiar flavour, as of wine, by which its origin may be recognized; raciness, piquancy. — *adj* **racial** (*rā'shl*, *-shyəl* or *-shi-əl*) of or relating to race. — *n* **ra'cialism** racism. — *n* and *adj* **ra'cialist** racist. — *adj* **racialis'tic**. — *adv* **ra'cially**. — *n* **raciā'tion** formation locally of new, distinct biological groups smaller than species. — *adv* **racily** (*rās'i-li*). — *n* **rac'ism** hatred, rivalry or bad feeling between races; belief in the inherent superiority of some races over others, *usu* with the implication of a right to be dominant; discriminative treatment based on such belief. — *n* and *adj* **rac'ist**. — **race hatred** animosity accompanying difference of race; **race memory** folk memory; **race relations** social relations between members of different races living in the same country or community; **race riot** a riot caused by perceived discrimination on the grounds of race; **race suicide** voluntary cessation of reproduction, leading to the extinction of the race; **racial unconscious** same as **collective unconscious** (qv under **collect**). [Fr, from Ital *razza*, of doubtful origin]

race[2] *rās*, *n* a fixed course, track or path over which anything runs; a channel bringing water to or from a millwheel; a groove in which anything runs (such as ball-bearings or a rope); a regular traverse of a fixed course, as of the sun; a rapid flow or current of the tides; a competitive trial of speed as by running, driving, sailing, etc; (in *pl*) a meeting for horse-racing; a competition in getting ahead of others figuratively; a running or racing place (*rare*); a run or onward rush (*archaic* and *Scot*). — *vi* to run, go, drive, sail, etc swiftly; to contend in speed with others; (of an engine, propeller, etc) to run wildly when resistance is removed. — *vt* to cause (a car, horse, etc) to race; to rush (an action); to contend in speed or in a race with. — *n* **ra'cer** a person who or that which races; any of several non-venomous N American snakes of the genus *Coluber*. — *n* **ra'cing**. — *adj* **ra'cy**. — **race'-ball** a ball held in connection with a race-meeting; **race'card** a programme for a race meeting; **race'course**, **race'path** or **race'track** a course for running races over; **race'-cup** a piece of plate forming a prize at a race; **race'goer** an attender at race meetings; **race'going**; **race'horse** a horse bred for racing; **race meeting** an organized occasion for horse-racing; **race'-walker**; **race'-walking** a form of racing in which the competitors walk as fast as possible, but must not run; **race'way** a millrace; a track for running races over; **racing bit** a light jointed ringbit; **racing car**; **racing certainty** a thing certain to happen. [ON *rās*; OE *rǣs*]

race[3] *rās*, (*Shakesp*) *n* a rootstock of ginger. [OFr *rais*, from L *rādīx*, *-īcis* a root]

race[4] *rās*, *n* a white streak down an animal's face. — Also **ratch** or **rach**. [Origin unknown]

race[5] *rās*, *vt* to scratch; to raze (*Spenser*); to erase (*Spenser*); to slash (*Shakesp*). — *n* a cut, slit or scratch. [An otherwise obs form of **raze**[2] or **rase**]

race[6] *rās*, (*Spenser*) *vt* to tear away or off, to pluck, snatch. — Also (*Shakesp*) **rase**. [OFr *arrachier*]

raceme *ra-*, *rə-* or *rā-sēm'*, or *ras'ēm*, (*bot*) *n* an indefinite formation in which stalked flowers are borne in acropetal succession on an unbranched main stalk; a similar group of spore-cases. — *n* **racemate** (*ras'i-māt*) a racemic mixture. — *n* **racemation** (*ras-i-mā'shən*) a gleaning or gathering of grapes; a residue; a cluster or bunch of anything, *esp* grapes. — *adj* **racemed'** (also *ras'* or *rās'*) in or having racemes. — *adj* **racemic** (*ra-sē'mik* or *-sem'ik*) applied to an acid obtained from a certain kind of grape, an optically inactive form of tartaric acid; hence applied to similar mixtures of dextrorotatory and laevorotatory enantiomorphs. — *n* **rac'emism** the quality of being racemic. — *n* **racemizā'tion** or **-s-** a change into a racemic form. — *vt* and *vi* **rac'emize** or **-ise**. — *adj* **racemose** (*ras'i-mōs*) of the nature of, or like, a raceme or racemes; of, in or having racemes; like a bunch of grapes. [L *racēmus* a bunch of grapes]

rache, **rach** or **ratch** *rach*, (*archaic*) *n* a dog that hunts by scent. [OE *racc* setter; ON *rakki*]

rachis or **rhachis** *rā'kis*, *n* the spine; an axis, eg of a feather, an inflorescence or a pinnate leaf, etc: — *pl* **rachises**, **rhachises** (*rak'i-sēz*), **rachides** or **rhachides** (*rāk'i-dēz*). — *adj* **ra'chial**. — *adj* **rachidial** (*rə-kid'*; *rare*) or **rachid'ian**. — *n* **rachilla** (*rə-kil'ə*) the axis of a grass spikelet. — *n* **rachischisis** (*ra-kis'ki-sis*; Gr *schisis* cleavage) a severe form of spina bifida. [Gr *rhachis*, *-ios*, or *-eōs* spine]

rachitis *ra-* or *rə-kī'tis*, (*med*) *n* rickets. — *adj* **rachitic** (*-kit'ik*). [Gr *rhachītis* inflammation of the spine, adopted by Dr Gleeson in 1650 in the belief that it was the etymon of **rickets**]

Rachmanism *rak'man-izm*, *n* the conduct of a landlord who charges extortionate rents for property in which very bad slum conditions prevail. — *adj* **Rach'manite**. [From the name of one such landlord exposed in 1963]

racial, etc, **racism**, etc. See under **race**[1].

raciness. See under **racy**[1].

rack[1] *rak*, *n* an instrument for stretching, *esp* an instrument of torture; an extreme pain, anxiety or doubt (*fig*); stress, *esp* of weather; a framework, grating, shelf, etc on or in which articles are laid or set aside; a grating from which farm animals, etc may pull down fodder; a bar or framework as for chaining a prisoner (*Spenser*); a bar with teeth to work into those of a wheel, pinion, cog, etc. — *vt* to stretch or move forcibly or excessively; to strain; to wrest, overstrain, distort; to torture; to practise rapacity upon; to extort (*Spenser*); to put in a rack; to separate (ore) by washing it on an inclined plane (*min ext*); to move or adjust by rack and pinion. — *adj* **racked** (also, *erron*, **wracked**) tortured, tormented; (in combination) denoting tortured or distressed by, as in *disease-racked*, etc. — *n* **rack'er**. — *n* and *adj* **rack'ing**. — **rack'-rail** a cogged rail, as on a rack-and-pinion railway; **rack'-railway** a mountain railway with a rack in which a cog-wheel on the locomotive works; **rack'-rent** a rent stretched to the utmost annual value of the property rented, an exorbitant rent; a rack-renter. — *vt* to subject to such rents. — **rack'-renter** a person who charges or pays rack-rent; **rack'work** a mechanism with a rack. — **(live at) rack and manger** (to live in) wasteful abundance; waste and destruction (*perh* from confusion with *rack and ruin*); **rack and pinion** a means of turning rotatory into linear or linear into rotatory motion by a toothed wheel engaging in a rack; **rack one's brains** to use one's memory or reasoning powers to the utmost; **rack up** to accumulate points (in a score). [Prob MDu *recke* (Du *rek*, *rak*) or LGer *reck*, *recke*, *rack*; cf ON *rakkr* straight, Ger *Rack* rail, *recken* to stretch; Eng **reach**[1]]

rack[2] *rak*, *n* same as **wrack**, destruction; a crash (*Milton*). — **rack and ruin** a state of neglect and collapse. [**wrack**[1], or ON *rek* wreckage]

rack[3] *rak*, *n* flying cloud (*Shakesp*); driving mist; a track; a shallow ford (*Scot*). — *vi* (*Shakesp*) to drift, to drive. [Appar ON *rek* drifting wreckage, or some related form; cf **wrack**, **wreck** and **wreak**; OE *wrecan* to drive]

rack[4] *rak*, *vt* to draw off from the lees. [Provençal *arracar*, from *raca* husks, dregs]

rack[5] *rak*, *n* the neck and spine of a forequarter of a carcass, *esp* as a cut of meat (*orig dialect*); a vertebra (*obs*); a horse's bones. — *n* **rack'abones** (*US*) a very thin person or animal. [Perh OE *hracca* occiput]

rack[6] *rak*, (now *esp US*) *n* a horse's gait at which the legs at the same side move nearly together. — *vi* to walk with such a gait. — *n* **rack'er**. [Origin obscure]

rack[7] *rak*, *n* aphetic for **arrack**. — **rack'-punch**.

rack[8] *rak*, *n* a young rabbit's skin. [Origin unknown]

racket[1] *rak'it*, *n* a bat with *usu* roughly elliptical head, of wood or metal strung with catgut or nylon, for playing tennis, badminton, etc; a snowshoe of similar design. — *vt* to strike with a racket. — *n sing* **rack'ets** a simplified derivative of the old game of tennis, similar to squash, played by two or four people in a four-walled court. — **rack'et-court**; **rack'et-ground**; **rack'et-press** a press for keeping a racket in shape; **rack'et-tail** a humming-bird with two long racket-shaped feathers. — *adj* **rack'et-tailed**. [Fr *raquette*, poss from Ar *rāhat*, colloq form of *rāha* the palm of the hand]

racket[2] *rak'it*, *n* din; clamour; hubbub; hurly-burly; fuss; noisy or hustling gaiety; dissipation; a noisy merry-making; a dodge; fraudulent, violent, or otherwise unscrupulous money-making activities; strain of excitement; responsibility; liability for expenses. — *vi* to make or engage in racket; to go about making a great, unnecessary noise (often with *about*); to have a full and exciting social life (*archaic*; often with *about*). — *vt* to disturb, stir or affect by racket: — *pr p* **rack'eting**; *pa t* and *pa p* **rack'eted**. — *n* **racketeer'** a person who extorts money or other advantage by threats or illegal interference. — *vi* to act as a racketeer. — *n* **racketeer'ing**. — *n* **rack'eter** a noisy or dissipated person. — *n* **rack'etry**. — *adj* **rack'ety** noisy; energetic and excitable. — **stand the racket** to endure the strain; to take the consequences or responsibility; to pay expenses. [Prob imit]

racket[3] or **rackett** *rak'it*, *n* a Renaissance or Baroque woodwind instrument developed in Germany, sounded through a double reed, the forerunner of the bassoon. [Ger *Rachett*, orig *raggett*, of uncertain origin]

raclette *rak-let'*, *n* a dish of melted cheese scraped from a large section of cheese while it is heated, served *esp* with jacket potatoes, *orig* from the Valais region of Switzerland. [Fr, a small scraper]

racloir *rä-klwär*, (*Fr*) *n* a scraper.

racon *rā'kon*, *n* a radar beacon. [*ra*dar and bea*con*]

raconteur *ra-kon-tûr'* or *rä-kɔ̃-tœr*, *n* a teller of anecdotes: — *fem* **raconteuse** (-*tœz*). — *n* **raconteur'ing**. [Fr]

racoon. See **raccoon**.

Racovian *rə-kō'vi-ən*, *n* a member of a group of 17c Polish Socinians whose seminary was at *Raków*. — Also *adj*.

racquet *rak'it*, *n*. Same as **racket**[1]. — **racq'uet ball** (*US*) a game played by two or four players in a walled court with rubber balls and short-handled strung rackets.

racy[1] *rās'i*, *adj* (of wine) having a distinctive flavour imparted by the soil; exciting to the mind by strongly characteristic thought or language; spirited; pungent; zestful; risqué. — *n* **ra'ciness** the quality of being racy. [**race**[1]]

racy[2]. See under **race**[2].

RAD *abbrev*: reflex and dilatation.

rad[1] *rad*, (*Spenser*) *pa t* and *pa p* of **read**[1], and *pa t* of **ride**.

rad[2] *rad*, (*Scot*) *adj* afraid. [ON *hræddr*]

rad[3] *rad*, *n* (also with *cap*) short form of **radical** (in politics). — *adj* (*slang*, *esp* and *orig US*) excellent, radically and admirably up to date (short for **radical**).

rad[4] *rad*, *n* a unit of dosage of any radiation, equal to 100 ergs of energy for one gram of mass of the material irradiated. [**rad(iation)**]

rad[5] *rad*, *n* short form of **radian**.

rad. *abbrev*: radius; *radix* (*L*) root.

RADA *rä'də*, *abbrev*: Royal Academy of Dramatic Art.

RADAR *abbrev*: Royal Association for Disability and Rehabilitation.

radar *rā'där*, *n* the use of high-powered radio pulses, reflected or regenerated, for locating objects or determining one's own position; equipment for sending out and receiving such pulses. — **radar altimeter** a high altitude radio altimeter; **radar beacon** a fixed radio transmitter whose signals enable an aircraft, by means of its radar equipment, to determine its position and direction; **ra'dar-gun** a gun-like device used by police which, when pointed at a moving vehicle and 'fired', records (by means of radar) the speed of the vehicle; **ra'darscope** a cathode-ray oscilloscope on which radar signals can be seen; **radar trap** a device using radar which enables the police to identify motorists exceeding the speed limit over a particular section of the road (see also **speed trap**). [Acronym from *ra*dio *d*etection *a*nd *r*anging, appropriately a palindrome word]

RADC *abbrev*: Royal Army Dental Corps.

raddle[1] *rad'l*, *n* a flexible rod or strip of wood used to make hurdles, fences or (with plaster) walls, by weaving between uprights; a hurdle, door, fence, etc so made; a hedge formed by interweaving the branches of trees; a wooden bar used in weaving. — *vt* to interweave; to thrash (*NEng*). [Anglo-Fr *reidele* rail]

raddle[2] *rad'l*, *n* reddle or ruddle (red ochre). — *vt* to colour or mark with red ochre; to rouge coarsely. — *adj* **radd'led** (of a person) aged and worsened by debauchery. — **radd'leman**. [See **ruddle**]

raddocke *rad'ək*, (*Shakesp*). Same as **ruddock**.

rade *rād*. *Scots* and *NEng* form of **rode**[1]. [See **ride**]

radge *raj*, (*Scot*) *adj* angry, obstreperous; sexually excited, lustful. [Variant of **rage**, perh influenced by Romany *raj*]

radial *rā'di-əl*, *adj* relating to a ray or radius; along, or in the direction of, a radius or radii; having rays, spokes or parts diverging from a centre; arranged like spokes or radii; near the radius of the arm (*med*). — *n* a radiating part; a radial artery, nerve, engine, plate, tyre, etc. — *n* **radiale** (-*ā'li*; L *ra-di-ä'le*) a wrist-bone in line with the radius: — *pl* **radia'lia**. — *n* **rādiality** (-*al'*) radial symmetry. — *n* **radialization** or **-s-** (*rād-yəl-ī-zā'shən*). — *vt* **ra'dialize** or **-ise** to arrange radially. — *adv* **rā'dially** in the manner of radii or of rays. — **radial artery** the smaller branch of the brachial artery at the elbow; **radial drill** (*eng*) a large drilling machine in which the drilling head is capable of radial adjustment along a horizontal arm; **radial engine** one with its cylinders radially arranged (as opposed to in line); **radial symmetry** symmetry about several planes intersecting in a common axis; **radial tyre** a radial-ply tyre; **radial velocity** the speed of motion along the observer's line of sight, *esp* to or from a star. — **radial-ply tyre** a tyre in which layers or plies of fabric in the carcass are wrapped in a direction radial to the centre of the wheel. [LL *radiālis*, from L *radius*]

radian *rā'di-ən*, *n* a constant unit of circular measure, nearly 57·3°, the angle between two lines which, when drawn from the centre of a circle, divide off on its circumference an arc equal to its radius. [L *radius*]

radiant *rā'di-ənt* or *rā'dyənt*, *adj* emitting rays; issuing in rays; transmitted by radiation; glowing; shining; with happy emotion, lit up, beaming. — *n* that which emits radiations; a point from which rays emanate; the centre from which meteoric showers seem to emanate; a straight line from a point about which it is conceived to revolve (*geom*). — *n* **rā'diance** or **rā'diancy** the state of being radiant; a measure of the amount of electromagnetic radiation being transmitted from or to a point (on a surface). — *adv* **rā'diantly**. — **radiant energy** energy given out as electromagnetic radiation; **radiant heat** heat transmitted by electromagnetic radiation. [L *radiāns*, *-antis*, pr p of *radiāre* to radiate, from *radius*]

radiata *rā-di-ä'tə*, *n* an *orig* Californian variety of pine tree, now grown *esp* in New Zealand for timber. — Also **radiata pine**.

radiate *rā'di-āt*, *vi* to emit rays; to shine; to issue in rays; to diverge from a point or points; to transmit without the use of cables, by radio. — *vt* to send out in or by means of rays; to communicate by radio, without wires; to broadcast. — *adj* (-*it*, -*ət* or -*āt*) having rays; having ray-florets; spreading like a ray or rays; radial; radially arranged; of or belonging to the Radiata. — *n* an animal of the Radiata. — *n pl* **Rādiā'ta** in Cuvier's obsolete classification, the lowest sub-kingdom of animals, radially symmetrical, including echinoderms, coelenterates, polyzoans, etc. — *adj* **rā'diated**. — *adv* **rā'diately**. — *n* **rādiā'tion** the or an act of radiating; the emission and diffusion of rays; that which is radiated; energy, *esp* nuclear rays, transmitted in electromagnetic waves; radial arrangement. — *adj* **rā'diātive** or **rādiā'tory**. — *n* **rā'diātor** that which radiates; an apparatus for radiating or diffusing heat, eg for warming a room, or cooling an engine; a radio transmitting aerial. — **radiation belts** see **Van Allen radiation belts**; **radiation oncologist** see **radiologist** under **radio-**; **radiation sickness** an illness due to excessive absorption of radiation in the body, marked by diarrhoea, vomiting, internal bleeding, decrease in blood cells, loss of teeth and hair, reduction of sperm in the male, etc. [L *radiāre* to shine, *radiātus* rayed, from *radius*]

radical *rad'i-kl*, *adj* relating to, constituting, proceeding from or going to the root; fundamental; original; intrinsic; inherent; thorough; primary; primitive; implanted by nature; not derived; proceeding from near the root (*bot*); of or concerning the root of a word (*linguistics*); of or concerning the roots of numbers (*math*); favouring, involving or necessitating thoroughgoing but constitutional social and political reform (*politics*; *usu* with *cap*); (with *cap*) of or relating to a political party holding such beliefs. — *n* a root, in any sense; a group of atoms behaving like a single atom and passing unchanged from one compound to another, now *usu* confined to electrically neutral entities as distinguished from charged ions (*chem*; also **rad'icle**); (with *cap*) an advocate of radical reform or member of the Radical party. — *n* **Rad'icalism** the principles or spirit of a Radical. — *n* **radicality** (*-kal'i-ti*). — *n* **radicalīzā'tion** or **-s-**. — *vt* and *vi* **rad'icalize** or **-ise** to make or become radical. — *adv* **rad'ically**. — *n* **rad'icalness**. — *adj* **rad'icant** rooting from the stem. — *adj* **rad'icāte** rooted; deeply rooted; firmly established; fixed. — *vt* to root; to plant or fix deeply and firmly. — *adj* **rad'icāted** rooted, established. — *n* **radicā'tion** rooting; implanting; rootedness; general character of the root-system. — *n* **rad'icel** (*-sel*) a rootlet. — *adj* **rad'icellose**. — *adj* **radicicolous** (*-sik'ə-ləs*) inhabiting or parasitic on roots. — *adj* **radiciform** (*rə-dis'*) like a root. — *adj* **radiciv'orous** root-eating. — *n* **rad'icle** a little root; the part of a seed that becomes the root; a rhizoid; a radical (*chem*). — *adj* **radic'ūlar** relating to a radicle, a rootlet, or the root of a tooth, nerve, etc. — *n* **rad'icūle**. — *adj* **radic'ulose** having many rootlets or rhizoids. — **radical axis** the locus of a point of equal potency with respect to two circles; **radical chic** (chiefly *US*) the trend amongst socialites of the late 1960s and early 1970s of mixing with and affecting the views, dress, style, etc of radicals; **radical mastectomy** see under **mastoid**; **radical sign** the symbol $\surd$, indicating a square root. — **free radical** see under **free**. [L *rādīx*, *-īcis* a root]

radicchio *rə-dē'ki-ō*, *n* a purple-leaved variety of chicory from Italy, used raw in salads. [Ital]

radices. See **radix**.

radicle. See **radical**.

radiesthesia *rā-di-es-thē'zi-ə*, *-zyə* or *-zhə*, *n* sensitivity to forms of radiation from any source, eg detecting water with a dowsing-rod, diagnosing illness with a pendulum, etc, considered an extrasensory power. — *n* **radiesthē'sist**. [L *radius* ray; New L *esthesia* feeling]

radii. See **radius**.

radio *rā'di-ō*, *n* a generic term applied to methods of signalling through space, without connecting wires, by means of electromagnetic waves generated by high-frequency alternating currents; a wireless receiving, or receiving and transmitting, set; a wireless message or broadcast: — *pl* **rā'dios**. — *adj* of, for, transmitted or transmitting by electromagnetic waves. — *vt* and *vi* to communicate by transmitting (a radio message). — **radio altimeter** see under **altimeter**; **radio amateur** a person licensed to send and receive radio messages privately on certain shortwave bands; **radio astronomy** astronomical study by means of radar; study of radio waves generated in space; **radio beacon** an apparatus that transmits signals for direction-finding; **radio communication** wireless telegraphy or telephony; **radio compass** a radio direction-finding instrument; **radio frequency** a frequency suitable for radio transmission, about 3kHz to 300GHz (**radio-frequency heating** heating, such as dielectric heating, by means of a radio-frequency electric current); **radio galaxy** a galaxy emitting a particularly high level of radio-frequency energy; **radio ham** (*slang*) a radio amateur; **radio microphone** a microphone with a miniature radio transmitter, and therefore not requiring any cable; **radio pill** a capsule which may be swallowed containing a tiny radio transmitter that will send out information about bodily processes; **radio spectrum** the range of radio frequencies; **radio star** a discrete source of radio waves in outer space, generally corresponding with no visual object and known only by radio astronomy; **radio station** a place where radio transmitters and (if radio-communication is involved) receivers are installed; a broadcasting company, association, etc; **radio telescope** an apparatus for the reception, analysis and transmission in radio astronomy of radio waves from and to outer space; **radio wave** an electromagnetic wave of radio frequency. [L *radius* a rod, spoke, radius, ray]

radio- *rā-di-ō-*, *combining form* (some of the following words may also be hyphenated) denoting: rays; radiation; radium; radius; radio, wireless; (of product or isotope) radioactive, as in **rādio-actin'ium** and **rādio-tho'rium**, both isotopes of thorium, or **rādioel'ement** (*chem*). — *adj* **rādioact'ive**. — *n* **rādioactiv'ity** spontaneous disintegration, first observed in certain naturally occurring heavy elements (radium, actinium, uranium, thorium) with emission of α-rays, β-rays, and γ-rays; disintegration effected by high-energy bombardment. — *n* **rādioaut'ograph** another term for **autoradiograph**. — *n* **radiobiol'ogy** the study of the effects of radiation on living tissue. — *n* **radiocar'bon** a radioactive isotope of carbon, *specif* carbon-14 (**radiocarbon dating** a method of establishing the age of any organic material, eg wood or paper, by measuring content of carbon-14). — *n* **rādiochem'istry** the chemistry of radioactive elements and compounds. — *n* **rādioel'ement** a radio-isotope. — *adj* **rādiogenic** (*-jen'ik*) produced by radioactive disintegration; suitable for broadcasting. — *n* **rādiogoniom'eter** a radio direction-finder. — *n* **rā'diogram** an X-ray photograph, a radiograph; a wireless telegram; (for **rādio-gram'ophone**) a combined wireless receiver and gramophone. — *n* **rā'diograph** (*-gräf*) a recorded image, *usu* a photograph, produced by X-rays; formerly, the wireless telegraph. — *n* **radiog'rapher** a technician involved in radiology, eg in the taking of radiographs or in radiotherapy. — *adj* **radiographic** (*-graf'ik*). — *n* **radiography** (*-og'rə-fi*) photography of interior of body or specimen by radiations other than light, such as X-rays, etc; formerly, radiotelegraphy; study of radioactivity. — *n* **ra'dioimmunoass'ay** (or *-ā'*) an immunoassay of a substance which has been labelled (qv) with a radioactive substance. — *n* **radio-ī'sotope** a radioactive isotope of a stable element. — *adj* **radiola'belled** labelled (qv) with a radioactive substance. — *n* **radiolocā'tion** position-finding by radio signals; radar. — *adj* **radiolog'ic** or **radiolog'ical**. — *n* **radiol'ogist** a doctor specializing in the use of X-rays and in methods of imaging the internal structure of the body for diagnosis and treatment of disease (now often called a **radiation oncologist**). — *n* **rādiol'ogy** the study of radioactivity and radiation or their application to medicine, eg as X-rays, or as treatment for certain diseases. — *n* **radioluminesc'ence** luminous radiation arising from radiation from a radioactive material. — *n* **rādiol'ysis** chemical decomposition induced by ionizing radiation. — *adj* **rādiolyt'ic**. — *n* **rādiometeor'ograph** same as **radiosonde**. — *n* **rādiom'eter** any instrument that measures radiant energy. — *adj* **rādiomet'ric**. — *adj* **radiomimet'ic** of drugs which imitate the physiological action of X-rays. — *n sing* **radion'ics** a form of healing at a distance using a form of dowsing for diagnosis. — *n* **rādionū'clide** any radioactive atom of an element identified by the number of neutrons and protons in its nucleus, and its energy state. — *n* **rā'diopager** a radio receiver which functions as a pager. — *adj* **radiopaque** (*-pāk'*) opaque to radiation (*esp* X-rays). — *n* **rā'diopaging**. — *n* **rā'diophōne** an instrument for producing sound by radiant energy; a radiotelephone. — *adj* **rādiophonic** (*-fon'ik*) (of music) produced electronically; producing electronic music. — *n sing* **rādiophon'ics**. — *n* **rādiophonist** (*-of'ə-nist*). — *n* **radioph'ony**. — *adj* **radioresist'ant** able to withstand considerable radiation doses without injury. — *n* **rā'dioscope** a machine used in **rādios'copy**, examination by X-rays, etc. — *adj* **rādiosen'sitive** quickly injured or changed by radiation. — *vt* **rādiosen'sitize** or **-ise** to make (eg cancer cells) more radiosensitive. — *n* **ra'diosonde** (Fr *sonde* plummet, probe) an apparatus for ascertaining atmospheric conditions at great heights, consisting of a hydrogen-filled balloon, radio transmitter(s), etc (also **rādiometeor'ograph**). — *n* **rādio-stron'tium** a radioactive isotope of strontium, *esp* strontium-90. — *n* **rādiotel'egram**. — *n* **rādiotel'egraph**. — *n* **rādio-teleg'raphy**. — *n* **rādiotelem'eter** see under **telemeter**. — *n* **rādiotel'ephone** a device which receives and transmits by means of radio waves (rather than wires) and which functions as a telephone (eg in cars and other vehicles). — *n* **rādioteleph'ony**. — *n* **rādio-tel'etype** a teleprinter that receives and transmits by radio. — *n* **rādiotherapeut'ics** or **rādio-ther'apy** treatment of disease, *esp* cancer, by radiation, eg by X-rays, etc. — *adj* **rādiotox'ic** of or relating to the toxic effects of radiation or radioactive material. — **radioactive waste** any radioactive waste material, *esp* spent fuel from a nuclear reactor (also called **radwaste**); **radiometric age** (*geol*) the radiometrically determined age of a fossil, mineral, rock, event, etc, *usu* given in years (also **absolute age**); **radiometric dating** (*geol*) the method of obtaining a geological age by measuring the relative abundance of radioactive parent and daughter isotopes in geological materials; **radionuclide imaging** (*radiol*) the use of radionuclides to image the physiology or anatomy of the body. [Ety as for **radio**]

Radiolaria *rā-di-ō-lā'ri-ə, n pl* an order of marine Protozoa, or unicellular animals, with fine radial tentacles for feeding and movement. — *adj* **radiola'rian**. — Also *n*. — **radiolarian ooze** a deep-sea deposit in which the siliceous skeletons of Radiolaria predominate. [LL *radiolus*, dimin of L *radius* radius]

radiothon *rā'di-ō-thon*, (*US*) *n* a very long radio programme used as a fund-raising event. [**radio** mara*thon*; cf **telethon**]

radish *rad'ish, n* a plant of the genus *Cruciferae*, especially *Raphanus sativus*; its pungent root, eaten raw as a salad vegetable. [Fr *radis*, from Provençal *raditz* or Ital *radice*, from L *rādīx*, *-īcis* a root]

radium *rā'di-əm, n* a radioactive metallic element (symbol **Ra**; atomic no 88) discovered by the Curies in 1898, found in pitchblende and other minerals, remarkable for its active spontaneous disintegration. — **radium A, B**, etc, successive products in the disintegration of radon; **radium bomb** an apparatus containing radium, emitting gamma rays for medical treatment (more commonly called **teleradium unit**); **radium emanation** radon. [L *radius* a ray]

radius *rā'di-əs, n* a straight line from the centre to the circumference of a circle or surface of a sphere (*geom*); a radiating line; anything placed like a radius, such as the spoke of a wheel, the movable arm of a sextant, etc; a radial plane of symmetry in a coelenterate; a line from a fixed point (eg the focus of a conic) to a point on a curve; the outer bone (in supine position) of the forearm in humans, or its equivalent in other animals; a barbule of a feather; the third vein of an insect's wing; a ray-flower or the ray-flowers of a head collectively (*rare*); a distance from a centre, conceived as limiting an area or range: — *pl* **radii** (*rā'di-ī*) or **ra'diuses**. — *adj* **ra'dial** see separate entry. — **radius vector** (*pl* **radii vectō'res** *-rēz*) a straight line joining a fixed point and a variable point. [L *radius* a rod, spoke, ray]

radix *rā'diks* or *rä'dēks, n* a root, root-number, root-word (*obs*); a source; a basis; the quantity on which a system of numeration, or of logarithms, etc is based: — *pl* **radices** (*rā'di-sez* or *rä-dē'kās*). [L *rādīx*, *-īcis* root]

radome *rā'dōm, n* a protective covering for microwave radar antennae. [*ra*dar *dome*]

radon *rā'don, n* a gaseous radioactive element (symbol **Rn**; atomic no 86), the first disintegration product of radium, radium emanation, formerly called *niton*. [**radium** and **-on**, as in *argon*, *xenon*, etc]

radula *rad'ū-lə, n* a mollusc's tongue or rasping ribbon: — *pl* **rad'ulae** (*-lē*). — *adj* **rad'ūlar**. — *adj* **rad'ūlate**. — *adj* **rad'ūliform** rasp-like. [L *rādula* a scraper, from *rādere*]

radwaste *rad'wāst*, (*esp US*) *n* radioactive waste. [*rad*ioactive *waste*]

RAEC *abbrev*: Royal Army Educational Corps.

RAeS *abbrev*: Royal Aeronautical Society.

Raetia and **Raetian**. See **Rhaetia**.

RAF *är-ā-ef'* or (*colloq*) *raf, abbrev*: Royal Air Force.

rafale *rä-fäl', n* a burst of artillery in quick rounds. [Fr, gust of wind]

raff *raf*, (*archaic*) *n* a heap, a quantity; riff-raff; one of the riff-raff; a rakish, flashy or blackguardly fellow. — *adj* raffish. — *adj* **raff'ish** (*raf'ish*) rakish, dashing; flashy. — *adv* **raff'ishly**. — *n* **raff'ishness**. [Cf **riff-raff**]

raffia *raf'i-ə, n* the Raphia palm or its leaf-bast. [**Raphia**]

raffinose *raf'i-nōs, n* a trisaccharide sugar. — *n* **raff'inate** liquid left after a desired solute has been extracted. [Fr *raffiner* to refine]

raffish, etc. See under **raff**.

raffle[1] *raf'l, n* an old game of dice, the stakes going to the thrower of a pair-royal; a lottery for an article. — *vt* to dispose of by raffle. — *vi* to engage in a raffle. — *n* **raff'ler**. — **raffle-ticket** a ticket with a number printed on it, bought by raffle participants and drawn to determine the winner(s). [Fr *rafle* a pair-royal]

raffle[2] *raf'l, n* a rabble; riff-raff; lumber; rubbish; a jumble; a tangle. [Cf **raff**]

raffle[3] *raf'l, vt* to notch; to crumple. [Ety uncertain]

Rafflesia *raf-lē'zi-ə, n* a genus (giving name to the family **Rafflesiā'ceae**, related to the birthwort family) of parasitic plants in Sumatra, Java, etc, one species having the largest known flowers, a yard across, carrion-scented, the rest of the plant reduced to threads within the tissues of its host-plant. [Named after Sir T Stamford *Raffles* (1781–1826), British governor in Sumatra (1818), who sent it to Brown, the botanist]

raft[1] *räft*, (*esp NAm*) *n* a large number, a heap; a crowd; a miscellaneous lot. [**raff**]

raft[2] *räft, n* a flat, floating mass of logs or other material (ice, vegetation, etc); a flat structure of logs, etc for support or for conveyance on water; a dense mass of floating waterfowl (*US*); a wide layer of concrete to support a building on soft ground. — *vt* to transport on a raft; to form into a raft; to cross, travel down, etc by raft. — *vi* to manage a raft; to travel by raft; to form into a raft; (of ice, etc) to pile up by overriding. — *n* **raft'er** a raftsman. — **raft'-bridge** a raft used as a bridge; a bridge supported on rafts; **raft'man** a raftsman; **raft'-port** (in ships) a large port for timber; **raft'-rope** a rope for towing blubber; **rafts'man** a person who works on a raft. [ON *raptr* rafter]

raft[3] *räft, obs pa t* and *pa p* of **reave**: in Keats *pa p* of **rive**.

rafter[1] *räf'tər, n* an inclined beam supporting a roof. — *vt* to equip with rafters; to plough so that a strip is overturned upon unploughed ground. — *adj* **raft'ered** having (*esp* visible) rafters. — *n* **raft'ering**. — **raft'er-bird** the spotted flycatcher. [OE *ræfter* a beam]

rafter[2] and **raftsman**. See under **raft**[2].

rag[1] *rag, n* a worn, torn or waste scrap of cloth; a tatter; a shred, scrap or tiny portion; a farthing (*old slang*); a jagged projection; a flag, handkerchief, sail, theatre curtain, garment, newspaper, or paper money (*contemptuously* or *playfully*); the pithy part of an orange, lemon, etc; a worthless or beggarly person; a person in a state of exhaustion; (in *pl*) tattered clothing; ragtime, or a piece of ragtime music. — *adj* of, for or dealing in rags. — *vt* to tear to rags; to make ragged; to perform in ragtime. — *vi* to become ragged, to fray; to dress (with *out* or *up*; *US archaic slang*): — *pr p* **ragg'ing**; *pa p* and *pa t* **ragged** (*ragd*). — *adj* **ragg'ed** shaggy; rough-edged; jagged; made or performed unevenly; raguly (*heraldry*); torn or worn into rags; wearing ragged clothes. — *adv* **ragg'edly**. — *n* **ragg'edness**. — *adj* **ragg'edy** ragged-looking. — *n* **ragg'ery** rags or ragged people collectively; clothes, *esp* women's (*slang*); raggedness. — *adj* **ragg'y** rough; ragged; of the nature of a rag. — **rag-and-bone'-man** a person who collects or deals in rags, bones, or other goods of little value; **rag-ba'by** (*archaic*) a rag-doll; **rag'bag** a bag for rags and thrown-away garments; a random or confused collection (*fig*); a slattern; **rag'bolt** a bolt with barbs to prevent withdrawal; **rag'-book** a child's book printed on cloth; **rag'-bush** a bush to which shreds of cloth are tied as offerings to the local spirit, often near a well;

rag'-doll a doll made of rags; a slattern; **rag'-dust** finely divided rags, used for making flock-paper; **rag'-fair** an old-clothes market; a kit inspection (*military slang*); **ragged-la'dy** *Nigella damascena*; **ragged-Rob'in** a campion (*Lychnis floscuculi*) with ragged-edged petals; **ragged school** (*hist*) a voluntary school for destitute children in the 19c; **ragged staff** (*heraldry*) a stick with branch stubs; **rag'head** (*derog slang*; *offensive*) an Arab; **rag'man** a person who collects or deals in rags; the devil; **rag'-money** (*slang*) paper money; **rag'-out** a newspaper article or headline reproduced in a later issue with a ragged edge as if torn out; an unofficial strike (*slang*); **rag'-paper** paper made from rags; **rag'-picker** a person who collects rags from bins, heaps, etc; **rag'-rolling** a technique, used in house decoration, of rolling a folded cloth over a specially painted surface to produce a randomly shaded effect. — *adj* **rags-to-rich'es** (of a story, etc) describing a person's progression from poverty to wealth. — **rag'tag** the rabble (also **ragg'le-tagg'le**). — *adj* of or like the rabble; ragged, disorderly. — **rag'time** a form of jazz music of Black American origin, with highly syncopated melody; a tune, song or dance in ragtime; **rag'timer**; **rag'top** (*US colloq*) a folding canvas roof on a sports car; a car with this, a convertible; **rag trade** (*colloq*) the trade concerned with designing, making and selling clothes; **rag'-trader** (*colloq*); **rag'weed** ragwort; any species of the composite genus *Ambrosia* (*US*); **rag'-wheel** a toothed wheel; a polishing-wheel made of cloth discs clamped together; **rag'-woman**; **rag'-wool** shoddy; **rag'worm** a pearly white burrowing marine worm (*Nephthys caeca*) used as bait by fishermen; **rag'wort** a common coarse yellow-headed composite weed (*Senecio jacobaea*) of pastures; any similar species of the genus with long rays (from the cut leaves). — **glad rags** see under **glad**; **rag-tag and bobtail** riff-raff. [OE *ragg*, inferred from the adj *raggig* shaggy; ON *rögg* shagginess, tuft]

rag[2] or **ragg** *rag*, *n* a rough hard stone of various kinds, *esp* one breaking in slabs; a large rough slate (3ft by 2). — **rag'stone**; **rag'work** undressed masonry in slabs. [Poss from **rag**[1]]

rag[3] *rag*, *vt* to rate; to banter; to assail or beset with silly questions, ridicule or horseplay. — *vi* to wrangle, argue; to indulge in a rag: — *pr p* **ragg'ing**; *pa t* and *pa p* **ragged** (*ragd*). — *n* an outburst of organized horseplay, *usu* in defiance of authority; riotous festivity, *esp* and *orig* of undergraduates (now, in British universities, associated with the raising of money for charity). — *n* **ragg'ing**. — *adj* **ragg'y** (*slang*) irritated. — **rag day** or **rag week** in British universities, the particular day or week during which money-making activities, such as processions, etc for charity are organized. — **lose one's rag** (*colloq*) to lose one's temper. [Perh shortened from **bullyrag**; perh from **rag**[1] as in *red rag*]

raga *rä'gə*, *n* a traditional Hindu musical form or mode, a rhythmic or melodic pattern used as the basis for improvisation; a piece composed in such a mode. [Sans *rāga* colour, tone (in music)]

ragamuffin *rag'ə-muf-in* or *-muf'*, *n* a ragged, disreputable child; (with *cap*) the name of a devil (*obs*). [Poss **rag**[1]]

rag'd or **ragde** *ragd*, (*Shakesp*) for **ragged**, shaggy, jagged; *perh* unruly; *poss* also (*rājd*) for **raged**, irritated (as if *pa p* of *vt*).

rage *rāj*, *n* madness; overpowering passion of any kind, such as desire or *esp* anger; inspired frenzy; ardour; a fit of any of these; a mania or craze (for something); a vogue (*colloq*); something in vogue; violence, stormy or furious activity; a flood (*Shakesp*); a party (*slang*, *esp Austr*). — *vi* to behave or speak with passion, *esp* with furious anger; to be violent; to storm; to be prevalent and violent; to scold (with *at* or *on*; *Scot*); to be violently bent on (*Milton*); to attend a party, etc, to have a good time (*slang*, *esp Austr*). — *vt* see **rag'd**. — *adj* **rage'ful**. — *n* **rā'ger**. — *adj* and *n* **rā'ging**. — *adv* **rā'gingly**. — **all the rage** very much in fashion. [Fr, from L *rabiēs*, from *rabere* to rave]

ragee. See **ragi**.

ragg. See **rag**[2].

ragged, **raggery** and **raggedy**. See under **rag**[1].

raggee. See **ragi**.

raggle *rag'l*, (*Scot*) *n* a groove in masonry, *esp* to receive the edge of a roof. — *vt* to make a raggle in. [Origin obscure]

raggle-taggle. See **rag-tag** under **rag**[1].

raggy. See under **rag**[1,3] and **ragi**.

ragi, **ragee**, **raggee** or **raggy** *rä'gē* or *rag'i*, *n* a millet (*Eleusine coracana*) much grown in India, Africa, etc. [Hindi (and Sans) *rāgī*]

ragini *rä'gi-nē*, *n* a modified raga. [Sans *rāgiṇī* coloured]

raglan *rag'lən*, *n* an overcoat with sleeve in one piece with the shoulder; any garment made in this style, *esp* knitted. — *adj* (of a sleeve) in one piece with the shoulder; (of a garment) having sleeves of this kind. [From Lord *Raglan* (1788–1855), British commander in the Crimea]

ragman[1] *rag'mən* or **ragment** *rag'mənt*, *n* a catalogue (*obs*); a document with pendent seals (*obs*); a rigmarole (*obs Scot*). — **Ragman Rolls** a collection of instruments by which the Scottish nobles, etc subscribed allegiance to Edward I. [Origin obscure]

ragman[2]. See under **rag**[1].

ragmatical *rag-mat'i-kl*, (*Fielding* and *Smollett*) *adj* apparently, riotous, disorderly. [Perh from **rag**[1], after **pragmatical**]

ragment. See **ragman**[1].

Ragnarök *rag'na-rək*, (*Scand mythol*) *n* the coming mutual destruction of the gods and the powers of evil, and the end of this world, to be superseded by a better. [ON *ragna rök* history or judgement of the gods, from *rögn*, *régin* gods, and *rök* reason, judgement, sophisticated into *ragna rökr* twilight of the gods, from *rökr* darkness]

ragout *ra-gōō'*, *n* a highly seasoned stew of meat and vegetables; a mixture. — *vt* to make a ragout of. [Fr *ragoût*, from *ragoûter* to restore the appetite]

ragstone and **ragwork**. See under **rag**[2].

ragtime, **ragweed**, **ragwheel**, **ragworm** and **ragwort**. See under **rag**[1].

raguly *rag'ū-li*, (*heraldry*) *adj* with projections like oblique stubs of branches. — Also **rag'ūled**. [Origin obscure]

rah or **'rah** *rä* or *rö*, *interj*, *n* and *vi*. Short form of **hurrah**.

Rahu *rä'hōō*, (*Hindu mythol*) *n* the demon that swallows the sun and moon at eclipses.

rai *rī*, *n* (also with *cap*) a modern, N African form of popular music, blending traditional Arabic and Spanish with Western folk music styles. [Ar *ra'y* opinion, view]

raid[1] *rād*, *n* a sudden swift inroad, *orig* by horsemen, for assault or seizure; an air attack; an invasion unauthorized by government; an incursion of police for the purpose of making arrests; an onset or onslaught for the purpose of obtaining or suppressing something; concerted selling by a group of speculators in order to lower the price of a particular stock (*stock exchange slang*). — *vt* to make a raid on. — *vi* to go on a raid. — *n* **raid'er** a person who raids; a raiding aeroplane. — **corporate raider** a person who buys up a large proportion of company's shares so as to be in a position to take it over or influence management policy; **dawn raid** see under **dawn**; **raid the market** to upset prices of stocks artificially for future gain. [Scots form of **road** (revived by Scott), from OE *rād* riding]

raid[2]. See **ride**.

raik *rāk*, (*Scot* and *NEng*) *n* course, journey; range; pasture. — *vi* to go; to range. [ON *reik* (n), *reika* (v) walk; coalescing later with **rake**[4]]

rail[1] *rāl*, *n* a bar extending horizontally or at a slope between supports or on the ground, often to form a support, a fence, a guard, a track for wheels, etc; the railway as a means of travel or transport; a horizontal member in framing or panelling (as in a door); the capping part of bulwarks; (in *pl*) a racecourse barrier; (in *pl*) railway shares. — *vt* to enclose or separate with rails; to provide with rails; to send by railway. — *vi* (*archaic*) to travel by railway. — *n* **rail'ing** fencing; fencing materials; (often in *pl*) a barrier or ornamental structure, *usu* of upright iron rods secured by horizontal connections. — *adj* **rail'less**. — **rail'bed** the roadbed of a railway track; **rail'bus** a light-weight railway coach powered by a bus-type diesel engine, or otherwise resembling a bus. — *adj* **rail'-borne** carried by railway. — **rail'-car** (*US*) a railway carriage; a self-propelled railway carriage; **rail'card** any of various cards entitling its holder (eg a young person, old age pensioner, etc) to reduced train fares; **rail'-fence** (*US*) a fence of wooden posts and rails; **rail'head** the furthest point reached by a railway under construction; the end of railway transport; **rail'man** or **rail'woman** a railway employee; **rail'-motor** a self-propelled railway carriage; **rail'road** (chiefly *NAm*) a railway. — *vt* (*colloq*) to force or push forward unduly (a person into a particular course of action, a bill through parliament, etc) (*orig US*); to get rid of, *esp* by sending to prison on a false charge. — **railroad car** (*US*) a railway carriage or a railway van or truck; **rail'roader** (*US*) a railway worker or official; **rail'-splitter** (*US*) a person who splits logs for fence-rails; **rail'way** a track laid with rails for wheels to run on, *esp* for locomotives with passengers and goods wagons; a system of such tracks together with their equipment and organization; the company owning such a system. — Also *adj*. — **rail'way-carriage** a railway vehicle for passengers; **rail'way-crossing** an intersection of railway lines or of road and railway, *esp* without a bridge; **rail'wayman** a railway employee; **rail'way-stitch** a name for various quickly worked stitches. — **off the rails** disorganized; not functioning; mad, deranged; morally degenerate. [OFr *reille*, from L *rēgula* a ruler]

rail[2] *rāl*, *vi* to scoff; to use vigorously or mockingly reproachful language; to banter; to revile (*usu* with *at* or *against*). — *vt* to bring or render by raillery. — *n* (*Spenser* **rayle**) reviling. — *n* **rail'er**. — *adj* and *n* **rail'ing**. — *adv* **rail'ingly**. — *n* **raillery** (*rāl'ər-i*; *archaic ral'*) railing or mockery; banter; playful satire. [Fr *railler*]

rail[3] *rāl*, *n* any bird of the genus *Rallus*, *esp* the water-rail, or other member of the family *Rallidae*, *esp* the corncrake or land-rail. [OFr *rasle* (Fr *râle*)]

rail[4] (*Spenser* **rayle** or **raile**) *rāl*, (*archaic*) *vi* to flow, gush. [Origin obscure]

rail[5] *rāl*, (*obs* except in **night-rail**) *n* a garment; a cloak; a neckerchief. — *n* **raill'y** (*Scott*) a jacket. [OE *hrægl*]

raiment *rā'mənt*, *n* (*archaic* or *poetic*) clothing. [**array-ment**]

rain[1] *rān*, *n* water that falls from the clouds in drops; a shower; a fall of anything in the manner of rain; (in *pl*) the rainy season in tropical countries. — *vi* to fall as or like rain; to send down rain. — *vt* to shower. — *n* **rain'iness**. — *adj* **rain'less**. — *adj* **rain'y**. — **rain'band** a dark band in the solar spectrum, due to water vapour in the earth's atmosphere; **rain'-bird** a bird, such as the green woodpecker and various kinds of cuckoo, supposed to foretell rain. — *adj* **rain'-bound** detained by rain. — **rain'bow** the coloured bow caused by refraction and internal reflexion of light in raindrops; any similar array of colours; a highly discoloured bruise (*slang*); a rainbow trout; a S American humming-bird, the cock with rainbow-coloured head. — *adj* of, or coloured like, the rainbow. — **rain'bow-chaser** a visionary, someone who tries to reach the end of the rainbow (**chase rainbows** to pursue an impossible aim); **rainbow coalition** a political alliance between minority groups or parties of varying opinions. — *adj* **rain'bow-coloured**. — **rainbow dressing** a gaudy display of flags on a ship. — *adj* **rain'bowed**. — *adj* **rain'bow-tint'ed**. — **rainbow trout** a finely marked and coloured trout (*Salmo gairdneri*) *orig* N American. — *adj* **rain'-bowy**. — **rain'-chamber** a compartment for condensing noxious fumes by spray; **rain'check** (*US*) a ticket for future use given to spectators when a game or a sports meeting is cancelled or stopped because of bad weather (**take a raincheck (on)** (*colloq*; *orig US*) to promise to accept an invitation (for) at a later date); **rain'-cloud** nimbus, a dense dark sheet of cloud that may shed rain or snow; **rain'coat** a light overcoat capable of protecting the wearer against moderate rain; **rain'date** (*US*) an alternative date set for an event in case of rain or bad weather; **rain'-doctor** a rainmaker; **rain'drop** a drop of rain. — *adj* **rained off** (of a sport, outdoor activity, etc) cancelled because of rain. — **rain'fall** a shower of rain; the amount (by depth of water) of rain that falls; **rain'forest** broad-leaved, evergreen tropical forest with very heavy rainfall; **rain'-gauge** an instrument for measuring rainfall; **rain'maker** a person in tribal societies who professes to bring rain; a high-powered employee who generates a great deal of income for his or her employers (*slang*); **rain'making** attempting to cause rainfall by techniques such as seeding clouds; **rain'-plover** the golden plover; **rain'-print** a little pit made by a raindrop in clay, etc, sometimes preserved in rocks. — *adj* **rain'proof** more or less impervious to rain. — *vt* to make rainproof. — *n* a rainproof overcoat. — **rain'-shadow** an area sheltered by hills from the prevailing winds and having a lighter rainfall than the windward side of the hills; **rain'-stone** a stone used in magic rites aimed at bringing rain; **rain'storm**. — *adj* **rain'tight** rainproof. — **rain'-tree** a S American tree (*Pithecolobium saman*) of the mimosa family, under which there is a constant rain of juice ejected by cicadas; **rain'-wash** the washing away of earth, etc by rain; downward creep of superficial deposits soaked in rain; matter so transported; **rain'water** water that falls or has fallen as rain; **rain'wear** articles of rainproof clothing. — **a rainy day** (*fig*) a possible future time of need; **chase rainbows** see **rainbow-chaser** above; **come rain or shine** whatever the weather or circumstances; **rain in** (of rain) to penetrate a roof, tent, badly-fitting window, etc; **right as rain** (*colloq*) perfectly in order; **take a raincheck (on)** see **raincheck** above. [OE *regn*; Du *regen*, Ger *Regen*; ON *regn*]

rain[2], **raine** (*Spenser*). Same as **reign**.

raird. See **reird**.

raise[1] *rāz*, *vt* to cause to rise; to make higher or greater; to lift; to exalt; to advance; to elevate; to cause to stand up or upright; to rouse; to stir up; to elate; to rear, grow or breed (children, animals, etc); to produce; to give rise to; to build, erect; to bring into being; to bring to life (from the dead); to utter (*esp* a question); to establish; to institute; to bring forward into consideration or notice; to bring into relief; to intensify; to call up; to cause (land) to rise in view by approaching (*naut*); to contact by radio; to levy, get together, collect (taxes, an army, etc); to cause (a lump) to swell; to extol; to remove, take off; to produce a nap on. — *n* a rising road; an increase in wages or salary (*colloq*; *esp NAm*). — *adj* **rais'able** or **raise'able**. — *n* **rais'er** someone who or that which raises a building, etc; the riser of a step. — *n* **rais'ing**. — **raised beach** (*geol*) an old sea-margin above the present water-level; **raised pastry** or **pie** a pastry or pie without support of a dish at the sides; **rais'ing-bee** (*US*) a gathering of neighbours to help in raising the frame of a house, etc. — **raise a hand to** to hit, or generally treat badly; **raise an eyebrow** or **raise one's eyebrows** to look surprised (at); **raise a siege** to abandon, or put an end to, a siege; **raise Cain** or **raise the roof** (*colloq*) to make a lot of noise; to be extremely angry; **raise hell** or **raise the devil** (*colloq*) to make a lot of trouble; **raise money on** to get money by pawning or selling, *esp* privately; **raise one's glass** to drink a health (to); **raise one's hat** to take one's hat off in salutation (to); **raise the market (upon)** (*stock exchange*) to bring about a rise in prices (to the disadvantage of); **raise the wind** (*slang*) to get together the necessary money by any means. [ME *reisen*, from ON *reisa*, causative of *rīsa* to rise; cf **rise** and **rear**[2]]

raise[2] *rāz*, (*NEng*) *n* a cairn. [ON *hreysi*]
raisin *rā'zn*, *n* a dried grape. [Fr, grape, from L *racēmus* a bunch of grapes]
raison d'état *rā-zɔ̃ dā-ta*, (*Fr*) *n* literally reason of state; the principle that national interests take precedence over strict individual rights, morality, etc.
raison d'être *rā-zɔ̃ detr'*, (*Fr*) *n* reason for existence (purpose or cause).
raisonné *rā-zon-ā*, (*Fr*) *adj* logically set out, systematically arranged, and (*usu*) provided with notes.
raisonneur *rā-zon-œr'*, *n* (in a play or novel) a character who embodies the author's point of view and expresses his or her opinions. [Fr, an arguer]
rait. Same as **ret**.
raita *rā-ē'tə* or *rī'tə*, *n* an Indian dish of chopped vegetables, *esp* cucumber, in yoghurt.
raiyat and **raiyatwari**. Same as **ryot** and **ryotwari**.
raj *räj*, *n* rule, sovereignty; government, *esp* (with *cap*) the British government of India, 1858–1947. — *n* **ra'ja** or **ra'jah** an Indian prince or king; a Malay chief. — *n* **ra'jaship** or **ra'jahship**. — *n* **raj'pramukh** (*-mo͝ok*) the head of a state or states union in the Democratic Republic of India. — *n* **Rajput** or **Rajpoot** (*räj'po͞ot*) a member of a race or class claiming descent from the original Hindu military and ruling caste. [Hindi *rāj*, *rājā*, *Rājpūt*, from Sans *rājan* a king (cognate with L *rēx*), and *putra* son]
Rajya Sabha *räj'yə sub'ə*, *n* the upper house of the Indian parliament. [Hindi *rajya* state, and *sabha* assembly]
rake[1] *rāk*, *n* a toothed bar on a handle, for scraping, gathering together, smoothing, etc; a tool for various purposes, toothed, notched or bladed and with a long handle (eg a croupier's implement for drawing in money); a wheeled field implement with long teeth for gathering hay, scraping up weeds, etc; a connected set (of railway carriages or wagons); an extremely thin person or horse. — *vt* to scrape, smooth, clear, break up, draw, gather, remove, cover, uncover, search, ransack, with a rake or as if with a rake; to cover (a fire) with ashes so as to keep smouldering; to graze, scrape; to pass over violently and swiftly; to fire (bullets, etc) across the entire line of one's enemy; to provide or take a view all over or completely through. — *vi* to work with or as if with a rake; to search minutely. — *n* **rā'ker** a person who rakes; a scavenger; a raking implement; (in games) a long, fast, low-flying shot (*perh* partly from **rake**[4]). — *n* and *adj* **rā'king**. — **rake'-off** monetary share, *esp* unearned or dishonest; **rake'shame** (*obs*) a base, dissolute wretch. — **rake in** (*colloq*) to acquire rapidly and in great quantity; **rake up** to revive from oblivion (*usu* something scandalous); to collect together. [OE *raca*; Ger *Rechen* rake; ON *reka* shovel]
rake[2] *rāk*, *n* a debauched or dissolute person, *esp* a man of fashion. — *vi* to lead a rake's life; to make a practice of lechery. — *n* **rā'kery** dissoluteness. — *adj* **rā'kish**. — *adv* **rā'kishly**. — *n* **rā'kishness**. [Shortening of **rakehell**]
rake[3] *rāk*, *n* inclination from the vertical or horizontal, eg of a ship's funnel, a theatre stage, etc; an angle, eg between the face of a cutting-tool and the surface on which it is working, or the wings and body of an aircraft. — *vi* to incline. — *vt* to slope; to cut aslant. — *n* **rā'ker** a sloping support or strut. — *adj* **rā'kish** with raking masts; swift-looking; pirate-like; dashing; jaunty. — *adv* **rā'kishly**. [Ety dubious]
rake[4] *rāk*, (now *dialect*) *vi* to proceed, *esp* swiftly; to roam, range about; (of a hawk) to fly wide; (of a dog) to follow the scent wanderingly along the ground. — *n* **rā'ker** a very fast pace; a plunge in betting. — *adj* **rā'king** advancing swiftly. [OE *racian* to go forward, hasten]
rake[5] *rāk*, (*NEng*) *n* a track, *esp* up a hill or in a gully or a pasture; a pasture; a journey, *esp* in fetching things; the amount carried at one journey, load, gang; an irregular, *usu* vertical, vein of ore; a string, eg of wagons. — *vi* (eg of sheep) to form into single file. [ON *rāk* stripe; partly coalescing with **raik**]
rakee. See **raki**.
rakehell *rāk'hel*, *n* an utterly debauched person. — *adj* **rake'hell** or **rake'helly**. — See also **rake**[2]. [Prob **rake**[1] and **Hell**, ie such as might be found by raking out hell]
raker. See under **rake**[1,3,4].
rakery. See under **rake**[2].
rakeshame. See under **rake**[1].
raki *räk'ē*, *n* an aniseed-flavoured spirit of Turkey and the E Mediterranean. — Also **rak'ee**. [Turk *rāqī*]
rakish, etc. See under **rake**[2,3].
rakshas *räk'shəs* or **rakshasa** *-shə-sə*, (*Hindu mythol*) *n* an evil spirit. [Sans *rākṣasa*]
raku *rä'-ko͞o*, *n* a type of Japanese coarse-grained, lead-glazed pottery fired at low temperature, used *esp* to produce tea bowls. [Jap, literally pleasure, enjoyment]
râle or **rale** *räl*, (*pathol*) *n* a sound from a diseased lung. [Fr]
rall. *ral*, (*music*) *abbrev*: rallentando.
rallentando *ral-ən-tan'dō*, (*music*) *adj* and *adv* becoming slower. — *n* a slowing: — *pl* **rallentan'dos**. — *abbrev* **rall**. [Ital, pr p of *rallentare* to slacken]
rallier. See under **rally**[1,2].
Rallus *ral'əs*, *n* the water-rail genus of birds, giving name to the family **Rall'idae**. — *adj* **rall'ine** (*-īn*). [Latinized from Fr *râle*]
rally[1] *ral'i*, *vt* to reassemble; to gather to one's support; to bring together for united effort; to muster (eg the faculties) by an effort; to pull together, revive. — *vi* to come together, *esp* from dispersal, or for renewed effort, or in support of a leader, friend or cause; to recover; to recover in some degree lost health, power, vigour, value, etc; (of a share price or currency value) to improve after a period of decline or decrease: — *pr p* **rall'ying**; *pa p* and *pa t* **rall'ied**. — *n* an assembly or reassembly for renewed effort; a gathering for a common purpose; a mass meeting; a competition to test skill in driving, and ability to follow an unknown route (*US* also **rall'ye**), or to test quality of motor vehicles (see also under **rely**); a pantomime mêlée; a temporary or partial recovery (from an illness, etc); a quick exchange of blows in boxing; a series of to-and-fro strokes in deciding a point, as in tennis. — *n* **rall'ier**. — *n* **rall'ying** long-distance motor-racing over public roads. — *n* **rall'yist**. — **rall'y-cross** motor-racing round a circuit consisting partly of paved road and partly of rough ground; **rall'ying-cry** a slogan to attract support for a cause, etc; **rall'ying-point** a place of assembly, *esp* for a mass meeting. — **rally round** to support, help someone in need. [OFr *rallier*, from pfx *re-* and *allier*; see **ally**[1]]
rally[2] *ral'i*, *vt* and *vi* to banter: — *pr p* **rall'ying**; *pa t* and *pa p* **rall'ied**. — *n* **rall'ier**. — *adv* **rall'yingly**. [Fr *railler*; cf **rail**[2]]
rallye. See **rally**[1].
Ralph *ralf* or *rāf*, *n* the imp of mischief in a printing-house. [Personal name, from OE *Rǣdwulf*]
RAM *abbrev*: random access memory (*ram*; *comput*); Royal Academy of Music.
ram *ram*, *n* a male sheep, a tup; Aries (*astrol*); a battering-ram; a ship's beak, a pointed device for striking holes in an enemy ship's hull; a warship with such a beak; a water-ram or hydraulic ram (see **hydraulic**); the falling weight of a pile-driver; the striking head of a steam-hammer; a piston applying pressure, operated by hydraulic or other power; a machine with such a piston; a rammer; an act of ramming. — *vt* to thrust roughly, cram (also *fig*); to block up; to beat hard; to drive hard down; to strike, batter or pierce with a ram; to strike or dash into violently: — *pr p* **ramm'ing**; *pa t* and *pa p* **rammed**. — *n* **ramm'er** a person who or that which rams, *esp* a tool for compressing earth before paving, etc. — *adj* **ramm'ish** rank in smell or taste (now *dialect*); lecherous, lustful (*obs*). — **ram'cat** a male cat; **ram'jet** or **ramjet engine** a simple form of aero-engine, consisting of forward air intake, combustion chamber and rear expansion nozzle, in which thrust is generated by compression due solely to forward motion; **ram'=raid** the action of smashing into shop windows, etc with

a stolen car and subsequent stealing of the goods inside. — *vi* and *vt* to perform such a raid (on). — **ram'raider**; **ram'-raiding**; **ram'rod** a rod for ramming down a charge into, or for cleaning, a gun-barrel; a stern, inflexible person; a strict disciplinarian. — *adj* rigid, inflexible; stern. — *vt* to push or drive with great force. — **ram's'-horn** the horn of a ram; any article made of or resembling this, eg a trumpet or snuff-box. — Also *adj*. — **ram-air turbine** a small turbine driven by air used as an emergency power source for aircraft, etc, or to provide power in guided weapons. [OE *ram, rom*; Ger *Ramm*]

r.a.m. *abbrev*: relative atomic mass.

Rāma *rä'mä, n* an incarnation of Vishnu. — *n* **Rāmāyana** (*rä-mä'yä-na*) the Sanskrit epic of *Rāma*.

Ramadan or **Ramadhan** *ram-ə-dän', n* the ninth month of the Muslim calendar, during which fasting is observed between dawn and dusk; the fast observed at this time. [Ar *Ramadān*]

ramakin. See **ramekin**.

ramal, ramate, etc. See under **ramus**.

Raman effect *räm'ən i-fekt', n* a change in frequency of light passing through a transparent medium, used in the study of molecules. [From Sir Chandrasekhara *Raman* (1888–1970), Indian physicist]

Ramapithecus *rä-ma-pith'i-kəs, n* an early Pliocene genus of primates, *poss* an ancestor of modern man, known from fossil remains found in N India. — *n* and *adj* **ramapith'ecine**. [**Rāma**, with reference to his birth as a prince of Oudh, and Gr *pithēkos* ape]

Rāmāyana. See **Rāma**.

ramble *ram'bl, vi* to go wherever one's fancy leads; to wander; to walk for recreation or pleasure; to wander in mind or discourse; to be desultory, incoherent or delirious; (of a plant, etc) to straggle or trail randomly. — *n* a roving about; an irregular, unorganized excursion; a walk for pleasure; rambling. — *n* **ram'bler** a person who rambles; a trailing climbing plant, *esp* a rose with small clustered flowers. — *n* and *adj* **ram'bling**. — *adv* **ram'blingly**. [ME *romblen*; appar connected with **roam**]

rambunctious *ram-bungk'shəs, adj* difficult to control, boisterous, exuberant. — *adv* **rambunc'tiously**. — *n* **rambunc'tiousness**. [Perh **rumbustious**]

rambutan *ram-bōō'tən, n* a sapindaceous tree (*Nephelium lappaceum*) of the same family as the lychee, found throughout SE Asia; its fruit with edible, translucent flesh and thick red shell covered with hooked hairs. [Malay *rambūtan*, from *rambut* hair]

RAMC *abbrev*: Royal Army Medical Corps.

ramcat. See under **ram**.

rameal and **rameous**. See under **ramus**.

Ramean. See **Ramism**.

ramee. See **rami**.

ramekin, ramequin or **ramakin** *ram'ə-kin, n* a mixture of cheese, eggs, etc baked in small moulds, or served on toast; a small, round, straight-sided baking dish or mould for single portions of food. [Fr *ramequin*, from obs Flem *rammeken*]

ramen *rä'-mən, n* a Japanese dish of clear broth containing vegetables, noodles and often pieces of meat. [Jap *rāmen*]

ramentum *ra-ment'əm, n* a chaffy scale, such as on ferns: — *pl* **rament'a**. [L *rāmentum* a scraping, from *rādere* to scrape]

rameous. See under **ramus**.

ramequin. See **ramekin**.

ramfeezle *ram-fē'zl, (Scot) vt* to weary out.

ramgunshoch *ram-gun'shohh, (Scot) adj* rough.

rami, ramie or **ramee** *ram'ē, n* a plant of the nettle family (*Boehmeria nivea*) long cultivated in China; its fibre, used for weaving, paper-making, etc; a garment made of this. — Also called **rhea** or **China grass**. [Malay *rami*]

ramification *ram-i-fi-kā'shən, n* branching; arrangement of branches; a single branch or part of a complex arrangement, or of a situation or problem, *esp* a consequence that must be taken into account. — *adj* **ram'iform** having a branched shape. — *vt* and *vi* **ram'ify** to divide into branches (also *fig*): — *pr p* **ram'ifying**; *pa t* and *pa p* **rami'fied**. [Ety as for **ramus**]

Ramilie, Ramillie *ram'i-li*, **Ramilies** or **Ramillies** *ram'i-liz, (hist) n* a name for several articles and modes of dress in fashion after Marlborough's victory at *Ramillies* (1706), *esp* a form of cocked hat, and a wig with a long plaited tail. — Also *adj*.

ramin *ram'in, n* a Malaysian tree of the genus *Gonystylus*; a hardwood obtained from this, commonly used in making moulding, frames, etc. [Malay]

Ramism *rā'mizm, n* the system of logic of Peter *Ramus* (1515–72). — *n* and *adj* **Rā'mean** or **Rā'mist**.

ramjet. See under **ram**.

rammer and **rammish**. See under **ram**.

rammy *ram'i, (Scot) n* a row, free-for-all fight. [Perh from Scots *rammle* an uproar, noisy drinking spree]

ramose and **ramous**. See under **ramus**.

ramp[1] *ramp, vi* to climb; to grow rankly; to rear as if climbing; to slope from one level to another; to rage; to dash about wildly. — *vt* to provide with a ramp; to bend into a ramp; to snatch; to rob; to hustle into paying a fictitious debt; to swindle; to increase (the price of something) dishonestly, and to a large extent (*usu* with *up*). — *n* an act of ramping; an inclined plane, a slope; a low hump made across a road, eg to slow down traffic; an inclined slip road (*NAm*); the slope of a wall-top, or anything similar, between two levels; an upwardly concave bend in a handrail; a swindle; a stunt worked for private profit; a worked-up excitement or craze, *esp* for some gain; an exploitation of a special situation to increase prices, etc; a romp, tomboy (*archaic*); a disorderly or loose woman (*archaic*). — *adj* **rampā'cious** (*Dickens*) rampageous. — *n* **rampall'ian** (*Shakesp*) a term of abuse. — *n* **ramp'er** a person who ramps, *esp* someone who makes a disturbance to cover the activities of others; a rampsman. — *n* **ramp'ing** (*business*) the practice of causing large, false increases in the price of shares, etc by dishonest means. — **ramps'man** (*slang*) a person who ramps bookmakers. [Fr *ramper* to creep, to clamber]

ramp[2] *ramp, n* a kind of wild onion native to N America; a ramson. [OE *wramsa*]

rampage *ram-pāj'* (*US* also *ram'*; *Scot* **rampauge** *-pöj'*), *n* turbulently or aggressively excited behaviour or rushing about. — *vi* to storm; to rush about wildly. — *adj* **rampā'geous**. — *n* **rampā'geousness**. — *n* **rampag'ing**. — **on the rampage** storming about, behaving wildly and violently in anger, exuberance, etc. [Ety as for **ramp**[1]]

rampant *ram'pənt, adj* rearing; standing in profile, on the left hindleg (*heraldry*); high-spirited; fierce; unrestrained; unchecked in growth or prevalence; (of an arch) having springers on different levels. — *n* **ramp'ancy**. — *adv* **ramp'antly**. [Ety as for **ramp**[1]]

rampart *ram'pärt* or *-pərt, n* a flat-topped defensive mound; that which defends. — *vt* to fortify or surround with ramparts. [Fr *rempart*, from OFr *rempar*, from *remparer* to defend, from L pfx *re-*, *ante*, and *parāre* to prepare]

rampauge. See **rampage**.

Ramphastos. See **Rhamphastos** under **rhamphoid**.

rampick *ram'pik* or **rampike** *-pīk*, (*archaic* and *US*) *n* a dead tree, or one decayed at the top, broken off or partly burned. — *adj* **ram'pick** or **ram'picked**. [Origin obscure]

rampion *ramp'yən* or *-i-ən, n* a bell-flower (*Campanula rapunculus*) whose root is eaten as a salad vegetable; any species of the related genus *Phyteuma*. [Cf Ital *raponzolo*, Ger *Rapunzel*, Fr *raiponce*]

rampire *ram'pīr*, (*archaic*) *n*. Same as **rampart**. — *adj* **ram'pired**.

ram-raid, etc and **ramrod**. See under **ram**.

ramshackle *ram'shak-l, adj* tumbledown; badly constructed or organized, etc. [Perh from *ramshackled*, pa p of an obs form of *ransackle* (see **ransha(c)kle**)]

ramson *ram'zən, n* (*orig pl* of the now *dialect* **rams**; *usu* in double *pl* form **ramsons**) wild or broad-leaved garlic. [OE *hramsa, hramse, hramsan* (pl)]

ramstam *ram'stam'*, (*Scot* and *NEng*) *adj* and *adv* headlong. [Poss **ram**]

ramus *rā'məs, n* a branch of anything, *esp* a nerve; a process of a bone; the mandible, or its ascending part; a feather barb: — *pl* **rā'mī**. — *adj* **rā'mal**, **rā'meal**, **rā'meous** or **rā'mous** of a branch. — *adj* **rā'mate**, **rā'mous** or **ramose** (*rə-mōs'* or *rā'mōs*) branched. — *adj* **ram'ūlar** of a branch. — *adj* **ram'ūlose** or **ram'ūlous** having ramuli. — *n* **ram'ūlus** a little branch: — *pl* **ram'ūlī**. [L *rāmus* a branch]

RAN *abbrev*: Royal Australian Navy.

ran *ran, pa t* of **run**.

Rana *rā'nə, n* the typical genus of frogs, giving name to the family **Ranidae** (*ran'i-dē*). — *adj* **ranarian** (*rə-nā'ri-ən*) froggy. — *n* **ranā'rium** a place where frogs are reared. — *adj* **raniform** (*ran'*) frog-like. — *adj* **ranine** (*rā'nīn*) of the under side of the tongue (seat of ranula). — *adj* **ranivorous** (*rə-niv'ər-əs*) frog-eating. — *n* **ranula** (*ran'ū-lə*) a cyst in the gland under the tongue (*poss* from an imagined resemblance to a small frog). [L *rāna*, dimin *rānula* a frog, ranula]

rana *rä'nä, n* a Rajput prince. [Hindi]

ranarium. See under **Rana**.

rance *rans*, (chiefly *Scot*) *n* a prop, shore; a bar. — *vt* to prop; to bar. [Fr *ranche*]

rancel. See **ranzel**.

ranch[1] *räntsh, ränsh* or *ra-, n* a stock farm, as in western N America, often taken to include its buildings and the people employed on it; an establishment for rearing any commercially-important animal, such as a *cattle ranch*, etc. — *vi* to own, manage or work on a ranch. — *adj* **ranched** (of a fur coat) made from skins of animals from a ranch. — *n* **ranch'er** or **ranch'man** a person who ranches. — *n* **ranchero** (*ran-chā'rō*, or *Sp rän-che'rō*; *pl* **ranche'ros**) in Mexico and the Southwestern US, a rancher. — *n* **rancheria** (*ran-chā-rē'ə*, or Sp *rän-che-rē'a*) a herdsmen's hut or village; a small village or settlement of Southwestern American, or Mexican, Indians; a rancherie (*obs*). — *n* **rancherie** (*ranch'ə-ri*) a Canadian Indian village or settlement, *esp* on a reserve. — *n* **ranch'ing**. — *n* **rancho** (*ran'chō*, or *Sp rän'chō*) a rude hut, or group of huts, *esp* for travellers; a ranch: — *pl* **ran'chos**. [Am Sp *rancho*, from Sp, mess, mess-room]

ranch[2] *räntsh, ränsh* or *ra-*, (*Dryden*) *vt* to tear. [Cf **race**[5]]

rancid *ran'sid, adj* rank in smell or taste, as of butter or oil that is going bad. — *n* **rancid'ity** or **ran'cidness**. [L *rancidus*]

rancour or *US* **rancor** *rang'kər, n* harboured bitterness of mind, speech, etc; deep-seated enmity; spite; virulence; sourness (*Shakesp*). — *adj* **ran'corous**. — *adv* **ran'corously**. [OFr, from L *rancor, -ōris* an old grudge, from *rancēre* to be rancid]

rand[1] *rand, n* a border, margin; a strip, *esp* of flesh or of leather; a ridge overlooking a valley (*SAfr ront* or *rand*); the basic unit of the S African decimal coinage (100 *cents*), introduced in 1961 as equivalent to ten shillings: — *pl* **rand** or **rands**. — **the Rand** the Witwatersrand goldfield. [OE and Du *rand* border]

rand[2] *rand, vi* an old form of **rant**.

R & A *abbrev*: Royal and Ancient (Golf Club of St Andrews).

randan[1] *ran-dan'* or *ran'dan, n* a din, uproar; riotous conduct; a spree. [Origin obscure]

randan[2] *ran-dan'* or *ran'dan, n* a boat rowed by three, the second with two oars. — Also **randan gig**. [Origin obscure]

R & B *abbrev*: rhythm and blues.

R & D *abbrev*: research and development.

randem *ran'dəm, n, adj* and *adv* a tandem with three horses.

randie. See **randy**.

randle-balk *ran'dl-bök*, **randle-perch** *-pûrch* or **randle-tree** *-trē*, (*Scot* and *NEng*) *n* a bar in a chimney for hanging pots; (**randle-tree**; *Scott*) applied to a tall, raw-boned woman. — Also **rann'el-balk**, **rann'ell-balk**, **rann'le-balk** or **ran'tle-balk**, etc. [Cf Norw *randa-tre*, from *rand* space above a fireplace]

random *ran'dəm*, also formerly (*Spenser* and *Shakesp*) **randon** *-dən, n* a rush, full speed (*obs*); uncontrolled or unguarded state, freedom (*Spenser*); chance (*archaic*); elevation of a gun (*obs*); irregular masonry. — *adj* haphazard, chance; fired at an elevation; uncontrolled; irregular. — *n* **randomīzā'tion** or **-s-**. — *vt* **ran'domize** or **-ise** to arrange or set up so as to occur in a random manner. — *n* **ran'domizer** or **-s-**. — *adv* **ran'domly** or **ran'domwise**. — **random access** (*comput*) access to any data in a large store of information without affecting other data; **random access memory** a computer memory that can be read from and written to by a program, and in which the data are accessed directly (not serially, as in magnetic tape; *abbrev* **RAM**); **random variable** (*statistics*) one which can take any from a range of values which occur randomly. [OFr *randon*, from *randir* to gallop]

R and R *abbrev*: (*colloq*; *orig US*) rest and recreation.

randy or **randie** *ran'di, adj* boisterous (*dialect*); aggressively or coarsely loud-spoken (*Scot*); sexually excited; lustful. — *n* (*Scot* and *NEng*) a violent beggar, *esp* a woman; a coarse virago; a romping girl. [Poss **rand**[2]]

ranee. See **rani**.

rang *rang, pa t* of **ring**[2,3].

rangatira *rang-ə-tē'rə, n* a Maori leader or chief. — *n* **rangatiratang'a** leadership, chieftaincy. [Maori]

range *rānj, vt* to set in a row or rows; to assign a place among others to; to classify; to arrange; to straighten, level, align; to traverse freely or in all directions; to sail along or about (*naut*); to bring to bear. — *vi* to lie in a direction; to extend; to take or have a position in a line, or alongside; to take sides; to lie evenly, align; to move, have freedom of movement, occur or vary within limits; to rove freely, in all directions; to beat about, as for game; to be inconstant, fluctuate; to have a range. — *n* a row or rank; a system of points in a straight line; anything extending in line, such as a chain of mountains or a row of connected buildings; a stretch of open country, *esp* one used for grazing; a north and south strip of townships six miles wide (*US*); line of lie; an act of ranging; scope, compass, extent, limits; movement, freedom of movement or variation between limits; space or distance between limits; the area or distance within which anything moves, can move, occurs, is possible, acts efficiently or varies; a place for practice in shooting; effective shooting distance of a gun, etc, ie between gun, etc and target; an enclosed kitchen fireplace fitted with appliances of various kinds. — *n* **ran'ger** a rover; a dog that beats the ground; a forest or park officer; a member of a body of troops, *usu* mounted and employed in policing an area; a soldier specially trained for raiding combat; (with *cap*) a member of a senior branch of the Girl Guide organization (also **Ranger Guide**); (with *cap*, in *pl*) a name sometimes taken by football clubs. — *n* **rang'ership**. — *n* **rang'iness**. — *adj* **ran'gy** disposed or well able to roam; roomy; long-legged and thin; mountainous (*Austr*). — **range'finder** an instrument for finding the distance of an object; same as **tacheometer**; **range'-finding**; **range'land** (often in *pl*) land suitable for grazing, but too dry for growing crops; **range** (or **ranging**) **pole** or **rod** a pole or rod used to mark positions in surveying. — **free-range** see under **free**. — **range oneself** to side (with), to take sides; (Fr *se ranger*) to settle down to reputable ways, *esp* on marrying. [Fr *ranger* to range, from *rang* a rank]

rangoli *rung-gō'li, n* a traditional Hindu form of decoration on floors or doorsteps, forming patterns of coloured sand and riceflour. [Hindi]

rani or **ranee** *rän'ē, fem* of **raja**. [Hindi *rānī*, from Sans *rājñī* queen, fem of *rājan*]

Ranidae, **raniform**, **ranine**, etc. See under **Rana**.

rank[1] *rangk*, *n* a row; a row of soldiers standing side by side (opposed to *file*); any row thought of as so placed (eg of squares along the player's side of a chessboard); (in *pl*) soldiers, *esp* private soldiers, (with *the*, private soldiers collectively); (in *pl*) persons of ordinary grade; a row of taxis awaiting hire; a place where taxis are allowed to stand for hire (also **taxi rank**); a set of organ pipes; arrangement in line; order, grade or degree; an official post ordered in superiority (*esp military*); position in society, etc; high standing, *esp* social. — *vt* to place in a line; to assign to a particular class or grade; to place on the list of claims against a bankrupt; to be superior to in position, grade, etc, outrank (*US*). — *vi* to have a place in a rank, grade, scale or class; to move in rank; to be admitted as a claim against the property of a bankrupt (*Scots law*). — *adj* **ranked** (*Shakesp*) *appar* bordered with rows. — *n* **rank'er** a person who serves or has served as a private soldier; an officer who has risen from the ranks. — *adj* **rank'ing** having a high military, political, etc position; highest in rank of those present. — *n* a position in a graded scale, a rating. — **break rank** or **ranks** (*esp military*) fall or move out of line; **close ranks** see under **close**[2]; **pull rank** to use one's rank to exert authority, get one's own way; **rank and file** common soldiers; ordinary people; those in an organization, etc not involved in its management; **take rank of** to take precedence over. [OFr *renc* (Fr *rang*), perh from OHGer *hring*, *hrinc* ring]

rank[2] *rangk*, *adj* strong, lusty, vigorous (*obs* or *dialect*); violent (*obs*); growing high and luxuriantly; coarsely or excessively overgrown; swollen (*Shakesp*); (of an amount of money) excessive (*law*); abundant (*Spenser*); dense (*Spenser*, now *NEng*); out-and-out, absolute, utter; over-productive; offensively strong-scented or strong-tasting; gross; foul; lustful, in heat (*Shakesp*); grossly obvious (*rare*); deep-cutting. — *adv* violently (*Spenser*); utterly (now *dialect*). — *adv* **rank'ly**. — *n* **rank'ness**. — **rank'-rī'der** a hard rider; a moss-trooper; a highwayman. — *adj* **rank'-rī'ding**. [OE *ranc* proud, strong]

ranke *rangk*, (Shakesp, *As You Like It* III. 3. 103) *n appar* a jog-trot (*perh* a misprint for **rack**[6]); passage otherwise explained as meaning a repetition of the same rhyme like a file (rank) of so many butterwomen.

Rankine *rang'kin*, *adj* of or designating an absolute scale of temperature on which the units are the same as those on the Fahrenheit scale. [After William J M *Rankine* (1820–72), Scottish engineer and scientist]

rankle *rangk'l*, *vi* to fester (*archaic*); to cause festering (*archaic*); to go on vexing, irritating or embittering. — *vt* to cause to fester; to envenom; to embitter. — *n* (*archaic*) a continual irritation. [OFr *rancler*, *raoncler*, from *draoncler*, appar from LL *dra*(*cu*)*nculus* an ulcer, dimin of L *dracō*, from Gr *drakōn* dragon]

rannel-balk, **rannell-balk**, **rannle-balk**, etc. See **randle-balk**, etc.

ransack *ran'sak* or *-sak'*, *vt* to search thoroughly; to plunder; to pillage. — *n* (*archaic*) eager search. — *n* **ran'sacker**. [ON *rannsaka*, from *rann* house, and *sœkja* to seek]

ransel. See **ranzel**.

ranshackle or **ranshakle** *ran-shak'l*, (*Scott*) *vt* to search, ransack. [Dialect Eng *ransackle*, *ram-*, from **ransack**]

ransom *ran'səm*, *n* redemption from captivity; price of redemption or reclamation; atonement, redemption (*relig*); an extortionate price. — *vt* to pay, demand or accept ransom for; to redeem; to redeem, atone (*relig*). — *adj* **ran'somable**. — *n* **ran'somer**. — *adj* **ran'somless**. — **a king's ransom** a very large sum of money; **hold to ransom** to retain until a ransom be paid; to blackmail into concessions (*fig*); **put to ransom** to offer to release for ransom. [Fr *rançon*, from L *redemptiō*, *-ōnis* redemption]

rant *rant*, *vi* to declaim bombastically; to storm or scold with great anger; to sing, play, or make merry, noisily. — *vt* to utter in a high-flown, self-important way. — *n* empty speechifying; bombast; a tirade; a noisy frolic (*Scot*); a lively tune. — *n* **ran'ter** a person who rants; an extravagant preacher; a member of a Commonwealth antinomian sect; (as a byname) a Primitive Methodist; a roisterer; a noisy musician (*Scot*). — *n* **ran'terism**. — *n* and *adj* **rant'ing**. — *adv* **rant'ingly**. [Obs Du *ranten* to rave; LGer *randen*, Ger *ranzen*]

rantipole *rant'i-pōl*, (*archaic*) *n* a wild, reckless person. — Also *adj* and *vi*. [Perh **rant**]

rantle-. See **randle-**.

ranula. See under **Rana**.

Ranunculus *rə-nung'kū-ləs*, *n* any plant of the buttercup genus *Ranunculus*: — *pl* **ranun'culī** or **ranun'culuses**. — *adj* **ranunculā'ceous** of the buttercup family (**Ranunculā'ceae**). [L *rānunculus*, dimin of *rāna* a frog]

ranz-des-vaches *rā̃-dā-väsh* or *rā̃s-*, *n* a French Swiss herdsman's song or alpenhorn melody. [Swiss Fr; *ranz*, of uncertain meaning, and Fr *des vaches* of the cows]

ranzel *ran'zl*, **rancel** or **ransel** *ran'sl*, *n* formerly in Orkney and Shetland, a search for stolen goods. — **ran'zelman**, etc (*Scott* **Ran'zellaar**) an official who did this. [Older Scot *ransell*; ON *rannsaka*; **ranshackle**]

RAOC *abbrev*: Royal Army Ordnance Corps.

raoulia *ra-ōō'li-ə*, *n* any plant of the *Raoulia* genus of large, white caespitose cushion plants (family *Compositae*) of New Zealand. [New L, from Étienne F L *Raoul* (died 1852)]

rap[1] *rap*, *n* a sharp blow; the sound of a knock; a crime or criminal charge (*slang*). — *vt* and *vi* to strike or knock sharply; to swear or testify, *esp* falsely (*obs slang*); to communicate or sound out by raps. — *vt* to censure, reprove (*colloq*); to utter sharply. — *vi* to rattle, patter: — *pr p* **rapp'ing**; *pa t* and *pa p* **rapped**. — *n* **rapp'er** a person who raps; a door-knocker; a great lie or oath (*archaic*); a spirit-rapper. — **rapp'ing** the process of loosening a pattern in a foundry mould by inserting in it and tapping a spike or similar object. — **rap sheet** (*slang*) a criminal record; a charge sheet. — **beat the rap** (*US slang*) to be acquitted of a crime; to avoid punishment; **take the rap** (*slang*) to take the blame or punishment, *esp* in place of another. [Imit]

rap[2] *rap*, *vt* to snatch; to grab; to carry away in spirit or with joy (*Shakesp*): — *pr p* **rapp'ing**; *pa p* **rapped** or **rapt**. [Perh partly related to MLGer *rappen*, Swed *rappa* to snatch; mainly a back-formation from **rapt**]

rap[3] *rap*, *n* an 18c Irish counterfeit halfpenny; as a type of worthlessness, a whit, *esp* in *not worth a rap*. [Origin obscure]

rap[4] *rap*, (*colloq*) *n* an informal talk, discussion, chat, etc; a rhythmic monologue delivered over a musical background; a type of music consisting of such monologues (also **rap music**). — *vi* to have a talk, discussion, etc; to get along well, sympathize; to deliver a rhythmic monologue to music. — *n* **rapp'er**. — *n* **rapp'ing**. — **rap artist** a performer of rap music; **rap group** (*US*) a group which meets for informal discussions; **rap session** an informal discussion. [Perhaps from **rapport**]

rap[5] *rap*, (*Austr*) *vt* (*usu* with *up*) to boost, commend, praise highly. — *n* a boost, acclamation, high praise. — Also **wrap**. [Appar erroneously from the obs sense of **rap**[2], to transport with joy, etc]

rapacious *rə-pā'shəs*, *adj* grasping; greedy for gain; living by taking prey. — *adv* **rapā'ciously**. — *n* **rapā'ciousness**. — *n* **rapacity** (*-pas'*). [L *rapāx*, *-ācis*, from *rapere* to seize and carry off]

rape[1] *rāp*, *n* rapine, plunder, seizure (*obs*); unlawful sexual intercourse (by force) with another person without that person's consent; violation, despoliation. — *vt* to seize and carry off (*obs*); to commit rape upon; to ravish or transport, as with delight (*obs*); to violate, despoil. — *n* **rā'per**. — *n* **rā'pist**. — *adj* **rā'ping** tearing prey (*heraldry*); ravishing, delighting (*obs*). — **date rape** see under **date**[1]; **statutory rape** see under **statute**. [Prob L *rapere* to snatch, confused with **rap**[2]]

rape[2] *rāp*, *n* a division of Sussex. [Origin obscure]

rape[3] *rāp*, *n* a plant (*Brassica napus*) closely related to the turnip and producing brilliant yellow flowers, cultivated for its herbage and oil-producing seeds; applied to various closely related species or varieties. — **rape cake** refuse of rapeseed after the oil has been expressed; **rape oil** or **rapeseed oil** oil expressed from rapeseed; **rape'seed**. [L *rāpa*, *rāpum* a turnip]

rape[4] *rāp*, *n* the refuse left after wine-making. [Fr *râpe*]

Raphanus *raf'ə-nəs*, *n* the radish genus. — *n* **raphania** (*rə-fā'ni-ə*) ergotism (attributed by Linnaeus to wild radish seeds). [Gr *rhaphanis*]

raphe *rā'fē*, *n* a seam-like junction; the ridge on the side of an anatropous ovule continuing the funicle to the chalaza; a broad connecting ridge, eg that between the halves of the vertebrate brain. — Also **ra'phé**. [Gr *rhaphē* a seam]

Raphia *rā'fi-ə* or *raf'i-ə*, *n* a genus of handsome pinnately-leaved palms; (without *cap*) raffia. [Malagasy]

raphis, **rhaphis** *rā'fis*, **raphide** or **rhaphide** *rā'fīd*, *n* a needle-like crystal, *usu* of calcium oxalate, occurring in plant cells: — *pl* **raphides** or **rhaphides** (*raf'i-dez* or *rā'fīdz*). [Gr *rhaphis*, *-idos* a needle, from *rhaptein* to sew]

rapid *rap'id*, *adj* swift; quickly accomplished; sloping steeply; requiring short exposure (*photog*). — *n* a very swift-flowing part of a river with steep descent and often broken water but no actual drop (*usu* in *pl*). — *n* **rapidity** (*rə-pid'i-ti*). — *adv* **rap'idly**. — *n* **rap'idness**. — **rapid fire** the firing of guns, asking of questions, etc in quick succession. — *adj* **rap'id-fire**. — **rapid eye movement** (*abbrev* **REM**) the rapid movement of the eyes in unison behind closed lids that accompanies phases of sleep during which dreams are particularly vivid; of or relating to this phase. [L *rapidus*, from *rapere* to seize]

rapier *rā'pi-ər*, *n* a long slender sword, suitable for thrusting. [Fr *rapière*]

rapine *rap'īn* or *-in*, *n* plundering; prey; ravishment, transport (*Milton*). [L *rapīna*, from *rapere* to seize]

rapist. See under **rape**[1].

raploch *rap'lohh*, (*Scot*) *n* and *adj* homespun. [Origin unknown]

rapparee *rap-ər-ē'*, *n* a wild Irish plunderer, *orig* of the late 17c. [Ir *rapaire* half-pike, robber]

rappee *ra-pē'*, *n* a coarse, strong-flavoured snuff. [Fr *râpé* rasped, grated, from *râper* to rasp]

rappel *rä-* or *rə-pel'*, *n* call to arms by the beating of a drum (*military*); abseiling. — *vi* same as **abseil**: — *pr p* **rappell'ing**; *pa t* and *pa p* **rappell'ed**. — *n* **rappell'ing**. [Fr]

rapper and **rapping**. See under **rap**[1].

Rappist *rap'ist* or **Rappite** *-īt*, *n* a Harmonist (qv), a follower of George *Rapp*.

rapport *ra-pör'*, *n* relation; connection; sympathy; emotional bond; spiritualistic touch. [Fr]

rapporteur *ra-pör-tœr'*, *n* a person whose task it is to carry out an investigation and/or draw up a report (for a committee, etc). — *n* **rapportage** (*ra-pör-täzh'*) the description of real events in writing; flat description, lacking in imagination. [Fr, from *rapporter* to bring back]

rapprochement *ra-prosh'mã*, *n* a drawing together; establishment or renewal of cordial relations. [Fr]

rapscallion *rap-skal'yən*, *n* a rascal; a low, mean wretch (*jocular*). [**rascal**]

rapt *rapt*, *adj* snatched or carried away (*archaic*); abducted (*archaic*); carried out of this world; transported, enraptured, entranced; wholly engrossed; very pleased, thrilled (*Austr* and *NZ colloq*). — *adv* **rapt'ly**. [L *raptus*, pa p of *rapere* to seize and carry off; but partly also pa p of **rap**[2]]

raptor *rap'tər*, *n* a rapist (*archaic*); a plunderer (*archaic*); a bird of prey (*esp* diurnal), member of the abandoned order **Raptores** (*-tō'rēz*). — *adj* **raptatō'rial** or **raptō'rial** predatory; adapted to predatory life. [L *raptor*, *-ōris* a plunderer, from *rapere* to seize]

rapture *rap'chər*, *n* a seizing and carrying away; extreme delight; transport; ecstasy; a paroxysm. — *vt* to enrapture. — *adj* **rap'tured**. — *adj* **rap'tureless**. — *n* **rap'turist**. — *vi* **rap'turize** or **-ise** to go into raptures. — *adj* **rap'turous**. — *adv* **rap'turously**. — **rapture of the deep** or **depth** nitrogen narcosis. [**rapt**]

rara avis *rā'rə ā'vis* or *rä'ra ä'wis*, (*L*) *n* a rare bird; a rare person or thing. [Juvenal, VI. 165]

ra-ra skirt *rä'rä skûrt*, *n* a very short gathered or pleated skirt, *orig* as worn by cheerleaders. [Prob from **hurrah**]

rare[1] *rār*, *adj* (of the atmosphere) thin; not dense; sparse; seldom encountered; uncommon; excellent; especially good; extraordinary; used as a mere intensive, *esp* in **rare and** (*colloq*). — *n* **rarefac'tion** (*rār-i-* or *rar-i-*) rarefying. — *adj* **rarefac'tive**. — *adj* **rar'efīable**. — *vt* and *vi* **rar'efy** to make or become less dense, to refine: — *pr p* **rar'efying**; *pa t* and *pa p* **rar'efied**. — *adv* **rāre'ly** seldom; choicely; remarkably well. — *n* **rāre'ness**. — *n* **rarity** (*rār'* or *rar'i-ti*) the state of being rare; thinness; something valued for its scarcity; uncommonness. — **rare bird** an exceptional person or thing; **rare'bit** (often called **Welsh rarebit**) melted cheese, with or without ale, on hot toast (also **rabbit** or **Welsh rabbit**); **rare earth** an oxide of a **rare-earth element**, any of a group of metallic elements (some of them rare) closely similar in chemical properties and very difficult to separate; now more *usu* a rare-earth element itself; **rare gas** inert gas. [Fr, from L *rārus*]

rare[2] *rār*, *adj* (of eggs) lightly cooked (*obs* or *dialect*); (of meat) underdone. [**rear**[3] influenced by **rare**[1]]

rare[3] *rār* or **rear** *rēr*, (*obs*) *adj* and *adv* early. — *adv* **rear'ly**. — *adj* **rare'-ripe** early ripe. [**rathe**]

rarebit. See under **rare**[1].

raree-show *rār'ē-shō*, *n* a show carried about in a box; a spectacle. [Appar representing a foreign pron of **rare show**]

raring *rā'ring*, *adj* eager (for), full of enthusiasm and sense of urgency, *esp* in phrase **raring to go**. [**rear**[2]]

rarity. See under **rare**[1].

RAS *abbrev*: Royal Astronomical Society.

ras *räs*, *n* a headland; an Ethiopian prince. [Ar *ras*, *ra's* head]

rascaille *räs-kä'i*, (*Scott*, etc) *n* and *adj* an archaic form of **rascal**, rabble.

rascal *räs'kl*, *n* the rabble (*obs*); one of the rabble (*obs*); a knave, rogue, scamp; (playfully) a fellow; a deer out of condition (*Shakesp*). — *adj* of the rabble; knavish; wretched; out of condition. — *n* **ras'caldom** the world or conduct of rascals. — *n* **ras'calism**. — *n* **rascality** (*-kal'*) the rabble; character or conduct of rascals. — *n* **rascallion** (*-kal'yən*) or **rapscall'ion** a rascal; a low, mean wretch. — *adj* **ras'cal-like**. — *adj* **ras'cally** (*superl*, *Shakesp*, **ras'calliest**). [OFr *rascaille* (Fr *racaille*) scum of the people]

rascasse *ras'kas*, *n*. Same as **scorpion fish** (see under **scorpion**).

raschel *räsh'əl*, *n* a type of light loosely-knitted fabric. [Ger *Raschelmaschine*, a kind of knitting-machine]

rase *rāz*. Same as **race**[3] or **raze**[2]. See also **race**[5,6] and **rise**.

rash[1] *rash*, *adj* over-hasty; lacking in caution; operating suddenly (*Shakesp*); calling for haste (*Shakesp*). — *adv* rashly. — *adv* **rash'ly**. — *n* **rash'ness**. [Cf Dan and Swed *rask*; Du and Ger *rasch* rapid]

rash[2] *rash*, *n* an outbreak of red spots or patches on the skin; a large number of instances of anything happening at the same time or in the same place. [Perh OFr *rasche* (Fr *rache*)]

rash[3] *rash*, (*obs*) *vt* to tear, drag. [OFr *arrachier* to uproot; cf **race**[6]]

rash[4] *rash*, (*Spenser*) *vt* to slash. [Variant of **raze**[2], **rase**, **race**[5]]

rash[5] *rash*, *vi* to dash, rush (*obs*). — *vt* (*Shakesp*) to stick, thrust forcibly. [Origin obscure]

rash[6] *rash*, *n* a Scots form of **rush**[2].

rasher *rash'ər*, *n* a thin slice of bacon. [Poss from **rash**[4]]

Raskolnik *ras-kol'nik*, (*hist*) *n* a dissenter from the Russian Orthodox Church. [Russ, from *raskól* separation]

rasorial *ra-* or *rə-sō'ri-əl*, or *-sö'ri-əl*, *adj* scraping the ground for food. — *n pl* **Rasō'res** (*-rēz*) an obsolete order, gallinaceous birds with or without the pigeons. [L *rāsor*, *-ōris* scraper]

rasp[1] *räsp*, *n* a coarse file; anything with a similar surface; a mollusc's tongue; an insect's stridulating apparatus; a risp at a door; a grating sound or feeling. — *vt* to grate as if with a rasp; to grate upon; to risp; to utter gratingly. — *vi* to have a grating effect; to scrape, as on a fiddle. — *n* **rasp'atory** a surgeon's rasp. — *n* **rasp'er** someone who, or that which, rasps; in hunting, a difficult fence (*colloq*). — *n* **rasp'ing** a filing; (in *pl*) fine breadcrumbs used as a coating for food before frying, etc. — *adj* grating, harsh. — *adv* **rasp'ingly**. — *adj* **rasp'y** rough. — **rasp'-house** (Du *rasphuis*) a former type of prison in Germany and Holland, where dye-wood was rasped. [OFr *raspe* (Fr *râpe*); perh Gmc]

rasp[2] *räsp*, (now *colloq* and *Scot*) *n* a raspberry. — *n* **raspberry** (*räz'bər-i*) the fruit of *Rubus idaeus*; the plant producing it; extended to some similar species; a sign of disapproval, *esp* a noise produced by blowing hard with the tongue between the lips (*slang*). — *adj* of, made with, or like raspberry. — **raspberry bush**; **raspberry jam tree** an Australian acacia (from the smell of its wood). [Earlier *raspis*; origin unknown]

rasse *ras'* or *ras'ə*, *n* a small civet, *Viverricula indica*. [Jav *rase*]

rast *räst* or *räst*, a Spenserian *pa p* of **race**[5,6] (= **raze**[2]).

Rastafarian or **Ras Tafarian** *ras-tə-fär'i-ən*, *n* a member of a West Indian (*esp* Jamaican) cult, which rejects western culture and ideas and regards Haile Selassie, the former Emperor of Ethiopia, as divine. — Also **Ras'ta** or **Ras'taman**. — *adj* **Rastafā'rian**, **Rastafari** (*-ä'ri*) or **Ras'ta** (all also without *cap*). [From Haile Selassie's title and name, *Ras Tafari*]

raster *ras'tər*, (*TV*) *n* a complete set of scanning lines appearing at the receiver as a rectangular patch of light on which the image is reproduced. [Perh from L *rāstrum*, as for **rastrum**]

rastrum *ras'trəm*, *n* a music-pen. [L *rāstrum* rake]

rasure or **razure** *rā'zhər*, *n* the act of scraping or shaving; erasure; obliteration. [L *rāsūra*]

rat[1] *rat*, *n* a genus (*Rattus*) of animals closely allied to mice, but larger; extended to various related or superficially similar animals; a renegade or turncoat (from the rat's alleged desertion of a doomed ship; *colloq*); a strike-breaker (*colloq*); someone who works for less than recognized wages (*colloq*); a miserable or ill-looking specimen (*colloq*); a despicable person (*colloq*). — *vi* to hunt or catch rats; to desert or change sides for unworthy motives; of a worker, to work as a rat: — *pr p* **ratt'ing**; *pa t* and *pa p* **ratt'ed**. — *adj* **rat'proof**. — *interj* **rats** (*slang*) expressing contemptuous incredulity, annoyance, etc. — *adj* **ratt'ed** (*slang*) drunk. — *n* **ratt'er** a killer of rats, *esp* a dog; a person who rats. — *n* **ratt'ery** apostasy; a place where rats are kept or are abundant. — *n* **ratt'ing** apostasy; rat-hunting. — Also *adj*. — *adj* **ratt'ish** rat-like; rat-infested. — *adj* **ratt'y** rat-like; rat-infested; wretched; unkempt, untidy; angry, irritable (*colloq*). — *adj* **rat'-arsed** (*vulg slang*) drunk. — **rat'bag** (*slang*) a term of abuse; a despicable person; **ratbite fever** a disease caused by infection with bacteria conveyed by the bite of a rat; **rat'-catcher** a professional killer of rats; unconventional hunting garb (*slang*); **rat'-catching**; **rat'-flea** a flea that infests rats; **rat'-guard** a metal disc put on a hawser to prevent rats from boarding a ship in port; **rat'-hole**; **rat'-hunting**; **rat'-kangaroo** the potoroo, a marsupial of various species about the size of a rabbit, related to the kangaroo; **rat'pack** (*slang*) a rowdy gang of young people; **rat'-pit** an enclosure where rats are worried by dogs; **rat'-poison** any poison for rats; **rat race** a continual round of hectic and futile activity; the scramble to get on in the world by fair means or foul; **rat'-run** (*colloq*) a minor road heavily used by traffic trying to avoid motorway congestion; **rats'bane** poison for rats, *esp* white arsenic; a name for many poisonous plants; **rat snake** any of several rodent-eating colubrid snakes, *esp* of the S Asian genus *Phytas*, or the N American *Elaphe*; **rat's'-tail** or **rat'-tail** the tail of a rat; anything like a rat's tail; a thin coherent dangling lock of hair; an excrescence on a horse's leg; (**rat'-tail**) the grenadier fish. — *adj* **rat's'-tail**, **rat'-tail** or **rat'-tailed** having a tail like a rat; like a rat's tail; (of a spoon) ridged along the back of the bowl. — **rat'-trap** a trap for catching rats; a toothed bicycle pedal. — Also *adj*. — **rat on** to inform against; to betray the interests of; to desert; **smell a rat** to have a suspicion that something is afoot. [OE *ræt*; cf Ger *Ratte*]

rat[2] *rat*, *vt* (in imprecations) used for **rot**. [Cf **drat**]

rata *rä'tə*, *n* a myrtaceous New Zealand tree (*Metrosideros robusta*) with hard red wood and bearing crimson flowers. [Maori]

ratable or **rateable** *rā'tə-bl*, *adj*. See under **rate**[1].

ratafia *rat-ə-fē'ə*, *n* a flavouring essence made with the essential oil of almonds; a cordial or liqueur flavoured with fruit-kernels; an almond biscuit or cake. [Fr; ety doubtful; cf **tafia**]

ratan *ra-tan'*, *n*. Same as **rattan**[1].

rataplan *rat-ə-plan'*, *n* a drumming sound. [Fr]

rat-a-tat *rat-ə-tat'*. Same as **rat-tat**.

ratatouille *rat-ə-too'i* or *ra-ta-twē'*, *n* a stew of tomatoes, aubergines, peppers, onions and other vegetables, with olive oil. [Fr, from *touiller* to stir]

ratbag. See under **rat**.

ratch[1] *rach*, *n* a ratchet; a ratchet-wheel. — *n* **ratch'et** a pawl and/or ratchet-wheel. — *vt* and *vi* to move by, or as if by, a ratchet mechanism, by steady, progressive degrees (with *up* or *down*). — **ratchet screwdriver** (*building*, etc) a screwdiver with a ratchet mechanism to make it operate in one direction only; **ratch'et-wheel** a wheel with inclined teeth with which a pawl engages. [Cf Ger *Ratsche*, Fr *rochet*]

ratch[2] *rach*, *n* same as **rache**. — *vi* to wander or prowl (often with *about*; *Scot* and *NEng*). [Ety as for **rache**]

ratch[3]. Same as **race**[4].

rate[1] *rāt*, *n* estimated amount or value (*Shakesp*); estimation (*Shakesp*); a fixed quantity (*obs*); price or cost; amount corresponding; ratio, *esp* time-ratio, speed; amount determined according to a rule or basis; a standard; a class or rank, *esp* of ships or sailors; manner, mode; extent, degree; (often in *pl*) an amount levied by a local authority according to the assessed value of property; a clock's gain or loss in unit time. — *vt* to allot (*Shakesp*); to calculate (*Shakesp*); to estimate; to value; to settle the relative rank, scale or position of; to esteem, regard as; to deserve, be worthy of; to value for purpose of rate-paying; to think highly of (*colloq*). — *vi* to be placed in a certain class. — *n* **rātabil'ity** or **rāteabil'ity**. — *adj* **rāt'able** or **rāte'able**. — *adv* **rāt'ably** or **rāte'ably**. — *n* **rāt'er** a person who makes an estimate; (in combination) a ship, etc of a given rate (such as *second-rater*). — *n* **rāt'ing** a fixing of rates; classification according to grade; the class of any member of a crew; a sailor of such a class; the tonnage-class of a racing yacht; the proportion of viewers or listeners who are deemed to watch or listen to a particular programme or network. — **ratable** (or **rateable**) **value** a value placed on a property, and used to assess the amount of rates payable to the local authority each year. — *vt* **rate'-cap**. — **rate'-capping** the setting by central government of an upper limit on the rate that can be levied by a local authority; **rate'-cutting** a lowering of charges to obtain traffic; **rated altitude** the height, measured in the international standard atmosphere, at which an aero-engine delivers its maximum power; **rated capacity** a general term for the output of a piece of equipment under specified conditions; **rate-determining step** (*chem eng*) the step, in a process involving a series of consecutive steps, with the slowest rate, largely determining the overall rate of the process; **rate fixing** the determination of the time allocated for a specific task, *usu* as a basis for remuneration; **rate'payer** a person who pays a local rate; **rate support grant** money contributed by central government to make up the difference between the rate levied and the amount required for local authority spending. — **at any rate** in any case, anyhow. [OFr, from LL (*pro*) *ratā* (*parte*) according to a calculated part, from *rērī*, *ratus* to think, judge]

rate[2] *rāt*, *vt* to scold; to chide; to reprove; to drive by scolding. — *vi* to scold. — *n* a reproof to a dog. [ME *raten*; origin obscure]

rate[3]. Same as **ret**.

ratel *rā'təl* or *rä'təl*, *n* an animal of the badger-like genus (*Ratel Mellivora*) of Africa and India, related to the gluttons. [Afrik; origin uncertain]

ratfink *rat'fingk*, (*derog slang*, *esp NAm*) *n* a mean, deceitful, despicable person. — Also *adj*. [**rat**[1] and **fink**]

rath[1] *räth* or **rathe** *rādh*, (*archaic*) *adj* quick; eager; early: — *compar* **rather** (*rädh'ər*; *Spenser*) earlier; *superl* **rath'est** (*obs* or *dialect*) earliest. — *adv* **rathe** (*rādh*; *Milton*) early: — *compar* **rather** (see **rather** below); *superl* (*obs*) **rath'est**. [Compar of archaic *rath* quick, ready, eager; OE *hræd* (rarely *hræth*) quick, *hræthe*, *hrathe* quickly; ON *hrathr*]

rath[2] *räth*, *n* a prehistoric hill fort. [Ir]

rathe. See **rath**[1].

rather *rä'dhər*, *adv* sooner, more quickly (*Shakesp*); more readily; more willingly; in preference; more than otherwise; more properly; somewhat, in some degree: — *irreg superl* **ra'therest** (*Shakesp*). — *interj* **ra'ther** (sometimes affectedly *rä-dhûr'*) I should think so; yes, indeed. — *adv* (*colloq*) **ra'therish**. — **the rather** all the more. [Compar of **rath**[1]; OE *hrathor*]

ratheripe *rādh'rīp* or **rathripe** *räth'rīp*, (*archaic* and *dialect*) *adj* early ripe. — *n* an early-ripening variety. [**rath**[1] and **ripe**[1]]

ratify *rat'i-fī*, *vt* to approve and sanction, *esp* by signature; to give validity or legality to; to confirm the correctness of (*obs*): — *pr p* **rat'ifying**; *pa t* and *pa p* **rat'ified**. — *n* **ratificā'tion**. — *n* **rat'ifier**. [Fr *ratifier*, from L *ratus*, pa p of *rērī* (see **rate**[1]), and *facere* to make]

ratine or **ratteen** *rat-ēn'*, *n* a rough, open dress-fabric. — Also **rat'iné** (*-i-nā*; Fr *ratiner* to frieze, put a nap on). [Fr *ratine*]

rating. See under **rate**[1].

ratio *rā'shi-ō* or *rāsh'yō*, *n* the relation of one thing to another of which the quotient is the measure; quotient; proportion; a portion, allowance (*rare*); (also **ratio decidendi**) the reason or principle on which a decision is based (*law*): — *pl* **rā'tios**. — **compound ratio** see under **compound**[1]; **inverse ratio** see under **inverse**. [L *ratiō*, *-ōnis* reason, from *rērī*, *ratus* to think]

ratiocinate *rat-* or *rash-i-os'i-nāt*, *vi* to reason. — *n* **ratiocinā'tion**. — *adj* **ratioc'inative** or **ratioc'inatory**. [L *ratiōcinārī*, *-ātus*]

ration *ra'shən*, or formerly *rā'shən*, *n* a fixed allowance or portion, *esp* of food and other provisions in time of shortage; (in *pl*) food (*colloq*). — *vt* to put on an allowance; to supply with rations; to restrict the supply of to so much for each. — **ra'tion-book** or **ra'tion-card** a book or card of coupons or vouchers for rationed commodities; **ra'tion-money** money in lieu of rations. [Fr, from L *ratiō*, *-ōnis*]

rational[1] *rash'ən-əl*, *adj* of the reason; endowed with reason; agreeable to reason; sane; intelligent; judicious; commensurable with natural numbers. — *n* a rational being or quantity; (in *pl*) rational dress, ie knickerbockers instead of skirts for women (*hist*). — *n* **rationale** (*rash-ə-näl'*) underlying principle; a rational account; a theoretical explanation or solution. — *n* **rat'ionalism** a system of belief regulated by reason, not authority; a disposition to apply to religious doctrines the same critical methods as to science and history, and to attribute all phenomena to natural rather than miraculous causes. — *n* **rat'ionalist**. — *adj* **rationalist'ic**. — *adv* **rationalist'ically**. — *n* **rationality** (*rash-ən-al'i-ti*) the quality of being rational; the possession or due exercise of reason; reasonableness. — *n* **rationalization** or **-s-** (*rash-nəl-ī-zā'shən*). — *vt* **rat'ionalize** or **-ise** to make rational; to free from irrational quantities; to conform to reason; to reorganize scientifically; to interpret rationalistically; to substitute conscious reasoning for unconscious motivation in explaining; to organize (an industry) so as to achieve greater efficiency and economy. — *vi* to think or argue rationally or rationalistically; to employ reason, rationalism or rationalization. — *adv* **rat'ionally**. — **rational dress** (*hist*) knickerbockers for women instead of skirts; **rational horizon** see under **horizon**; **rational number** a number expressed as the ratio of two integers. [L *ratiōnālis*, *-e*, from *ratiō*]

rational[2] *rash'ən-əl*, (*hist*) *n* the Jewish high-priest's breastplate; a bishop's vestment like the pallium. [L *ratiōnāle*, Vulgate translation of Gr *logion* oracle]

rationale[1]. See under **rational**[1].

rationale[2]. Obsolete form of **rational**[2].

ratite *rat'īt*, (*ornithol*) *adj* having a keel-less breastbone; of the **Ratitae** (*rä-tī'tē*), flightless birds — ostrich, rhea, emu, kiwi, etc. [L *ratis* raft]

ratlin, **ratline**, **ratling**, **rattlin**, **rattline** or **rattling** *rat'lin*, *rat'ling*, *n* any of the small lines forming steps of the rigging of ships. [Ety uncertain]

ratoo. See **ratu**.

ratoon *rat-* or *rət-ōōn'*, *n* a new shoot from the ground after cropping, *esp* of sugar-cane or cotton. — *vi* to send up ratoons. — *vt* to cut down so as to obtain ratoons. — *n* **ratoon'er** a plant that ratoons. [Sp *retoño* shoot]

rat-rhyme *rat'rīm*, (*Scot*) *n* a bit of doggerel; a screed.

rattan[1] or **ratan** *ra-tan'*, *n* any of various climbing palms, *esp* of the genus *Calamus*, with a very long thin stem; a cane made from the stem; the stems collectively as wickerwork. [Malay *rōtan*]

rattan[2] *rə-tan'*, *n* the continuous beat of a drum. [Imit]

rat-tat *rat'-tat'*, *n* a knocking sound. [Imit]

ratted. See under **rat**[1].

ratteen. Same as **ratine**.

ratten *rat'n*, *vt* to practise sabotage against (worker or employer). — *n* **ratt'ening** (found earlier than verb). [Origin uncertain]

ratter, **rattery**, **ratting**, etc. See under **rat**[1].

rattle *rat'l*, *vi* to make a quick succession or alternation of short hard sounds; to move along rapidly making such a sound; to chatter briskly and emptily. — *vt* to cause to rattle; to fluster, disconcert or irritate (*colloq*); to assail with rattling (*Shakesp*); to utter glibly, as by rote (often with *off*); to perform or push through to completion in a rapid, perfunctory or noisy manner; to scold loudly (*obs*). — *n* an instrument or toy producing a rattling sound when shaken; an instrument for making a whirring noise, formerly used by watchmen; a similar device used at festive gatherings; a dice-box (*old slang*); a plant whose seeds rattle in the capsule, applied to two scrophulaceous plants, **yellow-rattle** or cock's-comb (*Rhinanthus crista-galli*) and **red-rattle** or marsh lousewort (*Pedicularis palustris*); the rings of a rattlesnake's tail; a vivacious prattler; the sound of rattling; the crackling of paper; a sound in the throat of a dying person (also **death-rattle**); racket. — *n* **ratt'ler** a rattle; a coach (*old slang*); a rattlesnake (*colloq*); a telling blow (*colloq*); an excellent specimen of the kind (*colloq*). — *n* **ratt'ling**. — *adj* making a rattle; smart, lively; strikingly good (*colloq*). — Also *adv*. — *adj* **ratt'ly** making a rattling noise; inclined to rattle. — **ratt'lebag** a rattle or rattling apparatus; a person who causes commotion (*Scot*); **ratt'le-brain**, **ratt'le-head** or **ratt'le-pate** a shallow, voluble, volatile person. — *adj* **ratt'le-brained**, **ratt'le-headed** or **ratt'le-pated**. — **ratt'lesnake** a venomous American pit-viper (genus *Crotalus*) with rattling horny rings on the end of its tail; **ratt'le-trap** (*colloq*) a contemptuous name for any apparatus, equipment, finery, bric-à-brac; a rickety vehicle; the mouth. — **rattle someone's cage** (*colloq*) to stir someone up to anger or excitement. [ME *ratelen*; cf Ger *rasseln*, Du *ratelen* to rattle;

connection with OE plant names *hratele*, *hrætelwyrt* is questioned]

rattlin, **rattline** and **rattling**. Same as **ratlin**.

ratton *rat'n*, (now *NEng*) *n* a rat. [Fr *raton*]

ratty. See under **rat**[1].

ratu *rä'tōō*, *n* a local chief or ruler in Indonesia and Fiji. — Also **ra'too**.

raucle *rök'l*, (*Scot*) *adj* rough; vigorous; hale.

raucous *rö'kəs*, *adj* hoarse, harsh. — *adv* **rau'cously**. — *n* **rau'cousness**. — *adj* **raucid** (*rö'sid*; *Lamb*) raucous. [L *raucus* hoarse]

raught *röt*, *obs* or *archaic pa t* and *pa p* of **reach**[1,2] and **reck**.

raun (*Scott*). Same as **rawn**[1].

raunch[1] *rönsh*, (*Spenser*) *vt*. Same as **race**[6].

raunch[2]. See **raunchy**.

raunchy *rön'chi* or *rän'chi*, (*colloq*) *adj* coarsely or openly sexual; earthy, bawdy, lewd; carelessly untidy, shabby. — *n* **raunch** (*orig US*) coarseness, bawdiness. — *adv* **raunch'ily**. — *n* **raunch'iness**. [Origin unknown]

raunge *rönj*. Obsolete form of **range**.

Rauwolfia *rö-wol'fi-ə*, *n* a tropical genus of apocynaceous trees and shrubs, of which *Rauwolfia serpentina* and other species yield valuable drugs. [After the German botanist Leonhard *Rauwolf* (died 1596)]

RAuxAF *abbrev*: Royal Auxiliary Air Force.

ravage *rav'ij*, *vt* and *vi* to lay waste; to destroy; to pillage. — *n* devastation; ruin. — *n* **rav'ager**. [Fr *ravager*, from *ravir* to carry off by force, from L *rapere*]

RAVC *abbrev*: Royal Army Veterinary Corps.

rave[1] *rāv*, *vi* to rage; to talk as if mad or delirious; to write or speak with extreme enthusiasm (with *about*; *colloq*). — *vt* to utter wildly. — *n* infatuation (*colloq*); extravagant praise (*colloq*); a rave-up (*colloq*); an acid house party (qv under **acid**) (*slang*). — *adj* (*colloq*) extravagantly enthusiastic; crazy. — *n* **rā'ver** a person who raves; a lively, uninhibited person (*colloq*); a person attending an acid house party (*slang*). — *n* and *adj* **rā'ving**. — *adv* **rā'vingly**. — **rave'-up** (*colloq*) a lively celebration; a wild, uninhibited, thoroughly enjoyable party. — **raving mad** frenzied; very angry (*colloq*). [Perh OFr *raver*, which may be from L *rabere* to rave]

rave[2] *rāv*, *n* a side piece of a wagon. [Ety obscure]

rave[3] *rāv*, (*Scot*) *pa t* of **rive**.

ravel *rav'l*, *vt* to entangle; to disentangle, untwist, unweave, unravel (*usu* with *out*). — *vi* to become entangled; to be untwisted or unwoven; to search (with *into*; *obs*): — *pr p* **rav'elling**; *pa t* and *pa p* **rav'elled**. — *n* a tangle; a broken thread. — *n* **rav'elling** a ravelled out thread. — *n* **rav'elment**. [Appar Du *ravelen*]

ravel bread *rav'l bred*, (*obs* or *dialect*) *n* wholemeal bread, intermediate between white and brown. — Also **ravelled bread**. [Origin unknown]

ravelin *rav'lin*, (*fortif*) *n* a detached work with two embankments raised before the counterscarp. [Fr]

ravelment. See under **ravel**.

raven[1] *rā'vn*, *n* a large, glossy black species of crow (*Corvus corax*). — *adj* shiny black like a raven. — **rā'ven-bone** or **rā'ven's-bone** the gristle on the spoon of the brisket, formerly thrown to the ravens after a hunt; **rā'ven-duck** or **rā'ven's-duck** fine hempen sail-cloth. [OE *hræfn*; ON *hrafn*]

raven[2] *rav'in*, *n* same as **ravin** (*n*). — *vt* to take away by force (*obs*); to devour hungrily or greedily (*literary*). — *vi* to prey rapaciously (*on* or *upon*); to be intensely hungry; to hunger intensely (*for*); to roam about hungrily after prey. — *n* **rav'ener**. — *adj* **rav'ening**. — *adj* **rav'enous** plundering; rapacious; voracious; intensely hungry. — *adv* **rav'enously**. — *n* **rav'enousness**. [OFr *ravine* plunder, from L *rapīna* plunder]

ravin, **raven** or **ravine** *rav'in*, *n* rapine; preying; prey (*Spenser* and *Milton*). — *adj* (*Shakesp*) ravening. — *vt* and *vi* same as **raven**[2] (*v*). — *adj* **rav'in'd** (*Shakesp*) *prob* sated, gorged. [Ety as **raven**[2]]

ravine[1] *rə-vēn'*, *n* a deep, narrow gorge. — *adj* **ravined'** scored with ravines; trenched. [Fr, from L *rapīna* rapine, violence]

ravine[2]. See **ravin**.

ravioli *rav-i-ōl'ē*, *n* small, square pasta cases with a savoury filling of meat, cheese, etc. [Ital, pl of *raviòlo*]

ravish *rav'ish*, *vt* to seize or carry away by violence; to abduct; to snatch away from sight or from the world; to rape; to enrapture. — *n* **rav'isher**. — *adj* **rav'ishing** delightful; lovely; transporting. — *adv* **rav'ishingly**. — *n* **rav'ishment**. [Fr *ravir*, *ravissant*, from L *rapere* to seize and carry off]

raw *rö*, *adj* not altered from its natural state; not cooked or dressed; unwrought; not prepared or manufactured; not refined; not corrected; not mixed; having the skin abraded or removed (also *fig*); showing through the skin (*Spenser*); crude; hard, harsh, cruel; untrained; out of condition (*Spenser*); red and inflamed; immature; inexperienced; chilly and damp; naked; (of statistics, data for a computer, etc) not yet checked, sorted, corrected, etc. — *n* (with *the*) a skinned, sore or sensitive place; the raw state; that which is raw. — *adj* **raw'ish**. — *adv* **raw'ly**. — *n* **raw'ness**. — *adj* **raw'bone** (*Spenser*) or **raw'boned** with little flesh on the bones; gaunt. — **raw'head** or **raw'head-and-blood'y-bones** a bugbear or pair of bugbears to frighten children. — *adj* **raw'hide** of untanned leather. — *n* a rope or whip of untanned leather. — **raw material** material (often in its natural state) that serves as the starting-point of a manufacturing or technical process; that out of which something is or can be made, or may develop (*fig*); **raw silk** natural untreated silk threads; fabric made from these. — **a raw deal** harsh, inequitable treatment; **in the raw** in its natural state; naked. [OE *hrēaw*; Du *rauw*, ON *hrār*, Ger *roh*]

rawing. See **rowen**.

rawn[1] or **raun** *rön*, (*Scot*) *n* fish-roe; a female fish. [Cf Dan *ravn* roe]

rawn[2]. See **rowen**.

RAX *abbrev*: rural automatic exchange.

rax *raks*, (*Scot* and *NEng*) *vt* to stretch; to strain; to reach; to reach out, hand. — *vi* to stretch; to reach out. — *n* a stretch; a strain. [OE *raxan*]

ray[1] *rā*, *n* array (*obs*). — *vt* to array (*obs*); to dress (*obs*); to defile, dirty (*Shakesp*). [**array**]

ray[2] *rā*, *n* a line along which light or other energy, or a stream of particles, is propagated; a narrow beam; a gleam of intellectual light; a look or glance; a radiating line or part; the radially extended fringing outer part of an inflorescence; a supporting spine in a fin. — *vt* to radiate; to provide with rays. — *vi* to radiate. — *adj* **rayed**. — *adj* **ray'less**. — *n* **ray'let** a small ray. — **ray flower** or **floret** any of the small flowers radiating out from the margin of the flower head of certain composite plants; **ray'-fungus** a bacterium (*Actinomyces*) that forms radiating threads, some species pathogenic. — **ray of sunshine** a happy person, someone who cheers up others. [OFr *rais* (accusative *rai*), from L *radius* a rod]

ray[3] *rā*, *n* a skate, thornback, torpedo, or any similar flat-bodied elasmobranch fish. [Fr *raie*, from L *raia*]

ray[4]. Same as **re**[1].

rayah *rī'a*, (*hist*) *n* a non-Muslim subject of the Ottoman Empire. [Ar *ra'īyah*, from *ra'ā* to pasture]

Ray-Bans® *rā'banz*, *n pl* a type of sunglasses with dark green lenses and gold frames.

rayle or **rayne**. Obsolete or Spenserian spellings of **rail**[2,4], **rain**[2] or **reign**.

Rayleigh disc *rā'lē disk*, *n* a small light disc hung by a fine thread at an angle to a progressive sound wave, its deflection being used to measure the intensity of the sound. — **Rayleigh criterion** (*phys*) a criterion for the resolution of interference fringes, spectral lines and images; **Rayleigh wave** (*acoustics*) a non-dispersive surface wave on a solid body with a free surface. [After J W Strutt, Lord *Rayleigh* (1842–1919), English physicist]

raylet, etc. See under **ray**[2].

Raynaud's disease *rā'nōz di-zēz'*, (*med*) *n* constriction of the blood supply to digits due to a paroxymal disorder of the arteries, the fingers (or toes) turning white and then blue *usu* in response to cold or stress. — **Raynaud's**

phenomenon this condition in the context of an underlying disease of connective tissues. [Maurice *Raynaud* (1834–81), Fr physician]

rayon *rā'ən, n* a ray (*Spenser*); artificial silk fabric made from cellulose; (see **silk**). [Fr *rayon* ray]

raze[1] *rāz,* (*Shakesp*) *n.* Same as **race**[3].

raze[2] or **rase** *rāz, vt* to graze; to scrap; to erase; to slash, cut into ornamental devices; to lay (a building) level with the ground; to demolish. — *adj* **razed** or **rased**. [Fr *raser*, from L *rādere, rāsum* to scrape]

razee *rā-zē',* (*hist*) *n* a ship cut down by reducing the number of decks. — *vt* to remove the upper deck or decks of. [Fr *rasé* cut down]

razmataz. See **razzmatazz**.

razoo *rə-zōō',* (*Austr* and *NZ colloq*) *n* a (non-existent) coin of insignificant value, *esp* in phrases *not have a (brass) razoo, give someone every last razoo*, etc.

razor *rā'zər, n* a keen-edged implement for shaving. — *adj* (*fig*) sharp, keen, precise. — *adj* **rā'zorable** (*Shakesp*) fit to be shaved. — **rā'zor-back** a sharp ridge; a rorqual; a ridge-backed pig. — *adj* sharply ridged. — **rā'zor-bill** a species of auk, with a compressed bill; **rā'zor-cut** a haircut done with a razor. — *vt* **rā'zor-cut**. — **rā'zor-blade**; **rā'zor-edge** a very fine sharp edge, such as that on which a balance swings; a critically balanced situation; **rā'zor-fish** or **rā'zor-clam** a lamellibranch mollusc (genus *Solen*), with a shell like an old-fashioned razor handle; **rā'zor-shell** its shell, or the animal itself; **rā'zor-strop**; **razor wire** thick wire with sharp pieces of metal attached, used like barbed-wire, for fences, etc. — **Occam's razor** see under **Occamism**. [OFr *rasour*; see **raze**[2]]

razure. Same as **rasure**.

razz *raz,* (*slang*) *n* a raspberry. — *vt* and *vi* (*NAm*) to jeer (at).

razzamatazz. See **razzmatazz**.

razzia *raz'ya, n* a pillaging incursion, *esp* one carried out by N African Moors. [Fr, from Algerian Ar *ghāzīah*]

razzle-dazzle *raz'l-daz'l,* (*slang*) *n* a rowdy frolic or spree; dazzling show, confusion, etc. — Also **razz'le**. — **on the razzle** having a spree or bout of heavy drinking. [Appar from **dazzle**]

razzmatazz, **razmataz** *raz-mə-taz'* or **razzamatazz** *raz-ə-mə-taz', n* to-do, hullabaloo; razzle-dazzle.

RB *abbrev*: Republic of Botswana (IVR); Rifle Brigade.

Rb (*chem*) *symbol*: rubidium.

RBMK reactor *är-bē-em-kā ri-ak'tər, n* a graphite-moderated, boiling water-cooled, pressure-tube reactor, unique to the former USSR.

RC *abbrev*: Red Cross; Roman Catholic (Church); Taiwan (official name Republic of China) (IVR).

RCA *abbrev*: Central African Republic (*Republique Centafricaine*; IVR); Radio Corporation of America; Royal Canadian Academy; Royal College of Art.

RCAF *abbrev*: Royal Canadian Air Force.

RCB *abbrev*: Republic of the Congo (Brazzaville) (IVR).

RCD *abbrev*: residual current device.

RCGP *abbrev*: Royal College of General Practitioners.

RCH *abbrev*: Republic of Chile (IVR).

RCM *abbrev*: Regimental Court-martial; Royal College of Music.

RCMP *abbrev*: Royal Canadian Mounted Police.

RCN *abbrev*: Royal Canadian Navy; Royal College of Nursing.

RCO *abbrev*: Royal College of Organists.

RCOG *abbrev*: Royal College of Obstetricians and Gynaecologists.

RCP *abbrev*: Royal College of Physicians; Royal College of Preceptors.

RCR *abbrev*: Royal College of Radiologists.

RCS *abbrev*: Royal College of Science; Royal College of Surgeons; Royal Corps of Signals.

RCT *abbrev*: Royal Corps of Transport.

RCVS *abbrev*: Royal College of Veterinary Surgeons.

RD *abbrev*: (Naval) Reserve Decoration; refer to drawer (written on a returned bank cheque); Rural Dean.

Rd *abbrev*: Road (in addresses).

rd *abbrev*: rutherford.

RDA *abbrev*: recommended daily (or dietary) allowance.

RDC *abbrev*: Rural Development Council; (formerly) Rural District Council.

RDF *abbrev*: refuse-derived fuel.

RDX *abbrev*: Research Department Explosive (also called **cyclonite**).

RE *abbrev*: Reformed Episcopal; religious education (in schools); Royal Engineers; Royal Exchange; Royal Society of Etchers and Engravers.

Re. See **Ra**.

Re or **re** *abbrev*: rupee.

Re (*chem*) *symbol*: rhenium.

re[1] *rā,* (*music*) *n* the second note of the scale in sol-fa notation (also anglicized in spelling as **ray**). [See **Aretinian**]

re[2] *rē,* (*commercial jargon*) *prep* concerning, with reference to. [L *in rē* (abl of *rēs* thing) in the matter]

re- *rē-, pfx* denoting: again; again and in a different way. [L]

Words with the prefix **re-** are listed in the following text or in the separate panels.

're *r.* Short form of **are**.

reach[1] *rēch, vt* to stretch forth, hold out; to hand, pass; to deal, strike (*archaic*); to succeed in touching or getting; to communicate with; to arrive at; to extend to; to get at; to take, snatch, seize (*obs*); to stretch, lengthen out (*obs*). — *vi* to stretch out the hand; to extend; to amount; to attain to (*usu* with *for* or *after*); to succeed in going or coming: — *pa t* and *pa p* **reached** or (*obs*) **raught** (*röt*). — *n* act or power of reaching; extent of stretch; range, scope; the number of people estimated to be exposed at least once to a particular advertisement (*marketing*); artifice (*obs*); a stretch or portion between defined limits, as of a stream between bends; the distance traversed between tacks (*naut*); a bay (*obs*). — *adj* **reach'able**. — *n* **reach'er**. — *adj* **reach'ing**. — *adj* **reach'less** unattainable. — *adj* **reach'-me-down** ready-made. — *n* (often in *pl*) ready-made or second-hand attire; trousers. [OE *rǣcan* (pa t *rǣhte, rāhte*; pa p *gerǣht*); Ger *reichen* to reach]

reach[2] *rēch.* Obsolete or dialect form of **retch**[1].

react[1] *rē'akt', vt* to act a second, etc time.

react[2] *ri-akt', vi* to return an impulse in the opposite direction; to act in return; to act with mutual effect; to act in resistance; to swing back in the opposite direction; to respond to a stimulus; to undergo chemical change produced by a reagent; to act, behave; (of share prices) to fall sharply after a rise. — *n* **reac'tance** (*electronics*) the component of impedance due to inductance or capacitance. — *n* **reac'tant** (*chem*) a substance taking part in a reaction. — *n* **reac'tion** action resisting other action; mutual action; an action or change in an opposite direction; backward tendency from revolution, reform or progress; response to stimulus; the chemical action of a reagent; a physical or mental effect caused by medicines, drugs, etc; a transformation within the nucleus of an atom; acidity or alkalinity; feeling or thought aroused by, or in response to, a statement, situation, person, etc. — *adj* **reac'tional**. — *n* **reac'tionarism**. — *n* **reac'tionarist**. — *adj* **reac'tionary** of or favouring reaction, *esp* against revolution, reform, etc. — *n* a person who tends to

Some words with the prefix **re-**.

rēabsorb' *vt.*	**rēaccus'tom** *vt.*	**rēacquire'** *vt.*
rēabsorp'tion *n.*	**rēacquaint'** *vt.*	**rēac'tuate** *vt.*
rēacclī'matize or **-ise** *vt* and *vi.*	**rēacquaint'ance** *n.*	**rēadapt'** *vt* and *vi.*

oppose political change or who attempts to revert to past political conditions. — *n* and *adj* **reac'tionist** reactionary. — *adj* **reac'tive** of or relating to reaction; readily acted upon or responsive to stimulus; produced by emotional stress; relating to or having a reactance (*electronics*). — *adv* **reac'tively**. — *n* **reac'tiveness** or **reactiv'ity**. — *n* **reac'tor** someone who or that which undergoes a reaction; a device which introduces reactance into an electric circuit; a container in which a chemical reaction takes place; a nuclear reactor (qv under **nucleus**). — **reaction time** the interval between stimulus and reaction; **reaction turbine** a turbine in which the fluid expands progressively in passing alternate rows of fixed and moving blades, the kinetic energy continuously developed being absorbed by the latter. [LL *reagere*, *-actum*, from *agere* to do]

reactivate *rē-ak'ti-vāt*, *vt* to restore to an activated state. — *n* **reactivā'tion**. [re-]

reactive. See under **react**.

read[1] *rēd*, *vt* to advise (*archaic*; see **rede**); to make out; to interpret; to expound; to make known (*Spenser*); to declare; to name (*Spenser*); to solve; to look at and comprehend the meaning of written or printed words in; to understand as by interpretation of signs; to collect the meaning of; to go over progressively with silent understanding of symbols or with utterance aloud of words or performance of notes; to accept or offer as that which the writer intended; to learn from written or printed matter; to find recorded; to observe the indication of; to register, indicate; to teach, lecture on; to study; to impute by inference (as to read a meaning into); to retrieve (data) from a storage device (*comput*). — *vi* to perform the act of reading; to practice much reading; to study; to find mention; to give the reader an impression; to endure the test of reading; to deliver lectures; to have a certain wording: — *pa t* and *pa p* **read** (*red*). — *n* **read** (*rēd*) a spell of reading; reading-matter; an opportunity of reading (*Scot*); counsel, a saying, an interpretation (*Spenser*). — *adj* **read** (*red*) versed in books; learned. — *n* **readabil'ity** (*rēd-*). — *n* **read'ableness**. — *adj* **read'able** legible; easy to read; interesting without being of highest quality. — *adv* **read'ably**. — *n* **read'er** someone who reads or reads much; a person who reads prayers or passages of scripture, etc at a church service; a lecturer, *esp* a higher grade of university lecturer; a proof-corrector; a person who reads and reports on manuscripts for a publisher; a reading-book; a pocket-book (*thieves' slang*); a device which projects a large image of a piece of microfilm on to a screen, for reading; a document reader (*comput*). — *n* **read'ership** the post of reader in a university; the total number of readers (of a newspaper, etc). — *adj* **read'ing** addicted to reading. — *n* the action of the verb *read*; perusal; study of books; public or formal recital, *esp* of a bill before Parliament (see **first, second** and **third reading** below); the actual word or words that may be read in a passage of a text; the indication that can be read off from an instrument; matter for reading; lettering; an interpretation; a performer's conception of the meaning, rendering. — **reader advertisement** an advertising feature in a magazine which follows the style of the editorial part of the magazine, often with accompanying photographs or drawings; **readers' inquiry card** or **readers' service card** a business reply card bound into a magazine with numbers corresponding to advertised products; **read'-in** input of data to a computer or storage device; **reading age** reading ability calculated as equivalent to the average ability at a certain age; **read'ing-book** a book of exercises in reading; **read'ing-boy** (*printing*; *obs*) a reader's assistant; **read'ing-desk** a desk for holding a book or paper while it is read; a lectern; **read'ing-lamp** a lamp for reading by; **read'ing-machine** a reader for microfilm; a document reader (*comput*); **reading matter** printed material, eg books, magazines; **read'ing-room** a room for consultation, study or investigation of books in a library; a room with papers, periodicals, etc resorted to for reading; a proofreaders' room. — *adj* **read'-only** (*comput*) referring to a type of storage device whose contents have been built in and cannot be altered by programming. — **read'-out** output unit of a computer; the retrieval of data from a computer; data from a computer, printed or registered on magnetic tape or punched paper tape, or displayed on a screen; data from a radio transmitter. — **first, second** and **third reading** the three successive formal readings of a bill before parliament, when (in Britain) it is introduced, discussed in general, and reported on by a committee; **read between the lines** to detect a meaning not expressed but implied; **read into** to find in a person's writing, words, behaviour, etc (meanings which are not overtly stated and may not have been intended); **read off** to take as a reading from an instrument; **read (oneself) in** in the Church of England, to enter into possession of a benefice by reading the Thirty-nine Articles; **read out** to read aloud; to retrieve data from a computer, etc; **read someone's mind** to guess accurately what someone is thinking; **read up** to amass knowledge of by reading; **read-write head** (*comput*) in a disk drive, a head which can retrieve data and also record it; **read-write memory** (*comput*) one which allows retrieval and input of data; **take as read** (*red*) to presume; to understand to be, and accept as, true. [OE *rǣdan* to discern, read, from *rǣd* counsel]

read[2] *rēd*, *n* a ruminant's fourth stomach, the abomasum. [OE *rēad*]

ready *red'i*, *adj* prepared; dressed, attired (*obs*); willing; inclined; about or liable (to); dexterous; prompt; quick; handy; at hand; immediately available; direct. — *adv* readily (now only in *compar* and *superl*, **read'ier** and **read'iest**). — *n* (*usu* with *the*) the position of a firearm ready to be fired; ready money (*slang*; also in *pl*); time of, or for, making ready (*colloq*). — *vt* to make (*usu* oneself) ready. — *adv* **read'ily** willingly; quickly and without difficulty. — *n* **read'iness**. — In combination **ready-** or **ready-to-** ready to, as in **read'y-mix**, **read'y-to-eat'**, **read'y-to-sew'**, **read'y-to-wear'**, etc. — *adj* **read'y-made** made before sale, not made to order. — *n* a ready-made article, *esp* a garment. — *adj* **read'y-mix** (of cake, etc ingredients) prepared and blended so that *usu* only liquid need be added before cooking; (also **ready-mixed'**) (of concrete) mixed in the vehicle in which it is being transported to the site where it is to be used. — **ready money** money ready at hand; cash. — *adj* **read'y-money** paying, or for payment, in money on the spot. — *adj* **read'y-moneyed** or **read'y-monied** having, or of the nature of, ready money. — **ready reckoner** a book of tables used as a calculation aid, *esp* one giving the value of so many things at so much each, and interest on any sum of money from a day upwards; **read'y-wash** (*slang*) crack (cocaine). — *adj* **read'y-witted** quick-witted. — **at the ready** (of a firearm) ready to be fired; prepared for instant action; **make** or **get ready** to dress, put on one's clothes (*obs*); to prepare (*esp* a forme for printing); **ready, steady, go** words used by the starter of a race to the competitors. [OE (*ge*)*rǣde*; cf Ger *bereit*]

Some words with the prefix **re-**.

rēadaptā'tion *n*.	**rēadmiss'ion** *n*.	**rēadop'tion** *n*.
rēaddress' *vt*.	**rēadmit'** *vt*.	**rēadvance'** *n*, *vt* and *vi*.
rēadjust' *vt* and *vi*.	**rēadmitt'ance** *n*.	**rēad'vertise** *vt* and *vi*.
rēadjust'ment *n*.	**rēadopt'** *vt*.	**rēadver'tisement** *n*.

reaedify. Same as **re-edify**.

reafforest *rē-ə-for'ist*, *vt* to replant (a previously forested area) with trees. — *n* **reafforestā'tion**. [re-]

Reaganism *rā'gən-izm*, *n* the political policies and practices characteristic of Ronald *Reagan*, US President 1981–89, *esp* the advocacy of supply-side economics (**Rea'ganomics**). — *n* and *adj* **Rea'ganite**.

reagent *rē-ā'jənt*, *n* a substance with characteristic reactions, used as a chemical test. — *n* **reā'gency**. [See **react**]

reak[1] or **reik** *rēk*, (*obs*) *n* a prank, *usu* in *pl* **reaks** or **rex** (*reks*), sometimes with an allusion to L *rēx* king. [Origin obscure]

reak[2]. Obsolete spelling of **reck**.

real[1] *rē'əl* or *ri'əl*, *adj* actually existing; not counterfeit or assumed; true; genuine; sincere; authentic; relating to things fixed, eg lands or houses (*law*). — *adv* (*colloq*; *US* and *Scot*) really, quite, veritably. — *n* a real thing; that which is real; a realist. — *n pl* **realia** (*rē-ā'li-ə*; LL neuter *pl* of *realis* real) realities; objects, etc used as teaching aids to relate classroom work to real life. — *n* **rē'alism** the medieval philosophical doctrine that general terms stand for real existences (opposed to *nominalism*); the philosophical doctrine that in external perception the objects immediately known are real existences; the tendency to regard, accept or represent things as they really are (often in their most ignoble aspect); (often with *cap*) a style in art, literature, etc that seeks to present an unglamorized, unromanticized view of the world; literalness and precision of detail, with the effect of reality; the taking of a practical view in human problems. — *n* **rē'alist**. — *adj* **rēalist'ic** relating to the realists or to realism; lifelike. — *adv* **rēalist'ically**. — *n* **reality** (*ri-al'i-ti* or *rē-*) the state or fact of being real; that which is real and not imaginary; truth; verity; the fixed permanent nature of real property (*law*). — *adv* **rē'ally** in reality; actually; in truth. — *n* **rē'alness**. — *n* **rē'alo** a member of the less radical section of the German Green Party, advocating co-operation with other parties, industry, etc (cf **fundie**): — *pl* **rē'alos**. — Also *adj*. — *n* **re'altie** (*Milton*) sincerity, honesty. — **Realtor**® or **rē'altor** (*NAm*; irregularly formed) an agent for the buying and selling of landed property, *esp* one who is a member of the National Association of Real Estate Boards. — *n* **rē'alty** (*law*) land, with houses, trees, minerals, etc on it; the ownership of, or property in, lands (also, *esp NAm*) **real estate**. — **real account** one which records transactions relating to a tangible asset so that the value of the asset can be seen; **real ale** or **beer** beer which continues to ferment and mature in the cask after brewing. — *adj* **re'al-estate** (*esp NAm*) concerned with or dealing in property in land. — **real food** food that has not undergone commercial processing, does not contain additives, etc; **real image** see under **image**; **real income**, **wages**, etc income, wages etc measured in terms of their actual purchasing power; **real life** everyday life as lived by ordinary people, opposed to glamorous fictional life; **real number** any rational or irrational number; **real presence** see under **presence**; **real price** the price of a commodity measured in relation to changes in the general price level; **real school** (Ger *Realschule*, *rā-äl'shōō'lə*) a German school teaching modern languages, science, and technical subjects, not classics, the highest grade being the **real gymnasium** (Ger *Realgymnasium*, *rā-äl'gimnä'ziōōm*), opposed to the *gymnasium* proper, or classical school. — *adj* **real'time** (*comput*) relating to or designating a system in which the processing of data occurs as it is generated. — **for real** (*slang*) in reality; serious or seriously; intended to be carried out or put into effect; **get real** (*NAm slang*; *usu* in *imper*) to awaken to the realities of the situation; **the real Mackay** or **McCoy** the genuine article, *esp* good whisky (the expression has been variously explained); **the real thing** the genuine thing, not an imitation or a cheap substitute. [LL *reālis*, from L *rēs* a thing]

real[2] *rē'əl*, (*obs*) *adj* royal. — *n* **re'alty** (*obs*) royalty. — **real tennis** royal tennis, or tennis properly so called, not lawn-tennis (also **court tennis**). [OFr, from L *rēgālis* royal]

real[3] *rā-äl'* or *rē'əl*, (*hist*) *n* a quarter of a peseta; a former Spanish coin, one-eighth of a dollar. See also **reis**[2]. [Sp, from L *rēgālis* royal]

realgar *ri-al'gär* or *-gər*, *n* a bright red monoclinic mineral, arsenic monosulphide. [Medieval L, from Ar *rahj-al-ghār* powder of the mine or cave]

realia. See under **real**[1].

realign *rē-ə-līn'*, *vt* to align afresh; to group or divide on a new basis. — *n* **realign'ment**. [re-]

realize or **-ise** *rē'ə-līz*, *vt* to make real, or as if real; to bring into being or act; to accomplish; to convert into real property or money, *esp* to convert (an asset) into cash by selling; to obtain, as a possession; to feel strongly; to comprehend completely; to bring home to one's own experience; to provide a detailed artistic version of music where the composer has (as was often the case in the 17c and 18c) left much to be filled in by the performer; to provide the drawings for an animated cartoon. — *n* **realīzabil'ity** or **-s-** the ease with which an asset may be converted into cash. — *adj* **realī'zable** or **-s-** (or *rē'*) able to be realized; *specif* of an asset, able to be converted into cash. — *n* **realīzā'tion** or **-s-** (or *-li-*). — *n* **rē'alizer** or **-s-**. — *adj* **rē'alizing** or **-s-**. [Fr *réaliser*; see **real**[1]]

really[1] *rē-ə-lī'*, (*obs*) *vt* to rally; (*Spenser* **reallie**) to form again. [Obs Fr *realier* = *rallier*; see **rally**[1]]

really[2]. See under **real**[1].

realm *relm*, *obs* **reame** *rēm*, *n* a kingdom; a domain, province, region; a field of study or sphere of action. — *adj* **realm'less**. [OFr *realme*, from hypothetical LL *rēgālimen*, from L *rēgālis* royal]

realo. See under **real**[1].

realpolitik *rā-äl-po-lē-tēk'*, *n* practical politics based on the realities and necessities of life, rather than moral or ethical ideas. — *n* **realpolit'iker**. [Ger]

realtie, etc. See under **real**[1].

realty. See under **real**[1,2].

ream[1] *rēm*, *n* 20 quires; (in *pl*) a large quantity (*colloq*). — **printer's ream** 516 sheets of paper. [Ar *rizmah* a bundle]

ream[2] *rēm*, (*Scot*) *n* cream; froth. — *vi* to cream; to froth; to overflow. — *vt* to skim. — *adj* **ream'ing** (*Scot*) foaming; brimming. — *adj* **ream'y** creamy, frothy (*Scot*). [OE *rēam*]

ream[3] *rēm*, *vt* to enlarge the bore of. — *n* **ream'er** a rotating instrument for enlarging, shaping or finishing a bore; a spiral-bladed drill for enlarging root canals (*dentistry*). — **ream'ing-bit**. [Appar OE *rȳman* to open up, to make room, from *rūm* room]

reame *rēm*, (*Spenser*, etc) *n*. See **realm**.

rean. See **rhine**.

reanimate *rē-an'i-māt*, *vt* to restore to life; to infuse new life or spirit into. — *vi* to revive. — *n* **reanimā'tion**. [re-]

reanswer *rē-än'sər*, (*Shakesp*) *vt* to be equivalent to. [re-]

Some words with the prefix **re-**.

rēadvise' *vt* and *vi*.	**rēallocā'tion** *n*.	**rē-al'ter** *vt*.
rēaffirm' *vt*.	**rēallot'** *vt*.	**rē-alterā'tion** *n*.
rēaffirmā'tion *n*.	**rēallot'ment** *n*.	**rēamend'** *vt*.
rēall'ocate *vt*.	**rē-ally'** *vt* and *vi*.	**rēamend'ment** *n*.

reap *rēp*, *vt* to cut down, as grain; to clear by cutting a crop; to derive as an advantage or reward. — *n* **reap'er** a person who reaps; a reaping-machine. — **reap'ing-hook** a sickle; **reap'ing-machine** a machine for cutting grain; **reap'-silver** (*hist*) money paid in commutation for service in reaping. — **the grim reaper** (*fig*) death. [OE *rīpan* or *ripan*]

rear[1] *rēr*, *n* the back or hindmost part or position, *esp* of an army or fleet; a position behind; the buttocks (*euphem*); a public or school, etc lavatory (also in *pl*; *slang*). — *adj* placed behind; hinder. — *vt* (*Bunyan*) to attack in the rear. — *adj* **rear'most** last of all. — *adj* **rear'ward** or **rere'ward** in or toward the rear. — *adv* backward; at the back. — *n* (*archaic*) rear; rearguard (partly from Anglo-Fr *rerewarde*). — **rear admiral** an officer next below a vice-admiral, *orig* one in command of the rear; **rear'-arch**, **-dorse**, **-dos** and **-dorter** see under **rere-**; **rear'guard** (OFr *rereguarde*) the rear of an army; a body of troops protecting it. — *adj* from a defensive or losing position; from the rear, as characteristic of a rearguard. — **rear'-lamp** or **-light** a light carried at the back of a vehicle; **rear'-rank**; **rear-view mirror** a mirror that shows what is behind a vehicle. — **bring up the rear** to come last (in a procession, etc). [Aphetic for **arrear**; also partly from OFr *rere* (Fr *arrière*)]

rear[2] *rēr*, *vt* to raise, cause or help to rise; to set up or upright; to originate, to bring into being (*Spenser*); to erect; to build up; to lift up or off; to hold up; to take up; to take away (*Spenser*); to bring up; to breed and foster; to rouse, stir up (now *dialect*); to drive (a hunted animal) from cover (*obs*). — *vi* to rise up, tower (often with *up*); (of a quadruped) to rise on the hindlegs; be roused suddenly to anger, etc (*fig*). — *n* **rear'er**. — **rear'horse** a praying mantis (from its stance). — **rear its ugly head** (*fig*) (of a question, situation, etc) to arise unwelcomely. [OE *rǣran* to raise, causative of *rīsan* to rise]

rear[3] *rēr*, *adj* (now *obs* or *dialect*; see **rare**[2]) lightly cooked (*orig* applied to eggs). — *adj* **rear'-boiled**. — *adj* **rear'-roasted**. [OE *hrēr*]

rear[4]. Same as **rare**[3].

rearmouse. Same as **reremouse**.

reascend *rē-ə-send'*, *vt* and *vi* to ascend again; to go back up; to climb again. — *n* **rēascen'sion** or **rēascent'**. [**re-**]

reason *rē'zn*, *n* ground, support or justification of an act or belief; a premise, *esp* when placed after its conclusion; a motive or inducement; an underlying explanatory principle; a cause; the mind's power of drawing conclusions and determining right and truth; the exercise of this power; sanity; conformity to what is fairly to be expected or called for; moderation; fair treatment, eg satisfaction by a duel, or doing one's fair share in drinking (*archaic*); a remark, a sententious saying (*Shakesp*); proportion (*Spenser*). — *vi* to exercise the faculty of reason; to deduce inferences from premises; to argue; to debate; to converse (*Shakesp*). — *vt* to examine or discuss; to debate; to think out; to set forth logically; to bring by reasoning. — *adj* **rea'sonable** endowed with reason; rational; acting according to reason; agreeable to reason; just; not excessive; not expensive; moderate. — *adv* (now *illiterate*) reasonably. — *n* **rea'sonableness**. — *adv* **rea'sonably**. — *adj* **rea'soned** argued out. — *n* **rea'soner**. — *n* **rea'soning**. — *adj* **rea'sonless**. — **by reason of** on account of; in consequence of; **do someone reason** (*obs*) to give someone the satisfaction of a duel; to drink without shirking; **it stands to reason** it is obvious or logical; **listen to reason** listen to, and take heed of, the reasonable explanation, course of action, etc; **no reason but** (*Shakesp*) no reason for it being otherwise, hence, no possible alternative; **principle of sufficient reason** that nothing happens without a sufficient reason why it should be as it is and not otherwise; **pure reason** reason absolutely independent of experience; **within** or **in reason** within the bounds of what is possible, sensible, etc. [Fr *raison*, from L *ratiō*, *-ōnis*, from *rērī*, *ratus* to think]

reassure *rē-ə-shōōr'*, *vt* to assure anew; to reinsure; to give confidence to; to relieve apprehension or worry; to confirm. — *n* **reassur'ance**. — *n* **reassur'er**. — *adj* **reassur'ing**. — *adv* **reassur'ingly**. [**re-**]

reast[1], **reest** or **reist** *rēst*, *vi* to become rancid (*esp* of bacon). — *n* **reast'iness**, etc. — *adj* **reast'y**, etc. [ME *rest*, *reest*, rancid]

reast[2]. Same as **reest**[2].

reata or **riata** *rē-ä'tä*, *n* a lariat. [Sp, from *reater* to tie again]

reate *rēt*, *n* water-crowfoot. [Origin obscure]

reattribute *rē-ə-trib'ūt*, *vt* to judge (a work of art) to be by a different artist than that to whom it was previously attributed. — *n* **rēattribū'tion**. [**re-**]

Réau *abbrev*: Réaumur's thermometric scale.

Réaumur *rā-ō-mür*, *adj* (of a thermometer or thermometer scale) having the freezing-point of water marked 0° and boiling-point 80°. [From the French physicist, R A F de *Réaumur* (1683–1757), who introduced the scale]

reave, also (*orig Scot*) **reive** *rēv*, (*archaic*) *vt* and *vi* to plunder; to rob: — *pa t* and *pa p* **reft** (*obs* **raft**). — *n* **reav'er** or **reiv'er**. [OE *rēafian* to rob; cf Ger *rauben* to rob]

reback *rē-bak'*, *vt* to put a new back on. [**re-**]

re-bar *rē'bär*, *n* a steel bar in reinforced concrete. [*re*inforcing *bar*]

rebarbative *ri-bärb'ə-tiv*, *adj* repellent. [Fr *rébarbatif*, from *barbe* beard]

rebate[1] *ri-bāt'*, *vt* to reduce; to abate; to dull; to blunt; to repay a part of; to diminish by removal of a projection (*heraldry*). — *n* (or *rē'*) discount; repayment, refund. — *n* **rebāte'ment** abatement; reduction; discount; a narrowing (*Bible*). — *n* **re'bater**. [Fr *rabattre* to beat back, from pfx *re-* and *abattre* to abate]

rebate[2] *rē'bāt* or *rab'it*. Same as **rabbet**.

rebato *rə-bä'tō*, (*Shakesp*) *n* a stiff collar or support for a ruff: — *pl* **reba'toes**. — Also **reba'ter** or **raba'to** (*pl* **raba'toes**). [Fr *rabat*]

rebbe *re'bə*, *n* a rabbi or spiritual leader of a Hasidic Jewish group (also with *cap* as a title). [Yiddish, from Heb *rabbī*]

rebbetzin *reb'ət-sən*, *n* a rabbi's wife. [Yiddish]

rebec. See **rebeck**.

Rebecca *ri-bek'ə*, (*hist*) *n* the leader of those who demolished toll-gates in the **Rebecca riots** in Wales from 1843. — *n* **Rebecc'aism**. — *n* **Rebecc'aite**. [Alluding to Gen 24. 60]

rebecca-eureka *ri-bek'ə-ū-rē'kə*, *n* a secondary-radar system in which the interrogating installation is in an aircraft and the fixed beacon responder on the ground.

rebeck or **rebec** *rē'bek*, *n* a medieval instrument of the viol class shaped like a mandoline, *usu* with three strings. [OFr *rebec*, from Ar *rebāb*, *rabāb* (change of ending unexplained); other forms occur in European languages, including, in ME *ribibe* and *ribible*]

rebel *reb'(ə)l*, *n* a person who rebels; a person who resents and resists authority or oppressive conditions; someone who refuses to conform to the generally accepted modes of behaviour, dress, etc. — *adj* rebellious. — *vi*

Some words with the prefix **re-**.

rēannex' *vt.*	**rēappear'ance** *n.*	**rēappoint'ment** *n.*
rēannexā'tion *n.*	**rēapplicā'tion** *n.*	**rēappor'tion** *vt.*
rēappar'el *vt.*	**rēapply'** *vi.*	**rēappor'tionment** *n.*
rēappear' *vi.*	**rēappoint'** *vt.*	**rēapprais'al** *n.*

(*ri-bel'*; often with *against*) to renounce the authority of the laws and government, or to take up arms and openly oppose them; to oppose any authority; to revolt; to offer opposition; to feel repugnance: — *pr p* **rebell'ing**; *pa t* and *pa p* **rebelled'**. — *n* **reb'eldom**. — *n* **rebell'er** (now *rare*) — *adv* **reb'el-like** (*Shakesp*). — *n* **rebell'ion** (*-yən*) the or an act of rebelling; revolt. — *adj* **rebell'ious** engaged in rebellion; characteristic of a rebel or rebellion; inclined to rebel; refractory. — *adv* **rebell'iously**. — *n* **rebell'iousness**. [Fr *rebelle*, from L *rebellis* insurgent, from pfx *re-* and *bellum* war]

rebellow *rē-bel'ō*, (*Spenser*) *vi* to bellow in return; to echo back a loud noise. [**re-**]

rebid *rē-bid'*, *vt* and *vi* to bid again, *esp* (*bridge*) on the same suit as a previous bid. — *n* a renewed bid, *esp* on one's former suit. [**re-**]

rebind *rē'bīnd'*, *vt* to give a new binding to; to bind again: — *pa t*, *pa p* and *adj* **rēbound'**. [**re-**]

rebirth *rē-bûrth'*, *n* reincarnation; revival of, eg an interest; spiritual renewal. — *n* **rebirth'ing** a type of psychotherapy involving the reliving of the experience of being born, in order to release anxieties, etc. [**re-**]

rebite *rē-bīt'*, *vt* to freshen (a plate) by a new application of acid. [**re-**]

reboant *reb'ō-ənt*, (*poetic*) *adj* rebellowing; loudly resounding. — *n* **reboā'tion**. [L *reboāns*, *-antis*, pr p of *reboāre*, from *re* again, and *boāre* to cry aloud]

rebop. See **bebop**.

rebore *rē'bōr'* or *-bōr'*, *vt* to bore again (the cylinder of a car engine) so as to clear it. — Also *n*. [**re-**]

reborn *rē-börn'*, *p adj* born again (qv).

rebound[1]. See **rebind**.

rebound[2] *ri-bownd'*, *vi* to bound back from collision; to spring back (*literally* and *fig*); to re-echo; to recover quickly after a setback. — *vt* to throw back; to re-echo. — *n* (*rē'*) the or an act of rebounding. — **on the rebound** after bouncing; while reacting against a setback, disappointment, etc, *esp* in love affairs. [Fr *rebondir*; see **bound**[3]]

rebuff *ri-buf'*, *n* a blowing back (*Milton*); a sudden check, curb or setback; unexpected refusal or rejection; a snub or slight. — *vt* to beat back; to check; to repulse or reject; to snub. [OFr *rebuffe*, from Ital *ribuffo* a reproof, from Ital *ri-* (= L *re-*) back, and *buffo* puff]

rebuke *ri-būk'*, *vt* to check, restrain, beat back (*obs*); to put to shame (*archaic*); to reprove sternly. — *n* a check (*obs*); a putting to shame (*obs*); a reproach; stern reproof, reprimand. — *adj* **rebūk'able**. — *adj* **rebūke'ful**. — *adv* **rebūke'fully**. — *n* **rebūk'er**. — *adv* **rebūk'ingly**. [Anglo-Fr *rebuker* (OFr *rebucher*), from pfx *re-* and *bucher* to strike]

rebus *rē'bəs*, *n* an enigmatical representation of a word or name by pictures punningly representing parts of the word, as in a puzzle or a coat of arms; such a puzzle: — *pl* **re'buses**. [L *rēbus* by things, ablative pl of *rēs* thing]

rebut *ri-but'*, *vt* to drive back; to repel; to meet in argument or proof; to disprove; to refute. — *vi* to recoil (*Spenser*); to return an answer (*law*): — *pr p* **rebutt'ing**; *pa t* and *pa p* **rebutt'ed**. — *n* **rebut'ment**. — *adj* **rebutt'able**. — *n* **rebutt'al**. — *n* **rebutt'er** a person, or an argument, that rebuts; a defendant's reply to a plaintiff's surrejoinder (*law*). [OFr *rebo(u)ter*, *rebuter* to repulse; see **butt**[1]]

REC *abbrev*: regional electricity company.

rec *rek*, (*colloq*) *n* a recreation ground.

rec. *abbrev*: receipt; recipe; *recipe* (*L*) take; record.

recal. See **recall**.

recalcitrate *ri-kal'si-trāt*, *vt* and *vi* to kick back (*rare*). — *vi* (*usu* with *at* or *against*) to show strong objection or opposition; to be refractory. — *n* **recal'citrance** strong objection or opposition; refractoriness. — *adj* **recal'citrant** refractory; obstinate in opposition. — *n* a recalcitrant person. — *n* **recalcitrā'tion**. [L *recalcitrāre* to kick back, from *calx*, *calcis* the heel]

recalesce *rē-kal-es'*, *vt* to display again a state of glowing heat. — *n* **recales'cence** (*phys*) the renewed glowing of iron at a certain stage of cooling from white heat. — *adj* **recales'cent**. [L *re-* again, and *calēscere* to grow hot]

recall (rarely **recal**) *ri-kōl'*, *vt* to call back; to command to return; to bring back as by a summons; to remove from office by vote (*US*); to revoke; to call back to mind. — *n* act, power or possibility of recalling or of revoking; a signal or order to return; the calling back of a performer to the stage or platform by applause; a right of electors to dismiss an official by a vote (*US*); remembrance of things learned or experienced, *esp* in the phrase **total recall**, (power of) remembering accurately in full detail. — *adj* **recall'able** capable of being recalled. — *n* **recal'ment** or **recall'ment**. [**re-**]

recant *ri-kant'*, *vt* to retract. — *vi* to revoke a former declaration; to unsay what has been said, *esp* to declare one's renunciation of one's former religious belief. — *n* **recantā'tion** (*rē-*). — *n* **recant'er** (*ri-*). [L *recantāre* to revoke, from *cantāre* to sing, to charm]

recap *rē-kap'*. Short form of **recapitulate** and **recapitulation**.

recapitalize or **-ise** *rē-kap'i-təl-īz*, *vt* to supply again with capital. — *n* **rēcapitalīzā'tion** or **-s-**. [**re-**]

recapitulate *rē-kə-pit'ū-lāt*, *vt* to go over again the chief points of; (of an embryo) to repeat (stages in the development of the species) during embryonic development; to repeat (an earlier passage) in a musical work. — *n* **recapitūlā'tion** the act of recapitulating; summing up; the reproduction, in the developmental stages of an individual embryo, of the evolutionary stages in the life history of the race or type (*biol*); the final repetition of the subjects in sonata form after development (*music*). — *adj* **recapit'ūlātive** or **recapit'ūlatory** repeating again; of the nature of a recapitulation. [L *recapitulāre*, *-ātum*, from *re-* again, and *capitulum* heading, chapter, from *caput* head]

recaption *rē-kap'shən*, *n* reprisal; taking back by peaceable means goods, children, etc from someone who has no right to detain them (*law*). [**re-**]

recapture *rē-kap'chər*, *vt* to capture back, eg a prize from a captor; to recover by effort. — *n* the or an act of retaking; recovery; a thing recaptured. — *n* **recap'tor** or **recap'turer**. [**re-**]

recast *rē-käst'*, *vt* to cast or mould again or in a new form; to reconstruct, remould; to recalculate (*poetic*); to reassign parts in a theatrical production; to give (an actor) a different part: — *pa t* and *pa p* **recast'**. — *n* (*rē'käst* or *rē-käst'*) shaping again or afresh, reconstruction; that which has been shaped again or afresh. [**re-**]

recce *rek'i*, (*military slang*) *n* reconnaissance: — *pl* **recc'es**. — Also (*esp airforce*) **recc'ō**: — *pl* **recc'ōs**. — *vt* and *vi* (**recce**) to reconnoitre: — *pr p* **recc'eing**; *pa t* and *pa p* **recc'ed** or **recc'eed**.

reccy *rek'i*, (*military slang*) *n* another spelling of **recce**. — Also *vt* and *vi*: — *pr p* **recc'ying**; *pa t* and *pa p* **recc'ied**.

recd *abbrev*: received.

recede *ri-sēd'*, *vi* to go back, go farther off, become more distant (*lit* and *fig*); to go or draw back (from; *lit* and *fig*); to differ (from; *archaic*); to grow less, decline; to bend or slope backward; to give up a claim, renounce

Some words with the prefix **re-**.

rēappraise' *vt*.	**rēarm'** *vt* and *vi*.	**rēarrange'** *vt*.
rēappraise'ment *n*.	**rēarm'ament** *n*.	**rēarrange'ment** *n*.
rēapprais'er *n*.	**rēarous'al** *n*.	**rēarrest'** *n* and *vt*.
rēarise' *vi*.	**rēarouse'** *vt*.	**rēassem'blage** *n*.

a promise, etc. — *adj* **reced'ing**. [L *recēdere, recēssum*, from *re-* back, and *cēdere* to go, yield]

re-cede or **recede** *rē'sēd'*, *vt* to cede again or back. [**re-**]

receipt *ri-sēt'*, *n* receiving; place of receiving; capacity (*obs*); a written acknowledgment of anything received; that which is received; a recipe, *esp* in cookery (*archaic*); anything prepared after a recipe (*obs*). — *vt* to mark as paid; to give a receipt for (*usu NAm*). [OFr *receite, recete* (Fr *recette*), from L *recepta*, fem pa p of *recipere* to receive, with *p* restored after L]

receive *ri-sēv'*, *vt* to take, get or catch, *usu* more or less passively; to have given or delivered to one; to experience; to take in or on; to admit; to accept; to meet or welcome on entrance; to harbour (ideas, etc); to await in resistance; to bear the weight of; to experience, or learn of, and react towards; to accept as authority or as truth; to take into the body; to buy or deal in (stolen goods); to be acted upon by, and transform, electrical signals. — *vi* to be a recipient; to participate in communion (*Christian relig*); to receive signals; to hold a reception of visitors. — *n* **receivabil'ity** or **receiv'ableness**. — *adj* **receiv'able**. — *n* **receiv'al** (*rare*). — *adj* **received'** generally accepted. — *n* **receiv'er** a person who receives; an officer who receives taxes; a person appointed by a court to manage property under litigation, receive money, etc; an official receiver (see below); a person who receives stolen goods (*colloq*); a vessel for receiving the products of distillation, or for containing gases (*chem*); the glass vessel of an air-pump in which the vacuum is formed; an instrument by which electrical signals are transformed into audible or visual form, eg a telephone receiver; a receiving-set; a player on the offensive team eligible to catch forward passes (*Am football*); the catcher (*baseball*). — *n* **receiv'ership** the state of being in the control of a receiver; the office or function of a receiver. — *n* and *adj* **receiv'ing**. — **Received (Standard) English** the English generally spoken by educated British people and considered the standard of the language; **Received Pronunciation** the particular pronunciation of British English which is generally regarded as being least regionally limited, most socially acceptable, and is considered the standard (*abbrev* **RP**); **receiver general** an officer who receives revenues; **receiv'ing-house** a depot; a house where letters, etc are left for transmission; **receiv'ing-line** a number of people standing in line formally to receive a VIP, guests, etc on arrival; **receiv'ing-office** a branch post-office for receipt of letters, etc; **receiv'ing-order** formerly, an order putting a receiver in temporary possession of a debtor's estate, pending bankruptcy proceedings, now replaced by **bankruptcy order**; **receiv'ing-room** a room where patients, inmates, etc are received; **receiv'ing-set** apparatus for receiving radio communications; **receiv'ing-ship** a stationary ship for naval recruits. — **official receiver** an official appointed by the Department of Trade and Industry to manage the estate of a person, company, etc declared bankrupt, until a trustee has been appointed. [Anglo-Fr *receivre* (Fr *recevoir*), from L *recipere, receptum*, from *re-* back, and *capere* to take]

recency. See under **recent**.

recense *ri-sens'*, *vt* to revise critically. — *n* **recen'sion** a critical revision of a text; a text established by critical revision; a review. [L *recēnsiō, -ōnis*, from *re-* again, and *cēnsēre* to value, to assess]

recent *rē'sənt*, *adj* done, made, etc not long ago or not long past; fresh; modern; (with *cap*) of the present geological period, Post-Glacial. — *n* **rē'cency**. — *adv* **rē'cently**. — *n* **rē'centness**. [L *recēns, recentis*]

recept *rē'sept*, *n* an image or idea formed by repeated similar perceptions. [L *receptum*, pa p of *recipere* to receive, after *concept*, etc]

receptacle *ri-sep'tə-kl* also, eg *Shakesp*, *res'ip-tə-kl*, *n* that in which anything is or may be received or stored; the enlarged end of an axis bearing the parts of a flower or the crowded flowers of an infloresence; in flowerless plants, a structure bearing reproductive organs, spores or gemmae. — *adj* **receptacular** (*res-ip-tak'ū-lər*). — *n* **receptac'ulum** a receptacle: — *pl* **receptac'ula**. [L *receptāculum*, from *recipere, receptum* to receive]

receptibility and **receptible**. See under **reception**.

reception *ri-sep'shən*, *n* the act, fact or manner of receiving or of being received; taking in; the act or manner of taking up signals; the quality of received radio or television signals; a formal receiving, as of guests; a social function (eg *wedding reception*) at which guests are *usu* received formally; the part of a hotel, suite of offices, etc where visitors, guests, etc are received; a reception room; treatment on arrival; capacity for receiving (*Milton*). — *n* **recep'tionist** a person employed to receive callers, hotel-guests, patients, customers, etc and make arrangements. — *n* **receptibil'ity** (*ri-*) receivability. — *adj* **recept'ible** capable of receiving (with *of*); able to be received. — *adj* **recep'tive** capable of receiving; quick to receive or take in *esp* ideas; relating to reception or receptors. — *n* **recep'tiveness** or **receptivity** (*res-ep-tiv'i-ti*). — *n* **recep'tor** a receiver; an element of the nervous system adapted for reception of stimuli, eg a sense-organ or sensory nerve-ending; a chemical grouping on the surface of the cell to which a specific antigen may attach itself; a site in or on a cell to which a drug or hormone can become attached, stimulating a reaction inside the cell. — **reception centre** a building, office, etc where people are received for immediate assistance before being directed to specific centres of help, treatment, etc as in the case of drug-addicts or victims of fire, natural disasters, etc; **reception class** a class for the new intake of children at a school; **reception order** an order for the reception and detention of a person in a mental hospital; **reception room** a room for formal receptions; any public room in a house. [L *recipere, receptum* to receive]

recess *rē-ses'* or *rē'ses*, *n* a going back or withdrawing; retirement (*obs*); seclusion (*obs*); temporary cessation of business, *esp* the adjournment of a lawcourt, or of Parliament during a vacation; a break or interval during a school day (*NAm*); a holiday period during the academic year (*NAm*); part of a room formed by a receding of the wall; a niche or alcove; a secluded spot, a nook; a hidden, inner or secret place (often in *pl*); a small indentation or depression; a sinus. — *vt* to make a recess in; to put into a recess. — *vi* to adjourn. — *adj* **recessed'**. — *n* **recession** (*ri-sesh'ən*) the or an act of receding; withdrawal; the state of being set back; a slight temporary decline in a country's trade, *specif* one identified by two successive quarters without growth. — *adj* **recessional** (*ri-sesh'ən-əl*) a hymn sung during recession or retirement of clergy and choir after a service. — *adj* **recess'ional**. — *adj* **recessive** (*-ses'*) tending to recede; of an ancestral character, apparently suppressed in crossbred offspring in favour of the alternative character in the other parent, though it may be transmitted to later generations (*genetics*; also *n*); of stress, tending to move toward the beginning of the word (*linguistics*). — *adv* **recess'ively**. — *n* **recess'iveness**. — **recessed arch** one arch within another. [See **recede**]

Some words with the prefix **re-**.

rēassem'ble *vt* and *vi*.	**rēassess'** *vt*.	**rēassume'** *vt*.
rēassem'bly *n*.	**rēassess'ment** *n*.	**rēassump'tion**, *n*.
rēassert' *vt*.	**rēassign'** *vt*.	**rēattach'** *vt* and *vi*.
rēasser'tion *n*.	**rēassign'ment** *n*.	**rēattach'ment** *n*.

recession[1] *rē-sesh'ən, n* a ceding again or back. [**re-**]
recession[2]. See under **recess**.
Rechabite *rek'ə-bīt, n* a descendant of Jonadab, son of *Rechab*, who did not drink wine or dwell in houses (Jer 35. 6–7); a total abstainer from intoxicating drinks, *esp* a member of the order so named; a tent-dweller. — *n* **Rech'abitism**.
rechate (*Shakesp*). See **recheat**.
réchauffé *rā-shō'fā, n* a reheated dish; a fresh concoction of old material. [Fr]
recheat *ri-chēt'* or **rechate** *ri-chāt'*, (*Shakesp*) *n* a horn-call to assemble hounds. — *vi* to sound the recheat. [OFr *racheter*, *rachater* to reassemble]
recherché *rə-sher'shā, adj* carefully chosen; particularly choice; (too) far-fetched or tenuous; rare or exotic. [Fr]
rechie. See **reech**.
rechlesse *rech'lis*, (*Spenser*) *adj*. Same as **reckless**.
recidivism *ri-sid'i-vizm, n* the habit of relapsing into crime. — *n* and *adj* **recid'ivist**. [Fr *récidivisme*, from L *recidīvus* falling back]
recipe *res'i-pi, n* directions for making something, *esp* a food or drink; a prescription (*archaic*); a method laid down for achieving a desired end: — *pl* **rec'ipes**. [L *recipe* take, imperative of *recipere*]
recipient *ri-sip'i-ənt, adj* receiving; receptive. — *n* a person who or thing which receives. — *n* **recip'ience** or **recip'iency** a reception; receptivity. [L *recipiēns*, *-entis*, pr p of *recipere* to receive]
reciprocal *ri-sip'rə-kl, adj* acting in return; mutual; complementary; inverse; alternating; interchangeable; giving and receiving or given and received; expressing mutuality (*gram*); reflexive. — *n* that which is reciprocal; the multiplier that gives unity (*math*). — *n* **reciprocality** (*-kal'i-ti*). — *adv* **recip'rocally**. — *n* **recip'rocant** (*math*) a differential invariant. — *vt* **recip'rocāte** to give and receive mutually; to requite; to interchange; to alternate. — *vi* to move backward and forward; to make a return or interchange (*colloq*). — *n* **reciprocā'tion**. — *adj* **recip'rocātive** characterized by or inclined to reciprocation. — *n* **recip'rocātor** a person who or thing which reciprocates; a double-acting steam-engine. — *n* **reciprocity** (*res-i-pros'i-ti*) reciprocal action; mutual relation; concession of mutual privileges or advantages, *esp* mutual tariff concessions. — **reciprocal cross** (*biol*) a cross made both ways with regard to sex, ie A♂ x B♀ and B♂ x A♀; **reciprocal translocation** (*biol*) mutual exchange of non-homologous portions between two chromosomes; **reciprocating engine** an engine in which the piston moves to and fro in a straight line; **reciprocity principle** (*phys*) one stating that the interchange of radiation source and detector will not change the level of radiation at the latter, whatever the shielding arrangement between them. [L *reciprocus*]
recision *ri-sizh'ən, n* cutting back (*obs*); rescinding. [L *recīsiō*, *-ōnis*, from *recīdere* to cut off]
récit *rā-sē, n* a narrative, *esp* the narrative in a book as opposed to the dialogue; a book consisting largely of narrative; a solo part, for voice or instrument (*music*); a principal part in a concerted piece (*music*); a swell organ (*music*). [Fr]
recite *ri-sīt', vt* to repeat from memory; to declaim; to read aloud (*rare*); to narrate; to enumerate; to give (the details of); to repeat to a teacher, have heard a lesson in (*US*). — *vi* to give a recitation; to repeat, or have heard, a lesson (*NAm*). — *n* **recī'tal** the act of reciting; setting forth; enumeration; narration; a public performance of music, *usu* by one performer or composer, or of some particular character; that part of a deed which recites the circumstances (*law*). — *n* **recitation** (*res-i-tā'shən*) the or an act of reciting; a piece for declaiming; the repeating or hearing of a prepared lesson (*NAm*); hence a lesson generally (*NAm*). — *n* **recitā'tionist** a declaimer. — *n* **recitative** (*-tə-tēv'*) or **recitativo** (*re-sit-ä-tē'vō* or Ital *rā-chē-tä-tē'vō*; *pl* **recitati'vos**, Ital **recitati'vi** *-vē*) a style of song resembling speech in its succession of tones and freedom from melodic form; a passage to be sung in this manner. — *adj* in the style of recitative. — *n* **reciter** (*ri-sīt'ər*). — **recitā'tion-room** (*US*) a classroom; **recit'ing-note** the note on which, in a Gregorian chant, the greater part of a verse is sung. [L *recitāre*, from *citāre*, *-ātum* to call]
reck *rek*, (*usu* with a negative) *vt* to care, desire (with *infin*; *archaic*); to care about, heed; (used *impers*) to concern. — *vi* (*usu* with *of*) to care, concern oneself; (used *impers*) to matter: — *pa t* and *pa p* **recked**, *obs* or *archaic* **raught** (*röt*). — *n* care; heed. — **what reck?** (*Scot*) what does it matter? [OE *reccan*, *rēcan*; cf OHGer *ruoh* care, Ger *ruchlos* regardless]
reckan *rek'ən*, (*Scott*, ostensibly Cumberland dialect) *adj* or *pa p perh* **racked** or **ricked**.
reckless *rek'ləs, adj* careless; heedless of consequences; rash. — *adv* **reck'lessly**. — *n* **reck'lessness**. [**reck** and **less**]
reckling *rek'ling, n* the weakest, smallest or youngest of a litter or family. — *adj* puny. [Origin obscure; poss from ON *reklingr* an outcast]
reckon *rek'n* or *-ən, vt* to enumerate (*archaic*); to count; to calculate (often with *up*); to include (in an account); to place or class; to estimate, judge to be; to think, believe, suppose or expect; to attribute (to; *archaic*); to think much of (*slang*). — *vi* to calculate; to judge; to go over or settle accounts (with); to concern oneself (with); to count or rely (on or upon). — *n* **reck'oner**. — *n* **reck'oning** counting; calculation, *esp* of a ship's position; a tavern bill; settlement of accounts; judgment. [OE *gerecenian* to explain; Ger *rechnen*]
reclaim *ri-klām', vt orig* to call back (eg a hawk); to win back; to win from evil, wildness, waste or submersion; (*rē-klām'*) to claim back. — *vi* (*ri-klām'*) to exclaim in protest (*archaic*); to appeal (*Scots law*). — *n* recall; possibility of reform. — *adj* **reclaim'able**. — *adv* **reclaim'ably**. — *n* **reclaim'ant**. — *n* **reclaim'er**. [OFr *reclamer*, from L *reclāmāre*]
reclamation *rek-lə-mā'shən, n* the or an act of reclaiming; state of being reclaimed. [L *reclāmātiō*, *-ōnis*, from *reclāmāre*, from *clāmāre* to cry out]
réclame *rā-kläm, n* the art or practice by which publicity or notoriety is secured; publicity. [Fr]
recline *ri-klīn', vt* to lay on the back; to incline or bend (properly backwards). — *vi* to lean in a recumbent position, on back or side; (of the plane of a sundial) to make an angle with the vertical; to rely (on or upon; *archaic*). — *adj* or *adv* (*Milton*) recumbent. — *adj* **reclī'nable**. — *adj* **reclinate** (*rek'li-nāt*) bent down or back. — *n* **reclinā'tion** (*rek-li-*) reclining; bending back; angle of a dial with the vertical. — *adj* **reclīned'** recumbent; reclinate. — *n* **reclī'ner** someone who or something that reclines, *esp* a type of easy chair with a back that can be lowered towards a horizontal position. — *adj* **reclī'ning**. [L *reclīnāre*, *-ātum*, from *clīnāre* to bend]
recluse *ri-kloos', adj* enclosed, eg as an anchorite; secluded; retired; solitary. — *n* a religious devotee who lives shut up in a cell; a person who lives retired from the world. — *adv* **recluse'ly**. — *n* **recluse'ness** seclusion

Some words with the prefix **re-**.

rēattain' *vt*.	**rēawak'ening** *n*.	**rēbloss'om** *vi*.
rēattempt' *vt*, *vi* and *n*.	**rēbap'tism** *n*.	**rēboil'** *vt* and *vi*.
rēawake' *vt* and *vi*.	**rēbaptize'** or **-ise'** *vt*.	**rēborr'ow** *vt*.
rēawak'en *vt* and *vi*.	**rēbloom'** *vi*.	**rēbrace'** *vt*.

from society; retirement. — *n* **reclusion** (*-kloo'zhən*) religious seclusion; the life of a recluse; seclusion in prison. — *adj* **reclu'sive** (*-siv*) of or living in, etc seclusion. — *n* **reclu'sory** a recluse's cell. [L *reclūsus*, pa p of *reclūdere* to open, in later Latin, shut away, from *re-* back, away, and *claudere*]

recognize or **-ise** *rek'əg-nīz*, *vt* to know again; to identify as known or experienced before; to show sign of knowing (a person); to see or acknowledge the fact of; to acknowledge (that); to acknowledge the validity of (a claim); to acknowledge the status or legality of (eg a government); to allow someone to speak in court proceedings, formal debate, etc (*US*); to reward (meritorious conduct). — *n* **recognition** (*rek-əg-nish'ən*) the or an act of recognizing; state of being recognized; acknowledgment; acknowledgment of status; a sign, token or indication of recognizing; a return of the feu to the superior (*Scots law*). — *adj* **recognitive** (*ri-kog'*) or **recog'nitory**. — *adj* **recognīz'able** or **-s-** (or *rek'*). — *adv* **recognīz'ably** or **-s-** (or *rek'*). — *n* **recognizance** or **-s-** (*ri-kog'ni-zəns*) a recognition; acknowledgment; a token (*archaic*); (or *ri-kon'i-zəns*) a legal obligation entered into before a magistrate to do, or not to do, some particular act; money pledged for the performance of such an obligation. — *n* **recognizer** or **-s-** (*rek'əg-nīz-ər*, or *-nīz'ər*). [L *recognōscere* and OFr *reconoistre*, *reconoiss-*; see **cognosce** and **cognition**]

recoil *ri-koil'* (*Spenser* **recoyle**, **recule** or **recuile**) *vt* (*obs*) to force back. — *vi* to retreat, fall back (*archaic*); to revert (*obs*); to start back; to stagger back; to shrink in horror, etc; to rebound; (of a gun) to kick; to degenerate (*Shakesp*). — *n* retreat (*archaic*); a starting or springing back; rebound; the kick of a gun; change in motion of a particle caused by ejection of another particle, or (sometimes) by a collision (*nuc*). — *n* **recoil'er**. — *adj* **recoil'less**. — **recoil atom** an atom that experiences a sudden change of direction or reversal, after the emission from it of a particle or radiation; **recoil escapement** same as **anchor escapement** under **anchor**; **recoil nucleus** same as **recoil atom**. [Fr *reculer*, from *cul*, from L *cūlus* the hind parts]

recoin *rē-koin'*, *vt* to coin again, *esp* by melting and passing again through a mint. — *n* **recoin'age**. [**re-**]

recollect[1] *rek-əl-ekt'*, *vt* to recall to memory; to remember, *esp* by an effort; to absorb in mystical contemplation (*archaic*); to recall to the matter in hand, or to composure or resolution (*usu reflexive*). — *n* (*rek'*) a Franciscan friar of a reformed branch, aiming at detachment from creatures and recollection in God. — Also (*Fr*) **récollet** (*rā-kol-ā*). — *adj* **recollect'ed**. — *adv* **recollect'edly**. — *n* **recollect'edness**. — *n* **recollec'tion** (*rek-*) the act or power of recollecting; a memory, reminiscence; a thing remembered; mystical contemplation (*archaic*). — *adj* **recollec'tive**. — *adv* **recollec'tively**. — **recollected terms** (*Shakesp*) variously explained as: known by heart, picked, studied, lacking spontaneity. [L *recolligere* to gather again or gather up, from *colligere*; see **collect**]

recollect[2] or **re-collect** *rē'kol-ekt'*, *vt* to collect (*obs*); to gather together again; to summon up; to bring back again (*Milton*). [Partly **recollect**[1]; partly **re-** and **collect**]

recombine *rē-kəm-bīn'*, *vt* and *vi* to join together again. — *adj* and *n* **recombinant** (*ri-kom'bi-nənt*). — *n* **recombinā'tion** the act or result of recombining; the formation of new combinations of genes during meiosis by random assortment of chromosomes and by crossover (*biol*). — **recombinant DNA** genetic material produced by the combining of DNA molecules from different organisms (see also **genetic engineering** under **genetic**). [**re-**]

recomfort *ri-kum'fərt*, (*archaic*) *vt* to comfort; to console; to reinvigorate; to refresh. — *adj* **recom'fortless** (*Spenser*) comfortless. — *n* **recom'forture** (*Shakesp*) consolation. [**re-**]

recommend *rek-ə-mend'*, *vt* to commend, commit or consign (*archaic*); to commend or introduce as suitable for acceptance, favour, appointment or choice; to make acceptable; to advise; to inform (*Shakesp*). — *adj* **recommend'able**. — *adv* **recommend'ably**. — *n* **recommendā'tion**. — *adj* **recommend'atory**. — *n* **recommend'er**. [**re-**]

recompense *rek'əm-pens*, *vt* to return an equivalent to or for; to repay. — *n* (formerly **recompence**) return of an equivalent; that which is so returned; reward; retribution; requital. [OFr *recompenser*, from L *compēnsāre* to compensate]

reconcile *rek'ən-sīl*, *vt* to restore or bring back to friendship or union; to bring to agreement or contentment; to pacify; to make, or to prove consistent; to admit or restore to membership of a church; to adjust or compose; to regain, conciliate (*Spenser*); to reconsecrate (a desecrated holy place). — *n* **rec'oncilability** (or *-sīl'*). — *adj* **rec'oncilable** (or *-sīl'*). — *n* **rec'oncilableness** (or *-sīl'*). — *adv* **rec'oncilably** (or *-sīl'*). — *n* **rec'oncilement** (or *-sīl'*). — *n* **rec'onciler**. — *n* **reconciliā'tion** (*-sil-*). — *adj* **reconciliatory** (*-sil'i-ə-tər-i*). [L *reconciliāre*, *-ātum*, from *conciliāre* to call together]

recondite *ri-kon'dīt* or *rek'ən-dīt*, *adj* hidden; obscure; abstruse; profound. [L *recondere*, *-itum* to put away, from *re-* again, and *condere* to establish, store]

recondition *rē-kən-dish'ən*, *vt* to repair and refit; to restore to original or sound condition. [**re-**]

reconnaissance *ri-kon'i-səns*, *n* reconnoitring; a preliminary survey. — **reconnaissance in force** an attack by a large body to discover the enemy's position and strength. [Fr]

reconnoitre or (*esp NAm*) **reconnoiter** *rek-ə-noi'tər*, *vt* to examine with a view to military operations or other purpose; to remember (*obs*). — *vi* to make preliminary examination. — *n* a reconnaissance. — *n* **reconnoi'trer** or (*esp in NAm*) **reconnoi'terer**. [Fr *reconnoître* (now *reconnaître*), from L *rocognōscere* to recognize]

REconS *abbrev*: Royal Economic Society.

reconsider *rē-kon-sid'ər*, *vt* to consider (a decision, etc) again, with a view to altering or reversing it. — *n* **reconsiderā'tion**. [**re-**]

reconstitute *rē-kon'sti-tūt*, *vt* to constitute anew; to reorganize; to restore the constitution of (*esp* dried foods by adding water). — *adj* **reconstitūt'able**. — *adj* **reconstit'ūent** (*-kən-*). — *n* **reconstitū'tion** constituting afresh; refounding; restoration to original condition; theoretical reconstruction on the spot of the details of a crime. [**re-**]

reconstruct *rē-kən-strukt'*, *vt* to construct again; to rebuild; to remodel; to restore in imagination or theory. — *n* **reconstruc'tion** the act of reconstructing; a thing reconstructed; reorganization; a model representing a series of sections; a theoretical representation or view of something unknown; the upbuilding of moral and material public well-being after a great upheaval; (with *cap*) the process of restoring the Seceding States to the rights and privileges of the Union after the Civil War (*US*). — *adj* **reconstruc'tional**. — *adj* **reconstruc'tionary**. — *n* **reconstruc'tionist**. — *adj* **reconstruc'tive**. — *n* **reconstruc'tor**. — **reconstructive surgery** plastic surgery either to

Some words with the prefix **re-**.

rēbroad'cast *vt* and *n*.	**rēbutt'on** *vt*.	**rēchall'enge** *vt* and *n*.
rēbuild' *vt*.	**rēcal'culate** *vt*.	**rēcharge'** *vt*.
rēbur'ial *n*.	**rēcatch'** *vt* and *vi*.	**recharge'able** *adj*.
rēbur'y *vt*.	**rēcen'tre** *vt*.	**rēchart'** *vi*.

correct a disfigurement or make cosmetic changes to the body. **[re-]**

reconvalescence *ri-kon-vəl-es'əns*, (*archaic*) *n* recovery from illness. **[re-]**

reconvert *rē-kən-vûrt'*, *vt* to convert again to a former state, religion, etc. — *n* **reconver'sion**. **[re-]**

reconvey *rē-kən-vā'*, *vt* (of an estate, etc) to transfer again to a former owner. — *n* **reconvey'ance**. **[re-]**

record *ri-körd'*, *vt* to get by heart (*obs*); to go over in one's mind (*Spenser*); to repeat from memory (*Spenser*); to narrate, set forth (*archaic*); to sing in an undertone, practise quietly (*esp* of birds; *obs*); to call to mind (*archaic*); to set down in writing or other permanent form; to register (on an instrument, scale, etc); to trace a curve or other representation of; to perform before a recording instrument; to make a recording of (music, speech, etc); to mark, indicate; to bear witness to; to put on record (an offence, etc) without taking further measures against the offender; to register (as a vote or verdict); to celebrate. — *vi* to sing, warble, *esp* in quiet rehearsal (*obs*); to make a record. — *n* **record** (*rek'örd*, formerly *ri-körd'*) a register; a formal writing of any fact or proceeding; a book of such writings; past history; a witness, a memorial; memory, remembrance; anything entered in the rolls of a court, *esp* the formal statement or pleadings of parties in a litigation; a group of related fields forming a complete piece of information, such as a name and address, and constituting one of the basic elements of a file (*comput*); a curve or other representation of phenomena made by an instrument upon a surface; a disc (or formerly a cylinder) on which sound is registered for reproduction by an instrument such as a gramophone; a performance or occurrence not recorded to have been surpassed; a list of a person's criminal convictions. — *adj* not surpassed. — *adj* **record'able** (*ri-*) able to be recorded; worthy of record. — *n* **recordā'tion** (*Shakesp rek'*) remembrance; commemoration; recording. — *n* **record'er** (*ri-*) a person who records or registers, *esp* the rolls, etc of a city; (with *caps*) a judge of a city or borough court of quarter-sessions (*hist*); in England, a barrister or solicitor appointed as a part-time judge; a person who performs before a recording instrument; a recording apparatus; a fipple-flute, once called the 'English flute', much used in the 16c–18c and again in the 20c (from the *obs* meanings of the verb). — *n* **record'ership** the office of recorder or the time of holding it. — *n* **record'ing** a record of sound or images made for later reproduction, eg on magnetic tape, film or gramophone disc. — Also *adj*. — *n* **record'ist** a person who records (*esp* the sound for a cinema film). — **recorded delivery** a service of the Post Office in which a record is kept of the collection and delivery of a letter, parcel, etc; **recording angel** an angel supposed to keep a book in which every misdeed is recorded against the doer; **Record Office** a place where public records are kept; **rec'ord-player** a small, portable instrument for playing gramophone records, run on batteries or mains electricity, not spring-driven; a larger, more sophisticated, etc device for the same purpose; **rec'ord-sleeve** a cardboard case for a gramophone record. — **beat** or **break a** (or **the**) **record** to outdo the highest achievement yet recorded; **close the record** an act of a Scottish judge after each party has said all he or she wishes to say by way of statement and answer; **court of record** a court (such as the supreme court, county courts and others) whose acts and proceedings are permanently recorded, and which has the authority to fine or imprison persons for contempt; **for the record** (*colloq*) in order to get the facts straight; **go on record** to make a public statement; **off the record** not for publication in the press, etc (*adj* **off'-the-record**); **on record** recorded in a document, etc; publicly known; **public records** contemporary officially authenticated statements of acts and proceedings in public affairs, preserved in the public interest; **set the record straight** to put right a mistake or false impression; **trial by record** a common law mode of trial when a former decision of the court is disputed and the matter is settled by producing the record. [OFr *recorder*, from L *recordārī* to call to mind, get by heart, from *cor*, *cordis* the heart]

recount[1] *ri-kownt'*, *vt* to narrate the particulars of; to detail. — *n* **recount'al** (*ri-*). — *n* **recount'ment** (*Shakesp*) relation in detail. [OFr *reconter*, from *conter* to tell]

recount[2] or **re-count** *rē-kownt'* *vt* and *vi* to count over again. — *n* (*rē'kownt*) a second or new counting (as of votes). **[re-]**

recoup *ri-ko͞op'*, *vt* to deduct or keep back (from what is claimed by a counterclaim; *law*); to make good (a loss); to indemnify, compensate. — *n* **recoup'ment**. [Fr *recouper* to cut back, from *couper* to cut]

recoure or **recower** *ri-kowr'*, (*Spenser*) *vt*. Variant of **recover**. See also **recure**.

recourse *ri-kōrs'*, *-körs'*, *n* flowing back (*archaic*); withdrawal (*archaic*); recurrence (*archaic*); flow (*Shakesp*); return (*archaic*); freedom to return; access; resort; a source of aid or protection; right to payment, *esp* by the drawer or endorser of a bill of exchange not met by the acceptor. — *vi* (*Spenser*) to return, go back or revert in the mind. — **have recourse to** to go to for help, protection, etc; **without recourse** (*law* and *commerce*) a qualified endorsement of a bill or promissory note indicating that the endorser takes no responsibility for non-payment. [Fr *recours*, from L *recursus*, from *re-* back, and *currere*, *cursum* to run]

re-cover or **recover** *rē-kuv'ər*, *vt* to cover again. **[re-]**

recover *ri-kuv'ər*, *vt* to get or find again; to regain; to reclaim; to extract (a valuable substance) from an ore, etc, or (usable material) from waste; to bring back; to retrieve; to cure (*archaic*); to revive; to restore; to rescue; to succeed in reaching; to attain; to obtain as compensation; to obtain for injury or debt. — *vi* to regain health or any former state; to get back into position; to obtain a judgement (*law*). — *n* recovery (*obs*); possibility of recovery (*obs*); return to a former position, as in rowing or exercise with a weapon; the position so resumed. — *n* **recoverabil'ity**. — *adj* **recov'erable**. — *n* **recov'erableness**. — *n* **recoveree'** a person against whom a judgement is obtained in common recovery. — *n* **recov'erer** a person who recovers. — *n* **recov'eror** a person who recovers a judgement in common recovery. — *n* **recov'ery** the act, fact, process, possibility or power of recovering, or state of having recovered, in any sense; a verdict giving right to the recovery of debts or costs (*law*). — **recovery time** the minimum time interval between two separately-recorded events or states. — **common recovery** a former method of transferring an entailed estate by a legal fiction; **recover the wind of** (*Shakesp*) to get to windward of (so as to drive a hare into a toil, or take the wind out of someone's sails); to gain an advantage over. [OFr *recover*, from L *recuperāre*; see **recuperate**]

recower. See **recoure**.

recoyle. See **recoil**.

recpt *abbrev*: receipt.

recreant *rek'ri-ənt*, (*archaic*) *adj* surrendering; craven; false; apostate. — *n* a person who yields in combat; a

Some words with the prefix **re-**.

rēchart'er *vt* and *vi*.	**rēcir'culate** *vt* and *vi*.	**rēclose'** *vt*.
rēcheck' *vt* and *vi*.	**rēclassificā'tion** *n*.	**rēclothe'** *vt*.
rē'check *n*.	**rēclass'ify** *vt*.	**rēcode'** *vt*.
rēchrist'en *vt*.	**rēclimb'** *vt*.	**rēcolonizā'tion** or **-s-** *n*.

craven; a mean-spirited wretch; an apostate; a renegade. — *n* **rec'reance** or **rec'reancy**. — *adv* **rec'reantly**. [OFr, pr p of *recroire* to yield in combat, from LL *recrēdere* to surrender, from L *crēdere* to entrust]

recreate *rē-krē-āt'*, *vt* to create again; (in the following senses *rek'ri-āt*; *rare*) to reinvigorate; to refresh; to indulge, gratify or amuse by sport or pastime. — *vi* to take recreation. — *n* **recreation** (*rē-krē-ā'shən*) the act of creating anew; a new creation; (in the following senses *rek-ri-ā'shən*), refreshment after toil, sorrow, etc; pleasurable occupation of leisure time; an amusement or sport; a source of amusement. — *adj* **recreā'tional** (*rek-*). — *adj* **rĕcreā'tive** (and *rek'ri-ā-tiv*). — **recreational drug** one taken for its intoxicating effects, not for medical reasons; **recreational vehicle** one having living, sleeping, etc facilities in the back (often *abbrev* **RV**); **recreation ground** (*rek-*) an open area for games, sports, etc. [**re-**]

recrement *rek'ri-mənt*, *n* waste, dross; a secretion that is reabsorbed. — *adj* **recremental** (*-ment'l*). — *adj* **recrementitial** (*-mən-tish'l*). — *adj* **recrementi'tious**. [L *recrēmentum* dross, from *cernere* to sift]

recriminate *ri-krim'in-āt*, *vi* to charge an accuser. — *n* **recriminā'tion** act of accusing in return; countercharge. — *adj* **recrim'inative**. — *n* **recrim'inator**. — *adj* **recrim'inatory**. [L *crīmināri* to accuse]

recrudesce *rē-kroo-des'*, *vi* to break out afresh. — *n* **recrudesc'ence**. — *n* **recrudesc'ency**. — *adj* **recrudesc'ent**. [L *recrūdēscere*, from *crūdus* raw]

recruit *ri-kroot'*, *n* a reinforcement (*obs*); a new supply (of men, money, health, etc; *archaic*); renewal; restoration; a newly enlisted member, eg a soldier, police officer, etc. — *vi* to obtain fresh supplies; to recover in health or strength; to recoup expenses (*obs*); to enlist new soldiers. — *vt* to reinforce; to replenish; to restore; to reinvigorate; to enlist or raise. — *n* **recruit'al** renewed supply; restoration. — *n* **recruit'er**. — *adj* **recruit'ing**. — *n* **recruit'ment** the art or practice of recruiting, *esp* for employment; in deafness of neural cause, the distressing exaggeration of loud sounds, while soft sounds may be audible. — **recruiting ground** a place where recruits may be obtained. [Obs Fr *recrute* reinforcement, prob pa p fem of *recroître*, from L *recrēscere* to grow again]

recrystallize or **-ise** *rē-kris'təl-īz*, *vt* and *vi* to dissolve and reform (a crystalline substance), as when purifying chemical compounds. — *vi* (in metal) to replace deformed crystals by newly generated ones which absorb them. — *n* **recrystallīzā'tion** or **-s-**. [**re-**]

Rect *abbrev*: Rector; Rectory.

recta, **rectal**, etc. See under **rectum**.

rectangle *rek'tang-gl*, or *-tang'gl*, *n* a four-sided plane figure with all its angles right angles. — *adj* **rec'tangled** having a right angle. — *adj* **rectang'ūlar** of the form of a rectangle; at right angles; right-angled. — *n* **rectangūlar'ity**. — *adv* **rectang'ūlarly**. — **rectangular hyperbola** one whose asymptotes are at right angles; **rectangular solid** one whose axis is perpendicular to its base. [LL *rēct(i)angulum*, from L *angulus* an angle]

recti- *rekti-*, or before a vowel **rect-** *rekt-*, *combining form* denoting: right; straight. — *adj* **rectilineal** (*rek-ti-lin'i-əl*) or **rectilinear** (*rek-ti-lin'i-ər*; L *līnea* a line) in a straight line or lines; straight; bounded by straight lines. — *n* **rectilinearity** (*-ar'i-ti*). — *adv* **rectilin'early**. — *n* **rectipetality** (*rek-ti-pi-tal'i-ti*) or **rectipetaly** (*-pet'əl-i*; L *petere* to seek; *bot*) tendency to grow in a straight line. — *adj* **rectirostral** (*rek-ti-ros'trəl*; L *rōstrum* a beak) straight-billed. — *adj* **rectiserial** (*rek-ti-sēr'i-əl*; L *seriēs* a row) in straight rows. [L *rēctus* straight, right]

recti. See **rectus**.

rectify *rek'ti-fī*, *vt* to set right; to correct; to redress; to adjust; to purify by distillation (*chem*); to determine the length of (an arc); to change (an alternating current) to a direct current: — *pr p* **rec'tifying**; *pa t* and *pap* **rec'tified**. — *adj* **rec'tifiable**. — *n* **rectificā'tion**. — *n* **rec'tifier** a person who rectifies (*esp* alcohol); apparatus for rectifying (*esp* spirit, an alternating current, or electromagnetic waves). [Fr *rectifier*, from LL *rēctificāre*, from *facere* to make]

rectilineal, etc. See under **recti-**.

rection *rek'shən*, (*gram*) *n* syntactical government. [L *rēctiō*, *-ōnis* government]

rectipetality . . . to . . . **rectiserial**. See under **recti-**.

rectitis and **rectitic**. See under **rectum**.

rectitude *rek'ti-tūd*, *n* straightness (*obs*); rightness; uprightness; integrity. — *adj* **rectitū'dinous** manifesting moral correctness; over-obviously righteous. [Fr, from LL *rēctitūdō*, from L *rēctus* straight]

recto *rek'tō*, (*printing*) *n* the right-hand page of an open book, the front page of a leaf (opposed to *verso*): — *pl* **rec'tōs**. [L *rēctō* (*foliō*) on the right (leaf)]

recto- *rek'tō-*, *combining form* signifying of or relating to the rectum.

rector *rek'tər*, *n* a ruler, governor or controller (*obs*); in the Church of England, a clergyman of a parish where the tithes are not impropriate; an Episcopal clergyman with charge of a congregation in the United States or (since 1890) Scotland; the headmaster of certain schools in Scotland, *esp* those called academies; the chief elective officer of many Scottish (*Lord Rector*) and foreign universities; a college head (as at Lincoln and Exeter Colleges, Oxford; Science and Technology, London); an ecclesiastic in charge of a congregation, an important mission, a college or a religious house, *esp* the head of a Jesuit seminary (*RC*). — *adj* **rec'toral** of God as a ruler. — *n* **rec'torate** a rector's office or term of office. — *n* **rec'toress** or **rec'tress** a female rector; a rector's wife (*colloq*). — *adj* **rectorial** (*-tō'ri-əl*) of a rector. — *n* an election of a Lord Rector. — *n* **rec'torship**. — *n* **rec'tory** the province or residence of a rector. — **Rector Magnificus** the head of a German university. — **lay rector** a layman who enjoys the great tithes of a parish. [L *rēctor*, *-ōris*, from *regere*, *rēctum* to rule]

rectrix *rek'triks*, *n* a female governor (*rare*); a bird's long tail-feather, used in steering: — *pl* **rectrices** (*rek'tri-sēz* or *rek-trī'sēz*). — *adj* **rectricial** (*-trish'l*). [L *rēctrīx*, *-īcis*, fem of *rēctor*]

rectum *rek'təm*, *n* the terminal part of the large intestine: — *pl* **rec'ta** or **rec'tums**. — *adj* **rec'tal**. — *adv* **rec'tally**. — *n* **rectitis** (*rek-tī'tis*) inflammation of the rectum. — *adj* **rectitic** (*-tit'ik*). [L neuter of *rēctus* straight]

rectus *rek'təs*, (*anatom*) *n* a straight muscle: — *pl* **rec'tī**. [L]

recuile or **recule** *ri-kūl'* (*Spenser*). Same as **recoil**.

recumbent *ri-kum'bənt*, *adj* reclining; (of an organ, etc) resting against the anatomical structure from which it extends. — *n* **recum'bence** or **recum'bency**. — *adv* **recum'bently**. — **recumbent fold** (*geol*) an overturned fold with a more or less horizontal axial plane. [L *recumbere*, from *cubāre* to lie down]

recuperate *ri-koo'pər-āt* or *ri-kū'-*, *vt* and *vi* to recover from an illness, etc; to recover (a loss). — *adj* **recu'perable** recoverable. — *n* **recuperā'tion**. — *adj* **recu'perative** (*-ə-tiv*). — *n* **recu'perātor** an arrangement by which something lost is regained, such as the heat of

Some words with the prefix **re-**.

rēcol'onize or **-ise** *vt.*	**rēcommit'** *vt.*	**rēcompose'** *vt* and *vi.*
rēcommence' *vt* and *vi.*	**rēcommit'ment** *n.*	**rēcomposi'tion** *n.*
rēcommence'ment *n.*	**rēcommitt'al** *n.*	**rēcompress'** *vt.*
rēcommiss'ion *n*, *vt* and *vi.*	**rēcompact'** *vt.*	**rēcompress'ion** *n.*

waste gases in a furnace. — *adj* **recu'peratory**. [L *recuperāre* to recover]

recur *ri-kûr'*, *vi* to revert (*archaic*); to have recourse (*archaic*); to come up or come round again, or at intervals; to come back into one's mind: — *pr p* **recurr'ing** (or *-kur'*); *pa t* and *pap* **recurred'** (*-kûrd*). — *n* **recurr'ence** or **recurr'ency** (*-kur'*). — *adj* **recurr'ent** (*-kur'*) returning at intervals; running back in the opposite direction or toward the place of origin (*anatom*). — *adv* **recurr'ently**. — *n* **recur'sion** (*-kûr'*; *rare*) a going back, return. — *adj* (*math*; of a formula) enabling a term in a sequence to be computed from one or more of the preceding terms. — *adj* **recur'sive** (*math*; of a definition) consisting of rules which allow values or meaning to be determined with certainty. — **recurring decimal** a decimal fraction in which after a certain point one figure (*repeating decimal*) or a group of figures (*circulating*) is repeated to infinity. [L *recurrere*, from *currere* to run]

recure *ri-kūr'*, *vt* to cure, remedy, heal, bring back to a better state (*Spenser*, *Shakesp* and *Milton*); to recover, get back (*Spenser*). — *vi* (*obs*) to recover, get well. — *n* (*obs*) cure; recovery. — *adj* **recure'less** (*obs*) incurable. [Partly L *recūrāre* to cure, partly for **recoure** (qv)]

recurve *ri-kûrv'*, *vt* and *vi* to bend back. — *adj* **recurved'**. — *adj* **recurviros'tral** with up-bent bill. [L *recurvāre*; *rōstrum* beak]

recuse *ri-kūz'*, *vt* to reject, object to (eg a judge) (*archaic*). — *n* **recusance** (*rek'ū-zəns* or *ri-kū'zəns*; *rare*), **recusancy** (*-i*) or **recusant** (*rek'* or *ri-kū'*) a person (*esp* a Roman Catholic) who refused to attend the Church of England when it was legally compulsory (*hist*); a dissenter; a person who refuses, *esp* to submit to authority. — Also *adj*. — *n* **recusā'tion** (*law*) an objection or appeal. [L *recūsāre*, from *causa* a cause]

recycle *rē-sī'kl*, *vt* to pass again through a series of changes or treatment; to remake into something different; to cause (material) to be broken down by bacteria and then reconstitute it; to direct into a different channel. — *adj* **recy'clable**. — *n* **recy'clist**. [re-]

red[1] *red*, *adj* (*compar* **redd'er**; *superl* **redd'est**) of a colour like blood; extended traditionally to mean golden, and by custom to other colours more or less near red; having a red face (from shame, heat, embarrassment, etc; see also **red face** below); revolutionary, or supposedly revolutionary. — *n* the colour of blood; an object of this colour in a set of similar objects; a red pigment; red clothes; the red traffic-light, meaning 'stop'; a revolutionary or person who favours sweeping changes, variously applied to radical, republican, anarchist, socialist, communist, etc; a former squadron of the British fleet; a red cent. — *vt* **redd'en** to make red. — *vi* to grow red; to blush. — *adj* **redd'ish**. — *n* **redd'ishness**. — *adj* **redd'y**. — *adv* **red'ly**. — *n* **red'ness**. — **red admiral** a common butterfly (*Vanessa atalanta*) with reddish-banded wings; **red alert** a state of readiness for imminent crisis, eg war or natural disaster; **red algae** one of the great divisions of seaweeds, the *Rhodophyceae* or *Florideae*, containing a red pigment; **red ant** any of several reddish-coloured ants, *esp* the Pharaoh ant; **red'back** (*Austr*) a poisonous spider (*Latrodectus hasselti*) having a red strip on its back; **red'belly** the char, or other red-bellied fish; the slider, a terrapin; **red biddy** (*colloq*) a drink made of red wine and methylated spirit. — *adj* **red'-blood'ed** having red blood; abounding in vitality, and usually in crudity. — **red'-book** a book bound in red, *esp* a court-guide, peerage, directory of persons in the service of the state, official regulations, etc; **red'-box** a government minister's red-covered box for official papers; **red'breast** the robin; **red brick** a brick, made from clay containing iron compounds which are converted into ferric oxide. — *adj* **red'brick** (**redbrick university** a general name given to a later English type of university, *usu* one founded in the 19c or first half of the 20c, contrasted with Oxford and Cambridge). — **Red Brigade** any of a group of left-wing terrorist groups in Italy; **red'bud** the American Judas tree (*Cercis canadensis*), producing heart-shaped leaves and pink budlike flowers; **red cabbage** a purplish cabbage used for pickling; **red'cap** a goldfinch; a Scottish castle goblin (also **red'-cowl**); military policeman (*slang*); railway porter (*NAm*); **red card** (*football*) a red-coloured card that a referee holds up to show that he or she is sending a player off; **red carpet** a strip of carpet put out for the highly favoured to walk on; treatment as a very important person (*fig*). — *adj* **red'-car'pet** (*usu fig*). — **red cedar** a name for various species of *Cedrela* and of juniper; **red cent** a cent (formerly made of copper) considered as a very small amount (*colloq*; *esp US*); a whit; **red clay** a clayey deposit of oceanic abysses, stained reddish or brown by manganese and iron oxides; cave-earth; **red'coat** a British soldier (*hist*); an entertainment organizer at a Butlins holiday camp, wearing a red blazer as uniform; **red cock** (*fig*) an incendiary fire; **red corpuscle** an erythrocyte, a blood cell which carries oxygen in combination with the pigment haemoglobin, and removes carbon dioxide; **Red Crag** a middle division of the English Pliocene; **Red Crescent** the Red Cross Society in Islamic countries; **Red Cross** a red cross on a white ground, the national flag of England (in Spenser's **Redcross Knight**, representing holiness and the Church of England); the Swiss flag with colours reversed, the copyrighted symbol of an organization (known as **the Red Cross**) for tending sick, wounded in war, etc, enjoying privileges under the Convention of Geneva (1864); **redcurr'ant** the small red berry of a shrub of the Gooseberry genus. — *adj* **red'currant**. — **red deer** the common stag or hind, reddish-brown in summer; **Red Delicious** a red-skinned variety of eating apple; **Red Devils** (*colloq*) the Special Air Service; **red'-dog** the lowest grade of flour in high milling; **red dwarf** a red star of low luminosity; **Red Ensign** (*slang* **Red Duster**) a red flag with the Union Jack in the top left corner, till 1864 the flag of Red Squadron, now flown by British merchant ships; **red'-eye** the rudd; poor quality whisky (*US*); an overnight aeroplane journey (*NAm slang*; also *adj*); **red face** a blushing from embarrassment or disconcertion (*adj* **red'-faced**). — *adj* **red'-figure** or **red'-figured** designating a style of ancient Greek pottery in which the background is painted with a fine clay solution which turns and remains black after firing in a reducing atmosphere (cf **black-figure** under **black**). — **red'fish** a male salmon when, or just after, spawning; any of various red-fleshed fish, of the genus *Sebastes*; **red flag** a flag used as a signal of danger, defiance, no mercy, or an auction sale; the banner of socialism or of revolution; (with *cap*) a socialist's song; **red giant** a red star of high luminosity; **Red Guard** a member of a strict Maoist youth movement in China, *esp* active in the cultural revolution of the late 1960s; **red'-gum** an eruption of the skin in teething infants; a Eucalyptus (of various kinds) with red gum. — *adj* **red'-haired**. — **red hand** the bloody hand (see under **hand**). — *adj* and *adv* **redhand'ed** in the very act, or immediately after, as if with bloody hands. — **red'-hat** a cardinal; a cardinal's hat (award of this to cardinals

Some words with the prefix **re-**.

rēcondensā'tion *n*.	**rēcon'quer** *vt*.	**rēconsiderā'tion** *n*.
rēcondense' *vt* and *vi*.	**rēcon'quest** *n*.	**rēconsol'idate** *vt* and *vi*.
rēconfirm' *vt*.	**rēcon'secrate** *vt*.	**rēconsolidā'tion** *n*.
rēconnect' *vt*.	**rēconsecrā'tion** *n*.	**rēcontin'ue** *vt* and *vi*.

was discontinued 1969); a staff officer (*military slang*); **red'head** a person with red hair; any of several birds with reddish head, *esp* the pochard. — *adj* **red'-headed** having a red head or red hair; angrily excited (*slang*). — **red heat** the temperature at which a thing is red-hot. — *adj* **red'-heeled**. — **red herring** a herring cured and dried, of reddish appearance; a subject introduced to divert discussion or attention as a herring drawn across a track would throw hounds out. — *adj* **red'-hot** heated to redness; extreme; marked by extreme emotion of any kind; (of information) very recently received (*colloq*); (of a telephone line) very busy with calls (*colloq*); **red-hot poker** the plant Kniphofia or Tritoma. — **Red Indian** (*colloq*; *offensive*) an American Indian, *esp* of N America; **Red Lane** see under **lane**[1]. — *adj* **red'-latt'ice** (*Shakesp*) savouring of the alehouse (whose lattice was conventionally painted red). — **red lead** an oxide of lead (Pb_3O_4) of a fine red colour, used in paint-making (also called **minium**); **red'leg** (*Caribb*) a *derog* term for a poor white person, *esp* a descendant of original white settlers. — *adj* **red'-legged**. — *adj* **red'-letter** marked with red letters, as holidays or saints' days in the old calendars; deserving to be so marked, special. — **red light** a rear-light; a danger-signal; the red traffic-light, meaning 'stop'; a brothel (*colloq*). — *adj* **red'-light'** (*colloq*) of or relating to brothels, as in *red-light district*; *vt* **red'-line** to mark or cancel (a date, name, etc) by circling or scoring through with a red line; to subject to red-lining (see below). — *n* **red'-lining** (*colloq*; *orig US*) the practice of refusing credit to all those living in an area with a poor record of debt repayment. — *adj* **red'-looked** (*Shakesp*) having a red look; **red'-mad'** (*Scot*) stark mad. — **red'-man** or **red man** an American Indian (*archaic*); *prob* red mercuric sulphide (*alchemy*); **red meat** dark-coloured meat, eg beef and lamb; **red mud** a type of industrial waste resulting from alumina processing, consisting of silicone oxide, iron oxide, etc; **red mullet** see under **mullet**[1]; **red'-neck** (*US*) a *derog* term for a poor white farm labourer in the south-western states. — *adj* ignorant, intolerant, narrow-minded; pertaining to, or characteristic of, this class of labourers. — **red pepper** see under **pepper**; **red'-plague** or **-murrain** (*Shakesp*) bubonic plague; **red'poll** a name for two birds (*lesser* and *mealy redpoll*) related to the linnet; an animal of a red breed of polled cattle. — *adj* **red'-polled** having a red poll; red and polled. — **red rag** the tongue (*slang*); a cause of infuriation (as red is said to be to a bull); **red rattle** louse'-wort; **red ribbon** or **riband** the ribbon of the Order of the Bath; **red'root** a genus (*Ceanothus*) of the buckthorn family, *New Jersey tea*; **red rot** a disease of oaks, etc caused by *Polyporus*, the wood becoming brown and dry; **red salmon** any of various types of salmon with red flesh, *esp* **red sanders** a papilionaceous tree (*Pterocarpus santalinus*) of tropical Asia, with heavy dark-red heartwood, used as a dye, etc (see also **sandalwood**); **redsear**, **redshare** and **redshire** see **redshort**; **red seaweed** any of the red algae, *esp* one of the genus *Polysiphonia*; **red seed** the food of mackerel, small floating crustaceans, etc; **red'shank** a sandpiper with red legs; a Highlander or an Irishman (*colloq*; *derog*); (**red shank**) a polygonaceous annual plant with a red stem; **red shift** a shift of lines in the spectrum towards the red, considered to occur because the source of light is receding (see **Doppler's principle**, etc). — *adj* **red'-shifted**. — **Red Shirt** (*hist*) a follower of Garibaldi (1807–82), from his garb; a revolutionary or anarchist; **red'skin** (*derog slang*; *offensive*) a N American Indian; **red snapper** fish of the *Lutianidae* with reddish colouring, common off the east coast of America; **red snow** snow coloured by a microscopic red alga; **red spider** or **red spider mite** a spinning mite that infests leaves; **red squirrel** a squirrel of reddish-brown colour (*Sciurus vulgaris*) native to Europe and Asia, in Britain now rarely found outside the Scottish highlands; a small squirrel (*Sciurus hudsonicus*) of N America; **red'start** (OE *steort* tail) a European bird (*Ruticilla* or *Phoenicurus*) with a conspicuous chestnut-coloured tail; an American warbler, superficially similar; **red'streak** an apple with streaked skin; **red tape** the tape used in government offices to bind offical documents, etc; rigid formality of intricate official routine; bureaucracy. — *adj* **red'-tape**. — **red-tap'ism**; **red-tap'ist**; **red tide** a bloom of red dinoflagellates which colours the sea, etc red; **red'top** (*US*) a kind of bent grass (*Agrostis stolonifera*); **red'water** a cattle disease (also called **babesiasis** or **babesiosis** qqv) due to a protozoan parasite in the blood, that is transmitted by ticks and destroys the red blood cells, causing red-coloured urine to be passed; **red wine** wine coloured by (red) grape skins during fermentation (cf **rosé**); **red'wing** a thrush with reddish sides below the wings; **red'wood** a species of Sequoia with reddish wood much used commercially; any wood or tree yielding a red dye. — *adj* **red-wood'** or (*Scot*) **red-wud'** stark mad. — **in the red** overdrawn at the bank, in debt; **red out** to experience a red hazy field of vision, etc as a result of aerobatics; **Royal Red Cross** a decoration for nurses, instituted 1883; **see red** to grow furious; to thirst for blood; **see reds under the bed** (*colloq*) to be convinced that every misfortune, setback, etc is the result of communist infiltration; **the Red Planet** Mars. [OE *rēad*; cf Ger *rot*, L *ruber*, *rūfus*, Gr *erythros*, Gaelic *ruadh*]

red[2]. See **redd**[1,2].

redact *ri-dakt'*, *vt* to edit, work into shape; to frame. — *n* **redac'tion**. — *n* **redac'tor**. — *adj* **redactō'rial** (*re-* or *rē-*). [L *redigere*, *redactum*, to bring back, from pfx *red-*, and *agere* to drive]

redan *ri-dan'*, (*fortif*) *n* a fieldwork of two faces forming a salient. [OFr *redan*, from L *re-*, and *dēns*, *dentis* a tooth]

redargue *ri-där'gū*, (*obs* or *Scot*) *vt* to refute; to confute. [L *redarguere*, from *re*(*d*)- again, and *arguere* argue]

redd[1] or **red** *red*, (chiefly *Scot*) *vt* to put in order, make tidy; to clear up; to disentangle; to comb; to separate in fighting. — *vi* to set things in order, tidy up (*usu* with *up*): — *pr p* **redd'ing**; *pa t* and *pa p* **redd** or **red**. — *n* an act of redding; refuse, rubbish. — *adj* (*Scots law*) vacated. — *n* **redd'er**. — *n* **redd'ing**. — **redd'ing-up'** setting in order, tidying up; **redd'ing-comb** or **-kame** a hair-comb; **redd'ing-straik** a stroke received in trying to separate fighters. [Partly OE *hreddan* to free, rescue (cf Ger *retten* to rescue); prob partly from or influenced by OE *rǣdan* (see **rede, read**[1]); cf also **rid**[1]]

redd[2] or **red** *red*, *pa t* and *pa p* of **read**[1] (*Spenser*); same as **rede** (*pres* tense; *Scot*).

redd[3] *red*, (*Scot*) *n* fish or frog spawn; a spawning-place. [Origin obscure]

redden, etc. See under **red**[1].

reddendum *ri-den'dəm*, (*law*) *n* a reserving clause in a lease: — *pl* **redden'da**. — *n* **redden'do** (*Scots law*) service to be rendered or money to be paid by a vassal, or the clause in a charter specifying it: — *pl* **redden'dos**. [L, to be rendered, gerundive of *reddere*]

reddle and **reddleman**. See under **ruddle**.

rede *rēd*, *vt* an old spelling of **read**[1] retained as an archaism in the senses of 'to counsel or advise, expound, relate'. — *n* (*archaic*) advice; resolution;

Some words with the prefix **re-**.

rēconvene' *vt* and *vi*.	**rēdec'orate** *vt*.	**rēdefini'tion** *n*.
rēcross', *vt* and *vi*.	**rēdecorā'tion** *n*.	**rēdescend'** *vt* and *vi*.
rēdate' *vt*.	**rēded'icate** *vt*.	**rēdescribe'** *vt*.
redeal' *vt*, *vi* and *n*.	**redefine'** *vt*.	**rēdesign'** *vt*.

saying, tale; interpretation (*Browning*). — **rede'craft** (*archaic*) logic. — *adj* **rede'less** (*archaic*) without counsel or wisdom.

redeem *ri-dēm'*, *vt* to buy back; to act so as to settle or discharge (a burden, obligation, etc); to recover or free by payment; to free oneself from (a promise) by fulfilment; to ransom; to rescue, deliver, free; (of God or Christ) to deliver from sin; to get back; to reclaim; to exchange (tokens, vouchers, etc) for goods, or (bonds, shares, etc) for cash; to pay the penalty of; to atone for; to compensate for; to put (time) to the best advantage. — *n* **redeemabil'ity**. — *adj* **redeem'able**. — *n* **redeem'ableness**. — *adv* **redeem'ably**. — *n* **redeem'er**. — *adj* **redeem'ing**. — *adj* **redeem'less** not to be redeemed. — **the Redeemer** the Saviour, Jesus Christ. [L *redimere* (perh through Fr *rédimer*), from *red-* back, and *emere* to buy]

redeliver *rē-di-liv'ər*, *vt* to restore; to free again; to report the words of (*Shakesp*). — *n* **redeliv'erance**. — *n* **redeliv'erer**. — *n* **redeliv'ery**. [**re-**]

redemption *ri-dem'shən* or *-demp'shən*, *n* the act of redeeming; atonement. — *adj* **redemp'tible** (*rare*) redeemable. — *n* **redemp'tioner** an emigrant to N America bound to service until his or her fare was made up. — *n* **Redemp'tionist** a Trinitarian friar. — *adj* **redemp'tive**. — *n* **Redemp'torist** a missionary priest of a congregation founded by Alfonso Liguori in 1732 for work among the poor. — *adj* **redemp'tory**. — **redemption yield** (*finance*) the total return from a stock, including annual interest and any capital gain, calculated as a percentage of the price to be repaid at a fixed future date. [L *redimere*, *redemptum*; cf **redeem**]

redeploy *rē-di-ploi'*, *vt* to transfer (eg military forces, supplies, industrial workers) from one area to another. — Also *vi*. — *n* **redeploy'ment**. [**re-**]

redia *rē'di-ə*, *n* a form in the life-cycle of the trematodes: — *pl* **rē'diae** (*-ē*). [Named after Francesco *Redi* (died prob 1698), Italian naturalist]

Rediffusion® *rē-di-fū'zhən*, *n* a system by which television or radio programmes are transmitted by electricity along a wire rather than by direct broadcast.

redingote *red'ing-gōt*, *n* a long double-breasted (*orig* man's, later woman's) overcoat. [Fr, from Eng **riding=coat**]

redintegrate *red-in'ti-grāt*, *vt* to restore to wholeness; to re-establish. — *adj* restored; renewed. — *n* **redintegrā'tion** restoring to wholeness; the recurrence of a complete mental state when any single element of it recurs, eg when a piece of music reminds one of an occasion on which it was played (*psychol*). [L *redintegrāre*, *-ātum*, from *red-* again, and *integrāre* to make whole, from *integer*]

redisburse *rē-dis-bûrs'*, (*Spenser*) *vt* to refund. [**re-**]

redivivus *red-i-vī'vəs* or *re-di-wē'wŏŏs*, (*formal* or *literary*) *adj* resuscitated; come to life again. [L, from *red-* again, and *vivus* alive, from *vivere* to be alive]

redolent *red'ə-lənt*, *adj* fragrant; smelling (of, or with); suggestive (of), imbued (with). — *n* **red'olence** or **red'olency**. — *adv* **red'olently**. [L *redolēns*, *-entis*, from *red-* again, and *olēre* to emit smell]

redouble *ri-dub'l*, *vt* and *vi* to double; to repeat; to re-echo; to increase; (*rē'dub'l*) to double after previous doubling (*bridge*). — *n* (*rē'dub'l*) an act or fact or redoubling, as in bridge. — *n* **redoub'lement** (*ri-*). [**re-**]

redoubt[1] *ri-dowt'*, (*fortif*) *n* a fieldwork enclosed on all sides; an inner last retreat. [Fr *redoute*, from Ital *ridotto*, from LL *reductus* refuge, from L, retired, from *redūcere*; the *b* from confusion with **redoubt**[2]]

redoubt[2] *ri-dowt'*, *vt* to fear (*archaic*). — *adj* **redoubt'able** formidable; valiant. — *adj* **redoubt'ed** redoubtable (*archaic*). [OFr *redouter* to fear greatly, from L *re-* back, and *dubitāre* to doubt]

redound *ri-downd'*, *vi* to overflow (*Spenser*); to be in excess (*Milton*); to surge (*Spenser*); to be filled (*Spenser*); to flow back; to return; to rebound, be reflected or echoed; to turn, recoil, be reflected, as a consequence (to one's credit, discredit, advantage, etc); to conduce; to rise one above another in receding series (*Spenser*). — *vt* (*fig*) to cast, reflect. — *n* the coming back, as an effect or consequence, return. — *n* and *adj* **redound'ing**. [Fr *rédonder*, from L *redundāre*, from *red-* back, and *undāre* to surge, from *unda* a wave]

redowa *red'ō-va*, *n* a Bohemian dance; music for it, *usu* in quick triple time. [Ger or Fr, from Czech *rejdovák*]

redox *rē'doks*, *adj* of a type of chemical reaction in which one of the reagents is reduced, while another is oxidized. [*red*uction and *ox*idation]

redraft *rē-dräft'*, *n* a revised draft or copy; a new bill of exchange which the holder of a protested bill draws on the drawer or endorsers, for the amount of the bill, with costs and charges. — *vt* to make a revised draft of. [**re-**]

redress *ri-dres'*, *vt* to set right; to readjust; to restore (*Spenser*); to remedy; to compensate. — *n* relief; reparation. — *n* **redress'er** (*ri-*) a person who redresses abuses or injuries. — *adj* **redress'ive** (*Thomson*) affording redress. [Fr *redresser* (see **dress**); partly from **re-** and **dress**]

re-dress *rē'dres'*, *vt* and *vi* to dress again; to dress in different clothes. [**re-**]

redruthite *red'rŏŏth-īt*, *n* copper-glance, a mineral found at *Redruth* in Cornwall.

redshort *red'shört*, *adj* brittle at red-heat. — Also **red'sear**, **red'-share** or **red'-shire**. [Swed *rödskör*, from *röd* red, and *skör* brittle]

reduce *ri-dūs'*, *vt* to bring back (*archaic*); to restore to an old state (*archaic*); to bring into a new state (*archaic*); to put back into a normal condition or place (eg a dislocation or fracture) (*surg*); to change to another form; to express in other terms; to range in order or classification; to adapt, adjust; to translate; to put into (writing, practice, etc; with *to*); to bring into a lower state; to lessen; to diminish in weight or girth; to concentrate or thicken (a sauce) by boiling to evaporate water and reduce the volume; to weaken; to degrade (*military*); to impoverish; to subdue; to subject to necessity; to drive into (a condition; with *to*); to break up, separate, disintegrate; to disband (*military*; *obs*); to bring to the metallic state; to remove oxygen from, or combine with hydrogen, or lessen the positive valency of (an atom or ion) by adding electrons; to annul (*Scots law*). — *vi* to resolve itself; to slim, or lessen weight or girth. — *p adj* **reduced'** in a state of reduction; weakened; impoverished; diminished; simplified in structure. — *n* **reduc'er** a person who reduces; a means of reducing; a joint-piece for connecting pipes of varying diameter. — *n* **reducibil'ity**. — *adj* **reduc'ible** that may be reduced. — *n* **reduc'ibleness**. — *adj* **reduc'ing**. — *n* **reduc'tant** a reducing agent. — *n* **reduc'tase** an enzyme which brings about the reduction of organic compounds. — *n* **reduction** (*-duk'shən*) the act of reducing or state of being reduced; diminution; lowering of price; subjugation; changing of numbers or quantities from one denomination to another (*arith*); a settlement of S American Indians converted by the Jesuits to Christianity, and governed by them (*hist*). — *n* **reduc'tionism** the belief that complex data

Some words with the prefix **re-**.

rēdeterminā'tion *n*.	**rēdi'al** *vt* and *vi*.	**rēdirec'tion** *n*.
rēdeter'mine *vt*.	**rē'did'**. See **redo**.	**rediscount'** *vt*.
rēdevel'op *vt*.	**rēdip'** *vt*.	**redis'count** *n*.
rēdevel'opment *n*.	**rēdirect'** *vt*.	**rēdiscov'er** *vt*.

and phenomena can be explained in terms of something simpler. — *n* and *adj* **reduc'tionist**. — *adj* **reduc'tive** bringing back (*archaic*); reducing, narrowing, limiting. — *adv* **reduc'tively**. — *n* **reduc'tiveness**. — **reducing agent** (*chem*) a substance with a strong affinity for oxygen, or the like, serving to remove it from others; **reducing flame** a hot luminous blowpipe flame in which substances can be reduced; **reduction division** (*biol*) meiosis; **reduction works** smelting works. — **in reduced circumstances** (*euphem*) impoverished; **reduce to the ranks** to demote, for misconduct, to the condition of a private soldier. [L *redūcere*, *reductum*, from *re-* back, and *dūcere* to lead]

reductio ad absurdum *ri-duk'shi-ō ad ab-sûr'dəm* or *re-do͝ok'ti-ō ad ab-so͞or'do͝om*, reduction to absurdity; the proof of a proposition by proving the falsity of its contradictory; the application of a principle so strictly that it is carried to absurd lengths. [L]

reduit *rā-dwē*, *n* an inner fortified retreat for a garrison. [Fr *réduit*]

redundant *ri-dun'dənt*, *adj* surging (*Milton*); overflowing (*obs*); copious; over-copious; superfluous; (of a word or phrase) excessive, able to be removed from the sentence, etc without affecting meaning; (of workers) no longer needed and therefore dismissed. — *n* **redun'dance**. — *n* **redun'dancy** the state of being redundant; a dismissal, or a person dismissed, from a job because of redundancy; the presence of components which improve the reliability of a system (*comput*). — *adv* **redun'dantly**. — **redundancy payment** a minimum statutory payment to be made to an employee who is made redundant, its amount based on age, pay, and length of service. [L *redundāns*, *-antis*, pr p of *redundāre* to overflow]

reduplicate *ri-dū'pli-kāt*, *vt* to double; to repeat. — *vi* to double; to exhibit reduplication (*gram*). — *adj* doubled; showing reduplication (*gram*); in aestivation, valvate with edges turned outwards (*bot*). — *n* **reduplicā'tion** a folding or doubling; the doubling of the initial part, in inflection and word-formation, as in L *fefellī*, *perf* of *fallō*, Gr *tetypha*, *perf* of *typtō* (*gram*); the reduplicated element in a word; the combination of two rhyming, alliterative, etc words (the second sometimes a coinage for the purpose) to form one, as in *hurry-skurry*, *popsy-wopsy* or *mishmash*. — *adj* **redū'plicātive**. [L *reduplicāre*, *-ātum*, from *duplicāre* to double]

reduviid *rə-dū'vi-id*, *adj* belonging to the *Reduviidae* family of predaceous bugs. — *n* an insect of this family. [New L *Reduvi*us, and **-id**]

ree[1] *rē*. See **ruff**[2].

ree[2] *rē* or **reed** *rēd*, (*Scot*) *n* an enclosure, *esp* a (partially-) roofed walled yard, eg for coal, for wintering cattle, for confining sheep, etc. [Poss cognate with Du *rede* roadstead]

reebok *rā'bok*. *n* a South African antelope. [Du]

reech *rēch*. Same as **reek**. — *adj* **reech'y** (*Shakesp* **rechie** or **reechie**) smoky, grimy.

re-echo *rē-ek'ō*, *vt* to echo back; to repeat as if an echo. — *vi* to give back echoes; to resound. — *n* a re-echoing. [**re-**]

reed[1], **reede** (*Spenser*). Same as **rede**.

reed[2] *rēd*, *n* a tall stiff hard-culmed marsh or water grass of various kinds, *esp Phragmites communis*; a thing made, or formerly made, of a reed or reeds, eg a pen, an arrow, a measuring rod, a music pipe, the vibrating tongue of an organ-pipe or woodwind instrument (with or without the parts to which it is attached), a weaver's appliance for separating the warp threads and beating up the weft; thatching; a small reedlike moulding; a reed instrument; the metal reed of an organ pipe used as the plate of a capacitor for electronic amplification. — *adj* reedlike (*Shakesp*); having a vibrating reed (*music*); milled, ribbed. — *vt* to thatch. — *adj* **reed'ed** covered with reeds; having reed(s). — *adj* **reed'en** of reed. — *n* **reed'er** a thatcher. — *n* **reed'iness**. — *n* **reed'ing** the milling on the edge of a coin; a reed moulding. — *n* **reed'ling** the bearded titmouse. — *adj* **reed'y** abounding with reeds; resembling a reed; sounding as a reed instrument. — **reed'-band** a band of reed instruments; **reed'bed**; **reed'-bird** the bobolink; **reed bunting** a European bunting which breeds in marshy places and reedbeds; **reed'-drawing** the combing out of rough straw by means of a frame; **reed'-grass** a reedlike grass of various kinds (eg *Phalaris* or *Arundo*); **reed instrument** a woodwind with reed, such as a clarinet, oboe or bassoon; **reed'-knife** a tool for organ-tuning; **reed'mace** cat's-tail (*Typha*); **reed'-organ** a keyboard instrument with free reeds, such as the harmonium, or the American organ; **reed'-pheasant** the bearded titmouse; **reed'-pipe** an organ-pipe whose tone is produced by the vibration of a reed, the pipe acting as resonator; **reed'-rand** or **-rond** (*E Anglia*) a reed thicket; **reed'-sparrow** the reed-bunting; the sedge-warbler; **reed'stop** a set of reed-pipes controlled by a single organ-stop; **reed warbler** a warbler that frequents marshy places and builds its nest on reeds (also called **reed'-wren**, the **reed'-thrush** being a larger species (*greater reed-warbler*)). — **broken reed** (*fig*) a person who is too weak or unreliable to be depended upon; **free reed** a reed vibrating in an opening without touching the sides. [OE *hrēod*; cf Du *riet* and Ger *Riet*]

reed[3]. See **ree**[2].

re-edify *rē-ed'i-fī*, *vt* to rebuild. — (*Spenser*) **reæd'ifye**. — *n* **re-edificā'tion**. — *n* **re-ed'ifier**. [L *aedificāre* to build]

re-educate *rē-ed'ū-kāt*, *vt* to educate again; to change a person's (*esp* political) beliefs. — *n* **re-educa'tion**. — **re-education camp** a detention camp in some totalitarian states where dissidents and others are sent to be re-educated. [**re-**]

reedy. See under **reed**[2].

reef[1] *rēf*, *n* a chain of rocks at or near the surface of water; a shoal or bank; a gold-bearing lode or vein (*orig Austr*); the encasing rock of a diamond-mine, all ground in the mine other than diamondiferous (*SAfr*). — **reef'-builder** a coral-animal that forms reefs. [Du *rif*, from ON *rif*]

reef[2] *rēf*, *n* a portion of a sail that may be rolled or folded up. — *vt* to reduce the exposed surface of (a sail, etc); to gather up in a similar way. — *n* **reef'er** a person who reefs; a midshipman (*slang*); a reefing-jacket (also **reef'er-jacket**); a cigarette containing marijuana (*slang*). — *n* **reef'ing**. — **reef band** a strengthening strip across a sail; **reef'ing-jacket** a short thick double-breasted jacket; **reef'-knot** a flat knot used in tying reef points consisting of two loops passing symmetrically through each other; **reef point** a short rope on a reef band to secure a reefed sail. [ON *rif*]

reefer[1] *rē'fər*, (*slang*), *n* a refrigerated railway car; a refrigerated ship. [**refrigerator**]

reefer[2]. See under **reef**[2].

reek *rēk*, *n* smoke; vapour; fume; a smell, *esp* an offensive one. — *vi* to emit smoke, fumes, or (*esp* offensive) smell; to exhale. — *vt* to expose to smoke; to exhale. — *adj* **reek'ing**. — *adj* **reek'y** (or *Scot* **reek'ie**) smoky; smoked; reeking; foul (*Shakesp*). — **Auld Reekie** Edinburgh. [OE *rēc*; ON *reykr*, Ger *Rauch*, Du *rook* smoke; a Northern form; cf **reech**]

Some words with the prefix **re-**.

rēdiscov'erer *n*.	**rēdistil'** *vt*.	**rēdistrib'utive** *adj*.
rēdiscov'ery *n*.	**rēdistillā'tion** *n*.	**rēdivide'** *vt* and *vi*.
rēdissolu'tion *n*.	**rēdistrib'ute** *vt*.	**rēdivis'ion** *n*.
rēdissolve' *vt*.	**rēdistribu'tion** *n*.	**rēdo'** *vt*: — *pa t* **rēdid'**; *pa p* **rēdone'**.

reel *rēl*, *n* a cylinder, drum, spool, bobbin or frame on which thread, fishing-line, wire, cables, photographic film, etc may be wound; a length of material so wound; a loud rattling, a din (*Scot*); a whirl, a stagger; a lively dance, *esp* Highland or Irish; a tune for it, *usu* in 4–4, sometimes in 6–8 time; (in *pl*) revelry (*Shakesp*). — *vt* to wind on a reel; to take off by or from a reel; to draw (in) by means of a reel; to cause to whirl or roll (*Spenser*); to stagger along (*Shakesp*). — *vi* to whirl; to seem to swirl or sway; to totter; to stagger; (of eg line of battle) to waver; to rattle (*Scot*); to dance a reel. — *n* **reel'er** a person who reels; the grasshopper-warbler. — *n* and *adj* **reel'ing**. — *adv* **reel'ingly**. — **reel'man** (*Austr*) the member of a surf life-saving team who operates the reel on which the line is wound. — **off** or **right off the reel** in uninterrupted course or succession; without stop or hesitation; **reel off** to utter rapidly and fluently. — *adj* **reel'-to-reel'** (of recording equipment) using magnetic tape which is wound from one reel to another (as opposed to cassette or cartridge); (of a magnetic tape) which passes between two reels, as used with a reel-to-reel tape recorder; **Virginia reel** an American country-dance. [OE *hrēol*, but poss partly of other origin; Gaelic *righil* (the dance) may be from English]

reen. See **rhine**.

re-enact *rē-in-akt'*, *vt* to enact over again; to reconstruct in action. — *n* **re-enact'ment**. [**re-**]

re-enforce *rē-in-fōrs'* or *-förs'*, *vt* to enforce again; to reinforce (*rare*); to reassemble, rally (*Shakesp*). — *n* **re-enforce'ment** reinforcement. [**re-**]

re-enter *rē-en'tər*, *vt* and *vi* to enter again or afresh; (in engraving) to cut deeper. — *p adj* **re-en'tering** entering again; pointing inwards; reflex (*math*). — *n* **re-en'trance** the act or achievement of entering again; the fact of being re-entrant (in this sense also **re-en'trancy**). — *adj* **re-en'trant** re-entering (opposed to *salient*); reflex (*math*); returning upon itself at the ends (*electronics*). — *n* a re-entering angle; a valley, depression, etc running into a main feature; the concavity between two salients. — *n* **re-en'try** entering again, *esp* the action of a spacecraft entering the earth's atmosphere again; resumption of possession; the re-opening of an oil well for further drilling; a card allowing a hand to take the lead again. — **re-entry corridor** a narrow corridor, bounded by excessive heat below and low density above, ensuring safe re-entry for a spacecraft. [**re-**]

reest[1]. See **reast**[1].

reest[2], **reist** or **reast** *rēst*, (*Scot*) *vt* to dry or cure with smoke. — *vi* to be smoke-dried. [Origin obscure]

reest[3] or **reist** *rēst*, (*Scot*) *vi* (of a horse) suddenly to refuse to move, to baulk. — *n* a sudden fit of stubbornness. — *adj* **reest'y**. [Perh **rest**[1] or **arrest**]

reeve[1] *rēv*, (*hist*) *n* a high official, chief magistrate of a district; a bailiff or steward. [OE *gerēfa*; cf **grieve**[2] (*Scot*)]

reeve[2] *rēv*, *vt* to pass the end of a rope through; to pass through any hole; to thread one's way through; to fasten by reeving: — *pa t* and *pa p* **reeved** or **rove**. [Origin obscure]

reeve[3] *rēv*. See **ruff**[2].

ref *ref*, (*colloq*) *n*, *vt* and *vi* short form of **referee**: — *pr p* **reff'ing**; *pa t* and *pa p* **reffed**.

ref. *abbrev*: reference.

Ref. Ch. *abbrev*: Reformed Church.

refection *ri-fek'shən*, *n* refreshment or relief (*lit* and *fig*); a meal. — *vt* **refect** (*-fekt'*; back-formation) to refresh. — *vi* to take a meal. — *n* **refec'tion** (*zool*) in rabbits, hares and other herbivores, the habit of eating freshly-passed faeces. — *n* **refec'tioner** or **refectorian** (*rē-fek-tō'* or *-tö'ri-ən*) the officer in charge of the refectory and its arrangements. — *n* **refectory** (*ri-fek'tər-i*; sometimes *ref'ik-*) a dining-hall, *esp* in a monastery or convent. — **refectory table** a long narrow dining-table supported on two shaped pillars each set in a base; **Refection Sunday** Refreshment Sunday. [L *reficere*, *refectum*, from *facere* to make]

refel *ri-fel'*, (*obs*) *vt* to refute; to disprove; to confute; to repulse: — *pr p* **refell'ing**; *pa t* and *pa p* **refelled'**. [L *refellere*, from *fallere* to deceive]

refer *ri-fûr'*, *vt* to assign (to); to impute (to); to attribute (to); to bring into relation (to); to deliver, commit or submit (to); to hand over for consideration (to); to direct for information, confirmation, testimonials, or whatever is required (to); to direct the attention of (to); to postpone (*obs*); to recount (*archaic*); to direct to sit an examination again; to reproduce, represent (*obs*). — *vi* (with *to* in all cases) to have relation or application, to relate; to direct the attention; to turn for information, confirmation, etc; to turn, apply or have recourse; to make mention or allusion: — *pr p* **referr'ing**; *pa t* and *pa p* **referred'**. — *adj* **referable** (*ref'ər-ə-bl* or *ri-fûr'i-bl*; sometimes **referrable** *-fûr'* or **referrible** *-fer'*) that may be referred or assigned. — *n* **referee** (*ref-ə-rē'*; *colloq* shortening **ref**) a person to whom anything is referred; an arbitrator, umpire or judge; a person willing to provide a testimonial. — *vt* to act as referee for. — *vi* to act as referee. — *n* **ref'erence** the act of referring; a submitting for information or decision; the act of submitting a dispute for investigation or decision (*law*); relation; allusion; a person who is referred to; a testimonial; a person willing to provide this; a direction to a book or passage; a book or passage used for reference. — *vt* to make a reference to; to provide (a book, etc) with references to other sources. — *adj* (of a price, point on a scale, etc) providing a standard to which others may be referred for comparision. — *n* **referendary** (*-end'ə-ri*; *obs*) a referee; formerly a court official who was the medium of communication with the pope, emperor, etc. — *n* **referen'dum** the principle or practice of submitting a question directly to the vote of the entire electorate (*pl* **referen'da** or **referen'dums**). — *n* **ref'erent** the object of reference or discussion; the first term in a proposition. — *adj* **referential** (*-en'shl*) containing a reference; having reference (to); used for reference. — *adv* **referen'tially**. — *n* **referr'al** act or instance of referring or being referred, *esp* to another person or organization for, eg consideration, treatment, etc. — **reference book** a book to be consulted on occasion, not for consecutive reading; a pass book (*SAfr*); **ref'erence-mark** a character, such as *, †, or a superscript figure, used to refer to notes, etc; **referred pain** pain felt in a part of the body other than its source. — **terms of reference** a guiding statement defining the scope of an investigation or similar piece of work; the scope itself. [L *referre* to carry back, from *ferre* to carry]

reffo *ref'ō*, (*Austr slang*) *n* a refugee: — *pl* **reff'os**.

refigure *rē-fig'ər*, *vt* to represent again, reproduce (*Shakesp*); to restore to form; to recalculate. [**re-**]

refill *rē-fil'*, *vt* to fill again. — *n* (*rē'fil*) a fresh fill; a duplicate for refilling purposes. [**re-**]

refinancing *rē-fin-an'sing*, (*finance*) *n* payment of a debt by borrowing additional money. [**re-**]

refine *ri-fīn'*, *vt* to purify; to clarify; (*usu* with *out*) to get rid of (impurities, etc) by a purifying process; to free from coarseness, vulgarity or crudity; to make more cultured. — *vi* to become more fine, pure, subtle or

Some words with the prefix **re-**.

rē'do *n.*	**rē-elect'** *vt.*	**rē-eligibil'ity** *n.*
rēdraw' *vt* and *vi.*	**rē-elec'tion** *n.*	**rē-el'igible** *adj.*
rēdrive' *vt.*	**rē-el'evate** *vt.*	**rē-embark'** *vt* and *vi.*
rē-ed'it *vt.*	**rē-elevā'tion** *n.*	**rē-embarkā'tion** *n.*

cultured; to apply or affect subtlety or nicety; to improve by adding refinement or subtlety (with *on* or *upon*). — *adj* **refined'**. — *adv* **refin'edly** in a refined manner; with affected elegance. — *n* **refin'edness**. — *n* **refine'ment** the act or practice of refining; state of being refined; culture in feelings, taste and manners; an improvement; a subtlety; an excessive nicety. — *n* **refin'er**. — *n* **refin'ery** a place for refining. — *n* **refin'ing**. [L *re-* denoting change of state, and **fine**[1]]

refit *rē-fit'*, *vt* to fit out afresh and repair. — *vi* to undergo refitting. — *n* **re'fit**, **refit'ment** or **refitt'ing**. [**re-** and **fit**[1]]

reflag *rē-flag'*, *vt* to replace the national flag of (a ship) with that of a more powerful nation, so it sails under its protection; to change the country of registration of (a ship), *usu* for commercial advantage: — *pr p* **re-flagg'ing**; *pa t* and *pa p* **reflagged'**. [**re-**]

reflation *rē-flā'shən*, *n* increase in the amount of currency, economic activity, etc after deflation; a general increase, above what would normally be expected, in the spending of money. — *vt* (back-formation from *n*) **rēflate'**. — *adj* **reflā'tionary**. [**re-** and in*flation*]

reflect *ri-flekt'*, *vt* to bend or send back or aside; to throw back after striking; to give an image of in the manner of a mirror; to express, reproduce (*fig*); to cast, shed (eg credit or discredit) (*fig*); to consider meditatively (that, how, etc). — *vi* to bend or turn back or aside; to be mirrored; to cast a light (*Shakesp*); to meditate (on); to cast reproach or censure (on or upon); to bring harmful results. — *n* **reflect'ance** or **reflecting factor** ratio of reflected radiation to incident radiation. — *adj* **reflect'ed** cast or thrown back; turned or folded back; mirrored. — *n* **reflect'er** (*Swift*) a person who casts reflections. — *adj* **reflect'ing**. — *adv* **reflect'ingly** meditatively; with implication of censure. — *n* **reflection**, also (now chiefly in scientific use) **reflexion** (*ri-flek'shən*) a turning, bending or folding aside, back or downwards; folding upon itself; rebound; change of direction when an electromagnetic wave or sound-wave strikes on a surface and is thrown back; reflected light, colour, heat, etc; an image in a mirror; (production of) a mirror image of a line or figure (by reflecting it in an axis of symmetry); the conformal transformation in which a figure is reflected in a fixed line; the action of the mind by which it is conscious of its own operations; attentive consideration; contemplation; a thought or utterance resulting from contemplation; censure or reproach. — *adj* **reflec'tionless**. — *adj* **reflect'ive** reflecting; reflected; meditative. — *adv* **reflect'ively**. — *n* **reflect'iveness**. — *n* **reflectiv'ity** ability to reflect rays; reflectance. — *n* **reflec'togram** or **reflec'tograph** an image produced by reflectography. — *n* **reflectog'raphy** a technique used to detect underdrawing, etc in a painting, in which infra-red light is bounced off the lowest, gessoed layer and the resulting image viewed on a TV monitor. — *n* **reflect'or** a reflecting surface, instrument or body; a reflecting telescope. — **reflecting factor** see **reflectance** above; **reflecting microscope** one using a system of mirrors instead of lenses; **reflecting telescope** one (eg the Gregorian or Newtonian) which has a concave mirror instead of an object glass (lens or lenses). [L *reflectere*, *reflexum*, from *flectare* to bend]

reflet *rə-fle'* or *-flā'*, (*Fr*) *n* an iridescent or metallic lustre. [Ital *reflesso* reflection]

reflex *rē'fleks*, formerly *ri-fleks'*, *adj* bent or turned back; reflected; reciprocal; (of an angle) more than 180°; turned back upon itself; involuntary, produced by or concerned with response from a nerve-centre to a stimulus from without; illuminated by light from another part of the same picture (*painting*); using the same valve or valves for high- and low-frequency amplification (*radio*). — *n* reflection; reflected light; a reflected image; an expression, manifestation, outward representation; a reflex action; a reflex radio receiving set. — *vt* (*-fleks'*) to bend back; to project, direct (*Shakesp*). — *adj* **reflexed'** (*bot*) bent abruptly backward or downward. — *n* **reflexibil'ity**. — *adj* **reflex'ible**. — *adj* **reflex'ive** (*gram*) indicating that the action turns back upon the subject. — *adv* **reflex'ively**. — *n* **reflex'iveness** or **reflexiv'ity**. — *adv* **reflex'ly** (or *rē'*). — *n* **reflexol'ogy** the study of the body's reflexes as a guide to behaviour (*psychol*); a form of therapy for treating particular bodily ailments and general stress, carried out through massage on the soles of the feet, on the principle that specific areas of the feet relate to specific parts and organs of the body. — *adj* **reflexolog'ical**. — *n* **reflexol'ogist**. — **reflex anal dilatation** involuntary widening of the anus on examination; **reflex arc** the simplest functional unit of the nervous system, by which an impulse produces a reflex action; **reflex camera** one in which the image is reflected on to a glass screen for composing and focusing; **reflex light** a lens with a reflecting back, returning a beam of red light when the headlight, eg of a motor car, shines on it. [L *reflexus*, from *reflectere*; cf **reflect**]

reflow *rē-flō'*, *vi* to ebb; to flow again. — *n* **reflow'** or **reflow'ing** ebb; reflux. [**re-**]

refluent *ref'lo͝o-ənt*, (*rare*) *adj* flowing back; ebbing; tidal. — *n* **ref'luence** flowing back; ebb. [L *refluēns*, *-entis*, pr p of *refluere*, from *fluere*, *fluxum* to flow]

reflux *rē'fluks*, *n* a flowing back, an ebb; the process of boiling a liquid in a flask with a condenser attached so that the vapour condenses and flows back into the flask, avoiding loss by evaporation (*chem*; also *vi* and *vt*). [Ety as for **refluent**; L *fluxus*, *-ūs* a flow]

refocillate *ri-fos'il-āt*, (*obs*) *vt* to refresh, cherish. — *n* **refocillā'tion**. [L *refocillāre*, *-ātum* to cherish, from *focus* a hearth]

reforest *rē-for'ist*, *vt*. Same as **reafforest**. — *n* **reforestā'tion** same as **reafforestation**. [**re-**]

re-form *rē-förm'*, *vt* and *vi* to form again or anew. — Also **reform**. — *n* **rē-formā'tion**. — *adj* **rē-formed'**. [**re-**]

reform *ri-förm'*, *vt* to transform; to restore, rebuild (*Milton*); to amend; to make better; to remove defects from; to redress; to bring to a better way of life; to chastise (*Spenser*); to prune (*Milton*); to break up in reorganization, hence to disband, dismiss (*military hist*). — *vi* to abandon evil ways. — *n* amendment or transformation, *esp* of a system or institution; a stricter offshoot or branch of a religious order; an extension or better distribution of parliamentary representation. — *adj* **reform'able** (*-ri-*). — *n* **reformabil'ity**. — *n* **reformation** (*ref-ər-mā'shən*) the act of reforming; amendment; improvement; (with *cap*) the great religious revolution of the 16c, which gave rise to the various evangelical or Protestant organizations of Christendom. — *n* **reformā'tionist**. — *adj* **reformative** (*ri-förm'ə-tiv*) tending to produce reform. — *adj* **reform'atory** reforming; tending to produce reform. — *n* in the UK and US, formerly, an institution for reclaiming young delinquents. — *adj* **reformed'** changed; amended; improved; (with *cap*) Protestant, *esp* Calvinistic, in doctrine or polity. — *n* **reform'er** a person who reforms anything; someone who advocates political reform; (with *cap*) one of those who took part in the Reformation of the 16c. — *n* **reform'ism**. — *n* **reform'ist** a reformer; an advocate of reform, or of not very

Some words with the prefix **re-**.

rē-embod'iment *n*.	**rē-em'phasize** or **-ise** *vt*.	**rē-endow'** *vt*.
rē-embod'y *vt*.	**rē-encour'age** *vt*.	**rē-endow'ment** *n*.
rē-emerge' *vi*.	**re-endorse'** *vt*.	**rē-engage'** *vt* and *vi*.
rē-emer'gence *n*.	**re-endorse'ment** *n*.	**rē-engage'ment** *n*.

thoroughgoing reform. — **Reform flask** a salt-glazed stoneware flask made in the likeness of one of the figures connected with the 1832 parliamentary Reform Bill; **Reform Judaism** a form of Judaism, originating in the 19c, in which the Jewish Law is adapted so as to be relevant to contemporary life; **Reformed Presbyterian** Cameronian; **reform school** a reformatory. [L *refōrmāre, -ātum*, from *fōrmāre* to shape, from *fōrma* form]

reformado *ref-ör-mā'dō* or *-mä'dō*, (*hist*) *n* a disbanded or dismissed soldier; an officer whose company has been disbanded or who is for other reason without a command; a volunteer serving as an officer; a reformed person; a reformer: — *pl* **reforma'does** or **reforma'dos**. — Also **reformāde'** (*Bunyan*). — Also *adj*. [Sp *reformado* reformed]

refract *ri-frakt'*, *vt* of a medium, to deflect (rays of light, sound, etc passing into it from another medium); to produce by refraction (*rare*). — *adj* (*rare*) refracted. — *adj* **refract'able** refrangible. — *adj* **refrac'ted** deflected on passage into another medium; bent sharply back from the base (*bot*). — *adj* **refract'ing**. — *n* **refrac'tion**. — *adj* **refrac'tive** refracting; of refraction. — *n* **refractivity** (*rē-frak-tiv'i-ti*). — *n* **rēfractom'eter** an instrument for measuring refractive indices. — *n* **refrac'tor** (*ri-*) anything that refracts; a refracting telescope — **refracting telescope** one in which the principal means of focusing the light is an object glass; **refraction correction** (*astron*) the correction made in the calculation of the altitude of a star, planet, etc to allow for the refraction of its light by the earth's atmosphere; **refractive index** the ratio of the sine of the angle of incidence to that of the angle of refraction when a ray passes from one medium to another. — **angle of refraction** the angle between a refracted ray and the normal to the bounding surface; **double refraction** the separation of an incident ray of light into two refracted rays, polarized in perpendicular planes. [L *refringere, refrāctum*, from *frangere* to break]

refractory (formerly **refractary**) *ri-frak'tər-i*, *adj* unruly; unmanageable; obstinate; perverse; resistant to ordinary treatment, stimulus, disease, etc; *esp* difficult to fuse; fire-resistant. — *n* a substance that is able to resist high temperatures, etc, used in lining furnaces, etc. — *adv* **refrac'torily**. — *n* **refrac'toriness**. — **refractory period** (*biol*) for an organism or an excitable tissue, the period of zero response following a previous response. [L *refrāctārius* stubborn]

refrain[1] *ri-frān'*, *n* a burden, a line or phrase recurring, *esp* at the end of a stanza; the music of such a burden. [OFr *refrain*, from *refraindre*, from L *refringere*, from *frangere* to break]

refrain[2] *ri-frān*, *vt* to curb (*archaic*); to restrain (*archaic*); to abstain from (*Shakesp*); to keep away from (*obs*). — *vi* to keep oneself from action, forbear; to abstain (from; *obs* with *to*). [OFr *refrener*, from LL *refrēnāre*, from *re-* back, and *frēnum* a bridle]

refrangible *ri-fran'ji-bl*, *adj* that may be refracted. — *n* **refrangibil'ity** or **refran'gibleness**. [See **refract**]

refresh *ri-fresh'*, *vt* to make fresh again; to freshen up; to give new vigour, life, liveliness, spirit, brightness, fresh appearance, coolness, moistness, etc to. — *vi* to become fresh again; to take refreshment, *esp* drink (*colloq*). — *vt* **refresh'en** to make fresh again. — *n* **refresh'ener**. — *n* **refresh'er** a person who, or that which, refreshes; a cool drink (*colloq*); a fee paid to counsel for continuing his or her attention to a case, *esp* when adjourned; a douceur to encourage further exertions (*colloq*); a subsequent course of training or instruction to maintain or reattain one's former standard, study new developments, etc (also *adj*). — *adj* **refresh'ful** (*archaic*) full of power to refresh; refreshing. — *adv* **refresh'fully**. — *adj* **refresh'ing** pleasantly cooling, inspiriting, reviving or invigorating. — *adv* **refresh'ingly**. — *n* **refresh'ment** the or an act of refreshing; the state of being refreshed; renewed strength or spirit; that which refreshes, such as food or rest; (in *pl*) drink or a light meal. — **refresh'ment-room**; **Refreshment** or **Refection Sunday** the fourth Sunday in Lent, when the story of the loaves and fishes is read in English and RC churches. [OFr *refrescher*, from *re-*, and *freis* (fem *fresche*) fresh]

refrigerant *ri-frij'ə-rənt*, *adj* cooling; giving a feeling of coolness; refreshing. — *n* a freezing or cooling agent; that which gives a cool feeling. — *vt* **refrig'erāte** to freeze; to make cold; to make to feel cold; to expose (food, etc) to great cold for preservation. — *vi* to become cold. — *n* **refrigerā'tion**. — *adj* **refrig'erative** (*-rə-tiv*) cooling. — *n* **refrig'erator** (*-rā-tər*) an apparatus or chamber for producing and maintaining a low temperature (contracted to **fridge**, *esp* when in domestic use). — *adj* **refrig'eratory** (*-rə-tər-i*) cooling; refrigerative. — *n* (*archaic*) a refrigerator; a chamber in which ice is formed; a water-filled vessel for condensing in distillation. [L *refrigerāre, -ātum*, from *re-* (denoting change of state) and *frīgerāre*, from *frīgus* cold]

refringe *ri-frinj'*, *vt* (*obs*) to refract. — *n* **refring'ency** refractivity. — *adj* **refring'ent**. [L *refringere*; see **refract**]

reft *reft*, *pa t* and *pa p* of **reave**.

refuge *ref'ūj*, *n* shelter or protection from danger or trouble; an asylum or retreat; *specif* an establishment set up to provide emergency accommodation, protection, support, etc for eg battered wives; a street island for pedestrians; recourse in difficulty. — *vt* and *vi* (*archaic*) to shelter. — *n* **refugee** (*ref-ū-jē'*) a person who flees for refuge to another country, *esp* from religious or political persecution; a fugitive. — *n* **refugium** (*ri-fū'ji-əm*) a region that has retained earlier geographical, climatic, etc conditions, and thus becomes a haven for older varieties of flora and fauna: — *pl* **refū'gia** (*-ji-ə*). — **house of refuge** a shelter for the destitute. [Fr, from L *refugium*, from *fugere* to flee]

refulgent *ri-ful'jənt*, *adj* casting a flood of light; radiant; beaming. — *n* **reful'gence** or **reful'gency**. [L *refulgēns, -entis*, pr p of *refulgēre*, from *re-* (intensive) and *fulgēre* to shine]

refund[1] *ri-* or *rē-fund'*, *vt* to pour back (now *rare*); to repay. — *vi* to restore what was taken. — *n* **refund** (*rē'fund* or *ri-fund'*). — *adj* **refund'able**. — *n* **refund'er**. — *n* **refund'ment** (*ri-*). [L *refundere*, from *fundere* to pour]

refund[2] or **re-fund** *rē-fund'*, *vt* to fund anew; to replace (an old issue) by a new; to borrow so as to pay off (an old loan). [**re-**]

refurbish *rē-fûr'bish*, to renovate; to brighten up, redecorate. — *n* **refur'bishment**. [**re-**]

refuse[1] *ri-fūz'*, *vt* to decline to take or accept; to renounce; to decline to give or grant; (of a horse) to decline to jump over; to fail to follow suit to (*cards*); to decline to meet in battle; to hold back from the regular alignment in action (*military*). — *vi* to make refusal. — *adj* **refus'able** (*ri-*). — *n* **refus'al** the or an act of refusing; the option of taking or refusing; a thing refused. — *n* **refusenik** or **refusnik** (*ri-fūz'nik*; see **-nik**) formerly, a dissident Soviet citizen, *esp* a Soviet Jew wishing to emigrate; generally, a dissident (*colloq*). — *n* **refus'er**. [Fr *refuser*, from L *refūsum*, pa p of *refundere*, from *fundere* to pour; cf **refund**[1]]

Some words with the prefix **re-**.

rē-enlist' *vt* and *vi*.	**rē-erect'** *vt*.	**rē-examinā'tion** *n*.
rē-enlist'er *n*.	**rē-erec'tion** *n*.	**rē-exam'ine** *vt*.
rē-enlist'ment *n*.	**rē-estab'lish** *vt*.	**rē-exist'** *vi*.
rē-equip' *vt* and *vi*.	**rē-estab'lishment** *n*.	**rē-exist'ence** *n*.

refuse² *ref'ūs, adj* rejected as worthless; waste. — *n* that which is rejected or left as worthless; rubbish, waste. [Fr *refus*; see **refuse¹**]

refute *ri-fūt', vt* to disprove; to deny. — *adj* **refutable** (*ref'ūt-ə-bl* or *ri-fūt'ə-bl*). — *adv* **ref'utably** (or *ri-fūt'*). — *n* **refu'tal** or **refutā'tion** (*ref-*)the or an act of refuting; that which disproves. — *n* **refu'ter**. [L *refūtāre* to drive back]

regain *ri-* or *rē-gān', vt* to gain or win back; to get back to. — *n* recovery. — *adj* **regain'able**. — *n* **regain'er**. — *n* **regain'ment**. [Fr *regaigner* (now *regagner*)]

regal¹ *rē'gl, adj* royal; kingly. — *adj* **regalian** (*ri-gā'li-ən*; *archaic*) regal. — *n* **regalism** (*rē'gəl-izm*) royal supremacy, *esp* in Church matters. — *n* **re'galist**. — *n* **regality** (*ri-gal'i-ti*) state of being regal; royalty; sovereignty; a territorial jurisdiction formerly conferred by the king (*Scot hist*). — *adv* **re'gally**. — **regal lily** a variety of lily (*Lilium regale*) producing fragrant, white flowers. [L *rēgālis*, from *rēx* a king, from *regere* to rule]

regal² *rē'gl, n* a small portable organ. [Fr *régale*]

regale¹ *ri-gāl', vt* to feast; to treat to (stories, etc; with *with*); to give pleasure to. — *vi* (*archaic*) to feast. — *n* (*archaic*) a feast; a choice dish. — *n* **regale'ment**. [Fr *régaler*, from Ital *regalare*, perh from *gala* a piece of finery]

regale². See **regalia¹**.

regalia¹ *ri-gā'li-ə* or *rā-gä'li-a, n pl* royal privileges or powers, as (*hist*) that of enjoying the revenues of vacant sees, etc (*sing* **regale** *ri-gā'lē*); the insignia of royalty, ie crown, sceptre, etc; any insignia or special garb, such as that of the Freemasons. [L *rēgālis* royal, neuter sing *-e*, pl *-ia*]

regalia² *ri-gā'li-ə, n* a big cigar. [Sp, royal right]

regalism, regality, etc. See under **regal¹**.

regar. See **regur**.

regard *ri-gärd', vt* to look at; to observe; to heed; to look to; to esteem or consider; to esteem highly; to have kindly feelings for; to respect; to take into account; to have respect or relation to. — *vi* to look; to give heed. — *n orig* look; a thing seen (*Shakesp*); intention (*Shakesp*); attention with interest; observation; estimation; esteem; kindly, affectionate or respectful feeling; care; consideration; a thing to be considered; repute; respect; relation; reference; (in *pl*) in messages of greeting, respectful good will. — *adj* **regard'able** worthy of consideration. — *adj* **regard'ant** attentive; looking backward (*heraldry*). — *n* **regard'er**. — *adj* **regard'ful** heedful; respectful. — *adv* **regard'fully**. — *n* **regard'fulness**. — *prep* **regard'ing** concerning. — *adj* **regard'less** heedless; inconsiderate; without regard to consequences; careless (of). — *adv* nevertheless, anyway; despite or without concern for the consequences. — *adv* **regard'lessly**. — *n* **regard'lessness**. — **as regards** with regard to, concerning; **in regard of** or **to** (*archaic*) in comparison with; in reference to; out of consideration for (*Shakesp*); **in this regard** in this respect; **with regard to** concerning; so far as relates to. [Fr *regarder*, from *garder* to keep, watch]

regatta *ri-gat'ə, n* a yacht or boat race-meeting. [Ital (Venetian) *regata*]

regelation *rē-ji-lā'shən, n* freezing together again (as of ice melted by pressure when the pressure is released). — *vt* and *vi* **rē'gelāte**. [**re-** and L *gelāre* to freeze]

regency *rē'jən-si, n* the office, term of office, jurisdiction or dominion of a regent; a body entrusted with vicarious government; *specif* in French history, the minority of Louis XV, 1715–1723, when Philip of Orleans was regent; in British history, the years 1811–20, when the Prince of Wales (George IV) was Prince Regent. — *adj* of, or in the style prevailing during, the French or English regency. — *n* **rē'gence** (*obs*) government. — *adj* **regent** ruling; invested with interim or vicarious sovereign authority. — *n* a ruler; a person invested with interim authority on behalf of another; formerly in Scotland and elsewhere, a professor; a master or doctor who takes part in the regular duties of instruction and government in some universities. — *n* **rē'gentship**. — **rē'gent-bird** a bower-bird (*Sericulus*) named in honour of the Prince Regent. [L *regēns*, *-entis*, pr p of *regere* to rule]

regenerate *ri-jen'ər-āt, vt* to produce anew; to renew spiritually (*theol*); to put new life or energy into; to reform completely; to reproduce (a part of the body); to magnify the amplitude of an electrical output by relaying part of the power back into the input circuit (*electronics*); to produce again in the original form (*chem, nucleonics*, etc). — *vi* to undergo regeneration, to be regenerated. — *adj* (*-it* or *-āt*) regenerated, renewed; changed from a natural to a spiritual state. — *adj* **regen'erable**. — *n* **regen'eracy** (*-ə-si*). — *n* **regenerā'tion** renewal of lost parts; spiritual rebirth; reformation; recovery of waste heat or other energy that would have been lost; rebuilding or revitalizing of an area, eg the centre of a city. — *adj* **regen'erative**. — *adv* **regen'eratively**. — *n* **regen'erātor** someone who, or that which, regenerates; a chamber in which waste heat is, by reversal of draught, alternately stored up and given out to the gas and air entering. — *adj* **regen'eratory** (*-ə-tər-i*). [L *regenerāre*, *-ātum* to bring forth again, from *re-* again, and *generāre* to generate]

regent. See under **regency**.

regest *ri-jest', (Milton) n* a register. [See **register**]

reggae *reg'ā* or *rā'gā, n* a simple, lively, strongly rhythmic rock music of the W Indies, imported into Britain by immigrants in the mid-1960s.

reggo or **rego** *reg'ō, (Austr colloq) n*. Short form of (motor vehicle) **registration**.

regicide *rej'i-sīd, n* the killing or killer of a king. — *adj* **regicī'dal**. [L *rēx*, *rēgis* a king, on the analogy of **homicide, parricide**, etc]

régie *rā-zhē, (Fr) n* a system of government monopoly, *esp* in tobacco; the department concerned; tobacco sold by it.

regime or **régime** *rā-zhēm', n* regimen; system of government; a particular government; administration. [Fr, from L *regimen*]

regimen *rej'i-men, n* government; system of government; course of treatment, such as (*med*) a prescribed combination of diet, exercise, drugs, etc; grammatical government; prevailing system or set of conditions. — *adj* **regim'inal**. [L *regimen*, *-inis*, from *regere* to rule]

regiment *rej'mənt* or *rej'i-mənt, n* government (*archaic*); control (*archaic*); rule (*archaic*); regimen (*archaic*); a region under government (*archaic*); (often *rej'mənt*) a body of soldiers constituting the largest permanent unit, commanded by a colonel; a large number (*fig*). — *vt* (*rej'i-ment* or *-ment'*) to form into a regiment or regiments; to systematize, classify; to organize; to subject to excessive control. — *adj* **regimental** (*-i-ment'l*) of a regiment. — *n* (in *pl*) the uniform of a regiment. — *n* **regimentation** (*-i-men-tā'shən*). [LL *regimentum*, from L *regere* to rule]

regiminal. See under **regimen**.

regina *ri-jī'nə, n* queen; (with *cap*) title of a reigning queen (*abbrev* **R** in signature). — *adj* **reginal** (*-jī'nl*) of a queen; siding with a queen. [L *rēgīna*]

region *rē'jən, n* a tract of country; any area or district, *esp* one characterized in some way; the larger of the two local government administrative units in Scotland (see

Some words with the prefix **re-**.

rē-expand' *vt* and *vi*.	**rē-ex'port** *n*.	**rēfash'ion** *vt*.
rē-expan'sion *n*.	**rē-exportā'tion** *n*.	**rēfash'ionment** *n*.
rē-export' *vt*.	**rēface'** *vt*.	**rēfloat'** *vt*.

also **district**); a realm; a portion or division, as of the body; a portion of space; the atmosphere, or a division of it, *esp* the upper air (*Shakesp* and *Milton*); the heavens (*obs*). — *adj* (*Shakesp*) of the air. — *adj* **rē'gional**. — *n* **rē'gionalism** regional patriotism or particularism. — *n* **rē'gionalist**. — *n* **regionalīzā'tion** or **-s-** the dividing of England (in 1972) and Scotland (in 1973) into regions for local government administration. — *vt* **re'gionalize** or **-ise**. — *adv* **rē'gionally**. — *adj* **rē'gionary**. — **regional council** a council elected to govern the affairs of a region. — **in the region of** near; about, approximately. [Anglo-Fr *regiun*, from L *regiō*, *-ōnis*, from *regere* to rule]

régisseur *rā-zhē-sœr*, (*Fr*) *n* manager; stage manager; (in a ballet company) a director.

register *rej'is-tər*, *n* a written record or official list regularly kept; the book containing such a record; an entry in it; a recording or indicating apparatus, such as a cash register; a registrar (now *rare* or *US*); apparatus for regulating a draught; a register-plate; an organ stop or stop-knob; the set of pipes controlled by an organ stop, or a set of strings in a harpsichord; part of the compass of any instrument having a distinct quality of tone (also *fig*); the compass of an instrument or voice; the range of tones of a voice produced in a particular manner; the form of language used in certain circumstances, situations, or when dealing with certain subjects, eg legal, technical or journalistic; exact adjustment of position, as of colours in a picture, or letterpress on opposite sides of a leaf (*printing*); registration; an entry in a register; a certificate of registration; a device for storing small amounts of data (*comput*). — *vt* to enter or cause to be entered in a register; to record; to indicate; to put on record; to express; to represent by bodily expression; to adjust in register; to send by registered post. — *vi* to enter one's name (*esp* as a hotel guest); to correspond in register; to make an impression, reach the consciousness (*colloq*). — *adj* **reg'istered** recorded, entered or enrolled (as a voter, a letter requiring special precautions for security, etc); made with a register-plate. — *adj* **reg'istrable**. — *n* **reg'istrant** a person who registers, or has registered (a trademark, etc). — *n* **reg'istrar** (*-trär*, or *-trär'*) a person who keeps a register or official record; someone who makes an official record of births, deaths and marriages registered locally; a hospital doctor in one of the intermediate grades (**medical** or **surgical registrar**). — *n* **reg'istrarship** office of a registrar. — *n* **reg'istrary** (now only at Cambridge University) a registrar. — *n* **registrā'tion** the act or fact of registering; something registered; the act or art of combining stops in organ-playing. — *n* **reg'istry** registration; an office or place where a register is kept; a register; an entry in a register. — **Registered General Nurse** (*abbrev* **RGN**) a nurse who has passed the examination of the General Nursing Council for Scotland; **registered office** the officially recorded address of a company, to which legal documents, etc are sent; **registered post** a postal service in which a number is given to an item on payment of a registration fee, and compensation paid for loss or damage during delivery; **registered trademark** a trademark that has been officially registered to prevent it being used by others (*symbol* ®); **Register House** the building in Edinburgh where Scottish records are kept; **register office** a record-office; an employment office; the less common but strictly correct term for a registry office (see below); **reg'ister-plate** (in rope-making) a disc with holes to give each yarn its position; a chimney damper; **Reg'istrar-Gen'eral** an officer having the superintendence of the registration of all births, deaths and marriages; **registration number** the combination of letters and numbers shown on a motor vehicle's number plates, by which its ownership is registered; **registry office** an office for putting domestic servants in touch with employers; a registrar's office, (strictly, **register office**) where births, etc are recorded and civil marriages are celebrated. — **gross** or **net register** (**tonnage**) gross or net tonnage; **Lord Clerk-Register** an officer of the General Register House with duties concerned with the election of Scottish representative peers, formerly custodian of records and registers; **parish register** a book in which births, deaths and marriages are inscribed; **Registrar of Companies** the government official responsible for recording certain information about British companies, such as the memorandum of association, address of registered office, etc; **ship's register** a document showing the ownership of a vessel. [OFr *registre* or LL *registrum*, for L pl *regesta* things recorded, from *re-* back, and *gerere* to carry]

regius *rē'ji-əs* or *rā'gi-ōōs*, *adj* royal, eg **regius professor** one whose chair was founded by Henry VIII, or, in Scotland, by the Crown. — **regium donum** (*rē'ji-əm dō'nəm*) a former annual grant of public money to nonconformist ministers in England, Scotland, and *esp* Ireland. [L *rēgius*, from *rēx* king]

reglet *reg'lit*, *n* a flat, narrow moulding (*archit*); a fillet; a strip for spacing between lines (*printing*). [Fr *réglet*, dimin of *règle*, from L *rēgula* a rule]

regma *reg'mə*, (*bot*) *n* a fruit that splits into dehiscent parts: — *pl* **reg'mata**. [Gr *rhēgma*, *-atos* a breaking]

regnal *reg'nl*, *adj* of a reign. — *adj* **reg'nant** reigning (often after the noun, eg **queen regnant** a reigning queen, not a *queen consort*); prevalent. [L *rēgnālis*, from *rēgnum* a kingdom, *rēgnāns*, *-antis*, pr p of *rēgnāre* to reign]

regolith *reg'ə-lith*, *n* mantle-rock. [Gr *rhēgos* a blanket, and *lithos* a stone]

regorge *ri-* or *rē-görj'*, *vt* to disgorge, regurgitate; to swallow again (*rare*); to gorge to repletion (*Milton*). — *vi* to gush back. [**re-** and **gorge**; or Fr *regorger* to overflow, abound]

Reg. Prof. *abbrev*: Regius Professor.

regrate *ri-grāt'*, (*hist*) *vt* to buy and sell again in or near the same market, thus raising the price (formerly a criminal offence in England). — *n* **regrā'ter** or **regrā'tor** a person who regrates (*hist*); a middleman (*SW Eng*). — *n* **regrā'ting**. [OFr *regrater*; of doubtful origin]

regrede *ri-grēd'*, *vi* to retrograde (*rare*). — *n* **regrē'dience** (*Herrick*). [L *regredī*, from *re-*, and *gradī* to go]

regreet *ri-grēt'*, *vt* to greet in return; to greet again (*Shakesp*); to greet (*Shakesp*). — *vi* to exchange greetings. — *n* a greeting, *esp* in return; (in *pl*) greetings, salutation (*Shakesp*). [**re-**]

regress *rē'gres*, *n* passage back; return; reversion; backward movement or extension; right or power of returning; re-entry. — *vi* (*ri-gres'*) to go back; to recede; to return to a former place or state; to revert; to move from east to west (*astron*). — *vt* to cause to regress or return to a former state or condition. — *n* **regression** (*ri-gresh'ən*) the or an act of regressing; reversion; return towards the mean; return to an earlier stage of development, as in an adult's or adolescent's behaving like a child. — *adj* **regressive** (*ri-gres'iv*) going back; reverting; returning; (of taxation) in which the rate decreases as the amount to be taxed increases. — *adv* **regress'ively** in a regressive manner; by return. — *n* **regress'iveness** (*ri-*). — *n* **regressiv'ity** (*rē-*). — **regression therapy** (*psychol*) a therapeutic

Some words with the prefix **re-**.

rēflow'er *vi*.	**rēfoot'** *vt*.	**rēfortificā'tion** *n*.
rēflow'ering *n*.	**rēfor'mat** *vt*.	**rēfort'ify** *vt*.
rēfo'cus *vt*.	**rēform'ulate** *vt*.	**rēfound'** *vt*.

technique which aims to return a patient to the emotional state of a child in order to identify the causes of psychological problems. [L *regressus*, from *regredī*; see **regrede**]

regret *ri-gret'*, *vt* to remember with sense of loss or feeling of having done wrong; to wish otherwise: — *pr p* **regrett'ing**; *pa t* and *pa p* **regrett'ed**. — *n* sorrowful wish that something had been otherwise; sorrowful feeling of loss; compunction; an intimation of regret or refusal. — *adj* **regret'ful** feeling regret. — *adv* **regret'fully**. — *adj* **regrett'able** to be regretted. — *adv* **regrett'ably** in a regrettable way; I'm sorry to say, unfortunately. [OFr *regreter*, *regrater*; poss connected with **greet**[2]]

regt *abbrev*: regiment.

reguerdon *ri-gûr'dən*, (*Shakesp*) *n* reward. — *vt* to reward. [OFr *reguerdon*]

regula *reg'ū-lə*, *n* the rule of a religious order; a fillet, *esp* under the Doric taenia, below each triglyph (*archit*): — *pl* **reg'ulae** (*-lē*). [L *rēgula* a rule, from *regere* to rule]

regular *reg'ū-lər*, *adj* subject to a monastic rule (opposed to *secular*); governed by or according to rule, law, order, habit, custom, established practice, mode prescribed or the ordinary course of things; placed, arranged, etc at regular intervals in space or time; (of a marriage) celebrated by a church minister after proclamation of banns; normal; ordinary; habitual; constant; steady; uniform; periodical; duly qualified; inflected in the usual way, *esp* of weak verbs (*gram*); symmetrical, *esp* (*bot*) radially symmetrical or actinomorphic; having all the sides and angles equal or all faces equal, equilateral and equiangular, the same number meeting at every corner (*geom*); also (of a pyramid) having a regular polygon for base and the other faces similar and equal isosceles triangles; permanent, professional, or standing (*military*; opposed to *militia*, *volunteer* and *territorial*); (of a satellite) that keeps or scarcely deviates from a circular orbit around its planet (*astron*); thorough, out-and-out, *esp* (*US*) in party politics (*colloq*); of the same way of thinking as the speaker, hence ready to help or abet him or her, loyal, swell (*slang*); veritable (*colloq*). — *n* a member of a religious order who has taken the three ordinary vows; a soldier of the regular army; a regular customer; a loyal supporter of the party leader (*US politics*). — *n* **regularity** (*-lar'i-ti*) state, character or fact of being regular. — *n* **regularīzā'tion** or **-s-**. — *vt* **reg'ularize** or **-ise** to make regular. — *adv* **reg'ularly**. — *vt* **reg'ulate** to control; to adapt or adjust continuously; to adjust by rule. — *vi* to make regulations. — *n* **regulā'tion** the act of regulating; state of being regulated; a rule or order prescribed; a form of legislation used to bring the provisions of an Act of Parliament into force; in the EEC, a proposal from the commission which is approved by the council and immediately becomes law in all member states. — *adj* prescribed by regulation. — *adj* **reg'ulātive** tending to regulate. — *n* **reg'ulātor** a person who or thing which regulates; a controlling device, *esp* for the speed of a clock or watch; a change in the taxation rate introduced by the Chancellor of the Exchequer between budgets to regulate the economy. — *adj* **reg'ulatory** (*-lə-tər-i*). — **regulating rod** a fine control rod of a reactor (*nuc eng*); **regulatory gene** (*biol*) a gene involved in controlling the expression of other genes (cf **structural gene**). [L *rēgula* a rule, from *regere* to rule]

reguline. See under **regulus**.

Regulo® *reg'ū-lō*, *n* a thermostatic control system for gas ovens; loosely (with a given numeral) one of the graded scale of temperatures on a gas oven (also without *cap*).

regulus *reg'ū-ləs*, *n* an impure metal, an intermediate product in smelting of ores; antimony; (with *cap*) a first-magnitude star in Leo; the goldcrest genus of birds. — *adj* **reg'uline**. — *vt* **reg'ulize** or **-ise** to reduce to regulus. [L *rēgulus*, dimin of *rēx* a king]

regur or **regar** *rā'* or *rē'gər*, *n* the rich black cotton soil of the Indian subcontinent, full of organic matter. [Hindi *regar*]

regurgitate *ri-* or *rē-gûr'ji-tāt*, *vt* to cast out again; to pour back; to bring back into the mouth after swallowing. — *vi* to gush back. — *adj* **regur'gitant**. — *n* **regurgitā'tion**. [LL *regurgitāre*, *-ātum*, from *re-* back, and *gurges*, *gurgitis* a gulf]

reh *rā*, *n* an efflorescence of sodium salts on the soil in India, etc. [Hindustani]

rehab *rē'hab*, (chiefly *US*) *abbrev*: rehabilitate; rehabilitation; rehabilitation centre.

rehabilitate *rē-(h)ə-bil'i-tāt*, *vt* to reinstate, restore to former privileges, rights, rank, etc; to clear the character of; to bring back into good condition, working order or prosperity; to make fit, after disablement, illness or imprisonment, for earning a living or playing a part in the world; to rebuild or restore (a building or housing area) to good condition. — *n* **rehabilitā'tion**. — *adj* **rehabil'itative** tending to rehabilitate. — *n* **rehabil'itator**. [LL *rehabilitāre*, *-ātum*; see **habilitate**]

rehash *rē-hash'*, *n* something made up of materials formerly used, *esp* a restatement in different words of ideas already expressed by oneself or someone else. — Also *vt*. [**re-** and **hash**, (n)]

rehear *rē-hēr'*, *vt* to hear again; to retry (a lawsuit). — *n* **rehear'ing**. [**re-**]

rehearse *ri-hûrs'*, *vt* to repeat, say over or read aloud; to enumerate; to recount, narrate in order; to perform privately for practice or trial; to practise beforehand; to train by rehearsal. — *vi* to take part in rehearsal. — *n* **rehears'al** the or an act of rehearsing; repetition; enumeration; narration; a performance for trial or practice. — *n* **rehears'er**. — *n* **rehears'ing**. [OFr *rehercer*, *reherser*, from *re-* again, and *hercer* to harrow, from *herce* (Fr *herse*), from L *hirpex*, *-icis* a rake, a harrow]

reheat *rē-hēt'*, *vt* to heat again. — *n* (*rē'hēt*) a device to inject fuel into the hot exhaust gases of a turbojet in order to obtain increased thrust; the use of this. — *n* **reheat'er** a person who reheats; an apparatus for reheating. [**re-**]

rehoboam *rē-(h)ō-bō'əm*, *n* a large liquor measure or vessel (*esp* for champagne), the size of six normal bottles (*approx* 156 fluid oz). [*Rehoboam*, king of Israel]

rehouse *rē-howz'*, *vt* to provide with a new house or houses. — *n* **rehous'ing**. [**re-**]

rehydrate *rē-hī'drāt*, *vi* to absorb water after dehydration. — *vt* to add water to (a dehydrated substance); to enable a dehydrated person to absorb water. — *n* **rehydra'tion**. [**re-**]

Reich *rīhh*, *n* the German state; Germany as an empire (the **First Reich** Holy Roman Empire, 962–1806, **Second Reich** under Hohenzollern emperors, 1871–1918, and **Third Reich** as a dictatorship under the Nazi regime, 1933–45). — **Reichsbank** (*rīhhs'bängk*) the German state bank; **Reichsland** (*-länt*) imperial territory, ie Alsace-Lorraine, 1871–1919; **reichsmark** (*-märk*) the German monetary unit 1924–48 (see **mark**[2]); **Reichsrat**, earlier **Reichsrath** (*-rät*) the upper house of the parliament of the former Austrian Empire; a deliberative Council of the Weimar Republic in Germany (1919–33), representing the States; **Reichstag** (*-tähh*) the lower house of the parliament of Germany during

Some words with the prefix **re-**.

rēfoundā'tion *n.*	**rēframe'** *vt.*	**rēfū'elable** or **rēfū'ellable** *adj.*
rēfound'er *n.*	**rēfreeze'** *vt.*	**rēfur'bish** *vt.*
rēfrac'ture *n.*	**rēfū'el** *vt.*	**rēfur'nish** *vt* and *vi.*

the Second Reich and the Weimar Republic; the building in which it met. [Ger, OE *rīce* kingdom; cf **bishopric**]

Reichian *rīhh'i-ən, adj* of or relating to the theory or practice of Wilhelm *Reich*, Austrian-born psychiatrist (1897–1957), *esp* the concept of a universal, sexually-generated life energy called 'orgone'. — **Reichian therapy** (also without *cap*) therapy designed to release inhibited or disturbed energies by the use of massage, controlled breathing, etc (also called **bioenerget'ics**).

reif *rēf*, (*Scot*) *n* spoliation. [OE *rēaf*; cf **reave**]

reify *rē'i-fī, vt* to think of as a material thing; to convert into a material thing, to materialize. — *n* **reification** (*-fi-kā'shən*) materialization, turning into an object; depersonalization (*esp* in Marxist terminology). [L *rēs* a thing]

reign *rān, n* kingdom (*obs*); realm (*obs*); domain (*obs*); rule, actual or nominal, of a monarch; predominance; predominating influence; time of reigning. — *vi* to be a monarch; to be predominant; to prevail. [OFr *regne*, from L *rēgnum*, from *regere* to rule]

reik. Same as **reak**[1].

Reil's island. See **insula**.

reimbattell'd *rē-im-bat'ld*, (*Milton*) *pa p* drawn up again in battle array. [**re-**]

reimburse *rē-im-bûrs', vt* to repay; to pay an equivalent to for loss or expense. — *adj* **reimburs'able**. — *n* **reimburse'ment**. [LL *imbursāre*, from *in* in, and *bursa* purse]

reim-kennar *rīm'ken-ər, n* an enchanter or enchantress. [Appar invented by Scott, from Ger *Reim* rhyme, and *Kenner* knower]

reimplant *rē-im-plänt'*, (*med*) *vt* to replace severed body tissue, *esp* an organ or member, in its original site surgically. — *n* (*-im'-*) a section of the body which has been reimplanted. — *n* **reimplantā'tion**. [**re-**]

reimpression *rē-im-presh'ən, n* a second or later impression of an edition of a book, etc; a reprint. [**re-**]

rein[1] *rān, n* the strap or either half of the strap from the bit, by which a horse is controlled; (in *pl*) a device with a similar strap for guiding a small child (also called **walking reins**); any means of curbing or governing (*fig*). — *vt* to fasten or tie by the rein (*Shakesp*); to provide with reins; to govern with the rein; to restrain or control; to stop or check (with *in* or *up*). — *vi* to answer (*Shakesp*); to stop or slow up. — *adj* **rein'less** without rein or restraint. — **rein'-arm** and **rein'-hand** normally the left arm and hand respectively (opposed to *whip-hand*); **reins'man** a skilful horse-driver or rider. — **draw rein** to pull up, stop riding; **give rein** or **a free rein** or **the reins to** to allow free play to, apply no check to; **keep a tight rein (on)** to control closely; **rein back** to make a horse step backwards by pressure on the reins; (of a horse) to step backwards (also *fig*); **rein in** to check, stop; **take the reins** to take control. [OFr *rein, resne, rene* (Fr *rene*), perh through (hypothetical) LL *retina*, from L *retinēre* to hold back]

rein[2]. See under **reindeer** and **reins**.

reincarnate *rē-in-kär'nāt, vt* to cause to be born again in another body or form; to embody again in flesh. — *adj* (*poetic*) reborn. — *n* **rēincarnā'tion**. — *n* **rēincarnā'tionism** belief in reincarnation of the soul. — *n* **rēincarnā'tionist**. [**re-**]

reindeer *rān'dēr, n* a large heavy deer (genus *Rangifer*), wild and domesticated, of northern regions, antlered in both sexes, the N American variety (or species) called the caribou: — *pl* **rein'deer** or **rein'deers**. — Also (*rare*) **rein**. — **Reindeer Age** (*archaeol*) the Magdalenian; **reindeer moss** a lichen (*Cladonia rangiferina*), the winter food of the reindeer. [ON *hreinndȳri*, or ON *hreinn* (OE *hrān*) and **deer**]

reinette *rā-net'*. Same as **rennet**[2].

re infecta *rē* or *rā in-fek'tə* or *-tä*, (*L*) without finishing the business.

reinflation *rē-in-flā'shən, n* (excessive) reflation which, rather than stimulating the economy, causes further inflation. [**re-**]

reinforce *rē-in-fōrs'* or *-förs', vt* to enforce again (*rare*); to strengthen with new force or support; to strengthen; to increase by addition; to encourage (the response to a stimulus) by giving or not giving a reward (*psychol*). — *vi* (*Shakesp*) to get reinforcements. — *n* something that reinforces; a reinforced part near the rear of a gun. — *n* **reinforce'ment** the act of reinforcing; additional force or assistance, *esp* of troops (*usu* in *pl*). — **reinforced concrete** concrete strengthened by embedded steel bars or mesh. [Alteration by 17c, of **renforce**]

reinform *rē-in-förm', vt* to inform anew; to give form to again; to reanimate. [**re-**]

reinfund *rē-in-fund'*, (*Swift*) *vi* to flow in again. [**re-** and L *infundere*, from *fundere* to pour]

reins *rānz, n pl* (*rare* or *obs* in *sing*) the kidneys, *esp* as formerly believed to be the centre of emotion; the loins. [OFr *reins*, from L *rēn*, pl *rēnēs*]

reinstall *rē-in-stöl', vt* to install again. — *n* **reinstal'ment**. [**re-**]

reinstate *rē-instāt', vt* to instate again; to restore to or re-establish in a former station or condition. — *n* **reinstāte'ment**. — *n* **reinstā'tion** (*rare*). [**re-**]

reinsure *rē-in-shōōr', vt* to insure against the risk undertaken by underwriting an insurance; to insure again. — *n* **reinsur'ance**. — *n* **reinsur'er**. [**re-**]

reintegrate *rē-in'ti-grāt, vt* to integrate again; to redintegrate. — *n* **reintegrā'tion**.

reintermediation *rē-in-tər-mē-di-ā'shən, n* the return into the banking system of borrowing previously financed outside it to evade corset (qv) controls. [**re-**]

re-invent *rē-invent', vt* to invent again; to recreate in a different or spurious form. — *n* **re-inven'tion**. — **re-invent the wheel** to return, *usu* by a circuitous and complex process, to a simple device or method. [**re-**]

reinvest *rē-in-vest', vt* to clothe again; to endow again; to invest again (also *vi*). — *n* **reinvest'ment**. [**re-**]

reinvigorate *rē-in-vig'ər-āt, vt* to put new vigour into. — *n* **reinvigorā'tion**. [**re-**]

reioyndure (*Shakesp*). See **rejoin**[2].

reird *rērd* or **raird** *rārd*, (*Scot*) *n* an uproar, clamour, din. [OE *reord*]

reis[1] *rīs*. Same as **rice**[2].

reis[2] *rās, n pl* (*sing* **real** *rā-äl'*) an obsolete Portuguese and Brazilian money of account, 1000 reis making a *milreis*. [Port]

reist. Same as **reast**[1], or as **reest**[2,3].

reistafel. See **rijstafel**.

reiter *rī'tər*, (*hist*) *n* a German cavalry soldier. [Ger]

reiterate *rē-it'ər-āt, vt* to repeat; to repeat again and again. — *n* **reit'erance**. — *adj* **reit'erant** reiterating. — *adj* **reit'erate** or **reit'erated**. — *adv* **reit'eratedly**. — *n* **reiterā'tion** act of reiterating; the printing of the second side of a sheet. — *adj* **reit'erative**. — *n* a word expressing reiteration of utterance or act; a word formed by reduplication, the second element *usu* differing from the first (eg *helter-skelter*). [**re-**]

reive and **reiver**. Same as **reave** and **reaver**.

reject *ri-jekt', vt* to throw away; to discard; to refuse to accept, admit or accede to; to refuse; to renounce; (of the body) not to accept tissue, a transplanted organ, etc from another source (*med*). — *n* (*usu rē*) a person who or that which is rejected; an imperfect article, not

Some words with the prefix **re-**.

rēfū'sion *n*.	**rēgrade'** *vt*.	**rēgroup'** *vt*.
rēgath'er *vt* and *vi*.	**rēgrant'** *n* and *vt*.	**rēgrowth'** *n*.
rēgive' *vt*.	**rēgrind'** *vt*.	**rēhand'le** *vt*.

accepted for export, normal sale, etc, and often offered for sale at a discount. — *adj* **rejec'table** or **rejec'tible**. — *n pl* **rejectamen'ta** refuse; excrement. — *n* **rejec'tion**. — *adj* **rejec'tionist** (of a policy, attitude, etc) rejecting or clearly inclined towards rejection of eg an offer, proposal or (*esp* peace) plan; *specif* refusing to accept peace with Israel. — Also *n*. — *adj* **rejec'tive** tending to reject. — *n* **reject'or** or **reject'er**. [L *rejicere*, *rejectum*, from *re-* back, and *jacere* to throw]

rejig, re-jig *rē-jig'* or **rejigger** *-jig'ər*, *vt* to re-equip; to change or rearrange in a new or unexpected way that is sometimes regarded as unethical (*commerce*). — *n* **re'jig** or **re'-jig**.

rejoice *ri-jois'*, *vt* to make joyful (*archaic*); to gladden; to be joyful because of (*Shakesp*). — *vi* to feel joy (*archaic*); to exult; to make merry. — *adj* **rejoice'ful**. — *n* **rejoice'ment** rejoicing. — *n* **rejoic'er**. — *n* **rejoic'ing** act of being joyful; expression, subject or experience of joy; (in *pl*) festivities, celebrations, merry-makings. — *adv* **rejoic'ingly**. — **rejoice in** to be happy because of; to have (*facetious*). [OFr *resjoir*, *resjoiss-* (Fr *réjouir*), from L *re-*, *ex* and *gaudēre* to rejoice]

rejoin[1] *ri-join'*, (*law*) *vi* to reply to a charge or pleading, *esp* to a plaintiff's replication. — *vt* to say in reply, retort. — *n* **rejoin'der** (*ri-*) the defendant's answer to a plaintiff's replication (*law*); an answer to a reply; an answer, *esp* a sharp or clever one. [OFr *rejoindre*]

rejoin[2] *ri* or *rē-join'*, *vt* and *vi* to join again. — *n* **rejoin'dure** (*Shakesp* **reioyn'dure**) a joining again. **[re-]**

rejón *re-hhōn'*, (*Sp*) *n* a lance with a wooden handle, used in bullfighting: — *pl* **rejo'nes**. — *n* **rejoneador** (*re-hhōn-ā-ad-ör'* or *-ōr*) a mounted bullfighter who uses rejones: — *pl* **rejoneador'es**: — *fem* **rejoneador'a**. — *n* **rejoneo** (*re-hhōn-ā'ō*) the art of bullfighting on horseback using rejones.

rejourn *ri-jûrn'*, (*Shakesp*) *vt* to postpone, defer. [Cf **adjourn**]

rejuvenate *ri-jōō'vi-nāt*, *vt* to make young again; to restore to youthful condition or appearance or to activity; to restore (by uplift) to an earlier condition of active erosion (*geol*). — *vi* to rejuvenesce. — *n* **rejuvenā'tion**. — *n* **reju'venator**. — *vi* **rejuvenesce** (*-es'*) to grow young again; to recover youthful character; to undergo change in cell-contents to a different, *usu* more active, character (*biol*); to resume growth. — *vt* to rejuvenate. — *n* **rejuvenesc'ence**. — *adj* **rejuvenesc'ent**. — *vt* **reju'venize** or **-ise** to rejuvenate. **[re-** and L *juvenis* young, from *juvenēscere* to become young]

reke *rēk*, (*Spenser*) *vi* to reck. [OE *rēcan*]

rel. *abbrev*: related; relating; relation; relative.

relâche *rə-läsh*, (*Fr*) *n* relaxation; rest; no performance.

relapse *ri-laps'*, *vi* to slide, sink or fall back, *esp* into evil or illness; to return to a former state or practice; to backslide; to fall away. — *n* a falling back into a former bad state; the return of a disease after partial recovery (*med*). — *adj* **relapsed'** having relapsed. — *n* **relap'ser**. — *adj* **relap'sing**. — **relapsing fever** an infectious disease characterized by recurrent attacks of fever with enlargement of the spleen, caused by a spirochaete transmitted by ticks and lice. [L *relābī*, *relāpsus*, from *lābī* to slide]

relate *ri-lāt'*, *vt* to recount, narrate, tell; to give an account of (*Milton*); to bring back (*Spenser*); to refer, bring into connection or relation. — *vi* to date back in application (*law*); to have reference or relation; to connect; to get on well (with) (often with *to*; *colloq*); to discourse (*Shakesp*). — *adj* **relā'ted** narrated; referred (to) (*rare*); connected; allied by blood or marriage (also *fig*). — *n* **relā'tedness**. — *n* **relā'ter** a person who relates. — *n* **relā'tion** act of relating; state or mode of being related; narrative or recital; statement; an information (*law*); way in which one thing is connected with another; a quality that can be predicated, not of a single thing, but only of two or more together (*philos*); respect, reference; a relative by birth or marriage; (in *pl*) mutual dealings; (in *pl*) sexual intercourse (*euphem*). — *adj* **relā'tional** relating to, expressing, or of the nature of relation, *esp* syntactic relation in grammatical structures. — *adv* **relā'tionally**. — *n* **relā'tionism** (*philos*) the doctrine that relations have an objective existence; the doctrine of relativity of knowledge. — *n* **relā'tionist**. — *adj* **relā'tionless** kinless; unrelated. — *n* **relā'tionship** a state or mode of being related; relations; an emotional or sexual affair. — *adj* **relatival** (*rel-ə-tī'vl*) pertaining to relation, *esp* grammatical relation. — *adj* **rel'ative** (*-ə-tiv*) in or having relation; correlative; corresponding; having the same key-signature (*music*); relevant; comparative; not absolute or independent; relating, having reference (to); referring to an antecedent (*gram*). — *n* that which is relative; a relative word, *esp* a relative pronoun; a person who is related by blood or marriage. — *adv* **rel'atively**. — *n* **rel'ativeness**. — *n* **rel'ativism** relationism; a doctrine of relativity; the view that accepted standards of right and good vary with environment and from person to person. — *n* **rel'ativist**. — *adj* **relativis'tic** relating to relativity, or to relativism. — *n* **relativ'itist** a person who studies or accepts relativity. — *n* **relativ'ity** state or fact of being relative; (in *pl*) related aspects of pay, working conditions, etc between different jobs or the same job in different areas; a principle which asserts that only relative, not absolute, motion can be detected in the universe (Einstein's **Special Theory of Relativity**, 1905, starts from two fundamental postulates: a. that all motion is relative, b. that the velocity of light is always constant relative to an observer; his **General Theory of Relativity**, 1916, which embraces the Special Theory, deals with varying velocities or accelerations, whereas the Special Theory dealt with constant relative velocity, or zero acceleration, and it is much concerned with gravitation; in each case Einstein derived important equations and made predictions). — *vt* and *vi* **rel'ativize** or **-ise** to make or become relative. — *n* **relator** (*ri-lā'tər*) a person who relates; a narrator; a person who lays an information before the Attorney-General, enabling him to take action (*law*). — **relative abundance** a rough measure of population density, eg number of birds seen per hour, or the percentage of sample plots occupied by a species of plant (*ecol*); see **abundance** (*phys*); **relative aperture** (in a camera) the ratio of the diameter of the lens to the focal length *usu* expressed as the *f-number*; **relative atomic mass** the inferred weight of an atom of an element relatively to that of oxygen as 16 or, more recently, carbon-12 taken as 12; **relative density** the weight of any given substance as compared with the weight of an equal bulk or volume of water or other standard substance at the same, or at standard, temperature and pressure; **relative humidity** the ratio of the amount of water vapour in the air to the amount that would saturate it at the same temperature; **relative molecular mass** weight of a molecule relatively to that of an atom of carbon-12 taken as 12. — **relativity of knowledge** the doctrine that the nature and extent of our knowledge is determined not merely by the qualities of the objects known but necessarily by the conditions of our cognitive powers. [L *relātus*, *-a*, *-um*, used as pa p of *referre* to bring back, from *re* and *ferre*]

relative, etc. See under **relate**.

Some words with the prefix **re-**.

rēhand'ling *n*.	**rēheel'** *vt*.	**rēillume'** *vt*.
rēhang' *vt*: — *pa t* and *pa p* **rēhung'**.	**rēhȳdrā'tion** *n*.	**rēillum'ine** *vt*.
	rē-ignite' *vt*.	**rēimport'** *vt*.

relaunch *rē-lönch'* or *rē-lönsh'*, *vt* to reintroduce (a product or service) to the market, *usu* with some change to the item or its marketing. — Also *n* (*rē'lonch* or *rē'lonsh*). [**re-**]

relax *ri-laks'*, *vt* and *vi* to loosen; to slacken; to make or become less close, tense, rigid, strict or severe. — *n* a relaxing. — *adj* and *n* **relax'ant** laxative (*archaic*); (a substance) having the effect of relaxing. — *n* **relaxā'tion** (*re-* or *rē-*) the act of relaxing; the state of being relaxed; partial remission (*law*); release from outlawry (*Scots law*); recreation. — *adj* **relax'ative**. — *n* **relax'in** a hormone which has a relaxing effect on the pelvic muscles, and is used to facilitate childbirth. — *adj* **relax'ing** enervating. [L *relaxāre*, *-ātum*, from *laxus* loose]

relay[1] *ri-lā'*, also *rē'lā* or *rē'lā'*, *n* a fresh set of dogs in hunting (*archaic*); a supply of horses, etc to relieve others on a journey; a station for either of these; a relieving shift of men; a supplementary store of anything; a relay-race, or one of its stages; an electrically-operated switch employed to effect changes in an independent circuit; any device by which a weak electric current or other small power is used to control a strong one; a relayed programme, or act or fact of relaying it. — *vt* to place in, relieve, control, supply or transmit by relay; to rebroadcast (a programme received from another station or source). — *vi* to obtain a relay; to operate a relay: — *pa t* and *pa p* **relayed**. — **re'lay-race** a race between teams, each person running part of the total distance. [OFr *relais* relay of horses or dogs; origin obscure]

relay[2] *rē-lā'*, *vt* to lay again: — *pa t* and *pa p* **rēlaid'**. [**re-**]

rel.d *abbrev*: relative density.

release[1] *rē-lēs'*, *vt* to grant a new lease of. [Pfx **re-**]

release[2] *ri-lēs'*, *vt* to let loose; to set free; to let go; to relieve; to slacken; to undo; to remit; to relinquish; to surrender, convey, give up a right to (*law*); to make available, authorize sale, publication, exhibition, etc of; to make available for public knowledge. — *n* a setting free; liberation; discharge or acquittance; remission; mode of releasing; the giving up of a claim, conveyance; a catch for holding and releasing; authorization to make available on a certain date; a thing so made available; a film, video, gramophone record or other recording made available for sale by its production company (*esp* as *new release*). — *adj* **releas'able**. — *n* **releasee'** a person to whom an estate is released. — *n* **release'ment** release. — *n* **releas'er**. — *n* **releas'or** (*law*). [OFr *relaissier*, from L *relaxāre* to relax]

relegate *rel'i-gāt*, *vt* to banish; to consign (to a, *usu* unimportant, place or position); to remove to a lower league (*football*); to assign (to a class); to refer (to another or others) for decision or action; to refer (a person, for something, to another; *archaic*). — *adj* **rel'egable**. — *n* **relegā'tion**. [L *relēgāre*, *-ātum*, from *re-* away, and *lēgāre* to send]

relent *ri-lent'*, *vi* to melt (*obs*); to soften, become less severe; to give way (*Spenser* and *Milton*); to abate, slacken (*Spenser*); to slacken pace (*Spenser*). — *vt* to melt (*obs*); to soften, cause to relent (*Spenser* and *Burns*); to relax, moderate (*Spenser*); to slow down (*Spenser*); to regret, repent (*Spenser*). — *n* relenting; slowing (*Spenser*). — *n* and *adj* **relent'ing**. — *adj* **relent'less** unrelenting; inexorable; merciless, stern. — *adv* **relent'lessly**. — *n* **relent'lessness**. — *n* **relent'ment** (*rare*). [L *re-* back, and *lentus* sticky, sluggish, pliant]

relevant *rel'i-vənt*, *adj* bearing upon or applying to, the matter in hand, pertinent; related, proportional (to); sufficient legally. — *n* **rel'evance** or **rel'evancy**. — *adv* **rel'evantly**. [L *relevāns*, *-antis*, pr p of *relevāre* to raise up, relieve; from the notion of helping; cf **relieve**]

reliable, **reliant**, etc. See under **rely**.

relic *rel'ik*, *n* that which is left after loss or decay of the rest; a corpse (*usu* in *pl*; *archaic*); any personal memorial of a saint, held in reverence as an incentive to faith and piety (*RC*); a souvenir; a memorial of antiquity or object of historic interest; anything, such as a custom, that is a survival from the past. — Also (*archaic*) **rel'ique**. — **rel'ic-monger** a person who deals in or collects relics. [Fr *relique*, from L *reliquiae*; see **reliquiae**]

relict *rel'ikt*, *n* a relic (*obs*); a survivor or surviving trace (*archaic*); a widow (*archaic*); a species occurring in circumstances different from those in which it originated (*ecol*). — *adj* (*ri-likt'*) left behind; surviving; formed by removal of surrounding materials (*geol*). [L *relictus*, *-a*, *-um* left, pa p of *relinquere* to leave]

relide *ri-līd'*, (*Spenser*) for **relied**, *pa p* of *vt* (*obs*) **relie** to assemble, collect together. [**rely**]

relied and **relier**. See under **rely**.

relief *ri-lēf'*, *n* the lightening or removal of any burden, discomfort, evil, pressure or stress; release from a post or duty; a person who releases another by taking his or her place; that which relieves or mitigates; aid in danger, *esp* deliverance from siege; assistance to the poor; fresh supply of provisions; feeding or seeking food (*hunting*; *obs*); a certain fine paid to the overlord by a feudal tenant's heir on coming into possession (*hist*); release from obligation, or right to reimbursement of expenses thereby incurred (*Scots law*); anything that gives diversity; projection or standing out from the general surface, ground or level; a sculpture or other work of art executed in relief; appearance of standing out solidly; distinctness by contrast, *esp* in outline. — *adj* providing relief in cases of overloading, distress, danger or difficulty. — *adj* **relief'less**. — **Relief Church** a body that left the Church of Scotland because of oppressive exercise of patronage, organized in 1761, united with the United Secession Church in 1847 to form the United Presbyterian Church; **relief map** a map in which the form of the country is shown by elevations and depressions of the material used, or by the illusion of such elevations and depressions, or (loosely) by other means. [OFr *relef*, from *relever*; see **relieve**, also **rilievo**]

relieve *ri-lēv'*, *vt* to lift up (*Shakesp*); to bring, give or afford relief to; to release; to release from duty by taking the place of; to ease (eg a burden); (*reflexive*) to urinate or to defecate; to mitigate; to raise the siege of; to set off by contrast; to break the sameness of; to bring into relief; to feed (*obs*). — *adj* **reliev'able**. — *n* **reliev'er**. — *adj* **reliev'ing**. — **relieving arch** an arch in a wall to relieve the part below it from a superincumbent weight; **relieving officer** (*hist*) an official formerly appointed to superintend the relief of the poor. — **relieve someone of** to take from someone's possession, with or without that person's approval; to steal from someone; to free someone from (a necessity, restriction, etc). [OFr *relever*, from L *relevāre* to lift, relieve, from *levāre* to raise, from *levis* light]

relievo *ri-lē'vō*, also (from *Ital*) **rilievo** *rē-lyā'vō*, (*art*) *n* relief; a work in relief; appearance of relief: — *pl* **relie'vos** or **rilie'vi** (*-vē*). [Ital *rilievo*]

religieux *rə-lē-zhyø*, (*Fr*) *n* a monk or friar: — *fem* **religieuse** (*-zhyœz*) a nun.

religio- *re-lij'i-ō-*, *combining form* denoting: relating to religion or religious matters.

Some words with the prefix **re-**.

rēimpose' *vt.*	**rēindustrialīzā'tion** or **-s-** *n.*	**rēinhab'it** *vt.*
rēimposi'tion *n.*	**rēindus'trialize** or **-ise** *vt* and *vi.*	**rēinsert'** *vt.*
rēincrease' *vt.*	**rēinfuse'** *vt.*	**rēinser'tion** *n.*

religion *ri-lij'ən, n* belief in, recognition of or an awakened sense of a higher unseen controlling power or powers, with the emotion and morality connected with such; rites or worship; any system of such belief or worship; devoted fidelity; monastic life; a monastic order; Protestantism (*obs*). — *adj* **relig'ionary** (*rare*) religious. — *n* a member of a religious order; a Protestant (*obs*). — *n* **relig'ioner** a member of an order; a Protestant (*obs*). — *n* **relig'ionism** religiosity; bigotry. — *n* **relig'ionist** a person attached to a religion; a bigot; someone professionally engaged in religion, eg an evangelist (*US*). — *vt* **relig'ionize** or **-ise** to imbue with religion. — *vi* to make profession of being religious. — *adj* **relig'ionless**. — *adj* **religiose** (*-lij'i-ōs* or *-ōs'*) morbidly or sentimentally religious. — *n* **religiosity** (*-i-os'it-i*) spurious or sentimental religion; religious feeling. — *adj* **relig'ious** (*-əs*) of, concerned with, devoted to or imbued with religion; scrupulous; bound to a monastic life (*RC*); strict, very exact. — *n* a person bound by monastic vows. — *adv* **relig'iously**. — *n* **relig'iousness**. [L *religiō, -ōnis*, n, *religiōsus*, adj, perh connected with *religāre* to bind]

religiose, etc. See under **religion**.

religioso *rə-lij-i-ō'sō*, (*Ital*) *adj* and *adv* in a devotional manner (*music*).

reline *rē-līn'*, *vt* to mark with new lines; to renew the lining of. [**re-**]

relinquish *ri-ling'kwish*, *vt* to give up; to let go. — *n* **relin'quishment**. [OFr *relinquir*, *relinquiss-*, from L *relinquere*, *relictum*, from pfx *re-*, and *linquere* to leave]

relique *rel'ik* or *ri-lēk'*, *n* an archaic form of **relic**. — *n* **reliquaire** (*rel-i-kwār'*) or **rel'iquary** (*-kwər-i*) a receptacle for relics. — *adj* **rel'iquary** of relics; residual. [Fr]

reliquiae *ri-lik'wi-ē* or *re-lik'wi-ī*, *n pl* remains, *esp* fossil remains. [L, from *relinquere* to leave]

relish[1] *rel'ish*, *n* a flavour; characteristic flavour; enough to give a flavour; appetizing flavour; zest-giving quality or power; an appetizer, condiment; zestful enjoyment; gusto; pleasureful inclination. — *vt* to like the taste of; to be pleased with; to enjoy; to appreciate discriminatingly; to give a relish to; to taste, experience (*obs*). — *vi* to savour, smack; to have an agreeable taste; to give pleasure. — *adj* **rel'ishable**. [OFr *reles*, *relais* remainder, from *relaisser* to leave behind]

relish[2] or **rellish** *rel'ish*, *n* a musical ornament. — *vt* (*Shakesp*) to warble. [Origin obscure]

relive *rē-liv'*, *vt* and *vi* to live again; (*rē-līv'*) to revive (*Spenser*).

reliver *ri-liv'ər*, (*Shakesp*) *vt* to deliver back. [OFr *relivrer*; also **re-** and *liver* to deliver, *obs* and *dialect*]

rellish. See **relish[2]**.

relocate *rē-lō-kāt'*, *vt* to locate again; to move (a firm, workers, etc) to a different area or site. — *vi* to move one's place of business or residence. — *n* **relocā'tion**. [**re-**]

relucent *ri-lū'* or *ri-lōō'sənt*, (*archaic*) *adj* reflecting; shining. [L *relūcēns, -entis*, pr p of *relūcēre* to shine back]

reluct *ri-lukt'*, (*archaic*) *vi* to be unwilling (with *at*); to hold back. — *n* **reluc'tance** opposition, resistance (*Milton*); unwillingness; magnetomotive force applied to whole or part of a magnetic circuit divided by the flux in it. — *n* **reluc'tancy**. — *adj* **reluc'tant** struggling (*Milton*); unwilling; resisting. — *adv* **reluct'antly**. — *vi* **reluct'āte** to be reluctant. — *n* **reluctā'tion** (*rel-*) repugnance (*archaic*). [L *reluctārī*, from *re-* against, and *luctārī* to struggle]

relume *ri-lūm'* or *-lōōm'*, (*archaic*) *vt* to light or light up again; to rekindle. — *vt* (*archaic*) **relu'mine** (*-in*) to relume. [L *relūmināre*, from *lūmen, -inis* light]

rely *ri-lī'*, *vi* to rally (*obs*); to rest as on a support (*obs*); to depend confidently (on or upon): — *pr p* **rely'ing**; *pa t* and *pa p* **relied'**. — *n* **reliabil'ity**. — *adj* **relī'able** to be relied on, trustworthy. — *n* **relī'ableness**. — *adv* **relī'ably**. — *n* **relī'ance** trust; that in which one trusts. — *adj* **relī'ant**. — *n* **relī'er** (*Shakesp*). — **reliability test** or **trial** a public test of the qualities of motor vehicles (now known as a **rally**); **reliance loss** (*law*) the loss incurred by the plaintiff in a breach of contract action due to relying on the defendant's promise to enter into the contract. [OFr *relier*, from L *religāre* to bind back]

REM *rem*, *abbrev*: rapid eye movement. — **REM sleep** any of the phases of sleep accompanied by rapid eye movement.

rem *rem*, *n* a unit of radiation dosage, the amount which has the same effect as one rad of X-radiation. [*r*öntgen *e*quivalent *m*an or *m*ammal]

remain *ri-mān'*, *vi* to stay or be left behind; to continue in the same place; to dwell, abide (*Shakesp*); to be left after or out of a greater number; to continue in one's possession or mind; to continue unchanged; to continue to be; to be still to be dealt with (often without subject *it*); to await (*Spenser* and *Milton*). — *n* stay, abode (*Shakesp*); a surviving part (*archaic*). — *n* **remain'der** that which remains or is left behind after the removal of a part or after division; the residue, rest; balance of an account (*Shakesp*); an interest in an estate to come into effect after a certain other event happens (*law*); right of next succession to a post or title; residue of an edition when the sale of a book has fallen off. — *adj* (*Shakesp*) left over. — *vt* to sell (a book) as a remainder. — *n pl* **remains'** (occasionally with *sing* verb) that which is left; relics; a corpse; the literary productions of a dead person. — **remain'der-man** a person to whom a legal remainder is devised. [OFr *remaindre*, from L *remanēre*, from *re-* back, and *manēre* to stay]

remake *rē-māk'*, *vt* to make anew. — *adj* **rēmade'**. — *n* **rēmade'** or **rēmake'** a thing (eg a gutta golf ball) made over again from the original materials; (**rē'make**) something made again, *esp* (a new version of) a film. [**re-**]

remand *ri-mänd'*, *vt* to send back (*esp* a prisoner into custody or on bail to await further evidence). — *n* act of remanding; recommittal. — **remand centre** in the UK, a place of detention for those on remand or awaiting trial; **remand home** formerly a place where young people were detained as punishment. — **on remand** having been remanded. [OFr *remander*, or LL *remandāre*, from *mandāre* to order]

remanent *rem'ən-ənt*, *adj* remaining. — *n* a remainder; a remnant. — *n* **rem'anence** something that remains, *esp* (*phys*) the magnetization after an exciting magnetic field has been removed from ferromagnetic materials. — *n* **rem'anency**. — *n* **rem'anet** a remainder; a postponed case or parliamentary bill. [L *remanēns, -entis*, pr p, and *remanet*, 3rd pers sing pres indicative of *remanēre*]

remanié *rə-mä-nyā*, (*geol*) *n* a fossil or other relic of an older rock preserved as a fragment in a later deposit. [Fr, pa p of *remanier* to rehandle]

remark[1] *ri-märk'*, *vt* to mark out (*Milton*); to notice; to comment (that), or say incidentally (that). — *vi* to comment, make an observation (often with *on* or *upon*). — *n* noteworthiness; observation; comment; (also as Fr, **remarque'**) a marginal drawing or other distinguishing mark on an engraving or etching indicating an early state of the plate; a plate, print or proof bearing this special remark. — *adj* **remark'able** noteworthy; unusual, singular, strange, distinguished. — *n*

Some words with the prefix **re-**.

rēinspect' *vt.*	**rēinspir'it** *vt.*	**rēinter'pret** *vt.*
rēinspec'tion *n.*	**rēinter'** *vt.*	**rēinterpretā'tion** *n.*
rēinspire' *vt.*	**rēinter'ment** *n.*	**rēinter'pretative** *adj.*

a remarkable thing. — *n* **remark'ableness**. — *adv* **remark'ably**. — *adj* **remarked'** conspicuous; (also **remarqued'**) bearing a remark (eg of an etching). — *n* **remark'er**. [OFr *remarquer*, from *re-* (intensive) and *marquer* to mark]

remark[2] or **re-mark** *rē-märk'*, *vt* to mark again, *esp* in an examination. — *n* the act or an instance of marking something again. [**re-**]

remarque. See **remark**[1].

remaster *rē-mäs'tər*, *vt* to make a new master recording of. [**re-**]

rematch *rē'mach*, (*sport*) *n* a second match or return match. — Also *vt* (*rē-mach'*). [**re-**]

remblai *rã-ble*, *n* earth used to form a rampart, embankment, etc; stowage in a mine. [Fr]

remble *rem'bl* or *rem'l*, (*NE Eng*) *vt* to remove, clear. [Origin obscure]

Rembrandtesque *rem-bran-tesk'* or *-brən-*, *adj* like the work of *Rembrandt* (1606–69), *esp* in his contrast of high lights and deep shadows. — *adj* **Rem'brandtish**. — *n* **Rem'brandtism**.

REME *rē'mi*, *abbrev*: Royal Electrical and Mechanical Engineers.

remead. See **remedy**.

remeasure *rē-mezh'ər*, *vt* to measure anew; to retrace (*Spenser*). — *n* **remeas'urement**. [**re-**]

remedy *rem'i-di*, *obs* and *Scot* **remede**, **remeid** or **remead** (*ri-mēd'*), *n* any means of curing a disease, redressing, counteracting or repairing any evil or loss; reparation; redress; range of tolerated variation in the weight of a coin. — *vt* to cure (a person or diseased part) (*archaic*); to put right, repair, counteract: — *pr p* **rem'edying**; *pa t* and *pa p* **rem'edied**. — *adj* **remē'diable**. — *adv* **remē'diably**. — *adj* **remē'dial** tending or intended to remedy; of or concerning the teaching of slow-learning children. — *adv* **remē'dially**. — *adj* **remē'diat** or **remē'diate** (*Shakesp*) remedial. — *n* **remediā'tion**. — *adj* **rem'ediless** (formerly *-med'*) without remedy; incurable. — *adv* **rem'edilessly** (or *-med'*). — *n* **rem'edilessness** (or *-med'*). — **no remedy** (*Shakesp*) of necessity; **what remedy**? (*obs*) how can it be helped or avoided? [Anglo-Fr *remedie*, OFr *remede*, from L *remedium*]

remember *ri-mem'bər*, *vt* to keep in or recall to memory or mind; to mention, record (*obs*); to commemorate (*obs*); to bear in mind as something to be mentioned (*Shakesp*); to bear in mind as someone or something deserving of honour or gratitude, or as someone to be rewarded, tipped or prayed for; to remind (*archaic* or *dialect*); to recollect (*reflexive*; *Shakesp*); to occur to (*impers*; *archaic*); to regain one's good manners after a temporary lapse (*reflexive*); to recall to the memory of another (often as a greeting). — *vi* to have the power or perform the act of memory; to have memory (with *of*; *Shakesp* and *Milton*; now *Scot* and *US*). — *adj* **remem'berable**. — *adv* **remem'berably**. — *n* **remem'berer**. — *n* **remem'brance** memory; that which serves to bring to or keep in mind; a reminder; a souvenir; a memorandum; a memorial; the reach of memory; (in *pl*) a message of friendly greeting. — *n* **remem'brancer** a person who or thing which reminds; a recorder; an officer of exchequer responsible for collecting debts due to the Crown (**King's** or **Queen's Remembrancer**); an official representative of the City of London to Parliamentary committees, etc. — **Remembrance Sunday** the Sunday nearest to 11 November commemorating the fallen of the two World Wars (see **Armistice Day**). — **remember your courtesy** (*obs*) remember to put your hat on, which you have taken off in courtesy. [OFr *remembrer*, from L *re-* again, and *memor* mindful]

remen *rē'mən*, *n* a unit of measurement used by the ancient Egyptians (equivalent to 524cm or 20.62in), also known as a *royal cubit*. [Ancient Egyp]

remercy *ri-mûr'si*, (*obs*) *vt* to thank: — *pa t* (*Spenser*) **remer'cied**. [(O)Fr *remercier*]

remerge *rē-mûrj'*, *vt* to merge again. [**re-**]

remex *rē'meks*, *n* any of the large feathers of a bird's wing, either primary or secondary: — *pl* **remiges** (*rem'i-jēz*). — *vi* **remigate** (*rem'i-gāt*; *rare*) *to row*. — *n* **remigā'tion**. — *adj* **remigial** (*ri-mij'i-əl*). [L *rēmex*, *-igis* a rower]

remigrate *rem'i-grāt*, *vi* to change back; (also *rē-mī-grāt'*) to migrate again or back. — *n* **remigrā'tion** (*rem-i-* or *rē-mī-*). [**re-**]

remind *ri-mīnd'*, *vt* to put in mind (of), to cause to remember. — *n* **remind'er** that which reminds. — *adj* **remind'ful** mindful; reminiscent, prompting memories. [**re-** and **mind** *vt*]

remineralize or **-ise** *rē-min'ər-əl-īz*, (*med*) *vi* (of bone) to regain depleted minerals, eg calcium. — *n* **remineralizā'tion** or **-s-**. [**re-**]

reminiscence *rem-i-nis'əns*, *n* recollection; an account of something remembered; the recurrence to the mind of the past. — *vi* **reminisce** (*-nis'*; back-formation) to recount reminiscences. — *adj* **reminisc'ent** suggestive, remindful; addicted to reminiscences; pertaining to reminiscence. — Also *n*. — *adj* **reminiscen'tial** (*-sen'shl*) of or of the nature of reminiscence. — *adv* **reminisc'ently**. [L *reminīscēns*, *-entis*, pr p of *reminīscī* to remember]

remise *ri-mīz'*, *n* surrender of a claim (*law*); (*rə-mēz'*) an effective second thrust after the first has missed (*fencing*); a coach-house (*obs*); a livery-carriage (*obs*). — *vt* (*ri-mīz'*) to surrender. [Fr *remis*, *remise*, from *remettre*, from L *remittere* to send back, remit, relax]

remiss *ri-mis'*, *adj* negligent; slack; lax; lacking vigour. — *n* **remissibil'ity**. — *adj* **remiss'ible** that may be remitted. — *n* **remission** (*ri-mish'ən*) the or an act of remitting; slackening; abatement; relinquishment of a claim; the lessening of a term of imprisonment; pardon; forgiveness. — *adj* **remiss'ive** remitting; forgiving. — *adv* **remiss'ly**. — *n* **remiss'ness**. — *adj* **remiss'ory** of remission. [L *remittere*, *remissum*; see **remit**]

remit *ri-mit'*, *vt* to relax; to pardon (*archaic*); to refrain from exacting or inflicting; to give up; to desist from; to transfer; to transmit (money, etc); to put again in custody; to refer to another court or authority, etc; to refer for information; to send or put back. — *vi* (*esp* of pain, an illness, etc) to abate; to relax; to desist: — *pr p* **remitt'ing**; *pa t* and *pa p* **remitt'ed**. — *n* (*rē'mit* or *ri-mit'*) reference of a case or matter to another (*law*); scope, terms of reference; a matter submitted (to a conference or other body) for consideration (*politics*, *esp NZ*) — *n* **remit'ment** remission; remitting; remittance. — *n* **remitt'al** remission; reference to another court, etc. — *n* **remitt'ance** the sending of money, etc to a distance; the sum or thing sent. — *n* **remittee** (*-ē'*) the person to whom a remittance is sent. — *adj* **remitt'ent** remitting at intervals. — *adv* **remitt'ently**. — *n* **remitt'er** or **remitt'or** a person who makes a remittance. — **remitt'ance-man** a man dependent upon remittances from home; **remittent fever** a severe type of malaria in which the temperature falls slightly from time to time. [L *remittere*, *remissum*, from *re-* back, and *mittere* to send]

remnant *rem'nənt*, *n* a fragment or a small number surviving or remaining after destruction, defection, removal, sale, etc of the greater part; *esp* a remaining piece of cloth; a tag or quotation; a surviving trace; trace of a fact (*Scott*). — *adj* remanent, remaining. [**remanent**]

Some words with the prefix **re-**.

rēinterr'ogate *vt*.	**rēintroduc'tion** *n*.	**rēiss'ue** *vt* and *n*.
rēinterrogā'tion *n*.	**rēinvolve'** *vt*.	**rējudge'** *vt*.
rēintroduce' *vt*.	**rēiss'uable** *adj*.	**rēkin'dle** *vt* and *vi*.

remonetize or **-ise** *rē-mun'ə-tīz* or *-mon'*, *vt* to re-establish as legal tender. — *n* **remonetīzā'tion** or **-s-**. [**re-**]

remonstrance *ri-mon'strəns*, *n* a strong or formal protest, expostulation. — *adj* **remon'strant** remonstrating; (with *cap*) Dutch Arminian. — *n* a person who remonstrates; (with *cap*) a Protester (*Scot hist*); (with *cap*) a member of the Dutch Arminian party whose divergence from Calvinism was expressed in five articles in the Remonstrance of 1610. — *adv* **remon'strantly**. — *vi* **rem'onstrāte** (earlier *-mon'*) to make a remonstrance. — *vt* to say or (*obs*) state in remonstrance; to demonstrate (*obs*). — *adv* **rem'onstratingly**. — *n* **remonstrā'tion** (*rem-ən-*). — *adj* **remon'strative** or **remon'stratory** (*-strə-tər-i*) expostulatory. — *n* **rem'onstrator** (or *-mon'*). — **Grand Remonstrance** a statement of abuses presented to Charles I by the House of Commons in 1641. [L *re-* again, and *mōnstrāre* to point out]

remontant *ri-mon'tənt*, *adj* (of a plant) flowering more than once in the same season. — *n* a remontant plant, *esp* a rose. [Fr]

remora *rem'ə-rə*, *n* the sucking-fish, formerly believed to stop ships by attaching its sucker; an obstacle (*fig*). [L *remora* delay, hindrance, from *mora* delay]

remoralize or **-ise** *rē-mor'əl-īz*, *vt* to restore morality to. — *n* **remoralizā'tion** or **-s-**. [**re-**]

remorse *ri-mörs'*, *n* feeling of regret and guilt for past wrongdoing; compunction; pity, compassionate feeling (*Spenser*, *Shakesp* and *Milton*); mitigation (*Shakesp*); *prob* matter of conscience (*Shakesp*); bite (*Spenser*). — *adj* **remorse'ful** penitent; compassionate (*obs*). — *adv* **remorse'fully**. — *n* **remorse'fulness**. — *adj* **remorse'less** without remorse; cruel; without respite. — *adv* **remorse'lessly**. — *n* **remorse'lessness**. [OFr *remors* (Fr *remords*), from LL *remorsus*, from L *remordēre*, *remorsum* to bite again, from *re-* again, and *mordēre* to bite]

remote *ri-mōt'*, *adj* far removed in place, time, chain of causation or relation, resemblance or relevance; widely separated; very indirect; located separately from the main processor but having a communication link with it (*comput*). — *n* an outside broadcast (*TV* and *radio*, *esp US*) — *adv* **remote'ly**. — *n* **remote'ness**. — *n* **remō'tion** removal (*Shakesp*); remoteness (*rare*). — **remote control** control of a device from a distance by the making or breaking of an electric circuit or by means of radio waves; **remote handling equipment** (*nuc eng*) equipment enabling an operator to manipulate highly radioactive materials from behind a shield or from a safe distance; **remote job entry** (*comput*) input of data or programs to a computer from a distant input device (eg a card reader); **remote sensing** a method in which remote sensors are used to collect data for transmission to a central computer; observation and collection of scientific data without direct contact, *esp* observation of the earth's surface from the air or from space using electromagnetic radiation. [L *remōtus*, pa p of *removēre*; see **remove**]

remoud *ri-mo͞od'*, *pa t* (*Spenser*) for **removed**.

remoulade or **rémoulade** *rā-mo͞o-läd'*, *n* a sauce made with eggs, herbs, capers, etc, or sometimes with mayonnaise, and served with fish, salad, etc. [Fr dialect *ramolas* horseradish, from L *armoracea*]

remould *rē'mōld*, *n* a used tyre which has had a new tread vulcanized to the casing and the walls coated with rubber. — Also *vt* (*rē-mōld'*). — Cf **retread**. [**re-**]

remount *rē-mownt'*, *vt* and *vi* to mount again. — *n* a fresh horse or supply of horses. [**re-**]

remove *ri-mo͞ov'*, *vt* to put or take away; to transfer; to withdraw; to displace; to make away with; (in *passive*; *Thackeray*) of a dish on the table, to be succeeded (by). — *vi* to go away; to move house, change location. — *n* removal; the raising of a siege (*Shakesp*); absence (*Shakesp*); step or degree of remoteness or indirectness; in some schools, an intermediate class; promotion; a dish removed to make way for another, or taking the place of one so removed. — *n* **removabil'ity**. — *adj* **remov'able**. — *adv* **remov'ably**. — *n* **remov'al** the act of taking away; displacing; change of place; transference; going away; change of home or location; murder (*euphem*). — *adj* **removed'** remote; distant by degrees, as in descent or relationship. — *n* **remov'edness**. — *n* **remov'er** a person who or thing which removes; a person employed to convey furniture and other house contents from house to house. — **removal terms** (*Scot*) 28 May and 28 November, called Whitsunday and Martinmas. [OFr *remouvoir*, from L *removēre*, *remōtum*, from *re-* away, and *movēre* to move]

remuage *rə-mü-äzh'* or *-mo͞o-*, *n* the process of turning or shaking wine bottles so that the sediment collects at the cork end for removal. — *n* **remueur** (*rə-mü-œr'* or *-mo͞o-ûr'*) in wine-making, the person who turns the bottles. [Fr, from *remuer* to move or turn]

remuda *ri-mū'də* or *rā-mo͞o'dha*, *n* a supply of remounts. [Sp, exchange]

remunerate *ri-mū'nə-rāt*, *vt* to recompense; to pay for service rendered. — *adj* **remū'nerable**. — *n* **remūnerā'tion** recompense; reward; pay. — *adj* **remū'nerative** profitable. — *n* **remū'nerativeness**. — *n* **remū'nerātor**. — *adj* **remū'neratory** (*-ə-tər-i*) giving a recompense. [L *remunerārī* (late *-āre*), *-ātus*, from *mūnus*, *-eris* a gift]

remurmur *ri-mûr'mər*, *vt* and *vi* to echo, repeat, or resound in murmurs. [**re-**]

ren. See **run**.

renague. See **renegade**.

renaissance *ri-nā'səns*, *ren'i-säns* or *-säns'*, *n* a new birth; (with *cap*) the revival of arts and letters, the transition from the Middle Ages to the modern world. — *adj* of the Renaissance. — **Renaissance man** or **woman** a person who typifies the renaissance ideal of wide-ranging culture and learning. [Fr; cf **renascence**]

renal *rē'nl*, *adj* of the kidneys. [L *rēnālis*, from *rēnēs* (sing *rēn* is rare), the kidneys]

renascent *ri-nas'ənt*, also *-nās'*, *adj* coming into renewed life or vitality. — *n* **renasc'ence** being born anew; (with *cap*) Renaissance. [L *renāscēns*, *-entis*, pr p of *renāscī*, from *nāscī* to be born]

renay, **reney** *ri-nā'* or **reny** *ri-nī'*, (*obs*) *vt* to renounce, abjure, forswear; to deny: — *pr p* **renay'ing** or **reny'ing**; *pa p* **renayed'** or **renied'**. [OFr *renaier*, *renier*, from L *renegāre*]

rencounter *ren-kownt'ər*, or (*Fr*) **rencontre** *rā-kɔ̃-tr'*, *n* a chance meeting; an encounter; a casual combat; a collision; an informal meeting of scientists. — *vt* to meet; to encounter. [Fr *rencontre*]

rend *rend*, *vt* to tear asunder with force; to split; to tear away. — *vi* to become torn: — *pa t* and *pa p* **rent**. [OE *rendan* to tear]

render *ren'dər*, *vt* to give up; to give back, return, give in return; to make up; to deliver; to hand over; to give; to surrender; to yield; to tender or submit; to show forth; to represent or reproduce, *esp* artistically; to perform; to translate; to perform or pay as a duty or service; to present or betake (with *at*; *reflexive*); to cause to be or become; to melt; to extract, treat or clarify by melting; to plaster with a first coat. — *n* an act of rendering; that which is rendered. — *adj* **ren'derable**. — *n* **ren'derer**. — *n* **ren'dering** the action of the verb; a first coat of plaster, etc. — *n* **rendi'tion** surrender; rendering; a performance. [OFr *rendre*,

Some words with the prefix **re-**.

rēlet' *vt*: — *pa t* and *pa p* **rēlet'**.
rēlight' *vt* and *vi*.
rēload' *vt* and *vi*.
rēman' *vt*.
rēmarr'iage *n*.
rēmarr'y *vt* and *vi*.
rē'match *n*.
rēmint' *vt*.

from LL *rendere*, appar formed by influence of *prendere* to take, from L *reddere*, from *re-* back, and *dare* to give]

rendezvous *rä'dä-voo*, or *ron'di-*, *n* appointed meeting-place; a meeting by appointment; a general resort; an arranged meeting, and *usu* docking, of two spacecraft (*space tech*): — *pl* **rendezvous** (*-vooz*) or (*obs*) **rendezvous'es**. — *vi* to assemble at any appointed place: — *pa t* and *pa p* **rendezvoused** (*rä'dä-vood*, or *ron'di-*). [Fr *rendez-vous*, present yourselves, from *rendre* to render]

rendition. See under **render**.

rendzina *ren-dzē'nə*, *n* a fertile soil-type derived from a calcium-rich bedrock and typical of grass or open woodland in humid to semi-arid climates. [Russ, from Pol *redzina*]

renegade *ren'i-gād* or **renegate** *-gāt*, *n* a person who betrays or deserts a principle, party or religion; an apostate; a turncoat; *specif* a Christian convert to Islam. — Also **renegā'do** (or *-ä'dō*; *archaic*): — *pl* **renega'dos**. — *vi* **ren'egade** to turn renegade. — *adj* **ren'egade** or (now *dialect*) **ren'egate** apostate. — *n* **renegā'tion**. — *vt* **renege** or **renegue** (*ri-nēg'*, or *-näg'*) to renounce; to apostatise from. — *vi* to deny (often with *on*); to refuse (often with *on*); to revoke at cards. — Also **renig** (*-nig'*) or **renague** (*-näg'*; *Ir*). — *n* **reneg'er** or **reneg'uer**. [LL *renegātus*, from L *re-* (intensive) and *negāre*, *-ātum* to deny; partly through Sp *renegado*]

renew *ri-nū'*, *vt* to renovate; to transform to new life, revive; to begin again; to repeat; to make again; to invigorate; to substitute new for; to restore; to regenerate; to extend (eg the period of a loan, validity of a lease, etc). — *vi* to be made new; to begin again. — *adj* **renew'able**. — *n* (often in *pl*) any form of renewable energy (see below). — *n* **renew'al** renewing; short form of **urban renewal** (qv under **urban**). — *n* **renew'edness**. — *n* **renew'er**. — *n* **renew'ing**. — **renewable energy** an alternative source of energy, such as waves, wind or sun, that can be considered inexhaustible (also called **alternative energy**). [**re-** and **new** (*adj*)]

reney. See **renay**.

renfierst *ren-fērst'*, (*Spenser*) *pa p* made fierce. [Appar modelled on **renforce**]

renforce *ren-fōrs'* or *-förs'*, (*obs*) *vt* to reinforce; to force again. — *vi* to renew efforts: — (in *Spenser pa t* **re'nforst'**, *pa p* **renforst'**). [(O)Fr *renforcer*]

renga *ren'gə*. Same as **linked verse** (see under **link**[1]).

reni- *rē-ni-*, *combining form* denoting relating to the kidneys. [**renal**]

renied. See **renay**.

reniform *ren'i-förm*, *adj* kidney-shaped. [L *rēnēs* (sing *rēn*) the kidneys, and *fōrma* form: see **renal**]

renig. See **renegue** (under **renegade**).

renin *rē'nin*, *n* a protein enzyme secreted by the kidneys into the bloodstream, where it helps to maintain the blood pressure. [L *rēnēs* (sing *rēn*) the kidneys]

renitent *ri-nī'tənt* or *ren'i-tənt*, (*rare*) *adj* resistant; reluctant; recalcitrant. — *n* **renī'tency** (or *ren'*). [L *renītēns*, *-entis*, pr p of *renītī* to resist]

renminbi *ren-min-bē*, (also with *cap*) *n* the currency of the Peoples' Republic of China since 1948; a Chinese monetary unit, also called **yuan**, equal to 100 fen. [Chin *renmin* the people, and *bi* money]

renne *ren*, (*Spenser*) *vi* to run. — Also *pa p*. — *n* **renn'ing**. [See **run**]

rennet[1] *ren'it*, *n* any means of curdling milk, *esp* a preparation of calf's stomach. — **renn'et-bag** the fourth stomach of a ruminant. [OE *rinnan* to run; cf **earn**[2] and **yearn**[3]]

rennet[2] *ren'it*, *n* an apple of certain old varieties. [Fr *reinette*, *rainette*; origin uncertain]

rennin *ren'in*, *n* an enzyme found in gastric juice, which causes coagulation of milk. [*renn*et]

renormalization or **-s-** *rē-norm-əl-īz-ā'shən*, (*physics*) *n* a method of obtaining finite answers to calculations (rather than infinities) by redefining the parameters, *esp* of mass and charge. — *vt* **renorm'alize** or **-ise** to subject to or calculate using renormalization. [**re-**]

renounce *ri-nowns'*, *vt* to disclaim; to disown; to reject publicly and finally; to recant; to abjure. — *vi* to fail to follow suit at cards. — *n* a failure to follow suit. — *adj* **renounce'able**. — *n* **renounce'ment**. — *n* **renoun'cer**. [OFr *renuncer*, from L *renuntiāre*, from *re-* away, and *nuntiāre*, *-ātum* to announce]

renovate *ren'ō-vāt*, *vt* to renew or make new again; to make as if new; to regenerate. — *n* **renovā'tion**. — *n* **ren'ovātor**. [L *re-* again, and *novāre*, *-ātum* to make new, from *novus* new]

renown *ri-nown'*, *n* fame. — *vt* (*literary*) to make famous; to celebrate. — *adj* **renowned'** famous. — *n* **renown'er** (*Milton*) a person who gives another renown. [OFr *renoun* (Fr *renom*), from L *re-* again, and *nōmen* a name]

rensselaerite *ren'səl-ə-rīt* or *ren-səl-ā'rīt*, *n* a kind of firm-textured talc, used for carved or lathe-turned ornaments. [From Stephen Van *Rensselaer* (1764–1839), N American statesman]

rent[1] *rent*, *n* an opening made by rending; a fissure. — *vt* and *vi* (*obs* or *dialect*) to rend. — Also *pa t* and *pa p* of **rend**. [**rend**]

rent[2] *rent*, *n* periodical payment for use of another's property, *esp* houses and lands; revenue. — *vt* to hold or occupy by paying rent; to let or hire out for a rent; to charge with rent. — *vi* to be let at a rent. — *n* **rentabil'ity**. — *adj* **rent'able**. — *n* **rent'al** a rent-roll; rent; annual value; something rented or hired (*US*); a kindly (qv) tenant's lease (*Scot*). — *n* **rent'aller** (*Scot*) a kindly tenant. — *n* **rent'er** a tenant who pays rent; a person who lets out property; a farmer of tolls or taxes (*hist*); a theatre shareholder (*archaic*); a distributor of commercial films to cinemas. — **rent-a-** or before a vowel **rent-an-** (*facetious*; also without hyphens) *combining form* denoting: (as if) rented or hired, organized for a specific occasion or purpose, instantly or artificially created etc, as in **rent'-a-crowd**, **rent'-a-mob** or **rent'-an-army**. — **rental library** (*US*) a lending-library which takes fees for books borrowed; **rent boy** a young male prostitute; **rent'-charge** a periodical payment charged upon rent; **rent'-collector**; **rent'-day**. — *adj* and *adv* **rent'-free** without payment of rent. — **rent restriction** restriction of a landlord's right to raise rent; **rent roll** a list of property and rents; total income from property. — **for rent** (*orig US*) to let. [Fr *rente*, from L *reddita* (*pecūnia*) money paid, from *reddere* to pay; cf **render**]

rente *rät*, *n* annual income; (in *pl*; *rät*) French or other government securities or income from them. — *n* **rentier** (*rä-tyā*) a fund-holder; a person who has, or who lives on, an income from rents or investments. — Also *adj*. [Fr]

renunciation *ri-nun-si-ā'shən*, *n* the or an act of renouncing; self-resignation. — *adj* **renun'ciative** (*-shə-tiv*, *-syə-tiv* or *-si-ā-tiv*) or **renun'ciatory** (*-shə-tər-i* or *-si-ə-tər-i*). [L *renūntiāre* proclaim; see **nuncio**]

renverse *ren-vûrs'*, (*archaic*) *vt* to reverse; to upset: — *pa t* and *pa p* **renversed'** or **renverst'** (*Spenser*). — *n* **renversement** (*-vûrs'mənt*; *aeronautics*) *specif*, a half-roll and a half-loop in a combined manoeuvre; any aerial manoeuvre involving a reverse in direction of travel. [Fr *renverser*, from pfx *re-* and *enverser* to overturn]

Some words with the prefix **re-**.

remix *vt* (*rē-mix'*) and *n* (*rē'mix*).	**rēmod'ify** *vt*.	**rēnegō'tiable** *adj*.
rēmod'el *vt*.	**remort'gage** *vt* and *n*.	**rēnegō'tiate** *vt*.
	rēname' *vt*.	**rēnegōtiā'tion** *n*.

renvoi or (*esp* formerly) **renvoy** *ren-voi'*, Fr *rã-vwä*, *n* sending back by a government of an alien to his or her own country; a referring or relegation of a legal dispute to another jurisdiction. [Fr]

reny. See **renay**.

reopen *rē-ō'pn*, *vt* and *vi* to open again; to begin again. — **reopening clause** in collective bargaining, a clause enabling any issue in a contract to be reconsidered before the contract expires (also **reopener** or **reopener clause**). [**re-**]

reorient *rē-ō'* or *rē-ö'ri-ənt*, *adj* rising again. — *vt* (*-ent*) to orient again. — *vt* **reō'rientate** to reorient. — *n* **reōrientā'tion**. [**re-**]

rep[1] or **repp** *rep*, *n* a corded cloth. — Also **reps** (*reps*). — *adj* **repped** (*rept*) transversely corded. [Fr *reps*, perh from Eng **ribs**]

rep[2] *rep*, (*colloq*) *n* short form of: repertory (*theat*); repetition (*school*); representative (*esp commerce*); reprobate; reputation (early 18c and *US*).

rep[3] *rep*, *n* a unit of radiation dosage, now superseded by **rad**. [röntgen *e*quivalent *p*hysical]

rep[4] *rep*, *vi* (*commercial jargon*) to work or act as a commercial representative: — *pr p* **repp'ing**; *pa t* and *pa t* **repped**. — *n* **repp'ing**. [**rep**[2], from **represent**]

repaid *pa t* and *pa p* of **repay**.

repaint *rē-pānt'*, *vt* to paint over or again. — *n* (*rē'pānt*) a repainted golf ball. — *n* **repaint'ing**. [**re-**]

repair[1] *ri-pār'*, *vi* to take oneself; to go; to resort; to return (*Shakesp*). — *vt* (*Spenser*) to restore to its position; to withdraw. — *n* resort; place of resort; concourse. [OFr *repairer* to return to a haunt, from LL *repatriāre* to return to one's country, from L *re-* back, and *patria* native country]

repair[2] *ri-pār'*, *vt* to mend, fix, put right (something broken, out of order or condition, etc); to make amends for; to make good; to restore, refresh, revivify (*Shakesp*). — *n* restoration after injury, loss or deterioration; sound condition; condition in terms of soundness; a part that has been mended or made sound. — *adj* **repair'able** capable of being mended (*esp* of material things); liable to be repaired (with *by*; *law*). — *n* **repair'er**. — *n* **reparability** (*rep-ər-ə-bil'i-ti*). — *adj* **reparable** (*rep'ər-ə-bl*) capable of being made good or (*rare*) being mended; falling to be repaired. — *adv* **rep'arably**. — *n* **reparā'tion** repair; supply of what is wasted; amends; compensation, often (in *pl*) to a country after it has suffered by war. — *adj* **reparative** (*ri-par'ə-tiv*) or **repar'atory**. — **repair'man** a person who does repairs, *esp* on something mechanical; **repair'-shop**. [OFr *reparer*, from L *reparāre*, from *parāre* to prepare]

repand *ri-pand'*, (*bot* and *zool*) *adj* slightly wavy. [L *repandus*, from *re-* back, and *pandus* bent]

reparable, etc. See under **repair**[2].

repartee *rep-är-tē'*, *n* a ready and witty retort; skill in making such retorts. — *vt* and *vi* to retort with ready wit. [OFr *repartie*, from *repartir*, from *partir* to set out, from L *partīrī* to divide]

repartition *rep-ər-tish'ən*, *n* distribution; (*rē-pär-*) a second partition; a division into smaller parts. — *vt* (*rē-pär-*) to partition again or differently. [**re-**]

repass *rē-päs'*, *vt* and *vi* to pass again; to pass in the opposite direction. — *n* **repassage** (*rē-pas'ij*). [**re-**]

repast *ri-päst'*, (*formal*) *n* a meal; refreshment of sleep (*Spenser*). — *vt* and *vi* (*Shakesp*) to feed. — *n* **repas'ture** (*Shakesp*) food. [OFr *repast* (Fr *repas*), from LL *repastus*, from L *pascere*, *pastum* to feed]

repatriate *rē-* or *ri-pāt-ri-āt*, or *-pat'*, *vt* to restore or send (someone) back to his or her own country. — *n* a repatriated person. — *n* **repatriā'tion**. — *n* **repat'riator**. [LL *repatriāre*, *-ātum* to return to one's country, from L *patria*]

repay *rē-pā'* or *ri-pā'*, *vt* to pay back; to make return for; to recompense; to pay or give in return. — *vi* to make repayment: — *pr p* **repay'ing**; *pa t* and *pa p* **repaid'**. — *adj* **repay'able** that is to be repaid; due. — *n* **repay'ment**. [**re-**]

repeal *ri-pel'*, *vt* to revoke; to annul; to quash, repress, set aside (*Spenser* and *Milton*); to recall from banishment (*obs*); to try to have restored to favour (*Shakesp*). — *n* abrogation; (with *cap*) dissolution of the Union between Great Britain and Ireland called for by O'Connell (*hist*). — *adj* **repeal'able**. — *n* **repeal'er** a person who repeals; (with *cap*) an advocate of Repeal (*hist*). [OFr *rapeler*, from pfx *re-*, and *apeler* to appeal]

repeat *ri-pēt'*, *vt* to say, do, perform or go over again; to iterate; to quote from memory; to say off; to recount; to celebrate (*Milton*); to say or do after another; to tell to others, divulge; to cause to recur; to reproduce; to repeat the words or actions of (*reflexive*); to seek again (*obs*); to ask back (*obs*). — *vi* to recur; to make repetition; to strike the last hour, quarter, etc when required; to fire several shots without reloading; to rise so as to be tasted after swallowing; to vote (illegally) more than once (*US*). — *n* a repetition; a retracing of one's course; a passage repeated or marked for repetition (*music*); dots or other mark directing repetition; a unit of a repeated pattern; an order for more goods of the same kind; a radio or television programme broadcast for the second, third, etc time. — *adj* done or occurring as a repetition. — *adj* **repeat'able** able to be done again; fit to be told to others. — *adj* **repeat'ed** done again; reiterated. — *adv* **repeat'edly** many times repeated; again and again. — *n* **repeat'er** a person who, or thing which, repeats, or does a thing that he, she or it has done before; a decimal fraction in which the same figure (or sometimes figures) is repeated to infinity; a watch, clock or firearm that repeats; a ship that repeats an admiral's signals; an instrument for automatically retransmitting a message (*teleg*); a thermionic amplifier inserted in a telephone circuit (also **repeating coil**) or in a cable. — *n* and *adj* **repeat'ing**. — **repeat purchasing** (*marketing*) the buying of products that are used frequently, such as newspapers or bread. — **repeat oneself** to say again what one has said already. [Fr *répéter*, from L *repetere*, *repetītum*, from *re-* again, and *petere* to seek]

repechage *rep'ə-shäzh*, or Fr *rə-pesh-äzh*, (*sport*, *esp rowing* and *fencing*) *n* a supplementary heat or competition giving competitors eliminated in the first heat or earlier competitions a second chance to go on to the final. — Also *adj*. [Fr *repêchage* a fishing out again]

repel *ri-pel'*, *vt* to drive off or back; to repulse; to reject; to hold off; to provoke aversion in; to repudiate: — *pr p* **repell'ing**; *pa t* and *pa p* **repelled'**. — *n* **repell'ence** or **repell'ency**. — Also **repell'ance** or **repell'ancy**. — *adj* **repell'ent** driving back; able or tending to repel; distasteful. — *n* anything which repels. — *adv* **repell'ently**. — Also **repell'ant** and **repell'antly**. — *n* **repell'er**. — *adj* **repell'ing**. — *adv* **repell'ingly**. [L *repellere*, from *pellere* to drive]

repent[1] *ri-pent'*, *vi* to regret, be sorry for, or wish to have been otherwise, what one has done or left undone (with *of*); to change from past evil or misconduct; to feel contrition; to sorrow (*Spenser*). — *vt* (*reflexive* or *impers*) to affect with contrition or with regret (*archaic*); to regret or feel contrition for (an action). — *n* (*Spenser*) repentance. — *n* **repent'ance** the or an act of repenting; the state of being penitent. — *adj* **repent'ant** experiencing or expressing repentance. — *n* (*rare*) a

Some words with the prefix **re-**.

rēnum'ber *vt*.
rēoccupā'tion *n*.
rēocc'upy *vt*.
rēoffend' *vi*.
rēop'en *vt* and *vi*.
rēordain' *vt*.
rēor'der *vt*.
rēordinā'tion *n*.
rēorganizā'tion or **-s-** *n*.

penitent. — *adv* **repent'antly**. — *n* **repent'er**. — *adv* **repent'ingly**. [OFr *repentir*, from L *paenitēre* to cause to repent]

repent[2] *rē'pənt*, (*bot*) *adj* lying on the ground and rooting. — Also **rep'tant**. [L *repēns*, *-entis*, pr p of *repere* to creep]

repercuss *rē-pər-kus'*, *vt* (*obs*, or now *colloq*) to drive back, reflect, reverberate or have consequences. — *n* **repercussion** (*-kush'ən*) driving back; reverberation; echo; reflection; a return stroke, reaction or consequence. — *adj* **repercussive** (*-kus'iv*) driving back; reverberating; echoing; repeated. [L *repercutere*, *-cussum*, from *re-*, *per* and *quatere* to strike]

repertory *rep'ər-tər-i*, *n* a storehouse, repository; a stock of pieces that a person or company is prepared to perform. — Also *adj*. — *n* **repertoire** (*rep'ər-twär*; Fr *répertoire*) a performer's or company's repertory; a full set of the codes and instructions which a computer can accept and execute (*comput*). — **repertory theatre** a theatre with a repertoire of plays and a stock or permanent company of actors, called a **repertory company**. [LL *repertōrium*, from L *reperīre* to find again, from *parere* to bring forth]

repetend *rep'i-tend* or *rep-i-tend'*, *n* the figure(s) that recur(s) in a recurring decimal number (*math*); a recurring note, word, refrain, etc; anything that recurs or is repeated. — *adj* to be repeated. [L *repetendum* that which is to be repeated, from L *repetere* to repeat]

répétiteur *rā-pā-tē-tœr*, *n* a coach, tutor; a person who rehearses opera singers, etc. [Fr; cf **repeat**]

repetition *rep-i-tish'ən*, *n* the or an act of repeating; recital from memory; a thing repeated; power of repeating a note promptly. — *adj* **repeti'tional**, **repeti'tionary** or **repetitious** (*-tish'əs*) of the nature of, or characterized by, repetition. — *adj* **repetitive** (*ri-pet'i-tiv*) iterative; overmuch given to repetition. — *adv* **repeti'tiously** or **repet'itively**. — *n* **repeti'tiousness** or **repet'itiveness**. — **repetitive strain injury** inflammation of the tendons and joints of the hands and lower arms, caused by repeated performance of identical manual operations (*abbrev* **RSI**). [L *repetere*; see **repeat**]

rephrase *rē-frāz'*, *vt* to put in different words, *usu* so as to make more understandable, acceptable, etc. [**re-**]

repine *ri-pīn'*, *vi* to fret (with *at* or *against*); to feel discontent; to murmur. — *vt* (*obs*) to lament; to grudge. — *n* (*Shakesp*) a repining. — *n* **repīne'ment**. — *n* **repīn'er**. — *n* and *adj* **repīn'ing**. — *adv* **repīn'ingly**. [Appar from **pine**[2]]

repique *ri-pēk'*, *n* at piquet, the winning of thirty points or more from combinations in one's own hand, before play begins. — *vt* to score a repique against. — *vi* to score a repique. [Fr *repic*]

repla. See **replum**.

replace *ri-* or *rē-plās'*, *vt* to put back; to provide a substitute for; to take the place of, supplant. — *adj* **replace'able**. — *n* **replace'ment** the or an act of replacing; a person or thing that takes the place of another; the occurrence of a face or faces in the position where the principal figure would have a corner or edge (*crystallog*); the process by which one mineral gradually forms from another in crystalline form by solution and redeposition (*geol*). — *n* **replac'er** a substitute. — **replaceable hydrogen** hydrogen atoms that can be replaced in an acid by metals to form salts. [**re-**]

replant *rē-plänt'*, *vt* and *vi* to plant again. — *vt* to replace surgically (a severed limb, digit, etc). — *n* **replantā'tion**. [**re-**]

replay *rē-plā'*, *vt* to play again (a game, match, record, recording, etc). — *n* (*rē'plā*) a game or match played again; a recording played again, *esp* (also **action replay**) of a part of a broadcast game or match, often in slow motion. [**re-**]

replenish *ri-plen'ish*, *vt* to fill again; to fill completely; to stock abundantly; to people. — *adj* **replen'ished** (*Shakesp*) complete, consummate. — *n* **replen'isher** a person who replenishes; an apparatus for maintaining an electric charge. — *n* **replen'ishment**. [OFr *replenir*, *-iss-*, from *replein* full, from L *re-* again, and *plēnus* full]

replete *ri-plēt'*, *adj* full; completely filled; filled to satiety; abounding (with *with*). — *vt* to fill to repletion. — *n* **replete'ness** or **replē'tion** superabundant fullness; surfeit; fullness of blood (*med*); plethora. [L *replētus*, pa p of *replēre*, from *plēre* to fill]

replevy *ri-plev'i*, (*law*) *vt* to bail (*archaic*); to recover, or restore to the owner (goods distrained) upon pledge to try the right in legal proceedings. — *n* replevin. — *adj* **replev'iable** or **replev'isable** (*-i-səb-l*). — *n* **replev'in** replevying; a writ or action in such a case. — *vt* to recover by replevin (*Swift*, etc). [OFr *replevir*, from *plevir* to pledge]

replica *rep'li-kə*, *n* a duplicate, *esp* one by the original artist; a facsimile; a repeat (*music*). [Ital, from L *replicāre* to repeat]

replicate *rep'li-kāt*, *vt* to fold back; to repeat; to make a replica of; to reply. — *vi* (of molecules of living material) to reproduce molecules identical with themselves. — *n* (*music*) a tone one or more octaves from a given tone. — *adj* folded back. — *n* **replicā'tion** a reply; the plaintiff's answer to the defendant's plea; doubling back; copy, reproduction; reverberation, echo (*Shakesp*). — *n* **rep'licator**. — *n* **rep'licon** (*biol*) a part of a DNA molecule replicated from a single origin. — **replication fork** (*biol*) the site of simultaneous unwinding of duplex DNA and synthesis of new DNA. [L *replicāre*, *-ātum* to fold back, from *plicāre* to fold]

replum *rep'ləm* or *rē'pləm*, *n* a partition in a fruit formed by ingrowth of the placentas, as in Cruciferae: — *pl* **rep'la**. [L *replum* the upright in the frame of a folding door]

reply *ri-plī'*, *vt* to say in answer. — *vi* to answer; to respond in action, as by returning gunfire; to echo; to answer a defendant's plea: — *pr p* **reply'ing**; *pa t* and *pa p* **replied'**. — *n* an answer, response; a replication (*Scots law*); the answer in a fugue (*music*). — *n* **replī'er**. [OFr *replier*, from L *replicāre*; see **replicate**]

repo *rē'pō*, (*colloq*) *n* short form of **repossession**; a repurchase agreement (see under **repurchase**; *US finance*): — *pl* **rē'pōs**. — *n* **rē'pōman** a person employed to repossess unpaid-for goods.

repoint *rē-poynt'*, *vt* to repair (stone or brickwork) by renewing the mortar, etc. [**re-**]

répondez s'il vous plaît *rā-pɔ̃-dā sēl vo͞o ple*, or *abbrev* **RSVP** (*Fr*) please answer (this invitation).

repone *ri-pōn'*, (*Scots law*) *vt* to restore to office or status; to rehabilitate. [L *repōnere* to put back, from *pōnere* to put]

report *ri-pōrt'* or *-pört'*, *vt* to convey (*Spenser*); to bring back, as an answer, news or account of anything; to give an account of, *esp* a formal, official, or requested account; to state in such an account; to relate; to circulate publicly; to transmit as having been said, done or observed; to write down or take notes of, *esp* for a newspaper or radio or television programme; to lay a charge against; to echo back; (*reflexive*) to make personal announcement of the presence and readiness of. — *vi* to make a statement; to write an account of occurrences; to make a formal report; to report oneself; to act as a reporter. — *n* a statement of facts; a formal or official statement, such as of results of an

Some words with the prefix **re-**.

rēor'ganize or **-ise** *vt*.	**rēpag'inate** *vt*.	**rēpeo'ple** *vt*.
repack' *vt* and *vi*.	**rēpaginā'tion** *n*.	**rēperus'al** *n*.
rēpack'age *vt*.	**rēpā'per** *vt*.	**rēperuse'** *vt*.

investigation or matter referred; a statement on a school pupil's work and behaviour or the like; an account of a matter of news, *esp* the words of a speech; reporting, testimony (*Shakesp*); general talk; rumour; hearsay; repute (*Bible*); explosive noise. — *adj* **report'able**. — *n* **report'age** journalistic reporting, style or manner; gossip; a documentary presented through pictures (in film or photographs) without comment or written or spoken narrative. — *adv* **report'edly** according to report. — *n* **report'er** a person who reports, *esp* for a newspaper or legal proceedings. — *n* and *adj* **report'ing**. — *adv* **report'ingly** (*Shakesp*) by common report. — *adj* **reportō'rial** (*rep-ər-* or *-ör-*). — **reported speech** indirect speech; **reported verses** (Fr *vers rapportés*) verses that combine a number of parallel sentences by collocation of corresponding parts, such as Sidney's 'Virtue, beauty, and speech did strike, wound, charm, My heart, eyes, ears, with wonder, love, delight'; **report program** (*comput*) a program designed to search a file and print out an analysis of its data; **report stage** the stage at which a parliamentary bill as amended in committee is reported to the House, before the third reading. [OFr *reporter*, from L *reportāre*, from *re-* back, and *portāre* to carry]

repose *ri-pōz'*, *vt* to lay at rest; to rest (oneself) in confidence (on; *archaic*); to give rest to, refresh by rest; to place (eg confidence) in a person or thing; to place in trust. — *vi* to rest; to be still; to rely, place one's trust, be based (with *on* or *upon*; *archaic*). — *n* rest; quiet; stillness; calm; ease of manner; serenity; restful feeling or effect; a place of rest (*Milton*). — *n* **repōs'al** (*Shakesp* **repos'all**, another reading **repōs'ure**) reposing. — *adj* **repōsed'** calm; settled. — *adv* **repō'sedly**. — *n* **repōs'edness**. — *adj* **repōse'ful**. — *adv* **repōse'fully**. [Fr *reposer*, from LL *repausāre*; confused with **reposit**]

reposit *ri-poz'it*, *vt* to lay away, deposit. — *n* **reposition** (*rep-ə-zish'ən*) replacing; reinstatement (*Scot*); laying up. — *n* **repos'itor** an instrument for replacing a displaced organ. — *n* **repos'itory** a place or receptacle in which anything is deposited or contained; a collection or museum (now *rare*); a mart, *esp* for horses; an abode of souls (*archaic*); a tomb, sepulchre (*archaic*); a storehouse, magazine, as of information; a place of accumulation; a confidant. [L *repōnere*, *repositum* to put back, lay aside, from *pōnere* to put; confused with **repose**]

re-position or **reposition** *rē-pəz-ish'ən*, *vt* to put in a different position. [**re-**]

repossess *rē-pəz-es'*, *vt* to regain possession of; to take back (goods or property acquired on credit or by hire-purchase) because payment has not been made; to put again in possession. — *n* **repossession** (*-esh'ən*) the or an act of repossessing anything; a property, etc that has been repossessed. — *n* **rēpossess'or**. [**re-**]

repost. Same as **riposte**.

reposure. See under **repose**.

repoussé *rə-pōō-sā* or *-pōō'*, *adj* (of metal) raised in relief by hammering from behind or within; embossed. — *n* repoussé work; an article made from this. — *n* **repoussage** (*-säzh'*). — *n* **repoussoir** (*rə-pōō-swär*) a figure or object in the foreground of a painted, etc composition intended to draw the viewer's eye into the picture. [Fr, from *repousser* to push back]

repp. Same as **rep**[1].

repreeve (*Shakesp*). See **reprieve**.

reprehend *rep-ri-hend'*, *vt* to find fault with; to reprove. — *n* **reprehend'er**. — *adj* **reprehen'sible** blameworthy. — *adv* **reprehen'sibly**. — *n* **reprehen'sion** reproof; censure. — *adj* **reprehen'sive** containing reproof; given in reproof. — *adv* **reprehen'sively**. — *adj* **reprehen'sory**. [L *repraehendere*, *-hēnsum*, from *re-* (intensive) and *praehendere* to lay hold of]

represent *rep-ri-zent'*, *vt* to exhibit the image of; to use, or serve, as a symbol for; to stand for; to exhibit, depict, personate, show an image of, by imitative art; to act; to be a substitute, agent, deputy, member of parliament, etc, for; to correspond or be in some way equivalent or analogous to; to serve as a sample of, typify; to present earnestly to mind; to give out, make to appear, allege (that). — *adj* **represent'able** (*rep-ri-*). — *n* **representā'men** (*psychol*) the product of representation. — *n* **represent'ant** a representative. — *n* **representation** (*-zən-tā'shən*) act, state or fact of representing or being represented; anything which represents; an image; picture; dramatic performance; a mental image; a presentation of a view of facts or arguments; a petition, remonstrance, expostulation; a statement; assumption of succession by an heir (*law*); a body of representatives. — *adj* **representā'tional** (*rep-ri-zən-*) (*esp* of art) depicting objects in a realistic rather than an abstract form. — *n* **representā'tionalism** representational art; the doctrine that in the perception of the external world the immediate object represents another object beyond the sphere of consciousness (also **representā'tionism**). — *n* **representā'tionist**. — *adj* **representative** (*rep-ri-zent'ə-tiv*) representing; exhibiting a likeness; typical; relating to representation. — *n* a sample; a typical example or embodiment; a person who represents another or others, as a deputy, delegate, ambassador, member of parliament, agent, successor or heir; the head of a family (*Jane Austen*); a representative legislative body (*obs*). — *adv* **represent'atively**. — *n* **represent'ativeness**. — *n* **representee'** (*law*) a person to whom a representation has been made. — *n* **represent'er**. — *n* **represent'ment**. — *n* **represent'or** (*law*) a person who makes a representation in the course of contractual negotiations. — **representative peers** Scottish and Irish peers chosen by their fellows to sit in the House of Lords. — **House of Representatives** the lower branch of the United States Congress, consisting of members chosen biennially by the people; also of various State and other legislatures. [L *repraesentāre*, *-ātum*, from *praesentāre* to place before]

re-present *rē'pri-zent'*, *vt* to present again. — *n* **re'presentā'tion** or **rē'-present'ment**. [**re-**]

repress *ri-pres'*, *vt* to restrain; to keep under control; to put down; to banish to the unconscious. — *p adj* **repress'ed** having a tendency to repress unacceptable thoughts, feelings, etc. — *adj* **repress'ible**. — *adv* **repress'ibly**. — *n* **repression** (*-presh'ən*). — *adj* **repress'ive**. — *adv* **repress'ively**. — *n* **repress'or** someone or something that represses; a protein which binds to an operator site and prevents transcription of the associated gene (*biol*). [L *reprimere*, *repressum*, from *premere* to press]

re-press *rē'pres'*, *vt* to press again. [**re-**]

repriefe *ri-prēf'*, (*Spenser*) *n* reproach, insult, shame, reproof. — *vt* **reprieve** (*-prēv'*) to reprove. [Same root as **reproof**; for vowel see **prove**]

reprieve *ri-prēv'* (*Shakesp* **repreeve'**; *Spenser* **reprive** or **repryve** *-prīv'*) *vt* to delay the execution of; to give a respite to; to rescue, redeem. — *n* a suspension of a criminal sentence, *esp* a death sentence; interval of ease or relief. — *n* **repriev'al**. [Supposed to be from Anglo-Fr *repris*, pa p of *reprendre* to take back (see **reprise**); the *v* appar by confusion, perh with **reprieve** reprove]

reprimand *rep'ri-mänd* or *-mand*, *n* a severe reproof. — *vt* (also *-mänd'* or *-mand'*) to reprove severely, *esp* publicly or officially. [Fr *réprimande*, from L *reprimere*, *repressum* to press back, from *premere* to press]

Some words with the prefix **re-**.

rēplan' *vt* and *vi*.
rēpop'ulate *vt*.
rēpot' *vt*.
rēpott'ing *n*.
rēpro'grammable *adj*.
rēpro'gramme or (*NAm* and *comput*) **rēpro'gram** *vt*.
rēpublicā'tion *n*.
rēpub'lish *vt*.

reprime *ri-prīm'*, (*rare*) *vt* to repress. [See **repress**]

reprint *rē-print'*, *vt* to print again; to print a new impression of, *esp* with little or no change. — *vi* to be reprinted. — *n* **rē'print** a later impression (of eg a book); printed matter used as copy.

reprise (*Spenser* **reprize**) *ri-prīz'*, *vt* to gain anew (*obs*); to recapture (*obs*); to renew, repeat, reissue. — *n* a yearly charge or deduction; reprisal (*Dryden*); a renewed or alternating spell of action; (*-prēz'*) resumption of an earlier subject (*music*; also *vt*). — *n* **reprīs'al** seizure in retaliation; a prize (*Shakesp*); an act of retaliation; recapture; compensation. [Fr *reprise*, from *reprendre*, from L *repraehendere*]

reprivatize or **-ise** *rē-prī'vət-īz*, *vt* to return (a company, etc) to private ownership. — *n* **rēprivatizātion** or **-s-**. [**re-**]

reprive (*Spenser*). See **reprieve**.

repro *rē'prō* or *rep'rō*, *n* and *adj* short form of **reproduction**, *esp* designating modern copies of period styles of furniture. — *n* (*rē'prō*) short for **reproduction proof**: — *pl* **re'pros**.

reproach *ri-prōch'*, *vt* to upbraid, rebuke; to blame (oneself, etc; with *for* or *with*); to reprove gently; to bring into discredit; to cast (something) in someone's teeth (with *to*, *against*, also *on*; *Dryden*, etc). — *n* upbraiding; reproof; censure; disgrace; a source or matter of disgrace or shame. — *adj* **reproach'able**. — *n* **reproach'er**. — *adj* **reproach'ful** reproving; deserving of reproach, disgraceful (*obs*). — *adv* **reproach'fully**. — *n* **reproach'fulness**. — *adj* **reproach'less** irreproachable. — **above** or **beyond reproach** excellent, too good to be criticized; **the Reproaches** antiphons chanted in RC churches on Good Friday, in which Christ reproaches the Jewish people. [Fr *reprocher*, perh from L *prope* near; cf **approach**; or from *reprobāre*; see **reprobate**]

reprobate *rep'rō-bāt*, *adj* failing to pass a test (*esp* of silver) (*archaic*); base; rejected by God; given over to sin; depraved; unprincipled; condemnatory. — *n* a person rejected by God; an abandoned or profligate person; someone lost to shame; a villain or rogue; (often *joc*) a scamp. — *vt* to reject; to disapprove of; to censure; to disown (*obs*). — *n* **rep'robacy** (*-bə-si*) state of being a reprobate. — *n* **rep'robance** (*Shakesp*) reprobation. — *n* **rep'robāter**. — *n* **reprobā'tion** the act of reprobating; rejection; foreordination to eternal perdition; utter abandonment; severe censure or condemnation. — *adj* **rep'robātive** or **rep'robatory** condemnatory. — *n* **rep'robātor** (*Scots law*) an action to prove a witness perjured or biased. [L *reprobāre*, *-ātum* to reprove, contrary of *approbāre*, from *probāre* to prove]

reprocess *rē-prō'ses*, *vt* to process again, *esp* to remake used material, eg spent nuclear fuel, into a new material or article (see **fuel reprocessing** under **fuel**). [**re-**]

reproduce *rē-prō-dūs'*, *vt* to produce a copy of; to form again or afresh; to propagate; to reconstruct in imagination. — *vi* to produce offspring; to prove suitable for copying in some way; to turn out (well, badly, etc) when copied. — *n* **reprodū'cer**. — *adj* **reprodū'cible**. — *n* **reproduction** (*-duk'shən*) the or an act of reproducing; the act of producing new organisms, ie the whole process whereby life is continued from generation to generation; regeneration; a copy, facsimile; a representation. — Also *adj* (of furniture, etc). — *adj* **reproduc'tive**. — *adv* **reproduc'tively**. — *n* **reproduc'tiveness** or **reproductiv'ity**. — **reproduction proof** (*printing*) a high-quality proof made from strips of typeset copy and photographed to produce a plate for printing from (often *abbrev* as **repro proof** or **repro**). [**re-**]

reprography *ri-prog'rə-fi*, *n* the reproduction of graphic or typeset material, eg by photocopying. — *n* **reprog'rapher**. — *adj* **reprograph'ic**. [Fr *reprographie*]

reproof *ri-prōōf'*, *n* a reproving; rebuke; censure; reprehension; shame, disgrace (*Shakesp*); disproof (*obs*); (*rē-*) a second or new proof. — *vt* (*rē-*) to make waterproof again. — *n* **reproval** (*ri-prōō'vl*) reproof. — *vt* **reprove'** to rebuke; to censure, condemn; to disprove or refute (*obs*); to accuse or convict (of; *Bible*, AV). — *n* **repro'ver**. — *n* **repro'ving**. — *adv* **repro'vingly**. [OFr *reprover* (Fr *réprouver*), from L *reprobāre*; see **reprobate**]

repryve. See **reprieve**.

reps *reps*. See **rep**[1].

rept *abbrev*: receipt; report.

reptant. See **repent**[2] and **reptation**.

reptation *rep-tā'shən*, *n* the act of squirming along or up a smooth-walled narrow passage. — *adj* **rep'tant** (*old biol*) creeping. [L *reptāre* to creep]

reptile *rep'tīl*, *n* any animal of the class **Reptilia** (*-til'i-ə*), vertebrates with scaly integument, cold blood, right and left aortic arch, partly divided heart, single occipital condyle, pulmonary respiration and pentadactyl limbs (sometimes lacking), most laying shelled amniote eggs; a creeping thing; a base, malignant, abject or treacherous person. — *adj* creeping; like a reptile in nature. — *adj* **reptilian** (*-til'i-ən*) or **rep'tiloid**. — *adv* **reptil'ianly**. — *adj* **reptilif'erous** bearing fossil reptiles. — *adj* **reptil'ious** like a reptile. [LL *reptilis*, *-e*, from *repere* to creep]

republic *ri-pub'lik*, *n* the state (*archaic*); a form of government without a monarch, in which the supreme power is vested in the people and their elected representatives; a state or country so governed. — *adj* **repub'lican** of or favouring a republic; (with *cap*) of the Republican party. — *n* a person who advocates a republican form of government; (with *cap*) in US, *orig* an Anti-Federal, now a member of the political party opposed to the *Democrats*, and favouring an extension of the powers of the national government. — *n* **repub'licanism**. — *vt* **repub'licanize** or **-ise**. — **Republican era** the era adopted by the French after the downfall of the monarchy, beginning with 22 September 1792. — **republic of letters** the world of books and authors. [L *rēspublica* commonwealth, from *rēs* affair, and *publica* (fem) public]

repudiate *ri-pū'di-āt*, *vt* (of a husband) to divorce (*archaic*); to cast off, disown; to refuse or cease to acknowledge (debt, authority, claim, etc); to deny as unfounded (a charge, etc). — *adj* **repū'diable**. — *n* **repūdiā'tion**. — *n* **repūdiā'tionist** a person who favours repudiation of public debt. — *adj* **repū'diative**. — *n* **repū'diātor**. [L *repudiāre*, *-ātum*, from *repudium* divorce, from *re-* away, and the root of *pudēre* to be ashamed]

repugn *ri-pūn'*, *vt* to fight against, to oppose (*Shakesp*); to be repugnant to (*archaic*). — *vi* (*archaic*) to be repugnant. — *n* **repugnance** (*ri-pug'nəns*) inconsistency; aversion. — *n* **repug'nancy** repugnance (now chiefly *law*); opposition (*Shakesp*). — *adj* **repug'nant** inconsistent with (with *to*); (of things) incompatible; distasteful; disgusting; resisting, unwilling (*archaic*). [L *repugnāre*, from *re-* against, and *pugnāre* to fight]

repulse *ri-puls'*, *vt* to drive back; to beat off; to rebuff, reject. — *n* a driving back; a beating off; a check; a refusal; a rebuff. — *n* **repulsion** (*-pul'shən*) driving off; a repelling force, action or influence; driving force, effect or influence; action or effect; raison d'être. — *adj* **repul'sive** that repulses or drives off; repelling; cold, reserved, forbidding; causing aversion and disgust. —

Some words with the prefix **re-**.

rēpub'lisher *n.*	**rēreg'ister** *vt* and *vi.*	**rē'revise** *vt* and *n.*
rēpulp' *vt.*	**rēreg'ulate** *vt.*	**rē-roof'** *vt.*
rēquote' *vt* and *vi.*	**reregulā'tion** *n.*	**rēroute'** *vt.*

adv **repul'sively**. — *n* **repul'siveness**. [L *repulsus*, pa p of *repellere*, from *re-* back, and *pellere* to drive]

repunit *rep'ū-nit*, (*math*) *n* a number consisting of two or more identical integers, eg 22, 333. [*rep*eating *unit*]

repurchase *rē-pûr'chəs*, *vt* to purchase again, buy back. — Also *n*. — **repurchase agreement** (*finance*) one in which a seller of bonds, etc undertakes to buy them back after an agreed period. [**re-**]

repurify *rē-pūr'i-fī*, or **repure** *ri-pūr'*, *vt* to purify again; to refine thoroughly. [**re-**]

repute *ri-pūt'*, *vt* to account, deem. — Also (*archaic*) *vi* with *of*. — *n* general opinion or impression; attributed character; widespread or high estimation; fame. — *adj* **reputable** (*rep'ūt-ə-bl*) in good repute; respectable; honourable; consistent with reputation. — *adv* **rep'ūtably**. — *n* **reputā'tion** (*rep-*) repute; estimation; character generally ascribed; good report; fame; good name. — *adj* **rep'ūtātive** reputed; putative. — *adv* **rep'ūtātively** by repute. — *adj* **reputed** (*ri-pūt'id*) supposed, reckoned to be such; of repute. — *adv* **repūt'edly** in common repute or estimation. — *adj* **repute'less** (*Shakesp*) without good repute. — *n* **reput'ing** (*Shakesp*) pluming oneself. — **reputed owner** a person who has to all appearance the title to the property; **reputed pint** or **quart** that which is commonly called a pint or quart though not necessarily of legal standard (sometimes as little as half the legal amount). [L *reputāre*, *-ātum*, from *putāre* to reckon]

requere *ri-kwēr'*, (*Spenser*) *vt* to require.

request *ri-kwest'*, *n* the asking of a favour; a petition; a favour asked for; the state of being sought after. — *vt* to ask as a favour; to ask politely; to ask for. — *n* **request'er**. — **request note** an application for a permit to remove excisable goods; **request stop** a bus stop at which a bus will stop only if signalled to do so. — **Court of Requests** a former English court of equity, abolished 1641; a local small debt court, superseded by the County Court (called also *Court of Conscience*); **on request** if, or when, requested. [OFr *requeste* (Fr *requête*), from L *requīsītum*, pa p of *requīrere*, from *re-* away, and *quaerere* to seek]

requicken *rē-kwik'n*, (*Shakesp*) *vt* to give new life to. [**re-**]

requiem *rek'wi-əm* or *rē'kwi-əm*, *n* a mass for the rest of the soul of the dead; music for it; any music of similar character; rest (*obs*). [L, accusative of *requiēs*, from *re-* (intensive) and *quiēs* rest); first word of the introit]

requiescat *re-kwi-es'kat*, *n* a prayer for the rest of the soul of the dead. — **requiescat in pace** (*in pā'sē*, *pä'chā* or *pä'ke*) may he or she rest in peace (*abbrev* **RIP**). [L, third pers sing subjunctive of *requiescere*]

requight a Spenserian spelling of **requite**.

require *ri-kwīr'*, *vt* to ask (someone) a question (*obs*); to ask for (*obs*); to demand, exact; to direct (a person to do something); to request (*archaic*); to call for, necessitate. — *vi* to ask. — *adj* **requir'able**. — *adj* **required'** compulsory as part of a curriculum. — *n* **require'ment** a need; a thing needed; a necessary condition; a demand. — *n* **requir'er**. — *n* **requir'ing**. [L *requīrere*; partly through OFr *requerre*, later assimilated to L]

requisite *rek'wi-zit*, *adj* required; needed; indispensable. — *n* that which is required, necessary or indispensable. — *n* **req'uisiteness**. — *n* **requisi'tion** the act of requiring; a formal demand or request; a formal call for the doing of something that is due; a demand for the supply of anything for military purposes; a written order for the supply of materials; the state of being in use or service. — *vt* to demand a requisition from; to demand or take by requisition; to seize; to call in; to press into service. — *adj* **requisi'tionary**. — *n* **requisi'tionist** or **requis'itor** a person who makes a requisition. — *adj* **requis'itory**. [L *requīsītus*, pa p of *requīrere*; see **require**]

requite *ri-kwīt'*, *vt* to repay (an action); to avenge; to repay (a person, for); to retaliate on; to counterbalance, compensate for (*obs*): — *pa t* **requit'ed** (*Spenser* **requit'**); *pa p* **requit'ed** (*Shakesp* **requit'** or **requitt'ed**). — Also (*Spenser*) **requight** (*-kwīt'*). — *n* **requite'** (*rare*) requital. — *vt* **requit** (*-kwit'*; *obs*) to requite (*pa p*, *Shakesp*, **requitt'ed**). — *n* (*Burns*) requital. — *adj* **requī'table**. — *n* **requī'tal** the or an act of requiting; payment in return; recompense; reward. — *adj* **requite'ful**. — *adj* **requite'less** without requital, free. — *n* **requite'ment**. — *n* **requī'ter**. [**re-** and **quit**]

requoyle a Shakespearian spelling of **recoil**.

reradiate *rē-rā'di-āt*, *vt* to radiate again, *esp* as a result of having absorbed an amount of radiation previously. — *n* **reradiā'tion**. [**re-**]

rerail *rē-rāl'*, *vt* to replace on the rails. [**re-**]

rere- *rēr-*, *combining form* same as **rear**[1]. — *n* **rere'-arch** or **rear'-arch** an arch supporting the inner part of a wall's thickness, as in a splayed window. — *n* **rere'brace** (*-brās*; Fr *bras* arm) armour for the arm from shoulder to elbow. — *n* **rere'dorse**, **rere'dosse** or **rere'dos** (L *dorsum*, Fr *dos* back) a screen or panelling behind an altar or seat; a choir-screen; the back of a fireplace (*archaic*). — *n* **rere'dorter** (*hist*) a lavatory built behind a monastic dormitory. — *n* **rere'-supper** a late meal, after supper. — *adj* **rere'ward** rearward.

reread *rē-rēd'*, *vt* to read again: — *pa t* and *pa p* **re'read'** (*-red*). [**re-**]

reremouse or **rearmouse** *rēr'mows*, *n* a bat: — *pl* **rere'mice** or **rear'mice**. [OE *hrēremūs*, appar from *hrēran* to move, and *mūs* a mouse]

rerun *rē'run'*, *vt* to run (a race, etc) again; to broadcast (a radio or television series) again (also *fig*). — Also *n* (*rē'run*). [**re-**]

res or **rez** *rez*, (*US colloq*) short form of (N American Indian) **reservation**.

res. *abbrev*: research; reserve; residence; resolution.

resale *rē'sāl* or *rē-sāl'*, *n* the selling again of an article. — **resale price maintenance** the setting of a fixed minimum price on an article by the manufacturer (*abbrev* **RPM**). [**re-**]

resalgar *res-al'gər*, *obs* variant of **realgar**.

resat. See **resit**.

re-scale or **rescale** *rē-skāl'*, *vt* to plan or form on a new (*usu* reduced) scale. [**re-**]

reschedule *rē-shed'ūl* or *-sked'ūl*, *vt* to schedule again; to arrange a new time or timetable for; to rearrange (a country's debt repayment programme) *usu* to alleviate liquidity problems (*econ*). — *n* **resched'uling**. [**re-**]

rescind *ri-sind'*, *vt* to cut away; to annul, abrogate. — *n* **rescission** (*-sizh'ən*) abrogation; cutting off (*obs*). — *adj* **rescissory** (*-sis'ər-i*) annulling. [L *rescindere*, *rescissum*, from *rē* back, and *scindere* to cut]

rescore *rē'skōr'* or *-skōr'*, *vt* to rewrite a musical score for different instruments, voices, etc. [**re-**]

rescript *rē'skript*, *n* the official answer of a pope or an emperor to any legal question; an edict or decree; a rewriting. — Also *vt*. [L *rescrīptum*, from *re-*, and *scrībere*, *scrīptum* to write]

rescue *res'kū*, *vt* to free from danger, captivity or evil plight; to deliver forcibly from legal custody; to recover by force: — *pr p* **res'cuing**; *pa t* and *pa p* **res'cued**. — *n* the or an act of rescuing; deliverance from danger or evil; forcible recovery; forcible release from arrest or imprisonment; relief of a besieged place; a beach-rescue; a rescuer or rescuing party (*archaic*); a person or thing rescued; a bid (**rescue bid**) to bring one's

Some words with the prefix **re-**.

rēsalute' *vt*.	**rēseal'** *vt*.	**rēselect'** *vt*.
rēsay' *vt*: — *pa t* and *pa p* **rēsaid'**.	**rēseal'able** *adj*.	**rēselect'ion** *n*.
	rēseat' *vt*.	**rēsell'** *vt*: — *pa t* and *pa p* **rēsold'**.

partner out of a dangerous situation (*bridge*). — *adj* **res'cuable**. — *n* **res'cuer**. [OFr *rescourre*, from L *re-* and *excutere*, from *ex* out, and *quatere* to shake]

rescue-grass *res'kū-gräs*, *n* a S American brome-grass, *Bromus catharticus*. [Origin unknown]

research *ri-sûrch'*, *n* a careful search; investigation; systematic investigation towards increasing the sum of knowledge. — *vi* and *vt* to make researches (into or concerning); (**re-search** *rē'*) to search again. — *n* **research'er**. — *adj* **research'ful**. [Obs Fr *recerche* (mod Fr *recherche*); see **search**]

réseau *rā-zō'*, *n* a fine meshed ground for lacework; a network of lines for reference in star-photographs: — *pl* **réseaux** (*rā-zō'*) or **réseaus** (*rā-zōz'*). [Fr, network]

resect *ri-sekt'*, *vt* to cut away part of, *esp* the end of a bone. — *n* **resection** (*-sek'shən*) cutting away, *esp* bone (*surg*); a positional fix of a point by sighting it from three or more known stations (*surveying*). [L *resecāre*, *-sectum* to cut off, from *secāre* to cut]

Reseda *re'si-də* or *ri-sē'də*, *n* the mignonette genus, giving name to the family **Resedā'ceae**; (without *cap*; *re'*) a pale green colour (often as Fr **réséda** *rā-zā-dä*). — Also *adj*. [L *resēda*, said to be from *resēdā morbīs* assuage diseases, first words of a charm used in applying it as a poultice]

reseize *rē-sēz'*, (*Spenser*) *vt* to reinstate. [**re-** and **seise**]

resemble *ri-zem'bl*, *vt* to be like; to compare (*archaic*); to depict (*obs*). — *vi* to be like each other; to be like (with *to*; *archaic*). — *n* **resem'blance** likeness; appearance; an image. — *adj* **resem'blant**. — *n* **resem'bler**. — *adj* **resem'bling**. [OFr *resembler* (Fr *ressembler*), from *re-* again, and *sembler* to seem, from L *simulāre* to make like, from *similis* like]

resent *ri-zent'*, *vt* to take in, consider as an injury or affront; to feel joy or sorrow because of (*obs*); to receive (a person), well or badly (*obs*). — *vi* (*obs*) to savour (of). — *n* **resent'er**. — *adj* **resent'ful**. — *adv* **resent'fully**. — *adv* **resent'ingly**. — *adj* **resent'ive**. — *n* **resent'ment**. [OFr *ressentir*, from L *re-* in return, and *sentīre* to feel]

reserpine *ri-zûr'pin* or *-pēn*, *n* a drug obtained from *Rauwolfia serpentina* used against high blood pressure, and as a tranquillizer.

reserve *ri-zûrv'*, *vt* to hold back; to save up, *esp* for a future occasion or special purpose; to keep, retain; to preserve; to spare; to set apart; to book, engage. — *n* the keeping of something reserved; state of being reserved; that which is reserved; a reservation; a reserved store or stock; a reserve price; a tract of land reserved for a special purpose; in Canada, a N American Indian reservation; a substitute kept in readiness (*sport*); (*esp* in *pl*) a military force kept out of action until occasion serves; (*esp* in *pl*) a force not *usu* serving but liable to be called up when required; (often *pl*) resources of physical or spiritual nature available in abnormal circumstances; part of assets kept readily available for ordinary demands; (*usu* in *pl*) an unexploited quantity of a mineral (*esp* oil, gas or coal) calculated to exist in a given area; (in *pl*) amounts of gold and foreign currencies held by a country; artistic restraint; restrained manner; reticence; aloofness; a secret information withheld (*archaic*); limitation, restriction; a mental reservation. — *adj* kept in reserve; of a reserve or reserves. — *adj* **reserv'able**. — *n* **reservā'tion** (*rez-*) the act of reserving or keeping back, or keeping for oneself; an expressed or tacit proviso, limiting condition, or exception; something withheld; a tract of public land reserved for some special purpose, eg for preserving game, forest, etc; in the US, an area of land set aside by treaty for the use of a particular N American Indian tribe or group; the pope's retention to himself of the right to nominate to a benefice; a limitation; the booking of a seat, room, passage, etc; a booked seat, room, etc; the strip of grass, etc between the two roads of a dual carriageway; a clause of a deed by which a person reserves for himself or herself a right, interest, etc in a property he or she is granting, as that of ordinary rent (*law*). — *n* **reservatory** (*ri-zûrv'ə-tər-i*; *obs*) a receptacle; a reservoir. — *adj* **reserved'** reticent; uncommunicative; aloof in manner; booked; having the original colour of the surface or background (*ceramics*). — *adv* **reserv'edly**. — *n* **reservedness** (*ri-zûrvd'nis*). — *n* **reserv'ist** a member of a reserve force. — **reserve bank** any of the US Federal Reserve banks; a central bank holding reserves for other banks (*esp Austr* and *NZ*); **reserve currency** any stable and easily convertible foreign currency which a government holds in its foreign exchange reserves and uses to finance a large part of its international trade; **reserved list** a list of retired officers in the armed services who may be recalled for active service in the event of war; **reserved occupation** employment of national importance that exempts from service in the armed forces; **reserved word** (*comput*) a word with a specific use in a programming language that cannot therefore be used as an identifier, etc; **reserve price** the minimum price acceptable to the vendor of an article for sale or auction; **reserve ratio** (*econ*) the government-imposed minimum ratio that must be maintained by a bank between its total deposit liabilities and the cash reserves it retains with the central bank. — **judgement reserved** see under **judge**; **mental reservation** a reservation made mentally but not openly expressed; **reservation of the sacrament** the practice of reserving part of the consecrated bread of the eucharist for the communion of the sick; **without reserve** frankly, not holding back any information; fully, without reservation; without restrictions or stipulations regarding sale; without a reserve price. [OFr *reserver*, from L *reservāre*, from *re-* back, and *servāre* to save]

reservoir *rez'ər-vwär* or *-vwör*, *n* a receptacle; a store; a receptacle for fluids, *esp* a large basin, artificial lake or tank for storing water. — *vt* to store. — **reservoir rock** porous rock containing producible oil and/or gas. [Fr]

reset[1] *ri-set'*, (*Scot*) *vt* to harbour (*archaic*); to receive, knowing to be stolen. — Also *vi*. — *n* (*rē'*) harbouring of a proscribed person (*archaic*); receiving of stolen goods. — *n* **resett'er**. [OFr *recet(t)er*, from L *receptāre*, from *recipere* to receive]

reset[2] *rē-set'*, *vt* to set again. [**re-**]

res extincta *rāz eks-tingkt'ə*, (*law*) the thing does not exist, ie, the subject matter of a contract no longer or had never existed when it was drawn up, and therefore no contract will ensue. [L]

res gestae *rēz jes'tē* or *rās ges'tī*, (*L*) *n pl* exploits; facts relevant to the case and admissible in evidence (*law*).

reshuffle *rē-shuf'l*, *vt* to shuffle again; to rearrange, *esp* cabinet or government posts. — Also *n*. [**re-**]

resiant *rez'i-ənt* or *-ant*, (*obs* or *archaic*) *adj* and *n* resident. — *n* (*obs* or *archaic*) **res'iance**. [OFr *reseant*, pr p of *reseoir*, from L *residēre*]

reside *ri-zīd'*, *vi* to dwell permanently; to be in residence; to abide; to be vested; to inhere. — *n* **residence** (*rez'i-dəns*) the act or duration of dwelling in a place; the act of living in the place required by regulations or performance of functions; a stay in a place; a dwelling-place; a dwelling-house, *esp* one of some pretensions; that in which anything permanently inheres or has its seat. — *n* **res'idency** a residence; the official abode of a

Some words with the prefix **re-**.

rēsent'ence *vt*.	**rēshape'** *vt*.	**re-site'** *vt*.
rēsett'le *vt* and *vi*.	**rēship'** *vt* and *vi*.	**rēsole'** *vt*.
rēsett'lement *n*.	**rēship'ment** *n*.	**rēspell'** *vt*.

resident or governor of a protected state; an administrative district under a resident; a resident's post at a hospital, or the period during which it is held. — *adj* **res'ident** dwelling in a place for some time; residing on one's own estate, or the place of one's duties, or the place required by certain conditions; not migratory; not moving (*obs*); inherent. — *n* a person who resides; an animal that does not migrate; a doctor who works in, and *usu* resides at, a hospital to gain experience in a particular field; a registered guest at a hotel; a representative at a foreign court of lower rank than an ambassador (*hist*); a representative of a governor in a protected state; the governor of a residency or administrative district (*esp* in the former Dutch E Indies). — *n* **res'identer** (or *Scot -dent'*) an inhabitant. — *adj* **residential** (*-den'shl*) of, for, or connected with residence; suitable for or occupied by houses, *esp* of a better kind. — *adj* **residentiary** (*-den'shə-ri*) resident; officially bound to reside; relating to or involving official residence. — *n* an inhabitant; a person bound to reside, such as a canon. — *n* **residen'tiaryship**. — *n* **res'identship**. — *n* **resī'der**. [L *residēre*, from *re-* back, and *sedēre* to sit]

residue *rez'i-dū*, or *US* also *-do͞o*, *n* that which is left, remainder; what is left of an estate after payment of debts, charges and legacies (*law*). — *adj* **resid'ual** remaining as residue or difference; formed by accumulations of rock waste where the rock has disintegrated (*geol*). — *n* that which remains as a residue or as a difference; a payment to an artist, etc for later use of a film, etc in whch he or she appears. — *adj* **resid'uary** of, or of the nature of, a residue, *esp* of an estate. — *adj* **resid'uous** (*rare*) residual. — *n* **residuum** (*rə-zij'o͞o-əm -wəm*, or *rez-id'ū-əm*) a residue: — *pl* **resid'ua**. — **residual activity** in a nuclear reactor, the activity remaining after the reaction is shut down following a period of operation; **residual current device** a circuit-breaker used to protect electrical equipment or its operator; **residual value** (*finance*) the expected selling price of an asset at the end of its useful life. [L *residuum*, from *residēre* to remain behind]

resign *ri-zīn'*, *vt* to give up (one's position, employment, etc); to yield up; to submit calmly; to relinquish (often with *from*); to entrust. — *vi* to give up office, employment, etc; to submit (*rare*). — *n* **resignation** (*rez-ig-nā'shən*) the or an act of resigning; the state of being resigned or quietly submissive; the form by which a vassal returns the feu into the hands of a superior (*Scots law*). — *adj* **resigned** (*ri-zīnd'*) calmly submissive. — *adv* **resignedly** (*ri-zīn'id-li*). — *n* **resign'edness**. — *n* **resign'er**. — *n* **resign'ment**. [OFr *resigner*, from L *resignāre*, *-ātum* to unseal, annul, from *signāre* to seal, from *signum* a mark]

re-sign *rē-sīn'*, *vt* to sign again. **[re-]**

resile *ri-zīl'*, *vi* to recoil; to rebound; to recover form and position elastically; to draw back from a statement, agreement or course of action; to back out (*esp Scot*). [L *resilīre* to leap back, from *salīre* to leap]

resilient *ri-zil'i-ənt*, *adj* recoiling, rebounding; able to recover form and position elastically; able to withstand shock, suffering, disappointment, etc. — *n* **resilience** (*ri-zil'i-əns*) or **resil'iency** recoil; the quality of being resilient. — *adv* **resil'iently**. [L *resiliēns*, *-entis*, pr p of *resilīre*; see **resile**]

resin *rez'in*, *n* any of a number of substances or products obtained from the sap of certain plants and trees (*natural resins*), used in plastics, etc; any of a large number of substances made by polymerization or condensation (*synthetic resins*) which, though not related chemically to natural resins, have some of their physical properties, very important in the plastics industry, etc. — *vt* to treat with resin; to remove resin from; to rosin. — *n* **res'ināte** a salt of any of the acids occurring in natural resins. — *n* **res'iner** a resin gatherer. — *adj* **resinif'erous** yielding resin. — *n* **resinificā'tion**. — *vt* and *vi* **res'inify** to make or become a resin or resinous. — *vt* **res'inize** or **-ise** to treat with resin. — *adj* and *n* **res'inoid** (a substance) of, like or containing resin. — *n* **resinō'sis** abnormal flow of resin. — *adj* **res'inous** of, like, containing or of the nature of resin; of the lustre of resin; negative (as produced by rubbing a resin) (*electronics*; *obs*). — *adv* **res'inously**. [Fr *résine*, from L *rēsīna*]

resinata *rez-i-nā'tə*, *n* Greek white wine with resinous flavour. [L *rēsīnāta* (fem) resined]

resipiscence *res-i-pis'əns*, *n* recognition of error, change to a better frame of mind. — Also **resipisc'ency**. — *adj* **resipisc'ent**. [L *resipīscentia*, from *resipīscere*, from *re-* again, and *sapere* to be wise]

res ipsa loquitur *rēz ip'sə lok'wi-tər* or (*L*) *rās ip'sə lok'wi-to͝or*, (*law*) the thing speaks for itself, applied in cases in which the mere fact that an accident has happened is deemed to be evidence of negligence unless the defendant proves otherwise.

resist *ri-zist'*, *vt* to strive against, oppose; to withstand; to refuse; to hinder the action of; to be little affected by; to be distasteful to (*Shakesp*). — *vi* to make opposition. — *n* a protective coating, *esp* one on parts of a textile to protect the blank areas of the design that is being printed, an acid-proof coating on parts of a metal plate or a light-sensitive coating on a silicon wafer. — Also *adj*. — *n* **resis'tance** the act or power of resisting; opposition; the body's ability to resist disease; (with *cap*) an organization of (armed) opposition to an occupying enemy force, *esp* that of the French in World War II (also **resistance movement**); the opposition of a body to the motion of another; that property of a substance in virtue of which the passage of an electric current through it is accompanied with a dissipation of energy; an electrical resistor. — *n* **resis'tant** a person who, or thing which, resists. — *adj* **resis'tant** (less *usu* **resis'tent**) making resistance; (eg of parasites, germs, antibiotics, corrosion) withstanding adverse conditions. — *n* a person who, or thing which, resists. — *n* **resistibil'ity**. — *adj* **resis'tible**. — *adv* **resis'tibly**. — *adv* **resis'tingly**. — *adj* **resis'tive**. — *adv* **resis'tively**. — *n* **resistiv'ity** (*rez-*) capacity for resisting; (also **specific resistance**) a property of a conducting material expressed as resistance multiplied by cross-sectional area over length. — *adj* **resist'less** (*archaic*) irresistible; unable to resist. — *adv* **resist'lessly**. — *n* **resist'lessness**. — *n* **resist'or** anything that resists; a piece of apparatus used to offer electric resistance. — **resistance box** a box containing resistors; **resistance coil** a coil of wire used to offer resistance to the passage of electricity; **resistance movement** see above; **resistance pyrometer** or **thermometer** a device for measuring high temperatures by means of the variation in the electrical resistance of a wire as the temperature changes; **resistance thermometry** temperature measurement of this kind; **resistance welding** see under **weld**[2]. — **consumer** or **market resistance** unwillingness of consumers to buy marketed products (also **sales resistance**); **line of least resistance** the easiest course of action. [L *resistere*, from *re-* against, and *sistere* to make to stand]

resit *rē-sit'*, *vi* and *vt* to sit (an examination) again after failing: — *pa t* and *pa p* **resat'**. — *n* (*rē'*) an opportunity or act of resitting. **[re-]**

Some words with the prefix **re-**.

respray *vt* (*rē-sprā'*) and *n* (*rē'sprā*).	**rēstage'** *vt*.	**rēstock'** *vt*.
rēstaff' *vt*.	**rēstate'** *vt*.	**rēstring'** *vt*.
	rēstate'ment *n*.	**rēstruc'ture** *vt*.

res judicata *rēz jōō-di-kā'tə* or *rās yōō-di-kä'ta*, (*L*) *n* a case or suit already decided.

reskew or **reskue** (*Spenser*). Same as **rescue**.

resnatron *rez'nə-tron*, *n* a high-power, high-frequency tetrode. [*resona*tor and **-tron**]

resoluble *rez'əl-ū-bl*, *adj* that may be resolved, dissolved or analysed. — *adj* **resolute** (*rez'əl-ōōt* or *-ūt*) having a fixed purpose; constant in pursuing a purpose; determined. — *n* (*Shakesp*) a determined person. — *adv* **res'olutely**. — *n* **res'oluteness**. — *n* **resolution** (*rez-əl-ōō'shən* or *-ū-shən*) act of resolving; analysis; separation of components; melting; solution; the separation of an optically inactive mixture or compound into its optically active components (*chem*); the definition of a picture in TV or facsimile (measured by the number of lines used to scan the image of the picture); the smallest measurable difference, or separation, or time interval (*phys*, *electronics* and *nucleonics*); resolving power (qv); state of being resolved; fixed determination; that which is resolved; removal of or freedom from doubt; progression from discord to concord (*music*); a formal proposal put before a meeting, or its formal determination thereon; substitution of two short syllables for a long; the making visible of detail; the disappearance or dispersion of a tumour or inflammation. — *n* **re-solu'tion** (*rē-sol-*) renewed or repeated solution. — *n* **resolu'tioner** (*rez-əl-*) one who joins in or accepts a resolution. — *n* **Resolutioner** (*Scot hist*) a person who approved of the resolutions of 1650 admitting to civil and military office all persons except those excommunicate and hostile to the Covenant (opposed to *Protester*). — *adj* **res'olutive**. — *n* **resolvabil'ity**. — *adj* **resolvable** (*ri-zolv'*). — *vt* **resolve'** to separate into components; to make visible the details of; to analyse; to break up; to melt; to transform; to relax; to solve; to dissipate; to free from doubt or difficulty; to convince (of; *obs*); to assure (*obs*); to inform (*obs*); to answer (a question; *obs*); to dispel (fears; *Shakesp*); to pass as a resolution; to determine; to disperse (eg a tumour); to make (a discord) pass into a concord (*music*). — *vi* to undergo resolution; to come to a determination (often with *on* to indicate the course chosen); to decide to go to a place (with *on*; *Shakesp*); to take counsel (*Spenser*); to lapse (*law*). — *obs* senses also used reflexively. — *n* resolution; fixed purpose; firmness of purpose; solution (*obs*). — *adj* **resolved'** fixed in purpose. — *adv* **resolvedly** (*ri-zol'vid-li*) resolutely. — *n* **resol'vedness**. — *adj* **resol'vent** having power to resolve. — *n* that which causes or helps solution or resolution. — *n* **resol'ver**. — **resolving power** the ability of telescope, microscope, etc to distinguish very close, or very small, objects; the ability of a photographic emulsion to produce finely-detailed images. [L *resolvere*, *resolūtum*, from *re-* (intensive) and *solvere* to loose]

resolve, etc. See under **resoluble**.

resonance *rez'ən-əns*, *n* resounding; sonority; the sound heard in auscultation; sympathetic vibration; the ringing quality of the human voice when produced in such a way that sympathetic vibration is caused in the air-spaces in the head, chest and throat; the state of a system in which a large vibration (is) produced by a small stimulus of *approx* the same frequency as that of the system (*phys* and *electronics*); such a large vibration (*phys* and *electronics*); increased probability of a nuclear reaction when the energy of an incident particle or photon is around a certain value appropriate to the energy level of the compound nucleus; a property of certain compounds, in which the most stable state of the molecule is a combination of theoretically possible bond arrangements or distributions of electrons (*chem*); the complex of bodily responses to an emotional state, or of emotional responses to a situation. — *adj* **res'onant** resounding, ringing; of giving its characteristic vibration in sympathy with another body's vibration. — *adv* **res'onantly**. — *vi* **res'onate** to resound; to vibrate sympathetically. — *n* **res'onātor** a resonating body or device, such as for increasing sonority or for analysing sound. — **res'onance-box** a chamber in a musical instrument for increasing its sonority by vibration in sympathy with the strings. [L *resonāre*, *-ātum*, from *re-* back, and *sonāre* to sound]

resorb *ri-sörb'*, *vt* to absorb back. — *n* **resorb'ence** — *adj* **resorb'ent**. [L *resorbēre* to suck back]

resorcin *ri-zör'sin*, *n* a colourless phenol, $C_6H_4(OH)_2$, used in dyeing, photography and medicine. — Also **resor'cinol**. [**resin** and **orcin**]

resorption *ri-sörp'shən*, *n* resorbing, *esp* of a mineral by rock magma; the breaking-down and assimilation of a substance (*med*). — *adj* **resorp'tive**. [See **resorb**]

resort[1] *ri-zört'*, *vi* to revert (*obs*); to go (to); to betake oneself; to have recourse; to apply; to go or be habitually. — *n* act of resorting; a place much frequented; a haunt; that which one has or may have recourse to; concourse; thronging; repair. — *n* **resort'er** a frequenter. — **in the last resort** *orig* (a Gallicism, *en dernier ressort*), without appeal; *hence* as a last expedient. [OFr *resortir* (Fr *ressortir*) to rebound, retire, from *sortir* to go out; origin obscure]

resort[2] *rē-sört'*, *vt* to sort again or differently. [**re-**]

resound *ri-zownd'*, *vt* to echo; to sound with reverberation; to sound or spread (the praises of a person or thing). — *vi* to echo; to re-echo, reverberate; to sound sonorously. — *adj* **resound'ing** echoing; thorough, decisive, as in *resounding victory*. — *adv* **resound'ingly**. [**re-**]

resource *ri-sōrs'*, *-sörs* or *ri-z-*, *n* source or possibility of help; an expedient; (in *pl*) money or means of raising money; means of support; means of occupying or amusing oneself; resourcefulness. — *vt* to provide the (*esp* financial) resources for. — *adj* **resource'ful** fertile in expedients; clever, ingenious; rich in resources. — *n* **resource'fulness**. — *adj* **resource'less**. [OFr *ressource*, from *resourdre*, from L *resurgere* to rise again]

respeak *rē-spēk'*, (*Shakesp*) *vt* to echo. [**re-**]

respect *ri-spekt'*, *vt* to look to, regard, consider, take into account; to heed; to refer to, relate to, have reference to (*archaic*); to treat with consideration, refrain from violating; to feel or show esteem, deference, or honour to; to value (a thing) (*Shakesp*); to face, look at (*obs* and *heraldry*). — Also *vi*. — *n* heed (*Spenser*); an aspect (*obs*); a particular; a relation; reference; regard; consideration; partiality or favour towards (with *of*); deferential esteem; (often in *pl*) a greeting or message of esteem. — *n* **respectabil'ity**. — *vt* **respec'tabilize** or **-ise** to make respectable. — *adj* **respec'table** worthy of respect; considerable; passable; mediocre; of good social standing (*obs*); fairly well-to-do; decent and well-behaved; reputable; seemly; presentable; timidly or priggishly conventional. — *n* **respec'tableness**. — *adv* **respec'tably**. — *adj* **respec'tant** facing each other (*heraldry*); looking back. — *n* **respec'ter** a person who respects, *esp* in *respecter of persons*, someone who, or something that, singles out an individual or individuals for unduly favourable treatment (*usu* in *neg*). — *adj* **respect'ful** showing or feeling respect. — *adv* **respect'fully**. — *n* **respect'fulness**. — *prep* **respect'ing** concerning; considering. — *adj* **respec'tive** having respect; regardful, considerate (*Shakesp*); heedful; discriminating; respectful (*obs*); worthy of respect (*Shakesp*);

Some words with the prefix **re-**.

rēstyle' *vt.*	**rēsur'vey** *n.*	**rētell'** *vt*: — *pa p* **rētold'**.
rēsubmit' *vt.*	**resynchronizā'tion** or **-s-** *vt.*	**rētell'er** *n.*
rēsurvey' *vt.*	**resyn'chronize** or **-ise** *vt.*	**rētie'** *vt.*

relative; particular or several, relating to each distributively. — *adv* **respec'tively**. — *adj* **respect'less** regardless. — **respect of persons** undue favour, eg for wealth, etc; **in respect of** in the matter of; because of (*obs*); in comparison with (*obs*); **with respect to** with regard to. [L *respicere, respectum*, from *re-* back, and *specere* to look]

respire *ri-spīr'*, *vi* to breathe; to take breath. — *vt* to breathe; to exhale. — *adj* **respirable** (*res'pər-ə-bl* or *ri-spīr'ə-bl*) fit for breathing. — *n* **respiration** (*res-pər-ā'shən*) breathing; the taking in of oxygen and giving out of carbon dioxide, with associated physiological processes; a breath; a breathing-space. — *n* **res'pirātor** an appliance which provides artificial respiration (*med*); an appliance worn on the mouth or nose to filter or warm the air breathed; a gas mask. — *adj* **respiratory** (*res'pər-ə-tər-i* or *ri-spī'rə-tər-i*) of, relating to, or serving for, respiration. — *n* **respirom'eter** an apparatus for measuring breathing. [L *respīrāre, -ātum*, from *spīrāre* to breathe]

respite *res'pīt* or *-pit*, *n* temporary cessation of something that is tiring or painful; postponement requested or granted; temporary suspension of the execution of a criminal (*law*); delay in action (*obs*); leisure (*obs*). — *vt* to grant a respite to; to relieve by a pause (*obs*); to delay, put off; to grant postponement to; to prolong (*Shakesp*); to give up, cease from (*obs*). — *vi* to rest (from) (*obs*). [ME *respit*, from OFr (Fr *répit*), from L *respectus, respicere*; see **respect**]

resplend *ri-splend'*, *vi* to shine brilliantly. — *n* **resplend'ence** or **resplend'ency**. — *adj* **resplend'ent** shining, brilliant and splendid. — *adv* **resplend'ently**. [L *resplendēre*, from *re-* (intensive) and *splendēre* to shine]

respond *ri-spond'*, *vi* to answer; to utter liturgical responses; to act in answer; to react. — *n* a response to a versicle in liturgy; a half-pillar or half-pier attached to a wall to support an arch (corresponding to one at the other end of an arcade, etc). — *n* **respond'ence** response (*Spenser*); correspondence, agreement. — *n* **respond'ency** correspondence. — *adj* **respond'ent** answering; corresponding; responsive. — *n* a person who answers; a person who refutes objections; a defendant, *esp* in a divorce suit. — *n* **respondentia** (*res-pon-den'shə*) a loan on a ship's cargo, payable only on safe arrival. — *n* **respond'er, respons'er** or **respons'or** (*ris-*) a person who, or thing which, responds; the part of a transponder which replies automatically to the correct interrogation signal. — *n pl* **Respon'sa** a branch of rabbinical literature consisting of written decisions from authorities in reply to questions, problems, etc submitted to them (*n* **respon'sum** one of these decisions). — *n* **response'** an answer; an oracular answer; an answer made by the congregation to the minister or priest during divine service; a responsory; a reaction, *esp* sympathetic; the ratio of the output to the input level of a transmission system at any particular frequency (*electronics*). — *adj* **response'less**. — *n* **responsibil'ity** state of being responsible; a trust or charge for which one is responsible. — *adj* **respon'sible** liable to be called to account as being in charge or control; answerable (*to* a person, etc *for* something); deserving the blame or credit of (with *for*); governed by a sense of responsibility; being a free moral agent; morally accountable for one's actions; trustworthy; able to pay; respectable-looking; involving responsibility; correspondent (*obs*). — *adv* **respon'sibly**. — *n pl* **respon'sions** (*-shənz*) formerly, the first of three examinations for the BA degree at Oxford, 'smalls'. — *adj* **respon'sive** ready to respond; answering; correspondent; with responses. — *adv* **respon'sively**. — *n* **respon'siveness**. — *adj* **responsorial** (*ri-* or *rē-spon-sō'ri-əl* or *-sö'ri-əl*) responsive. — *n* an office-book containing the responsories. — *adj* **respon'sory** making answer. — *n* an anthem sung after a lesson; a liturgical response. — **response time** (*comput*) the time taken by a computer to reply to a command given to it by a user, eg to display a character on the screen after the corresponding key has been pressed. [L *respondēre, respōnsum*, from *re-* back, and *spondēre* to promise]

ressaldar. Same as **risaldar**.

rest[1] *rest*, *n* repose, refreshing inactivity; intermission of or freedom from motion or disturbance; tranquillity; repose of death; invigoration by resting (*Shakesp*); a place for resting; a prop or support (eg for a book, a billiard cue, a violinist's chin); motionlessness; a pause in speaking or reading; an interval of silence in music, or a mark indicating it. — *vi* to repose; to be at ease; to be still; to be supported (on); to lean (on); to put trust in (with *on*); to have foundation in (with *on*); to settle, alight; to remain; (*esp* of an actor or actress) to be temporarily unemployed (*colloq*; *facetious*). — *vt* to give rest to; to place or hold in support (on); to lean (on); to base (on); (*reflexive*) to give (oneself) rest or (*obs*) to rely (upon). — *n* **rest'er**. — *adj* **rest'ful** at rest; rest-giving; tranquil. — *adv* **rest'fully**. — *n* **rest'fulness**. — *n* and *adj* **rest'ing**. — *adj* **rest'less** unresting, not resting, sleeping or relaxing; never still; uneasily active; impatient (of) (*Pope*); impatient of inactivity or of remaining still; never-ceasing; unrestful, giving or allowing no rest. — *adv* **rest'lessly**. — *n* **rest'lessness**. — **rest'-centre** a place of shelter for numbers of people driven from their homes by an emergency; **rest'-cure** treatment consisting of inactivity and quiet; **rest'-day** a day of rest; the first day of a three days' visit; **rest'=home** an establishment for those who need special care and attention, eg invalids, old people, etc; **rest'-house** a house of rest for travellers; **rest'ing-place** a place of rest; a stair-landing; (**one's last resting-place** one's grave); **rest'ing-spore** a spore that can germinate after a period of dormancy; **rest'ing-stage** a state of suspended activity; **rest mass** (*phys*) the mass of an object when it is at rest; **rest room** a room in a building other than a private house with adjoining lavatories, etc; **rest stop** (*US*) a lay-by. — **at rest** stationary; in repose; free from disquiet; **lay to rest** to give burial to. [OE *rest, ræst*; Ger *Rast*, Du *rust*; converging and merging in meaning with **rest**[2,3]]

rest[2] *rest*, *n* remainder; all others; reserve fund; a rapid continuous series of returns (*tennis*, etc); a stake whose loss ends the game (*primero*). — *vi* to remain (see also **rest**[1]). — **for the rest** as regards other matters; **set up one's rest** (*archaic*) to make one's final stake; to take a resolution; to take up abode. [Fr *reste*, from L *restāre* to remain, from *re-* back, and *stāre* to stand]

rest[3] *rest*, (*hist*) *n* a contrivance on a breastplate to prevent the spear from being driven back. — *vt* (*Shakesp*) to arrest. [Aphetic for **arrest**]

restart *rē-start'*, *vi* and *vt* to start again. — *n* a fresh or subsequent start; (with *cap*) in the UK, a government scheme of courses, etc intended to help the unemployed find retraining or new employment. — *n* **rēstart'er**. [**re-**]

restaurant *rest'(ə-)-rã, -rong, -ront* or *-rənt*, *n* a place where food or meals are prepared and served, or are available, to customers. — *n* **restaurateur** (*res-tər-ə-tûr'* or *-tœr'*) the keeper of a restaurant. — *n* **restaura'tion** the business, skill or art of a restaurateur. — **res'taurant=car** a dining-car. [Fr, from *restaurer* to restore]

restem *rē-stem'*, (*Shakesp*) *vt* to force (a way) back against the current. [**re-**]

Some words with the prefix **re-**.

retile' *vt.*	**rētrain'** *vt* and *vi.*	**rētrim'** *vt.*
retime' *vt.*	**rētransfer'** *vt.*	**rētune'** *vt.*
retī'tle *vt.*	**rētrans'fer** *n.*	

rest-harrow *rest'-har-ō*, *n* a papilionaceous plant (genus *Ononis*) with long, tough, woody roots. [**rest**[3] and **harrow**[1]]

restiff *res'tif*, an obsolete form of **restive**.

restiform *res'ti-fôrm*, *adj* cordlike. [L *restis* a cord, and *fōrma* form]

restitute *res'ti-tūt*, (*archaic*) *vt* to restore. — *vi* (*archaic*) to make restitution. — *n* **restitū'tion** a restoring, return; compensation; (also **restitū'tionism**) restorationism (*esp US*). — *n* **restitū'tionist**. — *adj* **restitūtive** (*ri-stit'*, or *res'tit-*). — *n* **res'titūtor**. — *adj* **restit'ūtory**. [L *restituere*, *-ūtum*, from *re-*, and *statuere* to make to stand]

restitutio in integram *res-ti-tū'ti-ō in in-teg'rəm*, (*law*) the restoration of the parties to a contract to the relative positions occupied by them before the contract was made. [L]

restive *res'tiv*, *adj* inert (*obs*); unwilling to go forward; obstinate, refractory; uneasy, as if ready to break from control. — *adv* **res'tively**. — *n* **res'tiveness**. [OFr *restif*, from L *restāre* to rest]

restore *ri-stōr'* or *-stör*, *vt* to repair; to bring, put or give back; to make good; to reinstate; to bring back to a (supposed) former state, or to a normal state; to reconstruct mentally, by inference or conjecture. — *n* (*Spenser*) restitution. — *adj* **restor'able**. — *n* **restor'ableness**. — *n* **restoration** (*res-tō-rā'shən*, or *-tö-*, *-tə-*, *-to-*) the act or process of restoring; (*usu* with *cap*) a reinstatement of a monarch or monarchy (eg the Restoration of the Stuarts or the Bourbons); renovations and reconstruction (sometimes little differing from destruction) of a building, painting, etc; a reconstructed thing or representation. — *adj* (with *cap*) occurring during, or relating to, the period of the Restoration of Charles II. — *n* **restorā'tionism** (*theol*) the receiving of a sinner to divine favour; the belief that after a purgation all sinners and angels will be restored to the favour of God. — *n* **restorā'tionist** an adherent of restorationism, a universalist. — *adj* **restorative** (*ris-tor'ə-tiv* or *-tör'*) tending to restore, *esp* to strength and vigour. — *n* a medicine that restores. — *adv* **restor'atively**. — *n* **restor'er**. [OFr *restorer*, from L *restaurāre*, *-ātum*]

restrain *ri-strān'*, *vt* to hold back; to control; to subject to forcible repression; to tighten (*Shakesp*); to forbid (*Milton*). — *vi* (*rare*) to refrain. — *adj* **restrain'able**. — *adj* **restrained'** controlled; self-controlled; showing restraint; forbidden (*Shakesp*). — *adv* **restrain'edly**. — *n* **restrain'edness**. — *n* **restrain'er** a person who or thing which restrains; an ingredient of a photographic developer which checks the development and reduces the tendency to fog. — *n* and *adj* **restrain'ing**. — *n* **restraint'** the or an act of restraining; state of being restrained; a restraining influence; restriction; forcible control; artistic control or reticence; lack of liberty; reserve. — **restraint of princes** embargo; **restraint of trade** interference with free play of economic forces, eg by monopolies. [OFr *restraindre*, *restrai(g)n-*, from L *restringere*, *restrictum* from *re-* back, and *stringere* to draw tightly]

restrict *ri-strikt'*, *vt* to limit; to confine within limits; to limit circulation or disclosure of for security reasons. — *adj* **restrict'ed**. — *adv* **restrict'edly**. — *n* **restric'tion**. — *n* **restric'tionist** a person who favours restriction. — Also *adj*. — *adj* **restric'tive** restricting; tending to restrict; expressing restriction, as in relative clauses, phrases, etc that limit the application of the verb to the subject, eg *people who like historic buildings should visit Edinburgh*. — *adv* **restric'tively**. — *vt* **restringe** (*ri-strinj'*) to restrict. — *n* and *adj* **restrin'gent** astringent. — **restricted area** one from which the general public is excluded; one within which there is a speed limit; **restriction endonuclease** or **enzyme** an enzyme, widely used in genetic engineering, which can be used to divide genes into segments which can be combined with those of other species; **restrictive practice** a trade practice that is against the public interest, such as an agreement to sell only to certain buyers, or to keep up resale prices; used also of certain trade union practices, such as the closed shop, demarcation, working to rule, etc; **restrictive temperature** (*biol*) the temperature at which a temperature sensitive mutant organism will not grow (opposed to **permissive temperature**). [L *restringere*, *restrictum*]

restringe. See **restrict**.

resty *rest'i*, *adj* restive; sluggish (*Shakesp*); inoperative, ineffectual (*Spenser*). [**restive**, or partly **rest**[1]]

result *ri-zult'*, *vi* to issue (with *in*); to follow as a consequence; to rebound (*obs*); to be the outcome; to revert (*law*). — *n* consequence; outcome; outcome aimed at; quantity obtained by calculation; decision, resolution, eg of a council (*obs* and *US*); in games, the (*usu* final) score; in games, etc, a successful final score, a win, as in *get a result* (*colloq*). — *adj* **result'ant** resulting; resulting from combination (as of tones sounded together). — *n* a force compounded of two or more forces; a sum of vector quantities; a resultant tone; a result of combination. — *adj* **result'ative** expressing result. — *adj* **result'ful**. — *adj* **result'ing**. — *adj* **result'less**. — *n* **result'lessness**. [L *resultāre* to leap back, from *saltāre* to leap]

resume *ri-zūm'* or *-zōōm'*, *vt* to take back; to summarize, make a résumé of (*archaic*); to assume again; to take up again; to begin again. — *vi* to take possession again; to begin again in continuation. — *adj* **resum'able**. — *n* **résumé** (*rā-zü-mā* or *rez'ū-mā*; Fr *pa p*) a summary; (*rez'*) a curriculum vitae (*NAm*). — *n* **resumption** (*ri-zump'shən* or *-zum'*) the or an act of resuming. — *adj* **resumptive** (*-zump'* or *-zum'*). — *adv* **resump'tively**. [L *resūmere*, *-sūmptum*, from *re-*, and *sūmere* to take]

resupinate *ri-sōō'pin-āt* or *-sū'*, *adj* upside down by twisting (*bot*). — *n* **resupinā'tion**. — *adj* **resupine** (*rē-sū-pīn'* or *-sōō-*) lying on the back. [L *resupīnāre*, *-ātum*, and *resupīnus*, from *re-* back, and *supīnus* bent backward]

resurge *ri-sûrj'*, (*rare*) *vi* to rise again. — *n* **resur'gence**. — *adj* **resur'gent**. — *vt* **resurrect** (*rez-ər-ekt'*; back-formation) to restore to life; to revive; to disinter. — *vi* to come to life again. — *n* **resurrection** (*-ek'shən*) a rising from the dead, *esp* (with *cap*) that of Christ; resuscitation; revival; a thing resurrected; body-snatching (*hist*). — *adj* **resurrec'tional**. — *adj* **resurrec'tionary**. — *n* **resurrec'tionism**. — *n* **resurrec'tionist** or **resurrec'tion-man** (*hist*) a person who stole bodies from the grave for dissection. — *vt* **resurrec'tionize** or **-ise**. — *adj* **resurrect'ive**. — *n* **resurrect'or**. — **resurrec'tion-pie** a dish compounded of remnants of former meals; **resurrection plant** a plant that curls into a ball during a drought and spreads again when moist, such as the rose of Jericho, or some selaginellas. [L *resurgere*, *resurrēctum*, from *re-*, and *surgere* to rise]

resuscitate *ri-sus'i-tāt*, *vt* and *vi* to bring back to life or consciousness; to revive. — *adj* **resusc'itable**. — *adj* **resusc'itant**. — *n* a person who, or thing which, resuscitates. — *n* **resuscitā'tion**. — *adj* **resusc'itātive** tending to resuscitate; reviving; revivifying; reanimating. — *n* **resusc'itātor** a person who, or thing which, resuscitates; an oxygen-administering apparatus used to induce breathing after asphyxiation. [L *resuscitāre*, *-ātum*, from *re-*, *sus-*, *sub-* from beneath,

Some words with the prefix **re-**.

rē'tune *n.*	**rēū'nify** *vt.*	**rēurge'** *vt.*
rēturf' *vt.*	**rēūnificā'tion** *n.*	**rēūs'able** *adj.*
rē-type' *vt.*	**rēuphol'ster** *vt.*	**rēuse'** (*-ūz'*), *vt.*

and *citāre* to put into quick motion, from *ciēre* to make to go]

ret *ret*, **rate** or **rait** *rāt*, *vt* to expose to moisture. — *vt* and *vi* to soak; to soften, spoil or rot by soaking or exposure to moisture; to rot: — *pr p* **rett'ing, rāt'ing** or **rait'ing**; *pa t* and *pa p* **rett'ed, rāt'ed** or **rait'ed**. — *n* **rett'ery** a place where flax is retted. [Appar related to **rot**]

retable *ri-tā'bl*, *n* a shelf or ornamental setting for panels, etc behind an altar. [Fr *rétable*, from LL *retrōtabulum*]

retail *rē'tāl*, formerly (now *rare*) *ri-* or *rē-tāl'*, *n* the sale directly to the consumer, or in small quantities (cf **wholesale**). — *adj* in, of, engaged in or concerned with such sale. — *adv* by retail. — *vt* (*ri-* or *rē-tāl'*) to sell by retail; to repeat in detail; to put about, hand on by report. — *vi* to sell. — *n* **retail'er**. — *n* **retail'ment**. — **retail price maintenance** (*abbrev* **RPM**) same as **resale price maintenance** under **resale**. [OFr *retail* piece cut off, from *tailler* to cut]

retain *ri-tān'*, *vt* to keep; to hold back; to continue to hold; to keep up; to employ or keep engaged, eg by a fee paid; to keep in mind. — *adj* **retain'able**. — *n* **retain'er** a person who or thing which retains; a dependent of a person of rank, owing some service to him or her (*hist*); a family servant of long standing; an authorization; a retaining fee (in legal usage, **general** to secure a priority of claim on a counsel's services, **special** for a particular case). — *n* **retain'ership**. — *n* **retain'ment**. — **retaining fee** the advance fee paid to a lawyer to defend a cause; **retaining wall** a wall to hold back solid material, such as earth or (loosely) water (also called **revetment**). [Fr *retenir*, from L *retinēre*, from *re-* back, and *tenēre* to hold]

retake *rē-tāk'*, *vt* to take again; to take back, recapture: — *pa t* **retook'**; *pa p* **retā'ken**. — *n* (*rē'*) a second or repeated photographing or photograph, *esp* for a film. — *n* **retāk'er**. — *n* **retāk'ing**. [**re-**]

retaliate *ri-tal'i-āt*, *vt* to repay in kind (now *usu* an injury; sometimes *upon* a person). — *vi* to return like for like (*esp* in hostility). — *n* **retaliā'tion** return of like for like; imposition of a tariff against countries that impose a tariff. — *n* **retaliā'tionist**. — *adj* **retal'iātive**. — *n* **retal'iātor**. — *adj* **retal'iatory** (*-āt-ər-i* or *-ət-ər-i*). [L *retāliāre*, *-ātum*, from *re-*, and *tāliō*, *-ōnis* like for like, from *tālis* such]

retama *re-tä'mə*, *n* a name for various desert switch-plants, either papilionaceous or caesalpiniaceous, including Spanish broom. [Sp, from Ar *retām* (pl)]

retard *ri-tärd'*, *vt* to slow; to keep back development or progress of; to delay; to postpone (*rare*); to delay the timing of (an ignition spark). — *vi* to slow down; to delay. — *n* delay; lag. — *adj* **retar'dant** serving to delay or slow down a chemical reaction, such as rusting. — Also *n*. — *n* **retar'date** (*psychol*) a person who is mentally retarded or backward. — *n* **retardā'tion** (*rē-*) or **retard'ment** slowing; delay; lag. — *adj* **retardative** (*ri-tard'ə-tiv*). — *adj* **retar'datory**. — *adj* **retar'ded** delayed or slowed down; slow in development, *esp* mental, or having made less than normal progress in learning. — *n* **retar'der** retardant; a substance that delays or prevents setting of cement. — *n* **retard'ment** see **retardation** above. [L *retardāre*, *-ātum*, from *re-*, and *tardāre* to slow]

retch[1] *rech*, also *rēch*, *vi* to strain as if to vomit. — *n* an act of retching. [OE *hræcan*, from *hrāca* a hawking]

retch[2] *rech*, **retch'less**, etc. Obsolete forms of **reck**, etc.

retd *abbrev*: retired; returned.

rete *rē'tē*, (*anatom*) *n* a network, eg of blood-vessels or nerves. — *adj* **retial** (*rē'shi-əl*). [L *rēte* net]

retene *rē'tēn* or *ret'ēn*, *n* a hydrocarbon ($C_{18}H_{18}$) obtained from tar. — *n* **retinalite** (*ret'* or *ri-tin'*) a resinous-lustred serpentine. — *n* **retinis'pora** or **retinos'pora** a cypress or related conifer in a perpetuated juvenile form, once placed in a separate genus. — *n* **ret'inite** pitchstone (*obs*); a fossil resin. — *adj* **ret'inoid** resembling resin. — *n* (*biochem*) a chemical variant of vitamin A, with powerful effect when used as a drug. — *n* **ret'inol** an oil distilled from resin; vitamin A. [Gr *rhētinē* pine resin]

retention *ri-ten'shən*, *n* the act or power of retaining; memory; custody; inability to void or get rid of fluid, etc (*med*). — *n* **reten'tionist** a person who advocates the retaining of a policy, etc, *esp* that of capital punishment. — *adj* **reten'tive** retaining; tenacious; retaining moisture. — *adv* **reten'tively**. — *n* **reten'tiveness** or **retentiv'ity** (*rē-*). [L *retentiō*, *-ōnis*; OFr *retentif*; see **retain**]

retexture[1] *rē-teks'chər*, *n* weaving anew. [L *retexere* to weave anew, earlier to unweave]

retexture[2] *rē-teks'chər*, *vt* to treat (a material) so as to restore firmness lost through the action of spirit in the process of dry-cleaning. [**re-** and **texture** to give a texture to]

rethink *rē-thingk'*, *vt* to consider again and come to a different decision about. — Also *n* (*rē'thingk*). [**re-**]

retial. See under **rete**.

retiarius *rē-shi-ā'ri-əs* or *rā-ti-ä'ri-ōōs*, (*hist*) *n* a gladiator armed with a net. — *adj* **retiary** (*rē'shi-ər-i*) of nets; using a net as a weapon, as a gladiator or a spider. [L *rētiārius*, from *rēte* net]

reticella *re-ti-chel'ə*, *n* an early form of needlepoint lace produced in Italy in the 16c and 17c, made by working cutwork designs on a linen background. [Ital, dimin of *rete* net]

reticent *ret'i-sənt*, *adj* reserved or communicating sparingly or unwillingly. — *n* **ret'icence** or **ret'icency**. [L *reticēns*, *-ēntis*, pr p of *reticēre*, from *re-*, and *tacēre* to be silent]

reticle *ret'i-kl*, *n* an attachment to an optical instrument consisting of a network of lines of reference. — *adj* **reticular** (*ri-tik'ū-lər*) netted; netlike; reticulated; of the reticulum. — *adv* **retic'ularly**. — *adj* **retic'ulary**. — *vt* **retic'ulate** to form into or mark with a network; to distribute (eg water or electricity) by a network. — *vi* to form a network. — *adj* netted; marked with network; net-veined. — *adj* **retic'ulated** reticulate; (of masonry) consisting of lozenge-shaped stones, or of squares placed diamond-wise; (of rusticated work) having ridges of uniform width between irregular sinkings. — *adv* **retic'ulately**. — *n* **reticulā'tion** network; netlike structure. — *n* **reticule** (*ret'i-kūl*) a reticle; a small, woman's handbag, *esp* and *orig* of network. — *n* **retic'ulum** a network; the second stomach of a ruminant; (with *cap*) a southern constellation, also called the Net, between Hydrus and Dorado. — **reticulo-endothelial system** (*immunol*) the network of phagocytic cells extending throughout lymphoid and other organs which is involved in the uptake and clearance of foreign particles from the blood. [L *rēticulum*, dimin of *rēte* net]

retiform *rē'ti-fōrm*, *adj* having the form of a net. [L *rēte* net, and *fōrma* form]

retina *ret'i-nə*, *n* the sensitive layer of the eye: — *pl* **ret'inas** or **ret'inae** (*-nē*). — *adj* **ret'inal**. — *n* **retinī'tis** inflammation of the retina. — *n* **retinoblastōma** a cancerous tumour of the eye. — *n* **ret'inoscope** an optical instrument used in **retinos'copy**, examination of the eye by observing a shadow on the retina. — *n* **retinos'copist**. — *n* **retinula** (*ri-tin'ū-lə*) a cell playing the part of a retina to an ommatidium: — *pl* **retin'ulae**

Some words with the prefix **re-**.

rēuse' (*-ūs'*), *n*.
rēutt'er *vt*.
rēvac'cinate *vt*.
rēvaccinā'tion *n*.
rēval'idate *vt*.
rēvalida'tion *n*
rēvictual (*rē-vit'l*), *vt* and *vi*: — *pr p* **revict'ualling**; *pa t* and *pa p* **revict'ualled**.

(*-lē*). — *adj* **retin'ular**. — **retina camera** an instrument that photographs the minute blood-vessels at the back of the eye in full colour; **retinitis pigmentosa** (*pig-mən-tō'sə*) a familial and hereditary disease in which chronic and progressive degeneration of the choroid in both eyes causes progressive loss of vision. [LL *rētina*, appar from L *rēte* net]

retinaculum *ret-i-nak'ū-ləm*, *n* a connecting band; a means of retention; the apparatus that holds an insect's forewing and hindwing together; the sticky attachment of a pollen-mass, as in orchids: — *pl* **retinac'ula**. — *adj* **retinac'ūlar**. [L *retināculum* a holdfast, from *retinēre*; see **retain** and **retention**]

retinal. See under **retina**.

retinalite, retinispora, retinite, etc. See under **retene**.

retinitis and **retinoscopy**. See under **retina**.

retinue *ret'i-nū*, formerly *ri-tin'ū*, *n* a body of people accompanying and often attending an important person; a suite or train. [Fr *retenue*, fem pa p of *retenir*; see **retain**]

retinula, etc. See under **retina**.

retire *ri-tīr'*, *vi* to withdraw; to retreat; to recede; to withdraw from society, office, public or active life, business, profession, etc; to go into seclusion or to bed; to return (*obs*). — *vt* to withdraw; to draw back; to withdraw from currency; to cause to retire. — *n* (now *rare*) retirement; retreat (*obs*); a place of retirement (*obs*); return (*obs*); a signal to retreat. — *n* **retī'racy** (*US*) seclusion; enough to retire on. — *n* **retī'ral** giving up of office, business, etc; withdrawal. — *adj* **retired'** withdrawn; reserved in manner; secluded, sequestered; withdrawn from business or profession; recondite (*obs*). — *adv* **retīred'ly** (or *ri-tī'rid-li*). — *n* **retired'ness** (or *ri-tī'rid-nis*). — *n* **retī'ree** a person who retires or has retired from work. — *n* **retire'ment** the or an act of retiring; the state of being or having retired; solitude; privacy; a time or place of seclusion. — *n* **retī'rer**. — *adj* **retī'ring** reserved; unobtrusive; retreating; modest; given to someone who retires from a public office or service. — *adv* **retī'ringly**. — *n* **retī'ringness**. — **retired list** a list of officers who are relieved from active service but receive a certain amount of pay (**retired pay**); **retirement pension** (*UK*) a state pension paid to men of 65 and over, and women of 60 and over (formerly **old age pension**). [Fr *retirer*, from *re-* back, and *tirer* to draw]

retook. See **retake**.

retool *rē-tōōl'*, *vt* to re-equip with new tools (in a factory, etc; also *vi*); to remake, refashion (chiefly *US*). [**re-**]

retorsion. See under **retort**.

retort *ri-tört'*, *vt* to throw back; to return upon an assailant or opponent; to answer in retaliation; to answer sharply or wittily; to reject (*Shakesp*); to purify or treat in a retort (*chem*); to sterilize (food in sealed container) by heating it by steam, etc (*US*). — *vi* to make a sharp reply. — *n* retaliation; a ready and sharp or witty answer; the art or act of retorting; a vessel in which substances are placed for distillation, typically a flask with long bent-back neck. — *adj* **retor'ted** bent back; thrown back; turned back. — *n* **retor'ter**. — *n* **retortion** (*-tör'shən*; also **retor'sion**) retorting; bending, turning or casting back; retaliation. — *adj* **retor'tive**. [L *retorquēre*, *retortum*, from *re-* back, and *torquēre* to twist]

retouch *rē-tuch'*, *vt* to touch again; to touch up with the intention of improving. — *n* an act of touching up, *esp* of a photograph by pencil-work on the negative. — *n* **retouch'er**. [**re-**]

retour *ri-tōōr'*, *n* a return; an extract from chancery of the service of an heir to his or her ancestor (*Scots law*). — *vt* to return as heir; to return to chancery. [OFr *retour* return]

retrace *ri-* or *rē-trās'*, *vt* to trace back; to go back upon; to run over with the eye or in the memory; (*rē-*) to trace again; (*rē-*) to renew the outline of. — *adj* **retrace'able** (*ri-*). [Fr *retracer*]

retract *ri-trakt'*, *vt* to draw back; to withdraw; to revoke; to unsay; to undo (the previous move) (*chess*); to pronounce with tongue drawn back. — *vi* to take back, or draw back from, what has been said or granted. — *adj* **retrac'table** able to be retracted; that can be drawn up into the body or wings (*aeronautics*); that can be drawn up towards the body of a vehicle. — *n* **retractā'tion** (*rē-*) revoking; recantation. — *adj* **retrac'ted** drawn in; turned back; cancelled; revoked; pronounced with tongue drawn in. — *adj* **retrac'tile** (*-tīl*) that may be drawn back, as a cat's claws. — *n* **retractility** (*rē-trak-til'i-ti*). — *n* **retraction** (*ri-trak'-shən*) drawing back; retractation. — *adj* **retrac'tive** tending to retract; involving the reversal of the previous move (*chess*). — *adv* **retrac'tively**. — *n* **retrac'tor** a device or instrument for holding parts back, *esp* a surgical instrument for this purpose; a muscle that pulls in a part; a problem involving the reversal of the previous move (*chess*). [Mainly from L *retrahere*, *retractum*; partly from *retractāre*, *retractātum*, from *re-* back, and *trahere* to draw]

retraict, retrait and **retraite** *ri-trāt'*, *obs* forms of **retreat**.

retraitt. See **retrate**².

retral *rē'trəl* or *ret'rəl*, (*biol*) *adj* at or towards the rear. — *adv* **re'trally**. [L *retro* backwards]

retranslate *rē-trans-lāt'*, *-trəns-*, *-träns-*, or *-z-*, *vt* to translate anew; to translate back into the original language; to transfer back. — *n* **retranslā'tion**. [**re-**]

retransmit *rē-träns-mit'*, *vt* to transmit again; to transmit back; to transmit a stage further. — *n* **retransmiss'ion**. [**re-**]

retrate¹ *ri-trāt'*, (*Spenser*) *n* and *vi*. Same as **retreat**.

retrate² or **retraitt** *ri-trāt'*, (*Spenser*) *n* a portrait, portraiture. [Ital *ritratto*]

retread *rē-tred'*, *vt* to tread again: — *pa t* **retrod'**; *pa p* **retrodd'en**; to remould (a tyre): — *pa t* and *pa p* **retread'ed**. — *n* (*rē'tred*) a used tyre which has been given a new tread; someone or something returned to use, made useful again, eg a retired person who takes up new work, an MP who is returned to the Commons having previously lost his or her seat (*slang*); a soldier who fought in both the first and second World Wars (*Austr* and *US*). [**re-**]

retreat¹ *ri-trēt'*, *n* a withdrawal; an orderly withdrawal before an enemy, or from a position of danger or difficulty; a signal (by bugle or drum) for withdrawal or for retirement to quarters (*military*); recall of pursuers (*Shakesp*); retirement; seclusion; retirement for a time for religious meditation; a time of such retirement; a place of privacy, seclusion, refuge or quiet; an institution for the care and treatment of the elderly, the mentally ill, alcoholics etc. — *vi* to draw back; to relinquish a position; to retire; to recede. — *vt* (*rare*) to withdraw. — *n* **retreat'ant** a person taking part in a religious, etc retreat. [OFr *retret*, *-e*, pa p of *retraire*, from L *retrahere* to draw back]

re-treat or **retreat**² *rē-trēt'*, *vt* to treat again. [**re-**]

retree *ri-trē'*, *n* slightly damaged paper. [Perh Fr *retret*, *retrait*; see **retreat**]

retrench *ri-trench'* or *-trensh'*, *vt* to cut off, out or down; to protect by a retrenchment. — *vi* to cut down expenses. — *n* **retrench'ment** an act or instance of retrenching; economy; a work within another for

Some words with the prefix **re-**.

rēvis'it *vt* and *n*.	**rēvītalizā'tion** or **-s-** *n*.	**rēwind'** *vt*: — *pa t* and *pa p* **rēwound'**.
rēvis'itant *n*.	**rēvīt'alize** or **-ise** *vt*.	**rēwire'** *vt*.
rēvisitā'tion *n*.	**rēweigh'** *vt*.	

prolonging defence (*fortif*). [OFr *retrencher* (Fr *retrancher*), from *re-* off, and *trencher*; see **trench**]

retrial. See under **retry**.

retribute *ri-trib'ūt* or *ret'ri-būt*, *vt* to give in return; to give in return for. — *vi* to make requital. — *n* **retribution** (*ret-ri-bū'shən*) requital (now *esp* of evil). — *adj* **retrib'ūtive** (*ri-*) repaying; rewarding or punishing suitably. — *adv* **retrib'ūtively**. — *n* **retrib'ūtor**. — *adj* **retrib'ūtory**. [L *retribuere*, *-ūtum* to give back, from *re-* back, and *tribuere* to give]

retrieve *ri-trēv'*, *vt* to search for and fetch, as a dog does game; to recover, repossess; to rescue (from or out of); to save (time); to restore (honour or fortune); to make good (a loss or error); to return successfully (*tennis*), or to get possession of, (a shot, pass, etc which is difficult to reach) (*football*). — *vi* to find and fetch (as a dog does). — *n* retrieving. — *adj* **retriev'able**. — *n* **retriev'ableness**. — *adv* **retriev'ably**. — *n* **retriev'al** retrieving; the extraction of data from a file (*comput*). — *n* **retrieve'ment** (*rare*). — *n* **retriev'er** a dog (of a breed that can be) trained to find and fetch game that has been shot; a person who retrieves. — *n* and *adj* **retriev'ing**. [OFr *retroev-*, *retreuv-*, stressed stem of *retrover* (Fr *retrouver*), from *re-* again, and *trouver* to find]

retro or **Retro** *ret'rō* (*slang*) *adj* reminiscent of, reverting to, or recreating the past, *esp* for effect. — *n* design, style, etc which deliberately reverts to or recreates the past; short form of **retro-rocket**: — *pl* **ret'ros**. [Ety as for **retro-**]

retro- *ret-rō-* or *rē-trō-*, *combining form* denoting: backwards; behind. [L *retrō*]

retroact *rē-trō-akt'*, or *ret'rō-*, *vi* to act backward, or apply to the past (*law*); to react. — *n* **retroac'tion**. — *adj* **retroac'tive** applying to or affecting things past; operating backward. — *adv* **retroac'tively**. — *n* **retroactiv'ity**. [L *retroagere*, *-actum*, from *agere* to do]

retrobulbar *rē-trō-bul'bər* or *ret-rō-*, *adj* behind the eyeball. [**retro-** and L *bulbus* onion]

retrocede *ret-rō-* or *rē-trō-sēd'*, *vi* to move back or (*med*) inwards. — *vt* to cede back, grant back. — *adj* **retrocē'dent**. — *n* **retrocession** (*-sesh'ən*). — *adj* **retrocess'ive**. [L *retrōcēdere*, *-cēssum*, from *cēdere* to go, yield; partly from **retro-** and **cede**, or Fr *céder*]

retrochoir *rē'trō-kwīr* or *ret'rō-*, (*archit*) *n* an extension of a church behind the position of the high altar. [**retro-**]

retrocognition *ret-rō-kog-ni'shən*, *n* extrasensory knowledge of past events. [**retro-**]

retrod and **retrodden**. See under **retread**.

retrofit *ret'rō-fit*, *vt* to modify (a house, aircraft, nuclear reactor, etc) some time after construction by incorporating or substituting more up-to-date parts, etc: — *pr p* **ret'rofitting**; *pa t* and *pa p* **ret'rofitted**. — *n* **ret'rofit**. — *n* **ret'rofitting**. [**retro-**]

retroflex *ret'rō-fleks* or *rē'trō-*, *adj* bent back (also **retroflect'ed** or **ret'roflexed**); cacuminal (*phonetics*; also **ret'roflexed**). — *n* **retroflexion** or **retroflection** (*-flek'shən*). [LL *retroflexus*, from L *retro-* back, from L *flectere*, *flexum* to bend]

retrograde *ret'rō-grād* or *rē'trō-*, *adj* moving or directed backward or (*astron*) from east to west, relatively to the fixed stars; inverse; habitually walking or swimming backwards; degenerating; reverting; contrary (*Shakesp*). — *n* a person who goes back or degenerates; backward movement. — *vi* to go back or backwards, recede; to have a retrograde movement (*astron*). — *vt* to cause to go back. — *n* **retrogradation** (*-grə-dā'shən*) retrogression (*esp astron*). [L *retrōgradus* going backward, from *retrō-* backward, and *gradī*, *gressus* to go]

retrogress *ret'rō-gres*, *n* backward movement; degeneration. — *vi* **retrogress'** to retrograde, go backwards; to revert to an earlier, *esp* worse, state or condition. — *vt* to cause to retrogress. — *n* **retrogression** (*-gresh'ən*) a going backward or reversion; a decline in quality or merit; retrograde movement (*astron*). — *adj* **retrogress'ional** or **retrogress'ive**. — *adv* **retrogress'ively**. [L *retrōgressus* retrogression, from *retrō-* backward, and *gradī*, *gressus* to go]

retroject *ret'rō-jekt*, *vt* to throw backwards (opposed to *project*). — *n* **retrojec'tion**. [**retro-** and **project**]

retrolental *ret-rō-len'təl*, *adj* behind the or a lens, *esp* that of the eye. [**retro-**, and L *lēns*, *lentis* (see **lens**)]

retromingent *ret-rō-* or *rē-trō-min'jənt*, *adj* urinating backward. — *n* a retromingent animal. — *n* **retromin'gency**. [**retro-**, and L *mingere* to urinate]

retro-operative *ret-rō-* or *rē-trō-op'ər-ə-tiv*, *adj* retrospective in effect. [**retro-**]

retrophilia *ret-rō-fil'i-ə*, *n* love of anything, *esp* material objects, from, connected with or evoking the past. — *n* and *adj* **retrophil'iac**. [**retro-**]

retropulsion *ret-rō-* or *rē-trō-pul'shən*, *n* pushing backwards; a tendency in the paralysed to walk backwards. — *adj* **retropul'sive**. [**retro-**, and *pulsion* (*rare*), from L *pulsiō*, *-ōnis*]

retroreflector *ret-rō-rə-flect'ər*, *n* a device, placed on a satellite or a heavenly body, that reflects light or radiation back to its source. — *adj* **retroreflect'ive**. [**retro-**]

retro-rocket *ret'rō-rok-it* or *rēt'*, *n* a rocket whose function is to slow down, fired in a direction opposite to that in which a body, eg a spacecraft or an artificial satellite, is travelling. [**retro-**]

retrorse *ri-trörs'*, *adj* turned back or downward. — *adv* **retrorse'ly**. [L *retrōrsus*, from *retrōversus*]

retrospect *ret'rō-spekt* (or *rē'trō-*), *n* reference, regard; a backward view; a view or a looking back; a contemplation of the past. — *vi* to look back. — *vt* to look back on. — *n* **retrospec'tion**. — *adj* **retrospec'tive** looking back; relating to or of the nature of a retrospective; retroactive. — *n* an exhibition, etc presenting the life's work of an artist, musician, etc, or a representative selection thereof; an exhibition, etc which looks back over the history, development or earlier examples (of something). — *adv* **retrospec'tively**. [L *retrōspicere*, from L *specere*, *spectum* to look]

retroussé *rə-trōō's'ā* or *rə-trōō's'ā*, *adj esp* of the nose, turned up. — *n* **retroussage** (*-äzh'*) wiping aside of ink on an engraved plate to soften tones. [Fr *retrousser* (pa p *retroussé*) to turn up]

retrovert *ret-rō-*, *rē-trō-vûrt'* or *rē'trō-vûrt*, *vt* to turn back. — *n* **retrover'sion** a turning or falling back; backward displacement. [L *retrōvertere*, *-versum*, from *vertere* to turn]

retrovirus *ret'rō-vī-rəs*, *n* any of a group of eukaryotic viruses whose genetic material is encoded in the form of RNA rather than DNA and which are known to cause a number of diseases. [*re*verse *tr*anscriptase (the active enzyme in these viruses), and **virus**]

retry *rē-trī'*, *vt* to try again (judicially): — *pr p* **retry'ing**; *pa t* and *pa p* **retried'**. — *n* **rētrī'al**. [**re-**]

retsina *ret-sēn'ə*, *n* a Greek resin-flavoured wine. [Gr]

retted, **rettery** and **retting**. See under **ret**.

retund *ri-tund'*, *vt* to blunt. [L *retundere* to blunt]

return *ri-tûrn'*, *vi* to come or go back; to revert; to recur; to turn away (*Bible*); to continue with change of direction (*archit*). — *vt* to turn round (*Shakesp*); to make a turn at an angle (*archit*); to turn back (*Spenser*); to give, put, cast, bring or send back; to answer; to retort; to report officially; to report as appointed or elected; to elect to parliament; to give in return; to lead back or hit back (*sport*); to requite; to repay; to

---

Some words with the prefix **re-**.

rēwork' *vt.*	**rēwrite'** *vt*: — *pa t* **rēwrote'**;	**rē'write** *n.*
rēwrap' *vt.*	*pa p* **rēwritt'en**.	

respond to in a similar manner; to render; to yield; to come back over (*Shakesp*). — *n* the act of returning; a recurrence; reversion; continuation, or a continuing stretch, at an angle, *esp* a right angle (*archit*, etc); that which comes in exchange; proceeds, profit, yield; recompense; requital; an answer; an answering performance; a thing returned, *esp* an unsold newspaper; (in *pl*) a light-coloured mild tobacco (*orig* refuse); the rendering back of a writ by the sheriff, with a report (*law*); an official report or statement, eg of one's taxable income (*tax return*) or (*esp* in *pl*) of the votes cast in an election; election to parliament; a return ticket. — *adj* returning; for return; in return; at right angles. — *adj* **return'able**. — *n* **returnee'** someone who returns or is returned, *esp* home from abroad or war service. — *n* **return'er** a person who returns to paid employment after a period of absence, *esp* a woman doing so after having had children. — *n* **return'ik** (see **-nik**) a person, *esp* an E European, allowed or deciding to return to his or her country of origin after changes to its political system. — *adj* **return'less**. — **return crease** see under **crease**[1]; **returning officer** the officer who presides at an election; **return match** a second match played at a different venue by the same teams of players; **return order** (*law*) an order granted by a court at the request of a creditor to the effect that a consumer returns the goods to the creditor; **return shock** an electric shock due to induction sometimes felt after a lightning-flash; **return ticket** a ticket entitling a passenger to travel to a place and back to his or her starting-point. — **by return** or **return of post** by the next post leaving in the opposite direction; **many happy returns (of the day)** a conventional expression of good wishes said to a person on his or her birthday. [Fr *retourner*, from *re-* back, and *tourner* to turn]

re-turn *rē'tûrn'*, *vt* and *vi* to turn again or back. [**re-**]

retuse *ri-tūs'*, (*bot*) *adj* with the tip blunt and broadly notched. [L *retūsus*, from *retundere* to blunt]

reunion *rē-ūn'yən*, *n* a union, or a meeting, after separation; a social gathering of friends or persons with something in common. — *n* **reun'ionism**. — *n* **reun'ionist** a person in favour of the reuniting of the Anglican and Roman Catholic Churches. — Also *adj*. — *adj* **reunionis'tic**. [Fr *réunion*, from *re-* again, and *union* union]

reunite *rē-ū-nīt'*, *vt* and *vi* to join after separation. [**re-**]

Rev. *abbrev*: (the Book of) the Revelation of St John, Revelations (*Bible*); Reverend (also **Revd**); revise, revised or revision (also **rev.**).

rev *rev*, *n* a revolution in an internal-combustion engine. — *vt* to increase the speed of revolution in (often with *up*). — *vi* to revolve; to increase in speed of revolution: — *pr p* **revv'ing**; *pa t* and *pa p* **revved**. — *adj* **revved-up'** (*fig*) excited, eagerly anticipating something. [**revolution**]

revalenta *rev-ə-len'tə*, *n* lentil-meal. — Earlier **ervalen'ta**. [*Ervum lens*, Linnaean name of the lentil, from L *ervum* bitter vetch, and *lēns*, *lentis* lentil]

revalorize or **-ise** *rē-val'ər-īz*, *vt* to give a new value to, *esp* to restore the value of (currency). — *n* **rēvalorīzā'tion** or **-s-**. — *n* **rēvalūā'tion**. — *vt* **rēval'ue** to make a new valuation of; to give a new value to. [**re-**]

revamp *rē-vamp'*, *vt* to renovate, revise, give a new appearance to. — Also *n*. [**re-**]

revanche *ri-vänch'*, *n* revenge; a policy directed towards recovery of territory lost to an enemy. — *n* **revanch'ism**. — *n* **revanch'ist**. — Also *adj*. [Fr; connected with **revenge** (qv)]

Revd. See **Rev**.

reveal[1] *ri-vēl'*, *vt* to make known, as by divine agency or inspiration; to disclose; to divulge; to make visible; to allow to be seen. — *adj* **reveal'able**. — *n* **reveal'er**. — *n* and *adj* **reveal'ing**. — *n* **reveal'ment** revelation. [OFr *reveler* (Fr *révéler*), from L *revēlāre*, from *re-* back, and *vēlāre* to veil, from *vēlum* a veil]

reveal[2] *ri-vēl'*, *n* the side surface of a recess, or of the opening for a doorway or window between the frame and the outer surface of the wall. [OFr *revaler* to lower]

reveille *ri-val'i*, *ri-vel'i*, *ri-vāl'yi* or (*US*) *rev'ə-lē*, *n* the sound of the drum or bugle at daybreak to awaken soldiers; a summons to awake, get up or begin. [Fr *réveillez* awake, imperative of *réveiller*, from L *re-*, and *vigilāre* to watch]

revel *rev'l*, *vi* to feast or make merry in a riotous or noisy manner; to take intense delight, to luxuriate (with *in*). — *vt* to spend in revelry: — *pr p* **rev'elling**; *pa t* and *pa p* **rev'elled**. — *n* a riotous feast; merrymaking; a festival or (often in *pl*) occasion of merrymaking, dancing, masquerading, etc. — *n* **rev'eller**. — *n* **rev'elling**. — *n* **rev'elry** revelling. — **rev'el-rout** boisterous revelry; a crowd of revellers. — **Master of the Revels** an official organizer of entertainments, *esp* at court or in the Inns of Court. [OFr *reveler*, from L *rebellāre* to rebel]

revelation *rev-i-lā'shən*, *n* the act or experience of revealing; that which is revealed; a disclosure; an enlightening experience; divine or supernatural communication; **Revelation (of St John)** or, popularly, **Revelations** (*n sing*) the Apocalypse or last book of the New Testament. — *adj* **revelā'tional**. — *n* **revelā'tionist** a believer in divine revelation; a person who makes a revelation; the author of the Apocalypse or an apocalyptic book. — *adj* **rev'elātive**. — *n* **rev'elātor**. — *adj* **rev'elatory**. [L *revēlāre*, *-ātum*; see **reveal**[1]]

revenant *rəv-nã* or *rev'ə-nənt*, *n* a person who returns after a long absence, *esp* from the dead; a ghost. [Fr, pr p of *revenir* to come back]

revendicate *rē-vend'i-kāt*, *vt* to make formal claim to, or recover by such claim (eg lost territory); to endeavour to have unpaid-for and undamaged goods restored when the buyer is bankrupt. — *n* **revendicā'tion**. [Variant, through Fr, of **vindicate**]

revenge *ri-venj'*, *vt* to inflict injury in retribution for; (*esp reflexive*) to avenge. — *vi* to take vengeance: — *n* (the act of inflicting) malicious injury in return for injury received; the desire for retaliation of evil (also in *pl*; *Shakesp*); avenging (*Shakesp*); in games, opportunity of retaliation in a return game; punishment (*obs*). — *adj* **revenge'ful** ready to seek revenge. — *adv* **revenge'fully**. — *n* **revenge'fulness**. — *adj* **revenge'less**. — *n* **revenge'ment** (now *rare*). — *n* **reveng'er**. — *n* and *adj* **reveng'ing**. — *adv* **reveng'ingly**. — *adj* **reveng'ive** (*Shakesp*). [OFr *revenger*, *revencher* (Fr *revancher*) from L *re-*, and *vindicāre* to lay claim to]

revenue *rev'in-ū* (formerly also *ri-ven'ū*), *n* receipts or return from any source; income; the income of a state; a government department concerned with it. — *adj* **rev'enued**. — **revenue cutter** (*hist*) an armed vessel employed in preventing smuggling. — **Inland Revenue** revenue from excise, income tax, etc; the department of the civil service which collects this. [Fr *revenue*, pa p (fem) of *revenir* to return, from L *revenīre*, from *re-* back, and *venīre* to come]

reverb *ri-vûrb'* or **reverb unit** *ū'nit*, (*music*) *n* a device which creates an effect of reverberation, used in recording or with electrically amplified instruments. [Colloq abbrev of **reverberate** and **reverberation**]

reverberate *ri-vûr'bər-āt*, *vt* to beat or send back; to reflect; to echo; to heat in a reverberatory furnace. — *vi* to recoil, rebound; to be reflected; to re-echo; to resound. — *adj* reverberated (*poetic*); reverberating (*Shakesp*). — *vt* **reverb'** (after *Shakesp*). — *adj* **rever'berant** reverberating. — *n* **reverberā'tion**. — *adj* **rever'berātive** (or *-ət-*). — *n* **rever'berātor**. — *adj* **rever'beratory** (*-ət-ər-i* or *-āt-*). — **reverberation time** (*acoustics*) the time required for the decay of the average sound intensity in a closed room over an amplitude range of 60db; **reverberatory furnace** a furnace in which the flame is turned back over the substance to be heated. [L *reverberāre*, *-ātum*, from *re-* back, and *verberāre* to beat, from *verber* a lash]

revere *ri-vēr'*, *vt* to regard with high respect; to venerate. — *adj* **revēr'able**. — *n* **reverence** (*rev'ər-əns*) high respect; respectful awe; veneration; the state of being held in high respect; a gesture or observance of respect. — *vt* to venerate. — *n* **rev'erencer**. — *adj* **rev'erend** worthy of reverence; clerical; (with *cap*; *usu* written **Rev**) a title prefixed to the name of a member of the clergy. — *n* a member of the clergy. — *adj* **rev'erent** feeling or showing reverence. — *adj* **reverential** (*-en'shl*) proceeding from reverence; respectful; submissive. — *adv* **reveren'tially**. — *adv* **rev'erently**. — *n* **reverer** (*ri-vēr'ər*). — **His** (or **Your**) **Reverence** (now *Ir* or *playful*) a mode of referring to or addressing a member of the clergy; **Most Reverend** is used of an archbishop, **Right Reverend**, a bishop, or Moderator of the Church of Scotland, **Very Reverend**, a dean, a former Moderator, or (if a member of the clergy) a Scottish University principal; **Reverend Mother**, a Mother Superior of a convent; **save** or **saving (your) reverence** (*obs* contracted to **sir-reverence**) with all due respect to you — an apology for introducing an unseemly word or subject.) [OFr *reverer* (Fr *révérer*), from L *reverērī*, from *re-* (intensive) and *verērī* to feel awe]

reverie or **revery** *rev'ə-ri*, *n* an undirected train of thoughts or fancies in meditation; a fanciful notion (*archaic*); mental abstraction; a piece of music expressing such a state of mind. — *n* **rev'erist**. [Fr *rêverie*, from *rêver* to dream]

revers *ri-vēr'*, *US -vûr'* or *rə-ver'*, *n* any part of a garment that is turned back, such as a lapel: — *pl* **revers** (pronounced as *sing*, or *ri-vērz*). [Fr, from L *reversus*]

reverse *ri-vûrs'*, *vt* to turn the other way about, as upside down, outside in, in the opposite direction, etc; to invert; to set moving backwards; to overturn (a decision) on appeal to a higher court (*law*); to annul; to bring back (*Spenser*); to turn aside (*Spenser*). — *vi* to move backwards or in the opposite direction; to set an engine, etc moving backwards; to return (*Spenser*). — *n* the contrary, opposite; the back, *esp* of a coin or medal (opposed to *obverse*); a setback, misfortune, defeat; a back-handed sword-stroke; the or an act of reversing; a backwards direction; a direction or order opposite to normal; reverse gear. — *adj* contrary, opposite; turned about; acting in the contrary direction; reversing; back-handed (*obs*); of the rear (*military*). — *n* **rever'sal** the or an act of reversing. — *adj* **reversed'**. — *adv* **rever'sedly**. — *adj* **reverse'less** unalterable. — *adv* **reverse'ly**. — *n* **rever'ser** a person who, or thing which, reverses; a reversing device; a borrower on wadset (*Scots law*). — *n* **rever'si** (*-sē*) a game in which a captured piece is not removed from the board but turned upside down to show the captor's colour; reversis. — *n* **reversibil'ity**. — *adj* **rever'sible** able to be reversed (in any sense); of tissues, etc, able to be restored to a normal state (*med*). — *n* a fabric having both sides well finished. — *n* and *adj* **rever'sing**. — *n* **rever'sion** (*-shən*) the act or fact of reverting or of returning; anything which reverts or returns; the return, or the future possession, of any property after some particular event; the right to succeed to possession or office; a sum payable upon death; that which is left over, remains; the process by which a mutant phenotype is restored to normal by another mutation of the same gene, ie a back-mutation (*biol*). — *adj* **rever'sional**. — *adv* **rever'sionally**. — *adj* **rever'sionary** relating to reversion; of reversion; of the nature of a reversion. — *n* a person who has a reversion. — *n* **rever'sioner** a reversionary. — *n* **rever'sis** an old card-game in which the taker of fewest tricks wins. — *n* **rever'so** a verso; a back-handed sword-stroke: — *pl* **rever'sos**. — **reversal colour film** film in which the negative image in the respective colour layers is reversed in processing to give a positive transparency; **reverse** (or **reversed**) **discrimination** discrimination in favour of any group previously discriminated against; **reverse engineering** the taking apart of a competitor's product to see how it works, eg with a view to copying it or improving on it; **reverse gear** a gear combination which causes an engine, etc to go in reverse; **reverse genetics** the process of removing a gene from an organism, treating it in a known way, reinserting it, and testing the organism for any altered function; **reverse osmosis** (*chem*) purification of water by forcing it under pressure through a membrane impermeable to the impurities to be removed; **reverse pass** (*football*) a pass made when a player runs in one direction and passes in the other direction; **reverse printer** (*comput*) one capable of printing both from right to left and from left to right; **reverse takeover** (*business*) one in which the company that has been taken over controls the new organization; **reverse transcriptase** the enzyme in a retrovirus which makes a DNA copy of an RNA genome; **reverse yield gap** (*commerce*) the amount by which the average yield on the shares making up the Financial Times ordinary index, or the return on any particular stocks, falls short of the return on $2\frac{1}{2}$% consolidated annuities; **reversible reaction** a chemical reaction that can occur in both directions and, as a mixture of reactants and reaction products is obtained, is incomplete; **reversing layer** a layer of the sun's chromosphere that reverses bright lines of the spectrum to dark absorption lines; **reversing light** a light on the back of a motor vehicle which comes on when the vehicle is put into reverse gear, providing illumination for the driver, a warning to other road-users, etc. — **go into reverse** to engage reverse gear; to move backwards; **reverse the charges** to charge a telephone call to the person who receives it instead of to the caller. [L *reversāre* to turn round; partly through Fr]

revert *ri-vûrt'*, *vt* to turn back; to reverse. — *vi* to return; to fall back to a former state; to recur to a former subject; to return to the original owner or his or her heirs. — *adj* **rever'ted** reversed; turned backwards. — *adj* **rever'tible**. — *adj* **revert'ive** (*Thomson*). [L *re-* back, and *vertere* to turn]

revery. Same as **reverie**.

revest *ri-vest'*, *vt* to clothe again (*Spenser*); to vest again. — *vi* to vest again. — *n* **revest'iary** or **revest'ry** a vestry. [OFr *revestir*, or *re-* and *vestir*, from L *revestīre*, *vestīre* to clothe again, to clothe]

revet *ri-vet'*, *vt* to face with masonry, etc: — *pr p* **revett'ing**; *pa t* and *pa p* **revett'ed**. — *n* **revet'ment** a retaining wall, facing. [Fr *revêtir* to reclothe]

rêveur *re-vœr*, (*Fr*) *n* a daydreamer: *fem* **rêveuse** *re-vœz*.

revie *rē-vī'*, *vt* to stake more than an opponent has proposed on (eg the taking of a trick); to bandy (words) in emulation (*obs*). — *vi* to stake higher (*obs*): — *pr p* **rēvy'ing**; *pa t* and *pa p* **rēvied'**. — Also *n* (*obs*). [Fr *renvier*, from L *re-* and *invitāre* to invite]

review *ri-vū'*, *n* a viewing again (also **re-view** *rē'vū'*); a looking back, retrospect; a reconsideration; a survey; a revision; a critical examination; a critique; a periodical with critiques of books, etc; a display and inspection of troops or ships; the judicial revision of a higher court (*law*). — *vt* to see, view or examine again (also **rē-view'**); to look back on or over; to survey; to examine critically; to write a critique on; to inspect, eg troops; to revise. — *vi* to write reviews. — *adj* **review'able** capable of being reviewed. — *n* **review'al** a review of a book; reviewing. — *n* **review'er** a writer of critiques; a writer in a review. — **review body** a committee set up to review (salaries, etc); **review copy** a copy of a book sent by the publisher to a periodical for review. [Partly **re-** and **view**; partly Fr *revue*, pa p (fem) of *revoir*, from L *revidēre*, from *vidēre* to see]

revile *ri-vīl'*, *vt* to assail with bitter abuse. — *vi* to rail, use abusive language. — *n* revilement (*obs*). — *n* **revile'ment** the act of reviling; a reviling speech. — *n* **revil'er**. — *n* and *adj* **revil'ing**. — *adv* **revil'ingly**. [OFr *reviler*, from L *re-*, and *vīlis* worthless]

revindicate *ri-vin'di-kāt*, *vt* to claim and get back; to vindicate again. — *n* **revindicā'tion**. [**re-**]

revise *ri-vīz'*, *vt* to examine and correct; to make a new, improved version of; to study anew; to look at again (*obs*). — Also *vi*. — *n* the act of revising or being revised; review; a proof in which previous corrections have been incorporated (*printing*). — *adj* **revīs'able**

liable to revision. — *n* **revī'sal** revision. — *n* **revī'ser** (also **revī'sor**). — *n* **revision** (*-vizh'ən*) the act or product of revising. — *adj* **revi'sional** or **revi'sionary** relating to revision. — *n* **revi'sionism**. — *n* **revi'sionist** an advocate of revision (eg of a treaty, of established doctrines, etc); a Communist favouring modification of stricter orthodox Communism and evolution, rather than revolution, as a means of achieving world domination; (opprobriously) a Communist who does not hold to what some other Communist considers to be orthodox Communism (also loosely and *fig*); a reviser of the Bible. — *adj* **revī'sory**. — **Revised Version** an English translation of the Bible issued 1881–5 (Apocrypha 1895); **revising barrister** till 1918, a barrister appointed to revise the parliamentary voters' roll. [Fr *reviser* and L *revīsere*, from *re-* back, and *vīsere*, intensive of *vidēre* to see]

revive *ri-vīv'*, *vt* and *vi* to bring back or come back to life, vigour, being, activity, consciousness, memory, good spirits, freshness, vogue, notice, currency, use, the stage, or natural metallic form. — *n* **revīvabil'ity**. — *adj* **revī'vable**. — *adv* **revī'vably**. — *n* **revī'val** the act or fact of reviving; the state of being revived; recovery from languor, neglect, depression, etc; renewed performance, a restaged production, of a play, etc; renewed interest or attention; a time of extraordinary religious awakening or sometimes worked-up excitement; a series of meetings to encourage this; quickening; renewal; awakening. — *n* **revī'valism**. — *n* **revī'valist** a person who promotes religious, architectural or other revival; an itinerant preacher. — *adj* **revivalist'ic**. — *n* **revive'ment** (*rare*). — *n* **revī'ver** a person who, or thing which, revives; a renovating preparation; a stimulant (*slang*). — *n* and *adj* **revī'ving**. — *adv* **revī'vingly**. — *n* **revī'vor** (*law*) the revival of a suit which was abated by the death of a party or other cause. — **Gothic Revival** the reintroduction of Gothic style architecture in (and before) the 19c; **Romantic Revival** see under **romantic**; **Revival of Learning** the Renaissance. [L *revīvere* to live again, from *vīvere* to live]

revivescent. See **reviviscent**.

revivify *ri-viv'i-fī*, *vt* to restore to life; to put new life into; to reactivate. — *vt* and *vi* (*chem*) to revive, restore (eg metal) to its uncombined state: — *pr p* **reviv'ifying**; *pa t* and *pa p* **reviv'ified**. — *n* **revivificā'tion**. [LL *revīvificāre*, from *re-*, *vīvus* alive, and *facere* to make]

reviviscent *rev-i-vis'ənt* or *rē-vī-* or **revivescent** *-ves'ənt*, *adj* reviving. — *n* **revivisc'ence** or **revivisc'ency** (also **revivesc'ence** or **revivesc'ency**). [L *revīvīscere*, *-ēscere*]

revoke *ri-vōk'*, *vt* to recall, call back (now *rare*); to withdraw (*Spenser*); to check (*Spenser*); to annul; to retract. — *vi* to make revocations; to neglect to follow suit at cards. — *n* revocation, recall; the act of revoking at cards. — *adj* **revocable** (*rev'ō-kə-bl*). — *n* **rev'ocableness** or **revocabil'ity**. — *adv* **rev'ocably**. — Also **revō'kable**, etc. — *n* **revocā'tion** recall; the act of revoking. — *adj* **rev'ocatory**. — *n* **revoke'ment** (*Shakesp*) revocation. [L *revocāre*, from *vocāre* to call]

revolt *ri-vōlt'*, *vi* to renounce allegiance; to rise in opposition; to turn or rise in disgust, loathing or repugnance. — *vt* to turn back (*Spenser*); to cause to rise in revolt (*obs*); to inspire revulsion or repugnance in. — *n* a rebellion; insurrection; secession; revulsion (*Shakesp*); a rebel (*Shakesp*). — *adj* **revolt'ed** insurgent; shocked, outraged. — *n* **revol'ter**. — *adj* **revol'ting**. — *adv* **revol'tingly**. [Fr *révolter*, from L *re-* and *volūtāre*, frequentative of *volvere*, *volūtum* to turn]

revolute. See under **revolve**.

revolution *rev-əl-ōō'shən* or *-ū'*, *n* the act or condition of revolving; movement in an orbit, as distinguished from rotation; (less commonly) rotation; a complete turn by an object or figure, through four right angles, about an axis; a cycle of phenomena or of time; recurrence in cycles; turning over in the mind (*archaic*); mutation (*Shakesp*); a great upheaval; a complete change, eg in outlook, social habits or circumstances; a radical change in government; a time of intensified change in the earth's features (*geol*). — *adj* **revolu'tional** of revolution in movement. — *adj* **revolu'tionary** of, favouring, or of the nature of revolution, *esp* in government or conditions. — *n* a person who takes part in, supports or advocates a revolution. — *n* **revolu'tioner** (*hist*) a supporter of a revolution, *esp* that of 1688. — *n* **revolu'tionism**. — *n* **revolu'tionist** a supporter or advocate of revolution. — *vt* **revolu'tionize** or **-ise** to cause radical change, or a revolution, in; to make revolutionary. — **Revolutionary Calendar** the calendar used in France from 1793 to 1805 (see **Vendémiaire**, **Brumaire**, **Frimaire**, **Nivôse**, **Pluviôse**, **Ventôse**, **Germinal**, **Floréal**, **Prairial**, **Messidor**, **Thermidor** and **Fructidor**). — **the American Revolution** the change from the condition of British colonies to national independence effected by the thirteen states of the American Union in 1776; **the French Revolution** the overthrow of the old French monarchy and absolutism (1789); **the Revolution** the expulsion of James VII and II from the British throne (1688–9), and the establishment of a really constitutional government under William III and Mary. [LL *revolūtiō*, *-ōnis*]

revolve *ri-volv'*, *vt* and *vi* to roll back, return (*obs*); to ponder; to move about a centre; to rotate. — *n* turning, revolution; a part of the stage which can be revolved by hand or electrical means, providing one method of scene-changing (*theat*). — *adj* **revolute** (*rev'əl-ūt* or *-ōōt*; *bot*) rolled backward and *usu* downward. — *n* **revol'vency** revolution; a tendency to revolve. — *n* **revol'ver** a revolving device of various kinds; a pistol with a rotating magazine. — *n* and *adj* **revol'ving**. — **revolving credit** credit which is automatically renewed as the sum previously borrowed is paid back, so allowing the borrower to make repeated use of the credit so long as the agreed maximum sum is not exceeded; **revolving door** a door consisting of *usu* four leaves fixed around a central axis and standing within a cylindrical structure open at opposite sides to allow entrance and egress; (used *attrib*) designating the process whereby retiring government employees are offered senior consultative positions in companies with whom they had had contact through their previous job (*fig*). [L *revolvere*, *revolūtum*, from *volvere* to roll]

revue *ri-vū'*, *n* a loosely constructed theatrical show, more or less topical and musical. [Fr, review]

revulsion *ri-vul'shən*, *n* diversion to another part, *esp* by counter-irritation (*med*); withdrawal; disgust; a sudden change or reversal, *esp* of feeling. — *adj* **revul'sionary**. — *adj* **revul'sive** (*-siv*). [L *revellere*, *revulsum* to pluck back, from *vellere* to pluck]

revved, etc. See under **rev**.

Rev. Ver. *abbrev*: Revised Version.

revying. See **revie**.

rew *rōō* (*Spenser*). Same as **rue**[1,2] and **row**[1].

reward *ri-wörd'*, *n* that which is given in return for good (sometimes evil), or in recognition of merit, or for performance of a service. — *vt* to give or be a reward to or for; to give as a reward (*Bible*). — *adj* **reward'able** capable or worthy of being rewarded. — *n* **reward'ableness**. — *n* **reward'er**. — *adj* **reward'ful** yielding reward. — *adj* **reward'ing** profitable; yielding a result well worthwhile. — *adj* **reward'less** unrewarded. [OFr *rewarder*, *regarder*, from *re-* again, and *warder*, *garder* to guard; see **regard**, **guard** and **ward**]

rewarewa *rē'wə-rē'wə* or *rā'wə-rā'wə*, *n* a New Zealand tree (*Knightia excelsa*) whose wood is used in furniture-making (in NZ also called **honeysuckle**). [Maori]

reword *rē-wûrd'*, *vt* to repeat, re-echo (*Shakesp*); to put into different words. [**re-**]

rewth *rōōth* (*Spenser*). Same as **ruth**.

rex. See **reak**[1].

Rex *reks*, *n* king; the title used by a reigning king (*abbrev* **R** in signature); a type of cat of either of two varieties, Devon Rex or Cornish Rex with curly but thin coat (also **Rex cat**); a type of domestic rabbit in which the hair that would normally form the outer coat is shorter than that of the under coat (also **Rex rabbit**), one variety, **Astrex** (*as'treks*; *As*trakhan) having curly or wavy fur.

Reye's syndrome *rīz sin'drōm*, (*med*) *n* a rare, acute and often fatal disease of children, affecting the brain and the liver. [R D K *Reye* (1912–78), Australian paediatrician]

Reynard or **reynard** *rān'* or *ren'ärd*, or *-ərd*, *n* a fox, from the name given to the fox in the famous beast epic of LGer origin, *Reynard the Fox*. — In Spenser **Reyn'old**. [MDu *Reynaerd*, from OHGer *Reginhart*, literally strong in counsel]

Reynolds number *ren'əldz num'bər*, (*mech*) *n* a number designating type of flow of a fluid in a system, obtained from the product of the fluid's density, velocity and dimension at a particular point, divided by its viscosity. [Osborne *Reynolds* (1842–1912), British physicist]

rezone *rē-zōn'*, *vt* to alter (the boundaries of) a zone. [**re-**]

RF *abbrev*: radio frequency; *République française* (*Fr*) French Republic.

Rf (*chem*) *symbol*: rutherfordium.

RFA *abbrev*: Royal Fleet Auxiliary.

RFC *abbrev*: Royal Flying Corps (now **RAF**); Rugby Football Club.

RFU *abbrev*: Rugby Football Union.

RGG *abbrev*: Royal Grenadier Guards.

RGN *abbrev*: Registered General Nurse.

RGS *abbrev*: Royal Geographical Society.

Rgt *abbrev*: regiment.

RGV *abbrev*: Remote Guidance Vehicle.

RH *abbrev*: Republic of Haiti (IVR); Royal Highness.

Rh *symbol*: rhesus; rhodium (*chem*).

rh *abbrev*: right hand or right-hand.

RHA *abbrev*: Royal Hibernian Academy; Royal Horse Artillery.

rhabdus *rab'dəs*, *n* a rodlike sponge spicule. — *adj* **rhab'doid** rodlike. — *n* a rodlike body. — *n* **rhab'dolith** (Gr *lithos* stone) a calcareous rod in some Protozoa. — *n* **rhab'dom** (Gr *rhabdōma* bundle of rods) a fourfold rod in the compound eye of an arthropod. — *n* **rhab'domancy** (Gr *manteiā* divination) divination by rod, *esp* divining for water or ore. — *n* **rhab'domantist**. — *n* **rhabdomyō'ma** a tumour of striped muscle. — *n pl* **Rhabdoph'ora** the graptolites. — *n* **rhab'dosphere** an aggregation of rhabdoliths in oceanic ooze. [Latinized from Gr *rhabdos* rod]

rhachis, **rhachitis**. Same as **rachis**, **rachitis**.

Rhadamanthine *rad-ə-man'thīn*, *adj* rigorously just and severe, like *Rhadamanthus* (Gr *-os*), a judge of the lower world.

Rhaetia or **Raetia** *rē'shə* or *rē'shyə*, *n* (*hist*) a province of the Roman Empire, roughly Grisons and Tirol, to which Vindelicia was added. — *adj* and *n* **Rae'tian** or **Rhae'tian**. — *n* **Rhaetic** (*rē'tik*; *geol*) uppermost Trias (also **Keuper**) or (according to others) lowest Jurassic; Rhaeto-Romanic. — Also *adj*. — **Rhaeto-Roman'ic** a general name for a group of Romance dialects spoken from south-eastern Switzerland to Friuli (Romansch, Ladin and Friulian). — Also **Rhae'tic** or **Rhaeto-Romance'**. — Also *adj*.

rhagades *rag'a-dēz*, (*med*) *n pl* cracks or fissures in the skin. — *adj* **rhagad'iform**. [Gr *rhagas*, pl *rhagades* a tear, rent]

Rhamnus *ram'nəs*, *n* the buckthorn genus, giving name to the family **Rhamnā'ceae**. — *adj* **rhamnā'ceous**. [Latinized from Gr *rhamnos*]

rhamphoid *ram'foid*, *adj* hook-beak-shaped. — *n* **Rhamphast'os**, now *usu* **Ramphast'os**, the typical genus of toucans. — *n* **Rhamphorhynchus** (*ram-fō-ring'kəs*; Gr *rhynchos* snout) a genus of pterodactyls. — *n* **rhamphothē'ca** (Gr *thēkē* case) the horny sheath of a bird's bill. [Gr *rhamphos* a hooked beak]

rhaphe, **rhaphide** and **rhaphis**. Same as **raphe**, **raphide** and **raphis**.

rhapontic *ra-pon'tik*, *n* the common rhubarb, *Rheum Rhaponticum*. [LL *rhā ponticum* Pontic rhubarb; see **rhubarb**]

rhapsody *raps'ə-di*, *n* an epic or instalment of an epic recited at one sitting (*Gr hist*); a patching or stringing together of poems (*obs*); an orderless, unconnected composition, or collection of things said, beliefs, etc (*obs*); an ecstatic utterance of feeling; an irregular, emotional piece of music. — *n* **rhapsode** (*raps'ōd*) a reciter of Homeric or other epics. — *adj* **rhapsodic** (*-od'ik*) of rhapsodes or rhapsodies; of the nature of rhapsody. — *adj* **rhapsod'ical** rhapsodic; unrestrainedly enthusiastic, rapt. — *adv* **rhapsod'ically**. — *n* **rhaps'odist** a rhapsode; a person who rhapsodizes. — *vt* **rhaps'odize** or **-ise** (*-ə-dīz*) to piece together (*obs*); to recite in rhapsodies. — *vi* to write or utter rhapsodies. [Gr *rhapsōidiā* an epic, a rigmarole, from *rhaptein* to sew, and *ōidē* a song]

rhatany *rat'ə-ni*, *n* either of two S American caesalpiniaceous plants (species of *Krameria*); the astringent root of either plant. [Sp *ratania*, from Quechua *rataña*]

Rhea *rē'ə*, *n* the daughter of Uranus and Ge, wife and sister of Kronos (*Gr mythol*); the fifth satellite of Saturn. [Gr *Rhĕā*]

rhea[1] *rē'ə*, *n* rami. [Assamese *rihā*]

rhea[2] *rē'ə*, *n* a small flightless S American bird of the genus *Rhea*, resembling the ostrich. [**Rhea**]

Rheinberry. See under **Rhine**.

rhematic *rē-mat'ik*, *adj* of words or verbs; forming a word or words. [Gr *rhēma*, *-atos* word, verb]

Rhemish *rē'mish*, *adj* of *Rheims* (*Reims*) in NE France. — **Rhemish version** the English translation of the New Testament by Roman Catholics of the English college there (1582). — *n* **Rhē'mist** a translator of the Rhemish version.

Rhenish *ren'ish* or *rēn'ish*, *adj* of the river *Rhine*. — *n* (also **Rhenish wine**) Rhine wine, *esp* hock. — *n* **rhenium** (*rē'ni-əm*) a chemical element (symbol **Re**; atomic no 75) discovered by X-ray spectroscopy in Germany in 1925. [L *Rhēnus* the Rhine]

rheo- *rē'ō-* or *rē-ō'-*, *combining form* denoting current or flow. — *n* **rhē'ochord** or **rhē'ocord** a wire rheostat. — *adj* **rheolog'ic** or **rheolog'ical**. — *n* **rheol'ogist**. — *n* **rheol'ogy** the science of the deformation and flow of matter. — *n* **rheom'eter** an instrument for measuring a current of fluid; a galvanometer (*obs*). — *adj* **rheomet'rical**. — *n* **rhē'ostat** an instrument for varying an electric resistance. — *n* **rheotax'is** rheotropism. — *n* **rhē'otome** (*electronics*) an interrupter. — *n* **rhē'otrope** a commutator for reversing an electric current. — *adj* **rheotrop'ic**. — *n* **rheot'ropism** (*biol*) response to the stimulus of flowing water. [Gr *rheos* flow]

rhesus *rē'səs*, *n* a macaque, the bandar (*Macacus rhesus* or *Macaca mulatta*), a monkey of the Indian Subcontinent. — Also **rhesus monkey**. — **Rhesus factor**, **Rh-factor** or **Rh** any of a group of weakly antigenic agglutinogens *usu* found in human red blood cells and in those of rhesus monkeys, inherited according to Mendelian laws, **Rh-positive** people being those who have the factor, and **Rh-negative** those (a very much smaller number) who do not (a difference important in blood transfusion and as explaining haemolytic disease of the newborn). [Gr *Rhēsos*, a king of Thrace, arbitrarily applied]

rhet. *abbrev*: rhetoric.

rhetor *rē'tör*, *n* (*Gr hist*) a teacher of rhetoric; a professional orator. — *n* **rhetoric** (*ret'ər-ik*) the theory and practice of eloquence, whether spoken or written, the whole art of using language so as to persuade others; the art of literary expression, *esp* in prose; false, showy, artificial, or declamatory expression. — *adj* **rhetoric** (*ri-tor'ik*; *rare*) or **rhetor'ical** relating to rhetoric; oratorical; inflated, over-elaborate or insincere in style. — *adv* **rhetor'ically**. — *n* **rhetorician** (*ret-ər-ish'ən*) a person who teaches the art of rhetoric; an orator; a user of rhetorical language. — *vi* **rhetorize** or **-ise** (*re'*) to use rhetoric language (*obs*). — *vt* (*Milton*) to address rhetorically. — **rhetorical question** a question in form, for rhetorical effect, not calling for an answer. [Gr *rhētōr*]

rheum *rōōm*, *n* a mucous discharge, *esp* from the nose; tears (*poetic*); a cold in the head (*obs*); (in *pl*) rheumatic pains (*rare*); ill humour (*obs*). — *adj* **rheumatic** (*rōō-mat'ik*; *Shakesp rōō'*) of the nature of, relating to, apt to cause or affected with rheumatism or (*obs*) rheum. — *n* a person who suffers from rheumatism; (in *pl*) rheumatic pains (*colloq*). — *adj* **rheumat'ical**. — *adv* **rheumat'ically**. — *adj* **rheumat'icky**. — *n* **rheumatism** (*rōō'mə-tizm*) a condition characterized by pain and stiffness in muscles and joints (*dialect* **rheu'matiz**, **rheu'matize**, **rheu'matise** or **rheu'mateese**). — *adj* **rheu-matis'mal**. — *adj* **rheum'atoid** resembling rheumatism. — *adj* **rheumatolog'ical**. — *n* **rheumatol'ogist**. — *n* **rheumatol'ogy** the study of rheumatism. — *adj* **rheumed**. — *adj* **rheum'y** of or like rheum; (*esp* of air) cold and damp. — **rheumatic fever** an acute disease characterized by fever, multiple arthritis, and liability of the heart to be inflamed, caused by a streptococcal infection; **rheumatoid arthritis** a disease or diseases characterized by inflammation and swelling of joints, often leading to their complete stiffening. [Gr *rheuma*, *-atos* flow, from *rheein* to flow]

Rheum *rē'əm*, *n* the rhubarb genus. [Latinized from Gr *rhēon*]

rhexis *reks'is*, *n* rupture, *esp* of a blood-vessel. [Gr *rhēxis* breach]

RHF *abbrev*: Royal Highland Fusiliers.

Rh and **Rh-factor**. See **rhesus**.

RHG *abbrev*: Royal Horse Guards.

rhime. An *obs* spelling of **rhyme**.

rhin-. See **rhino-**.

Rhine *rīn*, *n* a river of W and Central Europe. — **Rhine'berry** or **Rhein'berry** the buckthorn berry; the buckthorn; **Rhine'grave** (*hist*) a count with possessions on the Rhine: — *fem* **Rhine'gravine** (*-ēn*; Du *Rijngrave*, now *-graaf*; feminine *Rijngravin*); **Rhine'stone** (also without *cap*) a rock-crystal; a paste diamond; **Rhine wine** wine made from grapes grown in the Rhine valley, *esp* hock. [Ger *Rhein*; Du *Rijn*]

rhine *rēn*, (*Somerset*, etc) *n* a ditch or watercourse. — Also spelt **reen**, **rean** or **rhyne**.

rhinencephalic and **rhinencephalon**. See under **rhino-**.

Rhineodon *rī-nē'ō-don* or **Rhinodon** *rī'nō-don*, *n* a gigantic shark of the Indian Ocean. [Gr *rhīnē* a file, a shagreen shark, and *odous*, *odontos* a tooth]

rhinitis. See under **rhino-**.

rhino[1] *rī'nō*, *n* short for **rhinoceros**: — *pl* **rhī'nos**.

rhino[2] *rī'nō*, (*archaic slang*) *n* money. — *adj* **rhinocerical** (*-ser'i-kl*; *archaic slang*) rich. [Connection with **rhino** and **rhinoceros** obscure]

rhino- *rīn-ō-*, or before a vowel **rhin-** *rīn-*, *combining form* denoting nose. — *adj* **rhī'nal** of the nose. — *n* **rhinencephalon** (*rīn-en-sef'ə-lon*; Gr *enkephalon* brain) the olfactory lobe of the brain. — *adj* **rhinencephalic** (*-al'ik*). — *n* **rhinī'tis** inflammation of the mucous membrane of the nose. — *n* **rhīnolalia** (*-lā'li-ə*; Gr *laliā* talk) nasal speech. — *n* **rhī'nolith** (Gr *lithos* stone) a concretion in the nose. — *adj* **rhīnolog'ical**. — *n* **rhīnol'ogist** a nose specialist. — *n* **rhīnol'ogy** the study of the nose; nasal pathology. — *n* **rhinopharyngitis** (*rī-nō-far-in-jī'tis*) inflammation of the nose and pharynx. — *n* **rhīnophyma** (*-fī'*; Gr *phȳma* growth, tumour) overgrowth of skin and subcutaneous tissue of the nose. — *adj* **rhīnoplas'tic**. — *n* **rhī'noplasty** plastic surgery of the nose. — *n* **rhinorrhagia** (*rī-nō-rā'jyə*; Ger *rhēgnynai* to break) excessive nose-bleeding. — *n* **rhīnorrhoea** (*-rē'ə*; Gr *rhoiā* flow) excessive mucous discharge from the nose. — *adj* **rhīnorrhoe'al**. — *n* **rhīnoscleroma** (*-sklē-rō'mə*) a disease with hard swelling in the nose, etc. — *n* **rhī'noscope** an instrument for examining the nose. — *adj* **rhīnoscop'ic**. — *n* **rhīnos'-copy**. — *n* **rhīnothē'ca** (Gr *thēkē* case) the sheath of a bird's upper mandible. — *n* **rhī'novirus** a virus belonging to a subgroup picornaviruses thought responsible for the common cold and other respiratory diseases. [Gr *rhīs*, *rhīnos* nose]

rhinoceros *rī-nos'ər-əs* or *ri-*, (*obs*) **rhinoc'erot** *-ot* or **rhinoc'erote** *-ōt*, *n* a large ungulate of several species in Africa and southern Asia, constituting a family (**Rhīno-cerot'idae** characterized by one or two horns on the nose: — *pl* **rhinoc'eroses**, (*obs*) **rhinocerotes** (*-ō'tēz*). — *adj* **rhinocerot'ic**. — **rhinoc'eros-beetle** a very large beetle (of various genera) with a large up-curved horn on the head; **rhinoc'eros-bird** an ox-pecker that alights on the rhinoceros; a hornbill. [Gr *rhīnokerōs*, from *rhīs*, *rhīnos* nose, and *keras* horn]

Rhinodon. See **Rhineodon**.

rhinolalia. . . **rhinotheca**. See under **rhino-**.

rhipidate *rip'i-dāt*, *adj* fan-shaped. — *n* **rhipid'ion** in the Greek Orthodox Church, the eucharistic fan or flabellum. — *n* **rhipid'ium** (*bot*) a fan-shaped cymose inflorescence. — *n pl* **Rhipip'tera** or **Rhipidop'tera** the Strepsiptera. [Gr *rhīpis*, *rhīpidos* a fan]

RHistS *abbrev*: Royal Historical Society.

rhizo- *rī-zō-*, or before a vowel **rhiz-** *rīz-*, *combining form* denoting root. — *adj* **rhīzan'thous** (*bot*) seeming to flower from the root. — *adj* **rhī'zic** of the root of an equation. — *n* **rhī'zine** (*-zin*) a lichen rhizoid. — *n* **rhizō'bium** (also with *cap*) a bacterium of the *Rhizobium* genus of bacteria, important in nitrogen fixation by leguminous plants: — *pl* **rhizō'bia**. — *n* **rhī'zocarp** (Gr *karpos* fruit) a water-fern or heterosporous fern; a plant with sporangia on rootlike processes; a perennial herb; a plant fruiting underground. — *adj* **rhīzocar'pic** or **rhīzocar'pous**. — *n* **rhī'zocaul** (Gr *kaulos* stalk) the rootlike stalk of a hydrozoan colony. — *n pl* **Rhīzo-ceph'ala** (Gr *kephalē* head) an order of *Cirripedes* parasitic on crabs. — *adj* **rhīzogen'ic**, **rhīzogenet'ic** or **rhīzog'enous** producing roots. — *n* **rhī'zoid** a short hairlike organ in the lower plants, serving as a root. — *adj* **rhīzoi'dal**. — *adj* **rhīzō'matous**. — *n* **rhī'zome** (Gr *rhizōma* a root-mass) a rootstock, an underground stem producing roots and leafy shoots. — *n* **rhī'zo-morph** (Gr *morphē* form) a rootlike mass of fungal hyphae. — *adj* **rhīzomorph'ous** having the form of a root. — *adj* **rhīzoph'agous** root-eating. — *adj* **rhīzo-ph'ilous** growing on roots. — *n* **Rhīzoph'ora** the mangrove genus, with great development of aerial roots, giving name to the family **Rhizophorā'ceae**. — *n* **rhī'zophore** a root-bearing structure, *esp* in *Selaginella*. — *n* **rhī'zoplane** the surface of a root together with the soil adhering to it. — *n* **rhī'zopod** any member of the **Rhīzop'oda**, protozoa with rootlike pseudopodia. — *n* **rhī'zopus** a mould of the *Rhizopus* genus. — *n* **rhī'zo-sphere** the region in the soil surrounding a plant's root system, affected by its excretions and characterized by considerable microbiological activity. [Gr *rhiza* root]

Rh-negative. See **rhesus**.

rho *rō*, *n* the seventeenth letter (P or *ρ*) of the Greek alphabet, corresponding to R; as a numeral $\rho' = 100$, $_{,}\rho = 100\,000$: — *pl* **rhos**. [Gr *rhō*]

rhod- *rōd-* or **rhodo-** *rō-dō-*, *combining form* signifying: rose; rose-coloured. — *n* **rhō'damine** (*-mēn*; see **amine**) a synthetic dyestuff, *usu* red, related to fluorescein. — *n* **rhō'danate** (in dyeing) a thiocyanate. — *adj* **rhōdan'ic** thiocyanic. — *vt* **rhō'danize** or **-ise** to electroplate with rhodium. — *adj* **rhō'dic** of rhodium in higher valency. — *n* **Rhodites** (*rō-dī'tēz*) a gallfly that forms bedeguars on the wild-rose. — *n* **rhō'dium** a metallic element (symbol **Rh**; atomic no 45) of the platinum group, forming rose-coloured salts. — *n* **rhodochrosite** (*rō-dō-krō'sīt*; Gr *rhodochrōs* rose-coloured) manganese spar, a pink rhombohedral mineral, manganese carbonate. — *n* **rhōdodaph'ne** (or *rod-*; *Spenser*; Gr *daphnē* laurel) oleander. — *n* **rhō'dolite** a pink or purple garnet (gemstone). — *n* **rhō'donite** a rose-red anorthic pyroxene, manganese silicate. — *n* **rhō'dophane** (Gr *phainein* to show) a red pigment in the retinal cones of birds, etc. — *n pl* **Rhōdophyceae** (*-fish'i-ē*; Gr *phȳkos* seaweed) the red seaweeds (including some forms that are neither red nor found in the sea), one of the main divisions of the algae, in which the chlorophyll is usually masked by a red pigment. — *n* **rhōdop'sin** (Gr *opsis* sight) visual purple. — *adj* **rhō'dous** of rhodium in lower valency. — *n* **Rhodymenia** (*rō-di-mē'ni-ə*; Gr *hymēn* a membrane) the dulse genus of red seaweeds. — **rhō'dium-wood** the scented wood of Canary Island convolvulus, yielding **oil of rhodium**. [Gr *rhodon* rose]

Rhode Island *rōd ī'lənd*, *n* an island of the United States, named from a supposed resemblance to the island of *Rhodes*; the state of which it forms part. — **Rhode Island red** an American breed of domestic fowl.

Rhodes *rōdz*, *n* an island and ancient city-state of the Aegean. — *n* and *adj* **Rhō'dian**. — **Rhodian laws** the earliest system of marine law; **Rhodian school** a school of Hellenistic sculpture, of which the Laocoön is the greatest product. [Gr *Rhodos*]

Rhodesia *rō-dē'zhyə* or *-zhi-ə*, also *-z-*, *-s-* or *-sh-*, *n* the former name of a region of southern Africa, named after Cecil John *Rhodes*, consisting of Zambia (formerly *Northern Rhodesia*) and Zimbabwe (formerly *Southern Rhodesia*, later simply *Rhodesia*). — *adj* and *n* **Rhodē'sian**. — **Rhodesian man** an extinct type of man represented by a skull found at Broken Hill, in Northern Rhodesia, in 1921; **Rhodesian ridgeback** (*rij'bak*) a hunting dog with a ridge of hair along the back.

rhodic . . . **rhodochrosite**. See under **rhod-**.

rhodie or **rhody** *rō'di*, (*colloq*) *n* rhododenron.

rhododendron *rōd-ə-den'dren* or *rod-ə-den'dren*, *n* any member of the *Rhododendron* genus of trees and shrubs of the heath family, with leathery leaves and large showy slightly zygomorphic flowers, some species being called *Alpine rose*. [Gr *rhodon* rose, and *dendron* tree]

rhodomontade. Same as **rodomontade**.

rhodonite . . . **rhodopsin**. See under **rhod-**.

rhodora *rō-dō'rə* or *-dö'*, *n* a N American species of Rhododendron, or separate related genus. [L *rhodōra* meadow-sweet, said to be a Gallic plant-name]

rhodous and **Rhodymenia**. See under **rhod-**.

rhody. See **rhodie**.

Rhoeadales *rē-ə-dā'lēz*, *n pl* an order of dicotyledons including poppies, Cruciferae, etc. — *n* **rhoe'adine** (*-dēn*) an alkaloid found in poppies. [Gr *rhoias, -ados* corn-poppy]

rhoicissus *rō-i-sis'əs*, *n* any climbing plant of the genus *Rhoicissuus* of the family Vitaceae, *esp* the **grape ivy** (*Rhoicissus rhomboidea* with rhomboid, toothed leaves, often grown as a foliage pot plant. [New L, from Gr *rhoia* pomegranate]

rhomb *rom* or *romb*, *n* an equilateral parallelogram (*usu* excluding the square); a lozenge-shaped object; anything that whirls, such as (*Milton*) the wheel of day and night (*obs*); a magic wheel; a rhombohedron (*crystallog*). — *n* **rhombencephalon** (*rom-bən-sef'ə-lon*; Gr *enkephalon* brain) the hind-brain. — *n* **rhombenporphyr** (*rom-bən-pör'fēr*; from Ger), **rhombenpor'phyry** or **rhomb'por'phyry** an intermediate, moderately fine-grained igneous rock with feldspar phenocrysts rhombic in section. — *adj* **rhombic** (*rom'bik*) shaped like a rhombus; orthorhombic (*crystallog*). — *adj* **rhombohē'dral** of a rhombohedron; trigonal (*crystallog*). — *n* **rhombohē'dron** (Gr *hedrā* seat) a crystal form of six rhombi, in the trigonal or hexagonal system, a hemihedral form of the hexagonal pyramid: — *pl* **rhombohē'dra** or **rhombohē'drons**. — *adj* **rhom'boid** like a rhombus; nearly square, with the petiole at one of the acute angles (*bot*). — *n* a figure approaching a rhombus, a parallelogram, *usu* one that is not a rhombus nor a rectangle. — *adj* **rhomboid'al** more or less like a rhomboid. — *n* **rhomboi'dēs** (*rare* or *obs*) a rhomboid. — *n* **rhom'bos** a bull-roarer: — *pl* **rhom'boi**. — *n* **rhom'bus** a rhomb (*geom*); an object shaped like a rhomb: — *pl* **rhom'bī** or **rhom'buses**. [Gr *rhombos* bull-roarer, magic wheel, rhombus]

rhonchus *rong'kəs*, *n* a bronchial sound, heard in auscultation: — *pl* **rhonch'ī**. — *adj* **rhonch'al** or **rhonch'ial** of rhonchus; of snoring. [Latinized from Gr *rhonchos* wheezing]

rhone. Same as **rone**.

rhopalic *rō-pal'ik*, *adj* (of a verse) having each word a syllable longer than the one before. — *n* **rhō'palism**. [Gr *rhopalikos* clublike, *rhopalon* a club]

Rhopalocera *rō-pəl-os'ə-rə*, *n pl* a sub-order of insects with clubbed antennae, ie butterflies as distinguished from moths. — *adj* **rhopaloc'eral** or **rhopaloc'erous**. [Gr *rhopalon* a club, and *keras* a horn]

rhotacize or **-ise** *rō'tə-sīz*, *vt* and *vi* to change to an *r*-sound (*esp* from *z*). — *n* **rhō'tacism** excessive, exceptional or exceptionable sounding of *r*; burring; a change or tendency to change to *r*. [Gr *rhōtakizein*, from *rhō* the Greek R]

rhotic *rō'tik*, (*phonetics*) *adj* r-pronouncing, ie denoting a dialect or accent, or speaking a dialect or with an accent, in which *r* is pronounced when it occurs before a consonant or before a pause. [Gr *rhō* the Greek R]

Rh-positive. See **rhesus**.

RHS *abbrev*: Royal Highland Show; Royal Historical Society; Royal Horticultural Society; Royal Humane Society.

rhubarb *rōō'bärb* or *-bərb*, *n* any species of the genus *Rheum*, of the dock family; the rootstock (chiefly of *Rheum officinale*) used for its purgative properties; the leaf-stalks (chiefly of *Rheum rhaponticum*) cooked and used as if fruit; a squabble, row, rumpus (*slang*) a word muttered repeatedly to give the impression of indistinct background conversation (*theat*); nonsense. — *n* **rhu'barbing** (*theat*) the use or practice of muttering rhubarb or a similar sound. — *adj* **rhu'barby**. — **monk's rhubarb** patience dock. [OFr *reubarbe*, from LL *rheubarbarum*, for *rhābarbarum*, from Gr *rhā* rhubarb, from *Rhā* the Volga, and L *barbarum* (neuter), from Gr *barbaron* foreign; influenced by *rhēum*, Gr *rhēon*]

rhumb *rum*, (*naut*) *n* a loxodromic curve; a course following such a fixed line; any point of the compass. — **rhumb'-line**; **rhumb'-course**; **rhumb'-sailing**. [Fr *rumb*, or Sp or Port *rumbo*, from L *rhombus*; see **rhomb**]

rhumba. Same as **rumba**.

rhus *rus*, *n* a plant of the sumach genus (*Rhus*) of the cashew-nut family. [L, from Gr *rhous*]

rhy (*Spenser*). Same as **rye**[1].

rhyme or (*archaic*) **rime** *rīm*, *n* in two or more words, identity of sound from the last stressed vowel to the end, the consonant or consonant group preceding not being the same in both or all cases; extended to other correspondences in sound, such as *head-rhyme* or alliteration, to inexact correspondences, such as *eye-rhyme*, and to variations such as French, *rich rhyme*, or *rime riche* (where the consonants immediately preceding the stressed vowel are alike), and *identical rhyme* (where like-sounding words of different meaning are used); a word or group of words agreeing in this way with another; versification, verses, a poem or a short piece of verse, in which this correspondence occurs at the ends of lines (or within the lines, in *internal rhyme*); a jingle. — *vi* to be in rhyme; to correspond in sound; to make or find a rhyme or rhymes; to harmonize; to chime; to make rhymes or verses. — *vt* to put into rhyme; to compose in rhyme; to use or treat as a rhyme. — *adj* **rhymed** or (*archaic*) **rimed** (*rīmd*) in rhyme. — *adj* **rhyme'less**. — *n* **rhy'mer** or (*archaic*) **ri'mer** a user of rhyme; a poet; an inferior poet; a minstrel. — *n* **rhyme'ster** a poetaster; a would-be poet. — *n* **rhym'ist** a versifier. — **rhyme'-letter** the alliterating letter; **rhyme-roy'al** (*appar* a commendatory name) a seven-line stanza borrowed by Chaucer from the French, its lines rhyming in the pattern *ababbcc*; **rhyme'-scheme** the pattern of rhymes in a stanza, etc; **rhyme'-word** a word used as a rhyme; **rhyming slang** a form of slang in which a word is replaced by another word, or part or all of a phrase, which rhymes with it. — **identical rhyme** and **rich rhyme** see **rhyme** above; **rhyme to death** to kill by incantations (as rats were supposed to be killed in Ireland); to pester with rhymes; **without rhyme or reason** without reasonable or sensible purpose or explanation (also in similar phrases, such as **neither rhyme nor reason**). [OFr *rime*, from L *rhythmus*, from Gr *rhythmos*; see **rhythm²**; associated and confused with OE *rīm* number]

rhyncho- *ringk-ō*, or before a vowel **rhynch-** *ringk-*, *combining form* denoting snout. — *n pl* **Rhynchobdell'ida** (Gr *bdella* leech) an order of leeches with proboscis but no jaw. — *n pl* **Rhynchocephalia** (*-si-fā'li-ə*; Gr *kephalē* head) a primitive order of reptiles extinct except for the New Zealand tuatara. — *n* **rhynch'ocoel** (*-sēl*; Gr *koilos* hollow) the cavity in which the proboscis of a nemertine lies. — *adj* **rhynch'odont** (Gr *odous*, *odontos* tooth) with toothed beak. — *n pl* **Rhynchonell'a** a genus of hinged brachiopods with prominent beak. — *n pl* **Rhynchoph'ora** (Gr *pherein* to bear) a group of beetles with snouts, the weevils. — *adj* **rhynchoph'orous** of or belonging to the Rhynchophora; snouted. — *n pl* **Rhynchō'ta** the Hemiptera. [Gr *rhynchos* a snout]

rhyne. See **rhine**.

Rhyniaceae *rī-ni-ā'si-ē*, *n pl* a family of very simple land plants (*Psilophytales*) found as Old Red Sandstone fossils at *Rhynie* in Grampian Region, Scotland.

rhyolite *rī'ō-līt*, *n* an acid igneous rock with a glassy or cryptocrystalline groundmass and generally phenocrysts of quartz and alkali-feldspar (called also *liparite*). — *adj* **rhyolitic** (*-lit'ik*). [Irregularly, from Gr *rhyax*, *-ākos* a (lava) stream, and *lithos* a stone]

rhyparography *rip-ə-rog'rə-fi*, *n* genre or still-life pictures, *esp* of sordid subjects. — *n* **rhyparog'rapher**. — *adj* **rhyparographic** (*-graf'ik*). [Gr *rhyparos* dirty, and *graphein* to write]

rhythm¹ *rīm*, an *obs* spelling of **rhyme**.

rhythm² *ridhm* or *rithm*, *n* regular recurrence, *esp* of stress or of long and short sounds; a pattern of recurrence; an ability to sing, move, etc rhythmically. — *adj* **rhyth'mal**. — *adj* **rhythmed** (*ridhmd* or *rithmd*). — *adj* **rhyth'mic** or **rhyth'mical**. — *n* **rhyth'mic** (also **rhyth'mics** *n sing*) the science or theory of rhythm. — *adv* **rhyth'mically**. — *n* **rhythmic'ity**. — *n* **rhyth'mist** a person skilled in rhythm. — *vt* **rhyth'mize** or **-ise** to subject to rhythm. — *vi* to act in or observe rhythm. — *adj* **rhythm'less**. — *n* **rhythmom'eter** a kind of metronome. — *n* **rhythmopoeia** (*-ō-pē'yə*; Gr *poieein* to make) the art of composing rhythmically. — *n* **rhyth'mus** rhythm. — **rhythm method** a method of birth control requiring the avoidance of sexual intercourse during the period in which conception is most likely to occur; **rhythm section** in a band, those instruments whose main function is to supply the rhythm (*usu* percussion, guitar, double-bass and piano); the players of such instruments. — **rhythm and blues** a type of music combining the styles of rock and roll and the blues. [L *rhythmus*, from Gr *rhythmos*, from *rheein* to flow; cf **rhyme**]

rhytidectomy *rī-ti-dek'tə-mi*, *n* an operation for smoothing the skin of the face by removing wrinkles, a face-lift. [Gr *rhytis* a wrinkle, and *ektomē* cutting out]

rhytina *ri-tī'nə*, *n* an aquatic mammal of the now extinct *Rhytina* genus of Sirenia (also called *Steller's sea-cow*). [Gr *rhytis* a wrinkle]

Rhytisma *rit-iz'mə*, *n* a genus of fungi that cause black spots on maple leaves. [Gr *rhytisma* a patch or darn]

rhyton *rī'ton*, *n* a drinking-cup or pottery horn (Greek, etc) with a hole in the point to drink by. — *pl* **rhy'ta**. [Gr *rhyton*, neuter of *rhytos* flowing]

RI *abbrev*: religious instruction; Republic of Indonesia (IVR); Rhode Island (US state); (Member of the) Royal Institute of Painters in Water Colours; Royal Institution.

RIA *abbrev*: Royal Irish Academy. — **RIAM** *abbrev*: Royal Irish Academy of Music.

ria *rē'ə*, (*geol*) *n* a normal drowned valley. [Sp *ría* river-mouth]

rial¹ *rī'əl*. Same as **ryal**.

rial² *rē'əl*, *rī'əl* or *rē-äl'*, *n* the unit of currency in Iran, Oman and (also **riyal** qv) Saudi Arabia and the Yemen Arab Republic. [Pers *rial*, Ar *riyal*; see **riyal**]

Rialto *rē-al'tō*, *n* a district and island of Venice, with a famous bridge over the Grand Canal. [Ital, contracted from *rivo alto* deep channel, or possibly *rialzato* raised]

RIAM. See **RIA**.

riant *rī'ənt*, *adj* laughing; merry. — *n* **rī'ancy**. [Fr, pr p of *rire*, from L *rīdēre* to laugh]

RIAS *abbrev*: Royal Incorporation of Architects in Scotland.

riata. See **reata**.

rib¹ *rib*, *n* any of the bones that curve round and forward from the backbone; a wife (from Gen 2. 21–23; *facetious*); a piece of meat containing one or more ribs; a curved member of the side of a ship running from keel to deck; a strengthening bar; a rodlike structure supporting or strengthening a membrane, such as one of the greater veins of a leaf, a nervure in an insect's wing, a member supporting the fabric of an aeroplane wing or of an umbrella; a bar of a grate (*Scot*); the shaft of a feather; any of the parallel supports of a bridge; the side of a guitar, violin, etc; a framing timber; a purlin; a raised band; a prominence running in a line; a ridge; a ridge raised in knitting, by alternating plain and purl stitches, or a similar ridge raised in weaving; the pattern of ribs so formed (also called **ribbing**); a moulding or projecting band on a ceiling. — *vt* to provide, form, cover or enclose with ribs; to plough with spaces between the furrows (**rib'-plough**): — *pr p* **ribb'ing**; *pa t* and *pa p* **ribbed**. — *adj* **ribbed** having ribs; ridged. — *n* **ribb'ing** an arrangement of ribs. — *adj* **ribb'y** having many or prominent ribs; nasty, seedy, squalid (*slang*). — *adj* **rib'less**. — *n* **rib'let** a small, narrow or shallow rib. — *adj* **rib'like**. — **rib'-bone** a rib; **rib'cage** the enclosing wall of the chest formed by the ribs, etc; **rib'-grass** the ribwort plantain. — *vt* **rib'-roast** (*obs*) to beat soundly. — **rib'-roaster** (*archaic*) a severe blow on the ribs; **rib-roast'ing** (*archaic*); **rib'-tickler** a very funny joke or story. — *adj* **rib'-tickling** very funny, inclining one to laugh uproariously. — **rib'-vaulting**; **rib'work**; **rib'wort** (or **ribwort plantain**) a common weed (*Plantago lanceolata*) with narrow, strongly ribbed leaves and short brown heads. — **false rib** one joined indirectly to the breastbone or (**floating rib**) not at all; **true rib** one joined directly by its cartilage. [OE *ribb* rib, *ribbe* ribwort; Ger *Rippe* rib]

rib² *rib*, (*slang*) *vt* to tease, ridicule, make fun of [Perh **rib¹**, from the tickling of one's ribs causing laughter]

RIBA *abbrev*: Royal Institute of British Architects.

ribald *rib'əld*, *n* a menial of the lowest grade (*obs*); a loose, low character (*obs*); an obscene speaker or writer. — *adj* low, base, mean; licentious; foul-mouthed or coarse; sometimes loosely, jeering, floutingly derisive. Also **rib'aud** or **ryb'auld** (*Spenser*). — *n* **rib'aldry** obscenity; coarse jesting. — Also **rib'audry** (*obs*) or **rybaudrye** (*-öd-ri*; *Spenser*). — *adj* **rib'audred** (*Shakesp*) an obscure word, perh for *ribaud-rid*, ridden by a ribald, or for *ribaldried*, composed of ribaldry. [OFr *ribald*, *ribaut* (Fr *ribaud*); origin uncertain]

riband or **ribband** *rib'ən* or *rib'ənd*, *n* a spelling of **ribbon**, used (now *esp* in *heraldry* or *sport*) in derivatives and compounds, eg **blue riband**.

ribattuta *rē-bät-tōō'tä*, (*music*) *n* the slow beginning of a trill. [Ital]

ribaud and **ribaudred**. See under **ribald**.

ribband. See **riband**.

ribble-rabble *rib'l-rab'l*, *n* a mob; gabble. [**rabble**]

ribbon *rib'ən*, *n* fine material, *usu* of silk or synthetic fibre, tightly woven in narrow bands or strips and used for decoration, trimming, etc; a strip of this or other material; anything resembling such a strip, such as a road or a stripe of colour; a torn strip, a tatter or shred; a watch-spring; an endless saw; a mollusc's radula; a strip of inking cloth, eg for a typewriter; a diminutive of the bend, one-eighth of its width (*heraldry*); (in *pl*) driving reins. — *adj* made of ribbon; of the shape of a ribbon, forming a narrow band or strip; having bands of different colours. — *vt* to decorate with, mark into, or make into ribbon; to stripe; to streak. — *n*

Ribb'onism an Irish secret society movement, at its height about 1835–55, opposed to the Orangemen, named from its badge, a green ribbon. — *n* **ribb'onry** ribbons collectively. — *adj* **ribb'ony**. — **ribbon building** or **ribbon-development** unplanned building, growth of towns, in long strips along the main roads; **ribb'onfish** a long, slender, laterally compressed fish of the family *Trachypteridae*, *esp* the oarfish; **ribb'on-grass** gardener's garters, a striped canary-grass; **Ribb'on-man** a member of the Ribbonism movement; **ribbon microphone** a microphone in which the sound is picked up by a thin metallic strip; **ribbon parachute** a parachute in which the canopy is made from light webbing, giving greater strength for deployment at high speed; **ribb'on-seal** a banded N Pacific seal; **ribb'on-weed** sugar-wrack; **ribb'on-worm** a nemertine. [OFr *riban*; origin obscure]

Ribes *rī'bēz*, *n* the black and red currant genus of the saxifrage family (generally including gooseberry), in some classifications giving name to a separate family **Ribēsiā'ceae**. [LL *ribes*, from Ar *rībās* sorrel]

ribibe *rib'ib* or *rib-īb'*, (*obs*) *n* a rebeck; an old crone. — *n* **ribible** (*ri-bib'l* or *ri-bī'bl*) a rebeck. [See **rebeck**]

ribose *rī'bōs*, (*chem*) *n* a pentose, $C_5H_{10}O_5$. — *n* **riboflavin** (*rī-bō-flā'vin*; L *flāvus* yellow) a member of vitamin B complex, in yellowish-brown crystals, promoting growth in children. — *n* **ribonuclease** (*ri-bō-nū'kli-ās* or *-āz*) an enzyme in the pancreas, etc, the first enzyme to be synthesized (1969). — *n* **ribonū'cleotide** a nucleotide containing ribose. — *adj* **ribosō'mal**. — *n* **ribosome** (*rī'bō-sōm*) a small particle, found in large numbers in all cells and composed of RNA and protein, on which protein synthesis takes place. — *n* **rī'bōzyme** an RNA-derived molecular displaying enzyme-like activity. — **ribonucleic acids** (*rī'bō-nū-klē'ik*) nucleic acids containing ribose, present in living cells, where they play an important part in the development of proteins (*abbrev* **RNA**); **ribosomal RNA** the major component of ribosomes. [From **arabinose**, by transposition of letters]

ribston or **ribstone** *rib'stən*, *n* (in full **Ribston pippin**) a variety of winter apple brought from Normandy to *Ribston Hall* in Yorkshire.

RIC *abbrev*: Royal Institute of Chemistry; Royal Irish Constabulary.

Ricardian *ri-kär'di-ən*, *adj* relating to David *Ricardo* (1772–1823), or his economic teaching. — *n* a follower of Ricardo.

Riccia *rik'si-ə*, *n* a genus of liverworts. [From the Italian botanist P Francisco *Ricci*]

rice[1] *rīs*, *n* a grass (*Oryza sativa*) grown in warm climates, *usu* in flooded paddy-fields; its grain, an important cereal food. — *vt* (*esp NAm*) to form soft food, *esp* cooked potatoes, into strands by passing through a ricer, sieve, etc. — *n* **rīc'er** (*esp NAm*) a kitchen utensil used for ricing food. — *adj* **rice'y** or **ri'cy**. — **rice'-beer** a fermented drink made from rice; **rice'-bird** the bobolink (as a feeder on true rice or so-called wild rice); the paddy bird or Java sparrow; **rice'-biscuit** a sweet biscuit made of flour mixed with rice; **rice cake** a light, *usu* round cake made from puffed rice grains, eaten alone or spread with other foods; **rice crispies** or **Rice Krispies**® puffed grains of rice, eaten *esp* as breakfast cereal; **rice'-field**; **rice flour**; **rice'-glue** a cement made by boiling rice flour in soft water; **rice'-grain** a marking like a grain of rice on the sun's photosphere; a decoration in pottery made by pressing rice or other seeds into the clay before firing; **rice'-grass** cord-grass; **rice milk** milk boiled and thickened with rice; **rice paper** sliced and flattened pith of an Asiatic tree of the Araliaceae; a similar material made from other plants, or from linen trimmings; **rice'-polishings** the parts rubbed off in milling rice; **rice pudd'ing**; **rice'-soup**; **rice'-water** an invalid's drink of water in which rice has been boiled; a cholera patient's evacuation, of similar appearance. — **Canada**, **Indian**, **water** or **wild rice** Zizania. [OFr *ris*, from L *oryza*, from Gr *oryza* a word of Eastern origin]

rice[2] *rīs*, (*obs* except *dialect*) *n* twigs or small branches collectively, brushwood; a twig or small branch. — Also **reis**. [OE *hrīs*; Ger *Reis*]

ricercar *rē-chər-kär'*, **ricercare** *-kä'rā* or **ricercata** *-kä'tä* (*music*) *n orig* a contrapuntal forerunner of the fugue; later, a very elaborate form of fugue. [Ital, from *ricercare* to seek again with effort]

rich *rich*, *adj* having many possessions; wealthy; fortunate in having any good thing; abundantly supplied or stocked; having any ingredient or quality in great abundance; productive; fertile; deep in colour; full-toned; full-flavoured; containing a high proportion of fat, sugar, fruit or seasonings; full; splendid and costly; sumptuous; elaborately decorated; ample; providing good opportunities for laughter, full of comic potential. — *vt* (*Shakesp*) to enrich. — *vi* (*obs*) to grow rich. — **-rich** *combining form* well-provided with a specified thing, as in *oil-rich*. — *vt* and *vi* **rich'en** to make or become richer. — *adv* **rich'ly**. — *n* **rich'ness**. — *adj* **rich'-left** (*Shakesp*) left heir to much wealth. [OE *rīce* great, powerful; Ger *reich*, Du *rijk*, Gothic *reiks*; perh reinforced by Fr *riche* rich]

Richardia *ri-chär'di-ə*, *n* an older name for *Zantedeschia*. [From the French botanists L C M *Richard* (1754–1821) and his son]

riches *rich'iz*, *n* (now *usu* treated as *pl*) wealth. (Also *Spenser*) **rich'esse**. [OFr *richesse*, from *riche* rich]

richt *rihht*, Scots form of **right**.

Richter scale *rik'tər* or *rihhtə'r skāl*, *n* a seismological scale of measurement. [From its inventor, Dr Charles F *Richter* (1900–85)]

ricin *rī'sin* or *ris'in*, *n* a highly toxic albumin found in the beans of the castor-oil plant. [See **Ricinus**]

Ricinulei *ris-i-nū'li-ī*, *n pl* the Podogona, a rare order of blind arachnids with male organs on the third leg. [L *ricinus* a tick]

Ricinus *ris'i-nəs*, *n* a genus of one species (*Ricinus communis*, castor-oil plant) of the spurge family. — *adj* **ricinolē'ic** (or *-ō'lē-ik*) relating to castor-oil, as in **ricinoleic acid** ($C_{18}H_{34}O_3$), an oily acid obtained from castor-oil. [L *ricinus* the castor-oil plant]

rick[1] *rik*, *n* a stack; a heap. — *vt* to stack. — *n* **rick'er** an implement for shocking hay. — **rick'-barton** a stack-yard; **rick'burner** an incendiary who fired stacks; **rick'-lifter**; **rick'stand** a flooring for a stack; **rick'stick** a toothed stick for combing thatch on a stack; **rick'yard**. [OE *hrēac*; ON *hraukr*]

rick[2] *rik*, *vt* and *n*. See **wrick**.

ricker *rik'ər*, *n* a spar or young tree-trunk. [Perh Ger *Rick* pole]

rickets *rik'its*, *n sing* a disease of children, characterized by softness of the bones caused by deficiency of vitamin D. — *adv* **rick'etily** shakily. — *n* **rick'etiness** unsteadiness. — *adj* **rick'ety** (formerly, now *rare* **rick'etty**) affected with rickets; feeble, unstable; tottery, threatening to collapse. [First recorded in SW England in the 17c, perh ME *wrikken* to twist; or Gr *rhachitis* (see **rachitis**)]

rickettsia *rik-et'si-ə*, *n* a member of the *Rickettsia* genus of micro-organisms found in lice and ticks and, when transferred to humans by a bite, causing typhus and other serious diseases, or of the family **Rickettsia'ceae** (*-ā'si-ē*), order **Rickettsia'les** (*-ā'lēz*), to which it belongs (also **Rickettsia body**): — *pl* **rickett'siae** (*-ē*) or **rickett'sias**. — *adj* **rickett'sial**. [After Howard Taylor *Ricketts* (1871–1910), US pathologist]

rickle *rik'l*, (*Scot*) *n* a loose heap; a rickety or ramshackle structure or collection. — *adj* **rick'ly**. [Poss Scand; connection with **rick**[1] very doubtful]

rick-rack or **ric-rac** *rik'rak*, *n* a decorative braid in even zigzag form, or openwork made with it. [**rack**[1]]

ricksha or **rickshaw** *rik'shä* or *-shö*, *n* a small two-wheeled, hooded carriage drawn by a man or men, or powered by a man on a bicycle (also **bicycle ricksha** or **rickshaw**) or motor-bicycle (also **auto ricksha** or **rickshaw**). — Also **jinrick'sha**, **jinrick'shaw** or **jinrik'isha**. [Jap *jin* man, *riki* power, and *sha* carriage]

ricochet *rik-ō-shā'*, *-shet'*, or *rik'*, *n* a glancing rebound or skip, such as that of a projectile flying low. — *vi* to glance; to skip along the ground: — *pr p* **ricocheting** (*-shā'ing* or *rik'*) or **ricochetting** (*-shet'ing* or *rik'*); *pa t* and *pa p* **ricocheted** (*-shād'* or *rik'*) or **ricochetted** (*-shet'id* or *rik'*). [Fr]

ricotta *ri-kot'ə*, *n* a type of soft Italian cheese of sheep's milk, often used in ravioli, lasagne, etc. [Ital, from L *recocta*, fem pa p of *recoquere* to cook again]

ric-rac. See **rick-rack**.

RICS *abbrev*: Royal Institution of Chartered Surveyors.

rictus *rik'təs*, (*zool*) *n* the gape, *esp* of a bird; the chink or aperture of a lipped corolla; unnatural gaping of the mouth, eg in horror. — *adj* **ric'tal** of the gape; at the corners of the mouth. [L *rictus*, *-ūs*]

rid[1] *rid*, *vt* to free; to deliver; to clear; to disencumber; to expel; to remove, eg by banishment or murder, make away with (*obs*): — *pr p* **ridd'ing**; *pa t* and *pa p* **rid** or **ridd'ed**. — *n* **ridd'ance** clearance; removal; disencumberment; deliverance; a thing that one is well rid of. — *n* **ridd'er**. — **a good riddance** a welcome relief; **get rid of** to disencumber oneself of; **rid way** (*Shakesp*) to cover ground, make progress. [ON *rythja* to clear; with senses converging upon **redd**[1]]

rid[2] and **ridden**. See **ride**.

riddle[1] *rid'l*, *n* a piece of verse, etc giving cryptic clues as to the identity of something which the hearer or reader is asked to name; a puzzling question; anything puzzling. — *vt* to solve; to puzzle. — *vi* to make riddles; to speak obscurely. — *n* **ridd'ler**. — *n* **ridd'ling** propounding of riddles; speaking in riddles. — *adj* enigmatic, obscure, puzzling; speaking in riddles; explaining riddles. — *adv* **ridd'lingly**. — *adj* and *adv* **riddl'e-like** (*Shakesp*). — **ridd'le-me-ree'** a fanciful modification of *riddle me a riddle*, or *riddle my riddle*. — *n* a rigmarole. [OE *rǣdelse*, from *rǣdan* to guess, to read, from *rǣd* counsel; cognate with Du *raad*, Ger *Rat*]

riddle[2] *rid'l*, *n* a large coarse sieve. — *vt* to pass through or sift with a riddle; to make full of holes like a riddle, as with shot. — *vi* to use a riddle; to sift. — *n* **ridd'ler**. — *n* **ridd'ling**. — *n pl* **ridd'lings** the less desirable part of anything, whether finer or coarser, separated by riddling and *usu* rejected; refuse. [OE *hriddel*, earlier *hridder*]

ride *rīd*, *vi* to travel or be borne on the back of an animal, on a bicycle, or in a vehicle, boat, on a broomstick, the waves, a whirlwind, etc (*usu* with *in*, *on* or *upon*); to float or seem to float buoyantly; to go on horseback on a raid (*archaic*), in procession, across a ford, etc; to serve as a cavalryman; to lie at anchor (*naut*); to remain undisturbed or unchanged; to sit or move as if on horseback; to turn, rest or grate upon something; to work up out of position; (of an animal, etc) to allow itself to be ridden; to weigh when mounted; to have sexual intercourse (*vulg slang*). — *vt* to traverse, trace, ford or perform on horseback, on a bicycle, etc; to sit on; to bestride; to sit on and control; to travel on; to control at will, or oppressively; to oppress, domineer over, badger, annoy; to improvise on (a theme) (*jazz*); to rest or turn on; to overlap; to mount upon; to sustain, come through, *esp* while riding at anchor (*naut*; also *fig*); to give a ride to, or cause to ride; to convey by vehicle (*US*); to have sexual intercourse with (*vulg slang*): — *pa t* **rōde**, *archaic* **rid**, *Scot* **raid** or **rade**; *pa p* **ridd'en**, *archaic* **rid** or **rode**. — *n* a journey on horseback, on a bicycle, or in a vehicle; the animal, vehicle, etc providing this; a spell of riding; an act of riding with particular regard to the rider's, driver's, etc degree of comfort or discomfort, etc; an experience or course of events of a specified nature, eg a *rough ride*; a fairground entertainment on or in which people ride; a road for horse-riding, *esp* one through a wood; an excise officer's district; an act of sexual intercourse (*vulg slang*); a sexual partner (*esp* female) (*vulg slang*). — *n* **rīdabil'ity** fitness for riding or driving, or for riding or driving along or across. — *adj* **rī'dable** or **ride'able**. — **-ridden** in combination, oppressed by the dominance or prevalence of a specified thing (eg **hag-ridden** or **cliché-ridden**). — *n* **rī'der** a person who rides or can ride; a commercial traveller (*obs*); a moss-trooper; an object that rests on or astride of another, such as a piece of wire on a balance for fine weighing; a clause or corollary added to an already complete contract or other legal document; a proposition that a pupil or candidate is asked to deduce from another; a gold coin bearing a mounted figure (Du and Flem *rijder*). — *adj* **rī'dered**. — *adj* **rī'derless**. — *n* **rī'ding** the action of the verb to ride; the art or practice of horse-riding; a track, *esp* through woodland, for riding on; an excise-officer's district; anchorage. — Also *adj*. — **ri'ding-boot** a high boot worn in riding. — *n pl* **ri'ding-breeches** breeches for riding, with loose-fitting thighs and tight-fitting legs. — **ri'ding-cloak**; **ri'ding-clothes**; **ri'ding-coat** a coat of a style worn by horse-riders; **ri'ding-committee** a committee of ministers sent by the General Assembly to carry out an ordination or induction, where the local presbytery refused to act, under the 18c Moderate domination in Scotland; **ri'ding-crop**; **ri'ding-glove**; **ri'ding-habit** a woman's dress for riding, *esp* one with a long skirt for riding side-saddle; **ri'ding-hood** a hood formerly worn by women when riding; **ri'ding-horse**; **ri'ding-in'terest** (*Scots law*) an interest depending on other interests; **ri'ding-light** (*naut*) a light hung out in the rigging at night when a vessel is riding at anchor; **ri'ding-master** a teacher of horse-riding; **ri'ding-rhyme** the heroic couplet, *perh* from Chaucer's use of it in the *Canterbury Tales*; **ri'ding-robe** a riding-habit; **ri'ding-rod** a light cane for equestrians; **ri'ding-school**; **ri'ding-skirt**; **ri'ding-suit**; **ri'ding-whip**. — **let (something) ride** to let (something) alone, not try to stop it; **ride a hobby** see under **hobby**[1]; **ride and tie** to ride and go on foot alternately, each tying up the horse, or leaving the bicycle by the roadside, and walking on (also *n*, *adv* and *vi* **ride'-and-tie'**); **ride down** to overtake by riding; to charge and overthrow or trample; **ride for a fall** to court disaster; **ride herd on** (*orig US*) to guard (a herd of cattle, etc) by riding on its perimeter; to control, keep watch on (*fig*); **ride (someone) off** (*polo*) to bump against (another player's horse) moving in the same direction; **ride out** to keep afloat throughout (a storm); to cut out from a herd by riding; to survive, get safely through or past (a period of difficulty, etc); **ride to hounds** to take part in fox-hunting; **ride up** (of a garment) to move gradually up the body out of position; **riding the fair** the ceremony of opening a fair by a procession; **take for a ride** to give (someone) a lift in a car with the object of murdering him or her in some remote place; to play a trick on, dupe. [OE *rīdan*; Du *rijden*, Ger *reiten*]

rident *rī'dənt*, (*literary*) *adj* laughing or smiling radiantly, beaming. [L *rīdēns*, *-entis*, pr p of *rīdēre* to laugh]

ridge *rij*, *n* the back (*obs*); the earth thrown up by the plough between the furrows; a strip of arable land, *usu* between furrows; a narrow elevation or raised strip along any surface; a rib on a knitted garment, etc; a long narrow top or crest; the horizontal line of a rooftop; a hill-range. — *vt* and *vi* to form into ridges; to wrinkle. — *adj* **ridged** having ridges. — *n* **ridg'er** a type of plough which forms furrows on either side of the blade. — *n* **ridg'ing** the forming of ridges; covering with ridge-tiles. — *adj* **ridg'y** having ridges. — **ridge'-back** Rhodesian ridgeback (qv under **Rhodesia**); **ridge'-bone** the spine; **ridge'-piece** or **ridge'-pole** the timber forming the ridge of a roof; **ridge'-rope** the central rope of an awning; **ridge'-tile** a tile shaped to cover the ridge of a roof; **ridge'way** a track along a hill-crest. [OE *hrycg*; ON *hryggr*, Ger *Rücken*, back]

ridgel or **ridgil** *rij'əl*, (now *dialect*) *n* a male animal with only one testicle in position or remaining. — Also **ridgling** (*rij'ling*) or **rig** (*rig*). — Northern form **rigg'ald**, **rig'ling** or **rig'lin** (*rig'*). [Appar from preceding, from the undescended testicle near the back]

ridicule[1] *rid'i-kūl*, *n* absurdity (*rare*); derision; mockery. — *vt* to laugh at; to make fun of; to deride; to mock. — *n* **rid'icūler**. — *adj* **ridic'ūlous** deserving or causing ridicule; absurd. — *adv* **ridic'ūlously**. — *n* **ridic'ūlousness**. [L *rīdiculus*, from *rīdēre* to laugh]

ridicule[2] *rid'i-kūl*, (now *dialect*) *n*. Same as **reticule**.

Riding *rī'ding*, *n* one of the three former divisions of Yorkshire; a political constituency (*Can*). [For *thriding*, from ON *thrithi* third]

riding. See under **ride**.

ridotto *ri-dot'ō*, *n* a public dancing party in the 18c and 19c: — *pl* **ridott'os**. [Ital]

RIE *abbrev*: Recognized Investment Exchanges.

riebeckite *rē'bek-īt*, (*mineralogy*) *n* a monoclinic amphibole, silicate of sodium and iron. [Named after the German traveller Emil *Riebeck* (1853–85)]

riel *rē'əl*, *n* the basic monetary unit (100 sen) of Cambodia (formerly Kampuchea).

riem *rēm*, *n* a rawhide thong. — *n* **riempie** (*rēm'pē*; dimin of *riem*) a long riem about the width of a shoelace, used as string, for the weaving of chair-backs and seats, etc. [Afrik]

Riemannian *rē-man'i-ən*, *adj* relating to the German mathematician Georg Friedrich Bernhard *Riemann* (1826–66), or to his work or concepts, *esp* to **Riemannian geometry**, the geometry of **Riemannian space**. (With certain nouns the adjective used is **Riemann**, as in **Riemann surface** or **Riemann integral**).

riempie. See **riem**.

rien ne va plus *ri-ɛ̃ nə va plōō*, (*Fr*) a term used by croupiers to indicate that no more bets may be placed. [Literally, nothing goes any more]

Riesling *rēz'ling*, *n* a type of grape grown *esp* in Germany; a dry white table wine produced from it. [Ger]

rieve. Same as **reave**.

riever. Same as **reaver**.

rifacimento *rē-fä-chi-men'tō*, *n* a recasting of a literary or musical work: — *pl* **rifacimen'ti** (*-tē*). [Ital]

rife *rīf*, *adj* prevalent; abounding; current. — Also *adv*. — *adv* **rife'ly**. — *n* **rife'ness**. [OE *rȳfe*, *rīfe*; Du *rijf*, ON *rīfr*]

riff *rif*, (*jazz* and *rock music*) *n* a phrase or figure played repeatedly. [Perh *refrain*]

riffle[1] *rif'l*, *n* a shallow section in a river where the water flows swiftly (*US*). — *vt* to turn or stir lightly and rapidly (eg the pages of a book), often in cursory search for something; to treat the pages of (a book) in this way (with *through*); to shuffle by allowing the corner of a card from one part of the pack to fall alternately with that of a card in the other. — Also *vi*. [Cf **ripple**[1]]

riffle[2] *rif'l*, *n* (eg in gold-washing) a groove or slat in a sluice to catch free particles of ore. [Cf **rifle**[2]]

riffler *rif'lər*, *n* a small file with curved ends used by sculptors, wood- or metalworkers, etc for intricate work. [Fr *rifloir*, from *rifler* to scrape or file]

riff-raff *rif'-raf*, *n* undesirable, common people, scum; rubbish. — *adj* rubbishy. [ME *rif and raf*, from OFr *rif et raf*]

rifle[1] *rī'fl*, *vt* to plunder; to ransack; to disarray; (of a hawk) to seize only the feathers of; to injure. — *n* **rī'fler**. [OFr *rifler*]

rifle[2] *rī'fl*, *vt* to groove spirally; (also *vi*) to shoot with a rifle. — *n* a firearm with a spirally grooved barrel. — *n* **rī'fling** the spiral grooving of a gun-bore. — **ri'fle-bird** or **ri'fleman-bird** an Australian bird of paradise; a New Zealand bushwren; **ri'fle-corps** a body of soldiers armed with rifles; **ri'fle-green** a dark green, the colour of a rifleman's uniform (also *adj*); **ri'fle-grenade** a grenade or bomb fired from a rifle; **ri'fleman** a soldier armed with a rifle; a rifle-bird; **ri'fle-pit** a pit to shelter riflemen; **rifle range** the range of a rifle; a place for rifle practice; **ri'fle-shot**. [OFr *rifler* to scratch; cf Ger *riefeln* and **rifle**[1]]

rift[1] *rift*, *n* a cleft; a fissure; a chink; a riven fragment (*Spenser*). — *vt* and *vi* to cleave, split. — *adj* **rift'less**. — *adj* **rift'y**. — **rift valley** a valley formed by subsidence of a portion of the earth's crust between two faults; **Rift Valley fever** an infectious disease of cattle and sheep in Africa, to which humans are also susceptible, characterized by high fever and hepatitis, and caused by a virus *prob* transmitted by mosquitoes. [Cf Dan and Norw *rift* a cleft]

rift[2] *rift*, (*Scot*) *vi* to belch. — Also *n*. [ON *ryfta*]

rifte *rift*, (*Spenser*) *pa p* of **rive**.

rig[1] *rig*, *vt* to fit with sails and tackling (*naut*); to fit up or fit out; to equip; to set up, set in working order; to dress, clothe (now *colloq*): — *pr p* **rigg'ing**; *pa t* and *pa p* **rigged**. — *n* the form and arrangement of masts, sails and tackling; an outfit; garb; general appearance; equipment; a team of horses and carriage (*NAm*); an articulated lorry (*colloq*, *esp NAm*); a well-boring plant, an oil rig. — *combining form* **-rigged** with masts and sails arranged in the manner indicated. — *n* **rigg'er** a person who rigs ships; a person who puts together and attends to the rigging of aircraft; someone who puts up and looks after the scaffolding and lifting apparatus, etc that is used for building operations and theatrical and musical productions, etc; outrigger; (in machinery) a narrow drum. — *combining form* **-rigger** denoting a ship rigged in the manner indicated. — *n* **rigg'ing** tackle; the system of cordage which supports a ship's masts and extends the sails; the system of wires and cords in an aircraft. — **rigg'ing-loft** a long workshop where rigging is fitted; the place in a theatre from which the scenery is manipulated; **rig'-out** an outfit. — **rig out** to provide with complete dress, full equipment, etc; **rig up** to dress or equip; to put up quickly from available, *esp* inadequate, materials. [Origin obscure; perh connected with Norw *rigga* to bind]

rig[2] *rig*, (*Scot* and *NEng*) *n*. Same as **ridge**. — *n* **rigg'ing** the roof. — **rigg'ing-tree** a roof-tree.

rig[3] *rig*, (*colloq*) *n* a frolic, prank; a trick, swindle. — *vt* to manipulate unscrupulously or dishonestly; to set up fraudulently. — *n* **rigg'ing** manipulating unscrupulously or dishonestly, as in *price-rigging*, *vote-rigging*, etc. — **run a rig** (now *dialect*) to play a trick (on). [Origin obscure]

rig[4] *rig*, *n* (now *dialect*) a wanton person. — *vi* to behave in a wanton manner; to romp about. — *adj* **rigg'ish** (*Shakesp*) wanton. [Origin obscure]

rig[5]. See **ridgel**.

rigadoon *rig-ə-dōōn'*, *n* a lively jig-like dance for one couple; the music for this. [Fr *rigaudon*]

rigatoni *rig-ətō'ni*, *n* pasta in the form of large, fluted tubes. [Ital, augmentative pl of *rigato*, pa p of *rigare* to draw lines, from *riga* line]

Rigel *rī'gəl* or *-jəl*, *n* a first-magnitude star appearing in the foot of the constellation Orion. [Ar *rijl* foot]

rigg *rig*, (*dialect*) *n* the dogfish. [Ety unknown]

riggald. See **ridgel**.

right[1] *rīt*, *adj* straight; direct; perpendicular; forming one-fourth of a revolution; with axis perpendicular to base; true; genuine; veritable; characteristic; truly judged or judging; appropriate; in accordance, or identical, with what is true and fitting; not mistaken; accurate; fit; sound; intended to be exposed (such as a side, eg of cloth); morally justifiable or incumbent; just; in accordance with what should be; equitable; justly to be preferred or commended; at or towards that side which corresponds to east when one is facing north, and at which in a majority of people is the better-developed hand (of a river, this side in relation to a person going downstream, or on the stage, from the point of view of an actor looking at the audience); worn or used by a part of the body, etc on the right side; sitting at the president's right hand (in Continental assemblies); hence, conservative or inclined towards conservatism, right-wing. — *adv* straight; straightway; quite; just, exactly; in a right manner; justly; correctly; very (*archaic* and *dialect* or in special phrases); to or on the right side. — *n* that which is right or correct; rightness; fair treatment; equity; truth; justice; just or legal claim; what one has a just claim to;

due; (in *pl*) a stag's brow, bez and trez antlers (*archaic*); territory (*Spenser*); the right hand; the right side; a glove, shoe, etc for the right hand, foot, etc; the region on the right side; the right wing; the conservatives. — *vt* to set right; to set in order; to rectify; to redress; to vindicate; to do justice to; to avenge; to set right side up or erect. — *vi* to recover an erect position. — *interj* expressing agreement, acquiescence or readiness. — *adj* **right'able** capable of being righted. — *vt* **right'en** (*archaic*) to set right. — *n* **right'er** a person who sets right or redresses wrong. — *adj* **right'ful** having a just claim; according to justice; belonging by right. — *adv* **right'fully**. — *n* **right'fulness** righteousness; justice. — *n* **right'ing**. — *adj* **right'ish**. — *n* **right'ist** an adherent of the political right, a conservative. — Also *adj*. — *adj* **right'less** (*Scot*) without rights. — *adv* **right'ly**. — *n* **right'ness**. — *interj* **righto'** (*pl* **rightos'**) or **right-oh'** (*colloq*) expressing acquiescence. — *adj* and *adv* **right'-ward** towards the right; more right-wing. — Also *n* (*rare*). — *adv* **right'wards**. — **right about** the directly opposite quarter (in drill or dismissal; also **right-about face**). — *adv* in the opposite direction. — *vi* to turn to face the opposite direction. — *adj* **right'-and-left'** having a right and a left side, part, etc; bilaterally symmetrical; on both sides; from both barrels. — *n* a shot or a blow from each barrel or hand. — *adv* on both sides; on all hands; towards one side, then the other; in all directions. — *adj* **right-ang'led** having a **right angle**, one equal to a fourth of a revolution. — **right ascension** see under **ascension**. — *adj* **right'-bank** on the right bank. — *adj* and *adv* **right'-down** out-and-out. — *adj* **right'-drawn** (*Shakesp*) drawn in a just cause. — *adj* **right'-hand** at the right side; towards the right; performed with the right hand; with thread or strands turning to the right; chiefly relied on (as *one's right-hand man*). — *adj* **right-hand'ed** using the right hand more easily than the left; with or for the right hand; with rotation towards the right, or clockwise. — *adv* towards the right. — **right-hand'edness**; **right-hand'er** a blow with the right hand; a right-handed person; **right-hand man** see **right-hand** above. — *n* and *adj* **Right Honourable** a title of distinction given to peers below the rank of marquis, to privy councillors, to present and past cabinet ministers, to certain Lord Mayors and Lord Provosts, etc. — *adj* **right'-lined** rectilinear. — *adj* **right-mind'ed** having a mind disposed towards what is right, just or according to good sense; sane. — **right-mind'edness**; **right-of-way'** a track over which there is a **right of way** (see below); the strip of land occupied by a railway track, a road, etc (*US*): — *pl* **right'-of-ways'** or **rights'-of-way'**. — *adj* **right-on'** absolutely correct; trendy, belonging to or in keeping with the latest social, moral, political etc ideas or fashions. — *n* and *adj* **Right Reverend** see under **reverend**. — **rights issue** (*commerce*) an issue of new shares which shareholders of a company may buy, *usu* below the market price, in proportion to their current holdings. — *adj* **right'-thinking** of approved opinions; right-minded. — *adj* **right-to-life'** (*esp NAm*) same as **pro-life**. — **right-to-life'r** (*esp NAm*) same as **pro-lifer**; **right whale** a whale of the typical genus Balaena, *esp* the Greenland whale; **right wing** the political right; the wing on the right side of an army, football pitch, etc. — *adj* **right'-wing** of or on the right wing; relating to the political right; (having opinions which are) conservative, opposed to socialism, etc. — **right'-wing'er** a player on the right wing; a person with right-wing views or who supports the right wing of a party, etc. — **all right** see under **all**; **at right angles** forming or in such a way as to form a right angle; **bill of rights** (often with *caps*) an accepted statement of the rights and privileges of the people or of individuals, which the government or state must not infringe (eg that embodied in the Bill of Rights, 1689, or in the US Constitution); **by rights** or (formerly **right**) rightfully; if all were right; **civil rights** see under **civil**; **do someone right** to do someone justice; to keep pace with someone in drinking; to drink someone's health; **have a right** (or **no right**) to be entitled (or not entitled); to be under a moral obligation (or no obligation) (*illiterate* or *dialect*); **have right** (*archaic*) to be right; **in one's own right** by absolute and personal right, not through another; **in one's right mind** quite sane; **in right of** by virtue of; by title vested in; **in the right** right; maintaining a justifiable position; **put** or **set to rights** to set in order; **right as a trivet** see under **trivet**; **right as rain** see under **rain**[1]; **right away** straightaway, immediately; without delay; **right down** plainly; **right, left and centre** same as **left, right and centre** under **left**; **right of common** (*law*) a right to take something from, or pasture animals on, the land of another; **right of entry** a legal right to enter a place; **right off** without delay; **right of way** the right of the public to pass over a piece of ground (see also **right-of-way** above); **right on** (*US*) an exclamation expressing enthusiastic agreement or approval (*adj* **right-on** see above); **right out** (*Shakesp*) outright; **right the helm** to put it amidships, in a line with the keel; **send**, etc **to the right about** (*colloq*) to dismiss summarily, or force to retreat; **she'll be right** (*Austr*) an expression of assurance or confidence. [OE *riht* (n and adj), *rihte* (adv), *rihten* (v); cf Ger *recht* and L *rēctus* straight, right]

right[2] (*Shakesp* and *Milton*) for **rite**.

righteous *rī'chəs*, *adj* just, upright; provoked or supported by a moral standpoint or premise; excellent, honest (*US slang*). — *adv* **right'eously**. — *n* **right'eousness** rectitude; a righteous act. [OE *rihtwīs*, from *riht* right, and *wīs* wise, prudent, or *wīse* wise, manner]

rigid *rij'id*, *adj* stiff; unbending; unyielding; rigorous; strict; (of an airship) having a rigid structure to maintain shape; (of a truck or lorry) not articulated. — *n* a strict or unyielding person (*rare*); a rigid airship. — *vt* and *vi* **rigid'ify** to make or become rigid: — *pr p* **rigid'ifying**; *pa t* and *pa p* **rigid'ified**. — *n* **rigid'ity**. — *vt* **rig'idize** or **-ise** to rigidify. — *adv* **rig'idly**. — *n* **rig'idness**. [L *rigidus*, from *rigēre* to be stiff]

Rigil *rī'gəl*, *-jəl*, or *rij'il*, *n* a first-magnitude double star in the foot of the Centaur, *usu* known as Alpha Centauri. [Cf **Rigel**]

riglin or **rigling**. See under **ridgel**.

rigmarole *rig'mə-rōl*, *n* a long rambling discourse; a long, complicated series of actions, instructions, etc, often rather pointless, boring or irritating. — *adj* prolix and incoherent. [**Ragman Roll**]

rigol or **rigoll** *rig'əl*, *n* a gutter or water-channel; a groove, *esp* an encircling groove; a circlet (*Shakesp*). [Fr *rigole* gutter, groove]

rigor *rī'gör* or *rig'ör*, *n* a sense of chilliness with contraction of the skin, a preliminary symptom of many diseases (*med*); failure to react to stimulus, under unfavourable conditions (*bot*); a rigid irresponsive state caused by a sudden shock, as when an animal is said to sham dead (*zool*); (*rig'ər*) another, chiefly American, spelling of **rigour**. — *n* **rigorism** (*rig'ər-izm*) extreme strictness; the doctrine that in doubtful cases the strict course should be followed. — *n* **rig'orist**. — *adj* **rig'orous** rigidly strict or scrupulous; exact; unsparing; severe; harsh, violent (*Spenser*). — *adv* **rig'orously**. — *n* **rig'orousness**. — *n* **rigour** (*rig'ər*) stiffness; hardness; rigor; severity; unswerving enforcement of law, rule or principle; strict exactitude; austerity; extreme strictness; severity of weather or climate. — **rigor mortis** (*mör'tis*, or *mor'tis*) (*L*) stiffening of the body after death. [L *rigor*, from *rigēre* to be stiff]

RIGS *abbrev*: regionally important geological site.

Rigsdag *rigz'dag* or *rēgz'däg*, *n* the former parliament of Denmark, replaced in 1953 by the Folketing. [Dan, from *rige* a kingdom, and *dag* a day, diet]

Rigveda *rig-vā'də* or *-vē'də*, *n* the first of the four Vedas. [Sans *ṛc* a hymn, and *veda* knowledge]

rigwiddie or **rigwoodie** *rig-wid'i*, *-wûd'i*, *-wud'i*, or *rig'*, (*Scot*) *n* a cart-horse's back-band. — *adj* lean and tough; stubborn; a vague word of reproach, with a suggestion of the *widdy*, or halter. [**rig**[2] and **widdy**(=**withy**)]

RIIA *abbrev*: Royal Institute of International Affairs.

rijstafel, **rijsttafel** or **reistafel** *rīs'tä-fəl*, *n* an Indonesian rice dish served with a variety of foods. [Du *rijst* rice, and *tafel* table]

rikishi *ri-kish'i*, *n* a sumo wrestler: — *pl* **rikish'i**. [Jap]

Riksdag *riks'dag*, *n* the parliament of Sweden. [Swed, from *rike* a kingdom, and *dag* a day, diet]

Riksmöl *riks'mol*, *n* former name for **Bokmål**. [Norw, from *riks*, genitive of *rik* kingdom, and *möl* language]

rile *rīl*, *vt* to annoy or irritate; to make angrily excited (also with *up*). — *adj* **riley** (*rī'li*; *US*) turbid, roily; irritable. [Variant of **roil**]

Riley *rī'li*: **the life of Riley** see under **life**.

rilievo. See **relievo**.

rill *ril*, *n* a very small brook; a runnel; a small trench; a narrow furrow on the moon or Mars (also **rille** from Ger *Rille*). — *vi* to flow in a rill or rills. — *n* **rill'et** a little rill. — **rill'mark** (*geol*) a marking produced by water trickling down a beach or bank. [Cf Du *ril*, Ger (orig LGer) *Rille* channel, furrow]

rillettes *ri-yet'*, *n pl* a French type of potted meat made by simmering shreds of lean and fat pork, etc till crisp, and pounding them to form a paste. [Fr]

RIM *abbrev*: Mauritania (*République Islamique de Mauretanie*; IVR).

rim[1] *rim*, *n* the outermost circular part of a wheel, not including the tyre; an edge, border, brim, or margin, *esp* when raised or more or less circular; an encircling band, mark or line. — *vt* to provide with a rim; to edge: — *pr p* **rimm'ing**; *pa t* and *pa p* **rimmed**. — *adj* **rim'less**. — *adj* **rimmed**. — **rim'-brake** a brake acting on the rim of a wheel; **rim'-lock** a lock mechanism in a metal case that is screwed to the inner face of a door (as opposed to a *mortise lock*); **rim'-shot** (*esp* in *jazz*) a drum-stroke which hits the rim and skin of the drum simultaneously. [OE *rima* (found in compounds)]

rim[2] *rim*, *n* a membrane (*obs*); the peritoneum (now *dialect*). [OE *rēoma*; cf **riem**]

rim[3] *rim*, (*vulg slang*) *vi* and *vt* to stimulate the anus (of), *esp* orally; to practise anilingus (on). — *n* **rimm'ing**. [Perh variant of **ream**[3]]

rima *rī'mə* or *rē'mə*, *n* a chink; *specif* the gap between vocal cords and arytaenoid cartilages: — *pl* **rimae** (*rī'mē* or *rē'mī*). — *n* **rime** (*rīm*; *obs*) a chink, fissure. — *adj* **rī'mose** (or *-mōs'*) or **rī'mous** full of chinks; covered with cracks. [L *rīma*]

rime[1] *rīm*, *n* hoar-frost or frozen dew; ice deposited by freezing of supercooled fog (*meteorol*). — *vt* to cover with rime. — *adj* **rī'my**. [OE *hrīm*; Du *rijm*, Ger *Reif*]

rime[2] and **rimer**, etc. Same as **ream**[3] and **reamer**, **rhyme** and **rhymer**, etc.

rime[3]. See **rima**.

rime riche *rēm rēsh*, (*Fr*) *n* literally rich rhyme (qv under **rhyme**). — **rime suffisante** (*sü-fē-zãt*; *Fr*) literally sufficient rhyme, corresponding to ordinary rhyme in English.

rimu *rē'moo͞*, *n* a coniferous tree of New Zealand, *Dacrydium cupressinum*. [Maori]

rin *rin*, a Scots form of **run**.

rind[1] *rīnd*, *n* bark; peel; crust; outside. — *vt* to bark. — *adj* **rīnd'ed**. — *adj* **rīnd'less**. — *adj* **rīnd'y**. [OE *rinde*; Du *rinde*, Ger *Rinde*]

rind[2] or **rynd** *rīnd*, *n* a fitting that supports an upper millstone, cross-shaped with expanded ends. [Cf MDu *rijn*, MLGer *rîn*]

rinderpest *rin'dər-pest*, *n* a malignant and contagious disease of cattle causing fever, severe diarrhoea, and discharges from the mucous membranes, etc. [Ger, cattle-plague]

rine *rīn*, (*Spenser*, etc) *n*. Same as **rind**[1].

rinforzando *rin-för-tsan'dō*, (*music*) *adj* with sudden accent. [Ital, reinforcing]

ring[1] *ring*, *n* a small, circular band, *esp* one of metal, worn on the finger, in the ear, nose, or elsewhere; any object, mark, arrangement, group or course of a similar form; an encircling band; a rim; a short cylinder for holding a table-napkin; a link of chain-mail; an encircling cut in bark; a zone of wood added in a season's growth, as seen in sections; a mark of fungus growth in turf (**fairy ring**); a flat crowd of very small satellites encircling Saturn; an annulus; a segment of a worm, caterpillar, etc; a closed chain of atoms; a system of elements in which addition is associative and commutative and multiplication is associative and distributive with respect to addition (*math*); a circular ripple; a circular earthwork or rampart; an arena; a space set apart for boxing, wrestling, circus performance, riding display of animals, etc; an enclosure for bookmakers at a racecourse; pugilism; prize-fighters or bookmakers with their associates collectively; a combination or clique, *esp* one organized to control the market or for other self-seeking purpose; a system operated by some antique dealers who refrain from bidding against each other at an auction, so that one of their number may buy cheaply, and then share the profit made by subsequent resale; a computer system suitable for local network use, with several microcomputers or peripheral devices connected by cable in a ring. — *vt* to encircle; to put a ring on or in; to put on in the manner of a ring; to cut a ring in the bark of; to cut into rings; to go in rings round; to excel, be the quickest sheep-shearer among (*Austr*). — *vi* to move in rings; to gather or be in a ring: — *pa t* and *pa p* **ringed**; formerly sometimes, and still in sheep-shearing competitions, **rung**. — *adj* **ringed** surrounded by, or marked with, a ring or rings; ring-shaped; composed of rings. — *n* **ringer** (*ring'ər*) a person who rings; a throw of a quoit that encircles the pin; a quoit so thrown; a person or thing of the highest excellence; the quickest, most expert of a group of shearers (*Austr*). — *n* and *adj* **ring'ing**. — *adj* **ring'less**. — *n* **ring'let** a little ring; a fairy ring; a fairy dance in a ring; a long curl of hair; a type of satyrid butterfly with small ring-marks on its wings. — *adj* **ring'leted**. — *n* **ring'ster** a member of a ring, *esp* in a political or price-fixing sense. — *adv* **ring'wise**. — **ring'-ar'mature** one with a ring-shaped core. — *vt* **ring'-bark** to strip a ring of bark from. — **ring binder** a loose-leaf binder with metal rings along the inside spine which open to hold perforated sheets of paper; **ring'bit** a horse's bit with rings at the ends; **ring'-bolt** a bolt with a ring through a hole at one end; **ring'bone** a bony callus on a horse's pastern-bone; the condition caused by this; **ring'-canal** a circular canal within the rim of a jellyfish; a circular vessel of the water-vascular system of echinoderms; **ring'-carrier** (*Shakesp*) a go-between; **ring circuit** (*electronics*) an electrical supply system in which a number of power-points are connected to the main supply by a series of wires, forming a closed circuit; **ring'-compound** a chemical compound with a closed chain; **ring'-cross** a circle with crossed diameters; **ring'-dance** a round dance; **ring'-dial** a portable sundial; **ring'-dott'erel** the ringed plover; **ring'-dove** the wood-pigeon, from the broken white ring or line on its neck; **ring'-dropping** a sharper's trick of pretending to find a dropped ring and selling it; **ring'-dyke** (*geol*) a dyke with more or less circular outcrop; **ringed'-plover** a ring-necked plover of various kinds; **ring'-fence** a fence continuously encircling an estate; a complete barrier; the compulsory reservation of funds for use within a specific, limited sector or department (of government, of a company, etc); the compulsory separation, for tax purposes, of a company's business interests in North Sea oil from their other business interests, to prevent them from paying less tax on their oil profits by setting against these profits any losses made in other businesses. — *vt* to enclose within a ring-fence; to apply a ring-fence to. — **ring'-fencing**; **ring'-finger** the third finger, *esp* of the left hand, on which the wedding-ring is worn; **ring fort** (*archaeol*) a type of defended dwelling-site of the Iron Age and later, enclosed within a strong circular wall; **ring'-gauge** a gauge in the form of a ring; either a collection of graded rings or a graduated stick for measuring ring- or finger-size; **ring'leader** a person who takes the lead in mischief or trouble; **ring main** (*electronics*) an electrical supply system in which the power-points and the mains are connected in a ring circuit; **ring'man** the ring-finger (*obs* or *dialect*); a bookmaker; **ring'-mark** a ring-shaped mark; **ring'-master** a person in charge of performances in a circus-ring; **ring'-money** money in the form of rings. — *adj* **ring'-necked** (*-nekt*) having the neck marked with a ring. — **ring network** (*comput*) one forming a closed loop of connected terminals; **ring ouzel** or **ousel** see under **ouzel**. — *adj* **ring'-porous** having annual rings marked by large pores. — **ring'-pull** the tongue of metal and the ring attached to it, which one pulls from or on the top of a can of beer, lemonade, etc to open it; **ring road** a road or boulevard encircling a town or its inner part; **ring roller** a type of roller consisting of a number of closely packed wheels on an axle, the rims of the wheels narrowing to form a wedge shape (also **Cambridge roller**); **ring rot** a disease of potatoes caused by the bacterium *Corynebacterium sepedonicum*, characterized by the browning and decay of the ring of vascular bundles in the tubers; **ring'-shake** a defect in timber, separation along the annual rings; **ring'side** the side of the prize-ring; **ring'sider** a spectator at prize-fights; **ringside seat** or **view** (*fig*) (a position which allows one to have) a very clear view. — *adj* **ring'-small** small enough to pass through a ring of standard size. — *n* stones of such a size. — **ring'-snake** a common English snake, the grass-snake (also **ringed snake**); a harmless American snake with yellow collar; **ring spanner** a spanner in the form of a notched ring in which diametrically opposite notches fit over the nut; **ring'stand** a stand for chemical vessels, with rings clamped to a vertical rod; a stand for finger-rings; **ring'-stopper** a rope for securing an anchor-ring to the cat-head. — *adj* **ring'-straked** (*Bible*) or **ring'-streaked** streaked in rings. — **ring'-tail** a studding-sail set upon the gaff of a fore-and-aft sail (*naut*); a light sail set abaft and beyond the spanker (*naut*); the female or young male of the hen-harrier, from a rust-coloured ring on the tail-feathers; (without *hyphen*) a ring-tailed cat (see **cacomistle**). — *adj* **ring'-tail** or **-tailed** (*-tāld*) having the tail marked with bars or rings of colour, as a lemur; having a prehensile tail curled at the end, as do certain species of opossum. — **ring'-taw** a game of marbles, with rings marked on the ground; **ring'-time** (*Shakesp*) time for giving rings; **ring'-walk** an encircling walk; **ring'-wall** an enclosing wall; **ring'way** a ring-road; **ring'-winding** winding that threads a ring; **ring'work** work executed in rings; **ring'worm** a skin disease characterized by ring-shaped patches, caused by fungi. — **hold** or **keep the ring** to watch a fight and keep others from interfering; **make** or **run rings round** to be markedly superior to; **ride** or **tilt at the ring** to practise the sport of riding rapidly and catching a hanging ring on a spear; **ring the shed** (*Austr*) to win a sheep-shearing competition; **throw one's hat into the ring** (*colloq*) to offer oneself as a candidate or challenger; to issue a challenge, institute an attack. [OE *hring*; ON *hringr*; Ger *Ring*, Dan and Swed *ring*]

ring² *ring*, *vi* to give a metallic or bell-like sound; to sound aloud and clearly; to give a characteristic or particular sound; to resound, re-echo; to be filled with sound, or a sensation like sound; to be filled with talk or news of (with *with*); to cause a bell or bells to sound, *esp* as a summons or signal. — *vt* to cause to give a metallic or bell-like sound; to sound in the manner of a bell; to summon, usher or announce by a bell or bells; to call on the telephone; to re-echo, resound, proclaim; to disguise (a stolen vehicle) by exchanging its frame, engine number, etc with those of a legitimate vehicle (*slang*): — *pa t* **rang**, (now *rare*) **rung**, (*obs*) **rong**; *pa p* **rung**. — *n* a sounding of a bell; the characteristic sound or tone, as of a bell or a metal, or of a voice; a ringing sound; a set of bells. — *adj* **ringed** (of a car) put together from parts of other cars (*slang*). — *n* **ring'er** a person who, or thing which, rings; a horse raced under the name of another horse, or an athlete or other contestant competing under a false name or otherwise disguised (*esp US*); an outsider, an impostor (*US slang*); (also **dead ringer**) a person or thing (almost) identical to some other person or thing (with *for*; *colloq*). — *n* and *adj* **ring'ing**. — *adv* **ring'ingly**. — **ring a bell** to begin to arouse a memory; **ring back** to telephone (a previous caller) in response to his or her call; to follow up a telephone call with a second one; **ring down** to give the signal for lowering the curtain (*theat*); (with *on*) to bring (something) to a close (*fig*); **ring in** to ring more rapidly before stopping, as a final intimation to lingering churchgoers; **ring in** or **out** to usher in or out (*esp* the year) with bell-ringing; **ringing tone** a telephone tone indicating to the caller that a telephone is ringing (ie not engaged or disconnected) at the number called; **ring off** to put an end to a telephone conversation by replacing the receiver; **ring out** to sound loudly, clearly and suddenly; **ring the bell** to achieve a great success (from the bell of a shooting-gallery bull's-eye); **ring the bells backward** to reverse the order of chimes; **ring true** to sound genuine (like a tested coin); **ring up** to summon by a bell; to call (someone) on the telephone; to enter (an amount, a total) in eg a shop till; **ring up the curtain** to give the signal for raising the curtain (*theat*); (with *on*) to open, set (something) in motion (*fig*). [OE *hringan*; ON *hringja*; Ger *ringen*; Dan *ringe*]

ring³ *ring*, *n* and *vi* an *obs* Scots form of **reign**: — *pa t* **rang**.

Ringelmann chart *ring'l-man chärt*, *n* a chart giving a scale of shades of grey against which density of smoke may be gauged. [After the deviser]

ringent *rin'jənt*, *adj* gaping. [L *ringēns*, *-entis*, pr p of *ringī*]

ringgit *ring'git*, *n* the unit of currency of Malaysia, comprising 100 sen. [Malay]

ringhals *ring'hals* or **rinkhals** *ringk'(h)als*, *n* a S African snake (*Haemachatus haemachatus*) which spits or sprays its venom at its victims. [Afrik *ring* a ring, and *hals* a neck]

rink *ringk*, *n* a course for tilting or racing; a portion of a bowling-green, curling pond, etc allotted to one set of players; a division of a side playing on such a portion; a piece of ice prepared for skating; a building or floor for roller-skating or ice-skating. — *vi* to skate on a rink. [Orig Scots; origin obscure]

rinky-dink *ring'ki-dingk*, (*US slang*) *n* something old-fashioned; something old and run down or worn out; something cheap, trite or trivial. — Also *adj*.

rinse *rins*, *vt* to wash lightly by pouring water in or over, or by dipping in water (also with *out*); to wash in clean water to remove soap traces; to apply a hair rinse to. — *n* an act of rinsing; liquid used for rinsing; a solution used in hairdressing, *esp* one to tint the hair slightly and impermanently. — *adj* **rins'able**, **rinse'able** or **rins'ible**. — *n* **rins'er**. — *adj* **rins'ing**. — *n pl* **rins'ings** liquid in which something has been rinsed. [OFr *rinser* (Fr *rincer*)]

rinthereout *rin'dhə-rōōt*, (*Scot*) *n* and *adj* vagrant; vagabond. **[run thereout]**

Rioja *rē-ō'hhä*, *n* a red or white Spanish table wine. [From La *Rioja*, a region in N Spain]

riot *rī'ət*, *n* wild revelry; debauchery; loose living; unrestrained squandering or indulgence; tumult; a great, *usu* boisterous, success; a disturbance of the peace by a crowd (legally three or more); a striking display of colour, etc; a wildly enjoyable or amusing event or occasion (*slang*); a hilarious person (*slang*). — *vi* to take part or indulge in riot; to revel. — *n* **rī'oter**. — *n* **rī'oting**. — *n* **rī'otise** (*-is*, *-ēz* or *-īz*) or **-ize** (*-īz*) (*obs*) riot, extravagance. — *adj* **rī'otous**. — *adv* **rī'otously**. — *n* **rī'otousness**. — *n* **rī'otry**. — **Riot Act** a statute designed to prevent riotous assemblies; a form of words read as a warning to rioters to disperse; **riot agent** a chemical substance such as tear gas used to control or disperse rioters; **riot police** police specially equipped with **riot gear** (shields, tear gas grenades, etc) for dealing with rioting crowds. — **read the riot act** (*fig*) to give vehement warning that something must cease; **run riot** to act or grow without restraint. [OFr *riot*, *riotte*]

RIP *abbrev*: *requiescat in pace*, (*L*) may he (or she) rest in peace.

rip[1] *rip*, *vt* to slash or tear open, apart, off or out; to make by such an action; to reopen (a wound; with *up*); to shred, tear into pieces (with *up*); to split or saw (timber) with the grain; to strip (a building or its roof); to utter explosively (with *out*). — *vi* to come apart in shreds; to break out violently; to rush, go forward unrestrainedly: — *pr p* **ripp'ing**; *pa t* and *pa p* **ripped** or (*archaic*) **ript**. — *n* a rent, tear; an unchecked rush. — *adj* **ripped** (*slang*) extremely drunk or high on drugs. — *n* **ripp'er** a person who rips; a tool for ripping; a person or thing especially admirable (*slang*, *esp Austr*). — *adj* **ripp'ing** (*slang*) excellent. — Also *adv*. — *adv* **ripp'ingly**. — **rip'cord** a cord for opening a balloon's gasbag or enabling a parachute to open; **rip'-off** (*slang*) (financial) exploitation; a theft, stealing, cheating, etc; a swindle, confidence trick; a film, etc that exploits the success of another by imitating it; **ripp'ing-saw** or **rip'-saw** a saw for cutting along the grain. — *adj* **rip'-roaring** wild and noisy. — **rip'snorter** (*slang*) a fast and furious affair or person; a gale. — *adj* **rip'snorting**. — *adj* **rip'stop** of a synthetic fabric (*esp* nylon), woven with a series of raised areas throughout to prevent or reduce ripping. — **let it rip** to allow an action or process to go on in an unrestrained or reckless way; **let rip** to express oneself, or to act, violently or without restraint; to make a sudden increase in speed, volume, etc; **rip off** (*slang*) to steal; to steal from; to exploit, cheat, overcharge, etc. [Uncertain; cf Fris *rippe*, Flem *rippen*, Norw *rippa*]

rip[2] *rip*, (*dialect*) *n* a wicker basket; a coop. — *n* **ripp'er** or **ripp'ier** (*obs*) a person who carries fish inland to sell. [ON *hrip* basket]

rip[3] *rip*, *n* an inferior horse; a disreputable person. [Poss **reprobate**]

rip[4] *rip*, *n* stretch of broken water (chiefly *US*); disturbed state of the sea. — **rip'tide** tidal rip. [Perh **rip**[1]]

rip[5] or **ripp** *rip*, (*Scot*) *n* a handful, *esp* a plucked handful, of grass or corn. [Poss **rip**[1]; connection with **reap** involves difficulty]

RIPA *abbrev*: Royal Institute of Public Administration.

riparian *rī-pā'ri-ən*, *adj* of or inhabiting a riverbank. — *n* an owner of land bordering a river. — *adj* **ripā'rial**. [L *rīpārius*, from *rīpa* a riverbank]

ripe[1] *rīp*, *adj* ready for harvest; arrived at perfection; fit for use; fully developed; finished; ready for a particular purpose or action; resembling ripe fruit; mature; (of cheese) mature, strong-smelling; (of language, etc) somewhat indecent or over-colourfully expressive; rich and strong in quality. — *vt* and *vi* to ripen. — *adv* **ripe'ly**. — *vt* and *vi* **rī'pen** to make or grow ripe or riper. — *n* **ripe'ness**. [OE *rīpe* ripe, *rīpian* to ripen; connected with *rīp* harvest, and perh **reap**; cf Du *rijp*, Ger *reif*]

ripe[2] *rīp*, (*Scot*) *vt* and *vi* to grope, search, ransack. — *n* **rī'per**. [OE *rȳpan* to rob]

ripeck. See **ryepeck**.

RIPHH *abbrev*: Royal Institute of Public Health and Hygiene.

ripidolite *rip-id'ō-līt*, or *rīp-*, *n* clinochlore. [Gr *rhīpis*, *-idos* fan]

ripieno *ri-pyā'nō*, (*music*) *adj* supplementary, reinforcing; for all, or nearly all, the orchestra or choir. — *n* a supplementary instrument or performer; same as **tutti** (n): — *pl* **ripie'nos** or **ripie'ni** (*-nē*). — *n* **ripie'nist** a supplementary instrumentalist. [Ital, full]

riposte *ri-post'* or *-pōst'*, *n* a quick return thrust after a parry (*fencing*); a repartee. — *vt* and *vi* to answer with a riposte. [Fr, from Ital *risposta* reply]

ripp, **ripper**, **rippier** and **ripping**. See under **rip** (various).

ripple[1] *rip'l*, *n* light fretting of the surface of a liquid; a little wave; a similar appearance on any surface; a type of ice cream with coloured syrup lightly mixed throughout to give a marbled appearance; small periodic variations in a steady current or voltage (*electronics*); a sound as of rippling water; (in *pl*) repercussions, reverberations. — *vt* to ruffle the surface of; to mark with ripples. — *vi* to move or run in ripples; to sound like ripples. — *n* **ripp'let** a small ripple. — *n* and *adj* **ripp'ling**. — *adv* **ripp'lingly**. — *adj* **ripp'ly**. — **ripple effect** a process in which a trend or situation spreads outward from its initial location to affect areas distant from it; **ripp'le-mark** an undulatory ridging produced in sediments by waves, currents and wind, often preserved in sedimentary rocks. — *adj* **ripp'le-marked**. [Origin obscure]

ripple[2] *rip'l*, *n* a toothed implement for removing seeds, etc from flax or hemp. — *vt* to clear of seeds by drawing through a ripple; to remove by a ripple. — *n* **ripp'ler**. [Cf LGer and Du *repel* a ripple, hoe, Ger *Riffel*]

Rippon *rip'ən*, (*obs*; in full **Rippon spur**) *n* a spur made at *Ripon*, once famous for the manufacture of such.

rip-rap or **riprap** *rip'rap*, *n* loose broken stones, used to form a foundation on soft ground or under water, or in the construction of revetments and embankments; a foundation formed of these. [From an obs word imit of the sound of repeated blows]

Ripstone pippin (*Dickens*) for **Ribstone pippin**.

ript. Same as **ripped** (see under **rip**[1]).

Ripuarian *rip-ū-ā'ri-ən*, *adj* applied to the Franks on the lower Rhine and their laws. — *n* a Ripuarian Frank. [Generally said to be from L *rīpa* a riverbank]

Rip Van Winkle *rip van wing'kl*, *n* a person very much behind the times, after a character of that name in a story by Washington Irving, who returned home after having slept in the mountains for twenty years.

risaldar *ris-äl-där'*, *n* the commander of a troop of Indian cavalry. [Hindi *risāldār*]

RISC *abbrev*: reduced instruction set computer (ie one having a central processor with a very small instruction set, allowing faster processing, etc).

rise *rīz*, *vi* to get up; to become erect, stand up; to come back to life; to become hostile; to revolt (often with *up*); to close a session; to break up camp; to raise a siege; to move upward; to come up to the surface; to fly up from the ground; to come above the horizon; to grow upward; to advance in rank, fortune, etc; to swell (*med*); (of dough) to swell under the action of yeast; to increase; to increase in price; to become more acute in pitch; to be excited; to be cheered; to come into view, notice or consciousness; to spring up; to take origin; to have source; to come into being; to extend upward; to tower; to slope up; to come to hand, chance to come; to respond (eg to provocation, or to a challenging situation); to excavate upward; to feel nausea (also *fig*). — *vt* to cause to rise; to surmount (*US*); to raise, view better by nearing (*naut*): — *pa t* **rose** (*rōz*), *Scot* **raise** or **rase** (*rāz*), *US dialect* **riz**; *pa p* **risen** (*riz'n*), *US dialect* **riz**. — *n* rising; ascent; a coming up to the surface, as that of a fish; the sport of making a butt of someone by deception; increase in height; vertical difference or amount of elevation or rising; increase of salary or price, etc; an upward slope; a sharpening of pitch; source, origin; occasion (*obs*); a response, *esp* an angry or excited one; the riser of a step; a shaft excavated from below. — *n* **rīs'er** a person who rises, *esp* from bed; that which rises; the upright portion of a step; a vertical pipe, eg in a building or an oil rig. — *n* **rīs'ing** the action or process of the verb in any sense; a revolt; a prominence; a swelling; a hill. — *adj* and *pr p* ascending: increasing; coming above the horizon; advancing; growing up; approaching the age of; quite as much as (*US*). — **rising tide** (*fig*) an increase in the frequency or occurrence of a specified thing, a growing trend or tendency. — **give rise to** to cause, bring about; **on the rise** in process of rising, *esp* in price; **rise and shine** a facetiously cheerful invitation or instruction to get out of bed briskly, *esp* in the morning; **rise from the ranks** to work one's way up from private soldier to commissioned officer; to become a self-made man or woman; **rise to it** or **rise to the bait** (*fig*, from fishing) to take the lure; **rise to the occasion** to prove equal to an emergency; **take a rise out of** to lure into reacting to provocation, or loosely, to make sport of; **take rise** to originate; **the rise of** (*US*) more than. [OE *rīsan*; ON *rīsa*, Gothic *reisan*, Ger *reisen*]

rishi *rish'i*, *n* a sage or poet. [Sans]

risible *riz'i-bl*, *adj* able or inclined to laugh; of laughter; ludicrous. — *n* **risibil'ity** laughter; inclination to laugh; faculty of laughter. [L *rīsibilis*, from *rīdēre*, *rīsum* to laugh]

risk, also (*obs*) **risque**, *risk*, *n* hazard, danger, chance of loss or injury; the degree of probability of loss; a person, thing or factor likely to cause loss or danger. — *vt* to expose to risk, endanger; to incur the chance of (an unfortunate consequence) by some action. — *n* **risk'er**. — *adj* **risk'ful**. — *adv* **risk'ily**. — *n* **risk'iness**. — *adj* **risk'y** dangerous, liable to accident or mishap; risqué (now *rare*). — **risk analysis** a methodical investigation process undertaken to assess the financial and physical risks affecting a business venture; **risk capital** see **venture capital** under **venture**; **risk'-money** allowance to a cashier to compensate for ordinary errors. — **at risk** in a situation or circumstances where loss, injury, physical abuse, etc are possible; susceptible (*adj* **at'-risk**); **run a risk** to be in, or get into, a risky situation; **run a** (or **the**) **risk of** to risk (failing, etc). [Fr *risque*, from Ital *risco*; origin uncertain]

risoluto *rē-zō-lōō'tō*, (*music*) *adj* and *adv* with emphasis, boldly. [Ital]

risorgimento *ri-sör-ji-men'tō*, *n* a revival, rebirth; (with *cap*) the Renaissance; (with *cap*) the liberation and unification of Italy in the 19c (*hist*): — *pl* **risorgimen'tos**. [Ital, from L *resurgere* to rise again]

risotto *ri-zot'ō*, *n* a dish of rice cooked in stock with meat or seafood, onions and other vegetables, and cheese, etc: — *pl* **risott'os**. [Ital, from *riso* rice]

risp *risp*, (*Scot*) *vt* to rasp; to grate. — *vi* to make a grating sound; to tirl. — *n* a rasp or coarse file; a baker's grater; a roughened bar, on which a ring is grated, used instead of a knocker or doorbell; a grating sound. — *n pl* **risp'ings** portions risped off. [ON *rispa* to scratch]

rispetto *rēs-pet'ō*, *n* a type of Italian folk-song with eight-line stanzas, or a piece of music written in the same style: — *pl* **rispet'ti** (*-tē*). [Ital]

risque. See **risk**.

risqué *rēs'kā* or *ris-kā'*, *adj* audaciously bordering on the unseemly. [Fr, pa p of *risquer* to risk]

Riss *ris*, (*geol*) *n* the third stage of glaciation in the Alps. — *adj* **Riss** or **Riss'ian**. [From a tributary of the Danube in Württemberg]

rissole *ris'ōl* or *rēs-ōl'*, *n* a fried ball or cake of minced seasoned meat or fish coated in breadcrumbs. [Fr]

risus *rī'səs* or *rē'sōōs*, *n* a laugh; a grin. — **risus sardonicus** (*sär-don'ik-əs* or *-ōōs'*; *pathol*) a sardonic grin, or drawing back of the corners of the mouth by spasm of the muscles, as in tetanus. [L *rīsus*, *-ūs* laugh]

rit or **ritt** *rit*, (*Scot*) *vt* to score; to scratch; to slit. — *n* a scratch; a slit. [ME *ritten*; cf Ger *ritzen*]

ritardando *rē-tär-dan'dō*, (*music*) *adj* and *adv* with diminishing speed. — *n* a ritardando passage; a slowing down: — *pl* **ritardan'dos**. [Ital]

rite *rīt*, *n* a ceremonial form or observance, *esp* religious; a liturgy. — *adj* **rite'less**. — **rite of passage**, **passage rite** or **rite de passage** (*rēt də pas-äzh*; *Fr*; *pl* **rites de passage**) a term, first used by the French anthropologist Arnold van Gennep, for any of the ceremonies (such as those associated with birth, puberty, marriage or death) which mark or ensure a person's transition from one status to another within society. [L *rītus*]

ritenuto *rit-ə-nū'tō*, (*music*) *adj* restrained, indicating a sudden slowing-down of tempo. — *n* a ritenuto passage: — *pl* **ritenū'tos**. [Ital, pa p of *ritenere* to restrain, hold back]

ritornello *rit-ör-nel'ō*, (*music*) *n* a short instrumental passage in a vocal work, eg a prelude or refrain; a passage for the whole orchestra in a concerto: — *pl* **ritornel'li** (*-lē*) or **ritornell'os**. — Also **ritornel'**, **ritornell'**, **ritornelle'** or **ritournelle'**. [Ital]

ritt. See **rit**.

ritter *rit'ər*, (*archaic*) *n* a knight. — *n* **ritt'-master** a captain of cavalry. [Ger *Ritter*, *Rittmeister*]

ritual *rit'ū-əl*, *adj* relating to, or of the nature of, rites. — *n* the manner of performing divine service, or a book containing it; a body or code of ceremonies; an often repeated series of actions; the performance of rites; a ceremonial. — *n* **rit'ualism** attachment of importance to ritual, *esp* with the implication of undue importance. — *n* **rit'ualist** a person skilled in or devoted to a ritual; a member of the High Church party in the Church of England. — *adj* **ritualist'ic**. — *adv* **ritualist'ically**. — *n* **ritualizā'tion** or **-s-**. — *vi* **rit'ualize** or **-ise** to practise or turn to ritualism. — *vt* to make ritualistic. — *adv* **rit'ually**. — **ritual abuse** child abuse involving elements of satanic ritual; **ritual choir** part of a church used as a choir; **ritual murder** the killing of a human being as part of a tribal religious ceremony. [L *rituālis*, from *rītus*; see **rite**]

Ritz *ritz*, *n* an expensive, stylish and luxurious establishment (often with *neg*). — *adj* **ritzy** (*rit'zi*; *slang*) stylish, elegant, ostentatiously rich. — **put on the Ritz** or **ritz** to get dressed up to impress; to dress or act ostentatiously. [The *Ritz* hotels]

riva *riv'ə* or *rēv'ə*, (*Shetland*) *n* a cleft in rock. [ON *rīfa*]

rivage *riv'ij* or *rīv'ij*, (*poetic*) *n* a bank, shore. [Fr, from L *rīpa* a bank]

rival *rī'vl*, *n* a person pursuing an object in competition with another; a person who strives to equal or excel another; a person for whom, or thing for which, a claim to equality might be made; a partner, fellow (*Shakesp*). — *adj* standing in competition; having similar pretensions or comparable claims. — *vt* to stand in competition with; to try to gain the same object against; to try to equal or excel; to be worthy of comparison with: — *pr p* **rī'valling**; *pa t* and *pa p* **rī'valled**. — *n* **rī'valess** (*archaic*) a female rival. — *n* **rīvality** (*-val'i-ti*) rivalry; equality (*Shakesp*). — *vi* **rī'valize** or **-ise** to enter into rivalry. — *adj* **rī'valless**. — *n* **rī'valry** the state of being a rival; competition; emulation; the feeling of a rival. — *n* **rī'valship** emulation. — *adj* **ri'val-hating** (*Shakesp*). [L *rīvālis*, said to be from *rīvus* river, as a person who draws water from the same river]

rive *rīv*, (*poetic* or *archaic*) *vt* to tear apart; to tear; to rend; to split; to discharge as if with rending (*Shakesp*); to pierce (*obs*); to plough up (*Scot*). — *vi* to tug, tear; to split: — *pa t* **rīved** or (*Scot*) **rave** (*rāv*); *pa p* **riven** (*riv'n*) or **rived** (*rīvd*), also *Spenser* **rive** (*riv*) and *Keats* **raft**. [ON *rīfa*]

rivel *riv'l*, (now *dialect*) *vt* and *vi* to wrinkle. — *adj* **riv'elled**. [OE *rifelede* rivelled]

river *riv'ər*, *n* a large stream of water flowing over the land; sometimes extended to a strait or inlet; a place for hawking (*archaic*); a stream in general. — *adj* of a river or rivers; dwelling or found in or near a river or rivers. — *adj* **riv'erain** (*-ān*) of a river or its neighbourhood. — *n* a riverside dweller. — *adj* **riv'ered** watered by rivers. — *n* **riv'eret** (*archaic*) a small river. — *adj* **riv'erine** (*-īn* or *-ēn*) of, on, or dwelling in or near a river. — *adj* **riv'erless**. — *adj* **riv'erlike**. — *adj* **riv'ery** of or like a river; having many rivers. — **riv'erbank**; **river basin** the whole region drained by a river with its affluents; **riv'er-bed** the channel in which a river flows; **river blindness** a W African disease, onchocerciasis (qv); **riv'er-boat** a boat with a flat bottom or shallow draft, for use on rivers; **riv'er-bottom** (*US*) alluvial land along the margin of a river; **riv'ercraft** small vessels that ply on rivers; **riv'er-dragon** Pharaoh (*Milton*, an allusion to Ezek 29.3); a crocodile; **riv'er-drift** old alluvia of rivers; **riv'er-driver** (*US*) a person who conducts logs downstream; **riv'er-flat** a piece of alluvial land by a river; **riv'erfront** land, quays, buildings, etc facing a river; **riv'er-god** the tutelary deity of a river;

riv'er-head the source of a river; **riv'er-hog** the capybara; an African wild pig; **riv'er-horse** the hippopotamus; the kelpie; a pole which a person sits astride to cross a river (*SAfr*); **riv'er-jack** (or **river-jack viper**) a W African viper; **riv'erman** a person who lives and works on or along a river; **riv'er-mouth**; **riv'er-mussel** a freshwater mussel; **river novel** same as **roman fleuve**; **riv'er-rat** a thief who prowls about a river; **riv'er-sand** sand from a river-bed; **riv'erscape** a picture of river scenery; **riv'erside** the bank or neighbourhood of a river. — *adj* beside a river. — **riv'er-terrace** a terrace formed when a river eats away its old alluvium deposited when its flood-level was higher; **riv'er-tide** the current of a river; the tide from the sea rising or ebbing in a river; **riv'er-wall** a wall confining a river within bounds; **riv'er-water**; **riv'erway** a river as a waterway; **riv'erweed** Podostemon; **riv'erworthiness**. — *adj* **riv'erworthy** fit to sail, etc on a river. [OFr *rivere* (Fr *rivière*), from L *ripārius* (adj), from *rīpa* bank; cf Ital *riviera*]

rivet[1] *riv'it*, *n* bearded wheat. [Origin obscure]

rivet[2] *riv'it*, *n* a bolt with a head at one end, used to join two or more pieces of metal, etc by hammering down the projecting, headless end. — *vt* to fasten with rivets; to fix immovably; to attract or fix (one's attention, etc) on something; to enthral or fascinate; to clinch or hammer out the end of: — *pr p* **riv'eting**; *pa t* and *pa p* **riv'eted** (formerly often **riv'etting** and **riv'etted**). — *n* **riv'eter** a person who rivets; a machine for riveting. — *n* **riv'eting**. — *adj* gripping, enthralling, arresting. — **riv'et-head**; **riv'et-hearth** a forge for heating rivets; **riv'et-hole** a hole to receive a rivet. [OFr *rivet*, from *river* to clinch; origin obscure]

riviera *riv-i-ā'rə*, *n* a warm coastal district reminiscent of the Riviera in France and Italy on the Mediterranean Sea.

rivière *rē-vyer* or *riv-i-er'*, *n* a necklace of diamonds or other precious stones, *usu* in several strings. [Fr, river]

rivlin *riv'lin*, (*Scot*) *n* a shoe moulded from untanned hide, worn with the hair to the outside; (in *pl*) tatters, rags. [OE *rifling*, ON *hriflinger* hide shoe]

rivo *rē'vō* or *rī'vō*, (*Shakesp*) *interj* a drinking-cry: — *pl* **ri'vos**.

rivulet *riv'ū-lit*, *n* a small river. [L *rīvulus*, dimin of *rīvus* a stream, perh through Ital *rivoletto*, from *rivolo*, from *rivo*]

rix-dollar *riks'-dol-ər*, (*hist*) *n* a silver coin, current in various European countries and colonies in the 16c–19c. [Obs Du *rijcksdaler* (Du *rijksdaalder*), from Du *rijk* kingdom (OE *rīce*), and *daler* dollar]

riyal *ri-yäl'*, *n* the unit of currency in Dubai and Qatar, and (also spelt **rial**, qv) in Saudi Arabia and the Yemen Arab Republic. [Ar *riyāl*, from Sp *real*; see **real**[3]]

riz *riz*, (*US dialect*) *pa t* and *pa p* of **rise**.

riza *rī'zə*, *n* an ornamental (*usu* silver) plate covering a Russian icon, with shaped holes through which to see the face and other features. [Russ, from OSlav, garment]

rizard. See **rizzer**[2].

rizzer[1], **rizzar** or **rizzor** *riz'ər*, (*Scot*) *vt* to dry, *esp* in the sun. — *n* a rizzered haddock. [Cf obs Fr *ressorer* to dry]

rizzer[2], **rizzar** *riz'ər*, **rizard** *riz'ərd* or **rizzart** *riz'ərt*, (*Scot*) *n* a red currant. [Earlier *razour*; origin unknown]

RJE (*comput*) *abbrev*: remote job entry. — **RJET** *abbrev*: remote job entry terminal.

RL *abbrev*: reference library; Republic of Lebanon (IVR); Rugby League.

RLC *abbrev*: (from April 1993) Royal Logistic Corps, incorporating former **RAOC**, **RCT**, etc.

RLO *abbrev*: returned letter office.

rly *abbrev*: railway.

RM *abbrev*: Republic of Madagascar (IVR); Resident Magistrate; Royal Mail; Royal Marines.

rm *abbrev*: ream (*printing*); room.

RMA *abbrev*: Royal Military Academy, Sandhurst.

RMetS *abbrev*: Royal Meteorological Society.

RMM *abbrev*: Republic of Mali (IVR).

RMN *abbrev*: Registered Mental Nurse.

RMO *abbrev*: Resident Medical Officer.

RMP *abbrev*: (Corps of) Royal Military Police.

rms (*math*) *abbrev*: root-mean-square.

RMT *abbrev*: (National Union of) Rail, Maritime and Transport Workers.

RN *abbrev*: Registered Nurse (*NAm*); Republic of Niger; Royal Navy.

Rn (*chem*) *symbol*: radon.

RNA (*biochem*) *abbrev*: ribonucleic acid.

RNAS *abbrev*: Royal Naval Air Service(s).

RNCM *abbrev*: Royal Northern College of Music.

RNIB *abbrev*: Royal National Institute for the Blind.

RNID *abbrev*: Royal National Institute for the Deaf.

RNLI *abbrev*: Royal National Lifeboat Institution.

RNR *abbrev*: Royal Naval Reserve.

RNT *abbrev*: Royal National Theatre (formerly **NT**).

RNVR *abbrev*: Royal Naval Volunteer Reserve.

RNZAF *abbrev*: Royal New Zealand Air Force.

RNZN *abbrev*: Royal New Zealand Navy.

RO *abbrev*: Romania (IVR).

ro *abbrev*: recto (*printing*); run out (*cricket*).

roach[1] *rōch*, *n* a silvery freshwater fish of the carp family, with pale red ventral and tail fins; applied to various N American fishes resembling this. — **as sound as a roach** perfectly sound. [OFr *roche*]

roach[2] *rōch*, (*naut*) *n* a concave curve in the foot of a square sail. — *vt* to arch; to cut short, trim (a horse's mane); to cut, or cut the hair or mane of, in an upright ridge. [Origin uncertain]

roach[3] *rōch*, *n* a cockroach (*US*); (the butt of) a marijuana cigarette (*slang*; *esp US*).

road (*Shakesp*, *Spenser*, etc, **rode**) *rōd*, *n* a ride, horseback journey (*Shakesp*); a raid, incursion (*Shakesp* and *Spenser*); a track suitable for wheeled traffic, *esp* for through communication (often in street-names); a highway; a roadway; a way of approach; course; a mine-passage; (often in *pl*) a roadstead; a railway (*US*); journeying; travelling, tour; dismissal (*colloq*); a prostitute (*Shakesp*). — *n* **road'ie** (*colloq*) a member of the crew who transport, set up and dismantle equipment for musicians, *esp* a rock group, on tour. — *adj* **road'less**. — *n* **road'ster** a horse, cycle or car suitable for ordinary use on the road; a coach-driver or other traveller by road (*obs*); an open car (*orig US*) with a rumble seat or large boot instead of a rear seat, and a single seat for two or three in front. — **road'-agent** (*US*) a highwayman; **road'-bed** the foundation of a railway track; the material laid down to form a road; **road'-block** an obstruction set up across a road, eg to prevent the escape of a fugitive; **road'-book** a guide-book to the roads of a district. — *adj* **road'-borne** carried by road. — **road'-bridge** a bridge carrying a road; **road'craft** knowledge and skill useful to drivers and other road-users; **road'-end** the place where a road branches off from another; **road fund licence** a round certificate, *usu* stuck on a vehicle's windscreen, showing that the vehicle excise duty (or *road fund licence fee*) payable on that vehicle has been paid; **road game** (*US*) a game played by a sports team while on tour; loosely, an away game; **road'header** a tunnelling machine used in mining which excavates with a combination of cutting heads and pressurized water jets; **road'-hog** a swinishly selfish or boorishly reckless motorist or other user of the road. — Also *vi*. — *adj* **road'-hoggish**. — **road'holding** the extent to which a motor vehicle holds the road when in motion; **road'house** a roadside public house, refreshment-room or inn catering for motorists, cyclists, etc; **road hump** any of a series of low ridges built into a road surface to slow traffic down, a sleeping policeman; **road'-maker**; **road'-making**; **road'man** a person who keeps a road in repair; a person who uses the roads, an itinerant; **road manager** the tour manager for a rock band or other group, entertainer, etc, responsible for organizing venues, equipment, crew, etc; **road'-map**; **road'-mender**; **road'-mending**; **road'-**

metal broken stones for roads; **road'-metalling**; **road pricing** the system of charging the driver of a vehicle for the use of a road (eg to reduce traffic in a city centre); **road movie** a film with a narrative based on a journey, the latter often undertaken as an escape and having no definite destination; **road'-roller** a heavy roller used on roads; **road'runner** the chaparral cock; **road'-scraper** an implement for clearing roads of loose material; **road'-sense** aptitude for doing the right thing in driving or road-using in general; **road'show** a touring group of theatrical or musical performers; (a live broadcast from one of a series of venues, presented by) a touring disc jockey and his or her retinue; a promotional tour undertaken by any body or organization seeking publicity for its policies or products; their performances; **road'side** the border of a road; wayside. — *adj* by the side of a road. — **road sign** a sign along a road, motorway, etc giving information on routes, speed limits, etc to travellers; **roads'man** a driver; a roadman; **road'stead** a place near a shore where ships may ride at anchor; **road'-surveyor** a person who supervises roads. — *vt* **road'-test** to test (a vehicle) on the road for performance and roadworthiness (also *fig*). — Also *n*. — **road'-train** (*Austr*) a number of linked trailers towed by a truck, for transporting cattle, etc; **road'-user**; **road'way** the way or part of a road or street used by traffic; the road surface. — *n pl* **road'works** the building or repairing of a road, or work involving the digging up, etc of part of a road. — **road'worthiness**. — *adj* **road'worthy** fit for the road. — **in** or **out of the** (or **one's**) **road** (chiefly *Scot*) in or out of, the way; **one for the road** a last alcoholic drink before setting off; **on the road** travelling, *esp* as a commercial traveller or a tramp; on the way to some place; **road up** road surface being repaired; **rule of the road** see under **rule**; **take the road** to set off, depart; **take to the road** to become a highwayman (*archaic*), or a tramp; to set off for, or travel to, somewhere. [OE *rād* a riding, raid; cf **raid** and **ride**]

roading. See under **rode**[3].

roadster and **roadstead**. See under **road**.

roam *rōm*, *vi* to rove about; to ramble. — *vt* to wander over; to range. — *n* a wandering; a ramble. — *n* **roam'er**. — *n* and *adj* **roam'ing**. [ME *romen*; origin obscure]

roan[1] *rōn*, *adj* bay or dark, with spots of grey and white; of a mixed colour, with a decided shade of red. — *n* a roan colour; a roan animal, *esp* a horse. [OFr *roan* (Fr *rouan*)]

roan[2] *rōn*, *n* grained sheepskin leather. — *adj* of roan. [Poss *Roan*, early form of *Rouen*]

roan[3]. Same as **rone**.

roar *rōr* or *rör*, *vi* to make a full, loud, hoarse, low-pitched sound, as a lion, fire, wind, the sea, cannon, etc; to bellow; to bawl; to guffaw; (of a diseased horse) to take in breath with a loud noise; to behave in a riotous, bullying, noisy manner (*obs*); to rush forward with loud noise from the engine. — *vt* to utter vociferously; to shout (encouragement, abuse, etc); to encourage by shouting (*esp* with *on*). — *n* a sound of roaring. — *n* **roar'er** a person who roars; a horse that roars as a result of disease; a roaring boy (*obs*). — *n* **roar'ing** the action of the verb in any sense; a disease of horses marked by roaring. — *adj* uttering or emitting roars; riotous; proceeding with very great activity or success. — *adv* **roar'ingly**. — *adj* **roar'y** or **roar'ie** (*Scot*) noisy; garish, too bright. — **roaring boy** (*obs*) a boisterous bullying reveller, swaggerer or brawler; **roaring drunk** very drunk (and typically rowdy); **roaring forties** see under **forty**; **the roaring game** curling. [OE *rārian*; but partly from MDu *roer* stir, disturbance]

roast *rōst*, *vt* to cook before a fire; to bake; to parch by heat; to heat strongly; to dissipate the volatile parts of (*esp* sulphur) by heat; to criticize excessively, even sarcastically; to banter (*slang*). — *vi* to undergo roasting; (of a person) to be very hot (*colloq*). — *adj* roasted. — *n* a joint, *esp* of beef, roasted or to be roasted; an operation of roasting; banter (*slang*). — *n* **roas'ter** apparatus for roasting; a pig, etc suitable for roasting; a very hot day (*colloq*). — *n* and *adj* **roast'ing**. — **roast'-beef**; **roast-beef plant** the fetid iris (from its smell); **roas'ting-jack** an apparatus for turning a joint in roasting; **roast'-meat**. — **cry roast-meat** (*archaic*) to publish one's good luck foolishly; **rule the roast** (mistakenly **roost**) to lord it, predominate. [OFr *rostir* (Fr *rôtir*); of Gmc origin]

roate. An old spelling (*Shakesp*) of **rote**[1].

rob[1] *rob*, *vt* to deprive wrongfully and forcibly; to steal from; to plunder; to deprive; to take as plunder; to carry off. — *vi* to commit robbery: — *pr p* **robb'ing**; *pa t* and *pa p* **robbed**. — *n* **robb'er** a person who robs. — *n* **robb'ery** theft from the person, aggravated by violence or intimidation; plundering. — **Robber Council** or **Synod** a council held at Ephesus in 449, afterwards repudiated, which reinstated Eutyches (from the violence of its proceedings); **robb'er-crab** a large coconut-eating land-crab of the Indian Ocean; a hermit-crab; **robb'er-fly** any fly of the *Asilidae*, large, bristly, insect-eating flies. — **daylight robbery** glaring extortion; **rob Peter to pay Paul** to deprive one person in order to satisfy another. [OFr *rober*, of Gmc origin; cf **reave**, OHGer *roubōn*, Ger *rauben*]

rob[2] *rob*, *n* a fruit syrup. [Ar *robb*]

robalo *rob'ə-lō*, *n* an American pike-like fish (*Centropomus*), of a family related to the sea-perches: — *pl* **rob'alos**. [Sp *róbalo* bass]

robe[1] *rōb*, *n* a gown or loose outer garment; a gown or dress of office, dignity or state; a rich dress; a woman's dress; a dressing-gown; (in *pl*) clothes, garb; a dressed bison hide, or the like. — *vt* to dress; to invest in robes. — *vi* to assume official vestments. — *n* **rob'ing** the putting on of robes or clothes; apparel; a trimming on a robe. — **robe-de-chambre** (*rob-də-shã-br'*; *Fr*) a dressing-gown: — *pl* **robes-de-chambre** (same pron); **robe'-maker** a maker of official robes; **rob'ing-room** a room in which official robes may be put on. — **Mistress of the robes** the head of a department in a queen's household; **the robe** or **the long robe** the legal profession. [Fr *robe*, orig booty; cf **rob**[1], **reave**, OHGer *raup* (Ger *Raub*) booty]

robe[2] or **'robe** *rōb*, *n* short for **wardrobe**.

roberdsman *rob'ərdz-man*, (*obs*) *n* a stout robber. — Also **rob'ertsman**. [Appar from *Robert*; allusion unknown]

robin[1] *rob'in*, *n* the redbreast or **robin redbreast** (*Erithacus rubecula*), a widely-spread singing bird with reddish-orange breast; extended to other birds eg a red-breasted thrush of N America (**American robin**). — **Robin Goodfellow** a mischievous English domestic spirit or brownie (also called *Puck*); **Robin Hood** a legendary medieval English outlaw who robbed the rich to give to the poor; **Robin-run'-in-the-hedge** or **Robin-run'-the-hedge** cleavers or goosegrass; ground-ivy; also various other hedgeside plants. [A form of *Robert*; cf *Jack*daw, and *Mag*pie]

robin[2] *rō'bin*, (*obs*) *n* trimming on a gown. •[**robing**]

Robinia *ro-bin'i-ə*, *n* any plant of the locust or false acacia genus (*Robinia*) of Papilionaceae. [From its introducer to cultivation, the Paris gardener Jean *Robin* (1550–1629)]

roble *rō'blā*, *n* a name for various species of oak (genus *Nothofagus*), and other trees. [Sp, from L *rōbur* oak]

roborant *rob'ər-ənt*, *n* a strengthening drug or tonic. — *adj* **rob'erant** or **rob'orating**. [L *rōborāns*, *-antis*, pr p of *rōborāre* to strengthen, invigorate]

robot *rō'bot*, *n* a mechanical man; a machine, now *esp* computer-controlled, able to perform complex physical tasks, eg welding; *esp* in S Africa, an automatic traffic signal. — *adj* **robot'ic**. — *n sing* **robot'ics** the branch of technology dealing with the design, construction and use of robots; a form of street dance in which a mechanical effect is achieved by making sharp movements keeping the body stiff (also called **robotic dancing**). — *vt* **rō'botize** or **-ise** to cause (a job, etc) to be done by, or (a house, etc) to be looked after by, a robot or robots. [Czech *robota* statute labour; from Karel Capek's play *RUR* (1920)]

roburite *rō'bər-īt*, *n* a flameless explosive, chlorinated dinitrobenzene with ammonium nitrate. [L *rōbur* strength]

robust *rō-bust'*, *adj* stout, strong and sturdy; constitutionally healthy; vigorous; thickset; over-hearty. — *adj* **robust'ious** (*-yəs*) robust; violent (*Shakesp*); strong or rough (*Milton*). — *adv* **robust'iously**. — *n* **robust'iousness**. — *adv* **robust'ly**. — *n* **robust'ness**. [L *rōbustus*, from *rōbur* strength, oak]

robusta *rō-bus'tə*, *n* coffee produced from the shrub *Coffea robusta*, grown *esp* in E Africa.

ROC *abbrev*: Royal Observer Corps.

roc *rok*, *n* an enormous bird described in Arabian legend, strong enough to carry off an elephant. — Also **rok**, **ruc** or **rukh** (*rōōk*). [Pers *rukh*]

rocaille *rō-kä'ē*, *n* artificial rockwork or similar ornament; scroll ornament; rococo. [Fr]

rocambole *rok'əm-bōl*, *n* a plant closely related to garlic. [Fr]

Roccella *rok-sel'ə*, *n* a genus of lichens, yielding archil and litmus. [Ital *orcella*, remodelled on *rocca* rock; see **archil**]

roch. See **rotch**.

Roche limit *rōsh* or *rosh lim'it*, (*astron*) *n* the lowest orbit which a satellite can maintain around its parent planet without being pulled apart by the tidal forces it creates. [Discovered by French astronomer Edouard *Roche* (1820–83)]

Rochelle *rō-shel'*, *n* properly **La Rochelle**, a town of France. — **Rochelle'-powder** seidlitz powder; **Rochelle'-salt** sodium potassium tartrate, discovered in 1672 by Seignette, a *Rochelle* apothecary.

roche moutonnée *rosh mōō-to-nā'*, (*geog*) *n* a smooth, rounded hummocky rock-surface due to glaciation: — *pl* **roches moutonnées** (same pron, or *-nāz*). [Fr *roche* a rock, and *moutonnée* a kind of wig; applied by De Saussure]

rochet *roch'it*, *n* a mantle (*obs*); a close-fitting surplice-like vestment worn by bishops and abbots. [OFr, of Gmc origin; cf Ger *Rock*, OE *rocc*]

rock[1] *rok*, *n* a large outstanding natural mass of stone; a natural mass of one or more minerals consolidated or loose (*geol*); any variety or species of such an aggregate; a diamond or other precious stone (*slang*); crack, the drug (*slang*); a stone, pebble or lump of rock (*US*); (in *pl*) testicles (*vulg slang*); a type of hard confectionary made in sticks; a sure foundation or support, anything immovable; a danger or obstacle (*fig*); for rockfish, rock pigeon or Plymouth Rock fowl; a coin (*US slang*). — *adj* of rock; found on, in or among rocks. — *vt* to stone (*US slang*); to clear of calcareous deposit. — *n* **rock'er** or **rock'ier** the rock dove. — *n* **rock'ery** a heap of soil and rock fragments in a garden, for growing rock plants. — *n* **rock'iness**. — *n* **rock'ling** a small fish of the cod family with barbels on both jaws. — *adj* **rock'y** full of rocks; like rocks; rough, difficult (*colloq*). — **rock'-alum** alum prepared from alunite; **rock'-badger** the Cape hyrax; a dassie; **rock'-basin** a lacustrine hollow in rock, excavated by glacier-ice; **rock'-bird** a puffin or other bird that nests or lives on rocks; **rock'-borer** any mollusc or other animal that bores into rocks; **rock bottom** bedrock; the very bottom, *esp* of poverty or despair. — *adj* the lowest possible; to, or at, the lowest possible level. — *adj* **rock'-bound** hemmed in by rock; rocky. — **rock'-brake** parsley-fern; **rock'-breaker** a machine for breaking stones; **rock'-butter** a butter-like exudation from rocks, containing alum; **rock cake** a small hard bun with irregular top; **rock candy** (*US*) the confectionary rock; **rock'-climber**; **rock'-climbing** mountaineering on rocky faces; **rock'-cod** a cod found on rocky sea-bottoms; a name for various Australian and other fishes, mostly of the sea-bass family; **rock'-cook** the small-mouthed wrasse; **rock'-cork** mountain cork; **rock'cress** a cruciferous plant of the genus *Arabis*; **rock crystal** colourless quartz, *esp* when well crystallized; **rock dove** a pigeon that nests on rocks, source of the domestic varieties; **rock drill** a tool for boring rock; **rock'-elm** an elm of N America with a corky bark; **Rock English** the Gibraltar dialect; **rock'-fall** a fall of rock; a mass of fallen rock; **Rock fever** undulant fever (from Gibraltar); **rock'fish** any of various types of fish that live among rocks or rocky bottoms; applied as a name to several such fishes, such as wrasse, striped bass, black goby; rock-salmon; **rock'-flour** finely divided rock material, such as is found under glaciers. — *adj* **rock'-forming** occurring as a dominant constituent of rocks. — **rock garden** a rockery; **rock'-guano** a rock phosphatized by percolations from guano. — *adj* **rock'-hewn** hewn out of rock. — **rock'-hopper** a crested penguin; **rock house** (*slang*) a crack- or cocaine-dealer's den; **rock'-lark** the rock-pipit; **rock'-leather** mountain leather; **rock-lizard** see **rock-scorpion** below; **rock lobster** see under **lobster**; **rock melon** (*Austr*) the cantaloupe; **rock'-oil** petroleum; **rock'-perch** a scorpion-fish; **rock pigeon** the rock dove; **rock'-pipit** a pipit inhabiting rocky coasts; **rock plant** a plant adapted to growing on or among rocks; **rock'-rabbit** a hyrax. — *adj* **rock'-ribbed** (*US*) unyielding. — **rock rose** a plant of either of the genera *Cistus* and *Helianthemum* of the family *Cistaceae*; **rock'-salmon** and **rock'-turbot** dogfish or wolf-fish when being sold as food fish; **rock salt** salt as a mineral, halite; salt in crystalline form; **rock'-scorpion** a person born in Gibraltar (also **rock'-lizard**); **rock snake** a python; a krait; **rock'-socks** an *orig* Japanese form of rubber socks, with a separate big-toe section, worn for walking over rocks, coral, etc. — *adj* **rock'-sol'id** steady; dependable; firm; unwavering; unbeatable. — **rock'-sparrow** a genus (*Petronia*) related to the true sparrow. — *adj* **rock-stead'y** absolutely steady. — **rock'-tar** petroleum; **rock'-temple** a temple hewn out of the solid rock; **rock tripe** an edible arctic lichen of various kinds; **rock'-vi'olet** a violet-scented alga growing on mountain rocks; **rock'water** water issuing from a rock; **rock'weed** bladderwrack or related seaweed growing on rocks; **rock'-wood** a wood-like asbestos; **rock wool** mineral wool, used as an insulating material; **rock'work** masonry in imitation of rock (*archit*); rocks in rockery; rock-climbing. — **on the rocks** penniless; (of whisky, etc) on ice; **Rocky Mountain goat** a white N American animal intermediate between goat and antelope; **the Rock** Gibraltar; **the Rockies** the Rocky Mountains. [OFr *roke*, from LL *rocca*]

rock[2] *rok*, (*archaic*) *n* a distaff. — *n* **rock'ing** (*Scot*) an evening party, *orig* for spinning. [ME *roc*; cf MDu *rocke*; ON *rokkr*; Ger *Rocken*]

rock[3] *rok*, *vt* and *vi* to sway to and fro, tilt from side to side; to startle, stagger (*colloq*). — *vi* to dance to, or play in, rock-and-roll style. — *n* a rocking movement; (also **rock music**) a form of music with a strong beat, which developed from rock-and-roll but which is more varied and often more complex in style, and less influenced by blues and country-and-western music; rock-and-roll. — *adj* pertaining to rock music or rock-and-roll. — *n* **rock'er** a person who rocks; an apparatus that rocks; a curved support on which anything rocks; a rocking-horse; a rocking-chair; (with *cap*) a member of a teenage faction of the 1960s who wore leather jackets, rode motor bicycles, and were rivals of the Mods; a rock-and-roll song (*colloq*); a mining cradle; a skate with curved blade; a 180°-turn in skating, so that the skater continues backwards in the same direction; a mezzotint engraver's tool for preparing a surface. — *adv* **rock'ily**. — *n* **rock'iness**. — *n* and *adj* **rock'ing**. — *adj* **rock'y** tending to rock; shaky; tipsy; unpleasant, unsatisfactory (*slang*). — **rock'abilly** a form of rock-and-roll with elements of hillbilly music; **rock-and-roll** see **rock-'n'-roll** below; **rocker panel** the part of a vehicle's bodywork below the door-sills of the passenger compartment; **rocker switch** an electric light, etc switch on a central pivot, the bottom being pushed back to switch on, the top to switch off; **rock'ing-chair** a chair mounted on rockers; **rock'ing-horse** the figure of a horse mounted on rockers or on some other supports which allow the horse to rock when ridden by a child; **rock'ing-stone** a logan, or finely poised boulder that can be made to rock; **rock'ing-tool** an engraver's tool for roughing a plate; **rock'-'n'-roll'** or **rock'-and-roll'** (also without *hyphens*) a simple form of music deriving from jazz, country-and-western and blues music, with a strongly accented, two-beat rhythm; dancing to the music; **rock'-shaft** in engines, a shaft that oscillates instead of revolving; **rock'steady** a 1960s style of dance music, *orig* from Jamaica, slow in tempo with a heavily stressed offbeat. — **off one's rocker** out of one's right mind; **rock the boat** to make things difficult for one's colleagues, create trouble. [OE *roccian*]

rockaway *rok'ə-wā*, *n* an American four-wheeled pleasure carriage, formerly made at *Rockaway*, New Jersey.

rockery. See under **rock**[1].

rocket[1] *rok'it*, *n* a cylinder full of inflammable material, projected through the air for signalling, carrying a line to a ship in distress, or for firework display; a missile projected by a rocket system; a system or vehicle obtaining its thrust from a backward jet of hot gases, all the material for producing which is carried within the rocket; a severe reprimand (*slang*). — *vi* to move like a rocket; (of a game bird) to fly straight up rapidly when flushed; (of eg prices) to rise very rapidly (*fig*); to come to an important position with remarkable speed (*fig*). — *vt* to attack with rockets. — *n* **rocketeer'** a rocket technician or pilot; a specialist in rocketry, *esp* a designer of rockets. — *n* **rock'eter** a game bird which rockets. — *n* **rock'etry** the scientific study of rockets. — **rocket engine** or **motor** a jet engine or motor which uses an internally stored oxidizer instead of atmospheric oxygen, for combustion; **rocket'-launcher**; **rocket plane** an aeroplane driven by rocket motor; **rocket range** a place for experimentation with rocket projectiles; **rocket scientist** (*stock exchange slang*) a person who devises schemes to take advantage of price differentials on money markets. [Ital *rocchetta*, of Gmc origin]

rocket[2] *rok'it*, *n* a cruciferous salad plant (*Eruca sativa*) of Mediterranean countries; extended to dame's violet (*Hesperis*) and other plants of the same family (**sea'-rocket** *Cakile*; **wall'-rocket** *Diplotaxis*; **yell'ow-rocket** winter-cress, *Barbarea*) or of other families (**blue'-rocket** monkshood; larkspur; **dy'er's-rocket** weld). [OFr *roquette*, from L *ērūca*]

rocklay. See **rokelay**.

rococo *rō-kō'kō* or *rō-kō-kō'*, *n* a style of architecture, decoration and furniture-making prevailing in Louis XV's time, marked by endless multiplication of ornamental details unrelated to structure, with rockwork, shells, scrolls and unsymmetrical broken curves, a lighter, freer development of the baroque; the equivalent of this style in other arts, *esp* music: — *pl* **rococos**. — *adj* in the style of rococo; florid, extravagant in style; grotesque; old-fashioned and odd (*obs*). [Fr, prob from *rocaille* rockwork]

rocquet *rok'it*, *n* a rochet. [OFr, a Northern form of *rochet*]

rod *rod*, *n* a long straight shoot; a slender stick; a slender bar of metal or other matter; such a metal bar forming part of the framework under a railway carriage (see also **ride the rods** below); a sceptre or similar emblem of authority; a stick or bunch of twigs as emblem or instrument of punishment; a stick or wand for magic or divination; a riding-crop; a slender pole or structure carrying a fishing-line; an angler using this; a measuring stick; a pole or perch ($5\frac{1}{2}$ yards, or $16\frac{1}{2}$ feet); a square pole ($272\frac{1}{4}$ sq ft); (of brickwork) 272 sq ft of standard thickness of $1\frac{1}{2}$ bricks or 306 cu ft; race or tribe (*Bible*); a rod-shaped body of the retina sensitive to light; a rod-shaped bacterium; a revolver, a pistol (*US slang*); a penis (*slang*). — *vt* to push a rod through (a drain, etc) so as to clear it: — *pr p* **rodd'ing**; *pa t* and *pa p* **rodd'ed**. — *n* **rodd'ing**. — *adj* **rod'less**. — *adj* **rod'like**. — *n* **rod'ster** (*archaic*) an angler. — **rod'fisher**; **rod'fishing**; **rod'man** or **rods'man** a person who holds, carries or uses a rod, *esp* an angler; **rod puppet** a glove puppet held on one hand, its arms being manipulated by rods held in the other hand. — **a rod in pickle** punishment in reserve; **kiss the rod** to accept punishment with submission; **make a rod for one's own back** to create trouble for oneself; **Napier's rods** see under **Napierian**; **ride the rods** (*US*) to travel illegitimately on the railway, supporting oneself on the rods (qv) of railway carriages. [OE *rodd*; cf ON *rudda* club]

rode[1] *rōd*, *pa t* of **ride**.

rode[2] *rōd*, (*Spenser* and *Shakesp*) *n* an old spelling of **road**. — *n* (*Shakesp*) **rode'way**.

rode[3] *rōd*, *vi* (*esp* of woodcock) to perform a regular evening flight. — *n* **rōd'ing** or **road'ing** a woodcock's evening flight. [Origin obscure]

rodent *rō'dənt*, *n* a mammal of the order **Rodentia** (*rō-den'shə* or *-shyə*), which have prominent incisor teeth and no canines, eg the squirrel, beaver or rat. — *adj* gnawing; belonging to the Rodentia. — *n* **roden'ticide** a substance that kills rodents. — *adj* **ro'dent-like**. — **rodent officer** an official rat-catcher. [L *rōdēns*, *-entis*, pr p of *rōdere* to gnaw]

rodeo *rō'di-ō* or *rō-dā'ō*, *n* a place where cattle are assembled; a round-up of cattle; an exhibition of cowboy skill; a contest suggestive of a cowboy rodeo involving eg motorcycles: — *pl* **ro'deos**. [Sp, from *rodear* to go round, from L *rotāre* to wheel]

rodgersia *ro-jûr'zi-ə*, *n* any of a group of flowering perennial herbs (family *Saxifragaceae*) native to E Asia, with large divided leaves and small, white panicled flowers. [John *Rodgers* (1812–82), US admiral]

rodomontade *rod-ō-mon-tād'*, *n* extravagant boasting. — *vi* to bluster or brag. — *n* **rodomontā'der**. [After the boasting of *Rodomonte* in Ariosto's *Orlando Furioso*]

roe[1] *rō*, *n* a mass of fish-eggs (also **hard roe**); the testis of a male fish containing mature sperm (also **soft roe**). — *adj* **roed** containing roe. — **roe'stone** oolite. [ME *rowe*; cf ON *hrogn*, MHGer *roge*, Ger *Rogen*]

roe[2] *rō*, *n* a small species of deer (also **roe'-deer**), sometimes applied to the female red deer. — **roe'buck** the male roe; **roe'buck-berry** or **roe'-blackberry** the stone-bramble. [OE *rā*, *rāha*; Ger *Reh*, Du *ree*]

Roe (Richard). See **Doe (John)**.

roemer *rōō'mər*, *n* a rummer. [Du]

roentgen. See **röntgen**.

rogation *rō-gā'shən*, (*eccles*) *n* an asking; supplication. — *adj* **rogatory** (*rog'ə-tə-ri*; **letters rogatory** see under **letter**). — **Rogation Days** the three days before Ascension Day, when supplications were recited in procession; **Rogation flower** the milkwort, which was carried in Rogation Day processions; **Rogation Sunday** that before Ascension Day; **Rogation Week** the week in which the Rogation Days occur. [L *rogātiō*, *-ōnis*, from *rogāre* to ask]

roger *roj'ər*, *n* (with *cap*) a male personal name; a goose (*cant slang*); a penis (*vulg slang*); a word used in signalling and radio-communication for R, in the sense of *r*eceived (and understood). — *vt* and *vi* (*vulg*) of a man, to copulate (with). — *n* **rog'ering**. — **Jolly Roger** the pirates' skull-and-crossbones flag; **Roger** (or **Sir Roger) de Coverley** (*də-kuv'ər-li*) an English country-dance (whence the name of the *Spectator* character). [Fr, of Gmc origin, equivalent to OE *Hrōthgār*]

Rogerian *roj-ēr'i-ən*, *adj* denoting a type of psychological therapy developed by Carl *Rogers* in the 1940s, in which the therapist tries to discover his patients' needs by involving himself in a positive and understanding relationship with them, by means of one-to-one counselling or group discussion.

rogue *rōg*, *n* a vagrant (*archaic*); an unprincipled person, a rascal; a wag; a mischievous person (often *playfully* or *affectionately*); a plant that falls short of a standard, or is of a different type from the rest of the crop; a variation from type; a horse, person or object that is troublesome, unruly or uncooperative; a savage elephant or other wild animal which lives apart from or has been driven from its herd. — *adj* mischievous; disruptive; diverging from type. — *vi* to act or behave as a rogue. — *vt* to cheat; to eliminate rogues or inferior plants from (a crop, etc). — *n* **roguery** (*rōg'ər-i*) rascally tricks; fraud; mischievousness; waggery. — *n* **rogue'ship** (*archaic*). — *adj* **roguing** (*rōg'ing*) roaming (*archaic*); behaving like a rogue. — *adj* **roguish** (*rōg'ish*) rascally; mischievous; waggish; villainous; confounded. — *adv* **rog'uishly**. — *n* **rog'uishness**. — *adj* **rog'uy** (*obs*). — **rogue elephant**; **rogue money** a former assessment in Scotland for the expense of catching, prosecuting and maintaining rogues; **rogues' gallery** a police collection of photographs of criminals; any group of disreputable people; **rogues' Latin** cant; **rogues' march** derisive music played at a drumming-out; **rogue value** (*comput*) a number or set of characters inserted at the end of a list of data indicating that no further items are to be input. [Cant; origin unknown]

roi fainéant *rwä fā-nā-ã*, (*Fr*) *n* a king without royal power (see **fainéant**).

roil *roil*, (now *dialect* and *US*) *vt* to make turbid or turbulent; same as **rile**. — *vi* to move turbulently, billow. — *adj* **roil'y** turbid. [Origin doubtful]

roin and **roinish**. Same as **royne**[1] and **roynish**.

roister or **royster** *rois'tər*, *n* a blusterer; a noisy reveller. — *vi* to bluster, swagger; to revel noisily. — *vi* **roist** or **royst** (back-formation from the noun) to roister. — *n* **rois'terer** or **roys'terer**. — *n* **rois'tering**. — *adj* **rois'terous** or **roys'terous**. — *adj* **rois'ting** or **roys'ting** blustering, boisterous; rousingly defiant (*Shakesp*). [OFr *rustre* a rough, rude fellow, from OFr *ruste*, from L *rusticus* rustic]

roji *rō'ji*, *n* a form of Japanese garden design incorporating a path of stepping stones which are sprinkled with water to concentrate the viewer's eye and mind on objects in the immediate field of vision. [Jap]

ROK *abbrev*: Republic of Korea (IVR).

rok. Same as **roc**.

roke *rōk*, (*dialect*) *n* a vapour; steam; mist; small rain; smoke. — *vt* and *vi* to steam; to smoke. — *adj* **rōk'y**. [Perh Scand]

rokelay or **rocklay** *rok'ə-lā* or *rok'lā*, (*Scot*) *n* a woman's short cloak, worn in the 18c. [Fr *roquelaire*; see **roquelaure**]

roker *rōk'ər*, *n* any ray other than skate, *esp* the thornback. [Perh Dan *rokke*, Swed *rocka* ray]

rokkaku *rō-kək'ō*, *n* a Japanese fighting kite used in competition: — *pl* **rokkak'u**. [Jap]

roky. See **roke**.

rolag *rō'lag*, *n* a roll of combed sheep's wool ready for spinning. [Gaelic *ròlag*, dimin of *rola* a roll]

Roland *rō'lənd*, *n* a hero of the Charlemagne legend; hence, a hero; a worthy match (with allusion to a drawn contest between Roland and his comrade-in-arms, Oliver). — **a Roland for an Oliver** tit for tat; as good as one got.

role or **rôle** *rōl*, *n* a part played by an actor; a function, part played in life or in any event. — **role model** a person whose character and behaviour, etc is imitated by others who would like to be in the same or a similar position or situation, etc; **role'-play** or **role'-playing** the performing of imaginary roles, *esp*, as a method of instruction, training or therapy, the acting-out of real-life situations in which the subject might find himself or herself. — *vt* and *vi* **role'-play**. [Fr]

Rolfing *rolf'ing*, *n* a therapeutic technique for correcting postural faults and improving physical wellbeing through manipulation of the muscles and connective tissue, so that the body is realigned symmetrically and the best use of gravity made in maintaining balance (also without *cap*). — *n* **Rolf'er** or **rolf'er** a practitioner of this technique. [Dr Ida *Rolf* (1897–1979), originator of the technique]

roll *rōl*, *n* a scroll; a sheet of paper, parchment, cloth or other material bent spirally upon itself into a nearly cylindrical form; a document in such form; a register; a list, *esp* of names; a spirally wound cake, or one of dough turned over to enclose other material; a small, individually-baked portion of bread formed into any of various shapes, that can be cut open and filled with other foods, preserves, etc; a revolving cylinder; a roller; a more or less cylindrical package, mass or pad; a cylindrical moulding; a volute; a bookbinder's tool with a small wheel for impressing designs; a part turned over in a curve; an act of rolling; a swaying about an axis in the direction of motion; a full rotation about an axis in the direction of motion, as an aeronautical manoeuvre; a continuous reverberatory or trilling sound; an undulation; a wavelike flow. — *vi* to move like a ball, a wheel, a wheeled vehicle or a passenger in one; to perform revolutions; to sway on an axis in the direction of motion; to turn over or from side to side; to swagger; to wallow; to go with a roll; to move in, on, or like waves; to flow; to undulate; to wander; to sound with a roll; to use a roller; to curl; to start; to get under way; to start operating; to make progress. — *vt* to cause to roll; to turn on an axis; (of the eyes) to move with a circular sweep; to wrap round on itself; to enwrap; to curl or to wind; to drive forward; to move upon wheels; to press, flatten, spread out, thin or smooth with a roller or between rollers; to round by attrition; to beat (a drum) rapidly; to rumble; to peal; to trill; to pour in waves; to wind (a clock; *Scot*); to attack and rob (*slang*); to rob (someone who is helpless, *esp* drunk or asleep; *NAm* and *NZ slang*); to have sexual intercourse with (*slang*, *esp NAm*). — *adj* **roll'able**. — *adj* **rolled**. — *n* **roll'er** a person who or thing which rolls; a revolving or rolling cylinder; a contrivance including a heavy cylinder or cylinders for flattening roads or turf; a long, coiled-up bandage (**roll'er-bandage**); a strap buckled round a horse to keep its blanket in place; a long heavy wave; a small solid wheel; a cylinder on which hair is wound to curl it; a kind of tumbler pigeon; a bird (*Coracias*) of a family related to the kingfishers, with a habit of flight like a tumbler pigeon (Ger *Roller*); a kind of canary with a soft trilling song; a Rolls-Royce car (*colloq*). — *adj* relating to, performed or carried out on roller-skates. — *n* **roll'ing**. — *adj* (of landscape) characterized by a gentle undulation; extremely rich (*slang*); staggering with drunkenness (*slang*); (of a contract, etc) subject to periodic review; occurring in different places in succession; (of planned events, etc) organized to take place successively, on a relay or rota system, with a steadily maintained or escalating effect. — *adj* **roll'about** podgy. — **roll'-bar** a metal bar that strengthens the frame of a vehicle, lessening the danger to the vehicle's occupants if the vehicle overturns; **roll'-call** the calling of a list of names, to ascertain attendance; **roll'collar** a collar of a garment turned back in a curve; **rolled gold** metal coated with gold rolled very thin; **rolled oats** oats which have been husked, steamed and flattened with rollers, used *esp* to make porridge; **roller bearing** a bearing consisting of two races between which a number of parallel or tapered rollers are located, *usu* in a cage, suitable for heavier loads than ball-bearings; **Roll'erblade®** or **roll'erblade** a type of roller-skate with wheels set in a line resembling the blade of an ice skate. — Also *vi*. — **roll'erblader**; **roll'erblading**; **roll'ercoaster** a type of switchback railway popular at carnivals, etc, along which people ride in open cars at great speed; an action or process moving at great speed and seemingly unstoppable (*fig*). — *vt* to direct or cause to move with great speed, *esp* in a set direction. — **roll'er-hockey** a form of hockey played by teams on roller-skates; **roll'er-skate** a skate with four wheels instead of a blade, set at the corners of the shoe. — Also *vi*. — **roll'er-skater**; **roll'er-skating**; **roll'er-towel** a continuous towel on a roller; **rolling launch** (*marketing*) the gradual introduction of a new product or service on the market; **roll'ing-mill** factory or machine for rolling metal into various shapes between rolls; **roll'ing-pin** a cylinder pushed between the hands for rolling out dough, etc; **roll'ing-stock** the stock or store of engines and vehicles that run upon a railway; **rolling stone** see phrases below. — *adj* **roll'neck** (of a jersey, etc) having a high neck which is made to be folded over loosely on itself; **roll'-on** (of a deodorant, etc) contained in a bottle which has a rotating ball in its neck, by means of which the liquid is applied to the skin; (of a boat, etc) roll-on-roll-off. — *n* a roll-on deodorant, etc; a corset that fits on by stretching. — *adj* and *n* **roll-on-roll-off'** (a ferry-boat, cargo boat, or ferry or cargo service) designed to allow goods vehicles to embark and disembark without unloading and passenger traffic to drive straight on and off. — **roll'out** the first public display of a prototype of an aircraft; the public launch or announcement of a new product or service (*fig*); that part of an aeroplane's landing during which it slows down after touch-down; **roll-over** see **roll over** below. — *adj* **roll'-top** (of a desk) having a flexible cover of slats that rolls up. — *adj* **roll'up** suitable for rolling up. — *n* an accumulator bet; a hand-rolled cigarette (*colloq*); attendance, turn-out (*Austr*); **roll-up fund** an offshore fund which returns interest earned from bank deposits back into the fund rather than paying it out to investors, so avoiding incurring income tax. — **a rolling stone gathers no moss** a wandering person does not grow rich, but is free from responsibilities and ties; **be rolling in** to have large amounts of (eg money); **heads will roll** severe punishments will be meted out, *esp* loss of status or office; **on a roll** (*colloq*, *esp US*) having continuing luck or success, on a winning streak; **Master of the Rolls** head of the Civil Division of the Court of Appeal (for England and Wales), formerly head of the Public Record Office, *orig* custodian of the court records (rolls); **roll along** to arrive by chance, or with a casual air; **rolled into one** combined in one person or thing; **roll in** to arrive in quantity; **roll in the hay** (*slang*) sexual intercourse or activity; **roll on** may (a specified event) come quickly; **roll over** to defer demand for the repayment of (a loan, etc); to defer indeterminately or indiscriminately (*n* and *adj* **roll'-over**); **roll up** (*colloq*) to assemble, arrive; **roll with the punches** (of a boxer) to move the body away to cushion the impact of the opponents blows (also *fig*); **strike off the roll** to remove the right to practise from (a doctor, solicitor, etc) after professional misconduct. [OFr *rolle* (noun), *roller* (verb), from L *rotula*, dimin of *rota* a wheel]

Roller. See under **Rolls-Royce**®.

rollick[1] *rol'ik*, *vi* to behave in a carefree, playful or boisterous manner. — *adj* **roll'icking** playful, boisterous; joyous, carefree. [Origin unknown]

rollick[2] *rol'ik*, (*slang*) *vt* to rebuke severely. — *n* a severe scolding. — *n* **roll'icking** (also **roll'ocking**). [Perh alteration of **bollock**]

rollmop *rōl'mop*, *n* a fillet of herring rolled up, *usu* enclosing a slice of onion, and pickled in spiced vinegar. [Ger *Rollmops*, from *rollen* to roll, and *Mops* a pug-dog]

rollock. See **rowlock**.

rollocking. See under **rollick**[2].

Rolls-Royce® *rōlz-rois'*, *n* a superior make of car, produced by *Rolls-Royce* Ltd (also *colloq* **Rolls** or **Roll'er**); anything thought of as being of superior quality (*fig*; also *adj*).

roly-poly *rōl'i-pōl'i*, *n* a pudding made of a sheet of dough, covered with jam or fruit, rolled up, and baked or steamed (also **roly-poly pudding**); a round, podgy person; an old game in which balls are bowled into holes or thrown into hats placed on the ground; any of several bushy plants, especially *Salsola kali*, that break off and roll in the wind (*Austr*). — *adj* round, podgy. [Prob **roll**]

ROM *rom*, (*comput*) *n* *r*ead-*o*nly *m*emory, a storage device whose contents cannot be altered by a programmer.

Rom. (*Bible*) *abbrev*: (the Letter to the) Romans.

rom *rom*, *n* a gypsy man: — *pl* **rom'a** or **rom'as**. [Romany, man, husband]

rom. *abbrev*: roman (type).

romage *rum'ij*, (*Shakesp*) *n* tumult. [**rummage**]

Romaic *rō-mā'ik*, *n* and *adj* modern Greek. — *n* **romā'ika** a modern Greek dance. [Mod Gr *Rhōmaikos* Roman (ie of the Eastern Roman Empire), from *Rhōmē* Rome]

romal *rō-mäl'* or **rumal** *ro͞o-mäl'*, *n* a handkerchief; a headcloth. [Pers *rūmāl*]

Roman *rō'mən*, *adj* relating to Rome, *esp* ancient Rome, its people, or the empire founded by them; relating to the Roman Catholic religion, papal; (without *cap*) of type, of the ordinary upright kind, as opposed to *italic*; (of numerals) written in letters (eg IV, iv, etc), as opposed to Arabic; (of handwriting) round and bold; (of a nose) high-bridged. — *n* a native or citizen of Rome; a Roman Catholic; (without *cap*) roman letter or type. — *adj* **Romanic** (*rō-man'ik*) of Roman or Latin origin; Romance. — *n* the Romance language or languages collectively. — *adj* **Ro'manish** (*usu derog*) Roman Catholic; reminiscent of, or having elements of, Roman Catholicism. — *n* **Ro'manism** Roman Catholicism or a slavish adherence to its doctrine. — *n* **Ro'manist** a Roman Catholic; a specialist in Romance philology or Roman law or antiquities. — *adj* Roman Catholic. — *adj* **Romanist'ic**. — *n* **Romanization** or **-s-** (*rō-mə-nī-zā'shən*). — *vt* **Ro'manize** or **-ise** to make Roman or Roman Catholic; to bring under Roman or Roman Catholic influence; to represent by the Roman alphabet. — *vi* to accept Roman or Roman Catholic ways, laws, doctrines, etc; to become Roman Catholic. — *n* **Ro'manizer** or **-s-**. — *combining form* **Romano-** (*rō-mä'nō-*) signifying: Roman; Romanized; Roman and (as in **Roma'no-Brit'ish**). — **Roman candle** a firework discharging a succession of white or coloured stars; a bad landing by aeroplane (*slang*); a landing by parachute when the parachute fails to open (*slang*). — *vi* to make such a landing. — *adj* **Roman Catholic** recognizing the spiritual supremacy of the Pope or Bishop of Rome. — *n* a member of the Roman Catholic Church. — **Roman Catholicism** the doctrines and polity of the Roman Catholic Church collectively; **Roman cement** a hydraulic cement made from calcareous nodules from the London Clay; **Roman Empire** the ancient empire of Rome, divided in the 4c into the Eastern and Western Empires (see also under **Holy**); **Roman law** the system of law developed by the ancient Romans, civil law; **Roman nettle** a nettle, rare in Britain, with female flowers in heads, traditionally introduced by the Romans; **Roman numerals** see **Roman** above; **Roman snail** the edible snail (*Helix pomatia*) much valued by the Romans. [L *Rōmānus*, from *Rōma* Rome]

roman *ro-mã'*, *n* a medieval romance, tale of chivalry; a novel. — **roman à clef** or **clefs**, **clé** or **clés** (*ro-mã-nä klā*; literally novel with a key) a novel with characters based on real people under disguised names; **roman à thèse** (*ro-mã-nä tez*) a novel that sets out to demonstrate a thesis or proposition; **roman à tiroirs** (*ro-mã-nä tēr'wär*; literally novel with drawers) a novel with an episodic structure, a picaresque; **roman fleuve** (*flœv*; literally river novel) a novel written as a series of self-contained narratives telling the story of a family or other social group over successive generations (also called **saga novel**). [Fr]

Romance *rō-mans'* or *rō'məns*, *n* a general name for the vernaculars that developed out of popular Latin, ie French, Provençal, Italian, Spanish, Portuguese, Romanian and Romansch, with their various dialects. — Also *adj*. — *n* **romance'** a tale of chivalry, *orig* one in verse, written in one of these vernaculars; any fictitious and wonderful tale; a fictitious narrative in prose or verse which passes beyond the limits of ordinary life; a Spanish historical ballad; a piece of romantic fiction; romantic fiction as a literary genre; a romantic occurrence or series of occurrences; a love affair;

romantic atmosphere or feeling; a leaning towards the romantic; an imaginative lie; romanticism; a composition of romantic character (*music*). — *vi* to write or tell romances; to talk extravagantly or with an infusion of fiction; to lie; to build castles in the air. — *n* **roman'cer**. — *adj* **roman'cical** (*Lamb*) dealing with romance. — *n* and *adj* **roman'cing**. [OFr *romanz*, from (hypothetical) LL *rōmānicē* (adv), in (popular) Roman language]

Romanes. See **Romany**.

Romanesque *rō-mən-esk'*, *adj* of the transition from Roman to Gothic architecture, characterized by round arches and vaults. — *n* the Romanesque style, art or architecture. [Fr]

Romani. See **Romany**.

Romanian *rō-mā'ni-ən*, **Rumanian** or **Roumanian** *roo-*, *adj* of or relating to *Romania* or its language. — *n* a native or citizen of Romania, or member of the same people; the Romance language of Romania. — Also (*archaic*) **Ruman** or **Rouman** (*roo'mən*). [Romanian *Romănia*, from L *Rōmānus* Roman]

Romanism, Romanize, etc. See under **Roman**.

Romansch, Romansh, Roumansch, Rumansch *rō-* or *roo-mansh'*, or *-mänsh'* or **Rumonsch** *-monsh'*, *n* and *adj* Rhaeto-Romanic; sometimes confined to the Upper Rhine dialects. [Romansch]

romantic *rō-man'tik*, *adj* relating to, or of the nature of, inclining towards, or savouring of, romance, *esp* feelings of love or the idea of sentimentalized love; fictitious; extravagant, wild; fantastic. — *n* a romanticist. — *adj* **roman'tical**. — *n* **romantical'ity**. — *adv* **roman'tically**. — *n* **roman'ticism** (*-sizm*) romantic quality, feeling, tendency, principles or spirit. — *n* **roman'ticist**. — *n* **romantic̄īzā'tion** or **-s-**. — *vt* **roman'ticize** or **-ise** (*-ti-sīz*) to make seem romantic. — *vi* to have or express romantic ideas. — **Romantic Revival** the late 18c and early 19c revolt against classicism or neo-classicism to a more picturesque, original, free and imaginative style in literature and art. [Fr *romantique*, from OFr *romant* romance]

Romany, Romani *rom'ə-ni* or *rōm'ə-ni*, also **Rommany** *rom'ə-ni*, *n* a gypsy; (also **Romanes** *rom'ə-nes*) the Indic language of the gypsies (in pure form not now common in Britain). — *adj* of Romanies or their language; gypsy. — **Romany rye** (*rī*) a man who associates with gypsies, though not one himself. [Gypsy, from *rom* man]

romaunt *rō-mönt'*, (*archaic*) *n* a romance. [OFr *romant*; see **Romance**]

Rome *rōm*, formerly *room*, *n* the capital of the Roman Empire, now of Italy; often used for the Roman Catholic Church or Roman Catholicism. — *adj* and *adv* **Rome'ward**. — *adv* **Rome'wards**. — *n* **Rōm'ic** a phonetic notation devised by Henry Sweet, based upon the original Roman values of the letters. — *adj* **Rōm'ish** Roman Catholic (*derog*); Roman (*obs*). — **Rome'-penny** or **-scot** (*obs*) Peter's penny; **Rome'-runner** (*obs*) a self-seeking cleric who had much resort to Rome. [L *Rōma*]

Romeo *rō'mi-ō*, *n* a young man very much in love; a Don Juan in the making: — *pl* **Rō'meos**. [Shakespearean character]

Rommany. See **Romany**.

romneya *rom'ni-ə*, *n* a plant of the *Romneya* genus of papaveraceous shrubs, with large white poppy-like flowers with yellow centres. [Thomas *Romney* Robinson (1792–1882), British astronomer and physicist]

romp *romp*, *vi* to frolic actively; to move along easily and quickly, *esp* in winning a race. — *n* a person, *esp* a girl, who romps; a tomboy; a vigorous frolic; a swift easy run. — *n* **romp'er** a person who romps; (*usu* in *pl*) a young child's garb for play (also **romp'er-suit'**). — *adv* **romp'ingly**. — *adj* **romp'ish**. — *adv* **romp'ishly**. — *n* **romp'ishness**. — **romp home** to win easily; **romp through** to do (something) quickly and easily. [**ramp**[1]]

roncador *rong-kə-dōr'* or *-dör'*, *n* a name for various fishes of the N American Pacific coast, *esp* of the maigre family, from the sounds they emit. [Sp, snorer]

rondache *ron-dash'* or *-däsh'*, *n* a buckler. [Fr]

rondavel *ron-dav'əl*, or *ron'*, *n* in S Africa, a round hut, *usu* with grass roof; a more sophisticated building of similar shape, used eg as a guest house. [Afrik *rondawel*]

ronde *rond*, *n* a script printing-type. [Fr, round (*fem*)]

rondeau *ron'dō* or *rɔ̃-dō*, *n* a form of poem characterized by closely-knit rhymes and a refrain, and, as defined in the 17c, consisting of thirteen lines, divided into three unequal strophes, not including the burden (repeating the first few words) after the eighth and thirteenth lines, brought into vogue by Swinburne; a rondo (*music*): — *pl* **ron'deaux** (*-dōz*). — *n* **ron'del** a verse-form of thirteen or fourteen lines on two rhymes, the seventh and thirteenth being identical with the first, and the eighth and (if present) the fourteenth with the second; a circular part or ornament in jewellery; a circular badge. — *n* **rondino** (*-dē'nō*; from *Ital dimin*) a short rondo: — *pl* **rondi'nos**. — *n* **ron'do** (*orig Ital*, from *Fr*) a musical composition whose principal subject recurs in the same key in alternation with other subjects, often the last movement of a sonata: — *pl* **ron'dos**. — *n* **rondolet'to** a short rondo: — *pl* **rondolet'tos**. [Fr *rondeau*, earlier *rondel*, from *rond* round]

rondure *rond'yər*, a Shakespearian form of **roundure**.

rone, roan or **rhone** *rōn*, (*Scot*) *n* a roof-gutter. [Origin unknown]

Roneo® *rō'ni-ō*, *n* a duplicating machine: — *pl* **Rō'neos**. — *vt* **rō'neo** to produce copies of by duplicating machine.

rong *rong* (*obs*) *pa t* of **ring**[2].

ronggeng *rong'geng*, *n* a Malaysian dancing-girl; a kind of dancing, often with singing, in Malaysia. [Malay *rônggeng*]

ronne and **ronning** (*Spenser*). Same as **run** (*infin* and *pa p*) and **running**.

ront or **ronte** (*Spenser*). Same as **runt**.

röntgen or **roentgen** *rœnt'yən*, also *rent'*, *ront'* or *runt'yən*, also *-gən*, (sometimes with *cap*), *adj* of the German physicist Wilhelm Conrad *Röntgen* (1845–1923), discoverer of the **röntgen rays** or X-rays (see **X**). — *n* the international unit of dose of X-rays or gamma rays, defined in terms of the ionization it produces in air under stated conditions. — *vt* **rönt'genize** or **-ise** to treat by röntgen rays. — *n* **rönt'genogram** a photograph made with these rays. — *n* **röntgenog'raphy** photography by these rays. — *n* **röntgenol'ogy** the study of the rays. — *n* **röntgenos'copy** observation by means of them. — *n* **röntgenother'apy** treatment of disease by means of them.

ronyon or **runnion** *run'yən*, (*Shakesp*) *n* a term of reproach to a woman. [Some connect with Fr *rogne* mange]

roo *roo*, (*Austr colloq*) *n* short form of **kangaroo**. — **roo bar** a strong metal bar or grid fitted to the front of a road vehicle as protection in case of collision with a kangaroo or other animal on an outback road, etc.

rood *rood*, *n* Christ's cross; a cross or crucifix, *esp* at the entrance to a church chancel; a rod, pole or perch, linear or square, varying locally in value; a quarter of an acre, or 0.10117 hectares. — **rood'-beam** a beam for supporting the rood; **Rood Day** (**Holy-rood Day** or **Rood'mas Day**) the feast of the Exaltation (14 September) or of the Invention (3 May) of the Cross; **rood'-loft** a gallery over the rood-screen; **rood'-screen** an ornamental partition separating choir from nave; **rood'-steeple** and **rood'-tower** the steeple and tower over the crossing of a church; **rood'-tree** (*obs*) Christ's cross. [OE *rōd* gallows, cross]

roof *roof*, *n* the top covering of a building or vehicle; a ceiling; the overhead surface, structure or stratum of a vault, arch, cave, excavation, etc; the upper covering of the mouth (the palate) or of any cavity; a dwelling; a culmination; a high or highest plateau (eg *the roof of the world*, the Pamir); an upper limit; an aeroplane's ceiling or limiting height: — *pl* **roofs**. — *vt* to cover with a roof; to shelter. — *adj* **roofed**. — *n* **roof'er** a person who makes or mends roofs; a roof-board; a letter of thanks for hospitality (*colloq*). — *n* **roof'ing** covering with a roof; materials for a roof; the roof itself; shelter. — *adj* for roofing. — *adj* **roof'less** (of a building) having no roof; (of a person) having neither permanent nor temporary accommodation, living on the streets. — *n* **roof'lessness**. — *adj* **roof'like**. — *adj* **roof'y** having a roof or roofs. — **roof'-board** a board lying under slates or tiles; **roof garden** a garden on a flat roof; **roof'guard** a device to prevent snow from sliding off a roof; **roof'-plate** a wall-plate that receives the lower ends of the rafters of a roof; **roof'-rack** a rack which may be fitted to the roof of a car, etc to carry luggage, etc; **roof'scape** a view of a skyline formed by the tops of buildings against the sky; **roof'top** the outside of a roof; **roof'tree** the ridge-pole; the roof. — **have a roof over one's head** to have somewhere to live; **hit** (or **go through**) **the roof** to become very angry; **raise the roof** to make a great noise or commotion; to hit the roof. [OE *hrōf*; Du *roef*]

rooinek *roi'nek*, *n* an Afrikaans nickname for a British or English-speaking person. [Afrik, red neck, from Du *rood nek*, from the complexion]

rook[1] *rŏŏk*, *n* a gregarious species of crow; a card sharp (*slang*); a simpleton (*obs*). — *vt* to fleece. — *n* **rook'ery** a breeding-place of rooks in a group of trees; a breeding-place of penguins, seals, etc; a crowded cluster of slum tenements (*archaic*); a place unpleasantly overcrowded with a particular group or type (*fig*); a disturbance (*slang* or *dialect*). — *adj* **rook'ish**. — *adj* **rook'y** (*Shakesp*) full of rooks, or *poss* black, murky (see **roky** under **roke**). [OE *hrōc*]

rook[2] *rŏŏk*, *n* a chess-piece which is moved in a vertical or horizontal line, its shape *usu* being that of a tower with battlements. [OFr *roc*, from Pers *rukh*]

rook[3] *rŏŏk* (*Shakesp*). Same as **ruck**[2].

rookie or **rooky** *rŏŏk'i*, (*slang*) *n* a raw beginner; a callow recruit; someone new to or inexperienced in eg a sport, sporting event, profession, etc. — Also *adj*. [Appar from **recruit**]

room *rōōm* or *rŏŏm*, *n* space; necessary or available space; space unoccupied; opportunity, scope or occasion; stead; a particular place; an assigned place, as in a theatre (*obs*); a seat (*Bible*); appointment, office; a holding of land (*obs*); a compartment; a chamber; a cottage sitting-room; company in a room. — *vt* and *vi* (chiefly *NAm*) to lodge; to share a room or rooms (with *with*). — *adj* **roomed** having rooms. — *n* **room'er** (*NAm*) a lodger, *usu* taking meals elsewhere. — *n* **roomette'** (*NAm*) a sleeping compartment in a train. — *n* **room'ful** as much or as many as a room will hold: — *pl* **room'fuls**. — *n* **room'ie** (*US colloq*) a room-mate. — *adv* **room'ily**. — *n* **room'iness**. — *n pl* **rooms** a set of rooms in a house, etc rented as a separate unit. — *adj* **room'some** (*obs*) roomy. — *adj* **room'y** having ample room; wide; spacious. — **room'-divider** a low wall or piece of furniture serving as one, dividing a room into two separate sections; **room'-fellow** (*archaic*) a person who shares a room; **room'ing-house** (*NAm*) a house with furnished rooms to let; **rooming-in'** (*NAm*) shared accommodation, *esp* for a mother and her newborn baby; **room'-mate** a fellow-lodger (*US*); a person who shares a room. — *adj* **room'-ridden** confined to one's room. — **room service** the serving of food, etc to people in their room(s) in a hotel, etc; **room temperature** the average temperature of a living-room, taken to be about 20°C. — **leave the room** (*euphem*) *esp* of children in school, to go to the toilet. [OE *rūm*; Ger *Raum*, Du *ruim*]

roon *rōōn* or **rund** *run(d)*, *rōōn(d)* or *rən(d)*, (*Scot*) *n* a list or selvage; a strip or thread of cloth. — Also (*Galt*) **royne** (*roin*). [Origin obscure]

roop[1] *rōōp*, *vi* (*Scot*) to make a hoarse sound. — *n* a hoarse sound; hoarseness. — *adj* **roop'it** or **roop'y** (*Scot*) hoarse. [Variant of **roup**[2]]

roop[2]. See **stoop**[4].

roosa. See **rusa**[2].

roose *rōōz* or (*Scot*) *rüz*, (*dialect*) *vt* to praise. [ME *rosen*, from ON *hrōsa* to praise]

roost[1] *rōōst*, *n* a perch or place for a sleeping bird; a henhouse; a sleeping-place; a bed; a set of fowls resting together; a loft or garret or its roof (*Scot*). — *vi* to settle or sleep on a roost or perch; to perch; to go to rest for the night. — *n* **roost'er** a domestic cock. — **come home to roost** to recoil upon oneself (**the chickens have come home to roost** one's actions have had unpleasant consequences for oneself); to return to a place (*usu* after travel) in order to settle down; **rule the roost** see under **roast**. [OE *hrōst*; Du *roest*]

roost[2] *rōōst*, (*Orkney* and *Shetland*) *n* a tidal race. [ON *röst*]

root[1] *rōōt*, *n* (ordinarily and popularly) the underground part of a plant, *esp* when edible; that part of a higher plant which never bears leaves or reproductive organs, ordinarily underground and descending, and serving to absorb salts in solution, but often above-ground, often arising from other parts, often serving other functions, though morphologically comparable (*bot*); the source, cause, basis, foundation or occasion of anything, eg an ancestor, or an element from which words are derived; an embedded or basal part, as of a tooth, a hair, a dam; a growing plant with its root; the factor of a quantity which, taken so many times, produces that quantity (*math*); any value of the unknown quantity for which an equation is true (*math*); the fundamental note on which a chord is built (*music*); (in *pl*) one's ancestry, family origins; (in *pl*) one's ethnic or cultural origins; (in *pl*) a feeling of belonging in a town, community, etc. — *vi* to fix the root; to be firmly established; to develop a root; to have sexual intercourse (*Austr* and *NZ slang*). — *vt* to plant in the earth; to implant deeply; to fix by the root; to have sexual intercourse with (*Austr* and *NZ slang*); to uproot (*usu* with *up*); to remove entirely by uprooting, clear away, eradicate, extirpate (*usu* with *out*). — *n* **root'age** the act of striking root; the state of being rooted; roothold; a root system. — *adj* **root'ed** having roots; fixed by roots or as by roots; firmly established. — *adv* **root'edly**. — *n* **root'edness**. — *n* **root'er**. — *adj* **root'less** having no roots; belonging nowhere, having no home and so constantly shifting about. — *n* **root'let**. — *adj* **root'like**. — *adj* **roots** expressing or concerned with one's ethnic or cultural identity; of or relating to roots music (see below). — *n* **root'siness**. — *adj* **root'sy** (*esp* of music) reminiscent of or incorporating traditional or folk styles. — *n* **root'y** abounding in, consisting of, or like roots; rank. — *adj* and *adv* **root-and-branch'** without leaving any part; thorough(ly), complete(ly). — **root'-ball** the spherical mass formed by the roots of a plant, with the surrounding soil; **root beer** a drink made from roots of dandelion, sassafras, etc. — *adj* **root'-bound** rooted to the ground (*Milton*); pot-bound. — **root canal** the narrow passage through which nerves and blood vessels enter the pulp-cavity of a tooth; **root'-cap** a sheath of cells at the tip of a root; **root cause** fundamental cause; **root'-climber** a plant that climbs by means of roots, such as ivy; **root crop** a crop of esculent roots; **root'-eater**. — *adj* **root'-fallen** fallen, by roots giving way. — *adj* **root'-fast** firmly rooted. — **root'-hair** a fine tubular outgrowth from a cell by which a young root absorbs water; **root'hold** maintenance of position by roots; a footing; **root'-house** a summer-house built of tree roots; a storehouse for potatoes, etc; **rooting compound** (*bot*) a preparation, containing plant growth substances, in which a cutting is dipped to promote root growth; **root'-knot** an enlargement of a root caused by a nematode; **root mean square** the square root of the sum of the squares of a set of quantities divided by the total number of quantities; **root nodule** (*bot*) the swelling on the root of a leguminous plant containing nitrogen-fixing bacteria; **root parasite** a plant parasitic on a root; **root pressure** an upward forcing of sap, shown by the bleeding of plants. — *vt* **root'-prune** to prune the roots of. — **root'=pruning**; **root'-rubber** rubber obtained from the roots of certain African apocynaceous plants; **root sheath** the sheath of the root of an orchid, hair, feather, etc; **roots music** popular music with a folk influence and a more or less discernible ethnic identity; **root'stock** rhizome, *esp* if short, thick, and more or less erect (*bot*); a source, ancestral form; **root system**; **root tubercle** a root nodule; **root vegetable** a vegetable which has an esculent root; the root itself. — **strike** or **take root** to root, to become established. [Late OE *rōt*, from ON *rōt*; Dan *rod*; Gothic *waurts*, OE *wyrt*]

root[2], earlier **wroot**, *rōōt*, *vt* to turn up with the snout. — *vi* (of pigs) to burrow into the ground with the snout; to grub; to rummage; to poke about. — *n* **root'er**. — *n* and *adj* **root'ing**. — *vt* and *vi* **root'le** to grub. [OE *wrōtan*, from *wrōt* a snout; see also **rout**[3]]

root[3] *rōōt*, (*orig US*) *vi* to shout, applaud, support or encourage (a contestant, etc) (with *for*). — *n* **root'er**. [Prob from **rout**[4]]

rootsiness and **rootsy**. See under **root**[1].

rooty[1] *rōōt'i*, (*military slang*) *n* bread. [Ety as for **roti**]

rooty[2]. See under **root**[1].

rope *rōp*, *n* a stout twist of fibre, wire, etc, technically over 1 inch round; a string of pearls, onions, etc; a glutinous stringy formation; a local lineal measure, 20 feet; a climbing party roped together. — *vt* to fasten, bind, enclose, mark off, or (*US* and *Austr*) catch with a rope; to hold back to avoid winning (*horse-racing*). — *vi* to form into a rope. — *adj* **rop'able** or **rope'able** (*Austr*; of cattle or horses) wild, unmanageable; very angry. — *adj* **roped** (*rōpt*). — *n* **rō'per** a rope-maker; a person who ropes a horse; a decoy (also **rō'per-in'**). — *n* **rōp'ery** ropework; trickery, knavery (*archaic*). — *adv* **rōp'ily**. — *n* **rōp'iness**. — *n* and *adj* **rōp'ing**. — *adj* **rō'py** or **rō'pey** stringy; glutinous; wrinkled like loops of rope; bad of its kind (*slang*). — **rope'-dance** a tight-rope performance; **rope'-dancer**; **rope'-drilling** boring by a drill alternately raised by a rope and then dropped; **rope'-house** a storehouse for ropes; a house where salt is crystallized from brine trickling along ropes; **rope'=ladder** a ladder of ropes; **rope'-machine**; **rope'-maker**; **rope'-making**. — *adj* **rope'-ripe** deserving to be hanged. — **rope's end** (*hist*) the end of a rope used for flogging. — *vt* (*hist*) to beat with a rope's end. — *adj* **rope'-soled** having a sole of rope. — **rope stitch** satin stitch worked in stitches laid diagonally side by side; **rope trick** a disappearing trick with a rope; *poss* a rhetorical figure, or, according to some, a trick deserving the gallows (*Shakesp*); **rope'-walk** a long narrow shed or alley for twisting strands into rope; **rope'-walker** a tight-rope performer; **rope'way** a means of transmission by ropes; **rope'work** a rope-walk or rope factory (also *n sing* **rope'works**); a system of ropes; **rope'-yarn** yarn for making ropes, or obtained by untwisting ropes; **roping=down'** (*colloq*) abseiling. — **give someone (enough) rope (to hang himself** or **herself)** to allow a person full scope to defeat his or her own ends; **know the ropes** see under **know**; **on the high ropes** elated; arrogant; **on the ropes** driven back against the ropes of a boxing ring; nearing defeat, desperate; **rope in** to bring in, enlist (*esp* someone who is reluctant); **ropes of sand** a bond with no cohesion; **the rope** capital punishment by hanging. [OE *rāp*; ON *reip*, Ger *Reif*]

roque. See **roquet**.

Roquefort *rok'fōr*, *n* a creamy, blue-veined, strong-flavoured cheese made from ewe's milk and matured in natural caves at *Roquefort* commune in S France.

roquelaure *rok'ə-lōr* or *-lör*, *n* a man's knee-length cloak worn in the 18c and early 19c. [Fr, after the Duc de *Roquelaure* (1656–1738)]

roquet *rō'kā*, *n* (in croquet) a stroke by which the player's ball strikes an opponent's. — *vt* to strike by a roquet. — *vi* to play a roquet. — *n* **roque** (*rōk*; back-formation) a version of croquet played in N America on a walled, hard-surfaced court. [Prob formed from **croquet**]

roquette *rō-ket'*, *n*. Same as **rocket**[2].

roral. See **roric**.

rore *rōr* or *rör*, an *obs* spelling (*Shakesp*) of **roar** (tumult).

roric *rō'* or *rō'rik*, **rorid** *rō'* or *rō'rid*, or **roral** *rō'* or *rō'rəl*, *adj* dewy. [L *rōs*, *rōris* dew]

ro-ro *rō'-rō*, *adj* and *n* short form of **roll-on-roll-off** (qv under **roll**): — *pl* **ro'-ros**.

rorqual *rör'kwəl*, *n* any whale of the genus *Balaenoptera* (finback). [Fr, from Norw *røyrkval*, from ON, literally red whale]

Rorschach test *rör'shak test*, *n* a test designed to show intelligence, personality and mental state, in which the subject interprets ink-blots of standard type. [Hermann *Rorschach* (1884–1922), Swiss psychiatrist]

rorty *rör'ti*, (*Austr colloq*) *adj* lively and enjoyable; rowdy. — *n* **rort** a racket; a lively or riotous party. — *vi* to falsify accounts, etc, commit fraud. — *n* **ror'ter** a spiv, a conman. [Ety doubtful]

rory or **rorie**. Same as **roary**.

Rosa *rōz'ə* or *roz'ə*, *n* the rose genus, giving name to the family **Rosā'ceae**. — *n* **rosace** (*rō-zās'* or *-zäs'*; from *Fr*; *archit*) a rosette; a rose-window. — *n* **rosacea** (*rō-zā'shi-ə*; *med*) same as **acne rosacea** qv under **acne**. — *adj* **rosaceous** (*rō-zā'shəs*) of the rose family; roselike. — *n* **rosā'rian** a rose-fancier. — *n* **rosā'rium** (*L*) a rose-garden. [L *rosa* rose; *rosāceus*, *roseus* rosy]

rosaker *ros-ā'kər*. *Obs* variant of **realgar**.

rosalia *rō-zä'lyä*, (*music*) *n* a series of repetitions of the same passage, each a tone higher. [Said to be from an Italian folksong, *Rosalia cara mia*]

rosaniline *rō-zan'i-lin*, *-lēn* or *-līn*, *n* a base derived from aniline, with red salts used in dyeing. [**rose**[2] and **aniline**]

rosarian and **rosarium**. See under **Rosa**.

rosary *rō'zər-i*, *n* a rose-garden or rose-bed (also **rō'sery**); a chaplet (*obs*); a series of prayers; a string of beads used by Roman Catholics as a guide to devotions. [L *rosārium* rose-garden]

rosa-solis *rō-zä-sō'lis*, (*obs*) *n* the sundew; a cordial, *orig* flavoured with sundew juice, afterwards with various spices. [Orig L *rōs sōlis* dew of the sun, altered to *rosa* rose]

roscid *ros'id*, (*rare*) *adj* dewy. [L *rōscidus*, from *rōs* dew]

Roscius *rosh'i-əs* or *rōs'ki-ōōs*, *n* a famous Roman actor (died 62 BC); hence, a great actor. — *adj* **Rosc'ian**. [L *Rōscius*]

rose[1], *pa t* of **rise**.

rose[2] *rōz*, *n* the flower of any species of the genus *Rosa*, national emblem of England; a shrub bearing it, mostly prickly, with white, yellow, pink, orange, or red flowers, numerous stamens and carpels, and achenes enclosed in the receptacle; extended to various flowers or plants in some way resembling the true rose (see eg **black hellebore** under **hellebore**, **guelder rose**, **rock rose** under **rock**[1]); a paragon; a rosette, *esp* on a shoe; a rose-cut stone; a rose-window; a perforated nozzle; a circular moulding from which eg a door-handle projects; a circular fitting in a ceiling from which an electric light flex hangs; the typical colour of the rose, pink or light crimson; (in *pl*) (in white-skinned peoples) the pink glow of the cheeks in health; erysipelas. — *adj* of, for or like the rose or roses; rose-coloured. — *vt* to make like a rose, in colour or scent. — *adj* **roseal** (*rō'zi-əl*) roselike. — *adj* **rō'seate** (*-zi-it* or *-zi-āt*) rosy; rose-scented; of roses; unduly favourable or sanguine. — *adj* **rosed** flushed (*Shakesp*); having a rose or roses. — *adj* **rose'less**. — *adj* **rose'like**. — *n* **rō'sery** a rose-garden (see **rosary**). — *n* **rosier** (*rō'zhər*; Fr *rosier*) or (*Spenser*) **rosiere** (*rō-zi-ār'*, *-ēr'*) a rose tree or bush. — *adv* **rō'sily**. — *n* **rō'siness**. — *adj* **rō'sy** of or covered in roses; roselike; rose-red; blooming; blushing; bright; hopeful; promising. — *n* (*old slang*) wine. — *vt* and *vi* to redden. — **rose'-apple** an E Indian tree of the clove genus; its edible fruit; **rose'bay** the oleander (also called **rosebay laurel** or **rose-laurel**); any rhododendron; **rosebay willow-herb** a willow-herb common where woods have been felled or land cleared by fire (also called **fireweed** qv); **rose'-beetle** the rose-chafer;

the rose-bug; **rose'bowl** an ornamental bowl for cut flowers; **rose'bud**; **rose'-bug** an American beetle that eats roses; **rose'bush**; **rose-camp'ion** a garden species of campion (*Lychnis coronaria*); **rose'-chafer** a beetle (*Cetonia aurata*) that eats roses. — *adj* **rose'-cheeked**. — **rose'-colour** pink. — *adj* **rose'-coloured** pink; seeing or representing things in too favourable a light. — **rose'-comb** a fowl's low red crest. — *adj* **rose'-combed**. — **rose'-cross** a cross within a circle; a Rosicrucian. — *adj* **rose'-cut** cut in nearly hemispherical form, with flat base and many small facets rising to a low point above. — **rose-di'amond** a rose-cut diamond; **rose'-drop** a rose-flavoured sweet; a red eruption on the nose; **rose-el'der** the guelder-rose; **rose'-engine** a lathe attachment for carving swirling patterns; **rose'finch** any of various finches of the genus *Carpodus* found in Europe and Asia, the males more or less covered with red or pink plumage, especially *Carpodus erythrinus*, the common rosefinch; **rose'fish** the bergylt; **rose'-garden**; **rose geranium** a pelargonium (*Pelargonium graveolens*) with small pink flowers and fragrant leaves; **rose'hip** the fruit of the rose. — *adj* **rose'-hued** (*archaic*) rose-coloured. — **rose'-knot** a rosette of ribbon, etc; **rose laurel** oleander; **rose'-leaf** the leaf of a rose; *usu* a rose-petal. — *adj* **rose'-lipped** having red lips. — **rose mallow** hollyhock; hibiscus; **rose noble** an old English gold coin with the figure of a rose; **rose oil** a fragrant oil expressed from rose petals. — *adj* **rose'-pink** rose-coloured; sentimental. — *n* a pink colour; a pink pigment. — **rose quartz** a rose-coloured quartz; **rose'rash** roseola. — *adj* **rose'-red** red as a rose. — **rose'-root** a stonecrop (*Sedum rosea*) with rose-scented root. — *adj* **rose'-tinted** rose-coloured (*lit* and *fig*). — **rose'tō'paz** a topaz coloured pink by heat; **rose'-tree** a standard rose; **rose'water** water distilled from rose petals. — *adj* sentimental; superfine. — **rose'-window** a round window with tracery of radiating compartments; **rose'wood** a valuable heavy dark-coloured wood of many trees, *esp* Brazilian and Indian species of Dalbergia (*Papilionaceae*), said to smell of roses when fresh-cut; **rose'wood-oil** oil of rhodium. — *adj* **ro'sy-bos'omed**. — *adj* **ro'sy-cheeked**. — *adj* **ro'sy-col'oured**. — **rosy cross** the emblem of the Rosicrucians; **ro'sy-drop** rose-drop. — *adj* **ro'sy-fing'ered** Homer's favourite epithet (*rhododaktylos*) of the dawn. — *adj* **ro'sy-foot'ed**. — **all roses** see **roses all the way** below; **bed of roses** see under **bed**[1]; **come out** (or **up**) **smelling of roses** to emerge from a series of events, etc seemingly innocent, with image untainted or undamaged; **look** or **see through rose-coloured** (or **rose-tinted** or **rosy**) **spectacles** or **glasses** to view matters over-optimistically; **rose of Jericho** a cruciferous plant (*Anastatica hierochuntica*) of N Africa and Syria, that curls in a ball in drought; **rose of Sharon** (in the Bible, *Song of Solomon*) *prob* a narcissus; now applied to a species of hibiscus, and to a species of Hypericum; **roses all the way** or **all roses** pleasant, happy; without difficulties, problems, etc; **under the rose** in confidence; privately; **Wars of the Roses** a disastrous dynastic struggle in England (1455–85) between the Houses of Lancaster and York, from their respective emblems, the red and the white rose. [OE *rōse*, from L *rosa*, prob from Gr *rhodeā* a rosebush, *rhodon* rose]

rosé *rō'zā*, *n* a pinkish table wine produced either by removing red grape skins, or by mixing red and white wines, early in fermentation (cf **red wine** under **red**). [Fr, literally pink]

roseal, **roseate**, etc. See under **rose**[2].

Roseland *rōz'lənd*, (*slang*) *n* the areas of SE England outside London. [*R*est *o*f *S*outh *E*ast and **land**, with deliberate suggestion of **rose**[1]]

rosella *rō-zel'ə*, *n* any of several varieties of Australian parakeet with brightly-coloured plumage, first observed at Rose Hill near Sydney. [For *rosehiller*]

roselle or **rozelle** *rō-zel'*, *n* an E Indian hibiscus.

rosemary *rōz'mə-ri*, *n* a small fragrant pungent Mediterranean labiate shrub (*Rosmarinus*), whose leaves are widely used as a flavouring in food, and in perfumes. [L *rōs marīnus* sea dew]

roseola *rō-zē'ə-lə*, *n* rose-coloured rash; German measles (also called **rubella**). [Dimin from L *roseus* rosy]

rosery. See **rosary**.

roset, **rosit**, **rozet** or **rozit** *roz'it*, (*Scot*) *n* a rosin. — *vt* to rosin. — *adj* **ros'ety** (sometimes **ros'etty**), etc. [**rosin**]

Rosetta stone *rō-zet'ə stōn*, *n* a tablet, found near Rosetta in Egypt in 1799, which carried the same inscription in hieroglyphics and demotic script and also in Greek and thus enabled a beginning to be made in deciphering hieroglyphics; any comparable first clue.

rosette *rō-zet'*, *n* a knot of radiating loops of ribbon or the like in concentric arrangement, *esp* worn as a badge showing affiliation, or awarded as a prize; a close radiating group of leaves, *usu* pressed to the ground; a rose-shaped ornament (*archit*); any structure, arrangement or figure of similar shape; a curve whose polar equation is $r = a \sin m^{\theta}$; a disc, *esp* of copper, formed by throwing water on molten metal; any of several diseases of plants (also **rosette disease**). — *adj* **rosett'ed**. [Fr, dimin of *rose*]

Rosh Hashanah *rosh hə-shä'nə*, *n* the Jewish festival of New Year. [Heb, literally head of the year]

Rosicrucian *roz'* or *rōz'i-kroo'sh(y)ən*, *n* a member of an alleged secret society whose members made great pretensions to knowledge of the secrets of Nature, transmutation of metals, elemental spirits, magical signatures, etc, affirmed to have been founded (1459) by Christian *Rosenkreutz*; a member of any of various modern esoteric quasi-religious fraternities. — Also *adj*. — *n* **Rosicru'cianism**. [Prob a Latinization of *Rosenkreuz* rose cross, L *rosa* rose, and *crux* cross]

Rosie Lee or **Rosy Lee** *rō'zi lē*, (*rhyming slang*) *n* tea.

rosier, **rosily** and **rosiness**. See under **rose**[2].

rosin *roz'in*, *n* a resin obtained when turpentine is prepared from dead pine wood, used to make waxes, varnishes, etc and for preparing the bows used to play stringed musical instruments (also called *colophony*). — *vt* to rub with rosin; to add rosin to. — *n* **ros'inate** a resinate. — *adj* **ros'ined**. — *adj* **ros'iny**. — **ros'in-oil** an oil distilled from rosin; **ros'in-plant** or **ros'in-weed** *Silphium* or compass-plant. [**resin**]

Rosinante or **Rozinante** *roz-in-an'ti*, *n* Don Quixote's horse; a pitiful, worn-out nag. [Sp *Roucinante*, explained as *rocin antes*, formerly a rouncy]

rosinate and **rosiny**. See under **rosin**.

rosit. See **roset**.

rosmarine[1] *roz'mə-rīn*, (*Spenser*) *n* a walrus, or a sea-monster supposed to lick dew off the rocks. [Dan *rosmar* walrus; influenced by **rosmarine**[2]]

rosmarine[2] *roz'mə-rīn* or *-rēn*, *n* rosemary (*Spenser*); sea dew (*Jonson*). [See **rosemary**]

Rosminian *ros-min'i-ən*, *adj* of Antonio *Rosmini*-Serbati (1797–1855), his philosophy, or the Institute of Charity founded by him. — Also *n*. — *n* **Rosmin'ianism**.

rosolio or **rosoglio** *rō-zō'lyō*, *n* a sweet cordial made with raisins (formerly, it is said, with sundew). [Ital *rosolio*, from L *rōs sōlis* dew of the sun]

RoSPA *ros'pə*, *abbrev*: Royal Society for the Prevention of Accidents.

rosser. Variant spelling of **rozzer**.

rost. An old spelling of **roast**.

rostellum *ros-tel'əm*, *n* a little beak; a beaklike outgrowth from an orchid column; the forepart of a tapeworm's head. — *adj* **rostell'ar** or **rostell'ate**. [L *rōstellum*, dimin of *rōstrum* beak]

roster *rōs'tər* or *ros'tər*, *n* a list of employees, army personnel, etc with assigned (turns of) duties; any roll of names (*colloq*). — *vt* to put in a roster. — *n* **ros'tering**. [Du *rooster*, orig gridiron (from the ruled lines), from *roosten* to roast]

rostrum *ros'trəm* or *rōs'troom*, *n* a beak; (properly in *pl*, **ros'tra**) a platform for public speaking, etc (from the *Rostra* in the Roman forum, adorned with the beaks of captured ships); a part resembling a beak (*biol*); a raised platform on a stage (*theat*); platform carrying a camera (*cinema* and *TV*). — *adj* **ros'tral** of or like a rostrum. — *adj* **ros'trāte** or **ros'trated** beaked. — *adj* **rostrocarinate** (*ros-trō-kar'in-āt*; L *carīna* keel) beaked and keeled. — *n* a supposed flint implement with beak and keel. [L *rōstrum* beak, from *rōdere*, *rōsum* to gnaw]

rosula *roz'ū-lə*, *n* a leaf-rosette. — *adj* **ros'ūlate** in a rosette. [LL dimin of L *rosa* rose]

rosy. See under **rose**[2].

Rosy Lee. See **Rosie Lee**.

ROT *abbrev*: registered occupational therapist.

rot *rot*, *vi* to putrefy; to decay; to become corrupt; to become weak; to suffer from wasting disease, *esp* in prison, or sheep-rot; to talk nonsense, to chaff (*slang*). — *vt* to cause to rot, to ret; to chaff (*slang*): — *pr p* **rott'ing**; *pa t* and *pa p* **rott'ed**. — *n* decay; putrefaction; corruption; collapse, disintegration (often *fig*); applied to various diseases of sheep, timber, etc; worthless or rotten stuff (*colloq*); nonsense (*colloq*). — *interj* expressing contemptuous disagreement. — *n* **rott'er** a thoroughly depraved or worthless person. — **rot'grass** soft grass, butterwort, pennywort or other plant reputed to cause sheep-rot; **rot'gut** bad liquor; **rot'stone** rottenstone. [OE *rotian*, pa p *rotod*; cf **rotten**[1]]

rota *rō'tə*, *n* a roster; a course, round, routine or cycle of duty, etc; (with *cap*) the Roman Catholic supreme ecclesiastical tribunal; a round, a canon, a rondo or other composition with much repetition. — *adj* **rō'tal**. — *n* **Rō'tameter**® a device for measuring the rate of flow of a fluid, in which a tapered float moves vertically in a transparent tube in accordance with the speed of flow. — *n* **rō'taplane** rotor plane. — *n* **Rōtarian** (*-tā'ri-ən*) a member of a Rotary club. — Also *adj*. — *n* **Rōtā'rianism**. — *adj* **rotary** (*rō'tər-i*) turning like a wheel; of the nature of rotation; working by rotation of a part; (with *cap*) of an international system of clubs, formed to encourage service to and within the community, with a wheel as a badge, each member being of a different occupation. — *n* a rotary apparatus; (with *cap*) a Rotary club; (with *cap*) Rotarianism; a traffic roundabout (*US*). — *adj* **rōtāt'able**. — *vt* and *vi* **rōtāte'** to turn like a wheel; to put, take, go or succeed in rotation. — *adj* **rō'tate** (*bot*) wheel-shaped; with united petals in a plane with almost no tube. — *n* **rotā'tion** a turning round like a wheel; succession in definite order, as of crops; recurrent order; the conformal transformation (qv) in which a particular arrangement is rotated about a fixed point (*math*, etc). — *adj* **rotā'tional**. — *adj* **rotative** (*rō'tə-tiv*). — *n* **rotā'tor** a person who, or thing which, rotates; a muscle which rotates a part of the body on its axis (*anatom*). — *adj* **rotatory** (*rō'tə-tər-i* or *rō-tāt'ər-i*) rotary. — *vt* **rō'tavate** or **rō'tovate** (back-formation) to till by means of a rotavator. — *n* **Rō'tavator**® or **Rō'tovator**® (*rot*ary culti*vator*; also without *cap*) a motor-powered, hand-operated soil-tilling machine. — *n* **rō'tavirus** a wheel-shaped virus causing gastroenteritis. — **rotary index** a filing box with a central, rotating spine to which index cards are attached at one edge and rolled vertically. [L *rota* a wheel, *rotāre*, *-ātum* to run]

ROTC *rot'si*, (*US*) *abbrev*: *R*eserve *O*fficers' *T*raining *C*orps.

rotch, rotche or **roch** *roch*, *n* the little auk. — Also **rotch'ie**. [Cf Du *rotje* petrel; Fris *rotgies*, pl of *rotgoes* brent-goose]

rote[1] *rōt*, *n* mechanical memory, repetition or performance without regard to the meaning. — *vt* (*Shakesp* **roate**) to fix by rote (according to others, to root); to discourse by rote. — **by rote** by repetition. [Origin obscure; L *rota* a wheel, and OFr *rote* road, have been conjectured]

rote[2] *rōt*, *n* a medieval stringed instrument. [OFr *rote* a fiddle, prob through Gmc from Celtic; Welsh *crwth*, Gaelic *cruit*]

rote[3] *rōt*, (now *US*) *n* the roar of surf. [Ety obscure]

rotenone *rō'ti-nōn*, *n* an insecticide and fish poison prepared from derris and other plants. [Origin unknown]

rother *rodh'ər*, (*Shakesp*, *emendation*) *n* an ox, cow. — **roth'er-beast**. [OE *hrȳther* an ox, a cow; cf Ger pl *Rinder* horned cattle]

roti *rō'tē*, *n* (in Indian and Caribbean cooking) a cake of unleavened bread; a kind of sandwich made of this wrapped around curried vegetables, seafood or chicken: — *pl* **rō'tis**. [Hindi, bread]

rotifer *rōt'if-ər*, *n* a wheel-animalcule, or member of the **Rotif'era**, minute aquatic animals whose rings of waving cilia suggest a rotating wheel. — *adj* **rotif'eral** or **rotif'erous**. [L *rota* a wheel, and *ferre* to carry]

rotisserie or **rôtisserie** *rō-tis'ə-ri* or *rō-tēs-rē*, *n* a cooking apparatus incorporating a spit; a shop or restaurant in which meats are cooked by direct heat. [Fr, cookshop, from *rôtir* to roast]

rotl *rot'l*, *n* a variable Levantine weight: — *pl* **rot'ls** or **ar'tal**. [Ar *ratl*]

rotograph *rō'tə-gräf*, *n* a photograph (eg of a manuscript) made directly by throwing a reversed image on a roll of sensitive paper. — *vt* to photograph by this method. [L *rota* a wheel, and Gr *graphein* to write]

rotogravure *rō-tō-grə-vūr'*, *n* a photogravure process using a rotary press; a print so produced. [L *rota* a wheel, and Fr *gravure* engraving]

rotolo *rō'tō-lō*, an Italian form of **rotl**: — *pl* **ro'tolos**.

rotor *rō'tər*, *n* a rotating part, *esp* of a dynamo, motor or turbine; a revolving cylinder for propulsion of a ship; a revolving aerofoil; a large, closed eddy sometimes formed under lee waves and associated with severe turbulence (*meteorol*). — **ro'torcraft** or **rotor plane** a helicopter or autogyro; **rotor ship**; **ro'tor-station** an aerodrome designed specially for helicopters. [For **rotator**]

Rotovator. See under **rota**.

rottan. See **rotten**[2].

rotten[1] *rot'n*, *adj* putrefied; decaying; affected by rot; corrupt; unsound; disintegrating; deplorably bad (*colloq*); miserably out of sorts (*colloq*). — *adv* **rott'enly**. — *n* **rott'enness**. — **rotten apple** a corrupt person; **rotten borough** a borough that still (till 1832) sent members to parliament though it had few or no inhabitants; **rott'enstone** a decomposed silicious limestone that has lost most of its calcareous matter, used for polishing metals. — *vt* to polish with rottenstone. [ON *rotinn*; cf **rot**]

rotten[2] or **rottan** *rot'n*. Same as **ratton**.

rotter, rotting, etc. See under **rot**.

Rottweiler *rot'vīl-ər*, *n* a large, powerfully built black German dog with smooth coat and tan markings on the chest and legs (also without *cap*); a rudely aggressive or brutish person (*fig*). — *adj* vicious and unscrupulous, brutal, as *Rottweiler politics*, etc. [*Rottweil*, in SW Germany]

rotula *rot'ū-lə*, *n* the knee-cap (*anatom*); a radial piece of Aristotle's lantern in sea-urchins (*zool*). [L *rotula*, dimin of *rota* a wheel]

rotund *rō-tund'*, *adj* round; rounded; nearly spherical; convexly protuberant; (of speech, etc) impressive or grandiloquent; plump. — *vt* to round. — *n* **rotund'a** a round (*esp* domed) building or hall. — *adj* **rotund'ate** rounded off; orbicular. — *n* **rotund'ity** roundness; a round mass. — *adv* **rotund'ly**. [L *rotundus*, from *rota* a wheel]

roturier *ro-tü-ryā*, *n* a plebeian. [Fr, prob from LL *ruptūra* ground broken by the plough, from L *rumpere*, *ruptum* to break]

ROU *abbrev*: Republic of Uruguay.

rouble or **ruble** *rōō'bl*, *n* the standard monetary unit of Russia and the countries formerly comprising the Soviet Union, equal to 100 kopecks. [Russ *rubl'*, perh from *rubit'* to cut; or Pers *rūpīya* a rupee]

roucou *rōō-kōō'*, *n* annatto. [Fr, from Tupi *urucú*]

roué *rōō'ā*, *n* a profligate, rake, debauchee. [A name given by Philippe, Duke of Orléans, Regent of France 1715–23, to his dissolute companions, from Fr *roué* broken on the wheel, from pa p of *rouer*, from *roue*, from L *rota* a wheel]

Rouen cross *rōō-ã kros*, *n* a cross in fretwork as a brooch or pendant. [*Rouen* in France]

rouge[1] *rōōzh*, *n* cosmetic powder used to redden the face, *orig* a mixture of safflower and talc; a polishing powder of hydrated ferric oxide (also **jeweller's rouge**); French red wine (for *vin rouge*). — *vt* to colour with rouge. — *vi* to use rouge; to blush. — **Rouge Croix** (*krwä*) and **Rouge Dragon** two of the pursuivants of the Heralds' College; **rouge-et-noir** (*rōōzh-ā-nwär*) a gambling card-game played on a table with two red and two black diamond marks on which stakes are laid (also called trente-et-quarante). [Fr *rouge*, from L *rubeus* red]

rouge[2] *rōōj* (*Eton*) *n* a scrimmage (*obs*); a touch-down in football. [Origin unknown]

rough *ruf*, *adj* uneven; rugged; unshorn; unshaven; unpolished; harsh; crude; unelaborated; without attention to minute correctness; (of a horse, etc) unbroken; coarse; rude; unrefined; ungentle; turbulent; aspirate; astringent; unpleasant, nasty (*colloq*); difficult, harrowing (*colloq*); feeling unwell, tired or hung over (*colloq*). — *adv* roughly; with roughness or risk of discomfort. — *n* rough state; that which is rough; rough ground, *esp* uncut grass, etc beside a golf fairway; a piece inserted in a horse's shoe to keep it from slipping; a hooligan, a rowdy; a crude preliminary sketch, etc. — *vt* to make rough; to ruffle; to roughen the shoes of; to shape roughly; to treat roughly (*usu* with *up*). — *n* **rough'age** refuse of grain or crops; bran, fibre, etc in food; coarse food that promotes intestinal movement. — *vt* **rough'en** to make rough. — *vi* to become rough. — *n* **rough'er** a person who performs preliminary operations. — *n* **rough'ie** a dry bough, *esp* one used as a torch (*Scott*); a rough or rowdy person (*slang*); an outsider in horse-racing or dog-racing (*Austr slang*); an unfair trick, twist or incident, etc (*Austr slang*). — *adj* **rough'ish**. — *adv* **rough'ly**. — *n* **rough'ness** the quality of being rough; a rough place; roughage (*US dialect*). — *n* **rough'y** same as **roughie**. — *adj* **rough'-and-read'y** ready to hand or easily improvised, and serving the purpose well enough; (of a person) lacking refinement or social graces but pleasant enough. — *adj* **rough'-and-tumb'le** haphazard and scrambling. — Also *adv*. — *n* a scuffle; haphazard struggling. — **rough breathing** in ancient Greek, the sound *h*. — *vt* **rough'cast** to shape roughly; to cover with roughcast. — *n* plaster mixed with small stones or shells, used to coat the outside walls of buildings. — *adj* coated with roughcast. — *adj* **rough'-coated** given an initial coat of plaster. — **rough cut** a roughly edited, preliminary version or sequence of a film; **rough diamond** see under **diamond**. — *vt* **rough'-draft** or **-draw** to draft roughly. — *vt* **rough'-dry** to dry without smoothing. — *adj* **rough'-footed** with feathered feet. — *adj* **rough'-grained** coarse-grained. — **rough grazing** uncultivated ground, used for pasture. — *vt* **rough-grind'** to grind roughly. — *vt* **rough-hand'le** to treat roughly. — *vt* **rough-hew'** (*Shakesp*) to hew or shape into a rough form. — **rough-hew'er**. — *adj* **rough-hewn'** shaped roughly; uncouth, unrefined. — **rough'-hound** a small species of dogfish; **rough'-house** (*orig US*; also **rough house**) a disturbance; a brawl. — *vi* to brawl; to make a disturbance. — *vt* to handle roughly, maltreat. — **rough justice** approximate justice, hastily assessed and carried out; a verdict or sentence that is appropriate, though formed without careful attention to the forms and processes of a legal code. — *adj* **rough'-legged** with feathered or hairy legs. — **rough'-neck** (*colloq*; *orig NAm*) an unmannerly lout; a hooligan or tough; a member of an oil rig crew employed to deal with equipment on the rig floor. — *vi* to work as a roughneck on an oil rig. — *adj* **rough'-out** a leather or a leather article, having the reverse side from the grain outermost. — **rough passage** a stormy sea voyage; a difficult, trying time. — *adj* **rough'-per'fect** nearly perfect in the memorizing of a part. — **rough puff-pastry** quick puff-pastry made without allowing the pastry to rest between the repeated rolling out and folding; **rough'-rider** a rider of untrained horses; a horse-breaker; an army riding-master's assistant; an irregular cavalryman. — *adj* **rough'shod** provided with horse-shoes with projecting nails to afford extra grip. — **rough shooting** shooting over moorland (mainly grouse). — *adj* **rough'-spoken** rough in speech. — **rough'-string** an intermediate support for the steps of a wooden stairway; **rough'-stuff** coarse paint laid on after the priming, and before the finish; violent behaviour; **rough trade** (*slang*) violent or sadistic male prostitute(s) or casual sexual partner(s), *esp* homosexual. — *adj* **rough'-wrought** shaped out or done roughly, or in a preliminary way. — **cut up rough** see under **cut**; **ride roughshod over** to set at nought, domineer over without consideration; **rough in** to sketch in roughly; **rough it** to live in rough or basic conditions (to which one is unaccustomed); to take whatever hardships come; **rough on** hard luck for; pressing hard upon; **rough out** to shape out roughly; **sleep rough** to sleep out-of-doors, *esp* because of being homeless. [OE *rūh* rough; Ger *rauch*, *rauh*, Du *ruig*]

rought *röt*, an *obs pa t* of **reck**.

rouille *rōō-ēy'*, *n* a Provençal sauce made from pounded red chillis, garlic and breadcrumbs blended with olive oil or stock, served *esp* with bouillabaise. [Fr, rust]

roul and **roule**. *Obs* forms of **roll**.

roulade *rōō-läd'*, *n* melodic embellishment (*music*); a run, turn, etc sung to one syllable (*music*); meat, cake or soufflé mixture served rolled up, *usu* with a filling (*cookery*). [Fr]

rouleau *rōō-lō'*, *n* a roll or coil, often of ribbon; a cylindrical pile or column of coins, blood corpuscles, or other discs: — *pl* **rouleaus** or **rouleaux** (*-lōz'*). [Fr]

roulette *rōōl-et'*, *n* literally a little roller or wheel; a game of chance in which a ball rolls from a rotating disc into one or other of a set of compartments answering to those on which the players place their stakes; a tool with a toothed disc for engraving rows of dots, for perforating paper, etc; a cylinder for curling hair or wigs; the locus of a point carried by a curve rolling upon a fixed curve (*geom*). [Fr]

roum *rōōm*, an old spelling of **room**. — *n* **roum'ing** (see **souming and rouming** under **soum**).

Rouman and **Roumanian**. See **Romanian**.

Roumansch. See **Romansch**.

rounce *rowns*, *n* in a hand printing-press, the apparatus, or its handle, for moving the carriage. [Du *ronse*]

rounceval *rown'si-vl*, *n* a giant (*obs*); a large, boisterous woman (*obs*); a marrow-fat pea. — *adj* (*obs*) gigantic. [Poss *Roncesvalles*, in the Pyrenees]

rouncy *rown'si*, (*archaic*) *n* a riding-horse; a nag. [OFr *ronci*]

round[1] *rownd*, (*archaic*) *vt* to whisper; to whisper to. — *vi* to whisper. [OE *rūnian* to whisper; cf **rune**]

round[2] *rownd*, *adj* having a curved outline or surface; approaching a circular, globular or cylindrical form; in a course returning upon itself; enveloping; with horizontal swing; plump; pronounced with lips contracted to a circle (*phonetics*); smooth and full-sounding; sonorous; well finished off; (of a sentence) periodic; approximate, without regarding minor denominations; (of a number) without fractions; full; not inconsiderable in amount; plain-spoken; candid; honest; unsparing; without mincing; (of pace) vigorous; (of a strong statement, etc) unqualified. — *adv* about; on all sides; every way; in a ring; in a curve; along the circumference; in rotation; from one to another successively; indirectly; circuitously; towards the opposite quarter; roundly (*Shakesp*); in the neighbourhood. — *prep* about; around; on every side of; all over; to every side of in succession; past, beyond. — *n* a round thing or part; a ring, circumference, circle or globe, *esp* the earth or the sky; a ladder rung or similar rounded connecting part; a whole slice of bread or toast; a sandwich made with two complete slices of bread; a cut of beef across the thigh-bone; a brewer's vessel for beer during fermentation; a projecting corner-turret (not necessarily round in shape); a carving in the round; a coil; a bend; a circuit; a course returning upon itself; a dance in a ring, or its tune; a canon sung in unison; a cycle or recurring series of events or doings; a complete revolution or rotation; an accustomed walk; a prescribed circuit; a patrol; a series of calls made by a doctor, postman, etc; a complete series of holes in golf; scope; routine; a volley, eg of firearms or applause; ammunition of one shot; a successive or simultaneous action of each member of a company or player in a game; a portion dealt around to each; a set of drinks bought at one time for all the members of a group; a subdivision of a bout, as in boxing; a defined stage in a competition; roundness; the condition of being visible from all sides, not merely in relief (*sculp*). — *vt* to make round; to surround; to go round; to turn round; to finish off; to give finish to. — *vi* to become round; to go round; to go the rounds. — *adj* **round'ed** made round or curved; (of a sound) round; finished, complete, developed to perfection. — *n* **round'edness**. — *n* **round'er** a person who or thing which rounds; a thing that is round (see also **roundure**); a person who goes the round of anything; (in *pl*) a bat-and-ball game in which players run from station to station; a complete circuit in this game. — *adj* **round'ing**. — *n* the process of raising (*up*) or lowering (*down*) a number to an approximation which has fewer decimal places (*comput*). — *adj* **round'ish**. — *adv* **round'ly**. — *n* **round'ness**. — *adj* **round'about** circuitous; indirect; cut evenly, without tails or train; plump. — *n* a circular revolving platform with handles, seats, etc at playgrounds, etc; a merry-go-round; a place where traffic circulates in one direction; a devious way; a round earthwork; a round dance; a short jacket (*US*). — *vi* to go round and round. — **roundaboutā'tion** or **roundaboutil'ity** (*facetious*). — *adv* **roundabout'edly** or **round'aboutly**. — **round'aboutness**; **round angle** same as **perigon**. — *adj* **round'arch** or **round'arched** having semicircular arches. — *adj* **round'-arm** with nearly horizontal swing of the arm. — *n* a throw made in this way. — *adj* **round'-backed**. — **round dance** a dance in a ring; a dance in which couples revolve about each other; **round'-down** an instance of rounding down (qv above under **rounding** *n*). — *adj* **round'-eared**. — *adj* **round'-eyed**. — *adj* **round'-faced**. — **round'-fish** any fish other than a flat fish; the carp; an American whitefish; **round game** a game, *esp* a card-game, in which each plays for his or her own hand; **round'hand** a style of penmanship in which the letters are well rounded and free; **Round'head** a supporter of Parliament during the English Civil War, a Puritan (from the close-cut hair). — *adj* **round'-headed** puritanical; having a round head, top or end; brachycephalic. — **round'house** a lock-up (*obs*); a cabin on the after part of the quarterdeck; an engine-house with a turntable (*US*); (a boxing style using) a wild swinging punch (*orig US*); **rounding error** (*comput*) an error in a computation caused by repeated rounding. — *adj* **round'-leaved**. — **round'-mouth** a cyclostome. — *adj* **round'-mouthed**. — *adj* **round'-nosed**. — **round robin** or **Robin** a paper with signatures in a circle, so that no one may seem to be a ringleader; any letter, petition, etc signed by many people; (in sports) a tournament in which each player plays every other player (also called **American tournament**). — *adj* **round'-shouldered** with shoulders bending forward from the back. — **rounds'man** a person who goes round *esp* one sent by a shopkeeper to take orders and deliver goods; a policeman who acts as a supervisor (*US*). — *adj* **round'-table** meeting on equal terms, like the inner circle of King Arthur's knights, who sat at a round table. — *adj* **round-the-clock'** lasting through the day and night, twenty-four-hour (also *adv*, without *hyphens*). — **round'-top** a mast-head platform; **round tower** a tall tapering tower of circular section, of early Christian origin, common in Ireland; **round-trip'** a trip to a place and back again; an instance of round-tripping (*colloq*). — *adj* (*esp NAm*) return. — **round-tripp'ing** (*colloq*) the financial practice of a company re-lending money at a rate higher than that at which they themselves have borrowed it; **round'-up** a driving together or assembling, as of all the cattle on a ranch, a set of people wanted by the police, a collection of facts or information, etc; an instance of rounding up (qv above under **rounding** *n*). — *adj* **round'-winged**. — **round'worm** a threadworm or nematode, a member of the *Nematoda*, unsegmented animals with long rounded body, mostly parasitic. — **bring round** see under **bring**; **come round** see under **come**; **get round to** to have the time or inclination to do (something) after delay; **go** or **make the rounds** to go or be passed from place to place or person to person; to circulate; to patrol; **in round numbers** or **figures** to the nearest convenient large number, ie ten, hundred, thousand, etc; roughly, approximately; **in the round** capable of being viewed from all sides, not merely in relief; taking everything into consideration; with all features, etc fully displayed; **round about** an emphatic form of round; the other way about; approximately; **round down** to lower (a number) to the nearest convenient figure, *usu* ten, hundred, etc; **round off** to finish off neatly; **round on** to turn on, attack verbally; **round out** to fill out to roundness; **round the bend** see under **bend**[1]; **round the twist** see under **twist**; **round the clock** see **round-the-clock** above; **round to** to turn the head of a ship to the wind; **round up** to ride round and collect; to gather in (wanted persons, facts, etc); to raise (a number) to the nearest convenient figure, *usu* ten, hundred, etc. [OFr *rund* (Fr *rond*), from L *rotundus*, from *rota* a wheel]

roundel *rown'dl*, *n* anything circular; a circle; a disc; a ladder rung; a ring-dance, a rondel; a round turret; a circular device (*heraldry*). — *n* **roun'delay** a song with a refrain; a dance in a ring. — *n* **roun'dle** a roundel. — *n* **round'let** (*-lit*) a little circle or disc. — *n* **rown'dell** (*Spenser*) a bubble. [OFr *rondel*, *-le*, *rondelet*, dimins of *rond* round]

roundure *rownd'yər* (*Shakesp* **round'er** or **rond'ure**) *n* roundness; a round form or space; a circle, circuit; a globe. [Fr *rondeur*, from *rond* round]

roup[1] *rowp*, (*Scot*) *n* a sale by public auction. — *vt* to sell by public auction; to sell up (with *out*). — **rouping'-wife** (*obs*) a woman auctioneer or buyer at auctions. [Scand]

roup[2] *ro͞op*, *n* an infectious disease of the respiratory passages of poultry; hoarseness (*Scot*). — *adj* **roup'it** (*Scot*). — *adj* **roup'y**. [Perh imit]

roup[3]. See **stoop**[4].

rousant. See under **rouse**[1].

rouse[1] *rowz*, *vt* to shake the feathers of (*orig reflexive*; *obs*); to ruffle, set up (*obs*); to start, as from cover or lair; to stir up; to awaken; to disturb (*rare*); to excite; to put in action; to haul in (eg a cable). — *vi* to shake oneself (*obs*); to rise from cover (*rare*); to stand erect (of hair; *Shakesp*); to awake; to be excited to action. — *n* a shake of the feathers, body, etc (*obs*); reveille. — *adj* **rous'ant** (*heraldry*) rising as a bird. — *n* **rouse'about** (*Austr*) an odd-job man on a sheep station. — *n* **rouse'ment** (*US*) religious excitement. — *n* **rous'er** a person who, or thing which, rouses; anything astonishing. — *adj* **rous'ing** awakening; stirring; vigorously active; great; violent. — *adv* **rous'ingly**. — *vt* **roust** to stir up; to rout out. — *vi* to move energetically. — *n* **roust'about** a wharf labourer (*NAm*); a person who does odd jobs (*NAm*); a rouseabout (*NAm* and *Austr*); a general labourer employed on an oil rig or in a circus. — *n* **roust'er** a roustabout. — **rouse on** (*Austr*) to reprove. [Origin obscure]

rouse[2] *rowz*, (*archaic*) *n* a carousal; a bumper. [Prob from **carouse**; poss Scand *rus* drunkenness]

roussette *ro͞o-set'*, *n* a fruit-bat; a dogfish. [Fr]

roust, **roustabout** and **rouster**. See under **rouse**[1].

rout[1] *rowt*, *n* a tumultuous crowd; a rabble; a pack, herd, or flock; a large party or reception (*archaic*); a fashionable evening gathering (*archaic*); a defeated body; an utter defeat; disorderly flight; a gathering of three or more people for the purpose of committing an unlawful act (*law*); disturbance; brawl; riot; clamour; a fuss. — *vi* to behave riotously. — *vt* to defeat utterly; to put to disorderly flight. — *n* (*archaic*) **rout'ing** going to receptions. — *adj* (*archaic*) **rout'ous**. — *adv* (*archaic*) **rout'ously**. — **rout'-cake** (*archaic*) a rich sweet cake formerly served at receptions; **rout'-seat** (*archaic*) a bench hired out for large social gatherings. [OFr *route*, from the pa p of L *rumpere*, *ruptum* to break]

rout[2] *rowt*, *vi* (now *Scot* and *dialect*) to snore. [OE *hrūtan*]

rout[3] *rowt*, *vt* (of a pig) to grub up; to scoop out; to turn up; to turn out, fetch out; to rummage out; to bring to light. — *vi* to grub; to poke about. — *n* **rout'er** a person or thing that routs; a tool of various styles for hollowing out, grooving, etc. [An irreg variant of **root**[2]]

rout[4] *rowt*, (*Scot* and *N Eng*) *vi* and *vt* to roar, bellow. [ON *rauta*]

route *rōōt* (formerly, now only *military*, *rowt*), *n* a way or course that is or may be traversed; marching orders; any regular journey; a regular series of calls, a round (*NAm*). — *vt* to fix the route of; to send by a particular route: — *pr p* **route'ing** or (*esp NAm*) **rout'ing**; *pa t* and *pa p* **rout'ed**. — **route'man** (*NAm*) a shopkeeper's roundsman; **route'-march** a long march of troops in training; **route-proving flight** a flight of aeroplanes sent out to test the possibilities and advantages of variants of a new service; **route'-step** an order of march in which soldiers are not required to keep step. [Fr, from L *rupta* (*via*) broken (way); see **rout**[1]]

routh or **rowth** *rowth*, (*Scot*) *n* abundance. — *adj* plentiful. — *adj* **routh'ie**. [Origin obscure]

routine *rōō-tēn'*, *n* regular, unvarying or mechanical course of action or round; the set series of movements gone through in a dancing, skating or other performance; a comedian's or singer's, etc act (*colloq*); a part of a program performing a specific and separate function (*comput*). — *adj* unvarying; keeping an unvarying round; forming part of a routine. — *n* **routineer'**. — *adv* **routine'ly**. — *n* **routi'nism**. — *n* **routi'nist** a person who advocates or is fond of routine. — *vt* **routinize'** or **-ise'** to render mechanical or uniform; to remove interest from. [Fr]

routous. See under **rout**[1].

roux *rōō*, (*cookery*) *n* a thickening made of equal quantities of butter and flour cooked together: — *pl* **roux** (*rōō* or *rōōz*). [Fr (*beurre*) *roux* brown (butter)]

ROV *abbrev*: remotely-operated vehicle.

rove[1] *rōv*, *vt* to wander over or through; to discharge (an arrow, etc) at random (*obs*). — *vi* to practise piracy (*obs*); to aim or shoot arrows, etc at random (with *at*; *obs*); to wander about; to ramble; to change about inconstantly; to troll with live bait. — *n* wandering; a mode of incomplete ploughing (*dialect*). — *n* **rō'ver** a pirate (*archaic*); a robber (*obs*); a random or distant mark (*archery*); an arrow for shooting at rovers (*obs*); a wanderer; an inconstant person; a croquet ball or player ready to peg out; formerly a member of a senior branch of the (Boy) Scout organization (also **rover scout**); a remotely-controlled vehicle for exploring the surface of the moon, etc. — *adj* **rō'ving** wandering; not confined to a particular place, eg *roving ambassador*, *roving commission*, etc. — Also *n*. — *adv* **rō'vingly**. — *adj* **rove'-over** (of a kind of verse in sprung rhythm) having an extra syllable at the end of one line, which forms a foot with the beginning of the next line. — **at rovers** (*archaic*) at a distant mark; at random; conjecturally; **have a roving eye** to tend to show a fleeting sexual interest in successive members of the opposite sex. [Partly at least from Du *rooven* to rob, *roofer* robber, from *roof* plunder; perh partly from a Midland form of obs N Eng *rave* to wander]

rove[2] *rōv*, *vt* to twist (cotton, wool, etc) slightly in preparation for spinning. — *n* a roved sliver. — *n* **rō'ver** a machine for roving; a person who operates it. — *n* **rō'ving** the process of giving the first twist to yarn; rove. [Origin obscure]

rove[3] *rōv*, *pa t* and *pa p* of **reeve**[2].

rove[4] *rōv*, *n* a metal plate or ring through which a rivet is put and clenched over. [ON *ró*]

rove-beetle *rōv'-bētl*, *n* the devil's coach-horse, or other beetle of the family *Staphylinidae*. [Cf Du *roof-kever*, literally reif chafer, from *roof* robbery]

row[1] *rō*, *n* a line or rank of people or things, eg seats, houses, turnips, etc; a series in line, or in ordered succession; often in street-names, of a single or double line of houses. — *vt* (*rare*) to set in or with a row or rows. — **row house** (*US*) a terraced house. — **a hard row to hoe** a destiny fraught with hardship; **death row** see under **death**; **in a row** in unbroken sequence; **twelve-tone row** or **twelve-note row** see under **twelve** and **serial**. [OE *rāw*; Ger *Reihe*, Du *rij*]

row[2] *rō*, *vt* to propel through water by making strokes with an oar or oars; to transport by rowing; to direct in a particular course of action, etc (*fig*); to achieve, render, perform or effect by use of oars; to take part in or race against in competitive rowing; to use (an oar) or make (a stroke) in rowing. — *vi* to work with the oar; to be moved by oars. — *n* an act or spell of rowing; a journey in a rowing-boat; a distance rowed. — *adj* **row'able** capable of being rowed or rowed on. — *n* **row'er**. — **row'-barge** (*hist*); **row'boat** (*US*); **row'ing-boat**; **rowing machine** an exercise machine with moveable seat and arms to simulate the action of rowing; **row'-port** (*naut*) a small square hole for an oar in a vessel's side. [OE *rōwan*]

row[3] *row*, *n* a noisy squabble; a brawl; a din, hubbub; a chiding or rebuking. — *vt* to rag, assail (*archaic*); to chide or scold. — *vi* to make a disturbance; to quarrel. [A late 18c word, poss a back-formation from **rouse**[2]]

row[4] *row*, *n* and *v* a Scots form of **roll**.

row[5] *row*, an *obs* or *dialect* form of **rough**.

rowan[1] *row'ən*, also *rō'ən*, *n* the mountain-ash (*Sorbus*, or *Pyrus*, *aucuparia*), a tree of the rose family with pinnate leaves; its small, red berrylike fruit. — **row'an-berry**; **row'an-tree**. [Cf Norw *raun*, Swed *rönn*]

rowan[2]. See **rowen**.

row-dow *row'-dow'* or **row-dow-dow** *row'-dow'-dow'*, *n* the sound of a drum. — *n* **rowdedow'** or **rowdydow'** hubbub. — *adj* **row'dy-dow'dy** uproarious. [Echoic]

rowdy[1] *row'di*, *n orig* a lawless American backwoodsman; a noisy, turbulent person. — *adj orig* of the nature of or belonging to a rowdy, lawless; noisy and disorderly, or having a tendency to behave so. — *adv* **row'dily**. — *n* **row'diness**. — *adj* **row'dyish**. — *n* **row'dyism**. [Origin unknown]

rowdy[2] *row'di*, (*obs slang*) *n* money.

rowdy-dow and **rowdy-dowdy**. See under **row-dow**.

rowel *row'əl*, *n* a small, spiked wheel on a spur; the rowel-head; a knob, ring or disc on a horse's bit; a disc used as a seton for animals. — *vt* to prick with the rowel: — *pr p* **row'elling**; *pa t* and *pa p* **row'elled**. — **row'el-head** the axis of a rowel; **row'el-spur** a spur with a rowel. [Fr *rouelle*, from LL *rotella*, dimin of L *rota* a wheel]

rowen *row'ən*, *n* a second mowing of grass in the same season, an aftermath. — Also **row'an**, **row'ing**, **raw'ing** or **rawn** (*rön*). [From a Northern form of OFr *regain*]

rowlock *rol'ək*, *rul'ək* or *rōl'ək*, *n* a contrivance serving as fulcrum for an oar. — Also **roll'ock** or **rull'ock**. [Prob for **oar-lock**, from OE *ārloc*]

rowme *rowm*, (*Spenser*) *n* a room; place, station. [**room**]

rownd. An *obs* spelling of **round**[1,2].

rowndell. See **roundel**.

rowt. Same as **rout**[3].

rowth. See **routh**.

Roxburghe *roks'bər-ə*, *n* a style of binding for books, with cloth or paper sides, plain leather back, gilt top, other edges untrimmed, named after the Duke of *Roxburghe* (1740–1804), book-collector.

Roy *roi*, (*Austr slang*; *derog*) *n* a fashion-conscious, young, Australian male. [From male given name *Roy*]

royal *roi'əl*, *adj* of, relating to or befitting a king or queen; kingly or queenly; being a king or queen; of a reigning family; founded, chartered or patronized by a king or queen; magnificent; of exceptional size or quality; of writing-paper, 19 by 24in, of printing-paper, 20 by 25in (**royal octavo** a book size $6\frac{1}{4}$ by 10in). — *n* a royal person (often in *pl* with *the*; *colloq*); a gold coin of various kinds; a sail immediately above the top gallant sail; the third (*orig* the second) tine of a stag; a stag with twelve or more points. — *n* **roy'alet** (*derog*, now *rare*) a petty king or other ruler. — *n* **roy'alism** support of the institution of monarchy. — *n* **roy'alist** (also with *cap*) an adherent of royalism, a monarchist; a cavalier during the English civil war; (in American history) a supporter of the British government during the American Revolution; (in French history) a supporter of the Bourbons. — Also *adj*. — *vt* **roy'alize** or **-ise** (*Shakesp*) to make royal or (*Milton*) royalist; to give royal character, sanction or status to. — *vi* to play the king. — *adv* **roy'ally**. — *n* **roy'alty** sovereignty; the state or office of a king or queen; royal or majestic character or quality; the person of the sovereign, majesty (*Shakesp*); the members of a royal family collectively or (*colloq*) any such member; a queen bee, queen termite, etc; sovereign rule, monarchy; royal authority; a right or prerogative granted by a king or queen, *esp* a right over minerals; a payment made by oil companies, etc to the owners of the mineral rights in the area in which they operate; payment to an author, composer, etc for every copy sold or every public performance of a particular work; the area of a royal domain, a realm; a royal burgh (*Scot*). — **Royal Academy** an academy of fine arts in London, founded in 1768, to which members and associates are elected (in very limited number); a teaching, degree-giving academy of music in London; **royal assent** see under **assent**; **royal blue** a bright, deep-coloured blue; **royal commission** (also with *caps*) a body of people nominated by the Crown to inquire into and report on a particular matter; **royal fern** (*Osmunda regalis*) the most striking of British ferns, with large fronds; **royal fish** a 'fish' that is the monarch's perquisite when cast ashore or caught near the land (whale, sturgeon, porpoise); **royal flush** see under **flush**[4]; **royal icing** a kind of hard icing made with egg white, used *esp* on rich fruit cakes; **royal jelly** a secretion produced by worker bees, the food of young larvae and of a developing queen bee; **royal marriage** (*bezique*) king and queen of trumps; **royal mast** (*naut*) the fourth and highest part of the mast, *usu* made in one piece with the top-gallant mast; **royal palm** a palm (*Oreodoxa regalis*) of the cabbage-palm genus; **Royal Peculiar** an ecclesiastical peculiar whose superior is the sovereign; **royal road** a short and easy way of circumventing difficulties; **royal standard** a banner bearing the British royal arms, flown wherever the monarch is present; **royal tennis** the earlier form of the game of tennis, distinguished from lawn tennis, and played in a walled court (also called **real** or **court tennis**); **royal warrant** an official authorization to supply goods to a royal household; **Royal We** (also without *caps*) a monarch's use of the first person plural when speaking of himself or herself. — **the Royals** formerly the first regiment of foot in the British Army (the Royal Scots); (without *cap*) see *n* above. [Fr, from L *rēgālis* regal]

royne[1] *roin*, (*Spenser*) *vi* to mutter, growl, roar. [Prob connected with **groin**[3]]

royne[2]. See **roon**.

roynish *roin'ish*, (*Shakesp*) *adj* scurvy, mangy; mean. [OFr *roigne* mange]

royst, royster, etc. Same as **roist, roister**, etc.

rozelle. Same as **roselle**.

rozet and **rozit**. See **roset**.

Rozinante. See **Rosinante**.

rozzer *roz'ər*, (*slang*) *n* a policeman. [Origin obscure]

RP *abbrev*: Received Pronunciation; Reformed Presbyterian; Regius Professor; Republic of the Philippines (IVR); retinitis pigmentosa; Royal Society of Portrait Painters.

RPB *abbrev*: recognized professional body.

RPG *abbrev*: role-playing game.

RPI *abbrev*: retail price index.

RPM *abbrev*: retail or resale price maintenance.

rpm *abbrev*: revolutions per minute.

RPN *abbrev*: reverse Polish notation.

RPO *abbrev*: Royal Philharmonic Orchestra.

RPR *abbrev*: *Rassemblement pour la République* (*Fr*), a neo-Gaullist, right-wing political party in France (formerly **UDR**).

RPS *abbrev*: Royal Photographic Society.

rps *abbrev*: revolutions per second.

RPT *abbrev*: registered physiotherapist; registered professional turner.

rpt *abbrev*: repeat; report.

RPV (*military*) *abbrev*: remotely-piloted vehicle, a miniature aircraft designed to identify the exact position of enemy targets.

RR *abbrev*: Right Reverend.

RRP *abbrev*: recommended retail price.

RS *abbrev*: Royal Society.

RSA *abbrev*: Republic of South Africa; Royal Scottish Academy or Academician; Royal Society of Arts.

RSAMD *abbrev*: Royal Scottish Academy of Music and Drama.

RSC *abbrev*: Royal Shakespeare Company; Royal Society of Chemistry.

RSFSR *abbrev*: Russian Federated Soviet Socialist Republic.

RSI *abbrev*: repetitive strain or stress injury.

RSJ *abbrev*: rolled steel joist.

RSL *abbrev*: Royal Society of Literature.

RSM *abbrev*: Regimental Sergeant-Major; Republic of San Marino (IVR); Royal School of Music; Royal Society of Medicine.

RSNC *abbrev*: Royal Society for Nature Conservation.

RSNO *abbrev*: Royal Scottish National Orchestra.

RSPB *abbrev*: Royal Society for the Protection of Birds.

RSPCA *abbrev*: Royal Society for the Prevention of Cruelty to Animals.

RSRE *abbrev*: Royal Signals and Radar Establishment.

RSSA *abbrev*: Royal Scottish Society of Arts.

RSSPCC *abbrev*: Royal Scottish Society for the Prevention of Cruelty to Children.

RSTM & H *abbrev*: Royal Society of Tropical Medicine and Hygiene.

RSV *abbrev*: Revised Standard Version (of the Bible).

RSVP *abbrev*: *répondez s'il vous plaît* (*Fr*), please reply.

RTA *abbrev*: road traffic accident.

RTE *abbrev*: *Radio Telefís Éireann* (*Ir Gaelic*), Irish Radio and Television.

Rt Hon. *abbrev*: Right Honourable.

RTPI *abbrev*: Royal Town Planning Institute.

Rt Rev. *abbrev*: Right Reverend.

RU *abbrev*: Republic of Burundi (IVR); Rugby Union; Russia (IVR; provisional).

Ru (*chem*) *symbol*: ruthenium.

ruana *ro͞o-ä'nə*, *n* a woollen outer garment resembling a poncho, worn in parts of S America. [Am Sp]

rub[1] *rub*, *vt* to apply friction to; to move something with pressure along the surface of; to move with pressure along the surface of something; to clean, polish or smooth by friction; to remove, erase or obliterate by friction (*usu* with *away*, *off* or *out*); to grind, sharpen, chafe or treat by friction; to cause to pass by friction (with *in*, *through*, etc); to impede (*Shakesp*); to irritate, fret; to take a rubbing of. — *vi* to apply, or move with, friction; to meet an impediment (*esp* in *bowls*); to chafe; to grate; to fret; to make shift, to get along somehow; to admit of being rubbed: — *pr p* **rubb'ing**; *pa t* and *pa p* **rubbed**. — *n* process or act of rubbing; an impediment, or a meeting with an impediment (*bowls*);

an inequality or uneven place; a difficulty; a hitch; an irritating experience. — *n* **rubb'ing** application of friction; experience of rubs (*Shakesp*); an impression of an inscribed surface produced by rubbing heel-ball or plumbago upon paper laid over it. — **rubb'ing-post** one for cattle to rub against; **rubb'ing-stone** a stone for smoothing; **rub'down** an act or experience of rubbing down; **rub'out** an act of rubbing out; a murder (*slang*); **rub'stone** a whetstone. — **rub along** (*colloq*) to get along, to manage somehow; to be on more or less friendly terms (with); **rub down** to rub from head to foot; to remove (a surface) by rubbing in order to repaint, etc; to search by passing the hands over the body; **rub in** to force into the pores by friction; to be unpleasantly insistent in emphasizing; **rub off on (to)** (*fig*) to pass to (another person or thing) by close contact, association, etc; **rub one's hands** to rub one's palms together, *esp* as a sign of satisfaction; **rub on** or **of the green** (*golf*) a chance outside interference with the ball (also *fig*); **rub out** to erase; to murder (*slang*); **rub shoulders** to come into social contact (with); **rub someone's nose in it** (*colloq*) to remind someone insistently of a mistake, fault, misdeed, etc; **rub** (or **rub up**) **the wrong way** to irritate by tactless handling; **rub up** to polish; to freshen one's memory of. [Cf LGer *rubben*]

rub[2]. See under **rubber**[2].

rub[3] *rub*, a Scots form of **rob**[1]: — *pa t* **rubb'it** or **rubb'et**.

rub-a-dub-dub *rub'ə-dub-dub'*, *n* the sound of a drum. [Echoic]

rubai *rōō-bä'ē*, *n* a Persian verse form consisting of four-line stanzas; *specif* (in *pl*, with *caps*) those written in Persia by Omar Khayyam in the late 11c or early 12c, and translated by Edward Fitzgerald in 1859: — *pl* **rubaiyat** (*rōō'bä-yat*). [Arabic *rubā'īyāt*, pl of *rubā'ī-yah* quatrain]

rubato *rōō-bä'tō*, (*music*) *adj*, *adv* and *n* (in) modified or distorted rhythm: — *pl* **ruba'ti** (*-tē*) or **ruba'tos**. [Ital, pa p of *rubare* to steal]

rubber[1] *rub'ər*, *n* a person who, or thing which, rubs or massages; an eraser; a thing for rubbing with, such as a hard brush, a file, a whetstone, emery-cloth, a coarse towel, etc; a rubbing part of a machine; a cabinet-maker's pad for polishing; a soft brick that can be cut and smoothed; an uneven place; a rub or impediment in bowls; a rebuff or irritating experience; caoutchouc, india-rubber, or a substitute; a piece of india-rubber, *esp* for erasing, or as part of a brake; (in *pl*) plimsolls or india-rubber overshoes (*orig US*); a rubberneck (*US*); a condom (chiefly *NAm*); (in *pl*) a sheep disease with heat accompanied by itchiness. — *adj* of, yielding or concerned with india-rubber. — *vt* to coat, cover or provide with rubber. — *vi* (*US*) to rubberneck. — *vt* **rubb'erize** or **-ise** to treat or coat with rubber. — *adj* **rubb'ery** resembling rubber in appearance or texture. — **rubber band** a thin loop of rubber used to hold things together; **rubber bullet** a hard rubber cylinder fired from a special type of gun, used in riot control; **rubber cement** an adhesive made of rubber dissolved in a solvent; **rubber cheque** or (*NAm*) **check** (*facetious*) a cheque that bounces; **rubber chicken circuit** (*US slang*) a lecture tour, round of political campaigning, etc characterized by the provision of bland, unappetizing food to the participants. — *adj* **rubb'er-cored** (of a golf ball) having a tightly wound band of rubber enclosed in a guttapercha cover. — **rubber goods** (*euphem*) condoms; **rubb'erneck** an over-inquisitive or gaping person; a tourist, *esp* one who sightsees from a tour coach. — *vi* (*slang*) to behave as a rubberneck. — *vt* (*slang*) to stare at. — **rubber plant** any of various plants from whose sap rubber is made, especially *Ficus elastica*, often grown as an ornamental pot-plant; **rubber room** (*US slang*) a room padded with foam rubber in a psychiatric hospital, etc; a tedious job with poor working conditions (*adj* **rubb'er-room**; *fig*); **rubber solution** a solution of rubber in naphtha or carbon disulphide, for repairing pneumatic tyres; **rubb'er-stamp** stamp of rubber for making inked impressions; a person unquestioningly devoted to routine or officialdom; an automatic or unthinking agreement or authorization; a person or people making such an agreement, etc. — *vt* to imprint with a rubber-stamp; to approve without exercise of judgment. — Also *adj*. — **rubber tree** a tropical American tree (*Hevea brasiliensis*) grown for its latex, a source of rubber; **rubb'erwear** rubber clothing. [Ety as for **rub**[1]]

rubber[2] *rub'ər*, *n* formerly in bowls (also **rubbers**, *sing* or *pl*), now chiefly in bridge and whist, the winning of, or play for, the best of three games (sometimes five); any spell of card-playing; used generally of a series of games in various sports, such as cricket, tennis, etc; a rub (*bowls*; see **rub**[1]). — Also **rub**. [Origin obscure]

rubberize, **rubbery**, etc. See under **rubber**[1].

rubbet. See under **rub**[3].

rubbish *rub'ish*, *n* fragments of ruined buildings, rubble; waste matter; litter; trash; trumpery; nonsense; a worthless or despicable person or people. — Also *adj*. — *vt* to criticize, think of or talk about as rubbish. — *adj* **rubb'ishing**. — *adj* **rubb'ishly** (*rare*). — *adj* **rubb'ishy** worthless; paltry; trashy. — **rubb'ish-heap**. [Origin obscure; appar connected with **rubble**]

rubbit. See under **rub**[3].

rubble *rub'l*, *n* loose fragments of rock or ruined buildings; undressed irregular stones used in rough masonry and in filling in; masonry of such a kind. — *adj* of rubble. — *adj* **rubb'ly**. — **rubb'le-stone**; **rubb'le-work** coarse masonry. [Origin obscure; cf **rubbish**]

rube *rōōb*, (*NAm slang*) *n* a country bumpkin; an uncouth, unsophisticated person. [*Reuben*]

rubefy *rōō'bi-fī*, *vt* to redden. — *adj* **rubefacient** (*-fā'shənt*) reddening. — *n* any external application that reddens the skin, *esp* a counter-irritant. — *n* **rubefaction** (*-fak'shən*) reddening. [L *rubefacere*, from *rubeus* red, and *facere* to make]

Rube Goldberg *rōō'bi gōld'bûrg* or **Goldbergian** *gōld-bûrg'i-ən*, (*NAm*) *adj*. Same as **Heath-Robinson**. [Reuben ('Rube') L Goldberg (1883–1970), US cartoonist]

rubella *rōō-bel'ə*, *n* German measles, an infectious disease producing a pink rash, like measles but milder, except for its possible effect on the foetus of an expectant mother infected early in pregnancy. — *n* **rubell'an** (or *rōō'*) an altered biotite. — *n* **rubell'ite** a red kind of mineral with varying composition, a red tourmaline. [Dimin from L *rubeus* red]

rubeola *rōō-bē'ə-lə*, *n* measles. [Dimin from L *rubeus* red]

rubescent *rōō-bes'ənt*, (*literally*) *adj* growing red; blushing. [L *rubescere* to grow red]

Rubia *rōō'bi-ə*, *n* the madder genus, giving its name to the **Rubiā'ceae**, a family of sympetalous dicotyledons related to the *Caprifoliaceae*. — *adj* **rubiā'ceous**. [L *rubia* madder, from *rubeus* reddish]

rubicelle *rōō'bi-sel*, *n* an orange-coloured spinel. [Fr, prob from *rubis* ruby]

Rubicon *rōōb'i-kon* or *-kən*, *n* a stream of Central Italy (*perh* the Fiumicino), separating Caesar's province of Gallia Cisalpina from Italia proper, its crossing by Caesar (49 BC) being thus a virtual declaration of war against the republic; (without *cap*) in piquet, the winning of a game before one's opponent scores 100. — *vt* (without *cap*) to defeat in this way. — **cross the Rubicon** (*fig*) to take a decisive, irrevocable step. [L *Rubicō*, *-ōnis*]

rubicund *rōō'bi-kund* or *-kənd*, *adj* ruddy. — *n* **rubicund'ity**. [L *rubicundus*, from *rubēre* to be red]

rubidium *rōō-bid'i-əm*, *n* a soft silvery-white metallic element (symbol **Rb**; atomic no 37). [L *rubidus* red (so called from two red lines in its spectrum)]

rubify (now *rare*). Same as **rubefy**.

rubiginous *rōō-bij'i-nəs*, *adj* rusty-coloured. — Also **rubig'inose** (*-nōs*). [L *rūbīgō* or *rōbīgō*, *-inis* rust]

Rubik's Cube® *rōō'biks kūb*, *n* a cube-shaped puzzle composed of 26 small pieces (cubes or partial cubes) with faces coloured in any of six colours, fixed to a central spindle that allows them to be rotated on three axes, the solved puzzle presenting a uniform colour on each face. [Developed by Ernö *Rubik*, Hungarian designer, in 1974]

rubin, **rubious**, etc. See under **ruby**.

ruble. See **rouble**.

rubric *roo'brik*, *n* red ochre (*obs*); a heading, guiding rule, entry or liturgical direction, *orig* one in red ink; a flourish after a signature; a thing definitely settled. — *adj* in red; ruddy; inscribed with book titles (*obs*). — *adj* **ru'brical**. — *adv* **ru'brically**. — *vt* **ru'bricate** to mark with red; to write or print in red; to make a red-letter saint; to provide with rubrics; to regulate by rubric. — *n* **rubricā'tion**. — *n* **ru'bricātor**. — *n* **rubrician** (*roo-brish'ən*) a person who follows, or is versed in, liturgical rubrics. [L *rubrīca* red ochre, from *ruber* red]

Rubus *roo'bəs*, *n* the raspberry and bramble genus of the rose family. [L *rubus* a bramble-bush]

ruby *roo'bi*, *n* a precious stone, a pure transparent red corundum; extended to other stones, such as varieties of spinel and garnet; the colour of a ruby, a deep crimson; (in *pl*) the lips (*poetic*); blood (*boxing slang*); a deep-red wine or port; ruby glass (see below); a type smaller than nonpareil and larger than pearl ($5\frac{1}{2}$ points; *printing*). — *adj* red as a ruby. — *vt* to redden: — *pr p* **ru'bying**; *pa t* and *pa p* **ru'bied**. — *adj* **ru'bied** red as a ruby. — *n* **ru'bin** or **ru'bine** (*-bin*; *Spenser*) a ruby. — *adj* **rubin'eous**. — *adj* **ru'bious** ruby, red, ruddy. — *adj* **ru'by-coloured**. — **ruby glass** glass coloured a deep red by the addition of mineral oxides. — *adj* **ruby-red'**. — **ruby silver** proustite; pyrargyrite; **ruby spinel** a ruby-red spinel (also *spinel-ruby*); **ru'by-tail** a gold-wasp, or cuckoo-fly; **ru'by-throat** a humming-bird with a ruby gorget. — *adj* **ru'by-throated**. — **ruby wedding** a fortieth wedding anniversary. [OFr *rubi* and *rubin*, from L *rubeus*, from *ruber* red]

RUC *abbrev*: Royal Ulster Constabulary.

ruc. Same as **roc**.

ruche *roosh*, *n* a frill of lace or other material, *esp* pleated. — *vt* to trim with a ruche. — *n* **ruch'ing**. [Fr; prob of Celtic origin]

ruck[1] *ruk*, *n* a wrinkle, fold or crease. — *vt* and *vi* to wrinkle or crease (often with *up*). — *n* **ruck'le** a pucker, crease. — *vt* and *vi* to pucker, crease. [ON *hrukka* a wrinkle]

ruck[2] *ruk*, *vi* to squat; to crouch down; to cower; to huddle. — *vt* (*Shakesp* **rook** *rook*, *reflexive*) to set squatting. [Prob Scand; cf Norw dialect *ruka* to crouch]

ruck[3] *ruk*, *n* a heap, stack or mass of anything, such as fuel, hay, etc; a multitude; the common run; (in Rugby football) a gathering of players around the ball when it is on the ground; (in Australian rules football) the three players who do not have fixed positions but follow the ball about the field. — *vt* to heap. — *vi* (in Rugby football) to form a ruck. [Prob Scand]

ruck[4] *ruk*, (*prison slang*) *n* a fight. [**ruckus**]

ruckle[1] *ruk'l*, (*Scot*) *n* a rattle in the throat; a gurgle. — *vi* to rattle; to gurgle. [Cf Norw dialect *rukl*]

ruckle[2]. See under **ruck**[1].

rucksack *rook'* or *ruk'sak*, or *-zak*, *n* a bag carried on the back by hikers, campers, etc. — *n* **ruck'seat** a folding seat with aluminium frame, attached to a rucksack for camping. [Ger dialect *ruck* (Ger *Rücken*) back, and Ger *Sack* bag]

ruckus *ruk'əs*, (*US*) *n* a disturbance. [Perh a combination of **ruction** and **rumpus**]

rucola *roo-kō'lə*, *n*. Same as **rocket**[2]. [Ital]

ructation *ruk-tā'shən*, (*obs*) *n* eructation. [L *ructāre* to belch]

ruction *ruk'shən*, (*colloq*; *esp* in *pl*) *n* a noisy disturbance; a rumpus, row. [Poss for **insurrection**]

rud *rud*, (*archaic* or *dialect*) *n* redness; flush; complexion; ruddle. — *vt* (*Spenser*) to redden: — *pa p* **rudd'ed**. [OE *rudu* redness, *rēodan* to redden]

rudas *roo'dəs*, (*Scot*) *n* a foul-mouthed old woman; a randy, a hag. — *adj* coarse. [Origin obscure]

rudbeckia *rud-* or *rood-bek'i-ə*, *n* any of the N American composite plants of the genus *Rudbeckia*, of the sunflower subfamily. [Named by Linnaeus in honour of Swedish botanist(s) *Rudbeck*, father and/or son]

rudd *rud*, *n* the red-eye, a fish closely related to the roach. [Prob OE *rudu* redness]

rudder *rud'ər*, *n* a steering apparatus; a flat structure hinged to the stern of a ship or boat for steering; a vertical control surface for steering an aeroplane to right or left; anything used for steering, such as an aquatic animal's tail; something, eg a principle, that guides a person in life (*fig*). — *adj* **rudd'erless**. — **rudd'er-fish** the pilot-fish, or other fish that accompanies ships. [OE *rōthor* oar; Ger *Ruder* oar]

ruddle *rud'l*, *n* red ochre. — *vt* to mark with ruddle; to rouge coarsely. — Also **radd'le** (*rad'l*) or **redd'le** (*red'l*). — **rudd'leman** a person who digs or deals in ruddle. — Also **radd'leman** or **redd'leman**. [Cf **rud**]

ruddock *rud'ək*, *n* the redbreast (now *dialect*); a gold coin (*obs slang*); a kind of apple (*obs*). [OE *rudduc*; cf **rud**]

ruddy *rud'i*, *adj* red; reddish; of the colour of healthy skin in white-skinned people; rosy, glowing, bright; bloody (*euphem*): — *compar* **rudd'ier**, *superl* **rudd'iest**. — *vt* to make red: — *pr p* **rudd'ying**; *pa t* and *pa p* **rudd'ied**. — *adv* **rudd'ily**. — *n* **rudd'iness**. [OE *rudig*; cf **rud** and **red**[1]]

rude *rood*, *adj* uncultured; unskilled; discourteously unmannerly; vulgar; harsh; crude; undeveloped; unwrought; coarse; rugged; rough; roughly or unskilfully fashioned; violent; (of health) robust. — *adv* (*rare*) rudely. — *n* (*slang*) a rude boy (see below). — *adv* **rude'ly**. — *n* **rude'ness**. — *n* **rud'ery** (*colloq*). — *n* **rudesby** (*roodz'bi*; *Shakesp*) an uncivil fellow. — *n* **rud'ie** (*slang*) a rude boy (see below). — *adj* **rud'ish**. — **rude boy** a youth who dresses in Mod-style clothing. [L *rudis* rough]

ruderal *roo'dər-əl*, (*bot*) *n* and *adj* (a plant) growing in wasteland or among rubbish. [L *rūdus*, *-eris* rubbish]

Rüdesheimer or **Rudesheimer** *rü'* or *roo'dəs-hī-mər*, *n* a white Rhine wine. [*Rüdesheim*, opposite Bingen]

rudie. See under **rude**.

rudiment *rood'i-mənt*, *n* (*usu* in *pl*) a first principle or element; anything in a rude or first state; an organ in the first discernible stage; often applied to an organ that never develops beyond an early stage (*biol*). — *adj* **rudimental** (*-ment'l*) rudimentary. — *adv* **rudimen'tarily**. — *n* **rudimen'tariness**. — *adj* **rudimen'tary** of rudiments; elementary; crude, primitive or makeshift; in an early or arrested stage of development (*biol*). [L *rudīmentum*, from *rudis* rough, raw]

rue[1] *roo*, *n* a strong-smelling shrubby Mediterranean plant (*Ruta graveolens*), with pinnately divided leaves and greenish-yellow flowers, punningly (see **rue**[2]) symbolic of repentance, compunction or compassion; any other member of its genus; extended with qualification to other plants (see **goat's-rue**, **meadow-rue** and **wall-rue**). — *adj* **rue'-leaved**. [Fr *rue*, from L *rūta*, from Peloponnesian Gr *rhȳtē*]

rue[2] *roo*, *n* (*archaic*) repentance; regret; sorrow; pity. — *vt* to cause to feel regret, grieve (*archaic*); to be sorry for; to repent of; to wish not to have been or happened; to feel compassion for. — *vi* to feel remorse or regret; to take pity; to change one's mind, contemplate backing out: — *pr p* **rue'ing** or **ru'ing**; *pa t* and *pa p* **rued**. — *adj* **rue'ful** sorrowful; piteous; deplorable; mournful; melancholy. — *adv* **rue'fully**. — *n* **rue'fulness**. — *n* **rue'ing** or **ru'ing** repentance. — **rue'-bargain** (*dialect*) a forfeit for withdrawing from a bargain. — **take the rue** (*Scot*) to change one's mind, *esp* about an intended marriage. [OE *hrēow* (noun), *hrēowan* (verb); cf Ger *Reue*, OHGer *hriuwa* mourning]

ruelle *rü-el'*, *n* the space between a bed and the wall; a bed-chamber where aristocratic French women held receptions in the morning in the 17c and 18c; a morning reception; in France, a narrow lane. [Fr, dimin of *rue* street]

ruellia *rōō-el'i-ə, n* any plant of the *Ruellia* genus of the acanthus family. [Named after the French botanist Jean *Ruel* (1479–1537)]

rufescent *rōō-fes'ənt,* (*bot* and *zool*) *adj* inclining to redness. [L *rūfescens, -entis,* pr p of *rūfescere* to turn reddish, from *rūfus* reddish]

ruff[1] *ruf, n* a frill, *usu* starched and pleated, worn round the neck, *esp* in the Elizabethan and Jacobean periods; an animal's or bird's collar of long hair or feathers; a ruffed breed of domestic pigeon. — *vt* to provide with a ruff; to ruffle (*Spenser*); to strike without securing (*falconry*). — *adj* **ruffed** (*ruft*) having a ruff. [Cf **ruffle**[1]]

ruff[2] *ruf, n* a kind of sandpiper, the male of which has an erectile ruff during the breeding season: — *fem* **reeve** (*rēv*) or **ree** (*rē*). [Poss **ruff**[1], but the fem is a difficulty]

ruff[3] *ruf, n* an old card-game similar to whist or trumps also called **ruff and honours**); an act of trumping. — *vt* and *vi* to trump. [Perh connected with OFr *roffle,* Ital *ronfa* a card-game]

ruff[4] *ruf, n* a low vibrating beat of a drum; applause, *esp* with the feet (*Scot*). — *vt* and *vi* to beat or be beaten with a ruff; to applaud (*Scot*). — *n* **ruff'-a-duff'** drumming. — *n* **ruff'le** a ruff of drums. — *vi* to ruff. [Prob imit]

ruff[5] *ruf,* a variant of **rough**.

ruff[6] or **ruffe** *ruf, n* the pope, a small freshwater fish of the perch family, with one dorsal fin. — *n* **ruff'in** (*Spenser*) the ruff. [Perh **rough**]

ruff[7] or **ruffe** *ruf,* (*obs*) *n* pitch or height of exaltation; elation; excitement. [Cf Swed *ruff* spirit]

ruffian *ruf'i-ən* or *ruf'yən, n* a brutal, violent person; a bully. — *adj* brutal; ruffianly; violent. — *vi* to behave like a ruffian. — *adj* **ruff'ianish**. — *n* **ruff'ianism**. — *adj* **ruff'ianly**. — *adj* **ruff'ian-like**. [OFr *ruffian* (Fr *rufien*); source obscure]

ruffin. See under **ruff**[6].

ruffle[1] *ruf'l, vt* to make uneven, disturb the smoothness of; to cause (feathers) to stand up or erect; to wrinkle; to disorder; to agitate; to turn the leaves of hastily; to disturb the equanimity of, to irritate, discompose. — *vi* to wrinkle; to grow rough; to flutter. — *n* a frill on a garment, *esp* at the wrist or neck; a bird's ruff; a ripple or disturbance on an otherwise even surface; annoyance; a quarrel; agitation. — *adj* **ruff'led** having a ruffle. — *n* **ruff'ler** a plate attached to a sewing-machine, for making ruffles. — *n* and *adj* **ruff'ling**. [Cf LGer *ruffelen*]

ruffle[2] *ruf'l,* (*archaic*) *vi* to struggle; to bluster; to swagger. — *vt* to handle roughly or offensively; to snatch (*Shakesp*). — *n* an encounter, a tumult; bustle (*Shakesp*). — *n* **ruff'ler** a beggar posing as a maimed soldier or sailor (*obs*); a swaggerer. [Origin obscure]

ruffle[3]. See under **ruff**[4].

ruffler. See under **ruffle**[1,2].

rufiyaa *rōō'fi-yä, n* the standard monetary unit of the Maldives (100 *laaris*). — Also **rupee** (qv).

rufous *rōō'fəs, adj* reddish or brownish-red. [L *rūfus,* related to *ruber* red]

rug[1] *rug, n* a coarse, rough, woollen fabric (*obs*); a thick, heavy floor-mat, *esp* for the hearth; a thick covering or wrap, eg for travelling; a toupee (*slang; orig* and *esp US*). — *adj* made of rug. — *n* **rugg'ing**. — **rug'-gown** a gown of rug; a watchman (*obs*). — *adj* **rug'-head'ed** (*Shakesp*) shock-headed. — **pull the rug (out) from under** (*fig*) to leave (a person) without support, defence, etc by a sudden action or discovery. [Cf Norw *rugga, rogga* coarse coverlet, Swed *rugg* coarse hair]

rug[2] *rug,* (*Scot*) *vt* to pull roughly. — *n* a tug; a haul, share. — *n* **rugg'ing**. [Prob Scand]

rug[3] *rug,* (*old slang*) *adj* secure; snug.

rugate. See **rugose**.

Rugby or **rugby** *rug'bi, n* a form of football using an oval ball which (unlike *Association*) permits carrying the ball. — Also (*colloq*) **rugg'er**. — **Rugby fives** the most usual version of fives (qv) played with a back, as well as front and side walls to the court; **Rugby football** or **Rugby Union football** the original form of the game, with 15 players; **Rugby League football** a modified form of the game subject to professional rules, with 13 players; **rugby shirt** or **jersey** a thick cotton shirt of a style worn for rugby, *usu* in a strong, single colour or stripes, with white collar and placket. [From *Rugby* school, Warwickshire]

rugelach or **ruggelach** *rōōg'ə-lahh,* (*Jewish cookery*) *n pl* small, crescent-shaped pastries filled with fruit, nuts, cheese, etc. [Yiddish *rugelekh,* pl of *rugele*]

rugged *rug'id, adj* rough; uneven; uncouth; toilsome; (of facial features) giving an appearance of strength or suggesting experience of (*esp* physical) hardships; sturdy and rough; massively irregular; robust, vigorous; stormy (now *US*). — *vt* **rugg'edize** or **-ise** to make rugged; to make so as to withstand rough handling. — *adv* **rugg'edly**. — *n* **rugg'edness**. — *adj* **rugg'y** (*dialect*) rough; uneven. [Prob related to **rug**[1]]

ruggelach. See **rugelach**.

rugger. See **Rugby**.

rugose *rōō'gōs* or *rōō-gōs', adj* wrinkled; covered with sunken lines. — Also **ru'gate** (*-gāt* or *-gət*; L *rugāre* to wrinkle) or **ru'gous**. — *adv* **ru'gosely** (or *-gōs'*). — *n* **rugosity** (*-gos'i-ti*). — *adj* **ru'gūlose** finely rugose. [L *rūgōsus,* from *rūga* a wrinkle]

ruin *rōō'in* or *rōō'in, n* downfall; collapse; overthrow; complete destruction; wreck; loss of fortune or means; bankruptcy; undoing; seduction or departure from chastity of life; a downfallen, collapsed, wrecked or irretrievably damaged state (often in *pl*); the cause of a person's ruin; broken-down remains, *esp* of a building (often in *pl*); devastation; inferior gin (*esp* as *blue ruin* and *mother's ruin*; *slang*). — *vt* to reduce or bring to ruin; to spoil. — *vi* (*archaic*) to fall headlong; to go to ruin. — *adj* **ru'inable**. — *vt* **ru'inate** to ruin, to destroy (*Shakesp*); to demolish (*archaic*); to reduce to poverty (*archaic*); to fling headlong (*Spenser; reflexive*). — *adj* (*archaic*) in ruins; ruined. — *n* **ruinā'tion** the or an act of ruining; the state of being ruined. — *adj* **ru'ined**. — *n* **ru'iner**. — *n* and *adj* **ru'ining**. — *adj* **ru'inous** fallen to ruins; decayed; bringing ruin; (of noise) of or resembling crashing (*Milton*). — *adv* **ru'inously**. — *n* **ru'inousness**. — **ruin agate** or **marble** agate or marble with irregular markings like ruins. [L *ruīna,* from *ruere* to tumble down]

ruing. See under **rue**[2].

rukh. Same as **roc**.

rule *rōōl, n* a straight-edged strip used as a guide in drawing straight lines or as a measuring-rod, or means of mechanical calculation; a type-high strip of metal for printing straight lines; a straight line printed or drawn on paper, etc; a dash; a straight-edge used for securing a flat surface in plaster or cement; a straight shaft of light (*Milton*); government; control; prevalence; that which is normal or usual; conformity to good or established usage; well-regulated condition; conduct (*obs*); misrule (*obs*); a principle; a standard; a code of regulations, such as of a religious order; a regulation, whether imposed by authority or voluntarily adopted; an order of a court; a guiding principle; a method or process of achieving a result; a regulation that must not be transgressed; a maxim or formula that it is generally best, but not compulsory, to follow; (in *pl*) an area around a prison in which privileged prisoners were allowed to live (*hist*); the privilege of living there (*hist*); (in *pl*) Australian football (see **Australian rules**). — *vt* to draw with a ruler; to mark with (*esp* parallel) straight lines; to govern; to control; to manage; to prevail upon; to determine or declare authoritatively to be; to determine, decree. — *vi* to exercise power (with *over*); to decide; to be prevalent; to stand or range in price. — *adj* **ru'lable** governable; allowable (*US*). — *adj* **rule'less** (*Spenser* **ru'lesse**) unruly, lawless; without rules. — *n* **ru'ler** a strip or roller for ruling lines; a person who rules. — *vt* to strike with a ruler. — *n* **ru'lership**. — *adj* **ru'ling** predominant; prevailing; reigning; exercising authority. — *n* a determination by a judge, *esp* an oral decision; the act of making ruled lines. — *adj* **ru'ly** orderly in behaviour. — **Rule 43** a UK prison rule allowing a prisoner who is thought to need protection from other prisoners to be held in solitary confinement; a prisoner held under this rule. — *adj* **rule-of-thumb'** according to rule of thumb (see below). — **as a rule** usually; **be ruled** take advice; **rule of faith** in polemical theology, the authoritative sources of the doctrines of the faith; **rule of the road** the regulations to be observed in traffic by land, water or air (eg in Britain drivers, riders and cyclists take the left side in meeting, and the right in overtaking); **rule of three** the method of finding the fourth term of a proportion when three are given; **rule of thumb** any rough-and-ready practical method; **rule** (or **rules**) **OK** (*slang*; *orig* a gang slogan, chiefly found in graffiti) to be dominant, have the ascendancy; **rule out** to exclude as a choice or possibility. [OFr *reule* (Fr *règle*), from L *rēgula*, from *regere* to rule]

rullion *rul'yən*, (*Scot*) *n* a rawhide shoe. [OE *rifeling*]

rullock. See **rowlock**.

ruly. See under **rule**.

rum[1] *rum*, *n* a spirit distilled from fermented sugar-cane juice or from molasses; intoxicating liquor generally (*US*). — *n* **rum'bo** rum-punch: — *pl* **rum'bos**. — *adj* **rumm'y**. — **rum baba** baba au rhum (see under **baba**); **rum'-blossom** or **rum'-bud** a pimple on the nose; **rum-butt'er** a mixture of butter and sugar with rum, etc; **rum-punch'** punch made with rum; **rum'-runner** (*hist*) a person involved in smuggling alcohol into the US during Prohibition, *esp* by boat; **rum'-running**; **rum'-shop**; **rum'-shrub** a liqueur of rum, sugar, lime or lemon juice, etc. [Perh from **rumbullion** or related form]

rum[2] *rum*, *adj* good (*obs slang*); queer, droll, odd, strange (*slang*). — *n* (*archaic*) a strange person. — *adv* **rum'ly**. — *adv* **rumm'ily**. — *n* **rumm'iness**. — *adj* **rumm'ish**. — *adj* **rumm'y**. — *n* **rum'ness**. [Cant]

rumal. See **romal**.

Ruman and **Rumanian**. See **Romanian**.

Rumansch and **Rumonsch**. See **Romansch**.

rumba or **rhumba** *rŏŏm'bə* or *rum'bə*, *n* a lively Afro-Cuban dance following a square pattern; a ballroom dance based on a modification of this; a piece of music for the dance. — *vi* to dance the rumba. [Sp]

rumbelow *rum'bi-lō*, *n* a meaningless word, occurring as a refrain in old sea-songs.

rumble[1] *rum'bl*, *vi* to make a low heavy grumbling or rolling noise; to move with such a noise; to be involved in a gang fight (*slang*, *esp NAm*). — *vt* to give forth, or to agitate or move, with such a sound; to inform against, betray to the police (*slang*). — *n* a sound of rumbling; low-frequency noise produced in vinyl disk recording when the turntable is not dynamically balanced (*acoustics*); a seat for servants behind a carriage, or for extra passengers in a two-seater car (also **rumble seat**); a quarrel, disturbance, gang fight (*slang*). — *n* **rum'bler**. — *n* and *adj* **rum'bling**. — *adv* **rum'blingly**. — *adj* **rum'bly**. — **rumble strip** one of a set of rough-textured strips set into a road surface to warn drivers (by tyre noise) of a hazard ahead; **rum'blede-thump** or **rum'bledethumps** (*Scot*) a dish of mashed potatoes with butter and seasoning, or mixed with cabbage or turnip; **rum'ble-tum'ble** a rumble seat; a lumbering vehicle; a tumbling motion. [Cf Du *rommelen*, Ger *rummeln*]

rumble[2] *rum'bl*, (*slang*) *vt* to grasp; to see through, discover the truth about. [Origin obscure]

rumblegumption. See **rumgumption**.

rumbo. See under **rum**[1].

rumbullion *rum-bul'yən*, (*obs*) *n* an older name for **rum**[1]. [Origin obscure]

rumbustious *rum-bust'yəs*, (*colloq*) *adj* boisterous. — Also (*archaic*) **rumbus'tical**. [Prob **robust**]

rume. A Shakespearian spelling of **rheum**.

rumelgumption. See **rumgumption**.

rumen *rŏŏ'men*, *n* the paunch or first stomach of a ruminant: — *pl* **ru'mina**. [L *rūmen*, *-inis* gullet]

Rumex *rŏŏ'meks*, *n* the dock and sorrel genus of *Polygonaceae*. [L *rumex*, *-icis* a kind of dart, also sorrel (from its hastate leaves)]

rumfustian *rum-fus'chən*, (*archaic*) *n* a hot drink, a kind of negus. [**rum**[1] and **fustian**]

rumgumption *rum-gum'shən* or *-gump'shən*, (*Scot*) *n* common sense. — Also **rumelgump'tion**, **rummelgump'tion**, **rumlegump'tion**, **rummlegump'tion** or **rumblegump'tion** (*rum'l-*).

rumina. See **rumen**.

ruminant *rŏŏ'min-ənt*, *n* an animal that chews the cud. — *adj* cud-chewing; meditative. — *n pl* **Ruminantia** (*-an'shyə* or *-shə*) the cud-chewing division of the even-toed ungulates. — *adv* **ru'minantly**. — *vi* **ru'mināte** to chew the cud; to regurgitate for chewing; to meditate (on or upon). — *vt* to chew over again; to muse on. — *adj* (*bot*) mottled as if chewed. — *adv* **ru'minātingly**. — *n* **rumina'tion**. — *adj* **ru'minative**. — *adv* **ru'minatively**. — *n* **ru'minātor**. [L *rūmināre*, *-ātum*, from *rūmen*, *-inis* the gullet]

rumkin[1] *rum'kin*, (*obs*) *n* a kind of drinking-vessel.

rumkin[2] *rum'kin*, *n* a tailless fowl. [Appar from **rump** and **-kin**]

rumlegumption. See **rumgumption**.

rummage *rum'ij*, *n orig* stowage of casks, etc in a ship's hold; a thorough search, eg by customs officers; an overhauling search; (*Shakesp* **romage**) commotion, upheaval. — *vt* to arrange, *orig* in a ship's hold (*archaic*); to ransack; to overhaul; to search; to stir. — *vi* to make a search. — *n* **rumm'ager**. — **rummage sale** (*esp NAm*) a sale at which buyers are allowed to rummage among the goods; any sale of odds and ends or unwanted goods. [Fr *arrumage* (now *arrimage*) stowage]

rummelgumption or **rummlegumption**. See under **rumgumption**.

rummer *rum'ər*, *n* a large drinking-glass; the quantity contained in this. [Du *roemer*; Ger *Römer*]

rummy[1]. See under **rum**[1,2].

rummy[2] *rum'i*, *n* a card-game in which cards are drawn from the stock and sequences, triplets, etc are laid on the table.

Rumonsch. See **Romansch**.

rumour or (*NAm*) **rumor**, *rŏŏ'mər*, *n* clamour, outcry (*archaic*); repute, renown (*Shakesp* and *Milton*); general talk, hearsay; gossip; a current story, *esp* unverified or based on partial evidence. — *vt* to circulate or make known by rumour. — *adj* **ru'morous** resounding (*archaic*); full of rumours; of the nature of rumours; vaguely heard. — *n* **ru'mourer**. — **rumour mill** a place or institution that continually creates or spreads rumours. [OFr, from L *rūmor*, *-ōris* a noise]

rump *rump*, *n* the hind part of an animal's body, the root of the tail with parts adjoining; a cut of beef between the loin and the round; (in birds) the uropygium; the buttocks; a remnant (*usu contemptuous*). — *vt* to turn one's back upon; to clean out of money (*Scot*). — *n* **Rump'er** (*Eng hist*) a member or supporter of the Rump Parliament (see below). — *n* **rum'ple** (*Scot*) a rump. — *adj* **rump'less**. — *n* **rump'y** a Manx cat; a tailless chicken. — **rump'-bone** the coccyx; **rump'-end**. — *adj* **rump'-fed** (*Shakesp*) *prob* with well-nourished rump. — **rump'le-bane** (*Scot*) rump-bone; **rump'-post** the share bone or pygostyle of a bird; **rump steak** beef steak cut from the thigh near the rump. — **the Rump** or **Rump Parliament** (*Eng hist*) the remnant of the Long Parliament, after Pride's expulsion (1648) of about a hundred Presbyterian royalist members. [Scand; cf Dan *rumpe*, Swed and Norw *rumpa*, ON *rumpr*, Ger *Rumpf*, Du *romp*]

rumple[1] *rum'pl*, *n* a fold, crease or wrinkle (now *rare*). — *vt* to crush out of shape, crease, wrinkle; to make uneven or disordered. [Du *rompel*; cf OE *hrimpan* to wrinkle]

rumple[2]. See under **rump**.

rumpus *rum'pəs*, *n* an uproar; a disturbance. — **rumpus room** (*orig NAm*) a room in which children can play freely.

rumpy. See under **rump**.

rumpy-pumpy *rump-i-pump'i*, (*slang*) *n* sexual intercourse. — Also **rump'y**.

rumti-iddity *rum-ti-id'i-ti*, **rumpti-iddity** *rump-ti-id'i-ti* or **rum-ti-tum** *rum'ti-tum'*, *interj* a meaningless refrain.

run *run*, formerly also **ren** *ren*; (*Scot*) **rin** *rin*, *vi* to proceed by lifting one foot before replacing the other; to go swiftly, at more than a walking pace; to hasten; to proceed quickly; to take oneself somewhere; to flee; to progress, *esp* smoothly and quickly; to go about freely; to ride at a running pace; to roll; to revolve; (of a film, video or audio tape, etc) to be rolling between spools, be playing or recording; to go with a gliding motion; to slip; to go on wheels; to travel, cover a distance; to make a short journey; to swim in shoals; to ascend a river for spawning; to ply; (of notes, words, etc) to have a definite sequence; (*esp* of a machine) to proceed through a sequence of operations, to work or go; to follow a course; (of a play or film) to be staged or screened regularly over a period of time; to flow; to spread, diffuse (*esp* of a colour), to spread through a fabric when wetted; (of a pipe, tap, etc) to emit or transmit a flow; to overflow, leak; (of a bath) to be being filled with water from the taps; to melt; to fuse; to curdle (now *dialect*); to have a course, stretch or extent; (of a bill, etc) to amount to, total (with *to*); to range; to average; to elapse; to tend; to come to be, become, pass (*archaic*); to be current; to be valid; to recur repeatedly or remain persistently (in the mind, in the family, etc); to come undone, eg by the dropping or breaking of a stitch or thread; to compete in a race; to be a candidate (*NAm*). — *vt* to cause to run; to chase, hunt; to drive forward; to thrust; to pierce; to drive; to pass quickly; to drive through (a red traffic light or stop signal; chiefly *NAm*); to range, run about or throughout; to hurry through; to enter, promote, put forward (eg a horse, candidate or protégé); to render, by running or otherwise; to conduct, manage; to follow; to traverse; to cause to extend, form in a line; to sew lightly and quickly; to shoot along or down; to perform, achieve or score by running, or as if by running; to flee or desert from; to incur; to risk and pass the hazard of; to smuggle; to have or keep current or running; to publish (a regular paper, magazine, etc); to publish (an article or advertisement) in a newspaper or magazine, *esp* in successive issues; to show (a film, video or TV programme); to compete with in a race; to press or put to it, in competition or difficulty; to coagulate; to fuse; to emit, discharge, flow with; to be filling (a bath) with water from the taps; to execute (a program; *comput*); to control the activities of (*esp* a spy): — *pr p* **runn'ing**; *pa t* **ran**; *pa p* **run**. — *n* an act, spell or manner of running; a journey, trip; distance, time or quantity run; a circuit of duty, such as a delivery round, etc; a continuous stretch, spell, series, or period; a shoal, migration or migrating body; a roulade (*music*); a spell of being in general demand; a rush for payment, as upon a bank; a unit of scoring in cricket; a batsman's passage from one popping-crease to the other; a circuit in baseball; flow or discharge; course; prevalence; the ordinary or average kind, the generality; a track; a path made by animals; a small stream (*US*); a range of feeding-ground; a tract of land used for raising stock (*Austr* and *NZ*); an enclosure for chickens, etc; freedom of access to all parts; the playing of a salmon; general direction; a ladder in knitting or knitted fabrics, *esp* stockings; the complete execution of a program, suite of programs or routine (*comput*); (in *pl*, with *the*) diarrhoea (*colloq*). — *adj* having been poured, smuggled or coagulated; having run. — *n* **run'let** a runnel. — *adj* **runn'able** (of a stag) fit for hunting. — *n* **runn'er** a person who, or thing which, runs or can run; a fugitive; a racer; a messenger; an agent; a tout; a person employed to collect information; a rooting stem that runs along the ground; a rope to increase the power of a tackle; a smuggler; a Bow Street officer (*hist*); a ring, loop, etc through which anything slides or runs; the part on which a sledge, a skate or a drawer slides; the passage by which metal is poured into a mould; a strip of cloth, *usu* embroidered, as a table ornament; a revolving millstone, *esp* the upper of a pair; a slice across a carcase of beef below the breast (*Scot*); a climbing plant of the kidney-bean genus *Phaseolus multiflorus*, (also called **runn'er-bean** or **scarlet-runn'er**); a breed of domestic duck also called **runner duck**); a vessel for conveying fish, oysters, etc; a long narrow strip of carpet used for passages and staircases. — *adj* **runn'ing** racing; habitually going at a run; current; successive; continuous; flowing; discharging; easy; cursive; itinerant; done at or with a run; hasty. — *n* the action of the verb; the pace; the lead; the competitive state. — *adv* **runn'ingly**. — *adj* **runn'y** inclined to run or liquefy. — **run'about** a gadabout; a vagabond; a small light car, boat or aeroplane; **run'around** a runabout (car); see also **get** and **give the runaround** (below); **run'away** a fugitive; a horse that bolts; a flight. — *adj* fleeing; done by or in flight; uncontrolled; overwhelming. — **run'-back** the area behind the base-line at either end of a tennis court; **run chart** (*comput*) a diagram prepared from a systems flowchart which represents the sequence of computer operations. — *adj* **run-down'** in weakened health; (of a building, etc) dilapidated. — *n* (*usu* **run'down**) a reduction in numbers; a statement bringing together all the main items, a summary (see also **run down** below). — *adj* **run'flat** (of a tyre) able to be safely driven on for a considerable distance when punctured, without sustaining further damage. — **run'-in** an approach; a quarrel, argument (*colloq*; see also **run in** below); **runner-up'** a competitor (*orig* a dog) that holds out to the last heat; the competitor next after the winner; any of a number of contestants coming close behind the winner: — *pl* **runners-up'**; **running back** (*Am football*) a back who is expected to advance the ball from the scrimmage by running with it; **running balance** one computed and shown every time a transaction or an alteration to an account occurs, such as in a bank statement (also called *continuous balance*); **running banquet** a slight or hasty collation; **running battle** a battle between pursuers and pursued; a continuing skirmish (also *fig*); **runn'ing-board** a footboard along the side of a motor car or (*US*) locomotive; **running commentary** a commentary accompanying a text; a broadcast description of a game or other event in progress; **running costs** the costs of materials and labour, etc required for the normal operation of a machine, office or business company; **running dog** (*derog*) in political jargon, a slavish follower; **running fight** a fight between pursuer and pursued; **running fire** (*military*) a rapid succession of firing; **running footman** a servant who ran before or alongside a horse-rider or carriage; **running gag** (*colloq*) a joke that continually reappears throughout a play, programme, etc; **runn'ing-gear** the wheels and axles of a vehicle; **runn'ing-hand** a cursive handwriting script produced without lifting the pen, etc between letters of the same word; **running head** same as **running title** below; **running knot** a knot that will form a noose on pulling; **running lights** the lights shown by vessels between sunset and sunrise; small lights at the front and rear of a car which remain on while the engine is running; **running mate** a runner who makes the pace for another; a horse teamed with another, or making the pace for another; the candidate for the less important of two associated offices, *esp* the candidate for the vice-presidency considered in relation to the presidential candidate (*US politics*); **running ornament** an ornament in which the design is continuous; **running repairs** minor repairs; **running rigging** (*naut*) all the rigging except the shrouds, stays and lower masthead pendants; **running sore** one which discharges pus; a continual irritation, a long-standing problem; **running stitch** a straight stitch worked in a line with stitches and spaces between of equal length, often used to gather fabric; **running time** the duration, *usu* given in minutes, of a cinema film; **running title** the title of a book, chapter, etc printed repeatedly in the upper margin of each or every alternate page; **run'-off** a race held to resolve a dead heat or other uncertain result (also *fig*); rainwater which drains into rivers, rather than being absorbed into the soil; urination (*slang*). — *adj* **run-of-the-mill'** constituting an ordinary fair sample, not selected; mediocre. — *adj* **run-on'** in verse, carrying the sense on beyond the end of the line (see also **run on** below). — *adj* **run'-resist** (of stockings or tights) knitted with a stitch which does not ladder readily. — **run'-through** an instance of running through (see **run through** below); **run time** the time needed for the execution of a computer program; **run-time error** (*comput*) same as **execution error**; **run-time system** (*comput*) a complete set of software which supports a high-level language and enables programs to be executed; **run'-up** an approach (*lit* and *fig*; see also **run up** below); **run'way** a trail, track or passageway; a firm strip of ground for aircraft to take off from and land on. — **do a runner** (*colloq*) to run away, *esp* to leave a shop, restaurant, etc quickly, without paying; **give (someone) the runaround** (*colloq*) to behave repeatedly in a vague, indecisive or deceptive way towards; to reply to a question or meet a request with evasion; **get the runaround** (*colloq*) to be treated in this way; **in the long run** in the end or final result; **in** or **out of the running** competing with or without a fair chance of success; **make** or **take up the running** to take the lead; to set the pace; **on the run** (*colloq*) pursued, *esp* by the police; **run across** to come upon by accident; **run after** to pursue; **run along** (*colloq*) off you go; **run a temperature** to be feverish; **run away with** to take away; to win (a prize, etc) easily; **run down** to pursue to exhaustion or capture; to collide with and knock over or sink; to treat or speak to disparagingly; to become unwound or exhausted; **run dry** to cease to flow; to come to an end; **run for it** (*colloq*) to attempt to escape, run away from; **run hard** or **close** to press hard behind; **run in** to go in; to arrest and take to a lock-up; to insert a word, etc, without making a break or new paragraph (*printing*); to bring (new machinery, a car, etc) into full working condition by a period of careful operation; **run in the blood** or **family** to be a hereditary characteristic or quality; **run into** to meet, come across; to extend into; **run into debt** to get into debt; **run it fine** to allow very little margin of time, etc; **run itself** (of a business enterprise, etc) to need little supervision or active direction; **run low** to run short; **run off** to cause to flow out; to take impressions of, to print; to repeat, recount; **run off one's feet** exhausted by overwork; **run off with** (*colloq*) to take away, steal; to elope with; **run on** to talk on and on; to continue in the same line, and not in a new paragraph (*printing*); to print extra copies of something, eg an advertisement for trade distribution; **run one's eyes over** to look at cursorily; **run out** to run short; to terminate, expire; to leak, let out liquid; to put out (a batsman or batswoman running between the wickets and not yet in his or her ground); dismissed thus; **run out of** to have no more of; **run out on** (*colloq*) to abandon, desert; **run over** to overflow; to overthrow; to go over cursorily; (of a road vehicle) to knock down (a person or animal); **run scared** (*slang*) to be frightened; **run short** to come to be short, lacking or exhausted; **run through** to pierce through with a sword, etc; to spend wastefully; to read or perform quickly or cursorily but completely; **run to** to be sufficient for; **run to earth** see under **earth**; **run to ground** see under **ground**[2]; **run together** to mingle or blend; **run to seed** see under **seed**; **run up** to make or mend hastily; to build hurriedly; to string up, hang; to send the ball rolling or flying low towards the hole (*golf*); to incur increasingly; **take a running jump** (*slang*) an expression of impatience, contempt, etc. [OE *rinnan, irnan, iernan* to run; causative *rennan* to curdle; see also **earn**[2]]

runagate *run'ə-gāt*, *n* a vagabond; a renegade; an apostate; a fugitive. — Also *adj*. [**renegade** influenced by **run** and **agate**[2]]

runch *runsh*, (*Scot* and *Eng*) *n* charlock; wild radish. [Origin obscure]

runcible *run'si-bl*, *adj appar* a nonsense-word of Edward Lear's, whose phrase *runcible spoon* has been applied to a pickle-fork with broad prongs and one sharp, curved prong.

runcinate *runs'in-āt*, (*bot*) *adj* with backward-pointing lobes. [L *runcina* a plane, formerly misunderstood as a saw]

rund. Same as **roon**.

rundale *run'dāl*, *n* a system of holding land in single holdings made up of detached pieces; land or a share of it so held. — Also *adj*. [**run** and *dale*, N Eng form of **dole**[1]]

rundle *run'dl*, *n* a round, a ladder rung; a ring, circle, disc or ball. — *adj* **run'dled**. [**roundel**]

rundlet *rund'lit* or **runlet** *run'lit*, (*archaic*) *n* a liquid measure equal to *approx* 15 gallons (US 18 gallons); a small barrel. [Fr *rondelet*]

rune *rōōn*, *n* any of the letters of the futhork or ancient Germanic alphabet; any of a set of tiles inscribed with such letters used for fortune-telling; a secret, a mystic symbol, sentence, spell or song; a song, stanza or canto of a Finnish poem, *esp* of the *Kalevala* (Finn *runo*, related to ON *rūn*). — *adj* **runed**. — *adj* **ru'nic** of, relating to, written in or inscribed with runes; ancient Scandinavian or Northern; in the style of ancient Northumbrian and Celtic interlacing ornament. — **rune'craft** knowledge of runes; **rune'-singer**; **rune'=stave** (OE *rūnstæf*) a runic letter. [OE and ON *rūn* mystery, rune; Gothic and OHGer *rūna*]

rung[1] *rung*, *n* a spoke; a crossbar or rail; a ladder round or step; a ship's floor-timber; a cudgel (*Scot*). [OE *hrung*; Ger *Runge*]

rung[2] *rung*. See **ring**[1,2].

rung[3] *rung*, *adj* having a ring through the nose. [**ring**[1]]

runic. See under **rune**.

runkle *rung'kl*, *n* a wrinkle, crease. — *vt* and *vi* to wrinkle; to crease. [Prob Scand; cf **ruck**[1] and **ruckle**[2]]

runlet[1]. See under **run**.

runlet[2]. See **rundlet**.

runnable. See under **run**.

runnel *run'l*, *n* a little brook. [OE *rynel*, dimin of *ryne* a stream, from *rinnan* to run]

runner and **running**. See under **run**.

runnet. Dialect variant of **rennet**[1].

runnion. See **ronyon**.

runny. See under **run**.

runrig *run'rig*, (*Scot*) *n* a form of land-tenure, the same as **rundale**. — Also *adj* and *adv*. [**run** and **rig**[2]]

runt *runt*, *n* a small, stunted or old ox or cow; a small pig, *esp* the smallest of a litter; anything undersized; a large breed of domestic pigeon; a dead tree-stump or trunk; a cabbage stem, *esp* withered; an apple core (*Scot*); a vague term of reproach, *esp* to the old or boorish. — *adj* **runt'ed**. — *adj* **runt'ish**. — *adj* **runt'y**. [Origin uncertain]

Runyonesque *run-yən-esk'*, *adj* in the style of the American writer A Damon *Runyon* (1884–1946), portrayer of gangsters in their milder moments.

rupee *rōō-pē'*, *n* monetary unit and nickel (*orig* silver) coin of India, Pakistan and Bhutan (equal to 100 paisas), Nepal (100 pice), and Sri Lanka, Mauritius, the Seychelles and the Maldive Islands (100 cents). [Urdu *rūpiyah*, from Sans *rūpya* wrought silver]

Rupert's drop *rōō'pərts drop*, *n* a tailed bulb formed by dropping molten glass in water, bursting when the tail is broken, reputedly discovered by Prince *Rupert* (1619–82).

rupestrian *rōō-pes'tri-ən*, *adj* composed of rock; inscribed on rock. [L *rūpēs* rock]

rupia *rōō'pi-ə*, *n* a skin ulcer covered by crusts of dried secretion and dead tissue. [Gr *rhypos* filth]

rupiah *rōō'pi-ə*, *n* the standard unit of currency of Indonesia (100 sen): — *pl* **ru'piah** or **ru'piahs**. [Hindi, rupee]

rupicoline *rōō-pik'ō-līn* or **rupicolous** *rōō-pik'ō-ləs*, *adj* rock-dwelling. [L *rūpēs* a rock, and *colere* to inhabit]

rupture *rup'chər*, *n* a breach, breaking or bursting; the state of being broken; breach of harmony, relations, or negotiations; a hernia, *esp* abdominal. — *vt* and *vi* to break or burst. — **rup'turewort** a caryophyllaceous plant (*Herniaria*), once thought to cure hernia. [LL *ruptūra*, from L *rumpere*, *ruptum* to break]

rural *rōō'rl*, *adj* of, relating to or suggesting the country or countryside. — *n* (*obs*) a country-dweller. — *n* **ru'ralism**. — *n* **ru'ralist**. — *n* **rurality** (*-al'i-ti*). — *n* **ruralizā'tion** or **-s-**. — *vt* **ru'ralize** or **-ise** to render rural. — *vi* to become rural; to adopt rural habits, way of life, etc, to rusticate. — *adv* **ru'rally**. — *n* **ru'ralness**. — *adj* **ruridecanal** (*rōō-ri-di-kā'nl*; sometimes *-dek'ən-l*) of a rural dean or deanery. — **rural dean** see under **dean**[2]. [L *rūrālis*, from *rūs*, *rūris* the country]

Ruritania *rōōr-i-tān'yə*, *n* a fictitious land of historical romance (in SE Europe) created by Anthony Hope; any idealistically exciting or romantic place, situation, etc. — *n* and *adj* **Ruritān'ian**.

rurp *rûrp*, (*orig US*) *n* a very small hook-like piton used in mountaineering. [Acronym of *r*ealized *u*ltimate *r*eality *p*iton]

ruru *rōō'rōō*, (*NZ*) *n*. Same as **mopoke**. [Maori]

rusa[1] *rōō'sə*, *n* any large E Indian deer of the genus *Rusa*, *esp* the sambar. — *adj* **ru'sine** (*-sīn*). [Malay *rūsa*]

rusa[2] or **roosa** *rōō'sə*, *n* an Indian grass (**rusa grass**) from which an aromatic oil (**rusa oil**) is distilled. [Hindi *rūsā*]

rusalka *rōō-sal'kə*, *n* a Russian water-nymph. [Russ]

ruscus *rus'kəs*, *n* any plant of the *Ruscus* genus of European evergreen shrubs (family *Liliaceae*). [L *rūscum* butcher's-broom]

ruse *rōōz*, *n* a trick, stratagem, artifice. — *adj* **rusé** (*rü-zā*; *Fr*) artful, deceitful, cunning. — **ruse contre ruse** (*rüz kɔ̃tr' rüz*; *Fr*) cunning against cunning; **ruse de guerre** (*də ger*; *Fr*) a stratagem of war. [OFr *ruse*, from *ruser*, *reüser* to get out of the way, double on one's tracks; see **rush**[1]]

rush[1] *rush*, *vi* to move forward with haste, impetuosity or rashness; to run with the ball, or gain ground by so doing (*Am football*). — *vt* to force out of place; to hasten or hustle forward, or into any action; to move, transport, drive or push in great haste; to capture, secure, surmount or pass by a rush; to provide a series of social entertainments for (a freshman) as an inducement to join a fraternity or sorority (*US*); to defraud (*colloq*); to overcharge (*colloq*). — *n* a swift impetuous forward movement; a sudden simultaneous or general movement (eg a *gold rush*); an onset; a stampede; a move to push through a line of defenders while in possession of the ball (*Rugby* and *Am football*); a migratory movement or body; a run upon, or sudden great demand for, anything; (in *pl*) an unedited print of a motion picture scene or series of scenes for immediate viewing by the film makers; the viewing of such a print; rapidly increased activity; bustling activity; a series of social entertainments provided for prospective members of a fraternity or sorority (*US*); a feeling of euphoria experienced after the taking of a drug, eg heroin or amphetamine (*slang*); a sound of rushing; a collective name for a group of pochards. — *adj* (*colloq*) done or needing to be done quickly, such as *rush job*, *rush order*, etc. — *n* **rushee'** (*US*) a prospective member of a fraternity or sorority taking part in a rush. — *n* **rush'er** a person who or thing which rushes; a player who specializes in rushing (*Am football*). — **rush hour** one of the times during the day of maximum movement of people or traffic (also *adj*). — **rush one's fences** to act precipitately. [Anglo-Fr *russcher*, OFr *reusser*, *reüser*, *ruser* (Fr *ruser*); see **ruse**]

rush[2] *rush*, *n* any plant of the grasslike marsh-growing genus *Juncus*; a stalk or round stalklike leaf of such a plant; extended to various more or less similar plants (see **bulrush**, **clubrush**, **Dutch rush**, **scouring-rush** and **wood-rush**); a rushlight, a rush wick; a type of something of no value or importance; a rush-ring (*Shakesp*). — *adj* of rush or rushes. — *vt* to make or strew with rushes. — *vi* to gather rushes. — *adj* **rush'en** (*archaic*) made of rushes. — *n* **rush'iness**. — *adj* **rush'like**. — *adj* **rush'y** rushlike; full of or made of rushes. — **rush'-bearing** a traditional annual festival in rural N England marked by carrying rushes to strew the local church; the day of this festival. — *adj* **rush'-bottomed** (of a chair etc) having a seat made with rushes. — **rush'-candle** or **rush'light** a candle or night-light having a wick of rush-pith; a small, feeble light. — *adj* **rush'-grown**. — **rush'-holder** a stand for a rushlight; **rush'-ring** a ring of plaited rush, formerly sometimes used as an improvised wedding-ring. — *adj* **rush'y-fringed**. [OE *risce*; Ger *Risch*]

rusine. See **rusa**[1].

rusk *rusk*, *n* a small, hard, crisp cake, made by rebaking slices of enriched bread, *esp* given to young children. [Sp *rosca* a roll, twist; origin unknown]

rusma *ruz'mə*, *n* a depilatory of lime and orpiment. [Appar Turk *khirisma*, from Gr *chrīsma* ointment]

russel *rus'l*, *n* a ribbed cotton and woollen material. — **russ'el-cord** a kind of rep made of cotton and wool. [Poss Flem *Rijssel* Lille]

Russellite *rus'əl-īt*, *n* a member of the International Bible Students' Association, or Jehovah's Witnesses, a millennialist sect founded by the American Pastor C T *Russell* (1852–1916). — Also *adj*.

russet *rus'it*, *n* a coarse homespun cloth or dress; a reddish-brown colour; a reddish-brown variety of apple (also **russet apple**). — *adj* made of russet; homespun, homely, rustic (*archaic*); reddish-brown; of brown leather. — *vt* and *vi* to make or become russet in colour. — *n* **russ'eting** a russet apple. — *adj* **russ'ety**. [OFr *rousset*, from L *russus* red]

Russian *rush'ən* or *rush'yən*, *adj* of *Russia*, its people or their language; of the former Soviet Union or its people. — *n* a native or citizen of Russia, or (formerly) the Soviet Union; the Slavonic language of most Russians, formerly the official language of the Soviet Union. — *n* and *adj* **Russ** (*rus*) Russian. — *adj* **Russia** (*rush'ə* or *-yə*) Russian. — *n* **russ'ia** russia leather. — *n* **Russ'ianism**. — *n* **Russ'ianist**. — *n* **Russianīzā'tion** or **-s-**. — *vt* **Russ'ianize** or **-ise** to give Russian characteristics to; to make Russian. — *n* **Russ'ianness**. — *n* **Russification** (*rus-i-fi-kā'shən*). — *vt* **Russ'ify** to Russianize. — *n* and *adj* **Russ'ky** or **Russ'ki** (*derog slang*, *esp NAm*) Russian. — *adj* **Russocen'tric** centred or focused on Russia, *esp* without due consideration of states allied to it, or (formerly) of other Soviet republics. — *n* **Russocen'trism**. — *n* and *adj* **Russocen'trist**. — *n* **Russ'ophil** or **Russ'ophile** a person who shows admiration for or is enthusiastic about the culture, language, political system, etc of Russia or (formerly) the Soviet Union (also *adj*). — *n* **Russoph'ilism**. — *n* **Russoph'ilist**. — *n* **Russ'ophobe** a person who dreads or hates the Russians, or (formerly) the Soviet Union, its citizens, political system, etc (also *adj*). — *adj* **Russophō'bic**. — *n* **Russoph'obist**. — *n* **Russophō'bia**. — **russia** (or **Russia**) **leather** a fine brownish-red leather with a characteristic odour; **Russian boots** wide-topped, calf-length leather boots; **Russian dressing** mayonnaise sharpened with chilli sauce, chopped pickles, etc; **Russian roulette** an act of bravado, *specif* that of loading a revolver with one bullet, spinning the cylinder, and firing at one's own head; **Russian salad** a salad of mixed vegetables, diced and served with a Russian dressing; **Russian tea** tea with lemon and no milk, *usu* served in a glass; **Russian thistle** or **tumbleweed** a tumbleweed (*Salsola kali teniufolia*) with narrow, prickly leaves, native to Russia; **Russian vine** a central Asian climbing plant (*Polygonum baldschuanicum*) of the knotgrass family, producing white or pink flowers. — *adj* **Russo-Byzan'-**

tine in or relating to the Byzantine style as developed in Russia.

Russniak *rus'ni-ak*, *n* and *adj* Ruthenian; Ukrainian or Little Russian. [Ruthenian *Rusnjak*]

rust *rust*, *n* the reddish-brown coating on iron exposed to moisture; any similar coating or appearance; a plant disease characterized by a rusty appearance, caused by various fungi of the *Uredineae*; a fungus causing such disease, notably *Puccinia graminis*, which attacks wheat; corrosion; injurious influence or consequence, *esp* of mental inactivity or idleness; the colour of rust. — *vi* to become rusty; to affect with rust; to become dull or inefficient by inaction. — *vt* to make rusty; to impair by time and inactivity. — *adj* **rust'ed**. — *adv* **rust'ily**. — *n* **rust'iness**. — *n* and *adj* **rust'ing**. — *adj* **rust'less** free from rust; proof against rust. — *adj* **rust'y** covered with rust; impaired by inactivity, out of practice; dull; affected with rust-disease; rust-coloured; of a rusty black; time-worn; rough; raucous; obstinate; discoloured. — **rust belt** those areas of the Midwestern and Northeastern US in which declining heavy industries, *esp* steel production, are concentrated (also with *caps*); extended to any similar area in other industrialized countries. — *adj* **rust'-belt** of or relating to such an area. — **rust'-bucket** (*colloq*) a badly rusted car. — *adj* **rust'-coloured**. — **rust fungus**. — *adj* **rust'-proof**. — *adj* **rust'-resistant**. — **rust'y-back** the scale-fern. — *adj* **rust'y-coloured**. — **rusty nail** (*colloq*) an alcoholic cocktail containing whisky and Drambuie®. [OE *rūst*; Ger *Rost*]

rustic *rus'tik*, *adj* of or characteristic of the country or country people; living in or belonging to the country; like, or like that of, country people; simple and plain; awkward; uncouth; unrefined; roughly made; made of rough branches; (of masonry) with sunken or chamfered joints, sometimes with roughened face. — *n* a peasant; a clown; a rough-surfaced brick or stone; rustic masonry; (in showjumping) a fence made of rough branches, etc. — *adj* and (*rare*) *n* **rus'tical**. — *adv* **rus'tically**. — *vt* **rust'icate** to send into the country; to banish for a time from town or college; to build in rustic masonry. — *vi* to live in the country; to become rustic. — *adj* **rust'icated**. — *n* **rusticā'tion**. — *n* **rust'icātor**. — *adj* **rusticial** (*-tish'l*; *Scott*, as a false archaism). — *n* **rust'icism** (*-sizm*) a rustic saying or custom. — *n* **rusticity** (*-tis'i-ti*) rustic manner; simplicity; rudeness. — *vt* and *vi* **rus'ticize** or **-ise** (*-ti-sīz*). — **rustic capitals** a type of Roman script using simplified, squared capital letters; **rus'tic-ware** a terra-cotta of a light brown paste, having a brown glaze; **rus'tic-work** rusticated masonry; summerhouses, etc of rough branches. [L *rūsticus*, from *rūs* (dialect) the country]

rustle *rus'l*, *vi* to make a soft, whispering sound, like that of dry leaves; to go about with such a sound; to stir about, hustle (*US*); to steal cattle (*US*). — *vt* to cause to rustle; to get by rustling (*US*). — *n* a quick succession of small sounds, as that of dry leaves; a rustling; bustle (*US*). — *n* **rus'tler**. — *n* and *adj* **rus'tling**. — *adv* **rus'tlingly**. — **rustle up** to arrange, gather together. [Imit; cf Flem *ruysselen*]

rustre *rus'tər*, (*heraldry*) *n* a lozenge pierced with a circular opening. — *adj* **rus'tred**. [Fr]

rusty[1]. See under **rust**.

rusty[2] *rust'i*, (now *dialect*) *adj*. Variant of **reasty**, etc (see under **reast**[1]).

rut[1] *rut*, *n* a furrow made by wheels; a fixed, often tedious, course difficult to get out of or depart from. — *vt* to furrow with ruts: — *pr p* **rutt'ing**; *pa t* and *pa p* **rutt'ed**. — *adj* **rutt'y**. — **in a rut** following a tedious routine from which it is difficult to escape. [Origin obscure; prob not Fr *route*]

rut[2] *rut*, *n* the annual period of sexual excitement in male deer; also in other male ruminants, such as sheep, goats, etc. — *vi* to be in such a period of sexual excitement. — *vt* (*Dryden*) to copulate with. — *n* and *adj* **rutt'ing**. — *adj* **rutt'ish** (*Shakesp*) lustful. — **rut'-time**. [OFr *ruit*, *rut*, from L *rugītus*, from *rugīre* to roar]

Ruta *rōō'tə*, *n* the rue genus of dicotyledons, giving its name to the family **Rutā'ceae** which is *usu* made to include the orange, etc. — *adj* **rutā'ceous**. [L *rūta*; see **rue**[1]]

rutabaga *rōō-tə-bā'gə*, (*NAm*) *n* the Swedish turnip. [Swed dialect *rotabagge*]

rutaceous. See under **Ruta**.

ruth *rōōth*, (*archaic*) *n* pity; remorse; sorrow; matter for pity; misfortune, calamity (*obs*). — *adj* **ruth'ful** pitiful, sorrowful; piteous, causing pity. — *adv* **ruth'fully**. [ME *ruthe*, *reuth*; see **rue**[2]; ending influenced by Scand, as ON *hryggth*]

Ruthenian *rōō-thēn'i-ən*, *n* a member of a branch of the Ukrainian people inhabiting both sides of the Carpathians; the language of the Ruthenians, a dialect of Ukrainian. — *adj* of or relating to the Ruthenians or their language. — Also (now *rare*) **Ruthēn'e** (*n* and *adj*).

ruthenium *rōō-thē'ni-əm*, *n* a metallic element (symbol **Ru**; atomic no 44) of the platinum group, found in the Ural Mountains. — *adj* **ruthē'nic** of or concerning ruthenium, *esp* with a high valency. — *adj* **ruthē'nious** of or concerning ruthenium, *esp* with a low valency. [LL *Ruthenia* Russia]

rutherford *rudh'ər-fərd*, *n* a unit of radioactive disintegration, equal to a million disintegrations a second (*abbrev* **rd**). — *n* **rutherford'ium** the name coined in the US for the transuranic element (symbol **Rf**; atomic no 104), called by the Russians *kurchatovium*. [After the physicist Baron *Rutherford* (1871–1937)]

ruthful etc. See under **ruth**.

ruthless *rōōth'ləs*, *adj* pitiless, brutal; severe, unsparing. — *adv* **ruth'lessly**. — *n* **ruth'lessness**. [**ruth** and **-less**]

rutilant *rōō'ti-lənt*, (*rare*) *adj* shining; glowing ruddily. [L *rutilāns*, *-antis*, pr p of *rutilāre* to be reddish]

rutile *rōō'tīl*, *n* a reddish-brown mineral of the tetragonal system, titanium oxide. — *adj* **rutilated** (*rōō'til-āt-id*) enclosing needles of rutile. [L *rutilus* reddish]

rutin *rōō'tin*, *n* a drug used against the fragility of small blood vessels. [Formed from **Ruta**]

rutter *rut'ər*, (*obs*) *n* a mercenary cavalryman. [MDu *rutter*, from OFr *routier*]

rutty, etc. See under **rut**[1].

RV *abbrev*: recreational vehicle; Revised Version (of the Bible).

RW *abbrev*: Right Worshipful; Right Worthy.

RWA *abbrev*: Rwanda (IVR).

RWS *abbrev*: Royal Society of Painters in Water Colours.

Rwy or **Ry** *abbrev*: Railway.

ry- in many words an old spelling of **ri-**.

RYA *abbrev*: Royal Yachting Association.

rya *rē'ə*, *n* a type of Scandinavian knotted-pile rug with a distinctive colourful pattern (also **rya rug**); the weave, pattern or style typical of a rya. — Also *adj*. [Swed, connected with Finn *ryijy*]

ryal or **rial** *rī'əl*, *adj* (*obs*) royal. — *n* a royal person; any of various coins, such as an old English gold coin worth about ten shillings, a Spanish real, and others (*hist*). [OFr *rial* royal]

rybat *rib'ət*, (*Scot*) *n* a dressed stone at the side of a door, window, etc. [Prob connected with **rebate**[2] and **rabbet**]

rybaudrye and **rybauld**. See **ribald**.

rye[1] *rī*, *n* a grass (*Secale*, especially *Secale cereale*) related to wheat and barley; its grain, used for making bread; rye grass; rye whisky. — *adj* of rye. — **rye'bread**; **rye coffee** a coffee substitute made from roasted grains of rye; **rye corn** (*Austr*) rye; **rye'flour**; **rye grass** a pasture and fodder grass (species of *Lolium*), with flat spikelets appressed edgewise in a two-rowed spike; **rye'-roll** a dark treacly cookie, understood not to be of rye. — *n* and *adj* **rye'-straw**. — **rye whisky** whisky distilled chiefly from rye; **rye wolf** (Ger *Roggenwolf*) an evil creature of German folklore lurking in the rye-fields. [OE *ryge*; ON *rugr*, Ger *Roggen* (also *Rocken*)]

rye[2] *rī*, *n* a gypsy word for gentleman. [Romany *rei*, *rai* lord]

ryepeck, **rypeck** or **ripeck** *rī'pek*, (*dialect*) *n* a pole used for mooring a punt. [Origin obscure]
ryfe *rīf*, (*Spenser*) *adj*. Same as **rife**.
ryke *rīk*, a Scots form of **reach**[1].
rymme an old spelling of **rim**[1,2].
rynd. Same as **rind**[2].
ryokan *rē-ō'kən*, *n* a traditional Japanese inn. [Jap]
ryot or **raiyat** *rī'ət*, *n* in the Indian subcontinent, a peasant. — *n* **ry'otwari** or **raiy'atwari** (*-wä-rē*) a system of land-tenure by which each peasant holds directly of the state. [Hindi *raiyat*, *raiyatwārī*, from Ar *ra'īyah* a subject]
rype *rü'pə*, *n* a ptarmigan: — *pl* **ry'per**. [Dan]
RYS *abbrev*: Royal Yacht Squadron.
RZS *abbrev*: Royal Zoological Society (**RZSE**, Royal Zoological Society of Edinburgh).

S

S or **s** *es*, *n* the nineteenth letter of the modern English alphabet, seventeenth in the Roman, a consonant, its usual sound a voiceless sibilant (ie pronounced *s*), but often voiced (ie pronounced *z*, and sometimes a voiceless palato-alveolar fricative (represented *usu* by *sh*), or voiced (as in *pleasure*); any mark or object of the form of the letter; as a medieval Roman numeral, S = 7 or 70; S̄ = 70 000. — **collar of SS** see **ess**.

S or **S.** *abbrev*: Sabbath; Saint; schilling (Austrian currency); siemens; Society; South; square; stokes; strangeness (*phys*); sun; Sweden (IVR). — **S4C** *abbrev* for *Sianel Pedwar Cymru*, the Welsh language television channel.

S *symbol*: sulphur (*chem*); (in the form **$**) dollar.

s or **s.** *abbrev*: second(s); shilling.

's *z* or *s*, a sentence element used to form the possessive of singular nouns (eg *John's*, *the dog's*), some pronouns (eg *one's*), and plural nouns not ending in *-s* or a similar sound (eg *the children's*); often also to form the plural lower-case letters (eg *m's*, of numbers (eg 3'*s*) or symbols ; a shortened form of **has** and **is** (eg *she's taken it*, *he's not here*); a shortened form of **us** (pronounced *s*; eg *let's go*).

SA *abbrev*: Salvation Army; sex-appeal; *Société anonyme* (Fr), limited liability company; Society of Antiquaries; Society of Arts; South Africa; South America; South Australia; *Sturm Abteilung* (Ger), literally, storm section, Nazi terrorist militia.

sa *abbrev*: *secundum artem* (*L*), according to art; *sine anno* (*L*), without date (literally, year).

sa' *sā*, *vt* an obsolete contraction of **save**.

Saam, Saame, Sabme, Sabmi or **Sami** *sä'mē*, *n* a Lapp: — *pl* **Saame** or **Samit**. — *adj* Lappish. [Lappish]

Saanen *sä'nən*, *n* a Swiss breed of white, short-haired goat; a goat of this breed. [*Saanen* a town in Switzerland]

sab[1] *sab*, (*Scot*) *n* a form of **sob**.

sab[2] *sab*, (*colloq*) *n* a saboteur.

Saba *sä'bä*, *n* the Sheba, an ancient people of Yemen. — *n* and *adj* **Sabaean** or **Sabean** (*-bē'ən*). — Also applied erroneously to adherents of Sabaism and of Sabianism. [Gr *Saba*, from Ar *Saba'*; Heb *Shebā*]

sabadilla *sab-ə-dil'ə*, *n* the seeds of a liliaceous plant, *Schoenocaulon officinale*, yielding the alkaloid veratrine. — Also **cebadill'a** or **cevadill'a**. [Sp *cebadilla*, dimin of *cebada* barley]

Sabaean. See under **Saba**.

Sabahan *sə-bä'hən*, *n* a citizen or inhabitant of *Sabah*, a Malaysian state (formerly North Borneo). — *adj* of, from or pertaining to Sabah.

Sabaism *sā'bā-izm*, *n* the worship of the host of heaven. [Heb *tsābā* host]

Sabal *sā'bal*, *n* an American genus of palms, the palmettos. [Origin unknown]

Sabaoth *sa-bā'oth*, (*Bible*) *n pl* armies, used only in the phrase, 'Lord of Sabaoth'; (*sab'əth*) erroneously for Sabbath (*Spenser*). [Heb *tsebāōth* (transliterated *sabaōth* in Gr), pl of *tsabā* an army]

sabaton *sab'ə-ton*, (*hist*) *n* a foot-covering, *esp* square- or round-toed, worn as part of a suit of armour; a shoe or half-boot made of cloth, etc. [Provençal *sabató*; cf **sabot**, Sp *zapata*]

Sabbath *sab'əth*, *n* (among the Jews) Saturday, set apart for rest from work; (among most Christians) Sunday; sometimes also used for the Muslim day of rest, Friday; a sabbatical year of the Jews; a time of rest; (also **sabb'at**) a witches' midnight meeting. — *adj* of or appropriate to the Sabbath. — *n* **Sabbatā'rian** a person who observes Saturday as Sabbath; a person who believes in or practises observance, or strict observance, of the Sabbath (Saturday or Sunday). — Also *adj* (sometimes without *cap*). — *n* **Sabbatā'rianism**. — *adj* **Sabb'athless**. — *adj* **sabbatic** (*sə-bat'ik*) or **sabbat'ical** (*-i-kəl*) pertaining to, or resembling, the Sabbath; enjoying or bringing rest; on or pertaining to leave from one's work (as in *sabbatical leave*, *sabbatical visit*, etc). — *n* a period of leave from one's work, *esp* for teachers and lecturers, also *esp* to undertake a separate or related project. — *adj* **sabb'atine** pertaining to Saturday. — *n* **sabb'atism** sabbatical rest; observance of the Sabbath. — *vt* **sabb'atize** or **-ise** to observe as a Sabbath. — *vi* to keep a Sabbath. — **Sabb'ath-breaker**; **Sabb'ath-breaking** (also *adj*); **Sabb'ath-day** (also *adj*); **Sabbath-day's journey** 2000 cubits, or about one kilometre, which a Jew was permitted to walk on the Sabbath; **Sabbath school** (chiefly *US*) a Sunday school; **sabbatical year** every seventh year, in which the Israelites allowed their fields and vineyards to lie fallow; a year off, for study, travel, etc. [Heb *Shabbāth*]

SABC *abbrev*: South African Broadcasting Corporation.

Sabean. See under **Saba**.

sabella *sə-bel'ə*, *n* a worm of the *Sabella* genus of tube-building sea-worms. [L *sabulum* sand]

Sabellian[1] *sə-bel'i-ən*, *n* and *adj* originally, Sabine; now generally used in a wide sense to include related ancient peoples and languages. [L *Sabellus*, poetic dimin of *Sabīnus*]

Sabellian[2] *sə-bel'i-ən*, *n* a follower of *Sabellius*, a Libyan priest of the 3c. — Also *adj*. — *n* **Sabell'ianism** the teaching of Sabellius, that Father, Son, and Holy Ghost are one and the same God in different aspects.

SABENA *abbrev*: *Société anonyme belge d'exploitation de la navigation aérienne* (Fr), Belgian World Airlines.

saber. *NAm* spelling of **sabre**.

Sabian *sā'bi-ən*, **Tsabian** *tsā-* or **Zabian** *zā'*, *n* an adherent of a religion or a group of religions (*esp* a semi-Christian sect of Babylonia) mentioned in the Koran as entitled to toleration, *prob* related to the Mandaeans; Mandaean; sometimes applied erroneously to a Sabaean, sometimes to an adherent of Sabaism. — Also *adj*. — *n* **Sā'bianism**. [Ar *Sābi'*]

sabin *sab'in* or *sā'bin*, (*phys*; now *obs*) *n* a unit of acoustic absorption, equal to the absorption, considered complete, of 1 sq ft of a perfectly absorbing surface. [From Wallace C *Sabine* (1868–1919), US physicist]

Sabine *sab'īn*, (*hist*) *n* a member of an ancient people of central Italy, united with the Romans about 300BC. — Also *adj*. [L *Sabīnus*]

Sabine's gull *sa-bēnz' gul*, *n* a small gull, *Larus sabini*, with a forked tail, grey and white plumage with black outer feathers on the wing-tips, and a black, yellow-tipped bill.

Sabin vaccine *sā'bin vak'sēn* or *-sin*, *n* a live-virus poliomyelitis vaccine taken orally. [Albert Bruce *Sabin*, US microbiologist (born 1906)]

sabkha, sabkhah *sab'kə* or *sab'hhə* or **sabkhat** *-kət* or *-hhət*, (*geol*) *n* a broad, salt-encrusted coastal plain, above the level of normal tides and subjected to only occasional flooding, common in Arabia. [Ar]

sable[1] *sā'bl*, *n* an arctic and subarctic marten, *esp Martes zibellina* of N Asia; its lustrous dark brown fur; a paintbrush made of its hair. — *adj* made of sable fur. [OFr; prob from Slav]

sable[2] *sā'bl*, *n* and *adj* black (*orig heraldry*, now chiefly *poetic*); dark. — *n* a sable antelope; (in *pl*) mourning garments. — *vt* to darken. — **sable antelope** a large predominantly black antelope of S and E Africa (*Hippotragus niger*), with long, ringed backward-curving horns. — *adj* **sa'ble-coloured**. [Fr *sable*; poss the same as **sable**[1]]

Sabme, **Sabmi**. See **Saame**.

sabot *sab'ō*, *n* a wooden shoe or clog, as formerly worn by the French peasantry; an attachment to guide a projectile through the bore of a firearm. — *n* **sabotier** (*sa-bo-tyā*) a wearer of wooden shoes; a Waldensian. [Fr]

sabotage (*sa-bo-täzh'*, now *usu sab'*, also *-tij*) malicious or deliberate destruction or damage of machinery, etc, by discontented workers, rebels, etc; action taken to prevent the fulfilment of any plan, aim, etc. — Also *vt* and *vi*. — *n* **saboteur** (*-tœr'*) a person who sabotages (*colloq* **sab**). [Fr *sabot*]

sabra *sä'brə*, *n* a native-born Israeli, not an immigrant. [Mod Heb *sābrāh*, a type of desert pear, prickly on the outside and soft inside]

sabre or (*NAm*) **saber** *sā'bər*, *n* a curved single-edged cavalry sword; a light sword used in fencing; a cavalry soldier armed with a sabre. — *vt* to wound or kill with a sabre. — *n* **sabreur** (*-rœr'*) a person, *esp* a cavalry soldier, who fights with a sabre. — **sa'bre-cut**. — *vi* **sa'bre-rattle**. — **sa'bre-rattling** an aggressive display of military power, military bluster intended to intimidate. — Also *adj*. — **sa'bre-tooth** any extinct feline carnivore of the Tertiary period, eg the **sabre-toothed tiger** (*Smilidon*), with extremely long upper canine teeth; **sa'bre-wing** a humming-bird of a group with bent outer primaries in the male. [Fr *sabre*, from Ger dialect *Sabel* (now *Säbel*); perh from Pol *szabla* or Hung *szablya*]

sabretache *sab'ər-tash*, *n* a flat bag slung from a cavalry officer's sword-belt. [Fr *sabretache*, from Ger *Säbeltasche*, from *Säbel* sabre, and *Tasche* pocket]

sabulous *sab'ū-ləs* or **sabulose** *sab'ū-lōs*, *adj* sandy; gritty; (of plants) growing in sandy places (also **sab'uline**). [L *sabulum* sand]

saburra *sə-bur'ə*, *n* a granular deposit, as in the stomach. — *adj* **saburr'al**. — *n* **saburrā'tion** (*med*) the application of hot sand as a treatment. [L *saburra* sand]

SAC *abbrev*: Strategic Air Command (in the US).

sac[1] *sak*, (*biol*) *n* a pouch or baglike structure. — *adj* **sacc'ate** pouched; pouchlike; gibbous; enclosed in a sac. — *adj* **sacciform** (*sak'si-förm*) or **sacc'ūlar** saclike. — *adj* **sacc'ūlate** or **sacc'ūlated** formed in a series of sac-like enclosures; enclosed in a sac. — *n* **saccūlā'tion**. — *n* **sacc'ūle** or **sacc'ūlus** a small sac, eg the smaller of two sacs in the vestibule of the ear: — *pl* **sacc'ūles** or **sacc'ūlī**. — *adj* **saccū'liform** in the shape of a small sac. — *adj* **sac'like** [Fr, from L *saccus* a bag; see **sack**[1]]

sac[2] *sak*, (*old Eng law*) *n* the conveyance to a lord of manor of certain rights of jurisdiction, eg holding courts. — *adj* **sac'less** (*Scott*) unchallengeable, not to be molested (see **sack'less** separate entry). — See also **soc**. [OE *sacu* strife, litigation]

sacaton *sak-ə-tōn* *n* a type of coarse perennial grass growing in alkaline regions of the Southern US, used for making hay. [Am Sp *zacatón*]

saccade *sa-käd'* or *sə-*, *n* the sharp lateral movement of the eye as it switches swiftly from one fixation point to another, eg in reading; a short rapid tug on a horse's reins; any short jerky movement. — *adj* **saccad'ic** jerky; consisting of or pertaining to saccades. — *adv* **saccad'ically**. [Fr *saccade* a jerk, from OFr *saquer* to pull]

sacchar- *sak-ər-*, **sacchari-** *sak-ə-ri-* or **saccharo-** *sak-ə-rō-*, *-rə-*, *combining form* denoting sugar. — *n* **sacch'arase** same as **invertase**. — *n* **sacch'arate** a salt of saccharic acid. — *adj* **sacch'arated** sugared, sweetened. — *adj* **sacchar'ic** of or obtained from saccharic acid, saccharin, or a saccharine substance. — *n* **sacch'aride** a carbohydrate; a compound with sugar. — *adj* **saccharif'erous** sugar-yielding. — *n* **sacchar'ification**. — *vt* **sacchar'ify** (or *sak'*) to convert or break down into sugar or sugars. — *n* **saccharim'eter** an instrument for testing the concentration of sugar solutions. — *n* **saccharim'etry**. — *n* **sacch'arin** or **sacch'arine** (*-in* or *-ēn*) an intensely sweet, white crystalline semi-soluble compound ($C_6H_4COSO_2NH$) used as an artificial sweetener; sickly sweetness (*fig*). — *adj* **sacch'arine** (*-īn*, *-ēn*) of sickly sweetness; sugary; of, containing, or of the nature of sugar or saccharine. — *n* **saccharinity** (*-in'i-ti*). — *n* **sacchariza'tion** or *-s-*. — *vt* **sacch'arize** or **-ise** to saccharify. — *adj* **sacch'aroid** or **saccharoid'al** (*geol*) like loaf-sugar in texture, *usu* applied to marbles and quartzites of fine to medium grain with closely interlocking crystals. — *n* **saccharom'eter** a hydrometer or other instrument for measuring concentration of sugar solutions. — *n* **Saccharomyces** (*-ō-mī'sēz*; Gr *mykēs* fungus) the yeast genus of ascomycete fungi. — *n* **sacch'arose** (*-ōs*) any carbohydrate, *esp* cane sugar. — *n* **Sacch'arum** the sugar-cane genus of grasses; (without *cap*) cane-sugar or its invert form. — **saccharic acid** an acid ($COOH(CHOH)_4COOH$), obtained by oxidation of sugar; **saccharic ester** an ester obtained from saccharic acid. [L *saccharum*, through Gr *sakcharon* sugar, ult from Sans *śarkarā* gravel, grit]

sacciform. See under **sac**[1].

saccos. Same as **sakkos**.

saccular, **sacculate**, etc. See under **sac**[1].

sacellum *sə-sel'əm*, *n* a tomb or monument in the form of a chapel within a church (*archit*); a little chapel; a roofless temple consecrated to an ancient Roman deity: — *pl* **sacell'a**. [L dimin of *sacrum* a holy place, from *sacer* consecrated]

sacerdotal *sas-ər-dō'tl*, *sak-*, *adj* priestly; sacerdotalist. — *n* **sacerdō'talism** the spirit, principles, etc of the priesthood; devotion to priestly interests; priestcraft; the belief that the presbyter is a priest in the sense of offering a sacrifice in the eucharist; the attribution to a priesthood of special or supernatural powers; excessive influence of priests over people's thoughts and actions (*derog*). — *n* **sacerdō'talist**. — *vt* **sacerdō'talize** or **-ise** to render sacerdotal. — *adv* **sacerdō'tally**. [L *sacerdōs*, *-ōtis* a priest, from *sacer* sacred, and *dare* to give]

sachem *sā'chəm*, (*US*) *n* a N American Indian chief, a sagamore; a political leader, *esp* one of the officials of Tammany Hall (qv). — *n* **sā'chemdom** or **sā'chemship**. — *adj* **sachemic** (*sā-chem'ik*). [Narraganset *sachim*]

Sachertorte *sähh'ər-tör-tə*, *zä-*, *-k-*, *n* a kind of sweet spiced chocolate cake made and served at *Sacher's* hotel in Vienna. — Also **Sacher torte**. [See **torte**]

sachet *sa'shā*, *n* a small *usu* plastic envelope, containing a liquid, cream, etc, such as shampoo; a small bag containing pot-pourri or other scented material; a bag for holding handkerchiefs, etc. [Fr]

sack[1] *sak*, *n* a large bag made of coarse fabric, thick paper, etc; a sackful; a varying, *usu* large measure of capacity; a woman's loose-fitting waistless dress (also **sack dress**); (with *the*) dismissal from employment (*colloq*); (with *the*) a form of the death penalty by which the criminal was condemned to be sewn up in a sack and drowned (*hist*); bed (*slang*); an instance of sacking (*Am football*). — *vt* to put into a sack; to dismiss from employment (*colloq*); to tackle (a quarterback) behind the line of scrimmage and before he or she can pass the ball (*Am football*). — *n* **sack'ful** as much as a sack will hold; a large quantity (*colloq*): — *pl* **sack'fuls**. — *n* **sack'ing** coarse cloth used in making sacks, sackcloth. — **sack'cloth** coarse cloth used for making sacks; coarse material, formerly worn in mourning or penance. — *adj* **sack-doudling** (*-dood'lin*; *Scott*) bagpiping (cf **doodle**[2] and Ger *Dudelsack*). — **sack race** one in which each runner's legs are encased in a sack; **sack tree** the upas (from the use of its inner bark to make sacks). — **hit the sack** (*slang*) to go to bed; **in sackcloth and ashes** showing extreme regret, penitence, etc (often *facetious*); in deep mourning; **sad sack** (*esp US slang*) a person who seems to attract mishap and disaster, a misfit. [OE *sacc*, from L *saccus*, from Gr *sakkos*; prob Phoenician]

sack[2] *sak*, *n* plundering or devastation (of a town or city); pillage. — *vt* to plunder; to pillage. — *n* **sack'age** (*rare*) or **sack'ing**. — *n* **sack'er**. [Fr *sac*; according to some the same as **sack**[1] (putting (one's loot) in a bag)]

sack[3] *sak*, *n* the old name of various dry white wines from Spain and the Canaries. — **sack'-poss'et** posset made with sack. — **burnt sack** mulled sack. [Fr *sec*, from L *siccus* dry]

sack[4] or **sacque** *sak*, (*hist*) *n* a woman's loose-fitting gown; a train of silk hanging from the shoulders of such a gown; a woman's hip-length coat with a loose-fitting back. [See ety for **sack**[1]; infl by Fr *sac*]

sackbut *sak'but*, *n* an early wind instrument with a slide like the trombone; a mistranslation of Aramaic *sabbekā*, the sambuca (*Bible*). [Fr *saquebute*, perh OFr *saquier* to draw out, and *bouter* to push]

sackless *sak'lis*, (*archaic* and *Scot*) *adj* innocent; guileless; feeble; dispirited (see also under **sac**[2]). [OE *sacléas*, from *sacu*; **sac**[2], **sake**[2]]

sacque. See **sack**[4].

sacra. See **sacrum**.

sacral[1] *sā'krəl*, *adj* of or relating to sacred rites. — *n* **sacralizā'tion** or **-s-** endowing something with sacred status or properties; treating something as if it were sacred. — See also **sacrum**. — *vt* **sac'ralize** or **-ise**. [L *sacrum* a sacred object]

sacral[2]. See under **sacrum**.

sacrament *sak'rə-mənt*, *n* a religious rite variously regarded as a channel to and from God or as a sign of grace, amongst Protestants generally *Baptism* and the *Lord's Supper*, amongst Roman Catholics and members of the Eastern Orthodox Church also *Confirmation*, *Penance*, *Holy Orders*, *Matrimony* and *Extreme Unction*; the Lord's Supper specially; the bread or wine taken in celebration of the Lord's Supper; a symbol of something spiritual or secret; a sign, token, or pledge of a covenant; a religious mystery; a Roman soldier's oath on enlistment; a pledge deposited by each party to a suit (*Roman law*); a solemn oath; an oath of purgation; materials used in a sacrament. — *vt* to bind by an oath. — *adj* **sacramental** (*-ment'l*). — *n* (*RC*) an act or object which may transmit or receive grace. — *n* **sacramen'talism**. — *n* **sacramen'talist** a person who attaches importance to the spiritual nature of the sacraments. — *adv* **sacramen'tally**. — *n* **sacramentā'rian** a person who holds a high or extreme view of the efficacy of the sacraments; someone who does not accept the real presence in the sacrament of the Lord's Supper (*obs*). — Also *adj*. — *n* **sacramentā'rianism**. — *adj* **sacramen'tary** pertaining to the sacrament or sacraments; sacramentarian. — *n* a book containing all the prayers and ceremonies used at the celebration of the RC sacraments; a person who denies the doctrine of the real presence. — **sacrament house** an ambry where the sacrament is kept. — **take the sacrament upon** or **to** to take communion in confirmation of (an oath). [L *sacrāmentum* an oath, pledge, from *sacrāre* to consecrate, from *sacer* sacred]

sacrarium *sā-krā'ri-əm*, *sa-krä'ri-ŏŏm*, *n* a place where sacred objects were kept, either in a temple or house (*Roman antiq*); the sanctuary of a church; the piscina (*RC Church*). — *pl* **sacra'ria**. [L *sacrārium*, from *sacer* holy]

sacred *sā'krid*, *adj* consecrated; devoted; set apart or dedicated to religious use, *esp* to God; holy; emanating from God; religious; entitled to veneration or worship; not to be violated, breached, etc; accursed (*rare*). — *adv* **sa'credly**. — *n* **sa'credness**. — **sacred ape** the hanuman of India; **sacred beetle** an Egyptian scarab; **sacred cat** the house cat of Egypt, sacred to Pasht or Bast; **Sacred College** the body of cardinals of the Roman Catholic Church; **sacred cow** (*colloq*) an institution, custom, etc, so venerated that it is above criticism; **sacred fish** oxyrhyncus; **Sacred Heart** (*RC*) the physical heart of Christ, adored with special devotion since the 18c; **sacred mushroom** any of various hallucinogenic mushrooms, eg of the genus *Psilocybe* of N and S America, and *Amanita* of Europe and Asia, used in religious rituals and ceremonies; a mescal button used in a similar way. [Pa p of obs *sacre*, from OFr *sacrer*, from L *sacrāre*, from *sacer*, sacred]

sacrifice *sak'ri-fīs*, sometimes (*esp poetic*) *-fīz*, *n* the slaughter of an animal, person, etc on an altar as an offering to a god; any offering, tangible or symbolic, to a god; Christ's offering of himself as mankind's saviour (*theol*); destruction, surrender, or foregoing of anything valued for the sake of anything else, *esp* a higher consideration; loss sustained by selling something at less than its value; a victim offered in sacrifice. — *vt* to offer up in sacrifice; to make a sacrifice of; to give up, surrender, for a higher good or for mere advantage; to make a victim of; to sell at a loss; to allow to come to destruction or evil. — *vi* to offer sacrifice(s). — *n* **sac'rificer**. — *adj* **sacrificial** (*-fish'l*) of or pertaining to sacrifice; (of an object or substance) protecting another from corrosion by its own exposure to and damage by the corrosive (as, eg, **sacrificial anode**, **sacrificial plate**, **sacrificial metal** (*technol*)). — *adv* **sacrifi'cially**. — *vt* and *vi* **sac'rify** (*obs*) to sacrifice: — *pa p* (*Spenser*) **sac'rifide**. — **sacrifice hit** (*baseball*) in baseball, a hit to enable another player to score or to gain a base. [L *sacrificium*, from *sacer* sacred, and *facere* to make]

sacrilege *sak'ri-lij*, *n* profanation or disregard of anything holy; the outrage of breaking into a place of worship and stealing from it; extreme disrespect for anything generally regarded as worthy of extreme respect. — *adj* **sacrilegious** (*-lij'əs*). — *adv* **sacrile'giously**. — *n* **sacrile'giousness**. — *n* **sacrilē'gist**. [Fr *sacrilège*, from L *sacrilegium*, from *sacer* sacred, and *legere* to gather]

sacring *sā'kring*, (*archaic*) *n* the act or ritual of consecration. — **sacring bell** (*RC Church*) a small bell rung to call attention to the more solemn parts of the service of the Mass. [**sacred**]

sacrist *sak'rist*, *sā'krist* *n* a sacristan; in a cathedral, someone who copied music for the choir and looked after the books (*hist*). — *n* **sacristan** (*sak'ri-stən*) an officer in a church who has care of the sacred vessels and other movables; a sexton. — *n* **sacristy** (*sak'*) an apartment in a church where the sacred utensils, vestments, etc, are kept; a vestry. [LL *sacrista*, *sacristānus* a sacristan, *sacristia* a vestry, from L *sacer* sacred]

sacro-. See under **sacrum**.

sacrosanct *sak'rō-sangkt*, *adj* inviolable, protected by sacred or quasi-sacred rules. — *n* **sacrosanc'tity**. or **sac'rosanctness**. [L *sacrōsanctus*, from *sacer* sacred, and *sanctus*, pa p of *sancīre* to hallow]

sacrum *sā'krəm* or *sak'rəm*, (*anatom*) *n* a triangular bone composed of five fused vertebrae (**sacral vertebrae**) wedged between the two innominate bones, so as to form the keystone of the pelvic arch in humans: — *pl* **sa'cra**. — *combining form* **sacr-** (sometimes before a vowel) or **sa'crō-** denoting sacrum. — *adj* **sa'cral**. — *n* **sacralgia** (*-ral'jə*, *-jyə*) pain in the sacrum or region of the sacrum. — *n* **sacraliza'tion** or **-s-** abnormal fusion of the sacrum with the fifth lumbar vertebra. — *adj* **sacrococcygeal** (*-kok-sij'i-əl*) relating to the sacrum and the coccyx. — *adj* **sacrocos'tal** connected with the sacrum and having the character of a rib (also *n*). — *adj* **sacrōil'iac** relating to the articulation of the sacrum and ilium. — *n* this joint. — *n* **sacroiliitis** (*-il-i-ī'tis*) inflammation of the sacroiliac joint. [L (*os*) *sacrum* holy (bone), so called for unknown reason]

SAD *abbrev*: seasonal affective disorder.

sad *sad*, (*compar* **sadd'er**, *superl* **sadd'est**) *adj* sorrowful; deplorable (often *joc*); (of baking) heavy, stiff, doughy; sober, dark-coloured; serious, earnest, grave (*archaic*); staid, sedate (*archaic*); steadfast, contrast (*obs*); heavy (*obs*); sated (*obs*). — *vt* **sadd'en** to make sad. — *vi* to grow sad. — *adj* **sadd'ish**. — *adv* **sad'ly** in a sad manner; unfortunately, sad to relate. — *n* **sad'ness**. — *adj* **sad'-eyed**, **sad'-faced** and **sad'-hearted**. — **sad'iron** a flatiron pointed at both ends; **sad sack** see under **sack**[1].

— **in sober sadness** in serious earnest. [OE *sæd* sated, weary; cf Du *zat*, Ger *satt*; L *sat*, *satis*]

saddhu. See **sadhu**.

saddle *sad'l*, *n* a seat for a rider on a horse, bicycle, etc; a pad for the back of a draught animal; anything of similar shape, eg a mountain col between two peaks; that part of the back of an animal on which the saddle is placed; a mark on that part; a butcher's cut including a part of the backbone with the ribs; the rear part of a male fowl's back; a worm's clitellum; the part of a lathe that slides on the bed, between the headstock and tailstock; a block surmounting one of the towers of a suspension bridge, supporting or fixing the suspension cables. — *vt* to put a saddle on; to encumber; to impose upon (someone) as a burden or encumbrance; (of a trainer) to be responsible for preparing and entering (a racehorse) for a race; to ride or mount (a horse, bicycle, etc) (*rare*). — *vi* to get into the saddle of a horse, bicycle, etc. — *adj* **sadd'leless**. — *n* **sadd'ler** a maker or seller of saddles and related goods; a soldier who has charge of cavalry saddles (also **sadd'ler-cor'poral** and **sadd'ler-ser'geant**); a saddle horse (*US colloq*). — *n* **sadd'lery** the occupation of a saddler; his shop or stock-in-trade; a saddle-room at a stables, etc. — **sadd'leback** a saddle-shaped hill, coping, animal or object; the great black-backed gull; the hooded crow; the male harp seal; a breed of goose; a breed of pig; a rare New Zealand wattlebird, *Philesturnus carunculatus*; a saddle roof. — *adj* (also **sadd'lebacked**) saddle-shaped; having a depression in the middle (of the back); having a saddle-shaped mark on the back; (of a coping) sloping from the middle to each side. — **sadd'lebag** a bag carried at, or attached to, the saddle. — *adj* (of furniture) upholstered in cloth in imitation of camels' saddlebags. — **saddle bar** a bar for supporting stained glass in a window; **saddlebill** or **saddle-bill stork** a large black and white stork, *Ephippiorhynchus senegalensis*, of sub-Saharan Africa, with a red and black bill that has a yellow saddle-like structure at the base; **saddle blanket** a folded blanket used as a saddle cloth; **sadd'lebow** (*-bō*) the arched front of a saddle; **sadd'lecloth** a cloth placed under a saddle to prevent rubbing. — *adj* **sadd'le-fast** firmly seated in the saddle. — **saddle feather** or **hackle** one of the long, slender feathers drooping from a male fowl's saddle; **saddle-girth** a band that holds the saddle in place; **saddle horse** a riding horse; **sadd'le-lap** the skirt of a saddle; **sadd'le-nose** flattening of the bridge of the nose, eg as a result of congenital syphilis. — *adj* **sadd'le-nosed**. — **saddle pillar** or **pin** the support of a cycle saddle, which fits a socket in the frame; **saddle reef** (*geol*) an ore depost occurring in concavo-convex formations of igneous rocks, *esp* in Australia; **saddle roof** a roof with a ridge and two gables; **sadd'leroom** a room where saddles and harness are kept. — *adj* **sadd'le-shaped** arched; concave and convex in sections at right angles to each other. — **saddle soap** a kind of oily soap used for cleaning and treating leather. — *adj* **sadd'le-sore** (of a rider) with buttocks and inner thighs sore or chafed from riding. — **saddle sore** a sore resulting from chafing of the saddle; **saddle spring** a spring supporting a cycle-saddle; **saddle stitch** needlework consisting of long stitches on the top surface and short stitches on the underside of the material; one such stitch; a method of stitching or stapling (a booklet, magazine, etc) together through the back centre fold. — *vt* and *vi* to sew using saddle stitch. — **sadd'letree** the frame of a saddle. — **in the saddle** in control; **put the saddle on the right horse** to impute blame where it is deserved; **saddle up** to saddle a horse; to mount (*SAfr*). [OE *sadol*, *sadel*; cf Du *zadel*, Ger *Sattel*]

Sadducee *sad'ū-sē*, *n* a member of a Jewish priestly and aristocratic party of traditionalists, whose reactionary conservatism resisted the progressive views of the Pharisees, and who rejected, among various other beliefs, resurrection of the body. — *adj* **Sadducaean** or **Sadducean** (*-sē'ən*). — *n* **Sadd'uceeism** or **Sadd'ucism** scepticism. [Gr *Saddoukaios*, from Heb *Tsadūqīm*, from *Zadok* the High Priest, the founder]

sadhe or **sade** *sä'dē*, *n* the eighteenth letter of the Hebrew alphabet (צ or ץ).

sadhu or **saddhu** *sä'dōō*, *n* a Hindu holy man, ascetic and mendicant. [Sans *sādhu*, from adj, straight, pious]

sadism *sā'dizm*, *n* pleasure, *esp* sexual satisfaction, obtained by inflicting pain or suffering on another person; love of cruelty. — *n* **sa'dist**. — *adj* **sadistic** (*sə-dis'*). — *n* **sadomasochism** (*sā-dō-mas'ə-kizm*) the combination of sadism and masochism in one person; pleasure, *esp* sexual gratification, obtained by inflicting pain on another person and having pain inflicted on one by another person. — *n* **sadomas'ochist**. — *adj* **sadomasochist'ic**. [Comte (called Marquis) de *Sade* (1740–1814), who died insane, notoriously depicted this form of pleasure in his novel]

sadza *sad'zə*, *n* a type of porridge made from maize flour, a staple food in southern Africa. [Shona]

SAE *abbrev*: Society of Automotive Engineers (in the US).

sae *sā*, *adv* Scottish form of **so**[1].

sae or **s.a.e.** *abbrev*: stamped addressed envelope.

saeculum or **seculum** *sek'ū-ləm*, *n* an astronomical or geological age. [L, a generation]

SAEF *abbrev*: Seaq Automatic Execution Facility. — See also **seaq**.

saeter *set'ər* or *sāt'*, *n* (in Norway) an upland meadow which provides summer pasture for cattle, and where butter and cheese are made; a hut on a saeter providing shelter for those looking after the animals. [Norw]

saeva indignatio *sē'və in-dig-nā'shi-ō* or *sī'wa*, also *sī'va in-dig-nä'ti-ō*, (*L*) fierce indignation.

safari *sə-fä'rē*, *n* an expedition, *esp* for hunting or animal-watching in Africa; a long expedition involving difficulty and requiring planning, *usu* in tropical climes. — *vi* to go on safari. — *n* **safar'ist** a person who goes on safari. — **safari park** an enclosed park where wild animals (mostly non-native) are kept uncaged on view to the public; **safari suit** a suit for men, boys, or women, typically of cotton and consisting of square-cut **safari jacket** with four pockets and a belt, and long or short trousers. [Swahili, from Ar *safarīya* a journey]

safe *sāf*, *adj* unharmed; free from danger; secure; sound, free from risk; certain, sure; reliable, trustworthy; cautious; good, fine (*slang*). — *n* a metal box, often set in a wall, secure against fire, thieves, etc; a ventilated box or cupboard for meat, etc; a condom (*NAm slang*). — *adv* in a safe manner or condition. — *vt* to make safe (*obs*); to bring safely (*Shakesp*). — *prep* (*Spenser*) save. — *adv* **safe'ly**. — *n* **safe'ness**. — *n* **safe'ty** (in Spenser often *sā'fi-ti*) the state or fact of being safe; a safety shot in snooker or billiards; a device designed to prevent injury, *esp* a safety catch; the defensive player placed furthest back in the field (*Am football*; also **safe'tyman**); a play in which the defensive team scores two points when an offensive player is tackled or downs the ball on or behind his own goal-line (*Am football*). — **safe'-blower**; **safe'-blowing** the forcing of safes, using explosives; **safe'-breaker** or **safe'-cracker**; **safe'-breaking** or **safe'-cracking** illegal opening of safes; **safe'-con'duct** a permit to pass or travel through an area with guarantee of freedom from interference or arrest. — *vt* (*-kon'*, *-dukt'*) to conduct (a person) safely; to give a safe-conduct to. — **safe'-deposit** or **safe'ty-deposit** a vault, etc providing safe storage for valuables; **safe'guard** a device, condition, or arrangement ensuring safety; a precaution; a safe-conduct. — *vt* to protect (*esp* interests or rights); to protect (eg native manufacturers and industry) against foreign competition. — **safe house** (*colloq*) a place (*esp* one kept by the intelligence services or care agencies) unknown to one's pursuers, where one can safely hide; **safe'-keeping** keeping in safety; safe custody; **safe light** a light used in a photographic darkroom, etc, which emits light of an intensity and colour which will not damage the materials being processed; **safe period** that part of the menstrual cycle during which conception is most unlikely; **safe seat** a parliamentary seat that the incumbent political party will almost certainly win again in an election; **safe sex** sexual intercourse minimizing the risk of transmission of disease, eg by the use of condoms; **safety arch** an arch built into the body of a wall to relieve the pressure of weight from above; **safety belt** a belt for fastening a workman, etc, to a fixed object while carrying out a dangerous operation; a belt for restraining the occupant of a seat in a car, aircraft, etc, a precaution against injury in a crash; **safety bicycle** a common low-wheeled bicycle; **safety bolt** the safety lock of a firearm; **safety cage** a cage with a safety catch to prevent it falling if the hoisting rope breaks (*mining*); (in a motor-vehicle chassis) a specially strengthened framework around the seating part to give maximum protection to driver and passengers in a crash (also **safety cell**); **safety-catch** any catch to provide protection against something, such as the accidental firing of a gun; **safety curtain** a fireproof curtain between stage and audience in a theatre; **safety factor** the ratio between the breaking stress in a member, structure, or material, and the safe permissible stress in it; **safety film** photographic or cinematographic film with a non-flammable or slow-burning base of cellulose acetate or polyester; **safety fuse** a slow-burning fuse that can be lit at a safe distance; a fuse inserted for safety in an electric circuit; **safety glass** a laminate of plastic between sheets of glass, used eg in vehicle windscreens; glass reinforced with wire, or otherwise toughened to avoid shattering (also **laminated glass**); **safety lamp** a miners' lamp that will not ignite inflammable gases; **safety light** a warning light; a light that will not readily cause a fire; **safety lock** a lock that cannot be picked by ordinary means; (in firearms) a device for preventing accidental discharge, a safety catch; **safety match** a match that can be ignited only on a specially prepared surface; **safety net** a net stretched beneath an acrobat, etc, during a rehearsal or performance, in case he or she should fall; any precautionary measure or means of protection from injury, hardship, etc; **safety officer** an official whose responsibility is to ensure that safety regulations are adhered to; **safety paper** paper difficult to imitate or tamper with without detection, such as that used for bank-notes; **safety pin** a pin in the form of a clasp with a guard covering its point; a pin for locking a piece of machinery or a device, eg that used to prevent detonation of a grenade, a mine, etc; **safety plug** an electrical plug that melts when the temperature rises too high; **safety razor** a razor incorporating a guard for the blade which prevents deep cutting of the skin; **safety rein** a rein for preventing a horse from running away; **safety shot** (in snooker and billiards) a shot in which the player purposely places the cue ball so that his opponent is prevented from scoring with his next shot; **safety valve** a valve that opens when the pressure becomes too great; any harmless outlet for pent-up emotion, energy, etc. — **be** or **err on the safe side** to choose the safer alternative; **place of safety order** a legal order, effective for not more than 28 days, allowing a child to be taken into care to avoid further or possible physical harm by parents, etc; **play safe** to act in a manner that minimizes the risk of defeat, injury or loss; to act in a cautious way; **safe and sound** secure and uninjured; **safe as houses** (*colloq*) very safe. [OFr *sauf*, from L *salvus*]

saffian *saf'i-ən*, *n* leather tanned with sumach and dyed in bright colours. [Russ *saf'yan*]

safflower *saf'lowr*, *n* a thistle-like composite plant (*Carthamus tinctorius*) cultivated in India; its dried petals, used in cosmetics and for making a red dye. — **safflower oil** an oil produced from this plant and used in cooking, etc. [Cf Du *saffloer*, OFr *saffleur*]

saffron *saf'rən*, *n* a species of crocus, *Crocus sativus*, wth purple flowers; its orange-coloured stigmas, dried and used as a dye and flavouring; an orange-yellow colour. — *adj* **saff'roned** coloured or flavoured with saffron. — *adj* **saff'rony** coloured somewhat like saffron or having a flavour like saffron. — *n* **saf'ranin** or **saf'ranine** any of various coal-tar dyes, giving various colours. — *n* **safronal** (*saf'rə-nəl*) a spicy-tasting chemical constituent of saffron. — **saffron cake** a cake flavoured with saffron. — **false**, **mock** or **bastard saffron** safflower; **meadow saffron** the autumn crocus, *Colchicum*; **saffron milk cap** an edible orange toadstool (*Lactarius deliciosus*). [OFr *safran*, from Ar *za'farān*]

SAfr *abbrev*: South Africa; South African.

safranin(e). See under **saffron**.

safrole *saf'rōl*, *n* a *usu* colourless oily liquid obtained from sassafras and used in perfumes, soaps and insecticides. [*sassafr*as and *-ol*]

sag *sag*, *vi* to bend, sink, or hang down, *esp* in the middle; to yield or give way, from or as if from weight or pressure; to flag; (of industrial activity, prices, etc) to decline; to droop; to move along in a slow, laboured manner; to move or drift to leeward: — *pr p* **sagg'ing**; *pa p* and *pa t* **sagged**. — *n* an act or instance of sagging; a part or area that sags, eg a depression in an area of glacial deposion. — *adj* sagging. — *n* and *adj* **sagg'ing**. — *adj* **sagg'y** inclined to sag. — **sag bag** a large bag filled with a substance, *usu* polystyrene granules, which allows it to be pushed into any shape and used as a chair, cushion, bed, etc. [Cf Swed *sacka* to sink down; LGer *sacken*, to sink]

saga[1] *sä'gə*, *n* a prose narrative of the deeds of Icelandic or Norwegian heroes in the old literature of Iceland; a body of legend about some subject; a series of novels dealing with the history of a family (also **saga novel**); a long, detailed story (*colloq*). — **sa'gaman** a narrator of Icelandic or Norwegian sagas. [ON *saga*; cf **saw**[3]]

saga[2]. See **sagum**.

sagacious *sə-gā'shəs*, *adj* keen in perception or thought; discerning and judicious; wise. — *adv* **sagā'ciously**. — *n* **sagā'ciousness** or **sagacity** (*-gas'i-ti*). [L *sagāx*, *-ācis*]

sagaman. See under **saga**[1].

sagamore *sag'ə-mör*, *n* a N American Indian chief. [Penobscot *sagamo*; cf **sachem**]

sagapenum *sag-ə-pē'nəm*, *n* a gum-resin, the juice of *Ferula persica*, formerly used to stimulate menstruation and as an antispasmodic. [Gr *sagapēnon*]

sagathy *sag'ə-thi*, (*obs*) *n* a lightweight fabric, a mixture of wool and silk or silk and cotton. [Origin unknown; cf Fr *sagatis*, Sp *sagatí*]

sage[1] *sāj*, *n* a garden labiate plant (*Salvia officinalis*) whose grey-green leaves are used as a flavouring; any plant of the *Salvia* genus, such as clary; extended to wood germander (*wood-sage*). — *adj* **sā'gy**. — **sage apple** an edible gall formed on Mediterranean sage; **sage'brush** a subshrub of the genus *Artemisia*, that grows in arid regions of N America; **sage cheese** a cheese flavoured and mottled with sage leaves; **sage Derby** a kind of sage cheese; **sage grouse** or **cock** a large N American grouse, *Centrocercus urophasianus*, that feeds on and lives in sagebrush; **sage'-green** greyish green, like sage leaves; **sage rabbit** a small hare found amongst sagebrush; **sage tea** an infusion of sage leaves, used domestically as a tonic; **sage'-thrash'er** the mountain mocking-bird. [OFr *sauge* (Ital *salvia*), from L *salvia*, from *salvus* safe]

sage[2] *sāj*, *adj* wise. — *n* a (*usu* old) man of great wisdom. — *adv* **sage'ly**. — *n* **sage'ness**. — **Seven Sages** see under **seven**. [Fr *sage*, ult from L *sapere* to be wise]

sagene *sə-jēn'*, *n* a fishing-net; a network. — *n* **sagenite** (*saj'ə-nīt* or *sə-jē'nīt*; *mineralogy*) rutile in the form of a network of needle-like crystals. — *adj* **sagenitic** (*saj-ə-nit'ik*). [Gr *sagēnē* drag-net]

saggar or **sagger** *sag'ər*, or **saggard** *sag'ərd*, or **segger** *seg'ər*, *n* a clay box in which pottery is packed for baking. [Perh **safeguard**]

sagged, **sagging**. See under **sag**.

sagger. See **saggar**.

saginate *saj'i-nāt*, *vt* to fatten (animals). — *n* **saginā'tion**. [L *sagīnāre* to fatten]

sagitta *sə-jit'ə, n* a keystone; a versed sine of an arc (*geom*); the middle stroke of the letter epsilon; (with *cap*) the Arrow, a northern constellation. — *adj* **sagittal** (*saj'it-l*) shaped like an arrow; like a sagitta; pertaining or parallel to the sagittal suture. — *adv* **sag'ittally**. — *n* **Sagittā'ria** the arrow-head genus. — *n* and *adj* **sagittar'ian** (of) a person born under Sagittarius. — *n* **Sagittā'rius** the Archer, a constellation and the ninth sign of the Zodiac; a person born between 23 Nov and 22 Dec, under this sign. — *n* **sag'ittary** a centaur; an archer. — *adj* **sag'ittate** or **sagitt'iform** (of leaves) shaped like an arrowhead with the barbs pointing backwards. — **sagittal suture** the serrated join between the two parietal bones forming the top and sides of the skull. [L *sagitta* an arrow]

sago *sā'gō, n* a nutritive cereal substance produced from the pith of the sago palm; **sago grass** a tall grass, *Paspalidum globoideum*, used as fodder for cattle in Australia; **sa'go-palm** any of various palms (*incl Metroxylon, Arenga, Caryota, Oreodoxa*) and certain cyclads, yielding sago. [Malay *sāgū*]

sagoin or **sagouin**. See **saguin**.

saguaro *sä-gwä'rō, n* a giant cactus, *Carnegiea gigantea*, of SW US and Mexico, with a tree-like trunk, white flowers and edible red fruits: — *pl* **sagua'ros**. [Mex Sp]

saguin, **sagoin** or **sagouin** *sag'win* or *sag-oin', n* a small S American monkey. [Fr *sago(u)in*, from Port *saguim*, from Tupí *saguin*]

sagum *sā'gəm, sag'ŏŏm n* a Roman military cloak: — *pl* **sa'ga**. [L *sagum*; prob Gaulish]

Saharan *sə-här'ən, adj* of, resembling, or characteristic of, the *Sahara* desert in N Africa.

Sahelian *sə-hē'li-ən* or *-hel'i-ən, adj* of or concerning the countries south of the Sahara desert, *incl* Chad, Niger, Mali and Mauretania, generally between the desert and savanna regions. [Ar *sāhel* coastal strip]

sahib *sä'ib, n* a form of address used in India to people of rank and, during the period of British rule, to Europeans; Sir or Mr; a European; a refined, cultured man (*colloq*): — *fem* **sah'iba** or **sah'ibah** (*rare*; see also **mem-sahib**). [Ar *sāhib*, orig, friend]

sai *sä'i, n* the capuchin monkey. [Tupí, monkey]

saibling *zīp'ling, n* a freshwater fish, the char. [Ger dialect]

saic, **saick**, or **saique** *sä-ēk'* or *sä'ik, n* a Levantine vessel like a ketch. [Fr *saïque*, from Turk *shāīqā*]

saice. Same as **syce**.

said[1] *sed, pa t* and *pa p* of **say**[1]. — *adj* previously- or already-mentioned.

said[2]. See **sayyid**.

saiga *sī'gə, n* a Eurasian antelope, *Saiga tatarica*, with a swollen nose ending in a pig-like snout. [Russ]

saikei *sī'kā', n* a Japanese miniature landscape of bonsai trees, etc, growing on rocks or stones; the art of cultivating such landscapes. [Jap *sai*, cultivation, and *kei* scenery]

saikless *sāk'lis, adj* a Scots form of **sackless**.

sail[1] *sāl, n* a sheet of canvas, framework of slats, or other structure, spread to catch the wind, so as to propel a ship, drive a windmill, etc; a specified type of sail on a boat or ship (often shortened to **s'l**), as in *foresail* or *fores'l*; sails collectively; a ship or ships; a trip in a vessel (which may or may not have sails); an act or distance of sailing; any sail-like organ or object; a wing, *esp* a hawk's; a submarine's conning-tower. — *vi* to progress, travel or make trips in sailing-craft or any other type of ship; to set out on a voyage; to glide or float smoothly along (*fig*). — *vt* to direct the course or movements of (a ship), navigate; to cause (a toy boat, etc) to sail; to pass over or along in a ship; to go through or get through effortlessly (*fig*). — *adj* **sail'able** navigable. — *adj* **sailed** having sails. — *n* **sail'er** a boat or ship that can sail in a stated manner. — *n* **sail'ing** travelling, or a journey, by sails or on water; (the time of) a ship's departure from port; the art or activity of directing a ship's course. — Also *adj*. — *adj* **sail'less**. — *n* **sail'or** a person who is employed in the management of a ship, *esp* one who is not an officer; a mariner, seaman; a navigator; a person regarded in terms of ability to tolerate the heaving motion of a ship (as in *good* or *bad sailor*); a sailor hat (*colloq*). — *n* **sail'oring** occupation as a sailor. — *adj* **sail'orless**. — *adj* **sail'orlike** or **sail'orly**. — **sail arm** one of the arms of a windmill; **sail'board** a small, light, flat-hulled sailing-craft *usu* consisting of a surfboard fitted with a single flexible mast, the sail being controlled by a hand-held boom; **sail'boarder** someone who goes in for sail-boarding; **sail'boarding** the sport of sailing a sailboard, windsurfing; **sail'-boat** (*esp NAm*) a (*usu* small) sailing-boat. **sail'cloth** a strong cloth used for sails; **sail'fish** a large game fish of the genus *Istiophorus*, related to the swordfish, with a large sail-like dorsal fin; another name for the basking shark; **sail'-flying** flying in a sailplane; **sailing boat** a boat moved by sails, though often having auxiliary motor power; **sail'ing-master** an officer in charge of navigation, *esp* of a yacht; formerly a warrant officer in the US navy; **sailing orders** instructions to the captain of a ship at setting forth on a voyage; **sailing ship** a ship driven by sails; **sail loft** a large room or loft with sufficient floor area to allow sails to be spread out while they are being made or repaired; **sail'-maker**; **sailor hat** a round hat with a wide, upcurved brim; **sail'or-man** a seaman; **sailor suit** a child's or woman's outfit resembling that of a sailor; **sail'plane** a glider that can rise with an upward current. — *vi* to fly in a sailplane. — **sail'room** a room aboard a vessel for storing sails in; **sail'-yard** the yard on which sails are extended. — **full sail** with all sails raised and filled with the wind; **good** (or **bad**) **sailor** a person who is unaffected (or made ill) by the motion of a ship; **make sail** to spread more canvas, raise more sails; **put on sail** to set more sails in order to travel more quickly (also *fig*); **sail close to** (or **near**) **the wind** see under **wind**; **sail under false colours** to pretend to be what one is not; **set sail** to spread the sails; to set forth on a voyage (with *for*); **shorten sail** to reduce its extent; **strike sail** to lower a sail or sails; to abate one's pretensions, eat humble pie; **trim one's sails** to adjust or modify one's plans, policy or opinion to take account of changed circumstances; **under sail** having the sails spread; propelled by means of sails. [OE *segel*; cf Du *zeil*, Ger *Segel*]

sail[2] *sāl, vi* to project. — *n* projection. [OFr *saillir* to jut, from L *salīre* to leap]

saim (*Scot*). See **seam**[2].

saimiri *sī-mē'rē, n* a squirrel-monkey. [Tupí *sai* monkey, and *miri* little]

sain *sān*, (*archaic*) *vt* to make the sign of the cross over; (by association with L *sānāre*) to heal. [OE *segnian*, from L *signāre*, from *signum* mark]

saine *sān*, a Spenserian form of the infinitive and the present indicative pl of **say**[1]; an editor's reading for **faine** (*Love's Labour's Lost* III. i. 88) taken as a *pa p* of **say**[1] (*Shakesp*).

sainfoin *sān'foin, n* a leguminous plant, *Onobrychis viciaefolia*, used as fodder. — Also **saint'foin**. [Fr *sainfoin*, prob from *sain* wholesome, and *foin* hay, from L *sānum fēnum*]

saint *sānt*, when prefixed to a name *sint, snt, adj* (or *n* in apposition) holy. — *n* a canonized person, a person formally recognized by the Christian (*esp* RC) Church as having lived a life of holiness and exceptional virtue, and to whom the right to be revered is therefore accorded; a person of outstanding virtue or kindness; an Israelite, a Christian, or one of the blessed dead (*Bible*); an angel (*Bible, Milton*); a member of various religious bodies, *esp* Puritans, as used of themselves or as a nickname; a sanctimonious person. — *vt* to make a saint of; to hail as saint. — *n* **saint'dom**. — *adj* **saint'ed** made a saint, canonized; like a saint; sacred; gone to heaven. — *n* **saint'ess**. — *n* **saint'hood**. — *adj* **saint'ish**. — *n* **saint'ism** the character or quality of a saint; sanctimoniousness. — *adj* **saint'like**. — *n* **saint'liness**. — *n* **saint'ling**. — *adj* **saint'ly** of, like, characteristic of, or befitting a saint. — *n* **saint'ship**. — **saint's day** a day set apart for the commemoration of a particular saint; **St Agnes's Eve** 20 January, when, according to tradition, having performed certain rites, one may dream of the person that will be one's husband or wife; **St Agnes's flower** the snowflake (qv); **St Andrew's cross** a cross in the form of the letter X; a white cross of this type on a blue background, as borne on the banner of Scotland; **St Andrew's Day** 30 November; **St Anthony's cross** the tau cross, a cross shaped like the Greek letter T; **St Anthony's fire** *prob* an old name for ergotism; see **Anthony**; **St Barbara's cress** yellow-rocket; **St Barnaby's thistle** a knapweed flowering about the saint's day (11 June); **St Bernard's dog** or **St Bernard** a breed of very large dogs, named after the hospice of the Great St Bernard, used, *esp* formerly, to rescue travellers lost in the snow; **St Crispin's Day** a shoemakers' festival, 25 October; **St Cuthbert's beads** and **St Cuthbert's duck** see **Cuthbert**; **St Dabeoc's heath** a rare Irish shrub; **St David's Day** 1 March; **St Elmo's fire** an electrical charge forming a glow around a church spire, ship's mast, etc, a corposant; **St George's cross** a red upright cross on a white background; **St George's Day** 23 April; **St Hubert's disease** another name for hydrophobia; **St Ignatius's bean** the poisonous seed of a plant (*Strychnos ignatii*) related to nux vomica; **St James's** the British royal court; **St John's bread** another name for the carob bean; **St John's Day** 27 December; **St Johnston's ribbon** or **tippet** the hangman's rope (*St Johnston* or *St John's toun* being Perth, associated in the 18c with hangings); **St John's wort** any of the plants of the *Hypericum* genus; **St Julien** an esteemed red Bordeaux wine from the Médoc region; **St Leger** a horse-race run annually at Doncaster, so called since 1778 from Colonel *St Leger*; **St Luke's summer** a spell of pleasant weather about the middle of October; **St Martin's evil** drunkenness; **St Martin's summer** a spell of mild, damp weather in late autumn; **St Nicholas's clerks** thieves; **St Patrick's Day** 17 March; **St Peter's fish** the dory; **St Peter's wort** square-stalked St John's wort; extended to several plants; **St Stephen's** Houses of Parliament; **St Swithin's Day** 15 July; **St Tibb's** (or **St Tib's**) **Eve** or **Tib(b)'s Eve** never; **St Trinian's** a fictitious girls' school created by the English cartoonist Ronald Searle (born 1920) and popularized in humorous films. — *adj* **St Trinian** of, pertaining to or typical of St Trinian's; applied to or denoting unruly or riotous behaviour, exploits, or spectacularly untidy dress, *usu* of schoolgirls (*colloq*). — *n* a pupil of St Trinian's. — **St Valentine's Day** 14 February (see also under **Valentine**); **St Vitus's dance** an old name for Sydenham's chorea. [Fr, from L *sanctus* holy]

saintfoin. See **sainfoin**.

saintpaulia *sānt-pö'li-ə*, *n* a tropical African flowering plant of the genus *Saintpaulia*, commonly grown as a pot plant, the African violet. — [New L, from Baron Walter von *Saint Paul* (1860–1910), who discovered it]

Saint-Simonism *sənt-* or *sint-sī'mən-izm*, *n* the socialist system of the French philosopher Comte de *Saint-Simon* (1760–1825). — *n* **Saint-Simō'nian** (also *adj*). — *n* **Saint-Simō'nianism**. — *n* **Saint-Si'monist**.

saique. See **saic**.

sair *sār*, Scots form of **sore**[1], **savour**, **serve**.

saist (*Spenser* and *Milton*). Same as **sayest** (see **say**[1]).

saith[1] *seth*, (*archaic*) *3rd pers sing present indicative* of **say**[1].

saith[2] or **saithe** *sāth*, *n* another name for the coalfish. [ON *seithr*]

Saiva *shī'və*, *sī'*, or **Shaiva** *shī'*, *n* a member of a sect devoted to the Hindu god Siva. — *n* **Sai'vism** or **Shai'vism**. — *n* **Sai'vite** or **Shai'vite**.

sajou *sä-zhōō'* or *-jōō'*, *n* a capuchin monkey. [Fr, from Tupí *sai* monkey, and augmentative *-uassu*]

Sakai *sä'kī*, *n* a group of forest tribes of Malaya; an individual of this group; their language, of the Mon-Khmer group: — *pl* **Sakai**. — Also *adj*.

sake[1] *sāk*, *n* a cause; account, behalf; advantage, benefit; purpose, aim, object. — **for goodness** (or **heaven's**, **pete's**, etc) **sake** an expression of frustration, irritation, urgency, etc. — **for old sake's sake** (*obs*) or **old time's sake** for the sake of old times or friendship, for auld lang syne; **for the sake of** for the purpose of; on account of. [OE *sacu* strife, a lawsuit; Du *zaak*, Ger *Sache*; OE *sacan* to strive, Gothic *sakan*; cf **sac**[2], **sackless, seek**]

sake[2] *sä'ki* or *sä'kē*, *n* a Japanese alcoholic drink made from fermented rice. — Also **saké** or **saki**. [Jap]

saker *sā'kər*, *n* a species of lanner falcon (*Falco cherrug*) used in falconry; an obsolete small cannon. — *n* **sa'keret** the male saker. [Fr *sacre*, prob from Ar *saqr*]

saki[1] *sä'ki* or *-kē*, *n* a S American monkey of the genus *Pithecia*, with a long bushy non-prehensile tail. [Fr, for Tupí *sai* or *saguin*; cf **sai, saguin**]

saki[2]. See **sake**[2].

sakieh, sakiyeh or **sakia** *sä'ki-yə*, *-ki-ə*, *n* an Eastern water wheel. [Ar *sāqiyah*]

sakkos *sak'os*, *n* an Eastern bishop's vestment like an alb or a dalmatic. — Also **sacc'os**. [Gr *sakkos* a bag]

saksaul. Same as **saxaul**.

Sakti *shäk'ti*, *shuk'*, *säk'* or **Shakti** *shäk'*, *shuk' shuk'tē*, (*Hinduism*) *n* the female principle, *esp* as personified in the wife of Siva or other god. — *n* **Sak'ta** or **Shak'ta** a worshipper of the Sakti. — *n* **Sak'tism** or **Shak'tism** [Sans *śsakti* divine energy]

sal[1] *säl*, a Northern form of **shall**.

sal[2]. See **sial**.

sal[3] *säl*, *n* a large N Indian tree, *Shorea robusta*, yielding valuable timber similar to teak. [Hind *sāl*]

sal[4] *sal*, (*chem* and *pharm*) *n* a salt. — **sal alembroth** (an alchemists' word of unknown origin) mercury ammonium chloride, also called *salt of wisdom*; **sal ammoniac** ammonium chloride; **sal prunella** or **sal prunelle** saltpetre cast in cakes; **sal volatile** (*vol-at'i-li*) ammonium carbonate, or a solution of it in alcohol and/or ammonia in water; smelling salts. [L *sāl* salt]

sal Atticum *sal at'i-kəm* or *säl at'i-kōōm*, (*L*) *n* Attic salt (see under **Attic**).

salaam *sä-läm'*, *n* a word and gesture of salutation in the East, chiefly among Muslims; obeisance; (in *pl*) greeting, compliments. — *vi* to perform the salaam, a low bow with the palm of the right hand on the forehead. — **salaam aleikum** peace be with you. [Ar *salām* peace; cf Heb *shālōm*]

salable, salableness, salably. See under **sale**[1].

salacious *sə-lā'shəs*, *adj* lustful; lecherous; arousing lustful or lecherous feelings. — *adv* **salā'ciously**. — *n* **salā'ciousness** or **salacity** (*-las'i-ti*). [L *salāx*, *-ācis*, from *salīre* to leap]

salad *sal'əd*, also (*archaic*) **sallad** and **sallet** *sal'it*, *n* a cold dish of vegetables or herbs (either raw or pre-cooked), generally mixed, with or without oil and vinegar or other dressing, sometimes including slices of egg, lobster, etc; a plant grown for or used in salads; a savoury seasoning (*obs*); a diverse or confused mixture. — *n* **sal'ading** herbs and vegetables for salads. — **fruit salad** see under **fruit**; **salad burnet** the common burnet; **salad cream** a type of bottled mayonnaise for dressing salad; **salad days** one's youth, *esp* if carefree and showing inexperience; **salad dressing** or **oil** sauce, olive-oil, etc used in dressing salads; [Fr *salade*, from L *sāl* salt]

salade. Same as **sallet**[1].

salade niçoise *sa-lad' nē-swäz'*, *n* a cold dish consisting of salad vegetables, French beans, hard-boiled eggs, anchovies, olives and herbs. [Fr, salad of Nice]

salal or **sallal** *sal'al*, *n* a NW American ericaceous shrub (*Gaultheria shallon*). — **salal berry** or **sallal berry** its edible fruit. [Chinook jargon]

salamander *sal'ə-man-dər* or *-man'*, *n* a member of a genus (*Salamandra*) of tailed amphibians, closely related to the newts; (in ancient myth) a lizard-like monster supposed to inhabit fire and able to quench it by the chill of its body; an elemental spirit believed by

Paracelsists to live in fire; a person who survives exposure to fire unscathed (*usu fig*); a poker used red-hot for kindling fires; a hot metal plate for browning meat, etc; a portable stove, used during the construction of a building, in a greenhouse, etc; a residual deposit of metal or slag on a furnace wall. — *adj* **salaman'der-like** (also *adv*). — *adj* **salaman'drian** or **salaman'drine**. — *adj* **salaman'droid** (also *n*). [Fr *salamandre*, from L *salamandra*, from Gr *salamandrā*; prob of Eastern origin]

salami *sə-lä'mi*, *n* a highly seasoned Italian sausage, *usu* sliced very thinly: — *pl* **salamis**. — **salami tactics** a policy of cutting away, one by one, undesirable elements, eg particular people from an organization; **salami technique** a fraud involving the deduction of almost indiscernible sums of money from numerous and scattered transactions (*esp comput*). [Ital, pl of *salame*, from an assumed Vulgar L *sālāre* to salt]

salamon. See **salmon**[2].

salangane *sal'əng-gān*, *n* a swiftlet (*Collocalia*) that builds edible nests. [Tagálog *salangan*]

salary *sal'ə-ri*, *n* a periodical payment (*usu* at longer intervals than a week) for one's (*usu* non-manual) labour. — *vt* to pay a salary to. — *n* **salariat** (*sə-lā'ri-ət*) the salary-earning class or body collectively. — *adj* **sal'aried**. — **sal'aryman** (in Japan) an office worker. [OFr *salarie* (Fr *salaire*), from L *salārium* salt-money, from *sāl* salt]

salband *säl'band* or *zäl'bänt*, (*geol*) *n* a crust or coating of mineral. [Ger *Salband* selvage, from *Selb* self, and *Ende* end]

salbutamol *sal-bū'tə-mol*, *n* a bronchodilator drug, used in the treatment of bronchial asthma, emphysema, etc.

salchow *sal'kō* or *-kov*, (*ice-skating*) *n* a jump in which the skater takes off from the inside back edge of one skate, spins in the air and lands on the outside back edge of the other skate. [From Ulrich *Salchow* (1877–1949), Swedish skater]

sale[1] *sāl*, *n* an act or instance of selling; the exchange of anything for money; the power or opportunity of selling; demand, volume of selling; the offer of goods at reduced prices for a limited period; the offer of goods at public auction; the state of being on offer to buyers. — *adj* intended for selling, in general, by auction, or *esp* at reduced prices. — *n* **saleabil'ity** or **salabil'ity**. — *adj* **sale'able** or **sal'able** suitable for selling; in good demand. — *n* **sale'ableness** or **sal'ableness**. — *adv* **sale'ably** or **sal'ably**. — **sale'-cat'alogue**; **sale price** price asked at a sale; **sale'ring** an enclosed area, often circular, at a market, where livestock for sale are paraded; **sale'room** or (*NAm*) **sales'room** a room where goods for sale, *esp* at auction, are displayed; **sales'clerk** (*NAm*) a sales assistant in a store or shop; **sales drive** a special effort to increase sales, using a variety of techniques; **sales engineer** a salesperson with technical knowledge of the company's product(s) or goods; **sales'man**, **sales'woman** or **sales'-person** a person who sells goods, *esp* in a shop; a commercial traveller; **sales'manship** the art of selling; skill in presenting wares in the most attractive light or in persuading purchasers to buy; **sales pitch** sales talk, *esp* the individual technique used by a salesperson; **sales resistance** unwillingness of potential customers to buy, or resistance to aggressive selling techniques; **sales talk** persuasive talk designed to effect a sale; **sales tax** (*esp NAm*) a tax levied on retail goods and services; **sale'yard** (*Austr* and *NZ*) an enclosure in which livestock for auction are kept. — **forced sale** a sale compelled by a creditor; **sale of work** a sale of things made by members of a church congregation, club or association to raise money; **sale or return** or **sale and return** an arrangement by which a retailer may return to the wholesaler any goods not sold. [Late OE *sala*, perh from ON *sala*]

sale[2] *sāl*, *n* sallow; wicker (*Spenser*). — Also **seal**. [Form of **sallow**[2]]

salep *sal'əp*, *n* dried orchid tubers; a food or drug prepared from them. [Turk *sālep*, from Ar]

saleratus *sal-ə-rā'təs*, (*NAm*) *n* potassium or sodium bicarbonate, used in raising agents such as baking-power. [L *sāl aerātus* aerated salt]

Salesian *sə-lē'shən*, *adj* of St Francis of *Sales* or his order, the Visitants. — *n* a follower of St Francis; a member of his order.

salet. See **sallet**[1].

salewd (*Spenser*) *pa t* of **salue**.

salfern *sal'fərn*, *n* gromwell (*Lithospermum arvense*).

Salian[1] *sā'li-ən*, *adj* pertaining to a tribe of Franks who established themselves along the Yssel river in the 4c. — *n* a member of this tribe. — *adj* **Salic** (*sal'ik* or *sā'lik*) or **Salique** (*sal'ik* or *sa-lēk'*). — **Salic law** a law among the Salian Franks limiting the succession of certain lands to males; a law so named by extension, excluding women from the succession to the French crown, first invoked in 1316. [L *Saliī* Salians]

Salian[2] *sā'li-ən*, *adj* pertaining to the *Saliī*, or priests of Mars in ancient Rome.

salic *sal'ik* or *sā'lik*, *adj* (of minerals) rich in silicon and aluminium. [*s*ilicon and *al*uminium]

Salic. See under **Salian**[1].

salicaceous *sal-i-kā'shəs*, *adj* of or belonging to the **Salicā'ceae**, a family of trees and shrubs *incl* the willows and poplars. — *n* **sal'icet** (*-set*) or **salicional** (*sə-lish'ə-nəl*) organ stops with tones like those of willow pipes. — *n* **salicetum** (*-sē'təm*) a thicket or plantation of willows: — *pl* **salicē'tums** or **salicē'ta**. — *n* **sal'icin** or **sal'acine** (*-sin*) a bitter crystalline glucoside ($C_{13}H_{18}O_7$) obtained from willow-bark, etc and used medicinally as an analgesic, etc. — *n* **salicyl'amide** an analgesic drug administered orally. — *n* **salicylate** (*sə-lis'i-lāt*) a salt of salicylic acid. — *vt* to treat with salicylic acid. — *adj* **salicylic** (*sal-i-sil'ik*; Gr *hȳlē* matter, material). — *n* **sal'icylism** poisoning due to overdose of salicylate-containing drugs such as aspirin. — **salicylic acid** an acid ($C_7H_6O_3$) *orig* prepared from salicin, and used in the manufacture of aspirin, fungicides, etc. [L *salix*, *salicis* a willow]

salices. See **salix**.

salicornia *sal-i-kör'ni-ə*, *n* any plant, such as glasswort, of the *Salicornia* genus of goosefoots, found on salt marshes and pebbly seashores, having jointed cactus-like stems. [Perh L *sāl* salt, and *cornū* a horn]

salient *sā'li-ənt*, *adj* outstanding, prominent, striking; projecting outwards (*archit*); leaping or springing (now *usu biol* or *heraldry*). — *n* an outward-pointing angle, *esp* of a fortification or line of defences. — *n* **sā'lience** (*Spencer* **saliaunce** onslaught) or **sā'liency**. — *n* and *adj* **salientian** (*-en'shyən*, *-shən*) (an animal of) the order **Salien'tia**, amphibians *incl* frogs and toads. — *adv* **sā'liently**. [L *saliēns*, *-entis*, pr p of *salīre*, to leap]

saliferous *sə-lif'ər-əs*, *adj* salt-bearing. [L *sāl*, *salis* salt, and *ferre*, to bear]

salify *sal'i-fī*, *vt* to combine or impregnate with, or form into, a salt: — *pr p* **sal'ifying**; *pa t* and *pa p* **sal'ified**. — *adj* **sal'ifīable**. — *n* **salificā'tion**. [Fr *salifier*, from L *sāl*, *salis* salt, and *facere* to make]

saligot *sal'i-got*, *n* another name for the water-chestnut. [Fr]

salimeter. Same as **salinometer** (qv under **saline**).

salina *sə-lē'nə* or *-lī'*, *n* a salt lagoon, lake, marsh, or spring. [Sp, from L *salīna* (in pl only), from *sāl* salt]

saline *sā'līn* or *sal'*, also *sə-līn'*, *adj* salt; salty; containing salt; of the nature of a salt; abounding in salt; of the salts of alkali metals and magnesium; adapted to an environment with salt. — *n* (*sə-līn'*, also *sā'līn*) a salina; a salt; an effervescent laxative powder; a salt solution, *esp* (*med*) an isotonic solution containing sodium chloride used as a plasma substitute, etc. — *n* **salinity** (*sə-lin'i-ti*). — *n* **salinometer** (*sal-i-nom'i-tər*) or **salim'eter** a hydrometer for measuring the amount of salt in a solution. [L *salīnus*, cf **salina**]

Salique. Same as **Salic** (see **Salian**[1]).

Salish *sā'lish*, *n* a group of N American Indian language dialects of the Mosan phylum spoken in the NW US and W Canada; (with *the*) the peoples speaking these dialects. — *adj* **Sa'lishan**.

saliva *sə-lī'və*, *n* spittle, a liquid secreted in the mouth to soften food and begin the process of digestion. — *adj* **salī'val** (*rare*). — *adj* **salivary** (*sal'i-vər-i* or *sə-lī'*) pertaining to, secreting, or conveying, saliva. — *vi* **sal'ivate** to produce or discharge saliva, *esp* in excess, *usu* in eager anticipation of food (also *fig*). — *vt* to cause to secrete excess of saliva. — *n* **salivā'tion** flow of saliva, *esp* in excess, and *esp* in anticipation (of food, etc). — **salivary gland** a saliva-secreting gland; **salivary gland chromosome** a giant, conspicuously banded chromosome found in the salivary glands of larvae of dipteran insects. [L *salīva*]

salix *sal'iks* or *sā'liks*, *n* any tree or plant of the willow genus *Salix*: — *pl* **salices** (*sal'i-sēz* or *sā'*). [L *salix*, *-icis*]

Salk vaccine *sök* or *sölk vak'sēn* or *-sin*, *n* the first vaccine developed against poliomyelitis, administered by injection. [Developed by Dr J E *Salk* (born 1914), US microbiologist, and others]

sallal. See **salal**.

salle *sal*, (*Fr*) *n* hall.

sallee or **sally** *sal'ē*, (*Austr*) *n* any of various species of acacia; a species of eucalyptus with pale-coloured bark, the snow gum. [From a native word, or **sally**[3]]

sallee-man *sal'ē-man*, *n* a Moorish pirate-ship (*obs*); a hydrozoan with a sail-like crest. — Also **sall'y-man**. — **sall'ee-rover**. [*Sallee*, on the coast of Morocco]

sallenders *sal'ən-dərz*, *n* a skin disease affecting the hocks of horses. [Cf Fr *solandre*]

sallet[1] or **salet** *sal'it*, *n* (in medieval armour) a light helmet extending over the back of the neck. — Also **salade** (*sä-läd'*). [Fr *salade*; cf Ital *celata*; perh from L *galea caelāta* engraved helmet]

sallet[2]. An archaic or dialect form of **salad**.

sallow[1] *sal'ō*, *adj* (*esp* of a person's skin) of a pale yellowish colour. — *vt* to make sallow. — *adj* **sall'owish**. — *n* **sall'owness**. — *adj* **sall'owy**. [OE *salo*, *salu*; cf OHGer *salo*]

sallow[2] *sal'ō*, *n* a willow, *esp* the broader-leaved kinds with comparatively brittle twigs, such as *Salix cinerea*, the common sallow. — *adj* **sall'owy**. — **sallow kitten** a small puss moth whose larva feeds on sallow; **sall'ow-thorn** sea-buckthorn. [OE (Anglian) *salh*, late stem *salg-* (WSax *sealh*, *sēales*); cf Ger *Sal*(*weide*), L *salix*]

sally[1] *sal'i*, *n* a sudden rushing forth of troops to attack besiegers; an outrush, a sortie; a going forth, excursion, outing, jaunt; a witty remark or retort; a projection; an angle cut into the end of a timber to allow it to rest on a cross-timber (*building*); a ship's leaping, bounding or swaying motion (*naut*). — *vi* (*archaic* or *facetious*; *usu* with *forth*) to rush out suddenly; to go or come forth, set off on an excursion, outing, etc; (of a ship) to sway, rock or bound (*naut*). — *vt* (*naut*) to rock (a ship) by running from side to side to urge it on: — *pr p* **sall'ying**; *pa t* and *pa p* **sall'ied**. — **sall'yport** a gateway or opening for making a sally from a fortified place; a large port for the escape of the crew from a fireship. [Fr *saillie*, from *saillir* (Ital *salire*), from L *salīre* to leap]

sally[2] *sal'i*, (*bell-ringing*) *n* the raising of a bell by a pull of the rope; the woolly grip of a bell rope. — *vt* to bring into position of sally. [Perh from **sally**[1]]

sally[3] *sal'i*, a variant of **sallee** and of **sallow**[2].

Sally Army *sal'i ärm'i*, (*colloq*) *n* the Salvation Army.

Sally Lunn *sal'i lun'*, *n* a sweet tea cake, *usu* served hot with butter. [From a girl who sold them in the streets of Bath, c1797]

sally-man. See **sallee-man**.

sallyport. See under **sally**[1].

salmagundi or **salmagundy** *sal-mə-gun'di*, *n* a dish of minced meat with eggs, anchovies, vinegar, pepper, etc; a medley, miscellany. [Fr *salmigondis*; origin obscure]

salmanazar or **salmanaser** *sal-man-ā'zər*, *n* (also with *cap*) a large wine bottle, *usu* holding the equivalent of 12 standard bottles. [Allusion to Shalmaneser, King of Assyria, II Kings 17. 3]

salmi or **salmis** *sal'mē*, *n* a ragout, *esp* of previously cooked game: — *pl* **salmis** (*sal'mē*). [Fr; perh from **salmagundi**, or from Ital *salame* sausage]

Salmo *sal'mō*, *n* the salmon and trout genus of fishes, giving name to the family **Salmonidae** (*sal-mon'i-dē*). — *n* **sal'monid**. — *n* and *adj* **sal'monoid**. [L *salmō*, *-ōnis* salmon]

salmon[1] *sam'ən*, *n* a large, soft-finned fish (*Salmo salar*), with silvery sides, that ascends rivers to spawn and is highly prized as a food and game fish; extended to many closely related fishes, and to some that resemble it superficially in some respects; the flesh of any of these as food; the colour of salmon flesh, a pinkish orange: — *pl* **salmon** or (in referring to different kinds of salmon) **salmons**. — *adj* salmon-coloured. — *n* **salm'onet** a samlet. — *n* **sal'monoid** (a fish) of the family *Salmonidae*, soft-finned fishes including the salmon, trout, etc. — *adj* and *n* **sal'monid** (of) any member of the suborder *Salmonoidea*. — **salm'onberry** a salmon-coloured N American raspberry, *Rubus spectabilis*; **salmon coble** a boat used on rivers and estuaries by salmon fishermen; **salm'on-colour** an orange-pink. — *adj* **salm'on-coloured**. — **salmon disease** a bacterial disease of salmon formerly attributed to a fungus (Saprolegnia); **salm'on-fisher**; **salmon fishery**; **salm'on-fishing**; **salmon fly** any artificial fly used in salmon-fishing; **salmon fry**; **salmon ladder** a series of steps built eg into the side of a river bed so as to permit salmon to pass upstream avoiding obstructions such as a dam, hydroelectric installation, etc; **salmon leap** a waterfall which salmon ascend by leaping; **salmon leister** or **spear** an instrument for spearing salmon; **salmon pink** (*adj* **salmon-pink'**); **salmon trout** a name applied to various forms of fish of the species *Salmo trutta*, resembling the salmon, *esp* the sea trout; applied to various kinds of trout and char (*US*). — **Burnett salmon** the Australian lungfish (from the Burnett River). [OFr *saumon*, from L *salmō*, *-ōnis*, from *salīre* to leap]

salmon[2] *sam'ən* or **salamon** *sal'ə-mən*, (*obs*) *n* supposed to mean the mass, as in the vagrants' inviolable oath *by* (*the*) *salmon*. [Origin obscure]

salmonella *sal-mə-nel'ə*, *n* a member of a large genus of rod-like bacteria (*Salmonella*), many of which are associated with poisoning by contaminated food: — *pl* **salmonell'as** or **salmonell'ae** (*-ē*). — *n* **salmonello'sis** food poisoning caused by infestation by Salmonella bacteria. [New L, from D E *Salmon*, (1850–1914) US veterinarian]

salmonet, salmonid, salmonoid. See under **salmon**[1].

Salomonic. Same as **Solomonic**.

salon *sal-ɔ̃* or *sal'on*, *n* a drawing-room; a reception room; a social gathering of distinguished people at the house of a lady of fashion, literary hostess, etc; a somewhat elegant shop or business establishment whose purpose is to provide cosmetic, hairdressing, etc services (eg *beauty salon*); a room or hall for the exhibiting of paintings, sculptures, etc; (with *cap*) a great annual exhibition of works by living artists in Paris. [Fr]

saloon *sə-lo͞on'*, *n* a large public room (for billiards, for hairdressing, for dancing, for exhibitions, etc); a large public cabin or dining-room for passengers on a ship, luxury train, etc; a saloon carriage; a saloon bar; an establishment where alcoholic drink is served (*NAm*); a motor car with two or four doors and enclosed compartment for driver and passengers, not an estate, coupé or sports model (also **saloon car**). — **saloon bar** an area in a public house, quieter and more comfortably furnished than the public bar, *usu* (*esp* formerly) separated from it; **saloon carriage** a railway carriage with its interior open from end to end, not divided into compartments, etc; **saloon deck** an upper deck on a ship reserved for saloon or first-class passengers; **saloon'-keeper** (*NAm*) a publican; **saloon passenger** a passenger entitled to use the principal cabin; a first-class passenger on board a ship; **saloon pistol** or **saloon rifle** one for use in a shooting gallery. [Fr *salon*]

saloop *sə-lo͞op'*, *n* a hot drink made from an infusion of salep, later from sassafras, formerly used as a tonic. [**salep**]

salop. A variant of **saloop**. — *adj* **salop'ian** (*Lamb*).

salopettes *sal'ə-pets*, *n pl* a type of ski suit consisting of *usu* quilted trousers extending to the chest and held up with shoulder-straps. [Fr]

Salopian *sə-lō'pi-ən* of or from Shropshire (formerly called *Salop*); of or from Shrewsbury School. — *n* a native or inhabitant of Shropshire; a person educated at Shrewsbury School. [*Salop*, from Anglo-Fr *Slop-pesberie*, from OE *Scrobbesbyrig*]

salpa *sal'pə*, *n* any free-swimming planktonic tunicate of the genus *Salpa*, having a transparent barrel-shaped body and lacking a larval stage: — *pl* **sal'pae** (*-pē*) or **sal'pas**. — Also **salp** (*salp*). — *n* and *adj* **sal'pian**. — *adj* **sal'piform**. [L from Gr *salpē*, a kind of fish]

salpicon *sal'pi-kon*, *n* a mixture of chopped meat, fish or vegetables, *esp* mushrooms or truffles, in a sauce, used in pâtés, or as fillings for pastries, etc. [Fr, from Sp *salpicar* to sprinkle with salt]

salpiglossis *sal-pi-glos'is*, *n* any plant of the genus *Salpiglossis*, some of which bear bright, trumpet-shaped flowers. [Gr *salpinx* a trumpet, and *glōssa* tongue]

salpinx *sal'pingks*, *n* the Eustachian tube, leading from the middle ear to the pharynx (*anatom*); either of the Fallopian tubes, leading from the ovary to the uterus (*anatom*); a trumpet or tuba of ancient Greece (*hist*). — *n* **salpingectomy** (*-pin-jek'tə-mi*) surgical removal of a Fallopian tube. — *adj* **salpingian** (*-pin'ji-ən*). — *adj* **salpingit'ic** of, or of the nature of, salpingitis. — *n* **salpingitis** (*-jī'tis*) inflammation of a tube, *esp* one or both Fallopian tubes. [Gr *salpinx*, *-ingos* a trumpet]

salsa *sal'sə*, *n* the name given to a type of rhythmic Latin-American big-band music, with elements of jazz and rock; a dance performed to this music; a spicy sauce made with tomatoes, onions, chillies and oil (*Mex cookery*). — *vi* to dance the salsa. — **salsa verde** Italian green sauce, made with anchovies, garlic, capers, oil and herbs. [Sp and Ital *salsa* sauce]

salse *sals*, (*geol*) *n* a mud volcano. [Fr, from Ital *salsa*, prob from *Sassuolo*, name of one near Modena]

salsify *sal'si-fi*, *n* the oyster-plant or vegetable oyster, a purple-flowered European composite plant, *Tragopogon porrifolius*, cultivated for its edible root tasting like oysters, and its tender spring shoots boiled like asparagus. — **black salsify** scorzonera, a plant like a dandelion, with an edible root. [Fr *salsifis*, prob from Ital *sassefrica*]

salsolaceous *sal'sə-lā'shəs*, (*bot*) *adj* of, characteristic of, or relating to the saltwort genus *Salsola* of the goosefoot family. [Obs Ital *salsola*, dimin of *salso*, from L *salsus* salt (adj)]

salsuginous *sal-so͞o'ji-nəs*, *adj* salty, brackish; growing in salty soil. [L *salsūgō*, *-inis* saltness]

SALT *sölt*, *abbrev*: Strategic Arms Limitation Talks or Treaty.

salt[1] *sölt*, *n* chloride of sodium, occurring naturally as a mineral (rock-salt) and in solution in sea-water, salt-water springs, etc, used as a condiment and preservative; a saltcellar; a compound in which metal atoms or electropositive radicals replace one or more of the replaceable hydrogen atoms of an acid, generalized to include the acid itself; piquancy, liveliness; dry or pungent wit; a saltmarsh or salting; an influx of salt water; a sailor, *esp* an experienced sailor; (in *pl*) smelling-salts; (in *pl*) Epsom salts or other salt or mixture of salts used medicinally, *esp* as a purgative; money collected at montem (qv). — *adj* containing salt; tasting of salt; seasoned or cured with salt; covered over with, or immersed in, salt water; growing in salt soil; inhabiting salt water; pungent; expensive, dear (*archaic slang*). — *vt* to sprinkle, season, preserve or impregnate with salt; to season, or add piquancy to; to acclimatize; to assign an excessive value to or in (*slang*); to add gold, ore, etc to (a mine, etc) in order to give a false appearance of riches (*mining slang*); to immunize (an animal) by inoculation, etc (*old*). — *adj* **salt'ed**. — **salt'er** a person who makes or deals in salt or salted foods; a dealer in gums, dyes, etc, a drysalter. — *adv* **salt'ily**. — *n* **salt'iness**. — *n* **salt'ing** the act of preserving, seasoning, etc with salt; a meadow flooded by the tides (sfx *-ing*, indicating a meadow in place-names); the montem (qv) ceremony. — *adj* **salt'ish**. — *adv* **salt'ishly**. — *n* **salt'ishness**. — *adj* **salt'less**. — *adv* **salt'ly**. — *n* **salt'ness**. — *adj* **salt'y** tasting of, containing, etc salt; piquant, racy, witty. — **salt bath** (*metallurgy*) a bath of molten salts in which steel is heated, hardened or tempered; **salt'box** a box for holding salt, *esp* one with a sloping clapper lid, once used as in burlesque music along with the marrow-bones, tongs, etc; **salt'bush** any shrubby plant (genus *Atriplex*) of the goosefoot family, of arid regions. — *adj* **salt'-butter** (*Shakesp*) fed on nothing better than salt butter, gross. — **salt cake** impure sodium sulphate; **salt'cat** a salt mixture given as a digestive to pigeons; **salt'cellar** (OFr *saliere*, from L *salārium*, from *sāl* salt) a container for holding salt when used as a condiment; a depression behind the collar-bone; **salt'-chuck** (*Can*) a body of salt water; **salt'-cote** (*obs*) a building where salt is prepared for use as a condiment; **salt dome** or **plug** (*geol*) a diapir formed by a column of rock salt forced up by pressure through upper rock stata; **salt'-fat** or (erroneously) **salt'-foot** formerly, a large saltcellar marking the class boundary at table; a pickling-tub; **salt'fish** (*Caribbean*) salted cod; **salt flat** a stretch of flat, salt-covered land left by the evaporation of an area of salt water; **salt'-glaze** a glaze produced on pottery by volatilization of common salt in the kiln; pottery produced with this glaze; **salt'-glazing**; **salt'-horse** (*slang*) and **salt'-junk** (*sailors' slang*) salt beef; **salt lake** an inland lake of saline water; **salt lick** a place to which animals go to obtain salt; a block of salt, often also containing other essential minerals, given to domestic animals as a dietary supplement; **salt marsh** land liable to be flooded with salt water; **salt'-mine** a mine of rock-salt; **salt'-money** an allowance for salt; money collected at montem (qv); **salt pan** a large basin for obtaining salt by evaporation; a natural depression in which salt accumulates or has accumulated by evaporation; **salt pit** a pit for obtaining salt by evaporation; **salt plug** see **salt dome**; **salt rheum** a discharge of mucus from the nose (*Shakesp*); eczema or other skin eruption (*NAm*; *old*); **salt spoon**; **salt spring** a brine spring. — *adj* **salt'water** of, containing or inhabiting salt water. — **salt'works** a place where salt is refined; **salt'wort** a fleshy, prickly plant of the genus *Salsola*, of the goosefoot family, eg *S. kali* found on sandy seashores; sometimes applied to the glasswort (*Salicornia*). — **above** (or **below**) **the salt** among those of high (or low) social class, the salt cellar formerly marking the boundary at table when all dined together; **lay, put** or **cast salt on someone's tail** to find or catch someone, from the jocularly recommended method of catching a bird; **like a dose of salts** (*colloq*) very quickly; **rub salt in a wound** to aggravate someone's sorrow, shame, regret, etc; **salt away** to store away; to hoard, *esp* in a miserly way; **salt down** to preserve with salt; to lay by, store up; **salt of sorrel** acid potassium oxalate, a solvent for removing ink-stains; **salt of tartar** a commercial name for purified potassium carbonate; **salt of the earth** the choice few of the highest excellence (from the Bible: Matt 5. 13); **salt of vitriol** sulphate of zinc; **salt of wisdom** sal alembroth; **salt of wormwood** potassium carbonate; **salt out** to obtain as a precipitate by adding a salt; **take with a grain** (or **pinch**) **of salt** to believe (something or someone) only with great reservations; **worth one's salt** valuable, useful, *orig* worth the value of the salt one consumes. [OE (Anglian) *salt* (WSax *sealt*); cf Ger *Salz*, also L *sāl*, Gr *hals*]

salt[2] *sölt*, (*obs*) *n* sexual desire, *esp* in bitches. — *adj* in heat; salacious. [L *saltus*, *-ūs* leap]

salt[3] *sölt*, *n*. See **sault**.

saltando *säl-tän'dō* or **saltato** *-tä'tō*, *adv* and *adj* arco saltando (qv). [Gerund and pa p respectively of Ital *saltare* to jump, skip]

saltant *sal'tənt* or *söl'tənt*, *adj* (of an organism) resulting from or exhibiting saltation (*biol*); dancing, jumping (*obs*); salient (*heraldry*). — *n* (*biol*) a changed or mutated form of an organism that has developed suddenly. — *vi* **sal'tate** to undergo saltation. — *n* **saltā'tion** a leaping or jumping; an abrupt variation or mutation (*biol*); the movement of a particle being transported by wind or water, resembling a series of leaps (*geol*). — *n* **saltāt'ionism** the process or concept of saltation, *specif* the evolutionary theory that new species come about by saltation. — *n* **saltāt'ionist** someone who supports saltationism as a theory. — *adj* **saltato'rial**, **saltato'rious** or **sal'tatory** of or for leaping or jumping (*biol*); of or displaying saltation. [L *saltāre*, *-ātum*, intens of *salīre* to leap]

saltarello *sal-tə-rel'ō*, *n* a lively Italian dance with a hop executed at the beginning of each measure; its music, in triple time: — *pl* **saltarell'os** or **saltarell'i**. [Ital *saltarello*, Sp *saltarelo*, from L *saltāre* to dance]

saltate, etc. See under **saltant**.

saltato. See **saltando**.

saltern *sölt'ərn*, *n* a salt-works. [OE *s(e)altern*, from s(*e*)*alt* salt, and *ærn* house]

saltier. See **satyr**, **saltire**.

saltigrade *sal'ti-grād*, *adj* progressing by leaps. — *n* a jumping spider. [L *saltus*, *-ūs* a leap, and *gradī* to go]

saltimbanco *sal-tim-bangk'ō*, (*obs*) *n* a mountebank, a quack: — *pl* **saltimbanc'os**. [Ital, from *saltare in banco* to leap on to a bench, so as to harangue a crowd; see also **mountebank**]

saltimbocca *sal-tim-bok'ə*, *n* and *adj* (of) an Italian dish of rolled slices of veal and ham, with cheese or herbs. [Ital, literally, it leaps into the mouth]

saltire or **saltier** *sal'* or *söl'tīr*, *n* an armorial emblem in the form of a St Andrew's cross (*heraldry*); loosely, the national flag of Scotland, a white St Andrew's cross on a blue background. — *adj* **sal'tirewise**. [OFr *saultoir*, *sautoir*, from LL *saltātōrium* a stirrup, from L *saltāre* to leap]

salto *sal'tō* or *säl'tō*, *n* a daring leap (*also fig*); a somersault (*gymnastics*): — *pl* **sal'tos**. — *vi* to perform a salto: — *pa p* and *pa t* **sal'toed**. [Ital, a jump, leap; also *salto mortale*, literally, a mortal leap, a somersault]

saltpetre or (*NAm*) **saltpeter** *sölt-pē'tər*, *n* potassium nitrate. — **saltpē'treman** (*hist*) someone authorized to search for saltpetre; someone who prepares saltpetre; **saltpe'tre-paper** touch-paper. — **Chile saltpetre** or **cubic saltpetre** sodium nitrate; **Norway saltpetre** calcium nitrate. [OFr *salpetre*, from LL *salpetra*, prob for L *sāl petrae* salt of stone]

saltus *sal'təs*, (*logic*) *n* a breach of continuity; a jump to a conclusion: — *pl* **saltuses**. [L, a leap, pl *saltūs*]

salubrious *sə-lōō'bri-əs* or *-lū'*, *adj* health-giving, promoting well-being; loosely, pleasant, decent, respectable. — *adv* **salu'briously**. — *n* **salu'briousness** or **salu'brity**. [L *salūbris*, from *salūs*, *salūtis* health]

salue *sal-ōō'*, or *-ū'*, also *sal'*, (*obs*) *vt* to salute. — *pa t* (*Spenser*) **salewd'** (also **sal'ued**, which may be for **salve'd**, hailed with *salve*, the Latin greeting). [Fr *saluer*, from L *salutāre*]

saluki *sə-lōō'kē* or *-gē*, *n* a tall, slender, silky-haired breed of dog, *orig* from Arabia and Persia. [Ar *seluqi*]

salutary *sal'ū-tər-i*, *adj* promoting health or safety; wholesome; containing, bringing, etc a timely warning. — *adv* **sal'ūtarily**. — *n* **sal'ūtariness**. [L *salūtāris*, from *salūs* health]

salute *sə-lōōt'* or *-lūt'*, *vt* to greet with words or (now *esp*) with a gesture or with a kiss; to honour formally by a discharge of cannon, striking of colours, or *esp* with any of various recognized gestures with the arm (*military*); to affect, act upon (*Shakesp*). — *vi* to perform the act of saluting, *esp* in the military manner. — *n* the act or position of saluting; a greeting, *esp* in the form of a gesture or a kiss; a complimentary discharge of cannon, dipping of colours, presenting of arms, etc, eg to honour a person or occasion. — *n* **salutation** (*sal-ū-tā'shən*) the act of, or words used in, greeting; a formal visit (*esp Roman hist*); a quickening (of the blood), excitement (*Shakesp*); the Angelic Salutation (see **ave**). — *adj* **salūtā'tional**. — *n* **salutatorian** (*sə-lōō-tə-tō'ri-ən* or *-tö'*) in American colleges, the graduand who pronounces the address of welcome. — *adv* **salu'tatorily**. — *adj* **salu'tatory**. — *n* an address of welcome, *esp* in American colleges; an audience chamber (*hist*). — *n* **salu'ter** someone who salutes; in Spain, someone who professed to work miracles in the name of St Catherine (Sp *saludador*; *hist*). [L *salūtāre*, *-ātum* (vb), and *salūs*, *salūtis* (n), and partly through Fr *salut*]

salutiferous *sal-ū-tif'ər-əs*, (*formal*) *adj* conducive to health or well-being. [L *salūtifer*, from *salūs*, *salūtis* health, and *ferre* to bring]

salvable, etc. See under **salve**[1].

salvage[1] *sal'vij*, *n* a reward paid by a ship's owner to those involved in its rescue, or the rescue of its cargo, from danger or loss; the raising of sunken or wrecked ships; the rescue of property from fire or other peril; the saving of waste material for utilization; anything saved in any of these ways. — *vt* to save from danger of loss or destruction; to manage to retain (one's pride, etc); to recover or save as salvage. — *adj* **sal'vageable**. — **sal'vage-corps** a body of men employed in salvage work. [LL *salvāgium*, from *salvāre* to save]

salvage[2] *sal'vij*, (*Spenser*, *Shakesp*, etc) *n* and *adj*. Same as **savage**.

salvarsan *sal'vər-san* or *sal-vär'san*, *n* a compound of arsenic, first used by Paul Ehrlich (1854–1915) as a remedy for syphilis (since superseded by antibiotics). [L *salvus* safe, whole, and Ger *Arsen* arsenic]

salve[1] *salv*, *vt* to salvage; to save (an opinion) from objection (*obs*); to vindicate (*obs*); to preserve unhurt or undamaged (*obs*); to explain by hypothesis (*obs*); to explain, clear up, harmonize (*obs*). — *n* a way out of a difficulty. — *n* **salvabil'ity**. — *adj* **salv'able**. — *n* **salvā'tion** the act of saving; the means of preservation from any serious evil; the saving of man from the power and penalty of sin, the conferring of eternal happiness (*theol*). — *n* **Salvā'tionism**. — *n* **Salvā'tionist** a member of the Salvation Army. — *n* **sal'vatory** a repository for safe storage. — *adj* (*rare*) saving. — *adj* (*obs*) **salvif'ic** or **salvif'ical** having the purpose or intention of saving. — *adv* (*obs*) **salvif'ically**. — **Salvation Army** an organization for the spread of religion among the poor, founded by William Booth in 1865. [LL *salvāre* to save; partly back-formation from **salvage**[1]]

salve[2] *säv*, *salv*, *n* a soothing ointment; a remedy; anything to soothe the feelings or conscience. — *vt* to anoint; to smear; to heal; to soothe. — *n* and *adj* **salv'ing**. [OE *s(e)alf* ointment; Ger *Salbe*, Du *zalf*]

salve[3] *sal'vi*, *sal'wā*, *interj* hail (addressed to one person). — *n* a greeting; a piece of church music beginning *Salve Regina* (*RC*). — *interj* and *n* **salvete** (*sal-vē'tē*, *sal-wā'tā*) (addressed to more than one person). [L *salvē*, imperative of *salvēre* to be well]

salver[1] *sal'vər*, *n* a tray or (silver) plate on which anything is presented. — *adj* **sal'ver-shaped** or **sal'verform** (*bot*) (of a corolla) having a long tube with terminal petals spread out flat. [Sp *salva*, the precautionary tasting of food, as by a prince's taster, hence the tray on which it was presented to the prince, from *salvar* to save, from LL *salvāre*]

salver[2]. See **salvor**.

salvia *sal'vi-ə*, *n* any labiate of the genus *Salvia*, *incl* sage. [L *salvia* sage]

salvific, etc. See under **salve**[1].

Salvinia *sal-vin'i-ə, n* a genus of water-ferns, giving name to a family **Salviniā'ceae**. — *adj* **salviniā'ceous**. [Named after Antonio Maria *Salvini* (1653–1729), Italian Greek scholar]

salvo[1] *sal'vō, n* a simultaneous discharge of artillery in salute or otherwise; a simultaneous discharge of bombs, etc; a sudden round of applause; a burst (of repeated criticisms, insults, attacks, etc): — *pl* **sal'vos** or **sal'voes**. [Ital *salva* salute, from L *salvē* hail]

salvo[2] *sal'vō, n* a saving clause, reservation (*esp law*); an excuse, pretext (*obs*); an expedient for saving appearances, avoiding offence, etc: — *pl* **sal'vos**. [L *salvō*, ablative of *salvus* safe, (one's right, honour, etc) being saved]

salvo jure *sal'vō jōō'rē*, also *sal'wō* or *yōō're*, (*L*) saving the right (the right being saved); without prejudice.

sal volatile. See under **sal**[4].

salvor or **salver** *sal'vər, n* a person who salvages.

SAM *sam, abbrev*: surface-to-air missile.

Sam. (*Bible*) *abbrev*: (the Books of) Samuel.

sam *sam*, (*Spenser*) *adv* together. [OE *samen*]

sama *sa'ma*, (*Jap*) *n* a title given to an exalted personage. Cf **san**[3].

samadhi *sə-mä'di, n* a state of super-awareness brought about by profound yogic meditation, in which the yogi becomes one with the object of the meditation. [Hindi]

saman *sa-män', n* the rain tree *Samanea Saman*, a member of the mimosa family. — Also **samaan'**. [Am Sp *samán*, from Carib *zamang*]

samara *sam'ə-rə* or *sə-mä'rə, n* a dry one-seeded fruit, with a wing-like appendage that facilitates distribution on air currents. — *adj* **sama'riform**. [L *samara, samera* elm seed]

Samaritan *sə-mar'i-tən, adj* of *Samaria*, in Palestine. — *n* a native of Samaria, an adherent of the religion of Samaria, differing from Judaism in that only the Pentateuch is accepted as holy scripture, with Moses the sole prophet of God; the Aramaic dialect of Samaria; a good Samaritan; a member of a voluntary organization formed to help people who are distressed or despairing, *esp* by talking to them on the telephone. — *n* **Samar'itanism**. — **Samaritan Pentateuch** a recension of the Hebrew Pentateuch accepted by the Samaritans as alone canonical. — **good Samaritan** a person who charitably gives help in need (from the Bible: Luke 10. 30–37). [L *Samāritānus*]

samarium *sə-mā'ri-əm, n* a metallic element (symbol **Sm**; atomic no 62) observed spectroscopically in samarskite. — *n* **samarskite** (*sə-mär'skīt*) a black mineral containing uranium. [Named in honour of Colonel *Samarski*, 19c Russian engineer]

Samaveda or **Sama-Veda** *sä-mä-vā'dä*, (*Hinduism*) *n* the name of one of the four books of the Veda, containing ritual chants for sacrifices. [Sans *Sāmaveda*]

samba *sam'bə, n* a Brazilian dance in duple time with syncopation; a ballroom dance developed from it; music for this dance. — *vi* to dance the samba. [Port]

sambal *säm'bäl, n* any of various foods served with curries in Malaysia and Indonesia, eg peppers, pickles, salt fish, coconut, etc. [Malay]

sambar or **sambur** *sam'bər, n* a large deer, *Cervus unicolor*, of S Asia, Indonesia and China. [Hindi *sābar*]

sambo[1] *sam'bō, n* the offspring of Black person and an American Indian or mulatto; a Black person,*esp* a man, sometimes used as a form of address (*offensive slang*): — *pl* **sam'bos**. [Sp *zambo*, said to be from L *scambus*, from Gr *skambos*, bow-legged; perh partly Fulah *sambo* uncle]

sambo[2] *sam'bō*, a from of wrestling using judo techniques. [Russ *sam*ozashchita *bez o*ruzhiya self-defence without weapons]

Sam Browne *sam' brown', n* a military officer's belt with a shoulder strap. [Invented by General Sir Samuel James *Browne* (1824–1901)]

sambuca *sam-bū'kə, n* an ancient musical instrument like a harp; an Indian liquorice-flavoured liqueur made from aniseed. [L *sambūca*, from Gr *sambȳkē*, prob an Asiatic word; cf Aramaic *sabbekā*]

sambur. Same as **sambar**.

same *sām, adj* identical (commonly with *as*, or a relative clause introduced by *that*; also with *with*); not different; unchanged; unvaried; (*esp* with *the*) mentioned before. — *pron* (*colloq*) the aforesaid, it, them, they, etc. — *n* (*rare*) an identical thing. — *adj* **same'ly** unvaried. — *n* **same'ness** being the same; tedious monotony. — *adj* **sā'mey** (*colloq*) (boringly) alike; monotonous. — **all the same** for all that, neverthless; **at the same time** still, however; **same here** (*colloq*) me too; **the same** the same thing or person; the aforesaid or aforementioned; in the same way. [OE *same* (only in phrase *swā same* likewise); Gothic *sama*; L *similis* like, Gr *homos*]

samekh *sä'mək* or *sam'ehh, n* the 15th letter of the Hebrew alphabet (ס).

samel *sam'l, adj* (of a brick, tile, etc) underburnt. [App OE pfx *sam-* half, and *ǣled* burned]

samen *sā'mən*, an obsolete Scots form of **same**.

samey. See under **same**.

samfoo or **samfu** *sam'fōō, n* an outfit worn by Chinese women, consisting of a jacket and trousers. [Cantonese]

Sami. See **Saam**.

Samian *sā'mi-ən, adj* of the Greek island of *Samos*. — *n* a native of Samos (also **Sa'miot** or **Sa'miote**). — **Samian earth** an argillaceous astringent soil; **Samian letter** the Pythagorean letter; **Samian stone** a goldsmiths' polishing stone; **Samian ware** brick-red or black earthenware pottery, with a lustrous glaze produced in Italy in the first century BC; a later imitation made in Roman Gaul and elsewhere in the Roman empire.

samiel *sā'mi-əl, n* a hot desert wind, the simoom. [Ar *samm* poison, and Turk *yel* wind]

Samiot, Samiote. See **Samian**.

samisen *sam'i-sen*, or **shamisen** *sham', n* a Japanese guitar-like instrument with three strings. [Jap]

samite *sam'īt, n* a kind of heavy silk fabric, often interwoven with gold or silver threads, used for clothing in medieval times. [OFr *samit*, from LL *examitum*, from Gr *hexamiton*, from *hex* six, and *mitos* thread]

samiti *sam'i-ti, n* (in India) an organization or committee of workers, *usu* involved in political activity. [Hindi]

samizdat *sam'iz-dat, n* in the former Soviet Union, the clandestine or illegal printing and distribution of underground literature, *usu* expressing views contrary to those endorsed by the state. — Also *adj*. [Russ *sam* self, and *izdatelstvo* publishing]

samlet *sam'lit, n* a young salmon. [**salmon**[1], and sfx **-let**]

samlor *sam'lör* or *-lōr, n* a three-wheeled vehicle common in Thailand, *usu* motorized and used as a taxi. [Thai]

Sammy *sam'i, n* a noodle (*slang*); an American expeditionary soldier (*military slang*; from *Uncle Sam*). [**Samuel**]

Samnite *sam'nīt, n* a member of an ancient people of central Italy, thought to be a branch of the Sabines, frequently in conflict with the Romans; their language; a Roman gladiator armed in the style of the Samnites. — Also *adj*. [L *Samnīs, -ītis*]

samnitis *sam-nī'tis*, (*Spenser*) *n* an unknown poisonous plant.

Samoed. See **Samoyed**.

samosa *sa-mō'sə, n* a small, fried, pastry turnover stuffed with spiced vegetables or meat, an Indian savoury: — *pl* **samo'sas** or **samo'sa**. [Hindi]

samovar *sam'ə-vär* or *-vär', n* a Russian metal urn for boiling water for making tea, etc, often elaborately decorated, traditionally heated by a central charcoal-filled pipe. [Russ *samovar*, literally, self-boiler]

Samoyed *sam-ō-yed'*, or *sam', n* a member of a Ugrian people of NW Siberia; their Ural-Altaic language; (*sa-moi'ed*) a breed of Siberian dog with a thick white coat and curled tail. — Also *adj* (*Milton* **Sam'oed**). — *adj* **Samoyed'ic**. [Russ *Samoyed*]

samp *samp*, (*NAm* and *SAfr*) *n* a coarsely ground maize; porridge made from it. [From Narranganset *nasaump*]

sampan *sam'pan*, *n* an Oriental skiff propelled by a sail or oar(s). — Also **san'pan**. [Chin *san* three, and *pan* board]

samphire *sam'fīr* or **sampire** *-pīr*, *n* an umbelliferous plant (*Crithmum maritimum*) of sea-cliffs, whose fleshy leaves are used in pickles; extended to other plants, eg *Inula crithmoides*, a plant related to elecampane (*golden samphire*), to glasswort (*marsh samphire*), to saltwort (*prickly samphire*). [Fr (*herbe de*) *Saint Pierre* Saint Peter('s herb)]

sampi *sam'pī*, *sam'pi* or *-pē*, *n* supposed name of a Greek numerical character, ϡ, (ͳ), or (ϡ), representing 900 and perhaps *orig* the same as the letter san. [Gr *sampī*]

sampire. See **samphire**.

sample *säm'pl*, *n* a specimen, a small portion to show the quality or nature of the whole; an example for imitation (*Spenser*, *Shakesp*) or (*obs*) warning. — *adj* serving as a sample. — *vt* to match (*obs*); to take, try or offer, a sample or samples of; (in popular music) to mix a (short) extract from one recording into a different backing rack; to record (a sound)and program it into a synthesizer which can then reproduce it at the desired pitch. — *n* **sam'pler** a collection of samples; the equipment that samples sound. — *n* **sam'pling** the taking, testing etc, of a sample; the examination and analysis of data obtained from a random group in order to deduce information about the population as a whole. — **sampling error** (*statistics*) variation due to a sample group necessarily giving only incomplete information about the whole population. [ME *essample*; see **example**]

sampler *säm'plər*, *n* an exemplar, type, pattern (*obs*); a test-piece of embroidery, commonly including an alphabet, with figures, names, etc. — *n* **sam'plery**. — **sam'pler-work**. [OFr *essemplaire*, from L *exemplar*; see **exemplar**]

samsara *səm-sä'rə*, *n* the never-ending cycle of birth and death and rebirth (*Hinduism*); the passage of a person's soul into another body or state (*Buddhism*). [Sans *saṁsāra* passing through]

samshoo or **samshu** *sam'shōō*, *n* a Chinese alcoholic drink made from fermented rice. [Pidgin; origin doubtful]

Samson *sam'sn*, *n* an abnormally strong man (from the biblical Hebrew champion of Judges 13–16). — **Samson's post** a strong post on a ship; a kind of mousetrap.

Samsonite® *sam'sən-īt*, *n* a kind of strong composite material, used to make luggage, etc.

samurai *sam'ōō-rī* or *-ū-rī*, (*Jap hist*) *n* a military retainer of a feudal Japanese nobleman; a member of the military caste in feudal Japan: — *pl* **sam'urai**. [Jap, from *samurau* to attend (one's lord)]

san[1] *san*, *n* a discarded letter of the Greek alphabet, Ϲ, *perh orig* the same as sampi. [Doric Gr *san* sigma]

san[2] *san*, (*old colloq*) *n* a sanatorium.

san[3] *san* or *sun*, *n* a Japanese title or form of address equivalent to Mr (or Mrs), placed after the name.

sanative *san'ə-tiv*, *adj* healing. — *n* **sanatō'rium** or (*esp NAm*) **sanitā'rium** (qv; imitation Latin) a hospital for convalescents and the chronically ill, *orig esp* for consumptives; a health farm, health resort or health station; a ward or building for the isolation and treatment of sick pupils at a boarding school, etc: — *pl* **sanato'riums** or **sanato'ria**. — *adj* **san'atory** healing; of healing. [L *sānāre*, *-ātum* to heal]

sanbenito *san-be-nē'tō*, *n* a garment, either yellow with a red cross worn by penitents in the Inquistion, or black with painted flames, devils, etc worn by impenitents at auto-da-fé: — *pl* **sanbeni'tos**. [Sp *San Benito* St Benedict, from its resemblance to St Benedict's scapular]

sancai *san'sī*, *n* in Chinese ceramics, a three-colour glaze. [Chin *san* three, and *cai* colour]

sancho or **sanko** *sang'kō*, *n* a W African guitar: — *pl* **san'chos** or **san'kos**. [Ashanti *osanku*]

sancho-pedro *sang'kō-pē'drō*, *n* a card game — the nine of trumps called **sancho**, the five **pedro**.

sanctify *sangk'ti-fī*, *vt* to make, declare, consider or show to be, sacred or holy; to set apart for sacred use; to free from sin or evil; to consecrate, bless; to invest with sacredness, blessedness or holiness; to sanction (*obs*): — *pr p* **sanc'tifying**; *pa t* and *pa p* **sanc'tified**. — *adj* **sanctifi'able**. — *n* **sanctificā'tion**. — *adj* **sanc'tified** made holy. — *adv* **sanc'tifiedly** (*-fī-id-li*). — *n* **sanc'tifier** (*-fī-ər*) a person who sanctifies; (*usu* with *cap*) the Holy Spirit. — *n* and *adj* **sanc'tifying**. — *adv* **sanc'tifyingly**. [Fr *sanctifier*, from L *sanctificāre*, from *sanctus* holy, and *facere* to make]

sanctimony *sangk'ti-mə-ni*, *n* holiness (*obs*); outward, affected, or simulated holiness. — *adj* **sanctimonious** (*-mō'ni-əs*) holy (*obs*); simulating holiness, *esp* hypocritically. — *adv* **sanctimō'niously**. — *n* **sanctimō'niousness**. [L *sanctimōnia*, from *sanctus*]

sanction *sangk'shən*, *n* motive, rationale for obedience to any moral or religious law (*ethics*); a penalty or reward expressly attached to non-observance or observance of a law or treaty (*law*); a military or economic measure taken by one country against another as a means of coercion (*politics*); the act of ratifying, or giving permission or authority; support; official permission, authority. — *vt* to give validity to; to authorize; to countenance, permit. — *n* **santioneer'** a person who advocates (*esp* political) sanctions. — **sanc'tions-busting** the breaching (*usu* by commercial concerns) of economic sanctions imposed on a country. [L *sanctiō*, *-ōnis*, from *sancīre*, *sanctum* to ratify]

sanctitude *sangk'ti-tūd*, *n* saintliness. [L *sanctitūdō*, *-inis*]

sanctity *sangk'ti-ti*, *n* the quality of being sacred or holy; purity; godliness; inviolability; saintship; (in *pl*) holy feelings, obligations, or objects. [L *sanctitās*, *-ātis* sanctity]

sanctuary *sangk'tū-ər-i*, *n* a holy place; a place of worship; the most holy part of a temple, church, etc; the chancel; a place affording immunity from arrest, persecution, etc; the privilege of refuge in such a place; a place of refuge or private retreat; a nature, animal, or plant reserve. — *vt* **sanc'tuarize** or **-ise** to afford sanctuary to. [L *sanctuārium*]

sanctum *sangk'təm*, (*esp* in the phrase *inner sanctum*) a sacred place; a (very) private room. — **sanctum sanctorum** the holy of holies; the inner chamber of the Jewish tabernacle; any specially reserved retreat or room (*colloq*). [L, from *sanctus* holy]

Sanctus *sangk'təs*, *n* the hymn *Holy, holy, holy* (from the Bible: Isaiah 6); music for it. — **sanctus bell** a bell rung at the singing of the Sanctus; a small bell rung to call attention to more solemn parts of the Mass (*RC Church*). [L]

sand *sand*, *n* a mass of rounded grains of rock, *esp* quartz; (in *pl*) a tract covered with this, as on a sea-shore or desert; (in *pl*) sandstones; (in *pl*) moments of time, from the use of the grains in an hourglass; firmness of character, grit (*NAm colloq*); a light yellowish-brown colour. — *adj* made of sand; of the colour sand. — *vt* to sprinkle, cover or mix with sand; to smooth or polish with abrasive material, *esp* sandpaper. — *adj* **sand'ed** sprinkled, covered, or mixed with sand; smoothed or polished with sandpaper, etc; yellow (*Shakesp*). — *n* **sand'er** a tool (*esp* power-driven) with an abrasive surface, or with a pad to which sandpaper, etc can be fitted, used to sand wood, etc. — *n* **sand'iness** sandy quality, *esp* in colour. — *n* **sand'ing**. — *n* **sand'ling** the launce or sand eel. — *adj* **sand'y** consisting of, covered with, containing, or like sand; measured by sand (*Shakesp*); coloured like sand, yellowish-beige. — **sand'bag** a bag of sand or earth, used *esp* to protect against bomb blasts, floods, etc; a small bag of sand, etc, used as a cosh; an engraver's leather cushion. — *vt* to provide with sandbags; to attack with a sandbag; to attack unexpectedly and with force; to obstruct or outmanoeuvre: — *pa t* **sand'bagged**. — **sand'bagger**; **sand'bank** a bank of sand in a river, river mouth, etc, often above water at low tide; **sand bar** a long sandbank in a river or the sea; **sand bath** a bath in sand; a vessel for heating without direct exposure to the source of heat; **sand bed** a layer of sand, *esp* one used in founding or moulding; a toper (*Scot*); **sand'-binder** a plant whose roots or rootstocks fix shifting sands; **sand'blast** a sand-laden wind; sand blown by a blast of air or steam under pressure for glass-engraving, finishing metal surfaces, cleaning stone and metal surfaces, etc. — Also *vt*. — **sand'blasting**. — *adj* **sand'-blind** see separate entry. — **sand blow** (*geol*) a sand volcano; **sand'box** a box for sand, eg for sprinkling on railway lines or roads; a sandpit; the explosive capsule of a tropical American tree (**sandbox tree**, *Hura crepitans*) of the spurge family, formerly used to sprinkle sand on wet ink; **sand'boy** a boy selling sand, proverbially happy; **sand break** sandy ground diversifying the country; **sand bunker**. — *vt* **sand'-cast** to cast in a mould of sand. — **sand'-casting**; **sand'castle** a model of a castle made by children at play on a beach or in a sandpit; **sand crack** a crack in a horse's hoof, often causing lameness; **sand dab** any of various kinds of small Pacific flatfishes often eaten as food; **sand dance** a dance performed on a sanded surface; **sand'-dart** a British noctuid moth; **sand'-devil** a small whirlwind; **sand dollar** a flat sea urchin of shallow coastal waters; **sand'-dune** a ridge of loose sand drifted by the wind; **sand eel** or **sand lance** the launce; **sand'-flag** a fissile sandstone; **sand flea** the chigoe or jigger; a sand-hopper; **sand'fly** a small biting midge (*Simulium*); a small moth-like midge (*Phlebotomus papatasii*) that transmits **sandfly fever**, an influenza-like viral infection; **sand'glass** a glass instrument, eg an hourglass, for measuring time by the running out of sand; **sand grain**; **sand grass** any grass that grows on sand; **sand'groper** (*Austr*) a pioneer at the time of the gold rush; a W Australian (*joc*); **sand grouse** any bird of the genera *Pterocles* and *Syrrhaptes*, with long pointed wings, once classified as grouse because of their feathered legs but now considered as a suborder (*Pterocletes*) related to pigeons; **sand'heap**; **sand'hill**; **sand'-hog** (*NAm slang*) a person who works on underground or under-water construction projects in an enclosed work area supplied with compressed air; **sand'-hopper** an amphipod crustacean (*Talitrus*, *Orchestia*, etc) of the seashore and tidal estuaries that jumps by suddenly straightening its bent body; **sand lance** the sand eel or launce; **sand'-lark** a name applied to various smaller shore birds; a sandpiper; **sand leek** the rocambole; **sand lizard** an oviparous lizard (*Lacerta agilis*) of Europe and S England; **sand'man** (with *the*) a fairy who supposedly puts children to sleep at bedtime by sprinkling sand on their eyes; **sand martin** a small European bird, *Riparia riparia*, of the martin family that nests in tunnels hollowed out of sandy banks; **sand mason** a tube worm that makes its tube out of sand; **sand mole** an African molerat, *Bathyergus*; **sand painting** the making of designs with coloured sand, as in various American Indian ceremonies; **sand'paper** the popular term for glasspaper, a stiff paper coated with powered glass, used as an abrasive; an early form of glasspaper, coated with sand. — *vt* to smooth or polish with sandpaper. — **sand'-peep** (*US*) any small sandpiper; **sand pipe** a tubular hollow in chalk, *usu* filled with clay, sand, etc from above; **sand'piper** the name for a large number of birds of the Scotopacidae family of ground-dwelling, wading birds intermediate between plovers and snipe, frequenting sandy shores and river banks and uttering a clear piping note; **sand'pit** a place from which sand is dug; an enclosure filled with sand for children to play in; **sand plough** a vehicle like a snow plough, for clearing roads, railway lines, etc of sand; **sand pride** a small river lamprey; **sand'pump** a pump for raising wet sand or mud; **sand saucer** the egg mass of certain sea snails; **sand'-screw** a burrowing amphipod (from its wriggling movements); **sand'shoe** a shoe for walking or playing on the sands in, *usu* with a canvas upper and rubber sole; **sand'-skipper** a sand-hopper; **sand'-snake** a short-tailed, boa-like genus (*Eryx*) of Old World snakes; **sand sole** see **lemon**[2]; **sand'spout** a moving pillar of sand drawn up by a whirlwind; **sand'-star** an ophiurid, *esp* of the short-armed kind, such as Ophiura; **sand'stone** a rock formed of compacted and hardened sand; **sand'storm** a storm of wind carrying along clouds of sand; **sand'sucker** the rough dab; **sand table** a tray for moulding sand on or for demonstration of military tactics; an inclined trough for separating heavier particles from a flow of liquid, as in ore-dressing, paper-making (also **sand trap**); **sand'-thrower** a tool for throwing sand on newly sized or painted surfaces; **sand trap** a bunker on a golf course; a sand table; **sand wasp** a solitary burrowing insect of several families related to the true wasps; **sand wedge** a golf club specially designed to hit the ball out of bunkers or sand traps; **sand'worm** the lugworm or other worm that lives on the sand; **sand'wort** any species of *Arenaria*, plants related to the chickweed; **sand'-yacht**, **sand'-yachting** see under **yacht**; **sand'y=lav'erock** (*Scot*) a sand-lark. [OE *sand*; Du *zand*, Ger *Sand*, ON *sandr*]

sandal[1] *san'dl*, *n* a type of footwear with an openwork upper, or consisting of a sole bound to the foot by straps; an ornate shoe or slipper; a strap for tying round a shoe; a slight rubber overshoe. — *adj* **san'dalled** wearing or fastened with sandals. — **sandal shoon** (*archaic*) sandals. [L *sandalium*, from Gr *sandalion*, dimin of *sandalon* sandal]

sandal[2] *san'dal*, *n* a long narrow N African boat. [Turk, Pers, and Ar]

sandal[3] *san'dl* or **sandalwood** *-wŏŏd*, *n* a compact and fine-grained very fragrant E Indian wood; the parasitic tree yielding it, *Santalum album* (**white sandalwood**), or other species; extended to other woods, such as red sanders and Barbados pride (*Adenanthera*), both called **red sandalwood**. [LL *santalum*, from Gr *sandanon*, from Sans *candana*, of Dravidian origin]

sandarach or **sandarac** *san'dər-ak*, *n* arsenic monosulphide, realgar; the resin (in full **gum sandarach** or **sandarac resin**) of the Moroccan **sandarach tree** (*Collitris quadrivalvis*) powdered to form pounce and used in making varnish. [L *sandaraca*, from Gr *sandarakē*, *-chē*]

sand-blind *sand'blīnd*, *adj* half-blind. [Prob OE pfx *sam-* half, and **blind**, affected by **sand**]

Sandemanian *san-di-mā'ni-ən*, *n* a follower of Robert *Sandeman* (1718–71), leader of a religious sect developed from the Glassites. — Also *adj*.

sander[1]. See **zander**.

sander[2]. See under **sand**.

sanderling *san'dər-ling*, *n* a species of sandpiper (*Crocethia alba*), without a hind toe. [Appar from **sand**]

sanders *san'* or *sän'dərz* or **san'derswood** *-wŏŏd*, *n* sandalwood, *esp* red sandalwood (**red sanders**; see under **red**). [OFr *sandre*, variant of *sandal*, *santal* sandalwood]

sandhi *sän'dē*, *n* (*linguistics*) modification of the sound of a word or affix caused by the context in which it is uttered. [Sans *saṁdhi* placing together]

Sandinista *san-di-nēs'tə*, *n* a member of the left-wing revolutionary movement in Nicaragua which overthrew President Samoza in 1979. — *n* **Sandinismo** (*-nēz'mō*) the beliefs and practices of the Sandinistas. [Named after the Nicaraguan rebel general Augusto César *Sandino*, murdered in 1933]

sandiver *san'di-vər*, *n* glass-gall, a scum formed on molten glass. [OFr *suin de verre*, literally, exudation of glass]

S and L *abbrev*: savings and loan (association).

sandling. See under **sand**.

S and M (*colloq*) *abbrev*: sado-masochistic (practices).

S and T *abbrev*: Signalling and Telecommunications.

sandwich *sand'wich*, *-wij*, *n* any sort of food between two slices of bread, said to be named from the fourth Earl of *Sandwich* (1718–92), who ate a snack of this kind in order not to have to leave the gaming-table; anything in a similar arrangement. — *vt* to lay or place between two layers; to fit tightly or squeeze between two others or two of another kind; to intercalate. — *adj* of the nature of, relating to or resembling, a sandwich or sandwich course. — **sandwich boards** a pair of advertising placards worn over the chest and back on shoulder straps by a person employed to walk the streets; **sandwich construction** (*aeronautics*) structural material, consisting of two thin skins either side of a thick core, having an exceptionally high stiffness/weight ratio; **sandwich course** an educational course consisting of alternating periods of study and paid employment; **sandwich technique** (*immunol*) a technique for the detection of antibody in histological preparations, involving the sandwiching of an antigen layer between the preparation and a layer of labelled antibody.

Sandy *san'di*, (*colloq*) *n* a Scot. [From *Alexander*]

sane *sān*, *adj* sound in mind; rational; sound in health (*rare*); sensible, reasonable. — *adv* **sane'ly**. — *n* **sane'ness**. [L *sānus*]

Sanforize or **-ise** *san'fər-īz*, *vt* to make (cotton or linen fabrics) proof against shrinking by mechanically compressing the fibres. [After *Sanford* L Cluett, US inventor of the process]

sang[1] *sang*, *pa t* of **sing**. — *n* a Scots form of **song**[1].

sang[2] *säng*, *n* a Chinese organ played by mouth. [Chin *shêng*]

sang[3] *sang*, *n* blood (*Scot*; in oaths; *heraldry sã*); anthrax (*vet*). [Fr, blood]

sangar or **sungar** *sung'gər*, *n* a stone breastwork; a look-out post. [Pushtu *sangar*]

sangaree *sang-gə-rē'*, *n* a W Indian drink of diluted and sweetened wine, similar to sangria. [Sp *sangría*]

sang-de-boeuf *sã-də-bœf'*, *n* a deep red colour, as found on old Chinese porcelain. [Fr, literally, ox-blood]

sangfroid *sã-frwä'*, *n* coolness, composure, self-possession. [Fr, literally, cold blood]

sanglier *sang'li-ər*, (*obs* and *heraldry*) *n* a wild boar. [Fr, from L *singulāris*, solitary]

sangoma *sang-go'mə*, (*SAfr*) *n* a witch doctor [Zulu *isangoma*]

Sangraal, **Sangrail** or **Sangreal** *sang-grāl'*, *sang'grāl* or *san-*, *n* the holy grail (see **grail**[3]). [**saint** and **grail**[3]]

Sangrado *sang-grä'dō* or *san-*, *n* a bloodletter, from Dr *Sangrado* in Le Sage's novel *Gil Blas*: — *pl* **Sangra'does**. [Sp *sangrador* one who lets blood]

sangria *sang'gri-ə* or *san-grē'a*, *n* a Spanish wine punch with fruit and soda water. [Sp *sangría*]

sangui- *sang-gwi-*, *combining form* denoting blood. — *adj* **sanguiferous** (*-gwif'ər-əs*; L *ferre* to bear) blood-carrying. — *n* **sanguificā'tion** blood-making. — *vi* **sang'uify** (*-fī*) to make blood. — *vt* to turn into blood. — *n* **sanguinaria** (*-gwi-nā'ri-ə*) the dried rhizome of the bloodroot *Sanguinaria* used as an emetic. — *adv* **sang'uinarily** (*-gwin-ə-ri-li*). — *n* **sang'uinariness**. — *adj* **sang'uinary** bloody. — *adj* **sanguine** (*sang'gwin*) (in old physiology) of the complexion or temperament in which blood was supposed to predominate over the other humours; ardent, confident and inclined to hopefulness; abounding in blood; blood-red; bloody; ruddy; florid; of blood (*rare*). — *n* a blood-red colour; a red chalk; a drawing in red chalks. — *vt* (*obs*) to colour blood-red; to stain with blood. — *adv* **san'guinely**. — *n* **sang'uineness**. — *adj* **sanguin'eous** of or having blood; blood-red; bloody; sanguine; full-blooded. — *n* **sanguin'ity** sanguineness. — *adj* **sanguin'olent** bloody. — *n* **Sanguisor'ba** (*-sör'bə*) the burnet genus (L *sorbēre* to absorb, from its supposed styptic quality). — *adj* **sanguiv'orous** or **sanguiniv'orous** feeding on blood (L *vorāre* to devour). [L *sanguis*, *-inis* blood; adjs *sanguineus*, *sanguinārius*, *sanguinolentus*; partly through Fr *sanguin*]

Sanhedrin *san'i-drin* or **Sanhedrim** *-drim*, also *-hed'*, (*hist*) *n* a Jewish council or court, *esp* the supreme council and court at Jerusalem. — *n* **San'hedrist** a member of the Sanhedrin. [Heb *sanhedrīn*, from Gr *synedrion*, from *syn* together, and *hedrā* a seat]

sanicle *san'ik-l*, *n* a woodland umbelliferous plant (in full **wood'-san'icle**; *Sanicula europaea*) with glossy leaves, headlike umbels, and hooked fruits; any plant of the genus; extended to various other plants. [OFr, perh from L *sānāre* to heal, from once-supposed power]

sanidine *san'i-dēn*, *n* a clear glassy variety of potash feldspar, *usu* tabular. [Gr *sanis*, *sanidos* a board]

sanies *sā'ni-ēz*, *n* a watery, *usu* foul-smelling discharge from wounds or sores, made up of serum, blood and pus. — *adj* **sa'nious**. [L *saniēs*]

sanify *san'i-fī*, *vt* to make healthy. [L *sānus* sound, and *facere* to make]

sanitary *san'i-tər-i*, *adj* pertaining to, or concerned with, the promotion of health, *esp* connected with drainage and sewage disposal; conducive to health. — *n* **sanitā'rian** a person who favours or studies sanitary measures. — Also *adj*. — *n* **sanitā'rianism**. — *adv* **san'itarily**. — *n* **san'itarist**. — *n* **sanitā'rium** (sham Latin; *esp NAm*) a sanatorium: — *pl* **sanita'ria** or **sanita'riums**. — *vt* **san'itate** (back-formation) to make sanitary; to furnish with sanitary appliances or ware. — *n* **sanitā'tion** measures for the promotion of health and prevention of disease, *esp* drainage and sewage disposal. — *n* **sanitā'tionist**. — *n* **sanitīzā'tion** or **-s-**. — *vt* **san'itize** or **-ise** to make sanitary; to make clinically or starkly, unwelcomingly clean; to clean up, make more acceptable by removing offensive elements, words, connotations, etc. — **sanitary engineer**; **sanitary engineering** the branch of civil engineering dealing with provision of pure water supply, disposal of waste, etc; **sanitary inspector** formerly, an official with responsibility for ensuring that standards of hygiene, etc were adhered to, both in commercial and domestic establishments (cf **environmental health officer**); **sanitary towel** a pad of absorbent material for wearing during menstruation, etc; **sanitary ware** coarse-glazed earthenware for sewer pipes; plumbing fixtures such as sinks, baths, lavatories, etc. [Fr *sanitaire*, from L *sānitās* health]

sanity *san'i-ti*, *n* health (*archaic*); soundness of mind; rationality. [L *sānitās*, from *sānus* healthy]

sanjak *san'jak*, *n* formerly, a subdivision of a Turkish vilayet or eyalet. [Turk *sancak* flag, sanjak]

San Jose scale *san hō-zā' skāl'*, *n* an E Asian scale insect, *Quadraspidiotus perniciosus*, introduced into the US, where it causes great damage to fruit trees.

sank *sangk*, *pa t* of **sink**.

Sankhya *säng'kyə*, *n* one of the six great systems of orthodox Hindu philosophy, teaching that salvation is gained through the eternal interaction between spirit and matter. [Sans *sāṁkhya*, literally, based on calculation]

sanko. See **sancho**.

sannie *san'i*, (*Scot colloq*) *n* a sandshoe.

sannup *san'əp*, *n* a married male N American Indian. [Abenaki *senanbe*]

sannyasi *sun-yä'si*, *n* a Hindu ascetic or hermit who lives by begging. — Also **sannya'sin**. [Hindi, from Sans *saṁnyāsin* one who has cast away (all worldly desires)]

sanpan. See **sampan**.

Sans. *abbrev*: Sanskrit.

sans *sã* or *sanz*, *prep* without. — **sans-appel** (*sãz-a-pel*) a person against whose decision there is no appeal; **sans cérémonie** (*sã-rā-mon-ē*) without ceremony, informally; **sans gêne** (*zhen*) at ease, unconstrained, unceremonious; **sans nombre** (*nɔ̃br'*; *heraldry*) repeated often, and covering the field; **sans phrase** (*fräz*) without phrases (of courtesy), without circumlocution; **sans souci** (*sōō-sē*) without care or worry. [Fr]

sansa *san'sə*. Same as **zanze**.

sansculotte *sã-kü-lot*, *n* in the French Revolution, the court party's nickname for an extreme republican (*appar* as wearing pantaloons instead of knee-breeches); hence generally, a strong republican, democrat, or violent revolutionary. — *n* **sansculotterie** (*-rē* or *-ə-rē*). — *adj* **sansculott'ic**. — *n pl* **sansculottides** (*-ēd'*) a proposed name (in honour of the most ardent revolutionaries) for the supplementary days in the French revolutionary calendar. — *n* **sansculott'ism**. — *n* **sansculott'ist**. [**sans**, and Fr *culotte* knee-breeches]

sansei *san'sā, n* a resident of the Americas born of the offspring of Japanese immigrant parents (cf **issei**, **nisei**). [Jap, third generation]

sanserif *san-ser'if, n* (*printing*)) a type without serifs. — Also *adj*. [**sans** and **serif**]

sansevieria *san-sev-i-ēr'i-ə, n* any liliaceous plant of the genus *Sansevieria*, *esp* a houseplant with sword-like leaves, known as *mother-in-law's tongue*, and *incl* plants yielding bowstring hemp. [Named after the Neapolitan inventor Raimondo di Sangro, Prince of *San Severo* (1710–71)]

Sansk. *abbrev*: Sanskrit.

Sanskrit or (old-fashioned) **Sanscrit**, *sans'krit, n* the ancient Indo-European literary language of India. — Also *adj*. — *adj* **Sanskrit'ic**. — *n* **Sans'kritist** a person skilled in Sanskrit. [Sans *saṁskṛta* put together, perfected, from *sam* together, and *karoti* he makes, cognate with L *creāre* to create]

sant *sant, n* (also with *cap* when used as title) a devout person, saint (*esp* in Sikhism). [Hindi]

Santa Claus *san'tə klöz', a* fat white-bearded old man dressed in a red coat or robe who by tradition brings children Christmas presents (also known as **Father Christmas**); an improbable source of improbable benefits. [Orig US modification of Du dialect *Sante Klaas* St Nicholas]

santal *san'təl, n* sandalwood. — *adj* **santalā'ceous** of or characteristic of the sandalwood genus *Santalum*, or sandalwood family *Santalaceae*. — *n* **san'talin** the colouring matter of red sandalwood. [Gr *santalon*]

santir *san-tēr'*, **santur** or **santour** *-tōōr', n* an Eastern dulcimer. [Ar *santīr*, Pers and Turk *sāntūr*]

santolina *san-tō-lē'nə, n* a plant of the *Santolina* genus of fragrant Mediterranean shrubs related to the camomile, with dissected leaves and clustered flower heads. [Ital *santolina*, from L *sanctus* holy, and *līnum* flax]

santon *san'ton, n* an Eastern dervish or saint. [Sp *santón*, from *santo* holy, from L *sanctus* holy]

santonica *san-ton'i-kə, n* the dried unexpanded flower-heads of a species of wormwood. — *n* **san'tonin** (*-tən-*) an anthelmintic extracted from it. [Gr *santonikon*, as found in the country of the *Santones* in Gaul]

santour, **santur**. See **santir**.

Saorstát Eireann *se'ər-stät e'ə-rən*, (*Ir*) *n* Irish Free State.

saouari. Same as **souari**.

sap[1] *sap, n* vital juice that circulates in plants; juice generally; sapwood; a saphead (*colloq*); a weak or foolish person (*colloq*); a plodding student (*colloq*); any object used as a bludgeon. — *vi* (*archaic colloq*) to play the part of a ninny; to be studious. — *vt* to drain or withdraw the sap from; to drain the energy from, exhaust; to strike with, or as if with, a sap. — *adj* **sap'ful** full of sap. — *adj* **sap'less**. — *n* **sap'lessness**. — *n* **sap'ling** a young tree (also *adj*) a young greyhound. — *n* **sapp'iness**. — *adj* **sapp'y**. — **sap'-green** a green paint made from the juice of buckthorn berries; its colour (also *adj*); **sap'head** (*colloq*) a fool, a weak or foolish person. — *adj* **sap'headed**. — **sap'wood** alburnum. [OE *sæp*; LGer *sapow* juice, Ger *Saft*]

sap[2] *sap, n* sapping; a trench (*usu* covered or zigzag) by which approach is made towards a hostile position. — *vt* to undermine or weaken. — *vi* to make a sap; to proceed insidiously: — *pr p* **sapp'ing**; *pa p* and *pa t* **sapped**. — *n* **sapp'er** someone who saps; a private in the Royal Engineers (formerly Royal Sappers and Miners). — **sap'head** the furthest point reached by a sap. [Ital *zappa* and Fr *sappe* (now *sape*); cf LL *sappa* a pick]

sapajou *sap'ə-jōō, n* a capuchin monkey; a spider monkey (*obs*). [Fr, from a Tupí name]

sapan. Same as **sappan**.

ɪ. See **serpigo**.

sa-pē'lē, n a wood resembling mahogany, used for ·ture; a W African tree of the genus *Entandrophragma* yielding this wood, *esp E. cylindricum*. [W African name]

saphead. See under **sap**[1,2].

saphena *sə-fē'nə*, (*anatom*) *n* either of two large superficial veins of the leg draining blood from the foot. — *adj* **saphe'nous**. [New L, from Ar *ṣāfin*]

saphir d'eau *sa-fēr dō*, (*mineralogy*) *n* an intensely blue variety of cordierite found in Ceylon. [Fr, water sapphire]

sapid *sap'id, adj* having a perceptible or decided taste; savoury; agreeable; relishing, exhilarating. — *n* **sapid'ity** or **sapidness**. — *adj* **sap'idless** (*Lamb*) insipid. [L *sapidus*, from *sapere* to taste]

sapient *sā'pi-ənt, adj* showing wisdom, sagacious (often *ironic*). — *n* **sa'pience** discernment, judgement; wisdom (often *ironic*). — **sāpiential** (*-en'shl*). — *adv* **sapien'tially**. — *adv* **sā'piently**. [L *sapientia*, from *sapere* to be wise]

sapindaceous *sap-in-dā'shəs, adj* of, belonging to, or characteristic of the *Sapindus* genus of plants, *incl* soapwort. [New L genus name *Sapindus*, from L *sāpō Indicus* Indian soap]

sapi-outan. See **sapi-utan**.

Sapium *sā'pi-əm, n* the tallow-tree genus of the spurge family.

sapi-utan or **sapi-outan** *sä-pi-ōō'tän, n* the wild ox of Celebes. [Malay *sāpi* cow, and *hūtan* wild, wood]

sapling. See **sap**[1].

sapodilla *sap-ə-dil'ə, n* a large evergreen sapotaceous tree of the W Indies, etc (*Achras zapota*); its edible fruit (also **sapodilla plum**); its durable timber. — Also called **naseberry**, **sapota**. [Sp *zapotilla*, dimin of *zapote*, from Nahuatl *tzapotl*]

saponaceous *sap-ə-nā'shəs, adj* soapy; soaplike. — *n* **sapogenin** (*-jen'in*) a compound derived from saponin, often used in synthesizing steroid hormones. — *n* **saponā'ria** any plant of the soapwort genus *Saponaria*. — *adj* **saponifiable** (*sap-on'i-fī'ə-bl*). — *n* **saponificā'tion** the process of turning into or forming soap; hydrolysis of esters into acid and alkali. — *vt* **sapon'ify** to convert (*esp* a fat) into soap. — *vi* to become soap; (of esters) to undergo hydrolysis into acid and alkali. — *pr p* **sapon'ifying**; *pa t* and *pa p* **sapon'ified**. — *n* **saponin** (*sap'ə-nin*) a glucoside derived from various plants such as soapwort, that gives a soapy froth. — *n* **sap'onite** a soapy amorphous silicate of magnesium and aluminium found in cavities in serpentine. [L *sāpō, -ōnis* soap, prob from Gmc]

sapor *sā'pör*, (*formal*) *n* a property of a substance that is perceived by the sense of taste; flavour. — *adj* **sā'porous** (*-pər-əs*). [L *sapor, -ōris*]

sapota *sə-pō'tə, n* another name for **sapodilla**. — *adj* **sapotā'ceous** of, belonging to, or characteristic of a family of tropical plants and trees (**Sapotā'ceae**), *incl* sapodilla, gutta-percha, etc. [Sp *zapote*, from Nahuatl *tzapotl*]

sappan or **sapan** *sap'an* or *-ən, n* brazil-wood (*Caesalpinia sappan*), *usu* **sapp'anwood** or **sap'anwood**. [Malay *sapang*]

sapped, **sapper**, **sapping**. See under **sap**[2].

sapperment *sap-ər-ment', interj* a German oath. [Ger *Sakrament* sacrament]

Sapphic *saf'ik, adj* of or pertaining to *Sappho*, a great Greek lyric poetess (c.600BC) of Lesbos; lesbian. — *n* (*usu* in *pl*; also without *cap*) verses in a form said to have been invented by Sappho in stanzas of four lines each, three *Lesser Sapphics* (–∪|–◡|–∪∪|–∪ |–◡) followed by an Adonic (–∪∪|–◡). — *n* **Sapph'ism** (also without *cap*) lesbianism, with which she was charged by ancient writers. — *n* **sapph'ist** a lesbian.

sapphire *saf'īr, n* a brilliant precious variety of corundum, generally of a beautiful blue; the blue colour of a sapphire. — *adj* made of sapphire; deep pure blue. — *adj* **sapph'ired** coloured with sapphire blue. — *adj* **sapph'irine** (*-ir-īn*) made of, or like, sapphire. — *n* a blue mineral, aluminium-magnesium silicate. — **sapph'ire-quartz** a blue quartz; **sapph'ire-wing** a blue-winged humming-bird. [OFr *safir*, from L *sapphīrus*, from Gr *sappheiros* lapis lazuli]

sapple *sap'l*, (*Scot*) *vt* to wash (clothes) by hand in soapy water. — *n pl* **sapples** soap suds.

sappy. See under **sap**[1].

sapro- *sap-rō-*, *-rə-* or *-ro'*, or before a vowel **sapr-** *combining form* denoting: rotten or decaying matter; putrefaction. — *n* **sapraemia** (*sap-rē'mi-ə*; Gr *haima* blood) blood poisoning resulting from the presence of toxins of saprophytic bacteria in the blood. — *adj* **saprae'mic**. — *n* **saprobe** (*sap'rōb*; Gr *bios* life) an organism living in foul water. — *adj* **saprobiot'ic** feeding on dead or decaying plants or animals. — *adj* **saprogenic** (*-jen'ik*) or **saprogenous** (*sə-proj'i-nəs*; Gr root of *gignesthai* to produce) growing on decaying matter; causing or caused by putrefaction. — *n* **saprolegnia** (*-leg'ni-ə*; Gr *legnon* border) any fungus of the genus *Saprolegnia*, one species of which grows on diseased salmon and was formerly thought to be the cause of the disease. — *n* **sap'rolite** (Gr *lithos* stone) a soft, partially decomposed rock that has remained in its original site. — *n* **sap'ropel** (*-pel*; Gr *pēlos* clay, mud) slimy sediment laid down in water, largely organic in origin. — *adj* **sapropel'ic** pertaining to, living in, or derived from, sapropel. — *n* **sapropel'ite** coal formed from sapropel. — *adj* **saproph'agous** (see **-phagous**) feeding on decaying organic matter. — *n* **sap'rophyte** (*-fīt*; see **-phyte**) a fungus or bacterium that feeds upon dead and decaying organic matter. — *adj* **saprophytic** (*-fit'ik*). — *adv* **saprophyt'ically**. — *n* **sap'rophȳtism**. — *adj* **saprozō'ic** (Gr *zōion* an animal) feeding on dead or decaying organic material. [Gr *sapros* rotten]

sapsago *sap-sā'gō* or *sap'sə-gō*, *n* a hard Swiss green cheese made from skimmed milk and melilot: — *pl* **sapsagos**. [Altered from Ger *Schabziger*, from *schaben* to scrape, and dialect Ger *ziger*, a kind of cheese]

sapsucker *sap'suk-ər*, *n* either of two N American woodpeckers (*Sphyrapicus*) which feed on the sap from trees. [**sap**[1] and **suck**]

sapucaia *sap-ōō-kä'yə*, *n* a Brazilian tree (*Lecythis*) whose urn-shaped fruit (monkey-pot) contains a number of finely-flavoured oval seeds or nuts. — **sapuca'ia-nut**. [Tupí]

SAR *abbrev*: synthetic aperture radar.

sar[1] *sär*. See **sargus**.

sar[2], **sa'r**, *sār*, (*Scot*) *n* and *vt* a form of **savour**: — *pr p* **sa'ring**; *pa t* **sared**.

saraband or **sarabande** *sar'ə-band*, *n* a slow Spanish dance, or dance-tune; a suite-movement in its rhythm, in 3–4 time strongly accented on the second beat (a dotted crotchet or minim). [Sp *zarabanda*]

Saracen *sar'ə-sən*, *n* a Syrian or Arab nomad; a Muslim, *esp* an opponent of the Crusaders; a Moor or Berber; a non-Christian (*obs*). — Also *adj*. — *adj* **Saracenic** (*-sen'ik*) or **Saracen'ical**. — *n* **Sar'acenism**. — **Saracenic architecture** a general name for Muslim architecture; **Saracen's-stone** same as **sarsen**. [OE *Saracene* (pl), from L *Saracēnus*, from late Gr *Sarakēnos*, perh from Ar *sharq* sunrise]

sarafan *sar-ə-fan'* or *sar'*, *n* a Russian peasant woman's cloak. [Russ]

Saran® *sə-ran'* *n* a thermoplastic resin based on a copolymer of vinylidene chloride and vinyl chloride, used in making fibre, moulded articles etc.

sarangi *sä'rung-gē*, *n* an Indian stringed instrument, played like a fiddle. [Hindi]

sarape. Same as **serape**.

Sarapis. See **Serapis**.

Saratoga *sar-ə-tō'gə*, (*US*) *n* (in full **Saratoga trunk**) a large travelling trunk. [*Saratoga Springs*, resort in New York State]

sarbacane *sär'bə-kān*, (*hist*) *n* a blowpipe for shooting animals, etc with. [Fr]

sarcasm *sär'kazm*, *n* language expressing scorn or contempt, often but not necessarily ironical; a jibe; the quality of such language. — *adj* **sarcas'tic** containing or inclined to sarcasm. — *adv* **sarcas'tically**. [L *sarcasmus*, from Gr *sarkasmos*, from *sarkazein* to tear flesh like dogs, to speak bitterly, from *sarx*, *sarkos* flesh]

sarcenchyme *sär-seng'kīm*, *n* a soft tissue of sponges with close-packed cells and reduced gelatinous matrix. — *adj* **sarcenchymatous** (*-kim'ə-təs*). [Gr *sarx*, *sarkos* flesh, and *enchyma* an infusion]

sarcenet. See **sarsenet**.

sarco- *sär'kō-*, *-kə-*, or *-ko'-*, or before a vowel **sarc-** *combining form* denoting flesh or fleshy tissue. — *n* **sarco'carp** (Gr *karpos* fruit; *bot*) the fleshy pericarp of a stone fruit. — *n* **sarcocystis** (*-sis'tis*; Gr *kystis* a bladder) a sporozoan of the genus *Sarcocystis*, parasitic in muscles of mammals. — *n* **sarcolemma** (*-lem'ə*; Gr *lemma* husk) the cell membrane enclosing a muscle fibre. — *n* **sarcol'ogy** (see **-logy**) the anatomy of the fleshy parts of the body. — *n* **sarc'omere** (*-mēr*; Gr *meros* part) a unit of myofibril of a muscle tissue. — *n* **sar'coplasm** the protoplasmic substance separating the fibrils in muscle fibres. — *adj* **sarcoplas'mic**. — *n* **Sarcoptes** (*-kop'tēz*; irreg, from Gr *koptein* to cut) a genus of small mites including *Sarcoptes scabiei*, the human itch mite. — *adj* **sarcop'tic**. — *adj* **sarcosaproph'agous** (*-sap-rof'ə-gəs*; Gr *sapros* rotten, and see **-phagous**) feeding on decaying fish. — *adj* **sarcous** (*sär'kəs*) of flesh or muscle. [Gr *sarx*, *sarkos* flesh]

sarcocolla *sär-kō-kol'ə*, *n* a Persian gum from *Astragalus* or other plants, reputed to heal wounds. [Gr *sarkokolla*, from *sarx*, *sarkos* flesh, and *kolla* glue]

sarcocystis. See under **sarco-**.

sarcode *sär'kōd*, *n* protoplasm, *esp* of protozoans. — *n* **Sarcodes** (*sär-kōd'ēz*) the Californian snow-plant genus. — *adj* **sarcodic** (*-kod'ik*) protoplasmic; flesh-like. — *n pl* **Sarcodina** (*-kō-dī'nə*) a class of Protozoa with pseudopodia. — *adj* **sar'coid** flesh-like. — *n* a fleshy tumour; short for sarcoidosis. — *n* **sarcoidō'sis** a chronic disease of unknown cause characterized by the formation of nodules in the lymph nodes, lungs, skin, etc. [Gr *sarkōdēs*, *sarkoeidēs*, from *sarx*, *sarkos* flesh, and *eidos* form]

sarcolemma, **sarcology**. See under **sarco-**.

sarcoma *sär-kō'mə*, *n* a tumour of connective tissue; any fleshy excrescence; a fleshy disc (*bot*): — *pl* **sarco'mas** or **sarcō'mata**. — *n* **sarcomatō'sis** a condition characterized by the formation of sarcomas in many areas of the body. — *adj* **sarcō'matous**. [Gr *sarkōma*, from *sarx*, *sarkos* flesh]

sarcomere. See under **sarco-**.

Sarcophaga *sär-kof'ə-gə*, *n* a genus of flesh-flies. — *adj* **sarcoph'agal** flesh-eating; of or relating to sarcophagi. — *adj* **sarcoph'agous** feeding on flesh. — *n* **sarcoph'agus** a limestone used by the Greeks for coffins, thought to consume the flesh of corpses; a stone coffin, *esp* one with carvings; a tomb or cenotaph of similar form: — *pl* **sarcoph'agi** (*-jī* or *-gī*) or **sarcoph'aguses**. [Gr *sarkophagos* flesh-eating, from *sarx*, *sarkos* flesh, and *phagein* (aorist) to eat]

sarcoplasm, **sarcoplasmic**, **Sarcoptes**, **sarcoptic**, **sarcosaprophagous**, **sarcous**. See under **sarco-**.

Sard *särd*, *n* and *adj* Sardinian. [L *Sardus*]

sard *särd* or **sardius** *sär'di-əs*, *n* a deep-red or brownish variety of chalcedonic silica. [L *sarda*, *sardius*, and Gr *sardion*, also *sardios* (*lithos*) the Sardian (stone), from *Sardeis* Sardis, in Lydia]

sardana *sär-dä'nə*, *n* a Catalan dance in a ring formation; the music for this, played *esp* on the flute and drum. [Catalan *sardana*]

sardel *sär-del'* or **sardelle** *-del'* or *-del'ə* *n* a small fish related to the sardine.

sardine[1] *sär-dēn'* or *sär'dēn*, *n* a young pilchard, commonly tinned in oil; applied at various times and places to other fishes. — **packed like sardines** crowded closely together. [Fr *sardine*, from Ital *sardina*, from L *sardīna*; Gr *sardīnos*, *sardīnē*]

sardine[2] *sär'dīn* or *-din*, *n* a biblical name for sard (stone). — Also *adj* (Revelations 4.3). — Also **sar'dius**. [Gr *sardinos* (*lithos*), from *sardios*; see **sard**]

Sardinian *sär-din'i-ən* or *-yən*, *adj* of the island or former kingdom of *Sardinia*, or of its inhabitants. — *n* a native, citizen, or member of the people of Sardinia; their language or dialect of Italian.

sardius. See **sard**.

sardonic *sär-don'ik*, *adj* mockingly scornful, heartless or bitter; sneering. — *adj* (*obs*) **sardō'nian**. — *adj* **sardon'ical**. — *adv* **sardon'ically**. [Fr *sardonique*, from L *sardonius*, from late Gr *sardonios*, doubtfully referred to *sardonion*, a plant of Sardinia (Gr *Sardō*) which was said to screw up the face of the eater]

sardonyx *sär'də-niks*, *n* an onyx with bands of cornelian or sard. [Gr *sardonyx*, from *Sardios* Sardian, and *onyx* a nail]

saree. See **sari**.

sargasso *sär-gas'ō*, *n* gulfweed; a floating mass or expanse of it, as in the **Sargasso Sea** in the North Atlantic: — *pl* **sargass'os**. [Port *sargaço*]

sargassum *sär-gas'əm*, *n* any brown seaweed of the genus *Sargassu*, of warm seas, with air sacs enabling it to float on the surface of the water. [New L; see **sargasso**]

sarge *särj*, (*colloq*) *n* sergeant.

sargus or **sargos** *sär'gəs*, *n* a fish (sea bream) of the genus *Sargus*. — Also **sar** and **sar'go** (*pl* **sar'gos**). [Gr *sargos*]

sari or **saree** *sär'ē*, *n* a Hindu woman's chief garment, a long cloth wrapped round the waist and passed over the shoulder and head. [Hindi *sārī*]

sarin *sär'in*, *n* a compound of phosphorus ($C_4H_{10}FPO_2$) used as a lethal nerve gas. [Ger]

sark *särk* or **serk** *serk*, *n* (*Scot*) a shirt or chemise; a surplice. — *n* (*Scot* and *NZ*) **sark'ing** a lining for a roof, *usu* of wood or felt. [OE *serc*; ON *serkr*]

sarky *sär'ki*, (*colloq*) *adj* sarcastic.

Sarmatia *sär-mā'shyə* or *-shi-ə*, *n* the ancient name for a region reaching from the Vistula and Danube to the Volga and Caucasus; Poland (*poetic*). — *n* and *adj* **Sarmā'tian**. — *adj* **Sarmatic** (*-mat'ik*).

sarment *sär'mənt*, *n* a cut twig or cutting (*obs*); a sarmentum; a long weak twig. — *adj* **sar'mentose** (*-tōz*), **sarmen'tous** or **sarmentaceous** (*-tā'shəs*) (of plants) having sarmenta or runners; creeping. — *n* **sarmen'tum** a stem in the form of a runner, as in the strawberry: — *pl* **sarment'a**. [L *sarmentum* a twig, from *sarpere* to prune]

sarnie or **sarney** *sär'ni*, (*colloq*) *n* a sandwich.

sarod *sa'rod*, *n* an Indian instrument like a cello, with strings that are plucked. [Hindi]

sarong *sə-rong'* or *sä'rong*, *n* a Malay skirtlike garment for a man or woman; a cloth for making it. [Malay *sārung*]

saros *sā'ros* or *sä'ros*, *n* an astronomical cycle of 6585 days and 8 hours, after which relative positions of the sun and moon recur; a Babylonian cycle of 3600 years. — *adj* **saronic** (*sə-ron'ik*). [Gr *saros*, from Babylonian *shāru* 3600]

sarpanch *sär'punch*, *n* an elected head of a village council in India. [Hindi *sar* head, and *panca* five]

sarracenia *sär-ə-sē'ni-ə*, *n* an American insectivorus flowering plant of the genus *Sarracenia* (family **Sarracenia'ceae**), with leaves modified to form pitchers for trapping insects. — *adj* **sarracenia'ceous** of or belonging to the Sarraceniaceae. [After Dr *Sarrazin*, 17c botanist, who sent them to Europe from Quebec]

sarrasin or **sarrazin** *sär'ə-zin*, *n* buckwheat. [Fr (*blé*) *sarrasin* Saracen (corn)]

sarrusophone *sə-rus'ə-fōn*, *n* a reed instrument of brass, devised by a 19c French bandmaster, *Sarrus*. [Gr *phōnē* voice]

sarsaparilla *sär-sə-pə-ril'ə* or *särs-pə-ril'ə*, *n* any tropical American plant of the genus *Smilax*; its dried root; a soft drink flavoured with this (*NAm*); a medicinal preparation from it; extended to various plants or roots of similar use. [Sp *zarzaparilla*, from *zarza* bramble (from Basque), and a dimin of *parra* vine]

SARSAT *sär'sat*, *abbrev*: Search and Rescue Satellite (which picks up emergency transmissions from international shipping, etc).

sarsen *sär'sn*, *n* a greywether. — Also **sars'den**, **sar'sen-stone** or **Sar'acen's-stone**. [Appar forms of **Saracen**]

sarsenet, **sarcenet** or **sarsnet** *särs'nit*, *-net*, *n* a thin tissue of fine silk. — *adj* made of sarsenet. [Anglo-Fr *sarzinett*, prob from *Sarzin* Saracen]

sartor *sär'tör*, (*facetious*) *n* a tailor. — *adj* **sartorial** (*-tō'ri-əl* or *-tö'*) of or relating to a tailor, tailoring, dress, or to the sartorius. — *adv* **sarto'rially**. — *adj* (*rare*) **sarto'rian**. — *n* **sarto'rius** (*anatom*) a narrow ribbon-like muscle at the front of the thigh, the longest muscle in the body, helping to flex the knee. [L *sartor* a patcher]

Sartrian *sär'tri-ən*, *adj* pertaining to the French philosopher, dramatist and novelist Jean-Paul *Sartre* (1905–1980). — *n* a follower or admirer of Sartre.

Sarum use *sā'rum ūs*, *n* the system of religious rites peculiar to Salisbury cathedral in medieval times. [*Sarum*, ancient name of Salisbury.]

sarus *sä'rəs*, *sā'rəs*, *n* an Indian crane. — Also **sarus crane**. [Hindi *sāras*]

Sarvodaya *sär-vō'da-ya*, *n* in India, the promotion of the welfare of the community as a whole. [Sans *sārva* all, and *udayā*, prosperity]

SAS *abbrev*: Special Air Service.

sa sa *sä sä'*, *interj* of incitement; a fencer's exclamation on thrusting. [Fr *ça ça*, there there]

sasarara. Same as **siserary**.

sash[1] *sash*, *n* a band or scarf worn round the waist or over the shoulder. — *vt* to dress or adorn with a sash. [Ar *shāsh*, a turban cloth]

sash[2] *sash*, *n* a frame, *esp* a sliding frame, for window panes. — *vt* to provide with sashes. — **sash cord** a cord attaching a weight to the sash in order to hold it open at any height; **sash weight** either of two counterweights in a sash window; **sash window** a window with a sash or sashes, as opposed to *casement window*. [Fr châssis]

sashay *sa-shā'*, (*colloq facetious*) *vi* to walk or move in a gliding or ostentatious way. — *n* an excursion. [Alteration of **chassé**]

sashimi *sash'i-mi*, *-ē'mi*, *n* a Japanese dish of thinly-sliced raw fish served with soy sauce, grated radish, etc. [Jap, literally, pierce flesh]

sasin *sas'in*, *n* the blackbuck or common Indian antelope. [Nepalese]

sasine *sā'sin*, (*Scots law*) *n* the act of giving legal possession of feudal property, infeftment. [Legal L *sasina*, a variant of **seisin**]

Sask. *abbrev*: Saskatchewan (Canadian province).

saskatoon *sas-kə-tōōn'*, *n* a small tree or shrub, *Amelanchier alnifolia*, of NW US and Canada; its edible purple fruit. [Cree *misáskwatomin*]

sasquatch *sas'kwach* or *-kwoch*, *n* in folklore, a large hairy manlike creature said to inhabit parts of W Canada. [Salish name]

sass *sas*, (*NAm colloq*) *n* impertinent talk or behaviour. — *vt* to be impertinent to. — *adj* **sass'y** impertinent. [**sauce**]

sassaby *sə-sā'bi*, *n* the bastard hartebeest, a large S African antelope. [Tswana *tsessébe*]

sassafras *sas'ə-fras*, *n* a tree (*Sassafras officinale*) of the laurel family, common in N America; the bark, *esp* of its root, a powerful stimulant; an infusion of it; extended to various plants with similar properties. — **sassafras nut** the pichurim bean (qv), whose oil smells like sassafras oil; **sassafras oil** a volatile aromatic oil distilled from sassafras. [Sp *sasafrás*]

Sassanid *sas'ə-nid*, *n* one of the **Sassan'idae**, the dynasty that ruled Persia from AD226–641. — *adj* **Sassā'nian**.

sassarara. Same as **siserary**.

sasse *sas*, (*obs*) *n* a sluice or lock. [Du *sas*]

Sassenach *sas'ə-nahh*, (*esp Scot*; *usu derog*) *n* an Englishman; a Lowlander. [Gaelic *Sasunnach* Saxon, English]

sassolite *sas'ə-līt*, *n* native boric acid, first found near *Sasso* (a province of Pisa). — Also **sass'olin**.

sassy. See under **sass**.

sastruga *sas-trōō'gə, n* one of the long parallel ridges of snow and ice that form on open wind-swept plains in snowy regions: — *pl* **sastru'gi** (*-gē*). [Russ *zastruga*]

SAT *abbrev*: scholastic aptitude test; South Australia Time; standard assessment task (*educ*).

Sat. *abbrev*: Saturday.

sat *sat, pa t* and *pa p* of **sit**.

Satan *sā'tən* (old-fashioned *sat'ən*), *n* the chief fallen angel, Lucifer; the chief evil spirit, adversary of God and tempter of men, the Devil; a devil. — Also **Satanas** (*sat'ən-as*), **Sathan** (*sā'thən*), **Sathanas** (*sath'*). — *adj* **satanic** (*sə-tan'ik*) or **satan'ical**. — *adv* **satan'ically**. — *n* (*rare*) **satan'icalness**. — *n* **sā'tanism** Satan-worship; devilish disposition. — *n* and *adj* **Sā'tanist**. — *n* **satanity** (*sə-tan'*) devilishness. — *n* **sātanol'ogy**. — *n* **sātanoph'any** (Gr *phainein* to show) an appearance of Satan. — *n* **sātanophō'bia** (see **-phobia**) fear of the Devil. — **Satanic abuse** the mental and physical (*esp* sexual) abuse of adults and children as part of the rituals associated with certain forms of Satanism; **Satanic school** Southey's name for Byron, Shelley, Keats and others whom he considered immoral because of their interest in the exotic and their rejection of orthodox Christianity; **Satan monkey** the black saki. [Gr and L *Satān, Satanās*, from Heb *sātān* enemy, from *sātan* to be adverse]

satang *sa-tang', n* a monetary unit of Thailand, one hundredth of a baht: — *pl* **satang'**. [Thai *satān*]

satara *sä-tä'rə* or *sat'ə-rə, n* a ribbed, hot-pressed and lustred woollen cloth. [*Sátára* in India]

satay *sat'ā, n* a Malaysian dish of marinated meat barbecued on skewers. — Also **sate**. [Malay]

SATB *abbrev*: soprano, alto, tenor, bass (when combined in choral music).

satchel *sach'l, n* a small bag, *usu* with shoulder strap(s), *esp* as traditionally carried by schoolchildren. — *adj* **satch'elled**. [OFr *sachel*, from L *saccellus*, dimin of *saccus*; see **sack**[1], **sac**[1]]

sate[1] *sāt, vt* to satisfy fully; to glut. — *adj* **sāt'ed**. — *adj* **sāte'less** insatiable. — *n* **sāt'edness**. [Blend of ME *sade* (cf **sad**) and L *sat* enough, or **satiate** shortened]

sate[2] *sat*, also (in rhyme) *sāt*, an archaic form of **sat**.

sate[3]. See **satay**.

sateen *sa-tēn', n* a glossy cotton or woollen fabric resembling *satin*.

satellite *sat'ə-līt, n* a body revolving around a planet, *esp* now a man-made device used for communication, etc (see **artificial satellite** below); a small piece of chromosomal material attached to a chromosome by a narrow filament (*biol*); a smaller companion to anything; a subordinate or dependent state, community, etc; an obsequious follower; an attendant. — Also *adj*. — *vt* to transmit by satellite. — *n* **satelles** (*sa-tel'ēz*; *obs*) a satellite: — *pl* **satell'ites** (*-i-tēz*; *Pope*). — *adj* **satellitic** (*-lit'ik*). — *vt* **sat'ellitize** or **-ise** to bring satellite(s) into use in (meteorology, broadcasting, etc). — **satellite broadcasting** or **television** broadcasting of television programmes via artifical satellite; **satellite dish** a saucer-shaped receiver for satellite television; **satellite state** or **country** one which relies on and obeys the dictates of a larger, more powerful state; **satellite town** a town, often a garden city, limited in size, built near a larger town to house excess population. — **artificial** or **earth satellite** any man-made body, *incl* spacecraft, launched by rocket into space and put into orbit round the earth. [L *satelles, satellitis* an attendant]

satem languages *sä'təm lang'gwij-əz, n pl* the group of Indo-European languages in which an original palatal consonant developed as a sibilant. — Cf **centum languages**. [From Avestic *satem* hundred (exemplifying the consonant so developed)]

Sathan(as), Sathanas. See **Satan**.

Sat Guru *sät gōō-rōō, n* a Sikh term for God, literally, the true guru. [Hindi]

sati. Same as **suttee**.

satiate *sā'shi-āt, vt* to gratify fully; to satisfy to excess. — *adj* glutted. — *n* **sātiabil'ity**. — *adj* **sā'tiable**. — *n* **sātiā'tion** or **satiety** (*sə-tī'ə-ti*) the state of being satiated; surfeit. [L *satiāre, -ātum*, from *satis* enough]

satin *sat'in, n* a closely woven silk with a lustrous and unbroken surface showing much of the warp. — *adj* of or like satin; clad in satin. — *vt* to make satiny. — *n* **satinet'** or **satinette'** (*Scott* **satinett'a**) a thin satin; a modification of satin with a slightly different weave; a cloth with a cotton warp and a woollen weft. — *adj* **sat'iny**. — **satin bird** an Australian bower-bird with satiny blue and black plumage; **satin finish** a satiny polish; **satin flower** a species of stitchwort; **satin paper** a fine, glossy writing paper; **satin sheeting** a twilled cotton and silk fabric with a satin surface; **satin spar** a satiny fibrous calcite, aragonite, or gypsum; **satin stitch** an embroidery stitch worked in adjacent parallel lines, giving a satiny appearance; **satin stone** a fibrous gypsum; **sat'inwood** a beautiful, smooth, satiny ornamental wood from India; the rutaceous tree (*Chloroxylon swietenia*) yielding it; extended to several more or less similar woods and trees. [Fr *satin*, appar from LL *sēta* silk (L *saeta* bristle), or from Ar *zaytūn*, from *Zaitūn* a town in China where it was produced]

satire *sat'īr, n* a literary composition, *orig* in verse, essentially a criticism of folly or vice, which it holds up to ridicule or scorn, its chief instruments being irony, sarcasm, invective, wit and humour; such writing as a genre; its spirit; the use of, or inclination to use, its methods; satirical denunciation or ridicule in which such methods are employed; (through confusion with **satyr**) a satirist (*obs*). — *adj* **satiric** (*sə-tir'ik*) or **satir'ical** pertaining to, or conveying, satire; sarcastic; abusive. — *adv* **satir'ically**. — *n* **satir'icalness**. — *n* **sat'irist** a writer of satire. — *vt* **satirize** or **-ise** (*sat'ər-īz*) to make the object of satire; to ridicule. — *vi* to write satire. [L *satira, satura* (*lanx*), full (dish), a medley]

satisfice *sat'is-fīs, vi* to aim for or achieve that which will satisfy or suffice, rather than a potential maximum. — *n* **sat'isficing**. [Alteration of **satisfy**]

satisfy *sat'is-fī, vt* to pay (a debt, etc) in full; to compensate or atone for; to give enough to; to be enough for; to supply fully; to fulfil the conditions of; to meet the requirements of; to make content; to free from doubt; to convince. — *vi* to remove the need or desire for more; to give contentment; to make payment or atonement: — *pr p* **sat'isfying**; *pa t* and *pa p* **sat'isfied**. — *n* **satisfaction** (*-fak'shən*) the act of satisfying; the state of being satisfied, contentment; payment; quittance; gratification; comfort; something which satisfies; atonement; reparation; the satisfying of honour, as by a duel; conviction. — *adv* **satisfac'torily**. — *n* **satisfac'toriness**. — *adj* **satisfac'tory** satisfying; giving contentment; such as might be wished; making amends or payment; atoning; convincing. — *adj* **sat'isfiable**. — *adj* **sat'isfied**. — *n* **sat'isfier**. — *adj* **sat'isfying**. — *adv* **sat'isfyingly**. — **satisfaction theory** (of the Atonement) the ordinary theory of Catholic orthodoxy that Christ made satisfaction to Divine justice for the guilt of human sin by suffering as the human representative, and that thus Divine forgiveness was made possible. [OFr *satisfier*, from L *satisfacere*, from *satis* enough, and *facere* to make]

satis verborum *sā'tis vûr-bō'rəm* or *-bö'* or *sat'is ver-* or *wer-bō'rōōm*, (*L*) enough of words; enough said.

sative *sā'tiv*, (*obs*) *adj* cultivated. [L *sativus*]

satnav *sat'nav*, (*informal*) *abbrev*: satellite navigation (system).

satori *sa-tō'rē* or *-tö', n* a state of sudden enlightenment, sought in Zen Buddhism. [Jap, from *toshi* be quick]

satrap *sat'rap, -rəp* or *sā'trap, n* a viceroy or governor of an ancient Persian province; a provincial governor, *esp* if powerful or ostentatiously rich; a tyrannical person. — *adj* **sat'rapal**. — *n* **sat'rapy** a satrap's province, office, or period of office. [Gr *satrapēs*, from Old Pers *khshathrapāvan-* country-protector]

sat sapienti *sat sap-i-en'tī* or *-tē*, (*L*) enough for the wise, a nod to the wise.

Satsuma *sat'sōō-mə* or *sat-sōōm'ə*, *n* a province of SW Japan. — **satsuma** or **satsuma orange** a thin-skinned seedless type of mandarin orange, or its tree; **Satsuma ware** a yellowish pottery with gilding and enamel made in Satsuma from the end of 16c.

saturate *sat'ū-rāt* or *sa'chə-rāt*, *vt* to soak; to imbue; to fill to the fullest extent possible; to satisfy all the valencies of (*chem*); to cover (a target area) completely with bombs dropped simultaneously. — *adj* (*-rət*, *-rāt*) saturated; pure in colour, free from dilution with white, grey or black. — *n* (*-rət*) a saturated compound (*chem*). — *adj* **sat'urable**. — *adj* **sat'urant** tending to saturate. — *n* a saturating substance. — *adj* **sat'urated** (of a solution) containing as much of a solute as can be dissolved at a particular temperature and pressure; (*esp* of a fat) containing no carbon-carbon double bonds in the molecule and consequently not susceptible to addition reactions (*chem*); thoroughly wet; soaked. — *n* **saturā'tion** the state of being saturated; the state of the atmosphere when fully saturated with water vapour at a given temperature; the state of a ferromagnetic material which has been magnetized to the fullest possible extent (*phys*); the conversion of an unsaturated compound to a saturated compound (*chem*); the condition where a field applied accross an ionization chamber is sufficient to collect all ions produced by incident radiation (*nuc eng*); the degree to which a colour departs from white and approaches a pure spectral wavelength, *desaturation* being the inverse of this (*phys*). — Also used as *adj*, meaning of very great, or greatest possible, intensity (eg *saturation bombing*). — *n* **sat'urātor**. — **saturated fat** an animal fat (*usu* solid, eg lard, butter) containing a high proportion of saturated fatty acids; **saturation coefficient** (*building*) the ratio between a building material's natural capacity to absorb moisture and its porosity; **saturation diving** diving to great depths using a chamber at the same temperature as the water, to which the diver can return frequently for rest spells, etc, thus reducing the frequency of (and hence time spent in) decompression; **saturation point** the point at which saturation is reached; dewpoint; the limit in numbers that can be taken in, provided with a living, used, sold, etc; the limit of emotional response, endurance, etc. [L *saturāre*, *-ātum*, from *satur* full, related to *satis* enough]

Saturday *sat'ər-di*, *n* the seventh day of the week, the Jewish Sabbath and the day dedicated by the Romans to Saturn. [OE *Sæter-*, *Sætern(es)dæg* Saturn's day]

Saturn *sat'ərn*, *n* the ancient Roman god of agriculture; commonly used for the Greek Kronos, with whom he came to be identified; the second in size and sixth in distance from the sun of the major planets, believed by the astrologers to induce a cold, melancholy, gloomy temperament; the metal lead (*alchemy*). — *n pl* **Saturnā'lia** (*Roman hist*) the festival of Saturn in mid-December, a time of great gift-giving and revelry when slaves had temporary freedom; hence (often as *n sing* without *cap*) an orgy. — *adj* **saturnā'lian** of the Saturnalia; riotously merry. — *n* **Satur'nia** (*sat-* or *sət-*) a genus of very large moths. — *adj* **Satur'nian** pertaining to Saturn, whose fabulous reign was called the golden age; hence happy, pure, simple; in the metre in which early Latin poems were written; of the planet Saturn. — *n* a person born under Saturn, or of saturnine temperament; the son of Saturn (Jupiter or Zeus); a fancied inhabitant of Saturn. — *adj* **satur'nic** (*med*) suffering from lead-poisoning. — *n* **saturniid** (*-ni-id*) any large tropical moth of the family *Saturniidae*, *incl* the emperor moth. — Also *adj*. — *adj* **sat'urnine** grave; gloomy; phlegmatic; caused or poisoned by lead. — *n* **sat'urnism** lead-poisoning. — *n* **sat'urnist** (*obs*) a gloomy person. — **Saturn's tree** an arborescent deposit of lead from a solution of a lead salt. [L *Sāturnus*, from *serere*, *satum* to sow]

satyagraha *sut'yə-gru-hə* or *-grä'*, *n orig*, Mahatma Gandhi's policy of passive resistance to British rule in India, now any non-violent campaign for reform. [Sans, reliance on truth]

satyr *sat'ər*, *n* a Greek god of the woodlands, with a tail and long ears, represented by the Romans as part goat; a very lecherous man; an orang-utan; a desert demon (*Bible*: *Isaiah*); any butterfly of the *Satyridae* family; (formerly, by confusion) a satire or satirist. — Shakespeare's **saltiers** (*The Winter's Tale* IV. 3. 336) is perhaps meant to mark a rustic confusion of satyr and saultier (jumper): — *fem* **sat'yra** or **sat'yress**. — *n* **sat'yral** (*heraldry*) a monster compounded of man, lion, and antelope. — *adj* **satyresque'**. — *n* **satyrī'asis** (*med*) morbid, overpowering sexual desire in men, corresponding to nymphomania in women. — *adj* **satyric** (*sə-tir'ik*) or **satyr'ical** of satyrs; having a chorus of satyrs. — *n* **sat'yrid** any butterfly of the family *Satyridae*, a sub-family of *Nymphalidae*, *incl* meadow-browns, heaths, marbled whites, etc. — *n* **sat'yrisk** a little satyr. — **satyr play** in ancient Greek drama, a play performed as comic relief after a series of three tragedies, in which the hero is presented with a chorus of satyrs. [L *satyrus*, from Gr *satyros*]

sauba *sä-ōō'bə* or *sö'bə*, *n* (also **sauba ant**) a S American leaf-carrying ant. [Tupí]

sauce *sös*, *n* any dressing poured over food; any (semi-) liquid mixture in which food is cooked and/or served; anything that gives relish; vegetables eaten with meat (*US*); stewed fruit (*N Am*); a solution of salt, etc, used in individual processes; a pert or impudent person (*obs*); pert or impertinent language or behaviour (*colloq*). — *vt* to add or give sauce to; to make piquant or pleasant; to be impertinent to; to rebuke (*Shakesp*); to make to pay dear (*Shakesp*); to belabour (*obs*). — *adv* **sauc'ily**. — *n* **sauc'iness**. — *adj* **sauc'y** (*compar* **sauc'ier**; *superl* **sauc'iest**) like or tasting of sauce; pert, forward; piquantly audacious, *esp* arousing sexual desire; (eg of a ship) smart and trim; disdainful; lascivious (*Shakesp*). — **sauce-alone'** the plant garlic-mustard; **sauce boat** a container from which sauce is poured over food; **sauce'box** (*colloq*) an impudent person; **sauce-crayon** (*sōs krā-yɔ̃*; Fr) a soft black pastel used for backgrounds; **sauce'pan** (*-pən*) a handled and *usu* lidded metal pan for boiling, stewing, etc, *orig* for sauces; **sauce'pan-fish** the king-crab. [Fr *sauce*, from L *salsa*, from *sallere*, *salsum* to salt, from *sāl* salt]

saucer *sö'sər*, *n orig*, a dish for salt or sauce; a shallow dish, *esp* one placed under a tea or coffee cup; anything of similar shape. — *n* **sau'cerful**: — *pl* **sau'cerfuls**. — **saucer eye** a large round eye. — *adj* **sau'cer-eyed**. — **flying saucer** see under **fly**. [OFr *saussiere*, from LL *salsārium*, from L *salsa* sauce]

sauch or **saugh** *söhh*, a Scots form of **sallow**[2].

saucisse *sō-sēs'* or **saucisson** *-ɔ̃*, (*military*) *n* a long canvas tube filled with powder for use as a fuse, eg when firing a mine. [Fr, sausage]

sauerbraten *sow'ər-brät-ən* or *zow'*, *n* a German dish of beef marinated in vinegar and braised. [Ger, sour roast]

sauerkraut *sow'* or *zow'ər-krowt*, *n* a German dish of cabbage allowed to ferment with salt, etc. — Also **sour'-crout**. [Ger, sour cabbage]

saufgard *söf-gärd'*, (*Spenser*) *n*. Same as **safeguard**.

sauger *sö'gər*, *n* a small N American pikeperch, *Stizostedion canadense*.

saul. A Scots form of **soul**.

saulge *söj*, (*Spenser*) *n*. Same as **sage**[1].

saulie *sö'li*, (*archaic Scot*) *n* a hired mourner. [Origin obscure]

sault *sölt*, *n* (also **salt**) a leap (*obs*); (*sōō*) a waterfall or rapid (*Can*). [Fr *saut*, 17c *sault*, from L *saltus*, *-ūs* leap]

sauna *sö'nə* or *sow'nə*, *n* (a building or room equipped for) a Finnish form of steam bath. [Finn]

saunt *sönt*, a Scots form of **saint**.

saunter *sön'tər*, *vi* to walk in a casual or leisurely manner; to wander about without purpose; to stroll; to dawdle (*obs*). — *n* a sauntering gait; a leisurely stroll. — *n*

saun'terer. — *n* **saun'tering**. — *adv* **saun'teringly**. [Origin obscure]

saurel *sō-rel'* or *sör'əl*, (*US*) *n* the horse-mackerel, scad. [Fr]

saurian *sö'ri-ən*, *adj* of or resembling a lizard; of, characteristic of, or belonging to the *Sauria*, an order of reptiles in former classification, *incl* the lizards. — *n* an old name for a lizard. — *adj* **saurischian** (*-is'ki-ən*; Gr *ischion* hip joint) of or belonging to the *Saurischia*, an order of Triassic dinosaurs *incl* the sauropods and theropods. — *n* any dinosaur of the *Saurischia*. — *adj* **saurog'nathous** (see **-gnathous**; *zool*) having a lizard-like arrangement of the palate-bones (as eg woodpeckers). — *adj* **saur'oid** lizard-like. — *n* **saur'opod** any gigantic quadrupedal herbivorous dinosaur of the suborder *Sauropoda*, one of the two main groups of lizard-hipped dinosaurs, *incl Apatosaurus* (*Brontosaurus*), *Diplodocus* and *Brachiosaurus*. — *adj* **saurop'odous**. — *n* and *adj* **saurop'sidan** (Gr *opsis* appearance) (a member) of the *Sauropsida*, one of the main divisions of Vertebrata *incl* birds and reptiles. — *n pl* **Sauropterygia** (*sö-rop-tər-ij'i-ə*; Gr *pterygion* a fin) an order of fossil reptiles, aquatic or amphibious, including Plesiosaurus. — *adj* **sauropteryg'ian**. — *n pl* **Saururae** (*-rōō'rē*; Gr *ourā* tail) an extinct (Jurassic) subclass of birds, with teeth and jointed tail (eg Archaeopteryx, etc). [Gr *saurā*, *sauros* a lizard]

saury *sö'ri*, *n* a long sharp-beaked, marine fish (*Scombresox saurus*) related to the garfish. [Perh Gr *sauros* lizard]

sausage *sos'ij*, *n* chopped or minced meat with fat, cereal, etc seasoned and stuffed into a length of intestine or now *usu* a synthetic tube-shaped casing, or formed into the shape of a tube; anything of similar shape. — **sausage bassoon** the rackett; **sausage dog** (*colloq*) a dachshund; **sausage machine** a machine that makes sausages by forcing meat into a continuous tube which is then divided into links; something (or someone) that produces identical items in a steady, monotonous manner; **sausage meat** meat prepared for making sausages; **sausage poisoning** (*old*) botulism (qv); **sausage roll** minced meat cooked in a roll of pastry; **sausage tree** a tropical tree (*Kigelia africana*) with bell-shaped flowers and sausage-shaped fruits. — **not a sausage** (*colloq*) nothing at all. [Fr *saucisse*, from LL *salsīcia*, from L *salsus* salted]

saussurite *sö-sū'rīt*, *n* a dull opaque mass of zoisite, albite, etc, formed by the alteration of feldspar. — *adj* **saussuritic** (*-it'ik*). [After H B de *Saussure* (1740–99), Swiss geologist]

saut *söt*, a Scottish form of **salt**[1].

sauté *sō'tā*, (*cookery*) *adj* fried lightly and quickly. — Also *vt*: — *pr p* **sau'téing** or **sau'téeing**; *pa p* and *pa t* **sau'téed**. — *n* a dish of food that has been sautéed: — *pl* **sautés** or **sautées**. [Fr *sauter* to jump]

Sauterne or **Sauternes** *sō-tûrn'* or *-tern'*, *n* sweet white wine produced at *Sauternes* in the Gironde, France.

sautoir *sō'twär*, *n* a long necklace, or pendant on a long chain or ribbon. [Fr, from LL *saltātōrium* a stirrup; cf **saltire**]

sauve qui peut *sōv kē pœ'*, (*Fr*) *n* a state of panic; a stampede. [Literally, save (himself) who can]

Sauvignon *sō'vē-nyɔ̃*, *n* a variety of grape *orig* grown in Bordeaux and the Loire valley; wine made from this grape variety.

savable, etc. See under **save**.

savage *sav'ij*, also (*obs*) **salvage** *sal'vij*, *adj* in a state of nature; untamed, wild; uncivilized; ferocious; furious. — *n* a human being in a wild, primitive or uncivilized state; a brutal, fierce, or cruel person; an enraged horse or other animal; a wild beast (*obs*; *rare*). — *vt* to make savage; to attack savagely, *esp* with the teeth. — *vi* (*obs*; *rare*) to play the savage. — *n* **sav'agedom** a savage state; savages collectively. — *adv* **sav'agely**. — *n* **sav'ageness** the state of being savage. **sav'agery** (*-ri* or *-ər-i*) fierceness; ferocity; uncivilized condition; wildness; savage behavour; savages collectively; wild ruggedness of landscape; wild, overgrowing vegetation (*obs*). — *n* **sav'agism**. [OFr *salvage*, from L *silvāticus* pertaining to the woods, from *silva* a wood]

savanna or **savannah** *sə-van'ə*, *n* a tract of level land, covered with low vegetation, treeless, or dotted with trees or patches of wood, as in tropical or subtropical Africa. — **savanna flower** a W Indian apocynaceous plant (*Echiles*); **savann'a-forest** parklands; **savann'a-sparr'ow** a N American sparrow (*Passerculus*); **savann'a-watt'le** fiddlewood. [Sp *zavana* (now *sabana*), said to be from Carib: not from *sábana* sheet]

savant *sa'vã* or *sä-vã'*, *n* a learned man, a scholar. — *adj* learned, accomplished. — **savant syndrome** the syndrome observed in an **idiot savant**. [Fr obs pr p of *savoir* to know]

savarin *sav'ər-in*, *n* a ring-shaped cake made with yeast, containing nuts, fruit, etc, and often flavoured with rum. [Named after Antheline Brillat-*Savarin* (died 1826), Fr politician and gourmet]

savate *sä-vät'*, *n* a method of boxing in which the feet (as well as the fists) are used. [Fr]

save *sāv*, *vt* to bring safe out of evil; to rescue; to bring or keep out of danger; to protect; to preserve; to prevent or avoid the loss, expenditure, or performance of, or the gain of by an opponent; to reserve; to spare; to deliver from the power of sin and from its consequences; to be economical in the use of; to hoard; to (enter an instruction to) store (data) on a tape or disk (*comput*); to prevent (a goal) from being scored; to obviate, to prevent; to be in time for (eg the post; *archaic*). — *vi* to act as a saviour; to be economical; to reserve *esp* money for future use. — *prep* except. — *conj* were it not that; unless. — *n* an act of saving, *esp* in games; a computer instruction to save material on to a tape or disk. — *adj* **sav'able**. — *n* **sav'ableness**. — *adj* **saved**. — *n* **sa'ver**. — *adj* **sa'ving** protecting; preserving; redeeming; securing salvation (*theol*); frugal; making a reservation (*esp law*); directed towards the avoidance of loss rather than the making of profit. — *prep* excepting. — *n* the action of the verb; something which is saved; (in *pl*) money laid aside for future use. — *adv* **sa'vingly**. — *n* **sa'vingness**. — **save'-all** a contrivance intended to save anything from being wasted or damaged; a pinafore or overall (*dialect*); a miser. — *adj* stingy. — *vt* **save'gard** (*Spenser*) to guard, protect. — **saving clause** a legal clause, or a statement, in which a reservation or condition is made; **saving game** a policy or procedure aimed rather at avoiding loss than at making a profit; **saving grace** see under **grace**; **savings and loan association** (*US*) a building society; **savings bank** a bank established to encourage thrift by taking small deposits, investing under regulations for safety, and giving compound interest; **savings certificate** a certificate of having invested a small sum in government funds. — **save appearances** to make hypothesis agree with observation (*astron*, *Milton*); to keep up an appearance of wealth, comfort, consistency, harmony, propriety, etc; **save as you earn** (*abbrev* **SAYE**) a government-operated savings scheme in which regular deductions are made from one's earnings; **save (some)one's bacon**, **save one's face**, **save the mark** see under **bacon**, **face**, and **mark**[1] (under **(God) bless the mark**); **save up** to accumulate or hold for some purpose by refraining from spending or using; **save you** (*archaic*) a greeting, God keep you. [Fr *sauver*, from L *salvāre*, from *salvus* safe]

saveloy *sav'ə-loi*, *n* a highly seasoned sausage, *orig* made of brains. [Fr *cervelat*, *cervelas* a saveloy, from Ital *cervellata*, from *cervello* brain, from L *cerebellum*, dimin of *cerebrum* the brain]

savey. See **savvy**.

savin or **savine** *sav'in*, *n* a species of juniper (*Juniperus sabina*) with very small imbricated leaves; its tops, yielding an irritant volatile oil, anthelmintic and abortifacient; extended to Virginian juniper ('red cedar') and other plants. [OFr *sabine*, from L *sabīna* (*herba*) Sabine (herb)]

saviour *sā'vyər*, *n* someone who saves from evil; (with *cap*) a title applied by Christians to Jesus Christ. [ME *sauveur*, from OFr *sauveour*, from L *salvātor*, from *salūs*, *salūtis* health, well-being, safety]

savoir-faire *sav-wär-fer'*, *n* the faculty of knowing just what to do and how to do it; tact. [Fr]

savoir-vivre *sav-wär-vē'vr*, *n* good breeding; knowledge of polite usages. [Fr]

savory *sā'vər-i*, *n* a labiate flavouring herb (genus *Satureia*, *esp Satureia hortensis*, summer savory, or *Satureia montana*, winter savory). [Appar from L *saturēia*]

savour or (*NAm*) **savor** *sā'vər*, *n* taste; odour; the distinctive quality of something; flavour; relish; repute (*Bible*). — *vi* to taste or smell (with *of*); to have a flavour; to have a suggestion (with *of*). — *vt* to flavour, season; to taste, smell; to be conscious of; to relish; to taste with conscious direction of the attention. — *adj* **sā'vorous** (*rare*) pleasant to the taste. — *adj* **sā'voured** having a savour. — *adv* **sā'vourily**. — *n* **sā'vouriness**. — *adj* **sā'vourless**. — *adv* **sā'vourly** (*obs*) relishingly; feelingly; understandingly. — *adj* **sā'voury** of good savour or relish; fragrant; having savour or relish; appetizing; salty, piquant or spiced (opposite to *sweet*; also *fig*); savouring of edification or holiness (*archaic*). — *n* a savoury course or dish or small item of food. [OFr *sav(o)ur* (Fr *saveur*), from L *sapor*, from *sapere* to taste]

Savoy *sə-voi'*, *n* a district of the former kingdom of Sardinia, now (and *usu* referred to by the French name **Savoie** (*sav-wa*)) a region of SE France, giving name to a former palace and sanctuary and to a theatre in London; (without *cap*) a winter cabbage with a large close head and wrinkled leaves, *orig* from *Savoy*. — *n* **Savoyard** (*sav'oi-ärd*) a native or inhabitant of Savoy, or of the Savoy precinct in London; (also without *cap*) a performer in, or devotee of, the Gilbert and Sullivan operas produced at the *Savoy* Theatre. — Also *adj*. [Fr *Savoie*, *Savoyard*]

savvy, **savvey** or **savey** *sav'i*, (*slang*) *vt* and *vi* to know; to understand. — *n* general ability; common sense; know-how, skill. — *adj* knowledgeable, shrewd. [Sp *sabe*, from *saber* to know, from L *sapere* to be wise]

SAW *abbrev*: surface acoustic wave.

saw[1] *sö*, *pa t* of **see**[2].

saw[2] *sö*, *n* any of numerous cutting tools with a toothed blade, of various shapes, used *esp* for cutting wood. — *vt* to cut with, or as with, or as, a saw; to play harshly or crudely (as a fiddler). — *vi* to use a saw; to make to and fro movements, as if with a saw: — *pa t* **sawed**; *pa p* **sawed** or (*usu*) **sawn**. — *adj* **sawed**. — *n* and *adj* **saw'ing**. — *adj* **sawn**. — *n* **saw'er** (*rare*). — *n* **saw'yer** a person who saws timber, *esp* at a sawpit; a stranded tree that bobs in a river (*NAm*). — **saw'bill** a merganser; a motmot; any of various humming-birds with serrated bils; **sawblade**; **sawbones** (*slang*) a surgeon or doctor; **saw'buck** (*NAm*) a sawhorse; a ten-dollar bill (*slang*); **saw doctor** a person who sharpens saw blades; **saw'dust** dust or small particles of wood, etc detached in sawing. — *vt* to sprinkle with sawdust. — *adj* **saw'dusty**. — **saw'-edge**. — *adj* **saw'-edged** serrated. — **saw'fish** a sharklike ray (*Pristis*) with a long, flattened, serrated jaw; **saw'-fly** a hymenopterous insect of various kinds with sawlike ovipositor; **saw'-frame** the frame in which a saw is set; **saw gate** or **saw kerf** the gap made by a saw; **saw'horse** a trestle for supporting wood that is being sawn; a straight-line diagram showing the three-dimensional structure of a molecule; **saw'mill** a mill for sawing timber. — *adj* **sawn'-off** (or **sawed'-off**) shortened by cutting with a saw; short in stature (*colloq*). — **saw'pit** a pit in which one sawyer stands while another stands above; **saw'shark** a shark (*Pristiophorus*) with a long flattened serrated jaw; **saw set** an instrument for turning saw-teeth to right and left; **saw'-tones** harsh notes; **saw'tooth**. — Also *adj*. — *adj* **saw'-toothed** serrated, like the edge of a sawblade. — **saw'-wort** a name for various composite plants with serrate leaves, eg *Serratula tinctoria*. [OE *saga*; Ger *Säge*]

saw[3] *sö*, *n* a saying; a proverb; a decree (*Spenser*). [OE *sagu*, from the root of *secgan* to say, tell]

saw[4] *sö*, a Scots form of **sow**[2] and of **salve**[2].

sawah *sa'wa n* an irrigated paddy-field. [Malay]

sawder *sö'dər*, *vt* to flatter, blarney. — *n* (*esp* in the phrase *soft sawder*) flattery. [Prob **solder**]

sawn *sön*, *pa p* of **saw**[2]; also (*Northern*) of **sow**[2]; (*Shakesp*) *perh* of **sow**[2], perh of **see**[1].

Sawney or **Sawny** *sö'ni*, *n* an old nickname for a Scotsman. [For *Sandy*, from *Alexander*]

sawney *sö'ni*, (*slang*) *n* a fool. [Origin obscure; perh developed from **zany**]

sawyer. See under **saw**[2].

sax[1] *saks*, *n* a chopper for trimming slates. [OE *sæx* (WSax *seax*) a knife]

sax[2] *saks*, (*colloq*) *n* short for **saxophone**.

sax[3] *saks*, a Scots form of **six**.

saxatile *sak'sə-tīl* or *-til*, *adj* rock-dwelling. [L *saxātilis*, from *saxum* a rock]

saxaul or **saksaul** *sak'söl*, *n* a low, thick, grotesquely contorted tree (*Haloxylon*) of the goosefoot family, found on the salt steppes of Asia.

Saxe *saks*, *adj* (of china, etc) made in, or characteristic of, Saxony; of a deep shade of light blue (also **Saxe blue**). — *n* Saxon blue, a dye colour; an albuminized paper (*photog*). [Fr *Saxe* Saxony]

saxhorn *saks'hörn*, *n* a brass wind-instrument having a long winding tube with a bell opening, invented by Antoine or Adolphe *Sax* (1814–94).

saxicavous *sak-sik'ə-vəs*, *adj* rock-boring. [L *saxum* a rock, and *cavāre* to hollow]

saxicolous *sak-sik'ə-ləs*, or **saxicoline** *sak-sik'ə-lēn*, *adj* living or growing among rocks. [L *saxum* a rock, and *colere* to inhabit]

saxifrage *sak'si-frij* or *-frāj*, *n* any plant of the London pride genus *Saxifraga*, alpine or rock plants with tufted foliage and small white, yellow or red flowers, giving name to the family **Saxifragā'ceae**; extended to other plants (see **burnet saxifrage**, **golden saxifrage**). — *adj* **saxifragā'ceous**. [L *saxifraga*, from *saxum* a stone, and *frangere* to break (from growing in clefts of rock, or, according to Pliny, from its supposed efficacy in breaking up a calculus in the bladder)]

saxitoxin *sak-si-tok'sin*, *n* a nerve poison found in molluscs feeding on dinoflagellates of the genus *Gonyaulax*. [*Saxi*domus giganteus, the Alaskan butter clam, from which the *toxin* has been isolated]

Saxon *saks'ən*, *n* a member of a N German people that conquered most of Britain in the 5c and 6c (including or excluding the Angles and Jutes); the language of that people on the Continent (Old Saxon) or in Britain (Anglo-Saxon, Old English); an English person or lowland Scots; someone whose native language is English; the English language; a native, inhabitant, or citizen of Saxony in the later German sense (now in S Germany). — *adj* pertaining to the Saxons in any sense, their language, country, or architecture. — *n* **Sax'ondom** the Anglo-Saxon or English-speaking world. — *n* **Saxonian** (*saks-ō'ni-ən*; *geol*) a stage name of West European Middle strata of the Permian. — *adj* **Saxonic** (*-on'ik*). — *n* **Sax'onism** a Saxon or English idiom; a preference for native English words, institutions, etc. — *n* **Sax'onist** a scholar in Old English. — *vt* and *vi* **Sax'onize** or **-ise** to make or become Saxon. — *n* **sax'ony** a soft woollen yarn or cloth. — **Saxon architecture** a style of building in England before the Norman Conquest, marked by the peculiar 'long and short' work of the quoins, projecting fillets running up the face of the walls and interlacing like woodwork, and baluster-like shafts between the openings of the upper windows resembling the turned woodwork of the period; **Saxon** or **Saxony blue** a dye produced by dissolving indigo in sulphuric acid; **Saxon Shore** (L *Litus Saxonicum*) in Roman times, the coast districts from Brighton to the Wash, peculiarly exposed to the attacks of the Saxons, or perhaps already partly settled by them, and so placed under the authority of a special officer, the 'Count of the Saxon Shore'. [L *Saxonēs* (pl); of Ger origin; cf OE *Seaxe*; Ger *Sachsen*; perh connected with OE *sæx* (WSax *seax*), OHGer *sahs* knife, short sword]

saxonite *saks'ən-īt*, *n* an ultrabasic igneous rock consisting of olivine and enstatite. [**Saxon** and *-ite*]

saxophone *sak'sə-fōn*, *n* a jazz, military and dance-band instrument with a reed, an S-shaped (properly metal) tube, and about twenty finger-keys. — *n* **saxophonist** (*-sof'ən-ist*). [*Sax*, the inventor (see **saxhorn**), and Gr *phōnē* the voice]

say[1] *sā*, *vt* to utter or set forth, as words or in words; to speak; to assert, affirm, state, declare; to express; to tell; to suppose as a hypothesis; to go through in recitation or repetition. — *vi* to make a statement; to speak; to declare, set forth in answer to a question: — *2nd pers sing present indicative* (*archaic*) **say'est** (*sā'ist* or **sayst** (*sāst*); *3rd pers sing* **says** (*sez* or *səz*) or (*archaic*) **saith** (*seth*); *pr p* **say'ing**; *pa p* and *pa t* **said** (*sed*); *2nd pers sing* (*archaic*) **said'est** (*sed'əst*) or **saidst** (*sedst*). — *n* something said; a remark; a speech; what one wants to say; opportunity of speech; a voice, part, or influence in a decision; a saw (*obs*). — *adv* approximately; for example. — *interj* (*NAm*) expressing surprise, protest, sudden joy, etc; used to introduce a rhetorical question (*esp* 18c *poetic*). — *adj* **say'able**. — *n* **say'er**. — *n* **say'ing** something said; an expression; a maxim. — **say'-so** an authoritative saying; authority; a rumour; hearsay. — **don't say** (*colloq*) surely it's not, let's hope it's not, the case that (eg *don't say I've no money with me!*); **I'll say!** (*colloq*) a response expressing wholehearted agreement; **I say!** an exclamation calling attention or expressing surprise, protest, sudden joy, etc; **it is said** or **they say** it is commonly reputed; **it says (that)** the text runs thus (*colloq*); **nothing to say for oneself** no defence of oneself to offer; no small-talk; **nothing to say to** no dealings or conversation with; **not to say** indeed one might go further and say; **says I, says you, he**, etc (in *illiterate* or *jocular* use) ungrammatical substitutes for said I, you, he, etc; **says you** *interj* expressing incredulity; **that is to say** in other words; **to say nothing of** not to mention; **to say the least** at least; without exaggeration; **what do you say to?** how about?; are you inclined towards?; **you can say that again** (*colloq*) you are absolutely right, I agree entirely; **you don't say!** (*colloq*) an astonished rejoinder, or ironic response to the obvious or unamusing. [OE *secgan* (*sægde, gesægd*); ON *segia*, Ger *sagen*]

say[2] *sā*, (*obs*; *Spenser, Shakesp*) *n*, *vt*, and *vi* an aphetic form of **assay**. — *n* **say'er**. — **say'-master**; **say'-piece**.

say[3] *sā*, (*archaic*) *n* a woollen fabric like serge. — *adj* made of say. — *n* **say'on** a medieval peasant's sleeveless jacket. [OFr *saie*, from L *saga*, pl of *sagum* military cloak]

SAYE *abbrev*: save as you earn.

sayne *sān*, (*Spenser*) *infinitive* and *pl* of *pr t* of **say**[1].

sayonara *sä-yo-nä'ra*, (*Jap*) *n* or *interj* good-bye.

sayyid, sayid or **said**, *sī'* or *sä'yid*, *sä'id*, also *sād*, *n* a descendant of Mohammed's daughter Fatima; an honorary title given to some Muslims. [Ar]

saz *saz*, *n* a stringed instrument of Turkey, N Africa and the Middle East. [Pers *sāz* a musical instrument]

sazerac® *saz'ə-rak*, *n* (*US*) a cocktail based on Pernod and whisky.

sazhen *sä-zhen'*, *n* a Russian measure, about 2 metres. [Russ]

Sb (*chem*) *symbol*: antimony.

sb. *abbrev*: substantive.

sbirro *zbir'rō*, *n* an Italian police officer: — *pl* **sbirr'i** (*-rē*). [Ital]

SBN *abrev*: Standard Book Number.

SBS *abbrev*: Special Boat Squadron.

'sblood *zblud*, (*archaic*) *interj* an exclamatory oath. [God's *blood*]

'sbodikins *zbod'ikinz*, or **'sbuddikins** *zbud'*, also **zbud** *zbud*, (*obs*) *interj* an exlamatory oath. [God's *body*]

SC *abbrev*: School Certificate (*Austr* and *NZ*); Signal Corps; South Carolina (US state).

Sc (*chem*) *symbol*; scandium.

sc (*printing*) *abbrev*: small capitals.

sc. *abbrev*: *scilicet* (*L*), namely; *sculpsit* (*L*), he/she sculpted (this work).

s/c *abbrev*: self-catering; self-contained.

scab *skab*, *n* vaguely, a skin disease, *esp* with scales or pustules, and *esp* one caused by mites (as in *sheep scab*); a fungal disease of various kinds in potatoes, apples, etc; a crust formed over a wound or sore, or in any of these diseases; a scoundrel (*derog*); a blackleg (*colloq*). — *vi* to develop a scab; to play the scab, act as a blackleg. — *adj* **scabbed** (*skabd* or *skab'id*) affected or covered with scabs; diseased with scab; vile, worthless (*archaic*). — *n* **scabb'edness**. — *n* **scabb'iness**. — *adj* **scabb'y**. [Appar from an ON equivalent of OE *scæb*, *sceabb* (see **shabby**) infl by association with L *scabiēs*]

scabbard *skab'ərd*, *n* a sheath, *esp* for a sword. — *vt* to sheathe. — *adj* **scabb'ardless**. — **scabbard fish** a long narrow fish (genus *Lepidopus*) having a whiplike tail. [ME *scauberc*, appar from Anglo-Fr *escaubers* (pl), prob Gmc]

scabble *skab'l*. Same as **scapple**.

scaberulous. *skə-ber'ū-ləs*, (*archaic*) *adj* somewhat scabrous. [From dimin of L *scaber* rough, scurfy]

scabies *skā'bēz* or *-biēz*, *n* a contagious skin infection caused by the itch mite, *Sarcoptes scabiei*, characterized by intense itching and the formation of vesicles and pustules. [L *scabiēs*, from *scabere* to scratch]

scabious *skā'bi-əs*, *n* any plant of the genus *Scabiosa* of the teasel family, such as the *Devil's-bit scabious*, long thought efficacious in treating scaly eruptions; a plant (*Jasione montana*; *sheep's*, or *sheep's-bit scabious*) of the bellflower family, of similar appearance. [L *scabiōsus*, from *scabiēs* the itch]

scablands *skab'ləndz*, (*geol*) *n pl* an area of bare, *usu* volcanic rock, in the NW US, that has been deeply channelled by glacial meltwaters. [**scab**]

scabrid *skab'rid*, (*archaic*) scabrous. — *n* **scabrid'ity**. [L *scabridus*, from *scaber* rough]

scabrous *skā'brəs*, *adj* rough; rough with projecting points; scurfy; harsh; beset with difficulties; bordering on the indecent. — *adv* **scab'rously**. — *n* **scā'brousness**. [L *scabrōsus*, *scabridus*, from *scaber* rough]

scad[1] *skad*, *n* a carangoid fish (genus *Caranx*, or *Trachurus*) with an armoured and keeled lateral line, superficially like a coarse mackerel, also called *horse mackerel*. [Appar Cornish dialect; perh **shad**]

scad[2] *skad*, (*esp US*; *colloq*) *n* (*usu* in *pl*) a large amount, a lot (*esp* of money.). [Of uncertain origin; poss from dialect *scald* multitude]

scaff *skaf*, *n* food (*Scot*); riff-raff (also **scaff'-raff**). [Perh Du or Ger *schaffen*, to procure food; cf **scoff**[2]]

scaffie *skaf'i*, (*Scot colloq*) *n* short for **scavenger**.

scaffold *skaf'əld*, *n* a temporary framework of platforms erected around a building, from which repairs, construction work, etc can be carried out; a raised platform, eg for performers, spectators, or executions; a raised framework, eg for hunters, or among some primitive peoples for disposal of the dead; a framework; (with *the*) capital punishment, hanging (*fig*). — *vt* to supply with a scaffold; to put on a scaffold; to sustain. — *n* **scaff'oldage** (*Shakesp* **scaff'olage**) a scaffolding; the gallery of a theatre. — *n* **scaff'older**. — *n* **scaff'olding** a framework of platforms for painters, builders, etc at work; materials for scaffolds; a frame, framework (*fig*); the erection of scaffolds. [OFr *escadafault* (Fr *échafaud*), of obscure origin; cf Ital *catafalco*.

scag or **skag** *skag*, *n* (*NAm slang*) heroin. [Origin obscure]

scaglia *skal'yə*, *n* an Italian limestone, *usu* reddish. [Ital *scaglia* scale]

scagliola *skal-iō'-lə*, *n* a polished imitation marble consisting of ground gypsum bound with glue. [Ital, dimin of *scaglia* a chip of marble]

scail. Same as **skail**.

scaith. See **scathe**.

scala *skā'lə* or *skä'lə*, *n* a ladder-like structure, such as any of the spiral canals of the cochlea: — *pl* **scā'lae** (*-lē* or *-lī*). — *adj* **scalar** (*skā'lər*) ladder-like; numerical; represented by a point in a scale; having magnitude only, not direction (*phys* and (*math*). — *n* a scalar quantity. — *adj* **scalariform** (*skə-lar'i-förm*) ladder-like. [L *scāla* a ladder]

scalade *skə-lād'* *n* an escalade. — Also **scala'do** (*-lā'dō*, *-lä'dō*): — *pl* **scala'dos**. [Ital *scalada*, from *scāla* a ladder]

Scalaria *skə-lā'ri-ə*, *n* the wentletrap genus. [Mod L, from *scāla* a ladder]

scalawag or **scallawag**. Same as **scallywag**.

scald[1] *sköld*, *vt* to injure with hot liquid or steam; to cook or heat short of boiling; to treat with very hot water; to burn, scorch (now *dialect*). — *vi* to be scalded; to be hot enough to scald. — *n* a burn caused by hot liquid. — *n* **scald'er**. — *n* and *adj* **scald'ing**. — *interj* **scald'ings** a cry of warning to get out of the way, as if of hot water. [OFr *escalder* (Fr *échauder*), from LL *excaldāre*, to bathe in warm water, from *ex* from, and *calidus* warm, hot]

scald[2], **scaldic**. Same as **skald**, **skaldic**.

scald[3] *sköld*, (*obs*) *adj* scabby; scurfy; paltry. — *n* scurf on the head; a scurvy fellow. — **scald'berry** the blackberry (from a belief that it causes scaldhead); **scald'-crow** (*Irish*) the hooded crow; **scald'fish** the smooth sole, *Argoglossus laterna*; **scald'head** a diseased scalp; scalp disease of various kinds. [For **scalled**]

scaldino *skal-* or *skäl-dē'nō*, *n* an Italian earthenware brazier: — *pl* **scaldi'ni** (*-nē*). [Ital *scaldare* to warm]

scale[1] *skāl*. Same as **skail**.

scale[2] *skāl*, *n* a graduated series or order; a graduated measure; a system of definite tones used in music; a succession of these performed in ascending or descending order of pitch through one octave or more; the compass or range of a voice or instrument; a numeral system; a system or scheme of relative values or correspondences; the ratio of representation to object; relative extent; a ladder (*obs*); a scaling-ladder (*Milton*); a flight of steps (*obs*). — *vt* to mount (as by a ladder); to climb; to change according to scale (often with *up* or *down*). — *vi* to mount. — *adj* **scal'able**. — *n* **scal'er** an instrument incorporating more than one **scaling circuit**, a device that counts very rapid pulses, by recording at the end of each group of specified numbers instead of after individual pulses; a scaling circuit itself. — *n* **scal'ing** climbing; adjustment to or in a scale. — **scale model** a model of something made in reduced size but accurate proportion; **scale stair** or **staircase** (*Scot*) stairs in straight flights; **scal'ing-ladder** a ladder for climbing the walls of a fortress, etc; a fireman's ladder. — **full-scale** see under **full**; **on a large, small**, etc **scale** in a great, small, etc way; **on the scale of** in the ratio of; **scale and platt** (*Scot*) stairs with straight flights and landings; **to scale** in proportion corresponding to actual dimensions. [L *scāla* a ladder, from *scandere* to mount]

scale[3] *skāl*, *n* a thin plate on a fish, reptile, etc; a readily detached flake; a lamina; an overlapping plate in armour; a small, flat, detachable piece of cuticle; a reduced leaf or leaf-base, often membranous, or hard and woody; a small flat structure clothing a butterfly's or moth's wing; the waxy shield secreted by a scale insect; an encrustation, *esp* that left inside a kettle, etc by hard water; a film, as on iron being heated for forging; a side piece of a razor or clasp-knife handle. — *vt* to clear of scales; to peel off in thin layers. — *vi* to come off in thin layers or flakes; to become encrusted with scale. — *adj* **scaled** having scales; cleared of scales. — *adj* **scale'less**. — *adj* **scale'like**. — *n* **scal'er** a person who scales fish, boilers, etc; an instrument for scaling, as for removing tartar from the teeth. — *n* **scal'iness**. — *n* **scal'ing** formation, peeling off, shedding, removal, or arrangement, of scales or scale; a scaled-off piece. — Also *adj*. — *adj* **scal'y** covered with scales; like scales; shabby; formed of scales; inclined to scale. — **scale'-arm'our** armour of overlapping scales; **scale board** a very thin slip of wood; **scale fern** a fern (*Ceterach officinarum*) whose back is densely covered with rusty-coloured scales; **scale fish** a dry-cured fish, such as haddock, hake, pollack; a fish with scales; **scale insect** any insect of the homopterous family *Coccidae*, in which the sedentary female fixes on a plant and secretes a waxy shield; **scale leaf** a scale that is homologically a leaf; **scale moss** a liverwort with small leaflike structures, as *Jungermannia*; **scale'work** imbricated ornament; **scal'y-bark** hickory; hickory-nut; **scal'y-leg** a disease of the legs and feet in poultry, caused by a mite. [ME *scāle*, from OFr *escale* husk, chip of stone, of Gmc origin; cf **scale**[4], **shale**, **shell**]

scale[4] *skāl*, *n* a balance pan; (*usu* in *pl*; by Shakespeare treated as *sing*) a balance; (in *pl*; *usu* with *cap*) Libra, a constellation and a sign of the zodiac. — *vt* to weigh; to weigh up. — *vi* to weigh or be weighed, as a jockey (often *scale in*). — **scale beam** the beam of a balance. — **tip the scale(s)** see under **tip**[4]. [A Northern form from ON *skāl* bowl, pan of balance; cf OE *scealu* shell, cup, Du *schaal*, Ger *Schale*, and **scale**[3]]

scale[5] *skāl*, (Shakesp, *Coriolanus I. i.* 97) *vt* variously explained as to spread, disseminate (see **skail**), to lay bare, make clear (see **scale**[3]) or as a misprint for **stale**.

scalene *skāl'ēn* or *skal-ēn'*, *adj* (of a triangle) with three unequal sides; (of a cone or cylinder) with the axis oblique to the base (*math*); denoting a neck muscle, the scalenus (qv; *anatom*). — **scalēnohē'dron** (*crystallog*) a hemihedral form bounded in the hexagonal system by twelve, in the tetragonal by eight, faces, each a scalene triangle. [Gr *skalēnos* uneven, and *hedrā* seat]

scalenus *skə-lē'nəs* or *skā-*, (*anatom*) *n* one of the paired muscles in the neck extending to the first and second ribs, being obliquely situated and unequal-sided: — *pl* **scaleni** (*-nī*. [New L, from LL *scalēnus*, from Gr *skalēnos*; see **scalene**]

scall *sköl*, (*obs*) *n* scabbiness, *esp* of the scalp. — *adj* scurvy; mean. — *adj* **scalled** (see **scald**[3]). [ON *skalli* bald head]

scallion *skal'yən*, *n* the shallot (*dialect*); the leek; an onion with a slim bulb; a spring onion. [ONFr *escalogne*, from L *Ascalōnia* (*cēpa*) Ascalon (onion)]

scallop *skol'əp* or *skal'əp*, *n* a bivalve (*esp* genus Pecten) having a sub-circular shell with sinuous radiating ridges and an eared hinge-line; a valve of its shell; a dish or other object of similar form; a shallow dish in which oysters, etc are cooked, baked, and browned; hence, the cooked oysters, etc themselves; a potato slice cooked in batter; one of a series of curves in the edge of anything; an escalope. — *vt* to cut into scallops or curves; to cook in a scallop with sauce and *usu* breadcrumbs. — *vi* to gather or search for scallops. — *adj* **scall'oped** having the edge or border cut into scallops or curves. — **scallop shell** the shell of a scallop, *esp* that of a Mediterranean species used (*esp hist*) as the badge of a pilgrim to the shrine of St James of Compostela. — Also **scoll'op**. [OFr *escalope*; of Gmc origin; cf Du *schelp* shell; Ger *Schelfe* husk]

scallywag *skal'i-wag*, **scallawag** or **scalawag** *-ə-wag*, *n* an undersized animal of little value; a good-for-nothing; a rascal, scamp; a Southerner who co-operated with the Republicans in the Reconstruction period (*US hist*). [Origin obscure; association with *Scalloway* in Shetland, in allusion to its small cattle or ponies, is regarded as a joke]

scalp[1] *skalp*, (*Scot* **scaup** *sköp*), *n* the skull (*obs*); the outer covering of the skull; the top or hairy part of the head; the skin on which the hair of the head grows; a piece of that skin torn off as a token of victory by some tribes of N American Indians (*hist*); a bare rock or mountain-top (*esp Scot*); a bed of oysters or mussels (*dialect*). —

vt to cut the scalp from; to buy cheap in order to resell quickly at a profit; to buy up and sell (theatre, travel, or other tickets) at inflated prices (*NAm*); to destroy the political influence of (*NAm*). — *n* **scalp'er**. — *n* **scalp'ing**. — *adj* **scalp'less**. — **scalp'ing-knife** a knife for scalping enemies; **scalp'ing-tuft** a scalp lock; **scalp lock** a long tuft of hair left unshaven as a challenge by N American Indians. [ME *scalp*; perh Scand; cf ON *skālpr*, sheath; cf **scallop**]

scalp[2] *skalp*, (*rare*) *vt* and *vi* to scrape; to cut; to engrave. — *n* **scalp'el** a small knife for dissecting or operating. — *adj* **scalpell'iform** shaped like a scalpel. — *n* **scalp'er** a scalprum; an engraver's scauper. — *adj* **scalp'riform** chisel-shaped. — *n* **scalp'rum** a surgeon's rasping instrument. [L *scalpere* to scrape, cut, and *scalper*, *scalprum*, dimin *scalpellum*, a knife]

scalpins *skal'pinz*, *n pl* small stones used for drainage in excavations, and as hardcore.

scaly. See under **scale**[3].

scam *skam*, (*esp NAm slang*) *n* a swindle.

scamble *skam'bl*, *vi* to scramble (for eg something scattered); to get along somehow (*obs*); to shamble (*dialect*); to sprawl (*dialect*). — *vt* to get together with effort (now *dialect*); to remove piecemeal; to scatter as for a scramble (*dialect*); to squander (*dialect*). — *n* **scam'bler** (*Scot*) a mealtime sponger. — *n* **scam'bling** (*obs*) scrambling; a haphazard meal. — Also *adj*. — *adv* **scam'blingly** strugglingly. — *n pl* **scam'bling-days** (*obs*) days of makeshift meals in Lent. [Origin obscure; appar related to **shamble** and **scramble**]

scamel *skam'l*, (*Shakesp*) *n* alleged to be a Norfolk name for the bar-tailed godwit; or a misprint for **staniel** or **stannel**.

scammony *skam'ən-i*, *n Convolvulus scammonia*, a twining Asian plant with arrow-shaped leaves; its dried root; a cathartic gum-resin obtained from its root or that of a substitute. [Gr *skammōniā*]

scamp[1] *skamp*, *vi* to go about idly (*dialect*); to take to the highway (as a robber; *obs*). — *n* a highwayman (*obs*); a rascal; a lively, tricky fellow. — *adj* **scamp'ish**. — *adv* **scamp'ishly**. — *n* **scamp'ishness**. [OFr *escamper* or Ital *scampare* to decamp]

scamp[2] *skamp*, *vt* to do or execute perfunctorily or without thoroughness. — *n* **scamp'er**. — *n* **scamp'ing**. — **scamp'-work**. [Poss ON *skemma* to shorten; cf **skimp**, **scant**]

scamper *skam'pər*, *vi* to run or skip about briskly; to decamp (*obs*). — *n* an act of scampering. [Related to **scamp**[1]]

scampi *skam'pi*, *n pl* crustaceans of the species *Nephrops norvegicus* (called the Norway lobster or Dublin (Bay) prawn), *esp* (treated as *sing*) when cooked (often in breadcrumbs) and served as a dish. [Pl of Ital *scampo* a shrimp]

scan *skan*, *vt* to analyse metrically (*prosody*); to recite so as to bring out the metrical structure (*prosody*); to examine critically or closely; to scrutinize; to judge (*obs*); to interpret, read (*Shakesp*); to make out; to examine all parts of in systematic order; (in television) to pass a beam over every part of in turn; to make pictorial records of (the body or part of it) by various techniques, eg ultrasonics (*med*); to examine data on (a magnetic disk, etc); to search out by swinging the beam (*radar*); to glance over quickly; loosely, to cast an eye negligently over; (*archaic*; in *pa p* **scand**) to climb, scale. — *vi* (*prosody*) to conform with the rules of metre; to analyse or recite verse metrically: — *pr p* **scann'ing**; *pa t* and *pa p* **scanned** (*archaic* **scand**). — *n* a scanning; the image, etc produced by scanning or by a scanner. — *n* **scann'er** a person who scans or can scan; a perforated disc (also **scann'ing-disc**) used in television (*obs*); the rotating aerial by which the beam is made to scan (*radar*); an instrument which scans, *esp* (*med*) one that makes an image of an internal organ. — *n* and *adj* **scann'ing**. — *n* **scan'sion** the act, art, or mode of analysing the metrical patterns of verse; scanning in television. — **scanning electron microscope** an electron microscope that produces a three-dimensional image, allowing the surface structure of a specimen to be examined (*abbrev* **SEM**); **scanning speech** (*med*) a speech disorder caused by cerebellar disease in which syllables are improperly separated and given equal stress. [L *scandere*, *scānsum* to climb]

Scand. or **Scan**. *abbrev*: Scandinavian.

scand. See **scan**.

scandal *skan'dl*, *n* anything that causes moral discredit or injury to reputation; something said which is injurious to reputation; a false imputation; malicious gossip; slander; opprobrious censure; a disgraceful fact, thing, or person; a shocked feeling; a stumbling-block to religious faith (*obs*); anything that brings discredit upon religion (*obs*). — *vt* (*obs*) to defame; to disgrace; to shock; — *n* **scandalīzā'tion** or **-s-**. — *vt* **scan'dalize** or **-ise** to give scandal or offence to; to shock; to disgrace (*obs*); to slander (*obs*). — *vi* (*rare*) to talk scandal. — *n* **scandal'izer** or **-iser**. — *adj* **scan'dalled** (*obs*) disgraceful; slandered. — *adj* **scan'dalous** giving scandal or offence; openly vile; defamatory. — *adv* **scan'dalously**. — *n* **scan'dalousness**. — **scan'dal-bearer** a propagator of malicious gossip; **scan'dalmonger** a person who spreads or relishes scandal. — *n* **scan'dalmongering**. — **scandal sheet** a newspaper with a reputation for publishing scandal or gossip; **scan'dalum magnā'tum** defamation of high personages (abbrev **scan. mag.**). [L *scandalum*, from Gr *skandalon* a stumbling-block]

scandent *skan'dənt*, *adj* (*esp* of plants) climbing. [L *scandēns*, *-entis*]

Scandinavian *skan-di-nā'vi-ən*, *adj* of, or characteristic of, *Scandinavia*, the peninsula divided into Norway and Sweden, but, in a historical sense, applying also to Denmark and Iceland; N Germanic (*philol*). — *n* a native of Scandinavia; a member of the dominant Nordic race of Scandinavia. — *n* and *adj* **Scan'dian**. — *adj* **Scan'dic**. [L *Scandināvia* (from Gmc word which did not have *n* before *d*), applied to the southern part of the peninsula, and its shortened form *Scandia*]

scandium *skand'i-əm*, *n* a rare metallic element (symbol **Sc**; atomic no 21) found in various rare minerals *incl* the Scandinavian mineral *euxenite* in which it was discovered in 1879, used in superconductors and lasers. [Scandinavian]

scan. mag. See under **scandal**.

scanner, **scansion**. See under **scan**.

scansorial *skan-sör'i-əl* or *-sōr'*, (*zool*) *adj* climbing, *esp* denoting birds of the old order *Scansores*; adapted for climbing, *esp* denoting a bird's foot having two forward-facing and two rear-facing toes. [L *scandere*, *scānsum* to climb]

scant *skant*, *adj* not full or plentiful; scarcely sufficient; deficient; short, poorly supplied; sparing. — *n* scarcity. — *adv* barely; scantily. — *vt* to stint; to restrict; to reduce; to dispense sparingly; to treat inadequately; to slight. — *n pl* **scant'ies** (*colloq*) underwear, *esp* women's brief panties. — *adv* **scant'ily**. — *n* **scant'iness**. — *n* (*rare*) **scant'ity**. — *adv* **scant'ly**. — *n* **scant'ness**. — *adj* **scant'y** meagre; deficient; skimped; lacking fullness; parsimonious. — **scant'-o'-grace** (*Scot*) a good-for-nothing. [ON *skamt*, neuter of *skammr* short]

scantle[1] *skan'tl*, (*obs*) *vt* to stint; to make scant; to shorten (sail). — *vi* to become scant. — *n* (*Shakesp*; variant reading for **cantle**) a portion. — *n* **scant'ling** a small portion. — *adj* petty. [Prob **scant**, with senses merging in **scantling**[1]]

scantle[2]. See under **scantling**[1].

scantling[1] *skant'ling*, *n* the dimensions of a cross-section, eg of timber used in building, shipbuilding, etc; a sample or pattern; a narrow piece of timber; a small quantity or amount (*archaic*); a gauge (*obs*). — *n* **scan'tle** a gauge for slates. — *vt* to adjust to measure. [OFr *escantillon*, *eschantillon*, of uncertain ety, senses merging in **scantle**]

scantling[2]. See under **scantle**[1].

scanty. See under **scant**.

scapa. See **scarper**.

scape[1] *skāp*, *n* an escape; an escapade; a transgression; a slip. — *vt* and *vi* (also **'scape**) to escape. — *adj* **scape'less** not to be escaped. — *n* **scape'ment** an escapement. — **scape'gallows** a person who deserves hanging; **scape'-grace** an incorrigible rascal; **scape'-wheel** an escape wheel. [**escape**]

scape[2] *skāp*, *n* a flower stalk rising from the ground, without foliage leaves (*bot*); the basal part of an antenna (*entomol*); the shaft or stem of a feather; the shaft of a column (*archit*). — Also **scapus** (*skā'pəs*): — *pl* **sca'p'i** (*-pī*). — *adj* **scape'less**. — *adj* **scapigerous** (*skə-pij'ər-əs*) having a scape. [L *scāpus* a shaft]

scape[3] *skāp*, *n* the cry of the snipe when flushed; the snipe itself. [Prob imit]

-scape *-skāp*, *sfx* indicating a type of scene or view, as in *seascape*, *streetscape*. [**landscape**]

scapegoat *skāp'gōt*, *n* a goat on which, once a year, the Jewish high-priest symbolically laid the sins of the people, and which was then allowed to escape into the wilderness (Lev 16); someone who is made to bear or take the blame for the failings, misfortunes or misdeeds of another. — *vt* to make into or treat as a scapegoat. — *n* **scape'goating** the practice of making (someone) into or using someone as a scapegoat, *esp* involving harsh or violent treatment; a psychological syndrome of this nature. [**escape** and **goat**]

scapegrace. See under **scape**[1].

scaphocephalus *skaf-ō-sef'ə-ləs -kef'*, *n* an abnormally long and narrow boat-shaped skull. — *adj* **scapho-cephal'ic** or **scaphoceph'alous**. — *n* **scaphoceph'aly**. [Gr *skaphē* a boat, and *kephalē* a head]

scaphoid *skaf'oid*, *adj* boat-shaped. — *n* **scaph'oid bone** or **scaphoid** a boat-shaped bone on the thumb side of the wrist or ankle joint, the navicular bone. [Gr *skaphē* a boat, and *eidos* form]

scaphopod *skaf'ə-pod* *n* a member of the class of marine molluscs *Scaphopoda* (tooth or tusk shells), in which the foot is trilobed or has a terminal disc and the mantle forms a tube enclosed by the tubular univalve shell. — Also *adj*. [Gr *skaphos* a spade, and *pous*, *podos* a foot]

scapi. See **scapus** under **scape**[2].

scapigerous. See under **scape**[2].

scapolite *skap'ə-līt*, *n* any of a group of rare minerals, silicates of aluminium, calcium, and sodium with some chlorine, crystallizing in the tetragonal system. [Gr *skāpos* a rod, and *lithos* a stone]

scapple *skap'l* or **scabble** *skab'l*, *vt* to work or shape (eg stone) roughly, without smoothing to a finish. [OFr *escapeler* to dress timber]

scapula *skap'ū-lə*, *n* the shoulder blade: — *pl* **scap'ulas** or **scap'ulae** (*-lē*). — *adj* **scap'ūlar** of the shoulder blade or shoulder. — *n orig* an ordinary working garb, now the mark of the monastic orders, a long strip of cloth with an opening for the head, worn hanging in front and behind over the habit; two pieces of cloth tied together over the shoulders, worn by members of certain lay confraternities (*RC Church*); a supporting bandage worn over the shoulder; any of the small feathers lying along the shoulder in birds. — *adj* and *n* **scap'ūlary** scapular. — *adj* **scap'ūlated** (*zool*) with noticeable scapular feathers. — *n* **scap'ūlimancy** or **scap'ūlomancy** (see **-mancy**) divination by means of the cracks appearing in a burning shoulder blade. — *adj* **scapūli-man'tic** or **scapūloman'tic**. [L *scapula* the shoulder blade]

scapus. See under **scape**[2].

scar[1] *skär*, *n* the mark left by a wound or sore; any mark or blemish; any mark, trace, or result of injury, eg of a material, moral or psychological, etc nature; a mark at a place of former attachment, eg of a leaf. — *vt* to mark with a scar. — *vi* to become scarred: — *pr p* **scarr'ing**; *pa t* and *pa p* **scarred**. — *adj* **scar'less** without scars; unwounded. — *adj* **scarred**. — *n* and *adj* **scarr'ing**. — *adj* **scarr'y**. [OFr *escare*, from L *eschara*, from Gr *escharā* a hearth, brazier, burn, scar]

scar[2] *skär* or **scaur** *skör*, *n* a precipitous bare place on a hill-face; a cliff; a reef in the sea. — *adj* **scarr'y**. [Appar ON *sker*, *skera* to cut]

scar[3] *skär* *n* (also **scar'fish**) a parrot-wrasse. — *n* **Scarus** (*skā'rəs*) the parrot-wrasse genus, giving name to the family **Scaridae** (*skar'i-dē*). [L *scarus*, from Gr *skaros*]

scar[4] or **scarre** *skär*, an archaic or Scots form of **scare**: — *pa t* and *pa p* **scarred** or **scarr'd**.

scarab *skar'əb*, *n* any scarabaeid beetle, *esp* a dung beetle, *Scarabaeus sacer*, the sacred beetle of the ancient Egyptians, or related species; a gem carved in the form of a beetle, used by the ancient Egyptians as an amulet, seal, etc; a term of abuse (*obs*). — *n* and *adj* **scarabaeid** (*skar-ə-bē'id*) or **scarabaean** (*-bē'ən*) (any lamellicorn beetle) of the family *Scarabaeidae*, *incl* the dung beetles, chafers, stag beetles, etc. — *n* **scarabae'ist** a person who studies scarabaeid beetles. — *adj* **scarabae'oid** resembling a scarabaeid. — *n* a scarabaeid or a gem carved in the shape of one. — *n* **scarabae'us** a beetle of the *Scarabaeus* genus of lamellicorn beetles, the typical genus of the *Scarabaeidae*: — *pl* **scarabae'uses** or **scarabaei** (*-bē'ī*). — *n* **scar'abee** (*archaic*) a scarabaeid beetle. — *n* **scar'aboid** a carved gem only vaguely resembling a beetle in shape; a scarabaeid. — Also *adj*. [L *scarabaeus*; cf Gr *kārabos*]

Scaramouch or **Scaramouche** *skar'ə-mo͞osh* or (*rare*) *-mowch*, *n* a stock character in an old Italian comedy, dressed in the black costume of a Spanish don, and characterized as a boastful coward; (without *cap*) a bragging, cowardly buffoon. [Fr *Scaramouche*, from Ital *Scaramuccia*]

scarce *skārs*, *adj* by no means plentiful; not often found; hard to get; in short supply; sparing (*obs*). — *adv* scarcely; with difficulty (*Milton*); hardly ever. — *adv* **scarce'ly** only just; not quite; not at all; scantily (*obs*). — *n* **scarce'ness**. — *n* **scarc'ity** the state or fact of being scarce; shortness of supply, *esp* of necessaries; dearth; deficiency; niggardliness (*obs*). — **make oneself scarce** (*colloq*) to leave quickly, unobtrusively, for reasons of prudence, tact, etc. [ONFr *escars* (Fr *échars*), niggardly, from a LL substitute for L *excerptus*, pa p of *excerpere*, from *ex* out, and *carpere* to pick]

scarcement *skārs'mənt*, (*Scot*) *n* a ledge formed by the setting back of a wall, buttress, or bank. [Poss from **scarce**]

scare *skār*, *vt* to startle, to frighten; to drive or keep off by frightening. — *vi* to become frightened. — *n* a fright; a panic; a baseless public alarm. — *adj* **scared** frightened. — *n* **scar'er**. — *adj* **scar'y** or **scare'y** frightening; timorous. — **scare'crow** anything set up to scare birds; a vain cause of terror, a bogy; a shabbily-dressed person; a person so thin that his or her clothes appear ill-fitting; **scared'y-cat** a term of abuse used, *esp* by children, in addressing someone who is afraid to undertake some dangerous or illicit act; a coward; **scare'-head**, **scare'-heading** or **scare'-line** a newspaper heading designed to raise a scare; **scare'monger** an alarmist, someone who causes panic by initiating or encouraging rumours of trouble; **scare'mongering**; **scare tactics** actions or words solely intended to intimidate. — **run scared** to panic; **scare the (living) daylights out of** or **scare the pants off** (both *colloq*) to frighten considerably; **scare up** to beat up (game) (*US* and *dialect*); to hunt out; to produce (eg a meal) quickly, to rustle up (*colloq*). [ME *skerre*, from ON *skirra* to avoid, from *skiarr* shy; vowel history obscure]

scarf[1] *skärf*, *n* a light, *usu* decorative piece of material thrown loosely on the shoulders about the neck, or tied around the head, etc; a muffler; a military or official sash; a band worn around the neck with ends hanging in front, formerly the mark of a clergyman of some degree of dignity, *esp* a nobleman's chaplain; hence, a chaplaincy; a veil; a necktie; a strip of woollen or other warm fabric to tie or tuck round the neck, a cravat; a sling for an injured limb (*obs*): — *pl* **scarfs** or **scarves**. — *vt* (*rare*) to cover, as if with a scarf; to wrap as a scarf does. — *adj* **scarfed** wearing a scarf, decorated with scarves. — *adv* **scarf'wise** in the manner of a scarf or sash, over the shoulder, diagonally across the chest and back, and secured under the arm. — **scarf'-pin** an ornamental pin worn in a scarf; a tie-pin; **scarf'-ring** an ornamental ring through which the ends of a scarf are drawn. [Perh ONFr *escarpe* (Fr *écharpe*) sash, sling]

scarf[2] *skärf*, *n* a joint between pieces placed end to end, cut so as to fit with overlapping like a continuous piece; an end so prepared; a longitudinal cut in a whale's carcase. — *vt* (also **scarph**) to join with a scarf-joint; to make a scarf in. — *n* **scarf'ing**. — **scarf'-joint**. [Perh Scand]

scarf[3] *skärf*, (*NAm slang*) *vt* to devour greedily (often with *up*, *down* or *out*). [Origin uncertain; perh variant of **scoff**]

scarfskin *skärf'skin*, *n* the surface skin. [Origin doubtful; perh **scarf**[1]; perh related to **scurf**]

Scaridae. See under **scar**[3].

scarify *skar'i-fī*, *vt* to make a number of scratches or slight cuts in; to break up the surface of (*esp* soil); to lacerate (the skin) with a series of small punctures, as in inoculation; to criticize harshly and severely: — *pr p* **scar'ifying**; *pa t* and *pa p* **scar'ified**. — *n* **scarification** (*-fi-kā'shən*). — *n* **scar'ificātor** a surgical instrument for scarifying; a scarifier. — *n* **scar'ifier** someone who scarifies; an implement for breaking the surface of the soil or of a road. [LL *scarīficāre*, *-ātum*, for L *scarīfāre*, from Gr *skarīphasthai*, from *skarīphos* an etching tool]

scarious *skā'ri-əs*, *adj* thin, dry, stiff, and membranous (*bot*); scaly, scurfy (*zool*). [Origin unknown]

scarlatina *skär-lə-tē'nə*, (*med*) *n* scarlet fever. [Ital *scarlattina*]

scarlet *skär'lit*, *n orig* a fine cloth, not always red; a brilliant red; a brilliant red cloth, garment, or garb, or its wearer. — *adj* of the colour scarlet; dressed in scarlet. — *vt* to redden. — **scarlet-bean** another name for the **scarlet runner**; **scarlet fever** an infectious streptococcal fever, *usu* marked by a sore throat, sickness and a scarlet rash, scarlatina; **scarlet geranium** a scarlet-flowered pelargonium; **scarlet hat** a cardinal's red hat; **scarlet letter** (*hist*) a scarlet-coloured letter A worn by women convicted of adultery in the Puritan communities of New England; **scarlet pimpernel** a flowering plant, *Anagallis arvensis*, of the primrose family, with small red, white or purple flowers that close when the weather is cloudy; **scarlet runner** a scarlet-flowered climber (*Phaseolus multiflorus*) of the kidney-bean genus, with edible beans; **scarlet woman** the woman referred to in the Bible (Rev 17), variously taken as pagan Rome, Papal Rome, or the world in its anti-Christian sense; a whore. [OFr *escarlate* (Fr *écarlate*), thought to be from Pers *saqalāt* scarlet cloth]

scarmoge *skär'məj*, *n* an archaic form of **skirmish**.

scarp[1] *skärp*, (*heraldry*) *n* a diminutive of the bend-sinister, half its width. [OFr *escarpe*; cf **scarf**[1]]

scarp[2] *skärp*, *n* an escarp; an escarpment. — *vt* to cut into a scarp. — *adj* **scarped**. — *n* **scarp'ing**. [Ital *scarpa*]

scarper *skär'pər*, (*slang*) *vi* to run away, escape, leave without notice. — Also **scar'pa** and **sca'pa**. [Ital *scappare* to escape; poss strengthened by Cockney *scapa*, from World-War-I rhyming slang *Scapa Flow* go]

scarph. See **scarf**[2].

scarpines *skär'pinz*, *n pl* an instrument of torture for the feet. — *n* **scarpet'to** a hemp-soled shoe or climbing boot: — *pl* **scarpet'ti** (*-tē*). [Ital *scarpino*, *scarpetto*, dimins of *scarpa* shoe]

scarre[1] *skär*, (*Shakesp*) *n* word of unknown meaning in *All's Well That Ends Well* (IV. 2. 38), probably a misprint, but never satisfactorily explained.

scarre[2]. See **scar**[4].

scarred, **scarring**, **scarry**. See under **scar**[1,2,4].

scart[1] *skärt*, (*Scot*) *vt* to scratch; to scrape. — *n* a scratch or scrape; a dash or stroke of a pen. — *adj* **scart'-free** (*Scot*). [See **scrat**]

scart[2], **scarth**. See **skart**.

Scarus. See **scar**[3].

scarves. See **scarf**[1].

scary. See **scare**.

scat[1] or **scatt** *skat*, (*hist*) *n* tribute; a tax; *esp* udaller's land-tax, in Orkney and Shetland, paid to the Crown. [ON *skattr*; cf OE *sceatt* money, Du *schat*, Ger *Schatz*]

scat[2] *skat*, (*colloq*) *interj* (used *orig* and *esp* to animals) be off! — *vt* to scare away. — *vi* to go away quickly: — *pr p* **scatt'ing**; *pa t* and *pa p* **scatt'ed**.

scat[3] or **skatt** *skat*, (*Devon and Cornish dialect*) *n* a blow; a throw or break; a spell; a sudden rain shower. — *adv* in collapse; to bankruptcy. — *n* **scatt'ing** pebble-dashing.

scat[4] or **skat** *skat*, *n* an animal dropping. — *adj* **scato-log'ical**. — *n* **scatol'ogy** the scientific study of excrement, as in (*pathol*) diagnosis by study of the faeces, or (*palaeontol*) classification or identification of fossils by study of their fossilized excrement; obscene literature; interest in or preoccupation with the obscene. — *adj* **scatoph'agous** (see **-phagous**) dung-eating. — *n* **scatoph'agy** (*-ji*) the practice of feeding on dung. [Gr *skōr*, *skatos* dung]

scat[5] *skat*, (*jazz*) *n* the use of nonsense syllables and other wordless effects in singing. — Also *adj*. — *vi* to sing in this way: — *pr p* **scatt'ing**; *pa t* and *pa p* **scatt'ed** [Perh imit]

scatch *skach*, *n* a stilt. [ONFr *escache* (Fr *échasse*); cf **skate**[1]]

scathe *skādh* (*Scot* **scaith**, **skaith** *skāth*; *Spenser* **scath** *skath*), *vt* (often in *neg*) to injure; to blast; to scorch with invective. — *n* (*archaic* or *dialect*) injury, harm. — *adj* **scathe'ful** hurtful. — *n* **scathe'fulness**. — *adj* **scathe'less** (*Scot* **scaith'less**, **skaith'less**) without injury. — *adj* **scath'ing**. — *adv* **scath'ingly**. [ON *skathe*; cf OE *sceatha* an injurer; Ger *Schade* injury]

scatole. Same as **skatole**.

scatological, **scatophagous**, etc. See under **scat**[4].

scatt. See **scat**[1].

scatter *skat'ər*, *vt* to disperse; to throw loosely about; to strew; to sprinkle; to dispel; to reflect or disperse irregularly (waves or particles). — *vi* to disperse; to fire shot loosely. — *n* a scattering; a sprinkling; dispersion; the extent of scattering. — *adj* **scatt'erable**. — *adj* **scatt'ered** dispersed irregularly, widely, in all directions, or here and there; thrown about; casually dropped (*archaic*); (of one's thoughts, etc) distracted. — *adv* **scatt'eredly** (*-ərd-li*). — *n* **scatt'erer**; **scatt'ering** dispersion; that which is scattered; a small proportion occurring sporadically; the deflection of the path of subatomic particles as a result of collisions with other particles or atoms *phys*); the deflection of light by the fine particles of solid, liquid or gaseous matter, from the main direction of the beam (*phys*); the deflection of radiation resulting from interactions between the photons radiated and the nuclei or electrons in the material through which the radiation is passing, or with another radiation field *phys*). — *adv* **scatt'eringly**. — *n* **scatt'erling** (*archaic*) a vagrant. — *adj* **scatt'ery** dispersed; sparse; giving an effect of scattering. — **scatt'erbrain** someone incapable of sustained attention or thought. — *adj* **scatter'brained**. — **scatt'ergood** a spendthrift; **scatt'er-gun** a shotgun; **scattering matrix** (*phys*) a matrix in which particles that result from high-energy collisions are made to scatter in various directions (also **S'-matrix**); **scatter rugs** and **cushions** small rugs and cushions which can be placed anywhere in the room. — *adj* **scatt'ershot** random, indiscriminate, wide-ranging, as is shot from a gun. — **elastic** and **inelastic scattering** see **elastic** and **inelastic collision** under **collide**. [Origin obscure; *scatered* occurs in the *OE Chronicle* (anno 1137); cf **shatter**]

scatted. See **scat**[2,5].

scattermouch *skat'ər-mowch*, (*sailors' old slang*) *n* any Latin or Levantine person. [**scaramouch** infl by **scatter**]

scatting. See **scat**[2,3,5].

scatty *skat'i*, (*colloq*) *adj* slightly crazy and unpredictable in conduct. — *n* **scatt'iness**. [Poss *scatter*brain]

scaturient *skat-ū'ri-ənt*, (*formal*) *adj* flowing out; gushing. [L *scatūriēns, -entis*, from *scatūrīre* to gush out]

scaud *sköd*, a Scots form of **scald**[1].

scaup *sköp*, *n* a mussel bed; any of various diving ducks of the genus *Aythya* that feeds on molluscs and crustaceans, *esp Aythya marila*, the male of which has a black, pale grey and white plumage (also **scaup duck**). [**scalp**[1]]

scauper *skö'pər* or **scorper** *skör'*, *n* a gouging chisel with a semicircular face, used by engravers and woodcarvers. [**scalper**]

scaur[1] *skör*, a Scots form of **scare**.

scaur[2]. Same as **scar**[2].

scaury *skö'ri* or *skö'*, (*Orkney* and *Shetland*) *n* a young gull. — Also **scou'rie** or **scow'rie**. [ON *skāri*]

scavage *skav'ij*, *n* a toll formerly levied in boroughs on goods offered for sale by outsiders; street refuse (*obs*). — *n* **scav'ager** the officer who collected the toll, later charged with keeping the streets clean. — *vt* **scav'enge** (*-inj* or *-inzh*; back-formation from **scavenger**) to cleanse; to remove impurities from (a substance) (*chem*). — *vi* to act as scavenger; to search (for useful items) among refuse. — *n* the sweeping out of waste gases from an internal-combustion engine. — *n* **scav'enger** (*-jər*) a person who searches for and gathers discarded items from garbage bins, etc; a person who cleans the streets; a person or apparatus that removes waste; an animal that feeds on garbage or carrion; someone who deals or delights in filth. — *vi* to act as scavenger. — *n* **scav'engering**. — *n* **scav'engery**. — *n* **scav'enging**. — **scavenge pump** in certain internal-combustion engines, an oil pump that returns used oil from the crank case to the oil tank. [Anglo-Fr *scawage* inspection; prob of Gmc origin; cf OE *scēawian* to inspect; see **show**]

scavenger[1] *skav'in-jər*, *n* a perversion of the name of *Skevington*, Lieutenant of the Tower under Henry VIII, inventor of an instrument of torture known as the **scavenger's**, or **Skevington's**, or **Skeffington's daughter**.

scavenger[2]. See under **scavage**.

scaw. Same as **skaw**.

scawtite *skö't'īt*, *n* a carbonate or silicate of calcium, occurring naturally as small colourless crystals. [*Scawt* Hill, Co. Antrim, where it is found]

scazon *skā'zon*, (*prosody*) *n* (also **scazon iambus**) a choliamb (qv): — *pl* **sca'zons** or **scazontes** (*skə-zon'tēz*). — *n* and *adj* **scazontic** (*skə-zon'tik*). [Gr *skazōn* limping]

ScB *abbrev*: *Scientiae Baccalaureus* (*L*), Bachelor of Science.

SCCL *abbrev*: Scottish Council for Civil Liberties.

SCD *abbrev*: *Scientiae Doctor* (*L*), Doctor of Science.

SCE *abbrev*: Scottish Certificate of Education.

sceat or **sceatt** *shat*, (*hist*) *n* a small silver (or gold) coin of Anglo-Saxon times: — *pl* **sceatt'as**. [OE]

scedule. See **schedule**.

scelerate *sel'ər-āt* or *-it*, (*obs*) *adj* wicked. — *n* (also **scelerat** after Fr *scélérat*) a villain. [L *scelerātus*, from *scelus* crime]

scena *shā'na*, *n* an operatic scene; an elaborate dramatic recitative followed by an aria: — *pl* **scene** (*shā'nā*). [Ital, from L *scēna, scaena*, from Gr *skēnē* tent, stage]

scenario *si-nä'ri-ō*, or *sē-* or *shā-*, *n* an outline of a dramatic work, film, etc, scene by scene; an outline of future development, or of a plan to be followed, which shows the operation of causes and where points of decision or difficulty occur; loosely, any imagined, suggested or projected sequence of events, plan of action, situation, etc: — *pl* **scena'rios**. — *n* **scena'rist**. — *n* **scenarizā'tion** or **-s-**. — *vt* **scenarize** or **-ise** (*-nä'rīz* or *-nā'*) to make a scenario of. — *n* **scenary** (*sē'nə-ri*; *obs*) disposition of scenes; scenery. [Ital, from L *scēnārius*, fom *scēna*; see **scena**]

scend. See **send**.

scene *sēn*, *n orig*, the stage; a stage performance (*obs*); the place of action in a play (hence in a story, an actual occurrence, etc); its representation on the stage; a painted slide, hanging, or other object, used for this purpose; a curtain, veil, or screen (*archaic*); a division of a play marked off by the fall of the curtain, by a change of place, or (in Latin, French, and some English plays) by the entry or exit of any important character; an episode; a dramatic or stagy incident, *esp* an uncomfortable, untimely, or unseemly display of hot feelings; a landscape, picture of a place or action; a view or spectacle; the activity, publicity, etc surrounding a particular business or profession, eg *the pop music scene* (*colloq*); one's area of interest or activity (*colloq*); a situation, state of affairs (*colloq*). — *vt* to set in a scene. — *n* **scēn'ery** dramatic action (*obs*); theatrical slides, hangings, etc collectively; views of beautiful, picturesque, or impressive country. — *adj* **scenic** (*sē'nik* or *sen'ik*) pertaining to scenery; having beautiful or remarkable scenery; belonging or relating to the stage or stage scenery; dramatic, theatrical; (of painting, sculpture, etc) representing a scene or incident, eg of historical action. — *adj* (*rare*) **scen'ical**. — *adv* **scen'ically**. — *adj* **scēnograph'ic** or **scēnograph'ical**. — *adv* **scēnograph'ically**. — *n* **scēnog'raphy** perspective drawing; scene-painting. — **scene dock** or **bay** the space where scenery is stored; **scene'man** a scene-shifter; **scene-of-crime officer** a police officer responsible for gathering evidence at the scene of a crime; **scene'-painter** a person who paints scenery for theatres; **scene'-shifter** a person who sets and removes the scenery in a theatre; **scenic railway** a miniature railway running through artificial representations of picturesque scenery; a roller-coaster, eg in an amusement park; **scenic reserve** (*NZ*) an area of picturesque scenery protected against development and accessible to the public for recreational purposes. — **behind the scenes** at the back of the visible stage; away from the public view (*lit* and *fig*); in a position to know what goes on; in private; **come on the scene** to arrive; **set the scene** to describe the background to an event, etc. [L *scēna, scaena*, from Gr *skēnē* a tent, stage building]

scène à faire *sen a fār*, *n* the climactic scene in a play or opera. [Fr, scene of action]

scent, earlier **sent**, *sent*, *vt* to track, find, or discern by smell, or as if by smell; to perfume. — *vi* to give forth a smell; to sniff; to smell. — *n* odour; sense of smell; a substance used for the sake of its smell, perfume; the smell left by an animal, etc, by which it may be hunted; paper strewn by the pursued in the game of hare and hounds. — *adj* **scent'ed** having a smell, fragrant; impregnated or sprinkled with perfume; endowed with a sense of smell. — *adj* **scent'ful** (*archaic*) odoriferous; with an acute sense of smell. — *n* and *adj* **scent'ing**. — *adj* **scent'less**. — **scent bag** a scent gland; a sachet; a bag of strong-smelling stuff dragged over the ground for a drag hunt; **scent bottle** a small bottle for holding perfume; **scent box**; **scent gland** a gland that secretes a substance of distinctive smell, for recognition, attraction, or defence; **scent organ** a scent gland; a smelling organ; **scent scale** on male butterflies' wings, a scale that gives off a scent. — **put** (or **throw**) **someone off the scent** to mislead someone. [Fr *sentir*, from L *sentīre* to perceive]

scepsis or (*esp US*) **skepsis** *skep'sis*, *n* philosophic doubt. [Gr *skepsis* query, doubt, hesitation, from *skeptesthai*; see **sceptic**]

sceptic or (*esp US*) **skeptic** *skep'tik*, *adj* (with *cap*) pertaining to the philosophical school of Pyrrho and his successors, who asserted nothing positively and doubted the possibility of knowledge; sceptical (*rare*). — *n* a person who doubts prevailing doctrines, *esp* in religion; a person who tends to disbelieve; (with *cap*) a Sceptic philosopher or adherent of the Sceptic school. — *adj* **scep'tical** or (*esp US*) **skep'tical** of or inclined to scepticism; doubtful or inclined towards incredulity. — *adv* **scep'tically** or (*esp US*) **skep'tically**. — *n* **scep'ticism** or (*esp US*) **skep'ticism** doubt; the doctrine that no facts can be certainly known; agnosticism; sceptical attitude towards Christianity; general disposition to doubt. [L *scepticus*, from Gr *skeptikos* thoughtful, from *skeptesthai* to consider]

sceptre or *US* **scepter** *sep'tər*, *n* a staff or baton carried as an emblem of monarchic authority; hence, monarchic authority itself. — *adj* **scep'tral** regal. — *adj* **scep'tred** or (*US*) **scep'tered** bearing a sceptre; regal. — *adj* **scep'treless** or (*US*) **scep'terless**. — *adj* **scep'try** (*Keats*) sceptred. [L *scēptrum*, from Gr *skēptron* a staff, from *skēptein* to prop, stay]

scerne *sûrn*, (*archaic*) *vt* to discern. [**discern**, or Ital *scernere*]

sceuophylax *skū-of'i-laks* or *sū-of'*, (*Greek Church*) *n* a sacristan. — *n* **sceuophylacium** (*-lā'si-əm*) a sacristy. [Gr *skeuos* a vessel, and *phylax* a watcher]

SCF *abbrev*: Save the Children Fund.

Sch. *abbrev*: schilling (qv); (also **sch.**) school.

schadenfreude *shä'dən-froi-də*, *n* malicious pleasure in the misfortunes of others. [Ger, from *Schade* hurt, and *Freude* joy]

Schafer's method *shā'fərz meth'əd n* a method of artificial respiration in which pressure is exerted on the prone patient's lower back at intervals of several seconds. — Cf **kiss of life**. [Sir Edward Sharpey-*Schafer* (1850–1935), Eng physiologist]

schalstein *shäl'shtīn*, *n* a slaty diabase tuff. [Ger, from *Schale* shell, scale, and *Stein* stone]

schanse *shan'sə*, **schanze** or **schantze** *shant'sə*, (*SAfr*) *n* a heap of stones used as a protection against rifle fire. [Du *schans*, *schantze*; see **sconce**[1]]

schappe *shap'ə*, *n* a fabric of waste silk with gum, etc partly removed by fermentation. — *vt* to subject to this process. [Swiss Ger]

schapska. See **chapka**.

schechita, shechita, shehita or **-tah** *she-hēt'a*, (*Judaism*) *n* the slaughtering of animals in accordance with rabbinical law. [Heb *shehītāh* slaughter]

schecklaton. See **checklaton**.

schedule *shed'ūl* or (*esp US*) *sked'ūl*, formerly (as in *Shakesp*) **scedule** *sed'ūl*, *n* a slip or scroll with writing; a list, inventory, or table; a supplementary, explanatory, or appended document; an appendix to a bill or act of parliament; a form for filling in particulars, or such a form filled in; a timetable, plan, programme, or scheme. — *vt* to make a schedule or enter in a schedule; to plan, appoint, arrange. — *adj* **sched'uled** entered in a schedule; planned, appointed, arranged (to happen at a specified time); (of a building) entered in a list of buildings to be preserved for historic or architectural reasons (see also **listed building** under **list**[2]). — *n* **sched'uler**. — **scheduled castes** (in India) the former untouchables; **scheduled territories** sterling area; **schedule tribes** (in India) aboriginal tribes officially given some protection and privileges. — **behind schedule** not keeping up to an arranged programme; late; **on schedule** on time. [OFr *cedule* (Fr *cédule*), from LL *sc(h)edula*, dimin of *scheda* a strip of papyrus, from Gr *schedē*]

Scheele's green *shā'ləz* or *shēlz grēn*, *n* a poisonous yellowish-green pigment, copper hydrogen arsenite, formerly used in wallpapers. [K W *Scheele*, who first prepared it; see ety for **scheelite**]

scheelite *shē'līt*, *n* a greenish or brownish mineral, calcium tungstate, crystallizing in the tetragonal system, an important source of tungsten. [From K W *Scheele* (1742–86), Swedish chemist, who investigated it]

schefflera *shef'lə-rə*, *n* any of various evergreen tropical or subtropical shrubs of the family *Auraliceae*, having large compound leaves and clusters of small flowers followed by berries.

schellum. Same as **skellum**.

schelm. Older form of **skelm**.

schema *skē'mə*, *n* a scheme, plan; a diagrammatic outline or synopsis; a mental picture of a thing in the imagination, which the mind uses to help perceive or understand it more clearly (*psychol*); a kind of standard or principle which the mind forms from past experiences, and by which new experiences can be evaluated to a certain extent: — *pl* **schē'mata**. — *adj* **schematic** (*ski-mat'ik*) or **schemat'ical** following, or involving, a particular plan or arrangement; representing something by a diagram, plan, etc. — *adv* **schemat'ically**. — *n* **schē'matism** form or outline of a thing; arrangement, disposition in a scheme. — *n* **schē'matist**. — *n* **schematizā'tion** or **-s-**. — *vt* **schē'matize** or **-ise** to reduce to or represent by a scheme. [Gr *schēma*, *-atos* form, from the reduced grade of the root of *echein* to have (as in the future *schēsein*)]

scheme *skēm*, *n* a systematic plan of action for achieving an end; a plan for building operations of various kinds, or the buildings, etc, constructed, or the area covered (eg *housing scheme*, *irrigation scheme*); a plan pursued secretly, insidiously, by intrigue, or for private ends; a project; a programme of action; a diagram of positions, *esp* (*astrol*) of planets; a table; a system; a rhetorical figure (*obs*); an escapade (*obs*). — *vt* to plan; to reduce to a system; to lay schemes for. — *vi* to form a plan; to lay schemes, to plot or intrigue; to indulge in an escapade (*obs*). — *n* **schē'mer**. — *n* and *adj* **schē'ming**. [**schema**]

schemozzle. See **shemozzle**.

Schengen agreement *sheng'gen ə-grē'mənt*, *n* an agreement between France, Germany, Belgium, Luxembourg and the Netherlands to remove all border controls between themselves and to exchange information on criminal activities, etc. [From the Luxembourg village of *Schengen*, where the agreement was first discussed.]

scherzo *sker'tsō* or *skûr'*, (*music*) *n* a lively busy movement in triple time, *usu* with a trio, now generally taking the place of the minuet in a sonata or a symphony: — *pl* **scher'zos** or **scher'zi** (*-tsē*). — *adj* and *adv* **scherzan'do** in a playful manner. — *n* a scherzando passage or movement: — *pl* **scherzan'dos** or **scherzan'di** (*-dē*). [Ital, from Gmc; cf Ger *Scherz* jest]

Scheuermann's disease *shoi'ər-mənz di-zēz'*, *n* a form of osteochondritis of the vertebrae affecting children and adolescents. [From H W *Scheuermann* (1877–1960), Danish surgeon]

schiavone *skyä-vō'nā*, *n* a 17c basket-hilted broadsword used by the Doge's bodyguard of Slavs. [Ital *Schiavoni* Slavs]

Schick (or **Schick's**) **test** *shik* (or *shiks*) *test*, *n* a test for susceptibility to diphtheria, made by injecting the skin with a measured amount of diphtheria toxin. [From Bela *Schick* (1877–1967), US paediatrician]

schiedam *skē'dam* or *-dam'*, *n* Holland gin, chiefly made at Schiedam (*s'hhē-däm'*), near Rotterdam.

Schiff's base *shifs bās*, *n* a benzylidene aniline. — **Schiff's reagent** a reagent for testing for the presence of aldehydes. [From Hugo *Schiff* (1834–1915), German chemist]

schiller *shil'ər*, (*geol*) *n* a peculiar bronze-like lustre in certain minerals, such as hypersthene, due to diffraction caused by minute plates of haematite, etc, developed in separation planes. — *n* **schillerīzā'tion** or **-s-** the development of such plates. — *vt* **schill'erize** or **-ise** to impart a schiller to. — **schiller spar** schillerized enstatite (bronzite). [Ger]

schilling *shil'ing*, *n* the Austrian standard monetary unit (100 *groschen*). [Ger; cf **shilling**]

Schilling test *shil'ing test*, (*med*) *n* a test to assess capacity to absorb vitamin B_{12} from the bowel, used in the diagnosis of pernicious anaemia. [From R F *Schilling* (born 1919), US physician]

schimmel *shim'l*, *n* a roan horse. [Ger, a white horse; also Du]

schindylesis *skin-di-lē'sis*, (*anatom*) *n* an articulation formed by the fitting of the crest of a bone into a groove in another. — *adj* **schindyletic** (*-let'ik*). [Gr *schindylēsis* cleaving]

schipperke *skip'ər-kə* or *-ki*, also *ship'* or *s'hhip'*, *n* a small tailless breed of dogs, *orig* used as watchdogs on Dutch barges. [Du, little boatman]

schism *sizm*, or *skizm*, *n* a breach, *esp* in the unity of a church; promotion of such a breach; a body so formed.

— *n* (*music*) **schisma** (*skiz'mə*) half the difference between twelve perfect fifths and seven octaves. — *n* **schismatic** (*siz-mat'ik* or *skiz-*) someone who favours a schism or belongs to a schismatic body; a Catholic who avoided penalties by occasional conformity (*RC*). — *adj* **schismat'ic** or **schismat'ical** tending to, favouring, or of the nature of, a schism. — *adv* **schismat'ically**. — *n* **schismat'icalness**. — *vi* **schis'matize** or **-ise** to practise schism; to make a schism. — **schism house** or **shop** (*old*, *esp* 19*c*) contemptuous Anglican terms for a nonconformist church. — **great Eastern** (or **Greek**) **schism** the separation of the Greek church from the Latin, finally completed in 1054; (**great**) **Western schism** the division in the Western church from 1378 to 1417, when there were antipopes under French influence at Avignon. [Gr *schisma* a split, rent, cleft, partly through OFr (*s*)*cisme*]

schist *shist*, *n* any crystalline foliated metamorphic rock not coarse and feldspathic enough to be called gneiss, such as mica-schist, hornblende-schist; sometimes extended to shaly rocks. — *adj* **schist'ose**. — *n* **schistosity** (*-os'i-ti*). — *adj* **schist'ous**. [Fr *schiste*, from Gr *schistos* split; pron due to German influence]

Schistosoma *shis-tə-sō'mə* or *skis-*, *n* a genus of blood flukes (also called **Bilharzia**, qv), some species of which are parasites of man. — *n* **schis'tosome** a member of the genus. — *n* **schistosomī'asis** a disease caused by infestation by schistosomes (also called **bilharziosis**). [Gr *schistos* split]

schizo *skit'sō*, (*colloq*) *n* and *adj* a schizophrenic: — *pl* **schiz'os**.

schizo- *skit'sō-*, *-sə-* or *-so'*, also *skid-zō*, etc and *skī-zō*, etc, or before a vowel **schiz-** *combining form* denoting cloven, a split or division. — *n* **Schizaea** (*-zē'ə*) a tropical genus of ferns giving name to the family **Schizaeā'ceae**, with sporangia splitting longitudinally by an apical annulus. — *adj* **schizaeā'ceous**. — *n* **schizanthus** (*-an'thəs*; Gr *anthos* flower) a Chilean flowering plant of the genus *Schizanthus*, frequently cultivated for its showy orchid-like blooms. — *adj* **schizo-affect'ive** marked by symptoms of schizophrenia and manic-depressiveness. — *n* **schi'zocarp** (*-kärp*; Gr *karpos* fruit; *bot*) a dry fruit that splits into several indehiscent one-seeded portions. — *adj* (*bot*) **schizocar'pous** or **schizocar'pic**. — *n* **schizogenesis** (*-jen'i-sis*; see **-genesis**) asexual reproduction by fission. — *adj* **schizogen'ic** or **schizogenetic** (*-ji-net'ik*) reproducing, reproduced, or formed by fission or splitting. — *adj* **schizog'onous**. — *n* **schizog'ony** (Gr *gonē*, generation) reproduction in protozoans by multiple fission. — *adj* **schizognathous** (*-og'nə-thəs*; see **-gnathous**) (of some birds) having the bones of the palate separate. — *adj* **schizoid** (*skit'soid* or *skid'zoid*; see **-oid**) showing qualities of a schizophrenic personality, such as asocial behaviour, introversion, tendency to fantasy, but without definite mental disorder. — *n* a schizoid person. — *adj* **schizoid'al**. — *n* **schizomycete** (*-sēt'*) any microscopic organism of the class **Schizomycetes**, *incl* the bacteria. — *adj* **schizomycet'ic** or **schizomycē'tous**. — *n* **schiz'ont** in protozoans, a mature trophozoite about to reproduce by schizogony. — *n* **schiz'ophrene** (*-frēn*; Gr *phrēn* mind) a person who suffers from schizophrenia. — *n* **schizophrenia** (*-frē'ni-ə*) a psychosis marked by introversion, dissociation, inability to distinguish reality from unreality, delusions, etc. — *n* **schizophrenic** (*-fren'ik*) a schizophrene. — Also *adj*. — *adj* **schizophrenet'ic** or **schizophrenet'ical**. — *adv* **schizophrenet'ically**. — *adj* **schizophrenogenic** (*-jen'ik*; see **-genic**) causing or tending to cause schizophrenia. — *adj* **schizophyceous** (*-fī'shəs* or *-fi'*) of or belonging to the **Schizophyceae** (*-fī'si-ē*; Gr *phykos* seaweed), a group of algae, bluish-green in colour, that grow in fresh or salt water, and can be responsible for the pollution of drinking-water. — *n* **schiz'ophyte** (*-fīt*; see **-phyte**) a plant of the **Schizoph'yta**, a group that multiply only by fission, *incl* bacteria and blue-green algae. — *adj* **schizophytic** (*-fit'ik*). — *n* **schi'zopod** (*-pod*; see **-pod**) a shrimp-like crustacean of the former order **Schizop'oda**, having each leg divided into exopodite and endopodite. — Also *adj*. — *adj* **schizop'odal** or **schizop'odous**. — *n* **schizothymia** (*-thī'mi-ə*; Gr *thymos* mind, temper; *psychiatry*) manifestation of schizoid traits within normal limits. — *adj* **schizothy'mic**. [Gr *schizein* to cleave]

schläger *shlā'gər*, *n* the sword used by students in some German universities where the duelling tradition has been preserved. [Ger, from *schlagen*, to beat]

schlemiel, **schlemihl** or **shlemiel** *shlə-mēl'*, (*slang*) *n* a clumsy person, a pitiful bungler, fool. [Yiddish, prob from *Shelumiel*, a biblical general notorious for losing battles, with spelling influenced by A von Chamisso's character Peter *Schlemihl* (1814)]

Schlemm's canal *schlemz kə-nal'*, (*anatom*) *n* a channel at the junction of the cornea and the sclera in the eye, through which aqueous humour drains. [From F *Schlemm* (1795–1858), German anatomist]

schlep, **schlepp** or **shlep** *shlep*, (*slang*) *vt* to carry or pull with effort; to drag: — *pr p* **schlepp'ing**; *pa t* and *pa p* **schlepped**. — *n* a clumsy, stupid, incompetent person; a person of no importance. — *n* **schlepp'er** or **shlepp'er** an incompetent or nonentity. — *adj* **schlepp'y**. [Yiddish]

schlich *shlihh*, (*mining*) *n* the finer portions of crushed ore, separated by water. [Ger]

schlieren *shlē'rən*, *n pl* streaks of mineral of different colour, structure, or composition in igneous rocks; visible streaks in a transparent fluid, caused by the differing refractive indices of fluid of varying density (*phys*). — **schlieren photography** the technique of photographing a flow of air or other gas, the variations in refractive index according to density being made apparent under a special type of illumination, often used in the testing of models in wind tunnels. [Ger, pl of *Schliere* streak]

schlimazel or **shlimazel** *shli-mä'zl*, (*US slang*) *n* a persistently unlucky person. [Yiddish; see **shemozzle**]

schlock or **shlock** *shlok'*, (*esp US slang*) *adj* of inferior quality. — *n* something of inferior quality, *esp* shoddy merchandise (also **schlock'er**). — *adj* **schlock'y**. [Yiddish]

schloss *shlos*, *n* a castle, palace, manor house. [Ger]

schlumbergera. See **Christmas cactus**.

schmaltz or **shmaltz** *shmölts* or *shmälts*, *n* mush; a production in music or other art that is very sentimental, or showy; sickly sentimentality. — *adj* **schmaltz'y** or **shmaltz'y** old-fashioned, old-style, outmoded; sentimental. [Yiddish, from Ger *Schmalz* cooking fat, grease]

schmeck or **shmek** *shmek'*, (*US slang*) *n* a taste or sniff; heroin (see also **smack**[4]). [Yiddish]

schmelz *shmelts*, *n* glass used in decorative work. [Ger *Schmelz* enamel]

schmo, **shmo** or **shmoe** *shmō*, (*US slang*) *n* a stupid or a boring person, a fool: — *pl* **schmoes** or **shmoes**. [Yiddish]

schmock. See **schmuck**.

schmoe. See **schmo**.

schmooze or **shmooze** *shmōōz*, or **shmoose** *shmōōs*, (*orig US slang*) *vi* to gossip, to chat in a friendly or intimate manner. — *n* (also **schmooz**) such a chat, *esp* at a social gathering. [Yiddish]

schmuck or **schmuck** *shmuk*, or **schmock** or **shmock** *shmok*, (*orig US slang*) *n orig*, a euphemism for penis; a pitiful, stupid or obnoxious person. [Yiddish, from Ger *Schmuck* ornament]

schmutter *shmut'ər*, (*slang*) *n* clothing; rag. [Yiddish *schmatte* rag]

schnapper *shnap'ər*, *n*. Same as **snapper** (Australian fish). [Germanized]

schnapps or **schnaps** *shnaps*, *n* any of various strong alcoholic drinks, *esp* Holland gin. [Ger *Schnapps* a dram]

schnauzer *shnowt'sər*, *n* a German breed of wire-haired terrier. [Ger *Schnauze* snout]

schnecken *shnek'ən*, (*esp NAm*) *n pl* sweet bread rolls containing nuts and flavoured with cinnamon: — *n sing* **schneck'e**. [Ger *Schnecke* snail (the bread being baked in a spiral shape reminiscent of a snail's shell]

Schneiderian *shnī-dē'ri-ən*, *adj* pertaining to the German anatomist Konrad Victor *Schneider* (1614–1680). — **Schneiderian membrane** the olfactory mucous membrane, studied by him.

schnell *shnel*, (*Ger*) *adj* quick. — *adv* quickly.

schnitzel *shnit'sl*, *n* a veal cutlet. — See also **Wiener schnitzel**. [Ger]

schnook *shnŏŏk*, (*orig US slang*) *n* a pathetic, timid or unfortunate person. [Yiddish, prob from Ger *Schnuck* small sheep]

schnorkel. See **snorkel**.

schnorrer *shnō'rər*, *shnö'* or *shno'*, (*US slang*) *n* a beggar. — *vi* **schnorr** (*shnōr* or *shnör*) to beg, *esp* in such a way as to make the giver feel in some way beholden. [Yiddish]

schnozzle *shnoz'əl*, (*slang*) *n* nose. [Yiddish]

schola cantorum *skō'lə kan-tō'rəm*, *n* a choir or choir school attached to a church, cathedral, etc; the part of a church, etc in which the choir is placed for services. [L, school of singers]

scholar *skol'ər*, *n* a pupil; a disciple; a student; (in times of less widespread education) someone who could read and write, or an educated person; someone whose learning (formerly *esp* in Latin and Greek) is extensive and exact, or whose approach to learning is scrupulous and critical; generally, a holder of a scholarship. — *adj* **schol'ar-like** like or befitting a scholar. — *n* **schol'arliness**. — *adj* **schol'arly** of or natural to a scholar; having the learning of a scholar; intended for serious students who already have some knowledge of the subject. — *adv* (*Shakesp*) as becomes a scholar. — *n* **schol'arship** scholarly learning; a foundation or grant for the maintenance of a pupil or student; the status and emoluments of such a pupil or student. — **scholar's mate** (*chess*) a simple mate accomplished in four moves. [OE *scōlere*, and (in part) OFr *escoler*, both from LL *scholāris*, from *schola*; see **school**[1]]

scholarch *skō'lärk*, *n* the head of a school, *esp* of philosophy. [Gr *scholarchēs*]

scholastic *skəl-as'tik* or *sko-*, *adj* pertaining to schools, universities, etc, or to teachers, teaching or students; subtle; pedantic. — *n* a teacher or scholar, one who adheres to the method or subtleties of the Medieval schools, a schoolman; a Jesuit who has taken first vows only; a university teacher (*esp* with implication of pedantry). — *adj* (*archaic*) **scholas'tical**. — *adv* **scholas'tically**. — *n* **scholas'ticism** (*-sizm'*) the aims, methods, and products of thought which constituted the main endeavour of the intellectual life of the Middle Ages; the method or subtleties of the schools of philosophy; the collected body of doctrines of the schoolmen. [Gr *scholastikos*, from *scholē*; see **school**[1]]

scholion *skō'li-on* or **scholium** *-əm*, *n* an annotation in the nature of an explanation or supplementary comment, such as those written in the margins of manuscripts of the classical authors; an observation or note added to a mathematical proposition: — *pl* **scho'lia**. — *n* **scho'liast** a writer of scholia; an annotator; a commentator. — *adj* **scholias'tic**. [Gr *scholion* (Mod L *scholium*), *scholiastēs*, from *scholē*; see **school**[1]]

school[1] *skōōl*, *n* a place for instruction; an institution for education, *esp* primary or secondary, or for the teaching of a specific subject or subjects (eg a *ballet school*); a division of such an institution; a building or room used for that purpose; the work of a such an institution; the time during which pupils, etc attend it; the body of pupils in it; the disciples of a particular teacher; a group of artists whose work shares a common style, from the circumstance of their having received instruction at the same place or under the same master, sometimes used by way of rough attribution where a work is by an unknown hand; those who hold a common doctrine or follow a common tradition; a particular environment or set of experiences seen as a training ground; a group of people meeting in order to play card games, *usu* for money (*slang*); a method of instruction; an instruction book (now *usu* in music); the body of instructors and students in a university, college, faculty, or department; a group of studies in which honours may be taken; (in *pl*) academic institutions; (in *pl*) an academic disputation; (in *pl*) the BA examinations at Oxford; (in *pl*) a university building comprising rooms for lectures, disputations or (in modern Oxford use) examinations. — *adj* of school, schools, or the schools. — *vt* to educate in a school; to train, to drill; to instruct; to coach in a part to be played; to teach overbearingly; to discipline; to admonish (*obs*). — *adj* **schooled** trained; experienced. — *n* **school'ery** (*archaic*) something taught, precepts. — *n* **school'ing** instruction or maintenance at school; tuition; training; discipline; school fees; reproof; reprimand. — *adj* and *adv* **school'ward**. — *adv* **school'wards**. — **school age** the age at which children attend school. — *adj* **school'-age**. — **school'bag** a bag for carrying schoolbooks; **school bell** a bell to announce time for school; **school board** formerly, an elected board of school managers for a parish, town, or district; now, a board made up of elected parents, teachers and community representatives with responsibility for the management of an individual school; **school book** a book used in school; **school'boy** a boy attending school. — Also *adj*. — *adj* **school'boyish**. — *adj* **school'-bred**. — **school'child**; **school'craft** learning; **school dame** the mistress of a dame-school (qv); **school'day** a day on which schools are open; (in *pl*) time of being a school pupil; **school'-divine**; **school'-divin'ity** scholastic or seminary theology; **school doctor** a schoolman; a schoolteacher (*obs*); a physician appointed to examine or attend the pupils of a school or schools; **school'fellow** someone taught at the same school at the same time as oneself; **school'-friend** someone who is or has been one's friend at school; **school'-friend'ship**; **school'girl** a girl attending school. — Also *adj*. — *adj* **school'girlish**. — *n* and *adj* **school'going**. — **school'house** a building used as a school; a house provided for a school-teacher (**school house** a headmaster's or headmistress's boarding-house; its boarders); **school'-inspector** an official appointed to examine schools; **school'-leaver**. someone who is leaving school because he or she has reached the statutory age, or the stage, for doing so. — *n* and *adj* **school'-leaving**. — **school'-ma'am** a school-marm; **school'maid** (*old*) a schoolgirl; **school'man** a philosopher or theologian of medieval scholasticism; a teacher or educator (*US*; *rare*); **school'-marm** (*colloq*; a form of **school-ma'am**) a schoolmistress (*NAm*); a prim pedantic woman (*colloq*). — *adj* **school'-marmish**. — **school'master** the master or one of the masters of a school; a tutor (*Shakesp*). — Also *vt* and *vi*. — *n* and *adj* **school'mastering**. — *adj* **school'masterish**. — *adj* **school'masterly**. — **school'mastership**; **school'-mate** a school-friend; a schoolfellow; **school'mistress** the mistress or one of the mistresses of a school; **school nurse** a registered nurse employed to visit schools and promote children's health through screening procedures, immunization, etc; **school phobia** an irrational fear of attending school; **school point** a point for scholastic disputation; **school'room** a school classroom; in a house, a room for receiving or preparing lessons in; **school ship** a training-ship. — *adj* **school'-taught** taught at school or in the schools. — **school'teacher** a person who teaches in a school; **school'teaching**; **school term** a division of the school year; a word or term in use in the schools or among schoolmen; **school'tide** schooldays; **school'time** the time at which a school opens, or during which it remains open; schooldays. — *adj* **school'-trained** trained at school. — **school'work**; **school year** the period of (more or less) continual teaching during the year comprising an academic unit during which a child or student remains in the same basic class, ie, in Britain, from autumn to early summer. — **old school** see under **old**; **the schoolmaster is abroad** a phrase of Brougham's implying that education and intelligence are now widely spread. [OE *scōl*, from L *schola*, from Gr *scholē* leisure, a lecture, a school]

school[2] *skōōl*, *n* a shoal of fish, whales, or other swimming animals; a flock, troop, assemblage (*esp* of birds). — *vi* to gather or go in schools. — *adj* going in schools. — *n* and *adj* **school'ing**. — **school'master** the leader of a school of whales, etc. [Du *school*; cf **shoal**[1]]

schoole (*Shakesp*, *Macbeth* I. 7. 6). Same as **shoal**[2] (*n*).

schooner *skōōn'ər*, *n* a sharp-built, swift-sailing vessel, generally two-masted, fore-and-aft rigged, or with top and topgallant sails on the foremast; a covered emigrant-wagon (also **prairie schooner**); a large beer glass (*esp NAm* and *Austr*); a large sherry glass. — *adj* **schoon'er-rigged**. [Early 18c (Massachusetts) *skooner*, *scooner*, said to be from a dialect Eng word *scoon* to skim]

schorl *shörl*, (*mineralogy*) *n* black tourmaline. — *adj* **schorlā'ceous**. — *n* **schorlomite** (*shör'lə-mīt*) a black variety of garnet rich in titanium dioxide. — **schorl'=rock** (*geol*) a rock composed of aggregates schorl and quartz. [Ger *Schörl*]

schottische *sho-tēsh'* or *shot'ish*, *n* a dance, or dance-tune, similar to the polka. [Ger (*der*) *schottische* (*Tanz*), (the) Scottish (dance); pron sham French]

Schottky defect *shot'ki dē'fekt*, *n* deviation from the ideal crystal lattice by removal of some molecules to the surface, leaving vacancies in the lattice; **Schottky effect** (*electronics*) the removal of electrons from the surface of a semiconductor when a localized field is present; **Schottky noise** see **shot noise** under **shot**[1]. [After Walter *Schottky* (1886–1976), German physicist]

schout *skowt*, *n* a municipal officer. [Du]

schrecklich *shrek'lihh*, (*Ger*) *adj* frightful. — *n* **Schreck'lichkeit** (*-kīt*) frightfulness.

schreech-owl. See under **shriek**.

Schrödinger equation *shrø'ding-ər ē-kwā'shən*, *n* a fundamental equation of wave mechanics which describes the behaviour of a particle in a field of force. [Erwin *Schrödinger*(1887-1961), Austrian physicist]

schtick, **schtik**. See **shtick**.

schtook, **schtuck**. See **shtook**.

schtoom. See **shtoom**.

schuit or **schuyt** *skoit*, *n* a Dutch flat-bottomed boat, used on canals and along the coast. [Du]

schuss *shōōs*, (*skiing*) *n* a straight slope on which it is possible to make a fast run; such a run. — *vi* to make such a run. [Ger]

schutzstaffel (abbrev **SS**) *shōōts'shtä-fəl*, (*Ger*) *n* Hitler's bodyguard of elite police later forming military units in Nazi Germany.

schuyt. See **schuit**.

schwa or **shwa** *shvä* or *shwä*, (*phonetics*) *n* an indistinct vowel sound; a neutral vowel (ə). — Cf **sheva**. [Ger, from Heb *schewa* a diacritic indicating lack of vowel sound]

Schwann cell *shvan sel*, (*zool*) *n* a large nucleated cell that lays down myelin in peripheral nerve fibres. [Theodor *Schwann* (1810–82), German physiologist]

schwärmerei *shver'mər-ī*, *n* sentimental enthusiasm, wild devotion, fanaticism. — *adj* **schwärmerisch** (*-ər-ish*) [Ger, swarming]

schwarzlot *shvarts'lōt*, *n* a type of black enamel decoration on glass, pottery and porcelain. [Ger, black lead]

Schwenkfelder *shvengk'fel-dər*, *n* a member of a religious sect, founded by Kaspar von *Schwenkfeld* (1490–1561). Also **Schwenkfeld'ian**.

sci. *abbrev*: science; scientific.

scia- *sī-ə* or *sī-a'*, *combining form* denoting shadow. See also words listed under **skia-**.

sciaenid *sī-ē'nid* or **sciaenoid** *sī-ē'noid*, *n* and *adj* (of or relating to) any member of the genus *Sciaena* or the family *Sciaenidae*, marine percoid tropical and subtropical fishes, *incl* the croakers and drums. [Gr *skiaina* a kind of fish]

sciamachy *sī-am'ə-ki n*. Same as **skiamachy** (qv under **skia-**).

sciarid *sī-ar'id*, *n* a minute, dark-coloured, two-winged fly of the family *Sciaridae*. — Also *adj*. [Gr *skiaros*, shady, dark-coloured, from *skia* shadow]

sciatic *sī-at'ik*, *adj* of, or in the region of, the hip. — Also **sciat'ical**. — *n* **sciat'ica** neuritis of the sciatic nerve. — **sciatic nerve** the major nerve of the leg, passing down the back of the thigh from the base of the spine. [LL *sciaticus*, fem *-a*, from Gr *ischion* hip-joint]

SCID (*med*) *abbrev*: severe combined immunodeficiency.

science *sī'əns*, *n* knowledge (*archaic*); knowledge ascertained by observation and experiment, critically tested, systematized and brought under general principles; a department or branch of such knowledge or study; a skilled craft (*obs*); trained skill, *esp* in boxing (now *usu jocular*). — *adj* **sci'enced** (*archaic*) versed, learned. — *adj* **sci'ent** (*archaic*) having science. — *adj* **sciential** (*-en'shl*; *rare*) of, having, or producing, science; scientific. — *adj* **scientif'ic** (L *facere*, to make) *orig* (of a syllogism) demonstrative, producing knowledge; of, relating to, based on, devoted to, according to, used in, or versed in, science. — Also (*rare*) **scientif'ical**. — *adv* **scientif'ically**. — *n* **sci'entism** the methods or mental attitudes of scientists; a belief that the methods used in studying natural sciences should be employed also in investigating all aspects of human behaviour and condition, eg in philosophy and social sciences; scientific or pseudo-scientific language. — *n* **sci'entist** a person who studies or practises any science, *esp* natural science. — *adj* **scientis'tic**. — *vt* **sci'entize** or **-ise** to treat in a scientific way — *n* **Scientol'ogist**. — *n* **Scientol'ogy**® a religious movement founded in the US in the 1950s by L Ron Hubbard, which claims that an individual's full spiritual potential may be realized through study and psychotherapy. — **science fiction** a literary genre dealing with speculative scientific and technological developments, *esp* the imaginative presentation, often set in the future, of people and environments on the earth, on other planets or in space (*colloq abbrev* **sci-fi** (*sī'-fī'*)); **science park** a centre for industrial research, etc attached to a university, set up for the purpose of co-operation between the academic and the commercial world; **scientific whaling** whaling carried out actually or ostensibly for the purposes of research. — **the (noble) science** the art of boxing. [L *scientia*, from *sciēns*, *-entis* pr p of *scīre* to know]

scienter *sī-en'tər*, (*legal*) *adv* having knowledge, being aware; knowingly, wilfully. [L]

sci.fa. *abbrev*: *scire facias* (*qv*).

sci-fi *sī'-fī'*, (*colloq*) *n* science fiction.

scilicet *sī'li-set* or *skē'li-ket*, *adv* to wit, namely (*abbrev* **scil**. or **sciz**.). [L *scīlicet*, from *scīre licet* it is permitted to know]

scilla *sil'ə*, *n* any plant of the squill genus *Scilla* of the lily family, *incl* some bright blue bell-shaped flowers. [L, from Gr *skilla* the officinal squill]

Scillonian *si-lō'ni-ən*, *adj* of, belonging to, concerning, the *Scilly* Isles, off the south-west coast of Britain. — *n* an inhabitant of these islands.

scimitar *sim'i-tər*, *n* a short, single-edged, curved sword, broadest at the point end, used by the Turks and Persians. [Poss through Fr *cimeterre* or Ital *scimitarra*, from Pers *shamshīr*; but doubtful]

scincoid *sing'koid* or **scincoidian** *-koi'di-ən*, *adj* resembling a skink. — *n* an animal resembling a skink. [Gr *skinkos* a skink, and see **-oid**]

scintigraphy *sin-tig'rə-fi*, *n* a diagnostic technique in which the pattern of gamma rays emitted by a radioactive isotope injected into the body is represented in diagrammatic form, and a record or map of the radioactivity in various parts of the body may be built up by scanning the body, section by section. — *n* **scint'igram** a diagram so produced. — *n* **scin'tiscan** a scintilliscan (qv). — *n* **scin'tiscanner** a device for producing scintiscans. [*scinti*llation, and **-graphy**, **-gram**]

scintilla *sin-til'ə*, *n* a spark; a hint, trace. — *adj* **scin'tillant** sparkling. — *vi* **scin'tillate** to sparkle; to be dazzlingly impressive or animated; to talk wittily. — *vt* to emit in sparks; to sparkle with. — *n* **scintillā'tion** a flash of light produced in a phosphor by an ionizing particle, eg an alpha particle, or a photon. — *n* **scin'tillātor** an instrument for detecting radioactivity. — *n* **scintill'-iscan** a scan made by scintigraphy. — *n* **scintillom'eter** an instrument for detecting and measuring radioactivity. — *n* **scintill'oscope** or **scintill'ascope** an instrument which shows scintillations on a screen, used to produce a scintigram. — **scintillation counter** a scintillometer. [L, a spark]

scio- *sī'ō-*, *sī'ə-* or *sī-o'*, *combining form* denoting shadow. — See also words listed under **skia-**.

sciolism *sī'ə-lizm*, *n* superficial pretensions to knowledge. — *n* **sci'olist** a pretender to science. — *adj* **sciolis'tic**. — *adj* **sci'olous**. [L *sciolus*, dimin of *scius* knowing, from *scīre* to know]

sciolto *shol'tō*, (*music*) *adj* and *adv* in a free manner. [Ital]

scion *sī'ən*, *n* a detached piece of a plant capable of propagating, *esp* by grafting; a young member of a family; a descendant, offshoot. [OFr *sion*, *cion*; origin obscure]

sciosophy *sī-os'ō-fi*, *n* a system of what claims to be knowledge but is without basis in ascertained scientific fact, such as astrology. [Gr *skiā* a shadow, and *sophiā* wisdom]

scire facias *sī'ri fā'shi-as* or *skē're fa'ki-äs*, (*law*) *n* a writ requiring a person to appear and show cause why a record should not be enforced, annulled or vacated (abbrev **sci. fa.**). [L *scīre faciās* make him to know]

scirocco. See **sirocco**.

Scirpus *sûr'pəs*, *n* the club-rush genus of the sedge family. [L, a rush]

scirrhus *skir'əs* or *sir'əs*, (*med*) *n* a hard swelling; a hard fibrous carcinoma. — *adj* **scirr'hoid** or **scirr'hous**. [Latinized from Gr *skirros*, *skīros* a tumour]

scissel *sis'l*, *n* metal clippings; scrap metal left when blanks have been cut out. — Also **sciss'il**. [OFr *cisaille*, from *ciseler*, from *cisel* a chisel; for the spelling cf **scissors**]

scissile *sis'īl*, *adj* capable of being cut; readily splitting. — *n* **scission** (*sish'ən* or *sizh'ən*) cutting; division; splitting; schism. — *n* **scissiparity** (*sis-i-par'i-ti*; L *parere* to bring forth) reproduction by fission. — *n* **scissure** (*sish'ər*) a cleft; a splitting, fissure; a rupture; a division; cutting. [L *scissilis*, *scissiō*, *-ōnis*, *scissūra*, from *scindere*, *scissum* to cut, to split, cleave]

scissors *siz'ərz*, *n pl* or (*rare*) *n sing* a cutting instrument with two blades pivoted to close together and overlap, *usu* smaller than shears; a position or movement like that of scissors; movement of the legs suggesting opening and closing of scissors (*gymnastics*, etc); (also **scissors hold**) locking the legs round body or head of an opponent (*wrestling*); a style of high jump in which the leg nearest the bar leads throughout; a pass executed on the run to another player who is crossing one's path (*Rugby football*). — *vt* **sciss'or** to cut with scissors. — *vi* (*Rugby football*) to execute a scissors pass. — *n* **sciss'orer** a scissors-and-paste compiler. — *adv* **sciss'or-wise**. — **sciss'or-bill** a skimmer; **scissor blade**; **scissor case**; **scissor cut**; **sciss'or-leg** a disability in which one leg is permanently crossed over the other, occurring in stroke victims and in certain brain-damaged children; **scissors-and-paste'** literary or journalistic matter collected from various sources with little or no original writing. — Also *adj*. — **scissors kick** a kick used in some swimming strokes in which the legs are moved in a scissorlike action; **sciss'ortail** an American fly-catcher; **sciss'or-tooth** a *usu* long, large tooth in a carnivore, used for tearing flesh. [OFr *cisoires*, from LL *cīsōrium* a cutting instrument, from *caedere*, *caesum* to cut; the spelling *sc-* is due to erroneous association with *scindere*, *scissum*; cf **scissile**]

scissure. See under **scissile**.

Scitamineae *sit-ə-min'i-ē*, *n pl* an order of monocotyledons *incl* the banana, ginger, Indian shot, and arrowroot families (also called **Musales**). — *adj* **scitamin'eous**. [Appar from L *scītāmenta* delicacies]

sciurine *sī-ūr'īn* or *sī'*, *n* a member of the genus *Sciurus* or family *Sciuridae* of rodents, *incl* the squirrels, marmots and chipmunks. — *adj* of, belonging to or characteristic of *Sciurus* or the *Sciuridae*. — *adj* **sciuroid** (*-ū'*). [L *sciūrus*, from Gr *skiouros*, from *skiā* shadow, and *ourā* tail]

sciz. See under **scilicet**.

SCL *abbrev*: Student of Civil Law.

sclaff *sklaf* or *skläf*, *n* a light slap or its sound (*Scot*); a stroke in which the sole of the club scrapes the ground before striking the ball (*golf*). — *vt* and *vi* to strike or play with a sclaff. [Imit]

sclate *sklāt* or *slāt*, *n* a Scots form of **slate**[1]. — **sclate'-stane** a piece of slate (such as money got from the Devil turned into).

sclaunder *sklön'dər*, **sclave**, **Sclav**, **Sclavonian**, etc obsolete forms of **slander**, **slave**, **Slav**, **Slavonian**, etc.

sclera *sklēr'ə*, *n* the outermost membrane of the eyeball, the sclerotic. — *adj* **sclē'ral**. — *n* **sclere** (*sklēr*; *zool*) a supporting element; a sponge spicule. — *n* **sclereid** or **sclereide** (*sklēr'i-id*; *bot*) a thick-walled cell. — *n* **sclerema** (*sklər-ē'mə*) hardening of (*esp* subcutaneous) tissues. — *n* **sclerenchyma** (*sklə-reng'ki-mə*; Gr *enchyma* in-filling) plant tissue consisting of cells with thick lignified walls; hard skeletal tissue, as in corals. — *adj* **sclerenchymatous** (*sklēr-eng-kim'ə-təs*). — *n* **sclerī'asis** hardening of tissue, scleroderma; a hard tumour; an induration. — *n* **sclē'rite** a hard skeletal plate or spicule. — *n* **scleritis** (*sklər-ī'tis*) sclerotitis. — *combining form* **sclero-** (*sklē-rō*, *-rə*, *sklərə'*) or (before a vowel) **scler-** (*skēr-* or *sklər-*) denoting hard; denoting the sclera. — *adj* **sclerocaulous** (*sklēr-ō-kö'ləs*). — *n* **sclē'rocauly** (Gr *kaulos* stem) possession of a hard, dry stem. — *n* **scleroderm** (*sklēr'*) a hard integument. — *n* **scleroder'ma** or **scleroder'mia** hardness and contraction of the body's connective tissue in which the skin becomes thickened by substitution of fibrous tissue for subcutaneous fat. — *adj* **scleroder'matous**, **scleroder'mic** or **scleroder'mous** hard-skinned; pertaining to a scleroderm or to sclerodermia. — *n* **scleroder'mite** the integument of a segment in arthropods. — *adj* **sclē'roid** (*bot* and *zool*) hard; hardened. — *n* **sclerō'ma** hardening; morbid hardening; a hardened area of mucous membrane or skin, eg forming nodules in the nose: — *pl* **scleromata** (*-rō'mə-tə*) or **sclero'matas**. — *n* **scleromalacia** (*-mə-lā'shi-ə*) thinning of the sclerotic coat resulting from inflammation. — *n* **sclerom'eter** an instrument for measuring the hardness of minerals. — *adj* **scleromet'ric**. — *n* **sclerophyll** (*sklēr'ə-fil*) a hard, leathery leaf; a woody plant, *esp* of hot, arid regions, with such leaves. — *adj* **sclerophyll'ous**. — *n* **sclero-ph'ylly** possession of sclerophylls. — *n* **scleroprō'tein** insoluble protein forming the skeletal parts of tissues. — *adj* **sclero'sal** affected with sclerosis. — *vt* **sclerose** (*sklə-rōs'* or *sklēr'*) to harden; to affect with sclerosis. — *vi* to become sclerotic. — *adj* **sclerosed** (or *sklēr'*). — *n* **sclerosis** (*sklə-rō'sis*) hardening; morbid hardening, eg of arteries by deposition of fatty plaques (*med*); hardening of tissue by thickening or lignification (*bot*): — *pl* **sclero'ses** (*-sēz*). — *adj* **sclerō'tal** sclerotic. — *n* a bony plate in the sclerotic of some animals. — *adj* **sclerot'ic** hard, firm, applied *esp* to the outer membrane of the eyeball; of sclerosis; sclerosed, affected with sclerosis. — *n* the sclera, the fibrous outer membrane of the eyeball (also **sclerotic coat**). — *n* **sclerotin** (*sklē'rə-tin*) (in insects) a protein in the cuticle that becomes hard and dark. — *n* **sclerotī'tis** inflammation of the sclerotic. — *adj* **sclerō'tioid** or **sclerō'tial** of, relating to, or resembling a sclerotium. — *n* **sclerotium** (*sklə-rō'shi-əm*) a hard, tuberlike body consisting of a compact mass of hyphae, the resting stage of many fungi: — *pl* **sclerō'tia**. — *vt* **scle'rotize** or **-ise** or (*zool*) to harden or darken. — *n* **sclerot'omy** (*med*) incision into the sclera. — *adj* **sclē'rous** hard or indurated; ossified or bony. — **disseminated sclerosis** an older name for **multiple sclerosis** (see under **multiple**). [Gr *sklēros* hard]

scliff or **skliff** *sklif*, (*Scot*) *n* a small segment or piece. [Imit]

sclim, sklim *sklim*, a Scots form of **climb**.

SCM *abbrev*: State Certified Midwife; Student Christian Movement.

SCODA *skō'də*, *abbrev*: Standing Conference on Drug Abuse.

scoff[1] *skof*, *n* mockery; a jibe, jeer; an object of derision. — *vi* to jeer (with *at*). — *vt* (*Shakesp*) to jeer at. — *n* **scoff'er**. — *n* and *adj* **scoff'ing**. — *adv* **scoff'ingly**. [Cf obs Dan *skof* jest, mockery, OFris *schof*]

scoff[2] or **skoff** *skof*, (*dialect* and *slang*) *vt* to devour; to plunder. — *vi* to feed quickly or greedily. — *n* food; a meal. [Appar **scaff**, reinforced by Afrik, from Du *schoft* a meal]

scofflaw *skof'lö*, (*US colloq*) *n* a person who is contemptuous of, or flouts, the law. [**scoff**[1] and **law**[1]]

scog. See **skug**[1].

Scoggin or **Scogan** *skog'ən*, *n* a popular 16c jestbook said to be the work of John Scogan, reputed to be court fool to Edward I; hence a buffoon.

scoinson *skoin'sən*. Same as **scuncheon**.

scold *skōld*, *n* a person, *usu* a woman, who constantly finds fault in a strident or clamorous manner; a scolding. — *vi* to brawl; to use abrasive language; to find fault vehemently or at some length. — *vt* to chide; to rebuke. — *n* **scold'er**. — *n* and *adj* **scold'ing**. — *adv* **scold'ingly**. — **scold's bridle** see **branks**.. [Appar ON *skāld* poet (through an intermediate sense, lampooner)]

scolecite *skol'ə-sīt* or *skōl'*, *n* a white mineral of the zeolite group, a hydrated silicate of calcium and aluminium. [**scolex** and **-ite**]

scolex *skō'leks*, *n* the head of a tapeworm having hooks and suckers by which it attaches itself to its host: — *pl* **scoleces** (*skō-lē'sēz*; erroneously **scō'lices**). — *n* **scolēcid** a worm of the *Scolecida*, the tapeworm class. — Also *adj*. — *adj* **scōleciform** (*-lēs'i-förm*). — *n pl* **Scōleciform'ia** the lugworm order. — *n* **scō'lecite** (*-sīt*) a member of the zeolite group of minerals. — *adj* **scōlecoid** (*-lē'koid*) like a scolex. [Gr *skolēx*, *-ēkos* a worm]

scolion. See **skolion**.

scoliosis *skol-i-ō'sis*, *n* abnormal curvature of the spine. — Also **scoliō'ma**. — *adj* **scoliotic** (*-ot'ik*). [Gr *skoliōsis*, from *skolios* crooked]

scollop[1]. Same as **scallop**.

scollop[2] *skol'əp*, *n* a flexible wooden rod, pointed at both ends, used in Ireland to pin down thatch. [Irish *scolb*]

scolopaceous *skol-ə-pā'shəs* *adj* of, belonging to, or characteristic of the genus *Scolopax* or family *Scolopacidae* of birds *incl* the woodcock and snipe. [Gr *scolopax*, *-akos* a woodcock]

scolopendra *skol-ə-pen'drə*, *n* a centipede of the genus *Scolopendra* of myriapods, *incl* large tropical centipedes up to a foot in length, giving name to the family *Scolopendridae*; a fabulous fish that vomited up the hook with its viscera, which it then re-swallowed. — *n* **scolopen'drid** any centipede of the family *Scolopendridae*. — *adj* **scolopen'driform** or **scolopen'drine**. — *n* **scolopen'drium** a fern with undivided leaves of the genus *Scolopendrium*, *incl* hart's-tongue, so called from the resemblance of the sori to a centipede. [Gr *skolopendra*]

Scolytus *skol'i-təs*, *n* the typical genus of **Scolytidae** (*-it'i-dē*), a family of bark-beetles. — *n* **scol'ytid** *n* a member of the *Scolytidae*. — Also *adj*. — *adj* and *n* **scol'ytoid**. [Gr *skolyptein* to strip]

Scomber *skom'bər*, *n* the mackerel genus, giving name to the family *Scombridae*. — *n* **Scom'bresox** (L *esox* pike) the skipper genus, giving name to the *Scombresocidae*. — *n* **scom'brid** a fish of the *Scombridae*. — Also *adj*. — *n* **scom'broid** a member of the *Scombroidea*, a suborder of marine spiny-finned fish *incl* the mackerel, tunny and swordfish. — Also *adj*. [L *scomber*, from Gr *skombros* a mackerel]

scomfish *skum'fish*, (*Scot*) *vt* to stifle; to disgust. [From *discomfish*, a by-form of **discomfit**, from the stem appearing in the Fr pr p]

sconce[1] *skons*, *n* a small protective fortification or earthwork; a shelter. — *vt* to entrench; to screen. — **build a sconce** to run up a debt (eg in a tavern) and have to keep away. [Du *schans*]

sconce[2] *skons*, (*archaic* and *dialect*) *n* the head; the crown of the head; brains, wits. [Origin obscure]

sconce[3] *skons*, *n* (at Oxford University) a fine imposed for some breach of university rules or etiquette (paid in ale or in attempting to drink a large amount of ale without taking a breath, or otherwise); a two-handled mug used for the purpose (holding about a quart); a forfeit. — *vt* to fine. [Origin obscure]

sconce[4] *skons*, *n* a candlestick or lantern with a handle; a bracket candlestick; a street wall-lamp. [OFr *esconse*, from LL *absconsa* a dark lantern, from *abscondere* to hide]

sconcheon. Same as **scuncheon**.

scone *skon*, sometimes anglicized as *skōn*, (*Scot*) *n* a flattish, *usu* round or quadrant-shaped plain cake of dough without much fat, with or without currants, baked on a girdle or in an oven. [Perh from Du *schoon* (*brot*) fine (bread)]

scontion. Same as **scuncheon**.

SCONUL *skō'nəl* or *-nōōl*, *abbrev*: Standing Conference of National and University Libraries.

scoog. See **skug**[1].

scoop *skōōp*, *n* a container for bailing water; a concave shovel or lipped container for skimming or shovelling up loose material; a kitchen utensil, a deeply concave spoon, often fitted with a mechanical device for unloading it, used for dispensing a serving of pulply food, eg ice cream or mashed potato; an instrument for gouging out apple-cores, samples of cheese, etc; anything of similar shape; an act of scooping; a sweeping stroke; a scooped-out place; anything got by or as by scooping, a haul; the forestalling of other newspapers in obtaining a piece of news; an item of news so secured (also *adj*). — *vt* to bail out; to lift, obtain, remove, hollow, or make with, or as if with, a scoop; to secure in advance of or to the exclusion of others. — *adj* **scooped**. — *n* **scoop'er** someone or something that scoops; an engraver's tool; another name for the avocet. — *n* **scoop'ful**: — *pl* **scoop'fuls**. — *n* **scoop'ing**. — *adj* **scooped'-out**. — **scoop neck** a low rounded neckline; **scoop'-net** a long-handled dipping net; a net for scooping along the bottom. — **scoop the pool** see under **pool**[2]. [Prob partly MLGer or MDu *schôpe* bailing-vessel, partly MDu *schoppe* shovel]

scoot[1] *skōōt*, *vt* and *vi* (*Scot*) to squirt. — *vi* to slip suddenly (*Scot*); to make off with speed (*colloq*); to travel on a scooter (*colloq*). — *n* a squirt (*Scot*); an act of scooting. — *n* **scoot'er** someone or something that scoots; a child's toy, a wheeled footboard with steering handle, pushed along with the foot; a small-wheeled motorcycle with a protective front fairing; a boat for sailing on ice and water (*US*); a swift motor-boat; a simple form of plough (*US*). [Prob from ON, related to **shoot**[1]]

scoot[2] *skōōt*, (*Scot*) *n* an insignificant person.

scop *skop*, *n* an Anglo-Saxon poet or minstrel: — *pl* **scopas**. [OE, jester, someone who scoffs; see also **scoff**[1]]

scopa *skō'pə*, *n* a brushlike tuft of hairs on the hind legs of bees, used for collecting pollen: — *pl* **sco'pae** (*-pē*). — *adj* **scō'pate** tufted. — *n* **scopula** (*skop'ū-lə*) a little tuft of hairs. — *adj* **scop'ulate**. [L *scōpae* twigs, a broom]

scope[1] *skōp*, *n* a point aimed at (*obs*); purpose or aim (*archaic*); range; field or opportunity of activity; capacity or room for action; potential or natural ability; spaciousness; a length of cable on an anchor that provides slack to allow a vessel to move with the tides, etc. [Ital *scopo*, from Gr *skopos* watcher, point watched, (*fig*) aim, from *skopeein* to view]

scope² *skōp*, *n* short for **microscope**, **telescope**, **horoscope**, etc; a visual display unit, *esp* a radar screen; a cinema (short for **bioscope**; *SAfr informal*). — *vt* to examine (the internal organs) with a viewing instrument.

-scope *-skōp*, *combining form* an instrument for viewing, examining, or detecting as in *telescope*, *oscilloscope*, *stethoscope*. [Gr *skopeein* to view]

Scopelus *skop'ə-ləs*, *n* a genus of deep-water fishes with laminous spots, giving name to the family *Scopelidae*. — *n* **scop'elid** or **scop'eloid** a member of the *Scopelidae*. — Also *adj*. [Gr *skopelos* a rock, thought by Cuvier to mean a kind of fish]

scopolamine *sko-pol'ə-mēn*, *n* an alkaloid obtained from plants of the genus *Scopolia* and other plants of the Solanaceae (see **hyoscine** under **Hyoscyamus**) with sedative properties, used eg to prevent muscle spasm and travel sickness and as a premedication before anaesthesia. [Named after *Scopoli* (1723–88), Italian naturalist; and **amine**]

scopophilia *skop-ə-fil'i-ə*, *n* the practice of obtaining sexual pleasure from things seen, as eg naked bodies. — *n* **scopophil'iac**. — *adj* **scopophil'ic**. [Gr *skopeein* to view, and **-philia**]

scopophobia *skop-ə-fō'bi-ə*, *n* fear of being looked at. [Gr *skopeein* to view, and **-phobia**]

Scops *skops*, *n* a genus of owls. [Gr *skōps*]

scoptophilia, **scoptophobia**. Same as **scopophilia**, **scopophobia**.

scopula, **scopulate**. See under **scopa**.

-scopy *-skə-pi*, *combining form* indicating viewing, examining, or observing, as in *autoscopy*, *poroscopy*, *ornithoscopy*. [Gr *skopeein* to view]

scorbutic *skör-bū'tik*, *adj* of, like, of the nature of, or affected with, scurvy. [LL *scorbūticus*, poss from MLGer *schorbuk*]

scorch¹ *skörch*, *vt* to burn slightly or superficially; to parch; to dry up, wither, or affect painfully or injuriously by heat or as if by heat; to wither with scorn, censure, etc. — *vi* to be burned on the surface; to be dried up; to cycle or drive furiously (*colloq*). — *n* an act of scorching; damage or an injury by scorching. — *adj* **scorched**. — *n* **scorch'er** a person who or thing which scorches; a day of scorching heat (*colloq*); something remarkable (*colloq*); anything stinging or caustic. — *n*, *adj* and *adv* **scorch'ing**. — *adv* **scorch'ingly**. — *n* **scorch'ingness**. — **scorched-earth policy** in warfare, the policy of destroying everything in an area that may be of use to an advancing army; any policy or manoeuvre in which action is taken to reduce useful assets in order to minimize their value to future occupants, owners, etc. [Perh ME *skorken*; cf ON *skorpna* to shrivel; poss affected by OFr *escorcher* to flay]

scorch² *skörch*, (*Shakesp*; *Scott*) *vt* to slash (in *Macbeth* III. 2. 13, *scotch'd* conjecturally read for *scorch'd* by L Theobald, 18c editor). [Perh **score**, infl by **scratch**]

scordato *skör-dä'tō*, (*music*) *adj* put out of tune. — *n* **scordatura** (*-tōō'rə*) a temporary departure from the normal tuning of a stringed instrument. [Ital]

score *skör* or *skōr*, *n* a notch, gash, or scratch; an incised line; a boldly drawn line, *esp* one marking a deletion; a line marking a boundary, starting-place, or defined position; an arrangement of music on a number of staves (*perh orig* with the bar divisions running continuously through all); a composition so distributed; music for a film, television or radio play or the music and songs for a stage or film musical; a notch in a tally; an account of charges incurred (as in a tavern) by tallies or (later) chalk marks or the like; a debt incurred; a reckoning, account; a grievance, grudge; the full total; the total or record of points made in a game; an addition made thereto; the result of a test or examination (*NAm*); a set of twenty (sometimes verging upon numeral *adj*); applied also to an indefinitely large number; twenty or twenty-one pounds in weight; a distance of twenty paces (*obs*); a fixed number (20 to 26) of tubs of coal. — *vt* to mark with or by scores; to record in or with a score; to make a score through as a mark of deletion (with *out*); to write as a score (*music*); to break down (a musical composition) into parts for individual (groups of) instruments, and write the appropriate music; to make as a score; to add to a score; to achieve; to enumerate; to record; to mark (a test or examination) (*NAm*); to rebuke or criticize harshly (*NAm*). — *vi* to keep or run up a score (*obs*); to make a point; to achieve a success; to be worth a certain number of points; (of a man) to succeed in having sexual intercourse (*slang*); to obtain illegal drugs (*slang*). — *n* **scor'er** a person who or thing that scores; someone who keeps the marks in a game. — *n* **scor'ing** the act of scoring; orchestration. — **score'board** or **scor'ing-board** a board on which the score is exhibited, as at cricket; **score'card**, **scor'ing-card** or **score'sheet** a card or sheet, for recording the score in a game; **score draw** (*esp football*) a result in which both teams have scored an equal number of points; **score'line** a score in a match, etc. — **go off at score** (*old*) to make a spirited start; **know the score** to know the hard facts of the situation; to know what is required, without having to be told; **on that score** as regards that matter; **pay off** (or **settle**) **old scores** to deal decisively with old grudges; **run up a score** to run up a debt; **score an own goal** (*colloq*) to do something unintentionally to one's own disadvantage; **score off** or **score points off** (*colloq*) to achieve a success against, get the better of. [Late OE *scoru*, from ON *skor*, *skora*; cf OE *sceran* (pa p *scoren*) to shear]

scoria *skö'ri-ə* or *skō'*, *n* dross or slag from metal-smelting; a piece of lava with steam-holes: — *pl* **sco'riae** (*-ri-ē*). — *adj* **sco'riac** or **scoriaceous** (*-ri-ā'shəs*). — *n* **scorificā'tion** reduction to scoria; assaying by fusing with lead and borax. — *n* **sco'rifier** a dish used in assaying. — *vt* **sco'rify** to reduce to scoria; to rid metals of (impurities) by forming scoria. — *adj* **sco'rious**. [L, from Gr *skōriā*, from *skōr* dung]

scorn *skörn*, *n* hot or extreme contempt; an expression, or the object, of contempt (*archaic*). — *vt* to feel or express scorn for; to refuse with scorn; to make a mock of (*obs*). — *vi* (*obs*) to scoff. — *n* **scorn'er**. — *adj* **scorn'ful**. — *adv* **scorn'fully**. — *n* **scorn'fulness**. — *n* **scorn'ing**. — **think scorn of** (*archaic*) to disdain or think beneath one. [OFr *escarn* mockery; of Gmc origin; cf OHGer *skern* mockery]

scorodite *skor'ə-dīt*, (*mineralogy*) *n* an orthorhombic hydrated arsenate of iron and aluminium. [Gr *skorodon* garlic, from its smell when heated]

scorpaenid *skör-pē'nid*, *n* a member of the genus *Scorpaena* or family *Scorpaenidae*, spiny-finned marine fish with large armoured heads, *incl* the scorpion fish and rock fish. — Also *adj*. — *adj* and *n* **scorpae'noid**. [Gr *skorpaina* a kind of fish]

scorper. See **scauper**.

Scorpio *skör'pi-ō*, *n* a constellation (the scorpion) between Libra and Sagittarius (also **Scor'pius**; *astron*); a sign of the zodiac; a person born between 14 Oct and 22 Nov, under the sign of Scorpio: — *pl* **Scor'pios**. [L, scorpion; see **scorpion**]

scorpioid *skör'pi-oid*, *adj* (*zool*) like a scorpion, or a scorpion's curled tail. — *n* (*bot*) a cincinnus or cicinnus, an inflorescence in which the plane of each daughter axis is at right angles, to right and left alternately, with its parent axis, that of the whole coiled in bud. [Gr *skorpios* scorpion, and **-oid**]

scorpion *skör'pi-ən*, *n* any arachnid of the genus *Scorpio* or order *Scorpionida* with head and thorax united, pincers, four pairs of legs, and a segmented abdomen including a tail with a venomous sting; a form of barbed scourge (*Bible*); an old contraption for hurling stones, a ballista; any person of virulent hatred or animosity; (with *cap*) the constellation or the sign Scorpio (*astron*). — *adj* **scorpion'ic**. — **scorpion fish** any of the family *Scorpaenidae*, having venomous spines on the fins; **scorpion fly** an insect of the order *Mecoptera* (from the male's scorpion-like tail); **scorpion grass** another name for forget-me-not; **scorpion spider** a whip scorpion. [L *scorpiō*, *-ōnis*, from Gr *skorpios* scorpion]

scorrendo *sko-ren'dō*, (*music*) *adj* gliding. [Ital]

scorse[1] *skōrs* or *skörs*, (*obs*) *vt* to chase. [Ital *scorsa* a run, from *scorrere*, from L *excurrere*]

scorse[2] *skōrs* or *skörs*, (*obs*) *n* exchange. — *vt* and *vi* to exchange (also **scourse**). — *n* **scors'er** someone who barters. [Poss from *horse-scorser* for **horse-courser**]

scorzonera *skör-zə-nē'rə*, *n* a plant of the genus *Scorzonera*, *esp Scorzonera hispanica* (black salsify). [Ital]

Scot *skot*, *n* a native or inhabitant of Scotland; a member of a Gaelic-speaking people of Ireland, afterwards also in Argyllshire (now part of Strathclyde) (*hist*). — *n* **Scotland** (*skot'lənd*) the country forming the northern member of the United Kingdom; Ireland (*hist*). — *n* **Scot'landite** naturally-occurring lead sulphite, first identified in Lanarkshire, Scotland. — *n* **Scott'y** or **Scott'ie** a nickname for a Scotsman; a Scotch terrier. — **Scotland Yard** the earliest or (New Scotland Yard) two more recent headquarters (1890 and 1967) of the Metropolitan Police; hence, the London Criminal Investigation Department. — **Irish Scot** (*obs*) a Highlander. [OE *Scottas* (pl), from LL *Scottus* and *Scōtus*; see also **Scotch, Scots, Scottish**]

Scot. *abbrev*: Scotland; Scottish.

scot *skot*, *n* (*hist*) a payment, *esp* a customary tax; a share of a reckoning (also **shot**). — *adj* **scot-free'** free from scot, untaxed (*hist*); entirely free from expense, injury, penalty, punishment, etc. — **scot and lot** an old local tax entitling all who paid to vote in parliamentary elections; an old legal phrase embracing all forms of tax; hence, all forms of responsibility, duty, etc. [OE *scot*, *sceot*; but prob partly from ON *skot*, and OFr *esco*; see **shot**[2], **escot**]

Scotch *skoch*, *adj* of or belonging to Scotland or the Scots, a term used outside Scotland, and by many Scots, though others prefer **Scottish**, of which it is a form, or **Scots**; applied to products or supposed products of Scotland, *esp* whisky; having the character popularly attributed to a Scotsman, an excessive leaning towards defence of oneself and one's property. — *n* Scotch whisky, or a glass of it; the Scots language; (as *pl*) the Scots. — *n* **Scotch'ness**. — *n* **Scot'chy** a nickname for a Scot. — *adj* having Scottish characteristics. — **Scotch attorney** (*W Indies*) a climber (*Clusia*) that strangles trees; **Scotch barley** hulled barley; **Scotch bluebell** the harebell; **Scotch bonnet** a round flat blue woollen cap with a tuft on the top; the fairy-ring mushroom; **Scotch broth** broth made with pearl barley, mutton or beef stock and plenty of various vegetables chopped small; **Scotch cart** (*SAfr*; *archaic*) a strong, springless, two-wheeled uncovered farm cart with one shaft; **Scotch catch** or **snap** (*music*) a short accented note followed by a longer, not peculiar to Scottish music; **Scotch collops** minced beef (sometimes called **scotched collops**); **Scotch cuddy** (Scot *cuddy* a donkey; *archaic*) a Scotch draper; **Scotch curlies** a variety of kale; **Scotch draper** (*archaic*) an itinerant dealer differing from a pedlar in not carrying his goods about with him; a credit itinerant draper (also **Scotch cuddy**); **Scotch egg** a hard-boiled egg (often cut in two) enclosed in sausage-meat and covered with breadcrumbs; **Scotch elm** the wych-elm (*Ulmus montana*); sometimes the common English elm (*Ulmus campestris*); **Scotch fiddle** (*archic*) scabies (from the movements of the fingers when scratching); **Scotch fir** Scots pine (see under **Scots**); **Scotch hand** a wooden bat for manipulating butter. — *adj* and *n pl* (*US*) **Scotch-Ir'ish** Irish of Scottish descent. — **Scotch kale** a variety of kale; **Scotch'man** a Scotsman; a florin (from a tradition of a Scotsman who benefited from its resemblance to a half-crown; *SAfr*; *obs*); **Scotch mist** a fine rain; something insubstantial, a phantom, *usu ironic*); **Scotch pancake** a drop-scone; **Scotch pebble** an agate or similar stone; **Scotch pine** Scots pine (see under **Scots**); **Scotch rose** the burnet rose (*Rosa spinosissima*); **Scotch snap** a Scotch catch (see above); **Scotch tape**® (*esp NAm*) a transparent tape, adhering to paper, etc when pressure is applied; **Scotch terrier** a rough-haired, prick-eared, strongly-built little dog (also **Scottish terrier**, **Scottie**, **Scotty**); **Scotch thistle** the cotton thistle, national emblem of Scotland (not native); **Scotch verdict** not proven; **Scotch'woman** a Scotswoman; **Scotch woodcock** scrambled eggs and anchovies on toast. — **Scotch and English** prisoners' base (qv under **prison**). [From **Scottish**]

scotch[1] *skoch*, *vt* to gash (*obs*); to score; (from Theobald's conjecture in *Macbeth*; see **scorch**[2]) to maim, to render harmless by crippling (without killing); to frustrate, put an end to; to quash. — *n* a gash (*obs*); a line marked on the ground (as for hop-scotch). [Origin unknown]

scotch[2] *skoch*, *n* a strut, wedge, block, etc, to prevent turning or slipping, as of a wheel, gate, ladder. — *vt* to stop or block; to frustrate (plans, etc). [Perh a form of **scratch**]

scoter *skō'tər*, *n* (also **scoter duck**) any of several northern sea ducks of the genus *Melanitta*, with black or mainly black plumage in the male. [Origin obscure]

Scotia *skō'shyə*, *-shə*, *n* (*poetic*) Scotland. — *adj* **Sco'tian** (*rare*). [LL *Scōtia*, *Scōticus*]

scotia *sko'ti-ə* or *-shi-ə*, (*archit*) *n* a concave moulding, *esp* at the base of an Ionic column. [Gr *skotiā*, from *skotos* darkness]

Scotic *skot'ik*, *adj* denoting the branch of English spoken in Scotland; relating to the ancient Scots, incomers from Ireland. — *adj* **Scot'ican** (formed after *Anglican*; *eccles*) of Scotland. [LL *Scōticus* from *Scōtus*]

Scotism *skō'tizm*, *n* the metaphysical system of Johannes Duns *Scotus* (c.1265–1308), a native of Maxton in Roxburghshire (not Duns, Berwickshire, Dunstane, Northumberland, or Down, Northern Ireland), who sought the foundation of Christian theology in practice, not in speculation, his theological descendants being the Franciscans, in opposition to the Dominicans, who followed Aquinas. — *n* **Scō'tist** a follower of Duns Scotus. — *adj* **Scotist'ic**.

Scoto- *skot-ō-*, *-ə-*, *-o'* *combining form* denoting Scotland and the Scots as in *Scotophobia*, or a Scottish element combined with another, as in *Scoto-Irish*, etc. — *n* **Scot'ophile** someone fond of Scotland and its people. — *n* **Scotophil'ia**. — *n* **Scot'ophobe** a hater of Scotland and its people. — *n* **Scot'ophōbia**. — *adj* **Scotopho'bic**. [LL *Scōtus* a Scot]

scoto- *skot-ō-*, *-ə-*, *-o'* or before a vowel **scot-**, *combining form* denoting dark, darkness. — *n* **scotodinia** (*-din'i-ə*; Gr *dīnos* whirling) dizziness with headache and impairment of vision. — *n* **scotoma** (*-ōm'ə*; *Gr skotōma* dizziness; *med*) an area of abnormal or absent vision within the visual field, a blind spot due to disease of the retina or optic nerve: — *pl* **scotō'mata** or **scotō'mas**. — *adj* **scotō'matous**. — *n* **scoto'meter** an instrument for identifying defects in the visual field. — *n* **scotō'mia** and **scot'omy** (*obs*) scotoma, in its obsolete sense of dizziness accompanied by dimness of vision. — *n* **scotōp'ia** vision in a dim light. — *adj* **scotop'ic** (*-op'*). [Gr *skotos* darkness]

Scots *skots*, *adj* Scottish (almost always used of money, measures, law, and language). — *n* any of the varieties of the Northern branch of English spoken in Scotland, *esp* that of Lowland Scotland preserved in the poetry of Burns and others (see also **Lallans**). — **Scots fir** Scots pine (see below); **Scots Greys** a famous regiment of dragoons, established in 1683, amalgamated with the 3rd Carabiniers in 1971; **Scots Guards** a Scottish force which served the kings of France from 1418 to 1759, nominally to 1830; a well-known regiment of Guards in the British army, formerly Scots Fusilier Guards; **Scots'man**; **Scots mile** see under **mile**; **Scots pine** (often called **Scots fir**) the only native British pine, *Pinus sylvestris*; **Scots pint** and **pound scots** see **pint**, **pound**[1]; **Scots'woman**. [Scot *Scottis* Scottish]

Scottice or **Scotice** *skot'i-sē, skot'i-kā, adv* in Scots. [L]

Scotticism or **Scoticism** *skot'i-sizm, n* a Scottish idiom; Scottish feeling. — *vt* **Scott'icize** or **-ise** to render Scottish; to put into Scots. [LL *Scotticus, Scōticus*]

Scottify or **Scotify** *skot'i-fī, vt* to make Scottish: *pr p* **Scot(t)'ifying**; *pa t* and *pa p* **Scot(t)'ified**. — *n* **Scottificā'tion** or **Scotificā'tion**. [**Scottish**]

Scottish *skot'ish, adj* of Scotland and the Scots. — *n* the English spoken in Scotland, *usu* Scots (qv); (as *pl*) the Scots collectively. — *vt* (*rare*) to put into the Scottish tongue. — *n* **Scott'ishness**. — **Scottish Certificate of Education** (in secondary education in Scotland) a certificate obtainable at Standard or Higher grades (see **Standard grade** and **Higher**) for proficiency in one or more subjects; **Scottish Office** the government department that deals with Scottish affairs and oversees the work of several Scottish government ministries and agencies. [OE *Scottisc*, from *Scottas*; see **Scot**]

SCOTVEC *skot'vek, abbrev*: Scottish Vocational Education Council.

scoug. Same as **skug**[1].

scoundrel *skown'drəl, n* an unprincipled or villainous person. — *adj* **scoun'drelly**. [Origin unknown]

scoup or **scowp** *skowp*, (*Scot*) *vi* to bound; to caper; to scamper. [Origin unknown]

scour[1] *skowr, vt* to clean, polish, remove, or form by hard rubbing; to scrub; to cleanse; to free from grease, dirt, or gum; to flush or cleanse by a current; to purge, *esp* drastically; to clear out; to punish (*fig*). — *vi* to scrub and polish; to serve or act as a purgative; (of livestock) to have diarrhoea. — *n* the action, place, or means of scouring; diarrhoea in cattle, etc; a swig of liquor (*Scot*). — *n* **scour'er** a person who scours; an instrument or container for scouring; a cathartic. — *n* **scour'ing** scrubbing; vigorous cleansing; clearing; erosion; purging; (often in *pl*) matter removed or accumulated by scouring. — Also *adj*. — **scouring rush** any of several horsetails or other plants whose rough stems were formerly used for scouring; **scouring stick** a rod for scouring a gun. [Prob MDu or MLG *schûren*, from OFr *escurer*, from L *ex cūrāre* to take care of]

scour[2] *skowr, vi* to rush or scurry along; to range about, *esp* in quest or pursuit. — *vt* to range over or traverse swiftly, vigorously, riotously, or in pursuit; to search thoroughly. — *n* **scour'er** or (*obs*) **scowr'er** (*hist*) a member of a roistering band that scoured the streets, maltreating watchmen and others. [Poss ON *skūr* storm, shower; cf **shower**]

scourer[1] *skowr'ər, n* a scout. [Aphetic from **discoverer**]

scourer[2]. See under **scour**[1,2].

scourge *skûrj, n* a whip; an instrument of divine punishment; a cause of widespread affliction. — *vt* to whip severely; to afflict. — *n* **scourg'er**. [Anglo-Fr *escorge*, from L *excoriāre* to flay, from *corium* leather (perh as made of a strip of leather, perh as a flaying instrument)]

scourie. See **scaury**.

scourse. See **scorse**[2].

Scouse *skows*, (*colloq*) *n* a native or inhabitant of Liverpool (also **scous'er**); the northern English dialect spoken in and around Liverpool; (without *cap*) a stew of hash, often made with meat scraps. [Short for *lobscouse* a vegetable stew, a sea dish]

scout[1] *skowt, n* watch, spying (*archaic*); someone, or (*obs* or *NAm*) a party, sent out to reconnoitre or bring in information; a (military) spy; a member of the Scout Association (formerly **Boy Scout**); (in the US) a member of the Girl Scouts (an organization similar to the Girl Guides); a patrolman on the roads; a person who watches or attends at a little distance; a fielder, as in cricket; a person (*usu* term of approbation; *slang*); a person who seeks out new recruits, sales opportunities, etc; a ship for reconnoitring; a small light aeroplane *orig* intended for reconnaissance; a light armoured car for reconnaissance (now *usu* **scout car**); a college servant (*esp* at Oxford). — *vt* to watch closely. — *vi* to act the scout; to reconnoitre (often with *about* or *around*). — *n* **scout'er** an adult working with instructors, etc, in the Scout Association. — *n* **scout'ing**. — **Scout Association** (formerly, the **Boy Scouts**) a worldwide movement for young people, intended to develop character and a sense of responsibility, founded (for boys) by Lord Baden-Powell in 1908; **scout car** see **scout** *n* above; **scout'craft** the knowledge and skill proper to a scout; **scout law** the code of rules of the Scout Association; **scout'master** the leader of a band of scouts, a scouter; formerly, an adult in charge of a troop of Boy Scouts; **scout's pace** alternately walking and running for a set number of paces. [OFr *escoute*, from *escouter*, from L *auscultāre* to listen]

scout[2] *skowt*, (*archaic*) *vt* to mock, flout; to dismiss or reject with disdain. [Cf ON *skūta* a taunt]

scout[3]. Same as **scoot**[2].

scouth or **scowth** *skōōth* or *skowth*, (*Scot*) *n* free range; scope; plenty.

scouther, **scowther** *skow'dhər* or **scowder** *skow'dər*, (*Scot*) *vt* to scorch, singe; to overheat; to toast slightly; to blight. — *vi* to drizzle; to threaten to rain or snow. — *n* a scorch or burn; a slight or flying shower. — *adj* **scou'thering**, **scow'dering** scorching, blighting. — *n* a scorching, blighting; a sprinkle of snow. — *adj* **scou'thery**. [Connected with **scald**[1]]

scow *skow, n* a flat-bottomed boat, *esp* a barge, or (*US*) a sailing yacht. [Du *schouw*]

scowder. See **scouther**.

scowl *skowl, vi* to contract the brows in a malevolent and menacing look; to look gloomy and threatening. — *n* a scowling look. — *adj* **scow'ling**. — *adv* **scow'lingly**. [Cf Dan *skule* to cast down the eyes, look sidelong]

scowp, See **scoup**.

scowrer. See **scour**[2].

scowrie. See **scaury**.

scowth. See **scouth**.

scowther. See **scouther**.

SCP *abbrev*: single-cell protein.

SCPS *abbrev*: Society of Civil and Public Servants.

SCR *abbrev*: Senior Common Room.

scr. *abbrev*: scruple (weight).

scrab *skrab*, (*archaic* and *dialect*) *vt* to scratch: — *pr p* **scrabb'ing**; *pa p* and *pa t* **scrabbed**. — *vt* and *vi* **scrabb'le** to scratch; to scrape; to scrawl. — *vi* to scramble. — *n* a scrawl. — *n* **scrabb'ler**. [Du *schrabben* to scratch, frequentative *schrabbelen*; cf **scrape**]

Scrabble® *skrab'l, n* a word-building game [**scrabble**]

scrae *skrā*, (*Scott*) *n*. Same as **scree**.

scrag[1] *skrag, n* a sheep's or (*slang*) human neck; the bony part of the neck; a lean person or animal. — *vt* to hang; to throttle; to wring the neck of; to grab by the neck: — *pr p* **scragg'ing**; *pa t* and *pa p* **scragged**. — *adj* **scragg'ed** (or *skragd*) scraggy. — *n* **scragg'edness**. — *adv* **scragg'ily**. — *n* **scragg'iness**. — *adj* **scragg'y** lean, skinny, and gaunt. — **scrag'-end** the scrag of a neck. [Prob **crag**[2]]

scrag[2] *skrag, n* a stump; a rough projection. — *adj* **scragg'ling**, **scragg'ly** or **scragg'y** irregular, unkempt, straggling. — *adv* **scragg'ily**. — *n* **scragg'iness**. — **scrag'-whale** a whale with a knobbed back. [Cf **scrog**]

scraich or **scraigh** *skrāhh*, (*Scot*) *vi* to screech; to make a scratchy sound. — *n* a screech; a scratchy sound. [Cf **scraugh, skreigh**]

scram[1] *skram*, (*slang*) *vi* (*esp* in the *imperative*) to be off: — *pr p* **scramm'ing**; *pa t* and *pa p* **scrammed**. [Perh **scramble**]

scram[2] *skram, adj* (*SW Eng*) puny; withered. — *vt* to benumb (*SW Eng*); to paralyse (*SW Eng*); to shut down (a nuclear reactor), *esp* in an emergency: — *pr p* **scramm'ing**; *pa t* and *pa p* **scrammed**. — *n* an emergency shut-down of a nuclear reactor. [Cf **scrimp**]

scram[3] or **scramb** *skram*, (*dialect*) *vt* to scratch with claws or nails. [From Du *schrammen*]

scramble *skram'bl, vi* to make one's way with disorderly struggling haste; to get along somehow; to clamber; to climb or grow upwards over a vertical surface; to dash or struggle for what one can get before others; (of a military aircraft or its crew) to take off immediately, as in an emergency. — *vt* to put, make, get or push together in a rough hasty manner; to change the frequency of (a transmission) so that it can be made intelligible only by means of an electronic decoding device; to beat (eggs) up and heat to thickness with milk, butter, etc; to make (a radiotelephone conversation) unintelligible by a device that alters frequencies; to order (a military aircraft or its crew) to take off immediately. — *n* an act or the action of scrambling; a disorderly performance; a dash or struggle for what can be had; an emergency take-off by a military aircraft; a form of motor or motorcycle trial on rough or hilly terrain. — *n* **scram'bler** a person who, or that which, scrambles, *esp* a telephone device. — *adj* **scram'bling**. — *n* the action of the verb scramble; participation in motorcycle, etc scrambles. — *adv* **scram'blingly**. — **scrambled eggs** eggs cooked as described above; the gold braid on a military officer's cap (*slang*). [Cf the dialect verb *scramb* to rake together with the hands]

scramjet *skram'jet*, *n* a jet engine in which compressed air drawn into the engine via turbo fans mixes with fuel to improve combustion at a supersonic speed. [*s*uper*s*onic *c*ombustion *ramjet*]

scran *skran*, (*colloq*) *n* food, provisions. — **bad scran to you** (*Irish*) bad luck to you. [Ety doubtful]

scranch *skranch* or *skransh*, *vt* to crunch. [Prob imit; cf Du *schransen* to eat heartily]

scrannel *skran'l*, (*archaic*) *adj* thin; meagre; squeaking; grating, scratchy (*Milton*). — *adj* **scrann'y** thin, scrawny.

scrap[1] *skrap*, *n* a small fragment; a piece of left-over food; a remnant; a cut-out picture, newspaper cutting, or the like, intended or suited for preservation in a scrapbook; residue after extraction of oil from blubber, fish, etc; metal clippings or other waste; anything discarded as worn-out, out of date, or useless. — *adj* consisting of, or of the value of, scrap. — *vt* to consign to the scrapheap; to discard, cease to use, do away with, abandon: — *pr p* **scrapp'ing**; *pa p* and *pa t* **scrapped**. — *adv* **scrapp'ily**. — *n* **scrapp'iness**. — *adj* **scrapp'y** fragmentary; disconnected, disorganized; made up of scraps. — **scrap'book** a blank book for pasting in scraps, cuttings, etc; **scrap'heap** a place where old iron or useless material is collected; a rubbish-heap (also *fig*); **scrap iron** or **scrap metal** scraps of iron or other metal, of use only for remelting; **scrap'-man, scrap merchant** or **scrap'-metal merchant** a person who deals in scrap metal; **scrap'yard** a scrap merchant's premises for the storing and processing of scrap metal. — **not a scrap** not even a tiny amount; **throw on the scrapheap** to reject as no longer useful (*lit* and *fig*). [ON *skrap* scraps; cf **scrape**]

scrap[2] *skrap*, (*slang*) *n* a fight, *usu* physical; a battle (*euphem*). — Also *vi* (*pr p* **scrapp'ing**; *pa t* and *pa p* **scrapped**). — *adj* **scrapp'y** belligerent; quarrelsome.

scrape *skrāp*, *vt* to press a sharp edge over; to move with a grating sound over; to smooth, clean, clear, reduce in thickness, abrade, graze, remove, form, collect, bring, render, by such an action; to get together, collect by laborious effort (often with *together* or *up*); to erase; contemptuously, to play (the fiddle). — *vi* to graze (with *against* or *on*); to scratch the ground; to grate; to make a grating sound; to draw back the foot in making a bow; to play the fiddle; to save as much as possible, enduring hardship thereby; to get with difficulty (with *through*, *along*, *home*, etc). — *n* an act, process, or period of scraping; a stroke of a violin, etc bow; a grating sound; a stroke (of a pen); a scraped place in the ground; a graze or abrasion, eg on the skin; a shave (*facetious*); a mass of earth scraped up, eg by a rabbit; a backward movement of one foot accompanying a bow; a scraping or thin layer; thin-spread butter or margarine; a fight or other conflict (*colloq*); a predicament that threatens disgrace or friction with authority (*colloq*). — *n* **scrāp'er** a person who scrapes; a scraping tool, instrument or machine; a fiddler (*derog*); a barber (*derog*); used to denote birds of the order *Rasores*, that scrape or scratch the ground. — *n* **scrāp'ie** a degenerative viral disease affecting the central nervous system of sheep, characterized by acute itching, the animals rubbing against trees, etc to relieve it. — *n* **scrāp'ing** the action of the verb; its sound; a thin piece scraped off. — **scrape'good** (*archaic*) a miser; **scrape'gut** (*archaic*) a fiddler; **scrape'penny** (*archaic*) a miser; **scrap'erboard** a clay-surface board on which drawings can be made by scraping tints off as well as applying them; such a drawing; this method of making drawings; **scraper ring** (*autos*) a ring fitted on the skirt of a petrol or oil-engine piston to prevent excessive oil consumption (also **oil-control ring**). — **bow and scrape** to be over-obsequious; **scrape acquaintance with** to contrive somehow to get to know; **scrape the bottom of the barrel** to utilize the very last of one's resources; to turn to something or someone as a last resort, reluctantly and perhaps not without humiliation. [OE *scrapian* or ON *skrapa*]

scrapie. See under **scrape**.

scrapple *skrap'əl*, (*US*) *n* a type of meat loaf made with scraps of meat or minced meat, *usu* pork, cornmeal, seasonings, etc, served sliced and fried. [**scrap**[1]]

scrat *skrat*, (*obs* or *dialect*) *vt* and *vi* to scratch. [ME *scratte*; origin doubtful]

Scratch *skrach*, *n* the Devil (also **Old Scratch**). [Cf ON *skratte* goblin, monster]

scratch *skrach*, *vt* to draw a sharp point over the surface of; to hurt, mark, render, seek to relieve an itch in, by so doing; to dig or scrape with the claws; to write hurriedly; to erase or delete (*usu* with *out*); to strike along a rough surface; to withdraw from a competition or (*esp* musical) engagement. — *vi* to use the nails or claws to inflict injury, relieve an itch, etc; to scrape; to make a grating or screechy noise; to retire from a contest or engagement; to get (along or through) somehow (*colloq*). — *n* an act, mark, or sound of scratching; a slight wound or graze; a scrawl; (formerly) the line in the ring up to which boxers were led to begin fighting — hence a test, trial, as in *come up to scratch* (qv below); the starting-point for a player or competitor without a handicap; a player or competitor who starts from scratch; a fluke, *esp* in billiards; a scratch-wig; cash, ready money (*slang*); (in *pl*) a disease in horses with the appearance of scratches on the pastern or ankle. — *adj* improvised; casual; hastily or casually got together; (of a player or competitor) having no handicap. — *n* **scratch'er**. — *adv* **scratch'ily**. — *n* **scratch'iness**. — *n* **scratch'ing** the action of the verb; the act of manipulating a gramophone record so that it plays a repeated beat or section of music. — *adv* **scratch'ingly**. — *adj* **scratch'less**. — *adj* **scratch'y** like scratches; uneven; ready or likely to scratch; irritable, bad tempered, tetchy (*esp US*); grating or screechy; itchy. — **scratch'back** a back-scratcher; **scratch brush** a wire brush, used eg in gilding and polishing metal. — *vt* **scratch'build** to build (*usu* models) from raw materials, as opposed to constructing from kits or buying ready made. — *n* **scratch'builder**. — *n* **scratch'building**. — *adj* **scratch'built**. — **scratch'-coat** a first coat of plaster, scratched to provide a key for the second coat; **scratch pad** a note-pad, jotter; **scratch test** (*med*) a test for allergy to a certain substance, made by introducing it to an area of skin that has been scratched; **scratch'-wig** a wig that covers only part of the head; **scratch'-work** sgraffito in plaster. — **come up to scratch** (*fig*) to reach an expected standard; to fulfil an obligation; **start from scratch** (*fig*) to start at the beginning; to embark on (a task, career, etc) without any advantages, experience or without any preparatory work having been done; **you scratch my back and I'll scratch yours** (*colloq*) do me a favour and I'll do you one in return. [Poss ME *cracchen* to scratch, modified by **scrat**]

scrattle *skrat'l*, (*West Country dialect*) *vi* to keep scratching; to scuttle. [Frequentative of **scrat**]

scraugh or **scrauch** *skröhh*, (*Scot*) *n* a raucous squawk. — *vi* to make a scraugh. [Imit]
scraw *skrö*, (*archaic*) *n* a thin sod or turf. [Irish *sgrath*]
scrawl *skröl*, *vt* and *vi* to draw or write illegibly, untidily or hastily; to scribble. — *n* untidy, illegible, or bad writing; a letter, etc, written thus; a small crab (*Lincolnshire dialect*; *Tennyson*). — *n* **scrawl'er**. — *n* and *adj* **scrawl'ing**. — *adv* **scrawl'ingly**. — *adj* **scrawl'y**. [Perh connected with **crawl**[1] or **sprawl**]
scrawm *skröm*, (*dialect*) *vt* to scratch. [Prob Du *schrammen* to graze]
scrawny *skrö'ni*, (*orig US*) *adj* unhealthily thin, scraggy; sparse, meagre.
scray or **scraye** *skrā*, *n* the tern. [Cf Welsh *ysgräell*]
screak *skrēk*, (*dialect*) *vt* to screech; to creak. — *n* a screech; a creak. — *adj* **screak'y**. [Cf ON *skrækja*]
scream *skrēm*, *vt* and *vi* to cry out in a loud shrill voice, as in fear or pain; to laugh shrilly and uncontrolledly; to shriek. — *vi* (of colours) to clash acutely (*colloq*); to be all too loudly evident (*colloq*); to move with a screaming noise. — *n* a shrill, sudden cry, as in fear or pain; a shriek; a loud whistling sound; anything or anyone supposed to make one scream with laughter (*colloq*). — *n* **scream'er** a person who screams; a large spur-winged S American bird (*crested* and *black-necked screamer*) with loud harsh cry; a different S American bird, the seriema (sometimes known as *crested screamer*); anything likely or intended to thrill with emotion, eg a sensational headline (*slang*); an exclamation mark (*printing slang*). — *adj* **scream'ing**. — *adv* **scream'ingly**. — **screaming farce** a highly ludicrous situation; **screaming habdabs** or **abdabs** see under **habdabs**; **screaming meemies** see **meemie**. [Late OE *scræmen*]
scree *skrē*, *n* a sloping mass of loose weathered rock at the base of a cliff or on the face of a mountain. [ON *skritha* a landslip, from *skrītha* to slide]
screech *skrēch*, *vi* to utter a harsh, shrill, and sudden cry or noise, or to speak in that way. — *vt* to utter in such tones. — *n* a harsh, shrill, and sudden cry, noise, or tone of voice. — *n* **screech'er** someone or something that screeches; the swift, barn-owl or other screeching bird. — *adj* **screech'y** shrill and harsh, like a screech. — **screech'-hawk** the nightjar; **screech'-martin** the swift; **screech'-owl** the barn-owl; a bringer of bad news; **screech'-thrush** the mistle-thrush; the fieldfare. [ME *scrichen*; cf **scritch**]
screed *skrēd*, *n* a shred; a strip; a border; a long passage, spoken or written; a drinking bout (*obs*); a band of plaster laid on the surface of a wall as a guide to the thickness of a coat of plaster to be applied subsequently (*building*); a layer of mortar finishing off the surface of a floor (also **screed'ing**); a strip of wood or metal for levelling off mortar, sand, etc; a rent, a tear (*Scot*). — *vt* to repeat glibly. — *vi* to tear; to make a shrill or tearing noise. — *n* **screed'er** a person whose job is to lay screeds on floors or walls. [OE *scrēade* shred]
screen *skrēn*, *n* a shield against danger, observation, wind, heat, light, or other outside influence; a piece of room furniture in the form of a folding framework or of a panel on a stand; a clothes horse (*Scot*); a large scarf or stole (*Ramsay*); a windscreen; a sheltering row of trees, shrubs, etc; a body of troops or formation of ships intended as a cover from the bulk of the army or fleet; a wall masking a building (also **screen wall**); a partial partition separating off part of a room, a church choir, or side chapel; a coarse sifting apparatus; in some cameras, a glass plate with a pattern of various kinds on it to aid in focusing; a glass plate with rules or dots of a given coarseness or frequency for printing half-tone photographs; a mosaic of primary colours for colour photography; the surface on which a cinema film, television image or slide projection is seen; a white board on the perimeter of a cricket ground, against which the batsman can pick out the ball moving towards him; a screen grid. — *vt* to shelter or conceal; to sift coarsely; to sort out by, or subject to, tests of ability, trustworthiness, desirability, etc; to test for illness, etc; to protect from stray electrical interference; to prevent from causing outside electrical interference; to project or exhibit on a cinema, television or slide screen or on cinema or TV screens generally; to make a motion picture of. — *vi* to show up on, or be suitable for, the screen. — *n* **screen'er**. — *n* **screen'ing**. — *n pl* **screen'ings** material eliminated by sifting. — **screen'-craft** the technique of making films; **screen door** (in the US) a frame of wood or metal with netting panels, to exclude insects when the door proper is open; **screen grid** an electrode placed between the control grid and anode in a valve, having an invariable potential to eliminate positive feedback and instability; **screening test** a test carried out on a large number of people to identify those who have, or are likely to develop, a specified disease; **screen'play** the written text for a film, with dialogue, stage directions, and descriptions of characters and setting; **screen printing** and **screen process** see **silk-screen printing**; **screen test** a trial filming to determine whether an actor or actress is suitable for cinema work; **screen'-wiper** a windscreen-wiper; **screen'-writer** a writer of screenplays. — **screen off** to hide behind, or separate by, a screen; to separate by sifting. [Appar related in some way to OFr *escran* (Fr *écran*) which may be, from OHGer *skirm*, *skerm* (Ger *Schirm*)]
screeve *skrēv*, (*slang*) *vt* and *vi* to write, *esp* begging letters; to draw on the pavement. — *n* a piece of writing; a begging letter. — *n* **screev'er**. — *n* **screev'ing**. [Prob Ital *scrivere*, from L *scrībere* to write]
screich, **screigh**. See **skreigh**.
screw *skrōō*, *n* a cylinder with a helical groove or ridge (the *thread*), used as a fastening driven into wood, etc by rotation (a *male screw*; for *female screw*, see **female**), mechanically or otherwise: anything of similar form; a screw propeller or ship driven by one; a thumbscrew, an instrument of torture; a corkscrew; a twisted cone of paper, or the portion of a commodity contained in it; a turn of the screw; pressure (*fig*); a twist; (*esp* in billiards and snooker) a spin imparted to a ball; a stingy person, an extortioner, a skinflint (*old slang*); a prison officer (*slang*); a broken-winded horse; an act of sexual intercourse (*vulg*); a sexual partner (*vulg*); salary, wages (*slang*). — *vt* to fasten, tighten, compress, force, adjust or extort by a screw or screws, a screwing motion, or as if by a screw; to apply a screw to; to twist; to turn in the manner of a screw; to pucker (often with *up*); to have sexual intercourse with (*vulg*); to practise extortion upon; to cheat, defraud or take advantage of (*slang*); to enter by means of a skeleton key (*slang*); to burgle, rob (*slang*). — *vi* to be capable of being screwed; to wind (with *in*, *up*, etc); to have sexual intercourse (*vulg*). — *adj* **screwed** messed up, spoiled; ruined, defeated; tipsy (*slang*). — *n* **screw'er**. — *n* and *adj* **screw'ing**. — *adj* **screw'y** (*colloq*) tipsy; eccentric, slightly mad (*colloq*). — **screw'ball** (*NAm*) a ball delivered with spin (*baseball*); a crazy person, an eccentric (*colloq*; *orig US*). — Also *adj*. — **screw bolt** a bolt with a screw thread; **screw cap** a lid that screws on to a container. — *adj* **screw'-down** closed by screwing. — **screw'driver** an instrument for turning and driving screws; a cocktail the principal ingredients of which are vodka and orange juice. — *adj* (of factories, assembly plants, etc) assembling components produced elsewhere, *usu* in a foreign country. — **screw eye** a screw formed into a loop for attaching rope, wire, etc; **screwing die** (*eng*) an internally threaded hardened steel block for cutting externally threaded screws or screwed pieces; **screwing machine** (*eng*) a form of lathe adapted for the continuous production of screws or screwed pieces by screwing dies; **screw jack** a jack for lifting heavy weights, operated by a screw; **screw nail** a nail with a screw thread; **screw'-pile** a pile for sinking into the ground, ending in a screw; **screw pine** a plant of the genus *Pandanus* or its family (from the screwlike arrangement of the leaves); **screw plate** (*eng*) a hardened steel plate in which a number of screwing dies

of different sizes are formed; **screw press** (*eng*) a press worked by a screw, for punching holes, etc; **screw propeller** a propeller with helical blades; **screw steamer** a steamer driven by a screw propeller; **screw thread** the helical ridge of a screw; **screw'top** a bottle with a stopper that screws in or on, *esp* a beer bottle of the kind with its contents. — also *adj*. — **screw'-worm** the larva of a dipterous fly (**screw-worm fly**) which develops under the skin of various animals, often causing death; **screw'-wrench** a tool for gripping screw heads. — **have a screw loose** to be defective (*esp* mentally); **put on** or **turn the screw** to apply (physical, moral, etc) pressure progressively; to exact payment; **put the screws on** to coerce; **screw it, them, you,** etc (*vulg slang*) an interjection expressing disgust, scorn, frustration, etc; **screw up** to twist or distort; to summon up (courage, etc); to disrupt, spoil or ruin (*colloq*); (*usu* passive) to cause to become nervous, emotionally disturbed, etc (*colloq*) (*n* **screw'-up** (*colloq*) a disaster, failure, mess or fiasco; a person who is a failure, whose life is a mess, etc). [Earlier *scrue*; appar OFr *escroue*, of obscure origin; prob connected with LG *schrûve*, Ger *Schraube*]

scribable, scribacious, etc. See under **scribe**.

scribble[1] *skrib'l, vt* and *vi* to scrawl; to write in a careless, illegible hand; to write paltry, ill-expressed material, *esp* copiously. — *n* careless writing; a scrawl. — *n* **scribb'lement**. — *n* **scribb'ler** (*derog*) a worthless author. — *n* **scribb'ling**. — *adv* **scribb'lingly**. — *adj* **scribb'ly**. — **scribb'ling-book, -pad, -paper**. [A frequentative of **scribe**, or LL *scrībillāre*, from L *scrībere* to write]

scribble[2] *skrib'l, vt* to comb (wool) roughly. — *n* **scribb'ler** a wool-combing machine; a person who tends it. — *n* **scribb'ling**. [Prob from LGer]

scribe *skrīb, n* an expounder and teacher of the traditional law and that of Moses (*Bible*); a writer; a public or official writer; a medieval clerk, amanuensis or secretary; a copyist; a penman, calligrapher; a pointed instrument to mark lines on wood, metal, etc. — *vt* to mark or score with a scribe, etc; to fit by so marking; to incise; to write. — *vi* to act as a scribe. — *adj* **scrī'bable** capable of being written upon. — *adj* **scribā'cious** (*archaic*) given to writing. — *n* (*archaic*) **scribā'ciousness**. — *adj* **scrī'bal**. — *n* **scrī'ber** a scribing tool, a scribe. — *n* **scrī'bing**. — *n* **scrī'bism**. [L *scrība* a scribe, and *scrībere* to write]

scriech. See **skreigh**.

scriene (*obs*). Same as **screen**.

scrieve[1] *skrēv*, (*Scot*) *vi* to glide swiftly along. [Prob ON *skrefa* from *skref* stride]

scrieve[2], **scrieve-board**. See under **scrive**.

scriggle *skrig'l, vi* to writhe; to wriggle. — *n* a wriggling. — *adj* **scrigg'ly**. [Cf **struggle**]

scrike *skrīk*, (*archaic* and *dialect*) *vi* to shriek. — *n* a shriek. [Prob Scand]

scrim *skrim, n* open fabric used in upholstery, bookbinding, for curtains, etc. [Ety obscure]

scrimmage *skrim'ij* or **scrummage** *skrum'ij, n* an untidy mêlée, a struggle; (in Rugby football) a scrum (*old*); (in American football) play between two teams beginning with the snap (qv) and ending when the ball is dead; a practice session of this; a line of scrimmage. — *vi* to take part in a scrimmage. — *n* **scrimm'ager** or **scrumm'ager**. — **line of scrimmage** or **scrimmage line** (*Am football*) an imaginary line, parallel to the goal lines, behind which the linemen of a team position themselves for start of play, and on which the end of the ball nearest that team's goal line rests. [A variant of **skirmish**]

scrimp *skrimp, adj* (*rare*) scanty; stinted. — *adv* (*obs*) barely. — *vt* to stint; to keep limited, often perforce. — *vi* to be sparing or niggardly, often perforce (*usu* in the phrase *scrimp and save*). — *adj* **scrimped**. — *adv* **scrimp'ily**. — *n* **scrimp'iness**. — *adv* **scrimp'ly** sparingly; scarcely. — *n* **scrimp'ness**. — *adj* **scrimp'y** scanty. [Cf Swed and Dan *skrumpen* shrivelled, OE *scrimman* to shrink]

scrimshander, scrimshandy. See **scrimshaw**.

scrimshank. See **skrimshank**.

scrimshaw *skrim'shö, n* a sailor's spare-time handicraft, such as engraving or carving fanciful designs on shells, whales' teeth, etc; anything crafted in this way. — Also **scrim'shander** or **scrim'shandy**. — *vt* and *vi* to work or decorate in this way. — *n* **scrim'shoner** someone who does scrimshaw. [Origin obscure]

scrimure *skrīm'yər*, (*obs*) *n* a fencer. [Fr *escrimeur*]

scrine or **scryne** *skrīn*, (*obs*) *n* a box or chest in which written records are kept; a shrine. [OFr *escrin*, from L *scrīnium* a chest; cf **shrine**]

scrip[1] *skrip, n* a writing; a scrap of paper or of writing; (for *subscription*) a preliminary certificate, as for shares allotted; share certificates, or shares or stock collectively; a dollar bill, money (*old US slang*); a paper token issued instead of currency in special eg emergency circumstances (*US*). — *n* **scripoph'ily** the collecting of bond and share certificates as a hobby, *esp* those of historical, etc interest; the items thus collected. — *n* **scrip'ophile** or **scripoph'ilist**. — **scrip issue** a bonus issue (qv at **bonus**). [**script** and **subscription**; partly perh **scrap**[1]]

scrip[2]. See **script**.

scrip[3] *skrip*, (*obs*) *n* a small bag; a satchel; a pilgrim's pouch. — *n* **scripp'age** the contents of a scrip. [Cf ON *skreppa* a bag, and OFr *escrep(p)e*]

Script. *abbrev*: Scripture.

script *skript, n* a piece of writing; the actors', director's, etc written copy of the text of a play, film, etc; a text for broadcasting; handwriting, or system or style of handwriting; a set of characters used in writing a language (such as *Cyrillic script*); type in imitation of handwriting; handwriting in imitation of type; an original document (*law*); a list of actors and their parts (*obs*); short for *manuscript* or *typescript*; short for *prescription* (also **scrip**; *slang*). — *vt* to write a script for, or make a script from (eg a novel), *esp* for broadcasting or the theatre or cinema. — *adj* **script'ed**. — **script'writer**. [L *scrīptum*, from *scrībere* to write]

scriptorium *skrip-tō'ri-əm* or *-tö'ri-əm, n* a writing-room, *esp* in a monastery: — *pl* **scripto'ria**. — *adj* **scripto'rial**. — *adj* **scrip'tory** (*-tər-i*) by, in, or relating to writing. [L *scrīptōrium*, from *scrībere* to write]

scripture *skrip'chər, n* handwriting; something written; (in *sing* or *pl*) the sacred writings of a religion, *esp* (with *cap*) the Bible; a biblical text (*rare*). — Also *adj*. — *adj* **scrip'tural** of, in or according to Scripture; of writing. — *n* **scrip'turalism** literal adherence to the Scriptures. — *n* **scrip'turalist** a person who adheres to the letter of Scripture; a student of Scripture (*obs*). — *adv* **scrip'turally**. — *n* **scrip'turism**. — *n* **scrip'turist** a person versed in Scripture; a person who bases his or her belief on the Bible and the Bible alone. — **scrip'ture-reader** (*hist*) a person who read the Bible in cottages, barracks, etc to those who could not read for themselves. [L *scrīptūra*, from *scrībere* to write]

scritch *skrich, n* a screech. — *vt* and *vi* to screech. — **scritch'-owl**. [ME *scrichen*, as **screech**]

scrive *skrīv*, or **scrieve** *skrēv*, (*Scot*) *vt* and *vi* to write, *esp* with copious fluency; to describe; to inscribe. — **scrive'board** or **scrieve'board** a shipbuilder's drawing board.

scrivener *skriv'nər*, (*hist*) *n* a scribe; a copyist; a person who draws up contracts, etc; a person who lends money at interest to others. — *n* **scriv'enership**. — *n* **scriv'ening** writing. — **scrivener's palsy** writer's cramp. [OFr *escrivain* (Fr *écrivain*), from LL *scrībānus*, from L *scrība* a scribe]

scrobe *skrōb*, (*entomol*) *n* a groove. [L *scrobis* ditch]

scrobicule *skrōb'i-kūl*, (*biol*) *n* a small pit or depression, as around the tubercles of a sea urchin. — *adj* **scrobicular** (*-bik'ū-lər*) relating to or surrounded by scrobicules. — *adj* **scrobic'ulate** (*-lət*) or **scrobic'ulated** pitted. [Dimin of L *scrobis* a ditch]

scrod *skrod*, (*NAm*) *n* a young cod or haddock. [Perh obs Du *schrood*, MDu *schrode*]

scroddled *skrod'ld*, *adj* (of pottery) made of clay scraps of different colours. [Cf LGer *schrodel* scrap]

scrofula *skrof'ū-lə*, *n* tuberculosis of the lymph nodes in the neck (also formerly called **king's evil**). — *adj* **scrof'ulous**. [L *scrōfulae*, from *scrōfa* a sow (supposed to be prone to it)]

scrog *skrog*, (*Scot* and *N Eng dialect*) *n* a stunted bush or small tree; a crabapple (the fruit or tree); a bushy place; scrubby wood; a broken branch; a branch of a tree (*heraldry*). — *adj* **scrogg'ie** or **scrogg'y** covered with scrogs; stunted. — **scrog'-apple** and **scrog'-bush** (or **-buss**) respectively the crabapple and crabapple tree. [Origin obscure]

scroll *skrōl*, *n* a roll of paper, parchment, etc; a ribbonlike decorative strip in painting, architecture, etc, partly coiled or curved, sometimes bearing a motto; a writing in the form of a roll; a draft or copy of a letter, etc (*Scot*); a list, roll or inventory; a spiral ornament or part, such as a flourish to a signature. — *vt* to set in a scroll; to draft (*Scot*); to roll into a scroll or scrolls; to cut into scrolls from a length of material; to move (a text, graphics, etc) up or down or from side to side in order to view data that cannot all be seen on a VDU at the same time (*comput*). — *vi* to curl; (of a text or graphics) to move up or down or from side to side (*comput*). — *adj* **scrolled** formed into a scroll; ornamented with scrolls; moved across a VDU screen as described above. — *adj* (*comput*) **scroll'ing**. — *adv* **scroll'wise**. — *n* **scroll'work** ornament in scrolls. — **scroll chuck** (*eng*) a self-centring chuck, *esp* a *three-jaw chuck* for holding round work; **scroll saw** a saw for cutting scrolls. [Earlier **scrowl(e)**, formed (perh as dimin) from **scrow**]

Scrooge *skrōōj*, *n* a miser. [From Ebenezer *Scrooge* in Dickens's *A Christmas Carol*]

scrooge. See **scrouge**.

scroop *skrōōp*, (*dialect*) *n* a scraping noise. — *vi* to make a scroop. [Imit]

scrophularia *skrof-ū-lā'ri-ə*, *n* a plant of the figwort genus *Scrophularia*. — *adj* **scrophulariaceous** (*-ā'shəs*) of, belonging to, or characteristic of the *Scrophulariaceae*, a family of sympetalous dicotyledons with zygomorphic flowers, *incl* foxglove, mullein, speedwell, eyebright. [L, scrofula (plant), from its being reputedly a cure for scrofula (qv)]

scrotum *skrō'təm*, *n* the bag of skin that contains the testicles in mammals. — *adj* **scrō'tal**. [L *scrōtum*]

scrouge, **scrowdge** *skrowj* or **scrooge** *skrōōj*, (*dialect*) *vt* and *vi* to squeeze; to crowd. — *n* **scroug'er** (*US archaic*) a whopper; something large. [Cf **scruze**]

scrounge *skrownj*, (*orig military slang*) *vt* to purloin; to cadge or beg, or obtain by cadging or begging. — *vi* to hunt around (with *for*); to sponge. — *n* **scroung'er**. — *n* **scroung'ing**. [Origin doubtful]

scrow *skrō*, *n* a scroll; (in *pl*) writings; a clipping or strip of hide or leather used in glue-making. [Anglo-Fr *escrowe*; see **escroll**, **escrow**, **scroll**]

scrowdge. See **scrouge**.

scrowl, **scrowle** *skrōl*. Old spellings of **scroll**.

scroyle *skroil*, (*obs*) *n* a wretch. [Origin doubtful]

scrub[1] *skrub*, *vt* to rub hard; to wash or clean by hard rubbing, eg with a stiff brush; to purify (*gas-making*); to cancel, abandon (plans, etc) (*slang*). — *vi* to use a scrubbing-brush; to make a rapid to-and-fro movement as if scrubbing; (of jockeys) to make a similar movement with the arms over a horse's neck to urge it forward (*horse-racing slang*): — *pr p* **scrubb'ing**; *pa t* and *pa p* **scrubbed**. — *n* an act of scrubbing; a worn or short-bristled brush or broom; a drudge. — *n* **scrubb'er** someone or something that scrubs; an apparatus for freeing gas from tar, ammonia, and hydrogen-sulphur combinations; any device that filters out impurities; an unattractive woman, or one with loose morals (*slang*). — *n* **scrubb'ing**. — **scrubb'ing-board** a wash-board; **scrubb'ing-brush** a brush with short stiff bristles for scrubbing floors, etc. — **scrub round** (*slang*) to cancel; to ignore intentionally; **scrub up** (of a surgeon, etc) to wash the hands and arms thoroughly before performing or assisting at an operation. [Perh obs Du *schrubben*, or a corresponding lost OE word]

scrub[2] *skrub*, *n* a stunted tree; stunted trees and shrubs collectively; brushwood; country covered with bushes or low trees, *esp* the Australian evergreen xerophytic dwarf forest or bush of eucalyptus, acacia, etc; hence, a remote place, far from civilization (*Austr colloq*); an undersized or inferior animal, *esp* one of indefinite breed; a player in a second or inferior team (*NAm*); a team of inferior players, or one with too few players (*NAm*); an insignificant or undersized person; anything small or insignificant. — *adj* insignificant; undersized; (of a team) improvised, hastily got together for the occasion (*NAm*); (of a player) in a second or inferior team (*NAm*). — *adj* **scrubb'ed** (*Shakesp*) stunted. — *n* **scrubb'er** (*Austr*) an animal that has run wild. — *adj* **scrubb'y** covered with scrub; stunted; insignificant. — **scrub bird** an elusive wren-like Australian bird (*Atrichornis*); **scrub'land** an area covered with scrub; **scrub rider** (*esp Aust*) a person who looks for cattle that stray into the scrub; **scrub turkey** or **scrub fowl** a type of ground-living bird of the Australian scrub, a mound-builder; **scrub typhus** a typhus-like disease caused by a parasitic microorganism and transmitted by a mite to humans (also called **tsutsugamushi disease**). — **the Scrubs** *colloq abbrev* for **Wormwood Scrubs**, an English prison. [A variant of **shrub**[1]]

scruff[1] *skruf*, *n* the nape (of the neck). [See **scuft**]

scruff[2] *skruf*, *n* scurf; an untidy, dirty person (*colloq*). — *n* **scruff'iness**. — *adj* **scruff'y** scurvy (*archaic*); untidy, dirty (*colloq*). [Metathetic variant of **scurf**]

scrum *skrum*, *n* a disorderly struggle, a mêlée; a closing-in of rival forwards round the ball on the ground, or in readiness for its being inserted (by the scrum half) between the two packs (*Rugby football*); a large number of people crushed into a relatively small space and jostling for position (*colloq*). — *vi* to form a scrum: — *pr p* **scrumm'ing**; *pa t* and *pa p* **scrummed**. — **scrum'-down** an act of forming a rugby scrum; **scrum half** (*Rugby football*) a half-back whose duty it is to put the ball into the scrum and secure it as soon as it emerges; **scrum'pox** (*Rugby slang*) impetigo spread by rugby players' faces rubbing together in the scrum. [Abbrev of **scrummage**; see **scrimmage**, **skirmish**]

scrummage. See **scrimmage**.

scrummy *skrum'i*, (*colloq*) *adj* scrumptious.

scrump, **skrump** *skrump*, or **scrimp** *skrimp*, (*dialect*) *vt* and *vi* to gather windfalls, hence to steal (apples) from orchards. — *n* anything shrivelled, small or undersized, *esp* an apple; an undersized person. — *n* **scrump'y** very strong cider made from small, sweet apples, *esp* as brewed in the West Country. [See **scrimp**]

scrumptious *skrump'shəs*, (*colloq*) *adj* delightful; delicious. — *adv* **scrump'tiously**. [Origin uncertain]

scrumpy. See under **scrump**.

scrunch *skrunch* or *skrunsh*, *vt* to crunch or crush, *esp* with relation to the noise produced. — *vi* (*esp* of paper, snow, hair, etc) to be crunched or crushed. — *n* the act or sound of scrunching. — *adj* **scrunch'y**. [Variant of **crunch**]

scrunt *skrunt*, (*Scot*) *n* anything stunted (eg an apple, a tree); a niggard. — *adj* **scrunt'y**.

scruple *skrōō'pl*, *n* a small weight (in apothecaries' weight, 20 grains, *abbrev* **scr.**); a sexagesimal division, as a minute of time or arc (*obs*); a very small quantity (*archaic*); a difficulty or consideration, *usu* moral, obstructing action, *esp* one turning on a fine point or one that is baseless; (in *pl*) moral standards, personal standards of decency which one adheres to; a doubt, disbelief or difficulty; protest, demur; scrupulousness. — *vi* to hesitate because of scruples. — *vt* to cause to feel scruples (*obs*); to question, doubt (*archaic*); to have scruples about (*archaic*); to hesitate. — *n* **scru'pler**. — *n* **scrupulosity** (*-pū-los'i-ti*). — *adj* **scru'pulous** directed by scruples; having scruples, doubts, or objections; extremely conscientious or exact; captious (*old*). — *adv* **scru'pulously**. — *n* **scru'pulousness**. — **make no scruple** (or **no scruples**) **about** or **make scruples about** to offer (no) moral objections to. [L *scrūpulus*, dimin of *scrūpus* a sharp stone, anxiety]

scrutin de liste *skrü-tɛ̃ də lēst*, (*Fr*) *n* a method of voting for the French Chamber of Deputies, in which the voter casts his or her ballot for any combination of the whole number of candidates for the department, as opposed to **scrutin d'arrondissement** (*dar-ɔ̃-dēs-mã*), in which method he or she votes only for local candidates. [List ballot, district ballot, from L *scrūtinium*; see **scrutiny**]

scrutiny *skroo'ti-ni*, *n* close, careful, or minute investigation or examination; a searching look; official examination of votes; examination of the catechumens (*hist*). — *adj* **scru'table** accessible to scrutiny, open to examination, observable. — *n* **scrutā'tor** a close examiner; a scrutineer. — *n* **scrutineer'** someone who makes a scrutiny, *esp* of votes. — *vt* and *vi* **scru'tinize** or **-ise** to examine closely. — *n* **scru'tinizer** or **-s-**. — *adj* **scru'tinizing** or **-s-**. — *adv* **scru'tinizingly** or **-s-**. — *adj* **scru'tinous**. — *adv* **scru'tinously**. [L *scrūtinium*, and *scrūtārī* to search even to the rags, from *scrūta* rags, trash]

scruto *skroo'tō*, (*theat*) *n* a kind of stage trap-door: — *pl* **scru'tos**. [Origin obscure]

scrutoire *skroo-twär'*, *-tōr'* or *-tör'*, *n*. Same as **escritoire**.

scruze *skrooz*, (*obs*; now *dialect*) *vt* to squeeze. [Perh **screw** combined with **squeeze**]

scry *skrī*, *vt* (*archaic* and *dialect*) to descry. — *vi* to practise crystal-gazing: — *pr p* **scry'ing**; *pa t* and *pa p* **scried**, (*Spenser*) **scryde**. — *n* **scry'er**. — *n* **scry'ing**. [Aphetic for **descry**]

scryne (*Spenser*). Same as **scrine**.

scuba *skoo'bə* or *skū'*, *n* an apparatus used by skin-divers, consisting of a breathing tube attached to a cylinder or cylinders of compressed air. — Also *adj*. — **scuba diver**; **scuba diving**. [*s*elf-*c*ontained *u*nderwater *b*reathing *a*pparatus]

scuchin, **scuchion**. Spenserian forms of **scutcheon**.

Scud *skud*, *n* a surface-to-surface missile of a kind made in the former Soviet Union. — *vt* to attack with Scud missiles (*colloq*; also *fig*).

scud[1] *skud*, *vi* (*esp* of clouds) to sweep along easily and swiftly; (*esp* of sailing vesels) to drive before the wind. — *vt* to cross swiftly: — *pr p* **scudd'ing**; *pa t* and *pa p* **scudd'ed**. — *n* an act or the action of scudding; driving cloud, shower or spray; a gust; a swift runner (*school slang*). — *n* **scudd'er**. — *vt* **scudd'le** to scuttle. [Perh alteration of *scut* rabbit's tail, hence meaning 'to run like a rabbit']

scud[2] *skud*, (*Scot*) *vt* to slap, to hit with a sharp, glancing blow: — *pr p* **scudd'ing**; *pa t* and *pa p* **scudd'ed**. — *n* a slap; (in *pl*) a spanking.

scud[3] *skud*, (*Scot*) *n* a state of nudity. — **in the scud** naked, without clothes. [Origin obscure]

scuddaler, **scudler**. Same as **skudler**.

scuddle. See under **scud**[1].

scudo *skoo'dō*, *n* an old Italian silver coin: — *pl* **scu'di** (*-dē*). [Ital, from L *scūtum* a shield]

scuff[1] *skuf*, *n* a form of **scruff**[1] or **scuft**.

scuff[2] *skuf*, *vt* and *vi* to shuffle, drag or scrape (the feet) on the ground; to brush, graze, scrape (*esp* shoes or heels while walking) or become grazed or scraped; to make or become shabby by wear. — *vt* (*NAm*) to prod at with the foot. — *n* the act or sound of scuffling; a scrape or scratch caused by scuffing. [Imit]

scuffle *skuf'l*, *vi* to struggle confusedly, *esp* while fighting; to shuffle. — *vt* to hoe, scarify; to shuffle; to poke at or scuff with the foot (*NAm*); to gather, scrape together (*esp* money) (with *up*; also *vi* with *up on*; *US*). — *n* a confused struggle; a thrust-hoe (*US*); an agricultural scuffler. — *n* **scuff'ler** a person who scuffles; an implement for scarifying the soil. [Cf Swed *skuffa* to shove; Du *schoffelen*; see **shove**, **shovel**, **shuffle**]

scuft *skuft*, (*dialect*) *n* the nape (of the neck). — Also **scuff** or **scruff**. [Poss ON *skopt*, *skoft* the hair]

scug. See **skug**[1].

scul, **scull**, **sculle** *skul*. Obsolete spellings of **school**[2].

sculduddry *skul-dud'ri*, **sculduddery** or **skulduddery** *-dud'ə-ri* (*Scot*, *facetious*) *n* breach of chastity; bawdy talk or writing. — *adj* bawdy. [Origin obscure]

sculduggery. Same as **skulduggery**.

sculk. Obsolete spelling of **skulk**.

scull[1] *skul*, *n* a short, light spoon-bladed oar for one hand, used in pairs; an oar used over the stern of a boat; a small, light rowing-boat propelled by sculls; an act or spell of sculling; (in *pl*) a race between small, light rowing-boats rowed by one person. — *vt* to propel with sculls, or with one oar worked like a screw over the stern. — *vi* to row using sculls. — *n* **scull'er** a person who sculls; a small boat pulled by one person with a pair of sculls. — *n* **scull'ing**. [Origin obscure]

scull[2] or **skull** *skul*, *n* a shallow basket for fish, etc. [Poss ON *skjōla* pail]

scull[3]. Obsolete spelling of **skull**[1].

scull[4], **sculle**. See **scul**.

scullery *skul'ər-i*, *n* a room for rough kitchen work, such as the cleaning of utensils; a kitchen (*obs dialect*). — **scull'ery-maid**. [OFr *escuelerie*, from L *scutella* a tray]

scullion *skul'yən*, *n* a servant employed for rough work (*archaic*); a mean, contemptible person. [Poss OFr *escouillon* a dish-cloth, from L *scōpa* a broom; or from Fr *souillon* scullion, infl by **scullery**]

sculp *skulp*, (*rare*) *vt* and *vi* to carve; to engrave; to sculpture. [L *sculpere*; not a back-formation from **sculptor**, **sculpture**]

sculp or **sculpt**. *abbrev*: *sculpsit* (qv); sculptor; sculpture.

sculpin *skul'pin*, (*NAm*) *n* the dragonet, a large-headed spiny fish of no commercial value; a good-for-nothing person or animal (*slang*). [Poss *Scorpaena*, a genus of spiny fishes]

sculpsit *skulp'sit* or *skoolp'sit*, (*L*) (he or she) sculptured (this work), sometimes appended to the signature of the sculptor (*abbrev* **sc.** or **sculp.**)

sculpt *skulpt*, *vt* and *vi* to carve or otherwise shape stone, or out of stone, to sculpture; to carve. [Fr *sculpter*, from L *sculpere* to carve; not a back-formation from **sculptor**, **sculpture**]

sculptor *skulp'tər*, *n* an artist in carving, *esp* in stone: — *fem* **sculp'tress**. — *adj* **sculp'tural** (*-chər-əl*). — *adv* **sculp'turally**. — *n* **sculp'ture** the art of carving, *esp* in stone; extended to clay-modelling or moulding for casting; work, or a piece of work, in this art; engraving (*obs*); shaping in relief; spines, ridges, etc, standing out from the surface (*biol*). — *vt* to carve, shape in relief; to represent in sculpture; to mould, or form, so as to have the appearance, or (*fig*) other quality, of sculpture; to modify the form of (the earth's surface). — *adj* **sculp'tured** carved; engraved; (of features) fine and regular like a classical sculpture; having ridges, etc on the surface (*bot* and *zool*). — *adj* **sculpturesque'**. — *n* **sculp'turing**. [L *sculptor*, *-ōris*, *sculptūra*, from *sculpere*, *sculptum* to carve]

scum *skum*, *n* matter coming to or floating on the surface of liquid, *esp* in the form of foam or froth; worthless, despicable people. — *vt* to remove the scum from. — *vi* to form or throw up a scum: — *pr p* **scumm'ing**; *pa t* and *pa p* **scummed**. — *n* **scumm'er** an instrument for removing scum. — *n pl* **scumm'ings** scum removed from a liquid. — *adj* **scumm'y**. — **scum'bag** (*vulg slang*) a condom (*esp US*); a general term of abuse. [Cf Dan *skum*, Ger *Schaum* foam]

scumber *skum'bər*, *skum'ər*, or **skummer** *skum'ər*, (*archaic*) *vt* and *vi* to defecate (used *esp* of a dog or fox). — *n* dung. [Prob OFr *descumbrer* to disencumber]

scumble *skum'bl*, *vt* (in painting and drawing) to soften the effect of (an outline or colour) by a very thin coat of opaque or semi-opaque colour, or by light rubbing or by applying paint with a dry brush. — *n* colour laid down in this way; the effect produced. — *n* **scum'bling**. [Frequentative of **scum**]

scumfish. Same as **scomfish**.

scuncheon *skun'shən*, **sconcheon** or **scontion** *skon'shən*, *skun'*, *n* the inner part of a door jamb or window frame. [OFr *escoinson*]

scunge *skunj*, (*dialect*) *vi* to slink about; to borrow or scrounge. — Also *vt*. — *n* a scrounger; a dirty, sneaky person; accumulated sticky dirt (*Austr* and *NZ*). — *adj* **scun'gy** (*Austr* and *NZ*) dirty; unkempt; sordid. [Cf **scrounge**]

scunner *skun'ər*, (*Scot*) *vi* to feel loathing. — *vt* to produce a feeling of loathing in; to disgust, nauseate. — *n* an object, or a manifestation, of loathing; an irritation or nuisance. — **take a scunner to** to take a strong dislike to. [Perh ME *scurn* to shrink; origin unknown]

scup *skup* or **scuppaug** *skup'ög* or *-ög'*, *n* the northern porgy, a common marine fish of Atlantic coastal waters of N America. [Narraganset *mishcuppauog*]

scupper[1] *skup'ər*, *n* (*usu* in *pl*) a hole allowing water to drain from a ship's deck. [Origin disputed]

scupper[2] *skup'ər*, (*colloq*) *vt* to do for; to ruin; to sink (a ship). [Perh connected with **scupper**[1]]

scuppernong *skup'ər-nong*, *n* a native American grape, *Vitis rotundifolia*, from the region of the *Scuppernong* river, N Carolina; a sweet wine made from it.

scur *skûr*. Same as **skirr**.

scurf *skûrf*, *n* small flakes or scales of dead skin, *esp* on the scalp, dandruff; an incrustation of flakes or scales. — *n* **scurf'iness**. — *adj* **scurf'y**. [OE *scurf*, *sceorf*]

scurrier. See **scurriour**.

scurril or **scurrile** *skur'il*, *adj* (*archaic*) like or worthy of a vulgar buffoon; indecently opprobrious or jocular. [L *scurrīlis*; see **scurrilous**]

scurrilous *skur'i-ləs*, *adj* indecently abusive and unjustifiably defamatory; characterized by vulgar or obscene humour. — *n* **scurrility** (*skə-ril'i-ti*). — *adv* **scurr'ilously**. — *n* **scurr'ilousness**. [L *scurrīlis*, from *scurra* a buffoon]

scurriour or **scurrier** *skur'i-ər*, (*obs*) *n* a scout. [See **discoverer**, **scourer**[1]]

scurry *skur'i*, *vi* to hurry briskly or in a panicky way; to scuttle. — *n* flurried haste; a flurry, as of snow; a short sprint race (*horse-racing*). [From **hurry-skurry**, reduplication of **hurry**; or back-formation of **scurrier**; or from **scour**[2].]

scurvy *skûr'vi*, *adj* scurfy; shabby; vile, contemptible. — *n* a disease caused by a deficiency of vitamin C when the diet is devoid of fresh fruit and vegetables, characterized by spongy and bleeding gums followed by subcutaneous bleeding. — *adv* **scur'vily** in a scurvy manner; meanly, basely. — *n* **scur'viness**. — **scurvy grass** a cruciferous plant (*Cochlearia officinalis*) used by sailors to treat scurvy; [**scurf**; the application to the disease helped by similarity of sound; see **scorbutic**]

scuse or **'scuse** *skūs*, *skūz*, *n* and *vt* aphetic for **excuse**.

scut *skut*, *n* a short erect tail, as in a hare, rabbit or deer; a hare; a contemptuous term for a (small) person (*dialect*). [Origin obscure]

scuta. Plural of **scutum** (see under **scute**).

scutage *skū'tij*, (*hist*) *n* a tax on a knight's fee, *esp* one in lieu of personal or military service. [LL *scūtāgium*, from L *scūtum* a shield]

scutal, scutate. See under **scute**.

scutch[1] *skuch*, *vt* to dress (eg flax) by beating; to switch. — *n* a tool for dressing flax, a swingle; a bricklayer's cutting tool. — *n* **scutch'er** a person, tool, or part of a machine that scutches; the striking part of a threshing-mill. — *n* **scutch'ing**. [Prob OFr *escousser* to shake off]

scutch[2] *skuch* or **scutch grass**. Forms of **quitch**[1] and **quitch grass** (see also **couch grass** under **couch**[2].)

scutcheon *skuch'ən*, *n* an aphetic form of **escutcheon**.

scute *skūt*, *n* a scutum; an écu, a French coin (*hist*); any coin of small value (*obs*); a hard exoskeletal plate (*zool*). — *adj* **scūt'al**. — *adj* **scūt'ate** protected by scutes or scuta; shield-shaped. — *adj* **scūt'iform**. — *n* **scūt'iger** a squire (*facetious*); a centipede of the genus *Scutigena*, giving name to the family *Scutigeridae*. — *n* **scūt'um** the oblong shield of Roman heavy-armed infantry (*hist*); a scute; the second tergal plate of the notum of an insect's thorax (*zool*): — *pl* **scūt'a**. [L *scūtum* a shield]

scutellum *skū-tel'əm*, *n* a scale of a bird's foot; the third tergal plate of the notum of an insect's thorax; a structure, supposed to be the cotyledon, by which a grass embryo absorbs the endosperm: — *pl* **scūtell'a**. — *adj* **scūtell'ar**. — *adj* **scūt'ellate**. — *n* **scūtellā'tion** (*zool*) the arrangement of scales or plates on an animal's body. [L *scutella* a tray, dimin of *scutra* a platter, confused in scientific use with *scūtulum*, dimin of *scūtum* a shield]

scutiform See under **scute**.

scutter *skut'ər*, *vi* to run hastily, scurry. — *n* a hasty run. [A variant of **scuttle**[3]]

scuttle[1] *skut'l*, *n* a shallow basket; a fireside container for coal. — *n* **scutt'leful**. [OE *scutel*, from L *scutella* a tray]

scuttle[2] *skut'l*, *n* an opening in a ship's deck or side; its lid; a shuttered hole in a wall, roof, etc; its shutter or trap-door. — *vt* to make a hole in, or open the lids of the scuttles of, *esp* in order to sink; to destroy, ruin (eg plans). — **scutt'lebutt** or **scuttle cask** (*hist*) a cask with a hole cut in it for drinking-water on board ship; a drinking fountain; rumour, gossip (*esp US slang*). [OFr *escoutille* hatchway]

scuttle[3] *skut'l*, *vi* to move or run with short rapid steps, scurry. — *n* an act of scuttling. — *n* **scutt'ler**. [**scud**]

scutum. See under **scute**.

scuzz *skuz*, (*NAm slang*) *n* dirt; seediness; something distasteful; an unpleasant, disreputable or worthless person (also **scuzz'ball**). — *adj* **scuzz'y**. [Origin uncertain]

scybalum *sib'ə-ləm*, *n* a lump or mass of hard faeces in the intestine: — *pl* **scyb'ala**. — *adj* **scyb'alous**. [Latinized from Gr *skybalon* dung]

scye *sī*, (*Scot* and *N Irish*) *n* an opening in a garment for the insertion of a sleeve. [Origin obscure]

Scylla *sil'ə*, (*Gr mythol*) *n* a six-headed monster who sat over a dangerous rock on the Italian side of the Straits of Messina, opposite **Charybdis**, and seized or drowned sailors from passing ships. — **between Scylla and Charybdis** (*usu fig*) forced to steer a perilous or hopeless course between two deadly dangers, avoidance of one meaning almost certain destruction by the other. [Gr *Skylla*]

scyphus *sīf'əs*, *n* a large ancient Greek drinking-cup; a cup-shaped structure (*bot*): — *pl* **scyph'ī**. — *adj* **scyph'iform**. — *n* **scyphis'toma** the segmenting polyp stage of a jellyfish (Gr *stoma* mouth): — *pl* **scyphis'tomas** or **scyphis'tomae**. — *n* **scyphozo'an** any of a class (*Scyphozoa* or *Scyphomedusae*) of medusoid coelenterates, a jellyfish. [Gr *skyphos* cup]

scytale *sit'ə-lē*, *n* a Spartan secret writing on a strip wound around a stick, unreadable without a stick of the same thickness. [Gr *skytalē* a staff]

scythe *sīdh*, *n* an instrument with a large curved blade and wooden handle, for mowing or cropping by hand; a blade attached to the wheel of a war chariot. — *vt* and *vi* to mow (down) with a scythe. — *adj* **scythed** armed or cut down with scythes. — *n* **scyth'er** a person who uses a scythe. — **scythe'man** a scyther; **scythe'-stone** a whet for scythes. [OE *sīthe*; cf ON *sigthr*, Ger *Sense*]

Scythian *sith'i-ən*, *adj* of *Scythia*, an ancient region N and E of the Black Sea, of its nomadic people, or of their language. — *n* a member of the people; the language of Scythia. — **Scythian lamb** the barometz plant.

SD *abbrev*: South Dakota (US state); Swaziland (IVR).

sd *sine die* (*L*), without a day, without (fixed) date.

SDA *abbrev*: Scottish Development Agency (now Scottish Enterprise).

S.Dak *abbrev*: South Dakota (US State).

SDI *abbrev*: Strategic Defense Initiative.

sdaine, sdayn. See **sdeigne**.

'sdeath *zdeth*, (*obs*) *interj* an obsolete oath. [God'*s death*]

sdeigne or **sdeign** *zdān*, (*obs*) *vt* and *vi* to disdain. — Also **sdein**, **sdaine** or **sdayn**. — *adj* **sdeign'full**. — *adv*

sdeign'fully. [Ital; *sdegnare*, aphetic for *disdegnare*; or Eng **disdain**]

SDLP *abbrev*: Social Democratic and Labour Party (of Northern Ireland).

SDP *abbrev*: (former) Social Democratic Party; social, domestic and pleasure (of motor insurance).

SDR *abbrev*: special drawing rights.

sdrucciola *zdrōōt'chō-la*, *adj* (of rhyme) triple. [Ital, slippery]

SE *abbrev*: Society of Engineers; south-east.

Se (*chem*) *symbol*: selenium.

SEA *abbrev*: Single European Act.

sea *sē*, *n* the great mass of salt water covering the greater part of the earth's surface, the ocean; any great expanse of water; a great (*esp* salt) lake, mainly in proper names; (a given height of) swell or roughness; a great wave; the tide; (with *the*) a maritime career; a seemingly limitless mass or expanse. — *adj* marine. — *adj* **sea'-like**. — *adv* in the manner of the sea. — *adj* and *adv* **sea'ward** towards the (open) sea. — *n* seaward side, direction or position. — *adj* and *adv* **sea'wardly**. — *adv* **sea'wards**. — **sea acorn** an acorn-shell; **sea adder** a pipefish; a marine stickleback; **sea air** the air at sea or at the seaside; **sea anchor** a floating anchor used at sea to slow a boat down, or maintain its direction; **sea anemone** a solitary soft-bodied polyp, *esp* of the order *Actiniaria*, typically having many tentacles around the mouth cavity; **sea ape** the sea otter; the thresher shark; a manatee; **sea aster** a flowering plant, *Aster tripolium*, of salt marshes; **sea'bank** the seashore; an embankment to keep out the sea; **sea bass** (*bas*) a perchoid marine fish of various kinds, *esp* of the *Serranidae* and the *Sciaenidae* families; **sea bat** a name for various fishes with long or outspread fins; **sea'-bather**; **sea'-bathing**; **sea beach**; **sea bean** the cacoon (*Entada*) or other seed cast up by the sea; a mollusc's operculum, worn as an amulet; **sea bear** the polar bear; the fur seal; **sea beast**. — *adj* **sea'-beat** or **-beaten** lashed by the waves. — **sea'bed** the bottom or floor of the sea; **sea beet** wild beet; **sea belt** another name for **sugar kelp**; **sea'bird** any marine bird; **sea biscuit** ship's biscuit, hardtack; **sea'blite** a salt-marsh plant (*Suaeda maritima*) of the goosefoot family; **sea blubber** a jellyfish. — *adj* **sea-blue'**. — **sea'board** the country or land bordering the sea. — Also *adj*. — **sea boat** a craft with reference to its seaworthiness in bad weather; **sea boots** long waterproof boots worn by sailors. — *adj* **sea'-born** produced by the sea. — *adj* **sea'borne** carried on or by the sea. — **sea'bottle** a translucent inflated seaweed (*Valonia*); bladderwrack; **sea bottom** the floor of the sea; **sea boy** (*Shakesp*) a sailor boy; **sea breach** an inroad of the sea; **sea bream** any fish of the *Sparidae* family, *esp Pagellus centrodontus* of European seas; also applied to any fish of the *Bramidae*, a family related to the mackerels; **sea breeze** a breeze from the sea, *esp* owing to convection in the daytime; **sea brief** see **sea letter** below; **sea buckthorn** a willow-like seaside shrub (*Hippophae rhamnoides*) of the family *Eleagnaceae*; **sea bun** a common name for the heart-urchin; **sea burdock** another name for clotbur (*Xanthium*); **sea butterfly** a pteropod, *Clione limacina*; **sea cabbage** sea kale; **sea calf** the common seal; **sea canary** the white whale; **sea cap** (*Shakesp*) a cap worn on shipboard; **sea captain** the captain of a merchant ship; **sea card** a compass card; a sea chart; **sea cat** a catfish; the great weever, a spring fish, *Trachinus draco*; the wolf fish or sea wolf, *Anarrhichas lupus*; a shark, *Scyllium catulus*; **sea change** (*Shakesp*) a change effected by the sea; a complete transformation; **sea chart**; **sea chest** a seaman's trunk; **sea cliff** a cliff fronting or formed by the sea; **sea coal** (*archaic*) coal in the ordinary sense, mineral coal not charcoal (possibly as first worked where exposed by the sea). — Also *adj*. — **sea'coast** the land adjacent to the sea; **sea cob** another name for a seagull; **sea'cock** a gurnard, a type of fish; a valve communicating with the sea through a vessel's hull; a bold sea rover; **sea colewort** sea kale; wild cabbage; **sea cook** a ship's cook (*son of a sea cook* being an abusive designation); **sea cow** the walrus (*archaic*); any sirenian, such as the dugong or manatee; the hippopotamus (*SAfr*; Du *zeekoe*); **sea'craft** skill in navigation; seamanship; any seagoing craft; **sea crow** a name of many birds, such as the skua, chough, cormorant; **sea cucumber** any burrowing echinoderm of the class *Holothuroidea*, with an elongated cucumber-like body, such as the trepang, bêche-de-mer; **sea dace** the bass; **sea devil** the devil fish (qv); **sea dog** a dogfish; the common or harbour seal (*old*); an old or experienced sailor; a pirate; a beast like a talbot with a dorsal fin and beaver's tail (*heraldry*); a luminous appearance over the horizon, presaging bad weather (cf **fog-bow**, **fog-dog**); **sea dotterel** another name for the turnstone; **sea dove** another name for the little auk; **sea dragon** any of various fishes, eg the dragonet and types of seahorse; **sea'drome** a floating aerodrome; **sea duck** any duck of the pochard group; **sea dust** dust deposited on the sea from a distant land; **sea eagle** any of several fish-eating eagles that live near the sea, such as *Haliaetus albicilla* the white-tailed eagle; **sea ear** an ormer (*Haliotis*); **sea eel** a conger; **sea egg** a sea urchin; **sea elephant** the elephant seal; **sea fan** an alcyonarian coral with a fanlike skeleton; **sea'farer** a traveller by sea, *usu* a sailor; **sea'faring**. — Also *adj*. — **sea feather** a feathery alcyonarian, the sea pen; **sea'-fight** a battle between ships at sea; **sea fir** a hydroid whose delicate branched structure resembles a fir; **sea'-fire** phosphorescence at sea; **sea fish** any salt-water or marine fish; **sea'-fish'er**; **sea'-fish'ing**; **sea floor** the bottom of the sea; **sea-floor spreading** (*geol*) the process by which new oceanic crust is generated at oceanic ridges by the convective upswelling of magma; **sea foam** the froth on the sea formed by the action of the waves; **sea fog** a fog on or coming from, the sea; **sea'folk** seafaring people; **sea'food** food got from the sea, *esp* shellfish; **sea'fowl** a seabird; **sea fox** another name for the thresher, or foxshark; **sea fret** a fog coming inland off the sea; **sea'front** the side of the land, of a town, or of a building that looks towards the sea; a promenade with its buildings fronting the sea; **sea froth** the foam of the sea; formerly, meerschaum; **sea furbelow** a brown seaweed (*Saccorhiza*) with a bulb of tentacular outgrowths above the primary holdfast; **sea gate** a seaward gate of a tidal basin, etc; an outlet to the sea; **sea gherkin** the sea cucumber, *Cucumaria saxicola*; **sea gillyflower** thrift; **sea ginger** millepore coral; **sea girdle** tangle, *esp Laminaria digitata*. — *adj* **sea'-girt** (*literary* and *poetic*) surrounded by sea. — **sea god** or **sea godd'ess** a god or goddess ruling over or dwelling in the sea. — *adj* **sea'-going** sailing on the seas; suitable for deep-sea voyages. — **sea gooseberry** a common ctenophore, *Pleurobranchia pileus*, like a gooseberry in shape; **sea gown** (*Shakesp*) a short-sleeved garment worn at sea; **sea grape** any plant of the genus *Ephedra*, or its fruit; seaside grape; another word for glasswort; gulfweed; (in *pl*) cuttlefish eggs in masses; **sea grass** a grass or grasslike plant growing by or in the sea, eg Enteromorpha, thrift, grasswrack, etc; **sea green** the bluish-green colour of some seas. — Also *adj* (**sea-green'**). — **sea-green incorruptible** a person sincerely and unshakably devoted to an ideal or purpose, *esp* in public life (*orig* used by Carlyle of Robespierre); **sea'gull** a gull; a casual dock-labourer not yet admitted to a union (*Austr* and *NZ*); a rugby player who hovers around the periphery of play waiting for the ball (*NZ*); **sea haar** a haar (qv). **sea hare** a tectibranch gasteropod, *Aplysia punctata*, with earlike tentacles; **sea'hawk** a skua; **sea heath** a wiry heath-like pink-flowered plant (*Frankenia laevis*) of salt marshes and chalk cliffs; **sea hedgehog** a sea urchin; a globe-fish; **sea'hog** a porpoise; **sea holly** a European plant, *Eryngium maritimum*, with spiny stems, that grows on seashores; **sea'horse** the fabulous hippocampus, a sea monster with the head and body of a horse and the tail of a fish; any marine fish of the genus *Hippocampus* with a prehensile tail and a horselike head, that swims in an upright position; the walrus (*archaic*); the hippopotamus (*obs*); **sea'-hound** dogfish; **sea ice**. — *adj* **sea'-island** (of cotton) of the kind grown on the islands off the coast of South Carolina. — **sea ivory** a lichen, *Ramalina siliquosa*, found on sea cliffs; **sea jelly** a jellyfish; **sea'kale** a fleshy, sea-green cruciferous seaside plant (*Crambe maritima*) cultivated for its blanched sprouts, eaten as food; **sea'kale beet** another name for chard; **sea'-keeping** maintenance of navigational control and stability, *esp* in rough seas; **sea king** a Viking chief who led raids on the coastal areas of Europe; a king of the merfolk; Poseidon or Neptune; **sea lace** a brown seaweed, *Chorda filum*; **sea lane** a navigable passage, delineated on charts, etc, between islands, ships, ice-floes, etc; an established route taken by ships at sea; **sea lark** any of various shore birds, eg the sandpiper; the rock pipit; **sea lavender** a salt-marsh plant of the plumbaginaceous genus *Limonium*; **sea law** maritime law, *esp* medieval customary law; **sea lawyer** (*naut slang*) a (low-ranking) sailor versed in the intricacies of maritime law, disputatiously standing on his rights, or finding fault with his superiors' decisions; a shark; **sea legs** ability to walk on a ship's deck when it is pitching; resistance to seasickness; **sea lemon** a type of sea slug, *Archidoris pseudoargus*, with a warty yellowish body; **sea lentil** gulfweed; **sea leopard** a spotted seal of the southern seas, *esp* of the genus *Ogmorhinus*; **sea letter** or **sea brief** formerly, a document listing a ship's place of origin and her cargo; a document issued to a neutral merchant vessel in wartime, allowing it to pass freely (also **sea pass** or **passport**); **sea lettuce** a seaweed, *Ulva lactuca*, with flat translucent green fronds, green laver (see under **laver**); **sea level** the mean level of the surface of the sea; **sea lily** see **crinoid**; **sea'line** a coastline; the sea horizon; **sea lion** a seal with external ears and with hind flippers turned forward; a lion with the tail of a fish (*heraldry*); **sea loach** a rockling; **sea loch** (*Scot*) a lakelike arm of the sea; **sea longworm** a nemertean worm (*Lineus*); **sea lord** (often with *caps*) a naval member of the Board of Admiralty, a division of the Ministry of Defence; **sea lung** a ctenophoran; **sea'maid** (*Shakesp*) a mermaid; **sea'man** a sailor; a man, other than an officer or apprentice, employed aboard ship; a merman. — *adj* **sea'manlike** showing good seamanship. — *adj* **sea'-manly** characteristic of a seaman. — **sea'manship** the art of handling ships at sea; **sea marge** or **margin** the shoreline; **sea'mark** a mark of tidal limit; any object serving as a guide to those at sea; **sea mat** hornwrack (*Flustra*), a common polyzoan like a flat horny seaweed; **sea maw** (now *Scot*) a sea-mew; **sea mell** an alleged variant of **sea mew**; **sea mew** any gull; **sea mile** a geographical or nautical mile; **sea milkwort** a primulaceous plant, *Glaux maritima*, of northern seashores, having small pink flowers; **sea monster** any huge maritime animal, *esp* fabulous; **sea moss** carrageen; seaweed; **sea'mount** a mountain under the sea of at least 3 000 ft; **sea mouse** an elliptical polychaet, *Aphrodite aculeata*, with coarse iridescent hairs and bristles along its sides; **sea nettle** a jellyfish; **sea nymph** a minor sea goddess; **sea oak** another name for **pod weed**; **sea onion** the sea squill; **sea orange** a large globose orange-coloured sponge (also called **sulphur sponge**); **sea otter** a N Pacific animal (*Enhydris lutris*) related to the true otters; its silvery brown fur, largely unobtainable since the widespread ban on otter-hunting; **sea owl** the lumpsucker; **sea parrot** another name for the puffin; **sea pass** see **sea letter** above; **sea passage** (the cost of) a journey by sea; **sea pen** a feather-like anthozoan coelenterate (*esp Pennatula*); a name for the squid's internal shell; **sea perch** a bass or other fish of the *Serranidae*; **sea pie** a baked dish of salt meat and vegetables eaten at sea; the oyster-catcher; **sea piece** a picture, poem or piece of music representing (a scene at) sea; **sea-pig** a porpoise; a dolphin; a dugong; **sea pike** a pike-like marine fish of various kinds — robalo, Belone, hake, etc; **sea pink** any of several perennial plants generally known as thrift; **sea'plane** an aeroplane with floats instead of wheels, for landing on water; **sea poacher** the pogge; **sea porcupine** another name for the globe fish (*Diodon*); **sea'port** a port or harbour on the sea; a place with such a harbour; **sea potato** another name for the heart-urchin, *Echinocardium cordatum*; **sea power** naval strength; a nation with great naval strength; **sea purse** the tough horny egg-case of certain sharks, skates or rays, a mermaid's purse; a small whirlpool formed by the meeting of two waves at an angle, dangerous to bathers (*US*); **sea purslane** see under **purslane**; **sea'-quake** a seismic disturbance at sea; **seaqua'rium** see **oceanarium**; **sea ranger** in the Girl Guide organization, a ranger who trains specially in seamanship and related matters; **sea'rat** a pirate; **sea raven** a large fish, *Hemitripterus americanus*, related to the bullhead; **sea reed** marram grass; **sea road** a designated route followed by ships, a sea lane; **sea robber** a pirate; **sea robin** an American fish (*esp* of the genus *Prionotus*) of the gurnard family, with red or brown colouring; **sea rocket** a fleshy cruciferous seaside plant (*Cakile*); **sea room** space to manoeuvre a ship safely; **sea rosemary** sea lavender; **sea rover** a pirate or pirate ship; **sea'-roving** piracy; **sea salmon** inaptly, coalfish or pollack; **sea salt** salt derived from seawater. — *adj* as salty as the sea. — **sea sand**; **sea satyre** a Spenserian sea monster; **sea'scape** a painting or photograph of the sea; **sea scorpion** a scorpion-fish, having a spiny head and fins; another name for the father-lasher (*Cottus scorpius*); **Sea Scout** a member of a marine branch of the Scout movement; **sea serpent** (*mythol*) an enormous marine animal of serpent-like form frequently seen and described by credulous sailors, imaginative landsmen and common liars; a sea snake; **sea shanty** same as **shanty**[2]; **sea'shell** the shell of a crustacean or mollusc; **sea'shore** the land immediately adjacent to the sea; the foreshore (*law*); **sea shrub** a sea fan. — *adj* **sea'sick** nauseous owing to the rolling movement of a vessel at sea; travel-worn (*Shakesp*). — **sea'sickness**; **sea'side** any area that borders the sea, *esp* one popular as a holiday resort. — Also *adj*. — **seaside grape** the grape tree (*Coccoloba*) or its fruit; **sea slater** a small crustacean, *Ligia oceanica*, resembling a woodlouse; **sea sleeve** a cuttlefish; **sea slug** a type of shell-less marine mollusc, a nudibranch; a sea cucumber; **sea snail** any snail-like marine gasteropod; an unctuous fish (*Liparis*) related to the lumpsucker; **sea snake** a snake that lives in the sea, *esp* of the very venomous family *Hydrophidae* of the Indian and Pacific oceans; a sea serpent; **sea snipe** the sandpiper; **sea'speak** (also with *cap*) a variety of English of restricted unambiguous vocabulary, used by mariners, navigators, etc for communication; **sea spider** a pycnogonid; **sea squill** a Mediterranean plant, *Urginea maritima*, of the lily family with an onion-like bulb, sea onion; **sea squirt** a marine animal shaped like a double-mouthed flask, an ascidian; **sea star** a starfish; **sea stick** a herring cured at sea; **sea storm**; **sea strand**; **sea surgeon** a tropical genus (*Acanthurus*) of spiny-finned fishes with a lancetlike spine ensheathed on each side of the tail; **sea swallow** a tern; the storm petrel; a flying fish; **sea swine** a porpoise; the ballan wrasse; **sea tangle** any of various kinds of brown seaweed, *esp* of genus *Laminaria*; **sea term** a nautical word; **sea trout** the salmon trout (*Salmo trutta*); extended to various other fishes of the genus *Cynoscion*, of US coastal waters; **sea turn** a gale from the sea; **sea turtle** a marine turtle; the black guillemot; **sea unicorn** a former name for the narwhal; **sea urchin** one of the *Echinoidea*, a class of echinoderms with a globular, ovoid, or heart-shaped, sometimes flattened body and shell of calcareous plates, without arms; **sea vampire** a giant ray, or devil-fish; **sea view** a view of the sea; a seascape; **sea wall** a wall to keep out the sea. — *adj* **sea'-walled** walled against or by the sea. — **sea'ware** seaweed; **sea'water** water of or from the sea; **sea wave**; **sea'way** progress through the waves; a heavy sea; a regular route taken by ocean traffic; an inland waterway on which ocean-going vessels can sail; **sea'weed** marine algae collectively; any marine alga; **sea whistle** a seaweed (*Ascophyllum nodosum*) whose bladders can be made into whistles; **sea'wife** a kind of wrasse; **sea wind**; **sea wing** a sail; **sea wolf** the wolf-fish; another name for the John Dory (also **loup de mer**, *lōō-də-mer*); the bass; the sea elephant (*obs*); a Viking; a pirate; **sea'woman** a mermaid; **sea'worm** any marine worm. — *adj* **sea'-worn** worn by the sea or by seafaring. — **sea'worthiness**. — *adj* **sea'worthy** (of a vessel) fit for sailing on the sea; able to endure stormy weather. — **sea wrack** coarse seaweeds of any kind; grasswrack. — **all at sea** totally disorganized; completely at a loss; **at full sea** at full tide; **at sea** away from land; on the ocean; disorganized, bewildered; **follow the sea** or **go to sea** to become a sailor; **heavy sea** a sea in which the waves run high; **molten sea** (*Bible*) the brazen laver of 1 Kings 7. 23–26; **short sea** a sea in which the waves are choppy, irregular, and interrupted; **the four seas** those bounding Great Britain; **the Seven Seas** see under **seven**. [OE *sǣ*; Du *zee*, Ger *See*, ON *sǣr*, Dan *sö*]

Seabee *sē'bē* (the letters *cb* phonetically represented), *n* a member of a US Navy *c*onstruction *b*attalion.

SEAC *sē'ak*, *abbrev*: School Examination and Assessment Council; South-East Asia Command.

seacunny *sē'kun-i*, *n* a lascar steersman or quartermaster. [Appar Pers *sukkānī*, from Ar *sukkān* rudder, confused with **sea** and **con**³]

seal¹ *sēl*, *n* a piece of wax, lead or other material, stamped with a device and attached as a means of authentication or attestation; a wafer, circular mark, or other substitute; a piece of wax, etc, stamped or not, used as a means of keeping something closed; the design stamped; an engraved stone or other stamp for impressing a device, or a trinket of similar form; an adhesive label, *esp* decorative, for a Christmas parcel, etc, sold for charity; a token or symbol to confirm a bargain, etc; any device which keeps something closed; an obligation to secrecy; an impression; a device to prevent the passage of a gas, air, water, etc; water in a gas-trap; a road surface sealed with bitumen, etc (*Austr* and *NZ*); an animal's, *esp* an otter's, footprint. — *vt* to put a seal on; to stamp; to fasten with a seal; to give confirmation of; to ratify; to close up, *esp* permanently or for a long time; to enclose; to decide, settle irrevocably; to set apart; to seal (a road surface) with bitumen, etc, to tarmac (*Aust* and *NZ*). — *vi* to set one's seal to something. — *n* **seal'ant** any device or (*esp* cement-like) substance used to seal a gap to prevent the passage of water, etc. — *adj* **sealed**. — *n* **seal'er** a person or thing that seals; a substance used to coat a surface for protection, impermeability, etc. — *n* **seal'ing**. — *adj* **sealed'-beam** (of car headlights) consisting of a complete unit sealed within a vacuum. — **sealed book** something beyond one's knowledge or understanding (also **closed book**); **seal'-engraving** the art of engraving seals; **seal'ing-wax** (also *obs* **seal'wax**) formerly beeswax, now *usu* a composition of shellac, turpentine, vermilion or other colouring matter, etc, for making decorative seals; **seal'-pipe** a dip-pipe; **seal ring** a signet-ring. — **Great Seal** (also without *caps*) the state seal of the United Kingdom; **Lord Privy Seal** formerly the keeper of the Privy Seal, now the senior cabinet minister without official duties; **Privy Seal** (also without *caps*) formerly, the seal appended to documents that were to receive, or did not require, authorization by the Great Seal, in Scotland used *esp* to authenticate royal grants of personal rights; **seal off** to make it impossible for any thing, person, to leave or enter (eg an area); **set one's seal to** or **on** to give one's authority or assent to; **the seals** symbolically the office of Lord Chancellor or of Secretary of State; **under seal** authenticated; **under sealed orders** under orders only to be opened at a stated time. [OFr *seel*, from L *sigillum*, dimin of *signum* a mark]

seal² *sēl*, *n* a member of the *Pinnipedia*, carnivorous marine mammals, *incl* the eared seals of the family *Otaridae* (sea lions and fur seals), and the true or earless seals of the family *Phocidae* (eg the grey seal, common seal, monk seal and elephant seal); sealskin. — *adj* made of seal or sealskin. — *vi* to hunt seals. — *n* **seal'er** a seal-fisher. — *n* **seal'ery** seal-fishery. — *n* **seal'ing**. — **seal'-fish'er** a hunter of seals; a sealing ship; **seal'-fish'ing**; **seal'point** a variety of Siamese cat, with a dark brown face, paws and tail; **seal rookery** a seals' breeding-place; **seal'skin** the prepared fur of the fur-seal, or an imitation (eg of rabbit-skin, or of mohair); a garment made of this. — Also *adj*. [OE *seolh* (genitive *sēoles*); ON *selr*]

seal³. Same as **seel**¹.

seal⁴ *sēl*, *vt* to tie up. — *n* a rope or chain for tying up an animal. [OE *sǣlan*, from *sāl* rope]

seal⁵. See **sale**².

seal⁶. See **seel**².

sealgh or **sealch** *selhh*, (*Scot*) *n* a seal (the animal). [**seal**²]

Sealyham *sēl'i-əm*, *n* (also without *cap*; in full **Sealyham terrier**) a long-bodied, short-legged, hard-coated terrier, first bred at *Sealyham* in Pembrokeshire.

seam¹ *sēm*, *n* a sewn join between edges of cloth; the turned-up edges of such a join on the wrong side of the work; the ornamentation of such a join; a piece of sewing work (*old*); a weld or other join between edges; a re-stitched surgical incision; a wrinkle; a stratum (of a mineral), *esp* if thin or valuable; (in cricket) seam bowling (*colloq*). — *vt* to join, provide, or mark with seams; to pick out the seams of. — *n* **seam'er** a person or thing that seams; a ball delivered by seam bowling (*cricket*). — *adj* **seam'less** without a seam or seams; unbroken, flowing (*fig*). — **seam allowance** (in dressmaking) the margin allowed for the seams along the edge of the pieces of a garment; **seam bowler**; **seam bowling** (*cricket*) bowling in which the seam of the ball is used in delivery to make the ball swerve in flight, or first to swerve and then to break in the opposite direction on pitching; **seaming lace** a lace, braid, etc, to insert in or cover seams; **seam'set** a tool for flattening seams in metal, etc; **seam welding** resistance welding of overlapping sheets of metal using wheels or rollers as electrodes; welding two pieces of sheet plastic along a line by dielectric heating. [OE *sēam*, from *sīwian* to sew; Du *zoom*, Ger *Saum*]

seam² or **seame** *sēm*, *n* grease (*Shakesp*); lard made from pork fat (*Scot* **saim** *sām*). — *vt* to grease. [OFr *saim*, OE *seime*; cf L *sagīna* stuffing, feasting]

seam³ *sēm*, (*obs* except *dialect*) *n* a pack-horse load (eg 8 bushels of grain, 9 pecks of apples, 120 lb of glass); a cartload. [OE *sēam* a burden, from LL *sauma*, from Gr *sagma* a pack-saddle]

seamster, **seamstress**, **seamstressy**. See **sempster**.

seamy *sē'mi*, *adj* having or showing seams; sordid; disreputable. — *n* **seam'iness**. — **seamy side** the wrong side of a garment (*Shakesp*); the disreputable, sordid or unpleasant side or aspect (of something, *esp* life). [**seam**¹]

sean *sēn*. Same as **seine**.

Seanad *shan'ədh* or **Seanad Eireann** *e'rən*, *n* the upper house of the legislature of the Republic of Ireland. [Irish, senate]

séance *sā'ās*, *n* a session or meeting of psychical researchers or spiritualists for the purpose of trying to contact the spirits of the dead or promote supernatural manifestations of various kinds. [Fr, from L *sedēre* to sit]

seannachie *shen'ə-hhē*, *n* a Highland or Irish genealogist and transmitter of family lore. — Also **seann'achy** or **senn'achie**. [Gaelic *seanachaidh*]

SEAQ or **Seaq** *sē'ak*, *abbrev*: Stock Exchange Automated Quotations.

seaquarium. See **oceanarium**.

sear¹ *sēr*, *n* the catch that holds a gun at cock or half-cock. — **tickle** or **tickled a th' sere** (*Shakesp*) ready to go off. [Cf OFr *serre*, from L *sera* a bar]

sear[2] *sēr*, *adj* (*poetic*) dry and withered (also **sere**); (*Spenser* **seare**) burning. — *vi* (rarely **sere**) to become sear. — *vt* to dry up; to scorch; to brand; to cauterize; to render callous or unfeeling. — *n* a mark of searing. — *adj* **seared**. — *n* **seared'ness**. — *n* and *adj* **sear'ing**. — *n* **sear'ness**. — **sear'ing-iron**. — **the sere, the yellow leaf** (*Shakesp*) the autumn of life. [OE *sēar* dry, *sēarian* to dry up; LGer *soor*, Du *zoor*]

searce *sûrs* or **search** *sûrch*, (*obs*) *vt* to sift. — *n* (*obs*) a sieve. [OFr *saas*; unexplained]

search *sûrch*, *vt* to explore all over in trying to find something; to examine closely; to examine for hidden articles; to ransack; to scrutinize (eg one's conscience); to probe; to penetrate all parts of (*archaic*); to put to the test; to seek (with *out*). — *vi* to make an examination, etc; to look or hunt (with *for*). — *n* the act or power of searching; a thorough examination; a quest; a search party (*obs*). — *adj* **search'able**. — *n* **search'er** a person who searches; a person appointed to search, eg a custom-house officer; an inspector of various kinds; a probe. — *adj* **search'ing** penetrating; thorough. — *adv* **search'ingly**. — *n* **search'ingness**. — *adj* **search'less** (*poetic*) unsearchable. — **search image** (*behav*) a predator's preconception of what its prey looks like and where it is to be found; **search'light** a lamp and reflector throwing a strong beam of light for illuminating a target or quarry by night; the beam of light so projected; **search party** a group of people sent out in search of somebody or something; **search warrant** a legal warrant authorizing the searching of a house, etc, *usu* by the police. — **right of search** the right of a warring country to search neutral ships for contraband of war; **search me** (*slang*) I don't know. [OFr *cerchier* (Fr *chercher*), from L *circāre* to go about, from *circus* a circle]

seare. See **sear**[2].

sease. See under **seize**.

season *sē'zn*, *n* one of the four natural divisions of the year, spring, summer, autumn and winter; the usual, natural, legal, or appropriate time, or time of year (for anything); any particular time; a limited period; a season ticket (*colloq*); seasoning (*obs*). — *vt* to mature; to temper, reduce somewhat; to bring into suitable condition, (eg wood by drying it out); to inure; to add herbs, spices, etc to, to make savoury, to flavour; to preserve from decay (*Shakesp*); to mature, confirm, imbue with the flavour of (*Shakesp*). — *vi* to become seasoned, mature or experienced. — *adj* **sea'sonable** appropriate to the particular season; timely. — *n* **sea'sonableness**. — *adv* **sea'sonably**. — *adj* **sea'sonal** according to the seasons; available only in certain seasons. — *n* **seasonal'ity** the quality of being seasonal. — *adv* **sea'sonally**. — *adj* **sea'soned**. — *n* **sea'soner**. — *n* **sea'soning** the process or act by which anything is seasoned; the process of acclimatization; herbs, spices, salt and pepper, added to food to improve its flavour; (in diamond-cutting) the charging of the laps or wheels with diamond-dust and oil; the process of coating dyed leather with liquid albumen. — *adj* **sea'sonless** without difference of seasons. — **seasonal affective disorder** (abbrev **SAD**) a depressive illness experienced by people in winter, thought to be due to the reduction in hours of daylight; **sea'soning-tub** a trough in which dough is set to rise; **season ticket** a ticket valid any number of times within a specified period. — **close** or **closed season** see under **close**[1]; **in season** ripe, fit and ready for use; (eg in the holiday trade) at the busiest time of the year; allowed to be killed; (of a bitch) ready to mate, on heat; fit to be eaten; **in season and out of season** at all times; **out of season** unripe, not normally grown; (eg in the holiday trade) at any other time than the busiest time of the year, or at the least busy time; inopportune. [OFr *seson* (Fr *saison*), from L *satiō*, *-ōnis* a sowing]

seasure. An obsolete spelling of **seizure**

seat *sēt*, *n* anything used or intended for sitting on; a chair, bench, saddle, etc; the part of a chair on which one sits; a mode of sitting, *esp* on horseback; a place where one may sit, in a theatre, church, etc, or a ticket for this; a right to sit; a parliamentary or local-government constituency; membership, eg of a committee; that part of the body or of a garment on which one sits; that on or in which something rests; site, situation; a place where anything is located, settled, or established; a post of authority; a throne; a capital city; station; a (*usu* country) abode, a mansion. — *vt* to place on a seat; to cause to sit down; to place in any situation, site, location, etc; to establish, fix; to assign a seat to; to provide with a seat or seats; to fit accurately; to make (a skirt, trousers, etc) baggy by sitting. — *vi* to sit or lie down (*obs*); to become baggy by sitting. — *adj* **seat'ed**. — *n* **seat'er** someone or something that seats. — *combining form* **-sea'ter** denoting a vehicle, sofa, etc, with seats for a specified number, as in *two-seater*. — *n* **seat'ing** the taking, provision, allocation or arrangement of seats; a supporting surface; fabric for covering seats. — *adj* **seat'less**. — **seat belt** (also **safety belt**) an adjustable belt for holding the occupant firmly in his or her aircraft seat, car seat, etc; **seat earth** a bed of clay underlying a coal seam; **seat rent** (*hist*) payment for a church sitting; **seat'-stick** a walking-stick that can be made to serve as a seat, a shooting-stick. — **by the seat of one's pants** instinctively, by intuition (*adj* **seat-of-the-pants'** instinctive); **lord of seat** a lord of Session; **lose one's seat** to fail to be re-elected to Parliament or local council; **take a seat** to sit down; **take one's seat** to take up one's allocated place, *esp* in Parliament. [ON *sǣti* seat; cf OE *sǣt* ambush]

SEATO *sē'tō*, *abbrev*: South-East Asia Treaty Organization.

seaward, seawardly, seawards. See under **sea**.

seaze. See **seize**.

sebaceous. See under **sebum**.

se-baptist *sē-bap'tist*, *n* a person who baptizes himself or herself. [L *sē* himself]

Sebat. See **Shebat**.

sebesten *si-bes'tən*, *n* an oriental boraginaceous tree (*Cordia*); its edible plumlike fruit; a preparation made from the fruit and used as medicine. [Ar *sabastān*]

sebum *sē'bəm*, *n* the fatty secretion that lubricates the hair and skin. — *adj* **sebaceous** (*si-bā'shəs*) like tallow; of, like, of the nature of, or secreting sebum. — *adj* **sebacic** (*-bas'*). — *n* **sebate** (*sē'bāt*) a salt of sebacic acid. — *adj* **sebif'erous** (*si-*) bearing fatty matter. — *adj* **sebif'ic** producing fatty matter. — *n* **seborrhoea** (*seb-ə-rē'ə*) excessive discharge of sebum from the sebaceous glands. — *adj* **seborrhoe'ic**. — **sebaceous cyst** a non-specific term for a cyst arising in a sebaceous gland (see also **steatoma, wen**); **sebaceous gland** a gland in the skin that secretes sebum; **sebacic acid** a dibasic acid, the esters of which are used in the production of resins and plasticizers. [L *sēbum* suet]

sebundy *si-bun'di*, *n* (in India) an irregular soldier or soldiers. [Urdu *sibandī*]

Sec. *abbrev*: Secretary.

sec[1] *sek*, *adj* (of wines) dry. [Fr]

sec[2] *sek*, *n* a secant; a second (of time) (*colloq*).

SECAM *sē'kam*, *abbrev*: *séquentiel couleur à mémoire* (*Fr*), a broadcasting system for colour television.

secant *sē'kənt* or *sek'ənt*, *adj* cutting. — *n* a cutting line; a straight line which cuts a curve in two or more places (*geom*); *orig* a straight line from the centre of a circle through one end of an arc to the tangent from the other end (*trig*); now (as a function of an angle) the ratio of the hypotenuse to the base of a right-angled triangle formed by dropping a perpendicular from a point on one side of the angle to the other (negative if the base is the side produced), in trigonometrical notation written **sec**. — *adv* **sec'antly**. [L *secāns*, *-antis*, pr p of *secāre* to cut]

secateurs *sek'ə-tûrz* or *-tûrz'*, *n pl* pruning-shears. [Pl of Fr *sécateur*, *from L secāre* to cut]

secco *sek'kō, adj (music)* unaccompanied; plain; (of wine, etc) dry. — *n* painting on dry plaster: — *pl* **sec'cos**. [Ital, dry, from L *siccus*]

secede *si-sēd', vi* to withdraw, *esp* from a party, religious body, federation, or the like. — *n* **secē'der** a country, etc which secedes; any of a body of Presbyterians (**Secession Church**) who seceded from the Church of Scotland about 1733. — *n* **secession** (*-sesh'ən*) the act of seceding; a body of seceders. — Also *adj*. — *adj* **secess'ional**. — *n* **secess'ionism**. — *n* **secess'ionist** a person who favours or joins in secession. — Also *adj*. — **War of Secession** the American Civil War. [L *sēcēdere, sēcēssum*, from *sē-* apart, and *cēdere* to go]

secern *si-sûrn', vt* to discriminate or distinguish; to secrete. — *n* and *adj* **secern'ent**. — *n* **secern'ment**. [L *sēcernere, sēcrētum* to separate]

secesher *si-sesh'ər*, or **secesh'**, (*US hist slang*) a secessionist (qv).

sech *sesh, n* a conventional abbrev of *h*yperbolic *sec*ant.

seckel or **seckle** *sek'l, n* a variety of pear. [From the American grower who originated it]

seclude *si-klood', vi* to shut off, *esp* from contact, association or influence. — *adj* **seclud'ed** kept apart from the rest of society; in a place not visible to, nor visited by, others, private (and *usu* quiet). — *adv* **seclud'edly**. — *n* **seclusion** (*si-kloo'zhən*) the act of secluding; the state of being secluded; retirement; privacy; solitude. — *n* **seclu'sionist**. — *adj* **seclu'sive** (*-siv*) tending to or favouring seclusion. [L *sēclūdere, -clūsum*, from *sē-* apart, and *claudere* to shut]

seco *sek'ō, (Sp) adj* (of wine) dry.

secodont *sek'ə-dont, (zool) adj* with cutting back teeth. — Also *n*. [L *secāre* to cut, and Gr *odous, odontos* tooth]

Seconal® *sek'ə-nəl, n* a hypnotic and soporific barbiturate.

second[1] *sek'ənd, adj* next after or below the first; other, alternate; additional; supplementary; another, as it were; inferior; subordinate; referring to the person or persons addressed (*gram*); singing or playing a part in harmony slightly below others of the same voice or instrument, as in *second soprano, second violin*; helpful, favouring (*obs*). — *adv* next after the first; in the second place, as the second matter, etc. — *n* a person or thing that is second or of the second class; a place in the second class or rank; a person who is second in rank, eg a Boy Scout or Cub Scout who is second-in-command in his patrol; second gear; a person who acts as an assistant to a boxer or duellist; a supporter; the 60th part of a minute of time, or of a minute of angular measurement (short form **sec**); a time interval variously measured (see under **atom**, **Ephemera**, **universe**): a very small amount of time (*colloq*; *esp* in short form **sec**); a second-class university degree (*colloq*); the second person (*gram*); the interval between successive tones of the diatonic scale (*music*); (in *pl*) goods of a second quality; (in *pl*) a second helping of food (*colloq*). — *vt* to follow; to act as second to (a boxer or a duellist); to back, give support to; to further; to assist; to encourage; to support (the mover of) a nomination or resolution; to sing or play second to (*music*); to follow up with another. — *adv* **sec'ondarily**. — *n* **sec'ondariness**. — *adj* **sec'ondary** subordinate; subsidiary; of lesser importance; of a second stage, *esp* of an electric circuit; not original, derivative; (of a disease or disorder) that results from or follows another; (of a voltage, magnetic field, etc) induced; (of education) between primary and higher or tertiary; (of a feather) growing in the second joint of the wing; (with *cap*; *geol*) Mesozoic, of the period between 225 million and 70 million years ago. — *n* a subordinate; a delegate or deputy; a feather growing in the second wing joint; a secondary colour; a malignant tumour that has spread from a primary cancer to another part of the body, a metastasis; (the coils and windings of) the second stage of a transformer, etc. — *n* **sec'onder** a person who seconds a motion, resolution, etc; a supporter; a member of a second group. — *adv* **sec'ondly** as regards the second matter. — **Second Advent** or **Second Coming** a second coming of Christ to earth; **second-ad'ventist** someone who expects a second coming of Christ; **secondary action** secondary picketing; **secondary alcohol** an alcohol containing the group CH·OH; **secondary battery** or **secondary cell** one on which the chemical action is reversible, and which can therefore be recharged; **secondary coil** one carrying an induced current; **secondary colour** one produced by mixing two primary colours; **secondary electron** an electron in a beam of secondary emission; **secondary emission** emission of electrons from a surface or particle caused by bombardment with electrons, etc, from another source; **secondary mineral** (*geol, min ext*) a mineral formed after the formation of the rock enclosing it; a mineral of minor interest in an ore-body undergoing exploitation; **secondary modern** formerly, a type of secondary school offering a less academic, more technical education than a grammar school (qv); **secondary picket**; **secondary picketing** the picketing by workers of a firm with which they are not directly in dispute but which has a trading connection with their own firm, in order to maximize the effects of a strike; **secondary production** (*ecol*) see **production**; **secondary (surveillance) radar** radar in which a responder is triggered by received pulses so that it retransmits a signal; **secondary school** any of various types of school for secondary education; **secondary sexual characteristics** (*zool*) features other than the reproductive organs which distinguish between the sexes; **secondary shut-down system** a system for shutting down a nuclear reactor should the control rods fail to do so; **secondary smoking** inhalation of tobacco smoke by non-smokers from smokers' cigarettes, etc, passive smoking; **second ballot** a system of election whereby a second vote is taken, the candidate or candidates who received fewest votes in the first ballot being eliminated; **second banana** a subordinate (*slang*; *orig* a vaudeville performer who played a secondary role). — *n* and *adj* **second-best'** next to the best (**come off second-best** to be in a position of disadvantage after a contest, to be the loser in a fight, etc). — **second chamber** in a legislature of two houses, the house with fewer powers, *usu* acting as a check on the other; **second childhood** mental weakness in extreme old age; **second class** the class next to, and in an inferior position relative to, the first. — *adj* **second-class'**. — **second-class citizen** a member of a group in the community which is not given the full rights and privileges enjoyed by the community as a whole; **second-class mail** or **post** mail sent at a cheaper rate either because of its character or because the sender is prepared to accept slower delivery; **second cousin** one who has the same pair of great-grandparents as oneself, but different grandparents; loosely, a first cousin's child, or a parent's first cousin (properly, first cousin once removed); **second degree** see under **degree**; **second floor** the floor above the first floor (see under **floor** for UK and NAm senses). — *adj* **sec'ond-floor**. — **second growth** a new growth of a forest after cutting, fire, etc; a second crop of grapes in a season. — *vt* and *vi* **sec'ond-guess'** (*colloq*; *orig US*) to judge, criticize, find fault with, using hindsight; to predict or anticipate (an action), or the future actions or behaviour of; to gain the advantage of, by forethought, anticipation, etc. — *adj* **second-hand'** derived from another; not original; already used by a previous owner; dealing in second-hand goods. — *adv* indirectly, at one remove; after use by a previous owner. — **second** (or **seconds**) **hand** a hand on a clock or watch that indicates seconds; **second home** a holiday home; a house owned in addition to one's main residence; a place where one feels as at home as in one's own house; **second-in-command'** the next under the commanding officer or other person in charge; **second-lieuten'ant** an army officer of lowest commissioned rank (formerly called an ensign or cornet); **second man** a man assisting the driver of a train (formerly, in steam trains, called the fireman); **second mate** or **second officer** an officer next in command to the first mate/officer on a merchant ship; **second mark** the character (″), used for seconds of arc or time or for inches; **second mortgage** a subsequent mortgage on an already-mortgaged property; **second nature** a deeply ingrained habit or tendency. — *adj* **second-rate**' inferior; mediocre. — **second-rat'er**; **second self** a person with whom one has the closest possible ties, almost intuitively sharing beliefs, attitudes, feelings and ways of behaving; **second sight** a gift of prophetic vision attributed to certain people, *esp* Scottish Highlanders; **seconds pendulum** a pendulum that makes one swing per second; **second storey** (*UK*) the first floor; **second strike** a counter-attack (in nuclear warfare) following an initial attack by an enemy. — *adj* **second-strike**' (of a nuclear weapon) specially designed so as to be ready to be used to strike back after a first attack by an enemy and to withstand such an attack. — **second string** an alternative choice, course of action, etc; **second thoughts** reconsideration. — *adj* **second-to-none**' supreme, best; unsurpassed. — **second wind** recovery of breath after a time, during prolonged exertion; the (former) Communist countries of the world regarded as a political and economic bloc. — **at second hand** through an intermediate source, indirectly; by hearsay; **every second** (**day**, **week**, etc) (on) alternate (days, weeks, etc), every other (day, week, etc). [Fr, from L *secundus*, from *sequī*, *secūtus* to follow]

second[2] *si-kond'*, *vt* to transfer (an officer) to another post or unit (*military*); to transfer (an employee) temporarily to another branch or company, *usu* to undertake some special task. — *n* **secondee** (*sek-on-dē'*) a person who is on secondment. — *n* **second'ment** temporary transfer to another position. [From the Fr phrase *en second* in the second rank (said of officers)]

seconde *si-kond'* or *sə-gɔ̃d* (*fencing*) *n* a position in parrying. [Fr]

secondo *si-kon'dō*, (*music*) *n* the lower part in a duet: — *pl* **secon'di** (*-dē*). [Ital]

sec. reg. *abbrev*: *secundum regulam* (*L*), according to the rule.

secret *sē'krət*, *adj* kept back from the knowledge of others; guarded against discovery or observation; unrevealed, unidentified; hidden; secluded; recondite, occult; preserving privacy. — *adv* (*poetic*) secretly. — *n* a fact, purpose, method, etc, that is kept undivulged; participation in the knowledge of such a fact; a nostrum (*obs*); anything unrevealed or unknown; the fact of being secret, secret quality, secrecy; a secret or private place (*obs*); a piece of armour hidden by clothes; the key or principle that explains or enables; an inaudible prayer, *esp* in the Mass; (in *pl*) external sex organs (*obs*). — *n* **secrecy** (*sē'krə-si*) the state or fact of being secret; concealment; seclusion; confidentiality; power or habit of keeping secrets; the keeping of secrets. — *n* **sē'cretage** treatment of furs with mercury before felting. — *vt* **secrete** (*si-krēt'*) to hide; to take away (*usu* an object) secretly; to form and emit by means of bodily functions (*biol* or *zool*). — *n* **secrē'tion** the act of secreting; that which is secreted, eg the substance produced by a gland; a mass of mineral matter formed by inward growth in a cavity. — *adj* **secrē'tional**. — *adj* **sē'cretive** (also *si-krē'tiv*) inclined to, fond of, secrecy; very reticent; indicative of secrecy. — *adv* **secretively**. — *n* **secretiveness**. — *adv* **sē'cretly** in secret; in concealment; (of prayers) inaudibly. — *n* **sē'cretness**. — *adj* **secrē'tory** (of a gland, etc) secreting. — **secret agent** someone employed in (the) secret service; **secret police** a police force which operates in secret, *usu* dealing with matters of politics, national security, etc; **Secret Service** a department of the US government service whose operations are covert, not disclosed; its activities; (without *caps*) espionage. — **in secret** with precautions against being known, found out, etc; in confidence, as a secret; secretly; **in on** (or **in**) **the secret** admitted to, participating in, or having knowledge of the secret; **keep a secret** not to divulge a secret; **of secret** (*Shakesp*) of a secret character; **open secret** see under **open**; **secret of** (or **secret de** *sə-krā də*) **Polichinelle** (Fr equivalent of the character Punchinello) something that is common knowledge. [L *sēcernere*, *sēcrētum*, from *sē-* apart, and *cernere* to separate]

secreta *si-krē'tə*, *n pl* products of secretion. [L, things secreted, neuter pl of *sēcrētus*, pa p of *sēcernere*; see **secret**]

secretaire *sek'ri-tār* or *sek-rə-ter'*, *n* a cabinet folding out to form a writing desk, an escritoire. — **secretaire à abattant** (*a a-ba-tã*) a writing cabinet with a desk flap that closes vertically. [Fr; cf **secretary**]

secretary *sek'ri-tə-ri*, *n* a person who types and deals with correspondence, and does general clerical and administrative work for a company or individual; a person employed to write or transact business for a society, company, etc; the minister at the head of certain departments of state; an ambassador's or government minister's assistant; a writing desk, a secretaire; secretary hand; secretary type. — *adj* **secretarial** (*-tār'i-əl*). — *n* **secretā'riat** or **secretā'riate** (*-ət*) secretaryship; a secretary's office; the administrative department of a council, organization, legislative or executive body; a body of secretaries. — *n* **sec'retaryship** the office, duties, or skills of a secretary. — **secretary bird** a long-legged snake-eating African bird of prey (*Serpentarius*), said to be named from the tufts of feathers at the back of its head like pens stuck behind the ear; **secretary-gen'eral** the chief administrator of an organization, eg the United Nations; **secretary hand** an old legal style of handwriting; **Secretary of State** a cabinet minister holding one of the more important folios; in the US, the foreign secretary; **secretary type** a type in imitation of secretary hand. [ME *secretarie*, from LL *sēcrētārius*, from L *sēcrētum*; see **secret**]

secrete, etc. See under **secret**.

secretin *si-krē'tin*, (*physiol*) *n* a hormone secreted by the duodenum, that stimulates the liver and pancreas. [L *sēcrētus*, pa p of *sēcernere* (see **secret**), and **-in**]

sect[1] *sekt*, *n* a body of followers, *esp* of an extreme political movement; a school of opinion, *esp* in religion or philosophy; a subdivision of one of the main religious divisions of mankind; an organized denomination, used *esp* by members of the established churches to express their disapproval of the less established or smaller; a dissenting body; a party; a class of people; a sex (*old*). — *adj* **sectā'rial** distinguishing a sect (*esp* in India). — *adj* **sectā'rian** of or pertaining to a a sect, or between sects; (of a crime, *esp* a murder) motivated solely by a hatred derived from religious bigotry; narrow, exclusive, rigidly adhering to the beliefs of a given sect; denominational. — *n* a member of a sect; a person strongly imbued with the characteristics of a sect, *esp* if bigoted. — *n* **sectā'rianism**. — *vt* **sectā'rianize** or **-ise**. — *n* **sectary** (*sek'tə-ri*) a follower, a votary; a member of a sect; a dissenter from the established faith. — *n* **sectā'tor** (*rare*) an adherent of a school or party. [L *secta* a school or following, from *sequī*, *secūtus* to follow, infl by *secāre* to cut]

sect[2] *sekt*, *n* (*Shakesp*) a cutting. — *adj* **sectile** (*sek'tīl*) capable of being cut with a knife without breaking. — *n* **sectil'ity**. [L *secāre*, *sectum* to cut]

sect. *abbrev*: section.

section *sek'shən*, *n* the act of cutting; a division; a portion; one of the parts into which anything may be considered as divided or of which it may be composed; the line of intersection of two surfaces; the surface formed when a solid is cut by a plane; an exposure of rock in which the strata are cut across (*geol*); a numbered subdivision in a body of law; a plan of anything represented as if cut by a plane or other surface; a thin slice for microscopic examination of a specimen; the act or process of cutting or the cut or division made (*surg*); a one-mile square of American public lands; a subdivision of a company, platoon, battery, etc; a number of men detailed for a special service; a district or region (*US*);

a subdivision of an orchestra or chorus, containing (players of) similar instruments or singers of similar voice; a frame for a honeycomb; a section mark (*printing*); a building plot (*NZ*). — *vt* to divide into sections; to draw a sectional plan of; to cut a section through (*surg*); to have (a person suffering from mental illness) confined in a mental hospital under the relevant section of mental health legislation. — *adj* **sec'tional** of a section; in section; of sectionalism; built up of sections. — *n* **sec'tionalism** a narrow-minded concern for the interests of a group, area, etc, at the expense of the general or long-term; class spirit. — *adj* **sec'tionalist** (also *n*). — *n* **sectionalizā'tion** or **-s-**. — *vt* **sec'tionalize** or **-ise** to make sectional; to divide into sections. — *adv* **sec'tionally**. — *n* **sectionizātion** or **-s-**. — *vt* **sec'tionize** or **-ise** to section; to cut sections or slices from (*bot*, etc). **sec'tion-cutter** an instrument for making sections for microscopic work; **section mark** the sign §, used to mark the beginning of a section of a book or as a reference mark. [L *sectiō*, *-ōnis*, from *secāre*, *sectum* to cut]

sector *sek'tər*, *n* a plane figure bounded by two radii and an arc; an object of similar shape, *esp* one for measuring angular distance (*astron*); a length or section of a fortified line, army front, guarded area, etc; a mathematical instrument consisting of two graduated rules hinged together, *orig* with a graduated arc; a telescope turning about the centre of a graduated arc; a division, section, eg of a nation's economic operations (as in *private* and *public sector*) or of military operations. — *vt* to divide into sectors. — *adj* **sec'toral**. — *adj* **sectorial** (*-tō'ri-əl* or *-tö'*) sectoral; adapted for cutting (*zool*). — *n* a tooth designed for flesh-eating; a vein in the wings of insects. — *n* **sectoriza'tion** or **-s-**. — *vt* **sec'torize** or **-ise** to divide into sectors. — **sector scan** (*radar*) a scan in which the antenna moves through only a limited sector. [L *sector*, from *secāre*, *sectum* to cut]

secular *sek'ū-lər*, *adj* pertaining to, or coming or observed once in, a lifetime, generation, century or age (in ancient Rome about 100 to 120 years); pertaining to the present world, or to things not spiritual; civil, not ecclesiastical; lay, not concerned with religion; (of clergy) not bound by monastic rules (as opposed to *regular*); of the secular clergy; lasting for a long time; age-long; age-old; appreciable only in the course of ages or over an extended period; occurring in cycles. — *n* a layman; a clergyman, such as a parish priest, not bound by monastic rules. — *n* **sec'ularism** the belief that the state, morals, education, etc, should be independent of religion; G J Holyoake's (1817–1907) system of social ethics. — *n* and *adj* **sec'ularist**. — *adj* **secularist'ic**. — *n* **secularity** (*-lar'*). — *n* **secūlarīzā'tion** or **-s-**. — *vt* **sec'ularize** or **-ise** to make secular. — *adv* **sec'ularly**. — **secular arm** the civil power, authority or courts; **secular games** (*Roman hist*) games held at long intervals; **secular hymn** a hymn for the secular games. [L *saeculāris*, from *saeculum* a lifetime, generation]

seculum. See **saeculum**.

secund *sē'kund*, also *sek'und* or *si-kund'*, *adj* (*bot*) (of eg leaves) all turned to or positioned on the same side. — *n* **sec'undine** (*-in* or *-īn*) the inner (rarely outer and second-formed) coat of an ovule; (in *pl*) the afterbirth. — **secundogeniture** (*-jen'*) inheritance of or by a second child or son. [L *secundus* following, second]

secundum *si-kun'dum* or *se-ko͞on'do͞om*, (*L*) following, according to. — **secundum artem** (*är'tem*) scientifically; professionally; **secundum regulam** according to rule (*abbrev* **sec. reg.**); **secundum ordinem** (*ör'di-nem*) in order; **secundum quid** (*kwid*) in some respects only.

secure *si-kūr'*, *adj* without care or anxiety; free from danger; safe; confident; over-confident, careless (*archaic*); assured; providing safety; stable; firmly fixed or held; in (police, etc) custody. — *adv* (*poetic*) in security. — *vt* to make safe or certain; to assure the possession of; to establish in security; to prevent (*obs*); to seize and guard; to get hold of; to contrive to get; to plight or pledge (*obs*); to guarantee; to fasten. — *vi* to make sure; to be, or make oneself, safe. — *adj* **secūr'able**. — *n* **secūr'ance** (*rare*). — *adv* **secure'ly**. — *n* **secure'ment**. — *n* **secure'ness**. — *n* **secūr'er**. — *n* **secūr'itan** (*obs*) someone who dwells in fancied security. — *n* **securitizā'tion** or **-s-** the procedure, practice or policy of making loans, mortages, etc into negotiable securities. — *vt* **secur'itize** or **-ise** to make (debts) into securities. — **secūr'ity** the state, feeling, or means of being secure; over-confidence, carelessness (*archaic*); protection from espionage, theft, attack, etc; staff providing such protection, etc; certainty; a pledge; a guarantee, a surety; a right conferred on a creditor to make him or her sure of recovering a debt; (*usu* in *pl*) a bond or certificate in evidence of debt or property. — *adj* providing security. — **secure unit** a government-run institution for the confinement of difficult or mentally disordered persons, juvenile offenders, etc; **security blanket** a blanket, piece of material, etc, that a child comes to depend upon for a sense of comfort and security; something that (irrationally) makes one feel secure or happy (*fig*); an official set of measures, a policy, etc, applied to conceal a matter of (often national) security; **Security Council** a body of the United Nations consisting of five permanent members (China, France, Russia, UK, USA, each with the right of veto) and six elected two-yearly members, charged with the maintenance of international peace and security; **security risk** a person considered from his or her political affiliations or leanings to be likely to divulge (*esp* state) secrets. [L *sēcūrus*, from *sē-* without, and *cūra* care]

securiform *si-kū'ri-förm*, *adj* axe-shaped. [L *secūris* axe, from *secāre* to cut, and **-form**]

Securitate *si-kūr-tä'tā*, *n pl* the secret police of Romania.

Secy *abbrev*: Secretary.

SED *abbrev*: Scottish Education Department.

sed, **se'd**. Miltonic spellings of **said** (*pa t* and *pa p*).

sedan *si-dan'*, *n* a covered chair for one person, carried on two poles (also **sedan chair**; *hist*); a litter; a palanquin; a large closed motor car, a saloon-car (*NAm* and *NZ*). [Appar not connected with *Sedan* in France; poss Ital *sedere* to sit]

sedate *si-dāt'*, *adj* composed; dignified or staid; slow in a boring or dignified way. — *vt* to calm or quieten by means of sedatives. — *adv* **sedāte'ly**. — *n* **sedāte'ness**. — *n* **sedā'tion** the act of calming, or state of being calmed, *esp* by means of sedatives. — *adj* **sedative** (*sed'ə-tiv*) calming; composing; allaying excitement or pain. — *n* a sedative drug or agent. [L *sēdātus*, pa p of *sēdāre* to still]

se defendendo *sē di-fen-den'dō* or *sā de-fen-den'dō*, (*L*) *adv* in self-defence.

sedent *sē'dənt*, *adj* seated. — *adv* **sedentarily** (*sed'ən-tər-i-li*). — *n* **sed'entariness**. — *adj* **sed'entary** sitting much and taking little exercise; requiring much sitting; inactive; stationary; not migratory; (eg of a spider) lying in wait, for prey, etc; (of animals) attached to a rock or other surface, and so moving very little (*zool*). — **sedentary soil** soil remaining where it was formed. [L *sedēns*, *-entis* (pr p), and *sedentārius*, from *sedēre* to sit]

Seder *sā'dər*, (*Judaism*) *n* the ceremonial meal and its rituals on the first night or first two nights of the Passover. [Heb, order]

sederunt *si-dē'runt*, *si-dā'rənt* or *sā-dā'ro͝ont*, *n* (in Scotland) a sitting, as of a court; a list of persons present. — **Acts of Sederunt** ordinances of the Court of Session. [L *sēdērunt* there sat (the following persons), from *sedēre* to sit]

sedes *sē'dēz* or *sed'ās*, (*L*) *n* a seat. — **sedes impedita** (*im-pə-dī'tə* or *im-ped'i-ta*) a papal or episcopal see where there is a partial cessation by the incumbent of his episcopal duties; **sedes vacans** (*vā'kənz*, *va'* or *wa'kanz*), also **sede vacante** (*sē'dē və-kan'ti*, *sed'e va-* or *wa-kan'te*; *ablative absolute*) a term of canon law to designate a papal or episcopal see when vacant.

sedge[1] *sej, n* any species of *Carex* or other plant of the *Cyperaceae*, a family distinguished from grasses by its solid triangular stems and leaf-sheaths without a slit; extended to iris and other plants; (also **sedge fly**) any of several mayflies or caddis flies common along rivers; an artificial fishing fly resembling a sedge fly. — *adj* **sedged** of sedge; bordered with sedge. — *adj* **sedg'y** of, like, or abounding with sedge. — **sedge'land**; **sedge warbler** (also **sedge bird** or **sedge wren**) a common British warbler of watery places. [OE *secg*; cf LGer *segge*]

sedge[2] *sej, n* See **siege**.

sedigitated *sē-dij'i-tā-tid, adj* six-fingered. [L *sēdigitus*, from *sex* six, and *digitus* finger]

sedilia *si-dil'i-ə, n pl* seats (*usu* three, often in niches) for the officiating clergy, on the south side of the chancel: — *n sing* **sedile** (*si-dī'li, se-dē'le*). [L *sedīle* (pl *sedīlia*) seat]

sediment *sed'i-mənt, n* solid matter that settles at the bottom of a liquid; dregs; a deposit; material deposited by water, wind or ice and formed into rock (*geol*). — *vt* to deposit as sediment; to cause or allow to deposit sediment. — *adj* **sedimentary** (*-men'tər-i*). — *n* **sedimentā'tion** deposition of sediment; the formation of sedimentary rocks. — *adj* **sedimentolog'ical**. — *n* **sedimentol'ogist**. — *n* **sedimentol'ogy** the study of sedimentary rock (*geol*). — **sedimentary rocks** those formed by accumulation and deposition of fragmentary materials or organic remains. [L *sedimentum*, from *sedēre* to sit]

sedition *si-dish'ən, n* insurrection (*archaic*); public speech or actions intended to promote disorder; vaguely, any offence against the state short of treason. — *n* **sedi'tionary** an inciter to sedition; inducement to attempt, otherwise than by lawful means, alteration in church or state. — *adj* **sedi'tious**. — *adv* **sedi'tiously**. — *n* **sedi'tiousness**. [OFr, from L *sēditiō, -ōnis*, from *sēd-* away, and *īre, itum* to go]

seduce *si-dūs', vt* to draw aside from party, belief, allegiance, service, duty, etc; to lead astray; to entice; to corrupt; to induce to have sexual intercourse. — *n* **sedūce'ment** the act of seducing or drawing aside; allurement. — *n* **sedū'cer** someone who seduces, *esp* in the sexual sense. — *n* and *adj* **sedū'cing**. — *adv* **sedū'cingly**. — *n* **seduction** (*si-duk'shən*) the act or practice of seducing; allurement. — *adj* **seduc'tive** tending or intended to seduce; alluring. — *adv* **seduc'tively**. — *n* **seduc'tiveness**. — *n* **seduc'tor** (*obs*) someone who seduces or misleads. — *n* **seduc'tress** a female seducer. [L *sēdūcere, sēductum*, from *sē-* aside, and *dūcere* to lead]

sedulous *sed'ū-ləs, adj* assiduous or diligent; painstaking. — *n* **sedulity** (*si-dū'li-ti*) or **sed'ulousness**. — *adv* **sed'ulously**. [L *sēdulus*, from *sē dolō* without deception, hence in earnest]

sedum *sē'dəm, n* any rock plant of the genus *Sedum*, with white, yellow or pink flowers. [L *sedum* houseleek]

see[1] *sē, vt* to perceive by the sense seated in the eye; to perceive mentally; to apprehend; to recognize; to realize; to understand; to learn; to be aware by reading; to look at; to judge, to deem; (with *in*) to find attractive about; to refer to; to ascertain; to regard as likely, or possible; to make sure of having; to wait upon, escort; to spend time with, or meet with regularly, *esp* romantically; to call on; to receive as a visitor; to meet; to consult; to experience; to witness; to meet and accept (another's bet) by staking a similar sum; to spend on seeing (*obs*; with *away*). — *vi* to have power of vision; to see things well enough; to look or inquire; to be attentive; to await further developments, to postpone any decision until more thought has been given to the matter; to consider: — *pa t* **saw** (also *illiterate* or *dialect* **see**, **seed** and **seen**); *pa p* **seen**. — *imperative* (in prefatory reference to a person or thing to be commented on) consider as an example, take, as in *See my brother, he's a great worker* (*colloq, esp Scot*); (passing into *interj*) look, behold. — *n* an act of seeing, a look. — *adj* **see'able**. — *n* **see'ing** sight; vision; clear-sightedness; atmospheric conditions for good observation (*astron*). — *adj* having sight, or insight; observant; discerning. — *conj* (also **seeing that**) since; in view of the fact that. — *n* **seer** (*sē'ər*) a person who sees; (*sēr*) a person who sees into the future: — *fem* **seer'ess**. — **see'ing stone** a scrying crystal. — *adj* **see'-through** (*esp* of fabrics) transparent. — **have seen better days** or **one's best days** to be now on the decline; **let me see** a phrase employed to express reflection; **see about** to consider; to do whatever is to be done about; to attend to; **see fit** to think it appropriate (to); **see in** to witness, greet, or celebrate the arrival of; **see off** to accompany (someone) at their departure; to reprimand (*slang*); to get rid of (*colloq*); **see one's way clear to** (*colloq*) to feel that one will be able to; **see out** to conduct to the door; to see to the end; to outlast; **see over** or **round** to look or be conducted all through (eg premises, property); **see red** see under **red**[1]; **see someone right** (*colloq*) to take care of someone, *usu* in the sense of giving them a tip or reward; **see the light** to experience a religious conversion; to come round to another's way of thinking, to come to understand and agree with someone (*usu facetious*); **see the back of** to be rid of or finished with (someone or something unpleasant, difficult, etc); **see things** see under **thing**; **see through** to participate in to the end; to back up till difficulties end; to understand the true nature of, *esp* when faults or bad intentions are concealed by a good appearance; **see to** to look after; to make sure about; **see what I can do** do what I can; **see you (later)** or **be seeing you** (*colloq*) goodbye for now; **well (or ill) seen** well (or ill) versed. [OE *sēon*; Ger *sehen*, Du *zien*]

see[2] *sē, n* a seat, *esp* of dignity or authority (*obs*); a throne, *esp* a bishop's (*archaic*); the office of bishop of a particular diocese; (wrongly according to some) a cathedral city, also a diocese. — **Holy See** the papal court. [OFr *se, sied*, from L *sēdēs, -is*, from *sedēre* to sit]

see[3] *sē, n* the third letter of the alphabet (C, c).

seecatch *sē'kach, n* an adult male Aleutian fur seal: — *pl* **see'catchie**. [Russ *sekach*, prob from Aleutian Indian]

seed[1] *sēd, n* a multicellular structure by which flowering plants reproduce, consisting of embryo, stored food, and seed-coat, derived from the fertilized ovule (*bot*); a small hard fruit or part in a fruit, a pip; a seedlike object or aggregate; semen (*literary* or *poetic*); spawn; the condition of having or proceeding to form seed; sown land; grass and clover grown from seed; a first principle; origin, beginning or germ; a crystal introduced to start crystallization; offspring, descendants, race; a small bubble in glass; a tournament player who has been seeded (*colloq*). — *vi* to produce seed; to run to seed. — *vt* to sow; to sprinkle, powder, dust; to remove seeds from; (in sports tournaments) to arrange (the draw) so that the best players do not meet in the early rounds; to deal with (the best players) in this way; to introduce particles of material (into something, eg a chemical solution) to induce crystallization or precipitation; *specif*, to induce rainfall, disperse a storm or freezing fog, etc, by scattering cloud with particles of an appropriate substance (also **cloud-seeding**). — *adj* **seed'ed** with the seeds removed; having seeds; bearing seed; full-grown; sown; showing seeds or carpels (*heraldry*); (of a tournament player) who has been seeded. — *n* **seed'er** a seed-drill; an apparatus for removing seeds from fruit; a seed-fish. — *adv* **seed'ily**. — *n* **seed'iness**. — *n* and *adj* **seed'ing**. — *adj* **seed'less**. — *adj* **seed'like**. — *n* **seed'ling** a plant reared from the seed; a young plant ready for planting out from a seedbed; a seed oyster. — Also *adj*. — *n* **seed'ness** (*obs*) sowing. — *adj* **seed'y** abounding with seed; having the flavour of seeds; not cleared of seeds; run to seed; worn out; out of sorts; shabby. — **seed bank** (*bot*) the total viable seed content of the soil; a collection of seeds in long-term storage, which can be germinated as required for breeding and study; **seed'bed** a piece of ground for receiving seed; an environment, etc, that fosters a particular thing (*esp* something considered undesirable); **seed'box** or **seed'case** a part of a plant in which the seeds are encased; **seed'cake** a cake flavoured with caraway seeds; **seed capital** (*finance*) capital provided to allow a new company to finance the costs of producing the business plan necessary to raise further capital for development; **seed'-coat** the hard protective covering of the seeds of flowering plants, the testa; **seed'-coral** coral in small irregular pieces; **seed'-corn** grain for sowing; assets likely to bring future profit; **seed'-drill** a machine for sowing seeds in rows; **seed'-field** a field in which seed is sown; **seed'-fish** a fish about to spawn; **seed'-lac** granular residues of lac after trituration; **seed'-leaf** a cotyledon, a leaf contained in a seed; **seed'lip** a sower's basket (OE *sǣdlēap* from *lēap*, *basket*); **seed'-lobe** a cotyledon; **seed money** money with which a project or enterprise is set up, seed capital; **seed'-oil** oil expressed from seeds; **seed'-oyster** a very young oyster; **seed'-pearl** a very small pearl; **seed'-plant** a spermatophyte or flowering plant; a plant grown from or for seed; **seed'-plot** a piece of nursery ground, a hotbed; **seed'-potato** a potato tuber for planting; **seeds'man** a dealer in seeds; a sower; **seed'-stalk** the funicle; **seed'-time** the season for sowing seeds; **seed'-vessel** a dry fruit; the ovary of a flower; **seed'y-toe** a disease of a horse's foot. — **go** or **run to seed** to grow rapidly and untidily in preparation for seeding, instead of producing the vegetative growth desired by the grower; to disappoint expectation of development; to become exhausted; to go to waste; (*usu* **go**) to become unkempt, shabby; **sow the seed(s) of** to initiate or engender. [OE *sǣd*; cf *sāwan* to sow; ON *sāth*; Ger *Saat*]

seed². See **see¹**.

seek *sēk*, *vt* to look for; to try to find, get, or achieve; to ask for; to aim at; to resort to, betake oneself to; to advance against; to try; to search, examine (*archaic*). — *vi* to make a search; to resort (*obs*): — *pa t* and *pa p* **sought** (*söt*). — *n* **seek'er** a person who seeks; an inquirer; a dissector's probing instrument; a telescopic finder; (with *cap*) a member of a 17c sect who sought for the true church. — **seek-no-furth'er** a reddish winter apple. — **seek after** to go in quest of; **seek for** to look for; **seek out** to look for and find; to find after much searching; to bring out from a hidden place; **sought after** in demand; **to seek** not to be found; lacking; at a loss to know (*archaic*; eg *What real good is, I am to seek*); defective (in; *archaic*). [OE *sēcan* (pa t *sōhte*, pa p *gesōht*); cf Ger *suchen*]

seel¹ *sēl*, *vt* to sew up the eyelids of (eg a hawk); to blindfold; to blind, hoodwink. [OFr *siller*, *ciller*, from *cil*, from L *cilium* eyelid, eyelash]

seel², **sele** or **seal** (*Scot* **seil**) *sēl*, (*dialect*) *n* happiness; good fortune; opportune time; season; time of day. — *adj* **seel'y** fortunate, happy, good (*obs*); simple, innocent (*Spenser*); pitiful, wretched, trifling; to be pitied, poor (*obs*); foolish (see **silly**). — **pass the seel of the day** to greet in passing. [OE *sǣl* time, due time, happiness; see **silly**]

seel³ *sēl*, (*naut* and *obs*) *vi* to heel over suddenly. — *n* a sudden heeling. [Origin obscure]

seeld *sēld*, **seeling**. Spenserian forms of **seld**, **ceiling**.

seely. See under **seel²**.

seem *sēm*, *vi* to appear; to appear to one; to appear to be; to be fitting (*obs*). — *vt* (*archaic*) to beseem, befit. — *n* **seem'er**. — *n* **seem'ing** appearance; semblance; a false appearance. — *adj* apparent; ostensible. — *adv* apparently; in appearance only (*esp* in combination, eg **seem'ing-sim'ple, seem'ing-virtuous**). — *adv* **seem'ingly** apparently; as it would appear. — *n* **seem'ingness**. — *adj* **seeme'lesse, seem'less** (*Spenser*) unseemly; indecorous. — *n* **seem'lihed** or **seem'lihead** (*Spenser* **seem'lyhed**) seemliness. — *n* **seem'liness**. — *adj* **seem'ly** (*compar* **seem'lier**; *superl* **seem'liest**) becoming; suitable; decent; handsome. — Also *adv* (*archaic*). — **it seems** it appears; it would seem; **it would seem** it turns out; I have been told. [ON *sǣma* to beseem]

seen. See **see¹**.

seep *sēp*, *vi* to ooze, percolate. — *n* a place or area where water or other liquid has oozed through the ground, seepage. — *n* **seep'age** the action of seeping; water or other liquid that has seeped. — *adj* **seep'y**. [Cf **sipe¹**]

seer¹ *sēr*, *n* an Indian weight of widely ranging amount, officially about 2 lb. [Pers *sīr*]

seer², **seeress**. See under **see¹**.

seer³. See **seir**.

seersucker *sēr'suk-ər*, *n* a thin crinkly Indian linen (or cotton) striped or checked fabric. [Pers *shīr o shakkar* literally milk and sugar]

seesaw *sē'sö*, *n* alternate up-and-down or back-and-forth motion; repeated alternation; a playground device, a plank balanced at its centre so that children sitting on either end can rise and sink alternately; the activity of rising and sinking on it. — *adj* (moving up and down) like a seesaw. — *adv* in the manner of a seesaw. — *vi* to play at seesaw; to move or go like a seesaw. — *vt* to make (something) go up and down like a seesaw. [Prob a reduplication of **saw²**, from a sawyer's jingle, from *See saw sack a down*]

seethe *sēdh*, *vi* to boil; to surge (*lit* or *fig*); to be agitated (by anger, excitement, etc). — *vt* to boil; to soak to a condition similar to that produced by boiling: — *pa t* **seethed** or (*archaic*) **sod**; *pa p* **seethed** or (*archaic*) **sodd'en**. — *n* **seeth'er**. — *n* and *adj* **seeth'ing**. [OE *sēothan* (pa t *sēath*, pl *sudon*; pa p *soden*); ON *sjōtha*, Ger *sieden*]

seewing. A Spenserian spelling of **suing** (see **sue**).

seg¹ *seg*, (*obs* or *dialect*) *n*. Same as **sedge¹**.

seg² *seg*, *n* a stud or small metal plate in the sole of a shoe to protect it from wearing down, *esp* at the toe or heel; a callus, *esp* at the base of the finger (*NW Eng dialect*). [ON *sigg* hard skin, a callus]

segar *si-gär'*, *n* a variant of **cigar**.

seggar. See **saggar**.

Seger cones *sāgər* or *zā'gər kōnz*, *n pl* (*eng*) small clay and oxide cones, used in furnaces to indicate the temperature reached, by softening and bending over within a particular temperature range.

seghol or **segol** *se-gōl'*, *n* a vowel-point in Hebrew with the sound of *e* in *pen*, placed under a consonant, thus (∴). — *n* **segh'ōlate** or **seg'ōlate** a disyllabic noun form with a tone-long vowel in the first and a short seghol in the second syllable. [Heb]

segment *seg'mənt*, *n* a part cut off; a portion; part of a circle, ellipse, etc, cut off by a straight line, or of a sphere, ellipsoid, etc, by a plane; a section; one of a linear series of similar portions, eg of a vibrating string between nodes, a somite or metamere of a jointed animal, or a joint of an appendage; a lobe of a leaf-blade not separate enough to be a leaflet; the smallest sound unit of speech (*phonetics*). — *vt* and *vi* (also *-ment'*) to divide or cut into segments. — *adj* **segmental** (*-ment'l*) of a segment; by segments; forming or formed of a segment, segments, arc, or arcs. — *adv* **segmen'tally**. — *adj* **seg'mentary** or **seg'mentate**. — *n* **segmentā'tion** the act or process of dividing into segments; an instance of this; the process of repeated cell division in a fertilized ovum, initially forming a solid mass of cells, followed by the diversification of cells into specific tissue types (*embryol*). — *adj* **segment'ed** (or *seg'*). — **segmental arch** an arch forming an arc of a circle whose centre is below the springing; **segmentation cavity** a blastocele. [L *segmentum*, from *secāre* to cut]

segno *sā'nyō*, (*music*) *n* a sign to mark the beginning or end of repetitions (:𝄋:): — *pl* **se'gnos**. [Ital, from L *signum* a mark]

sego *sē'gō*, *n* a showy liliaceous plant (*Calochortus*) of the western US: — *pl* **sē'gos**. [Ute Indian name]

segol. See **seghol**.

segreant *seg'ri-ənt*, (*heraldry*) *adj* generally understood to mean with raised wings. [Earlier *sergreant*; origin unknown]

segregate *seg'ri-gāt*, *vt* to set apart; to seclude; to isolate; to group apart. — *vi* to separate out in a group or groups or mass; to separate into dominants and recessives (*genetics*). — *adj* (*-gət*) set apart. — *n* (*-gət*) that which is segregated. — *adj* **seg'regable**. — *n* **segregā'tion** the act of segregating; the state of being segregated; dispersal (*obs*); separation of dominants and recessives in the second generation of a cross (*genetics*); the separation of hereditary factors from one another during spore formation (*bot*); the separation into patches or undistributed areas of impurities, inclusions, and alloying constituents in metals; a segregated mass or group; separation of one particular class of people from another, eg on grounds of race. — *n* **segregā'tionist** a believer in racial or other segregation. — *adj* **seg'regative** (*-gā-tiv*). [L *sēgregāre*, *-ātum*, from *sē-* apart, and *grex*, *gregis* a flock]

segue *sā'gwā*, (*music*) *vi* to proceed without pause, to follow on, *usu* as a musical direction (literally, it follows on, apprehended as an imperative) to proceed immediately with the next song, movement, etc (also *fig*): — *pr p* **se'gueing**; *pa t* and *pa p* **se'gued**. — *n* the term or direction to segue; the act or result of segueing; segued music (live or recorded); a compilation, *esp* in popular recorded music, in which tracks follow on continuously. [Ital]

seguidilla *seg-i-dēl'yä*, *n* a Spanish verse form of seven lines; a Spanish dance; a tune for it, in triple time. [Sp, dimin of *seguido* series]

sei *sā*, *n* (also **sei whale**) a kind of rorqual (*Balaenoptera borealis*). [Norw *sejhval* sei whale]

seicento *sā-chen'tō*, *n* (in Italian art, literature, etc) the seventeenth century. [Ital, abbrev of *mille seicento* one thousand six hundred]

seiche *sāsh* or *sesh*, *n* a periodic fluctuation from side to side of the surface of an enclosed or partly-enclosed body of water, such as a lake, harbour, etc, caused eg by changes in barometric pressure. [Swiss Fr]

Seidlitz powder *sed'lits pow'dər*, *n* a mixture of sodium bicarbonate, sodium potassium tartrate and tartaric acid, used as a laxative when dissolved in water. [*Sedlitz*, Bohemian village which produces a mineral water with a laxative effect]

seif *sāf* or *sīf*, *n* a long sand dune lying parallel to the direction of the wind that forms it. [Ar *saif* sword]

seignior *sā'* or *sē'nyər*, **seigneur** *sen-yœr*, *n* a feudal lord, lord of a manor, *esp* in France or French Canada. — *n* **seign'iorage** or **seign'orage** lordship; a right, privilege, etc, claimed by an overlord; an overlord's royalty on minerals; a percentage on minted bullion. — *n* **seign'i-oralty** seignory. — *adj* **seignio'rial**, **seigneu'rial**, **seigno-ral** (*sān'* or *sen'*) or **signo'rial** (*sin-*). — *n* **seign'iorship**. — *n* **seign'ory** or **seign'iory** feudal lordship; the council of an Italian city-state (*hist*); (also **seigneurie** *sen'yə-rē*) a domain. — **grand** (*grã*) **seigneur** a great lord; a man of aristocratic dignity and authority; **Grand Seignior** or **Signior** (*hist*) the Sultan of Turkey. [Fr *seigneur*, from L *senior*, *-ōris*, compar of *senex* old. In LL *senior* is sometimes equivalent to *dominus* lord]

seik *sēk*, *adj* a Scots form of **sick**.

seil[1]. Same as **sile**.

seil[2] (*Scot*). See **seel**[2].

seine *sān* or *sēn*, *n* a large vertical fishing-net whose ends are brought together and hauled (also **seine net**). — *vt* and *vi* to catch or fish with a seine. — Also **sean**. — *n* **sein'er**. — *n* **sein'ing**. — **seine boat**; **seine fishing**; **seine'-shooting** the casting of seine nets. [OE *segne*, from L *sagēna*, from Gr *sagēnē* a fishing-net]

seir or **seer** *sēr*, *n* a scombroid fish, *Cybidium guttatum*, of the eastern coastal waters of India. [Port *serra*, the name of the fish]

seise *sēz*, *vt* an old spelling of **seize**, still used legally in the sense of to put in possession (of property, etc): — *pa p* (*Spenser*) **seis'ed** reached, attained. — *n* **seis'in** or (*US*) **seizin** *orig* feudal possession, now possession in freehold; an object handed over as a token of possession; sasine (*Scots law*).

seism *sīzm*, (*rare*) an earthquake. [Gr *seismos*; see **seismo-**]

seismo- *sīz-mō-*, *-mə* or *-mo'* *combining form* denoting earthquake. — *adj* **seis'mal**, **seis'mic** or **seis'mical**. — *n* **seismicity** (*-mis'i-ti*) liability to or frequency of earthquakes. — *n* **seis'mism** earthquake phenomena. — *n* **seis'mogram** a seismograph record. — *n* **seis'mograph** an instrument for registering earthquakes. — *n* **seismog'rapher**. — *adj* **seismograph'ic** or **seismograph'ical**. — *n* **seismog'raphy**. — *adj* **seismolog'ic** or **seismolog'ical**. — *n* **seismol'ogist**. — *n* **seismol'ogy** the science and study of earthquakes. — *n* **seismom'eter** an instrument for measuring the intensity and duration of earthquakes. — *adj* **seismomet'ric** or **seismomet'rical**. — *n* **seismom'etry**. — *adj* **seismonas'tic**. — *n* **seis'-monasty** (Gr *nastos* pressed together, compressed; *bot*) response to mechanical shock. — *n* **seis'moscope** an instrument for detecting earthquakes. — *adj* **seismo-scop'ic**. — **seismic array** a system of seismographs, linked together and placed so as to increase sensitivity to the occurrence of earthquakes; **seismic prospecting** investigating the depth and character of subsurface rock formations by noting the travel times of reflected and refracted artificial shock waves; **seismic shock** or **wave** a vibration or shock wave resulting from earth movements. [Gr *seismos* a shaking, from *seiein* to shake]

seiten *sītən*, *n* wheat gluten, widely used in vegetarian and Far Eastern cookery.

seity *sē'i-ti*, *n* a self; selfhood, personal identity. [L *sē* oneself]

seize or (*old* or *legal*) **seise** (*Spenser*, *Shakesp*, *Milton*, **sease**, **seaze**, **ceaze**, etc) *sēz*, *vt* to grasp suddenly, eagerly, or forcibly; to take by force; to take prisoner; to apprehend; to take possession of; to take legal possession of; to lash or make fast (*naut*); to reach, attain (*naut* and *Spenser*). — *vi* to take hold, grasp (with *on* or *upon*); to penetrate (*Spenser*); (of mechanical parts) to jam or weld partially for want of lubrication. — *adj* **seiz'able**. — *n* **seiz'er**. — *n* **seiz'in** seisin (see **seise**). — *n* **seiz'ing** the action of the verb; a cord to seize ropes with (*naut*). — *n* **seizure** (*sē'zhər*) the act of seizing; a thing seized; capture; a sudden fit or attack of illness, *esp* a convulsion. — **be seized with** or **by** to have a sudden severe attack of (eg remorse, pneumonia); **seize** or **seise of** to put in possession of; **seized** or **seised of** in (legal) possession of; aware of; in the process of considering; **seize up** to jam, seize, become immovable or stuck. [OFr *seisir*, *saisir*, from LL *sacīre*, prob Gmc; cf OHGer *sazzan* to set, Ger *setzen*, Eng *set*]

sejant or **sejeant** *sē'jənt*, (*heraldry*) *adj* (*esp* of a quadruped) sitting (upright). [OFr *seiant*, Fr *séant*, pr p of *seoir*, from L *sedēre* to sit]

Sejm *sām*, *n* the unicameral parliament of the Polish People's Republic. [Pol, assembly]

sekos *sē'kos*, *n* a sacred enclosure. [Gr *sēkos*]

Sekt or **sekt** *sekt* or *zekt*, *n* a German sparkling wine. [Ger]

sel *sel*, (*Scot*) *n* self.

selachian *si-lā'ki-ən*, *n* any fish of the subclass *Selanchii*, *incl* sharks, rays, dogfish and skates. — Also *adj*. [Gr *selachos*]

seladang *se-lä'dang* or **sladang** *slä'dang*, *n* the gaur; the Malayan tapir. [Malay *seladang*, *saladang*]

selaginella *si-laj-i-nel'ə*, *n* a plant of the genus *Selaginella*, heterosporous club mosses constituting the family *Selaginellaceae*. [Dimin of L *selāgō*, *-inis* a plant mentioned by Pliny]

selah *sē'lä*, *n* in the Old Testament psalms, a Hebrew word probably meaning pause.

Selbornian *sel-bör'ni-ən*, *adj* of *Selborne* in Hampshire, or of Gilbert White (1720–93), author of *The Natural History and Antiquities of Selborne*; of Gault and

Upper Greensand (*geol*). — *n* a devotee of Gilbert White; the Gault and Upper Greensand.

selcouth *sel'kōōth*, (*obs*) *adj* strange, unfamiliar, marvellous. [OE *sel(d)cūth*, from *seldan* seldom, and *cūth* known, from *cunnan* to know]

seld *seld*, (*obs*) *adj* rare, uncommon. — *adv* seldom, rarely. — *adj* **seld'seen** (*obs*) rarely seen. — *adj* **seld'shown** (*Shakesp*) rarely shown. [See **seldom**]

seldom *sel'dəm*, *adv* rarely. — *adj* infrequent. — *n* **sel'domness**. — *adv* **sel'dom-times**. [OE *seldum*, altered (on the analogy of *hwīlum* whilom) from *seldan*; Ger *selten*]

sele. Same as **seel**[2].

select *si-lekt'*, *vt* to pick out from a number by preference; to free-select (*Austr*). — *adj* picked out; choice; exclusive. — *adj* **selec'ted**. — *n* **select'ee** a person who is selected, *esp* (*US*) a person selected for military service. — *n* **selec'tion** the act of selecting; a thing or collection of things selected; a pot-pourri (*music*); the process by which some individuals contribute more offspring than others to the next generation, in *natural selection* through intrinsic differences in fertility and survival, and in *artificial selection* through the breeder's choice of parents (*biol*); a horse selected as likely to win a race; a number or group of things from which to select; free-selection (*Austr*). — *adj* pertaining to or consisting of selection. — *adj* **selec'tive** having or exercising power of selection; able to discriminate, eg between different frequencies; choosing, involving, etc, only certain things or people. — *adv* **selec'tively**. — *n* **selectiv'ity** (*sel-*) ability to discriminate. — *n* **select'ness**. — *n* **select'or**. — *adj* **selecto'rial**. — **select committee** a number of members of parliament chosen to report and advise on some matter; **selective attention** see under **attention**; **selective mating** the selection of males, based on some outward characteristic (eg tail length in birds) and/or on competition between members of the same sex; **selective service** formerly, in the US, compulsory military service under which men were conscripted selectively; **selective weedkiller** a weedkiller that does not destroy garden plants; **select'-man** in New England towns, one of a board of officers chosen to manage local business. — **select out** (*US euphem*) to give (someone) the sack. [L *sēligere*, *sēlectum*, from *sē-* aside, and *legere* to choose]

selegiline *sə-leg'i-lēn*, *n* a drug used in the treatment of Parkinson's disease.

selenic *si-lē'nik* or *-len'ik*, *adj* of or relating to the moon (also **selenian** (*sə-lē'ni-ən*); of selenium in higher valency (**selenic acid** H_2SeO_4). — *n* **sel'enate** (*sel'i-nāt*) a salt of selenic acid. — *n* **selenide** (*sel'i-nīd*) a compound of selenium with an element or radical. — *adj* **selē'nious** or **selē'nous** of selenium in lower valency (**selenious acid** H_2SeO_3). — *n* **selenite** (*sel'i-nīt*) gypsum, *esp* in transparent crystals (anciently supposed to wax and wane with the moon); a salt of selenious acid. — *adj* **selenitic** (*sel-i-nit'ik*). — *n* **selenium** (*si-lē'*) a non-metallic element (symbol **Se**; atomic no 34) discovered by Berzelius in 1817 and named from its resemblance to tellurium. — *n* **selē'nograph** a delineation of the moon. — *n* **selenographer** (*sel-i-nog'rə-fər*). — *adj* **selenographic** (*si-lē-nə-graf'ik*) or **selenograph'ical**. — *n* **selenography** (*sel-i-nog'rə-fi*) mapping of the moon; the study of the moon's physical features. — *adj* **selēnolog'ical**. — *n* **selenol'ogist** a selenographer. — *n* **selenol'ogy** the scientific study of the moon. — *n* **selenomorphol'ogy** the study of the surface of the moon. — **selenium cell** a photoelectric cell dependent on the circumstance that light increases the electric conductivity of selenium. [Gr *selēnē* moon]

selenodont *si-lēn'ə-dont*, *adj* (of the molar teeth of certain animals) having crescent-shaped ridges on the crowns. — *n* an animal, such as a deer, having such ridges on the teeth. [Gr *selēne* moon, and *odous*, *odontos* tooth]

Seleucid *se-lū'sid*, *n* a member of the dynasty (**Seleu'cidae**) that ruled Syria from 312 to 65 BC, beginning with Alexander's general, *Seleucus* I (Nicator). — Also *adj*. — *adj* **Seleu'cidan**.

self *self*, *pronoun* loosely, oneself, myself, himself, etc. — *n* personality, ego; a side of one's personality; identity; what one is; self-interest; a self-coloured plant or animal; a thing (*esp* a bow) made in one piece: — *pl* **selves** (*selvz*) or, of things in one colour or one piece, **selfs**. — *adj* very, same, identical (*archaic*); own (*archaic*); uniform in colour; made in one piece; made of the same material. — *vt* to fertilize by the same individual (self-fertilize) or by the same strain (inbreed). — *n* **self'hood** personal identity; existence as a person; personality; selfishness (*rare*). — *n* **self'ing** (*biol*) self-fertilization or self-pollination. — *adj* **self'ish** chiefly or wholly concerned with one's own welfare and interests, *usu* when accompanied by a disregard for others; tending to perpetuate or duplicate itself in the genome without affecting the host or phenotype (*genetics*). — *adv* **self'ishly**. — *n* **self'ishness**. — *n* **self'ism** concentration upon self; the selfish theory of morals, that people act from the consideration of what will give them the most pleasure. — *n* **self'ist**. — *adj* **self'less** having no regard to self, altruistic. — *n* **self'lessness**. — *n* **self'ness** egotism; personality. — **one self** (*Shakesp*) one and the same, one only; **one's self** see **oneself**; **second self** see under **second**. [OE *self*; Du *zelf*; Ger *selbe*, Gothic *silba*]

self- *self-*, *combining form* indicating: action upon the agent; action by, of, in, in relation to, etc, oneself or itself; automatic action. — *n* **self-aban'donment** disregard of self. — *n* **self-abase'ment** self-humiliation. — *n* **self-abnegā'tion** renunciation of one's own interest; self-denial. — *adj* **self-absorbed'** wrapped up in one's own thoughts or affairs. — *n* **self-absorp'tion** the state of being self-absorbed; self-shielding (*phys*). — *n* **self-abuse'** self-deception (*Shakesp*); revilement of oneself; masturbation. — *n* **self-abus'er**. — *n* **self-accusā'tion**. — *adj* **self-accus'atory**. — *adj* **self-acknow'ledged** — *adj* **self'-act'ing** automatic. — *n* **self-ac'tion** spontaneous or independent action. — *n* **self-activ'ity** an inherent power of acting. — *n* **self-actualizā'tion** or **-s-** (*psychol*) the realization of one's whole personality and one's understanding and development of all its aspects. — *adj* **self-addressed'** addressed to oneself. — *adj* **self-adhē'sive** able to stick to a surface without the use of (additional) glue, etc. — *adj* **self-adjust'ing** requiring no external adjustment. — *adj* **self-admin'istered**. — *n* **self-admirā'tion**. — *n* **self-advance'ment**. — *n* **self-advert'isement**. — *n* **self-ad'vertiser**. — *n* **self-ad'vocacy** the act or practice or representing oneself, *esp*, in the US, the practice of mentally handicapped people taking control of their own affairs rather than automatically being represented by non-handicapped people. — Also *adj*. — *n pl* **self'-affairs** (*Shakesp*) one's own affairs. — *adj* **self-affec'ted** (*Shakesp*) self-loving. — *adj* **self-affrigh'ted** (*Shakesp*) frightened at oneself. — *n* **self-affirma'tion** assertion of the existence of the self. — *n* **self-aggrand'izement** or **-s-**. — *adj* **self-aggrand'izing** or **-s-**. — *n* **self'-anal'ysis**. — *adj* **self-anneal'ing** (of metals such as lead, tin, and zinc) recrystallizing at air temperature and so able to be cold-worked with little or no strain-hardening. — *n* **self-annihilā'tion** the losing of one's sense of individual existence when contemplating the divine; a sense of union with God. — *adj* **self-anoin'ted**. — *n* **self-applause'**. — *adj* **self-appoint'ed**. — *n* **self-appreciā'tion**. — *n* **self-approbā'tion**. — *n* **self-appro'val**. — *adj* **self-approv'ing**. — *adj* **self-assem'bly** (of furniture, etc) in parts of sections for assembly by the purchaser. — *adj* **self-assert'ing** or **self-assert'ive** given to asserting one's opinion or to putting oneself forward. — *n* **self-asser'tion**. — *adj* **self-assumed'** assumed by one's own act. — *n* **self-assump'tion** conceit. — *n* **self-assū'rance** assured self-confidence. — *adj* **self-assured'**. — *adj* **self-aware'**. — *n* **self-aware'ness**. — *adj* **self-bal'ancing** balancing without outward help; stable. — *adj* **self-bast'ing** (*cookery*) not requiring to be basted by hand. — *adj* (*archaic*) **self-begot'** or

self'-begott'en being its own parent, as is the phoenix. — *n* **self-betray'al**. — *n* **self-bind'er** a reaping-machine with automatic binding apparatus; a portfolio that grips loose sheets. — *adj* **self'-blind'ed**. — *adj* **self'-born'** born of itself, as is the phoenix. — *n* **self-boun'ty** native goodness. — *n* **self-breath'** (*Shakesp*) one's own utterances. — *adj* **self-built'** or **self-build'** built, or to be built, by the purchaser or owner. — *n* **self-capac'itance** capacitance. — *adj* **self-cat'ering** (of a holiday, accommodation, etc) in which one cooks, etc for oneself. — *adj* **self-cen'tred** fixed independently; preoccupied with oneself; selfish. — *n* **self-certifica'tion** in Britain, a system, introduced in 1982, by which an employee declares, on a pre-printed form and without needing the authorization of a doctor, that an absence from work (for up to seven days) was due to illness. — *n* **self-char'ity** (*Shakesp*) self-love. — *adj* **self-clean'ing**. — *adj* **self-clōs'ing** shutting automatically. — *n* **self-cock'er** a firearm in which the hammer is raised by pulling the trigger. — *adj* **self-cock'ing**. — *adj* **self-collec'ted** self-possessed. — *n* **self-col'our** uniform colour; natural colour. — *adj* **self-col'oured**. — *n* **self-command'** self-control. — *n* **self-commit'ment**. — *n* **self-commun'ion** communing with oneself, introspective meditation. — *n* **self-compar'ison** (*Shakesp*) the setting of oneself against another. — *adj* **self-compat'ible** (*bot*) (of a plant) capable of self-fertilization. — Also *n*. — *n* **self-complā'cence** satisfaction with oneself, or with one's own performances. — *adj* **self-complā'cent**. — *n* **self-conceit'** an over-high opinion of oneself, one's own abilities, etc; vanity. — *adj* **self-conceit'ed**. — *n* **self-conceit'edness**. — *n* **self-concentrā'tion** concentration of one's thoughts upon oneself. — *n* **self-con'cept** one's concept of oneself. — *n* **self-concern'**. — *n* **self-condemna'tion**. — *adj* **self-condemned'** condemned by one's own actions or out of one's own mouth. — *adj* **self-condemn'ing**. — *adj* **self-confessed'** openly acknowledging oneself as such. — *n* **self-con'fidence** confidence in, or reliance on, one's own powers; self-reliance. — *adj* **self-con'fident**. — *adv* **self-con'fidently**. — *adj* **self-confi'ding** self-reliant. — *n* **self-congratulā'tion**. — *adj* **self-congrat'ulatory** congratulating oneself. — *adj* **self-con'jugate** (*math*) conjugate to itself. — *adj* **self-con'scious** conscious of one's own mind and its acts and states; irrationally believing oneself to be the subject of close observation by others, and embarrassed as a result. — *n* **self-con'sciousness**. — *n* **self-con'sequence** self-importance. — *adj* **self-con'sequent**. — *adj* **self-consid'ering** deliberating with oneself. — *n* **self-consist'ency** consistency of each part with the rest; consistency with one's principles. — *adj* **self-consis'tent**. — *adj* **self-con'stituted** constituted by oneself. — *adj* **self-consūmed'**. — *adj* **self-consūm'ing** consuming oneself, or itself. — *adj* **self-contained'** wrapped up in oneself, reserved; calmly independent, not needing the company or reassurance of others; (of a house, flat, room, etc) complete in itself. — **self-contempt'**. — *n* **self-content'** self-satisfaction, complacency. — *n* **self-contradic'tion** the act or fact of contradicting oneself; a statement whose terms are mutually contradictory. — *adj* **self-contradic'tory**. — *n* **self-control'** power of controlling oneself. — *adj* **self-convict'ed** convicted by one's own acts or words. — *n* **self-convic'tion**. — *adj* **self'-correct'ing**. — *adj* **self-cov'ered** (*Shakesp*) either dissembling, or revealed in one's true colours. — *n* **self-creāt'ed**. — *n* **self-creā'tion**. — *adj* **self-crit'ical**. — *n* **self-crit'icism** critical examination and judgement of one's own works and thoughts. — *n* **self-cult'ure** development and education of one's personality by one's own efforts. — *adj* **self-damn'ing**. — *n* **self-dan'ger** (*Shakesp*) personal risk. — *n* **self-deceit'** or **self-decep'tion** deceiving of oneself, *esp* with regard to one's true feelings or motives. — *adj* **self-deceit'ful**. — *adj* **self-deceived'**. — *n* **self-deceiv'er**. — *adj* **self-defeat'ing** that defeats its own purpose. — *n* **self-defence'** defending one's own person, rights, etc (**art of self-defence** *orig* boxing, now used more loosely to refer to any of various martial arts). — *n* **self-degradā'tion**. — *n* **self-delight'** delight in one's own being or thoughts. — *n* **self-delu'sion** the delusion of oneself by oneself. — *n* **self-denī'al** forbearing to gratify one's own appetites or desires. — *adj* **self-deny'ing**. — *adv* **self-deny'ingly**. — *n* **self-depen'dence**. — *adj* **self-depen'dent**. — *adj* **self-dep'recating**. — *adj* **self-deprēc'iating** lowering its (or one's) own value; undervaluing oneself or itself. — **self'-despair'** a despairing view of one's own nature, prospects, etc. — *n* **selfe'-despight'** (*Spenser*) injury to oneself. — *adj* **self-destroy'ing**. — *vi* **self-destruct'** (of a spacecraft, etc) to disintegrate or explode automatically through the operation of a timing-device, etc. — Also *adj*. — *n* **self-destruc'tion** the destruction of anything by itself; suicide. — *adj* **self-destruc'tive**. — *n* **self-determinā'tion** determination without extraneous impulse; direction of the attention or will to an object; the power of a population to decide its own government and political relations or of an individual to live his or her own life. — *adj* **self'-deter'mined** and **self'-deter'mining**. — *adj* **self-devel'oping**. — *n* **self-devel'opment**. — *adj* **self-devōted**. — *n* **self-devōtion** self-sacrifice. — *adj* **self-direc'ted**. — *n* **self-direc'tion**. — *n* **self-direc'tor**. — *n* **self-dis'charge** (*elec eng*) loss of capacity of a primary cell or accumulator as a result of internal leakage; loss of charge in a capacitor due to finite insulation resistance between plates. — *n* **self-dis'cipline**. — *adj* **self-disliked'**. — *n* **self-dispar'agement**. — *adj* **self-displeased'**. — *n* **self-dispraise'**. — *n* **self-dissocia'tion** (*chem*) the splitting into ions of the molecules of certain highly polar liquids. — *n* **self-distrust**. — *adj* **self-doc'umenting** (of a computer program) that informs the user how to use the program as it runs. — *n* **self-doubt'**. — *n* **self-dramatizā'tion** or **-s-** presentation of oneself as if a character in a play; seeing in oneself an exaggerated dignity and intensity. — *adj* **self-drive'** (of a hired motor vehicle) to be driven by the hirer. — *adj* **self-driv'en** driven by its own power. — *adj* **self-ed'ucated** educated by one's own efforts. — *n* **self-efface'ment** keeping oneself in the background out of sight; withdrawing from notice or rights. — *adj* **self-effac'ing**. — *adj* **self-elect'ed** elected by oneself or itself. — *adj* **self-elect'ing** or **self-elect'ive** having the right to elect oneself or itself, as by co-option of new members. — *n* **self-elec'tion**. — *adj* **self-employed'** working independently in one's own business, or on a freelance basis. — *n* **self-employ'ment**. — *n* **self'-end** (*obs, esp* 17c) a selfish motive or object. — *adj* **self-endeared'** self-loving. — *n* **self-enjoy'ment** internal satisfaction. — *n* **self-enrich'ment**. — *n* **self-esteem'** good opinion of oneself; self-respect. — *n* **self-ev'idence**. — *adj* **self-ev'ident** obvious, evident without proof. — *adj* **self-evolved'**. — *n* **self-examinā'tion** a scrutiny into one's own state, conduct, etc; examination of one's own body in order to detect changes or abnormalities, *esp* by women of their breasts. — *n* **self'-example** one's own example. — *adj* **self-excīt'ing** or **self-excit'ed** (*elec*) (of an electrical machine) itself supplying the exciting current. — *adj* **self-ex'ecuting** (*legal*) automatically coming into effect, not needing legislation to enforce. — *n* **self-exer'tion**. — *adj* **self-ex'iled**. — *n* **self-exist'ence**. — *adj* **self-exist'ent** existing of or by oneself or itself, independent of any other cause. — *adj* **self-explan'atory** or **self-explain'ing** obvious, understandable without explanation, self-evident. — *n* **self-explicātion**. — *n* **self-express'ion** the giving of expression to one's personality, as in art. — *vi* **self-express'**. — *adj* **self-faced'** undressed or unhewn, *esp* of a stone showing a natural cleavage. — *adj* **self-fed'** fed by itself or automatically; fed upon itself. — *n* **self-feed'er** a device for supplying anything automatically, *esp* a measured amount of foodstuff for cattle, etc. — *adj* **self-feed'ing**. — *n* **self-feel'ing** one's personal experience. — *adj* **self-fer'tile** or **self-fer'tilizing** made fertile or fertilizing by its own pollen or sperm. — *n* **self'-fertilīzā'tion** or **-s-**. — *n* **self-fertil'ity**. — *adj* **self-fig'ured** of one's own devising. — *n* **self-fill'er** a fountain pen that can be filled without a dropping-tube. — *adj* **self-finan'cing** (of a business, enterprise, etc) requiring no finance from outside sources, eg loans, etc. — *adj* **self-flatt'ering**. — *n* **self-flatt'ery**. — *adj* **self-fo'cusing**. — *adj* **self-forget'ful** unselfishly forgetful of oneself or one's own interests. — *adv* **self-forget'fully**. — *adj* **self'-fulfill'ing**. — *n* **self-fulfil'ment**. — *adj* **self-gen'erating**. — *adj* **self-giv'ing**. — *adj* **self-glazed'** (of pottery, etc) glazed in one tint or colour. — *n* **self-glorificā'tion**. — *adj* **self-glō'rious** boastful. — *adj* **self-gov'erning**. — *n* **self-gov'ernment** self-control; autonomy; government without outside interference; democracy. — *adj* **self-gra'cious** gracious towards oneself or spontaneously gracious. — *adj* **self-har'ming**. — *n* **self-hate'** or **self-hāt'red**. — *n* **selfheal** see separate entry. — *n* **self-heal'ing** spontaneous healing; healing oneself. — Also *adj*. — *n* **self-help'** doing things for oneself without assistance from others. — Also *adj*. — *adj* **self-het'erodyne** (*electronics*) autodyne. — *n* **self'-hood** see under **self**. — *n* **self-humiliā'tion**. — *n* **self-hypnō'sis** or **self'-hyp'notism**. — *n* **self-iden'tity** identity of a thing with itself; the conscious realization of the individual identity. — *n* **self-im'age** an individual's view of his or her own personality and abilities. — *n* **self-immolā'tion** offering oneself up in sacrifice; suttee. — *n* **self-import'ance** an absurdly high sense of one's own importance; pomposity. — *adj* **self-import'ant**. — *adv* **self-import'antly**. — *n* **self-improve'ment** improvement, by oneself, of one's status, education, job, etc. — *adj* **self-imposed'** taken voluntarily on oneself. — *n* **self-impregnā'tion** impregnation of a hermaphrodite by its own sperm. — *adj* **self-incompat'ible** having reproductive organs that cannot function together. — *adj* **self'-induced'** induced by oneself; produced by self-induction (*electronics*). — *n* **self-induc'tance** the property of an electric circuit whereby self-induction occurs. — *n* **self-induc'tion** the property of an electric circuit by which it resists any change in the current flowing in it (cf **mutual induction**). — *adj* **self-induc'tive**. — *n* **self-indul'gence** undue or unhealthy gratification of one's appetites or desires. — *adj* **self'-indul'gent**. — *n* **self-infec'tion** infection of the entire organism from a local lesion. — *adj* **self'-inflict'ed** inflicted by oneself on oneself. — *vi* **self-inject'**. — *n* **self-injec'tion**. — *n* **self-insū'rance** the practice of laying aside funds from income, etc to cover losses, rather than taking out an insurance policy. — *n* **self-in'terest** private interest; regard to oneself or one's own advantage. — *adj* **self-in'terested**. — *adj* **self-invī'ted** invited by nobody but oneself. — *adj* **self-involved'** wrapped up in oneself or one's own thoughts; inwoven into itself. — *n* **self-judge'ment**. — *n* **self-justificā'tion**. — *adj* **self-jus'tifying** justifying oneself; automatically arranging the length of the lines of type (*printing*). — *adj* **self-killed'**. — *n* **self-kill'er**. — *adj* **self-know'ing**. — *n* **self-knowl'edge** knowledge of one's own nature or personality. — *adj* **self-left'** left to oneself. — *adj* **self-lev'elling** automatically adjusting so as to be level. — *n* **self'-life** self-existence; life only for oneself. — *adj* **self-light'ing** igniting automatically. — *adj* **self'-like** exactly similar. — *adj* **self-lim'ited** (*pathol*) running a definite course. — *adj* **self-liq'uidating** (of a loan, business enterprise, etc) yielding sufficient increase to pay for its own redemption, initial outlay, etc. — *adj* **self-load'ing** (of a gun) automatically reloading itself. — *adj* **self-lock'ing** locking automatically. — *adj* **self-lost'** lost or damned through one's own fault. — *n* **self-love'** the love of oneself; tendency to seek one's own welfare or advantage; desire of happiness. — *adj* **self-lov'ing**. — *adj* **self-lum'inous** emitting a light of its own. — *adj* **self-made'** made by oneself; risen from poverty or obscurity to a high position by one's own exertions. — *n* **self-man'agement** self-control; the management of a factory, etc, by its own workers. — *n* **self-mas'tery** self-command; self-control. — *n* **self-mett'le** (*Shakesp*) natural spirit. — *adj* **self-misused'** denigrated by oneself. — *n* **self-mock'ery**. — *n* **self-mo'tion** spontaneous motion. — *adj* **self-mo'tivated** or **self-mo'tivating** naturally enterprising; motivated by inherent energy, enthusiasm, ambition, etc, without external impetus. — *adj* **self-mo'ving** moving spontaneously from within. — *n* **self-mur'der** suicide. — *n* **self-mur'derer**. — *adj* **self-mur'dering**. — *n* **self-neglect'**. — *n* **self-observā'tion** (*psychol*) the observation of one's own behaviour, personality, mental processes, etc. — *adj* **self-occ'upied**. — **self-offence'** (*rare*) an attack on, or injury to, oneself; one's own offence (*Shakesp*). — *adj* **self-o'pening** opening of its own accord; opening automatically. — *adj* **self'-op'erating**. — *n* **self-opin'ion** high, or unduly high, opinion of oneself or of one's own opinion. — *adj* **self-opin'ionated**, **self-opin'ionative** or **self-opin'ioned** obstinately adhering to one's own opinion. — *adj* **self-ordained'**. — *n* **self-par'ody** parody of oneself or one's own work. — *adj* **self-perpet'uating**. — *adj* **self-pī'ous** hypocritical. — **self-pit'y** pity for oneself. — *adj* **self-plant'ed** planted without human agency. — *adj* **self-plea'sing**. — *adj* **self-poised'** balanced without outside help. — *n* **self-pollinā'tion** the transfer of pollen to the stigma of the same flower (or sometimes the same plant or clone). — *n* **self-pollu'tion** (*archaic*) masturbation. — *n* **self-por'trait** a portrait of oneself executed by oneself. — *n* **self-por'traiture**. — *adj* **self-possessed'** having self-possession. — *n* **self-possess'ion** collectedness of mind; calmness. — *adj* **self-pow'ered**. — *n* **self-praise'** the praise of oneself by oneself. — *n* **self-prepara'tion**. — *adj* **self-prepared'**. — *n* **self-preservā'tion** care, action, or instinct for the preservation of one's own life. — *adj* **self-preser'vative** or **self-preser'ving**. — *n* **self-pride'** self-esteem. — *adj* **self-proclaimed'**. — *adj* **self-produced'**. — *adj* **self-professed'**. — **self-prof'it** private interest. — *adj* **self-prop'agating** propagating itself when left to itself. — *adj* **self-propelled'**. — *n* **self-propell'ing** carrying its own means of propulsion. — *n* **self-propul'sion**. — *n* **self-protec'tion** self-defence. — *adj* **self-protect'ing**. — *adj* **self-protec'tive**. — *adj* **self-pru'ning** naturally shedding twigs. — *n* **self-pub'licist** someone who actively creates or seeks publicity for himself or herself. — *n* **self-public'ity**. — *n* **self-pun'ishment**. — *adj* **self-ques'tioning**. — *adj* **self-raised'** raised by oneself; grown without cultivation. — *adj* **self-rais'ing** (of flour) already mixed with a raising agent (also, *esp NAm*, **self-ris'ing**). — **self-realīzā'tion** or **-s-** attainment of such development as one's mental and moral nature is capable of. — *adj* **self-record'ing** recording its own readings. — *adj* **self-rec'tifying** (*radiol*) (of an X-ray tube) automatically adjusting the direction of radiation when an alternating voltage is applied between target and cathode. — *adj* **self-referr'ing** (of eg literature) containing references to (other parts of) itself. — *n* **self-regard'** self-interest; self-respect, *esp* exaggerated. — *adj* **self-regard'ing**. — *adj* **self-reg'istering** self-recording. — *adj* **self-reg'ulating** regulating itself. — *n* **self-regulā'tion**. — *adj* **self-regulāt'ory** (or *reg'*). — *n* **self-relī'ance** reliance on one's own abilities, resources, etc. — *adj* **self-relī'ant**. — *adj* **self-rely'ing**. — *n* **self-renunciā'tion** self-abnegation. — *adj* **self-repeat'ing**. — *n* **self-repose'**. — *n* **self-repress'ion** repression of one's own desires or of expression of one's personality. — *n* **self-reproach'** blaming oneself or finding fault with one's own actions. — *n* **self-reproof'** or **self-reprov'ing** reproof of conscience. — *n* **self-repug'nance**. — *adj* **self-repug'nant** self-contradictory; inconsistent. — **self-repug'nant** self-contradictory; inconsistent. — *n* **self'-resem'blance** (*Spenser*) appearance of being what one really is. — *n* **self-respect'** proper respect for oneself or one's own character. — *adj* **self-respect'ful**. — *adj* **self-respect'ing**. — *adj* **self-restrained'** restrained by one's own will. — *n* **self-restraint'** a refraining from excess; self-control. — *adj* **self-reveal'ing**. — *n* **self-revelā'tion**. — *n* **self-rev'erence** great self-respect. — *adj* **self-rev'erent**. — *n* **self-right'eous** having a high opinion of one's own virtue; pharisaical. — *n* **self-right'eousness**. — *adj* **self-right'ing** (*esp* of a boat, etc) righting itself when capsized. — *adj* **self-rig'orous** rigorous towards oneself. — *adj* **self-ris'ing** see **self-raising** above. — *adj* **self-rolled'** (*Milton* **self-rowld'**) coiled on itself. — *n* **self-rule'**. — *adj* **self-rul'ing**. — *n* **self-sac'rifice** foregoing one's own needs, etc for the sake of others. — *adj* **self-sac'rificing**. — *n* **self'-same** the very same. — *n* **self-same'ness**. — *n* **self-satisfac'tion**. — *adj* **self-sat'isfied** satisfied with oneself, one's efforts, etc; inordinately proud of oneself, smug; unwisely resting on one's laurels. — *adj* **self-sat'isfying** giving satisfaction to oneself. — *adj* **self-schooled'**. — *adj* **self-seal'ing** (of envelopes, etc) that can be sealed by pressing two adhesive surfaces together; (of tyres) that seal automatically when punctured. — *n* **self-seed'er** a plant that propagates itself from its own seeds shed around it. — *n* **self-seek'er** someone who looks mainly to his or her own interests or advantage; a device which automatically tunes a radio to required wavelengths by means of a push-button control. — *n* and *adj* **self-seek'ing**. — *n* **self-ser'vice** helping oneself, as in a restaurant, petrol station, etc. — Also *adj*. — *adj* **self-ser'ving** taking care of one's own interests before and *usu* to the prejudice of those of other people. — Also *n*. — *adj* **self-severe'** (*Milton*). — *n* **self-shield'ing** (*phys*) in large radioactive sources, the absorption in one part of the radiation arising in another part. — *adj* **self-slain'**. — *n* **self-slaugh'ter**. — *adj* **self-slaugh'tered**. — *n* **self-slay'er**. — *n* **self-sov'ereignty** sovereignty over, or inherent in, oneself. — *vi* **self'-sow** (of *esp* cultivated plants) to disperse and sow seeds naturally without human agency. — *adj* **self-sown'**. — *adj* **self-stan'ding** independent, standing or functioning alone, without support. — *n* **self-star'ter** an automatic contrivance for starting a motor; a car or other vehicle fitted with one; a person with initiative and drive. — *adj* **self-ster'ile** unable to fertilize itself. — *n* **self-steril'ity**. — *n* **self-stud'y** study on one's own, without a teacher. — *adj* **self-styled'** called by oneself; pretended. — *adj* **self-subdued'** (*Shakesp*) subdued by one's own power. — *adj* **self-substan'tial** (*Shakesp*) composed of one's own substance. — *n* **self-suffi'ciency**. — *adj* **self-suffi'cient** requiring nothing to be brought from outside; requiring no emotional, etc support from others. — *adj* **self-suffic'ing**. — *n* **self-sugges'tion** autosuggestion. — *n* **self-support'**. — *adj* **self-support'ed**. — *adj* **self-support'ing** able to support or maintain oneself without outside help; of independent means, paying one's way; (of plants, structures, etc) able to stand up without support(s). — *n* **self'-surren'der** a yielding up of oneself or one's will. — *adj* **self-survi'ving** surviving as a mere ruin of itself. — *adj* **self-sustained'** sustained by one's own power. — *adj* **self-sustain'ing**. — *n* **self-sustain'ment**. — *n* **self-sustenance** and **self-sustentā'tion**. — *adj* **self-synch'ronizing** or **-s-** (*elec eng*) (of a synchronizing machine) that may be switched to alternating current without being in exact synchronism with it. — *adj* **self-tapp'ing** (of a screw) made of hard metal with a thread that either deforms a softer metal as it is driven in or grips thin sheets of metal within the thread. — *adj* **self-taught**. — *adj* **self-temp'ted**. — *adj* **self-think'ing** thinking for oneself. — *n* **self-tor'ment**. — *adj* **self-torment'ing**. — *n* **self-torment'or**. — *n* **self'-tor'ture**. — *adj* **self-trained'**. — **self-transformā'tion**. — *n* **self-treat'ment**. — *n* **self-trust'** self-reliance; confidence in one's own faithfulness to oneself (*Shakesp*). — *adj* **self-una'ble** (*Shakesp*) insufficient in oneself. — *n* **self-understand'ing**. — *n* **self-vindicā'tion**. — *n* **self-vī'olence** suicide. — *n* **self-will'** obstinacy. — *adj* **self-willed'**. — *adj* **self-wind'ing** (of a watch) wound by the wearer's spontaneous movements, or by opening and shutting the case; automatically wound by electricity. — *n* **self-wor'ship**. — *n* **self'-worth** (one's idea of) one's own worth, usefulness, etc; self-esteem. — *n* **self-wrong'** (*Shakesp*) injury done to one by oneself. [OE *self*; Du *zelf*, Ger *selbe*, Gothic *silba*]

-self *-self*, *combining form* used to form reflexive and emphatic pronouns: — *pl* **-selves** (*-selvz*). — **be oneself, himself, herself**, etc, to be in full possession of one's powers; to be (once more) at one's best or as normal; to be alone (*Scot*); **by oneself**, etc, alone.

selfheal *self'hēl*, *n* a spreading labiate European plant, *Prunella vulgaris*, with bright purple, pink or white flowers — widely believed to be a healer of wounds and infections. [**self** and **heal**[1]]

selictar *se-lik'tär*, *n* a sword-bearer. [Turk *silihdār*, from Pers *silahdār*, from Ar *silh* weapon]

Seljuk *sel-jo͞ok'*, *n* a member of any of the Turkish dynasties (11c–13c) descended from *Seljūq* (grandfather of Togrul Beg); a Turk subject to the Seljuks. — *adj* **Seljuk'** or **Seljuk'ian**.

selkie. See **silkie**.

sell[1] *sel*, *vt* to give or give up for money or other equivalent; to betray; to impose upon, trick; to promote the sale of; to make acceptable; to cause someone to accept (eg an idea, plan); to convince (someone) of the value of something; to praise, to cry up (*obs*). — *vi* to make sales; to be sold, to be in demand for sale: — *pa t* and *pa p* **sold**. — *n* (*colloq*) a deception; a disappointment or let-down; an act of selling; a particular quality emphasized in order to sell; stocks to be sold; an order to sell stocks. — *adj* **sell'able** that can be sold. — *n* **sell'er** a person who sells; that which finds a sale; a selling race or plate (*colloq*). — **sell-by date** a date, indicated on a manufactuer's or distributor's label, after which goods, *esp* foods, are considered no longer fit to be sold (also *fig*); **sellers'** or **seller's market** one in which sellers control the price, demand exceeding supply; **sell'ing-pla'ter** a horse fit only to race in a selling race (also *fig*); **sell'ing-price** the price at which a thing is sold; **selling race** or **plate** a race the winning horse of which must be put up for auction at a price previously fixed (cf **claiming race**); **sell'-out** a betrayal; a show, performance, etc for which all seats are sold. — **sell someone a bargain** (*Shakesp*) see under **bargain**; **sell down the river** to play false, betray; **sell off** to sell cheaply in order to dispose of (*n* **sell'-off**); **sell on** to sell (what one has bought) to someone else; **sell one's life dearly** to do great injury to the enemy before one is killed; **sell out** to dispose entirely of; to sell one's commission; to betray; **sell short** to belittle, disparage; to sell (stocks, etc) before one actually owns them, when intending to buy at a lower price; **sell the pass** to betray a trust; **sell up** to sell the goods of, for debt; to sell all; **to sell** for sale. [OE *sellan*, to give, hand over; ON *selja*, Gothic *saljan*]

sell[2] or **selle** *sel*, *n* a seat (*archaic*); a saddle (*obs*). [OFr *selle*, from L *sella*, from *sedēre* to sit]

sell[3] *sel*, *n* a Scots form of **self**: — *pl* **sells**.

sella *sel'ə*, (*anatom*) *n* (also **sella turcica** *tûr'ki-kə*) a saddle-shaped area in the sphenoid bone enclosing the pituitary gland. [L, a seat, saddle]

selle. See **sell**[2].

Sellotape® *sel'ə-tāp*, (also without *cap*) *n* (a brand of) *usu* transparent adhesive tape. — *vt* to stick with Sellotape.

seltzer *selt'sər*, *n* a mineral water from Nieder-*Selters* near Wiesbaden in Germany, or an imitation of it. — *n* **selt'zogene** (*-sə-jēn*) a gazogene.

selva *sel'və*, *n* (*usu* in *pl* **sel'vas**) a wet forest in the Amazon basin. [Sp, Port, from L *silva* wood]

selvage or **selvedge** *sel'vij*, *n* a differently finished edging of cloth; a border, *esp* one sewn or woven so as not to fray. — *vt* to border. — *n* **sel'vagee** (or *-jē'*) a marked hank of rope, used as a strap or sling. [**self** and **edge**]

selves *selvz*, *pl* of **self**.

SEM *abbrev*: scanning electron microscope.

Sem. *abbrev*: Seminary; Semitic.

sem. *abbrev*: semester; semicolon.

semantic *si-man'tik*, *adj* relating to meaning, *esp* of words. — *n sing* **seman'tics** the area of linguistics dealing with the meaning of words; the meaning attached to words or symbols (*comput*). — *n pl* (loosely) differences in, and shades of, meaning of words. — *n* **seman'teme** a unit of meaning, a word or the base of a word, that conveys a definite idea. — *adv* **seman'tically**. — *n*

seman'ticist. — *n* **sememe** (*se'mēm* or *sē'mēm*) a unit of meaning, *usu specif* the smallest linguistically analysable unit. — **semantic error** (*comput*) an error which results in an ambiguous or erroneous meaning in a program; **semantic memory** a computer memory that recalls vast blocks of information corresponding to whole areas of human knowledge, eg language or mathematics, rather than specific items of data. [Gr *sēmantikos* significant]

semantide *si-man'tīd*, (*biol*) *n* a molecule carrying information, eg in a gene or messenger RNA.

semantron *si-man'tron*, *n* a wooden or metal bar that is struck with a mallet, used instead of a bell in Orthodox churches and in mosques: — *pl* **seman'tra**. [Gr *sēmantron* sign, signal]

semaphore *sem'ə-fōr* or *-för*, *n* a signalling apparatus, an upright with arms that can be turned up or down — often the signaller's own body and arms with flags; this system of signalling. — *vt* and *vi* to signal in this way. — *adv* **semaphor'ically**. [Fr *sémaphore*, from Gr *sēma* sign, signal, and *-phoros* bearing, bearer]

semasiology *si-mā-zi-ol'ə-ji* or *-si-*, *n* the science of semantics. — *adj* **semasiolog'ical**. — *adv* **semasiolog'ically**. — *n* **semasio'logist**. [Gr *sēmasia* meaning]

sematic *si-mat'ik*, (*biol*) *adj* (of an animal's colouring) serving for recognition, attraction, or warning. [Gr *sēma* sign]

semble[1] *sem'bl*, *vi* (*obs*) to seem; to be like (with *to*). —*vt* (*obs*) to pretend; to make a picture or image of. — *adj* (*obs*) **sem'blable** resembling, similar, like. — *n* (*obs*) one's like, fellow, equal; something similar. — *adv* **sem'blably** in like manner. — *n* **sem'blance** a likeness or copy; outward appearance; an apparition; an image. — *adj* (*archaic*) **sem'blant** resembling; seeming. — *n* (*obs*) semblance; cheer, countenance, entertainment; demeanour. — *adj* **sem'blative** (*obs*) resembling or seeming; simulative. [Fr *sembler* to seem, to resemble, from L *simulāre*, from *similis* like]

semble[2] *sem'bl*, *vt* to bring together, collect, *esp* as some female moths do males by scent. — **sembling box** (*entomol*) a collector's box enclosing a captive female. [Aphetic from **assemble**]

semé or **semée** *sem'ā*, *sem'i*, (*heraldry*) *adj* strewn or scattered over with small bearings, powdered. — Also **sem'éed**. [Fr, pa p of *semer*, from L *sēmināre* to sow]

semeio-, *combining form*. See **semio-**.

semeion *sē-mī'on*, *n* in ancient prosody, the unit of time; one of the two divisions of a foot; a mark of metrical or other division: — *pl* **semei'a**. [Gr *sēmeion* sign]

semeiotic and **semeiotics**. See **semiotics**.

sememe. See under **semantic**.

semen *sē'men*, *n* the liquid that carries spermatozoa. — See also **seminal**. [L *sēmen*, *-inis* seed]

semester *si-mes'tər*, *n* an academic half-year course or term. — *adj* **semes'tral** or **semes'trial** half-yearly. [L *sēmēstris*, from *sex*, six, and *mēnsis* a month]

semi- *sem'i-*, *pfx* denoting: half; (loosely) nearly, partly, incompletely. — *n* **sem'i** (*colloq*) a semi-detached house; a semi-trailer or semi-truck (*NAm*); a semibajan (also **sem'ie**); a semi-finished (qv) article of steel, copper, etc. — *n* **sem'iangle** a half-angle. — *adj* **semi=ann'ual** (chiefly *NAm*) half-yearly. — *adv* **semi-ann'ually**. — *adj* **semi-ann'ular** half-ring shaped. — *adj* **semi-aqua'tic** (*esp* of plants) living near or in water. — *n* and *adj* **semi-Ā'rian** homoiousian. — *n* **semi-Ā'rianism**. — *adj* **semi-a'rid**. — *adj* **semi-attached'** partially bound. — *adj* **semi-automat'ic** partly automatic but requiring some tending by hand. — *n* **sem'i-axis** a half-axis. — *n* **semi-bā'jan** (*hist*, *Scot univ*) a second-year student. — *n* and *adj* **semi-barbā'rian**. — *n* **semi=bar'barism**. — *n* **semibold'** (*printing*) a typeface between medium and bold; matter printed in this. — Also *adj*. — *n* **sem'ibrēve** half a breve (2 minims or 4 crotchets). — *n* **sem'ibull** a pope's bull issued between election and coronation. — *n* **semicar'bazide** a base ($H_2N{\cdot}CO{\cdot}NH{\cdot}NH_2$) reacting with aldehydes and ketones to form **semicar'bazones**. — *adj* **semi-centenn'ial** occurring at the completion of fifty years. — *n* (*US*) a jubilee. — *n* **semichōr'us** half, or part of, a chorus; a passage sung by it. — *n* **sem'icircle** half a circle, bounded by the diameter and half the circumference. — *adj* **sem'icircled**. — *adj* **semicir'cular** (**semicircular canals** three curved tubes of the inner ear concerned with balance or equilibrium, with each canal registering movement on a different plane). — *adv* **semicir'cularly**. — *n* **sem'icirque** (*poetic*) a semicircular hollow; a semicircle. — *n* **sem'icolon** (or *-kō'lon*) the point (;) marking a division greater than the comma. — *n* **semicō'ma** a condition approaching coma. — *adj* **semico'matose**. — *adj* **semiconduct'ing**. — *n* **semiconductiv'ity**. — *n* **sem'iconduct'or** any solid, non-conducting at low temperatures or in pure state, which is a conductor at high temperatures or when very slightly impure; formerly, any substance with electrical conductivity between that of metals and of non-conductors. — *adj* **semicon'scious**. — *adj* **semicrys'talline** or **semicrystall'ic** having, or being, a partly crystalline structure. — *n* **sem'icyl'inder** a longitudinal half-cylinder. — *n* **sem'idem'isem'iquaver** half a demisemiquaver. — *adj* **semidepō'nent** (*gram*) passive in form in the perfect tenses only. — Also *n*. — *adj* **semi=detached'** partly separated; joined by a party wall to one other house only; associated with, but not wholeheartedly committed to, a particular group, political doctrine, etc. — *n* a semi-detached house. — *n* **semi=diam'eter** half the diameter, *esp* the angular diameter. — *adj* **semi-diur'nal** accomplished in twelve hours; pertaining to half the time or half the arc traversed between rising and setting. — *adj* **semi-divine'** half-divine; of, or of the nature of, a demigod. — *n* **semidocument'ary** a cinema film based on real events but with an invented plot and dialogue. — Also *adj*. — *n* **semi-dome'** half a dome, *esp* as formed by a vertical section. — *adj* **semidomes'ticated** partially domesticated; half-tame. — *adj* **semi-doub'le** (of flowers) having only the outermost stamens converted into petals. — *n* such a flower; a religious festival less solemn than a double (*eccles*; qv). — *adj* **semi-dry'ing** (of oils) thickening without completely drying on exposure. — *n* **semi-ellipse'** half of an ellipse, bounded by a diameter, *esp* the major axis. — *adj* **semi-ellip'tical**. — *n* **semi-ev'ergreen** a plant which is evergreen in its original habitat but not completely so in other places it now grows, dropping leaves in severe weather conditions. — Also *adj*. — *adj* **semifī'nal** (in competitions, sports contests, etc) denoting the contest immediately before the final. — *n* a last round but one. — *n* **semifī'nalist** a competitor in a semifinal. — *adj* **semi=fin'ished** partially finished, *specif* of metal shaped into rods, sheets, etc, in preparation for further processing into finished goods. — *adj* **semiflu'id** nearly solid but able to flow to some extent. — Also *n* (*sem'-*). — *adj* **semiglob'ular**. — *n* **semi-grand'** a square piano with a curtailed keyboard. — Also *adj*. — *n* and *adj* **semi=im'becile**. — *adj* **semi-independ'ent** not fully independent. — *n* **semi-ju'bilee** the twenty-fifth anniversary. — *n* **sem'i-latus rectum** (*geom*) half the latus rectum, terminated at the focus. — *adj* **semi-liq'uid** half-liquid. — *n* and *adj* **semilit'erate** (a person) barely able to read and write. — *adj* **sem'i-log** or **semi=logarith'mic** (of graph paper, graphs, etc) having an arithmetical scale on the *x*-axis and a logarithmic scale on the *y*-axis (also called **single-log** or **-logarithmic**; cf **log-log** or **double-log**). — *adj* **semilu'cent** half-transparent. — *adj* **semilu'nar** or **semilu'nate** half-moon-shaped (as the **semilunar valves** of the aorta and pulmonary artery which prevent regurgitation of blood into the heart). — *n* **sem'ilune** (*-lōōn*) a half-moon-shaped object, body, or structure. — *n* **semimanufac'ture** a manufactured product, material, etc, used to make an end-product. — *adj* **semimen'strual** half-monthly. — *n* **semi-met'al** (*obs*) a metal that is not malleable. — *adj* **semi-month'ly** (chiefly *NAm*) half-monthly. — *n* a half-monthly periodical. — *adj* **semi=**

mute' with speech impaired by loss of hearing. — Also *n*. — *adj* **semi-nūde'** half-naked. — *adj* **semi-occā'sional** (*NAm*) occurring now and then. — *adv* **semi-occā'sionally**. — *adj* **semi-offic'ial** partly official. — *adv* **semi-offic'ially**. — *n* **semi-ō'pal** a dull variety of opal. — *adj* **semi-opaque'** partly opaque. — *adj* **semiovip'arous** (*zool*) giving birth to partially developed young. — *adj* **semipal'mate** (*mət*, *-māt*) or **semipalmā'ted** half-webbed; partly web-footed. — *n* **semipalmā'tion**. — *n* **semipar'asite** a partial parasite, feeding partly independently. — *adj* **semiparasit'ic**. — *n* **sem'iped** (*prosody*) a half-foot. — *n* and *adj* **Semi-Pelā'gian**. — *n* **Semi-Pelā'gianism** the middle course between Augustinian predestination and Pelagian free-will. — *adj* **semi-pellu'cid** imperfectly transparent. — *n* **semiperim'eter** half the perimeter. — *n* **semi-permeabil'ity**. — *adj* **semi-per'meable** permeable by a solvent but not by the dissolved substance. — *n* **sem'iplume** a feather with an ordinary shaft but a downy web. — *n* **semipor'celain** a coarse ware resembling porcelain. — *adj* **semipost'al** (chiefly *US*; *philately*) denoting an issue of postage stamps the profits of which are donated to charity. — *adj* **semi-prec'ious** (*mineralogy*) valuable, but not valuable enough to be considered a gemstone. — *n* **sem'iquāver** half a quaver. — *adj* **semi-rig'id** (of an airship) having a flexible gas-bag and a stiffened keel. — *n* **sem'i-ring** a half-ring. — *adj* **semi-sag'ittate** shaped like half an arrowhead. — *n* and *adj* **Semi-Sax'on** (*obs*) Early Middle English (c.1150–1250). — *adj* **semi-skilled'**. — *adj* **semi-soft'** (of cheese) fairly soft. — *adj* and *n* **semisol'id** (a substance) of a consistency between liquid and solid. — *adj* and *n* **semisubmers'ible** (denoting) a floating oilrig (used mainly for exploratory drilling) which has the greater part of its structure below the water. — *adj* **semiterete'** half-cylindrical. — *n* **sem'itone** half a tone, one of the lesser intervals of the musical scale, as from B to C. — *adj* **semiton'ic**. — *n* **semi-trail'er** or **semi-truck'** (*NAm*) an articulated trailer or lorry. — *n* **semitranspa'rency**. — *adj* **semitranspa'rent** imperfectly transparent. — *adj* **semi-trop'ical** subtropical. — *adj* **semi-tū'bular** like half of a tube divided longitudinally. — *adj* **semi-un'cial** (of writing) intermediate between uncial and minuscule. — *n* a semi-uncial letter. — *n* **sem'ivowel** a sound having the nature of both a vowel and a consonant; a letter representing it, in English, chiefly *w* and *y*, and sometimes used of the liquid consonants *l* and *r*. — *n* **semi-water-gas** see under **water**. — *adj* **semi-week'ly** issued or happening twice a week. — Also *n* and *adv*. [L *sēmi-* half-; cf Gr *hēmi-*, OE *sam-*]

Sémillon *sā-mē-yɔ̃*, *n* a grape variety grown worldwide, used to produce various wines, *incl* Sauternes.

seminal *sem'i-nl*, *adj* pertaining to, or of the nature of, seed or semen; of or relating to the beginnings, first development, of an idea, study, etc, rudimentary; generative; notably creative or influential in future development. — *n* **seminal'ity** germinating principle; germ. — *adv* **sem'inally**. — *vt* **sem'ināte** to sow; to propagate. — *n* **seminā'tion** sowing; seed-dispersal; seeding. — *adj* **seminif'erous** seed-bearing; producing or conveying semen. — **seminal fluid** semen. [L *sēmen*, *-inis* seed]

seminar *sem'i-när*, *n* a group of advanced students working in a specific subject of study under a teacher; a class at which a group of students and a tutor discuss a particular topic; a discussion group on any particular subject. — *adj* **seminarial** (*-ā'ri-əl*) of a seminary. — *n* **seminā'rian** or **sem'inarist** (*-ə-rist*) a student in a seminary or in a seminar; a Roman Catholic priest educated in a foreign seminary; a teacher in a seminary. — *n* **sem'inary** (*-ə-ri*) a breeding-place; a place of origin and fostering, a nursery; formerly, a pretentious name for a school (*esp* for young ladies); now, *usu* a theological college providing training and instruction to ministers, priests, rabbis, etc; a seminary-educated priest (*obs*). — *adj* seminal; of, relating to or educated in a seminary. [L *sēminārium* a seed-plot, from *sēmen* seed]

Seminole *sem'i-nōl*, *n* a native American of a group that is a branch of the Creek people, *orig* in Florida, now mostly in Oklahoma. [Creek *Simánole* literally runaway]

semio- or **semeio-**, *sē-mi-ə*, *sem-i-ə*, *-o'* *combining form* denoting sign. — *n* **semiochem'ical** a chemical produced by an animal, eg in a scent gland, and used as a means of signalling its presence, readiness to mate, etc. — *adj* **semiolog'ical**. — *n* **semiol'ogist**. — *n* **semiol'ogy** the science or study of signs or signals, *esp* of spoken or written words as signs and their relationships with the objects, concepts, etc they refer to (*linguistics*); the scientific study of signs and symptoms (*pathol*). — See also **semiotics**. [Gr *sēmeion* sign]

semiotics or **semeiotics** *sē-mi-ot'iks* or *sem-i-*, *n sing* the study of signs and symptoms, symptomatology or semiology (*pathol*); the study of signs, signals and symbols, *esp* in language and communication, semiology. — *adj* **semiot'ic** or **semeiot'ic**. — *n* **semioti'cian** or **semeioti'cian**. [Gr *sēmeiōtikos*, from *sēmeion* a sign]

semis *sē'mis* or *sā'mis*, *n* a bronze coin of the ancient Roman republic, half an as. [L *sēmis*, *sēmissis*]

semitar, **semitaur**. *Obs* spellings of **scimitar**.

Semite *sem'* or *sēm'īt*, *n* a member of any of the peoples said (in the Bible: Gen 10) to be descended from Shem, or speaking a Semitic language. — *adj* **Semitic** (*si-mit'ik*). — *n* any Semitic language. — *n sing* **Semit'ics** the study of Semitic languages, etc. — *n* **Sem'itism** a Semitic idiom or characteristic; Semitic ways of thought; the cause of the Semites, *esp* the Jews. — *n* **Sem'itist** a Semitic scholar. — *n* **Semitīzā'tion** or **-s-**. — *vt* **Sem'itize** or **-ise** to render Semitic in language, religion, or otherwise. — **Semitic languages** Assyrian, Aramaic, Hebrew, Phoenician, Arabic, Ethiopic, and other ancient languages of this Afro-Asiatic sub-family. [Gr *Sēm*, Shem]

semmit *sem'it*, (*Scot*) *n* a vest or undershirt.

Semnopithecus *sem-nō-pi-thē'kəs*, *n* the genus of monkeys to which the entellus monkey belongs. [Gr *semnos* honoured, and *pithēkos* an ape]

semolina *sem-ə-lē'nə* or *-lī'nə*, *n* the particles of fine, hard wheat that do not pass into flour in milling, used to make puddings, thicken soups, etc. [Ital *semolino*, dimin of *semola* bran, from L *simila* fine flour]

semper *sem'pər* or *-per*, (*L*) *adv* always. — **semper fidelis** always faithful; **semper idem** (*ī'dem*, *id'em* or *ē'dem*; *masc* and *neuter*) always the same: — *fem* **semper eadem** (*ē'ə-* or *e'a-*); **semper paratus** (*pə-rā'təs* or *pa-rä'to͝os*) always ready.

sempervivum *sem-pər-vī'vəm*, *n* any succulent plant of the family *Crassulaceae*, *incl* the house-leek and various ornamental plants. [New L, from L *sempervīvus* ever-living]

sempiternal *sem-pi-tûr'nl*, (chiefly *poetic*) *adj* everlasting. — *adv* **sempiter'nally**. — *n* **sempiter'nity**. — *n* **sempiter'num** (*obs*) a durable woollen cloth. [L *sempiternus*, from *semper* always, ever]

semple *sem'pl*, *adj* a Scottish form of **simple**, *esp* meaning not of gentle birth.

semplice *sem'plē-che*, (*music*) *adj* and *adv* simple or simply, without embellishments. [Ital]

sempre *sem'pre*, (*music*) *adv* always, in the same manner throughout. [Ital, from L *semper* always]

sempster *sem'stər*, or **seamster** *sem'* or *sēm'*, *n* (*orig fem*) a person who sews: — *fem* later **semp'stress** or **seam'stress**. — *n* **semp'stering**, **semp'stressing** and **semp'stress-ship**. — *n* **seam'stressy** (*Sterne*) sewing, needlework. [OE *sēamestre*; see **seam**[1]]

semsem *sem'sem*, *n* sesame. [Ar *simsim*]

Semtex® *sem'teks*, *n* a very powerful kind of plastic explosive.

semuncia *si-mun'shyə* or *-shə*, *n* a Roman half-ounce; a bronze coin, an as in its ultimate value. — *adj* **semun'cial**. [L *sēmuncia*, from *sēmi-* half, and *uncia* a twelfth]

SEN *abbrev*: Special Educational Needs; State Enrolled Nurse.

Sen. *abbrev*: senate; senator; senior.

sen[1] *sen, n* a hundredth part of the Japanese yen and the currencies of SE Asian countries; a coin of this value: — *pl* **sen**. [Chin *ch'ien* coin]

sen[2] *sen, n* a monetary unit in SE Asia, one-hundredth of a rupiah, a ringgit, or a riel; a coin of this value. [**cent**]

sen. (*music*) *abbrev*: *senza* (*Ital*), without.

sena *sä'-nä, n* in India, an army, *esp* used of paramilitary political organizations representing various castes. [Hindi]

senary *sēn'* or *sen'ər-i, adj* of, involving or based on, six. — *n* a set of six; a senarius. — *n* **senarius** (*si-nā'ri-əs*) a verse of six iambs or equivalents: — *pl* **sena'rii** (*ri-ī*). [L *sēnārius*, from *sēnī* six each, from *sex* six]

senate *sen'it, n* the governing body of ancient Rome; a legislative or deliberative body, *esp* the upper house of a national or state legislature; a body of venerable or distinguished people; the governing body of certain British universities (in older Scottish univerities, **Senā'tus Academ'icus**). — *n* **senator** (*sen'ə-tər*) a member of a senate (**Senator of the College of Justice** a Lord of Session (see under **lord**)). — *adj* **senatorial** (*sen-ə-tō'ri-əl* or *-tö'ri-əl*). — *adv* **senato'rially** with senatorial dignity. — *n* **sen'atorship**. — **sen'ate-house** the meeting-place of a senate. — **senā'tus con'sult** or **senā'tus consultum** (*kən-sul'təm*) a decree of the senate, *esp* in ancient Rome. [L *senātus* council of elders, from *senex, senis* an old man]

senatus populusque Romanus *sə-nā'təs pop'ūl-əs-kwē rōmā'nəs* or *sen-ä'tōōs pop-ōōl-ōōs'kwe rō-mä'nōōs*, (*L*) the Roman senate and people (*abbrev* **SPQR**).

send *send, vt* to cause, direct, or tell to go; to propel; to cause to be conveyed; to dispatch; to forward; to grant; (*orig* of jazz) to rouse (someone) to ecstasy. — *vi* to dispatch a message or messenger (often with *for*); to pitch into the trough of the sea (*naut*; sometimes **scend** or **'scend**, as if aphetic from *ascend* or *descend*): — *pa t* and *pa p* **sent**; *naut* **send'ed**. — *n* a messenger (*Scot*); one or more escorts sent ahead of a bridegroom to fetch the bride (*Scot*); an impetus or impulse; the sound or a movement of breaking waves, a swash. — *n* **send'er** a person who sends; a transmitting instrument. — *n* **send'ing** dispatching; pitching; transmission; that which is sent. — **send'-off** a gathering to express good wishes at departing or starting a journey; **send'-up** a process of making fun of someone or something; a play, film, novel, etc, doing this. — **send down** to send to prison (*colloq*); to expel from university; **send for** to require, direct or request by message (someone or something) to come or be brought; **send in** to submit (an entry) for a competition, etc; **send off** (in football, etc) to order (a player) to leave the field and take no further part in the game, *usu* after an infringement of the rules; **send on** to send in advance; to readdress and repost (a letter or package); **send round** to circulate; **send up** to make fun of; to sentence to imprisonment (*colloq*); **send word** to send an intimation. [OE *sendan*; ON *senda*, Gothic *sandjan*, Ger *senden*]

sendal *sen'dəl, n* a thin silk or linen; a garment made of this. [OFr *cendal*, prob from Gr *sindōn*; see **sindon**]

Seneca *sen'i-kə, n* an Iroquois Indian of a tribe in New York state; their language. — *adj* **Sen'ecan**. — **Seneca oil** crude petroleum, used by them for medicinal purposes. [From Du *Sennecaas* (*pl*), collective name for this and related tribes]

Senecan *sen'i-kən, adj* of or in the manner of Lucius Annaeus *Seneca*, Stoic philosopher and writer of declamatory tragedies (c.4 BC–AD 65).

senecio *se-nē'shi-ō* or *-si-ō, n* any composite plant of the genus *Senecio*, distributed throughout most parts of the world, *incl* groundsel and ragwort and many cultivated varieties (cf **cineraria**): — *pl* **senē'cios**. [L *senex* an old man, from the hoary pappus]

senega *sen'i-gə, n* an American milkwort, *Polygala senega*; its dried root used as an expectorant and reputed by the *Seneca* Indians to be an antidote for snakebites (also **senega snakeroot**).

senescent *si-nes'ənt, adj* verging on or characteristic of old age; ageing. — *n* **senesc'ence** the process of growing old, *esp* (*biol*) the physical changes such as slowing down of metabolism and breakdown of tissues that are characteristic of this process. [L *senēscēns, -entis*, pr p of *senēscere* to grow old, from *senex* old]

seneschal *sen'i-shl* (*hist*) *n* a steward; an administrative and judicial title still retained for certain cathedral officials and a judicial position on Sark (Channel Islands). — *n* **sen'eschalship**. [OFr (Fr *sénéchal*), of Gmc origin, literally old servant; cf Gothic *sineigs* old, *skalks*, OE *scealc* servant]

sengreen *sen'grēn, n* the house-leek. [OE *singrēne*, evergreen, house-leek, periwinkle, from pfx *sin-* one, always (cf L *semel* once), *grēne* green; cf Ger *Sin(n)grüne* periwinkle]

Senhor *se-nyōr'* or *-nyör', fem* **Senhora** *se-nyō'rə* or *-nyör'ə* and **Senhorita** *-yə-r-ē'tə, n* the Portuguese forms corresponding to the Spanish **Señor**, **Señora** and **Señorita**.

senile *sēn'īl* or (*esp NAm*) *se'nīl, adj* characteristic of or accompanying old age; showing the decay or imbecility of old age. — *adv* **sēn'ilely**. — *n* **senility** (*si-nil'i-ti*) old age; the imbecility of old age; a state of deterioration or decay. — **senile dementia** mental decay in old age, senility. [L *senīlis*, from *senex, senis* old]

senior *sēn'yər, adj* elder; older or higher in standing; more advanced; first. — *n* a person who is senior; a fourth-year student at college (*US*). — *n* **seniority** (*sē-ni-or'i-ti*) the state or fact of being senior; priority by age, time of service, or standing; a body of seniors or senior fellows. — **senior citizen** an old age pensioner; **senior common room** see under **junior**; **senior optime** see **optime**; **senior service** the navy. [L *senior, -ōris*, compar of *senex* old]

senna *sen'ə, n* any tropical shrub of the genus *Cassia*; a laxative drug obtained from its dried leaflets and fruits (**senna pods**). — **senna tea** an infusion of senna. — **bladder senna** a papilionaceous shrub (*Colutea*) with similar properties. [Ar *sanā*]

sennachie. Same as **seannachie**.

sennet *sen'it*, (*Shakesp*) *n* a trumpet or woodwind announcement of a ceremonial entrance or exit; a fanfare. [Appar a form of **signet**]

sennight or **se'nnight** *sen'īt*, (*archaic*) *n* a week. [**seven** and **night**]

sennit *sen'it* or **sinnet** *sin'it, n* a flat braid or cordage made from several strands of rope, straw or grass. [Origin uncertain]

Senonian *si-nō'ni-ən*, (*geol*) *n* a name applied to the stratigraphic subdivision European Upper Cretaceous. — Also *adj*. [L *Senonēs*, a tribe of central Gaul]

Señor *se-nyōr'* or *-nyör', n* a gentleman; (in address) sir; (prefixed to a name) Mr: — *fem* **Señora** (*se-nyō'rə* or *-nyö'*) a lady; madam; (as a title) Mrs. — *n* **Señorita** (*sen-yə-rē'tə* or *-yö-*) a young lady; Miss. [Sp, from L *senior* older]

Senoussi. See **Senussi**.

sens *sens, adv* (*obs*) since.

sensate *sen'sāt, adj* endowed with physical sensation; perceived by the senses. [LL *sensātus*, from L *sensus* sense]

sensation *sen-sā'shən, n* consciousness of a physical experience, resulting from a certain bodily condition or resulting from stimulation of a sense organ (cf **perception**); function or operation of any of the senses; an effect on the senses; power of sensing; an emotion or feeling, *esp* of a specified kind; a thrill; a state, or matter, of general excited interest in the public, audience, etc; melodramatic quality, style or method; enough to taste, as of an alcoholic drink (*slang*). — *adj* **sensātional** causing or designed to cause a strong emotional reaction, *esp* excitement or horror; excellent (*colloq*); related to sensation or the senses. — *n* **sensā'tionalism** the doctrine that our ideas originate solely in sensation (*philos*); the use of melodramatic style or lurid details in order to achieve a sensational effect. — *n* **sensā'tionalist**. — *adj* **sensātionalist'ic**. — *adv* **sensā'tionally**. — *n* **sensā'tionism**. — *n* **sensā'tionist** and **sensā'tion-monger** a dealer in the sensational. [From Med L *sensātiō*, *-ōnis*, from L *sensus* sense]

sense *sens*, *n* faculty of receiving sensation, general or particular; subjective consciousness; inward feeling; impression; opinion; mental attitude; discernment; understanding; appreciation; feeling for what is appropriate; discerning feeling for things of some particular kind; (*usu* in *pl*) one's right wits; soundness of judgement; reasonableness; sensible or reasonable discourse; that which is reasonable; plain matter of fact; the realm of sensation and sensual appetite; a sense-organ (*Shakesp*); a meaning, *esp* any of a range of meanings that a word or phrase may convey; interpretation; purport; gist; direction (*esp* in *geom*, after Fr *sens*). — *adj* pertaining to a sense or senses. — *vt* to have a sensation, feeling, or appreciation of; to appreciate, grasp, comprehend; to become aware (that); (of computers) to detect (eg a hole, constituting a symbol, in punched card or tape). — *adj* **sensed** having meaning of a specified kind, etc. — **sense'ful** significant; full of good sense. — *adj* **sense'less** unconscious; without good sense; meaningless. — *adv* **sense'lessly**. — *n* **sense'lessness**. — *n* and *adj* **sen'sing**. — *n* **sen'sism** sensationalism (*philos*). — *n* **sen'sist**. — **sense datum** what is received immediately through the stimulation of a sense organ (also called **sensum** *sen'səm*: — *pl* **sen'sa**); **sense organ** a structure specially adapted for the reception of stimuli, such as eye, ear and nose; **sense perception** perception by the senses. — **five senses** the senses of sight, hearing, smell, taste, and touch; **bring someone to his or her senses** to make someone recognize the facts; to let someone understand that his or her behaviour must be mended; **come to one's senses** to regain consciousness; to start behaving sensibly (again); **common sense** see under **common**; **in a sense** in a sense other than the obvious one; in a way; after a fashion; **in** or **out of one's (right) senses** in or out of one's right wits or normal rational condition; **make sense** to be understandable, sensible or rational; **make sense of** to understand; to see the purpose in, or explanation of; **sixth sense** an ability to perceive what lies beyond the powers of the five senses; **take leave of one's senses** to go mad, start behaving unreasonably or irrationally. [L *sensus*, from *sentīre* to feel]

sensibilia *sen-si-bil'i-ə*, *n pl* whatever may be perceived by the senses. [L, neuter pl of *sensibilis*]

sensible *sen'si-bl*, *adj* having or marked by good sense, reasonable, judicious; perceptible by sense; perceptible, appreciable; easily perceived, evident; having the power of sensation; physically conscious; sensitive, easily or readily affected or altered; cognizant, aware (*of*); having sensibility (*obs*). — *n* an object of sense; that which is perceptible. — *n* **sensibil'ity** sensitiveness, sensitivity; capacity of feeling or emotion; readiness and delicacy of emotional response; sentimentality; (*usu* in *pl*) feelings that can be hurt. — *n* **sen'sibleness**. — *adv* **sen'sibly** in a sensible manner; to a sensible or perceptible degree; so far as the senses show. — **sensible horizon** the visible horizon; **sensible note** (*music*) a leading note. [ME, from OFr, from L *sensibilis*]

sensile *sen'sīl*, *adj* sentient; capable of affecting the senses. [L *sensilis*, from *sentīre* to feel]

sensillum *sen-sil'əm*, *n* in insects, a small sense organ on the integument: — *pl* **sensill'a**. [New L, dimin of L *sensus* sense]

sensitive *sen'si-tiv*, *adj* having power of sensation; feeling readily, acutely, or painfully; capable of receiving stimuli; reacting to outside influence; ready and delicate in reaction; sensitized; susceptible to the action of light (*photog*); pertaining to, or depending on, sensation; (of documents, etc) with secret or controversial contents. — *n* someone who or that which is sensitive, or abnormally or excessively sensitive. — *adv* **sen'sitively**. — *n* **sen'sitiveness** or **sensitiv'ity** response to stimulation of the senses; heightened awareness of oneself and others within the context of personal and social relationships; abnormal responsiveness eg to an allergen; degree of responsiveness to electric current, or radio waves, or to light; (of an instrument) readiness and delicacy in recording changes. — **sensitive flame** a flame that rises or falls in response to sound; **sensitive plant** a plant, *esp Mimosa pudica*, that shows more than usual irritability when touched or shaken, by movements of leaves, etc; a person who is easily upset. [ME, from OFr, from Med L *sensitīvus*]

sensitize or **-ise** *sen'si-tīz*, *vt* to render sensitive, or more sensitive, or sensitive in a high degree. — *n* **sensitizā'tion** or **-s-**. — *adj* **sen'sitized** or **-s-**. — *n* **sen'sitizer** or **-s-** [*sensit*ive and **-ize**]

sensitometer *sen-si-tom'-i-tər*, *n* an instrument for measuring sensitivity, eg of photographic films. [*sensit*ive and **-meter**]

sensor *sen'sər*, *n* a device that detects a change in a physical stimulus and turns it into a signal which can be measured or recorded, or which operates a control. [**sense** and **-or**]

sensori- *sen'sə-ri* or **senso-** *sen'sō* or *-sə-*, *combining form* indicating the senses, as in *sensorineural*, *sensorimotor*, and *sensoparalysis*. — **sensorimotor development** (*behav*) the development of co-ordination between perception and action, eg hand-eye co-ordination.

sensorial. See **sensorium** and **sensory**.

sensorium *sen-sō'ri-əm* or *-sō'* (*biol*) *n* the area of the brain that is the seat of sensation; the brain; the mind; the nervous system: — *pl* **senso'riums** or **senso'ria**. — *adj* **senso'rial** relating to the sensorium. [LL, from L *sēnsus* felt]

sensory *sen'sə-ri adj* of the senses or sensation. — *adj* **senso'rial** sensory. — *adv* **sen'sorily**. — **sensory deprivation** the reduction to a minimum of all external stimulation reaching the body, a situation used in psychological experiments and sometimes as a method of interrogation. [L *sensōrius*, from L *sentīre* to feel]

sensual *sen'-sū-əl* or *-shōō-əl*, *adj* of the senses, as distinct from the mind; not intellectual or spiritual; connected with gratification, *esp* undue gratification of bodily sense; tending to arouse sexual appetite; carnal; lewd; voluptuous. — *n* **sen'sualism** sensual indulgence; the doctrine that all our knowledge is derived originally from sensation, sensationalism (*philos*); the regarding of the gratification of the senses as the highest end. — *n* **sen'sualist** a person given to sensualism or sensual indulgence; a debauchee; a believer in the doctrine of sensualism. — *adj* **sensualist'ic**. — *n* **sensual'ity** the quality of being sensual; indulgence in sensual pleasures. — *n* **sensualīzā'tion** or **-s-**. — *vt* **sen'sualize** or **-ise** to make sensual; to debase by carnal gratification. — *adv* **sen'sually**. — *n* **sen'sualness**. [LL *sensūalis*, from L *sensus* sense]

sensum. See **sense-datum** under **sense**.

sensuous *sen'sū-əs*, *adj* of or pertaining to the senses without implication of lasciviousness or grossness (apparently coined by Milton to distinguish this sense from those of **sensual**); alive to the pleasures of sensation; connected with sensible objects; (of pleasure) experienced through the senses. — *adv* **sen'suously**. — *n* **sen'suousness**. [L *sensus*]

Sensurround® *sen'sə-round*, *n* a system of sound reproduction used *esp* in films, in which low-frequency output produces physical sensations in the audience and creates the impression of involvement in the action portrayed on screen.

sent[1]. An obsolete spelling of **scent** *n*, *vt*, and *vi*, smell; sense.

sent[2] *sent*, *pa t* and *pa p* of **send**.

sentence *n* determination of punishment pronounced by a court or a judge; a judgement, opinion or decision; a number of words making a complete grammatical structure, in writing generally begun with a capital letter and ended with a full stop or its equivalent; an assertion in logic or mathematics; a maxim, aphorism (*archaic*); a group of two or more phrases forming a musical unit; sense, meaning, matter (*obs*). — *vt* to pronounce sentence or judgement on; to condemn. — *n* **sen'tencer**. — *adj* **sentential** (*-ten'shl*). — *adv* **senten'tially**. — *adj* **senten'tious** full of meaning; aphoristic, abounding in maxims; tending to moralize. — *adv* **senten'tiously**. — *n* **senten'tiousness**. — **open sentence** a sentence which, having an undefined variable is, as it stands, neither true nor false (*math*). [Fr, from L *sententia*, from *sentīre* to feel]

sentient *sen'shyənt* or *shənt*, *adj* conscious; capable of sensation; aware; responsive to stimulus. — *n* that which is sentient; a sentient being or mind. — *n* **sen'tience** or **sen'tiency**. [L *sentiēns*, *-entis*, pr p of *sentīre* to feel]

sentiment *sen'ti-mənt*, *n* a thought or body of thought tinged with or influenced by emotion; an opinion, attitude or judgement; a thought or feeling expressed in words; a maxim; emotion; feeling bound up with some object or ideal; regard to ideal considerations; sensibility, refined feelings, *esp* as expressed in art or literature; consciously worked-up or partly insincere feeling; sentimentality, mawkishness; a toast, *esp* epigrammatically expressed, proposed for drinking (*old*). — *adj* **sentimental** (*-men'tl*) pertaining to or expressive of sentiment; easily feeling and expressing tender emotions, *esp* love, friendship and pity; providing or designed to provoke such emotions, *esp* in large measure and without sublety; closely associated with, or moved (to tears) by, fond memories of the past. — *n* **sentimentality** (*-men-tal'-i-ti*) or **sentimen'talism**, the state or quality of being sentimental; the tendency to indulge in sentiment or the affectation of fine feelings; an act or statement that is sentimental; sloppiness. — *n* **sentimen'talist**. — *vi* **sentimen'talize** or **-ise** to behave sentimentally; to indulge in sentimentality. — *vt* to make sentimental; to treat sentimentally. — *adv* **sentimen'tally**. [LL *sentīmentum*, from L *sentīre* to feel]

sentinel *sen'ti-nl*, *n* a person posted on guard, a sentry; a character indicating the occurrence of a specified condition, eg the end of a magnetic tape (*comput*). — *adj* acting as a sentinel. — *vt* to watch over; to post as a sentinel; to supply with a sentinel or sentinels. — *vi* to keep guard: — *pr p* **sen'tinelling**; *pa t* and *pa p* **sen'tinelled**. — **sentinel crab** a crab of the Indian Ocean with long eyestalks. [Fr *sentinelle*, from Ital *sentinella* watch, sentinel]

sentry *sen'tri*, *n* a sentinel; a member of the armed forces set to guard eg a gate or entrance; the watch or guard kept by such a soldier, etc. — **sentry box** a box-like shelter with an open front, in which a sentry can stand for protection from rain, etc; **sen'try-go** a sentry's patrol or duty; a watchtower (*obs*). [Ety obscure, perh shortening of obs *centrinell*, *centronel*, *var of* **sentinel**]

Senussi or **Senusi** *sen-ōō's'ē*, *n* a member of a Muslim sect or confraternity, chiefly in NE Africa, founded by Sidi Mohammed ben Ali es-Senussi (d 1860; named from the *Senus* Mountains): — *pl* **Senuss'i** or **Senuss'is**. — Also **Senouss'i**.

senvy *sen'vi*, (*obs*) *n* mustard (the plant or seed). [OFr *senevé*, from L *sināpi*, from Gr *sināpi* mustard]

senza *sen'tsä*, (*music*) *prep* without (*abbrev* **sen.**). [Ital]

SEO *abbrev*: Senior Executive Officer.

Sep or **Sep.** *abbrev*: September.

sep. *abbrev*: separate.

sepad *sə-päd'*, *vt* to suppose; to warrant. [A ghost word; from J M Barrie's mishearing of *I'se* (= I sal) *uphaud*, I shall uphold]

sepal *sep'l*, also *sēp'l*, *n* any of the separate parts of a flower calyx. — *adj* **sep'alous** having sepals. — *adj* **sep'aline** (*-īn*) or **sep'aloid** of the form of sepals. — *n* **sep'alōdy** (Gr *eidos* form) transformation of other flower parts into sepals. [Fr *sépale*, invented by N J de Necker (1790) from Gr *skepē* cover]

separate *sep'ə-rāt*, *vt* to divide; to part; to sunder; to sever; to disconnect; to disunite; to remove; to isolate; to keep apart; to seclude; to set apart for a purpose; to shut off from cohabitation, *esp* by judicial decree; to remove cream from, using a separator. — *vi* to part; to cease to live together as a (*esp* married) couple; to withdraw; to secede; to come out of combination or contact; to become disunited. — *adj* (*sep'ə-rit* or *sep'rit*) separated; divided; apart from another; distinct. — *n* an offprint; (in *pl*) items of dress, eg blouse, skirt, etc, forming separate parts of an outfit. — *n* **separability** (*-ə-bil'i-ti*). — *adj* **sep'arable** that may be separated or disjoined. — *n* **sep'arableness**. — *adv* **sep'arably**. — *adv* **sep'arately**. — *n* **sep'arateness**. — *n* **separā'tion** act of separating or disjoining; the state of being separate; disunion; chemical analysis; cessation of cohabitation by agreement or judicial decree, without a formal dissolution of the marriage tie. — *n* **sep'aratism** (*-ə-tizm*) or **separā'tionism**. — *n* and *adj* **sep'aratist** a person who withdraws or advocates separation from an established church, federation, organization, etc (also **separā'tionist**); a dissenter; an Independent (*hist*); (by Unionists) a person who advocates Home Rule; a believer in separate authorship of parts, *esp* of the Homeric poems. — *adj* **sep'arative** (*-ə-tiv*) tending to separate. — *n* **sep'arātor** a person who or thing which separates; a machine for separating cream from milk by whirling. — *n* **separatory** (*sep'ər-ə-tər-i*) an instrument for separating. — *adj* having the function of separating. — *n* **sep'arātrix** a separating line, solidus. — *n* **separā'tum** a separate offprint. — **separate development** segregation of different racial groups, each supposed to progress in its own way; **separate maintenance** a provision made by a husband for his separated wife; **separation allowance** a government allowance to a serviceman's wife and dependents. [L *sēparāre*, *-ātum*, from *sē-* aside, and *parāre* to put]

Sephardim *si-fär'dēm* or *-dim*, (*Judaism*) *n pl* the Jews of Spanish, Portuguese or N African descent; loosely, Oriental Jews. — *n* **Sephar'di** a member of the Sephardim; the pronunciation of Hebrew used by them. — Also *adj*. — *adj* **Sephar'dic**. [Heb *sephāradhī*, from *sephāradh* a region (thought to be Spain) mentioned in Obad 20, to which Jews were exiled]

sephen *sef'en*, *n* a stingray. [Ar *safan* shagreen]

sepia *sē'pi-ə*, *n* cuttlefish ink; a cuttlefish, *esp* of *Sepia* or a related genus; a pigment made from it, or an artificial imitation; its colour, a fine brown; brownish tone produced in certain, *esp* early, photographic processes; a sepia drawing or photograph. — *adj* of the colour of sepia; done in sepia. — *n* **sē'piolite** (Gr *lithos* stone) meerschaum. — *n* **se'piost** or **sepiostaire'** (*-stār*; Fr *sépiostaire*, from Gr *osteon* bone) or **se'pium** cuttlebone. [L, from Gr *sēpiā* cuttlefish]

sepiment *sep'i-mənt*, *n* a hedge, a fence. [L *saepīmentum* a hedge]

sepiolite, **sepiost**, **sepiostaire**, **sepium**. See under **sepia**.

sepmag *sep'mag*, *adj* (of a film, television programme, etc) having sound recorded on separate magnetic tape which is then synchronized with the film, etc as it is run. [*sep*arate and *mag*netic]

sepoy *sē'poi*, (*hist*) *n* an indigenous soldier or policeman in India during British rule. [Urdu and Pers *sipāhī* horseman]

seppuku *se-pōō'kōō*, *n* hara-kiri. [Jap]

seps *seps*, *n* a skink of the genus *Seps* with a serpentlike body, the serpent-lizard; a very venomous snake mentioned by classical writers. [Gr *sēps*]

sepsis *sep'sis*, (*med*) *n* putrefaction; invasion by pathogenic bacteria: — *pl* **sep'sēs**. [Gr *sēpsis* putrefaction]

Sept or **Sept.** *abbrev*: September.

sept *sept*, *n* (*orig* in Ireland) a division of a tribe; a clan. — *adj* **sept'al**. [Prob for **sect**[1], infl by L *saeptum*]

sept- *sept-*, **septi-** *sep-ti* or **septem-** *sep-tem'-* or *sep'təm-*, *combining form* denoting the quantity or amount seven. — *adj* **septemfid** (*sep'təm-fid*; root of L *findere* to cleave) seven-cleft. — *n* **septemvir** (*sep-tem'vir*; L *vir* man) one of a board of seven: — *pl* **septem'virī** or **septem'virs**. — *n* **septem'virate** the office of a septemvir; a board of septemviri; a group of seven men. — *adj* **septilateral** (*sep-ti-lat'ə-rəl*; L *latus*, *lateris* a side) seven-sided. — *n* **septillion** (*sep-til'yən*; modelled on **million**) the seventh power of a million; the eighth power of a thousand (*NAm*). [L *septem*]

septa, **septal**. See under **septum**.

septa'rium *sep-tā'ri-əm*, *n* a nodule of mineral substance with a network of cracks filled with another mineral: — *pl* **septā'ria**. — *adj* **septārian**. [Mod L, from L *septum*]

septate *sep'tāt*, *adj* partitioned; divided by septa. — *n* **septā'tion** division by partitions or septa. [**septum**]

September *səp-* or *sep-tem'bər*, *n* the ninth (*orig*, in the calendar of ancient Rome, the seventh) month of the year. — *adj* **Septem'berish**. — *n* **Septem'brist** a participator in the September massacres of royalist prisoners in Paris, 2–7 Sept 1792 (*Fr hist*); a supporter of the successful rising of 1836 in Portugal. — *n* **Sep'tembrizer** or **-s-** a Septembrist (*Fr* and *Port hist*); a partridge-shooter, *esp* one active in September. — **September people** (*informal euphem*) people of late middle age or older. [L *September*, *-bris*]

septenarius *sep-ti-nā'ri-əs*, *n* a seven-foot verse, *esp* a trochaic tetrameter catalectic. — *adj* **septenary** (*sep-tē'nə-ri* or *sep'tə-nə-ri*) numbering or based on seven. — *n* a seven, set of seven (*esp* years); a septenarius. [L *septēnārius* of seven]

septennium *sep-ten'i-əm*, *n* a period of seven years: — *pl* **septenn'ia**. — *n* **septenn'ate** a period of seven years. — *adj* **septenn'ial**. — *adv* **septenn'ially**. — **Septennial Act** a statute of 1716, in force till 1911, limiting the length of a parliament to seven years. [L *septennis*, from *annus* a year]

septentrion *sep-ten'tri-ən*, (*archaic*) *n* the north. — *n pl* **septen'trions** or **septentriō'nēs** the seven stars of the Plough; the Great Bear. — *adj* **septen'trion** (*archaic*), **septen'trial** (*obs*) or **septen'trional** northern. — *adv* **septen'trionally**. [L *septentriōnēs*, ie *septem triōnēs* the seven plough-oxen]

septet or **septette** *sep-tet'*, *n* a musical composition for seven performers; a set of seven (*esp* musicians). [Ger *Septett*, from L *septem*]

sept-foil *set'foil*, *n* the tormentil plant; a figure divided by seven cusps (*archit*). [Fr *sept* seven, and OFr *foil*, from L *folium* a leaf]

septic *sep'tik*, *adj* affected by bacteria from a diseased wound, putrefying; caused by such bacteria. — *n* **septicaemia** (*sep-ti-sē'mi-ə*; Gr *haima* blood) the presence of pathogenic bacteria in the blood. — *adv* **sep'tically**. — *n* **septicity** (*-tis'i-ti*). — **septic tank** a tank, *usu* below ground, in which sewage is decomposed by anaerobic bacteria. [Gr *sēptikos*, from *sēpein* to putrefy]

septicidal *sep-ti-sī'dəl*, (*bot*) *adj* with splitting of septa, as when a fruit dehisces by separation of the carpels. [**septum** and L *caedere* to cut]

septiferous, **septiform**. See under **septum**.

septifragal *sep-ti'frə-gl*, (*bot*) *adj* with separation of the outer walls of the carpels from the septa. [**septum** and root of L *frangere* to break]

septilateral, **septillion**. See under **sept-**.

septimal *sep'ti-ml*, *adj* relating to or based on the number seven. — *n* **septime** (*sep'tēm*; *fencing*) the seventh parrying position. — *n* **sep'timole** (*-mōl*; *music*) a group of seven notes to be played in the time of four or six. [L *septimus* seventh, from *septem* seven]

septleva *set'lə-vä*, (*cards*) *n* (in the game of basset) seven times as much added to the first stake. [Fr *sept-et-le-va* seven and the first stake]

Septrin® *sep'trin*, *n* an antibacterial drug.

septuagenarian *sep-tū-ə-ji-nā'ri-ən*, *n* a person seventy years old, or between seventy and eighty. — *adj* of that age. — *adj* **septuagenary** (*-ə-jē'nər-i* or *-aj'i-nə-ri*) consisting of or relating to seventy. — *n* a person seventy years old. [L *septuāgēnārius*, from *septuāgēnī* seventy each]

Septuagesima *sep-tū-ə-jes'i-mə*, *n* the third Sunday before Lent (also **Septuagesima Sunday**), *appar* in continuation of the sequence Quadragesima, Quinquagesima, etc. [L *septuāgēsimus*, *-a*, *-um* seventieth]

Septuagint *sep'tū-ə-jint*, *n* the Greek Old Testament, traditionally attributed to 72 translators at Alexandria in the 3c BC, *usu* written **LXX**. — *adj* **Septuagin'tal**. [L *septuāgintā*, from *septem* seven]

septum *sep'təm*, (*biol* and *anatom*) a partition or dividing structure in a cavity, tissue, etc: — *pl* **sept'a**. — *adj* **sept'al**. — *adj* **septif'erous** having partitions. — *adj* **sep'tiform** in the form of a partition. [L *saeptum* (used in pl) a fence, enclosure, from *saepīre* to fence, enclose]

septuor *sep'tū-ör*, *n* a septet. [Fr, from L *septem*, after *quattuor*]

septuple *sep'tū-pl*, also *-tū'*, *-to͝o-* or *-to͞o'*, *adj* sevenfold. — *vt* to multiply sevenfold. — *n* **sep'tūplet** one of seven children (or animals) born at a single birth; a group of seven notes played in the time of four or six, a septimole (*music*). [LL *septuplus*, from L *septem* seven; cf **quadruple**]

sepulchre or (*US*) **sepulcher** *sep'əl-kər*, *n* a tomb; a recess in a church, *usu* in the north chancel wall, or a structure placed in it, to receive the reserved sacrament and the crucifix from Maundy Thursday or Good Friday till Easter (**Easter sepulchre**); burial. — *vt* (formerly sometimes *si-pul'kər*) to entomb; to enclose as a tomb. — *adj* **sepulchral** (*si-pul'krəl*) of, or of the nature of, a sepulchre; as if of or from a sepulchre; funereal, gloomy, dismal; hollow-toned. — *adj* **sepul'chrous** (*rare*). — *adj* **sepul'tural**. — *n* **sep'ulture** the act of burial in a sepulture; a tomb or burial-place. — *vt* to entomb. — **whited sepulchre** see under **white**. [L *sepulcrum*, *sepultūra*, from *sepelīre*, *sepultum* to bury]

seq. *abbrev*: *sequens* (*L*), following: — *pl* **seqq**. *sequentes* or *sequentia*.

sequacious *si-kwā'shəs*, *adj* ready to follow a leader or authority; compliant; pliant; observing logical sequence or consistency. — *n* **sequā'ciousness** or **sequacity** (*si-kwas'i-ti*). [L *sequāx*, *sequācis*, from *sequī* to follow]

sequel *sē'kwəl*, *n* that which follows; followers (*obs*); successors (*obs*); consequences; upshot; a resumption of a story already complete in itself, in book, play, film, etc form; sequence (*Shakesp*); an allowance to mill servants in thirlage (*Scots law*). — *n* **sequela** (*si-kwē'lə*) any abnormal condition following or relating to a previous disease; the psychological, etc after-effect of any trauma: — often in *pl* **sequē'lae** (*-lē*). [L *sequēla*, from *sequī* to follow]

sequence *sē'kwəns*, *n* a state or fact of being sequent or consequent; succession; order of succession; a series of things following in order; a succession of quantities each derivable from its predecessor according to a law (*math*); a set of three or more cards consecutive in value; that which follows; consequence; successive repetition in higher or lower parts of the scale or in higher or lower keys (*music*); (in cinematography) a division of a film more or less equivalent to a scene in a stage play; (in liturgics) a hymn in rhythmical prose, sung after the gradual and before the gospel. — *vt* to place in sequence; to discover or determine the sequence or order of. — *n* **se'quencer** any device which arranges or determines the order of a number of events, operations, items or data, etc, in a sequence; a device connected to a synthesizer that can memorize sequences of notes. — *n* **se'quencing** (*biochem*) the process of determining the order of amino acids in a protein or of nucleotides in DNA or RNA. — *adj* **sē'quent** following; consequent; successive; consecutive. — *n* a follower (*Shakesp*); that which follows. — *adj* **sequential** (*si-kwen'shl*) in, or having, a regular sequence; sequent; (of data) stored one after another (*comput*). — *n* **sequentiality** (*-shi-al'i-ti*). — *adv* **sequen'tially**. — **sequential access** (*comput*) a method of finding data in a file by reading through the file from the beginning (cf **direct access**). — **sequence of tenses** the relation of tense in subordinate clauses to that in the principal clause. [L *sequēns, -entis*, pr p of *sequī* to follow]

sequester *si-kwes'tər*, *vt* to set aside; to seclude; to set apart; to confiscate; to remove (property, etc) from someone's possession until a dispute can be settled, creditors satisfied, etc; to hold the income of (a vacant benefice) for the benefit of the next incumbent; to sequester the estate or benefice of; to remove or render ineffective (a metal ion) by adding a reagent that forms a complex with it (eg as a means of preventing or getting rid of precipitation in water). — *vi* (*obs*) to seclude oneself. — *n* (*sek'wis-tər*; *Shakesp*) seclusion. — *adj* **seques'tered** retired, secluded. — *adj* **seques'trable**. — *n* **seques'trant** (*chem*) a substance which removes an ion or renders it ineffective, by forming a complex with the ion. — *vt* **sequestrate** (*sek'*, *sēk'*, or *si-kwes'*) to sequester; to vest (the property, assets, etc of a bankrupt individual) in a trustee for distribution amongst creditors (*Scots law*); to render (a person) bankrupt (*Scots law*). — *n* **sequestrā'tion** (*sek-*, *sēk-*) the act of sequestering; the process of vesting a bankrupt's property, assets, etc, with a trustee for distribution amongst creditors, bankruptcy (*Scots law*); the action of a sequestrant (*chem*); a portion of diseased or dead tissue detached from, or joined abnormally to, surrounding healthy tissue (*med*). — *n* **seq'uestrātor**. — *n* **seques'trum** (*pathol*) a fragment of dead or diseased bone that has become detached from healthy bone, as in osteomyelitis: — *pl* **seques'tra**. [LL *sequestrāre, -ātum*, from L *sequester* a depositary, from *secus* apart]

sequin *sē'kwin*, *n* a spangle used to decorate a garment; an old Italian gold coin. — *adj* **se'quined** or **se'quinned**. [Fr, from Ital *zecchino*, from *zecca* the mint; of Ar origin]

sequoia *si-kwoi'ə*, *n* either of two gigantic Californian conifers, the redwood, *Sequoia sempervirens*, and the big tree or giant sequoia, *Sequoiadendron giganteum* (formerly *Sequoia gigantea*, also Wellingtonia), that can grow to heights of 100 metres and may take 2000 years to reach their mature height. [After the Cherokee Indian scholar *Sequoiah*]

ser. *abbrev*: serial; series; serine; sermon.

sera. See **serum**.

sérac or **serac** *sā-rak'* or *sā'rak*, *n* one of the cuboidal or pillarlike masses into which a glacier breaks on a steep incline. [Swiss Fr, *orig* a kind of white cheese]

serafile. See under **serried**.

serafin. Same as **xerafin**.

seraglio *sə-rä'li-ō*, *se-* or *-lyō*, *n* women's quarters in a Muslim house or palace; a harem; a collection of wives or concubines; an enclosure; a Turkish palace, *esp* that of the sultans at Constantinople: — *pl* **sera'glios**. [Ital *serraglio*, from L *sera* a door-bar, confused with Turk *saray*, *serāī* a palace]

serai *se-rä'i*, *n* a khan or caravanserai; erroneously, a harem, a seraglio. [Turk (orig Pers) *saray*, *serāī*]

serail *se-rāl'*, *n* a seraglio. [Fr *sérail*]

seral. See under **sere**[3].

serang *se-rang'*, *n* a boatswain on an Oriental, *esp* Indian, ship. [Pers *sarhang* a commander]

serape or **sarape** *sə-rä'pā*, *n* a *usu* brightly coloured woollen riding-blanket, often worn around the shoulders by Mexican men. [Mex Sp *sarape*]

seraph *ser'əf*, *n* a six-winged celestial being (from the Bible: Isaiah 6); an angel of the highest of the nine orders; a person of angelic character or mien: — *pl* **ser'aphs** or **ser'aphim** (*-im*), formerly also **ser'aphin**, **ser'aphins** or **ser'aphims**, the plurals in *-im* and *-in* also occurring as *obs sing*. — *adj* **seraphic** (*-af'*) or **seraph'ical** of or like a seraph; serene, blissful. — *adv* **seraph'ically**. — *n* **ser'aphine** (*-ēn*) a keyboard reed instrument, precursor of the harmonium. — **Seraphic Doctor** St Bonaventura; St Teresa; **Seraphic Father** St Francis; **Seraphic Order** the Franciscans. [Heb *Serāphīm* (pl)]

seraphin[1]. Same as **xeraphin** (see **xerafin**).

seraphin[2]. See **seraph**.

Serapis or **Sarapis** *sə-* or *se-rā'pis*, *n* a god of the Greeks of Egypt, identified with Apis and Osiris. — *n* **Serapeum** (*ser-ə-pē'əm*) a temple of Serapis. — *adj* **Serapic** or **Sarapic** (*-ap'ik*). [Gr *Sarāpis*, later (also L) *Serāpis*]

seraskier *ser-as-kēr'*, *n* a Turkish commander-in-chief or war minister. — *n* **seraskier'ate** the office of seraskier. [Turk pron of Pers *ser'asker*, from *ser* head, and Ar *'asker* army]

Serb *sûrb*, or **Serbian** *sûr'bi-ən*, *n* a native or citizen of Serbia (formerly a kingdom, then a constituent republic of Yugoslavia, now an independent republic); a member of the people principally inhabiting Serbia; the South Slav language of Serbia. — *adj* of Serbia, its people, or their language. — *n* **Serbo-Cro'at** or **Serbo-Croatian** (*-krō-ā'shən*) a member of the South Slavonic branch of the Indo-European family of languages, spoken in Serbia, Croatia, etc. — Also *adj*. [Serb *Srb*]

Serbonian *sər-bō'ni-ən*, *adj* like *Sirbōnis*, *Serbōnis*, a now dry lake in the NE corner of Egypt, 'Where armies whole have sunk' (*Paradise Lost*, II. 594).

SERC *abbrev*: Science and Engineering Research Council.

serdab *sər-däb'*, *n* an underground chamber; a secret chamber in an ancient Egyptian tomb. [Pers *sard* cold, and *āb* water]

Sercial *sûr'si-əl*, a Riesling-like grape variety used to make the driest Madeira wine. [Fr]

sere[1]. See **sear**[1,2].

sere[2] *sēr*, (*obs*) *n* a claw. [OFr *serre*, from *serrer* to hold]

sere[3] *sēr*, *n* a series of ecological communities succeeding each other and representing stages in the biological development of an area. — *adj* **sēr'al**. — **seral community** an ecological community which is not stabilized but represents a stage in a succession. [L *seriēs* series]

serein *sə-rɛ̃'*, *n* in the tropics, fine rain falling from an apparently cloudless sky after sunset. [Fr, from L *sērum* evening, from *sērus* late]

serenade *ser-i-nād'*, *n* a composition like a symphony, *usu* lighter in tone and in more movements; a song or tune suitable for or suggestive of the evening, *esp* one with a romantic theme sung or played under a lady's window by a suitor; the performing of such a song or tune in this way. — *vt* to entertain with a serenade. — *vi* to perform a serenade. — *n* **serenā'der**. — *n* **serenata** (*-i-nä'tä*) a (symphonic) serenade; a pastoral cantata. — *n* **ser'enate** (*Milton*) a serenade. [Fr *sérénade*, and Ital *serenata*, prob from Ital *sereno* open air, from L *serēnus* clear, cloudless; meaning infl by L *sērus* late]

serendipity *ser-ən-dip'i-ti*, *n* the faculty of making fortunate or beneficial discoveries by accident. — *n* **serendip'itist** a person who believes in serendipity; a person who has this faculty. — *adj* **serendip'itous** discovered by luck or chance; pertaining to or having serendipity. — *adv* **serendip'itously**. [*Serendip*, a former name for Sri Lanka. Horace Walpole coined the word (1754) from the title of the fairy-tale 'The Three Princes of Serendip', whose heroes 'were always making discoveries, by accidents and sagacity, of things they were not in quest of']

serene[1] *sə-rēn'*, *adj* calm; unclouded; unruffled; (with *cap*) an adjunct to the titles of members of some European royal families (translating Ger *Durchlaucht* Serenity). — *n* (*poetic*) calm brightness; serenity; serene sky or sea; pure air. — *vt* (*archaic*) to tranquillize; to clear. — *adv* **serēne'ly**. — *n* **serēne'ness**. — *n* **serenity** (*-ren'i-ti*). — **all serene** (*colloq*) everything as it should be; all right; **drop serene** (*Milton*) gutta serena or amaurosis, a kind of blindness. [L *serēnus* clear]

serene[2] *ser'ēn* or *sə-rēn'*, (*obs*) *n* a supposedly unwholesome night dew; serein. [**serein**]

Serevent® *ser'ə-vent*, *n* a tradename for the bronchodilator drug salmerol, a beta-2 agonist used to control asthma.

serf *sûrf*, *n* a person in modified slavery, *esp* one bound to work on the land; a villein: — *pl* **serfs**. — *n* **serf'age**, **serf'dom**, **serf'hood** and **serf'ship**. — *adj* **serf'ish**. — *adj* **serf'like**. [Fr, from L *servus* a slave]

Serg. *abbrev*: Sergeant.

serge[1] *sûrj*, *n* a strong twilled fabric, now *usu* of worsted. — *adj* of serge. [Fr, from L *sērica* silk; see **seric**]

serge[2]. See **cerge**.

sergeant or **serjeant** *sär'jənt*, *n orig* a servant; an officer who made arrests (*obs*); (*usu* with *g*) a non-commissioned officer next above a corporal; (with *g*) an officer of police; (*usu* with *g*) alone or as a prefix, designating certain officials; (with *j*) formerly, a barrister of highest rank (in full **serjeant-at-law'**). — *n* **ser'geancy** or **ser'jeancy** office or rank of sergeant or serjeant. — *n* **ser'geantship** or **ser'jeantship**. — *n* **ser'jeantry** serjeanty. — *n* **ser'jeanty** a condition of tenure by service in person to the king (**grand serjeanty**) or rendering some small object (**petty serjeanty**). — **sergeant-** (or **serjeant-**)**at-arms'** an officer of a legislative body or the Court of Chancery, for making arrests, etc; **sergeant-drumm'er** drum-major; **ser'geant-fish** a fish with stripes, *esp* the cobia (*Rhachicentron*) of the SE US, related to the mackerel; **sergeant-mā'jor** formerly, an officer of rank varying from major to major-general; now, the highest non-commissioned officer (**company sergeant-major** the senior warrant officer in a company; **regimental sergeant-major** a warrant officer on the staff of a battalion, regiment, etc); **sergeant first class** in the US army, a sergeant below a master sergeant. — **Common Serjeant** in London, an assistant to the Recorder, a judge of the quarter-session court. [Fr *sergent*, from L *serviēns*, *-entis*, pr p of *servīre* to serve]

Sergt *abbrev*: Sergeant.

serial, **seriate**, **seriatim**. See **series**.

seric *serik*, (*rare*) *adj* silken; (with *cap*) Chinese. — *adj* **sericeous** (*sə-rish'əs*) silky; covered with soft silky appressed hairs (*bot*); with a silky sheen. — *n* **sericin** (*ser'i-sin*) the gelatinous protein substance found in raw silk. — *n* **ser'icite** a silky soapy potash mica. — *adj* **sericitic** (*-sit'ik*). — *n* **sericitīzā'tion** or **-s-** conversion (*esp* of orthoclase) into sericite. — *n* **sericterium** (*-tē'ri-əm*; *entomol*) a silk or spinning gland, as in the silkworm: — *pl* **sericte'ria**. — *n* **ser'iculture** the breeding of silkworms for production of raw silk. — Also **sericiculture** (*ser'i-si-kul-chər*). — *n* **sericul'turist** or **sericicul'turist**. — *n* **ser'igraph** a print made by silk-screen process. — *n* **serig'rapher**. — *adj* **serigraph'ic**. — *n* **serig'raphy**. [Gr *sērikos*, from *Sēres* the Chinese people who produced silk in ancient times]

sericon *ser'i-kon*, *n* conjectured to be a red (or black) tincture in alchemy.

sericulture. See under **seric**.

seriema *ser-i-ē'mə* or *-ā'mə*, *n* either of two S American birds of the family *Cariamidae*, related to the cranes and the rails, somewhat like a small crested crane in form (also, now obsolescent, **caria'ma**). [Tupí *çariama*]

series *sē'rēz* or *-riz*, rarely *sē'ri-ēz*, *n* a set of things in line or in succession, or thought of in this way; a set of things having something in common, eg of books in similar form issued by the same publishing house; a set of things differing progressively; the sum where each term of a sequence is added to the previous one (*math*); a taxonomic group (of various rank); a geological formation; succession; sequence; linear or end-to-end arrangement; a set of notes in a particular order, taken, instead of a traditional scale, as the basis of a composition, eg the twelve-note row of twelve-tone music: — *pl* **se'ries**. — *adj* **se'rial** forming a series; in series; in a row; in instalments; of publication in instalments; using series as the basis of composition (*music*); (of supernumerary buds) one above another. — *n* a publication, *esp* a story, in instalments; a motion picture, television or radio play appearing in instalments. — *n* **se'rialism** (*music*) serial technique, or use of it. — *n* **se'rialist** a writer of serials, or of serial music. — *n* **seriality** (*-al'i-ti*). — *n* **serializā'tion** or **-s-** publication in instalments; the use of notes and/or other elements of music in regular patterns. — *vt* **se'rialize** or **-ise** to arrange in series; to publish serially. — *adv* **se'rially**. — *adj* **se'riate** (*-ət*) in rows. — *vt* (*-āt*) to arrange in a series, or in order. — *adv* **se'riately**. — *n* **seriā'tion**. — **serial killer** a person who murders several people over a period, often killing the victims in the same way or choosing victims of the same type, sex, age, etc; **serial number** the individual identification number marked on each one of a series of identical products; **serial port** (*comput*) a socket in a computer by means of which it can be connected to a peripheral device such as a printer; **serial technique** the technique of music based on series; **serial time** time regarded as an infinite regression of successive times, each needed for the description of its predecessor (J W Dunne, 1875–1949); **series winding** (in an electric motor) a winding of the armative coil and field-magnet coil so that they are in series with the external circuit. — *adj* **series-wound'**. — **arithmetical series** (*math*) a series progressing by constant difference; **geometrical series** (*math*) a series progressing by constant ratio; **in series** (*phys*) of electric components, connected in such a way that a current flows through them. — Cf **in parallel**. [L *seriēs*, from *serere*, *sertum* to join]

seriatim *sē-ri-ā'tim*, (*L*) in succession, one after another, one by one. [Med L, from L *serēs*; see **series**]

serif *ser'if*, *n* a short decorative foot at the end of a stroke on a printed character; any of the styles of type or print which feature such feet. — Also (*rare*) **ser'iph** and **cer'iph**. [Origin obscure; poss Du *schreef* stroke]

serigraph, **serigrapher**, etc. See under **seric**.

serin *ser'in*, *n* any of various small finches of the genus *Serinus*, *incl* the canary. — *n* **serinette'** a small barrel-organ for training songbirds. [Fr, canary]

serine *ser'ēn*, *sēr'ēn* or *-in*, *n* an amino acid ($HOCH_2CH(NH_2)COOH$), found in protein and synthesized in the body. [From *ser*icin and **-ine**]

seringa *sə-ring'gə*, *n* a Brazilian tree (*Hevea*) yielding rubber; mock-orange (*Philadelphus*). [Port; see **syringa**]

serious *sē'ri-əs*, *adj* grave; staid; earnest; disinclined to lightness of mood; in earnest; not to be taken lightly; showing firmness of intention or commitment; approaching the critical or dangerous; concerned with weighty matters; professedly religious; significant, notable, or in significant quantities, as in *serious money* (*colloq*). — *adj* **se'riocom'ic** or **seriocom'ical** partly serious and partly comic. — *adv* **se'riously** in a serious manner; extremely, as in *seriously rich* (*colloq*). — *n* **se'riousness**. [LL *sēriōsus*, from L *sērius* grave, weighty]

seriph. See **serif**.

serj. or **serjt**. *abbrev*: serjeant.

serjeant. See **sergeant**.

serk. See **sark**.

serkali *ser-käl'ē*, *n* (in Africa) the Government; (in Africa) white rulers. [Swahili]

sermon *sûr'mən*, *n* a discourse, *esp* one delivered, or intended to be delivered, from the pulpit, on a Biblical text; a written version of this; a harangue, reproof or moralizing lecture. — *vt* and *vi* (*rare*) to preach; to discourse. — *n* **sermoneer'** or **ser'moner** (both *rare*) a preacher; a sermonizer. — *n* **sermonet'** or **sermonette'** a brief sermon. — *adj* **sermonic** (*-mon'ik*) or **sermon'ical**. — *n* **ser'moning**. — *vi* **ser'monize** or **-ise** to compose sermons; to preach. — *vt* to preach to. — *n* **ser'monizer** or **-s-**. [L *sermō*, *sermōnis* speech, prob ult from *serere* to join]

sero- *sē-rō-*, *-rə-*, *-ro'*, *combining form* denoting serum. — *adj* **serolog'ical**. — *adv* **serolog'ically**. — *n* **serol'ogist**. — *n* **serol'ogy** the study of serums, their constituents and properties. — *adj* **seroneg'ative** (of an individual whose blood has been tested for a specific disease) showing no serological reaction. — *adj* **seropos'itive**

showing a serological reaction indicating the presence of a virus or disease, such as AIDS. — *adj* **seropu'rulent** (*pathol*) containing a mixture of serum and pus, as in infected blisters. — *n* **seropus** (*sē'rō-pus*) a mixture of serum and pus. — *n* **serotaxon'omy** serological analysis sas a source of information for taxonomic classification. — *n* **serother'apy** treatment or prevention of disease by injecting blood serum containing known antibodies. — **serological typing** a technique based on antibody–antigen reactions, for the identification of pathogenic organisms when morphological differentiation is difficult or impossible, serotyping.

seroconvert *sē-rōkən-vûrt'*, *vi* to produce specific antibodies in response to the presence of an antigen, such as a virus or vaccine. — *adj* **seroconvert'ed**. — *n* **seroconver'sion**. [**sero-** and **convert**]

seron or **seroon** *si-rōn'*, *-ron'* or *-rōōn'*, (*archaic*) *n* a crate or hamper; a bale wrapped in hide. [Sp *serón*]

seronegative, **seropositive**, **seropurulent**. See under **sero-**.

serosa *si-rō'zə*, (*zool*) *n* an epithelial layer formed in the development of an insect's egg; a serous membrane, such as the peritoneum (see **serous**): — *pl* **serō'sas** or **serō'sae** (*-zē*). [Mod L; fem of *serōsus*, from *serum* (see **serum**)]

serosity. See **serous**.

serotherapy. See under **sero-**.

serotine *ser'ə-tīn* or *-tin*, *n* a large insectivorous bat, *Eptesicus serotinus*, of Europe, N Africa and SE Asia (also **serotine bat**). — *adj* (*biol*) late in occurrence, development, flowering, etc (also **serotinal** *si-rot'i-nəl*). — *adj* **serotinous** (*si-rot'i-nəs*). [L *sērōtinus*, from *sērus* late]

serotonin *sē-rə-tō'nin*, (*biochem*) *n* a compound that occurs throughout body tissue, *esp* in the brain, intestinal tissue and blood platelets, acting as a neurotransmitter and powerful vasoconstrictor. — Also called **5-hydroxytrypramine**. [**sero-**, *ton*ic and **-in**]

serotype *sē'rō-tīp*, *n* a group or category of bacteria or other microorganisms that have a certain set of antigens in common or against which common antibodies are produced; the combination of antigens by which such a group is categorized. — *vt* to classify according to the composition of antigens. — *n* **ser'otyping** serological typing. [**sero-** and **-type**]

serous *sē'rəs*, *adj* of, relating to, like or consisting of serum; watery. — *n* **seros'ity**. — **serous membrane** a serosa, a thin membrane, moist with serum, lining a cavity and enveloping the viscera within, such as the peritoneum or pericardium. [L *serōsus*, from *serum*; see **serum**]

serow *ser'ō*, *n* either of two SE Asian goat-antelopes, the mainland serow (*Capricornis sumatrensis*), and the smaller Japanese or Taiwanese serow (*Capricornis crispus*). [Lepcha (Tibeto-Burman language) *sa-ro*]

serpent *sûr'pənt*, *n* formerly, any reptile or creeping thing, *esp* if venomous; (with *the*) Satan as the tempter (*Old Testament*); a snake (*literary* and *dialect*); a treacherous or malicious person; an obsolete wooden leather-covered bass wind instrument shaped like a writhing snake; a firework that writhes like a serpent when ignited; (with *cap*) a northern constellation. — *adj* serpentlike. — *adj* **serpentiform** (*-pent'*) snake-shaped. — *adj* **ser'pentine** (*-tīn*) snakelike; winding; tortuous. — *n* a winding track; an old kind of cannon; a soft, *usu* green mineral, a hydrated magnesium silicate, occurring in winding veins and in masses, formed by alteration of olivine, etc; a rock, commonly an altered peridotite, composed mainly of the mineral serpentine. — *vt* and *vi* to wind; to insinuate. — *adv* **ser'pentinely**. — *adj* **serpentinic** (*-tin'ik*). — *n* and *adj* **ser'pentīning**. — *adv* **serpentī'ningly**. — *n* **serpentinite** (*-pen'*) a rock composed mainly of serpentine. — *n* **serpentinizā'tion** or **-s-**. — *vt* **ser'pentinize** or **-ise** to convert into serpentine. — *adj* **serpentī'nous** of serpentine; winding. — *vi* **ser'pentize** or **-ise** to wind. — *vt* to cause to wind. — *adj* and *adv* **ser'pentlike**. — *n* **ser'pentry** serpents collectively. — **ser'pent-eater** the secretary bird; the markhor; **serpent god** or **goddess** a deity in the form of a snake; a deified snake; **serpentine verse** a line that begins and ends with the same word (from the figure of a snake with its tail in its mouth, common as a symbol of eternity); **ser'pent-liz'ard** the lizard Seps; **ser'pent-star** a brittle-star; **ser'pent-stone** an ammonite; a snake-stone; **ser'pent-worship**. — **the old serpent** Satan. [L *serpēns*, *-entis*, pr p of *serpere* to creep; cf Gr *herpein*]

serpigo *sər-pī'gō*, (*pathol*) *n* (*Shakesp* **sapego** or **suppeago**) any spreading or creeping skin disease, *specif* ringworm: — *pl* **serpigines** (*-pij'in-ēz*) or **serpī'goes**. — *adj* **serpiginous** (*-pij'*) (of certain skin lesions) having an indented or wavy margin. [LL *serpīgō*, from L *serpere* to creep]

SERPS or **Serps** *sûrps*, *abbrev*: state earnings-related pension scheme.

serpula *sûr'pū-lə*, *n* a marine polychaete worm of the family *Serpulidae*, that constructs and lives within a twisted calcareous tube: — *pl* **ser'pulae** (*-lē*). — *n* **ser'pulite** a fossil resembling a worm-tube. [L, a snake, from *serpere* to creep]

serr, **serre**. See under **serried**.

serra *ser'ə*, *n* a sawlike organ (*zool*); anything sawlike (*L*); a mountain-range (*Port*): — *pl* **serr'ae** (*-ē*) or **serr'as**. — *n* **serradill'a** or **serradell'a** (*Port*) a species of clover grown as fodder. — *n* **serr'an** a fish of the genus Serranus, or its family. — *n* **Serranus** (*sə-rā'nəs*) the typical genus of **Serranidae** (*-ran'i-dē*), a family of percoid fishes, *incl* the sea perches, sea basses and groupers. — *n* **serranid** (*ser'ən-id*) or **serr'anoid** a member of the Serranidae. — Also *adj*. — *n* **serrasal'mo** (L *salmō* salmon) a fish of the piranha genus *Serrasalmo*: — *pl* **serrasal'mos**. — *vt* **serrate'** to notch. — *adj* **serrā'ted** or **serr'āte** notched like a saw; with sharp forward-pointing teeth (*bot* and *zool*). — *n* **serrā'tion** saw-edged condition; (*usu* in *pl*) a sawlike tooth. — *adj* **serratiros'tral** (L *rōstrum* beak) saw-billed. — *adj* **serratulate** (*sə-rat'ū-lāt*) minutely serrate. — *n* **serrature** (*ser'ə-chər*) serration. — *n* (*anatom*) **serrā'tus** one of several muscles of the thorax. — *adj* **serricorn** (*ser'*; L *cornū* horn) having serrate antennae. — *adj* **serr'ulate** or **serr'ulated** finely serrated. — *n* **serrulā'tion**. [L and Port (from L) *serra* a saw]

serrate, **serrated**, etc. See under **serra**.

serried *ser'id*, *adj* close-set; packed or grouped together without gaps. — *vt* **serr** or **serre** (*sûr*) to press close; to close the ranks of. — *n* **serrefile** or **serafile** (*ser'ə-fīl*; see **file**[1]) a file of officers or men detailed to ride in rear of the rear rank of a squadron when in line; a soldier so detailed. — *vt* and *vi* **serr'y** to close together. [Fr *serrer* or its pa p *serré*, from L *sera* bar, lock]

serrulate, etc. See under **serra**.

serry. See under **serried**.

Sertoli cells *sûr-tō'li selz*, *n pl* specialized nutritive cells which initiate the formation of seminiferous tubules in the testes and which nourish the developing sperm. [From E Sertoli, Ital histologist]

sertularian *sûr-tū-lā'ri-ən*, *n* any hydroid coelenterate of the common genus *Sertularia*, having a double row of sessile hydrothecae. — Also *adj*. [Mod L, from dimin of *serta* garland]

seruewe (ie **servewe**). Spenserian spelling of **surview**.

serum *sē'rəm*, *n* a watery liquid, *esp* that which separates from coagulating blood; blood serum containing antibodies, taken from an animal that has been inoculated with bacteria or their toxins, used to immunize people or animals; the watery part of a plant fluid: — *pl* **sē'rums** or **sē'ra**. — **serum albumin** an albumin (or combination of albumins) that makes up more than half the protein in blood plasma and maintains the osmotic pressure of the blood; **serum globulin** a globulin (or combination of globulins) containing most of the antibodies in blood plasma; **serum hepatitis** a virus infection of the liver, *usu* transmitted by transfusion of infected blood or use of contaminated instruments, *esp* needles, consequently often occurring in drug addicts; **serum sickness** a hypersensitivity reaction that sometimes occurs after injection of foreign serum, with fever, rashes, and enlargement of the lymph nodes; **serum therapy** serotherapy (see under **sero-**). [L *serum* whey]

serval *sûr'vl, n* a slender long-legged African cat (*Felis serval*), with a spotted coat. [Port (*lobo*) *cerval*, literally deer-like wolf]

servant *sûr'vənt, n* someone who is hired to perform service, *esp* personal or domestic service of a menial kind, or farm labour, for another or others; a person who is in the service of the state, the public, a company, or other body; someone who serves in any capacity; a ministrant; formerly, a man conventionally accepted by a lady (called his *mistress*) as binding himself to devoted attendance, a lover; in formal letter-writing, formerly in greeting and leave-taking, now *usu* jocularly, applied in seeming humility to oneself; a designation formerly used in the US for a slave; (in *pl*) formerly a designation conceded by a great personage to a company of actors, to evade legal difficulties. — *vt* (*rare*) to subject. — *adj* **ser'vantless**. — *n* **ser'vantry** (*rare*) servants collectively. — *n* **ser'vantship** the position or relation of a servant. — **ser'vant-girl**, **ser'vant-lass** or **ser'vant-maid** a female domestic servant; **ser'vant-man** a male servant; **servants' hall** a servants' dining- and sitting-room. — **civil servant** a member of the civil service (see **civil**). [Fr, pr p of *servir*, from L *servīre* to serve]

serve *sûrv, vt* to be a servant to; to be in the service of; to worship (*obs*); to work for; to render service to; to perform service for or under; to perform the duties or do the work connected with; (of a male animal) to copulate with (the female); to attend as assistant; to be of use to or for; to avail; to suffice for; to satisfy; to further; to minister to; to attend to the requirements of; to supply; to provide with materials; to provide with quarry (*falconry*); to help to food, etc; to present (food) in a specified manner; to send or bring to table; to deal; to put into action, bring to bear (*archaic*); to put into play by striking (*tennis*, etc); to treat, behave towards; to be opportune to; to conform one's conduct to; to undergo, work out, go through; to bind (rope, etc) with cord, etc in order to strengthen (*esp naut*); to deliver or present formally, or give effect to (*law*); to operate or maintain in operation (a gun, etc) (*military*); to declare (heir) (*Scots law*). — *vi* to be a servant; to be in service or servitude; to render service; to be a member, or take part in the activities, of an armed force; to perform functions; to wait at table; to attend to customers; to act as server, eg at RC Mass; to answer a purpose, be of use, do; to be opportune or favourable; to suffice. — *n* service of a ball in tennis, etc; a piece of (*esp* light-hearted) verbal abuse or mockery (*Austr slang*). — *n* **ser'ver** a person who serves, *esp* at meals or tennis; a person who acts as assistant to a priest during Mass; a salver; a fork, spoon, or other instrument for distributing or helping at table; (in computer networks) a specialized machine that stores communal files, processes electronic mail, provides printing facilities, etc. — *n* **serv'ery** a room or rooms adjoining a dining-room, from which meals and drinks are served and in which utensils are kept. — *n* and *adj* **serv'ing**. — **serving mallet** (*naut*) a mallet with a grooved head used in serving ropes; **serv'ing-man** (*archaic*) a manservant. — **serve as** to act as; to take the place of; **serve someone a trick** to play a trick on someone; **serve someone right** (of something unpleasant) to be no more than deserved; **serve one's time** to pass through an apprenticeship or a term of office (see also **time-served**, etc under **time**); **serve out** to deal or distribute; to punish; to get even with, take revenge on; **serve the** (or **one's**) **turn** to suffice for one's immediate purpose or need; **serve time** to undergo a term of imprisonment, etc; **serve up** to bring to table (also *fig*). [Fr *servir*, from L *servīre* to serve]

servewe. A Spenserian spelling of **surview**.

Servian[1] (*obs*). Same as **Serbian**.

Servian[2] *sûr'vi-ən, adj* of *Servius* Tullius, legendary king of Rome.

service[1] *sûr'vis, n* the condition or occupation of a servant or of any person who serves; work; the act or mode of serving; employ; employment in the armed forces, or in any public organization or department; the personnel so employed; the force, organization, or body employing it (in *pl usu* the fighting forces); that which is required of its members; that which is required of a feudal tenant; performance of a duty or function; actual participation in warfare; a warlike operation; a performance of religious worship; a liturgical form or office or a musical setting of it; a good turn, good offices, benefit to another or others; duty or homage ceremonially offered, as in health-drinking, correspondence, or greeting; use; hard usage; availability; disposal; supply, eg of water, public transport, etc; expediting; waiting at table; that which is served, a course; the order of dishes; a complete set, eg of dishes for a particular meal; supplementary activities for the advantage of customers; the checking, and (if necessary) repairing and/or replacing of parts, of machinery, etc to ensure efficient operation; (in tennis, squash, badminton, etc) the right of a player to serve the ball, the act of so doing, or the manner, style or game in which an individual player serves; the cost of interest and sinking-fund charges; cord or other material for serving a rope. — *adj* of the army, navy, or air force; (sometimes in *pl*) of the army, navy and air force collectively; for the use of servants; providing services rather than manufactured products (see eg **service industry** below). — *vt* to provide or perform service for (eg motor cars). — *n* **serviceabil'ity** or **ser'viceableness**. — *adj* **ser'viceable** able or willing to serve; advantageous; useful; capable of rendering long service, durable. — *adv* **ser'viceably**. — *adj* **ser'viceless**. — **service agreement** a type of employment contract, *usu* between an employer and a senior employee; **service area** a place by a motorway or major road where facilities such as filling stations, garages, restaurants and toilets are available; the range covered by a radio or television transmitter; **service book** a book of forms of religious service; a prayer book; **service car** (*NZ*) a bus used on long-distance journeys; **service ceiling** the altitude above sea level in standard atmospheric conditions, at which the rate of ascent of an aircraft falls to a specified rate (cf **absolute ceiling**); **service charge** a charge made for service in a restaurant or hotel, *usu* a percentage of the bill; **service contract** a service agreement; **service court** in tennis, the area outside of which a served ball must not fall; **service flat** a flat in which domestic service is provided, its cost being included in the rent; **service hatch** one connecting dining-room to kitchen, etc, through which dishes, etc, may be passed; **service industry** an industry which provides a service rather than a product, eg catering, entertainment, transport; **service line** the boundary of the service court, in tennis 21 feet from the net; **ser'viceman** or (*fem*) **ser'vicewoman** a member of a fighting service; **service mark** a mark, emblem, device, etc used to identify a certain service, such as catering, insurance, etc and reserved for the exclusive use of providers of that service; **service pipe** and **service wire** a branch from a gas, electric, etc main to a building; **service reservoir** a reservoir for supplying water to a particular area; **service road** a minor road parallel to a main road, providing access to local facilities, eg shops, without obstructing the main road; **service room** a room in a club or hotel where visitors' requirements are attended to; **service station** an establishment providing general services, *esp* the supply of fuel for motorists. — **active service** service of a soldier, etc, in the field (widely interpreted by the authorities); **at your service** at your disposal; also a mere phrase of civility; **civil service** see under **civil**; **have seen service** to have fought in war; to have been put to long or hard use. [Fr, from L *servitium*]

service[2] *sûr'vis, n* (also **service tree**) a Eurasian tree (*Sorbus domestica*) similar to the rowan, with apple- or pear-shaped fruits used since Roman times to make an alcoholic drink (also called **sorb**); a related European tree (**wild service**), *Sorbus torminalis*, somewhat like a maple, with clusters of rounded fruits. [OE *syrfe*, perh from L *cerevisia* the cider-like drink made from its fruit, perh from L *sorbus*]

serviceberry *sûr'vis-be-ri, n* any of several N American trees or shrubs of the genus *Amelanchier*, having clusters of white flowers and edible red or purple berries (also called **shadbush, shadblow, Juneberry**); the sweet fruit of several species (also called **shadberry, Juneberry**).

servient *sûr'vi-ənt*, (*law*) *adj* subordinate; subject to a servitude or easement (qv). [L *serviēns, -entis*, pr p of *servīre* to serve]

serviette *sûr-vi-et'*, (*orig Scot*, now general, but regarded by the socially sensitive as vulgar or non-U) *n* a table-napkin. [Fr]

servile *sûr'vīl, adj* pertaining to slaves or servants; slavish; fawning or submissive; cringing; controlled, subject; slavishly or unintelligently imitative; expressing mere grammatical relations. — *n* (*rare*) a servile person. — *adv* **ser'vilely**. — *n* **ser'vilism** (*-vil-izm*) systematic or habitual servility; servile spirit; a system based on slavery or advocacy of it. — *n* **servility** (*-vil'i-ti*) servitude; slavishness of manner or spirit; slave-like deference. [L *servīlis*, from *servus* a slave]

Servite *sûr'vīt, n* a member of the mendicant order of Servants of the Virgin, founded at Florence in 1233.

servitor *sûr'vi-tər, n* a person who serves; a servant (chiefly *poetic*); a person who serves in war (*obs*); an assistant, apprentice, lawyer's clerk, assistant school-master, or the like (*Scot, obs*); a follower or adherent; formerly, at Oxford University, an undergraduate partly supported by the college, his duty being to wait on the fellows and gentlemen commoners at table; at Edinburgh University, a classroom janitor: — *fem* **ser'vitress**. — *adj* **servito'rial**. — *n* **ser'vitorship**. [LL *servītor, -ōris*, from L *servīre* to serve]

servitude *sûr'vi-tūd, n* a state of being a slave or (now *rare*) servant; slavery; subjection; compulsory labour; subjection to irksome conditions; a burden on property obliging the owner to allow another person or thing an easement (*legal*). [L *servitūdō*]

servo *sûr'vō, adj* and *combining form* denoting a system in which the main mechanism is set in operation by a subsidiary mechanism and is able to develop a force greater than the force communicated to it. — *n* **ser'vocontrol** (in aircraft) a reinforcing mechanism for the pilot's effort, *usu* a small auxiliary aerofoil. — *adj* **servomechan'ical**. — *n* **ser'vomechanism** a closed-cycle control system in which a small input power controls a larger output power in a strictly proportionate manner. — *n* **ser'vomotor** a motor using a servomechanism. [L *servus* a servant, slave]

servus servorum Dei *sûr'vəs sûr-vō'rəm, -vö'rəm, dē'ī, ser'vŏŏs, -wŏŏs, ser-vō'rŏŏm, -wō', de'ē*, (*L*) a servant of the servants of God (a title adopted by the popes).

sesame *ses'ə-mi, n* a plant, *Sesamum indicum*, probably native to SE Asia, cultivated for its seeds which yield a light edible oil (**sesame oil**; also called **benne** or **gingili oil**). — *adj* **ses'amoid** shaped like a sesame seed. — *n* (*anatom*) (in full **ses'amoid bone**) a small rounded bone formed in the substance of a tendon, eg in the flexor tendon of the big toe. — Also *adj*. — **sesame grass** gama-grass; **sesame seed**. — **open sesame** see under **open**. [Gr *sēsamē* a dish of sesame (Gr *sēsamon*)]

sese. See **sessa**.

seseli *ses'ə-li, n* a plant of the genus *Seseli* of the Umbelliferae family. [Gr *seseli* a name for several umbellifers of this and other genera]

sesey. See **sessa**.

sesqui- *ses'kwi-, combining form* denoting the ratio of one and a half to one, or (*chem*) one and an *n*th to one. — *adj* **sesquialter** (*-al'tər*; L *alter* second) as three to two. — *n* **sesquial'tera** (*music*) a perfect fifth; three notes against two; an organ stop reinforcing harmonics. — *n* **sesquicar'bonate** a salt composed of a carbonate and a hydrogen carbonate. — *n* **sesquicente'nary** or **sesqui-centenn'ial** a hundred and fiftieth anniversary. — Also *adj*. — *n* **sesquiox'ide** an oxide with three atoms of oxygen to two of the other constituent. — *adj* **sesqui-pedā'lian** or **sesquip'edal** (L *sēsquipedālis*, from *pēs, pedis* foot) tending to use long or cumbersome words; (of words) long, pedantic or polysyllabic (after *sesqui-pedalia verba* in Horace's *Ars Poetica*, words a foot and a half long). — *n* **sesquipedā'lianism** or **sesquipe-dality** (*-pi-dal'i-ti*). — *adj* **sesquip'licate** (*math*; L *sēsquiplex, -plicis*) of, or as, the square roots of the cubes. — *n* **sesquisul'phide** a compound with three atoms of sulphur to two of the other element or radical. — *n* **sesquiter'pene** any of a group of terpene derivatives of the empirical formula $C_{15}H_{24}$. — *n* **sesquiter'tia** (*music*) a perfect fourth; four notes against three. [L *sēsqui*, from *sēmisque*, from *sēmis* (for *sēmi-as*) half a unit, and *que* and]

Sess. *abbrev*: Session.

sess *ses, n* Same as **cess**.

sessa *ses'ə*, or **sesey** *ses'ē*, (*Shakesp*) *interj* of disputed meaning. — Other readings are **caese, cease**; **ceas, sese**. [Poss reduplication of *sa*; poss Sp *cesa*, or Fr *cessez*, cease]

sessile *ses'īl* or *esp NAm ses'il, adj* stalkless; sedentary; fixed or stationary. — *adj* **sess'ile-eyed**. — **sessile oak** a native British oak, *Quercus petraea*, distinguished from the English oak by its stalkless acorns (also called **durmast oak**). [L *sessilis* low, squat, from *sedēre, sessum* to sit]

session *sesh'ən, n* an act of sitting (*obs*); a seated position (*obs*); the enthronement of Christ at God's right hand; a sitting, series of sittings, or time of sitting, eg of a court or public body; the time between the meeting and prorogation of Parliament; a school year (sometimes a school day); (in Scotland) a division of the academic year; the kirk session; formerly, the Court of Session; (in *pl*) quarter-sessions; a period of time spent engaged in any one activity (*colloq*). — *adj* **sess'ional**. — *adv* **sess'ionally**. — **sess'ion-clerk** the official who records the transactions of a kirk session; **sess'ion-house** a building where sessions are held; the room where a kirk session meets; **session singer** or **musician** a person who provides vocal or instrumental backing at recording sessions. — **Court of Session** the supreme civil court of Scotland. [Fr, from L *sessiō, sessiōnis*, from *sedēre, sessum* to sit]

sesspool. Same as **cesspool**.

sesterce *ses'tərs, n* a Roman coin, the *sestertius*, worth 2½ asses, later 4 asses. — *n* **sester'tium** (*-shi-əm*) a Roman money of account equal to 1000 sesterces: — *pl* **sester'tia**. [L *sestertius* two and a half, from *sēmis* half, and *tertius* third; *sestertium*, prob orig genitive pl for *mille sestertium* a thousand sesterces]

sestet, sestett or **sestette** *ses-tet', n* a group of six; the last six lines of a sonnet; a composition for six performers (*music*; also **sestett'o**: — *pl* **sestett'os**). [Ital *sestetto*, from *sesto* from L *sextus* sixth]

sestina *ses-tē'nə*, (*poetry*) *n* an old verse form of six six-lined stanzas having the same end-words in different orders, and a triplet introducing all of them. — Also **sestine** (*-tēn'*). [Ital, from L *sextus* sixth]

seston *ses'ton, n* a very small plankton organism. [Gr *sēston*, from *sēthein* to strain, filter]

set *set, vt* to put, place, or fix in position or required condition; to dispose, array, arrange; to restore (a broken bone) to its normal alignment; to apply; to cause to be; to plant; to stake; to embed; to frame; to mount; to beset or bestow about; to stud, dot, sprinkle, variegate; to put in type (*printing*); to compose (type); to form or represent, eg in jewels; to adjust to show the correct (or a specified) time, etc; to spread, lay, cover (a table) with the food, dishes, etc for a meal, or (*Scot* and *dialect*) to cover the table with the food, dishes, etc for (a meal); to regulate; to appoint; to ordain; to assign; to prescribe; to propound; to put on a course, start off; to incite, direct; to put in opposition; to posit; to cause to become solid, coagulated, rigid, fixed, or motionless; to begin to form (eg a fruit or seed); to rate, value; to pitch (eg a tune); to compose or fit music to; to position (sails) to catch the wind ; to arrange (hair) in a particular style when wet, so that it will remain in it when dry; to seat (*obs* and *dialect*); to put (a hen) on eggs; to put (eggs) under a hen; (of a gundog) to indicate by crouching; to sharpen (eg a razor); to defeat (one's opponent's contract) *usu* by a stated number of tricks (*bridge*); to escort (*Northern dialect*); to lease or let to a tenant (*esp Scot*); to become, befit (chiefly *Scot*); conversely, to appear to advantage in (*Scot*). — *vi* to go down towards or below the horizon, to decline; to offer a stake; to become rigid, fixed, hard, solid, or permanent; to coagulate; (of a broken bone) to knit; to settle down; (of eg bone) to begin to develop; to have, take or start along a course or direction; to dance in a facing position; to acquire a set or bend; (of dogs) to point out game; to apply or betake oneself; to hang in position; to be in session; to sit (now *obs* or *dialect*): — *pr p* **sett'ing**; *pa t* and *pa p* **set**. — *adj* in any of the senses of the participle; prescribed; deliberate, intentional; prearranged; formal; settled; fixed; rigid; determined; regular; established; ready. — *n* a group of persons or things, *esp* of a type that associate, occur, or are used together or have something in common; a clique, coterie, exclusive group; a complete series, collection, or complement; a company performing a dance; a series of dance movements or figures; a complete apparatus, *esp* for receiving radio or television signals; an act, process, mode, or time of setting; a setting; an inclination; a direction; the scenery, properties, etc set up for a scene (*theat*, etc); the place where filming takes place (*cinematog*); any collection of objects, called 'elements', defined by specifying the elements (*math*); the basic haploid complement of chromosomes (*biol*); habitual or temporary form, posture, carriage, position, or tendency; the items performed by a singer or band at a concert; a group of games in which the winning side wins at least six, with such additional games as may be required in the case of deuce (*tennis*); a set hairstyle; the hang of a garment; a young plant-slip, bulb or tuber, for planting; a gun dog's indication of game; bodily build (now *dialect*); permanent effect of strain; the constitution of a burgh; (for the following senses, **set** or **sett**): the number of a weaver's reed, determining the number of threads to the inch; the texture resulting; a square or a pattern of tartan; a paving-block of stone or wood; a tool for setting in various senses; a badger's burrow; a lease or letting (*Scot*); a mining lease or area worked (*Cornwall*, etc); a place with fixed fishing-nets. — *n* **set'ness**. — *n* **sett'er** someone who or something that sets; a dog that sets; a dog of a breed derived from the spaniel and (probably) pointer; a person who finds victims for thieves, etc; a spy. — *n* **sett'ing** the act of someone who sets; the direction of current; fixation; surroundings; environment; a level of power, volume, etc, to which a machine or other device can be set; mounting of jewellery; the period of time in which a play, novel, etc, is set; adaptation to music; music composed for a song, poem, etc; a system of dividing pupils in mixed-ability classes into ability groups for certain subjects only; the period of play after a game has been set (to two, three or five) (*badminton*). — **set'-aside** (also **land set-aside**) the practice or policy of taking agricultural land out of production (**set-aside scheme** *specif* that introduced to reduce EC grain surpluses, with compensatory payments to farmers); **set'back** a check, reverse, or relapse; a disappointment or misfortune; a receding section in the upper part of a tall building; **set'-down** a rebuff or snub; a rating; **set'line** any of various kinds of fishing-line suspended between buoys, etc, and having shorter baited lines attached to it; **set'-off** a claim set against another; a cross-claim which partly offsets the original claim; a counterbalance; an ornament; a contrast, foil; a setting forth; an offset (*archit* and *printing*); **set'-out** an outfit; preparations; a display of dishes, dress, etc; company or clique; **set piece** a piece of theatrical scenery with a supporting framework, distinguished from a side-scene or drop-scene; an elaborately arranged display in fireworks; a painstakingly prepared performance; in football, etc, a (carefully planned and executed piece of team-work at a) corner or free kick. — *adj* **set'-piece**. — **set point** (*tennis, etc*) a point which wins a set; **set pot** a fixed boiler or copper; **set'screw** a screw used to prevent relative motion by exerting pressure with its point; **set speech** a studied oration; **set square** a right-angled triangular drawing instrument. — *adj* **set'-stitch'd** (*Sterne*) *perh* embroidered. — **set terms** deliberately chosen, *usu* outspoken language; **setter-forth'**; **setter-off'**; **setter-on'**; **setter-out'**; **setter-up'**; **setting lotion** a lotion containing gum or resin used to fix or set a hairstyle; **set-to'** a bout; a fight or argument; a hot contest: — *pl* **set-tos'** or **set-to's'**; **set'-up** the arrangement, organization, configuration or structure of anything; the place where an instrument for measuring, surveying, recording, etc is set up; a situation, the outcome of which has been prearranged, eg on in which someone is made a victim (*slang*); a shot, forming part of a scene, consisting of part of the action, close-up or location, etc (*film*); bodily carriage and physique. — See also **set up** below. — **dead set** determined (on); indisputable (*Austr slang*); **set about** to begin, take in hand; to attack; to spread (rumours); **set against** to assail; to compare or balance; **set alight, set light to, set fire to** or **set on fire** to cause to break into flame and burn; **set apart** to put aside, or out of consideration; to separate, distinguish; **set aside** to put away or to one side; to reject, annul; to reserve, lay by; to take (agricultural land) out of production, to leave fallow; **set at naught** see under **naught**; **set back** to check, delay, hinder, reverse; to cost (in money; *slang*); to place at some distance behind; to surprise, take aback; **set by** to lay up; to put aside; to value or esteem, to care (*archaic*); **set down** to lay on the ground; to put in writing, record; to appoint a time for (*Shakesp*); to judge, esteem, regard; to snub; to pitch, encamp (*Shakesp*); to attribute, ascribe; to lay down authoritatively; to stop and allow (passengers) to alight from a taxi, bus, car, etc; **set eyes on** to see, catch sight of; **set fair** (of weather) steadily fair; (of future prospects, outlook, etc) settled and secure; likely, to all appearances (to do the desired thing); **set fire to** see **set alight** above; **set forth** to exhibit, display; to state, expound, declare; to praise, recommend; to publish; to start on a journey; **set free** to release, liberate; **set going** to put in motion; **set hand to** to set to work on; **set in** to begin; to become prevalent or established; (of wind, etc) to run landwards (*naut*); **set in hand** to undertake; to set someone about doing; **set little, much**, etc, **by** to regard or value little, much, etc; **set off** to start off; to send off; to show in relief or to advantage; to counterbalance; to make an offset, mark an opposite page; to mark off, lay off; **set on** to attack or incite to attack; to instigate; bent or determined upon; **set oneself** to bend one's energies; **set oneself against** to oppose; **set one's face against** see under **face**; **set one's hand to** to start work on, set about; to sign; **set one's heart on** see under **heart**; **set one's teeth** to clench the teeth, as in strong resolution; **set on fire** see **set alight** above; **set on foot** to set going, to start; **set out** to start, go forth; to display; to begin with an intention; to expound; to mark off; to adorn; to equip and send forth; **set sail** see under **sail**; **set to** to affix; to apply oneself; to set (eg a bone) (*Shakesp*); **set (a game) to two, three or five** (*badminton*) to set, in the final stages of a game, a new deciding score of two, three, or five points; **set up** to erect; to put up; to exalt, raise up (**set you, him**, etc **up** (*Scot*; *ironic*) what a cheek you've, he's, etc, got!); to arrange; to begin; to enable to begin; to place in view; to put in type; to begin a career, *esp* in one's own business; to make pretensions; to arrange matters so as to implicate, incriminate, embarrass or make a fool of (another person) (*slang*; *n* **set'-up**); **set upon** to set on; determined on. [OE *settan*; cognate with Ger *setzen*, ON *setja*, Gothic *satjan*; *settan* is the weak causative of *sittan* to sit; the noun is from the verb, but may be partly from OE *set* seat, partly from OFr *sette*, from L *secta* sect]

seta *sē'tə*, *n* a bristle; a bristle-like structure; the stalk of a moss capsule: — *pl* **se'tae** (*-tē*). — *adj* **setaceous** (*si-tā'shəs*) or **setose** (*sē'tōs* or *-tōs'*). — *adj* **setif'erous** or **setig'erous** bearing bristles. — *adj* **set'iform**. [L *saeta* (*sēta*) bristle]

se-tenant *sə-tə-nã*, (*philately*) *adj* denoting two or more stamps joined together in an unsevered row or block, (at least) one of which differs (eg in design or value) from the other(s). [Fr, holding together]

SETI *abbrev*: search for extraterrestrial intelligence.

seton *sē'tn*, *n* a thread or similar filament passed through the skin as a counter-irritant and means of promoting drainage; a flow obtained in this way. [LL *sētō*, *-ōnis*, appar from L *sēta*, *saeta* bristle]

sett. See **set**.

settee[1] *se-tē'*, *n* a long seat with a back. [Prob **settle**]

settee[2] *se-tē'*, *n* a single-decked Mediterranean vessel with a long prow and lateen sails. [Prob Ital *saettia*]

setter[1], **setting**. See under **set**.

setter[2] *set'ər*, (chiefly *Northern dialect*) *vt* to treat with a seton of setterwort root. — *n* a flow so produced in cattle. — **sett'erwort** stinking hellebore. [Perh from MLGer]

settle *set'l*, *n* a long high-backed bench; a ledge (*Bible*). — *vt* to place in a stable, secure, restful or comfortable situation; to adjust; to lower; to compact, cause to subside; to regulate; to fix, arrange; to establish, set up, or install (eg in residence, business, marriage, a parish); to colonize; to make clear; to determine; to decide; to put beyond doubt or dispute; to restore to good order; to quiet; to compose; to secure by gift or legal act; to create successive interests in, use or income going to one person while the corpus of the property remains another's; to make final payment of; to dispose of, put out of action, stun, kill. — *vi* to alight; to come to rest; to subside; to sink to the bottom (or form a scum); to dispose oneself; to take up permanent abode; to become stable; to fix one's habits (often with *down*); to grow calm or clear; to come to a decision or agreement; to adjust differences; to settle accounts (often with *up*). — *adj* **sett'leable**. — *adj* **sett'led**. — *n* **sett'ledness**. — *n* **sett'lement** act of settling; the state of being settled; payment; arrangement; the placing of a religious minister in a parish; a subsidence or sinking; a settled colony; a local community; an establishment of social workers aiming at benefit to the surrounding population; a settling of property, an instrument by which it is settled, or the property settled, *esp* a marriage-settlement; residence in a parish or other claim for poor-relief in case of becoming destitute. — *n* **sett'ler** someone who settles; a colonist; a decisive blow, argument, etc. — *n* **sett'ling**. — *n* **sett'lor** (*law*) a person who settles property on another. — **sett'le-bed** a settle that may be converted to a bed; **settler's clock** (*Austr*) a name formerly used for the kookaburra; **settling day** a date fixed by the stock exchange for completion of transactions; **settling pond** a man-made pond into which water containing effluent from a mine, etc is discharged and in which harmful sediment is deposited. — **settle for** to agree to accept (*usu* as a compromise); **settle in** to adapt to a new environment; to prepare to remain indoors for the night; **settle with** to come to an agreement with; to deal with. [OE *setl* seat, *setlan* to place; the verb may be partly from, or influenced by, late OE *sehtlian* to reconcile]

setule *set'ūl*, *n* a small seta or bristle. — *adj* **set'ulose** or **set'ulous**. [Mod L *setula*, dimin of *seta*]

setwall *set'wol*, *n orig* zedoary; now, valerian. — Also **setuale** (*-ū-āl*; *Spenser*), **cet'ywall**, etc. [OFr *citoual*, from LL *zedoāria*, from Ar *zedwār*]

seven *sev'n*, *n* the cardinal number next above six; a symbol representing it (7, vii, etc); a set of that number of people or things; a shoe or other article of a size denoted by that number; a card with seven pips; a score of seven points, tricks, etc; the seventh hour after midday or midnight; the age of seven years. — *adj* of the number seven; seven years old. — *adj* **sev'enth** last of seven; next after the sixth; equal to one of seven equal parts. — *n* a seventh part; a person or thing in seventh position; a tone or semitone less than an octave; a note at that interval. — *adv* **sev'enthly** in the seventh place. — **seven-a-side'** a form of Rugby football played by seven players on each side instead of fifteen (also called **sev'ens**). — Also *adj*. — *adj* **sev'en-day** for seven days. — *adj* and *adv* **sev'enfold** in seven divisions: seven times as much. — *adj* **sev'en-league** taking seven leagues at a stride, as the ogre's boots acquired by Hop-o'-my-Thumb. — **sev'enpence** the value of seven pennies. — *adj* **sev'enpenny** costing or worth sevenpence. — *n* a sevenpenny book, bus-ticket, etc. — *n* and *adj* **sev'en-score**. — **seventh day** Saturday. — *adj* **sev'enth-day** observing Saturday as Sabbath (**Seventh-day Adventists** a sect that expect the second coming of Christ and observe Saturday as the Sabbath). — **Seven against Thebes** the war of seven heroes to reinstate Polynices in Thebes against Eteocles; **Seven Champions of Christendom** St George for England, St Andrew for Scotland, St Patrick for Ireland, St David for Wales, St Denis for France, St James for Spain, St Anthony for Italy; **seven deadly sins** pride, covetousness, lust, anger, gluttony, envy, and sloth; **Seven Sages** Solon of Athens, Thales of Miletus, Pittacus of Mitylene, Bias of Priene in Caria, Chilon of Sparta, Cleobulus tyrant of Lindus in Rhodes, and Periander tyrant of Corinth; an Eastern cycle of tales in which seven wise men contend in story-telling against a woman for the life of a belied prince; **Seven Seas** the Arctic, Antarctic, North and South Atlantic, North and South Pacific, and Indian Oceans; all the seas of the world generally; **Seven Sleepers** seven Christian youths at Ephesus said to have slept walled up in a cave c.AD 250 to 447; **Seven Stars** the planets known to the ancients; the Plough; the Pleiades; **seventh heaven** see under **heaven**; **seven hills of Rome** the hills on which ancient Rome was built, the Aventine, Caelian, Capitoline, Esquiline, Palatine, Quirinal and Viminal; **Seven Wonders of the World** the seven monuments regarded as the most remarkable of the ancient world, the Pyramids, the Hanging Gardens of Babylon, the Temple of Artemis at Ephesus, Phidias's statue of Zeus at Olympia, the Mausoleum at Halicarnassus, the Colossus of Rhodes, and the Pharos of Alexandria; **seven-year itch** a tendency towards sexual infidelity, held in jocular tradition to be common after about seven years of marriage; **Seven Years' War** the struggle for Silesia between Frederick the Great and the Empress Maria Theresa (1756–63). [OE *seofon*; Du *zeven*, Ger *sieben*, Gothic *sibun*, Gr *hepta*, L *septem*]

seventeen *sev-n-tēn'*, or *sev'*, *n* and *adj* seven and ten. — *adj* **sev'enteen-hund'er** (*Burns*) woven with a reed of 1700 divisions, ie fine linen. — *adj* and *n* **sev'enteenth** (or *-tēnth'*). — *adv* **seventeenth'ly**. [OE *seofontīene*, from *seofon* seven, and *tīen* ten]

seventy *sev'n-ti*, *n* and *adj* seven times ten: — *pl* **sev'enties** the numbers seventy to seventy-nine; the years so numbered in a life or any century; a range of temperature from seventy to just less than eighty degrees. — *adj* **sev'entieth** last of seventy; next after the sixty-ninth; equal to one of seventy equal parts. — *n* a seventieth part; a person or thing in seventieth position. — **seventy-eight'** an old type of gramophone record designed to be played at 78 revolutions per minute, standard before the introduction of long-playing microgroove records (*usu* written **78**). — **the Seventy**

the Jewish Sanhedrim; the disciples sent out in Luke 10; the Septuagint translators (often written **LXX**). [OE *(hund)seofontig*]

sever *sev'ər, vt* and *vi* to separate; to divide, part; to cleave, split; to detach. — *adj* **sev'erable**. — *n* **sev'erance**. — **severance pay** an allowance granted to an employee on the termination of his or her employment. [ME *severen*, from MFr *severer*, from L *sēparāre* to separate]

several *sev'ə-rəl, adj* various; sundry; more than one (*usu* more than three), but not very many; separate; particular; distinct; different; belonging or pertaining distributively, not jointly (*law*); privately owned. — *n* privately owned land, *esp* enclosed pasture (*hist*); private property (*archaic* or *legal*); a detail, particular (*Shakesp*); an individual person (*Shakesp*). — *pronoun* a few. — *adj* and *adv* **sev'eralfold**. — *adv* **sev'erally** separately; respectively. — *n* **sev'eralty** separateness; individual ownership of property, *esp* land (*law*). — **in several** separately, individually. [OFr, from L *sēparāre* to separate]

severe *si-vēr', adj* rigorous, harsh; very strict; conforming to a rigorous standard; unsparing; hard to endure; dangerous; grave, acute or very bad; critical; stern; austerely restrained or simple in appearance. — *adv* **sevēre'ly**. — *n* **sevēre'ness**. — *n* **severity** (*si-ver'i-ti*). — **severe combined immunodeficiency syndrome** a severe form of congenital immunological deficiency in which both T and B lymphocytes are absent (*abbrev* **SCID**). [L *sevērus*]

severy *sev'ə-ri*, (*archit*) *n* a compartment of vaulting. [OFr *civoire*, from L *cibōrium*; see **ciborium**]

Sèvres *sev'r', adj* (of porcelain) made at *Sèvres*, near Paris. — *n* Sèvres porcelain.

sevruga *si-vroo͞'gə, n* a species of sturgeon, *Acipenser stellatus*, of the Black and Caspian seas; a delicately-flavoured caviare obtained from it.

sew[1] *sō, vt* to join, attach, enclose, or work on with a needle and thread, with wire, or with a sewing-machine. — *vi* to work with a needle and thread, sewing-machine, or in any similar way: — *pa t* **sewed** (*sōd*); *pa p* **sewn** (*sōn*) or **sewed**. — *n* **sew'er**. — *n* **sew'ing** the act of sewing; something that is being sewn. — **sew'ing-machine** a machine for sewing fabric, leather, etc. — **sew up** to enclose or close up by sewing; to complete satisfactorily, or secure a satisfactory result (*slang*); to tire out, bring to a standstill, nonplus, or make drunk (*slang*). [OE *sīwian*, *sēowian*; from OHGer *siuwen*, Gothic *siujan*]

sew[2] (*Spenser*). Same as **sue**.

sew[3] *sū, vt* (*dialect*) to drain. — *vi* to ooze (*dialect*); to be aground (*naut*). — *n* **sew'age** refuse or waste carried off by sewers. — *n* **sewer** (*soo͞'ər* or *sū'ər*, *old-fashioned shōr* or *shör*) a channel (*esp* underground) for receiving the discharge from house-drains and streets. — *vt* to provide with sewers. — *n* **sew'erage** a system, or the provision, of sewers; sewage; **sew'ering**. — **sew'age-farm** a place where sewage is treated to render it suitable for use as manure; also, a farm on which sewage is used as fertilizer; **sew'age-works** a place where sewage is treated and purified before being discharged into a river or the sea; **sew'er-gas** the contaminated air of sewers produced by the decomposition of sewage; **sew'er-rat** the brown rat. [OFr *essever* to drain off, from L *ex* out, and *aqua* water]

sewel. See **shewel**.

sewellel *si-wel'əl, n* the mountain beaver, *Aplodontia rufa*, a squirrel-like burrowing rodent of NW coastal regions of N America. [Chinook *shewallal* a robe of its skin]

sewen. See **sewin**.

sewer[1] *sū'ər*, (*hist*) *n* a high-ranking servant who superintended the service at table in medieval England; later, an officer of the royal household. [OFr *asseour*, from *asseoir* to set down, from L *ad* to, and *sedēre* to sit]

sewer[2]. See under **sew**[1].

sewer[3], **sewerage**. See under **sew**[3].

sewin, **sewen** *sū'in, n* the Welsh and Irish name for a sea-trout grilse. [Origin unknown]

sewn. See **sew**[1].

sex *seks, n* the sum of the characteristics which distinguish an animal or plant as male or female; the quality of being male or female; either of the divisions according to this, or its members collectively; the whole area connected with this distinction; sexual intercourse, or behaviour, feelings, desires, etc associated with it. — Also *adj*. — *vt* to ascertain the sex of. — *adj* **sexed** (*sekst*) having sex; being male or female; having sexual desires or urges to a specified degree (as in **over-**, **under-**, **highly-**, etc **sexed**). — *n* **sex'er** a person who ascertains the sex of domestic fowl, etc. — *n* **sex'iness**. — *n* **sex'ism** discrimination against, stereotyping of, patronizing or otherwise offensive behaviour towards anyone (*orig* women) on the grounds of sex. — *n* and *adj* **sex'ist**. — *adj* **sex'less** of neither sex; without sex; without sexual feelings; devoid of sexual attractiveness. — *n* **sex'lessness**. — *adj* **sexolog'ical**. — *n* **sexol'ogist**. — *n* **sexol'ogy** the study of (human) sexual behaviour and relationships. — *adj* **sex'ūal** of, by, having or characteristic of, sex, one sex or other, or organs of sex. — *n* **sex'ūalism** emphasis on sex. — *n* **sex'ūalist**. — *n* **sexūal'ity**. — *vt* **sex'ūalize** or **-ise** to make sexual; to attribute sexual significance to. — *adv* **sex'ūally**. — *adj* **sex'y** (of a person) sexually attractive, stirring sexual interest in others; stimulating sexual instincts; involved in, or concerned with, sexual activity, *esp* sexual intercourse; (of an object, idea, etc) exciting, attractive, fascinating, tempting (*slang*). — **sex aid** any of various articles and devices used to prompt or increase sexual arousal artificially, as sold in sex shops; **sex appeal** the power of attracting, *esp* of exciting sexual desire in others; **sex bomb** (*colloq*) a person, *esp* female, with a lot of sex appeal; **sex cell** an egg cell or sperm; **sex'-change** (*esp* of humans) a changing of sex, *usu* achieved by the surgical transformation and/or re-creation of sexual organs. — Also *adj*. — **sex chromosome** the chromosome that determines sex; **sex'-determinātion** the biological process by which the sex of a new organism is determined; **sex drive** the natural impulse and appetite for sexual relations. — *adj* **sexed-up'** made sexy or extra sexy; sexually excited. — **sex hormones** hormones produced by the gonads that control the development of sexual characteristics; **sex intergrade** an intersex; **sex kitten** a young woman (mischievously) playing up her sex appeal. — *adj* **sex'-limited** developed only in one sex; **sex'-linked** (of a trait, disorder, etc) inherited along with sex, that is, by a factor located in the sex chromosome. — **sex'pot** (*slang*) a person of very great or obvious physical attraction; **sex'-reversal** change from male to female or female to male in the life of the individual; **sex shop** a shop selling articles connected with sexual arousal, behaviour, etc. — *adj* **sex'-starved** deprived of the pleasures and satisfactions of sexual activity. — **sex** (or **sexual**) **therapist** a person who deals with problems relating to sexual intercourse; **sex** (or **sexual**) **therapy**; **sexual abuse** the subjection of a person to sexual activity likely to cause physical or psychological harm; **sexual athlete** someone who performs sexual intercourse skilfully and/or frequently; **sexual harassment** that consisting of misplaced and unwelcome sexual advances, remarks, etc, *esp* from a senior colleague in the workplace; **sexual intercourse** the uniting of sexual organs, *esp* involving the insertion of the male penis into the female vagina and the release of sperm; **sexually transmitted disease** venereal disease; **sexual preference** a preference for homosexual (or heterosexual) relations; **sexual reproduction** the union of gametes or gametic nuclei preceding the formation of a new individual; **sexual selection** the province of natural selection in which preference for mates having certain characters comes into play; **sexual system** the Linnaean system of plant classification according to sexual organization. — **the sex** (*archaic*) the female sex, women. [L *sexus*, *-ūs*]

sex-, *seks-* or **sexi-** *sek-si, combining form* denoting six. — *adj* **sex'fid** cleft in six. — *n* **sex'foil** a window, design, etc, with six lobes or leaves. — *adj* **sexivā'lent** (or *sek-siv'ə-lənt*) or **sexvā'lent** (*chem*) of a valency of six. — *adj* **sexloc'ūlar** with six compartments. — *adj* **sexpart'ite** parted in six; involving six participants, groups, etc. [L *sex* six]

sexagenarian *sek-sə-ji-nā'ri-ən, n* a person sixty years old, or between sixty and seventy. — *adj* of that age. — *adj* **sexagenary** (*sek-sə-jē'nər-i* or *-saj'in-ər-i*) of, containing, based on, sixty; sexagenarian. — *n* a sexagesimal fraction; a sexagenarian. [L *sexāgēnārius*, from *sexāgēnī* sixty each]

Sexagesima *sek-sə-jes'i-mə, n* the second Sunday before Lent (also **Sexagesima Sunday**), *appar* so named on the false analogy of Quadragesima, etc. — *adj* **sexages'imal** pertaining to, or based on, sixty. — *n* a sexagesimal fraction. — *adv* **sexages'imally** by sixtieths. [L *sexāgēsimus, -a, -um* sixtieth]

sexcentenary *sek-sin-tēn'ər-i* or *-ten'ər-i, n* a 600th anniversary or a celebration of this. — Also *adj.*

sexennial *sek-sen'yəl, adj* lasting six years; recurring every six years. — *adv* **sexenn'ially**. [L *sex* six, and *annus* year]

sexer ... to ... **sexology**. See under **sex**.

sexpert *seks'pûrt*, (*colloq*; *esp US*) *n* an expert in sexual behaviour. [**sex** and **expert**]

sexploitation *seks-ploi-tā'shən, n* the exploitation of sex for commercial gain in films and other media. [**sex** and **exploitation**]

sext *sekst, n* (prayers said at) *orig* the sixth, now the fourth, canonical hour of the divine office, at midday (*RC*); a sixth (*music*): an organ stop giving the twelfth and the tierce (a sixth apart). [L *sextus* sixth, from *sex* six]

sextan *seks'tən*, (*med*) *adj* (of the paroxysms of a fever) recurring every fifth day (sixth by old reckoning). [From Med L *sextana* (*febris*) (fever) of the sixth (day)]

sextant *seks'tənt, n* the sixth part of a circle or its circumference, a sector or an arc of 60°; an instrument with an arc of a sixth of a circle, for measuring angular distances, *esp* a navigating instrument incorporating a small telescope (with *cap*; also **Sex'tans** *-tənz*) a constellation, lying over the equator; (also **sex'tans** *-tənz*) a Roman bronze coin worth a sixth of an as (*hist*). — *adj* **sextantal** (*-tant'l*). [L *sextāns, -antis* a sixth]

sextet, **sextett**, **sextette** *seks-tet', n* altered forms (partly through Ger) of **sestet**.

sextile *seks'tīl* or *-til*, (*astrol*) *n* a position 60° apart on the zodiacal chart (also **sextile aspect**). [L *sextīlis* sixth]

sextillion *seks-til'yən, n* the sixth power of a million; the seventh power of 1000 (*US*). [For *sexillion*, after **billion**, etc]

sextodecimo *seks-tō-des'i-mō, n* a book or a size of book made by folding each sheet into sixteen leaves: — *pl* **sextodec'imos**. — Also *adj.* — See also **sixteenmo** under **sixteen**. [L (*in*) *sextō decimō* (in) one-sixteenth]

sextolet *seks'tə-let*, (*music*) *n* a group of six notes performed in the time of four. [Ger *Sextole*, from L *sex*]

sexton *seks'tən, n* an officer who rings a church bell, attends the clergyman, digs graves, etc; a burying beetle (also **sexton beetle**). — *n* **sex'toness** a female sexton. — *n* **sex'tonship**. [**sacristan**]

sextuor *seks'tū-ör, n* a sextet. [Fr, from L *sex*, after *quattuor* four]

sextuple *seks'tū-pl, adj* sixfold. — *n* six times as much. — *vt* and *vi* to increase or multiply sixfold. — *n* **sex'tūplet** a sextolet (*music*); one of six children born at a single birth. [LL *sextuplus*]

sexual, **sexy**, etc. See under **sex**.

sey *sī*, (*Scot*) *n* part of a carcase of beef *incl* the sirloin. [Origin obscure]

seyen, **seysure**. Shakespearean spellings of **scion**, **seizure**.

Seyfert galaxy *sī'fərt* or *sē'fərt gal'ək-si*, (*astron*) *n* one of a small class of galaxies with intensely bright nuclei and inconspicuous spiral arms. [After Carl *Seyfert* (1911–60), US astrophysicist]

sez. Slang spelling of **says**.

Sezary syndrome *sez'ə-ri sin'drōm*, (*med*) *n* a rare condition in which abnormal growth of lymphocytes occurs in the skin, liver and lymph nodes.

SF *abbrev*: science fiction; signal frequency; Sinn Fein.

sf *abbrev*: sforzando.

SFA *abbrev*: Scottish Football Association; Sweet Fanny Adams (= nothing at all; *slang*).

sferics. See **spherics**[1].

SFO *abbrev*: Serious Fraud Office.

'sfoot *sfo͝ot*, (*Shakesp*) *interj* for **God's foot**, an exclamatory oath.

sforzando *sför-tsän'dō* or **sforzato** *sför-tsä'tō*, (*music*) *adj* and *adv* forced, with sudden emphasis (*abbrev* **sf** and **sfz**, or marked >, ∧). — Also *n*: — *pl* **sforzan'dos** or **sforzan'di** (*-dē*), **sforza'tos** or **sforza'ti** (*-tē*). [Ital, pr p and pa p of *sforzare* to force, from L *ex* out, and LL *fortia* force]

sfumato *sfo͞o-mä'tō*, (*painting* and *drawing*) *n* a misty, indistinct effect achieved by gradually blending together areas of different colour or tone: — *pl* **sfuma'tos**. [Ital, pa p of *sfumare* to shade off, from L *ex* out, and *fūmāre* to smoke]

sfx *abbrev*: suffix.

sfz. *abbrev*: sforzando.

SG *abbrev*: Solicitor-General.

sg *abbrev*: specific gravity.

SGHWR *abbrev*: steam-generating heavy water reactor.

sgian-dubh *skē'ən-do͞o', n.* Same as **skene-dhu**.

SGP *abbrev*: Singapore (IVR).

sgraffito *zgräf-fē'tō, n* decorative work in which different colours are revealed by removal of parts of outer layers of material (plaster, slip, etc) laid on; pottery with such decoration: — *pl* **sgraffi'ti** (*-tē*). [Ital, from L *ex-*, and Ital *graffito*, qv]

Sgt *abbrev*: Sergeant.

sh *sh, interj* hush: — *pl* **sh's**.

s/h *abbrev*: shorthand.

shabble *shab'l*, (*Scot*) *n* an old rusty sword. [Cf Ital *sciabola*, Pol *szabla*, and **sabre**]

shabby *shab'i, adj* dingy or dirty; (of eg clothes) threadbare or worn; having a look of poverty; (of behaviour) unworthy, discreditable or contemptible; low; paltry. — *adv* **shabb'ily**. — *n* **shabb'iness**. — *adj* **shabb'y-genteel** keeping up or affecting an appearance of gentility, though really very shabby. — *n* **shabby-gentil'ity**. [Obs or dialect *shab* scab, from OE *sceabb*]

shabrack *shab'rak*, (*hist*) *n* a trooper's housing or saddle-cloth. — Also **shab'racque**. [Ger *Schabracke*, prob from Turk *çāprāq*]

Shabuoth, **Shavuoth** *shav-ū'oth* or *-ot*, or **Shavuot** *-ot, n* the Jewish Feast of Weeks, celebrated on the 50th day after Passover, *orig* marking the end of harvest, now generally taken as a commemoration of the giving of the Law to Moses. — Also called **Pentecost**. [Heb *shabuot(h)* weeks]

shack *shak, n* a roughly-built hut. — **shack up** (with *with*; *slang*; *usu* of unmarried sexual partners) to live together, or set up house together. [US; origin obscure]

shacko. See **shako**.

shackle *shak'l, n* a prisoner's or slave's ankle-ring or wrist-ring, or the chain connecting a pair; (in *pl*) fetters, manacles; a hindrance, constraint; a hobble; a staple-like link, closed with a pin; the curved movable part of a padlock; a coupling of various kinds. — *vt* to fetter; to couple; to hamper. — **shack'le-bolt** the pin of a shackle; **shack'le-bone** (*Scot*) the wrist. [OE *sceacul*]

shad *shad, n* an anadromous fish related to the herring; extended to various other similar but unrelated fishes. — *adj* **shad'-bellied** flat-bellied, *opp* to *pot-bellied*; (of a coat) sloping away gradually in front. — **shad'berry** the fruit of the **shad'bush**, the Juneberry (*Amelanchier*), a N American rosaceous shrub flowering at shad spawning-time. [OE *sceadd*]

shaddock *shad'ək*, *n* an Oriental citrus fruit like a very large orange, the pomelo; the tree that bears it. [Introduced to the W Indies c.1700 by a Captain *Shaddock*]

shade[1] *shād*, *n* partial or relative darkness; interception of light; obscurity; a shadow; a momentary facial expression; a place or area from which sunlight is excluded; shelter from light or heat; that which casts a shadow; a screen; a window-blind (*US*); a cover to modify or direct the light from a lamp; an inverted glass vessel formerly put over a clock or ornament; a projecting cover to protect the eyes from glare; (in *pl*; *slang*) sunglasses; an awning for a shop-window; a lace head-covering (*obs*); a variety or degree of colour; a hue mixed with black; the dark part of a picture; a slight difference or amount; (in *pl*) the darkness of the underworld, the abode of the dead, Hades; the disembodied soul; a ghost (*literary*). — *vt* to screen; to overshadow; to mark with gradations of colour or shadow; to soften down; to darken; to shadow, represent (*obs*); to lower (eg a price) very slightly (*orig US*). — *vi* to pass imperceptibly (*away*, *into*, etc). — *adj* **shā'ded**. — *adj* **shade'less**. — *adv* **shā'dily**. — *n* **shā'diness**. — *n* **shā'ding** the marking of shadows or shadowlike appearance; the effect of light and shade; fine gradations; nuances; toning down; modification of sound by anything put on top of an organ-pipe; the generation of a non-uniform background level in an image by a television camera tube; slight lowering of prices. — *adj* **shā'dy** having, or in, shade; sheltered from light or heat; underhand, disreputable (*colloq*); shadowy, mysterious, sinister. — **shade card** a card illustrating the various shades available in a certain type of paint; **shade plant** a plant adapted to light of low intensity; **shade tree** a tree planted to give shade. — **in the shade** sheltered from strong light; overlooked, forgotten, in relative obscurity; **on the shady side of** (*colloq*) over (a specified age); **put in the shade** to outdo completely; **shades of** an exclamation greeting something which reminds one in some way of (a specified person or thing). [OE *sceadu*; see **shadow**]

shade[2] *shād*, (*Scot*) *vt* to part (the hair). [Northern form of **shed**[1]]

shadoof or **shaduf** *shä-dōōf'*, *n* a device for raising water by a bucket on a counterpoised pivoted rod. [Egyp Ar *shādūf*]

shadow *shad'ō*, *n* shade cast by the interception of light by an object; the dark figure so projected on a surface, mimicking the object; the dark part of a picture; a reflected image; a mere appearance; an unreal thing; a representation; a person or thing wasted away almost to nothing; an inseparable or constant companion; a spy or detective who follows one; shade; protective shade, shelter; darkness; gloom; trouble; a ghost, spirit. — *adj* unreal; feigned; existing only in skeleton; inactive, or only partly active, but ready for the time when opportunity or need arises; denoting, in the main opposition party, a political counterpart to a member or section of the party in power. — *vt* to shade; to cloud or darken; to indicate obscurely, vaguely, or in dim outline (*usu* with *forth*); to typify; to hide; to attend like a shadow, follow and watch; to maintain a position close to, follow every movement of; to shadowcast. — *vi* to cast a shadow; to darken. — *n* **shad'ower**. — *n* **shad'owiness**. — *n* **shad'owing**. — *adj* **shad'owless**. — *adj* **shad'owy** shady; like a shadow; symbolic; secluded, dim; unsubstantial. — **shadow box** a frame or boxlike structure (often with shelves and a clear protective front) used to display articles; **shad'ow-boxing** sparring practice with an imaginary opponent; making a show of opposition or other action, as a cover for taking no effective steps; **shadow cabinet** a body of opposition leaders meeting from time to time and ready to take office should their party assume power. — *vt* **shad'owcast** (in microscopy) to cast shadows of projecting parts of (a specimen) by exposing to a stream of vapour of a heavy metal. — **shad'owcasting**; **shadow effect** a loss of signal strength in broadcast transmissions due to the topography of a region; **shadow fight** a fight between or with shadows or imaginary enemies; **shadow figure** a silhouette; **shad'owgraph** an image produced by throwing a shadow on a screen; a radiograph; **shadow mark** the trace of an archaeological site revealed by observation from the air; **shadow play** one in which the spectators see only shadows on a screen (also **shadow pantomime**); action which is merely symbolic or which mimics real or effective action. — **afraid of one's own shadow** extremely timid; **may your shadow never grow less** may you continue to prosper; **shadow of death** the darkness of death; the threatening approach of darkness or death. [OE *sceadwe*, genitive, dative and accusative of *sceadu* (**shade** representing the nominative); cf OHGer *scato*, Gr *skotos* darkness]

SHAEF *shāf*, *abbrev*: Supreme Headquarters Allied Expeditionary Force.

Shafiite *shaf'i-īt*, *n* a member of one of the four principal sects of the Sunnites, or orthodox Muslims. [Ar *Shāfi'ī* the name of the founder]

shaft *shäft*, *n* anything long and straight; a stem; an arrow; a missile (*esp fig*); the main, upright, straight, or cylindrical part of anything; the part of a cross below the arms; the part of a column between the base and the capital; the rachis of a feather; the thill of a carriage on either side of the horse; a straight handle; a pole; a ray or beam of light; a rotating rod that transmits motion; a well-like excavation or passage; the penis (*vulg slang*); a woman's body (purely as a sexual object) (*US vulg slang*). — *vt* to have sexual intercourse with (a woman) (*vulg slang*); to dupe, swindle, treat unfairly (*slang*). — *adj* **shaft'ed**. — *n* **shaft'er** or **shaft'-horse** a horse harnessed between shafts. — *n* **shaft'ing** the action of the verb in either sense; a system of shafts. — *adj* **shaft'less**. — **make a shaft or a bolt of it** to venture and take what comes of it, the shaft and the bolt being the arrows of the longbow and the crossbow respectively. [OE *sceaft*; perh partly Ger *Schacht* pit-shaft]

shag *shag*, *n* a ragged mass of hair, or anythng similar; a long coarse nap; a kind of tobacco cut into shreds; the green cormorant (*appar* from its crest), or other species; an act of sexual intercourse (*vulg slang*); a partner, *usu* female, in sexual intercourse (*vulg slang*); a whore (*vulg slang*); a US dance related to the jitterbug but with shuffling footwork, first popular in the 1950s and 60s; a lively dance of the 1930s. — *adj* shaggy; shaggy-haired. — *vt* to make shaggy. — *vi* (*archaic*) to hang in shaggy clusters. — *vt* and *vi* to have sexual intercourse (with) (*vulg slang*). — *vi* to dance the shag: — *pr p* **shagg'ing**; *pa t* and *pa p* **shagged** (*shagd*). — *adj* **shagged** (*shagd*) shaggy, rough (also *shag'id*); tired out, exhausted, as if from strenuous lovemaking (often with *out*) (*colloq*). — *n* **shagg'edness**. — *adv* **shagg'ily**. — *n* **shagg'iness**. — *adj* **shagg'y** long, rough, and coarse; having long, rough, coarse hair, wool, vegetation, etc; unkempt; rugged. — **shag'-bark** a kind of hickory tree. — *adj* **shag'-** (or **shagge'-**)**eared** (*Shakesp*) hairy-eared. — **shaggy cap**, **shaggy ink-cap** or **shaggy mane** an edible fungus (*Coprinus comatus*) with a white, cylindrical, shaggy-scaled cap; **shaggy-dog story** (from the shaggy dog featured in many) a whimsically long-drawn-out story humorous because of its length and the inconsequence of its ending. — *adj* **shag'-haired**. — *adj* **shag'pile** (*esp* of carpets) having a pile of long, thick fibres. [OE *sceacga*; cf ON *skegg* a beard]

shagreen *shə-grēn'*, *n* a granular leather made from horse's or donkey's skin; the skin of shark, ray, etc, covered with small nodules (formerly **chagrin'**). — *adj* **shagreen'** or **shagreened'** of, or covered with, shagreen. [Fr *chagrin*, from Turk *sagri* horse's rump, shagreen]

shagroon *shə-grōōn'*, *n* an early settler in New Zealand of other than British origin. [Perh Irish *seachrān* wandering]

shah *shä*, *n* the king of Persia (now Iran) (*hist*); also formerly of certain other Eastern countries. [Pers *shāh*]

shaikh. Same as **sheikh**.

shairn. Same as **sharn**.

Shaitan *shī-tän'*, *n* Satan; (without *cap*) an evil spirit; a devilish person or animal; a dust storm. [Ar *shaitān*, from Heb (see **Satan**)]

Shaiva. See **Saiva**.

shake *shāk*, *vt* to move with quick, short, often violent to-and-fro movements; to brandish; to cause to tremble or to totter; to disturb the stability of; to cause to waver; to disturb; to dismay; to unnerve, shock; to alert, rouse, summon (*slang*); to put, send, render or cause to be, by shaking; to scatter or send down by shaking; to split; to get rid of (*US*; *old*). — *vi* to be agitated; to tremble; to shiver; to shake hands; to trill (*music*); to happen (*slang*): — *pa t* **shook** or *obs* **shāked** and **shākt**; *pa p* **shāk'en** or *obs* **shāked, shākt** and **shook**. — *n* a shaking; tremulous motion; a damaging or weakening blow; a shaken-up drink (*esp* a milkshake); a trillo, rapid alternation of two notes a tone or semitone apart, commonly ending with a turn (*music*); a fissure or crack (*esp* in rock or in growing timber); a moment (*colloq*). — *adj* **shake'able** or **shāk'able**. — *adj* **shāk'en**. — *n* **shāk'er** a person who shakes; a person who makes things happen, as in the phrase *mover and shaker*; a device for shaking (eg drinks); a perforated container from which something, eg flour, is shaken; (with *cap*; in *pl*) a name popularly applied to an American religious sect, the United Society of Believers in Christ's Second Appearing, as a result of their ecstatic dancing, also formerly to Quakers and sects whose religious fervour manifested itself in violent trembling. — *n* **Shāk'erism**. — *adv* **shāk'ily**. — *n* **shāk'iness**. — *n* and *adj* **shāk'ing**. — *adj* **shāk'y** shaking or inclined to shake; loose; tremulous; precarious; uncertain; wavering; unsteady; frail from old age or illness; full of cracks or clefts. — **shake'-bag** a fighting cock turned out of a bag; a large fighting cock; **shake'down** a temporary bed (*orig* made by shaking down straw); a trial run, operation, etc to familiarize personnel with procedures and machinery (chiefly *US*; *colloq*); an act of extortion or blackmail (*slang*); a thorough search of a person or place *esp* by the police (*slang*); **shake'-out** a drastic reorganization or upheaval; a recession in a particular commercial or industrial activity, *esp* when accompanied by cutbacks in the workforce or closure of individual businesses; **shake'-rag** (*obs*) a disreputable ragged man; **shake'-up** a disturbance or reorganization (*colloq*); **shaking palsy** a name for Parkinson's disease. — **great shakes** or **no great shakes** of great account or of no account; **shake a leg** (often *imperative*; *colloq*) to hurry up, get moving; **shake down** (*slang*) to extort money from by threats or blackmail; to search thoroughly; to frisk (a person for weapons, drugs, etc); to go to bed (*esp* in a temporary bed); to settle by shaking; to cheat of money at one stroke; **shake hands with** to greet (someone) by clasping his or her hand *usu* with an up-and-down movement; to seal a bargain, acknowledge an agreement, settle differences, etc, with (someone) in this way; **shake** or **shiver in one's shoes** to be so afraid that one's body, *esp* one's legs, quiver with fear; **shake off** to get rid of, often by shaking (also *fig*); to get away, escape, from (someone or something that is following, pursuing, etc); **shake off** (or **shake**) **the dust from one's feet** see Matt 10. 14) to leave hurriedly or gladly (*lit* and *fig*); **shake one's head** to turn one's head from side to side as an indication of reluctance, rejection, denial, disapproval, etc; **shake one's sides** to laugh uproariously; **shake out** to empty or cause to spread or unfold by shaking; **shake up** to rouse, mix, disturb, loosen by shaking; to reorganize (*colloq*); to upbraid (*Shakesp*); **two shakes (of a lamb's tail**, etc) (*colloq*) a very short time. [OE *sc(e)acan*]

Shakespearian or **Shakespearean** *shāk-spē'ri-ən*, *adj* of or relating to William *Shakespeare* (1564–1616), or his literary works, etc. — *n* a student of Shakespeare. — *n* **Shakespeariana** (*-i-ä'nə*) items, writings or lore relating to Shakespeare. — **Shakespearian sonnet** see under **sonnet**.

shako or **shacko** *shak'ō*, *n* a tall, nearly cylindrical military cap with a plume: — *pl* **shak'os** or **shak'oes**. [Hung *csákó*]

Shakta, Shakti, Shaktism. See **Sakti**.

shakudo *shak'o͞o-dō* or *-dō'*, *n* an alloy of copper and a small percentage of gold, used in Japanese decorative art, *esp* in sword fittings, to give a blue-black patina. — *adj* made of or with shakudo. [Jap]

shakuhachi *shak-o͞o-hach'ē* or *shäk-o͞o-häch'ē*, *n* a Japanese end-blown bamboo flute. [Jap]

shale[1] *shāl*, *n* clay rock splitting readily into thin layers along the bedding-planes. — *adj* **shā'ly**. — **shale mine**; **shale'-miner**; **shale oil** oil distilled from oil-bearing shales. [Ger *Schale* lamina; or from **shale**[2]]

shale[2] *shāl*, (*Shakesp*) *n* a shell or husk. — *vt* to shell. [OE *sc(e)alu*; cf **scale**]

shall *shal* or *shəl*, *vt orig* expressing debt or moral obligation, now used with the infinitive of a verb (without *to*) to form (in sense) a future tense, expressing in the first person mere futurity (as **will** does in the second and third), in the second and third implying also promise, command, decree, or control on the part of the speaker (rules for use of *shall*, *will*, are often ignored); must, will have to, is to, etc (in 2nd and 3rd persons, and interrogatively 1st); may be expected to, may chance to, may well (in all persons); may in future contingency, may come to (in all persons): — no *participles*; *2nd pers sing* (*archaic*) **shalt**; *3rd pers sing* **shall**; *pa t* **should** (*sho͝od* or *shəd*); *2nd pers sing* (*archaic*) **shouldest** or **shouldst**. [OE *sculan*, pr t *sceal*, *scealt*, *sceal*; pa t *sceolde*; cf Ger *soll*, Gothic *skal*, ON *skal*]

shalli. See **challis**.

shallon *shal'ən*, *n* salal.

shalloon *shə-lo͞on'*, *n* a light woollen fabric used for coat linings, etc. [OFr *chalon*; perh made at *Châlons-sur-Marne*]

shallop *shal'əp*, *n* formerly, a heavy fore-and-aft-rigged boat; a dinghy; a small or light boat. [Fr *chaloupe*; cf **sloop**]

shallot or **shalot** *shə-lot'*, *n* a species of onion (*Allium ascalonicum*) with clusters of garlic-flavoured, oval bulbs. — Also **eschalot** (*e-shə-lot'*, *esh'*). [OFr *eschalote*, variant of *escalogne*; see **scallion**]

shallow *shal'ō*, *adj* of no great depth, concavity, profundity or penetration; superficial. — *adv* at or to no great depth. — *n* a shallow place; (in *pl* with *the*) the shallow part (of the sea, etc). — *vt* to make shallow. — *vi* to grow shallow. — *n* and *adj* **shall'owing**. — *adv* **shall'owly** simply, foolishly; in a shallow or superficial manner. — *n* **shall'owness**. [ME *schalowe*, perh related to **shoal**[2]]

shalm. Same as **shawm**.

shalom *shal-ōm'* or *shal-om'*, (*Heb*) *interj* (in full **shalom aleichem** *ə-lāhh'əm*) peace (be with you), a greeting or valediction used *esp* by Jewish people.

shalot. See **shallot**.

shalt *shalt*, *2nd pers sing* of **shall**.

shalwar *shul'vär* or *shal'war*, *n* loose-fitting trousers worn (by both sexes) in many parts of S Asia. — **shalwar-kameez'** a S Asian outfit (for men and women) of loose-fitting trousers and a long tunic. [Urdu *shalwār*, Hindi *salvar*, from Pers *shalwar*; Urdu *kamis*, from Ar *qamīs* shirt]

shaly. See under **shale**[1].

sham *sham*, *n* a hoax, imposture (*obs*); a counterfeit, pretence. — *adj* pretended; false. — *vt* to pretend; to feign; to impose upon (*obs*). — *vi* to make false pretences; to pretend to be (as *to sham dead* or *sick*): — *pr p* **shamm'ing**; *pa t* and *pa p* **shammed**. — *n* **shamm'er**. — **sham Abraham** see under **Abraham-man**. [First found as slang, late 17c; prob derived from **shame**]

shama *shä'mə*, *n* an Indian songbird of the thrush family. [Hindi *śāmā*]

shaman *shäm'an* or *-ən*, *n* a doctor-priest or medicine man working by magic, *esp* a priest of Asian Shamanism: — *pl* **sham'ans**. — Also *adj*. — *adj* **shaman'ic**. — *n* **Sham'anism** (also without *cap*) the religion of certain peoples of N Asia, based essentially on magic and sorcery as practised by shamans. — *n* **sham'anist**. — *adj* **shamanist'ic**. [Russ, from Tungus *saman*, ult from Sans *śrama* religious practice]

shamateur *sham'ə-tœr* or *-tūr*, *n* a person rated as an amateur in sport who yet makes gains from playing or competing. — Also *fig*. — *n* **sham'ateurism**. [**sham**, and **amateur**]

shamba *sham'bə*, *n* (in E Africa) any farm, plot or smallholding used for growing crops. [Swahili]

shamble[1] *sham'bl*, *vi* to walk with an awkward, unsteady gait; to shuffle. — *n* a shambling gait. — *n* and *adj* **sham'bling**. — *adj* **sham'bly**. [Poss from **shamble**[2], in allusion to its trestle-like legs]

shamble[2] *sham'bl*, *n* a butcher's market stall; (in *pl*; *usu* treated as *n sing*) a flesh-market, hence, a slaughterhouse. — *n sing* **sham'bles** a place of carnage (*fig*); a mess or muddle (*colloq*). — *adj* **shambol'ic** (*slang*) chaotic. [OE *scamel* (Ger *Schemel*) stool, from LL *scamellum*, dimin of *scamnum* a bench]

shame *shām*, *n* the humiliating feeling of having appeared unfavourably in one's own eyes, or those of others, by shortcoming, offence, or unseemly exposure, or a similar feeling on behalf of anything one associates with oneself; susceptibility to such feeling; fear or scorn of incurring disgrace or dishonour; modesty; bashfulness; disgrace, ignominy; disgraceful wrong; a cause or source of disgrace; a thing to be ashamed of; an instance or a case of hard or bad luck (*colloq*); those parts of the body that it is felt to be immodest to expose (*archaic*). — *interj* how shameful, what a disgrace!; an expression of affection, warmth or sympathy (*SAfr*). — *vt* to make ashamed; to disgrace; to cause to seem humiliatingly poor or paltry by greater excellence; to drive or compel by shame. — *vi* to be ashamed. — *adj* **shame'able** or **sham'able**. — *adj* **shamed** ashamed. — *adj* **shame'ful** disgraceful. — *adv* **shame'fully**. — *n* **shame'fulness**. — *adj* **shame'less** immodest, brazen; done without shame. — *adj* **shame'lessly**. — *n* **shame'lessness**. — *n* **shā'mer** someone who or that which causes shame. — *adj* **shame'faced** (alteration of **shame'fast**, OE *scamfæst*) very modest or bashful; showing shame; abashed. — *adv* **shame'facedly** (*-fāst-li* or *fā'sid-li*). — **shame'facedness** (formerly **shame'fastness**) modesty. — *adj* **shame'-proof** insensible to shame. — *adj* **shame'worthy**. — **for shame** an interjectional phrase, you should be ashamed; **put to shame** to disgrace, *esp* by excelling; **shame on (you, them, etc)** (you, they, etc) should be ashamed; **tell the truth and shame the devil** put the devil to disgraceful defeat by boldly telling the truth; **think shame** to be ashamed. [OE *sc(e)amu*; Ger *Scham*]

shamianah or **shamiana** *shä-mē-ä'nə*, *n* (in India) a large tent, awning or canopy. — Also **shamiya'nah**. [Hindi *shāmiyāna*; from Pers]

shamisen. See **samisen**.

shammes *shä'məs* or **shammash** *shamash'*, (*Judaism*) *n* a caretaker of a synagogue with a similar role to a sexton's; a candle used to light the candles of the menorah: — *pl* **shammos'im** or **shammash'im**. [Yiddish, from Heb *shāmmāsh*, from Aramaic *shemāsh* to serve]

shammy *sham'i*, *n* (in full **shammy leather**) a soft leather, *orig* made from chamois skin, now *usu* from sheepskin, by working in oil; a piece of it, used for polishing, etc. — Also *adj*. — *vt* **sham'oy** (or *-moi'*) to prepare (skins) by working oil into them. [**chamois**]

shampoo *sham-pōō'*, *vt* to massage; to wash and rub (the scalp and hair) with special lathering preparation; to clean (a carpet, etc) by rubbing with detergent: — *pa t* and *pa p* **shampooed'** or **shampoo'd'**. — *n* an act or process of shampooing; a preparation for the purpose: — *pl* **shampoos'**. — *n* **shampoo'er**. [Hindi *čapnā* to squeeze]

shamrock *sham'rok*, *n* the national emblem of Ireland, a trifoliate leaf or plant; (in living popular tradition) the lesser yellow trefoil; (in English poetry) often wood-sorrel; according to some, white clover, hop-trefoil, black medick, or some other (or any) leaf or plant with three leaflets. [Ir *seamróg*, Gaelic *seamrag*, dimin of *seamar* trefoil]

shamus *shā'məs* or *shä'*, (*old US slang*) *n* a detective: — *pl* **sha'muses**. [Perh from Yiddish *shammes* a sexton, caretaker, with influence from Irish *Seamas* James]

shan. See **shand**.

Shan *shän*, *n* a member of a Mongoloid people of China, Thailand, Burma, and Assam, related to the Thais; their Sino-Tibetan language. — Also *adj*.

shanachie *shan'ə-hhē*. Same as **seannachie**.

shand *shand*, or **shan** *shan*, (*obs criminals' slang*) *n* a base or counterfeit coin. [From dialect *shan* paltry]

Shandean *shan'di-ən* or *shan-dē'ən*, *adj* characteristic of Tristram *Shandy* or the Shandy family, or their creator Laurence Sterne. — *n* a person of Shandean character.

shandry *shan'dri*, (*N Eng*) *n* a light cart on springs. — *n* **shan'drydan** (*-dri-dan*) a shandry; an old-fashioned chaise; a rickety vehicle. [Origin unknown]

shandy *shan'di*, *n* a mixture of beer and ginger beer or lemonade. — Also (*esp US*) **shan'dygaff**. [Origin unknown]

Shang *shang*, *n* a Chinese dynasty (17c–11c BC). — *adj* of the dynasty, its time or *esp* its pottery, bronzes, etc.

shanghai[1] *shang-hī'*, *vt* to drug or make drunk and send to sea as a sailor; to trick into performing an unpleasant task: — *pr p* **shanghai'ing**; *pa t* and *pa p* **shanghaied'** or **shanghai'd'**. — *n* **shanghai'er**. [*Shanghai* in China]

shanghai[2] *shang-hī'*, (*Austr* and *NZ*) *n* a catapult. — *vt* to shoot with a shanghai. [Ety uncertain]

Shangri-la *shang'gri-lä*, *n* an imaginary pass in the Himalayas, an earthly paradise, described in James Hilton's *Lost Horizon* (1933); hence, any remote or imaginary paradise.

shank *shangk*, *n* the leg from knee to foot; the corresponding part in other vertebrates; the lower part of the foreleg, *esp* as a cut of meat; a shaft, stem, straight or long part; the part of a shoe connecting sole with heel; the leg of a stocking; a long-handled ladle for molten metal; an act of shanking a golfball; the end, latter part (*dialect*). — *vi* to be affected with disease of the footstalk (*bot*); to take to one's legs (also *vt* with *it*). — *vt* to dispatch unceremoniously (*Scot*); to strike (the ball) by mistake with the part of the club where the clubhead meets the shaft (*golf*). — *adj* **shanked** having a shank; affected with disease of the shank or footstalk (*bot*). — **shank'bone**. — **on Shanks's pony, mare, nag**, etc, on foot. [OE *sc(e)anca* leg; Du *schonk*, LGer *schanke*]

shanny *shan'i*, *n* the smooth blenny, *Lipophrys pholis*, a small marine fish found in inshore waters and rock pools. [Origin obscure]

shan't or **sha'n't** *shänt*, (*colloq*) a contraction of **shall not**.

shantung *shan-tung'* or *-tōōng'*, *n* a plain rough cloth of wild silk; a similar cotton or rayon fabric. [*Shantung* province in China]

shanty[1] *shan'ti*, *n* a roughly built hut; a ramshackle dwelling; a rough public house or (*hist*) a place selling alcohol illicitly (*Austr*). — **shan'tyman** a man, *esp* a logger, who lives in a shanty; **shan'tytown** a town, or an area of one, where housing is makeshift and ramshackle. [Perh Fr *chantier* a timber-yard (in Canada a woodcutters' headquarters); perh Irish *sean tig* old house]

shanty[2] or **shantey** *shan'ti*, *n* a rhythmical song with chorus and solo verses (often extempore) sung by sailors while heaving at the capstan, etc. — Also **chanty**, **chantie** or **chantey**. — *n* **shan'tyman** the solo-singer in shanties. [Said to be from Fr *chantez* (imperative) sing]

SHAPE *shāp*, *abbrev*: Supreme Headquarters Allied Powers Europe.

shape *shāp*, *vt* to form; to fashion; to mould into a particular shape or form; to give form to; to embody; to plan, devise; to direct; to determine; to purpose (*obs*). — *vi* to take shape; to develop; to give promising signs; to conduce (*Shakesp*); to become fit: — *pa t* **shaped**, (*obs* **shope** *shōp*); *pa p* **shāped** (*archaic* **shāp'en**). — *n* form; figure; disposition in space; guise; form or condition; that which has form or figure; an apparition; a pattern; a mould (*cookery*); a jelly, pudding, etc, turned out of a mould. — *adj* **shāp'able** or **shape'able**. — *adj* **shaped** having a shape, or a definite, determinate, or adapted shape, often in combination, as in *L-shaped*. — *adj* **shape'less** of ill-defined or unsatisfactory shape; without shape; purposeless (*Shakesp*). — *n* **shape'lessness**. — *n* **shape'liness**. — *adj* **shape'ly** having an attractive, well-proportioned shape or figure. — *adj* **shap'en** fashioned; definitely shaped. — *n* **shap'er** someone or something that shapes; (in management) a decisive, somewhat bullying leader who carries others along with his or her dynamism (*informal*). — *n* and *adj* **shap'ing**. — **shape tape** (*colloq*) a music or video cassette tape in which instructions are given for a series of exercises designed to promote fitness, improve one's figure, etc; **shape'-up** (*NAm*) formerly, a method of hiring workers, *esp* dockers, for a single day's work by selecting the number of men needed from an assembly gathered for this purpose. — **in any shape or form** at all; **in good shape** or **in shape** in good condition; **in the shape of** in the guise of; of the nature of; **out of shape** deformed, disfigured; in poor physical condition, unfit; **shape one's course** to direct one's way; **shape up** to assume a shape; to develop, to be promising; **take shape** to assume a definite form or plan; to be embodied or worked out in practice. [OE *sceippan*, pa t *scōp*, pa p *scapen*, to create, form, with new present developed from the pa p influenced by the noun *gesceap* creation, form; cf ON *skapa*, Ger *schaffen*, *schöpfen*]

shaps *shaps*, *n pl* short form of **chaparajos**.

sharawaggi or **sharawadgi** *shar-ə-waj'i*, *n* (in design, architecture, etc), the use of irregularity, discordance or incongruity for deliberate, artful, contrastive effect. [Used orig in the late 17c in the context of Chinese landscape gardening, ety uncertain]

shard[1] *shärd*, (*Shakesp*) *n* a piece of cow dung. — *adj* **shard'ed** (*archaic*) sheltered under dung. — **shard beetle** a dor beetle, laying its eggs in cow dung. — *adj* **shard'-borne** (see separate article). [Cf **sharn**]

shard[2] *shärd* or **sherd** *shûrd*, *n* a gap (now *dialect*); a boundary water (*archaic*); a scrap, broken piece, *esp* of pottery. [OE *sceard* cleft, potsherd; cf *sceran* to cut; Ger *Scharte* notch]

shard[3] *shärd*. Same as **chard**.

shard[4] *shärd*, (*zool*) *n* a tough or hard sheath or shell, such as a beetle's wingcase. [From a misunderstanding of Shakespeare's **shard-borne**]

shard[5] or **shar'd** *shärd*, (*Spenser*) *pa t* and *pa p* of **share**[1,2].

shard-borne *shärd'börn* or *-bōrn*, *adj* born in dung (*Shakesp*); later used as meaning borne on elytra. [**shard**[1]; cf **shard**[4]]

share[1] *shār*, *n* a part allotted, contributed, owned or taken; a part cut off (*archaic*); a division, section, portion; a fixed and indivisible section of the capital of a company. — *vt* to divide into shares; to apportion; to give or take a share of; to participate in; to have in common. — *vi* to have, receive, or give a share. — *n* **shar'er**. — *n* **shar'ing**. — **share bone** the pubis; **share'-capital** money derived from the sale of shares in a business, and used for carrying it on; **share certificate** a certificate issued to a shareholder by a company indicating ownership of its shares; **share'cropper** (*esp US*) a tenant farmer who supplies, in lieu or rent, a share of the crop. — *vi* **share'crop**. — **shared logic** (*comput*) a shared facility in which the central processing unit is shared by several terminals; **shared ownership** a type of house ownership shared between the householder and a housing association; **share'-farmer** (*esp Austr*) a tenant farmer who pays a share of the proceeds as rent; **share'holder** a person who owns a share or shares, *esp* in a company; **share'holding**; **share index** an index showing the movement of shares in companies trading on a stock exchange; **share'man** or **shares'man** a fisherman who shares profits with the owners; **share'milker** (*NZ*) a sharefarmer on a dairy farm; **share option** a scheme enabling employees to buy shares in their company at less than the market rate; **share'-out** a distribution in or by shares; **share'-pusher** a person who seeks to sell shares otherwise than through recognized channels, eg by dubious advertisement, etc; **share shop** a shop or special area in a bank, etc where shares are traded quickly and informally without investment advice; **share'ware** (*comput*) software readily available for a nominal fee. — **go shares** (*colloq*) to share something with others; **lion's share** see under **lion**; **share and share alike** give everyone his or her due share; in equal shares. [OE *scearu*; cf **shear**]

share[2] *shār*, *n* a ploughshare, or the corresponding part of another implement. — *vt* to cut, cleave: — *pa t* and *pa p* **shared**, (*Spenser*) **shard** (*shärd*). [OE *scear*; cf **share**[1], and **shear**]

Sharia *shə-rē'ə* or **Shariat** *shə-rē'ət*, *n*. Same as **Sheria**, **Sheriat**. — Also without *cap*.

sharif. See **sherif**.

shark *shärk*, *n* a general name for elasmobranchs other than skates, rays, and chimaeras, voracious fishes with a fusiform body, lateral gill-slits, and a mouth on the under side; sometimes confined to the larger kinds, excluding the dogfishes; an extortioner; a financial swindler; an underhand or predatory dealer; a sharper. — *vi* and *vt* (*archaic*) to obtain by swindling. — *n* **shark'er**. — *n* **shark'ing**. — **shark oil** oil from shark's liver, used like cod-liver oil; **shark patrol** (*esp Austr* and *US*) a regular patrol of the waters close to bathing beaches by boats, aircraft, etc, to look for sharks; **shark'skin** a woollen or worsted suiting in twill weave; a heavy rayon material with dull finish; shagreen; **shark'sucker** a remora. [Origin doubtful; Ger *Schurke* scoundrel, Austrian Ger *Schirk* sturgeon, Fr dialect *cherquier* to seek, L *carcharus* dogfish, from Gr *karcharos* jagged, have been suggested]

sharn *shärn*, (*Scot* and *dialect*) *n* cow dung or dung generally. — *adj* **sharn'y**. — **sharny peat** a cake of cow dung mixed with coal. [OE *scearn*; cf ON *skarn*]

sharon fruit *shar'ən froōt*, *n* a persimmon. [From the *Sharon* valley in Israel where it is esp grown]

sharp *shärp*, *adj* cutting; piercing; penetrating; acute; having a thin edge or fine point; affecting the senses as if pointed or cutting; severe; harsh; keen; eager; hungry (*Shakesp*); alive to one's own interests; barely honest; of keen or quick perception; alert; fit, able; pungent, sarcastic; brisk; abrupt; having abrupt or acute corners, etc; sudden in onset; clear-cut; unblurred; well-defined; stylish (*slang*); too dressy, overly smart or fashionable in dress (*slang*); high in pitch, or too high (*music*); raised a semitone (*music*); voiceless (*obs phonetics*). — *adv* high or too high in pitch; punctually, precisely; sharply. — *n* a note raised a semitone; the symbol for it; the key producing it; sharpness (*Milton*); a long slender needle; a small sword or duelling-sword; (in *pl*) hard parts of wheat, middlings; (in *pl*) sword-fighting in earnest; a sharper. — *vt* and *vi* (*obs* or *dialect*) to sharpen. — *vt* and *vi* **sharp'en** to make or become sharp in any sense. — *n* **sharp'ener**. — *n* **sharp'er** a cheat or hoaxer, *esp* someone who cheats at cards. — *n* **sharp'ie** a flat-bottomed, two-masted vessel with triangular sails, formerly of the US Atlantic coast; one of a set of stylishly dressed teenagers (*Austr* and *NZ*). — *n* and *adj* **sharp'ing** cheating. — *adj* **sharp'ish**. — *adv* **sharp'ly**. — *n* **sharp'ness**. — *adj* **sharp'-cut** well-defined; clear-cut. — *adj* **sharp'-edged**. — *adj* **sharp'-eyed**. — *adj* **sharp'-**

ground ground to a sharp edge. — *adj* **sharp'-looking** (*Shakesp*) hungry-looking. — *adj* **sharp'-nosed** having a pointed nose; with a keen sense of smell. — *adj* **sharp'-pointed**. — **sharp practice** unscrupulous dealing, verging on dishonesty. — *adj* **sharp'-set** hungry; keen in appetite for anything, *esp* food or sexual indulgence; (of a tool, etc) set with a sharp edge. — *adj* **sharp'-shod** (of a horse) having spikes in the shoes to prevent slipping. — **sharp'shooter** an expert marksman; a soldier, policeman, etc employed as a marksman; (loosely) someone with a talent for scoring in any sport; **sharp'shooting**. — *adj* **sharp-sight'ed** having acute sight; shrewd. — **sharp-tailed grouse** a grouse of western Canada and US whose middle tail-feathers are longer than the rest. — *adj* **sharp-tongued'** critical, sarcastic, harsh in speech. — *adj* **sharp-toothed'**. — *adj* **sharp-witt'ed** having an alert intelligence, wit or perception. — **at the sharp end** in the position of greatest difficulty, danger, stress, etc, in any activity; **look sharp** be quick; hurry up; **sharp's the word** be brisk. [OE *scearp*; ON *skarpr*, Ger *scharf*]

Shar-Pei *shär-pā*, *n* a large muscular dog of a Chinese breed, with a distinctive wrinkled nose. [Chin dialect, sand fur]

shash[1] *shash*. The earlier spelling of **sash**[1].

shash[2] *shash*, (*telecomm*) *n* noisy interference (to a sound or picture signal). [Imit]

shashlik or **shashlick** *shash-lik'* or *shash'-*, *n* a type of lamb kebab. [Russ *shashlyk*]

Shasta daisy *shas'tə dā'zi*, *n* a composite flowering plant, *Chrysanthemum maximum*, with large, yellow-centred, white daisylike flowers. [From Mount *Shasta*, California]

shaster *shas'tər*, or **shastra** *shäs'trä*, (*Hinduism*) *n* a holy writing. [Sans *śāstra*, from *śās* to teach]

shat. See **shit**.

shatter *shat'ər*, *vt* to scatter (*archaic*); to dash to pieces; to wreck. — *vi* to break into fragments. — *n* a fragment; an impaired state. — *adj* **shatt'ered** (*colloq*) exhausted; extremely upset. — *adj* **shatt'ery** brittle. — **shatt'er-brain** or **shatt'er-pate** a scatterbrain. — *adj* **shatt'er-brained**. — *adj* **shatt'erproof**. [Perh LGer; cf **scatter**]

shauchle *shöhh'l*, (*Scot*) *vi* to shuffle. — *vt* to put out of shape or make down-at-heel. — *n* a shuffling gait; a down-at-heel shoe. — *adj* **shauch'ly**. [Origin obscure]

shave *shāv*, *vt* to scrape or pare off a superficial slice, hair (*esp* of the face), or other surface material from; to tonsure; to remove by scraping or paring; to pare closely; to graze the surface of; to plunder, fleece. — *vi* to remove hair with a razor; to pass or escape with little margin: — *pa p* **shaved** or *archaic* **shā'ven**. — *n* the act or process of shaving; a paring; a narrow miss or escape (*esp* in *close shave*); a paring or slicing tool. — *n* **shave'ling** a tonsured cleric. — *adj* **shā'ven** shaved; tonsured; close-cut; smoothed. — *n* **shā'ver** a person who shaves; an electric razor; a barber; a sharp or extortionate dealer; a chap, a youngster (*colloq*). — *n* **shā'vie** (*Scot*) a trick. — *n* **shā'ving** the act of scraping or using a razor; a thin slice, *esp* a curled piece of wood planed off. — **shave'-grass** Dutch rush; **shā'ving-brush** a brush for lathering the face before shaving; **shā'ving-soap** soap for lathering in preparation for shaving; **shā'ving-stick** a cylindrical piece of shaving-soap. [OE *sc(e)afan*; Du *schaven*, Ger *schaben*]

Shavian *shā'vi-ən*, *adj* pertaining to the dramatist George Bernard *Shaw* (1856–1950). — *n* a follower or admirer of Shaw.

Shavuot, **Shavuoth**. See **Shabuoth**.

shaw[1] *shö*, *n* a small wood. [OE *sc(e)aga*; ON *skōgr*, Dan *skov*]

shaw[2] *shö*, (*Scot*) *n* the above-ground parts of a potato plant, turnip, etc; show, appearance, display. [Scot form of **show**]

shawl *shöl*, *n* a loose knitted or other covering for the shoulders, wrapping a baby in, etc. — *vt* to wrap in a shawl. — *n* **shawl'ie** or **shawl'ey** (*Irish*) a working woman, *esp* a fisherwoman, who habitually wears a shawl. — *n* **shawl'ing**. — *adj* **shawl'less**. — **shawl collar** a large rolled collar tapering from the neck to (near) the waistline; **shawl pattern** the pine-cone pattern used on Kashmir shawls and imitated on Paisley shawls in the 19c; **shawl waistcoat** a waistcoat with a large prominent pattern like that of an oriental or Paisley shawl. — **Paisley shawl** see under **paisley**. [Pers *shāl*]

shawm *shöm* or **shalm** *shäm*, *n* a musical instrument, a predecessor of the oboe, having a double reed and a flat circular piece against which the lips are rested. [OFr *chalemie*, *-mel*, from L *calamus* reed]

Shawnee *shö-nē'*, *n* a N American Indian of an Algonquin tribe now mostly in Oklahoma; the language of this tribe. — **shawnee'-wood** a species of *Catalpa*. [Shawnee *Shawunogi*]

shay *shā*, *n*. A *colloq* form of **chaise**.

shaya. See **chay**[2].

shchi or **shtchi** *shchē*, *n* cabbage soup. [Russ]

she *shē* (or when unemphatic *shi*), *nominative* (also, irregularly, ungrammatically or dialectally, *accusative* or *dative*) *fem pronoun* of the 3rd *pers*: the female (or thing spoken of as female) named before, indicated, or understood (*pl* **they**). — *n* (*nominative*, *accusative* and *dative*) a female (*pl* **shes**). — *adj* female (*esp* in combination, as in **she'-ass**, **she'-bear**, **she'-devil**). [Prob OE *sēo*, fem of the definite article, which in the 12c came to be used instead of the pronoun *hēo*]

s/he. A form representing *she or he*.

shea *shē*, *shē'ə*, *n* an African tree (**shea'-tree**, *Butyrospermum parkii*) whose seeds (**shea'-nuts**) yield **shea'-butt'er**, used as a food and in soap manufacture. [Mungo Park's spelling of Mandingo (WAfr language) *si*]

sheading *shē'ding*, *n* one of the six divisions or districts of the Isle of Man. [**shedding**]

sheaf *shēf*, *n* a bundle of things bound side by side, *esp* stalks of corn; a bundle of papers; a bundle of (*usu* 24) arrows: — *pl* **sheaves** (*shēvz*). — *vt* **sheaf** or **sheave** to bind in sheaves. — *vi* to make sheaves. — *adj* **sheaf'y**. — *adj* **sheaved** in sheaves; flared; perh, made of straw (*Shakesp*). [OE *scēaf*; cf Ger *Schaub*, Du *schoof*]

sheal[1], **sheel**, **shiel** *shēl* or **shill** *shil*, (*Shakesp*) *vt* to shell or husk. — **sheal'ing-** (or **sheel'ing-**, etc) **hill** a hill where grain is winnowed by the wind. [Related to **shell**, **shale**, **scale**]

sheal[2], **shealing**. Same as **shiel**[2], **shieling**.

shear *shēr*, *vt* to cut, or clip, *esp* with shears; to cut superfluous nap from; to achieve or make by cutting; to tonsure; to reap with a sickle (*Scot*); to subject to a shear (*eng* and *phys*); to strip, fleece (also *fig*). — *vi* to separate; to cut; to penetrate; to reap with a sickle (*Scot*): — *pa t* **sheared** or (*archaic* and *poetic*) **shore**; *pa p* **shorn**, also, less commonly in ordinary senses, but always of deformation and *usu* of metal-cutting, **sheared**. — *n* a shearing or clipping; a strain, stress, or deformation in which parallel planes remain parallel, but move parallel to themselves (*eng* and *phys*). — *n* **shear'er** a person who shears sheep; a reaper (*Scot*). — *n* **shear'ing**. — *n* **shear'ling** a sheep that has been shorn for the first time; the fleece of such a sheep, *usu* of inferior quality. — *n pl* **shears** *orig* scissors (also *Scot*); now a larger pair of clippers, or any scissorlike cutting instrument, with a pivot or spring; a hoisting apparatus (see **sheers** under **sheer**[2]). — **shear force** a force that tends to cause sliding of adjacent layers relative to each other, in a material; **shear'-hog** a shearling; **shear'-hulk** and **shear'leg** see under **sheer**[2]; **shearing shed** (*Austr* and *NZ*) a building in which sheep are shorn, *esp* one specially equipped with several power-driven shears, shearing platforms and wool-baling machines; **shear'man** a textile worker who shears superfluous nap from cloth; **shear pin** a pin, which, as a safety mechanism, will shear and halt a machine or power-transmission when the correct load or stress is exceeded; **shear'-steel** steel suitable for making shears, etc; **shear'water** a seabird of the genus *Puffinus*, related to the petrels, that skims the water when flying low; **shear zones** (*geol*) bands in metamorphic rocks consisting of crushed and brecciated material and many parallel fractures. [OE *sceran*; ON *skera* to clip, Ger *scheren* to shave]

shears *shērz*, (*eng*) *n pl* another name for **ways** (see under **way**[2]).

'sheart *särt*, (*obs*) *interj* for **God's heart**, an exclamatory oath.

sheatfish *shēt'fish* or **sheath'fish** *shēth'*, *n* the wels, a large fish (*Silurus glanis*, the American catfish) introduced into European rivers; any related fish. [Ger *Scheidfisch*; *see* **sheath**]

sheath *shēth*, *n* a case for a sword or blade; a close-fitting (*esp* tubular or long) covering; a woman's close-fitting tubular dress (also **sheath dress**); a clasping leaf-base, or any similar protective structure; an insect's wing-case; a contraceptive device for men, a condom: — *pl* **sheaths** (*shēdhz*). — *vt* **sheathe** (*shēdh*) to put into or cover with a sheath or casing. — *adj* **sheathed** (*shēdhd*) having, or enclosed in, a sheath. — *n* **sheath'ing** (*-dh-*) that which sheathes; casing; the covering of a ship's bottom. — *adj* **sheath'less**. — *adj* **sheath'y** (*-th-* or *-dh-*) sheathlike. — **sheath'bill** either of two Antarctic seabirds (*Chionis*) having a white plumage and a horny sheath at the base of the bill; **sheath dress** see **sheath** above; **sheathfish** see **sheatfish**; **sheath knife** a knife encased in a sheath. — *adj* **sheath'-winged** (*zool*) coleopterous. — **sheathe the sword** (*literary*) to end war. [OE *scēath*, *scǣth*; Ger *Scheide*, ON *skeithir*]

sheave[1] *shēv*, *n* a shive, slice, slab; a grooved wheel, pulley-wheel; a fragment; a speck, particle of impurity, as in paper. [Related to **shive**]

sheave[2], **sheaves**, etc. See **sheaf**.

Sheba *shē'bə*. Same as **Saba**.

shebang *shi-bang'*, (*slang*, *orig US*) *n* a room, house, shop, hut, etc; a vehicle; affair, matter, etc, *esp* in the phrase *the whole shebang*. [Of uncertain origin; perh connected with **shebeen** or Fr *cabane*]

Shebat *shē'bät*, *n* the fifth (ecclesiastically eleventh) Jewish month, parts of January and February. — Also **Se'bat**. [Heb *Sh'bāt*]

shebeen *shi-bēn'*, *n* an illicit liquor shop; (in Ireland) illicit, *usu* home-made, alcohol. — *vi* to keep a shebeen. — *n* **shebeen'er**. — *n* **shebeen'ing**. [Anglo-Irish]

Shechinah *shi-kī'nə*, *n* Same as **Shekinah**.

shechita, **schechitah**. See **schechita**.

shecklaton. See **checklaton**.

shed[1] *shed*, *vt* to part, separate; to cast off; to give, give away; to drop; to emit; to pour forth; to cast, throw (eg light); to impart; to cause effusion of; to spill (*dialect*); to besprinkle (*archaic*). — *vi* to fall off; to disperse (*archaic*): — *pr p* **shedd'ing**; *pa t* and *pa p* **shed**. — *n* (*obs* or *dialect*) a parting. — *adj* cast; spilt, emitted. — *n* **shedd'er** a person who or thing that sheds; an animal that moults or casts hair; a female salmon or the like after spawning. — *n* **shedd'ing**. [OE *scādan*, *scēadan* (strong verb), to separate; Ger *scheiden*]

shed[2] *shed*, *n* a structure, often open-fronted, for storing or shelter; an outhouse. — *n* **shedd'er** (*NZ*) a person who milks cows in a milking shed. [Appar a variant of **shade**]

she'd *shēd* (*colloq*). A contraction of **she had** or **she would**.

sheel, **sheeling**. See under **sheal**[1].

sheen *shēn*, *n* shine; lustre; radiance; a very thin slick of oil (on water); glistening attire (*poetic*). — *adj* (*rare* or *poetic*) beautiful; bright; shining. — *vi* (*obs* except *Scot*) to shine; to gleam; to have a lustre. — *adj* **sheen'y** lustrous; glistening. [OE *scēne* (WSax *sciene*, *scȳne*) beautiful; Du *schoon*, Ger *schön*; infl by **shine**]

sheeny *shēn'i*, (*hist slang*; *offensive*) *n* (also with *cap*) a Jew; a pawnbroker. — *adj* Jewish; fraudulent; (of money) base. [Origin unknown]

sheep *shēp*, *n* a beardless, woolly, wild or domestic ruminant animal (*Ovis*) of the goat family; the skin of such an animal, with or without the woolly coat; someone who is like a sheep, in being eg a member of a flock (or congregation), a creature that follows meekly, is at the mercy of the wolf or the shearer, displays tameness of spirit, etc: — *pl* **sheep**. — *adj* **sheep'ish** like a sheep; embarrassed through having done something foolish or wrong. — *adv* **sheep'ishly**. — *n* **sheep'ishness**. — *n* **sheep'o** (*Austr* and *NZ*) a farm worker who drives sheep into pens for shearing: — *pl* **sheep'os**. — *adj* **sheep'y** (*rare*) sheeplike. — **sheep'-biter** a dog that bites or worries sheep; *prob* an oppressive supervisor (*Shakesp*). — *adj* **sheep'-biting** given to biting sheep; (*fig archaic*) sneaking, thieving. — Also *n*. — **sheep'cote** an enclosure for sheep; **sheep'-dip** a disinfectant insecticidal preparation used in washing sheep; a place for dipping sheep, *specif* the trough of disinfectant through which they are driven; inferior liquor (*slang*); **sheep'dog** a dog trained to watch or drive sheep, or of a breed used for that purpose; a chaperon (*slang*). — *adj* **sheep'-faced** sheepish, bashful. — **sheep'-farmer**; **sheep'fold**; **sheep'-hook** a shepherd's crook; **sheep ked** a wingless fly (*Melophagus ovinus*) that sucks sheep's blood; **sheep'-louse** a louse (*Trichodectes*) that infests sheep; loosely, a sheep ked: — *pl* **sheep'-lice**; **sheep'-master** an owner of sheep; **sheep meat** mutton or lamb; **sheep'-pen**; **sheep'-plant** vegetable sheep; **sheep'-pox** a contagious eruptive disease of sheep, resembling smallpox; **sheep'-rot** liver rot; **sheep'-run** a tract of grazing country for sheep; **sheep's'-bit** or **sheep's scabious** a campanulaceous plant (*Jasione*) with blue heads resembling scabious; **sheep scab** a mange in sheep transmitted by mites; **sheep'-scor'ing** the counting of sheep (**sheep-scoring numerals** numerals of Welsh origin, used by shepherds, knitters, and in counting-out rhymes by children); **sheep's'-eyes** a wishful amorous look; **sheep's fescue** a temperate tufted pasture grass (*Festuca ovina*); **sheep's'-foot** a printer's claw-hammer; **sheep'shank** a sheep's leg; something of slender importance (*Scot*); a nautical knot for shortening a rope; **sheep's'-head** the head of a sheep, *esp* as food (also *adj*); a dolt; an American fish related to the porgie; **sheep'shearer**; **sheep'shearing**; **sheep'-silver** money paid in commutation of some right connected with sheep; **sheep'skin** the skin of a sheep, with or without the fleece attached; an item made from it eg a rug, horse's noseband, coat, etc); leather or parchment prepared from it. — Also *adj*. — **sheep station** (*Austr*) a large sheep farm; **sheep'-stealer**; **sheep'-stealing**; **sheep tick** strictly, a tick (*Ixodes ricinus*), a parasite of sheep (and other animals, *incl* man); commonly, a sheep-ked; **sheep'walk** a range of pasture for sheep; **sheep'-wash** a sheep-dip. — *adj* **sheep'-whistling** (*Shakesp*) tending sheep. — **black sheep** the disreputable member of a family or group; **separate the sheep from the goats** to identify (*esp* by some test) the superior members of any group. [OE *scēap*; Ger *Schaf*]

sheer[1] *shēr*, *adj* bright, clear (*archaic*); thin; pure; unmingled; mere, downright; plumb; unbroken; vertical or very nearly vertical. — *adv* clear; quite; plumb; vertically. — *n* a very thin fabric. — *adv* **sheer'ly** completely, thoroughly, wholly, etc. [ME *schēre*, perh from a lost OE equivalent of ON *skærr* bright]

sheer[2] *shēr*, *vi* (with *off* or *away*) to deviate; to take oneself off, *esp* to evade something disagreeable; to swerve. — *vt* to cause to deviate. — *n* a deviation; an oblique position; the fore-and-aft upward curve of a ship's deck or sides. — *n pl* **sheers** or **shears** an apparatus for hoisting heavy weights, having legs or spars spread apart at their lower ends, and hoisting tackle at their joined tops. — **sheer'-hulk** or **shear'-hulk** an old dismantled ship with a pair of sheers mounted on it; popularly, a mere hulk, as if from **sheer**[1]; **sheer'leg** or **shear'leg** one of the spars of sheers; (in *pl*) sheers. [Partly at least another spelling of **shear**; perh partly from the LGer or Du equivalent, *scheren* to cut, withdraw]

sheet[1] *shēt*, *n* a large wide expanse or thin piece of something; a large broad piece of cloth, *esp* for a bed, a penitent, or a corpse; a piece of paper, *esp* large and broad; a section of a book printed on one piece of paper, a signature; as much copy as will fill a sheet; a pamphlet, broadsheet, or newspaper; a sail (*poetic*); a sill (**intrusive sheet**; *geol*); sheet-rubber; one of the separate pieces or planes that make up a surface; aircraft structural material under 6·35 mm (0·25 inches) thick, thinner than 'plate'. — *adj* in the form of a sheet; printed on a sheet. — *vt* to wrap or cover with, or as if with, a sheet; to provide with sheets; to form into sheets. — *vi* to form or run in a sheet; (of rain) to fall fast and heavily. — *adj* **sheet'ed** wrapped or covered with a sheet (*esp* of a corpse); (eg of a cow) marked with a white band or belt; spread out like a sheet. — *n* **sheet'ing** cloth for sheets; protective boarding or metal covering; formation into sheets. — *adj* **sheet'y**. — **sheet-copp'er, -i'ron, -lead', -met'al, -rubb'er, -tin'**, etc, copper, iron, etc, in thin sheets. — *vt* and *n* **sheet'-feed**. — **sheet'-feeder** (*comput* and *word processing*) a storage cassette that feeds single sheets of paper into a printer as required; **sheet'-glass** a kind of crown-glass made in a cylinder and flattened out; **sheet lightning** the diffused appearance of distant lightning; **sheet music** music written or printed on (unbound) sheets. [OE *scēte* (WSax *scīete*), *scēat*; cf **sheet**[2]]

sheet[2] *shēt*, (*naut*) *n* a rope attached to the lower corner of a sail; (in *pl*) the part of a boat between the thwarts and the stern or bow. — **sheet bend** a type of knot used *esp* for joining ropes of different sizes. — **a sheet** (or **three sheets**) **in** or **to the wind** half-drunk (or drunk). [OE *scēata* corner; related to **sheet**[1]]

sheet-anchor *shēt'angk'ər*, *n* an extra anchor for an emergency (*naut*); a chief support; a last refuge. [Formerly *shut-*, *shot-* or *shoot-anchor*; origin doubtful]

Sheffield plate *shef'ēld plāt*, *n* a type of metalware developed in Sheffield and produced between the mid 18c and mid 19c, of copper coated with silver. [*Sheffield*, city in S Yorkshire, and **plate**]

shehita or **shehitah**. See **schechita**.

sheikh or **sheik** *shāk* or *shēk*, *n* an Arab chief; a girl's young man or ideal film hero (*old slang*); a Hindu convert to Islam. — *n* **sheikh'a** the chief wife or consort of a sheikh; a high-class Arab lady. — *n* **sheikh'dom** or **sheik'dom** a sheikh's territory. [Ar *shaikh*, from *shākha* to be old]

sheila *shē'lə*, *n* a young girl or a woman (*Austr colloq*); a white Teddy girl (*SAfr*). [From proper name]

sheiling. Same as **shieling** (qv under **shiel**[2]).

shekel *shek'l*, *n* a Jewish weight (about 14 grams) and coin of this weight; the standard unit of currency of Israel (100 *agorot*); (in *pl*) money (*slang*). [Heb *sheqel*, from *shāqal* to weigh]

Shekinah or **Shechinah** *shi-kī'nə*, (*Judaism*) *n* the divine presence. [Heb *shekīnāh*, from *shākan* to dwell]

shelduck *shel'duk*, *n* (*fem* or generic) any of various large ducks (genus *Tadorna*) with bold black, brown and white plumage (in the breeding season) and red feet and bill. — Also **sheld'duck, shell'duck, shiel'duck**, and (*esp masc*) **shel'drake, shell'drake, shiel'drake**. [Prob dialect *sheld* (cf Du *schillede*) variegation, and **duck, drake**]

shelf *shelf*, *n* a board fixed horizontally on a wall, in a bookcase, cupboard, etc, for laying things on; a shelfful; a terrace; a ledge; a shoal; a sandbank: — *pl* **shelves** (*shelvz*). — *vt* to shelve. — *n* **shelf'-ful** enough to fill a shelf: — *pl* **shelf'-fuls**. — *adj* **shelf'like**. — *adj* **shelf'y**. — **shelf'-catalogue** a library catalogue arranged by shelves; **shelf ice** ice extending from the land out to sea; **shelf'-life** the length of time a product can be stored without deterioration occurring; **shelf'-mark** an indication on a book of its place in a library; **shelf'room** space or accommodation on shelves; **shelf'talker** a marketing device, eg a notice or mini-poster, attached to a shelf in a shop, to promote a specific product. — **off the shelf** immediately available, in stock; of a company, registered only in order to be sold; **on the shelf** no longer likely to have the opportunity to marry; removed from further prospect of employment. [OE *scylf* shelf, ledge, pinnacle, or LGer *schelf*; perh partly from some other source]

shell *shel*, *n* a hard outer covering, *esp* of a shellfish, a tortoise, an egg, or a nut; a husk, pod, or rind; a shelled mollusc; an outer framework; the outer, often waterproof or showerproof, layer of a lined garment such as a jacket, coat, trousers, etc; a crust; a hollow sphere or the like; a mere outside, empty case, or lifeless relic; any frail structure; a type of light racing boat; a light coffin; a conch trumpet; a lyre of tortoise-shell; an explosive projectile shot from a cannon, large gun, etc; a cartridge containing explosive for small-arms, fireworks, etc; a piece of quicklime; in some schools, an intermediate class (from one that met in an apse at Westminster). — *adj* of, with, or like shell or shells. — *vt* to separate from the shell; to case; to throw, fire, etc shells at. — *vi* to peel, scale; to separate from the shell. — *adj* **shelled** having a shell; separated from the shell, pod, etc. — *n* **shell'er**. — *n* **shell'ful**. — *n* **shell'iness**. — *n* **shell'ing**. — *adj* **shell'-less**. — *adj* **shell'-like** resembling a mollusc's shell; used as an epithet for the ear (*poetic* or *jocular*). — *n* (*slang*) an ear. — *adj* **shell'y** of or like shell or shells; abounding in shells; having a shell; testaceous. — **shell'back** an old sailor; a sailor who has crossed the equator; **shell'bark** a hickory with peeling bark; **shell bean** (*US*) a bean removed from, and eaten without, its pod; any of various bean plants suitable for this. — *adj* **shell'bound** (of a baby bird, etc) unable to escape from the shell. — **shell company** a little-known or failing company through which a major company conducts business clandestinely; **shell'-crater** a hole in the ground made by a bursting shell; **shell'fire** bombardment with shells; **shell'fish** a shelled aquatic invertebrate, *esp* a mollusc or crustacean, or such animals collectively; **shell game** (*NAm*) thimblerig; **shell heap** (*archaeol*) a heap of domestic refuse consisting mainly of shells, associated with peoples who live on shellfish; **shell'-hole** a shell-crater; **shell'-ice** ice no longer supported by water; **shell'-jack'et** a tight, short military jacket; **shell'-lime** lime made from seashells; **shell'-lime'stone** a limestone mainly consisting of shells; **shell'-marl** a white, earthy lacustrine deposit; **shell'-mon'ey** wampum; **shell mound** a shell heap; **shell ornament** a decoration based on the form of a shell; **shell parrakeet** or **parrot** the budgerigar; **shell-pink'** a pale yellow-tinged shade of pink. — Also *adj*. — *adj* **shell'proof** able to resist shells or bombs. — **shell'-sand** sand consisting in great part of calcareous organic remains; **shell'shock** mental disturbance due to war experiences, once thought to be caused by the bursting of shells; mental disturbance due to similar violent, etc experiences. — *adj* **shell'shocked**. — **shell star** (*astron*) a star surrounded by a gaseous shell; **shell suit** a type of lightweight tracksuit with a crinkly nylon outer layer and a cotton lining; **shell'work** work composed of or adorned with shells; **shell'ycoat** (*Scot*) a water goblin dressed in shells; a sheriff's messenger. — **come out of one's shell** to cease to be shy and reticent; **electron shell** see under **electron**; **shell out** (*slang*) to pay up; to pay out, spend. [OE *scell* (WSax *sciell*); Du *schil*, ON *skel*]

she'll *shēl*, (*colloq*). A contraction of **she shall** or **she will**.

shellac *shə-lak'* or *shel'ak*, *n* lac (qv) in thin plates, obtained by melting seed-lac, straining and dropping, formerly used for making gramophone records; an old gramophone record whether or not made of shellac; loosely, lac, the resin, used eg as a spirit varnish. — *vt* to coat with shellac; (*shə-lak'*) to trounce, defeat decisively (*NAm*): — *pr p* **shellacking**; *pa t* and *pa p* **shellacked**. — *n* **shellacking**. — Also **shell'-lac**. [**shell** and **lac**, transl of Fr *laque en écailles* lac in scales]

Shelta *shel'tə*, *n* a secret jargon used by vagrants in Britain and Ireland. [*Shelrū*, poss a perversion of OIrish *béulra* language]

shelter *shel'tər*, *n* a shielding or screening structure, *esp* against weather; (a place of) refuge, retreat, or temporary lodging in distress; asylum; screening; protection. — *vt* to screen; to shield; to afford asylum, protection or lodging to; to harbour. — *vi* to take shelter. — *adj* **shel'tered** affording shelter. — *n* **shel'terer**. — *n* and *adj* **shel'tering**. — *adj* **shel'terless**. — *adj* **shel'tery** affording shelter. — **shelter belt** a row of trees providing shelter from the wind; **sheltered housing** housing for the elderly or disabled consisting of separate units with a resident housekeeper and/or warden to look after the tenants' wellbeing; **shelter tent** (in the US army) a tent for two men. [Origin obscure]

sheltie or **shelty** *shel'ti*, *n* a Shetland pony or sheepdog. [Perh ON *Hjalti* Shetlander]

shelve *shelv*, *vt* to furnish with shelves; to place on a shelf; to put aside, postpone. — *vi* to slope, incline. — *n* a ledge; a shelf. — *n pl* **shelves** (*pl* of **shelf** and of **shelve**). — *n* **shelv'ing** provision of, or material for, shelves; shelves collectively; the act of putting on a shelf or setting aside; a slope. — *adj* shallowing; sloping. — *adj* **shel'vy** having sandbanks; overhanging. [See ety for **shelf**]

Shema *shə-mä'*, *n* a Jewish prayer representing a declaration of faith, recited morning and evening. [Heb, hear]

Shemite. Earlier form of **Semite**.

shemozzle *shi-moz'l*, (*slang*) *n* a mess; a scrape; a rumpus. — Also **shimozz'le**, **shlemozz'le**, **schemozz'le**. — *vi* to make off. [Yiddish, from Ger *schlimm* bad, Heb *mazzāl* luck; cf **schlimazel**]

shenanigan *shi-nan'i-gən*, (*slang*; *usu* in *pl*) *n* trickery, underhand dealings; mischief, antics. [Origin unknown]

shend *shend*, (*archaic* or *poetic*) *vt* to put to shame; to disgrace; to reproach, chide; to punish; to discomfit; to injure: — *pa t* and *pa p* **shent**. [OE *scendan* to disgrace]

she-oak *shē'-ōk*, (*Austr*) *n* an evergreen tree of the genus Casuarina, adapted for dry conditions. [**she**, denoting inferior, and **oak**, from its grain]

She'ol or **Sheol** *shē'ōl*, (*Old Testament*) *n* the place of departed spirits, the abode of the dead; (also without *cap*) hell. [Heb *she'ōl*]

shepherd *shep'ərd*, *n* a person who tends sheep (*fem* **shep'herdess**); a swain; a pastor; (with *cap*) a small moon orbiting Saturn (*astron*). — *vt* to tend or guide as or like a shepherd; to watch over, protect the interests of, or one's own interests in. — *vi* to tend sheep. — *adj* **shep'herdless**. — *n* **shep'herdling** a little shepherd. — **Shepherd kings** the Hyksos; **shepherd** (or **shepherd's**) **check**, **plaid** or **tartan** (cloth with) a small black-and-white check; **shepherd's club** another name for mullein; **shepherd's cress** a small cruciferous plant, *Teesdalia*; **shepherd's glass** or **weather glass** the scarlet pimpernel; **shepherd's myrtle** butcher's-broom; **shepherd's needle** Venus's comb; **shepherd's pie** a dish of meat cooked with mashed potatoes on the top; **shepherd's-purse** a cosmopolitan cruciferous weed with flat obcordate pods (*Capsella bursa-pastoris*); **shepherd's rod** the small teasel. — **the Good Shepherd** Jesus Christ (from the Bible: John 10. 11). [OE *scēaphirde*; see **sheep** and **herd**]

sherardize or **-ise** *sher'ərd-īz*, *vt* to coat with zinc by heating with zinc-dust in a vacuum. [From *Sherard* Cowper-Coles, the inventor of the process]

Sheraton *sher'ə-tən*, *n* a kind or style of furniture designed by Thomas *Sheraton* (1751–1806). — Also *adj*.

sherbet *shûr'bət*, *n* an effervescent drink, or powder for making it; a kind of water-ice; a fruit-juice drink; beer (*Austr colloq*). [Turk and Pers *sherbet*, from Ar; cf **shrub**², **syrup**]

sherd *shûrd*, *n*. See **shard**².

shere. A Spenserian spelling of **sheer**¹.

Sheria *shə-rē'ə* or **Sheriat** *shə-rē'ət*, *n* (also without *cap*) the body of Islamic religious law. — Also **shari'a** or **shari'at**. [Turk *sherī'at* law]

sherif or **shereef** *shə-rēf'*, *n* a descendant of Mohammed through his daughter Fatima; a prince, *esp* the Sultan of Morocco; the chief magistrate of Mecca. — Also **sharif'**. — *adj* **sherif'ian** or **shereef'ian**. [Ar *sharīf* noble, lofty, illustrious]

sheriff *sher'if*, *n* the king's representative in a shire, with wide judicial and executive powers (*hist*); (in England) the chief officer of the crown in the county, with duties chiefly honorary rather than judicial; (in Scotland) the chief judge of the sheriff court of a town or region; (in the US) an elected officer of a county, mainly responsible for maintaining peace and order, attending courts, guarding prisoners, serving processes and executing judgements. — *n* **sher'iffalty** shrievalty. — *n* **sher'iffdom** the office, term of office, or territory under the jurisdiction of a sheriff; (in Scotland) one of the six divisions of the judicature, made up of sheriff court districts. — *n* **sher'iffship** the office of sheriff. — **sheriff clerk** (in Scotland) the registrar of the sheriff's court, who has charge of the records of the court, organizes its work, etc: — *pl* **sheriff clerks**; **sheriff court** (in Scotland) a court having jurisdiction over civil and most criminal cases; **sheriff depute** (in Scotland) till the abolition of the heritable jurisdictions in 1748, a lawyer who acted as deputy for the sheriff; thereafter sometimes applied to the sheriff or sheriff principal: — *pl* **sheriff deputes**; **sheriff officer** (in Scotland) an officer connected with the sheriff-court, who is responsible for raising actions, enforcing decrees, ensuring attendance of witnesses, etc; **sheriff principal** (in Scotland) the chief judge of a sheriffdom; **sheriff's post** (*hist*) a painted post at a sheriff's door for affixing proclamations; **sheriff substitute** a Scottish acting sheriff, appointed by the crown, in most cases resident in his judicial district: — *pl* **sheriffs substitute**. — **high sheriff** an English sheriff proper; the chief executive officer of a district (*US*); **honorary sheriff substitute** one who may act in the absence of the sheriff substitute; **un'der-sheriff** an English sheriff's deputy who performs the execution of writs. [OE *scīrgerēfa*, from *scīr* shire, and *gerēfa* reeve; cf **reeve**, **grieve**², Ger *Graf* count]

sherlock *shûr'lok* *n* a detective; (also with *cap*) someone who shows highly developed powers of observation and deduction, as did the detective, Sherlock Holmes, in the stories of Conan Doyle (1859–1930), often used ironically.

Sherpa *shûr'pə*, *n* one of an eastern Tibetan people living high on the south side of the Himalayas, renowned for their skills as mountaineers and guides; their Tibetan language; (also without *cap*) an aide to, or personal representative of, a head of government participating in a summit conference, and concerned with negotiations behind the scenes and with drafting agreements, communiques, etc: — *pl* **Sher'pa** or **Sher'pas**. [Tibetan *shar* east, and *pa* inhabitant]

sherris *sher'is*, (*archaic*) *n* sherry. — **sherr'is-sack** sack imported from *Xeres* (now **Jerez**).

sherry *sher'i*, *n* a fortified wine from the neighbourhood of Jerez de la Frontera in Spain; a wine of this type from various regions of the world, *incl* Australia, S Africa, Cyprus, etc. — **sherry-cobb'ler** a drink made up of sherry, lemon, sugar, ice, etc; **sherry party** a *usu* informal gathering at which sherry is served. [*Xeres*, earlier form of *Jerez*]

sherwani *shûr-wä'ni*, *n* in India, a man's knee-length coat buttoning up to the chin: — *pl* **sherwa'nis**. [Hindi]

she's *shēz*, (*colloq*). A contraction of **she is** or **she has**.

shet *shet*, *obs* or *dialect* form of **shut**.

Shetland *shet'lənd*, (also without *cap*) *adj* pertaining to the Shetland Islands off the N coast of Scotland. — *n* **Shet'lander**. — *adj* **Shetlan'dic**. — *n* Shetland dialect. — **Shetland pony** a small, hardy pony with a thick coat, originating in the Shetland Islands (also **shel'tie**); **Shetland sheep** a breed of sheep of Shetland and formerly Aberdeenshire; **Shetland sheepdog** a breed of dog developed in the Shetland Islands resembling the collie, though smaller in size and with a thicker coat (also **shel'tie**); **Shetland wool** a fine loosely twisted wool obtained from Shetland sheep.

sheuch or **sheugh** *shōōhh*, (*Scot*) *n* a ditch or drain. — *vt* to plant temporarily. [**sough**[2]]

sheva *shə-vä'*, *n* (in Hebrew grammar) a point or sign (:), under a consonant, indicating absence of vowel; a neutral vowel sound, a schwa (*phonetics*). [Heb *shewā*]

Shevuoth *shev'-ū-oth*, *n*. Another spelling of **Shabuoth**.

shew *shō* or *shōō*. An archaic spelling of **show**: — *pa p* **shewn** (*shōn*).

shewbread or **showbread** *shō'bred*, *n* the twelve loaves placed each Sabbath on the table beside the altar of incense in the sanctuary of the tabernacle by the Jewish priests in ancient Israel. [After Ger *Schaubrot*, transl Heb *lechem pānīm* bread of the presence]

shewel *shōō'əl*, (*obs* or *dialect*) *n* a scarecrow; a device to scare deer. — Also **sew'el**. [Connected with **shy**[1]]

SHF or **shf** *abbrev*: superhigh frequency.

Shia or **Shiah** *shē'ə*, *n* the branch of Islam, or a collective name for its adherent sects, that recognizes Ali (Mohammed's cousin and son-in-law) and his successors as the true imams; a member of this branch of Islam, a Shiite. — *n* **Shiism** (*shē'izm*). — *n* **Shiite** (*shē'īt*) a member of this (now chiefly Iranian) sect. — Also *adj*. — *adj* **Shiitic** (*-it'ik*). [Ar *shī'a* sect]

shiatsu or **shiatzu** *shi-at'sōō*, *n* acupressure, a Japanese healing and health-promoting therapy using massage with fingers, palms, etc. [Jap, literally, finger pressure]

shibah. See **shivah**.

shibboleth *shib'ə-leth*, *n* the criterion, catchword or catchphrase of a group, party or sect by which members may be identified; a slogan; a peculiarity of speech; the Gileadite test-word to distinguish an Ephraimite, who could not pronounce *sh* (from the Bible: Judg 12. 5–6); any such test. [Heb *shibbōleth* an ear of corn, or a stream]

shibuichi *shi-bōō-i'chē*, *n* an alloy of three parts copper to one part silver, widely used in Japanese decorative art to give a silver-grey patina. — *adj* made of or with shibuichi. [Jap *shi* four, *bu* part, and *ichi* one]

shicker *shik'ər*, (*esp Austr* and *NZ slang*) *n* strong drink, liquor; a drunk. — *adj* **shick'ered** drunk. [Yiddish *shikker*, from Heb]

shicksa. Same as **shiksa**.

shidder *shid'ər*, (*Spenser*) *n* a female animal. [**she** and **deer**; cf **hidder**]

shied. See **shy**[1,2].

shiel[1]. Same as **sheal**[1].

shiel[2] or **sheal** *shēl*, (chiefly *Scot*) *n* a hut, shieling. — *n* **shiel'ing** or **sheal'ing** a rough hut near summer pasture used as shelter by shepherds or people tending cattle; a summer pasture. [Prob from a lost OE equivalent of ON *skāli* hut]

shield *shēld*, *n* a piece of armour, a broad plate carried to deflect weapons, *esp* one with a straight top and tapering curved sides; a protective plate, screen, pad, or other guard; the outer protective covering of certain animals, such as the carapace of a tortoise; any protective device; a tubular framework that supports the ground and protects workers during tunnelling; a shield-shaped design or object, eg an escutcheon used for displaying arms, or a piece of plate awarded as a prize; the large stable area of Pre-Cambrian rocks that forms the central part of a continent; a policeman's badge (*US*). — *vt* to protect by sheltering; to hide from view; to ward off; to forfend (*Shakesp*). — *n* **shiel'der**. — *n* **shiel'ding** (*nuc eng*; *radiol*) protective use of materials of low atomic number to thermalize strong neutron beams, or of concrete, lead or other heavy materials to shield against radiation. — *adj* **shield'less**. — *adj* **shield'like**. — *n* **shield'ling** a protected person. — **shield'-arm** the left arm; **shield'-bearer** an attendant who carries a warrior's shield; **shield bug** any heteropterous insect of the superfamily *Pentatomoidea*, typically having flat, broad bodies shaped like heraldic shields; **shielded line** (*elec eng*) a line or circuit shielded from external interference by highly conducting or magnetic material; **shielded pair** (*telecomm*) a balanced pair of insulated wires encased in a cable which prevents external interference; **shield fern** any evergreen or semi-evergreen fern of the genus *Polystichum* with scales covering the spore-producing pinnae; **shield'-hand** the left hand; **shield ivy** a variety of common ivy, *Hedera helix*, with heart-shaped leaves (also called **sweetheart ivy**); **shield law** (*NAm*) a law that protects journalists from being forced to reveal confidential information relating to sources, etc; **shield'-maid**, **-maiden** or **-may** an Amazon; a Valkyrie; **shield pond** or **shielding pond** (*nuc eng*) a deep tank of water used to shield operators from highly radioactive materials stored and manipulated at the bottom of it. — *adj* **shield'-shaped**. — **shield volcano** (*geog*) a volcano with a broad, gently sloping dome formed by successive eruptions of lava; **shield'wall** a defence of interlocked shields. — **shield of brawn** the thick skin of a pig's side, *esp* when stuffed with meat. [OE *sceld* (WSax *scield*); Ger *Schild*, ON *skjöldr*, protection]

shieldrake, **shieldduck**. See under **shelduck**.

shieling. See **shiel**[2].

shier, **shies**, **shiest**. See under **shy**[1,2].

shift *shift*, *vt* to change; to change the clothes of (*archaic* or *dialect*); to change the position of; to remove; to dislodge; to transfer; to evade (*obs*); to rid; to quit; to swallow, consume (*slang*); to sell, get rid of by selling (*slang*); to put off. — *vi* to manage, get on, do as one can; to change; to change position; to fluctuate; to change one's clothes (*archaic* or *dialect*); to take appropriate or urgent action; to move; to go away; to move quickly (*colloq*); to undergo phonetic change. — *n* an expedient; an artifice or contrivance; a group of people who work for a specific period within a working day, alternating with other groups; the time worked by such a group; a change; a change of position or direction; a change in the direction of the wind (*naut*); a general or bodily displacement of a series (as of lines in the spectrum, consonant or vowel sounds, faulted strata); displacement of an ordered set of data to the left or right (*comput*); the movement of two or more offensive players at the same time before the snap (*Am football*); (in violin-playing) any change of position of the hand on the fingerboard; a removal; the gear change in a motor vehicle (chiefly *NAm*); a woman's undergarment, a smock, chemise or slip (*old*); a loose dress, roughly triangular or oblong; provision of clothes or (*archaic*) other things for use in rotation or substitution. — *adj* **shift'ed**. — *n* **shift'er** someone who shifts, *esp* a scene-shifter; someone who resorts to shifts, tricks, evasions, or sophistry. — *adv* **shif'tily**. — *n* **shift'iness**. — *n* **shift'ing**. — *adj* moving about; unstable; shifty. — *adj* **shift'less** without a smock (*archaic*); without resource or expedient; inefficient; feckless. — *adv* **shift'lessly**. — *n* **shift'lessness**. — *adj* **shift'y** evasive, tricky, suggesting trickery; dubious, shady, furtive; ready with shifts or expedients. — **shif'ting-boards** partitioning to prevent shifting of cargo; **shifting cultivation** a system of cultivating land, in which an area is cleared and farmed until the fertility of the soil is exhausted, then abandoned for a new area; **shifting register** same as **shift register**; **shifting spanner** an adjustable spanner; **shift key** a key on a typewriter or computer keyboard used to bring a different set of letters (eg capitals) into use; **shift register** (*comput*) a register (qv) which carries out shifts on data (bits or digits); **shift work** (a system of) working in shifts; **shift worker**; **shift working**. — **shift about** to move from side to side; to turn right round to the opposite point; **shift down** or **up** (chiefly *NAm*) to change down or up a gear (also *fig*); **shift for oneself** to depend on one's own resources; **shift one's ground** (*usu fig*) to change the position one has taken, eg in a discussion. [OE *sciftan* to divide, allot; ON *skipta*]

shigella *shi-gel'ə*, *n* a rod-shaped bacterium of the genus *Shigella*, in particular *Shigella dysenteriae*, which causes bacillary dysentery. — *n* **shigellosis** (*shi-gə-lō'sis*) infestation of the intestinal tract by shigella, causing bacillary dysentry. [After K *Shiga* (1870–1957), the Japanese bacteriologist who discovered it]

shih tzu *shē dzōō*, *n* a small long-haired dog bred from the Chinese Pekingese and the Tibetan lhasa apso. [Chin *shi zī goū*]

Shiism, Shiite, Shiitic. See under **Shia**.

shiitake *shi-i-tä'kā*, *n* the large dark brown mushroom (*Lentinus edodes*) widely used in Oriental cookery, cultivated on tree logs: — *pl* **shiita'ke**. [Jap *shii* a type of tree, and *take* mushroom]

shikar *shi-kär'*, (*Anglo-Ind*) *n* hunting, *esp* of big game; game, booty; sport. — *n* **shikar'ee** or **shikar'i** a hunter, *esp* of big game; a professional, *esp* indigenous, hunting guide; a sportsman. [Urdu, from Pers *shikār*]

shiksa or **shikse** *shik'sə*, *n* a non-Jewish girl or woman. [Yiddish]

shill[1]. See **sheal**[1].

shill[2] *shil*, (*slang*; *esp NAm*) *n* an accomplice to a tradesman, etc, who poses as a genuine customer to encourage trade or interest; a gambler's or con man's sidekick; a decoy. — Also *vi*. [Prob abbrev of **shillaber**]

shillaber *shil'ə-bər*, (*old US slang*) *n* an enthusiastic or satisfied customer; a shill. [Origin uncertain]

shillelagh *shi-lā'li* or *-lā'lə*, *n* in Ireland, an oak or blackthorn cudgel, or any similar stout club, etc. — Also **shilla'lah**. [*Shillelagh*, an oak wood in County Wicklow, Ireland, or *sail* willow, and *éille* (genitive) thong]

shilling *shil'ing*, *n* a coin or its value, 12 old pence, equivalent to 5 (new) pence (*hist*); (in Kenya, Tanzania, Uganda, etc) a coin worth 100 cents. — *adj* costing or offered for a shilling; also in combination, as in *two'-shilling*, *three'-shilling*, etc. — *adj* **shill'ingless**. — *n* **shill'ingsworth** as much as can be purchased for a shilling. — **shilling mark** a solidus sign; **shilling shocker** or **shilling dreadful** a short sensational story or novel, *orig* one published at a shilling. — **take the (king's** or **queen's) shilling** (*hist*) to enlist as a soldier by accepting a recruiting officer's shilling, a practice discontinued in 1879. [OE *scilling*, Ger *Schilling*]

shilly-shally *shil'i-shal'i*, *vi* to be indecisive; to hesitate; to vacillate. — *adv* indecisively. — *n* vacillation; someone who vacillates. — **shill'y-shall'ier**. — *n* **shill'y-shallying**. [A reduplication of *shall I?*]

shilpit *shil'pit*, (*Scot*) *adj* sickly-looking; puny; insipid; watery; inferior. [Ety uncertain]

shily. See under **shy**[1].

shim *shim*, *n* a thin slip of metal, wood, etc, used to fill in space or to adjust parts. — *vt* to fill in or adjust using a shim or shims. — **shim rod** (*nuc eng*) a coarse control rod of a reactor. [Ety uncertain]

shimaal *shi-mäl'*, *n* in the Middle East, a hot dry north wind that carries sand in desert regions.

shimmer *shim'ər*, *vi* to gleam tremulously, to glisten. — *n* **shimm'er** or **shimm'ering** a tremulous gleam. — *adj* **shimm'ery**. [OE *scimerian*, from *scimian* to shine; Ger *schimmern*]

shimmy[1] or **shimmey** *shim'i*, (*colloq*) *n* a chemise.

shimmy[2] *shim'i*, *n* a body-shaking dance (also **shimm'y-shake**); a shaking of the hips; vibration in a motor vehicle or an aeroplane. — *vi* to dance the shimmy, or make similar movements; to vibrate. [Origin uncertain]

shimozzle. See **shemozzle**.

shin *shin*, *n* the forepart of the leg below the knee; the lower part of a leg of beef. — *vi* to swarm, climb by gripping with the hands and legs (*usu* with *up*); to use one's legs, hasten along. — *vt* to climb by gripping with the hands and legs; to kick on the shins. — **shin'-barker** a dog that barks at one's shins; **shin'bone** the tibia; **shin'plaster** (*US*; now *obs*) *orig*, a brown-paper patch for a sore on the shin; paper money of low value. [OE *scinu* the shin; Du *scheen*; Ger *Schiene* a thin plate]

shindig *shin'dig*, (*colloq*) *n* a lively celebration or party; a row. [Cf **shindy**]

shindy *shin'di*, (*colloq*) *n* a row, rumpus. — **kick up a shindy** to make a disturbance. [Perh **shinty**]

shine *shīn*, *vi* to give off or reflect light; to beam with steady radiance; to glow; to be bright; to be clear or conspicuous; to excel. — *vt* to cause to shine; to direct the light of (a torch, etc): — *pa t* and *pa p* **shone** (*shon*) or (*archaic*, or in the sense 'polished') **shined**. — *adj* (*archaic*) sheen. — *n* brightness; lustre; a dash, brilliant appearance; an act or process of polishing; fine weather; a party (*old slang*); a shindy (*old slang*). — *adj* **shine'less**. — *n* **shīn'er** a person who or thing that shines; a coin, *esp* a sovereign (*old slang*); a small fish of various kinds with glittering scales; a black eye (*slang*). — *n* **shīn'iness**. — *adj* **shīn'ing** bright or gleaming; excellent or distinguished. — *adv* **shīn'ingly**. — *n* **shīn'ingness**. — *adj* **shīn'y** having a bright or polished surface or appearance; lustrous, glossy. — *n* a shiny or bright object; (with *the*) money (*old slang*). — Also *adv* (*Spenser*). — **shine at** to be very good at; **take a shine to** (*colloq*) to fancy, take a liking to; **take the shine out of** or **off** (*slang*) to outshine, eclipse; to take the brilliance or pleasure-giving quality out of. [OE *scīnan*; Ger *scheinen*; in some senses perh a different word; cf **shindy**]

shiness. See under **shy**[1].

shingle[1] *shing'gl*, *n* a thin tile, *usu* of wood, laid on a roof or the sides of a building, in overlapping rows; these tiles collectively; a board; a small signboard or plate (*US*); a style of haircut in which the hair is cut short in overlapping layers, emphasizing the shape of the head at the back. — *vt* to cover with shingles; to cut in the manner of a shingle. — *adj* **shing'led**. — *n* **shing'ler**. — *n* **shing'ling** shingles collectively; the act or process of laying shingles; the act or process of cutting hair in a shingle; the state or condition of overlapping in the manner of shingles. — *adj* **shing'le-roofed**. [LL *scindula* a wooden tile, from L *scindere* to split]

shingle[2] *shing'gl*, *n* coarse gravel; small rounded pebbles found *esp* on beaches; a bank or bed of gravel or stones. — *adj* **shing'ly**. [Origin obscure]

shingles *shing'glz*, *n sing* the disease *Herpes zoster*, in which acute inflammation of nerve ganglia produces pain and a series of blisters along the path of the nerve, *esp* in the area of the waist and ribs, but sometimes round the head and face. [L *cingulum* a belt, from *cingere* to gird]

shinne *shin*, *n*. An *archaic* form of **chin**.

shinny[1]. See **shinty**.

shinny[2] *shin'i*, (*NAm*) *vi* to shin (*usu* with *up*, *down*, etc). [**shin**]

Shinto *shin'tō*, *n* the Japanese nature and hero cult, the indigenous religion of the country. — *n* **Shin'tōism**. — *n* **Shin'tōist**. [Jap, from Chin *shin tao*, from *shin* god, and *tao* way, doctrine]

shinty *shin'ti*, or **shinny** *shin'i*, *n* a game similar to hockey, of Scottish origin, played by teams of 12; the slim curved club (the caman, also **shin'ty-stick**) or leather-covered cork ball (or substitute) used in this game. [Perh from Gaelic *sinteag* a bound, pace]

shiny. See under **shine**.

ship *ship*, *n* a large sea-going vessel using engines or sails, formerly *esp* a square-rigged sailing vessel with bowsprit and three masts; a racing-boat with eight oars; any floating craft (*also fig*); an aircraft or airship; a spaceship; a ship's crew. — *vt* to put, receive, or take on board; to send or convey by ship; to send by land or air; to dispatch, send (off); to engage for service on board; to fix or place in position. — *vi* to embark; to travel by ship; to engage for service on board ship: — *pr p* **shipp'ing**; *pa t* and *pa p* **shipped**. — *n* **ship'ful**. — *adj* **ship'less**. — *n* **ship'ment** the act of putting on board; a consignment, *orig* by ship, now extended to other forms of transport. — *adj* **shipped** provided with a ship or ships (*archaic*); embarked. — *n* **shipp'er** a person or company that sends goods by ship or aircraft. — *n* **shipp'ing** ships collectively; accommodation on board ship; (the act of) putting aboard ship; transport by ship, the business of a shipper; a voyage (*archaic*). — **ship** (or **ship's**) **biscuit** a hard biscuit formerly used as a staple food for sailors aboard ship, hardtack; **ship'board** a ship's side, hence a ship. — *adj* occurring on board a ship. — **ship** (or **ship's**) **boy** a boy that serves on a ship; **ship'-breaker** a person or company that breaks up old ships; **ship'broker** a broker for the sale, insurance, etc, of ships; **ship'builder** a person or company that constructs ships; **ship'building**; **ship canal** a canal large enough for ships; **ship** (or **ship's**) **carpenter** a carpenter employed on board ship or in a shipyard; **ship** (or **ship's**) **chandler** a dealer in supplies for ships; **ship chandlery**; **ship fever** a form of typhus fever; **ship'-holder** a remora; **ship'lap** an arrangement of boards or plates, used *esp* on a ship's hull, in which the lower edge of one overlaps the upper edge of the adjacent one. — Also *vt* and *vi*. — **ship letter** a letter sent by a private vessel, not by the mail boat; **ship'load** the actual or possible load of a ship; **ship'man** (*archaic*) a sailor; a skipper; a pilot: — *pl* **ship'men**; **ship'master** the captain of a ship; **ship'mate** a fellow sailor; **ship money** (*hist*) a tax imposed by the sovereign to raise money to build a fleet of ships, *esp* that raised without authorization of parliament by Charles I from 1635 onwards; **ship'-of-the-line'** (before steam navigation, a man-of-war large enough to take a place in a line of battle; **ship'-owner** the owner of, or owner of a share in, a ship or ships; **shipping agent** a person or company that manages the administrative business of a ship on behalf of the owner; **shipping articles** articles of agreement between the captain and his crew; **shipping clerk** a person employed by a shipper to deal with the receiving and dispatching of goods; **ship'pound** in the Baltic ports, twenty lispounds; **ship railway** a railway for carrying ships overland. — *adj* **ship'-rigged** having three masts with square sails and spreading yards. — **ship's biscuit** see **ship biscuit**. — *adj* **ship'shape** in a seamanlike condition; trim, neat, proper. — **ship's husband** see under **husband**; **ship's papers** documents that a ship is required to carry; **ship'-tire** (*Shakesp*) a shiplike headdress; **ship'way** a sliding way for launching ships; a support for ships under examination or repair; a ship canal; **ship'worm** a wormlike lamellibranch mollusc (*esp* of the family *Teredinidae*) that makes shell-lined tunnels in submerged wood; **ship'wreck** a wrecked ship; the wreck or destruction (*esp* by accident) of a ship; destruction, ruin, disaster; wreckage (*rare*). — *vt* to wreck; to cause to undergo shipwreck; to cause ruin or destruction to. — *vi* to suffer or undergo shipwreck or destruction. — **ship'wright** a wright or carpenter employed in shipbuilding; **ship'yard** a yard where ships are built or repaired. — **on shipboard** upon or within a ship; **ship a sea** or **ship water** to have a wave come over the side of a ship or boat; **ship it green** to ship waves, not mere spray; **ship of the desert** the camel; **ship the oars** to put the oars in the rowlocks; to bring the oars into the boat; **ship water** see **ship a sea**; **take ship** or **shipping** to embark; **when one's ship comes home** or **in** when one becomes rich. [OE *scip*; Gothic *skip*, ON *skip*, Ger *Schiff*]

-ship *-ship*, *sfx* denoting: a condition or state, eg *friendship*, *fellowship*; position, rank, status, eg *lordship*, *kingship*; a specified type of skill, eg *craftsmanship*, *scholarship*; a group of people having something in common, eg *membership*. [OE *-scipe*, connected with **shape**]

shipment, etc. See under **ship**.

shippen or **shippon** *ship'n*, (*dialect*) *n* a cowhouse, cattle-shed. [OE *scypen*; cf **shop**]

shippo *ship-ō'*, *n* Japanese cloisonné ware. [Jap *shippô* seven precious things, hence something beautiful]

shir. See **shirr**.

shiralee or **shirralee** *shir'ə-lē*, (*Austr*; now *obs*) *n* a swagman's bundle. [Origin uncertain, perh from an Aboriginal word]

Shiraz *shi'räz*, *n* a variety of red grape now grown chiefly in Australia; the dark, tannic red wine made from this grape. — Also called (in France) **Syrah**. [From *Shiraz* a city in Iran]

shire *shīr* (in combination *-shir* or *-shər*), *n* an administrative district of England formed for mainly taxation purposes by the Anglo-Saxons; a county; formerly, applied also to certain smaller districts, as with *Richmondshire* and *Hallamshire*; a rural district having its own elected council (*Austr*). — **shire horse** a large, strong draught-horse with fringes of hair on the lower legs, once bred chiefly in the Midland shires; **shire'man** a sheriff; **shire'-moot** (OE *scīrgemōt*; *hist*) the court of the shire in medieval England; **shire'-reeve** a sheriff (see ety at **sheriff**). — **the Shires** (often *shērz*) those English counties whose names end in *-shire* particularly (for hunting) Leicestershire, Rutlandshire (later Rutland), Northamptonshire, and part of Lincolnshire. [OE *scīr* office, authority]

shirk *shûrk*, *vt* to evade (work, a duty, responsibility, etc). — *vi* to go or act evasively; to avoid work or duty. — *n* a person who shirks. — *n* **shirk'er**. [Cf **shark**]

Shirley poppy *shûr'li pop'i*, *n* a garden variety of the common poppy first produced at *Shirley* vicarage, Croydon.

Shirodkar's operation *shi'rod-kärz op-ə-rā'shən*, (*obstetrics*) *n* an operation in which the neck of the womb is closed with a suture to prevent miscarriage. [N V Shirodkar (1900–71), Indian obstetrican]

shirr, shir *shûr*, *n* a puckering or gathering. — *vt* to pucker, make gathers in; to draw (fabric) into a series of parallel gathered rows using elastic thread; to bake (eggs broken into a dish). — *adj* **shirred**. — *n* **shirr'ing**. [Origin unknown]

shirra *shir'ə*, *n* an obsolete Scots form of **sheriff**.

shirt *shûrt*, *n* a man's loose sleeved garment for the upper part of the body, typically with a fitted collar and cuffs; a woman's blouse of similar form; an undershirt; a nightshirt; a close covering. — *vt* (now *rare*) to put a shirt on. — *n* **shirt'ing** cloth for shirts. — *adj* **shirt'less**. — **shirt'band** the neckband of a shirt; **shirt button**; **shirt dress** a straight dress with a collar like a shirt's, resembling an elongated shirt; a shirtwaister (*US*); **shirt frill** a frill on the breast of a shirt; **shirt front** the breast of a shirt, *esp* a starched false one, a dickey; **shirt'lifter** (*derog slang*) a male homosexual; **shirt pin** an ornamental pin fastening a shirt at the neck; **shirt'-sleeve**; **shirt stud**; **shirt tail** the longer flap at the back of a shirt; **shirt'waist** (*US*) a woman's blouse; **shirt'waister** a tailored dress with a shirtwaist top. — **Black Shirt** or **Black'shirt** a fascist; **boiled shirt** a white shirt (with starched front); **Brown Shirt** or **Brown'shirt** a Nazi; **get** or **have one's** (or **someone's**) **shirt out** (*old slang*) to become (or make someone else) angry (from the dishevelment of uncontrolled rage); **in one's shirt** wearing nothing but a shirt, or nothing over the shirt; **in one's shirtsleeves** with one's jacket or jersey off; **keep one's shirt on** to keep calm; **lose one's shirt** to lose all one has; **put one's shirt on** to bet all one has on; **Red Shirt** a follower of Garibaldi. [OE *scyrte*; cf **short**]

shirty *shûr'ti*, (*colloq*) *adj* ill-tempered, annoyed. — *adv* **shirt'ily**. — *n* **shirt'iness**. [From *get* or *have someone's shirt out*; see under **shirt**]

shish kebab. See under **kebab**.

shit *shit* or (*dialect*, *euphem* or *jocular*) **shite** *shīt*, (*vulg*) *n* faeces, excrement; the act of defecating; a contemptuous term for a person; rubbish, nonsense; marijuana or heroin (*drug-user's slang*). — *vi* to evacuate the bowels, defecate. — *vt* to produce by defecating (also *fig*); (*reflexive*) to defecate over one's person, soil (oneself): — *pr p* **shitt'ing** or **shī'ting**; *pa t* and *pa p* **shit**, **shitt'ed**, **shī'ted** or **shat**. — *interj* expressing anger, disgust, disappointment, etc. — *n* **shitt'iness**. — *adj* **shitt'y** soiled with or like shit; very bad or unpleasant. — **shit'head** a contemptible or unpleasant person; a drug-user, *esp* a user of marijuana (*slang*); **shit'hole** a filthy or dilapidated place or establishment. — *adj* **shit-hot'** (*usu* of a person) very good, excellent, first-rate, admirable. — **shit'-stirrer** someone who causes unnecessary trouble. — **bull'shit** see under **bull**[1]; **have a shit** to defecate; **in (the) shit** (*slang*) in trouble; **no shit**

(*US slang*) no fooling; you amaze me (often *ironic*); **shit oneself** (*slang*) to be very scared; **the shits** (*slang*) diarrhoea; **when the shit hits the fan** (*slang*) when real trouble or conflict begins. [OE *scitan* to defecate]

shittim *shit'im*, *n* (in full **shitt'im wood**; *Old Testament*) the wood of the **shitt'ah (tree)**, believed to be a species of acacia; applied also to various other trees. [Heb *shittāh*, pl *shittīm*]

shiv. See **chiv**.

Shiva. See **Siva**.

shivah or **shibah** *shiv'ə*, (*Judaism*) *n* a period of mourning observed for seven days after a funeral. [Heb, seven days]

shivaree *shiv-ə-rē'*, (*NAm*) *n* a variant of **charivari**.

shive *shīv*, *n* a slice, eg of bread (*Scot*); a thin flat cork or bung; (in *pl*) pale yellow or brown splinters of undigested wood particles in wood pulp or paper; (in *pl*) small particles of vegetable or woody matter found in flax fibres or newly-shorn wool (*textiles*). [ME *schive*; cf ON *skīfa*; Du *schijf*, Ger *Scheibe*]

shiver[1] *shiv'ər*, *n* a splinter or small fragment (now *rare*); a flake or splinter of stone. — *vt* and *vi* to shatter. — *adj* **shiv'ery** brittle. — **shiver my timbers** a stock nautical exclamation uttered by stage sailors, etc. [Early ME *scifre*; cf **shive, sheave**; Ger *Schiefer*]

shiver[2] *shiv'ər*, *vi* to quiver; to tremble; to make an involuntary muscular movement as with cold; (of sails) to tremble or shake when a sailing vessel is brought close to the wind (*naut*). — *vt* to cause to quiver or tremble. — *n* a shivering movement or feeling. — *n* **shiv'erer**. — *n* and *adj* **shiv'ering**. — *adv* **shiv'eringly**. — *adj* **shiv'ery** inclined to shiver or to cause shivers. — **shiver in one's shoes** see **shake**; **the shivers** (*colloq*) a shivering fit; the ague; a thrill of horror or fear. [ME *chivere*]

shiver[3] *shiv'ər*, (*dialect*; *esp Scot*) a cold sore. [Perh **shiver**[2]]

shivoo *shə-vōō'*, (*Austr colloq*) *n* a (noisy) party or social occasion. [From N Eng dialect *sheevo* a shindy; perh connected with Fr *chez vous* at your house]

shlemiel. See **schlemiel**.

shlemozzle. See **shemozzle**.

shlep. See **schlep**.

shlimazel. See **schlimazel**.

shlock. See **schlock**.

SHM or **shm** (*phys*) *abbrev*: simple harmonic motion.

shmaltz. See **schmaltz**.

shmo. See **schmo**.

shmock. See **schmock** under **schmuck**.

shmoose, **shmooze**. See **schmooze**.

shmuck. See **schmuck**.

shoal[1] *shōl*, *n* a multitude of fishes, etc, swimming together; a flock, swarm, great assemblage. — *vi* to gather or go in shoals, swarm. — *adv* **shoal'wise** in shoals. [OE *scolu* troop, prob from MDu *schōle* troop, group; cf **school**[2]]

shoal[2] *shōl*, *adj* shallow. — *n* an area of shallow water; a sandbank, *esp* one exposed at low tide. — *vi* to become shallow; to sail into shallow water (*naut*). — *vt* to sail into (water of decreasing depth); to make shallow. — *n* **shoal'ing**. — *n* **shoal'ness**. — *adj* **shoal'y** (of a stretch of water) full of shallows; (of a vessel's draught) shallow, and therefore capable of sailing in shoal water (*naut*). — **shoal mark** an indication of shoal water; **shoal water**. [OE *sceald* shallow]

shoat or **shote** *shōt*, *n* a young pig, *esp* one that has just been weaned. [From ME; connected with Flem *shote*]

shochet *shohh'ət*, *n* a slaughterer qualified to kill cattle or poultry according to prescribed Jewish ritual: — *pl* **shoch'etim** (*-tim*). [Heb *shōḥēt*, pr p of *shāḥat* to slaughter]

shock[1] *shok*, *n* a violent impact, *orig* of charging warriors; a dashing together; a shaking or unsettling blow; a sudden shaking or jarring as if by a blow; a blow to the emotions or its cause, an unpleasant surprise; outrage at something regarded as improper; a convulsive excitation of nerves, eg by electricity; a state of extreme physical collapse, a suspension of the body's voluntary and involuntary functions caused by trauma, a surgical operation, or excessive sudden emotional disturbance; a stroke of paralysis, eg resulting from cerebral haemorrhage (*colloq*). — *vt* to meet or assail with a shock; to shake or impair by a shock; to give a shock to; to cause to feel outrage, indignation, disgust, horror, etc. — *vi* to outrage feelings; to collide with violence. — *adj* (*journalism*) sensational, surprising, unexpected, as in *a shock result*. — *adj* **shock'able**. — *n* **shockabil'ity**. — *adj* **shocked**. — *n* **shock'er** (*colloq*) a sensational story, film or play; any remarkably unpleasant or offensive person or thing. — *adj* **shock'ing** giving a shock; revolting to the feelings, *esp* to oversensitive modesty; execrable; deplorably bad. — *adv* (*colloq*) deplorably. — *adv* **shock'ingly**. — *n* **shock'ingness**. — **shock'-absorber** a device for absorbing shock, such as the telescopic oleo leg in aircraft landing gear or (erroneously) the dampers between the chassis and axles in a motor vehicle; **shocking pink** an extremely vivid, glaring shade of pink. — *adj* **shock'-proof** protected in some way from giving, or suffering the effects of, shock or impact; unlikely to be upset, or to feel moral outrage; **shock'stall** (*aeronautics*) loss of lift at high speed caused by the formation of shock waves on an aircraft's wings; **shock tactics** *orig* tactics of cavalry attacking in masses and depending for their effect on the force of impact; any course of action aimed at achieving an object by means of suddenness and overwhelming force (*fig*); **shock therapy** or **treatment** the use of electric shocks in the treatment of mental disorders; the use of violent measures to change someone's way of thinking (*fig*); **shock troops** troops trained or selected for attacks demanding exceptional physique and bravery; **shock wave** a wave of the same nature as a sound wave but of very great intensity, caused eg by an atomic explosion, earthquake or by a body moving with supersonic velocity; the reaction to a sensation or a scandal, thought of as spreading in ever-widening circles. — **shock horror** (*colloq*) an ironic expression used in response to something purporting to shock. — *adj* **shock'-horror** used eg of banner headlines and other sensationalistic devices of the tabloid press. [Appar Fr *choc* (noun), *choquer* (verb) to strike, or perh directly from a Gmc source; cf Du *schok*]

shock[2] *shok*, *n* a stook, or propped-up group of sheaves; three score, sixty. — *vt* to set up in shocks. — *n* **shock'er**. [ME *schokke*; the corresponding word in some Gmc languages has come to mean sixty]

shock[3] *shok*, *n* a mass of thick, shaggy hair; (also **shock dog**) a poodle or other dog with long shaggy fur (*obs*). — Also *adj*. — **shock'-head**. — *adj* **shock-head'ed**. [Poss from **shock**[2]; cf **shough**]

shod. See **shoe**.

shoddy *shod'i*, *adj* inferior and pretentious; cheap and nasty; sham; made of shoddy; badly made or executed. — *n* woollen fibre obtained by shredding refuse woollen rags; cloth made of it, alone or mixed; anything inferior seeking to pass for better than it is. — *adv* **shodd'ily**. — *n* **shodd'iness**. [Origin unknown]

shoder *shōd'ər*, *n* a set of skins in which goldleaf is beaten the second time (see **cutch**[2]). [From obs Fr *chaucher* to press; ult from L *calx* heel]

shoe *shōō*, *n* a stiff outer covering for the foot, not coming above the ankle (or in US not much above); a rim of iron nailed to a hoof; anything in form, position, or use like a shoe, as in a metal tip or ferrule, a piece attached where there is friction, a drag for a wheel, the part of a brake that comes in contact with the wheel, etc, the block by which an electric tractor collects current; the short bent part at the bottom of a downpipe that directs water away from the wall (*building*); a box-like device for dispensing playing-cards singly (*gambling*): — *pl* **shoes** (*shōōz*); also, *archaic* and *dialect* **shoon** (*shōōn*, *Scot shün* or *shin*). — *vt* to put shoes or a shoe on: — *pr p* **shoe'ing**; *pa t* and *pa p* **shod** (*shod*) or **shoed** (*shōōd*). — *adj* **shod**. — *n* **shoe'ing**. — *adj* **shoe'less**. —

n **shoer** (*shōō'ər*) a person who shoes horses. — **shoe'bill** a large African wading bird (*Balaeniceps rex*) with a heavy bill (also called **shoebill stork, whale-head, whale-headed stork**); **shoe'black** someone who polishes shoes, a bootblack; **shoe brush**; **shoe buckle**; **shoe'horn** a curved implement with a handle used for easing the heel into the back of a shoe; anything serving to facilitate something else (*old*). — *vt* (*fig*) to fit, squeeze or compress into a tight or insufficient space. — **shoe-lace** a cord passed through eyelet holes to fasten a shoe; **shoe latchet** a thong for fastening a shoe, sandal, etc; **shoe leather** leather for shoes; shoes generally; **shoe'-maker** a person who makes (now more often only sells or mends) shoes and boots; **shoe'making**; **shoe nail** a nail for fastening a horseshoe; a nail for a shoe sole; **shoe peg** a peg for fastening parts of a shoe together; **shoe'shine** (the act of) polishing shoes; the shiny appearance of polished shoes; **shoe shop**; **shoe'string** a shoelace (*US*); a minimum of money or capital. — *adj* operated, produced, etc on a minimum of money or capital; petty, paltry (*US*). — **shoestring fungus** the honey fungus (qv); **shoe tie** a (fancy) shoelace; **shoe'tree** a support, *usu* of wood or metal, inserted in a shoe when it is not being worn, in order to preserve its shape. — **another pair of shoes** (*colloq*) quite a different matter; **be in, fill** or **step into someone's** (or **a dead man's**) **shoes** to be in, or succeed to, someone's place; **die in one's shoes** to die by violence, *esp* by hanging; **on a shoestring** with an extremely small amount of capital. [OE *scōh* (pl *scōs*); Gothic *shōhs*, Ger *Schuh*]

shofar *shō'fär*, (*Judaism*) *n* a wind instrument made from a ram's horn, blown in Jewish religious ceremonies and in ancient times as a call to battle, etc: — *pl* **shō'fars** or **shōfroth** (*-frōt'*). — Also **shophar**. [Heb *shōphār* ram's horn]

shog *shog*, (chiefly *dialect*) *vi* to shake; to sway, swing; to jog; to move on, go away. — *vt* to shake; to push aside: — *pr p* **shogg'ing**; *pa t* and *pa p* **shogged**. — *n* a jog, shock. [ME *shogge*, perh related to **shock**[1] and OHGer *scoc* a swing]

shoggle *shog'l*, (*dialect*) *vt* to shake, rock. — *vi* to wobble, shake. — *adj* **shogg'ly**. [Cf **shoogle, shog**]

shogi *shō'gē*, *n* the Japanese form of chess. [Jap *shōgi*]

shogun *shō'gōōn* or *-gōōn*, (*Jap hist*) *n* any of the hereditary military governors who were the effective rulers of Japan from the 12c until the 1860s. — *adj* **shō'gunal**. — *n* **shō'gunate** the office, jurisdiction or state of a shogun. [Jap, from *sho* to lead, and *gun* army]

shoji *shō'jē*, *n* a screen of paper covering a wooden framework, forming a wall or sliding partition in Japanese homes: — *pl* **sho'ji** or **sho'jis**. [Jap, from *sho* to separate, and *ji* a piece]

shola[1] *shō'lə*, *n* a thicket or jungle in S India. [Tamil *çolai*]

shola[2]. Same as **sola**[2].

sholom. Same as **shalom**.

Shona *shō'nə*, *n* a group of African peoples living south of the Zambesi; any member of the group; any language spoken by the group; (**Union Shona**) a literary language designed for use by the whole group.

shone *shon*, *pa t* and *pa p* of **shine**.

shoneen *shō'nēn* (*Irish derog*) *n* an Irishman who imitates the ways and manners of the English. [From Irish *Seoinín*, dimin of *Seon* John (a generic name for an Englishman)]

shonky *shongk'i*, (*Austr slang*) *adj* underhanded, illicit; unreliable. [Perh from offensive *shonk* Jew, a mean, money-grubbing person]

shoo *shōō*, *interj* an exclamation used to scare away birds, animals, etc. — *vi* to cry 'Shoo!' — *vt* to drive away by shouting 'Shoo!'; to cause or allow (a horse) to win a race (*US slang*); to fix (a race) so that a particular horse wins (*US slang*). — *n* **shoo'-in** (*US slang*) a horse that is allowed to win; any certain winner of a race, competition, etc; a sure thing. — **shoo'fly** (*US*) a child's toy, a rocker consisting of a seat with end boards shaped and painted like animals; **shoo'fly pie** (*US*) a sweet open pie filled with molasses and baked. [Instinctive; cf Ger *schu*, Gr *sou*]

shoogie *shōōg'ē* or *shōōg'ē*, (*Scot dialect*) *vi* to swing, sway back and forth. — *n* a swing (as of a pendant); a swaying movement. [Cf **shoogle, shog**]

shoogle *shōōg'l*, (*Scot*) *vi* to shake, joggle; to sway, rock back and forth. — *vt* to shake, joggle. — *n* a swaying, rocking motion. — *adj* **shoog'ly**. [Cf **shog, shoggle**]

shoo-in. See **shoo**.

shook[1] *shōōk*, *pa t* of **shake**.

shook[2] *shōōk*, *n* a bundle of sheaves, a shock, stook; a set of cask staves and heads, or of parts for making a box, etc. [Origin unknown]

shool[1] or **shoole** *shōōl*, (*dialect* and *old slang*) *vi* to saunter about, skulk; to go about begging; to sponge. — Also **shule**. [Perh Irish]

shool[2] *shōōl* or *shōl*, (*Scot shül* or *shil*), *n* and *v* a dialect form of **shovel**.

shoon. See **shoe**.

shoot[1] *shōōt*, *vt* to dart; to let fly with force; to discharge (a bullet, missile, etc); to hit, wound, or kill in this way; to precipitate, launch forth; to tip out, dump; to cast; to kick or hit at goal (*games*); to score, for a hole or the round (*golf*); to thrust forward; to pull (one's shirt cuffs) forward so that they project from the sleeves of one's jacket; to slide along; to slide (a bolt) across or back; to put forth in growth; to crystallize; to pass rapidly through, under, or over; to pass through (traffic lights at red) without stopping; to photograph, *esp* for motion pictures; to variegate (*usu* in *pa p*); to inject (*esp* oneself) with (a drug) (*slang*); to play (a round of golf, game of pool, etc); to detonate. — *vi* to dart forth or forward; (of a cricket ball) to be propelled forward keeping low in to the batsman, after pitching; to send darting pains; to sprout; (of vegetables) to bolt; to elongate rapidly; to jut out far or suddenly; to begin, *esp* to speak one's mind or to tell what one knows (*colloq*; *usu* in *imperative*); to tower; to send forth a missile, etc; to discharge a shot or weapon; to use a bow or gun in practice, competition, hunting, etc; to crystallize: — *pa t* and *pa p* **shot**; see also **shott'en**. — *n* a shot (*archaic*); a shooting; a shooting match, party, expedition; a shooting pain; a movement of the shuttle; a weft thread; the shooting of a film; a photographic modelling session; new growth; a sprout; the stem and leaf parts of a plant; a dump; a chute (see **chute**[1]). — *adj* **shoot'able** capable of being shot, or shot over. — *n* **shoot'er** a cricket ball that shoots (see above); a gun, etc (*colloq*); someone who shoots, a hired killer, etc (*colloq*). — *n* **shoot'ing** the action of the verb in any sense; a twinge of quick pain; the killing of game with firearms over a certain area; the right to do so; the district so limited; the planing of edges that are to be joined. — Also *adj*. — **shoot'ist** (*slang*; now *esp US*) someone who shoots; a skilled marksman. — **shoot-'em-up** (*informal*; *orig US*) a film, television programme or computer game featuring or involving scenes of violent action, gunfights, etc; **shooting board** a board for steadying a piece of wood for shooting; **shooting box** or **lodge** a small house in the country for use in the shooting season; **shooting brake** (*old*) an estate car; **shooting gallery** a long room used for practice or amusement with firearms; a place where addicts gather to inject drugs (*slang*); **shooting iron** (*slang*) a firearm, *esp* a revolver; **shooting jacket** a short coat for shooting in; **shooting range** a place for shooting at targets; **shooting script** (*film*) a final version of a script with instructions for the cameraman indicating the order in which scenes will be shot; **shooting star** (*informal*) a meteor; **shooting stick** a printer's tool used for locking and unlocking formes by tapping the quoins; a walking stick with a two-part handle that opens out to form a seat; **shooting war** actual war as distinct from cold war; **shoot'-out** a gunfight, *esp* to the death or other decisive conclusion (also *fig*). — **get shot of** (*slang*) to get rid of; **have shot one's bolt** see under **bolt**[1]; **shoot a line** (*slang*) to brag, exaggerate (*n* **line'-shooter**); **shoot down** to kill, or to bring down (an aeroplane) by shooting; to rout, defeat; **shoot down in flames** (*slang*) to reprimand severely; to destroy, humiliate, *esp* by the strength of one's argument; **shoot from the hip** (*colloq*) to speak bluntly or hastily, without preparation or without concern for the consequences (*adj* **shoot'-from-the-hip'**); **shoot home** to hit the target (also *fig*); **shoot it out** to settle (a dispute, competition, etc) conclusively by shooting (also *fig*); **shoot off** to discharge a gun; to begin; to rush away; **shoot oneself in the foot** (*colloq*) to harm one's own interests by ineptitude; **shoot one's mouth off** see under **mouth**; **shoot the breeze** to chat inconsequentially; **shoot the crow** (*slang*) to leave without paying; **shoot the sun** (*naut*) to take the sun's altitude; **shoot the works** (*slang*) to risk one's all on one play (*gambling*); hence, to make one's maximum effort; **shoot through** (*slang*; *esp Austr*) to go, depart in haste; **shoot up** to kill or injure by shooting; to grow very quickly; to inject (a drug, *esp* heroin) (*slang*); **the whole (bang) shoot** or **shooting-match** (*colloq*) the whole lot. [OE *scēotan*; Du *schieten*, Ger *schiessen*; in some senses merging with Fr *chute* fall]

shoot². Same as **shoat**.

shop *shop*, *n* a building or room in which goods are sold; a spell of shopping, *esp* for food and/or household items; a place where mechanics work, or where any kind of industry is pursued; a place of employment or activity, *esp* a theatre; prison (*old slang*); talk about one's own business. — *vi* to visit shops, *esp* for the purpose of buying. — *vt* to imprison, or cause to be imprisoned (*slang*); to betray or inform against (someone) to the police, etc (*slang*); to give employment to (*obs*): — *pr p* **shopp'ing**; *pa p* **shopped**. — *n* **shopahol'ic** a compulsive shopper (see **-aholic**). — *n* **shop'ful**. — *n* **shopp'er** a person who shops; a shopping bag or basket. — *n* **shopp'ing** the activity of visiting shops to buy or see goods; goods thus bought. — *adj* for shopping. — *adj* **shopp'y** commercial; having many shops; given to talking shop; concerning one's own pursuit. — **shop assist'ant** a person who serves customers in a shop; **shop bell** a bell, fitted to the door of a shop, that rings when the door is opened; **shop'board** a counter; a bench on which tailors work; **shop'-boy** or **-girl** *esp* formerly, a boy or girl employed in a shop; **shop'breaker** a person who breaks into a shop; **shop'-breaking**; **shop floor** that part of a factory, etc, housing the production machinery and in which that part of the workforce directly involved with production is employed; the people who work on the shop floor, *esp* those workers organized in a union. — *adj* **shop'-floor**. — **shop'front** the part of a shop, with display windows, etc, that faces on to the street. — *adj* **shop-in-shop'** (of a supplier of particular goods or services) having a retail outlet within a larger shop or store. — **shop'-keeper** a person who keeps a shop of his or her own; **shop'keeping**; **shop-lifter**; **shop-lifting** stealing from a shop; **shop'man** a man who serves in a shop; a shopkeeper (*rare*); a workshop man (*US*); **shopping bag** or **basket** a receptacle for goods bought; **shopping-bag lady** same as **bag lady** under **bag**; **shopping centre** a place where there is a concentration of shops of different kinds; **shopping list** a list of items to be bought; a list of items to be obtained, done, acted upon, considered, etc (*fig*); **shopping mall** see under **mall**; **shopping precinct** see under **precinct**; **shop sign** a sign over a shop indicating the occupier's name and trade. — *adj* **shop'soiled** somewhat faded or worn by display in a shop (also *fig*). — **shop steward** a representative of factory or workshop hands elected from their own number; **shop walker** a shop employee who walks about in a shop to see customers attended to; **shop window** a window of a shop in which wares are displayed; any means of displaying what is on offer to advantage. — *adj* **shop'worn** shopsoiled (also *fig*). — **all over the shop** (*informal*) dispersed all around; **on the shop floor** among the workers in a factory or workshop; **set up shop** to open a trading establishment; to begin operations generally; **shop around** to compare prices and quality of goods at various shops before making a purchase; **shut up shop** to close a shop, etc, at the end of a working day, week, etc; to close a business permanently; **talk shop** to talk about one's own work or business; **the Shop** the former Royal Military Academy at Woolwich; **the wrong shop** (*colloq*) the wrong place to look for eg sympathy or help. [OE *sceoppa* a treasury]

shope *shōp*, *obs pa t* (*Spenser*) of **shape**.

shophar. See **shofar**.

shoran *shōr'an*, *n* a system of navigation in an aircraft or other vehicle using the measurement of the time taken for dispatched radar signals to return from two known fixed points. [*Sho*rt *ra*nge *n*avigation]

shore¹ *shōr* or *shör*, *n* the land bordering on the sea or a great expanse of water; the foreshore. — *vt* to set on shore. — *adj* **shore'less** having no shore, unlimited, boundless. — *adj* and *adv* **shore'ward**. — *adv* **shore'-wards**. — **shore'bird** any of various birds that live on the shore or close to water, a wader; **shore boat** a boat plying near or to the shore; **shore crab** a crab (*Carcinus maenas*) very common between tidemarks; **shore due** (*Scot*) a harbour due; **shore effect** (*telecomm*) horizontal refraction of a radio wave as it crosses a shoreline, causing direction-finding errors (also **coast-line effect**). — *adj* **shore'-going** going, or for going, ashore; land-dwelling. — **shore leave** leave of absence granted to members of a ship's crew to go ashore; **shore'line** the line of meeting of land and water; a rope connecting a net with the land; **shore'man** a dweller on the shore; a landsman; (*US* also **shores'man**) a person who has an onshore job connected with fishery; **shore'side** the neighbourhood of the shore. — Also *adj*. — **shore'weed** a plant (*Litorella lacustris*) of the plantain family found on lake margins. — **on shore** on the land; ashore. [ME *schore*; cf Du *schoor*, *schor*]

shore² *shōr* or *shör*, *n* a temporary prop used to support a wall, excavation, etc, to prevent slipping, sagging, etc. — *vt* to prop (often with *up*; also *fig*). — *n* **shor'er**. — *n* **shor'ing** supporting by shores; a set of props. [MDu *schōre* prop; related to ON *skortha*]

shore³ *shōr* or *shör*, (*Scot*) *vt* to warn, threaten; to offer. — *n* threatening, menace. [Origin obscure]

shore⁴ *shōr* or *shör*, (*archaic* and *dialect*) *n* a sewer, drain, *usu* (as *Shakesp*) **common-shore**. [Perh **sewer**; perh **shore¹**]

shore⁵ *shōr* or *shör*, (*Austr* and *NZ* or *archaic*) *pa t* of **shear**.

shorn *shörn*, *pa p* of **shear**.

short *shört*, *adj* of little length, tallness, extent, or duration; in the early future (as *short day*, *date*); concise; curt or abrupt; snappish; (of pastry, etc) crisp yet readily crumbling; brittle; on the near side; (of memory) not retentive; failing to go far enough or reach the standard or level required; deficient; lacking (in); scanty, in inadequate supply; in default; unable to meet engagements; pertaining to the sale of what one cannot supply; not being in possession of shares, etc at the time of sale in anticipation of a fall in prices before their delivery date (*finance*); in accentual verse, loosely, unaccented (*prosody*); (of an alcoholic drink) undiluted with water, neat (*colloq*); having short wool; (of glass) fast-setting; (of metal) brittle (*min ext*); (of certain fielding positions) relatively near the batsman (*cricket*); (of a bowled ball) bouncing at some distance from the batsman (*cricket*). — *adv* briefly; abruptly; curtly; without leaving a stump; on this or the near side; at a disadvantage (eg *taken short*); see **sell short** under **sell**. — *n* that which is short; shortness, abbreviation, summary; a short circuit; (in *pl*) short trousers (ie thigh-length, as opposed to ankle-length); (in *pl*) undershorts (*US*); (in *pl*) the bran and coarse part of meal, in mixture; (in *pl*) short-dated securities; a short film subordinate to a main film in a programme; a drink of spirits (*colloq*); (in *pl*) a deficiency (*NAm*). —

vt to short-change. — *vt* and *vi* to shorten (*obs*); to short-circuit; to fall short of, or perhaps cause to fail (*archaic*). — *n* **short'age** a lack, deficiency. — *vt* **short'en** to make shorter; to make to seem short or to fall short; to draw in or back; to check; to make friable (by adding butter, lard, etc); to put (a baby) in short clothes (*old*). — *vi* to become shorter. — *n* **short'ener**. — *n* **short'ening** making or becoming shorter; fat for making pastry short. — *n* **short'ie** or **short'y** (*colloq*) a very short person, garment, etc. — Also *adj*. — *adj* **short'ish**. — *adv* **short'ly** soon; briefly; curtly; for a short time (*rare*); a little; with shortness in that which is indicated. — *n* **short'ness**. — *adj* **short'arm** (*boxing*, etc; of a blow) using a bent (rather than extended) arm. — **short'bread** a brittle crumbling biscuit of flour, butter and sugar; **short'cake** shortbread or other friable cake; a light cake, prepared in layers with fruit between, served with cream (*orig NAm*). — *vt* **short-change'** to give less than the correct change to; to deal dishonestly with (a person). — *adj* pertaining to cheating. — **short-chan'ger**; **short circuit** a new and unwanted path of comparatively low resistance accidentally created between two points of a circuit, often causing damage to components (*electr*); an artificial connection between two normally separate tubular organs or parts (*surg*). — *vt* **short-cir'cuit** to establish a short circuit in; to interconnect where there was obstruction between (*surg*); to provide with a short cut (*fig*). — *vi* to cut off current by a short circuit; to save a roundabout passage. — **short clothes** or **short coats** formerly, the shortened skirts of a child when the first long clothes are left off. — *vt* **short'-coat** (*old*) to put into short coats. — **short'coming** the circumstance of coming or falling short; a neglect of, or failure in, duty; a defect, failing; **short commons** minimum rations. — *adj* **short'-cord** (*elec eng*) (of an armature winding) employing coils whose span is less than the pole pitch. — **short covering** (*stock exchange*) the buying of securities, etc, to cover a short sale; the securities, etc, bought for this purpose. — **short cut** a shorter route than the usual. — *vi* **short'-cut** to use a shorter route (also *fig*). — *adj* and *n* denoting tobacco cut in short shreds. — *adj* **short'-dāted** (of a bill) having little time to run from its date; (of securities) redeemable in under five years. — **short-day plant** (*bot*) one that will flower only if the daily period of light is shorter than some critical length (cf **day-neutral plant**, **long-day plant**); **short division** division without writing down the working out; **short'fall** the fact or amount of falling short; **short fuse** (*colloq*) a quick temper; **short game** (*golf*) play on and around the green(s); **short'gown** (*old Scot*) a woman's short jacket; **short'hand** a system of writing in which whole words and phrases are represented by (combinations of) simple strokes, used for recording speech at speaking pace; writing of such a kind. — Also *adj*. — *adj* **short-hand'ed** short of an adequate number of workers; with a small or reduced number on the team, in the crew, etc. — *adj* **short'-haul** involving transportation, etc, over (relatively) short distances. — *vt* **short'-head** (*colloq*) to beat by a short head (see phrases below). — Also *adj*. — *adj* **short'hold** (*law*) in Britain, of or being a tenancy of one to five years. — **short'horn** any of the various types of beef and dairy cattle developed from a short-horned breed originating in NE England, *usu* having red and white, roan or white coat (also called **Durham**); **short leg** (*cricket*) the fielder or the field near (and in line with) the batsman on the leg side. — *adj* **short'-life** having a short duration, existence, etc. — **short list** (see also **leet**[1]) a list of candidates for an office, post, etc from which the successful candidate will be selected. — *vt* **short'-list** to include (someone) in a short list. — *adj* **short'-lived** (or *-līvd*) living or lasting only for a short time. — **short measure** less than the amount promised or paid for; **short metre** (*poetry*) a form of four-line stanza of which the first, second and last lines have six syllables and the third line eight; **short odds** (in betting) a nearly even chance, favourable odds in terms of risk, unfavourable in terms of potential gain. — *adj* **short-oil** see **oil length** under **oil**. — **short order** (*NAm*) (an order for) food that can be prepared quickly. — *adj* **short'-order**. — *adj* **short'-priced** having short odds. — *adj* **short'-range** of or relating to a short distance or period of time. — **short rib** a floating rib; **short sale** a sale of something which the seller does not yet own; **short score** a musical score with some of the parts omitted; **short sea** (*naut*) one in which the distance between the wave crests is comparatively short; **short selling** see **sell short** under **sell**; **short sheep** short-woolled sheep; **short shrift** see under **shrift**. — *adj* **short-sight'ed** able to see clearly only those objects that are relatively near, myopic; lacking foresight. — *adv* **short-sight'edly**. — **short-sight'edness**; **short slip** (*cricket*) the fielder, or the field, near the batsman on the off side behind the wicket. — *adj* **short-spō'ken** curt in speech. — *adj* **short-staff'ed** having a reduced or inadequate number of staff. — *adj* **short-stā'ple** (of wool, cotton, etc fibre) short. — **short'stop** (*baseball*) the fielding position (or the defending player positioned) between the second and third base; **short story** a work of prose narrative shorter than a novel and *usu* concentrating on a single episode or experience and its effect; **short'sword** a sword with a short blade. — *adj* **short-tem'pered** easily moved to anger, quick-tempered. — **short tennis** a form of tennis for young children, using a smaller court and modified equipment and rules. — *adj* **short'-term** extending over a short time; concerned with the immediate present and future as distinct from time further ahead. — **short-term'ism** (a tendency towards) the adopting of only short-term views, solutions to problems, etc. — *n* and *adj* **short-term'ist**. — **short-term memory** (*psychol*) a section of the memory with limited capacity, capable of storing information for a short time only. — **short time** (the condition of) working fewer than the normal number of hours per week. — *adj* **short'-time**. — **short track** a shortened form of **short-track (speed)skating**, the sport of individual, relay and pursuit speedskating on an indoor ice track over any of several distances between 500m and 5000m; **short wave** a radio wave with a frequency of between 10m and 100m. — *adj* **short'-wave**. — *adj* **short-wind'ed** soon becoming breathless. — **by a short head** by a distance less than the length of a horse's head; narrowly, barely (*fig*); **caught** or **taken short** (*colloq*) having a sudden, uncontrollable need to urinate or defecate; **cut short** see under **cut**; **draw the short straw** to be given an unpleasant task, duty, etc, or the most unpleasant of several; **fall short** see under **fall**; **for short** as an abbreviation; **go short** (*colloq*) to have an insufficient amount (*esp* of money or food); **have someone by the short and curlies** (*vulg slang*) to have someone over a barrel, at one's mercy, in a position difficult to wriggle out of; **in short** in a few words, briefly; **in short supply** not available in desired quantity, scarce; **in the short run** over a brief period of time; **make short work of** to settle or dispose of promptly; **run short** see under **run**; **short and sweet** surprisingly or gratifyingly brief, used eg of a speech expected to be of greater length (and tedium); (ironically) curt or abrupt; **short for** a shortened form of; **short of** less than; without going so far as; having insufficient supplies of; **short on** (*colloq*) deficient in; **stop short** to come to a sudden standstill; **taken short** see **caught short** above; **take** (or **take up**) **short** to take by surprise or at a disadvantage; to interrupt curtly; **the short and the long (of it)** (*Shakesp*) same as **the long and the short** (under **long**[3]) [ME, from OE *sc(e)ort*; related to OHGer *scurz*, ON *skera* to cut]

Shoshone *shō-shō'nē*, *n* (a member of) an American Indian people of the West Central area of the US; their Aztec-Tanoan language. — Also **Shosho'ni**.

shot[1] *shot*, *pa t* and *pa p* of **shoot**. — *adj* hit or killed by shooting; exhausted (*colloq*); ruined (*colloq*); elongated by rapid growth; advanced (in years; *archaic*);

with warp and weft of different colours, as in *shot silk*; showing a play of colours; rid (with *of*; *colloq*). — *n* (*farming*) a reject animal from a herd or flock.

shot[2] *shot*, *n* an act of shooting; a blast; an explosive charge; a single photographic exposure, or a length of cinematic film taken without a break with a single camera; a camera's range or extent of view, as in *out of shot*; a stroke, throw or hit in sports and games; an attempt; a spell; a turn; a guess; the casting of a net; a set of nets or length of net cast; an aggressive remark; an injection (*colloq*); a dram (*colloq*); a person that shoots, a marksman; a projectile, *esp* one that is solid and spherical, without bursting charge; a cannonball; a weight for putting (*athletics*); a bullet; a small pellet of which several are shot together; such pellets collectively; the launch of a rocket to a specified destination; flight of a missile, or its distance; range, reach; a plot of land; (also **scot**) a payment, *esp* of a bill or one's share of a bill; a contribution. — *vt* to load with shot: — *pr p* **shott'ing**; *pa t* and *pa p* **shott'ed**. — *adj* **shott'ed**. — **shot'-blasting** the cleaning of metal, etc, by means of a stream of shot; **shot'-clog** (*obs*) a simpleton who is only tolerated for his willingness to pay the bill; **shot'firer** (*min ext*) in blasting, the worker who fires the charge. — *adj* **shot'-free** scot-free; safe from shot. — **shot'gun** see separate entry; **shot'hole** a hole made by a shot, or in timber by a boring insect, or in a leaf by a fungus; a hole in a wall for shooting from; a hole bored in rock for a blasting charge; **shot'maker** (*sport*, *esp tennis* and *golf*) a person who produces winning, attacking or skilful shots or strokes; **shot'-making**; **shot noise** (*electronics*) inherent noise resulting from variations in the current output of an electronic device caused by the random pulses of electron emission from the electrode (also called **flicker noise**, **Schottky noise**). — *adj* **shot'proof** proof against shot. — **shot'put** the athletics event of putting the shot; **shot tower** formerly, a tower where small shot is made by dropping molten lead into water from a given height; **shot window** (*obs*) *appar* a hinged or casement window. — **a shot across the bows** one thus directed so as to warn a ship off rather than damage it (often *fig*); **a shot in the arm** an injection in the arm (*med*); a revivifying injection, eg of money, new effort, renewed confidence, fresh talent (*fig*); **a shot in the dark** a random guess or wild speculation; **big shot** (*colloq*) a person of importance; **call the shots** see under **call**[1]; **have a shot** (with *at*) (*colloq*) to have a try or go (at something); to jeer or carp (at someone) (*Austr*); **hotshot** see under **hot**; **like a shot** instantly, quickly; eagerly, willingly; **stand shot** (*obs* and *dialect*) to pay the bill; **still have shot in the** (or **one's**) **locker** to be still potent; to have something yet in reserve. [OE *sc(e)ot*, *gesc(e)ot*; cf **shoot**]

shote, **shot** or **shotte** *n*. Variant spellings of **shoat**.

shotgun *shot'gun*, *n* a smooth-bore gun for firing shot at relatively short range, used *esp* for shooting birds and other small game, clay pigeons, etc. — *adj* pertaining to a shotgun; involving coercion or duress (eg *shotgun merger*, *shotgun wedding*); covering a wide field in random, haphazard fashion with resultant hit-and-miss effect. — **ride shotgun** to protect a vehicle and its occupants from attack by riding on it (or following close behind it) bearing a firearm or firearms (also *fig*).

shott *shot*, (*geog*) *n* in N Africa and the Middle East, a shallow watercourse or lake that tends to dry up in certain seasons.

shotten *shot'n*, *old* or *dialect pa p* of **shoot**. — *adj* (of a herring, etc) having ejected the spawn and of little food value; effete, exhausted, worthless; bursting or shooting out, as something violently dispersed.

shottle. See **shuttle**[2].

shough or (*Shakesp*) **showghe** *shog*, *shok* or *shuf*, *n* a shaggy kind of lapdog. [Perh **shock**[3]]

should *sho͝od*, *pa t* of **shall**. [OE *sceolde*]

shoulder *shōl'dər*, *n* the part of a human or other vertebrate animal's body around the junction with the arm or forelimb; the upper joint of an animal's foreleg as a cut of meat; part of a garment covering the shoulder; a coat-hanger (*old*); a bulge, protrusion, offshoot, etc resembling the human shoulder, eg near the summit of a mountain; a curve like that between the shoulder and the neck or side, as on a stringed instrument; either edge of a road, *usu* applied to the unpaved strip on which vehicles do not normally travel; the flat surface on a piece of type from the foot of the bevel to the body (*printing*); the part of a ring where the setting joins the band (*jewellery*); the part of a characteristic curve where levelling off is perceptible (*electronics*). — *vt* to thrust with the shoulder; to take upon the shoulder or in a position of rest against the shoulder; to undertake; to take responsibility for; to set shoulder to shoulder; to fashion with a shoulder or abutment; to embezzle from or defraud (one's employer) (also *vi*; *old slang*). — *vi* to jostle. — *adj* **shoul'dered** having a shoulder or shoulders. — *n* and *adj* **shoul'dering**. — **shoulder bag** a bag suspended from a strap worn over the shoulder; **shoulder belt** a belt that passes across the shoulder; **shoulder blade** the broad, flat, blade-like bone forming the back of the shoulder, the scapula; **shoulder bone** shoulder blade; **should'er-clapper** (*Shakesp*) a bailiff; **shouldered arch** (*archit*) a lintel supported over an opening, eg for a door, by corbels; **shoulder girdle** the pectoral girdle. — *adv* **shoul'der-height** as high as the shoulder. — *adj* and *adv* **shoulder-high'** as high as the shoulder. — **shoulder joint**; **shoulder knot** a knot worn as an ornament on the shoulder; a bailiff (*old slang*); **shoulder mark** (*US*) a badge of naval rank worn on the shoulder; **shoulder note** (*printing*) a note at the upper outside margin of a page level with the first line of type; **shoulder-of-mutton sail** a triangular sail; **shoulder pad** a pad inserted into the shoulder of a garment to raise and square it; **shoulder plane** a rebate plane with reversed cutting bevel, used in woodworking for fine trimming. — *adj* **shoul'der-shotten** (*Shakesp*) with a dislocated or sprained shoulder. — **shoulder slip** a sprain of the shoulder. — *adj* **shoul'der-slipped**. — **shoulder strap** a strap worn on or over the shoulder, *esp* one that holds up a garment, etc; a narrow strap of cloth edged with gold lace worn on the shoulder with uniform to indicate rank (*US*). — **cold shoulder** see under **cold**; **put one's shoulder to the wheel** to set to work in earnest, as if to get a coach out of the mire; **shoulder arms** (*military*) (of soldiers on parade, etc) to bring a firearm, etc to an upright position close to the right side of the body; **shoulder to shoulder** side by side; close together united, in unity; **(straight) from the shoulder** frank(ly) and forceful(ly). [OE *sculdor*; Ger *Schulter*, Du *schouder*]

shouldest, **shouldst**. See **shall**.

shouldn't *sho͝od'ənt*, (*colloq*) a contraction of **should not**.

shout *showt*, *n* a loud cry; a call; a call for a round of drinks (*slang*); a turn to buy a round of drinks (*slang*); a term used by the emergency services (fire-fighters, police and ambulance) for a call-out (*slang*). — *vi* to utter a shout; to speak in a raised, *esp* angry, voice (with *at*); to stand drinks all round (*slang*). — *vt* to utter with or as a shout. — *n* **shout'er**. — *n* and *adj* **shout'ing**. — *adv* **shout'ingly**. — **shouting match** (*colloq*) a quarrel or argument in which both sides loudly insult each other; **shout'line** (*informal*) a short line of text, *usu* printed in bold type, drawing attention to a major selling point in an advertisement or promotional material. — **all over bar the shouting** (of a happening, contest, etc) as good as over, virtually finished or decided; **go on the shout** (*orig Austr*; *slang*) to go on a drinking bout, drink to excess; **shout down** to make (another speaker) inaudible by shouting or talking loudly; **within shouting distance** nearby; within reach. [Ety doubtful, poss as **scout**[2], connected with ON *skuta* a taunt]

shouther *sho͞o'dhər*, Scots form of **shoulder**.

shove *shuv*, *vt* and *vi* to thrust; to push; to jostle; to place roughly or hastily. — *n* a push, thrust. — *n* **shov'er**

someone or something that shoves; a punning form of **chauffeur**. — **shove'-groat** (*obs*) shovelboard (also *adj* as in **shove-groat shilling** a smooth-worn shilling suitable for playing shovelboard); **shove-half'penny** a gambling game similar to shovelboard. — **shove off** to push (a boat) from the shore; to go away (*colloq*). [OE *scūfan*; Du *schuiven*, Ger *schieben*]

shovel *shuv'l*, *n* a broad spadelike tool for scooping, the blade *usu* curved up at the sides; (a part of) a machine having a similar shape or function; a scoop; a shovelful; a shovel hat. — *vt* to move with, or as if with, a shovel; to gather in large quantities. — *vi* to use a shovel: — *pr p* **shov'elling**; *pa t* and *pa p* **shov'elled**. — *n* **shov'elful** as much as a shovel will hold: — *pl* **shov'elfuls**. — *n* **shov'eller** or (*US*) **shov'eler** someone who shovels; a dabbling duck (*Anas clypeata*) of marshes and muddy shallows, with a long, rounded, spadelike bill (*usu* **shov'eler**). — **shovel hat** a hat with a broad brim, turned up at the sides, and projecting in front, as formerly worn by Anglican clergy; **shov'elhead** a shark (*Sphyrna tiburo*) of the hammerhead family, having a flattish shovel-like head; a shovelnose; **shov'elnose** a freshwater sturgeon (*Scaphorhynchus platorhynchus*) of N American rivers, having a broad shovel-like snout. [OE *scofl*, from *scūfan* to shove]

shovelboard *shuv'l-börd* or **shuffle-board** *shuf'l-börd*, *n* an old game in which a coin or other disc was driven along a table by the hand; a modern development played in America; a deck game played with wooden discs and cues; a table for the game; a shove-groat shilling (*Shakesp*). [Appar **shove** and **board**, confused with **shovel** and **shuffle**]

show or (now rarely) **shew** *shō*, *vt* to present to view; to exhibit, display or set forth; to cause or allow to be seen or known; to instruct by demonstrating; to prove; to manifest; to indicate; to usher or conduct (with *in*, *out*, *over*, *round*, *up*, etc). — *vi* to appear; to come into sight; to be visible; to arrive, turn up (*slang*): — *pa t* **showed** or (rarely) **shewed** (*shōd*); *pa p* **shown** or (rarely **shewn** (*shōn*), or **showed** or (rarely) **shewed**. — *n* an act of showing; display; exhibition; a sight or spectacle; an entertainment; parade; a demonstration; appearance; plausibility; pretence; a sign, indication; an indication of the presence of oil or gas in an exploratory well; performance; any thing, affair or enterprise (*colloq*); in childbirth, a small discharge of blood and mucus at the start of labour; a chance, opportunity (*NAm*, *Austr* and *NZ*). — *adj* of the nature of, suitable for, or connected with, a show; for show. — *n* **shower** (*shō'ər*). — *adv* **show'ily**. — *n* **show'iness**. — *n* **show'ing** the act of displaying, pointing out, etc; appearance; performance; a setting forth, representation. — *adj* **show'y** cutting a dash; making a show; ostentatious; gaudy; flashy. — **show bill** a bill or poster announcing a play or show; **show'boat** a river boat, *usu* a paddle-steamer, serving as a travelling theatre. — *vi* to behave in an ostentatious manner; to show off. — **show'boater**; **show'box** a showman's box out of which he takes his materials; **show'bread** see **shewbread**; **show business** the entertainment business, *incl* theatre, film and television. — Also (*informal*) **show'biz** or **show biz** (*adj* **show'-bizzy**). — **show card** a shopkeeper's advertising card; a card of patterns; a show bill; **show'case** a glass display case for a museum, shop, etc; any setting in which something or someone can be displayed to advantage (also *adj*). — *vt* to display, exhibit. — **show'down** in poker, the exposure of players' cards face up on the table at the end of a game; the name of a card game similar to poker; an open disclosure of plans, means, etc; a confrontation or clash by which a contested issue, argument, etc may be finally settled; **show'girl** a girl who takes part in variety entertainments *usu* as a dancer or singer; **show'ground** a plot of land on which an outdoor show is held; **show house** a decorated and furnished house, used to show prospective buyers, as an example of the type of house available on a new or incomplete housing estate; **show'jumper** a horse or rider in a showjumping competition; **show'jumping** a competition in which a succession of riders on horseback have to jump a series of obstacles of different kinds (also *adj*); **show'man** a person who exhibits, or owns, a show; a person who is skilled at public display and self-advertisement. — *adj* **show'manly**. — **show'manship** skilful display, or a talent for it; **show'-off** a person who behaves in an ostentatious manner in an effort to win admiration or public attention; **show'piece** something considered an especially fine specimen of its type, etc; an exhibit, something on display, etc; **show'place** a place visited or shown as a sight; a place where shows are exhibited; **show'room** a room where goods or samples are displayed; **show-stopper** see **stop the show** below; **show trial** one held purely for propaganda, the charges often being false, and the confession forcibly extracted; **show'yard** a yard for cattle shows. — **for show** for the sake of outward appearances; to attract notice; **give the show away** to let out a secret; **good** (or **bad**) **show** well (or not well) done; fortunate (or unfortunate) occurrence or circumstances; **run the show** (*colloq*) to take or be in charge; to take over, dominate; **show a leg** (*colloq*) to get out of bed; **show and tell** an activity of young schoolchildren in which an object is brought to the class by each child to be displayed and described, demonstrated and talked about; **show fight** to show a readiness to resist; **show forth** to manifest, proclaim; **show off** to display or behave ostentatiously; **show of hands** a vote indicated by raising hands; **show up** to expose; to appear to advantage or disadvantage; to show (*esp* faults) clearly by contrast; to embarrass, put to shame (*colloq*); to be present; to appear, arrive (*colloq*); to lodge, hand in, as a school exercise; **steal the show** to win the most applause; to attract the most publicity or admiration; **stop the show** to be applauded with so much enthusiasm as to interrupt the show, play, etc (hence *n* **show'stopper** the act, line, etc, so applauded); to have a sensational effect. [OE *scēawian* to look; from Du *schouwen*, Ger *schauen* to behold]

showbiz. See under **show**.

shower *show'ər* or *showr n* a short fall of rain, etc; a fall of drops of liquid; a fall, flight, or accession of many things together, such as meteors, sparks, arrows, blows, volcanic dust or (*esp NAm*) wedding gifts, gifts for an expected baby, etc; a party at which gifts are presented (*NAm*); a device with a nozzle for spraying water to wash the body; a wash thus taken; a booth or compartment containing such a device; an attack, a pang (*obs*); a large number of fast particles arising from a high-energy particle; a disparaging term applied to any particular group of people one disapproves of (*slang*). — *vt* and *vi* to drop in a shower or showers; to sprinkle; to water. — *vi* to wash under a shower. — *adj* **shower'ful**. — *n* **shower'iness**. — *n* and *adj* **shower'ing**. — *adj* **shower'less**. — *adj* **shower'y** marked by showers; raining by fits and starts. — **shower bath** (*old*) a bathroom shower, or a wash taken under one; **shower curtain** a plastic curtain drawn around a person taking a shower. — *adj* **shower'proof** impervious to showers. — *vt* to render showerproof. — **shower tray** a moulded plastic or tiled tray with a drain hole used for standing in while taking a shower. [OE *scūr*; ON *skūr*, Ger *Schauer*]

showghe. See **shough**.

shoyu *shō'ū*, a rich soy sauce made from soya beans naturally fermented with wheat or barley, used as flavouring in oriental, *esp* Japanese, cookery. [Jap *shōyu*]

shpt. *abbrev*: shipment.

shr. (*stock exchange*) *abbrev*: share(s).

shraddha. See **sraddha**.

shrank *shrangk*, *pa t* of **shrink**.

shrapnel *shrap'nl*, *n* a shell filled with musketballs with a bursting-charge, invented by General *Shrapnel* (1761–1842), or any later improved version of this; such shells collectively; pieces scattered by the bursting of a shrapnel or other shell.

shred *shred*, *n* a scrap, fragment; a paring, *esp* a curled paring; a ragged strip. — *vt* to prune (*obs*); to cut or cut off; to cut, tear or scrape into shreds. — *vi* to be reduced to shreds: — *pr p* **shredd'ing**; *pa t* and *pa p* **shredd'ed** or **shred**. — *adj* **shredd'ed**. — *n* **shredd'er** a device or machine for shredding eg vegetables, waste paper. — *n* **shredd'ing**. — *adj* **shredd'y**. — *adj* **shred'less**. — **shred'-pie** mince-pie. [OE *scrēade*, ult from Germanic base *skraud-*, *skreud-*, *skrud-* cut; cf **screed**, **scroll**, **shroud**; Ger *Schrot*]

shreek, **shreik**, and **shriech**. *Obs* spellings of **shriek**.

shrew *shrōō*, *n* a small mouselike insectivorous mammal of the family *Soricidae*, with a long snout, formerly thought to be venomous to cattle, a shrewmouse; an evil being (*obs*); a brawling, troublesome person, in later use only a woman, a scold. — *vt* (*Shakesp*) to curse, beshrew. — *adj* **shrew'ish** of the nature of a shrew or scold; ill-natured. — *adv* **shrew'ishly**. — *n* **shrew'ishness**. — **shrew mole** any of various moles of Asia and N America having a long snout and tail; **shrew'mouse** a shrew: — *pl* **shrew'mice**. [OE *scrēawa* a shrewmouse]

shrewd *shrōōd*, *adj* showing keen practical judgement, astute; wily, crafty; evil, hurtful, spiteful, ill-natured, ill-conditioned, mischievous (*obs* or *dialect*); severe, hard (*obs*); formidable (*obs*); uncomfortably near the mark; biting, keen, piercing (*archaic*); shrewish, vixenish (*obs*). — *adv* (*Shakesp*) keenly. — *n* **shrewd'ie** (*colloq*) a shrewd person. — *adv* **shrewd'ly**. — *n* **shrewd'ness**. [**shrew**]

Shri. See **Sri**.

shriche-owl. See under **shriek**.

shriech. See **shriek**, **shritch**.

shriek *shrēk*, *n* a shrill outcry; a wild piercing scream; an exclamation mark (*slang*). — *vi* to utter a shriek. — *vt* to utter shriekingly. — Also **shreek** (*Shakesp*, *Spenser*), **shreik** (*Milton*), **shriech** (*Spenser*). — *n* **shriek'er**. — *n* and *adj* **shriek'ing**. — *adv* **shriek'ingly**. — **shriek'-owl**, also (*Spenser*) **shriech-**, **shriche-**, etc, **schreech-** (*Shakesp*) a screech-owl. [Cf **screak**, **screech**]

shrieval *shrē'vl*, *adj* pertaining to a sheriff. — *n* **shriev'alty** the office, term of office, or area of jurisdiction, of a sheriff. [*shrieve*, obs form of **sheriff**]

shrieve *shrēv*. Same as **shrive**.

shrift *shrift*, *n* (*archaic*) *orig* a prescribed penance; absolution; confession; a confessional (*Shakesp*). — **short shrift** short time for confession before execution; summary treatment of a person or a matter. [OE *scrift*, from *scrīfan* to shrive]

shright *shrīt*, (*Spenser*) *n* a shriek. — See also **shritch**. [Perh a misreading of Chaucer, *Troilus* IV, 1147]

shrike[1] *shrīk*, *n* a butcher-bird, any passerine bird of the family *Laniidae*, some species of which prey on smaller birds and small mammals, impaling them on thorns or barbed wire for later consumption. [Perh from OE *scrīc* thrush, MLGer *schrīk* corncrake; cf **shriek**]

shrike[2] *shrīk*, *vi* to shriek (*archaic*); (of birds) to pipe (*obs* or *dialect*). — *n* (*archaic*) a shriek. [Cf **scrike**, **shriek**]

shrill *shril*, *adj* high-pitched and piercing; keen; excessively strident. — *adv* shrilly; often in combination, as in **shrill-shrik'ing** (*Shakesp*). — *n* a piercing sound. — *vt* and *vi* to sound or cry shrilly. — *n* and *adj* **shrill'ing**. — *n* **shrill'ness**. — *adj* **shrill'y**. — *adv* **shril'ly**. — *adj* **shrill-gorged'** (*Shakesp*) shrill-voiced. — *adj* **shrill-tongued'**. — *adj* **shrill-voiced'**. [Cf LGer *schrell*, whence prob Ger *schrill*]

shrimp *shrimp*, *n* a small edible crustacean, *esp* a decapod of *Crangon* or related genera; the colour of a shrimp, a bright pink; a very small or puny person (*colloq*). — *vi* to fish for shrimps. — *n* **shrimp'er**. — *n* and *adj* **shrimp'ing**. — *adj* **shrimp'y**. — **shrimp plant** a small Mexican plant (*Justicia brandegeana*), of the acanthus family with shrimp-like, pendent bracts enclosing small white flowers; **shrimp net**. [Cf **scrimp**, and OE *scrimman* to shrink]

shrine *shrīn*, *n orig* a chest or cabinet; a container for relics or the place in which such a container is kept; the tomb of a saint or other holy person; a place hallowed by its association with a sacred object or person; a niche, alcove or shelf for a religious image; an image (*Shakesp*). — *vt* to enshrine. — *adj* **shrī'nal**. — *adj* **shrīne'like**. [OE *scrīn*, from L *scrīnium* a case for papers, from *scrībere* to write]

shrink *shringk*, *vi* to contract; to become smaller in size or extent; to shrivel; to wither; to dwindle; to give way; to draw back, retreat; to withdraw; to show or feel repugnance or reluctance; to recoil; to shrink-wrap (*colloq*). — *vt* to cause to contract, shrink or dwindle; to withdraw; to fix by allowing to contract: — *pa t* **shrank** or (*old*) **shrunk**; *pa p* **shrunk** or **shrunk'en**. — *n* an act of shrinking; contraction; withdrawal or recoil; a psychiatrist, contracted from **headshrinker** (*slang*, *orig US*). — *adj* **shrink'able**. — *n* **shrink'age** a contraction into a smaller compass; extent of such diminution; in meat marketing, the loss of carcase weight during shipping, preparation for sale, etc; in manufacturing, etc, the loss of goods resulting from pilfering, breakages, etc. — *n* **shrink'er**. — *adj* **shrink'ing**. — *adv* **shrink'ingly**. — *adj* **shrunk** or **shrunk'en** contracted, reduced, shrivelled. — **shrink'pack** a shrink-wrapped package. — *adj* **shrink'-proof** or **shrink-resis'tant** that will not shrink on washing. — **shrink'-resistance**. — *vt* **shrink'-wrap** to package (goods) in a clear plastic film that is subsequently shrunk (eg by heating) so that it fits tightly (also *n*). — **shrinking violet** see under **violet**. [OE *scrincan*, *scranc*, *gescruncen*]

shritch *shrich*, (*obs* or *dialect*) *vi* to shriek, screech (*pa t*, *Spenser* **shright** *shrīt*). — *n* (*Spenser* **shriech**) a shriek. — **shritch'-owl** screech-owl. [Cf **scritch**]

shrive *shrīv*, also (after *Spenser*) **shrieve** *shrēv*, (*RC Church*) *vt* to hear a confession from and give absolution to; to confess; to disburden by confession or otherwise. — *vi* to receive or make confession: — *pa t* **shrōve**, **shrīved** or **shrieved** (*shrēvd*); *pa p* **shriven** (*shriv'ən*), **shrīved** or **shrieved**. — *n* **shrī'ver** a confessor. — *n* **shrī'ving** (*Spenser*) shrift. — **shrī'ving-time** (*Shakesp*) time for confession. [OE *scrīfan* to write, to prescribe penance, from L *scrībere*]

shrivel *shriv'l*, *vi* and *vt* to contract into wrinkles; to lose or cause to lose potency, vitality, etc: — *pr p* **shriv'elling** or (*US*) **shriv'eling**; *pa t* and *pa p* **shriv'elled** or (*US*) **shriv'eled**. [Cf Swed dialect *skryvla* to wrinkle]

shroff *shrof*, (*Anglo-Ind*) *n* in the East, a banker, money-changer, or moneylender; in the Far East, an expert who identifies and separates base coin from that which is genuine. — *vt* to examine or test (money) in order to detect base coin. — *vi* to practise money-changing. — *n* **shroff'age** commission for such examination. [Ar *sarrāf*]

shroud[1] *shrowd*, *n* a garment, clothes (*obs*); a garment or piece of cloth used to wrap a corpse, a winding-sheet; (with *cap*; with **the**) a long piece of linen stained with the imprint of a crucified body, preserved in Turin, Italy, as the shroud of Jesus but shown by scientific tests to be probably a medieval fake; an enveloping or protective covering, screen, shelter, or shade; (in *pl*) a set of ropes from the masthead to a ship's sides to give lateral support to the mast; an extension from the rear of a fixed aerofoil surface covering the leading edge of eg a flap hinged to it (*aeronautics*); a streamlined covering used to protect the payload during launch (*space*); an extension of the metal parts in electrical devices (subject to high voltages) to protect the insulating dielectric (*telecomm*). — *vt* to enclose in a shroud; to cover, envelop; to hide; to shelter. — *vi* to take shelter. — *adj* **shroud'ed**. — *n* and *adj* **shroud'ing**. — *adj* **shroud'less** without a shroud. — *adj* **shroud'y** giving shelter. — *adj* **shroud-laid'** (of a rope) having four strands twisted round a central strand or heart. —

shroud line any one of the cords of a parachute by which the load is suspended from the canopy. [OE *scrūd*; ON *skrūth* clothing, gear, from Gmc base *skraud-*, *skreud-*, *skrud-* cut; see also **shred**]

shroud[2] *shrowd*, (*dialect*) *n* (*usu* in *pl*) a branch; loppings. — *vt* to lop. [Prob same as **shroud**[1] from the root meaning of cut]

shrove *shrōv*, *pa t* of **shrive**.

Shrove *shrōv*, *n* (*obs*) Shrovetide. — *vi* (*obs*) **shrove** to celebrate Shrovetide (*go a-shroving*, to go round singing for money at Shrovetide). — **Shrove'tide** the days preceding Ash Wednesday; **Shrove Tuesday** the day before Ash Wednesday. [Related to OE *scrīfan* to shrive]

shrow *shrō*, **shrowd** *shrōd*, (*Shakesp*). Forms of **shrew**, **shrewd**.

shrub[1] *shrub*, *n* a low woody plant smaller than a tree, a bush, *esp* one with little or no trunk; a scrub (*obs*). — *vt* to lop; to cudgel (*obs*). — *adj* **shrubb'eried**. — *n* **shrubb'ery** a plantation or growth of shrubs. — *n* **shrubb'iness**. — *adj* **shrubb'y** of, like, having the character of, a shrub; covered with shrubs. — *adj* **shrub'less**. — *adj* **shrub'like**. [OE *scrybb* scrub]

shrub[2] *shrub*, *n* a mixed drink of lemon or other citrus fruit juice, sugar, spices and a spirit, *esp* rum; a cordial of fruit juice (eg raspberry) and vinegar (*US*). [Ar *sharāb*, for *shurb* drink, cf **sherbet**, **syrup**]

shrug *shrug*, *vi* to shudder, shiver (*rare* or *obs*); to raise (and lower) the shoulders in an abrupt movement, a gesture expressive of doubt, indifference, etc. — *vt* to shrink; to raise (the shoulders) in a shrug: — *pr p* **shrugg'ing**; *pa t* and *pa p* **shrugged**. — *n* a jerk; an expressive raising of the shoulders. — **shrug off** to shake off, get rid of; to show indifference to or dismiss as unimportant (eg responsibility, a difficulty). [Origin obscure]

shrunk, **shrunken**. See under **shrink**.

sht. *abbrev*: sheet(s).

shtchi. See **shchi**.

shtetl or **shtetel** *shtet'əl*, *n* formerly, a Jewish community in an Eastern European town or village: — *pl* **shtet'lach** (*-läk*) or **shtetls**. [Yiddish, small town, from MHGer *stetel*, dimin of *stat* town]

shtg. *abbrev*: shortage.

shtick, **schtick** or **schtik** *shtik*, (*slang*) *n* a familiar routine, line of chat, etc, adopted by, and associated with, a particular comedian, etc; an attention-catching device. [Yiddish *shtik* piece, part, slice, from MHGer *stücke*]

shtook, **schtook**, **shtuck** or **schtuck** *shto͝ok*, (*slang*) *n* trouble, bother. — **in shtook**, etc (*slang*) in trouble. [Origin unknown]

shtoom, **schtoom**, **shtum**, **shtumm** or **stumm** *shto͞om*, (*slang*) *adj* silent, dumb, quiet. — **keep** or **stay shtoom**, etc remain silent, be quiet. [Yiddish, from Ger *stumm* silent]

shtup *shto͝op*, (*slang*) *vt* and *vi* to have sexual intercourse (with), to copulate: — *pr p* **shtupp'ing**; *pa t* and *pa p* **shtupped**. [Yiddish, from Ger *stupsen* to push]

shubunkin *sho͞o-bung'kin* or *-bo͝ong'*, *n* a type of variegated large-finned goldfish. [Jap]

shuck *shuk*, (*NAm*) *n* a husk, shell, or pod. — *vt* to remove the shuck from; to strip or peel off or away, to discard (with *off*). — *n* **shuck'er**. — *n* **shuck'ing**. — *interj* **shucks** (*slang*) a mild exclamation expressive of disappointment, irritation or embarrassment. — **not worth shucks** (*slang*) worthless. [Origin unknown]

shudder *shud'ər*, *vi* to shiver, eg from cold or horror; to vibrate. — *n* a tremor caused by cold or horror; an act or instance of vibrating or trembling. — *n* and *adj* **shudd'ering**. — *adv* **shudd'eringly**. — *adj* **shudd'ersome**. — *adj* **shudd'ery**. [From ME *shod(d)er*, from MLGer *schöderen*; cf OHGer *skutten* to shake]

shuffle *shuf'l*, *vt* to mix at random (*esp* playing-cards); to jumble; to put (*out*, *in*, *off*, etc) surreptitiously, evasively, scramblingly, or in confusion; to manipulate unfairly; to patch up; to drag (the feet) along without lifting them clear; to perform with such motions. — *vi* to mix cards in a pack; to scramble; to behave shiftily; to shift ground; to evade fair questions; to move by dragging the feet along; to shamble; to dance the shuffle. — *n* act of shuffling; a shuffling gait or dance; an evasion or artifice. — *n* **shuff'ler**. — *n* and *adj* **shuff'ling**. — *adv* **shuff'lingly**. — **shuff'le-cap** an old game in which the stake is money shaken in a cap. — **shuffle off** to thrust aside, put off, wriggle out of. [Early modern; cf **scuffle**, **shove**, **shovel**; LGer *schüffeln*]

shuffleboard. See **shovelboard**.

shufti or **shufty** *shuf'ti*, (*colloq*) *n* a look, glance. [Colloq Ar *shufti* have you seen?, from *shaffa* to see]

shul *sho͞ol*, *n* a synagogue: — *pl* **shuln** or **shuls**. [Yiddish, from MHGer *schuol* school]

shun *shun*, *vt* to avoid deliberately: — *pr p* **shunn'ing**; *pa t* and *pa p* **shunned**. — *adj* **shun'less** (*Shakesp*) not to be shunned. — *adj* **shunn'able**. — *n* **shunn'er**. — **upon the shun** bent on evading notice. [OE *scunian*]

'shun *shun*, (*military colloq*) *interj* attention!

shunamitism *sho͞o'nə-mit-izm*, *n* rejuvenation of an old man by means of a young woman. [Abishag the *Shunammite* (I Kings 1. 3)]

shunt *shunt*, *vt* and *vi* to turn or move aside; to move (railway rolling-stock) to another track, *esp* a side track; to divert or be diverted by means of a shunt (*electronics* or *med*). — *vt* to bypass; to sidetrack; to shelve; to get rid of; to crash (a car) (*slang*). — *vi* (*colloq*) to be off. — *n* an act of shunting; a conductor connected in parallel with eg a measuring instrument, diverting part of an electric current; a switch; a passage (resulting from congenital abnormality or created surgically) in which two anatomical channels are connected and blood (or, in the brain, cerebrospinal fluid) is diverted from one to the other (*med*); a road accident, crash, mishap (*orig motor-racing slang*). — *n* **shunt'er**. — *n* and *adj* **shunt'ing**. — *adj* **shunt'-wound** (of an electric motor, etc) having the field and armature circuits connected in parallel. — **shunt'-winding** [Perh connected with **shun**]

shura *sho͞o'rə*, *n* in Afghanistan, a traditional consultative or law-making council.

shush *shush*, *vt* and *vi* to (cause to) be quiet. — *interj* hush! be quiet!

shut *shut*, *vt* to place so as to stop an opening; to stop or cover the opening of; to lock; to fasten; to bar; to forbid entrance into; to bring together the parts or outer parts of; to confine; to catch or pinch in a fastening; to end the operations of (a business, etc); to shoot (eg a bolt; *obs*). — *vi* to become closed; to be capable of being closed; to close in; (of a business, etc) to cease to operate: — *pr p* **shutt'ing**; *pa t* and *pa p* **shut**. — *adj* made fast; closed; rid (with *of*; *colloq*). — *n* an act or time of shutting. — **shut'down** a temporary closing, eg of a factory; the reduction of power in a nuclear reactor to the minimum, *usu* carried out as a safety or emergency measure; **shut'-eye** (*colloq*) sleep; **shut'-in** (*NAm*) a disabled person confined indoors; **shut'-off** a device that stops the flow or operation of something; a stoppage. — *adj* **shut'-out** intended to exclude, as (*bridge*) a bid to deter opponents from bidding (also *n*). — **shut away** to keep hidden or repressed; to isolate; to confine; **shut down** to close down, or stop the operation of, often temporarily; **shut in** to enclose, to confine; to settle down, or fall (said, eg, of evening); **shut off** to exclude; to switch off; to stop the flow of; **shut one's eyes to** to ignore; to refuse to acknowledge (*esp* something disagreeable); **shut out** to prevent from entering; to hide or screen from view; to prevent (the opposing team) from scoring; **shut up** to close finally or completely; to confine; to cease speaking (*colloq*); to reduce to silence. [OE *scyttan* to bar; cf *scēotan*, to shoot]

shutter *shut'ər*, *n* something or someone that shuts; an external or internal cover for a window, *esp* one of a (*usu* wooden or metal) hinged pair; a device for regulating the opening of an aperture, as in photography and cinematography; a removable cover, gate, or piece of shuttering. — *vt* to close or fit with a shutter or shutters. — *adj* **shutt'ered**. — *n* **shutt'ering** closing and fitting with a shutter; material used as shutters; temporary support for concrete work. — *n* **shutter'bug** (*slang*) a camera or photographic enthusiast. [**shut**]

shuttle[1] *shut'l*, *n* an instrument used for shooting the thread of the woof between the threads of the warp in weaving or through the loop of thread in a sewing-machine; anything that makes similar movements; rapid movement to and fro between two points; a shuttle service or the vehicle, craft, etc, used for this; a shuttlecock — *vt* and *vi* to move to and fro like a shuttle; to move or travel regularly between two points. — *adv* **shutt'lewise** to and fro like a shuttle. — **shutt'lecock** a lightweight cone consisting of a rounded cork stuck with feathered flights (or a moulded plastic version of this) to be driven to and fro with battledores or badminton rackets; the game played with battledores; something tossed to and fro repeatedly. — *vt* and *vi* to shuttle. — **shuttle diplomacy** the exercise, undertaken by an intermediary, of travelling to and fro between two heads of states, in order to bring about agreement between them; **shuttle service** a train or other transport service moving constantly between two points. [OE *scytel* dart; *scēotan* to shoot; Dan and Swed *skyttel*]

shuttle[2] *shut'l* or **shottle** *shot'l*, (*esp Scot*) *n* a small drawer, *esp* in a cabinet or chest. [Perh **shut**; perh OE *scyttel* bolt, bar]

shwa. See **schwa**.

shy[1] *shī*, *adj* shrinking from notice or approach; bashful; chary; disposed to avoidance (with *of*; also used in combination, as in *workshy*); secluded; warily reluctant; unproductive; scanty; short, lacking (with *of*) (*NAm colloq*); of doubtful repute; (*esp* in poker) short in payment: — *compar* **shy'er** or **shi'er**, *superl* **shy'est** or **shi'est**. — *vi* to recoil, to shrink (with *away*, *off*); to start aside, like a horse from fear. — *vt* to shun: — *3rd pers sing* **shies** (*shīz*); *pr p* **shy'ing**; *pa t* and *pa p* **shied** (*shīd*). — *n* a sudden swerving aside: — *pl* **shies**. — *n* **shi'er** or **shy'er**. — *adj* **shy'ish**. — *adv* **shy'ly** or **shi'ly**. — *n* **shy'ness** or (*obs*) **shi'ness**. — **shy'-cock** a cock not easily caught. — **fight shy of** to shrink from. [OE *scēoh* timid; cf **skeigh**, MHGer *schiech*]

shy[2] *shī*, *vt* and *vi* to fling, toss: — *3rd pers sing* **shies**; *pr p* **shy'ing**; *pa t* and *pa p* **shied**. — *n* a throw; a fling; a gibe; an attempt, shot; a thing to shy at: — *pl* **shies**. — *n* **shi'er** or **shy'er**. [Origin obscure]

Shylock *shī'lok*, *n* a ruthless creditor; an avaricious, grasping person. [From Shylock in *The Merchant of Venice*]

shyster *shī'stər*, (*slang*) *n* an unscrupulous or disreputable lawyer; an unscrupulous practitioner in any profession or business. [Appar from **shy**[1] in sense of 'of doubtful repute']

SI *abbrev*: Système International (d'Unités), the modern scientific system of units (**SI units**), used in the measurement of all physical quantities, the principal units being the metre, kilogram, second, ampere, kelvin, candela, and mole.

si *sē*, (*music*) *n* the seventh note of the scale, a later addition to the six Aretinian syllables, but superseded by *ti*. [Perhaps from the initial letters of *S*ancte *I*oannes, the last line of the hymn from which the Aretinian (qv) syllables were taken]

sial *sī'al* or *-əl*, *n* the lighter upper part of the earth's continental crust composed of rocks rich in *si*lica and *al*umina. — Also **sal** (*sal*). — *adj* **sial'ic**.

siala- *sī-ə-lə-* or *sī-al'ə-*, or **sialo-** *sī-ə-lō-*, *-lə-*, or *sī-al'ō-*, *-lə-*, or *sī-ə-lo'*, or **sial-** *sī'əl-*, *sī-al'-*, *combining form* denoting saliva. — *adj* **sial'ic** of or relating to saliva. — *adj* **sī'aloid** resembling saliva. — *n* **sialagogue** or **sialogogue** (*sī-al'ə-gog*; Gr *agōgos* leading) anything that stimulates a flow of saliva. — Also *adj*. — *adj* **sialagog'ic** or **sialogog'ic**. — *n* **sial'ogram** an X-ray of the salivary tract. — *n* **sialog'raphy**. — *n* **sial'olith** (Gr *lithos* a stone) a calculus in a salivary gland. — *n* **sialorrhoe'a** (Gr *rhoiā* flow) excessive secretion of saliva, ptyalism. — **sialic acid** (*biochem*) any of a group of amino sugars that form covalently linked sugar residues in glycoproteins. [Gr *sialon* saliva]

sialic. See under **sial** and **siala-**.

sialon *sī'ə-lon*, *n* any of various ceramic materials consisting of silicon, aluminium, oxygen, and nitrogen. [From the chemical symbols of the constituent elements, *Si*, *Al*, *O*, *N*]

siamang *sē'ə-mang* or *syä'mang*, *n* a large black gibbon, *Symphalangus* (or *Hylobates*) *syndactylus*, found in Sumatra and the Malay Peninsula. [Malay]

Siamese *sī-ə-mēz'*, *adj* of *Siam*, the former name of Thailand. — *n* a native, or citizen, or the language of Siam; a Siamese cat. — *vt* **siamese'** or **-eze'** to join (eg pipes) in a way suggestive of the union of Siamese twins (*old*). — **Siamese cat** a domestic fawn-coloured cat, with blue eyes and a small head, probably descended from the jungle cat of India, Africa, etc; **Siamese fighting fish** a brilliantly-coloured freshwater fish of the genus Anabas (*Betta splendens*) of SE Asia — the males have elongated sail-like fins and are extremely pugnacious; **Siamese twins** *orig* a set of Chinese twins (1811–74), born in Siam, joined from birth by a fleshy ligature; any set of twins thus joined; inseparables (*fig*).

SIB *abbrev*: Securities and Investments Board.

sib (*Spenser* **sybbe**, *Scott* **sibb**) *sib*, *n* kinship (*rare*); kindred (*rare*); a kinsman or kinswoman; a blood relation; a brother or sister; a group descended from one ancestor (*anthropol* or *genetics*). — *adj* akin, related by blood; (of canaries) inbred. — *n* **sib'ling** a person who has a parent or an ancestor in common with oneself; a person who has both parents in common with oneself, a brother or sister. — Also *adj* — *n* **sib'ship** a group of sibs; blood-relationship; clan-relationship. [OE *sibb* relationship, *gesibb* related; Ger *Sippe*]

sibilate *sib'i-lāt*, *vt* and *vi* to pronounce (words) with, or produce, a hissing sound. — *n* **sib'ilance** or **sib'ilancy**. — *adj* **sib'ilant** hissing; pronounced with a hissing sound. — *n* a hissing consonant sound, as of *s* and *z*. — *adv* **sib'ilantly**. — *n* **sibilā'tion**. — *n* **sib'ilator**. — *adj* **sib'ilatory** (*-ə-tə-ri*) or **sib'ilous**. [L *sībilāre*, *-ātum* to hiss]

sibling. See under **sib**.

sibyl *sib'il*, *n* (also with *cap*) any of several female oracles or prophets of ancient Rome, Greece, Babylonia, Egypt, etc, each believed to be inspired by an individual deity; loosely, a prophetess, witch or female fortune-teller; an old crone. — *adj* **sib'ylline** (*-īn*). — *adj* **sibyll'ic** or **sibyl'ic**. — *n* **Sib'yllist** a believer in the Sibylline prophecies. — **Sibylline Books** prophetic books offered to Tarquinius Superbus by the Cumaean Sibyl, of which he ultimately bought three for the price he had refused to give for nine, these three being held in the Capitol and referred to by the ancient Roman senate in times of emergency and disaster; a later set made after the first collection was destroyed by fire in 83BC. [Gr *Sibylla*]

sic[1] *sik*, *adj* a Scots form of **such**. — *adj* **sicc'an** (for *sic kin* such kind) such; (in exclamations) what, what a. — *adj* **sic'like** suchlike. — *adv* in like manner.

sic[2] *sik* or *sēk*, (*L*) so, thus — printed within brackets in quoted matter to show that the original is being faithfully reproduced even though incorrect or apparently so. — **sic passim** (*pas'im*) so throughout, a phrase used to indicate that a word, spelling, etc has been printed in the same form throughout in a book, article, etc.

sic[3]. Same as **sick**[2].

Sican *sik'ən*, *n* a native of Sicily. — *n* and *adj* **Sicanian** (*-ā'ni-ən*). [L *Sīcānus*, *Sıcānus*, from Gr *Sıkanos*]

siccan. See under **sic**[1].

siccar. Same as **sicker**.
siccative *sik'ə-tiv*, *adj* drying. — *n* a drying agent. — *n* **siccity** (*sik'si-ti*) dryness. [L *siccus* dry]
sice[1] *sīs* or **size** *sīz*, *n* the number six in a game of dice. [OFr *sis*]
sice[2]. Same as **syce**.
Sicel *sis'əl* or *sik'əl* or **Siceliot** *si-sel'i-ot* or *-kel'*. See **Sikel**.
sich *sich*, *adj* an archaic form of **such**.
Sicilian *si-sil'yən* or *-sil'i-ən*, *adj* of *Sicily*; denoting a cloth of cotton and mohair. — *n* **siciliano** (*si-sil-yä'nō*) a Sicilian pastoral dance, dance tune, or movement, in 6-8 or 12-8 time: — *pl* **sicilia'nos**. — **Sicilian Vespers** the massacre of the French in Sicily in 1282, beginning, according to a late tradition, at the first stroke of the vesper-bell.
siciliana *sē-chē-lyä'nä*, (*Ital*) *n* a siciliano: — *pl* **sicilia'ne** (*-nā*). [Ital, Sicilian]
sicilienne *si-si-lyen'*, (*Fr*) *n* a ribbed silk fabric; a siciliano. [Fr, Sicilian]
sick[1] *sik*, *adj* unwell, ill; diseased; vomiting or inclined to vomit; pining; mortified; thoroughly wearied; out of condition; sickly; of or for the people who are ill; (of humour, comedy, a joke, etc) gruesome, macabre, tending to exploit topics not normally joked about, such as illness, death, etc; disappointed (*colloq*). — *vi* (*Shakesp*) to grow sick. — *vt* (*colloq*) to vomit (with *up*). — *vt* **sick'en** to make sick; to disgust; to make weary of anything. — *vi* to become sick; to be disgusted (with *at*); to become disgusting or tedious; to become weakened. — *n* **sick'ener**. — *n* and *adj* **sick'ening**. — *adv* **sick'eningly**. — *n* **sick'ie** (*colloq*) a day's sick leave (*Austr* and *NZ*); a sick person, whether mentally or physically (*NAm*). — *adj* **sick'ish**. — *adv* **sick'ishly**. — *n* **sick'ishness**. — *adj* **sick'lied**. — *adv* **sick'lily**. — *n* **sick'liness**. — *adj* **sick'ly** inclined to be ailing; feeble; languid; pallid; suggestive of sickness; slightly or insipidly sickening; mawkish; of sickness or the sick. — *adv* in a sick manner; feebly. — *vt* (*obs*) to make sickly-looking, impart an unhealthy hue to; to make sentimental or mawkish. — *n* **sick'ness**. — *n* **sick'o** (chiefly *NAm*) a mentally ill person; a crazy or deranged person; a pervert. — *adj* perverted; macabre. — **sick bag** a small paper bag, provided for each passenger on an aircraft, which may be used by those suffering from travel sickness to vomit into; **sick bay** a compartment for sick and wounded on a ship (also **sick berth**); an infirmary or sanatorium at a boarding-school, etc; **sick'bed** a bed on which someone lies sick; **sick benefit** or **sickness benefit** a benefit paid to someone who is out of work through illness; **sick building** a building in which inadequate ventilation or air-conditioning causes its occupants to experience a set of symptoms, such as headaches, dizziness and general fatigue (**sick-building syndrome**). — *adj* **sick'-fallen** (*archaic*) struck with sickness; **sick-feath'ered** (of birds) with immature feathers at moulting. — **sick flag** a quarantine flag; **sick headache** a headache with nausea; **sick leave** leave of absence owing to sickness; **sick list** a list of the sick. — *adj* **sick'-listed** entered on the sick list. — *adj* **sick'-making** (*colloq*) sickening. — **sick note** (*informal*) in Britain, a note (signed either by the employee or the employee's doctor) given to an employer to certify that absence from work was due to illness; **sick'nurse** a nurse who attends the sick; **sick'nurs'ing**; **sick'-out** (*NAm* and *Caribbean*) a form of industrial action in which all workers at a particular factory, workplace, etc, absent themselves simultaneously on the pretext of sickness; **sick'room** or **sick chamber** a room to which one is confined by sickness. — *adj* **sick-thought'ed** (*Shakesp*) lovesick. — *adj* **sick-tired'**. — **be sick** to vomit; **sick as a dog** (*colloq*) vomiting profusely and unrestrainedly; **sick as a parrot** (*colloq*) extremely disappointed; **sicken for** to show early symptoms of; **sick (and tired) of** tired of; wearied to the point of disgust by; **sick to one's stomach** about to vomit. [OE *sēoc*; Ger *siech*, Du *ziek*]
sick[2] *sik*, *vt* to set upon, chase; to incite (eg a dog) to make an attack (on). [A dialect variant of **seek**]
sicker or **siccar** *sik'ər*, *adj* (*archaic* and *Scot*) sure, certain, firm. — *adv* (*archaic*) surely, certainly. — *adv* **sick'erly** (*Scot*). — *n* **sick'erness** (*Scot*). [OE *sicor*, from L *sēcūrus*; Ger *sicher*]
sickle[1] *sik'l*, *n* an implement with a curved blade and a short handle, for cutting crops, etc, a reaping-hook; a sickle feather. — *adj* **sick'led** bearing a sickle. — **sick'lebill** a bird of paradise, humming-bird, etc, with a sickle-shaped bill; **sickle-cell** (or **-celled**) **anaemia** (also called **sickle'mia**) a severe hereditary anaemia, affecting mainly Black people, in which the production of abnormal haemoglobin causes the red blood cells to become distorted into a sickle shape — these abnormal cells are then destroyed by the body's defence systems resulting in anaemia; **sickle-cell trait** a mild, *usu* symptomless, condition with some of the characteristics of sickle-cell anaemia; **sickle feather** a cock's elongated tail feather; **sick'leman** a reaper. — *adj* **sick'le-shaped**. [OE *sicol*, *sicel*, perh from L *secula*, from *secāre* to cut]
sickle[2] *sik'l*, (*Shakesp*) *n* a shekel. [OFr *sicle*, from Heb *sheqel*]
Siculian *si-kū'li-ən*, *adj* of the *Sicul̄ī* (*L*), or Sikels, an ancient people that colonized Sicily from Italy. — Also *n*.
Sida *sī'də*, *n* any plant of the Queensland hemp genus *Sida*, of the mallow family, tropical herbs yielding a fibre. [Gr *sidē* a plant name]
sidalcea *si-dal'si-ə*, *n* a plant of the genus *Sidalcea* of the mallow family, a herbaceous perennial with tall spikes of white, pink, or purple flowers. [Mod L from Gr *sidē* a kind of plant, and *alkea* mallow]
siddhi *sid'i*, *n* (in Hinduism, Buddhism and Jainism) the supernatural powers that come with the spiritual perfection attained by meditation, etc. — Also with *cap* and in *pl*. — *n* **sidd'ha** someone who has attained perfection (also **sid'ha**). — **siddha yoga** see **maha yoga**. [Sans, fulfilment]
siddur *si'dōōr*, (*Judaism*) *n* a Jewish prayer book used in daily liturgy: — *pl* **siddur'im** or **-im'**. [Heb *siddūr* order, arrangement]
side[1] *sīd*, *n* a line or surface forming part of a boundary; the part near such a boundary; a surface or part turned in some direction, *esp* one more or less upright, or one regarded as right or left, not front or back, top or bottom; the part of the body between armpit and hip; half of a carcase divided along the medial plane; either of the extended surfaces of anything in the form of a sheet; a page; a portion of space lying in this or that direction from a boundary or a point; the father's or mother's part of a genealogy; a department or division, eg of a school or prison; an aspect; a direction; a particular district; a border or bank; the slope of a hill; the wall of a vessel or cavity; any party, team, interest, or opinion opposed to another; part (as in *on my side*, for my part); the womb (*Milton*); a spin given to a ball causing it to swerve and regulating its angle of rebound (*billiards*, etc); a pretentious air, arrogance (*slang*); a speech in a play; a television channel (*colloq*). — *adj* at or toward the side; sideways; subsidiary. — *vi* to ally oneself with a particular side in an argument, etc, to take sides (with *with*). — *vt* to cut into sides; to thrust or set aside; to adjudge or assign to one side or other (*Shakesp*); to assign in this way to (*Shakesp*); to be on the side next to (*archaic*). — *adj* **sid'ed** having sides; flattened on one or more sides. — *combining form* **-sided** having a (specified) number or kind of sides, as in *three-sided*, *many-sided*, *unequal-sided*. — *adj* and *adv* **side'ling** sideways; with a slope. — *adj* **side'long** oblique; sloping; tilted; sideways. — *adv* in the direction of the side; obliquely; on the side. — *n* **sid'er** someone who takes a side. — *adj* and *adv* **side'ward**. — *adv* **side'wards**. — *adj* and *adv* **side'ways** or **side'wise** toward or on one side. — *n* **sid'ing** a short railway track for shunting or lying by. — *n* and *adj* taking sides. —

side'arm (*usu* in *pl*) a weapon worn at the side or in a belt; **side'band** (*radio*) a frequency band above or below the carrier frequency, containing additional frequencies constituting the information to be conveyed, introduced by modulation; **side'bar** (*NAm*) a short newspaper article alongside, and dealing in detail with some aspect of, a longer article; **side'-bar** (in South Africa) solicitors, as opposed to barristers (who belong to the bar); **side'board** a side table (*archaic*); a piece of dining-room furniture for holding plates, etc, often with drawers and cupboards; a board at the side, eg of a cart; (in *pl*) side whiskers; **side'bones** ossifications of the lateral cartilages of a horse's hoof; **side box** a box at the side of a theatre; **side'burns** short side whiskers, a modification of the rather more extensive growth pioneered by General *Burnside* of America; **side'car** a jaunting car; a small car attached to the side of a motorcycle *usu* for the carriage of a passenger; a kind of cocktail consisting of brandy, orange liqueur and lemon juice; **side chain** (*chem*) a chain of atoms forming a branch attached to a ring; **side comb** a small comb in the hair at the side; **side cutting** an excavation along the side of a railway or canal to get material for an embankment; **side dish** a supplementary dish; **side door** a door at the side of a building or of a main door. — *vt* **side'-dress** to place fertilizers on or in the soil near the roots of (a crop, etc). — **side drum** a small double-headed drum with snares, slung from the drummer's side or from a stand; **side effect** a subsidiary effect; an effect, often undesirable, additional to the effect sought; **side glance** a sidelong glance; a passing allusion; **side issue** something subordinate, incidental, not important in comparison with main issue; **sidekick** (*colloq*) a partner, deputy; a special friend; **side'light** a light carried on the side of a vessel or vehicle; a window above or at the side of a door; a window, as opposed to a skylight; light coming from the side; any incidental illustration; **side'line** a line attached to the side of anything; a branch route or track; a subsidiary trade or activity; (in *pl*) (the area just outside) the lines marking the edge of a football pitch, etc, hence, a peripheral area to which spectators or non-participants are confined. — *vt* to remove (a player) from a team and confine to the sidelines; to suspend from normal operation or activity; to confine to a peripheral area; to relegate (someone) to a minor, peripheral position, prevent his or her participation in the main or most important area of activity, *esp* in business. — *adj* **side'lined**. — **side'lock** a lock of hair at the side of the head; **side'man** (*jazz*) one of the members of a band or orchestra, other than the leader or featured artist, who performs occasional solo passages demonstrating virtuosity on a particular instrument: — *pl* **side'men**; **side'note** a comment written in a margin. — *adj* and *adv* **side-on'** with a side facing forwards or leading. — **side'path** a byway, footpath or sidewalk; **side plate** a small plate used for food, such as bread or salad, which accompanies the main meal; **side post** a doorpost; a post supporting a roof at the side; **side'road** a by-road; **side'saddle** a saddle designed for women wearing long riding habits, on which the rider sits with both legs on the same side (also *adv*); **side'saddle flower** a N American pitcher plant, *Sarracenia*; **side'shoot** (*bot*); **side'show** an exhibition subordinate to a larger one; any subordinate or incidental activity; **side'slip** an oblique offshoot; a bastard (*obs*); a skid; a lateral movement of an aircraft; a side-on downward slide (*skiing*). — *vi* to slip sideways. — **sides'man** a deputy churchwarden; a partisan (*archaic*). — *adj* **side'-splitting** extremely funny, making one laugh till one's sides ache. — **side'step** a step taken to one side; a step attached to the side. — *vi* to step aside. — *vt* to avoid, as by a step aside. — *adj* **side'stream** (of exhaled cigarette, cigar or pipe smoke) that which is inhaled involuntarily by non-smokers. — **side'street** a minor street, *esp* if opening off a main street; **side'stroke** a stroke given sideways; a stroke performed by a swimmer lying on his or her side; **side'swipe** a blow dealt from the side, not struck head-on; a criticism made in passing, incidentally to the main topic. — *vt* to deal (someone) a sideswipe. — *n* **side'swiper**. — **side table** a table used as a sideboard, or placed against the wall, or to the side of the main table; **side'track** a railway siding. — *vt* to divert or turn aside; to shelve. — **side view** a view on or from one side; **side'walk** (*NAm*) a pavement or footpath; **side'wall** the side portion of a tyre, between tread and wheel rim. — *adj* **side'-wheel** with paddle wheels at the side. — **side'wheeler** a side-wheel paddle steamer; **side whiskers** hair grown by a man down either side of the face, in front of the ears; **side wind** a lateral wind; indirect means; **side'winder** a rattlesnake (*Crotalus cerastes*) of the southern US that progresses by lateral looping motions; the name of an air-to-air missile directed at its target by means of a homing device. — **bit on the side** see under **bit**[1]; **choose sides** to pick teams; **get on the right** (or **wrong**) **side of** to gain (or lose) the regard, approval, favour, etc of; **let the side down** to fail one's colleagues, associates, etc, by falling below their standard; **on the side** in addition to or apart from ordinary occupation, income, etc, *esp* applied to dishonest or underhand dealings; **on the short, long, tight**, etc, **side** rather too short, long, etc; **put on one side** to shelve; to set apart; **put on side** (*colloq*) to assume pretentious airs; **right** (or **wrong**) **side** the side intended to be turned outward (or inward); **side by side** close together; abreast; **split one's sides** see under **split**; **take sides** to range oneself with one party or other; **the other side** the spiritual world, to which one passes after death; **this side of** between here and (somewhere specified); short of. [OE *sīde*, from Ger *Seite*, Du *zijde*]

side[2] *sīd*, (now *dialect*; *Shakesp*) *adj* long. — *adj* and *adv* **side'long** (*Spenser*). [OE *sīd* ample]

sidereal *sī-dē'ri-əl*, *adj* of, like, or relating to the stars. — *adj* **sideral** (*sid'ər-əl*) sent from the stars, said *esp* of a malign influence. — *vt* **sid'erate** to blast or strike. — *n* **siderā'tion** (*now rare*) a blast, blight, or stroke; sudden paralysis of (any part of) the body; erysipelas. — *n* **sid'erostat** a mirror, or telescope with a mirror, for reflecting the rays of a star in a constant direction, on the principle of the coelostat. — **sidereal day** the time the earth takes to make a revolution on its axis, relative to the time between two successive transits of a particular star; **sidereal month** see under **month**; **sidereal time** time based on the sidereal day; **sidereal year** see under **year**. [L *sīdus*, *sīderis* a star, constellation]

sidero- *sid'ə-rō-* or *-rə* or **sider-** *sid'ər-*, *combining form* denoting iron. — *n* **siderite** (*sid'ə-rīt*) chalybite, or ferrous carbonate, one of the ores of iron; a meteorite mainly of metallic iron. — *adj* **sideritic** (*-it'ik*). — *n* **sid'erolite** (Gr *lithos* stone) a meteorite made up partly of stone and partly of iron. — *n* **sideropēn'ia** (*med*) deficiency of iron. — *n* **sid'erophile** (*geol*) an element with a weak affinity for oxygen and sulphur but soluble in molten iron, whose geochemical distribution is influenced by this quality (also *adj*). — *adj* **siderophil'ic**. — *n* **siderō'sis** lung disease caused by breathing in iron or other metal particles. [Gr *sidēros* iron]

siderostat. See under **sidereal**.

sidesman, **siding**, etc. See under **side**[1].

sidha. See under **siddhi**.

sidle *sīd'l*, *vi* to go or edge along (sideways), *esp* in a furtive or ingratiating manner. [Prob back-formation from *sideling* sideways]

SIDS *abbrev*: sudden infant death syndrome.

siege *sēj*, *n* the act or process of surrounding a town or fortress, cutting off its supply lines and subjecting it to persistent attack with the intention of forcing surrender by its defenders and capturing it; any persistent attack, offensive, attempt to gain control, etc; a long period of persistent illness or troubles; a seat or throne (*archaic*); rank, distinction or class (*obs*); a privy (*obs*); dung (*Shakesp*); a mason's or bricklayer's workbench (*build-*

ing); the floor of a pot furnace or tank furnace (*glass*); a company of herons or bitterns (also **sedge**). — *vt* to besiege. — *n* **sieg'er** a besieger. — **siege'-artillery** or **siege'-gun** heavy artillery or a gun designed for use in sieges rather than in the field; **siege basket** a gabion; **siege'craft** the art of the besieger; **siege economy** an economy in which imports are restricted in order to protect national industries and production; **siege mentality** a mental state in which one imagines one is constantly under attack; **siege piece** a coin, generally of imperfect workmanship, issued in a besieged place; a siege-gun; **siege train** a train of artillery for besieging a place; **siege'works** a besieger's engineering works. — **lay siege to** to besiege; **state of siege** a condition of suspension of civil law or its subordination to military law. [OFr *sege* (Fr *siège*) seat, from L *sēdēs* seat]

Sieg heil *sēg hīl*, (*Ger*) victory hail — a Nazi salute.

sield *sēld*. A Spenserian spelling of **ceiled**.

siemens *sē'menz*, *n* the unit of electrical conductance (an SI additional unit; *abbrev* **S**), the equivalent of mho and reciprocal of ohm. [After Sir William *Siemens* (1823–83), German-born British inventor and industrialist]

sien *sī'ən*, (*Shakesp*) *n*. Same as **scion**.

Sienese or **Siennese** *sē-ə-nēz'*, *adj* of *Siena* (also Sienna) or its school of painting. — *n* a native of Siena. — *n* **sienna** (*sē-en'ə*) a fine pigment made from ferruginous ochreous earth, browny-yellow when *raw*, warm reddish-brown when *burnt* (ie roasted); its colour.

sient *sī'ənt*, (*archaic*) *n*. Same as **scion**.

sierra *si-er'ə*, *n* a mountain range, *esp* in Spanish-speaking countries and the US. — *adj* **sierr'an**. [Sp, from L *serra* saw]

siesta *si-es'tə*, *n* a midday or afternoon nap. [Sp, from L *sexta* (*hōra*) sixth (hour)]

sieth. A Shakespearian spelling of **scythe**.

sieve *siv*, *n* a utensil with a meshed or perforated bottom for sifting or straining, generally finer than a riddle; a refuse-basket (*Shakesp*). — *vt* and *vi* to sift. — **sieve plate** (*bot*) a perforated area by which a sieve tube connects with another; **sieve tube** (*bot*) a conducting element in phloem, consisting of rows of thin-walled cells with perforations. — **sieve of Eratosthenes** (*er-ə-tos'then-ēz*; *math*) a method of finding prime numbers, by listing all positive integers from 2 up to some given number, leaving the first number, 2, but crossing out all its multiples, leaving the second remaining number, 3, but crossing out all its multiples, and so on; **have a head** (or **memory**) **like a sieve** to be very forgetful. [OE *sife*; Ger *Sieb*]

sievert *sē'vərt*, *n* the SI unit (*abbrev* **Sv**) of radiation dose equivalent (see under **dose**), equal to one joule per kilogram (or 100 rems). [R M *Sievert* (1896–1966), Swedish physicist]

sifaka *si-fä'kə*, *n* a lemur, typically long-tailed and black and white (genus *Propithecus*), native to Madagascar. [Malagasy]

siffle *sif'l*, *vi* to whistle, hiss. — *n* **siffleur** (*-flœr*) and **siffleuse** (*-flœz*) respectively, a male or female professional whistler. [Fr *siffler*, from L *sībilāre*]

sift *sift*, *vt* to separate eg by passing through a sieve; to remove lumps from in this way; to sprinkle eg from a sieve; to examine closely and discriminatingly. — *vi* to use a sieve; to pass through, or as if through, a sieve, to filter; (with *through*) to go through or investigate item by item. — *n* a sifting. — *n* **sift'er**. — *n* **sift'ing** putting through a sieve; separating or sprinkling by a sieve; (in *pl*) material separated by a sieve and rejected. — *adj* **sift'ing**. — *adv* **sift'ingly**. [OE *siftan*, from *sife* a sieve]

Sig. *abbrev*: signor; signore.

sig. *abbrev*: signature.

sigh *sī*, *vi* to produce a long, deep, audible respiration expressive of yearning, dejection, relief, etc; (of the wind, etc) to make a sound similar to this. — *vt* to utter, regret, while away, bring, or render, with sighs. — *n* an act of, or the sound made by, sighing. — *n* **sigh'er**. — *adj* **sigh'ful**. — *adj* **sigh'ing**. — *adv* **sigh'ingly**. — **sigh for** to yearn for. [Prob a back-formation from the weak pa t of ME *siche*, from OE (strong) *sīcan*; Swed *sucka*]

sight[1] *sīt*, *n* the faculty of seeing, vision; an opportunity or act of seeing; a view, glimpse; estimation, judgement; a beginning or coming to see; an instrumental observation, eg an astronomical altitude observation using sextant and chronometer to determine a ship's position when out of sight of land; visual range; anything that is seen; a spectacle; an object of especial interest; perusal; anything unsightly, odd or ridiculous in appearance; a visor (*Shakesp*); a guide to the eye on a gun or optical or other instrument; a sight-hole; skill, insight (*obs*); a great many or a great deal (*colloq*). — *vt* to catch sight of; to view; to take a sight of; to adjust the sights of (a gun, etc). — *vi* to take a sight. — *adj* **sight'able**. — *adj* **sight'ed** having sight, not blind; (of a gun, etc) equipped with a sight. — *combining form* **-sighted** denoting sight of a particular kind, as in *long-sighted*. — *n* **sight'er** a practice shot in archery, etc. — *n* **sight'ing** an instance or the act of taking or catching sight. — *adj* **sight'less** blind; invisible (*Shakesp*); unsightly (*Shakesp*). — *adv* **sight'lessly**. — *n* **sight'lessness**. — *n* **sight'liness**. — *adj* **sight'ly** pleasing to look at; comely. — *adj* **sight'worthy** worth looking at. — **sight'-hole** an aperture for looking through; **sight'line** the line from the eye to the perceived object; (in *pl*) the view afforded, eg of the stage in a theatre or the screen in a cinema; **sight'-player**, **-reader** and **-singer** someone who can read or perform music at first sight of the notes; **sight'-playing**, **-reading** and **-singing**. — *vi* and *vt* **sight'-read**. — *vi* **sight'-sing**. — **sight screen** (*cricket*) a large (*usu* white) screen placed on the boundary behind the bowler, providing a backdrop against which the batsman can more easily see the approaching ball. — *vi* **sight'see** to go about visiting sights, buildings, etc of interest. — **sight'seeing**; **sight'seer** (*-sē-ər*); **sights'man** a local guide, cicerone. — **at first sight** when seen initially and without the benefit of a detailed study or investigation; **at** or **on sight** without previous view or study; as soon as seen; on presentation; (of a bill, draft, etc, payable) as soon as presented; **at so many days' sight** (of a bill, draft, etc, payable) so many days after it is presented; **catch sight of** to get a glimpse of, begin to see; **in sight** within view, visible; (also **within sight**; with *of*) in a position to see, or be seen from or by; close at hand, expected soon; **keep sight of** or **keep in sight** to keep within seeing distance of; to remain in touch with; **know by sight** to recognize or be familiar with by appearance; **lose sight of** to cease to see; to get out of touch with; **out of sight** (with *of*) not in a position to be seen (from or by) or to see; out of range of vision; not visible, hidden; beyond comparison, marvellous (*colloq*); **put out of sight** to remove from view; to eat or drink up (*slang*); **raise one's sights** to set oneself a more ambitious target; **set one's sights on** to aim for (eg a specified goal); **sight for sore eyes** a most welcome sight; **sight unseen** without having seen the object in question. [OE *sihth*, *gesiht*; Ger *Sicht*]

sight[2] *sīt*. An old *pa t* of **sigh**.

sigil *sij'il*, *n* a seal, signet; a magical mark or sign. — *n* **sigillā'rid** (*geol*) any fossil lycopod tree of the genus *Sigillaria*, having parallel rows of seal-like leaf-scars and found chiefly in coal deposits. — *n* and *adj* **sigillā'rian**. — *adj* **sig'illary** (*-ə-ri*) pertaining to a seal. — *adj* **sig'illate** sealed; with seal-like impressions. — *n* **sigillā'tion**. [L *sigillum*, dimin of *signum* sign]

sigisbeo *sē-jēs-bā'ō* or *si-jis-*, *n*. Same as **cicisbeo**: — *pl* **sigisbe'i** (*-ē*). [Ital]

sigla *sig'lə*, *n pl* abbreviations, symbols and signs, as used in manuscripts, seals, etc. [L, *pl* of *siglum*, dimin of *signum* sign]

sigma *sig'mə*, *n* the eighteenth letter (Σ, early form C; σ, or when final, ς) of the Greek alphabet, corresponding to S; as a numeral σ' = 200, ͵σ = 200 000; the symbol Σ, used in mathematical notation to indicate summation of the numbers or quantities given. — *adj* **sig'mate** (*-māt*) shaped like Σ, C, or S. — *vt* to add σ or ς to. — *adj* **sigmatic** (*-mat'ik*) characterized by σ. — *n* **sigmā'tion** (*-shən*) the adding of σ or ς at the end of a syllable. — *n* **sig'matism** repetition of the *s*-sound. — *n* **sig'matron** a machine consisting of two accelerators (cyclotron and betatron; see under **accelerate**), for the generation of very high-energy X-rays. — *adj* **sig'moid** or **sigmoid'al** C-shaped; S-shaped. — *adv* **sigmoid'ally**. — *n* **sigmoid'ectomy** (*surg*) removal of the sigmoid colon. — *n* **sigmoid'oscope** an instrument inserted through the anus and used for examining the interior of the rectum and sigmoid colon. — *n* **sigmoid'oscopy**. — **sigma particles** (*phys*) three hyperons of medium mass, having respectively positive, neutral and negative charge; **sigmoid flexure** (*zool*, etc) a C-shaped or S-shaped bend; (also **sigmoid colon**) the S-shaped terminal part of the descending colon that leads to the rectum. [Gr *sīgma*]

sign *sīn*, *n* a gesture expressing a meaning; a signal; a mark with a meaning; a symbol; an emblem; a token; a portent; a miraculous token; an ensign, banner (in *pl* insignia; *archaic*); an indication of positive or negative value, or that indicated; a device marking an inn, etc (formerly also a house) instead of a street number; a board or panel giving a shopkeeper's name or trade, etc; an effigy (*obs*); a mere semblance (*obs*); an indication; an outward or objective indication of a disorder or disease, perceptible to an examining doctor (cf **symptom**); a trail or track of a wild animal, perceptible to a tracker; a trace; a twelfth part (30°) of the zodiac, bearing the name of, but not now coincident with, a constellation. — *vt* to indicate, convey, communicate, direct or mark by a sign or signs; to mark; to attach a signature to; to write as a signature; to designate by signature; to engage by signature; to betoken (*archaic*); to cross, make the sign of the cross over; to make the sign of. — *vi* to make a sign; to sign one's name; to use sign language; to bode, promise (*obs*). — *n* **sign'age** another term for **sign'ing** (see below); the arrangement or design of a sign or signs; signs collectively. — *n* **signary** (*sig'nə-ri*) a system of symbols, as an alphabet or syllabary. — *n* **sign'er**. — *n* **sign'ing** the use of sign language (*esp* by the deaf) as a means of communication; an act or instance of this. — *adj* **sign'less**. — **sign'board** a board bearing a notice or serving as a shop or inn sign; **sign language** a means of communication using finger and hand movements, used eg by the deaf; **sign-man'ual** a signature, *esp* a king's; **sign'-painter** a person who paints signs for shops, etc; **sign'post** a post for an inn sign; a fingerpost or post supporting road signs; an indication, clue. — *vt* to provide with a signpost; to point out as a signpost does, clearly, conspicuously or so obviously as to seem to be catering for imbeciles. — **sign'-writer** an expert in lettering for shop signs, etc; **sign'-writing**. — **sign away** to transfer or relinquish by signing; **sign in** or **out** to sign one's name on coming in, going out; **sign off** to record departure from work; to stop work, etc; to discharge from employment; to announce the end of broadcasting or a broadcast; to signal that one does not intend to bid further (*bridge*); **sign of the cross** a gesture of tracing the form of a cross as an invocation of God's grace; **sign on** to engage (*vt* or *vi*) for a job, etc, by signature (also **sign up**); to record arrival at work; to register for unemployment benefit (*colloq*); **sign on the dotted line** to give one's consent, thereby binding oneself, to a proposed scheme, contract, etc; to do this docilely or without proper investigation; **sign out** see **sign in**; **sign up** see **sign on**. [Fr *signe*, from L *signum*]

signal *sig'nl*, *n* a token; an intimation, eg of warning, conveyed over a distance; a transmitted effect conveying information; the apparatus used for the purpose; a piece of play intended to give information to one's partner (*cards*); an intimation of, or event taken as marking, the moment for action; an initial impulse. — *vt* to intimate, convey, or direct by signals; to signalize. — *vi* to make signals: — *pr p* **sig'nalling** or (*US*) **sig'naling**; *pa t* and *pa p* **sig'nalled** or (*US*) **sig'naled**. — *adj* remarkable; notable. — *vt* **sig'nalize** or **-ise** to mark or distinguish signally. — *n* **sig'naller** or (*US*) **sig'naler**. — *n* **sig'nalling** or (*US*) **sig'naling**. — *adv* **sig'nally** notably. — **signal box** a railway signalman's cabin or an automatic or semi-automatic control point for the signals for all railway lines in a section; **signal letters** (*naut*) four letters by which an individual ship may be identified; **sig'nalman** a person who transmits signals; a person who operates railway signals. — **signal peptide** a short N-terminal peptide sequence involved in the passage of a protein across a membrane (also **signal sequence**); **signal-to-noise ratio** (*acoustics*) the relationship, *usu* expressed in decibels, between the wanted signal and the unwanted background noise. [Fr *signal*, from L *signum*]

signary. See under **sign**.

signatory. See under **signature**.

signature *sig'nə-chər*, *n* a signing; a signed name; a distinctive mark or stamp; an indication of key, also of time, at the beginning of a line of music, or where a change occurs; a letter or numeral at the foot of a page to indicate sequence of sheets; a sheet so marked; the pages formed by such a sheet when folded and cut; in a plant, a distinctive feature of shape or marking once believed (according to the **doctrine of signatures**) to be a symbolic indication of its (*esp* medicinal) properties, a kidney-shaped leaf, for instance, indicating the plant's capacity to cure kidney disease; a signature tune; the indication of the presence of eg an aeroplane on a radar screen or a submarine on a sonar screen. — *n* **sig'natory** a person who has signed a document, agreement, treaty, etc. — Also *adj*. — **signature tune** a tune used to introduce, and hence associated with, a particular radio or television programme, group of performers, etc. [LL *signātūra*, from L *signāre*, *-ātum* to sign]

signet *sig'nit*, *n* a small seal; the impression of such a seal; a signet ring; one of the royal seals for authenticating grants (for **Writer to the Signet** see under **write**). — *vt* to stamp or authenticate with a signet. — *adj* **sig'neted**. — **signet ring** a ring with a signet. [From Med L *signētum* a small seal, from *signum*]

signeur. A Shakespearean spelling of **senior**. — *n* **sign'eurie** (*Shakesp*) seniority. — *n* **sign'ieur** (*Shakesp*) seigneur.

signify *sig'ni-fī*, *vt* to be a sign for; to mean; to denote, betoken; to indicate or declare. — *vi* to be of consequence: — *pr p* **sig'nifying**; *pa t* and *pa p* **sig'nified**. — *adj* **sig'nifiable**. — *n* **signif'icance** (*-i-kəns*) meaning; import; the quality of being significant (also **signif'icancy**); a value of probability at which a particular hypothesis is held to be contradicted by the results of a statistical test (*statistics*). — *adj* **signif'icant** having a meaning; full of meaning; important, worthy of consideration; indicative. — *n* that which carries a meaning; a sign. — *adv* **signif'icantly**. — *n* **signif'icate** a thing signified. — *n* **significā'tion** meaning; that which is signified; importance. — *adj* **signif'icative** (*-kə-tiv*) indicative; significant. — *adv* **signif'icatively**. — *n* **signif'icātor** (*astrol*) a planet ruling a house. — *adj* **signif'icatory** (*-kə-tər-i*). — *n sing* **signif'ics** the science of meaning. — *n* **sig'nifier**. — **significance test** (*statistics*) a test which is used to demonstrate the probability that observed patterns cannot be explained by chance; **significant figures** or (*esp NAm*) **significant digits** (*math*) the figures 1 to 9, or ciphers occurring medially (the following numbers are expressed to three significant figures — 3·15, 0·0127, 1·01). [L *significāre*, *-ātum*, from *signum* a sign, and *facere* to make]

Signor, **Signior** *sē'nyör* or **Signore** *sēnyō'rā* or *-nyö'*, *n* an Italian title or form of address equivalent to *Mr* or *Sir*; (without *cap*) a gentleman: — *pl* **sig'nors** or **signo'ri**. — *n* **Signora** (*sē-nyō'rə* or *-nyö'*) feminine of *Signor*, Mrs, madam; (without *cap*) a lady: — *pl* **signo're**. — *n* **Signorina** (*sē-nyə-rē'nə* or *-nyö-*) Miss; (without *cap*) an unmarried lady, a young lady: — *pl* **signori'ne** (*-nā*). — *n* **signoria** (*-rē'ä*; *hist*) a seignory, the governing body of an Italian city-state. — *n* **si'gnory** seignory; a signoria. — *n* **Signorino** (*sē-nyə-rē'no*) Master; (without *cap*) a young man, young gentleman: — *pl* **signori'ni**. — **Grand Signior** see under **seignior**. [Ital *signor, signore*]

signorial. See under **seignior**.

sijo *sē'jō*, *n* a Korean verse form of three lines each of four groups of syllables, *orig* sung with musical accompaniment. [Korean, literally, melody of the times]

sika *sē'kə*, *n* a deer, *Cervus nippon* (of the subfamily *Cervidae*), of Japan and E Asia, similar to the fallow deer in size and with a spotted coat in summer. [Jap *shika*]

sike[1] or **syke** *sīk*, (*Scot*) *n* a rill or small ditch. [Northern, from OE *sīc*]

sike[2]. Spenserian spelling of **sic**[1].

Sikel *sik'əl*, *n* and *adj* Siculian. — *adj* **Sikelian** (*-el'*). — *n* **Sikel'iot** an ancient Greek colonist in Sicily. — Also **Sicel**, **Sicelian**, **Siceliot**. [Gr *Sikelos, Sikeliōtēs*]

Sikh *sēk* or *sik*, *n* an adherent of a monotheistic religion established in the 16c by those former Hindus who rejected the authority of the Vedas, taking the Granth as their scripture; a Sikh soldier in the Indian army. — Also *adj*. — *n* **Sikh'ism**. [Hindi, disciple]

sikorsky *si-kör'ski*, *n* (also with *cap*) any of various helicopters that are versions of the first successful helicopter that flew in 1939, designed by Igor Sikorsky (1889–1972), Russian-born US aeronautical engineer.

silage *sī'lij*, *n* any green crop (such as grass or clover) harvested, compressed, fermented and stored for use as animal fodder, ensilage. — *vt* to harvest and store (a green crop) in this way: — *pr p* **si'laging** or **si'lageing**. [**ensilage**, after **silo**]

silane *si'lān*, *n* a gas, silicon hydride, Si_1H_4, used in the production of semiconductors; also applied to a group of silicon hydrides *incl* disilane and trisilane. [From **silica** and **-ane**]

Silastic® *si'l-astik*, *n* a flexible silicone rubber, used in the manufacture of artifical limbs, etc. — Also without *cap*.

sild *sild*, *n* a young herring. [Norw]

sile or **seil** *sīl*, (*dialect*) *vt* to strain. — *vi* to rain heavily. — *n* a strainer (also **sī'ler**). [Scand; cf Swed and Norw *sila* to pass through a strainer]

silen. See **silenus**.

silence *sī'ləns*, *n* absence of sound, stillness; omission of, or abstention from, sounding, speech, mention, or communication; a time of such absence or abstention; a state of not, or no longer, being spoken about; taciturnity; the state of being forgotten, oblivion; secrecy; (of distilled spirits) flavourlessness, odourlessness. — *vt* to cause to be silent. — *interj* be silent. — *adj* **si'lenced** brought to silence; (of a priest) forbidden to preach. — *n* **si'lencer** a person who or a thing that silences; a device for reducing the sound of escaping gases by gradual expansion, used, eg for small-arms and internal combustion engines. — *adj* **si'lent** noiseless; without sound; unaccompanied by sound; refraining from speech, mention, or divulging; taciturn; not pronounced; (of distilled spirit) without flavour or odour; inoperative; (of the new moon) not yet visible (*Milton*). — *n* a time of silence (*archaic*); a silent film. — *adv* **si'lently**. — *n* **si'lentness**. — **silent film** a cinema film which has no accompanying synchronized soundtrack; **silent majority** those, in any country the bulk of the population, who are assumed to have sensible, moderate opinions though they do not trouble to express them publicly; **silent partner** a sleeping partner (qv). [L *silēre* to be silent]

silene *sī-lē'ni*, *n* a flowering plant of the genus *Silene* (of the family *Caryophyllaceae*), *incl* the campions, catchfly and many cultivated species. [Mod L, prob from L *Sīlēnus*; see **silenus**]

silent, etc. See under **silence**.

silentiary *sī-len'shi-ə-ri*, *n* an official who calls for silence, *esp* (*hist*) an official of the Byzantine court; someone who observes or recommends silence. [From L *silentiarius* a confidential servant, privy counsellor]

silentium altum. See **altum silentium**.

silenus *sī-lē'nəs*, *n* a woodland god or elderly satyr (*pl* **sile'ni** *-nī*); (with *cap*) the chief of the satyrs, foster-father of Bacchus, represented as a pot-bellied, bald, snub-nosed old man; (with *cap*) the lion-tailed macaque genus. — Also **si'len** (*-lin*). [L *Sīlēnus*, from Gr *Seilēnos*]

silesia *sī-lē'zhə*, *n* a thin, twilled cotton or linen used for lining clothes, etc, *orig* made in *Silesia* (now part of Poland).

silex *sī'leks*, *n* silica of quartz; a heat-resistant and shock-resistant glass formed of fused quartz. [L *sılex, silicis* flint]

silhouette *sil-ōō-et'*, *n* a pictorial representation of an object or *esp* a person, in profile, consisting of an outline filled in with black; an image of anything against a lighter background in which only the outline is seen in detail; an outline. — *vt* to represent or show in silhouette. [Étienne de *Silhouette* (1709–67), French minister of finance in 1759; reason disputed]

silica *sil'i-kə*, *n* silicon dioxide or silicic anhydride, occurring in nature as quartz, chalcedony, etc, and (amorphous and hydrated) as opal. — *adj* composed of silica. — *n* **sil'icate** one of the largest group of minerals, all of which are composed of silicon, oxygen and one or more metals, with or wihout hydrogen; any salt of silicic acid or derived from silicon. — *vt* to combine, coat, or impregnate with silica or silicates. — *adj* **siliceous** or **silicious** (*-ish'əs*) of or containing silica. — *adj* **silicic** (*-is'ik*) pertaining to, or obtained from, silica (**silicic acid** a general name for a group of acids, eg **orthosilic'ic**, H_4SiO_4; **metasilic'ic**, H_2SiO_3). — *n* **sil'icide** (*-sīd*) a compound of silicon and another element. — *adj* **silicicolous** (*-sik'*; L *colere* to cultivate, inhabit) growing on siliceous soil. — *adj* **silicif'erous** containing silica. — *n* **silicification** (*si-lis-i-fi-kā'shən*). — *adj* **silicified** (*-lis'*). — *vt* **silic'ify** to render siliceous; to impregnate or cement with or replace by silica. — *vi* to become siliceous. — *n* **sil'icon** (*-kon* or *-kən*) a non-metallic element (symbol **Si**; atomic no 14), most abundant of all except oxygen, forming grey crystals or brown amorphous powder and having semiconducting properties, *orig* called **silicium** (*-lis'* or *-lish'*). — *n* **sil'icone** any of a number of extremely stable organic derivatives of silicon, used in rubbers, lubricants, polishes, etc. — *n* **silicosis** (*-kō'sis*) a lung disease caused by the prolonged inhalation of silica dust. — *n* and *adj* **silicot'ic**. — **silicon chip** see under **chip**; **silicon valley** a district or area in which there is a concentration of information technology industries (from the *orig Silicon Valley* in California). [L *silex, silicis* flint]

silicle, **silicula**, etc. See under **siliqua**.

siliqua *sil'i-kwə* or **silique** *si-lēk'*, (*bot*) *n* a type of dry fruit consisting of a long, somewhat cylindrical pod of two carpels divided by a partition, which splits to allow the seeds to escape, characteristic of cruciferous plants. — *n* **silicula** (*-ik'ū-lə*) a dry fruit consisting of a short, broad pod of similar structure to a siliqua. — Also **sil'icle** or **sil'icule**. — *adj* **silic'ulose**. — *adj* **sil'iquose**. [L *siliqua* pod, dimin *silicula*]

silk *silk*, *n* a fibre produced by the larva of a silkworm moth, mainly of fibroin coated with sericin, formed by the hardening of a liquid emitted from spinning-glands; a similar fibre from another insect or a spider; an imitation (**artificial silk**) made by forcing a viscous solution of modified cellulose through small holes; a thread, cloth, garment, or clothing made from such fibres; the silk gown, or the rank, of a queen's (or king's) counsel; hence, a QC or KC (*informal*); the styles of maize; silky lustre in the ruby, etc. — *adj* of or pertaining to silk; silky (*Shakesp*). — *vt* to cover or clothe with silk. — *adj* **silk'en** of, like or clad in silk; glossy; soft and smooth; ingratiating; luxurious. — *vt* to make silken. — *adv* **silk'ily**. — *n* **silk'iness**. — *adj* **silk'y**. — **silk cotton** the silky seed-covering of *Erio-*

dendron anfractuosum and other trees of the family Bombacaceae; **silk gland** a gland (at a silkworm's mouth, on a spider's abdomen) from which silk is spun; **silk'-grass** a name for various plants with fibrous leaves, eg *Karatus* (Bromeliaceae), Yucca, Agave; **silk'grower** a breeder of silkworms for silk; **silk hat** a top hat; **silk'-man** (*Shakesp*) a dealer in silks; **silk'-screen** a print produced by the **silkscreen process**, a printmaking process in which silk (or now more usually a manmade fibre) is stretched and attached to a frame with stencils attached to the underside of the fabric mesh, colour then being forced through the upper side of the mesh, using a rubber squeegee, on to those areas of the print not blocked out by the stencil; **silk'tail** the waxwing; **silk'-thrower** or **-throwster** a person who makes raw silk into thread; **silk'weed** another name for **milk-weed**; **silk'worm** any of various moths (*esp Bombyx mori*) whose larva produces silk; opprobriously, a wearer of silk (*obs*); someone who haunts draper's shops without buying (*obs*); **silk'worm-gut** the drawn-out glands of the silkworm. — **take silk** to become a QC or KC. [OE *seolc*, from L *sēricum*; see **Seric**]

silkie or **silky** (*Scot*) *n* a seal (the animal). — Also **selkie** (*sel'ki*). [Old Scottish *selich*, OE *seolh*]

sill or **cill** *sil*, *n* a horizontal length of timber, stone, etc at the foot of an opening, eg for a door, window, embrasure, port, dock-entrance, etc; the bottom of a title-page, a plough, a ledge; a bed of rock (*mining*); a sheet of intrusive rock more or less parallel to the bedding (*geol*). [OE *syll*; ON *syll*; Ger *Schwelle*]

sillabub. Same as **syllabub**.

silladar *sil'ə-där*, *n* an irregular cavalryman. [Urdu and Pers *silāhdār*]

siller *sil'ər*, *n* a Scots form of **silver**, *usu* used in the sense of money. — Also *adj*.

Sillery *sil'ə-ri*, *n* champagne from *Sillery*, near Rheims.

sillimanite *sil'i-mən-īt*, *n* a mineral, Al_2SiO_5, aluminium silicate in the form of orthorhombic crystals, occurring in argillaceous metamorphic rocks. — See also **fibrolite**. [After Benjamin *Silliman* (1779–1864), US scientist]

sillock *sil'ək*, (*N Scot*) *n* a young coalfish. [Cf ON *silungr* a small salmon]

silly *sil'i*, *adj* feeble-minded; witless, foolish, stupid; lacking in good sense; not well thought out; frivolous; nonsensical, absurd; dazed, stunned (eg from a blow); harmless (said of eg sheep); defenceless (*archaic*); simple, humble (*obs*); pitiable, feeble (*obs*); (of a fielding position) very near the batsman (*cricket*). — *n* a silly person. — *adv* **sill'ily**. — *n* **sill'iness**. — **silly-bill'y** (*colloq*) a foolish person; **sill'y-how** (*archaic* and *Scot*; OE *hūfe* headdress) a (child's) caul; **silly money** (*colloq*) absurdly or unthinkably large quantities of cash; **silly season** a time of year, *usu* late summer, when newspapers print trivial matter for want of more newsworthy material. [OE *sælig*; see **seely**]

silo *sī'lō*, *n* a pit or airtight chamber for storing grain, or for ensilage, or for storing other loose materials; a storage tower above ground, typically tall and cylindrical; an underground chamber housing a guided missile ready to be fired: — *pl* **si'los**. — *vt* to put or keep in a silo: — *pa p* **si'lo'd** or **si'loed**. [Sp from L *sīrus*, from Gr *siros*, *sīros*, *seiros* a pit]

silphium *sil'fi-əm*, *n* a plant (*perh* the umbelliferous *Ferula tingitana*) imported from Cyrenaica by the Greeks for use as a food and in medicine (*hist*); (*cap*) a genus of American composites, compass-plants: — *pl* **sil'phia** or **sil'phiums**. [L, from Gr *silphion*]

silt *silt*, *n* fine sediment deposited by a body of water. — *vt* to choke, block, cover, etc with silt (with *up*). — *vi* to become silted up. — *n* **siltā'tion**. — *adj* **silt'y**. — **silt'stone** rock formed of hardened silt. [ME *sylt*; cf Dan and Norw *sylt* salt marsh]

Silurian *sil-ōō'ri-ən* or *-ū'*, *adj* of the *Sil'urēs*, an ancient British tribe, or the district around the Welsh/English border which they inhabited; applied by Murchison in 1835 to the geological period of the Palaeozoic Era preceding the Devonian. — Also *n*. — *n* **sil'urist** (also with *cap*) a Silurian, a name adopted by the poet Henry Vaughan (1621 or -22–95).

silu'rid *sil-ōō'rid* or *-ū'-*, *n* any freshwater fish of the family *Siluridae*, including the European catfish, wels or sheatfish, *Silurus glanis*, having an elongated, slimy, scaleless body and a long anal fin. — *Also adj*. — *adj* **silu'roid**. [L *silūrus*, from Gr *silouros*]

silva or **sylva** *sil'və*, *n* the assemblage of trees in a region: — *pl* **sil'vas, syl'vas, sil'vae** or **syl'vae** (*-vē*). — See also **sylvan**. [L *sylva* (sometimes *sylva*) a wood]

silver *sil'vər*, *n* a white precious metal (symbol **Ag**, for L *argentum*; atomic no 47); silver money; silverware; cutlery, sometimes even when not of silver; a silver medal. — *adj* of or like silver; silver-coloured; clear and ringing in tone. — *vt* to cover with silver; to make silvery. — *vi* to become silvery. — *n* **sil'veriness**. — *n* **sil'vering** coating with, or of, silver or quicksilver. — *vt* **sil'verize** or **-ise** to coat or treat with silver. — *n* **sil'verling** (*Bible*) a small silver coin. — *adv* **sil'verly** with the appearance or sound of silver. — *adj* **sil'vern** (*poetic*) made of silver; silvery. — *adj* **sil'very** like silver; silver-coloured; light in tone; having a clear ringing sound. — **Silver Age** the reign of Zeus, second of the ages of the world, following and less innocent than the Golden Age of Kronos (*Gr* and *Roman mythol*); in Latin literature, the time of Martial, Tacitus and Juvenal; **sil'verback** an older male gorilla with grey hair on its back and flanks; **sil'ver-bath** (*photog*) a solution of a silver salt, or a vessel for it, for sensitizing plates; **sil'ver-beater** a person who beats silver into foil; **silver bell** any of various deciduous trees or shrubs of the genus *Halesia*, native to N America and China, having bell-shaped silvery-white flowers (also called **snowdrop tree**); **sil'verbill** the name of two species of the genus *Lonchura* of weaver-finches, with a silvery sheen to their bills; **silver birch** a species of birch, *Betula pendula*, with silvery-white peeling bark; **silver fir** a European fir, *Abies alba*, with shiny needles, green on top and silvery beneath — an important timber tree; a small Japanese fir, *Abies veitchii*, with notched needles banded with silver underneath; **sil'verfish** any wingless primitive insect of the genus *Lepisma* (order *Thysanura*), eg *L. saccharina*, which feeds on starch in wallpaper, bookbindings, etc; a silvery-white goldfish, or other silvery fish; **silver foil** silver leaf; **silver fox** an American red fox in a colour phase in which the fur is black with white tips; this fur; **silver gate** see **gate**; **silver-gilt'** gilded silver. — Also *adj*. — **sil'ver-glance** native sulphide of silver; **sil'ver-grain** medullary rays in longitudinal section; **silver iodide** a yellow powder that darkens when exposed to light, is used in photography, is scattered on clouds to cause rainfall, and has various medical uses; **silver jubilee** a twenty-fifth anniversary; **Silver Latin** that written by authors of the Silver Age; **silver leaf** silver beaten into thin leaves; a disease of plum trees; **silver lining** a redeeming aspect of an otherwise unpleasant or unfortunate situation; **silver medal** (in athletics competitions, etc) the medal awarded as second prize. — *adj* **sil'ver-mount'ed**. — **silver nitrate** a poisonous colourless crystalline salt that turns grey or black in the presence of light or organic matter, and has uses in photography, as an antiseptic, etc; **silver paper** silver foil; (*usu*) tinfoil (sometimes with a backing of greaseproof paper); fine white tissue paper; **silver pheasant** a white-tailed Chinese pheasant, introduced to Europe, etc; **silver plate** utensils, *esp* tableware, made of silver; electroplate. — *adj* **silver-plā'ted**. — **sil'ver-point** the process or product of drawing with a silver-tipped pencil; **silver salmon** the cohoe; **silver screen** the cinema screen; **silver service** a method of serving food in restaurants, etc, in which the waiter or waitress uses a spoon and fork held in one hand to transfer food from the serving dish to the diners' plates; **sil'verside** a cut of beef taken from the rump, below the aitchbone; **sil'versides** any small fish of the family *Atherinidae*, eg *Atherina presbyter*, the sand smelt; **sil'verskin** the fine skin of a coffee bean;

sil'versmith a worker in silver; **sil'versmithing**; **silver steel** a type of carbon steel containing silicon, manganese and chromium, and low in phosphorus and sulphur; **sil'ver-stick** a palace officer, from his silvered wand; **silver'tail** (*Austr informal*) a wealthy socialite; a social climber. — *adj* **sil'ver-tongued** plausible, eloquent. — **silver tree** a silvery-leaved S African proteaceous tree (*Leucadendron argenteum*). — *adj* **sil'ver-voiced**. — **silver wedding** the twenty-fifth wedding anniversary; **sil'verweed** a creeping plant (*Potentilla anserina*) with silvery leaves and yellow flowers whose starchy roots were used as food from prehistoric times; **silver white** see **China white** under **white**. — *adj* **sil'ver-white** of a lustrous greyish white colour. — **born with a silver spoon in one's mouth** born to affluence; **tree of silver** see under **tree**. [OE *silfer*, *seolfor*; ON *silfr*, Ger *Silber*]

silvestrian, silviculture. See **sylvan**.

sim. See **Simeonite**.

sima *sī'mə*, *n* the part of the earth's crust underlying the sial. [From *si*licon and *ma*gnesium]

simar, simarre *si-mär'*. Same as **cymar**.

simaruba or **simarouba** *sim-ə-roo'bə*, *n* any tropical American tree of the *Simaruba* genus, *esp Simaruba amara* of Brazil, Guyana, etc; the bark of *Simaruba amara* that contains quassine and is used medicinally. — *adj* **simaruba'ceous** or **simarouba'ceous** of, belonging or relating to the *Simarubaceae*, a family of tropical trees related to the *Rutaceae*. [Carib name]

simazine *sim'ə-zēn*, *n* (also with *cap*) an organic herbicide used as a general weedkiller.

Simeonite *sim'i-ən-īt*, *n* a follower of Charles *Simeon* (1759–1836); a low-churchman or evangelical — often shortened to **sim**.

simi *sim'i*, *n* (in East Africa) a short two-edged sword or large knife. [Swahili *sime*]

simian *sim'i-ən*, *adj* of the apes; apelike. — Also *n*. — *adj* (*rare*) **sim'ial** or **sim'ious**. [L *sīmia* ape]

similar *sim'i-lər*, *adj* (with *to*) like; resembling; exactly corresponding in shape, without regard to size (*geom*). — *n* **similarity** (*-lar'i-ti*). — *adv* **sim'ilarly**. [Fr *similaire*, from L *similis* like]

simile *sim'i-li*, (*rhetoric*) *n* a figure of speech in which a person or thing is described by being explicitly likened to another, *usu* preceded by *as* or *like*; the use of such figures of speech: — *pl* **sim'iles**. — *adj* **sim'ilātive** expressing similarity. — *vt* **sim'ilize** or **-ise** to liken. — *vi* to use simile. — *n* **simil'itude** likeness; semblance; comparison; parable. [L neuter of *similis* like]

simillimum *si-mil'i-mum*, *n* (in homoeopathy) a remedy chosen because it would produce in a healthy person the same symptoms as those exhibited by the patient. [L, neuter superlative of *similis* like]

similor *sim'i-lör*, *n* a yellow alloy used for cheap jewellery. [Fr, from L *similis* like, and *aurum* gold]

simious. See under **simian**.

simitar. Same as **scimitar**.

simkin or **simpkin** *sim'kin*, (*Anglo-Ind*) *n* an Urdu corruption of **champagne**.

Simmental *zim'ən-täl*, *n* a breed of cattle, *orig* native to Switzerland, used in many parts of Europe for meat and milk. — Also **Simm'enthal** or **Simm'enthaler** (*-tä-lər*). [From the *Simmental* or Simme valley]

simmer *sim'ər*, *vi* and *vt* to boil gently. — *vi* to be close to an outburst of emotion, *esp* anger. — *n* a simmering state. — **simmer down** to calm down. [Earlier *simper*; origin unknown]

'simmon *sim'ən*, *n* short for **persimmon**.

simnel *sim'nl*, *n* a sweet fruit cake *usu* covered with marzipan and traditionally eaten at Easter, or sometimes Christmas or Mothering Sunday. — Also **sim'nel-bread** or **-cake**. [OFr *simenel*, from L *siminellus* fine bread, from *simila* fine flour]

Simon Pure *sī'mən pūr'*, *n* the real person (or thing). — *adj* **sī'mon-pure** real, genuine. [From a character in Susannah Centlivre's comedy, *A Bold Stroke for a Wife*]

simony *sī'mə-ni* or *sim'ə-ni*, *n* the buying or selling of an ecclesiastical benefice. — *n* **simō'niac** a person guilty of simony. — *adj* **simonī'acal**. — *adj* (*obs*) **simō'nious**. — *adv* **simonī'acally**. — *n* **si'monist** a person who practises or defends simony. [*Simon* Magus (from the Bible: Acts 8)]

simoom *si-mōōm'* or **simoon** *-mōōn'*, *n* a hot suffocating desert wind in Arabia and N Africa. [Ar *samûm*, from *samm* to poison]

simorg. Same as **simurg**.

simp. See **simpleton** under **simple**.

simpai *sim'pī*, *n* the black-crested langur of Sumatra. [Malay]

simpatico *sim-pat'i-kō*, (*colloq*) *adj* sympathetic in the sense of congenial. [Ital and Sp]

simper *sim'pər*, *vi* to smile in a silly, weak or affected manner. — *n* a silly or affected smile, or one displaying or suggestive of weakness. — *n* **sim'perer**. — *adj* **simp'ering**. — *adv* **simp'eringly**. [Cf Norw *semper* smart]

simpkin. See **simkin**.

simple *sim'pl*, *adj* consisting of one thing or element; not complex or compound; in or relating to simple time (*music*); not divided into leaflets (*bot*); easy; plain; unornate; unpretentious; mean, sorry; mere, sheer; ordinary; unlearned or unskilled; of humble rank or origin; unaffected; artless; guileless; unsuspecting; credulous; weak in intellect; silly. — *n* (*archaic*) a simple or humble person (also used collectively) or thing; a simpleton; an irreducible component of a compound; a medicine having only one constituent; hence a medicinal plant. — *vi* (*archaic*) to gather medicinal plants. — *n* **sim'pleness**. — *n* (*archaic*) **sim'pler** a gatherer of medicinal plants. — *n* **sim'plesse** (*Spenser*) simplicity. — *n* **sim'pleton** a weak or foolish person, one easily imposed on (colloq short form **simp**, *esp NAm*). — *n* **simplicity** (*-plis*). — *n* **simplificā'tion** the process, or an instance, of making simple or simpler. — *adj* **sim'plificātive**. — *n* **simp'lificātor** and **sim'plifier**. — *vt* **sim'plify** to make simple, simpler, or less difficult: — *prp* **sim'plifying**; *pa t* and *pa p* **sim'plified**. — *n* (*archaic*) **sim'pling** the act or process of gathering medicinal herbs. — *n* **sim'plism** affected simplicity; oversimplification of a problem or situation. — *n* (*archaic*) **sim'plist** a person having an expert knowledge of simples or medicinal herbs. — *adj* **simplis'tic** tending to oversimplify, making no allowances for the problems and complexities that exist or inevitably arise; naïve. — *adv* **simplis'tically**. — *adv* **sim'ply** in a simple manner; considered by itself; alone; merely; without qualification; veritably; absolutely; really (*colloq*). — **simple fraction** a fraction that has whole numbers as numerator and denominator; **simple fracture** see **fracture**; **simple harmonic motion** (*phys*) the motion of a particle subjected to a force which is proportional to the displacement of the particle from a fixed point and is directed towards that point (*abbrev* **SHM**). — *adj* **simple-heart'ed** (*archaic*) guileless; frank, sincere. — **simple interest** interest calculated on the principal only. — *adj* **simple-mind'ed** lacking intelligence; foolish. — **simple-mind'edness**; **simple sentence** a sentence with one predicate; **simple time** (*music*) any measure or time in which there are two, three or four beats to the bar (See also **compound time**). [Fr *simple*, and L *simplus*, *simplex*]

simplex *sim'pleks*, *n* a figure with the minimum number of vertices for space of a particular number of dimensions (eg a triangle in 2-dimensional space) (*geom*); a simple word, as opposed to a compound word (*linguistics*): — *pl* **sim'plices** (*-pli-sēz*). — *adj* simple, single; allowing transmission and reception in one direction only (*comput* and *telecomm*). [L]

simpliciter *sim-plis-i-tər*, *-plik'i-ter*, (*L*) *adv* simply, not relatively; naturally, unconditionally.

simplicity, simplify, etc. See under **simple**.

simpliste *sɛ̃-plēst*, *sim-plēst'* or *sim'plist adj* simplistic, naïve. [Fr]

simul *sim'əl*, (*chess*) *n* a short form of **simultaneous**. — Also *adj*.

simulacrum *sim-ū-lā'krəm*, *n* an image; a semblance, superficial likeness: — *pl* **simula'cra** or **simula'crums**. — Also **simulacre** (*-lā'kər*). [L *simulācrum*]

simulate *sim'ū-lāt*, *vt* to feign; to have or assume a false appearance of; to mimic; to re-create the conditions of, for the purposes of training or experimentation. — *adj* feigned. — *adj* **sim'ulant** simulating; mimicking (*biol*). — *n* a simulator. — *adj* **sim'ular** counterfeit; feigned. — *n* (*archaic*) a person or thing that simulates. — *adj* **sim'ulated** (of a material, eg fur, leather, wood) not of such a material but made (*usu* in an inferior material) to look like it; not genuine, feigned. — *n* **simulā'tion** feigning; mimicry; the making of working replicas or representations of machines or the re-creation of a situation, environment, etc, for demonstration or for analysis of problems. — *adj* **sim'ulātive**. — *n* **sim'ulātor** someone who or something that simulates; a device used for simulating required conditions, etc, eg for training purposes. — *adj* **sim'ulatory**. — **simulated pearl** a bead resembling a pearl. [L *simulāre*, *-ātum*; cf **similar**, **simultaneous**]

simulcast *sim'əl-käst*, *n* a programme broadcast simultaneously on radio and television or, on two or more radio wavebands or television channels; the transmission of such a programme. — Also *vt*. [*simul*taneous and broad*cast*]

simulium *si-mū'li-əm*, *n* a small black blood-sucking fly of the genus *Simulium*, of tropical regions, that breeds in fast-flowing streams. — *n pl* **Simulī'idae** (*-dē*) the family of flies of which the *Simulium* is the type-genus, some species of which are the carriers of diseases such as onchocerciasis. [L *simulāre* to imitate]

simultaneous *sim-əl-tā'nyəs* or (*NAm*) *sīm'ul-*, *adj* being or happening at the same time; (of equations) satisfied by the same roots (*math*). — *n* (*chess*) an exhibition in which one player plays several opponents at once (*usu* shortened to **simul**). — *n* **simultaneity** (*-tə-nē'i-ti* or *-nā'-*) the quality of being simultaneous, coincidence; a basic consequence of relativity, that two events that are simultaneous for one observer may occur at different times for another observer in another reference frame moving relative to the first (*phys*). — *adv* **simultā'neously**. — *n* **simulta'neousness**. — **simultaneous translation** a simultaneously running translation of a speaker's or actor's words into the language, or respective languages, of audience members, *esp* relayed through hand-held earphones. [L *simul* at the same time]

simurg or **simurgh** *si-mōōrg'* or *-mûrg'*, or **simorg** *-mörg*, *n* a monstrous bird of Persian fable. [Pers *sīmurgh*]

sin[1] *sin*, *n* moral offence or shortcoming, *esp* from the point of view of religion; the condition of offending in this way; an offence generally; a shame or pity (*old colloq*). — *vi* to commit sin (often with *against*). — *vt* to commit; to burden with sin (as in *sin one's soul*); to bring, drive, or render by sin (hence *sin one's mercies*, to be ungrateful): — *pr p* **sinn'ing**; *pa t* and *pa p* **sinned**. — *adj* **sin'ful** tainted with sin; wicked; involving sin; morally wrong. — *adv* **sin'fully**. — *n* **sin'fulness**. — *adj* **sin'less**. — *adv* **sin'lessly**. — *n* **sin'lessness**. — *n* **sinn'er**. — *vt* (with *it*; *Pope*) to act as a sinner. — **sin bin** (in ice-hockey, etc) an enclosure to which a player is sent for a statutory length of time when suspended from a game for unruly behaviour; a room or other place to which disruptive school pupils are sent. — **sin'-eater** (*hist*) a person who by eating bread and salt at a funeral was supposed to take upon himself the sins of the dead person, so that the soul might be delivered from purgatory. — *adj* **sin'-eating**. — **sin'-offering** a sacrifice in expiation of sin; **sin tax** (*esp US*) a tax levied on items such as cigarettes and alcohol. — **live in sin** (*old*) to cohabit in an unmarried state; **original sin** see under **origin**. [OE *synn*; ON *synth*; Ger *Sünde*; perh L *sōns*, *sontis* guilty]

sin[2] or **sin'** *sin*, *prep*, *conj*, and *adv* (*archaic* or *Scot*) since. — **long sin** (*Spenser*) for a long time in the past. [Shortened from **sithen**]

sin[3]. See **sine**[1].

sin[4] *sēn*, *n* the 21st letter of the Hebrew alphabet (שׁ).

Sinaean *sin-ē'ən* (*rare*) *adj* Chinese. [LL *Sīnae*, Gr *Sīnai* Chinese (pl)]

Sinaitic *sī-nā-it'ik*, *adj* of Mount *Sinai*.

Sinanthropus *sin-* or *sīn-an'thrə-pəs* or *-thrō'*, *n* Peking (fossil) man. [Gr *Sīnai* (the) Chinese, and *anthrōpos* man]

sinapism *sin'ə-pizm*, *n* a mustard plaster. [Gr *sināpi*]

sinarchism *sin'är-kizm* or **sinarquism** *sin'är-kizm* or *-kwizm*, *n* (also with *cap*) the fascist movement in Mexico prominent around the time of the Second World War. — *n* and *adj* **sin'archist** or **sin'arquist**. [Sp *sinarquismo*, from *sin* without, and *anarquismo* anarchism]

since *sins*, *adv* from that time on; after that time; past; ago. — *prep* after; from the time of. — *conj* from the time that; seeing that; because. [ME *sins*, *sithens*; see under **sith**[1]]

sincere *sin-sēr'*, *adj* pure, unmixed; unadulterated; unfeigned; genuine; free from pretence; the same in reality as in appearance. — *adv* **sincēre'ly**. — *n* **sincēre'ness** or **sincerity** (*-ser'*). — **yours sincerely** used in moderately formal conclusion to a letter. [Fr *sincère*, from L *sincērus* clean]

sinciput *sing'si-put*, (*anatom*) *n* the forepart of the head or skull: — *pl* **sin'ciputs** or **sincip'ita**. — *adj* **sincip'ital**. [L, from *sēmi-* half, and *caput* head]

sind. See **synd**.

Sindhi or **Sindi** *sin'dē*, *n* a native or inhabitant of *Sind*, in SE Pakistan; the Indic language spoken mainly in Sind. — Also *adj*.

sindon *sin'dən* (*archaic*) *n* fine (*esp* linen) cloth, or a garment, etc, made from it; a shroud, *esp* that preserved as Jesus's at Turin, Italy. — *n* **sindonol'ogy** the study of this shroud and its history. — *n* **sindonol'ogist**. — *n* **sindonoph'any** (Gr *phainein* to show) the periodic exhibiting of this shroud to the public. [Gr *sindōn* fine cloth, winding sheet]

sine[1] *sīn*, (*math*) *n* (as a function of an angle) the ratio of the side opposite it (or its supplement) in a right-angled triangle to the hypotenuse (short form **sin**); *orig* the perpendicular from one end of an arc to the diameter through the other. — *adj* **sinical** (*sin'i-kl*). — **sine curve** a curve showing the relationship between the size of an angle and its sine, a sinusoid; **sine wave** any oscillation whose graphical representation is a sine curve. [L *sinus* a bay]

sine[2]. Same as **syne**[1,2].

sine[3] *sī'nē* or *si'ne*, (*L*) *prep* without. — **sine die** (*dī'ē* or *di'ā*) without a day (appointed); of a meeting or other business, indefinitely adjourned; **sine dubio** (*dū'bi-ō* or *dōōb'i-ō*) without doubt; **sine prole** (*prō'lē* or *prō'le*) without issue, without children; **sine qua non** (*kwā non* or *kwä nōn*) an indispensable condition.

sinecure *sī'ni-kūr* or *sin'*, *n* a benefice without cure of souls; an office without work, a cushy job. — Also *adj*. — *n* **sin'ecurism**. — *n* **sin'ecurist**. [L *sine* without, and *cūra* care]

sinew *sin'ū*, *n* a piece of strong fibrous tissue that joins a muscle to a bone, a tendon; physical strength, muscle; (often *pl*) (a source of) strength or power of any kind. — *vt* (*poetic*) to bind as if by sinews; to strengthen. — *adj* **sin'ewed**. — *adj* **sin'ewless**. — *adj* **sin'ewy**. — **sinews of war** money. [OE *sinu*, genitive *sinwe*]

sinfonia *sin-fō'ni-ə*, *sin-fō-nē'ə*, *n* a symphony; a symphony orchestra. — *n* **sinfonietta** (*-nyet'ə*) a simple, or light, little symphony; a small symphony orchestra. — **sinfonia concertante** (*kon-chər-tan'ti*) an orchestral work with parts for more than one solo instrument. [Ital]

sing *sing*, *vi* to utter melodious sounds in musical succession in articulating words; to perform songs; to emit more or less songlike sounds; to give a cantabile or lyrical effect; (of the ears) to ring; to be capable of being sung; to write poetry (*literary*); to confess, to turn informer, to squeal (*slang, esp NAm*). — *vt* to utter or perform by voice, musically; to chant; to celebrate; to proclaim, relate, in song or verse or in comparable manner; to bring, drive, render, pass, etc by singing: — *pa t* **sang** or (now rarely) **sung**; *pa p* **sung**. — *adj* **sing'able**. — *n* **sing'ableness**. — *n* **sing'er** a person, bird, etc, that sings; a person who sings as a profession; an informer (*slang, esp NAm*); a poet (*obs*). — *n* **sing'ing**. — *adv* **sing'ingly**. — **singer-song'writer** a person who performs songs that he or she has also written; **sing'ing-bird** a songbird; **singing flame** a flame that gives a musical note in a tube; **sing'ing-gallery** a gallery occupied by singers; **sing'ing-hinny** (*Northern*) a currant cake that hisses on the girdle; **sing'ing-man** (*Shakesp*) a man employed to sing, eg in a church choir; **singing master** a teacher of singing; **singing sand** musical sand; **singing telegram** a method of delivering a greeting by employing a person specializing in this service to sing the greeting to the recipient; **sing'-sing'** (in New Guinea) a tribal get-together for singing, dancing and feasting; **sing'song** a ballad; jingly verse; (monotonous) up-and-down intonation; an informal gathering of friends at which there is singing; a meeting for community singing. — *adj* of the nature of singsong. — *vt* and *vi* to sing, speak or utter, in a singsong way. — **all-sing'ing-all-dan'cing** (*colloq*) incorporating the full range of features and elaborations; **sing along** (*orig US*) of an audience, to join in the familiar songs with the performer (with *with*; *n* **sing'along**); **sing another song** or **tune** to change to a humbler tone; to express an opinion different from that of someone else, or *esp* from one's own earlier one, to change one's mind; **sing out** to call out distinctly, to shout; to inform, peach (*colloq*); **sing small** to assume a humble tone. [OE *singan*; Ger *singen*, Gothic *siggwan*]

sing or **sing**. *abbrev*: singular.

singe *sinj*, *vt* to burn on the surface; to scorch; to remove by scorching. — *vi* to become scorched: — *pr p* **singe'ing**; *pa t* and *pa p* **singed**. — *n* a burning on the surface; a slight burn. — **singed cat** a person who is better (in any respect) than outward appearance suggests. [OE *sen(c)gan*]

Singhalese. See **Sinhalese**.

single *sing'gl*, *adj* consisting of one only or one part; unique, individual; one-fold; uncombined; unmarried; for the use of or sufficient for one; (of combat) man-to-man; slight, poor (*Shakesp*); (of ale) weak, small; undivided; unbroken; determined; (of a flower) without development of stamens into petals, or having ligulate instead of tubular florets; sincere, honest (*rare*); (of a travel ticket) valid for the outward journey only, not return. — *adv* singly. — *n* anything single; (*usu* in *pl*) an unmarried, unattached person; (in *pl*; in tennis, etc) a game played by one against one; a hit for one run (*cricket*); a talon of a hawk; a gramophone record with *usu* only one tune, or other short recording, on each side; a one-pound or one-dollar note. — *vt* to separate; to pick (out); to pick out challengingly (*Milton*); to take aside; to thin. — *vi* (*Spenser*) to come forth alone. — *n* **sing'lehood** the state of being unmarried. — *n* **sing'leness** (*-gl-nis*). — *n* **sing'let** (*-glit*) a thing that is single; an undershirt or sleeveless vest; a state in which there are no unpaired electrons (*chem*). — *n* **sing'leton** (*-gl-tən*) a single card of its suit in a hand; anything single. — *n* **sing'ling** (*-gling*). — *adv* **sing'ly** (*-gli*) one by one; alone; by oneself. — *adj* **sing'le-acting** (of a reciprocating engine, etc) acting effectively in one direction only. — *adj* **sing'le-action** (of a firearm) having a hammer which requires to be cocked manually before firing. — Also *n*. — *adj* **sing'le-breasted** with one thickness over the breast and one row of buttons. — *adj* **sing'le-chamber** having one legislative house. — **single cream** cream with a low fat-content that will not thicken when beaten; **sing'le-cross** (*genetics*) a first-generation hybrid of two inbred lines; **single-deck'er** a vessel or vehicle, *esp* a bus, with only one deck. — *adj* **single-digit** of a number or percentage smaller than ten. — **sing'le-end** (*Scot*) a one-room dwelling, *esp* in a tenement; **single-entry** a system of book-keeping in which each entry appears only once on one side or other of an account. — *adj* **sing'le-eyed** one-eyed; devoted, unselfish. — *adj* **sing'le-figure**. — **single figures** a score, total, etc, of any number from 1 to 9; **single file** see under **file**; **sing'le-foot** (*dressage*) a brisk walking pace with each foot striking the ground separately, a rack or amble. — *adj* and *adv* **single-hand'ed** by oneself: unassisted; with or for one hand. — *adj* **single-heart'ed** sincere; without duplicity; dedicated, devoted in one's attitude. — *adv* **single-heart'edly**. — **single house** (*Scot*) a house one room deep; **single-lens reflex (camera)** see **reflex camera**. — *adj* **single-mind'ed** ingenuous; bent upon one sole purpose. — **single-mind'edness**; **single parent** a mother or father bringing up children alone (hence **single-parent family**). — *adj* **sing'le-phase** (of an alternating electric current) requiring one outward and one return conductor for transmission. — **singles bar** or **club** one *esp* for unmarried or unattached people, where friendships (and implicitly sexual relationships) can be formed; **single-seat'er** a car, aeroplane, etc fitted with one seat only. — *adj* **sing'le-sex** (of schools, etc) for pupils, members, etc of one sex only. — **single soldier** (*Scott*) a private. — *adj* **sing'le-soled** having one thickness of sole. — *vt* **single-step'** (*comput*) to carry out a single instruction on (a program). — **sing'lestick** (*-gl-stik*) a fighting stick for one hand; a fight or game with singlesticks; **single tax** a tax on ground-rent or land-values to supersede all other taxes; **single ten** (*Shakesp*) the ten of a card suit; **sing'le-wicket** cricket with one wicket, and with one batsman at a time. — **single transferable vote** see under **transfer**. [OFr, from L *singulī* one by one]

singletree *sing'gl-trē*, *n*. Same as **swingletree**.

sing-sing, singsong. See under **sing**.

singspiel *sing'spēl* or Ger *zing'shpēl*, *n* a semi-dramatic representation in dialogue and song. [Gr, from *singen* to sing, and *Spiel* play]

singular *sing'gū-lər*, *adj* single; unique; proper; private; denoting or referring to one; pre-eminent; pre-eminently good or efficacious; extraordinary; peculiar; strange; odd. — *adv* singularly. — *n* an individual person or thing; the singular number or a word in the singular number (*gram*). — *n* **singularīzā'tion** or **-s-**. — *vt* **sing'ularize** or **-ise** to make singular; to signalize. — *n* **sing'ularism** a philosophy that recognizes one principle only, opposed to *pluralism*. — *n* **sing'ularist** someone who affects singularity; an upholder of singularism. — *n* **singularity** (*-lar'i-ti*) the fact or state of being singular; peculiarity; individuality; oddity; oneness; anything curious or remarkable; a point in space-time at which matter is compressed to an infinitely great density (*astron*). — *adv* **sing'ularly** in a singular manner; peculiarly; strangely; singly; pre-eminently (*archaic*). [L *singulāris*]

singult *sing'gult*, (*archaic*) *n* a sob. — *n* **singult'us** (*med*) hiccuping. [L *singultus* a sob]

sinh *shīn* or *sīn-āch'*, (*math*) *n* a conventional abbreviation of *hyperbolic sine*.

Sinhalese *sin'hə-lēz* or *-lēz'* or **Singhalese, Cingalese** *sing'gə-lēz, -lēz'*, also **Sinhala** *sin'hə-lə*, *adj* of the majority population of Sri Lanka (formerly Ceylon); of or in their language, similar to Pali. — *n* a member of the Sinhalese people; their language. [Sans *Siṁhala* Ceylon]

Sinic *sin'ik*, *adj* Chinese. — *n* **Sin'icism** (*-sizm*) a Chinese custom, idiom, etc. — *vt* and *vi* **sin'icize** or **-ise** to make or become Chinese or of Chinese character. [From Med L *Sinicus* Chinese; see also **Sinaean**]

sinical. See under **sine**[1].

sinister *sin'is-tər*, formerly also *-is'*, *adj* suggestive of threatened evil, ominous; malign; underhand; left or on the left side; on the left side from the point of view of the bearer of the shield, not the beholder (*heraldry*), and similarly sometimes in description of an illustration, etc; inauspicious; unlucky; misleading (*obs*). — *n* **sinisterity** (*-ter'*; *rare*) left-handedness; sinister quality. — *adv* **sin'isterly**. — *adv* **sin'isterwise**. — *adj* **sin'istral** turning to the left; left-handed; (of flatfish) lying left side up; (of a shell) coiled contrary to the normal way. — *n* a left-handed person. — *n* **sinistral'ity**. — *adv* **sin'istrally**. — *adj* **sinistrous** (*si-nis'* or *sin'is-*) inauspicious; sinister (*obs*). — *adv* **sinistrously**. [L, left, on the left side]

sinistrodextral *si-nis-trō-deks'trəl*, *adj* moving, going or extending from left to right. [**sinister** and **dexter**]

sinistrorse *sin-is-trörs'* or *sin'*, (*biol*) *adj* (of a climbing plant) rising spirally and turning to the right, ie crossing an outside observer's field of view from right to left upwards (like an ordinary spiral stair). — Also **sinistrors'al**. — *adv* **sinistrors'ally**. — *adv* **sinistrorse'ly**. [L *sinistrōrsus*, *sinistrōversus* towards the left side, from *sinister* left, and *vertere*, *versum* to turn]

sink *singk*, *vi* to become submerged, wholly or partly; to subside; to fall slowly; to go down passively; to pass to a lower level or state; to penetrate or be absorbed; to slope away, dip; to diminish; to collapse; to be or become withdrawn inwards. — *vt* to cause or allow to sink; (*golf*, etc) to cause (the ball) to run into the hole (*colloq*); to suppress; to degrade; to conceal; to appropriate surreptitiously; to excavate; to let in, insert; to abandon; to abolish; to merge; to pay (a debt); to lose under the horizon; to invest, *esp* unprofitably or beyond easy recovery; to damn or ruin (*esp* in imprecation); to drink quickly (*colloq*): — *pa t* **sank** or (now rarely) **sunk**; *pa p* **sunk** or **sunk'en**. — *n* a kitchen or scullery trough or basin with a drain, for washing dishes, etc; a receptacle or drain for filth or dirty water; a place where things are engulfed or where foul things gather; a cesspool; a depression in a surface; an area without surface drainage; a swallow-hole (*geol*); a shaft; a natural or artificial means of absorbing or discharging heat, fluid, etc (*phys*, etc). — *n* **sink'age** the process of sinking; amount of sinking; a sunken area or depression; shrinkage. — *n* **sink'er** a person who sinks; a weight for sinking anything, such as a fishing-line; a doughnut (*US informal*); a mistletoe root. — *n* and *adj* **sink'ing**. — *adj* **sink'y** yielding underfoot. — **sink'hole** a hole for filth; a swallow-hole (*NAm*); **sinking fund** a fund formed by setting aside income to accumulate at interest to pay off debt; **sink unit** a fitting consisting of sink, draining-board, with cupboards, etc underneath. — **sink in** to be absorbed; to be understood. [OE *sincan* (intransitive verb); Ger *sinken*, Du *zinken*]

sink-a-pace or **sinke-a-pace**. Same as **cinque-pace**.

sinner, etc. See under **sin²**.

sinnet *sin'it*. Same as **sennit**.

Sinn Fein *shin fān*, *n* a political movement and party in Ireland championing a republic, opposing partition and later campaigning for reunification. — *n* **Sinn Fein'er**. — *n* **Sinn Fein'ism**. [Irish, we ourselves]

sinningia *sin-in'ji-ə*, *n* any Brazilian plant of the genus *Sinningia* of the *Gesneriaceae* family, *esp Sinningia speciosa*, popularly known as gloxinia and grown in greenhouses for its bell-shaped, velvety flowers. [W *Sinning*, German gardener]

Sino- *sī-nō-*, *-nə-*, *sin-* *pfx* denoting Chinese, as in *Sino-American*. — *n* **Si'nologue** a person with knowledge of Chinese language, culture, etc, a Sinologist. — *adj* **Sinolog'ical** (*-loj'*). — *n* **Sinologist** (*-ol'ə-jist*). — *n* **Sinol'ogy** the study of Chinese language, culture, etc. — *n* and *adj* **Si'nophil** or **Si'nophile** (someone who is) friendly to the Chinese or attracted by Chinese culture. — *n* **Sinoph'ily** or **Sinoph'ilism**. [Gr *Sīnai* Chinese (pl)]

sino- *sin'ō-* or *sī'nō-*, *pfx* denoting sinus.

sinoekete. See **synoecete**.

sinopia *si-nō'pi-ə*, *n* a reddish-brown pigment used for one of the preparatory drawings of a fresco, obtained from **sin'opite**, an iron ore; a drawing so made. — Also **sinō'pis**. [L *sinopis* sinopite]

sinsemilla *sin-sə-mil'ə*, *n* marijuana containing high levels of the narcotic tetrahydrocannabinol; the plant, a seedless female strain of *Cannabis sativa*, from which it is obtained. [Am Sp *sin* without, and *semilla* seed]

sinsyne *sin-sīn'*, (*Scot*) *adv* since that time. [**sin²** and **syne**]

sinter *sin'tər*, *n* a deposit from hot springs. — *vt* to heat (a mixture of powdered metals) sometimes under pressure, to the melting-point of the metal in the mixture which has the lowest melting-point, the melted metal binding together the harder particles. — *vi* to coalesce under heat without liquefaction. — *adj* **sin'tery**. [Ger *Sinter*; cf **cinder**]

sinuate *sin'ū-āt* or **sinuated** *sin'ū-ā-tid*, *adj* having a wavy edge or margin; winding; sinuous. — *adv* **sin'uately**. — *n* **sinuā'tion**. [L *sinuātus* curved, bent, from *sinus* bend]

sinuous *sin'ū-əs*, *adj* wavy; bending in a supple manner. — *adj* **sinuose** (*sin'ū-ōs*) sinuous. — *n* **sinuosity** (*-os'*). — *adv* **sin'uously**. — **sin'uousness**. [L *sinuōsus*, from *sinus*, bend]

sinus *sī'nəs*, *n* an air-filled cavity in the bones of the skull, connecting with the nose; a narrow cavity through which pus is discharged; a cavity; an indentation; a notch between two lobes in a leaf (*bot*): — *pl* **si'nuses**. — *n* **sinusī'tis** or **sinuī'tis** (*sī-nū-*) inflammation of a sinus, *esp* one in the skull communicating with the nose. — *adj* **sinupall'ial** (*sī-nū-*) or **sinupall'iate** (of certain bivalve molluscs) having an indented pallial line for the retraction and expansion of the pallial siphons. — *n* **sinusoid** (*sī'nə-soid*) the curve of sines ($y = a \sin x$); a small blood vessel in certain organs, such as the liver, heart, etc. — *adj* **sinusoid'al**. — *adv* **sīnusoid'ally**. [L *sinus*, *-ūs* a bend, fold, bay]

Sioux *sōō*, *n* an American Indian of a tribe now living in the Dakotas, Minnesota, and Montana; any of the group of languages spoken by them: — *pl* **Sioux** (*sōō* or *sōōz*). — Also *adj*. — *adj* **Siou'an** pertaining to the Sioux, or to a larger group to which the Sioux belong; pertaining to the languages of this group. — *n* the group of languages spoken by the Siouan peoples. [Fr, from a native word]

sip *sip*, *vt* and *vi* to drink, or drink from, in small quantities by action of the lips: — *pr p* **sipp'ing**; *pa t* and *pa p* **sipped**. — *n* the act of sipping; the quantity sipped at once. — *n* **sipp'er** someone who or something that sips; a drinking straw (*NAm*). [Cf **sup**; OE *sypian*; LGer *sippen*]

sipe¹ *sīp*, (*dialect*) *vi* to soak through; to seep or ooze. — Also **sype**. [OE *sipian* to soak]

sipe² *sīp*, *n* a tiny groove or slit in the tread of a tyre, aiding water dispersal and improving the tyre's grip. [From **sipe¹**]

siphon or **syphon** *sī'fən*, *n* a bent tube or channel by which a liquid may be drawn off over a higher point to a lower level; a tubular organ for intake and output of water, as in lamellibranchs; an aerated-water bottle that discharges by a siphon. — *vt* (often with *off*) to convey, remove by means of (or as if by means of) a siphon; to divert (funds, money, etc). — *n* **sī'phonage**. — *adj* **sī'phonal** or **sīphon'ic**. — *n pl* **Sīphonap'tera** the flea order of insects. — *adj* **sī'phonate** having a siphon. — *n* **sī'phonet** an aphid's honeydew tube. — *n* **sīphon'ogam** a seed plant. — *n* **sīphonog'amy** (*bot*) fertilization by pollen tube. — *n* **sī'phonophore** (or *sī-fon'*) a colonial hydrozoan of the order *Siphonophora*. — *n* **sīphonostele** (*-stē'lē* or *-stēl'*; *bot*) a hollow cylinder of vascular tissue. — *n* **sī'phuncle** a tube connecting the chambers of a nautilus; a siphonet. [Gr *sīphōn*, *siphōn* siphon]

Siporex® *sip'ər-eks*, *n* a material used by builders, and also by artists, a form of aerated concrete, which can be sawn, etc.

sippet *sip'it*, *n* a morsel, *esp* of bread to be eaten with soup. — *vt* and *vi* **sipp'le** to sip at leisure. [Cf **sip** and **sup**]

sipunculid *sī-pungk-ū-lid*, *n* any marine worm of the group *Sipunculacea*, having a retractile proboscis. — Also *adj*. — *n* and *adj* **sipunc'uloid**. [Mod L, from L *siphunculus* a little pipe]

si quis *sī* or *sē kwis*, *n* a public notice, *esp* one announcing the impending ordination of a parish priest, allowing for objections to be raised. [L *sī quis* if anybody (wants, knows, has found, etc)]

sir *sûr*, *n* a word of respect (or disapprobation) used in addressing a man; a gentleman; (with *cap*) prefixed to the Christian name of a knight or baronet; (with *cap*) a word of address to a man in a formal letter; formerly used as a translation of L *dominus*, bachelor of arts (as distinguished from *magister*, master of arts). — *vt* to address as 'sir': — *pr p* **sirr'ing**; *pa t* and *pa p* **sirred**. [OFr *sire*, from L *senior* an elder]

Sir. (*Bible*) *abbrev*: (the Apocryphal Book) Wisdom of Jesus the son of Sirach (also called *Ecclesiasticus*).

sircar or **sirkar** *sər-kär'* or *sûr'*, (*Anglo-Ind*) *n* the state or government; the authorities; a province or district; an Indian clerk or factotum. — Also **circar**. [Urdu *sarkār* a superintendent, from Pers *sar* head, and *kār* agent]

sirdar *sər-där'* or *sûr*, *n* a military leader in India and other Eastern countries; a commander-in-chief, *specif* (formerly) the British commander-in-chief of the Egyptian army. [Urdu *sardār*, from Pers *sar* head, and *dār* holding]

sire *sīr*, *n* a father, *esp* of a horse or other animal; an ancestor; a master, lord, man of high rank (*obs*); a term of address to a king (*hist*); a senior or elder (*obs*). — *vt* (of animals) to father. [See **sir**]

siren *sī'rən*, *n* a signalling or warning instrument that produces sound by the escape of air or steam through a rotating perforated plate; a fascinating woman, insidious and deceptive; a bewitching singer; (with *cap*) one of certain sea nymphs, part woman, part bird, whose seductive songs lured sailors to their deaths on rocks (*Gr mythol*); a mermaid; any eel-like amphibian of the family *Sirenidae*, having no hind legs and with external gills. — Also *adj*. — *adj* **sirē'nian** of, relating or belonging to the *Sirenia*, an order of aquatic mammals now represented by the dugong and the manatee. — *n* a member of this order, having paddlelike forelimbs and no hind limbs. — *adj* **sirenic** (*-ren'*). — *vt* **sire'nize** or **-ise** to bewitch, allure or enchant. — **siren suit** a close-fitting trousered overall *orig* designed for use in air raids. [Gr *Seirēn*]

sirgang *sûr'gang*, *n* a green Asiatic jay-like bird. [Prob from native name]

sirih or **siri** *sē'ri*, *n* betel. [Malay *sīrih*]

Sirius *sir'i-əs*, *n* the Dogstar. — *adj* **Sir'ian**. — *n* **sirī'asis** sunstroke. [L *Sīrius*, from Gr *Seirios*]

sirkar. See **sircar**.

sirloin or rarely **surloin** *sûr'loin*, *n* the upper part of a loin of beef. [From a by-form of OFr *surlonge*, from *sur* over, and *longe* (cf **loin**)]

sirname. Same as **surname**.

sirocco *si-rok'ō* or **scirocco** *shi-rok'ō*, *n* a hot, dry, dusty and gusty wind blowing from N Africa to the north Mediterranean coast, becoming moist further north; any oppressive south or south-east wind; a wind from the desert; a drying machine: — *pl* **sirocc'os** or **scirocc'os**. — Also **siroc'** or **sciroc'**. [Ital *s(c)irocco*, from Ar *sharq* east wind]

sirrah *sir'ə*, *n* (*archaic*) sir (used in anger or contempt). — **sirree'** (*sûr-ē'*; *US*) a form of sir or sirrah used for emphasis, *esp* with *yes* or *no*. [An extension of **sir**]

sir-reverence *sə-rev'ə-rəns*, (*obs*) a corruption of the phrase *save reverence*, used apologetically when anything vulgar or disgusting has to be mentioned. — *n* (a piece of) excrement.

sirup. See **syrup**.

sirvente *sēr-vât'*, *n* a medieval verse form of satirical or heroic character as composed and performed by troubadours. [Fr]

SIS *abbrev*: Satellite Information Services; (in New Zealand) Security Intelligence Service.

sis or **siss** *sis*, (*esp NAm*) *n* a contracted form of **sister** (used in addressing a girl). — *n* and *adj* **siss'y** (*orig* chiefly *NAm*) cissy. — *adj* **siss'ified** cissy.

-sis *-sis*, *n sfx* signifying: action, process; condition caused by: — *pl* **-ses** (*-sēz*). [Gr]

sisal *sī'səl* or *sī'zəl*, *n* (also **sis'al-hemp** or **-grass**) agave fibre, used for making rope, etc. [First exported from *Sisal*, in Yucatán]

siserary or **sisserary** *sis-ər-ā'ri*, *n* a scolding; a blow. — Also **sasarara** or **sassarara**. — **with a siserary** suddenly; on the spot. [Corruption of **certiorari**]

siskin *sis'kin*, *n* a yellowish-green Eurasian finch, *Carduelis spinus*. [Ger dialect *sisschen*; appar Slav]

siss. See under **sis**.

sisserary. See **siserary**.

sissoo *sis'ōō*, *n* a papilionaceous Indian timber tree (*Dalbergia*) or its wood. [Hindi *sīsū*]

sissy. See under **sis**.

sist *sist*, (*Scots law*) *vt* to stop, stay; to cite, summon. — *n* a stay. [L *sistere* to make to stand]

sister *sis'tər*, *n* a daughter of the same parents; a half-sister; formerly, a sister-in-law; a female fellow; a member of a sisterhood; a nun; a senior nurse, *esp* one in charge of a ward. — *adj* of the same origin; fellow; built on the same model. — *vt* to be a sister to; to call sister. — *n* **sis'terhood** the act or state of being a sister; the relationship of sister; a society, *esp* a religious community, of women; a set or class of women. — *adj* **sis'tering** (*Shakesp*) neighbouring. — *adj* **sis'terless**. — *n* **sis'terliness**. — *adj* **sis'terly** like or befitting a sister; kind; affectionate. — **sister hook** one of a pair of hooks that close each other; **sis'ter-in-law** a husband's or wife's sister, or a brother's wife; a husband or wife's brother's wife: — *pl* **sis'ters-in-law**. — *adj* **sis'terlike**. — **sister-chromatid exchange** reciprocal exchange of DNA between the chromatids of a single chromosome. [Appar ON *systir*; OE *sweostor*; Du *zuster*, Ger *Schwester*]

Sistine *sis'tīn* or *-tēn* or *-tin*, *adj* of Pope *Sixtus*, *esp* Sixtus IV (1471–84) or V (1585–90). — **Sistine Chapel** the Pope's chapel in the Vatican, built by Sixtus IV; **Sistine Madonna** a picture by Raphael of the Madonna with Sixtus II (257–8).

sistrum *sis'trəm*, *n* an ancient Egyptian wire rattle used in Isis-worship: — *pl* **sis'tra**. [L *sīstrum*, from Gr *seistron*]

Sisyphean *sis-i-fē'ən*, *adj* relating to *Sisyphus*, king of Corinth, condemned in Tartarus to roll ceaselessly up a hill a huge stone which would roll back to the foot of the hill again each time he neared the top; hence, endless, laborious and futile.

sit *sit*, *vi* to rest on the buttocks and thighs with the upper body more or less vertical; (of birds) to perch; to brood; to have a seat, eg in parliament; to be in session; to reside; to be a tenant; to be located, have station or (of the wind) direction; to pose, be a model; to undergo an examination, be a candidate; to weigh, bear, press; to be disposed in adjustment, hang, fit; to befit. — *vt* to seat; to have a seat on, ride; to undergo or be examined in; (often in combination) to stay in or with in order to look after, as in *babysit*: — *pr p* **sitt'ing**; *pa t* and *pa p* **sat**, (*archaic*) **sate** (*sat* or *sāt*). — *n* a mode or spell of sitting. — *n* **sitt'er** someone who sits; someone who sits as a model for an artist or with a medium; someone who takes responsibility for looking after a child at home while its parents are out, a babysitter; also, someone who looks after a house, pet, etc in the absence of its owner; a sitting bird; an easy shot; an easy dupe (*slang*); anything difficult to fail in; a sitting-room (*slang*). — *n* **sitt'ing** the state of being seated or act of taking a seat; a period of being seated; brooding on eggs; a clutch; one or two or more groups into which a large number of diners are divided, or the period set aside for each group to occupy the dining-room, etc; a continuous meeting of a body; a spell of posing for an artist, etc; a seat; a church seat. — *adj* seated; brooding; in the course of a parliamentary session. — **sit'-down** a spell of sitting. — *adj* (of a meal) that one sits down to; (of a strike) in which workers down tools but remain in occupation of the plant, workshop, etc. — **sit'fast** a lump in a horse's skin under the saddle; **sit'-in** the occupation of a building, etc, as an organized protest against some (alleged) injustice, etc (also *adj*); **sitt'er-in** a babysitter; **sitt'ing-room** a room in which members of a family commonly sit; a space for sitting; **sitting target** an easy target or victim; **sitting tenant** the tenant currently occupying a property; **sit'-upon** (*colloq*) the buttocks. — **sit at** to live at the rate of expense of; **sit back** to take no active part, or no further active part; **sit by** to look on without taking any action; **sit down** to take a seat; to pause, rest; to take up positions prior to beginning a siege; to accept meekly (with *under*); **sit in** to act as a baby-sitter; to be present as a visitor, and (*usu*) take part, eg at a conference or discussion; to have or take part in a sit-in; **sit on** or **upon** to hold an official inquiry regarding; to repress, check or delay dealing with (*slang*); **sit out** to sit apart without participating; to sit to the end of; to outstay; **sit tight** to maintain one's seat; to keep one's position quietly and unobtrusively; **sitting pretty** see under **pretty**; **sit under** to be in the habit of hearing the preaching of (a particular priest, minister, etc); **sit up** to rise from a recumbent to a sitting position, or from a relaxed to an erect seat; to become alert or startled; to remain up instead of going to bed; to keep watch during the night. [OE *sittan*; Ger *sitzen*, L *sedēre*]

sitar *si-tär'*, *n* a Hindu plucked-string instrument with a long neck and a rounded body. — Also **sittar'**. [Hindi *sitār*]

sitatunga *si-tə-tōōng'gə* or *-tung'gə*, also **situtun'ga** *si-tə-* or *si-tōō-*, *n* a species of African antelope, *Tragelaphus spekei*, notable for its elongated hooves which allow it to walk on marshy ground. [Swahili]

sitcom *sit'kom*, (*colloq*) *n* a *sit*uation *com*edy.

site *sīt*, *n* the situation, *esp* of a building, town, etc; the area or ground occupied or set apart for a building, etc; an area set aside for some specific purpose, activity, etc; posture (*obs*). — *vt* to locate, position. — **site-specific mutagenesis** the possibility of altering a DNA sequence at a defined position, eg by synthesizing an alternative sequence and reinserting it into the host chromosome. [L *situs* situation, from *sineri*, *situs* to be placed, from *sinere* to allow]

sith[1] *sith*, (*Shakesp*) *adv*, *prep* and *conj* since. — Also **sith'en**, (*Spenser*, *Shakesp*) **sith'ence** and **sith'ens**. [OE *siththan*, for *sīth than* (instrumental), after that; cf **since**, **syne**[1]]

sith[2], **sithe** or **sythe** *sīdh n* time: — *pl* **sith**, **sithes** or **sythes**. [OE *sīth* time]

sithe[1] *sīdh*, (*archaic*) *n* and *vt*. Same as **scythe**.

sithe[2] *sīdh*, *n* and *vi*. An obsolete or dialect form of **sigh**.

sithe[3]. See **sith**[2].

sithen, **sithence**, **sithens**. See **sith**[1].

sitiology, **sitiophobia**. See under **sitology**.

Sitka spruce *sit'kə sprōōs*, *n* a spruce tree, *Picea sitchensis*, with sharp blue-green needles — grown for its timber in both N America and Europe. [*Sitka* in Alaska]

sitology *sī-tol'ə-ji* or **sitiology** *sit-i-ol'ə-ji*, *n* dietetics. — *n* **sitophō'bia** or **sitiophō'bia** morbid aversion to food. [Gr *sītos*, dimin *sītion* grain, food]

sitrep *sit'rep*, (*colloq*) *n* a report on the current military position (also *fig*). [*sit*uation *rep*ort]

Sitta *sit'ə*, *n* the nuthatch genus. — *adj* **sitt'ine**. [Gr *sittē* nuthatch]

sittar. See **sitar**.

sitter, **sitting**, etc. See under **sit**.

sittine. See under **Sitta**.

Sittlichkeit *zit'lihh-kīt*, (*Ger*) *n* morals, morality; that which is becoming or suitable.

situate *sit'ū-āt*, *vt* to set, place, locate; to circumstance. — *adj* (*-ū-it*; now *esp law*) situated. — *adj* **sit'uated** set, located; circumstanced. — *n* **situā'tion** location; place; position; momentary state; condition; a set of circumstances, a juncture; a critical point in the action of a play or the development of the plot of a novel; office, employment. — *adj* **situā'tional**. — **situation comedy** a comedy, now *esp* in a television or radio series in which the same characters appear in each episode, which depends for its humour on the behaviour of the characters in particular, sometimes contrived, situations (*colloq* short form **sitcom**); **situation ethics** see under **ethic**. [LL *situātus*, from L *situere*, to place]

situla *sit'ū-lə* (*antiq*) *n* a bucket: — *pl* **sit'ūlae** (*-lē*). [L]

situs *sī'təs*, *n* position; the normal position of an organ in the body: — *pl* **sī'tus** (*-z*). [L, site, position]

situtunga. See **sitatunga**.

sit. vac. *sit vak*, *abbrev*: situation vacant: — *pl* **sits vac**.

sitz-bath *sits'-bäth*, *n* a therapeutic hip-bath in hot water. [Ger *Sitzbad*]

sitzkrieg *sits'krēg* or *zits'krēhh*, *n* the period (September 1939 to May 1940) of comparative military quiet at the opening of World War II, or any similar period in any war. [Ger *sitzen* to sit, and *Krieg* war; cf **blitzkrieg**]

Sium *sī'əm*, *n* the water-parsnip genus. [Gr *sion*]

Siva *shē'və*, *sē'*, or *shi'və*, *si' n* the third god of the Hindu triad, destroyer and reproducer. — Also **Shiva** (*shē'və* or *shi'və*). — *n* **Si'vaism** or **Shi'vaism**. — *adj* **Sivaist'ic** or **Shivaist'ic**. — *n* **Si'vaite** or **Shi'vaite**. — *n* **Sivapithē'cus** (or *-pith'*) an Indian Miocene fossil anthropoid. — *n* **Sivathē'rium** a gigantic giraffe-like Indian Pliocene fossil animal. [Sans *śsiva* friendly, gracious]

Sivan *sē-vän'*, *n* the ninth month of the Jewish civil year, third of the ecclesiastical year, part of May and June. [Heb *sīwān*]

siver. See **syver**.

siwash *sī'wosh*, (also with *cap*; *NW US derog colloq*) *n* a NW American Indian. — Also *adj*. [Chinook, from Fr *sauvage* wild]

six *siks*, *n* the cardinal numeral next above five; a symbol representing it (6, vi, etc); a set of that number; an article of size denoted by it; a playing-card with six pips; a score of six points, tricks, etc; the sixth hour after midnight or after midday; a six-cylinder engine or car; a six-syllable line; a division of a Brownie Guide or Cub Scout pack; the age of six years. — *adj* of the number six; six years old. — *n* **six'er** anything counting for six, eg a hit at cricket, or indicated by six; the leader of a Brownie Guide or Cub Scout six. — *adj* and *adv* **six'fold** in six divisions: six times as much. — *adj* **sixth** last of six; next after the fifth; equal to one of six equal parts. — *n* a sixth part; a person or thing in sixth position; an interval of five (conventionally called six) diatonic degrees (*music*); a combination of two tones separated by such an interval (*music*). — *adv* **sixth'ly** in the sixth place. — *adj* **six'-day** of or for six days (ie *usu* excluding Sunday). — *adj* **six'-foot** measuring six feet. — **six'-foot'er** a person six feet tall; **six'-gun** a six-shooter; **six'-pack** a pack which comprises six items sold as one unit, *esp* a pack of six cans of beer; **six'pence** a coin worth six old pence; its value. — *adj* **six'penny** costing or worth sixpence; cheap; worthless. — *n* formerly, a sixpenny book. — n and *adj* **six'score**. — **six'-shooter** a six-chambered revolver; **sixth form** (the classes studying in) the (*usu*) two years of preparation for A-level examinations in England or, in Scotland, the one year of preparation for higher level examinations and sixth-year studies; **sixth-form college** a school which provides the sixth-form education for the pupils of an area. — **at sixes and sevens** in disorder; **hit** or **knock for six** to overcome completely; to take by surprise; **long** or **short sixes** candles weighing six to the pound, about 8 or 4 inches long respectively; **six (of one) and half a dozen (of the other)** equal, attributable to both parties equally; having alternatives which are considered equivalent, equally acceptable, etc; **Six Nations** a more recent N American grouping of the Five Nations (qv) and the Tuscaroras; **the Six Counties** Northern Ireland. [OE *siex*; Ger *sechs*; Gaelic *sé*; L *sex*, Gr *hex*, Sans *ṣaṣ*]

sixain or **sixaine** *sik-sān'*, (*prosody*) *n* a stanza of six lines. [Fr]

sixte *sikst*, (*fencing*) *n* a parry with hand on guard opposite the right breast, sword point a little raised to the right. [Fr]

sixteen *siks-tēn'* or *siks'tēn*, *n* and *adj* six and ten. — *n* **sixteen'er** a verse of sixteen syllables. — *n* and *adj* **sixteen'mo** sextodecimo, written 16mo: — *pl* **six-teen'mos**. — *adj* **sixteenth'** (or *siks'*) last of sixteen; next after the fifteenth; equal to one of sixteen equal parts. — *n* a sixteenth part; a person or thing in sixteenth position. — *adv* **sixteenth'ly**. [OE *siextēne* (*-tīene*); see **six** and **ten**]

sixty *siks'ti*, *adj* and *n* six times ten: — *pl* **six'ties** the numbers sixty to sixty-nine; the years so numbered in a life or century; a range of temperature from sixty to just less than seventy degrees. — *adj* **six'tieth** last of sixty; next after the fifty-ninth; equal to one of sixty equal parts. — *n* a sixtieth part; a person or thing in sixtieth position. — **sixty-four-(thousand-)dollar question** (from a US quiz game), the final and most difficult question one has to answer, from the sixty-four-(thousand-)dollar top prize money awarded; hence, a hard question to answer, the supreme or crucial question. [OE *siextig*]

size[1] *sīz*, *n* bigness; magnitude; any of a series of graded measurements into which eg clothes, shoes, are divided; an allowance (*obs*); a portion of food and drink (*obs*); an assize (*obs*). — *vt* to arrange according to size; to measure; formerly at various universities, to get (food or drink) on credit. — *vi* (*rare*) to draw a size; to assume size. — *adj* **sī'zable** or **size'able** of a considerable size. — *n* **sī'zar** (also **sī'zer**) at Cambridge and Dublin, a student receiving a college allowance towards expenses. — *n* **sī'zarship**. — *adj* **sized** having a particular size (often in combination, as in *medium-sized*). — *n* **sī'zer** a measurer; a gauge; a thing of considerable or great size (*slang*). — *n* **sī'zing** sorting by size. — *n* **sī'zism** or **sī'zeism** discrimination against fat people. — *n* and *adj* **sī'zist** or **sī'zeist**. — **size-exclusion chromatography** chromatographic separation of particles according to size, a solid phase of material of restricted pore size functioning as a molecular sieve. — **of a size** of the same size; **size up** to take mental measure of (also *fig*); **the size of it** (*colloq*) an assessment of the present situation or state of affairs obtaining. [**assize**]

size[2] *sīz*, *n* a weak glue or gluey material used for stiffening paper or rendering it sufficiently water-resistant to accept printing-ink without over-absorption, for stiffening fabric and for preparing walls before plastering or wallpapering. — *vt* to cover or treat with size. — *adj* **sized**. — *n* **sī'zer**. — *n* **sī'ziness**. — *n* **sī'zing** application of size, or material for the purpose. — *adj* **sī'zy**. [Origin obscure]

size[3] *sīz*. Same as **sice**[1].

sizel *siz'l*. Same as **scissel**.

sizzle *siz'l*, *vi* to make a hissing sound of frying; to be in a state of intense emotion, *esp* anger or excitement (*colloq*). — *vt* and *vi* to fry, scorch, sear. — *n* a hissing sound; extreme heat. — *n* **sizz'ler** a sizzling heat or day; a thing strikingly fierce or effective. — *n* **sizz'ling** a hissing. — *adj* very hot; very striking. — *adv* **sizz'ingly**. [Imit]

SJ *abbrev*: Society of Jesus.

sjambok *sham'bok*, (*SAfr*) *n* a whip of dried hide. — *vt* to flog. [Afrik, from Malay *samboq*, from Urdu *chābuk*]

Sjögren's syndrome *sher'grenz sin'drōm*, *n* a condition, often associated with rheumatoid arthritis and lupus erythematosus, in which secretion from the mucous membrane becomes deficient, with resulting dryness of eg the mouth and eyes. [HSC *Sjögren*, 20c Swedish opthalmologist]

ska *skä*, *n* a form of Jamaican music similar to reggae. [Origin obscure]

skail, **scail** or **scale** *skāl*, (*Scot*) *vt* and *vi* to disperse; to scatter; to spill. [Ety doubtful; prob not connected with Gaelic *sgaoil*]

skaines mate *skānz māt*, (*Shakesp*) *n perh* a companion, a scapegrace.

skaith. See **scathe**.

skald or **scald** *sköld*, *n* a poet; a Scandinavian bard. — *adj* **skald'ic** or **scald'ic**. — *n* **skald'ship** or **scald'ship**. [ON *skāld*]

skank *skangk*, *vi* to dance to reggae music, lifting the knees up in rapid, jerky movements. — *n* such a dance, or a spell of this kind of dancing — *n* **skank'ing**.

skart, **scart** *skärt*, **scarth** or **skarth** *skärth*, (*Scot*) *n* a cormorant. [ON *skarfr*]

skat[1] *skät*, *n* a three-handed card game using 32 cards. [OFr *escart* laying aside]

skat[2]. Same as **scat**[1].

skat[3]. See **scat**[4].

skate[1] *skāt*, *n* a sole or sandal mounted on a blade (for moving on ice); the blade itself; a boot with such a blade fixed to it; a roller-skate; a spell of skating. — *vi* to go on skates. — *n* **skā'ter**. — *n* **skā'ting**. — **skate'board** a narrow board made of wood, fibreglass, etc, mounted on roller-skate wheels, on which the user balances and rides, *usu* in a standing position; **skate'-boarder**; **skate'boarding**; **skatepark** an area set aside for skateboarding, *usu* including specially designed ramps, obstacles, etc; **skā'ting-rink**. — **get one's skates on** (*colloq*) to hurry; **skate on thin ice** see under **ice**; **skate over** (*fig*) to hurry over lightly; **skate around** (*fig*) to avoid discussing or answering directly. [Du *schaats*, from ONFr *escache* stilt, from LGer *schake* shank]

skate[2] *skāt*, *n* a large edible kind of ray of tropical and temperate waters (*Raia batis*, or related species). [ON *skata*]

skatole *skat'ōl* or *skā'tōl*, *n* a crystalline compound (C_9H_9N) found in faeces and coal tar. [Gr *skōr*, *skatos* dung]

skatt. Same as **scat**[3].

skaw, **scaw** *skö*, *n* a low cape or headland (in place names). [ON *skagi*]

skean. See **skene**.

skear and **skeary**. Dialect forms of **scare** and **scary**.

skedaddle *ski-dad'l*, (*colloq*) *vi* to run off hurriedly. — *n* a hasty flight. — *n* **skedadd'ler**. [Ety uncertain]

skeechan *skē'hhən*, (*Scot*) a kind of beer made by mixing malt liquor, a by-product of the brewing process, with treacle. [Gaelic *caochan* fermented liquor]

skeely *skē'li*, (*Scot*) *adj* skilful. [**skill**]

skeer and **skeery**. Dialect forms of **scare** and **scary**.

skeesicks *skē'ziks*, (*US*) *n* a rascal.

skeet *skēt*, *n* a form of clay-pigeon shooting. [ON *skōta* to shoot]

skeeter *skēt'ər*, (*US*) *n* a colloq short form of **mosquito**.

Skeffington's daughter. See **scavenger**[1].

skeg or **skegg** *skeg*, (*naut*) *n* (in early sailing vessels) a short length of keel projecting aft beyond the sternpost to protect the rudder; (in steamships) an extension or projection from the keel to protect the propellers; (in modern yachts) a short keel used in conjunction with a fin keel; a stabilizing fin projecting from the underside at the rear of a surfboard or sailboard. [Du *scheg* cutwater, from Scand]

skegger *skeg'ər*, *n* a young salmon, a salmon fry. [Scand; perhaps related to **skeg**]

skeigh *skēhh*, (*Scot*) *adj* shy; coy; aloof; skittish. [Cf OE *scēoh* shy]

skein *skān*, *n* a loosely tied coil or standard length of thread or yarn; a tangle (also *fig*); a web; a loose or confused bundle of things; a flock of wild geese in flight; the chromosomal network in a cell when at the mitosis stage (*old cytology*). [OFr *escaigne*]

skelder *skel'dər*, *vi* and *vt* to beg or obtain (money) by begging; to swindle, cheat. [Cant; perh perverted from Du *bedelen* to beg]

skeleton *skel'i-tn*, *n* the internal or external framework of bones of a person or an animal; the veins of a leaf; a framework or outline of anything; a scheme reduced to its essential or indispensable elements; a workforce, etc reduced to its lowest strength; an emaciated person or animal (*colloq*). — Also *adj*. — *adj* **skel'etal**. — *adj* **skeletogenous** (*-toj'*) skeleton-forming. — *vt* **skel'etonize** or **-ise** to reduce to a skeleton or minimum framework; to create the basic framework for. — **skeleton key** a key with its serrated edge or the shaped part of its bit filed down, so that it can open many locks; **skeleton shrimp** a ghostly-looking amphipod (*Caprella*); **skeleton suit** (*hist*) an early 19c boy's suit with the trousers buttoning over the coat. — **skeleton in the cupboard**, **closet**, **house**, etc a hidden domestic sorrow or shame. [Gr *skeleton* (*sōma*), dried (body), from *skellein* to dry]

skelf *skelf* (*Scot* and *N Eng*) a splinter of wood, *esp* one that becomes embedded in the skin. [Prob from obs Du *schelf*]

skell *skel*, (*slang*) *n* a homeless person who lives on the streets, often obtaining money, etc by begging. [Prob from **skelder** or **skellum**]

skellie. See **skelly**.

skelloch *skel'əhh*, (*Scot*) *vi* to yell. — *n* a yell.

skellum, **schellum** or **skelum** *skel'əm*, (*dialect* and *Scot*) *n* a ne'er-do-well; a scamp, rascal. [Du *schelm* a rogue; cf **skelm**]

skelly[1] or **skellie** *skel'i*, (*Scot*) *vi* to squint. — *n* a sideways glance. — *adj* (also **skelly-eyed'**) cross-eyed. [Prob ON; cf OE *sceolh* squint]

skelly[2] *skel'i*, *n* a freshwater white fish, *Coregonus lavaretus*, of the Lake District, a local variation of the powan with spotted flanks.

skelm or **schelm** *skelm*, (*SAfr*) *n* a rascal. [Du *schelm*, Ger *Schelm*]

skelp *skelp*, (*Scot* and *N Eng*)) *vt* to slap. — *vi* to move briskly along; to bound along. — *n* a slap. — *adj* **skelp'ing** very big or full; smacking; lusty. — *n* a smacking. [Gaelic *sgealp* a slap with the palm of the hand]

skelter *skel'tər*, *vi* to scurry. — *n* a scurry.

skene *skēn* or **skean** *skē'ən*, *n* an Irish or Highland dagger, knife, or short sword. — **skene-dhu** or **skean-dhu** (*-do͞o'*) a dirk, a dagger stuck in the stocking in full Highland dress; **skene-occle** (*-ok'l*) a dirk, dagger or knife carried in the sleeve. [Irish and Gaelic *sgian* knife, *dhu* black, *achlais* armpit]

skeo. Same as **skio**.

skep *skep*, *n* a large round basket of wickerwork or straw; a beehive, *esp* one made of straw. — *vt* to collect into a hive: — *pr p* **skepp'ing**; *pa t* and *pa p* **skepped**. — *n* **skep'ful**. [ON *skeppa* bushel]

skeptic, **skepsis**. Same as **sceptic**, **scepsis**.

sker. Same as **skirr**.

skerrick *sker'ik*, (*dialect*; *esp NAm*, *Austr* and *NZ*) *n* a minute quantity, a scrap (chiefly in the phrase **not a skerrick**). [Ety uncertain]

skerry *sker'i*, *n* a reef of rock or a small rocky island. [ON *sker*]

sketch *skech*, *n* a drawing, slight, rough, or without detail, *esp* as a study towards a more finished work; an outline or short account; a short and slightly constructed play, dramatic scene, musical entertainment, etc; a short descriptive essay. — *vt* to make or give a sketch of; to outline, or give the principal points of. — *vi* to practise sketching. — *n* **sketchabil'ity**. — *adj* **sketch'able** worth sketching. — *n* **sketch'er**. — *adv* **sketch'ily**. — *n* **sketch'iness**. — *adj* **sketch'y** like a sketch; incomplete, slight, vague; imperfect, inadequate. — **sketch'book** or **sketch book** a book of or for sketches (in drawing, literature or music). [Du *schets*, prob from Ital *schizzo*, from L *schedium* an extempore, from Gr *schedios* offhand]

skeuomorph *skū'ə-mörf*, *n* a decoration or decorative feature in architecture, etc, derived from the nature of the material (originally) used, or the way of working it; a retained but no longer either functional or incidental characteristic of an artefact, eg the 'casting seams' knapped on to a flint knife, imitated from those on a cast bronze knife (*archaeol*); also applied to modern decorative features such as the imitation stitching on plastic upholstery. — *adj* **skeuomorph'ic**. — *n* **skeuomorph'ism**. [Gr *skeuos* vessel, tool, and *morphe* shape]

Skevington's daughter. See **scavenger**[1].

skew[1] *skū*, *adj* oblique; biased; assymetrical; (of statistics or a curve representing them) not symmetrical about the mean. — *adv* awry. — *n* obliquity. — *vt* and *vi* to set, go, or look obliquely. — *adj* **skewed** distorted; skew. — *n* **skew'ness**. — **skew'back** (*archit*) the part or inclined surface on which a segmented arch abuts; **skew bridge** a bridge having its arch or arches set obliquely on its abutments. — *adj* and *adv* **skew-whiff'** (*colloq*) crooked, awry. [Appar ONFr *eskiu*(*w*)*er*, from OFr *eschuer*; see **eschew**; or MDu *schuwe* to shun; cf **shy**]

skew[2] *skū*, *n* the coping or a coping-stone of a gable. — **skew'-corbel**, **skew'-put** or **skew'-table** the corner-stone supporting the coping of a gable. [OFr *escu*, from L *scūtum* a shield]

skewbald *skū'böld*, *adj* (of an animal, *esp* a horse) marked in white and another colour (not black). — *n* a skewbald horse. [From **skew**[1] and pie**bald**]

skewer *skū'ər*, *n* a long pin of wood or metal, *esp* for holding pieces of meat together for cooking. — *vt* to fasten or pierce with a skewer; to transfix. [**skiver**]

ski *skē*, (formerly also *shē*) *n* a long narrow runner *orig* of wood, now also of metal or manmade materials, fastened to the foot to enable the wearer to slide across snow, etc: — *pl* **skis** or **ski**. — *vi* to travel on skis: — *pr p* **ski'ing**; *pa t* and *pa p* **skied** or **ski'd**. — *adj* **ski'able** (of a surface) in a condition suitable for skiing on. — *n* **ski'er**. — *n* **ski'ing**. — **ski'bob** a vehicle resembling a bicycle used for gliding down snow-slopes, consisting of a short front-pivoting ski, turned by handlebars, and a longer fixed rear ski with a seat attached. — Also *vi*. — **ski'bobbing**; **ski bum** (*colloq*) a devotee of skiing who travels the world seasonally in search of snowy conditions; **ski'-flying** ski-jumping from a high take-off point, so that a longer time is spent in the air; **skijoring** (*-jōr'* or *-jör'*) or (*Norw*) **skikjöring** (*shihh-yûr'ing*) the sport of being towed on skis by a horse or motor vehicle; **ski'-jump** a steeply sloping, snow-covered track ending in an elevated platform from which a skier jumps; a jump by a skier from such a platform; **ski'-jumper**; **ski'-jumping**; **ski'-kiting** water-skiing holding on to a bar on a kitelike device; **ski lift** and **ski tow** devices for taking skiers uphill; **ski pants** tightly-fitting trousers made of stretch fabric and having a strap which is worn under the foot, *orig* designed for skiing but now more often worn as everyday wear; **ski run** a slope for skiing on; **ski school**; **ski slope**; **ski stick** one of a pair of sticks, *usu* pointed with a disc near the tip, used by skiers for balance or propulsion; **ski'-touring** the sport of journeying on skis across country, as distinct from downhill skiing on a particular slope. [Norw, from ON *skīth* snow-shoe, piece of split wood; OE *scīd*]

skia- *skī'ə-* or *skī-a'*, or **scia-** *sī-ə-* or *sī-a'-*, *combining form* denoting shadow. — *n* **ski'agram** or **ski'agraph** a shadow picture or photograph, eg an X-ray photograph. — *n* **skiamachy** (*-am'ə-ki*; Gr *machē* a fight) a sham fight; a fight with shadows. — *n* **skias'copy** retinoscopy. — *n* **ski'atron** a cathode-ray tube in which an electron beam varies the transparency of a phosphor, which is illuminated from behind so that its image is projected on to a screen. [Gr *skiā* a shadow]

skid *skid*, *vi* to slide along without rotating, as does a wheel to which a brake has been applied; to slip, *esp* sideways; (of an aeroplane) to slide sideways when banking; to slip or slide losing grip or traction. — *vt* to check with a skid; to cause to skid: — *pr p* **skidd'ing**; *pa t* and *pa p* **skidded**. — *n* a side-slip; a skidding; a support on which something rests, is brought to the desired level, or slides; an aeroplane runner; a ship's wooden fender; a shoe or other device to check a wheel on a down-slope. — *n* **skid'der** a person or thing that skids; a tractor with thick tyres used for hauling logs (*forestry*). — **skid lid** (*slang*) a crash helmet; **skid pan** or

pad a piece of slippery ground on which motorists can learn to control a skidding car; **skid'pan** (*slang*) a drag for a wheel (also *fig*). — *adj* **skid'proof** (of a road surface, tyre, etc) designed to prevent skids. — **skid row** or **road** (*esp NAm*) a squalid quarter where vagrants, chronic drunks, etc live. — **put the skids on** or **under** (*slang*) to cause to hurry; to put a stop to, thwart; **the skids** (*fig*; *colloq*) a downward path. [Prob related to **ski**]

Ski-doo®, skidoo *ski-doo'*, *n* a motorized sledge, fitted with tracks at the rear and steerable skis at the front.

skier[1]. See under **ski**.

skier[2] and **skiey**. See under **sky**.

skiff[1] *skif*, *n* a small light boat. [Related to **ship**]

skiff[2] *skif*, (*Scot*) *vi* and *vt* to skim. — *n* a skimming or grazing movement or blow; a slight touch; a sketch; a puff. [Prob imit]

skiffle[1] *skif'l*, *n* a strongly accented jazz type of folk-music played by guitars, drums, and often unconventional instruments, etc, at the height of its popularity about 1957. [Origin obscure]

skiffle[2] *skif'l*, (*dialect*) *n* light rain, drizzle. [Prob from **skiff**[2]]

skijoring, **skikjöring**. See under **ski**.

skill *skil*, *n* expertness; a craft or accomplishment; (in *pl*) aptitudes and competencies appropriate for a particular job; expert knowledge (*archaic*); reason (*Shakesp*); discrimination (*obs*). — *vt* and *vi* (*archaic*) to matter; to make (a difference); to signify. — *adj* **skil'ful** or (*NAm*) **skill'ful**. — *adv* **skil'fully** or (*NAm*) **skill'fully**. — *n* **skil'fulness** or *NAm* **skill'fulness**. — *adj* **skilled** expert; skilful; (of a job) requiring special training. — *adj* **skill'-less** or **skil'less**. — *adj* **skill'y** or **skeel'y** (*Scot*) skilful. — **skill'centre** in Britain, a Government-funded training establishment to assist those who wish to develop new occupational skills; **skills gap** a situation in which there are insufficient numbers of workers with the appropriate level of training in the skills required by industry; a shortage of skilled workers. [ON *skil* distinction, *skilja* to separate]

skillet *skil'it*, *n* a small, long-handled pan; a frying-pan (*esp NAm*). [Origin doubtful]

skilligalee, **skilligolee**. See **skilly**.

skilling[1] *skil'ing*, *n* an obsolete coin of Scandinavian countries, of small value. [Dan]

skilling[2]. See **skillion**.

skillion *skil'yən*, (*Austr*) *n* an outhouse or lean-to, *esp* one with a sloping roof. — Also **skill'ing**. — **skillion roof** a roof slanting out from the wall of a building. [Eng dialect *skilling* an outhouse, lean-to]

skilly[1] *skil'i*, *n* thin gruel. — Also **skilligalee'** or **skilligolee'**. [Ety uncertain]

skilly[2]. See under **skill**.

skim *skim*, *vt* to remove floating matter from the surface of; to remove (floating matter) from the surface of a liquid (often with *off*; also *fig*); to glide lightly over; to read superficially, skipping parts. — *vi* to pass over lightly; to glide along near the surface; to become coated over: — *pr p* **skimm'ing**; *pa t* and *pa p* **skimmed**. — *n* the act of skimming; skimmed milk. — *n* **skimm'er** someone who or something that skims; a utensil for skimming milk; an apparatus for clearing water of floating debris or pollutants, eg in a swimming pool; a seabird (genus *Rhyncops*) that skims the water. — *n* **skimm'ing**. — *adv* **skimm'ingly**. — **skimmed milk** or **skim milk** milk from which the cream has been skimmed. [Appar related to **scum**]

skimble-skamble *skim'bl-skam'bl*, (*archaic*) *adj* wild, rambling, incoherent. [A reduplication of **scamble**]

skimmia *skim'i-ə*, *n* any Asiatic shrub of the genus *Skimmia*, cultivated for its holly-like leaves and fragrant panicles of flowers. [Jap *shikimi*]

skimmington *skim'ing-tən*, *n* (in rural Britain) the old custom of forming a burlesque procession to ridicule an unfaithful husband or nagging wife. [Origin unknown]

skimp *skimp*, *vt* and *vi* to scrimp; to stint. — *adj* scanty, spare. — *adv* **skimp'ily**. — *adj* **skimp'ing**. — *adv* **skimp'ingly**. — *adj* **skimp'y** (of clothes) scanty; stingy, mean. [Poss **scamp**[2] combined with **scrimp**]

skin *skin*, *n* the natural outer covering of tissue of a person or an animal; a hide; a thin outer layer or covering; the outer surface other than fabric of an aircraft (*aeronautics*); an integument; a membrane; a wine vessel made of an animal's skin; a drum (*slang*); short for **skinhead** (qv below) (*slang*). — *adj* of skin. — *vt* to cover with a skin; to strip the skin from; to swindle or fleece. — *vi* to become covered with skin, or with any membranous layer; to slip through or away: — *pr p* **skinn'ing**; *pa t* and *pa p* **skinned**. — *n* **skin'ful** (*colloq*) as much alcoholic drink as one can hold. — *adj* **skin'less**. — *adj* **skinned** stripped of skin; having skin, *esp* (in combination) of a specified type or quality, as in *fair-skinned, thick-skinned*. — *n* **skinn'er** a person who prepares hides. — *n* **skinn'iness**. — *adj* **skinn'y** of or like skin; thin, *esp* unattractively thin, too thin; (of a pullover, etc) tight-fitting (*colloq*). — *adj* **skin'-deep** superficial; shallow, not deeply fixed. — **skin'-diver** *orig*, a naked pearl-diver; a person involved in skin-diving; **skin'-diving** diving and swimming under water, with breathing equipment carried on the back, not wearing the traditional diver's helmet and suit, and not connected with a boat; **skin effect** the tendency, increasing with frequency, for an alternating current to be greater in the surface layer of a conductor; **skin'flick** (*slang*) a cinema film in which there is much nudity and sexual activity, *esp* a (cheaply made) pornographic film; **skin'flint** a very niggardly person; **skin'food** a cosmetic intended to nourish the skin; **skin game** a swindling trick; **skin'head** a young person with closely cropped hair, *esp* applied to a member of a gang wearing simple, severe clothes and displaying aggressive anti-establishment behaviour; **skin magazine** (*slang*) a magazine featuring photographs of naked women (or men). — *vi* **skinn'y-dip** (*esp NAm*) to bathe naked. — **skinn'y-dipper**; **skinn'y-dipping**; **skinn'y-rib** (*informal*) a tight-fitting sweater of ribbed wool or similar fibre. — Also *adj*. — *vi* **skin'-pop** (*slang*) to inject drugs. — **skin'-popping**; **skin test** a test made by applying a substance to, or introducing a substance beneath, a person's skin, to test for an allergy, immunity from a disease, etc. — *adj* **skin'-tight** fitting close to the body, like a skin. — *n* (in *pl*) tights. — **skin wool** wool from a dead sheep. — **by** or **with the skin of one's teeth** very narrowly; **get under someone's skin** to annoy someone; to interest someone seriously, to become an obsession with someone; **no skin off one's nose** (*colloq*) a matter about which one feels unconcerned or indifferent because it does not harm or inconvenience one, or because it may be to one's benefit; **save one's skin** to save one's life. [ON *skinn*; late OE *scinn*]

skink[1] *skingk*, *vi* and *vt* to pour out. — *n* (*Scot*) alcoholic drink. — *n* **skink'er**. — *adj* **skink'ing** (*Scot*) thin, watery. [Perh LGer *schenken*; cf OE *scencan*; Ger *schenken*]

skink[2] *skingk*, *n* any lizard of the family *Scincidae*, of Africa and Asia, with an elongated body and short limbs. [L *scincus*, from Gr *skinkos*]

skink[3] *skingk*, *n* (*Scot*) soup, *orig* made with stock from a shin of beef, now *usu* made with fish; a shin of beef. [MDu *schenke*, LGer *schinke*]

skinny. See under **skin**.

skint *skint*, (*slang*) *adj* without money, hard up. **[skinned]**

skio or **skeo** *skyō*, (*Orkney* and *Shetland*) *n* a hut; a shed: — *pl* **skios** or **skeos**. [Norw *skjaa*]

skip[1] *skip*, *vi* to progress by hopping on each foot alternately; to spring or hop lightly; to make jumps over a twirling rope; to pass lightly, inattentively, etc (with *through*, *over*, etc); to pass discontinuously. — *vt* to overleap; to omit; to cut, not go to (eg a class): — *pr p* **skipp'ing**; *pa t* and *pa p* **skipped**. — *n* an act of skipping; a belt of inaudibility in wireless transmission; a college servant in some older universities. — *n*

skipp'er a person who skips; a dancer; a young and thoughtless person (*Shakesp*); a hairy-bodied butterfly of the family *Hesperiidae*, with wings of the same length as its body, so called because of its short jerky flight; the saury. — *adj* **skipp'ing** flighty, giddy. — *n* the art or activity of jumping over a twirling rope. — *adv* **skipp'ingly**. — *adj* **skipp'y** (*informal*) frolicsome; exuberant. — **skip'jack** a pert fop (*archaic*); any of a number of species of fish that jump out of, or swim at the surface of, the water, such as the bonitos, the bluefish, the saurel, and either of two species of tuna (the **skipjack tuna**, *Katsuwonus pelamis*, and the **black skipjack**, *Euthynnus yaito*); another name for the click beetle; a jumping toy made of a fowl's wishbone (*hist*); **skip'-kennel** (*obs*) a lackey; **skipp'ing-rope** a rope for skipping with; **skip-tooth saw** a saw from which alternate teeth are cut away; **skip zone** an area round a broadcasting station where transmissions cannot be received. — **skip it!** (*colloq*) never mind, forget it! [Cf ON *skopa* to run]

skip[2] *skip*, *n* a box or truck for raising minerals from a mine; a large container for transporting building materials, etc, theatrical costumes or refuse. [**skep**]

skip[3] *skip*, *n* the captain of a rink in bowls or curling. — *vt* and *vi* to act as a skip: — *pr p* **skipp'ing**; *pa t* and *pa p* **skipped**. [**skipper**]

skipjack. See **skip**[1].

skipper[1] *skip'ər*, *n* a ship's captain; the captain of an aeroplane; the captain of a team. — *vt* to act as skipper. — **skipper's daughters** white-topped waves. [Du *schipper*]

skipper[2]. See under **skip**[1].

skipper[3] *skip'ər*, (*old cant*) *n* a barn, outhouse, etc, *esp* as a sleeping-place for vagrants. — *vi* to sleep rough in barns, etc. — *n* **skipp'ering** (*current slang*) sleeping rough. [Perh Cornish *sciber* or Welsh *ysgubor* barn]

skippet *skip'it*, *n* a flat box for protecting a seal (eg of a document). [Origin unknown]

skirl *skirl* or *skûrl*, (*Scot*) *vt* and *vi* to shriek or sing shrilly. — *vi* to make the sound of the bagpipes. — *n* a shrill cry; the sound of the bagpipes. — *n* **skirl'ing** a shrill sound. — **skirl-in-the-pan'** the noise of frying; a fried dish. [Scand]

skirmish *skûr'mish*, *n* a minor irregular fight between small or marginal parties. — *vi* to fight slightly or irregularly. — *n* **skir'misher**. — *n* **skir'mishing**. [OFr *escarmouche*]

skirr, **sker**, **scur** or **squirr** *skûr*, *vt* to scour, search, range over (*Scot*); to send skimming. — *vi* (*Shakesp*) to scurry. [Origin doubtful]

skirret *skir'it*, *n* a water parsnip (*Sium sisarum*) with edible roots. [ME *skirwhit*, as if *skire white*, pure white, but perh altered from OFr *eschervis*]

skirt *skûrt*, *n* a garment, or part of a garment, generally a woman's, that hangs from the waist; the lower part of a gown, coat, or other garment or anything suggesting this; a saddle-flap or saddle-lap; a midriff (of meat); a rim, border, margin; a part of, or attachment to, an object that suggests a skirt, eg the flap of material hanging down around the base of a hovercraft to contain the air-cushion, or a similar flap around a racing-car; the lower edges of a sheep's fleece (*Austr* and *NZ*); a woman (*offensive slang*; also **bit of skirt**). — *vt* to border; to pass along the edge of; to scour the outskirts of. — *vi* to be on or pass along the border (*usu* with *along*, *around*, etc); (of dogs) to leave the pack (*hunting*). — *adj* **skirt'ed** wearing or having a skirt. — *n* **skir'ter** someone who removes skirts from fleeces (*Austr* and *NZ*); a huntsman who dodges his jumps by going round about. — *n* **skir'ting** material for skirts; skirting-board; (in *pl*) dirty wool from the skirts of a fleece. — Also *adj*. — *adj* **skirt'less**. — **skirt'-dancing** dancing characterized by the waving of flowing skirts; **skir'ting-board** the narrow board next to the floor round the walls of a room. — **divided skirt** trousers made to look like a skirt. [ON *skyrta* a shirt, kirtle; cf **shirt**]

skit *skit*, *n* a satirical sketch in dramatic or literary form; a humorous hit; a hoax; a sudden slight shower of rain or snow, etc (*dialect*). — *vi* **skite** or **skyte** (*skīt*; *Scot*) to dart or glide obliquely. — *n* a glancing blow; a spree; a trick; a queer person. [Perh related to ON *skjōta* to shoot]

skite *skīt*, (*Austr slang*) *vi* to boast. — *n* a boastful person. [**blatherskite**]

skitter *skit'ər*, *vi* to skim over the surface of water; to fish by drawing the bait over the surface; to scamper lightly. [Perh from **skite** (see **skit**)]

skittish *skit'ish*, *adj* unsteady; light-headed; frivolous; frisky, playful; lively; volatile; changeable; wanton; coy (*rare*). — *adv* **skitt'ishly**. — *n* **skitt'ishness**. [Perh connected with **skit**]

skittle *skit'l*, *n* a pin for the game of **skittles**, a form of ninepins in which a ball or cheese (see **cheese**[1]) is used. — *vt* to knock down. — **skitt'le-alley**, **skitt'le-ball**, **skitt'le-ground** — **beer and skittles** see under **beer**; **skittle out** (*cricket*) to dismiss (batsmen) quickly. [Prob alteration of **kail**[1] (see ety for **squail**), through intermediate *kittle*; see **kittle-pins**]

skive[1] *skīv*, *vt* to pare or split leather. — *n* **skī'ver** split sheepskin leather; a person or machine that skives. — *n* **skī'ving**. [ON *skīfa*; cf **shive**]

skive[2] *skīv*, (*colloq*) *vt* and *vi* (often with *off*) to evade (a duty, work, etc). — Also *n*. — *n* **skī'ver**. — *adj* **skī'vy**. [Origin uncertain]

skiver *skiv'ər*, (*dialect*) *n* and *vt* same as **skewer**. [Origin unknown]

skivie *skī'vi*, (*obs Scot*) *adj* deranged; askew. [Cf ON *skeifr*]

skivvy[1] *skiv'i*, (*colloq*) *n* a disrespectful word for a (*esp* female) domestic servant; a drudge. — *vi* to work as a skivvy, to drudge. [Origin uncertain]

skivvy[2] *skiv'i*, *n* a man's undervest (*esp NAm slang*); a knitted cotton polo-necked sweater (*Austr* and *NZ*). [Ety uncertain]

sklate *sklāt*, Scottish form of **slate**[1].

sklent *sklent*, Scottish form of **slant**[1].

skliff. Same as **scliff**.

sklim. Same as **sclim**.

skoal *skōl* or **skol** *skol*, *interj* hail!; a friendly exclamation in salutation before drinking, etc. [ON *skāl*; Norw *skaal* a bowl, Swed *skå*; cf **scale**[3,4]]

skoff. See **scoff**[2].

skokiaan *skö'ki-än*, (*SAfr*) *n* a strong home-brewed drink made from yeast. [Afrik]

skol. See **skoal**.

skolion or **scolion** *skō'li-on* or *skol'*, *n* a short drinking-song of ancient Greece, taken up by the guests in irregular succession: — *pl* **skō'lia** or **scō'lia** (or *skol'*). [Gr *skolion*]

skolly or **skollie** *skol'i*, (*SAfr derog*) *n* a Coloured hooligan, *esp* a member of a gang. [*Afrik*, prob from Du *schoelje* rascal]

skoosh *sko͞osh*, (*Scot*) *vt* and *vi* to squirt, spurt. — *n* a squirt or spurt. [Imit]

skran. Same as **scran**.

skreen. Same as **screen** (*esp* in the sense of partition of wood or stone).

skreigh, **skriech**, **skriegh**, **screich**, **screigh** or **scriech** *skrēhh*, (*Scot*) *n* and *v* (to) screech, shriek. — **skreigh of day** cock-crow, daybreak. [Imit improvement upon **screak**]

skrik *skrik*, (*SAfr*) *n* a fright. [Afrik, from Du *schrik* fright]

skrimmage. Same as **scrimmage**.

skrimp. See **scrump**.

skrimshank or **scrimshank** *skrim'shangk*, (*military slang*) *vi* to evade work or duty. — *n* evasion of work. — *n* **skrim'shanker**. [Origin obscure]

skrump. See **scrump**.

skry, **skryer**. Same as **scry**, **scryer**.

Skt or **Skr** *abbrev*: Sanskrit.

skua *skū'ə*, *n* any of several large predatory gull-like birds of the genus *Stercorarius*. [ON *skūfr*]

skudler, **scuddaler** or **scudler** *skud'lər*, (*Shetland*) *n* the leader of a band of guisers; the conductor of a festival. [Origin obscure]

skug[1] or **scug** *skug* (*Scot* **scoug**, **scoog** *skŏŏg* or **scog** *skog*), *n orig* shadow; shelter. — *vt* and *vi* to shelter. [ON *skuggi* shadow]

skug[2] *skug*, (*dialect*) *n* a squirrel.

skulduddery. See **sculduddery**.

skulduggery or (*NAm*) **skullduggery** *skul'dug-ə-ri*, *n* underhand malpractices; trickery. [Perh **sculduddery**]

skulk *skulk*, *vi* to sneak out of the way; to lurk; to malinger. — *n* **skulk** or **skulk'er** a person who skulks. — *n* and *adj* **skulk'ing**. — *adv* **skulk'ingly**. — **skulk'ing-place**. [Scand, as in Dan *skulke*]

skull[1] *skul*, *n* the bony case that encloses the brain; the head, the brain (*colloq*); a skullcap, *esp* of metal; a crust of solidified metal on a ladle, etc. — **skull'cap** a close-fitting brimless cap; a protective cap of metal for the top of the head; the top of the skull; any labiate plant of the genus *Scutellaria*, with helmet-like calyx. — **skull and crossbones** see **crossbones** under **cross**. [ME *scolle*; perh Scand]

skull[2]. See **scull**[2].

skulpin. Same as **sculpin**.

skummer. See **scumber**.

skunk *skungk*, *n* a small American musteline animal, typically with a black and white coat and a squirrel-like tail, that emits an offensive fluid from a gland near its anus; its fur; a despised person (*abusive slang*). — *vt* (*US*) to defeat without allowing to score. — **skunk'bird** or **skunk-black'bird** the bobolink (from its colouring); **skunk cabbage** a foul-smelling plant (*Symplocarpus foetidus*) of the arum family. [Algonkian *segonku*]

Skupshtina *skŏŏp'shti-nə*, *n* the national assembly of Serbia and Montenegro (*hist*), later of the former Yugoslavia. [Serb]

skurry. Same as **scurry**.

skutterudite *skŏŏt'ər-ŏŏ-dīt*, *n* a cubic mineral, cobalt arsenide. [*Skutterud* in Norway, a source]

skuttle. Same as **scuttle**.

sky *skī*, *n* the apparent canopy over our heads; the heavens; the weather; the upper rows of pictures in a gallery; sky-blue: — *pl* **skies**. — *vt* to raise aloft; to hit high into the air; to hang above the line of sight: — *3rd pers sing* **skies**; *pr p* **sky'ing**; *pa t* and *pa p* **skied**. — *n* **sky'er** or **skī'er** (*cricket*) a hit high into the air. — *adj* **sky'ey** or **skī'ey** of the weather; of or like the sky. — *adj* **sky'ish** (*Shakesp*) like or approaching the sky, lofty. — *adj* and *adv* **sky'ward**. — *adv* **sky'wards**. — *adj* **sky'-aspiring** (*Shakesp*). — *n* and *adj* **sky-blue'** light blue like the sky. — *adj* **sky'born** of heavenly birth. — *adj* **sky'-bred**. — *adj* **sky'clad** naked. — *adj* **sky'-coloured**. — **sky'diver**; **sky'-diving** or **-jumping** jumping by parachute as a sport, using a special steerable parachute, and delaying opening it for a specified time. — *adj* **sky-high'** (*esp* of prices) very high. — Also *adv*. — **sky'hook** a hook at the end of a length of cable and hung beneath eg a helicopter, used to attach a load; a type of grappling-iron used by climbers to secure a rope above, on a sheer face. — *vt* **sky'jack** (*colloq*) to hijack (an aeroplane). — *n* **sky'jacker**; **sky'jacking**; **sky'lab** an orbiting experimental space-station, *specif* (with *cap*) that launched and manned by the US, 1973-74; **sky'lark** the common lark. — *vi* to frolic boisterously. — *vt* to trick. — **sky'larker**; **sky'larking** running about the rigging of a ship in sport; frolicking; **sky'light** a window in a roof or ceiling; light from or in the sky; light through the bottom of an empty glass; **sky'line** the horizon; a silhouette or outline against the sky; **sky'man** a paratrooper; **sky marshal** an armed plain-clothes officer on an air-flight, having the job of protecting passengers and dealing with hijacking attempts; **sky parlour** (*old colloq*) an attic; **sky pilot** (*slang*) a clergyman, a military chaplain; **sky'rocket** a firework that bursts high in the sky. — *vi* to shoot up high; to rise high and fast. — **skysail** (*skī'sl*) a square sail above the royal on a square-rigged ship; **sky'scape** a view or a picture of the sky; **sky'scrāper** a very lofty building; a triangular skysail; anything very high; **sky sign** an elevated advertising sign, eg a neon sign on a high building; **sky'-surfing** the sport of free-falling from an aeroplane with a modified surfboard attached to the feet, which is used to ride the air currents. — *adj* **sky'-tinc'tured** of the colour of the sky. — **sky troops** paratroopers; airborne troops; **sky wave** a radio wave reflected from the ionosphere; **sky'way** a route for aircraft; **sky'-writing** tracing of words by smoke from an aircraft. — **the sky's the limit** (*colloq*) there are no restrictions on amount or extent (of something); **to the skies** (*colloq*) in a lavish or vociferously enthusiastic manner as in *applaud to the skies*. [ON *ský* cloud]

Skye *skī*, *n* (in full, **Skye terrier**) a small long-haired Scotch terrier. [From the island of *Skye*]

skyr *shür* or *skēr*, *n* curds; a yoghurt-like curd cheese. [Scand, from ON]

skyre *skīr*, (*Scot*) *vi* to shine, be gaudy, flaunt. [Origin obscure]

skyte. Same as **skite** (see **skit**).

SL *abbrev*: Sergeant-at-Law; Solicitor at Law.

slab[1] *slab*, *n* a plane-sided plate; a large thick slice of cake, etc; an outer plank sawn from a log; a thin flat piece of stone, etc. — *vt* to cut slabs from; to form into slabs; to cover with slabs. — *adj* **slabbed**. — *adj* **slab'-sided** (*NAm*) flat-sided; tall and lank. — **slab'stone** flagstone. [Origin obscure]

slab[2] *slab*, *adj* semi-liquid, viscous. — *n* mud. — *n* **slabb'iness**. — *adj* **slabb'y** muddy. [Scand; cf Norw, Swed *slabb* wet filth]

slabber *slab'ər*, *vi* to slaver, to drivel. — *vt* to beslaver, beslobber, or beslubber; to gobble sloppily and grossly. — *n* **slabb'erer**. — *adj* **slabb'ery**. [Cf LGer and Du *slabberen* and **slobber**]

slack[1] *slak*, *adj* lax or loose; not firmly extended or drawn out; not holding fast; remiss; promiscuous (*slang*); not strict; not eager or diligent, inattentive; not busy; not violent or rapid, slow; pronounced with wide, not tense, tongue (*phonetics*). — *adv* in a slack manner; partially; insufficiently. — *n* the slack part of a rope, belt, etc; a time, occasion, or place of relaxed movement or activity; a slack-water haul of a net; (in *pl*) long, loose trousers for casual wear. — *vi* **slack** or **slack'en** to become loose or less tight; to be remiss; to abate; to become slower; to fail or flag; to be inactive or lax. — *vt* to make slack or less tight; to loosen; to slow, retard; to be remiss or dilatory in; to relax; to slake (lime). — *n* and *adj* **slack'ening**. — *n* **slack'er** an idler; a person who is reprehensibly inactive; a shirker. — *adv* **slack'ly**. — *n* **slack'ness**. — *vt* **slack'-bake** to half-bake. — *adj* **slack-hand'ed** remiss. — **slack jaw** (*slang*) impudent talk; **slack rope** a loosely stretched rope for a funambulist; **slack water** turn of the tide; a stretch of still or slow-moving water. — *adj* pertaining to slack water. — **slack away** to ease off freely; **slack in stays** (of a ship, etc) slow in going about; **slack off** or **slacken off** to ease off; **slack up** or **slacken up** to ease off; to slow. [OE *slæc* (*sleac*); cf Swed *slak*, ON *slakr*]

slack[2] *slak*, *n* coal dross. [Cf Ger *Schlacke*]

slack[3] *slak*, (*Scot*) *n* a cleft between hills; a boggy place. [ON *slakki* dell]

sladang. Same as **seladang**.

slade[1] *slād*, *n* a little valley or dell; a piece of low, moist ground. [OE *slæd* dell]

slade[2] *slād*, Scots *pa t* of **slide**.

slae *slā*, a Scots form of **sloe**.

slag[1] *slag*, *n* solid scum on molten metal; vitrified cinders; scoriaceous lava; coal-mining waste; a piece of slag. — *vt* and *vi* to form into slag. — *adj* **slagg'y**. — **slag heap** a small hill of coalmining waste; **slag wool** fibre made from molten slag, mineral wool. [MLGer *slagge*; cf Ger *Schlacke* dross]

slag[2] *slag*, (*slang*) *n* a slovenly or dissolute woman (or, more recently, man). [**slag**[1]]

slag[3] *slag*, (*slang*) *vt* to criticize, mock, deride (*esp* with *off*): — *pr p* **slagg'ing**; *pa t* and *pa p* **slagged**. [**slag**[1]]

slag[4] *slag*, (*Austr slang*) *n* spit. — *vi* to spit: — *pr p* **slagg'ing**; *pa t* and *pa p* **slagged**. [Prob **slag**[1]]

slaid *slād*. Same as **slade**[2].

slain *slān*, *pa p* of **slay**.

slàinte *slän'chə*, (*Gaelic*) *interj* good health!

slairg *slārg*, (*Scot*) *vt* to spread or smear sloppily. — *vi* to eat messily. — *n* a dollop; a smear. [Cf Ger dialect *schlarggen* to smear]

slaister *slās'tər*, (*Scot* and *N Eng*) *n* a sloppy mess; wet slovenly work. — *vt* to bedaub. — *vi* to do anything in a wet, dirty, slobbery way. — *adj* **slais'tery**. — *n* slops; drudgery. [Origin obscure]

slake[1] *slāk*, *vt* to quench; to extinguish; to deaden; to moisten; to refresh with moisture; to hydrate (eg lime); to abate, mitigate, allay, reduce, moderate (*poetic*); to slacken. — *vi* to become slaked; to subside; to abate; to die down. — *adj* **slake'less** that cannot be slaked. [OE *slacian*, *sleacian* to grow slack, from *slæc*, *sleac* slack]

slake[2] *slāk*, (*Scot*) *vt* and *vi* to lick, smear, daub. — *n* a slabbery daub; a smear. [ON *sleikja* to lick; Ger *schlecken* to lick]

slake[3] *slāk*, (*Northern*) *n* mud; slime; a mudflat.

slalom *slä'ləm*, *n* a race in which tactical skill is required, *esp* a downhill or zigzag ski-run among posts or trees, or between hanging poles in canoes. — *vi* and *vt* (*fig*) to move in a zigzag course. [Norw]

slam[1] *slam*, *vt* or *vi* to shut or strike with violence and noise; to bang; to censure, harshly criticize (*colloq*): — *pr p* **slamm'ing**; *pa t* and *pa p* **slammed**. — *n* the act or sound of slamming; a harsh criticism (*colloq*). — *adv* with a slam (also *fig*). — *n* **slamm'er** (*slang*) prison; a slam dancer. — *adv* **slam'-bang** (chiefly *NAm*) a variant of **slap-bang**); carelessly. — **slam dancer**; **slam dancing** (at, *esp* heavy metal, rock concerts) the practice of leaping in the air and crashing into others in the crowd (also **slamm'ing**); **slamming stile** (*building*) the upright member of a door-case against which the door shuts and into which the bolt of a rim lock engages. [Cf Norw *slemma*]

slam[2] *slam*, *n* an old card-game, also called ruff or trump; (in whist) the winning of every trick; (in bridge), the winning of every trick (*grand slam*) or of all but one (*small* or *little slam*). — *vt* to inflict a slam upon. [Origin unknown]

slammakin *slam'ə-kin*, or **slammerkin** *slam'ər-*, (*obs*) *n* a loose gown; a slovenly-dressed woman, a slattern. — *adj* slovenly. [Origin obscure]

slander *slän'* or *slan'dər*, *n* a false or malicious report; injurious defamation by spoken words or by looks, signs, or gestures (distinct from *libel*; *law*); defamation whether spoken or written (*Scots law*); calumny. — *vt* to defame; to calumniate. — *n* **slan'derer**. — *adj* **slan'derous**. — *adv* **slan'derously**. — *n* **slan'derousness**. [OFr *esclandre*, from L *scandalum*, from Gr *skandalon* snare, scandal]

slane *slān*, *n* a turf-cutting spade. [Irish *sleaghan*]

slang[1] *slang*, *n orig* a jargon of thieves and disreputable people; the jargon of any class, profession, or set; words and usages not forming part of standard language, only used very informally, *esp* in speech. — Also *adj*. — *vt* (*colloq*) to scold, vituperate. — *adv* **slang'ily**. — *n* **slang'iness**. — *n* **slang'ing** a scolding. — Also *adj*. — *adv* **slang'ingly**. — *adj* **slang'ish**. — *adj* **slang'ular** (*Dickens*). — *adj* **slang'y**. — *vt* and *vi* **slang'-whang** to rail, to rant. — **slang'-whanger**. — **slanging match** a bitter verbal quarrel, *usu* involving an exchange of insults. — **back-slang** see under **back**[1]. [Of cant origin; connection with **sling**[1] very doubtful]

slang[2] *slang*, (*old slang*) *n* a short weight or measure; a travelling show, or performance (*obs*); a hawker's licence. — *n* **slang'er** a hawker; a dealer in illegal drugs (*US slang*). [Cant; origin obscure]

slang[3] *slang*, *n* a watch chain; any chain; (in *pl*) leg-irons, fetters. [Perh Du *slang* snake]

slangish, slangular, slangy. See **slang**[1].

slant[1] *slänt* or *slant*, *vt* and *vi* to slope; to turn, strike, fall, obliquely; to be biased. — *vt* to bias in a certain direction in presentation. — *n* a slope; obliquity; a sloping surface, line, ray, or movement; a divergence from a direct line; a glance (*NAm colloq*); a jibe; a point of view, way of looking at a thing; bias; a chance (*slang*). — *adj* sloping; oblique; inclined from a direct line. — *adj* **slant'ed** biased, prejudiced. — *adj* **slantendic'ūlar** or **slantindic'ūlar** (*jocular colloq*) oblique; neither horizontal nor perpendicular. — *adj* **slant'ing**. — *adv* **slan'tingly, slant'ingways, slant'ly, slant'ways** or **slant'wise**. — *adj* **slant'-eyed** having slanting eyes; Chinese, Japanese or SE Asian (*offensive*). — **slant rig** (*min ext*) a rig with facilities for digging at an angle from the vertical. [ME *slent*; cf Norw *slenta*, Swed *slinta* to slope, slip]

slant[2] *slänt* or *slant*, *n* a transitory breeze. [Earlier *slent*; Scand; cf Norw *slett*]

slap[1] *slap*, *n* a blow with the hand or anything flat; the sound made by this; a snub, rebuke; stage make-up (*theat slang*); hence, make-up generally. — *vt* to give a slap to; to bring or send with a slap; to rebuke (also with *down*); to apply without much care or attention (*usu* with *on*): — *pr p* **slapp'ing**; *pa t* and *pa p* **slapped**. — *adv* with a slap; suddenly, violently; directly, straight. — *n* **slapp'er** someone who or something that slaps; a whopper, a thing very big of its kind (*slang*). — *adj* **slapp'ing** (*slang*) whopping. — *adv* **slap'-bang** violently, all at once; directly, straight. — *adj* dashing, violent. — *n* a cheap eating-house; a simple firework that makes a noise when thrown down. — *adv* **slap'-dash** in a hasty, careless way. — *adj* hastily and carelessly done. — *n* roughcast; careless work. — *vt* to do in a hasty, imperfect manner; to roughcast. — *adj* **slap-happy'** (*colloq*) recklessly or boisterously happy; slap-dash, happy-go-lucky; punch-drunk. — **slap'jack** (*US*) a flapjack, griddle-cake; a card game in which players try to win the pack by being the first to slap a hand over the jack, as it is turned over on top of the pile; **slap'shot** (in ice hockey) a fast powerful shot; **slap'stick** a harlequin's double lath that makes a noise like a slap; (also **slapstick comedy**) knockabout low comedy or farce. — *adj* **slap'-up** (*colloq*) first-class, lavish, sumptuous. — **slap and tickle** (*colloq*) amorous frolicking, with kissing, petting, etc; **slap in the face** (*colloq*) an insult or rebuff; **slap on the back** (*colloq*) a mark of congratulations; **slap on the wrist** (*colloq*) a mild reprimand. [Related to LGer *slapp*, Ger *Schlappe*; imit]

slap[2] *slap*, (*Scot*) *n* a gap in a fence, wall, hedge, etc; a hill pass; a passage in a salmon cruive; hence the weekly close time when the passage is open. — *vt* to breach; to pierce. [Du or LGer *slop*]

slash[1] *slash*, *vt* to cut by striking with violence and often at random; to make long cuts in; to slit so as to show lining or material underneath; to lash; to criticize very harshly; to crack (eg a whip); to cut down, reduce drastically or suddenly (*colloq*); to clear by felling trees. — *vi* to strike violently and at random with a cutting or sharp instrument; to strike right and left. — *n* a long cut; a slant or solidus (/); a cut at random; a cut in cloth to show colours or material underneath; a stripe on a non-commissioned officer's sleeve; débris of trees (*NAm*); a forest clearing, *esp* littered with débris (*NAm*). — *adj* **slashed** cut with slashes; gashed. — *n* **slash'er** a person who or thing that slashes; a machine for sizing warp threads (*weaving*); a circular saw for slicing logs into regular lengths. — *n* **slash'ing** a slash or slashes; the felling of trees as a military obstacle; felled trees; a clearing. — *adj* cutting mercilessly, unsparing; dashing; very big, slapping. — **slash-and-burn'** a method of agriculture in which trees and natural undergrowth are cut down and burned, leaving the soil bare before cultivation begins. [Perh OFr *esclachier* to break; or connected with **lash**]

slash[2] *slash*, (*US*) *n* a low-lying, swampy area. [Poss alteration of **plash**[3]]

slash[3] *slash*, (*vulg slang*) *vi* to urinate. — *n* an act of urinating. [Cf Scot *slash* a large splash, poss from OFr *esclache*]

slat[1] *slat*, *vt* and *vi* to strike, beat; to flap. — *n* a sudden sharp blow. [Poss ON *sletta* to slap, splash]

slat[2] *slat*, *n* a slate or roofing slab (*dialect*); a thin strip of wood, etc. — *adj* **slatt'ed** having, or composed of, slats. [OFr *esclat*]

slatch *slach*, (*naut*) *n* the slack parts of a cable or rope lying outside a ship.

slate[1] *slāt*, *n* a fine-grained argillaceous rock which by regional metamorphism has developed a cleavage along close-spaced planes independent of the bedding, *usu* a dull blue, grey, purple, or green; a slab of this material (or a substitute) for roofing, or for writing on with chalk; a preliminary list (eg of political candidates; *esp NAm*); slate-colour. — *adj* of slate; slate-coloured, dull dark blue. — *vt* to cover with slate; to enter on a slate; to clear (hide) of fine hair with a slater; to enter on a list; to note down for nomination or appointment (*US*); to propose; to schedule (*US*). — *adj* **slat'ed** covered with slates. — *n* **slat'er** a person who covers roofs with slates; a tool with a slate blade for removing fine hair from hides; a woodlouse (*dialect*, *Austr* and *NZ*). — *n* **slat'iness**. — *n* **slat'ing** covering with slates; a covering of slates; materials for slating. — *adj* **slat'y** of or like slate. — **slate axe** a slater's sax; **slate club** an informally organized communal fund to which members contribute regularly, as insurance against hard times or savings towards eg Christmas expenses. — *adj* **slate'-coloured** dark greenish or bluish grey. — *adj* **slate-grey'** or **-gray'** of a light slate colour. — **slate pencil** a cut or turned stick of soft slate, compressed slate powder, or pyrophyllite, for writing on slate; **slate'-writer**; **slate'-writing** in spiritualism, the mysterious process of producing writing on a covered slate; **slaty cleavage** (*geol*) fissility like that of slate along planes independent of bedding. — **a clean slate** see under **clean**; **a slate loose** (*slang*) a slight mental derangement; **on the slate** (*colloq*) on credit; **wipe the slate clean** to allow a person to make a fresh start in a job, relationship, etc by ignoring past mistakes, crimes, etc. [OFr *esclate*; cf **slat**[2]]

slate[2] *slāt*, *vt* to abuse; to review or comment on very unfavourably; to reprimand; to bait with dogs (*dialect*); to set on (*dialect*). — *n* **slā'ting**. [From the ON word answering to OE *slǣtan* to bait]

slather *sladh'ər*, (*esp NAm* and *dialect*) *n* a large quantity. — *vt* to slop or smear; to squander. — **open slather** (*Austr* and *NZ*) carte blanche, a free rein; a free-for-all. [Origin uncertain]

slattern *slat'ərn*, *n* a dirty, untidy or slovenly woman. — *vi* **slatt'er** (*dialect*) to be untidy or slovenly. — *vt* (*dialect*) to spill, splash, slop about. — *n* **slatt'ernliness**. — *adj* **slatt'ernly** slovenly. — Also *adv*. — *adj* **slatt'ery** (*dialect*) sloppy: slovenly. [Appar **slat**[1]]

slaughter *slö'tər*, *n* the killing of animals, *esp* for food; the killing of great numbers, *usu* of people; wanton or inexcusable killing, *esp* of the helpless; carnage; butchery; bodies of the slain. — *vt* to kill in any of these ways. — *adj* **slaugh'terable** fit or due for slaughter. — *n* **slaugh'terer**. — *adj* **slaugh'terous** inclined to slaughter, murderous; destructive. — *adv* **slaugh'terously**. — *n* **slaugh'tery** (*rare*) slaughter; a slaughterhouse. — **slaugh'terhouse** a place where animals are killed prior to being butchered; **slaugh'terman** a man employed in killing or butchering animals. [ON *slātr* butchers' meat, whence *slātra* to slaughter (cattle)]

Slav *släv*, *n* a person whose language is Slavonic, ie belongs to that division of the Indo-European tongues that includes Russian, Polish, Wendish, Czech, Slovak, Serbian, Slovenian, and Bulgarian. — *adj* **Slav** or **Slav'ic**. — *n* **Slav'dom** the Slavs collectively, the Slavonic world. — *vt* **Slav'ify** to assimilate to the Slavs. — *n* **Sla'vism** a Slavonic idiom used in another language; enthusiasm for Slavic ways or culture; anything characteristic of the Slavs. — *n* **Slavonia** (*slə-* or *slä-vō'ni-ə*) a region bounded by the Danube, Sava, and Drava. — *adj* **Slavo'nian** of Slavonia; Slav. — Also *n*. — *adj* **Slavonic** (*-von'ik*) of the group of languages indicated above, or the peoples speaking them. — *n* the forerunner of the group of languages indicated above, or the umbrella term for the group. — *vt* **Slavon'icize** or **-ise** or **Slav'onize** or **-ise** to make Slavonic. — *adj* **Slav'ophil** or **Slav'ophile** favourable or friendly to Slavs. — Also *n*. — *adj* **Slav'ophobe** hostile to Slavs. — Also *n*. [Med L *Sclavus*, from Late Gr *Sklabos*, from the stem of Slav *slovo* word, *sloviti* to speak; cf **Slovene**]

slave *slāv*, *n* a person kept as property, *usu* made to work as a servant; a person who is submissive under domination; a person who is submissively devoted to another; a person whose will has lost power of resistance, *esp* to an influence, drug, etc; a person who works extremely hard, as if in bondage, a drudge; a mechanism controlled by another mechanism, eg in computing, by the central processor, or by remote control; a master-slave manipulator (qv under **master**). — Also *adj* — *vi* to work like or as a slave: to drudge. — *vt* to enslave; to treat as a slave; *perh* make subservient to one's own views (*Shakesp*: *King Lear* IV, 1, 69). — *n* **slāv'er** a slave-trader; a ship employed in the slave-trade. — *n* **slāv'ery** the state of being a slave or enslaved; the institution of ownership of slaves; drudgery. — *n* **slāv'ey** (*colloq*) a domestic drudge, a maid of all work. — *adj* **slāv'ish** of or belonging to slaves; befitting a slave; servile; abject; servilely following or conforming (eg to fashion); laborious. — *adv* **slāv'ishly**. — *n* **slāv'ishness**. — *n* **slāvoc'racy** (*esp US hist*) slave-owners collectively; their power, interests, etc. — *n* **slāv'ocrat**. — **slave ant** an ant captured and kept as a worker in a community of another species; **slave'-driver** a person who superintends slaves at their work; a hard taskmaster (*fig*); **slave'-fork** a long and heavy forked branch fixed on a slave's neck to prevent escape; **slave'holder** an owner of slaves; **slave'holding**; **slave'-hunt** a hunt after runaway slaves or after people to enslave; **slave labour** (the work of) people employed as slaves (*lit* and *fig*); **slave ship** a ship used for transporting slaves; **slave states** those states of the American Union which maintained domestic slavery before the Civil War — Delaware, Maryland, Virginia, North and South Carolina, Georgia, Florida, Alabama, Mississippi, Louisiana, Texas, Arkansas, Missouri, Kentucky, and Tennessee; **slave trade** or **slave traff'ic** the buying and selling of slaves; **slave'-trader** or **slave-traff'icker**. [OFr (Fr) *esclave*, orig a Slav]

slaver[1] *slav'ər* or *esp Scot slāv'ər*, *n* spittle running from the mouth, *esp* in anticipation of food. — *vi* to let spittle run out of the mouth; to drivel; to fawn over (a person), *esp* with lust. — *vt* to beslobber. — *n* **slav'erer**. — *adj* **slav'ering**. — *adv* **slav'eringly**. — *adj* **slav'ery** slabbery. [Related to **slabber**]

slaver[2]. See under **slave**.

Slavic. See under **Slav**.

slavocracy, **slavocrat**. See under **slave**.

Slavonian, **Slavonic**, etc. See under **Slav**.

slaw *slö*, *n* cabbage salad. [Du *sla*, from *salade*]

slay *slā*, (*literary* and *archaic*) *vt* and *vi* to kill: — *pa t* **slew** (*slo͞o*); *pa p* **slain** (*slān*). — *vt* (*colloq*) to amuse very much; to impress greatly: — *pa t* **slayed**, sometimes **slew**; *pa p* **slayed**. — *n* **slay'er**. [OE *slēan* to strike, to kill; ON *slā*, Gothic *slahan*, Ger *schlagen* to strike]

sld *abbrev*: sailed.

sleave *slēv*, *n* (*Shakesp*) a fine filament that can be separated from a silk fibre. — *vt* (*dialect*) to separate (eg threads). — *adj* **sleaved** used in the term **sleaved silk**, floss silk. [OE *slǣfan* to divide]

sleazy *slē'zi*, *adj* slatternly (*colloq*); squalid, *esp* in sexual ways (*colloq*). — *n* **sleaze** (*back-formation*) sleaziness (*colloq*); a sleazy person, *esp* a man (*slang*). — *adv* **sleaz'ily**. — *n* **slea'ziness**. — **sleaze'ball** (also **sleaze'-bag**) (*slang*) a sleazy person, *esp* an unprincipled man who tries to take advantage of women. [Origin doubtful]

sled *sled*, *n* a sledge, *esp* a small one; a drag or wheelless structure for conveying goods, *esp* on snow, formerly for taking the condemned to execution. — *vt* to convey by sled. — *vi* to go on a sled: — *pr p* **sledd'ing**; *pa t* and *pa p* **sledd'ed**. — *adj* **sledd'ed** (*Shakesp*) having sleds. — *n* **sledd'ing**. [MDu or MLGer *sledde*; Ger *Schlitte*, ON *slethi*; cf **sledge**[1], **sleigh, slide**]

sleded. See **sleided**.

sledge[1] *slej*, *n* a conveyance with runners for sliding on snow; a framework without wheels for dragging goods along; an iron- or flint-studded board for threshing corn (*hist*). — *vt* and *vi* to convey, or travel, by sledge. — *n* **sledg'er**. — *n* **sledg'ing**. — **sledge'-chair** a chair mounted on runners for ice. [MDu *sleedse*; cf **sled**]

sledge[2] *slej*, *n* a sledgehammer. — *n* **sledg'ing** (*cricket slang*, *esp Austr*) the practice of baiting batsmen in order to spoil their concentration. — **sledge'hammer** a large heavy hammer wielded in both hands. [OE *slecg*, from *slēan* to strike, slay]

slee *slē*, Scots form of **sly**.

sleech *slēch*, *n* slimy mud; a mudflat. — *adj* **sleech'y**. [Origin uncertain]

sleek *slēk*, *adj* pleasingly smooth; glossy; having an oily, plastered-down look; insinuating, slick in manner; suggestive of material wealth; prosperous in appearance. — *vt* to make smooth or glossy; to calm or soothe. — *vi* to glide. — *adv* smoothly, oilily. — *vt* **sleek'en** to make sleek. — *n* **sleek'er** a moulding tool for smoothing over small irregularities in the mould (also **smooth'er**). — *n* **sleek'ing**. — *adj* **sleek'it** (*Scot*) smooth, sleek; sly, cunning, sneaking. — *adv* **sleek'ly**. — *n* **sleek'ness**. — *adj* **sleek'y** smooth; sly, untrustworthy. — *adj* **sleek'-headed**. — **sleek'stone** a polishing stone. [A later form of **slick**]

sleep *slēp*, *vi* to take rest by surrendering consciousness; to slumber; to be motionless, inactive, or dormant; to appear still or restful; to take or have the nocturnal position, to display nyctitropism (*bot*); to be dead (*euphem*); to rest in the grave (*euphem*); (of a limb) to go or be numb from pressure, etc; (of a top) to spin steadily without movement of the axis. — *vt* to spend (time) in sleep; to enjoy a period of (sleep, as cognate object); to outsleep; to provide, contain sleeping accommodation for: — *pa t* and *pa p* **slept** (*slept*). — *n* the state of being asleep; a period of sleeping; dormancy; death (*euphem*); vertical disposition of leaves at night, nyctitropism (*bot*); mucous matter which collects at the corners of the eyes (*colloq*). — *n* **sleep'er** a person who sleeps; a horizontal beam supporting and spreading a weight, *esp* a support for railway rails; a sleeping-car; a compartment or berth in a sleeping-car; a sleeping tablet (*colloq*); a Communist (or other) agent who spends a long time (often years) establishing himself or herself as an inoffensive citizen preparing for the moment when he or she will be required to pass on information, spy for a foreign power, etc; someone or something not recognized for what it is; a record, film, etc which becomes popular after an initial period of not being so, or an item whose true value is not recognized and which is sold too cheaply as a result (*colloq*). — *adj* (*Scot*) **sleep'ery** or **sleep'ry** sleepy. — *adv* **sleep'ily**. — *n* **sleep'iness**. — *n* **sleep'ing** sleep; abeyance. — *adj* in a state of, occupied with, or for, sleeping; dormant. — *adj* **sleep'less** without sleep; unable to sleep. — *adv* **sleep'lessly**. — *n* **sleep'lessness**. — *adj* **sleep'y** inclined to sleep, drowsy; drowsy; inducing or suggesting sleep; partially decayed internally, *esp* of a pear, soft and lacking juice. — **sleeping bag** a quilted bag for sleeping in, used by travellers, campers, etc; **sleeping berth**; **sleeping car, carr'iage** or **coach** a railway carriage with berths for sleeping in; **sleeping draught** a drink containing a drug to induce sleep; **sleeping partner** a person who has money invested in a business but takes no part in its management; **sleeping pill** one containing a sleep-inducing drug; **sleeping policeman** a low transverse hump built into the surface of a road, intended to slow down traffic; **sleeping sickness** a deadly disease of tropical Africa, characterized by headache, great drowsiness, and exhaustion, caused by a trypanosome introduced by the bite of a tsetse-fly; sometimes erroneously applied to sleepy-sickness; **slee'ping-suit** or **sleep'suit** a baby's all-in-one garment for sleeping in; **sleep learning** see **hypnopaedia**; **sleep'-out** (*Austr* and *NZ*) a partitioned-off section of a veranda for use as a sleeping area; **sleep' walker** a person who walks in his or her sleep, a somnambulist; **sleep'walking**; **sleep'y-head** a lazy or sleepy-looking person; **sleepy hollow** a very quiet place, from *A Legend of Sleepy Hollow*, by Washington Irving; **sleep'y-sick'ness** encephalitis lethargica, a feature of which is great drowsiness; formerly applied to sleeping sickness. — **get to sleep** to manage to fall asleep; **go to sleep** to fall asleep; (of a limb) to become numb through pressure or positioning that cuts off the blood supply; **in one's sleep** while asleep; **on sleep** (*Bible*) asleep; **put to sleep** to anaesthetize; to kill (an animal) painlessly (*euphem*); **sleep around** to be sexually promiscuous; **sleep in** to oversleep, wake or get up later than intended; to sleep later than usual; **sleep off** to recover from (eg a hangover) by sleeping; **sleep on** to consider overnight, postpone a decision on; **sleep together** to have sexual relations with each other; **sleep with** to have sexual relations with. [OE *slǣpan* (verb), *slǣp* (noun); Ger *Schlaf*, Gothic *slēps*]

sleet *slēt*, *n* rain mingled with snow or hail; a coating of ice formed when rain or sleet freezes on a cold surface (*US*). — *vi* to hail or snow simultaneously with rain. — *n* **sleet'iness**. — *adj* **sleet'y**. [Prob an unrecorded OE (Anglian) *slēt*; Ger *Schlosse* a hailstone]

sleeve *slēv*, *n* the part of a garment covering, or partially covering, the arm; a tube into which a rod or other tube is inserted; a tube, *esp* of a different metal, fitted inside a metal cylinder or tube, as protection or to decrease the diameter (*eng*); a thin cardboard container for a gramophone record; a wind-sock; a drogue. — *vt* to provide with sleeves. — *adj* **sleeved** having sleeves; (in combination) having sleeves of a stated type, as in *long-sleeved*. — *adj* **sleeve'less** without sleeves; futile, vain (see **errand**). — *n* **sleev'er** an old, *esp* Welsh, measure for beer, containing about three quarters of a pint; a straight-sided beer glass. — *n* **sleev'ing** tubular flexible insulation for threading over bare conductor wires. — **sleeve board** a small board for ironing sleeves; **sleeve dog** (*old-fashioned*) a little dog that could be carried in the sleeve; **sleeve fish** the squid; **sleeve'hand** (*Shakesp*) a wristband; **sleeve notes** the text on a record sleeve; **sleeve nut** a double nut for attaching the joint-ends of rods or tubes; **sleeve** or **sleeved waistcoat** a long-sleeved waistcoast, as worn by hotel porters, etc. — **keep something up one's sleeve** to keep something, eg information, in secret reserve; **laugh in** or **up one's sleeve** to laugh privately or unperceived; **roll up one's sleeves** to get down wholeheartedly to a job, *esp* an unpleasant manual one; **wear one's heart on one's sleeve** see under **heart**. [OE (Anglian) *slēfe* (WSax *sliefe*)]

sleeveen *slē'veen*, (*Irish*) *n* a crafty, smooth-talking person. [Irish *slíbhín*]

sleezy. Same as **sleazy**.

sleided and **sleded** *slēd'id*, (*Shakesp*) *adj appar* irregular forms of **sleaved**.

sleigh *slā*, *n* (*esp NAm*) a sledge. — *vi* to travel by sleigh. — *n* **sleigh'er**. — *n* **sleigh'ing**. — **sleigh bell** a small bell attached to a sleigh or its harness. [Du *slee*]

sleight (*obs* **slight**) *slīt*, *n* cunning: dexterity; an artful trick; a juggling trick; trickery; a design, device, pattern (*Spenser*). — **sleight of hand** deceptive movement of the hands, *esp* in order to conceal or remove something, as in conjuring, legerdemain. — Also *adj* (**sleight'-of-hand**). [ON *slǣgth* cunning, *slǣgr* sly]

slender *slen'dər, adj* thin or narrow; slim; slight. — *vt* and *vi* **slen'derize** or **-ise** to make or become slender. — *adv* **slen'derly**. — *n* **slen'derness**. [Origin obscure]

slept *slept, pa t* and *pa p* of **sleep**.

sleuth *slo͞oth, n* a relentless tracker, a detective (*esp joc*); a bloodhound, a sleuth-hound (*obs*); a track or trail (*obs*). — *vt* and *vi* to track. — **sleuth'-hound** a bloodhound or other dog trained to track people; a detective. [ON *slōth* track]

slew[1] *slo͞o, pa t* of **slay**.

slew[2] or **slue** *slo͞o, vt* and *vi* to turn about the axis; to swing round, *esp* suddenly and uncontrollably. — *n* a turn, twist or swing round; a position so taken. — *adj* **slewed** or **slued** (*slang*) tipsy. — **slew rate** (*electronics*) the rate at which an amplifier can respond to a change in input level. [First recorded as a sailor's word: origin unknown]

slew[3] or **slue** *slo͞o,* (*NAm colloq*) *n* a large number or amount. [Irish *slua* a multitude]

sley *slā, n* a weaver's reed. [OE *slege*, from *slēan* to strike]

slice *slīs, n* a thin broad piece or segment; a flat or broad-bladed instrument of various kinds, *esp* a broad knife for serving fish; a slash, swipe; a sliced stroke (*golf*); a share (of something) (*colloq*); a representative section. — *vt* to cut into slices; to cut a slice from; to cut as a slice; (in golf) to strike or play so as to send the ball curving to the right (left for left-handed players). — *vi* to slash; to cut in the manner of slicing; (of a boat) to move through the water in a smooth, cutting manner; to slice a stroke (*golf*). — *n* **slī'cer**. — *n* and *adj* **slī'cing**. [OFr *esclice*, from OHGer *slīzan* to split]

slick *slik, adj* sleek; smooth; smooth-tongued, glib; adroit; trim, smart. — *adv* smoothly; glibly; deftly; quickly; altogether. — *n* a smooth place or surface; a slicker; a film or expanse of spilt oil; a smooth racing-car tyre; a glossy magazine. — *vt* to polish, make glossy; to tidy up; to smooth (hair; with *back* or *down*). — *vt* **slick'en** to smooth, polish. — *n* **slick'er** a smoothing tool; a waterproof, *esp* oilskin (*US*); a swindler, shifty person; a sophisticated city-dweller. — *adj* **slick'ered**. — *n* **slick'ing**. — *adv* **slick'ly**. — *n* **slick'ness**. — **slick'enside** (*geol*) a smooth, polished or striated rock surface produced by friction. — *adj* **slick'ensided**. — **slick'stone** a sleekstone. [ME *sliken*, from OE *slician*, (in composition) to smooth]

slid See under **slide**.

'slid *slid,* (*archaic*) *interj* for **god's lid** (eyelid), an exclamatory oath.

slidder *slid'ər, vi* to slip, slide. — *n* a steep path or trench down a hillside. — *adj* **slidd'ery** slippery. [OE *slidor* slippery, *sliderian* to slip]

slide *slīd, vi* to slip or glide; to pass along, over, down, etc smoothly; to glide or slip in a standing position (without skates or snowshoes) over ice or other slippery surface; to lapse, fall out of use; to pass quietly, smoothly, or gradually; to take its own course; to decamp (*colloq*). — *vt* to cause to slip or glide along: — *pa t* **slid** (*slid*), (*obs*) **sli'ded**, (*Scot*) **slade**, **slaid**; *pa p* **slid**, (*obs*) **sli'ded**, (*rare*) **slidd'en**. — *n* a slip; a polished slippery track (on ice); a chute or shoot; a slippery sloping surface, eg in a park, for children to slide down; a bed, groove, rail, etc, on or in which a thing slides; a sliding part, eg of a trombone; a sliding clasp, *esp* for women's hair; a flat piece of glass for mounting objects for the microscope; a case (*dark slide*) for photographic plates or its sliding cover; a translucent photograph for projection on a screen, a transparency; a sliding lid; a sledge; a runner; a sliding seat, *esp* in a rowing boat; a landslip; a gliding from one note to another (*music*); a falling (in value, popularity, etc); (with **the**) a rhythmic dance. — *n* **slīd'er** a person who or thing that slides; a sliding part; ice-cream between wafers (*Scot*); a red-bellied terrapin. — *n* and *adj* **slīd'ing**. — *adv* **slīd'ingly**. — **slide guitar** a method of playing the guitar using a metal tube which is drawn across the frets; **slide rest** (*eng*) an apparatus for carrying the cutting-tool of a lathe, etc; **slide rule** a mechanical calculating device consisting of two logarithmic graduated scales sliding one against the other (also **slid'ing-rule**); **slide trombone** a trombone; **slide valve** a valve in which openings are covered and uncovered by a sliding part; **sliding keel** a centreboard; **sliding scale** a scale, eg of taxes, varying according to variation in something else, eg prices; a slide rule; **sliding seat** a racing-boat seat, moving with the swing of the rower's body. — **let slide** to take no action over; to allow to deteriorate through negligence. [OE *slīdan* to slide]

'slife *slīf,* or **'slight** *slīt,* (*archaic*) *interj* for **God's life** or **light**, exclamatory oaths.

slight[1] *slīt, adj* smooth (*obs*); flimsy; lacking solidity, massiveness, weight, significance; slim; slender; trifling; small; slighting (*obs*). — *adv* slightly; slightingly, meanly. — *vt* to smooth (*obs*); to raze, level to the ground (*archaic*); to ignore or overlook disrespectfully; to insult; to toss contemptuously (*Shakesp*). — *n* contemptuous indifference; discourteous disregard; an affront by showing neglect or lack of respect. — *adj* **slight'ing**. — *adv* **slight'ingly**. — *adj* **slight'ish**. — *adv* **slight'ly**. — *n* **slight'ness**. — **(not) in the slightest** (not) at all; **slight off** (*Shakesp*) to put off, set aside, with contempt; **slight over** to ignore. [Cf OE *eorthslihtes* close to the ground; ON *slēttr*, OLGer *slicht* plain, Du *slecht* bad, Ger *schlecht* bad]

slight[2]. Old spelling of **sleight**.

slily *slī'li, adv*. See under **sly**.

slim *slim, adj* (of people) attractively thin; slender; only slight; crafty (reintroduced from Afrik, now again *rare*): — *compar* **slimm'er**; *superl* **slimm'est**. — *n* (also with *cap*) the name used in Africa for AIDS (from the severe weight loss associated with the disease). — *vt* to make thin; to decrease (*fig*). — *vi* to make oneself more slender, by dieting, taking exercise, etc; (of a company, etc) to become more efficient or economical, *esp* by reducing the workforce: — *pr p* **slimm'ing**; *pa t* and *pa p* **slimmed**. — *adv* **slim'ly**. — *n* **slimm'er**. — *n* **slimm'ing**. — *adj* **slimm'ish**. — *n* **slim'ness**. — *adj* **slim'sy** (*US*) frail, flimsy. — *adj* **slim'line** slim, or conducive to slimness (also *fig*). — **slimmers' disease** anorexia nervosa. — **slim down** to make or become slimmer or more economical (*adj* **slimmed-down'**). [Du, LGer, Fris *slim* crafty; Dan *slem* worthless, Ger *schlimm* bad]

slime *slīm, n* any very fine, thin, slippery, or gluey mud-like substance, *esp* when considered unpleasant; bitumen (*obs*); any thick organic semi-liquid secretion, such as mucus; matter, *esp* as forming the human body; moral filth; obsequiousness, oily servility; (in *pl*) finely crushed ore in mud form. — *vt* to smear or cover with slime; to grind to slime; to clear of slime. — *vi* to go or move slimily. — *adv* **slim'ily**. — *n* **slim'iness**. — *adj* **slim'y** thick and slow-flowing, only semi-liquid; covered with slime; disgusting; obsequiously servile (*colloq*). — **slime'ball** (*slang*) a disgusting person. — Also *adj*. — **slime fungus** or **slime mould** a myxomycete; **slime pit** a hole where bitumen is obtained; a pit for receiving metallic slimes. [OE *slīm*; Ger *Schleim*]

sling[1] *sling, n* a strap or pocket with a string attached to each end, for hurling a stone; a catapult; a ballista; a loop for hoisting, lowering, or carrying a weight; a hanging support for an injured arm or foot; a strap attached to something for carrying it; an act of throwing; a sweep or swing. — *vt* to throw with a sling; to hang loosely; to put up (a hammock, etc); to move or swing by means of a rope; to hurl, toss or fling (*colloq*); to pass, give, etc (*slang*). — *vi* to discharge, eg stones, from a sling; to bound along with swinging steps: — *pa t* and *pa p* **slung**. — *n* **sling'er**. — **sling'back** or **slingback shoe** one without a covering for the heel, supported by a strap fastening round the heel; **sling fruit** a fruit that ejects its seeds by elastic tissue; **sling'shot** (*NAm*) a catapult; **sling'stone** a stone for throwing from a sling. — **sling ink** (*slang*) to write for the press; **sling off at** (*Austr* and *NZ colloq*) to jeer at; **sling one's hook** (*slang*) to go away, remove oneself.

[Prob from several sources; cf ON *slyngva* to fling, OE *slingan* to wind twist, LGer *sling* noose]

sling[2] *sling*, *n* an *orig* American drink, spirits and water sweetened and flavoured. [Perh **sling**[1] in the sense of toss off; poss Ger *schlingen* to swallow]

slink *slingk*, *vi* to go sneakingly or ashamedly; (of an animal, *esp* a cow) to miscarry. — *vt* to slip; to droop; (of an animal, *esp* a cow) to give birth to prematurely: — *pa t* and *pa p* **slunk**. — *n* a prematurely born calf or other animal; its flesh or hide; a bastard child; a slinking gait. — *adj* prematurely born; lean, starved; mean. — *n* **slink'er**. — *adj* **slink'y** slinking; lean; sinuous; close-fitting. — **slink butcher** a dealer in slink and diseased meat; **slink'skin** the skin of a slink, or leather made from it; **slink'weed** rosebay willow-herb or other plant believed to cause cows to slink. [OE *slincan*; LGer *slinken*]

slinter *slin'tər*, (*Austr* and *NZ colloq*) a dodge or trick. — Also *obs* **slen'ter**. [Du *slenter*]

slip[1] *slip*, *vi* to escape; to move quietly, easily, unobtrusively or stealthily; to glide; to get out of position accidentally; (of animals, *esp* horses) to give birth prematurely; to slide, fall, etc, *esp* accidentally; to lose one's former skill, grip, or control of the situation (*colloq*); to lose one's footing; to make a slight mistake inadvertently rather than from ignorance; to lapse morally; (of a motor clutch) to fail to engage correctly. — *vt* to cause or allow to slide or fall; to put with a sliding motion; to convey quietly or secretly; to let pass; to let slip; to cast; to disengage, let loose; to escape from or elude; (of animals, *esp* horses) to give birth to prematurely; to dislocate (a spinal disc): — *pr p* **slipp'ing**; *pa t* and *pa p* **slipped** or (formerly) **slipt**. — *n* an act of slipping; an inadvertent mistake; a slight error or transgression; a lapse, *esp* in morals or principles; an escape; an incline, sloping down to the water; a slight dislocation; a landslide; a pillow case; a garment easily slipped on, *esp* one worn under a dress, a full-length version of a petticoat; a leash; the difference between the pitch of a propeller and the distance actually travelled; any of three fielders (*first slip*, *second slip*, *third slip*) positioned on the off side somewhat behind the wicket-keeper or (often in *pl*) their position (*cricket*); the runner of a sledge; (in *pl*) the place at the side of the stage for slipping scenery from; the side of a theatre gallery. — *n* **slipp'age** (the extent of) failure to reach a set target; the act, an instance or the amount of slipping. — *adj* **slipp'er** (*archaic*) slippery. — *adv* **slipp'erily**. — *n* **slipp'eriness** or **slipp'iness**. — *adj* **slipp'ery** or **slipp'y** so smooth, wet or slimy as to allow or cause slipping; elusive; evasive; apt to slip; unstable; uncertain, unpredictable. — **slip angle** in vehicles, the attitude angle; **slip'-board** a board sliding in grooves; **slip'-carriage** or **slip-coach** a railway carriage that can be left behind without stopping the train; **slip'case** a boxlike case for a book or set of books, open at one end to leave the spine(s) visible; **slip'-dock** a dock with a slipway; **slip form** (*building*) a form that can be moved slowly as work progresses (*adj* **slip'form**); **slipform paver** a machine for laying continuously a concrete road surface; **slip gauge** (*eng*) an accurately ground rectangular block used to measure with great accuracy the distance between components or faces; **slip'knot** a knot that adjusts tightness by slipping along a rope; a knot easily untied by pulling an end. — *adj* **slip'-on** or **slip'-over** slipped on or over; (of a garment) slipped easily over the head without unbuttoning. — *n* a garment easily slipped on; a garment slipped over the head. — **slipped disc** see **disc**; **slippery elm** a N American elm; its mucilaginous bark used as a demulcent; **slip'rail** (*Austr*) a movable rail serving as a gate; a gap closed by such a rail; **slip road** a local bypass; a road by which vehicles move off or on to a motorway. — *adj* **slip'shod** shod with slippers, or with shoes down at the heel; slovenly; careless, carelessly executed. — **slip'-shoe** (*obs*) a slipper; **slip stitch** a concealed sewing stitch used on hems, facings, etc in which only a few threads of the material forming the main body of the garment are caught up by the needle for each stitch; **slip'stream** the stream of air driven back by an aircraft propeller or the stream of air behind any (*usu* quickly) moving vehicle or other object. — *vt* and *vi* to follow (another car, bicycle, etc) closely and thus benefit from the decreased wind resistance created by its slipstream. — **slip'-string** (*obs* or *dialect*) a rogue, someone who richly deserves hanging. — Also *adj*. — **slip'-up** (*colloq*) an error or failure; **slip'way** a pier in a dock or shipyard that slopes down into the water. — **give someone the slip** to escape from someone, *usu* by cunning; **let slip** to reveal accidentally; to miss (an opportunity); **look slippy** (*colloq*; *esp in imperative*) to be quick, to hurry; **slip a cable** or **mooring** to let a cable or mooring go overboard instead of waiting to weigh anchor; **slip off** to fall off; to take off quickly; to go away quietly; **slip of the tongue** or **pen** a word, etc said, or written, in error when something else was intended; **slip on** to put on loosely or in haste; **slip one's ways** (*Scot*) to make one's way quietly; **slip the cable** to die; **slip up** to make a mistake, to fail (*colloq*); to deceive or disappoint (*Austr*). [Perh LGer or Du *slippen*; but OE has *slipor* slippery, and *slȳpescōh* slipper]

slip[2] *slip*, (*obs*) *n* a counterfeit coin. [Perh **slip**[1]]

slip[3] *slip*, *n* a cutting; a descendant; a young or slender person; a young pig (*dialect* and *Austr*); a small sole (fish); a strip; anything slender or narrow; a small piece of paper, etc for a memorandum, or for indexing, etc; a galley proof; a memorandum giving details of the kind of cover required, to be signed by the underwriters (*insurance*). — *vt* to take cuttings from; to tear obliquely (*heraldry*). [Perh MDu or MLGer *slippe* strip]

slip[4] *slip*, *n* a creamy paste of clay and water for coating, decorating and casting pottery. — **slip'ware** pottery decorated with slip. [OE *slipa* or *slypa* slime, paste]

slipe *slīp*, *n* a skip or sledge (*mining*); a runner. [Appar LGer *slîpe*]

slippage. See under **slip**[1].

slipper *slip'ər*, *n* a shoe easily slipped on, *esp* a loose indoor shoe; a person who slips; (*esp* formerly) a device attached to a wheel eg of a coach to slow its speed when going downhill; the runner of a sledge. — *vt* to provide with slippers; to beat with a slipper. — *adj* **slipp'ered**. — **slipper animalcule** see **Paramecium**; **slipper bath** a partially covered bath, shaped like a slipper; (*esp* formerly) one of a number of single baths for hire at public baths; **slipper limpet** an American mollusc (*Crepidula*) with a somewhat slipperlike shell; **slipper orchid** any terrestrial orchid of the genus *Cypripedium*, with flowers made up of fused lateral sepals, a large dorsal sepal and a conspicuous slipperlike lip (see also **lady's slipper**); **slipper satin** fine satin with a dull finish; **slipper socks** thick *esp* patterned socks with a reinforced sole, for use as slippers; **slipp'erwort** a S American genus of flowering plants, calceolaria. [Ety as for **slip**[1]]

slippery, **slipshod**, **slipstream**, etc. See under **slip**[1].

slipslop *slip'slop*, *n* sloppy stuff; twaddle; a malapropism (from Mrs *Slipslop* in Fielding's *Joseph Andrews*); a person who commits malaproprisms; a loose sandal. — *adj* **slip'sloppy**.

slipt. See **slip**[1].

slipware. See under **slip**[3].

slish *slish*, (*Shakesp*) *n* a cut. [**slash**]

slit *slit*, *vt* to make a long cut in, *esp* lengthwise; to split; to cut into strips: — *pr p* **slitt'ing**; *pa t* and *pa p* **slit**. — *n* a long cut; a narrow opening. — *adj* cut with a long opening, *esp* lengthwise; cut open; having a slit. — *n* **slitt'er**. — **slit pocket** an overcoat pocket with a slit to give access to a pocket within; **slit trench** (*military*) a narrow trench for one person or a few people. [ME *slitten*, appar related to OE *slītan*; Ger *schlitzen*]

slither *slidh'ər*, *vi* to slide, *esp* on the belly. — *adj* slippery. — *n* a scree. — *adj* **slith'ery** slippery. [**slidder**]

slive *slīv*, (*dialect*) *vt* and *vi* to slip: — *pa t* **slove** or **slived**; *pa p* **slived** or **sliven** (*sliv'ən*). [Cf OE *slēfan* to slip (on)]

sliver *sliv'ər* or *slī'vər*, *vt* to split, tear off lengthwise or slice thinly. — *n* a thin or small piece cut or torn off, a slice or splinter; a continuous strand of loose untwisted wool or other fibre. [OE (*tō-*)*slīfan* to cleave]

slivovitz *sliv'ə-vits*, *n* a dry plum brandy. — Also **sliv'ovic** (*-vits*), **sliv'ovica** (*-sə*) or **sliv'owitz**. [Serbo-Croat *šljivovica*, from *šljiva* plum]

sloan *slōn*, (*Scot*) *n* a snub; a reproof. [Ety uncertain]

Sloane Ranger *slōn rān'jər*, *n* a young person, typically upper- or upper-middle-class and female, favouring expensively casual clothing suggestive of rural pursuits, speaking in distinctively clipped tones, evincing certain predictable enthusiasms and prejudices and resident (during the week) in the *Sloane* Square area of London or a comparable part. — Also **Sloane**. [Coined in mid-1970s by P Yorke, punning on *The Lone Ranger* a television cowboy hero]

slob *slob*, *n* sludge, mud, ooze; a mud-flat; a slovenly, lazy person (*slang*); a person with wealth but no refinement, a boor (*slang*). — *adj* **slobb'ish**. — *n* **slobb'ishness**. — *adj* **slobb'y**. — **slob ice** (*Can*) sludgy floating ice; **slob'land** a mudflat; reclaimed alluvial land. [Irish *slab*]

slobber *slob'ər*, *vt* and *vi* to slaver. — *adj* **slobb'ery**. [Cf Du *slobberen* to eat or work in a slovenly way; **slabber**, **slubber**]

slockdolager, **-iger**, **-oger**. See **sockdologer**.

slocken or **sloken** *slok'n* or *slōk'n*, (*Scot*) *vt* to quench; to slake; to moisten; to extinguish. [ON *slokna* to go out]

sloe *slō*, *n* the blackthorn fruit or bush. — *adj* of blackthorn wood; made with sloes; black. — **sloe'bush**. — *adj* **sloe'-eyed** dark-eyed, slant-eyed, or both. — **sloe gin** gin flavoured by having sloes steeped in it; **sloe'thorn**; **sloe'tree**. [OE *slā*, *slāg* or *slāh*; Du *slee*]

slog *slog*, *vt* and *vi* to hit hard. — *vi* to work or walk doggedly, with great effort: — *pr p* **slogg'ing**; *pa t* and *pa p* **slogged**. — *n* a hard blow (generally with little regard to direction); a strenuous spell of work; something which requires strenuous, *esp* protracted, effort. — *n* **slogg'er**. [Origin uncertain]

slogan *slō'gən*, *n* a party political catchword; an advertising catch-phrase; *orig*, a clan war-cry. — *n* **sloganeer'** an enthusiastic inventor and user of slogans. — *vi* to invent or make heavy use of slogans. — *n* **sloganeer'ing**. — *vi* **slo'ganize** or **-ise** to utter or repeat slogans, *esp* as a substitute for reasoned discussion. — *n* **slo'ganizing** or **-s-**. [Earlier **slog(h)orne**, **sloggorne**; said to be from Gaelic *sluagh* army, and *gairm* cry; see **slughorn(e)**]

sloid. See **sloyd**.

sloken. See **slocken**.

slo-mo *slō'-mō'*, (*colloq*) *n* and *adj* slow-motion.

sloom *sloom*, (*NEng dialect*) *n* slumber. — *vi* to slumber. — *adj* **sloom'y**. [OE *slūma*]

sloop *sloop*, *n* a light boat; a one-masted cutter-rigged vessel, differing from a cutter in having proportionally smaller sails and sometimes no bowsprit; (also **sloop'-of-war**) formerly a vessel (of whatever rig) between a corvette and a gun vessel, under a commander, carrying from ten to eighteen guns. [Du *sloep*; cf **shallop**]

sloosh *sloosh*, (*colloq* or *dialect*) *vt* to wash or rinse with (*usu* large quantities of) water or other liquid (often with *out*); to pour (*usu* large quantities of) water or some other liquid (over). — *vi* (of a quantity of liquid) to make or move with a rushing, splashing, pouring sound. — *n* a washing or rinsing with water, etc; an act or instance of pouring, or the sound of this. [Prob imit]

sloot. See **sluit**.

slop[1] *slop*, *n* slush; spilled liquid; a puddle; (in *pl*) bedpan waste; (in *pl*) weak or insipid liquor or semi-liquid food, *esp* as fed to pigs; (in *pl*) wishy-washy sentiment. — *vt* and *vi* to spill; to splash with slops; to slobber. — *vt* to wash away. — *vi* to walk carelessly in slush or water: — *pr p* **slopp'ing**; *pa t* and *pa p* **slopped**. — *adv* **slopp'ily**. — *n* **slopp'iness**. — *adj* **slopp'y** wet or muddy; wishy-washy, watery; (of work or language) slipshod; over-sentimental; maudlin. — **slop'-basin** or **slop'-bowl** a basin for waste liquids at table; **slop'-bucket** or **slop'-pail** a pail for removing bedroom slops or used by prisoners to slop out. — **slop out** (of a prisoner) to take away and empty out bedpan waste; to take slops from (a cell). [OE (*cū-*)*sloppe* (cow-)droppings (cowslip), from *slūpan* to slip]

slop[2] *slop*, *n* a loose garment — gown, cassock, smock-frock, etc; (in *pl*) wide baggy trousers or breeches; the wide part of these; (in *pl*) poor quality ready-made clothing; (in *pl*) clothes and bedding issued to seamen. — *adj* **slop'-built** jerry-built. — **slop'-chest** a supply of clothing taken on board a ship to sell to seamen; a seaman's chest for keeping clothes and bedding in; **slop'-clothing**; **slop'-pouch**; **Sloppy Joe** (*slang*) a large, loose sweater; a runny mixture of minced beef and sauce served on a half roll (*US*); **slop'-seller**; **slop'-shop** a shop for ready-made clothes; **slop'work** the making of slop-clothing; cheap inferior work. [Cf OE *oferslop* loose outer garment; MDu *slop*; ON *sloppr*]

slop[3] *slop*, (*obs*) *n* a policeman. [Back-slang]

slope *slōp*, *n* an incline; an inclined surface; an inclined position; an inclination, upward or downward slant. — *adj* slanting (*poetic*); moving on a slope (*Milton*). — *adv* aslant. — *vt* to form with a slope, or obliquely; to put in a sloping position or positions; to turn downwards, to bow. — *vi* to have or take a sloping position or direction; to move down a slope; to decamp or disappear (*slang*). — *adv* **slope'wise** obliquely. — *adj* **slop'ing**. — *adv* **slop'ingly**. — *adj* **slop'y** sloping. — **at the slope** (of a rifle) on the shoulder with the barrel sloping back and up; **slope arms** to place or hold a rifle at the slope; **slope off** (*slang*) to go away, *esp* suddenly or furtively, to decamp. [Aphetic from **aslope**, from OE *āslopen* pa p of *āslūpan* to slip away]

sloppy. See under **slop**[1,2].

slops. See under **slop**[1,2].

slosh *slosh*, *n* slush; a watery mess; a heavy blow (*slang*). — *vi* to flounder or splash in slush; to loaf around (*NAm*); to hit (*slang*). — *vt* to splash; to hit hard, beat (*slang*). — *adj* **sloshed** (*colloq*) drunk, intoxicated. — *n* **slosh'ing** (*space tech*) the bulk motion of liquid propellants in their tanks, particularly at launch. — *adj* **slosh'y**. [**slush**]

slot[1] *slot*, *n* a bar or bolt; a crosspiece that holds other parts together. [LGer or Du *slot* lock]

slot[2] *slot*, *n* the hollow down the middle of the breast (now *Scot*); a long narrow depression or opening, such as one to receive a coin, an armature winding or part of a mechanism, or opening in an aerofoil or into the conduit of an electric or cable tramway or railway; a slit; a (*usu* regular) place or position in eg a radio or television programme or schedule of programmes; a niche in an organization; a point in an airport's timetable at which a given aircraft may take off. — *vt* to make a slot in, provide with a slot; to pass through a slot; to put into a slot; to fit into a small space (*lit* or *fig*; with *in* or *into*). — *vi* to fit into a slot in something (with *in* or *into*); to fit into a story, puzzle, etc (*fig*): — *pr p* **slott'ing**; *pa t* and *pa p* **slott'ed**. — *n* **slott'er** a person or machine that cuts slots. — **slot-car racing** racing on a track by tiny model cars powered and controlled electrically; **slot machine** one operated by inserting a coin in a slot, such as a vending machine or a fruit machine; **slotted aerofoil** any aerofoil having an air passage (or slot) directing the air from the lower to the upper surface in a rearward direction; **slotting-machine** a machine for cutting slots. [OFr *esclot*]

slot[3] *slot*, *n* tracks, *esp* a deer's footprints. — *vt* to track. [OFr *esclot*, from ON *slōth*; cf **sleuth**]

sloth *slōth* or *sloth*, *n* laziness, sluggishness; a slow-moving, tree-dwelling, tropical American edentate mammal. — *vt* and *vi* to spend (time) in sloth. — *adj* **sloth'ful** inclined to sloth, inactive, lazy. — *adv* **sloth'fully**. — *n* **sloth'fulness**. — **sloth bear** a black Indian bear (*Melursus ursinus*), with a long snout. [ME *slawthe*, altered from OE *slǣwth*, from *slāw* slow]

slouch *slowch*, *n* a loose, ungainly stooping gait; a stoop; a droop; an inefficient person (*US slang*); a slouch hat. an awkward, ungainly person. — *adj* drooping. — *vi* to go or carry oneself slouchingly; to droop. — *vt* to turn down the brim of (a hat). — *n* **slouch'er**. — *adj* **slouch'ing**. — *adj* **slouch'y**. — **slouch hat** a soft, broad-brimmed hat. — *adj* **slouch'-hatted**. — **be no slouch** (*colloq*) (of a person) to be very good, efficient, etc (*usu* with *at*). [Cf ON *slōkr* a slouching fellow]

slough[1] *slow*, *n* a hollow filled with mud; a marsh; (*sloo͞*) a backwater, a marshland creek (*US*). — *adj* **sloughed** (*slowd*) bogged down or swallowed up in a slough. — *adj* **slough'y**. — **the Slough of Despond** (the state of) extreme despondency, great depression. [OE *sloh*]

slough[2] *sluf*, *n* a cast skin; a coating; dead tissue in a sore. — *vi* to come away as a slough (with *off*); to cast the skin; to develop a slough. — *vt* to cast off, eg a snake's skin. — *adj* **slough'y**. [ME *sloh*; origin uncertain]

Slovak *slō'vak* or *slō-vak'*, *n* a member of a Slavonic people living East of the Czechs; their language. — Also *adj*. — *adj* **Slovakian** (-*vak'* or -*vāk'*). [Slovak *Slovák*]

slove. See **slive**.

sloven *sluv'n*, *n* a person carelessly or dirtily dressed or slipshod in work. — Also *adj*. — *adj* **slov'enlike**. — *n* **slov'enliness**. — *adj* and *adv* **slov'enly**. — *n* **slov'enry** (*Shakesp*) slovenliness. [Cf ODu *slof*, *sloef*, LGer *sluf* slow, indolent]

Slovene *slō-vēn'* or *slō'vēn*, *n* a member of a branch of the Southern Slavs found chiefly in Slovenia, formerly the northernmost constituent republic of Yugoslavia and now an independent republic, and in adjoining areas. — Also *adj*. — *n* and *adj* **Slovē'nian**. [OSlav *Slovēne*]

slow *slō*, *adj* not fast, not quick; late; behind in time; not hasty; not ready; not progressive; (of wit and intellect) dull; (of a road lane) for slow-moving traffic; (of business) slack; (of a cooker, etc) heating gently, cooking slowly; lessening the speed of the ball, players, etc (*sport*); acting, etc slowly; (of photographic film) comparatively less sensitive to light. — *n* anything that is slow. — *adv* (or in compounds) slowly. — *vt* to delay, retard, or reduce the speed of. — *vi* to reduce speed. — *n* **slow'ing** a lessening of speed. — *adj* **slow'ish**. — *adv* **slow'ly**. — *n* **slow'ness**. — **slow'back** (*obs*) a lazy person; **slow burn** a slow or delayed but finally strong response, reaction, etc. — *adj* **slow'-burn**. — **slow'coach** a person who works, moves, etc slowly and who lags behind; a slow or sluggish person; **slow cooker** an electric casserole dish that cooks at very low power over a long period; **slow-down** see **slow down** below. — *adj* **slow'-footed** moving with a slow pace. — *adj* **slow'-gaited** (*Shakesp*) accustomed to walk slowly. — **slow handclap** see under **hand**; **slow march** a march at a slow pace. — *vi* **slow'-march**. — **slow match** a slowly burning rope for firing explosives. — *adj* **slow-mo'tion** much slower than normal or (*cinematograph*) actual motion. — *adj* **slow-mov'ing**. — **slow neutron** same as **thermal neutron**. — *adj* **slow'-paced**. — **slow'poke** (*esp US*) an irritatingly slow person, a slowcoach. — *adj* **slow-release'** (of a medicinal capsule, fertilizer, etc) releasing its active ingredient little by little over a period of time. — *adj* **slow-sight'ed**. — **slow virus** a transmissible agent which may take years to induce symptoms. — **go slow** and **go-slow** see under **go**[1]; **slow down** or **up** to go more slowly (*n* **slow'-down** and **slow'-up**). [OE *slāw*; Du *slee*, ON *sljōr*]

slow-hound *slō'hownd*, *n appar* a form of **sleuth-hound**, assimilated to **slow**.

slowworm *slō'wûrm*, *n* the blindworm, a harmless snake-like legless lizard. [OE *slāwyrm*, prob from root of *slēan* to strike, and *wyrm* worm, assimilated to **slow**]

sloyd or **sloid** *sloid*, *n* a Swedish system of using woodwork to teach basic manual skills, co-ordination, etc. [Swed *slöjd* dexterity; cf **sleight**]

SLR *abbrev*: single-lens reflex; self-loading rifle.

slub[1] or **slubb** *slub*, *vt* to twist (fibre) after carding to prepare it for spinning. — *n* a piece of fibre twisted in this way. — *n* **slubb'er**. — *n* **slubb'ing**.

slub[2] *slub*, *n* a lump in yarn. — *adj* lumpy, knobbly in texture. — *adj* **slubbed** or **slubb'y**. [Origin obscure]

slubb. See under **slub**[1].

slubbed. See **slub**[2].

slubber[1] *slub'ər*, *vt* to smear, soil or daub; to perform hurriedly and carelessly, to slur over; to gobble. — *vi* to wallow. — *n* **slubberdegull'ion** a dirty, slovenly person. — *n* and *adj* **slubb'ering**. — *adv* **slubb'eringly**. [Du *slobberen* to lap, LGer *slubbern*]

slubber[2]. See under **slub**[1].

slubby. See under **slub**[2].

sludge *sluj*, *n* soft mud or mire; half-melted snow; a slimy precipitate, such as from sewage; a dark yellowish or brownish green. — *adj* **sludg'y** miry; muddy. [Cf **slush**]

slue. Same as **slew**[2,3].

slug[1] *slug*, *n* a heavy, lazy person; a land mollusc with a rudimentary shell or none at all; a sea slug; anything slow-moving. — *vi* to be inert; to go sluggishly; to hunt for slugs. — *vt* to make sluggish. — *n* **slugg'ard** a person who is habitually inactive. — Also *adj*. — *vt* **slugg'ardize** or **-ise** (*Shakesp*) to make lazy. — *adj* **slugg'ish** habitually lazy; slothful; slow-moving, slow-acting, etc; inactive. — *adv* **slugg'ishly**. — *n* **slugg'ishness**. — **slug'-a-bed** or **slugg'abed** (*Shakesp*) a person who lies in bed a long time. [Cf Norw dialect *slugg* a heavy body, *sluggje* a slow heavy person, Swed dialect *slogga* to be sluggish]

slug[2] *slug*, *n* a lump of crude ore (*mining*); a lump of metal, *esp* one for firing from a gun; a bullet (*colloq*); see **fuel rod** (*nuc eng*); a metal token used in a slot machine; a solid line or section of type cast by a composing machine (*printing*); a strip of metal thicker than a lead, for separating type (*printing*); the gravitational unit of mass, *approx* 32·174 pounds (= 14·5939 kg) in the **slug-foot-second** system (47·88 kg in slug-metre-second reckoning). [Perh connected with **slug**[1] or **slug**[3]]

slug[3] *slug*, *vt* and *vi* to slog; to fling heavily. — Also *n*. — *n* **slugg'er**. — **slug'fest** (Ger *Fest* festival, celebration) a match, struggle, characterized by heavy blows. [Cf **slog**]

slug[4] *slug*, (now *esp US*) *n* a gulp, a swallow; an alcoholic drink. [Poss Gaelic *slug* a gulp]

sluggard, **sluggish**, etc. See under **slug**[1].

slughorn or **slughorne** *slug'hörn*, *n* an old form of **slogan**; by Chatterton (followed by Browning) imagined to be a musical instrument not unlike a hautboy, or a kind of clarion.

sluice *sloo͞s*, *n* a structure with a gate for stopping or regulating flow of water; a floodgate or watergate; a regulated outlet or inlet; a drain or channel for water; a trough for washing gold from sand, etc; an act of sluicing. — *vt* to let out or drain by a sluice; to wet or drench copiously; to wash in or by a sluice; to flush or swill by flinging water on; to dash with water. — *adj* **sluic'y** streaming as from a sluice; sluicelike; soaking. — **sluice'gate**. [OFr *escluse* (Fr *écluse*), from LL *exclūsa* (*aqua*) a sluice, ie (water) shut out, pa p of L *exclūdere* to shut out]

sluit *slü'it* or *sloo͝t*, (*SAfr*) *n* a narrow water channel. — Also **sloot**. [Du *sloot* ditch]

slum[1] *slum*, *n* an overcrowded, squalid neighbourhood. — *vi* to visit slums, *esp* for pleasure; (also *vt* with *it*) to adopt a lower standard of social behaviour, a less sophisticated level of cultural or intellectual activity, etc than is or would be normal for oneself. — *n* **slumm'er**. — *n* **slumm'ing**. — *adj* **slumm'y**. — **slum'-dweller**; **slum'lord** (*esp NAm*) a landlord of slum dwellings. [Cant]

slum[2] *slum*, *n* the non-lubricating part of crude oil.

slumber *slum'bər*, *vi* to sleep, *esp* lightly; to be inattentive or inactive (*fig*). — *vt* to spend in slumber. — *n* light sleep; repose. — *n* **slum'berer**. — *adj* **slum'berful**. — *n* and *adj* **slum'bering**. — *adv* **slum'beringly**. — *adj*

slum'berless. — *adj* **slum'berous** or **slum'brous** inviting or causing slumber; sleepy. — *adv* **slum'berously** or **slum'brously**. — *adj* **slum'bersome**. — *adj* **slum'bery** or **slum'bry** sleepy, drowsy. — **slum'berland** the state of slumber; **slumber party** (*NAm*) a gathering of girls at one house where they spend the night, *usu* including eating, playing music and discussion, all in their nightwear. [ME *slūmeren*, from OE *slūma* slumber]

slummock *slum'ək*, *vi* to move slowly and awkwardly. — *n* (*dialect* or *colloq*) a slovenly person, *esp* a woman, a slut.

slummy. See **slum**[1].

slump[1] *slump*, *vi* to fall or sink suddenly into water or mud; to fail or fall through helplessly; (of prices, trade, etc) to fall suddenly or heavily; to flop, to relax carelessly and completely; to plump (*obs*). — *n* a boggy place; a sinking into mud, etc; the sound so made; a (time of) sudden or serious fall of prices, business, etc (as opposed to *boom*). — *adj* **slump'y** marshy. — **slumpflā'tion** an economic situation in which there is a marked decline in investment in industry, at the same time as a marked rise in inflation. — *adj* **slumpflā'tionary**. — **slump test** (*civ eng*) a test for determining the consistency of concrete by measuring subsidence in a cone of known dimensions. [Cf Norw *slumpe* to slump or plump, LGer *schlump* marshy place]

slump[2] *slump*, (*Scot*) *vt* to throw into a lump or mass, to lump. — *vi* to flow lumpily. — *n* a gross amount, a lump. — **slump sum** a lump sum. [Cf LGer *slump*, Du *slomp* mass]

slung *slung*, *pa t* and *pa p* of **sling**[1]. — **slung'-shot** a weight attached to a cord, used as a weapon.

slunk *slungk*, *pa t* and *pa p* of **slink**.

slur *slûr*, *n* an aspersion, stain, imputation of blame or wrongdoing; disparagement; discredit to one's reputation; a slight; a blur; a running together resulting in indistinctness in writing or speech; a smooth or legato effect (*music*); a curved line indicating that notes are to be sung to one syllable, played with one bow, or with a smooth gliding effect; a gliding movement in dancing (*obs*); a gliding throw in cheating with dice (*obs*); thin mud (*dialect*). — *vt* to disparage, cast aspersions on; to smear or besmirch (*dialect*); to glide over slyly so as to mask or to avoid attracting attention; to blur; to sound (*esp* speech) indistinctly; to sing or play legato; to go through perfunctorily; to slip glidingly out of the dice-box (*obs*); to cheat (*obs*). — *pr p* **slurr'ing**; *pa t* and *pa p* **slurred**. — *adj* **slurred**. — *n* **slurr'y** (*slur'i*) a thin paste or semi-fluid mixture, eg a thin liquid cement, liquid waste from farm animals, liquid waste or residue from mining, coal-washing, etc. [Origin obscure, perh different words that have run together]

slurb *slûrb*, (*informal*) *n* an area combining the appearance and qualities of a *sl*um and a sub*urb*.

slurp *slûrp*, *vt* to drink (liquid) or eat (semi-liquid food) noisily. — *vi* to flow with, or produce the sound of, a slurp or slurps. — *n* the noise produced by, or similar to that produced by, slurping food or drink. — *n* **slurp'er**. [Du *slurpen* or *slorpen* to sip audibly, gulp]

slurry. See under **slur**.

sluse. A Miltonic spelling of **sluice**.

slush *slush*, *n* liquid mud; melting snow; a protective coating for metal; worthless sentimental drivel or gush. — *vt* to splash or cover with slush; to sluice, wash by throwing water; to fill the joints of (brick, etc) with mortar (with *up*). — *vi* to splash in slush. — *adj* **slush'y**. — **slush fund** or **money** (*slang*, *orig US*) a fund of money used, *usu* corruptly, in political campaigning and propaganda, bribery, undeclared commissions, etc. [Cf **slosh**]

slut *slut*, *n* a dirty, untidy woman; a promiscuous or otherwise disreputable woman; a bitch, female dog (*archaic*); a greased rag used as a candle (*obs*). — *adj* **slutt'ish**. — *adv* **slutt'ishly**. — *n* **slutt'ishness** or **slutt'ery**. [Cf Ger dialect *schlutt*(*e*)]

sly *slī*, *adj* skilful in doing anything (*esp* anything wrong) without being observed; cunning; wily; secretive; surreptitious; done with artful dexterity; with hidden meaning; illicit (*Austr*); expert (*obs* or *dialect*); cunningly made (*obs*). — *compar* **sly'er** or **sli'er**; *superl* **sly'est** or **sli'est**. — *adj* **sly'ish**. — *adv* **sly'ly** (also **slī'ly**). — *n* **sly'ness**. — **sly'boots** a sly or cunning person or animal. — **on the sly** surreptitiously. [ON *slægr*; cf **sleight**; cf Ger *schlau*]

slype *slīp*, *n* a passage between walls, *esp* a covered passage from a cloister between transept and chapterhouse. [Perh **slip**[3]]

SM *abbrev*: sadomasochism (also **s-m** or **s/m**); Sergeant-Major; Short Metre.

Sm (*chem*) *symbol*: samarium.

sma *smö*, (*Scot*) *adj* small.

smack[1] *smak*, *n* taste; a distinctive or distinguishable flavour; a trace or tinge; a mere tasting, enough to taste. — *vi* to taste or have the flavour (of); to have a suggestion or trace (of) (*fig*). [OE *smæc*]

smack[2] *smak*, *n* a small decked or half-decked coaster or fishing vessel, *usu* rigged as a cutter, sloop, or yawl; a fishing vessel containing a well in which fish can be kept alive (*esp US*). [Du *smak*; Ger *Schmacke*]

smack[3] *smak*, *vt* to strike smartly, to slap loudly; to kiss roughly and noisily; to make a sharp noise with (eg the lips by first compressing and then parting them); to taste with relish or with a smacking sound. — *vi* to make such a sound. — *n* a sharp sound; a crack; a slap; a hearty kiss. — *adv* sharply, straight, absolutely. — *n* **smack'er** (*slang*) a £1 sterling; a dollar; an enthusiastic or exaggerated kiss. — *n* and *adj* **smack'ing**. [Prob imit; Du or LGer *smakken* to smite, Ger *schmatzen* to smack]

smack[4] *smak*, (*slang*) *n* heroin. [Perh Yiddish *schmeck*, with same meaning]

smacker, **smacking**. See under **smack**[3].

smaik *smāk*, (*Scot*) *n* a contemptible fellow, a rascal.

small *smöl*, *adj* little in size, extent, quantity, value, power, importance, or degree; slender; narrow; fine in grain, texture, gauge, etc; unimposing, humble; (of thought or action) ungenerous, petty, ignoble; short of the full standard; dilute; operating on no great scale; soft or gentle in sound; minor. — *n* a small thing, portion or piece; the narrow part (eg of the back); small-coal; (in *pl*) small-clothes; (in *pl*; *euphem* and *joc*) underclothes; (in *pl*) formerly at Oxford, the examination called Responsions (corresponding to little go at Cambridge); a size of roofing slate, 12 × 8in (305 × 203mm). — *adv* in a low tone; gently; in small pieces; on a small scale; only slightly (*Shakesp*). — *vt* and *vi* (*rare*) to make or become small. — *adj* **small'ish**. — *n* **small'ness**. — **small ads** classified advertisements; **small ale** ale with little malt and unhopped; **small'-and-earl'y** (*colloq*; *Dickens*, etc) an informal evening party; **small'-arm** (*usu* in *pl*) a weapon that can be carried by a person, *esp* a handgun or short weapon; **small beer** see under **beer**[1]. — *adj* **small'-bore** (of a firearm) having a barrel with a small bore, of a calibre not more than ·22in. — **small calorie** see **calorie**; **small capitals** (*colloq* **small caps**) capital letters of the height of lower case; **small change** coins of low value; hence, someone or something of little importance; **small chop** (*WAfr*) snacks served with drinks; **small circle** see under **circle**; **small'-clothes** knee-breeches, *esp* those of the close-fitting 18c form; **small'-coal** coal in small pieces; **small craft** small vessels generally; **small debts** (in Scotland) debts up to £750, recoverable in the Sheriff Court; **smallest room** (*euphem*) a lavatory, *esp* in a house; **small fry** a small person; an unimportant or insignificant person (or people); **small'-hand** writing such as is ordinarily used in correspondence; **small'holder**; **small'-holding** a holding of land smaller than an ordinary farm, *esp* one provided by the local authority; the working of such land; **small hours** hours immediately after midnight; **small intestine** see **intestine**; **small lady** a size of roofing slate, 14 × 12 in (356 × 305mm); **small letter** (*usu* in *pl*) a lower-case letter. — *adj* **small-mind'ed** petty. — **small pica** see **pica**; **small'-pipes** the form of bagpipes played *esp* in southern Scotland and northern England, smaller than the Highland bagpipes and with the bag inflated by bellows under the arm rather than by air from the lungs; **small potatoes** (*orig NAm*) someone or something (*esp* a sum of money) of little importance, value, significance, etc; **small'pox** (*orig pl*) a contagious, febrile disease, characterized by fever and pockmarks on the skin; **small'sat** (*informal*) a relatively small, inexpensive communications satellite; **small screen** television (*adj* **small'-screen**); **small sword** a light thrusting sword for fencing or duelling; **small talk** light or trifling conversation. — *adj* **small'-time** (*slang*) unimportant; insignificant. — *adj* **small'-town** provincial, petty; naïve, unsophisticated. — **small wares** small articles such as tape, braid, buttons and hooks; trifles. — **by small and small** (*Shakesp*) little by little; **feel small** to feel insignificant, cheap, ashamed, etc; **in a small way** with little capital or stock; unostentatiously, on a small scale; **in small** on a small scale; **in the smallest** (*Shakesp*) in the least; **look small** to look silly or insignificant; to be snubbed; **small=tooth comb** a comb with a row of fine teeth on each side; an arrangement for minute investigation (*fig*); **the small print** (the location of) the fine but important details of a contract, etc, *usu* printed very small. [OE *smæl*; Ger *schmal*]

smallage *smöl'ij*, *n* wild celery. [**small**, and Fr *ache*, from L *apium* parsley]

smalm. See **smarm**.

smalt *smölt*, *n* glass coloured with cobalt oxide; its powder, used as a pigment; its deep blue colour; smalto. — *adj* deep blue. — *n* **smalt'ite** a cubic mineral, $(Co,Ni)As_2$, cobalt arsenide. — *n* **smalto** (*smöl'tō*; *zmäl'tō*) coloured glass or enamel for mosaic work; a cube of it: — *pl* **smaltos** or **smalti** (*-tē*). [Ital *smalto*, from OHGer *smalzjan* (Ger *schmelzen*) to melt]

smaragd *smar'agd*, (*archaic*) *n* emerald. — *adj* **smar-ag'dine** (*-din*, *-dēn* or *-dīn*) emerald green. — *n* **smarag'dite** a mineral, a green amphibole. [L *smaragdus*, from Gr *smaragdos*]

smarm *smärm*, (*obs*) **smalm** *smäm*, *vt* and *vi* to smear, daub or plaster (*dialect*); to sleek. — *vi* to fawn ingratiatingly and fulsomely; to be unctuous. — *n* smarminess. — *adv* **smarm'ily** or (*obs*) **smalm'ily**. — *n* **smarm'iness** or (*obs*) **smalm'iness**. — *adj* **smarm'y** or (*obs*) **smalm'y**. [Origin obscure]

smart *smärt*, *vi* to feel or be the location of a prolonged stinging pain (also *fig*); to be punished. — *vt* to cause to smart. — *n* a smarting pain; smart money; a dandy (*old slang*). — *adj* sharp and stinging; brisk; acute, witty; clever, brainy; pert, vivacious; trim, spruce, fine; fashionable; keen, quick, and efficient in business; considerable (*esp US*); technologically advanced (*comput*); computer-guided or electronically controlled, as in *smart house*, *smart bomb*, etc (*colloq*). — *adv* smartly. — *vt* and *vi* **smart'en** to make or become smart, to brighten (with *up*). — *adj* **smart'ish**. — *adv* (*colloq*) quickly. — *adv* **smart'ly**. — *n* **smart'ness**. — *n* **smart'y** or **smart'ie** (*usu ironic* or *contemptuous*) a would-be smart person. — **smart Al'ick**, **Al'eck**, **Al'ec** or **alec** a would-be clever person or one too clever for their own good. — Also *adj* (with *hyphen*). — **smart'ass** or **smart'arse** (*derog slang*) a smarty. — Also *adj*. — **smart bomb** or **missile** a bomb or missile that is able to alter its direction and/or find its target using computer-aided or electronically-controlled guidance and detection systems; **smart card** a plastic card like a banker's card fitted with a microprocessor (including a memory) rather than a magnetic strip, used in commercial transactions, telecommunications, etc, its design intended to combat fraud; **smart drug** a non-technical name for a drug that can radically enhance mental powers, a cognitive enhancer; **smart missile** see **smart bomb**; **smart money** money paid by a recruit for his release before being sworn in (*obs*); money paid for escape from any unpleasant situation or engagement; excessive damages; money allowed to soldiers and sailors for wounds, or to employees for injuries received (*obs*); money staked or invested by experienced or clever gamblers or investors; the people staking or investing this money; **smart'-tick'et** (*obs*) a certificate granted to someone entitled to smart money; **smart'-weed** water pepper, from its acridity; **smart'ypants** or **smart'y-boots** (*colloq*; *pl* the same) a smarty. — **look smart** (*colloq*) to be quick, to hurry. [OE *smeortan*; Du *smarten*]

smash *smash*, *vt* to dash or shatter violently; to ruin, to cause to fail; to strike overhand with great force (*tennis*, etc). — *vi* to fly into pieces; to be ruined, to fail; to be dashed or shattered violently; to smash a tennis ball, etc. — *n* an act or occasion of smashing, destruction, ruin, bankruptcy; an accident, *esp* in road traffic; a smash hit; cash (*slang*). — *adj* **smashed** (*slang*) drunk or under the influence of drugs. — *n* **smash'er** a person or thing that smashes; a person who passes bad money (*old slang*); anything great or extraordinary (*slang*); a person of dazzling charm (*slang*). — *n* **smasheroo'** (*slang*) a person or thing of superlative quality, importance, etc, eg a smash-hit. — Also *adj*. — *n* **smash'ing**. — *adj* crushing, shattering; dashing; strikingly good, wonderful (*slang*). — *adj* and *n* **smash=and-grab'** (a robbery) effected by smashing a shop-window and grabbing goods. — **smash hit** (*slang*) an overwhelming success, *esp* in entertainment of any kind; **smash'-up** a serious accident. [Imit; cf Swed dialect *smaske* to smack]

smatch *smach*, (*obs*) *n* smack, taste; tincture (*Shakesp*); touch; smattering. — *vi* to smack, have a flavour. — *vt* to smack of. [**smack**[1]]

smatter *smat'ər*, *n* a smattering. — *vi* to talk superficially; to have a superficial knowledge; to dabble. — *vt* to talk or utter smatteringly; to dabble in. — *n* **smatt'erer**. — *n* **smatt'ering** a scrappy, superficial knowledge. — *adv* **smatt'eringly**. [ME *smateren* to rattle, to chatter; connections doubtful]

SMD (*electronics*) *abbrev*: surface-mounted device.

SME *abbrev*: Suriname (IVR).

smear *smēr*, *n* grease (*obs*); a rub with, or a mark or patch of, anything sticky or oily; the matter so applied, *esp* to a slide for microscopic study; a fine glaze for pottery; a slur, defamatory accusation. — *vt* to anoint; to spread something sticky or oily over; to apply in a smear or smears; to rub smearily; to defame. — *adv* **smear'ily**. — *n* **smear'iness**. — *adj* **smear'y** sticky; greasy; ready to smear; showing smears. — **smear campaign** a series of verbal or written attacks intended to defame or discredit; **smear'-dab** see **lemon**[2]; **smear tactics** tactics employed in a smear campaign; **smear test** a test involving the microscopic study of a smear, as for example a cervical smear (qv). [OE *smeru* fat, grease; Ger *Schmer* grease; ON *smjör* butter]

smeath. See **smee**.

smectic *smek'tik*, (*chem*) *adj* used of a substance whose state is intermediate between solid and liquid and whose atoms or molecules are oriented in parallel planes. [L *smecticus* cleansing, from Gr *smektikos* detergent, (from the soapy consistency of a smectic substance)]

smectite *smek'tīt*, *n* the family of minerals that are consituents of clays, *incl* bentonite, fuller's earth and saponite. [See **smectic**)]

smeddum *smed'əm*, *n* fine powder; spirit, mettle (*Scot*). [OE *smed(e)ma*, *smeodoma* fine flour]

smee *smē*, **smeath** or **smeeth** *smēth*, (*dialect*) *n* names for various ducks — smew, pochard, wigeon, pintail.

smeech *smēch* (*SW Eng dialect*) and **smeek** *smēk* (Scots) forms of **smoke**.

smeeth. See **smee**.

smegma *smeg'mə*, *n* a sebaceous secretion, *esp* that under the foreskin. [Gr *smēgma*, *-atos* soap]

smell *smel*, *n* the sense by which the odours of gases, vapours and very finely divided substances are perceived, located in the higher animals in the mucous membrane of the nose; the specific sensation excited by such a substance; the property of exciting it; an act or instance of exercising the sense; a pleasant scent or (often) an unpleasant one; a smack, savour, sense, property of suggesting, intimation (*fig*). — *vi* to affect the sense of smell; to have an odour (*esp* unpleasant), or an odour (of); to have or use the sense of smell; to have a savour, give a suggestion (of something) (*fig*). — *vt* to perceive, detect, find, by smell (often with *out*); to take a smell at; to impart a smell to; to emit a smell of: — *pa t* and *pa p* **smelled** or **smelt**. — *n* **smell'er**. — *n* **smell'iness**. — *n* and *adj* **smell'ing**. — *adj* **smell'-less**. — *adj* **smell'y** having an unpleasant smell. — **smell'-feast** (*obs*) a sponger; **smelling bottle** a bottle of smelling-salts or the like; **smell'ing-salts** a preparation of ammonium carbonate with lavender, etc, used as a stimulant in cases of fainting, etc; **smell'-trap** a drain-trap. — **smell a rat** see under **rat**[1]; **smell at** to sniff at, take a smell at; **smelling of roses** see under **rose**[2]; **smell of** to have the smell of; to savour of; **smell out** to find out (eg a scandal) by prying; to detect by witchcraft (*SAfr*). [Very early ME *smel*, prob OE but not recorded]

smelt[1] *smelt*, *n* any fish of the family *Osmeridae*, related to the salmon family, with a cucumber-like smell; any of various similar fish, such as those of the family *Retropinnidae* of Australia and Tasmania. [OE *smelt*]

smelt[2] *smelt*, *vt* to melt in order to separate metal from ore. — *n* **smel'ter**. — *n* **smel'tery** a place for smelting. — *n* **smel'ting**. — **smel'ting-furnace**, **-house**, **-works**. [Prob MLGer or MDu *smelten*; cf Norw *smelta*, Swed *smälta*]

smelt[3] *smelt*, (*obs slang*; *Scott*) *n* a half-guinea. [Origin obscure]

smeuse *smūs* or *smūz*, *n* a dialect form of **meuse**[1].

smew *smū*, *n* a sea duck, a small species of merganser. [Origin uncertain]

smicker *smik'ər*, (*obs*) *adj* beautiful; smirking, wanton. — *vi* to look amorously. — *n* **smick'ering** an amorous inclination. — *adv* **smick'ly** amorously. [OE *smicer* beautiful]

smicket *smik'it*, *n* a smock. [Prob dimin]

smiddy *smid'i*, a Scots form of **smithy**.

smidgen, **smidgeon** or **smidgin** *smij'ən* or *-in*, (*colloq*) *n* a very small amount. [Ety uncertain]

smifligate *smif'li-gāt*. Same as **spiflicate**.

smight. A Spenserian spelling of **smite**.

smilax *smī'laks*, *n* any plant of the genus *Smilax*, of the lily family, mostly climbers with net-veined leaves, some yielding sarsaparilla; a southern African twining plant of the asparagus family, with bright green foliage, much used by florists as decoration. [Gr *smīlax*]

smile *smīl*, *vi* to express amusement, slight contempt, favour, pleasure, etc by a slight drawing up of the corners of the lips; to look joyful; to be favourable (*fig*); to drink, *esp* whisky (*old slang*). — *vt* to express, drive (away), etc, by smiling; to smile at (*Shakesp*); to give (a smile). — *n* an act of smiling; the expression of the features in smiling; favour (*fig*); a drink, a treat (*old slang*). — *adj* **smile'ful**. — *adj* **smile'less**. — *n* **smil'er**. — *n* **smil'et** (*Shakesp*) a little smile. — *n* and *adj* **smil'ing**. — *adv* **smil'ingly**. — *n* **smil'ingness** the state of being smiling. — **smile at** to show amusement at, disregard of; **smile on** (*fig*) to show favour to, be propitious to. [ME *smīlen*; poss from LGer]

smilodon *smīl'ə-don*, *n* a member of an extinct genus (*Smilidon*) of large, short-limbed, sabre-toothed tigers which inhabited the Americas during the Pleistocene period. [LL, from Gr *smilē* a knife, and *odous*, *odontos* a tooth]

smir. See **smur**.

smirch *smûrch*, *vt* to besmear or dirty; to sully. — *n* a stain. [Earlier *smorch*, supposed to be from OFr *esmorcher* to hurt, influenced by **smear**]

smirk *smûrk*, *vi* to smile affectedly, smugly or foolishly; to look affectedly soft. — *n* an affected, smug or foolish smile. — *adj* **smirk** trim, spruce. — *adv* **smirk'ingly**. — *adj* **smirk'y** simpering. [OE *smercian*]

smirr. See **smur**.

smit[1] *smit*, (*obs* or *poetic*) *pa t* and *pa p* of **smite**.

smit[2] *smit*, (*Northern dialect*) *vt* to stain, mark with ruddle, infect. — *n* a stain (*obs*); ruddle, a mark on sheep, infection (*Northern dialect*). — *adj* **smitt'le** (*Northern dialect*) infectious. [OE *smittian* to befoul or infect, intensifier of *smītan* to smear; *smitte* spot]

smite *smīt*, (*literary* or *archaic*) *vt* to strike; to beat; to kill; to overthrow in battle; to affect with feeling; to afflict. — *vi* to strike; to meet forcibly: — *pa t* **smōte** or (*archaic* or *poetic*) **smıt**); *pa p* **smitt'en** or (*archaic* or *poetic*) **smit**. — *n* **smī'ter**. — **smite off** to cut off. [OE *smītan* to smear]

smith *smith*, *n* a person who forges metals with a hammer; a worker in metals; (often in combination) a person who makes anything. — *vt* to forge; to fashion. — *vi* to work as a smith. — *n* **smith'ery** a smithy; smith's work, smithing. — *n* **smithy** (*smidh'i* or *smith'i*) a smith's workshop. — *vt* and *vi* to smith. — **smith'craft**. [OE *smith*; Ger *Schmied*]

smithereens *smidh-ə-rēnz'*, *n pl* shivers, tiny fragments. — Also **smith'ers**. — *vt* (*rare*) **smithereen'** to break into tiny pieces; to shatter. — Also *fig*. [Ir *smidirín*, dimin of *smiodar* a fragment]

Smithsonian parity *smith-sō'ni-ən par'i-ti*, *n* parity agreed for major currencies at an international conference at the *Smithsonian* Institution, Washington, in 1971.

smithsonite *smith'sən-īt*, *n* a white mineral, carbonate of zinc, occurring in calcareous rocks. — Also called **calamine**. [After James *Smithson* (1765–1829), British chemist and mineralogist]

smithy. See under **smith**.

smitten *smit'n*, *pa p* of **smite** (*literary* or *archaic*); obsessed (with), in love (with) (*colloq*).

smittle. See under **smit**[2].

SMM *abbrev*: *Sancta Mater Maria* (*L*), Holy Mother Mary.

SMMT *abbrev*: Society of Motor Manufacturers and Traders.

SMO *abbrev*: Senior Medical Officer.

smock *smok*, *n* a woman's shift, a chemise (*archaic*); an outer garment of coarse white linen formerly worn by farm workers in the south of England; a loose, protective garment, *usu* of coarse cloth, worn by artists, etc; a loose dress worn by pregnant women; a woman or wench (*obs*). — *vt* to clothe in a smock; to decorate with smocking. — *n* **smock'ing** honeycomb stitching, as on the yoke and cuffs of a smock. — *adj* **smock'-faced** pale-faced. — **smock'-frock** a farm-worker's smock; **smock mill** a windmill with a fixed tower and revolvable cap above it bearing the sails (also called **tower mill**); **smock'-race** (formerly) a race run by women or girls for the prize of a smock. [OE *smoc*]

smog *smog*, *n* smoky fog. — *adj* **smogg'y**.

smoile or **smoyle** *smoil*, old forms of **smile**.

smoke *smōk*, *n* the gases, vapours, and fine particles that are emitted by burning material; solid particles suspended in a gas; fumes; vapour; fog; a cloud or column of fumes; something which may be smoked — tobacco, a cigarette, or a cigar (*colloq*); an instance or spell of smoking; S African brandy (**Cape smoke**); tear gas (*colloq*). — *vi* to exhale or emit smoke, vapour, dust, etc; to reek; to send smoke (*esp* in a wrong direction); to move like smoke; to dash along in a cloud of smoke, vapour, spray, or dust; to suffer (*orig* at the stake), to smart; to take into the mouth and puff out the smoke of tobacco or something similar; to permit, or lend itself to, smoking. — *vt* to dry, scent, preserve, fumigate, suffocate, blacken, taint, drive or render by smoke; to inhale and emit the smoke from; to scent out, suspect, have an inkling of (*archaic*); to observe (*archaic*); to quiz, ridicule (*archaic*); to thrash (*archaic*). — *adj* **smok'able** fit to be smoked. — *adj* **smoked**. — *adj* **smoke'less** (eg of a fuel) emitting no smoke; containing little or no smoke. — *adv* **smoke'-lessly**. — *n* **smoke'lessness**. — *n* **smok'er** apparatus for emitting smoke; a person who smokes tobacco; a smoking carriage or compartment; a person who smoke-dries meat, or an apparatus for doing this; a smoking concert. — *adv* **smok'ily**. — *n* **smok'iness**. — *n* and *adj* **smok'ing**. — *n* **smok'o** (*pl* **smok'os**) a smoke-ho. — *adj* **smok'y** giving out smoke; like smoke; coloured like or by smoke; filled, or liable to be filled, with smoke; tarnished or made unattractive or offensive by smoke; suspicious (*archaic*). — *n* (*Scot*) a smoked haddock. — **smoke abatement** (measures directed to) reducing the amount of smoke in the atmosphere of towns; **smoke alarm** a device that detects smoke from a fire in a room, building, etc and sounds a warning bell or buzzer; **smoke'-ball** a shell emitting smoke as a screen or to drive out an enemy; **smoke'-black** lampblack; **smoke'board** a board suspended before the upper part of a fireplace to prevent the smoke coming out into the room; **smoke'-bomb** a bomb that emits smoke on bursting; **smoke'-box** part of a steam boiler where the smoke is collected before passing out at the chimney; **smoke'bush** or **smoke'tree** a sumach with light feathery or cloudlike panicles; **smoke'-consumer** an apparatus for burning all the smoke from a fire; **smoke control area** one in which the emission of smoke from chimneys is prohibited; **smoke detector** a device that activates an alarm when it detects smoke in the air, a smoke alarm. — *adj* **smoke'-dried**. — *vt* **smoke'-dry** to cure or dry by means of smoke. — **smoke helmet** a head-covering for fire-fighters or others who work in dense smoke; **smoke-ho'** (*Austr*) *orig* a break for a smoke during the working day, now a rest, a tea-break; **smoke hole** a fumarole; a hole allowing smoke to escape; **smoke'hood** a protective hood that prevents the wearer from inhaling smoke and poisonous fumes, eg from a fire on a plane; **smoke'house** a building where meat or fish is cured by smoking, or where smoked meats are stored; **smoke'-jack** a contrivance for turning a spit by means of an ascending current of air (*hist*); a muddled brain (*obs*); **smokeless fuel** a fuel that is permitted in a smoke control area; **smokeless zone** (*colloq*) a smoke control area. — *adj* **smoke'proof** impervious to smoke. — **smoke'-room** a smoking room (see below); **smoke-room story** one unsuitable for telling elsewhere; **smoke'-sail** a small sail hoisted to drive off the smoke from the galley; **smoke'screen** a cloud of smoke raised to conceal movements (also *fig*); **smoke signal** (often in *pl*) a signal or message conveyed by means of patterns of smoke (also *fig*); **smoke'stack** the funnel of a ship or railway engine; a (*usu* tall industrial) chimney; **smoke stack industry** a traditional heavy industry, *esp* one employing methods of production and technology that adversely affect the environment; **smoke test** a method of testing for leaks in drain pipes or chimneys by introducing dense smoke, often by using a smoke-bomb. — *adj* **smoke'tight** impervious to smoke. — **smoketree** see **smokebush**; **smoke tunnel** a wind tunnel into which smoke is put at certain points in order to make wind effects visible; **smoking cap** and **smoking jacket** a light ornamental cap and jacket formerly worn by smokers; **smoking carriage, compartment** or **room** a railway carriage, compartment or room, set apart for smokers; **smoking concert** a concert at which smoking (euphemistically) is allowed; **smoky quartz** Cairngorm stone. — **end** or **go up in smoke** (of eg hopes) to vanish; (of eg plans) to come to nothing; **like smoke** very quickly; **sell smoke** (L *fūmum vendere*, to make empty promises) to swindle; **smoke out** to discover; to drive out of a hiding place by smoke or fire; **the (Big) Smoke** (*colloq*; also without *caps*) a metropolitan area characterized by atmospheric pollution, *esp* London; the (nearest) city or major town (*orig* a phrase used by the Australian aborigines), now *esp* Melbourne or Sydney. [OE *smoca* (noun), *smocian* (verb); Ger *Schmauch*]

smoko. See under **smoke**.

smolder. American spelling of **smoulder**.

smolt *smōlt*, *n* a young river salmon when it is bluish along the upper half of the body and silvery along the sides. [Orig Scot; see **smout**[2]]

smooch *smo͞och*, (*colloq*) *vi* to kiss or pet. [Origin uncertain; poss related to **smouch**[1]]

smoor. See **smore**.

smoot *smo͞ot*, (*slang*) *n* a compositor who does odd jobs in various printing houses. — *vi* to work in this way. [Origin obscure]

smooth *smo͞odh*, *adj* having an even surface; without roughness of texture or taste; evenly spread; glossy; hairless; of even consistency; slippery; gently flowing; easy; bland; fair-spoken; charming, perhaps self-consciously so; classy or elegant (*slang*). — *adv* smoothly. — *vt* to make smooth, not rough, lumpy, etc; to free from obstruction, difficulty or harshness; to reduce from a diphthong to a simple vowel; to remove by smoothing (often with *away*; often *fig*); to calm or soothe; to blandish; to make (difficulties or problems) seem less serious or less important (often with *over*). — *vi* to become smooth; to flatter, blandish or behave ingratiatingly (also *vt* with *it*; *Shakesp*). — *n* a smooth place, part or side; an act of smoothing. — *vt* **smooth'en** to make smooth. — *n* **smooth'er** a person or thing that smooths; a smoothing tool, a sleeker; a flatterer (*obs*). — *n* **smooth'ie** (*slang*) a plausible or smooth-spoken person; a person elegant or suave in manner or appearance, *esp* insincerely or excessively so; a thick drink of smooth consistency made with puréed fruit, milk, yoghurt or ice cream (*NAm*, *Austr* and *NZ*). — *n* and *adj* **smooth'ing**. — *adj* **smooth'ish**. — *adv* **smooth'ly**. — *n* **smooth'ness**. — *adj* **smooth'-bore** (of a firearm) not rifled (also **smooth'-bored**). — *n* a gun with a smooth-bored barrel. — *adj* **smooth'-browed** with unwrinkled brow. — *adj* **smooth'-chinned** beardless. — *adj* **smooth'-coated** not shaggy-haired. — **smooth dab** see **lemon**[2]. — *adj* **smooth-ditt'ied** (*Milton*) set to words that smoothly fit the tune or, possibly, having a smooth ditty, or set of words; **smooth'-faced** having a smooth face or surface; pleasant-looking; beardless; unwrinkled; plausible. — **smoothing iron** a flatiron; **smoothing plane** a small fine plane used for finishing. — *adj* **smooth'-leaved**. — **smooth muscle** unstriated muscular tissue (eg in the walls of the intestines) whose action is slow rhythmic contraction and relaxation, independent of the will. — *adj* **smooth'-paced** having a regular easy pace. — **smooth'pate** a bald person (*archaic*). — *adj* **smooth'-shod** having shoes without spikes. — *adj* **smooth'-spoken** or **smooth'-tongued** conciliatory, plausible, flattering, or soft in speech. [OE *smōth* (usu *smēthe*)]

smørbrød *smōr'bro͞o* or *smœr'brō*, (*Norw*) or **smørrebrød** *smœr'ə-brœdh* or *smör'ə-bröd*, (*Dan*) *n* literally, bread and butter; hors d'œuvres served on slices of buttered bread.

smore *smōr* or *smör*, or **smoor** *smo͞or*, (*Scot*) *vt* and *vi* to smother or suffocate; to put out (a fire or light). — *n* **smoor** smoke. [OE *smorian*]

smörgåsbord *smör'gas-börd* or *smœr'gōs-bo͞ord*, *n* a Swedish-style table assortment of hors d'œuvres and many other dishes to which one helps oneself. [Swed]

smørrebrød. See **smørbrød**.

smorzando *smört-san'dō* or *zmort-sän'dō*, or **smorzato** *-sä'tō*, (*music*) *adj* and *adv* with a gradual fading away; growing slower and softer. [Ital; gerund and pa p of *smorzare* to tone down, extinguish]

smote *smōt*, *pa t* of **smite**.

smother *smudh'ər*, *vt* to suffocate by excluding the air, *esp* by a thick covering; to stifle (*lit* and *fig*); to envelop closely; to cover up thickly; to suppress; to conceal. — *vi* to be suffocated or suppressed; to smoulder. — *n* smoke; thick floating dust; a smouldering fire or condition; a welter; suffocation. — *adj* **smoth'ered**. — *n* **smoth'erer**. — *n* **smoth'eriness**. — *n* and *adj* **smoth'ering**. — *adv* **smoth'eringly**. — *adj* **smoth'ery** tending to smother; stifling. — **smothered mate** or **smother mate** (*chess*) checkmate by a knight, the king having been prevented from moving by the positions of his own forces; **smother'-fly** an aphis. [ME *smorther*, from OE *smorian* to smother; cf **smore**]

smouch[1] *smowch*, (*dialect*) *n* a smack, a hearty kiss. — *vt* to kiss. [Cf Ger *Schmutz*]
smouch[2] *smowch* or **smouse** *smowz*, *n* a Jew (*obs slang*); a pedlar (*SAfr*). — *vi* (*SAfr*) to trade as a pedlar. — *n* **smous'er** (*SAfr*) a pedlar. [Afrik *smous*, perh from Heb *sh'mū'ōth* news]
smouch[3] *smowch*, *vt* to filch. — *vi* to cheat.
smouch[4] *smowch*, *n* a form of **smutch** and **smudge**.
smoulder *smōl'dər*, *vt* to smother. — *vi* to burn slowly or without flame; to linger on in a suppressed or hidden state. — *n* smother; smouldering fire. — *n* and *adj* **smoul'dering**. — *adj* **smoul'dry** (*Spenser*). [ME *smolder*; origin obscure]
smouse, smouser. See **smouch**[2].
smout[1] *smowt*. Same as **smoot**.
smout[2] or **smowt** *smowt*, *n* Scots form of **smolt**; a small person or child.
smoyle *smoil*. An old form of **smile**.
smudge[1] *smuj*, *n* a smear; a blur; a rubbed blot. — *vt* to smear; to blur; to soil; to daub. — *n* **smudg'er**. — *adv* **smudg'ily**. — *n* **smudg'iness**. — *adj* **smudg'y**. [Cf **smutch**]
smudge[2] *smuj*, *n* a choking smoke; fuel for obtaining smoke. — *vt* to fumigate with smoke. — *adj* **smud'gy** smoky. — **smudge box, pot**, etc a container for or of materials which produce smoke to protect people, plants, etc against insects, etc. [Origin obscure]
smug[1] *smug*, *adj* neat, prim, spruce; smooth; sleek; affectedly smart; offensively self-complacent. — *n* a smug person; an industrious student who does not take part in social activities (*obs university slang*). — *vt* to make trim. — *adv* **smug'ly**. — *n* **smug'ness**. — *adj* **smug'-faced**. [Connection with LGer *smuk* trim is unlikely, as the *g* presents difficulty]
smug[2] *smug*, (*slang*) *vt* to seize without ceremony; to steal; to hush up. [Origin obscure]
smuggle[1] *smug'l*, *vt* to import or export illegally or without paying duty; to convey secretly. — *adj* **smugg'led**. — *n* **smugg'ler** a person who smuggles; a vessel used in smuggling. — *n* and *adj* **smugg'ling**. [LGer *smuggeln*; Ger *schmuggeln*]
smuggle[2] *smug'l*, *vt* to fondle or cuddle. [Origin obscure]
smur *smûr*, **smirr** or **smir** *smir*, (*Scot*) *n* fine misty rain, — *vi* to drizzle, rain very finely. — *adj* **smurr'y** or **smirr'y**.
smut *smut*, *n* soot; worthless or bad coal; a flake or spot of dirt, soot, etc; a black spot; a disease of plants, *esp* cereals, giving an appearance of soot; the fungus causing it; mildly obscene conversation, remarks, material, etc. — *vt* to soil, spot or affect with smut; to become smutty. — *adj* **smutt'ed**. — *adv* **smutt'ily** — *n* **smutt'iness**. — *adj* **smutt'y** stained with smut; affected with smut disease; mildly obscene. — **smut fungus** any member of the *Ustilaginales*, an order of Basidiomycetes, parasitic on plants, causing smut and bunt. [Cf LGer *schmutt*; Ger *Schmutz* dirt]
smutch *smutch*, *vt* to smut; to sully. — *n* a dirty mark; soot; grime; a stain. [Cf **smudge**[1]]
smytrie *smīt'ri*, (*Scot*) *n* a collection of small things. [Cf Flem *smite*]
SN *abbrev*: Senegal (IVR).
Sn (*chem*) symbol: *stannum* (*L*), tin.
sn *abbrev*: *secundum naturam* (*L*), according to nature.
snab. See **snob**.
snabble. See **snaffle**.
snack *snak*, *n* a snap, bite (*dialect*); a share; a small quantity, a taste; a light meal. — *vi* to snap (*Scot*); to share (*obs*); to eat a snack. — **snack'-bar** or **snack'-counter** a place where light meals can be bought. — **snack on** to make a light meal from. [Cf MDu *snacken* to snap; **snatch**]
snaffle *snaf'l*, *n* a jointed bit for horses (less severe than the curb). — *vt* to put a snaffle on; to control by a snaffle; (the following meanings *slang*; also **snabb'le**) to arrest; to capture; to purloin; to get possession of. — **snaff'le-bit**; **snaff'le-bridle**; **snaff'le-rein**; **snaff'ling-lay** the trade of highwayman. [Ety doubtful; cf Du *snavel*, Ger *Schnabel* beak, mouth]
snafu *sna-foō'*, (*NAm slang, orig military*) *n* chaos. — *adj* chaotic. [*s*ituation *n*ormal — *a*ll *f*ouled (or *f*ucked) *u*p]
snag *snag*, *n* a stump, eg of a branch or tooth; a jag; a short tine; an embedded tree, dangerous for boats; hence, a catch, a (hidden) obstacle or drawback; a caught thread in a stocking; (*usu pl*) sausage (*Austr slang*). — *vt* to catch on a snag; to tear on a snag; to hack so as to form snags; to clear of snags: — *pr p* **snagg'ing**; *pa t* and *pa p* **snagged**. — *adj* **snagged**. — *adj* **snagg'y**. [Cf ON *snagi* peg]
snaggletooth *snag'l-tōōth*, *n* a broken, irregular or projecting tooth: — *pl* **snagg'leteeth**. — *adj* **snagg'le-toothed**. [Appar from **snag** and **tooth**]
snail *snāl*, *n* any terrestrial or air-breathing gasteropod mollusc with a well-developed coiled shell; extended to other shelled gasteropods and (*dialect*) to slugs; a sluggish person or animal; a snail wheel; medick of various kinds (from its coiled pods). — *vi* to crawl, go very slowly (also *vt* with *it*). — *n* **snail'ery** a place where edible snails are bred. — *adj* and *adv* **snail'-like**. — *adj* **snail'y**. — **snail darter** a small American freshwater fish (*Percina tanasi*); **snail'-fish** the fish also called the sea-snail; **snail flower** any flower pollinated by snails. — *adj* **snail'-paced**. — **snail'-shell**. — *adj* **snail'-slow**. — **snail's pace** a very slow speed; **snail wheel** a cam that controls the striking of a clock. — **giant African snail** a 10-inch snail, a serious plant pest except in its place of origin, East Africa. [OE *snegl*, *snægl*, *snǣl*]
'snails *snālz*, (*obs*) *interj* for **God's nails**, an exclamatory oath.
snake *snāk*, *n* a serpent, or member of the *Ophidia*, a class of elongated limbless (or all but limbless) scaly carnivorous reptiles, often venomous, with forked tongue, no eyelids or external ears, and teeth fused to the bones that bear them; an ungrateful or treacherous person (in allusion to one of Aesop's fables); a wretch or drudge; anything snakelike in form or movement; an apparatus for blasting a passage through a minefield; (formerly) the band (narrower than the *tunnel* allowed by the IMF on the world market) within which the relative values of certain EC currencies were allowed to float. — *vi* to move sinuously or follow a winding course; to creep. — *vt* to drag. — *adj* **snake'like**. — *adv* **snake'wise** in the manner of a snake. — *adv* **snāk'ily**. — *n* **snāk'iness**. — *adj* **snāk'ish**. — *n* **snāk'ishness**. — *adj* **snāk'y**. — **snake'bird** the darter; the wryneck; **snake'bite** the bite of a venomous snake; the condition or symptoms of a victim of a snakebite; a drink made of lager and cider in equal measures; **snake'-charmer** a person who handles snakes and gets them to perform rhythmical movements; **snake cult** serpent-worship; **snake dance** a religious dance of the Hopi Indians in which snakes are handled; **snake eel** an eel without a tail fin; **snake fence** (*US*) a worm fence; **snake fly** a neuropterous insect (*Raphidia*) with a necklike prothorax. — *adj* **snake'-hipped** slim-hipped. — **snake'-house** a place where snakes are kept; **snake'-oil** any substance or mixture without medicinal value but sold as medicine; **snake'-pit** (*fig*) a mental hospital; a place, or circumstances, characterized by disordered emotions and relationships; **snake'root** bistort, milkwort, *Aristolochia*, or any other plant whose root has been thought good for snakebites; **snake's'-head** fritillary; **snake'skin** the skin of a snake, *esp* when made into leather. — Also *adj*. — **snake'stone** a fossil ammonite; a stone thought to cure snakebite; **snake'-weed** bistort; **snake'wood** letterwood. — **snake in the grass** (*fig*) someone who injures furtively; a lurking danger; **snakes and ladders** a board game played with counters and dice in which 'ladders' afford short cuts to the finish, but 'snakes' oblige players to descend to nearer the starting-point. [OE *snaca*]
snap *snap*, *vi* to make a bite (often with *at*); to speak tartly in sudden irritation; to grasp (with *at*); to shut suddenly, eg by a spring; to make a sharp noise; to go with a sharp noise; to break suddenly. — *vt* to bite suddenly; to seize, secure promptly (*usu* with *up*); to

answer or interrupt sharply (often with *up*); to shut with a sharp sound; to cause to make a sharp sound; to send or put with a sharp sound; to say snappishly (sometimes with *out*); to break suddenly; to pass (the ball) from the line of scrimmage back to the quarterback (*Am football*); to take an instantaneous photograph of, *esp* with a hand-held camera: — *pr p* **snapp'ing**; *pa t* and *pa p* **snapped**. — *n* an act, instance, or noise of snapping; a small catch or lock; an earring (*rare*); (in *pl*) a kind of handcuffs; a share; a scrap; a whit; a snack; a crack; a crisp, ginger biscuit (also **gingersnap**); a quick, crisp, incisive, epigrammatic quality in style; lively energy; a brief theatrical engagement (*slang*); an easy and profitable place or task; a sharper, a cheat (*old slang*); a riveter's or glass-moulder's tool; a snapshot; a sudden cold spell (also **cold snap**); a type of card game in which the first player to shout 'snap' on spotting a matching pair of cards wins all the cards on the table; the play that involves snapping the ball (*Am football*). — *adj* sudden, unexpected; offhand; (of a decision or judgement) made on the spur of the moment without deep consideration of all possibilities; snapping shut. — *adv* with a snap. — *interj* used in claiming cards in the game of snap; also, on meeting or discovering two matching items, circumstances, etc. — *n* **snapp'er** an animal that snaps; someone who snaps or snaps up; an attachment at the end of a whiplash to make it crack; a snapping-turtle; any fish of the family *Lutjanidae*, related to the basses; (also **schnapper**) any of several highly esteemed food-fish of the family *Sparidae*, found in Australian and New Zealand waters; a Christmas or party cracker (*NAm*). — *adv* **snapp'ily**. — *n* and *adj* **snapp'ing**. — *adv* **snapp'ingly**. — *adj* **snapp'ish** inclined to snap; quick and tart. — *adv* **snapp'ishly**. — *n* **snapp'ishness**. — *adj* **snapp'y** snappish; snapping; having the quality of snap; instantaneous; smart, fashionable, polished (as in *snappy dresser*). — *adj* **snap'-brim** (of a hat) having a brim that turns down springily. — **snap'dragon** a plant (genus *Antirrhinum*) of the figwort family whose flower when pinched and released snaps like a dragon; a Christmas game of snatching raisins out of burning brandy; **snap'-fastener** a press-fastener, a press-stud; **snap'-link** a link with a side opening closed by a spring; **snapp'ing-turtle** a large aggressive American freshwater tortoise; **snap'shooter**; **snap'shooting**; **snap'shot** a hasty shot; a photograph taken quickly and informally, with simple equipment; an instant record of an event, situation, etc at a particular time, *esp* a stage in a process or sequence (*fig*; also *adj*); a visual record of the placement of stored data at a specific stage in a program run (*comput*). — **look snappy, make it snappy** (*colloq*) to hurry; **Scotch snap** see under **Scotch**; **snap into it** to get going quickly; **snap out of it** (*colloq*) to give (eg a mood or habit) up at once; **snap someone's head** or **nose off** to answer irritably and rudely; **snap up** to take or purchase eagerly and quickly. [Prob Du *snappen* to snap; Ger *schnappen*]

snaphaunce *snap'häns* or *-höns*, **snaphance** *-häns* or *-hans* or **snaphaunch** *-hönsh*, (*obs*) *n* a freebooter; a flintlock or a weapon with one; a spring catch or trap. [Cf Du *snapshaan*, from *snappen* to snap, and *haan* a cock]

snapper[1] *snap'ər*, (*Scot*) *n* a stumble; a slip in conduct; a scrape. — *vi* to stumble. [Cf Ger dialect *schnappen* to stumble]

snapper[2]. See under **snap**.

snar *snär*, (*Spenser*) *vi* to snarl. [Cf Du and LGer *snarren*]

snare *snār*, *n* a running noose for trapping; a trap; an allurement, temptation, entanglement or moral danger; a loop for removing tumours, etc; a string stretched across the lower head of a side-drum. — *vt* to catch, entangle or trap in a snare; to remove with a snare. — *n* **snar'er**. — *n* **snar'ing**. — *adj* **snar'y**. — **snare'-drum** a side-drum. [OE *sneare* or ON *snara*; prob partly from Du *snaar* or LGer *snare*]

snark *snärk*, *n* an imaginary animal created by Lewis Carroll (1876).

snarl[1] *snärl*, *vi* to make a surly resentful noise with a show of teeth; to speak in a surly manner. — *vt* to utter snarlingly. — *n* an ill-natured growling sound or facial expression; an act of snarling. — *n* **snarl'er**. — *n* and *adj* **snarl'ing**. — *adv* **snarl'ingly**. — *adj* **snarl'y**. [**snar**]

snarl[2] *snärl*, *n* a knot; a tangle; a knot in wood. — *vt* to ensnare (*dialect*); to tangle; to raise with a snarling-iron. — *vi* to tangle. — *adj* **snarled**. — *n* **snarl'er**. — *n* **snarl'ing**. — **snarl'ing-iron** or **-tool** a curved tool for raised work in hollow metalware. — **snarl up** (used *esp* in *pa p* and *participial adj* forms) to make muddled or tangled and thus stop operating, moving, etc smoothly (*n* **snarl'-up** a tangle; a traffic jam). [**snare**]

snash *snash*, (*Scot*) *n* insolence, abusive language. — *vi* to talk impudently. [Prob imit]

snaste *snāst*, (now *dialect*) *n* a wick; a candle-snuff. [Origin obscure]

snatch *snach*, *vt* to seize suddenly; to pluck away quickly; to grab; to take as opportunity occurs. — *vi* to make a snap or seizure. — *n* a snap (*Shakesp*); an act of snatching or snatching at; a grab; a short spell; a fragment, eg of song or verse; a snack; a catch (of the voice) (*Shakesp*); a quibble (*Shakesp*); (in weight-lifting) a type of lift in which the weight is raised from the floor to an overhead position in one movement. — *n* **snatch'er**. — *adv* **snatch'ily** or **snatch'ingly**. — *adj* **snatch'y** irregular. — **snatch block** a block with a side opening for the bight of a rope; **snatch'-purse** or **-thief** a thief who snatches; **snatch squad** a group of policemen, etc who force a sudden quick passage into eg a disorderly or rioting crowd in order to arrest trouble-makers or ringleaders; a swift, organized sally by a group of people in order to seize something. — **snatch at** to try to snatch or seize. [ME *snacchen*; poss related to **snack**]

snath *snath*, **snathe** *snādh*, **snead** *snēd*, **sneath** *snēth* or **sned** *sned*, *n* the curved handle or shaft of a scythe. [OE *snǣd* a scythe handle, a slice]

snazzy *snaz'i*, (*slang*) *adj* very attractive or fashionable; flashy. [Origin obscure]

SNCF *abbrev*: *Société Nationale des Chemins de Fer français* (*Fr*), French national railways.

snead. See **snath**.

sneak *snēk*, *vi* to go furtively or meanly, to slink or skulk; to cringe; to behave meanly; to tell tales. — *vt* to pass furtively; to steal (*slang*): — *pa t* and *pa p* **sneaked** or (*NAm* or *colloq*) **snuck**. — *n* a sneaking person; a person who sneaks or sneaks away; a sneaking thief; a tell-tale; a ball bowled along the ground (*cricket*). — *n* **sneak'er** a person who or thing that sneaks; a soft-soled, *usu* canvas, shoe; a sandshoe. — *adv* **sneak'ily**. — *n* **sneak'iness**. — *adj* **sneak'ing** mean, crouching; secret, underhand, not openly avowed; lurking under other feelings. — *adv* **sneak'ingly**. — *adj* **sneak'ish** befitting a sneak. — *adv* **sneak'ishly**. — *n* **sneak'ishness**. — *n* **sneaks'by** (*archaic*) a sneak. — *adj* **sneak'y** sneaking; cunning. — **sneak'-cup** in some editions of Shakespeare (*Henry IV Part One*, III. 3. 99), probably a misreading of a blurred **sneakeup** (see **sneak-up**) in the first quartos, but by some taken to be a correction and explained as one who balks his cup, or a stealer of cups; **sneak preview** a special private screening or viewing of a film, exhibition, etc before it is officially released, made available, etc to the public; **sneak'-raid** a bombing or other raid made under conditions of concealment; **sneak'-thief** a thief who steals through open doors or windows without breaking in; **sneak'-thievery**; **sneak'-up** a sneak, shirker or skulker. [Connection with OE *snīcan* to crawl is obscure]

sneap *snēp*, *vt* to nip, pinch; to put down, repress, snub. — *n* a snub, check. — *adj* **sneap'ing** (*Shakesp*). [Earlier *snape*, from ON *sneypa*]

sneath. See **snath**.

sneb and **snebbe**. Old forms of **snib**[1], **snub**.

sneck[1] *snek*, (*Northern*) *n* a latch; a door-catch. — *vt* to fasten with a sneck. — **sneck drawer** someone who lifts the latch; an insinuating or crafty person. — Also **sneck draw**. — **sneck'-drawing**. — Also *adj*. [Cf **snack**, **snatch**]

sneck[2]. See **snick**[1].

sneck up. See **snick up**.

sned[1] *sned*, *vt* to cut; to lop; to prune. [OE *snǣdan*]

sned[2]. See **snath**.

snee *snē*, (*obs*) *vi* to cut. — **snick and snee** or **snick** (or **stick**) **or snee** see **snickeersnee**. [Du *snijden* to cut]

sneer *snēr*, *vi* to show cynical contempt by the expression of the face, as by drawing up the lip (sometimes with *at*); to express such contempt in other ways; to grin (*obs*). — *vt* to utter sneeringly; to sneer at (*obs*); to render or drive by sneering. — *n* a sneering expression; an act of sneering. — *n* **sneer'er**. — *n* and *adj* **sneer'ing**. — *adv* **sneer'ingly**. — *adj* **sneer'y**. [Perh related to Fris *sneere* to scorn]

sneesh *snēsh*, (*Scot*) *n* a pinch of snuff; snuff. — *n* **sneesh'in**, **sneesh'ing** or **sneesh'an** snuff; a pinch of snuff. — **snee'shin-mull** a snuff box. [Poss **sneeze**, **sneezing**; or imit; cf **snush**]

sneeze *snēz*, *vi* to make a sudden, involuntary and audible expiration through the nose and mouth, due to irritation of the inner nasal membrane. — *n* an act of sneezing. — *n* **sneez'er**. — *n* **sneez'ing**. — *adj* **sneez'y**. — **sneeze box** (*slang*) a snuffbox; **sneeze'weed** an American composite plant (*Helenium*); **sneeze'wood** a S African meliaceous timber tree (*Ptaeroxylon*), or its wood, whose sawdust causes sneezing; **sneeze'wort** a species of yarrow (*Achillaea ptarmica*) once used as a substitute for snuff; white hellebore. — **not to be sneezed at** not to be despised. [ME *snesen*, *fnesen*, from OE *fnēsan* to sneeze; Du *niezen*]

snell[1] *snel*, (*Scot*) *adj* (of eg wind or weather) keen, sharp or severe. — *adv* **snel'ly**. [OE *snell* active; Ger *schnell* swift]

snell[2] *snel*, (*angling*) *n* a short piece of hair, gut, etc attaching a hook to a line. — *vt* to attach (a hook) to a line. [Origin obscure]

Snell's law. See under **law**[1].

SNG *abbrev*: synthetic natural gas.

snib[1]. Same as **snub**.

snib[2] *snib*, (chiefly *Scot*) *n* a small bolt; a catch for a window-sash. — *vt* to fasten with a snib. [Cf LGer *snibbe* beak]

snick[1] *snik*, (*Scott* **sneck** *snek*), *vt* to cut out, snip, nick; to deflect slightly by a touch of the bat (*cricket*). — *n* a small cut; a glancing stroke in cricket. — **snick and/or snee** see **snickersnee**. [Origin doubtful]

snick[2] *snik*, *n*, *vt*, and *vi* click. [Imit]

snicker *snik'ər*, *vi* to snigger; to nicker or neigh. — *vt* to say gigglingly. — *n* a giggle. [Imit; cf **nicker**[1], **snigger**[1]]

snicker-snack *snik'ər-snak'*, *n* a word coined by Lewis Carroll to evoke the sound of a slicing blade. [Imit; also cf **snickersnee**]

snickersnee *snik'ər-snē*, *n* a large knife for fighting; fighting with knives (*obs*). — *vi* (*obs*) to fight with knives. — Also earlier **snick'-a-snee**, **snick and snee**, **snick** (earlier **stick**) **or snee**. [Appar Du *steken* to thrust, and *snijden* to cut]

snicket *snik'it*, (*dialect*) *n* a narrow passage or back street; a ginnel. [Origin obscure]

snick up *snik up'*, (*Shakesp*) *vi* (*usu imper*) go hang. — Also **sneck up**.

snide *snīd*, *adj* sham; counterfeit; base; mean; dishonest; derogatory in an insinuating way; showing malice. — Also *n*. — *adv* **snide'ly**. — *n* **snide'ness**. [Ety doubtful]

sniff *snif*, *vt* to draw in with the breath through the nose; to smell; to suspect or detect by smell or as if by smell. — *vi* to draw in air sharply and audibly through the nose; to draw up mucus or tears escaping into the nose; to smell tentatively; to express disapprobation with reticence by a slight sound in the nose; to snuffle; to inhale a dangerous or addictive substance (eg glue or cocaine). — *n* an act or a sound of sniffing; a smell; a small quantity inhaled by the nose; a slight intimation or suspicion (*fig*). — *n* **sniff'er**. — *adj* (of a dog, apparatus, etc) trained, designed, etc to seek out or locate (*esp* illicit or dangerous substances) by smell. — *adv* **sniff'ily**. — *n* **sniff'iness**. — *n* and *adj* **sniff'ing**. — *adv* **sniff'ingly**. — *vi* **sniff'le** to snuffle slightly, to sniff. — *n* an act of sniffling; the sound made by sniffling; (often in *pl* with **the**) a slight cold; (often in *pl* with **the**) liquid mucus running out of or blocking the nose. — *n* **sniff'ler** someone who sniffles; a slight breeze. — *adj* **sniff'y** inclined to be disdainful. — **not to be sniffed at** not to be despised. [Imit; cf **snuff**[1]]

snift *snift*, *vi* to sniff or snivel; to blow out steam, etc. — *vt* and *vi* **snift'er** to sniff. — *n* a sniff; (in *pl*) blockage of the nasal passages in catarrh, the sniffles; a dram (*slang*); a strong breeze; a brandy-glass (*US*). — *adj* **snift'y** (*slang*) having a tempting smell; inclined to sniff in disdain. — **snift'er-** or **snift'ing-valve** an air valve of a cylinder, etc. [Ety as for *sniff*]

snig *snig*, (*dialect*) *n* a river eel, *esp* an immature (olive and yellow) eel. — *vt* to drag a load with chains or ropes. — *vt* **snigg'er** to catch (salmon) with a weighted hook. — *vi* **snigg'le** to fish for eels by thrusting the bait into their hiding places; to fish for salmon, etc, by striking with a hook. — *vt* to catch in this way. — *n* a baited hook. — *n* **snigg'ler**. — *n* **snigg'ling**. [Origin obscure]

snigger[1] *snig'ər*, *vi* to laugh in a half-suppressed way, often derisively or mockingly. — *vt* to say with a snigger. — *n* a half-suppressed laugh. — *n* **snigg'erer**. — *n* and *adj* **snigg'ering**. — *adv* **snigg'eringly**. [Imit]

snigger[2]. See under **snig**.

snip *snip*, *vt* to cut eg with scissors; to snatch or snap (*obs*): — *pr p* **snipp'ing**; *pa t* and *pa p* **snipped**. — *n* a small cut, eg with scissors; a small shred; a small, slender or despicable person; a small piece; a notch, slit or slash; the sound of a stroke of scissors; a white or light patch or stripe on a horse, *esp* on the nose; a share; a tailor (*slang*); a certainty; a bargain. — *n* **snipp'er**. — *n* **snipp'ing** a clipping. — *adj* **snipp'y** fragmentary; stingy; snappish. — *n pl* **snips** hand-shears for sheet metal. — **snip-snap'** the action or sound of scissors; quick snappy dialogue. — Also *adj*, *adv*, *interj* or *vi*. — **snipp'er-snapper** a whipper-snapper. — **snipt taffeta fellow** (*Shakesp*) one who goes about in slashed silk. [LGer or Du *snippen*; Ger dialect *schnippen*]

snipe *snīp*, *n* any of several wading birds of the genus *Gallinago*, breeding in marshes and having a long straight bill; any of several similar or related species; a fool or contemptible person (*Shakesp*); the butt of a cigar or cigarette (*US slang*); a sniping shot; a verbal attack, criticism: — *pl usu* **snipe** of the bird, **snipes** of species of the bird, and in other senses. — *vi* to shoot snipe for sport, go snipe-shooting; to shoot at individuals from a position of (*usu* distant) cover; to attack or criticize, *esp* from a position of security (*fig*; often with *at*). — *vt* to pick off by rifle-fire from (*usu* distant) cover. — *n* **snip'er**. — *n* **snip'ing**. — *adj* **snip'y** snipe-like; snipe-beaked; frequented by snipe. — **snipe'fish** the trumpet fish. [Prob Scand; the OE word is *snīte*]

snipper. See under **snip**.

snippet *snip'it*, *n* a little piece snipped off; a scrap, of literature, news, etc. — *n* **snipp'etiness**. — *adj* **snipp'ety** trivial, fragmentary. [**snip**]

snip-snap-snorum *snip-snap-snö'rəm*, *n* a children's game of turning up cards, to the calls of 'snip', 'snap' and 'snorum'. [LGer *snipp-snapp-snorum*]

snirt *snirt* or *snûrt*, (*Scot*) *n* a smothered laugh. — *vi* **snirt'le** to snicker. [Imit]

snitch *snich*, (*slang*) *n* the nose; a fillip on the nose (*obs*); an informer. — *vi* to inform or sneak. — *vt* (*colloq*) to pilfer. — *n* **snitch'er** an informer; (*usu* in *pl*) a handcuff (*obs slang*).

snivel *sniv'l*, *n* mucus of the nose; a sniff; a hypocritical snuffle; cant. — *vi* to run at the nose; to sniff; to snuffle; to whimper or cry. — *vt* to utter with snivelling: — *pr p* **sniv'elling**; *pa t* and *pa p* **sniv'elled**. — *n*

sniv'eller. — *adj* **sniv'elling**. — *adj* **sniv'elly**. [OE *snofl* mucus]

SNO *abbrev*: Scottish National Orchestra (now **RSNO** Royal Scottish National Orchestra).

snob *snob*, *n* a person who sets too much value on social standing, wishing to be associated with the upper class and their mores, and treating those viewed as inferior with condescension and contempt; someone having similar pretensions as regards specified tastes, such as *wine snob*, *intellectual snob*; a shoemaker, shoemaker's apprentice, cobbler (*old colloq* and *dialect*; *Scot* **snab**); a townsman (*Cambridge University slang*); a person of ordinary or low rank (*obs*); an ostentatious vulgarian (*obs*); a blackleg, scab (*obs*). — *n* **snobb'ery** snobbishness; snobbish behaviour. — *adj* **snobb'ish**. — *adv* **snobb'ishly**. — *n* **snobb'ishness**. — *n* **snobb'ism**. — *adj* **snobb'y**. — *n* **snob'ling** a little snob. — *n* **snoboc'racy** or **snobboc'racy** snobs as a powerful class. — *n* **snobog'rapher**. — *n* **snobog'raphy** the description of snobs and snobbery. [Orig slang]

SNOBOL *snō'böl*, *n* String Oriented Symbolic Language, a high-level computer language for handling strings of symbols.

Sno-cat *snō'kat*, *n* a type of motorized, tracked vehicle for use on snow. [From **snow** and **caterpillar**]

snod *snod*, (*Scot*) *adj* smooth, neat, trim, snug. — *vt* to trim, set in order (with *up*): — *pa t* and *pa p* **snodd'ed** or **snodd'it**. [Poss connected with ON *snothinn* bald]

snoek. See **snook**[2].

snog *snog*, (*slang*) *vi* to embrace, cuddle, kiss, indulge in lovemaking. — Also *n*. [Origin obscure]

snoke. See **snook**[1].

snood *snōōd*, *n* a band for the hair, once worn by unmarried women in Scotland as the badge of virginity; an ornamental hairnet supporting the back of a woman's hair; a tube of knitted or other material worn as a hood; the length of fine line, gut, etc, by which a fish hook is fixed to the line. — *vt* to bind, dress or fasten with or in a snood. — *adj* **snood'ed**. [OE *snōd*]

snook[1] *snōōk*, **snoke** *snōk* or (*Scot*) **snowk** *snowk*, *vi* to snuff or smell about; to lurk, prowl or sneak about. [ME *snoken* to lurk, from MLGer *snoken*, orig from Scand]

snook[2] *snōōk*, *n* any of several marine fishes — the cobia, robalo, garfish, or (in S Africa and now elsewhere also **snoek** *snōōk*) the barracouta (*Thyrsites atun*). [Du *snoek* pike]

snook[3] *snōōk* or *snōōk*, *n* the gesture of putting the thumb to the nose with the fingers held upright and spread out, to express derision, defiance, etc. — Also **snooks**. — **cock a snook** to make that gesture (also *fig*). [Origin obscure]

snooker *snōōk'ər*, *n* a variety of the game of pool, played with 15 red balls, 1 white cue ball and 6 balls of other colours, the object being to pocket the non-white balls in a certain order and gain more points in so doing than one's opponent; a situation in snooker where the path between the cue ball and the ball to be played is blocked, forcing an indirect shot to be played. — *vt* to render a direct stroke impossible for; to thwart (a person or plan) by placing an obstacle in the way (*fig*). [Popularly believed to be a coinage, at the game's inception in India in 1875, from old military slang *snooker* a raw cadet, perh from **snook**[1]]

snool *snōōl*, (*Scot*) *n* someone who submits tamely to wrong or oppression. — *vt* to keep in subjection; to snub. — *vi* to be tamely submissive. [Ety doubtful]

snoop *snōōp*, (*slang*) *vi* to go about sneakingly, to pry. — Also *n*. — *n* **snoop'er**. — *adj* **snoop'y**. — **snoop'erscope** (*US*) a device which converts infrared radiation reflected from an object into an image on a fluorescent screen, used for locating or identifying objects in darkness. [Du *snoepen* to eat, steal]

snoot *snōōt*, *n* the nose (*slang*); an expression of contempt; a snobbish person (*slang*). — *vt* to regard contemptuously. — Also *vi*. — *n* **snoot'ful** (*colloq*) enough alcohol to make one drunk. — *adj* **snoot'ily**. — *n* **snoot'iness**. — *adj* **snoot'y** (*colloq*) haughtily supercilious, snobbish. [Cf Du *snuit* snout, face]

snooze *snōōz*, *vi* to doze, take a nap. — *n* a nap; something boring and soporific (*slang*). — *n* **snooz'er**. — *adj* **snooz'y**. — **snooze button** a device on an alarm clock which stops the alarm and allows a few minutes respite before it sounds again. [Origin obscure; perh orig slang]

snoozle *snōō'zl*, (*colloq* and *dialect*) *vi* to nuzzle and then sleep. — *vt* to thrust nuzzlingly. [Cf **snooze** and **nuzzle**[1]]

snore *snōr* or *snör*, *vi* to breathe roughly and hoarsely during sleep with vibration of the uvula and soft palate, or of the vocal chords; to snort. — *vt* to pass in snoring; to render by snoring. — *n* a noisy breathing of this kind; a boring person, thing or event (*slang*). — *n* **snōr'er**. — *n* **snōr'ing**. [Imit; cf **snort**]

snorkel *snör'kl*, *n* a retractable tube or set of tubes by means of which a submarine takes in air and releases exhaust gases; a short stiff tube with a mouthpiece, by means of which a submerged swimmer can breathe. — Also **schnor'kel** (*shnör'*). — *n* **snor'keler**. — *n* **snor'kelling** swimming with a snorkel. [Ger *Schnörkel* a spiral ornament]

snort *snört*, *vi* to force air with violence and noise through the nostrils, as horses do; to snore (*Shakesp*); to inhale a powdered drug, eg cocaine, through the nose (*slang*). — *vt* to express by or utter with a snort; to force out, as by a snort; to inhale (a powdered drug, *esp* cocaine) through the nose (*slang*). — *n* an act or sound of snorting; a quick drink (*slang*); the snorkel on a submarine. — *n* **snort'er** someone who or something that snorts; anything characterized by extreme force, *esp* a gale (*colloq*); anything exceptional, eg in size, strength (*colloq*). — *n* and *adj* **snort'ing**. — *adv* **snort'ingly**. — *adj* **snort'y** snorting; inclined to snort (*colloq*); contemptuous and ready to take offence. [Imit]

snot *snot*, *n* nasal mucus; a contemptible person. — *vt* and *vi* (chiefly *dialect*) to blow the nose. — *vi* **snott'er** to breathe through an obstruction in the nostrils; to sob, snuffle, blubber. — *n* the wattles of a turkey cock; snot (*Scot*). — *n* **snott'ery** snot, filthiness. — *adj* (*Scot*) snotty, foul with snot. — *adv* **snott'ily**. — *n* **snott'iness**. — *adj* **snott'y** like, or foul with, snot; superciliously stand-offish, with the nose in the air; mean, of no importance. — *n* (*naval slang*) a midshipman (also **snott'ie**). — *adj* **snott'y-nosed**. [OE *gesnot*; *snȳtan* to blow the nose; cf Du *snot*; allied to **snout**]

snotter *snot'ər*, (*naut*) *n* the fitting that supports the inboard end or heel of a sprit (qv). [Origin obscure]

snout *snowt*, *n* the projecting muzzle of an animal, *esp* a pig; any similar projection; the lower end of a valley glacier (*geog*); a cigarette, tobacco (*prison slang*); a police informer (*slang*). — *vt* to provide with a snout. — *adj* **snout'ed**. — *adj* **snout'y** like a snout; snouted; haughtily supercilious (see **snooty**). — **snout beetle** another name for **weevil**. [ME *snūte*, prob from unrecorded OE; cf Swed *snut*; Ger *Schnauze*, Du *snuit*; also **snot**]

snow[1] *snō*, *n* atmospheric vapour frozen in crystalline form, whether in single crystals or aggregated in flakes; a snowfall; a mass or expanse of snow; a winter; any substance resembling snow, such as carbonic acid snow (frozen carbon dioxide); snowlike specks on the screen caused by electrical interference (*TV* and *radar*); anything white, such as hair (*fig*); a white-fleshed variety of apple; linen, *esp* drying or bleaching (*old slang*); cocaine, morphine, heroin (*slang*). — *adj* of snow. — *vi* to shower snow; to fall as snow or like snow. — *vt* to shower like snow; to strew as with snow; to whiten, whiten the hair of (*fig*); (with *up* or *under*) to bury, block, shut in or overwhelm, with or as if with snow; to mislead, persuade, overwhelm or convince with insincere and complex information (*NAm slang*). — *adv* **snow'ily**. — *n* **snow'iness**. — *adj* **snow'ish** resembling snow. — *adj* **snow'less**. — *adj* **snow'like**. —

adj **snow'y** abounding or covered with snow; white, like snow; pure. — **snow'ball** a ball made of snow pressed hard together, used as a missile, *esp* by children; a snowball tree; a dance begun by one couple who then separate and choose new partners, and so on until everyone present is dancing; a drink of advocaat and lemonade; a round white pudding, cake, or sweetmeat; (*ironically*) a Black person, chimney-sweep, etc; something that grows like a snowball rolled in snow, *esp* a distribution of begging letters, each recipient being asked to send out so many copies; a mixture of cocaine and heroin (*slang*). — *vt* to throw snowballs at. — *vi* to throw snowballs; to grow greater ever more quickly. — **snowball tree** a deciduous flowering shrub of the genus *Viburnum*, eg *Viburnum plicatum* having dense rounded heads of sterile white flowers; **snow'berry** the white berry of a N American shrub (*Symphoricarpos albus*) of the honeysuckle family; the shrub itself; **snow'bird** any finch of the N American genus *Junco*, white underneath, familiar in winter; applied to various other birds that appear in winter; one of these birds; a person who regularly moves to, or holidays in, a warmer climate in winter (chiefly *US slang*); a cocaine addict or user (*slang*). — *adj* **snow'-blind**. — **snow blindness** amblyopia caused by excessive exposure to ultraviolet light reflected from snow; **snowblink** a reflection from fields of snow, like iceblink; **snow'blower** a snow-clearing machine which takes in the snow in front of it and blows it to the side of the road; **snow board** (*building*) a horizontal board fixed above a roof gutter to prevent snow falling off in a mass (also **gutter board** or **snow guard**); **snow'boarding** skiing on a **snowboard**, a board, similar to a skateboard but without wheels, on which the user balances, guiding the board with movements of the feet and body; **snow'boot** a boot or overshoe for walking in snow. — *adj* **snow'bound** shut in or prevented from travelling by snow. — **snow box** a theatrical apparatus for representing a snowfall; **snow brake** a fern (*Pteris ensiformis*) with dark green fronds marked with greyish-white along the mid-rib; **snow'-broth** melted or melting snow; **snow bunting** a black-and-white (in summer partly tawny) bunting (*Plectrophenax nivalis*), of the Arctic regions, a winter visitor in Britain; **snow bush** a small evergreen shrub (*Breynia nivosa* or *Phyllanthus nivosus*), having rounded green leaves with white marbling; (also **snow'bush**) any of several white-flowered ornamental N American shrubs; **snow cannon** see **snow gun**; **snow'cap** a cap of snow as on the polar regions or a mountain-top. — *adj* **snow'-capped** or **snow'-capt**. — **snow'drift** a bank of snow drifted together by the wind; **snow'drop** a drooping white flower of early spring, or a plant (of the genus *Galanthus*, *esp G. nivalis*) of the amaryllis family that bears it; **snow'-dropper** or **snow'-gatherer** (*old slang*) a linen thief; **snowdrop tree** the fringe tree; any of several American styraceous trees or shrubs of the genus *Halesia* with white, pendent bell-shaped flowers (also called **silver bell**); **snow'-eyes** an Innuit device to prevent snow blindness, a piece of wood with slits; **snow'fall** a fall of snow; the amount falling in a given time. — *adj* **snow'-fed** (of a stream, etc) begun or increased by melted snow. — **snow fence** a paling fence erected to prevent snow drifting on to a road, railway, etc; **snow'field** a wide expanse of snow, *esp* where permanent; **snow finch** an Alpine bird like the snow bunting; **snow'flake** a feathery clump of snow crystals; any of several flowering plants of the genus *Leucojum*, cultivated for their white or pink flowers that resemble the snowdrop; (also **snow'fleck** or **snow'flick**) the snow bunting; **snow flea** a springtail living in or on snow; **snow'-goggles** goggles to guard against snow blindness; snow-eyes; **snow goose** a white Arctic American goose (*Anser* or *Chen caerulescens*), with black-tipped wings; **snow guard** a snow board; **snow gun** or **cannon** a device for spreading artificial snow on to ski slopes; **snow'hole** a hole dug in snow as a temporary shelter; **snow'ice** ice formed from freezing slush or compacted snow; **snow-in-summ'er** a white-flowered, mat-forming garden mouse-ear chickweed, *Cerastium tomentosum* or *biebersteinii*; **snow job** (*NAm slang*) an attempt to mislead, persuade or convince by means of insincere or flattering words, exaggeration, inaccurate or complex information, etc; **snow leopard** the ounce (*Panthera uncia*), an animal related to the leopard, found in the mountainous regions of Central Asia; **snow'line** the level or line above or beyond which an area, *esp* an upland area, is under permanent snow; **snow'man** a figure resembling a person fashioned from packed snow; the abominable snowman (see under **abominate**); **snow'mobile** (*-mə-bēl*) a motorized sleigh or a tractorlike vehicle capable of travelling over snow; **snow-on-the-mount'ain** a N American annual plant, *Euphorbia marginata*, cultivated for its ornamental leaves which become edged and veined with white as the plant matures; **snow pea** another name for the mangetout or sugar pea; **snow plant** a red Californian saprophyte (*Sarcodes sanguinea*) of the wintergreen family that grows through snow in mountainous regions; the organism of **red snow** (see under **red**); **snow'plough** an implement for clearing snow from roads and railways; a skiing position in which the skis form a V, with the tips touching, used to slow down or stop. — *vi* (in skiing) to assume the snowplough position. — **snow'scape** a snowy landscape; **snow'shoe** a wooden or metal frame, broad at the front and tapering at the back, with a network of thongs, strapped to the foot for walking on snow; a ski (*obs*). — *vi* to walk or travel on snowshoes. — **snowshoe rabbit** or **snowshoe hare** a N American hare, white in winter, brownish with white feet in summer; **snow'slip** a small avalanche of snow; **snow'storm**; **snow'-water** water from melted snow; **snow'surfing** the sport of skiing downhill on a large single ski controlled like a surfboard. — *adj* **snow-white'** as white as snow; spotless, pure. — **snow'-wreath** a snowdrift; **snowy egret** a small white American egret, *Egretta thula*; **snowy owl** a great white owl of northern regions. — **not a snowball's chance (in hell** or **in an oven)** (*colloq*) no chance at all; **snowed in** or **up** blocked or isolated by snow; **snowed under with** overwhelmed with a heap or rapid accumulation of. [OE *snāw*; Ger *Schnee*, L *nix, nivis*]

snow[2] *snō*, *n* a vessel like a brig, with a trysail-mast. [Du *snaauw*]

snowk. See **snook**[1].

SNP *abbrev*: Scottish National Party.

Snr or **snr** *abbrev*: senior.

snub *snub*, *vt* to rebuke; to take up, cut short, rebuff, in a humiliating or mortifying manner; to check or stop; to bring to a sudden stop, eg to bring (a boat, unbroken horse, etc) to a stop by means of a rope secured to a post or stake; to cut or break short: — *pr p* **snubb'ing**; *pa t* and *pa p* **snubbed**. — *n* an act of snubbing; a check; a snub nose; (*archaic* **snubbe**) a stub, snag, knob. — *adj* flat, broad, blunt and turned up; (of a polyhedron) having undergone secondary truncation (*geom*). — *n* **snubb'er** someone who snubs; a device for stopping a rope; a shock absorber (*NAm*). — *n* and *adj* **snubb'ing**. — *adv* **snubb'ingly**. — *adj* **snubb'ish** or **snubb'y** inclined to snub or check; somewhat snub. — **snubbing post** a post for passing a rope round, so as to stop a boat or horse; **snub cube** (*geom*) a polyhedron obtained by repeated truncation of a cube, have 38 faces, six of which are squares, the rest being equilateral triangles; **snub nose** a short, blunt turned-up nose. — *adj* **snub'-nosed** having a snubnose; having a blunt end or front. [ON *snubba* to chide, snub]

snuck *snuk*, a *dialect* or *NAm colloq pa t* and *pa p* of **sneak**.

snudge[1] *snuj*, (*obs*) *vi* to be snug and quiet. [Origin obscure]

snudge[2] *snuj*, *vi* to save in a miserly way. — *n* a mean stingy person. [Origin unknown]

snuff[1] *snuf*, *vi* to draw in air violently and noisily through the nose; to sniff; to smell at anything doubtfully; to take snuff. — *vt* to draw into the nose; to smell, to examine, suspect, or detect by smelling. — *n* a powdered preparation of tobacco or other substance for inhaling through the nose; a pinch of snuff or act of snuffing; a sniff; resentment, huff. — *n* **snuff'er**. — *n* **snuff'iness**. — *n* and *adj* **snuff'ing**. — *adj* **snuff'y** like, smelling of, soiled with or showing traces of, snuff; touchy, huffy. — **snuff'box** a small lidded (*usu* metal) box for snuff; **snuffbox bean** the cacoon; **snuff'-colour** or **snuff'-brown** a yellowish or greyish brown, slightly paler than bistre. — *adj* **snuff'-coloured**. — **snuff'=dipper**; **snuff'-dipping** *orig* in the US, the practice of rubbing the teeth and gums with a wet stick dipped in snuff; now, the practice of sucking a pinch or sachet of snuff held between the gum and the inside of the cheek; **snuff mill** a factory or a hand-mill for grinding tobacco into snuff; a snuff-mull; **snuff'-mull** a snuffbox (see **mill**[1]); **snuff'-paper** (*Scott*; *contemptuous*) bank notes; **snuff spoon** a spoon for taking snuff from a snuffbox; **snuff'-taker**; **snuff'-taking**. — **take it in snuff** (*Shakesp*) to take offence, to be angered by; **up to snuff** alert, knowing, not likely to be taken in or imposed upon; up to scratch, in good order; of a high or suitable standard. [MDu *snuffen*; Ger *schnaufen* to snuff]

snuff[2] *snuf*, *n* the sooty burnt part of a wick; a worthless or offensive residue; a heel-tap. — *vt* to remove the snuff from; to make brighter; to put out as with snuffers (with *out*; also *fig*). — *n* **snuff'er** (in later use **snuffers**, or **pair of snuffers**) an instrument like a pair of scissors for removing snuffs from the wicks of candles or oil-lamps; an instrument with a cap-shaped part for extinguishing candles; an attendant, *esp* in a theatre, who snuffed candles. — **snuff'-dish** a dish or tray for candle snuffs; **snuff film**, **movie** or **video** an illegal, *usu* pornographic, film or video recording depicting scenes of violence and torture climaxing in the actual killing of an unsuspecting member of the cast. — **snuff it** (*slang*) to die; **snuff out** (*slang*) to kill or be killed. [ME *snoffe*; connection with **snuff**[1] and with LGer *snuppen*, Ger *schnappen*, is obscure]

snuffle *snuf'l*, *vi* to breathe hard or in an obstructed manner through the nose; to sniff; to speak through the nose. — *vt* to sniff; to say or utter nasally. — *n* an act or sound of snuffling; a snuffling tone; cant; (in *pl*) an obstructed condition of the nose, *esp* in infants. — *n* **snuff'ler** (*snuf'lər* or *snuf'l-ər*). — *n* and *adj* **snuffling** (*snuf'ling* or *snuf'l-ing*). — *adj* **snuff'ly**. [Frequentative of **snuff**[1]; cf **snivel** and Du *snuffelen*, Ger *schnüffeln*]

snug *snug*, *adj* lying close and warm; comfortable; sheltered; not exposed to view or notice; in good order; compact; fitting close. — *n* a snuggery. — *vi* to lie close. — *vt* to make snug; to stow away snugly: — *pr p* **snugg'ing**; *pa t* and *pa p* **snugged**. — *n* **snugg'ery** a snug room or place, *esp* a bar-parlour or (*dialect*) a separate small compartment in a bar. — *vi* **snugg'le** to nestle. — *vt* to hug close; to wrap close. — *adv* **snug'ly**. — *n* **snug'ness**. [Origin obscure]

snush *snush*, (*obs*) *n* snuff. — *vt* and *vi* (*obs*) to snuff. [Poss imit; cf **sneesh**, Dan and Swed *snus*]

snuzzle *snuz'l*, (*dialect*) *vi* to grub or root; to rub or poke and sniff; to nuzzle. [Cf **nuzzle**[1] and **snoozle**]

snye or **sny** *snī*, (*Can*) *n* a side channel of a river. [From CanFr *chenail*, from Fr *chenal* channel]

SO *abbrev*: Signal Officer; special order; Staff Officer; standing order.

so[1] *sō*, *adv* merging in *conj* or *interj* in this, that, or such manner, degree, or condition; to such an extent; likewise; accordingly; well; therefore; in due course, thereupon, thereafter; as; soever; thus; for the same or the said reason; in a high degree; as has been stated; provided; in case; in order that (*colloq*); be it; that will do; very good; so what? (see under **what**). — **so'-and-so** this or that person or thing; such-and-such a person or thing; used to replace a descriptive oath (*colloq*; also *adj*). — *adj* **so'-called** styled thus, *usu* implying doubt or denial of the meaning or implications of the following term, or a wish to disassociate oneself from the implications of the term. — **so many** such-and-such a number of; **so much** such-and-such an amount; in such a degree; to such an extent; such an amount (of); that amount of; an equal amount. — **and so on** or **and so forth** (or as one phrase **and so on and so forth**) and more of the same or the like; and the rest of it; **just so** exactly right, impeccable; quite so; **or so** or thereabouts; approximately; **quite so** just as you have said, exactly; **so as** in such a manner as or that; in order (with *to*; *colloq*); if only, on condition that; **so be it** used to express acceptance or resignation; **so far** to that, or to such an, extent, degree, or point; **so far so good** everything is all right up to this point; **so long**! and **so long as** see under **long**[3]; **so much as** as much as; even; **so much for** that disposes of; that is the end of; no more of; **so much so** to such an extent (that); **so so** see **so-so** (separate entry); **so that** with the purpose that; with the result that; if only; **so then** thus then it is, therefore; **so to say** (or **speak**) if one may use that expression; **so what**? see under **what**. [OE *swā*; ON *svā*, Gothic *swa*, Ger *so*]

so[2] *sō*. See **sol**[1].

s.o. (*stock exchange*, *finance*) *abbrev*: seller's opinion; shipping order.

soak *sōk*, *vt* to steep in a liquid; to drench; to saturate; to absorb (liquid) (with *up*; also *fig*); to draw through the pores; to bathe thoroughly (*NAm*); to beat, pummel (*slang*); to overcharge, tax heavily, etc (*slang*). — *vi* to be steeped in a liquid; to pass through pores; to drink (*usu* alcohol) to excess, to guzzle; to soften by heating: — *pa p* **soaked**, rarely **soak'en**. — *n* the process or act of soaking; a drenching; a marshy place; a heavy or habitual drinker. — *n* **soak'age** the process or period of soaking; liquid that has percolated. — *n* **soak'er** someone who or something that soaks; a small piece of sheet lead used to form a watertight joint with slates or tiles at a chimney or wall where it projects above the surface of a roof. — *n* and *adj* **soak'ing**. — *adv* **soak'ingly**. — **soak'away** a depression or excavated pit into which water percolates. [ME *soke*, from OE *socian*, a weak verb related to *sūcan* to suck]

soap *sōp*, *n* an alkaline salt of a higher fatty acid; *esp* such a compound of sodium (*hard soap*) or potassium (*soft soap*) which reacts with water to produce a lather that acts as a cleaning agent in washing; smooth words, flattery (*obs slang*; cf **soft soap**); money, *esp* used for bribery and other secret political purposes (*US slang*); girls or women collectively, *esp* as sex objects (*slang*); a soap opera. — *vt* to rub with soap; to flatter. — *n* **soap'er** (*NAm*) a soap opera. — *n* **soap'ie** (*Austr*) a soap opera. — *adv* **soap'ily**. — *n* **soap'iness**. — *n* **soap'land** (*slang*) a red-light district. — Also *adj*. — *adj* **soap'less**. — *adj* **soap'y**. — **soap'-ball** soap made into a ball, often with starch, as an emollient; **soap'bark** a S American rosaceous tree (*Quillaja saponaria*), or its bark, used as a substitute for soap; **soap'berry** the fruit of *Sapindus saponaria*, a S American tree, or related species, used as a substitute for soap; **soap boiler** a manufacturer of soap; **soap boiling**; **soap'box** a box for packing soap; such a box used as an improvised platform by a speaker or campaigning politician in the street, etc; **soap bubble** a globe of air enclosed in a film of soap suds; **soap dish**; **soap flakes**; **soap opera** a sentimental, melodramatic radio or television serial concerned with the day-to-day lives of the members of a family or other small group (also *fig*; *orig* American and often sponsored by soap manufacturers); broadcast drama of this sort; **soap powder**; **soap'root** any of certain species of *Gypsophila*, *Saponaria*, and other plants whose roots can be used as a substitute for soap; **soap'stone** a popular name for steatite, or French chalk, a compact kind of talc with a greasy or soapy feel; **soap'suds** soapy water, *esp* when frothy; **soap test** a test for determining hardness of water by amount of standard soap solution required to make a lather;

soap' tree the soapbark tree, the soapberry tree, or other yielding saponin; **soap'-works** a factory manufacturing soap; **soap'wort** a tall herb (*Saponaria officinalis*, or other species) of the pink family, whose roots and leaves contain saponin. [OE *sāpe*; Du *zeep*, Ger *Seife*]

soar *sōr* or *sör*, *vi* to rise or fly high in the air; to rise to a great height (*lit* or *fig*); to glide high in the air, *esp* on a rising current; to increase rapidly in number or amount. — *vt* to reach, traverse, or accomplish in upward flight. — *n* **soar'er**. — *n* and *adj* **soar'ing**. — *adv* **soar'ingly**. — *adj* **soar'away** making spectacular progress. [Fr *essorer* to expose to air, raise into air, from L *ex* out, and *aura* air]

soar[2] and **soare**. See **sore**[2].

Soave *swä'vā* or *sō-ä'vā*, *n* a dry, pale white wine from a small region east of Verona in NE Italy. [From the town of *Soave*]

Soay *sō'ā* or in full **Soay sheep** (*shēp*), *n* a breed of small, wild, dark-coloured sheep found *esp* on the island of *Soay* in the Outer Hebrides; one of this breed.

SOB or **S.O.B**. See **s.o.b**.

sob *sob*, *vi* to catch the breath convulsively in distress or other emotion; to make a similar sound; to weep noisily. — *vt* to utter with sobs; to bring (oneself) to a certain state by sobbing: — *pr p* **sobb'ing**; *pa t* and *pa p* **sobbed**. — *n* a convulsive catch of the breath; any similar sound. — *n* and *adj* **sobb'ing**. — *adv* **sobb'ingly**. — **sob sister** (*slang*) an actor, writer, etc who seeks to arouse sentimental feelings in his or her audience, readers, etc; a journalist who answers questions in a woman's magazine; **sob story** a pitiful tale told to arouse sympathy; **sob stuff** cheap and extravagant pathos, to stir tears; maudlin or highly sentimental stories, films or scenes. [Imit]

s.o.b. *abbrev*: son of a bitch. — Also **S.O.B**. or **SOB**.

sobeit *sō-bē'it*, (*archaic*) *conj* provided. [**so be it**]

sober *sō'bər*, *adj* not drunk; temperate, *esp* in use of intoxicants; moderate; restrained; without excess or extravagance; serious; sedate; quiet in colour; sombre; sane, rational (*obs*); poor, feeble (*Scot*). — *vt* to make sober (often with *up*). — *vi* to become sober (often with *up*). — *adj* **so'bering** making sober; causing to become serious, grave or thoughtful. — *adv* **so'beringly**. — *vt* **so'berize** or **-ise** to make sober. — *adv* **so'berly**. — *n* **so'berness** or **sobriety** (*sō-* or *sə-brī'i-ti*) the state or habit of being sober; calmness; gravity. — *adj* **so'ber-minded**. — *n* **so'ber-mindedness** the state of being sober-minded; freedom from inordinate passion; calmness. — *n* **so'bersides** a sedate, serious-minded and solemn person: — *pl* **so'bersides**. — *adj* **so'ber-suited** dressed in sombre-coloured clothes. [Fr *sobre*, from L *sōbrius*, from *sē-* apart, not, and *ēbrius* drunk]

sobole *sō'bōl* or **soboles** *sob'ō-lēz*, (*bot*) *n* a creeping underground stem producing roots and buds: — *pl* **sob'ōlēs**. — *adj* **sobolif'erous** having soboles. [L *sobolēs*, *subolēs* a shoot, from *sub* under, and the root of *alere* to nourish, sustain]

Sobranje *sō-brän'ye*, *n* the national assembly of Bulgaria. — Also **Sobran'ye**. [Bulg]

sobriquet *sō'bri-kā* or **soubriquet** *sōō'-*, *n* a nickname; an assumed name. [Fr *sobriquet*, earlier *soubriquet* a chuck under the chin]

Soc. *abbrev*: Socialist; Society.

soc *sok*, (*law*; *hist*) *n* the right of holding a local court. — *n* **soc'age** or **socc'age** feudal tenure of lands by service fixed and determinate in quality (other than military service); a payment made by a socager. — *n* **soc'ager** or **soc'man** a tenant by socage (also **sōke'man**). — *n* **soke** (*sōk*) soc; a district under a particular jurisdiction. — *n* **soke'manry** tenure by socage. — *n* **sōk'en** a district under a particular jurisdiction. [OE *sōcn* inquiry, jurisdiction, franchise]

soca *sō'kə*, *n* a variety of Caribbean calypso music incorporating elements of American soul music and having a strong pounding rhythm. — Also **sokah**. [*so*ul and *ca*lypso]

so-called *sō'köld*, *adj*. See under **so**[1].

soccer *sok'ər*, (*colloq*) *n* association football. — *n pl* **socceroos'** (*soccer* and kangar*oos*) the Australian national association football team.

socdolager, **-iger**, **-oger**. See **sockdologer**.

sociable *sō'shə-bl*, *adj* tending to live in groups or communities, rather than in isolation; companionable; favourable to social intercourse; friendly, fond of others' company. — *n* a four-wheeled open horse-drawn carriage with side seats facing each other; a seat, tricycle, aeroplane, etc, for two people side by side; a social (*US*). — *n* **sociabil'ity** or **so'ciableness**. — *adv* **so'ciably**. [Fr, from L *sociābilis*, from *sociāre* to write, from *socius* companion]

social *sō'shl*, *adj* relating to life in an organized community; relating to welfare in such a community; growing or living in communities; relating to, or characterized by, friendly association; convivial; gregarious, sociable; relating to fashionable circles; sympathetic (*obs*). — *n* an informal party or gathering of a club, church, etc; (with **the**) social security (*colloq*). — *n* **so'cialism** the theory, principle, or scheme of social organization which places the means of production of wealth and the distribution of that wealth in the hands of the community. — *n* **so'cialist** an adherent of socialism. — Also *adj*. — *adj* **socialist'ic**. — *adv* **socialist'ically**. — *n* **so'cialite** (*colloq*) a person having a place in fashionable society. — *n* **sociality** (*sō-shi-al'i-ti*) the quality or fact of being social; social relations, association, or intercourse; sociability; a social function or formality. — *n* **socialīzā'tion** or **-s-** the act or process of socializing; the process by which infants and young children become aware of society and their relationships with others. — *vt* **so'cialize** or **-ise** to render social; to put on a socialistic footing. — *vi* (*colloq*) to behave in a sociable manner, eg at parties, etc; to spend time in the company of others. — *adv* **so'cially**. — *n* **so'cialness**. — *n* **so'ciate** (*-shi-āt*; *archaic*) an associate. — Also *adj*. — *n* **socia'tion** a plant community; the smallest area in which a full range of plants making up such a plant community may be found. — *adj* **so'ciātive** expressing association. — **social anthropologist**; **social anthropology** the branch of anthropology which deals with the culture, customs and social structure of (*esp* primitive) societies; **Social Charter** in the EC, a proposed charter laying down the conditions of employment of workers across the Community, *incl* minimum pay, maximum working hours, etc; **social climber** (often *derog*) a person who tries to become accepted into a higher social stratum by a deliberate policy of getting to know and associating with people belonging to it; **social contract** or **compact** the voluntary agreement between individuals upon which an organized society, its rights, functions, and the relationships within it are founded; **social credit** (*econ*) a movement stressing the element of unearned increment in the returns of industry and advocating the achievement of social well-being by the stable adjustment of production and consumption through monetary reform; (with *cap*) a theory that the government should distribute national dividends in order to spread purchasing power and thus increase consumption (regarded as a benefit); **social democracy** the practices and policies of socialists who believe that socialism can and should be achieved by a gradual and democratic process; **social democrat** a supporter of social democracy; (with *caps*) a member or supporter of a Social Democratic party. — *adj* **social democratic**. — **social dumping** the practice of reducing wage rates and conditions of employment in order to attract or keep investment; **social engineer**; **social engineering** the furtherance of social change and the development of social institutions in accordance with an overall plan; **social evil** *specif*, prostitution (*archaic*); any factor which has a damaging, unhealthy or negative effect on or with society as a whole; **social fund** in Britain, a social security fund from which discretionary loans or grants may be made (*esp* for basic household items) to those in extreme need; **social insurance** state insurance by compulsory contributions against sickness, unemployment, and retirement; **social ownership** (*euphem*) nationalization; **social science** the scientific study of human society and behaviour, including such disciplines (the *social sciences*) as anthropology, sociology, economics, political science and history; **social secretary** one who is responsible for organizing the social activities of a person, club, association, etc; **social security** security against sickness, unemployment, retirement, provided by a social insurance scheme; income support; **social service** welfare work (also in *pl*); (in *pl*) the public bodies carrying out such work; **Social War** the war (90–88 BC) of Rome's Italian allies (*Socii*) against Rome for admission to Roman citizenship; **social whale** the ca'ing whale (see under **ca'**); **social work** any of various forms of welfare work intended to promote the well-being of those regarded as socially disadvantaged; **social worker**. — **socialism of the chair** professorial socialism, the doctrines of a school of political economists (c.1872) in Germany whose aim was mainly to better the condition of the working-classes by factory acts, savings banks, insurance against sickness and old age, etc. [L *socius* a companion]

société anonyme *so-syā-tā a-no-nēm*, (*Fr*) *n* literally, anonymous society; joint-stock company.

society *so-sī'it-i*, *n* fellowship, companionship; company; association; a community; the conventions and opinions of a community; the fashionable world; a corporate body; any organized association. — *adj* of fashionable society. — *adj* **soci'etal** pertaining to society, social. — *adv* **soci'etally**. — **the Society of Jesus** see **Jesuit**. [OFr *societé*, from L *societās*, from *socius* a companion]

Socinian *sō-sin'i-ən*, *adj* pertaining to or following Laelius (1525–62) and Faustus (1539–1604) *Socinus*, uncle and nephew, Italian Unitarians. — Also *n*. — *n* **Socin'ianism**.

socio- *sō'si-ō-* or *sō'shi-ō-*, *combining form* denoting social, of or pertaining to society, as in *sociocultural*, *socioeconomic*, *sociopolitical*. — *adj* **sociobiolog'ical**. — *n* **sociobiol'ogist**. — *n* **sociobiol'ogy** a scientific discipline combining biology and the social sciences which attempts to establish that social behaviour and organization in humans and animals has a genetic basis and is to be explained in terms of evolution and genetics. — *n* **so'ciogram** (*-gram*) a chart representing personal interrelationships within a social group. — *n* **so'ciolect** (*linguistics*) a variety of language used by members of a particular social class or group. — *n* **socioling'uist**. — *adj* **sociolinguis'tic** of or pertaining to sociolinguistics; pertaining to language as it functions as a social tool. — *n sing* **sociolinguis'tics** the study of language as it functions in society and is affected by social and cultural factors. — *n* **sociologese'** the jargon of sociology. — *adj* **sociolog'ical** or **sociolog'ic** pertaining to sociology; dealing or concerned with social questions and problems of human society; social. — *n* **sociol'ogism** a concept or explanation taking into consideration social factors only, disregarding others. — *n* **sociol'ogist**. — *adj* **sociologis'tic**. — *n* **sociol'ogy** the study of the origin, development, structure and functioning of human society. — *adj* **sociomet'ric**. — *n* **sociom'etrist**. — *n* **sociom'etry** the measurement of social phenomena; the study of personal interrelationships within a social group. — *n* **so'ciopath** a person suffering from a personality disorder characterized by asocial or antisocial behaviour, such as a psychopath. — *adj* **sociopath'ic**. — *n* **sociop'athy**. [L *socius* a companion]

sock[1] *sok*, *n* a covering for the foot and part or all of the lower leg; an insole placed in a shoe for warmth, to improve the fit, etc; a light shoe, worn by Greek Roman actors of comedy (*obs* except *hist* and allusively; cf **buskin**); a windsock; anything resembling a sock in shape or function. — *n* **sockette** (*soket'*) a covering for the foot only. — **knock the socks of** (*informal*) to surpass, defeat, overtake, etc in competitions; **pull up one's socks** to brace oneself for doing better; **put a sock in it** (*slang*; *usu imperative*) to become silent, stop talking. [OE *socc*, from L *soccus*]

sock[2] *sok*, (*dialect* and *slang*) *vt* to thrust hard; to strike hard; to drub, thrash. — *n* a violent blow, *esp* with the fist. — *adj* **sock'ō** (*US* and *theat slang*) excellent, successful, knockout; having an impact, full of energy. — *n pl* **socks** a beating, *esp* in the phrase *give someone socks*. — **sock it to** (*slang*) to speak, behave, etc in a manner that creates an impact on. [Ety dubious]

sock[3] *sok*, *n* a ploughshare. [OFr *soc*, from Celtic, Bret *souc'h*, Gaelic *soc*]

sockdologer or **sockdolager** *sok-dol'ə-jər*, also **soc-**, **sog-**, **slock-**, **-dolager**, **-doliger** (*old US slang*) *n* a conclusive argument; a hard or decisive blow; anything unusually big, a whopper. [Cf **sock**[2]; influenced by **doxology** as the closing act of a service]

socket *sok'it*, *n* a hollow into which something is inserted or into which something fits, such as the receptacle of the eye, of a bone, of a tooth, of the shaft of an iron golf club, the hollow of a candlestick, etc; a device in which an electric plug or light bulb may be inserted to make a connection; a stroke with the socket of a golf club. — *vt* to provide with or place in a socket; to strike with the socket (*golf*): — *pr p* **sock'eting**; *pa t* and *pa p* **sock'eted**. — *adj* **sock'eted**. — **socket chisel** a robust chisel with a socketed metal shaft into which the wooden handle is fitted; **socket head screw** a screw with a hexagonal recess in its head, turned by means of a hexagonal bar formed into a key (also **cap screw**); **socket spanner** a spanner with a socketed head made to fit over a nut or a bolt; **socket wrench** a wrench with a handle to which a variety of socketed heads can be fitted. [OFr *soket*, dimin of *soc*; see **sock**[3]]

sockette. See under **sock**[1].

sockeye *sok'ī*, (in full **sockeye salmon**) *n* a Pacific salmon, *Oncorhynchus nerka*, of coastal areas from Japan to California. — Also called **red** or **blueback salmon**. [By folk ety from Am Ind *sukai* the fish of fishes, the native name on the Fraser River]

socking *sok'ing*, (*colloq*) *adj* huge, whacking (*usu* followed by *great*). [Prob **sock**[2]]

socle *sō'kl* or *sok'l*, (*archit*) *n* a plain face or plinth at the foot of a wall, column, etc. [Fr, from Ital *zoccolo*, from L *socculus*, dimin of *soccus* a shoe]

Socratic *sō-krat'ik* or *so-*, *adj* pertaining to *Socrates*, the celebrated Greek philosopher (c.469–399 BC), to his philosophy, or to his method of teaching, by a series of simple questions revealing to his interlocutors their own ignorance. — *n* a follower of Socrates. — *adv* **Socrat'ically**. — *vi* **Socratize** or **-ise** (*sōk'rə-tīz* or *sok'*) to practise the Socratic method. — **Socrat'ic irony** (*philos*) a means by which a questioner pretends to know less than a respondent, when actually he knows more; **Socrat'ic method** (*philos*) a method of questioning unaffected by preformed conclusions, used by Socrates to expose feeble arguments or develop latent ideas in his pupils.

sod[1] *sod*, *n* a turf, *usu* one cut in rectangular shape; sward; the ground (*poetic*). — *adj* of sod. — *vt* to cover with sod. — *adj* **sodd'y** covered with sod; turfy. — **sod'buster** (*US*) a farmer who works the soil. [MLGer *sode*; Ger *Sode*]

sod[2] *sod*. See **seethe**.

sod[3] *sod*, (chiefly *UK* and *Austr vulg slang*) *n* an obnoxious person — *usu* applied to a man or boy; a non-pejorative term for a chap or fellow, now also sometimes applied to a woman or girl, as in the phrase *you lucky sod!*. — *interj* (*vulg*) a term expressing annoyance, exasperation, etc (sometimes behaving as a verb with *it*, *him*, etc as object). — *adj* **sodd'ing**. — **sod off** (*vulg*; *usu imperative*) to go away; **Sod's law** (*facetious*) the precept that states that the most inconvenient thing is the most likely to happen, or if there is a possibility that something will go wrong, it will. [Abbrev of **sodomite**]

soda *sō'də*, *n* any of a number of common sodium compounds, *incl* sodium oxide (Na_2O), sodium hydroxide (*caustic soda*), sodium carbonate (*washing-soda*), and sodium bicarbonate (*baking soda*); soda water (*colloq*); a fizzy drink made of soda water with flavouring, ice-cream, etc (*NAm*). — *adj* of or containing soda or sodium. — *adj* **sodaic** (*sō-dā'ik*) containing or relating to soda. — *n* **so'dalite** a cubic mineral, a complex feldspathoid consisting of sodium aluminium silicate and sodium chloride in crystalline form, occurring in igneous rocks. — *n* **so'damide** (*-mīd*) a compound ($NaNH_2$) formed when ammonia gas is passed over hot sodium (also called **sodium amide**). — *adj* **so'dic**. — **soda ash** anhydrous sodium carbonate in powdered form for commercial use; **soda fountain** (*NAm*) an apparatus for supplying soda water; a shop or counter where sodas, ice-cream, etc are served; **soda jerk** or **soda jerker** (*NAm slang*) a person who serves at a soda fountain; **soda-lake** a lake containing and depositing a large amount of sodium salts; **soda lime** a mixture of caustic soda and quicklime; **soda nitre** sodium nitrate (also called **Chile saltpetre, nitratine**); **soda pop** (*US*) a carbonated soft drink of any flavour; **soda scone** a scone made with baking soda; **soda-siphon** a siphon which dispenses soda water; **soda water** water (now commonly without sodium bicarbonate) charged with carbon dioxide. [Ital and LL *soda*; origin doubtful]

sodain, sodaine. *Obs* spellings of **sudden**.

sodality *sō-dal'i-ti*, *n* a fellowship or fraternity. [L *sodālitās*, from *sodālis* a comrade]

sodden *sod'n*, *pa p* of **seethe**. — *adj* soaked thoroughly; boggy; doughy, not well baked; bloated or saturated with drink; boiled (*rare*). — *vt* and *vi* to make or become sodden; to soak. — *n* **sodd'enness**. — *adj* **sodden-witt'ed** (*Shakesp*) heavy, stupid.

soddy. See under **sod**[1].

sodger *so'jər*, *n* a dialect word for **soldier**.

sodium *sō'di-əm*, *n* a bluish-white alkaline metal (symbol **Na**; atomic no 11), occurring in nature in combination, eg as a nitrate, chloride, etc. — **sodium amytal** (*am'i-tal*; ® with *caps*) a sodium salt used as a barbiturate drug; **sodium ascorbate** a compound used as a meat preservative and also in the treatment of vitamin C deficiency; **sodium benzoate** a compound used as an antiseptic and as a food preservative; **sodium bicarbonate** see under **bicarbonate**; **sodium carbonate** a soluble compound widely used in the making of glass, ceramics, etc and as a cleaning agent; **sodium chlorate** a colourless crystalline compound used in explosives, as an antiseptic, and as weedkiller; **sodium chloride** common table salt, occurring naturally as halite and in seawater; **sodium cromoglycate** a drug which blocks the release of histamine, used to treat asthma and various allergies; **sodium hydroxide** caustic soda, manufactured by treating quicklime with a solution of hot sodium carbonate, and used as a reagent, in the manufacture of soap, rayon and sodium compounds; **sodium lamp** a street lamp using sodium vapour and giving orange or yellow light; **sodium nitrate** a white crystalline solid compound used in explosives, as a fertilizer and food preservative (also called **soda nitre**); **sodium pump** (*biochem*) a mechanism by which sodium is removed through cell membranes, eg in the axon of a neurone and certain kidney cells, the energy for the process being derived from the breakdown of ATP; **sodium thiosulphate** a white soluble substance used as a fixer in photography. [**soda**]

Sodom *sod'əm*, *n* one of the 'cities of the plain' (in the Bible: Gen 18 and 19); any place of utter depravity (*fig*). — *n* **Sod'omite** (*-īt*) an inhabitant of Sodom; (without *cap*) someone who practises sodomy. — *adj* **sodomitic** (*-it'ik*) or **sodomit'ical**. — *adv* **sodomit'ically**. — *vt* **sod'omize** or **-ise** to practise sodomy upon. — *n* **sod'omy** anal intercourse (with a man or woman) or copulation with an animal, imputed to the inhabitants of Sodom. — **apple of Sodom** see under **apple**.

SOE *abbrev*: Special Operations Executive.

soever *sō-ev'ər*, *adv* generally used to extend or render indefinite the sense of (and *esp* as *combining form* **-soever** added to) *who*, *what*, *where*, *how*, etc.

sofa *sō'fə*, *n* a long upholstered seat with back and arms. — **sofa bed** a piece of furniture serving as a sofa by day, a bed at night; **sofa table** a narrow table with a flap at each end, used as a writing-table from c.1790. [Ar *suffah* a raised platform used as a bench]

sofar *sō'fär*, *n* a method of calculating the location of an underwater explosion from measurements of the time taken for the sound vibrations to reach three widely separated shore stations (used in searching for survivors, who drop into the sea). [*so*und *f*ixing *a*nd *r*anging]

soffioni *sof-yō'nē*, *n pl* volcanic steam-holes. [Ital]

soffit *sof'it*, *n* a ceiling, now generally restricted to the ornamented underside of a stair, entablature, archway, etc. [Ital *soffitto*, from L *suffixus*, pa p of *suffigere* to fasten beneath, from *sub* under, and *figere* to fix]

Sofi, Sofism. See **Sufi, Sufism**.

S. of S. (*Bible*) *abbrev*: Song of Songs or Song of Solomon.

soft *soft*, *adj* easily yielding to pressure; easily cut; easily scratched (*mineralogy*); malleable; yielding; not rigorous enough; (of sounds) not loud, low; not glaring; diffused; slightly blurred; weak in muscle or mind; out of training; smooth; pleasing or soothing to the senses; tender; mild; politically moderate, not radical or extreme, as in *soft left*; sympathetic; gentle; effeminate; unable to endure rough treatment or hardship; (relatively) unprotected; (of a vehicle) unarmoured (*military*); gently moving; easy; (of water) free from calcium and magnesium salts; (of coal) bituminous; (of money) paper rather than metallic; (of paper) unsized; rainy (*dialect*); pronounced with a somewhat sibilant sound, not guttural or explosive; voiced or sonant; (of silk) freed from natural gum; (of diet) consisting of semi-liquid and easily-digestible foods; apt to fall in price; (of drugs) not habit-forming in an obvious degree; (of radiation) having short wavelengths and therefore not highly penetrating; (in computer typesetting and word-processing) of a space or hyphen that can be automatically removed when its environment changes to make it redundant. — *n* a softy, a fool; (in *pl*) soft commodities. — *adv* softly; gently; quietly. — *vt* (*Spenser*) to soften. — *interj* (*archaic*; also **soft you**) hold; not so fast. — *vt* **soften** (*sof'n*) to make soft or softer; to mitigate; to tone down, make smoother or less glaring. — *vi* to grow soft or softer. — *n* **softener** (*sof'nər*). — *n* **softening** (*sof'ning*). — *n* **soft'ie** a softy. — *adj* **soft'ish** rather soft. — *n* **soft'ling** (*archaic*) a weakling; an effeminate man or boy; a soft object. — *adv* **soft'ly**. — *adj* (*Spenser*) soft; slack in enterprise. — *n* **soft'ness**. — *n* **soft'y** a silly person, a weak fool; someone who is soft-hearted or sentimental. — **soft'back** or **soft'cover** a paperback. — Also *adj*. — **soft'ball** an American game similar to baseball, played on a smaller diamond with a soft ball; the ball itself. — *adj* **soft-billed'**. — *adj* **soft-bod'ied**. — *vt* **soft'-boil**. — *adj* **soft-boiled'** boiled not long enough to be quite solid; soft-hearted (*colloq*). — *adj* **soft-cen'tred**. — **soft commodities** foodstuffs, coffee, cotton, etc, as opposed to metals. — *adj* **soft-con'scienc'd** (*Shakesp*) having a not very rigorous conscience. — *adj* **soft'-core** (of obscene or pornographic material) not explicit, blatant or graphic. — **soft currency** one unstable in value in the international money-market through fluctuation in its gold backing; **soft drink** a non-alcoholic drink. — *adj* **soft-finned'** without fin-spines. — **soft focus** (*photog*, *cinematog*) deliberate slight blurring of a picture or scene. — *adj* **soft-foot'ed** softly treading. — **soft fruit** small, stoneless, edible fruit, such as berries and currants; **soft furnishings** curtains, coverings, rugs, etc; **soft'-goods** cloth and cloth articles (as opposed to *hardware*, etc); **soft'-grass**

a worthless grass (*Holcus mollis* or other species) similar to oats; **soft'head** a simpleton. — *adj* **soft-head'ed**. — *adj* **soft-heart'ed** kind, generous; tender-hearted. — **soft hyphen** (in word-processing) one inserted in a word only if necessary for word division at the end of a line; **soft landing** a landing by a spacecraft, etc without uncomfortable or damaging impact (also *fig*); **soft lens** a flexible contact lens of a hydrophylic material which allows some oxygen to reach the cornea; **soft line** a flexible or lenient attitude, policy, etc; **soft loan** one without conditions attached; a cheap or interest-free loan, *usu* to a developing country. — *adj* **softly-soft'ly** cautious, careful, delicate. — *adj* **softly-spright'ed** (*Shakesp*) tame-spirited. — **soft mark** see under **mark**; **soft meat** regurgitated food given by pigeons to their young. — *adj* **soft'-nosed** (of a bullet) with a tip that expands on striking. — **soft option** an alternative that is easy to carry out, undergo, etc; **soft palate** the fleshy back part of the palate. — *adj* **soft'paste** (of porcelain) made of a paste of various kinds requiring less heat in firing than china clay (also *n* **soft paste**). — **soft pedal** a pedal for reducing tone in the piano, *esp* by causing the hammer to strike only one string (*una corda*). — *vt* and *vi* **soft-ped'al** to play with the soft pedal down; to subdue, tone down, avoid emphasizing or alluding to (*slang*). — **soft power** (*esp US*) the power of a nation to influence others by displaying the advantages of its own cultural, social, financial, etc systems without the use of military power; **soft radiation** (*radiol*) radiation which has very limited penetrating power; **soft rock** a form of rock music, *usu* rhythmically complex, highly melodious and low in volume; **self-rock geology** (*colloq*) the geology of sedimentary rocks; **soft rot** a bacterial disease of plant tissues which reduces them to soft, mushy, foul-smelling rot; **soft sawder** or **sowder** flattery. — *vt* to flatter, blarney. — **soft science** any of the scientific disciplines in which rules or principles of evaluation are difficult to obtain, such as social sciences (cf **hard science** under **hard**[1]). — *adj* **soft-sect'ored** (*comput*) (of a floppy disk) formatted by means of an electronic control system and software (cf **hard-sectored**). — **soft'-sect'oring**; **soft sell** selling or sale by preliminary softening up or other indirect method; mild persuasion, or mildly persuasive tactics. — *adj* **soft-sell'**; **soft'-shell** or **-shelled'** having a soft shell; moderate in policy or principles. — **soft'-shell** a soft-shell crab, clam, or river-turtle; a moderate. — *adj* **soft'-shoe** characteristic of or pertaining to a form of tap-dancing done in soft-soled shoes; **soft'-slow** (*Shakesp*) soft and slow. — **soft soap** a kind of soap containing potash; flattery; blarney. — *vt* **soft'-soap** to rub or cover with soft soap; to flatter for some end. — **soft sore** chancroid, a sexually-transmitted disease resulting in enlargement and ulceration of the lymph nodes in the groin. — *adj* **soft-spo'ken** having a mild or gentle voice; affable; suave; plausible in speech. — **soft spot** see under **spot**; **soft thing** an easy task; a snug job; **soft top** a convertible car with a fabric roof. — *adj* **soft-top**. — **soft touch** see under **touch**; **soft underbelly** the vulnerable part; **soft'ware** computer programs that control the operation of computer hardware (qv); computer program (or analogous) accessories (other than the actual parts of a computer, etc); video cassettes and discs; material recorded in microform; **software engineering** the production of reliable software and its maintenance and modification for particular applications; **software house** a commercial organization specializing in the design of software programs; **soft wheat** a variety of wheat with soft kernels and a high starch content, suitable for making biscuits, pastry, etc; **soft'wood** timber of a conifer (also *adj*). — **be** or **go soft on** to be lenient with; **softening of the brain** a softening of brain tissues; marked deterioration of mental faculties (*colloq*); **soften up** to lessen resistance in (*colloq*); to wear down by continuous shelling and bombing. [OE *sōfte*, *sēfte*; Du *zacht*, Ger *sanft*]

softa *sof'tə*, *n* a Muslim theological student, attached to a mosque. [Turk *sōfta*]

sog *sog*, *n* (*dialect*) a soft wet place. — *vt* and *vi* to soak. — *adj* **sogged**. — *adv* **sogg'ily**. — *n* **sogg'iness**. — *n* and *adj* **sogg'ing**. — *adj* **sogg'y** soaked; soft or heavy with moisture; boggy; soppy; sultry; spiritless. [Ety dubious]

SOGAT *sō'gat*, now properly **SOGAT 82** *abbrev*: Society of Graphical and Allied Trades.

sogdolager, **-iger**, **-oger**. See **sockdologer**.

soger *sō'jər*, *n* a dialect word for **soldier**.

sogged, **soggy**, etc. See under **sog**.

soh. See **sol**[1].

so-ho or **soho** *sō-hō'*, (*Shakesp*) *interj* a form of call from a distance, a huntsman's halloo. [Anglo-Fr]

soi-disant *swä-dē-zã*, *adj* self-styled, pretended, would-be. [Fr]

soigné, *fem* **soignée**, *swa-nyā*, *adj* well-groomed; elegantly simple; carefully done. [Fr]

soil[1] *soil*, *n* the ground; the mould in which plants grow; the mixture of disintegrated rock and organic material which nourishes plants; land, country. — *adj* having soil. — *adj* **soil'-bound** attached to the soil. — **soil creep** (*geol*) the very slow but continuous movement of soil and rock fragments down a slope; **soil mechanics** a branch of civil engineering concerned with the ability of different soils to withstand the use to which they are put; **soil science** the study of the composition and uses of soil. [OFr *soel*, *suel*, *sueil*, from L *solum* ground]

soil[2] *soil*, *n* dirt; dung; filth; sewage; a spot or stain; a wallowing-place (*obs*); a watery place where a hunted animal takes refuge. — *vt* to make dirty; to stain; to manure. — *vi* to become dirty or stained; to tarnish. — *adj* **soiled**. — *n* **soil'iness** (*rare*) stain; foulness. — *n* and *adj* **soil'ing**. — *adj* **soil'less** destitute of soil. — *n* (*archaic*) **soil'ure** stain; pollution. — *adj* **soil'y**. — **soil pipe** an upright pipe which carries away waste water and sewage from a building into a sewer or drain. [OFr *soil*, *souil* (Fr *souille*) wallowing-place]

soil[3] *soil*, *vt* to feed (livestock) on fresh-cut green food; to purge by so doing; to fatten. — *n* **soil'age** green fodder for livestock. [OFr *saouler*, from *saol*, *saoul*, from L *satullus*, from *satur* full; or from **soil**[2]]

soirée *swär'ā* or *swör'ā*, *n* an evening party; an evening social meeting with tea, etc. [Fr, from *soir* evening, from L *sērus* late]

soixante-neuf *swa-sãt-nøf*, (*Fr*) *n* a sexual position in which both partners simultaneously orally stimulate each other's genitalia. [Literally sixty-nine, from the position adopted]

soja. See **soy**.

sojourn *so'* or *su'jərn* or *-jûrn'*, *vt* to stay for a day; to dwell for a time. — *n* a temporary residence. — *n* **so'journer**. — *n* **so'journing** or **so'journment**. [OFr *sojourner*, from L *sub* under, and *diurnus* of a day, from *diēs* a day]

Soka Gakkai *sō-kə gak'ī*, *n* a Japanese Buddhist sect and political party, characterized by militant nationalism. [Jap, value creating society]

soke, **sokeman**, **soken**. See under **soc**.

Sol *sol*, *n* the sun personified, Helios or Phoebus; gold (*alchemy*); the tincture or (*heraldry*); (without *cap*; *sōl*) the Peruvian monetary unit (one-tenth of a libra), and formerly a coin bearing a sun with rays: — *pl* **soles** (*sō'lās*) or **sols** (*sōlz*). [L *sōl* sun]

Sol. or **Solr** *abbrev*: Solicitor.

sol[1] *sol*, *n* the fifth note of the scale in sol-fa notation. — Also **so** or **soh** (*sō*).

sol[2] *sol*, *n* a colloidal suspension in a liquid (cf **gel**). — *n* **solā'tion** liquefaction of a gel. [Short for **solution**]

sol[3] *sol*, *n* an old French coin, one-twentieth of a livre. [OFr *sol* (now *sou*), from L *solidus* solid]

sol. *abbrev*: solution.

sola[1] *sō-lä'*, *interj* a cry to a person at a distance.

sola[2] *sō'lə*, *n* spongewood, an Indian papilionaceous plant (*Aeschynomene aspera* or *paludosa*, also known as the *hat-plant*); its pithlike stems used in making lightweight hats. — Also **sō'lah**. — *adj* of sola. — **sola hat, helmet** or **topi** a sun helmet made of sola pith (also, incorrectly, **solar**). [Hindi *śolā*]

sola[3]. See **solus**.

solace *sol'is* or *sol'əs*, *n* consolation, comfort in distress; pleasure, amusement; a source of comfort or pleasure. — *vt* to comfort in distress; to console; to allay. — *vi* to take comfort. — *n* **sol'acement**. — *adj* **solacious** (*-ā'shəs*; *archaic*) giving solace. [OFr *solas*, from L *sōlātium*, from *sōlārī*, *-ātus* to comfort in distress]

solah. See **sola**[2].

solan *sō'lən* or **solan goose** (*gōōs*), *n* an old name for the gannet. [Scand *soland*; ON *sūla*]

solanaceous. See under **solanum**.

solander *sō-lan'dər*, *n* a box in the form of a book, invented by the Swedish botanist Daniel *Solander* (1736–82).

solanine. See under **solanum**.

solano *sō-lä'nō*, *n* a hot, dust-laden south-easterly wind in Spain: — *pl* **sola'nos**. [Sp, from L *sōlānus* (*ventus*), the east wind, from *sōl* the sun]

solanum *sō-lā'nəm*, *n* any herbaceous plant of the genus *Solanum*, *incl* the potato, bittersweet and certain nightshades. — *adj* **solanā'ceous** of, related or belonging to the *Solanaceae*, a family of dicotyledonous flowering plants with fused petals, many of which contain poison and/or tropane alkaloids used in medicine, and *incl* potato, tomato, peppers, tobacco, henbane and certain nightshades. — *n* **solanine** (*sol'*- or *sōl'ə-nēn*) a glucoside obtained from potato sprouts and other solanaceous plants. [L *sōlānum* nightshade]

solar[1] *sō'lər*, *adj* of, from, like, or pertaining to the sun; measured by the sun; influenced by the sun; powered by energy from the sun's rays; with branches radiating like the sun's rays. — *n* (also **sō'ler**, **sollar** or **soller** *sol'ər*; OE *solor*, or OFr *soler*; *archaic*) an upper room; a garret; a landing between ladders in a mine. — *n* **solarimeter** (*-im'it-ər*) a device for measuring solar radiation. — *n* **sō'larism** excessive use of solar myths in the explanation of mythology. — *n* **sō'larist**. — *n* **solā'rium** a sundial; a place for sunbathing or equipped with sunbeds: — *n* **sōlarīzā'tion** or **-s-** the act, process, or effect of solarizing; the reversal of an image by over-exposure (*photog*); the interruption of photosynthesis by long exposure to bright light (*bot*). — *vt* **sō'larize** or **-ise** to expose to sunlight or affect by such exposure, *esp* excessive or injurious exposure. — *vi* to be so affected. — **solar battery** a battery of solar cells; **solar cell** a photoelectric cell converting the energy of sunlight into electric power; **solar day**, **time** and **year** see under **day**, **time** and **year**; **solar energy** energy obtained from the sun's rays, *esp* when used for home-heating, etc; **solar flare** a short-lived bright outburst in the sun's chromosphere, generally associated with sun spots and often the cause of radio and magnetic disturbances on earth; **solar furnace** a furnace using sunlight (guided and focused by a system of mirrors) as a heat source; **solar heating** a method of providing hot water, *esp* for domestic heating systems, by collecting heat radiated by the sun in water passed through solar panels; **solar microscope** an apparatus for projecting an enlarged image; **solar myth** a sun-myth, or a myth allegorizing the course of the sun; **solar noise** a hissing background noise heard in radio communication, due to radiation from the sun and its atmosphere; **solar panel** a panel of solar cells, *esp* when used to provide domestic heating or power for spacecraft, etc; **solar plexus** (*anatom*) a network of sympathetic nerves high in the back of the abdomen (so called from its radiating nerves; also called **coeliac plexus**); **solar power** solar energy (*adj* **sō'lar-powered**); **solar prominences** large prominent or protruding parts of the great volumes of heated gas surrounding the sun; **solar salt** salt got by evaporation of seawater by the sun; **solar system** the sun with its attendant bodies — major and minor planets, meteors, comets, satellites; **solar time** see under **time**; **solar wind** charged particles emitted by the sun, travelling at about one and a half million kilometres an hour. [L *sōlāris* solar, *sōlārium* a sundial, from *sōl* the sun]

solar[2] *sō'lər*. See **sola**[2].

solation. See under **sol**[2].

solatium *sō-lā'shi-əm* or *sō-lä'ti-ōōm*, *n* (*esp law*) compensation for disappointment, inconvenience, wounded feelings: — *pl* **sola'tia**. [L *sōlātium*]

sold[1] *sōld*, *pa t* and *pa p* of **sell**[2]. — **sold on** extremely enthusiastic or convinced about.

sold[2] *sold*, *n* (*Spenser*) pay, remuneration. — Also **solde** (*Meredith*). [Fr *solde*, from L *solidus* a piece of money]

soldado *sōl-dä'dō*, *n* a soldier: — *pl* **solda'dos**. [Sp]

soldan *sol'dən*, (*archaic*) *n* a sultan, *esp* of Egypt. [Fr; see **sultan**]

soldatesque *sol-də-tesk'*, *adj* soldierlike. [Fr, from *soldat* a soldier]

solde. See **sold**[2].

solder *sōl'dər* or *sol-*, *NAm* also *sod'ər* or *sōd'ər*, *n* a fusible alloy for uniting metals. — *vt* to attach with solder; to join; to mend, patch up. — *vi* to adhere. — *n* **sol'derer**. — *n* **sol'dering**. — **soldering iron** a tool with a pointed or wedge-shaped copper bit for use in soldering. [OFr *soudre*, *souldure*, from *souder*, *soulder* to consolidate, from L *solidāre* to make solid]

soldi. See **soldo**.

soldier *sōl'jər* or *sōld'yər*, *n* a person engaged in military service; a private; a person of military skill; a low-ranking member of a criminal organization, such as the Mafia, *esp* one who carries out shootings and other violent acts (*slang*); a shirker (*naut*); an ant, or white ant, of a specialized fighting caste; a scarlet, pugnacious, or armoured animal of various kinds (beetle, fish, etc); a red herring (*slang*); the ribwort plantain (used by children for a game of soldiers); a diligent worker for a cause; a brick set upright in a wall; a narrow strip of bread-and-butter or toast, *esp* for a child to eat (*colloq*). — *vi* to serve as a soldier; to shirk. — *n* **sol'diering**. — *adj* **sol'dierlike** having the appearance of a soldier; soldierly. — *adv* in the manner of a soldier. — *n* **sol'dierliness**. — *adj* **sol'dierly** befitting a soldier; having the qualities of or befitting a soldier. — *n* **sol'diership** the state or quality of being a soldier; military qualities; martial skill. — *n* **sol'diery** soldiers collectively; a military body or class; military qualities. — **soldier crab** a hermit crab; **soldier of fortune** a mercenary; someone ready to serve anywhere for pay or his or her own advancement. — **old soldier** see under **old**; **soldier on** to continue doggedly in face of difficulty or discouragement. [OFr *soldier*, from L *solidus* a piece of money, the pay of a soldier]

soldo *sol'dō*, *n* a former Italian coin, one-twentieth of a lira: — *pl* **sol'di** (*-dē*). [Ital, from L *solidus*]

sole[1] *sōl*, *n* the underside of the foot; the bottom of a boot or shoe; the undersurface of a golf club head; the floor of an oven or furnace; a sill (now *dialect*); the bottom, understructure, floor, or undersurface of various things; a thrustplane (*geol*). — *vt* to put a sole on. — **sole'plate** a bed-plate or similar object. [OE and OFr *sole*, from L *solea* sole, sandal, from *solum* bottom]

sole[2] *sōl*, *n* an elliptical flatfish of the genus *Solea*, *esp Solea solea*, the European or Dover sole, having a twisted mouth with teeth on the underside only and dorsal and anal fins that extend to the tail. — *n* **solenette** (*sōl-net'* or *sōl-ə-net'*) a small European species of sole, *Buglossidium luteum*, with distinctive dark-coloured rays on the dorsal and anal fins. — **lemon-sole** see under **lemon**[2]. [Fr *sole*, from L *solea*]

sole[3] *sōl*, *adj* alone; only; without husband or wife (*law*); without another; solitary; consisting of one person; exclusive; uniform. — *adv* **sole**. — *adv* **sole'ly** alone; only; singly. — *n* **sole'ness**. [Fr, from L *sōlus* alone]

sole[4] *sōl*, (*Shakesp*) *vt* to pull (by the ears). — Also (*dialect*) **sowl, sowle** or **soole** (*sowl*, *sēl*, or *sōōl*). [Origin obscure]

solecism *sol'i-sizm*, *n* a breach of syntax or a nonstandard grammatical usage; any absurdity, impropriety, or incongruity; a breach of good manners or etiquette. —

n **sol'ecist**. — *adj* **solecist'ic** or **solecist'ical**. — *adv* **solecist'ically**. — *vi* **sol'ecize** or **-ise** to commit a solecism or solecisms. [Gr *soloikismos*, said to come from the corruption of the Attic dialect among the Athenian colonists (*oikizein* to colonize) of *Soloi* in Cilicia]

solein. An old form (*Spenser*) of **sullen**.

solemn *sol'əm*, *adj* attended with or marked by special (*esp* religious) ceremonies, pomp, or gravity; attended with an appeal to God, as an oath; grave; in serious earnestness; with formal dignity; awed; awe-inspiring; stately; pompous; glum; sombre. — *vt* **solemnify** (*sə-lem'ni-fī*) to make solemn. — *n* **solemnity** (*-lem'ni-ti*) a solemn ceremony; high seriousness; affected gravity. — *n* **solemnization** or **-s-** (*sol-əm-nī-zā'shən*). — *vt* **sol'emnize** or **-ise** (*-nīz*) to perform religiously or solemnly; to celebrate with rites; to make solemn. — *n* **sol'emnizer** or **-s-**. — *adv* **sol'emnly**. — *n* **sol'emnness** (also **sol'emness**). — **solemn mass** high mass. [OFr *solempne*, *solemne* (Fr *solennel*), from L *sollemnis* customary, appointed]

solenodon *sō-len'ə-don*, *n* either of two shrewlike West Indian insectivorous mammals with elongated snouts and hairless tails, growing to about two feet in length. [New L, from L *sōlēn*, from *Gr sōlēn* a pipe]

solenoid *sōlə-noid*, *n* a cylindrical coil of wire, acting as a magnet when an electric current passes through it, converting electrical energy to mechanical energy. — *adj* **solenoid'al**. — *adv* **solenoid'ally**. [From Gr *sōlēn* a pipe, and sfx **-oid**]

solenette. See under **sole**[2].

soler. See **solar**[1].

solera *sō-lā'rä*, *n* a system of sherry production involving blending wines of various ages from a series of graded casks to achieve uniformity; collectively, the casks used in this process. — Also *adj*. [Sp, from L *solus* ground, base]

soles. See **Sol**.

soleus *sō'li-əs*, (*anatom*) *n* a broad flat muscle, in the calf of the leg beneath the gastrocnemius, that flexes the foot. [New L, from L *soles* sole]

sol-fa *sol'fä'*, (*music*) *n* a system of syllables (*do* or *ut*, *re*, *mi*, *fa*, *sol* or *so*, *la*, *si* or *ti*) representing and sung to the notes of the scale. — *adj* belonging to the system. — *vt* and *vi* to sing to sol-fa syllables: — *pr p* **sol-faing** (*-fä'ing*); *pa t* and *pa p* **sol-faed** or **-fa'd** (*-fäd'*). — *n* **sol-fa'ism** singing by syllables; solmization. — *n* **sol-fa'ist** a teacher, practiser, or advocate of solmization. — *n* **solfège** (*-fej'*; *Fr*) solfeggio. — **solfeggio** (*-fed'jō*; *Ital*) an exercise in sol-fa syllables: — *pl* **solfeggi** (*-fed'jē*) or **solfeggios**. — **tonic sol-fa** see under **tonic**. [**sol**[1] and **fa**]

sol-gel or **solgel** *sol'jel*, *adj* of or pertaining to alteration between **sol** and **gel** states.

solfatara *sol-fä-tä'rə*, *n* a volcanic vent emitting only gases, *esp* one emitting acid gases (hydrochloric acid and sulphur dioxide): — *pl* **solfata'ras**. — *adj* **solfata'ric**. [From the *Solfatara* (literally sulphur-mine, sulphur-hole) near Naples, from Ital *solfo* sulphur]

solfeggio. See **sol-fa**.

solferino *sol-fə-rē'nō*, *n* the colour of rosaniline, a purplish-red, discovered soon after the battle of *Solferino* in Italy (1859): — *pl* **solferi'nos**.

Sol.-Gen. *abbrev*: Solicitor-General.

soli. See **solo**.

solicit *sō-lis'it*, *vt* to petition; to importune; to seek after; to call for, require; to invite or urge to immorality; to incite; to conduct, manage; to extract gently (*obs*). — *vi* to petition; to act as solicitor; (of prostitutes) to make advances so as to win custom; (of beggars) to importune for alms. — *n* (*Shakesp*; another reading **solic'ity**) a solicitation. — *n* **solic'itant** a person who solicits (also *adj*). — *n* **solicitā'tion** a soliciting; an earnest request; an invitation. — *n* **solic'iting** any action of the verb, *esp* (of prostitutes) the making of advances. — *n* **solic'itor** a person who is legally qualified to act for another in a court of law (*esp* formerly a court of equity); a lawyer who advises, prepares deeds, manages cases, instructs counsel in the higher courts, and acts as an advocate in the lower courts; a person who asks earnestly; a canvasser (*NAm*). — *n* **solic'itorship**. — *adj* **solic'itous** soliciting or earnestly asking or desiring; anxious; concerned; considerate; careful. — *adv* **solic'itously**. — *n* **solic'itousness** or **solic'itude** the state of being solicitous; anxiety or uneasiness of mind; trouble. — **Solic'itor-Gen'eral** in England, the law officer of the crown next in rank to the Attorney-General — in Scotland, to the Lord-Advocate. [L *sōlicitāre*, *sollicitāre*, from *sō-*, *sollicitus*, from *sollus* whole, and *citus* aroused, from *ciēre* to cite]

solid *sol'id*, *adj* resisting change of shape, having the particles firmly cohering (as opposed to *fluid*; distinguished from *liquid* and *gaseous*); hard; compact; full of matter; not hollow; strong; having or pertaining to three dimensions; substantial; worthy of credit; weighty; of uniform undivided substance; financially sound, wealthy; reliable; sensible; unanimous; unbroken; unvaried. — *n* a substance, body, or figure that is solid; a solid mass or part. — *n* **solidare** (*sol'i-dār*; *Shakesp*) a small coin. — *n* **sol'idarism** (*-də-rizm*). — *n* **sol'idarist** an advocate of solidarity. — *n* **solidarity** (*-dar'i-ti*) unity of interests, aims, opinions, etc. — *adj* **sol'idary** (*-dər-i*) marked by solidarity; jointly responsible; joint and several. — *vt* **sol'idate** (*rare*) to consolidate. — *adj* **solidifiable** (*sə-lid'i-fī-ə-bl*). — *n* **solidificā'tion**. — *vt* **solid'ify** to make solid or compact. — *vi* to grow solid: — *pr p* **solid'ifying**; *pa t* and *pa p* **solid'ified**. — *adj* **sol'idish**. — *n* **sol'idism** the doctrine that refers all diseases to alterations of the solid parts of the body. — *n* **sol'idist** a believer in solidism. — *n* **solid'ity** the state of being solid; fullness, substance, actuality; strength or firmness, moral or physical; soundness, sturdiness; volume; a solid thing (*Shakesp*). — *adv* **sol'idly**. — *n* **sol'idness**. — **solid colour** a colour covering the whole of an object; a uniform colour. — *adj* **sol'id-hoofed** (of animals) with uncloven hoofs. — **solid matter** (*printing*) matter set without leads between the lines; **solid propellant** (*space*) rocket propellant in solid state, *usu* in caked, plastic-like form. — *adj* **sol'id-state** of, consisting of, or relating to solid substances; of, consisting of or relating to semiconductor materials (and their electrical properties); **solid-state light** light produced by means of a semiconductor device; **solid-state physics** a branch of physics which covers all properties of solid materials, now *esp* electrical conduction in crystals of semiconductors, and superconductivity and photoconductivity. — **solid of revolution** a solid figure regarded as formed by a plane figure turning round on an axis; **solid with** packed tight with; on a firm footing of understanding with; supporting fully. [L *solidus*, *-a*, *-um* solid]

solidago *sol-id-äg'o*, *n* goldenrod, any herbaceous composite plant of the genus *Solidago*, typically having plumelike clusters of golden-yellow flowers. [New L, from Med L *soldago*, from *soldāre* to strengthen (from its supposed healing qualities)]

solidum *sol'i-dum*, *n* the die of a pedestal (*archit*); a complete sum (*Scots law*). [See ety for **solid**]

solidungulate *sol-id-ung'gū-lāt*, (*zool*) *adj* having uncloven hoofs. — Also **solidung'ulous**. [L *solidus* solid, and *ungula* a hoof]

solidus *sol'i-dəs*, *n* the stroke, oblique or slash (/), a sign used for various purposes, as in writing fractions and to separate alternatives, ratios, etc (eg 3/4, and/or); a line in a constitutional diagram, eg of alloys, indicating the temperatures at which solidification is completed or melting begins (*chem*; cf **liquidus**); a Roman gold coin introduced by Constantine, later called the *bezant*; a medieval silver coin of 12 denarii: — *pl* **solidi** (*-dī*). [ME, from LL *solidus* (*nummus*) a solid (coin); used to denote the former English shilling, representing the old lengthened *s* (£. s. d. = *librae*, *solidii*, *denarii* pounds, shillings, pence]

solifidian *sō-li-fid'i-ən, (Christian relig) n* a person who maintains that only faith can bring redemption. — Also *adj.* — *n* **solifid'ianism**. [L *sōlus* only, and *fidēs* faith]

solifluxion or **solifluction** *sol-i-fluk'shən, (geol) n* the slow movement of soil or scree down a slope resulting from alternate freezing and thawing. [L *solum* soil, and *fluxiō, -ōnis* flow]

Solifugae *sol-i-fū'jē, n pl* an order of spider-like arachnids, with head and three-jointed thorax distinct. [See **Solpuga**; modified by popular association with L *sōl* the sun, and *fugere* to flee]

soliloquy *so-, sō-* or *sə-lil'ə-kwi, n* an act of talking to oneself; a speech of this nature made by a character in a play, etc. — *vi* **solil'oquize** or **-ise** to speak to oneself; to utter a soliloquy in a play, etc. — *n* **solil'oquizer** or -s-, or **solil'oquist**. [L *sōliloquium*, from *sōlus* alone, and *loquī* to speak]

solion *sol'ī-ən* or *-ī'on, n* a low-frequency amplifier that controls the flow of ions in solution. [*sol*ution and **ion**]

soliped *sol'i-ped, n* an animal with uncloven hoofs. — *adj* **sol'iped** or **solip'edous**. [L *sōlus* alone, and *pēs, pedis* a foot]

solipsism *sol'ip-sizm, (philos) n* the theory that holds that self-existence is the only certainty, otherwise described as absolute egoism, the extreme form of subjective idealism. — *n* and *adj* **sol'ipsist**. — *adj* **solipsis'tic**. — *adv* **solipsis'tically**. [L *sōlus* alone, and *ipse* self]

solitaire *sol-i-tār', n* a recluse; a game played by one person with a board and balls, pegs, etc; patience (the card game) (*esp NAm*); a gemstone, *esp* a diamond, set by itself; a large loose silk necktie as worn in the 18th century; a gigantic flightless pigeon (*Pezophaps solitarius*) of Rodriguez, extinct since the 18th century; an American or West Indian fly-catching thrush. — **solitaire board** a board with cups, holes, etc for playing solitaire. [Fr, see **solitary**]

solitary *sol'i-tər-i, adj* alone; single, separate; living alone, not social or gregarious; without company; remote from society; retired, secluded; lonely; growing singly (*bot*). — *n* someone who lives alone; a hermit; solitary confinement (*colloq*). — *n* **solitarian** (*-tā'ri-ən*) a hermit. — *adv* **sol'itarily**. — *n* **sol'itariness**. — **solitary confinement** imprisonment in a cell by oneself. [L *sōlitārius*, from *sōlus* alone]

solito *sol'i-tō, (music) adv* in the usual manner. [Ital]

soliton *sol'it-ən, (phys) n* a solitary wave; a quantum which corresponds to a solitary wave in its transmission. [**solitary**]

solitude *sol'i-tūd, n* solitariness; absence of company; a lonely place or desert. — *n* **solitūdinā'rian**. — *adj* **solitūd'inous**. [L *sōlitūdō*, from *sōlus*]

solivagant *sō-liv'ə-gənt, adj* wandering alone. — Also *n.* [L *sōlus* alone, and *vagāns, -antis* wandering]

solive *so-lēv', n* a joist or beam of secondary importance. [Fr, from L *sublevāre* to support]

sollar, soller. See **solar**[1].

solleret *sol'ər-et, n* a jointed steel shoe worn as part of protective armour. [OFr, dimin of *soler* slipper]

solmization or **-isation** *sol-mi-zā'shən, (music) n* sol-faing; a recital of the notes of the gamut. [**sol**[1] and **mi**]

solo *sō'lō, n* a piece or passage for one voice or instrument, accompanied or unaccompanied; any performance in which no other person or instrument participates; a single-seater motorcycle or bicycle as opposed to motorcycle with side-car, tandem, etc; a card game (**solo whist**) based on whist, in which various declarations are made and the declarer may or may not have a partner: — *pl* **sō'lōs** or (*music*) **soli** (*sō'lē*). — *adj* performed, or for performances, as a solo; performing a solo; for one; single. — *adv* alone. — *vi* to fly solo; to play (a) solo. — *n* **sō'lōist**. — **solo parent** (*Austr* and *NZ*) a single parent; **solo stop** an organ stop for imitating a solo performance on another instrument. [Ital, from L *sōlus* alone]

Solomon *sol'ə-mən, n* a person of unusual wisdom, from *Solomon*, king of Israel (from the Bible: 1 Kings 3. 5–15). — *adj* **Solomonian** (*-mō'ni-ən*) or **Solomonic** (*-mon'ik*). — **Solomon's seal** any species of *Polygonatum*, a genus of the lily family, with small dangling greenish flowers (*perh* from the scars on the rootstock); a symbol formed of two triangles interlaced or superposed, forming a six-pointed star.

Solon *sō'lon, n* a famous lawgiver of Athens (594 BC), one of the Seven Sages; a sage; a wiseacre; a Congressman or member of any other legislative assembly (*US*). — *adj* **Solō'nian**.

solonchak *sol-on'chak, n* a pale or grey soil-type found in arid to subhumid, poorly drained conditions. [Russ, salt marsh, from *sol* salt]

solonetz or **solonets** *sol-on-ets', n* an alkaline soil-type having a hard, dark subsoil under a thin friable topsoil, formed by the leaching of salts from a solonchak. — *adj* **solonet'zic**. — *n* **soloniza'tion** or **-s-** the process by which a solonetz is formed. [Russ, salt not produced by boiling]

so-long or **so long** *sō-long', (colloq* or *slang) interj* goodbye. [Prob **so**[1] and **long**[3]; poss **salaam**]

Solpuga *sol-pū'gə n* a genus of very venomous Solifugae. — *n* and *adj* **solpu'gid** (a member) of the genus. [L *solpūga, salpūga, solipūga, solipugna*, a venomous animal supposedly the same, a word originating in Spain]

Solr *abbrev*: Solicitor.

solstice *sol'stis, n* the time when the sun reaches its maximum distance from the equator (*summer solstice* when it touches the tropic of Cancer, about 21 June; the *winter solstice* when it touches that of Capricorn, about 21 December); the turning-point then reached. — *adj* **solstitial** (*-stish'l*) pertaining to, or happening at, a solstice, *esp* at the summer solstice. — *adv* **solstit'ially**. [Fr, from L *sōlstitium*, from *sōl* the sun, *sistere, statum* to make to stand, from *stāre*]

soluble *sol'ū-bl, adj* capable of being solved, dissolved, or resolved. — *n* **solūbil'ity** (a measure of) the ability of a substance to dissolve. — *n* **solubilizā'tion** or **-s-**. — *vt* **sol'ubilize** or **-ise** to render soluble; to make more soluble. — *n* **sol'ūte** a dissolved substance. — *adj* (*sol'* or *-ūt'*) loose; free; not adhering; dissolved. — *n* **solution** (*səl-ōō'shən* or *-ū'shən*) the act of solving or dissolving; the condition of being dissolved; the preparation resulting therefrom; the separating of parts; abnormal separation; an explanation; the removal of a doubt; the solving of, answer to, a problem; the crisis of a disease; a breach (as of continuity); the payment of a debt, or similar discharge of an obligation; a solution of rubber. — *vt* to mend or cement with rubber solution; to apply or treat with a solution, to solve (a problem) (*esp NAm*). — *adj* **solutional** (*-ōō'* or *-ū'*). — *n* **solu'tionist** a solver (as of puzzles). — *adj* **sol'ūtive** tending to dissolve; laxative. — **solution of triangles** (*trig*) finding the values of the remaining sides and angles, some being given. [L *solvere, solūtum* to loosen]

solum *sō'ləm, n* ground, soil; a piece of ground. [L *solum* the ground]

solus *sō'ləs, adj* alone, *orig* in dramatic directions: — *fem* form **sō'la**. [L *sōlus* alone]

Solutrean or **Solutrian** *sol-ōōt'ri-ən* or *-ūt'* or *-trē', adj* belonging to an upper Palaeolithic European culture which succeeded the Aurignacian and preceded the Magdalenian. [*Solutré*, in Saône-et-Loire, where objects of this culture have been found]

Solvay process *sol'vā prō'ses, n* a process for manufacturing sodium carbonate in which carbon dioxide is passed through a concentrated solution of sodium chloride saturated with ammonia with the resulting precipitate of sodium bicarbonate being heated to produce the carbonate. [After Ernest *Solvay* (1838–1922), Belgian chemist]

solve *solv, vt* to unbind; to dissolve; to settle; to clear up or explain; to find an answer to or a way out of. — *n* **solvabil'ity**. — *adj* **sol'vable** capable of being solved; capable of being paid, dissolved, or resolved (*rare* or *obs*); solvent (*obs*). — *n* **sol'vate** a definite combination of solute and solvent. — *vt* and *vi* to (cause to) undergo solvation. — *n* **solvā'tion** the association of the molecules of a solvent with solute ions or molecules. — *n* **sol'vency**. — *adj* **sol'vent** able to solve or dissolve; able to pay all debts. — *n* a substance that dissolves another; that component of a solution which is present in excess, or whose physical state is the same as that of the solution; something which provides a solution. — *n* **sol'ver**. — **solvent abuse** self-intoxication by inhaling the fumes given off by various solvents — adhesives, petrol, etc. [L *solvere* to loosen, prob from *sē-*, *se-* aside, and *luere* to loosen]

solvitur ambulando *sol'vi-tōōr am-bū-lan'dō*, (*L*) literally, it is solved by walking (ie the problem of reality of motion); hence, the problem is solved by practical experiment, by actual performance.

Som. *abbrev*: Somerset.

soma[1] *sō'mə*, *n* (also with *cap*) a plant (perhaps an asclepiad), or its intoxicating juice, used in ancient Indian religious ceremonies, and personified as a god. [Sans *soma* (Avestan *haoma* juice)]

soma[2] *sō'mə*, *n* an imaginary perfect drug described by Aldous Huxley in *Brave New World*; (with *cap*; ®) a drug which relieves pain and is a muscle-relaxant. [**soma**[1]]

soma[3] *sō'mə*, *n* the body; the body of an animal or plant excluding the germ-cells (*biol*): — *pl* **somas** or **somatas**. — *n* **somascope** (*sō'mə-skōp*; Gr *skopeein* to view) an instrument using ultrasonic waves converted into a television image to show the character of diseased internal tissues of the body. — *adj* **somatic** (*-mat'ik*). — *adv* **somat'ically**. — *n* **so'matism** (*-mə-tizm*) materialism. — *n* **so'matist** (also *adj*). — *adj* **somatogenic** (*sō-mə-tō-jen'ik*) originating in body cells. — *adj* **somatolog'ic** or **somatolog'ical**. — *n* **somatol'ogy** the science of the properties of matter; the science of the human body. — *n* **so'matoplasm** protoplasm of the somatic cells. — *n* **so'matopleure** (*-plōōr*; Gr *pleurā* side) the outer body wall or the layer that gives rise to it. — *n* **somatostatin** (*sō-mə-tō-stat'in*) a polypeptide hormone, produced in the brain and pancreas, which appears to inhibit the secretion of certain other hormones, *esp* growth hormone. — *adj* **somatotens'ic** that which restores the equilibrium of an organism (applied *esp* to certain plants when eaten as food). — *n* **somatotōn'ia** a pattern of temperament and body type in which alertness and aggression are combined with mesomorphic build. — *adj* **somatotonic** (*-ton'*). — *adj* **somatotrop'ic** or **somatotroph'ic** promoting bodily growth. — *n* **somatotrop'in** or **somatotroph'in** a polypeptide growth hormone. — *n* **somat'otype** a type consisting of a physical build paired with a particular temperament. — *vt* to place with regard to somatotype. — *adj* **somital** (*sō'mi-tl*) or **somit'ic**. — *n* **so'mite** (*zool*) a body segment of a vertebrate embryo or of a segmented invertebrate. — **somatic cell** one of the non-reproductive cells of the body, as distinct from the reproductive or germ cells; **somatic cell hybrid** a cell formed by fusion of two somatic cells from the same or different species; **somatic mutation** a mutation occurring in the genes of somatic cells, and therefore not inheritable. [Gr *sōma* body]

soman *sō'mən*, *n* an organophosphate nerve agent developed for use in chemical warfare, causing sweating, vomiting, convulsions and death, if inhaled.

sombre or *NAm* **somber** *som'bər*, *adj* dark and gloomy; melancholy, dismal. — *vt* and *vi* to make or become sombre. — *adv* **som'brely**. — *n* **som'breness**. — *adj* **som'brous** sombre. [Fr *sombre* (cf Sp *sombra* shade), perh from L *sub* under, and *umbra* a shade]

sombrerite *som-brā'rīt*, *n* rock-guano. [*Sombrero* in the West Indies]

sombrero *som-brā'rō*, *n* a broad-brimmed hat, *esp* as worn in Mexico: — *pl* **sombre'ros**. [Sp, hat, from *sombra* shade]

some *sum*, *indefinite pronoun* an indefinite part of the whole number or quantity; (a) certain (undetermined) one(s); a great deal (*NAm*); a good deal more, *esp* as *and then some* (*esp NAm*); one, one or other (*obs*). — *adj* one or other; in an indefinite number or quantity; a little; not a little; considerable; a certain; certain unspecified; several; a few; in approximate number, length, etc, more or less; remarkable, outstanding, of note (*colloq*, *esp US*; also *ironical*). — *adv* somewhat, in some degree, rather, a little (*dialect*); very much (*NAm*); sometimes (*Shakesp*). — *n* (or *pronoun*) **some'body** some person; a person of importance: — *pl* **some'bodies**. — *adv* **some'day** at an unspecified time in the future. — *adv* **some'deal** or **some'dele** (*archaic*) in some degree, somewhat. — *adv* **some'gate** (*Scot*) somewhere, somehow. — *adv* **some'how** in some way or other. — *n* (or *pronoun*) **some'one** somebody. — *adv* **some'place** (*NAm*) somewhere. — *n* (or *pronoun*) **some'thing** an undefined thing; a thing of some account; a portion. — *adv* in some degree. — *adj* that is some account. — Also used as substitute for any word (*n*, *adj* or *v*) or component of any word forgotten, indefinite or avoided. — **-something** *combining form* indicating an unspecified or unknown number greater than or in addition to, as in *thirty something*. — *adv* **some'time** at a time not fixed; at one time or other; formerly. — *adj* former; late. — *adv* **some'times** at times; now and then; sometime (*obs*). — *adj* (*Shakesp*) sometime. — *adv* **some'way**, **some'ways** or **some'wise** in some way; somehow. — *adv* **some'what** in some degree. — *n* an unfixed quantity or degree; something. — *adv* **some'when** (*rare*) some time or other. — *adv* **some'-whence** (*rare*). — *adv* **some'where** in or to some place. — *adv* **some'while** or **some'whiles** (*rare*) sometimes. — *adv* **some'whither** (*rare*). — *adv* **some'why** (*rare*). — **someone else** some other person; **someone else's** some other person's. [OE *sum*; Gothic *sums*, ON *sumr*]

-some[1] *-sum* or *-səm*, *sfx* (1) forming adjectives with the meaning full of, eg *troublesome*, *wholesome*; (2) forming nouns denoting a group with a certain number of members, eg *twosome*, *threesome*. [OE *-sum*; Ger *-sam*; cf **same**]

-some[2] *-sōm*, *sfx* forming nouns denoting a body, eg *chromosome*. [Gr *soma* body]

somersault or **summersault** *sum'ər-sölt*, *n* a leap or other movement in which a person (or animal) turns heels over head. — *vi* to turn a somersault. — Also sometimes **som'erset**. [OFr *sombre saut* (Fr *soubresaut*), from L *suprā* over, and *saltus*, *-ūs* a leap, from *salīre* to leap]

somital, **somite**, **somitic**. See under **soma**[3].

sommelier *som'ə-lyā*, *n* a butler; a wine waiter or steward in a restaurant. [Fr]

somnambulance *som-nam'bū-ləns*, *n* sleepwalking. — *adj* and *n* **somnam'būlant**. — *adj* **somnam'būlar** or **somnam'bulary**. — *vi* **somnam'būlate** to walk in one's sleep. — *n* **somnambūlā'tion**. — *n* **somnam'būlātor** or **somnam'būle** a sleepwalker. — *adj* **somnam'būlic**. — *n* **somnam'būlism** walking in sleep; a hypnotic trance in which acts are performed that are not remembered afterwards. — *n* **somnam'būlist**. — *adj* **somnambūlis'tic**. [L *somnus* sleep, and *ambulare* to walk]

somnial *som'n-yəl*, *adj* (*rare*) pertaining to dreams. — *vt* **som'niate** to dream. — Also *vi* to make drowsy, stupefy. — *adj* **som'niative** or **som'niatory**. [L *somnus* sleep]

somnifacient *som-ni-fāshənt* or *-shi-ənt*, *adj* sleep-inducing or promoting. — Also **somnif'erous** or **somnif'ic**. — *n* a somnifacient drug. [L *somnus* sleep, and *faciens*, *facientis* pr p of *facēre* to do]

somniloquence *som-nil'ə-kwəns*, **somniloquism** *-nil'ə-kwizm* or **somniloquy** *-nil'ə-kwi*, *n* (the act of) talking in one's sleep. — *n* **somnil'oquist**. — *vi* **somnil'oquize or -ise**. [L *somnus* sleep, and *loquī* to talk]

somnolence *som'nə-ləns*, *n* sleepiness, drowsiness. — Also **som'nolency**. — *adj* **som'nolent**. — *adv* **som'nolently**. — *adj* **somnolesc'ent** half-asleep. [ME *sompnolence*, from OFr, from L *somnolentia*, from *somnus* sleep]

son *sun, n* a male child or offspring; formerly extended to a son-in-law; a descendant, or one so regarded or treated; a disciple; a native or inhabitant; the product of anything; a familiar (sometimes patronizing) mode of address to a boy or to a male younger than oneself. — *adj* **son'less**. — *n* **sonn'y** a little son; a familiar mode of address to a boy. — *n* **son'ship** the state or character of a son. — **son'-in-law** a daughter's husband; formerly, a stepson: — *pl* **sons'-in-law**. — **son of** (*often facetious*) a person (or thing) that is a derivative, copy or product of an original; **son of a bitch** see **sonofabitch**; **son of a gun** see under **gun**; **son of man** a man; applied to Jesus Christ or the Messiah; **son of the manse** a minister's son; **the Son** the second person in the Trinity, Jesus Christ. [OE *sunu*; Du *zoon*, Ger *Sohn*]

sonant *sō'nənt*, (*phonetics*) *adj* voiced; syllabic. — *n* a voiced sound; a syllabic consonant. — *n* **so'nance** a sounding. — *n* **so'nancy** sonant character. [L *sonāns -antis*, pr p of *sonāre* to sound]

Sonar *sō'nər, n orig*, the American equivalent of Asdic; (without *cap*) natural equipment that provides echo location in bats and some marine animals; (without *cap*) echo-sounding equipment in general. — **sonar buoy** same as **sonobuoy**. [*so*und *n*avigation *a*nd *r*anging]

sonata *sə-* or *so-nä'tə*, (*music*) *n orig*, an instrumental composition; a composition *usu* of three or more movements designed chiefly for a solo instrument. — *n* **sonatina** (*son-ə-tē'nə*) a short sonata. — **sonata form** the form usual in the first movement of a sonata or symphony, divided into three sections: exposition, development and recapitulation. [Ital, fem pa p of *sonare*, from L *sonāre* to sound]

sonce. See **sonse**.

sondage *sɔ̃-däzh, n* a trial bore or excavation (*mining* and *archaeol*); a sounding (*naut*); sounding out of opinion, an opinion poll. [Fr]

sonde *sond, n* any device for obtaining information about atmospheric and weather conditions at high altitudes. [Fr]

sondeli *son'de-li, n* the Indian musk shrew. [Kanarese *sundili*]

sone *sōn, n* a unit of sound on a scale such that the numerical value is proportional to the perceived loudness. [L *sonus* sound]

soneri *son'* or *sōn'ə-rē, n* cloth of gold. [Hindi *sonā* gold]

son et lumière *son ā lüm'yər'* or *-yar', n* a dramatic spectacle presented after dark, involving lighting effects on natural features of the country or on a chosen building and an appropriate theme illustrated by spoken words and by music. [Fr]

song[1] *song, n* that which is sung; a short poem or ballad suitable for singing or set to music; the melody to which it is sung; an instrumental composition of similar form and character; singing; the melodious outburst of a bird; any characteristic sound; a poem, or poetry in general; a theme of song; a habitual utterance, manner, or attitude towards anything; a fuss; a mere trifle (as in **going for a song** being sold for a trifling sum). — *adj* **song'ful** abounding in song; melodious; songlike; like singing; ready to break into song. — *adv* **song'fully**. — *n* **song'fulness**. — *adj* **song'less**. — *adj* **song'like**. — *n* **song'ster**, *fem* **song'stress**, a singer. — **song'bird** a bird that sings; any bird of the suborder Oscines; **song'book** a service-book (*obs*); a book of songs; **song'craft** (*rare*) the art of writing or singing songs; **song cycle** a sequence of songs connected in subject; **song'fest** see **fest**; **song form** the form of composition usual in songs; **song'man** (*Shakesp*) a singer; a choir singer; **song school**; **song'smith** a composer of songs; **song sparrow** an American songbird (*Melospiza melodia*); **song thrush** the mavis or throstle (see also **thrush**[1]); **song'-writer** one who composes music and/or words for (*esp* popular) songs. — **make a song (and dance) about** to make overmuch of; to make an unnecessary fuss about; **on song** (*colloq*) performing well, on form; **Song of Songs** or **of Solomon** Canticles, a book of the Old Testament long attributed to Solomon. [OE *sang*, from *singan* to sing; Gothic *saggws*, ON *söngr*]

song[2] *song*, (*Spenser*) *pa t* of **sing**.

sonic *son'ik, adj* pertaining to or using sound waves; travelling at about the speed of sound. — *n sing* **son'ics** the study of the technological application of sounds, *esp* supersonic waves. — **sonic bang** or **boom** (*aeronautics*) a loud double report caused by shock waves projected outward and backward from the leading and trailing edges of an aircraft as it reaches supersonic speed; **sonic barrier** the sound barrier; **sonic mine** an acoustic mine. [L *sonus* sound]

sonne. An obsolete spelling of **son** or **sun**.

sonnet *son'it, n* formerly, a short (*esp* lyrical) poem; a short poem of fourteen lines of ten or eleven syllables, rhymed according to one or other of certain definite schemes, forming an octave and a sestet, properly expressing two successive phases of one thought. — *vi* to write sonnets. — *vt* to celebrate in sonnets. — *adj* **sonn'etary**. — *n* **sonneteer'** a writer of sonnets; a poetaster (*obs*). — *vi* **sonn'etize** or **-ise** to compose sonnets. — **sonnet sequence** a connected series of sonnets composed by one poet. — **Petrarchan** (or **Petrarchian**) **sonnet** one rhymed *abbaabba cdcdcd*; **Miltonic** *abbaabba cdecde*; **Shakespearian** *ababcdcd efefgg*. [Ital *sonetto*, dimin of *suono*, from L *sonus* a sound]

Sonnite. See **Sunna**.

sonny. See under **son**.

sono- *son'ō-, combining form* meaning sonic. — *n* **sonobuoy** (*son'ō-boi* or *NAm -bōō-ē*) sonar equipment dropped to float on the sea and pick up underwater noise, eg from a submarine, and to transmit bearings of the source to aircraft. — *n* **son'ogram** a visual representation of a sound produced by a sonograph (*acoustics*); a sonogram produced by ultrasonography (*med*). — *n* **son'ograph** an instrument for scanning and recording sound and its component frequencies. — *n* **sonog'rapher**. — *n* **sonog'raphy**. [L *sonus* sound]

sonofabitch *sun'əv-ə-bich'*, (*slang*; *esp NAm*) *n* son of a bitch, an abusive term of address or of description, or vulgar exclamation: — *pl* **sons of bitches**.

sonorous *sə-nō'rəs* or *son'ə-rəs, adj* sounding, *esp* loudly, deeply, impressively, etc; full-sounding; sounding or ringing when struck. — *n* **son'orant** (*phonetics*) a frictionless continuant or nasal (*l, r, m, n, ng*) capable of fulfilling a vocalic or consonantal function; the consonants represented by *w* and *y*, having consonantal or vocalic articulations. — *n* **sonority** (*sō-* or *sə-nor'i-ti*) sonorousness; type, quality, etc, of sound. — *adv* **sono'rously** (or *son'*). — *n* **sono'rousness** (or *son'*) sonorous quality or character. [L *sonōrus*, from *sonor, -ōris* a sound, from *sonāre* to sound]

sonse or **sonce** *sons*, (*Scot*) *n* good luck; abundance. — *adj* **sons'y** or **sons'ie** bringing luck; comely; comfortable-looking; good-natured; plump, buxom; robust. [Gaelic *sonas* good fortune]

sontag *son'tag* or *zōn'tähh, n* a woman's knitted cape, tied down round the waist. [From the famous German singer Henriette *Sontag* (1806–1854)]

sonties *son'tiz*, (*Shakesp*, in an oath) *n pl* prob for **sanctities**.

soogee or **soogie** *sōō'jē* or *-ji*, (*naut*) *n* a solution of soap, soda, etc for cleaning the decks and paintwork of a ship. — Also **soo'jey** or **su'jee**. — *vt* to clean, wash, *esp* with soogee. [Perh connected with Hindi *suji* a type of gruel; or poss from Jap *sōji* cleaning]

sook[1] *sŏŏk, n* a soft, timid or cowardly person (*slang, esp Austr*); someone who sucks up fawningly, a toady (*Brit dialect*). [Perh from earlier *suck(-calf)*, a hand-reared calf, infl by Scot pronunciation of **suck**.]

sook[2]. Same as **souk**.

soole. See **sole**[4].

soom *sōōm*, a Scots form of **swim**.

soon *sōōn, adv* (*compar* **soon'er**, *superl* **soon'est**) in a short time; without delay; early; readily; willingly. — *adv* **soon'est** (*telegraphese* and *military jargon*) as soon as possible, immediate. — **no sooner** . . . **than** immediately; **soon at** (*Shakesp*) about; **sooner or later** eventually. [OE *sōna*]

soop *sōōp*, (*Scot*) *vt* to sweep. — *n* **soop'ing** (*Scot*). — *adv* **soop'stake** (*Shakesp*) with a sweep of the stakes (another reading **swoop'-stake-like**). [ON *sōpa*; cf **sweep**, **swoop**]

soot[1] *sōōt*, *n* a black deposit from imperfect combustion of carbonaceous matter (wood, coal, etc); a smut. — *vt* to cover, smear, dirty, clog, or treat with soot. — *n* **soot'erkin** (*now rare*) an imaginary afterbirth of which Dutch women were reported to be delivered, thought to be the offspring of the stoves over which they huddled; a Dutchman; a Black person; a chimney-sweep; anything supplementary, fruitless, or imperfect. — *adv* **soot'ily**. — *n* **soot'iness**. — *adj* **soot'less**. — *adj* **soot'y**. — **soot'flake** a smut of soot; **sooty mould** a disease of plants in which a dark-coloured fungus grows on the sticky secretions of certain insects. [OE *sōt*; Dan *sod*]

soot[2] or **soote** *sōōt*, *adj* and *n* (*obs*) sweet. — *adv* (*Spenser*) sweetly. [ODu *soet* sweet]

sooterkin. See under **soot**[1].

sooth *sōōth*, *n* truth, verity, reality (*archaic*); blandishment (*Shakesp*); an augury, foretokening (*obs*; *Spenser* **soothe**). — *adj* true; truthful; smooth, soft (*Keats*). — *adv* in truth; indeed. — *adj* **sooth'fast** truthful, honest, faithful. — *adv* **sooth'fastly**. — *n* **sooth'fastness**. — *adj* **sooth'ful** truthful; faithful. — *adv* **sooth'ly** or **sooth'lich** (*Spenser*) truly, indeed. — *vi* **sooth'say** to foretell, to divine. — *n* a prediction; (*Spenser* **soothsay'**) an omen. — *n* **sooth'sayer** (*Spenser -sā'*) someone who foretells, a diviner or prognosticator; a truth-teller (*obs*). — *n* **sooth'saying**. [OE *sōth* truth, true; ON *sannr*]

soothe[1] *sōōdh*, *vt* to calm, comfort, compose, tranquillize; to appease; to allay, soften; to blandish, cajole, flatter; to gloss over (*obs*); to prove or declare true (*obs*); to confirm, support, back up (*obs*). — *vi* to have a tranquillizing effect. — *n* **sooth'er** someone who, or something that, soothes; a dummy teat for a baby, a comforter or pacifier. — *vt* (*Irish*) to flatter, blandish. — *n* and *adj* **sooth'ing**. — *adv* **sooth'ingly**. [OE (*ge*)*sōthian* to confirm as true, from *sōth* true]

soothe[2]. See **sooth**.

sootily, **sootiness**, **sooty**. See under **soot**[1].

SOP *abbrev*: significant other person (eg a cohabiting partner); standard operating procedure.

sop *sop*, *n* bread or other food dipped or soaked in liquid; a puddle; a soaking; a propitiatory gift or concession (from the drugged sop the Sibyl gave to Cerberus to gain passage for Aeneas to Hades, *Aeneid* 6. 420). — *vt* to steep in alcohol; to take up by absorption (with *up*); to soak. — *vi* to soak in, percolate; to be soaked: — *pr p* **sopp'ing**; *pa t* and *pa p* **sopped**. — *adv* **sopp'ily**. — *n* **sopp'iness**. — *n*, *adj*, and *adv* **sopp'ing**. — *adj* **sopp'y** drenched; thoroughly wet; sloppily sentimental. [OE *sopp* (noun), *soppian* (verb); prob connected with *sūpan* to sup]

sop. *abbrev*: soprano.

soph *sof*, *n* a short form of **sophister** and of **sophomore**.

sopherim *sō'fə-rim*, *n pl* the scribes, the expounders of the Jewish oral law. — *adj* **sopheric** (*-fer'ik*). [Heb *sōferīm*]

Sophi. Same as **Sophy**.

sophism *sof'izm*, *n* a plausibly deceptive fallacy. — *n* **soph'ist** a captious or intentionally fallacious reasoner; *orig* one of a class of public teachers of rhetoric, philosophy, etc, in ancient Greece. — *n* **soph'ister** a sophist (*Shakesp*); *esp* formerly, a second- or third-year student at certain British universities, or a third- or fourth-year student at Dublin and others. — *adj* **sophis'tic** or **sophis'tical** pertaining to, or of the nature of, a sophist or sophistry; fallaciously subtle. — *adv* **sophis'tically**. — *n* **soph'istry** (an instance of) plausibly deceptive or fallacious reasoning; the art of reasoning speciously. [Gr *sophiā* wisdom, *sophisma* skill]

sophisticate *so-fis'ti-kāt*, *vt* to give a fashionable air of worldly wisdom to; to make (eg a machine) highly complex and efficient; to make sophistic; to adulterate, falsify. — *vi* to practise sophistry. — *adj* **sophis'ticāte** or **sophis'ticāted** very refined and subtle; devoid or deprived of natural simplicity, complex; with qualities produced by special knowledge and skill; (of a person) accustomed to an elegant, cultured way of life; with the most up-to-date devices; worldly-wise; adulterated, falsified. — *n* **sophis'ticāte** a sophisticated person. — *n* **sophisticā'tion**. — *n* **sophis'ticātor**. [Med L *sophisticāre* to adulterate, from *sophisticus* sophistic; see **sophism**]

sophistry. See under **sophism**.

Sophoclean *sof-ō-klē'ən*, *adj* pertaining to *Sophocles*, the Athenian tragic poet (c.496–c.406 BC).

sophomore *sof'ə-mör*, (*esp US*) *n* a second-year student. — Also *adj*. — *adj* **sophomoric** (*-mor'*) or **sophomor'ical** of a sophomore; bombastic. [Prob from *sophom* (obs form of *sophism*) and *-or*, as if from *sophos* wise, and *mōros* foolish]

Sophy *sō'fi*, (*obs*) *n* the shah of Persia. [From the *Çafī* or Safawi dynasty (1502–1736) descended from Çafi-ud-dīn]

sopite *sō-pīt'*, (*now rare*) *vt* to dull, lull, put to sleep; to put an end to. [L *sōpītus*, pa p of *sōpīre* to put to sleep, calm, settle]

sopor *sō'pör*, (*pathol*) *n* unnaturally deep sleep. — *adj* **soporiferous** (*sop-* or *sōp-ər-if'ər-əs*) inducing sleep. — *adv* **soporif'erously**. — *n* **soporif'erousness**. — *adj* **soporif'ic** inducing sleep (also *fig*). — *n* a sleep-inducing agent. — *adj* **sop'orōse** or **sop'orous** sleepy. [L *sopor*, *-ōris* deep sleep, and *ferre* to bring, *facere* to make]

sopped, **sopping**, **soppy**. See under **sop**.

sopra *sō'pra*, (*music*) *adv* above. [Ital, from L *suprā* above]

soprano *sə-prä'nō*, *n* the highest variety of voice, treble; a singer with such a voice; a part for such a voice: — *pl* **sopra'nos** or **sopra'ni** (*nē*). — *adj* of, or possessing, a treble voice or a part for it; in a group of instruments of the same type but of different sizes, that with the range close to the range of a soprano voice. — *adj* **sopranino** (*sō-prə-nē'nō*) (of an instrument) higher than the corresponding soprano. — Also *n*: — *pl* **soprani'nos** or **soprani'ni**. — *n* **sopra'nist** a soprano singer. [Ital, from *sopra*, from L *suprā* or *super* above]

SOR *abbrev*: sale or return.

sora *sō'rə* or *sö'*, *n* a N American short-billed rail (*Porzano carolina*). — Also **so'ree**. [Indian name]

sorage. See under **sore**[2].

soral. See under **sorus**.

Sorb *sörb*, *n* a Wend. — *n* and *adj* **Sor'bian** or **Sor'bish** Wendish. [Ger *Sorbe*; cf **Serb**]

sorb[1] *sörb*, *n* the service tree, the wild service tree, or (sometimes) the rowan tree; its fruit (also **sorb'-apple**). — *n* **sor'bate** a salt of sorbic acid. — **sorbic acid** an acid obtained from the rowanberry, used in food preservation. [L *sorbus* (the tree), *sorbum* (the fruit)]

sorb[2] *sörb*, *vt* to absorb or adsorb. — *adj* **sorbefacient** (*-i-fā'shənt*) promoting absorption. — Also *n*. — *n* and *adj* **sor'bent**. [L *sorbēre* to suck in, and *faciēns*, *-entis*, pr p of *facere* to make]

sorbaria *sörb-ā'ri-ə*, *n* any shrub of a small Asiatic genus (*Sorbaria*) of deciduous shrubs of the family *Rosaceae*, with long pinnate leaves and large clusters of white flowers. [L *sorbus*; see **sorb**[1]]

sorbate. See under **sorb**[1].

sorbefacient, **sorbent**. See under **sorb**[2].

sorbet *sör'bət* or *sör'bā*, *n* sherbet; water-ice. [Fr, from Ital *sorbetto*; cf **sherbet**]

Sorbian. See under **Sorb**.

sorbic acid. See under **sorb**[1].

Sorbish. See under **Sorb**.

sorbite *sorb'īt* (*metallurgy*), *n* a fine-grained constituent of steel formed of ferrite and cementite, produced by tempering martensite at over 450°C. — *adj* **sorbit'ic**. — *n* **sorbitiza'tion** or **-s-**. — *vt* **sorb'itize** or **-ise** to turn (a metal) into a form containing sorbite.

sorbitol *sör'bi-tol*, *n* a white crystalline substance ($C_6H_8(OH)_6$) derived from (and used as a substitute for) sugar. [**sorb**[1]]

sorbo rubber *sör'bō rub'ər*, *n* a spongy type of rubber. [From **absorb**]

Sorbonne *sor-bon'*, *n* a theological college of the medieval university of Paris, founded in 1253 by Robert of *Sorbon*, long dominant in matters of doctrine, suppressed 1792, revived 1808, seat of the faculties of science and letters (arts). — *adj* **Sorbon'ical** or **Sorbonn'ical**. — *n* **Sor'bonist** or **Sor'bonnist** a doctor or student of the Sorbonne.

sorbus *sörb'əs*, *n* any plant of a large genus of deciduous shrubs and trees (*Sorbus*) of the family *Rosaceae*, *incl* the service tree and the rowan: — *pl* **sorb'uses**. [L; see **sorb**[1]]

sorcery *sör'sə-ri*, *n* divination by the assistance of evil spirits; enchantment; magic; witchcraft. — *n* **sor'cerer**, *fem* **sor'ceress**. — *adj* **sor'cerous**. [OFr *sorcerie*, from L *sors*, *sortis* lot]

sord[1] *sörd* or *sörd*, (*Milton*) *n* a form of **sward**.

sord[2] *sōrd* or *sörd*, *n* a flock of mallard. [OFr *sordre*, from L *surgere* to rise]

sordamente. See under **sordo**.

sordid *sör'did*, *adj* dirty, squalid; mean; meanly avaricious; mercenary; of low or unworthy ideals. — *adv* **sor'didly**. — *n* **sor'didness**. [L *sordidus* dirty]

sordo *sör'dō*, (*music*) *adj* muted, damped: — *fem* **sor'da**. — *adv* **sordamente** (*-dä-men'tā*) gently, softly. — *n* **sordino** (*-dē'nō*) a mute or damper to soften or deaden the sound of an instrument: — *pl* **sordini** (*-nē*). — **con sordino** with mute; **senza sordino** without mute. [Ital, from L *surdus* deaf, noiseless]

sore[1] *sōr* or *sör*, *n* a painful or tender injured or diseased spot; an ulcer or boil; grief; an affliction. — *adj* wounded; tender; readily sensitive to pain; irritable; touchy; painful; afflicted; vexed; irritated; causing pain; painful to contemplate; grievous (*archaic* or *Bible*); aching (*Scot*); bringing sorrow or regret; aggrieved (*colloq*). — *adv* painfully; grievously; severely; distressingly; in distress; hard; eagerly; very much. — *vt* to make sore; to wound. — *adv* **sore'ly**. — *n* **sore'ness**. — **sore'head** (*orig* and *esp NAm*) someone discontented, eg with his reward; an irritable or grumpy person. — *adj* **sore'head'ed**. — **sore point** a subject about which someone feels touchy, angry or aggrieved. — **a sore thumb** something obtrusive, too painful or too awkward to be ignored; **stick out like a sore thumb** (*colloq*) to be painfully obvious, noticeable, etc. [OE *sār*; Ger *sehr* very, ON *sārr* sore]

sore[2], **soar** or **soare** *sōr* or *sör*, (*obs*) *adj* sorrel, reddish-brown; (of hawks, etc) in the reddish-brown first-year plumage. — *n* a hawk in its first year (*obs*); a buck in its fourth year (*Shakesp*). — *n* **sor'age** the first year of a hawk. [Anglo-Fr and OFr *sor* (Fr *saur*, *saure*) sorrel, reddish; cf **sorrel**[2]]

soredium *sō-rē'di-əm* or *sö-*, *n* a small vegetative reproductive body in lichens, consisting of a few algal cells enclosed in fungal hyphae: — *pl* **sorē'dia**. — *adj* **sorē'dial** or **sorē'diate**. [Gr *sōros* a heap]

soree. See **sora**.

sorehon *sōr'hon* or *sör'*, *n* an ancient Irish exaction of free accommodation by a lord from a freeholder or tenant. [See **sorn**]

sorel and **sorell** See **sorrel**[2].

sorex *sō'reks* or *sö'*, *n* any member of the common shrew genus *Sorex*, of the family *Soricidae*. — *adj* **soric'ident** (L *dēns*, *dentis* tooth) having teeth like the shrew. — *adj* **soricine** (*sor'i-sīn* or *-sin*) of the shrew; shrewlike. — *adj* **sor'icoid** (*-koid*) shrewlike. [L *sōrex*, *-icis* shrew; cf Gr *hyrax*]

sorghum *sör'gəm*, *n* any grass of the tropical Old World genus (*Sorghum*) of grasses closely related to sugarcane, including durra and Kaffir corn; molasses made from its juice (*US*). — *n* **sor'go** or **sor'gho** a variety of durra from which sugar is prepared (**sweet sorghum**, or Chinese sugarcane): — *pl* **sor'gos** or **sor'ghos**. [Ital *sorgo*, prob from an E Ind word, or poss from (unattested) vulg L *Syricum* (*grānum*) Syrian (grain)]

sori. See **sorus**.

soricident, **soricine**, **soricoid**. See under **sorex**.

sorites *sō-rī'tēz* or *sö-*, (*logic*) *n* a string of propositions in which the predicate of one is the subject of the next (or the same in reverse order); a sophistical puzzle on the model of 'How many grains make a heap?'. — *adj* **sorit'ic** or **sorit'ical**. [Gr *sōreitēs*, from *sōros* a heap]

sorn *sörn*, (*Scot*) *vi* to obtrude oneself as an uninvited guest. — *n* **sor'ner**. — *n* **sorn'ing**. [Obs Irish *sorthan* free quarters]

soroban *sör'ə-bän*, *n* a Japanese abacus. [From Jap, from Chin words meaning 'calculating board']

soroche *so-rō'chā*, *n* mountain sickness. [Sp, from Quechua *surúcht* antimony (present in the Andes and formerly believed to cause the sickness)]

Soroptimist *sor-opt'i-mist*, *adj* of an international organization of clubs for professional women. — *n* a member of one of these clubs. [L *soror* sister, and **optimist**]

sororal *sor-ō'rəl*, *-ö'*, or **sororial** *-ri-əl*, *adj* sisterly; of or of the nature of a sister. — *n* **soro'rate** (or *sor'ər-āt*) a custom that allows or requires marriage with a wife's sister. — *adv* **soro'rially**. — *n* **sororicide** (*-or'i-sīd*; L *caedere* to kill) the killing or killer of a sister. — *n* **sorority** (*sor-or'i-ti*) a sisterhood; a women's academic society (*US*). — *vi* **sororize** or **-ise** (*sor'ər-īz*) to associate in a sisterly way. — *n* **sorō'sis** (*US*) a women's club. [L *soror* sister]

sorosis *so-*, *sö-* or *sə-rō'sis*, *n* a fleshy fruit formed from a crowd of flowers, as the pineapple. [Gr *sōros* a heap]

sorption *sörp'shən*, *n* ab*sorption* and/or ad*sorption*.

sorra. See **sorrow**.

sorrel[1] *sor'l*, *n* any of the acid-tasting species of herbs of the dock genus, *Rumex* (**common sorrel** *Rumex acetosa*; **sheep's sorrel** *Rumex acetosella*; **French** or **Roman sorrel** *Rumex scutatus*) or the related *Oxyria digyna* (**mountain sorrel**); applied also to other plants such as roselle and wood-sorrel. — **salts of sorrel** a very poisonous combination of potassium acid oxalate and oxalic acid. [OFr *sorele*, *surele* (Fr *surelle*), from *sur* sour, from OHGer *sûr* (Ger *sauer*) sour]

sorrel[2] *sor'l*, *adj* reddish-brown or light chestnut. — *n* a reddish-brown colour; a sorrel horse; (also **sorel** or **sorell** *sōr'el* or *sör'*; *Shakesp*) a buck in its third year. [OFr *sorel*, from *sor* (Fr *saur*, *saure*) sorrel; poss LGer; cf **sore**[2]]

sorrow *sor'ō*, *n* grief, sadness; affliction; pain of mind; lamentation; a person or thing causing any such state of mind; the devil (in imprecations, as an emphatic negative, and applied as a term of abuse; *Irish* **sorra**). — *vt* and *vi* to grieve. — *adj* **sorr'owed** (*Shakesp*) accompanied with sorrow. — *n* **sorr'ower**. — *adj* **sorr'owful** full of sorrow; causing, showing, or expressing sorrow; sad; dejected. — *adv* **sorr'owfully**. — *n* **sorr'owfulness**. — *n* and *adj* **sorr'owing**. — *adj* **sorr'owless** free from sorrow. [OE *sorg*, *sorh*; Ger *Sorge*, ON *sorg*]

sorry *sor'i*, *adj* regretful; expressing pity, sympathy, etc; (often merely formally) apologetic; distressing; poor, miserable, wretchedly bad, contemptible, worthless: — *compar* **sorr'ier**; *superl* **sorr'iest**. — *interj* expressing (often slight) apology; (as a question) I beg your pardon?, what did you say? (*colloq*). — *adv* **sorr'ily**. — *n* **sorr'iness**. — *adj* **sorr'yish**. [OE *sārig* wounded, from *sār* pain; Du *zeerig*; influenced in meaning by **sorrow**, but not connected in origin]

sort *sört*, *n* a class, kind, or species; quality or rank; one, a specimen or instance, of a kind (often ungrammatically in the singular with *these* or *those*, to denote examples of this or that kind); something of the nature but not quite worthy of the name; a letter, stop, or other character in a fount of type; manner; a person (*colloq*); a woman, *esp* an attractive one (*slang*, *orig Austr*); a company, group, collection, parcel (*obs*); a lot (in sortilege) (*Shakesp*). — *vt* to separate into lots or classes; to group, classify, arrange; to pick out, select;

to put in good order; to adjust, put to rights, attend to (*Scot*); to geld; to beat, punish (*colloq*); to deal effectively with (*esp* in a vague threat) (*colloq*); to provide (*Scot*); to procure (*Scot*); to allot, assign (*Shakesp*); to dispose (*Shakesp*); to befit (*rare*). — *vi* to come about, turn out (*obs*); to fit, accord (*rare*); to agree (*Scot*); to consort (*dialect*). — *adj* **sort'able** capable of being sorted; assorted; suitable, befitting (*rare*). — *n* **sort'ance** (*Shakesp*) suitableness, agreement. — *n* **sortā'tion** a sorting out. — *n* **sort'er** someone who (or something which) separates and arranges (eg letters). — *n pl* **sort'es** (*-ēz* or *-ās*) divination by chance opening of the Bible, Homer, Virgil, etc. — *n* and *adj* **sort'ing**. — *n* **sorti'tion** the casting of lots. — *n* **sort'ment** a sorting out; an assortment. — **after a sort** to some extent; **a good sort** a decent fellow; **in a sort** in a manner; **in some sort** in a way; as it were; **in sort** in a body (*Shakesp*); inasmuch (*Spenser*); **of a sort** or **of sorts** vague, rough, inexact; inferior; **out of sorts** out of order, slightly unwell; with some sorts of type in the fount exhausted (*printing*); **sort of** (*colloq*; used adverbially and parenthetically) as it were; to an extent; rather; **sort out** to classify, separate, arrange, etc; to deal with, punish, etc; **that's your sort** that's right; well done; go on. [L *sors*, *sortis* a lot, *sortīrī* to draw lots; partly through OFr]

sortie *sör'ti*, *n* a sally from a besieged party to attack their besiegers; a raiding excursion. — *vi* to sally. [Fr, from *sortir* to go out, to issue]

sortilege *sor'ti-lij*, *n* divination by drawing lots. — *n* **sortil'eger**. — *n* **sortil'egy**. [L *sortilegus* a diviner]

sorus *sō'rəs* or *sö'*, (*bot*) *n* a cluster of sporangia or soredia: — *pl* **so'rī**. — *adj* **so'ral**. [Gr *sōros* a heap]

SOS *es-ō-es'*, *n* an appeal for help or rescue, *esp* at sea by Morse code (...---...). — *vi* to make such an appeal. [Chosen for ease of transmission in Morse]

so-so (or **so so**) *sō'sō*, *adj* neither very good nor very bad; tolerable; indifferent. — Also *adv*. [**so**[1]]

soss *sos*, (*dialect*, *esp Scot*) *n* a mess; a dish of sloppy food; a puddle; a heavy fall; a plump. — *vt* to dirty; to slobber up; to throw carelessly about. — *vi* to plump down; to splash about. — *adv* plump. — *n* **soss'ing**. [Imit]

sostenuto *sos-te-nōō'tō* or *-nū'*, (*music*) *adj* sustained. — *adv* with full time allowed for each note. [Ital]

SOT *abbrev*: stay-on-tab (see under **stay**).

sot[1] *sot*, *n* a fool (*obs*); someone stupefied by alcohol; a habitual drunkard. — *vi* to play the sot. — *adj* **sott'ed** besotted. — *n* **sott'ing**. — *adj* **sott'ish** like a sot; foolish; stupid with drink. — *adv* **sott'ishly**. — *n* **sott'ishness**. [OFr *sot*]

sot[2] *sot* or *sut*, (*Scot*) *adv* the emphatic correlative of *not*, meaning on the contrary, etc, used to contradict a negative assertion. [Variant of **so**[1] influenced by **not**]

Sotadic *sō-tad'ik*, or **Sotadean** *sō-* or *so-tə-dē'ən*, *adj* pertaining to *Sōtadēs*, a lascivious and scurrilous Greek poet (fl. 276 BC), or his writings, or his metre; coarse and scurrilous; palindromic. — *n* a satire in his manner; a catalectic tetrameter of ionics *a majore* (see **Ionic**).

soterial *sō-tē'ri-əl*, (*theol*) *adj* pertaining to salvation. — *adj* **sōtēriolog'ical**. — *n* **sōtēriol'ogy** the doctrine of salvation. [Gr *sōtēriā* salvation, from *sōtēr* a saviour]

Sothic *sō'thik*, *adj* of or pertaining to Sirius. — **Sothic cycle** or **period** a period of 1460 years, after which the beginning of the Egyptian year of 365 days again coincides with the beginning of the **Sothic year**, which was reckoned from the heliacal rising of Sirius. [Egyptian name of Sirius, given in Gr as *Sōthis*]

Sotho *sōō'tōō* or *sō'tō*, *n*. See **Basuto**.

sotted, etc. See under **sot**[1].

sottisier *so-tēz-yā*, *n* a collection of jokes, ridiculous remarks, quotes, etc. [Fr, from *sottise* folly]

sotto voce *sot'tō vō'che*, *adv* in an undertone or aside. [Ital, below the voice]

sou *sōō*, *n* a French five-centime piece (*hist*); a tiny amount of money. [Fr, from L *solidus*; cf **sold**[2], **soldier**, **soldo**]

souari or **saouari** *sow-ä'ri*, *n* a tropical American tree (*Caryocar*) yielding a durable timber and edible butternuts. — **soua'ri-nut** or **saourari-nut** see **butternut** under **butter**[1]. [Fr *saouari*, from Galibi]

soubise *sōō-bēz'*, *n* an 18c cravat; a sauce made from, or a side dish of, puréed onions. [Fr, after the French Marshal Prince de *Soubise* (1715–87)]

soubrette *sōō-bret'*, *n* a pert, coquettish, intriguing maidservant in comedy (*theatre*); a singer of light songs of similar character; a maidservant, lady's maid. [Fr, from Provençal *soubreto* (fem), coy]

soubriquet. See **sobriquet**.

souce, **souct**. Old spellings (*Spenser* and *Shakesp*) of **souse**[2], **soused**.

souchong *sōō-shong'* or *sōō-chong'*, *n* a fine sort of black China tea. [Chin *hsiao* small, and *chung* sort]

Soudanese. Same as **Sudanese**.

souffle *sōō'fl*, (*med*) *n* a murmuring sound heard in auscultation. [Fr]

soufflé *sōō'flā*, *n* a light dish, properly one made with eggwhites whisked into a froth. — *adj* prepared in this style. [Fr, pa p of *souffler*, from L *sufflāre* to blow]

sough[1] *sow* or *suf*, or (*Scot*) *sōōhh*, *vi* to sigh, as the wind does. — *vt* to whine out; to sigh out; to hum. — *n* a sighing of the wind; a deep sigh; a vague rumour; a whining tone of voice. — **keep a calm sough** to keep quiet. [OE *swōgan* to rustle]

sough[2] *suf*, *n* a drain, sewer, adit. — **sough'ing-tile** a drain-tile. [Cf Flem dialect *zoeg* a small ditch]

sought *söt*, *pa t* and *pa p* of **seek**.

souk *sōōk*, *n* among Eastern Muslim people, a market-place. — Also **suk**, **sukh** or **suq**. [Ar *sūq*]

soukous *sōō'kōōs*, *n* a form of Central African dance music, originating in Zaire, heavily influenced by Latin American rhythms. (From Fr *secouer* to shake]

soul *sōl*, *n* that element of a being which thinks, feels, desires, etc, regarded by some as distinct from the physical, material form, and as immortal; a spirit, embodied or disembodied; the ego; innermost being or nature; moral and emotional nature, power, or sensibility; nobleness of spirit or its sincere expression; a complete embodiment or exemplification; the essential part; essence; an element; an indwelling or animating principle; the moving spirit, inspirer, leader; a person (*colloq*); the lungs of a goose, etc; a violin sound-post; (also **soul music**) the popular music *orig* and *esp* of black Americans, typically emotional and earthy, a blend of blues, jazz, gospel and pop elements; life (*obs*). — *adj* of or relating to soul music; of or characteristic of black Americans or their food, music, culture, etc. — *interj* by or upon my soul. — *adj* **souled** having a soul, *esp*, in compounds, of this or that kind. — *adj* **soul'ful** having or expressive of deep or elevated feeling or emotion. — *adv* **soul'fully**. — *n* **soul'fulness**. — *adj* **soul'less** without a soul; (of a person) lacking animation, spirit, or nobleness of mind; (of a place, etc) empty, lifeless, bleak; (of a job) mechanical, dehumanized. — *adv* **soul'lessly** in a soulless manner. — *n* **soul'lessness**. — **soul brother** or **sister** a fellow Black person. — *adj* **soul'-confirming** (*Shakesp*) ratifying the devoting of the soul. — **soul'-cūrer** (*Shakesp*) a parson. — *adj* **soul'-destroying** (of a task, situation, etc) extremely monotonous, unrewarding, etc. — *adj* **soul'-fearing** (*Shakesp*) terrifying the soul. — **soul food** (*US colloq*) food such as chitterlings, cornbread, etc, traditionally eaten by black Americans of the Southern states; **soul'-force** (a term for) satyagraha. — *adj* **soul'-killing** (*Shakesp*). — **soul mate** a person to whom one is deeply emotionally or spiritually attached; **soul music** see **soul** above; **soul'-search'ing** a critical examination of one's actions, motives, etc. — Also *adj*. — **soul'-shot**, **-scot** or **-scat** a payment to the church on behalf of a dead person, a funeral payment. — *adj* **soul'-sick** morally diseased. — **soul'-sleeper** a psychopannychist.

— *adj* **soul'-stirring**. — **upon my soul!** an exclamation of surprise, etc. [OE *sāwol*; Ger *Seele*]

souldan. An old form of **soldan**.

souldier. An old spelling of **soldier**.

soum or **sowm** *sōōm*, (*Scot*) *n* the proportion of sheep or cattle suitable for any pasture; pasture for one cow or its equivalent in sheep, etc. — *vt* and *vi* to determine in terms of soums. — *n* **soum'ing**. — **souming and rouming** the determination of the number of soums appropriate to a common pasture, and their apportionment (according to ability to supply fodder through winter) to the various roums or holdings. [Form of **sum**]

sound[1] *sownd*, *adj* safe; whole; uninjured, unimpaired; in good condition; healthy; wholesome; (of sleep) deep; whole or solid; (of eg a beating) thorough; well-founded; well-grounded; trustworthy; of the right way of thinking, orthodox. — *adv* soundly, completely fast (as in sleep). — *adv* **sound'ly**. — *n* **sound'ness**. — **sound as a bell** see under **bell**[1]. [OE *gesund*; Ger *gesund*]

sound[2] *sownd*, *n* a strait; a fish's swimming bladder. [OE *sund* swimming]

sound[3] *sownd*, *n* the sensation of hearing; a transmitted disturbance perceived or perceptible by the ear; *esp* a tone produced by regular vibrations (as opposed to *noise*); mere noise, without meaning or sense or distinguished from sense; a mental impression; quality or level of noise; (in *pl*) music, *esp* popular (*slang*); spoken commentary, music, etc accompanying visual material such as filmed news footage (*broadcasting* and *cinematog*); radio, as opposed to television (*broadcasting*); earshot. — *vi* to give out a sound; to resound; to be audible; to be sounded; to be famed; to give an impression on hearing; to call, as by trumpet; to tend (*obs*). — *vt* to cause to make a sound; to produce, utter or make the sound of; to utter audibly; to pronounce; to announce, publish, proclaim, celebrate, signal or direct by sound; to mean (*obs*); to examine by percussion and listening (see also **sound**[4]); to tease, goad, provoke (*US slang*). — *n* **sound'er** that which sounds; a telegraph-receiving instrument in which Morse signals are translated into sound signals. — *n* **sound'ing** emission of sound; a signal by trumpet, bell, alarm, etc; examination by percussion. — *adj* making a sound; sonorous; resounding; having a magnificent sound. — *adv* **sound'ingly**. — *adj* **sound'less**. — *adv* **sound'lessly**. — **sound barrier** (*aeronautics*) a resistance met at or about the speed of sound when power required to increase speed rises steeply; **sound'bite** or **sound'-bite** a brief segment on television news in which a reporter, or political figure, etc delivers a short succinct report or statement; **sound board** a thin resonating plate of wood or metal in a musical instrument; (in an organ) the apparatus that conveys the air from the windchest to the appropriate pipes; a sounding board; **sound boarding** boards between joists carrying pugging to make a floor soundproof; **sound body** a resonance box; **sound bow** the thick edge of a bell, against which the hammer strikes; **sound box** a resonance box; part of a gramophone supporting the diaphragm; **sound broadcasting** or **radio** broadcasting by radio as opposed to television; **sound-carrier** a medium, such as a record, tape or compact disc, on which sound is recorded; **sound effects** sounds other than dialogue or music used in films, radio and television; **sound engineer** (*broadcasting*, etc) one responsible for sound; **sound film** a cinema film with a sychronized soundtrack; **sound hole** an *f*-shaped hole in the belly of a stringed musical instrument; **sounding board** a structure for carrying a speaker's voice towards the audience; a soundboard; any person, object or institution used to test the acceptability or effectiveness of an idea, plan, etc; **sound'man** a member of a television or film crew whose job it is to record sound; **sound mixer** the person who controls the tone and volume of sound(s) to be recorded for a motion picture, gramophone record, etc; the machine used in performing this task; **sound poem** a poem consisting of a series of euphonic syllables; **sound poet**; **sound post** a short post connecting the belly and back of a violin, etc, under the bridge. — *adj* **sound'proof** impenetrable by sound. — *vt* to render soundproof. — **sound'-proofing**; **sound radio** sound broadcasting; **sound ranging** (*acoustics*) the calculation of position by timing the arrival of sound waves from (three or more) known positions; **sound shadow** a region of silence behind a barrier to sound; **sound shift** a series of regular changes in stop-consonants differentiating Germanic from other Indo-European languages, or (*second shift*) High German from other Germanic; **sound spectrogram** a record produced by a **sound spectrograph**, an electronic instrument which makes a graphic representation of the qualities of a sound, eg frequency, intensity, etc; **sound spectrography**; **sound stage** the soundproof area of a motion-picture studio on which the actors perform and sets are built; **sound system** an electronic system, *incl* amplifier, speakers and one or more devices for playing recorded sound; a highly sophisticated or accessorized music system, eg a mobile discothèque; **sound'track** (on a cinema film) the magnetic tape on which sounds are recorded; a recording of the sound (*esp* musical) accompaniment to a film; **sound wave** a longitudinal disturbance propagated through air or other medium. — **sound off** (**about** or **on**) to speak loudly and freely (about or on), *esp* in complaint; to boast. [ME *soun*, from Anglo-Fr, from L *sonus*; for *d* cf **pound**[3]]

sound[4] *sownd*, *vt* to measure the depth of; to probe; to examine with a sound (*med*); to try to discover the inclinations, thoughts, etc, of (*esp* with *out*). — *vi* to take soundings; to dive deep (of eg a whale). — *n* (*med*) a probe for examining the bladder, etc. — *n* **sound'er** a person who sounds; apparatus for taking soundings. — *n* **sound'ing** the action of something which or someone who sounds; an ascertained depth; (in *pl*) waters in which an ordinary sounding line will reach the bottom; a test or measurement of depth, *esp* of water by means of an echo-sounder or sounding line; penetrating a particular environment to obtain sample readings, eg of temperature; (*usu* in *pl*; also with *out*) sample testing of opinion, inclination, etc, *usu* of an unofficial kind. — **sounding lead** the weight at the end of a sounding line; **sounding line** a line with a plummet at the end for soundings; **sounding rocket** a rocket devised to gather high-altitude meteorological data and to radio it back to earth; **sounding rod** a rod for measuring water in a ship's hold. [OE *sund-* (in compounds), cf **sound**[2]; or perh OFr *sonder* to sound, which may be from Gmc]

sound[5] *sownd*, (*obs*) *n* and *vi*. Same as **swound**. See **swoon**.

sounder *sown'dər*, *n* a herd of pigs; a young boar. [OFr *sundre*; of Gmc origin; cf OE *sunor*]

soup *sōōp*, *n* any liquid food made by stewing pieces of meat, vegetables or grains; loosely, anything resembling soup in consistency, etc; a photographic developer (*slang*); stolen plate melted down (*slang*); nitroglycerine (*US slang*). — *n* **soup'er** in Ireland, someone who dispenses soup as a means of proselytizing; a person really or supposedly converted in this way. — *adj* **soup'y**. — *adj* **soup'ed-up** (*slang*) (of eg an engine) having had the power increased; enlivened. — **soup kitchen** a place for supplying soup to the poor; a mobile kitchen (*military*); **soup maigre** (or **meagre**) a thin fish or vegetable soup, originally for fast days; **soup plate** a large deep plate for serving soup; **soup'-spoon** a spoon with a large, rounded bowl for taking soup; **soup'-ticket** a ticket entitling someone to eat at a soup kitchen; **soup tureen**. — **in the soup** in difficulties or trouble; **soup up** (*slang*) to increase the power of; to enliven; **the ticket for soup** (*slang*) the ticket (qv). [OFr *soupe*; cf **sop**]

soupçon *sōōp-sɔ̃*, *n* a hardly perceptible quantity, a dash. [Fr, suspicion]

souple[1] *sōōp'l*, *adj* a dialect form of **supple**[1]; (of silk) lightly scoured; clever (*Scot*). — *vt* to make supple or souple.
souple[2] *sōōp'l*, *n* a Scots form of **swipple**; a cudgel (*Scott*).
sour *sowr*, *adj* having an acid taste or smell; turned, rancid or fermented; rank; (of animals) heavy, strong; cold and wet; embittered, crabbed, or peevish; disagreeable; inharmonious (*lit* and *fig*); bad, unsuccessful; containing sulphur compounds. — *vt* to make sour; to treat with dilute acid. — *vi* to become sour. — *n* an acid drink, such as a gin or whisky cocktail that contains lemon or lime juice; an acid solution used in bleaching, curing skins, etc. — *n* **sour'ing** the process of turning or becoming sour; vinegar; the crab-apple; treatment with dilute acid in bleaching. — *adj* **sour'ish**. — *adv* **sour'ishly**. — *adv* **sour'ly**. — *n* **sour'ness**. — *adj* **sour'-cold** (*Shakesp*). — **sour cream** cream soured by a ferment; **sour'-crout** see **sauerkraut**; **sour'dough** leaven; a piece of dough reserved to leaven a new batch; in Canada and Alaska, an old-timer. — *adj* **sour'-eyed** morose-looking. — **sour gas** (*min ext*) natural gas containing impurities, mainly hydrogen sulphide; **sour'-gourd** the cream of tartar tree; a tropical grass related to millet; sorrel; **sour grapes** disdain, peevishly affected, for something one would have liked to have, participate in, etc; **sour mash** (*US*) new mash mixed with old to increase acidity and promote fermentation; **sour'puss** (*slang*) a sour-tempered person. [OE *sūr*; Ger *sauer*, ON *sūrr*]
source *sōrs* or *sörs*, *n* a spring; the head of a stream; an origin; a rise; (*Spenser* **sourse**) *perh* a surging; an originating cause; something from which anything rises or originates; a book or document serving as authority for history, or furnishing matter or inspiration for an author; any person, publication, etc, providing information. — *vt* (in *passive*) to come from, originate; to obtain (from a particular source). — *n* **sourc'ing**. — **source'book** a book of original documents for (*esp* historic) study; **source code** a computer code that requires translation by a compiler before it can be executed by the computer (cf **object code**). [OFr *sorse* (Fr *source*), from *sourdre*, from L *surgere* to rise]
sourdeline *sōōr'də-lēn*, *n* a small bagpipe. [Fr]
sourdine *sōōr-dēn'*, (*music*) *n* a mute or sordino. [Fr; cf **sordino** under **sordo**]
sourock *sōō'rək*, (*Scot*) *n* sorrel (the plant). [**sour**]
sourse. See **source**.
soursop *sow'ər-sop*, *n* a W Indian tree of the *Anona* species; its large, sour, pulpy fruit. [**sour** and **sop**]
sousaphone *sōō'zə-fōn*, *n* a large tubalike brass wind instrument invented by the American bandmaster and composer J P *Sousa* (1854–1932).
sous-chef *sōō'shef*, *n* a chef next in rank to the head chef in a hotel, restaurant, etc. [Fr *sous* under, and **chef**]
souse[1] or **sous** *sows*, (*obs*) *n*. Same as **sou**: — *pl* **souse** or **sous'es**.
souse[2] *sows*, *vt* to pickle; to marinade and cook in spiced wine or vinegar; to plunge, immerse or duck; to drench or soak; to make drunk; to dash; to fling down; to smite; to swoop down upon. — *vi* to be drenched or soaked; to wash oneself thoroughly; to get drunk; to strike; to impinge; to fall heavily; to swoop like a hawk. — *n* pickled meat, *esp* pig's feet or ears; an ear (*dialect* or *facetious*); pickling liquid; a plunge in pickling or other liquid; a ducking or drenching; a wash; a sluicing with water; a getting drunk (*slang*); a drunkard (*US*); a heavy blow or fall; a thump; an impact; a rising from the ground, taking wing (in the falconer's phrase *at souse*, *at the souse*, when the hawk gets a chance of striking); hence, the downward swoop of a bird of prey. — *adv* with a plunge; with a heavy impact; plump; suddenly. — *adj* **soused** pickled; very wet; drunk (*slang*). — *n* and *adj* **sous'ing**. — Also **souce**, **sowce**, **sowse**, **sowsse** in old writers. [Partly OFr *sous*, *souce*, from OHGer *sulza*, from the root of **salt**[1]; partly imit (cf German *Saus*); partly **source** in its old sense of rising]
souslik. Same as **suslik**.
sout (*Spenser*). Same as **soot**[1].
soutache *sōō-täsh'*, *n* a narrow braid used for trimming. [Fr]
soutane *sōō-tän'*, *n* a cassock. [Fr, from Ital *sottana*, from L *subtus* beneath]
soutar. See **souter**.
souteneur *sōōt'nœr*, *n* a prostitute's bully or exploiter. [Fr, supporter, protector; cf **sustain**]
souter *sōō'tər*, (*Scot*) *n* a shoemaker, a cobbler. — Also **sow'ter** or **sou'tar**. — *adj* **sou'terly**. — **souter's clod** (*Scott*) a brown wheaten roll. [OFr *sūtere* (ON *sūtari*), from L *sūtor*, from *suere* to sew]
souterrain *sōō-te-rɛ̃* or *sōō'tə-rān*, *n* an underground chamber; an earth-house. [Fr]
south *sowth*, *adv* in the direction directly opposite to (ie 180° from) north. — *n* the point of the horizon, the region, or the part, in that direction; the south wind; (with *cap* and **the**); the Southern States of the USA. — *adj* lying towards the south; forming the part, or that one of two, that is towards the south; blowing from the south; (of a pole of a magnet, *usu*) south-seeking. — *vi* (*sowdh*) to move or veer towards the south; to cross the meridian. — *n* **souther** (*sowdh'ər*) a south wind or gale. — *vi* (*sudh'ər*) to move or veer towards the south. — *adj* **southering** (*sudh'*). — *n* **southerliness** (*sudh'*). — *adj* and *adv* **southerly** (*sudh'*) towards or (of wind) from the south. — *adj* **southern** (*sudh'*) of the south; in the south or in the direction toward it; (of wind) from the south; (with *cap*) of, from or pertaining to the South — *n* a southerner. — *n* **southerner** (*sudh'*) a native or inhabitant of the south; (with *cap*) an inhabitant of the US South. — *n* **southernism** (*sudh'*) a form of expression peculiar to the south, *esp* the Southern States of the US. — *vt* **southernize** or **-ise** (*sudh'*) to render southern in character. — *adj* **southernly** (*sudh'*) southerly. — *adv* towards the south. — *adj* (*superl*) **south'ermost** (*rare*) or **southernmost** (*sudh'*). — *n* **southing** (*sowdh'*) distance, deviation, tendency or motion to the south; meridian passage. — *adj* (*superl*) **south'most**. — *adj* **southron**, **Southron** or **Southroun** (*sudh'rən*; *Scot*) southern, *esp* English as distinguished from Scots. — *n* a southerner; an Englishman; the English of England. — *adj*, *adv* and *n* **southward** (*sowth'wərd* or (*naut*) *sudh'ərd*). — *adj* and *adv* **south'wardly**. — *adv* **south'wards**. — *adj* **southbound** (*sowth'*) travelling in a southward direction. — *adj* and *adv* **south-east'** (or *sowth'*) midway between south and east. — *n* the direction midway between south and east; the region lying in, the wind blowing from, that direction. — **south-east'er** a strong wind from the south-east. — *adj* and *adv* **south-east'erly** towards or (of wind) from the south-east. — *adj* **south-east'ern** belonging to, or being in, the south-east, or in that direction. — *adj* and *adv* **south-east'ward** towards the south-east. — *n* the region to the south-east. — *adj* and *adv* **south-east'wardly**. — *adj* **south-east'wards**. — **Southern Cross** a conspicuous southern constellation with four bright stars placed crosswise; **southernwood** (*sudh'*) an aromatic S European shrub (*Artemisia abrotanum*), of the wormwood genus; **southland** (*sowth'*) the south (also *adj*); **south'lander**. — *adj* (*colloq*) **south'paw** left-handed; (in boxing) leading with the right hand. — *n* (*colloq*) a left-handed person, *esp* in sport; a boxer who leads with his right hand. — *adj* **south'-pōlar**. — **south pole** the end of the earth's axis in Antarctica; its projection on the celestial sphere (*astron*); (*usu*) the south-seeking pole of a magnet (logically the north-seeking); **South Sea** the Pacific ocean. — *adj* **south-seeking** (*sowth'*) turning towards the earth's magnetic south pole. — *n*, *adj* and *adv* **south-south-east'** in a direction midway between south and south-east. — *n*, *adj* and *adv* **south-south-west'** in a direction midway between south and south-west. — *adj* and *adv* **south-west** (*sowth'* or *sow'*, also *-west'*) midway between south and west. — *n* the direction between south and west; the region lying that way; the wind blowing from that direction. — **south-west'er** a gale from the south-west (see also separate entry

sou'wester). — *adj* **south-west'erly** toward or (of wind) from the south-west. — *adj* **south-west'ern** belonging to, or lying in, the south-west or in that direction. — *adj, adv* and *n* **south-west'ward**. — *adj* and *adv* **south-west'wardly**. — *adv* **south-west'wards**. — **south by east** (or **west**) one compass point east (or west) of south. [OE *sūth*; Ger *süd*, ON *suthr*]

Southcottian *sowth-kot'i-ən*, *n* a follower of Joanna *Southcott* (1750–1814) who was expected to give birth to a Shiloh or Prince of Peace. — Also *adj*.

Southdown *sowth'down*, *adj* pertaining to the *South Downs* in Hampshire and Sussex, the famous breed of sheep so named, or their mutton. — *n* a sheep of this breed, or its mutton.

southerly, **southern**, etc. See under **south**.

Southern blot *suth'ərn blot*, (*biol*) *n* a technique for the identification and isolation of DNA fragments. [From its pioneer, E M Southern (1938–), British molecular biologist]

southsay, etc. Same as **soothsay**, etc.

souvenir *sōō'və-nēr* or *-nēr'*, *n* a memento; an item kept as a reminder of a place, occasion, etc. — *vt* (*Austr* and *NZ*; *colloq*) to collect as a 'souvenir', to steal, purloin. [Fr *souvenir*, from L *subvenīre* to come up, to come to mind, from *sub* under, and *venīre* to come]

sou'-wester *sow-wes'ter*, *n* a gale from the south-west (*colloq*; *esp naut*); a waterproof hat with a large flap at the back of the neck, as worn by seamen. [Orig *southwester*]

souvlaki *sōōv-lä'kē*, or **souvlakia** *ki-a*, *n* a Greek dish of lamb, similar to a shish kebab: — *pl* **souvla'ki** or **souvla'kia**. [Gr *soubláki*, pl *soublákia*, dimin of *soúbla* a skewer]

sov. See **sovereign**.

sovenance *sōō'və-näns*, (*archaic*) *n* remembrance, memory. [OFr *sovenance* (Fr *souvenance*, from *so(u)venir*, see **souvenir**]

sovereign *sov'rin* or *sov'rən*, *n* a supreme ruler or head; a monarch; an Irish mayor (*obs*); a gold coin (from the time of Henry VII to Charles I worth 22s. 6d. to 10s., from 1817–1914 a pound sterling; *colloq* short form **sov** *sov*). — *adj* supreme; excelling all others; having supreme power residing in itself, himself or herself; of sovereignty; highly efficacious. — *adv* **sov'ereignly** supremely; as a sovereign. — *n* **sov'ereignty** pre-eminence; supreme and independent power; the territory of a sovereign or of a sovereign state. [OFr *sovrain* and Ital *sovrano*, from L *super* above]

soviet *sō'vi-ət* or *sov'yet* *n* a council, *esp* one of those forming the machinery of local and national government in the former Union of Soviet Socialist Republics, the local councils elected by workers, peasants, and soldiers, the higher councils consisting of deputies from the lower. — *adj* (with *cap*) of or relating to the USSR. — *adj* **soviet'ic**. — *n* **so'vietism** the principles and practices of a soviet government, *specif* communism; a characteristic mannerism indicative of soviet ideology. — *vt* **so'vietize** or **-ise** to transform to the soviet model. — *adj* **Sovietolog'ical** (also without *cap*). — *n* **Sovietol'ogist** (also without *cap*) a person making a special study of the theory and practice of government in the USSR and of Soviet affairs. — **Supreme Soviet** see under **supreme**. [Russ *sovet* council]

sovran *sov'ran*, *n*. An *archaic* and *poetic* form of **sovereign**. — *adv* **sov'ranly**. — *n* **sov'ranty**.

sow[1] *sow*, *n* a female pig; the female of various other animals, eg the badger; an abusive term for a fat, lazy, greedy, or sluttish person, *esp* a woman; a main channel for molten iron, leading to metal pigs (qv); the metal solidified there; a movable shed for protecting besiegers (*military hist*). — **sow'back** (*geol*) same as **hogback**; **sow'bread** a cyclamen, *esp Cyclamen europaeum*, so called because its tubers are eaten by pigs; **sow bug** (*NAm*) a woodlouse. — *adj* **sow'-drunk** (*colloq*) beastly drunk. — *n* and *adj* **sow'-skin**. — **sow thistle** a thistle-like genus of plants (*Sonchus*) with milky juice, yellow flowers and prickly leaves. [OE *sū*, *sugu*; Ger *Sau*, ON *syr*; L *sūs*, Gr *hȳs*]

sow[2] *sō*, *vt* to scatter on, or put in, the ground; to plant by strewing; to scatter seed over; to spread, strew, disseminate. — *vi* to scatter seed for growth: — *pa t* **sowed** (*sōd*); *pa p* **sown** (*sōn*) or **sowed**. — *n* **sow'er**. — *n* **sow'ing**. — **sow the seeds of** to initiate or implant. [OE *sāwan*; Ger *säen*, ON *sā*, Gothic *saian*]

sowans. See **sowens**.

sowar *sō-wär'*, (*Anglo-Ind*) *n* an Indian trooper, mounted policeman, or attendant. — *n* **sowarr'y** or **sowarr'ee** a mounted retinue, cavalcade. [Urdu *sawār* horseman]

sowce. See **souse**[2].

sowens or **sowans** *sō'ənz*, (*Scot*) *n pl* a dish made from the farina remaining among the husks of oats, flummery. [Supposed to be from Gaelic *sùghan*, the liquid of sowens, from *sùgh* juice]

sowf, **sowff**. See **sowth**.

sowl, **sowle**. See **sole**[4].

sowm. See **soum**.

sownd[1] *sownd*, (*Spenser*) *vt appar*, to wield.

sownd[2] *sownd*, (*Spenser*) *n*. Same as **swound**, **swoon**.

sowne *sown*, (*Spenser*) *n*. Same as **sound**[3].

sowp *sowp*, (*Scot*) *n* a spoonful, sip, small drink. [ON *saup*; cf **sop**, **sup**]

sowse or **sowsse** *sows*, (*Spenser*; *Shakesp*) *v* and *n*. Same as **souse**[2].

sowter. See **souter**.

sowth *sowth*, (*Scot*) *vi* and *vt* to whistle or hum over softly. — Also **sowf** or **sowff** (*sowf*). [Scots forms of obs *solf*, from Fr *solfier* to sol-fa]

sox *soks*, *n pl*. A slang spelling of **socks**.

soy *soi*, or **soya** *sō'yə* or *soi'ə*, also **soja** *sō'yə* or *sō'jə*, *n* a dark, salty sauce made from fermented soy beans and wheat flour (also **soy** (or **soya**) **sauce**); the soy bean, rich in oil and protein; the eastern Asiatic papilionaceous plant (*Glycine soja*, *Glycine hispida* or *max*) producing it. — *adj* made from soy beans or soy flour. — **soy** (or **soya**) **bean**; **soy** (or **soya**) **flour**. [Jap *shō-yu*, colloq *soy*, Du *soya*, *soja*, from Chin *shi-yu* salt bean oil]

soyle *soil*, (*Spenser*) *n* apparently body or prey. [Unexplained]

Soyuz *sö'yōōz*, (*space*) *n* a vehicle used by the former USSR for ferrying crews to and from its orbiting space stations. [Russ *soyúz* union]

sozzle *soz'l*, *vt* (*NAm* and *dialect*) to splash; to make sloppy; to intoxicate; to perform sluttishly. — *n* (*NAm* and *dialect*) slops; sluttishness; a slattern. — *adj* **sozz'led** (*colloq*) drunk. — *adj* **sozz'ly** (*NAm* and *dialect*) sloppy. [Cf **soss**]

SP *abbrev*: starting price.

sp *abbrev*: *sine prole* (*L*), without issue.

sp. *abbrev*: species (*pl* **spp**.); spelling.

spa *spä*, formerly *spö*, *n* a mineral spring; a resort where such a spring is located; a heated bath or pool of aerated water (also **spa bath** or **pool**); a device which circulates water or some other solution in which parts of the body may be immersed or bathed, such as *foot spa*. — *vi* to stay at a spa. — *n* **spa'ing**. — **spa town**. [*Spa* in Belgium]

SPAB *abbrev*: Society for the Protection of Ancient Buildings.

space *spās*, *n* that in which material bodies have extension; a portion of such; room; intervening distance; an interval; an open or empty place; regions remote from the earth; an interval between lines or words; a type used for making such an interval (*printing*); an interval between the lines of the stave (*music*); see **mark** (*telecomm*); a portion, extent, or interval of time; a short time; opportunity, leisure (*colloq*). — *vt* to make, arrange, or increase intervals between. — *vi* (*Spenser*) to walk about. — *adj* **spaced**. — *adj* **space'less**. — *n* **spac'er** someone who, or something which, spaces; an instrument for reversing a telegraphic current; a space bar; a space traveller or spacecraft (*science fiction*); a spacer plate (see below). — *adj* **spacial** (*spā'shl*) spatial.

— *n* **spacing** (*spās'ing*) a space or spatial arrangement; the existence or arrangement of spaces, or of objects in spaces. — *adj* **spacious** (*spā'shəs*) of a great extent or area; ample; roomy; wide; broad in scope. — *adv* **spa'ciously**. — *n* **spa'ciousness**. — *adj* **spac'y** or **spac'ey** (*slang*; chiefly *NAm*) dreamy; behaving as if spaced out; eccentric, unconventional. — **space age** the present time when exploration of, and ability to travel in, space up to the limit of and beyond the earth's atmosphere are increasing. — *adj* **space'-age** characteristic of the space age; very modern, up-to-date, using sophisticated modern technology. — **space band** a wedge for justifying the line in mechanical type-setting; **space bar** a bar on a typewriter or computer keyboard which is pressed to insert a space. — *adj* **space'borne** carried through space; effected or operated in space. — **space cadet** a trainee spaceman or spacewoman; a space-travel enthusiast; a person habitually high on drugs; **space'craft** a vehicle, manned or unmanned, designed for putting into space, orbiting the earth, or reaching other planets. — *adj* **space'faring** concerned with or engaged in space travel. — Also *n*. — **space heater** a device which warms the air in a room or similar enclosed area; **space-heat'ing**; **Space Invaders®** an electronic video game, involving 'shooting' at graphic representations of supposed invaders from outer space; **space lattice** an arrangement of points in three-dimensional space at the intersections of equally spaced parallel lines — such as the arrangement of atoms in a crystal disclosed by X-ray spectroscopy; **space'man** or **space'woman** a traveller in space; **space medicine** branch of medicine concerned with effects of conditions in space on the human body; **space'plane** a craft (eg HOTOL and the space shuttle) designed to take off like a plane, enter into space orbit (eg to deliver pay-loads) and return to earth landing horizontally like a glider; **space platform** or **space station** a platform in space planned as an observatory and/or a landing-stage in space travel; **space probe** a spacecraft designed to obtain, and *usu* transmit, information about the environment into which it is sent; **spacer plate** (*archaeol*) a flat bead, eg of jet or amber, with several parallel holes, for separating the threads of a multi-string necklace; **space'ship** a spacecraft; **space shuttle** a spacecraft designed to transport men and materials to and from space stations, in-orbit experiments, satellite repair, etc; **space station** see **space platform**; **space'suit** a suit specially designed for use in space travel; **space-time'** normal three-dimensional space plus dimension of time, modified by gravity in relativity theory; **space-time continuum** physical space or reality, regarded as having four dimensions (length, breadth, height and time) in which an event can be represented as a point fixed by four co-ordinates; **space travel**; **space traveller**; **space travelling**; **space vehicle** see under **vehicle**; **space walk** an excursion by an astronaut outside his or her craft while in space. — *vi* **space'-walk**. — **space writer** a writer paid according to the space filled; **spacious times** days of expansion (in knowledge, trade, etc) and scope (for discovery, adventure, and the like), as in the reign of Queen Elizabeth I. — **space out** to set wide apart or wider apart; to lapse into a drugged, dazed, delirious or light-headed state; **spaced out** (*slang*) in a dazed or stupefied state (as if) caused by the taking of drugs. [Fr *espace*, from L *spatium*; Gr *spaein* to draw]

spadassin *spad'ə-sin*, *n* a swordsman, a bravo. [Fr, from Ital *spadaccino*, from *spada* a sword]

spade[1] *spăd*, *n* a broad-bladed digging tool; a whaler's knife; a spade's depth or spit. — *vt* to dig or remove with a spade. — *n* **spade'ful** as much as a spade will hold: — *pl* **spade'fuls**. — *adj* **spade'like**. — *n* **spa'der**. — **spade bone** another name for the scapula; **spade'fish** a marine fish (*Chaetodipterus*, *esp Chaetodipterus faber*) of N American coastal waters, having a deep, flattened body; **spade foot** a rectangular, spade-shaped furniture foot; **spade guinea** a guinea with spade-shaped shield, coined 1787–99; **spade'man** or **spades'man** a worker with the spade; **spade'work** preparatory drudgery. — **call a spade a spade** to speak plainly without euphemism. [OE *spadu*, *spædu*; related to Gr *spathē* (see **spade**[2])]

spade[2] *spăd*, *n* a playing card with black leaf-shaped (on Spanish cards sword-shaped) pips; (*offensive*) a Black or other coloured person. — **in spades** (*orig US slang*) extremely, emphatically; to a great(er) extent. [Sp *espada* sword, from L *spatha*, from Gr *spathē* a broad blade]

spade[3]. See **spado**.

spade[4]. See **spayad**.

spadger *spaj'ər*, (*slang*) *n* a sparrow. [Form of **sparrow**]

spadices, **spadiceous**, etc. See under **spadix**.

spadille *spə-dil'*, *n* the ace of spades in the games of ombre and quadrille. — Also (*obs*) **spadill'o** or **spadill'io**. [Fr, from Sp *espadilla*, dimin of *espada*; see **spade**[2]]

spadix *spā'diks*, (*bot*) *n* a fleshy spike of flowers: — *pl* **spādices** (*-dī'sēz*). — *adj* **spadiceous** (*spā-dish'əs*) having, like, of the nature of, a spadix; coloured like a date; shaped like a palm branch. — *adj* **spadicifloral** (*spā-dī-si-flō'rəl* or *-flö'*) having flowers in a spathe, as do arum, palms, and some other monocotyledons. [Gr *spādix*, *-īkos* a torn-off (palm) branch, in L date-coloured, bay]

spado *spā'dō* or *spä'*, *n* a castrated or impotent person or animal: — *pl* **spadones** (*spä-dō'nēz* or *-nās*), **spā'dos** or **spā'does**. — Also (*rare*) **spade**. [L *spadō*, *-ōnis*, from Gr *spadōn*, *-ōnos*, from *spaein* to pull, tear]

spadroon *spə-drōōn'*, (*hist*) *n* a cut-and-thrust sword; swordplay with it. [Fr (Genevan dialect) *espadron*]

spae *spā*, (*Scot*) *vt* and *vi* to foretell, divine. — *n* **spā'er**. — **spae'man**; **spae'wife** a, *usu* old, woman supposed to be able to tell the future. [ON *spā*]

spag *spăg*, (*Austr offensive slang*) *n* an Italian person. — *adj* pertaining to anything Italian. [From *spag*hetti]

spageric. See **spagyric**.

spaghetti *spä-* or *spə-get'i*, *n* pasta in the form of long cordlike strings intermediate between macaroni and vermicelli. — *adj* denoting similarity to spaghetti, *esp* in terms of numerous intertwining strands, etc. — **spaghetti bolognese** (*bol-on-yāz'* or *bol-ən-āz'*), in full **spaghetti alla bolognese** (*al-a*), spaghetti served with a meat and tomato sauce; **spaghetti western** a film about the American west, *usu* made in Europe by an Italian director, characterized by a violent and melodramatic content and a baroque style. [Ital, pl of *spaghetto*, dimin of *spago* a cord]

spagyric or **spagyrical** *spə-jir'ik*, *-əl*, *adj* alchemical. — *n* **spagyr'ic** or **spagyrist** (*spaj'ər-ist*) an alchemist. — Also **spagir'ic**, **spager'ic**, etc. [Prob coined by Paracelsus]

spahi or **spahee** *spä'hē*, *n* formerly, a Turkish or French Algerian cavalryman. [Turk (from Pers) *sipāhi*; cf **sepoy**]

spain. See **spane**.

spairge. See **sparge**.

spake *spāk*. See **speak**.

spald. See **spauld**.

spale *spāl*, (*Scot*) *n* a splinter; a chip. [See **spall**[1]]

spall[1] *spöl*, *vt* and *vi* to split or splinter, to chip. — *n* a chip or splinter, *esp* of stone. — *n* **spallā'tion** (*phys*) a nuclear reaction in which bombardment by high-energy particles produces a large number of disintegration particles not entirely identifiable. — *n* **spall'ing** the breaking off of fragments of stone or concrete from a surface, *usu* caused by water ingress through fine cracks (*building*, *civ eng*); the process of breaking off splinters from a block of stone being dressed. — *vt* and *vi* **spalt** to split, splinter. — *adj* brittle. — *adj* **spalt'ed**. [Cf ME *spalden* to split; Ger *spalten*]

spall[2], **spalle**. See **spauld**.

spalpeen *spal-pēn'*, *n* a rascal, a mischievous fellow; a boy. [Irish *spailpín* a (migratory) labourer]

spalt, **spalted**. See under **spall**[1].

Spam® *spam*, *n* a type of luncheon meat made from pork, spices, etc. — *adj* **spammy** tasting of, containing or like spam or luncheon meat; loosely, bland, unexciting, corny (*colloq*). [*Sp*iced *ham*]

span[1] *span*, *n* the total spread or stretch; the distance between abutments, piers, supports, etc, or the portion of a structure (eg a bridge) between; the distance between the wing tips of an aeroplane; a stretch of time, *esp* of life; the space from the end of the thumb to the end of the little finger when the fingers are extended; nine inches. — *vt* to stretch over; to arch over; to bridge; to encompass; to measure by spans; to measure: — *pr p* **spann'ing**; *pa t* and *pa p* **spanned**. — *adj* **span'less** that cannot be spanned or measured. — **span'-counter** or **span'-farthing** a game in which one tries to throw a counter or coin within a span of one's opponent's. — **span loading** (*aerodynamics*) the gross weight of an aircraft divided by the square of the span. — *adj* **span'-long** of the length of a span. — **span roof** a roof with equal slopes. [OE *spann*; cf Ger *Spanne*]

span[2] *span*, *n* a pair of horses; a team of oxen. — *vt* to yoke; to wind up (*obs*). [Du and LGer *span*]

span[3] *span*, *adj* fresh, short for **span new** quite new, new as a fresh-cut chip. — **spick and span** see under **spick**[1]. [ON *spān-nӯr*, from *spān* chip (cf **spoon**[2]), *nӯr* new]

span[4] *span*. See **spin**.

spanaemia *span-ē'mi-ə*, *n* deficiency of red corpuscles in the blood. — *adj* **spanae'mic**. [Gr *spanos* lacking, and *haima* blood]

spancel *span'sl*, *n* a hobble, *esp* for a cow. — *vt* to hobble. — *adj* **span'celled**. [Du or LGer *spansel*, from *spannen* to stretch]

spandex *span'deks*, *n* a synthetic elastic fibre made chiefly from polyurethane; (with *cap*; ®) a fabric made from this fibre. [Metathesis of **expand**]

spandrel or **spandril** *span'drəl*, *n* the space between the curve of an arch and the enclosing mouldings, string-course, or the like (*archit*); a self-contained area of surface space (*esp* triangular) available for decorative use, eg in graphic design or forming part of a structure. [Poss connected with **expand**]

spane, **spain** or **spean** *spān*, (*Scot*) *vt* to wean. [MDu or MLGer *spanen*, or OFr *espanir*; cf Ger *spänen*]

spang[1] *spang*, *n* a glittering ornament (*obs*); a clasp (*archaic*). — *vt* (*obs*) to sprinkle with spangs. — *n* **spangle** (*spang'gl*) a small, thin, glittering plate of metal; a sequin; a sparkling speck, flake, or spot. — *vt* to decorate with spangles. — *vi* to glitter. — *adj* **spang'led**. — *n* **spang'ler**. — *n* **spang'let** (*Shelley*). — *n* and *adj* **spang'ling**. — *adj* **spang'ly**. [OE *spang* clasp; cf Du *spang*, Ger *Spange*, *Spängel*]

spang[2] *spang*, (*dialect, esp Scot*) *n* a bound; a leap; a sudden movement or blow; a bang. — *vi* to bound, spring. — *vt* to dash; to fling; to throw or cause to spring into the air. — *adv* (*NAm*) bang, exactly, straight, absolutely. — **spang'-cockle** the flicking of a marble, etc, from the forefinger with the thumbnail. — *vt* **spang'hew** to fling into the air, *esp* in a seesaw game using a plank, *orig* from a practice of torturing frogs using a stick. [Origin obscure, perhaps connected with **spring**[1] and **spank**[2]]

spangle, etc. See under **spang**[1].

Spaniard *span'yərd*, *n* a native or citizen of *Spain*; a Spanish ship (*archaic*). [ME *Spaignarde*, from OFr *Espaignart*]

spaniel *span'yəl*, *n* a kind of dog, *usu* liver-and-white, or black-and-white, with large pendent ears; a fawning person. — *adj* like a spaniel; fawning, mean. — *vt* (*Shakesp*) to follow or fawn on like a spaniel. — *vi* (or *vt* with *it*) to play the spaniel. — *adj* and *adv* **span'iel-like**. — **Blenheim spaniel** a red-and-white spaniel named from the Duke of Marlborough's seat; **Cavalier King Charles spaniel** a larger variety of King Charles spaniel; **clumber spaniel** a lemon-and-white spaniel formerly bred at *Clumber*, Notts; **field-** or **land-spaniel** hunting breeds (eg *cockers*, *springers*); **(Irish) water-spaniel** a (liver-coloured) spaniel for retrieving water fowl; **King Charles spaniel** a black-and-tan spaniel, made fashionable by *Charles II*; **Sussex spaniel** a golden-liver or brown spaniel; **toy spaniel** any of the smaller breeds (eg *Blenheim*, *King Charles*). [OFr *espaigneul* (Fr *épagneul*), from Sp *Espanôl* Spanish]

spaniolate *span'yō-lāt*, or **spaniolize** or **-ise** *-līz*, *vt* to hispanicize. [OFr *Espaignol* a Spaniard]

Spanish *span'ish*, *adj* of or pertaining to *Spain*. — *n* the language of Spain. — **Spanish bayonet** a yucca with straight sword-shaped leaves; **Spanish broom** a Mediterranean shrub (*Spartium junceum*) resembling broom, with showy yellow fragrant flowers; **Spanish chalk** soapstone, French chalk; **Spanish chestnut** the true chestnut; **Spanish cress** a species of pepperwort; **Spanish customs** see **Spanish practices** below; **Spanish dagger** *Yucca gloriosa*; **Spanish fly** the blister beetle, *Lytta vesicatoria*; a preparation made from the dried bodies of these beetles yielding cantharides (qv) formerly used medicinally to produce blisters or as an aphrodisiac; **Spanish fowl** a breed of domestic hen, also called *white-faced black Spanish*; **Spanish grass** esparto; **Spanish influenza** a severe form of influenza, which, first noted in Spain, spread all over the world in 1918; **Spanish Inquisition** see under **inquisition**; **Spanish juice** extract of liquorice root; **Spanish Main** (ie mainland) the mainland coast of the Caribbean Sea; often (popularly) the Caribbean Sea itself; **Spanish moss** any of various plants which grow in tropical and subtropical areas in long, trailing strands from tree branches — *esp Usnea longissima* or *Tillandsia usneoides*; **Spanish needles** an American weed of the bur-marigold genus with hooked fruits; **Spanish omelette** an omelette made with various vegetables; **Spanish onion** a large mild type of onion. — *n pl* **Spanish practices** or **customs** irregular or restrictive practices by a group of workers, such as overmanning and excessive overtime, which are costly, inefficient, etc (*orig* called **old Spanish practices** or **customs**). — **Spanish sheep** a merino; **Spanish soap** Castile soap; **Spanish topaz** an orange-brown variety of quartz (not a true topaz) used as a gemstone; **Spanish walk** the piaffer gait in horsemanship; **Spanish windlass** (*esp naut*) a stick or short bar used in ropemaking to twist and tighten the strands. — **ride the Spanish mare** (*naut hist*) to bestride the boom as a punishment; **walk Spanish** to compel or be compelled to walk on tiptoe, lifted by the collar and the seat of the trousers — hence, to proceed or act under duress or compulsion. [*Spain*, with vowel-shortening]

spank[1] *spangk*, *vt* and *vi* to move or drive briskly. — *n* **spank'er** a person or thing that spanks; any person or thing particularly striking or dashing; a fore-and-aft sail on the aftermost mast of a sailing ship (*naut*); a gold coin (*obs slang*). — *adj* **spank'ing** spirited, going freely; (of a wind) fresh and brisk; striking, beyond expectation; very; very large. — *adv* **spank'ingly**. [Poss back-formation from **spanking**]

spank[2] *spangk*, *vt* to strike with the flat of the hand, to smack. — *n* a loud slap, *esp* on the buttocks. — *n* **spank'ing**. [Prob imit]

spanner *span'ər*, *n* a wrench for nuts, screws, etc; an instrument for winding up a spring (*obs*). — **throw a spanner in the works** to cause confusion or difficulty, upset plans. [Ger *Spanner*, from *spannen* to stretch; cf **span**[1]]

spansule *span'sūl*, *n* a type of pill, generally a capsule containing grains coated with varying amounts of a soluble substance, so that the medicine is released into the body slowly over a period of time. [**span**[1] and cap*sule*]

spar[1] *spär*, *n* a rafter; a pole; a bar or rail (chiefly *Scot*; also *archaic* **sparre**); an undressed tree stem of medium girth; a general term for masts, yards, booms, gaffs, etc (*naut*). — *vt* to fasten with a spar (also *archaic* **sperre**); to fasten; to shut; to fit with spars. — **spar deck** (*naut*) a temporary deck laid in any part of a ship; a light upper deck of a flush-decked ship. [OE *gesparrian* to bar; Du *spar* (noun) *sperren* (verb); ON *sparri*; Ger *sperren* (verb)]

spar[2] *spär, n* any transparent to translucent, lustrous, non-metallic mineral, with clean cleavage planes (*esp* in compounds, eg *calc-spar, fluorspar, feldspar*); a crystal or fragment of this; an ornament made of it. — *adj* **sparry** (*spär'i*) of or like spar. [MLGer *spar*, related to OE *spærstān* gypsum]

spar[3] *spär, vi* to box, or make the actions of boxing; to dispute, argue; (of gamecocks) to fight with spurs: — *pr p* **sparr'ing**; *pa t* and *pa p* **sparred**. — *n* a boxing match or demonstration; a cock fight; a dispute. — *n* **sparr'er**. — *n* **sparr'ing**. — **sparring partner** a person, *usu* another boxer, with whom a boxer practises; a friend with whom one enjoys lively arguments. [Perh OFr *esparer* (Fr *éparer*) to kick out; prob Gmc]

sparable *spar'ə-bl, n* a small headless nail used by shoemakers. [Altered from **sparrow-bill** from its shape]

Sparagmite *spär-ag'mīt*, (*geol*) a general name for the late Precambrian rocks of Scandinavia, containing conglomerates, quartzites, breccias and arkoses. — *adj* **sparag'matic**. [**spar**[2] and stal*agmite*]

sparaxis *spar-ak'sis, n* any plant of the S African *Sparaxis* genus of cormous iridaceous plants, having colourful star-shaped flowers with lacerated spathes. [LL, from Gr *sparassein* to tear, lacerate]

spard *spärd*. Archaic form of **spared**.

spare[1] *spār, vt* to do without, part with voluntarily; to afford; to allow oneself, concede to oneself (*archaic*); to abstain from using; to refrain from hurting, injuring, punishing, killing or ending; to treat mercifully; to relieve or save from; to avoid; to avoid incurring; to use frugally (*archaic*); to save, hoard (*obs*). — *vi* (*archaic* or *rare*) to be frugal; to refrain; to be merciful. — *adj* not in actual use; not required; kept or available for others or for such purposes as may occur; lean; frugal, scanty, meagre; sparing. — *adv* sparely. — *n* a spare part, thing or person; a duplicate kept or carried for emergencies, etc; (in skittles or tenpin bowling) overturning all the pins with the first two balls — ie with a ball to spare (a *double spare*, with first ball only); the score for so doing. — *adj* **spare'less** unmerciful. — *adv* **spare'ly**. — *n* **spare'ness**. — *n* **spār'er**. — *adj* **spār'ing** tending or wanting to make savings, frugal, economical. — *adv* **spār'ingly**. — *n* **spār'ingness**. — **spare part** a part for a machine ready to replace an identical part if it becomes faulty (**spare-part surgery** surgery involving the replacement of organs, by transplants or artificial devices); **spare rib** a piece of pork consisting of ribs with a little meat adhering to them; **spare room** a bedroom that is not normally used, available for visitors; **spare time** leisure time (*adj* **spare'-time**); **spare tyre** an extra tyre for a motor vehicle, carried in case of a puncture; a roll of fat around the midriff (*colloq*). — **go spare** (*slang*) to become furious or frenzied; **to spare** over and above what is required. [OE *sparian* to spare, *spær* sparing; Ger *sparen*]

spare[2] *spār*, (now *Scot*) *n* the opening or slit at the top of a skirt, pair of trousers, etc. [Origin obscure]

sparganium *spär-gā'ni-əm, n* a plant of the bur-reed genus *Sparganium* that grows in marshes and shallow water, typically having straplike leaves and globelike flower-heads made up of either male or female flowers. [Gr *sparganion*]

sparge *spärj*, or (*Scot*) **spairge** *spārj, vt* to sprinkle (with moisture). — *n* **spar'ger** a sprinkler. [L *spargere* to sprinkle]

spar-hawk *spär'-hök, n*. Same as **sparrow hawk**.

sparid or **sparoid** *spar'id* or *-oid, n* any marine fish of the family *Sparidae*, *incl* the sea breams, porgies, dentex, etc, with slim streamlined bodies and well-developed teeth adapted to their individual feeding habits. [Gr *sparos* the fish sargus]

spark *spärk, n* a glowing or glittering particle; anything of this appearance or character, eg easily extinguished, ready to cause explosion or burning hot; a flash; an electric discharge across a gap; anything active or vivid; a bright sprightly person; a small diamond (*slang*); an electrician (*slang*; see also **sparks** below); a lover, a beau (*archaic*). — *vi* to emit sparks; to produce a spark; to sparkle; to play the gallant or lover (*archaic*). — *vt* to cause to begin, kindle or animate (often with *off*). — *adj* **spark'ish** jaunty, showy. — *adv* **spark'ishly**. — *adj* **spark'less**. — *adv* **spark'lessly**. — *n* **spark'let** a small spark. — *n sing* **sparks** a ship's wireless operator (*naut slang*); an electrician (*slang*; also **spark** or *esp Austr* **spark'ie**). — *adj* **spark'y**. — **spark chamber** a radiation detector, consisting of a chamber containing inert gas and electrically-charged metal plates, in which tracks of particles can be detected and studied by photographing the spark caused by their ionization of the gas; **spark coil** an induction coil; a connection of high resistance used to prevent sparking in electrical apparatus; **spark gap** the space between electrodes across which electric sparks pass; apparatus with such a space; **spark plug** or **spark'ing-plug** in an internal-combustion engine, a plug carrying wires between which an electric spark passes to fire the explosive mixture of gases. — **make sparks fly** to cause or arouse sudden anger; **spark off** see **spark** (*vt*) above; **spark out** (*slang*) to fall asleep; to pass out; to die (*adj* **sparked out**). [OE *spærca*, *spearca*; Du *spark*]

sparke *spärk*, (*Spenser*) *n* a weapon of some kind, perhaps an error for **sparthe**.

sparkle *spärk'l, n* a little spark; glitter; scintillation; emission of sparks; the appearance of effervescence (as of carbon dioxide in wine); vivacity; spirited animation; scintillating wit. — *vi* to emit sparks; to glitter; to effervesce with small shining bubbles; to be bright, animated, vivacious or witty. — *vt* to cause to sparkle; to throw out as, in, or like sparks. — *n* **spark'ler** that which sparkles; a diamond or other gem (*slang*); a small firework that gives off a shower of tiny sparks and which can be held in the hand. — *n* and *adj* **spark'ling**. — *adv* **spark'lingly**. — *adj* **spark'ly** having sparkles; sparkling. — *n* (*colloq*) something that sparkles: — *pl* **spark'lies**. — **sparkling wine** wine that effervesces, either as a result of secondary fermentation or by the introduction of carbon dioxide. [Dimin and frequentative of **spark**]

sparling *spär'ling*, **sperling** or **spirling** *spûr'* or *spir'ling, n* a dialect (*esp Scot*) name for the smelt. [Partly OFr *esperlinge* (of Gmc origin), partly MLGer *spirling* or MDu *spierling*]

sparoid. See **sparid**.

sparre. See **spar**[1].

sparrer, **sparring**, etc. See under **spar**[3].

sparrow *spar'ō, n* any member of a family of small finchlike birds of the genus *Passer* and related genera (eg *Passer domesticus*, the house sparrow, and *Passer montanus* tree sparrow); extended to many other, *usu* brown, birds, such as the hedge sparrow. — **sparr'ow-bill** see **sparable**. — **sparr'ow-hawk** any member of the *Accipiter* genus of long-legged, short-winged falcons, similar to, but smaller than, the goshawks, that prey on smaller birds. [OE *spearwa*; Gothic *sporwa*, ON *spörr*, Ger *Sperling*]

sparrow-grass or **sparrow grass** *spar'ō-gräs*, (*dialect* and *colloq*) *n* a corruption of **asparagus**. — Also **spara'-grass**.

sparry. See under **spar**[2].

sparse *spärs, adj* thinly scattered; scanty. — Also *adv*. — *adv* **spars'edly** (now *rare*). — **sparse'ly**. — *n* **sparse'ness**. — *n* **spars'ity**. [L *sparsus*, pa p of *spargere* to scatter; Gr *speirein* to sow]

spart *spärt, n* esparto; Spanish broom (*obs*). — *n* **sparterie** (*-ə-rē*; *Fr*) articles made of esparto. [L *spartum* Spanish broom, esparto, and Sp *esparto*]

Spartacist *spär'tə-sist, n* a follower of *Spartacus*, leader of the slaves that revolted against Rome in the Third Slave War (73–71 BC); a German communist of extreme type in the revolution of 1918.

spartan *spär'tən, adj* simple, hardy, rigorous, frugal, laconic, militaristic, despising culture — ie characteristic of the ancient Greek city of *Sparta*, capital of

Laconia; bleak, rigorous, austere. — *n* someone or something displaying spartan qualities; (with *cap*) a citizen or native of Sparta or Laconia. [Gr *Spartē* (Doric *Spartā*)]

sparteine *spar'tē-ēn* or *-in*, *n* an oily alkaloid ($C_{15}H_{26}N_2$), obtained from the branches of the common broom plant and the seeds of the lupin, sometimes used to treat heart irregularities. [New L *Spartium*, from Gr *spartos* broom]

sparterie. See under **spart**.

sparth or **sparthe** *spärth*, (*archaic*) *n* a long battleaxe. [ON *spartha*]

spasm *spaz'm*, *n* a sustained involuntary muscular contraction; a sudden convulsive action, movement, or emotion; a brief period, a spell (*colloq*); a section of a performance, eg a verse of a song, stanza of a poem, etc (*jocular slang*). — *vi* to go into spasm; to experience a spasm or spasms. — *adj* (*rare*) **spasmat'ic** or **spasmat'ical**. — *adj* **spasm'ic**. — *adj* **spasmod'ic** or **spasmod'ical** relating to, or occurring in, spasms; convulsive; intermittent. — *adv* **spasmod'ically**. — *n* **spas'modist** (*rare*) a person whose work is spasmodic. — **Spasmodic School** a group of English poets, P J Bailey, Sydney Dobell, Alexander Smith, etc, whose works are marked by over-strained and unnatural sentiment and expression. [Gr *spasma*, *-atos*, and *spasmos*, *-ou* convulsion; adj *spasmōdēs*, from *spaein* to draw, convulse]

spastic *spas'tik*, *adj* of the nature of spasm; characterized or affected by spasms, as in *spastic colon*; spasmodic; awkward, clumsy, useless (*derog slang*). — *n* a person affected with spastic paralysis; a useless or stupid person (*derog slang*). — *adv* **spas'tically**. — *n* **spasticity** (*-tis'i-ti*) tendency to spasm. — **spastic paralysis** permanent muscle constriction or involuntary jerky muscle movement caused by injury to the muscle-controlling part of the brain. [Gr *spastikos*, from *spaein* to draw, convulse; see ety at **spasm**]

spat[1] *spat*, *pa t* and *pa p* of **spit**[2].

spat[2] *spat*, *n* the spawn of shellfish; a shellfish larva. — *vi* and *vt* to spawn. — *n* **spat'fall** a mass of planktonic shellfish larvae which has settled on the seabed prior to developing into adults; the location or occurrence of this settlement. [ME; origin uncertain]

spat[3] *spat*, *n* a slap (*rare*); a large drop, as of rain; a splash, spattering; a petty quarrel. — *vt* (*rare*) to slap, to strike lightly. — *vi* to engage in a petty quarrel. [Prob imit; cf Du *spat* spot, stain, spatter]

spat[4] *spat*, *n* a short gaiter; a fairing covering an aircraft wheel. **[spatterdash]**

spatangoid *spa-* or *spə-tang'oid*, *n* a heart urchin, a member of the *Spangoidea*, an order of more or less heart-shaped sea urchins with eccentric anus. [Gr *spatangēs* a kind of sea urchin]

spatchcock *spach'kok*, *n* a fowl just killed that is dressed and cooked at once; a fowl slit lengthways, opened out, and cooked (*usu* grilled) flat. — *vt* to treat in this way; to interpolate, insert (words, a sentence, etc) hastily into a narrative, etc. [Prob **dispatch** and **cock**[1]; cf **spitchcock**]

spate *spāt*, (*orig Scot* and *NEng dialect*) *n* a flood; a sudden rush or increased quantity. — Also **speat** (*rare*). — **in spate** (of a river) in a swollen, fast-flowing condition. [Origin doubtful]

spathe *spādh*, (*bot*) *n* a sheathing bract, *usu* a conspicuous one enclosing a spadix. — *adj* **spathaceous** (*spə-thā'shəs*) or **spathed** (*spādhd*) having a spathe. [Gr *spathē* a broad blade]

spathic *spath'ik*, (*mineralogy*) *adj* of the nature of, or like, spar; lamellar. — *adj* **spath'ose** (or *-ōs'*) spathic. — **spathic iron** another name for **siderite**. [Ger *Spat(h)* spar]

spathiphyllum *spə-thi'fi-lum*, *n* any araceous tropical plant of the genus *Spathiphyllum* (eg *Spathiphyllum wallisii*, the peace lily) with lance-shaped leaves and fleshy white spadices of flowers in white spathes. [New L, from Gr *spathē* a broad blade, and *phyllon* leaf]

spathulate *spath'ū-lāt*. Same as **spatulate**.

spatial or **spacial** *spā'shl*, *adj* relating to space. — *n* **spatiality** (*spā-shi-al'i-ti*). — *adv* **spā'tially**. — *adj* **spatiotemp'oral** of space-time or space and time together. [L *spatium* space]

Spätlese *shpāt'lā-zə*, (*Ger*) *n* literally, a late harvest; a sweet white wine made from grapes harvested after the main vintage (also without *cap*).

spattee *spat-ē'*, *n* a protective outer stocking or long gaiter. [**spat**[1] and **puttee**]

spatter *spat'ər*, *vt* to throw out or scatter upon or about; to sprinkle, *esp* with mud or liquid. — *vi* to fly or fall in drops; to fall, rain down or fly about. — *n* a spattering; something spattered. — **spatt'erdash** roughcast (*US*); an old type of long gaiter or legging to protect the trouser leg from being spattered with mud, etc; **spatt'erdock** (*US*) the yellow waterlily of the genus *Nuphar*; **spatt'erwork** reproduction of designs by covering the surface with the pattern and spattering colour on the parts exposed. [Cf Du and LGer *spatten*]

spatula *spat'ū-lə*, *n* a broad, blunt, flexible blade or flattened spoon. — *adj* **spat'ular**. — *adj* **spat'ulate** shaped like a spatula; broad and rounded at the tip and tapering at the base. — *n* **spat'ule** a spatula. [L *spatula*, *spathula*, dimin of *spatha*, from Gr *spathē* a broad blade]

spauld *spöld*, (now chiefly *Scot*) *n* the shoulder; the shoulder of an animal used as food; a limb. — Also **spald**, **spall**, **spaul** or (*Spenser*) **spalle**. — **spauld'-bone** shoulder-blade; **spauld'-ill** the cattle disease black-quarter. [OFr *espalde* (Fr *épaule*), from L *spatula* (see **spatula**)]

spavin *spav'in*, (*vet*) *n* a disease of the hock joint of horses, resulting from inflammation, in which a bony growth (**bone** or **bony spavin**), or distension of the tissues and veins associated with the joint (**bog spavin**), occurs; the growth or enlargement so formed. — *n* **spavie** (*spā'vē*; *Scot*) spavin. — *adj* **spav'ined** affected with spavin; lame; broken down, decrepit. [OFr *espa(r)vain* (Fr *éparvin*)]

spaw *spö*, **spaw'-well**. Obsolete forms of **spa**, **spa-well**.

spawl *spöl*, (*archaic*) *n* spittle, slaver, saliva. — *vi* to spit (also *fig*). [Origin unknown]

spawn *spön*, *n* a mass of eggs laid in water; fry; brood; (contemptuously) offspring; mushroom mycelium. — *vt* to produce as spawn; (contemptuously) to generate, *esp* in mass. — *vi* to produce or deposit spawn; to teem; to come forth as or like spawn. — *n* **spawn'er**. — *n* and *adj* **spawn'ing**. — *adj* **spawn'y** of or like spawn; lucky (*slang*). — **spawn brick** or **cake** a consolidated cake of horse dung with mushroom spawn; **spawn'ing-bed** or **-ground** a bed or place in the bottom of a stream on which fish deposit their spawn. [OFr *espandre* to shed, from L *expandere* to spread out]

spay[1]. See **spayad**.

spay[2] *spā*, *vt* to remove or destroy the ovaries of (a female animal). [Anglo-Fr *espeier*, from *espee* (Fr *épée*) sword]

spayad *spā'ad*, **spayd**, **spade** *spād* or **spay** *spā*, (*obs*) *n* a male deer in his third year. [Origin obscure]

SPCK *abbrev*: Society for Promoting Christian Knowledge (now **USPG**).

SPD *abbrev*: *Sozialdemokratische Partei Deutschlands*, the German Social Democratic Party.

speak *spēk*, *vi* to utter words; to talk or converse; to make a speech; to sound; to give voice; to give expression, information, or intimation by any means. — *vt* to pronounce; to utter; to express; to declare; to mention; to describe (*archaic*); to hail or communicate with; to use or talk in (a language); to bring or render by speaking: — *pa t* **spoke** or (*archaic* or *dialect*) **spake**; *pa p* **spō'ken** or (*archaic*) **spoke**. — *combining form* **-speak** (*colloq*) a particular jargon or style of language, such as *techno-speak*, *doublespeak*, *airspeak*, *seaspeak*, etc. — *adj* **speak'able** able or fit to be spoken or expressed in speech; able to speak (*rare*). — *n* **speak'er** a person who speaks; the president (*orig* the mouthpiece) of a legislative body, such as the House of

Commons; a loudspeaker. — *n* **speak'ership** the office of speaker. — *n* **speak'ing** the act of expressing ideas in words; conversation, discussion. — *adj* uttering or transmitting speech; seeming to speak, lifelike. — *adj combining form* **-speaking** able to speak a particular language, as in *English-speaking*. — *adv* **speak'ingly**. — **speak'easy** (*US*) during Prohibition, an illicit bar selling alcohol, a shebeen; **speak'erphone** a type of telephone using a combined loudspeaker and microphone; **speaking clock** a British telephone service which states the exact time when dialled; **speak'ing-tube** a tube for speaking through to another room; **speak'ing-voice** the kind of voice normally used in speaking. — **on speaking terms** see under **term**; **so to speak** as one might put it, as it were; **speak a ship** to hail and speak to someone on board her; **speak fair** (*archaic*) to address in conciliatory terms; **speak for** to speak on behalf of or in favour of; to be a proof of or witness to; to bespeak or engage; **speak in tongues** see under **tongue**; **speak one's mind** see under **mind**; **speak out** to speak boldly, freely, unreservedly, or so as to be easily heard (*n* **speak'out**); **speak the same language** see under **language**; **speak to** to converse with, address; to rebuke, scold; to attest, testify to; to comment on, discuss; **speak up** to speak so as to be easily heard; to state one's opinions boldly; **to speak of** worth mentioning. [Late OE *specan* (for *sprecan*); Ger *sprechen*]

speakerine *spēk-rēn*, (*old TV* and *radio*) *n* a female announcer or programme hostess. [Fem form of *speaker* announcer, from Eng **speaker**]

speal *spēl*, *n*. See **spule**.

spean. See **spane**.

spear *spēr*, *n* a long weapon made of a pole with a pointed head; a barbed fork for catching fish; anything sharp or piercing; a spearman; a spire; a spiky shoot or blade; a reed. — *vt* to pierce with a spear. — *adj* **speared** armed with the spear. — *adj* **spear'y**. — **spear'fish** marlin or any similar large game fish; **spear grass** a name for many spearlike grasses; **spear gun** an underwater hunting gun which fires spears; **spear'head** the head of a spear; the front of an attack (also *fig*). — Also *vt*. — **spear'man** a man armed with a spear; **spear'mint** a common garden mint used in cooking and flavouring; **spear'-point**; **spear'-running** a tourney; **spear'-shaft**; **spear side** the male side or line of descent (opposite of *spindle side*, or *distaff side*); **spear thistle** a common thistle (*Cnicus lanceolatus* or *Cirsium lanceolatum*); **spear'-thrower** a throwing stick; **spear'wort** any of various Eurasian plants of the genus *Ranunculus* with lance-shaped leaves, eg *Ranunculus lingua* **greater spearwort**, and *Ranunculus flammula*, **lesser spearwort**. [OE *spere*; Ger *Speer*; with some senses from **spire**[1]]

speat. See **spate**.

spec[1] *spek*, *n* a *colloq* shortening of **speculation**. — *adj* **spec-built** (of houses, etc) built as a speculative investment by the builder. — **on spec** as a gamble, on the chance of achieving something.

spec[2] *spek*, *n* a *colloq* shortening of **specification**.

speccy *spek'i*, (*colloq*) *n* and *adj* (someone who is) bespectacled. [Cf **specs**, **spectacle**]

special *spesh'l*, *adj* particular; peculiar; distinctive; exceptional; additional to ordinary; detailed; intimate; designed for a particular purpose; confined or mainly applied to a particular subject. — *n* any special or particular person or thing; any person or thing set apart for a particular duty — a constable, a railway train, etc; a dish offered exceptionally as an addition to a restaurant menu, often at a lower price; a newspaper extra, a dispatch from a special correspondent. — *n* **spec'ialism** (devotion to) some particular study or pursuit. — *n* **spec'ialist** a person whose work, interest or expertise is concentrated on a particular subject; an organism with a narrow range of food and habitat preferences (*ecol*). — *adj* **specialist'ic**. — *n* **speciality** (*spesh-i-al'i-ti*) or *NAm* **specialty** (*spesh'əl-ti*) the particular characteristic skill, use, etc of a person or thing; a special occupation or object of attention. — *n* **specialīzā'tion** or **-s-**. — *vt* **spec'ialize** or **-ise** to make special or specific; to differentiate; to adapt to conditions; to specify; to narrow and intensify; to become or be a specialist in (with *in*). — *vi* to become or be a specialist; to become differentiated; to be adapted to special conditions. — *n* **spec'ializer** or **-s-**. — *adv* **specially** (*spesh'ə-li*). — *n* **spec'ialogue** a mail order catalogue aimed at a specific target group of customers. — *n* **spec'ialty** something special or distinctive; any special product, article of sale or of manufacture; any special pursuit, department of study, etc; speciality (chiefly *NAm* or *med*); a special contract for the payment of money; a deed under seal (*law*). — **Special Air Service** (*abbrev* **SAS**) a regiment of the British Army specializing in operations behind enemy lines, etc; **special area** an earlier name for **development area**; **Special Branch** a British police department which deals with political security; **special constable** see under **constable**; **special correspondent** a person employed to send reports to a particular newspaper, agency, etc; **special delivery** the delivery of mail by special messenger outside normal delivery times; **special hospital** a secure hospital for mentally ill patients who are also dangerous; **Special Drawing Rights** (also without *caps*; *abbrev* **SDR** or **SDRs**) a reserve of International Monetary Fund assets which members of the fund may draw on in proportion to their IMF contributions; **special licence**, **offer**, **pleading**, **verdict** see under **licence**, etc; **special school** a school designed for the teaching of children with particular needs, *esp* the mentally or physically handicapped; **Special Theory of Relativity** see under **relate**. — **in special** (*archaic*) in particular; especially. [L *speciālis*, from *speciēs* species]

spécialité de la maison *spās-yal-ē-tā də la mez-ʒ*, *n* the dish regarded by a restaurant as its best and most distinctive. [Fr, speciality of the house]

speciate, **specation**. See **species**.

specie *spē'shē* or *-shi-ē*, *n* coined money. — **in specie** in coin; in kind. [L, ablative of *speciēs* kind; formerly used of payment or requital in the same kind (*in speciē*]

species *spē'shēz* or *shi-ēz*, *n* a group of individuals having common characteristics, specialized from others of the same genus (*logic*); a group (sometimes rather arbitrarily defined) of closely allied mutually fertile individuals showing constant differences from allied groups, placed under a genus (*biol*); a kind, sort, type; outward appearance, visible form (*obs* except *theol*); a eucharistic element; a visual image (*obs*): — *pl* **spē'cies**. — *n* **speciā'tion** formation of new biological species, *incl* formation of polyploids. — *vt* **spē'ciate**. — *n* **speciesism** (*spē'shēz-izm*) the assumption that man is superior to all other species of animals and that he is therefore justified in exploiting them to his own advantage. — *n* **spe'ciesist**. — *n* **speciocide** (*spē'shē-ə-sīd*) the destruction of a whole animal species. [L *speciēs*, pl *-ēs* appearance, kind, species, from *specere* to look at]

specif. *abbrev*: specific; specifically.

specify *spes'i-fī*, *vt* to mention particularly; to make specific; to set down as required: — *pr p* **spec'ifying**; *pa t* and *pa p* **spec'ified**. — *adj* **spec'ifiable** (or *-fī'*). — *adj* **specific** (*spi-sif'ik*) of special application or origin; specifying; precise; constituting or determining a species; pertaining to or peculiar to a species; (of a parasite) restricted to one particular host; (of a stain) colouring certain structures or tissues only; (of a physical constant) being the ratio per unit volume, area, (or *esp*) mass, etc. — *n* a remedy or medicine for a particular disease or part of the body; anything that is specific, *esp* a specific detail or factor. — *adj* **specif'ical**. — *adv* **specif'ically**. — *vt* **specif'icate** to specify. — *n* **specificā'tion** (*spes-*) making, becoming, or being specific; the act of specifying; any point or particular specified; a detailed description of requirements, etc; the description of his or her invention presented by an inventor applying for a patent. — *n* **specificity** (*spes-i-fis'i-ti*). — *adj* **spec'ified**. — **specific**

gravity relative density; **specific heat** or **specific heat capacity** (*phys*) the number of heat units necessary to raise the unit of mass of a given substance one degree in temperature; **specific impulse** a measure of the efficiency of a rocket engine, the ratio of the thrust obtained to the fuel consumed, *usu* per second; **specific name** in biological nomenclature, the name of the species, ie the second name, the first being the generic name. [OFr *specifier*, from LL *specificāre*, from L *speciēs* kind, and *facere* to make]

specimen *spes'i-min*, *n* an object or portion serving as a sample, *esp* for purposes of study, collection or consideration; a remarkable type; a urine, blood or tissue sample (*med*); derogatorily, a person (*colloq*). — *adj* for use as, or of the nature of, a specimen; representative. [L *specimen*, from *specere* to see]

specious *spē'shəs*, *adj* beautiful (*obs*); showy; looking good at first sight; plausible, but wrong or inaccurate in reality. — *n* **speciosity** (*-shi-os'i-ti*) or **spe'ciousness**. — *adv* **spe'ciously**. [L *speciōsus* showy, from *speciēs* form, from *specere* to look at]

speck[1] *spek*, *n* a small spot; a particle. — *vt* to spot. — *adj* **speck'less**. — *adj* **speck'y**. [OE *specca*]

speck[2] or **spek** *spek*, *n* (now chiefly *US* and *SAfr*) fat; bacon; blubber from a whale. — *n* **specktioneer** or **specksioneer** (*spek-shən-ēr'*) the chief harpooner in whale-fishing. [Ger *Speck*, Du *spek* fat; cf OE *spic* fat bacon]

speckle *spek'l*, *n* a little spot, *esp* of colour; a grainy pattern on or forming a photographic image, caused by atmospheric interference (*astron* and *phys*). — *vt* to mark with speckles. — *adj* **speck'led**. — *n* **speck'ledness**. — **speckle interferogram** a visual record produced by speckle interferometry; **speckle interferometry** (*astron* and *phys*) a method of obtaining information, *esp* a visual image, of a distant stellar object by the processing and analysis of a number of short-exposure speckle photographs. [Dimin of **speck**[1]]

specktioneer. See under **speck**[2].

specs *speks*, (*colloq*) *n pl* a pair of **spectacles**. — Also **specks**.

spectacle *spek'tə-kl*, *n* a sight; a show, pageant or exhibition; (in *pl*) a pair of lenses (for correcting the eyesight) mounted in frames with side-pieces to grip the temples; (in *pl*) a marking (on an animal) resembling spectacles. — *adj* **spec'tacled** wearing spectacles; having rings around the eyes (*fig*). — *adj* **spectacular** (*-tak'ū-lər*) of the nature of, or marked by, display; sensational, extremely impressive. — *n* a theatrical show, *esp* on television, or any display, that is large-scale and elaborate. — *n* **spectacularity** (*-lar'i-ti*). — *adv* **spectac'ularly**. — **pair of spectacles** (*cricket*) a duck in both innings. [L *spectāculum*, from *spectāre*, *-ātum*, intensive of *specere* to look at]

spectator *spek-tā'tər*, *n* a person who looks on: — *fem* (*rare*) **spectā'tress** or **spectā'trix**. — *vi* **spectate'** (*back-formation*) to look on. — *adj* **spectatorial** (*-tə-tō'ri-əl* or *-tö'*). — *n* **spectā'torship** the action, office, or quality of a spectator. — **spectator sport** a sport that has great appeal for spectators. [L *spectātor*, from *spectāre* to look]

spectra. See under **spectrum**.

spectral, **spectrality**. See under **spectre** and **spectrum**.

spectre or *NAm* **specter** *spek'tər*, *n* an apparition; a ghost, phantom; a haunting fear or premonition. — *adj* **spec'tral** relating to, or like, a spectre. — *n* **spectral'ity** the state of being spectral; a spectral object. — *adv* **spec'trally**. — *adj* **spectrolog'ical**. — *adv* **spectrolog'ically**. — *n* **spectrol'ogy** the study of ghosts. — **spectre bat** a leaf-nosed bat; **spectre crab** a glass crab; **spectre insect** a phasmid; **spectre lemur** the tarsier; **spectre shrimp** a skeleton shrimp. [Fr *spectre*, from L *spectrum*, from *specere* to look at]

spectro- *spek'trō* or *-tro'*, *combining form* signifying: spectre; spectrum.

spectrum *spek'trəm*, *n* an after-image; the range of colour produced by a prism or diffraction grating; any analogous range of radiations in order of wavelength; range of frequencies of sound or a sound; the range of effectiveness of a drug, *esp* an antibiotic (*pharmacol*); range of opinions, activities, etc (*fig*): — *pl* **spec'tra**. — *adj* **spec'tral** relating to, or like, a spectrum. — *n* **spectral'ity**. — *n* **spec'trochemistry** chemical spectroscopy. — *n* **spec'trogram** a photograph of a spectrum; a sound spectrogram (see under **sound**[3]). — *n* **spec'trograph** a spectroscope designed for use over a wide range of frequencies (well beyond visible spectrum) and recording the spectrum photographically (see also **mass spectrograph** under **mass**[1]). — *adj* **spectrograph'ic** or **spectrograph'ical**. — *n* **spectrog'raphy**. — *n* **spectrohē'liogram** a photograph of the sun by monochromatic light. — *n* **spectrohē'liograph** an instrument for taking it. — *n* **spectrohē'lioscope** a similar instrument with which one can observe an image of the whole solar disc in the light of a single particular wavelength. — *adj* **spectrolog'ical**. — *adv* **spectrolog'ically**. — *n* **spectrol'ogy** the science of the spectrum or spectrum analysis. — *n* **spectrom'eter** an instrument for measuring refractive indices; one used for measurement of wavelength or energy distribution in a heterogeneous beam of radiation (see also **mass spectrometer** under **mass**[1]). — *adj* **spectromet'ric**. — *n* **spectrom'etry**. — *n* **spectrophotom'eter** an instrument for measuring intensity of each colour or wavelength present in an optical spectrum. — *n* **spectrophotom'etry**. — *n* **spec'troscope** a general term for an instrument (*spectrograph*, *spectrometer*, etc) used in spectroscopy, the basic features of which are a slit and collimator for producing a parallel beam of radiation, a prism or grating for 'dispersing' different wavelengths through differing angles of deviation, and a telescope, camera or counter tube for observing the dispersed radiation. — *adj* **spectroscop'ic** or **spectrosocop'ical**. — *adv* **spectroscop'ically**. — *n* **spectroscopist** (*spek-tros'kə-pist* or *spek'trə-skop-ist*). — *n* **spectros'copy** (or *spek'*) the study of spectra. — **spectral type** (*astron*) one of the different groups into which stars can be classifed according to characteristics of their spectra; **spectroscopic binary** (*astron*) a binary star whose components are too close to be resolved visually, but can be resolved spectroscopically; **spectrum analysis** determination of chemical composition by observing the spectrum of light or X-rays coming from or through the substance. [L *spectrum* an appearance, from *specere* to look at]

specular *spek'ū-lər*, *adj* mirrorlike; having a speculum; by reflection; visual; giving a wide view. — **specular iron** a brilliant steely crystallized haematite; **specular stone** any transparent or semitransparent mineral, such as mica, selenite, talc. [L *speculāris*, from *speculum* a mirror, and *specula* a watch-tower]

speculate *spek'ū-lāt*, *vi* to reflect; to theorize; to make conjectures or guesses; to take risk in hope of gain, *esp* in buying and selling. — *vt* to look at or into, view, examine (*lit* or *fig*; *archaic*); to observe (*archaic*); to view in a mirror (*obs*); to make conjectures about (*obs*). — *n* **speculā'tion** act of speculating or its result; theorizing; conjecture; mere guesswork; a more or less risky investment of money for the sake of unusually large profits; a card game in which trumps are bought and sold; vision (*obs*); viewing (*obs*); an observer (*Shakesp*). — *n* **spec'ulātist** a speculative philosopher; a speculator. — *adj* **spec'ulātive** (or *-ət-*) of the nature of, based on, given to, speculation or theory. — *adv* **spec'ulatively**. — *n* **spec'ulativeness**. — *n* **spec'ulātor** someone who speculates in any sense; a watchman, lookout (*archaic*). — *adj* **spec'ulatory** exercising speculation; adapted for spying or viewing (*archaic*). — *n* (*rare*) **spec'ulātrix** a female speculator. [L *speculātus*, pa p of *speculārī*, from *specula* a lookout, from *specere* to look at]

speculum *spek'ū-ləm*, *n* a mirror; a reflector, *usu* of polished metal; an instrument for inserting into and holding open a cavity of the body so that the interior may be inspected (*med*); a bright patch on a wing, *esp* a duck's: — *pl* **spec'ula**. — **speculum metal** an alloy of copper and tin, with or without other ingredients, which can be highly polished and used for mirrors, lamp reflectors, etc. [L *speculum* a mirror, from *specere* to look at]

sped *sped*, *pa t* and *pa p* of **speed**.

speech *spēch*, *n* that which is spoken; language; the power of speaking; manner of speaking; a continuous spoken utterance; a discourse, oration; talk; colloquy; mention; the sounding of a musical instrument; parole (qv) (*linguistics*); a rumour (*obs*); a saying (*obs*). — *vt* and *vi* (*rare* or *dialect*) to harangue. — *adj* **speech'ful** loquacious; expressive. — *n* **speech'fulness**. — *n* **speechificā'tion** (*colloq*). — *n* **speech'ifier**. — *vi* **speech'ify** to make speeches, harangue (implying contempt). — *adj* **speech'less** destitute or deprived of the power of speech. — *adv* **speech'lessly**. — *n* **speech'lessness**. — **speech act** (*philos* and *linguistics*) an utterance, such as a directive, defined in terms of the content, the intention of the speaker and the effect on the listener; **speech community** a community based on a common language or dialect; **speech'craft** philology; rhetoric; **speech'-crī'er** (*hist*) a hawker of broadsides giving hanged criminals' dying speeches; **speech day** the public day at the close of a school year, or on which prizes won during the previous year are presented; **speech'maker** someone who speaks, or is accustomed to speaking, in public; **speech'making**; **speech reading** lip-reading; **speech recognition** the understanding of an individual's speech patterns, or of continuous speech, by a computer; **speech'-song** (*music*) sprechgesang; **speech therapy** treatment of speech and language defects; **speech'-train'ing** training in clear speech. [Late OE *spēc*, *spǣc*, OE *sprēc*, *sprǣc*; Ger *Sprache*]

speed *spēd*, *n* quickness, swiftness, dispatch; the rate at which a distance is covered; the time taken for a photographic film to accept an image; amphetamine (*slang*); success, good fortune (*archaic*); a help to success (*archaic*). — *vi* to move quickly; to hurry; to drive at high, or at dangerously, unduly, or illegally high, speed; to succeed, fare (*archaic*). — *vt* to send swiftly; to push forward; to hasten; to betake with speed; to urge to high speed; to set or regulate the speed of; to give or bring success to, to further (*archaic*); to send forth with good wishes (*archaic*); to bring to an end or finished state (*archaic*); to bring to a sorry plight, to do for (in *passive*; *archaic*): — *pa t* and *pa p* **sped** (also **speed'ed**). — *n* **speed'er** someone who or something that speeds or promotes speed. — *adj* **speed'ful**. — *adv* **speed'fully**. — *adv* **speed'ily**. — *n* **speed'iness** quickness. — *n* **speed'ing** success; promotion, furtherance; progressive increase of speed (often with *up*); motoring at excessive speed. — Also *adj*. — *adj* **speed'less**. — *n* **speedom'eter** a device indicating the speed at which a vehicle is travelling (*colloq* shortening **speed'o**, *pl* **speed'os**). — *n* **speed'ster** a speedboat; a fast (sports) car; someone who speeds, *esp* in driving. — *adj* **speed'y** swift; prompt; soon achieved. — **speed'ball** a team sport with eleven players a side, combining many elements of soccer, basketball and rugby; a mixture of cocaine and opiates, *esp* heroin or morphine (*slang*); **speed'balling** (*slang*) injecting or sniffing speedball; **speed'boat** a very swift motorboat; **speed'boating**; **speed bump** a low hump across a road intended to slow down traffic; **speed'-cop** (*slang*) a policeman who watches out for motorists who are exceeding a speed limit; **speed' limit** the maximum speed at which motor vehicles may be driven legally on certain roads; **speed merchant** (*slang*) someone who drives a motor vehicle exceedingly fast; **speed reading** a technique of very rapid reading, by which words are taken in in phrases or other groups instead of singly; **speed'skating** a sport in which two or more ice- or roller-skaters race on a track for a number of separate distances, the winner being the skater who accumulates the fewest overall time points; **speed trap** a section of road over which the police (often using radar) check the speed of passing vehicles and identify drivers exceeding the limit (see also **radar trap**); **speed'-up** an acceleration, *esp* in work; **speed'way** a road for fast traffic; the sport of motorcycle racing on a short oval cinder track; such a track; **speed'well** any species of the scrophulariaceous genus *Veronica*, typically blue-flowered, with posterior petals united and lacking a posterior sepal; **Speedwriting**® a type of shorthand, in which letters of the alphabet stand for words or sounds, as *u* for you; **speedy cut** or **cutting** injury to a horse's foreleg by the opposite shoe. — **speed up** to quicken the rate of working. [OE *spēd*; Du *spoed*]

speel[1] *spēl*, (*Scot*) *vt* and *vi* to climb. — *n* a climb. — *n* **speel'er** an acrobat (*obs*); a climber; a climbing-iron. [Poss LGer *speler* a performer]

speel[2] *spēl*, (*Northern dialect*) *n* a splinter of wood, etc. [Scand, cf Norw *spela*, *spila*, Swed *spjela*, *spjele*]

speir or **speer** *spēr*, (*Scot*) *vt* and *vi* to ask, inquire. — *n* **speir'ings** or **speer'ings** news. [OE *spyrian* to inquire after, *spor* a trace]

speisade. See **lance speisade** under **lance prisado**.

speiss *spīs*, *n* a mass of arsenides and commonly antimony compounds, a first product in smelting certain ores. — **speiss cobalt** smaltite. [Ger *Speise*]

spek. See **speck**[2].

spekboom *spek'bōm*, *n* a S African succulent shrub of the purslane family. [Du, bacon tree]

spelaean or **spelean** *spi-lē'ən*, *adj* cave-dwelling. — *adj* **spelaeological** or **speleological** (*spē-li-ə-loj'i-kl* or *spel-*). — *n* **spelaeol'ogist** or **speleol'ogist**. — *n* **spelaeol'ogy** or **speleol'ogy** the scientific study of caves; exploration of caves. — *n* **spelaeo'them** or **speleo'them** a term for depositional features, such as stalactites and stalagmites, found in caves. [Gr *spēlaion* cave]

speld *speld* or **spelder** *spel'dər*, (*Scot*) *vt* to spread open or sprawlingly; to slit and lay open. — *n* **spel'ding** or **speld'ring**, or **spel'din** or **speld'rin** a haddock (or other fish) split open and dried. [Cf ME *spalden* to split; Ger *spalten*]

spelean, etc. See **spelaean**, etc.

spelikin. See **spill**[2].

spelk *spelk*, (*Northern dialect*) *n* a splinter, of wood, etc. [OE *spelc*]

spell[1] *spel*, *n* a magic formula; a magic influence; enchantment; entrancement. — *vt* to say a spell over; to bind with a spell; to enchant. — *vi* (*obs*) to discourse. — *adj* **spell'ful** magical. — *vt* **spell'bind** (*back-formation*). — **spell'binder** an orator, *usu* political or evangelical, who holds his or her audience spellbound; any person or thing that entrances. — *adj* **spell'bound** bound by a spell; entranced. [OE *spell* narrative, discourse, *spellian* to speak, announce; cf Gothic *spill*, ON *spjall* tale]

spell[2] *spel*, *vt* to read laboriously, letter by letter; to name or set down in order the letters of; to constitute or represent orthographically; to make out, come to understand; to scan; to signify, indicate, amount to (*fig*). — *vi* to spell words, *esp* correctly; to contemplate (*poetic*); to express or hint a desire: — *pa t* and *pa p* **spelled** or **spelt**. — *n* a mode of spelling. — *adj* **spell'able**. — *n* **spell'er**. — *n* **spell'ing**. — *adv* **spell'ingly** letter by letter. — **spell'down** (*US*) a spelling competition; **spelling bee** a spelling competition; **spelling book** a book for teaching to spell; **spell'check** a program in a word-processor that checks the accuracy of the operator's spelling (also *adj*); **spelling pronunciation** (*linguistics*) a pronunciation of a word that, as a side-effect of literacy, closely represents its spelling, superseding the traditional pronunciation, eg *forehead* as *för'hed* (*orig for'id*). — **spell backward** to spell in reverse order; perversely to mispresent or misconstrue the qualities of; **spell baker** to do something difficult, probably because *baker* was one of the first disyllables in old spelling books; **spell it out** or **spell out** to be extremely specific in explaining something. [OFr *espeller* (Fr *épeler*), of Gmc origin; cf **spell**[1]]

spell[3] *spel*, *vt* to take the place of at work; to relieve, give a rest to; to take a turn at. — *vi* to take turns; to rest: — *pr p* **spell'ing**; *pa t* and *pa p* **spelled**. — *n* a shift; a turn at work; a bout, turn; a short time; a stretch of time; a rest; a fit (of irritation, illness, etc). [OE *spelian* to act for another: cf Du *spelen*, Ger *spielen* to play]

spell[4] *spel*, (*dialect*) *n* a splinter; a rung; a trap for throwing up the knur in knur and spell. [Perh **speld**; but cf Ger *spellen* to split]

spellikin, **spellican**. See under **spill**[2].

spelt[1] *spelt*, *n* an inferior species of wheat (*Triticum spelta*), grown in the mountainous parts of Europe. [OE *spelt*]

spelt[2]. See **spell**[2].

spelter *spel'tər*, *n* zinc, *esp* impure zinc. [Cf LGer *spialter*]

spelunker *spi-lun'kər*, *n* a person who explores caves as a hobby. — *n* **spelunk'ing**. [From L *spēlunc*, *-a*, from Gr *spēlynx* a cave]

spence *spens*, *n* a larder (*dialect*); a pantry (*dialect*); an inner room, parlour (*Scot*). [OFr *despense* a buttery, from *despendre*, from L *dispendere*]

spencer[1] *spens'ər*, *n* a kind of wig; a short double-breasted overcoat; a woman's short undergarment, formerly over-jacket. [After various persons of the name]

spencer[2] *spens'ər*, *n* (in ships and barques) a fore-and-aft trysail abaft the fore and main masts. [Perh the name Spencer]

Spencerian *spen-sē'ri-ən*, *adj* pertaining to the synthetic philosophy or evolutionary cosmology of Herbert *Spencer* (1820–1903). — *n* a follower of Spencer. — *n* **Spencē'rianism**.

spend *spend*, *vt* to expend; to pay out; to give, bestow, employ, for any purpose; to shed; to consume; to use up; to exhaust; to waste; to pass (time, etc). — *vi* to make expense: — *pa t* and *pa p* **spent**. — *n* an act of, or the sum of money available (*usu* on a regular basis) for, spending. — *adj* **spen'dable**. — *n* **spen'der**. — *n* **spen'ding**. — *adj* **spent** used up; exhausted; (of fish) exhausted by spawning; (of a mast or yard) broken during bad weather (*naut*). — **spend'all** a spendthrift; **spending money** pocket money; **spend'thrift** someone who spends the savings of thrift; a prodigal. — *adj* excessively lavish. — **spent force** a person or thing whose former strength, usefulness, etc, is exhausted. — **spend a penny** (*euphem*) to urinate. [OE *spendan*, from L *expendere* or *dispendere* to weigh out]

Spenglerian *speng-glēr'i-ən*, *adj* of or pertaining to the German historian Oswald *Spengler* (1880–1936) and his work, *esp* the theory that all world civilizations are subject to the same inevitable cycle of growth and decline. — *n* a follower of Spengler.

Spenserian *spen-sē'ri-ən*, *adj* pertaining to Edmund *Spenser* (1552–99) or *esp* his stanza in *The Faerie Queene*, of eight decasyllabic lines and an Alexandrine, rhymed *ababbcbcc*.

spent *spent*. See under **spend**.

speos *spē'os*, *n* a grotto-temple or tomb: — *pl* **spe'oses**. [Gr, cave]

Spergula *spûr'gū-lə*, *n* the spurrey genus of plants, related to chickweed. — *n* **Spergulā'ria** the related sandwort-spurrey genus. [LL]

sperling *spûr'ling*. Same as **sparling**.

sperm *spûrm*, *n* semen; spermatozoa; any generative substance; eggs, spawn, brood, offspring (*obs*); the chalaza of a hen's egg (formerly believed to be contributed by the cock) (*obs*); a sperm whale; sperm oil; a sperm candle; spermaceti. — **-sperm** *combining form* denoting seed. — *adj combining forms* **-spermal** and **-spermous**. — For some compounds beginning **sperma-** or **spermo-** see **spermato-** below. — *n* **sper'maduct** or **sper'miduct** a duct conveying spermatozoa. — *n* **spermā'rium** (*pl* **spermā'ria**) or **sper'mary** the male germ gland. — *combining form* **spermat-** see **spermato-** below. — *n* **spermatothē'ca** or **spermathē'ca** (Gr *thēkē* receptacle) in female insects, etc, a receptacle in which sperms received are stored. — *adj* **spermathē'cal**. — *adj* **spermat'ic** or **spermat'ical** of, pertaining to, associated with or conveying sperm; generative. — *n* **spermat'ic** a spermatic vessel. — *n* **sper'matid** a cell that develops directly into a spermatozoon. — *n* **spermatium** (*-mā'shəm*) a non-motile male gamete in red seaweeds; a sporelike structure, part of the reproductive system in some fungi and lichens: — *pl* **spermā'tia**. — *combining form* **spermato-** *spûrmə-tō* or *spûr-mə-to'*, or **spermat-** denoting (1) sperm; (2) organs or ducts conveying, or associated with, sperm. — *n* **sper'matoblast** (Gr *blastos* a shoot) a spermatid. — *adj* **spermatoblas'tic**. — *n* **sper'matocele** (Gr *kēlē* tumour) a cystic swelling of the testicle arising from the epididymis and containing sperm. — *n* **sper'matocyte** (Gr *kytos* vessel) a male sex cell that gives rise to spermatids or develops into an antherozoid. — *n* **spermatogenesis** (*-jen'*) or **spermatogeny** (*-ə-toj'i-ni*) the process of sperm production in the testes. — *adj* **spermatogenet'ic**, **spermatogen'ic** or **spermatog'enous**. — *n* **spermatogonium** (*-gō'ni-əm*) one of the cells that by repeated division form the spermatocytes. — *n* **sper'matophore** a case enclosing the spermatozoa of certain crustaceans, molluscs and amphibians. — *n* **spermat'ophyte**, **sperm'aphyte** or **sperm'ophyte** any member of the *Spermatophyta*, one of the four phyla of the plant kingdom, *incl* all seed-bearing plants. — *adj* **spermatophytic** (*-fit'ik*; also **sperma'phytic** or **spermo'phytic**). — *n* **spermatorrhoe'a** or **spermatorrhe'a** (Gr *rhoiā* flow) involuntary discharge of semen. — *adj* **spermatozō'al**, **spermatozō'an** or **spermatozō'ic**. — *n* **spermatozō'id** or **spermatozō'on** (Gr *zōion* animal; *pl* **spermatozō'a**) a male sex cell, any of the millions contained in semen. — *adj* **sper'mic** spermatic. — *adj* **spermicī'dal**. — *n* **sper'micide** any substance which kills spermatozoa. — *n* **sper'miogenesis** same as **spermatogenesis**. — For some compounds beginning **spermo-** see **spermato-** above. — *n* **sper'mogone** or **spermogō'nium** (*pl* **spermogō'nia**) a flask-shaped structure in some fungi and lichens in which spermatia are produced. — *adj* **sper'mous** spermatic; of, derived from, or relating to the sperm whale. — **spermatic artery** (*anatom*) either of two arteries that supply blood to the testes; **spermatic cord** (*anatom*) the cord, consisting of the vas deferens, blood vessels and nerves, that runs from the abdominal cavity to the testicle; **sperm bank** a refrigerated store of semen for use in artificial insemination; **sperm candle** a candle made from spermaceti; **sperm cell** a male gamete; **sperm count** a measure of male fertility found by estimating the concentration of spermatozoa in semen; **sperm oil** oil from the sperm whale; **sperm'-whale** the cachalot, *Physeter catodon*, a whale from which spermaceti is obtained. [Gr *sperma*, *-atos* seed, semen, from *speirein* to sow]

spermaceti *spûr-mə-set'i*, *n* a waxy matter obtained mixed with oil from the head of the sperm whale and others. — Also *adj*. [L *sperma cētī* (genitive of *cētus* a whale, from Gr *kētos*) whale's sperm, from a wrong notion of its origin]

spermarium, **spermatic**, etc. See **sperm**.

spermophile *spûr'mō-fil* or *-fīl*, *n* a ground squirrel (*Spermophilus*, *Citellus*, etc), a N American rodent related to the true squirrels and regarded as a pest in many areas. [Gr *sperma* seed, and *phileein* to love]

sperre *spûr*, (*Spenser*) *vt* to bolt, bar. — In Shakespeare, *Troilus and Cressida*, Prologue, line 19, **stirre** is probably a misprint for **sperre**. [**spar**[1]]

sperrylite *sper'i-līt*, *n* a white lustrous metallic mineral, platinum diarsenide in cubic crystalline form. [After F L *Sperry*, with Gr *lithos* stone]

sperse *spûrs*, (*archaic*) *vt* and *vi* an aphetic form of **disperse**: — *pa t* and *pa p* (*Spenser*) **sperst**; also **spersed**.

sperthe. Same as **sparth**.

spessartite *spes'ärt-īt* or **spessartine** *-īn*, *n* a dark, orange-red garnet, a silicate of manganese and aluminium, used as a gemstone. [From *Spessart* in Bavaria]

SPET or **Spet** *spet*, *abbrev*: single photon emission tomography. — **SPET scanner** a scanner used to pinpoint areas of the cerebral cortex that are not functioning, by measuring the blood flow.

spet *spet*, (*archaic* and dialect) *vt* and *vi* a form of **spit**².

spetch *spech*, *n* a piece of hide, undressed leather used in making glue. [Northern dialect *speck* a patch of leather or cloth]

Spetsnaz or **Spetznaz** *spets'naz*, *n* a select intelligence unit in the former Soviet Union, specializing in undercover activities, counter-insurgency tactics, raids, etc. — Also without *cap*. — *adj* (*usu* without *cap*) of or pertaining to the Spetsnaz. [Russ]

spew or (*archaic*) **spue** *spū*, *vt* to vomit. — *vi* to vomit; to ooze, run. — *n* vomited matter; a marshy spot (*dialect*). — *n* **spew'er**. — *n* **spew'iness**. — *adj* **spew'y** boggy (*dialect*); awful, despicable (*Austr slang*); very angry (*Austr*). [OE *spīwan*, *spīowan* to spit; Du *spuwen*, Ger *speien*; also L *spuere*, Gr *ptyein*]

SPF *abbrev*: sun protection factor (of a sunscreen, lotion, etc).

SPG *abbrev*: Special Patrol Group.

sp.gr. *abbrev*: specific gravity (now relative density).

sphacelus *sfas'ə-ləs*, (*pathol*) *n* (an instance of) necrosis, mortification. — *vt* **sphac'elate** to cause, or affect with, gangrene or mortification. — Also *vi*. — *adj* **sphac'elate** or **sphac'elated** necrosed; dark and shrunken, as rye affected with ergot (*bot*). — *n* **sphacelā'tion**. [Gr *sphakelos* convulsive movement, painful spasm, gangrene]

sphaere, **sphaer**. Obsolete forms of **sphere**.

sphaeridium *sfē-rid'i-əm*, *n* a minute spheroidal body on the surface of a sea urchin, perhaps a sense organ: — *pl* **sphaerid'ia**. — *n* **sphae'rite** a hydrous aluminium phosphate. — *n* **sphaerocō'baltite** cobalt carbonate, occurring in rounded masses. — *n* **sphaerocrys'tal** a rounded crystalline mass. — *n* **sphaerosid'erite** concretionary clay ironstone. [Gr *sphaira* a ball]

sphagnum *sfag'nəm*, *n* any moss of the genus *Sphagnum* of boggy areas in temperate regions, forming peat as it decays and used in horticulture, etc for its water-retentive properties. — Also called **peat moss** or **bog moss**. — *adj* **sphagnic'olous** (L *colere* to inhabit) living in peat moss. — *n* **sphagnol'ogist**. — *n* **sphagnol'ogy** the study of the sphagnum mosses. — *adj* **sphag'nous**. [Gr *sphagnos* a name for various plants]

sphairistike *sfī-ris'ti-ki*, *n* the name under which lawn tennis was patented in 1874 by Walter Wingfield, and by which it was quite widely known for a time. [Gr *sphairistike techne* the art of playing ball, from *spahira* ball]

sphalerite *sfal'ər-īt*, (*mineralogy*) *n* zinc blende, a lustrous black or brown crystalline zince sulphide, the commonest source of zinc. [Gr *sphaleros* deceptive, from its resemblance to galena]

spheare or **sphear**. Archaic forms of **sphere**.

sphendone *sfen'do-nē*, (*archaeol*) *n* a headband or fillet worn by women in ancient Greece; an elliptical or semi-elliptical auditorium. [Gr *sphendonē* a sling]

sphene *sfēn*, *n* the mineral titanite, occurring as wedge-shaped crystals in igneous and metamorphic rocks. — *adj* **sphē'nic** wedgelike. — *n pl* **Sphenisciformes** (*sfē-nis-i-för'mēz*) the penguin order of birds. — *n* **Sphē'nodon** (Gr *odous*, *odontos* a tooth) the genus, also known as *Hatteria*, to which the tuatara (qv) belongs; (without *cap*) an animal of this genus. — *n* **sphē'nogram** a cuneiform character. — *adj* **sphē'noid** wedge-shaped, applied to a set of bones at the base of the skull. — *n* a sphenoid bone; a wedge-shaped crystal form of four triangular faces. — *adj* **sphenoid'al**. [Gr *sphēn*, *sphēnos* a wedge]

sphere *sfēr*, *n* a solid figure bounded by a surface of which all points are equidistant from a centre, any cross-section of which is a circle; its bounding surface or the space enclosed by it; the apparent sphere of the heavens, upon which the stars are seen in projection; any one of the concentric spherical shells which were once supposed to carry the planets in their revolutions; a circle of society or class, *orig* of the higher ranks (as if a planetary sphere); domain, scope, range; a field of activity; condition of life; a world, mode of being; a ball, globe; a spherical object, *esp* a planet; an orbit (*archaic*). — *vt* to round; to place in a sphere; to encompass; to send about. — *adj* **sphēr'al**. — *adj* **sphered**. — *adj* **sphere'less**. — *adj* **sphere'like**. — *adj* **spheric** (*sfer'ik*) or **spher'ical** of a sphere or sphere; having the form of a sphere. — *n* **spherical'ity**. — *adv* **spher'ically**. — *n* **spher'icalness** or **sphericity** (*-is'i-ti*) the state or quality of being spherical. — *n* **sphеristē'rion** (Gr *sphairistērion*) a room or court for ball games. — *n* **spher'ocyte** an abnormal red blood cell that is spherical rather than disc-shaped. — *n* **spher'ocytosis** the presence of spherocytes in the blood, as in certain haemolytic anaemias. — *n* **sphē'roid** a body or figure nearly spherical, but not quite so — a form of ellipsoid (*prolate spheroid*, a slightly lengthened sphere; *oblate spheroid*, a slightly flattened sphere). — *adj* **sphēroi'dal**. — *n* **sphēroidi'city**. — *n* **sphēroidizā'tion** or **-s-**. — *vt* **sphēr'oidize** or **-ise** to develop spherulitic or granular structure in. — *n* **sphērom'eter** an instrument for measuring curvature of surfaces. — *adj* **spherūlar** (*sfer'*). — *n* **spher'ūle** a small sphere or spherical object. — *n* **spher'ūlite** a radiating spherical group of minute crystalline fibres occurring in certain rocks. — *adj* **spherūlitic** (*-lit'ik*). — *adj* **sphē'ry** spherical, round; belonging to the celestial spheres. — **spherical aberration** (*phys*, *optics*) loss of image definition which occurs when light strikes a lens or mirror with a spherical surface; **spherical angle** an angle formed by arcs of great circles on the surface of a sphere; **spherical geometry** the branch of geometry dealing with the properties of figures on the surface of spheres; **spherical polygon** a closed figure bounded by three or more arcs of great circles on the surface of a sphere; **spherical triangle** a three-sided figure on the surface of a sphere, bounded by arcs of great circles; **spherical trigonometry** the branch of trigonometry concerned with the measurement of these. — **music** (or **harmony**) **of the spheres** the music, inaudible to mortal ears, produced according to Pythagoras by the motions of the celestial spheres in accordance with the laws of harmony; **sphere of influence** any region over which one nation has a dominant influence. [Gr *sphaira*]

spherics¹ or *NAm* **sferics** *sfe'riks* or *sfē'*, *n pl* a shortened form of **atmospherics**.

spherics² *n sing* the geometry and trigonometry of the sphere.

sphincter *sfingk'tər*, (*anatom*) *n* a ringlike muscle whose contraction narrows or shuts an orifice, eg the anus. — *adj* **sphinc'teral**, **sphincterial** (*-tē'ri-əl*) or **sphincteric** (*-ter'ik*). [Gr *sphinktēr*, from *sphingein* to bind tight]

sphingomyelin *sfin-go'-mī-ə-lin*, (*biol*) *n* a phospholipid derived from sphingosine, occurring in cell membranes. [From Gr *sphingein* to bind, and **myelin**]

sphingosine *sfin-go'-sīn*, (*biol*) *n* a hydrophobic amino alcohol, a component of sphingomyelins and cerebrosides. [From Gr *sphingein* to bind, and **-ine**']

Sphinx or **sphinx** *sfingks*, *n* a monster of Greek mythology, with the head of a woman and the body of a lioness, that lay outside Thebes and proposed riddles to travellers, strangling those who could not solve them; any similar monster or representation of one, *esp* any of numerous massive stone statues built by the ancient Egyptians; an enigmatic or inscrutable person (from the facial expression of the huge stone sphinx at Gîza): — *pl* **sphinx'es** or **sphinges** (*sfin'jēz*). — *n* and *adj* **sphingid** (*sfin'jid*) (a member) of the *Sphingidae*, the hawk moth family, so called because the posture of its larvae resembles that of the sphinx. — *adj* **sphinx'like**. — **sphinx moth** (*NAm*) the hawk moth. [Gr, from *sphingein* to draw tight]

sphragistic *sfrə-jist'ik*, *adj* pertaining to seals and signets. — *n sing* **sphragist'ics** the study of seals and signets. [Gr *sphrāgistikos*, from *sphrāgis* a seal]

sphygmus *sfig'məs*, *n* the pulse. — *adj* **sphyg'mic**. — *n* **sphyg'mogram** a sphygmograph record. — *n* **sphyg'-**

mograph an instrument for recording the pulse, showing the rate and strength of the beats. — *adj* **sphygmograph'ic**. — *n* **sphygmog'raphy**. — *adj* **sphyg'moid** resembling a pulse. — *n* **sphygmol'ogy** the science or study of the pulse. — *n* **sphygmōmanom'eter** or **sphygmom'eter** an instrument for measuring arterial blood pressure, consisting of an inflatable cuff for the arm connected to a column of mercury which indicates systolic and diastolic pressure in millimetres. — *n* **sphyg'mophone** an instrument that records and transmits pulse beats as sounds. — *n* **sphyg'moscope** an instrument for making arterial pulsations visible. [Latinized from Gr *sphygmos* pulse]

spial *spī'əl* (*obs*) *n* observation, watch; a spy, a scout. [Aphetic from **espial**]

spic, **spick** or **spik** *spik*, (*esp US derog slang*) *n* a person from a Spanish-speaking American country, or of Mexican, S American, etc, origin; a member of one of the Mediterranean races. [Origin uncertain]

spica *spī'kə*, *n* a bandage wound around an injured limb in repeated figures-of-eight forming a series of overlapping V-shapes suggesting an ear of barley; in birds, a spur: — *pl* **spicae** or **spicas**. — *adj* **spī'cate** or **spī'cated** (*esp bot*) in, having, or forming a spike; spikelike. — *n* **spicilege** (*spī'si-lij*; L *spīcilegium*, from *legere* to gather) a gleaning; an anthology. — *n* **spicula** (*spik'ū-lə*) a spicule, prickle, or splinter. — *adj* **spic'ūlar** of the nature of or like a spicule. — *adj* **spic'ūlate** having spicules. — *n* **spic'ūle** a minute needlelike body, crystal, splinter, or process; a small splinter of bone (*med*); one of the spikelike forms seen forming and re-forming on the edge of the sun, caused by ejections of hot gas several thousand miles above its surface. — *n* **spic'ūlum** a little spine; a spicula; a snail's dart: — *pl* **spic'ūla**. [L *spīca* an ear of corn]

spiccato *spik-kä'tō*, (*music*) *adj* and *adv* half staccato. — *n* spiccato playing, or a spiccato passage: — *pl* **spicca'tos**. [Ital]

spice *spīs*, *n* any aromatic and pungent vegetable substance used as a condiment and for seasoning food — pepper, cayenne pepper, pimento, nutmeg, mace, vanilla, ginger, cinnamon, cassia, etc; such substances collectively or generally; a characteristic smack, flavour; anything that adds piquancy or interest; an aromatic odour; sweetmeats (*dialect*); a touch, tincture (*fig*). — *vt* to season with spice; to tincture, vary, or diversify. — *adj* **spiced** impregnated with a spicy odour; seasoned with spice; over-scrupulous (*obs*). — *n* **spīc'er** (*obs*) a dealer in spices or drugs. — *n* **spīc'ery** spices in general; a repository of spices; spiciness. — *adv* **spīc'ily**. — *n* **spīc'iness**. — *adj* **spīc'y** producing or abounding with spices; fragrant; pungent; piquant, pointed; racy; risqué; showy. — **spiceberry** any of several plants having spicy edible berries, eg a small American tree, *Eugenis rhombea*, with black or orange fruits; the fruit of this tree; **spice box** a box, often ornamental, for keeping spices; **spice'bush** an aromatic American shrub (*Lindera benzoin*) of the laurel family; **spice cake** any spiced cake. [OFr *espice* (Fr *épice*), from LL *speciēs* kinds of goods, spices, from L *speciēs* a kind]

spicilege. See under **spica**.

spick[1] *spik*, *n* a nail, a (wooden) spike. — *adj* tidy, fresh. — **spick and span** trim and speckless (like a newly cut spike or a newly split chip); **spick and span new** brand-new. [**spike**[2]]

spick[2]. See **spic**.

spicknel. See **spignel**.

spicule, etc. See under **spica**.

spicy. See under **spice**.

spide. An obsolete spelling of **spied** (see **spy**).

spider *spī'dər*, *n* an arachnid of the order *Araneae*, the body divided into two distinct parts, an unsegmented cephalothorax with four pairs of legs, and a soft unsegmented abdomen with spinnerets; formerly, a light high-wheeled horse-drawn carriage (in full **spider phaeton**); a frying pan, properly one with feet; any of various spiderlike radiating structures, instruments, tools, etc; a rest for a cue in billiards, *specif* one with legs arched wide and offering several cueing positions; an arrangement of elastic straps with hooks attached, used to fasten luggage, etc, on to the roof-rack of a car or on to a motorcycle, etc. — *adj* **spi'derlike**. — *adj* **spī'dery** spiderlike; abounding in spiders. — **spider crab** a crab with long thin legs; **spider flower** an annual plant of the genus *Cleome*, bearing clusters of white or pink flowers with long stamens reminiscent of spider's legs; **spider hole** (*military*) a hole in the ground to conceal a sniper; **spider leg** a long thin leg. — *adj* **spi'der-legged**. — **spider line** a thread of silk spun by a spider; any fine thread in an optical instrument, for measurement, position-marking, etc; **spi'derman** a building worker who erects the steel structure of a tall building; **spider mite** any web-spinning mite of the family *Tetranychidae*, feeding on, and often a serious pest of, plants, eg the **red spider mite** (*Panonychus ulmi*); **spider monkey** an American monkey of the genus *Ateles*, with long slender legs and tail; **spider plant** any of various plants of the genus *Chlorophytum*, with spiky, variegated leaves, *esp Chlorophytum comosum* which grows new plantlets on trailing stems; spiderwort; **spider spanner** see **spider wrench**; **spider stitch** a stitch in lace or netting in which threads are carried diagonally and parallel to each other; **spider wheel** (in embroidery) a circular pattern with radiating lines; **spi'derwork** lace worked by spiderstitch; **spi'derwort** any plant of the American commelinaceous genus *Tradescantia*, *esp Tradescantia virginica*, with deep-blue or reddish-violet flowers; **spider wrench** or **spanner** a box-spanner having heads of different sizes at the ends of radial arms. [OE *spīthra*, from *spinnan* to spin; cf Dan *spinder*, Ger *Spinne*]

spie. (In *Spenser*, *Milton*, etc) an archaic spelling of **spy**.

spied. See **spy**.

spiegeleisen *spē'gl-ī-zn*, *n* a white cast-iron containing manganese, largely used in the manufacture of steel by the Bessemer process. [Ger, from *Spiegel*, from L *speculum* a mirror, and Ger *Eisen* iron]

spiel *spēl* or *shpēl*, *n* a (*esp* plausible) story or line of talk. — *vi* to talk glibly, tell the tale. — Also *vt*. — *n* **spiel'er** a person with a glib, persuasive line of talk; a swindler or a card sharper; a gambling den (*criminal slang*). [Ger *spielen* to play]

spies. See **spy**.

spiff *spif*, *adj* (*dialect*) smart, spruce. — Also **spiff'y**. — *adj* **spiff'ing** (*old-fashioned colloq*) excellent. [Origin obscure]

spiflicate or **spifflicate** *spif'li-kāt*, (*esp schoolboy slang*) *vt* to destroy; to quell; to confound; to handle roughly. — *n* **spiflicā'tion** or **spifflicā'tion**.

Spigelia *spī-jē'li-ə*, *n* the pink-root genus of Loganiaceae. — *adj* **Spigē'lian** of van der Spiegel or of Spigelia; applied to the *lobulus Spigelii*, one of the lobes of the liver. [From the Belgian Adrian van der *Spiegel* (1578–1625)]

spight *spīt*, *v* and *n* (*Spenser* and *Shakesp*). Same as **spite**.

spignel *spig'nl*, *n* baldmoney or meu, a European plant, *Meum athamanticum*, of mountainous regions. — Also (*obs*) **spick'nel**. [Origin obscure]

spigot *spig'ət*, *n* a peg for a vent hole or peg used to close the opening of a tube or pipe; a tap or faucet (*NAm*); an interface (*comput*). [Provençal *espigot*, from L *spīculum*]

spik. See **spic**.

spike[1] *spīk*, *n* an ear of corn; an inflorescence in which sessile flowers or spikelets are arranged on a long axis (*bot*); a kind of lavender (**spike lavender**). — *vi* to develop a spike. — *n* **spike'let** (in grasses, etc) a small crowded spike, itself forming part of a greater inflorescence. — **spike grass** *Uniola* or other American grass with conspicuous spikelets; **spike oil** the oil of spike lavender; **spike-rush** any of several sedges of the genus *Eleocharis*, closely related to the true sedges, with stiff tufted stems and solitary spikelets. [L *spīca* an ear of corn]

spike[2] *spīk*, *n* a hard thin pointed object; a large nail; a sharp metal projection, eg one of those forming a row along the top of a railing, etc; a sharp-pointed metal rod set upright on a base, on which to impale documents requiring attention, etc; (in *pl*) spiked shoes, worn, *esp* by athletes, to prevent slipping; a bayonet (*military slang*); a workhouse or its casual ward (*old slang*); a dosshouse (*UK slang*); an electric impulse, *esp* a very brief, potentially damaging surge of power on an electronic circuit. — *vt* to fasten, set, pierce or damage with a spike or spikes; to make (eg a gun) useless, *orig* by driving a spike into the vent; to frustrate, put a stop to; to make (a drink) stronger by adding spirits or other alcohol (*colloq*); to contaminate (eg food) by the addition of a harmful substance; to reject (a news article, etc) (*journalism*); to inject with a drug. — *vi* to form a spike or peak; to inject oneself with a drug. — *adj* **spiked**. — *adv* **spīk'ily**. — *n* **spīk'iness**. — *adj* **spīk'y** having or provided with spikes; having a sharp point; irritable, acerbic; characterized by irritable, difficult or jarring disagreements or incidents. — **spike'fish** (*US*) a kind of sailfish; **spike heel** a very narrow metal heel on a woman's shoe; **spike'-nail** a large small-headed nail. [OE *spīcing* a spike-nail; poss from L *spīca* an ear of corn]

spike[3] *spīk*, *n* a very High-Church Anglican, an Anglo-Catholic. — *n* **spīk'ery**. — *adj* **spīk'y** very High-Church. [From **spiky** see under **spike**[2]]

spikenard *spīk'närd*, *n* an aromatic oil or balsam yielded by an Indian valerianaceous herb (*Nardostachys jatamans*; also called **nard**) or a synthetic substitute for this; the plant itself. — **ploughman's spikenard** a European and N African spikenard with yellow flowers and aromatic roots (*Inula conyza*). [L *spīca nardī*]

spile *spīl*, *n* a plug; a spigot; a pile for a foundation; a stake, or post for fencing. — *vt* to pierce and provide with a spile; to shape (the timbers of a wooden vessel or the ribs of a steel vessel) to form a gradual slope towards the bow and/or stern (*naut*). — *n* **spī'ling**. — **soft spile** in beer-making, a wooden peg driven into a cask to allow carbon dioxide to escape during secondary fermentation. [Cf LGer *spile*, Du *spijl*, Ger *Speil*]

spilikin. See under **spill**[2].

spilite *spī'līt*, (*geol*) *n* a fine-grained igneous rock of basaltic composition, often developed as submarine lava-flows. — *adj* **spilitic** (*-it'ik*). — *n* **spī'losite** a spotted slate, formed by contact metamorphism. [Gr *spilos* a spot]

spill[1] *spil*, *vt* to allow to run out of a container; to shed; to waste; to throw from a vehicle or the saddle (*colloq*); to empty from the belly of a sail or empty of wind for reefing; to overlay as if by spilling (*Spenser*); to kill (*obs*); to destroy (*obs*). — *vi* to overflow; to be shed; to be allowed to fall, be lost, or wasted; to come to grief or ruin (*obs*): — *pa t* and *pa p* **spilled** or **spilt**. — *n* a fall, a throw; a spilling. — *n* **spill'age** the act of spilling; that which is spilt. — *n* **spill'er**. — *n* **spill'ing**. — *n* **spilth** spilling; anything spilt or poured out lavishly; excess. — **spilling line** a rope for spilling the wind out of a square sail; **spill'over** an overflow (also *fig*); **spill'stream** an overflow channel; a bayou; **spill'way** a passage for overflow water. — **spill over** to overflow (also *fig*); **spill the beans** to divulge information, or a secret, whether inadvertently or not. [OE *spillan*; Du *spillen*, ON *spilla* to destroy]

spill[2] *spil*, *n* a spile; a thin strip of wood or paper for lighting a candle, a pipe, etc. — *n* **spill'ikin**, **spilikin** or **spellican** a small slip of wood, ivory, etc, to be picked out from a heap without disturbing the others in the game of **spillikins**. [Connection with **spile** or with **spell**[4] doubtful]

spillage, etc. See under **spill**[1].

spilosite. See **spilite**.

spilt *spilt*, *pa t* and *pa p* of **spill**[1]. — Also *adj*.

spilth. See under **spill**[1].

spin *spin*, *vt* to draw out and twist into threads; to draw out a thread as spiders do; to form by spinning; to draw out; to make to last (*usu* with *out*); to send hurtling; to twirl, set revolving rapidly; to fish with a swivel or spoon-bait; to reject at an examination (*slang*). — *vi* to practise the art or trade or perform the act of spinning; to rotate rapidly; to whirl; to hurtle; to go swiftly, *esp* on wheels; to spirt; to stream vigorously; to lengthen out, last (*usu* with *out*); to fish with rotating bait: — *pr p* **spinn'ing**; *pa t* **spun**, *archaic* **span**; *pa p* **spun**. — *n* act or result of spinning; a rotatory motion; a cycle ride; a short trip in a motor car; a spurt at high speed; a spiral descent (*lit* and *fig*); a period of time, an experience (*Austr* and *NZ colloq*); (of a subatomic particle) quantized angular momentum in the absence of orbital motion (*phys*); (of a nucleus) quantized angular momentum including contributions from the orbital motion of nucleons (*phys*); confused excitement; the sum of five dollars (*Austr*). — *n* **spin'ar** (*astron*) a rapidly spinning galactic body. — *n* **spinn'er** someone who or something that spins; a spider (*Shakesp*); a spinneret; a spinning-machine; a ball with imparted spin, causing it to swerve or break (*cricket*); a spin-bowler; an artificial fly that revolves in the water (*fishing*); a rotating display stand (eg for books) in a shop, etc; a spin doctor (qv). — *n* **spinn'eret** a spinning organ in spiders, etc; a plate with holes from which filaments of plastic material are expressed (also **spinnerette**). — *n* **spinn'erule** (*-ə-rōōl* or *-rūl*) one of the tubules of a spinneret. — *n* **spinn'ery** a spinning-mill. — *n* and *adj* **spinn'ing**. — **spin'-bowling** (*cricket*) a style of bowling in which the ball is give a twisting motion by the bowler's wrist or fingers, in order to make its speed and direction as it rises after striking the ground unpredictable; **spin'-bowler**; **spin doctor** or **spin'-doctor** (*orig US*) someone (often a public relations expert) employed by a politician, etc to influence public opinion; **spin-dri'er** or **spin-dry'er** a device that dries washed clothes without wringing, to a point ready for ironing, by forcing the water out of them under pressure of centrifugal force in a rapidly revolving drum. — *vt* **spin-dry'**: — *pa t*, *pa p* **spin-dried'** or **spun-dry'**. — *n* **spin'-dry**. — **spinn'ing-house** (*hist*) a place of correction where lewd and incorrigible women were made to spin; **spinn'ing-jenny** a machine by which a number of threads can be spun at once; a cranefly (*dialect*); **spinn'ing-mill** a factory where thread is spun; **spinning mule** an early form of spinning machine; **spinning top** see **top**[2]; **spinn'ing-wheel** a machine for spinning yarn, consisting of a wheel driven by the hand or by a treadle, which drives one or two spindles; **spin'-off** a process of transference of business on the US stock-market; a by-product that proves profitable on its own account; an incidental benefit. — Also *adj*. — **spin'out** a spinning skid that throws a motor vehicle off the road, track, etc; **spin stabilization** the stabilizing of the flight of a projected bullet, space rocket, etc, by giving it a spinning motion. — **flat spin** a state of panic; **spin a yarn** to tell a story; **spin out** to prolong, protract; (of a vehicle) to execute a spinning skid and leave the road, etc. [OE *spinnan*; Ger *spinnen*]

spina bifida *spī'nə bif'id-ə*, *n* a congenital defect in which one or more vertebrae fail to unite during the embryo stage, resulting in exposure of part of the spinal cord and often permanent paralysis. [See **spine** and **bifida**]

spinach *spin'ij* or *-ich*, *n* a plant (*Spinacia oleracea*) of the goosefoot family; its young leaves used as a vegetable; extended to various other plants. — *adj* **spinaceous** (*spin-ā'shəs*). — **spin'ach-beet** a kind of beet used like spinach. [OFr *espinage*, *espinache*; of doubtful origin, poss from L *spīna*, poss Ar *isfināj*]

spinal, **spinate**. See under **spine**.

spinar. See under **spin**.

spindle *spin'dl*, *n* the pin by which thread is twisted; a pin on which anything turns; the fusee of a watch; anything very slender; a spindle-shaped structure containing longitudinally-running microtubules, formed within the nucleus or cytoplasm during mitosis and meiosis (*biol*). — *vi* to grow long and slender. — *n* **spin'dling** a person or thing too long and slender; a slender shoot. — *adj* long and slender. — *adj* **spin'dly** disproportionally long and slender. — *adj* **spin'dle-legged** or **spin'dle-shanked** having long thin legs, like spindles. — *n pl* **spin'dle-legs** or **spin'dle-shanks** long slim legs; hence (as *n sing*) a person with long thin legs. — **spindle moulder** (*building*) a machine with a revolving spindle to which cutters of various shapes can be fixed; **spindle oil** very light and fluid lubricating oil. — *adj* **spin'dle-shaped** shaped like a spindle, thickest in the middle and tapering to both ends. — **spindle shell** a gasteropod (*Fusus*) with a spindle-shaped shell; **spindle side** the female side or line of descent, distaff side (opposite of *spear side*); **spindle tree** a shrub (*Euonymus europaeus*) of the *Celastraceae*, whose hard-grained wood was used for making spindles; **spindle whorl** a heavy ring giving momentum to the spindle. [OE *spinel*, from *spinnan* to spin; Ger *Spindel*]

spindrift *spin'drift*, *n* the spray blown from the crests of waves. [See **spoon**[1] and **drift**]

spine *spīn*, *n* a thorn, *esp* one formed by a modified branch or leaf; a long sharp process of a leaf; a thin, pointed spike, *esp* in fishes; the spinal column; any ridge extending lengthways; heartwood; the back of a book. — *n* **spī'na** the spinal column; a quill of a spinet; a lengthwise barrier in a Roman circus (*antiq*). — *adj* **spī'nal** of the backbone. — *adj* **spī'nate** or **spined** having a spine or spines. — *adj* **spine'less** having no spine; weak; vacillating; lacking courage, *esp* moral courage. — *adv* **spine'lessly**. — *n* **spine'lessness**. — *n* **spīnesc'ence**. — *adj* **spīnesc'ent** tapering or developing into a spine; tending to become spinous; somewhat spiny. — *adj* **spīnif'erous** thornbearing. — *adj* **spī'niform** like a thorn. — *adj* **spīnig'erous** bearing spines. — *adj* **spī'nigrade** moving by means of spines, as an echinoderm does. — *n* **spī'niness**. — *adj* **spī'nose** (or *-nōs'*) full of spines; thorny. — *n* **spīnos'ity** thorniness. — *adj* **spī'nous** spinose; like a thorn or spine in appearance (*anatom*, etc). — *adj* **spin'ūlāte**. — *n* **spinūle** (*spin'* or *spīn'*; *biol*) a small or minute spine. — *adj* **spinūlesc'ent**. — *adj* **spinūlif'erous**. — *adj* **spin'ūlōse** or **spin'ūlous**. — *adj* **spī'ny** full of spines; thorny; troublesome; perplexed. — **spina bifida** see separate entry; **spinal anaesthesia** injection of an anaesthetic into the spinal canal, producing suppression of sensation in part of the body but not unconsciousness; loss of sensation in part of the body due to injury to, or disease of, the spinal cord; **spinal canal** a passage running through the spinal column, containing the spinal cord; **spinal column** in vertebrates, the articulated series of vertebrae extending from the skull to the tip of the tail, forming the axis of the skeleton and enclosing the spinal cord; **spinal cord** or **chord** the main neural axis in vertebrates; **spine-bashing** (*Austr slang*) loafing, lying down, sleeping; **spine-basher**; **spine'-chiller** a frightening story, thought or happening. — *adj* **spine'-chilling**. — *adj* **spine'-tingling** that which causes a frisson of fear, pleasure or excitement. — **spiny anteater** an echidna. [L *spīna* a thorn]

spinel *spi-nel'* or *spin'əl*, *n* any mineral of a group of aluminates, ferrates, and chromates of magnesium, iron, zinc, etc crystallizing in octahedra. — **spinel ruby** ruby spinel, a variety of magnesian spinel with the colour of a true ruby. [Ital *spinella*]

spinescence, etc. See under **spine**.

spinet or **spinette** *spin'it* or *spi-net'*, *n* a musical instrument like a small harpsichord. — Also **spinnet**. [Ital *spinetta*, poss from maker G *Spinetti* (fl. 1500)]

spiniferous. See under **spine**.

spinifex *spin'*, *spīn'i-feks*, *n* a sharp-pointed Australian grass (genus *Spinifex*), of arid regions, whose spiny heads blow about and disseminate seed; popularly applied in Australia to porcupine grass. [L *spīna* spine, and the root of *facere* to make]

spiniform, **spinigerous**, etc. See under **spine**.

spink[1] *spingk*, (now *dialect*) *n* a finch, *esp* the chaffinch. [Perh imit]

spink[2] *spingk*, *n* the lady's smock or cuckoo flower. [Ety dubious]

spinnaker *spin'ə-kər*, (*naut*) *n* a three-cornered lightweight sail normally set forward of a yacht's mast to increase sail area when running before the wind or on a broad reach — on racing yachts the spinnaker has a great deal of flow in the belly of the canvas and is often brightly coloured. [Perh from **spin** and **moniker** or from *spinxer* a word coined when it was first introduced on the yacht *Sphinx* in the 1870s]

spinner, **spinneret**, etc. See under **spin**.

spinnet. See **spinet**.

spinney or **spinny** *spin'i*, *n* a copse or small clump of trees: — *pl* **spinn'eys** or **spinn'ies**. [OFr *espinei*, from L *spīnētum* a thorn hedge, thicket, from *spīna* thorn]

spino- *spī-nō-*, *combining form* signifying spine.

spinode *spī'nōd*, (*geom*) *n* a cusp or stationary point of a curve. [L *spīna* thorn, and *nōdus* knot]

spinose, **spinous**, etc. See under **spine**.

Spinozism *spi-nōz'izm*, (*philos*) *n* the doctrines of Benedict *Spinoza* (1632–77), *esp* the definitions, axioms and theorems of his metaphysical treatise *Ethics*; the pantheistic monism of Spinoza. — *n* **Spinō'zist** a follower of Spinoza or adherent of Spinozism. — *adj* **Spinōzis'tic**.

spinster *spin'stər*, *n* an unmarried woman; an old maid; a woman fit for the spinning-house (*obs*); a spinner (*obs* and *Shakesp*). — *n* **spin'sterdom** the world of old maids collectively. — *n* **spin'sterhood**. — *adj* **spinsterial** (*-stē'ri-əl*). — *adj* **spinstē'rian**. — *adj* **spin'sterish**. — *adj* **spin'sterly**. — *n* **spin'stership**. — *n* **spin'stress** a woman who spins; a spinster. [**spin**, and sfx **-ster**]

spintext or **spin-text** *spin'tekst*, *n* a clergyman, a long-winded preacher. [**spin** and **text**]

spinthariscope *spin-thär'i-skōp*, *n* an instrument for counting alpha particles by observing the sparks produced by their impact on a fluorescent screen. [Gr *spintharis* a spark, and *skopeein* to observe]

spinule, **spiny**, etc. See under **spine**.

spiracle *spīr'ə-kl*, *n* a breathing hole (*zool*); a vent, orifice, passage (*geol*). — *adj* **spīracular** (*-ak'ū-lər*). — *adj* **spīrac'ulate**. — *n* **spīrac'ulum**: — *pl* **spīrac'ula**. [L *spīrāculum*, from *spīrāre* to breathe]

spiraea or (*esp NAm*) **spirea** *spī-rē'ə*, *n* a plant or shrub of the rosaceous genus *Spiraea*, having flattened or plume-shaped heads of small pink or white flowers. [Gr *speiraiā* privet, from *speira* a coil (from its coiled fruits)]

spiral, etc. See under **spire**[1,2].

spirant *spī'rənt*, (*phonetics*) *adj* fricative, open, produced by narrowing without stopping the air passage. — *n* a spirant consonant (including or excluding nasals, liquids, and semi-vowels). — *n* **spīrā'tion** breathing; the procession of the Holy Ghost (*theol*). [L *spīrāre* to breathe]

spiraster, **spirated**. See under **spire**[2].

spire[1] *spīr*, *n* a tapering or conical body, *esp* a tree-top; a flower spike; a tall slender architectural structure tapering to a point; a shoot, sprout; a stalk, *esp* a long slender one; a reed or reedlike plant (also collectively); a deer's tine; a spike; a cone; a summit, peak. — *vi* to sprout; to shoot up. — *vt* to furnish with, or form into, a spire; to put forth as a shoot or fruit (*Spenser*). — *adj* **spīr'al** (*rare*) towering and tapering. — *n* **spir'alism** advancement through, or the concept of, a spirally structured career (or social, etc) system. — *n* **spir'alist** someone engaged in spiralism; loosely, an ambitious person. — *adv* **spir'ally**. — *adj* **spired** having a spire; tapering, conical; peaked; spiked; sprouted. — *n* **spire'less**. — *adv* **spire'wise**. — *adj* **spīr'y** shooting into spires; spire-like; tapering; abounding in spires. — **spiral ratchet screwdriver** a ratchet screwdriver which can be made to turn in either direction by downward pressure on a sleeve which applies torque to helical groves in the shaft; **spire'-steeple** a steeple with a spire. [OE *spīr* shoot, stem; cf **spike, spine**]

spire[2] *spīr*, *n* a coil; a spiral; the spiral part of a shell, excluding the body-whorl. — *vi* to wind, mount, or proceed in spirals. — *adj* **spīr'al** winding like the thread of a screw; with parts arranged in spirals (*bot*). — *n* a spiral line, course, or object; a curve (*usu* plane), the locus of a point whose distance from a fixed point varies according to some rule as the radius vector revolves (*math*); a helix; a gradual but continuous rise or fall, as of prices. — *vi* to go in a spiral; (of stocks and shares) to decrease in value uncontrollably (*informal*). — *vt* to make spiral. — *adj* **spīr'aliform** in or based on the shape of a spiral. — *n* **spīrality** (*-al'i-ti*). — *adv* **spīr'ally**. — *n* **spīras'ter** (Gr *astēr* star) a coiled sponge spicule with radiating spines. — *adj* **spīr'āted** spirally twisted. — *n* **spīr'ēme** in mitosis, the coiled thread formed by nuclear chromatin. — *adj* **spīr'ic** like a tore or anchor-ring. — *n* a curve, the plane section of a tore. — *adj* **spīrill'ar**. — *n* **spīrillō'sis** infection with a spirillum. — *n* **spīrill'um** any rigid, spiral-shaped bacterium of the genus *Spirillum*, eg *Spirillum minus* that causes rat-bite fever: — *pl* **spīrill'a**. — *adj* **spī'roid** with the form of, or like, a spiral. — *adj* **spīr'y** spirally coiled. — **spiral arm** an arm of a spiral galaxy; **spiral galaxy** (*astron*) one of a large class of galaxies, with two spiral arms emerging from a bright central ellipsoidal nucleus about which they rotate; **spiral staircase** a staircase in the form of a spiral, with a central column around which the steps are built. [Gr *speira* a coil, a tore]

spirit *spir'it*, *n* vital principle; the principle of thought; the soul; a disembodied soul; a ghost; an incorporeal being; a kidnapper (*obs*); enthusiasm; actuating emotion, disposition, frame of mind; a leading, independent, or lively person; animation; verve; courage; mettle; real meaning; essence, chief quality; a breath of wind (*archaic* or *poetic*); a breath (*obs*); a breathing (*Gr gram*); (*usu* in *pl*) a formerly supposed subtle substance in the body; (in *pl*) cheerful or exuberant vivacity; (in *pl*) state of mind, mood; (in *pl*) mental powers (*obs*); (in *pl*) spirituous liquor; (the following also in *pl*, sometimes with verb in *sing*) a distilled liquid; an aqueous solution of ethyl alcohol; a solution in alcohol. — *vt* to give spirit to; to inspirit, encourage, cheer; to convey away secretly, to kidnap (often with *away*, *off*). — *adj* **spir'ited** full of spirit, life, or fire; animated; possessed by a spirit. — *adv* **spir'itedly**. — *n* **spir'itedness**. — *adj* **spir'itful**. — *n* **spir'iting** the action of someone who spirits in any sense; the offices of a spirit or sprite. — *n* **spir'itism** spiritualism; animism. — *n* **spir'itist**. — *adj* **spiritist'ic**. — *n* **spir'itless** without spirit, cheerfulness, or courage; dejected; dead. — *adv* **spir'itlessly**. — *n* **spir'itlessness**. — *adj* **spir'itous** of the nature of spirit, pure; ardent, spirituous. — *n* **spir'itousness**. — *adj* **spir'itūal** of, of the nature of, relating to, spirit, a spirit, spirits, the mind, the higher faculties, the soul; highly refined in thought and feeling, habitually or naturally looking to things of the spirit; incorporeal; ecclesiastical, religious; witty, clever, as a Gallicism; spirituous (*obs* or *rare*). — *n* that which is spiritual; a Black American religious song. — *n* **spir'itualism** the condition of being spiritual; the philosophical doctrine that nothing is real but soul or spirit; the doctrine that spirit has a real existence apart from matter; the interpretation of a varied series of abnormal phenomena as for the most part caused by spiritual beings acting upon specially sensitive persons or mediums (also **spiritism**). — *n* **spir'itualist** someone who has a regard only to spiritual things; (sometimes with *cap*) someone who holds the doctrine of spiritualism or spiritism. — *adj* **spiritualist'ic**. — *n* **spirituality** (*-al'i-ti*) state of being spiritual; that which is spiritual; property held or revenue received in return for spiritual service (*hist*); the clergy (*hist*). — *n* **spiritualīzā'tion** or **-s-**. — *vt* **spir'itualize** or **-ise** to make spiritual; to imbue with spirituality; to refine; to free from sensuality; to give a spiritual meaning to. — *n* **spir'itualizer** or **-s-**. — *adv* **spir'itually**. — *n* **spir'itualness** the state or quality of being spiritual. — *n* **spir'itualty** (*obs* or *hist*) spirituality; the clergy. — *adj* **spirituel**, also *fem* (indiscriminately used) **spirituelle** (*spē-rē-tü-el*; *colloq spir-it-ū-el'*) showing refined and witty grace and delicacy. — *n* **spirituos'ity** spirituous character; immateriality. — *adj* **spir'ituous** sprightly (*obs*); spiritual (*obs*); of the nature of, or containing, a volatile principle (*archaic*); alcoholic. — *n* **spir'ituousness**. — *n* **spiritus** (*spīr'* or *spir'i-təs* or *spē'ri-tŏŏs*) spirit; a breathing (*Gr gram*; **spiritus asper** rough breathing, **spiritus lenis** smooth breathing). — *adj* **spir'ity** (*dialect* or *colloq*) spirited; spirituous. — **spir'it-blue** aniline blue; **spirit duck** another name for the bufflehead, from its rapid diving; **spirit duplicator** one that uses a solution of alcohol in the copying process; **spirit gum** a preparation used by actors for attaching false beards, etc; **spirit lamp** lamp burning methylated or other spirit to give heat; **spirit level** a glass tube nearly filled with *usu* alcohol, showing perfect levelness when the bubble is central; **spirit master** the master sheet used in a spirit duplicator; **spirit photography** the taking of photographs of people in which other shadowy figures appear; **spirit rapper** someone who claims to receive messages from disembodied spirits by raps or knocks; **spir'it-rapping**. — *adj* **spir'it-stirring** rousing the spirit. — **spirit varnish** shellac or other resin in a volatile solvent, *usu* alcohol; **spirit world** the world of disembodied spirits. — **animal spirits** a form of energy formerly believed to be sent along the nerves from the brain in order to cause sensation and motion; hence, constitutional liveliness; **Holy Spirit** or **the Spirit** see **Holy Ghost** under **holy**; **in spirits** cheerfully vivacious; **out of spirits** depressed; **spirit** (or **spirits**) **of ammonia** sal volatile; **spirit** (or **spirits**) **of salt** hydrochloric acid in water; **spirit** (or **spirits**) **of wine** alcohol. [L *spīritus* a breath, from *spīrāre* to breathe]

spiritoso *spir-it-ō'sō*, (*music*) *adj* and *adv* with spirit. [Ital]

spirling. See **sparling**.

spiro-[1] or **spir-** *spī'rō-*, *combining form* denoting spiral, as in *spirochaete*. [Gr *speira* a coil]

spiro-[2] *spī'rō-*, *combining form* denoting breathing, respiration. — *n* **spī'rogram** a record obtained from a spirograph. — *n* **spī'rograph** an instrument for recording breathing movements. — *n* **spīrog'raphy**. — *n* **spīrom'eter** an instrument for measuring lung capacity. — *adj* **spīromet'ric**. — *n* **spīrom'etry**. — *n* **spī'rophore** (Gr *phoros* a bringing) an apparatus for inducing artificial respiration by means of an airtight case for the body and an air pump. [L *spīrāre* to breathe]

spirochaete *spīrō-kēt*, *n* a spirally coiled bacterium (*Spirochaeta* and related genera) lacking a rigid cell wall, the cause of syphilis and other diseases. — *n* **spirochaet'aemia** the presence of spirochaetes in the blood, as in the later stages of syphilis. — *n* **spirochaetō'sis** infection with a spirochaete, as in syphilis, relapsing fever, etc. [Gr *speira* a coil, and *chaitē* hair, mane]

spirogyra *spī-rō-jī'rə* or *-gī'*, *n* any freshwater alga of the genus *Spirogyra* with chlorophyll in spiral bands. [Gr *speira* a coil, and *gȳros* a ring]

spiroid. See under **spire**[2].

spironolactone *spīr-ōnō'lak-tōn*, *n* a synthetic corticosteroid drug used in the treatment of hypertension and as a diuretic. [**spiro-**[2], **-no-**, and **lactone**]

spirt[1] *spûrt*, *vi* to shoot out forcibly, or in a fine strong jet. — *vt* to squirt in a fine strong jet. — *n* a sudden fine jet. [Origin uncertain; cf Ger dialect *spirzen* to spit; **spurt**]

spirt[2] *spûrt*, (*Shakesp*) *vi* to sprout, shoot up. [OE *sprytan*; cf **sprout**]

spirtle. Same as **spurtle**.

spiry. See under **spire**[1,2].

spissitude *spis'i-tūd*, (*now rare*) *n* density. [L *spissitūdō*, from *spissus* thick]

spit[1] *spit*, *n* a long thin rod, *usu* of metal, on which a joint of meat, etc is skewered for roasting; a sword (*joc*); a long narrow tongue of land or sand running into the sea; a wire or spindle holding a spool in a shuttle. — *vt* to transfix; to string on a rod or wire: — *pr p* **spitt'ing**; *pa t* and *pa p* **spitt'ed**. — *adj* **spitt'ed**. — *n* **spitt'er** a young deer with unbranched antlers. — *n* **spitt'ing** (an act of or) the action of piercing. [OE *spitu*; Du *spit*, Ger *Spiess*]

spit[2] *spit*, *vt* to throw out from the mouth; to eject with violence; to utter with hate, scorn or violence; to spawn. — *vi* to throw out saliva from the mouth; to rain in scattered drops; to make a spitting sound; to sputter; to feel or be furious (*colloq*): — *pr p* **spitt'ing**; *pa t* and *pa p* **spat**, *archaic* **spit**, *obs pa p* **spitt'en** or **spitt'ed** (*Bible*). — *n* saliva, spume; a light fall of rain or snow; an exact replica (*slang*; *usu dead* or *very spit*, from the phrase *as like him as if he had spit him out of his mouth*). — *n* **spitt'er**. — *n* **spitt'ing** the act of ejecting saliva; the ejection of oxygen, with drops of molten metal, when silver or platinum heated in air cools slowly; the resulting surface appearance. — Also *adj*. — *n* **spitt'le** spit, saliva. — *n* **spittoon'** any (*usu* bucket-like) container for spitting in, formerly a common feature of public houses, etc. — **spit box** a spittoon; **spit curl** (*colloq*) a curl pressed flat on the temple; **spit'fire** that which emits fire, eg a volcano, cannon; (with *cap*) a type of fighting aeroplane used in World War II; a hot-tempered person, *esp* a woman; **spitting image** (form of *dialect spitten image* — for *spit and image*) the exact likeness of (see above); **spitt'lebug** or **spittle insect** a froghopper or frothfly. — **spit and polish** cleaning up of uniform and equipment, *esp* to excess; ceremony and formality; **spit and sawdust** of or referring to a floor left rough and covered with sawdust, wood chippings, etc, or *esp* a bar having this type of floor; also, the character, quality, etc, of such a bar, spartan earthiness; **spit blood** or **feathers** to rage, be furious; **spit (it) out** to speak out, tell (it). [Northern OE *spittan*, ON *spȳta*, Ger dialect *spitzen*, *spützen*]

spit[3] *spit*, *vt* and *vi* to dig; to plant with a spade. — *n* a spade's depth; this amount of earth, a spadeful. [OE *spittan*, or (M)Du and (M)LGer *spit*]

spital. See **spittle**[2].

spitchcock *spich'kok*, *n* an eel split and broiled. — *vt* to split and broil (an eel). [Orig unknown; cf **spatchcock**]

spitcher *spit'chə*, (*naval slang*) *adj* done for. [Maltese *spicċċa*, pronounced *spitch'a* finished, ended]

spite *spīt*, *n* grudge; lasting ill-will; hatred; a cause of vexation (*archaic*). — *vt* to vex; to thwart; to hate. — *adj* **spite'ful** full of spite; wanting or intended to vex or injure another; malignant. — *adv* **spite'fully**. — *n* **spite'fulness**. — **in spite of** in opposition to all efforts of, in defiance of, in contempt of; notwithstanding; **spite (of)** despite. [**despite**]

spitten. Obsolete *pa p* of **spit**[2].

spitter. See under **spit**[1,2].

spittle[1], **spittoon**. See under **spit**[2].

spittle[2], also **spital**, *spit'l*, (*archaic*) *n* a hospital, *esp* for foul diseases, a lazar-house. — **spitt'le-house**. [**hospital**]

spitz *spits*, *n* a Pomeranian dog; a group of breeds of dog generally having long hair, pointed ears and a tightly curled tail, *incl* husky, samoyed, Pomeranian, etc. [Ger]

spiv *spiv*, (*slang*) *n* a flashy black-market hawker; someone who makes money by dubious means; an idler. — *n* **spivv'ery** the world or the practices of spivs. — *adj* **spivv'y**. [Back-formation of dialect *spiving* smart; perh connected with **spiff**]

splanchnic *splangk'nik*, (*zool*) *adj* visceral, intestinal. — *n* **splanch'nocele** (*-sēl*; Gr *koilos* hollow) a visceral cavity; the posterior part of the coelom. — *n* **splanch'nology** the study of the viscera. [Gr *splanchnon*, pl *splanchna* entrails]

splash *splash*, *vt* to spatter, as with water or mud; to throw (liquid) about unevenly or scatteringly; to dash liquid on or over; to effect by or with splashing; to variegate as if by splashing; to display, print very prominently. — *vi* to dabble; to dash liquid about; to move or go with a throwing about of liquid; to fly about dispersedly; (of bullets) to throw about fragments or molten metal on striking. — *n* the dispersion of liquid suddenly disturbed, as by throwing something into it or by throwing it about; liquid thrown on anything; a spot formed by or as if by throwing liquid; a little soda water, tonic, etc (with a spirit); lead thrown about by a bullet on striking; ostentation, publicity, display; an instance of this; a sensation, excitement, dash; a prominently printed slogan or (a story, article, introduced by such a) headline. — *n* **splash'er** someone who, or something that, splashes; a guard against splashing; a board attached to the foot for walking on mud. — *adv* **splash'ily**. — *n* and *adj* **splash'ing**. — *adj* **splash'y** splashing; with splashing; wet and muddy; full of puddles; ostentatious, showy. — **splash'-back** a piece of glass, plastic, etc, or area of tiles covering the part of a wall behind a wash basin to protect against splashing; **splash'board** a mudguard; a dashboard; **splash'down** (the moment of) the landing of a spacecraft on the sea. — *adj* **splash'proof**. — **splash down** (of spacecraft) to land on the sea at the end of a mission; **splash out (on)** (*colloq*) to spend a lot of money (on). [**plash**]

splat[1] *splat*, *n* a thin strip forming the upright middle part of a chair back. [**plat**[3]]

splat[2] *splat*, *n* the sound made by a soft, wet object striking a surface. — *vi* to strike a surface with a splat; to cause (droplets of molten metal) to strike and spread over a metal surface, driven by shock waves (*metallurgy*). — *adv* with this sound. — *n* **splatt'ing**. — **splat cooling** or **splat quenching** the technical process of cooling metal rapidly by splatting. [Onomatopoeic]

splatch *splach*, (*Scot* and *US*) *n* a splash or clot of dirt or colour; a splotch. — *vt* to splotch. [Cf **splotch**]

splatter *splat'ər*, *vt* and *vi* to spatter; to splash; to sputter. — *n* a splash; a spattering. — **splatter film** or **movie** (*slang*) a film in which graphic scenes of gory mutilation, amputation, etc are depicted, employing various special effects. [Cf **spatter**]

splay[1] *splā*, *vt* and *vi* to display (*obs*); to slope, slant, or bevel (*archit*); to spread out. — *n* a slant or bevel, as of the side of a doorway, window, etc. — *adj* having a splay; turned outwards. — *adv* with a splay. — **splay foot** a flat foot turned outward. — *adj* **splay'-foot** or **-footed**. — *adj* **splay'-mouthed** wide-mouthed. [**display**]

splay[2] *splā*, (*NAm slang*) *n* marihuana. [Origin obscure]

spleen *splēn*, *n* a soft, pulpy, ovoid organ close to the stomach, that produces lymphocytes in the newborn and contains phagocytes which remove worn-out blood cells and other waste matter from the bloodstream — once thought the seat of anger and melancholy; hence various meanings (mostly in *Shakesp* and more or less *obs*) such as spite, boredom, ill-humour, melancholy, mirth, caprice, impulse, high spirit. — *adj* **spleen'ful**. — *adj* **spleen'ish**. — *adj* **spleen'less**. — *adj* **spleen'y** (*Shakesp*). — *adj* **splē'native** (*obs*) hot-tempered. — *n* **splenec'tomy** (*splin-*; Gr *ek* out, and *tomē* a cutting) surgical excision of the spleen. — *adj* **splenetic** (*splin-et'ik*; formerly *splēn'i-tik*) of the spleen; affected with spleen; bad-tempered, irritable or irritated, peevish; melancholy. — *n* a splenetic person. — *adj* **splenet'ical**. — *adv* **splenet'ically**. — *adj* **splenic** (*splē'nik* or *splen'*) of the spleen. — *n* **splenī'tis** (*splin-*) inflammation of the spleen. — *n* **splēnīzā'tion** or **-s-** conversion (eg of the lung) into a spongy, spleenlike substance. — *n* **splēnomeg'aly** (Gr *megas*, *megalē*, *mega* big) enlargement of the spleen. — **spleen'stone** (*obs*) jade; **spleen'wort** any fern of the genus *Asplenium*; **splenic fever** anthrax. [L *splēn*, from Gr *splēn*]

splendent *splen'dənt*, (*archaic*) *adj* brightly shining; brilliant, magnificent, gorgeous; renowned (*fig*). [L *splendens*, *-ent-* pa p of *splendēre* to shine]

splendid *splen'did*, *adj* brilliant, resplendent; magnificent; excellent (*colloq*). — *adj* (*obs*) **splendid'ious** — *adv*

splen'didly. — *n* **splen'didness**. — *adj* **splen'didous** (*obs*). — *adj* **splendif'erous** (now only *colloq*). — *adj* **splen'dorous** or **splen'drous**. — *n* **splen'dour** or (*NAm*) **splendor** (*-dər*) brilliance; magnificence. [L *splendēre* to shine, *splendidus*, *splendor*]

splendide mendax *splen'di-dā men'daks*, (*L*) splendidly false, nobly lying, untruthful for a good reason. [Horace *Odes III*. 11. 35]

splenectomy, **splenetic**, etc. See under **spleen**.

splenial *splē'ni-əl*, *adj* splint-like; of the splenium or the splenius. — *n* **splē'nium** (*anatom*) the round padlike posterior border of the *corpus callosum*, the bundle of fibres uniting the two cerebral hemispheres. — *n* **splē'nius** (*anatom*) a large thick muscle on the back of the neck. [Gr *splēnion* pad, compress]

splenic, **splenomegaly**, etc. See under **spleen**.

spleuchan *splōōhh'ən*, (*Scot* and *Ir*) *n* a tobacco pouch; a purse. [Gaelic *spliùc(h)an*]

splice *splīs*, *vt* to unite by interweaving the strands; to join together by overlapping; to unite, *esp* (*slang*; also *vi*) in matrimony. — *n* the act of splicing; a joint made by splicing; the part of the handle of a cricket bat, etc that fits into the blade. — *n* **splicer**. — **sit on the splice** (*cricket slang*) to bat defensively, with no attempt to gain runs; **splice the mainbrace** (*naut slang*) to serve out an allowance of alcohol spirits; to partake of alcoholic spirits. [Du (now dialect) *splissen*]

spliff *splif*, (*slang*, *esp Rastafarian*, *orig W Indian*) *n* a marijuana cigarette, a joint; the act of smoking such a cigarette. [Origin uncertain]

spline *splīn*, *n* a key to make a wheel and shaft revolve together; a thin strip or slat. — *vt* to put splines on. [Orig E Anglian]

splint *splint*, *n* a strip, slip of wood, lath; a splinter; an overlapping strip in armour; a contrivance for holding a broken bone, etc, in position; a bony enlargement on a horse's leg along the line of the splint bone between knee and fetlock; the growth of such an enlargement; splint coal. — *vt* to put in splints. — *n* **splint'er** a piece of wood, metal, etc, split off, *esp* a needlelike piece; a slender strip of wood, *esp* one used as a torch; a splint (*obs*). — *vt* and *vi* to split into splinters. — *vt* (*Shakesp*) to put in splints, hence join, piece. — *adj* **splint'ery** made of, or like, splinters; apt to splinter. — **splint armour** armour of narrow overlapping plates; **splint bone** a small bone alongside the cannon bone in the horse, etc, the second or the fourth metacarpal or metatarsal (also **splent bone**); the fibula; **splint coal** a hard coal of uneven fracture that does not cake; **splinter group** a group formed by a breakaway from a larger body. — *adj* **splint'er-proof** proof against the splinters of bursting shells or bombs, or against splintering. — **splintery fracture** (*mineralogy*) the property of breaking with a surface like broken wood; **splint'wood** sapwood. [MDu *splinte* (Du *splint*) or (M)LGer *splinte*, *splente*; Du and LGer *splinter*, Ger *Splenter*]

split *split*, *vt* to break in pieces, wreck; to rend; to cleave lengthwise; to divide, share; to disunite; to divulge (*colloq*). — *vi* to be dashed to pieces (often with *up*); to suffer shipwreck; to divide or part asunder (often with *up*); to divulge secrets (*colloq*); to divide one's votes instead of plumping; to burst with laughter; to go at full speed; to leave, to make oneself scarce (*slang*); to break off relations (with) (*slang*; often with *up*): — *pr p* **splitt'ing**; *pa t* and *pa p* **split**, *Shakesp*, etc **splitt'ed**. — *n* a crack or rent lengthwise; a schism; a half-bottle of aerated water, etc, a half-glass of spirits; (in *pl*) the acrobatic feat of going down to the floor with the legs spread out laterally or one forward and one back; a division, share-out (*usu* of money, stolen goods, etc) (*colloq*); a kind of rough suede made from an inner separated layer of hide, so having the same finish on both sides (also **split leather**); a sweet dish, *usu* of sliced-open fruit and cream, ice-cream, etc; a piece of wood split for kindling or basket weaving (*Can*); a split-level house or apartment (*US*); a split time. — *adj* having been split; having a split or break. — *n* **splitt'er** someone who, or that which, splits; someone who splits hairs in argument, classification, etc; a splitting headache (*colloq*). — *adj* **splitt'ing** rending; cleaving; ear-splitting; (of a headache) very severe; very rapid. — *adj* **split'-brain** (*zool*) of or involving separation of the cerebral hemispheres by dividing the corpus callosum. — **split cane** bamboo split to form triangular strips then glued to form a hexagonal rod, used to make strong but flexible fishing rods; **split end** the end of a hair that has split; an offensive end player who lines up some distance from the formation (*Am football*); **split image** a bisected image, produced in a focusing system in which the two halves are displaced if the camera is out of focus (*photog*); a spitting image (also **splitt'ing image**); **split-image rangefinder** an optical device, used to assist camera focusing, in which the image is split when out of focus and whole when focused; **split infinitive** an infinitive with an adverb between 'to' and the verb, as in *to boldly go*; **split leather** see **split** above. — *adj* **split-lev'el** on more than one level (see also below). — **split mind** a mental disorder in which the thoughts may become separated from the emotions; loosely, a divided or dual opinion or feeling (about something). — *adj* **split'-new** (*Scot*) brand-new. — **split'-off** (*US finance*) an exchange of the stock in a subsidiary company with part of the stock in the parent company; **split pea** see under **pea**[1]; **split personality** dual personality; **split pin** a pin made of a doubled piece of metal formed into a ring at the head to give tension and *usu* inserted in a hole in a bolt to hold a nut, etc, firmly; **split ring** a ring made up of two or more loops of metal that may be stretched apart, as for keeping keys together; **split screen** a cinematic technique of showing different scenes simultaneously on separate parts of the screen, also used in television; a facility whereby separate areas of the screen may be used to display and carry out separate functions simultaneously (*comput*). — *adj* **split'-screen**. — **split second** a fraction of a second. — *adj* **split'-second** timed to a fraction of a second. — **split-seconds hand** a double seconds hand in a chronograph, of which first one and then the other member can be stopped by pressing a button; **split shift** a working shift divided into two separate periods during the day; **split time** the time indicated by the split-seconds hand of a chronograph. — **full split** at full speed; **split hairs** see under **hair**; **split investment trust** see under **trust**; **split-level house** a one-storey house with rooms on more than one level; **split on** (*colloq*) to betray, give (a person) away; **split on a rock** to meet some unforeseen and disastrous difficulty, to go to ruin; **split one's sides** to laugh immoderately; **split the difference** to divide equally the sum of matter in dispute, to take the mean. [Du *splitten*, related to *splijten*, Ger *spleissen*]

splodge, **splodgily** etc. See under **splotch**.

splore *splōr* or *splör*, (*Scot*) *n* a frolic; a spree; an escapade; a row; a scrape. [Origin obscure]

splosh *splosh*, *n*, *vi* and *vt* a *usu* humorous variant of **splash**.

splotch *sploch* or **splodge** *sploj*, *n* a big or heavy splash, spot, or stain. — *vt* to mark with splotches or splodges. — *vi* to trudge flounderingly or splashily. — *adv* **splotch'ily** or **splodg'ily**. — *n* **splotch'iness** or **splodg'iness**. — *adj* **splotch'y** or **splodg'y**. [Perh connected with OE *splott* spot]

splurge *splûrj*, *n* any boisterous or extravagant display; a bout of extravagance. — *vi* to make such a display; to spend a lot of money (on). — *adj* **splur'gy**. [Imit]

splutter *splut'ər*, *vi* to eject drops; to scatter ink upon a paper, as a bad pen does; to scatter liquid with spitting noises; to articulate confusedly as in rage. — *vt* to utter splutteringly. — *n* an act or noise of spluttering. — *n* **splutt'erer**. — *n* and *adj* **splutt'ering**. — *adv* **splutt'eringly**. — *adj* **splutt'ery**. [Prob imit; cf **sputter**]

Spode *spōd*, *n* (also without *cap*) a porcelain made with addition of bone-ash by Josiah *Spode* (1754–1827) at Stoke-on-Trent. — Also *adj*.

spodium *spō'di-əm*, (*now rare*) *n* powder obtained fom various substances by calcination; bone-black. [Gr *spodos*, dimin *spodion* ashes]

spodo- or **spod-** *spŏd'ō*, *combining form* signifying ashes, dross. — *n* **spōdō'gram** (*bot*) a preparation of the ash from (the section of) a plant, used in investigating structure in microscopy. — *n* **spodomancy** (*spod'ə-man-si*) divination by means of ashes. — *adj* **spodoman'tic**. [Gr *spodos* ashes]

spodumene *spŏd'ū-mēn*, (*mineralogy*) *n* a monoclinic pyroxene, a silicate of aluminium and lithium occurring in granite pegmantites. [From Gr *spodoumenos* (contracted participle) burnt to ashes, from its appearance under the blowpipe]

spoffish or **spoffy** *spof'ish* or *spof'i*, (*archaic*) *adj* fussy, officious. [Origin obscure]

spoil *spoil*, *vt* to mar; to impair; to make useless; to treat over-indulgently; to harm the character by so doing; to take by force (*archaic*); to plunder; to despoil; to strip; to deprive; to corrupt; to destroy, end (*Shakesp*). — *vi* to go bad; to deteriorate; to practise spoliation: — *pa t* and *pa p* **spoiled** or (only in sense of damage) **spoilt**. — *n* (*usu* in *pl*) plunder, booty; acquisitions, prizes; spoliation; pillage; a cast or stripped-off skin; remains of an animal body; material cast out in excavation; damage, impairment (*rare*); a thing spoiled in making (*rare*). — *n* **spoil'age** the act of spoiling; waste by spoiling; material so wasted. — *adj* **spoiled**. — *n* **spoil'er** any thing or person that spoils; an aerodynamic device fitted to the wings of an aircraft to reduce lift and assist descent; a similar device fitted to motor vehicles, *esp* racing and sports cars, to lessen drag and reduce the tendency to become unstable through a lifting effect at high speeds; an electronic device incorporated in a piece of recording equipment which prevents unauthorized recording, *usu* by using a **spoiler signal** which renders useless any recording made; a newspaper article, speech, etc intended to lessen the impact of another published or made on the same subject elsewhere (*slang*); a third candidate in a two-way political election, whose only effect is to reduce the number of votes for one of the main candidates (*US*). — *adj* **spoil'ful** (*Spenser* **spoylefull**) plundering. — **spoil bank** or **heap** a deposit of spoil; **spoil'five** a card game drawn or *spoiled* if no player wins three out of five tricks; **spoils'man** someone who looks for profit out of politics or who advocates the spoils system (*US*); **spoil'sport** someone who stops or interferes with sport or other people's pleasure; a meddler; **spoils system** (chiefly *US*) the practice of appointing supporters of the political party gaining or in power, to nonelective public offices, on the principle that 'to the victor belong the spoils'; **spoilt paper** in a ballot, a voting paper marked, *esp* deliberately, in such a way as to render it invalid. — **spoiling for** (a fight, etc) more than ripe or ready for; intent on. [OFr *espoille*, from L *spolium* spoil]

spoke[1] *spōk*, *pa t* of **speak**.

spoke[2] *spōk*, *n* one of the radiating bars of a wheel. — *adv* **spoke'wise**. — **spoke'shave** a two-handled planing tool for curved work. — **put a spoke in someone's wheel** to thwart or hinder someone. [OE *spāca*; Du *speek*, Ger *Speiche*]

spoken *spōk'n*, *pa p* of **speak**. — Used in combination to denote speech or speaking, as in *plain-spoken*, *soft-spoken*. — **spo'ken for** chosen, reserved; romantically attached, not free or single (*colloq*).

spokesman *spōks'mən* or **spokes'person**, *fem* **spokes'-woman**, *n* a person who speaks for another, or for others: — *pl* **spokes'men**, **spokes'persons** or **spokes'-people**, *fem* **spokes'women**. — [**speak** and **man**[1], **person**, **woman**]

spolia opima *spō'li-ə ōp'i-mə* or *spo'li-a* or *op-ē'ma*, (*L*) the richest spoils — the arms taken in single combat by a leader from a leader; hence supreme achievement.

spoliate *spō'li-āt*, *vt* and *vi* to despoil, to plunder. — *n* **spōliā'tion**. — *adj* **spō'liātive** serving to take away or diminish. — *n* **spō'liātor**. — *adj* **spō'liatory** (*-ə-tər-i*). [L *spoliāre*, *-ātum*, from *spolium* spoil]

spondee *spon'dē*, (*prosody*) *n* a foot of two long syllables. — *adj* **spondaic** (*-dā'ik*). — *adj* **spondā'ical**. [L *spondēus* (*pēs*), from Gr *spondeios* (*pous*) (a foot) used in the slow solemn hymns sung at a *spondē* or drink-offering, from *spendein* to pour out, make a libation]

spondulicks, **spondoolicks** or **spondulix** *spon-dōō'liks*, (*orig US*; *slang*) *n pl* money. [From Gr *spondylikos*, from *spondylos* a seashell used as currency]

spondyl *spon'dil*, (*zool*) *n* a vertebra; a thorny oyster (*Spondylus*). — *adj* **spondylit'ic** affected by spondylitis. — *n* a person suffering from spondylitis. — *n* **spondylī'tis** (*med*) inflammation of the synovial joints of the backbone. — *n* **spondylolisthē'sis** a partial dislocation of the (*usu* lower) vertebrae in which a vertebra slips forward over the one below. — *n* **spondylol'ysis** disintegration of one or more vertebrae. — *n* **spondylō'sis** vertebral ankylosis. — *n* **spondylō'syndēsis** surgical fusion of the joints between the vertebrae. — *adj* **spon'dylous**. [Gr *sp*(*h*)*ondylos* a vertebra]

sponge *spunj*, *n* any member of the phylum *Porifera*, sessile aquatic animals with a single cavity in the body, with numerous pores; the fibrous skeleton of such an animal, remarkable for its power of holding water; a piece of such a skeleton, or a synthetic substitute, used for washing, absorbing, etc; a swab for a cannon; any spongelike substance, such as leavened dough, a cake or pudding or swampy ground; a bedeguar; a hanger-on or parasite (*colloq*); a drunkard (*colloq*); an application of a sponge; the life or behaviour of a sponger upon others (*colloq*). — *vt* to wipe, wipe out, soak up or remove with a sponge; to drain, as if by squeezing a sponge; to gain by the art of the parasite. — *vi* to suck in, as a sponge does; to fish for sponges; to live on others parasitically (often with *on* or *off*). — *adj* **spon'geable**. — *adj* **spongeous** (*spun'jəs*) spongy. — *n* **spong'er** a person who uses a sponge; a sponge fisher; a sponge fishing boat; an apparatus for sponging cloth; a sponge or parasite. — *adj* **spongicolous** (*spun-* or *spon-jik'ə-ləs*; L *colere* to inhabit) living in association with, *usu* within, a sponge. — *adj* **spon'gi-form** like or related to a sponge. — *adv* **spon'gily** in a spongy way or manner. — *n* **spongin** (*spun'jin*) a horny substance in the skeletons of various sponges. — *n* **spon'giness**. — *adj* **spongiose** (*spun'* or *-ōs'*). — *adj* **spongious** (*spun'jəs*). — *adj* **spongoid** (*spong'goid*). — *n* **spongologist** (*spong-gol'ə-jist*). — *n* **spongol'ogy** the science of sponges. — *adj* **spongy** (*spun'ji*) absorptive; porous; wet and soft; drunken; (of vehicle suspension, brakes, etc) lacking firmness or responsiveness. — **sponge'bag** a waterproof bag for carrying a sponge; (in *pl*) checked or striped trousers. — *adj* checked. — **sponge bath** a washing of the body by or from a sponge, as for a sick or bedridden person; **sponge cake** a very light sweet cake of flour, eggs, and sugar; **sponge cloth** a cotton cloth of open texture similar to a sponge; **sponge'-down** see **sponge down** below; **sponge finger** a finger-shaped sponge cake; **sponge fisher**; **sponge fishing**; **sponge rubber** rubber processed into spongelike form; **sponge'ware** (*ceramics*) pottery, etc on which patterns, colours, etc are applied using a sponge; **sponge'wood** sola, an Indian plant also known as the hat plant; **spon'ging-house** or **spun'ging-house** (*obs*) a bailiff's lodging-house for debtors in his custody before their committal to prison; **spongy parenchyma** (*bot*) a loose tissue in leaves with much intercellular space; **spongy platinum** or **platinum sponge** platinum in a finely divided state. — **set a sponge** to leaven a small mass of dough for use in leavening a large quantity; **sponge down** to clean or wipe with a sponge (*n* **sponge'-down**); **throw up** (or **in**) **the sponge** to acknowledge defeat by throwing into the air the sponge with which a boxer is rubbed down between rounds (cf **throw in the towel**); to give up any struggle. [OE *sponge*, *spunge*, and OFr *esponge*, from L *spongia*, from Gr *spongiā*]

sponsal *spon'sl*, *adj* spousal. — *n pl* **sponsā'lia** espousals.

sponsible *spon'si-bl*, (now *dialect*) *adj* aphetic for **responsible** in the sense of respectable.

sponsing. See **sponson**.

sponsion *spon'shən*, *n* the act of becoming surety for another; an agreement or promise made on behalf of another, *esp* by an individual on behalf of his or her government. — *adj* **spon'sional**. [L *spondēre*, *spōnsum* promise]

sponson *spon'sn*, *n* a platform extending out from a ship's deck, for mounting a gun, a paddle, wheel, etc; a wing section giving extra lift; an air-filled tank on the side of a canoe to give buoyancy; a structure to give a seaplane stability on the water. — Also **spon'sing**. [Ety dubious]

sponsor *spon'sər*, *n* a person who promises solemnly for another; a surety; a godfather or godmother; a promoter; a person or organization financing an event, a broadcast, etc in return for self-advertisement at the event, etc; a person or organization who promises to pay a specified sum to a person for taking part in a fund-raising event or activity on behalf of a charity, etc. — *vt* to act as a sponsor. — *adj* **sponso'rial**. — *n* **spon'sorship**. [L *spondēre*, *spōnsum* promise]

spontaneous *spon-tā'nyəs* or *-ni-əs*, *adj* of one's free will; acting by its own impulse or natural law; produced of itself; impulsive; unpremeditated. — *n* **spontaneity** (*-tə-nē'i-ti* or *-nā'i-ti*). — *adv* **spontā'neously**. — *n* **spontā'neousness**. — **spontaneous abortion** miscarriage; **spontaneous combustion** catching fire by causes at work within, *esp* slow oxidation of a mass of matter; **spontaneous behaviour** (*behav*) behaviour occurring in the apparent absence of any stimuli; **spontaneous generation** the production of living organisms from dead matter; **spontaneous remission** recovery without treatment. [L *spontāneus*, from *sponte* of one's own accord]

sponte sua *spon'te sōō'ä*, (*L*) of one's own accord, unsolicited.

spontoon *spon-tōōn'*, *n* a small-headed halberd formerly carried by some infantry officers. [Fr *sponton*, from Ital *spontone*, from *punto*, from L *punctum* a point]

spoof *spōōf*, (*slang*) *n orig*, a hoaxing game invented and named by Arthur Roberts (1852–1933), comedian; a card game; a parody, take-off, satire; ejaculated semen (*Austr*). — *adj* bogus. — *vt* and *vi* to hoax; to parody. — *n* **spoof'er**. — *n* **spoof'ery**.

spook *spōōk*, *n* a ghost; a spy, an undercover agent (*slang*, *orig US*). — *vi* to play the spook; to take fright; (of a horse) to shy away. — *vt* to frighten, startle. — *adj* ghostly. — *n* **spook'ery** things that are spooky; matters pertaining to spooks. — *adv* **spook'ily**. — *n* **spook'iness**. — *adj* **spook'ish** or **spook'y**. [Appar LGer; cf Ger *Spuk*, Du *spook*]

spool *spōōl*, *n* a cylinder, bobbin or reel on which yarn, etc is wound. — *vt* and *vi* to wind on spools. — *n* **spool'er**. [LGer *spôle*; Du *spoel*, or ONFr *espole*; Ger *Spule*]

spoom, spooming. See **spoon**[1].

spoon[1] *spōōn*, *vi* to scud before the wind; to run before a gale with reduced canvas (*old naut*). — Also **spoom**. — *adj* **spoom'ing** (*Keats*) foaming. — *n* **spoon'drift** light spray borne on a gale. — Also (*orig Northern*) **spin'drift**. [Origin unknown]

spoon[2] *spōōn*, *n* an (eating, or serving, etc) instrument with a shallow bowl and a handle; anything of similar shape, such as an oar; (a stroke with) a wooden-headed golf club with the face slightly hollowed; a spoonbait (*colloq*); the wooden spoon (*Cambridge*; see under **wood**[1]); a simpleton; courtship, *esp* when mawkish or sentimental; a person who engages in such courtship. — *vt* to transfer with, or as if with, a spoon; to shove, scoop, or hit softly up into the air, instead of striking cleanly and definitely; to court, *esp* in a sentimental way; to fish with a spoonbait; to pack together like spoons. — *vi* to indulge in (*esp* sentimental) courtship; to fish with a spoonbait. — *n* **spoon'ful** as much as fills a spoon; a small quantity: — *pl* **spoon'fuls**. — *adv* **spoon'ily**. — *adv* **spoon'ways** or **spoon'wise** like spoons packed closely together. — *adj* **spoon'y** or **spoon'ey** silly; foolishly and demonstratively fond. — *n* someone who is spoony. — **spoon'bait** or **spoon'hook** a lure on a swivel, used in trolling for fish; **spoon'bill** any bird of a family (*Plataleidae*) similar to the ibises, with long, flat, broad bill, spoon-shaped at the tip; a shoveller (genus *Spatula*). — *adj* **spoon'-fed** or **spoon'fed** fed with a spoon; artificially fostered (*fig*); taught by doled-out doses of cut-and-dried information. — *vt* **spoon'-feed**. — **born with a silver spoon in one's mouth** see under **silver**. [OE *spōn* sliver, chip, shaving, Ger *Span* chip, ON *spānn*, *spōnn* chip, spoon]

spoonerism *spōō'nər-izm*, *n* a transposition of initial sounds of spoken words, eg 'shoving leopard' for 'loving shepherd'. [Rev W A *Spooner* (1844–1930), a noted perpetrator of transpositions of this kind]

spoor *spōōr*, *n* a track, *esp* of a hunted animal. — *vt* and *vi* to track. — *n* **spoor'er**. [Du *spoor*, a track; cf OE and ON *spor*, Ger *Spur*; also **speir**]

spoot *spōōt*, (*Orkney*) *n* the razor-shell mollusc.

sporadic *spor-ad'ik*, *adj* scattered; occurring here and there or now and then; occurring casually. — Also (*rare*) **sporad'ical**. — *adv* **sporad'ically**. [Gr *sporadikos*, from *sporas*, *sporados* scattered, from *speirein* to sow]

spore *spōr* or *spör*, (*biol*) *n* a unicellular asexual reproductive body; sometimes extended to other reproductive bodies. — *adj* **sporangial** (*spor-an'ji-əl*). — *n* **sporan'giole** or **sporan'giolum** (or *-jī'*; *pl* **sporan'giola**) a sporangium containing one or few spores. — *n* **sporan'giophore** the part that bears sporangia. — *n* **sporan'giospore** a spore developed in a sporangium. — *n* **sporan'gium** (*pl* **sporan'gia**) a hollow, walled structure or sac in which spores are produced. — Also **spore case**. — *n* **spor'idesm** (Gr *desmos* a bond) a multicellular body or group of spores, of which every cell is capable of germinating. — *adj* **sporid'ial**. — *n* **sporid'ium** (*pl* **sporid'ia**) a spore borne on a promycelium. — *n* **spor'ocarp** (Gr *karpos* fruit) a structure containing the sori and sporangia in aquatic ferns; a multicellular structure in which spores are formed in certain fungi, algae, etc. — *n* **spor'ocyst** a rounded, thick-walled structure produced, as by protozoans, in the process of sporulation; the cyst-like larva of a trematode. — *adj* **sporocyst'ic**. — *n* **sporogen'esis** production of or by spores. — Also **sporogeny** (*-oj'*). — *adj* **sporog'enous** producing spores. — *n* **sporogonium** (*-gō'*; *pl* **sporogo'nia**) the capsule or asexual generation in mosses and liverworts. — *n* **spor'ophore** a spore-bearing stalk or structure, as in fungi. — *adj* **sporophor'ic** or **sporoph'orous**. — *n* **spor'ophyll** or **spor'ophyl** (Gr *phyllon* leaf) a leaf (often modified) that bears sporangia. — *n* **spor'ophyte** (Gr *phyton* plant) the spore-bearing or asexual generation in the lifecycle of a plant. — *adj* **sporophytic** (*-fit'ik*). — *n* **sporotrichosis** (*spōr-ō-trik-ō'sis*) a chronic skin infection caused by *Sporothrix schenckii*, a fungus of moss and other plants, resulting in ulcers and nodules in the lymph glands. — *n* **sporozō'an** any parasitic protozoan of the class *Sporozoa*, reproducing by spores, including the causal organisms of malaria and pébrine. — Also *adj*. — *n* **sporozō'ite** (Gr *zōion* an animal) a minute, mobile, pre-adult, *usu* infective spore developed by sporozoans. — *adj* **spor'ūlar**. — *vi* **spor'ūlate** to produce spores. — *n* **sporūlā'tion** formation or production of spores; breaking up into spores. — *n* **spor'ule** a small spore. [Gr *sporā* a seed, from *speirein* to sow]

sporran *spor'ən*, *n* an ornamental pouch of leather and/or fur worn hanging in front of the kilt as part of Scottish Highland dress. [Gaelic *sporan*]

sport *spōrt* or *spört*, *n* recreation; a pastime; play; a game or activity, *esp* one involving physical exercise; a specific, *esp* outdoor, amusement, activity or recreation; success in or pleasure from shooting, fishing, or the like; amusement, fun, good-humoured mirth; mockery, contemptuous mirth; an object of mockery, a laughing-stock; a plaything (*esp fig*); dalliance, amorous behaviour; a person of sportsmanlike character, a good fellow; a form of address, used *esp* between males (*Austr* and *NZ*); an animal or plant that varies singularly and spontaneously from the normal type. — *vi* to enjoy oneself, have a good time; to frolic (also *vt* with *it*); to play (*archaic*); to take part in a specific amusement, activity or recreation, *esp* outdoor; to make fun (of) (often with *with*); to trifle (with); to deviate from the normal (*biol*). — *vt* to wear, use, exhibit, set up, publicly or ostentatiously; to wager; to squander (often with *away*; *rare*); to amuse (*obs*); to force open (*obs*). — *adj* see **sports**. — *n* **sportabil'ity** (*rare*) sportiveness. — *adj* **sport'able** (*rare*). — *n* **sport'ance** (*rare*) play. — *n* **sport'er** someone who sports; a sportsman. — *adj* **sport'ful** full of sport; merry; full of jesting. — *adv* **sport'fully**. — *n* **sport'fulness**. — *adv* **sport'ily**. — *n* **sport'iness**. — *adj* **sport'ing** relating to, engaging in, or fond of sports or gambling; willing to take a chance; sportsmanlike; (in the UK) pertaining to one of the two major classes of dogs recognized by the Kennel Club (the other being *non-sporting*), comprising hounds, gundogs, and terriers; (in the US) pertaining to one of the six recognized groups of breeds, essentially comprising the gundogs (as opposed to hounds, terriers, etc). — *adv* **sport'ingly**. — *adj* **sport'ive** inclined to sport; playful; merry; amorous, wanton. — *adv* **sport'ively**. — *n* **sport'iveness**. — *adj* **sport'less** (*rare*) without sport or mirth; sad. — *n pl* **sports** a meeting for races and other competitive events. — *adj* of, or suitable for, sport, eg *sports shoes*. — Also (*esp NAm*) **sport**. — *adj* **sport'y** sportsmanlike (*colloq*); (of a person) who enjoys, takes part in or is proficient at sport; (of a car) that looks or handles like a sports car; stylish, lively. — **sporting chance** as good a chance of winning or being successful as of losing or failing; **sporting house** a public house, hotel, etc, patronized by sportsmen or gamblers (*archaic*); a brothel (*euphem*; *esp US*); **sports car** a low car, *usu* for two, capable of attaining high speed; **sports'caster** or **sport'caster** (*TV* and *radio*; *orig US*) a commentator on a sports programme; **sports coat** (*NAm*, *Austr* and *NZ*) a sports jacket; **sports ground** an area with equipment and facilities designed for, *esp* competitive, outdoor sports; **sports injury** any injury that is sustained or arises during participation in sports; **sports jacket** a man's jacket, *usu* tweed, for casual wear; **sports'man**, **sports'person** or (*fem*) **sports'woman** someone who practises, or is skilled in, sport; someone who shows fairness and good humour in sport. — *adj* **sports'manlike**. — **sports'manship**; **sports medicine** the branch of medicine concerned with the treatment of medical disorders, injuries, etc related to sport, and with assessment and improvement of fitness; **sports shirt** a man's casual shirt; **sports'wear** clothing designed to be worn for sport; designer clothes, *esp* matching separates, for casual wear; **sports'writer** a journalist who writes on sporting matters; **sports'writing**. — **sport one's oak** see under **oak**. [Aphetic for **disport**]

sporular, **sportulate**, etc. See under **spore**.

sposh *sposh*, (*US*) *n* slush. — *adj* **sposh'y**. [Imit]

SPOT *spot*, *abbrev*: *S*atellite *P*robatoire pour l'*O*bservation de la *T*erre (a French satellite that gathers information by remote sensing).

spot *spot*, *n* a mark made by a drop of something wet; a blot; a small discoloured or differently coloured place; a locality, place or limited geographical area; precise place, location; an eruption on the skin, a pimple; a moral flaw; one of the marked points on a billiard table, from which balls are played; a relatively dark area on the surface of the sun; a small quantity of anything (*colloq*); a spotlight (*informal*); a white pigeon with a spot on the forehead; a name for various American fishes; a job, piece (of work) (*obs*); a place of entertainment; a place on eg a television or radio programme; a turn, performance, *esp* a short one; an awkward position or situation; a spot deal or commodity (*finance*). — *vt* to mark with spots; to tarnish, eg a reputation; to reprehend (*Spenser*); to pick out, detect, locate, identify, discern (*colloq*); to free from spots (often with *out*); to place on a spot, as in billiards; to allow or yield an advantage, concession, etc to, *esp* in order to give (an opponent) an even chance of winning (*informal*). — *vi* to become spotted; (of fabric) to be susceptible to spotting; to rain slightly, with few and intermittent drops (*usu* as *spot with rain*) (*colloq*): — *pr p* **spott'ing**; *pa t* and *pa p* **spott'ed**. — *adj* on the spot, random (see **spot check** below); of monetary or commodity transactions, etc, to be paid (*usu* in cash) or delivered immediately (as in *spot market*, *spot price*, etc); involving payment in cash only. — *adj* **spot'less** without a spot or blemish; very clean; untainted; pure. — *adv* **spot'lessly**. — *n* **spot'lessness**. — *adj* **spott'ed**. — *n* **spott'edness**. — *n* **spott'er** someone who or something (such as a plane) that spots, observes or detects. — *adv* **spott'ily**. — *n* **spott'iness**. — *n* **spott'ing**. — *adj* **spott'y**. — **spot advertising** advertising by means of brief items, *usu* in dramatized form, on television or radio. — *adj* **spot'-barred** (*billiards*) under the condition that the spot stroke may not be played more than twice consecutively. — **spot cash** money down; **spot check** a check made without prior warning; a check of random samples to serve in place of a general check (*vt* **spot'-check**); **spot dance** a dance after which a prize is given to the couple spotlighted when the music stopped; **spot dealer** (*commerce*) one dealing in the spot market; **spot height** on a map, a number giving the height above mean sea level at that point; **spot kick** a kick made from the penalty spot, eg in rugby; **spot'light** a, *usu* powerful, light that projects a circle of light on an actor, a small part of a stage, or that illuminates a small area; any adjustable, focused-beam lamp, such as a car lamp additional to fixed lights; a focusing of attention (*fig*). — *vt* to turn the spotlight on; to draw attention to (*fig*). — **spot market** (*commerce*) a market in which commodities are bought and sold for cash or immediate delivery. — *adj* **spot-on'** (*colloq*) on the target; exactly right, accurate; precisely what is required, excellent. — **spot stroke** (*billiards*) a stroke by which the player pockets the red ball from the spot, leaving his own ball in position to repeat the stroke; **spotted dick** a pudding or loaf with currants; **spotted dog** a Dalmatian dog; a spotted dick; **spotted fever** any of several febrile diseases, such as cerebrospinal fever and Rocky Mountain spotted fever, characterized by small spots on the skin; **spotted flycatcher** a European songbird (*Muscicapa striata*). — *vt* **spot'-weld** to join metal with single circular welds. — *n* a weld of this kind. — **spot'-welder**. — **in a spot** in a difficult situation; **knock (the) spots off** to surpass or outdo easily; **on the spot** at the very place; there and then; alert, equal to the occasion; in difficulty or danger (eg *put on the spot*, *orig* to doom to be murdered) (*adj* **on-the-spot'**); **soft spot** (*colloq*) affectionate feeling or weakness (for); **tight spot** (*colloq*) a dangerous or difficult situation; **weak spot** (*colloq*) a weakness; an area in which one is not knowledgeable. [Cf obs Du, LGer, *spot*, ON *spotti*]

-spot *-spot*, *verb combining form* signifying to note or identify. — *noun combining form* **-spotter** as in *train-spotter*. — *noun combining form* **-spotting**. [Ety as for **spot**]

spouse *spows* or *spowz*, *n* a husband or wife. — *vt* (*obs*) to betroth; to marry. — *n* **spous'age** marriage. — *adj* **spous'al** nuptial; matrimonial. — *n* (*usu* in *pl*) nuptials; marriage. — *adj* **spouse'less**. [OFr *spus(e)*, *espous(e)* (Fr *époux*, fem *épouse*), from L *spōnsus*, pa p of *spondēre* to promise]

spout *spowt*, *vt* to throw out in a jet; to declaim; to pawn (*obs slang*). — *vi* to issue in a jet; to blow as a whale; to declaim (*derog*). — *n* a projecting lip or tube for discharging liquid from a container, a roof, etc; a gush, discharge, or jet; an undivided waterfall; a waterspout;

the blowing or the blow hole of a whale; a chute; a lift in a pawnshop (*obs*); hence, a pawnshop (*obs*). — *n* **spout'er** someone who, or that which, spouts; a declaimer; a spouting oil well; a spouting whale; a whaling ship. — *n* **spout'ing** the action of the verb; a rainwater downpipe or the system of rainwater downpipes on the outside of a building (*NZ*). — *adj* **spout'less**. — *adj* **spout'y**. — **spout'-hole** a blow-hole. — **up the spout** (*slang*) pawned; failed, gone wrong, ruined; pregnant. [ME *spouten*; cf Du *spuiten* to spout, ON *spýta* to spit]

spoylefull (*Spenser*). See **spoil**.

SPQR *abbrev*: *Senatus Populusque Romanus* (*L*), the Senate and the People of Rome.

SPR *abbrev*: Society for Psychical Research.

sprachgefühl *sprahh'gə-fül*, *n* an instinctive feeling and aptitude for a language, its essential character, word patterns, usage, etc. [Ger *Sprache* language, and *Gefühl* feeling]

sprack *sprak*, (*W Midland* and *SW dialect*) *adj* vigorous, sprightly, alert. — Also (after the pronunciation of Sir Hugh Evans, *The Merry Wives of Windsor* IV. 1. 85) **sprag**. [Origin obscure]

sprackle *spräk'l* or **spraickle** *sprāk'l*, (*Scot*) *vi* to clamber. [Origin obscure]

sprad *sprad*, (*obs*) *pa p* of **spread**.

sprag[1] *sprag*, *n* a mine prop; a bar inserted to stop a wheel; a device to prevent a vehicle from running backwards. — *vt* to prop, or to stop, by a sprag: — *pr p* **spragg'ing**; *pa t* and *pa p* **spragged**. [Origin obscure]

sprag[2]. See **sprack**.

spraickle. See **sprackle**.

spraid. See **spray**[3].

sprain *sprān*, *vt* to overstrain the muscles of. — *n* a wrenching of a joint with tearing or stretching of ligaments. [Connection with OFr *espreindre* to squeeze out, is disputed]

spraint *sprānt*, *n* (*usu* in *pl*) otter's dung. [OFr *espraintes* literally, pressed out]

sprang *sprang*, *pa t* of **spring**[1].

sprangle *sprang'gəl*, (now *US* and *dialect*) *vi* to sprawl; to straggle; to ramify; to struggle. — *n* a straggle. [ME *spranglen*]

sprat *sprat*, *n* a fish like the herring, but much smaller; a term of contempt (*Shakesp*). — **sprat'-weather** the dark days of November and December. — **a sprat to catch a mackerel, herring** or **whale** a small risk taken in order to make a great gain. [OE *sprot*; Du *sprot*, Ger *Sprotte*]

sprattle *sprat'l*, (*Scot*) *vi* to scramble. [Cf Swed *sprattla*]

sprauchle *spröhh'l*, (*Scot*). A later form of **sprackle**.

sprauncy *sprön'si*, *adj* smart, dapper. [Origin obscure, poss connected with dialect *sprouncey* cheerful, jolly]

sprawl *spröl*, *vi* to toss or kick the limbs about (*archaic*); to lie, fall or crawl with limbs spread out; to straggle. — *vt* to spread stragglingly. — *n* a sprawling posture, movement, or mass. — *n* **sprawl'er**. — *adj* **sprawl'ing**. — *adj* **sprawl'y**. [OE *sprēawlian* to move convulsively]

spray[1] *sprā*, *n* a cloud of small flying drops; an application or dispersion of such a cloud; an apparatus or a preparation for so dispersing. — *vt* to sprinkle in or with fine mistlike jets. — *n* **spray'er**. — *adj* **spray'ey**. — *adj* **spray'-dried**. — **spray drift** spray, *esp* a chemical pesticide or herbicide, which remains suspended in the air and is blown away from the original site of spraying by the wind; **spray drying** the rapid drying of a liquid by spraying it into a flow of hot gas; **spray gun** a device for applying paint, etc, by spraying. — *adj* **spray'-on** applied in a spray, *usu* by an aerosol. — **spray paint** paint that is applied in the form of a spray, *usu* an aerosol. — *vt* **spray'-paint** to use spray paint (on something); to apply with spray paint. — **spray'-painting**; **spray steel** steel made by pouring molten iron through a ring of oxygen jets, a method of rapidly oxidizing impurities. [MDu *sprayen*]

spray[2] *sprā*, *n* a shoot or twig, *esp* one spreading out in branches or flowers; an ornament, casting, etc, of similar form. — *vi* to spread or branch in a spray. — *adj* **spray'ey** branching. [Poss connected with **sprig** or with OE *spræc* twig]

spray[3] *sprā*, **spreathe**, **spreethe** *sprēdh*, **spreaze** or **spreeze** *sprēz*, (*SW dialect*) *vt* and *vi* to chap, roughen, *usu* in *pa p* **sprayed**, **spraid**, etc. [Origin obscure]

sprayey. See **spray**[1,2].

spread *spred*, *vt* to cause to extend more widely or more thinly; to scatter or disseminate abroad or in all directions; to stretch; to extend, *esp* over a surface; to apply (a soft substance) by smoothing it over a surface; to open out so as to cover a wider surface; to force apart; to overlay; to set with provisions, as a table. — *vi* to extend or expand; to be extended or stretched; to become bigger or fatter; to open out; to go or be forced further apart; to unfold; to be capable of being spread; to be propagated, circulated or disseminated: — *pa t* and *pa p* **spread**. — *n* extent; compass; reach; expanse; an expanded surface; the act or degree of spreading; an expansion; the process of becoming bigger or fatter; an array of food, a feast; anything for spreading on bread; a cover, *esp* a bedcover; a ranch (*NAm*); a double page, ie two facing pages (*printing*); a large property with grounds (*colloq*); the gap between the bid and offer price of shares (*stock exchange*). — *adj* extended; (of sounds) made with the lips stretched sideways (*phonetics*); (of a gemstone) flat and shallow. — *n* **spread'er** a machine for spreading bulk materials, eg *manure spreader*; a spatula or similar implement for spreading, eg butter, paint, etc; a device for spreading and keeping apart parallel objects, eg rails, electric wires; someone who, or something that, spreads. — *n* and *adj* **spread'ing**. — *adv* **spread'ingly**. — **spread eagle** a heraldic eagle with the wings and legs stretched out, the emblem of the USA; (anything adopting or placed in) a position in which the limbs are stretched out; a skating figure. — *adj* **spread'-eagle** in, or adopting, the position of a spread eagle; bombastic, boastful, and frothy, *esp* in American patriotism. — *vt* to tie up with outstretched limbs; to spread out; to outrun. — *vi* to cut, do or make, spread eagles; to lie, fall, etc, with outstretched limbs; to talk in spread-eagle strain. — **spread-ea'gleism**. — *adv* **spread-ea'glewise**. — **spread'-over** an act of spreading out; an elastic distribution of working hours; **spread'sheet** or **spread'sheet program** (*comput*) a program with which data, formatted in rows and columns of cells, can be viewed on a screen and manipulated to make projections, calculations, etc. — **spread a plate** (*horse-racing*) (of a horse) to lose a shoe or racing plate, *esp* before or during a race; **spread one's wings** to try one's powers or capabilities; to increase the area of one's activities. [OE *sprǣdan*; Du *spreiden*, Ger *spreiten*]

spreagh *sprähh* or *sprehh*, *n* a prey; a foray, cattle raid. — *n* **spreagh'ery** or **sprech'ery** (*sprehh'*) cattle-stealing; petty possessions, *esp* plunder. [Gaelic *spréidh* cattle]

spreathe, **spreaze**. See **spray**[3].

sprechery. See under **spreagh**.

sprechgesang *shprehh'gə-zang*, (*music*) *n* a style of vocalization between singing and speaking, originated by Arnold Schoenberg. — *n* **sprech'stimme** (*-shtim-ə*) music using this form of vocalization. [Ger, speaking-song, speaking voice]

spreckled *sprek'ld*, (now *dialect*) *adj* speckled. [Cf obs Ger *gespreckelt*]

spred, **spredd**, **spredde**. *Obs* spellings of **spread** (*pr t*, *pa t* or *pa p*). — Also **spredd'en**.

spree *sprē*, *n* a merry frolic; a drunken bout; a bout of self-indulgence or other enjoyable activity; a gathering or party at which a prospective bride displays her wedding gifts (*old-fashioned Scot*). — *vi* to carouse. [Orig slang]

spreethe, **spreeze**. See **spray**[3].

sprent *sprent*, (*archaic*) *adj* sprinkled. [Pa p of obs *sprenge*, from OE *sprengen*, *sprengan*, causative of *springan* to spring]

sprew. See **sprue**[3].

sprig *sprig*, *n* a small shoot or twig; a scion, a young person (*usu disparagingly*); an ornament like a spray; a headless or almost headless nail, a brad; a spriglike object, ornament, or design, *esp* embroidered or applied. — *vt* to embroider with representations of twigs; to nail with sprigs: — *pr p* **sprigg'ing**; *pa t* and *pa p* **sprigged**. — *adj* **sprigged**. — *adj* **sprigg'y** full of or like sprigs. [Origin obscure]

spright *sprīt*, *n* a variant of **sprite**, *obs* except perhaps in the sense of a supernatural being, impish person. — *vt* (*Shakesp*) to haunt. — *adj* **spright'ful** (*obs*) spirited. — *adv* **spright'fully** (*Shakesp*). — *n* **spright'fulness** (*obs*). — *adj* **spright'less** (*obs*) spiritless. — *n* **spright'liness**. — *adj* **spright'ly** vivacious; animated; lively; brisk; ghostly (*Shakesp*).

spring[1] *spring*, *vi* to move suddenly, as by elastic force; to bound; to start up suddenly; to break forth; to appear; to issue; to come into being; to take origin; to sprout; to dawn (*Bible*); to branch off; to begin to arch; to give way, split, burst, explode, warp, or start. — *vt* to cause to spring up; to start; to release the elastic force of; to let off, allow to spring; to cause to explode; to make known suddenly (with *on* or *upon*); (of a leak) to open; (of a mast) to crack; to bend by force, strain; to start from an abutment, etc (*archit*); to leap over; to set together with bevel-joints; to attach or fit with springs; to procure the escape of (a prisoner) from jail (*slang*): — *pa t* **sprang**; *pa p* **sprung**. — *n* a leap; a sudden movement; a recoil or rebound; elasticity; an elastic contrivance *usu* for setting in motion or for reducing shocks; a source of action or life; rise; beginning; cause or origin; a source; an outflow of water from the earth; the time of beginning (*Shakesp*); the dawn (*Bible*); (often with *cap*) the season when plants spring up and grow — in Northern temperate regions roughly February or March to April or May, astronomically from the spring equinox to the summer solstice; a shoot (*obs*); a youth (*Spenser*); copse (*obs*); undergrowth (*Spenser*); high water; spring tide; a lively dance tune (*Scot*); a Norwegian dance or dance tune; a flock of teal; the springing of an arch; a split, bend, warp, etc, *esp* a crack in a mast. — *adj* of the season of spring; sown, appearing, or used in spring; having or worked by a spring. — *n* (*archaic*) **spring'al** or **spring'ald** an active young man, a youth. — *n* **spring'er** someone who or something that springs; a kind of spaniel, useful in copses; the bottom stone of an arch (*archit*); a spring chicken (chiefly *NAm*); a springing cow; a spring salmon. — *adv* **spring'ily**. — *n* **spring'iness**. — *n* **spring'ing** the act of leaping, sprouting, starting, rising, or issuing; the beginning of curvature of an arch; a place of branching; providing with springs. — *adj* leaping; arising; dawning; sprouting; with the freshness of youth; resilient; starting; beginning to curve. — *adj* **spring'less**. — *n* **spring'let** a little spring. — *adj* **spring'like**. — *adj* **spring'y** elastic; resilient; abounding with springs. — See also **sprung**. — **spring balance** or (*esp NAm*) **spring scale** an instrument for weighing by the elasticity of a spiral spring; **spring beauty** an American flowering plant *Claytonia virginica* of the purslane family; **spring beetle** a click beetle. — *adj* **spring'-bladed** (of a knife) having a blade that springs out on pressure of a button. — **spring'board** a springy board for jumping or diving from; anything which serves as a starting point, or from which one can launch ideas, projects, etc; **spring'bok** a S African antelope, *Antidoras marsupalis*, that moves in leaps when alarmed (also **spring'buck**); (with *cap*) a S African international sportsman (from emblems of sporting teams, originally the 1906 rugby team; shortened to **Bok**); hence also any South African, *esp* when overseas; **spring box** a box or barrel in which a spring is coiled; the frame of a sofa, etc, in which the springs are set; **spring'-carriage** and **spring'-cart** one mounted on springs; **spring chicken** a young chicken, *usu* between two and ten months old, particularly tender when cooked (chiefly *NAm*; also **spring'er**); a young, lively, sometimes naïve, person. — *vt* and *n* **spring-clean'**. — **spring'-clean'er**; **spring'-clean'ing** a thorough cleaning (*esp* of a house), *usu* in spring; **spring clip** a spring-loaded clip; **spring fever** spring lassitude (*facetious*); restlessness; **spring'haas** (*-häs*; *pl* **spring'haas** or **spring'hase**; *Du*; also **spring hare**) a S African nocturnal rodent, *Pedetes capensis*; **spring'halt** (*vet*) a jerking lameness in which a horse suddenly twitches up his leg or legs (also called **string'-halt**); **spring hare** see **springhaas**; **spring'head** a fountainhead, source; a head- or end-piece for a carriage spring. — *adj* **spring'-heeled** having springs on one's heels, as in **spring-heeled Jack**, supposed to do great leaps and play pranks or commit robberies. — **spring'house** (*esp US*) a larder, dairy, etc, built over a spring or brook in order to keep the contents cool; **springing cow** a cow about to calf; **spring'keeper** a salamander; **spring ligament** a ligament of the sole of the foot; **spring line** a mooring line (*naut*); one of the strips of rubber, steel or wood inserted in and running down the handle of a cricket bat, hockey stick, etc. — *adj* **spring-load'ed** having or operated by a spring. — **spring lock** a lock in which the bolt is spring-loaded; one that opens when a spring is touched; **spring mattress** a mattress of spiral springs in a frame; **spring onion** a type of onion, its small bulb and long leaves being eaten raw in salads; **spring roll** a deep-fried Chinese savoury pancake enclosing a mixture of vegetables, pork, prawns, etc; **spring'tail** any member of the *Collembola* order of primitive, wingless insects; **spring'tide** springtime; **spring tide** a tide of maximum amplitude after new and full moon, when the forces of the sun and moon act in the same direction; any great rush or flood (*fig*); **spring'time** the season of spring; **spring'water** water of or from a spring; **spring wheat** wheat sown in the spring, rather than autumn or winter; **spring'wood** secondary wood with larger and thinner-walled elements formed in spring and early summer; **spring'wort** a root thought to be magical, *perh* mandrake. — **spring a leak** to begin to leak; **spring a mine** to cause it to explode. [OE *springan*; Ger *springen*]

spring[2]. See **springe**[1].

springal, springald. See under **spring**[1].

springe[1] *sprinj*, *n* a snare with noose and spring; a gin. — Also **spring** (*spring*). — *vt* to snare in a springe: — *pr p* **spring'ing**; *pa t* and *pa p* **springed** (*sprinjd*). — *n* **springle** (*spring'gl*) a snare. [Earlier *sprenge*, from a probable OE *sprencg*; cf **sprent, spring**[1]]

springe[2] *sprinj*, (*George Eliot*) *adj* active, nimble. [Ety unknown]

sprinkle *spring'kl*, *vt* to scatter in small drops or particles; to scatter on; to baptize with a few drops of water; to strew, dot, diversify. — *vi* to scatter in drops. — *n* an aspersorium or utensil for sprinkling. — *n* **sprin'kle** or **sprin'kling** the act of someone who sprinkles; a small quantity sprinkled (also *fig*); (in bookbinding) the mottling of the edges of pages by scattering a few drops of colour. — *n* **sprin'kler** any thing or person that sprinkles; any of various devices for scattering water in drops, eg over growing plants, as fire extinguishers, etc (**sprinkler system** a system of such fire extinguishers which operate automatically on a sudden rise in temperature). [Frequentative from OE *sprengan*, the causative of *springan* to spring; cf Ger *sprenkeln*]

sprint *sprint*, *n* a short run, row, cycle or race at full speed. — *vi* to run at full speed. — *vt* to perform a sprint over (a given distance). — *n* **sprin'ter**. — *n* **sprin'ting**. [Cf ON *spretta*, Swed *spritta*]

sprit *sprit*, (*naut*) *n* a spar set diagonally to extend a fore-and-aft sail. — **spritsail** (*sprit'sl*) a sail extended by a sprit. [OE *sprēot* pole; Du *spriet* and Ger *Spriet* sprit]

sprite *sprīt*, *n* a goblin, elf, imp, impish or implike person; (in computer graphics) an icon formed of pixels, which can be moved around a screen by means of a software program. — *adj* **sprite'ly** see under **spright**. [OFr *esprit*; cf **spirit**, **spright**]

spritsail. See under **sprit**.

spritzer *sprit'zər*, *n* a drink of white wine and soda water. [Ger *spritzen* to spray, squirt]

spritzig *shprit'zig*, (*Ger*) *adj* sparkling (*esp* of wine). — *n* a slightly sparkling (*usu* German) white wine; the tangy quality of such a wine.

sprocket *sprok'it*, *n* a tooth on the rim of a wheel or capstan for engaging the chain; a toothed cylinder for driving a film, tape, etc; a sprocket wheel; a piece of wood used to build a roof out over eaves. — **sprocket wheel** a wheel with sprockets. [Origin unknown]

sprod *sprod*, (*Northern dialect*) *n* a young salmon in its second year. [Origin obscure]

sprog *sprog*, *n* a recruit (*RAF slang*); a child, infant (*colloq*). [Poss a reversed portmanteau form of **frog spawn** or a recruit's confusion of **sprocket** and **cog**[2]]

sprong *sprong*, (*archaic*) *pa t* and *pa p* of **spring**[1].

sprout *sprowt*, *n* a new growth; a young shoot; a side bud, as in **Brussels sprouts** (see under **Brussels**); a scion, descendant; sprouting condition. — *vi* to shoot; to push out new shoots. — *vt* to put forth as a sprout or bud; to cause to sprout; to remove sprouts from (*dialect*). — *adj* **sprout'ed**. — *n* and *adj* **sprout'ing**. [OE *sprūtan* (found in compounds), Du *spruiten*, Ger *spriessen*]

spruce[1] *sprōōs*, *adj* smart; neat, dapper; over-fastidious, finical. — *adv* sprucely. — *vt* to smarten. — *vi* to become spruce or smart (often with *up*). — *adv* **spruce'ly**. — *n* **spruce'ness**. [Prob from **spruce**[2], from 'spruce leather' a fine soft leather used for making jackets (obtained from *Pruce* or Prussia) in the 16c]

spruce[2] *sprōōs*, *n* any conifer of the genus *Picea*, with long shoots only, four-angled needles, and pendulous cones; its wood; spruce beer. — *adj* of spruce or its wood. — **spruce beer** a drink made from a fermentation of sugar or treacle and the green tops of spruce; **spruce fir** the spruce tree; extended to some other trees; **spruce pine** a name given to various American pine trees; extended to some varieties of spruce. [OE *Spruce* Prussia, altered from *Pruce*, via OFr from L *Prussia*]

sprue[1] *sprōō*, *n* a passage by which molten metal runs into a mould; the metal that solidifies in it, also called *dead-head*. [Origin obscure]

sprue[2] *sprōō*, *n* infantile thrush (*obs*); either of two disorders, *tropical sprue* and coeliac disease, in which the intestines fail to absorb nutrients adequately. — **tropical sprue** a disease characterized by loss of appetite and weight, diarrhoea, inflammation of the mouth and tongue, and atrophy of the lining of the small intestine. [Du *spruw*]

sprue[3] or **sprew** *sprōō*, (*esp SE dialect*) *n* very thin, inferior asparagus.

sprug *sprug*, (*Scot*) *n* a sparrow.

spruik *sprōōk*, (*Austr* and *NZ*) *vi* (of a showman, etc) to harangue people in public. — *n* **spruik'er**. [Origin uncertain]

spruit *sprāt*, *sprü'it* or *sprīt*, (*SAfr*) *n* a small, deepish watercourse, dry except during and after rains. [Du, sprout]

sprung *sprung*, *pa t* and *pa p* of **spring**[1]. — *adj* strained; split; loosed; furnished with springs; tipsy (*colloq*). — **sprung rhythm** a poetic rhythm close to the natural rhythm of speech, with mixed feet, and frequent single stressed syllables.

sprush *sprōōsh* or *sprush*, *adj*, *adv*, and *vt* a Scots form of **spruce**.

spry *sprī*, *adj* nimble; agile: — *compar* **spry'er**; *superl* **spry'est**. — *adv* **spry'ly**. — *n* **spry'ness**. [Origin doubtful]

SPUC *abbrev*: Society for the Protection of the Unborn Child.

spud *spud*, *n* a small narrow digging tool with a spadelike blade; a stumpy person or thing; a blunt needle used to remove foreign bodies embedded in the eye (*med*); a support for earth-moving or drilling machinery; a potato (*slang*). — *vt* and *vi* to dig with a spud; (to position (machinery) in order) to start excavating or drilling (eg an oil-well). — *n* **spudd'ing** or **spudd'ing-in** the process of starting to excavate or drill (eg an oil-well by boring a hole in the seabed). — *adj* **spudd'y** podgy. — **spud'-bashing** (*slang*) peeling potatoes; **spudding bit** (*min ext*) a large drill bit for making an initial bore hole, eg into which the casing of an oil-well is cemented. [Origin obscure]

spue. An old-fashioned spelling of **spew**.

spuilzie. See **spulzie**.

spule *spûl* or *spül*, (*Scot*) *n* the shoulder. — Also **speal** (*spēl*). — **spule'bane**, **spule'bone** or **spule'blade**. [Relation to **spauld** obscure]

spulzie, **spuilzie**, **spulye** or **spulyie** *spül'yi*, (*Scot*) *n* spoliation. — *vt* and *vi* to plunder. [See **spoil**]

spume *spūm*, *n* foam; scum. — *vi* to foam. — *vt* to throw up or off as foam or scum. — *n* **spūmesc'ence**. — *adj* **spūmesc'ent** foamy, frothing. — *adj* **spū'mous**. — *adj* **spū'my**. [L *spūma*, from *spuere* to spew]

spun *spun*, *pa t* and *pa p* of **spin**, and *adj*. — *adj* **spun'-out** unduly lengthened. — **spun silk** a fabric made from waste silk fibres, sometimes mixed with cotton; **spun sugar** sugar spun into fine fluffy threads, as in candy floss; **spun'yarn** a line or rope made from one or more yarns twisted (not laid) into a cord.

spunge *spunj*, *obs* spelling of **sponge**. — **spun'ging-house** see under **sponge**.

spunk *spungk*, *n* spirit, mettle, courage, pluck; a small but spirited person (*dialect*); a spark (*dialect*, *esp Scot*); a match (*dialect*); a fungus from which tinder is made (*dialect*); touchwood, tinder (*obs*); semen (*vulg*). — *vi* to take light, flame up (*archaic*); to fire up; to show spirit (*usu* with *up*; *US*); to come to light (*Scot*; with *out*). — *n* **spunk'ie** (*Scot*) a will-o'-the-wisp; a fiery or mettlesome person; whisky (*Burns*). — *n* **spunk'iness**. — *adj* **spunk'y** spirited; fiery-tempered. [Cf Ir *sponc* tinder, sponge, from L *spongia* a sponge, from Gr *spongiā*]

spur *spûr*, *n* a goading instrument on a horse rider's heel; incitement, stimulus; a hard sharp projection; a claw-like projection at the back of a cock's or other bird's leg; an artificial substitute for this on a gamecock; a short, *usu* flowering or fruit-bearing, branch; a great lateral root; ergot; a tubular pouch at the base of a petal; an expansion of a leaf base; anything that projects in the shape of a spur, eg an extension from an electrical circuit; a lateral branch, as of a hill range; a siding or branch line of a railway; a strut; a structure to deflect the current from a bank. — *vt* to apply the spur to; to urge on; to provide with a spur or spurs; to prune into spurs. — *vi* to press forward with the spur; to hasten; to kick out: — *pr p* **spurr'ing**; *pa t* and *pa p* **spurred**. — *adj* **spur'less**. — *adj* **spurred** having or wearing spurs or a spur; in the form of a spur; urged; (eg of rye) affected with ergot. — *n* **spurr'er** — *n* **spurr'ier** a maker of spurs. — *n* and *adj* **spurr'ing**. — *adj* **spurr'y** like, of the nature of, or having a spur. — *vt* **spur'-gall** (*Shakesp*) to gall or wound with a spur. — **spur gear** or **wheel** a gear wheel with straight teeth parallel to its axis, as used in **spur gearing**, a system of such gears connecting two parallel shafts. — *adj* **spur'-heeled** having a long straight hind claw. — **spur leather** a strap for fastening a spur; **spur rowel** the rowel of a spur; **spur'-roy'al**, **-ry'al** or **-rī'al** a former English fifteen-shilling piece of gold, bearing a star like a spur rowel; **spur'way** (*dialect*) a bridle road; **spur'-whang** (*Scot*) a spur leather; **spur wheel** see **spur gear**. — *adj* **spur'-winged** with a horny spur on the pinion of the wing. — **gilt spurs** a mark of knighthood; **on the spur of the moment** without premeditation; **set spurs to** to apply the spur to (a horse) and ride off quickly; to urge on; to hasten the progress of; **win one's spurs** to gain distinction by achievement; *orig* to earn a knighthood. [OE *spura*, *spora*; ON *spori*, Ger *Sporn*]

spurge *spûrj*, *n* any species of *Euphorbia*, a genus of very varied habit, with milky, generally poisonous, juice, and an inflorescence (*cyathium*) of flowers so reduced as to simulate a single flower. — **spurge'-laurel** a European evergreen shrub (*Daphne laureola*) with yellowish-green flowers, thick leaves, and poisonous berries. [OFr *espurge* (Fr *épurge*), from L *expurgāre* to purge, from *ex* off, and *purgāre* to clear]

spurious *spūr'i-əs*, *adj* not genuine; false; sham; forged; simulating but essentially different; bastard, illegitimate. — *n pl* **spūr'iae** (*-i-ē*) in birds, feathers of the bastard wing. — *n* **spurios'ity**. — *adv* **spūr'iously**. — *n* **spūr'iousness**. [L *spurius* false]

spurling *spûr'ling*. Same as **sparling**.

spurn *spûrn*, *vt* to reject with contempt; to tread, *esp* in contempt; to kick (*archaic*). — *vi* to trip (*obs*); to kick (often with *at* or *against*; *archaic*). — *n* a kick or kicking (*archaic*); disdainful rejection. — *n* **spurn'er**. — *n* and *adj* **spurn'ing**. [OE *spornan*, *spurnan*, related to **spur**]

spurne *spûrn*, (*Spenser*) *vt* to spur.

spurrey, sometimes **spurry**, *spur'i*, *n* any plant of the genus *Spergula*; applied to related plants, *Spergularia rubra* (*sand spurrey*) and *Sagina nodosa* (knotted pearlwort or *knotted spurrey*). [Du *spurrie*]

spurrier, **spurry**[1]. See under **spur**.

spurry[2]. See **spurrey**.

spurt *spûrt*, *vt* to spout, or send out in a sudden stream or jet. — *vi* to gush out suddenly in a small stream; to flow out forcibly or at intervals; to make a sudden short intense effort. — *n* a sudden or violent gush; a jet; a short spell, *esp* of intensified effort, speed, etc. [Variant of **spirt**[1]]

spurtle *spûr'tl*, (*Scot*) *n* a stick for stirring porridge; a sword (also **spur'tle-blade**). [Origin doubtful]

sputa. See **sputum**.

sputnik *spŏŏt'nik*, *n* any of a series of man-made earth satellites launched by the former Soviet Union. [After the Russian *Sputnik* ('travelling companion') 1, the first such satellite, put in orbit in 1957]

sputter *sput'ər*, *vi* to spit or throw out moisture in scattered drops, to splutter; to speak rapidly and indistinctly, to jabber, to stutter; to make a sputtering noise. — *vt* to spit out or throw out in or with small drops; to utter hastily and indistinctly; to remove atoms from a cathode by positive ion bombardment, the unchanged atoms being deposited on a surface, and the process being used for coating glass, plastic, another metal, etc, with a thin film of metal. — *n* an instance of, or the process or sound of sputtering; matter sputtered out. — *n* **sputt'erer**. — *n* and *adj* **sputt'ering**. — *adv* **sputt'eringly**. — *adj* **sputt'ery**. [Imit; cf Du *sputteren*, and **spit**[2]]

sputum *spū'təm*, *n* matter spat out: — *pl* **spū'ta**. [L *spūtum*, from *spuere* to spit]

sp. vol. *abbrev*: specific volume.

spy *spī*, *n* a secret agent employed to watch others or to collect information, *esp* of a military nature; a spying; a look; an eye (*fig*): — *pl* **spies**. — *vt* to watch, observe, investigate, or ascertain secretly (often with *out*); to catch sight of, make out; to discover. — *vi* to play the spy: — *pr p* **spy'ing**; *pa t* and *pa p* **spied**; *3rd pers present indicative* **spies**. — *n* **spy'al** (*Spenser*) a spy (see **spial**). — *n* and *adj* **spy'ing**. — **spy'glass** a small hand-held telescope; **spy'hole** a peephole, eg in a door; **spy'master** a person who controls and coordinates the activities of undercover agents; **spy'-money** money paid for secret intelligence; **spy'plane** an aeroplane specially equipped to collect information on enemy positions, military manoeuvres, etc. — **spy in the cab** (*colloq*) a tachograph fitted in a lorry or truck. [OFr *espie* (noun), *espier* (verb); cf **espy**]

spyre. *Obs* spelling (*Spens*) of **spire**[1].

sq. *abbrev*: *sequens* (*L*) following: — *pl* **sqq** *sequentes* or *sequentia*; (or **Sq.**) square or Square (in addresses).

sqn *abbrev*: squadron.

Sqn Ldr *abbrev*: squadron leader.

squab *skwob*, *adj* fat, clumsy; unfledged, newly hatched; shy, coy; curt, abrupt (*obs*); having a squab. — *n* a young pigeon or rook; a fledgling; a young chicken (*US*); a short stumpy person (*colloq*); a soft thick cushion; a padded sofa or ottoman; a carriage cushion; the back part of a motor car seat. — *vt* to upholster or stuff thickly and sew through in places. — *vi* to fall heavily. — *adv* plump and squashily. — *adj* **squabb'ish** thick, heavy. — *adj* **squabb'y** squat. — **squab pie** a pie made of mutton or pork, onions, and apples. [Poss Scand; cf Swed dialect *sqvabb* loose flesh, *sqvabbig* flabby]

squabash *skwə-bash'*, (*colloq*) *vt* to crush, smash, defeat. — *n* a crushing blow. — *n* **squabash'er**. [Prob **squash**[1] and **bash**]

squabbish. See under **squab**.

squabble *skwob'l*, *vi* to dispute in a noisy manner; to wrangle. — *n* a noisy, petty quarrel; a brawl. — *n* **squabb'ler**. [Cf Swed dialect *sqvabbel*]

squabby. See under **squab**.

squacco *skwak'ō*, *n* a small crested European heron, *Ardeola valloides*: — *pl* **squacc'os**. [Ital dialect *sguacco*]

squad *skwod*, *n* a small group of soldiers drilled or working together; any working party; a set or group; a number of players trained in readiness for the selection of a team (*sport*). — *n* **squadd'ie** or **squadd'y** (*military colloq*) a private, an ordinary soldier. — **squad car** a police car. — **awkward squad** a body of recruits not yet competent in drill, etc. [Fr *escouade*; cf Sp *escuadra*, Ital *squadra*]

squadron *skwod'rən*, *n* a body of soldiers drawn up in a square (*obs*); a detachment, body, group; a division of a regiment, *esp* a cavalry regiment, under a major or captain; a section of a fleet under a flag-officer; a group of aeroplanes forming a unit under one command. — *vt* to form into squadrons. — *adj* **squad'ronal**. — *adj* **squad'roned**. — **squad'ron-lead'er** an air force officer corresponding in rank to a lieutenant-commander or major; **squadrone (volante)** (*skwa-drō'nā* (*vō-län'tā*); Ital, flying squadron) an early 18c Scottish political party opposed to the Argathelians. [Ital *squadrone*, from *squadra* square]

squail *skwāl*, *n* a counter for playing squails; (in *pl*) a parlour-game similar to tiddlywinks, in which small discs are snapped from the edge of the table to a centre mark; (in *pl*) ninepins; a stick for throwing. — *vi* to throw sticks (as at birds or fruit). — *vt* to pelt with sticks; to hit by throwing a stick. — *n* **squail'er** a throwing-stick. — *n* **squail'ing**. [Cf **kail**[1] (obs *skail*, *skayle*), a ninepin]

squalene *skwā'lēn*, (*biochem*) *n* a symmetrical triterpine, an intermediate in the synthesis of cholesterol, present in mammalian and plant tissue (formerly called **spinacene**). [From New L *squalus*, genus name of the shark in which it was originally found]

squalid *skwol'id*, *adj* filthy, foul; neglected, uncared-for, unkempt; sordid and dingy; poverty-stricken. — *n* **squalid'ity**. — *adv* **squal'idly**. — *n* **squal'idness**. — *n* **squal'or** the state of being squalid; dirtiness; filthiness. [L *squālidus* stiff, rough, dirty, from *squālor*, *-ōris*]

squall *skwöl*, *vi* to cry out violently; to yell; to sing loudly and unmusically; (of wind) to blow in a squall. — *vt* to sing or utter loudly and unmusically. — *n* a loud cry or yell; a brief violent storm or sudden strong wind. — *n* **squall'er**. — *n* and *adj* **squall'ing**. — *adj* **squall'y** of, abounding in, or disturbed with, squalls or gusts of wind; gusty, blustering; threatening a squall. — **white squall** see under **white**. [Prob imit]

squaloid *skwā'loid*, *adj* of or pertaining to sharks of the suborder *Squaloideae*; like a shark. [L *squālus* a sea fish of the shark or dogfish group]

squalor. See under **squalid**.

squama *skwā'mə* or *skwä'mə*, *n* a scale; a scalelike structure; a thin plate of bone; the exopodite of an antenna in *Crustacea*: — *pl* **squa'mae** (*-mē* or *-mī*). — *n pl* **Squamā'ta** (*skwə-*; *zool*) an order of reptiles comprising snakes and lizards. — *adj* **squā'mate** scaly. — *n* **squamā'tion** (*skwə-*) scaliness; the mode of arrangement of scales. — *n* **squame** (*skwām*) a scale or squama. — *n* **squamell'a** (*skwə-*) a little scale. — *adj* **squā'miform** like a scale. — *n* **squamosal** (*skwə-mō'sl*) a paired membrane bone of the vertebrate skull, the squamous portion of the temporal bone. — Also *adj.* — *adj* **squā'mose** or **squā'mous** scaly; (of epithelium) consisting of a layer of flattened scalelike cells. — *n* **squāmos'ity**. — *n* **squamula** (*skwam'ū-lə* or *skwām'*). — *n* **squam'ule** a little scale. — *adj* **squam'ūlose**. — **squamous cell carcinoma** a tumour of the flattened, scalelike cells in the skin. [L *squāma* a scale]

squander *skwon'dər*, *vt* to spend lavishly or wastefully; to scatter, disperse (*obs*). — *vi* (*obs*) to wander, roam, straggle; to scatter. — *n* (*rare*) a squandering. — *adj* **squan'dered**. — *n* **squan'derer**. — *n* and *adj* **squan'dering**. — *adv* **squan'deringly**. — *n* **squandermā'nia** (*slang*) a spirit of reckless expenditure (eg in a government). [Origin obscure]

square *skwār*, *n* a geometric figure having four equal sides and four right angles; an object, piece, space, figure, of approximately that shape, eg a windowpane, paving-stone, space on a chessboard, a silk headscarf; an open space, commonly but not necessarily of that shape, in a town, along with its surrounding buildings; a rectangular block of buildings (*US*); a body of troops drawn up in that form; the product of a quantity multiplied by itself (*math*); the yoke of a garment (*Shakesp*); a unit of flooring, 100 square feet; an instrument for drawing or testing right angles; a carpenter's measure; a piece of timber cut square, of side up to six inches; a canon, standard, criterion, rule (*obs*); squareness; quartile aspect (*old astron*); due proportion; order; honesty, equity, fairness; quarrel, dissension (*obs*); possibly part, compartment (*Shakesp, King Lear* I, 1.); an unopened cotton flower (*US*); a person of boringly traditional outlook and opinions, *esp* in musical taste or dress (*slang*). — *adj* having or approaching the form of a square; relatively broad, thick-set; right-angled; (in football, etc) in a line, position, etc, across the pitch; equal to a quantity multiplied by itself; measuring an area in two dimensions, ie length multiplied by width or breadth; exact, suitable, fitting; true, equitable, fair, honest; even, leaving no balance, equal in score; directly opposed; complete, unequivocal; solid, full, satisfying; (of taste in music, dress, etc) boringly traditional and orthodox (*slang*); bourgeois in attitude (*slang*). — *vt* to make square or rectangular, *esp* in cross-section; to make nearly cubical; to form into squares; to construct or determine a square equal to; to multiply by itself; to reduce to any given measure or standard, to adjust, regulate; to bring into accord, reconcile; to place at right angles with the mast or keel (*naut*); to make equal; to pay; to bribe; (with *with*) to get (someone's) agreement, approval or permission for something. — *vi* to suit, fit; to accord or agree; to adopt a position of offence and defence, as a boxer does (often with *up to*; see also below); to swagger (*obs*); to make the score or account even. — *adv* at right angles; solidly; directly; evenly; fairly, honestly. — *adj* **squared**. — *adv* **square'ly**. — *n* **square'ness**. — *n* **squar'er** someone who or something that squares; a fighting, quarrelsome person, or perhaps a swaggerer (*Shakesp*). — *adv* **square'wise**. — *n* and *adj* **squar'ing**. — *adj* **squar'ish**. — **square'-bashing** parade-ground drill (*military slang*); **square bracket** a bracket. — *adj* **square'-built** of a form suggesting squareness; broad in proportion to height. — **square centimetre, metre**, etc, an area equal to that of a square whose side measures a centimetre, metre, etc. — *adj* **square-cut** cut in a square shape; (of a person's chin) having a strong, squared outline; **square dance** (*esp NAm*) a folk dance done by a group of four couples in a square formation (also *vi* **square'-dance**); **square'-dancing**; **square deal** (*colloq*) a fair and honest arrangement, transaction, etc; **square'-face** (*SAfr*) gin (from the shape of the bottle); **square foot, inch, mile**, etc an area equal to that of a square whose side measures a foot, etc; **square'head** (*old derog slang*) a Scandinavian or German; **square knot** a reef knot; **square leg** (*cricket*) a fielder to the left of (right of), and in line with, a right-handed (left-handed) batsman; the position of this player; **square matrix** (*math*) a matrix with an equal number of rows and columns; **square meal** a full, satisfying meal; **square measure** a system of measures for surfaces, its unit the square of the lineal unit; **square mile** see **square foot**; (*usu* with *caps*) the City of London, *specif* the area around and *incl* the Bank of England; financial life, activities, etc in the City of London (*fig*); **square number** a number the square root of which is an integer. — *adj* **square'-pierced** (*heraldry*) having a square opening so as to show the field. — *adj* **square-rigged'** (*naut*) having square sails extended by yards suspended by the middle at right angles to the masts, the opposite of *fore-and-aft*. — **square-rigg'er** (*naut*) a square-rigged ship; **square root** a number or quantity which being multiplied by itself produces the quantity in question, eg 3 *is the square root of* 9; **square'-sail** (*-sl'*; *naut*) a four-sided sail extended by yards suspended by the middle generally at right angles to the mast; **square shooter** (chiefly *US colloq*) a frank and honest person; **square shooting**. — *adj* **square-shoul'dered** with broad, straight shoulders. — *adj* **square-toed'** (of shoes, etc) ending square at the toes. — **square'-toes** (*pl*) square-toed shoes; (*sing*) an old-fashioned, punctilious person (*archaic*). — **back to square one** back to the original position with the problem, etc, unchanged; **how squares go** (*obs*) what is doing; how things are going; **on the square** at right angles; openly, honestly; an expression identifying someone as a member of the Freemasons (*slang*); **square off** (*colloq*) to adopt an offensive or defensive stance, as in boxing before any blows are struck; **square away** to set (sails) at right angles to the keel (*naut*); to make neat and tidy (*NAm*); **square up** (*colloq*) to settle (a bill, account, etc); **square up to** to face up to and tackle; **squaring the circle (quadrature of the circle)** finding a square of the same area as a circle — for hundreds of years this was attempted by Euclidean means (ie with straight-edge and compass) until in 1882 it was proved impossible; any impossible task. [OFr *esquarre* (Fr *équerre*), from L *ex* and *quadra* a square]

squarial *skwār'i-əl*, *n* a flat diamond-shaped (as opposed to round) aerial for receiving satellite television broadcasts. [**square** and **aerial**]

squarrose *skwar'ōs*, *skwor'ōs* or *-ōs'*, (*biol*) *adj* rough with projecting or deflexed scales, bracts, etc; standing out straight or deflexed. [L *squarrōsus* scurfy]

squarson *skwär'sn*, *n* a clergyman who is also a squire or landowner in his parish. — *n* **squar'sonage** his residence. [*squ*ire and *parson*]

squash[1] *skwosh*, *vt* to press into pulp; to crush flat; to squeeze; to put down, suppress; to snub or crush. — *vi* to form a soft mass as from a fall; to crowd; to squelch; to become crushed or pulpy. — *n* an unripe peascod (*Shakesp*); anything soft and unripe or easily crushed; a crushed mass; a drink made from fruit juice; a crushed condition; a close crowd; a squeezing; a game for two or four players played with a small rubber ball, which is struck with a racket against the walls of an enclosed court (also **squash rackets** or **racquets**); a soft rubber ball for playing squash. — *adv* with a squash. — *adj* **squash'able**. — *n* **squash'er**. — *adv* **squash'ily**. — *n* **squash'iness**. — *adj* **squash'y** pulpy; squelching; sopping. — **squash tennis** a game for two players similar to squash rackets (see above) but played with an inflated ball and larger rackets. [OFr *esquacer* (Fr *écacher*) to crush, from L *ex* intensifying, and *quassāre* to shatter; see **quash**]

squash[2] *skwosh*, (*NAm*) *n* the fruit of various marrow-like plants of the genus *Cucurbita*, with edible flesh, vegetable marrow; any of the plants bearing such fruit. [Narragansett *askutasquash*]

squat *skwot*, *vi* to crouch down on the hams or heels; to hunch or crouch small and low like an animal; to settle on land or in unoccupied buildings without legal right, or (*Austr hist*) to settle on land with a view to acquiring legal title. — *vt* to cause to squat: — *pr p* **squatt'ing**; *pa t* and *pa p* **squatt'ed**. — *adj* crouching; short and thick, dumpy. — *n* the act of squatting; a building in which people are squatting (*colloq*). — *n* **squat'ness**. — *n* **squatt'er** someone who squats; a large landowner (*Austr*). — *n* **squatt'iness**. — *vt* and *vi* **squatt'le** to squat down. — *n* **squattoc'racy** (*Austr*) the powerful land-owning class. — *adj* **squatt'y** short and thick. — **squat shop** a business, *usu* selling cheap goods, that occupies an empty or disused shop illegally, pays no rent or rates and trades for the time taken by the owner to obtain an eviction order from a court. [OFr *esquatir* to crush, from L *ex*, intensifying, and *coactus*, pa p of *cōgere* to force together]

squatter[1] *skwot'ər*, *vi* to splash along. — *n* a fluttering; a splashing, spattering. [Prob imit]

squatter[2], **squattle**, **squatty**. See under **squat**.

squaw *skwö*, *n* a native American woman, *esp* a wife. — **squaw'man** a white man with a native American wife. [Massachusett *squa*]

squawk *skwök*, *n* a croaky call or cry; a loud complaint or protest (*slang*); a signal on a radar screen identifying an aircraft and its flight level (*slang*). — *vi* to utter a squawk; to complain loudly (*slang*). — *vt* to utter with a squawk. — *n* **squawk'er**. — *n* and *adj* **squawk'ing**. — *adj* **squawk'y**. — **squawk box** (*slang*) an intercom or telephone with loudspeaker. [Imit]

squeak *skwēk*, *vi* to give forth a high-pitched nasal-sounding note or cry, or produce a similar noise; to inform or confess (*slang*). — *vt* to utter, sing or render squeakily. — *n* a squeaky sound; a narrow escape; a bare chance; the slimmest of margins; a tiny amount; a feeble newspaper (*old slang*). — *n* **squeak'er** someone who or something that squeaks; a young bird; an informer; a squeaking toy. — *n* **squeak'ery**. — *adv* **squeak'ily**. — *n* **squeak'iness**. — *n* and *adj* **squeak'ing**. — *adv* **squeak'ingly**. — *adj* **squeak'y**. — *adj* **squeak'y-clean** *orig*, of wet hair, so clean that it squeaks when pulled; spotlessly clean; (often slightly *derog*; of a person) impeccable, wholesome, virtuous, above criticism or reproach. — **squeak through** to succeed, pass, win, etc only by a narrow margin. [Imit; cf Swed *sqväka* to croak, Ger *quieken* to squeak]

squeal *skwēl*, *vi* to utter a high-pitched cry of some duration; to cry out in pain; to complain; to turn informer (*slang*). — *vt* to utter, sing, render or express with squealing. — *n* a high sustained cry. — *n* **squeal'er** someone who or something that squeals, *esp* a piglet or a bird of various kinds, eg a young pigeon; an informer (*slang*). — *n* and *adj* **squeal'ing**. [Imit; cf Swed dialect *sqväla* to cry out]

squeamish *skwēm'ish*, *adj* feeling nauseous, sick; easily nauseated; easily shocked, disgusted, or offended; fastidious; coy; reluctant from scruples or compunction. — *adv* **squeam'ishly**. — *n* **squeam'ishness**. [ME *scoymous*, from Anglo-Fr *escoymous*; ety dubious]

squeegee *skwē'jē* or *-jē'* or **squilgee** *skwil'jē*, *n* an implement with a blade or pad of rubber, leather, etc, for clearing water or mud from decks, floors, windows, etc or used to apply ink in screen printing; a photographer's roller or brush for squeezing out moisture from wet prints or negatives. — *vt* to clear, press, or smooth with a squeegee. [Appar **squeeze**]

squeeze *skwēz*, *vt* to crush, press hard, compress; to grasp tightly; to embrace; to force by pressing; to effect, render, or put by pressing; to crush the juice or liquid from; to force to discard winning cards; to fleece, extort from; to take a rubbing of. — *vi* to press; to crowd; to crush; to force a way; to yield to pressure. — *n* the act of squeezing; pressure; a restriction or time of restriction (*usu* financial or commercial); a crowded assembly; an embrace; a close grasp; a portion withheld and appropriated as by an official; a rubbing; a few drops obtained by squeezing; play that forces an opponent to discard a potentially winning card (also **squeeze play**; *bridge*). — *n* **squeezabil'ity**. — *adj* **squeez'able**. — *n* **squeez'er** someone who squeezes; an instrument, machine or part for squeezing; a playing card marked in the corner with suit and value. — *n* and *adj* **squeez'ing**. — *adj* **squeez'y** squeezable; confined, cramped, contracted. — **squeeze'-box** (*informal*) a concertina, accordion; **squeezy bottle** or (*esp US*) **squeeze bottle** a flexible plastic bottle, eg for washing-up liquid, that is squeezed to force out the contents. — **squeeze home** to win, succeed, etc with difficulty or narrowly. [Origin obscure]

squegging *skweg'ing*, (*electronics* and *telecomm*) *n* a type of oscillation in which the oscillations build up to a certain value and then stop for a time before resuming. — Also *adj*. — *vi* **squeg** (back-formation) to oscillate intermittently or irregularly. — *n* **squegg'er** a squegging oscillator. [Orig uncertain, poss from *self-quenching*]

squelch *skwelch* or *skwelsh*, *n* a gurgling and sucking sound as of walking in wet mud; a heavy blow on, or fall of, a soft body; its sound; a pulpy mass; a disconcerting or quashing retort or rebuff; a circuit which automatically controls the audio-frequency amplifier of a radio receiver in accordance with certain input characteristics, eg to suppress background noise at very low signal levels; the operation of this circuit. — *vi* to make, or walk with, the sound of a squelch. — *vt* to crush under heel; to put down, suppress, snub, crush. — *n* **squelch'er** someone who or something that squelches; an overwhelming blow, retort, etc. — *n* and *adj* **squelch'ing**. — *adj* **squelch'y**. [Imit; cf **quelch**]

squeteague *skwi-tēg'*, *n* an Atlantic American spiny-finned food fish of the genus *Cynoscion*, misnamed salmon or trout. [Narragansett *pesukwiteaug*, literally, they make glue]

squib *skwib*, *n* a firework, consisting of a paper tube filled with explosive powder, which burns noisily and explodes; a short piece of satire, a lampoon; a paltry fellow (*archaic*). — *vt* to aim squibs at; to lampoon. — *vi* to write lampoons; to use squibs; to sound or skip about like a squib. — *n* and *adj* **squibb'ing**. — **damp squib** see under **damp**. [Perh imit]

SQUID *skwid*, (*phys*) *abbrev*: superconducting *q*uantum *i*nterference *d*evice (any of several devices used to measure extremely small currents, voltages and magnetic fields).

squid *skwid*, *n* any large-headed cephalopod mollusc, *esp* of the genera *Loligo* and *Ommastrephes*, with a long tapering body, ten tentacles and triangular tail fins; a bait or lure of, or in imitation of, a squid; an anti-submarine mortar; a pound sterling, a quid (*colloq slang*); a lead puck used in the game of octopush: — *pl* **squid** or **squids**. — *vi* to fish with a squid. [Origin obscure]

squidge *skwij*, *vt* to squeeze or squash (something soft, moist, pulpy, etc). — *n* something soft, wet and gooey. — *adj* **squid'gy** squashy; soft, wet and springy; gooey. [Imit]

squier. See **squire**[2].

squiffer *skwif'ər*, (*slang*) *n* a concertina.

squiffy *skwif'i*, (*colloq*) *adj* tipsy. — Also **squiff**. [Origin unknown]

squiggle *skwig'l*, *vi* to squirm, wriggle; to make wriggly lines. — *n* a twist, wriggle, or wriggly line. — *adj* **squigg'ly**. [Imit, or poss from *squ*irm and *wriggle*]

squilgee. See **squeegee**.

squill *skwil*, *n* any plant of the liliaceous genus *Scilla*, eg spring squill, *Scilla verna*, with strap-like leaves and blue star-shaped flowers; the sea onion (*Urginea maritima*), formerly included in that genus; (*usu* in *pl*) its dried bulbs used as a diuretic and expectorant; a mantis shrimp of the genus *Squilla* (also **squill'a**). [L *squilla*, *scilla* sea onion, shrimp, from Gr *skilla* sea onion]

squinancy *skwin'ən-si*, (*obs*) *n* quinsy, suppurative tonsillitis. — **squinancy wort** a species of woodruff, *Asperula* *cynamchica*, once thought good for quinsy. [LL *squinanchia*, a combination of Gr *synanchē* sore throat, and *kynanchē* (see **cynanche**)]

squinch *skwinch* or *skwinsh*, (*archit*) *n* an arch or other support across a re-entrant or interior angle. [**scuncheon**]

squinny *skwin'i* or **squiny** *skwī'ni*, (*Shakesp* and *dialect*) *vi* to squint, peer, look askance. [Prob related to **squint**].

squint *skwint*, *adv* obliquely, to one side. — *adj* looking obliquely; looking askance; squinting; strabismic; oblique; indirect. — *vi* to look obliquely; to have the eyes focusing in different directions, either by purposely crossing them, or by strabismus; to have a side reference or allusion; to glance aside or casually; to glance (*colloq*); to give an impresson of disapproval in one's glance. — *vt* to cause to squint; to direct or divert obliquely. — *n* the act or habit of squinting; strabismus; an oblique look; a glance; a peep; an oblique reference, hint, tendency, or aim; an oblique opening in a wall, eg a hagioscope. — *n* **squint'er**. — *n* and *adj* **squint'ing**. — *adv* **squint'ingly**. — **squint'-eye** or **squint'=eyes** someone who squints. — *adj* **squint'-eyed**. [Aphetic for **asquint**; perh related to Du *schuinte* slope, slant, from *schuin* sideways, sloping]

squiny. See **squinny**.

squire[1] *skwīr*, *n* an esquire, an aspirant to knighthood attending a knight (*hist*); a man who escorts or attends a lady; an English or Irish landed gentleman, *esp* of old family; a title applied to a justice of the peace, local judge, etc (*US*); in some parts of Britain, a form of sometimes ironically respectful address. — *vt* to escort or attend. — *n* **squire'age** or **squir'age** landed gentry collectively. — Also **squiral'ity** or **squir'alty**. — *n* **squire'arch** or **squir'arch**. — *adj* **squirearch'al**, **squirarch'al**, **squirearch'ical** or **squirarch'ical**. — *n* **squire'archy** or **squir'archy** the rule of or government by squires; squires collectively and their social or political power. — *n* **squire'dom**. — *n* **squireen'** (Ir *dimin sfx -ín*; *Anglo-Ir*) a petty squire, a squireling. — *n* **squire'hood**. — *adj* and *adv* **squire'like** or **squire'ly**. — *n* **squire'ling** a squire of small possessions. — *n* **squire'ship**. — *n* **squir'ess** a squire's wife. — **squire of dames** a man who devotes himself to the ladies, from a character in Spenser (*Faerie Queene* III. 7. 53). [**esquire**]

squire[2] or **squier** *skwīr*, (*Spenser* and *Shakesp*) *n* a carpenter's square or rule; a canon, rule. — **by the squire** precisely. [See **square**]

squirm *skwûrm*, *vi* to writhe or move with wriggling motion; to display or feel deep discomfort or distress, as from guilt, pain, embarrassment, etc. — *n* a wriggle. — *adj* **squirm'y**. [Prob imit]

squirr. Same as **skirr**.

squirrel *skwir'əl*, *n* a nimble, bushy-tailed arboreal rodent (*Sciurus* or kindred genus); the pelt of such an animal; a person who hoards things (*fig*). — *adj* made of squirrel pelts. — *vt* to hoard (*usu* with *away*). — *adj* **squirr'elly** or **squirr'ely** like a squirrel; nervous, jumpy. — **squirrel cage** a cage with a treadwheel for a squirrel (or other small animal); any seemingly endless and purposeless situation, task, etc; in an induction motor, a rotor whose winding suggests this; **squirrel fish** any of various brightly-coloured marine fishes of the family *Holocentridae* of shallow tropical waters, so called because their large eyes resemble those of the squirrel; **squirrel monkey** a small golden-haired S American monkey, *Saimiri sciureus*; **squirrel shrew** a tree shrew; **squirr'el-tail** a grass (*Hordeum marinum*) of European marshland with long hairlike awns (in full **squirrel-tail grass**); a broad-tailed lobworm (*Walton*); a cap of squirrel skins, with a tail hanging down behind. [OFr *escurel*, from LL *scurellus*, dimin of L *sciūrus*, from Gr *skiouros*, from *skiā* shade, and *ourā* tail]

squirt *skwûrt*, *vt* to throw out in a jet; to splash or spray with (water, etc) from a jet. — *vi* to spirt. — *n* an instrument for squirting; a jet; an unimportant and irritatingly pretentious person (*slang*). — *n* **squirt'er**. — *n* and *adj* **squirt'ing**. — **squirt gun** (*NAm*) a water pistol or spray gun; **squirting cucumber** a Mediterranean cucurbitaceous plant (*Ecballium elaterium*) that squirts out its ripe seeds. [Cf LGer *swirtjen*, *swürtjen*]

squish *skwish*, *vi* to make a squelching or squirting sound. — *n* the sound of squishing; bosh (*dated slang*); marmalade (*public school slang*). — *adj* **squish'y**. — **squish lip system** a type of diesel engine combustion chamber designed to lessen fumes and noise pollution. [Imit]

squit *skwit*, (*slang*) *n* a contemptible person; nonsense. [Cf **squirt**]

squitch *skwich*, *n* quitch grass.

squitters *skwit'ərs*, (*colloq slang*) *n pl* (with **the**) diarrhoea. [Cognate with **squirt**]

squiz *skwiz*, (*Austr* and *NZ slang*) *n* a quick, close look. [Perh **squint** and **quiz**]

SR *abbrev*: Southern Region.

Sr *abbrev*: senior; Señor; Sir; Sister.

Sr (*chem*) *symbol*: strontium.

sr (*math*) *abbrev*: steradian.

sraddha or **shraddha** *srä'dä* or *shrä'dä*, (*Hinduism* and *Buddhism*) *n* an offering to the manes of an ancestor. [Sans *śsrāddha*]

SRC: *abbrev*: Student Representative Council.

SRCh *abbrev*: State Registered Chiropodist.

Sri or **Shri** *shrē*, in India, a title of great respect given to a man, now generally used as the equivalent of *Mr*. [Sans *śsrī* majesty, holiness]

SRN *abbrev*: State Registered Nurse.

SRO *abbrev*: self-regulatory organization.

SRU *abbrev*: Scottish Rugby Union.

SS *abbrev*: Saints; *Schutzstaffel* (*Ger*), Hitler's bodyguard.

ss *abbrev*: screw steamer; steamship.

SSA *abbrev*: standard spending assessment (a government assessment of the funds that a local authority will require for its services in a given year).

SSAFA *abbrev*: Soldiers' Sailors' and Airmen's Families Association.

SSC *abbrev*: *Societas Sanctae Crucis* (*L*), Society of the Holy Cross; Solicitor in the Supreme Court (of Scotland).

SSD *abbrev*: *Sanctissimus Dominus* (*L*), Most Holy Lord (the Pope).

SSE *abbrev*: south-south-east.

SSM *abbrev*: surface to surface missile.

SSN *abbrev*: Standard Serial Number.

SSP *abbrev*: statutory sick pay.

SSR *abbrev*: Soviet Socialist Republic.

SSSI *abbrev*: site of special scientific interest.

SST *abbrev*: supersonic transport.

SSW *abbrev*: south-south-west.

St or **St.** *abbrev*: Saint; Strait; Street.

st or **'st** *st*, *interj* hush; a sound made to attract someone's attention: — *pl* **st's**.

'st *st*, a shortened form of **hast**.

st. *abbrev*: stone (the weight).

stab *stab*, *vt* to wound or pierce by driving in a pointed weapon; to give a sharp pain (also *fig*); to roughen (brickwork) with a pick so as to provide a key for plaster (*building*); to pierce near the back edges, for the passage of thread or wire (*bookbinding*). — *vi* to thrust or pierce with a pointed weapon: — *pr p* **stabb'ing**; *pa t* and *pa p* **stabbed**. — *n* an act of stabbing; a wound with a pointed weapon. — *n* **stabb'er**. — *n* and *adj* **stabb'ing**. — *adv* **stabb'ingly**. — **have a stab at** (*colloq*) to have a go at, attempt; **stab in the back** (*lit* and *fig*) to injure in a treacherous manner. [Origin uncertain; cf **stob**]

Stabat Mater *stā'bat mā'tər* or *stä'bat mä'ter*, *n* a Latin hymn commemorating the sorrows of the Virgin Mary; a musical setting of it. [From its opening words, the mother stood]

stabile, **stability**, **stabilize**, etc. See under **stable**[1].

stable[1] *stā'bl*, *adj* standing firm; firmly established; durable; firm in purpose or character; constant; not ready to change; not radioactive. — *n* **stab'ilate** (*biol*) a population preserved in a viable state though subjected to extraordinary conditions, eg micro-organisms subjected to freezing. — *adj* **stā'bile** (*-bīl* or *-bil*) stable (*rare*); not moving; not fluctuating; not decomposing readily, eg under moderate heat. — *n* an abstract art construction of metal, wire, wood, differing from a mobile in having no movement. — *n* **stability** (*stəbil'i-ti*) the state of being stable; steadiness; fixity; the power of recovering equilibrium; the fixing by vow of a monk or nun to one convent for life. — *n* **stabilization** or **-s-** (*stab-, stāb-i-lī-zā'shən*, or *-li-*). — *n* **sta'bilizātor** or **-s-**. — *vt* **stabilize** or **-ise** (*stab'* or *stāb'*) to render stable or steady; to fix; to fix the value of; to establish, maintain, or regulate the equilibrium of. — *n* **stab'ilizer** or **-s-** anything that stabilizes; an additional plane or other device for giving stability to an aircraft; a gyroscope or other means of steadying a ship; any measure, such as progressive taxation, reduction of subsidy, etc, taken to control production, restrict fluctuations in prices, etc (*econ*); a substance that retards chemical action, eg an additive to food; (in *pl*) an extra pair of small wheels attached to (*usu* the back wheels of) a child's bicycle. — *n* **stā'bleness**. — *adv* **stā'bly**. — **stable equilibrium** the condition in which a body will return to its old position after a slight displacement. [Fr, from L *stabilis*, from *stāre* to stand]

stable[2] *stā'bl*, *n* a building for horses, or sometimes other animals; a set of horses kept together; a horse-keeping establishment, organization or staff (as a horse-keeping establishment often *pl* in form but treated as *sing*); a number of skilled trained (*esp* young) people who work together under one head or one manager; a group of commercial (*esp* publishing) enterprises under the same ownership or management; an establishment in which a group of Japanese sumo wrestlers live and receive training; (in *pl*) a cavalry soldier's duty in the stable, or the call summoning to it. — *vt* to put or keep in a stable. — *vi* to live in a stable, or as if in a stable. — *n* **sta'bler** (*Scot* or *archaic*) a stable-keeper, an inn-keeper. — *n* **sta'bling** the act of putting into a stable; accommodation for horses, cattle, cycles, etc. — **sta'bleboy** or **sta'bleman** someone who works at a stable; **stable companion** (*colloq*) someone who lodges in the same place or is a member of the same club, etc; **stable fly** a two-winged, blood-sucking fly, *Stomoxys calcitrans*, a common pest of man and domestic animals; **stable lad** or **lass** someone whose job is to look after the horses at a racing-stable; **sta'blemate** a horse from the same stable as another; anything manufactured, originated, produced, etc, in the same place as another (eg different models of the same car), or a person from the same club, etc as another (*fig*). — **out of the same stable** having the same background, training, etc. [OFr *estable* (Fr *étable*), from L *stabulum*, from *stāre* to stand]

stablish *stab'lish*, *vt*. An archaic form of **establish**.

staccato *stə-kä'tō* or *stäk-kä'tō*, (*music*) *adj* and *adv* with each note detached or disconnected (opposite of *legato*). — *n* a staccato performance, manner, or passage: — *pl* **stacca'tos**. — *adj* and *adv* (*superl*) **staccatis'simo**. [Ital, pa p of *staccare*, for *distaccare* to separate]

stachys *stā'kis*, *n* any labiate plant of the genus *Stachys*, *esp Stachys byzantium* or *lanata*, lamb's-tongue, or *Stachys officinalis*, betony. [New L, from Gr *stachys* ear of corn]

stack[1] *stak*, *n* a large built-up pile (eg, of hay, corn, wood, etc or of goods or equipment); a group or cluster of chimneys or flues, or a single tall chimney; the chimney or funnel of a steamer, steam-engine, etc; an isolated pillar of rock, often rising from the sea; a set of compactly arranged bookcases for storing books not on the open shelves of a library; a temporary storage area for data in a computer memory; a pyramid of three rifles, etc; an ordered, built-up pile; a standard quantity of gambler's chips bought at one time; aircraft waiting to land and circling at definite heights according to instructions; a large amount (*colloq*). — *vt* to pile into a stack; to shuffle or arrange the order of (cards) for cheating; to arrange (aircraft waiting to land) in a stack (see above). — *adj* **stacked** piled in a stack; (of shoe-heels) made of horizontal layers of leather; (of a woman) having a large bust (*slang*; also **well-stacked**'). — *n* **stack'er** a person who stacks; a machine for stacking (eg products in a factory). — *n* **stack'ing**. — **stack'room** in a library, a room where books are stored in stacks; **stack** or **stacking system** a modular hi-fi system which stacks one component on top of the other; **stack'yard** a yard for stacks. — **stack against** (or **in favour of**) to arrange (circumstances) to the disadvantage (or advantage) of (**have the cards stacked against** (or **in favour of**) to be faced with circumstances arranged in this way); **stack up** to pile or load high. [ON *stakkr* a stack of hay]

stack[2]. See **stick**[1].

stacket *stak'it*, (*obs Scot*) *n* a palisade. [Du *staket*]

stacte *stak'tē*, (*Old Testament*) *n* a sweet-smelling spice, liquid myrrh, used in incense by the ancient Hebrews. — *n* **stactom'eter** or **staktom'eter** a pipette with a hollow bulb in the middle for counting drops. [Gr *staktos*, *-ē*, *-on* dropping]

stadda *stad'ə*, *n* a combmaker's double-bladed handsaw. [Origin unknown]

staddle *stad'l*, *n* a support, *esp* for a stack of hay, etc; the bottom of a stack; a small tree left unfelled; a stump left for coppice. — **staddle stone** a low mushroom-shaped arrangement of a conical and flat, circular stone, used as a support for a hay stack. [OE *stathol* foundation; Ger *Stadel*]

stade. See **stadium**.

stadholder. See **stadtholder**.

stadia[1] *stā'di-ə*, (*surveying*) *n* a graduated rod used in measuring distances at one observation, by the angle subtended by the distance between two hairs (**stadia hairs** or **lines**) in the telescope (also **stadia rod**); the telescope so used (*US*). [Ety dubious]

stadia[2], **stadial**. See under **stadium**.

stadium *stā'di-əm*, *n* a race course, sports ground; an ancient Greek measure of length equivalent to 184 metres or $606\frac{3}{4}$ feet; a stage in development (eg of a glacier, culture, geological or evolutionary period); a stage in the course of a disease (*med*): — *pl* **stā'dia** or **stadiums**. — *n* **stade** (*stād*) a stadium. — *n* **stād'ial** a substage within a period of glaciation or the life of a glacier during which the temperature drops or the ice advances. — *adj* of or pertaining to a stage, stadium or stadial. [Latinized from Gr *stadion*]

stadtholder *stat'hōl-dər* or *stät'* or **stadholder** *stad'* or *städ'*, *n* a Dutch viceroy or provincial governor; the head of the Dutch republic (*hist*). [Du *stadhouder*, literally, stead-holder (Ger *Statthalter*, Fr *lieutenant*), from *stad* place (now only town), and *houder* holder; spelling influenced by Ger *Stadt* town]

staff *stäf*, *n* a stick carried in the hand; a prop or support; a long piece of wood; a pole; a flagstaff; a long handle; a stick or ensign of authority; a token authorizing an engine driver to proceed along a section of single-track railway; a set of lines and spaces on which music is written or printed; a stanza; (in a watch or clock) the spindle of a balance wheel (these meanings have *pl* **staffs** or **staves** *stāvz*; see also **stave**); a body of officers who help a commanding officer, or perform special duties; a body of people employed in an establishment, *usu* on management, administration, clerical, etc, work as distinct from manual; the body of teachers or lecturers in a school, college, university, etc (these three meanings have *pl* **staffs** *stäfs*). — *adj* (or in combination) belonging or attached to the staff; applied also to officers on the staff of a commanding officer, at central headquarters, etc. — *vt* to provide with a staff. — *n* **staff'er** a member of the permanent staff of a business, etc, *usu* as opposed to temporary or casual employees; a member of the editorial staff of a newspaper (*journalism*). — **staff college** (*military*) a college that trains officers for staff appointments; **staff corps** (*military*) a body of officers and men assisting a commanding officer and his staff; formerly a body that supplied officers to the Indian army; **staff duty** (*military*) the occupation of an officer who serves on a staff, having been detached from his regiment; **staff notation** musical notation in which a staff is used, as opposed to the tonic sol-fa system; **staff nurse** a nurse immediately below a sister in rank; **staff officer** (*military*) an executive officer serving on a staff; **staff'room** a room for the use of the staff, as of a school; **staff sergeant** (*military*) a non-commissioned officer serving on a regimental staff; **staff surgeon** a navy surgeon of senior grade; an army surgeon on the staff of a hospital, not with his regiment; **staff'-sys'tem** a block-system that uses a staff; **staff'-tree** any of various American shrubs and climbing plants of the family *Celastraceae* (**staff'=tree family**) *incl* bittersweet and burning bush. — **staff of life** staple food, *esp* bread. [OE *stæf*, ON *stafr*, Ger *Stab*]

staffage *sta-fäzh'*, *n* decorative accessories in a picture, or subordinate additions in any work of art. [Sham Fr, from Ger *staffieren* to garnish]

Staffs. *stafs*, *abbrev*: Staffordshire.

stag *stag*, *n* a male deer, *esp* a red deer over four years old; a male of various kinds (cock, turkey-cock, etc); a man who goes to dances, etc, unaccompanied by a woman; a stag party (*US*); (*Scot* **staig** *stāg*) a colt or stallion; (*Scot* **staig**) an animal castrated in maturity; a person who applies for shares in order to sell them at once at a profit (*stock exchange slang*); an informer (*obs slang*). — *adj* male; of or for males. — *vt* to follow, dog, shadow. — *vi* to deal as a stag (also *vt* with *it* or *the market*; *stock exchange slang*); (of a man) to go as a stag. — *n* **stagg'ard** a deer, *esp* a red deer, in its fourth year. — **stag beetle** any beetle of the family *Lucanidae*, from the large antlerlike mandibles of the males; **stag'=dance** one of men only. — *adj* **stag-head'ed** (of a tree) dying back giving an antlerlike appearance. — **staghorn fern** *Platycerium* a fern with antlerlike leaves; **staghorn moss** common club moss; **stag'hound** the buck hound; the Scottish deerhound; **stag hunt**; **stag party** or **night** a party for men only, *esp* one held for a man about to be married. [OE *stagga* stag; cf ON *steggr*, cock-bird, gander]

stage *stāj*, *n* an elevated platform, *esp* for acting on; the theatre; theatrical representation; the theatrical calling; any scene or field of action; a place of rest on a journey or road; the portion of a journey between two such places; one of a series of divisions of a bus route for which there is a fixed scale of fares; a point reached in, or a section of, life, development, or any process; a subdivision of a geological series or formation; one of the sections in a rocket jettisoned during flight; one of the elements in a complex piece of electronic equipment; (in a microscope, etc) the support for an object to be examined; a tier, shelf, floor, storey; a tiered structure for plants; a scaffold; a stagecoach. — *adj* pertaining to the stage, acting or the theatre; as conventionally represented on the stage (eg *a stage rustic*). — *vt* to represent or put on the stage; to contrive dramatically, organize and bring off. — *vi* (or *vt* with *it*) to travel by stages or by stagecoach (*obs*). — *adj* **staged** in storeys or tiers; put on the stage. — *n* **sta'ger** someone who has had much experience in anything, an old hand (*old stager*); a stage-horse; an actor (*archaic*). — *n* **sta'gery** theatrical contrivances. — *adv* **sta'gily**. — *n* **stag'iness**. — *n* **sta'ging** scaffolding; stagecoaching; putting on the stage; the jettisoning of any of the stages of a rocket. — *adj* **sta'gy** or **sta'gey** savouring of the stage, acted, assumed, affected; of a style or level of competence in acting such that the artificiality is apparent. — **stage'coach** formerly, a coach that ran regularly with passengers from stage to stage; **stage'coaching**; **stage'coachman**; **stage'craft** skill in the technicalities of the theatre; **stage direction** in a copy of a play, an instruction to the actor to do this or that; **stage door** the actors' entrance to a theatre; **stage effect** theatrical effect; **stage fever** a passion to go on the stage; **stage flower** a flower exhibited on a tiered stand; **stage fright** nervousness before an audience, *esp* for the first time (also *fig*); **stage hand** a workman employed about the stage; **stage horse** a stagecoach horse. — *vt* **stage-man'age** (back-formation; used *lit*; also *fig*) to arrange (an event) effectively as if it were a stage scene. — **stage'-manager** a person who superintends the production of plays, with general charge behind the curtain; **stage'-name** a name assumed professionally by an actor or actress; **stage play** a play played or intended to be played on a stage, as opposed to on radio or television; **stage'-player**. — *n pl* **stage rights** legal rights to perform a play. — *adj* **stage'-struck** passionate about all things theatrical, *esp* with a strong desire to act. — **stage whisper** an audible utterance conventionally understood by the audience to represent a whisper; a loud whisper meant to be heard by people other than the person addressed; **staging area** or **base** a point for the assembly of troops en route for an operation; **staging post** a regular point of call on an air route. — **stage left** (or **right**) at the left (or right) of the stage, facing the audience. [OFr *estage* (Fr *étage*) a storey of a house, from inferred LL *staticus*, from L *stāre* to stand]

stagflation *stag-flā'shən*, *n* an economic situation in which there is stagnation in industrial output and consumer demand at the same time as a marked rise in inflation. — *adj* **stagflā'tionary**. [*stag*nant and **in***flation*]

staggard. See under **stag**.

stagger *stag'ər*, *vi* to reel; to go reeling or tottering; to waver. — *vt* to cause to reel; to give a shock to; to cause to waver; to nonplus, confound; to dispose alternately or variously, or to arrange so that one thing or part is ahead of another. — *n* a staggering; a wavering; a staggered arrangement (eg in aircraft, *positive* where the upper plane of a biplane is advanced, *negative* where the lower); (in *pl*, often treated as *sing*) giddiness, also any of various kinds of disease causing horses, sheep, etc, to stagger (**grass** or **stomach staggers**, an acute indigestion; **mad** or **sleepy staggers**, an inflammation of the brain). — *adj* **stagg'ered**. — *n* **stagg'erer**. — *n* and *adj* **stagg'ering**. — *adv* **stagg'eringly**. [Earlier *stacker*, from ON *stakra*, frequentative of *staka* to push]

Stagirite or erroneously **Stagyrite** *staj'i-rīt*, *n* a native or inhabitant of *Stagira* (Gr *Stagīros*) in Macedonia, *esp* in reference to Aristotle (384–322 BC).

stagnant *stag'nənt*, *adj* (of water) still, standing, without current; (of water) foul, unwholesome, or dull from stillness (also *fig*); inert. — *n* **stag'nancy**. — *adv* **stag'nantly**. — *vi* **stagnate'** (or *stag'*-) to be or become stagnant. — *n* **stagnā'tion** — **stagnation point** the point at or near the nose of a body in motion in a fluid, where the flow divides. [L *stagnāre*, *-ātum*, from *stagnum* pond]

stagy. See under **stage**.

Stagyrite. See **Stagirite**.

Stahlhelm *shtäl'helm*, *n* a German old soldiers' conservative nationalist and militaristic organization after World War I. — *n* **Stahl'helmer** or **Stahl'helmist**. [Ger, steel helmet]

Stahlian *stäl'i-ən*, *adj* pertaining to Georg Ernst *Stahl* (1660–1734), German physician, or his animism. — *n* **Stahl'ianism** or **Stahl'ism**.

staid *stād*, *adj* steady; sober, grave or sedate, often implying a dull or boring quality; permanent (*rare*). — *adv* **staid'ly**. — *n* **staid'ness**. [**stayed**, from pa t and pa p of **stay**]

staig. See **stag**.

stain *stān*, *vt* to impart a new colour to; to tinge; to dye; to impregnate with a substance that colours some parts so as to show composition and structure; to tarnish; to sully; to bring reproach on; to deprive of colour (*obs*); to pale by comparison (*obs*). — *vi* to take or impart a stain. — *n* a dye or colouring matter; discoloration; a spot; the taint of guilt; pollution; a cause of reproach; shame. — *adj* **stained**. — *n* **stain'er**. — *n* and *adj* **stain'ing**. — *adj* **stain'less** free from stain; not liable to stain, rust, or tarnish. — *adv* **stain'lessly**. — *n* **stain'lessness**. — **stained glass** glass painted with certain pigments fused into its surface; **stainless steel** a steel that will not rust, containing 8 to 25 per cent of chromium. **[distain]**

stair *stār*, *n* a series of steps, *usu* in *pl*, a flight from landing to landing, but in Scotland, in *sing*, the whole series from floor to floor; one such step. — *adj* **staired** having, or arranged like, stairs. — *adv* **stair'wise** by steps; in the manner of a stair. — **stair carpet** a long carpet for stairs; **stair'case** the structure enclosing a stair; stairs with banisters, etc. — *vi* (*slang*) (of an individual who has a house in a shared-ownership scheme) to buy that part of the property which he did not previously own, thus achieving full ownership, and then sell the house on the open market. — **stair'casing**; **stair'foot** the level place at the foot of stairs; **stair'head** the level place at the top of stairs; **stair'lift** a lift, mounted on the wall of a staircase in a house, on which a disabled person sits to be carried upstairs (and downstairs); **stair rod** a rod for holding a stair carpet in place; **stair'way** a staircase; a passage by stairs; **stair'well** the well of a staircase; **stair'work** backstairs intriguing. — **below stairs** in the basement; among the servants. [OE *stǣger*, from *stīgan* to ascend; Ger *steigen* to climb, Norw *steg* step]

staithe or **staith** *stāth*, (*N Eng dialect*) *n* a wharf; a structure for shipping coal; an embankment. [OE *stæth* bank, and ON *stöth* landing-stage]

stake[1] *stāk*, *n* a stick or pole pointed at one end; a post; a post to which someone condemned to be burned was tied (*hist*); hence, death or martyrdom by burning; a tinsmith's anvil. — *vt* to fasten to or with, to protect, shut, support, furnish, pierce, with a stake or stakes; to mark the bounds of with stakes (often with *off* or *out*). — **stake boat** a boat anchored as a marker for a boat race, or to which other boats may be moored; **stake net** a net hung on stakes. — **stake a claim** (*for* or *to*) to intimate one's right to or desire to possess; **stake out** (*colloq*) to place (a person, etc) under surveillance (*n* **stake'-out**). [OE *staca* stake]

stake[2] *stāk*, *vt* to deposit as a wager; to risk, hazard; to furnish, supply, fit out, whether free or in expectation of return (with *with* or *to*; *orig US*). — *n* anything pledged as a wager; a prize; anything to gain or lose; an interest, concern; the condition of being at hazard; a grubstake; (in *pl*) a race for money staked or contributed. — **at stake** hazarded; in danger; at issue. [Perh MDu *staken* to place]

stakhanovite *stə-kan'ō-vīt*, *n* a worker who has received recognition for his or her part in increasing the rate of production in a factory, etc. — Also *adj*. — *n* **stakhan'ovism**. [G *Stakhanov*, a Russian miner]

stalactite *stal'ək-tīt* or *sta-lak'tīt*, *n* an icicle-like pendant of calcium carbonate, formed by the evaporation of water percolating through limestone, as on a cave roof; the material it is composed of; anything of similar form. — *adj* **stalac'tic**, **stalac'tical**, **stalac'tiform**, **stalactī'tal**, **stal'actīted** (also *-ak'*), **stalactitic** (*-tit'ik*; the usual *adj*), **stalactit'ical**, **stalactitiform** (*-tīt'*) or **stalactitious** (*-tish'əs*). — *adv* **stalactit'ically**. — *n* **stal'agmite** (also *-ag'*) an upward-growing conical formation on the floor, formed by the drip from the roof or from a stalactite. — *adj* **stalagmitic** (*-mit'ik*) or **stalagmit'ical**. — *adv* **stalagmit'ically**. — *n* **stalagmom'eter** an instrument for determining surface tension by drops. — *n* **stalagmom'etry**. [Gr *stalaktos*, *stalagma*, *stalagmos* a dropping, from *stalassein* to drip]

stalag *stal'ag*, *shtä'lak* or *shtä'lähh*, *n* a German camp for prisoners of war (non-commissioned officers and men). [Ger *Stamm* base, and *Lager* camp]

stalagmite. See under **stalactite**.

stal'd *stöld*, (*archaic*) *pa p* of **stall**[1].

stale[1] *stāl*, *adj* no longer fresh; past the best; out of condition by over-training or overstudy; impaired by lapse of time; tainted; vapid or tasteless from age; (of liquor) old, clear, and strong (*obs*). — *vt* and *vi* to make or become stale, over-familiar, or insipid. — *adv* **stale'ly**. — *n* **stale'ness**. [Perh from the root *sta-*, as in **stand**]

stale[2] *stāl*, *n* a decoy bird (*dialect*); a thief's accomplice, acting as a decoy (*obs*); a lure; a low prostitute employed as a decoy by thieves, or generally (*Shakesp*); a stalking-horse, cover to a real purpose (*Shakesp*); a pretext; a lover made a butt of by or for one preferred. [Cf Anglo-Fr *estal*, *-e* pigeon used to entice a hawk, OE *stælhrān* decoy-reindeer, Ger *Stellvogel* decoy-bird; prob from root of OE *stellan* to place]

stale[3] *stāl*, *n* urine, now *esp* of horses. — *vi* to urinate. [Cf Du *stalle*, Ger *Stall*, OFr verb *estaler*]

stale[4] *stāl*, (*dialect*) *n* a handle, shaft; a stalk. [OE *stalu*, appar part of a harp]

stale[5] *stāl*, (now *rare* or *obs*) *n* and *vt* stalemate. — **stale'mate** an unsatisfactory draw resulting when a player not actually in check has no possible legal move (*chess*); an inglorious deadlock. — *vt* to subject to a stalemate. [Cf Anglo-Fr *estale*, perh from Eng **stall**]

stale[6]. See **steal**[1].

Stalinism *stä'lin-izm*, *n* the rigorous rule of the Soviet Communist dictator Josef *Stalin* (1879–1953), *esp* in its concentration of all power and authority in the Communist world in the former Soviet Union. — *n* and *adj* **Sta'linist**.

stalk[1] *stök*, *n* the stem of a plant; a slender connecting part; a shaft; a tall chimney. — *vt* to remove the stalk from. — *adj* **stalked** having a stalk. — *adj* **stalk'less**. — *adj* **stalk'y** running to stalk; like a stalk. — *adj* **stalk'-eyed** having the eyes on stalks. [Dimin from the root of OE *stela*, *stalu* stalk]

stalk[2] *stök*, *vi* to stride stiffly or haughtily; to go after game, keeping under cover; to follow a person, *esp* an enemy, in a similar manner. — *vt* to approach under cover; to stalk over or through (a tract of country, etc). — *n* an act of stalking; a stalking gait. — *n* **stalk'er**. — *n* and *adj* **stalk'ing**. — **stalk'ing-horse** a horse or substitute behind which a hunter hides while stalking game; anything put forward to mask plans or efforts. [OE (*bi*)*stealcian*, frequentative of **steal**[1]]

stalko *stö'kō*, (*Anglo-Ir*) *n* a gentleman without fortune or occupation: — *pl* **stalk'oes**. [Perh Ir *stócach* idler]

stall[1] *stöl*, *n* a standing-place; a stable, cowshed, or the like; a compartment for one animal; a bench, table, booth or stand for the display or sale of goods, or used as a working-place; a church seat with arms, *usu* one of those lining the choir or chancel on both sides, reserved for cathedral clergy, for choir, for monks, or for knights of an order; an office entitling one to such a seat; a doorless pew; an individual seat with arms in a theatre, etc, *esp* (in *pl*) on the ground floor; a working place in a mine; a covering for a finger (as in *fingerstall*); a starting stall (qv at **start**); an instance of stalling in aircraft or engine; a standstill; (*Scot* **staw**) a surfeit. — *vi* to put or keep in a stall; to induct, install; to bring to a standstill; to cause (an aeroplane) to fly in such a way that the angle between the aerofoils and the direction of motion is greater than that at which there is maximum lift, and so lose control; to stop (an engine) by sudden braking, overloading, etc; to cause (a vehicle) to become stuck in mud or snow; (*esp* in Scots form **staw**) to surfeit; (*Spenser* in *pa p* **stal'd** *stöld*) to release on payment by instalments. — *vi* to dwell (*obs*); to inhabit a stall; to share a dwelling (*obs*); to come to a standstill; to stick in mud or snow; (of an aircraft or engine) to be stalled. — *n* **stallage** (*stöl'ij*) rent paid for erecting a stall in a fair or market. — *adj* **stalled** kept or fed in a stall; fatted; having a stall or stalls; stuck; sated (*Scot* **stawed**). — *n* **stall'ing** stabling. — *n* **stall'inger** or **stallenger** (*-in-jər*; *hist*) a keeper of a stall; a person who paid for the privilege of trading in a burgh of which he was not a freeman. — *adj* **stall'-fed** (of domestic animals) fed and fattened in a stall. — *vt*

stall'-feed to confine (an animal) to its stall and fatten it. — **stall'ing-ken'** (*obs cant*) a house for receiving stolen goods; **stall'man** a keeper of a stall, *esp* a bookstall; **stall'master** (Ger *Stallmeister*) a master of horse; **stall plate** a plate with a knight's arms affixed to his stall. [OE *stall*, *steall*, ON *stallr*, Ger *Stall*]

stall[2] *stöl*, *n* a ruse, trick; an evasive manoeuvre; a decoy, *esp* someone who diverts attention from a criminal action. — *vt* to delay or obstruct; to stave off (with *off*). — *vi* to hang back, play for time; to be obstructive, evasive or deceptive. [**stale**[2]]

stallage, stallenger, stallinger. See under **stall**[1].

stallion[1] *stal'yən*, *n* an uncastrated male horse, *esp* one kept for breeding. [OFr *estalon* (Fr *étalon*), from OHGer *stal* stall]

stallion[2] *stal'yən*, (*obs*) *n* a courtesan (*Hamlet*; another reading, *scullion*). [Fr *estalon*; cf **stale**[2]]

stallion[3] (*Shakesp*). Same as **staniel**.

stalwart *stöl'wərt*, *adj* stout, strong, sturdy; determined or committed in support or partisanship. — *n* a resolute person. — Also (*archaic*) **stal'worth** (*-wərth*). — *adv* **stal'wartly**. — *n* **stal'wartness**. [Orig Scots form (popularized by *Scott*) of *stalworth*, from OE *stælwierthe* serviceable, from *stǣl* place (from *stathol* foundation), and *wierthe* worth]

stamen *stā'mən*, *n* the pollen-producing part of a flower, consisting of anther and filament: — *pl* **stā'mens** or **stamina** (*stam'i-nə*). — *adj* **stā'mened** having stamens. — *adj* **stam'inate** having stamens but no carpels, male. — *adj* **staminif'erous** (*stam-* or *stām-*) having stamens. — *n* **stam'inode** or **staminō'dium** a sterile stamen. — *n* **stam'inody** metamorphosis of other parts into stamens. — *adj* **stam'inoid** like, or metamorphosed into, a stamen. [L *stāmen*, *stāminis* a warp thread (upright in an old loom), from *stāre* to stand]

stamina[1] *stam'in-ə*, *n* sustained energy, staying power, whether physical, mental or emotional. [Pl of *stamen* warp, understood as the threads of life spun out by the Fates]

stamina[2]. See under **stamen**.

stammel *stam'l*, (*hist*) *n* a kind of woollen cloth, *usu* dyed red, and used to make underclothes; the bright red colour of this cloth. — *adj* of stammel; bright red. [Fr *estamel*, or independently formed ME *stamin*, from OFr *estamin*, both from L *stāmina* warp threads]

stammer *stam'ər*, *vi* to falter in speaking; to speak with involuntary hesitations, to stutter. — *vt* to utter falteringly or with a stutter. — *n* involuntary hesitation in speech, a stutter; a faltering mode of utterance. — *n* **stamm'erer**. — *n* and *adj* **stamm'ering**. — *adv* **stamm'eringly**. [OE *stamerian*; Du *stemeren*]

stamnos *stam'nos*, *n* an ancient Greek short-necked jar: — *pl* **stam'noi**. [Gr]

stamp *stamp*, *vt* to bring the foot forcibly down upon; to trample; to bring the sole of (the foot) down flat, heavily or with force; to impress, imprint, or cut with a downward blow, as with a die or cutter; to mint, make or shape by such a blow; to fix or mark deeply; to crush, grind or pound (ore, etc); to impress with a mark attesting official approval, ratification, payment, etc; to affix an adhesive stamp to; to attest, declare, prove to be; to characterize. — *vi* to bring the foot down forcibly and noisily; to walk with a heavy tread. — *n* the act of stamping; an impression; a stamped device, mark, imprint; an adhesive paper used as a substitute for stamping, *esp* one affixed to show that postage has been paid; attestation; authorization; a coin (*Shakesp*); pounded maize (*SAfr*); cast, form, character; distinguishing mark, imprint, sign, evidence; an instrument or machine for stamping; national insurance contributions, formerly (and for some self-employed still) recorded by sticking a stamp on to an official card (*colloq*). — *n* **stamp'er**. — *n* and *adj* **stamp'ing**. — **Stamp Act** an act of parliament imposing or regulating stamp duties, *esp* that of 1765 imposing them on the American colonies; **stamp album** a book for keeping a collection of postage stamps in; **stamp collector** formerly, a receiver of stamp duties; a person who makes a hobby of collecting postage stamps; **stamp duty** a tax on legal documents, its payment being confirmed by the affixation of a stamp; **stamp-hinge** see under **hinge**; **stamp'ing-ground** an animal's usual resort; a person's habitual place of resort; **stamping machine** a machine used for stamping coins, in the stamping of brasswork, or in crushing metallic ores; **stamp mill** or **stamping mill** a machine for crushing ores; **stamp note** a certificate from a customs officer for goods to be loaded as freight of a ship; **stamp office** an office where stamp duties are received and stamps issued; **stamp paper** paper bearing a government revenue stamp. — **stamp out** to put out, extinguish by tramping; to extirpate; to make by stamping from a sheet with a cutter. [ME *stampen*, from an inferred OE *stampian* from the same root as *stempan*; Ger *stampfen*]

stampede *stam-pēd'*, *n* a sudden mass rush of a panic-stricken herd; a headlong scramble by a crowd of people; any mass rush to do something. — *vi* to rush in a stampede. — *vt* to send rushing in a stampede. — Also *n* and *vt* (*obs*) **stampē'do**. [Sp *estampida* crash, from *estampar* to stamp]

stance *stans*, *n* a posture adopted in standing; the standing position of someone about to play the ball in golf, etc; a point of view taken, an attitude; a place occupied by market stalls, a taxi rank, etc (*Scot*); a stanza (*obs*). [Fr *stance* (now meaning 'stanza'), from Ital *stanza* a stopping-place, station, from L *stāre* to stand]

stanch[1], *stänch* or *stänsh* or **staunch** *stönch* or *stönsh*, *vt* to stop the flowing of (*esp* blood); to quench, allay. — *vi* (*Bible*) to cease to flow. — *n* a styptic; a floodgate. — *adj* **stanch'able** or **staunch'able**. — *n* **stanch'er** or **staunch'er**. — *n* **stanch'ing** or **staunch'ing**. — *adj* **stanch'less** or **staunch'less** that cannot be quenched or stopped. [OFr *estancher* (Fr *étancher*), from LL *stancāre* to stanch, from L *stagnāre* to be or make stagnant, from *stagnum* a pond]

stanch[2]. See **staunch**[1].

stanchel, stancher. See under **stanchion**.

stanchion *stän'shən* or *stan'shən*, *n* an upright beam, bar, rod, shaft, etc acting as a support, a strut. — *vt* to support by means of, or fasten to, a stanchion. — Also (*Scot*) **stanchel** (*stän'* or *stān'*) or **stan'cher**. — *adj* **stan'chioned**. [OFr *estançon*, from *estance* prop, from L *stāre* to stand]

stanck *stangk*, (*Spenser*) *adj* faint. [Ital *stanco*]

stand *stand*, *vi* to be, become, or remain upright, erect, rigid, or still; to be on, or rise to, one's feet; to be a particular height, as in *He stands six feet tall*; to be steadfast; to have or take a position; to assume the attitude and duties of (guard, sentinel); to be or remain; to be set or situated; to be likely, be in a position (to lose or gain something); to come to a stop, be stationary or remain still; used with *and* to introduce a second verb, eg *stand and stare*; to be set down; to hold a course or direction (with *for*; *naut*); to hold good; to endure, continue to exist; to be, at the moment in question, as in *the score stands at* 3 *to* 1, *as things stand*; to be a representative, representation or symbol (with *for*); to be a candidate (with *for*); (of a vehicle) to park, wait (*NAm*). — *vt* to withstand; to tolerate; to endure; to sustain; to suffer, undergo; to abide by; to be at the expense of, offer and pay for; to station, cause to stand; to set erect, in place, or in position: — *pa t* and *pa p* **stood**; *Scot* **stood'en**, **studd'en**; *infinitive*, *Spenser*, **stand'en**. — *n* an act, manner, or place of standing; a taking up of a position for resistance; resistance; an attitude or position adopted; the partnership of any two batsmen at the wicket, the period of time of the partnership, or the runs made during it (*cricket*); a standing position; a standstill; a stoppage; a post, station; a stall or position occupied by a trader or an organization at an exhibition, for the display of goods, etc; a place, sometimes under cover, for awaiting game; a place for vehicles awaiting hire; a structure, with or without a roof, with sitting or standing accommodation for spectators, eg at a football or rugby game; a stop on tour to give one or more performances, or the place where it is made (*theat*); a platform; a witness-box (*NAm*); a base or structure for setting things on; a piece of furniture for hanging things from; a company of plovers; a complete set, *esp* (*Scot*) a suit of clothes or armour; a shearer's position in a shed (*Austr* and *NZ*); a standing growth or crop; a young tree left standing; a tub or vat. — *n* **stand'er**. — *adj* **stand'ing** established; settled; permanent; fixed; stagnant; erect; having a base; done as one stands; from a standing position, without preliminary movement (eg *standing jump, standing start*). — *n* the action of someone who or something that stands; duration or continuance; a place to stand in or on; position, status or reputation in one's profession or in society; a current ranking within a graded scale, *esp* in sport; a right or capacity to sue or maintain an action. — *adj* **stand'-alone** (*comput*) (of a system, device, etc) that can operate unconnected to and unaided by any other. — **stand'-by** that which, or someone whom, one relies on or readily resorts to; something or someone available for use in an emergency (see also **on stand-by** below). — *adj* (of an airline passenger, ticket, fare, etc) occupying, or for, an aircraft seat not booked in advance but taken as available, *usu* with some price reduction, at the time of departure. — **stand'er-by** (*Shakesp*) a bystander: — *pl* **stand'ers-by**; **stand first** (*journalism*) an introductory paragraph in bigger and/or bolder type summarizing the contents of a newspaper or magazine article; **stand'-in** a substitute; **standing bed** a high bedstead, not a truckle bed; **standing committee** one permanently established to deal with a particular matter; **standing joke** a subject that raises a laugh whenever it is mentioned; **standing-off dose** (*radiol*) the absorbed dose after which occupationally exposed radiation workers must be transferred to duties not involving further exposure; **standing order** an instruction from a customer to his or her bank to make regular payments from his or her account (also called **banker's order**); an order placed with a shopkeeper, etc for the regular supply of a newspaper or other goods; a military order with long-term application; (in *pl*) regulations for procedure adopted by a legislative assembly (also **standing rules**); **standing ovation** a burst of applause from an audience that rises to its feet in its enthusiasm; **standing rigging** the fixed ropes in a ship; **stand'ing-room** room for standing, without a seat; **standing stone** (*archaeol*) a great stone set erect in the ground, thought to be of religious significance to prehistoric peoples; **standing wave** the pattern of maxima and minima when two sets of oppositely travelling waves of the same frequency interfere with each other (*phys*); (in *pl*) a long-lasting layered cloud-formation seen in hilly regions (*meteorol*); **stand'-off** a rugby half-back who stands away from the scrum as a link between scrum-half and the three-quarters (also **stand-off half**); a tie, draw or deadlock (*NAm*); any object that stands, projects or holds another a short distance away, eg on a ladder, an attachment that holds it away from the surface supporting it. — *adj* **stand'off** standoffish (*NAm*); (of a missile) capable of being released at a long distance from its target. — *adj* **standoff'ish** inclined to hold aloof, keep others at arm's-length. — **stand-off'ishness**; **standpatt'er** (*US*) someone who refuses to accept or consider change; a political diehard; **stand-patt'ism**; **stand'pipe** an open vertical pipe connected to a pipeline, to ensure that the pressure head at that point cannot exceed the length of the pipe; a pipe fitted with a tap, used to obtain water, eg from an attached hose; **stand'point** a viewpoint; **stand'still** a complete stop. — *adj* stationary; unmoving; forbidding or refraining from movement. — **stand'-to** a precautionary parade or taking of posts. — *adj* **stand'-up** erect; done or taken in a standing position; (of a fight) in earnest; delivering, or consisting of, a comic monologue without feed or other support. — *n* something that stands upright, either independently or with a support to hold it in position; a broken date (between two people) (*colloq*). — **all standing** everything remaining as it stands; without unrigging; fully clad; **it stands to reason** it is only logical to assume; **make a stand** to halt and offer resistance; **one-night stand** see under **one**; **on stand-by** in readiness to provide assistance, or work, in an emergency; **stand against** to resist; **stand by** to support; to adhere to, abide by; to be at hand; to hold oneself in readiness; to prepare to work at; **stand down** to leave the witness box; (*esp* of a member or members of the armed forces) to go off duty; to withdraw from a contest or from a controlling position (*vi* and *vt*): — *pa p* **stood down**; **stand fast** to be unmoved; **stand fire** to remain steady under the fire of an enemy (also *fig*); **stand for** to be a candidate for; to direct the course towards (*naut*); to be a sponsor for; to represent, symbolize; to champion; to put up with, endure (*colloq*); **stand from** (*naut*) to direct the course from; **stand in** to cost; to become a party; to have an understanding, be in league; to deputize, act as a substitute (with *for*); **stand in with** to support, act together with; **stand low** (*printing*) to fall short of the standard height; **stand off** to keep at a distance; to direct the course from (*naut*); to forbear compliance or intimacy (*Shakesp*); to suspend temporarily from employment: — *pa p* **stood off**; **stand off and on** (*naut*) to sail away from shore and then towards it; **stand on** to continue on the same tack or course (*naut*); to insist on; to set store by (see also under **ceremony**); to behove; to found upon; **stand one's ground** to maintain one's position; **stand one's hand**, **stand sam** (*colloq*), **stand shot** and **stand treat** to treat the company, *esp* to drinks; **stand on one's own (two) feet** to manage one's own affairs without help; **stand out** to project, to be prominent; not to comply, to refuse to yield, take an independent stand (with *against* or *for*); **stand over** to keep (someone who is working, etc) under close supervision; to postpone or be postponed; **stand pat** (*US*) to play one's hand in poker as it was dealt, without drawing any cards; to adhere to an established, *esp* political, principle, resisting all compromise (*fig*); **stand to** to fall to, set to work; to back up; to uphold; to take up a position in readiness for orders; **stand up** to get to one's feet; to take position for a dance; to be clad (with *in*); to fail to keep an appointment with (*colloq*); **stand up for** to support or attempt to defend; **stand upon** to stand on; to attack (*Bible*); **stand up to** to meet (an opponent, etc) face to face, to show resistance to; to fulfil (an obligation, etc) fairly; to withstand (hard wear, etc); **stand well** to be in favour; **stand with** to be consistent. [OE *standan*; Gothic *standan*; cf Ger *stehen*, Gr *histanai* to place, L *stāre* to stand]

standard *stand'ərd*, *n* an established or accepted model; (often in *pl*) a principle of behaviour or morality; a criterion; a definite level of excellence or adequacy required, aimed at, or possible; an overall level achieved; an authorized model for a unit of measurement; the legally required weight and purity of the metal used in coins; the commodity, eg gold or silver, that is taken as the basis of value in a currency; a measure of wood in board form, equivalent to 4·7 cubic metres, 165 cubic feet or 1980 board feet (board foot = a piece of wood one foot square and one inch thick); a flag or military symbolic figure on a pole, marking a rallying point; a rallying point (also *fig*); a long tapering flag notched and rounded at the end, bearing heraldic symbols and fixed in the ground (*heraldry*); a flag generally; a regimental flag; a standard-bearer; a standing shrub or tree not trained on an espalier or a wall; a fruit tree or other tree grafted and trained so as to have an upright stem without branches; an upright post, pillar, stick; a tree left growing amidst coppice; a song or piece of music that has remained popular over the years; a class or grade in an elementary school; the uppermost petal of a papilionaceous flower; a streaming wing feather; a structure erected at a conduit (*obs*);

an accepted authoritative statement of a church's creed; that which stands or is fixed. — *adj* serving as or conforming to a standard; of the normal, regular quality, size, etc, without additions or variations; of accepted and enduring value; growing as a standard; standing upright. — *n* **standardīzā'tion** or **-s-**. — *vt* **stand'ardize** or **-ise** to make, or keep, of uniform size, shape, etc. — *n* **stand'ardizer** or **-s-**. — **standard assessment task** (*educ*) in England and Wales, a component of the standardized testing procedures employed, as part of the national curriculum, to determine a pupil's level of attainment in a particular subject (*abbrev* **SAT**); **standard atmosphere** 101 325 newtons per sq metre, or 1 013 250 dynes per sq centimetre; a standard of measurement of atmospheric conditions used in comparing the performance of aircraft (*aeronautics*, etc); **stand'ard-bearer** a person who carries a standard or banner; an outstanding leader; **standard bread** bread made with flour containing 80 per cent of the whole-wheat including germ and semolina; **Stand'ardbred** a breed of horse *orig* developed in the US as harness racehorses for trotting or pacing to a standard minimum speed; (also without *cap*) a horse of this breed. — Also *adj*. — **standard candle** see **candle**; **standard deviation** in a frequency distribution, the root of the average of the squares of the differences from their mean of a number of observations, used as a measure of dispersion; **standard English** the form of English taught in schools, etc, and used, *esp* in formal situations, by the majority of educated English-speakers; **standard error** standard deviation; standard deviation divided by the root of the number of observations in a sample; **Standard grade** a form of examination introduced into Scotland in 1989, intended to replace O grade, and to assess candidates' application rather than merely their assimilation of knowledge; a subject offered, or satisfactory assessment obtained, at Standard grade; **standardized mortality rate** (*med*) the ratio of observed to expected deaths in a subpopulation (*abbrev* **SMR**); **standard lamp** a lamp on a tall support; **standard solution** a solution of known concentration, used for purposes of comparison, commonly containing the equivalent, in grammes, of the solute to a litre of solution (*normal solution*) or some simple fraction (as *decinormal*, one-tenth normal); **standard temperature and pressure** a temperature of 0°C and a pressure of 101 325 N/m^2 (*abbrev* **stp**); **standard wing** a bird of paradise of the Moluccas with a pair of erectile white feathers at the bend of the wing. — **(international) standard book number** a number allotted to a book by agreement of (international) publishers which shows area, publisher and individual title (*abbrev* **ISBN**). [OFr *estandart*; prob connected either with **extend** or **stand**, and in any case influenced by or partly from **stander**]

standee *stan-dē'*, (*esp US*) *n* a person standing as opposed to sitting, eg on a bus when all the seats are occupied. [**stand** and sfx **-ee**]

standgale *stand'gāl*, *n* a corrupt form of **staniel**.

standish *stan'dish*, (*archaic*) *n* an inkstand. [Poss for *stand-dish*]

stane *stān*. Scots form of **stone**.

stang[1] *stang*, *n* a stake, pole. — **riding the stang** punishment by being carried astride of a stang. [ON *stöng*; cf OE *stæng*, Du *stang*]

stang[2] *stang* or *stöng*, (*Scot*) *vi* to sting. — *n* a sting. [ON *stanga* to prick]

stanhope *stan'əp* or *-hōp*, *n* a light open one-seated carriage first made for Fitzroy *Stanhope* (1787–1864). — **Stanhope press** a printing press invented by the third Earl *Stanhope* (1753–1816).

staniel, stanyel *stan'yəl* or **stannel** *stan'l* (*Shakesp* **stallion** *stal'yən*), *n* the kestrel. [OE *stāngella*, literally, stone yeller]

Stanislavski method or **system** *stan-i-släf'ski*, *n* method acting (qv). [K *Stanislavski* (1863–1938), Russian actor and director]

stank[1] *stangk*, *pa t* of **stink**.

stank[2] *stangk*, (chiefly *Scot*) *n* a ditch, a pool; a dam; a drain in the street. [OFr *estanc* a pond, from L *stagnum* a pond]

Stanley knife® *stan'lē nīf*, *n* a type of trimming knife with a hollow metal handle into which a renewable, extremely sharp blade is fitted, used for trimming various materials, such as carpet, hardboard, etc. [From F T *Stanley*, US businessman, who founded the Stanley Rule and Level Company in 1843]

stann- *stan-*, *combining form* signifying tin. — *n* **stann'ary** (*-ə-ri*) a tin-mining district (*esp* the **Stannaries** in Cornwall and Devon). — Also *adj*. — *n* **stann'ate** a salt of stannic acid. — *n* **stannā'tor** one of the members of the Stannary Parliament. — *adj* **stann'ic** (*stan'ik*; *chem*) relating to tin in its quadrivalent state. — *adj* **stannif'erous** tin-bearing. — *n* **stann'ite** (*stan'it*) a mineral composed of tin, copper, iron, and sulphur, occurring in tin-bearing veins (*mineralogy*); a salt of stannous hydroxide, $Sn(OH)_2$, acting as a weak acid (*chem*). — *n* **stann'otype** a photo-mechanical process in which an exposed and developed bichromated film is coated with tinfoil and used directly for pressure printing. — *adj* **stann'ous** of bivalent tin. — **Stannary Courts** courts (abolished 1896) for the tinners of the Stannaries; **Stannary Parliament** the ancient parliament of tinners, comprising twenty-four representatives (stannators) for all Cornwall, reconvened in 1974 after a lapse of more than 200 years; **stannic acid** H_2SnO_3. [L *stannum* tin]

stannel, stanyel. See **staniel**.

stanza *stan'zə* (*Shakesp* **stanze** or **stan'zo** (*pl* **stan'zoes** or **-zos**)), *n* a group of lines of verse forming a definite pattern, *usu* constituting one of a series of units in a poem; a pattern so composed. — *adj* **stanzā'ic**. [Ital *stanza*, from L *stāre* to stand]

stap *stap*, *vt* an obsolete affectation for **stop**, *esp* in the sense of choke or obstruct; also (*stap* or *stäp*) a Scots form, in the senses of stuff, thrust, cram.

stapedectomy, stapedial, stapedius. See under **stapes**.

stapelia *stə-pē'li-ə*, *n* any succulent plant of the carrion flower genus *Stapelia*, native to S Africa, having toothed, four-angled stems and large, star-shaped, blotched flowers that smell of carrion. [After the Dutch botanist J B van *Stapel* (d 1636)]

stapes *stā'pēz*, *n* the stirrup-shaped bone, the innermost ossicle of the middle ear that articulates with the incus: — *pl* **stā'pēs** or **stapē'dēs**. — *n* **stapedectomy** (*stap-i-dek'tə-mi*) the surgical removal of the stapes. — *adj* **stapedial** (*stə-pē'di-əl*). — *n* **stape'dius** the muscle of the stapes. [LL *stapēs*, *-edis* a stirrup]

staph. See **staphylococcus** under **staphylo-**.

staphylo- *staf'i-lō* or **staphy-** *staf'i*, *combining form* denoting: (1) uvula; (2) resembling a bunch of grapes. — *adj* **staph'yline** like a bunch of grapes. — n **staphylī'tis** inflammation of the uvula. — *adj* **staphylococc'al**. — *n* **staphylococc'us** (Gr *kokkos* a grain) a Gram-positive spherical bacterium of the genus *Staphylococcus*, found in clustered masses and producing exotoxins which can cause serious infections such as osteomyelitis, pneumonia, boils, abscesses, etc (*colloq* shortening **staph**; *pl* **staphylococc'i**). — *n* **staphylō'ma** abnormal protrusion of the sclera or of the cornea. — *n* **staphylo'plasy** (*surg*) plastic surgery involving the soft palate and the uvula. — *n* **staphylorrh'aphy** (Gr *rhaphē* stitching) the operation of uniting a cleft palate. [Gr *staphylē* a bunch of grapes, a swollen uvula]

staple[1] *stā'pl*, *n* a leading commodity or raw material; a main element (as of diet, reading, conversation); unmanufactured wool or other raw material; textile fibre, or its length and quality; a settled mart or market (*medieval hist*). — *adj* constituting a staple; leading, main. — *vt* to grade (wool, cotton, etc) according to staple. — *n* **stā'pler** a merchant of a staple; a person who grades and deals in wool. — **merchant of the staple**

a member of a medieval association of merchants privileged to trade in a staple commodity, *esp* wool, at the **staple town** (or **towns**) appointed by the king. [OFr *estaple*, from LGer *stapel* heap, mart]

staple[2] *stā'pl*, *n* a U-shaped rod or wire for driving into a wall, post, etc as a fastening; a similarly-shaped piece of wire that is driven through sheets of paper and compressed, to fasten them together; the curved bar, etc that passes through the slot of a hasp, receives a bolt, etc; the metallic tube to which the reed is fastened in the oboe, etc. — *vt* to fasten with a staple. — *n* **stā'pler** an instrument for (dispensing and) inserting staples into papers, etc. — **stapling machine** a machine that stitches paper with wire. [OE *stapol* post, support; cf **staple**[1]]

staple[3] or **stapple** *stap'l*, (*Scot*) *n*. See **stopple**[2].

star[1] *stär*, *n* any of those heavenly bodies visible by night that are really gaseous masses generating heat and light, whose places are relatively fixed (**fixed stars**); more loosely, these and the planets, comets, meteors and even, less commonly, the sun, moon and earth; a planet as a supposed influence, hence (*usu* in *pl*) one's luck, or an astrologer's summary of planetary influences; an object or figure with pointed rays, most commonly five; an asterisk; a starfish; a radial meeting of ways; a star-shaped badge or emblem, denoting rank, honour or merit, used eg in grading or classification, as in *three-star general*, *four-star petrol*, *five-star* (ie luxurious) *hotel*; a white mark on an animal's forehead, *esp* a horse's; a pre-eminent or exceptionally brilliant person; a leading performer, or one supposed to draw the public; a networking conformation in which the central control point is linked individually to all workstations (*comput*). — *adj* of stars; marked by a star; leading, pre-eminent, brilliant. — *vt* to make a star of; to have (a specified person) as a star performer; to mark with a star; to shatter or crack in a radiating form; to set with stars; to bespangle. — *vi* to shine, as a star; to attract attention; to appear as a principal or star performer: — *pr p* **starr'ing**; *pa t* and *pa p* **starred**. — *n* **star'dom** the state of being or status of a star performer, *esp* of stage or screen. — *adj* **star'less**. — *n* **star'let** a kind of starfish (*Asterina*); a little star; a young film actress, *esp* one hailed as a future star. — *adj* and *adv* **star'like**. — *adj* **starred** adorned or studded with stars; influenced by or having a star; decorated or marked with a star; turned into a star; star-shaped; radially cracked, fissured. — *adv* **starr'ily**. — *n* **starr'iness**. — *n* and *adj* **starr'ing**. — *adj* **starr'y** abounding or adorned with stars; consisting of, or proceeding from, the stars; like, or shining like, the stars. — **star anise** a Chinese evergreen tree (*Illicium*) of the magnolia family, with aromatic oil; the star-shaped dried seed pods of this tree, imparting an aniseed flavour when used in cookery; **star'-apple** the edible fruit of the West Indian sapotaceous tree *Chrysophyllum cainito*; **star billing** prominent display of the name of a performer, etc on posters, etc. — *adj* **star'-bright'** bright as a star or with stars. — **star catalogue** a list of stars, with their places, magnitudes, etc. — *adj* **star'-crossed** or (*archaic*) **star'-crost** thwarted by the stars; ill-fated. — **star'drift** a common proper motion of a number of fixed stars in the same region; **star'dust** cosmic dust, meteoric matter in fine particles; distant stars seen like dust grains; an imaginary dust that blinds the eyes to reality and fills them with romantic illusions. — *adj* glittering, romantic, magical. — **star'fish** any member of the Asteroidea, a class of echinoderms with five arms merging in a disc, and tube-feet on the under surface; sometimes extended to the ophiuroids; **star fruit** the fruit of the carambola tree, star-shaped in cross-section. — *vi* **star'-gaze**. — **star'gazer** an astrologer; an astronomer; someone who gazes at the sky, or in abstraction; a dreamer or wool-gatherer; a small supplementary sail set above the moonsail and skysail on a square-rigged ship; any fish of the family *Uranoscopidae* with upward-looking eyes set on top of its head, enabling it to see when it conceals itself in the sand on the sea bottom; **star'gazing**; **stargazey pie** a savoury Cornish fish pie in which whole fish are baked in pastry with their heads protruding through the crust; **star grass** a name for many grasslike plants with star-shaped flowers or leaf arrangement (see also **star**[2]). — *adj* **star'-led** guided by a star. — **star'light** light from the stars; an unknown plant, otherwise called astrophel or penthia (*Spenser*). — *adj* of or with starlight; lighted by the stars; bright as a star. — *adj* **star'lit** lighted by the stars. — **star map** a map showing the positions of stars; **star'monger** an astrologer; **star-nosed mole** a N American aquatic mole (*Condylura cristata*) with a starlike fringe of sensory tentacles around its nose. — *adj* **star'-pav'd** (*Milton*) paved with stars; **star'-proof** (*Milton*) impervious to starlight. — **star'-read** (*Spenser*) astronomy. — *adj* **starr'y-eyed** out of touch with reality; innocently idealistic; radiantly happy. — **star ruby** or **star sapphire** a ruby or sapphire manifesting asterism. — *adj* **star'-shaped** shaped like a conventional star, with pointed rays. — **star shell** a shell that explodes high in the air, lighting up the scene; **star'shine** starlight; **star sign** a sign of the zodiac. — *adj* **star'-spang'led** spangled or studded with stars (**Star-spangled Banner** the Stars and Stripes; the American national anthem). — **star'spot** an area of relative darkness on the surface of a star; **star'stone** a sapphire, ruby, or other stone showing asterism. — *adj* **star'-studded** covered with stars; (of the cast of a film, play, etc) having a high proportion of famous performers. — **star thistle** a species of *Centaurea* with radiating spiny bracts; **star trap** a stage trap of several wedge-shaped pieces meeting in a centre; **star turn** the chief item in an entertainment; a pre-eminent performer; **Star Wars** (also without *caps*) a colloquial term for the Strategic Defence Initiative (qv). — Also *adj*. — **star wheel** a spur wheel with V-shaped teeth; **star'wort** any plant of the genus *Aster* (not the China aster); stitchwort; a waterplant (**water starwort** *Callitriche*). — *adj* **star-ypointing** (*stär'-i-point'ing*; *Milton*; incorrectly formed; see **y-** *pfx*) pointing to the stars. — **see stars** (*colloq*) to see spots of light, as a result eg of blow on the head; to be in a dazed condition; **star of Bethlehem** a plant (*Ornithogalum*) of the lily family with yellow starlike flowers; **Star of David** the Jewish religious symbol — Solomon's-seal (see second meaning of this); **star-of-the-earth** buck's-horn plantain, *Plantago coronopus*, so called because its serrated leaves radiate outwards along the ground; **star-of-the-night** Clusia; **Stars and Stripes** the flag of the United States of America, with thirteen stripes alternately red and white, and a blue field containing as many stars as there are states. [OE *steorra*; cf **stern**[3], Ger *Stern*, L *stēlla* (for *sterula*), Gr *astēr*]

star[2] or **starr** *stär*, (*Scot*) *n* *Ammophila* or any other coarse seaside grass, sedge, or rush. — Also **star grass** or **starr grass** (see also under **star**[1]). [ON *stǫrr*]

staragen *star'ə-gən*, (*obs*) *n* the tarragon plant. [Cf Sp *estragón*, Fr *estragon* tarragon]

starboard *stär'bərd* or *-börd*, *n* the right-hand side of a ship. — *adj* and *adv* of, to, towards, or on, the right. — *vt* to turn to the right (see note at **port**[1]) — opposite of *port*. [OE *stēorbord*, from *stēor* steering, and *bord* board, side of a ship (ancient Gmc ships being steered by a paddle at the right side)]

starch *stärch*, *n* the principal reserve food material stored in plants, chemically a carbohydrate, $(C_6H_{10}O_5)_x$ used in laundry as a stiffener; stiffness, formality. — *adj* made of starch; stiff, rigid, formal. — *vt* to stiffen or stick with starch. — *adj* **starched**. — *adv* **starchedly** (*stärcht-* or *stärch'id-*). — *n* **starched'ness** (or *-id-*). — *n* **starch'er**. — *adv* **starch'ily**. — *n* **starch'iness**. — *adj* **starch'y** of or like starch; stiff, formal, strait-laced, prim; precise. — **starch blocker** a slimming aid which is thought to prevent the body from digesting starch. — **starch'-grain** a rounded or irregular mass of starch in the plastids of plants; **starch gum** dextrin; **starch**

hyacinth grape hyacinth, from its smell; **starch paper** a test paper for iodine, coated with starch and potassium iodide. — *adj* **starch'-reduced** (of bread, etc for the use of slimmers) containing less than the usual amount of starch. [OE *stercan* to stiffen, inferred from *sterced-ferhth* stiff-spirited; cf Ger *Stärke* strength, vigour, starch, and **stark**]

Star Chamber *stär chām'bər*, *n* a court (abolished 1641) with a civil and criminal jurisdiction, which met in the old council chamber at Westminster and was empowered to act without a jury and to use torture; (also without *caps*) generally, an over-zealous or secret inquiry or investigation; a closed meeting in which important decisions, resolutions, etc are made, *esp* on matters of public concern; a group of senior ministers of the British Cabinet, who meet occasionally to decide how government spending is to be allocated amongst various ministries. [Prob named from the gilt *stars* on the ceiling, not from the Jewish bonds (*starrs*) kept in it]

stare[1] *stār*, *vi* to look with a fixed gaze; to glare; to be insistently or obtrusively conspicuous, to be all too obvious. — *vt* to put into a particular state by staring. — *n* a fixed look. — *n* **star'er** someone who stares; (in *pl*; *old-fashioned colloq*) a lorgnette. — *n*, *adj* and *adv* **star'ing**. — *adv* **star'ingly**. — **stare down** or **out** to force (someone) to drop his or her gaze through the steadiness and power of one's own; **stare (someone) in the face** to be perfectly evident; to be imminent or apparently inevitable. [OE *starian*, from root seen in Ger *starr* rigid; also in Eng **stern**[1]]

stare[2] *stär*, *n* a starling. [OE *stær*]

staretz or **starets** *stär'ets*, *n* (in Russia) a holy man, a religious teacher or spiritual advisor. [Russ *starets*]

stark *stärk*, *adj* stern; harsh; plain, bare, unadorned; sheer; out-and-out; harshly apparent; all too clear; stark-naked (qv). — *adv* utterly. — *vt* and *vi* (*archaic*) to stiffen. — *vt* and *vi* (*obs* or *dialect*) **stark'en** to make or become stark. — *adj* **starkers** see **stark-na'ked**. — *adv* **stark'ly**. — *n* **stark'ness**. [OE *stearc* hard, strong; ON *sterkr*, Ger *stark*]

stark-naked *stärk'-nā'kid*, *adj* utterly naked; quite bare (shortened to **stark** or (*colloq*) **stark'ers**). — Earlier (now *dialect*) **start'-na'ked**. [ME *stert-naked*, from OE *steort* tail, and *nacod* naked; influenced by **stark**]

starlet. See under **star**.

starling[1] *stär'ling*, *n* a bird (*Sturnus vulgaris*), with black, brown-spotted, iridescent plumage, a good mimic; any other member of its genus, *Sturnus*, or family, *Sturnidae*. [OE *stærling*, dimin of *stær*, see **stare**[2]]

starling[2] *stär'ling*, *n* piling protecting a bridge pier. [Prob for *staddling* from **staddle**]

starn. Same as **stern**[3]; also (*naut* or *dialect*) for **stern**[2].

starnie. See **stern**[3].

starosta *stär'os-tə*, (*hist*) *n* a Russian village headman; a Polish noble holding a **star'osty** or domain bestowed by the crown. [Russ and Polish *starosta* elder]

starr[1]. See **star**[2].

starr[2] *stär*, *n* a Jewish deed or bond, eg of acquittance of debt. [Heb *sh'tār* a writing]

starrily, **starry**, etc. See under **star**[1].

START *stärt*, *abbrev*: Strategic Arms Reduction Talks (or Treaty).

start *stärt*, *vi* to begin, commence; to shoot, dart, move suddenly forth, or out; to spring up or forward; to strain forward; to break away; to make a sudden involuntary movement as of surprise or becoming aware; to spring open, out of place, or loose; to begin to move; (of a car, engine, etc) to begin to work, to fire, combust; to set forth on a journey, race, career; to take to grumbling, to begin an argument, quarrel, etc (*colloq*). — *vt* to begin; to set going; to set on foot; to set up; to cause to begin (doing something); to conceive (a baby) (*colloq*); to drive (an animal or bird) from a lair or hiding-place; to cause or undergo displacement or loosening of; to startle (*obs*); to break in (a young horse); to pour out or shoot. — *n* a beginning; a beginning of movement, *esp* of a journey, race or career; a setting in motion; the time or place at which something starts, eg a race; a help in or opportunity of beginning; an advantage in being early or ahead; the extent of such an advantage in time or distance; a sudden movement; a sudden involuntary motion of the body; a startled feeling; a queer occurrence (*colloq*); a spurt, spasm, burst; a beginning of building work on a new house site (*esp* as *house* or *housing starts*). — *n* **start'er** one of the competitors or horses assembled for the start of a race; a person who gives the signal for starting; a dog that drives out game; an apparatus or device for starting a machine, such as that (also called **self-starter**) for starting an internal-combustion engine; anything used to begin a process, such as a bacterial culture in making butter or cheese; (also in *pl*) the first course of a meal (see also **for starters** below); a potentially successful or profitable idea, project, etc (*commercial jargon*). — *adj* **start'ful** apt to start. — *n* and *adj* **start'ing**. — *adv* **start'ingly** (*Shakesp*) by starts. — *adj* **start'ish** apt to start, skittish. — **starter home** a small house or flat built, or considered by the seller, to suit and be affordable by a first-time buyer, *esp* a young couple; **starting block** (*usu* in *pl*) a device for helping a sprinter make a quick start to a race, consisting of a framework with blocks of wood or metal attached, on which the sprinter braces his feet; **starting gate** a movable barrier behind which the runners in a horse race are contained till the start; starting stalls (*US*); **starting hole** a hiding place; an evasive trick; **starting point** the point from which anything starts, or from which motion begins; **starting post** the post or barrier from which the competitors start in a race; **starting price** odds on a horse when the race begins (*colloq abbrev* **SP**); **starting stalls** a line of compartments in which runners wait before the start of a horse race, fitted with gates that are sprung open at the start; **start'-up** an upstart (*Shakesp*); a rustic half-boot or short legging (*obs*); the process of setting up a company or business; such a company or business. — Also *adj*. — **for a start** in the first place, as a preliminary consideration; **for starters** (*colloq*) as the first course of a meal; in the first place, for a start; **give (someone) a start** to give (someone) an advantage at the start of, or in beginning, an enterprise, race, etc; to startle (someone); to give (someone) a job, *esp* a manual job (*colloq*); **start a hare** see under **hare**; **start in** to begin; **start (in) on** (*colloq*) to turn on, scold, berate; **start out** to begin; to begin a journey; **start over** (*NAm*) to begin again from the beginning, start all over again; **start up** to rise suddenly; to come suddenly into notice or being; to set in motion; to set up, initiate, establish (*n* **start'-up** see above); **to start with** at the beginning; in the first place, as a primary consideration. [ME *sterten*; closely related to Du *storten* to plunge, Ger *stürzen*]

startle *stärt'l*, *vt* to surprise or frighten suddenly; to cause to start with alarm; to take aback; to cause to awake with a start. — *vi* to start with alarm; to awake with a start; (of a horse) to shy. — *n* sudden alarm or surprise. — *adj* **start'led**. — *n* **start'ler**. — *n* and *adj* **start'ling**. — *adv* **start'lingly**. — *adj* **start'lish** or **start'ly** apt to start. — **startle colours** (*zool*) bright colours on the bodies of animals or wings of birds which often resemble vertebrate eyes and act as an anti-predator device. [ME *stertle*, from OE *steartlian* to stumble, struggle, kick, or formed afresh from **start**]

start-naked. See **stark-naked**.

starve *stärv*, *vi* to die, now only of hunger or (chiefly *Scot* and *N Eng dialect*) cold; to suffer extreme hunger (or cold); to be in want (with *for*); to deteriorate (*obs*). — *vt* to cause to die of hunger; to afflict with hunger (or cold); to deprive of food; to force, subdue or cure by depriving of food; to deprive (with *of*). — *n* **starvā'tion** (attributed to Lord Melville, 1775). — *adj* **starved**. — *n* **starve'ling** a lean, hungry, weak, or pining person, animal, or plant. — Also *adj*. — *n* and *adj* **starv'ing**. [OE *steorfan* to die; Du *sterven*, Ger *sterben* to die]

stash *stash*, (*colloq*) *vt* to stow in hiding (often with *away*); to stop, desist, quit (*old slang*). — *n* a secret store, or its hiding-place; a hidden store of a drug, or the drug itself (*slang*; *esp US*). [Origin obscure]

stashie. See **stooshie**.

stasidion, **stasimon**, etc. See under **stasis**.

stasis *stā'sis* or *stas'is*, (also **-stasis** *-stə-sis*, *combining form*; chiefly *med*) *n* cessation, arrest, *esp* of growth, of blood-circulation or bleeding, or of the contents of the bowels; (maintenance of) a state of equilibrium, or a constant state; in punctuated equilibrium, the period of equilibrium or no change in evolution (interrupted by a period of rapid change) (*palaeontol*, *biol*). — *n* **stasid'ion** (*Mod Gr dimin*) a stall in a Greek church. — *n* **stas'imon** (Gr, stationary) in Greek tragedy, an ode sung after the chorus had taken their places, or without interruption by dialogue: — *pl* **stas'ima**. — *n* **stas'i-morphy** structural modification by arrested development. [Gr *stasis* stoppage, stationariness]

stat. *abbrev*: *statim* (*L*), immediately.

-stat *-stat*, *combining form* designating a regulating device that causes something to remain constant or stationary, as in *barostat*, *hygrostat*, *thermostat*. [Gr *-statēs* causing to stand, from *histanai* to cause to stand]

statant *stā'tənt*, (*heraldry*) *adj* standing on four feet. [L *stāre* to stand]

state *stāt*, *n* a condition; a perturbed condition of mind (*colloq*); a mode of existence; a set of circumstances that exist at any time; a phase or stage; an impression taken at a stage of progress in engraving or etching or in printing a book; status; station in life; high station; grave import (*Shakesp*); pomp, display, ceremonial dignity; a seat of dignity (*Shakesp*); a canopy (*Milton*); an estate, order, or class in society or the body politic; hence (in *pl*) the legislature (*hist*); an exalted personage (*Milton*); public welfare; the constitution; a republic (*obs*); the civil power; a political community under one government; one of a number of political communities forming a federation under a central government; the territory of such a community; high politics; an interest in property (*Spenser*); property, estate (*Shakesp*); a body of men united by profession; a statement, report (now chiefly *military*). — *adj* of, belonging to, or relating to, the state or a federal state; run or financed by the state; public; ceremonial; pompous; affectedly solemn and mysterious; magnificent. — *adv* or *adj* (*Spenser*) explained in old gloss as stoutly (*perh* pompous). — *vt* to set forth; to express the details of; to set down fully and formally; to assert, affirm; to install, establish, endow, place in a condition (*esp* favourable; *archaic*); to set in state; to specify; *perh* to determine the value of (*Milton*); to settle. — *adj* **stāt'able** capable of being stated. — *adj* **stāt'al** of a federal state. — *adj* **stāt'ed** settled; established; declared; regular; circumstanced (*obs*). — *adv* **stāt'edly**. — *n* **state'hood** the status of a state. — *adj* **state'less** without nationality; unworthy to be accounted a state; without pomp. — *n* **state'lessness**. — *adv* **state'lily**. — *n* **state'liness**. — *adj* **state'ly** showing state or dignity; majestic, greatly impressive. — *adv* majestically; loftily. — *n* **state'ment** the act of stating; that which is stated; a formal account, declaration of facts, etc; an instruction in a source language or any directive input to a program that converts a source language into machine code (*comput*); a financial record, eg one issued regularly by a bank to a customer, stating his or her personal balance and detailing debits and credits; (in the UK) a written undertaking, legally binding, by an education authority to provide certain stated resources in the education of a particular child with learning difficulties. — *adj* **state'mented**. — *n* **state'-menting**. — *n* **stāt'er**. — *adj* **state'wide**. — *n* **stāt'ism** (the belief in) state control of economic and social affairs. — *n* and *adj* **stāt'ist** (see also separate entry). — *adj* **state-aid'ed** receiving contributions from the state. — **state bank** (in the USA) a bank that is awarded its charter by a state government; **state cabin** a stateroom on a ship; **state'craft** the art of managing state affairs; **State Department** the US government department dealing with foreign affairs; **state house** (*usu* with *caps*) the building in which a state legislature sits; (sometimes with *cap*) a building where state ceremonies are held; a house built by the government for renting (*NZ*); **stately home** a large, fine old house, *esp* one open to the public; **state paper** an official paper or document relating to affairs of state; **state prison**; **state prisoner** a prisoner confined for offence against the state; **state religion** a religion recognized by the state as the national religion; **state'room** a private cabin or railway compartment; **state school** one controlled by a public authority, and financed by taxation; **States General** the representative body of the three orders (nobility, clergy, burghers) of the French kingdom (*hist*); the Dutch parliament. — *adj* and *adv* **State'side** (*colloq*; also without *cap*) of, in, towards or to the USA. — **states'man**, *fem* **states'-woman** a person skilled in government; a person who takes an important part in governing the state, *esp* with wisdom and broad-mindedness; a person who farms his or her own estate, a small landholder (*N Eng*). — *adj* **states'manlike** or **states'manly** befitting a statesman. — **states'manship**; **states'person**; **state trial** a trial for an offence against the state; **state trooper** (in the US) a member of a state police force. — *adj* **state'wide** (*US*) applied throughout the state. — **Council** (or **House**) **of States** see under **council**; **lie in state** (of a corpse) to be laid out in a place of honour before being buried; **State Enrolled Nurse** (*abbrev* **SEN**) a nurse who has passed a particular examination of the General Nursing Council of England and Wales or the General Nursing Council of Scotland (see also **State Registered Nurse** below); **state of affairs** or **events** a situation, set of circumstances; **state of play** the situation as it currently stands; **state of repair** physical condition, soundness; **state of the art** the level or position at a given time, *esp* the present, of generally accepted and available knowledge, technical achievement, etc in a particular field, etc; the level of technological development as yet unsurpassed in a particular field (*adj* **state-of-the-art'**); **state of the Union message** (in the US) an annual report by the President, required by statute, on the state of the nation and on legislative plans; **State Registered Nurse** (*abbrev* **SRN**) in England and Wales, a nurse who has passed a more advanced examination of the General Nursing Council of England and Wales than a State Enrolled Nurse (for Scotland, see **Registered General Nurse** under **register**); **States of the Church** (*hist*) an area of central Italy ruled by the popes as a temporal domain (also **Papal States**); **the States** the United States; **turn State's evidence** see under **evident**. [L *status*, *-ūs*, from *stāre*, *statum* to stand; partly through OFr (see **estate**)]

stater *stā'tər*, *n* an ancient Greek standard coin of various kinds, the gold daric, silver tetradrachm, etc. [Gr *statēr*, orig a pound weight, from *histanai* to set, establish, weigh]

static *stat'ik* or **statical** *stat'i-kəl*, *adj* pertaining to statics; pertaining to bodies, forces, charges, etc, in equilibrium; stationary; stable; resting; acting by mere weight; pertaining to sense of bodily equilibrium. — *n* **stat'ic** statics (*obs*); atmospheric disturbances in radio reception; white specks or flashes on a television picture; crackling on a vinyl record; static electricity. — *adv* **stat'ically**. — *n sing* **stat'ics** the science of forces in equilibrium. — **static electricity** electrical charges that are stationary, not moving along in a current; **static line** a cord joining a parachute pack to the aircraft so that when the wearer of the pack jumps, the parachute is automatically opened; **static memory** (*comput*) random access memory in which information is retained as long as power is maintained. [Gr *statikos* bringing to a standstill, from *histanai* to cause to stand, to place in the balance, weigh]

statice *stat'i-sē*, *n* any plumbaginaceous plant of the sea lavender genus (*Limonium*), many of which are cultivated for their everlasting flowers. [L, thrift, from Gr *statikē*, fem of *statikos* (see **static**), in medical usage meaning astringent]

statim *sta'tim*, (*L*) *adv* immediately, at once.

station *stā'shən*, *n* a standing still (now *rare*); a mode of standing; position; a chosen fixed point; a standing-place; a fixed stopping-place, *esp* one on a railway with associated buildings and structures; a place set apart and equipped for some particular purpose; a place where a person stands; a local office, headquarters, or depot; a branch post office (*US*); a habitat; an actual spot where a species has been found; an assigned place or post; an assigned region for naval duty; a place in India where officials and officers reside; a stock farm (*Austr* and *NZ*); position in life (*esp* a high position) or in the scale of nature; a holy place visited as one of a series, *esp* one of (*usu* fourteen) representations of stages in Christ's way to Calvary, disposed around a church interior or elsewhere (*RC*). — *adj* of a station. — *vt* to assign a station to; to set; to appoint to a post, place, or office. — *adj* **sta'tional**. — *n* **sta'tionariness**. — *adj* **sta'tionary** still; unmoving; fixed; static, not changing; settled; permanently located; continuously resident. — Also *n*. — *n* **sta'tioner** (L *statiōnārius* a shopkeeper, in the Middle Ages a university bookseller, distinguished from an itinerant) a bookseller or publisher (*obs*); a dealer in writing-materials and the like. — *adj* **sta'tionery** belonging to a stationer. — *n* the goods sold by a stationer. — **Stationers' Hall** the hall in London of the Company of Stationers, who until the passing of the Copyright Act in 1842 enjoyed an absolute control over printing and publishing; **Stationery Office** an office for providing books, stationery, etc, to government offices and for arranging the printing of public papers; **station hand** (*Austr*) a man employed on a station; **station house** a lock-up at a police station; a police station (*US*); a small railway station; **sta'tion-master** or **sta'tion-manager** the person in charge of a railway station; **station wagon** (*NAm*, *Austr* and *NZ*) an estate car. [L *statiō*, *-ōnis*, from *stāre* to stand]

statism. See under **state**.

statist *stā'tist*, *n* a statesman; a politician; an advocate of statism (qv under **state**); a statistician.

statistic *stə-tist'ik*, *n* (in *pl*) tabulated numerical facts, *orig* those relating to a state, or (with *sing* verb) the classification, tabulation, and study of such facts; one such fact; a statistician. — *adj* **statist'ical** of, concerned with, or of the nature of, statistics. — *adv* **statist'ically**. — *n* **statistician** (*stat-is-tish'ən*) a person skilled in statistics; a compiler or student of statistics. — **statistical mechanics** (*phys*) theoretical predictions of the behaviour of a macroscopic system by applying statistical laws to the behaviour of component particles. [Ital *statista* and Ger *Statistik*, from L *status* state]

stative *stā'tiv*, *adj* permanent, fixed (now only of a Roman camp); indicating a physical state or reflex action (of certain Hebrew verbs); indicating a state, as opposed to an action, etc (*linguistics*). [L *statīvus*, from *stāre* to stand]

stato- *stat'ō-*, *combining form* signifying standing. — *n* **statocyst** (*stat'ō-sist*; Gr *kystis* bladder) an organ of equilibrial sense in crustaceans and other invertebrates, containing statoliths; a cell with starch grains by which a plant is supposed to be sensitive to gravity. — *n* **stat'olith** (Gr *lithos* stone) a starch grain or other free solid body in a statocyst. — *n* **stat'oscope** a sensitive barometer for detecting minute differences. [Gr *statos* set, placed]

stator *stā'tər*, (*mech*, *elec eng*) *n* a stationary part within which a part rotates. [L *stator* stander]

statue *stat'ū*, *n* a representation (*usu* near or above life-size) of a human or animal form in the round. — Also (*obs*) **stat'ua**. — *adj* **stat'uary** of, relating to, or suitable for sculpture; sculptured; statuesque. — *n* sculpture; statues. — *adj* **stat'ued** furnished with statues; sculptured. — *adj* **statuesque** (*-esk'*) like a statue; (of a person, *esp* a woman) tall and well-proportioned in figure, or dignified and imposing in appearance. — *adv* **statuesque'ly**. — *n* **statuesque'ness**. — *n* **statuette'** a small statue, figurine. [L *statua*, from *statuere* to cause to stand, from *stāre*]

stature *stach'ər* or *stat'yər*, *n* body height; eminence. — *adj* **stat'ured** having a stature. [L *statūra*]

status *stā'təs*, *n* a state of affairs; condition; standing; position, rank, importance, in society or in any group; high rank or standing; a person's legal position or classification with regard to marriage, citizenship, etc: — *pl* (*rare*) **status** (*-tūs*) or **statuses**. — **status symbol** a possession or a privilege considered to mark a person out as having a high position in his social group. [L *status*]

status quo *stā'təs* or *stat'ōōs kwō*, (*L*) *n* the existing condition, unchanged situation; (also **status quo ante**; *an'ti*) the condition or situation existing before a particular change. [Literally, the state in which]

statute *stat'ūt*, *n* a law expressly enacted by the legislature (as distinguished from a customary or common law); a written law; the act of a corporation or its founder, intended as a permanent rule or law; a bond or other proceeding based on a statute; a hiring-fair (*obs*). — *adj* **stat'utable** prescribed, permitted, recognized by, or according to statute. — *adv* **stat'utably**. — *adv* **stat'utorily**. — *adj* **stat'utory** of or relating to statute; prescribed, enacted or recognized by statute; depending on statute for its authority; so common or frequent as to seem the rule (as though prescribed by statute; *colloq*). — *adj* **sta'tute-barred** disallowed by the statute of limitations. — **statute book** a record of statutes or enacted laws; **statute cap** (*Shakesp*) a kind of cap enjoined by statute (1571) to be worn on Sundays by all below a certain rank; **statute labour** (*old*) compulsory labour on roads, etc; **statute law** law in the form of statutes (also **statutory law**); **statute mile** see under **mile**; **statutory rape** (*US*) the criminal offence of having sexual intercourse with a girl who is below the age of consent. — **statute of limitations** a statute prescribing the period of time within which proceedings must be taken to enforce a right or bring a legal action; **Statute of Westminster** an act (1931) of the United Kingdom parliament conferring independent sovereign status on the self-governing dominions. [L *statūtum* that which is set up, from *statuere*]

staunch[1] *stönch* or *stönsh* or **stanch** *stänch* or *stänsh*, *adj* firm in principle, pursuit, or support; trusty, hearty, constant, loyal, zealous; stout and firm; watertight; seaworthy. — *adv* **staunch'ly**. — *n* **staunch'ness**. [OFr *estanche*; see **stanch**[1]]

staunch[2] (*vt*). See **stanch**[1].

staurolite *stör'ə-līt*, *n* (*mineralogy*) a silicate of aluminium with ferrous oxide, magnesia, and water, sometimes occurring as twinned cruciform crystals. — *adj* **staurolitic** (*-lit'ik*). [Gr *stauros* cross, and *lithos* stone]

stauroscope *stör'ə-skōp*, *n* an optical instrument for studying the structure of mineral crystals under polarized light. — *adj* **stauro'scopic**. [Gr *stauros* cross, and *skopeein* to look at]

stave *stāv*, *n* one of the strips of wood of which a barrel or tub is made; a staff, rod, bar, shaft, *esp* wooden, as the rung of a ladder; a staff (*music*); a stanza, verse of a song. — *vt* to break a stave or the staves of (a boat or barrel; with *in*); to break; to burst inward (with *in*); to drive off, as with a staff; to delay, ward off or keep back (with *off*); to put together, repair or fit with staves; to sprain, jar violently (fingers, toes, etc) (*Scot*). — *vi* to thrust onward (*Scot*); to break up: — *pa t* and *pa p* **staved** or **stove**. [By-form of **staff**]

stave-church *stāv'-chûrch*, *n* an ancient Norwegian wooden church supported on masts, with gabled roofs rising one above another. [Norw *stav-kirke*, from *stav* staff, stave, and *kirke* church]

staves *stāvz*, *pl* of **staff** and of **stave**.

stavesacre *stāvz'ā-kər*, *n* a tall larkspur whose seeds were formerly used against lice. [OFr *stavesaigre*, from LL *staphisagria*, from Gr *staphis* raisins, and *agrios* wild]

staw *stö*, a Scots form of **stall**[1] (*n* and *vt*) and **stole** (*pa t* of **steal**[1]).

stay[1] *stā*, *vi* to remain, continue to be, in a place, position or condition; to reside temporarily, as in *stay at a hotel*; to live, dwell (*Scot* and *SAfr*); to wait in order to participate in or be present at; to pause, wait, tarry; to be kept waiting; to wait, attend as a servant (*Shakesp*); to stop, cease, desist (*archaic*); to stand firm (*archaic*); to hold out, last, endure; (in a race, etc) to maintain one's pace over a long distance; to keep pace or keep up (with *with*); (in poker) to match a bet in order to stay in the game. — *vt* to reside, remain for a specific period, as in *stay for a week*; to hold, restrain, check the action of; to delay or hinder; to stop, suspend, discontinue or postpone (judgement, proceedings, etc); to hold in abeyance; to endure or remain to the end; to satisfy, appease or allay; to quell, suppress (*archaic*); to stop for, be stopped by (*archaic*); to detain (*archaic*); to await (*archaic*): — *pa t* and *pa p* **stayed**. — *n* (a period of) staying, temporary residence; a visit; a sojourn; a suspension or postponement of legal proceedings; a check or restraint; the act of stopping or being stopped; staying power, endurance; an obstacle (*obs*); a permanent state (*obs*). — *n* **stay'er** a person or animal (*esp* a horse or greyhound) of good lasting or staying qualities for a race. — *adj* **stay-at-home** keeping much at home; tending or preferring to stay at home, in one's own area or country; untravelled, unadventurous. — *n* a stay-at-home person. — **stay'away** (*SAfr*) a strike; a person participating in a strike; **staying power** the ability to continue or sustain effort, *esp* over a long period, without flagging; **stay-on tab** a ring-pull that does not pull entirely off, but bends into the can; **stay stitching** (*dressmaking*) a line of stitching in the seam allowance to prevent stretching and fraying of the fabric. — **be here** (or **have come**) **to stay** to have become permanent or established; **stay on** to remain, tarry after the normal or expected time for departing; **stay over** (*colloq*) to remain overnight, stay the night; **stay out** to remain away from home; to remain throughout or beyond the end of; **stay put** not to move from the place or position in which one has been put; **stay someone's hand** (*literary*) to stop someone on the point of doing something; **stay the course** to endure to the end of the race or other trial of one's stamina and staying power. [From Anglo-Fr *estaier* to stay, from OFr *ester*, from L *stāre* to stand]

stay[2] *stā*, *n* a prop or support; one of a number of strips of bone or metal sewn into a corset to stiffen it; (in *pl*) a corset thus stiffened. — *vt* to prop or support (with *up*); to sustain, comfort, strengthen (with *up*; *archaic* or *literary*); to cause to rely or depend (with *upon*; *archaic*). — *adj* **stay'less** without stays; unsupported. — **stay bolt** a bolt or rod binding together opposite plates; **stay lace** a lace for fastening a corset; **stay'-maker** a maker of corsets. [OFr *estaye*]

stay[3] *stā*, (*naut*) *n* a rope bracing a mast, etc, a guy; a brace generally. — *vt* to brace or support (a mast, etc) using stays. — *vi* to bring the head of a sailing vessel up to the wind in order to tack or go about; (of a mast) to incline (forward). — *n* **staysail** (*stā'sl*) a triangular, auxiliary fore-and-aft sail spread or set on a stay. — **at short (or long) stay** (of an anchor cable) taut and leading to the anchor at a steep (or acute) angle near (or at some distance away from) the bow; **in stays** (of a sailing vessel during tacking) hanging with head to windward without moving to the opposite tack, or **miss** (or **refuse**) **stays** with head falling back on the original tack. [OE *staeg*; cf ON *stag*, MLGer *stach*, Norw *stagle* wooden post]

stayne, stayre. Old spellings (*Spenser*, etc) of **stain**, **stair**.

stays. see **stay**[2].

STD *abbrev*: sexually transmitted disease; subscriber trunk dialling.

std *abbrev*: standard.

Ste *abbrev*: *Sainte* (*Fr*), *fem* of *saint*.

stead *sted*, *n* the place, function, role or position of another, as in *act in someone's stead*; service, avail, advantage, as in **stand someone in good stead** to be advantageous to someone; a space of time (*Spenser*); circumstances, case, condition (*Spenser*). — *vt* to avail, help, serve (*archaic*); to fulfil in substitution (*Shakesp* **steed up**): — *pa t* and *pa p* **stead'ed** or **stead** (*sted*). [OE *stede* place]

steadfast *sted'fäst*, *adj* firm; constant; resolute; steady. — *adv* **stead'fastly**. — *n* **stead'fastness**. [OE *stede faest*]

steadicam® *sted'i-kam*, (*cinematog*) *n* a device for steadying a hand-held camera, consisting of a shoulder and waist harness with a shock-absorbing arm attached, to which the camera is fitted.

steading *sted'ing*, *n* the range of building surrounding a farmhouse, a farmstead. [OE *stede* place]

steady *sted'i*, *adj* standing firmly; fixed; stable; constant; resolute; consistent; regular; uniform; sober, industrious; (with *to*) (of a hound) seldom diverted from the trail of (a deer, hare, etc); (with *from*) (of a horse or hound) seldom distracted, upset or diverted by (another animal, a noise, etc): — *compar* **stead'ier**; *superl* **stead'iest**. — *vt* to make steady; to support; to make or keep firm: — *pr p* **stead'ying**; *pa t* and *pa p* **stead'ied**. — *n* a rest or support, as for the hand, a tool, or a piece of work; a regular boyfriend or girlfriend (*colloq*) — *interj* be careful!; keep calm!; hold the present course (*naut*); see **ready, steady, go!** under **ready**. — *adj* **stead'y-going** having or showing steady habits or action. — **steady state** a state or condition of dynamic equilibrium with entropy at its maximum (*phys*); any oscillation system that continues unchanged indefinitely (*telecomm*); **steady-state theory** (*astron*) in cosmology, a theory that asserts the universe is in a steady state, being infinitely old and containing the same density of matter at all points and all times, with new matter being created to compensate for the space left by the observed expansion of the universe (cf **big-bang theory**; see also **continuous creation**). — **go steady** (*colloq*) (*esp* of a boy and girl not yet engaged to be married) to have a steady relationship, to go about regularly together; **steady on**! keep calm!; don't be so foolish, hasty, etc. [OE *stede*]

steak *stāk*, *n* any of several cuts of beef graded for frying, braising, stewing, etc; a slice of meat (*esp* hindquarters of beef) or fish. — **steak'house** a restaurant specializing in fried or grilled beefsteaks; **steak knife** a knife with a serrated blade for eating steak; **steak tartare** minced beef steak served raw mixed with onions, raw egg and seasonings (also **tartar steak**). [ON *steik*; *steikja* to roast on a spit]

steal[1] *stēl*, *vt* to take by theft, *esp* secretly; to take, gain or win, by beguiling talk, by contrivance, unexpectedly, insidiously, gradually, or furtively; to snatch; to hole (a long putt) by a delicate stroke — the opposite of *gobble* (*golf*); to gain (a base) without the help of a hit or error (*baseball*); to put surreptitiously, smuggle. — *vi* to practise theft; to take feloniously; to pass quietly, unobtrusively, gradually, or surreptitiously: — *pa t* **stole** (*obs* **stale**; *Scot* **staw**, **stealed** or **stealt**); *pa p* **stō'len** (*obs* **stōle**; *Milton* **stōln**; *Scot* **stown**, **stealed** or **stealt**). — *n* (*colloq*) an act of stealing, a theft; something acquired by theft; a bargain, a snip; the stealing of a base (*baseball*). — *n* **steal'er**. — *n* and *adj* **steal'ing**. — *adv* **steal'ingly**. — **steal a march on** see under **march**[2]; **steal a marriage** to marry secretly; **steal someone's thunder** to make use of another's invention against him or her (as when John Dennis's stage thunder was used in a rival's play); to rob someone of the opportunity of achieving a sensational effect by forestalling him or her; **steal the show** see under **show**. [OE *stelan*; related to Ger *stehlen*, Du *stelen*, Swed *stjäla*, Dan *stjæle*]l

steal[2], **steale**, **steel**, **stele** or **steil** *stēl*, (*dialect* and *Spenser*) *n* a handle, shank, shaft. [OE *stela* stalk, cf Ger *Stiel*; connected with **stale**[4]]

stealed, **stealt**. See **steal**[1].

stealth *stelth*, *n* a theft (*Spenser*, *Shakesp*); a thing stolen (*Milton*); secret or unobtrusive going or passage (*Shakesp*); secret procedure or manner; furtiveness. — *adj* (*military jargon*) of, using, or associated with technological means of avoiding detection, such as (in aircraft) reducing noise, infra-red emissions, radar reflections and (in personnel) wearing clothing that reduces the risk of observation by infra-red night-sights. — *vt* and *vi* to approach (an enemy, etc) without being detected, as certain martial arts experts are trained to do. — *adv* **stealth'ily**. — *n* **stealth'iness**. — *n* **stealthing** the act or process of approaching, eg an enemy, without being detected. — *adj* **stealth'y** acted or acting with stealth; furtive. [From **steal**[1]]

steam *stēm*, *n* water in the form of a gas or vapour, or of a mist or film of liquid drops; a steamed dish; steam power; a spell of travel by steam power; energy, force, spirit (*colloq*). — *adj* of, for, using or worked by steam; outdated, old-fashioned, not using the latest technology (*facetious*). — *vi* to rise or pass off in steam or vapour; to emit or generate steam, vapour, or smell; to move by means of steam power; to move fast (*colloq*). — *vt* to expose to steam, apply steam to; to cook by means of steam; to exhale (smoke from a pipe) (*old slang*). — *adj* **steamed**. — *n* **steam'er** a steamship; a cooking apparatus for steaming food; one of a gang of muggers that attack by the method of steaming (*slang*); stewed kangaroo flavoured with pork (*Austr slang*). — *n* **steam'ie** (*Scot*) a public laundry. — *adv* **steam'ily**. — *n* **steam'iness**. — *n* **steam'ing** the action or process of emitting, moving by, applying, or cooking by, steam; a form of mugging used by gangs, eg on the London Underground, who rush en masse through crowds, snatching whatever they can (*slang*). — *adj* (*colloq*) in an advanced state of drunkenness. — *adj* **steam'y** of, like, full of, covered with, as if covered with, or emitting, steam or vapour; erotic, sexy, lubricious (*colloq*). — **steam bath** a steam-filled compartment, eg one at a Turkish bath, etc in which to refresh oneself by sweating, etc, or one in a laboratory for sterilizing equipment; **steam'boat**, **steam'ship** or **steam vessel** a vessel driven by steam; **steam boiler** a boiler for generating steam; **steam car** a car propelled by steam; **steam chest** (*eng*) a chamber above a steam boiler serving as a reservoir for steam and in which the slide valve works; **steam coal** coal suitable for raising steam. — *adj* **steam'-driv'en**. — **steam engine** any engine worked by steam; **steamer duck** a large duck of S America whose swimming action is suggestive of the motion of a steamer with a paddle wheel on each side; **steam gauge** a pressure gauge for steam; **steam governor** the governor (qv) of a steam engine; **steam hammer** a vertical hammer worked by steam. — *vt* and *vi* **steam'-haul** to draw (a conveyance for goods, passengers, etc) along rails by means of chains, etc attached to a stationary steam engine. — **steaming lights** (*naut*) compulsory white navigation lights carried on the masts of all vessels at sea, indicating their presence (and course) at night; **steam iron** an electric iron having a compartment in which water is heated to provide steam to dampen fabrics for easier ironing; **steam jacket** a hollow casing formed around a steam engine cylinder and supplied with steam to prevent condensation of the steam in the main cylinder; **steam launch** a large steam driven boat; **steam locomotive** a self-propelled steam engine and boiler mounted on a wheeled frame, such as a railway engine; **steam navvy** or **shovel** an excavator driven by steam; **steam packet** a steam vessel plying between certain ports; **steam port** an opening from the valve-face to the cylinder of a steam engine for the passage of steam; **steam power** the force or agency of steam when applied to machinery; **steam radio** (*facetious*) sound radio, considered old-fashioned in comparison with television; **steam'-roller** a steam engine with heavy rollers for wheels, used in road-mending, etc; any weighty crushing force (*fig*). — *vt* (*colloq*) to crush (objections, etc); to force (eg legislation through parliament, etc). — **steam room** a room filled with steam, for use as a steam bath; **steam shovel** see **steam navvy** above. — *adj* **steam'tight** impervious to steam. — **steam trap** a contrivance for allowing the passage of water but not of steam; **steam turbine** an engine in which expanding steam acts on blades attached to a drum; **steam whistle** a whistle sounded by the passage of steam. — **full steam ahead** forward at the greatest speed possible; with maximum effort; **get up steam** to build up steam pressure; to collect one's forces; to become excited; **let off steam** to release steam into the atmosphere; to work off energy; to give vent to anger or annoyance; **run out of steam** (*colloq*) to be forced to stop through loss of impetus, strength or energy; **steam open** to soften the gum of, and peel open (sealed envelopes) under exposure to steam; **steam up** (of windows, etc) to become or cause to become dimmed with condensed vapour; (as *pa p* **steamed up**) indignant (*slang*); **under one's own steam** by one's own unaided efforts. [OE *stēam*; Du *stoom*]

stean[1], **steane** or **steen** *stēn*, (*dialect* or *archaic*) *n* a stone or earthenware container with two handles. [OE *stǣne*]

stean[2]. See **steen**[1].

steane. See **stean**[1].

steapsin *stē'ap-sin*. Same as **lipase**.

stear, **steard**, **stearage**, **stearsman**. Obsolete spellings of **steer**[2], **steered**, etc.

stearsmate. Another spelling of **steersmate**.

stear- *stē'ər-* or *-ar'*, also **steato-** or **steat-** *-ət'ō* or *-at'-*, *combining form* denoting suet, fat, fatty tissue. — *n* **stearate** (*stē'ər-āt*) a salt of stearic acid. — *adj* **stearic** (*stē-ar'ik*) of stearin (**stearic acid** a solid fatty acid $C_{17}H_{35}COOH$) derived from animal and vegetable fats. — *n* **ste'arin** (*stē'ə-rin*) glyceryl ester of stearic acid; a mixture of stearic and palmitic acids (also **ste'arine**); the solid part of a fat. — *adj* **ste'arine** (*-rīn*) (of candles, etc) made of stearin. — *n* **steatite** (*stē'ə-tīt*) soapstone. — *adj* **steatitic** (*-tit'ik*). — *n* **steat'ocele** (Gr *kēlē* tumour) a fatty tumour in the scrotum. — *n* **steatō'ma** a tumour of a sebaceous gland or sebaceous cyst. — *adj* **steatom'atous**. — *n* **steatopygia** (*stē-ə-tō-pī'ji-ə* or *-pij'i-ə*; Gr *pygē* buttock) the accumulation of fat in the buttocks. — *adj* **steatopygous** (*-tō-pī'gəs* or *-top'i-gəs*) fat-buttocked. — *n* **steatorrhoea** or **steatorrhea** (*stē-ə-tə-rē'ə*; Gr *rhoia* a flow) accumulation of abnormal levels of fat in the faeces. — *n* **steatō'sis** fatty degeneration; the accumulation of fat in hepatocytes, occurring eg in pregnancy, alcoholism and as a side effect of some drugs [Gr *steār*, *steātos* suet, tallow]

steare *stēr*, (*archaic*). Same as **steer**[1].

steato-, **steat-**. See **stear-**.

sted, **stedd**, **stedde**, **stede** (*Spenser*) or **steed** (*Shakesp*). Obsolete forms of **stead** (*n* and *vt*).

stedfast an obsolescent spelling (*Shakesp*, *Milton*, etc) of **steadfast**.

steddy, **steedy**. Old spellings of **steady**.

steed[1] *stēd*, *n* a horse, *esp* a spirited horse. [OE *stēda* stud horse, stallion; cf OE *stōd* stud; Ger *Stute* stud mare, *Gestüt* stud]

steed[2]. See **sted**.

steek *stēk*, (*Scot*) *n* a stitch. — *vt* and *vi* to stitch. — *vt* to pierce; to fasten; to shut: — *pa t* and *pa p* **steek'it**. [Partly at least OE *stice* stitch, puncture; perh partly confused with **stick**[1]]

steel[1] *stēl*, *n* iron containing a little carbon, with or without additional ingredients; a weapon of steel, a sword (*literary*); a rough-surfaced steel implement for sharpening knives; a piece of steel, eg for stiffening a corset; a steel engraving; extreme hardness, staying power, trustworthiness (*fig*); formerly, any chalybeate medicine; (in *pl*) bonds and shares of steel companies (*stock exchange*). — *adj* of or like steel. — *vt* to cover, point or edge with steel; to harden; to nerve; to make obdurate. — *adj* **steeled** made of, covered, protected, provided or edged with, steel; hardened; nerved. — *n* **steel'iness**. — *n* **steel'ing**. — *adj* **steel'y** of or like steel.

— **steel band** a West Indian band, using steel drums, etc. — *n* and *adj* **steel'-blue** grey-blue like a reflection from steel. — *adj* **steel'-clad** clad in armour. — **steel collar** (or **steel-collar worker**) a term applied to a robot, used in manfacturing industry, *esp* in the automation of assembly-lines, to carry out tasks formerly done by a worker or workers; **steel drum** a percussion instrument *usu* made from the top of an oil drum, hammered out into a bowl-like shape and faceted so as to produce different notes (also called **steel pan**); **steel'-engraving** the act or process of engraving on steel plates; an impression or print resulting from this; **steel erector** a spiderman. — *n* and *adj* **steel'-grey'** or **steel-gray'** bluish-grey like steel. — *adj* **steel-head'ed**. — **steel'man** (more often in *pl* **steel'men**) a worker in the steel industry; **steel pan** see **steel drum**; **steel plate** a plate of steel; one on which a design is engraved; a print from it. — *adj* **steel-plat'ed** plated with steel. — **steel trap** one with steel jaws and spring; **steel wool** steel shavings used for cleaning and polishing; **steel'work** work executed in steel; a framework for (part of) a building, made of steel; (in *pl*) a factory where steel is made; **steel'worker**; **steel'working**. [OE *stȳle*; Ger *Stahl*]

steel[2]. See **steal**[2].

steelbow *stēl'bō*, (*Scots law*) *n* stock and goods received from a landlord with obligation to return a like amount and value when the lease expires; a contract or tenure on these terms. — Also *adj*. [**steel**[1], in the sense of rigidly fixed, and obs *bow*, from ON *bū* stock of cattle]

steeld. See **stell**.

steeled. See **steel**[1], and **stellar**.

steelyard *stēl'yärd*, *n* a weighing machine consisting of a lever with a short arm for the thing weighed and a long graduated arm on which a single weight moves. [Prob **steel**[1] and **yard**[1], but suggested or fixed in use by the *Steelyard* or *Stâlhof* (LGer; properly sample yard, mistranslated steel yard), the Hanse headquarters in London]

steem *stēm*, (*archaic*) *vt*. Same as **esteem**; also same as **steam**.

steen[1], **stean** or **stein** *stēn*, *vt* to line (a well or other excavation) with stone. — *n* such a lining. — *n* **steen'ing**, **stean'ing** or **stein'ing** such a lining or the process of making it. [OE *stǣnan*]

steen[2]. See **stean**[1].

steenbok *stān'* or *stēn'bok*, *n* a small S African antelope, *Raphicerus campestris*. — Also **steinbock**. [Du from *steen* stone, and *bok* buck]

steenbras *stēn'bras*, (*SAfr*) *n* any of several edible estuarine S African fish. [Afrik, from Du *steen* stone, and *brasem* bream]

steenkirk *stēn'kûrk*, (*hist*) *n* a neckcloth or cravat with long lace ends. — Also **steinkirk**. [From the battle of *Steenkerke*, 3 August 1692, in which the French won a victory over the English]

steep[1] *stēp*, *adj* lofty (*obs*); rising or descending with great inclination; precipitous; headlong; difficult; excessive, exorbitant (*colloq*); a lot to ask anyone to believe, exaggerated, incredible (*colloq*). — *n* a precipitous place. — *vt* (*SW England*) to cause to stoop, slope. — *vi* to rise or fall precipitously. — *vt* and *vi* **steep'en** to make or become steeper. — *n* **steep'iness** (*obs*). — *adj* **steep'ish**. — *adv* **steep'ly**. — *n* **steep'ness**. — *adj* **steep'y** (*poetic*) steep. — *adj* **steep'-to** (*naut*) going down precipitously into the water. [OE *stēap*; cf **stoop**[1]]

steep[2] *stēp*, *vt* to soak; to wet thoroughly; to saturate; to imbue. — *vi* to undergo soaking or thorough wetting. — *n* a soaking process; a liquid for steeping anything in; rennet. — *n* **steep'er** someone who steeps; a vessel for steeping in. [ME *stepen*; perh connected with **stoup**[1]]

steeple *stēp'l*, *n* a church or other tower with or without, or including or excluding, a spire; a structure surmounted by a spire; the spire alone. — *adj* **steep'led** having a steeple or steeples or the appearance of steeples. — **steep'lebush** the spirea plant, *esp* the American spiraea or hardhack; **steep'lechase** *orig* an impromptu horse race with some visible church steeple as goal; a horse race across country; a horse race over a course with obstacles to be jumped; a race of this kind run on foot. — *vi* to ride or run in a steeplechase. — **steep'lechaser**; **steep'lechasing**; **steep'le-crown** a high conical hat. — Also *adj*. — *adj* **steep'le-crowned**. — **steeple fair** (*obs*) a market held in the grounds of a vicarage, manse, etc; **steeple hat** a steeple-crowned hat; **steeple house** (*obs*) a church building; **steep'lejack** a person who repairs steeples and high chimneys. [OE *stēpel*, *stȳpel*, *stīpel*, from root of **steep**[1]]

steer[1] *stēr*, *vt* to move (a vehicle or ship) in the direction desired by means of a steering wheel, helm or similar device; to guide; to govern, control the course of. — *vi* to direct a ship, vehicle, etc in its course; to move, follow a course, in response to the wheel, helm, etc. — *n* an act of steering, as in *a bum steer* (*US*), a piece of misinformation. — *adj* **steer'able**. — *n* **steer'age** the act or practice of steering; the effect of a rudder on the ship; course; government; apparatus for steering; part (in front of the great cabin) from which a ship used to be steered; part of a passenger ship with lowest fares (also *adj*). — *n* **steer'er**. — *n* **steer'ing** an act of or the process of steering; the mechanism or interconnected parts that make up a steering system. — **steerage way** (*naut*) sufficient movement of a vessel to allow the rudder to grip the water thus enabling it to be controlled by the helm; **steering column** in a motor vehicle, the shaft on which the steering wheel or handlebars are mounted; **steering committee** a group who decide what measures shall be brought forward and when; **steering gear** the mechanism that transmits motion from the steering wheel, etc so that a vehicle, aircraft, etc may be steered; **steering wheel** the wheel by which a ship's rudder is turned, or a motor car, etc is guided; **steers'man** or (*obs*) **steers'mate** the person who steers a vessel, a helmsman. — **steer clear of** to avoid. [OE *stēoran*, *stȳran* to steer]

steer[2] *stēr*, *n* a young ox, *esp* a castrated one from two to four years old. — *n* **steer'ling** a little or young steer. [OE *stēor*; Ger *Stier*]

steer[3] *stēr*, *n*, *vt* and *vi* a Scots form of **stir**[1]. — *n* **steer'y** (*Scott*) commotion.

steeve[1] *stēv*, *n* the angle of elevation, *esp* of a bowsprit, in relation to the horizontal. — *vt* and *vi* to incline to the horizon. [Origin unknown]

steeve[2] or **stieve** *stēv*, (*Scot*) *adj* stiff, firm; sturdy. — Also *adv*. — *adv* **steeve'ly** or **stieve'ly**. [ME *stef*; ety doubtful]

steeve[3] *stēv*, (*naut*) *vt* to stuff, pack tightly (cargo, eg cotton) into a ship's hold. — *n* a derrick or spar with a block on the end for packing cargo into a ship's hold. — *n* **steev'ing**. [Perh Fr *estiver*, from L *stīpāre* to stuff]

stegano-, *steg'ən-ə-* or *-o* or **stego-** *steg'ə-* or *-o-*, *combining form* signifying covered, roofed, hidden, watertight. — *n* **steganogram** (*steg'ən-ə-gram*) or **steganograph** a cryptogram. — *n* **steganographer** (*-og'*) a person who works with ciphers. — *adj* **steganograph'ic**. — *n* **steganog'raphist**. — *n* **steganog'raphy**. — *n* **steg'anopod** (Gr *pous*, *podos* foot) any bird of the *Steganopodes*, the pelican order of birds, with all four toes webbed together. — *adj* **steganop'odous**. — *n* **stegno'sis** constriction of the pores and vessels; constipation. — *adj* **stegnot'ic**. — *adj* **stegocarp'ous** (Gr *karpos* fruit) with a lidded capsule. — *n pl* **Stegocephalia** (*-se-fā'li-ə*; Gr *kephalē* head) an extinct order of amphibians (Labyrinthodon, etc) having the skull protected by bony plates. — *adj* and *n* **stegocephā'lian**. — *adj* **stegocephalous** (*-sef'ə-ləs*). — *n* **stegodon** or **stegodont** (*steg'ə-don* or *-dont*; Gr *odons*, *odontos* tooth) an extinct mammal with ridged teeth, related to the mastodon and the elephant. — *n* **stegoph'ilist** a person who climbs buildings for sport. — *n* **steg'osaur** (Gr *sauros* lizard) any of several ornithischian, quadrupedal, herbivorous dinosaurs of the Jurassic period, having armour of various kinds made up of bony plates. — *adj* **stego-**

saur'ian. — *n* **Stegosaur'us** (also without *cap*) a member of the class of stegosaurs, having two lines of kite-shaped plates along the backbone. [Gr *steganos* covered, watertight, *stegein* to cover, hold water, protect, hide, *stegnoein* to make costive, *stegos* roof]

steil. See **steal**[2].

stein[1] *stēn*, *stīn* or *shtīn*, *n* a large beer mug, often earthenware and frequently with a hinged lid; the amount held by such a mug. [Ger]

stein[2], **steining**. See **steen**[1].

Steinberger *stīn'bûr-gər* or *shtīn'ber-hhər*, *n* an esteemed white Rhine wine, from *Steinberg*, near Wiesbaden.

steinbock *stīn'bok*, *n* the Alpine ibex; another name for **steenbok**. [Ger *Stein* stone, and *Bock* buck]

stele[1] *stē'lē*, *n* an upright stone slab or tablet (also **stē'la**); (*stē'lē* or *stēl*) the central cylinder (vascular bundles with pith and pericycle) in stems and roots of the higher plants (*bot*): — *pl* **stē'lae**. — *adj* **stē'lar** or **stē'lene**. [Gr *stēlē*, from root of *histanai* to set, stand]

stele[2]. See **steal**[2].

stelene. See **stele**[1].

stell *stel*, *vt* to establish (a law) (*obs*); to fix, post (*Scot*); to delineate (*obs* or *archaic*; *Shakesp*). — *pa p* **steeld** (*steld*). — *n* (*Scot*) an enclosure (*usu* a ringwall) for sheltering sheep, etc. — *adj* **stelled** fixed (see also under **stellar**). [OE *stellan* to fix, put]

stellar *stel'ər*, *adj* of the stars; of the nature of, relating to, belonging to or characteristic of a star; starry; relating to a star performer or performance; excellent (*slang*). — *n* **stell'arator** (*stellar* and gener*ator*) a twisted torus in which plasma can be confined by a magnetic field, used for producing thermonuclear (ie stellar) power by nuclear fusion. — *adj* **stell'ate** star-shaped; with branches radiating from a point; with sides that intersect one another, giving a starlike effect, as in the pentagram. — *adj* **stellā'ted** stellate; starred. — *adv* **stell'ately**. — *n* **stellerid** or **stelleridan** (*zool*) an old name for starfish. — Also *adj*. — *adj* **stellif'erous** having or bearing stars or starlike marks or forms. — *adj* **stell'ified**. — *adj* **stell'iform** star-shaped. — *vt* **stell'ify** to turn into a star; to set among the stars; to set with stars (*obs*). — *n* **stell'ifying**. — *adj* **stell'ūlar** or **stell'ūlate** like a little star or little stars; set with little stars. — **stellar evolution** the sequence of events and changes covering the entire life-cycle of a star; **stellar wind** material radiating from the atmosphere of a very hot star. [L *stēlla* a star]

Stellenbosch *stel'ən-bosh*, (*military slang*) *vt* to relegate to a post where incompetence matters less; to supersede. [From *Stellenbosch*, Cape of Good Hope, such a dumping-ground]

stelliferous, etc. See under **stellar**.

stellion *stel'yən*, *n* an E Mediterranean lizard (*Agama stellio*) with starry spots. [L *stēlliō*, *-ōn-* from *stēlla* star]

stellionate *stel'yən-āt*, (*Scot law*) *n* a fraud for which there is no specific name. [L *stēlliōnatus* fradulent person, from *stēlliō*, *-ōn*, from *stēlla* star]

stellular, **stellulate**. See under **stellar**.

stem[1] *stem*, *n* the leaf-bearing axis of a plant; a stalk; anything stalklike, such as the slender vertical part of a written musical note, or of a wine glass, or the winding shaft of a watch; an upright stroke of a letter; the main line (or sometimes a branch) of a family; a race or family; the base of a word, to which inflectional suffixes are added (*philol*). — *vt* to provide with a stem; to deprive of stalk or stem. — *vi* to grow a stem; to spring, take rise. — *adj* **stem'less**. — *n* **stem'let**. — *adj* **stemmed**. — **stem cell** (*histology*) a generalized parent cell that gives rise to cells that specialize; **stem cup** a Chinese porcelain goblet first produced in the Ming Dynasty, having a roomy bowl mounted on a stem that broadens to form the base; **stem ginger** the underground stem of the ginger plant; **stem stitch** an overlapping stitch used in embroidery; **stem'wīnder** (*US*) a keyless watch. [OE *stemn*, *stefn*; Ger *Stamm*; perh connected with **stand**]

stem[2] *stem*, *n* a curved timber at the prow of a ship; the forepart of a ship. — *vt* to make slight headway or hold position against (a contrary tide or current); hence, to make way against, breast; to ram. — *n* **stem'son** a curved timber behind the apron of a wooden-hulled ship. — **from stem to stern** from one end of a vessel to the other; throughout. [ON *stemn*, *stefn*; cf LGer, Du *steven*, ON *stamn*, *stafn*]

stem[3] *stem*, *vt* to stop, check; to dam; to plug or tamp (*mining*); to staunch; to slow down by pushing the heels apart (*skiing*): — *pr p* **stemm'ing**; *pa t* and *pa p* **stemmed**. — *n* (in skiing) the process of stemming, used in turning. — *n* **stemm'er** (*mining*) a metal bar used to tamp down a charge in a blasting hole. — *n* **stemm'ing**. — **stem turn** (*skiing*) a turn performed by stemming one ski and bringing the other ski down parallel with it. [ON *stemma*, OHGer *stemmen*]

stembuck *stem'buk* or **stembok** *-bok*. Same as **steenbok**.

steme *stēm*, (*archaic*) *vt* for **steam**, ie evaporate.

stemma *stem'ə*, *n* a garland; a scroll; a pedigree, family tree; a diagrammatic tree drawn up (using the internal evidence of manuscripts, etc) to show the descent and relationships of the texts of a literary work; an ocellus: — *pl* **stemm'ata**. — *adj* **stemm'atous**. — *vt* **stemme** (*stem*; *Spenser*) to encircle. [Gr *stemma*, usu in pl *stemmata*]

stempel or **stemple** *stem'pl*, *n* a crosstimber in a shaft, as support or step. [Cf Ger *Stempel*]

stemson. See under **stem**[2].

sten. See **stend** and **sten gun**.

stench *stench* or *-sh*, *n* a stink. — *vt* (*rare*) to cause to stink. — *adj* **stench'y**. — **stench trap** a device to prevent the rise of gases in drains. [OE *stenc* smell (good or bad); cf **stink**; Ger *Stank*]

stencil *sten'sl* or *sten'sil*, *n* a plate perforated with a design, lettering, etc from which copies are made by applying paint, etc through it on to paper or other material; the design or lettering so produced; a piece of waxed paper, etc, on which letters are cut by typewriter or stylus so that ink will pass through. — *vt* to produce (lettering or a design) from a stencil; to mark or decorate (a material) using a stencil: — *pr p* **sten'cilling** or *US* **sten'ciling**; *pa t* and *pa p* **sten'cilled** or *US* **sten'ciled**. — *adj* **sten'cilled**. — *n* **sten'ciller**. — *n* **sten'cilling**. — **stencil plate**. [OFr *estinceller* to spangle, from *estincelle*, from L *scintilla* a spark]

stend *stend*, (*Scot*) *vi* to bound, stride vigorously. — *n* a bound or great stride; a dart of pain. — Also **sten**. [Poss L *extendere*]

stengah *steng'ga*, *n* a drink of whisky and soda, a stinger. [Malay *se tengah* one half]

sten (also **Sten**) **gun** *sten gun*, *n* a small lightweight machine-gun. [*S*hepherd and *T*urpin, the designers, and *En*field, as in **bren gun**]

stenlock *sten'lək*, (*Scot*) *n* a coalfish; an overgrown coalfish. [Origin doubtful]

steno- *sten-ō-* or *-ə-*, *combining form* denoting narrow, constricted, contracted. — *n* **stenocar'dia** (Gr *kardia* heart) another name for the heart disease *angina pectoris*. — *n* **sten'ochrome** (*-krōm*; Gr *chrōma* colour) a print by stenochromy. — *n* **sten'ochromy** (or *-ok'rə-mi*) printing in several colours at one printing. — *n* **sten'ograph** a shorthand character or report; a machine for writing shorthand, operated by keyboard. — *vt* to write in shorthand. — *n* **stenog'rapher** (*NAm*) a shorthand typist. — *adj* **stenograph'ic** (*sten-ə-graf'ik*). — *adv* **stenograph'ically**. — *n* **stenog'raphist**. — *n* **stenog'raphy** the art, or any method, of writing very quickly; shorthand. — *adj* **stenopaeic** (*-pē'ik*; Gr *opaios* holed, *opē* an opening) with a narrow opening (also **stenopā'ic**). — *adj* **steno'phyllous** (*bot*) having narrow leaves. — *adj* **stenosed** (*sti-nōst'*; *med*) contracted as a result of disease. — *n* **stenō'sis** (*med*) constriction, narrowing of a tube or passage; constipation: — *pl* **stenōsēs**. — *adj* **stenotic** (*sti-not'ik*). — *adj* **sten'otopic** (*ecology*) able to tolerate only a small degree of environmental change (also **sten'otropic**). — *n* **Sten'otype**® (*sten'ə-tīp*) a form of typewriter used for recording speech in phonetic shorthand. — *n* **sten'otypist**. — *n* **sten'otypy**. [Gr *stenos* narrow]

stent[1] *stent*, *n*, *vt* and *vi*. Same as **stint**[1], with meanings shading off into those of **stent**[2].

stent[2] *stent*, (*Scot*) *n* assessment; valuation; tax. — *vt* to assess; to tax; to levy. — *n* **stent'or** or **stent'our** stentmaster. — **stent'master** a person who determines the amount of tax to be paid. [**extent**, or OFr *estente*; see also **stent**[1] and **stint**[1]]

stentorian *sten-tō'ri-ən*, *adj* (of a voice) loud, powerful, carrying. [*Stentōr* the loud-voiced Greek herald in Homer's *Iliad*]

stentour. See under **stent**[2].

STEP *step*, *abbrev*: Special Temporary Employment Programme.

step *step*, *n* a pace; a movement of the leg in walking, running, or dancing; the distance so covered; a footstep, footfall; a footprint; gait; a small space; a short walk or journey; a degree of a scale; a stage upward or downward; one tread of a stair; a rung of a ladder; a doorstep; something to put the foot on in mounting or dismounting; a stairlike rise or drop in level; a stage on the way up or down; a move towards an end or in a course of proceeding; coincidence in speed and phase; a support for the end of a mast, pivot, etc; (in *pl*) walk, direction taken in walking; (in *pl*) a stepladder (often a **pair of steps**); (in *pl*) a flight of stairs. — *vi* to advance, retire, mount, or descend by taking a step or steps; to pace; to walk; to walk slowly or gravely; to walk a short distance. — *vt* to perform by stepping; to measure by pacing; to arrange or organize in a steplike formation or arrangement, stagger; to set (foot) (*old US*); to fix (a mast, etc): — *pr p* **stepp'ing**; *pa t* and *pa p* **stepped** (also (*archaic*) **stept**). — *n* **stepp'er**. — *adv* **step'wise** in the manner of steps. — *adj* **step'-cut** (of diamonds and other stones) cut in steplike facets. — **step dance** a dance involving an effective display of steps by an individual dancer; **step'dancer**; **step'dancing**; **step'-down** a decrease in rate, quantity, output, etc. — *adj* reducing voltage; decreasing by stages. — **step fault** (*geol*) one of a series of parallel faults throwing in the same direction; **step function** (*math*) a function which makes an instant change in value from one constant value to another with an infinite number of harmonics present; **step'-in** a garment that is put on by being stepped into, *esp* one that needs no fastening. — Also *adj*. — **step'ladder** a ladder with flat treads and a hinged prop; **stepped-index fibre** (*telecomm*) an optical fibre in which there is an abrupt transition from the higher refractive index of the information-bearing core to the lower refractive index of the cladding (cf *graded-index fibre*); **stepp'ing-stone** a large stone in a shallow stream, etc stepped on to cross the stream, etc; a means to gradual progress (*fig*); **step rocket** one made in sections operating successively and then discarded; **step stone** a door step; **step'-up** an increase in rate, quantity, output, etc. — *adj* increasing or changing by steps; raising voltage. — **break step** to change the sequence of right and left foot, so as to get out of step; **in step** with simultaneous putting forward of the right (or left) feet in marching, etc (with others); in conformity or agreement (with others); **out of step** not in step; not in conformity, at odds (with others); **keep step** to continue in step; **step by step** gradually, little by little; **step down** to withdraw, retire, resign, from a position of authority, etc; to decrease the voltage of; to reduce the rate of; **step in** or **step into** to enter easily or unexpectedly; to intervene; **step on** to put or press the foot down on; to crush or subdue; **step on it** (*slang*; see also under **gas** and **juice**) to hurry; **step out** to go out a little way; to increase the length of the step and so the speed; to have a busy social life; **step out of line** to depart from the usual, or accepted, course of action; **step short** to shorten the length of one's step; **step up** to come forward; to build up into steps; to raise by a step or steps; to increase the voltage of; to increase the rate or level of; **take steps** to take action; **watch one's step** to go carefully, *esp* with a view to not giving offence or cause for complaint. [OE (Mercian) *steppe* (WSax *stæpe*); Du *step*, Ger *Stapfe*]

step- *step-*, *pfx* indicating relationship by a second or subsequent marriage or mating. — *n* **step'bairn** (*Scot*) *n* stepchild. — *n* **step'brother** or **-sister** the son or daughter of a stepfather or stepmother. — *n* **step'child**, **-daughter** or **-son** a wife's or husband's but not one's own child, daughter or son. — *n* **step'dame** (*archaic*) stepmother. — *n* **step'father** a mother's husband not one's own father. — *n* **step'mother** a father's wife not one's own mother; a bird that hatches another's eggs. — *n* **step'-parent**. — *n* **step'-parenting**. [OE *stēop-* (as in *stēopmōdor*), orig meaning orphan; Ger *stief-*]

stephane *stef'ə-nē*, *n* an ancient Greek headdress like a diadem. [Gr *stephanē*, from *stephein* to encircle]

stephanite *stef'ə-nīt*, *n* a brittle silver ore, composed of silver, sulphur, and antimony. [After Archduke *Stephan* (1817–67)]

stephanotis *stef-ə-nō'tis*, *n* any asclepiad plant of the genus *Stephanotis*, of Madagascar, etc, cultivated for their waxy, scented flowers. [Gr *stephanōtis* fit for a wreath, from *stephanos* a crown, wreath]

stepney *step'ni*, (*old slang*) *n* a spare wheel (often *fig*); a mistress, *esp* that of a white slaver. [Said to be from the name of a street where the wheels were made]

steppe *step*, *n* a dry, grassy, generally treeless, uncultivated and sometimes salt plain, as in central Europe and in Asia. [Russ *step'*]

stept. See **step**.

ster. *abbrev*: sterling.

-ster *-stər*, *sfx* used to denote a person with a particular characteristic, as in *youngster*, or activity, as in *mobster*, *prankster*, etc. [OE sfx *-estre*]

steradian *sti-rā'di-ən*, *n* a unit of measurement for solid angles, the angle subtended at the centre of a sphere by an area on its surface numerically equal to the square of the radius. [Gr *stereos* solid, and **radian**]

stercoraceous *stûrk-ə-rā'shəs*, (*esp med*) *adj* of, relating to, like or of the nature of faeces. — *adj* **sterc'oral** stercoraceous. — *n* **sterc'oranism** formerly, a name for the belief that the sacramental bread is digested and evacuated like other food. — *n* **sterc'oranist**. — *adj* **stercorā'rious** or **sterc'orary**. — *vt* **sterc'orate** to evacuate the bowels. [L *stercus*, *-oris* dung]

sterculia *stər-kū'li-ə*, *n* any tree or shrub of the genus *Sterculia* (family *Sterculiaceae*) related to the mallows, including kola and cacao. [L *Sterculius* god of manuring, from *stercus* dung, from the stinking flowers]

stere *stēr*, *n* a timber measure, a cubic metre (about 35·315 cubic feet), used as *combining form* as in *decastere*, 10 steres, *decistere*, a tenth of a stere. [Fr *stère*, from Gr *stereos* solid]

stereo *stēr'i-ō* or *ster'i-ō*, *n* stereophonic reproduction of sound; stereoscopic vision; a piece of stereophonic equipment, such as a record-player, tape recorder, etc; a unit comprising such pieces: — *pl* **ster'eos**. — *adj* stereophonic; stereoscopic.

stereo- *stēr'i-ō-* or *ster'i-ō-*, *combining form* meaning solid, hard, three-dimensional. — *n* **stereoacū'ity** the degree to which a person is aware of the separation of objects along the line of sight. — *n* **ster'eobate** (root of Gr *bainein* to go, walk) a substructure, foundation. — *adj* **stereobatic** (*-bat'ik*). — *adj* **ster'eoblind** having two-dimensional rather than normal three-dimensional vision. — *n* **ster'eocard** a card on which a pair of stereoscopic pictures are mounted. — *n* **stereochem'istry** the study of the spatial arrangement of atoms in molecules. — *n* **ster'eochrome** (Gr *chrōma* colour). — *n* **ster'eochrōmy** mural painting fixed with waterglass. — *n* **stereoflu'oroscope** a fluoroscope giving a three-dimensional view. — *n* **ster'eogram** a picture or diagram suggestive of solidity; a stereographic double picture; *esp* formerly, a radiogram for reproducing stereophonic records. — *n* **ster'eograph** a stereogram (in first two senses). — *adj* **stereograph'ic**. — *n*

stereog'raphy. — *n* **stereoī'somer** an isomer having the same chemical composition, molecular weight and structure, but differing spatial arrangement of atoms. — *adj* **stereoīsomer'ic**. — *n* **stereoīsom'erism**. — *n* **ster'eome** mechanical tissue in plants. — *n* **stereom'eter** an instrument for measuring specific gravity or for measuring solids. — *adj* **stereomet'ric** or **stereomet'rical**. — *adv* **stereomet'rically**. — *n* **stereom'etry**. — *adj* **stereophon'ic** giving the effect of sound from different directions in three-dimensional space. — *adv* **stereophon'ically**. — *n* **stereoph'ony** stereophonic reproduction of sound. — *n* **stereops'is** (Gr *opsis* vision) binocular stereoscopic vision. — *n* **stereopt'icon** a double projecting lantern, by means of which the one picture dissolves into another. — *n sing* **stereop'tics** the optics of stereoscopy. — *n* **ster'eoscope** an instrument by which the images of two pictures differing slightly in point of view are seen one by each eye and so give an effect of solidity. — *adj* **stereoscop'ic**. — *adv* **stereoscop'ically**. — *n* **stereos'copist**. — *n* **stereos'copy**. — *adj* **stereoson'ic** stereophonic. — *adj* **stereospecif'ic** relating to, or (of atoms) having, a fixed spatial arrangement. — *adj* **stereotac'tic** or **stereotac'tical** (Gr *tassein* to arrange) of stereotaxis (*biol*); (also **stereotax'ic**) relating to the precise location of particular brain structures by three-dimensional survey (*med*). — *n* **stereotax'ia** (*med*) the electrical destruction of a small area of brain tissue, using stereotactic methods, to relieve disorders such as epilepsy and Parkinsonism. — *n* **stereotax'is** the reaction of an organism to the stimulus of contact with a solid body (*biol*); stereotaxia. — *n* **stereot'omy** (Gr *tomē* a cut) section-cutting of solids; stone-cutting. — *adj* **stereotrop'ic**. — **stereot'ropism** (Gr *tropos* a turn) the tendency to bend or turn in response to contact with a solid object. — *n* **ster'eotype** a solid metallic plate for printing, cast from a mould (made of papier-mâché or other material) of composed type; the art, method, or process of making such plates; a fixed conventionalized or stock image, or a person or thing that conforms to it. — *adj* pertaining to, or done with, stereotypes. — *vt* to make a stereotype of; to print with stereotypes; to characterize or categorize (*esp* a person) too readily or simplistically. — *adj* **ster'eotyped** transferred as letterpress from set-up movable type to a mould, and thence to a metal plate; fixed, unchangeable, as opinions; conventionalized, conforming to a stock image or cliché. — *n* **ster'eotyper**. — *adj* **stereotyp'ic** or **stereotyp'ical**. — *n* **ster'eotyping**. — *n* **ster'eotypy** the producing of stereotype plates; the repetition of senseless movements, actions or words in cases of insanity, etc (*med*). [Gr *stereos* solid]

steric *ster'ik*, *adj* relating to the spatial arrangement of atoms in a molecule. [Gr *stereos* solid, and sfx **-ic**]

sterigma *ster-ig'mə*, (*bot*) *n* a stalk that bears a sporangium, basidiospore or conidium: — *pl* **sterig'mata**. [Gr *stērigma* support]

sterile *ster'īl* or (*US*) *-il*, *adj* unfruitful; barren; not producing, or unable to produce, offspring, fruit, seeds, or spores; (of a flower) without pistils; (of a glume) not subtending a flower; sterilized; destitute of ideas or results. — *n* **ster'ilant** a sterilizing agent. — *n* **steril'ity** the quality of being sterile; unfruitfulness, barrenness, in regard to reproduction. — *n* **sterilization** or **-s-** (*ster-i-lī-zā'shən*). — *vt* **ster'ilize** or **-ise** to cause to be fruitless; to deprive of power of reproduction; to destroy micro-organisms in. — *n* **ster'ilīzer** or **-s-** one who, or that which, sterilizes; any apparatus for destroying germs. [L *sterilis* barren]

sterlet *stûr'lit*, *n* a small sturgeon. [Russ *sterlyad*]

sterling[1] *stûr'ling*, *n* an old English silver penny (*obs*); English, Scottish, or British money of standard value. — *adj* of sterling or standard English money; genuine, authentic; of authority; of thoroughly good character, solidly worthy and reliable; (of silver) of standard quality, ie containing at least 92·5 per cent silver (*usu* alloyed with copper). — **sterling area** a group of countries with currencies tied to sterling and freely settling transactions among themselves through London; **sterling effective rate** see under **effect**. [Prob a coin with a star, from OE *steorra* star, from some early Norman pennies being so marked]

sterling[2] *stûr'ling*. Same as **starling**[2].

Sterling *stûr'ling*, *n* a submachinegun that fires bursts or single shots, and does not jam. [From the makers' name]

stern[1] *stûrn*, *adj* severe; austere; rigorous; hard, unyielding, inflexible; unrelenting. — Also *adv* (*archaic*). — *adv* **stern'ly**. — *n* **stern'ness**. [OE *styrne*]

stern[2] *stûrn*, *n* the hind part of a vessel; the rump or tail; steering-gear, helm, the steersman's place (*obs*; *Shakesp*). — *vt* to back, to row backward. — *n* **stern'age** (*Shakesp*) sterns collectively. — *adj combining form* **-sterned** having a stern of a specified type. — *adj* **stern'most** farthest astern. — *adv* **stern'ward** (also *adj*) or **sternwards**. — **stern'board** backward motion of a ship; loss of way in tacking; **stern'-chase** a chase in which one ship follows directly in the wake of another; **stern'-chaser** a cannon in the stern of a ship; **stern'fast** a rope or chain for making fast a ship's stern to a wharf, etc. — *adv* **stern-fore'most**. — **stern frame** the framework of a ship's stern; **stern'port** a port or opening in the stern of a ship; **stern'post** the aftermost timber of a ship, supporting the rudder; **stern'sheet** (*usu* in *pl*) the part of a boat between the stern and the rowers; **stern'son** the hinder extremity of a ship's keelson, to which the sternpost is bolted; **stern'way** the backward motion of a vessel; **stern-wheel'er** (*US*) a small vessel with one large paddlewheel at the stern. — *n pl* **stern'works** hinder parts. [ON *stjōrn* a steering, or lost OE equivalent]

stern[3] *stûrn* or *stern* or **starn** *stärn*, (*obs* and *Scot*) *n* a star. — *n* (*dimin*) **starn'ie**. [ON *stjarna*]

sternite, etc. See under **sternum**.

sternson. See under **stern**[2].

sternum *stûr'nəm*, *n* the breastbone in humans, and the corresponding bone in other vertebrates; the under part of a somite in arthropods. — *adj* **ster'nal**. — *n* **sternal'gia** (*med*; Gr *algos* pain) pain around the sternum, angina pectoris. — *adj* **sternal'gic**. — *n* **ster'nebra** (modelled on *vertebra*) a segment of the breastbone. — *n* **ster'nite** the ventral plate of a segment in arthropods. — *adj* **sternit'ic**. — *adj* **ster'notribe** (Gr *tribē* a rub) pollinated by touching an insect's under surface. [Latinized from Gr *sternon* chest]

sternutation *stûr-nū-tā'shən*, *n* sneezing. — *adj* **sternū'tative** or **sternū'tatory** that causes sneezing. — *n* a substance that causes sneezing. — Also **ster'nūtātor**. [L *sternūtāre*, intensive of *sternuere* to sneeze]

sterol *stēr'ol* or *ster'*, *n* a solid higher alcohol, such as *cholesterol* or *ergosterol*. — *n* **stēr'oid** (or *ster'*) any of a class of compounds including the sterols, bile acids, adrenal hormones, sex hormones, vitamin D, etc. — **steroid receptors** discrete regions in the cell responsible for DNA binding, steroid binding, and gene activation and repression; **steroid regulated genes** sets of genes whose expression is modulated by steroid hormones, resulting in the altered physiology of the target tissue. [See **cholesterol**]

stertorous *stûr'tər-əs*, *adj* with a snoring sound. — *adv* **ster'torously**. — *n* **ster'torousness**. [L *stertere* to snore]

sterve *stûrv*, *vt* and *vi* an old form (*Spenser*) of **starve**, to starve, to die.

stet *stet*, *vt* to restore after marking for deletion: — *pr p* **stett'ing**; *pa t* and *pa p* **stett'ed**. [L, let it stand, 3rd pers sing present subjunctive of *stāre* to stand; written on a proof-sheet with dots under the words to be retained]

stethoscope *steth'ə-skōp*, (med) *n* an instrument with which to listen to the sounds produced by the heart, lungs, etc, with a hollow circular part that is applied to the body wall, from which sound is transmitted by tubes into earpieces. — *adj* **stethoscopic** (*-skop'ik*). — *adv* **stethoscop'ically**. — *n* (*rare*) **stethoscopist** (*-os'kə-*

pist). — *n* **stethos'copy**. [Gr *stēthos* chest, and *skopeein* to look at, examine]

Stetson *stet'sn, n* a man's felt hat with a broad brim and a soft, high crown. [Maker's name]

stevedore *stēv'ə-dōr* or *-dör, n* a person who loads and unloads shipping vessels. — *vt* and *vi* to load and unload (cargo or a ship). [Sp *estibador* packer, from *estibar* to stow, from L *stīpāre* to press]

steven *stev'n, n* a voice (now *dialect*); an outcry (*Spenser*). [OE *stefn* voice]

stevengraph *stēv'n-gräf, n* a silk picture woven in colours. [T *Stevens*, American weaver of the 19c]

stew[1] *stū, n* a dish of food, *esp* meat with vegetables, cooked in water or a stock; a hole, a fix (*colloq*); a state of mental agitation (*colloq*); an overheated or sweaty state (*colloq*); a hot bath (*old-fashioned*); a room for hot-air baths (*old-fashioned*); a boiling pot (*Spenser* and *Shakesp*); (*usu* in *pl*) a brothel, or prostitutes' quarter; a prostitute (*obs*); someone who studies hard, *esp* unintelligently (*old slang*). — *vt* to simmer or boil slowly with some moisture; to over-infuse (eg tea); to keep in a swelter or narrow confinement; to bathe in sweat; to bathe in hot air or water. — *vi* to swelter, *esp* in a confined space; to be cooked by stewing; to be in a state of worry or agitation (*colloq*); to study hard (*old slang*). — *adj* **stewed** cooked by stewing; (of tea) over-infused; drunk (*colloq*). — *n* **stew'er**. — *n* and *adj* **stew'ing**. — *adj* **stew'y** like a stew; sweltering. — **stew'-can** (*naval slang*) a destroyer; **stew'pan** or **stew'pot** a pan or pot used for stewing. — **in a stew** in a state of worry, agitation; **stew in one's own juice** to be left to reap the consequences of one's own actions. [OFr *estuve* (Fr *étuve*) stove; prob connected with **stove**[1]]

stew[2] *stū, n* a fish pond; a fish tank; an artificial oyster bed. — **stew'pond**. [OFr *estui* (Fr *étui*)]

steward *stū'ərd, n* a person who manages the domestic concerns of a family or institution; one who superintends another's affairs, *esp* an estate or farm; the person who oversees catering arrangements and general passenger comfort on a ship, aircraft, etc; a male member of the team responsible for these; a college caterer; someone who helps in arrangements, marshalling, etc, at races, a dance, a wedding, an entertainment; an overseer; a foreman; the treasurer of a congregation, guild, society, etc; a shop steward. — *fem* (in ships, aircraft, etc) **stew'ardess**. — *n* **stew'ardship** or **stew'ardry** the office of a steward; management; the individual's function in the practical work of the Christian church involving obligation to give a share of his time and goods to others. — *n* **stew'artry** (*Scot*) a stewardship, or the extent of a stewardship, applied nominally to the county of Kirkcudbright (now part of Dumfries and Galloway). — **stewards' enquiry** (*horse-racing*) an examination of the evidence relating to an allegation of contravention of the rules of racing, carried out by the stewards after a race — the result is signalled by the hoisting of flags on the racecourse. — **Lord High Steward** one of the great officers of state, and anciently the first officer of the crown in England. [OE *stig-weard*, from *stig* hall ('sty'), and *weard* ward, keeper]

stey *stī*, (*Scot*) *adj* steep. [Cf **stile**[1], **stirrup**]

stg *abbrev*: sterling.

sthenic *sthen'ik, adj* strong, robust; morbidly active (*med*). [Gr *sthenos* strength]

stiacciato *sti-ə-chi-ä'to*, (*sculpture*) *n* very low relief, as on coins. [Ital]

stibble *stib'l, n* a Scots form of **stubble**. — *n* **stibb'ler** a horse turned out to feed on stubble; a person who cuts the handfuls left by the reaper; a probationer (*Scott*).

stibium *stib'i-əm, n* antimony. — *adj* **stib'ial**. — *n* **stib'ialism** antimony poisoning. — *n* **stib'ine** (*-ēn* or *-īn*) antimony hydride, a poisonous gas. — *n* **stib'nite** native antimony trisulphide. [L, from Gr *stibi, stimmi*, from Egypt *stm* (Coptics *stēm*)]

sticcado *stik-ä'dō* or **sticcato** *-tō, n* a kind of xylophone: — *pl* **sticcados, sticcadoes, sticcatos** or **sticcatoes**. [Perh Ital *steccato* palisade]

stich *stik, n* a line of verse, or section of prose of comparable length. — *n* **stichar'ion** (Gr *sticharion*) a Greek vestment like the Western alb. — *n* **stichē'ron** a short hymn. — *adj* **stich'ic** of or pertaining to stichs. — *n* **stichid'ium** (*bot*) a branch producing tetraspores, in red seaweeds: — *pl* **stichid'ia**. — *n* **stichol'ogy** metrical theory. — *adj* **stichomet'ric** or **stichomet'rical**. — *adv* **stichomet'rically**. — *n* **stichom'etry** (*prosody*) measurement by lines; division into lines (often of a prose text into lines that mimic verse, units of meaning with a regular rhythm); a statement of such measurements. — *n* **stichomythia** (*-mith'*; Gr *stichomȳthiā*) dialogue in alternate lines. — *adj* **stichomyth'ic**. — *n* **stich'os** a stichometric line of a manuscript, etc; a verse or versicle (*Gr Church*): — *pl* **stich'oi**. — *combining form* **-stichous** signifying having a certain number of lines or rows, eg *distichous*. [Gr *stichos* a row, from *steichein* to march]

stick[1] *stik, vt* to pierce, transfix; to stab; to spear; to thrust; to fasten by piercing; to insert; to set in position; to set or cover with things fastened on; to cause to adhere, fix with an adhesive; to endure (*esp* with *it*) (*colloq*); to function successfully (*colloq*); to bring to a standstill or nonplus; to leave someone (with) (something unpleasant) (*colloq*); (*usu* passive) to confine. — *vi* to be fixed by insertion; to jut, protrude; to adhere; (of a charge or accusation) to be accepted as valid; to become or remain fixed; to remain; to be detained by an impediment; to jam; to fail to proceed or advance; to scruple; to hold fast, keep resolutely (with *to*): — *pa t* **stuck**, *Scot* **stack**; *pa p* **stuck**, *Scot* **stick'it**. — *n* a stoppage (*obs*); a difficulty (*archaic*); a hitch; adhesiveness. — *n* **stickabil'ity** (*colloq facetious*) the ability to stick at something, persistence, perseverence. — *n* **stick'er** a person who kills pigs, etc; a person who or thing that sticks; a piercing weapon (*colloq*); a person or thing difficult to get rid of; someone who is constant or persistent; a gummed label or poster; a poser; a piano jack; an upright rod that transmits motion from an organ key. — *vt* to apply stickers (gummed labels) to. — *adv* **stick'ily**. — *n* **stick'iness**. — *n* and *adj* **stick'ing**. — *adj* **stick'y** adhesive; tenacious; gluey; muggy; difficult (*colloq*); unpleasant (*colloq*). — *vt* to make sticky. — **stick'ing-plaster** an adhesive plaster for covering wounds; **sticking-point** the point beyond which a thing cannot proceed; **stick'-in-the-mud** an old fogey. — Also *adj*. — **stickit minister** (*Scot*) a licentiate who never gets a pastoral charge; **stick'jaw** a cloggy pudding or sweetmeat; **stick pin** (*US*) a tie-pin; **stick'ybeak** (*Austr* and *NZ colloq*) a Nosey Parker; **sticky end** an unpleasant end, disaster. — *adj* **stick'y-fing'ered** (*colloq*) prone to pilfering. — **sticky wicket** a difficult situation to cope with. — *adj* **stuck-up'** self-importantly aloof. — **get stuck in** (or **into**) (*colloq*) to deal with, consume, attack in a vigorous, aggressive, eager, etc manner; **stick around** (*colloq*) to remain or linger; **stick at** to hesitate or scruple at (often with *nothing*); to persist at; **stick by** to be firm in supporting, to adhere closely to; **stick 'em up!** hold up your hands (or be shot)!; **stick in** (*Scot*) to persevere assiduously; also (of a dressing, etc) to adhere to a wound; **stick in one's throat** or **craw** to be difficult, or against one's conscience, for one to countenance; **stick it to** to overcharge systematically; to gain a victory over (someone); **stick one's neck out** see under **neck**; **stick or snee** see **snickersnee**; **stick out** to project; to be obvious; to continue to resist; **stick out for** to insist upon; **stick to** to persevere in holding to; **stick together** to be allies; to support each other; **stick up** to stand up; to waylay and plunder (*esp US*; *n* **stick'-up**); **stick up for** to speak or act in defence of; **stick with** to remain with; to force (a person) to cope with (something unpleasant) — often in *passive*, ie **be stuck with**; **stuck for** unable to proceed because of the lack of;

stuck on (*colloq*) enamoured of. [OE *stician*; cf **stick**[2], **stitch**]

stick[2] *stik*, *n* a rod of wood, *esp* for walking with or for beating; a twig; anything shaped like a rod of wood; a timber tree or trunk; a piece of firewood; a tally; an instrument for beating a percussion instrument; an instrument for playing hockey or another game; a bow for a fiddle, or the wooden part of it; a person of stiff manner; a person who lacks enterprise; a rod; any oblong or cylindrical piece; a control rod of an aeroplane; a group of bombs, or of paratroops, released at one time from an aeroplane; a piece of furniture, *esp* one of few (*usu* in *pl*); a ray of a fan; a support for a candle; (in *pl*) hurdles in steeplechasing; a printer's composing stick; a stickful; blame, criticism (*slang*). — *adj* in the form of a stick; made of sticks. — *vt* to support (a plant) with sticks; to arrange in a composing stick (*printing*): — *pa t* and *pa p* **sticked**. — *n* **stick'ful** (*printing*) as much as a composing stick holds. — **stick force** (*aeronautics*) the force exerted on the control column by the pilot when applying aileron or elevator control; **stick insect** a twiglike phasmid insect; **stick'leader** the leader of a stick of paratroops; **stick'work** skill in using one's stick in any game played with one; **sticky ends** single-stranded ends of DNA that has been cut with a restriction endonuclease, able to pair with complementary ends on, and thus joining, other fragments. — **beat to sticks** to defeat and surpass utterly; **big stick** force, coercion; **carrot and stick** see under **carrot**; **give someone stick** (*slang*) to censure or punish someone; **in a cleft stick** in a dilemma; **right** (or **wrong**) **end of the stick** a true (or mistaken) understanding of the situation; **the sticks** rural areas, the backwoods; **up sticks** (*colloq*) to move, go and live somewhere else, make off. [OE *sticca*; ON *stika*]

stickit (*Scot*). See **stick**[1].

stickle[1] *stik'l*, *vi* to regulate a contest (*obs*); to mediate (*obs*); to interpose (*obs*); to contend, stand up (with *for*); to be scrupulous or obstinately punctilious. — *vt* to compose (*obs*); to stop contention between (*obs*); to contend (*obs*); to scruple. — *n* **stick'ler** a punctilious and pertinacious insister or contender, *esp* for something trifling; a regulator or umpire, a mediator (*obs*, *excl dialect*); a second (*obs*); a backer (*obs*). — *adj* or *adv* **stick'ler-like** (*Shakesp*). [Prob ME *stightle*, from OE *stihtan* to set in order]

stickle[2] *stik'l*, (*SW Eng dialect*) *adj* steep; rapid. — *n* a rapid. [OE *sticol* steep]

stickleback *stik'l-bak*, *n* a small spiny-backed river-fish. [OE *sticel* sting, prick, and **back**[1]]

sticky. See under **stick**[1].

stiction *stik'shən*, *n* the frictional force occurring when one surface is set against another. [**stick** and **friction**]

stiddie *stid'i*. Same as **stithy**.

stie. An old spelling of **sty**[2,3].

stieve. Same as **steeve**[2].

stiff *stif*, *adj* not easily bent; rigid; lacking suppleness; moved or moving with difficulty or friction; dead; approaching solidity; thick, viscous, not fluid; dense, difficult to mould or cut; resistant; difficult; tough, tiring, arduous; pertinacious; stubborn; formidable; (of an alcoholic drink) strong; (of a breeze) blowing strongly; firm, high, or inclining to rise (in price, etc); excessive; not natural and easy; constrained; formal; keeping upright (*naut*); certain (not to run, to win, to lose; *slang*); unlucky (*esp Austr*); (*predicatively*) to an extreme degree, as in *bore* or *scare someone stiff*. — *adv* stiffly; stark; very, extremely (*colloq*). — *n* (*slang*) someone who or something that is stiff; a corpse; a good-for-nothing; a racehorse that is a notably poor bet; a customer who fails to tip; a negotiable paper; a forged paper; an illegal letter sent or received by a prisoner. — *vt* (*slang*) to cheat; to rob; to fail to tip; to murder; to cause to fail, get nowhere (also *vi*). — *vt* and *vi* **stiff'en** to make or become stiff or stiffer. — *n* **stiff'ener** a person who or thing that stiffens; a strong alcoholic drink (*colloq*); a cigarette-card or the like, used to stiffen a package. — *n* and *adj* **stiff'ening**. — *adj* **stiff'ish**. — *adv* **stiff'ly**. — *n* **stiff'ness** the state or quality of being stiff; in a mechanical vibrating system, the restoring force per unit of displacement (the reciprocal of **compliance**). — **stiff bit** a horse's jointless bit. — *adj* **stiff'-hearted** (*Bible*) obstinate, stubborn. — **stiff neck** a condition affecting the neck muscles, making it painful to turn the head; torticollis. — *adj* **stiff'-necked** obstinate; haughty; formal and unnatural. — **stiff'-necked'ness**. — **stiff'ware** (*comput jargon*) software that is no longer flexible, having been customized or having incomplete documentation or an obscure function and therefore being difficult to modify or remove without risk to other programs. — **a stiff upper lip** see under **lip**; **stiff with** (*colloq*) full of, crowded with. [OE *stīf* stiff; Du *stijf*, Ger *steif*]

stifle[1] *stī'fl*, *vt* to stop the breath of by foul air or other means; to make breathing difficult for; to suffocate, smother; to choke down; to suppress; to repress; to make stifling. — *vi* to suffocate. — *n* a stifling atmosphere, smell, or condition. — *adj* **sti'fled**. — *n* **sti'fler** someone who stifles; the gallows. — *n* and *adj* **sti'fling** (*-fling*). — *adv* **sti'flingly**. [Origin obscure]

stifle[2] *stī'fl*, *n* the joint of a horse, dog, etc, corresponding to the human knee. — **stifle bone** the knee-cap; **stifle-joint**. [Connection with **stiff** doubtful]

stigma *stig'mə*, *n* a disgrace or reproach attached to a person; a mark of infamy; any special mark; a spot; a scar; a mark on the skin indicative of a particular disease; a spot sensitive to light; the part of a carpel that receives pollen (*bot*); a spiracle; a pore; (in *pl*) the marks of Christ's wounds or marks resembling them, claimed to have been impressed on the bodies of certain holy people, notably Francis of Assisi in 1224: — *pl* **stig'mata** (or, *esp* in religion, *-mä'tə*); also (*esp bot* or in sense of *disgrace* or *reproach*) **stig'mas**. — *adj* **stigmā'rian** (also *n*). — *adj* **stigmatic** (*-mat'ik*) of, pertaining to, of the nature of, a stigma; marked or branded with a stigma; giving infamy or reproach; anastigmatic, or not astigmatic. — *n* a person who bears the stigmata; someone who is branded (*Shakesp stig'*, with deformity). — *adj* **stigmat'ical**. — *adv* **stigmat'ically**. — *adj* **stigmatif'erous** (*bot*) stigma-bearing. — *n* **stig'matism** impression of the stigmata; anastigmatism. — *n* **stig'matist** someone impressed with the stigmata. — *n* **stigmatīzā'tion** or **-s-** act of stigmatizing; the production of stigmata or of bleeding spots on the body, as by hypnotism. — *vt* **stig'matize** or **-ise** to mark with a stigma or the stigmata; to brand, denounce, describe condemnatorily (with *as*). — *n* **stig'matophilia** excessive enthusiasm for stigmata, ie tattooing or body piercing. — *n* **stig'matophilist**. — *adj* **stig'matose**. — *n* **stig'mē** (*Gr palaeog*) a dot used as a punctuation mark. [Gr *stigma*, *-atos* tattoo-mark, brand, *stigmē* a point]

stilb *stilb*, *n* the CGS unit of intrinsic brightness, one candela/cm^2. — *n* **stilbene** (*stil'bēn*) a crystalline hydrocarbon, used in dye-manufacture. [Gr *stilbein* to shine]

stilbestrol. See **stilboestrol**.

stilbite *stil'bīt*, *n* a pearly zeolite. [Gr *stilbein* to shine]

stilboestrol or *US* **stilbestrol** *stil-bēs'trəl*, *n* a synthetic oestrogen. [Gr *stilbos* glistening and **oestrus**]

stile[1] *stīl*, *n* a step, or set of steps, built into a wall or fence. [OE *stigel*; cf OE *stīgan*, Ger *steigen* to mount]

stile[2] *stīl*, *n* an upright member in framing or panelling. [Perh Du *stijl* pillar, doorpost]

stile[3]. An older spelling of **style**.

stilet. See **stylet** (under **style**).

stiletto *sti-let'ō*, *n* a dagger with a narrow blade; a pointed instrument for making eyelets; a stiletto heel: — *pl* **stilett'os**. — *vt* to stab with a stiletto: — *pr p* **stilett'oing**; *pa t* and *pa p* **stilett'oed**. — **stiletto heel** a high, thin heel on a woman's shoe. — *adj* **stilett'o-heeled**. [Ital, dimin of *stilo* a dagger, from L *stilus* a style]

still[1] *stil*, *adj* motionless; inactive; silent; calm; quiet; not sparkling or effervescing; continual, constant (*Shakesp*). — *vt* to quiet; to silence; to appease; to restrain. — *vi* to become still. — *adv* without motion; up to the present time or time in question; as before; yet, even (*usu* with a *compar*); even so, even then; nevertheless, for all that; inactively; quietly; always, constantly (*archaic*). — *n* calm; quiet; an ordinary photograph, or one taken from a cinematographic film and used for publicity, etc purposes. — *n* **still'er** someone who, or something which, stills or quiets, or prevents splashing over. — *n* and *adj* **still'ing**. — *n* **still'ness**. — *adj* **still'y** (*poetic*) still; quiet; calm. — *adv* **stil'ly** (*archaic*) silently; gently. — **still air range** the theoretical ultimate range of an aircraft without wind and with allowances only for take-off, climb to cruising altitude, descent and alighting; **still'birth** the birth of an already dead child (or animal); anything born without life. — *adj* **still'born** dead, or in suspended animation, when born (also *fig*). — **still hunt** or **hunting** (*US*) stalking. — *vt* and *vi* **still'-hunt** (*US*). — **still'-hunter** (*US*) — **still life** the class of pictures representing inanimate objects; a picture of this class: — *pl* **still lifes**. — Also *adj* **still'-life** relating to the representation of inanimate objects. — *adj* **still-peer'ing** (*Shakesp*) *perh* a misprint for **still-piecing** (ie repairing) or **still-piercing**. — **still'-stand** a standstill (*Shakesp*); an armistice (*obs*). — *adj* **still-video** (*photog*) of or pertaining to (an image photographed by) a camera incorporating a disc drive — the image(s) are held on floppy disc and may be transferred direct to a computer. — **still and on** (*Scot*), or **still and all** (*colloq*) nevertheless. [OE *stille*, quiet, calm, stable; Du *stil*, Ger *still*]

still[2] *stil*, *vt* to exude or cause to fall by drops; to distil. — *vi* to fall in drops. — *n* an apparatus for distillation. — *n* **still'er** a distiller. — **still'-head** the head of a still; **still'house** (*US*) a distillery; **still'room** a room, in a large house, where liquors, preserves, etc are kept, and where tea, etc is prepared for the table; a housekeeper's pantry; **still'room-maid**. [Aphetic for **distil**]

stillage *stil'ij*, *n* a frame, stand, or stool for keeping things off the floor; a boxlike container for transporting goods; a cask stand. — *n* **still'ing** or **still'ion** a cask stand. [Prob Du *stellage*, *stelling*, from stellen to place]

stillatory *stil'ə-tər-i*, *n* a still; a distillery. [LL *stillātōrium*, from L *stillāre* to drip, *stilla* a drop]

stillicide *stil'i-sīd*, *n* a drip; eavesdrop; an urban servitude for allowing one's eavesdrop to fall on a neighbour's ground (otherwise forbidden; *Roman law*). [L *stillicidium*, from *stilla* drop, and *cadere* to fall]

stilling, stillion. See under **stillage**.

Still's disease *stilz di-zēz'*, *n* a disease of children causing arthritis leading to ankylosis, possibly a type of rheumatoid arthritis. [First described by Sir G F *Still*, English physician, 1868-1941]

Stillson wrench® *stil'sən rench* or *rensh*, *n* an adjustable wrench whose grip is tightened by pressure on the handle. [D C *Stillson*, 1830–99, US inventor]

stilly. See under **still**[1].

stilpnosiderite *stilp-nō-sid'ər-īt*, *n* limonite. [Gr *stilpnos* shining, and *sidēros* iron]

stilt *stilt*, *n* a thin wooden prop with a foot rest enabling one to walk supported high above the ground; any tall support, eg for keeping a house above water-level; a plough handle (now *dialect*); a very long-legged wading bird (*Himantopus candidus* or other species) related to the avocets (also **stilt'bird** or **plov'er**). — *vt* to raise on stilts or as if on stilts. — *adj* **stilt'ed** stiff and pompous; laboured and unnatural; elevated on stilts; (of an arch) springing from above the capital (*archit*). — *adv* **stilt'edly**. — *n* **stilt'edness**. — *n* **stilt'er**. — *n* **stilt'iness**. — *n* **stilt'ing**. — *adj* **stilt'ish** or **stilt'y**. — **stilt'-walker**. [ME *stilte*; cf Du *stelt*, Ger *Stelze*, Swed *stylta*]

Stilton *stil'tən*, *n* a rich white, often blue-veined, cheese first sold chiefly at *Stilton* in Cambridgeshire.

stime; **stimie, stimy**. Same as **styme**; **stymie**.

stimpmeter *stimp'mē-tər*, (*golf*) *n* in the US, a device for measuring the speed of a putting green.

stimulus *stim'ū-ləs*, *n* a sting or stinging hair (*archaic*); an action, influence, or agency that produces a response in a living organism; anything that rouses to action or increased action: — *pl* **stim'ulī**. — *adj* **stim'ulable** responsive to stimulus. — *n* **stim'ulancy**. — *adj* **stim'ulant** stimulating; increasing or exciting vital action. — *n* anything that stimulates or excites; a stimulating drug; an alcoholic liquor. — *vt* **stim'ulate** to incite; to instigate; to excite; to produce increased action in (*physiol*). — *vi* to act as a stimulant. — *adj* **stim'ulating**. — *n* **stimulā'tion**. — *adj* **stim'ulātive** tending to stimulate. — *n* that which stimulates or excites. — *n* **stim'ulātor** a person who stimulates; an instrument for applying a stimulus. [L *stimulus* a goad]

stimy. See **styme**.

sting[1] *sting*, *n* in some plants and animals a weapon (hair, modified ovipositor, tooth, etc) that pierces and injects poison; the act of inserting a sting; the pain or the wound caused; any sharp, tingling, or irritating pain or its cause (also *fig*); the point of an epigram; the pain inflicted by wounding words, etc; stinging power; pungency; a goad; an incitement; (a substantial sum of money gained through) a deception, theft, etc (*slang*); a trap for criminals set up by the police (*slang*). — *vt* to pierce, wound, pain, or incite with or as if with a sting; to goad or incite (with *into*); to rob, cheat, or involve in expense (*slang*). — *vi* to have or use a power of stinging; to have a stinging feeling: — *pa t* and *pa p* **stung**. — *adj* **stinged** having a sting. — *n* **sting'er** someone who or something that stings; anything stinging or pungent; see also separate entry below. — *n* and *adj* **sting'ing**. — *adv* **sting'ingly**. — *adj* **sting'less**. — *adj* **sting'y** (*colloq*). — **sting'bull** or **sting'fish** the weever; **stinging nettle** a common plant of the genus *Urtica*, with stinging hairs; **sting'-ray** or (*US* and *Austr*) **stingaree** (*sting'gə-rē*, *-ə-rē* or *-rē'*) a ray (*Trygon* or related genus) with a formidable barbed dorsal spine on its tail. — **sting in the tail** an unlooked-for final unpleasantness or irony; **take the sting out of** (*colloq*) to soften the pain of (*lit* and *fig*). [OE *sting* puncture, *stingan* to pierce]

sting[2] *sting*, (*Scot*) *n* a pole. — **sting and ling** with a rope slung from a pole; by force (*fig*). [OE *steng*]

stingaree. See under **sting**[1].

stinger[1] *sting'ər*, *n* same as **stengah**; (*esp US*) a cocktail containing brandy and white crème de menthe. [**stengah**, influenced by **sting**[1]]

stinger[2]. See under **sting**[1].

stingo *sting'gō*, *n* strong malt liquor (*obs slang*); vigour, energy, punch (*colloq*; also *adj*): — *pl* **stin'gos**. [**sting**[1]]

stingy[1] *stin'ji*, *adj* niggardly; bad-tempered (*dialect*). — *adv* **stin'gily**. — *n* **stin'giness**. [Prob **sting**[1]]

stingy[2]. See under **sting**[1].

stink *stingk*, *vi* to give out a strong, offensive smell; to be offensive, have a bad reputation, suggest or imply evil or dishonesty (*fig*). — *vt* to impart a bad smell to (a room, etc; with *out*); to drive by a bad smell (with *out*, etc): — *pa t* **stank** or **stunk**; *pa p* **stunk**. — *n* an offensive smell; an outraged reaction, a furore; (in *pl*) chemistry or science, a science master (*schoolboy slang*). — *n* **stink'ard** someone who stinks, an offensive person (*rare* or *obs*); a name given to various foul-smelling animals, eg the **stinking badger** of Java. — *n* **stink'er** a person or thing that stinks; a disagreeable person or thing (*colloq*); a stinkard; a fulmar or petrel that ejects a foul-smelling oil from its stomach (*sailor's slang*). — *adj* **stink'ing** which stinks (*lit* and *fig*). — *adv* very, extremely, *esp* as in *stinking rich*, *stinking drunk* (*colloq*). — Also (*rare*) *n*. — *adv* **stink'ingly**. — **stink ball** or **stink pot** (*hist*) a ball or jar filled with a stinking, combustible mixture, used to create a suffocating smoke when boarding an enemy's vessel; **stink'bird** see **hoatzin**; **stink bomb** a *usu* small bomblike container which releases foul-smelling gases when exploded; **stink'horn** a stinking gasteromycete fungus, *Phallus impudicus*; **stink'stone** a limestone that gives a fetid urinous smell when rubbed; **stink'wood** the foul-smelling wood of various trees, *esp* the lauraceous *Ocotea bullata* of S Africa. — **like stink** (*colloq*) very much, to a great extent; intensely; **raise a stink** to complain; to cause trouble, *esp* disagreeable publicity; **stink out** (*colloq*) to drive out by a bad smell; to fill (a room, etc) with a bad smell. [OE *stincan* to smell (well or bad)]

stinko *sting'kō*, (*slang*) *adj* drunk.

stint[1] *stint*, *vt* to limit; to check (*archaic*); to restrain (*archaic* or *dialect*); to stop (*obs*); to allot, apportion (*archaic*); to set as a task or as a day's work (*archaic*); to restrict (*obs*); to keep short; to be niggardly with or towards; to allot stingily; to spare; to serve successfully, get with foal, lamb, etc. — *vi* to cease, stop (*obs*); to be sparing, go short (*dialect*). — *n* cessation of action, motion, etc (*obs*); limit (*obs*); restraint, restriction; proportion allotted, fixed amount; allowance; a set task; a (conventional) day's work. — *adj* **stint'ed**. — *adv* **stint'edly**. — *n* **stint'edness**. — *n* **stint'er**. — *n* and *adj* **stint'ing**. — *adv* **stint'ingly**. — *adj* **stint'less**. — *adj* **stint'y**. [OE *styntan* to dull, from *stunt* stupid; cf **stent**[1], **stunt**[1]]

stint[2] *stint*, *n* any small wading bird of the genus *Calidris* (eg the little stint, *Calidris minuta*, and Temminck's stint, *Calidris temminckii*) that *usu* winters in Africa and is a passage migrant in Britain. [Origin obscure]

stinty. See under **stint**[1].

stipa *stī'pə*, *n* any grass of the feather grass genus *Stipa*. [L *stipa* tow]

stipe *stīp*, *n* a stalk, *esp* of the fruiting body of a fungus, a fern-leaf, a pappus, or an ovary. — Also **stipes** (*stī'pēz* or *stē'pes*; *pl* **stipites** *stip'i-tēz* or *stē'pi-tās*). — *adj* **stipitate** (*stip'*). [L *stīpes*, *-itis* post, stock]

stipel *stī'pl*, (*bot*) *n* a stipule-like appendage at the base of a leaflet. — *adj* **stipellate** (*stī'pəl-āt* or *stip-el'āt*) having stipels. [Dimin from **stipule**]

stipend *stī'pənd*, *n* a soldier's pay; a salary, *esp* a Scottish parish minister's (*Scot stēp'ənd*); a periodical allowance. — *adj* **stipendiary** (*sti-pen'di-ə-ri* or *stī-*) receiving a stipend. — *n* a person who performs services for a salary, *esp* a paid magistrate. — *vt* **stipen'diate** to provide with a salary. [L *stīpendium*, from *stips* payment, dole, *pendere* to weigh]

stipes, **stipites**, **stipitate**. See under **stipe**.

stipple *stip'l*, *vt* to engrave, paint, draw, etc, in dots or separate touches. — *n* painting, engraving, etc, in this way; the effect so produced; a brush for stippling. — *adj* **stipp'led**. — *n* **stipp'ler**. — *n* **stipp'ling**. [Du *stippelen*, dimin of *stippen* to dot]

stipulaceous, **stipular**, etc. See under **stipule**.

stipulate *stip'ū-lāt*, *vt* to set or require as a condition of an agreement; to specify, insist on, as an essential part of an agreement (with *for*); to guarantee (*rare*). — *vi* to make stipulations; to become surety (*obs*). — *n* **stipulā'tion** act of stipulating; a contract; a condition of agreement; a requiring of such a condition. — *n* **stip'ulator**. — *adj* **stip'ulatory** (*-lə-tər-i*). [L *stipulārī*, *-ātus*, prob from Old L *stipulus* firm, connected with *stīpāre* to press firm, but thought by some to be from *stipula* straw, from the ancient custom of breaking a straw to seal a bargain]

stipule *stip'ūl*, *n* a paired, *usu* leafy, appendage at a leaf base. — *adj* **stipulā'ceous**. — *adj* **stip'ular** or **stip'ulary**. — *adj* **stip'ulāte** or **stip'uled**. [L *stipula* straw, stalk, dimin of *stīpes*; new meaning assigned by Linnaeus]

stir[1] *stûr* (*Scot* **steer** *stēr*, *Spenser* **stire** or **styre** *stīr*), *vt* to set in motion; to move around; to move (something, *esp* in liquid or powder form) around by continuous or repeated, *usu* circular, movements of a spoon or other implement through it, eg in order to mix its constituents; to disturb; to rouse; to move to activity; to excite; to move, raise, moot (eg a question) (*now rare*). — *vi* to make a movement; to begin to move; to be able to be stirred; to go about; to be active or excited; (*esp* in *pr p*) to be out of bed; to go forth; to cause trouble or dissension (*colloq*): — *pr p* **stirr'ing**; *pa t* and *pa p* **stirred**. — *n* movement; slight movement; activity; commotion; sensation; an act of stirring. — *adj* **stir'less** without stir. — *adj* **stirred**. — *n* **stirr'er** a person who or thing that stirs; a person that stirs up trouble, a troublemaker (*slang*). — *n* and *adj* **stirr'ing**. — *adv* **stirr'ingly**. — **stir'about** (*Anglo-Ir*) porridge; a bustle or commotion; a bustling person. — *adj* busy, active. — *vt* and *vi* **stir'-fry** to fry (food) rapidly while stirring it in the pan. — **stir abroad**, **forth** or **out** (*old-fashioned* or *dialect*) to go out of doors; **stir up** to excite; to incite; to arouse; to mix by stirring. [OE *styrian*; Du *storen*, Ger *stören* to disturb]

stir[2] *stûr*, **stirrah** or **stirra** *stir'ə*, (*Scot*) *n* apparently corruptions of **sir** and **sirrah**, applied to both sexes.

stir[3] *st ur*, (*slang*) *n* prison. — *adj* **stir-crā'zy** (*NAm*) unbalanced from confinement, *esp* in prison. [Perh OE *stēor*, *stȳr* punishment, or various Romany words, eg *stiraben*, *steripen*]

stire *stīr*, an archaic form of **steer**[2] and **stir**[1].

stirk *stûrk*, *n* a yearling or young ox or cow. [OE *stirc* calf]

Stirling engine *stûr'ling en'jin*, *n* a closed-cycle external-combustion engine using heated air (devised by Dr Robert *Stirling*, d 1878), or a more sophisticated 20c version using, eg, helium under pressure.

stirps *stûrps*, *n* (a person and his or her descendents forming) a branch of a family (*esp law*); pedigree; a category in biological classification, eg (*zool*) a superfamily, family or subfamily, or (*bot*) a rootstock that retains characteristics in cultivation: — *pl* **stirpes** (*stûr'pēz* or *stir'pās*). — Also **stirp**: — *pl* **stirps**. — *n* **stirp'iculture** selective breeding. [L *stirps*, *stirpis*]

stirrah, **stirra**. See under **stir**[2].

stirre. See **sperre**.

stirrup *stir'əp*, *n* a support for a rider's foot, *usu* consisting of a metal hoop suspended on a strap from the saddle; a foot-rest, clamp or support of more or less similar shape or function; the stirrup bone; a short rope hanging from a yard on a square-rigged sailing vessel, having a thimble in its lower end for supporting a footrope (*naut*). — **stirrup bone** the stapes; **stirrup cup** a drink taken on horseback on departing, or arriving; a container in the form of a fox's head from which a stirrup cup was drunk (*rare*); **stirrup iron** the metal part of a stirrup, *usu* regarded as the stirrup itself; **stirrup leather** or **strap** the strap of a stirrup; **stirrup pump** a portable water pump held in position by the foot in stirrup-like bracket, for fighting small fires. [OE *stigrāp*, from *stīgan* to mount, and *rāp* rope]

stishie. See **stooshie**.

stitch *stich*, *n* a complete movement of the needle in sewing, knitting, surgery, etc; a loop or portion of thread, etc, so used; a surgical suture; a mode of stitching or knitting; a fastening with thread or wire through all sections (*bookbinding*); the least scrap of clothing, sails, etc; a sharp pricking pain in the side brought on by running, etc; a ridge of land (*dialect*); a shock of corn (*dialect*). — *vt* to join, adorn, or enclose with stitches. — *vi* to sew. — *adj* **stitched**. — *n* **stitch'er**. — *n* **stitch'ery**. — *n* **stitch'ing**. — **stitch'craft** the art of needlework; **stitch'work**; **stitch'wort** any plant of the chickweed genus *Stellaria*, *esp* the greater stitchwort, *Stellaria holostea*, once thought good for easing stitches in the side. — **a stitch in time (saves nine)** a timely repair or corrective measure (avoids the need for more extensive repairs or measures); **drop a stitch** (in knitting) to let a stitch fall off the knitting needle; **in stitches** in pained helplessness with laughter; **stitch up** (*slang*) to incriminate by informing on; to swindle. [OE *stice* prick; cf **stick**[1]]

stithy *stidh'i* or **stiddie** *stid'i*, (*archaic* or *dialect*) *n* an anvil; a smithy. — *vt* to forge on an anvil. [ON *stethi*; Swed *städ* an anvil]

stive *stīv*, (*dialect*) *vt* and *vi* to enclose or be enclosed in a close hot place; to stifle, suffocate. — *adj* **stived** or **stived'-up** without fresh air. — *adj* **stiv'y** stuffy. [Cf **stew**[1]]

stiver *stī'vər*, *n* formerly, a Dutch coin *approx* equivalent in value to a penny; a very small coin or sum; the smallest possible amount. [Du *stuiver*]

stivy. See under **stive**.

stoa *stō'ə*, *n* in ancient Greece, a portico or covered colonnade; *esp* the public ambulatory, *Stoa Poikilē* (the Painted Porch), in Athens where Zeno gave his lectures — *pl* **sto'as**, **sto'ae** or **sto'ai** (-ī). [Gr *stoā*]

stoat *stōt*, *n* a small carnivorous mammal, *Mustela erminea*, of the weasel family distinguishable by its black-tipped tail — in colder northern regions its coat often turns white in winter and it is then called ermine. [ME *stote*]

stob *stob*, (*Scot*) *n* a stake, stump, or stub; an awl. [Variant of **stub**]

stobie pole *stōbi pōl*, (*Austr*) *n* a steel and concrete pole for supporting electricity wires. [Name of design engineer]

stoccado *stok-ä'dō* or **stoccata** *-tə*, *n* a straight thrust in fencing: — *pl* **stocca'dos** or **stocca'tas**. [Ital *stoccata* thrust, stab, from *stocco* rapier, from Ger *Stock* stick]

stochastic *stə-kas'tik*, *adj* conjectural (*obs*); random. [Gr *stochastikos* skilful in aiming]

stocious *stō'shəs*, *adj* a variant spelling of **stotious**.

stock[1] *stok*, *n* a fund; capital of a company, divisible into shares, or a unit of ownership of a company, consisting of a group of shares; supply, store, equipment; raw material, equipment, etc for use or in hand, as in *rolling stock*, *film stock* (unused film) etc; a supply of goods, material or equipment for sale; the animals kept on a farm; shares of a public debt; (in *pl*) public funds; a tally for money paid to the exchequer (*obs*); a repertoire of plays done by a stock company (see below); repute, estimation (*fig*); the undealt part of a pack of cards or set of dominoes; liquor from simmered meat, bones, etc used as a basis for soups, stews, etc; a trunk or main stem; the perennial part of a herbaceous plant; the rooted trunk that receives a graft, rootstock; a log; a post; a block; a stump; an upright beam; the wooden part of a gun; a handle; a part to which others are attached; any cruciferous garden plant of the genus *Matthiola* having heavily-scented spikes of flowers (see also **Virginia stock**); anything fixed and solid; an intrusive boss (*geol*); a stocking (*archaic* or *dialect*); a stiff band worn as a cravat, often fastened with a buckle at the back; (in *pl*) a device for holding a delinquent by the ankles, and often wrists; (in *pl*) a framework on which a ship is built, keel blocks; the horizontal crosspiece of certain old types of anchor set a right angles to the arms; a box or trough; a fireside ledge (*dialect*); the original progenitor; source; race; kindred; family. — *vt* to store or supply with (goods, etc); to keep (goods) in stock for sale; to put in the stocks; to fit (a gun) with a stock; to supply or furnish with stock (eg a river with fish); to keep (a cow) unmilked before selling; to root up (trees, etc); to stunt the growth of (a plant or animal) (*dialect*). — *vi* (of a plant) to send out new shoots; to take in or lay up a stock or supply (*usu* with *up*); (of a plant or animal) to be stunted in growth (*dialect*). — *adj* concerned with stock or stocks; kept in stock; conventionally used, standard; banal, trite; used for breeding purposes; used or intended for livestock. — *n* **stock'er** an animal kept while being fattened or matured for slaughter (*NAm*); a person who stocks or makes stocks. — *n* **stock'ist** a person who keeps a commodity in stock. — *adj* **stock'less**. — **stock agent** (*Austr* and *NZ*) a dealer in livestock; **stock appreciation** (*econ*) business profit from increase in the value of goods held in stock; **stock'-breeder** a person who raises livestock; **stock'breeding**; **stock'broker** a stock exchange member who buys and sells stocks or shares for clients, having been officially superseded in the British Stock Exchange, on 27 October 1986, by the broker/dealer, combining the jobs of stockbroker and stockjobber (**stockbroker belt** the area outside a city, *esp* that to the south of London, in which wealthy businessmen live); **stock'broking**; **stock car** a specially-adapted and strengthened ordinary saloon car used for a type of racing (**stock car racing**) in which cars are often damaged or destroyed in collisions; **stock company** (*NAm*) a joint-stock company; a permanent repertory company attached to a theatre; **stock cube** a cube of compressed meat, fish or vegetable extract used for making stock; **stock dove** a dove (*Columba oenas*), like a small wood-pigeon — so called from its habit of nesting in tree stumps or rabbit burrows, or from the (errroneous) supposition that it represents the ancestor of the domestic breeds; **stock exchange** a building for the buying and selling of stocks and shares; an association of people transacting such business; (with *caps*) the institution in London where such business is done; **stock farm** a farm specializing in the rearing of livestock; **stock-farmer** a farmer who rears livestock; **stock-gill'yflower** an old name for the garden flower, stock; **stock'holder** someone who holds stocks in the public funds, or in a company; a person who owns livestock (*Austr*); **stock'horse** (*Austr*) a horse trained for working with sheep and cattle; **stock'-in-trade** all the goods a shopkeeper has for sale; standard equipment or devices necessary for a particular trade or profession; a person's basic intellectual and emotional resources (often implying inadequacy or triteness); **stock'jobber** a stock exchange member who deals only with other members (in some special group of securities), his job having been abolished in the British Stock Exchange on 27 October 1986, with the introduction of the job of broker/dealer, combining the jobs of stockbroker and stockjobber; a stockbroker (*US*); an unscrupulous speculator; **stock'jobbery**; **stock'jobbing**; **stock'list** a list of stocks and current prices regularly issued; **stock'man** (*esp Austr*) a man in charge of livestock; **stock market** a stock exchange; stock exchange business; **stock'pile** an accumulated reserve supply. — Also *vt*. — **stock'piling** accumulating reserves, eg of raw materials; **stock'pot** a pot in which stock for soup is made and kept; **stock rider** (*Austr*) a herdsman on horseback; **stock'room** a storeroom; a room in a hotel for the display of commercial travellers' wares; **stock route** (*Austr* and *NZ*) a right of way for travelling stock; **stock saddle** a type of saddle with a high pommel and low curved seat, as *orig* used by American cowboys. — *adj* and *adv* **stock-still'** utterly still (as a post or log). — **stock'take** an act of stocktaking. — Also *vi*. — **stock'taking** inventorying and valuation of stock; **stock whip** a herdsman's whip with short handle and long lash; **stock'yard** a large yard with pens, stables, etc, where cattle are kept for slaughter, market, etc. — **in** (or **out of**) **stock** available (or not available) for sale; **on the stocks** in preparation but unfinished; **stockbrokers' Tudor** (*archit*) imitation Tudor; **stocks and stones** inanimate idols; **take stock (of)** to make an inventory of goods on hand; to make an estimate of; **take stock in** to trust to, attach importance to. [OE *stocc* a stick; Ger *Stock*]

stock[2] *stok*, (*Shakesp*) *n* a stoccado. [Ital *stocco* rapier]

stockade *stok-ād'*, *n* a barrier of stakes. — *vt* to surround with a stockade for defence. [Fr *estacade*, from Sp *estacada*; cf **stake**[1]]

stock and horn *stok' ənd hörn*, *n* a primitive Scottish musical instrument made of a cow's horn, a sheep's thigh bone or elder pipe, with stops and a single reed. — Also called **stock in horn** or **stockhorn**. [OE (Northumbrian) *stocc* trumpet]

stockfish *stok'fish*, *n* unsalted dried hake, cod, etc, commonly beaten with a stick before cooking. [Prob Du *stokvisch*]

Stockholm syndrome *stok'hōm sin'drōm*, (*psychol*) *n* a mental condition sometimes experienced by hostages and kidnap victims in which positive feelings develop towards their captors which are difficult to reconcile with normal moral standards, *esp* after their release. [Named after the seige of a bank in Stockholm in 1973 in which bank robbers took hostages]

stockinet or **stockinette** *stok-i-net'*, *n* an elastic knitted fabric for undergarments, etc. [Poss orig *stocking-net*]

stocking *stok'ing, n* a close-fitting covering for the whole leg, *usu* made of fine knitted fabric, worn by women; a close-fitting covering for the foot and lower leg, made from knitted wool or similar fibre, as worn by men in Highland dress; distinctive colouring or feathering of an animal's leg. — *adj* **stock'inged** wearing stockings (but *usu* not shoes). — *n* **stock'inger** (*-ing-ər*) a maker of stockings. — *adj* **stock'ingless**. — **stocking filler** a small present for a Christmas stocking; **stock'ing-foot'** the foot of a stocking; **stocking frame** a knitting machine; **stocking mask** a nylon stocking pulled over the head to distort and so disguise the features; **stocking-sole'**; **stock'ing-stitch** a style of knitting in which a row of plain stitch alternates with a row of purl; **stocking stuffer** (*NAm*) a stocking filler. — **in one's stocking-feet** or **-soles** with stockings or socks but no shoes. [**stock**[1], in archaic sense of *stocking*, perh from comparison of the *stocks* to a pair of leggings]

stockwork *stok'wərk*, (*min ext*) *n* a mass of veins, impregnations, etc of ore that can be worked as one deposit. [Anglicized from Ger *Stockwerk*]

stocky *stok'i, adj* sturdy, thickset. — *adv* **stock'ily**. — *n* **stock'iness**. [**stock**[1], in the sense of a stout piece of wood, and sfx *-y*]

stodge *stoj, vt* to stuff, cram or gorge with food; to sate (*archaic*); to bog (*archaic*). — *vi* (*archaic*) to trudge or plod through mud, etc; to work doggedly (with *at*). — *n* cloggy stuff; heavy, often uninteresting, food. — *n* **stodg'er** a heavy, dull, spiritless, or unenterprising person. — *adv* **stodg'ily**. — *n* **stodg'iness**. — *adj* **stodg'y** heavy and cloggy; solemnly dull. [Perh imit]

stoechiology, stoechiometry, etc. See **stoichiology**.

stoep *stōōp*, (*SAfr*) *n* a platform along the front, and sometimes the sides, of a house, an open porch; a verandah. [Du; cf **step**]

stogy, stogey or **stogie** *stō'gi*, (*US*) *n* a long, inexpensive cigar. [From Cone*stoga*, Pennsylvania]

Stoic *stō'ik, n* a disciple of the philosopher Zeno (d c.261 BC), who taught in the *Stoa Poikilē* (Painted Porch) at Athens; (without *cap*) a stoical person. — *adj* **Stō'ic** or **Stō'ical** pertaining to the Stoics, or to their opinions; (without *cap*) indifferent to pleasure or pain; (without *cap*) uncomplaining in suffering. — *adv* **stō'ically**. — *n* **stō'icalness**. — *n* **stō'icism** (*-sizm*) the philosophy of the Stoics; indifference to pleasure or pain; limitation of wants; austere impassivity; uncomplaining fortitude in suffering. [Gr *Stōikos*, from *stoā* a porch]

stoichiology, stoicheiology or **stoechiology** *stoi-kī-ol'ə-ji, n* the branch of biology that deals with the elements comprising animal tissues. — *adj* **stoichiolog'ical, stoicheiolog'ical** or **stoechiolog'ical**. — *n* **stoichiometry, stoicheiometry** or **stoechiometry** (*stoi-kī-om'i-tri*) the branch of chemistry that deals with the numerical proportions in which substances react. — *adj* **stoichiomet'ric, stoicheiomet'ric** or **stoechiomet'ric**. [Gr *stoicheion* an element]

stoit *stoit*, (*Scot*) *vi* to bounce; to stumble, stagger, lurch. — Also **styte**. — *vi* **stoit'er** (*Scot*) to stagger; to falter in speech. [Perh Du *stuiten* to bounce]

stoke *stōk, vt* to feed with fuel. — *vi* to act as stoker. — *n* **stok'er** a person who or thing which feeds a furnace with fuel. — **stoke'hold** a ship's furnace chamber; a stokehole; **stoke'hole** the area around the mouth of a furnace; the space allotted to the stokers; a hole in a reverberatory furnace for introducing a stirring tool. — **stoke up** to fuel a fire or furnace (also *fig*); to have a good large meal (*colloq*). [Du *stoker* stoker, from *stoken* to stoke]

stokes *stōks, n* the CGS unit of kinematic viscosity. — Also (*esp US*) **stoke**: — *pl* **stokes**. — **Stokes' law** either of two laws in physics: (1) the frequency of luminescence excited by radiation is usually less than the frequency of the radiation which excites it; (2) the force needed to move a sphere through a viscous fluid is directly proportional to the velocity of the sphere, its radius, and the viscosity of the fluid. [Sir G *Stokes* (1819–1903), British physicist]

STOL *stol, n* a system by which aircraft land and take off over a short distance; an aircraft operating by this system. — See also **VTOL** — **STOL'port** an airport for such aircraft. [*s*hort *t*ake-*o*ff and *l*anding]

stole[1] *stōl, pa t* and *obs pa p* of **steal**[1].

stole[2] *stōl, n* a narrow ecclesiastical vestment worn on the shoulders, hanging down in front; a woman's outer garment of similar form; loosely, a gown, a surplice. — *adj* **stoled** (*stōld*) wearing a stole. [OE *stole*, from L *stola* a Roman matron's long robe, from Gr *stolē* equipment, garment, from *stellein* to array]

stolen *stōl'ən, pa p* of **steal**[1]. — Also *adj*. — *adv* (*archaic*) **stol'enwise** by stealth.

stolid *stol'id, adj* impassive; showing little or no interest; unemotional. — *n* **stolid'ity** or **stol'idness**. — *adv* **stol'idly**. [L *stolidus*]

stollen *shtol'ən, n* rich, sweet German bread made with raisins, etc and coated with icing sugar. [Ger, a prop, strut, from the shape of the loaf]

stolon *stō'lən, n* a runner, a shoot from the base of a plant, rooting and budding at the nodes (*bot*); a stemlike structure or budding outgrowth from a colony (*zool*). — *adj* **stōlonif'erous** producing stolons. [L *stolō, -ōnis* twig, sucker]

STOLport. See **STOL**.

stoma *stō'mə, n* a mouthlike opening in some animals (*zool*); a pore by which gases pass through the epidermis of the green parts of a plant (*bot*); the artificial opening of a tube that has been brought to the abdominal surface, as in colostomy (*surg*): — *pl* **stō'mata**. — *adj* **stomal**. — *adj* **stomatal** (*stōm'* or *stom'ə-tl*) or **stomat'ic**. — *n* **stomatī'tis** inflammation of the mucous membrane of the mouth. — *n* **stomatodaeum** (*-dē'əm'*; Gr *hodaios* on the way) in embryology, the invagination that forms the anterior part of the digestive tract. — *adj* **stomatogas'tric** of or pertaining to the mouth and stomach, or the upper alimentary tract. — *n* **stomatol'ogy** study of the mouth. — *n* **stom'atoplasty** plastic surgery of the mouth. — *n* **stom'atopod** a crustacean of the order *Stomatopoda*, the mantis shrimps, with legs mostly near the mouth. — *combining form* **-stomous** denoting a particular kind of mouth. — **stoma therapist** or **stoma-care nurse** (*med*) a nurse specially trained in the care of surgical stomata. [Gr *stoma, -atos* mouth]

stomach *stum'ək, n* the strong muscular bag into which food passes from the gullet, and where some initial digestion takes place; the cavity in any animal for the digestion of its food; (loosely) the belly (also *euphem*); appetite, relish for food, inclination generally; disposition, spirit, courage, pride, spleen. — *vt* to bear or put up with; to digest; to turn the stomach of (*archaic*); to resent (*archaic*); to find offensive (*archaic*). — *adj* of the stomach. — *adj* **stom'achal**. — *adj* **stom'ached**. — *n* **stom'acher** (*-chər* or *-kər*) a covering or ornament for the chest, *esp* one worn under the lacing of a bodice. — *n* **stom'achful** as much as the stomach will hold (*pl* **stom'achfuls**). — *adj* (*archaic*) spirited; haughty; obstinate; resentful; angry. — *n* **stom'achfulness**. — *adj* **stomachic** (*stəm-ak'ik*) of the stomach; promoting digestion. — *n* a stomachic medicine. — *adj* **stomach'ical**. — *adj* **stom'achless**. — *adj* **stom'achous** (*archaic*) resentful; haughty; spirited; courageous. — *adj* **stom'achy** (*archaic* or *dialect*) haughty; easily offended; spirited; paunchy. — **stom'achache**; **stomach pump** a syringe with a flexible tube for withdrawing fluids from the stomach, or injecting them into it. [OFr *estomac*, L *stomachus*, Gr *stomachos* throat, later stomach, from *stoma* a mouth]

stomatal, stomodaeum, etc. See under **stoma**.

stomp *stomp, vi* to stamp the feet; to dance the stomp (*colloq*). — *n* an early jazz composition with heavily accented rhythm; a lively dance with foot stamping (*colloq*); an act of stamping the feet. — *n* **stom'per**. [Variant of **stamp**]

-stomy *-stəm-i, combining form* denoting a surgical operation to form a new opening into an organ, as in *jejunostomy, ileostomy*. [Gr *stoma* a mouth]

stond *stond, n* a Spenserian form of **stand**.

stone *stōn, n* a detached piece of rock, *usu* small; the matter of which rocks consist; a gem; a shaped piece of stone designed for a particular purpose; a mirror (*Shakesp*); a concretion; a diseased state characterized by formation of a concretion in the body; (now *rare slang*) a testicle; a hard fruit kernel; the hard seed of any of several fruits; the colour of stone, *usu* a dull, light brownish-grey; (with *pl usu* **stone**) a standard weight of 14 lb avoirdupois (other stones have been in use, as that of 24 lb for wool, 22 lb for hay, 16 lb for cheese, etc); a tombstone; a hailstone; a printer's table for imposing. — *adj* of stone; of the colour of stone; of stoneware; of the Stone Age; (of an animal) not castrated (*rare*). — *vt* to pelt with stones; to remove stones from (fruit); to lay or wall with stones; to rub or sharpen with a stone; to turn to stone (*Shakesp*). — *vi* to form a stone. — *adj* **stoned** having or containing a stone or stones; with the stone or stones removed; very drunk, or very high on drugs (*slang*). — *adj* **stone'less**. — *adj* **ston'en** or **ston'ern** (*obs* or *dialect*) of stone. — *n* **ston'er** a person who stones; used in combination to denote a person who weighs, or a horse that carries, so many stone. — *adv* **ston'ily**. — *n* **ston'iness**. — *n* **ston'ing**. — *adj* **ston'y** of or like stone; abounding with stones; hard; pitiless; obdurate; rigid; petrifying; stony-broke. — **Stone Age** a stage of culture before the general use of metal, divided into the Old Stone Age (Palaeolithic) and the New (Neolithic). — *adj* **Stone'-Age** or **stone'-age** (often *fig*). — **stone axe** an axe made of stone; a two-edged axe for cutting stone. — *adj* **stone'-blind** completely blind. — **stone bass** a large marine perch (*Polyprion americanus*) of the Atlantic, Mediterranean and Tasman Sea, reputed to frequent wrecked ships (also called **wreck fish**); **stone'boat** (*NAm*) a low sled for carrying rocks or other heavy objects; **stone boiling** a primitive method of boiling water by putting hot stones in it; **stone'borer** or **stone'-eater** any boring mollusc; **stone bramble** a bramble (*Rubus saxatilis*) of rocky places; **stone'brash** a soil of finely-broken rock; **stone'break** another name for saxifrage; **stone'-breaker** a person who or thing that breaks stones; a stone-crushing machine. — *adj* **stone-broke** see **stony-broke** below. — **stone canal** a calcified vertical tube in the water-vascular system of echinoderms; **stone'cast** or **stone's-cast** a stone('s) throw; **stone cell** (*bot*) a cell not much longer than it is broad, with thick lignified walls; **stone'chat** a little black, ruddy and white European songbird (*Saxicola torquata*) of gorse heathland, with a call resembling the sound of two stones being banged together; **stone circle** a circle of prehistoric standing stones; **stone coal** mineral coal, as opposed to charcoal; any hard coal; anthracite. — *adj* **stone-cold'** cold as a stone (**stone-cold sober** completely free of (*esp* alcohol-induced) excitement or passion, utterly sober). — *n* and *adj* **stone'-colour** light brownish-grey. — *adj* **stone'-coloured**. — *adj* **stone-crazy** or **stone-mad** completely crazy or mad. — **stone'crop** any plant of the crassulaceous genus *Sedum*; any similar plant that grows on rocks and walls; **stone curlew** a large ploverlike wading bird (*Burhinus oedicnemus*), that habitually nests on stony ground (also called **thick-knee**); **stone'cutter** a person who hews stone; a machine for dressing stone; **stone'-cutting**. — *adj* **stone'-dead** dead as a stone, completely lifeless. — **stone'-deaf** completely deaf. — **stone dresser** a person who prepares stones for building, a stonemason; **stone falcon** or **stone hawk** the merlin, from its habit of using a stony outcrop as a 'plucking-post'; **stone'fish** any poisonous tropical scorpaenid fish of the family Synanceiidae, which resembles a stone on the seabed; **stone'fly** a plecopterous insect (*Perla*) whose larvae live under stones in streams; **stone fruit** any fruit with a stone, a drupe. — *adj* **stone'ground** (of flour) ground between millstones. — **stone hammer** a hammer for breaking stones; a hammer with a stone head; **stone'hand** (*printing*) an imposer, a person who sets the type in the chase. — *adj* **stone'-hard** (*Shakesp*) as hard as a stone. — **stone'horse** (*rare*) a stallion; **stone-lil'y** a fossil crinoid; **stone loach** a scaleless, bottom-living fish, *Noemacheilus barbatulus*, of European rivers, and sometimes lakes; **stone marten** a white-breasted marten (*Martes foina*) of European woodland (also called **beech marten**); its highly valued fur; **stone'mason** a mason who works with stone; **stone'masonry**; **stone parsley** an umbelliferous plant (*Sison amomum*) similar to parsley, with aromatic seeds; **stone'-pine** a Mediterranean pine (*Pinus pinea*) with umbrella-shaped branches and edible seeds or nuts; **stone pit** a quarry; **stone plover** another name for the stone curlew; **stone'rag** or **stone'raw** (OE *ragu* lichen) a lichen (*Parmelia saxatilis*) yielding a dye; **stone saw** a toothless saw for cutting stone; **stone'shot** a stone's-throw; stones or a stone used as shot; **stone snipe** a N American plover, *Totanus melanoleucus*; **stone's'-throw** the distance a stone may be thrown, hence, a fairly short distance. — *adv* and *adj* **stone'-still** (*Shakesp*) as still as a stone. — *vi* **stonewall'** to hold up progress, (in parliament) by obstructing discussion, (in cricket) by playing extremely defensively. — **stonewall'er**; **stonewall'ing**; **stone'ware** a coarse kind of pottery baked hard and glazed; a high-fired, vitrified, non-porous ceramic material or objects made of it. — *adj* **stone'-washed** (of new clothes) given an old faded appearance using small pieces of pumice. — **stone'work** work in (*usu* dressed) stone; **stone'wort** any plant of the *Characeae* (from the limy crust); stone parsley. — *adj* **stony-broke'** (*slang*) penniless, or nearly so (also **ston'y**, **stone-broke'**). — *adj* **stony-heart'ed** hard-hearted. — **leave no stone unturned** to do everything that can be done in order to secure the effect desired; **mark with a white stone** to mark as particularly fortunate; **stone me!** and **stone the crows!** (*slang*) expressions of astonishment. [OE *stān*; Ger *Stein*, Du *steen*]

stonen, stonern. See under **stone**.

stong. Old form of **stung**.

stonied (*Spenser*). See **stony**[1].

stonker[1] *stong'kər*, (*slang*) *vt* to kill, destroy, overthrow, thwart. — *n* **stonk** (*stongk*; *military slang*; back-formation) intense bombardment. [Ety dubious]

stonker[2] *stong'ker*, (*slang*) *n* an extremely big, impressive, etc one of its kind, a whopper. — *adj* **stonk'ing**. [Presumably **stonker**[1]]

stonn and **stonne**. Old forms of **stun**.

stony[1] *ston'i*, (*obs*) *vt* aphetic for **astony** (see **astonish**; *pa p*, *Spenser*, **ston'ied**).

stony[2]. See under **stone**.

stood *stŏŏd*, *pa t*, *pa p*, **stooden** *-ən*, (*Scot*) *pa p*, of **stand**.

stooge *stōōj*, (*slang*) *n* a performer speaking from the auditorium; an actor who feeds lines to a comedian, etc and is used as the butt of the jokes; a subordinate or drudge; a scapegoat. — Also *vi*. — **stooge around** (*old-fashioned*) to wander about leisurely, purposelessly, or idly. [Origin unknown]

stook *stŏŏk*, *n* a group of sheaves, set up in the field. — *vt* to set up in stooks. — *n* **stook'er**. [Cf LGer *stuke* bundle]

stool *stōōl*, *n* a chair, seat of authority or dignity, throne (*obs*); a seat without a back; a low support for the feet or knees; formerly, a seat used in evacuating the bowels; hence, defecation; (*usu* in *pl*) faeces; a stand; a tree or shrub cut back to ground level and allowed to produce new shoots (*bot*); a stump from which sprouts shoot up; a growth of shoots; the wicket in stoolball; a piece of wood to which a bird is fastened as a decoy in hunting. — *vi* to evacuate the bowels (*archaic*); to put forth shoots; to lure wildfowl with a stool. — *n* **stoolie** see **stool pigeon** below. — **stool'ball** an old game resembling cricket; **stool pigeon** a decoy pigeon; a decoy; a police informer (shortened form **stool'ie**; *slang*). — **fall between two stools** to lose both possibilities by hesitating between them, or trying for both; **stool of repentance** a place, *esp* in Scottish churches, where delinquents, *esp* fornicators, were exposed. [OE *stōl*; Ger *Stuhl*; cf Ger *stellen* to place]

stoop[1] *stōōp*, *vi* to bend the body forward; to lean forward; to submit; to descend from rank or dignity; to condescend; to lower oneself by unworthy behaviour; (of a bird of prey) to swoop down. — *vt* to bend, incline, lower, or direct downward. — *n* a bending of the body; inclination forward; descent; condescension; a swoop. — *adj* **stooped** having a stoop, bent. — *n* **stoop'er**. — *adj* **stoop'ing**. — *adv* **stoop'ingly**. [OE *stūpian*; ON *stūpa*; the vowel preserved by the following *p*]

stoop[2]. See **stoup**[1].

stoop[3] *stōōp*, (*US*) *n* a raised platform, verandah, porch, or set of outside steps leading to the front door of a house. [See **stoep**]

stoop[4] or **stoup** *stōōp*, *n* a post (*dialect*); a prop, supporter, patron (*Scot*); a massive supporting pillar of coal in a mine (*dialect*). — **stoop and roop** or **stoup and roup** (*Scot*) stump and rump, completely. [ON *stolpi* post]

stoope. See **stoup**[1].

stoor[1] or **stour** *stōōr*, **sture** *stûre* or **stowre** *stowr*, (*obs*) *adj* great, formidable; stiff, harsh, austere; stubborn, obstinate, surly. [Partly ME *stūr* harsh (cf MLGer *stûr*), partly OE *stōr*, great]

stoor[2] *stōōr*. See **stour**[2].

stooshie *stōōsh'i*, (*Scot*) *n* fuss, ado, disturbance; frolic. — Also **stash'ie**, **stish'ie** or **stush'ie**. [Poss from aphetic form of **ecstasy**]

stop *stop*, *vt* to cause to cease; to bring to a standstill; to hinder or prevent the passage of; to prevent; to cease from, leave off, discontinue; to obstruct; to snuff, block, plug, choke, close up (often with *up*); to thrust, cram (*obs* except as Scots **stap**); to bring down, hit with a shot; to withhold; to restrain; to limit the vibrating length of, *esp* by pressure of a finger (*music*); to punctuate; to pinch off (the tip of a growing stem) (*hortic*); to adjust the aperture of, with a diaphragm (*photog*); to place a pause in, *esp* at the end of a line or couplet (*prosody*); to make fast by lashing (*naut*). — *vi* to come to a standstill, halt; to cease; to desist; to come to an end; to stay, tarry, sojourn (*colloq*): — *pr p* **stopp'ing**; *pa t* and *pa p* **stopped**. — *n* act of stopping; the state of being stopped; cessation; a halt; a pause or interruption; a halting-place; hindrance; obstacle; a contrivance that limits motion; a card that interrupts the run of play; a diaphragm (*photog* and *optics*); an aperture setting (*photog*); the stopping of an instrument or string; a fret on a guitar, etc; a fingerhole, a key for covering it, or other means of altering pitch or tone; a set of organ pipes of uniform tone quality; a knob operating a lever for bringing them into use; a mechanism on a harpsichord for bringing particular strings into play; a sound requiring complete closure of the breath passage, a mute (*phonetics*; also **stop'-consonant**); a punctuation mark; a stud on a football boot (*Austr*); the angle between the forehead and muzzle in a dog or cat, taken as an indication of proper structure in breeding and showing. — *adj* **stop'less**. — *n* **stopp'age** act of stopping; the state of being stopped; a stopping of work, as for a strike; obstruction; an amount stopped off pay. — *adj* **stopped**. — *n* **stopp'er** a person who stops; that which stops; a plug; a plug (*usu* glass) for a bottle; a short rope for making something fast (*naut*). — *vt* to close or secure with a stopper. — *n* **stopp'ing** the action of one who or that which stops in any sense (**double stopping** simultaneous stopping of and playing on two strings); stuffing or filling material, *esp* for teeth. — **stop-and-search'** a police policy of random searching of people in the streets, to look for concealed weapons, etc *usu* during or just after a period of civil disobedience. — Also *adj*. — **stop'bank** (*NZ*) an embankment to prevent flooding; **stop bath** a substance in which a photographic negative or print is immersed in order to halt the action of the developing solution; **stop'cock** a short pipe opened and stopped by turning a key or handle; loosely, the key or handle; **stop codon** (*biol*) one of several specific codons which signal the end of a protein-coding sequence in DNA or RNA, and which cause termination of protein synthesis; **stop-frame camera** a film camera that can be adjusted to take a reduced number of frames, used in creating the effect of pixillation (qv); **stop'gap** a temporary expedient or substitute. — Also *adj*. — *adj* **stop-go'** (of policy) alternately discouraging and encouraging forward movement. — *n* a stop-go economic policy, etc. — **stop'light** a brake light on a vehicle (*NAm*); a traffic light. — *adj* **stop'-loss** (*stock exchange*) of or relating to an order to a stockbroker to sell shares when their value drops below a certain level, to minimize losses. — **stop'-off** or **stop'off** a stopover; **stop'over** a break in a journey, *esp* a short stay overnight in the course of a journey; **stoppage time** (*sport*) injury time; **stopp'ing-out** selective use (of a protective covering against acids in etching, against light in photography) to create special effects; **stopp'ing-place**; **stopping power** (*phys*) the energy loss resulting from a particle traversing a material; **stop'-press** or **stop press** late news inserted in a newspaper after printing has begun; a space for it. — Also *adj*. — **stop'watch** an accurate watch readily started and stopped, used in timing a race, etc. — **pull out all the stops** to do one's utmost, using all one's energy and efforts; **stop down** (of a camera lens) to reduce the size of the aperture; **stop the show** see under **show**; **stop off**, **stop over**, **stop in** or (*NAm*) **stop by** to break one's journey, pay a visit to (*usu* with *at*); **stop thief** a cry for help to catch a thief. [OE *stoppian* found in the compound *forstoppian* to stop up, from L *stuppa* tow, from Gr *styppē*]

stope[1] *stōp*, *n* a steplike excavation in mining. — *vt* to excavate, or extract in this way. — *n* **stop'ing**. [Perh connected with **step**]

stope[2]. See **stoup**[1].

stopple[1] *stop'l*, (*rare*) *n* a stopper; a plug. — *vt* to stopper, plug. [**stop**]

stopple[2] *stop'l*, *n* a tobacco-pipe stem. — Also (*Scot*) **stap'ple** or **stap'le**. [MDu *stapel* stem]

storable, **storage**. See under **store**.

storax *stō'raks*, *n* the resin of any of the tropical trees or shrubs of the genus *Styrax*, once used in medicine; now that of *Liquidambar orientale* (*liquid storax*). [L *storax*, from Gr *styrax*]

store *stōr* or *stör*, *n* a hoard; a stock laid up for future use; sufficiency or abundance (of eg necessities); keeping; a storehouse, warehouse; a shop; a co-operative shop or one with many departments or branches; an animal being fattened for the market; livestock; value, esteem; a computer memory unit, in which programme and data are stored; (in *pl*) supplies of provisions, ammunition, etc, for an army, ship, etc. — *adj* and *adv* (*archaic* and *dialect*) in abundance. — *adj* of a store; (of animals) bought or kept for fattening, as in *store cattle*, *store lambs*, etc; sold or purchased in a shop. — *vt* to furnish or supply; to lay up, keep in reserve; to deposit in a repository; to give storage to; to put (data) into a computer memory. — *adj* **stor'able**. — *n* **stor'age** placing, accommodation, reservation, or safe-keeping, in store; reservation in the form of potential energy; the keeping of information in a computer memory unit; charge for keeping goods in store. — *n* **stor'er**. — **storage battery** an accumulator; **storage capacity** the maximum amount of information that can be held in a computer store; **storage device** any of several pieces of computer equipment, such as magnetic disks, on which data may be stored; **storage heater** an electric heater with a large thermal capacity that accumulates and stores heat during the off-peak periods and releases it over a longer period; **stored program** (*comput*) a program wholly contained and capable of being altered, in store; **store farm** (*Scot*) a stock farm, a cattle farm; **store farmer**; **store'front** (*NAm*) the façade of a shop or store; **store'house** a house for storing goods of any kind; a repository; a treasury; **store'keeper** a man in charge of stores, eg in a warehouse; a shopkeeper (chiefly *NAm*); **store'keeping**; **store'man** a storekeeper (*NAm*); a person who looks after stores or a storeroom; **store'room** a room in which stores are kept; space for storing; **store ship** a vessel used for carrying naval stores. — *adj* **in-store** within a shop or store. — **in store** in hoard for future use, ready for supply; in reserve, awaiting, imminent; **set** or **lay (great) store by** to value greatly. [OFr *estor*, *estoire*, from L *īnstaurāre* to provide]

storey or *esp NAm* **story** *stō'ri* or *stö'*, *n* all that part of a building on the same floor; a tier: — *pl* **stor'eys** or **storys**. — *adj* **stor'eyed** or **sto'ried** having storeys. — **first**, **second**, etc **storey** the ground, first, etc, floor. [Prob same word orig as **story**[1]]

storge *stör'gē* or *-jē*, *n* natural, *esp* parental, affection. [Gr]

storiated, **storiette**, **storiology**, etc. See under **story**[1].

storied. See under **story**[1] and **storey**.

stork *störk*, *n* any large wading bird of the family *Ciconiidae*, with a sturdy bill and legs, eg the white stork (*Ciconia ciconia*), widely distributed in Europe, Asia and Africa; the bringer of babies (*facetious*). — **stork's'bill** or **stork's bill** any plant of the genus *Erodium* closely related to the geraniums, having elongated beaked fruits and small, *usu* saucer-shaped, pink, yellow or purplish-red flowers. [OE *storc*; Ger *Storch*]

storm *störm*, *n* a violent disturbance of the weather with high winds and *usu* rain, snow, hail and/or thunder and lightning; a tempest; a wind of force 10 on the Beaufort scale reaching speeds of 64 to 72 knots, just short of a hurricane (*meteorol*); any intense meteorological phenomenon; a heavy fall of snow, rain, hail, etc; a violent commotion or outbreak of any kind; a paroxysm; a violent, direct assault (*military*). — *vi* to be stormy; to rage; to rush violently or in attack; to upbraid angrily (often with *at*). — *vt* to take or try to take by assault; to disturb by a storm. — *adj* **storm'ful** stormy. — *adv* **storm'fully**. — *n* **storm'fulness**. — *adv* **storm'ily**. — *n* **storm'iness**. — *n* and *adj* **storm'ing**. — *adj* **storm'less**. — *adj* **storm'y** having many storms; agitated with violent winds; boisterous; violent; passionate. — **storm beach** shingle or sand thrown up by heavy seas beyond the level of normal tides. — *adj* **storm-beat'en** beaten by repeated storms. — **storm belt** an area extending around the earth in which storms are frequent; **stormbird** a petrel. — *adj* **storm'bound** delayed, cut off, confined to port by storms. — **storm cellar** an underground shelter affording protection against hurricanes, etc; **storm centre** the position of lowest pressure in a cyclonic storm; any focus of controversy or strife; **storm cloud**; **storm'-cock** the missel thrush; **storm collar** a high collar on a coat, jacket, etc that may be fastened tightly around the neck; **storm cone** a black canvas cone or cones hoisted, eg at coastguard stations, as a storm signal, the position of the cone or cones signifying the direction of the wind; **storm cuff** an extra elasticated cuff let into the cuff opening of a jacket, etc, to give extra warmth and protection; **storm door** an additional outer door used as protection in stormy weather; **storm drain** a large drain for carrying away large volumes of rainwater; **storm glass** a tube containing a solution supposed to change appearance with the weather; **storm jib** (*naut*) a small, strong sail carried at the front of the mast in very bad weather; **storm lantern** a lantern with flame protected from wind and weather; **storm petrel** or (popularly) **stormy petrel** see under **petrel**. — *adj* **storm'proof** proof against storms or storming. — **storm sail** a storm trysail; **storm shutter** an outside window shutter; **storm signal** a signal hoisted in warning of the approach of a storm. — *adj* **storm'-stayed** hindered from proceeding by storms. — **storm surge** an unusual, rapid rise in tide level caused by a combination of low pressure over the sea and strong onshore winds. — *adj* **storm'-tossed** tossed about by storms; much agitated by conflicting passions. — **storm trooper**. — *n pl* **storm troops** shock troops; a body formed in Germany by Adolf Hitler, disbanded 1934. — **storm trysail** a small strong sail replacing the mainsail in very bad weather; **storm warning**; **storm window** a window raised above the roof, slated above and at the sides; an additional outer casement. — **a storm in a teacup** a great commotion in a narrow sphere, or about a trifle; **go down a storm** (*colloq*) to be received with great enthusiasm; **take by storm** to take by assault; to captivate totally and instantly (*fig*). [OE *storm*; ON *stormr*; from root of **stir**[1].]

stornello *stör-nel'ō*, *n* an Italian folk verse form, *usu* of three lines and often beginning with an invocation of a flower: — *pl* **stornell'i** (*-ē*). [Ital, literally, turning aside]

Storting or **Storthing** *stōr'ting* or *stör'*, *n* the legislative assembly of Norway, comprising the Lagting and Odelsting. [Norw *stor* great, and *ting* (ON *thing*) assembly]

story[1] *stō'ri* or *stö'*, *n* history (*obs*); legend; a narrative of incidents in their sequence; a fictitious narrative; a tale; an anecdote; the plot of a novel or drama; a theme; an account, report, statement, allegation; a news article; a lie, a fib (*colloq*). — *vt* to tell or describe historically, to relate (*rare*); to adorn (a pot, etc) with scenes from history. — *vi* to relate (*rare*). — *adj* **sto'riated** decorated with elaborate ornamental designs (also **historiated**). — *adj* **sto'ried** told or celebrated in a story; having a history; adorned with scenes from history. — *n* **storiette'** or **storyette** a short tale. — *n* **storiol'ogist**. — *n* **storiol'ogy** the scientific study of folk tales. — *n* and *adj* **sto'rying**. — **sto'ryboard** (a board on which is mounted) a series of rough sketches showing the sequence of film images to be used in an advertisement, cinema film, televison programme, etc; **sto'rybook** a book of tales true or fictitious, *esp* one for children. — *adj* unreal, fantastic; rather luckier or happier than in real life. — **sto'ryline** the main plot of a novel, film, television series, etc, or line along which the plot is to develop; **sto'ryteller** a person who relates tales; a liar (*colloq*); **sto'rytelling**. — **end of story** (*colloq*) the matter or discussion is closed; **the same old story** an often-repeated event or situation; **the story goes** it is generally said. [Anglo-Fr *estorie*, from L *historia*]

story[2]. See under **storey**.

stoss *stos*, *n* the side of a hill, crag, or other feature facing upstream or towards the flow of a glacier. — **stoss and lee** a type of glaciated landscape in which only those parts facing the flow of the glacier show erosion. [Ger, from *stossen* to push, thrust]

stot[1] *stot*, (*dialect*) *n* a bullock, steer; a stupid, clumsy person. [OE *stot* horse]

stot[2] *stot*, (*Scot*) *vi* to bound, bounce; to stagger, walk unsteadily; to walk with a springy step. — *vt* to cause to bounce. — *n* a bounce, spring; a sharp blow; rhythm, beat. — *n* **stott'er** a stagger, stumble; a person or thing that is admired, a smasher. [Origin obscure]

stotinka *sto-tingk'ə*, *n* a Bulgarian unit of currency, worth one hundredth of a lev: — *pl* **stotin'ki**. [Bulg]

stotious *stō'shəs*, (*Ir* and *Scot*) *adj* drunk. [Origin uncertain: poss from **stot**[2]]

stotter. See under **stot**[2].

stoun *stōōn*, (*Spenser*) *vt*: — *pa t* and *pa p* **stound**. Same as **stun**.

stound[1] or **stownd** *stownd* or *stōōnd*, (*archaic* and *Scot*) *n* a period of time, moment; a time of trouble; a pang, an ache; an assault, stroke; a shock; a din. — *vi* to shoot like a pang; to ache, throb. [OE *stund*]

stound[2] *stownd* or *stōōnd*, (*Spenser*) *vt* to stun, astound. — *n* a stunned or astounded condition. [**stoun** or **astound**]

stoup[1] or **stoop** *stōōp* (*Shakesp* **stoope** or **stope** *stōp*), *n* a bucket (*obs*); a drinking vessel (*archaic*); a vessel for holy water. [Cf ON *staup* and Du *stoop*; OE *stēap*]

stoup[2]. See **stoop**[4].

stour[1]. See **stoor**[1].

stour[2], **stowre** or **stoor** *stowr* or *stōōr*, *n* battle, assault; tumult; turmoil; dust (*Scot*). — *adj* **stour'y** (*Scot*) dusty. [OFr *estour* tumult]

stoush *stowsh*, (*Austr* and *NZ*) *n* a fight, a brawl; a war. — *vt* and *vi* to fight. [Variant of Scot **stooshie**]

stout *stowt*, *adj* resolute; dauntless; vigorous; enduring; robust; strong; thick; fat; fierce (*obs*); proud, arrogant (*obs*); unyielding (*obs* or *dialect*); stubborn (*obs*). — *adv* stoutly. — *n* strong dark beer flavoured with malt or barley. — *vt* and *vi* **stout'en** to make, or grow, stout or stouter. — *adj* **stout'ish**. — *adv* **stout'ly**. — *n* **stout'ness**. — *adj* **stout-heart'ed**. — *adv* **stout-heart'edly**. — **stout-heart'edness**. [OFr *estout* bold, from Du *stout*; Ger *stolz* proud]

stouth *stōōth*, (*obs Scot*) *n* theft. — *n* **stouth'rie** or **stouth'erie** theft; stolen goods; provision, furniture. — *n* **stouth'rief** (*old Scots law*) theft with violence (later only in a dwelling-house). — **stouth and routh** plenty, abundance (cf **stoop and roop** under **stoop**[4]). [ON *stuldr* theft]

stovaine *stō-vā'in* or *stō'* or *-vān'*, *n* a local anaesthetic, a substitute for cocaine, used for spinal analgesia. [**stove**[1], Eng transl of the name of Prof Furneau, who first prepared it]

stove[1] *stōv*, *n* a closed heating or cooking apparatus; a fire-grate; a kiln or oven for various manufacturing operations; a hot-air bath (*archaic*); a heated room or chamber (*archaic*); a hothouse. — *vt* to put, keep, heat, or dry in a stove; to stew (*Scot*). — *n pl* (*Scot*) **stov'ies** stewed potatoes; a thick stew of potatoes, lard, onions and sausage meat or corned beef; Irish stew. — *n* **stov'ing** drying a specially prepared paint quickly by application of heat. — **stove enamel** a type of heatproof enamel produced by heating an enamelled article in a stove; **stove'pipe** a metal pipe for carrying smoke and gases from a stove; a tall silk hat (*colloq*; in full **stovepipe hat**); **stove plant** a hothouse plant. [OE *stofa*; Ger *Stube*]

stove[2] *stōv*, *pa t* and *pa p* of **stave**. — Also used as *pr t*.

stover *stō'vər*, (*archaic*) *n* fodder. [Aphetic for **estover**]

stovies. See under **stove**[1].

stow[1] *stō*, *vt* to place, put, lodge; to put away; to store; to put under hatches; to put down one's throat (*joc*); to desist from (*stow it* stop it; *slang*); to pack; to have room for; to arrange. — *vi* (with *away*) to hide as a stowaway; to be able to be stowed away when not in use. — *n* **stow'age** act or manner of stowing; the state of being laid up; room for stowing; a place for stowing things; money paid for stowing goods; things stowed. — *n* **stow'er**. — *n* **stow'ing**. — **stow'away** a person who hides in a ship, etc to get a passage. — *adj* travelling as a stowaway; that can be packed up and stored, carried, etc. — **stow'down** the process of stowing down in a ship's hold. [OE *stōw* place]

stow[2] *stōō*, (*Scot*) *vt* to crop. [ON *stūfr* stump]

stown *stown*, a Scots form of **stolen**. — *adv* **stown'lins** or **stow'lins** (*Scot*) by stealth.

stownd. See **stound**[1].

stowre. See **stoor**[1] and **stour**[2].

STP *abbrev*: *Sanctae Theologiae Professor* (*L*), Professor of Theology.

stp *abbrev*: standard temperature and pressure.

str *abbrev*: steamer.

str. *abbrev*: strong.

strabism *strā'bizm* or **strabismus** *strə-biz'məs*, *n* a muscular defect of the eye, preventing parallel vision; a squint. — *adj* **strabis'mal**, **strabis'mic** or **strabis'mical**. — *n* **strabismom'eter** (*strab-iz-*) or **strabom'eter** an instrument for measuring strabismus. — *n* **strabot'omy** (Gr *tomē* a cut) the surgical operation for the cure of squinting. [Gr *strabos* and *strabismos* squinting; cf *strephein* to twist]

stracchino *strä-kē'nō*, *n* a North Italian soft cheese: — *pl* **stracchi'ni** (*-nē*). [Ital, from *stracco* weak]

strack. See **strike**.

strad. See **Stradivarius**.

straddle *strad'l*, *vi* to part the legs wide; to sit, stand, or walk with legs far apart; to seem favourable to both sides, to be noncommittal (*colloq*). — *vt* to bestride; to set (the legs) far apart; to overshoot and then shoot short of, in order to get the range; to cover the area of with bombs; to adopt a noncommittal attitude or position towards. — *n* act of straddling; a noncommittal position; a stock transaction in which the buyer obtains the privilege of either a *put* or a *call*; a vertical timber in a mine supporting a set; the combination of a shot beyond the mark and one short of it; a style of high jump in which the legs straddle the bar while the body is parallel to it. — *adv* astride. — **straddle carrier** a high self-propelled vehicle which can straddle a container and lift, carry, and deposit where required. — *adj* **stradd'le-legged** having the legs wide apart. [Frequentative of **stride**]

stradiot *strad'i-ot*, (*hist*) *n* a Venetian light horseman from Albania or Greece. [Ital *stradiotto*, from Gr *stratiōtēs* soldier]

Stradivarius *strad-i-vä'ri-əs* or *-vā'* or **Stradivari** *-vä'rē*, *n* a stringed instrument, *usu* a violin, made by Antonio *Stradivari* (1644–1737) of Cremona (*colloq* short form **strad**).

strae *strā*, *n* a Scots form of **straw**[1]. — **strae death** natural death in bed.

strafe or **straff** *sträf* or (*esp NAm*) *strāf*, (originally war slang of 1914) *vt* to punish; to bombard; to assail; to rake with machine-gun fire from low-flying aeroplanes. — *n* an attack. [Ger *strafen* to punish, used in the phrase *Gott strafe England* God punish England, a German slogan of World War I]

straggle *strag'l*, *vi* to wander from the main group or course; to linger behind; to be absent without leave but not long enough to be counted a deserter; to stretch dispersedly or sprawlingly; to grow irregularly and untidily. — *n* a straggling line or group; a person who straggles, a straggler; a stray; a vagrant. — *n* **stragg'ler**. — *n* **stragg'ling** (*phys*) variation of energy or range of particles in a beam passed through absorbing material, resulting from random interactions. — Also *adj*. — *adv* **stragg'lingly**. — *adj* **stragg'ly** straggling; irregularly spread out. [Origin obscure]

straicht. See **straucht**.

straight[1] *strāt*, *adj* uncurved; in a right line; direct; upright; flat, horizontal; in good order; accurate; frank and honourable; respectably conducted; balanced, even, square; settled; downright; normal; with all debts and favours repaid, even; conventional in tastes, opinions, etc (*slang*); heterosexual (*slang*); in sequence (*poker*); (of games, sets won) in succession (*tennis*); (of a theatrical part) not comic; (of a drink, *esp* alcohol) undiluted, neat; uninterrupted; consistent; not under the influence of, or not in the habit of taking, drugs (*slang*). — *n* a straight condition; good behaviour; a straight line, part, course, flight, *esp* the last part of a racecourse; a sequence of five cards, irrespective of suit, or the hand containing it (*poker*); a heterosexual person (*slang*). — *adv* in a straight line; directly; all the way; immediately; upright; outspokenly; honestly. — *vt* and *vi* **straight'en** to make or become straight. — *n* **straight'ener** something that straightens; a bribe (*criminal slang*). — *adv* **straight'-forth** directly forward; straight away, immediately. — *adj* **straight'ish**. — *adv* **straight'ly** in a straight line or manner; directly. — *n* **straight'ness**. — *adv* **straight'way** (*archaic*) directly; immediately; without loss of time. — Also **straight'ways**. — **straight angle** a right angle (*obs*); two right angles. — *adj* **straight'-arm** (of a Rugby tackle) with the arm extended straight, illegally. — *adj* **straight'away** straight forward. — *adj* **straight'=cut** (of tobacco) cut lengthwise of the leaf; cut in a straight line. — **straight'edge** a strip or stick for testing straightness or drawing straight lines; **straight fight** (*esp* in politics) a contest in which only two individuals or sides take part. — *adj* **straightfor'ward** going forward in a straight course; without digression; without evasion; easy to understand, not complex; honest; frank. — *adv* straightforwardly. — *adv* **straightfor'wardly**. — **straightfor'wardness**. — **straight man** an actor who acts as stooge to a comedian. — *adj* **straight'-out** (*NAm*, *esp* in party politics) out-and-out; see also **straight out** below. — *adj* **straight'-pight** (*Shakesp*) straight, erect. — **straight play** a play without music; a serious drama as opposed to a comedy; **straight talk** a candid outspoken talk; **straight talking**; **straight ticket** see under **ticket**; **straight tip** a racing tip that comes straight from the owner or trainer; inside information that can be relied on. — **go straight** to give up criminal activities; **keep a straight bat** (*fig*) to behave honourably; **keep a straight face** to refrain from smiling; **straight away** immediately; **straighten out** to disentangle, resolve; **straight from the shoulder** frankly, without equivocation (also *adj* **straight-from-the-shoulder**); **straight off** straight away, without hesitation (*colloq*); **straight out** frankly, directly; **straight up** honestly, really (*colloq*; often *interrog*); **the straight and narrow** the virtuous or law-abiding way of life. [OE *streht*, pa p of *streccan*; see **stretch**]

straight[2]. See **straucht**.

straight[3]. See **strait**.

straik[1] *strāk*, *n* and *v* a Scots form of **stroke**[1,2]. — *n* (*Scott*) proportion of malt in brewing.

straik[2]. See **strake**[2].

strain[1] *strān*, *vt* to stretch; to draw tight; to draw with force; to exert to the utmost; to injure by overworking; to force unnaturally, unduly, or wrongly; to exalt emotionally; to change in form or bulk by subjecting to a stress; to constrain (*obs*); to urge, insist upon, press for (*Shakesp*); to press to oneself, embrace; to squeeze, press; to grip, grasp tightly; to compress; to restrain; to squeeze out, express; to sing or play; to filter or sieve (*esp* coarsely). — *vi* to make violent efforts; to tug; to retch; to have difficulty in swallowing or accepting (with *at*); to make efforts at evacuation of the bowels; to be percolated or filtered. — *n* the act of straining; a violent effort; an injury by straining, *esp* a wrenching of the muscles; any change of form or bulk under stress; pitch, height; a section of a melody; a melody; an outpouring or flow of language; emotional tone, key, manner. — *adj* **strained** having been strained; tense, forced or unnatural. — *adv* **strain'edly** (or *strānd'li*). — *n* **strain'er** someone who or something that strains; a sieve, colander, etc. — *n* and *adj* **strain'ing**. — **strain gauge** a device for measuring strain (deformation) in a machine or structure; **strain hardening** a process by which metal is deformed in order to increase its hardness; **straining sill** (*building*) a piece of timber lying on the tie-beam of a timber roof and butting against the bottoms of the queen posts; **strain viewer** (*phys*) an eyepiece or projector of a polariscope. — **strain a point** to waive a doubt or principle. [OFr *estraindre*, from L *stringere* to stretch tight]

strain[2] *strān*, *n* offspring (*archaic*); breed, race, stock, line of descent; natural, *esp* inherited, tendency or element in one's character; a variety of bacterium or other organism; kind, type (*archaic*). [Appar OE (*ge*)*strēon* gain, getting, begetting (see **strene**), with altered vowel by confusion with **strain**[1]]

straint *strānt*, (*Spenser*) *n* pressure. [**strain**[1], on the model of **constraint**, etc]

strait *strāt*, *n* a narrow part, place, or passage, *esp* (often in *pl*) by water; (*usu* in *pl*) difficulty, distress, hardship. — *adj* (*obs* or *rare*) close; narrow; strict; rigorous; hard-pressed, needy; sparing in giving; tight (*Shakesp*). — *adv* (*obs* or *rare*) tightly; closely; narrowly; strictly; rigorously; with hardship. — *vt* (*obs* or *rare*) to tighten; to narrow; to put in a difficulty; to reduce to hardship. — *vt* **strait'en** to distress; to put into difficulties; to run short; to narrow (*archaic*); to confine (*archaic*); to tighten (*obs*). — *vi* (*archaic*) to narrow. — *adj* **strait'ened**. — *adv* **strait'ly** (*obs* or *archaic*) tightly; narrowly; closely; strictly. — *n* **strait'ness** (*rare*). — **strait'jacket** a garment for restraining a person with violent tendencies, consisting of a padded jacket with arms crossing in front and tying behind; anything which inhibits freedom of movement or initiative (*fig*). — *adj* **strait-laced'** narrow in principles of behaviour; prudish. [OFr *estreit* (Fr *étroit*), from L *strictus*, pa p of *stringere* to draw tight]

strak. See **strike**.

strake[1] *strāk*, *obs pa t* of **strike**.

strake[2] or **straik** *strāk*, *n* a stripe (*archaic*); a strip; a line of planking or plating in a ship, running the length of the hull; a section of a cartwheel rim; a trough for washing ore. [Related to **stretch**, coalescing with **streak**[1]]

stramaç. See **stramazon**.

stramash *strə-mash'*, (*Scot*) *n* a tumult, disturbance; a broil; wreck. — *vt* to wreck, smash. [Perh an elaboration of **smash**]

stramazon or **stramaç** *stram'ə-zon* or *-son*, (*obs*) *n* a downward cut in fencing. [Ital *stramazzone*, and Fr *estramaçon*]

stramineous *strə-min'i-əs*, *adj* strawy; light, worthless; straw-coloured. [L *strāmineus*, from *strāmen* straw]

strammel *stram'l*. See **strummel**.

stramonium *strə-mō'ni-əm*, *n* the thorn apple; a drug similar to belladonna obtained from its seeds and leaves and used to treat asthma and nervous disorders. [New L, poss from a Tatar word]

stramp *stramp*, (*Scot*) *vt* and *vi* to tread, stamp, or trample. — *n* a stamp of the foot.

strand[1] *strand*, *n* a shore or beach (*poetic*); a landing-place (*archaic*). — *vt* and *vi* to run aground. — *adj* **strand'ed** driven on shore; left helpless without further resource. — **strandflat** in Norway, a gently sloping coastal platform extending seaward; **strandwolf** the brown hyena (*Hyaena brunnea*), that scavenges along the shores in S Africa. [OE *strand*; Ger *Strand*, ON *strönd* border]

strand[2] *strand*, *n* a yarn, thread, fibre, or wire twisted or plaited with others to form a rope, cord, or the like; a thread, filament; a tress. — *vt* to break a strand of (*archaic*); to insert a strand in (*archaic*); to form of strands. — *adj* **strand'ed** (of a fur garment) made by resewing skins after they have been cut diagonally into strips; (of a rope) having one of its strands broken. [Origin obscure]

strand[3] *strand*, (*Scot*) *n* a rivulet; a gutter. [Origin obscure]

strange *strānj*, *adj* foreign (*Shakesp*); alien; from elsewhere; not of one's own place, family, or circle; not one's own; not formerly known or experienced; unfamiliar (often with *to*); interestingly unusual; odd; surprising; not easy to explain; (of an elementary particle) exhibiting strangeness; estranged; like a stranger; distant or reserved; unacquainted, unversed (often with *to*); crazy, silly, stupid (*Austr colloq*); exceedingly great, exceptional (*obs*). — *adv* **strange'ly**. — *n* **strange'ness** the quality of being strange; a property of certain elementary particles, conserved in strong but not in weak interactions and represented by a quantum number (**strangeness number**) equal to the particle's hypercharge number minus its baryon number (*phys*). — *n* **strān'ger** a foreigner; a person whose home is elsewhere; a person unknown or little known; a person who is outside one's familiar circle or kindred; a visitor; a new-born child (*humorous*); a non-member; an outsider; a person not concerned; a person without knowledge, experience, or familiarity (with *to*). — *vt* (*Shakesp*) to make a stranger. — **strange matter** (*phys*) a hypothetical form of matter composed of up, down and strange quarks; **strangeness number** see **strangeness**; **strange quark** (*phys*) one of six categories of quark, having a charge of -1/3, spin of 1/2 and mass of 195; **strange particles** kaons and hyperons, which have a non-zero strangeness (qv) number; **strangers' gallery** a public gallery, *esp* in the House of Commons. — **make it strange** (*Shakesp*) to make difficulties, show reluctance. [OFr *estrange* (Fr *étrange*), from L *extrāneus*, from *extrā* beyond]

strangle *strang'gl*, *vt* to kill by compressing the throat, to throttle; to choke; to kill (*obs*); to constrict; to choke back, suppress, stifle; to impede or prevent the development of. — *n* (*rare*) **strang'lement**. — *n* **strang'ler**. — *n pl* **strang'les** a contagious bacterial disease of horses caused by infection with streptococci (also called *equine distemper*). — **strang'lehold** a choking hold in wrestling; complete power over a person or situation that prevents any freedom of action; **strang'le-weed** a name applied to various parasitic plants, eg dodder, broomrape, that have a strangling effect on crop plants. [OFr *estrangler* (Fr *étrangler*), from L *strangulāre*; see **strangulate**]

strangulate *strang'gū-lāt*, *vt* to strangle; to compress (eg a vein) so as to suppress or suspend circulation or other function. — *adj* **strang'ulated** strangled; constricted, much narrowed. — *n* **strangulā'tion**. [L *strangulāre*, *-ātum*, from Gr *strangalaein* to strangle, *strangos* twisted]

strangury *strang'gū-ri*, (*med*) *n* severe pain in the urethra with intense desire to pass urine or painful passage of a few drops of urine. [L *strangūria*, from Gr *strangouriā*, from *stranx* a drop, trickle, and *ouron* urine]

strap *strap*, *n* a narrow strip, *usu* of leather or similar material; a thong; a strop (*obs* or *dialect*); a metal band or plate for holding things in position; a narrow flat projection, as on a strap-hinge; a looped band; a string or long cluster; anything strap-shaped; an application of the strap or tawse in punishment; a barber (*slang*, after Hugh *Strap* in Smollett's *Roderick Random*); a term of abuse to a woman (*Anglo-Ir*); credit, *esp* for liquor (*old slang*). — *vt* to beat or bind with a strap; to strop; to hang (*Scot*); to make suffer from scarcity, *esp* of money; to allow credit for (goods) (*old slang* or *dialect*). — *vi* to work vigorously; to suffer strapping, or be capable of being strapped: — *pr p* **strapp'ing**; *pa t* and *pa p* **strapped**. — *adj* **strap'less** without a strap or straps, *esp* (of woman's dress) without shoulder-straps. — *n* **strapp'er** a person who works with straps, *esp* a groom; an energetic worker; a tall robust person (*colloq*); a whopping lie. — *n* **strapp'ing** fastening with a strap; materials for straps; strengthening bands; a thrashing. — *adj* tall and robust. — *adj* **strapp'y** having (many) straps (used *esp* of clothing and footwear). — **strap'-game** the game of fast-and-loose. — *vi* **strap'-hang**. — **strap'-hanger** a standing passenger in a train, bus, etc, who holds on to a strap for safety; **strap hinge** a hinge fastened by a long leaf or flap; **strap'line** (*publishing*) a subsidiary headline in a newspaper or magazine, *esp* one beneath the title; **strap'-oil** (*old slang*) a thrashing. — *adj* **strap'-shaped**. — **strap work** (*archit*) ornamentation of crossed and interlaced fillets; **strap'wort** a seaside caryophyllaceous plant (*Corrigiola littoralis*) of SW England, etc, with strap-shaped leaves. — **strapped for** (*slang*) short of (*esp* cash). [Northern form of **strop**]

strapontin *stra-pɔ̃-tɛ̃*, (*Fr*) *n* a folding seat, as in a taxi, theatre, etc.

strappado *strap-ā'dō* or *-ä'dō*, *n* a form of torture in which the victim was hoisted on a rope tied around the wrists and then allowed to drop with a sudden jerk to the length of the rope: — *pl* **strappa'dos**. — *vt* to torture or punish by the strappado. [Sham Spanish, from Ital *strappata*, from *strappare* to pull]

strapper, etc. See under **strap**.

strass *stras*, *n* paste for making false gems. [Josef *Strasser*, its inventor]

strata *strā'tə* or *strä'*, *pl* of **stratum**.

stratagem *strat'ə-jəm*, *n* a plan for deceiving an enemy or gaining an advantage; any artifice generally. [Fr *stratagème*, from L, from Gr *stratēgēma* a piece of generalship, trick; see **strategy**]

strategy *strat'i-ji*, *n* generalship, or the art of conducting a campaign and manoeuvring an army; any long-term plan; artifice or finesse generally. — *adj* **strategic** (*strət-ēj'ik*) or **strate'gical** pertaining to, dictated by, of value for, strategy. — *adv* **strateg'ically**. — *n sing* **stratē'gics** (*esp* military) strategy. — *n* **strat'egist** a person skilled in strategy. — **Strategic Defence Initiative** a strategic defence system proposed by the US involving laser-equipped satellites deployed in space for destroying enemy missiles (*abbrev* **SDI**; also called **Star Wars**); **strategic materials** and **strategic metals** materials or metals used for military purposes or necessary for carrying on a war; **strategic position** a position that gives its holder a decisive advantage. [Gr *stratēgia*, from *stratēgos* a general, from *stratos* an army, and *agein* to lead]

strath *strath*, *n* in the Highlands of Scotland, a broad valley. [Gaelic *srath* a valley, from L *strāta* a street]

strathspey *strəth-spā'*, *n* a Scottish dance, similar to and danced alternately with the reel; a tune for it, differing from the reel in being slower, and abounding in the jerky motion of dotted notes and semiquavers. [*Strathspey*, the valley of the *Spey*]

stratify, etc. See under **stratum**.

stratocracy *strat-* or *strət-ok'rə-si*, *n* military rule or despotism. — *n* **stratocrat** (*strat'ō-krat*). — *adj* **stratocrat'ic**. — *adj* **stratonic** (*-on'ik*) of an army. [Gr *stratos* an army]

stratum *strā'təm* or *strä'*, *n* a layer; a bed of sedimentary rock; a layer of cells in living tissue; a region determined by height or depth; a level of society: — *pl* **stra'ta**. — *adj* **strati'culate** (of rocks) composed of thin parallel strata. — *n* **stratificā'tion** (*strat-*). — *adj* **stratifica'tional**. — *adj* **strat'ified**. — *adj* **strat'iform** layered; forming a layer. — *vt* **strat'ify** to deposit, form or arrange in layers; to classify according to a graded scale (*science* and *social science*). — *vi* to form, settle, compose into levels or layers: — *pr p* **strat'ifying**; *pa t* and *pa p* **strat'ified**. — *n* **stratig'rapher** or **stratig'raphist**. — *adj* **stratigraph'ic** or **stratigaph'ical**. — *adv* **stratigraph'ically**. — *n* **stratig'raphy** the geological study of strata and their succession; stratigraphical features. — *adj* **stra'tose** in layers. — *n* **stratosphere** (*strat'* or *strāt'ō-sfēr*) a region of the atmosphere beginning about $4\frac{1}{2}$ to 10 miles up, in which temperature does not fall as altitude increases. — *adj* **stratospheric** (*-sfer'ik*) of or in the stratosphere; (of prices, etc) extremely high (*informal*). — *adj* **stra'tous** of stratus. — *n* **stra'tus** a wide-extended horizontal sheet of low cloud. — **stratificational grammar** (*linguistics*) a model that views language as a system of related layers of structure; **stra'to-cū'mulus** a cloud in large globular or rolled masses, not rain-bringing; **stra'topause** the transitional layer between the stratosphere and the mesosphere; **strat'otanker** a type of aeroplane which refuels other planes at high altitudes. [L *strātum*, *-ī*, *strātus*, *-ūs* something spread or laid down, from *strātum* neuter pa p of *sternere* to spread out, lay down]

straucht or **straught** *ströhht*, (*Scot*) *vt* a form of **stretch**; *esp* in the sense to lay out (a corpse). — *adj* and *adv* a form of **straight**[1]. — Also (*adj*, *adv*) **straicht** or **straight** (*strehht*).

straunge *strönj*, (*archaic*) *adj*. Same as **strange**, in the sense foreign, borrowed.

stravaig *strə-vāg'*, (*Scot*) *vi* to wander about idly. — *n* **stravaig'er**. [Cf **stray** and **extravagant**]

straw[1] *strö*, *n* the stalk of corn; dried stalks, etc, of corn, or of peas or buckwheat, etc used as fodder, bedding, packing, for making hats, etc; a narrow tube for sucking up a beverage; a straw hat (*old-fashioned*); a trifle, a whit. — *adj* of straw; of the colour of straw. — *adj* **straw'en** (*archaic*) of straw. — *adj* **straw'like**. — *adj* **straw'y** of or like straw. — **straw'board** a thick cardboard, made of straw; **straw boss** (*US*) an assistant, temporary, or unofficial foreman; **straw'-breadth** the breadth of a straw. — *n* and *adj* **straw'-colour** delicate brownish-yellow. — *adj* **straw'-coloured**. — **straw'-flower** or **straw flower** any Australian composite flowering plant of the genus *Helichrysum*, *esp* *Helichrysum bracteatum* (or *macranthum*) with everlasting flowers in a wide variety of colours. — *adj* **straw'-hat** (*US*) of or pertaining to summer theatre. — **straw man** a man of straw (see under **man**[1]); **straw poll** an unofficial vote taken to get some idea of the general trend of opinion; **straw'-stem** the fine stem of a wine glass pulled out from the material of the bowl, instead of being attached separately; a wine glass having such a stem; **straw wine** a sweet wine obtained from grapes dried on straw; **straw'worm** another name for a caddis fly larva. — **catch, clutch** or **grasp at straws** or **at a straw** to resort to an inadequate remedy in desperation; **last straw** see under **last**[4]; **man of straw** see under **man**[1]; **straw in the wind** a sign of possible future developments. [OE *strēaw*; Ger *Stroh*; cf **strae, strew**]

straw[2] *strö*, *vt* an archaic form of **strew**: — *pa t* **strawed**; *pa p* **strawed** or **strawn**.

strawberry *strö'bə-ri* or *strö'bri*, *n* the fruit (botanically the enlarged receptacle) of any species of the rosaceous genus *Fragaria*, related to *Potentilla*; the plant bearing it. — *adj* of the colour (pinkish-red) or flavour of strawberries. — *n* and *adj* **strawberry blonde** (a woman with hair that is) reddish-yellow. — **strawberry cactus** a clump-forming cactus, *Mammillaria prolifera*, with pale yellow flowers and red strawberry-flavoured berries; **strawberry leaf** the leaf of the strawberry plant; symbolically (*esp* in *pl*) the rank of duke or duchess, from the ornaments like strawberry leaves on a duke's (also a marquess's or earl's) coronet; **strawberry mark** a reddish birthmark; **strawberry roan** a horse with a reddish brown coat flecked with white; **strawberry tomato** the Cape gooseberry; **strawberry tree** *Arbutus unedo*, a small tree of the heath family, with red berries. — **barren strawberry** a Potentilla distinguished from the wild strawberry by its dry fruit. [OE *strēawberige*, possibly from the chaffy appearance of the achenes]

strawen, strawy. See under **straw**[1].

stray *strā*, *vi* to wander; to wander away, *esp* from control, or from the right way; to digress; to get lost. — *vt* (*Shakesp*) to set astray. — *n* a domestic animal that has strayed or is lost; a straggler; a waif; anything occurring casually, isolatedly, or out of place; a body of strays (*archaic*); a common; (in *pl*) atmospherics; a straying (*Shakesp*). — *adj* gone astray; casual; isolated. — *adj* **strayed** wandering, gone astray. — *n* **stray'er**. — *n* and *adj* **stray'ing**. — *n* **stray'ling** a stray. — **stray field** (*elec eng*) a magnetic field set up around electric machines or current-carrying conductors that has no use and may interfere with the operation of measuring instruments, etc; **stray radiation** (*phys*) direct and secondary radiation from irradiated objects that has no use. [OFr *estraier* to wander, from L *extrā* beyond, and *vagārī* to wander]

streak *strēk*, *n* an irregular stripe; the colour of a mineral in powder, seen in a scratch; a scratch; a strain, vein, interfused or pervading character; a line of bacteria, etc (placed) on a culture medium; the line or course as of a flash of lightning; a rush, swift dash; a dash made by a naked person through a public place (*colloq*); a course or succession, as of luck. — *vt* to mark with streaks. — *vi* to become streaked; to rush past; to run naked, or in a state of indecent undress, in public (*colloq*). — *adj* **streaked** streaky, striped. — *n* **streak'er** a person or thing that streaks; a person who runs naked through a public place (*colloq*). — *adv* **streak'ily**. — *n* **streak'iness**. — *n* **streak'ing**. — *adj* **streak'y** marked with streaks, striped; fat and lean in alternate layers; uneven in quality. — **like a streak** like (a flash of) lightning. [OE *strica* a stroke, line, mark; Ger *Strich*; cf **strike**]

stream *strēm*, *n* a small body of running water; a river or brook, *esp* a rivulet; a flow or moving succession of anything; a large number or quantity coming continuously; a division of pupils on the roll of a school consisting of those of roughly equal ability or similar bent, or those following a particular course of study; any similar division of people; a current; a drift; a tendency. — *vi* to flow, issue, or stretch, in a stream; to pour out abundantly; to float out, trail; to wash earth, etc in search of ore. — *vt* to discharge in a stream; to wave, fly; to wash (earth, etc) for ore; to divide (pupils, etc) into streams. — *n* **stream'er** a flag, ribbon, plume, or the like streaming or flowing in the wind; a luminous beam or band of light, as of the aurora; one who washes detritus for gold or tin; a large bold headline (*journalism*); a narrow roll of coloured paper that streams out when thrown. — *adj* **stream'ered**. — *n* **stream'iness**. — *n* and *adj* **stream'ing**. — *adv* **stream'ingly**. — *adj* **stream'less** not watered by streams; waterless; without a current. — *n* **stream'let** or **stream'ling** a little stream. — *adj* **stream'y** abounding in streams; flowing in a stream. — **stream anchor** a small anchor used in warping or for stemming an easy current; **stream'-gold** placer-gold; **stream'-ice** pieces of drift ice swept down in a current; **stream'line** a line followed by a streaming fluid; the natural course of air streams. — *vt* to make streamlined. — *adj* **stream'lined** having boundaries following streamlines so as to offer minimum resistance; a term of commendation with a variety of meanings, such as efficient, without waste of effort, up-to-the-minute, of superior type, graceful (*colloq*). — **stream'-tin** tin-ore found in alluvial ground. — **on stream** see **on-stream** under **on**; **stream of consciousness** the continuous succession of thoughts, emotions, and feelings, both vague and well-defined, that forms an individual's conscious experience, often used to describe a narrative style which imitates this, as in James Joyce's *Ulysses*. [OE *strēam*; Ger *Strom*, ON *straumr*]

streek *strēk*, *vt* and *vi* a Northern form of **stretch**, not confined to Northern use; *esp* (*vt Scot*) in the sense to lay out for burial.

streel *strēl*, (*Ir*) *vi* to trail; to stream; to wander. [Cf Irish *straoillim* to trail]

street *strēt*, *n* a paved road; a road lined with houses, broader than a lane, including or excluding the houses and the footways; those who live in a street or are on the street; (with *cap*) used in street names; a passage or gap through or among anything. — *adj* of or characteristic of the streets, *esp* in densely populated cities, or of the people who frequent them, *esp* the poor, the homeless, prostitutes, petty criminals, etc (also in compounds). — *n* **street'age** (*US*) a toll for street facilities. — *adj* **street'ed** having streets. — *n* **street'ful**: — *pl* **street'fuls**. — *adv* and *adj* **street'ward** (*-wərd*) towards or facing the street. — *adv* **street'wards**. — *adj* **street'y** savouring or characteristic of the streets. — **street arab** see **Arab**; **street'boy** a boy who lives mainly on the street; **street'car** (*NAm*) a tramcar; **street credibility** (often abbreviated as **street cred**) trust, believability, popularity, support or trust from the man in the street; convincing knowledge of popular fashions, modes of speech, etc. — *adj* **street-cred'ible** (*colloq* short form **street-cred'**). — **street cries** the slogans of hawkers; **street door** the door of a house that opens on to the street; **street furniture** the various accessorial public items sited in the street, eg litter bins, parking meters, road signs; **street hockey** (*orig US*) a type of hockey played on roller skates, *orig* in the street; **street'keeper** an official formerly employed to keep order in a street or streets; **street'lamp** or **street'light** one set high on a lamppost to light a street. — *adj* **street'-level** at ground level; in or pertaining to the urban street environment, *esp* street-trading; pertaining to the general population. — Also *n*. — **street name** a common or slang name for an illegal drug. — *adj* **street'-raking** (*Scott*) ranging the streets. — **street'-room** space enough in the street; **street'scape** a scene or view of a street; the specific characteristics of, or improvements made to, a street. — *adj* **street'smart** (*NAm*) streetwise. — **street smarts** (*NAm slang*) the quality of being streetsmart; **street sweeper** a person who or machine that sweeps the streets clean; **street theatre** dramatic entertainments performed in the street; **street value** the cash value of an item when sold directly to the customer in the street, *esp* illegally or on the black market; **street'walker** any one who walks in the streets, *esp* a prostitute who solicits in the street. — *n* and *adj* **street'walking**. — *adj* **street'wise** familiar with the ways, needs, etc of the people who live and work on the city streets, eg the poor, the homeless, the petty criminals, etc; experienced in, and able to cope with, the harsher realities of city life; cynical; wily. — **not in the same street as** much inferior to; **on the street** (*slang*) homeless, destitute; **on the streets** (*slang*) practising prostitution; **streets ahead of** far superior to; **streets apart** very different; **up one's street** (*fig*) in the region in which one's tastes, knowledge or abilities lie. [OE *strǣt* (Du *straat*, Ger *Strasse*, Ital *strada*), from L *strāta* (*via*) a paved (way), fem form of *strātus*, pa p of *sternere* to spread out]

Strega® *strā'gə*, *n* a sweet, orange-flavoured Italian liqueur.

streight *strīt*. An archaic form of **strait** and **straight**[1].

streigne. An old spelling of **strain**[1].

strelitz *strel'its*, *n* a soldier of the Muscovite guards, abolished by Peter the Great: — *pl* **strel'itzes** or **strel'itzi**. [Russ *strelets* bowman]

strelitzia *strel-it'si-ə*, *n* a plant of the S African genus *Strelitzia*, of the banana family, with large showy flowers. [From Queen Charlotte, wife of George III, of the house of Mecklenburg-*Strelitz*]

strene *strēn*, (*Spenser*) *n* a form of **strain**[2], in the sense race.

strength *strength*, *n* the quality, condition, or degree of being physically or mentally strong; the power of action or resistance; the ability to withstand great pressure or force; force; degree or intensity; vigour; potency; a beneficial characteristic; complement (as of a workforce, team, etc); a military force; the number on the muster roll, or the normal number; the point, the truth (*Austr* and *NZ*). — *vt* **strength'en** to make strong or stronger; to confirm. — *vi* to become stronger. — *n* **strength'ener**. — *n* and *adj* **strength'ening**. — *adj* **strength'ful**. — *adj* **strength'less** without strength. — **get the strength of** (*esp Austr* and *NZ*) to comprehend; **go from strength to strength** to move successfully forward, through frequent triumphs or achievements; **on the strength of** in reliance upon; founding upon. [OE *strengthu*, from *strang* strong]

strenuous *stren'ū-əs*, *adj* active; vigorous; urgent; zealous; requiring exertion. — *n* (*rare*) **strenuity** (*stri-nū'i-ti*). — *n* **strenuosity** (*stren-ū-os'i-ti*) or **stren'uousness**. — *adv* **stren'uously**. [L *strēnuus*]

strep. See **strepto-**.

strepent *strep'ənt*, (*rare*) *adj* noisy. — *adj* **strep'erous** loud; harsh-sounding. — *adj* **strep'itant** loud; noisy; clamorous. — *n* **strepitā'tion**. — *adj* **strep'itous**. [L *strepere* to make a noise; frequentative *strepitāre*]

Strephon *stref'on* or *-ən*, *n* a love-sick shepherd in Sir Philip Sidney's *Arcadia*; any love-sick swain.

strephosymbolia *stref-ō-sim-bō'li-ə*, *n* a visual disorder in which items are seen in mirror image; a reading problem in which letters, symbols, words, etc are reversed, transposed or confused. [LL, from Gr *strephein* to twist, turn, and *symbolon* a symbol]

strepitant, etc, and **strepitous**. See under **strepent**.

strepitoso *strep-i-tō'sō*, (*music*) *adj* noisy, boisterous. — Also *adv*. [Ital; see **strepent**]

strepsipterous *streps-ip'tə-rəs*, *adj* of, relating or belonging to an order of insects (*Strepsiptera*) parasitic in other insects, the females wormlike, the males with twisted forewings. [Gr *strepsis* a twist, and *pteron* a wing]

strepto- *strep'tō-*, *combining form* denoting bent, flexible, twisted quality. — *n* **streptocarpus** any flowering plant of the Cape primrose genus *Streptocarpus*, with foxglove-shaped flowers. — *adj* **streptococcal** (*-kok'l*) or **streptococcic** (*-kok'sik*). — *n* **Streptococcus** (*-kok'əs*; Gr *kokkos* a grain) a genus of bacteria forming bent chains, certain species of which can cause scarlet fever, pneumonia, etc; (without *cap*) any bacterium of this genus (*colloq* short form **strep**): — *pl* **streptococ'ci** (*-kok'sī* or *-kok'i-*). — *n* **streptokin'ase** a generic thrombolytic drug, used to treat heart attack victims. — *n* **streptomycin** (*-mī'sin*; Gr *mykēs* fungus) an antibiotic drug obtained from the bacterium *Streptomyces griseus*, used as the first effective drug treatment for tuberculosis, and in the treatment of certain rare infections such as tularaemia, brucellosis and glanders. — *n* **streptosol'en** an evergreen solanaceous flowering shrub of the genus *Streptosolen*, with panicles of tubular orange flowers. — **strep throat** (*med*) an informal name for an acute streptococcal infection of the throat. [Gr *streptos* twisted, flexible]

Strepyan *strep'i-ən*, *adj* of the oldest known Palaeolithic culture. [*Strépy*, a village near the Belgian town of Charleroi, where stone implements of this stage occur]

stress *stres*, *n* hardship, straits (*obs*); strain; a constraining influence; physical, emotional or mental pressure; force; the system of forces applied to a body; the insistent assigning of weight or importance; emphasis; relative emphasis placed on a syllable or word; distraint (*law*). — *vt* to apply stress to; to subject to stress or strain; to lay stress on; to emphasize. — *adj* **stressed**. — *adj* **stress'ful**. — *adj* **stress'less**. — *n* **stress'or** an agent or factor that causes stress. — *adj* **stressed-out** (*colloq*) exhausted or incapacitated by psychological stress. — **stressed-skin construction** that of aircraft structures in which the skin carries a large proportion of the loads; **stress fracture** (*med*) a fracture of a bone resulting from repetitive jarring, most commonly occurring in runners and other athletes; **stress mark** a mark used to indicate that a written syllable is stressed when spoken. [Aphetic for **distress**; prob partly also from OFr *estrece*, from L *strictus*, from *stringere* to draw tight]

stretch *strech*, *vt* to extend (in space or time); to draw out; to expand, make longer or wider by tension; to spread out; to reach out; to exaggerate, strain, or carry further than is right; to lay at full length; to lay out; to place so as to reach from point to point or across a space; to hang by the neck (*slang*). — *vi* to be drawn out; to reach; to extend (with *over*, *across*, etc); to be extensible without breaking; to straighten and extend fully one's body and limbs; to exaggerate; to go swiftly. — *n* the act of stretching; the state of being stretched; reach; extension; utmost extent; strain; undue straining; exaggeration; extensibility; a single spell; a continuous journey; an area, expanse; a straight part of a course; a term of imprisonment (*slang*); a stretch limo (*slang*). — *adj* capable of being stretched. — *adj* **stretched**. — *n* **stretch'er** a person who stretches; anything used for stretching eg gloves, hats, etc; a frame for stretching a painter's canvas; a frame for carrying the sick or wounded; a rower's footboard; a crossbar or horizontal member; a brick, stone, sod, sandbag, etc, laid horizontally with others in the forming of a wall; an exaggeration or lie. — *vt* to transport (a sick or injured person) by stretcher; (with *off*) to carry (*esp* an injured player) from the field of play on a stretcher. — *adj* **stretch'less** no longer liable to stretch. — *adj* **stretch'y** able, apt, or inclined to stretch. — **stretch'er-bearer** a person who carries injured from the field; **stretch'er-bond** or **stretch'ing-bond** a method of building with stretchers only, the joints of one course falling between those above and below; **stretching course** a brick course entirely of stretchers; **stretching frame** a machine for stretching cotton rovings; a frame on which starched fabrics are dried; **stretching iron** a currier's tool for dressing leather; **stretch limo** (*informal*; in full **stretch limousine**) a luxurious, custom-made limousine that has been lengthened to provide extra seating, etc. — **at a stretch** continuously, without interruption; with difficulty; **stretch a point** to go further, *esp* in concession, than the strict rule allows; **stretch one's legs** to take a walk, *esp* for exercise. [OE *streccan*]

stretto *stret'ō*, (*music*) *n* part of a fugue in which subject and answer are brought closely together; (also **strett'a**: — *pl* **strett'e** *-tā*) a passage, *esp* a coda, in quicker time: — *pl* **strett'i** (*-ē*). [Ital, contracted]

strew *stro͞o*, *vt* to scatter loosely; to cover dispersedly; to spread (*rare*); to level (*poetic*): — *pa t* **strewed**; *pa p* **strewed** or **strewn**. — *n* an assemblage of things strewn. — *n* **strew'age**. — *n* **strew'er**. — *n* **strew'ing**. — *n* **strew'ment** (*Shakesp*) strewings. [OE *strewian*, *streowian*]

strewth *stro͞oth*, *interj* an oath (from *God's truth*).

stria *strī'ə* or *strē'a*, *n* a fine streak, furrow, or threadlike line, *usu* parallel to others; one of the fillets between the flutes of columns, etc (*archit*): — *pl* **stri'ae** (*strī'ē* or *strē'ī*). — *vt* **strī'ate** to mark with striae. — *adj* **strī'ate** or **strī'ated**. — *n* **striā'tion**. — *n* **striā'tum** the *corpus striatum*, the great ganglion of the forebrain. — *n* **strī'ature** mode of striation. — **striated muscle** a voluntary muscle, or muscular tissue, whose fibres are transversely striated. [L *stria* a furrow, flute of a column]

strich *strich*, (*archaic*) *n* the screech-owl. [L *strix*, prob modified by **scritch**]

stricken *strik'n*, (*literary* and *poetic*, or in certain compounds such as *grief-stricken*) *adj* struck, affected; afflicted. [Archaic pa p of **strike**]

strickle *strik'l*, *n* an instrument for levelling the top of a measure of grain or shaping the surface of a mould; a template; a tool for sharpening scythes. — *vt* to level (a measure of grain) or shape the surface of (a mould) with a strickle. [OE *stricel*]

strict *strikt*, *adj* exact; rigorous; allowing no laxity; austere; observing exact rules, regular; severe; exactly observed; thoroughgoing; tight (*Shakesp*); narrow (*archaic*); stiff and straight (*bot*); close, intimate (*obs*); restricted. — *adj* **strict'ish**. — *adv* **strict'ly**. — *n* **strict'ness**. — *n* **strict'ure** an adverse remark or criticism; strictness (*Shakesp*); abnormal narrowing of a passage (*med*); a binding; a closure; tightness. — *adj* **strict'ured** abnormally narrowed. [L *strictus*, pa p of *stringere* to draw tight]

stridden. See under **stride**.

stride *strīd*, *vi* to walk with long steps; to take a long step; to straddle. — *vt* to stride over; to cover (a distance) by striding: — *pa t* **strōde**; *pa p* **stridd'en** (*strid'n*). — *n* a long step; a striding gait; the length of a long step; stride piano (*jazz*); (in *pl*) trousers (*slang*, *esp Austr*). — *vi* **striddle** (*strid'l*) to straddle (back-formation from *stridling*). — *adv* **stride'ways** or **stridling** (*strid'*; *dialect*) astride. — *adv* **stride'legs** or **stride'legged** (*Scot*) astride. — **stride piano** (*jazz*) a rhythmic style of piano-playing derived from ragtime, popularized in Harlem during the 1920s. — **be into**, **get into** or **hit one's stride** to achieve one's normal or expected level of progress, efficiency, degree of success, etc; **make great strides** to make rapid progress; **take in one's stride** to accomplish without undue effort or difficulty. [OE *strīdan* to stride]

strident *strī'dənt*, *adj* (of a voice) loud and grating; urgent, commanding attention. — *n* **strī'dence** or **strī'dency**. — *adv* **strī'dently**. — *n* **strī'dor** a harsh shrill sound; a harsh whistling sound of obstructed breathing (*med*). — *adj* **stridūlant** (*strid'*) stridulating; pertaining to stridor. — *adv* **strid'ulantly**. — *vi* **strid'ūlate** to make a chirping or scraping sound, like a grasshopper. — *n* **stridūlā'tion** the act of stridulating. — *n* **strid'ūlātor** an insect that makes a sound by scraping; the organ it uses. — *adj* **strid'ūlatory**. — *adj* **strid'ūlous**. [L *strīdēre* and *strīdere* to creak]

stridling. See under **stride**.

stridulant ... **to** ... **stridulous**. See under **strident**.

strife *strīf*, *n* contention or conflict; variance; striving; any sort of trouble, hassle. — *adj* **strife'ful**. — *adj* **strife'less**. — *n* **strift** (*strift*; *archaic*) a struggle. — *adj* **strife'-torn** severely disrupted, damaged, etc by conflict. [OFr *estrif*; see **strive**]

strig *strig*, (*S Eng dialect*) *n* a stalk. — *vt* to remove the stalk from: — *pr p* **strigg'ing**. [Origin obscure]

striga *strī'gə*, *n* a stria; a bristle, *usu* an appressed bristle (*bot* and *zool*): — *pl* **strigae** (*strī'jē*). — *adj* **strī'gate** or **strī'gose** (or *-gōs'*; *bot* and *zool*) marked with streaks; having bristles. [L *striga* a swath, a furrow, a flute of a column]

Striges *strī'jēz*, *strig'ās* or **Strigiformes** *strij-i-för'mēz*, *n pl* in some classifications, the order comprising the owls. — *adj* **strig'iform**. — *adj* **strī'gine** owl-like; of the owls. [L *strix*, *strigis* an owl]

strigil *strij'il*, *n* (in ancient Greece and Rome) a scraper used to clean the skin after bathing; (in bees) a mechanism for cleaning the antennae. [L *strigilis*]

strigine. See under **Striges**.

Strigops *strī'gops* or **Stringops** *string'gops*, *n* the kakapo or owl-parrot genus. [Gr *strinx* or *strix*, *stringos* owl, and *ōps* face]

strigose. See under **striga**.

strike *strīk*, *vt* to give a blow to or with; to hit, smite; to come into forcible contact with; to deal, deliver, or inflict; to bring forcibly into contact; to impel; to put, send, move, render, or produce by a blow or stroke; to render as if by a blow; to impress; to impress favourably; to afflict; to assail, affect; to affect strongly or suddenly; to mark off; (of a line, path, etc) to draw, describe, give direction to; to arrive at, estimate, compute, fix, settle (as a balance, an average, prices); to make (a compact or agreement), to ratify; to occur to; to assume (a pose or an attitude); to lower (eg a sail, flag, tent); to take down the tents of (*strike camp*); to dismantle; to sound by percussion or otherwise; to announce by a bell; to come upon, reach; to stamp; to coin; to print; to delete, cancel; to constitute (*orig* by cutting down a list); to broach (*Shakesp*); to fight (a battle) (*Shakesp*); to blast, bewitch; to hook (a fish) by a quick turn of the wrist; to smooth (*dialect*); to strickle (*dialect*); to stroke (*obs* and *Bible*). — *vi* to make one's way; to set out; to take a direction or course; to dart, shoot, pass quickly; to penetrate; to jerk the line suddenly in order to impale the hook in the mouth of a fish; to put forth roots; to chance, alight, come by chance; to interpose; to deal or aim a blow, perform a stroke; to sound or be sounded or announced by a bell; to hit out; to seize the bait; to strike something, as a rock, sail, flag; to attempt to hook the ball (*Rugby football*); to touch; to run aground; to surrender; to go on strike; to blast, blight (*Shakesp*): — *pa t* and *pa p* **struck**. — *n* a stroke, striking; an attack, *esp* by aircraft; a raid; the direction of a horizontal line at right angles to the dip of a bed (*geol*); a find (as of oil), a stroke of luck; a cessation of work, or other obstructive refusal to act normally, as a means of putting pressure on employers, etc; the part that receives the bolt of a lock; (in tenpin bowling) the knocking down of all the pins with the first ball bowled, or the score resulting from this; a ball missed by the batter, or a similar event counting equivalently against the batter (*baseball*); the position of facing the bowling, licence to receive the next delivery (*cricket*); blackmail, *esp* by introducing a bill in the hope of being bought off (*old US slang*); the quantity of coins, etc made at one time; a strickle; a proportion of malt (cf **straik**). — *n* **strik'er** someone who or something that strikes; a footpad (*Shakesp*); a batsman (*baseball*); a forward, attacker, *esp* one whose task is to attempt to score goals (*football*); the batsman facing the bowling (*cricket*). — *n* **strik'ing**. — *adj* that strikes or can strike; impressive, arresting, noticeable. — *adv* **strik'ingly**. — *n* **strik'ingness**. — *adj* **strike'bound** closed or similarly affected because of a strike. — **strike'breaker** a person who works during a strike or who does the work of a striker, *esp* if brought in with a view to defeating the strike; **strike'breaking**; **strike fault** (*geol*) a fault parallel to the strike; **strike force** a force designed and equipped to carry out a strike (*military*); a special police unit trained to strike suddenly and forcefully to suppress crime; **strikeout** see **strike out**; **strike pay** an allowance paid by a trade union to members on strike; **strike zone** (*baseball*) the area above home plate extending from the batter's knees to his or her armpits; **striking circle** (*hockey*) the area in front of goal from within which the ball must be hit in order to score; **striking price** (*stock exchange*) a stipulated price at which a holder may exercise his or her put or call option. — **be struck off** (of doctors, lawyers, etc) to have one's name removed from the professional register because of misconduct; **on strike** taking part in a strike; (of a batsman) facing the bowling (*cricket*); **strike a match** to light it by friction or a grazing stroke; **strike at** to attempt to strike, aim a blow at; **strike back** to return a blow; to backfire, burn within the burner; **strike down** to fell; to make ill or cause to die; **strike hands** to join or slap together hands in confirmation of agreement; **strike home** to strike right to the point aimed at (also *fig*); **strike in** to enter suddenly; to interpose; to agree, fit (*obs*); **strike into** to enter upon suddenly, to break into; **strike it rich** (*colloq*) to make a sudden large financial gain, eg through discovering a mineral deposit, etc; **strike off** to erase from an account, to deduct; to remove (from a roll, register, etc); to print; to separate by a blow; **strike oil** see under **oil**; **strike out** to efface; to bring into light; to direct one's energy and efforts boldly outwards; to swim away; to dismiss or be dismissed by means of three strikes (*baseball*); to fail completely (*colloq*; *esp NAm*; *n* **strike'out**); to remove (testimony, an action, etc) from the record (*law*); to strike from the shoulder; to form by sudden effort; **strike root** see under **root**[1]; **strike through** to delete with a stroke of the pen; **strike up** to begin to beat, sing, or play; to begin (eg an acquaintance); **struck on** enamoured of; **take strike** (*cricket*) (of a batsman) to prepare to face the bowling. [OE *strīcan* to stroke, go, move]

Strimmer® *strim-ər*, *n* a machine for cutting grass, *esp* in areas inaccessible to a lawn mower, using a filament or length of strong cord (instead of a blade) that rotates rapidly within a protective guard.

Strine *strīn*, (*colloq*) *n* a jocular name given to Australian English in terms of its vernacular pronunciation (with frequent assimilation, elision, etc). — *adj* Australian. [Alleged pron of *Australian*, coined by Alastair Morrison (pseudonym Afferbeck Lauder), *esp* in his book *Let Stalk Strine*]

string *string*, *n* a small cord or a piece of it; cord of any size; a hangman's rope; a piece of anything for tying; anything of similar character, such as a tendon, nerve or fibre; a leash; a shoelace (*NAm*); a stretched piece of catgut, silk, wire, or other material in a musical instrument; (in *pl*) the stringed instruments played by a bow in an orchestra or other combination; (in *pl*) their players; the cord of an archery bow; in theoretical physics, a minute, one-dimensional entity in space (see **string theory** below); the thread of a necklace or the like; anything on which things are threaded; a filing cord; a set of things threaded together or arranged as if threaded; a train, succession, file, or series; (of horses, camels, etc) a drove or number; a long bunch; the buttons strung on a wire by which the score is kept; (*billiards*); hence, the score itself; a sloping joist supporting the steps in wooden stairs; a string course; a hoax (*slang*); (in *pl*) awkward or undesirable conditions or limitations. — *adj* of, like or for string or strings. — *vt* to fit or furnish with a string or strings; to put in tune (*poetic*); to make tense or firm; to tie up; to hang; to extend like a string; to put on or in a string; to take the strings or stringy parts off; to hoax, humbug (*slang*). — *vi* to stretch out into a long line; to form into strings; (of glues, etc) to become stringy; to be hanged (*Scot*); (in billiards) to drive the ball against the end of the table and back, to decide who is to begin: — *pa t* and *pa p* **strung**. — *adj* **stringed** (*stringd*) having strings; of stringed instruments. — *n* **stringer** (*string'ər*) someone who or that which strings; a horizontal member in a framework (*archit*); an interior horizontal plank, supporting the beam ends of a ship (*naut*); a narrow mineral vein; a journalist employed part-time by a newspaper or news agency to cover a particular (*esp* remote) town or area. — *adv* **string'ily**. — *n* **string'iness**. — *n* **string'ing**. — *adj* **string'less**. — *adj* **string'y** consisting of, or abounding in, strings or small threads; fibrous; capable of being drawn into strings; like string or a stringed instrument. — **string-bag'** a bag made of string, or (**string'-bag**) for holding string; **string band** a band of stringed instruments; **string bass** a double bass; **string bean** the French bean; **string'board** a board facing the well-hole of a staircase, and receiving or covering the ends of the steps; **string course** a projecting horizontal course of bricks or line of mouldings running quite along the face of a building; **string figure** a structure of string looped around the fingers in a symmetrical pattern that can be altered by manipulation, as in cat's-cradle; **string pea** a pea with edible pods; **string piece** a long, heavy, *usu* horizontal timber used to support a framework; the string of a staircase; **string quartet** a musical ensemble of two violins, a viola and a cello; music for such an ensemble; **string theory** (*phys*) the theory that all fundamental particles in the cosmos arise from strings (invisibly small, one-dimensional, elastic entities) and that the characteristic properties of each particle are determined by the vibration and rotation of the string, much in the same way as the tension, etc of a violin string determines the sound produced — further developed as **superstring theory** a supersymmetrical version of the original theory; **string tie** a narrow necktie of uniform width; **string vest** a vest made of a netlike fabric; **string'y-bark** one of a class of Australian eucalypts with very fibrous bark. — **highly-strung** see under **high**; **more than one string to one's bow** (capable of or expert in) more than one area of knowledge, function, etc; **no strings** or **no strings attached** with no conditions or limitations (*adj* **no'-strings**); **on a string** under complete (*esp* emotional) control; kept in suspense; **pull (the) strings** to use influence behind the scenes, as if working puppets (*n* **string'-pulling**); **string along** (*vt*) to string, fool; to give someone false expectations; (*vi*) to go along together, cooperate; **string out** (*colloq*) to be under the influence of or addicted to a drug; **string up** to hang by the neck (*colloq*); **strung out** (*orig US*) suffering from drug-withdrawal symptoms; weak, ill or distressed as a result of drug addiction; addicted to a drug; **strung up** nervously tensed. [OE *streng*; cf Du *streng*, Ger *Strang*, ON *strengr*]

stringent *strin'jənt*, *adj* tight; binding; rigorous; demanding close attention to detail, set procedure, etc; characterized by difficulty in finding money. — *n* **strin'gency**. — *adv* **strin'gently**. — *n* **strin'gentness**. [L *stringēns*, *-entis*, pr p of *stringere* to draw together]

stringendo *strin-jen'dō*, (*music*) *adj* and *adv* (played) with increasing speed. [Ital]

stringer. See under **string**.

stringhalt *string'hölt*, *n* a catching up of a horse's legs, *usu* of one or both hindlegs, caused by a muscle spasm in the hock. — Also **spring'halt**. [Appar **string** (sinew) and **halt**[2]]

Stringops. See under **Strigops**.

stringy. See **string**.

strinkle *string'kl*, (*Scot*) *vt* to sprinkle. — *n* **strink'ling**. [Cf **sprinkle**]

strip *strip*, *vt* to pull, peel, or tear off; to doff; to divest; to undress; to reduce to the ranks; to deprive of a covering; to skin, to peel, to husk; to lay bare, expose; to deprive; to clear, empty; to dismantle; to clear of fruit, leaves, stems, midribs, or any other part; to press out the last milk from (a cow, etc) or obtain milk in this way; to press out the roe or milt from; to handle as if milking a cow; to cut in strips; to put strips on; to outstrip, press (*obs*); to remove a constituent from a substance by boiling, distillation, etc (*chem*); to break the thread of (a screw, etc) or a tooth of (a gear); to unload (*esp* a container or lorry). — *vi* to undress; to perform a striptease; (of a screw) to be stripped of the thread; to come off; to go swiftly (*obs*): — *pr p* **stripp'ing**; *pa t* and *pa p* **stripped**. — *n* a long narrow piece; a long thin piece of rolled metal, such as *steel* *strip*; a narrow space in a newspaper in which a story is told in pictures (also **strip cartoon**); a lightweight uniform, *esp* one displaying the club colours, for running, football, etc; a striptease; an airstrip; a row of three or more connected stamps. — *n* **stripp'er** someone who or something that strips; a striptease artist. — *n pl* **stripp'ings** the last milk drawn at a milking. — **strip cartoon** see **strip** (*n*); **strip cell** a secure room without furnishings or fittings, in eg a psychiatric hospital, in which seriously disturbed patients are confined; **strip club** one which regularly features striptease artists; **strip joint** (*informal*) a strip club; **strip'-leaf** tobacco stripped of stalks; **strip lighting** lighting by means of long fluorescent tubes; **strip map** a map showing a long narrow strip of country, used *esp* by airmen; **strip mill** a mill where steel is rolled into strips; **strip mine** an opencast mine in which the overburden is removed (stripped) before the valuable ore is excavated; **stripped atom** an ionized atom from which one or more electrons have been removed; **strip-po'ker** poker in which losses are paid by removing articles of clothing; **strip search** a search of a person's body (for hidden items, eg drugs, contraband) for which their clothes are removed. — Also *vt*. — **strip'tease** an act of undressing slowly and seductively, *esp* as entertainment. — **strip down** to dismantle, remove parts from; **strip off** (*colloq*) to take one's clothes off; **strip out** (*commerce*) to remove (one or more items) from a balance sheet, *usu* to give a truer picture of a firm's trading and financial position. [OE *strȳpan*; Ger *streifen*; perh partly from other sources]

stripe *strīp*, *n* a blow, *esp* with a lash; a band of colour; a chevron on a sleeve, indicating non-commissioned rank or good behaviour; a striped cloth or pattern; a strip; a strain; a kind, particular sort (*US*); magnetic sound track(s) on cinema film for sound-film reproduction. — *vt* to make stripes on; to mark with stripes; to lash. — *adj* **striped** having stripes of different colours; marked with stripes. — *adj* **stripe'less**. — *n* **stripes** (*old colloq*) a tiger. — *adj* **strip'ey** stripy. — *n* **strip'iness**. — *n* **strip'ing**. — *adj* **strip'y** stripelike; having stripes. [Perh different words; cf Du *streep* (earlier *strijpe*); Ger *Streif* stripe, ON *strīp* striped fabric, Du *strippen* to whip]

stripling *strip'ling*, (*literary* and *facetious*) *n* a youth. [Dimin of **strip**]

stripper. See under **strip**.

stripy. See under **stripe**.

strive *strīv*, *vi* to contend; to be in conflict (with *against*); to struggle (with *for*); to endeavour earnestly (with *to*); to make one's way with effort: — *pa t* **strove** (*strōv*), *Shakesp* **strīved**; *pa p* **striven** (*striv'n*), *Shakesp* **strove**, *Bible* **strīved**. — *n* **striv'er**. — *n* and *adj* **striv'ing**. — *adv* **striv'ingly**. [OFr *estriver*; poss Gmc, from the root of **stride**, or of Ger *streben* to strive]

stroam *strōm*, (*dialect*) *vi* to wander idly about; to stride. [Perh **stroll** and **roam**]

strobic *strob'ik*, *adj* like a spinning-top; spinning or seeming to spin. — *n* **strobe** (*strōb*) the process of viewing vibrations with a stroboscope; a stroboscope or stroboscopic light. — *n* **stroboscope** (*strob'* or *strōb'ə-skōp'*) an optical toy giving an illusion of motion from a series of pictures seen momentarily in succession; an instrument for studying rotating machinery or other periodic phenomena by means of a flashing lamp which can be synchronized with the frequency of the periodic phenomena so that they appear to be stationary. — *adj* **stroboscopic** (*strob-* or *strōb-ə-skop'ik*). — **stroboscopic** (more commonly **strobe**) **lighting** periodically flashing light, or the equipment used to produce it. [Gr *strobos* a whirling, from *strephein* to twist]

strobila *stro-bī'lə*, (*biol*) *n* (in the lifecycle of jellyfishes) a chain of segments, cone within cone, that separate to become medusoids; a chain of segments forming the body of a tapeworm: — *pl* **strobī'lae** (*-lē*). — *adj* **strobilaceous** (*strob-i-lā'shəs*) of or like a strobile; bearing strobiles. — *vi* **strob'ilate** to undergo strobilation. — *adj* of the nature of a strobilus. — *n* **strobilā'tion**, **strobilīzā'tion** or **-īsā'tion** production or reproduction by strobilae. — *n* **strobile** (*strob'* or *strōb'īl* or *-il*) a strobila; a strobilus. — *adj* **strobiliform** (*-il'*), **strob'iline** or **strob'iloid**. — *n* **strobī'lus** a close group of sporophylls with their sporangia, a cone; a scaly spike of female flowers, as in the hop: — *pl* **strobī'li** (*-lī*). [Gr *strobīlē* a conical plug of lint, *strobīlos* a spinning-top, whirl, pine cone, from *strobos* (see foregoing)]

stroboscope, etc. See under **strobic**.

stroddle *strod'l*, (*obs* or *dialect*). Same as **straddle**.

strode *strōd*, *pa t* of **stride**.

strodle *strod'l* (*obs* or *dialect*). Same as **straddle**.

stroganoff *strog'ən-of*, *adj* (of meat) cut thinly and cooked with onions, mushrooms and seasoning in a sour cream sauce, as in *beef stroganoff*; also applied to vegetables cooked in this way, as in *mushroom stroganoff*. — *n* a dish cooked in this way. [After Count Paul *Stroganoff*, 19c Russ diplomat]

stroke[1] *strōk*, *n* an act or mode of striking; a hit or attempt at hitting; a blow; a striking by lightning; a reverse; damage to part of the brain caused by diminished blood flow or leakage of blood through the walls of blood vessels, leading to (often permanent) impairment of sensation, function or movement in those parts controlled by the damaged area; the striking of a clock or its sound; a dash or line; a touch of pen, pencil, brush, etc; a trait (*obs*); a beat, pulse; a sudden movement or occurrence; a particular named style or manner of swimming; a single complete movement in a repeated series, as in swimming, rowing or pumping; a stroke oar; a single action towards an end; an effective action, feat, achievement. — *vt* to put a stroke through or on; to cross (commonly with *out*); to row as stroke in or for; to row at the rate of. — *vi* to row as the stroke-oar; to make a stroke, as in swimming. — **stroke oar** the aftmost oar in a boat; its rower, whose stroke leads the rest; **stroke play** (*golf*) scoring by counting the total number of strokes played (rather than the number of holes won). — **off one's stroke** operating less effectively or successfully than usual; **on the stroke (of)** punctually (at). [OE (inferred) *strāc*; cf Ger *Streich*]

stroke[2] *strōk*, *vt* to rub gently in one direction; to rub gently in kindness or affection; to put or direct by such a movement; to reassure or flatter with attention (*NAm*); to milk, strip; to tool in small flutings; to whet; to set in close gathers; to strike, move (a ball, etc) smoothly. — *n* an act of stroking. — *n* **strok'er**. — *n* **strok'ing**. [OE *strācian*, from *strāc* stroke (noun); cf Ger *streichen* to rub]

stroke[3] *strōk* or **stroken** *strōk'n*, *obs* forms (*Spenser* and *Shakesp*) of **struck**.

stroll *strōl*, *vi* to walk at a leisurely pace; to saunter; to wander from place to place. — *n* a leisurely walk; a stroller (*NAm*). — *n* **stroll'er** a person who strolls; a wanderer; a saunterer; a vagrant; an itinerant; a pushchair (*NAm*). — *n* and *adj* **stroll'ing**. — **strolling player** (*hist*) an itinerant actor. — **stroll on**! an exclamation of surprise, disbelief (often used ironically). [Perh Ger *strolchen* (obs *strollen*), from *Strolch* vagrant]

stroma *strō'mə*, *n* a supporting framework of connective tissue (*zool*); a dense mass of hyphae in which a fungus fructification may develop (*bot*); the denser part of a blood-corpuscle, chloroplast, etc: — *pl* **strōm'ata**. — *adj* **strōmatic** (*-mat'ik*) or **strō'matous**. — *n* **stromatolite** a rocky, greenish-brown mass, often dating from Precambrian times, consisting of calcium carbonate precipitated by dense mounds of microbes living in warm, shallow water. [Gr *strōma* a bed, mattress]

stromb *strom* or *stromb*, *n* a very large gasteropod related to the whelk; its shell with short spire and expanded lip. — *adj* **strombūlif'erous** bearing spirally coiled organs or parts. — *adj* **strombū'liform** shaped like a spinning top; spirally twisted. — *n* **strom'bus** the stromb, any gasteropod mollusc of the genus *Strom-*

bus; a spirally coiled pod. [Gr *strombos* a spinning-top, snail, whirlwind]

strond *strond*, (*Spenser* and *Shakesp*) *n*. Same as **strand**[1].

strong *strong*, *adj* powerful; forcible; forceful; (of wind) fast-moving; vigorous; hale; robust; of great staying power; firm; resistant; difficult to overcome; steadfast; excelling; efficient; of great tenacity of will and effective in execution; able, competent; well-skilled or versed; rich in resources or means to power; well provided; numerous; numbering so many; of vigorous growth; stiff, coarse, and abundant, indicating strength; (of language) without ambiguity, obscurity, or understatement; (of language) intemperate, offensive and unseemly; gross; violent; grievous; having great effect; intense; ardent and convinced; performed with strength; powerfully, or unpleasantly powerfully, affecting the senses; rank; vivid; marked; (of a syllable) stressed, emphasized; bold in definition; in high concentration; showing the characteristic properties in high degree; (of prices, markets, currency) steady or tending to rise; (of Germanic and similar verbs) showing vowel variation in conjugation (*gram*); (of Germanic nouns and adjectives) having a stem originally ending in a vowel or a consonant other than *n*; of the strongest type of interaction between nuclear particles, occurring at a range of less than (approximately) 10^{-15} cm and accounting for the stability of the atomic nucleus (*phys*): — *compar* **stronger** *strong'gər*; *superl* **strongest** *strong'gist*. — *adv* strongly (*rare*); very (*obs*). — *adj* **strongish** (*strong'gish*). — *adv* **strong'ly**. — **strong'arm** a person who uses violence. — *adj* by, having, or using, physical force. — *vt* to treat violently, show violence towards. — **strong'box** a safe or strongly made coffer for valuables; **strong drink** alcoholic liquors; **strong flour** or **wheat** one rich in gluten, giving bread that rises well; **strong force** (*phys*) the force that binds quarks together and holds neutrons and protons together to form atomic nuclei; **strong head** power to withstand alcohol or any dizzying influence; **strong'hold** a fastness or fortified refuge; a fortress; a place where anything is in great strength; **strong interaction** an interaction between particles completed in a time of the order of 10^{-23}s, such an interaction binding protons and neutrons together in the nuclei of atoms. — *adj* **strong'-knit** firmly jointed or compacted. — **strong language** swearing; plain, emphatic language; **strong'man** a person who performs feats of strength, in a circus, etc; a person, group, etc that wields political, economic, etc power; **strong meat** solid food, not milk (*Bible*, *Heb* 5. 12 and 14); anything tending to arouse fear, repulsion, etc. — *adj* **strong-mind'ed** resolute, determined, having a vigorous mind. — **strong-mind'edness**; **strong'point** (*military*) a favourably situated and well-fortified defensive position; **strong point** that in which one excels, one's forte; **strong'room** a room constructed for the safe-keeping of valuables or prisoners. — **a strong stomach** resistance to nausea; **come on strong** see under **come**; **going strong** see under **going**[2]. [OE *strang* strong; ON *strangr*, Ger *streng* tight]

strongyle or **strongyl** *stron'jil*, *n* a blunt rhabdus; a parasitic threadworm (*Strongylus* or kindred genera). — *adj* and *n* **stron'gyloid**. — *n* **strongyloidiasis** (*-dī'ə-sis'*) an intestinal disease caused by infestation with a type of tropical or subtropical threadworm of the genus *Strongyloides*, *esp Strongyloides stercoralis*. — *n* **strongylō'sis** infestation with strongyles. [Gr *strongylos* round]

strontia, **strontian**, **strontianite**. See under **strontium**.

strontium *stron'shi-əm*, *sh-əm* or *stron'ti-əm*, *n* an element (symbol **Sr**; atomic no 38), a yellow metal found in celestine. — *n* **stron'tia** its oxide. — *n* **stron'tian** (*-shi-ən*) (loosely) strontium, strontia or strontianite. — Also *adj*. — *n* **stron'tianite** its carbonate, an orthorhombic mineral (first found in 1790 near *Strontian* (*stron-tē'ən*) in Argyllshire). — **strontium-90** a radioactive isotope of strontium, an important element in nuclear fallout; **strontium unit** a measure of the concentration of strontium-90 in organic material (*abbrev* **SU**).

strook or **strooke** *strŏŏk*, *obs pa t* and *pa p* (*also* **strook'en**) of **strike**. — *n* **strooke** (*strōk*; *obs*) a stroke.

strop[1] *strop*, *n* a strip of leather, etc, for sharpening razors; a rope or band round a dead-eye (*naut*). — *vt* to sharpen on a strop: — *pr p* **stropp'ing**; *pa t* and *pa p* **stropped**. [Older form of **strap**, from OE *strop*, prob from L *struppus* a thong]

strop[2] *strop*, (*slang*) *n* censure, criticism, *esp* in the phrase *give someone strop*. [Perh back-formation from **stroppy**]

strophanthus *strof-* or *strōf-an'thəs*, *n* a plant of the African and Asiatic genus *Strophanthus*, of the periwinkle family; its dried seeds used in medicine or yielding poison used to make poison arrows. — *n* **strophan'thin** a very poisonous glucoside in its seeds. [Gr *strophos* twisted band, and *anthos* flower, from the ribbonlike prolongation of the petals, twisted in bud]

strophe *strof'i* or *strōf'i*, (*prosody*) *n* (in a Greek play) the song sung by the chorus as it moved towards one side, answered by an exact counterpart, the **an'tistrophe**, as it returned; part of any ode answered in this way; (loosely) a stanza. — *adj* **stroph'ic**. [Gr *strophē* a turn]

strophiole *strof'i-ōl*, (*bot*) *n* a caruncle. — *adj* **stroph'iolate** or **stroph'iolated**. [Gr *strophiolon* a fringe, from *strophos* a twisted band]

stroppy *strop'i*, (*colloq*) *adj* quarrelsome, bad-tempered; rowdy, obstreperous and awkward to deal with. [Perh **obstropalous**]

strossers *stros'ərz*, (*Shakesp*) *n pl* trousers. [Cf **trousers**]

stroud *strowd*, (*obs* or *rare*) *n* a blanket made for trading with American Indians. — *n* **stroud'ing** its material, coarse wool. [Prob made at *Stroud*, Gloucestershire]

stroup *strŏŏp*, (*Scot*) *n* a spout, nozzle, eg of a kettle, jug, pump, etc; a water tap. — *n* **stroup'ach** or **stroupan** a drink of tea. [Cf Swed *strupe* throat]

strout *strowt*, (*dialect*) *vi* to bulge, swell; to stand out, protrude; to flaunt; to strut. — *vt* to cause to protrude. [OE *strūtian* to protrude]

strove *strōv*, *pa t* of **strive**.

strow, **strower**, **strowing**. Same as **strew**, **strewer**, **strewing**: — *pa t* **strowed**; *pa p* **strown**.

stroy *stroi*, (*obs* or *dialect*) *vt* to destroy. — *n* (*Bunyan*) destruction. **[destroy]**

struck. See under **strike**.

structure *struk'chər*, *n* the manner or (*obs*) act of putting together; construction; the arrangement of parts; the manner of organization; a thing constructed; an organic form. — *vt* to organize, build up; to construct a framework for; to allot to (a linguistic element) its function or syntactical relationship. — *adj* **struc'tural**. — *n* **struc'turalism** the belief in and study of unconscious, underlying patterns in thought, behaviour, social organization, etc. — *n* **struc'turalist**. — Also *adj*. — *adv* **struc'turally**. — *n* (*rare*) **structurā'tion** forming (something) into or applying an organized structure to (something), creating a formal structure. — *adj* **struc'tured** having a certain structure; having a definite structure or organization. — *adj* **struc'tureless**. — **structural formula** a chemical formula showing the arrangement of atoms in the molecule and the bonds between them; **structural gene** a gene specifying the amino acid sequence of a protein needed for cell structure or metabolism (cf **regulatory gene**); **structural isomerism** (*chem*) the property of substances which are isomeric (qv) and differ in molecular structure, often having distinct physical and chemical properties (contrast with **stereoisomerism**); **structural linguistics** the study of language in terms of the interrelations of its basic phonological, morphological and semantic units; **structural psychology** a type of psychology dealing with the nature and arrangement of mental states and processes; **structural steel** a strong mild steel suitable for construction work; **structural unemployment** unemployment due to changes in the structure of society or of a particular industry. [L *structūra*, from *struere*, *structum* to build]

strudel *strōō'dl* or *shtrü'dl*, *n* very thin pastry enclosing fruit, or cheese, etc. [Ger, eddy, whirlpool, from the way the pastry is rolled]

struggle *strug'l*, *vi* to strive vigorously in resistance, contention, or coping with difficulties; to make great efforts or exertions; to contend strenuously; to make one's way with difficulty; to move convulsively. — *n* a bout or course of struggling; strife; a hard contest with difficulties; a convulsive movement. — *n* **strugg'ler**. — *n* and *adj* **strugg'ling**. — *adv* **strugg'lingly**. [ME *strogelen*; origin unknown]

Struldbrug *struld'brug*, *n* one of a class among the Luggnaggians in Swift's *Gulliver's Travels*, endowed with immortality, but doomed to decrepitude after eighty, and most wretched. [A capricious coinage]

strum *strum*, *vt* and *vi* to sound the strings of a guitar, etc with a sweep of the hand; to play in this way (rather than plucking individual strings): — *pr p* **strumm'ing**; *pa t* and *pa p* **strummed**. — *n* a strumming. [Cf **thrum**]

struma *strōō'mə*, *n* scrofula or a scrofulous tumour (*pathol*); goitre (*pathol*); a cushionlike swelling (*bot*): — *pl* **stru'mae** (*-mē* or *-mī*). — *adj* **strumatic** (*strōō-mat'ik*), **strumose** (*strōō'mōs*) or **stru'mous**. — *n* **strumī'tis** inflammation of the thyroid gland. [L *strūma* a scrofulous tumour]

strummel *strum'l* or **strammel** *stram'l*, (*obs slang*) *n* straw; hence, hair. [Cf L *strāmen* straw]

strumose, **strumous**. See under **struma**.

strumpet *strum'pit*, (*archaic*) *n* a whore. — *adj* like a strumpet; inconstant; false. — *vt* to make a strumpet of; to call a strumpet. [Origin obscure]

strung *strung*, *pa t* and *pa p* of **string**.

strunt[1] *strunt*, (*Scot*) *vi* to strut. [Cf Norw *strunta*]

strunt[2] *strunt*, (*Scot*) *n* alcoholic liquor. [Ety dubious]

strunt[3] *strunt*, (*Scot*; often in *pl*) *n* the huff, the sulks. [Origin unknown]

strut[1] *strut*, *vi* to walk stiffly in vanity or self-importance; to walk in an ostentatious, swaggering manner; to stand stiffly upright (*obs*); to flaunt, glory (*obs*); to bulge, protrude (*obs*): — *pr p* **strutt'ing**; *pat* and *pa p* **strutt'ed**. — *n* a strutting gait. — *n* **strutt'er**. — *n* and *adj* **strutt'ing**. — *adv* **strutt'ingly**. — **strut one's stuff** (*slang*; *orig US*) to dance; to show off one's talent (at a public activity, etc); to show off generally. [OE *strūtian* or some similar form; see **strout**]

strut[2] *strut*, *n* a rod or member that resists pressure; a prop. — *vt* to support as, or with, a strut or struts. [Cf LGer *strutt* rigid, and **strut**[1]]

struthious *strōō'thi-əs*, *adj* (of birds) resembling or related to the ostrich or belonging to the order of flightless birds (*Struthiones*) to which the ostrich belongs. — *adj* and *n* **stru'thioid**. [L, from Gr *strouthiōn* an ostrich]

strychnine *strik'nēn*, *n* a very poisonous alkaloid ($C_{21}H_{22}O_2N_2$) obtained from the seeds of the nux vomica plant. — *vt* to poison with strychnine. — *n* **strych'nia** (now *rare*) strychnine. — *adj* **strych'nic**. — *n* **strych'ninism** or **strych'nism** strychnine poisoning. [Gr *strychnos* nightshade (of various kinds)]

stub *stub*, *n* a short piece (eg of a cigarette or a pencil) left after the larger part has been used; something blunt and stunted; a counterfoil; a stump; (also **stub'-nail**) a short thick nail or worn horseshoe nail, *esp* in *pl*, old nails used as scrap. — *vt* to strike as against a stub; to extinguish by pressing the end on something (often with *out*); to remove stubs from; to grub (up); to wear or cut to a stub; to wound with a stub: — *pr p* **stubb'ing**; *pa t* and *pa p* **stubbed**. — *adj* **stubbed** cut or worn to a stub; cleared of stubs; stumpy; blunt. — *n* **stubb'iness**. — *adj* **stubb'y** abounding with stubs; short, thick, and strong. — *n* (*Austr*) a small, squat beer bottle or the beer it contains. [OE *stubb*, *stybb*]

stubble *stub'l*, *n* a stump of reaped corn; such stumps collectively; straw; a reaped field; unshaven growth of beard. — *adj* **stubb'led** stubbly. — *adj* **stubb'ly** like or covered with stubble. — *adj* **stubb'le-fed** fed on the natural grass growing among stubble. — **stubble field**; **stubble goose** a goose fed on stubble; **stubble rake** a rake with long teeth for raking stubble. [OFr *estuble*, from LL *stupula*, from L *stipula*; see **stipule**]

stubborn *stub'ərn*, *adj* obstinate, *esp* unreasonably or troublesomely so; pertinacious; refractory; hard to work or treat; inflexible (*lit* and *fig*); rigid. — *vt* (*obs*) to make stubborn. — *adv* **stubb'ornly**. — *n* **stubb'ornness**. [Connection with **stub** is obscure]

stubby. See under **stub**.

STUC *abbrev*: Scottish Trades Union Congress.

stucco *stuk'ō*, *n* any kind of plaster or cement used to coat exterior walls or make architectural mouldings; a decorative work on a building done in stucco (*pl* **stucc'ōs**). — *vt* to face or overlay with stucco; to form in stucco: — *pa t* and *pa p* **stucc'oed** or **stucc'ō'd**. — *n* **stucc'ōer** a worker or dealer in stucco. [Ital *stucco*; from OHGer *stucchi* crust, coating]

stuck[1]. See under **stick**[1].

stuck[2] *stuk*, (*Shakesp*) *n* a thrust. [**stock**[2]]

stuck-up *stuk-up*, (*colloq*) *adj* snobbish, arrogant.

stud[1] *stud*, *n* a horse-breeding establishment; the animals kept there; a collection of horses or other animals, or of cars, belonging to the same owner; a stud horse; a sexually potent or active man, or one who thinks he is (*slang*). — *adj* kept for breeding; of a stud. — **stud'book** a record of horses' (or other animals') pedigrees; **stud'farm** a horse-breeding farm; **stud groom** a groom at a stud, *esp* the head groom; **stud horse** a stallion kept for breeding; **stud poker** a variety of the game of poker in which bets are placed on hands containing some cards dealt face up. — **at stud** or **out to stud** being used for breeding purposes. [OE *stōd*; cf **steed**[1]; Ger *Stute* mare, *Gestüt* stud]

stud[2] *stud*, *n* a wooden post (*obs*); a tree trunk (*Spenser*); a spur, stump, or short branch; an upright in a timber framework or partition; a crosspiece strengthening a link in a chain; one of several rounded projections on the soles of certain types of (*esp* sports) footwear, improving the grip; a projecting boss, knob, or pin; a large-headed nail; a stud bolt; a type of fastener consisting of two interlocking discs; the height of a room (*US*). — *vt* to adorn, set, or secure with studs; to set at intervals: — *pr p* **studd'ing**; *pa t* and *pa p* **studd'ed**. — *adj* **studd'ed**. — *n* **studd'ing**. — **stud bolt** a bolt with a thread on each end, screwed into a fixed part at one end, receiving a nut on the other; **stud'work** brickwork walls between studs; studded leather. [OE *studu* post]

studden. See **stand**.

studdingsail or **studding-sail** *stun'sl* or *stuns'l*, *n* a narrow additional sail set at the outer edges of a square sail when wind is light and abaft the beam. — Also **stun'sail** or **stuns'l**. [Origin unknown]

studdle *stud'l*, *n* a post; a prop. [OE *stodla*]

student *stū'dənt*, *n* a person who studies; a person devoted to books or to any study; a person who is enrolled for a course of instruction, *esp* at a higher or further education establishment; an undergraduate; a member of the foundation of Christ Church, Oxford, answering to a fellow elsewhere; the holder of a studentship; a school pupil; a person learning a specified profession, etc (as *student teacher*, *student nurse*). — *n* **stu'dentry** students collectively. — *n* **stu'dentship** an endowment for a student in a college; in Christ Church, Oxford, the equivalent of a fellowship; the condition or time of being a student. — *adj* **studied** (*stud'id*) well considered; deliberately contrived, designed; over-elaborated with loss of spontaneity; well prepared by study; well read; versed. — *adv* **stud'iedly**. — *n* **stud'iedness**. — *n* **stud'ier**. — *n* **studio** (*stū'di-ō*) an artist's workroom; a workshop for photography, cinematography, radio or television broadcasting, the making of sound recordings, etc: — *pl* **stu'dios**. — *adj* **studious** (*stū'di-əs*) devoted to or assiduous in study; studied; painstaking or painstakingly carried out; deliberate. — *adv* **stu'diously**. — *n* **stu'diousness**. — *vt* **study** (*stud'i*) to apply the mind to in order to acquire knowledge or skill; to examine; to consider; to scrutinize; to look contemplatively at; to take into consideration; to consider the wishes, advantage, feelings of; to devise; to think out; to instruct (*Shakesp*). — *vi* to apply the mind closely to books, nature, acquisition of learning or of skill; to take an educational course; to rack one's mind; to muse, meditate, reflect: — *pr p* **stud'ying**; *pa t* and *pa p* **stud'ied**. — *n* an object of endeavour, solicitude, or mental application; (in *pl*) related objects of mental application or departments of knowledge; a state of consideration; attentive and detailed examination; a scrutiny; a reverie; application of the mind to the acquisition of knowledge or skill; a department of knowledge; a preliminary essay towards a work of art; an exercise in art; a musical composition serving as an exercise in technique; a presentation in literature or art of the results of study; a room devoted to study, actually or ostensibly; the committing to memory, hence a memorizer (*theatre*); inclination; interest; zeal. — **studio couch** a couch, sometimes without a back, that can be converted into a bed; **studio flat** a small flat consisting of one main room, or an open-plan living area; **studio pottery** pottery individually produced by the potter in a studio, rather than factory-made; **study group** a group of people studying a specific subject, who meet informally at regular intervals to discuss their work or some other topic. [L *studēre* (pr p *studēns, -entis*) to be zealous, from *studium* (OFr *estudie*; Ital *studio*) zeal, study]

studio, study, etc. See under **student**.

stuff *stuf*, *n* stuffing, filling (*obs*); matter; substance; essence; material; a preparation used or commodity dealt in in some particular industry or trade; garden produce; cloth, *esp* woollen; a medicinal mixture; goods; luggage; provision; furniture; money; literary or journalistic copy; liquor (**good stuff** often whisky); a broad category or collection of indeterminate or unspecified things (*colloq*); rubbish; nonsense; indecent matter (*obs*). — *adj* (*archaic*) woollen. — *vt* to garrison (*obs*); to store, furnish (*Shakesp*); to provision (*obs*); to line; to be a filling for; to fill very full; to thrust in; to crowd; to cram; to obstruct, clog; to cause to bulge out by filling; to fill (eg a fowl) with seasoning; to fill the skin of (an animal) so as to reproduce the living form; to hoax (*slang*); (of a man) to have sexual intercourse with (*vulg*); to load (a freight container); (in electronics manufacturing, etc) to assemble the internal components of a machine in its external casing; to defeat very convincingly (*slang*). — *vi* to feed gluttonously; to practise taxidermy. — *adj* **stuffed** provisioned; well stored; filled; filled out with stuffing; clogged in nose or throat, etc (often with *up*). — *n* **stuff'er**. — *adv* **stuff'ily**. — *n* **stuff'iness**. — *n* **stuff'ing** that which is used to stuff or fill anything, straw, sawdust, feathers, hair, etc; savoury ingredients put into meat, poultry, etc, in cooking. — *adj* **stuff'y** badly ventilated, musty; stifling; stout, sturdy (*Scot*); stodgy (*slang*); strait-laced; sulky (*US*); (of a nose) blocked up with mucus, etc. — **stuffed shirt** a pompous, unbendingly correct person, *esp* if of little real importance; **stuff gown** a gown of stuff, not silk, *esp* that of a junior barrister; **stuffing box** a device for preventing leakage of gases or liquids along a reciprocating rod or rotating shaft, consisting of a ring-shaped chamber packed to provide a pressure-tight seal. — **and stuff** (*colloq*) and that sort of thing or rubbish; **bit of stuff** (*offensive slang*) a girl or woman considered sexually; **do one's stuff** to do what is expected of one; **get stuffed!** (*vulg slang*) *interj* expressing anger, derision, contemptuous dismissal, etc; **hot stuff** (*colloq*) denoting a very attractive, effective, etc person or thing; **knock the stuffing out of** to reduce (an opponent) to helplessness; **know one's stuff** to have a thorough knowledge of the field in which one is concerned; **stuff it** (or **them**, **you**, etc; *vulg slang*) *interj* expressing disgust, scorn, frustration, etc; **that's the stuff!** excellent!; (**a drop of**) **the hard stuff** (some) strongly alcoholic drink, *esp* whisky. [OFr *estoffe* stuff, from *estoffer* to furnish, equip, from Gmc *stopfōn*, earlier *stoppōn*, from LL *stuppāre* to plug, stop up, from L *stuppa*, from Gr *styppē* coarse fibres, tow]

stuggy *stug'i*, (*dialect*) *adj* thick-set, stout.

stull *stul*, (*mining*) *n* a horizontal prop in a stope. — *n* **stulm** (*stulm*) an adit; a small draining-shaft. [Cf Ger *Stollen*]

stultify *stul'ti-fī*, *vt* to dull the mind of; to cause to appear foolish or ridiculous; to destroy the force of, as by self-contradiction; to allege or prove to be of unsound mind (*law*): — *pr p* **stul'tifying**; *pa t* and *pa p* **stul'tified**. — *n* **stultificā'tion**. — *n* **stul'tifier**. [L *stultus* foolish]

stum *stum*, *n* must, grape-juice unfermented; new wine used to revive dead or vapid wine; a mixture used to impart artificial strength, etc, to weak beer or wine; wine revived by the addition of stum or by a second fermentation. — *vt* to renew or doctor with stum; to fume (eg a cask of liquor) with burning sulphur: — *pr p* **stumm'ing**; *pa t* and *pa p* **stummed**. [Du *stom* must, from *stom* mute; Ger *stumm* dumb]

stumble *stum'bl*, *vi* to take a false step or come near to falling in walking; to move or speak unsteadily or with hesitations; to err; to lapse into wrongdoing; to flounder; to come upon by chance or error (with *across* or *on*). — *vt* to disconcert. — *n* a trip; a false step; a lapse; a blunder. — *n* **stum'bler**. — *adv* **stum'blingly**. — *adj* **stum'bly** apt to stumble or to cause stumbling. — **stum'blebum** (*slang*; *orig* and *esp US*) an awkward, inept, ineffectual person; **stum'bling-block** an obstacle; a cause of perplexity or error. [ME *stomble*, *stumble*; cf Norw *stumla*, and **stammer**]

stumer *stū'mər*, (*slang*) *n* a counterfeit coin or note; a forged or worthless cheque; a sham; a dud; a failure, bankruptcy; a horse sure to lose; a stupid mistake, clanger; a stupid person (*Scot*). [Origin obscure]

stumm *stŏŏm*. Same as **shtoom**.

stummel *stum'l*, *n* the bowl and adjacent part of a pipe. [Ger]

stump *stump*, *n* the part of a felled or fallen tree left in the ground; a short thick remaining basal part, *esp* of anything that projects; a short thick branch; a leg (*facetious*); a wooden leg; anything stumpy; a stumping walk or its sound; a pencil of soft material for softening hard lines, blending, etc; one of the three sticks forming (with the bails) a wicket (*cricket*); a challenge to perform a feat (*US*); a tree stump or similar, used as a platform, eg by a public speaker. — *adj* reduced to a stump; stumpy. — *vt* to reduce to a stump; to remove stumps from; (of the wicket-keeper; sometimes with *out*) to dismiss by breaking the wicket when the striker is out of his or her ground (*cricket*); to clear out of money (*slang*); to nonplus, foil, defeat; to soften or tone with a stump; to walk over or strike heavily and stiffly; to traverse (an area) making political speeches; to dare, challenge (*US*). — *vi* to walk stiffly and heavily, as if on wooden legs; to make political speeches from improvised platforms. — *n* **stump'age** (*US*) standing timber, its monetary value, or money paid for it. — *n* **stump'er**. — *adv* **stump'ily**. — *n* **stump'iness**. — *n sing* **stumps** (*cricket*) the end of play. — *adj* **stump'y** short and thick; full of stumps (*US*). — *n* (*slang*) cash. — **stump orator** one who speaks from an improvised platform, *usu* with an implication of rant; (in the US) a political public speaker in general; **stump oratory**; **stump speech**; **stump work** elaborate raised embroidery of the 15c–17c using various materials and raised by stumps of wood or pads of wool. — **draw stumps** (*cricket*) to end play (also *fig*); **on the stump** engaged in a (political) speech-making tour, campaign; **stir one's stumps** to move, be active; **stump up** to pay up, fork out. [Cf Du *stomp*, MLGer *stump*, ON *stumpr*, Ger *Stumpf*]

stun *stun*, *vt* to render unconscious by a blow or similar; to stupefy or daze, eg with din or sudden emotion; to abrade, bruise: — *pr p* **stunn'ing**; *pa t* and *pa p* **stunned**. — *n* a shock, stupefying blow; stunned condition. —

adj (of a weapon) designed to stun rather than kill. — *n* **stunn'er** someone who or something that stuns; a person or thing supremely excellent (*colloq*); a very attractive person (*colloq*). — *n* **stunn'ing** stupefaction. — *adj* stupefying, dazing; supremely excellent (*colloq*); very attractive (*colloq*). — *adv* **stunn'ingly**. — **stun grenade, gun**, etc one designed to stun its target temporarily without causing serious injury. [OFr *estoner* (Fr *étonner*) to astonish; cf OE *stunian* to make a din, from *stun* a din]

Stundist *stŏŏn'dist*, *n* a member of a Russian Protestant evangelical sect. — *n* **Stun'dism**. [Ger *Stunde* hour, lesson, from their Bible-reading meetings]

stung *stung*, *pa t* and *pa p* of **sting**[1].

stunk *stungk*, *pa t* and *pa p* of **stink**.

stunkard *stungk'ərd*, (*Scot*) *adj* sulky; sullen. [Origin obscure]

stunsail, stuns'l *stun'sl*. See **studdingsail**.

stunt[1] *stunt*, *vt* to hinder from growth, to dwarf, check. — *n* a check in growth; a stunted animal. — *adj* **stunt'ed** dwarfed. — *n* **stunt'edness**. [OE *stunt* dull stupid; ON *stuttr* short]

stunt[2] *stunt*, *n* a difficult, often showy, performance, enterprise, or turn; anything done to attract attention. — Also *adj*. — *vi* to perform stunts. — **stunt'man** one paid to perform dangerous and showy feats (*esp* a stand-in for a film actor). [Perh a variant of **stint**[1], **stent**[1]; cf **stunt**[1]; or perh Ger *Stunde* hour, lesson]

stupa *stōō'pə*, *n* a dome-shaped Buddhist memorial shrine, a tope. [Sans *stūpa*]

stupe[1] *stūp*, (*archaic*) *n* a medicated piece of tow or cloth used in fomentation. — *vt* to treat with a stupe. [L *stūpa* for *stuppa*, from Gr *styppē* tow]

stupe[2]. See **stupid**.

stupefy *stū'pi-fī*, *vt* to make stupid or senseless (as with alcohol, drugs, etc); to stun with amazement, fear, etc. — *vi* to become stupid or dull: — *pr p* **stū'pefying**; *pa t* and *pa p* **stū'pefied**. — *adj* **stupefacient** (*-fā'shənt*) stupefying. — *n* a stupefying drug. — *n* **stupefaction** (*-fak'shən*) the act of stupefying; the state of being stupefied; extreme astonishment. — *adj* **stupefac'tive** stupefying. — *adj* **stu'pefied**. — *n* **stu'pefier**. — *adj* **stu'pefying**. [L *stupēre* to be struck senseless, and *facere* to make]

stupendous *stū-pen'dəs*, *adj* astounding; astoundingly huge; often used as a *colloq* term of approbation or admiration. — *adv* **stupen'dously**. — *n* **stupen'dousness**. — *adj* **stu'pent** (*rare*) astounded; dumbfounded. [L *stupendus*, gerundive, and *stupēns*, *-entis*, pr p of *stupēre* to be stunned]

stupid *stū'pid*, *adj* stupefied or stunned; senseless; insensible; deficient or dull in understanding; showing lack of reason or judgement; foolish; dull; boring. — *n* (*colloq*) a stupid person (also *colloq* **stupe**). — *n* **stupid'ity** or **stu'pidness**. — *adv* **stu'pidly**. [L *stupidus*]

stupor *stū'pər*, *n* torpor; lethargy; a state of near-unconsciousness (as caused by alcohol, drugs, etc). — *adj* **stu'porous**. [L *stupor*, *-ōris*, from *stupēre*]

stuprate *stū'prāt*, (*archaic*) *vt* to ravish, violate. — *n* **stuprā'tion**. [L *stuprāre*, *-ātum*]

sturdy *stûr'di*, *adj orig*, giddy; impetuous, violent, rough (*obs*); refractory; obstinate; resolute; robust; stout; firmly built or constructed. — *n* gid, a disease of sheep characterized by staggering, due to a bladderworm in the brain; a sturdy person. — *adj* **stur'died** affected with sturdy. — *adv* **stur'dily**. — *n* **stur'diness**. [OFr *estourdi* (Fr *étourdi*) stunned, giddy]

sture. See **stoor**[1].

sturgeon *stûr'jən*, *n* any member of a genus (*Acipenser*) of large fishes of N temperate waters, with a cartilaginous skull, long snout, heterocercal tail, and rows of bony shields on the skin, yielding caviar and isinglass. [Anglo-Fr from OFr *estourgeon*, of Gmc origin (OHGer *sturjo*)]

Sturge-Weber syndrome *sterj-web'er sin'drōm*, *n* a rare congenital condition in which abnormal distension and knotting of the blood vessels in part of the brain (causing weakness on the opposite side of the body, seizures, etc) is associated with a large purple birthmark spreading over one side of the face, including the eye. [W A *Sturge* (1850–1919) and F P *Weber* (1863–1962), British physicians]

Sturmabteilung *shtŏŏrm'ap-tī-lŏŏng*, *n pl* storm-troops (qv), Brownshirts. [Ger *Sturm* storm, and *Abteilung* division]

Sturmer *stûr'mər* or **Sturmer Pippin** (*pip'in*), (also without *caps*) *n* a variety of dessert apple named after *Sturmer*, a village in Essex where it was developed; an apple of this variety.

Sturm und Drang *shtŏŏrm ŏŏnt drang*, *n* a German literary movement of the latter half of the 18c, characterized by realism, extravagant passion and rousing action; storm and stress, turmoil. [Ger, literally storm and stress, title of a play by German dramatist F M von Klinger (1752–1831)]

sturnus *stûr'nəs*, *n* any bird of the starling genus (*Sturnus*) giving name to the family **Stur'nidae** (*-ni-dē*). — *adj* **stur'nine** or **stur'noid**. [L *sturnus* starling]

sturt *stûrt*, (chiefly *Scot*) *n* contention, strife, annoyance; a disturbance. — *vt* to trouble, annoy, disturb. — *vi* to start with fear. [**strut**]

stushie. See **stooshie**.

stutter *stut'ər*, *vi* and *vt* to speak, say, or pronounce with spasmodic repetition of (*esp* initial) sounds, *usu* consonants; to stammer. — *n* a speech impediment characterized by such repetition. — *n* **stutt'erer**. — *n* and *adj* **stutt'ering**. — *adv* **stutt'eringly**. [A frequentative of obs dialect *stut* to stutter, ME *stutten*; cf ON *stauta*; Ger *stossen*]

STV *abbrev*: Scottish Television; Single Transferable Vote.

sty[1] or **stye** *stī*, *n* a small inflamed swelling at the edge of the eyelid, caused by bacterial infection. — Also called (*med*) **hordeolum**. [Obs or dialect *stian*, *styan*, from OE *stīgend*, from *stīgan* to rise]

sty[2] *stī*, (*obs*) *vi* to mount, rise, climb. — Also **stye** or **stie**. — *n* a path; a ladder. [OE *stīgan* to mount, rise, ascend, *stīg* path, and ON *stige* path, OE *stīge* ascent or descent]

sty[3] or rarely **stye** *stī*, *n* a pen for pigs; any extremely filthy place; any place of gross debauchery: — *pl* **sties** or **styes**. — *vt* and *vi* to put or keep in a sty: — *pr p* **sty'ing**; *pa t* and *pa p* **stied** or **styed**. [OE *stig* pen, hall; Ger *Steige*]

stye. See **sty**[1,2,3].

Stygian *stij'i-ən* or *-yən*, *adj* of the *Styx*, one of the rivers of Hades, across which Charon ferries the spirits of the dead (*Gr mythol*); hellish, infernal, gloomy; black as the Styx. — **Stygian oath** an inviolable oath, like that of the gods, by the Styx. [Gr *Styx*; cf *stygein* to hate]

stylar, stylate. See under **style**.

style *stīl*, *n* the manner of writing, mode of expressing thought in language or of expression, execution, action or bearing generally; a literary composition (*obs*); the distinctive manner peculiar to an author or other; the particular custom or form observed, as by a printing house in optional matters (*style of the house* or *house style*), or by lawyers in drawing up deeds; designation; manner, form, fashion, *esp* when considered superior or desirable; an air of fashion or consequence; a kind or type; a slender structure of various kinds (*biol*); the slender part of the pistil of a flower connecting the stigma and the ovary (*bot*); a hand, pointer, index; the gnomon of a dial; a pointed instrument for writing on wax tablets; a similar instrument or tool of various kinds, such as a graver, a blunt probe, a tracing or cutting point; a mode of reckoning dates, ie *Old Style*, according to the Julian calendar, as in Britain till 1752, Russia till 1917, and *New Style*, according to the Gregorian calendar, adopted in Britain by omitting eleven days, 3th to 13th September 1752. — *vt* to arrange or dictate the fashion or style of; to designate. — *adj* and *adv combining form* **-style** in the style of, resembling. — *adj* **sty'lar**. — *adj* **sty'late** having a style or a persistent style. — *adj* **style'less**. — *n* **sty'let** or **stī'let** a probe; a wire in a catheter; a small bristlelike process (*biol*); an engraving tool; a writing instrument; a piercing part of an insect's jaws; a stiletto. — *adj* **stylif'erous** (*bot* and *zool*) bearing a slender structure of various kinds. — *adj* **sty'liform** (*bot* and *zool*) shaped like a style or a bristle. — *adj* **sty'lish** displaying style; fashionable; showy; imposingly smart. — *adv* **sty'lishly**. — *n* **sty'lishness**. — *n* **sty'list** a person with a distinctive and fine (*esp* literary, etc) style; a person who creates or arranges a style, *esp* in hairdressing. — *adj* **stylist'ic**. — Also *n*. — *adv* **stylist'ically**. — *n sing* **stylis'tics** the science of the variations in language, including the effective values of different words, forms, and sounds, that constitute style in the literary and also the wider sense. — *n* **stylīzā'tion** or **-s-**. — *vt* **sty'lize** or **-ise** to conventionalize; to give an elaborate, *esp* non-naturalistic, style to. — *adj* **sty'loid** (*bot* and *zool*) like a style or bristle; forming a slender process. — *n* a spiny process, *esp* that of the temporal bone in the skull. — **style'book** a book of forms for deeds, etc, or rules for printers and editors. — **in style** in a grand manner. [L *stilus* a writing instrument, literary composition or style, confused with Gr *stȳlos* a column; in some senses perh from the Gr word]

stylite *stī'līt*, *n* one of a class of ascetics that lived on the tops of pillars in ancient times. [Gr *stȳlītēs*, from *stȳlos* a pillar]

stylize, -ise. See under **style**.

stylo. See under **stylography**.

stylobate *stī'lō-bāt*, (*archit*) *n* a continuous pedestal supporting a row of columns. [Gr *stȳlobatēs*, from *stȳlos* a column, and *batēs* someone who treads, from the root of *bainein* to walk]

stylography *stī-log'rə-fi*, *n* a mode of writing or engraving with a style. — *n* **styl'ograph** (*stī'lə-gräf*; *colloq* short form **sty'lō**: — *pl* **sty'lōs**) a pencil-like pen from which ink is liberated by pressure on a needle-point. — *adj* **stylographic** (*-graf'ik*). — *adv* **stylograph'ically**. [Gr *stȳlos* a style, and *graphein* to write]

styloid. See under **style**.

stylolite *stī-lol'īt*, (*geol*) *n* an irregular suture-like boundary creating columnar formations in some limestones and evaporites, *usu* independent of the bedding planes, and probably formed by pressure-controlled solution followed by redeposition. — *adj* **styloli'tic**. [Gr *stȳlos* pillar, and **-lite**]

stylometry *stī-lom'ə-tri*, *n* a method of studying literary style and development by means of statistical analysis. [Gr *stȳlos* a style, and *metron* a measure]

stylopized or **-s-** *stī'lop-īzd*, *adj* (of eg bees) infested with a strepsipterous parasite of the *Stylops* or a similar genus.

stylopodium *stī-lō-pō'di-əm*, (*bot*) *n* the swollen disc-shaped or conical base of the style in umbelliferous plants. [Gr *stȳlos* pillar (as if style), and *podion*, dimin of *pous*, *podos* foot]

stylus *stī'ləs*, *n* the cutting needle used in making gramophone records; a durable needle (eg sapphire- or diamond-tipped) for replaying a disc recording; same as **style** in the sense of the writing instrument or similar: — *pl* **styli** (*stī'lī*) or **sty'luses**. [Ety as for **style**]

styme or **stime** *stīm*, (*Scot*) *n* a glimmer or glimpse (of light); a tiny amount, jot, particle, etc. — *vi* to peer. — *n* **stymie, stimie** or **stimy** (*stī'mi*) a purblind person (*Scot*); a situation on the putting-green, once difficult to overcome, in which an opponent's ball blocks the way to the hole, the rules now allowing the obstructing ball to be lifted and its position marked (*golf*); hence, a situation from which it is difficult or impossible to proceed. — *vt* to put in such a situation (also **lay someone a stymie**); to frustrate, thwart, prevent, obstruct, block, stop: — *pa t* and pa p **sty'mied**. — Also *adj*. [Origin obscure]

styptic *stip'tik*, *adj* drawing together; astringent; checking bleeding, haemostatic. — *n* a styptic agent. — *n* **styp'sis** the use, action, etc of a styptic or styptics. — *adj* **styp'tical**. — *n* **stypticity** (*-tis'i-ti*). — **styptic pencil** a healing agent for minor cuts, *esp* sustained during shaving. [Gr *stȳptikos*, from *stȳphein* to contract]

styrax *stī'raks*, *n* any tropical or subtropical styracaceous tree or shrub of the genus *Styrax*, eg *Styrax officinalis* (see **storax**). — *adj* **styraca'ceous** of, related or belonging to the storax family *Styracaceae*, chiefly American and Asian trees and shrubs with leathery, alternate leaves and often fragrant, bell-shaped white flowers. [Gr *styrax*]

styre. See **stir**[1].

styrene *stī'rēn* or *stēr'ēn*, *n* an unsaturated hydrocarbon obtained from essential oils (such as the balsam storax) and coal-tar, forming thermoplastics (**styrene resins**) on polymerization. [Gr *styrax*; cf **storax**]

Styrofoam® *stī'rə-fōm*, *n* (also without *cap*) a type of expanded plastic made from polystyrene.

suable *sū'* or *sōō'ə-bl*, *adj* that may be sued. — *adv* **su'ably**. — *n* **suabil'ity**.

suasion *swā'zhən*, *n* persuasion. — *adj* **sua'sible** (*-si-bl*). — *adj* **sua'sive** (*-siv*). — *adv* **sua'sively**. — *n* **sua'siveness**. — *adj* **sua'sory**. [L *suāsiō*, *-ōnis*, from *suādēre* to advise]

suave *swäv* (formerly *swāv*), *adj* (of a person, *esp* a man) polite, sophisticated and smoothly affable, *esp* superficially so; smooth, bland. — *adv* **suave'ly**. — *n* **suavity** (*swäv'i-ti*). [Fr, from L *suāvis* sweet, agreeable]

suaveolent *swə-vē'ə-lənt*, (*rare*) *adj* fragrant. [L *suāveolēns*, *-entis*, from *suāvē* sweetly, and *olēns* smelling]

sub. *abbrev*: subject.

sub- *sub-* or *səb-*, *pfx* (1) under, underneath, underlying, below, at the bottom of; (2) subordinate, subsidiary, secondary; (3) part of, a subdivision of; (4) almost, partially, nearly, somewhat imperfectly, bordering on, deviating slightly from; (5) secretly, covertly; (6) (*chem*) in smaller proportion; (7) in the style of but inferior to, as in *sub-Chaplin*, *sub-Beethoven* (*informal*). — *n* **sub** (*colloq*) a subordinate; a subaltern; a sub-editor; a sublieutenant; a subsidiary; a subway; a subscription (also **subs**); a subscriber; a substitute; a submarine; subsistence money, hence a loan, an advance payment. — *vi* (*colloq*) to act as a sub; to work as a substitute; to work as a newspaper subeditor. — *vt* (*colloq*) to subedit: — *pr p* **subb'ing**; *pa t* and *pa p* **subbed**. — *n* **subb'ing** (*colloq*) the advancing of part of the wages while the work is going on. [L *sub* under, near; in composition, in some degree, secretly]

Words with the prefix **sub-** are listed in the following text or in the separate panels.

subacid *sub-as'id*, *adj* somewhat or moderately acid or sour (*lit* and *fig*). — *n* **subacid'ity** or **subac'idness**. — *adv* **subac'idly**. [**sub-** (4)]

subact *sub-akt'*, *vt* to work up (as in cultivation, the process of digestion, etc); to subdue. — *n* **subac'tion** (*-shən*). [L *subactus*, pa p of *subigere*, from *sub* under, and *agere* to drive, do]

Some words with **sub-** prefix; see **sub-** entry for numbered senses.

sub'abbot *n* (2).
subabdom'inal *adj* (1).
subac'etate *n* (6).
subac'rid *adj* (4).
subadmin'istrative *adj* (2).
subadmin'istrator *n* (2).
subaf'fluent *adj* (4).
suba'gency *n* (2).
suba'gent *n* (2).
subag'gregate *n* and *adj* (6).
subaggrega'tion *n* (6).
suballi'ance *n* (2).
suballoca'tion *n* (3).
subang'ular *adj* (4).
subantarc'tic *adj* (4).
subappear'ance *n* (2).
subarbor'eal *adj* (1 and 4).
subarboresc'ent *adj* (1 and 4).
subarc'tic *adj* (4).
sub'area *n* (2 and 3).
subar'id *adj* (4).

subacute *sub-ə-kūt'*, *adj* slightly or moderately acute; (of a disease) not acute but progressing more rapidly than chronic (*med*). — *adv* **subacute'ly**. [**sub-** (4)]

subadar. See under **subah**.

subadult *sub-ad'ult* or *sub-ə-dult'*, *adj* (*usu* of an animal) fully or almost fully grown but not yet having developed all the adult characteristics; adolescent. — *n* an individual at subadult stage. [**sub-** (4)]

subaerial *sub-ā-ē'ri-əl*, *adj* in the open air; occurring on the land at or near the earth's surface, as opposed to underground or under water. — *adv* **subāē'rially**. [**sub-** (1)]

subah *sōō'bä*, *n* a province of the Mogul empire; a subahdar. — *n* **subahdar** or **subadar** *orig* the governor of a subah; a native officer in an Indian regiment corresponding to a captain. — *n* **subahdar'y** or **su'bahship** the office of subahdar. [Hindi and Pers]

subalpine *sub-al'pīn*, *adj* bordering on the alpine; at the foot of or on the lower slopes of the Alps. [**sub-** (4) and (1)]

subaltern *sub'əl-tərn* (*NAm*, except in logic, *usu sub-öl'tərn*), *adj* (of military officers) under the rank of captain; particular (*logic*); being at once a genus and a species of a higher genus (*logic*); ranked successively (*rare*); subordinate, of inferior status; occupied by, or having the status of, a vassal (*archaic*). — *n* a subaltern officer; a proposition differing from another in quantity alone (both being affirmative or both negative, but one universal, the other particular) (*logic*); a subordinate. — *n* **subalter'nant** (*logic*) a universal in relation to the subaltern particular. — *n* **subalter'nate** (*logic*) a particular proposition in relation to the subaltern universal. — *adj* subservient, lesser in status, etc; intermediate between alternate and opposite (*bot*). — *n* **subalternation** (*sub-öl-tər-nā'shən*) the relation between a universal and particular of the same quality. — *n* **subalter'nity** subordinate position. [L *subalternus*, from *sub* under, and *alter* another]

subapical *sub-ā'pi-kəl* or *-ap'i-*, *adj* below the apex. [**sub-** (1)]

subapostolic *sub-ap-os-tol'ik*, *adj* of the time just after that of the apostles. [**sub-** (4)]

subaquatic *sub-ə-kwat'ik*, *adj* under water (also **sub-ā'queous**); partially aquatic (*zool* and *bot*). — *adj* **suba'qua** or **sub-a'qua** of or relating to underwater sport. [**sub-** (1) and (4)]

subarachnoid *sub-ə-rak'noid*, (*anatom*) *adj* below the arachnoid membrane; of, relating to or occurring in the space between the arachnoid membrane and the pia meninges of the brain. [**sub-** (1)]

subarcuate *sub-är'kū-āt*, *adj* somewhat arched; with two or more arches under a main arch (*archit*). — *n* **subarcūā'tion**. [**sub-** (4) and (1)]

subarrhation or **subarration** *sub-ə-rā'shən*, *n* an ancient mode of betrothal in which a ring or gift, *esp* of money, was bestowed by the man upon the woman. [L *subarr(h)ātiō*, *-ōnis*, from *sub* under, and *arr(h)a* earnest-money]

subassembly *sub-ə-sem'bli*, (*eng*) *n* an assembled unit that may be incorporated with others in a more complex assembly. — *vt* **subassem'ble**. [**sub-** (2)]

subastral *sub-as'trəl*, *adj* beneath the stars, terrestrial. [**sub-** (1)]

subatom *sub-at'əm*, *n* a constituent part of an atom. — *adj* **subatom'ic** relating to particles constituting the atom or processes that occur within the atom or at less than atomic level. — *n sing* **subatom'ics** the study of these particles and processes. [**sub-** (3)]

subaudition *sub-ö-dish'ən*, (*esp gram*) *n* a sense understood or implied without being expressed. [**sub-** (5)]

subbase *sub'bās*, *n* the lowest part of a base (*archit*); a division of a military base. — *adj* **subbasal** (*sub'bās'əl*) near or below the base. [**sub-** (1) and (3)]

subbie *sub'ē*, (*colloq*) *n* a subcontractor, *esp* one working for a main contractor in the construction industry. — Also **subby**.

Subbuteo® *sub-oo'ti-ō*, *n* a version of table football in which individual toy players mounted on hemispherical bases are flicked with the fingers.

subcalibre or (*NAm*) **subcaliber** *sub-kal'i-bər*, *adj* (of ammunition) of a calibre less than the firearm or barrel used to fire it. [**sub-** (4)]

subcarrier *sub-kar'i-ər*, (*telecomm*) *n* a modulated frequency used to modulate (with others) a main carrier wave. [**sub-** (2)]

subcartilaginous *sub-kär-ti-laj'in-əs*, *adj* composed partly of cartilage; situated under a cartilage. [**sub-** (4) and (1)]

subcellular *sub-sel'ū-lər*, (*biol*) *adj* occurring within a cell; smaller than a cell. [**sub-** (3) and (6)]

subception. See **subliminal perception** under **subliminal**.

subchanter *sub'chänt'ər*, *n* a precentor's deputy; an officer or lay member of a cathedral who assists in chanting the litany. [**sub-** (2)]

subclavian *sub-klā'vi-ən*, (*anatom*) *adj* and *n* (any of the arteries, nerves, etc) situated or passing under the clavicle. — *adj* **subclavic'ular**. [**sub-** (1) and **clavicle**]

subclimax *sub-klī'maks*, (*ecol*) *n* a relatively stable plant community or system at some stage of a succession preceding climax. [**sub-** (4)]

subclinical *sub-klin'i-kəl*, *adj* (of a disease) not sufficiently developed to be detectable by usual clinical methods. [**sub-** (4)]

subcompact *sub-kom'pakt*, (*NAm*) *n* a small car, such as a sports car. [**sub-** (2)]

subconscious *sub-kon'shəs*, *adj* dimly conscious; distant from the focus of attention but capable of being consciously recalled; (of memories, motives, intentions, thoughts, etc) of which the individual is only dimly aware but which exert an influence on his or her behaviour. — *n* the subconscious mind or activities. — *adv* **subcon'sciously**. — *n* **subcon'sciousness**. [**sub-** (4)]

subcontinent *sub-kon'ti-nənt*, *n* a large portion of a continent with a character of its own (a term formerly applied to South Africa, later to India); a large landmass not large enough or distinct enough to be called a continent. — *adj* **subcontinent'al**. — **Indian subcontinent** the area covered by India, Pakistan, Bangladesh, Sikkim, Bhutan and Nepal. [**sub-** (2), (4) and (1)]

subcontract *sub-kon'trakt*, *n* a contract subordinate to another contract, as for the subletting of work. — *vi* **subcontract'** to let out or undertake work under a subcontract. — *vt* to engage one or more parties as subcontractor(s) to carry out (work forming all or part of an original contract); to undertake (work) under a subcontract. — *n* **subcontract'ing**. — *n* **subcontract'or**. [**sub-** (2)]

subcontrary *sub-kon'trə-ri*, (*logic*) *adj* (of a particular proposition in relation to another differing only in quality) such that at least one must be true. — *n* a subcontrary proposition. — *n* **subcontrarī'ety**. [**sub-** (4)]

subcostal *sub-kost'əl*, *adj* near or under a rib or the ribs; behind or near the costa. — *n* the subcostal nervure or vein of an insect's wing (also **subcost'a**). [**sub-** (1)]

sub'article *n* (2 and 3).
subassocia'tion *n* (2).
subatmospher'ic *adj* (1 and 4).
subau'dible *adj* (1).
subaud'io *adj* (4).
subau'ral *adj* (4).
subauric'ular *adj* (1).
subav'erage *adj* (1).
subax'illary (or *-l'*) *adj* (1).
subbase'ment *n* (1).
sub'branch *n* (2 and 3).
sub'breed *n* (3).
sub'bureau *n* (2).
subcab'inet *n* (1).
subcan'tor *n* (2).
subcap'sular *adj* (4).
subcar'dinal *n* (2).
sub'caste *n* (3).
subcat'egory *n* (3).
subcau'dal *adj* (1).
subcav'ity *n* (1).

subcritical *sub-krit'i-kl, adj* of insufficient mass to sustain a chain reaction (*phys*); below the critical temperature for hardening metals. [**sub-** (1)]

subculture *sub-kul'chər, n* a social, ethnic or economic group with a particular character of its own within a larger culture or society; a culture (eg of a micro-organism) derived from a pre-existing one. — *adj* **sub'cul'tural**. [**sub-** (2) and (3)]

subcutaneous *sub-kū-tā'ni-əs, adj* beneath or just under the skin. — *adv* **subcuta'neously**. [**sub-** (1)]

subdeacon *sub-dē'kən, n* a member of the order of the ministry next below that of deacon, preparing the vessels, etc at the eucharist. — *n* **subdea'conry**. — *n* **subdea'conship**. [**sub-** (2)]

subdelirious *sub-də-lir'i-əs, adj* mildly or intermittently delirious. — *n* **subdelir'ium**. [**sub-** (4)]

subdew. An *obs* form of **subdue**.

subdivide *subdi-vīd', vt* and *vi* to divide into smaller divisions; to divide again. — *n* **subdivid'er**. — *adj* **subdivisible** (*-viz'*). — *n* **subdivision** (*-vizh'ən*). — *adj* **subdivis'ional**. — *adj* **subdivī'sive**. [**sub-** (3)]

sub divo *sub dī'vō, so͞ob dē'vō* or *-wō*, (*L*) *adv* under the sky; in the open air. — Also **sub Jove** (*jō'vē, yō've* or *-we*) under Jupiter (the god of the sky or heavens).

subdolous *sub'dō-ləs*, (*rare*) *adj* crafty. [L pfx *sub-*, in sense of somewhat, and *dolus* a wile]

subdominant *sub'dom'i-nənt, n* the fourth degree of the diatonic scale, eg F in the scale of C (*music*); something that is partially or not quite dominant. — *adj* not quite ranking as dominant; partially dominant. [**sub-** (1) and (4)]

subduce *sub-dūs', vt* (*obs*) to withdraw. — *vt* **subduct** (*-dukt'*) to withdraw, take away (now *rare*); to abstract or take away secretly or surreptitiously (*rare*); to lift up; to cause subduction. — *vi* to take something away (now *rare*); to undergo subduction. — *n* **subduc'tion** a withdrawal, subtraction (now *rare*); the action or process of one part of the earth's crust moving underneath another. — **subduction zone** the Benioff zone. [L *sub*, and *dūcere, ductum* to lead, take]

subdue (*Spenser* **subdew**) *sub-dū', vt* to overcome, conquer; to overpower; to subject; to make (a person or animal) submissive; to bring (land) under cultivation; to allay; to reduce the intensity, degree, etc of; to quieten; to tone down; to achieve (*Spenser*). — *adj* **subdu'able**. — *n* **subdu'al**. — *adj* **subdued'** toned down; quiet, restrained; dejected, in low spirits; passive. — *adv* **subdued'ly** (or *-dū'id-li*). — *n* **subdued'ness**. — *n* **subdue'ment**. — *n* **subdu'er**. [OFr *souduire*, from L *subdūcere*; see **subduce**]

subduple *sub-dū'pl* or *sub'dū-pl, adj* in the ratio of one to two. — *adj* **subdū'plicate** (of a ratio) expressed as the ratio of square roots. [LL *subduplus*]

subdural *sub-dū'rəl* or *-do͞o'rəl*, (*anatom*) *adj* below the dura mater; of, relating to or occurring in the space between the dura mater and the arachoid membrane of the brain. [**sub-** (1)]

subedar. Same as **subahdar**; see under **subah**.

subedit *sub-ed'it, vt* to select and edit material for (a newspaper); also, to assist in editing. — *n* **subed'itor**. — *adj* **subeditorial** (*-tōr'* or *-tör'*). — *n* **subed'itorship**. [**sub-** (2)]

subentire *sub-en-tīr'*, (*bot*) *adj* (of a leaf or other flat plant member) with very faintly indented margin. [**sub-** (4)]

suber *sū'bər*, (*bot* and *chem*) *n* the bark of the cork tree; cork. — *n* **su'berate** a salt of suberic acid. — *adj* **subē'reous** or **suberic** (*-ber'ik*) of cork (**suberic acid** an acid, $HOOC{\cdot}(CH_2)_6COOH$, obtained by the action of nitric acid on cork). — *n* **su'berin** the complex of fatty substances that form the chemical basis of cork tissue making it waterproof and resistant to decay. — *n* **suberīzā'tion** or **-s-** the deposition of suberin in the cell walls of cork. — *vt* **su'berize** or **-ise** to deposit suberin in (cell walls) thus forming cork. — *adj* **su'berose** or **su'berous** like or having the appearance of cork. [L *sūber, -eris* the cork oak]

subfamily *sub'fam'i-li*, (*bot* and *zool*) *n* a taxonomic division of a family, of one or more genera. [**sub-** (3)]

subfeu *sub'fū*, (*hist*) *n* a feu granted to a vassal. — *vt* **subfeu'** to make a subinfeudation of. — *n* **subfeudā'tion** subinfeudation. — *adj* **subfeud'atory**. [**sub-** (2)]

subfloor *sub'flōr* or *-flör, n* a rough floor forming the foundation for the finished floor. [**sub-** (1)]

subframe *sub'frām, n* the frame on which the coachwork of a motor car is built (cf **chassis**); a frame built into a wall to which a door- or window-frame is fixed. [**sub-** (1)]

subfusc or, less commonly, **subfusk** *sub'fusk* or *sub-fusk'*, *adj* dusky; sombre. — *n* dark, formal clothes worn in combination with the academic gown, *esp* at Oxford University. — *adj* (*rare*) **subfusc'ous**. [L *subfuscus* dark brown, from *sub* under, and *fuscus* tawny]

subgenus *sub-jē'nəs*, (*bot* and *zool*) *n* a taxonomic division of a genus: — *pl* **subgenera** (*-jen'ə-rə*) or **subge'nuses**. — *adj* **subgener'ic**. — *adv* **subgener'ically**. [**sub-** (3)]

subglacial *sub-glā'si-əl* or *-glā'shəl, adj* at the base or bottom of a glacier. — *adv* **subgla'cially**. [**sub-** (1)]

subgrade *sub'grād, n* levelled ground under the foundations of a road or a railway. [**sub-** (1)]

subgum *sub-gum', n* and *adj* (of) a Chinese-style dish consisting of mixed vegetables, and sometimes diced meat or seafood. [Chin *sháp kám* literally, mixture]

subhastation *sub-has-tā'shən*, (*obs* or *hist*) *n* sale by public auction. [L *sub* under, and *hasta* a lance (set up by the Romans as a sign that an auction was to be held)]

subhedral *sub-hēd'rəl*, (*geol*) *adj* showing some traces of crystal form, hypidiomorphic. [**sub-** (4)]

subhuman *sub-hū'mən, adj* less than human, not quite human; of or designating animals that are below the human race in evolutionary development. [**sub-** (4)]

subhumid *sub-hū'mid, adj* (of a climate) too wet for xerophytic vegetation but not wet enough for tree growth. [**sub-** (4)]

subimago *sub-im-ā'gō, n* a stage in the life history of a mayfly, emerging from the last aquatic nymph already winged but before the last moult: — *pl* **subimagines** (*-i-mā'jin-ēz* or *-gin-*) or **subimā'gōs**. — *adj* **subima'ginal**. [**sub-** (4)]

subincision *sub-in-sizh'ən, n* the formation of an opening into the urethra by incision of the underside of the penis, as a puberty rite practised by some trible peoples. — *vt* **subincise'** to perform subincision upon. [**sub-** (1)]

subindicate *sub-in'di-kāt*, (*obs*) *vt* to hint. — *n* **subindicā'tion**. — *adj* **subindic'ative**. [**sub-** (4)]

subinfeudation *sub-in-fū-dā'shən, n* the granting of land by a feudal tenant or vassal to a subtenant who became his vassal; the tenure so granted or established. — *vt* and *vi* **subinfeu'date**. — *adj* and *n* **subinfeud'atory**. [**sub-** (2)]

subintelligitur *sub-in-tel-i'ji-tər* or *so͞ob-in-tel-i'gi-to͞or, n* an implication that is understood without necessarily being stated. — Also **subintellec'tion** or **subintell'igence**. [L, literally it is more or less understood, from *sub* in the sense of covertly, and *intelligere* to understand]

subintrant *sub-in'trənt*, (*med*) *adj* (of fevers) with paroxysms succeeding close upon one another. [**sub-** (4)]

subceil'ing *n* (1).
subceles'tial *adj* (1).
sub'cellar *n* (1).
subcent'ral *adj* (1 and 4).
sub'chapter *n* (2 and 3).
sub'charter *n* (2).
sub'chelate *adj* (6).
sub'chief *n* (2).
sub'chloride *n* (6).
sub'chord *n* (1).
sub'circuit *n* (2).
subciviliza'tion *n* (4).
subciv'ilized *adj* (4).
sub'claim *n* (2).
sub'class *n* (3).
sub'clause *n* (2).
subcommiss'ion *n* (2 and 3).
subcommiss'ioner *n* (2 and 3).
subcommitt'ee *n* (2 and 3).
subcomm'unity *n* (3).
subcontig'uous *adj* (4).

subintroduce *sub-in-trō-dūs'*, *vt* to bring in surreptitiously or subtly. [**sub-** (5)]

subinvolution *sub-in-və-lū'shən* or *-lōō'*, (*med*) *n* partial or complete failure of the uterus to return to its normal size in the six weeks following childbirth. [**sub-** (4)]

subirrigation *sub-ir-i-gā'shən*, *n* irrigation by underground pipes; irrigation from beneath. — *vt* **subirr'igate**. [**sub-** (1)]

subitaneous *sub-i-tā'ni-əs*, (*rare*) *adj* sudden; hasty; hastily made. [L *subitāneus*, from *subitus* sudden]

subitize or **-ise** *sub'i-tīz*, (*psychol*) *vt* to perceive or be capable of perceiving (the number of items in a group) at a glance without actually counting. — *vi* (of the number of items in a group) to be perceived in this way. [L *subitus* sudden, and **-ize**]

subito *sōō'bi-tō*, (*music*) *adv* suddenly; immediately; in haste. [Ital]

subj. *abbrev*: subject; subjective; subjunctive.

subjacent *sub-jā'sənt*, *adj* underlying; (of a rock mass) having no perceptible base, bottomless (*geol*). [L *subjacēns*, *-entis*, from *sub* under, and *jacēre* to lie]

subject *sub'jikt*, *adj* (often with *to*) under rule, government, jurisdiction, or control; owing allegiance; under obligation; subordinate; subservient; dependent; liable; exposed; prone, disposed; cognizable; dependent upon condition or contingency; underlying, spread out below (*obs*). — *adv* conditionally (with *to*). — *n* a person who is subject; a person who is under, or who owes allegiance to, a sovereign, a state, a feudal superior, etc; a citizen; a body of such persons (*Shakesp*); a thing over which a legal right is exercised; a piece of property (*Scot*); a substance (*obs*); something having inherent attributes; a thing existing independently; the mind regarded as the thinking power (as opposed to the *object* about which it thinks); that of which something is predicated, or the term denoting it (*logic*); that part of a sentence or clause denoting the person or thing about which something is said (*gram*); a topic; a matter of discourse, thought, or study; a department of study; a theme; a person or thing on which any operation is performed; a person or thing that is treated or handled; matter for any action or operation; a ground; a sufferer from disease, a patient; a dead body for dissection (*anatom*); a person peculiarly sensitive to hypnotic influence; the person or thing that an artist or photographer seeks to represent or express; a picture representing action and incident; a theme or phrase around which a movement of music is built. — *vt* **subject** (*səb-jekt'*) to make subject; to make liable; to subordinate; to submit; to subdue; to lay open. — *adj* **subject'ed** made subject; subjacent (*obs*). — *vt* **subject'ify** to make subjective. — *n* **subjec'tion**. — *adj* **subject'ive** relating to the subject; derived from, expressive of or existing in one's own consciousness; personal, individual; influenced by or derived from personal taste or opinion and lacking impartiality or objectivity; nominative (*gram*); introspective. — *n* (*gram*) the subjective case. — *adv* **subject'ively**. — *n* **subject'iveness**. — *n* **subject'ivism** (*philos*) a term used loosely to denote any view, statement, etc in which the truth of the statement, etc depends or is founded on the mental state or reactions of the individual making it, and not on objective reasoning. — *n* and *adj* **subject'ivist**. — *adj* **subjectivist'ic**. — *adv* **subjectivist'ically**. — *n* **subjectiv'ity**. — *n* **subjectiviza'tion** or **-s-**. — *vt* **subject'ivize** or **-ise**. — *adj* **sub'jectless**. — *n* **sub'jectship** the state of being subject. — **subject catalogue** in a library, a catalogue of books arranged according to subjects dealt with; **subject heading**; **subjective idealism** (*philos*) a view that what is perceived exists only when and because it is perceived, subjectivism; **subject matter** the subject, theme or topic; **sub'ject-ob'ject** (*philos*) the immediate object of cognition, or the thought itself; **sub'ject-super'ior** a superior who is himself the subject of a sovereign. [L *subjectus* thrown under, from *sub* under, and *jacere* to throw]

subjoin *sub-join'*, *vt* (*formal*) to add at the end or afterwards, to append. — *n* **subjoin'der** (*Lamb*) a remark following on another. — *n* **subjunc'tion** the act or fact of subjoining. [**sub-** in addition, and **join**]

sub Jove. See **sub divo**.

sub judice *sub jōō'di-sē* or *sŏŏb ū'di-ke*, (*formal* or *law*) *adj* under (judicial) consideration; before, but not yet decided by, a judge or court (and therefore not able to be discussed or reported). [L]

subjugate *sub'jōō-gāt*, *vt* to bring under the yoke; to bring under power or domination; to make subservient; to conquer. — *n* **subjugā'tion**. — *n* **sub'jugātor**. [L *subjugāre*, *-ātum*, from *sub* under, and *jugum* a yoke]

subjunctive *səb-jungk'tiv*, *adj* subjoined, added to something; (of a verb) in a mood or form expressing condition, hypothesis, or contingency (*gram*). — *n* the subjunctive mood; a subjunctive form; a verb in the subjunctive mood (eg *if I WERE you*, *far BE it from me* etc). — *adv* **subjunct'ively**. [L *subjunctīvus*, from *sub*, and *jungere*, to join]

subkingdom *sub'king-dəm*, (*bot* and *zool*) *n* a taxonomic division of a kingdom; a phylum. [**sub-** (2)]

Sublapsarian *sub-lap-sā'ri-ən*, *n* (also without *cap*) a believer in Sublapsarianism. — Also *adj*. — *n* **Sublapsā'rianism** (also without *cap*) a doctrine of moderate Calvinists, that God permitted the fall of Adam without preordaining it. [L *sub* in some degree, and *lāpsus* a fall]

sublate *sub-lāt'*, *vt* to remove (*obs*); to deny, contradict (*logic*); to resolve in a higher all-embracing unity by combining thesis and antithesis in a synthesis (*philos*). — *n* **sublā'tion**. [L *sublātum*, used as supine of *tollere* to take away, from *sub-* in sense of away, and *lātum*]

sublease *sub'lēs*, *n* an underlease or lease by a tenant to another. — *vt* and *vi* **sublease'**. — *n* **sublessee'** the holder of a sublease. — *n* **subless'or** a person who or organization that grants a sublease. [**sub-** (2)]

sublet *sub-let'*, *vt* and *vi* to sublease: — *pa t* and *pa p* **sublet'**. — *n* a subletting. — *n* **sublett'er**. — *n* **sublett'ing**. [**sub-** (2)]

sublieutenant *sub-lef-ten'ant* or (*US*) *-lōō-*, *n* a naval officer ranking with an army lieutenant — formerly *mate*, or *passed midshipman*. [**sub-** (2)]

sublime *səb-līm'*, *adj* exalted, lofty; majestic; supreme; of the highest or noblest nature; awakening feelings of awe and veneration; raised up, lifted on high (*archaic*); of proud or supercilious aspect or bearing (*literary*); just under the skin (*anatom*). — *n* that which is sublime; a pinnacle of achievement, surpassing excellence, the lofty or grand, in thought, arrangement or style; the supreme degree. — *vt* to raise up, to exalt; to transmute into something higher; to object to or obtain by sublimation; to deposit as a sublimate; to purify by (or as if by) sublimation. — *vi* to undergo sublimation. — *adj* **sublīm'able**. — *vt* **sublimate** (*sub'lim-āt*) to elevate; to sublime; to purify by sublimation; to transmute into something higher; to direct unconsciously (a primitive impulse such as an aggressive or sexual impulse) into a higher or more socially acceptable action; to direct into a higher channel. — *n* (*-mət*; *chem*) a product of

subcontin'uous *adj* (4).	**subcrust'al** *adj* (1).	**subdi'alect** *n* (3).
sub'cool *adj* (1).	**subdean'** *adj* (2).	**subdis'trict** *n* (3).
subcor'date *adj* (4).	**subdean'ery** *n* (2).	**sub'dorsal** *adj* (1 and 4).
subcor'tex *n* (1 and 4).	**subdeca'nal** *adj* (2).	**subeconom'ic** *adj* (1).
subcort'ical *adj* (1 and 4).	**subder'mal** *adj* (1).	**sube'qual** *adj* (4).
subcrā'nial *adj* (1).	**subdia'conal** *adj* (2).	**subequato'rial** *adj* (4).
sub'crust *n* (1).	**subdia'conate** *n* (2).	**suberect'** *adj* (4).

sublimation, *esp* a corrosive sublimate. — *adj* (*-mət*) sublimed or sublimated. — *adj* **sub'limated**. — *n* **sublimā'tion** the change from solid to vapour without passing through the liquid state, *usu* with subsequent change back to solid (*chem*); purification by this process; a sublimate; elevation; ecstasy; the acme, height; transmutation into something higher; the unconscious diversion towards higher aims or more socially acceptable actions of the energy derived from an instinct which is denied gratification, such as an aggressive or sexual impulse. — *adj* **sublimed** (*səb-līmd'*). — *adv* **sublime'ly**. — *n* **sublime'ness**. — *n* and *adj* **sublīm'ing**. — *n* **sublimity** (*səb-lim'*) loftiness; elevation; grandeur; nobleness of nature, thought, execution; the emotion of awe and veneration; that which evokes it; the summit, height, acme. — *vt* **sub'limize** or **-ise** (*rare*) to make sublime; to exalt; to purify, refine. [L *sublimis* in a high position, exalted, from *sublimāre, -ātum* to exalt; origin unknown]

subliminal *sub-lim'in-əl, adj* beneath the threshold of consciousness, subconscious; (of stimuli, images, etc) of insufficient intensity or duration to produce a response or register in the conscious mind. — *n* a subliminal message, image, stimulus, etc. — *adv* **sub-lim'inally**. — **subliminal advertising** the insertion of subliminal images into the run of a cinema film, television programme, etc in order to exert subconscious influences on the viewer; **subliminal perception** (*behav*) a controversial hypothesis that suggests that external stimuli presented below the level of conscious awareness may influence or affect behaviour (also called **subcep'tion**). [L *sub* under, and *līmen, -inis* threshold]

sublinear *sub-lin'i-ər, adj* under the line; nearly linear (*bot*). — *n* **sublineā'tion** underlining. [**sub-** (1) and (4)]

sublingual *sub-ling'gwal, adj* under the tongue. [**sub-** (1)]

sublittoral *sub-lit'ə-rəl, adj* growing, living or occurring near but not on the shore, whether on land or at sea; of or pertaining to the zone of the sea between the lowest mark of ordinary tides and the edge of the continental shelf. — *n* a sublittoral zone. [**sub-** (4)]

sublunary *sub-lōō'nər-i, adj* under the moon; earthly; of this world; between (the orbit of) the moon and the earth, under the moon's influence. — Also **sublu'nar**. [**sub-** (1)]

sublunate *sub-lōō'nāt, adj* approaching, or nearly in, the form of a crescent. [**sub-** (4)]

subluxation *sub-luks-ā'shən,* (*med*) *n* partial dislocation or displacement, eg of a bone in a joint or tooth in its socket. [**sub-** (4)]

submachine-gun *sub-mə-shēn'-gun, n* a light machine-gun, *usu* one fired from the hip or shoulder. [**sub-** (4)]

subman *sub'man, n* an animal not quite a man; a primitive or subnormal type of human being. [**sub-** (4)]

submarginal *sub-mär'ji-nəl, adj* near the margin; below the minimum necessary; (of land) that cannot be farmed profitably. [**sub-** (4)]

submarine *sub'mə-rēn, adj* under the sea; under the surface of or on the bed of the sea. — *n* a submersible vessel, *esp* for warfare; a submarine organism or dweller; a large sandwich consisting of a long bread roll split lenthwise and filled with meat, cheese, salad, etc (*NAm*). — *vt* to attack by submarine. — *vi* (of the occupant of a vehicle) to be subjected to the submarine effect. — *n* **submarin'er** (or *-mar'in-*) a member of the crew of a submarine. — **submarine canyon** (*geol*) a trench on the continental shelf, sometimes with tributaries; **submarine effect** one in which the occupant of a vehicle simultaneously moves forward and slides out from under the seat belt, *esp* during a collision, rendering him or her vulnerable to an increased risk of injury. [**sub-** (1)]

submaxillary *sub-maks'il-ə-ri* or *-il'ə-, adj* of or under the lower jaw. — *n* a nerve, artery, etc situated below the lower jaw. [**sub-** (1)]

submediant *sub-mē'di-ənt,* (*music*) *n* the sixth degree of the diatonic scale, eg A in the scale of C major. [**sub-** (1)]

submental *sub-ment'əl, adj* below the chin; of the submentum. — *n* **subment'um** the basal part of the lower lip in insects. [L *sub* under, and *mentum* chin]

submerge *səb-mûrj', vt* to put under the surface of liquid; to sink; to cover over with liquid; to overwhelm; to conceal, suppress. — *vi* to sink under the surface of liquid. — *adj* **submerged'** sunk; entirely under the surface of liquid; growing under water, submersed; obscured, concealed; swamped. — *n* **submerge'ment** (*rare*). — *n* **submerg'ence** submersion. — *n* **submergibil'ity**. — *adj* **submerg'ible** submersible. — *vt* **submerse** (*-mûrs'*) to submerge. — *adj* **submersed'** (*bot*) growing (almost) entirely under water. — *n* **submers'ibility**. — *adj* **submers'ible** capable of being submerged at will. — *n* a submersible boat. — *n* **submer'sion** (*-shən*) the act of submerging; the state or fact of being submerged. [L *submergere, -mersum*, from *sub* under, and *mergere* to plunge]

submicron *sub-mī'kron, n* a particle visible by ultra-microscope but not by the ordinary microscope (50–2000 angstrom units). [**sub-** (1)]

subminiature *sub-min'i-chər, adj* smaller than miniature; (of a camera) of a very small size, for taking photographs on 16mm film. — *n* a subminiature camera or component. [**sub-** (1)]

submit *sub-mit', vt* (often with *to*) to yield, resign; to subordinate; to subject; to offer, lodge or refer for decision, consideration, sanction, arbitration, etc; to put forward in respectful (eg legal) debate; to lower, lay down (*obs*). — *vi* to yield; to surrender; to be subjected to; to be resigned; to consent. — *pr p* **submitt'ing**; *pa t* and *pa p* **submitt'ed**. — *adj* **submiss'** (*archaic*) submissive; subdued, low-toned. — *adj* **submiss'ible**. — *n* **submission** (*-mish'ən*) an act of submitting; a reference, or agreement to refer, to arbitration; a view submitted; resignedness, submissiveness; a surrender; a confession (*Shakesp*). — *adj* **submiss'ive** willing or ready to submit; yielding. — *adv* **submiss'ively**. — *n* **submiss'iveness**. — *adv* **submiss'ly** (*archaic*). — *n* **submiss'ness** (*archaic*). — *adj* **submitt'ed**. — *n* **submitt'er**. — *n* and *adj* **submitt'ing**. [L *sub* beneath, and *mittere, missum* to send]

submontane *sub-mon'tān, adj* under or at the foot of a mountain range. [**sub-** (1)]

submucosa *sub-mū-kō'sə, n* the connective tissue underlying a mucous membrane: — *pl* **submucosae** (*-sē*). — *adj* **submucō'sal** or **submū'cous**. [**sub-** (1)]

submultiple *sub-mul'ti-pl,* (*math*) *n* a number that will divide another number exactly without a remainder, an aliquot part, a factor. [LL *submultiplus*]

subnascent *sub-nas'ənt* or *-nās', adj* growing beneath (*obs*); growing up from beneath. [L *subnāscēns, -entis*]

subneural *sub-nūr'əl,* (*anatom*) *adj* beneath a main neural axis or cord in the nervous system. [**sub-** (1)]

subniveal *sub-niv'i-əl, adj* under snow. — Also **subniv'ean**. [**sub-** (1), and L *nix, nivis* snow]

subnormal *sub-nör'məl, adj* less than normal; (of a person) having intellectual powers that fall below a given point on a standardized intelligence test; (of a person) having

subfacto'rial *n* (2).
subfer'tile *adj* (4).
subfertil'ity *n* (4).
sub'field *n* (3).
sub'freezing *adj* (1).
sub'genre *n* (3).
subglobose' *adj* (4).
subglob'ular *adj* (4).
subgoal' *n* (3).
sub'group *n* (3).
subharmon'ic *n* and *adj* (3).
subhead' or **sub'heading** *n* (2).
subin'dustry *n* (3).
subinsinua'tion *n* (4 and 5).
subinspec'tor *n* (2).
subinspec'torship *n* (2).
sublan'ceolate *adj* (4).
sub'language *n* (3).
suble'thal *adj* (4).
sublibra'rian *n* (2).
subman'ager *n* (2).

intellectual powers so underdeveloped that he or she is not capable of looking after him- or herself. — *n* (*geom*) the projection of the normal on the axis. — *n* **subnormal'ity**. [**sub-** (4) and (1)]

subnuclear *sub-nū'kli-ər*, (*phys*) *adj* referring to particles within the nucleus of an atom. [**sub-** (3)]

suboccipital *sub-ok-sip'it-əl*, (*anatom*) *adj* below or behind the occiput, or the occipital lobe. [**sub-** (1)]

suboctave *sub-ok'tāv*, *n* the octave below; (also **suboctave coupler**) an organ coupler that gives an octave below. [**sub-** (1)]

suboctuple *sub-ok-tū'pl* or *sub-ok'tū-pl*, *adj* in the ratio of one to eight. [LL *suboctuplus*]

suboperculum *sub-o-pûr'kū-ləm*, *n* (in fishes) a bone below and partly behind the gill cover. — *adj* **suboper'cular**. [**sub-** (1)]

suborbital *sub-ör'bi-təl*, *adj* below the orbit of the eye (*anatom*); of less than a complete orbit. [**sub-** (1)]

subordinary *sub-ör'di-nə-ri*, (*heraldry*) *n* a less honourable armorial charge. [**sub-** (2)]

subordinate *sub-ör'di-nāt* or *-nit*, *adj* lower in order, rank, nature, power, importance, etc; dependent; under the orders or authority of another person; submissive (*obs*); lower in a series of successive divisions; underlying. — *n* a person who or thing that is subordinate or ranked lower; a person who works under another. — *vt* (*-nāt*) to place in a lower order; to consider of less value; to subject. — *n* **subor'dinancy** subordination. — *adv* **subor'dinately**. — *n* **subor'dinateness**. — *n* **subordinā'tion** arrangement in a series of successive orders; the disposition of successive recessed arches in an archway (*archit*); the act of subordinating or placing in a lower order; the state of being subordinate; inferiority of rank or position; submission and obedience to authority. — *n* **subordinā'tionism** the doctrine according to which the second and third Persons of the Trinity are subordinate to the first. — *n* **subordinā'tionist**. — *adj* **subor'dinātive**. — **subordinate clause** (*gram*) a clause which cannot function as a separate sentence in its own right, but performs an adjectival, adverbial or nominal function; **subordinating conjunction** (*gram*) a conjunction which introduces a subordinate clause. [LL *subordinātus*, from *sub-* under, and *ordināre* to ordain]

suborn *səb-örn'*, *vt* to bribe or procure to commit perjury or other unlawful or wrongful act; to prepare, provide, or achieve by stealthy means. — *n* **subornā'tion** (*sub-ör-*). — *n* **suborn'er** (*səb-*). [L *sub-* in the sense of secret, and *ornāre* to equip]

subpanation *sub-pan-ā'shən*, (*rare*) *n* the doctrine that the body and blood of Christ are locally and materially present in the eucharist under the form of bread and wine. [L *sub* under, and *pānis* bread]

subplot *sub'plot*, *n* a subsidiary plot coinciding with the main action in a play or story. [**sub-** (2)]

subpoena *sub-* or *sə-pē'nə*, *n* a writ commanding attendance (eg of a witness) or submission (eg of a document) as evidence in court. — *vt* to serve with such a writ: — *pa t* and *pa p* **subpoe'na'd** or **subpoe'naed**. [L, under a penalty]

subpopulation *sub-pop-ū-lā'shən*, *n* a subdivision of a statistical population. [**sub-** (3)]

subreference *sub-ref'ə-rens*, *n* an incomplete or surreptitious reference; an appeal by a veiled understanding. [**sub-** (5)]

subreption *sub-rep'shən*, (*formal* and *law*) *n* procuring an advantage or benefit by misrepresentation or concealment of the truth, *esp* an ecclesiastical benefit, or (*Scots law*) a gift of escheat (cf **obreption**). — *adj* **subreptitious** (*-tish'əs*) obtained by subreption; surreptitious. — *adj* **subrep'tive** surreptitious; arising out of obscure and unconscious suggestions of experience (*philos*). [L *subreptiō*, *-ōnis*, from *sub-* secretly, and *rapere* to snatch; cf **surreptitious**]

subrogate *sub'rō-gāt* or *-rə-*, *vt* to substitute; to put in place of another party as successor to that party's rights (*law*). — *n* **subrogā'tion**. [See ety for **surrogate**]

sub rosa *sub rō'zə* or *sŏŏb ro'zä*, (*L*) literally, under the rose (a traditional symbol of secrecy); hence, privately, confidentially.

subroutine *sub'rōō-tēn'*, *n* a self-contained part of a complete computer program which performs a specific task and which can be called into use at any time throughout the running of the main program. [**sub-** (2)]

subs. See under **sub-**.

subsacral *sub-sāk'rəl*, *adj* below (in man in front of) the sacrum. [**sub-** (1)]

subscapular *sub-skap'ū-lər*, *adj* below (in man in front of) the shoulder-blade. — *n* a subscapular vessel or nerve. [**sub-** (1)]

subscribe *səb-skrīb'*, *vi* (*usu* with *to*) to sign one's name; to assent, agree; to contribute money; to put one's name down as a purchaser or donor; to make periodical payments by arrangement; to make acknowledgment; to undertake to answer; to submit (*Shakesp*). — *vt* to sign, *orig* and *esp* at the bottom; to write beneath (*archaic*); to profess to be (by signing); to declare assent to; to make a signed promise of payment for or regular contributions to; to set down, declare, in writing (*Shakesp*); to give up by signing (*Shakesp*). — *adj* **subscrīb'able**. — *adj* **subscrībed'**. — *n* **subscrīb'er**. — *n* and *adj* **subscrīb'ing**. — *adj* and *n* **subscript** (*sub'skript*) (a character) written or printed beneath the normal line of script or type, *esp* in chemistry, mathemetics, etc (eg the number 2 in H_2O). — *n* **subscrip'tion** an act of subscribing; that which is subscribed; a membership fee; a contribution to a fund, society, etc; a method of sale to subscribers; a raising of money from subscribers; advance ordering, *esp* of a book or magazine before publication; an advance order, *esp* for a book or magazine before publication; a signature; assent, sanction, endorsement; submission (*Shakesp*). — *adj* **subscrip'tive**. — **subscriber set** (*comput*) a modem; **subscriber station** (*comput*) a connection for transmission of data linking an outside location with a central office; **subscriber trunk dialling** a dialling system in which subscribers in exchanges in many countries of the world can dial each other directly (*abbrev* **STD**); **subscription library** a lending library run commercially and funded by members' subscriptions; **subscription television** pay television. [L *subscrībere*, from *sub* beneath, below, and *scrībere* to write]

subsea *sub'sē*, *adj* occurring, used, etc, under the surface of the sea. [**sub-** (1)]

subsecive *sub'si-siv*, (*obs* or *rare*) *adj* remaining over; spare. [L *subsecīvus*, from *sub* after, and *secāre* to cut]

subsellium *sub-sel'i-əm*, *n* a seat in a Roman amphitheatre; a misericord: — *pl* **subsell'ia**. [L, a low bench, from *sub* below, and *sella* seat]

subsensible *sub-sen'si-bl*, *adj* below the range of sense. [**sub-** (4)]

submandib'ular *adj* (1).
sub'matrix *n* (3).
submicromin'iature *adj* (4).
submicroscop'ic *adj* (4).
submin'iaturize or **-ise** *vt* (4).
submol'ecule *n* (3).
subnat'ural *adj* (4).
subocean'ic *adj* (1).
soboc'ular *adj* (1).
sub'office *n* (2 and 3).
sub'officer *n* (2 and 3).
subor'der *n* (3).
subor'dinal *adj* (4).
subo'vate *adj* (4).
subox'ide *n* (6).
subpar'allel *adj* (4).
sub'phrenic *adj* (1).
subphy'lum *n* (3).
subpolar' *adj* (4).
sub-post'master, *fem* **sub-post'mistress**, *n* (3).
sub-post'-office *n* (3).

subsequence[1]. See under **subsequent**.

subsequence[2] *sub'sē'kwəns*, *n* a sequence (*esp math*) that forms part of another sequence. [**sub-** (3)]

subsequent *sub'si-kwənt*, *adj* following or coming after; (of a stream, river, etc) flowing approximately at right angles to the original slope of the land, *usu* along the line of a fault, distinguished from *consequent* and *obsequent*. — Also *adv* (with *to*) after. — *n* **sub'-sequence**. — *adj* **subsequential** (*-kwen'shl*) subsequent. — *adv* **sub'sequently**. [L *subsequēns*, *-entis*, pr p of *subsequī*, from *sub* under, after, and *sequī* to follow]

subsere *sub'sēr*, (*ecol*) *n* a secondary sere occurring when a sere has been interrupted. [**sub-** (3)]

subserve *sub-sûrv'*, *vt* to help forward. — *vi* to help in a subordinate way; to be subordinate (*obs*). — *n* **sub-ser'vience** or **subser'viency**. — *adj* **subser'vient** obsequious; slavish; subserving; serving to promote, instrumental; subject, subordinate. — *n* a subservient person or thing. — *adv* **subser'viently**. [L *subservīre*, from *sub* under, and *servīre* to serve]

subset *sub'set*, *n* a set that forms part of a larger set, *specif* a set *x* is a subset of *y* if and only if *x* is an element of *y* (*math*); a functionally or structurally different population of cells within a single cell type (*immunol*); short for subscriber set (*comput*). [**sub-** (3)]

subshrub *sub'shrub*, *n* a low-growing shrub. — *adj* **subshrubb'y**. [**sub-** (4)]

subside *səb-sīd'*, *vi* to settle, sink down; to fall into a state of quiet or calm; to diminish in intensity, amount, extent, etc, to become less. — *n* **subsidence** (*sub'si-dəns*; often *səb-sī'dəns*) or (*rare*) **sub'sidency** (or *-sī'*) the process of subsiding, settling, or sinking. [L *subsīdere*, from *sub* down, and *sīdere* to settle]

subsidy *sub'si-di*, *n* aid in the form of money; a grant of public money in aid of some enterprise, industry, etc, or to support or keep down the price of a commodity, or from one state to another; a special parliamentary grant of money to the king (*hist*); a payment exacted by a king or feudal lord (*hist*); assistance (*obs*). — *adv* **subsid'iarily**. — *n* **subsidiar'ity** the state or quality of being (a) subsidiary; the concept of a central governing body permitting its member states, branches, etc to take decisions on issues best dealt with at local or subsidiary level. — *adj* **subsid'iary** furnishing a subsidy, help, or additional supplies; aiding; subordinate; relating to or depending on subsidies. — *n* someone who or something which aids or supplies; an assistant; a subordinate; a subsidiary company. — *vt* **sub'sidize** or **-ise** to provide with a subsidy, grant, or regular allowance; to purchase the aid of, to buy over. — **subsidiary company** one of which another company holds most of the shares; **subsidiary troops** mercenaries. [L *subsidium*, orig troops stationed behind in reserve, aid, from *sub* under, and *sīdere* to settle]

subsist *səb-sist'*, *vi* to have existence (often with *in*); to have the means of living (often with *on*); to remain, continue; to consist or be inherent; to hold out, stand fast (*Milton*). — *n* **subsist'ence** the state of being subsistent; real being; the means of supporting life; livelihood. — *adj* (used eg of an allowance, wage) providing the bare necessities of living. — *adj* **sub-sist'ent** subsisting; having real being; inherent. — *adj* **subsistential** (*sub-sis-ten'shl*). — **subsistence farming** farming in which land will yield just enough to support the farmer leaving little or nothing to be sold; **subsistence level** the level of income which will purchase bare necessities only; **subsistence money** or **allowance** a portion of wages paid in advance for immediate needs, colloquially known as a **sub**; a special allowance for exceptional circumstances; **subsistence wage** one fixed at subsistence level. [L *subsistere* to stand still, from *sub* under, and *sistere* to stand]

subsizar *sub-sīz'ər*, *n* a Cambridge undergraduate (now only at certain colleges) ranking below a sizar. [**sub-** (1)]

subsoil *sub'soil*, *n* a layer of broken or partly weathered rock underlying the soil, *esp* that part below the layer normally used in cultivation. — *vt* to turn up or loosen the subsoil of. — *n* **sub'soiler** a plough for subsoiling. — *n* **sub'soiling** ploughing the subsoil. [**sub-** (1)]

subsolar *sub-sōl'ər*, *adj* directly under the sun, as a point on the earth's surface where the sun is vertically overhead. [**sub-** (1)]

subsong *sub'song*, *n* a low-volume, often unstructured, song produced by certain songbirds before the full song of the breeding season. [**sub-** (4)]

subsonic *sub-son'ik*, *adj* having, or (capable of) travelling at, a speed slower than that of sound. [**sub-** (4)]

sub specie *sub spē'shi-ē* or *sŏŏb spek'i-ā*, *adv* (*L*) under the appearance or aspect (of). — **sub specie aeternitatis** (*ē-tûr-ni-tāt'is* or *ī-ter-ni-tät'is*) (seen) under the aspect of eternity (*Spinoza*); hence, as it essentially is.

subst. *abbrev*: substantive (*gram*); substitute.

substage *sub'stāj*, *n* apparatus under the stage of a microscope; a division of a stage (*esp geol*). — Also *adj*. [**sub-** (1) and (3)]

substance *sub'stəns*, *n* something in which qualities or attributes exist, the existence to which qualities belong; that which makes anything what it is; the principal part; gist; subject-matter; body; matter, material; a kind of matter, *esp* one of definite chemical nature; amount (*Shakesp*); wealth, property; solidity, body; solid worth; foundation, ground; marihuana or other illegal drug (*euphem slang*). — *adj* **substantial** (*səb-stan'shl*) of or having substance; being a substance; essential; actually existing; real; corporeal, material; solid; stable; solidly based; durable; enduring; firm, stout, strong; considerable in amount; bulky; well-to-do, wealthy, influential; of firm, solid or sound value. — *n* **substan'tialism** the theory that there is a real existence or substratum underlying phenomena. — *n* **substan'tialist**. — *n* **substantiality** (*-shi-al'i-ti*). — *vt* **substan'tialize** or **-ise** to give reality to. — *adv* **sub-stan'tially**. — *n* **substan'tialness**. — *vt* **substan'tiate** (*-shi-āt* or *-si-āt*) to make substantial; to embody; to prove or confirm. — *n* **substantiā'tion**. — *adj* **sub-stantival** (*sub-stən-tī'vl*) of, or of the nature of, a substantive. — *adv* **substantī'vally**. — *adj* **sub'stantive** (*-tiv*) relating to substance; expressing existence; real; of real, independent importance; substantival; (of dyes) taking effect without a mordant; definite and permanent; considerable in amount. — *n* (*gram*) a noun or noun-like item. — *adv* **sub'stantively**. — *n* **sub'stantive-ness**. — *n* **substantiv'ity** substantiality; affinity for a dyestuff. — *vt* **sub'stantivize** or **-ise** (or *-stan'*) to turn into a noun. — **substance abuse** (*euphem*) a general term for the inappropriate use of substances such as alcohol, solvents, drugs, etc, often leading to dependency or other harmful effects. — **in substance** in general; in the most important aspects. [L *substantia* substance, essence, property, from *sub* under, and *stāre* to stand]

substation *sub'stā-shən*, *n* a subordinate station, *esp* a switching, transforming, or converting electrical sta-

subpo'tent *adj* (4).
subpre'fect *n* (2).
subpre'fecture *n* (2).
subprin'cipal *n* (2).
sub'prior, *fem* **subpri'oress**, *n* (2).
sub'program *n* (2 and 3).
subre'gion *n* (3).
subre'gional *adj* (3).
sub'ring *n* (2).
sub-Sahar'an *adj* (1).
subsample' *n* and *vt* (3).
sub'schema, *pl* **sub'schemata**, *n* (3).
sub'section *n* (3).
subser'ies *n* (3).
sub'sessile *adj* (4).
subset' *n* (3).
subspe'ciality *n* (2).
sub'species *n* (3).
subspecif'ic *adj* (3).
subspecif'ically *adv* (3).
subspi'nous *adj* (4).
substan'dard *adj* (1 and 2).
sub'state *n* (2 and 3).
subster'nal *adj* (1).

tion intermediate between the generating station and the low-tension distribution network. [**sub-** (2)]

substellar *sub-stel'ər, adj* directly under a star, applied eg to a point on the earth's surface where the star is vertically overhead; under the influence of a star. [**sub-** (1)]

substitute *sub'sti-tūt, n* one put in place of another; a thing used instead of another; a deputy; a proxy (*Shakesp*); an heir (*law*); a person entitled to receive an hereditary peerage if no male heir is produced. — *vt* to use instead of, or put in place of, another (often with *for*); to appoint as deputy; to nominate in remainder. — *vi* (*orig US*) to act as substitute. — *n* **substit'uent** something that may be, or is, substituted, *esp* one atom or radical replacing another in a molecule. — Also *adj*. — *adj* **substitū'table**. — *adj* **sub'stituted**. — *n* **substitū'tion** the act of substituting; the condition of being a substitute; the substituting of one atom or radical for another without breaking up the molecule (*chem*); the replacement of one idea by another, as a form of defence mechanism (*psychiatry*); the replacement of one kind of metrical foot by another, eg for emphasis (*prosody*); a rule of inference in which an expression replaces a variable throughout a theorem (*math*); delegation (*Shakesp*). — *adj* **substitū'tional** or **substitū'tionary**. — *adv* **substitū'tionally**. — *adj* **sub'stitūtive**. — *adv* **sub'stitutively**. — *n* **substitutiv'ity**. — **substitution product** a substance obtained by substitution of so many equivalents for certain atoms or groups. [L *substituere, -ūtum*, from *sub* under, and *statuere* to set]

substract *səb-strakt', vt* (now *illiterate*) to subtract. — *n* **substrac'tion** (now *illiterate*). — *n* **substrac'tor** (*Shakesp*) a detractor. [LL *substrahere, substractum*, for L *subtrahere*, after the model of **abstract**]

substrata, substrate, etc. See under **substratum**.

substratosphere *sub-strat'ō-sfēr, n* the region of the atmosphere below the stratosphere and over $3\frac{1}{2}$ miles above the earth. [**sub-** (4)]

substratum *sub-strā'təm* or *-strä', n* a basis, foundation, ground; the material in which a plant grows or on which an animal moves or rests; an underlying layer, *esp* of rock or soil: — *pl* **substra'ta**. — *adj* **substrā'tal** or **substrā'tive**. — *n* **sub'strate** a substratum; a base; a medium on which an organism can grow (*biol*); a solid object to which a plant, such as seedweed, is attached; a body of material on or in which integrated circuits or circuit elements are fabricated (*electronics*); the substance or substances on which an enzyme can act; the substances used by a plant in respiration (*bot*). [L *substernere, -strātum*, from *sub* under, and *sternere* to spread]

substruct *sub-strukt', vt* to build beneath, lay as a foundation. — *n* **substruc'tion**. — *adj* **substruc'tural**. — *n* **sub'structure** an understructure; a foundation, a supporting structure. [**sub-** (1)]

substyle *sub'stīl, n* the straight line on which the style of a dial is erected. — *adj* **sub'stylar** (or *-stī'*). [**sub-** (1)]

subsultive *sub-sult'iv* or **subsultory** *-ər-i, adj* (*rare*) moving by sudden leaps or starts; twitching. — *adv* **subsult'orily**. — *n* **subsult'us** (*med*) an abnormal convulsive or twitching movement, *usu* of the muscles. [L *subsultāre* to jump, hop, from *sub* up, and *salīre* to leap]

subsume *sub-sūm', vt* to take in under a more comprehensive term or proposition; to include in something larger; to take over (*officialese*). — *adj* **subsum'able**. — *n* **subsumption** (*səb-sump'shən*). — *adj* **subsump'tive**. [L *sub* under, and *sūmere* to take]

subtack *sub'tak', n* a sublease in Scotland. — *n* **sub'tack'sman** a holder (of land) by subtack. [**sub-** (2)]

subtangent *sub'tan'jənt*, (*geom*) *n* (of a curve) the projection of the tangent on the axis. [**sub-** (1)]

subteen *sub'tēn*, (chiefly *NAm*) *n* and *adj* (of or for) a child younger than thirteen years. [**sub-** (1)]

subtemperate *sub'tem'pər-it* or (*rare*) *-āt, adj* slightly colder than temperate, cold-temperate. [**sub-** (4)]

subtend *səb-tend', vt* to be opposite to (as a hypotenuse is to a right-angle) or to extend under (as a chord does an arc) (*geom*); to be situated immediately below (as a leaf is to a bud in its axil) (*bot*). — *n* **subtense'** a subtending line. — *adj* placed so as to subtend an angle, as a rod or bar used as a distance base in tacheometry. [L *sub* under, and *tendere, tentum* or *tēnsum* to stretch]

subter- *sub'tər-, combining form* signifying under, as in *subterhuman, subterjacent*. [L]

subterfuge *sub'tər-fūj, n* an evasive device, as used in discussion or argument; action taken, or manoeuvres made, to evade, conceal or obscure; a refuge (*obs*). [L *subter* under, and *fugere* to take flight]

subternatural *sub-tər-nach'rəl, adj* below that which is considered natural, less than natural. [L *subter* under, and **natural**]

subterranean *sub-tə-rā'ni-ən, adj* underground; operating underground; hidden, working, etc, in secret. — *n* a person who or thing that is subterranean. — *n* **sub'terrane** or **sub'terrain** an underground chamber, room or dwelling. — *adj* **subterrā'neous** underground. — *adv* **subterrā'neously**. — *adj* **subterrene'** underground. — *n* an underground dwelling; the underworld. — *adj* and *n* **subterres'trial** (a person or thing) existing underground. [L *sub* under, and *terra* the earth]

subtext *sub'tekst, n* a footnote (*obs*); an underlying theme in literature. [**sub-** (1)]

subthreshold *sub-thresh'ōld*, (*psychol*) *adj* not sufficient to produce a specified response; subliminal. [**sub-** (1)]

subtil and **subtile**. Archaic forms of **subtle**.

subtitle *sub'tī-tl, n* (in a book, etc) an additional or second title; a half-title; a repetition of the title at the head of the text; (*usu* in *pl*) wording superimposed on a film or television picture, eg a printed translation at the foot of the screen of dialogue that is in a language foreign to the viewers or other descriptive text similarly displayed (cf **supertitle**). — *vt* to provide with a subtitle or subtitles. [**sub-** (2)]

subtle *sut'l, adj* tenuous, slight; elusive, impalpable; showing or calling for fine discrimination; delicate, refined; overrefined or overrefining, rarefied; abstruse; crafty, artful; insidious, devious; ticklish, tricky (*Shakesp*). — *n* **subtilīzā'tion** or **-s-** (*sut-*). — *vt* **subtilize** or **-ise** (*sut'*) to rarefy, refine; to make subtle. — *vi* to refine, use subtlety. — *n* **subt'leness** or **subt'lety** the state or quality of being subtle; a subtle trick or refinement; an ornamental device in sugar (*obs*; *cookery*). — *adv* **subt'ly**. [OFr *soutil* and its source L *subtīlis*, from *sub* under, and *tēla* a web]

subtonic *sub-ton'ik*, (*music*) *n* the seventh degree of the diatonic scale, the leading note. [**sub-** (1)]

subtopia *sub-tō'pi-ə*, (*derog*) *n* an area of sprawling housing estates spreading into the countryside, in which suburban dwellers enjoy some aspects of rural living while clinging to urban amenities. — *adj* **subto'pian**. [Coined in the 1950s by I Nairn; from **suburb** and **Utopia**]

subtract *səb-trakt', vt* to withdraw, remove; to withhold; to take from another quantity so as to find the

sub'surface *adj* (1).	**sub'total** *n* and *vt* (3).	**subvari'ety** *n* (3).
sub'system *n* (2).	**subtreas'urer** *n* (2).	**sub'vassal** *n* (2).
sub'tenancy *n* (2).	**subtreas'ury** *n* (2).	**subver'tebral** *adj* (1).
subten'ant *n* (2).	**subtriang'ular** *adj* (4).	**subver'tical** *adj* (4).
subten'ure *n* (2).	**sub'tribe** *n* (3).	**subvit'reous** *adj* (4).
subter'minal *adj* (4).	**sub'type** *n* 3).	**subwar'den** *n* (2).
sub'tidal *adj* (4).	**subu'nit** *n* (3).	**sub'zon'al** *adj* (1).
subtor'rid *adj* (4).	**subur'sine** *adj* (4).	**sub'zone** *n* (3).

difference (*math*). — *n* **subtract'er** (*comput*) a device performing subtraction using digital signals. — *n* **subtrac'tion** withdrawal, removal; withholding, *esp* in violation of a right; the operation of finding the difference between two quantities by taking one from the other (*math*). — *adj* **subtract'ive** indicating, tending towards or of the nature of subtraction; negative. — *n* **subtract'or** a light filter to eliminate a particular colour. — **subtractive process** (*image technol*) the basis of all modern colour photography and colour printing, in which the red, green and blue components of a subject are reproduced as separate images in complementary or subtractive colours, ie cyan, magenta and yellow, which are superimposed to produce the final print. [L *sub-* (in the sense of away), and *trahěre*, *tractum* to draw]

subtrahend *sub'trə-hend*, (*math*) *n* that which is to be subtracted (cf **minuend**). [L *sub-* away, and *trahendus* requiring to be drawn (gerundive of *trahěre* to draw]

subtriplicate *sub-trip'li-kit* or *-kāt*, *adj* expressed by the cube root. [LL *subtriplus* in the ratio of one to three]

subtrist *sub-trist'*, (*archaic*) *adj* somewhat sad. [L *sub-trīstis*, from *sub* in some degree, and *trīstis* sad]

subtropical *sub-trop'i-kl* or **subtropic** *-trop'ik*, *adj specif* of, from or characteristic of those areas (the **subtropics**) lying between the Tropic of Cancer and 40°N and the Tropic of Capricorn and 40°S, *esp* the climatic conditions of these areas; (loosely) of, having or resembling near-tropical climate. — *adv* **subtrop'ically**. [**sub-** (4)]

subtrude *sub-trōōd'*, *vi* to push in stealthily. [L *sub-* in sense of secretly, and *trūdere* to thrust]

subucula *sub-ū'kū-lə* or *sōōb-ōō'kōō-la*, *n* in ancient Rome, a man's undergarment or shirt; in the early English Church, a kind of cassock worn under the alb. [L *subūcula*, from *sub* under, and the root of *induere* to put on, and *exuere* to take off]

subulate *sū'bū-lāt*, (*biol*, *esp bot*) *adj* long, narrow and tapering to a point, awl-shaped. [L *sūbula* an awl]

subumbrella *sub-um-brel'ə*, *n* the undersurface of a jellyfish's umbrella. — *adj* **subumbrell'ar**. [**sub-** (1)]

subungulate *sub-ung'gū-lət*, *n* and *adj* (a member) of the **Subungulā'ta**, a classification of animals which are related to, but whose evolution diverged from, the *Ungulata* before the development of the hoof, consisting of four orders *incl* the elephants, hydraxes, sea cows and aardvark. [**sub-** (4)]

suburb *sub'ərb*, *n* a district or community adjoining a town or city, *esp* one having relatively low-density housing and open space as characteristic features; (in *pl*) the outskirts of a town; outskirts generally. — *adj* suburban; characteristic of the suburbs. — *adj* **suburban** (*səb-ûr'bən*) situated or living in the suburbs; typical of the suburbs; without the good qualities either of town or country; provincial, narrow in outlook; cosily traditional or unadventurous in tastes, as in the stereotypical suburbanite. — *n* someone living in a suburb. — *n* **subur'banism** the state of being suburban. — *n* **subur'banite** a person who lives in the suburbs. — *n* **suburbanity** (*sub-ər-ban'i-ti*) suburban quality; suburbanism; a suburban place. — *n* **suburbanizā'tion** or **-s-**. — *vt* **subur'banize** or **-ise** to make suburban. — *n* **subur'bia** (often used pejoratively) the suburban world. — *adj* **suburbicā'rian** being near the city, *esp* of the dioceses and churches of the cardinal bishops in the suburbs of Rome. [L *suburbium*, from *sub* under, near, and *urbs* a city]

subvention *səb-ven'shən*, *n* a grant of money in aid, eg public money or an ex-gratia payment from one company in a group to another. — *adj* **subven'tionary**. [L *subventiō*, *-ōnis* a coming to help, from *sub* from below, and *venīre*, *ventum* to come]

sub verbo. See **sub voce**.

subvert *səb-vûrt'*, *vt* to overthrow, overturn, ruin (eg principles, a political system, etc); to pervert or corrupt (a person). — *n* **subver'sal**. — *vt* (*obs*) **subverse'** (*pa p* and *adj* in *Spenser* **subverst'**). — *n* **subver'sion** overthrow, ruin; perversion, corruption. — *adj* **subver'sive** or less commonly **subver'sionary** tending to overthrow or subvert. — *n* a subversive person, *esp* politically. — *n* **subvert'er**. [L *sub* under, and *vertere*, *versum* to turn]

subviral *sub-vī'rəl*, *adj* referring to, or caused by, a structural part of a virus. [**sub-** (3)]

subvocal *sub-vō'kəl*, *adj* (of words) formed in speech order in the mind with or without accompanying (inaudible) movements of the speech organs. [**sub-** (1)]

sub voce *sub vō'sē*, *sōōb vō'ke* or *wō'* or **sub verbo** *vûr'bō* or *wûr'*, (*L*) literally, under the voice or word — used as a reference in dictionaries, etc (*abbrev* **sv**).

subway *sub'wā*, *n* a tunnel for pedestrians; an underground passage for water-pipes, gas-pipes, sewers, etc; an underground railway. [**sub-** (1)]

subzero *sub-zē'rō*, *adj* less than zero, *esp* of temperature. [**sub-** (1)]

succade *suk-ād'*, *n* fruit or vegetable candied or in syrup. [Anglo-Fr *sukade*, perh from L *succus* juice]

succedaneum *suk-si-dā'ni-əm*, *n* (*esp med*) a substitute: — *pl* **succeda'nea** (*-ni-ə*). — *adj* **succedā'neous** (*esp med*) serving as a substitute. [L, neuter of *succēdāneus*, from *succēdere* to come after]

succeed *sək-sēd'*, *vt* to come after, follow; to follow up or in order; to take the place of (*esp* in office, title, or possession); to inherit (*Shakesp*); to cause to succeed (*obs*). — *vi* to follow in order; to take the place of another (often with *to*); to devolve, pass in succession (*Shakesp*); to turn out (*archaic*); to turn out well; to prosper; to obtain one's wish or accomplish what is attempted; to avail, be successful (with *in*); to approach (*obs*). — *n* **succeed'er** someone who is successful; a successor. — *adj* **succeed'ing**. — *n* **success** (*sək-ses'*) an act of succeeding; the state of having succeeded; upshot (*obs*); prosperous progress, achievement, or termination; prosperity; attainment of wealth, influence or acclaim; a successful person, book, affair, etc; sequence (*obs*); succession (*obs*). — *adv* **success'antly** (*Shakesp*) in succession. — *adj* **success'ful** resulting in success; achieving, having achieved, or having, the desired effect or outcome; prosperous, flourishing. — *adv* **success'fully** with success; with promise of success (*Shakesp*). — *n* **success'fulness**. — *n* **succession** (*-sesh'ən*) a coming after or following; a coming into another's place; a sequence in time or place; law, recognized mode, right, order or turn, of succeeding one to another; (in Roman and Scots law) the taking of property by one person in place of another; rotation of crops; heirs collectively; posterity; a set of strata which represents an unbroken chronological sequence (*geol*); in an ecological community, the sequence of changes as one set of species succeeds another. — *adj* **success'ional**. — *adv* **success'ionally**. — *n* **success'ionist** a believer in the necessity of Apostolic succession. — *adj* **success'ionless**. — *adj* **successive** (*sək-ses'iv* or *Shakesp suk'*) coming in succession or in order; hereditary (*obs*). — *adv* **success'ively**. — *n* **success'iveness**. — *adj* **success'less**. — *adv* **success'lessly**. — *n* **success'lessness**. — *n* **success'or** a person who, or thing which, succeeds or comes after; a person appointed to succeed. — *n* **success'orship**. — **succession duty** a tax imposed on succession to property, varying with the degree of relationship; **succession house** a forcing-house in a graded series, in which plants are moved on from one to the next; **succession states** states resulting from the break-up of previously existing countries, such as those established after the break-up of the Austro-Hungarian empire; **success story** (the record of) a person's, company's, etc rise to prosperity, fame, etc. — **in succession** following one another, one after another; **plant succession** a series of vegetation types following one another in the same region. [OFr *succeder*, from L *succēdere*, *-cēssum*, from *sub-* in sense of near, next after, and *cēdere* to go]

succentor *sək-sent'ər*, *n* a subordinate cantor; a bass soloist in a choir. [L *succentor*, from *succinere*, from *sub* under, and *canere* to sing]

succès *sük-se*, (*Fr*) *n* success. — **succès fou** (*fōō*) literally, success with wild enthusiasm; extraordinary success. — **succès de scandale** (*də skã-dal*) success of a book, dramatic entertainment, due not to merit but to its connection with or reference to a topical scandal; **succès d'estime** (*des-tēm*) a success of esteem or approval; success with more honour than profit.

success, etc. See under **succeed**.

succi. See **succus**.

succinate. See under **succinic**.

succinct *sək-* or *suk-singkt'*, *adj* girded up (*archaic* and *poetic*); close-fitting (*archaic* and *poetic*); brief and precise, concise. — *adv* **succinct'ly**. — *n* **succinct'ness**. — *n* **succincto'rium** or **succinct'ory** a band embroidered with an Agnus Dei, worn hanging from the girdle by the pope on some occasions. [L *succinctus*, from *sub* up, and *cingere* to gird]

succinic *suk-sin'ik*, *adj* of, relating to or derived from amber. — *n* **suc'cinate** a salt of succinic acid. — *n* **suc'cinite** amber, *esp* a variety from which succinic acid was originally obtained. — *n* **suc'cinyl** either of two chemical groups of succinic acid. — **succinic acid** an acid, $C_4H_6O_4$, occurring in plant resins such as amber, in various animal tissues, etc. [L *succinum* amber]

succise *suk'sīs*, (*bot*) *adj* (of leaves, etc) ending abruptly below, as if cut off. [L *succisus* cut below]

succor. A *NAm* spelling of **succour**.

succory *suk'ər-i*, *n*. Another name for **chicory**.

succose. See under **succus**.

succotash *suk'ō-tash*, *n* a stew of green Indian corn and beans and sometimes pork. [Narragansett *msiquatash*]

Succoth. Same as **Sukkoth**.

succour or (*NAm*) **succor** *suk'ər*, *vt* to aid in distress; to relieve. — *n* aid; relief. — *adj* **succ'ourable**. — *n* **succ'ourer**. — *adj* **succ'ourless**. [Anglo-Fr *socorre*, from L *succurrere* to run to help, from *sub* up, and *currere* to run]

succous. See under **succus**.

succubous *suk'ū-bus*, (*bot*) *adj* having the lower leaf-margin overlapping the leaf below. [L *sub* under, and *cubāre* to lie]

succubus *suk'ū-bəs*, also **succuba** *-bə*, *n* a devil supposed to assume a female body and have sex with men in their sleep; a strumpet (*archaic*): — *pl* **succ'ubuses** or **succ'ubī**, also **succ'ubae** (*-bē*) or **succ'ubas**. — *adj* **succ'ubine**. [L *succuba* a whore, from *sub* under, and *cubāre* to lie]

succulent *suk'ū-lənt*, *adj* juicy; sappy; juicy and fleshy, or (loosely) merely fleshy (*bot*). — *n* a plant, such as a cactus, that stores water in its stem and leaves. — *n* **succ'ulence** or **succ'ulency**. — *adv* **succ'ulently**. [L *sūculentus*, from *sūcus* juice]

succumb *sə-kum'*, *vi* to give way or sink under pressure, difficulty, temptation, etc (often with *to*); to yield; to die. [L *sub* under, and *cumbere* to lie down]

succursal *suk-ûr'sl*, *adj* subsidiary, *usu* applied to a religious establishment; branch. — *n* a branch or subsidiary establishment. [Fr, from L *succurrere* to succour]

succus *suk'əs*, *n* juice; any fluid secretion from a plant or animal, eg from a gland; extracted juice: — *pl* **succi** (*suk'sī*). — *adj* **succ'ose** or **succ'ous**. [L *sūcus*, *succus* juice]

succuss *suk-us'*, *vt* to shake up. — *n* **succussā'tion** a shaking up, violent shaking; the trotting of a horse (*obs*). — *n* **succussion** (*-ush'ən*) an act or instance of shaking; a method of diagnosis in which a patient is shaken to detect the presence of an abnormal quantity of fluid in a body cavity, eg the pleural cavity (*med*); the splashing sound made by such fluid when the patient moves suddenly or is deliberately shaken. — *adj* **succuss'ive**. [L *succutere*, *succussum* to toss up, from *sub* up, and *quatere* to shake]

such *such*, *adj* of that kind, a similar kind, or the same kind (often followed by *as* or by a clause beginning with *that*); so characterized; of what kind; what (exclamatorily); so great; mentioned earlier; some particular but unspecified. — *adv* so (preceding the indefinite article if any). — *pronoun* such a person, persons, thing, or things; the before-mentioned; that. — *adj* **such'like** of such a kind. — *pronoun* suchlike persons or things (or person or thing). — *n* **such'ness** (*archaic*) quality. — *adv* **such'wise** in such a manner. — *adj* **such'-and-such** this or that, some, some or other (before the indefinite article if any). — *pronoun* such-and-such a person. — **as such** as it is described; in a particular capacity; **such as** for example; **such as it is** being what it is (and no better); **such that** in such a way, to such an extent, etc that. [OE *swilc*; cognate with Gothic *swaleiks*; cf **so**[1] and **like**[1]]

suck *suk*, *vt* to draw into the mouth by producing a partial vacuum with the lips and tongue; to draw (milk or some other liquid) from with the mouth; to apply to or hold, roll about or squeeze in the mouth; to draw or render by suction; to absorb, draw in; to extract; to imbibe; to drain, exhaust. — *vi* to draw in with the mouth; to suck milk from the breast; to draw in or up by suction; to make a noise of sucking; to draw in air as a dry pump; to draw in; to be repellent or contemptible (*slang*, *orig US*). — *n* an act or spell of sucking; milk drawn from the breast; suction; a short drink, *esp* a dram of spirits (*old slang*). — *adj* **sucked**. — *n* **suck'er** a person who, or thing which, sucks; a sucking-pig, new-born whale, or other unweaned animal; a sucking-fish; an American freshwater fish related to the carps, that feeds by sucking up small animals from the bottom; a sucking or adhesive organ; a device that adheres, draws water, etc by suction, such as a pump piston; a sweet or lollipop (*colloq*); a shoot rising from an underground stem or root and developing into a new plant; a new shoot; a parasite, toady or sponge; a hard drinker (*old slang*); a gullible person, one taken advantage of (*colloq*); a person who is drawn to, or who has a weakness for, a specified thing (*colloq*). — *vt* to strip off superfluous shoots from; to dupe, make a sucker of (*esp US*). — *vi* (of a plant) to develop suckers. — *adj* **suck'ered** having suckers. — *n* and *adj* **suck'ing**. — **suck'er-punch** (*US slang*) a quick, surprise punch, *esp* from behind. — *vt* (*US slang*) to give (someone) a sudden unexpected punch. — **suck'-hole**, **suck''ole** or **suck'-holer** (*Austr slang*) an ingratiating, servile, fawning, obsequious person; **suck-in'** (*slang*, *orig US*) a disconcerting disappointment; **suck'ing-fish** the remora or any other fish with an adhesive disc, eg a lumpsucker; **sucking louse** a bloodsucking wingless insect of the order *Anoplura*; **suck'ing-pig** a young milk-fed pig. — **be a sucker for** (*colloq*) to be unable to resist; **suck in** to absorb; to engulf; to take in, deceive (*slang*); **suck face** (chiefly *US slang*) to kiss; **suck off** (*slang*) to perform fellatio or cunnilingus on; **sucks**! or **sucks to you**! an expression of derision, contempt, etc; **suck up to** (*slang*) to flatter, be ingratiatingly nice to. [OE *sūcan*, *sūgan*; Ger *saugen*, Du *zuigen*, Swed *suga*; cf L *sūgere*]

sucken *suk'n*, (*old Scots law*) *n* the district or population thirled to a mill; thirlage; an area of jurisdiction or field of operation. — *n* **suck'ener** a tenant under the sucken or thirlage system. [**soken** (see **soc**)]

sucket *suk'it*, an *obs* form of **succade**. — **sucket spoon** or **fork** an old table implement, spoon at one end, fork at the other.

suckle *suk'l*, *vt* to feed by allowing to suck milk from the breast or other mamma. — *vi* to take milk in this way. — *n* **suck'ler** an animal that suckles; a suckling. — *n pl* **suck'lers** (*dialect*) heads of clover. [Prob back-formation from **suckling**]

suckling *suk'ling*, *n* an unweaned child or animal; the act of giving suck; clover, also honeysuckle (*dialect*). — *adj* giving suck; putting to suck; sucking. [**suck**]

sucralfate *sōō'krəl-fāt*, *n* a drug used in the treatment of peptic ulcer.

sucre *sōō'krā*, *n* the standard monetary unit of Ecuador (100 *centavos*). [Named after Antonio José de *Sucre* (1795-1830)]

sucrose *sōō'* or *sū'krōs*, *n* a disaccharide carbohydrate ($C_{12}H_{22}O_{11}$), occurring in beet, sugar cane and other plants; sugar, cane sugar (*colloq*). — *n* **su'crase** same as **invertase**. — *n* **sucrier** (*sü-kri-ā*; *Fr*) a table vessel for sugar, *usu* of porcelain, etc. [Fr *sucre* sugar]

suction *suk'shən*, *n* the act or power of sucking or of drawing or adhesion by reducing pressure of air; the removal of unwanted material, liquid or semi-liquid, from the body using a syringe, hollow needle or mechanical pump (*med*). — *adj* (*zool*) **sucto'rial** (adapted for) sucking or adhering. — *n* and *adj* (*zool*) **sucto'rian** (a member) of the **Sucto'ria**, a subclass of *Ciliata*. — **suction lipectomy** a technique used in cosmetic surgery in which unwanted fat is removed through a suction instrument inserted through a small skin incision; **suction pump** a pump for raising fluids by suction; **suction** (or **suctional**) **stop** (*phonetics*) a stop consonant in which the contact of the articulating organs is followed by an inrush of air; a click or implosive. [L *sūgere*, *suctum*; related to **suck**]

sucurujú *sōō-kōō-rōō-zhōō'*, *n* a S American Indian name for the anaconda.

sud. See **suds**.

sudamina *sōō-* or *sū-dam'i-nə*, (*pathol*) *n pl* whitish vesicles due to retention of sweat in the sweat ducts or upper layers of skin: — *n sing* **sudamen** (*-dā'mən*). — *adj* **sudam'inal**. [L *sūdāmen*, pl *sūdāmina*, from *sūdāmina*, from *sūdāre* to sweat]

Sudanese *sōō-dən-ēz'* or *sōō'dən-ēz*, *n* a native or inhabitant of the *Sudan*, a republic of NE Africa, or of the region south of the Sahara and Libyan deserts: — *pl* **Sudanese**. — *adj* of or pertaining to the Sudan or its inhabitants. — *n* **Sudan'ic** a group of languages spoken in the Sudan. — *adj* of or relating to these languages; of or relating to the Sudan. — **Sudan grass** a sorghum, *Sorghum vulgare sudanensis*, grown for hay and fodder.

sudate *sū'dāt* or *sōō'*, (*rare*) *vi* to sweat. — *n* **sudā'rium** or **su'dary** (*-də-ri*) a cloth for wiping sweat, *esp* the veil or handkerchief of St Veronica, believed to have retained miraculously the image of Christ's face. — *n* **sudā'tion** sweating; sweat; a watery exudation from plants. — *n* **sudatorium** (*-də-tö'ri-əm*) a hot room (such as in an ancient Roman bathhouse) which induces sweating. — *n* **su'datory** (*-tə-ri*) a sudatorium; a drug which induces sweating. — *adj* of sweat; inducing sweating. [L *sūdāre*, *-ātum* to sweat]

sudd *sud*, *n* a mass of vegetation floating on water in NE Africa, particularly on the White Nile where it may obstruct navigation; a temporary dam. [Ar *sudd* obstruction]

sudden *sud'n*, *adj* without warning or apparent preparation; unexpected; hasty; abrupt; prompt; swift in action or production; glancing quickly; improvised. — *adv* suddenly. — *adv* **sudd'enly**. — *n* **sudd'enness** or (*rare Scot*) **sudd'enty**. — **sudden death** (*sport*) an extended period of play to settle a tied contest, ending when one of the contestants scores. — **all of a sudden** all at once, suddenly; **sudden infant death syndrome** see **cot death**; **sudden unexplained death syndrome** a mysterious condition, particularly affecting young men of SE Asian origin, in which sudden death occurs from unknown causes, and *usu* without previous symptoms of illness (*abbrev* **SUDS**). [Anglo-Fr *sodain*, from L *subitāneus* sudden, from *subitus* approaching stealthily, from *subīre*, *-itum*, from *sub* in the sense of 'secretly', and *īre* to go]

sudder *sud'ər*, (*Anglo-Ind*) *adj* chief, supreme. — *n* a supreme court. [Ar *çadr* chief]

Sudeck's atrophy *sōō'deks at'rəf-i*, *n* local osteoporosis that develops rapidly in a hand or foot as a result of injury, infection, etc. [P H M *Sudeck* (1866–1938), German surgeon]

sudor *sū'dör*, *sōō'* or *-dər*, (*med*) *n* sweat. — *adj* **su'doral**. — *adj* **sudorif'erous** inducing or secreting sweat. — *adj* **sudorif'ic** causing sweat. — *n* a diaphoretic. — *adj* **sudorip'arous** secreting sweat. — *adj* **su'dorous** sweaty. [L *sūdor*, *-ōris* sweat]

Sudra *sōō'drə*, (*Anglo-Ind*) *n* a member of the fourth and lowest of the great Hindu castes. [Sans *śsūdra*]

SUDS *abbrev*: sudden unexplained death syndrome (qv under **sudden**).

suds *sudz*, *n pl* froth of soapy water (rarely in *sing* **sud**); beer (*NAm slang*). — *vt* to wash in soap suds,to lather. — *vi* (*NAm*) to lather, form suds. — *n* **sud'ser** (*slang*; *journalese*) a soap opera. — *adj* **sud'sy**. [Prob from MDu *sudse* marsh, swamp; connected with **seethe**, **sodden**]

sue *sū* or *sōō*, (*Spenser* **sew**) *vt* to follow, pursue (*obs*); to prosecute at law; to petition for, apply for; to court (*archaic*). — *vi* to make legal claim; to make application; to entreat; to be a wooer (*Shakesp*); to do service (*obs*): — *pr p* **su'ing**; *pa t* and *pa p* **sued**. — *n* **sueabil'ity** same as **suability**. — *adj* **sue'able** same as **suable**. — *n* **su'er**. — *n* and *adj* **su'ing**. — **standing to sue** (*law*) the right to bring a case to court. [OFr *suir* (Fr *suivre*), from L *sequī*, *secūtus* to follow]

suede or **suède** *swād* (Fr *sü-əd*), *n* undressed kidskin or other leather with a soft unglazed nap finish, used eg for gloves and shoe uppers; the colour of undressed kidskin, a light beige. — Also *adj*. — *vt* to give a suede finish to (leather or cloth). — *n* **suedette'** a fabric made with a velvet-like nap resembling suede. [Fr (*gants de*) *Suède*, (gloves of) Sweden]

suet *sū'it* or *sōō'it*, *n* a solid fatty tissue, accumulating around the kidneys and omentum of the ox, sheep, etc. — *adj* **su'ety** of or resembling suet; (of a person's face or complexion) fatty and having a pallor resembling suet. — **suet pudding** a boiled pudding, savoury or sweet, made with suet. [OFr *seu* (Fr *suif*), from L *sēbum* fat]

suffect *su'fekt*, *adj* (of a Roman consul or his office) additional, ie elected during the official year. [L *suffectus*, pa p of *sufficere* substitute]

suffer *suf'ər*, *vt* to undergo; to endure; to tolerate; to be affected by; to permit (*Bible* and *archaic*); to inflict pain on (*Shakesp*). — *vi* to feel or undergo pain, grief, privation, etc; to sustain loss or disadvantage; to be injured; to undergo a punishment or penalty, such as death or martyrdom; to be the object of an action. — *adj* **suff'erable**. — *n* **suff'erableness**. — *adv* **suff'erably**. — *n* **suff'erance** tacit or unwilling assent; toleration; capacity to endure pain, injury, etc; suffering (*archaic*); patient endurance (*archaic*). — *n* **suff'erer**. — *n* and *adj* **suff'ering**. — **on sufferance** tolerated with reluctance. [L *sufferre* to sustain, from *sub* in the sense of 'up from underneath', and *ferre* to carry]

suffete *suf'ēt*, *n* one of the chief administrative officials of ancient Carthage. [L *sūfes*, *-etis*, from a Punic word]

suffice *sə-fīs'*, *vi* to be enough; to be competent or adequate. — *vt* to satisfy. — *n* **suffic'er**. — *n* **sufficience** (*sə-fish'əns*; *archaic*) sufficiency; capacity; ability; competence; sustenance. — *n* **sufficiency** (*sə-fish'ans-i*) the state of being sufficient; a sufficient quantity or supply; means enough for a comfortable living; adequate ability, competence, capacity (*obs* or *archaic*). — *adj* **suffic'ient** adequate for the purpose; sufficing; effective; being a sufficient condition (*logic*); competent (*archaic*). — *n* a sufficient quantity, enough. — *adv* **suffic'iently**. — *adj* **suffic'ing**. — *n* **suffisance** (*suf'i-zəns*; *obs*) sufficiency; satisfaction; enjoyment. — **sufficient condition** (*logic*) a condition or proposition whose existence assures the truth of, or leads to the occurrence of, a further condition. — **suffice it to say** let it be enough to say. [Through Fr, from L *sufficere* to suffice, from *sub* below, and *facere* to make]

suffigance *suf'i-gans*, (Shakesp, *Much Ado About Nothing*) *n* Dogberry's blunder for **suffisance** (qv under **suffice**).

suffisance. See under **suffice**.

suffix *suf'iks*, *n* an affix attached to the end of a root, stem or word (*gram*); an index placed after and below a symbol, such as *n* in x_n (*math*). — *vt* **suffix'** (also *suf'iks*) to add as a suffix; to subjoin. — *adj* **suff'ixal**. — *n* **suffixā'tion** or **suffix'ion**. [L *suffīxus*, from *sub* under, and *fīgere* to fix]

sufflate *sə-flāt'*, (*archaic*) *vt* and *vi* to inflate. — *n* **sufflā'tion**. [L *sufflare*]

suffocate *suf'ə-kāt*, *vt* and *vi* to choke by stopping or obstructing the passage of air to the lungs; to stifle, eg in hot, airless conditions. — *adj* (*Shakesp*) suffocated. — *n* and *adj* **suff'ocāting**. — *adv* **suff'ocātingly**. — *n* **suffocā'tion**. — *adj* **suff'ocātive** tending to suffocate. [From pa p of L *suffōcare*, from *sub* under, and *faucēs* the throat]

Suffolk *suf'ək*, *n* an English breed of large, well-muscled, black-faced sheep without horns; a sheep of this breed. — **Suffolk punch** see **punch**[1].

suffragan *suf'rə-gən*, *n* an assistant, a bishop's coadjutor; any bishop in relation to his metropolitan. — Also *adj*. — *n* **suff'raganship**. [LL *suffrāgāneus* assistant, supporting, from L *suffrāgium* a vote]

suffrage *suf'rij*, *n* the right or power to vote; a vote; supporting opinion, sanction; a prayer, *esp* for the dead, or in a litany. — *n* **suffragette** (*suf-rə-jet'*; *hist*; an improperly formed word) a woman (in the late 19c and early 20c) who sought, sometimes by extreme methods, to obtain voting rights for women. — *n* **suffraget'tism**. — *n* **suff'ragism**. — *n* **suff'ragist** a believer in the right (eg of women) to vote. [L *suffrāgium* a vote]

suffruticose *sə-froo͝t'i-kōs*, (*bot*) *adj* herbaceous with a woody persistent stem-base. — Also **suffructes'cent**. [L *sub* under, and *frutex*, *-icis* a shrub]

suffumigate *sə-fū'mi-gāt*, *vt* to fumigate from below. — *n* **suffumigā'tion**. [L *sub*, and *fūmigāre*]

suffuse *sə-fūz'*, *vt* to spread over or through, or cover, eg with a liquid or a tint; to permeate. — *adj* (*sə-fūs'*; *bot*) spread out on the substratum. — *n* **suffū'sion** (*-zhən*). — *adj* **suffū'sive** (*-siv*). [L *sub* underneath, and *fundere*, *fūsum* to pour]

Sufi *so͞o'fē*, *n* an adherent of various Muslim orders or groups that aspire to a state of union with God through mystical contemplation, a Muslim mystic: — *pl* **Su'fis**. — *n* **Su'fism**. — *adj* **Su'fic** or **Sufist'ic**. [Ar *çūfī*, prob man of wool, from *çuf* coarse wool (as worn by ascetics)]

sugar *sho͝og'ər*, *n* a sweet substance (*sucrose* or *cane sugar*, $C_{12}H_{22}O_{11}$) obtained chiefly from cane and beet; extended to any water-soluble, crystalline monosaccharide or oligosaccharide, eg fructose, lactose, glucose, etc; a measure (eg a lump, teaspoonful) of sugar; money (*slang*); a term of endearment (*colloq*); flattery (*slang*); heroin or LSD (*slang*). — *adj* made with or of sugar; sweet (*Shakesp*). — *vt* to sprinkle, coat, mix, or sweeten with sugar. — *adj* **sug'ared** sweetened or coated with sugar; sugary. — *n* **sug'ariness**. — *n* **sug'aring** sweetening with sugar; coating trees with sugar as a method of collecting insects; formation of sugar or syrup by boiling maple sap (also **sugaring off**; *NAm*). — *adj* **sug'arless**. — *adj* **sug'ary** like sugar in taste or appearance; having or containing much sugar; cloyingly sweet, sickly, over-sentimental. — **sug'arally** or **sug'arallie** (*-al'i*; *Scot*) liquorice; **sugar apple** the sweetsop fruit; **sug'ar-baker** (*obs*) a sugar refiner; also a confectioner; **sugar basin** or **bowl** a small basin for holding sugar at table; **sugar bean** the lima bean; **sugar beet** any variety of common beet, *esp* the variety *Rapa*, grown for sugar; **sugar bird** a S African bird, *Promerops cafer*, that sucks nectar from flowers; **sugar bush** (*US*) an area of woodland with a preponderance of sugar maples; **sugar candy** sugar in large crystals (also **rock candy**); a sweet, confection (*US*); **sug'arcane** or **sugar cane** a tall woody grass (*Saccharum officinarum*) of tropical and semitropical regions, cultivated in the West Indies, the southern USA, Australia, and elsewhere, one of the chief sources of sugar; **sugar charcoal** a pure form of charcoal obtained from sucrose. — *adj* **sugar-coat'ed** coated with sugar. — **sug'ar-cube** or **-lump** a small square block of sugar; **sugar daddy** a wealthy, elderly or middle-aged man who lavishes money or gifts on a young woman or young homosexual man, *usu* in return for sexual favours or companionship; **sugar diabetes** diabetes mellitus. — *adj* **sugar'-free** containing no sugar. — **sugar glider** an Australian possum, *Petauras breviceps*, with winglike flaps of skin enabling it to make long gliding jumps between trees; **sugar grass** sweet sorghum; **sugar gum** a eucalyptus, *Eucalyptus cladocalyx*, with sweet-tasting foliage; **sug'arhouse** a factory, etc where sugar or maple syrup is made; **sugar kelp** a type of kelp, *Laminaria saccharina*, a source of mannitol (also called **sea belt**); **sug'arloaf** a loaf or hard mass of refined sugar, *usu* more or less conical (see also **loaf sugar**); a hill, hat, or other object of similar form; **sugar-lump** see **sugar-cube**; **sugar maple** a N American maple (*Acer saccharum* or related species) from whose sap maple syrup or maple sugar is made; **sugar mill** a machine for pressing out the juice of the sugar cane; **sugar mimic** any substance, either occurring naturally or developed synthetically, which mimics certain sugars in plant or animal cells; **sugar mite** a mite infesting unrefined sugar; **sugar palm** a palm (of various species) yielding sugar; **sugar pea** another name for **mangetout**; **sugar pine** a tall Western American pine (*Pinus lambertiana*) with sugary heartwood; **sug'arplum** a small round boiled sweet; something pleasing, such as a compliment; a term of endearment; **sug'ar-refī'ner**; **sug'ar-refī'nery**; **sug'ar-refī'ning**; **sugar sifter** a container for sugar with a perforated top, enabling the sugar to be sprinkled; **sugar soap** an alkaline cleansing or stripping preparation for paint surfaces; **sugar tongs** small tongs for lifting sugar-lumps at table. — **heavy sugar** (*slang*) big money; **sugar of lead** lead acetate, sweet and poisonous, used as a mordant for dyeing and printing textiles, and as a drier for paints and varnishes; **sugar the pill** to compensate somewhat for an unpleasant prospect, unwelcome imposition, etc. [OFr (Fr) *sucre*, from Ar *sukkar*, from Sans *sharkarā*; the *g* unexplained; cf **saccharin**]

suggest *sə-jest'* or (*US*) *səg-jest' vt* to introduce indirectly to the thoughts; to call up in the mind; to put forward (a plan, hypothesis, thought, etc); to give an impression of; to tempt (*Shakesp*); to insinuate (*Shakesp*); to influence hypnotically. — *vi* to make suggestions. — *n* **suggest'er**. — *n* **suggestibil'ity**. — *adj* **suggest'ible** capable of being suggested, or of being influenced by suggestion, *esp* hypnotic. — *n* **suggest'ion** (*-yən*) process or act of suggesting; a hint; a proposal; an indecent proposal; incitement, temptation; information without oath, not being pleadable (*law*); a false or underhand representation (*obs*); communication of belief or impulse to a hypnotized person. — *n* **suggest'ionism** treatment by suggestion; the theory that hypnotic effects are entirely due to the action of suggestion. — *n* **suggest'ionist**. — *adj* **suggest'ive** containing a hint; tending to suggest or evoke, evocative; awaking the mind; stimulating; pertaining to hypnotic suggestion; tending to awake indecent mental images or thoughts (*colloq euphem*). — *adv* **suggest'ively**. — *n* **suggest'iveness**. [L *suggerere*, *-gestum*, from *sub* under, and *gerere* to carry]

sugging *sug'ing*, (*commercial jargon*) *n* selling under the guise of market research, a deprecated technique in which a salesperson obtains information as though for a survey before advancing a sales offer. [Appar acronymic for *s*elling *u*nder the *g*uise]

sui *so͞o'ī*, *so͞o'ē* or *so͞o'ē*, (*L*) of himself, herself, itself. — **sui generis** (*jen'ər-is* or *ge'ne-ris*) of its own kind, the only one of its kind; **sui juris** (*jo͞or'is* or *ūr'*) having full legal capacity to act; (in Roman law) having the rights of a freeman.

suicide *sū'i-sīd* or *so͞o'*, *n* the act of killing oneself intentionally; a person who kills himself or herself intentionally. — Cf **parasuicide**. — *adj* **suicī'dal**. — *adv* **suicī'dally**. — *n* **suicidol'ogist**. — *n* **suicidol'ogy** the study of suicide. — **suicide jockey** (*slang*) an utterly reckless driver (as though suicidal); **suicide pact** an agreement between (*usu* two) people to kill themselves together. — **commit suicide** to kill oneself. [L *suī* of himself, and *caedere* to kill]

suid *sū'id* or *so͞o'*, *n* any member of the pig family *Suidae*, *incl* wild pigs such as the wild boar and wart-hog of the Old World, and domestic pigs of the genus *Sus*. — *adj* and *n* **suid'ian**. — *adj* **su'illine**. [L *sūs*, *suis* pig, adj *suillus*, *suilla*, *suillum*]

suint *so͞o'int* or *swint*, *n* perspiration of sheep that dries in the wool and which consists of fatty matter and potassium salts. [Fr, from *suer* to sweat, from L *sūdāre*]

suit *sūt* or *so͞ot*, *n* the process or act of suing; an action at law; courtship; a petition; a series or set; a sequence; a set of cards of the same denomination, in the pack or in one player's hand; a number of articles made to be worn together, eg a set of clothes or armour; matching trousers (or skirt) and jacket, sometimes with a waistcoat; such an outfit for a specified occasion or purpose; a business manager or accounts executive (as contrasted with ordinary workers or creative individuals) (*slang*); (used contemptuously) a bureaucratic functionary or administrative official (*slang*); pursuit (*obs*); a suite (*obs*). — *vt* to provide or furnish; to fall in with the requirements of; to fit; to become, look attractive on; to please; to attire (*obs*). — *vi* to agree; to match or be fitting. — *n* **suitabil'ity**. — *adj* **suit'able** that suits; fitting; agreeing; adequate. — *n* **suit'ableness**. — *adv* **suit'ably**. — *adj* **suit'ed** dressed, clothed; matched, appropriate. — *n* **suit'ing** (sometimes in *pl*) cloth suitable for making suits. — *n* **suit'or** a person who sues; a petitioner; a man seeking the love of a woman, or her hand in marriage: — *fem* (*rare*) **suit'ress** a female suitor. — *vi* (*archaic*) to be or act as a suitor. — **suit'case** a portable oblong travelling case for carrying suits, clothes, etc. — **follow suit** to play a card of the suit led; to do the same; **strong suit** something one is specially good at; **suit yourself** do what you like. [Fr *suite*; cf **sue** and **suite**]

suite *swēt*, *n* a train of followers or attendants; a set, as of furniture or rooms; a sequence of instrumental movements, *usu* dance tunes, in related keys; a sequel. [Fr, from a LL form of L *secūta*, fem pa p of *sequī* to follow]

suitor, suitress. See under **suit**.

suivante *swēv'ənt*, *n* a waiting woman or lady's maid; a confidential maid. [Fr]

suivez *swē-vā*, (*music*) follow (the solo part, a direction to accompanist(s)). [Fr]

sujee. See **soogee**.

suk, sukh. See **souk**.

sukiyaki *so͞o-kē-yä'kē* or *skē-ä-kē*, *n* a Japanese dish of thinly-sliced beef, vegetables, soya sauce, etc, cooked quickly together, often at the table. [Jap]

sukkah or **succah** *suk'ä* or *so͝ok'ə*, *n* a hut or shelter roofed with branches, used by the orthodox Jews as temporary living accommodation during the festival of Sukkoth. [Heb, hut, tabernacle; see also **Sukkoth**]

Sukkoth *suk'əth*, *suk'ət* or *so͞o'kəs*, or **Sukkot** *suk'ət*, *n* an eight-day Jewish harvest festival beginning on the 15th day of Tishri and commemorating the wanderings of the ancient Israelites in the wilderness, the Feast of Tabernacles. — Also **Succ'oth**. [Heb pl *sukkōth* huts, tents]

sulcus *sul'kəs*, *n* a groove, furrow or fissure; a groove or furrow between two convolutions of the brain (*anatom*): — *pl* **sul'ci** (*-sī*). — *adj* **sul'cal** (*-kl*) of a sulcus; grooved; furrowed. — *vt* **sul'calize** or **-ise** to furrow. — *adj* **sul'cate** or **sul'cated** furrowed, grooved; with parallel longitudinal furrows. — *n* **sulcā'tion**. [L *sulcus* a furrow]

sulfa, **sulfate**, **sulfide**, **sulfite**, **sulfo- sulfone**, **sulfur**. See **sulpha**, **sulphate**, **sulphide**, **sulphite**, **sulpho-**, **sulphone**, **sulphur**.

sulfadoxine *sul-fə-dox'in*, *n* a drug used to prevent and treat malaria.

sulfurate, **sulfuric** etc. US spellings of **sulphurate**, **sulphuric**, etc.

sulk *sulk*, *vi* to be sullen, silent or aloof, *esp* out of petty resentment or bad temper. — *n* someone who sulks; (often in *pl*) a fit of sulking. — *adv* **sulk'ily**. — *n* **sulk'iness**. — *adj* **sulk'y** sullen; inclined to sulk. — *n* a light two-wheeled horse-drawn vehicle for one person. [Prob from the root seen in OE *āseolcan* to slack, be slow, pa p *āsolcen*]

sullage *sul'ij*, *n* filth; refuse, sewage; scum; scoria; silt. [Perh connected with **sully**]

sullen *sul'ən*, *adj* gloomily angry and silent; malignant, baleful; dull, dismal. — *adv* sullenly. — *adv* **sull'enly**. — *n* **sull'enness**. [Appar through an OFr derivative from L *sōlus* alone]

sully *sul'i*, *vt* to soil; to tarnish; to mar or stain; to pollute or defile. — *vi* (*archaic*) to be or become soiled: — *pr p* **sull'ying**; *pa t* and *pa p* **sull'ied**. — *n* a spot; tarnish. [OE *sylian* to defile, from *sol* mud; or from OFr *souiller* to soil]

sulph- *sulf-* or **sulpho-** *sul'fō-* (also, chiefly *US*, **sulf-** or **sulfo-**), *pfx* denoting sulphur.

sulpha or (*US*) **sulfa** *sul'fə*, *adj* of a class of synthetic antibacterial drugs, the sulphonamides. — *n* any drug of this class. [*sulpha*nilamide]

sulphacetamide or (*US*) **sulfacetamide** *sul-fə-sēt'a-mīd*, *n* a sulphonamide used in eye drops against conjunctivitis, etc. [*sulpha*, *cet*yl and *amide*]

sulphadiazine or (*US*) **sulfadiazine** *sul-fə-dī'ā-zēn* or *-zin*, *n* a sulphonamide, $C_{10}H_{10}N_4O_2S$, used, *usu* in combination with an antibiotic, in the treatment of pneumonia, meningitis, etc. [*sulpha* and *diazine*]

sulphamethoxazole or (*US*) **sulfamethoxazole** *sul-fə-meth-ok'sə-zōl*, *n* a sulphonamide, $C_{10}H_{11}N_3O_3S$, used with trimethoprim in the combination drug co-trimoxazole, to treat various infections such as bronchitis, pneumonia, etc. [*sulpha*, *meth*yl and is*oxazole*]

sulphanilamide or (*US*) **sulfanilamide** *sul-fə-nil'a-mīd*, *n* a white crystalline compound, $C_6H_8N_2O_2S$, formerly used as an antibacterial drug. [*sulpha*, *anil*ine and *amide*]

sulphatase or (*US*) **sulfatase** *sul'fə-tāz*, *n* any of a group of enzymes found in microorganisms and animal tissue that help to break down sulphuric acid esters.

sulphate or (*US*) **sulfate** *sul'fāt*, *n* a salt of sulphuric acid. — *vt* to form a deposit of lead sulphate on; to treat or impregnate with sulphur or a sulphate. — *vi* to become sulphated. — *n* **sulphā'tion** or (*US*) **sulfā'tion**. [Fr, from New L *sulfātum*]

sulphathiazole or (*US*) **sulfathiazole** *sul-fə-thī'ə-zōl*, *n* a sulphonamide formerly used in human medicine against staphylococcal infection (now only used in veterinary medicine). [*sulpha* and *thiazole*]

sulphhydryl or (*US*) **sulfhydryl** *sulf-hi'dril*, *n* a chemical group, SH, characteristic of sulphur-containing compounds and present in certain proteins, coenzymes, etc. [*sulph-* and *hydryl*]

sulphide or (*US*) **sulfide** *sul'fīd*, *n* a compound of an element or radical with sulphur; a salt of hydrosulphuric acid. [**-ide**]

sulphinpyrazone *sul-fin-pī'rə-zōn*, *n* a drug used to treat gout.

sulphinyl or (*US*) **sulfinyl** *sul'fə-nil*, *n* the bivalent chemical group, SO.

sulphite or (*US*) **sulfite** *sul'fīt*, *n* a salt of sulphurous acid. — **sulphite pulp** in paper-making, wood chips treated with calcium or magnesium acid sulphite. [**-ite**[4]]

sulpho- or (*US*) **sulfo-**. See **sulph-**.

sulphone or (*US*) **sulfone** *sul'fōn*, *n* any of a class of substances consisting of two organic radicals combined with SO^2. — *n* **sulphon'amide** or (*US*) **sulfon'amide** an amide of a sulphonic acid, any of a group of drugs with antibacterial action. — *n* **sul'phonate** or (*US*) **sul'fonate** a salt or ester derived from a sulphonic acid. — *vt* to convert (*esp* an aliphatic or aromatic compound) into a sulphonic acid by treating with sulphuric acid; to introduce the sulphonic group, SO_2OH, into (an organic compound). — *n* **sulphona'tion** or (*US*) **sulfona'tion**. — **sulphon'ic** (or *US* **sulfon'ic**) **acid** any of a group of organic acids containing the group SO_2OH, used in the manufacture of phenols, dyes, etc. [Ger *Sulfon*]

sulphonium or (*US*) **sulfonium** *sul-fō'ni-əm*, *n* the positively charged group, SH_3, its salts or derivatives. [**sulph-** and sfx *-onium*, as in *ammonium*]

sulphonylurea *sul-fŏn-il-yo͞o-ri-ə*, *n* a synthetic compound used to reduce the level of glucose in the blood in diabetes mellitus. [*sulphonyl* a bivalent chemical group, and *urea*]

sulphur or (*US*) **sulfur** *sul'fər*, *n* a yellow nonmetallic element (symbol S; atomic no 16), very brittle, fusible and inflammable, occurring in nature uncombined, as metal sulphides such as galena and pyrite, or as sulphur-containing compounds, used in the manufacture of sulphuric acid, in vulcanization of rubber and as a constituent of certain drugs; the colour of sulphur, a bright yellow. — *adj* composed of sulphur. — *vt* to treat or fumigate with sulphur. — *vt* **sul'phurate** (*-fū-rāt*) to combine with, or subject to the action of, sulphur. — *n* **sulphura'tion**. — *n* **sulphura'tor**. — *adj* **sulphureous** (*-fū'ri-əs*) sulphury; sulphur-yellow. — *adv* **sulphu'reously**. — *n* **sulphu'reousness**. — *n* **sul'phuret** (*-fū-ret*) (*obs*) a sulphide. — *vt* to impregnate, treat or combine with sulphur: — *pr p* **sul'phuretting** or (*esp US*) **-eting**; *pa t* **sul'phuretted** or (*esp US*) **-eted**. — *adj* **sul'phuretted** combined with sulphur. — *adj* **sulphu'ric** containing sulphur in relatively high valency (as opposed to *sulphurous*). — *n* **sulphuriza'tion** or **-s-**. — *vt* **sul'phurize** or **-ise** to sulphurate. — *adj* **sul'phurous** (*-fūr-* or *-fər-*) pertaining to, resembling or containing sulphur; containing sulphur in relatively low valency (*chem*; *-fū'rəs*); of or pertaining to hellfire, infernal, satanic; fiery; blasphemous. — *adj* **sulphury** (*sul'fər-i*) like sulphur. — **sulphur bacteria** bacteria that liberate sulphur from hydrogen sulphide, etc and ultimately form sulphuric acid; **sul'phur-bottom** the blue whale (from the yellowish spots on its underside); **sulphur dioxide** a pungent, colourless, non-flammable gas, SO_2, formed when sulphur burns, a major pollutant when discharged into the atmosphere in waste from industrial processes and used in the manufacture of sulphuric acid, in bleaching, disinfecting and preserving; **sulphuretted hydrogen** hydrogen sulphide; **sulphuric acid** oil of vitriol, a very corrosive acid, H_2SO_4, an important heavy chemical used extensively in industry; **sulphurous acid** an unstable acid, H_2SO_3, used as a food preservative and bleaching agent; **sulphur trioxide** a corrosive substance, SO_3, the anhydride of sulphuric acid; **sulphur tuft** a poisonous fungus (*Hypholoma fasciculare*) with a yellowish cap. [L *sulphur*, *sulfur*, *sulpur*, *-uris*]

sultan *sul'tən*, *n* a Muslim ruler, *esp* (*hist*) the former head of the Ottoman empire; a despot; a small white (*orig* Turkish) variety of domestic fowl with feathered legs and feet. — *n* **sultana** (*sul-* or *səl-tä'nə*) a sultan's wife or concubine; a sultan's mother, sister or daughter; a fiddle strung with wires in pairs; a small, pale, seedless raisin. — *n* **sul'tanate** the rank or office of sultan; the territory ruled over by a sultan. — *n* **sul'taness**. — *adj* **sultanic** (*sul-tan'ik*). — *n* **sul'tanship**. — **sweet sultan** a name given to two annual species of *Centaurea*, *Centaurea moschata* and *Centaurea suaveolens*. [Ar *sultān*]

sultry *sul'tri*, *adj* humid and oppressive, sweltering; hot with anger; passionate, voluptuous; (of language) lurid, verging on the indecent, indelicate (*dated slang*). — *adv* **sul'trily**. — *n* **sul'triness**. [**swelter**]

Sulu *so͞o'lo͞o*, *n* a member of a Muslim people of the *Sulu* Archipelago in the SW Philippines; their Malayan language. — Also *adj*.

sulu *so͞o'lo͞o*, *n* a length of cloth worn in Fiji, etc as a sarong. [Fijian]

sum *sum*, *n* total, whole; the aggregate, whole amount; the result of addition; amount; a quantity of money; a problem in addition, or in arithmetic generally; chief points; substance or result; summation; height, culmination, completion. — *vt* (often with *up*) to add, to make up the total of; to be an epitome of, exemplify; to summarize; to reckon up, form an estimate of; to complete the development of, bring to perfection (*obs*). — *vi* (with *up*) to summarize or make a summing-up; to do sums: — *pr p* **summ'ing**; *pa t* and *pa p* **summed**. — *n* **sum'mand** (or *-and'*) an addend; part of a sum. — *n* **summation** see separate entry. — *adj* **sum'less** not to be summed or counted; incalculable. — *adj* **summed**. — *n* **summ'er**. — *n* and *adj* **summ'ing**. — **summing-up'** a recapitulation or review of the leading points, *esp* a judge's summary survey of the evidence given to a jury before it withdraws to consider its verdict; **sum total** complete or final sum. — **in sum** in short; to sum up; **sum and substance** the gist; the essence; **sum of things** the public weal; the universe. [OFr *summe*, from L *summa*, from *summus* highest]

sumac or **sumach** *so͞o'*, *sho͞o'* or *sū'mak*, *n* any tree or shrub of the genus *Rhus*, *esp Rhus coriaria*; the leaves and shoots used in dyeing. [Fr *sumac* or LL *sumach*, from Ar *summāq*]

sumatra *so͞o-mä'trə*, *n* a short, violent squall in or near the Straits of Malacca, coming from *Sumatra*.

Sumerian *so͞o-mēr'i-ən*, *adj* of or relating to the ancient civilization, people, language, etc of the region of *Sumer* in southern Babylonia (*fl* 3500BC). — *n* a native of Sumer; the language or its cuneiform script.

summa *sum'ə*, *n* a treatise giving a summary of a whole subject: — *pl* **summ'ae** (*-ē*). — *adj* **summar** (*sum'ər*; *Scot*) summary. — *n* **summ'ist** a writer of summae; an epitomist. — **Summar Roll** a list of cases requiring dispatch. [L *summa* sum]

summa cum laude *sum'ə kum lö'dē* or *so͞om'ä ko͞om low'de*, (*L*; *laus*, *laudis* praise) *adv* and *adj* with greatest distinction.

summand. See under **sum**.

summar. See under **summa**.

summary *sum'ə-ri*, *n* an abstract, abridgment or compendium; a shortened form of a story or report, etc summing up the main points. — *adj* condensed; short; brief; compendious; done by a short method; without unnecessary formalities or delay, without further application to the court. — *adv* **summ'arily**. — *n* **summ'ariness**. — *n* **summ'arist** someone who summarizes. — *vt* **summ'arize** or **-ise** to present in a summary or briefly. — **summary offence** (*law*) one which is tried by a magistrate. [L *summārium*, from *summa* sum]

summat *sum'ət*, a dialect form of **something**, **somewhat**.

summate *sum'āt*, *vt* to add together. [Back-formation from **summation**]

summation *sum-ā'shən*, *n* the process of finding the sum, addition; accumulation; an aggregate; a summing-up, summary. — *adj* **summā'tional**. — *adj* **summ'ative** additive. [Med L *summātio*, from *summare* to sum up, from L *summa* sum]

summer[1] *sum'ər*, *n* the warmest season of the year; the period between the summer solstice and the autumn equinox; a spell of warm weather (see **Indian**, **St Luke's**, **St Martin's summer**); a year of age or time (*poetic*); a time of peak maturity, heyday. — *adj* of, for or occurring in summer. — *vi* to pass the summer. — *vt* to keep through the summer. — *n* **summ'ering**. — *adj* **summ'erlike**. — *adj* **summ'erly** warm and bright like summer. — *adj* **summ'ery** like summer; suitable for summer. — **summer cypress** the burning bush, a Eurasian goosefoot, *Kochia scoparia*; **summ'erhouse** a small building in a garden for sitting in in good weather; a summer residence; **summer pudding** a pudding made of seasonal soft fruit and bread; **summer savory** see **savory**; **summer school** a course of study held during the summer. — *adj* **summ'er-seeming** (*Shakesp*) perhaps hot and transient, like summer. — **summer solstice** the solstice that occurs around 21 June in the northern hemisphere (December in the southern); **summer stock** (*US*) a summer season of plays presented by a repertory company; summer theatres collectively; **summ'ertide** (*archaic* or *poetic*) the summer season; **summ'ertime** the summer season; **summer time** time adopted (for daylight-saving purposes) one hour in advance of Greenwich Time between March and October. — *adj* **summ'er-weight** (of clothes) light enough to be worn in summer. — **summ'erwood** wood with smaller and thicker-walled cells than springwood, formed late in the growing season. [OE *sumer, sumor*; Du *zomer*, Ger *Sommer*]

summer[2] *sum'ər, n* a pack-horse, a sumpter (*obs*); a great horizontal beam or lintel, *esp* supporting a floor or roof (also **summ'er-tree**). [See **sumpter**]

summer[3]. See under **sum**.

summersault, summerset. Same as **somersault, somerset**.

summist. See under **summa**.

summit *sum'it, n* the highest point or degree; the top, apex; a summit conference. — *adj* **summ'ital**. — *n* **summiteer'** a participant in summit conferences. — *adj* **summ'itless**. — *n* **summ'itry** the practice or technique of holding summit conferences. — **summit conference, talks** or **meeting** a conference between heads of states; sometimes extended to mean a conference between heads of lesser organizations; **summ'it-level** the highest level. [OFr *sommette, somet* (Fr *sommet*), dimin of *som*, from L *summum* highest]

summon *sum'ən, vt* to call up, forth, or together; to call upon to appear (eg in court) or to do something; to rouse, gather (eg strength or energy). — *adj* **summ'onable**. — *n* **summ'oner** someone who summons; an officer who serves summonses; an apparitor. — *n* **summ'ons** a summoning or an authoritative call; a call to appear (*esp* in court); a call to surrender: — *pl* **summ'onses**. — *vt* to serve with a summons. [OFr *somoner*, from L *summonēre*, from *sub-* secretly, and *monēre* to warn: sense partly from OE *somnian* to assemble]

summum bonum *sum'əm bō'nəm* or *sŏŏm'ŏŏm bo'nŏŏm*, (*L*) *n* the chief good (as the ultimate ethical objective).

summum genus *sum'əm jē'nəs* or *sŏŏm'ŏŏm gen'əs, n* the highest division in a classification; a genus that cannot be categorized under a higher genus (*logic*). [New L]

sumo *sōō'mō, n* a traditional Japanese sport, a form of wrestling, in which a contestant wins if he succeeds in forcing his opponent out of the ring or causes him to touch the ground within it with any part of his body other than the soles of his feet: — *pl* **su'mos**. — *n* **sumotō'ri** a sumo wrestler: — *pl* **sumotō'ri** or **sumotō'ris**. [Jap *sumō*]

sump *sump, n* a bog, pool, puddle (now *dialect*); a pit or depression into which liquid drains, such as the lowest point of a mine into which water drains, a depression into which seawater drains at a salt work; a reservoir for liquid *esp* the lower part of the crankcase in an internal-combustion engine serving as a receptacle for oil. [Du *somp*; Ger *Sumpf*]

sumph *sumf*, (*Scot*) *n* a stupid person, a simpleton; a surly, sullen person. — *adj* **sumph'ish**. — *n* **sumph'ishness**. [Origin unknown]

sumpit *sum'pit* or **sumpitan** *sum'pit-an, n* a Malay blowpipe made from a hollow cane and used for shooting (*esp* poisonous) arrows. [Malay]

sumpsimus *sump'si-məs, n* a correct expression used in place of one that is popularly used but is strictly incorrect. [L *sūmpsimus*, see **mumpsimus**]

sumpter *sump'tər* or *sum'tər*, (*archaic*) *n* a packhorse or mule. [OFr *sommetier*, a packhorse driver, from Gr *sagma* a pack, saddlebag, *sattein* to pack]

sumptuary *sump'tū-ər-i* or *sum'tū-ər-i, adj* pertaining to or regulating expense; relating to the control or moderation of extravagance. [L *sumptuārius*, from *sumptus* cost]

sumptuous *sum'* or *sump'tū-əs, adj* costly; magnificently luxurious. — *n* **sumptuos'ity**. — *adv* **sump'tūously**. — *n* **sump'tūousness**. [L *sūmptus* cost, from *sūmere, sūmptum* to take]

Sun. *abbrev*: Sunday.

sun *sun, n* the star which is the gravitational centre around which the planets, etc revolve, and the source of light and heat to our planetary system (often with *cap*); its heat and light; the position of this star or the time when it is visible in the sky; sunshine; any star around which planets, etc revolve; a representation of the sun, often with a human face; a person or thing likened to the sun, eg in splendour, glory, as the central body in a system, etc; a year, or a day (*archaic* and *poetic*); sunrise; sunset. — *vt* to expose to the sun's rays; to warm, etc in sunshine. — *vi* to be exposed or expose oneself to the sun's rays; to bask in sunshine: — *pr p* **sunn'ing**; *pa t* and *pa p* **sunned**. — *adj* **sun'less**. — *n* **sun'lessness**. — *adj* **sun'like**. — *adj* **sunned** exposed to the sun or sunshine. — *adv* **sunn'ily**. — *n* **sunn'iness**. — *adj* **sunn'y** of, from, like or lighted, coloured or warmed by the sun; genial; cheerful. — *adj* and *adv* **sun'ward** towards the sun. — *adv* **sun'wards**. — *adv* **sun'wise** in the direction of the sun's apparent revolution. — *adj* **sun-and-plan'et** geared so that one wheel moves round another. — **sun animalcule** a heliozoan. — *vi* **sun'bake** (*Austr*) to sunbathe. — Also *n*. — *adj* **sun'baked** baked or dried by the heat of the sun. — **sun'bath** or **sun'bathe** exposure of the body to the sun's rays, *esp* in order to tan the skin. — *vi* **sun'bathe**. — **sun'bather** (*-bādh-*); **sun'-bathing**; **sun'beam** a shaft of sunlight. — *adj* **sun'-beamed**. — *adj* **sun'beamy**. — **sun bear** a small black bear (*Helarctos malayanus*) of forest areas of SE Asia, with a crescent-shaped yellowish-white patch at the front of its neck. — *adj* **sun'beat** or **sun'beaten** continually exposed to the sun. — **sun'bed** a unit consisting of a couch with sunlamps for obtaining an artificial suntan; a sunlounger; **sun'belt** a region with a warm, sunny climate, a preferred place to live; a favoured area generally; (*often cap*; also **Sun Belt**) the Southern States of the US; **sun'berry** a dark red edible fruit, a hybrid resulting from a cross between a blackberry and a raspberry; the plant producing this fruit; **sun'bird** any of the *Nectariniidae*, a family of small, often brightly-coloured, tropical birds related to honey-eaters and superficially like hummingbirds; **sun bittern** a S American wading bird (*Eurypyga helias*) with brilliant many-coloured markings; **sun'blind** a shade or awning for a window. — *adj* **sun'-blind** blinded by the sun. — **sun'-blink** (*Scot*) a gleam of sunshine; **sun'block** a sunscreen that completely protects the skin from the sun's ultraviolet rays; **sun bonnet** a light bonnet projecting beyond the face at the top and sides to provide protection from the sun; **sun'bow** a bow or arc of rainbow-like colours that is made by the sun shining through spray or mist, eg of a waterfall. — *adj* **sun'bright** bright as the sun. — **sun'burn** reddening of the skin and tenderness caused by excessive exposure to the sun's ultraviolet rays; tanning of the skin. — *vt* to burn or tan by exposure to the sun. — *vi* to become sunburned. — *adj* **sun'burned** or **sun'burnt**. — **sun'burst** a strong outburst of sunlight; something, eg a jewel or ornament, resembling the rayed sun. — *adj* **sun'-clad** clothed in radiant light. — **sun crack** a crack formed in clayey ground as it dries in the sun, often preserved in rocks; **sun cult** worship of a sun-god or of the sun. — *adj* **sun'-cured** cured in the sun. — **sun dance** a N American Indian ceremonial dance, performed in honour of the sun; **sun deck** or **sun'deck** the upper deck of a passenger ship that is exposed to the sun; a roof, balcony or terrace used for sunbathing; **sun'dew** an insectivorous bog plant (*Drosera*); **sun'dial** a device for telling the time by a shadow cast by the gnomon on a graduated flat surface; **sun disc** or (*esp NAm*) **sun disk** the visible disc of the sun; a winged disc, an ancient Egyptian symbol of the sun-god; **sun'dog** a mock sun or parhelion; **sun'down** sunset; a woman's broad-brimmed hat (*US colloq*); **sun'downer** in Australia, a loafer or tramp who arrives at a place in time for a meal and lodging, but too late to do any work in exchange; a government official who practises a profession after hours (*US*); an alcoholic drink taken after sunset. — *adj* **sun'drenched** exposed to long periods of hot sunshine. — **sun'dress** a low-cut dress, leaving the arms, shoulders and back exposed to the sun. — *adj* **sun'-dried** dried in the sun. — **sun'drops** an American evening primrose of the genus *Oenothera*, with flowers that open at or around sunrise. — *adj* **sun'-expelling** (*Shakesp*) keeping off the sun. — *adj* **sun'fast** (chiefly *NAm*) (of dye, fabric or garment colour) not fading in the sunlight. — **sun'fish** any of various N American perch-like fishes of the family *Centrarchidae*, eg the largemouth bass, smallmouth bass and pumpkinseed, all having rounded, often brightly-coloured bodies and differing from the perches in that they build nests and care for their young; any large marine fish of the family *Molidae*, *esp Mola mola*, of temperate and tropical seas, having a deep almost oval body and teeth fused to form a sharp beak; **sun'flower** a composite plant (*Helianthus*) or its large head with yellow rays and edible seeds from which an oil is extracted; **sun'glass** a burning-glass. — *n pl* **sun'glasses** dark-lensed spectacles used to protect the eyes against strong sunlight. — **sun'glow** the glow in the sky before sunrise and after sunset; **sun'-god** a god personifying or concerned with the sun; **sun'hat** a hat with a brim to shade the face; **sun'lamp** a lamp that gives out ultraviolet rays, used curatively or to induce artificial suntan; a lamp producing a very bright light, used in film-making; **sun'light** the light of the sun. — *adj* **sun'lit** lighted by the sun. — **sun lounge** or (*US*) **sun parlor** a room with large windows, or a glass wall, to admit the maximum sunlight; **sun'lounger** an upholstered couch for sunbathing; **sun myth** a solar myth; **sunny side** a pleasant or cheerful part or point of view; the better side; an age less than one specified, as *on the sunny side of fifty* (see also below); **sun parlor** see **sun lounge**; **sun picture** or **print** (*obs*) a photograph. — *adj* **sun'proof**. — **sun protection factor** the effectiveness of a sunscreen in protecting the skin from the sun's ultraviolet rays, *usu* indicated by a number on a scale of 1 to 12 or 15 (*abbrev* **SPV**); **sun'ray** a sunbeam, ray of sunshine; **sunray pleats** tapering knife pleats giving a flared effect to skirts, etc; **sun'rise** or **sun'rising** the rising or first appearance of the sun above the horizon; the time or colour-effects of this rising; the east; **sunrise industry** a new and rapidly-growing industry, often based on electronics; **sun'roof** or **sunshine roof** a section in a car roof that can be slid open to admit light and air; **sun room** a sun lounge; **sun'screen** a lotion, cream, etc, that prevents sunburn by screening the skin from ultraviolet rays; **sun'set** or **sun'setting** the setting or going down of the sun; the time or phenomenon of this; the west; **sun'shade** a parasol; an awning; **sun'shine** bright sunlight; brightness; prosperity; geniality; an informal term of address, often used in a gently scolding or ironic tone. — *adj* **sun'shine** sunshiny; fair-weather. — **sunshine recorder** an instrument for recording duration of sunshine; **sunshine roof** see **sunroof**. — *adj* **sun'shiny** bright with sunshine; pleasant; bright like the sun; genial. — **sun'spot** a relatively dark patch on the surface of the sun; a place with a very warm sunny climate; **sun spurge** a spurge (*Euphorbia helioscopia*) supposed to turn with the sun, a common weed; **sun'stone** aventurine feldspar; **sun'stroke** a medical condition of general collapse caused by prolonged exposure to intense sunlight, which can result in delirium, convulsions and coma. — *adj* **sun'struck** affected with sunstroke. — **sun'suit** a child's outfit for playing in the sun, leaving most of the body exposed; **sun'tan** a browning of the skin as a result of exposure to the sun; (in *pl*) a light-coloured military uniform for summer wear (*US*). — *adj* **sun'tanned**. — **sun'trap** a sheltered, sunny place; **sun'up** sunrise; **sun visor**; **sun worship** adoration or deification of the sun; **sun worshipper** or **sun'worshipper** an adherent of sun worship; a person who spends long periods of time sunbathing. — **a place in the sun** a place or opportunity for good living or attaining prosperity; **a touch of the sun** mild sunburn; mild sunstroke; **between** (in *Shakesp* **'twixt**) **sun and sun** or **from sun to sun** between sunrise and sunset; **catch the sun** to be sunburnt; **have been in the sunshine** or **have the sun in one's eyes** to be drunk; **sunny side up** (*colloq*) (of an egg) fried on one side only, so that the yolk is visible; **take the sun** to ascertain the sun's meridian altitude; to walk or laze in the sun; **under the sun** on earth. [OE *sunne*; ON *sunna*, OHGer *sunnô*]

sundae *sun'dā* or *-di*, *n* an ice-cream with syrup or crushed fruit; a mixed nougat or confection. [Perh **Sunday**]

sundari *sun'də-rē*, *n* an East Indian sterculiaceous timber-tree (*Heritiera*). — Also **sun'dra**, **sun'dri** or **sun'der**. [Sans *sundarī*]

Sunday *sun'dā* or *sun'di*, *n* the first day of the week, anciently dedicated to the sun, now regarded as the Sabbath by most Christians; a newspaper published on Sundays. — *adj* of, for or occurring on Sunday. — **Sunday best** one's best clothes; **Sunday driver** someone who drives a car at weekends only, hence, an unpractised and incompetent driver. — *adj* **Sun'day-go-to-meeting** appropriated to Sunday and church-going. — **Sunday painters** people who paint seriously but in their spare time; **Sunday punch** (*NAm colloq*) a powerful punch intended to knock out one's opponent (also *fig*); **Sunday saint** someone whose religion or morality is confined to Sundays; **Sunday school** a school for religious (*orig* general) instruction for children on Sunday. — **a month of Sundays** a long time. [OE *sunnan dæg*; Ger *Sonntag*; transl of L *diēs sōlis* day of the sun]

sunder[1] *sun'dər*, (*archaic* and *poetic*) *vt* and *vi* to separate; to part. — *n* **sun'derance**. — *adj* **sun'dered**. — *n* **sun'derer**. — *n* and *adj* **sun'dering**. — *n* **sun'derment**. — **in sunder** (*Bible*) asunder. [OE *syndrian* to separate, *sundor* separate; ON *sundr* asunder]

sunder[2], **sundra**, **sundri**. See **sundari**.

sundew, **sundial**, etc. See under **sun**.

sundry *sun'dri*, *adj* separate; more than one or two; several; miscellaneous, various; varied (*Shakesp*). — *n pl* **sun'dries** sundry things; miscellaneous small things, *esp* things of low or little value. — **all and sundry** all collectively and individually. [OE *syndrig*; cf **sunder**[1]]

sunfast, **sunfish**, **sunflower**. See under **sun**.

Sung *sōōng*, *n* a Chinese dynasty (960–1279). — *adj* of the dynasty, or its culture, including its pottery.

sung *sung*. See **sing**.

sungar. See **sangar**.

sunglass, **sunglasses**, **sun-god**, **sun hat**. See under **sun**.

sunk[1] *sungk*, **sunken** *sungk'n*. See **sink**.

sunk[2] *sungk*, (*Scot*) *n* a turf seat; a pad; a bank; an overweight person. — *n* **sunk'ie** a little stool. [Origin unknown]

sunket *sung'kit*, (*Scot*) *n* (*usu* in *pl*) a dainty or delicacy. [From *sumquhat*, Scots form of **somewhat**]

sunlamp ... to ... **sun myth**. See under **sun**.

sunn *sun*, *n* an E Indian leguminous shrub (*Crotalaria juncea*) that yields a tough fibre used in rope-making, etc; this fibre (also **sunn hemp**). [Hindi *san*]

Sunna or **Sunnah** *sōōn'ə* or *sun'ə*, *n* the traditional root of Muslim law, based on biographical stories about Muhammad, constituting a secondary source of revelation to that which is written down in the Koran. — *n* **Sunn'i** (*-ē*) one of the two main branches of Islam, accepting the authority of the Sunna; a member of this (also **Sunn'ite**). — *n* **Sunn'ism** the teachings and beliefs of orthodox Muslims. [Ar *sunnah*]

sunny ... to ... **sun worshipper**. See under **sun**.

suo jure *sōō'ō jōō'rē* or *sōō'ō yōō'rē*, (*esp law*) *adv* in one's own right. [L]

suo loco *sōō'ō lō'kō* or *sōō'ō lo'kō*, (*esp law*) *adv* in one's (or its) rightful place. [L]

Suomi *sōō'ə-mi*, *n* Finland or the Finnish language. — *n pl* the Finns. — *adj* **Suo'mic** or **Suo'mish**.

suovetaurilia *sū-ov-i-tö-ril'i-ə* or *sōō-o-we-tow-rē'li-a*, *n pl* a Roman sacrifice of a sheep, a pig, and an ox. [L *sūs* pig, *ovis* sheep, and *taurus* ox]

sup *sup*, *vt* to take (a liquid) into the mouth, to drink; to eat with a spoon (*Scot*); to provide supper for (*Shakesp*). — *vi* to eat the evening meal (*archaic*); to sip (*Bible*): — *pr p* **supp'ing**; *pa t* and *pa p* **supped**. — *n* a small mouthful, as of a liquid. [OE *sūpan*; ON *sūpa*,

Ger *saufen* to drink; partly from OFr *soper*, *souper* (Fr *souper*) to take supper]

sup. *abbrev*: superfine; superior; superlative (also **superl.**); supine; supplement; *supra* (*L*), above; supreme.

supawn. See **suppawn**.

Sup.Ct. *abbrev*: Superior Court; Supreme Court.

supe. See **super²**.

super¹ *sōō'pər* or *sū'pər*, *adj* of superior quality; exceptionally good; delightful. — *n* something of superior quality or grade, such as a grade of petrol. — *interj* (*colloq*) good, lovely, smashing! [L, above]

super² *sōō'pər* or *sū'pər*, a *colloq* short form of superfine, superintendent and supernumerary, *esp* a supernumerary actor (also **supe**).

super- *sōō-pər-* or *sū-pər-*, *pfx* denoting: (1) above or over; (2) beyond, exceeding, exceedingly, surpassing all others; (3) of greater size, strength, extent, power, quantity, etc; (4) in addition, extra; (5) in greater proportion (*chem*). [L *super* above; cf **over**, Gr *hyper*]

Words with the prefix **super-** are listed in the following text or in the separate panels.

superable. See under **superate**.

superabound *sōō-* or *sū-pər-ə-bownd'*, *vi* to be more, very, or excessively abundant. — *n* **superabun'dance**. — *adj* **superabund'ant**. — *adv* **superabund'antly**. [**super-** (2)]

superadd *sōō-* or *sū-pər-ad'*, *vt* to add over and above. — *n* **superaddi'tion**. — *adj* **superaddi'tional**. [L *superaddere*, from *super* and *addere*]

superalloy *sōō-* or *sū-pər-al'oi*, *n* an alloy that has good stability at 600°C to 1000°C. [**super-** (3)]

superaltar *sōō-* or *sū-pər-ölt'ər*, *n* a slab of stone used as a portable altar to be laid on the top of an unconsecrated altar; a structure over an altar. [**super-** (1)]

superannuate *sōō-* or *sū-pər-an'ū-āt*, *vt* to set aside or cause to retire on account of age; to pension off. — *adj* (*-ət*; *rare*) superannuated. — *n* (*-ət*; *rare*) a superannuated person. — *adj* **superann'uable**. — *adj* **superann'ūated**. — *n* **superannūā'tion** the act or state of superannuating; a pension; a regular contribution paid by an employee towards a pension. [L *super* above, and *annus* year]

superate *sōō'* or *sū'pər-āt*, *vt* (*obs*) to overcome, outdo, or surmount. — *adj* **su'perable** capable of being overcome, outdone, surmountable. — *adv* **su'perably**. — *n* **superā'tion**. [L *superāre* to go over, surmount]

superb *sōō-* or *sū-pûrb'*, *adj* proud, haughty (*obs*); magnificent; gorgeous; triumphantly effective; supremely excellent (*colloq*). — *n* (*rare*) **superb'ity**. — *adv* **superb'ly**. — *n* **superb'ness**. [L *superbus* proud]

supercalender *sōō-* or *sū-pər-kal'ən-dər*, *vt* to give a high polish to (paper, cloth, etc) by calendering. — *n* a machine for this. — *adj* **supercal'endered**. [**super-** (3)]

supercargo *sōō-* or *sū-pər-kär'gō*, *n* a person in a ship placed in charge of the cargo and superintending all commercial transactions of the voyage: — *pl* **supercar'goes**. — *n* **supercar'goship**. [**super-** (1)]

supercharge *sōō-* or *sū-pər-chärj'*, *vt* to fill to excess; to charge above the normal; to add pressure to; to charge exorbitantly, overcharge; to place as an overcharge (*heraldry*). — *n* **su'percharge** an excessive, exorbitant, or greater than normal charge; a charge borne upon an ordinary or other charge (*heraldry*). — *n* **su'percharger** a device for increasing the pressure in an internal combustion engine. [**super-** (2)]

supercherie *sü-per-shə-rē*, *n* deception; hoax; fraud. [Fr]

superciliary *sōō'* or *sū'pər-sil'i-ər-i*, *adj* of, on or near the eyebrow; marked above the eye. — *n* a superciliary ridge or mark. [L *supercilium*, from *super* above, and *cilium* eyelid]

supercilious *sōō-* or *sū-pər-sil'i-əs*, *adj* disdainfully superior in manner; overbearing (*obs*); superciliary (*rare*). — *adv* **supercil'iously**. — *n* **supercil'iousness**. [Ety as for **superciliary**]

superclass *sōō'* or *sū'pər-kläs*, (*biol*) *n* a taxonomic category that consists of a number of related classes between a class and a subphylum or phylum. [**super-** (3)]

supercluster *sōō-* or *sū-pər-klus'tər*, (*astron*) *n* a large cluster of galaxies. [**super-** (3)]

supercoil *sōō'* or *sū'pər-koil*, *n* a complex coil formed by intertwining strands of protein or DNA. — *adj* **su'percoiled**. [**super-** (3)]

supercold *sōō-* or *sū'pər-kōld*. Same as **cryogenic**.

supercollider *sōō-* or *sū-pər-kə-lī'dər*, *n* an extremely powerful particle accelerator. [**super-** (3)]

supercolumnar *sōō-* or *sū-pər-kə-lum'nər*, (*archit*) *adj* above a column or colonnade; with one colonnade above another. — *n* **supercolumniā'tion**. [**super-** (1)]

supercomputer *sōō-* or *sū-pər-kəm-pū-tər*, *n* a powerful computer which can perform a large number of mathematical calculations very quickly. [**super-** (3)]

superconduct *sōō-* or *sū-pər-kən-dukt'*, *vi* to conduct electricity without resistance. — *adj* **superconduc'ting**. — *adj* **superconduc'tive**. — *n* **superconductiv'ity** complete loss of electrical resistance shown by certain pure metals and alloys at temperatures approaching absolute zero and by certain ceramics at higher temperatures. — *n* **superconduc'tor** a substance having superconductivity. [**super-** (3)]

supercontinent *sōō-* or *sū-pər-kon'ti-nənt*, *n* any of the vast land-masses from which the continents were originally formed. [**super-** (3)]

supercool *sōō-* or *sū-pər-kōōl'*, *vt* to cool (a liquid) below normal freezing-point without freezing or crystallization occurring. — *vi* to become supercooled. — *adj* (*colloq*; *esp NAm*) (of a person) extremely calm, unflappable, imperturbable; having admirable or excellent qualities to a supreme degree. [**super-** (2)]

supercritical *sōō-* or *sū-pər-krit'i-kəl*, *adj* capable of sustaining a chain reaction such that the rate of reaction increases (*nuclear phys*); (of an aerofoil, aircraft's wing) moving slower than sound while the surrounding air moves faster than sound, hence permitting increased lift and speed. [**super-** (2)]

superdense *sōō'* or *sū'pər-dens*, (*astron*) *adj* extremely dense. — **superdense theory** big-bang theory.

superdominant *sōō'* or *sū'pər-dom'i-nənt*, (*music*) *n* the submediant.

super-duper *sōō'pər-dōō'pər*, (*colloq*) *adj* superlatively fine or great; marvellous. [Reduplication of **super**]

superego *sōō-* or *sū-pər-ē'gō*, or *-eg'ō*, (*psychol*) *n* the strong unconscious inhibitory mechanism which criticizes the ego and causes it pain and distress when it accepts unworthy impulses from the id. [**super-** (1)]

superelevation *sōō-* or *sū-pər-el-ə-vā'shən*, *n* excess in height; the difference in height between the opposite sides of a road or railway on a curve. [**super-** (2), (1)]

supereminent *sōō-* or *sū-pər-em'i-nənt*, *adj* of a degree of eminence or excellence surpassing all others. — *n* **superem'inence**. — *adv* **superem'inently**. [**super-** (2)]

supererogation *sōō-* or *sū-pər-er-ō-gā'shən*, *n* doing more than is required. — *vi* (*obs*) **superer'ogate**. — *adj* **supererogatory** (*-ə-rog'ə-tər-i*). — Also (*rare*) **superer'ogant** or **supererog'ative**. — **works of supererogation** (*RC*) works which, not absolutely required of each

Some words with **super-** prefix; see **super-** entry for numbered senses.

superabsorb'ent *adj* (2).	**superbrain'** *n* (3).	**superclean'** *adj* (2).
superac'tive *adj* (2).	**superbrat'** *n* (2).	**supercon'fidence** *n* (2).
superacute' *adj* (3).	**superbright'** *adj* (2).	**supercon'fident** *adj* (2).
superambi'tious *adj* (2).	**supercau'tious** *adj* (2).	**supercrim'inal** *n* and *adj* (3).
superbold' *adj* (3).	**supercelest'ial** *adj* (1) and (2).	**superdaint'y** *adj* (2).

individual for salvation, may be done for the sake of greater perfection, affording the church a store of surplus merit, to eke out the deficient merit of others. [L *super* above, and *ērogāre*, *-ātum* to pay out]

superette *sōō-* or *sū-pər-et'*, (*orig Austr* and *NAm*) *n* a small local supermarket. [*super*market, and dimin sfx *-ette*]

superfamily *sōō'* or *sū'pər-fam-i-li*, *n* a taxonomic group of related families between a suborder or order and a family. [**super-** (3)]

superfatted *sōō-* or *sū-pər-fat'id*, *adj* (of soap) having an excess of fat, so that there is no free alkali. [**super-** (5)]

superfecta *sōō-* or *sū-pər-fek'tə*, (*NAm*) *n* a type of bet (eg on a horserace) in which the better must select the first four finishers in the correct order. [**super-** (3) and **perfecta**]

superfecundation *sōō-* or *sū-pər-fē-kən-dā'shən* or *-fek-ən-*, *n* fertilization of two or more eggs produced at the same time by successive depositions of sperm, often from different males; fertilization of a large number of eggs. [**super-** (3)]

superfetation *sōō-* or *sū-pər-fē-tā'shən*, *n* fertilization of a second ovum some time after the start of a pregnancy, resulting in two foetuses of different age in the same uterus, normal in some animals and believed by some to have occurred in women; superabundant production or accumulation. — *vi* **superfē'tate**. [L *superfētāre*, from pfx *super-* over, and *fētus* a fetus]

superficial *sōō-* or *sū-pər-fish'l*, *adj* of, on or near the surface; not thorough or careful; not deep or profound; lacking sincerity or richness of personality, *esp* being concerned only with outward appearances. — *n* that which is, or those who are, superficial; (in *pl*) surface characteristics. — *n* **superficiality** (*-fish-i-al'i-ti*). — *vt* **superfic'ialize** or **-ise** to make superficial. — *vi* to deal superficially. — *adv* **superfic'ially**. — *n* **superfic'ialness**. [LL *superficiālis*, from L *superficiēs*; see next entry]

superficies *sōō-* or *sū-pər-fish'i-ēz*, *n* a surface, that which has length and breadth but no thickness (*geom*); a bounding or outer surface; a surface layer; a surface area; external features, appearance: — *pl* **superfic'ies**. [L *superficiēs*, from *super*, and *faciēs* face]

superfine *sōō'* or *sū'pər-fīn*, *adj* of specially fine size or quality (short form **super**); overly fastidious or proper. — *n* **su'perfineness**. [**super-** (2)]

superfluid *sōō-* or *sū-pər-flōō'id*, *adj* relating to, or demonstrating, superfluidity. — *n* **superfluid'ity** a phenomenon observed in a form of helium (*helium II*), obtained below 2·19 K, in which internal friction is negligible. [**super-** (3)]

superfluous *sōō-* or *sū-pûr'flōō-əs*, *adj* above what is enough; redundant; unnecessary. — *n* **superfluity** (*-flōō'*) the state of being superfluous; a thing that is superfluous; superabundance. — *adv* **super'fluously**. — *n* **super'fluousness** superfluity. — *n* **su'perflux** (*Shakesp*) superfluity. [L *superfluus* overflowing, from *super*, and *fluere* to flow]

superfoetation. Same as **superfetation**.

superfrontal *sōō-* or *sū-pər-frun'tl*, *n* a covering hanging over the upper edge of an altar frontal. [**super-** (1)]

superfuse *sōō-* or *sū'pər-fyōōz'*, *vt* to pour over (something else) (*obs*); to supercool. — *n* **superfu'sion**. [**super-** (1) and (2)]

super G *sōō-* or *sū-pər-jē'*, (*skiing*) *n* a competitive event similar to giant slalom but skied over a longer distance with greater intervals between the gates. [*super-* in the sense of 'greater', and giant (slalom)]

supergene *sōō'* or *sū'pər-jēn*, *n* a cluster of genes along a chromosome that may act as a unit in meiosis but may have unrelated functions. [**super-** (3)]

supergiant *sōō'* or *sū'pər-jī-ənt* or *-jī'ənt*, *n* a very bright star of enormous size and low density, such as Betelgeuse and Antares. [**super-** (3)]

superglacial *sōō-* or *sū-pər-glā'si-əl* or *glā'shəl*, *adj* occurring or originating on the surface of a glacier. [**super-** (1)]

superglue *sōō'* or *sū'pər-glōō*, *n* a very strong and quick-acting impact adhesive. — *vt* and *vi* to stick with superglue. [**super-** (3)]

supergrass *sōō'* or *sū'pər-gräs*, (*slang*) *n* a police informer who has given information leading to the arrest of a great number of criminals. [**super-** (2)]

supergravity *sōō-* or *sū-pər-grav'i-ti*, *n* a supersymmetrical theory of gravitation. [**super-** (3)]

supergroup *sōō'* or *sū'pər-grōōp*, *n* a pop group made up of established solo artists; an internationally successful pop group. [**super-** (2)]

superheat *sōō-* or *sū-pər-hēt*, *vt* to heat to excess; to heat (steam, etc) above the temperature of saturation; to heat (a liquid) above normal boiling-point without vaporization. — *n* the state of being superheated; the amount of superheating. — *n* **superheat'er**. [**super-** (2)]

superheavy *sōō-* or *sū-pər-hev'i*, *adj* having an atomic number or weight heavier than the heaviest known. — *n* a superheavy element. [**super-** (2)]

superhero *sōō'* or *sū'pər-hē-rō*, *n* any of various comic-book heroes with supernormal or superhuman powers. [**super-** (2)]

superheterodyne *sōō-* or *sū-per-het'ər-ə-dīn*, *adj* of a type of radio or TV reception in which the incoming signal is mixed with a locally generated signal giving output of a signal of carrier frequency, but containing all the original modulation, which is then amplified and demodulated. — *n* a superheterodyne receiver. [**super-** (3)]

superhigh frequency. See **frequency** under **frequent**.

superhighway *sōō'* or *sū'pər-hī-wā*, (*NAm*) *n* a wide road for fast motor-traffic; a motorway, expressway. [**super-** (3)]

superhive *soo'* or *sū'pər-hīv*, *n* a detachable upper compartment of a beehive. [**super-** (1)]

superhuman *sōō-* or *sū-pər-hū'mən*, *adj* above man; greater than, or exceeding, the power, strength, capability, etc of man; more or higher than human. — *n* **superhūman'ity**. — *vt* **superhū'manize** or **-ise**. — *adv* **superhū'manly**. [**super-** (1) and (2)]

superhumeral *sōō-* or *sū-pər-hū'mə-rəl*, *n* any ecclesiastical vestment worn on the shoulders. [**super-** (1)]

superimpose *sōō-* or *sū-pər-im-pōz'*, *vt* to set on the top of something else; to place one over another; to establish in superaddition. — *adj* **superimposed'**. — *n* **superimposi'tion**. [**super-** (1)]

superincumbent *sōō-* or *sū-pər-in-kum'bənt*, *adj* resting on the top; overlying; overhanging; exerted from above. — *n* **superincum'bence** or **superincum'bency**. — *adv* **superincum'bently**. [**super-** (1)]

superinduce *sōō-* or *sū-pər-in-dyōōs*, *vt* to bring in over and above, or in supersession of, something else; to superadd. — *n* **superinduce'ment** or **superinduc'tion**. [**super-** (1)]

superinfection *sōō-* or *sū-pər-in-fek'shən*, *n* an infection arising during and in addition to another infection and caused by a different (or a different variety of the same) microorganism. — *vt* **superinfect'**. [**super-** (4)]

superintend *sōō-* or *sū-pər-in-tend'*, *vt* to supervise; to exercise supervision over; to control or manage. — *n* **superinten'dency** the office or district of a superintendent; the act or process of superintending (also

superessen'tial *adj* (2).	**superexc'ellent** *adj* (2).	**superord'inary** *adj* (1) and (2).
superev'ident *adj* (2).	**superfast'** *adj* (2).	**superpa'triot** *n* (2).
superexalt' *vt* (2).	**supergun'** *n* (3).	**superpa'triotism** *n* (2).
superexaltā'tion *n* (2).	**superher'oine** *n* (2).	**superpol'ymer** *n* (3).
superexc'ellence *n* (2).	**superim'portant** *adj* (2).	**superpraise'** *vt* (2).

superintend'ence). — *adj* **superinten'dent** superintending. — *n* a person who superintends; an overseer; the head of a Sunday school; (in some Protestant churches) a clergyman having the oversight of the clergy of a district; a police officer above a chief inspector; the head of a police department (*US*); (in the RSPCA) a rank between commander and chief inspector; the administrator of a local school system (*US*); the caretaker of a building (*NAm*). — *n* **superinten'dentship**. — *adj* **superintend'ing**. [Ecclesiastical L *superintendēre*; see **super-** (1) and **intend**]

superior *sōō-* or *sū-pē'ri-ər*, *adj* upper; higher in nature, place, rank, or excellence; better (with *to*); surpassing others; beyond the influence, rising above (with *to*); supercilious or uppish; (often *patronizingly*) very worthy and highly respectable; of wider application, generic; set above the level of the line (*printing*); (of an ovary) inserted on the receptacle above the other parts (*bot*); (of other parts) seeming to arise above the ovary (*bot*). — *n* a person or thing superior to others; the head of a religious house, order, etc; the feudal lord of a vassal; a person to whom feu-duty is paid (*Scots law*): — *fem* **supe'rioress** the head of a nunnery. — *n* **superiority** (*-or'i-ti*) quality or state of being superior; pre-eminence; advantage; the right which the superior enjoys in the land held by the vassal (*Scots law*). — *adv* **supe'riorly** in a superior manner or position. — *n* **supe'riorship**. — **superior court** a court intermediate between an inferior court (eg a magistrate's or district court) and a high court; **superiority complex** (*psychol*) overvaluation of one's worth, often affected to cover a sense of inferiority; **superior planets** those more distant from the sun than the earth is. [L, compar of *superus* on high, from *super* above]

superjacent *sōō-* or *sū-pər-jā'sənt*, *adj* lying above. [L *super*, and *jacēns*, *-entis*, pr p of *jacēre* to lie]

superjet *sōō'* or *sū'pər-jet*, *n* a supersonic jet aircraft. [*super*sonic and *jet*]

superl. *abbrev*: superlative.

superlative *sōō-* or *sū-pûr'lə-tiv*, *adj* raised above others or to the highest degree; superior to all others; most eminent; expressing the highest degree (*gram*). — *n* the superlative or highest degree (*gram*); an adjective or adverb in the superlative degree; any word or phrase of exaggeration. — *adv* **super'latively**. — *n* **super'lativeness**. [L *superlātīvus*, from *super*, and *lātus* carried]

superloo *sōō-* or *sū-pər-lōō'*, (*colloq*) *n* a type of public lavatory offering a greater number of facilities and a high level of luxury, or one which is fully automated, self-cleaning, etc. [**super-** (3)]

superluminal *sōō-* or *sū-pər-lōō'min-əl*, or *-lū-*, *adj* faster than the speed of light; travelling, or able to travel, at such speed. [**super-** (2)]

superlunar *sōō-* or *sū-pər-lōō'nər* or **superlunary** *-lōō'nə-rē*, *adj* above the moon; not of this world, celestial. [**super-** (1)]

superman *sōō'* or *sū'pər-man*, *n* ideal man; a man with exceptional strength or ability; a fictional character with superhuman powers. [**super-** (2)]

supermarket *sōō'* or *sū'pər-mär-kit*, *n* a large, mainly self-service, retail store selling food and other household goods (sometimes shortened to **su'permart**). [**super-** (3)]

supermassive *sōō-* or *sū-pər-mas'iv*, (*astron*) *adj* (of stars) having an extremely high mass, extremely heavy. [**super-** (2)]

supermini *sōō'* or *sū'pər-mi-ni*, *n* a small car with a good standard of performance and comfort. [**super-** (3)]

supermundane *sōō-* or *sū-pər-mun'dān*, *adj* above worldly things. [**super-** (1)]

supernaculum *sōō'* or *sū'pər-nak'ū-ləm*, (*old slang*) *adv* to the last drop. — *n* liquor of the best kind; anything excellent of its kind; a drinking of alcohol in a single draught; a full glass, a bumper. — *adj* **supernac'ular**. [Sham L *super naculum* on the nail, from L *super*, and Ger *Nagel* nail; from the old custom of turning the glass up to show that no more is left than will stand on the thumbnail]

supernal *sōō-* or *sū-pûr'nl*, (*poetic*) *adj* on high; celestial; of a higher world; exalted; topmost. — *adv* **super'nally**. [L *supernus*, from *super*]

supernatant *sōō-* or *sū-pər-nā'tənt*, *adj* floating or swimming above; (of a liquid) overlying a sediment. [L *supernatāns*, *-antis*, from *super*, and *natāre* to swim, float]

supernational, **supernationalism**. See **supranational**.

supernatural *sōō-* or *sū-pər-nach'ə-rəl*, or *-nat'yə-*, *adj* above or beyond nature; not according to the laws of nature; miraculous; magical; spiritual; occult. — *n* that which is supernatural; a supernatural being. — *n* **supernat'uralism** supernatural character or agency; the belief in the influence of the supernatural in the world. — *n* **supernat'uralist** a believer in the supernatural. — *adj* of or pertaining to the supernatural. — *adj* **supernaturalist'ic**. — *vt* **supernat'uralize** or **-ise** to bring into the supernatural sphere. — *adv* **supernat'urally**. — *n* **supernat'uralness**. — *n* **su'pernature** the supernatural. [**super-** (1)]

supernormal *sōō-* or *sū-pər-nör'məl*, *adj* beyond what is normal; in greater number, amount, concentration, etc, than the normal. — *n* **supernormal'ity**. — *adv* **supernor'mally**. [**super-** (1) and (2)]

supernova *sōō-* or *sū-pər-nō'və*, *n* a very brilliant nova resulting from an explosion which blows the star's material into space, leaving an expanding cloud of gas: — *pl* **supernō'vae** (*-vē*) or **supernō'vas**. [L *super-* above, and **nova**]

supernumerary *sōō-* or *sū-pər-nū'mər-ər-i*, *adj* over and above the stated, usual, normal or necessary number. — *n* a supernumerary person or thing; an actor without speaking parts. [LL *supernumerārius*, from L *super*, and *numerus* number]

superoctave *sōō'* or *su'pər-ok-tiv*, *n* an organ coupler giving an octave higher; an organ stop two octaves above the principal. [**super-** (1)]

superorder *sōō-* or *sū-pər-ör-dər*, (*biol*) *n* a taxonomic category of related orders between an order and a subclass or sometimes class. — *adj* **superord'inal** pertaining to a superorder. [**super-** (1)]

superordinate *sōō-* or *sū-pər-örd'in-it*, *adj* superior in rank or condition; in the relation of superordination. — *n* a superior in rank or condition. — *vt* (*-āt*) to make superordinate. — *n* **superordinā'tion** (*logic*) the relation of a universal proposition to a particular proposition in the same terms. [**super-** (1) and (2)]

superorganic *sōō-* or *sū-pər-ör-gan'ik*, *adj* above or beyond the organic, psychical; pertaining to a higher organization, social. — *n* **superorg'anism** a highly organized social community perceptible as a single organism (eg a colony of bees). [**super-** (1) and (2)]

superovulation *sōō-* or *sū-pər-ov-ū-lā'shən*, *n* the production of a larger number of ova than usual, eg under stimulus of injected hormones. — *vi* **superovū'late**. [**super-** (3)]

superoxide *sōō'* or *sū'pər-oks-īd*, *n* any of various oxides having two oxygen atoms. [**super-** (5)]

superphosphate *sōō-* or *sū-pər-fos'fāt*, *n* an acid phosphate; a mixture of calcium sulphate and calcium acid phosphate chiefly used as a fertilizer. [**super-** (5)]

superrefine' *vt* (4).
superrefined' *adj* (4).
superrich' *adj* (2).
supersafe' *adj* (2).
supersafe'ty *n* (2).
supersales'man *n* (3).
su'persalt *n* (5).
superscreen *n* and *adj* (1) and (3).
su'persell *n* (3).
supersen'sitive *adj* (2).
supersen'sitiveness *n* (2).
supersen'sory *adj* (2).
supersen'sual *adj* (2) and (3).
supersharp' *adj* (2).
su'persleuth *n* (2).

superphylum *sōō'* or *sū'pər-fi-ləm*, (*biol*) *n* a taxonomic category of related phyla between a phylum and a kingdom. [**super-** (3)]

superphysical *sōō-* or *sū-pər-fiz'i-kəl*, *adj* beyond or above the physical world, its laws or phenomena. [**super-** (1)]

superplastic *sōō-* or *sū'pər-plas'tik*, or *-pläs'*, *adj* and *n* (a metal or alloy) that is extremely pliable, or capable of being moulded without fracturing, at high temperatures. — *n* **superplastic'ity**. [**super-** (2)]

superplus *sōō'* or *sū'pər-plus*, (*obs*) *n* surplus.

superpose *sōō-* or *sū-pər-pōz'*, *vt* to bring, or suppose to be brought, into coincidence (*geom*); to place vertically over or on something else. — *adj* **superpos'able**. — *adj* **superposed'**. — *n* **superposi'tion** act of superposing; state of being superposed; that which is above anything. [**super-** (1)]

superpower *sōō'* or *sū'pər-powr* or *-pow-ər*, *n* a very powerful state, often applied to the USA and the former USSR. [**super-** (2) and (3)]

superrealism *sōō-* or *sū-pər-rē'əl-izm*, *n* (in art) a style that transcends realism; surrealism; also applied to photo-realism. — *n* and *adj* **superre'alist**. [**super-** (1) and (2)]

super-royal *sōō-* or *sū-pər-roi-əl*, *adj* (of paper-size) larger than royal. [**super**[1] and **royal**]

supersaturate *sōō-* or *sū-pər-sat-ū-rāt* or *-sa-chə-rāt*, *vt* to saturate beyond the normal point; to increase the concentration of beyond saturation. — *adj* **supersat'ūrated**. — *n* **supersaturā'tion**. [**super-** (2) and (3)]

supersaver *sōō'* or *sū'pər-sā-vər*, *n* anything offered at a specially reduced price, *esp* a bus, rail or airplane fare. [**super-** (2)]

superscribe *sōō-* or *sū-pər-skrīb'*, *vt* to write or engrave above, on the top or on the outside of something; to address (eg a letter); to sign at the top. — *adj* **su'perscript** (*-skript*) written above; superior (*printing*). — *n* the superscription, address (*archaic*); a superior character (*printing*). — *n* **superscrip'tion** the act of superscribing; that which is superscribed. [L *super* above, and *scrībere*, *scrīptum* to write]

supersede *sōō-* or *sū-pər-sēd'*, *vt* to set aside, discard; to set aside in favour of another, supplant; to come or put in the room of, to replace; to desist or refrain from (*obs*); to override (*obs*). — *vi* (*obs*) to refrain, desist. — *n* **superse'deas** (*-di-as*; *law*) a writ to stay proceedings, or to suspend the powers of an officer (from the use of the Latin *2nd pers sing present subjunctive*, you are to desist). — *n* **superse'dence**. — *n* **superse'der**. — *n* **supersedere** (*-si-dē'ri* or *sōō-per-se-dā're*, *infinitive*) a private agreement among creditors, under a trust-deed, to supersede or sist diligence for a certain period (*Scots law*); an order of court granting protection to a debtor. — *n* **supersē'dure**. — *n* **supersession** (*-sesh'ən*). [L *supersedēre* to sit above, refrain from, from *super* above, and *sedēre*, *sessum* to sit]

supersensible *sōō-* or *sū-pər-sens'i-bl*, *adj* above the range, beyond the reach, or outside the realm, of the senses. — *adv* **supersen'sibly**. [**super-** (1) and (2)]

superserviceable *sōō-* or *sū-pər-sûr'vis-ə-bəl*, *adj* officious. — *adv* **superserv'iceably**. [**super-** (2)]

supersession. See under **supersede**.

supersonic *sōō-* or *sū-pər-son'ik*, *adj* above the audible limit; too high-pitched for human hearing (ultrasonic); faster than the speed of sound; travelling, or capable of travelling, at such a speed. — *n* a supersonic wave; (in *pl*) the study of such waves. — *adv* **superson'ically**. — **supersonic boom** a shock wave produced by an object moving supersonically; **supersonic-combustion ramjet** see **ramjet**. [L *super* above, and *sonus* sound]

supersound *sōō'* or *sū'pər-sownd*, *n* sound vibrations too rapid to be audible. [**super-** (1) and (2)]

superstar *sōō'* or *sū'pər-stär*, *n* an extremely popular and successful star of the cinema, popular music, etc. — *n* **superstar'dom**.

superstate *sōō'* or *sū-pər-stāt*, *n* a state or organization having governing power over subordinate states. [**super-** (3)]

superstition *sōō-* or *sū-pər-stish'ən*, *n* false worship or religion; an ignorant and irrational belief in supernatural agency, omens, divination, sorcery, etc; a deep-rooted but unfounded general belief; a rite or practice proceeding from superstitious belief or fear (*obs*). — *adj* **superstit'ious**. — *adv* **superstit'iously**. — *n* **superstit'iousness**. [L *superstitiō*, *-ōnis*]

superstore *sōō'* or *sū'pər-stör*, *n* a large supermarket, which *usu* sells many different goods in addition to food. [**super-** (3)]

superstring, superstring theory. See under **string**.

superstructure *sōō'* or *sū'pər-struk-chər*, *n* the part of a building above the foundations, or of a ship above the main deck; any thing or concept based or founded on another. — *vt* **superstruct'** to build on something else as a foundation. — *n* **superstruc'tion**. — *adj* **superstruct'ive**. — *adj* **superstruct'ural**. [**super-** (1)]

supersubtle (or *obs* **supersubtile**) *sōō-* or *sū-pər-sut'l*, *adj* overly subtle; extremely subtle. — *n* **supersub'tlety**. [**super-** (2)]

supersymmetry *sōō-* or *sū-pər-sim'i-trē*, (*particle phys*) *n* a theory that attempts to link all four fundamental forces, and postulates that each force emerged separately during the expansion of the very early universe. — *adj* **supersymmet'rical**. [**super-** (3)]

supertanker *sōō'* or *sū'pər-tang-kər*, *n* a large tanker, *esp* one used for transporting crude oil. [**super-** (3)]

supertax *sōō'* or *sū'pər-taks*, *n* an extra or additional tax on large incomes (term not in official use). [**super-** (4)]

superterranean *sōō-* or *sū-pər-tər-ān'i-ən*, *adj* living or situated on the earth's surface. [**super-** (1)]

superterrestrial *sōō-* or *sū-pər-ti-res'tri-əl*, *adj* above the earth; above worldly things. [**super-** (1)]

supertitle *sōō-* or *sū'pər-tī-tl*, *n* a surtitle. [**super-** (1)]

supertonic *sōō-* or *sū'pər-ton'ik*, (*music*) *n* the second degree of the diatonic scale, eg D in the scale of C. [**super-** (1)]

supervene *sōō-* or *sū-pər-vēn'*, *vi* to come in addition, or closely after. — *n* **supervēn'ience**. — *adj* **supervēn'ient** supervening. — *n* **supervention** (*-ven'shən*). [L *super* above, and *venīre*, *ventum* to come]

supervise *sōō'* or *sū'pər-vīz*, *vt* to oversee, manage or direct the operation of; to watch over, control. — *vi* to read over (*Shakesp*). — *n* (*Shakesp*) reading over. — *n* **supervī'sal** (*rare*). — *n* **supervisee** (*-vīz-ē'*) a person who is supervised. — *n* **supervision** (*-vizh'ən*) act of supervising; inspection; control. — *n* **supervisor** (*-vī'zər*; also *sōō'* or *sū'*) a person who supervises; an overseer; an inspector; an elected local government official (*US*); a spectator (*Shakesp*). — *n* **supervī'sorship**. — *adj* **supervī'sory** pertaining to, or having, supervision. [L *super* over, and *vidēre*, *vīsum* to see]

supervolute *sōō'* or *sū'pər-vo-lūt'*, or *-lōōt'*, (*bot*) *adj* convolute. [**super-** (2)]

superwoman *sōō'* or *sū'pər-wōō-mən*, *n* an exceptionally strong, talented or energetic woman, *esp* one who successfully combines a career with bringing up children and household duties; a fictional woman with superhuman powers. [**super-** (2)]

supine *sōō'* or *sū'pīn*, or *-pīn'*, *adj* lying on the back; leaning backward, inclined, sloping; negligently inert; indolent; passive. — *n* a Latin verbal noun in *-tum* (*first supine*, an old accusative) or *-tū* (*second supine*, an old locative), possibly as formed from the stem of the passive participle; the English infinitive with *to*. — *vt* **su'pinate** (*-pin-āt*) to place (the hand) palm upward or

supersoft' *adj* (2).
supersophis'ticated *adj* (2).
superspe'cies *n* (3).
su'perspeed *n* (3).
su'perspy *n* (2).
superstra'tum *n* (1).
supersubstan'tial *adj* (2).
supersweet' *adj* (2).
superthin' *adj* (2).
supervir'ulent *adj* (2).
su'perweapon *n* (3).

forward (opposite of *pronate*). — *n* **supinā'tion** the placing or holding of the palm of the hand upward or forward. — *n* **su'pinator** a muscle that extends from the elbow to the shaft of the radius that supinates the forearm and hand. — *adv* **supine'ly**. — *n* **supine'ness**. [L *supīnus* supine; related to *sub* under, and *super* over]

supp. or **suppl.** *abbrev*: supplement.

suppawn or **supawn** *sə-pön'*, *n* a kind of porridge made with maize flour boiled in water. [Natick (see under **Algonkian**) *saupáun* softened]

suppeago *sə-pē'gō*. See **serpigo**.

suppedaneum *sə-pə-dā'ni-em*, *n* a support under the foot of a crucified person: — *pl* **suppedā'nea** (*-ni-ə*). [L, footstool, from neuter of *suppedaneus* beneath the foot]

supper *sup'ər*, *n* a light meal eaten in the evening; a late-night snack taken in addition to and later than the main evening meal. — *vt* (*archaic*) to provide with supper. — *adj* **supp'erless**. — **supper cloth** a tablecloth, larger than a teacloth, on which supper is served; **supp'ertime** the time at which supper is usually eaten. [OFr *soper* (Fr *souper*)]

supping. See **sup**.

supplant *sə-plänt'*, *vt* to oust; to supersede; to dispossess and take the place of; to overthrow, to lay low (*Milton*); to uproot (*Shakesp*). — *n* **supplantation** (*sup-lən-tā'shən*). — *n* **supplant'er**. [L *supplantāre* to trip up, from *sub* under, and *planta* the sole]

supple[1] *sup'l*, *adj* pliant; lithe; yielding; fawning (*archaic*). — *vt* (*rare*) to make supple; to make soft or compliant. — *vi* (*rare*) to become supple. — *n* **supp'leness**. — *adv* **supp'lely** or **supp'ly**. — **supp'lejack** any of various tropical shrubs with pliant or twining stems; a pliant cane. [Fr *souple*, from L *supplex* bending the knees, from *sub* under, and *plicāre* to fold]

supple[2] *so͝op'l*, a Scots form of **swipple**. — See also **souple**[2].

supplement *sup'li-mənt*, *n* that which supplies a deficiency or fills a need; that which completes or brings closer to completion; an extra part added (later) to a publication, giving further information or listing corrections to earlier mistakes; a special part of a periodical publication accompanying an ordinary part; the quantity by which an angle or an arc falls short of 180° or a semicircle. — *vt* **supplement** (*-ment'*; also *sup'li-mənt*) to supply or fill up; to add to. — *adj* **supplement'al** or **supplement'ary** added to supply what is needed; additional. — Also *n*. — *adv* **supplement'ally** or **supplement'arily**. — *n* **supplementā'tion**. — *n* **supplement'er**. — *n* **supplē'tion** a supplement; the adding of a word to supply a missing form of a conjugation, etc, such as *went* for the past tense of *to go* (*gram*). — *adj* **supp'letive** or **supp'letory** supplemental. — **supplementary benefit** a state allowance paid each week to those with low incomes in order to bring them up to a certain established level (now called **income support** in the UK). [L *supplēmentum* a filling up, *supplēre* to fill up]

supplial. See under **supply**[1].

suppliance. See under **suppliant**[1] and **supply**[1].

suppliant[1] *sup'li-ənt*, *adj* supplicating; asking earnestly; entreating. — *n* a humble petitioner. — *n* **supp'liance** supplication. — *adv* **supp'liantly**. [Fr *suppliant*, pr p of *supplier*, from L *supplicāre*; see **supplicant**]

suppliant[2], **supplier**. See under **supply**[1].

supplicant *sup'li-kənt*, *adj* supplicating; asking submissively. — *n* a person who supplicates or entreats earnestly. — *n* **supp'licat** (in the English universities) a petition. — *vt* and *vi* **supp'licate** to entreat earnestly; to petition; to pray. — *adj* **supp'licating**. — *adv* **supp'licatingly**. — *n* **supplicā'tion** act of supplicating; an earnest or humble petition; (in ancient Rome) a solemn service or day decreed for giving formal thanks to the gods for victory, etc; earnest prayer or entreaty, *esp* in liturgies, a litany petition for some special blessing. — *adj* **supp'licatory** containing supplication or entreaty; humble. — *n* **supplicā'vit** formerly, a writ issued by the King's Bench or Chancery for taking the surety of the peace against a person. [L *supplicāre*, *-ātum*, from *supplex*; see **supple**[1]]

supply[1] *sə-plī'*, *vt* to make good; to satisfy; to provide, furnish; to fill, occupy (as a substitute); to serve instead of; to supplement (*obs*); to reinforce, to help (*obs*); to fill up a deficiency in (*obs*): — *pr p* **supply'ing**; *pa t* and *pa p* **supplied'**. — *n* act of supplying; that which is supplied or which supplies a need; amount provided or in hand; available amount of a commodity; amount of food or money provided (used generally in *pl*); a source of water, electricity, etc; a parliamentary grant for expenses of government; a person who takes another's duty temporarily, a substitute, *esp* a teacher. — *n* **supplī'al** the act of supplying. — *n* **supplī'ance** (*Shakesp*) supplying, something to fill up time, pastime, gratification. — *adj* **supplī'ant** (*Shakesp*) supplementary, reinforcing. — *n* **supplī'er**. — *n* **supply'ment** (*Shakesp*) replenishment, supplementing. — **supply day** in the House of Commons, a day in which backbenchers may debate and vote on government expenditure; **supply-side economics** (an economic policy based on) the cutting of taxes in order to stimulate production, in the belief that supply creates demand; **supply'-sider** an advocate of supply-side economics. — **Commissioners of Supply** a former administrative and rating authority in Scotland, superseded by the County Council. [OFr *suppleier*, *supplier* (Fr *suppléer*), from L *supplēre* to fill up]

supply[2]. See under **supple**[1].

support *sə-pōrt'* or *-pört'*, *vt* to bear the weight of; to hold up; to endure; to sustain; to maintain; to keep going; to corroborate; to make good; to uphold; to back up; to second; to contend for; to represent in acting; to maintain a loyal interest in the fortunes of (*esp* a sporting team), *usu* by regular attendance at matches; to perform as an introduction to (the main performer in a musical concert); to supply with means of living; to show an interest in the activities of, eg by attendance at meetings, etc; to nourish; to strengthen. — *n* act or fact of supporting or upholding; a person who or thing that supports, sustains, or maintains; maintenance; backing; a prop; an actor playing a subordinate part with a star. — *adj* **support'able** capable of being held up, carried, sustained, or maintained. — *n* **support'ableness**. — *adv* **support'ably**. — *n* **support'ance** (*Shakesp*) support. — *n* **support'er** a person who or thing that supports; an adherent; a defender; a person who attends matches and watches with interest the fortunes of a team; the supporting act or acts at a pop concert; a figure on each side of the escutcheon (*heraldry*). — *n* and *adj* **support'ing**. — *adj* **support'ive**. — *adj* **support'less**. — *n* (*rare*) **support'ment**. — *n* (*rare*) **support'ress**. — *n* (*rare*) **support'ure**. — **support hose**, **stockings** or **tights** elasticated hose; **supporting act**, **film** or **programme** a film, films, acts, etc accompanying the main film or star performance in a variety show; **support level** or **area** (on the stock market) the price level below which a commodity does not decline, as it then becomes an investment proposition; **support worker** a worker, *esp* in health care, who carries out various tasks under the supervision of registered practitioners. [L *supportāre*, from *sub* up, and *portāre* to bear]

suppose *sə-pōz'*, *vt* to incline to believe; to conceive, imagine, guess; to assume provisionally or for argument's sake; to imply, presuppose; (*esp* in *passive*) to expect in accordance with rules or conventions; to expect (*Milton*); to believe (*Shakesp*); to place underneath (*obs*); to substitute fraudulently (*obs*). — *n* a supposition; an instance of supposing or saying 'suppose'; expectation (*Shakesp*). — *adj* **suppo'sable**. — *adv* **suppo'sably**. — *n* **suppo'sal** supposition; notion (*Shakesp*); proposal (*obs*). — *adj* **supposed** (*-pōzd'*; also *-pōz-id*) generally believed to be (often implying doubt or disagreement on the part of the speaker); assumed; conjectured; feigned (*Shakesp*); supposititious (*obs*); placed below, or having a note below, the fundamental of the chord (*music*). — *adv* **suppo'sedly** according to supposition. — *n* **suppo'ser**. — *n* **suppo'sing**. — **suppose** and **supposing** (*imperative*, introducing an expression of proposal or conjecture) if; what if; (**suppose**) even if (*Scot*); (**supposing**) how about. [Fr *supposer*, from pfx *sup-* (*sub-*), and *poser*; see **pose**[1], and cf **compose**, **dispose**, etc]

supposes *sə-pōz'iz*, (*Shakesp*, *Taming of the Shrew*, V. 1. 120) *n pl* perhaps substitutes, or substitutions, or suppositions. See repeated play on the word in Shakespeare's source, Gascoigne's *Supposes* (and its original, Ariosto's *I Suppositi*).

supposition *sup-ə-zi'shən*, *n* an act of supposing; that which is supposed; assumption; presumption, opinion. — *adj* **supposi'tional** hypothetical; conjectural; supposed. — *adv* **supposi'tionally**. — *adj* **supposi'tionary** suppositional. — *adj* **suppositious** (*-zi'shəs*; *rare*) suppositional; *usu* used erroneously for *supposititious*. — *adj* **supposititious** (*sə-poz-i-tish'əs*) secretly and cunningly substituted for another; spurious; suppositional. — *adv* **suppositi'tiously**. — *n* **suppositi'tiousness**. — *adj* **suppos'itive** (*-i-tiv*) suppositional. [L *suppōnere*, *-positum* to set under, substitute, from *sub*, and *pōnere* to put]

suppository *sə-poz'i-tə-ri*, *n* a medicated plug inserted in the rectum, vagina or urethra, and left to melt. [L *suppositōrium*; see ety for **supposition**]

suppress *sə-pres'*, *vt* to crush, put down; to subdue; to hold back, *esp* from publication, circulation, divulgation, expression or development; to check, stop, restrain; to hold in; to moderate; to leave out; to hold or press down (*Spenser*); to ravish (*Spenser*). — *n* **suppress'ant** a substance, eg a drug, that suppresses rather than eliminates. — Also *adj*. — *adj* **suppressed'**. — *adv* **suppress'edly**. — *adj* **suppress'ible**. — *n* **suppression** (*-presh'*) act of suppressing; stoppage; concealment. — *adj* **suppress'ive** tending to suppress; subduing. — *n* **suppress'or** a person who suppresses anything; a device for suppressing anything, eg the echo of one's own voice on a telephone, electrical interference with television reception. — **suppressor grid** (*electronics*) a grid between the anode and screen of a pentode valve to repel secondary electrons back to the anode; **suppressor mutation** (*biol*) a base change which suppresses the effect of mutations elsewhere. [L *supprimere*, *suppressum*, from *sub* under, and *premere* to press]

suppurate *sup'ū-rāt*, *vi* to gather or discharge pus. — *n* **suppurā'tion**. — *adj* **supp'urātive**. — *n* a suppurative agent. [L *sub* under, and *pūs*, *pūris* pus]

Supr. *abbrev*: Supreme.

supra- *sōō'prə-* or *sū'prə-*, *pfx* signifying above. — *adj* **supra-ax'illary** arising above an axil. — *adj* **suprachias'mic** (*anatom*) above the chiasm (*esp* in **suprachiasmic nucleus** a small area in the hypothalmus thought to regulate the biological clock). — *adj* **supraciliary** (*-sil'*) above the eyebrow. — *adj* **supracost'al** above or on a rib. — *adj* **supracrust'al** (of rocks) on or near the surface, above the earth's crust. — *n* **Supralapsarian** (*-laps-ā'ri-ən*; L *lāpsus* fall) one of a class of Calvinists who make the decree of election and predestination to precede the Creation and the Fall (as opposed to *Sublapsarian*). — Also *adj*. — *n* **Supralapsā'rianism**. — *adj* **supralu'nar** beyond the moon; very lofty. — *n* **supramol'ecule** a cluster of molecules, *usu* created artificially. — *adj* **supramun'dane** above the world. — *adj* **supranat'ional** overriding national sovereignty; in or belonging to more than one nation (also, less commonly, **supernational**). — *n* **supranat'ionalism** (also, less commonly **supernationalism**). — *adj* **supraor'bital** above the orbit of the eye. — *adj* **suprapu'bic** above the pubic bone. — *adj* **suprarē'nal** above the kidneys (**suprarenal capsules** or **glands** the adrenal glands; **suprarenal extract** an extract from these used in the treatment of haemorrhage, Addison's disease, etc). — *adj* **suprasegmen'tal** (*phonetics*) representing or continuing through two or more speech sounds. — *adj* **suprasens'ible** above the reach of the senses. — *adj* **supratemp'oral** transcending time; of the upper part of the temples or temporal region. [L *suprā* above]

supreme *sū-* or *sōō-prēm'*, *adj* highest; greatest; most excellent. — *n* the highest point; the highest authority. — *n* **suprem'acism** (belief in) the supremacy of one particular group of people. — *n* **suprem'acist** a believer in or supporter of supremacism. — *n* **supremacy** (*-prem'ə-si*) state of being supreme; supreme position or power. — *n* **Suprematism** (*sōō-prem'ə-tizm*; also without *cap*) an extreme form of cubism using very simple geometrical shapes. — *n* and *adj* **Suprem'atist** (also without *cap*). — *adv* **supremely** (*-prēm'*). — *n* **supreme'ness** or **supremity** (*-prem'*). — **Supreme Being** a superior deity; God; **Supreme Court** in the US, the highest Federal court having jurisdiction over all lower courts; elsewhere, the highest court of a nation or state; in England and Wales, a court consisting of the Crown Court, High Court and Court of Appeal (in full **Supreme Court of Judicature**); **supreme sacrifice** the giving up of one's life; **Supreme Soviet** the legislature of the former USSR, consisting of two bodies, the Council of the Union, in which each deputy represented so many of the population, and the Council of Nationalities, in which each deputy represented one of the Republics or other distinct regions within the USSR. [L *suprēmus*, superlative of *superus* high, from *super* above]

suprême or **supreme** *sü-prem*, *sū-* or *sōō-prēm'*, *n* a rich cream sauce; a dish of meat, *esp* breast of chicken, served in this sauce. [Fr]

supremo *sū-* or *sōō-prē'mo*, *n* a supreme head; a leader with unlimited powers: — *pl* **supre'mos**. [Sp, from L *suprēmus* highest]

Supt *abbrev*: Superintendent.

suq. See **souk**.

sur *sür*, (*Fr*) *prep* on, above. — **sur le tapis** (*lə ta-pē*) literally, on the carpet (as a table cover), hence, under discussion, the subject of talk; **sur place** (*plas*) on the spot.

sur- *sûr-*, *pfx* signifying over, above, beyond. [Fr, from L *super*]

sura[1] or **surah** *sōō'rə*, *n* a chapter of the Koran. [Ar *sūra*, *sūrah* step]

sura[2] *sōō'rə*, *n* fermented palm sap. [Sans *surā*]

suraddition *sûr-ə-dish'ən*, (*Shakesp*) *n* an additional title or designation. [**sur-**]

surah[1] *sū'* or *sōō'rə*, *n* a soft twilled silk or artificial fabric. — Also *adj*. [Possibly from *Surat*]

surah[2]. See **sura**[1].

sural *sū'rl*, *adj* pertaining to the calf of the leg. [L *sūra* the calf]

suramin *sōō'rə-min*, *n* a drug, *usu* administered by slow intravenous injection, used in the treatment of trypanosomiasis.

surance *shōōr'əns*, (*Shakesp*) *n* assurance.

surat *sōō-rat'* or *sōō'*, *n* coarse uncoloured cotton; anything that is of inferior quality (*old slang*). [*Surat*, in India]

surbahar *sür-ba-här'*, *n* an Indian stringed instrument, larger than a sitar. [Bengali]

surbase *sûr'bās*, (*archit*) *n* a cornice or series of mouldings above the base of a pedestal, etc. — *adj* **surbased** (*-bāst'*) of an arch, lower than half the span. — *n* **surbase'ment**. [**sur-**]

surbate *sûr-bāt'*, *vt* (*Spenser sûr'*) to bruise (the hoofs or feet) with walking, make footsore: — *pa p* **surbat'ed** or (*Spenser*) **surbet'**. [OFr *surbatu* excessively beaten, but with the meaning of Fr *solbatu*]

surbed *sûr-bed'*, (*obs*) *vt* to set on edge (applied to a stone with reference to the grain; *masonry*). [**sur-**]

surbet. See **surbate**.

surcease *sûr-sēs'*, (*archaic*) *vi* to cease. — *vt* to desist or refrain from; to end, put a stop to. — *n* cessation. [OFr *sursis*, pa p of *surseoir*, from L *supersedēre* to refrain from; cf **supersede**; spelling influenced by **cease**]

surcharge *sûr-chärj'*, *vt* to exact a surcharge from; to overcharge; to overload; to overburden; to overstock; to saturate; to print over the original printing; to disallow; to charge with overwhelming force (*Spenser*). — *n* **sur'charge** (or *-chärj'*) an overcharge; an extra charge; an excessive load; an overloaded condition; an amount not passed by an auditor, which must be refunded; a new valuation or cancel-mark printed on or over a stamp; that part of a bank of earth, or its depth, lying above the top of a retaining wall. — *adj* **surcharged'**. — *n* **surcharge'ment**. — *n* **surcharg'er**. [**sur-**]

surcingle *sûr'sing-gl*, *n* a girth or strap for holding a saddle on an animal's back; the girdle of a cassock. — *vt* to gird, fasten, or thrash with a surcingle. [OFr *surcengle*, from L *super*, and *cingulum* a belt]

surcoat *sûr'kōt*, *n* a medieval outer garment, *usu* sleeveless, often with heraldic devices, worn by men and women over armour or ordinary dress; an undershirt or waistcoat (*esp Scot*). [OFr *surcote*, *surcot*, from *sur* over, and *cote* garment]

surculus *sûr'kū-ləs*, (*bot*) *n* a sucker. — *adj* **sur'culose** having or producing suckers. [L *sūrculus* a twig]

surd *sûrd*, *adj* that cannot be expressed in rational numbers (*math*); voiceless (*phonetics*); deaf (*obs*); senseless (*obs*). — *n* an irrational quantity (*math*); a voiceless consonant (*phonetics*); someone who is deaf to persuasion, rational argument, etc. — *n* **surd'ity** deafness. [L *surdus* deaf]

sure[1] *shŏŏr*, *adj* secure; safe; fit to be depended on; unerring; stable; bound in alliance (*esp* by betrothal or marriage; *obs*); certain; assured; confident beyond doubt; without other possibility. — *interj* (*colloq*) certainly, undoubtedly, yes. — *adv* (now chiefly *Irish* or *NAm*, except in combination and in conventional phrases) surely. — *adv* **surely** firmly; confidently; safely; certainly; assuredly; as it would seem (often *ironic*). — *n* **sure'ness**. — *n* **sure'ty** certainty; safeguard; legal security against loss; a person who becomes legally responsible for another's liabilities; a sponsor. — *vt* (*Shakesp*) to be security for. — *n* **sure'tyship**. — *adj* **sure-enough'** (*US*) genuine, real. — *adj* **sure'-fire** (*colloq*) infallible. — *adj* **sure'footed** not liable to stumble, nimble. — *adv* **surefoot'edly**. — **surefoot'edness**; **sure thing** a certainty, certain success; (as *interj*) certainly, beyond doubt. — **be sure** do not omit; **for sure** certainly; of a certainty; **make sure** see under **make**[1]; **stand surety for** to act as guarantor for; **sure enough** no doubt; in very fact; accordingly; there's no denying; **to be sure** certainly; I admit. [OFr *sur*, *seur* (Fr *sûr*), from L *sēcūrus*; see **secure**]

sure[2]. An old spelling of **sewer** (see under **sew**[3]).

Sûreté *sür-tā*, (*Fr*) *n* the French criminal investigation department.

surety. See under **sure**[1].

SURF *sûrf*, (*nuc eng*) *abbrev*: spent unreprocessed fuel.

surf *sûrf*, *n* surging water or waves rushing up a sloping beach; sea foam. — *vi* to bathe in or ride on surf. — *n* **surf'er**. — *n* **surf'ie** (*Austr*) a young, *usu* unemployed, person who spends a great deal of time surfing. — *n* **surf'ing** the sport of riding breaking waves on a surfboard or in a surf canoe; any similar sport using a surfboard, such as snow surfing, sky surfing, etc. — *adj* **surf'y**. — **surf'-bather**; **surf'-bathing** bathing in surf; **surf'bird** an American Pacific shorebird (*Aphriza virgata*) related to sandpipers; **surf'board** a long narrow board used in surfing; **surf'boarding**; **surf boat** a boat for use in surf; **surf canoe** a slalom canoe or a kayak used for surfing; **surf'caster**; **surf'casting** fishing from the shore by casting into surf; **surf duck** the scoter; **surf'fish** any fish of a Western American viviparous perchoid family, *Embiotocidae*, that inhabit coastal waters (also called **surfperch**); **surf'man** a man skilful in handling boats in surf; **surf'perch** see **surf'fish**; **surf'-riding** riding on a surfboard. [Origin obscure]

surface *sûr'fis*, *n* the outer boundary or face of anything; the outside or upper layer; a flat, two-dimensional geometric figure that has length and breadth but no thickness; area; outer appearance, character or texture; an aerofoil. — *adj* of, on, or near a surface; superficial. — *vt* to apply a surface or finish to. — *vi* to bring or rise to the surface; to be exposed or revealed, to become apparent (*NAm colloq*); to regain consciousness (*colloq*); to get out of bed (*colloq*). — *adj* **sur'faced** having this or that kind of surface. — *n* **sur'facer** a person or thing that smooths or levels a surface. — *n* **sur'facing** giving a surface to anything; material for a surface layer; washing surface deposits for gold. — *adj* **sur'face-active** able to alter the surface tension of liquids (see also **surfactant**). — **surface activity** the alteration to the surface tension of liquids due to superactive substances; **sur'face-craft** a floating, not submersible, craft; **surface mail** mail sent otherwise than by air; **sur'faceman** a workman who keeps a railway bed in repair; **surface noise** the noise produced by the friction of a stylus on a record; **surface plate** (*eng*) a rigid cast-iron plate whose surface is accurately scraped flat, used eg to test the flatness of other surfaces; **surface structure** (*linguistics*) the formal structure of sentences, *esp* when broken down into their constituent parts; **surface tension** that property in virtue of which a liquid surface behaves like a stretched elastic membrane, clinging to the sides of a container. — *adj* **surface-to-air'** (of a missile, etc) travelling from a base on the ground to a target in the air. — Also *adv*. — *adj* and *adv* **surface-to-sur'face**. — **sur'face-vessel**; **surface water** drainage water; **surface wind** (*meteorol*) the wind at a standard height of 10m (33ft) above ground; **surface worker** a person engaged in any of the ancillary jobs in a coalmine not done underground. [Fr, from *sur*, from L *super*, and *face*, from L *faciēs* face]

surfactant *sər-fak'tənt*, *n* a substance, eg a detergent, which reduces surface tension; a wetting agent; a substance secreted by the pneumocytes lining the alveoli of the lungs that prevents the walls of the alveoli from sticking together; a substance administered as a substitute for this, eg to premature babies whose lungs are not fully developed. [*surf*ace-*act*ive *agent*]

surfeit *sûr'fit*, *n* overfulness; gorging; gluttony; excess; an excessive meal; sickness or satiety caused by overeating or overdrinking. — *vt* to feed or fill to satiety or disgust. — *vi* to indulge to excess, *esp* in food and drink (*archaic*); to suffer from excess (*obs*). — *adj* **sur'feited**. — *n* **sur'feiter**. — *n* and *adj* **sur'feiting**. [OFr *surfait* excess, from L *super* above, and *facere* to make]

surficial *sûr-fish'l*, (*geol*) *adj* superficial, subaerial. [**surface**, altered in analogy with *superficial*]

surg. *abbrev*: surgeon; surgery; surgical.

surge[1]. An old spelling (*Shakesp*) of **cerge**.

surge[2] *sûrj*, *n* an uprush, boiling or tumultuous movement of liquid; a sudden increase of power; a great wave; a swell; a sudden oscillation; a jerk on a rope; (of spacecraft) movement in the direction of travel. — *vi* to well up; to heave tumultuously; to slip back; to jerk. — *vt* to send in surges; to slack suddenly. — *adj* **surge'ful**. — *adj* **surge'less**. — *adj* **sur'gent**. — *n* and *adj* **sur'ging**. — *adj* **sur'gy**. [L *surgere* to rise]

surgeon *sûr'jən*, *n* a person who treats injuries or diseases by manual operations; an army or naval doctor; a ship's doctor; a surgeonfish. — *n* **sur'geoncy** or **sur'geonship** the office or employment of a surgeon in the army or navy. — *n* **sur'gery** the art and practice of a surgeon; a doctor's or dentist's consulting-room; a doctor's or dentist's time of consultation; a set, *usu* regular, time when a member of parliament, local councillor, etc, is available to his or her constituents for consultation. — *adj* **sur'gical** of, pertaining to, or used in surgery; (of a garment or appliance) designed to correct a physical deformity; incisive; precise. — *adv* **sur'gically**. — **sur'geonfish** any member of the family *Acanthuridae*, tropical fishes having razor-sharp spines on their tails, *incl* the tangs and unicorn fishes; **surgeon general** the senior officer in the medical branch of the service (*military*); head of the public health service (*US*); **surgeon's knot** a knot like a reef knot but with a double turn in the first part (used in ligaturing a cut artery); **surgical boot** or **shoe** a boot or shoe designed to correct deformities of the foot; **surgical neck** (*anatom*) the constriction of the shaft of the humerus below the head, a frequent site of fractures; **surgical shock** see **shock**; **surgical spirit** methylated spirit with small amounts of castor oil and oil of wintergreen. [Anglo-Fr *surgien*; see **chirurgeon**]

surgy. See under **surge**[2].

suricate *sū'* or *sōō'ri-kāt*, *n* a S African animal of the civet family, the slender-tailed meerkat. [From Du *surikat*; of uncertain origin]

Surinam *sū- or sōō-ri-nam'*, also *sū'* or *sōō'*, *n* a republic, *orig* a Dutch colony, in northern S America. — **Surinam poison** fish poison obtained from a S American papilionaceous plant, *Tephrosia*; **Surinam toad** a S American amphibian that hatches its eggs in pits in its back.

surjection *sûr-jek'shən*, (*math*) *n* a mapping function in which all the elements in one set correspond to all the elements in another set. — See also **bijection**, **injection**. [**sur-** and L *jacēre* to throw]

surloin. Same as **sirloin**.

surly *sûr'li*, *adj* morose; gruff and grumpy; rough and gloomy; haughty (*Shakesp*); refractory. — *adv* (*Shakesp*) surlily. — *adv* **sur'lily**. — *n* **sur'liness**. [From obs *sirly* haughty, from **sir** and **like**[1]]

surmaster *sûr'mäs-tər*, (*archaic*) *n* the second master or deputy head in a school: — *fem* **sur'mistress**. [**sur-**]

surmise *sər-mīz'*, *n* allegation (*obs*); suspicion; conjecture. — *vt* to imagine; to suspect; to conjecture, guess. — *adj* **surmis'able**. — *n* **surmis'al**. — *n* **surmis'er**. — *n* and *adj* **surmis'ing**. [OFr, from *surmettre* to accuse, from L *super* upon, and *mittere* to send]

surmistress. See under **surmaster**.

surmount *sər-mownt'*, *vt* to mount above; to be on or go to the top of; to surpass; to get the better of, overcome. — *adj* **surmount'able**. — *adj* **surmount'ed** surpassed; overcome; higher than half the span (*archit*); having another figure laid over (*heraldry*). — *n* **surmount'er**. — *n* and *adj* **surmount'ing**. [OFr *surmunter* (Fr *surmonter*), from LL *supermontāre*; see **mount**[2]]

surmullet *sər-mul'it*, *n* a species of red mullet, admired by the Romans for its colour-changes as it died. [Fr *surmulet*]

surname *sûr'nām*, *n* an additional name (*archaic*); a family name. — *vt* to name by a surname. — *adj* **surnom'inal**. [On the analogy of Fr *surnom*, from Eng **name** and L *nōmen*, *-inis*]

surpass *sər-päs'*, *vt* to go or be beyond; to exceed; to excel. — *adj* **surpass'able**. — *adj* **surpass'ing** passing beyond others; excellent in a high degree. — Also (*obs* or *poetic*) *adv*. — *adv* **surpass'ingly**. — *n* **surpass'ingness**. [Fr *surpasser*, from *sur-*, and *passer* to pass]

surplice *sûr'plis*, *n* a white linen vestment worn over the cassock. — *adj* **sur'pliced** wearing a surplice. [Fr *surplis*, from LL *superpellicium* an overgarment, from *pellis* skin]

surplus *sûr'pləs*, *n* that which is left over; remainder; excess over what is required; excess of revenue over expenditure. — Also *adj*. — *n* **sur'plusage** surplus; superfluity. [Fr, from LL *superplūs*, from *super*, and *plūs* more]

surprise *sər-prīz'*, *n* a catching, or being caught, unawares; the emotion caused by anything sudden or contrary to expectation; anything that causes or is intended to cause this emotion. — Also *adj*. — *vt* to come upon suddenly or unawares; to capture by an unexpected assault; to lead or bring unawares, to betray (with *into*); to strike with wonder or astonishment; to confuse; to seize (*obs*). — *vi* (*formal*) to cause surprise. — *n* **surpris'al** an act of surprising. — *adj* **surprised'**. — *adv* **surpris'edly**. — *n* **surpris'er**. — *n* and *adj* **surpris'ing**. — *adv* **surpris'ingly**. — *n* **surpris'ingness**. — **much** (or **greatly**, etc) **to one's surprise** causing one great surprise; **surprise, surprise** ironic exclamation of surprise. [OFr (Fr) fem pa p of *surprendre*, from L *super*, and *prehendere* to catch]

surquedry *sûr'kwi-dri*, (*Spenser*) *n* arrogance. — Also (*obs*) **sur'quedy**. [OFr *surcuiderie*, from *surcuidier*, from L *super* above, and *cōgitāre*, *-ātum* to think]

surra *sōō'rə*, (*vet*) *n* a trypanosome disease of the blood in horses, etc, in E Asia. [Marathi *sūra* wheezing]

surrealism *sər-ē'ə-lizm*, *n* a movement in art and literature, begun in France around 1919, that sought to resolve the contradictory conditions of dream and reality into an absolute reality by various techniques, thus escaping the dominance of reason and conscious control. — *adj* **surre'al**. — *adj* and *n* **surre'alist**. — *adj* **surrealist'ic**. — *adv* **surrealist'ically**. [Fr *surréalisme*, from *sur* above, and *réalisme* realism]

surrebut *sur-i-but'*, (*law*) *vi* to reply to a defendant's rebutter. — *n* **surrebutt'al** a plaintiff's evidence or presentation of evidence, in response to a defendant's rebuttal. — *n* **surrebutt'er** the plaintiff's reply, in common law pleading, to a defendant's rebutter. [**sur-**]

surreined *sûr'ānd*, *adj* overridden. [Appar **sur-** and **rein**[1]]

surrejoin *sur-i-join'*, (*law*) *vt* and *vi* to reply to a defendant's rejoinder. — *n* **surrejoind'er** a plaintiff's reply to a defendant's rejoinder. [**sur-**]

surrender *sə-ren'dər*, *vt* to deliver over; to relinquish; to yield up; to resign. — *vi* to yield oneself up; to yield. — *n* the act of surrendering. — *n* **surrenderee'** a person to whom a legal surrender is made. — *n* **surren'derer**. — *n* **surren'deror** (*law*) a person who makes a surrender. — *n* **surren'dry** (*obs*) a surrender. — **surrender value** the amount to be paid to an insured person who surrenders his or her policy. [Anglo-Fr *surrender*, OFr *surrendre*, from *sur-*, and *rendre*; see **render**]

surreptitious *sur-əp-tish'əs*, *adj* done by stealth or fraud; stealthy. — *adv* **surrepti'tiously**. [See **subreption**]

surrey *sur'i*, (*US*) *n* a light four-wheeled horse-drawn vehicle for four, *usu* with two seats. [Developed from a vehicle used in *Surrey*]

sur-reyn'd. A Shakespearian spelling of **surreined**.

surrogate *sur'ō-git* or *-gāt*, *n* a substitute; a deputy, *esp* of an ecclesiastical judge; a deputy of a bishop who grants marriage licences; a judge of probate (*US*, *local*); a person or thing standing, eg in a dream, for another person or thing, or a person who fills the role of another in one's emotional life (eg *mother surrogate*; see also **surrogate mother** below). — *n* **surr'ogacy** the state of being a surrogate; use of a surrogate, *esp* of a surrogate mother. — *n* **surr'ogateship**. — *n* **surrogā'tion** subrogation. — *n* **surrogā'tum** a substitute (*obs*); something that stands in place of something else, eg a price instead of the thing itself (*Scots law*). — **surrogate mother** a woman who bears a baby for another (*esp* childless) couple, after either (artificial) insemination by the male or implantation of an embryo from the female; **surrogate motherhood**. [L *surrogāre*, *-ātum*, from *sub* in the place of, and *rogāre* to ask]

surround *sə-rownd'*, *vt* to overflow (*obs*); to go or extend all around; to encompass, environ; to encircle; to be the background situation to, or make up the context or environment of; to maintain around (oneself) a following of people or collection of things; to make a circuit of (*rare*). — *n* an act of surrounding (*esp* hunted animals); a border, *esp* the floor or floor-covering around a carpet; an ornamental structure fitted around (eg an open fire). — *adj* **surround'ing** encompassing; neighbouring. — *n* an encompassing; (in *pl*) environment, things round about. — **surround sound** any form of stereophonic sound reproduction using three or more speakers to give an effect of sound coming from all directions. [OFr *suronder*, from L *superundāre* to overflow, from *super*, and *unda* wave; confused with **round**[2]]

surroyal *sə-roi'əl*, *n* any tine of a stag's horn above the royal. [**sur-**]

surtarbrand. See **surturbrand**.

surtax *sûr'taks, n* an additional tax; tax payable on incomes above a certain high level (term not in official use in this sense). — *vt* to tax additionally; to charge surtax. [**sur-**]

surtitle *sûr'tī-tl, n* a printed translation of the libretto of an opera in a language foreign to the audience, projected above the proscenium arch. [**sur-**]

surtout *sər-tōō'* or *-tōōt', n* an overcoat (*obs*); a lady's hood (*obs*); a close-bodied 19c frock coat; a raised portion of the parapet of a work at the angles, to protect from enfilade fire (*fortif*). [Fr, from LL *supertōtus* an outer garment, from L *super*, and *tōtus* all]

surturbrand or **surtarbrand** *sûr'tər-brand, n* lignite found interbedded with lavas in Iceland. [Icel *surtarbrandr*, from *Surtar*, genitive of *Surtr* name of a fire-giant, and *brandr* brand]

surucucu *sōō-rōō-kōō-kōō', n* a S American Indian name for the bushmaster snake.

surveillance *sər-vā'ləns* or *-lyəns, n* a watch kept over someone or something, *esp* over a criminal (and his or her activities) by the police; vigilant supervision; superintendence. — *n* **surveill'ant**. — *vt* **surveille** (*-vāl'*; back-formation; *US*) to observe, keep under surveillance. — **surveillance radar** a plan-position indicator radar showing the position of aircraft within an air-traffic control area. [Fr, from *surveiller*, from *sur*, and *veiller* to watch, from L *vigilāre*]

survew, survewe. Spenserian spellings of **surview**.

survey *sər-vā', vt* to view comprehensively and extensively; to examine in detail; to examine (a building) in order to assess structural soundness or determine value; to measure (land heights and distances in an area) for mapping purposes; to perceive, spy (*Shakesp*). — *n* **sur'vey** (also *-vā'*) a general view, or a statement of its results; an inspection; collection of data for mapping; an organization or body of people for that purpose; superintendence. — *n* **survey'al**. — *n* **survey'ance**. — *n* **survey'ing**. — *n* **survey'or** an overseer; a measurer of land; an inspector of buildings, their structure, state of repair, etc; an inspector (of roads, of weights and measures, of customs duties, etc). — *n* **survey'orship**. [OFr *surveoir*, from L *super* over, and *vidēre* to see]

surview *sər-vū', vt* to survey, look over; to command a view of. [**sur-**]

survive *sər-vīv', vt* to live or exist after or in spite of; to outlive. — *vi* to remain alive or in existence. — *n* **survivabil'ity**. — *adj* **survi'vable**. — *n* **survi'val** a surviving or living after; anything that continues to exist after others of its kind have disappeared, or after the time to which it naturally belongs. — *adj* (*esp* of standard equipment) designed to help one to survive exposure to extreme cold or other dangerous conditions. — *n* **survi'valism**. — *n* **survi'valist** a person who takes measures to ensure their own survival after a catastrophic event, or measures for their own personal protection from attack, robbery, etc. — Also *adj*. — *n* **survi'vance** survival; succession or right to succeed on surviving the present holder. — *adj* **survi'ving**. — *n* **survi'vor**. — *n* **survi'vorship**. — **survival curve** (*radiol*) a curve showing the percentage of organisms surviving at different times after subjection to a large radiation dose. — **survival of the fittest** the longer average life of the fittest members of a (*esp* animal) community in the struggle for existence, and the consequent transmission of healthy or otherwise favourable characteristics to later generations. [Fr *survivre*, from L *super* beyond, and *vīvere* to live]

Surya *sōōr'yə, n* the Hindu sun-god. [Sans]

Sus. (*Bible*) *abbrev*: (the Apocryphal Book of) Susanna.

sus *sus,* (*slang*) *n* a suspect; suspicion; suspicious behaviour, eg loitering with intent. — *vi* (*slang*) to arrest for suspicious behaviour: — *pa t* and *pa p* **sussed**. — Also **suss**. — **sus** (or **suss**) **laws** laws allowing a person to be arrested on suspicion of having committed a crime. — **sus** (or **suss**) **out** (*slang*) to investigate; to find out, discover. [**suspect** or **suspicion**]

susceptible *sə-sep'ti-bl, adj* (*usu* with *to*) open to, admitting of; suffering readily (from), prone (to); capable of receiving; impressionable, easily influenced or persuaded; easily affected by emotion (*esp* amatory). — *n* **suscep'tance** (*phys*) the imaginary part of the admittance. — *n* **susceptibil'ity** or **suscep'tibleness**. — *adv* **suscep'tibly**. — *adj* **suscep'tive** capable of receiving or admitting; readily admitting. — *n* **suscep'tiveness**. — *n* **susceptiv'ity** (*sus-*). — *n* **suscep'tor** (*obs*) a sponsor. — *n* **suscip'ient** a recipient, *esp* of a sacrament. — *adj* receiving. [L *suscipere*, *susceptum* to take up, from *sus-* (*subs-*) up, and *capere* to take]

suscipient. See under **susceptible**.

suscitate *sus'i-tāt, vt* to excite, rouse. — *n* **suscitā'tion**. [L *suscitāre*, *-ātum*, from *sus-* (*subs-*) under, and *citāre* to arouse]

sushi *sōō'shi, n* a Japanese dish of small cakes of cold rice and fish, vegetables, etc, and a vinegar sauce. [Jap]

suslik *sus'lik* or *sōōs'lik, n* a spermophile, zizel, or ground squirrel. [Russ]

suspect *səs-pekt', vt* to mistrust; to imagine to be guilty; to doubt; to be ready to believe, but without sufficient evidence; to incline to believe the existence, presence, or agency of; to have an inkling of; to conjecture. — *vi* to imagine guilt, to be suspicious. — *n* suspicion (*archaic*); (*sus'pekt*) a person suspected. — *adj* suspected. — *adj* **suspect'able**. — *adj* **suspect'ed**. — *adv* **suspect'edly**. — *n* **suspect'edness**. — *adj* **suspect'ful** suspicious. — *adj* **suspect'less** unsuspicious; unsuspected. [L *suspicere*, *suspectum* to look at secretly or askance, from *su-* (*sub-*), and *specere* to look]

suspend *səs-pend', vt* to hang; to make to depend; to keep from falling; to put or hold in a state of suspense or suspension; to make to stop for a time; to defer; to defer or stay (eg a sentence) (*law*); to debar from any privilege, office, emolument, etc, for a time; to sustain into a following chord, producing discord (*music*); to hold in an indeterminate state. — *adj* **suspen'ded**. — *n* **suspend'er** someone who or something that suspends; a strap to support a sock or stocking; (in *pl*) braces for trousers (*NAm*). — **suspended animation** temporary slowing down to an absolute minimum of the body's principal functions, eg in hibernation; **suspended sentence** a sentence of imprisonment not served unless the offender commits another crime; **suspen'der-belt** a woman's undergarment with stocking suspenders attached. — **suspend payment** publicly to stop paying debts from insolvency. [L *suspendere*, *-pēnsum*, from pfx *sus-* (*subs-*), and *pendere*, to hang]

suspense *səs-pens', n* intermission; cessation; deferring (eg of judgement); a state or atmosphere of nervous or excited uncertainty; indecision. — *adj* in suspense; (*Milton* **suspens'** or **suspence'**) suspended, held back. — *n* **suspens'er** something, eg a film or book, that is filled with suspense. — *adj* **suspense'ful**. — *n* **suspensibil'ity**. — *adj* **suspen'sible**. — *n* **suspen'sion** (*-shən*) act of suspending; interruption; delay; temporary debarment from office or privilege; a temporary or conditional withholding; holding a note from a chord into the next chord (*music*); a discord so produced (*music*); a mixture of a fluid with dense particles which are prevented from settling by viscosity and impact of molecules (*chem*); (in a motor vehicle or railway carriage) the system of springs, etc, supporting the chassis on the axles. — *adj* **suspen'sive**. — *adv* **suspen'sively**. — *n* **suspen'soid** (*chem*) a colloid dispersed with difficulty, yielding an unstable solution that cannot be reformed after coagulation. — *n* **suspen'sor** a chain of cells to which a plant embryo is fixed (*bot*); a suspensory bandage. — *adj* **suspensorial** (*sus-pen-sō'ri-əl* or *-sö'*). — *n* **suspenso'rium** that which holds up a part, *esp* the arrangement joining the lower jaw to the cranium in vertebrates below mammals. — *adj* **suspen'sory** suspending; having the power or effect of delaying or staying; of the suspensorium. — *n* a suspensorium. — **suspense account** an account in which items are entered which cannot at once be placed in an ordinary account; **suspension bridge** a bridge with roadway hanging on cables themselves suspended from heavier cables stretched between elevated piers; **suspension building** building round a concrete core and from the top downward; **suspension culture** (*biol*) a method of culturing large quantities of cells by keeping them in vessels continually stirred and aerated. [Ety as for **suspend**]

supercollate *sus-pər-kol'āt*, (*facetious*) *vt* to hang. [*sus. per col.*, abbrev for L *suspendātur per collum* let him be hanged by the neck]

suspicion *səs-pish'ən*, *n* act of suspecting; the state of being suspected; the imagining of something without evidence or on slender evidence; inkling; mistrust; a slight quantity, minute trace, eg of spirits (*colloq*); ground for suspicion (*Shakesp*). — *vt* (*dialect* and *US dialect*) to suspect. — *adj* **suspi'cionless**. — *adj* **suspi'cious** full of suspicion; showing suspicion; inclined to suspect; giving ground for suspicion; liable to suspicion, doubtful. — *adv* **suspi'ciously**. — *n* **suspi'ciousness**. — **above** (or **beyond**) **suspicion** too honest, virtuous, etc, to be suspected of a crime or fault; **on suspicion (of)** suspected (of); **under suspicion** suspected. [L *suspīciō*, *-ōnis*; see **suspect**]

suspire *səs-pīr'*, (*archaic* or *poetic*) *vi* to sigh; to breathe. — *vt* to breathe forth. — *n* **suspiration** (*sus-pə-rā'shən*) sighing. — *adj* **suspirious** (*səs-pir'i-əs*) breathing labouredly; sighing. [L *suspīrāre*, from *su-* (*sub-*), and *spīrāre* to breathe]

suss. See **sus**.

sussarara. Same as **siserary**.

sustain *səs-tān'*, *vt* to hold up; to bear; to support; to provide for; to maintain; to sanction; to keep going; to keep up; to support the life of; to prolong. — *n* (*Milton*) means of sustenance. — *n* **sustainabil'ity** that which is capable of being sustained; in ecology, the amount or degree to which the earth's resources may be exploited without deleterious effects. — *adj* **sustain'able**. — *adj* **sustained'**. — *adv* **sustain'edly**. — *n* **sustain'er** a person who, or thing that, sustains; the main motor in a rocket, continuing with it throughout its flight (cf **booster**). — *n* and *adj* **sustain'ing**. — *n* **sustain'ment** act of sustaining; sustenance. — *n* **sustenance** (*sus'ti-nəns*) that which sustains; maintenance; nourishment. — *adj* **sustentac'ūlar** supporting. — *n* **sustentac'ūlum** a supporting part or structure. — *vt* **sus'tentāte** to sustain. — *n* **sustentā'tion**. — *adj* **sustentative** (*sus'tən-tā-tiv* or *səs-ten'tə-tiv*) sustaining. — *n* **sus'tentātor** a sustaining part or structure. — *n* **susten'tion** the act of sustaining. — *adj* **susten'tive**. — *n* **sus'tinent** sustaining. — **sustaining pedal** a pedal on a piano which sustains the note(s) played by allowing the strings to continue vibrating. [L *sustinēre*, from pfx *sus-* (*subs-*), and *tenēre* to hold; partly through OFr *sustenir* (Fr *soutenir*)]

sustenance, **sustentacular**, **sustentation**, **sustinent**, etc. See under **sustain**.

Susu *sōō'sōō*, *n* a Negroid people of W Africa, living mainly in Mali, Guinea and Sierra Leone; a member of this people; its language.

susurrus *sū-* or *sōō-sur'əs*, (*poetic*) *n* a murmuring; a whisper; a rustling. — *adj* **susurr'ant**. — *vi* **su'surrate**. — *n* **susurrā'tion**. [L *susurrus*]

sutile *sū'*, *sōō'tīl* or *-til*, (*rare*) *adj* done by stitching. [L *sūtilis*, from *suere* to sew]

sutler *sut'lər*, (*hist*) *n* a person who sells liquor or provisions to soldiers in camp or garrison; a camp-hawker. — *n* **sut'lery** a sutler's work or stall. — *vi* **sutt'le** to trade as a sutler. [Du *zoetelaar* (earlier *soeteler*)]

sutor *sū'*, *sōō'tör* or *-tər*, (*archaic*) *n* a cobbler. — *adj* **suto'rial** or **suto'rian** relating to cobbling or to sewing. [souter; or directly from L *sūtor*, *-ōris* cobbler]

sutra *sōōt'rə*, *n* (in Sanskrit literature) an aphoristic rule or book of aphorisms on ritual, grammar, metre, philosophy, etc; (in Buddhist sacred literature) any of a group of writings including the sermons of Buddha and other doctrinal works. [Sans *sūtra* thread]

suttee or **sati** *sut'ē* or *sut-ē'*, *n* an Indian widow who burned herself on her husband's funeral pyre; the Hindu custom of so doing. — *n* **suttee'ism**. [Sans *satī* a true wife]

suttle[1] *sut'l*, (*obs*) *adj* light (*esp* of weight when tare is subtracted). [**subtle**]

suttle[2] *sut'l*, (*Milton*) *adj* subtle. — *n* **sutt'letie** subtlety. — *adv* **sutt'ly**. [**subtle**]

suttle[3]. See under **sutler**.

suture *sū'*, *sōō'chər* or *-tūr*, *n* a seam; a stitching; the stitching of a wound; the thread, etc for this; a junction or meeting of margins, *esp* of bones or of carpels; a line of dehiscence; a line of union. — *vt* to stitch up. — *adj* **su'tural**. — *adv* **su'turally**. — *n* **suturā'tion**. — *adj* **su'tured**. [L *sūtūra* a seam, from *suere* to sew]

suum cuique *sōō'əm kwī'* or *kī'kwi* or *sōō'ōōm kōō-ē'kwe*, (*L*) to each his own.

suversed *sū-vûrst'*, (*obs*; *trig*) *adj* versed of the supplement. [From the contraction *sup.* (meaning 'supplement') versed]

suzerain *sōō'zə-rān* or *sū'*, *n* a feudal lord; supreme or paramount ruler; a state having supremacy over another. — *adj* paramount. — *n* **su'zerainty** the position or power of a suzerain. [Fr, formed in imitation of *souverain* from *sus-* over, from L *sūsum* (for *sūrsum*, *subvorsum*)]

SV *abbrev*: *Sancta Virgo*, (*L*) Holy Virgin; *Sanctitas Vestra*, (*L*) Your Holiness.

Sv *abbrev*: sievert.

sv or **s.v.** *abbrev*: *sub verbo*, (*L*) under the word; *sub voce*, (*L*) under that heading.

svarabhakti *svä-rä-bäk'tē*, *n* development of a vowel between consonants. [Sans *svara* vowel, and *bhakti* separation]

Svarga. See **Swarga**.

svastika *svas'tik-ə*, *n*. See **swastika**.

svelte *svelt*, *adj* attractively slim; slender and graceful; lissom, lithe; (in art) free, easy, light and bold. [Fr]

Svengali *sven-gä'lē*, *n* a person who exerts total mental control over another, *usu* for evil ends. [Name of the evil hypnotist in George du Maurier's novel *Trilby*]

SW *abbrev*: short wave; small women or women's (clothing size); south-west; south-western.

SWA *abbrev*: South-West Africa (Namibia) (also IVR).

swab *swob*, *n* a mop for cleaning or drying floors or decks; a brush for wetting foundry moulds; a sponge or the like for cleaning the bore of a firearm; a bit of cotton-wool or the like for mopping up blood or discharges, applying antiseptics, cleaning a patient's mouth, or taking a specimen of a bodily secretion for examination; a specimen so taken; a naval officer's epaulette (*old slang*); a lubber or clumsy fellow (*old slang*); in an old form of whist, a card entitling its holder to a share of the stakes. — *vt* to mop with a swab: — *pr p* **swabb'ing**; *pa t* and *pa p* **swabbed**. — *n* **swabb'er** a person who uses a swab; a mop for cleaning ovens; a swab in whist as formerly played; (in *pl*) whist so played (also **whisk and swabbers**). — *n* **swabb'y** (*US slang*) a seaman, *esp* a new recruit. [Du *zwabber* swabber]

swack *swak* or *swäk*, (*Scot*) *adj* pliant; nimble. [Cf LGer *swak*, Du *zwak*; Ger *schwach* weak]

swad *swod*, (*dialect*) *n* a country lout; a soldier. — *n* **swadd'y** a soldier, *esp* a militiaman. [Perh Scand, or from **squad**, **squaddy**]

swaddle *swod'l*, *vt* to swathe; to bandage; to wrap (an infant) tightly in strips of cloth, as was formerly done to soothe or prevent over-exertion; to thrash, beat soundly (*obs*). — *n* swaddling-clothes; a bandage. — *n* **swadd'ler** (*Anglo-Ir colloq*) a Methodist or Protestant in general. — **swadd'ling-band** or **swadd'ling-clothes** (*Bible*) a strip or strips of cloth for swaddling an infant. [OE *swæthel*, *swethel* bandage; cf **swathe**[1]]

swaddy. See under **swad**.

Swadeshi *swä-dā'shē*, (*hist*) *n* a pre-Independence Indian nationalist movement, promoting home industries and boycott of foreign, *esp* British, goods; a product made in India. — Also *adj*. — *n* **Swade'shism**. [Bengali, own country]

swag *swag*, *vi* to sway; to sag; (often with *it*) to travel around carrying a bundle, as a vagrant or in search of work (*Austr slang*): — *pr p* **swagg'ing**; *pa t* and *pa p* **swagged**. — *n* a swagging; a festoon; a subsidence, as of ground over a mine; a depression; a bundle of possessions carried by someone travelling on foot (*esp Austr*); plunder (*slang*). — *n* **swagg'ie** (*Austr slang*) a swagman. — *adj* **swag'-bellied** having a pendulous belly. — **swag'-belly** a pendulous belly; someone whose belly swags; **swag'man** (*Austr*) a man who carries his swag about with him, *esp* in search of work; **swag'shop** (*slang*) a place where cheap and trashy goods are sold; **swags'man** a swagman; a burglar's accomplice who carries the plunder (*slang*). [Related to **sway**; prob Scand]

swage[1] *swāj*, *n* a grooved or moulded border (*obs*); any of several tools including a tool in two grooved parts, for shaping metal. — *vt* to shape with a swage; to reduce the cross-section of a rod or tube, eg by forcing it through a tapered aperture between two grooved dies. — **swage block** a block with various holes, grooves, etc, for use in metalworking. [OFr *souage*]

swage[2] *swāj*, (*Milton*) *vt* to assuage. [Anglo-Fr *suagier*, from L *suāvis*, mild or aphetic for **assuage**]

swagger *swag'ər*, *vi* to walk with a blustering or overweening air of superiority and self-confidence; to brag noisily or ostentatiously; to behave arrogantly. — *vt* to do, bring or render by swaggering. — *n* a swaggering gait, manner, mien or behaviour. — *adj* (*slang*) ostentatiously fashionable; smart. — *n* **swagg'erer**. — *n* and *adj* **swagg'ering**. — *adv* **swagg'eringly**. — **swagg'er-cane** or **-stick** a short military cane; **swagger coat** a coat that flares loosely from the shoulders. [**swag**]

Swahili *swä-hē'li*, *n* the people of Zanzibar and the opposite coast; one of them; loosely, their language (*Kiswahili*), a Bantu tongue modified by Arabic, spoken in Kenya, Tanzania and other parts of East Africa. [Ar *sawāhil*, pl *sāhil* coast, with sfx]

swain *swān*, (*poetic*, often *ironic*; also *archaic*) *n* a young man; a peasant or rustic; a lover or suitor. — *n* **swain'ing** love-making. — *adj* **swain'ish** boorish. — *n* **swain'ishness** boorishness. [ON *sveinn* young man, servant; OE *swān*]

swale[1] *swāl*, (*local*) *n* a shady spot; shade; a sunken or marshy place. — *adj* **swāl'y**. [Cf ON *svalr* cool]

swale[2] *swāl*, *vi* to sway.

swale[3], **swaling**. See **sweal**.

SWALK *swölk* or *swalk*, *abbrev*: sealed with a loving kiss (written on the back of an envelope containing a love-letter).

swallet. See under **swallow**[2].

swallow[1] *swol'ō*, *n* a small long-winged migratory bird (*Hirundo rustica*), often with a forked tail, that catches insects on the wing; any bird of its genus or family; extended to various unrelated birds of similar form or habits. — **swall'ow-dive** a dive during which one's arms are outstretched to the sides. — Also *vi*. — **swall'ow-tail** a forked tail; a long-tailed dress coat; a butterfly of the family *Papilionidae* with prolongations of the hind wings; a barbed arrow; a pennon; a swallow-tailed bird (eg the humming-bird and the kite). — *adj* **swall'ow-tailed** with a forked and pointed tail. — **swall'ow-wort** an asclepiad (*Cynanchum* or *Vincetoxicum*), from the swallow-tailed appearance of its paired pods; hence any asclepiad; greater celandine (qv under **celandine**). [OE *swalwe*, *swealwe*; Ger *Schwalbe*]

swallow[2] *swol'ō*, *vt* to take into the stomach through the gullet by a muscular movement of the throat; to engulf or subsume (often with *up*); to take in; to accept, sit down under (eg an affront); to stifle or repress (eg tears or one's pride); to believe credulously. — *vi* to perform the action of swallowing something. — *n* an abyss; a swallow hole; a throat; an act of swallowing; a gulp; a quantity swallowed at once; capacity for swallowing; the aperture in a block, between the sheave and frame, through which the rope runs (*naut*). — *n* **swall'et** a swallow hole. — *n* **swall'ower**. — **swallow hole** a funnel or fissure through which surface water passes underground, *esp* in limestone (also called **sink hole**). [OE *swelgan* (verb), *geswelg* (noun); cf Ger *schwelgen*]

swam *swam*, *pa t* (and *Shakesp*, etc, *pa p*) of **swim**.

swami *swä'mē*, *n* a Hindu idol; a Hindu religious instructor, *esp* (often with *cap*) as a form of address; a mystic. [Hindi *svāmī* lord, master]

swamp *swomp*, *n* a tract of wet, spongy (in the USA often tree-clad) land; low waterlogged ground. — *vt* to cause to sink or become stuck in a swamp (also *fig*); to cause (eg a boat) to fill with water; to overwhelm, inundate. — *vi* to become swamped. — *adj* of, or of the nature of, swamp; living or growing in swamps. — *n* **swamp'er** (*US*) a person who lives or works in the swamps. — *n* **swamp'iness**. — *adj* **swamp'y**. — **swamp boat** a flat-bottomed boat with a raised aeroplane engine for travelling over swamps; **swamp cypress** a deciduous conifer, *Taxodium*, of swamps in the Southern USA; **swamp fever** leptospirosis; a viral disease of horses (also called **equine infectious anaemia**); malaria (*US*); **swamp gas** marsh gas; **swamp'land**; **swamp oak** Casuarina. [Perh from LGer; prob related to OE *swamm* mushroom, Ger *Schwamm* sponge, fungus]

swan *swon*, *n* any species of *Cygnus*, a genus of large, graceful, stately, long-necked aquatic birds; one of these birds. — *vi* (*colloq*) to swim, move, glide, etc like a swan; to swan about (see below). — *adj* **swan'like**. — *n* **swann'ery** a place where swans are kept or bred. — *n* (*colloq*) **swann'ing**. — *adj* **swann'y** swanlike. — **swan'-goose** the China goose; the coscoroba swan (*Coscoroba coscoroba*) of S America; **swan'herd** someone who tends swans; **swan'-hopping** (*erron*) swan-upping; **swan'-maiden** (in Germanic folklore) a maiden who can become a swan by putting on her feather-garment; **swan'-mark** the notch made on the swan's upper mandible, as a mark of ownership; **swan'-mussel** a large freshwater mussel; **swan'-neck** an S-shaped bend or piece; **swans'-down** or **swans'down** the under-plumage of a swan; a soft woollen or mixed cloth; a thick cotton with a soft nap on one side; **swan'-shot** a shot of large size, like buckshot; **swan'skin** or **swan'-skin** the unplucked skin of a swan; a soft, nappy, fine-twilled fabric; **swan'-song** or **swan song** the fabled song of a swan just before its death; a writer's or musician's last work; one's last work or final appearance; **swan'-upping** an annual expedition up the Thames for the marking of young swans belonging to the Dyers' and Vintners' Companies (those belonging to the crown being unmarked) (see *vt* **up**). — **swan about** or **around** (*colloq*) to move about aimlessly, or gracefully; **swan in** or **up** (*colloq*) to arrive, either aimlessly or gracefully; **swan off** (*colloq*) to wander off, or depart, in a nonchalant, relaxed or oblivious manner. [OE *swan*; Ger *Schwan*, Du *zwaan*]

swang *swang*, (*Wordsworth*) a rare *pa t* of **swing**.

swanherd. See under **swan**.

swank *swangk*, *n* (*colloq*) ostentation; pretentiousness; a person who swanks. — *vi* (*colloq*) to show off; to swot (*archaic*). — *adj* slender, pliant (*Scot*); agile (*Scot*); smart, swanky (*colloq*). — *n* **swank'er**. — **swankey**, **swankie** see **swanky**. — *adj* **swank'ing** strapping, vigorous and strong; showing off (*colloq*); showy (*colloq*). — *n* **swank'y** (*Scot*) an active, smart, vigorous person; poor thin beer or any sloppy drink, even sweetened water and vinegar. — Also **swank'ey**, **swank'ie**. — *adj* (*colloq*) ostentatiously smart. — **swank'pot** a swanker (*colloq*). [Cf OE *swancor* pliant, MHGer *swanken* to sway]

swap or **swop** *swop*, *vt* to barter; to give in exchange; to exchange; to strike (as a bargain); to strike, hit (*obs*);

to slam, plump, slap down (*dialect*); to reap (corn, etc) close to the ground (*dialect*). — *vi* to barter; to exchange one for another, carry out a mutual exchange; to smite (*obs*); to flop (*rare*): — *pr p* **swapp'ing** or **swopp'ing**; *pa t* and *pa p* **swapped** or **swopped**, also (formerly) **swapt** or **swopt**. — *n* an exchange; something which is exchanged or offered in exchange; an exchange (of a sum of money) at different rates (*finance*); a swap option (*finance*); a swap line (*econ*); a blow, stroke (*obs*). — *adv* (*dialect*) suddenly. — *n* **swapp'er** or **swopp'er** a person who swaps; a very big thing, a whopper (*old slang*). — *n* and *adj* **swapp'ing** or **swopp'ing**. — **swap line** (*econ*) a lending arrangement between central banks; **swap meet** a gathering at which collectors, dealers, etc trade or barter; **swap option** (*finance*) a transaction in which debt liabilities are exchanged, eg a fixed-interest loan contract for one with a floating rate; **swap'-shop** a shop, meeting, etc where goods are exchanged for other goods or services rather than for money. [ME *swappen*; perh imit; or connected with **sweep** or **swoop**]

SWAPO *swä'pō*, *abbrev*: South-West Africa People's Organization.

swaption *swop'shən*, (*finance*) *n* a swap option (see under **swap**).

swaraj *swä-räj'*, (*Ind hist*) *n* self-government, independence, home-rule. — *n* **swaraj'ism** (formerly) the policy of Indian political independence. — *n* **swaraj'ist** an advocate of this. [Sans *svarājya*, from *sva* own, and *rājya* rule]

sward *swörd*, (*usu poetic*) *n* the grassy surface of land; green turf. — Also **swarth**. — *vt* (*usu in passive*) to cover with sward. — *adj* **sward'ed** or **sward'y** covered with sward. [OE *sweard* skin, rind; Du *zwoord*, Ger *Schwarte*]

sware *swār*, *archaic pa t* of **swear**.

swarf[1] *swörf*, **swarve** *swärv*, **swerf** *swûrf*, or **swerve** *swûrv* (*Scot*), *vi* to faint. — *n* **swarf** or **swerf** a swoon.

swarf[2] *swörf*, *n* grit from an axle, etc; stone or metal grindings, filings, turnings, etc. [ON *svarf* file-dust]

Swarga or **Svarga** *swär'gä* or *swur'gə*, *n* heaven; Indra's paradise. — Also (*Southey*) **Swer'ga**. [Sans *Svarga*]

swarm[1] *swörm*, *n* a body of bees going off to found a new community; a throng of insects or other small animals; a throng (of people, or of inanimate objects), *esp* one on the move, eg a mass of meteorites travelling through space; a colony, offshoot. — *vi* to go off in a swarm; to occur or come in swarms; to abound, teem. — *vt* to cause to swarm; to throng (chiefly *US* except in *passive*). — *n* **swarm'er**. — *n* and *adj* **swarm'ing**. — **swarm'-spore** or **-cell** a free-swimming generally ciliated asexual reproductive body (*bot*); an active germ produced by sporulation in Protozoa (*zool*). [OE *swearm*; Ger *Schwarm*]

swarm[2] *swörm*, *vt* and *vi* to climb (eg a pole or tree) by clasping with arms and legs. [Origin unknown]

swart *swört* or **swarth** *swörth*, *adj* (*archaic* or *dialect*) black; dusky; blackening, hence, malignant, baleful. — *n* **swarthiness** (*swör'dhi-nis*). — *adj* **swarthy** (*swör'dhi*) blackish; dark-complexioned. — *n* **swart'ness**. — *adj* (*obs*) **swart'y**. — **swart'-back** (ON *svartbakr*) the great black-backed gull; **swart star** (*Milton*) *appar* the Dog-star, in reference to its appearance in the summer, when the sun darkens the skin. [OE *sweart*; ON *svartr*, Ger *schwarz* black]

swarth *swörth*. Same as **sward**, **swart** or (*Shakesp*) **swath**[1].

swarty. See under **swart**.

swarve. See **swarf**[1].

swash[1] *swosh*, *n* slush; pig-wash; a wash of liquid, eg of water over a beach; the action or sound of splashing liquid; a dash; a heavy blow; a clashing or dashing sound; a swashbuckler (*archaic*); swaggering (*archaic*). — *adv* with a splash, heavy blow, or with a clashing or dashing sound. — *vt* and *vi* to dash; to splash; to clash. — *n* **swash'er** (*Shakesp*) a blusterer. — *n* and *adj* **swash'ing** slashing, crushing; blustering. — *adj* **swash'y** slushy. — **swash'buckler** a person who clashes a sword on a buckler; hence, a bully, a blusterer; a dare-devil. — *adj* **swash'buckling** of or resembling a swashbuckler; adventurous, exciting. [Imit]

swash[2] *swosh*, *n* (*obs*) a piece of turner's work with mouldings oblique to the axis; a flourish on a letter. — *adj* (*printing*) (of letters) ornamental italic, with decorative strokes that end in a flourish, used only at the beginning or end of a word. — **swash plate** (*eng*) a disc set obliquely on a revolving axis; **swash'work** turner's work cut obliquely. [Origin unknown]

swastika *swos'ti-kə* or *swas'*, also **svastika** *svas'*, *n* an ancient and worldwide symbol, a Greek cross with arms bent at a right angle, *esp* clockwise (see also **fylfot**), emblematic of the sun, good luck, anti-semitism or Nazism. — See also **gammadion**. [Sans *svastika*, from *svasti* wellbeing, from *su* good, and *asti*, he is]

swat[1] *swot*, *vt* to hit smartly or heavily. — *n* a sharp or heavy blow; a swatter. — *n* **swatt'er** an instrument consisting of a flexible shaft with a wide, flat, flaplike head, with which to swat flies. [**squat**]

swat[2] *swot* or *swöt*, (*Scot* and *Spenser*) *pa t* of **sweat**.

swat[3]. See **swot**.

swatch *swoch*, *n* a sample, *esp* of cloth, or of carpet, wallpaper, etc. — **swatch'book** a collection of swatches bound together into book form. [Origin unknown]

swath[1] *swöth* or *swoth* or **swathe** *swādh*, *n* a band of mown ground or of grass or corn cut by the scythe or mowing-machine, or ready for these; a broad band; the sweep of a scythe or mowing-machine. — *vt* **swathe** (*Canada*) to cut and leave (grain) lying in swathes to ripen on the ground. — *adj* **swathy** (*swöth'i* or *swādh'i*). [OE *swæth* and *swathu* track; Du *zwade*]

swath[2] *swoth*, (*Shakesp*) *n*. Same as **swathe**[1].

swathe[1] *swādh*, *vt* to bind round, envelop; to bandage. — *n* a bandage; a wrapping. — *n pl* **swath'ing-clothes** (*Shakesp*; or another reading, **swath'ling-** or **swoth'-ling-clouts**) swaddling-clothes. [OE *swathian*]

swathe[2], **swathy**. See **swath**[1].

swats *swots*, (*Scot*) *n* new ale. [OE *swatan* (pl) beer]

swatter[1] *swot'ər* or *swat'ər*, (*dialect*) *vi* to squatter; to splash or spill about. [Cf **squatter**]

swatter[2]. See under **swat**[1].

sway *swā*, *vt* to cause to move swingingly or sweepingly from side to side, *usu* slowly; to cause to lean or incline; to divert; to influence by power or moral force; to wield (*archaic*); to govern, hold sway (*archaic*); to control (*archaic*); to have a preponderating influence upon (*archaic*); (*usu* with *up*) to hoist (*naut*). — *vi* to swing; to oscillate; to swerve; to incline to one side; to have preponderating weight or influence; to rule (*archaic* or *poetic*); to proceed, bend one's course (*Shakesp*); to advance in hostility (*Spenser*). — *n* directing force or influence; preponderance, dominance; rule, supremacy; a swinging or sweeping motion; a motion to and fro or back and forth; a swerve; rotation (*Shakesp*); (in thatching) a hazel lath laid horizontally to hold down the straw or reed. — *adj* **swayed** or **sway'-back** (eg of a horse) bent down in the back. — *n* **sway'er**. — *n* and *adj* **sway'ing**. — **sway'back** a nervous disease of lambs causing difficulty in walking or standing (see also above). — **hold sway (over)** to have power, authority (over). [Perh from a lost OE word, or the corresponding ON *sveigja* to bend, swing; prob partly from LGer *swâjen* (Ger *schweien*) to swing]

swayl, **swayling**. See **sweal**.

Swazi *swä'zē*, *n* a racially mixed people inhabiting Swaziland and parts of the Eastern Transvaal of South Africa; a member of this people; its language. [*Mswati*, a former king of this people]

swazzle or **swozzle** *swoz'l*, *n* an instrument consisting of two convex pieces of metal with a tape stretched between them, placed in the mouth to make the voice of Mr Punch in a Punch and Judy show. [Perh from Ger *schwätzeln* to chatter, tattle]

sweal, **sweel** *swēl*, **swale** or **swayl** *swāl*, (*dialect*) *vt* to scorch; to singe; to roast in the skin; to burn off (eg heather and gorse, or soot in a chimney); to cause (a candle) to gutter; to waste away. — *vi* to be burning hot; (of a candle) to gutter. — *n* and *adj* **sweal'ing, swal'ing** or **swayl'ing**. [OE *swǣlan* (vt), *swelan* (vi) to burn]

swear *swār*, *vi* to take or utter an oath; to utter imprecations; (eg of a cat) to utter defiant noises (*colloq*); to give evidence on oath (*rare*). — *vt* to assert, promise, agree to, confirm or value, on oath; to assert loudly or boldly; to invoke (*Shakesp*); to administer an oath to; to put on oath; to bind by oath; (now *usu* **swear in**) to admit to office by an oath; to bring, put or render by swearing: — *pa t* **swore** (*swör* or *swōr*), *archaic* **sware**; *pa p* **sworn** (*swörn* or *swōrn*) or *archaic* and *illiterate* **swōre**. — *n* an expression that is formally an oath or a curse, or bad language generally (*colloq*); a bout of swearing, bad language (*colloq*); an oath (*archaic*). — *n* **swear'er**. — *n* and *adj* **swear'ing**. — *adj* **sworn** attested; bound by oath; having taken an oath; devoted, inveterate, confirmed, as if by oath. — **swear'-word** a word that is considered bad language. — **swear at** to hurl oaths and curses at; to be very incongruous with, *esp* in colour (*colloq*); **swear by** to invoke as witness to an oath; to put complete confidence in; **swear in** to inaugurate by oath; **swear off** to renounce, promise to give up; **swear to** to affirm or identify on oath. [OE *swerian*; Du *zweren*, Ger *schwören*]

sweard *swērd*, (*Spenser*) *n*. Same as **sword**.

sweat *swet*, *n* the moisture excreted by the skin; moisture exuding or seeming to exude from anything; a state, fit or process of exuding sweat; exercise or treatment inducing sweat; sweating sickness (*obs*); labour, long, hard work; drudgery; fidgety anxiety; a soldier (*slang*). — *vi* to give out sweat or moisture; to do difficult, strenuous work (*colloq*); to toil, drudge for poor wages; to exude; to become coated with moisture; to worry, be anxious (*colloq*); to suffer penalty, smart (*obs*). — *vt* to give forth as, or like, sweat; to cause to sweat; to heat (fruit, meat, etc) slowly so as to extract the juices (*cookery*); to squeeze money or extortionate interest from; to exact the utmost from; to wring evidence or confession from (*US slang*); to extract undue gains from, eg by removing gold from a coin; to compel to do hard work for meagre wages; to unite by the partial fusion of metal surfaces; to wet or soil with sweat: — *pa t* and *pa p* **sweat'ed** (or **sweat**). — *adj* **sweat'ed**. — *n* **sweat'er** a person who or animal, etc that sweats; a cause of sweating, eg a diaphoretic medicine; a (heavy) jersey for leisure wear, intervals in exercise, etc (*orig* one for reducing weight by sweating); someone who sweats coins or workers; a London street ruffian in Queen Anne's time who prodded and threatened passers-by with his sword. — *n* **sweat'iness**. — *n* and *adj* **sweat'ing**. — *adj* **sweat'y**. — **sweat band** the leather or similar band inside a man's hat; a band worn to absorb perspiration from the forehead; an absorbent wristlet worn by eg tennis players to prevent sweat running down to their hands; **sweat cooling** (*aeronautics*) cooling a component by evaporating fluid through a porous layer; **sweated labour** hard work obtained by exploitation; **sweat'er-girl** (*colloq*) a woman with a large bust, *usu* one wearing a tight-fitting sweater; **sweat gland** any of the glands producing sweat; **sweating sickness** an epidemic disorder (*usu* fatal) which ravaged Europe and *esp* England in the 15c and 16c, a violent inflammatory fever, with a fetid perspiration over the whole body; **sweating system** the practice of working poor people at starvation wages, for long hours, at home or in unhealthy rooms; **sweat'pants** (*esp US*) trousers of (*usu* thick) cotton material, with drawstring or elasticated waist and cuffs, as worn by athletes when warming up or after exercise; **sweat'-shirt** or **sweat'shirt** a long-sleeved knitted cotton sweater, *usu* fleecy on the inside; **sweat shop** a factory or shop using sweated labour; **sweat'suit** or **sweat suit** a loose-fitting suit consisting of sweater and trousers, *usu* close-fitting at wrist and ankle, worn by athletes, etc. — **in a cold sweat** (*fig*) in a state of terror or anxiety; **no sweat** (*US colloq*) words used to signify assent, or indicating that something will present no problems; **sweat blood** to work or worry extremely hard; **sweat it out** (*slang*) to endure, live through a time of danger, etc. [OE *swǣtan* to sweat; cf Ger *schweissen*; the OE noun was *swāt*]

sweath-band *swēth'-band*, (*Spenser*) *n* a swaddling-band. [**swathe**[1]]

Swede *swēd*, *n* a native or citizen of *Sweden*; (without *cap*) a Swedish turnip, a large buff-flowered, glaucous-leaved kind with yellow flesh. — *adj* **Swēd'ish**. — *n* the Scandinavian language of Sweden; (as *pl*) the natives or people of Sweden.

Swedenborgian *swē-dn-bör'ji-ən*, *n* a follower of Emanuel *Swedenborg*, a Swedish religious teacher (1688–1772), who claimed to be in direct contact with the spiritual world, and whose followers founded the New Jerusalem Church. — Also *adj*. — *n* **Swedenbor'gianism**.

swee or **swey** *swē*, (*Scot*) *n* a sway, swerve or lurch; a children's swing; the horizontal iron bar which could be swung over an old fireplace, on which cooking vessels were hung. — *vt* and *vi* to sway; to swing. [**sway**]

sweel. See **sweal**.

sweeney todd *swē'ni tod*, or **sweeney**, *n rhyming slang* for **flying squad** in the British police force, *esp* in London.

sweeny *swē'ni*, (*vet*) *n* atrophy of the shoulder muscles of a horse, eg following nerve injury. [OE *swindan* to pine away, disappear]

sweep *swēp*, *vi* to pass swiftly or forcibly, *esp* with a swinging movement or in a curve; to move with trailing or flowing drapery, hence with pomp, indignation, etc; to extend in a long curve; to range systematically or searchingly; to row with sweeps. — *vt* to pass something brushingly over; to elicit by so doing (*poetic*); to pass brushingly; to wipe, clean, move or remove with a broom; to carry along or off with a long brushing stroke, swiftly and/or with force; to wipe out or remove at a stroke (often with *away* or *up*); to perform with a sweeping movement; to trail with a curving movement; to drag as with a net or rope; to describe, generate or swing through (eg a curve, angle or area); to range or move over exploratively or searchingly; to row with sweeps: — *pa t* and *pa p* **swept**. — *n* the or an act of sweeping; a swinging movement, swing; onrush, surge; impetus; a clearance; range, compass; a curved stair; a curved drive in front of a building; that which is swept, sweepings; a sweepstake; a pump-handle; a long oar; a wire drag used in searching for shoals, mines, etc; a chimneysweep; a blackguard (*old slang*); sweepback (*aeronautics*). — *n* **sweep'er** a person who, or thing which, sweeps; (in association football) a player in front of the goalkeeper who assists the defence. — *n* **sweep'ing** the action of the verb in any sense; (*usu* in *pl*) things collected by sweeping, rubbish. — *adj* performing the action of sweeping in any sense; of wide scope, wholesale, indiscriminate. — *adv* **sweep'ingly**. — *n* **sweep'ingness**. — *adj* **sweep'y** swaying, sweeping, curving. — **sweep'back** (*aeronautics*) the angle at which an aeroplane wing is set back relatively to the axis; **sweep'-net** or **-seine** a long net paid out in a curve and dragged ashore; an insect net with a handle; **sweep'-saw** a turning-saw (qv under **turn**); **sweep'stake** or **sweep'stakes** a method of gambling by which participators' stakes are pooled, numbers, horses, etc assigned by lot, and prize(s) awarded accordingly on decision of event; such a prize, race, etc (for *adv* see **soopstake**); **sweep'-washer** a person who recovers gold or silver from the sweepings of refineries. — *adj* **swept'back** sweptwing. — *adj* **swept'wing** (of an aircraft, etc) having wings that are swept back. — **make a clean sweep (of)** to clear out completely; to win all the awards, prizes, etc; **sweep the board** see under **board**. [Prob from a lost OE word related to *swāpan* to sweep, and *geswǣpe* sweepings; cf **soop** and **swoop**]

sweer or **sweir** *swēr*, (*Scot*) *adj* slothful; loth. — Also **sweered**, **sweert** or **sweirt**.— *n* **sweir'ness**. [OE *swǣr*, *swǣre* heavy, grievous, sluggish; cf Ger *schwer*]

sweet *swēt*, *adj* having one of the fundamental varieties of taste, that of sugar, honey, ripe fruits (distinguished from *salt*, *acid* or *sour*, *bitter*, *dry*); sugary; pleasing to the taste, senses or feelings; fragrant; clear and tuneful; smoothly running; easy, free from harshness, benign; (of water) fresh, not salt; (of milk) fresh, not tainted; (of wine, ale, etc) not dry or bitter, retaining a sugary or fruity flavour; wholesome; gracious; amiable; mild, soft, gentle; delightful, charming (*colloq*); all right, satisfactory (*Austr colloq*); dear, beloved (*archaic*); ingratiating, often insipidly; cloying or sickly in taste, smell, etc; more or less enamoured (with *on* or *upon*; *colloq*). — *adv* sweetly. — *n* that which is sweet; a sweet dish (pudding, fruit, etc) as a course; a sweetmeat, confection, *esp* a boiled sweet (see under **boil**[1]); (a form of address used to) a beloved person; (in *pl*) wines and cordials sweetened with syrup. — *vt* (now *rare*) to sweeten. — *vt* **sweet'en** to make sweet; to mitigate something unpleasant; to pacify, make (a person) agreeable (often with *up*). — *n* **sweet'ener** a substance that sweetens, *esp* one not containing sugar; a person who sweetens; a bribe (*slang*). — *n* **sweet'ening**. — *n* **sweet'ie** or **sweet'y** a sweetmeat, item of confectionery; a sweetheart (*colloq*); (**sweetie**; often with *cap*) a large, seedless citrus fruit with greenish-yellow skin, its pulp sweeter than that of the grapefruit. — *n* **sweet'ing** a sweet apple; a darling (*archaic*). — *adj* **sweet'ish**. — *n* **sweet'ishness**. — *adv* **sweet'ly**. — *n* **sweet'ness**. — **sweety** see **sweetie** above. — *adj* **sweet'-and-sour'** cooked with sugar and vinegar or lemon juice; (in Oriental cookery) having a seasoning of sugar, vinegar, soy sauce, etc. — *adj* **sweet'-and-twen'ty** both fair and young (after *Shakesp*, who perhaps meant only sweet indeed; see **twenty** for intensive use). — **sweet'-bay** the laurel (*Laurus nobilis*); a kind of magnolia (*US*); **sweet'bread** the pancreas (*stomach sweetbread*), or sometimes the thymus (*neck sweetbread*), *esp* as a food; **sweet'-brier** or **-briar** a wild rose with fragrant foliage (*Rosa rubiginosa*); **sweet chestnut** see **chestnut**; **sweet Cicely** an aromatic umbelliferous plant (*Myrrhis odorata*); **sweet'corn** a sweet variety of maize; the yellow kernels of this, eaten as a vegetable; **sweetfish** see **ayu**; **sweet'-flag** an aromatic araceous pond-plant (*Acorus calamus*); **sweet'-gale** bog-myrtle, a low-growing aromatic shrub found in bogs; **sweet gas** hydrocarbon gas without sulphur compounds; **sweet'-heart** a lover or beloved. — *vt* and *vi* to court. — **sweetheart agreement**, **contract**, etc an agreement between a trade union and an employer that excessively favours the employer, and is often concluded without the consent of higher-ranking trade union officials; **sweet'ie-pie** (*colloq*) a term of endearment; **sweet'ie-wife** (*Scot*) a woman who sells sweets; (*esp* of an effeminate man) a gossip, scandalmonger. — *adj* **sweet'meal** (of biscuits) made of whole meal and sweetened. — **sweet'meat** any confection made wholly or chiefly of sugar; any sweet food (*obs*); **sweet'-oil** olive-oil; rape-oil; any oil of mild pleasant taste; **sweetpea'** a S European papilionaceous garden plant (*Lathyrus odoratus*) with bright-coloured fragrant flowers; **sweet pepper** see under **pepper**; **sweet potato** batata, a tropical and subtropical twining plant (*Ipomoea batatas*) of the convolvulus family; its large sweetish edible tuber. — *adj* **sweet-sa'voured**. — *adj* **sweet-scent'ed** having a sweet smell. — **sweet'sop** a tropical American evergreen (*Anona squamosa*); its pulpy fruit; **sweet spot** (*sport*) the spot on a golf club, tennis or squash racket, etc where, for best effect and control, the ball should ideally make contact; **sweet'-stuff** confectionery; sweetheart (*colloq*, as a term of address); **sweet talk** flattery, persuasion. — *vt* **sweet'-talk** (*colloq*) to coax, flatter, persuade. — *adj* **sweet-tem'pered** having a mild, amiable disposition. — *adj* **sweet-toothed'** fond of sweet things. — *adj* **sweet'-water** freshwater. — **sweet'water** a very sweet white grape; **sweet william** a garden pink (*Dianthus barbatus*) with bearded petals; **sweet willow** any of various trees, eg bay-leaved sweet willow (*Salix pentandra*); sweet-gale; **sweet'wood** a name for various S American and W Indian lauraceous trees; **sweet'-wort** (in beer-making) sweet-flavoured wort, before the addition of hops. — **a sweet tooth** a fondness for sweet things; **sweetness and light** an appearance of mildness, reasonableness, etc. [OE *swēte*; Ger *süss*, Gr *hēdys*, L *suāvis*, Sans *svādu* sweet]

sweir, **sweirt**, etc. See **sweer**.

swelchie *swelhh'i*, (*Orkney*) *n* a whirlpool; a tidal race. [ON *svelgr*, cf **swallow**[2]]

swell *swel*, *vi* to expand; to increase in volume; to be inflated; to bulge out; to grow louder; to rise into waves; to heave; to well up; to rise and fall in loudness; to be bombastic; to be elated or dilated with emotion; to give a feeling of expansion or welling up. — *vt* to augment; to expand; to dilate; to fill full; to louden; to elate: — *pa t* **swelled**; *pa p* **swelled** or **swollen** (*swōln* or *swōl'ən*), sometimes **swōln**. — *n* act, power, habit or condition of swelling; distension; a heaving; a bulge; an enlargement (*rare*); a loudening; a device in an organ for varying tone; a crescendo followed by a diminuendo (*music*); an area of gently rising ground, an incline; a dandy, a fashionable or finely dressed person (*slang*); a member of the governing class, a bigwig, an adept (*slang*). — *adj* (*slang*, *esp US*) a vague word of commendation (as being of, of the nature of, or befitting a swell). — *n* **swell'dom** (*slang*) the fashionable world. — *adj* **swelled**. — *n* **swell'er**. — *adj* and *n* **swell'ing**. — *adv* **swell'ingly**. — *adj* **swell'ish** (*slang*) foppish, dandified. — *adj* **swollen** (*swōl'ən*). — **swell box** (in an organ) a chamber containing a set of pipes or reeds, which is opened or closed by the swell; **swelled head** self-conceit, *esp* in someone carried away by success. — *adj* **swelled-head'ed**, **swell-head'ed** or **swollen-head'ed** conceited. — **swell'-mob** (*obs slang*) well-dressed pickpockets collectively; **swell-mobs'man** (*obs slang*); **swell organ** the pipes enclosed in the swell box. [OE *swellan*; Ger *schwellen*]

swelt *swelt*, *vi* to die (*obs* or *dialect*); to faint (*Spenser*, *obs Scot*); to swelter (*obs*); to pass like a fever (*Spenser*): — *pa t* **swelt'ed** or (*Spenser*) **swelt**. — *vi* **swelt'er** to endure great heat; to sweat copiously or feel faint or oppressed by heat; to exude (in *passive*; *archaic*). — *vt* to overpower, as with heat; to exude (*archaic*; *Shakesp*). — *n* a sweltering; a sweating; sweltered venom (*archaic*). — *adj* **swelt'ered**. — *n* and *adj* **swelt'ering**. — *adj* **swelt'ry** sultry; oppressive or oppressed with heat. [OE *sweltan* to die]

swept *swept*, *pa t* and *pa p* of **sweep**. — **sweptback** and **sweptwing** see under **sweep**.

swerf. See **swarf**[1].

Swerga. See **Swarga**.

swerve[1] *swûrv*, *vi* to turn aside; to deviate, *esp* to change course suddenly; to give way, shrink (*Milton*); to swarm, scramble (*Dryden*). — *vt* to deflect; to cause (a ball) to swerve in the air. — *n* a turning aside; a (sudden) deviation; a deflection; a ball that swerves in the air (*cricket*); the act or trick of making it do so (*cricket*). — *adj* **swerve'less** unswerving. — *n* **swerv'er**. — *n* and *adj* **swerv'ing**. [ME; the OE *sweorfan* to rub, file, scour, is not known to have had this sense]

swerve[2]. See **swarf**[1].

sweven *swev'n*, (*obs*) *n* a dream. [OE *swefn*]

swey. See **swee**.

SWG or **swg** *abbrev*: standard wire gauge, (a measure in) the UK scale of standard wire thicknesses.

swidden *swid'ən*, (*agric*) *n* an area of land made cultivable by cutting or burning off the vegetative cover. [ON *svithin*, pa p of *svitha* to burn]

swift[1] *swift*, *adj* fleet; rapid; speedy; prompt. — *adv* swiftly. — *n* a bird (*Apus apus* or *Cypselus apus*) superficially like a swallow but structurally nearer the humming-birds and goatsuckers; any bird of its genus or family; the common newt (now *dialect*); a reel for winding yarn; the main cylinder of a carding-machine; a rapid (*obs*). — *n* **swift'let** a bird (genus *Collocalia*) a species of swift, the builder of edible nests. — *adv* **swift'ly**. — *n* **swift'ness**. — *adj* **swift'-foot** or **-footed**. — *adj* **swift'-winged**. [OE *swift*, from same root as **swoop**]

swift[2] *swift*, (*naut*) *vt* to tighten with a rope. — *n* **swift'er** a rope used to tighten or keep a thing in its place. [Prob Scand or LGer]

Swiftian *swif'ti-ən*, *adj* of, or in the style of, the (*esp* satirical) writings of Jonathan *Swift* (1667–1745), Anglo-Irish writer and cleric.

swig[1] *swig*, *n* (*naut*) a pulley with ropes not parallel. — *vt* to tighten by hauling at right angles (*naut*); to castrate (eg a ram) by ligature. [Prob connected with **swag**]

swig[2] *swig*, *n* a deep draught of (*esp* alcoholic) drink; toast and ale (*archaic*); a wassail (*Oxford*). — *vt* to take a swig or swigs of or from. — *vi* to drink, take swigs: — *pr p* **swigg'ing**; *pa t* and *pa p* **swigged**. — *n* **swigg'er**. [Origin unknown]

swill *swil*, *vt* or *vi* to rinse (often with *out*); to dash water over or around; to wash; to drink greedily or in quantity. — *n* a large draught of liquor; hogwash. — *n* **swill'er**. — *n* and *adj* **swill'ing**. — **swill'-tub** a tub for hogwash. [OE *swilian* to wash]

swim *swim*, *vi* to propel oneself in water (or other liquid); to float; to come to the surface; to travel or be conveyed by water; to be suffused; to be immersed or steeped; to glide smoothly; to be dizzy. — *vt* to pass or cross by swimming; to cover (a distance) by swimming; to cause to swim or float; to test for witchcraft by immersion (*hist*): — *pr p* **swimm'ing**; *pa t* **swam** (*swam*) or *old-fashioned* **swum**; *pa p* **swum** (*Shakesp*, etc, **swam**). — *n* an act, performance or spell of swimming; any motion like swimming; the general movement or current of affairs; a crossing-place for swimmers (*local*); a place where many fishes swim; the air-bladder of a fish (*obs*). — *adj* **swimm'able** capable of being swum. — *n* **swimm'er**. — *n* **swimm'eret** a crustacean's abdominal appendage used in swimming. — *n* and *adj* **swimm'ing**. — *adv* **swimm'ingly** in a gliding manner as if swimming; smoothly, successfully (*colloq*). — *n* **swimm'ingness** the state of swimming; a melting look, tearfulness. — *adj* **swimm'y** inclined to dizziness. — **swim'-bladder** a fish's air-bladder; **swimm'ing-bath** (also in *pl*) an indoor swimming-pool; **swimm'ing-bell** a medusoid modified as a swimming organ; **swimming costume** swimsuit; **swimm'ing-pond**; **swimm'ing-pool** an artificial pool for swimming in; **swim'suit** a garment worn for swimming; now *esp* a one-piece woman's garment of stretch fabric, covering the torso only; **swim'wear** (in shops, fashion magazines, etc) garments worn for swimming. — **in the swim** in the main current (of affairs, business, etc); **swim with** (or **against**) **the stream** or **tide** to conform to (or go against) normal behaviour, opinions, etc. [OE *swimman*; Ger *schwimmen*]

swindge (*Milton*; *Shakesp* — also in **swindge'-buckler**). Same as **swinge**[1] and **swinge-buckler**.

swindle *swin'dl*, *vt* and *vi* to cheat. — *n* a fraud; anything not really what it appears to be. — *n* **swin'dler** a cheat. — *n* and *adj* **swin'dling**. — **swin'dle-sheet** (*facetious*) an expense account. [Ger *Schwindler* a giddy-minded person, swindler, from *schwindeln* to be giddy]

swine *swīn*, *n* a pig; a term of strong abuse; a sensual person (*archaic*): — *pl* **swine**. — *n* **swine'hood** the status of a swine. — *n* **swin'ery** a place where pigs are kept; swinishness; swine collectively. — *adj* **swin'ish** of or like swine; sensual (*archaic*); filthy; voracious; beastly. — *adv* **swin'ishly**. — *n* **swin'ishness**. — *adj* **swine'-drunk** (*Shakesp*) bestially drunk. — **swine fever** hog-cholera, a highly contagious disease of pigs due to a virus; **swine'=fish** the wolf-fish; **swine'herd** (*archaic*) a person who herds pigs; **swine'-keeping**; **swine'-pox** a form of chicken-pox; a viral skin disease of pigs; **swine's cress** a cruciferous weed of waste places (*Senebiera* or *Coronopus*); applied to various other plants; **swine's succory** a small plant (*Arnoseris*) related to chicory; **swine'stone** stinkstone; **swine'-sty** (*archaic* or *dialect*) a pig-sty; **swine vesicular disease** a highly contagious viral disease of pigs, causing sores on the skin of the feet, legs and mouth. [OE *swīn* a pig; Ger *Schwein*, L (adj) *suīnus*, from *sūs*, Gr *hȳs*]

Swing *swing*, (*hist*) *n* a fictitious captain in whose name rick-burners sent threatening letters to users of threshing-mills about 1830–33; the movement, operations or methods of the rick-burners. — Also *adj*. — *n* **swing'ism**.

swing *swing*, *vi* to sway or wave to and fro, as a body hanging freely; to amuse oneself on a swing; to oscillate; to hang; to be hanged; to sweep, wheel, sway; to swerve; to move with a swaying gait; (of a ship) to turn round (eg to test the compass); to attract, excite or be perfectly appropriate to place or mood (*slang*); (of a person) to be thoroughly responsive (to jazz, any of the arts or any aspect of living) (*slang*); to be lively or up-to-date (*slang*); to take part in sexual activity on an uncommitted basis (*slang*). — *vt* to cause to swing; to set swinging; to control; to sway; to hurl, whirl; to brandish (eg a weapon); to transport in suspension (eg an object suspended from a crane); to move in a sweep; (of a bell) to sound or send out (sound) by swinging; to indicate by an oscillation; to impart swing to; to perform as swing-music; to fix up so as to hang freely; to influence the result of (eg a doubtful election, decision, etc) in favour of an individual or party; to arrange, fix (*slang*): — *pa t* **swung**, *rarely* **swang**; *pa p* **swung**. — *n* an act, manner, etc or spell of swinging; oscillating, waving, sweeping; motion to and fro; shift from one position, etc to a markedly different one (*lit* and *fig*); the sweep or compass of a swinging body; the sweep of a golf club, bat, or the like; sway; scope, free indulgence; impetus; vigorous sweeping rhythm; big-band jazz music with strong rhythm and improvisations, as played in the 1930s and 1940s (also **swing'-music**); a suspended seat or carriage for the amusement of swinging; a reversal of fortune; the movement of voters from one party to another as compared with the previous election. — *n* **swing'er** (*swing'ər*) a person or thing that swings; a ball bowled so as to swerve in the air (*cricket*); a badly-centred gramophone record; a lively and up-to-date person (*slang*); a person engaging freely in sexual activity, *usu* in groups (*slang*); either of the middle pair in a team of six horses; a Hindu votary who swings from hooks in his flesh. — *n* **swinging** (*swing'ing*) the act of moving to and fro in suspension, *esp* as a pastime; hanging (*colloq*); the practice of unrestrained sexual activity, *esp* in groups, swapping partners, etc (*slang*); hanging by hooks, as by a Hindu devotee. — *adj* swaying; turning; with a swing; having a free easy motion; with it, fully alive to, and appreciative of, the most recent trends and fashions in living (*colloq*); up-to-date (*colloq*); lively (*colloq*); sexually promiscuous, *esp* indulging in partner-swapping or group sex (*slang*). — *adv* **swing'ingly**. — *n* **swingom'eter** a device which shows the direction and extent of the current swing of the counted votes in an election. — *adj* **swing'y** (*colloq*) having swing. — **swing'-back** a reaction; a camera back that can be tilted; **swing'boat** a boat-shaped swinging carriage for fairs, etc; **swing'-bridge** a bridge that may be opened by swinging it to one side; **swing'-by** the passing of a spacecraft near a planet in order to use its gravitational field to change course; **swing-door'** a door (*usu* one of a pair) that opens either way and swings shut by itself; **swing'-handle** a pivoted (*esp* arched) handle; **swing'ing-boom** (*naut*) the spar that stretches the foot of a lower studding-sail; **swing'ing-post** the post to which a gate is hung; **swing-music** see **swing** above; **swing'-plough** a plough without a fore-wheel under the beam; **swing'-shelf** a hanging shelf; **swing shift** (*US*) the work shift between the day and night shifts (eg from mid-afternoon till midnight); the workers allocated to this shift; the workers employed to take irregular shifts over a seven-day week to enable other workers to work a regular five-day week; **swing'stock** an upright timber, with a blunt upper edge for swingling flax on (also **swing'ing-block**); **swing'-swang** a complete (to and fro) oscillation; **swingtail cargo aircraft** an aircraft with tail that swings aside to give access to the full cross-section of the fuselage for rapid loading and unloading of cargo; **swing'tree** a whippletree; **swing'-wheel** the wheel that drives a clock pendulum; **swing'-wing (aircraft)** variable-geometry aircraft. — **in full swing** in fully active operation; in mid-career; **swings and roundabouts** a situation in which advantages and disadvantages cancel each other out; **swing the lead** see under **lead**[2]. [OE *swingan*; Ger *schwingen*]

swinge[1] *swinj*, *vt* to beat (*archaic* or *dialect*); to chastise (*obs*); to lash, sway, flourish (*obs*): — *pr p* **swinge'ing**. — *adj* (*colloq*) **swinge'ing** great, huge, thumping; severe, drastic. — *adv* **swinge'ingly**. — *n* (*colloq*; *archaic* and *rare*) **swinger** (*swinj'ər*) any great or astonishing person or thing; a bold lie, a whopper. — **swinge'buckler** (*obs*) a swashbuckler. [ME *swenge*, from OE *swengan* to shake, causative of *swingan* to swing]

swinge[2] *swinj*, (*Spenser*) *vt*. Same as **singe**.

swingism. See under **Swing**.

swingle *swing'gl*, *n* a scutching tool; the swipple of a flail. — *vt* to scutch. — *n* **swing'ling**. — **swing'le-bar** or **swing'letree** a whippletree; a swing-stock; **swing'lehand** a scutching tool; **swing'ling-stock** a swing-stock. [Cf OE *swingell* stroke, scourge, rod, and MDu *swinghel*]

swingometer. See under **swing**.

swinish, etc. See under **swine**.

swink *swingk*, (*archaic*) *vi* to toil. — *n* toil. — *adj* **swinked** (*Milton* **swink't**) toil-worn, fatigued. [OE *swinc* (noun), *swincan* (verb)]

swipe *swīp*, *n* a sweeping stroke; a swath (*archaic*). — *vt* to purloin, steal (*colloq*); to strike with a swipe; to pass (a credit or debit card, etc) through an electronic reading terminal; to gulp (*archaic slang*). — *vi* to make a swipe; to sweep for old anchors. — *n* **swip'er**. — *n* **swipes** (*slang*) bad or spoilt beer; small beer. — *adj* **swip'ey** (*rare*) fuddled with malt liquor. [OE *swipian* to beat]

swipple *swip'l*, *n* a swingle or striking part of a flail. [Cf **swipe** and **sweep**]

swire *swīr*, *n* a neck (*obs*); (in place names) a hollow between two hills. [OE *swēora* (Northern *swīra*) neck]

swirl *swûrl*, *n* an eddy; a whirl; a curl. — *vt* to whirl; to wind. — *vi* to eddy; to whirl; to spin. — *adj* **swirl'y**. — **swirl vanes** (*aeronautics*) vanes that cause a swirling motion in the air entering a gas-turbine combustion chamber. [Orig Scot; cf Norw dialect *svirla*]

swish[1] *swish*, *n* a prolonged and rushing sibilant sound, such as is produced by branches being swept to and fro by the wind, or by fabric brushing along the ground; dashing spray; a cane or birch. — *vt* to whisk with a swish; to flog, thrash. — *vi* to make or go with a swish. — *adv* with a swish. — *n* **swish'er**. — *n* and *adj* **swish'ing**. — *adj* **swish'y**. [Imit]

swish[2] *swish*, (*slang*) *adj* smart, stylish. [Origin unknown]

Swiss *swis*, *adj* of or from *Switzerland*. — *n* a native or citizen of Switzerland; the High German dialect spoken by most of the Swiss: — *pl* **Swiss** (formerly **Swiss'es**). — *n* (*archaic*) **Swit'zer** a Swiss; a Swiss (or other) mercenary or member of a bodyguard. — **Swiss chard** see under **chard**; **Swiss cheese plant** a tropical climbing plant (*Monstera deliciosa*) with large, thick, perforated leaves, often grown as a house plant; **Swiss Guards** a body of Swiss mercenaries in the French guards from 1616, wiped out in the Revolution; the Pope's bodyguard; **Swiss roll** a thin cake of sponge rolled up with jam, cream, etc; a flexible floating pier. [Fr *Suisse*, OHGer *swīz*]

swissing *swis'ing*, *n* ordinary calendering of cloth. [Origin unknown]

switch *swich* (*Shakesp* **swits** *swits*), *n* a long flexible twig; a tapering riding-whip; a rod, cane; an application of a switch; a brushing blow; a whisk, jerk; a tool for beating eggs or cream; a tress, *usu* false; the tuft of an animal's tail; a movable rail for shunting; a changeover (*esp* in cards to another suit, led or called); a device for making, breaking or changing an electric circuit; a switchboard; a turn of a switch. — *vt* to strike with a switch; to drive with, or as if with, a switch; to whisk, jerk, lash; to beat up, whip (eg an egg or cream); to prune; to shunt; to divert; to turn (off, on, or to another circuit); to race (a horse) under the name of another horse. — *vi* to use a switch; to turn aside; to change over; to whisk. — *n* **switch'ing**. — *adj* **switch'y**. — **switch'back** *orig* a zigzag mountain railway on which the train shunted back at each stage; an up-and-down track on which cars rise by the momentum gained in coming down; an up-and-down road (also *fig*); **switch'blade** or **switchblade knife** a flick-knife; **switch'board** a board or frame bearing apparatus for making or breaking an electric current or circuit; a board for connecting telephones; **switch'gear** the apparatus that controls the switches in the electric circuits of a power station; **switch'man** a pointsman; **switch'over** the action of the verb; a changeover; **switch'-plant** a plant with long slim green shoots, the leaves reduced or sparse; **switch selling** the practice of arousing the interest of a prospective buyer by offering a low-priced article, then describing the shortcomings of the cheap article and trying to sell the customer a more expensive one. — **switched on** aware of and responsive to all that is most up-to-date (*colloq*); under the influence of drugs (*colloq*). [Earlier *swits* (*Shakesp*), *switz*; prob from Du or LGer]

switchel *swich'l*, (*NAm*) *n* treacle-beer, a drink of molasses and water, etc; (in Newfoundland) cold tea. [Origin unknown]

swith *swith*, (*obs*) *adv* quickly; at once. — *interj* away. [OE *swīthe* very]

swither *swidh'ər*, (*Scot*) *vi* to be undecided. — *n* indecision; flurry. [Poss OE *swethrian* to subside]

swits. See **switch**.

Switzer. See under **Swiss**.

swive *swīv*, (*archaic*) *vt* to make love to, have sexual intercourse with (a female). [Appar OE *swifan*, see **swivel**]

swivel *swiv'l*, *n* a ring or link that turns round on a pin or neck; a swivel-gun. — *vt* and *vi* to turn on a pin or pivot: — *pr p* **swiv'elling**; *pa t* and *pa p* **swiv'elled**. — **swiv'elblock** a block on which a swivel is mounted; **swiv'el-chair** a chair with a seat that swivels round; **swiv'el-eye** (*colloq*) a squint-eye; **swiv'el-gun** a gun that turns on a pivot; **swiv'el-hook** a hook secured to anything by means of a swivel. [OE *swīfan* to move quickly, to turn round]

swivet *swi'vit*, (*dialect*) *n* a state of nervous agitation. [Origin unknown]

swiz *swiz* or **swizzle** *swiz'l*, (*slang*) *n* a fraud; a great disappointment. — *vt* to defraud, cheat. [Poss **swindle**]

swizzle[1] *swiz'l*, (*colloq* and *dialect*) *vi* to drink to excess. — *vt* to mix or swirl, as with a swizzle-stick. — *n* a mixed or compounded drink containing rum or other spirit. — **swizzle'-stick** a stick or whisk used to mix a swizzle. [Origin unknown]

swizzle[2]. See **swiz**.

SWL (*UK*) *abbrev*: safe working load (for eg a derrick).

swob, **swobber**, etc. Same as **swab**, **swabber**, etc.

swollen *swōl'ən* or *swōln*, *pa p* of **swell**, and *adj*.

swoln. See **swell**.

swoon *swōōn*, also (*archaic* and *poetic*) **sound** *sownd*, **swoun** *swown* or **swound** *swownd* (*Spenser* **swownd** or **swone**), *n* a fainting fit; a sleep (*Spenser*). — *vi* to faint; to be languorous, give a feeling of fainting (*poetic*); to subside (*poetic*). — *adj* **swooned** in a swoon. — *n* and *adj* **swoon'ing**. — *adv* **swoon'ingly**. [Prob from ME *iswowen*, from OE *geswōgen* (pa p; other parts unknown) in a swoon, wrongly analysed as *in swoon*]

swoop *swōōp*, *vi* to come down with a sweeping rush; to rush suddenly; to sweep along (*obs*). — *vt* (*obs*) to pounce on, to snatch with a sweep, *esp* on the wing. — *n* an act of swooping; a sudden onslaught. — *adv* **swoop'stake-like** see under **soop**. — **at one fell swoop** (*Shakesp*, *Macbeth*, IV. 3. 219) by one terrible blow; (also **in** or **with**) by one complete decisive action; suddenly. [Appar OE *swāpan* to sweep; perh influenced by **soop**]

swoosh *swŏŏsh*, *n* a noise of or resembling a rush of air, water, etc. — *vi* to make this noise. [Prob imit, or from **swish**[1] and **swoop**]

swop, **swopper**, **swopping**, **swopt**. See **swap**.

sword *sörd* or *sōrd*, *n* a weapon with a long blade, sharp on one or both edges, for cutting or thrusting; a blade or flat rod resembling a sword; a swordfish's snout; destruction or death by the sword or by war; war; military force; the emblem of vengeance or justice, or of authority and power; (in *pl*) a suit in the tarot pack. — *vi* (*archaic*) to wield a sword. — *n* **sword'er** (*archaic*) a gladiator; an assassin, a cut-throat; a swordsman. — *adj* **sword'less**. — *adj* **sword'like**. — *adj* **sword'-and-buck'ler** fought or armed with sword and buckler. — **sword'-arm** and **-hand** the arm, and hand, that wield the sword; **sword'-bayonet** a bayonet shaped somewhat like a sword, and used as one; **sword'-bean** an Indian papilionaceous plant (genus *Canavalia*) with long sword-shaped edible pods; its seed; **sword'-bearer** a public officer who carries the sword of state; **sword'-belt** a belt from which the sword is hung; **sword'-bill** a S American humming-bird with a bill longer than its body; **sword'-blade** the blade of a sword; **sword'-breaker** an old weapon for grasping and breaking an adversary's sword; **sword'-cane** or **-stick** a hollow cane or stick containing a sword; **sword'craft** swordsmanship; military power; **sword'-cut** a cut with the edge of a sword; a wound or scar so produced; **sword'-dance** a dance performed sword in hand or among or over swords; **sword'-dollar** (*hist*) a Scottish silver coin of James VI, worth 30s Scots (2s 6d English), with a sword on the reverse; **sword'fish** a large fish (Xiphias or other genus of the family Xiphiidae) with upper jaw compressed and prolonged as a stabbing weapon; **sword'-grass** a name for many plants with sword-shaped leaves; **sword'-guard** the part of a sword-hilt that protects the bearer's hand; **sword'-knot** a ribbon tied to the hilt of a sword; **sword'-law** government by the sword; **sword'man** a swordsman; a fighting man; **sword'play** fencing; **sword'player**. — *adj* **sword'proof** capable of resisting the blow or thrust of a sword. — **sword'-rack** a rack for holding swords. — *adj* **sword'-shaped**. — **swords'man** a man skilled in the use of a sword; **swords'manship**; **sword-stick** see **sword-cane**; **sword'-swallower** a performer who seems to swallow swords; **sword'-tail** a small Central American freshwater Cyprinodont fish with a swordlike tail-lobe. — **cross swords with** see under **cross**; **put to the sword** (of armies, etc; *hist*) to kill (prisoners, etc) by the sword; **sword of Damocles** (*dam'ə-klēz*) imminent calamity (from *Damocles*, the Syracuse courtier, forced to sit through a feast with a sword suspended over his head by a single hair). [OE *sweord*; Ger *Schwert*]

swore, **sworn**. See **swear**.

SWOT (*marketing*) *abbrev*: strengths, weaknesses, opportunities and threats (considered in the analysis of a product).

swot or **swat** *swot*, (*slang*) *vt* and *vi* to study hard: — *pr p* **swott'ing** or **swatt'ing**; *pa t* and *pa p* **swott'ed** or **swatt'ed**. — *n* hard study; a person who swots. — *n* **swott'er** or **swatt'er**. — *n* **swott'ing** or **swatt'ing**. [**sweat**]

swothling-clouts. See under **swathe**[1].

swoun, **swound**. See **swoon**. — (*Spenser*) **swoune**, **swownd**, **swowne**.

swounds, **'swounds**. Same as **zounds**.

swozzle. See **swazzle**.

SWP *abbrev*: Socialist Workers' Party.

SWRI *abbrev*: Scottish Women's Rural Institute.

swum *swum*, *pa p* and old-fashioned *pa t* of **swim**.

swung *swung*, *pa t* and *pa p* of **swing**. — **swung dash** (*printing*) the sign ~ used to represent a word that has already been printed.

swy *swī*, (*Austr slang*) *n* the Australian game of two-up (also **swy game** or **swy'-up**): a two-year prison sentence. [Ger *zwei* two]

SY *abbrev*: Seychelles (IVR).

sy-. See **syn-**.

Syalon® *sī'ə-lon*, *n* a hard, strong, light, ceramic material for use in high-temperature environments, eg gas turbines and car engines. [*si*licon, *al*umina, *o*xy*n*itrides (its components)]

Sybarite *sib'ə-rīt*, *n* an inhabitant of *Sybaris*, a Greek city in ancient Italy, on the Gulf of Tarentum, noted for luxury; a person devoted to luxury. — Also *adj*. — *adj* **Sybaritic** (*-rit'ik*) or **Sybarit'ical**. — *adj* **Sybarīt'ish**. — *n* **Sy'barītism**. — All words also without *cap*.

sybbe. See **sib**.

sybil. Same as **sibyl**.

sybo, **syboe** or **sybow** *sī'bō* or *sī'bi*, (*Scot*) *n* a cibol; a young or spring onion: — *pl* **sy'boes** or **sy'bows**. [**cibol**]

sybotic *sī-bot'ik*, (*rare*) *adj* pertaining to a swineherd. — *n* **sybotism** (*sib'ə-tizm*). [Gr *sybōtēs* swineherd, from *sȳs* swine, and *boskein* to feed, tend]

sycamine *sik'ə-mīn*, (*Bible*) *n* the mulberry-tree. [Gr *sȳkaminos*, of Semitic origin, influenced by *sȳkon* a fig]

sycamore *sik'ə-mōr* or *-mör*, *n* a kind of fig-tree (now often **syc'omore** or **sycomore fig**); in England, the great maple (*Acer pseudo-platanus*) called in Scotland the plane (formerly **sycomore**); (in the USA) any true plane (*Platanus*). [Gr *sȳkomoros*, from *sȳkon* a fig, and *moron* black mulberry]

syce, **sice** or **saice** *sīs*, (*esp India*) *n* a groom, mounted attendant; a chauffeur. [Ar *sā'is*]

sycee *sī-sē'*, *n* silver ingots used as Chinese money. — Also **sycee silver**. [Chin *sí sz'*]

sycomore. See **sycamore**.

syconium *sī-kō'ni-əm*, (*bot*) *n* a multiple fruit in which the true fruits (the pips) are enclosed in a hollow fleshy receptacle, eg the fig. [Gr *sȳkon* a fig]

sycophant *sik'ō-fənt* or *sik'ə-*, also *-fant*, *n* a servile flatterer; a common informer (*Gr hist*). — *n* **syc'ophancy** the behaviour of a sycophant; obsequious flattery; servility; mean tale-bearing (*Gr hist*). — *adj* **sycophantic** (*-fant'ik*) or (*obs*) **sycophant'ical**. — *adv* **sycophant'ically**. — *adj* **syc'ophantish** (or *-fant'ish*). — *adv* **syc'ophantishly**. — *vi* **syc'ophantize** or **-ise** to play the sycophant. — *n* **syc'ophantry** the arts of the sycophant. [Gr *sȳkophantēs* an informer, swindler, confidential agent, from *sȳkon* a fig, and *phainein* to show; variously but unsatisfactorily explained]

sycosis *sī-kō'sis*, (*med*) *n* inflammation of the hair follicles, *esp* of the beard. [Gr *sȳkōsis* a fig-shaped ulcer, from *sȳkon* a fig]

Sydneysider *sid'ni-sīd-ər*, *n* a person who comes from or is resident in *Sydney*, Australia, or the surrounding area.

sye *sī*, (now *dialect*) *vt* to strain. — *n* a sieve; a milk-strainer. [OE *sīon*, *sēon* to strain]

syen. A Shakespearian spelling of **scion**.

syenite *sī'ən-īt*, *n* a coarse-grained plutonic rock composed of orthoclase and a ferromagnesian mineral, *usu* hornblende. — *adj* **syenitic** (*-it'ik*) relating to *Syene* in Egypt; pertaining to syenite. [L *syēnītēs* (*lapis*) a hornblende granite (not syenite) found at Aswan (Gr *Syēnē*)]

SYHA *abbrev*: Scottish Youth Hostels Association.

syke. See **sike**[1].

syker *sik'ər*, (*Spenser*) *adv* surely. [**sicker**]

syl. *abbrev*: syllable; syllabus.

syl-. See **syn-**.

syllable *sil'ə-bl*, *n* a word or part of a word uttered by a (more or less) single effort of the voice, and into which a word can be divided for the purposes of linguistic analysis; (loosely, *usu* with a *neg*) a single sound or word, a murmur. — *vt* to express by syllables, to utter articulately. — *n* **syll'abary** a (system of writing composed of a) set of symbols representing syllables. — Also **syllabā'rium**. — *adj* **syllabic** (*sil-ab'ik*) of or constituting a syllable or syllables; syllable by syllable. — *adj* (*obs*) **syllab'ical** syllabic. — *adv* **syllab'ically**. — *vt* **syllab'icate** to syllabify. — *n* **syllabicā'tion** syllabification. — *n* **syllabicity** (*-is'i-ti*). — *n pl* **syllab'ics** verse patterned not by stresses but by syllables. — *n* **syllabificā'tion** pronunciation as a syllable; division into syllables. — *vt* **syllab'ify** to divide into syllables. — *n* **syll'abism** use of a syllabary; division into syllables. — *vt* **syll'abize** or **-ise** to form or divide into syllables; to sing to syllables. — *adj* **syll'abled** having (in compounds, so-many) syllables. — **syllabic verse** or **metre** syllabics. — **in words of one syllable** (*colloq*) very simply, bluntly. [L *syllaba*, from Gr *syllabē*, from *syn* with, and *lab-*, root of *lambanein* to take; *-le* as in principle, participle]

syllabub or (now *rarely*) **sillabub** *sil'ə-bub*, *n* a dish of cream curdled (eg with wine), flavoured and frothed up; anything frothy or insubstantial. [Origin obscure]

syllabus *sil'ə-bəs*, *n* an abstract or programme, eg of a series of lectures or a course of studies; either of two catalogues of doctrinal positions or practices condemned by the RC Church (produced in 1864 and 1907): — *pl* **syll'abuses** or **syll'abi** (*-bī*). [Originally a misprint for L *sittybas*, accusative plural of *sittyba*, Gr *sittubā* a book-label]

syllepsis *sil-ep'sis*, *n* a figure in rhetoric by which a word does duty in a sentence in the same syntactical relation to two or more words but has a different sense in relation to each: — *pl* **syllep'ses** (*-sēz*). — *adj* **syllep'tic** or **syllep'tical**. — *adv* **syllep'tically**. [Gr *syllēpsis* a taking together, from *syn* together, and the root of *lambanein* to take]

syllogism *sil'ō-jizm* or *sil'ə-jizm*, *n* a logical argument in three propositions, two premises and a conclusion that follows necessarily from them; deductive reasoning; a clever, subtle or specious argument. — *adj* **syllogistic** (*-jist'ik*) or **syllogist'ical**. — *n* **syllogist'ic** (often *pl*) the branch of logic concerned with syllogisms. — *adv* **syllogist'ically**. — *n* **syllogization** or **-s-** (*-jī-zā'shən*). — *vi* **syll'ogize** or **-ise** to reason by syllogisms. — *vt* to deduce syllogistically. — *n* **syll'ogizer** or **-s-**. [Gr *syllogismos*, from *syllogizesthai*, from *syn* together, and *logizesthai* to reckon, from *logos* speech, reason]

sylph *silf*, *n* a spirit of the air; a sylphlike being; a slim person; a kind of humming-bird. — *n* **sylph'id** or **sylph'ide** a little sylph. — Also *adj*. — *adj* (*Meredith*) **sylph'idine**. — *adj* **sylph'ish**, **sylph'-like** or **sylph'y**. [Coined by Paracelsus]

sylvan *sil'vən*, *adj* (*literary* and *poetic*) of woods or woodland; wooded, tree-lined; romantically rural, arcadian. — *n* a wood-god; a forest-dweller. — *adj* **sylvat'ic**. — *adj* **sylves'trian**. — *adj* **sylvicul'tural**. — *n* **syl'viculture** forestry. — All these words are often found spelt with *i*. [L *silva* (sometimes *sylva*) wood.]

sylvaner *sil-vä'nər*, (often with *cap*) *n* a German grape, used in making white wine; wine made from this grape. [Ger]

sylvanite *sil'vən-īt*, *n* a mineral, telluride of gold and silver. [Tran*sylvania*, where it is found]

sylvia *sil'vi-ə*, *n* any warbler of the genus *Sylvia*, that gives its name to a family *Sylviidae* or subfamily *Sylviinae* of the thrush family. — *adj* **syl'viīne**. [L *silva* a wood]

Sylvian *sil'vi-ən*, *adj* of *Sylvius*, ie either the French anatomist Jacques Dubois (1478–1555), or Franz de la Boë (1614–72), the Dutch-German iatrochemist. — **Sylvian fissure** (*anatom*) a deep lateral fissure in the cerebrum, discovered apparently by the latter.

sylviculture, etc. See under **sylvan**.

sylvine *sil'vēn* or **sylvite** *sil'vīt*, *n* native potassium chloride, a source of potash. — *n* **syl'vinite** (*-vin-īt*) a rock composed of sylvine and rock salt. [Formerly called digestive salt of *Sylvius*]

sym. *abbrev*: symbol; symmetrical; symphony; symptom.

sym-. See **syn-**.

symar. Same as **cymar**.

symbiosis *sim-bi-ō'sis*, *n* a mutually beneficial partnership between organisms of different kinds (*biol*); *esp* such an association where one lives on or within the other. — *n* **sym'biont** (*-bi-ont*) an organism living in symbiosis. — *adj* **symbiotic** (*-bi-ot'ik*). — *adv* **symbiot'ically**. [Gr *syn* together, and *bios* livelihood]

symbol *sim'bl* or *-bəl*, *n* an emblem; a sign used to represent something; that which by custom or convention represents something else; a type (*obs*); a creed, compendium of doctrine, or a typical religious rite, such as the eucharist (*theol*); an object or act representing an unconscious or repressed conflict (*psychol*). — *vt* to symbolize. — *adj* **symbolic** (*-bol'ik*) or **symbol'ical**. — *adv* **symbol'ically**. — *n* **symbol'icalness**. — *n sing* **symbol'ics** study of creeds. — *n* **sym'bolism** representation by symbols or signs; a system of symbols; use of symbols; use of symbols in literature or art; (often with *cap*) a late 19c movement in art and poetry that treated the actual as an expression of something underlying; symbolics. — *n* and *adj* **sym'bolist**. — *adj* **symbolist'ic** or **symbolist'ical**. — *n* **symbolīzā'tion** or **-s-**. — *vt* **sym'bolize** or **-ise** to be symbolic of; to represent by symbols; to combine (*obs*); to formulate in a creed. — *vi* (*obs*) to agree. — *n* **sym'bolizer** or **-s-**. — *adj* **sym'bolled** symbolized; bearing symbols. — *n* **symbolog'raphy** symbolic writing or representation. — *n* **symbol'ogy** (for **symbolol'ogy**) the study or use of symbols. — *n* **symbolol'atry** (Gr *latreiā* worship) undue veneration for symbols. — **symbol grocer**, etc (*marketing*) a member of an independent group (**symbol group**) of retail grocers, etc who join together to obtain improved discounts and prices from suppliers, and display a common symbol or logo on their shops, packaging, etc; **symbolic logic** a branch of logic which uses symbols instead of terms, propositions, etc in order to clarify reasoning. [Gr *symbolon* a token, from *syn* together, and *ballein* to throw]

symbole. An old spelling of **cymbal**.

symitar, **symitare**. *Obs* spellings of **scimitar**.

symmetallism or (*US*) **symmetalism** *si-met'ə-lizm*, *n* a monetary system in which an alloy of two or more metals in a fixed proportion is used as the standard of currency; advocacy of this system. — *adj* **symmetallic** (*-mi-tal'ik*). [Gr *syn-* together, and **metal**]

symmetry *sim'i-tri*, *n* exact correspondence of parts on either side of a straight line or plane, or about a centre or axis; balance or due proportion; beauty of form; disposition of parts, eg the method of arrangement of constituent parts of the animal body; the quality of remaining unchanged despite transformations in the surrounding environment or structure (*phys*). — *adj* **symm'etral** of symmetry. — *n* **symmetrian** (*si-met'ri-ən*) a person who studies or theorizes on the due proportions of things. — *adj* **symmet'ric** or **symmet'rical** having symmetry; actinomorphic (*bot* and *zool*). — *adv* **symmet'rically**. — *n* **symmet'ricalness**. — *n* **symmetrīzā'tion** or **-s-**. — *vt* **symm'etrize** or **-ise** to make symmetrical. — *n* **symmetrophō'bia** (Gr *phobos* fear) fear or dislike of symmetry. [Gr *symmetriā*, from *syn* together, and *metron* a measure]

sympathectomy *sim-pəth-ek'tə-mi*, (*surg*) *n* excision of part of a sympathetic nerve. [From **sympathetic**, and Gr *ektomē* excision]

sympathin *sim'pə-thin*, (*biochem*) *n* a substance, secreted by sympathetic nerve-endings, which constricts and dilates blood vessels. [From **sympathetic**]

sympathique *sɛ̃-pa-tēk*, (*Fr*) *adj* to one's taste, congenial, evoking a sense of affinity or harmony.

sympathy *sim'pə-thi*, *n* community of feeling; power of entering into another's feelings or mind; harmonious understanding; compassion, pity; affinity or correlation whereby one thing responds to the action of another or to action upon another; agreement; (often in *pl*) a feeling of agreement or support, or an expression of this. — *adj* **sympathet'ic** feeling, inclined to or expressing sympathy; in sympathy; acting or done in sympathy; induced by sympathy (as sounds in a resonating body); congenial; compassionate; of the sympathetic nervous system (see below); (a Gallicism) able to awake sympathy. — *adj* **sympathet'ical** (*obs*) sympathetic. — *adv* **sympathet'ically**. — *vi* **sym'pathize** or **-ise** to be in sympathy; to feel with or for another; to be compassionate; to be in accord, correspond. — *vt* (*Shakesp*) to be in sympathy, accord or harmony with; to combine harmoniously; to represent or understand sympathetically; *perh* to affect all alike. — *n* **sym'pathizer** or **-s-**. — *adj* (*med*) **sympatholyt'ic** inhibiting the action of the sympathetic nervous system. — *n* a drug which has this effect. — *adj* (*pharmacol*) **sympathomimet'ic** mimicking the action of the sympathetic nervous system. — *n* a drug which does this. — **sympathetic ink** see under **ink**; **sympathetic magic** magic depending upon a supposed sympathy, eg between a person and his or her name or portrait, between rainfall and libations; **sympathetic nervous system** a system of nerves supplying the involuntary muscles and glands, *esp* those originating from the cervical, thoracic and lumbar regions of the spinal cord; sometimes also including those from the brain and the sacral region (the **parasympathetic nervous system**); **sympathy** (or **sympathetic**) **strike** a strike in support of other workers, not in furtherance of the strikers' own claims. — **in sympathy (with)** in agreement (with), in support (of). [Gr *sympatheia*, from *syn* with, and *pathos* suffering]

sympatric *sim-pat'rik*, (*biol*) *adj* (eg of species) of, occurring in, or from the same geographical region, or overlapping regions, but which do not interbreed (cf **allopatric**). [**sym-**, Gr *patrā* fatherland, with suffix *-ic*]

sympetalous *sim-pet'ə-ləs*, (*bot*) *adj* having the petals united. — *n pl* **Sympet'alae** (*-lē*) a main division of dicotyledons, typically having united petals. [Gr *syn* together, and *petalon* leaf]

symphile *sim'fīl*, (*entomol*) *n* an animal of another kind kept as a guest or domestic animal in an ants' or termites' nest. — *n* **sym'philism** (*-fil-izm*) or **sym'phily**. — *adj* **sym'philous**. [Gr *symphiliā* mutual friendship, from *syn* together, and *philos* a friend]

symphony *sim'fə-ni*, *n* harmony, *esp* of sound; an orchestral composition on a great scale in sonata form (*music*); an instrumental portion of a primarily vocal work (*archaic*); a symphony orchestra; an *obs* name for various musical instruments (bagpipe, drum, hurdy-gurdy, virginal). — *adj* **symphonic** (*sim-fon'ik*). — *n* **symphō'nion** a combination of piano and harmonium. — *adj* **symphonious** (*-fō'ni-əs*) agreeing or harmonizing in sound; accordant; harmonious. — *n* **sym'phonist** a composer or (rarely) performer of symphonies. — **symphonic poem** a large orchestral composition in programme music with the movements run together; **symphony orchestra** a large orchestra comprising strings, woodwind, brass and percussion, capable of performing symphonies. [Gr *symphōniā* harmony, orchestra, from *syn* together, and *phōnē* a sound]

Symphyla *sim'fi-lə*, *n* a class or order of arthropods linking the bristle-tails with the centipedes. — *adj* **sym'phylous**. [Gr *symphȳlos* of the same race, from *syn* with, and *phȳlē*, *phȳlon* a race, clan]

symphysis *sim'fi-sis*, *n* the union or growing together of parts, concrescence (*zool*); union of bones by fusion, cartilage or ligament (*anatom*); a place of junction of parts (*bot* and *zool*). — *adj* **symphyseal** or **symphysial** (*sim-fiz'i-əl*). — *n* **symphyseot'omy** or **symphysiot'omy** (Gr *tomē* a cut; *surg*) the operation of cutting through the pubic symphysis. — *adj* **symphytic** (*-fit'ik*) by fusion. — *n* **Sym'phytum** the comfrey genus of the borage family, *perh* from its supposed virtue of closing wounds or healing fractures. [Gr *symphysis*, from *syn* with, and *phyein* to grow]

sympiesometer *sim-pi-i-zom'i-tər*, *n* a barometer with a gas instead of a vacuum; an instrument for measuring the pressure of a current. [Gr *sympiesis* a pressing together, from *syn* with, *piezein* to press, and *metron* a measure]

symplast *sim'pläst* or *-plast*, (*bot*) *n* the continuous network of protoplasts, linked by plasmodesmata, bounded by the cell membrane. [**sym-** and *-plast* (from Gr *plastos* formed, from *plassein* to form)]

symploce *sim'plō-sē*, (*rhetoric*) *n* the repetition of a word at the beginning and another at the end of successive clauses. [Gr *symplokē* an interweaving, from *syn* with, and *plekein* to weave]

sympodium *sim-pō'di-əm*, (*bot*) *n* a stem involved in sympodial growth: — *pl* **sympo'dia**. — *adj* **sympo'dial**. — *adv* **sympo'dially**. — **sympodial growth** a pattern of growth in which a shoot ceases to grow and one or more of the lateral buds next to the apical bud grow(s) out and repeat(s) the pattern. — Cf **monopodial growth**. [Gr *syn* together, and *pous*, *podos* foot]

symposium *sim-pō'zi-əm*, *n* a conference; a collection of views on one topic; a meeting for (*orig* philosophical) conversation; a drinking party (*hist*): — *pl* **sympō'sia**. — *adj* **sympō'siac** or **sympō'sial**. — *n* **sympō'siarch** (*-ärk*; Gr *archos* leader) the master, director, etc of the feast or conference. — *n* **sympō'siast** a person who takes part in a symposium. [Latinized from Gr *symposion*, from *syn* together, and *posis* drinking]

symptom *simp'təm* or *sim'təm*, *n* a subjective indication of a disease, ie something experienced by the patient, not outwardly visible (*med*); any abnormal sensation, or emotional expression or thought, accompanying disease or disorder of body or mind (*med*); (loosely) any objective evidence of disease or bodily disorder; a characteristic sign or indication of the existence of a state. — *adj* **symptomat'ic** or (now *rare*) **symptomat'ical**. — *adv* **symptomat'ically**. — *vt* **symp'tomatize** or **-ise** to be a symptom of. — *n* **symptomatol'ogy** the study of symptoms; the symptoms of a patient or a disease taken as a whole. — *adj* **symptomolog'ical**. — *n* **symptō'sis** wasting; emaciation. — *adj* **symptotic** (*-tot'ik*). [Gr *symptōma*, *symptōsis*, from *syn* with, and root of *piptein* to fall]

syn. *abbrev*: synonym; synthetic.

syn-, **sy-**, **syl-**, **sym-** or **sys-** *pfx* signifying together, with. [Gr *syn* with]

synadelphite *sin-ə-del'fīt*, (*mineralogy*) *n* a manganese aluminium arsenate. [Gr *syn* with, and *adelphos* brother, as found along with similar minerals]

synaeresis *sin-ē'rə-sis*, *n* the running together of two vowels into one or into a diphthong (*phonetics*); the spontaneous expulsion of liquid from a gel (*chem*). [Gr *syn* together, and *hairesis* taking, from *haireein* to take]

synaesthesia *sin-ēs-thē'zi-ə* or *-zhyə*, *n* sensation produced at a point different from the point of stimulation; a sensation of another kind suggested by one experienced (eg in colour-hearing). — *adj* **synaesthet'ic**. [Gr *syn* together, and *aisthēsis* sensation]

synagogue *sin'ə-gog*, *n* an assembly of Jews for worship and for instruction in the Torah; a Jewish place of worship. — *adj* **syn'agogal** (*-gō-gl*) or **synagog'ical** (*-gog'* or *-goj'i-kl*). [Gr *synagōgē*, from *syn* together, and *agōgē* a bringing, from *agein* to lead]

synallagmatic *sin-a-lag-mat'ik*, *adj* mutually or reciprocally obligatory. [Gr *synallagmatikos*, from *synallagma* a covenant, from *syn* together, and *allagma* exchange]

synaloepha *sin-ə-lē'fə*, (*gram*) *n* the melting of a final vowel or diphthong into the initial vowel or diphthong of the next word. [Latinized from Gr *synaloiphē*, from *synaleiphein* to coalesce, smear together, from *syn* together, and *aleiphein* to anoint]

synandrium *sin-an'dri-əm*, (*bot*) *n* a mass of united stamens. — *adj* **synan'drous** having united stamens. [Gr *syn* together, and *anēr* a man (male)]

synangium *sin-an'ji-əm*, *n* an arterial trunk (*anatom*); a group of united sporangia (found in Marattiaceae) (*bot*). [Gr *syn* together, and *angeion* a vessel]

synantherous *sin-an'thər-əs*, (*bot*) *adj* syngenesious. [Gr *syn*, and **anther**]

synanthesis *sin-an-thē'sis*, (*bot*) *n* simultaneous ripening of stamens and stigmas. — *adj* **synanthet'ic**. — *adj* **synan'thic** showing synanthy. — *adj* **synan'thous** synanthic; flowering and leafing simultaneously. — *n* **synan'thy** abnormal fusion of flowers. [Gr *syn* together, and *anthēsis* flowering, from *anthos* a flower]

synaphea or **synapheia** *sin-ə-fē'ə*, (*prosody*) *n* metrical continuity between verses in a system, so that they can be scanned as one verse, as in anapaestics, with possibility of elision at the end of a line. [Gr *synapheia*, from *syn* together, and *haph-*, root of *haptein* to join]

synaposematism *sin-ap-ō-sē'mə-tizm*, (*biol*) *n* warning coloration common to a number of dangerous species in the same region. — *adj* **synaposematic** (*-mat'ik*). [Gr *syn* together, and **aposematism**]

synapsis *sin-aps'is*, *n* the pairing of chromosomes of paternal and maternal origin before the reducing division (*biol*); a synapse (*med*): — *pl* **synaps'es** (*-ēz*). — *n* **synapse'** (also *sin'* or *sīn'*; *med*) an interlacing or enveloping connection of one nerve-cell with another. — *n* **synapt'ase** emulsin. — *n* **synapte** (*sin-ap'tē*) in the Greek Church, a litany. — *adj* **synapt'ic**. [Gr *synapsis* contact, junction, from *syn* together, and *haptein* to fasten; *synaptē* (*euchē*, a prayer), joined together]

synarchy *sin'ər-ki*, *n* joint sovereignty. [Gr *synarchiā*, from *syn* with, and *archein* to rule]

synarthrosis *sin-ər-thrō'sis*, (*anatom*) *n* immovable articulation: — *pl* **synarthroses** (*-sēz*). — *adj* **synarthrō'dial**. — *adv* **synarthrō'dially**. [Gr *synarthrōsis*, from *syn* together, and *arthron* a joint; also *arthrōdiā* a flattish joint]

synastry *sin-as'tri*, (*astrol*) *n* a coincidence of stellar influences; comparison of the horoscopes of two or more people. [Gr *syn* together, and *astron* a star]

synaxis *si-nak'sis*, *n* in the early Church, meeting for worship, *esp* for the eucharist. — *n* **synaxā'rion** (*Gr Ch*) a lection containing an account of a saint's life. [Gr *synaxis* a bringing together, from *syn* together, and *agein* to lead]

sync or **synch** *singk*, *n*, *vi* and *vt* short for **synchronization** and **synchronise**. — **in sync** synchronized; running together correctly, sharing a common rhythm, time, pattern, etc; matching, harmonious; **out of sync** (or **synch**) not synchronized; having different and jarring rhythms; (loosely) ill-matched (with *with*).

syncarp *sin'kärp*, (*bot*) *n* a compound fruit formed from two or more carpels, of one or more than one flower. — *adj* **syncarpous** (*sin-kär'pəs*) of or having united carpels. — *n* **syn'carpy**. [Gr *syn* together, and *karpos* a fruit]

syncategorematic *sin-kat-i-gor-i-mat'ik*, (*linguistics*) *adj* not able to form a term without other words. — *adv* **syncategoremat'ically**. [Gr *synkatēgorēmatikos*, from *syn* with, and *katēgorēma* predicate]

synch. See **sync**.

synchondrosis *sing-kon-drō'sis*, (*anatom*) *n* connection of bones by cartilage: — *pl* **synchondro'ses** (*-sēz*). [Gr *synchondrōsis*, from *syn* with, and *chondros* a cartilage]

synchoresis *sing-kō-rē'sis*, (*rhetoric*) *n* a concession, *esp* one made for the sake of a more effective retort. [Gr *synchōrēsis*, from *synchōreein* to agree, yield ground, from *syn* with, and *chōros* space]

synchro *sin'krō*. See **synchronized swimming** (under **synchronal**).

synchrocyclotron *sing-krō-sī'klō-tron*. See under **accelerate**.

synchroflash *sing'krō-flash*, (*photog*) *n* a mechanism which synchronizes the opening of a camera shutter with the peak of brilliance of a flash bulb. [*synchronized flash*]

synchromesh *sing'krō-mesh*, *adj* of a gear in which the speeds of the driving and driven members are automatically synchronized before coupling, so as to avoid shock and noise in gear-changing. — *n* such a gear. [*synchronized mesh*]

synchronal *sing'krə-nl*, *adj* coinciding in time. — *adj* **synchronic** (*-kron'ik*) or **synchron'ical** synchronous; concerned with the study of a subject (*esp* a language) at a particular period, without considering the past or the future (opposed to *diachronic*). — *adv* **synchron'ically**. — *n* **synchronicity** (*-is'i-ti*). — *n* **synch'ronism** coincidence in time; simultaneity; keeping time together; occurrence of similar phrases at the same time; exhibition of contemporary history in one scheme; the bringing together of different parts of a story (occurring at different times) in one picture or work of art. — *adj* **synchronis'tic** or (*rare*) **synchronis'tical**. — *adv* **synchronis'tically**. — *n* **synchronīzā'tion** or **-s-**. — *vi* **syn'chronize** or **-ise** to coincide or agree in time. — *vt* to cause to coincide or agree in time; to time together or to a standard; to represent or identify as contemporary; to make (the soundtrack of a film) exactly simultaneous with the picture (*TV* and *cinema*). — *n* **synch'ronizer** or **-s-** that which, or someone who, synchronizes; a synchroscope; a unit for maintaining synchronism when transmitting data between two devices (*comput*). — *n* **synchronol'ogy** chronological arrangement side by side. — *adj* **synch'ronous** simultaneous; contemporary; keeping time together. — *adv* **synch'ronously**. — *n* **synch'ronousness**. — *n* **synch'rony** simultaneity. — **synchronized swimming** (also *colloq* **synchro swimming** or **synch'ro**) a sport in which a swimmer or group of swimmers performs a sequence of gymnastic and balletic movements in time to music; **synchronous motor** an electric motor whose speed is exactly proportional to the frequency of the supply current; **synchronous orbit** geostationary orbit; **synchronous transmission** (*comput*) transmission of data along communication lines at a fixed rate and in a continuous string. [Gr *syn* together, and *chronos* time]

synchroscope *sin'krō-skōp*, (*elec eng*) *n* an instrument which indicates the difference in frequency between two AC supplies. [*synchro*nism, and **-scope**]

synchrotron *sing'krō-tron*, (*phys*) *n* a type of very high-energy particle accelerator. — **synchrotron radiation** electromagnetic radiation emitted by charged particles passing through magnetic fields, produced in the form of a very intense polarized beam, with important uses for analysing the structure and behaviour of substances. [Gr *syn* together, *chronos* time, and electr*on*]

synchysis *sing'ki-sis*, *n* confusion of meaning due to unusual arrangement (*rhetoric*); fluidity of the vitreous humour of the eye (*pathol*). [Gr, from *syn* together, with, and *cheein* to pour]

synclastic *sin-klas'tik*, (*geom*) *adj* having the same kind of curvature in all directions. [Gr *syn* together, and *klastos* broken]

syncline *sin'klīn*, (*geol*) *n* a fold in which the beds dip downwards towards the axis. — *adj* **synclīn'al**. — *n* a syncline. — *n* **synclinorium** (*-kli-nō'ri-əm* or *-nö'*) a great synclinal structure carrying minor flexures: — *pl* **synclino'ria**. [Gr *syn* together, and *klīnein* to cause to lean]

Syncom *sin'kom*, *n* one of a series of communication satellites in a synchronous orbit. [*syn*chronous *com*munications satellite]

syncope *sing'kə-pi*, *n* the elision of a letter or syllable from the middle of a word; a fainting fit caused by a sudden fall of blood pressure in the brain (*med*); a cutting short (*rare*); syncopation (*obs*). — *adj* **sync'opal** of syncope. — *vt* **sync'opate** to shorten by cutting out the middle (of a word); to alter the rhythm of (music, etc) temporarily by transferring the accent to a normally unaccented beat. — *adj* **sync'opated**. — *n* **syncopa'tion**. — *n* **sync'opātor**. — *adj* **syncopic** (*sing-kop'ik*). — *adj* **syncopt'ic**. [Gr *synkopē* a cutting up, cutting short, syncope, from *syn* together, and *koptein* to cut off]

syncretism *sing'kri-tizm* or *sin'*, *n* reconciliation of, or attempt to reconcile, different systems of belief, *esp* of different forms of Christianity, by German Lutheran Georg Calixtus (1586–1656); fusion or blending of religions, as by identification of gods, taking over of observances, or selection of whatever seems best in each (*usu derog*); illogical compromise in religion; the fusion of *orig* distinct inflectional forms of a word (*hist linguistics*). — *adj* **syncretic** (*sin-krē'tik* or *sing-*). — *n* **syn'cretist**. — *adj* **syncretis'tic**. — *vt* and *vi* **syncretize** or **-ise** (*sing'kri-tīz*). [Gr *synkrētismos* a confederation (orig appar of *Cretan* communities)]

syncytium *sin-sit'i-əm*, (*biol*) *n* a multinucleate cell; a tissue without distinguishable cell-walls: — *pl* **syncyt'ia**. — *adj* **syncyt'ial**. [Gr *syn* together, and *kytos* a vessel]

synd or **sind** *sīnd*, (*Northern*) *vt* (*esp* with *out*) to rinse; to wash out or down. — *n* a rinsing; a washing down with liquor. — *n pl* **synd'ings** or **sind'ings**. — Also **syne** (*Burns*). [Origin obscure]

synd. *abbrev*: syndicate.

syndactyl *sin-dak'til*, (*zool*) *adj* having fused digits, as do many birds and lower mammals. — *n* **syndac'tylism**. — *adj* **syndac'tylous**. — *n* **syndac'tyly**. [Gr *syn* together, and *daktylos* finger, toe]

synderesis. See **synteresis**.

syndesis *sin'di-sis*, *n* (*obs*) a binding; synapsis (*biol*). — *adj* **syndetic** (*-det'ik*) or **syndet'ical** connective; of a construction in which clauses are connected by conjunctions (*gram*). — *adv* **syndet'ically**. [Gr *syndesis*, from *syn* together, and *deein* to bind]

syndesmosis *sin-des-mō'sis*, (*zool*) *n* the connection of bones by ligaments: — *pl* **syndesmo'ses** (*-sēz*). — *adj* **syndesmotic** (*-mot'ik*). [Gr *syndesmos*, from *syn* together, and *desmos* a bond]

syndet *sin'det*, *n* *syn*thetic *det*ergent.

syndetic, etc. See under **syndesis**.

syndic *sin'dik*, *n* a person chosen to transact business for others, *esp* the accredited legal representative of a corporation, society or company; a member of a committee of the Senate of Cambridge University; (at various times and places) a magistrate or mayor; (in ancient Greece) an advocate, delegate or judge. — *adj* **syn'dical** (**syndical chamber** or **union** a French trade-union). — *n* **syn'dicalism** a development of trade-unionism which originated in France, aiming at putting the means of production in the hands of unions of workers. — *n* **syn'dicalist**. — Also *adj*. — *adj* **syndicalist'ic**. — *n* **syn'dicate** (*-di-kət*) a body of syndics; a council; the office of a syndic; a body of people chosen to watch the interests of a company, or to manage a bankrupt's property; a combination of people for some common purpose or interest; an association of business people or companies to undertake a project requiring a large amount of capital; an association of criminals who organize and control illegal operations; a combined group of newspapers. — *vt* (*-kāt*) to control, effect, or publish by means of a syndicate; to sell (eg an article) for simultaneous publication in a number of newspapers or periodicals; to sell radio or TV programmes for broadcasting by many different radio or TV stations; to join in a syndicate; to judge, censure (*obs*). — *vi* to join in a syndicate. — *n* **syndicā'tion**. — *n* **syn'dicātor**. [Gr *syndikos*, from *syn* with, and *dikē* justice]

syndrome *sin'drōm* (or formerly *sin'drə-mi* or *-mē*, *sin'drō-mi* or *-mē*), *n* concurrence, *esp* (*pathol*) of symptoms; a characteristic pattern or group of symptoms; a pattern or group of actions, feelings, observed happenings, etc, characteristic of a particular problem or condition. — *adj* **syndromic** (*-drom'ik*). [Gr *syndromē*]

syndyasmian *sin-di-az'mi-ən*, (*anthropol*) *adj* pairing, applied to a form of family founded on a loose temporary marriage. [Gr *syndyasmos* coupling]

syne[1] *sīn*, (*Scot*) *adv* then, next; afterwards, later; ago, since (as in *auld lang syne*). [**sithen**]

syne[2]. See **synd**.

synecdoche *sin-ek'də-kē* or *-ki*, (*rhetoric*) *n* a figure of speech in which a part is used to refer to the whole, or vice versa, as in *wiser heads* used to mean wiser people. — *adj* **synecdochic** (*-dok'ik*) or **synechdoch'ical**. — *adv* **synecdoch'ically**. — *n* **synec'dochism** use of synecdoche; use of part for the whole in sympathetic magic. [Gr *synekdochē*, from *syn* together, and *ekdechesthai* to receive]

synechia *sin-e-kī'ə* or *sin-ē'ki-ə*, (*pathol*) *n* abnormal adhesion, *esp* of the iris to the cornea or to the lens. [Gr *synecheia* continuity, from *syn* together, and *echein* to hold]

synecology *sin-ē-kol'ə-ji*, *n* the ecological study of communities of plants or animals. — *adj* **synecolog'ic** or **synecolog'ical**. — *adv* **synecolog'ically**. — *n* **synecol'ogist**. [Gr *syn* together, (**syn-**) and **ecology**]

synecphonesis *sin-ek-fō-nē'sis*, (*phonetics*) *n* synizesis. [Gr *syn* together, and *ekphōnēsis* pronunciation, from *ek* out, and *phōnē* voice, utterance]

synectics *sin-ek'tiks*, *n sing* the study of processes leading to invention, with the end aim of solving practical problems, *esp* by a **synectics group**, a miscellaneous group of people of imagination and ability but varied interests. — *adj* **synec'tic**. — *adv* **synec'tically**. [Gr *synektikos* fit for holding together]

synedrion *sin-ed'ri-on*, *n* a judicial assembly; (*specif*) a sanhedrin. — Also **syned'rium**: — *pl* (of both) **syned'ria**. — *adj* **syned'rial**. [Gr *syn* together, and *hedrā* seat]

syneidesis *sin-ī-dē'sis*, (*hist theol*) *n* conscience as passing judgement on past acts (as opposed to *synteresis*). [Gr *syneidēsis* conscience, from *syn* with, together, and *eidenai* to know]

syneresis. Same as **synaeresis**.

synergy *sin'ər-ji*, *n* combined or co-ordinated action. — *adj* **synergetic** (*-jet'ik*) or **syner'gic** working together. — *n* **syner'gid** (*bot*) either of the two cells in the embryo-sac that seem to guide the pollen-tube. — *n* **synergism** (*sin'* or *-ûr'*) the doctrine (ascribed to Melanchthon) that the human will and the Divine Spirit are two efficient agents that co-operate in regeneration (*theol*); increased effect of two substances, *esp* drugs, obtained by using them together; (more generally) the working together of a number of individuals for greater effect. — *n* **syn'ergist** (or *-ûr'*) a substance which increases the effect of another (eg pesticide); a muscle, etc that acts with another. — *adj* **synergist'ic**. — *adv* **synergist'ically**. — *vi* **syn'ergize** or **-ise** to act as a synergist (with another substance). [Gr *synergiā* co-operation, from *syn* together, and *ergon* work]

synesis *sin'ə-sis*, *n* syntax having regard to meaning rather than grammatical form. [Gr, sense]

synfuel *sin'fū-əl*, *n* any type of fuel synthesized from a fossil fuel. [*syn*thetic and **fuel**]

syngamy *sing'gə-mi*, (*biol*) *n* free interbreeding; union of gametes. — *adj* **syngamic** (*sin-gam'ik*) or **syngamous** (*sing'gə-məs*). [Gr *syn* together, and *gamos* marriage]

syngas *sin'gas*, *n* a mixture of hydrogen and carbon monoxide, from which various hydrocarbons (eg methanol and gasoline) can be synthesized. [*syn*thesis and **gas**]

syngeneic *sin-ji-nē'ik* or *-nā'ik*, (*immunol*) *adj* genetically identical. [Gr *syngeneia* kinship]

syngenesis *sin-jen'i-sis*, *n* (*biol*) reproduction by fusion of male and female elements, the offspring being derived from both parents. — *n pl* **Syngenesia** (*sin-ji-nē'si-ə*) in the Linnaean system, a class of plants with syngenesious stamens, corresponding to the Compositae. — *adj* **syngene'sious** (*bot*) having the anthers united in a tube around the style, as in Compositae. — *adj* **syngenetic** (*-net'ik*) of or by syngenesis; (of minerals) formed contemporaneously with the enclosing rock. [Gr *syn* together, and *genesis* formation, generation]

syngnathous *sin-* or *sing'gna-thəs*, also *sing'nath-*, (*zool*) *adj* (of certain fish) having the jaws fused to form a tubular structure. — *n pl* **Syngnathidae** (*sin-* or *sing-gnath'i-dē*, also *sing-nath'*) the pipefish family. [Gr *syn* together, and *gnathos* jaw]

syngraph *sing'gräf*, (*rare*) *n* a writing, eg a contract, signed by both or all of the parties to it. [Gr *syn* together, and *graphein* to write]

synizesis *sin-i-zē'sis*, *n* the union into one syllable of two vowels without forming a recognized diphthong (*phonetics*); contraction of chromatin towards one side in karyokinesis (*cytology*). [Gr *synizēsis* a collapse, from *syn* with, together, and *hizein* to seat, to sit down]

synkaryon *sin-kar'i-ən*, (*biol*) *n* a cell nucleus formed by the fusion of two separate nuclei, or (as in fungal hypha) a pair of nuclei in close association. [Gr *syn* together, and *karyon* kernel]

synod *sin'əd*, *n* an ecclesiastical council; a Presbyterian church court intermediate between presbytery and the General Assembly; the supreme court of the former United Presbyterian Church; conjunction (*astron*; *obs*). — *adj* **syn'odal** of, of the nature of, or done in a synod. — *n* a payment made by a clergyman on the occasion of a synod, or at a visitation. — *adj* **synodic** (*-od'ik*) or **synod'ical** synodal; pertaining to conjunction (*astron*); from conjunction to conjunction (see **synodic month** under **month**). — *adv* **synod'ically**. — **synodic period** (*astron*) the time between two successive conjunctions of a heavenly body with the sun; **syn'odsman** a lay member of a synod. — **General Synod of the Church of England** the governing body set up in 1970 giving the laity more say in the decisions of the Church. [Gr *synodos* a meeting, conjunction, from *syn* together, and *hodos* a way]

synoecete *sin-ē'sēt* or **sinoekete** *-kēt*, *n* a guest tolerated with indifference in an ants' or termites' nest. — *n* **synoeciosis** (*-si-ō'sis*) the rhetorical figure of coupling opposites. — *adj* **synoecious** (*-ē'shəs*) or **synoicous** (*-oi'kəs*; *bot*) having antheridia and archegonia in the same group. — *n* **synoe'cism** union of communities or cities. — *vt* and *vi* **syn'oecize** or **-ise** (*-ē-sīz*) to unite in one community or city-state. — *n* **synoecology** (*-kol'ə-ji*) same as **synecology**. [Gr *synoikia* a living together, community, *synoiketēs* a house-fellow, *synoikizein* to unite in one community, from *syn* with, and *oikeein* to dwell]

synonym *sin'ə-nim*, *n* a word having the same meaning as another in the same language (*usu* very nearly the same meaning); a word or term used as an alternative to another of the same meaning; a systematic name to which another is preferred as valid (*biol*). — *adj* **synonymatic** (*sin-on-i-mat'ik*), **synonym'ic** or **synonym'ical** of, consisting of, relating to, etc synonyms. — *n* **synonym'icon** a dictionary of synonyms. — *n* **synon'ymist** a person who studies synonyms, or the different names of plants and animals. — *n* **synonym'ity** the fact or quality of being synonymous. — *vt* **synon'ymize** or **-ise** to be synonymous with, or a synonym for; to give, or analyse, the synonyms of (*rare*); (loosely) to exemplify, embody (*colloq*). — *adj* **synon'ymous** having the same meaning. — *adv* **synon'ymously**. — *n* **synon'ymousness**. — *n* **synon'ymy** rhetorical use of synonyms; a setting forth of synonyms; a list of synonyms. [Gr *synōnymon*, from *syn* with, and *onoma* a name]

synop. *abbrev*: synopsis.

synopsis *sin-op'sis*, *n* a general view; a summary or outline (*esp* of a book): — *pl* **synop'sēs**. — *vt* **synop'size** or **-ise** to make a synopsis of. — *adj* **synop'tic** or **synop'tical** affording or taking a general view of the whole. — *adv* **synop'tically**. — *n* **synop'tist** one of the writers of the Synoptic Gospels. — *adj* **synoptis'tic**. — **Synoptic Gospels** those of Matthew, Mark and Luke, which can readily be said to have been written from a common point of view. [Gr *synopsis*, from *syn* with, together, and *opsis* a view]

synostosis *sin-os-tō'sis*, (*anatom*) *n* complete union of bones: — *pl* **synosto'ses** (*-ēz*). [Gr *syn* with, together, and *osteon* bone]

synovia *sin-ō'vi-ə*, *n* (*physiol*) a viscous, glair-like lubricating fluid in the joints and in the tendon sheaths and capsular ligaments surrounding joints. — *adj* **syno'vial**. — *adj* **synovitic** (*-vit'ik*) pertaining to synovitis. — *n* **synovī'tis** (*med*) inflammation of a synovial membrane. — **synovial membrane** (*anatom*) a membrane of connective tissue that lines tendon sheaths and capsular ligaments and secretes synovia. [Appar an arbitrary coinage of Paracelsus, who applied it more generally]

synroc *sin'rok*, *n* a type of synthetic rock developed especially to fuse with radioactive waste and remain stable over geological time, for burial deep underground. [*syn*thetic *roc*k]

syntactic, **syntagma**, etc. See under **syntax**.

syntan *sin'tan*, *n* a *syn*thetic *tan*ning agent.

syntax *sin'taks*, *n* grammatical structure in sentences; one of the classes in some RC schools; systematic order or arrangement of elements; a set of rules for combining the elements of a programming language into permitted constructions (*comput*). — *adj* **syntac'tic** or **syntac'tical**. — *adv* **syntac'tically**. — *n* **syntag'ma** or (*rare*) **syntagm** (*sin'tam*) a systematic body, system or group; a word or words constituting a syntactic unit (*linguistics*): — *pl* **syntag'mata** or (*rare*) **syntagms**. — *adj* **syntagmat'ic**. — *n* **syntag'matite** a kind of hornblende. [Gr *syntaxis*, from *syn* together, and *tassein* to put in order]

syntectic, **syntectical**. See under **syntexis**.

syntenosis *sin-tə-nō'sis*, (*zool*) *n* the connection of bones by tendons: — *pl* **syntenoses** (*-ō'sēz*). [Gr *syn* with, and *tenōn* a sinew]

synteresis *sin-ti-rē'sis*, *n* conscience as a guide to future action (as opposed to *syneidesis*). — Also **synderē'sis** (from the later *Gr* pronunciation). [Gr *syntērēsis* observation, from *syn* with, and *tēreein* to watch over]

syntexis *sin-tek'sis*, *n* (*rare*) liquefaction; melting; wasting. — *adj* (*obs*) **syntec'tic** or **syntec'tical**. [Gr *syntēxis*, from *syn* with, and *tēkein* to melt]

synth *sinth*, *n* short for synthesizer. — Also *adj*.

synthesis *sin'thi-sis*, *n* building up; putting together; making a whole out of parts; the combination of separate elements of thought into a whole; reasoning from principles to a conclusion (as opposed to *analysis*): — *pl* **syn'theses** (*sēz*). — *n* **syn'thesist** someone who makes a synthesis. — *vt* **syn'thesize** or **-ise** to put together in synthesis; to form by synthesis. — *n* **syn'thesīzer** or **-s-** a person who, or thing which, synthesizes; a computerized instrument for generating sounds, often beyond the range of conventional instruments, used *esp* in making electronic music. — *adj* **synthetic** (*-thet'*) or **synthet'ical** pertaining to, consisting in, or formed by, synthesis; artificially produced but of similar nature to, not a mere substitute for, the natural product; not sincere, sham (*colloq*). — *n* **synthet'ic** a synthetic substance. — *adv* **synthet'ically**. — *n* **synthet'icism** the principles of synthesis, a synthetic system. — *vt* **syn'thetize** or **-ise** to synthesise. — *n* **syn'thetīzer** or **-s-**, or **syn'thetist**. — **synthesis gas** syngas (see separate entry); **synthetic aperture radar** a radar system that produces finely detailed images, an increased antenna aperture being obtained by integrating individual readings from the same area as the aircraft or spacecraft moves over it (*abbrev* **SAR**); **synthetic drug** a drug made in the laboratory, whether one occurring naturally or an artificial one; **synthetic languages** those that use inflectional forms instead of word order, prepositions, etc to express syntactical relationships; **synthetic philosophy** Herbert Spencer's system, a fusion, as he thought, of the different sciences into a whole. [Gr *synthesis*, from *syn* with, together, amd *thesis* a placing]

synthon *sin'thon*, (*chem*) *n* (within a molecule to be synthesized) a constituent part which can be readily used in the synthesis process. [*synth*etic and i*on*]

synthronus *sin'thrə-nəs*, (*eccles hist* or *Gr Ch*) *n* the seat of the bishop and his presbyters, behind the altar. [Gr *syn* together, and *thronos* a throne]

syntony *sin'tən-i*, *n* (*elec eng*; *old*) tuning, or agreement in resonance frequency, of radio apparatus. — *adj* **syntonic** (*sin-ton'ik*) tuned together (*music*); showing a normal emotional response to one's environment (*psychol*). — *n* **syn'tonin** (*biol*) a substance similar to fibrin, found in muscle. — *vt* **syn'tonize** or **-ise** (*elec*) to adjust to agree in frequency. — *adj* **syn'tonous** (*music*) syntonic. [Gr *syn* together, and *tonos* tone]

sype. Same as **sipe**[1].

sypher *sī'fər*, (*carpentry*) *vt* to lay (the chamfered edge of a plank) over that of another to make a flush surface. [Variant of **cipher**]

syphilis *sif'i-lis*, (*med* and *pathol*) *n* a contagious venereal disease due to infection with a micro-organism *Spirochaeta pallida* (*Treponema pallidum*). — *adj* **syphilit'ic**. — *n* a person suffering from syphilis. — *n* **syphilīzā'tion** or -s-. — *vt* **syph'ilize** or **-ise** to inoculate or infect with syphilis. — *adj* **syph'iloid** like syphilis. — *n* **syphilol'ogist**. — *n* **syphilol'ogy** the study of syphilis. — *n* **syphilō'ma** a syphilitic tumour. — *n* **syphilophō'bia** a morbid dread of syphilis. [Title of Fracastoro's Latin poem (1530), whose hero *Syphilus* is infected]

syphon and **syren**. Same as **siphon** and **siren**.

SYR *abbrev*: Syria (IVR).

Syrah *sīr'ə*, *n* a red wine grape; (also without *cap*) wine made from this. [The ancient Persian City of *Shiraz*, where the grape is supposed to have originated]

Syriac *sir'i-ak*, *n* the ancient Aramaic dialect of *Syria*; a modern form of this dialect still spoken in the Middle East and in the USA. — Also *adj*. — *n* **Syr'iacism** (*-ə-sizm*), **Syr'ianism**, **Syr'iasm** or (*rare*) **Syr'ism** a Syriac idiom. — *adj* **Syr'ian** relating to Syria. — *n* a native or citizen of Syria. — *n* **Syr'iarch** (*-ärk*; Gr *Syriarchēs*; *hist*) the chief priest in Roman Syria. — *n* **Syrophoenicia** (*sī-rō-fi-nish'yə*; *hist*) a Roman province between Lebanon and the coast. — *n* and *adj* **Syrophoeni'cian**.

syringa *sir-ing'gə*, *n orig* (and still popularly) the mock-orange; the lilac; (with *cap*) after Linnaeus, the generic name of the lilac. [New L, from Gr *syrinx* (from its stems being used for pipes; see ety for **syrinx**)]

syringe *si-rinj'*, *n* an instrument for injecting or extracting fluids. — *vt* and *vi* to clean, spray or inject with a syringe. [Ety as for **syrinx**]

syringeal ... to ... **syringotomy**. See under **syrinx**.

syrinx *sir'ingks*, *n* Pan-pipes; the vocal organ of birds; a fistula or fistulous opening (*pathol*); a rock-cut tunnel, as in Egyptian tombs (*archaeol*): — *pl* **syringes** (*-in'jēz*) or **syr'inxes**. — *adj* **syringeal** (*-in'ji-əl*). — *n* **syringitis** (*-jī'tis*; *med*) inflammation of the Eustachian tube. — *n* **syringomyelia** (*si-ring-gō-mī-ē'li-ə*; Gr *myelos* marrow; *pathol*) a chronic, progressive disease of the spinal cord, causing paralysis and loss of sensitivity to pain and temperature. — *n* **syringotomy** (*sir-ing-got'ə-mi*; *surg*) cutting of a fistula. [Gr *sȳrinx*, *-ingos* Pan-pipes, channel, tube]

syrlye. An old form (*Spenser*) of **surly**.

Syrophoenicia, **Syrophoenician**. See under **Syriac**.

Syrphus *sûr'fəs*, *n* a genus of wasp-like flies that hover and dart, giving the name to the family **Syr'phidae** (*-fi-dē*). — *n* and *adj* **syr'phid**. [Gr *syrphos* gnat]

syrtis *sûr'tis*, (*Milton*) *n* a patch or area of quicksand: — *pl* **syr'tes** (*-tēz*). [L *Syrtēs*, Gr *Syrtides* (singular of each *Syrtis*), name of two sandy bays of N Africa, from Gr *sȳrein* to draw, sweep along]

syrup *sir'əp*, *n* a saturated solution of sugar boiled to prevent fermentation; any thick sweet liquid; a sugar-flavoured liquid medicine; cloying sweetness (*fig*; *colloq*). — *vt* to make into syrup; to cover, fill, etc with syrup. — Also (*esp US*) **sir'up**. — *adj* **syr'upy**. — **golden syrup** the uncrystallizable part left over from the manufacture of crystallized sugar, a golden-yellow, clear syrup used in baking, etc. [Fr *sirop*, from Ar *sharāb*; cf **shrub**[2] and **sherbet**]

sys-. See **syn-**.

sysop *sis'op*, (*comput*) *n* short for **system operator**, a person who runs an on-line bulletin board, keeping information on the system up-to-date and dealing with faults and queries.

syssarcosis *sis-är-kō'sis*, (*zool* and *anatom*) *n* the connection of one bone with another by intervening muscle: — *pl* **syssarcoses** (*-ō'sēz*). [Gr *syn* together, and *sarx* flesh]

syssitia *si-sit'i-ə* or *-sish'*, *n* the ancient Spartan custom of eating the main meal together in public. [Gr *syssītiā*, from *syn* together, and *sītos* food]

systaltic *sis-tal'tik*, *adj* alternately contracting and dilating, pulsatory. [Gr *systaltikos* depressing; cf **systole**]

system *sis'tim* or *-təm*, *n* anything formed of parts placed together or adjusted into a regular and connected whole; a set of things considered as a connected whole; a group of heavenly bodies moving mainly under the influence of their mutual attraction (*astron*); a set of bodily organs of similar composition or concurring in function; the bodily organism; one of the great divisions of the geological strata, subordinate only to the division into Palaeozoic, Mesozoic and Cainozoic; a plan of action; a method of procedure; a method of organization; an organized set of computer components (hardware) which interact to allow the processing of data; the operating procedures and computer hardware and software required to process data in a given application; methodicalness; a systematic treatise; (with *the*, often with *cap*) society seen as a soulless and monolithic organization thwarting individual effort; a group of (Greek) verses; a body of doctrine; a theory of the universe; a full and connected view of some department of knowledge; an explanatory hypothesis; a scheme of classification; a manner of crystallization. — *adj* **systemat'ic** or **systemat'ical** pertaining to, consisting of, for the purpose of, observing, or according to system; methodical; habitual; intentional. — *adv* **systemat'ically**. — *n* **systematician** (*-ə-tish'ən*). — *n sing* **systemat'ics** the science of classification; the study of classification of living things in accordance with their natural relationships. — *n* **sys'tematism**. — *n* **sys'tematist**. — *n* **systematīzā'tion** or -s- or **systemīzā'tion** or -s-. — *vt* **sys'tematize** or **-ise**, **sys'temize** or **-ise** to reduce to a system. — *n* **sys'tematizer** or -s-. — *n* **systematol'ogy**. — *adj* **sys'temed**. — *adj* **systemic** (*-tem'ik*) pertaining to the bodily system or to a system of bodily organs; affecting the body as a whole; (of a pesticide, etc) spreading through all the tissues, without harming the plant but making it toxic to the insect, etc; (of a herbicide) spreading through all the tissues of a plant and killing it. — *adj* **sys'temless** without system; not exhibiting organic structure. — **system building** building using standardized factory-produced components. — *adj* **sys'tem-built**. — **sys'tem-maker** or **-monger** someone unduly fond of constructing systems; **systems analysis**; **systems analyst** a person who analyses the operation of a scientific, commercial, industrial, etc procedure, *usu* with a computer, in order to plan more efficient methods, better use of equipment, or the introduction of computers into the operation; **systems engineering** a branch of engineering that uses information theory and systems analysis to design integrated systems; **systems flowchart** (*comput*) a flowchart designed to analyse the operation of a computing system with a view to improving it; **systems program** (*comput*) a software program which controls the operation of a computer system (as opposed to an *applications program*); **systems software** (*comput*) a set of programs used to run the operating system of a computer, making it usable and controlling its performance. [Gr *systēma*, from *sy-*, *syn-* together, and the root of *histanai* to set]

systole *sis'to-lē* or *-tə-lē*, *n* rhythmical contraction, *esp* of the heart (as opposed to *diastole*; *physiol*); collapse of the nucleus in mitosis; the shortening of a long syllable (*gram*). — *adj* **systolic** (*-tol'ik*). [Gr *systolē*, from *syn* together, and *stellein* to place]

systyle *sis'tīl*, (*archit*) *adj* having an intercolumniation of two diameters. — *n* such an arrangement; a building or part constructed in this way. [Gr *systȳlos*, from *sy-*, *syn-* together, and *stȳlos* a column]

sythe (*Spenser*). See **sith**[2].

syver or **siver** *sī'vər*, (*Scot*) *n* a drain; a grating over a drain. [Perh a form of **sewer** (see **sew**[3])]

syzygy *siz'i-ji*, *n* conjunction or opposition; the period of new or full moon (*astron*); a dipody (*classical prosody*): — *pl* **syz'ygies**. — *adj* **syzyg'ial**. [Gr *syzygiā* union, coupling, from *sy-*, *syn-* with, together, and *zygon* a yoke]

Szekely *sek'ə-li*, *n* a Transylvanian Magyar. — Also **Szekel** (*sekl*) or **Szekler** (*sek'lər*). [Hung *sēkel* to reside]

T

T, t *tē, n* the twentieth letter in the modern English alphabet, eighteenth in the Roman, *usu* sounded as a voiceless stop produced with the tip of the tongue in contact with teeth, gums or palate; an object or mark in the form of the letter T (also **tee**); as a medieval Roman numeral T = 160, T̄ = 160 000. — **T'-band'age** a bandage composed of two strips fashioned in the shape of the letter T; **T'-bar** a metal bar with cross-section in the shape of the letter T; a type of ski-lift (also **T'-bar lift**); **T'-bone** a bone shaped like a T, *esp* in a large steak cut from the sirloin of beef; **T'-cart** a four-wheeled, horse-drawn carriage, *usu* used for pleasure-trips, with a T-shaped body; **T'-cell** a type of lymphocyte involved in cellular immunity, that matures (in mammals) in the *t*hymus gland, eg a *cytotoxic T-cell* able to kill virus-infected cells; **T'-cloth** a plain cotton made for the India and China market, stamped with a T; **T'-cross** a tau cross; **T'-group** (*psychol*) (sensitivity-*t*raining *group*) an encounter group whose purpose is to improve the communication skills of individual members by discussion and analysis of the roles that they each adopt habitually in their dealings with others; **T'-junction** a road junction in the shape of a T; **T'-lymphocyte** a T-cell; **T'-plate** a T-shaped plate, eg for strengthening a joint in a wooden framework; **T'-rail** a rail with T-shaped cross-section. — *adj* **T'-shaped**. — **T'-shirt** see under **tee**[1]; **T'-square** a T-shaped ruler; **T'-strap** a T-shaped strap on a shoe. — **marked with a T** branded as thief; **to a T** with perfect exactness.

T or **T.** *abbrev*: tenor (*music*); Thailand (IVR).

T *symbol*: surface tension; tera-; tesla (*phys*); tritium (*chem*).

't a shortened form of **it**.

t- or **t'** an obsolete shortened form of **to** before a vowel, as in Spenser **tadvance** to advance, **tasswage** to assuage; N of England dialect form of **the**.

t or **t.** *abbrev*: tare (see **tare**[2]); temperature; tense; ton(s); transitive; troy (weight).

t *symbol*: time.

TA *abbrev*: Territorial Army.

Ta (*chem*) *symbol*: tantalum.

ta *tä*, (*colloq*) *interj* (used to or by young children, or affectedly) thank you.

Taal *täl*, (*archaic*) *n* (with **the**) Afrikaans or Cape Dutch. [Du, speech]

TAB *abbrev*: Totalizator Agency Board, the off-course betting statutory authority (*Austr* and *NZ*); typhoid-paratyphoid A and B (vaccine).

tab[1] *tab, n* a small tag, flap or strap attached to something; a loop for hanging something up by, etc; a loop for drawing a stage curtain; hence, a stage curtain; an insignia distinguishing a staff officer, on the collar of his or her uniform (*military*); a small auxiliary aerofoil on eg a rudder or aileron, which helps control the aircraft in flight; the bill, tally, cost, check (chiefly *NAm*). — *adj* **tabbed**. — *vt* to fix a tab to: — *pr p* **tabb'ing**; *pa t* and *pa p* **tabbed**. — **keep tabs on** see under **keep**; **pick up the tab** (chiefly *NAm colloq*) to pay the bill. [Ety doubtful]

tab[2] *tab, n* short for **tablet**.

tab[3] *tab, n* short for (typewriter) **tabulator**. — *vt* short for **tabulate**.

Tabanus *tə-bā'nəs, n* the gadfly genus. — *n* **tabanid** (*tə-bā'-nid*) any member of this blood-sucking genus, or of its family **Tabanidae** (*tə-ban'i-dē*), *incl* eg the horsefly. [L *tabānus*]

tabard, also formerly **taberd** *tab'ərd, n* a medieval peasant's overcoat (*hist*); a knight's sleeveless or short-sleeved coat (*hist*); a herald's coat or tunic bearing a coat-of-arms; a woman's outer garment, a sleeveless tunic. — *n* **tab'erdar** a scholar of Queen's College, Oxford, from the gowns they wore, now applied to the holders of some scholarships at that college. [OFr *tabart*]

tabaret *tab'ə-ret, n* an upholsterer's silk fabric, with alternate stripes of watered and satin surface. [Orig tradename, prob formed from **tabby**]

Tabasco® *tə-bas'kō, n* a hot pepper sauce. [*Tabasco* state in Mexico]

tabasheer or **tabashir** *tab-ə-shēr', n* a siliceous substance sometimes found in crude form in hollows of bamboos (also prepared by chemical processes) and used in Eastern medicine. [Hindi, Pers, Ar *tabāshīr*]

tabbinet. See under **tabby**.

tabbouleh *ta-bōō'le, n* a Mediterranean salad introduced from Lebanon, made with cracked wheat, tomatoes, cucumber, mint, parsley, lemon juice and olive oil. [Ar *tabbūla*]

tabby *tab'i, n* a coarse waved or watered silk fabric; an artificial stone; a tabby-cat; a gossiping, interfering woman (*colloq*); a girl or woman (*Austr slang*). — *adj* brindled. — *vt* to water (silk, etc) or cause to look wavy: — *pr p* **tabb'ying**; *pa t* and *pa p* **tabb'ied**. — *n* **tabb'inet** or **tab'inet** a more delicate kind of tabby resembling damask, used for window curtains. — *n* **tabb'yhood**. — **tabby cat** a brindled cat, *esp* a greyish or brownish cat with dark stripes; sometimes (*perh* from *Tabitha*) a female cat; an old maid; a spiteful gossiping woman. [Fr *tabis*, appar from *'Attābiy*, a quarter in Baghdad where it was made]

tabefaction *tab-i-fak'shən*, (*pathol*; *rare*) *n* wasting away, emaciation. — *vt* and *vi* **tab'efy**. [L *tābēs* wasting away, and *facere* to do]

tabellion *tə-bel'yən, n* an official scrivener in the Roman empire and elsewhere. [LL *tabelliō, -ōnis*, from L *tabella* tablet, dimin of *tabula* a board]

taberdar. See under **tabard**.

tabernacle *tab'ər-na-kl, n* a tent or movable hut; the tent carried by the Jews through the desert, used as a temple and to house the Ark of the Covenant (*hist*); the human body as the temporary abode of the soul; a place of worship, *esp* temporary or dissenting; a receptacle for the vessel containing the pyx (*RC*); a canopied niche or seat (*eccles*); a canopy; a reliquary; a socket for a mast (*naut*). — *vi* to sojourn. — *vt* to put or enshrine in a tabernacle. — *adj* **tab'ernacled**. — **tabernacular** (*-nak'ū-lər*). — **tab'ernacle-work** ornamental work over niches, stalls, etc, with canopies and pinnacles, or any work in which this forms a characteristic feature. — **Feast of Tabernacles** (also called **Feast of Ingathering** or **Sukkoth**) a Jewish harvest festival, commemorating the sojourn in tents in the wilderness. [L *tabernāculum*, dimin of *taberna* a hut]

tabes *tā'bēz*, (*pathol*) *n* wasting away; tabes dorsalis. — *n* **tabescence** (*tə-bes'əns*) wasting; shrivelling. — *adj* **tabesc'ent**. — *adj* **tabetic** (*-bet'ik*) or **tab'id**. — *n* **tabet'ic**. — **tabes dorsalis** (*dör-sā'lis*) a complication of syphilis, appearing many years after infection, in which degeneration of the spinal cord causes muscular incoordination, severe pains in the trunk and legs and incontinence (also called **locomotor ataxia**); **tābōparē'sis** an effect of syphilitic infection of the nervous system in which there are symptoms of tabes dorsalis and general paralysis of the insane. — See also **tabefaction**, **tabefy**. [L *tābēs, -is*]

tabi *tab'ī, n* a sock, worn with Japanese sandals, with a thick sole and a division for the big toe. [Jap]

tabinet. Same as **tabbinet** (qv; see under **tabby**).

tabla *tab'lə* or *-lä*, *n* an Indian percussion instrument, a pair of small drums played with the hands. [Hindi]

tablanette *tab-lə-net'*, *n* a variant of the card game cassino. [Perh from Fr *table nette* clean table]

tablature *tab'lə-chər*, *n* an old notation for lute music, etc, with a line for each string and letters or figures to indicate the stopping, used with modifications for other instruments; a tablet; a painting, picture, pictorial representation or work. [L *tabula* a board]

table *tā'bl*, *n* an article of furniture consisting of a flat top on legs, a pillar or trestles, for use at meals, work, play, for holding things, etc (often in combination, as in *work-table*, *gaming-table*, etc); a flat surface, such as a plateau; a slab or board; a layer; a compact scheme of numerical information, words, facts etc, *usu* in columns; (in *pl*) a collection of these for reference; a syllabus or index; a condensed statement; a slab with or for an inscription; a slab inscribed with laws; (in *pl*) a code of law (eg the *Twelve Tables of ancient Rome*); a writing tablet (*esp* in the *obs* phrase *a pair of tables*); supply of food, entertainment; the company at a table; the soundboard of a violin, guitar or similar instrument; a string-course (*archit*); a panel; a board for painting on; a picture; a broad flat surface on a cut gem; a tabular crystal; a board for a game, eg chess; each half of a folding board; (in *pl*) a backgammon board, or the game itself (*obs*); a quadrangular space on the palm of the hand (*Shakesp*); a flat gravestone supported on pillars; a board or committee; a dispensing of the communion; a projecting part of a scarfed joint. — *adj* of, for, like or relating to a table or meals. — *vt* to put forward (a bill, order, proposal, etc) for discussion in parliament or some formal meeting; to postpone discussion of (a bill, etc) for some time or indefinitely (*US*); to tabulate; to lay on the table; to pay down; to board. — *vi* to board. — *adj* **tabled** (*tā'bld*) flat-topped; having a smooth sloping surface of dressed stone; having a table or tables. — *n* **ta'bleful** as much as a table will hold. — *adj* and *adv* **ta'blewise** in the form or in the manner of a table; (of the communion table) not altarwise. — *n* **ta'bling** tabulation; the presenting of a bill, order, proposal, etc for discussion; playing at tables or backgammon; board; provision of tables; scarfing; a broad hem on the skirt of a sail to reinforce it. — **ta'ble-beer** light beer for common use; **ta'ble-book** a book of writing tablets, memorandum book or notebook; an ornamental book intended to lie on a table; a book of tables; **ta'blecloth** a cloth for covering a table, *esp* at meals; **ta'ble-cover** a cloth for covering a table, *esp* at other than meal-times. — *adj* **ta'ble-cut** (of gems) cut with a flat top. — **table-d'hôte** (*tä-bl'-dōt*; *Fr*, host's table) a meal at a fixed price (as at a hotel): — *pl* **tables-d'hôte** (*tä-bl'-dōt*). — Also *adj*. — **table football** a version of football played on a table with small metal, etc players *usu* suspended on rods, that are turned and spun to strike the ball; **table game** a board game; **table knife** a knife for cutting one's meat, etc with at the table; **ta'bleland** an extensive region of elevated land with a flat or undulating surface; a plateau; **ta'ble-leaf** an extension to a table-top, hinged, drawn out or inserted; **table licence** a licence to serve alcoholic drinks with meals only; **table linen** linen tablecloths, napkins, etc; **ta'ble-maid** a woman who sets the table and waits; **table manners** social behaviour at the table during meals; **ta'ble-mat** a mat placed under dishes on a table; **table money** an allowance (*esp* in the services) for official entertainment; a restaurateur's euphemism for *cover-charge*; **ta'ble-music** music in parts that can be read by performers at each side of a table; **table napkin** a cloth (or paper substitute) used at table to protect the clothes and to wipe fingers and lips; **ta'ble-rapping** knocking or tapping sounds on a table, attributed by spiritualists to the spirits of the dead attempting to communicate with the living; **table salt** fine salt suitable for use at table; **ta'ble-skittles** a game in which a suspended ball is swung to knock down pegs set up on a board; **ta'blespoon** one of the largest spoons used at table, for serving food; **ta'blespoonful** as much as will fill a tablespoon: — *pl* **ta'blespoonfuls**; **ta'ble-sport** (*Shakesp*) the butt of the company at table; **ta'ble-talk** familiar conversation, as at table, during and after meals; **table tennis** a game like lawn tennis played on a table using hollow balls of celluloid or similar light material; **ta'bletop** the top of a table; a flat top. — *adj* **ta'bletopped**. — **ta'ble-turning** movements of tables (or other objects) attributed by spiritualists to the agency of spirits, and by the sceptical to collective involuntary muscular action; the practice of turning tables (see **turn the tables** below); **ta'bleware** dishes, spoons, knives, forks, etc for table use; **table water** a mineral water suitable for the table; **table wine** an ordinary wine *usu* drunk with a meal; **ta'ble-work** (*printing*) the setting of type for tables, columns of figures, etc. — **at table** at a meal; **fence the tables** see under **fence**; **lay on the table** to table (a bill, etc; see **table** *vt*, above); **Lord's table** see under **lord**; **turn the tables** to bring about a complete reversal of circumstances, from the idea of players at backgammon changing sides; **under the table** not above board, illicit; hopelessly drunk (*colloq*). [Partly OE *tabule*, *tabele*, partly OFr (and Fr) *table*, both from L *tabula* a board]

tableau *tab'lō*, *n* a picture or vivid pictorial impression; a suddenly created dramatic situation; a tableau vivant; a moment or scene in which the action is 'frozen' for dramatic effect (*theat*): — *pl* **tableaux** (*tab'lōz*). — **tableau curtains** theatre curtains drawn back and up, to give a draped effect when opened; **tableau vivant** a 'living picture', a motionless representation, often of some famous scene from history, by living people in costume: — *pl* **tableaux vivants** (*tä-blō-vē-vā*). [Fr dimin of *table*]

tablet *tab'lit*, *n* a small, flattish slab, eg of soap; a small flat cake of any solid material, *esp* medicinal; a device that converts the movement of a specially adapted pen or mouse (qv) into digital or analog signals, allowing graphic designs to be displayed on a visual display unit (*comput*); a slab or stiff sheet for making notes on; a pad of writing paper (*orig US*); a panel, *esp* inscribed or for inscription; an inscribed plate hung up in fulfilment of a vow; a brittle confection of sugar and condensed milk, made in slabs (*Scot*). — *vt* to provide with, inscribe on, or make into, a tablet. [OFr *tablete*, dimin of *table*]

tablier *tab'li-ā*, *n* an apron; part of a girl's or woman's dress resembling an apron; an overall buttoning behind. [Fr]

tabloid *tab'loid*, *n* a newspaper of small format, measuring *approx* 30 × 40cm (about 12 × 16in), *usu* rather informal or sensationalistic in style and with many photographs; anything in a concentrated form, a summary. — *adj* of, for, or in the form of, tabloid newspapers; (of eg television programmes) designed to appeal to a mass audience; concentrated. — *adj* **tab'loidy** (*colloq*). [From *Tabloid*, trademark for a medicine in tablet form]

taboggan. See under **toboggan**.

taboo or **tabu** *tə-bōō'*, *adj* subject to taboo; forbidden, *esp* because holy or unclean. — *n* any recognized or general prohibition, interdict, restraint, ban, exclusion or ostracism; *orig* a Polynesian (or other) system of prohibitions connected with things considered holy or unclean; any one of these prohibitions: — *pl* **taboos'** or **tabus'**. — *vt* to place under taboo; to forbid approach to or use of: — *pr p* **taboo'ing** or **tabu'ing**; *pa t* and *pa p* **tabooed'** or **tabued'**. [Tongan *tabu* (pronounced *tä'bōō*) holy, unclean]

tabor or **tabour** *tā'bər*, *n* a small drum like a tambourine without jingles, *usu* played with a stick held in one hand, to accompany a pipe held in the other (*hist*); a taborer. — *vi* and *vt* to play on a tabor; to beat or drum. — *n* **tā'borer** (*Spenser* **tabrere** *ta-brēr'*) a person who beats the tabor. — *n* **taborin** or **tabourin** (*tab'ə-rin* or *-rēn*) a small drum longer in body than the tabor, used in a similar way. — *n* **tabouret** or in *US* **taboret** (*tab'ə-ret* or *tä-bōō-rā*) a low stool, *orig* drum-shaped; an embroidery frame, a tambour. — *n* **tabret** (*tab'rit*; *hist*) a small tabor. [OFr *tabour*; an Oriental word]

Taborite *tā'bər-īt*, *n* a Hussite of Žižka's party, opposed to the Calixtines or Utraquists. — Also *adj*. [*Tabor* in Bohemia, founded by them as headquarters]

tabour, **tabourin**, etc, **tabret**. See **tabor**.

tabu. See **taboo**.

tabula *tab'ū-lə*, *tab'ōō-la*, *n* a writing-tablet; an altar frontal (*eccles*); a flattened structure; a horizontal partition in corals: — *pl* **tab'ulae** (*-lē*, *-lī*). — **tabula rasa** (*tab'ū-lə rā'zə* or *tab'ōō-la rä'sa*) a smoothed or blank tablet; a clean slate (*lit* and *fig*); a mind not yet influenced by outside impressions and experience: — *pl* **tabulae** (*-lē*, *-lī*) **rasae** (*-sē*, *-sī*). [L, writing table]

tabular *tab'ū-lər*, *adj* of, in the form of, like or according to, a table or tablet; laminated; platy; horizontally flattened. — *n* **tabularīzā'tion** or **-s-**. — *vt* **tab'ularize** or **-ise** to tabulate. — *adv* **tab'ularly**. — *vt* **tab'ulate** to reduce to or lay out in the form of a table or synopsis. — *adj* tabular; having tabulae. — *n* **tabulā'tion**. — *n* **tab'ulātor** a person who or a machine which tabulates data; a device in a typewriter which sets and then finds automatically the margins needed in tabular work; a machine which prints lists or tables of data very rapidly from punched cards, etc, on to continuous paper (*comput*). — *adj* **tab'ulatory** (*-lə-tə-ri*). — **tabular spar** another name for **wollastonite**. [L *tabula* table]

tabun *tä-bōōn'*, *n* (also with *cap*) an organic phosphorus compound, $C_5H_{11}N_2O_2P$, which can be used as a nerve gas. [Ger]

tacahout *tak'ə-howt*, *n* a gall on the tamarisk, a source of gallic acid. [From Berber]

tacamahac *tak'ə-mə-hak*, *n* a gum-resin yielded by several tropical trees; the balsam poplar, or its resin. — Also **tac'mahack**. [From Nahuatl]

TACAN, **Tacan** or **tacan** *tak'an*, *n* an electronic system of air navigation which gives an aircraft a direct reading of distance and bearing from a ground-based transmitter. [*tac*tical *a*ir *n*avigation]

tac-au-tac *tak'-ō-tak'*, (*fencing*) *n* the parry combined with the riposte; also a series of close attacks and parries between fencers of equal skill. [Fr]

tace[1] *tā'sē* or *ta'kā*, *imperative* be silent. — **tacet** (*tā'set* or *ta'ket*; *music*) is silent (marked on a score as an instruction for a particular singer or instrument). — **tace is Latin for a candle** a phrase understood as requesting or promising silence. [L *tacē*, imperative, *tacet*, 3rd person singular present indicative, of *tacēre* to be silent]

tace[2]. See **tasse**.

tach or **tache** *tach*, (*Bible*) *n* a fastening or clasp. [OFr *tache*, cf **tack**[1] and **attach**]

tache[1] *tash*, (*colloq*) *n* short for **moustache**.

tache[2]. Same as **tach**.

tacheometer *tak'i-om'i-tər*, *n* a surveying instrument for rapid measurement of points on a survey, such as distance, elevation, etc. — *adj* **tacheomet'ric** or **tacheomet'rical**. — *n* **tacheom'etry**. [Fr *tachéomètre*, from Gr *tache-*, oblique stem of *tachys* swift, and of *tachos* speed, and *-mètre* -meter]

tachinid *tak'i-nid*, *n* any dipterous bristly fly of the family *Tachinidae* whose larvae are parasites of other insects and are therefore useful as a biological control of insect pests. — Also *adj*. [New L *Tachina* genus name, from Gr *tachinos* swift, from *tachos* swiftness]

tachism *tash'izm* or **tachisme** *ta-shēzm*, *n* a mid-20c movement in abstract painting characterized by irregular splotches and dabs of colour apparently applied at random for dramatic or emotional effect rather than to represent or express. — *n* and *adj* **tach'ist** or **tachiste** (*-shēst*). [Fr *tache* blob (of paint)]

tachistoscope *tə-kis'tə-skōp*, *n* an instrument that flashes visual images, sentences, etc onto a screen for brief, exactly measured intervals of time, used eg to test speed of perception and comprehension, and to increase reading speed. [Gr *tachistas*, superlative of *tachys* swift, and **-scope**]

tacho *tak'ō*, (*colloq*) a tachograph or tachometer: — *pl* **tach'os**.

tacho- *tak-ō-*, *-ə-*, *-o'-*, *combining form* denoting speed. — *n* **tach'ogram** a record made by a tachograph. — *n* **tach'ograph** a recording tachometer; a tachogram; an instrument fitted to commercial vehicles to record mileage, speed, number and location of stops, etc. — *n* **tachom'eter** a device showing speed of rotation; an instrument for measuring the velocity of machines or currents. — *adj* **tachomet'ric** or **tachomet'rical**. — *n* **tachom'etry**. [Gr *tachos* speed]

tachy- *tak-i-*, *combining form* denoting fast, rapid. — *n* **tachycar'dia** abnormal rapidity of heartbeat. — *n* **tach'ygraph**, **tachyg'rapher** or **tachyg'raphist** a shorthand writer, a stenographer or practitioner of tachygraphy. — *adj* **tachygraph'ic** or **tachygraph'ical**. — *n* **tachyg'raphy** shorthand, *esp* that used by the ancient Greeks and Romans; the abbreviated form of Greek and Latin found in medieval manuscripts. — *n* **tach'ylyte** (also **tach'ylite**; Gr *lytos* melted, because easily fused; *mineralogy*) a black opaque glass occurring as a thin selvage to intrusive basalt. — *adj* **tachylytic** or **tachylitic** (*-lit'ik*). — *n* **tachym'eter** a tacheometer (qv). — *adj* **tachymet'ric** or **tachymet'rical**. — *n* **tachym'etry**. — *n* **tachyphasia** (*-fā'zi-ə*; Gr *phasis* utterance) or **tachyphrasia** (*-frā'zi-ə*; Gr *phrasis* speed) abnormally rapid or voluble speech. — *n* **tachypnoea** or (*US*) **tachypnea** (*-ip-nē'ə*; Gr *-pnoia* breathing) abnormally rapid respiration. [Gr *tachys* swift]

tachyon *tak'i-on*, (*phys*) a theoretical elementary particle moving faster than light. [Gr *tachys* swift, and **-on**]

tacit *tas'it*, *adj* unspoken; understood or implied without being expressed directly; silent. — *adv* **tac'itly**. — *n* **tac'itness**. [L *tacitus* silent, unspoken, unspeaking, from *tacēre* to be silent]

taciturn *tas'i-tûrn*, *adj* disinclined to speak, reticent, uncommunicative. — *n* **taciturn'ity**. — *adv* **tac'iturnly**. [L *taciturnus*, from *tacitus* silent, unspoken or unspeaking]

tack[1] *tak*, *n* a short, sharp nail with a broad head; a long loose temporary stitch; a fastening strip; a rope or other fastening for the lower windward corner of a sail (*naut*); the corner itself (*naut*); the course of a sailing ship with respect to the side of the sail against which the wind is blowing (*naut*); an alternate course in zigzag to take advantage of wind blowing from the side when sailing to windward (*naut*); a course of action; a direction taken in argument, thinking, etc; a change of policy, a strategical move; something tacked on; stickiness. — *vt* to attach or fasten, *esp* in a loose, hasty or impermanent manner, eg by tacks or long loose stitches; to append or affix (with *on*); to change the course of (a sailing ship) by a tack (*naut*); to steer (a sailing ship) by tacking. — *vi* to change the course or tack of a ship by shifting the position of the sails (*naut*); to zigzag; to shift one's position, to veer; to change one's position or behaviour, often abruptly. — *adj* **tacked**. — *n* **tack'er**. — *n* **tack'et** (*Scot* and *dialect*) a hobnail. — *adj* **tack'ety**. — *adv* **tack'ily**. — *n* **tack'iness**. — *n* **tack'ing** proceeding by tacks (*naut*); fastening; fastening by tacks; introducing into a bill (*esp* a money bill) provisions beyond its natural scope (*politics*). — *adj* **tack'y** slightly sticky. — *adj* **tacked'-on**. — **tack hammer** a light hammer for driving in tacks; **tack'-weld** to join (pieces of metal) with several welds placed some distance apart; **tack'-welding**. — **change tack** to change course, take a new direction; **on the right** (or **wrong**) **tack** following the right (or wrong) course of action, train of thought, etc. [OFr *taque*, doublet of *tache* (see **tach**)]

tack[2] *tak*, *n* food generally, fare, *esp* of the bread kind, such as *hard tack* (ship's biscuit), *soft tack* (loaves). [Origin uncertain]

tack[3] *tak*, *n* the sound of a sharp tap. [Imit]
tack[4] *tak*, *n* riding harness, saddles, bridles, etc. — **tack room** a room in or near a stable where tack is kept. [**tackle**]
tack[5]. see under **tacky**[1].
tack[6] *tak*, (*Scot*) *n* a tenure; a lease; a leased tenement; a spell; a take or catch. — **tacks'man** (*Scot*) a lessee; in the Scottish Highlands, a person who holds a lease and sublets. [See **tak** and **take**]
tack[7] *tak*, (*dialect*) *n* any distinctive flavour, smack.
tacker, tacket. tackety. See under **tack**[1].
tackiness. See under **tack**[1] and **tacky**[1].
tacking. See under **tack**[1].
tackle *tak'l*, *n* the ropes, rigging, etc of a ship (*naut*; *tāk'l*); tools, gear, weapons, equipment (for sports, etc); ropes, etc for raising heavy weights; a pulley; the act of gripping; an act of tackling (*football*); the player (also **right** or **left tackle**) positioned one from the end (respectively right or left) on the scrimmage line (*Am football*). — *vt* to seize or take hold of; to grapple with; to come to grips with; to begin to deal in earnest with; to confront, encounter, challenge; to harness. — *vt* and *vi* (*Rugby football*) to seize and stop or (*association football*) intercept (a player who has possession of the ball) in an effort to get the ball away. — *adj* **tackled** (*tak'ld*) fitted with harness or tackle; made of ropes (*Shakesp*). — *n* **tack'ler**. — *n* **tack'ling** furniture or apparatus belonging to the masts, yards, etc, of a ship; harness for drawing a carriage; tackle or instruments; grappling. [Cf LGer *takel*]
tacky[1] *tak'i*, (*slang*) *adj* (*orig US*) shabby; sleazy; vulgar, gaudy, in bad taste. — *n* (*US*) a poor ill-conditioned horse or person. — *n* **tack** any shabby, vulgar or gaudy object or collection of objects; tackiness. — *adv* **tack'ily**. — *n* **tack'iness**. [Origin uncertain]
tacky[2]. See under **tack**[1].
tacmahack. See under **tacamahac**.
taco *tä'kō*, *n* in Mexican cooking, a very thin rolled pancake with a meat filling, *usu* fried crisp: — *pl* **ta'cos**. [Mex Sp]
taconite *tak'ə-nīt*, *n* a sedimentary rock containing enough iron to make it a low-grade iron ore. [*Taconic* Mountains in NE United States]
tact *takt*, *n* adroitness in managing the feelings of persons dealt with; fine perception in seeing and doing exactly what is best in the circumstances; the stroke in keeping time (*music*). — *adj* **tact'ful**. — *adv* **tact'fully**. — *n* **tact'fulness**. — *adj* **tact'less**. — *adv* **tact'lessly**. — *n* **tact'lessness**. [L *tactus*, *-ūs*, from *tangere*, *tactum* to touch]
tactic *tak'tik* or **tactical** *tak'ti-kəl*, *adj* relating to taxis or tactism, or to tactics; (**tactical**) skilful, adroit, calculated; (**tactical**; of weapons, bombing, etc) used to support military or naval operations. — *n* **tac'tic** a system, or a piece, of tactics. — *adv* **tac'tically**. — *n* **tactician** (*-tish'ən*) a person skilled in tactics. — *n* **tactic'ity** (*chem*) the stereochemical arrangement of units in the main chain of a polymer. — *n sing* **tac'tics** the science or art of manoeuvring in presence of the enemy. — *n pl* the means adopted to achieve an end; purposeful procedure. — *n* **tac'tism** (*biol*) taxis. — **tactical voting** the practice of voting for a political party one does not support in order to prevent the election of a party one is even more opposed to. [Gr *taktikos* fit for arranging, from *taktos* ordered, verbal adj of *tassein* to arrange]
tactile *takt'īl*, *adj* perceptible by touch; relating to the sense of touch; concerned in perception by touch; suggestive of touch. — *n* **tact'ilist** (*-i-list*) a painter who aims at tactile effects. — *n* **tactil'ity**. [L *tactilis*, from *tangere*, *tactum* to touch]
taction *tak'shn*, (*rare*) *n* contact, touch. [L *tactiō*, *-iōnis*, from *tangere*, *tactum* to touch]
tactual *takt'ū-əl*, *adj* relating to or derived from the sense of touch. — *n* **tactūal'ity** tactual quality. — *adv* **tact'ually**. [L *tactus*, *-ūs* touch, from *tangere*, *tactum* to touch]
tad *tad*, (*colloq*, *esp NAm*) *n* a small amount; a little lad. [Short for **tadpole**]
taddie *tad'i*, (*Austr colloq*) a tadpole.
Tadjik. See under **Tajik**.
tadpole *tad'pōl*, *n* the larva of a toad or frog, or (rarely) of an ascidian. — **Tadpole and Taper** political hacks, from characters in Disraeli's *Coningsby*. [OE *tāde* toad, and **poll** (head)]
Tadzhik. See under **Tajik**.
tae *tā*, a Scots form of **toe**, **to** and **too** (meaning 'also'). — Also in phrase *the tae* for *that ae*, the one (adjectivally). [See **tone**[2] and **tother**]
taedium, an obsolete spelling of **tedium**. — **taedium vitae** (*tē'di-əm vī'tē* or *tī'di-ōōm vē'tī* or *wē'tī*; *L*) weariness of life.
tae kwon do *tā kwon dō*, *n* a Korean martial art, similar to karate. [Korean *tae* kick, *kwon* fist, and *do* method]
tael *tāl*, *n* Chinese *liang* or ounce, about 38g (1 lb 3oz); a money of account (not normally a coin) in China, *orig* a tael weight of pure silver. — **tael bar** a gold bullion measure used in the Far East (1, 5 or 10 tael weight). [Port, from Malay *tail* weight]
ta'en *tān*, a contraction of **taken**.
taenia or (*US*) **tenia** *tē'ni-ə*, *n* a ribbon or fillet; the fillet above the architrave of the Doric order (*archit*); a ribbon-like structure; any member of the tapeworm genus *Taenia*: — *pl* **tae'niae** (*-ni-ē*) or **tae'nias**. — *n* **taen'iacide** (*-sīd*) a substance that destroys tapeworms. — *n* **taen'iafuge** (*-fūj*) a substance, eg a drug, for expelling tapeworms from the body. — *n* **taenī'asis** infestation with tapeworms. — *adj* **tae'niate** or **tae'nioid** like a ribbon or a tapeworm. [L, from Gr *tainiā* a band]
TAFE *tāf*, *abbrev*: Technical and Further Education.
tafferel. See under **taffrail**.
taffeta *taf'i-tə* or **taffetas** *taf'i-tas*, *n* a thin glossy silk fabric; loosely applied to various similar or mixed fabrics. — *adj* made of taffeta; florid, over-dainty (*Shakesp*). — Also **taffety** (*taf'i-ti*). [Through Fr or LL from Pers *tāftah* woven, from *tāftan* to twist]
taffrail *taf'ril*, *n* the rail round the stern of a ship; the upper part of a ship's stern timbers. — Also **taff'erel**. [Du *tafereel* a panel, from *tafel* a table]
Taffy *taf'i*, (*slang*) *n* a Welshman. [From *Dafydd*, Welsh form of David]
taffy *taf'i*, *n* toffee; flattery, blarney (*US*).
tafia or **taffia** *taf'i-ə*, *n* a type of rum. [Perh a W Indian name, but cf Malay *tāfiā*]
tag[1] *tag*, *n* a tab; a label, *esp* a tie-on label; an identifying mark or sign; a symbol or signature used by a graffiti-writer, eg as a message, means of identification, etc (*slang*); an electronic tag (qv under **electronic**); a label or marker giving summarized information, descriptions, attributes, etc which apply to the text following (or if one of a pair, also preceding) it (*comput*); the metal or plastic point of a lace; any small thing tacked or attached to another; a flap, or a loose or flapping end; a flap of a slashed garment; a shred; a stray, matted or dirty lock, eg of a sheep's wool; the tip of an animal's tail; the tail-end (eg of the batting order in cricket); a trite (*esp* Latin) quotation; a moral to a story; the closing words of a play, etc, *usu* addressed to the audience; a refrain; a vehicle licence plate (*US*); a parking ticket (*US*); the rabble, the common people (*obs*); anything mean; a piece of brightly coloured wire, fabric, etc tied to the end of the body of an artificial fly (*angling*); (in *pl*) a footman's shoulder-knot. — *vt* to put a tag or tags on; to attach as a tag; to put a signature or similar mark on (*slang*); to mark (text) with tags (*comput*); to fit with an electronic tag; to tack, fasten, append; to remove tags from; to dog or follow closely; to give (a driver or vehicle) a parking ticket (*US*); to replace an atom in (a molecule or compound) by a radioactive isotope, for the purpose of identification. — *vi* to make tags, to string words or ideas together; to go behind as a follower (with *on* or *along*): — *pr p* **tagg'ing**; *pa t* and *pa p* **tagged**. — *n*

taggee' a person wearing an electronic tag (qv under **electronic**). — *n* **tagg'er**. — *n pl* **tagg'ers** thin sheet-iron or sheet-steel coated with tin. — *n* **tagg'ing**. — *adj* **tagg'y** (of eg wool) matted into tags. — **tag day** (*NAm*) a flag day; **tag'-end** (*esp NAm*) the fag-end, tail-end; **tagged atom** a radioactive isotopic atom of a tracer element; **tag line** (*US*) a punch line; a watchword, slogan; **tag question** an interrogative clause (eg *can't you?*) added to the end of a statement to invite agreement (also **question tag**); **tag'rag** the rabble (*old*); a fluttering rag, a tatter. — Also *adj*. — **tag'-tail** a worm with a tail like a tag. — **tag along** (with *with*) to follow, accompany or trail after someone, *esp* when uninvited; **tag rag and bobtail** rag-tag and bobtail. [Origin obscure]

tag² *tag*, *n* the children's game of tig; the act of putting out a runner by touching him or her with the ball or the hand holding the ball (*baseball*). — *vt* to tig; to put out (a runner) by a tag (*baseball*): — *pr p* **tagg'ing**; *pa t* and *pa p* **tagged**. — **tag wrestling** a contest between two teams of two wrestlers, in which only one wrestler from each team is in the ring at any one time and may be replaced by the wrestler outside the ring after touching the latter's hand. [Ety doubtful]

Tagálog or **Tagalog** *tə-gä'log*, *n* a people of the Philippine Islands; their Austronesian language. — Also *adj*.

tagetes *tə-jē'tēz*, *n* a plant of the Mexican and S American *Tagetes* genus of composites with yellow and orange flowers, *incl* the French marigold and African marigold: — *pl* **tagē'tes**. [L *Tagēs*, an Etruscan god]

taghairm *tə-gûrm'*, *n* (in the Scottish Highlands) divination; *esp* inspiration sought by lying in a bullock's hide behind a waterfall. [Gaelic]

Tagliacotian. See under **Taliacotian**.

tagliarini *täl-yə-rē'ni*, *n* pasta cut into flat, very thin strips. [Ital]

tagliatelle *tal-yə-tel'i*, *tä-lya-tel'ā*, *n* pasta made in long ribbons. [Ital]

taglioni *tal-yō'nē*, *n* an early-19c overcoat. [Named after a family of dancers]

tagma *täg'mə*, (*zool*) *n* any of the distinct regions of the body in arthropods and other animals with segmented bodies, eg, in insects, the head, thorax or abdomen: — *pl* **tag'mata**. [Gr, a grouping or arrangement, from *tassein* to arrange]

tagmeme *tag'mēm*, (*linguistics*) *n* any of the positions in the structure of a sentence into which a certain class of grammatical items can fit. — *adj* **tagmē'mic**. — *n sing* **tagmē'mics** the analysis of the grammar of a language based on the arrangement or positions of the spoken elements. [Gr *tagma* arrangement, order]

taguan *ta'gwan* or *tä'gwän*, *n* a large E Indian flying squirrel. [Tagálog]

taha *tä'hä*, *n* a S African weaver bird. [Zulu *taka*]

tahina *tə-hē'nə* or **tahini** *-nē*, *n* an oily paste made of crushed sesame seeds. [Ar, from *ṭaḥana* to grind]

Tahitian *tä-hē'shən*, *adj* of or relating to *Tahiti* in the S Pacific. — *n* a native or inhabitant of Tahiti; the Polynesian language of Tahiti.

tahr or **tehr** *tär*, *n* a beardless Himalayan wild goat (*Hemitragus jemlahicus*) that frequents forest peaks. [Appar its name in the W Himalaya, confused with Nepali *thār*; see **thar**]

tahsil *tä-sēl'* or *tähh-sēl'*, *n* in India, a division of a district for revenue and certain other purposes. — *n* **tahsildar'** an officer of a tahsil. [Hindi *taḥsīl*, from Ar]

Tai or **T'ai**. Same as **Thai**.

tai *tī*, *n* a Japanese sea bream. [Jap]

taiaha *tī'ə-hä*, *n* a Maori weapon in the form of a carved staff, now held during ceremonial public speaking. [Maori]

t'ai chi *tī chē'* or **t'ai chi chu'an** (*chwän'*), *n* a Chinese system of exercise and self-defence in which good use of co-ordination and balance allows effort to be minimized. [Chin, great art of boxing]

Taig *tāg*, (*offensive slang*) *n* (in Northern Ireland) a Catholic. [Variant of *Teague*, orig used as nickname for any Irishman]

taiga *tī'gə*, *n* marshy pine forest spreading across much of subarctic N America and Eurasia, with tundra to the north and steppe to the south. [Russ *taigá*]

taigle *tā'gl*, (*Scot*) *vt* to entangle or hinder. — *vi* to linger or loiter; to trudge. [Cf Swed (Bornholm) *taggla* to disorder]

tail¹ *tāl*, *n* the posterior extremity of an animal, *usu* a slender prolongation beyond the anus; a bird's train of feathers; a fish's caudal fin; anything of similar appearance, position, etc; the back, lower, rear, latter, downstream, weaker or inferior part or prolongation of anything (often *opp* to the *head*); the rear, stabilizing part of an aircraft, *incl* tailplane, fin and control surfaces, or of a rocket, missile, etc; the stem of a note in written music; a downward extension of a letter; a retinue, suite; a queue; a train; anything long and trailing or hanging, such as a catkin, the luminous train of a comet or long curl or braid of hair; (*usu* in *pl*) the reverse of a coin; (in *pl*) the depleted uranium produced during enrichment (*nuc eng*); the end of a shoal sloping into deeper water; the weaker batsmen at the end of a team's batting order (*cricket*); (often in *pl*) the skirts of a garment (*old*); (in *pl*) a tailcoat; (in *pl*) evening dress, *incl* a tailcoat; in Turkey, a horse-tail, formerly a mark of rank; a person engaged to follow and keep a constant watch on someone (*colloq*); the route or course taken by someone running away (*colloq*); the margin at the bottom of the page, or the bottom edge of the page (*printing*); the buttocks, backside (*colloq*); the female genitalia or the penis (*slang*); sexual intercourse (*slang*); a woman (*slang*). — *vt* to provide with a tail; to be a tail to; to remove the tail or stalk from; to grip or drag by the tail; to join end to end; to insert or incorporate the end of (a tile, brick, timber, etc) into a wall or other support; to herd (*Austr*); to follow closely, shadow. — *vi* to taper (often with *off* or *away*); to lessen or deteriorate slowly (with *off* or *away*); to straggle; to show the tail. — *adj* **tailed**. — *n* **tail'ing** the inner covered end of a projecting brick or stone in a wall (*building*); a winter sport in which a tail-like string of luges is drawn along by a horse-sleigh; (in *pl*) refuse, dregs; (in *pl*) the rejected or washed away portion of an ore (*min ext*); (in *pl*) the higher boiling fraction in a distillation process. — *adj* **tail'less** having no tail. — *adj* **tail'-like**. — **tail'back** a line of traffic stretching back from anything obstructing or slowing down traffic flow; **tail'board** a movable board at the back of a cart, wagon or lorry; **tail'-boom** a longitudinal strut supporting the tail of an aeroplane; **tail'-coat** a man's formal coat, cutaway at the front and with narrow tails at the back; **tail covert** any of a bird's covert feathers covering the bass of its tail feathers; **tail'-end** the fag-end, final and/or inferior part; (in *pl*) inferior corn sorted out from better; something that comes at the end; **tail-end Charlie** (*colloq*) a person who comes at the end; **tail-en'der** (*colloq*) someone or something coming at the end; **tail'-feather** one of the rectrices or stiff rudder-feathers of a bird's tail, used in steering; a feather on a bird's back forming a train, as in the peacock; **tail'-fly** (*fishing*) the fly at the end of the leader; **tail'gate** lower gate of a lock; a tailboard; a door at the back of a car that opens upwards on hinges at its top edge; a jazz style of playing *esp* the trombone. — *vt* to drive dangerously close behind (another vehicle; *slang*) — Also *vi*. — **tail'gater** a person who tailgates; **tail'-lamp** or **tail'-light** a *usu* red light carried at the back of a train, tram, car or other vehicle (*esp NAm*); **tail'piece** a piece at the tail or end; an engraving, design, etc occupying the bottom of a page, eg at the end of a chapter; a strip of ebony, etc to which the ends of the strings are attached in a fiddle; **tail'pipe** an exhaust pipe (of a car; *US*); the suction-pipe in a pump. — *vt* to tie a tin can or similar object to the tail of (a dog) to frighten or annoy it (the precise force of 'pipe' being unknown). — **tail'plane** a horizontal aerofoil on the tail of an aircraft; **tail'race** the channel in which water runs away below a mill-wheel, or from a hydraulically-operated machine, etc; **tail'-rhyme** or **tailed rhyme** a verse form in which two or more rhymed lines are followed by a shorter line that does not rhyme with the others; **tail'-rope** a rope attached to the rear part of anything; **tail'skid** a support under the tail of an aeroplane on the ground; (in a motor vehicle) a skid starting with the rear wheels; **tail'spin** a spiral dive of an aeroplane; an uncontrolled downward spiral; a state of panic or frenzy (*colloq*); **tail'stock** a slidable casting mounted on a lathe, aligned with the headstock, used to support the free end of the piece being worked on; **tail'wheel** a wheel at the rear of a vehicle, *esp* that under the rear end of an aircraft; **tail wind** a wind blowing in the same direction as one is travelling in. — **a bit** (or **piece**) **of tail** (*offensive slang*) a woman; **not make head or tail of** to make no sense of; **on someone's tail** following someone very closely; **tail off** to become gradually less or fewer; **tail of the eye** the outer corner of the eye; the margin of the field of vision; **the tail wagging the dog** (*colloq*) a situation in which the less important element or factor controls or influences the more important; **turn tail** to turn round (and run off); **twist the lion's tail** to irritate Britain; **with the tail between the legs** in a state of dejection after chastisement or humiliation, like a beaten cur. [OE *tægl*, *tægel*; Gothic *tagl* hair]

tail[2] *tāl*, (*law*) *n* limitation of inheritance to certain heirs. — *adj* limited. — **tail male** limitation to male heirs. — **in tail** subject to such a limitation. [Fr *taille* cutting]

tailard. See under **tailor**[2].

taileron *tā'lə-ron*, (*aeronautics*) *n* either part of a two-piece tailplane whose two halves can operate either together or differentially. [**tail**[1] and **aileron**]

taille *tī*, (*hist*) *n* a tax levied by a French king or overlord on his subjects, or on lands held from or under him: — *pl* **tailles** (*tī*). [Fr, from OFr *taillier* to cut or shape]

tailleur *ta-yûr'*, *n* a woman's tailored suit. [Fr]

taillie. See under **tailzie**.

tailor[1] *tā'lər*, *n* a person whose business is to cut out and make outer garments, *esp* for men (*fem* **tail'oress**); any of several fish, *incl* the bluefish and the Australian skipjack (*Teninodon saltator*); a teller stroke (*bell-ringing*; *esp dialect*). — *vi* to work as a tailor. — *vt* to make clothes for; to fit with clothes; to fashion by tailor's work; to make or adapt so as to fit a special need exactly. — *adj* **tail'ored** tailor-made; wearing well-tailored clothes; well cared for. — *n* **tail'oring**. — **tail'or-bird** any Asian warbler of the genus *Orthotomus* (*esp O. sutorius*) that sews leaves together to form a nest. — *adj* **tail'or-made** made by a tailor, *esp* of plain, close-fitting garments for women; exactly adapted (for a purpose). — *n* a tailor-made garment; a factory-made cigarette, not one rolled by hand (*colloq*). — *vt* **tail'ormake** (*orig* and *esp US*) to make especially to suit a particular purpose or person, etc. — **tailor's chalk** a small piece of French chalk used by tailors and dressmakers to mark the position of seams, darts, etc on cloth; **tailor's tack** a long loose stitch used eg to hold fabric to a pattern during cutting, or to mark the position of seams, darts, etc prior to fitting. [Anglo-Fr *taillour* (Fr *tailleur*), from LL *tāliātor*, *-ōris*, from *tāliāre* to cut]

tailor[2] *tā'lər*, (*Shakesp*, *Midsummer Night's Dream* II. 1. 54) *interj* variously explained as referring to a tumble backwards (*opp* to *header*), to the tailor-like squatting position that results, or as the obsolete **tailard**, a person with a tail.

tailzie, **tailye** or **taillie** *tāl'yi*, *tā'li*, (*law*) *n* Scots forms of **tail**[2]; entail.

Taino *tī'nō*, *n* a member of an extinct Indian tribe of the W Indies (*pl* **Tai'nos** or collectively **Tai'no**); the language spoken by this people. — Also *adj*.

taint *tānt*, *n* a stain or blemish; pollution; infection; a tincture of some evil quality; a contaminating or corrupting influence; a latent or incipient defect or corruption; attaint (*obs*); a hit in tilting (*obs*); tint, tinge (*obs*); — *vt* to affect or imbue with anything objectionable; to contaminate or infect; to impart a taint to, to tarnish; to attaint (*obs*); to touch in tilting (*obs*); to tint, tinge (*obs*). — *vi* to become infected or rotten; to go bad; to weaken, wilt, wither. — *adj* **taint'ed**. — *adj* **taint'less**. — *adv* **taint'lessly**. — *n* **taint'ure** defilement. — **taint'-worm** (*Milton*) some worm supposed to infect cattle. [Partly aphetic for **attaint**; partly OFr *taint* (Fr *teint*), from L *tinctus*, *-ūs*, from *tingere*, *tinctum* to wet, dye]

'taint *tānt*, (*slang* or *illiterate*) contraction of **it is not**.

taipan[1] *tī'pan*, *n* a large venomous Australian snake, *Oxyuranus scutellatus*. [Aboriginal name]

taipan[2] *tī'pan*, *n* a foreigner living in China and head of a foreign business there. [Chin]

T'ai-p'ing *tī-ping'*, *n* the new order that Hung-hsiu Ch'üan sought to found in central and N China; a participator in his rebellion (1851–65). [Chin *t'ai p'ing* great peace or great harmony]

taira. See under **tayra**.

taisch or **taish** *tīsh*, *n* (in the Scottish Highlands) an apparition or voice, *esp* of someone about to die; second-sight. [Gaelic *taibhis*, *taibhse* apparition]

tait[1]. Same as **tate**.

tait[2] *tāt*, (*Austr*) *n* the honey possum (*Tarsipes*). [Aboriginal name]

taiver. See under **taver**[1,2].

taivert. See under **taver**[2].

taj *täj*, *n* a crown; a dervish's tall conical cap. [Ar and Pers *tāj* crown]

Tajik, **Tadjik** or **Tadzhik** *taj'ik*, *n* a people of Iranian race living in Afghanistan and Turkestan; a member of this people; its dialect, resembling Farsi. — Also *adj*. [Pers, a Persian]

tajine *ta-zhēn'*, a conical clay pot used in N African cooking; any stew cooked in such a pot. [Fr dimin of **taj**]

tak *tak* or *täk*, a Scots form of **take**.

taka *tä'kə*, *n* the standard unit of currency in Bangladesh (100 *poisha*). [Bengali]

takahe *tä'kə-hē*, *n* a large flightless bird (*Notornis* or *Porphyrio mantelli*) of the rail family with brilliant blue-green plumage, a heavy pink bill and a large red shield on its forehead, thought to be extinct until 1948 when a small population was discovered on S Island, New Zealand. [Maori]

takamaka *tak'ə-mak-ə*. Same as **tacamahac**.

take *tāk*, *vt* to lay hold of; to get into one's possession; to seize, catch, capture; to captivate; to receive or come to have willingly or by an act of one's own; to pay for, buy or rent; to appropriate; to assume, adopt; to accept; to receive; to admit; to submerge (*Scot*); to have normally assigned to one; to find out, come upon, surprise, detect; to swallow or inhale; to eat or drink, often habitually; to apply to oneself; to obtain; to engage, secure; to seek and receive; to have recourse to; to make use of; to deal with or react to in a specified way; to teach (a subject or class); to attend a course in; to undertake (a course) or attend (a regular class) in some subject; to visit; to call for, necessitate, use up; to remove; to cause to go; to subtract; to convey; to carry with one; to escort; to detract; to derive; to understand; to apprehend; (with *it*) to assume, suppose; to mistake; to conceive or think of; to accept as true; to tolerate or endure; to ascertain; to observe or measure; to ascertain something from; to execute, perform; to set down; to portray; to photograph; to charge oneself with; to declare solemnly; to strike; to come upon and affect; to bewitch or charm; to blight; to put an end to (someone's, or one's own, life); to cheat, swindle or deceive (*colloq*); to deliver, give (*obs*); to have sexual intercourse with (*archaic*); to betake. — *vi* to have the intended effect; to be effective, to work; (of plants, *esp* grafted buds) to begin to grow shoots (cf **strike**); to please the public; to betake oneself, begin; (of a fish) to bite ; to make a capture or acquisition; to be capable of being taken; to become, fall, eg ill (*colloq*); to freeze (*NAm*); to cast a spell (*Shakesp*): — *pa t* **took**; *pa p* **tā'ken**. — *n* an act of taking, or of catching (eg the ball in rugby, etc); a capture; quantity taken on one occasion; the amount of money taken, eg from a business enterprise, admission charges, etc; the amount of film (eg one scene) photographed, music recorded, etc at any one time (*cinematog*); amount of copy set up by a printer at one time; a sign on the body (eg a rash) that a vaccine has been successful; a successful tissue graft. — *adj* **take'able** or **tā'kable**. — *adj* **tā'ken** (with *with*; *colloq*) impressed or attracted by. — *n* **tā'ker**. — *n* **tā'king** the action of the verb in any sense; (*usu* in *pl*) that which is taken, receipts; plight (*Spenser*); bewitchment, malignant influence (*Shakesp*); agitation, perplexity (*colloq*). — *adj* captivating; alluring; infectious, catching. — *adv* **tā'kingly**. — *n* **tā'kingness**. — *adj* **tā'ky** (*old colloq*) attractive. — *adj* **take'away** (of cooked food) sold for consumption away from the place of sale; (of a restaurant) selling such food. — *n* such a restaurant; a takeaway meal. — **take'-down** a humiliation; **take-home pay** pay after deduction of tax, etc; **take'-in** a deception, fraud or disappointment of hopes; **take'-leave** leave-taking; **take'-off** a burlesque mimicking; the place, act or mode of leaving the ground for a jump, dive or flight (also *fig*); a drawback; **take-off rocket** (*aeronautics*) a rocket used to assist the acceleration of an aircraft at take-off. — *adj* **take'out** (*NAm*) takeaway. — *n* and *adj* (*bridge*) (of or designating) a conventional bid asking one's partner to bid a different suit. — **take'over** the acquirement of control of a business by purchase of a majority of its shares. — Also *adj*. — **take'-up** the fact, or an instance, of taking up (ie using or accepting, or picking up). — Also *adj*. — **take-up rate** the number of people, as a percentage of the total number eligible, who claim a benefit to which they are entitled or who accept an offer; **tāking-off'** removal, assassination. — Many phrases with **take** are given below; others are covered in the entries for their other elements. — **on the take** engaged in small-scale dishonest making of profit; **take after** to resemble (eg a parent) in appearance or characteristics; **take against** to take a dislike to; to oppose; **take apart** to separate into component parts; to defeat convincingly (*colloq*); to criticize or scold severely; **take away** to subtract; to carry somewhere else, remove; **take back** to retract, withdraw; to carry back (mentally) in time; to return to an original position; to move (text) to the previous line (*printing*); **take down** to go above in class; to demolish, pull down or dismantle; to take to pieces; to report or write down to dictation; (of a man) to escort (a lady) to the dining-room; (also, more *usu*, **take down a peg**) to humiliate to some degree; to reduce; to lower; **take effect** to come off, succeed; to come into force; **take five** (or **ten**) (*colloq*) to take a short break of five (or ten) minutes; **take for** to suppose to be, *esp* wrongly; **take fright** see under **fright**; **take heed** to be careful; to pay attention; **take in** to enclose; to comprise; to annex; to grasp, realize or understand; to accept as true; to cheat; to subscribe for, buy regularly; to receive into one's home eg as a guest or lodger; to accept (work, eg washing) for doing in one's own home for payment; to tighten, contract, make smaller; to furl; to admit; to subdue; to visit (a place) or go to (a show, etc) *esp* as part of an itinerary or plan (*US*); (of a man) to conduct (a lady) to the dining-room; **take in hand** to undertake; to undertake to reform, help or guide (someone); **take into one's head** to be seized with a notion; **take in vain** to use (eg God's name) with unsuitable levity; **take it** to assume; to endure punishment or bad luck without giving way or collapsing under the strain (*colloq*); **take it from me** you can believe me, believe me when I say; **take it from there** to deal with a situation appropriately, at whatever point it falls to one to do so; **take it or leave it** to accept something with all its disadvantages, or else do without it; **take it out of** to exhaust the strength or energy of; to exact the utmost from; **take it out on** to make (an innocent person or object) suffer for one's anger or frustration; to vent one's bad temper, anger, etc on; **take me with you** (*Shakesp*) let me understand what you mean; **take notice** to observe; to show that observation is made; (with *of*) to remark upon; **take off** to remove, detach; to mimic; to leave the ground for a jump or flight; to begin a rapid improvement, expansion, or surge in popularity; to depart or set out (*colloq*); to swallow; **take on** to receive aboard; to agree to do, to undertake; to assume or acquire; to take into employment; to be very upset or distraught (*colloq*); to accept a challenge from (*esp* a stronger opponent); (of ideas, etc) to gain acceptance; **take out** to remove from within; to extract; to go out with, escort; to obtain (eg a licence) on application; to receive an equivalent for; to copy (*Shakesp*); to kill, destroy or defeat (*slang*); to bid a different suit from (one's partner) (*bridge*); **take over** to receive by transfer; to convey across; to assume control of; to move (text) to the following line (*printing*); **takeover bid**; **takeover bidder**; **take someone out of himself** or **herself** to make someone forget his or her problems or worries; **take someone up on** to accept someone's offer or challenge with respect to; to challenge someone over (a statement, point, etc); **take to** to make for, take oneself off to; to adapt oneself to; to become fond of, to begin to do regularly as a habit; **take to pieces** to separate into component parts; **take to task** to call to account, reprove; **take to wife** (*archaic*) to marry; **take up** to lift, to raise or collect; to pick up for use; to absorb; to accept (an offer); to adopt the practice, study, etc, of, begin to go in for; to begin to patronize, seek to advance; to become interested in and begin to do; to discuss with; to shorten (a garment); to engross, occupy or fill fully; to interrupt sharply; to arrest; to resume; to take in hand; to buy up; to settle, compound (a quarrel) (*Shakesp*); to reprove (*Shakesp*); to cope with (*Shakesp*); to obtain on credit (*Shakesp*); (*usu* in passive) to interest, please (with *about* or *with*); to borrow; to secure, fasten; **take upon oneself** to assume; to presume; to take responsibility for; to undertake; to feign, make believe (*Shakesp*); **take up with** to begin to associate with, form a connection with. [Late OE *tacan* (pa t *tōc*) to touch, take, from ON *taka* (pa t *tōk*; pa p *tekinn*)]

takhi or **taki** *tak'i*, *n* a rare wild horse (*Equus Przewalskii*) native to the Mongolian steppes, with a reddish-brown coat, stiff black mane and white muzzle. [Native Mongolian name]

takin *tä'kin* or *tä-kēn'*, *n* a large horned, hoofed mammal (*Budorcas taxicolor*) of the Himalayas, China, etc, related to the goats and antelopes. [Tibetan]

tala *tä'la*, *n* a traditional rhythmic pattern in Indian music. [Sans, hand-clapping]

talak. See under **talaq**.

talapoin *tal'ə-poin*, *n* (a title of respect for) a Buddhist monk, *esp* of Pegu, Myanmar (formerly Burma); a small green W African guenon monkey (*Cercopithecus talapoin*). [Port *talapão*, from Old Peguan *tala pôi* my lord]

talaq or **talak** *ta-läk'*, *n* (under Islamic law) a form of divorce. [Ar *talāq* divorce]

talar, **talaria**. See under **talus**[1].

talant and **talaunt**. Spenserian forms of **talon**.

talayot *tä-lä'yot*, (*archaeol*) *n* a prehistoric *usu* unchambered stone monument of the Balearic Islands. [Balearic Sp for Sp *atalaya* an outlook, from Ar *al talā'i* the vanguard]

talbot *töl'bət*, *n* a breed of broad-mouthed large-eared hound, *usu* white, now extinct. [Poss from the *Talbot* family]

talbotype *töl'bə-tīp*, *n* calotype, invented by William Henry Fox *Talbot* (1800–77).

talc *talk*, *n* talcum powder; a very soft, pliable, greasy, silvery-white, foliated, granular or compact mineral, acid magnesium silicate, found in magnesium-rich rocks and dolomitic limestones. — *vt* to apply or treat with talc: — *pr p* **talc'ing** (*talk'*) or **talck'ing**; *pa t* and *pa p* **talc'ed** (*talkt*) or **talck'ed**. — *adj* **talc'ose**, **talc'ous**, **talc'y** (*talk'*) or **talck'y**. — *n* **talc'um** talc. — **talc schist** a schistose rock composed essentially of talc, with accessory minerals; **talcum powder** purified powdered talc, *usu* perfumed, applied to the skin to absorb moisture. [Fr *talc* or LL *talcum*, from Ar *talq*, from Pers *talk*]

tale *tāl*, *n* an act of telling; a narrative, story; a false story; a mere story; (in *pl*) things told idly or to get others into trouble; number, total (*archaic*); reckoning (*archaic*); discourse, talk (*obs*). — *adj* **tale'ful** full of stories. — **tale'bearer** someone who gossips idly or maliciously passes on (*esp* discreditable) information about others, *esp* to someone in authority; **tale'bearing**. — Also *adj*. — **tale'-teller** a teller of stories, narrator; a talebearer. — **be in a** (or **one**) **tale** (*archaic*) to be in full agreement; **old wives' tale** a superstitious or misleading story, explanation or precept; any extraordinary tale that makes demands on one's credulity; **tell a tale** to disclose something important; **tell one's** (or **its**) **own tale** to speak for oneself or itself; **tell tales** to gossip or pass on (discreditable) information about others, to be a talebearer; **tell tales out of school** to reveal confidential matters. [OE *talu* story, number; Ger *Zahl* number]

talea *tä'li-ə*, (*music*) *n* a recurring rhythmic pattern in isorhythmic medieval motets: — *pl* **taleae** (*tä'li-ē*). [L, literally, stick or cutting]

talegalla *tal-i-gal'ə*, *n* the brush turkey, *Talegalla* (or *Alectura*) *lathami*. [Malagasy *talèva* the purple coot, and L *gallus* a cock]

talent[1] *tal'ənt*, *n* any natural or special gift; special aptitude or ability; eminent ability short of genius; persons of special ability; young girls or young men, *esp* attractive, handsome, etc (*colloq*); disposition; *orig*, an ancient unit of weight and of money — 60 minas or 6000 drachmas, or about 38kg (Aeginetan talent), 25kg (Euboic), 26kg (Attic) of gold or silver; hence (from the parable, Matt 25. 14–30) faculty; (*Shakesp* **tallent**) *perh* wealth, abundance, or *perh* golden tresses. — *adj* **tal'ented** possessing talent or aptitude. — *adj* **tal'entless**. — **talent scout** or **tal'ent-spotter** someone whose business is to discover and recruit talented people, *esp* in entertainment and sport. — *vi* and *vt* **tal'ent-spot**. [L *talentum*, from Gr *talanton* a balance, a talent]

talent[2]. An old form (*Shakesp*, *Scott*, now *dialect*) of **talon**.

taler. See under **thaler**.

tales *tā'lēz*, (*orig pl*; *law*) *n* the filling up, from those who are present, of a deficiency in the number of jurors. — **talesman** (*tā'lēz-mən* or *tālz'mən*) a bystander chosen to make up a deficiency in a jury. — **pray a tales** to plead that the number of jurors be completed in this way. [From the phrase *tālēs de circumstantibus* such of the bystanders; *tālēs*, pl of L *tālis* such]

tali. See **talus**[1].

Taliacotian or **Tagliacotian** *tal-yə-kō'shən*, *adj* pertaining to the Italian surgeon Gasparo *Tagliacozzi* or *Taliacotius* (1546–99), or his rhinoplastic operation.

taligrade *tal'i-grād*, (*zool*) *adj* walking on the outside of the feet. [L *talus* ankle, and *gradus* step]

talion *tal'i-ən*, (*legal hist*) *n* like for like; retaliation. — *adj* **talion'ic**. [L *tāliō*, *-ōnis* like punishment, from *tālis* such]

talipes *tal'i-pēz*, *n* club foot. — *adj* **tal'iped** (*-ped*) having a club foot. — Also *n*. [L *tālus* ankle, and *pēs* foot]

talipot or **talipat** *tal'i-pot*, *-pat*, *-put*, *n* an E Asian palm (*Corypha*) with large, hand-shaped leaves. [Sinh *talapata*, from Sans *tālī* palmyra palm, and *pattra* leaf]

talisman *tal'is-mən*, or *-iz-*, *n* an object supposed to be indued with magical powers and able to protect, bring good fortune, etc to the possessor; an amulet or charm: — *pl* **tal'ismans**. — *adj* **talismanic** (*-man'ik*) or **talisman'ical**. [Ar *tilsam*, from Gr *telesma* payment, certificate, later completion, rite, consecrated object, from *teleein* to complete, fulfil, consecrate]

talk *tök*, *vi* to speak, to express or communicate in spoken words; to converse; to have a discussion (often with *about*); to chat or gossip; to be able to speak; to speak indiscreetly; to divulge secrets, part with (*esp* incriminating) information, eg to the police (*colloq*); to speak pompously or bombastically; (of eg money, wealth, etc) to have influence, be effective (*colloq*). — *vt* to utter; to speak about; to mean, have in mind, as in *we're talking millions here* (*colloq*; *esp US*); to speak in (a language); to bring or render by talking. — *n* conversation; discussion; gossip or rumour; mention of possibility or proposal; a general theme, eg of gossip or a conversation; utterance; pompous or bombastic speech (*colloq*); a short informal address; (in *pl*) detailed and extended discussions; a particular way of speaking. — *adj* **talk'able** easy to converse with; to be talked about. — *n* **talkabil'ity**. — *n* **talk'athon** (*colloq*, *orig US*) a long-drawn-out discussion, debate, talking session etc. — *adj* **talk'ative** given to much talking. — *adv* **talk'atively**. — *n* **talk'ativeness**. — *n* **talk'er**. — *n* **talk'ie** (*old-fashioned colloq*; commonly in *pl*) a talking film, cinematograph picture accompanied by sound. — *n* and *adj* **talk'ing**. — *adj* **talk'y** talkative. — **talk'back** a two-way radio system; a phone-in (*Austr* and *NZ*); **talk'ee-talk'ee** or **talk'y-talk'y** a corrupt dialect; chatter; a little harangue. — Also *adj*. — **talk'fest** (*colloq*; *esp US*) an informal meeting for discussion; **talk'-in** (a gathering for the purpose of) an informal yet intensive discussion; **talking book** a recording of a reading of a book, *esp* for use by the blind; **talking head** a person talking on television, viewed in close-up, contrasted with programmes with more action; **talk'ing-machine** a machine to produce imitation speech; **talk'ing-point** a matter of or for talk; **talking shop** (*colloq*) a meeting or a place for discussion, as opposed to decision or action (also **talk shop**); **talk'ing-to** a reproof, ticking-off; **talk-show** see **chatshow** (under **chat**[1]); **talk'-you-down** an apparatus by means of which instructions are given to aircraft pilots to help them to land. — **know what one is talking about** (*colloq*) to be an expert; **look who's talking** (*ironic*) you're a fine one to be saying that; **now you're talking** (*colloq*) now you are saying something I want to hear, or something important or to the point; **talk against time** to keep on talking merely to fill up time, as often happens in parliament; **talk at** to address remarks to indirectly; to talk to incessantly, without waiting for a response; to address pompously; **talk back** to reply impudently; to reply on a two-way radio system; **talk big** to talk boastfully or over-confidently; **talk down** to speak or argue more loudly or aggressively than, and so silence; to talk as though to people inferior to oneself in intellect or education; to bring (an aircraft) to a landing by radioed instructions from the ground (**talk-down system** the apparatus and procedures for doing this); **talk the hindlegs off a donkey** see under **donkey**; **talking of** apropos of, now that mention has been made of; **talk into** to persuade; **talk out** to defeat (a parliamentary bill or motion) by going on speaking until it is too late to vote on it; to resolve (a difference of opinion) by thorough discussion; **talk over** to persuade, convince; to discuss, consider together; **talk round** to talk of all sorts of related matters without tackling (the subject at issue); to bring to one's way of thinking by talking persuasively; **talk shop** see under **shop**; **talk tall** to boast; **talk to** to address; to rebuke; **talk turkey** see under **turkey**; **talk up** to speak boldly; to praise, *esp* to arouse interest in; to make much of; **you can't** (or **can**) **talk** (*colloq*) you are in no position to criticize or disagree. [ME *talken*, frequentative of **tell**]

tall *töl*, *adj* high in stature, *esp* higher than average; long, *esp* in a vertical direction; lofty; (*usu* of a person) of a stated height, as in *six feet tall*; great, remarkable; (of talk) bombastic, inflated in style; hardly to be believed (as in *tall tale*); doughty, stout (*obs*). — *adj* **tall'ish**. — *n* **tall'ness**. — **tall'boy** a high chest of drawers, one portion superimposed on another or on a dressing-table; a glass with a long stem; a long narrow top for a smoky chimney; **tall copy** a book with ample margins above and below; **tall hat** a top hat; **tall men** (*obs*) loaded dice; **tall order** see under **order**; **tall-poppy syndrome** (*Austr colloq*) the tendency or desire to cut any successful or prominent person down to size; **tall ship** a square-rigged ship. — **a tall man of his hands** a deft worker; a sturdy fighter; **talk tall** and **walk tall** see under **talk** and **walk**. [Appar OE *getæl* prompt]

tallage *tal'ij*, *n* a tax levied by the Norman and Angevin kings on their demesne lands and towns, or by a feudal lord on his tenants (*hist*); an aid, toll or rate. — *vt* to levy a tax upon. — *adj* **tall'iable** subject to tallage. — *vt* **tall'iate** to lay a tallage upon. [OFr *taillage*, from *tailler* to cut or to tax]

tallat, **tallet** or **tallot** *tal'ət*, (*W of England*) *n* a loft. [Welsh *taflod*, from LL *tabulāta* flooring]

tallent. See under **talent**[1].

tallet. See **tallat**.

talliable and **talliate**. See **tallage**.

tallier. See **tally**.

tallith *tal'ith*, *n* the Jewish prayer shawl. [Heb *tallūth*]

tall-oil *täl'oil*, *n* an oily liquid which is a by-product of chemical wood pulp, used in the manufacture of paints, linoleums, soaps, etc. [Swed *tallolja*, from *tall* pine, and *olja* oil]

tallot. See **tallat**.

tallow *tal'ō*, *n* fat, grease; rendered fat, *esp* of cattle and sheep, used eg for making soap and candles; any coarse, hard fat. — *adj* of, for or like tallow. — *vt* to grease with tallow; to produce tallow. — *adj* **tall'owish**. — *adj* **tall'owy**. — **tall'ow-candle** a candle made of tallow; **tall'ow-catch** (*Shakesp*) *perh* a receptacle for tallow, or a lump (keech) of tallow; **tall'ow-chandler** a dealer in tallow candles, etc; **tall'ow-dip** a candle made by dipping a wick in tallow; **tall'ow-face** (*Shakesp*) a person with a pasty yellow face. — *adj* **tall'ow-faced**. — **tallow tree** any of various trees (eg *Sapium*, *Pentadesma*, *Aleurites*) yielding a thick oil or vegetable tallow, or a substance capable of making candles. [ME *talgh*; cf Ger *Talg*]

tally *tal'i*, *n* a score or account, *esp* one kept by notches or marks; a mark made in recording or scoring an account; credit, tick; a full number or total score; a number taken as a unit in computation; a stick notched to mark numbers or keep accounts; half of such a stick split across the notches, serving as receipt or record (*hist*); a corresponding part, a counterpart; a distinguishing mark; a label; a plant-label; a tag: — *pl* **tall'ies**. — *adv* (*old slang*) in concubinage. — *vt* to keep score, count, calculate or mark down by tally; to mark or provide with a label or tally; to notch or mark as a tally; to reckon; to match, adapt. — *vi* to correspond, match, agree; to deal on credit: — *pr p* **tall'ying**; *pa t* and *pa p* **tall'ied**. — *n* **tall'ier**. — **tally clerk** a checker of ship's cargoes against a list; **tall'yman** a person who keeps a tallyshop; a salesman for a tallyshop; someone who keeps a tally; someone who lives with a woman without marriage (*old slang*): — *fem* **tall'ywoman**; **tall'yshop** a shop where goods are sold on credit to be paid for by instalments, the seller having one account-book which tallies with the buyer's; **tall'y-system** or **-trade** a method of dealing on credit for payment by instalments. — **live tally** (*old slang*) to cohabit without marriage. [Anglo-Fr *tallie*, from L *tālea* a stick]

tally-ho *tal-i-hō'*, *interj* the huntsman's cry signifying that a fox has been sighted. — *n* a cry of tally-ho; a four-in-hand coach: — *pl* **tally-hos'**. — *vt* to greet with tally-ho: — *pr p* **tally-ho'ing**; *pa t* and *pa p* **tally-ho'd** or **tally-ho'ed**. — *vi* to call tally-ho. [Cf Fr *taïaut*]

talma *tal'mə*, *n* a loose cloak or cape. [From F J *Talma* (1763–1826), the actor]

Talmud *tal'mo͝od* or *-mud*, (also without *cap*) *n* the fundamental code of Jewish civil and canon law, the *Mishnah* and the *Gemara*. — *adj* **Talmud'ic** or **Talmud'ical**. — *n* **Tal'mudist** a scholar of the Talmud. — *adj* **Talmudist'ic**. [Heb *talmūd* instruction, from *lāmad* to learn]

talon *tal'ən*, *n* a hooked claw or finger; an ogee moulding (*archit*); the part of the bolt of a lock that the key presses on when it is turned; cards remaining after the deal, the stock; a detachable printed part of a form or certificate, *esp* of bearer bonds entitling the holder to apply for a new sheet of coupons (*stock exchange*). — *adj* **tal'oned**. [Fr *talon*, from LL *tālō*, *-ōnis*, from L *tālus* the heel]

Talpa *tal'pə*, *n* the mole genus of the family **Tal'pidae** (*-pi-dē*); (without *cap*) an encysted tumour on the head, a wen. [L, a mole]

taluk *tä-lo͞ok'*, **taluka** or **talooka** *tä-lo͞ok'ə*, (*Ind admin*) *n* a hereditary estate; a subdivision of a district for revenue purposes, a collectorate. — *n* **taluk'dar** holder of a taluk. [Hindi *ta'alluq* estate]

talus[1] *tā'ləs*, *n* the ankle bone or astragalus: — *pl* **tā'lī**. — *n* **tā'lar** a robe reaching the ankles. — *n pl* **talaria** (*tə-lā'ri-ə*) winged sandals, or wings on the ankles, as of Hermes in Greek mythology. [L *tālus* ankle]

talus[2] *tā'ləs*, *n* the sloping part of a work (*fortif*); a scree formed from frost-shattered rocks (*geol*); a slope (*archaic*). [Fr, from LL *talutium* a slope]

talweg. Same as **thalweg**.

TAM *abbrev*: television audience measurement.

tam. See **Tam o' Shanter**.

tamale *tä-mäl'i*, *n* a highly seasoned Mexican dish of meat, chilli sauce and maize dough wrapped *usu* in a corn husk and steamed or baked. Also **tamal'**. [Sp *tamal* (pl *tamales*), from Nahuatl *tamalli*]

tamandua *tä-män'dū-ä* or *-dwä'*, *n* a S American anteater smaller than the antbear. — Also **tamandu'**. — *n* **tamanoir** (*tä-mä-nwär'*; Carib *tamanoa*, same root as *tamanduà*) the great antbear. [Port *tamanduá*, from Sp *tamándoa*, from Tupí *tamanduà*]

tamanu *täm'ä-no͞o*, *n* a lofty gamboge tree of the East Indies and Pacific Islands, its trunk yielding tacamahac. [E Ind]

tamara *tam'ə-rə*, *n* a mixture of cinnamon, cloves, coriander, etc.

tamarack *tam'ə-rak*, *n* (the wood of) the American or black larch. [Am Ind]

tamarau, **tamarao** *tam'ə-row* or **timarau** *tim'ə-row*, *n* a small wild buffalo (*Bubalus* (or *Anao*) *mindorensis*) native to Mindora in the Philippines, with thick brown hair and short horns. [Tagálog]

tamari *ta-mä'ri*, *n.* a concentrated sauce made of soya beans and salt. [Jap]

tamarillo *tam-ə-ril'ō*, *n.* Same as **tree tomato**.

tamarin *tam'ə-rin*, *n* any small Central and S American monkey of the genera *Saguinus* and *Leontopithecus*, related to the marmosets. [Fr, from Carib]

tamarind *tam'ə-rind*, *n* a large tropical caesalpiniaceous tree (*Tamarindus indica*) which bears yellow flowers and long brown seed pods; its wood; its pod, filled with a pleasant, slightly acid, sweet, reddish-black pulp used in making drinks and medicines. [Ar *tamr-Hindī* date of India]

tamarisk *tam'ə-risk*, *n* a plant of the genus **Tam'arix** giving name to a family (**Tamaricā'ceae**; *-ri-kā'si-ē*) of xerophytic plants with slender branches and pink and white flowers, one species a naturalized shrub of S English seashores. [L *tamariscus*, *tamarix*]

tamasha *tə-mä'shä*, (*Ind*) *n* an entertainment, show; fuss. [Ar and Pers *tamāshā*]

tambac. See **tombac**.

tamber *tam'bər*, *n.* Anglicized form of **timbre**.

tambour *tam'bo͞or*, *n* a drum of any of various types, eg the bass drum, or a single-headed tambourine-like instrument, *usu* without jingles; a circular embroidery frame for keeping the fabric being worked taut; a rich gold and silver embroidery; embroidery done on a tambour; a cylindrical stone forming part of a column or the centre of a Corinthian capital (*archit*); the drum of a recording instrument; a vestibule in a church porch, etc; palisading to defend a gate, etc; a flexible top (eg of a desk) or front (eg of a cabinet) made of narrow strips of wood fixed closely together on canvas, the whole sliding in grooves; a sloping buttress or projection for deflecting a ball in eg real tennis and fives. — *vt* to embroider on a tambour. — *vi* to do tambour-work. — *n* **tambour'a** an Eastern stringed instrument, used to produce a drone (also **tambura**). — *n* **tambourin** (*tã-bo͞o-rɛ̃*) a Provençal dance or dance-tune with drone bass; a long, narrow drum used *esp* to accompany this. — *n* **tambourine** (*tam-bə-rēn'*) a shallow single-headed drum with jingles fitted round its rim, played on by beating or tapping with the hand. — Also (*Spenser*) **tam'burin**. — *n* **tambourin'ist**. [Fr *tambour* drum; Pers *tanbūr*, and Ar *tunbūr* tamboura]

tambura. See under **tambour**.

tame *tām*, *adj* having lost native wildness and shyness; cultivated; domesticated; (of land, crops, etc) improved by cultivation (*US*); gentle; spiritless; without vigour; dull, flat, uninspiring; wonted, accustomed (*Shakesp*). — *vt* to make tame or domestic; to make gentle; to subdue; to reclaim. — *vi* to become tame. — *n* **tamabil'ity** or **tameabil'ity**. — *adj* **tam'able** or **tame'able**. — *n* **tam'ableness** or **tame'ableness**. — *n* **tame'less**. — *n* **tame'lessness**. — *adv* **tame'ly**. — *n* **tame'ness**. — *n* **tam'er**. — *n* **tam'ing**. — **tame cat** (*US*) a person who is happy to be completely dominated by another. [OE *tam*; Ger *zahm*; Gr *damaein*, L *domāre* to tame]

Tamil *tam'il*, *n* a member of a Dravidian people of SE India and N, E, and central Sri Lanka; the language of this people. — *adj* **Tam'il**, **Tamil'ian**, **Tamil'ic** or **Tamūl'ic**.

tamin, **tamine** *tam'in*, *n* a thin worsted fabric, with a highly glazed finish. [Fr *étamine*; cf **stammel**]

tamis *tam'is*, *n* same as **tammy**¹. — *n* **tamise** (*tä-mēz'*) a name for various thin woollen fabrics. [Fr]

Tammany Hall *tam'ə-ni höl*, *n* a Democratic political society, notorious for its corrupt influence in New York city politics in the 19c (also **Tamm'any**); the building it met in, leased to the Democratic party of New York. — *adj* **Tamm'any**. — *n* **Tamm'anyism**. — *n* **Tamm'anyite**. [From an Indian chief, *Tammanend*, who is said to have signed the treaty with Penn]

tammar *tam'ər*, *n* a small scrub wallaby (*Macropus eugenii*) native to S and SW Australia. [Aboriginal]

Tammie Norie *tam'i nō'ri*, (*Scot*) *n* the puffin.

Tammuz *tam'o͞oz* or *-uz*, *n* a Babylonian, Sumerian and Assyrian sun-god, identified with Adonis (also called **Thammuz**); the tenth month of the Jewish civil year, fourth of the ecclesiastical.

tammy¹ *tam'i*, *n* a strainer; a glazed woollen or mixed fabric. [Appar same as **tamis**, or perh **tamin**]

tammy² *tam'i*, *n* a Tam o' Shanter.

Tam o' Shanter *tam-ə-shan'tər*, *n* the hero of Burns's poem of the same name; a cap with broad circular flat top (*colloq* **tam** or **tamm'y**).

tamoxifen *tam-ok'si-fen*, *n* a drug which inhibits the effect of oestrogen, used *esp* in the treatment of advanced breast cancer, and now also thought to have useful preventive effects in certain women at relatively high risk of developing breast cancer.

tamp *tamp*, *vt* to stop up (a shot hole) with earth, etc after the explosive has been introduced; to ram down so as to consolidate (eg ballast on a railway track); to pack round. — *n* **tamp'er** a person who, or thing which, tamps; an instrument for pressing down tobacco in a pipe; a casting round the core of a nuclear weapon to delay expansion and act as a neutron reflector. — *n* **tamp'ing** the act of filling up a hole for blasting; the material used. — **tamp down** (*colloq*) to bend the thumb over the neck of a guitar and hold down (one or more bass strings) with it. [Perh back-formation from *tampin*, variant of **tampion**]

tamper¹ *tam'pər*, *vi* (*usu* with *with*) to interfere unwarrantably or damagingly; to meddle; to work, contrive or practise; to have secret or corrupt dealings. — *vt* (*obs*) to temper (eg clay). — *n* **tam'perer**. — *n* **tam'pering**. — *adj* **tamper-ev'ident** (of packaging) designed in such a way that it is obvious when it has been tampered with. — *adj* **tamp'er-proof** (of locks, etc) that cannot be tampered with. — *adj* **tamper-resist'ant**. [A by-form of **temper**]

tamper², **tamping**. See under **tamp**.

Tampico *tam-pē'kō*, *n* a port in Mexico. — **Tampico fibre** istle.

tampion *tam'pi-ən*, or **tompion** *tom'pi-ən*, *n* a plug, *esp* a protective plug placed in the muzzle of a gun when not in use. [Fr *tampon*, from *tapon* a plug of cloth]

tampon *tam'pon*, *n* a plug of cotton or other absorbent material inserted into a wound or orifice to control haemorrhage, etc or into the vagina to absorb menstrual flow; an inking-pad; a two-headed drumstick. — *vt* to plug with a tampon. — *n* **tamponade'** (*-nād'*) or **tam'ponage** surgical use of a tampon. [A reintroduction from Fr; see ety for **tampion**]

tam-tam *tum'-tum* or *tam'-tam*, *n* a gong, *esp* one used in an orchestra; *esp* formerly, a tom-tom. [**tom-tom**]

tamworth *tam'wûrth*, (also with *cap*) *n* a breed of long-bodied pigs with golden-red hair. [*Tamworth* in Staffordshire, where the breed originated]

Tamulic. See under **Tamil**.

tan¹ *tan*, *n* a suntan; a tawny brown colour; a lightish brown colour, beige (*US*); oak bark or other material used for tanning; spent bark. — *adj* tawny or (*US*) beige. — *vt* to convert into leather by steeping in vegetable solutions containing tannin, or mineral salts, or synthesized chemicals; to treat with tan or tannin; to make brown, suntanned or tawny; to beat (*colloq*). — *vi* to become tanned: — *pr p* **tann'ing**; *pa t* and *pa p* **tanned**. — *n* **tan'ling** (*Shakesp*) someone tanned by the sun. — *adj* **tann'able**. — *n* **tann'age** tanning; that which is tanned. — *n* **tann'ate** a salt of tannic acid. — *adj* **tanned**. — *n* **tann'er**. — *n* **tann'ery** a place where hides, etc are tanned. — *adj* **tann'ic** of, relating to or produced by tan or tannin. — *n* **tann'in** a colourless, amorphous, bitter substance derived from gallnuts, sumach, many barks and other vegetable matter, used in tanning and dyeing, and occurring in wines (*esp* red), giving a distinctive flavour. — *n* **tann'ing** the art or practice of tanning or converting skins and hides into leather. — Also *adj*. — **tan'-balls** tanner's used bark pressed into lumps for fuel; **tan'bark** any bark good for tanning; **tan'-bed** (*hortic*) a bark bed. — *adj* **tan'-coloured**. — **tan'-liq'uor**, **-ooze** or **-pickle** an aqueous extract of tanbark; **tannic acid** tannin; **tan'-pit** or **-vat** a vat in which hides are steeped with tan; **tan'-ride** a riding track laid with tan; **tan'yard** a tannery, or a part of it. — **flowers of tan** see under **flower**. [OE *tannian* (found in pa p *getanned*), *tannere* tanner; also OFr *tan*, from Bret *tann* oak]

tan² *tan*, (*trig*) *n* a conventional short form for **tangent**.

tana¹, *tä'nə*, *n* a military or police station in India. — Also **ta'nna**, **ta'nnah**, **tha'na**, **tha'nah**, **tha'nna** or **tha'nnah**. — *n* **ta'nadar** or **tha'nadar** an officer in charge of a tana. [Hindi *thānā*, *thāna*]

tana² *tä'nə*, *n* a mainly terrestrial tree shrew (*Lyonogale tana*) of Sumatra and Borneo. [Malay (*tūpai*) *tāna* ground (squirrel)]

Tanach *ta'nahh*, *n* the three divisions of the Jewish Old Testament, comprising the Law, Prophets and Hagiographa, taken as a whole. [Vocalization of the Heb acronym *TNK*, *torah* law, *nebhī'īm* prophet, and *kethūbhīm* (other) writings]

tanager *tan'ə-jər*, *n* any passerine bird of the S American family subfamily *Thraupinae*, closely related to the buntings, the males having brightly-coloured plumage. — *n* **Tan'agra** a genus of this family. — *adj* **tan'agrine**. [Tupí *tangará*]

Tanagra *tan'ə-grə*, *n* a town of ancient Boeotia; (without *cap*) a terracotta figurine made there.

tanaiste *tön'ish-tä*, *n* the deputy prime minister of the Republic of Ireland. [Ir, second, next, deputy; cf **tanist**]

tanalized or **tanalised** *tan'ə-līzd*, (*building*) *adj* (of timber) treated with **Tan'alith**®, a proprietary preservative.

tandem *tan'dəm*, *n* a bicycle, tricycle, etc for two people, one behind the other; an arrangement of two things, one placed behind the other, *orig* of two horses harnessed singly one behind the other; a vehicle with such a team of horses. — Also *adj*. — *adv* one behind the other; in the position of horses harnessed singly one behind the other. — *adv* **tan'demwise**. — **tandem roller** a road roller with front and back rollers of approximately the same diameter. — **in tandem** with one behind the other; together or in conjunction. [Punning application of L *tandem* at length]

tandoori *tan-* or *tun-dōōr'i*, *n* a type of Indian cooking in which meat, vegetables, etc are baked over charcoal in a clay oven. — Also *adj*. — *n* **tandoor'** a clay oven. [Hindi *tandoor* a clay oven]

tane[1] or **ta'ne**. Obsolete spellings (*Spenser* and *Shakesp*, etc) of **ta'en** (**taken**).

tane[2] *tān*, (*Scot*) *pronoun* one (**the tane** for *that ane*, the one). [See **tae**, **tone**[2], **tother**]

T'ang or **Tang** *tang*, *n* a Chinese dynasty (AD 618–907). — *adj* of this dynasty, its period or its poetry and art, *esp* pottery, etc. [Chin]

tang[1] *tang*, *n* a biting, characteristic or extraneous flavour, after-taste or smell; a smack, tinge or hint; pungency; a projecting piece or shank; a point, sting or spike; part of a tool that goes into the haft; a prong; a barb; a sea-surgeon. — *adj* **tanged** (*tangd*) with a tang; barbed. — *adj* **tangy** (*tang'i*) having a fresh or sharp taste or smell (also *fig*). [ON *tange* point, tang]

tang[2] *tang*, *n* a ringing sound; a twang. — *vt* to cause to ring; to utter ringingly (*Shakesp*). — *vi* to ring. [Imit; influenced by next word]

tang[3] *tang*, *n* coarse seaweed. [Cf Norw and Dan *tang*]

tanga *tang'gə*, *n* a brief string-like bikini; (women's or men's) briefs consisting of a waistband and a triangle of fabric at front and back, so that the hips are left exposed at either side.

tangelo *tan'ji-lō*, *n* a hybrid between *tang*erine orange and pom*elo*: — *pl* **tan'gelos**. [Portmanteau word]

tangent *tan'jənt*, *adj* of or involving a tangent; touching without intersecting. — *n* a line that touches a curve; the limiting case of a secant when the two points of intersection coincide; (often *abbrev* **tan**; as a function of an angle) the ratio of the side of a right-angled triangle opposite the given angle to the side opposite the other acute angle (*trig*) (the tangent of an obtuse angle is equal numerically to that of its supplement, but has the negative sign); the striking-pin of a clavichord. — *n* **tan'gency** (*-jən-si*) fact of being tangent; a contact or touching. — *adj* **tangential** (*-jen'shəl*) of a tangent; in the direction of a tangent; peripheral, irrelevant (*fig*). — *n* **tangentiality** (*tan-jen-shi-al'i-ti*). — *adv* **tangen'tially** or **tangen'tally** in the direction of a tangent. — **tangent galvanometer** a galvanometer with a vertical circular coil and a horizontal magnetic needle, which measures a current passed through it by assessing the magnetic field produced which deflects the needle. — **at a tangent** in the direction of the tangent; in a divergent train of thought or action; in continuation in the momentary direction instead of following the general course. [L *tangens*, *-entis*, pr p of *tangere* to touch]

tangerine *tan'jə-rēn* or *-rēn'*, *n* a mandarin orange, *esp* a small, flattish, loose-skinned variety; the colour of this fruit, a reddish orange; (with *cap*) a native of *Tangier* on the coast of Morocco. — *adj* tangerine-coloured or -flavoured; (with *cap*) of Tangier.

tanghin *tang'gin*, *n* a Madagascan poison, formerly used to test the guilt of someone suspected of a crime; the apocynaceous tree yielding it. — *n* **tangh'inin** its active principle. [Malagasy *tangèna*]

tangi *tan'ji*, *n* a Maori ceremony of mourning, a funeral. [Maori *tangihanga*]

tangible *tan'ji-bl*, *adj* perceptible by the touch; capable of being possessed or realized; material, corporeal. — *n* (*usu pl*) a tangible thing or asset, ie physical property as opposed to goodwill. — *n* **tangibil'ity** or **tan'gibleness**. — *adv* **tan'gibly**. [L *tangibilis*, from *tangere* to touch]

tangie *tang'i*, *n* an Orcadian water-spirit, appearing as a seahorse, or man covered with seaweed. [From **tang**[3]]

tangle[1] *tang'gl*, *vt* to form into, involve in, or cover with, a confused interwoven mass; to entangle; to hamper or trap (*colloq*). — *vi* to become tangled; (with *with*) to become involved in conflict or argument (*colloq*); (with *with*) to embrace (*colloq*). — *n* a tangled mass or condition; a perplexity or complication; a naturalist's dredge consisting of bundles of frayed rope or similar material; involved relations, conflict, argument. — *adj* **tang'led**. — *n* **tang'lement**. — *n* **tang'ler**. — *adj* **tang'lesome**. — *n* and *adj* **tang'ling**. — *adv* **tang'lingly**. — *adj* **tang'ly** tangled; inclined to tangle. — **tang'lefoot** (*US*) whisky, intoxicating liquor; **tangle net** a long net, anchored to the sea bed at both ends; **tangle'-netter** a fishing boat using a tangle net. [Appar from earlier *tagle*; see **taigle**]

tangle[2] *tang'gl*, *n* coarse seaweed, *esp* the edible Laminaria. — *adj* **tang'ly**. — **tang'le-picker** the turnstone (qv under **turn**); **tan'gleweed** tangle. [Appar connected with ON *thöngull* Laminaria stalk, from *thang* bladder-wrack]

tangle[3] *tang'gl*, (*Scot*) *n* any tall and limp person or thing; an icicle. — *adj* long and limp. — *adj* **tang'ly**. [Origin obscure]

tango[1] *tang'gō*, *n* a ballroom dance or dance-tune in 4-4 time, of Argentinian origin, characterized by long steps and pauses: — *pl* **tan'gos**. — *vi* to dance the tango: — *pr p* **tang'going**; *pa t* and *pa p* **tang'oed**. — *n* **tang'oist**. [Sp, a S American Negro festival or dance]

tango[2] *tang'gō*, *n* (in international communications) a code word for the letter *t*.

tangram *tan'gram*, *n* a Chinese puzzle, a square cut into seven pieces that will fit together in various ways. [Origin obscure]

tangun *tang'gun*, *n* the Tibetan piebald pony. [Hindi *tāghan*, from Tibetan *rtanān*]

tangy. See under **tang**[1].

tanh *tansh* or *than*, *n* a conventional short form for *h*yperbolic *tan*gent.

tanist *tan'ist*, (*hist*) *n* a Celtic chief's heir elect. — *n* **tan'istry** the system of succession by a previously elected member of the family. [Ir *tánaiste*, Gaelic *tànaiste* heir, successor]

taniwha *tan'i-fä*, *n* a mythical Maori monster, *usu* a water monster. [Maori]

tank *tangk*, *n* a large basin or cistern; a reservoir of water, oil, etc; an armoured, enclosed, armed vehicle moving on caterpillar wheels; a receptacle for developing solutions (*photog*); the amount held in a tank, a tankful; a prison or prison cell (*US slang*); a pool, pond, reservoir (*Ind* and *Austr*); a pond (*US*). — *vt* to store in a tank; to plunge into a tank; to defeat, thrash (*slang*). — *vi* to drink heavily (with *up*; *slang*); to refuel (often with *up*; *colloq*); to travel (*esp* to drive) at great speed or relentlessly; to lose or drop points, games, etc deliberately (*tennis slang*). — *n* **tank'age** storing in tanks; charge for such storage; the capacity of a tank or tanks; residue from tanks; a fertilizer derived from the dried residues of animal carcases. — *adj* **tanked** (*slang*; often with *up*) drunk. — *n* **tank'er** a ship or heavy vehicle that carries liquids, *esp* oil in bulk; an aircraft that refuels others. — *n* **tank'ful**: — *pl* **tank'fuls**. — *n* **tank'ing** a defeat, a thrashing (*slang*); waterproof material included in an underground structure to prevent infiltration of subsoil water (*building*, *civ eng*). — **tank'buster** (*military slang*) a jet aircraft designed to attack and destroy tanks; **tank'busting**; **tank'-car** or **-wagon** a railway wagon for carrying oil or other liquid in a large tank; **tank engine** a locomotive that incorporates its own tanks for carrying water and coal (without the need for a tender); **tank farm** an area with tanks for storing oil; **tank'-farmer**; **tank'-farming** hydroponics; **tank furnace** (*glass*) a furnace consisting of a large 'box' of refractory material, which can hold up to 200 tonnes of glass; **tank top** a sleeveless pullover, *usu* with a low round neckline, worn over a shirt, etc;

tank'-trap an obstacle large enough to stop a military tank. [Port *tanque*, from L *stagnum* a pool]

tanka[1] *tang'kə* or *täng'kä*, *n* (also with *cap*) the boat population of Canton, inhabiting **tank'a-boats**. — Also **tan'kia**. [Chin]

tanka[2] *tang'kə*, *n* a waka, a Japanese poem of five lines and 31 syllables, the first and third lines having five syllables and the others seven: — *pl* **tan'ka** or **tan'kas**. [Jap *tan* short, and *ka* verse]

tankard *tangk'ərd*, *n* a large mug-like vessel, *usu* with a handle and sometimes a hinged lid, used *esp* for drinking beer from; the amount contained in a tankard. — **cool-tankard** see under **cool**. [Cf MDu *tanckaert*]

tankia. See under **tanka**[1].

tanky *tang'ki*, (*slang*) *n* a hard-line communist, a strict follower of Marxist-Leninism. [Perh from **tank**, because of hard-line communist reluctance to condemn Soviet intervention (using *tanks*) in Afghanistan in 1979]

tanling. See under **tan**[1].

tanna. See under **tana**[1].

tannable, **tannage**. See under **tan**[1].

tannah. See under **tana**[1].

tannate, **tanned**. See under **tan**[1].

tanner[1] *tan'ər*, (*old slang*) *n* a sixpence.

tanner[2], **tannery**, **tannic**, **tannin**, etc. See under **tan**[1].

Tannoy® *tan'oi*, *n* a sound-reproducing and amplifying system. — *vt* **tann'oy** to call by, use, or make a sound by, Tannoy.

tanrec. See **tenrec**.

tansy *tan'zi*, *n* a bitter, aromatic roadside composite plant (*Tanacetum vulgare*) with small heads of tubular yellow flowers, the leaves having formerly been used in cookery and medicine; extended to other plants, such as ragwort, silverweed and yarrow; a pudding or cake flavoured with tansy, eaten at Easter. — **like a tansy** exactly right. [OFr *tanasie*, through LL from Gr *athanasiā* immortality]

tantalate. See under **tantalum**.

Tantalean, **Tantalian**, **Tantalic**. See under **Tantalus**.

tantalic, **tantalite**, **tantalous**. See under **tantalum**.

tan'talize or **-ise** *tan'tə-līz*, *vt* to torment by presenting something desirable but keeping it out of reach; to entice or provoke frustratingly; to torture or tease laboriously into unnatural form (*obs*). — *n* **tan'talism** the punishment of Tantalus; a tormenting. — *n* **tantalīzā'tion** or **-s-**. — *n* **tan'talizer** or **-s-**. — *n* and *adj* **tan'talizing** or **-s-**. — *adv* **tan'talizingly** or **-s-**. [Tantalus]

tantalum *tan'tə-ləm*, *n* a metallic element (symbol **Ta**; atomic no 73), acid-resistant and useful for electronic and surgical parts. — *n* **tan'talate** a salt of tantalic acid. — *adj* of or containing tantalum. — *n* a black mineral, the main ore from which tantalum is derived. — *adj* **tan'talous** of or containing trivalent tantalum. — **tantalic acid** an acid ($HTaO_3$) that forms salts or tantalates; **tantalum lamp** an electric lamp with tantalum filament. [**Tantalus**, from its inability to absorb water]

Tantalus *tan'tə-ləs*, *n* a son of Zeus punished in Tartarus (for revealing secrets of the gods) by having to stand in water that ebbed when he attempted to drink, overhung by grapes that drew back when he reached for them; (without *cap*) a case in which alcohol decanters are visible but locked up; (without *cap*) any bird of the wood-ibis genus *Tantalus*. — *adj* **Tantā'lean**, **Tantā'lian** or **Tantalic** (*-tal'ik*) of Tantalus. — **Tan'talus-cup** a philosophical toy, with a siphon within the figure of a man whose chin is on a level with its bend.

tantamount *tan'tə-mownt*, *adj* (with *to*) amounting to as much or to the same; equivalent; equal in value or meaning. [Anglo-Fr *tant amunter* to amount to as much]

tantara *tan-tä'rä*, *n* a blast on the trumpet or horn. — Also **tantara'ra**. [Imit]

tanti *tan'tī* or *tan'tē*, (*archaic*) *adj* worth while. [L, of so much worth; genitive of *tantum*, neuter of *tantus* so much]

tantivy *tan-tiv'i*, (*rare* or *archaic*) *adv* at full gallop; headlong. — *n* a hunting cry; a rapid rush; a nickname for a Tory High Churchman (*hist*). — *adj* headlong; High Church Tory (*hist*). — *interj* expressive of galloping or (later) expressive of the sound of the hunting-horn. [Imit]

tant mieux *tã myø*, (*Fr*) so much the better.

tanto *tan'tō*, (*Ital*; *music*) *adv* so much, too much. [L *tantum* so much]

tantony. See under **Anthony**.

tanto uberior *tan'tō ū-bē'ri-ər* or *ōō-be'ri-or*, (*L*) so much the richer.

tant pis *tã pē*, (*Fr*) so much the worse.

Tantra or **tantra** *tan'-* or *tun'trə*, *n* any of a number of Hindu and Buddhist writings giving religious teaching and ritual instructions (including the use of incantations, diagrams, etc); the teaching of the Tantras. — *adj* **Tan'tric** or **tan'tric**. — *n* **Tan'trism** the teaching of the Tantras. — *n* **Tan'trist**. [Sans *tantra* thread, fundamental doctrine]

tantrum *tan'trəm*, *n* a sudden fit of childish, uncontrolled bad temper or rage. [Origin unknown]

Tantum ergo *tan'təm ûr'gō*, or *tan'tōōm er'gō*, the fifth stanza of the Latin hymn 'Pange, lingua, gloriosi corporis mysterium', written for the office of the Festival of Corpus Christi, which St Thomas Aquinas drew up in 1263. [From its opening words]

taoiseach *tē'shohh*, *n* the prime minister of the Republic of Ireland. [Ir, chief, leader]

Tao *tä'ō*, *tow* or *dow*, *n* (in Taoism) the absolute entity which is the source of all existence and change; (in Confucianism and some other philosophies) the way to be followed, right or proper conduct. [Chin, way, path]

Taoism *tä'ō-izm*, *tow'izm* or *dow'izm*, *n* the philosophical system set forth in the *Tao Te Ching* (ascribed to the legendary Chinese philosopher Lao-tzu, *perh* born 604 BC), and other works; a religious system combining Taoist philosophy with magic and superstition and the worship of many gods. — *n* and *adj* **Ta'oist**. — *adj* **Taoist'ic**. [Tao]

tap[1] *tap*, *n* a gentle knock or its sound; a protective piece on a shoe heel; a shoe sole (*dialect*); a metal piece attached to the sole and heel of a shoe for tap-dancing; tap-dancing; (in *pl*) a signal (*esp* a bugle call) for putting lights out, also used at military funerals (*orig US military*). — *vt* and *vi* to knock gently. — *vi* to walk making a tapping sound; to tap-dance. — *vt* to provide or repair with a tap: — *pr p* **tapp'ing**; *pa t* and *pa p* **tapped**. — *adj* **tapp'able**. — *n* **tapp'er** a person who taps; a person who soles and heels; an instrument or part that taps; a decoherer. — *n* and *adj* **tapp'ing**. — **tap'-dance**. — Also *vi*. — **tap'-dancer**; **tap'-dancing** dancing characterized by rhythmical striking of dancer's tapped shoes on the floor; **tap'-in** an act of striking the ball in the air with the hand, so that it goes into the basket (*basketball*); a very short, light putt required to put the ball into the hole (*golf*); **tap'-kick** (*Rugby football*) a light kick which starts play from a penalty, with the same team keeping possession of the ball; **tap'-shoe** a tapped shoe for tap-dancing. [OFr *taper*]

tap[2] *tap*, *n* a hole or short pipe with a valve for running off a fluid; a peg or stopper on a barrel, etc; a taproom; any particular liquor drawn through a tap; a screw for cutting an internal thread; a taproot; a device, which when attached to a telephone line, enables, eg the police, security forces, etc secretly to listen to conversations; an instance of tapping a telephone wire; (often in *pl*) tap stock. — *vt* to pierce, so as to let out fluid; to broach; to draw off; to draw upon, *esp* for the first time (*fig*); to attach a receiver to (a telephone line) in order secretly to overhear conversations; to eavesdrop on (a conversation) by this means; to get supplies, information, etc from; to get money from (*slang*); to supply with a tap, or with a screw-thread. — *vi* to act as a tapster: — *pr p* **tapp'ing**; *pa t* and *pa p* **tapped**. — *n* **tapp'er** someone who taps trees, etc; a milking-machine. — *n* **tapp'ing** the act or art of drawing out or running off a fluid; an operation for removal of liquid from the body. — *n* **tap'ster** a person who draws liquor, a barperson. — **tap'-bolt** a screwed-in bolt; **tap'-cinder** slag produced in a puddling furnace; **tap'-dressing** well-dressing; **tap'-house** a tavern; **tap issue** tap stocks; **tap'lash** poor or weak liquor, *esp* stale beer; the dregs from a cask; **tap'room** a room where beer is served from the tap or cask; **tap'root** a strong main root growing down vertically; **tap stock** government bonds, etc to which the public can subscribe at any time; **tap water** water from a household tap. — **on tap** kept in cask (*opp* to *bottled*); continuously and readily available (*fig*); **tap into** (*comput*) to gain unauthorized access to (a company's computer system, files, etc). [OE *tæppa* tap, *tæppestre* (female) tapster; Du *tap*, Ger *Zapfen* tap]

tap[3] *tap*, *n* a Scots form of **top**. — *adj* **tapp'it** crested. — **tapp'it-hen** a crested hen; a drinking vessel with a knob on the lid, of capacity variously stated at 1, 3 or 6 imperial quarts; a wine-bottle size equivalent to *approx* three standard bottles, 2.27 litres, used *esp* for port; **taps'man** a servant in overall charge of others; chief of a company of drovers. — **take one's tap in one's lap** (*Scot*) to bundle up (one's flax or tow for the distaff) and go home.

tap[4] *tap*, *n* an Indian malarial fever. [Pers]

tapa[1] or **tappa** *tä'pə*, *n* paper-mulberry bark; a fabric made from this. [Polynesian generally]

tapa[2] *tä'pa*, *n* (*usu* in *pl*) a light savoury snack or appetizer, *esp* one based on Mediterranean, *esp* Spanish, foods and cooking techniques: — *pl* **ta'pas**. — **tapas bar** a bar where tapas are served along with alcoholic drinks. [Sp]

tapaculo *tä-pä-koo'lō* or **tapacolo** *tä-pä-kō-lō'*, *n* a small S American passerine bird (family *Rhinocryptidae*) with a tilted tail: — *pl* **tapacu'los** or **tapaco'los**. [Sp *tapaculo*, from *tapa* cover (imperative), and *culo* posterior]

tapadera *tä-pä-dä'rə* or **tapadero** *tä-pä-dä'rō*, *n* the leather guard in front of a Mexican stirrup: — *pl* **tapader'as** and **tapader'os**. [Sp, lid, cover, from *tapar* to cover]

tape *tāp*, *n* material woven in long narrow bands; a strip of such material, used for tying up, connecting, sticking, etc; a strip of material stretched across the track at the winning-line of a race; a ribbon of paper printed by a recording instrument, as in telegraphy; a flexible band that guides the sheets (*printing*); a tape measure; magnetic tape; a tape recording or cassette; liquor (*slang*). — *vt* to provide, fasten, bind or measure with a tape; to tape-record; to get the range or measure of; to deal out, or use, sparingly (*Scot*). — *adj* **tape'able**. — *adj* **tape'less**. — *adj* **tape'like**. — *adj* **tā'pen** (*rare*) made of tape. — *n* **tā'per** a person who works with tapes. — *n* **tā'pist** a red-tapist. — **tape deck** a machine for recording sound on tape and playing tape-recorded sound through a separate amplifier as part of a hi-fi system; a tape drive; **tape drive**, **deck** or **transport** (*comput*) a mechanism within a computer or peripheral device which moves magnetic tape across the recording and playback heads; **tape grass** any plant of the genus *Vallisneria*; **tape'line** or **tape measure** a flexible measuring strip of tape, steel or other material; **tape'-loop** a length of magnetic tape or film with the ends joined together to form an endless strip, allowing a recording to be continuously repeated; **tape luring** the luring and subsequent capture of a seabird by playing tape-recordings of its call from beaches and cliffs. — *vt* **tape'-lure**. — **tape machine** a telegraphic instrument by which messages received are automatically printed on a tape; **tape punch** (*comput*) a device which encodes data by punching holes in paper tape; **tape reader** a device which senses data recorded on paper or magnetic tape and converts it into a form suitable for computer processing. — *vt* **tape'-record** to record (sound) using a tape recorder. — **tape recorder** an instrument for recording sound on magnetic tape and subsequently reproducing it; **tape'-recording** the act or process of recording sound on magnetic tape; (**tape recording**) a magnetic tape on which sound has been recorded; the sound so recorded; **tape'script** a tape-recorded reading of a complete text; **tape streamer** (*comput*) a continuous loop of magnetic tape for use in a tape drive, used for backing up information. — *adj* **tape'-tied** tied up with tape; bound with, or by, red tape (see under **red**[1]). — **tape transport** see **tape drive** above; **tape'worm** a ribbon-shaped segmented parasitic worm, any cestode, but *esp* of *Taenia* or related genus. — **breast the tape** in winning a foot-race, to pass through or break with one's chest the tape stretched across the track at the winning-line; **have something** or **someone taped** to have a thorough understanding of someone or something; **magnetic tape** see under **magnet**; **red tape** see under **red**[1]. [OE *tæppe* tape, fillet]

tapenade *tap-ə-näd'*, *n* a paste made from capers, anchovies and black olives, seasoned with olive oil and lemon juice, used in French (*esp* Provençal) cooking. [Provençal *tapéo* capers]

taper *tā'pər*, *n* a long thin waxed wick or spill; a feeble light; lengthwise diminution in width; gradual leaving off; a wax-candle (*obs*). — *adj* tapering. — *vi* to become gradually smaller towards one end; to diminish slowly in size, quantity or importance (with *off*). — *vt* to make to taper. — *adj* **tā'pered** tapering; lighted by tapers (*literary*). — *n* **tā'perer** a person who carries a taper. — *n* and *adj* **tā'pering**. — *adv* **tā'peringly**. — *n* **tā'perness**. — *adv* **tā'perwise**. — **taper pin** (*eng*) a pin, used as a fastener, very slightly tapered to act as a wedge; **taper roller bearing** (*eng*) a roller bearing able to sustain end thrust by the use of tapered rollers. [OE *tapor*]

tapestry *tap'is-tri*, *n* an ornamental textile used for the covering of walls and furniture, etc, and for curtains, made by passing coloured threads or wools through a fixed-warp fabric; a picture or design made of this; a machine-made imitation of this; anything like a tapestry in being intricate and with many closely-interwoven elements (*fig*). — *adj* of tapestry (*Milton* **tap'stry**). — *vt* to hang with tapestry; to work or represent in tapestry. — *adj* **tap'estried**. — **tapestry moth** a moth of the Tineidae family (*Trichophaga tapetzella*), with brown, white-tipped forewings. [Fr *tapisserie*, from *tapis* a carpet, from LL *tapētium*, from Gr *tapētion*, dimin of *tapēs*, *-ētos*, prob of Iranian origin]

tapet *tap'it*, (*Spenser*) *n* a piece of tapestry. [L *tapēte*, perh through OE *tæppet*]

tapeti *tap'ə-ti*, *n* the Brazilian rabbit. [Tupí]

tapetum *tə-pē'təm*, *n* a layer of cells surrounding spore mother-cells (*bot*); the light-reflecting pigmentary layer of the retina (*zool*): — *pl* **tapē'ta**. — *adj* **tapē'tal**. [L *tapētum*, from Gr *tapēs*, *-ētos* carpet]

taphephobia or **taphophobia** *taf-ə-fō'bi-ə*, *n* morbid fear of being buried alive. [Gr *taphē* burial, *taphos* grave, and **phobia**]

taphonomy *tə-fon'ə-mi*, *n* the study or science of how plants and animals die, decay and become buried, fossil or fossilized. — *adj* **taphonom'ic** or **taphonom'ical**. — *n* **taphon'omist** an expert or specialist in taphonomy. [Gr *taphos* grave, and **-nomy**]

taphrogenesis *taf-frō-gen'ə-sis*, (*geol*) *n* vertical movements of the Earth's crust resulting in the formation of major faults and rift valleys. [*taphros* pit, and **genesis**]

tapioca *tap-i-ō'kə*, *n* a farinaceous substance made by heating cassava; extended to a kind of sago and a preparation of potato starch; a pudding made from tapioca. — **pearl-tapioca** see under **pearl**[1]. [Tupí-Guaraní *tipyoca*, from *tipi* juice, and *ok* to squeeze out]

tapir *tā'pər*, *n* a large odd-toed hoofed mammal with a short flexible proboscis, several species of which are found in S America, Malaya, etc. — *adj* **tā'piroid**. [Tupí *tapira*]

tapis *tä'pē*, also *tap'is*, (*obs*) *n* a covering, hanging, etc of tapestry or the like. — **on the tapis** on the table; under consideration. [Fr]

tapist. See under **tape**.

tapotement *tə-pōt'mənt, tä-pot-mã*, *n* the use of light taps in massage. [Fr]

tappa. See **tapa**[1].

tappet *tap'it*, *n* a projection that transmits motion from one part of a machine to another by tapping, *esp* in an internal-combustion engine from the camshaft to the valves. — **tapp'et-loom**, **-mōtion**, **-ring**, **-rod**, etc. [**tap**[1]]

tappice *tap'is*, *vi* to lie low. — *vt* to hide. [Fr *tapir*, *tapiss-*]

tappit, **tappit-hen**, **tapsman**. See under **tap**[3].

tapsalteerie *tap-sl-tē'ri* or **tapsieteerie** *tap-si-tē'ri*, *adv*, *adj* and *n*, Scots forms of **topsyturvy**.

tapstry *tap'stri* (*Milton*). See **tapestry**.

tapu *tä'pōō*. Same as **taboo**. [Maori]

tar[1] *tär*, *n* a dark, viscous mixture obtained by destructive distillation of wood, coal, peat, etc; a natural bituminous substance of similar appearance (mineral tar). — *vt* to smear, coat or treat, with tar: — *pr p* **tarr'ing**; *pa t* and *pa p* **tarred**. — *n* **tarriness** (*tär'i-nis*). — *n* and *adj* **tarr'ing**. — *adj* **tarr'y** (*tär'i*) of, like, covered or soiled with tar. — **tar'-box** a shepherd's box for tar as salve for sheep; a shepherd; **tar'boy** a person who, during the shearing of sheep, puts tar or antiseptic on cuts; **tar'-brush** a brush for applying tar; **tar'-heel** (*US slang*) a North Carolinian; **tarmacad'am** or **tar'mac** (also **Tarmac**® in *US*) a road surfacing of broken stone covered or mixed with tar; (**tar'mac**) the runways of an airport. — *vt* **tar'mac** to surface with tarmacadam: — *pr p* **tar'macking**; *pa t* and *pa p* **tar'macked**. — **tar'-paper** heavy paper treated with tar, used as a building material; **tar pit** (*geol*) an outcrop where natural bitumen occurs; **tarr'y-breeks** (*Scot*) a sailor. — *adj* **tarr'y-fingered** thievish. — **tar'-sand** a deposit of sand or sandstone saturated with bitumen, from which petroleum can be extracted; **tar'-seal** (*NZ*) a tarmacadam surface on a road; a road so surfaced. — *vt* to seal the surface of (a road) by covering with tarmacadam. — **tar'-spot** a black spot of Rhytisma; **tar'-water** a cold infusion of tar in water, once popular as a medicine; **tar'weed** a name for various heavy-scented American composites. — **tar and feather** to smear with tar and then cover with feathers as a punishment; **tarred with the same brush** or **stick** having the same defects; **touch of the tar-brush** (*derog*) a certain amount of eg Negro blood resulting in darkish skin. [OE *teru*, *teoro*; Ger *Teer* (from LGer), and Du *teer*]

tar[2] *tär*, (*colloq*) *n* a sailor. [Perh for **tarpaulin**]

tar[3] (*Shakesp* **tarre**) *tär*, *vt* to set on, incite to fight. [Connected with OE *tergan* to worry]

tara *tä'rə*, *n* a variety of bracken found in New Zealand and Tasmania, with an edible rhizome. — Also **ta'ra-fern**. [Perh a native Tasmanian name]

taradiddle. See **tarradiddle**.

tarakihi *ta-rə-kē'hē, -kē'ē*, or **terakihi** *te-rə-*, *n* a morwong. [Maori]

taramasalata *tar-ə-mə-sə-lä'tə*, *n* a Greek dish, a pink creamy paste made of grey mullet or smoked cod's roe with olive oil and garlic. [Mod Gr, from *taramas* preserved roe, and *salata* salad]

tarand *tar'ənd*, (*obs*) *n* a northern beast fabled to change colour like the chameleon; a reindeer. [Gr *tarand(r)os* a reindeer or (probably) elk]

tarantara. See under **taratantara**.

tarantas or **tarantass** *tä-rən-täs'*, *n* a four-wheeled, horse-drawn Russian vehicle mounted on poles. [Russ *tarantas*]

tarantella *tar'ən-tel'ə*, *n* a lively Neapolitan dance (in triplets for one couple), once thought a remedy for tarantism; a tune for it. — *n* **tar'antism** (*med hist*) an epidemic dancing mania *esp* prevalent in S Italy from the 15c to the 17c, popularly thought to be caused by the tarantula bite. [*Taranto*, in S Italy]

tarantula *tə-ran'tū-lə*, *n* a large venomous S European hairy wolf spider (*Lycosa tarentula*), once supposed to cause tarantism; any of various large hairy spiders of the family *Theraphosidae*, whose bite is painful but not generally venomous to man; (in America) applied to large venomous spiders of the bird-catching family (*Aviculariidae*); (in Africa) a biting but not venomous solpugid; (in Australia) applied to several large harmless laterigrade spiders, *esp* the huntsman spider; (with *cap*) a genus of pedipalps. — **tarantula juice** (*US*) bad whisky. [Med L *tarantula*, from Ital *tarantola*, from Gr *Taras*, *-antos* Tarentum, Taranto]

taratantara *tär-ə-tan'tə-rə*, or *-tan-tä'rə*, *n* the sound of a trumpet or trumpet fanfare. — Also *interj*, *adj*, *adv*, *vt*, and *vi*. — Also **taran'tara**. [Imit]

taraxacum *tə-raks'ə-kəm*, *n* a plant of the dandelion genus *Taraxacum*; its root and rootstock, a tonic laxative. [Appar from Ar *tarakhshaqōq*, from Pers *talkh chakōk*, assimilated to Gr *taraxis* disturbance]

tarboggin. See under **toboggan**.

tarboosh, **tarboush** or **tarbush** *tär-bōōsh'*, *n* a fez, a hat worn by Muslim men, sometimes as the base of a turban. [Ar *tarbūsh*]

tarcel. See **tercel**.

Tardenoisian *tär-di-noi'zi-ən*, (*archaeol*) *adj* belonging to a stage of culture represented by flint implements found at *Tardenois*, Aisne, France, transitional between Palaeolithic and Neolithic.

tardigrade *tär'di-grād*, *adj* slow-paced; of or pertaining to the Tardigrada. — *n* a member of the Tardigrada. — *n pl* **Tardigrā'da** a class of arthropods found in water, ditches, etc, the bear-animalcules; formerly the sloths. [L *tardus* slow, and *gradī* to step]

tardy *tär'di*, *adj* slow; sluggish; behindhand; too long delayed; late; caught at fault (*obs*). — *vt* (*Shakesp*) to retard. — *adv* **tar'dily**. — *n* **tar'diness**. — *adj* **tar'dive** (*-div*) late in development. — **tardive dyskinesia** (*med*) a condition caused by long-term use of some tranquillizers, characterized by loss of muscle control leading to eg involuntary facial and head movements and excessive salivating. — *adj* **tar'dy-gaited** (*archaic*) slow-paced. [Fr *tardif*, from L *tardus* slow]

tare[1] *tār*, *n* a vetch of various kinds, *esp* of the lentil-like group; a weed, *prob* darnel (*Bible*). [Origin obscure]

tare[2] *tār*, *n* the weight of a vessel, wrapping or container, which subtracted from the gross weight gives the net weight; an allowance made for this; the weight of an empty vehicle, without cargo, passengers, fuel, etc. — *vt* to ascertain or allow for the tare of. — *n* **tar'ing** the calculating of a tare. [Fr, from Sp *tara*, from Ar *tarhah* thrown away]

tare[3] *tār*, *archaic pa t* of **tear**[2].

targa top *tär'gə top*, *n* a removable hard roof on a car, which fits into the boot when not in use. — *adj* **targa-topp'ed**.

targe[1] *tärj*, *n* a shield, *esp* a light shield. [OFr *targe*, from ON *targe* shield]

targe[2] *tärj*, (*Scot*) *vt* to cross-examine; to supervise strictly; to reprimand; to thrash. [Origin unknown]

target *tär'git*, *n* a round or shield-like mark to shoot at for practice or competition; an object aimed at (also *fig*); a butt or focus (eg of unkind remarks or actions); a result to be aimed at; a shooting score; a neck and breast of lamb; a small buckler or round shield (*hist*); a surface on which electrons impinge at high velocity, such as the fluorescent screen of a cathode-ray tube; a plate in a television camera tube on which external scenes are focused and scanned by an electron beam; a reflecting object which returns radiated pulse energy to the receiver of a radar system (*radar*); a sight on a levelling staff; an American railway signal. — *adj* chosen as a target, aimed at. — *vt* to aim; to aim at; to make, or identify as, a focus, target or victim: — *pr p* **tar'geting**; *pa t* and *pa p* **tar'geted** — *adj* **tar'getable** which can be aimed, or aimed at. — *adj* **tar'geted** selected as a target, aimed at; provided with a shield (*hist*). — *n* **targeteer'** (*hist*) a person armed with a shield, a peltast. — **target acquisition** see under **acquire**;

target area an area containing a target, or which is a target, eg of missiles; **target cell** (*immunol*) an antigen-bearing cell which is the target of attack by lymphocytes or a specific antibody; **target language** the language into which a text is to be translated; **target man** (*football*) a tall forward player to whom high passes can be made; **target practice** repeated shooting at a target to improve one's aim. — **on target** on the correct course for a target; on schedule. [OFr *targuete*; cf **targe**[1]]

Targum *tär-gōōm'* or *tär'gəm*, *n* any Aramaic version or paraphrase of the Old Testament: — *pl* **Targums**. — *adj* **Targumic** (*tär-gōō'mik*, *-gū'mik* or *-gum'ik*) or **Targum'ical**. — *n* **Targum'ist** a writer of a Targum; a student of the Targums. — *adj* **Targumist'ic**. [Chaldean *targūm* interpretation]

tariff *tar'if*, *n* a list or set of customs duties; a customs duty levied on particular goods (eg at a hotel); (a list of) standard rates charged for a service, eg electricity or insurance; a menu. — *vt* to set a tariff on. — *n* **tarifficā'tion** the fixing of a tariff; conversion (eg of import restrictions) into a tariff. — *adj* **tar'iffless**. — **tariff-reform'er** a person who favoured the early 20c movement for **Tariff Reform** or Protection opposed to Free Trade; **tariff wall** a barrier to the flow of imports made by high rates of customs duties. [Ital *tariffa*, from Ar *ta'rīf* explanation, from *'arafa* to explain]

taring. See under **tare**[2].

tarlatan *tär'lə-tən*, *n* an open, stiff, transparent muslin. [Fr *tarlatane*; origin doubtful]

tarmac, **tarmacadam**. See under **tar**[1].

tarn *tärn*, *n* a small mountain lake. [ON *tjörn*]

tarnal *tär'nl*, and **tarnation** *tär-nā'shən*, (*US slang*) *adj* and *adv* softened forms of **eternal** and **damnation**, *appar* influenced by each other. — *adv* **tar'nally**.

tarnish *tär'nish*, *vt* to dull, discolour, render iridescent, diminish the lustre of, etc by exposure to the air, etc; to sully or impair. — *vi* to become dull; to lose lustre. — *n* loss of lustre; a surface discoloration or iridescence on metal or mineral; a stain or blemish; a film of oxide, sulphide, etc. — *adj* **tar'nishable**. — *adj* **tar'nished**. — *n* **tar'nisher**. [Fr *ternir*, *terniss-*, from *terne* dull, wan; poss Gmc]

taro *tä'rō*, *n* a plant (genus *Colocasia*) of the arum family, widely cultivated for its edible rootstock in the islands of the Pacific: — *pl* **ta'ros**. — Also called **eddo**. [Polynesian]

tarot *tar'ō*, *n* a card of a type originating in Italy with an allegorical picture; a set consisting of 100 such cards used in card games and *esp* fortune-telling; (*usu* in *pl*) a game played with tarots together with cards of the ordinary suits. — Formerly also **taroc** or **tarok** (*tar'ok*). [Fr *tarot*, from Ital *tarocco*]

tarp *tärp*, (*US* and *Austr*) short for **tarpaulin**.

tarpan *tär'pan*, *n* a small wild horse of the steppes of S European Russia, long extinct but now somewhat restored by selective breeding and introduced into Poland, not identical with the takhi (Przewalski's horse). [Tatar]

tarpaulin *tär-pö'lin*, *n* strong linen or hempen cloth waterproofed with tar or otherwise; a sheet of it; a sailor's waterproof hat; a sailor (*colloq*); a sea-bred officer (*obs*). — Also **tarpaul'ing**. — Also *adj*. [Appar **tar**[1] and **palling**, from **pall**[1]]

Tarpeian *tär-pē'ən*, *adj* of *Tarpeia*, according to legend a Roman officer's daughter who betrayed the Capitol at Rome to the Sabines and was buried beneath the **Tarpeian Rock** on the Capitoline Hill, from which traitors were thrown.

tarpon *tär'pən*, *n* a very large fish (*Tarpon* or *Megalops*) related to the herring, popular with anglers on the Florida and Gulf coasts. [Origin unknown]

tarradiddle or **taradiddle** *tar-ə-did'l*, *n* a fib, a lie; nonsense. [Appar founded on **diddle**]

tarragon *tar'ə-gən*, *n* an aromatic herb (genus *Artemisia*), whose leaves are used for flavouring vinegar, sauces, etc. [Ar *tarkhūn*, perh from Gr *drakōn* a dragon]

Tarragona *tar-ə-gōn'ə*, *n* a strong dry red Spanish wine used in blending or as a substitute for port. [Province in Catalonia]

tarras *tar'əs*, *n* Spenserian for **terrace**. See also **trass**.

tarre. See **tar**[3]. — Also (*Spenser*) for **tar**[1].

tarriance, **tarrier**, **tarrow**. See under **tarry**[2].

tarrock *tar'ək*, *n* a seabird of various kinds (applied to different ones in different areas). [Origin obscure]

tarry[1] *tär'i*. See under **tar**[2].

tarry[2] *tar'i*, *vi* to linger; to loiter; to delay; to stay behind; to sojourn; to wait. — *vt* (*archaic*) to await: — *pr p* **tarr'ying**; *pa t* and *pa p* **tarr'ied**. — *n* (*archaic*) delay; sojourn, stay. — *n* **tarr'iance** (*archaic*) tarrying; delay; waiting; a sojourn. — *n* **tarr'ier** a person who tarries or delays. — *vi* **tarr'ow** (*tär'ō*; *Scot*) to hesitate; to be unwilling. [History obscure; the form agrees with OE *tergan* to irritate, the meaning with OFr *tarier*]

tarsal[1], **tarsel** *tär'sl*. See **tercel**.

tarsal[2], **tarsalgia**. See under **tarsus**.

tarsia *tär'si-ə* or *tär-sē'ä*, *n* intarsia (qv). — Also **tar'sia-work**. [Ital]

tarsier *tär'si-ər* *n* a lemuroid monkey (genus *Tarsius*) of the E Indies, nocturnal, tree-dwelling, with large eyes and long tarsal bones. — *adj* **tar'sioid** like the tarsier; of the tarsier genus *Tarsius*. [*Fr*, *from tarre* tarsus]

Tarsipes *tär'si-pēz*, *n* the genus represented by the honey mouse or honey possum, a long-snouted Australian honey-sucking phalanger with feet like a tarsier. — *n* **tar'siped** a marsupial of the genus *Tarsipes*. [New L *tarsus* tarsus, and L *pes* foot]

tarsus *tär'səs*, *n* the bones forming part of the foot to which the leg is articulated; (in birds) sometimes applied to the tarsometatarsus; (in insects) the five-jointed foot; a plate of connective tissue at the edge of the eyelid: — *pl* **tar'sī**. — *adj* **tar'sal** relating to the tarsus or ankle. — *n* a bone of the tarsus. — *n* **tarsalgia** (*-sal'ji-ə*) pain in the instep. — *adj* **tarsometatar'sal**. — *n* **tarsometatar'sus** a bird's shank-bone, the combined metatarsals and distal tarsals. [Gr *tarsos* the flat of the foot]

tart[1] *tärt*, *adj* sharp; biting; acidulous. — *adj* **tart'ish**. — *adv* **tart'ly**. — *n* **tart'ness**. [OE *teart*]

tart[2] *tärt*, *n* a dish of pastry distinguished from a pie either by being uncovered or by having a sweet, not savoury, filling; a girl (*offensive slang*); a prostitute (*derog slang*). — *n* **tart'iness**. — *n* **tart'let** a small tart. — *adj* **tart'y** (*slang*) like a tart; vulgar, cheaply and blatantly provocative (*esp* of a woman or woman's clothing, etc). — **tart up** (*colloq*) to make more showy or striking, *esp* in a superficial, meretricious or inartistic way; to smarten up (*adj* **tart'ed-up**). [OFr *tarte*]

Tartan® *tär'tən*, *n* a material used to lay tracks for athletic events, usable in all weathers.

tartan[1] *tär'tən*, *n* a woollen (or other) checked material; any of a large variety of checked patterns, as worn by Highland clans of Scotland, each the distinctive mark of an individual clan. — *adj* of tartan; checked in tartan; Scottish, *esp* referring to self-consciously Scottish artefacts or attitudes (*derog*). — *adj* **tar'taned** clad in tartan. — *n* **tartanā'lia** or **tar'tanry** (*derog*) artefacts, imagery, etc that are self-consciously Scottish. [Poss from MFr *tiretaine* linsey-woolsey]

tartan[2] *tär'tən*, *n* a Mediterranean vessel with lateen sail. — Also **tartane** (*tär-tän'*). [Fr *tartane*, poss from Ar *tarīdah* a small ship]

tartana *tär-tä'nə*, *n* a little covered wagon. [Sp]

Tartar[1] *tär'tər*, *n* a Tatar; the Turkic language spoken by the Tatars; (without *cap*) a formidable, rough, unmanageable or ferocious person; (without *cap*) a person who unexpectedly turns the tables on his or her assailant. — Also *adj*. — *n* and *adj* **Tartarian** (*-tā'ri-ən*) Tartar, Tatar. — *adj* **Tartaric** (*-tar'ik*) of the Tartars. — *adj* **Tar'tarly** like a Tartar; (without *cap*) ferocious. — *n* **Tartary** Tatary, qv under **Tatar**. — **Tartarian lamb** barometz. [See **Tatar**]

Tartar[2]. See under **Tartarus**.

tartar *tär'tər*, *n* recrystallized and partially purified argol, chiefly acid potassium tartrate (with calcium tartrate, etc); a deposit of calcium phosphate and other matter on the teeth. — *adj* **tartareous** (*-tā'ri-əs*) of or like tartar; with rough crumbly surface (*bot*). — *adj* **tartaric** (*tär-tar'ik*) of or derived from tartar (**tartaric acid**, $C_4H_6O_6$, prepared from argol or found naturally in plants and fruit). — *n* **tartarizā'tion** or **-s-**. — *vt* **tar'tarize** or **-ise** to treat, mix or combine with tartar. — *n* **tar'trate** a salt of tartaric acid. — *n* **tar'trazine** (*-zēn*) a yellow dye used in textiles, food and drugs. — **tartar emetic** a compound of potassium, antimony, carbon, hydrogen and oxygen, used in dyeing and in medicine. — **cream of tartar** purified argol, used in baking powder, etc. [LL *tartarum*, perh from Ar]

Tartare. See under **Tartarus**.

tartare *tä-tär'*, *n* (also **tartare sauce** or **tartar** (*tär'tər*) **sauce**) a mayonnaise dressing with chopped pickles, olives, capers, etc added, *usu* served with fish. [Fr *sauce tartare*, from **Tartar**[1]]

tartareous. See under **tartar**.

tartaric. See under **tartar**.

Tartarie. See under **Tartarus**.

tartarize. See under **tartar**.

Tartarus *tär'tə-rəs*, *n* in Homer, a deep and sunless abyss, as far below Hades as earth is below heaven; a place for the punishment of evil-doers in Hades; hell. — Also (*Spenser* and *Shakesp*) **Tar'tar**, and (*Spenser*) **Tar'tare**, **Tar'tarie** and **Tar'tary**. — *adj* **Tartarean** (*-tā'ri-ən*). [L, from Gr *Tartaros*]

Tartary. See under **Tartar** and **Tartarus**.

tartine *tär-tēn'*, (*Fr*) *n* a slice of bread with butter or jam.

tartrate, tartrazine. See under **tartar**.

Tartuffe or **Tartufe** *tär-tüf'*, *-tōōf' n* a hypocritical person who pretends to be deeply religious. — *adj* **Tartuff'ian**, **Tartuf'ian**, **Tartuff'ish** or **Tartuf'ish**. — *n* **Tartuff'ism** or **Tartuf'ism**. [From the character in Molière's *Tartuffe* (3-act version 1664, 5-act 1669)]

tarty. See under **tart**[2].

tarwhine *tär'wīn* or *tär'hwīn*, *n* an Australian sea-bream. [Aboriginal]

Tarzan *tär'zan*, *n* a man of great strength and agility. [From the hero of stories by Edgar Rice Burroughs (1875–1950) about a man brought up by apes]

Tas. *abbrev*: Tasmania.

tasar *tus'ər*. Same as **tusser**.

taseometer *tas-i-om'i-tər*, *n* an instrument for measuring strains in a structure. [Gr *tasis*, *-eōs* a stretching, and *metron* measure]

Taser® *tā'zər*, (*orig* and *esp US*; also without *cap*) *n* a small gunlike device which fires electrified darts or barbs, used to immobilize or stun eg an attacker. — *vt* to immobilize or stun with a Taser. — *adj* **Tas'ered**. [From the fictitious *T*om *S*wift's *e*lectric *r*ifle, after *laser*]

tash[1] *täsh*, (*Scot*) *vt* to soil; to blemish; to disfigure; to disarray. [Fr *tacher*]

tash[2] *tash*, (*colloq*) *n* short for **moustache**.

Tashi Lama *tash'i lä'mə*, *n* another name for **Panchen Lama**. [*Tashi*, the name of the monastery of which this lama is the head]

tasimeter *tə-sim'i-tər*, *n* an instrument for measuring changes in pressure, etc by variations in electrical conductivity. — *adj* **tasimet'ric**. [Gr *tasis* a stretch, and *metron* measure]

task *täsk* or *task*, *n* a piece or amount of work set or undertaken (sometimes an *esp* burdensome, difficult or unpleasant one); a single piece of work to be processed (*comput*). — *vt* to burden with heavy or difficult work; to put (a person's skills or capacity) fully or severely to the test; to assign a task or (eg military) mission to; to allocate as a task; to tax (*Shakesp*). — *n* **task'er** a person who imposes or performs a task; a person who does piece-work. — *n* **task'ing** task-work. — **task'-force** or **task'-group** a group formed by selection from different branches of the armed services to carry out a specific task; a similar group within the police force; a working party (qv) for a civilian purpose; **task'master** a person who allots tasks *esp* involving hard, regular or continuous work: — *fem* **task'mistress**; **task'-work** work done as a task, or by the job. — **take (someone) to task** to rebuke (someone). [OFr *tasque* (Fr *tâche*), from LL *tasca*, *taxa*, from L *taxāre* to rate]

taslet. See under **tasse**.

TASM *abbrev*: tactical air-to-surface missile.

Tasmanian *tas-* or *taz-mā'ni-ən*, *adj* of *Tasmania*, island state of Australia discovered in 1642 by Abel Janszoon *Tasman*. — *n* a native or citizen of Tasmania. — **Tasmanian devil** a small ferocious marsupial of the Tasmanian dasyure family, *Sarcophilus harrisii*; **Tasmanian myrtle** a Tasmanian and Victorian evergreen beech; **Tasmanian wolf** (or **tiger**) the thylacine, a striped wolflike dasyure of Tasmania, now virtually extinct.

TASS *tas*, *abbrev*: Technical, Administrative and Supervisory Section (of the **AUEW**); *Telegrafnoye Agentsvo Sovietskovo Soyuza* (*Russ*), telegraph agency of the former Soviet Union, now replaced by **ITAR-TASS**.

tass[1] *täs*, (*dialect*) *n* a mow, a heap. [OFr *tas*, poss from Du]

tass[2] *tas*, *n* a drinking-cup; a small drink. — *n* **tass'ie** (*Scot*) a small cup. [Fr *tasse*, from Ar *tāss* cup]

tasse or **tace** *tas*, *n* (in plate armour) one of a series of overlapping pieces forming a kind of skirt. — *n* **tas'let** or **tass'et** a tasse. [OFr *tasse*, *tasselet*, *tassete*]

tassel[1] *tas'l*, *n* an ornamental hanging tuft of threads; an inflorescence of similar appearance, *esp* of maize; a ribbon book-mark; a clasp or fastening (*Shakesp*); a gold or silver plate on a vestment. — *vt* to provide with tassels; to remove the tassels from. — *vi* (eg of maize) to form tassels, flower: — *pr p* **tass'elling**, or (*US*) **tass'eling**; *pa t* and *pa p* **tass'elled**, or (*US*) **tass'eled**. — *adj* **tass'elled**. — *n* **tass'elling**. — *adj* **tass'elly**. [OFr *tassel*; origin doubtful]

tassel[2]. See under **torsel**.

tassel[3], **tassell**, **tassell-gent** and **tassel-gentle**. See under **tercel**.

tasset. See under **tasse**.

tassie. See under **tass**[2].

taste *tāst*, *n* the act of tasting; the particular sensation caused by a substance on the tongue; the sense by which we perceive the flavour of a thing; the quality or flavour of anything; a small portion; an experience; discernment of, or accordance with, what is socially right or acceptable; the faculty by which the mind perceives the beautiful or elegant; fine perception; choice, predilection, liking; the act of testing (*obs*). — *vt* to try, or to perceive, by the sense located in the tongue and palate; to try or test by eating or drinking a small amount; to eat or drink a small amount of; to partake of; to experience, perceive; to try, test (*obs*); to relish, enjoy (*archaic*); to enjoy carnally (*Shakesp*); to give a flavour to (*rare*). — *vi* to try or perceive by the mouth; to have a flavour (with *of*); to act as taster; to have experience. — *adj* **tāst'able**. — *adj* **tāst'ed** having a taste. — *adj* **taste'ful** full of taste; having a pleasant or a high relish; showing good taste. — *adv* **taste'fully**. — *n* **taste'fulness**. — *adj* **taste'less** without taste; without good taste; insipid. — *adv* **taste'lessly**. — *n* **taste'lessness**. — *n* **tāst'er** someone skilful in distinguishing flavours by the taste; someone employed to test the innocuousness of food by tasting it before serving it to his or her master or mistress (*hist*); any implement or device used to obtain samples for tasting; a publisher's reader (*colloq*); an extract or sample (*colloq*). — *adv* **tāst'ily**. — *n* **tāst'iness**. — *n* **tāst'ing**. — *adj* **tāst'y** savoury, appetizing; tasteful (*colloq*). — **taste bud** a group of cells on the tongue sensitive to taste. — Also **taste bulb**. — **good taste** intuitive feeling for what is aesthetically or socially right; **to one's taste** to one's liking, agreeable to one. [OFr *taster* (Fr *tâter*), as if from a LL frequentative of L *taxāre* to touch, handle, estimate, from *tangere* to touch]

tastevin *tāst'* or *tast'vɛ̃*, *n* a small shallow cup used for tasting wine. [Fr]

tat[1] or **tatt** *tat*, *vt* to make by tatting. — *vi* to make tatting. — *n* **tatt'ing** knotted lace edging made by hand with a shuttle from sewing-thread; the act or process of making this. [Origin uncertain]

tat[2] *tät*, *n* E Indian hempen matting. [Hindi *ṭāṭ*]

tat[3] or **tatt** *tat*, *n* pretentious odds and ends of little real value, eg in an antique shop; tawdry or shabby articles *esp* clothes; a rag, *esp* an old one. — *vt* to touch up. — *adv* **tatt'ily**. — *n* **tatt'iness**. — *adj* **tatt'y** cheap, of poor quality; untidy; shabby; (of clothes or ornament) fussy; precious, and often bogus. [**tatter**]

tat[4] *tat*, *n*. See under **tattoo**[3].

tat[5] *tat*, *n* a tap. — *vt* to touch, tap; to flog. [Cf **tap**[1], and see **tit**[2]]

tat[6]: **tit for tat** See under **tit**[2].

ta-ta *tä-tä'*, (*childish* and *colloq*) *interj* good-bye.

tatami *ta-tä'mi*, *n* a type of mat, of a standard size, made from rice stalks, used as a floor-covering in Japanese houses. [Jap]

Tatar *tä'tər*, *n orig* a member of any of certain Tungusic tribes in Chinese Tartary; extended to any of the Mongol, Turkish and other warriors who swept over Asia and Europe; loosely, one of the mixed inhabitants of Tartary, Siberia and the Russian steppes, *incl* Kazan Tartars, Crim Tartars, Kipchaks, Kalmucks, etc; any of the languages spoken by the Tatars, belonging to the Turkic group of languages; a speaker of a Turkic language. — Also *adj*. — *adj* **Tatarian** (*tä-tā'ri-ən*) or **Tataric** (*-tar'ik*) of the Tatars; of the Turkic group of languages. — *n* **Ta'tary** or **Tar'tary** (*hist*) a name given from the 14c by W European peoples to a vast, ill-defined area of E Europe and Asia, inhabited by Tatars. [Turk and Pers *Tatar*; association with Gr *Tartaros* hell, seems to have suggested the form **Tartar**]

tate or **tait** *tāt*, (*Scot*) *n* a small portion, pinch, tuft.

tater *tā'tər*, *n* a colloquial form of **potato**. — Also **tā'tie**.

tath *täth*, (*dialect*) *n* cattle dung; coarse tufted grass that grows where it has fallen. — *vt* to manure. — *vi* to drop dung. [ON *tath*]

tatin *ta-tɛ̃*, (also with *cap*) *adj* denoting a kind of tart made with fruit (*esp* apples and pears) which has been caramelized, and baked with the pastry on top of the fruit instead of beneath it. [*Tatin*, the name of two French sisters who invented it in the early years of the 20c]

tatler. See under **tattle**.

tatou *ta'to͞o* or *-to͞o'*, *n* an armadillo, *esp* the giant armadillo. [Tupí *tatú*]

tatouay *ta'to͞o-ā*, *n* a large armadillo (*Cabassous unicinctus*) of tropical S America. [Sp *tatuay*, from Guaraní *tatu* armadillo, and *ai* lazy, worthless]

tatpurusha *tat-po͝o'ro͞o-shə*, *n* a class of compound words in which the first element modifies the second by standing to it in various types of relationship, eg possession, as in *goatskin*, location, as in *fieldmouse*, as the object of an action, as in *guitar-player*, and as agent, as in *man-made*; a compound of this class. [Sans *tatpuruṣa* literally, his servant]

tatt[1], **tattily, tattiness, tatty**. See under **tat**[3].

tatt[2]. See **tat**[1].

tatter *tat'ər*, *n* a torn shred; a loose hanging rag. — *vt* to tear to tatters. — *vi* to fall into tatters. — *adj* **tatt'ered**. — *adj* **tatt'ery** ragged. — **in tatters** ragged; ruined. [Cf Icel *töturr*]

tatterdemalion *tat-ər-di-mā'lyən*, or **tatterdemallion** *-di-mal'yən*, *n* a tattered person, a ragamuffin. — *adj* ragged, tattered, scarecrowlike. [From *tattered* or *tatter*, with termination of uncertain formation]

Tattersall's *tat'ər-sölz*, *n* a famous London horse market and haunt of racing-men, founded 1766 by Richard *Tattersall* (1724–95); a sweepstake or lottery agency with headquarters at Melbourne, Australia (*colloq* **Tatts**). — **Tattersall** (a fabric with) a pattern of checks like that of the horse-blankets *orig* used at Tattersall's horse-market. — Also **Tattersall check**.

tattie *tat'i*, *n* a Scots form of **potato**. — **tatt'ie-bogle** a scarecrow; **tatt'ie-claw** potato soup; **tatt'ie-lifting** or **-howk'ing** the potato harvest; **tatt'ie-shaw** the part of a potato plant above the ground.

tatting. See **tat**[1].

tattle *tat'l*, *n* idle talk, chatter; gossip. — *vi* to talk idly, chatter; to gossip, tell tales or secrets. — *vt* to tell, give away, in tattle. — *n* **tatt'ler** (formerly **tat'ler**) an indiscreet talker; a chatterer, a gossip; any (*esp* American) bird of the Totaninae family, so-called because of their loud cry. — *n* and *adj* **tatt'ling** chattering; tale-telling. — *adv* **tatt'lingly**. — **tatt'le-tale** (chiefly *NAm*) a tell-tale. [Used by Caxton to translate MDu *tatelen*; imit]

tattoo[1] *tə-to͞o'*, *n* a beat of drum or other signal calling soldiers to quarters; a drumming; a military entertainment, with marching, displays of prowess, etc, held at night. — **the devil's tattoo** drumming with the fingers on a table, etc, absent-mindedly or impatiently. [Du *taptoe*, from *tap* tap (of a barrel), and *toe* to, in the sense of shut]

tattoo[2] *tə-to͞o'*, earlier **tatu** *tə-to͞o'* and **tattow** *-tow'*, *n* a design marked on the skin by pricking in colouring matter. — *vt* to mark (the skin) in this way; to produce (a design) in this way: — *pa t* and *pa p* **tattooed'**. — *n* **tattoo'er** or **tattoo'ist**. [Tahitian *ta'tau*, Marquesan *ta'tu*]

tattoo[3] *tut'o͞o*, *n* a native-bred Indian pony. — Short form **tat** (*tat*). [Hindi *ṭaṭṭū*]

tattow. See **tattoo**[2].

Tatts. See **Tattersall's**.

tatty[1]. See under **tat**[3] and **taut**[2].

tatty[2] *tat'i*, *n* an Indian mat of bamboo, cuscus-grass roots, etc, *esp* one kept wet in a doorway or window to cool the air. [Hindi *ṭaṭṭī*]

tatu. See **tattoo**[2].

tau *tow*, *n* the nineteenth letter (Τ, τ) of the Greek alphabet, corresponding to T; a tau cross; as a numeral $\tau' = 300$, $\tau = 300\,000$; a tau particle. — **tau cross** a T-shaped cross, St Anthony's cross; **tau particle** (*phys*) a lepton of mass 3600 times greater than that of an electron; **tau staff** a staff with a cross-piece at the top like a crutch. [Gr *tau*, of Semitic origin]

taube *tow'bə*, *n* a German monoplane with recurved wings (1914–18 war). [Ger, dove]

taught[1] *töt*, *pa t* and *pa p* of **teach**.

taught[2]. See **taut**[1].

tauld *töld*. A Scots form of **told** (*pa t* and *pa p*).

taunt[1] *tönt*, *vt* to goad or provoke in a wounding way; to censure or reproach sarcastically or contemptuously. — *vi* to jibe. — *n* a wounding jibe; an object of taunts (*Bible*) — *n* **taunt'er**. — *n* and *adj* **taunt'ing**. — *adj* **taunt'ingly**. [Poss OFr *tanter*, from L *tentāre* to tempt; or Fr *tant pour tant* tit for tat]

taunt[2] *tönt*, (*naut*) *adj* (*esp* of the masts of ships) very tall. [Origin unknown]

taupe *tōp*, *n* and *adj* (of) a brownish-grey colour. [Fr, mole, from L *talpa*]

taupie. See **tawpie**.

Taurean. See under **Taurus**[1].

taurean *tö'rē-ən* or *tö-rē'ən*, or **tauric** *tö'rik*, *adj* of or relating to a bull. [L *taurus* bull]

tauriform *tö'ri-förm*, *adj* having the form of a bull. [L *taurus* bull, and **-form**.]

taurine[1] *tö'rīn*, *adj* of a bull; bull-like. [L *taurīnus*, from *taurus* bull]

taurine[2] *tö'rēn*, *n* a neutral crystalline compound occurring *esp* in invertebrates. [L *taurus* bull (because discovered in the bile of cattle), and **-ine**']

tauro- *tö-rō-*, *-rə-*, *-ro'-*, *combining form* denoting a bull. — *n* **taurobō'lium** (Gr *taurobolion*, from *bolē* a throw or stroke) the sacrifice of a bull, eg as in the ancient Phrygian cult of Cybele; an artistic representation of this. — *n* **tauromachy** (*-rom'ə-ki*; Gr *tauromachiā*, from *machē* fight) bullfighting; a bullfight. — *adj* **tauromā'chian**. — *adj* **tauromor'phous** (Gr *morphē* form) bull-shaped. [L *taurus* and Gr *tauros* bull]

Taurus[1] *tö'rəs* or *tow'ro͞os*), *n* the Bull, a sign of the zodiac and a constellation formerly coinciding with it;

a person born between 21 April and 21 May, the sign of Taurus. — *n* and *adj* **Tau'rean** (or *-rē'ən*) (relating to) a person born under Taurus. [L *taurus* and Gr *tauros* bull]

Taurus[2] *tö'rəs*, (*stock exchange*) *abbrev*: an acronym for *t*ransfer and *au*tomated *r*egistration of *u*ncertified *s*tock, a computerized system of share settlement, without the need for share certificates, abandoned March 1993.

taut[1] (*obs* **taught**) *töt*, *adj* tightly drawn; tense; in good condition. — *vt* and *vi* **taut'en** to tighten. — *adv* **taut'ly**. — *n* **taut'ness**. [Prob connected with **tow**[1] and **tight**[1]]

taut[2] or **tawt** *töt*, (*Scot*) *vt* and *vi* to mat, tangle. — *adj* **taut'it**. — *adj* **tawt'ie** or **tatt'y**. [Cf OE *tætteca* rag]

taut- *töt-*, or **tauto-** *tö-tō-*, *tö-tə-* or *tö-to'-*, *combining form* denoting the same. — *n* **taut'ochrone** (*-krōn*; Gr *chronos* time) a curve such that a particle travelling along it under gravity reaches a fixed point in the same time, no matter where it starts. — *n* **tautoch'ronism**. — *adj* **tautoch'ronous**. — *n* **tautologic** (*-loj'*) or **tautolog'ical**. — *adv* **tautolog'ically**. — *n* **tautol'ogism**. — *n* **tautol'ogist**. — *vi* **tautol'ogize** or **-ise** to use tautology. — *adj* **tautol'ogous** (*-ə-gəs*) tautological. — *adv* **tautol'ogously**. — *n* **tautol'ogy** (Gr *tautologia*, from *tautologos* saying the same thing, from *legein* to say) use of words, *esp* as an error of style, that repeat something already implied in the same statement, etc, as in *all at once she suddenly remembered*. — *n* **taut'omer** (*chem*) (Gr *meros* part) a readily interconvertible isomer. — *adj* **tautomer'ic**. — *n* **tautom'erism**. — *adj* **tautomet'ric** or **tautomet'rical** exactly corresponding in arrangement of syllables. — *n* **taut'onym** (Gr *onyma* name) in a biological nomenclature, a taxonomic name in which the specific name repeats the generic. — *adj* **tauton'ymous**. — *adj* **tautophon'ic** or **tautophon'ical**. — *n* **tautoph'ony** (Gr *phōnē* sound) repetition of a sound. [Gr *tauto*, for *to auto* the same]

tautog *tö-tog'*, *n* a labroid fish (*Tautoga onitis*) of the N American Atlantic coast. [Narragansett *tautauog*]

taver[1] or **taiver** *tā'vər*, (*Scot*) *n* (often in *pl*) a shred, tatter. [Cf Norw and Dan *tave*]

taver[2] or **taiver** *tā'vər*, (*Scot*) *vi* to wander about aimlessly; to rave. — *adj* **ta'vert** or **tai'vert** muddled; fuddled, bewildered; stupid. [Cf Norw *tava* to toil, fumble]

tavern *tav'ərn*, (*usu archaic* or *literary*) *n* a public house or inn. — *n* **tav'erner** a publican. [OFr (Fr) *taverne*, from L *taberna* shed, stall, tavern, from the root of *tabula* a board]

taverna *tə-vûr'nə*, *n* in Greece, a type of guesthouse with a bar, popular as holiday accommodation. [Adopted into Mod Gr; see **tavern**]

TAVR *abbrev*: Territorial and Army Volunteer Reserve (replaced in 1979 by **TA**).

taw[1] *tö*, *n* a large or choice marble; a game of marbles; the line shot from at marbles. [Origin unknown]

taw[2] *tö*, *vt* to prepare (skins) for white leather by soaking, salting, stretching and paring; to flog (*obs*). — *n* (*obs*) tawed leather; a thong or whip. — *n* **taw'er** a maker of white leather. — *n* **taw'ery** a place where skins are dressed. — *adj* **taw'ie** (*Scot*) tractable. — *n* **taw'ing**. [OE *tawian* to prepare; Du *touwen* to curry; OHGer *zawjan* to make, prepare]

tawa[1] *tä'wə*, *n* an evergreen tree (*Beilschmiedia tawa*) of the Lauraceae family, with slender branches and graceful foliage, bearing a damsonlike fruit, native to New Zealand. [Maori]

tawa[2] *tä'wə*, *n* a griddle used in Indian cookery. — Also **tava** or **tavah** (*tä'və*). [Hindi and Punjabi *tava* griddle, frying-pan]

tawdry *tö'dri*, *adj* showy without taste or worth; gaudily adorned. — *n* trumpery; a tawdry-lace (*obs*) — *adv* **taw'drily**. — *n* **taw'driness**. — **taw'dry-lace'** (*obs*) a woman's silk necktie (in *Spenser* a waist-belt) such as was sold at St Audrey's Fair at Ely (17 October); gaudy adornment. [From *St Audrey* (ie Æthelthrȳth, daughter of Anna, King of E Anglia), who thought a tumour in her throat a punishment for having worn jewelled necklaces]

tawer, **tawery**, **tawie**. See under **taw**[2].

tawny, *tö'ni*, *adj* and *n* brownish yellow or orange. — *n* a port of a rich brownish-orange colour. — Also **taw'ney**. — *n* **taw'niness**. — **tawny eagle** a tawny-coloured eagle of Africa and Asia (*Aquila rapax*); **tawny owl** a tawny-coloured European owl (*Strix aluco*). [Fr *tanné*, pa p of *tanner* to tan]

tawpie or **taupie** *tö'pi*, (*Scot*) *n* a clumsy, heedless or inefficient girl. [Cf Norw *taap* a halfwit]

taws or **tawse** *töz*, (*esp Scot*) *n sing* or *n pl* a leather strap, *usu* cut into strips at the end, for corporal punishment. [Poss pl of **taw**[2], n]

tawt, **tawtie**. See under **taut**[2].

tax *taks*, *vt* to levy a tax on (people, businesses, incomes or goods); to register or enrol for fiscal purposes (*Bible*: Luke 2. 1–5); to make heavy demands on; to accuse, charge (*usu* with *with*); to assess (costs) (*law*); to examine (accounts) in order to allow or disallow items. — *n* a contribution to revenue exacted by the state from individuals or businesses; a burden, drain or strain (with *on* or *upon*); a charge, accusation (*obs*). — *n* **taxabil'ity**. — *adj* **tax'able**. — *adv* **tax'ably**. — *n* **taxā'tion**. — *adj* **tax'ative** taxing; of taxing. — *adj* **taxed**. — *n* **tax'er** (also **tax'or**). — *n* **tax'ing** imposition of taxes; the practice of mugging a person for his or her fashionable footwear (*street slang*; *orig US*); censure, satire (*obs*). — *adj* demanding; onerous. — *adj* **tax'less**. — **tax allowance** a sum which is deducted from total income to arrive at taxable income; **tax avoidance** legal evasion of payment of tax; **tax break** (*informal*) an opportunity legally available for reducing one's tax obligations; **tax cart** or **taxed cart** (*hist*) a light spring-cart (*orig* paying a lower tax, later none); **tax'-collector**. — *adj* **tax-deduct'ible** (of expenses, etc) that may be deducted from one's income before it is assessed for tax. — **tax disc** a paper disc displayed on a motor vehicle's windscreen to show that the road tax has been paid for a given period; **tax evasion** illegal evasion of payment of tax. — *adj* **tax-exempt'** not liable to taxation. — **tax exile** a person living abroad so as not to pay high taxes; **tax'-farmer** (*esp hist*) a tax-gatherer who pays a fixed sum for the right to collect taxes, retaining the revenue as income. — *adj* and *adv* **tax=free'** without payment of tax. — **tax'-gatherer**; **tax haven** a country or state where taxes are low; **tax holiday** a period during which a government makes tax concessions available to business, eg to encourage exports; **tax loss** a loss that can be offset against taxable future profits; **tax'ing-master** an officer of a court of law who examines bills of costs; **tax'man** (*colloq*) a tax-collector; tax-collectors collectively; **tax'-payer** a person who pays tax or taxes; a person who is liable to taxation; a building put up for the express purpose of earning money to pay tax on the land (*US*). — *adj* **tax'-paying**. — **tax point** the date on which value-added tax becomes payable; **tax relief** the cancelling of part of the income tax due; **tax reserve certificate** a government receipt for money deposited that may later be used, with certain advantages, for payment of tax; **tax return** a yearly statement of one's income, from which the amount due in tax is calculated; **tax shelter** a financial arrangement made in order to pay the minimum taxation. — *adj* **tax'-sheltered** of or produced by a tax shelter; of or involving investments legally exempt from tax. — **tax threshold** the level of income at which tax starts to be payable. [Fr *taxe* a tax, from L *taxāre* to handle, value, charge]

taxa. See **taxon**.

Taxaceae, **taxaceous**. See **Taxus**.

taxameter. See **taximeter**.

taxes (*tak'siz*) *pl* of **tax** or (*tak'sēz*) *pl* of **taxis**.

taxi *tak'si*, *n* (also **tax'icab**) a motor car, *usu* fitted with a taximeter, licensed to carry passengers on request to a specified destination; any other vehicle available for hire, such as a boat or small aircraft: — *pl* **tax'is** or **tax'ies**. — *vi* to travel by taxi; (of an aeroplane) to run along the ground, or (or a seaplane) over the surface of water, before take-off or after landing, at low speed under its own power. — *vt* to run (an aeroplane) along the ground in this way; to send or convey by taxi: — *pr p* **tax'ying** or **tax'iing**; *pa t* and *pa p* **tax'ied**; *3rd pers sing present indicative* **tax'ies**. — **taxi dancer** a person, *usu* a woman, hirable as a partner, dance by dance, in a dance hall; **tax'i-driver**; **tax'iman** a taxi-driver; **taxi rank** or (*US*) **taxi stand** a place where taxis congregate for hiring; **taxi track** or **tax'iway** at an airport or aerodrome, a specially prepared track used for ground movement of aircraft, eg from runways to terminals, etc. [Shortening of **taximeter cab**]

taxiarch. See under **taxis**.

taxidermy *tak'si-dûr-mi*, *n* the art of preparing, stuffing and mounting the skins of animals and birds so that they present a lifelike appearance. — *adj* **taxider'mal** or **taxider'mic**. — *vt* **tax'idermize** or **-ise**. — *n* **tax'idermist**. [Gr *taxis* arrangement, and *derma* a skin]

taximeter *tak'si-mē-tər* or *tak-sim'i-tər* (*obs* **taxameter**), *n* an instrument attached to a cab for indicating (distance travelled and) fare due. [Fr *taxe* price, and **-meter**]

taxis *tak'sis*, *n* return to position of displaced parts by means of manipulation only (*surg*); movement of a whole organism, eg a bacterium in response to stimulus (*biol*); arrangement or order; a division of an ancient Greek army (in Athens the contingent from a phyle): — *pl* **tax'ēs**. — *n* **tax'iarch** (*-i-ärk*) the commander of an ancient Greek taxis. [Gr, from *tassein* to arrange]

taxon *tak'sən* or *tak'son*, *n* a biological category, a taxonomic group (eg *species*) or its name: — *pl* **tax'a**. [Back-formation from *taxonomy*]

taxonomy *tak-son'ə-mi*, *n* classification or its principles; classification of plants or animals, *incl* the study of means by which formation of species, etc takes place. — *n* **taxon'omer** a taxonomist. — *adj* **taxonom'ic** or **taxonom'ical**. — *adv* **taxonom'ically**. — *n* **taxon'omist**. [Gr *taxis* order, and *-nomia* distribution]

taxor. See under **tax**.

Taxus *tak'səs*, *n* the yew genus of conifers, giving name to the family **Taxā'ceae** (*-si-ē*). — *adj* **taxā'ceous** of, relating to or belonging to the Taxaceae. — *n* **Taxō'dium** (Gr *eidos* form) the swamp-cypress genus. — *n* **tax'ol** (also with *cap*) (*pharmacol*) a drug obtained from the bark of the Pacific yew (*Taxus brevifolia*), possibly of value as a tumour-suppressant. [L *taxus* yew]

tay *tā*, (*dialect, esp Ir*) *n* tea.

tayberry *tā'bə-ri*, *n* a hybrid plant, a blackberry crossed with a raspberry; the fruit of this plant. [*Tay*side in Scotland, where it was first produced]

tayra or **taira** *tī'rə*, *n* a large S American member (*Eira barbara*), of the weasel family. [Tupí *taira*]

Tay-Sachs disease *tā-saks' diz-ēz'*, *n* a congenital disorder, prevalent in Ashkenazi Jews, caused by a faulty gene, in which progressive degeneration of nerve cells in the brain and spinal cord cause mental retardation, blindness, paralysis and *usu* an early death in childhood. — Also called **amaurotic familial idiocy**. [W *Tay* (1843–1927), British doctor and B *Sachs* (1858–1944), US neurologist]

tayassuid *tä-yə-sōō'id*, *n* any member of the peccary family *Tayassuidae* of New World pigs (together with the suids they comprise the suborder *Suina*). [From *tayassu* (the common peccary), from Tupí *tayaçu*]

tazza *tat'sə*, *n* a shallow cup mounted on a circular foot; a saucer-shaped bowl: — *pl* **taz'ze** (*-sā*) or **taz'zas**. [Ital, cup; cf **tass**[2]]

TB *abbrev*: torpedo boat; tubercle bacillus; tuberculosis.

Tb (*chem*) *symbol*: terbium.

tbsp *abbrev*: tablespoonful (*pl* **tbsps**).

Tc (*chem*) *symbol*: technetium.

TCD *abbrev*: Trinity College, Dublin.

tch-. For some words see **ch-**.

tchick *chik* or *ch'*, *n* a sound made by pressing the tongue against the roof of the mouth and then drawing back one side, as in urging a horse on. — *vi* to make such a sound. [Imit]

tchoukball *tchōōk'böl*, *n* a game, invented in the 1970s, in which the object is to prevent the ball (thrown by the opposing team against a highly sprung net) from landing when it rebounds, physical contact with other players being against the rules. [Imit of the sound of the ball hitting the net]

TCP *abbrev*: *t*richloro*p*henylmethyliodisalicyl, a proprietary germicide.

TD *abbrev*: *Teachda Dála*, Member of the Dáil; Territorial Decoration.

Te (*chem*) *symbol*: tellurium.

te. See under **ti**[1].

tea *tē*, formerly *tā*, *n* a tree (*Camellia sinensis*, family Theaceae) cultivated in China, Assam, etc; its dried and prepared leaves, buds and shoots; a beverage made by infusing the leaves in boiling water; extended to any of various substitutes (see **Labrador**, **Paraguay**, etc); the leaves of any plant infused as a beverage; more rarely, a similar preparation of animal origin (eg **beef-tea**); a cup of tea; an afternoon meal or light refreshment at which tea is generally served; a cooked meal taken in the early evening, high tea (*UK*); marijuana (*old US slang*). — *vi* (*colloq*) to take tea. — *vt* (*colloq*) to provide tea for: — *pr p* **tea'ing**; *pa t* and *pa p* **tead** or **tea'd** — **tea bag** a bag containing tea leaves for infusion; **tea ball** chiefly in US, a perforated metal ball-shaped container to hold the tea leaves for infusion; **tea'berry** wintergreen; a wintergreen berry; **tea biscuit** any of various kinds of sweetish biscuits, often eaten with tea; **tea'board** a tea tray; **tea bread** light sweet bread or buns to be eaten with tea; **tea break** a break for tea during the working day; **tea caddy** or **tea canister** an airtight box or jar for holding tea; **tea cake** a glazed currant bun, *usu* eaten toasted; **tea ceremony** in Japan, the ceremonial making and serving of tea; **tea chest** a tall wooden container with a metal lining, in which tea is packed for transporting; **tea clipper** (*hist*) a fast sailing-ship in the tea trade; **tea cloth** a small tablecloth; a tea towel, a drying-up cloth; **tea cosy** a thick cover for a teapot to keep the tea hot; **tea'cup** a *usu* medium-sized bowl-shaped cup designed for drinking tea out of; **tea'cupful** the amount held by a teacup, about 140ml (5fl oz): — *pl* **tea'cupfuls**; **tea dance** a thé dansant; **tea'-dealer** a buyer and seller of tea; **tea dish** an old name for a teacup; **tea'-drinker**; **tea equipage** apparatus for making and serving tea with all that accompanies it; **tea fight** (*slang*) a tea party; **tea garden** a plantation of tea; an open-air restaurant for tea and other refreshments; **tea gown** a loose gown formerly worn at afternoon tea at home; **tea house** a restaurant in China, Japan, or other eastern countries where tea, etc is served; **tea kettle** a kettle for boiling water for tea; **tea lady** a woman who makes and serves tea in an office or factory; **tea lead** lead with a little tin for lining tea chests; **tea leaf** a leaf of tea; (*usu* in *pl*) a small piece of such a leaf, *esp* when it has been used in making tea; (*rhyming slang*) a thief; **tea meeting** a public social meeting at which tea is drunk; **tea party** a social gathering at which tea is served; the people present; **tea plant**; **tea plantation**; **tea'-planter** the owner or cultivator of a tea plantation; **tea'pot** a spouted vessel for pouring out tea; **tea room** a restaurant where tea and light refreshments are served; a room used for refreshment and informal conversation by the staff or members of an establishment; **tea rose** a hybrid rose, derived from *Rosa odorata*, with a scent resembling that of tea; **tea service** or **tea set** a set of utensils for serving tea; **tea shop** a shop where tea is sold; a restaurant in which teas are served; **Teas'made**® small machine with an alarm clock or timer which makes tea *usu* by the pot at a preset time; **tea'spoon** a small spoon used with a teacup; the amount held by a teaspoon, used eg as a measure in cookery; **tea'spoonful**: — *pl* **tea'spoonfuls**; **tea'-strainer** a small strainer to catch tea leaves when pouring tea; **tea table** a table at which tea is drunk; the company at tea; **tea'-taster** an expert who judges tea by tasting it; **tea'-tasting**. — *n pl* **tea things** the tea pot, cups, etc. — **tea'time** the time in the afternoon or early evening when tea is taken. — Also *adj*. — **tea towel** a cloth for drying crockery, kitchen utensils, etc; **tea tray** a tray for carrying tea things; **tea tree** the common tea plant or shrub; a name of Australian plants of the Myrtaceae family (*Melaleuca*, *Leptospermum*; also called **manuka**) the leaves of which were formerly used to make a type of tea; an African solanaceous shrub (*Lycium*) said to have been labelled by mistake; **tea trolley** or (*NAm*) **tea wagon** a small tiered table on wheels from which afternoon tea, etc is served; **tea urn** a large closed urn with a tap, often also a heating device, for making tea in quantity. — **another cup of tea** a very different thing; **black tea** tea which has been fermented between rolling and firing (heating with charcoal in a sieve); (*usu* **not) for all the tea in China** (not) for any reward whatever; **green tea** tea which is fired immediately after rolling; **high tea** an early evening meal with tea and eg meat, eggs, fish, or a savoury dish; **one's cup of tea** (*colloq*) what is to one's taste or appeals to one; **Russian tea** tea with lemon and no milk *usu* served in a glass; **tea and sympathy** (*colloq*) hospitality and kind words offered to someone in trouble, as being the only, albeit *usu* inadequate, help one can give. [S Chinese *te*, the common form being *ch'a* or *ts'a*]

teach *tēch*, *vt* to impart knowledge or art to; to impart the knowledge or art of; to guide the studies of; to exhibit so as to impress upon the mind; to show; to direct; to accustom; to counsel; to be an object lesson to (someone) to do or not to do something in future; to force home the desirability or undesirability of (particular conduct, etc) to. — *vi* to impart knowledge or give instruction as one's profession: — *pa t* and *pa p* **taught** (*töt*). — *n* **teachabil'ity**. — *adj* **teach'able** capable of being taught; willing and quick to learn, responsive to teaching. — *n* **teach'ableness**. — *n* **teach'er** a person whose profession, or whose talent, is the ability to impart knowledge, practical skill, or understanding. — *adj* **teach'erless**. — *adj* **teach'erly**. — *n* **teach'ership**. — **teach'ing** the act, practice or profession of giving instruction; doctrine; instruction. — *adj* occupied with giving instruction; instructive. — *adj* **teach'less** (*archaic*) incapable of being taught. — **teacher-gov'ernor** a teacher who has also been elected to his or her school's board of governors; **teach'-in** a long public debate consisting of a succession of speeches by well-informed persons holding different views on a matter of general importance, *usu* with discussion, etc; **teaching aid** any object or device used by a teacher to help to explain or illustrate a subject; **teaching hospital** a hospital in which medical students are trained; **teaching machine** any mechanical device capable of presenting an instructional programme; **teaching practice** a trainee teacher's temporary period of teaching in a school, *usu* under supervision. — **teach school** (*US*) to be a teacher in a school; **teach (someone) a lesson** to bring home to (someone) his or her folly; **that'll teach you, him**, etc (*colloq*) that (unpleasant experience) will teach you, him, etc to behave better, be more careful, etc next time. [OE *tǣcan* to show, teach; cf Ger *zeigen* to show; Gr *deiknynai* to show]

teachie. Obsolete form of **tetchy**.

tead or **teade** *tēd*, (*Spenser*) *n* a torch. [L *taeda*]

teagle *tē'gl*, (*dialect*) *n* a hoist or lift; a baited line for catching birds. — *vt* to hoist or catch with a teagle. [Prob a form of **tackle**]

Teague *tēg*, *n* an old nickname for an Irishman. [*Tadhg*, an Irish name, Thady]

teak *tēk*, *n* a verbenaceous tree (*Tectona grandis*) of India, Malaya, etc; its hard and durable wood; the yellowish brown colour of its wood; any of several trees or their wood, resembling, or used as a substitute for, teak. — **African teak** an African euphorbiaceous tree, *Oldfieldia africana*; **bastard teak** dhak; **white teak** a Flindersia. [Malayalam *tēkka*]

teal *tēl*, *n* any of several kinds of small freshwater duck, *esp Anas crecca*, with variegated plumage and distinctive chestnut and green head in the male; a dark greenish-blue colour: — *pl* **teals** or **teal**. [ME *tēle*, prob from OE; cf Du *teling*, *taling*]

team *tēm*, *n* a set of people constituting one side in a competitive game, a side; a set of people working in combination; a set of animals harnessed together; a set of animals with the vehicle to which they are harnessed, an equipage, a turn-out; a stock of animals; a string of flying ducks, geese, etc; a brood, a litter (*obs* or *dialect*); a chain, *esp* for hauling a plough, etc (*dialect*). — *vt* to join together in order to make a team or co-operative effort (with *with*); to match (clothes, etc; often with *with*); to harness (animals) in a team, to yoke; to draw or convey with a team (*NAm*). — *vi* to drive a team. — *adj* **teamed** (*Spenser* **tem'ed** and **teem'ed**) harnessed in a team. — *n* **team'er** a teamster. — *n* **team'ing** driving a team; work apportioned to a team; transport by team; removal of excavated material from cutting to bank. — *n* **team'ster** a person who drives a team; a truck-driver (*US*). — *adv* **team'wise** harnessed together. — **team effort** a co-operative endeavour, teamwork; **team game** an *esp* outdoor game played by *usu* two teams in opposition; **team'-mate** a fellow member of a team; **team spirit** the spirit of willingness to co-operate with others and work, etc as (a member of) a team; **team teaching** instruction given by a team of teachers organized as a team, rather than by individual teachers in individual classes; **team'work** work done by organized division of labour; co-operation, pulling together, regard to success of the enterprise as a whole rather than personal exploits or achievement. — **team up with** to join forces with. [OE *tēam* child-bearing, brood, team; in related languages a bridle, rope, draught of a net; cf OE *tēon* to draw]

Tean. See **Teian**.

teapoy *tē'poi*, *n* a small table with a three-legged or four-legged base; (by confusion with **tea**) a tea-caddy. [Hindi *tīn*, *tīr*- three, and Pers *pāi* foot]

tear[1] *tēr*, *n* a drop of liquid secreted by the lachrymal gland that moistens and cleans the eye, or overflows from it as a manifestation of emotion, *esp* sorrow; an exuding drop; a blob, bead, pear-shaped drop; a small flaw or cavity, as in glass. — *adj* **tear'ful** brimming with, ready to shed, or shedding, tears, crying; inclined to cry, lachrymose; emotion-filled, productive of tears. — *adv* **tear'fully**. — *n* **tear'fulness**. — *adj* **tear'less** shedding no tears, dry-eyed; sorrowless. — *adj* **tear'y** tearful. — **tear bag** the lachrymal gland; the tear-pit; **tear bottle** (*archaeol*) a small bottle once thought to contain mourners' tears; **tear drop** a tear; **tear duct** the opening at the inner corner of the eye by which tears drain into the nose, the lachrymal duct. — *adj* **tear'-falling** (*Shakesp*) shedding tears. — **tear gas** a gas or volatile substance that blinds temporarily by provoking tears. — *vt* (**tear'-gas**) to use tear gas on. — **tear gland** the lachrymal gland; **tear'-jerker** an extravagantly sentimental song, book, film, etc, inviting pity, grief, sorrow. — *adj* **tear'-jerking**. — **tear pit** (in deer) a gland below the eye secreting a waxy substance; **tear shell** a shell that disperses tear gas; **tear smoke** a lachrymatory vapour that (as *opp* to tear gas) is visible. — *adj* **tear'-stained** (of the face or cheeks) streaked with tracks left by tears. — **bored to tears** bored beyond endurance; **in tears** weeping; **without tears** by an easy or painless method. [OE *tēar*; Gothic *tagr*; Gr *dakry*]

tear[2] *tār*, *vt* to draw apart or separate with violence; to rend, rip, lacerate; to cause pain, bitterness, etc to; to make (a hole, rent, etc) by tearing. — *vi* to move or act with violence; to rush, move very quickly; to rage; to become torn: — *pa t* **tore** (*tör* or *tōr*), *archaic* **tare**; *pa p* **torn** (*törn* or *tōrn*). — *n* an act of tearing; a rent or hole torn in something; a rush (*slang*); a spree. — *adj*

tear'able. — *n* **tear'er** someone who or something which tears; a boisterous person (*slang*). — *adj* **tear'ing** great, terrible, rushing. — **tear'away** a reckless and *usu* violent young person. — *adj* impetuous, reckless; of or relating to a tearaway. — **tear'sheet** a page, eg in a magazine, perforated to facilitate its removal for reference, etc; **tear'-strip** a narrow perforated strip on a paper or card wrapper which can be pulled away to facilitate opening; **tear webbing** webbing in which two adhering layers form a fold that will tear apart so as to lessen the violence of a sudden strain. — **tear a** (or **the**) **cat** (*obs*) to rant; **tear apart** (*colloq*) to criticize vehemently or destructively; to search (eg a room) thoroughly; **tear a strip off (someone)** or **tear (someone) off a strip** (*slang*) to reprimand (someone); **tear away** to remove by tearing; to remove (oneself) reluctantly; **tear down** to demolish violently; **tear into** to attack physically or verbally; to scold furiously; **tear off** to remove by tearing; to depart hurriedly; to compose or produce hurriedly; **tear one's hair** formerly, to be reduced by grief or rage to tearing out handfuls of one's hair; to reach an extreme pitch of frenzy and frustration; **tear up** to remove violently from a fixed state; to pull to pieces; **that's torn it** see under **torn**. [OE *teran*; cf Ger *zehren*]

tease *tēz*, *vt* to make fun of, to disconcert for one's own amusement; to plague, irritate, *esp* playfully, mischievously or unkindly; to arouse sexual desire in (someone) but refuse to satisfy it; to tantalize; to subject to banter; to open out the fibres of; to comb or card (wool, etc); to scratch (cloth) with teasels, so as to raise a nap; to raise a nap on; to backcomb (the hair). — *n* a person given to teasing; an act of teasing. — *n* **teas'er** any person who teases; a tricky question; a riddle, conundrum; an introductory, appetite-whetting advertisement (*US*); a male horse used to arouse a mare's interest before the selected stallion is put to her. — *n* and *adj* **teas'ing**. — *adv* **teas'ingly**. [OE *tǣsan* to card]

teasel *tēz'l*, *n* a plant of the genus *Dipsacus*, *esp Dipsacus fullonum*, with prickly flowers; its dried flower-head, with hooked bracts used in raising a nap on cloth; an artificial substitute for its head. — *vt* to raise a nap on with the teasel: — *pr p* **teas'elling** or (*US*) **teas'eling**; *pa t* and *pa p* **teas'elled** or (*US*) **teas'eled**. — *n* **teas'eller** or **teas'eler**. — *n* **teas'elling** or **teas'eling**. — Also **teaz'el** or **teaz'le**. [OE *tǣsel*, from tǣsan; see **tease**]

teat *tēt*, *n* the small protuberance through which the mammalian young suck the milk; a similarly-shaped piece of rubber through which milk is sucked from a baby's or young animal's feeding-bottle; a nipple. — *adj* **teat'ed** having a teat or teats. [OE *titt*, *tit*; influenced by OFr *tete* (Fr *tette*)]

teaze. An obsolete spelling of **tease**.

teazel and **teazle**. See under **teasel**.

tebbad *teb'ad*, *n* a sandstorm. [Cf Pers *tab* fever, and *bād* wind]

Tebeth *teb'eth*, *n* the tenth month of the Jewish ecclesiastical, and fourth of the secular, year, parts of December and January. — Also **Tebet** or **Tevet** (both *tevet'*). [Heb *Tēbēth*]

Tebilize® or **-ise** *teb'il-īz*, *vt* to treat (cotton and linen fabrics) by a finishing process that prevents shrinking and creasing.

TEC or **Tec** *abbrev*: Training and Enterprise Council.

'tec *tek*, (*colloq*) *n* a detective.

tech *tek*, (*colloq*) *n* a technical college.

tech. *abbrev*: technical; technology.

technetium *tek-nē'shi-əm*, *n* a chemical element (symbol **Tc**; atomic no. 43), the first element to be produced artificially. [Gr *technētos* artificial, from *technē* art]

technic *tek'nik*, *n* technology; (often in *pl*) technicality, technique. — *n* **technician** (*-nish'ən*) a person skilled in a practical or mechanical art; a person who does the practical work in a laboratory, etc. — *n* **tech'nicism** (too great) an emphasis on or concern with practical results or method. — *n* **tech'nicist** a technician. — *vt* **tech'nicize** or **-ise** to render technical or technological. — *n pl* **tech'nics** technical details or procedure. — *n sing* technology; the study of industry. [Gr *technikos*, from *technē* art, skill]

technical *tek'ni-kəl*, *adj* relating to a practical or mechanical art or applied science; industrial; belonging to, or in the language of, a particular art, department of knowledge or skill, or profession; so called in strict legal or technical language; being so by virtue of a strict application or interpretation of the rules; caused by a mechanical problem or failure; of or relating to a market whose prices are influenced by internal factors (such as supply and demand) rather than external ones (such as general economic conditions) (*finance*). — *n* **technical'ity** a technical term of expression; a technical point, a point of strictly correct procedure, etc; the state of being technical. — *adv* **tech'nically**. — *n* **tech'nicalness**. — **technical chemistry** industrial chemistry; **technical college** a college of further education that specializes in technical subjects, such as industrial skills, secretarial work, etc; **technical foul** (*sport*) a foul that does not involve physical contact; **technical hitch** a mechanical fault that brings a broadcast, etc, to a temporary halt; **technical knockout** (*boxing*) a defeat on the referee's decision that the losing contestant, though not actually knocked out, is unable to continue the fight. [Gr *technikos* (see **technic**), and sfx *-al*]

Tech'nicolor® *tek'ni-kul-ər*, *n* a process of colour photography in motion pictures in which films of the same scene, using different filters, are projected simultaneously. — *adj* **tech'nicolour** (modelled on above) in artificially or exaggeratedly bright, colours; garishly romanticized. — *adj* **tech'nicoloured**. — **technicolour yawn** (*vulg slang*) vomit, in reference to its variegated appearance.

technique *tek-nēk'*, *n* a skilled procedure or method; a knack or trick of doing something; proficiency, refinement, in artistic performance. [Fr, from Gr *technikos*; see **technic**]

techno *tek'nō*, (*colloq*) *n* short for **technomusic**.

techno- *tek-n-ō*, *tek-nə-* or *tek-no'-*, *combining form* denoting: craft, art, eg *technography*; technical, technological or technology, eg *technophobia*, *technomania*. — *n* **tech'nobabble** (*colloq*) technical jargon, specialized words, acronyms and abbreviations used to describe modern technology, *esp* computer hardware and software. — *n* **technoc'racy** government or management by technical experts; a state, etc, so governed; a body of technical experts in political control; **tech'nocrat** a member of a technocracy; a believer in technocracy. — *adj* **technocrat'ic**. — *n* **tech'nofear** (*colloq*) technophobia. — *n* **technog'raphy** the study and description of the arts, crafts and sciences in their historical and geographical contexts. — **technomā'nia** a mania for technology. — *n* **technomā'niac**. — *n* **tech'nomusic** (*colloq*) popular music that makes use of electronic effects, *esp* loud and unmelodic. — *n* **tech'nophile** a person who likes and promotes technology. — *n* **tech'nophobe** a person who fears and dislikes technology. — *n* **technophō'bia**. — *adj* and *n* **technophō'bic**. — *n* **tech'nopole** a place where high-technology industries are concentrated. — *n* **technop'olis** a society ruled by technology; a geographical area where projects in technological research and development are concentrated. — *n* and *adj* **technopol'itan**. — *n* **tech'nostress** stress resulting from over-involvement with computers. — *n* **tech'nostructure** the people in control of technology in a society. [Gr *technē* art, skill]

technology *tek-nol'ə-ji*, *n* the practice of any or all of the applied sciences that have practical value and/or industrial use; technical methods in a particular area of industry or art; technical nomenclature; technical means and skills characteristic of a particular civilization, group or period. — *adj* **technolog'ical**. — *adv* **technolog'ically**. — *n* **technol'ogist**. — **technological fix** or **technological optimum** (often used pejoratively) the reliance on technological processes and developments to solve human problems. [Gr *technē* art, skill, and **-logy**]

techy. See **tetchy**.

teckel *tek'l*, *n* a dachshund. [Ger]

tectibranch *tek'ti-brangk*, (*zool*) *n* any member of the **Tectibranchiā'ta**, opisthobranch molluscs with gill covered by the mantle, *incl* eg the sea slugs. — *n* and *adj* **tectibranch'iate**. [L *tegere*, *tēctum* to cover, and *branchiae* gills]

tectiform *tek'ti-fŏrm*, *adj* roof-like; roofing. [L *tēctum* a roof, and *fōrma* shape]

tectonic *tek-ton'ik*, *adj* relating to building; relating to structural changes in the earth's crust caused by upheavals and other movements within it (*geol*). — *adv* **tecton'ically**. — *n sing* **tecton'ics** building as an art; structural geology (see also **plate tectonics**). — *n pl* the constructive arts; structural features. — **tectonic plate** (*geol*) one of several rigid plates forming the earth's crust, continually shifting slightly in relation one to another. [Gr *tektōn* a builder]

tectorial *tek-tō'ri-əl* or *-tö'ri-əl*, (*anatom*) *adj* covering. — **tectorial membrane** the membrane covering the organ of Corti in the inner ear. [L *tectōrius*, from *tegere*, *tectum* to cover]

tectrix *tek'triks*, *n* a feather covering the quill bases on a bird's wings and tail (also called **covert**): — *pl* **tec'trices** (*-sēz* or *-trī'sēz*). — *adj* **tectricial** (*-trish'l*). [L *tectrix*, *-īcis*, fem of *tector*, *-ōris* a coverer, plasterer, from *tegere* to cover]

tectum *tek'təm*, (*anatom*) *n* the roof of the midbrain. [L *tectum* roof, canopy]

Ted *ted*, *n* (also without *cap*; *colloq*) a Teddy boy or girl.

ted *ted*, *vt* to spread (new-mown grass) for drying: — *pr p* **tedd'ing**; *pa t* and *pa p* **tedd'ed**. — *n* **tedd'er** a person who teds; an implement for tedding. [Prob from a lost OE *teddan*; cf Icel *tethja* to manure]

teddy[1] *ted'i n* (in full **teddy bear**) a furry, stuffed toy bear. [From Theodore (*Teddy*) Roosevelt, a famous hunter and President of USA (1901–1909)]

teddy[2] *ted'i*, *n* a one-piece undergarment for a woman, combining panties and chemise. — Also **tedd'ie**. [Perh a use of **teddy**[1]]

Teddy boy *ted'i boi*, *n* an unruly adolescent, *orig* in the 1950s, affecting a dandyish style of dress reminiscent of Edward VII's time. — **Teddy girl** the Teddy boy's female companion and counterpart in conduct; **Teddy suit**. [**Edward**]

tedesco *te-des'kō*, *adj* German: — *pl* **tedes'chi** (*-kē*); *fem* **tedes'ca** (*-ka*): — *pl* **tedes'che** (*-kā*). [Ital]

Te Deum *tē dē'əm* or *tā dā'ŏŏm*, *n* a famous Latin hymn of the Western Church, expressing praise and thanksgiving; a musical setting of it. [From its first words, *Tē Deum laudāmus* thee, God, we praise]

tedium *tē'di-əm*, *n* the quality of being tiresome or wearisome, *usu* because long-drawn-out or slow in progress; monotony; irksomeness; boredom. — Also **tae'dium** (*obs*). — *n* **tedios'ity**. — *adj* **te'dious** tiresomely long; long-winded; montonous; boring. — *adv* **te'diously**. — *n* **te'diousness**. — *adj* (*Scot*) **te'disome** or **te'diousome**. — *adj* (*Scott*) **te'dy**. [L *taedium*, from *taedēre* to weary]

tee[1] *tē*, *n* the twentieth letter of the alphabet (T, t); a T-shaped object or mark. — **tee shirt** or **T'-shirt** a slip-on shirt, typically of knitted cotton, with short sleeves and no collar or buttons, shaped like a letter T when laid flat; **tee'-square** see under **T**. — **to a tee** exactly, to a perfection.

tee[2] *tē*, *n* a small plastic or wooden support for the ball, with a concave top, used when it is first played at each hole (*golf*); the strip of ground (also **tee'ing-ground**) where this is done; the mark aimed at in quoits or curling. — *vt* (often with *up*) and *vi* (with *up*) to place (the golf ball) on the tee: — *pr p* **tee'ing**; *pa t* and *pa p* **teed** or **tee'd**. — **tee'-marker** (*golf*) a marker on the ground indicating the forward limit of the teeing-ground; **tee'-off** (*golf*) the strip of ground where tees are placed and where play begins at each hole; the act of hitting the golf ball from the tee to begin play at a hole (also **teeing-off'**). — **tee off** to start play with a shot from the tee (*golf*); generally, to start proceedings, make the opening move, etc (*colloq*); **tee up** to prepare (oneself or something) (with *for*). [False singular from orig form *teaz*, itself of uncertain origin]

tee[3] *tē*, *n* the umbrella-shaped finial of a dagoba. [Burmese *h'ti* umbrella]

tee-hee or **te-hee** *tē'hē'*, *interj* expressing derision or merriment. — *n* a laugh, titter. — *vi* to titter: — *pr p* **tee-hee'ing**; *pa t* and *pa p* **tee-heed'**. [Written representation of a titter or snigger]

teel. See under **til**.

teem[1] *tēm*, *vi* to be full, abound (with *with*); to abound, be plentiful; to bear or be fruitful; to be pregnant (*obs*). — *vt* (*obs*) to bring forth (young). — *adj* **teem'ful**. — *adj* **teem'ing** swarming, overrun (with *with*); full of creatures, people, etc, crowded; plentiful, copious, present in vast numbers. — *adj* **teem'less** (*rare*) barren. [OE *tīeman*, from *tēam*; see **team**]

teem[2] *tēm*, *vi* to pour, fall in torrents (with *down*); to flow copiously. — *vt* to pour, empty. — *n* **teem'er**. [ON *tœma* to empty; cf **toom**]

teemed (*Spenser*). See under **team**.

teen[1] *tēn*, *n* any number or year of age, etc, from thir*teen* to nine*teen* (*usu* in *pl*); a teenager (*colloq*). — *adj* belonging to people in their teens, teenage. — *adj* **teen'āge** in the teens; of or appropriate to someone in the teens. — *adj* **teen'āged**. — **teen'āger** a person between thirteen and nineteen years old inclusive; **tee'ny-bopper** (*colloq*) a young teenager, *esp* a girl, who follows enthusiastically the latest trends in pop music, clothes, etc. [OE sfx *-tīene*, from *tīen* ten]

teen[2], **teene** or **tene** *tēn*, (*archaic*) *n* injury; affliction; grief; anger; pains. [OE *tēona*, injury, anger, grief]

teend. See under **tind**.

teene[1] *tēn*, (*Spenser*) *vt appar* to allot.

teene[2]. See **teen**[2].

teeny *tē'ni*, (*colloq*) *adj* tiny. — Also (often *facetious*) **teen'sy** (*tēn'zi*), **teensy-weensy** (*-wēn'zi*), **teen'tsy** (*tēn'-tsi*), **teen'ty** (*tēn'ti*) and **teen'y-ween'y** (*-wē'ni*).

teepee. See **tepee**.

teer *tēr*, (*technical* or *dialect*) *vt* to plaster; to daub; to spread. [OFr *terer*, from *terre* earth]

Teeswater *tēz'wö-tər*, *n* a breed of large hornless sheep with long-fibred fleece, developed in the Tees valley in the NE of England. [District of County Durham]

tee-tee[1] *tee'-tee'* (*colloq*) *adj* teetotal. — *n* teetotaller. [The abbrev **TT** (qv)]

tee-tee[2]. Same as **titi**[1].

teeter *tē'tər*, *vi* to sway as if about to fall, wobble; to move unsteadily; to vacillate, hestitate, waver; to see-saw (*US*). — *vt* to cause to teeter. — *n* a see-saw. — **teet'er-board** a see-saw; (also **teet'er-tott'er**) a board which throws one into the air when someone else jumps on the opposite end of it. [ME *titeren* to totter]

teeth *tēth*, *pl* of **tooth**.

teethe *tēdh*, *vi* to develop or cut (*esp* milk) teeth. — *vt* to provide with teeth. — *n* and *adj* **teething** (*tēdh'ing*). — **teething ring** a ring of plastic, bone, etc for a baby to chew when teething; **teething troubles** pain and irritation caused by the cutting of teeth; mechanical difficulties encountered on first using a new machine, etc or in the early stages of any undertaking. [From **teeth**, pl of **tooth**]

teetotal *tē-tō'tl*, *adj* abstaining totally from alcoholic drink; out-and-out, complete (*dialect*). — *n* a total abstainer; a principle, movement or pledge of total abstinence (*rare*). — *n* **teetō'talism**. — *n* **teetō'taller** a total abstainer from alcoholic drink. — *adv* **teetō'tally**. [*Teetotally* prob established first as a facetious or emphatic reduplicative form of *totally*; *teetotal* subsequently used in a speech advocating abstinence by Richard Turner of Preston in 1833]

teetotum *tē-tō'təm*, (*hist*) *n* a small spinning top inscribed with letters, or a gambling game played with it, decided by the letter that came uppermost, T standing for L *tōtum*, all, ie take all the stakes; any small top twirled by the fingers: — *pl* **teeto'tums**. [Orig *T totum*, ie a *totum* (= this kind of top) with a *T* on one face]

tef or **teff** *tef, n* an Ethiopian cereal grass, *Eragrostis tef.* [Amharic *ṭêf*]

tefillin or **tephillin** *tə-fē'lin*, (*Judaism*) *n pl* phylacteries, or the texts quoted on them. — *sing* **tefill'ah** or **tephill'ah** (*-fē'lə*). [Heb, from *tephillāh* prayer]

TEFL *tef'l, abbrev*: Teaching English as a Foreign Language.

Teflon® *tef'lon, n* a trademark for *polytetrafluoroethylene*, as used eg to coat the inside of cooking pans to render them non-stick. — *adj* (*facetious, orig US*; *specif* of politicians, statesmen, etc) to whom the blame for incompetence, dubious dealings, etc somehow fails to adhere, attaching itself instead to others.

teg or **tegg** *teg, n* a sheep (or *obs* a doe) in its second year; the fleece of a sheep in its second year. [Perh Scand]

tegmen *teg'mən, n* a covering; the inner coat of a seed covering (*bot*); the leathery forewing in *Orthoptera*, the cockroaches and related insects: — *pl* **teg'mina**. — *adj* **tegmental** (*-men'təl*). — *n* **tegment'um** a scale protecting a bud: — *pl* **tegment'a**. [L *tegere* to cover]

teguexin *te-gwek'sin, n* a large black and yellow S American lizard, *Tupinambis teguexin*. — Also called **tegu** (*teg'ōō*). [Aztec *tecoixin*]

tegula *teg'ū-lə, n* a scale at the base of the forewing in some insects; a flat roofing-tile: — *pl* **teg'ūlae** (*-lē*). — *adj* **teg'ūlar** of, like or overlapping like tiles or slates. — *adv* **teg'ūlarly**. — *adj* **teg'ūlāted** composed of plates overlapping like tiles. [L *tegula* a tile, from *tegere* to cover]

tegument *teg'ū-mənt, n* the skin or other natural covering of an animal or plant body, an integument. — *adj* **tegūment'al** or **tegūment'ary**. [L *tegumentum*, a covering, from *tegere* to cover]

te-hee. See **tee-hee**.

tehr *tār*. Same as **tahr**.

Teian or **Tean** *tē'ən, adj* of Teos in ancient Ionia, or of Anacreon, a native of Teos. [Gr *Tēios* Teian, from *Teōs* Teos]

teichopsia *tī-kop'si-ə, n* temporary blurring of vision, or partial blindness, with the appearance of a multi-coloured zigzag of light before the eye, accompanying migraine. [Gr *teichos* wall, and *opsis* sight]

te igitur *tē ij'i-tər*, or *tā ig'i-tōōr, n* the first paragraph of the canon of the mass; a service-book on which oaths were taken. [L *tē igitur*, thee therefore (the first words)]

teil *tēl, n* the linden or lime tree. — **teil tree** the lime; the terebinth (*Bible*). [OFr *teil*, from L *tilia*]

teind *tēnd, n* in Scotland, a tithe. — *vt* to assess or take a tithe on. [A form of **tenth**, **tithe**]

teinoscope *tī'nə-skōp*, (*obs*) *n* a combination of prisms which magnify or diminish the linear dimensions of objects while at the same time correcting chromatic aberration. [Gr *teinein* to stretch, and **-scope**]

teknonymy *tek-non'i-mi, n* the naming of the parent from the child. — *adj* **teknon'ymous**. [Gr *teknon* a child, and *onyma, onoma* a name]

tektite *tek'tīt, n* a type of small glassy stone, of uncertain and perhaps extra-terrestrial origin, found in certain areas of the earth (*incl* Australia, where it is known as **australite**). [Gr *tēktos* molten]

tel (*n*). See **tell²**.

tel. *abbrev*: telephone.

tel-. See **tele-**.

tela *tē'lə* or *tā'lä, n* a web, weblike structure or tissue: — *pl* **tē'lae** (*-lē* or *tā'lī*). — *adj* **tē'lary** web-spinning. [L *tēla*]

telaesthesia or (*US*) **telesthesia** *tel-ēs-thē'zi-ə, -zhi-ə, n* an abnormal impression, eg of perception of objects or occurrences beyond the normal range of the senses. — *adj* **telaesthetic** or (*US*) **telesthetic** (*-thet'ik*). [**tele-** (1), and Gr *aisthēsiā* sensation]

telamon *tel'ə-mən*, (*archit*) *n* a man's figure used as a supporting pillar: — *pl* **telamones** (*-mō'nēz*). [Gr mythological hero, *Telamōn*, from *tlēnai* to endure, bear]

telangiectasis *tel-an-ji-ek'tə-sis*, or **telangiectasia** *-tā'zi-ə, -tā'zhi-ə*, (*pathol*) *n* dilatation of the small arteries or capillaries. — *adj* **telangiectatic** (*-ek-tat'ik*). [Gr *telos* end, *angeion* a vessel, and *ektasis* extension]

telary. See under **tela**.

Telautograph® *tel-ö'tə-gräf, n* a telegraph for reproducing the movement of a pen or pencil and so transmitting writings or drawings; one for transmission of images by electric scanning. — *adj* **telautographic** (*-graf'ik*). — *n* **telautography** (*-tog'rə-fi*). [**tele-** (1), **auto-** and **-graph**]

teld *teld*, (*Spenser*) *pa t* and *pa p* of **tell**. — (*Scot*) **teld**, **tell'd** and **telt**.

tele- *tel-i-*, (also **tel-**) *combining form* denoting: (1) far, distant, over a distance; (2) television; (3) telephone. [Gr *tēle* far]

tele-ad *tel'i-ad, n* a classified advertisement submitted to a newspaper, etc by telephone. [**tele-** (3) and **advertisement**]

telearchics. See under **telecontrol**. [**tele-** (1), and Gr *archein* to rule]

telebridge *tel-i'brīj, n* a television broadcast of a discussion between studio audiences in different countries linked by satellite. [**tele-** (1)]

telecamera *tel'i-kam-ə-rə, n* a television camera (see under **camera**).

telecast *tel'i-käst, n* a *tele*vision broad*cast*. — *vt* to transmit by television: — *pr p* **tel'ecasting**; *pa t* and *pa p* **tel'ecast** or **tel'ecasted**. — *n* **tel'ecaster**.

telechir *tel'i-kēr, n* a form of robot controlled by telecommand by an operator who has feedback from electronic sensors, eg television cameras. — *adj* **telechir'ic**. [**tele-** (1), and Gr *cheir* hand]

telecine *tel-i-sin'i, n* transmission of filmed material by television; the equipment required for this. [**tele-** (2) and **cine-**]

telecom *tel'i-kom* or **telecoms** *-komz, n sing*. Short for **telecommunication** or **telecommunications**.

telecommand *tel'i-kə-mänd, n* the operation of machinery by remote electronic control. [**tele-** (1)]

telecommunication *tel-i-kə-mū-ni-kā'shən, n* communication of information, in verbal, written, coded or pictorial form, by telephone, telegraph, cable, radio, television. — *n sing* **telecommunica'tions** the science of technology of such communication. [**tele-** (1)]

telecommute *tel-i-kə-mūt', vi* to work at home, communicating with the office by telephone, computer link, etc. — *n* **telecommū'ter**. — *n* **telecommū'ting**. [**tele-** (3)]

teleconference *tel-i-kon'fər-əns, n* a meeting between people physically separated but linked by video, audio and/or computer facilities. — *n* **telecon'ferencing** the practice of holding such conferences, or the technology involved. [**tele-** (1)]

telecontrol *tel-i-kon-trōl', n* control of mechanical devices remotely, either by radio (as of ships and aircraft), by sound waves, or by beams of light. — Also *n sing* **telearchics** (*-ark'*). [**tele-** (1)]

teleconverter *tel-i-kən-vûr'tər*, (*image technol*) *n* a supplementary lens system for converting a camera lens to a much greater focal length. [**tele-** (1)]

telecottage *tel'-i-kotij-, n* a building or room in a rural area with electronic equipment, services, etc for teleworking, often shared by a number of local residents. — *n* **tel'ecottaging**. [**tele-** (1)]

teledu *tel'ə-dōō, n* a small short-tailed carnivorous Indonesian mammal (*Mydaus javanesis*), which can give off a strong, offensive odour, the stinking badger of Java or stinkard. [Jav]

telefax *tel'i-faks, n* fax, a facsimile of a document. — *vt* to send (a copy of a document) by fax machine. [**tele-** (3)]

téléférique *tā-lā-fār-ēk*, (*Fr*) *n* a light aerial cable car, *esp* one electrically propelled.

telefilm *tel'i-film, n* a motion picture made specially for subsequent television transmission. [**tele-** (2)]

telega *tel-eg'ə* or *tel-yeg'ə, n* a four-wheeled Russian wagon, without springs. [Russ]

telegenic *tel-i-jen'ik*, *adj* having a presence, appearance and manner suitable for television. [**tele-** (2), modelled on **photogenic**]

telegnosis *tel-i-nō'sis* or *-ig-nō'sis*, *n* the knowledge of events taking place far away, not obtained in any normal way. — *adj* **telegnos'tic**. [**tele-** (1), and **-gnosis**]

telegony *ti-leg'ə-ni*, *n* the (imaginary) transmitted influence of a previous mate on the offspring of a female by a later mate. — *adj* **telegon'ic** or **teleg'onous**. [**tele-** (1), and Gr *gonos* begetting]

telegram *tel'i-gram*, *n* a message sent by telegraph and *usu* presented in printed form (in UK since 1981 only available for international messages). — *adj* **telegrammat'ic** or **telegramm'ic** of or like a telegram. [**tele-** (1), and **-gram**]

telegraph *tel'i-gräf*, *n* a combination of apparatus for transmitting information to a distance, now almost exclusively by electrical impulses; a telegraph board; used as the name of a newspaper; a message sent by telegraph (*obs*). — *vt* to convey or announce by telegraph; to send a message by telegraph to (a person or place); to signal; to give a premature indication of something to come. — *vi* to signal; to send a telegram. — *n* **telegrapher** (*ti-leg'rə-fər*) a telegraphist. — *n* **telegraphese** (*ti-leg-rə-fēz'*; *facetious*) the jargon or contracted idiom used in telegrams. — *adj* **telegraphic** (*-graf'ik*). — *adv* **telegraph'ically**. — *n* **teleg'raphist** a person who works a telegraph. — *n* **teleg'raphy** the science or art of constructing or using telegraphs. — **telegraph board** a scoreboard or information board that can be read at a distance, used at matches, athletics meetings, races, etc; **telegraph cable** a cable containing wires for transmitting telegraphic messages; **telegraphic address** a shortened address registered for use in telegraphing; **telegraph plant** an Indian papilionaceous plant (*Desmodium gyrans*) whose leaves jerk spontaneously in different directions, like semaphore arms; **telegraph pole** a pole supporting telegraph wires; **telegraph wire** a wire for carrying telegraphic messages. [**tele-** (1) and **-graph**]

Telegu. See under **Telugu**.

telejournalist *tel-i-jûr'nə-list*, *n* a journalist working in television. — *n* **telejourn'alism**. [**tele-** (2)]

telekinesis *tel-i-ki-nē'sis*, *-kī-*, *n* the production of motion at a distance by willpower or thought alone. — *adj* **telekinetic** (*-net'ik*). [**tele-** (1), and **kinesis**]

telemark *tel'i-märk*, (*skiing*) *n* a sudden turn on the outer ski, first practised at *Telemark* in Norway. — *vi* to execute a telemark.

telemarketing. See **teleselling**.

telematics *tel-i-mat'iks*, *n sing* the transmission of computerized information over long distances. — *adj* **telemat'ic**. [**tele-** (1), and infor*matics*]

Telemessage® *tel'i-mes-ij*, *n* a message sent by telex or telephone, superseding the telegram. [**tele-** (1)]

telemeter *ti-lem'i-tər*, *n* an instrument for measuring distances (*surveying*); a photographer's rangefinder; an instrument for measuring an electrical or other quantity and signalling the measurement to a distant point (also called **radiotelem'eter**). — *vt* to record and signal by telemeter. — *adj* **telemetric** (*tel-i-met'rik*). — *n* **telem'etry**. [**tele-** (1), and **-meter**]

telencephalon *tel-en-sef'ə-lon*, (*zool*) *n* part of the forebrain in vertebrates, comprising the cerebral hemispheres, the olfactory lobes and the olfactory bulbs. — *adj* **telencephal'ic**. [Gr *telos* end, and **encephalon**]

teleo-[1] *tel-i-ō*, *-ə-*, or *-o'*, *combining form* denoting perfect, complete. [Gr *teleios* perfect, complete]

teleo-[2] *tel-i-ō*, *-ə-*, *-o'*,- or *tē-*, *combining form* denoting end, purpose. [Gr *telos*, *teleos* end]

teleology *tel-i-ol'ə-ji* or *tē-li-*, *n* the doctrine of the final causes of things; interpretation of phenomena in terms of their purpose rather than possible causes. — *adj* **teleologic** (*-ə-loj'ik*) or **teleolog'ical**. — *adv* **teleolog'ically**. — *n* **teleol'ogism**. — *n* **teleol'ogist**. [**teleo-**[2], and **-logy**]

teleonomy *tel-i-on'ə-mi*, or *tē-li-*, *n* the characteristic of being governed by an overall purpose. — *adj* **teleonom'ic**. [**teleo-**[2], and **-nomy**]

Teleosaurus *tel-i-ə-sö'rəs*, *n* a Jurassic genus of fossil crocodiles. — *n* **tel'eosaur** an animal of this genus. — *adj* and *n* **teleosau'rian**. [**teleo-**[1], and *sauros* a lizard]

Teleostei *tel-i-os'ti-ī* *n pl* the bony fishes with well-developed bones. — *n* and *adj* **tel'eost** or **teleos'tean**. [**teleo-**[1], and *osteon* bone]

Teleostomi *tel-i-os'tə-mī*, *n pl* fishes with membrane bones in the skull, jaws, etc, all ordinary fishes except the sharks and rays. — *n* **tel'eostome** (*-stōm*). — *adj* **teleos'tomous**. [**teleo-**[1], and *stoma* mouth]

telepathy *ti-lep'ə-thi*, *n* communication between mind and mind otherwise than through the known channels of the senses. — *n* **telepath** (*tel'i-path*) a telepathic subject. — *vt* and *vi* to communicate by telepathy. — *adj* **telepath'ic**. — *adv* **telepath'ically**. — *n* **telep'athist** a person who believes in or practises telepathy. — *vt* **telep'athize** or **-ise** to affect or act upon through telepathy. — *vi* to communicate or become aware through telepathy. [**tele-** (1), and Gr *pathos* feeling]

telepheme *tel'i-fēm*, *n* a telephone message. [**tele-** (3), and Gr *phēmē* a saying]

téléphérique. Same as **téléférique**.

telephone *tel'i-fōn*, *n* an instrument for reproducing sound at a distance, *esp* by means of electricity; *specif* an instrument with a microphone and a receiver mounted on a handset, for transmitting speech; the system of communication which uses these instruments. — Also *adj*. — *vt* to contact and speak to by telephone; to convey (a message, etc) by telephone. — *vi* to make a telephone call. — *n* **tel'ephōner**. — *adj* **telephonic** (*-fon'ik*). — *adv* **telephon'ically**. — *n* **telephonist** (*ti-lef'ə-nist*) a person who operates a switchboard or works as an operator in a telephone exchange. — *n* **teleph'ony** telephonic communication. — **telephone answering machine** an answerphone; **telephone book** or **directory** a book listing the names, addresses and numbers of telephone subscribers; **telephone box**, **booth** or **kiosk** a *usu* enclosed place with a telephone for public use; **telephone exchange** a central office where telephone lines are connected; **telephone number** a number which identifies a particular telephone and is dialled to make connections with it; (often in *pl*) a very large number or amount (*esp* of money; *colloq*); **telephone-tapping** see **tap**[2]. [**tele-** (1), and Gr *phōnē* a sound]

telephoto *tel-i-fō'tō*, *adj* a shortening of **telephotographic**. — **telephoto lens** a lens of long focal length for obtaining large images of distant objects.

telephotography *tel-i-fə-tog'rə-fi*, *n* photography of distant objects by means of suitable lenses; erroneously, phototelegraphy. — *n* **telepho'tograph**. — *adj* **telephotograph'ic**. [**tele-** (1)]

teleplay *tel'i-plā*, *n* a play written to be performed on television. [**tele** (2)]

telepoint *tel'i-point*, *n* a device located in eg a public place that activates any portable cordless telephones being carried within a certain radius of it, enabling those carrying them to make calls. [**tele-** (3)]

teleport *tel'i-pört*, (*psychol*) *vt* to move by telekinesis. — *n* **teleportā'tion**. [**tele-** (1)]

teleprinter *tel-i-print'ər*, *n* a telegraph transmitter with typewriter keyboard. [**tele-** (1)]

teleprocessing *tel-i-prō'ses-ing*, *n* the use of a computer to process data transmitted from distant points. [**tele-** (1)]

teleprompter *tel-i-promp'tər*, *n* a device located out of view of the audience by which a television speaker or actor sees a projection of what he or she is to say. [**tele-** (2)]

teleradium unit. See under **radium**.

telerecording *tel-i-ri-kör'ding*, *n* recording for broadcasting by television; a television transmission from a recording. — *vt* **telerecord'**. [**tele-** (2)]

telergy *tel'ər-ji*, *n* a physical force assumed to be at work in telepathy. — *adj* **teler'gic** (*-ûr'jik*) working at a distance, as in telepathy. — *adv* **teler'gically**. [**tele-** (1), and Gr *ergon* work]

telesale. See under **teleselling**.

telescience *tel'i-sī-əns*, (*astronautics*) *n* the performing of scientific experiments at a distance, controlled remotely by the experimenter. [**tele-** (1)]

telescope *tel'i-skōp*, *n* an optical instrument for viewing objects at a distance. — *vt* to drive or slide one into another like the movable joints of a telescope; to compress, shorten, make smaller, etc, to compact, crush. — *vi* to collapse part within part, like a telescope; to be compressed or compacted. — *adj* **telescopic** (*-skop'ik*) or **telescop'ical** of, performed by, or like a telescope; seen only by a telescope; sliding, or arranged, like the joints of a telescope; capable of retraction and protrusion. — *adv* **telescop'ically**. — *adj* **telescop'iform**. — *n* **telescopist** (*ti-les'kə-pist*) a person who uses a telescope. — *n* **Telescōp'ium** (*astron*) the Telescope, a small southern constellation between the constellations of *Ara* and *Corona Austrinus*. — *n* **teles'copy** the art of constructing or of using the telescope. — **telescopic shaft** (*eng*) an assembly of two or more tubes sliding one within the other to provide a hollow shaft of variable length; **telescopic sight** a telescope on a gun used as a sight. [**tele-** (1), and **-scope**]

telescreen *tel'i-skrēn*, *n* a television screen. [**tele-** (2)]

teleselling *tel'i-sel-ing*, *n* the selling of goods or services by using the telephone to seek customers (also called **telemark'eting**). — *n* **tel'esale** a sale made on the telephone. [**tele-** (3)]

teleseme *tel'i-sēm*, *n* a signalling apparatus with an indicator. [**tele-** (1), and Gr *sēma* a sign]

teleservices *tel'i-sûr-vis-əz*, *n pl* information, etc services available to users of teletext and viewdata systems. [**tele-** (2)]

telesis *tel'i-sis*, *n* the activity of making use of natural and social processes for the achievement of a particular purpose. [Gr, fulfilment, from *teleein* to accomplish, fulfil, from *telos* end, purpose]

telesm *tel'ezm*, *n* a talisman. — *adj* **telesmat'ic** or **telesmat'ical**. — *adv* **telesmat'ically**. [Gr *telesma*; see **talisman**]

telesoftware *tel-i-soft'wār*, (*comput*) *n* software which is transmitted to users by means of a teletext or viewdata system. [**tele-** (2)]

telespectroscope *teli-spek'trə-skōp*, *n* a combination of a telescope and a spectroscope, used for observing and analysing the radiation given off by heavenly bodies. [**tele-** (1), and **spectroscope**]

telestereoscope *tel-i-stē'ri-ə-skōp*, *n* a binocular optical instrument used for viewing distant objects stereoscopically. [**tele-** (1), and **stereoscope**]

telesthesia. See **telaesthesia**.

telestic *ti-les'tik*, *adj* relating to the mysteries. [Gr *telestikos*, from Gr *teleein* to fulfil, consummate, initiate, perform, from *telos* end, rite, etc]

telestich *ti-les'tik*, *tel'i-stik*, *n* a poem or block of words in which the final letters of each line spell a name or word. [Gr *telos* end, and *stichos* row]

teletex *tel'i-teks*, *n* a means of transmitting written data, similar in principle to telex (qv), but using more modern, high-speed electronic apparatus. [**tele-** (1), **text**]

teletext *tel'i-tekst*, *n* a computer-based information-retrieval system which allows current, regularly updated, news and information in the form of text and graphics to be transmitted by television companies in the form of coded pulses which can be decoded by a special adaptor for viewing on a page-by-page basis on a conventional television. [**tele-** (2)]

telethon *tel'ə-thon*, (*orig US*) *n* a very long television programme, *esp* one seeking to raise money for a charity, or support for eg a political candidate. [*tele*vision mara*thon*]

teletron *tel'i-tron*, *n* a cathode-ray tube for synthesis of television images. [**tele-** (2), and **-tron**]

Teletype® *tel'i-tīp*, *n* a type of teleprinter. — *vt* to send (a message) by Teletype. — *vi* to operate a Teletype. — **Teletype'setter®** a telegraphic machine which delivers its message as a perforated roll that can be used to actuate a type-setting machine; **teletype'writer** (*US*) a teleprinter. [**tele-** (1), and **type**]

teleutospore *ti-lū'tō-spōr* or *-spör*, *n* a thick-walled winter spore of the rust fungi, producing a promycelium on germination. [Gr *teleutē* completion, and *sporā* seed]

televangelist *tel-i-van'ji-list*, *n* (*esp* in US) an evangelical, *esp* fundamentalist, preacher with a regular slot on television. — *adj* **televangel'ical**. — *n* **televan'gelism**. [**tele-** (2), and **evangelist**]

televérité *tel-i-ver'i-tā*, *n* the televising of scenes from actual life in order to convey a heightened realism. — See also **cinéma vérité** under **cinema**. [**tele-** (2), modelled on **cinéma vérité**]

television *tel-i-vizh'ən*, *n* the transmission by radio waves, and reproduction on a screen, of visual images, *usu* accompanied by sound; an apparatus (also **television set**) incorporating a screen, for receiving these; television broadcasting in general; those occupations concerned with television broadcasting. — *Abbrev* **TV**. — Also *adj*. — *vt* and *vi* **tel'eview** to view by television. — *n* **tel'eviewer** a television watcher. — *vt* and *vi* **tel'evise** (*tel'i-vīz*) to transmit by television. — *n* **tel'eviser**. — *adj* **televi'sional** or **televi'sionary** of or relating to television. — *n* **televī'sor** a receiver for television. — *adj* **televi'sual** relating to television; suitable for televising, telegenic. — *adv* **televis'ually**. [**tele-** (1)]

teleworker *tel'ə-wûr-kər*, *n* a telecommuter. — *n* **tel'eworking**. [**tele-** (3)]

telewriter *tel-i-rī'tər*, *n* a telegraph instrument that reproduces handwriting. [**tele-** (1)]

telex *tel'eks*, *n* an international telegraphic service whereby subscribers hire the use of teleprinters; a teleprinter used in this service; a message transferred by this service. — *vt* to send (someone) (a message) by telex. [*tele*printer and *ex*change]

telfer, etc. See under **telpher**.

telic. See under **telos**.

teliospore *tēl'i-ə-spör*. Same as **teleutospore**. [**telium**, and **spore**]

telium *tē'li-əm*, *n* the cluster of spore cases of the rust fungi, producing teleutospores: — *pl* **tē'lia**. — *adj* **tē'lial**. [New L, from Gr *teleios* finished]

tell[1] *tel*, *vt* to utter, to express in words; to narrate; to disclose or make known; to inform; to discern or distinguish (with *from*); to explain; to order, direct, instruct; to assure; to count (votes); to count out (*archaic*); to bid (goodbye; *US*). — *vi* to give an account (with *of*); to have an effect (with *on*); to have weight; to make an effective story; to give an indication, be evidence (with *of*); to give away secrets; to play the informer; to know definitely; to have an influence or be evidence (with *against*): — *pa t* and *pa p* **tōld**, (*Scot*) **teld**, **tell'd** or **telt**. — *adj* **tell'able** capable of being told; fit to tell. — *n* **tell'er** a person who tells or narrates; a person who counts votes; a clerk whose duty it is to receive and pay money, *esp* in a bank; one of the strokes made by a church bell ringing a funeral knell (also, *esp dialect*, **tailor**). — *n* **tell'ership**. — *adj* **tell'ing** effective; significant, meaningful. — *n* numbering; narration; instruction, orders. — *adv* **tell'ingly**. — **telling-off'** a reprimand; **tell'-tale** or **tell'tale** a person who reports the private concerns or misdeeds of others; a tattler (bird); anything revealing or betraying; any of several indicators or monitors; a recording clock; a strip of material outside the playing area at the foot of the front wall of a squash court, which makes a distinctive sound when hit; one of the lengths of wool sewn or tied on a yacht's sail to indicate airflow (*naut*). — *adj* blabbing; revealing, betraying; indicating. — **as far as one can tell** judging from information available so far; **I tell you** or **I'm telling you** I assure you, I insist; **take a telling** to do as one is asked without having to be told again; **tell apart** to distinguish between; **tell me another** (*colloq*) used to express disbelief; **tell off** to reprimand (*colloq*); to count off and detach on some special duty; **tell on** (*colloq*) to betray, inform on or give away secrets about; **tell a tale** to be revealing; **tell the time** to read the time on a clock or watch; **there's no telling** one cannot possibly know or predict; **you're telling me** (*interj*; *colloq*) I know that only too well. [OE *tellan*; ON *telja*, Ger *zählen* to number]

tell[2] or **tel** *tel*, *n* in Arab lands, a hill or ancient mound formed from the accumulated debris from earlier mud or wattle habitations. [Ar *tall*]

tellar, **teller**. Same as **tiller**[2].

tellen. See **tellin**.

teller. See **tellar** and under **tell**[1].

Tellima *tel'i-mə*, *n* a genus of hardy herbaceous perennials of the saxifrage family. [New L]

tellin or **tellen** *tel'in*, *n* any bivalve mollusc of the *Tellina* genus, with thin, delicate shells tinted yellow or pink, living in estuaries. — *adj* **tell'inoid**. [New L *Tellina*, the name of the genus, from *tellinē* a shellfish]

Tellus *tel'əs*, *n* the Roman earth goddess; (also without *cap*) the earth. — *adj* **tell'ūral** pertaining to the earth. — *n* **tell'ūrate** a salt of telluric acid. — *adj* **tell'ūretted** combined with tellurium. — *adj* **tellū'rian** terrestrial. — *n* an inhabitant of the earth; a tellurion. — *adj* **tellū'ric** of or from the earth; of tellurium in higher valency (*chem*; **telluric acid** a white crystalline acid (H_2TeO_4) produced when tellurium is oxidized by hydrogen peroxide). — *n* **tell'ūride** a compound of tellurium with another element or radical. — *n* **tellū'rion** or **tellū'rian** an apparatus representing the earth and sun, demonstrating the occurrence of day, night, the seasons, etc. — *n* **tell'ūrite** native oxide of tellurium (*mineralogy*); a salt of tellurous acid (*chem*). — *n* **tellū'rium** a rare, silvery, non-metallic element (symbol **Te**; atomic no 52, *appar* so named by Klaproth (1798) as the counterpart of his previous discovery of uranium). — *vt* **tell'ūrize** or **-ise** to combine with tellurium. — *n* **tellūrom'eter** an electronic instrument used to measure survey lines by measurement of the time required for a radar signal to echo back. — *adj* **tell'ūrous** of tellurium in lower valency (**tellurous acid** a weak, unstable acid (H_2TeO_3) containing tetravalent tellurium). [L *Tellūs*, *-ūris*]

telly *tel'i*, (*colloq*) *n* television.

telocentric *tel-ə-sen'trik*, (*genetics*) *adj* (of a chromosome) having the centromere at one end of the chromosome. [Gr *telos* end, and **-centric**]

telomere *tel'ə-mēr*, (*genetics*) *n* the structure which terminates the arm of a chromosome, protecting the chromosome against gene loss and decay. [Gr *telos* end, and *meros* part]

telophase *tel'ō-fāz*, *n* in mitosis, the stage of reconstruction of nuclei after separation of daughter chromosomes. — *adj* **telopha'sic**. [Gr *telos* completion, and *phasis* phase]

telos *tel'os*, *n* aim, purpose, ultimate end. — *adj* **tel'ic** expressing purpose; purposive. [Gr *telos* end, purpose]

telpher *tel'fər*, *n* a system of automatic electric transport, *esp* using cars or containers suspended from overhead cables; a car or carrier in such a system. — Also **telfer**. — *adj* pertaining to a system of telpherage. — *vt* to transport by means of a telpher system. — *n* **tel'pherage** any system of automatic electric transport, a telpher; an electric ropeway or cableway system; overhead traction in general. — Also **tel'ferage**. — *adj* **tel'pheric** or **tel'feric**. — **tel'pherline**; **tel'pherman**; **tel'pherway**. [Irreg coined by Fleeming Jenkin, from Gr *tēle* far, and *phoros* bearing, from *pherein* to bear]

telson *tel'sən*, (*zool*) *n* the terminal or hindmost segment of a crustacean or arachnid. [Gr *telson* a headland in ploughing; cf *telos* end]

Telstar *tel'stär*, *n* a satellite launched on 10 July 1962, used to relay television pictures and telephone conversations across the Atlantic.

telt *telt* (*Scot*), *pa t* and *pa p* of **tell**[1].

Telugu *tel'o͞o-go͞o* or *tel'ə-go͞o*, *n* a Dravidian language of SE India; one of the people speaking it: — *pl* **Tel'ugus**, **Tel'ugu**. — Also **Telegu** (*tel'ə-go͞o*). — Also *adj*.

TEM (*phys*) *abbrev*: transmission electron microscope.

Temazepam *tə-mā'zi-pam*, (also without *cap*) *n* a drug used to treat insomnia, also used as a sedative before operations.

temblor *tem'blör*, (esp *US*) *n* an earthquake or earth tremor: — *pl* **tem'blors** or **temblores** (*-blör'āz*). [Am Sp, from Sp *tremblar* to tremble, shake]

teme. An obsolete spelling of **team**.

temenos *tem'ə-nos*, *n* a place dedicated to a god, a sacred precinct. [Gr, shrine, from *temnein* to cut off]

temerity *ti-mer'i-ti*, *n* rashness; unreasonable contempt for danger. — *adj* **temerarious** (*tem-ə-rā'ri-əs*; *rare* or *literary*) rash, reckless. — *adv* **temerā'riously**. — *adj* **tem'erous** rash. — *adv* **tem'erously**. [L *temeritās*, *-ātis*, and *temerārius*, from *temere* by chance, rashly]

temp *temp*, (*colloq*) *n* a temporarily-employed secretarial or other office worker. — *vi* to work as a temp. [**temporary**]

temp. *abbrev*: temperature; temporal; temporary; *tempore* (*L*), in the time of.

Tempe *tem'pē*, *n* the valley of the Pēneios (Peneus) in Thessaly, praised by the classic poets for its unsurpassed beauty; hence, any place of choice beauty. — *adj* **Tempē'an**. [Gr *Tempē* (*Tempea*)]

tempeh *tem'pā*, *n* a high-protein food prepared by incubating soya beans with a fungus to bring about fermentation, made *esp* in Japan and Indonesia. [Indonesian *tempe*]

temper *tem'pər*, *n* temperament, disposition; a habitual or transitory frame of mind; mood; composure; self-control; uncontrolled anger; a fit of ill-humour or rage; the hardness, elasticity, etc of a metal; proper mixture or balance of different or contrasting qualities; constitution of the body; lime or other substance used to neutralize the acidity of cane-juice. — *vt* to modify by blending or adding a lesser ingredient; to moderate, soften; to harden (steel) by heating to red heat and quenching, or, after this, to heat moderately and cool slowly, or to perform both these actions; to adjust, attune; to tune; to tune the notes on (a piano or other keyboard instruments) so that the intervals between them are correct, or to adjust the pitch of the notes of (a scale) (*music*); to mix in proper proportions; to bring to a favourable state of mind. — *vi* to become tempered; to tamper, meddle (*Shakesp*); to soften (*Shakesp*). — *adj* **tem'perable** capable of being tempered. — *n* **temperabil'ity**. — *adj* **tem'pered** having a certain specified disposition or temper; (of eg steel) brought to a certain temper; tuned or adjusted to some mean, or to equal, temperament (*music*). — **-tem'pered** *adj combining form* possessed of, or showing, a specified disposition of temper, as in *ill-tempered*, *bad-tempered*, *sweet-tempered*, etc. — *adv combining form* **-tem'peredly**. — *n combining form* **-tem'peredness**. — *n* **tem'perer**. — *n* and *adj* **tem'pering**. — **(in a) bad temper** (in) an angry or sulky mood; **(in a) good temper** (in) a cheerful frame of mind; **keep one's temper** to remain composed, restrain one's anger; **lose one's temper** to lose restraint, break out in anger; **out of temper** in an irritable mood; angry. [L *temperāre* to temper, restrain, moderate, mix, partly through OE *temprian* to moderate]

tempera *tem'pə-rə*, (*art*) *n* an emulsion, *esp* made with egg yolk, used as a medium for powdered pigments; the paint so produced; the technique of painting with this paint; distemper. [Ital, from L *temperāre* to mix proportionately]

temperalitie *tem-pə-ral'iti*, (*Shakesp*, 2 *Henry IV*, II. 4. 25) *n* Mistress Quickly's elaboration of temper, frame of mind.

temperament *tem'prə-ment*, *n* disposition, personality, *esp* with regard to emotional make-up; high excitability, nervous instability, and sensitiveness; an adjustment made to the intervals between notes on a keyboard to allow modulation to any key (*music*); any of the recognized types of physical and mental make-up, believed to be controlled by the humours, ie choleric or bilious, sanguine, melancholy, phlegmatic (*obs physiol*); combination or predominance of humour (*obs physiol*); state with respect to combination or predominance of qualities (*obs*); proportioned mixture; climate (*obs*); internal constitution or state; tempering (*archaic*); compromise (*archaic*). — *adj* **temperament'al** relating to temperament; of a volatile, excitable temperament, given to extreme swings of mood; (of a machine etc) working erratically, unreliable. — *adv* **temperament'ally**. — *adj* **temperament'ful**. — **equal temperament** (*music*) a tuning adjustment by which the octave on a keyboard is divided into twelve equal intervals. [L *temperamentum* the mixing of things in proper proportion]

temperance *tem'pə-rəns*, *n* moderation, *esp* in the indulgence of the natural appetites and passions, or, in a narrower sense, moderation in the use of alcoholic liquors, and even entire abstinence from them. — *adj* advocating or consistent with temperance in or abstinence from alcoholic drinks. — **temperance hotel** (*hist*) one at which no alcohol is supplied. [L *temperantia* sobriety, moderation]

temperate *tem'pə-rət*, *adj* moderate; self-restrained, *esp* in appetites and passions; abstemious; moderate in temperature, neither very hot nor very cold. — *vt* (*obs* or *rare*) to temper; to moderate; to restrain. — *adv* **tem'perately**. — *n* **tem'perateness**. — *adj* **tem'perative** having a moderating influence. — **temperate phage** (*biol*) a bacteriophage which integrates its genome into that of its host, where it lies dormant for many generations; **temperate zones** the parts of the earth of moderate temperature between the tropics and the polar circles. [L *temperātus*, pa p of *temperāre* to restrain, modify]

temperature *tem'prə-chər*, *n* degree of hotness of a body, etc or medium (eg air, water) ascertainable by means of a thermometer; a body temperature above normal, fever; condition determining interchange of heat between bodies; the degree of warmth or friendliness in an interchange or relationship; the degree of enthusiasm, excitement or animation generated during debate; tempering; tempered condition; mixture; constitution; proportion. — **absolute temperature** see under **absolute**; **temperature coefficient** (*biol*) the ratio of the rate of any reaction or process at a given temperature to the rate at a temperature 10°C lower (also $\mathbf{Q_{10}}$); **temperature-humidity index** an index measuring temperature and humidity with regard to human discomfort; **temperature inversion** (*meteorol*) anomalous increase in temperature with height in the troposphere; **temperature-sensitive mutant** (*biol*) a mutant organism able to grow at one temperature (the *permissive temperature*) but unable to do so at another (the *restrictive temperature*). — **have a temperature** to have a raised body temperature, a fever; **take someone's temperature** to use a thermometer to ascertain someone's body temperature, as part of diagnosis. [L *temperātūra* appropriate measure, proportion]

tempest *tem'pist*, *n* a violent wind storm; a violent commotion or agitation. — *vt* (*Milton*) to stir violently. — *adj* **tempestive** (*-pest'iv*) timely; seasonable. — *adj* **tempest'ūous** stormy, turbulent; wild, passionate. — *adv* **tempest'ūously**. — *n* **tempest'ūousness**. — *adj* **tem'pest-beaten**, **tem'pest-tossed** or **tem'pest-tost** (*Shakesp*) driven about by storms. [OFr *tempeste*, from a LL form of L *tempestās* a season, tempest, from *tempus* time]

tempi. See under **tempo**.

Templar *tem'plər*, *n* a member of a religious and military order (**Knights Templar** or **Knights Templars**) founded in 1119 for the protection of the Holy Sepulchre and pilgrims going there, extinguished 1307–14; (also without *cap*) a student or lawyer, living or with chambers, in the Temple, London; a member of a US order of Freemasons; see also under **good**. [Med L *templārius* of the temple]

templar. See under **temple**[1].

template or **templet** *tem'plit*, *n* a thin plate cut to the shape required, used as a guide in cutting wood, metal, etc; a pattern cut in card or plastic for shaping pieces of cloth for patchwork; any model from which others form, are produced, etc; a mould shaped to a required outline from which to execute moulding; a timber or small beam used to spread the load in a wall; the coded instructions for the formation of a further molecule carried by a molecule of DNA, etc (*biochem*). [Earlier form was *templet*, perh a Fr dimin of L *templum* a small timber]

temple[1] *tem'pl*, *n* a building or place dedicated to, or regarded as the house of, a god; a place of worship; in France, a Protestant church; (with *cap*) the headquarters of the Knights Templar on or near the site of Solomon's temple in Jerusalem; (with *cap*) in London, two inns of court (*Inner* and *Middle Temple*) on the site once occupied by the Knights Templar, with the Knights' church; a synagogue, *esp* of Reform or Conservative Judaism (*US*); a building or place thought of as the centre of an activity or interest. — *adj* **tem'plar** of a temple. — *adj* **tem'pled**. [L *templum*]

temple[2] *tem'pl*, *n* the flat portion of either side of the head above the cheekbone. [OFr, from L *tempus*, *-oris*]

temple[3] *tem'pl*, *n* a pair of rollers fitted to the sides of a loom to keep the cloth at full width and suitably tensioned as it is woven. [ME, from L *templum* a small timber]

templet. See under **template**.

tempo *tem'pō*, (*music*) *n* time; speed and rhythm: — *pl* **tem'pos** or **tem'pi** (*-pē*). [Ital]

tempolabile *tem-pō-lā'bīl*, (*chem*) *adj* tending to change with time. [*tempus*, *-oris* time, and *lābilis*, from *lābī* to slip]

temporal[1] *tem'pə-rəl*, *adj* relating to time; relating to time in this life or world (*opp* to *eternal*); worldly, secular, or civil (*opp* to *spiritual*, *sacred* or *ecclesiastical*); relating to tense or the expression of time (*gram*); lasting for a short time. — *n* **temporality** (*-al'i-ti*) the state or fact of being temporal; what relates to temporal welfare; (*usu* in *pl*) secular possessions, revenues of an ecclesiastic proceeding from lands, tithes, etc. — *adv* **tem'porally**. — *n* **tem'poralness**. — *n* **tem'poralty** the laity; lay peers; (*usu pl*) worldly possessions. [*L temporālis*, from *tempus*, *-oris* time]

temporal[2] *tem'pə-rəl*, (*anatom*) *adj* relating to or close to the temples on either side of the head. — *n* a bone, muscle or scale in that position. — **temporal lobe** a lobe at the side of each cerebral hemisphere by the temple, concerned with hearing and speech. [L *tempus*, *-oris*; see **temple**[2]]

temporaneous *tem-pə-rā'ni-əs*, (*obs*) *adj* lasting only a relatively short time, temporary; relating to time, temporal. [L *temporāneus* opportune, timely, from *tempus*, *-oris* time]

temporary *tem'pə-rə-ri*, *adj* lasting for a time only; transient, impermanent; provisional. — *n* a person employed temporarily (see also **temp**): — *pl* **tem'poraries**. — *adv* **tem'porarily**. — *n* **tem'porariness**. [L *temporārius* lasting briefly, from *tempus*, *-oris* time]

tempore *tem'pə-rē*, *tem'por-e*, (*L*) in the time of.

temporize or **-ise** *tem'pə-rīz*, *n* to comply with the demands of the moment, yield to circumstances; to use delaying tactics, behave so as to gain time. — *n* **temporizā'tion** or **-s-**. — *n* **tem'porizer** or **-s-**. — *n* and *adj* **tem'porizing** or **-s-**. — *adv* **tem'porizingly** or **s-**. [Fr *temporiser*, from L *tempus*, *-oris* time]

tempt *tempt*, *vt* to try or tend to persuade, *esp* to do wrong; to entice or invite; to dispose, incline; to attract; to make trial of, test the virtue of (*archaic*, *Bible* or *literary*). — *n* **temptabil'ity**. — *adj* **temp'table**. — *n* **temp'tableness**. — *n* **temptā'tion** the act of tempting; the state of being tempted; that which tempts; enticement to do wrong; trial. — *adj* **temptā'tious** (*rare*) seductive. — *n* **temp'ter** a person or being who tempts, *esp* (with *cap*) the devil: —*fem* **temp'tress**. — *n* **temp'ting**. — *adj* attractive, enticing. — *adv* **temp'tingly**. — *n* **temp'tingness**. [OFr *tempter*, from L *tentāre*, an intensive of *tendere* to stretch]

'tempt or **tempt**. Aphetic for **attempt**.

tempura *tem'pōō-rə*, *n* a Japanese dish of seafood or vegetables deep-fried in batter.

tempus fugit *tem'pəs fū'jit* or *tem'pōōs fōō'git*, (*L*) time flies.

temse or **tems** *tems*, *temz*, (*now dialect*) *n* a sieve, strainer. — *vt* to sift. [OE *temesian* to sift; cf Du *tems*]

temulence *tem'ū-ləns*, (*rare*) *n* intoxication. — Also **tem'ulency**. — *adj* **tem'ulent**. — *adv* **tem'ulently**. [L *tēmulentus* drunk]

ten *ten*, *n* the cardinal number next above nine; a symbol or numeral representing it (x, X or 10); a set of that number of things or persons; used indefinitely, a large number; an article of a size denoted by 10; a card with ten pips; a score of ten points, tricks, etc; the tenth hour after midday or midnight; the age of ten years. — *adj* of the number ten; amounting to ten; ten years old. — *adj* and *adv* **ten'fold** in ten divisions; ten times as much. — *n* **tenn'er** (*colloq*) a ten-pound note; a ten-dollar bill; ten years. — *adj* **tenth** the last of ten; next after the ninth; equal to one of ten equal parts. — *n* a tenth part; a tenth part of the annual profit of a church living; a person or thing in tenth position; an octave and a third (*music*); a note at that interval (*music*). — *adv* in tenth position; as the tenth point, etc — *adv* **tenth'ly**. — *adj* **ten'-foot** measuring ten feet. — **Ten Commandments** see under **command**; **ten-gallon hat** (*US*) a cowboy's broad-brimmed hat; **ten-minute rule** a parliamentary procedure by which a member makes a short speech (lasting no more than ten minutes) requesting permission to introduce a bill; **ten'pence** an amount in money equal to ten pennies; **ten-pence** (or **ten-penny) piece** in Britain, a coin worth 10 pence (also **tenpenny-piece'**). — *adj* **ten'penny** offered for, or sold at, tenpence. — **tenpenny nail** formerly, a nail sold at tenpence a hundred; a large nail; **tenpin bowling** or **ten'pins** a game like skittles, in which the aim is to knock down ten target pins standing at the end of a long lane by rolling a heavy ball at them; **ten-point'er** a stag with ten points or tines. — *adj* **ten'-pound** weighing, worth, sold or offered for, ten pounds. — **ten-pound'er** something weighing or worth ten pounds; a person who was a voter by virtue of occupying property worth ten pounds a year (*hist*). — *adj* **ten'-score** two hundred. — *adj* **tenth'-rate** of very poor quality. — **long ten** the ten of trumps in catch-the-ten. [OE (Anglian) *tēn*, *tēne* (WSax *tīen*, *tīene*); Ger *zehn*, Welsh *deg*, L *decem*, Gr *deka*, Sans *daśa*]

tenable *ten'ə-bl* (*archaic tēn'-*), *adj* capable of being retained, kept or defended. — *n* **tenabil'ity** or **ten'ableness**. [Fr *tenable*, from tenir to hold]

tenace *ten'ās*, *-is*, (*cards*) *n* the combination in one hand of the cards next above and next below the other side's best in the suit. [Sp *tenaza* pincers]

tenacious *ti-nā'shəs*, *adj* retentive; (with *of*) holding fast to; clinging; sticking firmly; cohesive; tough; stubborn, obdurate, determined. — *adv* **tenā'ciously**. — *n* **tenā'ciousness** or **tenacity** (*-nas'i-ti*). [L *tenāx*, *-ācis*, from *tenēre* to hold]

tenaculum *ti-nak'ū-ləm*, *n* a surgical hook or forceps for picking up blood-vessels; a band of muscle or fibrous tissue that holds, eg an organ, in place (*anatom*): — *pl* **tenac'ula** (*-lə*). [L *tenāculum* holder, pincers]

tenaille *ti-nāl'*, (*fortif*) *n* an outwork in the main ditch in front of the curtain. — Also **tenail'**. — *n* **tenaillon** (*ti-nal'yən*) a work to strengthen the side of a small ravelin. [Fr, from L *tenāculum* pincers, from *tenēre* to hold]

tenant *ten'ənt*, *n* a person who occupies property owned by another, in return for rent, service, etc; a person who has, on certain conditions, temporary possession of any place; an occupant; someone who possesses land or property by private ownership (*law*). — *vt* to hold as a tenant; to occupy. — *vi* to dwell. — *n* **ten'ancy** a temporary occupation or holding of land or property by a tenant; time of such holding; the property held by a tenant; possession by private ownership. — *adj* **ten'antable** fit to be tenanted; in a state of repair suitable for a tenant. — *adj* **ten'antless**. — *n* **ten'antry** the state or time of being a tenant; a set or body of tenants, *esp* of the same landlord. — **ten'antship**. — **tenant-at-will'** a tenant who holds property only so long as the proprietor wills; **tenant farmer** a farmer who rents a farm; **tenant-in-chief'** a tenant holding lands directly from the sovereign; **tenant right** the right of a tenant, *esp* that of a customary tenant, to sit continuously at a reasonable rent, the right to receive compensation for his or her interest from the incoming tenant, and for all permanent or unexhausted improvements from the landlord; **tenants' association** an organization of tenants, eg on a housing estate, who work to improve housing conditions, amenities, etc on that estate; **tenants' charter** a document listing the legal rights of local-authority and housing-association tenants, *incl* right of tenancy. [Fr *tenant*, pr p of *tenir*, from L *tenēre* to hold]

tench *tench* or *tensh*, *n* a dark bronze-green to brown freshwater fish (*Tinca tinca*) of the carp family, its mouth bearing a pair of short barbels used in sensing prey. [OFr *tenche* (Fr *tanche*), from L *tinca*]

tend[1] *tend*, *vt* to attend to, take care of; to mind; to watch over or stand by and perform services for or connected with; to minister to, wait upon; to escort (*Shakesp*). — *vi* to pay attention (with *to*, *esp US*); to wait on, attend to (with *on*, *upon*; *old*); to attend, hearken (*Shakesp*); to be in waiting or readiness (*Shakesp*); to wait, attend (*Shakesp*). — *n* **ten'dance** tending; expectation (*Spenser*); attendants collectively (*Shakesp*). — *adj* **ten'ded**. — *n* **ten'der** a person who tends; a small craft that attends a larger; a carriage attached to a locomotive to carry fuel and water. — **tend out on** (*US*) to attend or attend to. [Aphetic for **attend**]

tend[2] *tend*, *vi* to be apt or prone (to do something); to move or incline in some direction; to be directed to any end or purpose; to conduce. — *n* **ten'dence** or **tendenz** (*ten-dents'*; *Ger*) tendency (*esp* in composition, tendentious). — *n* **ten'dency** a trend, drift, inclination; proneness; a faction within a particular political movement. — *adj* **tenden'tious** purposely tending or angled; with an object; biased, *esp* towards controversy. — Also **tenden'tial** or **tenden'cious**. — *adv* **tenden'tiously**. — *n* **tenden'tiousness**. [L *tendere* and Fr *tendre* to stretch]

tender[1]. See under under **tend**[1].

tender[2] *ten'dər*, *vt* to offer for acceptance, *esp* to offer in payment; to proffer. — *vi* to make a tender. — *n* an offer or proposal, *esp* one in writing offering to provide a particular service for a particular price; the paper containing it; the thing offered; a formal offer to save the consequences of non-payment or non-performance (*law*). — *n* **ten'derer**. — *n* **ten'dering**. — **legal tender** see under **legal**; **put out to tender** to invite tenders for a particular job. [Fr *tendre* to stretch, reach out]

tender[3] *ten'dər*, *adj* soft, delicate, fragile; easily chewed, not tough; easily impressed or injured; not hardy; gentle; youthful, vulnerable; sensitive, *esp* to pain or sorrow; painful when touched or pressed; requiring gentle or tactful handling; easily moved to pity, love, etc; careful not to hurt; kind, sympathetic; considerate, careful (with *of*; *archaic*); pathetic; expressive of, of the nature of, or arousing the softer passions; compassionate, loving, affectionate; (of porcelain) soft-paste; scrupulous, chary; beloved (*Shakesp*); (of a ship) apt to lean over under sail. — *vt* (*obs* or *dialect*) to cherish; to value, have respect to; to make tender; to treat with tenderness (*Shakesp*); to feel tenderness for (*Shakesp*). — *n* care, regard, concern (*Shakesp*); tender feeling, fondness (now *usu* in Fr form **tendre**, *tâdr'*). — *vt*

ten'derize or **-ise** to break down the connective tissue of (meat) so as to make it tender, either by pounding or by applying a chemical or marinade. — *n* **ten'derizer** or **-s-** a pounding instrument or a substance that tenderizes meat. — *n* **ten'derling** a person coddled too much, an effeminate person; one of the first horns of a deer. — *adv* **ten'derly**. — *n* **ten'derness**. — *adj* **ten'der-dying** (*Shakesp*) dying young. — **ten'derfoot** (*orig* and *esp US*) a person not yet hardened to life in the prairie, mining-camp, etc; a newcomer; a greenhorn, beginner; formerly, a boy scout or girl guide who has passed only the first tests: — *pl* **ten'derfoots** or **ten'derfeet**. — *adj* **tender-heart'ed** compassionate, easily touched or moved. — *adv* **tender-heart'edly**. — **tender-heart'edness**. — *adj* **tender-heft'ed** (*Shakesp*) *perh* set in a tender bodily 'haft' or frame. — **ten'derloin** the tenderest part of the loin of beef, pork, etc, close to the lumbar vertebrae; a district where bribes to the police and other forms of corruption are extremely common (*US slang*). [Fr *tendre*, from L *tener*]

tendon *ten'dən*, *n* a cord, band or sheet of fibrous tissue attaching a muscle to a bone or other structure. — *n* **tendinitis** or **tendonitis** (*-ī'tis*) inflammation of a tendon. — *adj* **ten'dinous**. [LL *tendō*, *-inis* or *-ōnis*, appar from Gr *tenōn*, *-ontos* sinew, tendon; cf *teinein* to stretch; *d* suggested by L *tendere*]

tendovaginitis. See **tenovaginitis**.

tendre. See under **tender**[3].

tendril *ten'dril*, *n* a plant's coiling threadlike climbing organ (leaf, leaflet or shoot); anything resembling a tendril, such as a curl of hair. — *adj* **ten'drillar** or **ten'drillous**. — *adj* **ten'drilled**. [Ety doubtful; cf Fr *tendrillon* shoot]

tendron *ten'drən*, *n* a shoot, sprout; (in *pl*) cartilages of the ribs. [Fr]

tene. See under **teen**[2].

tenebrae *ten'i-brē*, *ten'e-brī*, *n pl* (*RC*; also with *cap*) matins and lauds of the following day sung on the Wednesday, Thursday and Friday of Holy Week — candles are extinguished one by one at the end of each psalm with the final psalm being sung in darkness. [L, darkness]

tenebrific *ten-i-brif'ik*, *adj* producing darkness. [L *tenebrae* darkness, and *facere* to make]

tenebrio *ti-neb'ri-ō*, *n* a night spirit; a night prowler; (with *cap*) the mealworm genus of beetles, giving name to the family **Tenebrionidae** (*-on'i-dē*): — *pl* **teneb'rios**. [L *tenebriō* a person who lurks in the dark, from *tenebrae* darkness]

tenebrious. See under **tenebrose**.

tenebrism *ten'ə-brizm*, (*art*) *n* the 17c Italian and Spanish naturalist school of painting, *esp* of Caravaggio, characterized by large expanses of shadow. — *n* and *adj* **ten'ebrist**. [L *tenebrae* darkness]

tenebrose *ten'i-brōz*, **tenebrious** *tə-neb'ri-əs* or **tenebrous** *ten'i-brəs*, *adj* dark, gloomy. — *n* **teneb'rity** or **tenebros'ity**. [L *tenebrae* darkness]

tenement *ten'i-mənt*, *n* a dwelling or habitation, or part of it, used by one family; one of a set of apartments in one building, each occupied by a separate family; a building divided into dwellings for a number of families (*Scot* and *US*)); a holding, by any tenure; anything held, or that may be held, by a tenant. — *adj* **tenemental** (*-ment'l*). — *adj* **tenement'ary**. — **tenement building**; **tenement house**. [LL *tenementum*, from L *tenēre* to hold]

tenendum *ti-nen'dəm*, *n* that clause in a deed wherein the tenure of the land is defined and limited. [L neuter of *tenendus*, gerundive of *tenēre* to hold]

tenesmus *ti-nes'məs*, (*med*) *n* a continuous or frequently recurring desire to defecate, with painful and ineffectual straining to empty the bowels. [Latinized from Gr *teinesmos*, from *teinein* to strain]

tenet *ten'et* (also *tē'nit*) *n* any opinion, principle or doctrine which a person holds or maintains as true. [L *tenet*, (he) holds, from *tenēre* to hold]

tenfold. See under **ten**.

Tengku. See under **Tunku**.

tenia, tenioid, etc. Variant spellings of **taenia, taenioid**, etc.

Tenn. *abbrev*: Tennessee (US state).

tennantite *ten'ən-tīt*, *n* a mineral composed of sulphur, arsenic and copper, *usu* with iron. [Named after Smithson *Tennant* (1761–1815), English chemist]

tenné *ten'ā*, (*heraldry*) *n* and *adj* orange-brown. — Also **tenn'y**. [Obs Fr; cf **tawny**]

tenner. See under **ten**.

tennis *ten'is*, *n* lawn tennis (qv); an ancient game played with ball, rackets (*orig* palms of the hands), and net, in a specially constructed building or enclosed court (distinguished from lawn-tennis, which was derived from it, as **close, court, real** (ie genuine, original), or (in Australia from the late 19c) **royal** tennis). — **tenn'is-ball**; **tenn'is-court**; **tennis elbow** an inflamed condition of the muscle that extends the wrist, at the point where it arises at the elbow, caused by over-exercise; **tenn'is-match**; **tenn'is-player**; **tenn'is-racket**; **tenn'is-shoe**. — **short tennis** see under **short**. [Prob Fr *tenez*, (Anglo-Fr *tenetz*) imperative of *tenir* to take, receive]

tenno *ten'ō*, *n* the formal title of the emperor of Japan, *esp* in his capacity as a divine leader. [Jap]

tenny. See under **tenné**.

tenon *ten'ən*, *n* a projection at the end of a piece of wood, etc, inserted into the socket or mortise of another, to hold the two together. — *vt* to fix or fit with a tenon. — *n* **ten'oner**. — **tenon saw** a thin backsaw for tenons, etc. [Fr *tenon*, from *tenir* to hold, from L *tenēre*]

tenor (*obs* or *old-fashioned* **tenour**) *ten'ər*, *n* the adult male voice intermediate between baritone and alto; in early polyphonic music the part maintaining the melody, often assigned, in counterpoint singing, to this voice; a person who sings tenor; the part next above the bass in a vocal quartet; an instrument, eg the viola or recorder, of corresponding compass; the largest and lowest-pitched bell in a full peel; continuity of state; general run or course; the value of a bank-note or bill (*hist*); the proportion of ore mineral in an ore; general purport, drift; the subject referred to by a metaphor; the exact wording of a document (*law*); an exact transcript of a document (*law*). — Also *adj*. — *n* **ten'orist**. — *n* **tenoroon'** an obsolete tenor bassoon. — **tenor clef** the C clef placed on the fourth line; **tenor cor** the mellophone (see under **mellow**); **tenor drum** a snareless drum intermediate between a side drum and a bass drum, used *esp* in military bands. [L *tenor* a course followed or held to, from *tenēre* to hold]

tenorite *ten'ə-rīt*, *n* melaconite, black copper ore (CuO), found in volcanic regions (*orig* on Vesuvius) and copper veins. [Named after G *Tenore*, President of the Naples Academy, 1841]

tenorrhaphy *ti-no'rə-fi*, (*med*) *n* the repairing of a split or torn tendon by sutures. [Gr *tenōn* tendon, and *raphē* suture]

tenosynovitis *ten-ō-sī-nə-vī'tis*, (*med*) *n* painful inflammation and swelling of a tendon, associated with repetitive movements. [Gr *tenōn* tendon, and **synovitis**]

tenotomy *tə-not'ə-mi*, *n* surgical cutting of a tendon. — *n* **tenot'omist**. [Gr *tenōn* tendon, and *tomē* a cut]

tenovaginitis *ten-ō-va-ji-nī'tis*, or **tendovaginitis** *ten-dō-*, *n* inflammation or thickening of the fibrous wall of the sheath surrounding a tendon, *esp* in the hand. [Gr *tenōn* or L *tendō* tendon, and **vaginitis**]

tenour. See under **tenor**.

tenpence, etc. See under **ten**.

tenrec *ten'rek*, or **tanrec** *tan'rek*, *n* a large Madagascan insectivore of the **Tenrecidae** (*-res'i-dē*) family (*esp Tenrec ecaudatus*) similar to the hedgehog. [Malagasy *t(r)àndraka*]

TENS *abbrev*: transcutaneous electrical nerve stimulation (see under **transcutaneous**).

tense[1] *tens*, *n* time in grammar, the form of a verb to indicate the time of the action. — *adj* **tense'less**. [OFr *tens* (Fr *temps*), from L *tempus* time]

tense[2] *tens*, *adj* stretched tight; strained or producing strain; rigid; pronounced with the tongue tightened or narrowed (*phonetics*). — *vt* and *vi* to make or become tense. — *adv* **tense'ly**. — *n* **tense'ness** state of being tense. — *n* **tensibil'ity**. — *adj* **tens'ible** capable of being stretched. — *adj* **tens'ile** (*-sīl*, or *esp US -sil* or *-səl*) tensible; of or relating to stretching. — *n* **tensility** (*-sil'i-ti*). — *n* **tensim'eter** an instrument for measuring vapour pressure. — *n* **tensiom'eter** an instrument for measuring tension, tensile strength, the moisture content of soil. — *n* **tensiom'etry** the branch of physics relating to tension, tensile strength, etc. — *n* **tension** (*ten'shən*) stretching; a pulling strain; stretched or strained state; strain generally; formerly, pressure in gases or vapours; electromotive force; a state of barely suppressed emotion, such as excitement, anxiety or hostility; a feeling of strain with resultant symptoms (*psychol*); strained relations between persons; opposition between conflicting ideas or forces; a device for regulating the tautness of a string, thread in a sewing machine, etc; the looseness with which a person knits. — *vt* to subject to tension. — *adj* **ten'sional**. — *adv* **ten'sionally**. — *adj* **ten'sionless**. — *n* **tens'ity** tenseness. — *adj* **tens'ive** giving the sensation of tenseness or stiffness. — *n* **tens'or** (*anatom*) a muscle that tightens a part; a mathematical or physical entity represented by components which depend in a special way on the choice of a co-ordinate system. — **tensile strength** the strength of a material when being stretched, expressed as the greatest stress it can resist before breaking; **tensile test** (*eng*) a test performed on a metal or other material to determine its tensile characteristics; **tension rod** a structural member subjected to tensile stress only. [L *tensus*, pa p of *tendere* to stretch]

tenson *ten'sn*, *n* a competition in verse between two troubadours before a court of love; a subdivision of the piece of verse so composed. — Also **ten'zon**. [Fr, from L *tensiō*, *-ōnis* a struggle]

tensor. See under **tense**[2].

tent[1] *tent*, *n* a portable shelter of canvas or other cloth stretched on poles and attached to the ground by pegs; anything resembling a tent, eg (*med*) an enclosure within which to regulate the oxygen supply to a patient; a temporary field pulpit; a common shelter spun by a company of caterpillars. — *vi* to camp in a tent; to camp temporarily. — *vt* to cover or shelter (as if) with a tent; to lodge in tents. — *n* **tent'age** tents collectively; material for making tents. — *adj* **ten'ted** covered with tents; formed like a tent; (of a settlement or camp) dwelling in tents. — *n* **tent'er** someone who lives in a tent. — *n* **tent'ful** as many as a tent will hold. — *n* **tent'ing**. — *adj* (*Keats*) having the form of a tent. — *adj* **tent'less**. — *adv* **tent'wise**. — **tent'-bed** a camp-bed, a bed with a canopy hanging from a central point; **tent caterpillar** any of several caterpillars which build communal shelters in trees; **tent coat, tent dress** etc, a coat, dress, etc shaped like a circular tent, narrow at the shoulders and wide at the hem; **tent'-cloth** cloth suitable for tents; **tent dress** a type of full waistless dress that flares from shoulder to hem in a tent-like shape; **tent'-fly** a flap forming a door to a tent; a subsidiary outer roof to a tent; **tent'-guy** a stay or guy rope for a tent; **tent'-maker**; **tent peg** or **tent pin** a strong notched peg driven into the ground to fasten a tent; **tent'-pegging** the sport of riding at full speed and trying to bear off a tent peg on the point of a lance; **tent pole** a pole to support a tent; **tent'-preaching** open-air preaching; **tent rope** a rope for securing a tent to a peg. [Fr *tente*, from L *tendere*, *tentum* to stretch]

tent[2] *tent*, *n* a plug or roll of soft material for dilating a wound or keeping open an orifice (*med*); a probe (*obs*). — *vt* to dilate or keep open with a tent (*med*); to probe (*obs*). [Fr *tente*, from L *tentāre* to try]

tent[3] *tent*, *n* a deep-red Spanish wine. [Sp *tinto*, from L *tinctus*, pa p of *tingere* to dye]

tent[4] *tent*, (*Scot*) *n* heed. — *vt* to take heed or notice of, attend to. — *n* **tent'er** a person who tends, *esp* to a machine. — *adj* **tent'ie** or **tent'y** wary, attentive. [Aphetic for **attent** and **intent**]

tent[5] *tent*, *n* (*obs*) an embroidery or tapestry frame. — **tent stitch** an embroidery stitch made in parallel series diagonally to the canvas threads; tent-work; **tent'-work** work in tent stitch. [Origin obscure, perh related to **tent**[1]; cf ME *tent* to stretch, **tenter**[1], and L *tendere*, *tentum*]

tentacle *ten'tə-kl*, *n* a slender flexible organ, *esp* in invertebrates, for feeling, grasping, etc; any sensitive filament in insectiverous plants used in the capture of prey, eg the gland-tipped leaf hairs of the sundew plant; anything resembling a tentacle, *esp* in its ability to grasp or feel. — Also **tentaculum** (*-tak'ū-ləm*; *pl* **tentac'ūla**). — *adj* **ten'tacled**. — *adj* **tentac'ūlar**. — *adj* **tentac'ūlate**. — *adj* **tentacūlif'erous**. — *adj* **tentac'ūloid**. — *n* **tentac'ūlite** (*palaeontol*) a ringed conical Silurian and Devonian fossil, apparently a pteropod. [L *tentāre* to feel]

tentation *ten-tā'shən*, *n* an old form of **temptation**; a method of adjusting by a succession of trials (*mech*). [L *tentātiō*, *-ōnis*, from *tentāre* to test]

tentative *ten'tə-tiv*, *adj* done or made provisionally and experimentally; cautious, hesitant, diffident. — *n* an experimental attempt. — *adv* **ten'tatively**. — *n* **ten'tativeness**. [L *tentāre* to try]

tenter[1] *ten'tər*, *n* a frame for stretching cloth, *esp* so that it retains its shape while drying; a tenterhook; a hook. — *vt* to stretch on hooks. — **ten'terhook** a sharp, hooked nail to fasten cloth to a tenter; a hook. — **on tenterhooks** in impatient suspense. [Appar connected with Fr *tenture* hangings, and L *tendere* to stretch]

tenter[2]. See under **tent**[1,4].

tenth. See under **ten**.

tentie. See under **tent**[4].

tentigo *ten-tī'gō*, *n* priapism; morbid lasciviousness. — *adj* **tentiginous** (*-tij'i-nəs*). [L *tentīgō*, *-inis*, from *tendere* to stretch]

tentorium *ten-tō'ri-əm*, *ten-tö'ri-əm*, *n* a sheet of the dura mater stretched between the cerebrum and the cerebellum (*anatom*); the internal chitinous skeleton of an insect's head. — *adj* **tento'rial**. [L *tentōrium* a tent, from *tendere* to stretch]

tenty. See under **tent**[4].

tenue *tə-nü*, *n* bearing, carriage; manner of dress. [Fr]

tenuirostral *ten-ū-i-ros'trəl*, *adj* (of a bird) slender-billed. [L *tenuis* thin, and *rōstrum* bill]

tenuis *ten'ū-is*, *ten'ōō-is*, *n* an unaspirated voiceless stop consonant, such as *k*, *p* or *t*: — *pl* **ten'ues** (*-ēz*, *-ās*). [L, thin]

tenuity. See under **tenuous**.

tenuous *ten'ū-əs*, *adj* thin; slender; slight, insubstantial; rarefied. — Also (*rare*) **tenū'ious**. — *adv* **ten'uously**. — *n* **tenū'ity** or **ten'uousness**. [L *tenuis* thin; cf *tendere* to stretch]

tenure[1] *ten'yər*, *n* holding, occupation; time of holding; the holding of an appointment in a university or college for an assured length of time after a period of probation; conditions on which property is held; a tenant's rights, duties, etc. — *adj* **ten'urable** (of a university post) giving tenure. — *adj* **ten'ured** (of *esp* a university lecturer) having tenure. — *adj* **tenūr'ial**. — *adv* **tenūr'ially**. — **tenure track** (*NAm*) a career path, *usu* in higher education, with a guarantee of tenure after a given number of years' service or probationary period. [Anglo-Fr *tenure*, from *tenir* to hold]

tenure[2] (*Shakesp*) for **tenor**.

tenuto *te-nōō'tō*, (*music*) *adj* and *adv* sustained. — *n* a sustained note or chord: — *pl* **tenu'tos**. [Ital, pa p of *tenere* to hold]

tenzon. See under **tenson**.

teocalli *tē-ō-kal'i*, *tē-ə-kal'i* or *tā-ō-kal'yi*, *n* a Mexican pyramid temple. [Nahuatl, from *teotl* god, and *calli*, house]

teosinte *tē-ō-sin'ti*, *n* a tall grass (*Euchlaena mexicana*), related to maize, a native of the southern US and

Mexico, often used as a fodder crop. [Nahuatl, from *teotl* god, and *centli* ear of corn]

tepal *tē'pəl* or *tep'əl*, (*bot*) *n* one of the subdivisions of a perianth that is not clearly differentiated into a calyx and a corolla. [Fr *tépale*, changed from *pétale* petal, influenced by *sépale* sepal]

tepee, **teepee**, or **tipi** *tē'pē* or *ti-pē'*, *n* an American Indian tent formed of skins, etc, stretched over a frame of converging poles. [Sioux *tīpī* dwelling]

tepefy *tep'i-fī*, *vt* and *vi* to make or become tepid. — *n* **tepefac'tion**. [L *tepefacere*, from *tepēre* to be tepid, and *facere* to make]

tephigram *tē'fi-gram*, *n* (*meteorol*) a diagram on which information about vertical variation of atmospheric conditions is plotted. [*t*, for temperature, *phi*, former symbol for entropy, and **-gram**]

tephra *tef'rə*, *n* ash and debris ejected by a volcano. [Gr *tephrā* ashes]

tephrite *tef'rīt*, *n* a fine-grained basaltic rock containing a feldspathoid as well as feldspar, but no olivine. — *adj* **tephritic** (*-rit'ik*). — *n* **teph'roite** (*-rō-īt*) an ashy-grey or reddish silicate of manganese. — *n* **teph'romancy** (see **-mancy**) divination by ashes, *esp* those left after a sacrifice. [Gr *tephrā* ashes, *tephros* ash-coloured]

tepid *tep'id*, *adj* moderately warm, lukewarm; lacking enthusiasm, half-hearted. — *n* **tepidā'rium** (or *-dä'ri-ōōm*) a warm room between the cold and hot rooms of a Roman bath. — *n* **tepid'ity** or **tep'idness**. — *adv* **tep'idly**. [L *tepidus*, from *tepēre* to be warm]

tequila or **tequilla** *tə-kē'lə*, *n* a Mexican alcoholic drink made from an agave plant (*Agave tequilana*). [From a district of Mexico]

Ter. *abbrev*: Terrace (in street names); Territory.

ter- *tûr-*, *combining form* thrice, three, threefold. [L, thrice]

tera- *ter'ə-*, *combining form* denoting ten to the twelfth power (formerly *megamega*), as in *terawatt*.

teraflop *ter'ə-flop*, (*comput*) *adj* able to perform a trillion calculations per second, as in *teraflop chip* a computer chip, and *teraflop machine* a computer, able to perform this number of calculations per second. [**tera-**]

terai *tə-rī'*, *n* a wide-brimmed double-crowned ventilated felt hat, first worn in the *Terai* (Tarái), India.

terakihi. See under **tarakihi**.

teraph *ter'əf*, *n* in ancient Jewish religion and divination, an image of some sort, such as a household deity: — *pl* **ter'aphim** (also used as *sing*). [Heb]

teras *ter'əs*, (*biol* and *pathol*) *n* a monstrosity: — *pl* **ter'ata**. — *n* **ter'atism** a monster; a malformed person or animal, *esp* in the foetal stage. [Gr *teras*, *-atos* monster]

terato- *ter-ə-tō-*, *-tə-* or *-to'-*, *combining form* denoting monster, congenital malformation. — *n* **terat'ogen** (*-jen*) an agent that raises the incidence of congenital malformation. — *n* **teratogen'esis**. — *adj* **teratogen'ic** producing monsters; causing abnormal growth (in a foetus). — *n* **teratog'eny** (*-toj'i-ni*) the production of monsters. — *adj* **teratolog'ic** or **teratolog'ical**. — *n* **teratol'ogist**. — *n* **teratol'ogy** the study of biological malformations or abnormal growths; a collection of tales and myths about fantastic monsters. [Gr *teras*, *-atos* monster]

teratoid *ter'-ə-toid*, (*biol*) *adj* monstrous. [Gr *teras*, *-atos* monster]

teratoma *ter-ə-tō'mə* (*med*) *n* a tumour consisting of tissue not normally found at that site, occurring *esp* in the testis or ovary: — *pl* **teratō'mata**. — *adj* **teratō'matous**. [Gr *teras*, *-atos* monster]

terbium *tûr'bi-əm*, *n* a rare metal (symbol **Tb**; atomic no 65) found in certain yttrium minerals. — *adj* **ter'bic**. [From *Ytterby*, Sweden, place of discovery]

terce *tûrs*, *n* a widow's right, where she has no conventional provision, to a life-rent of a third of the husband's heritable property (*Scots law*); one of the seven canonical hours of the divine office, taking place at the third hour of the day (9 am) (also **tierce**; *eccles*). [See **tierce**]

tercel *tûr'səl*, **tiercel** *tēr'səl*, **tarcel**, **tarsal**, **tarsel** *tär'səl*, **tassel** or **tassell** *tas'əl*, *n* a male hawk. — *n* **terc'elet** or **tierc'elet** a tercel. — **ter'cel-gent'le** (*Scott*), **tass'el-gentle** (*Shakesp*) and **tass'ell-gent** (*Spenser*) a male peregrine falcon; **ter'cel-jerkin** a male gerfalcon. [OFr *tercel*, from L *tertius* third, perh as being one-third smaller than the female, or from the belief that the male hawk hatched from the last egg of three]

tercentenary *tûr-sən-tē'nə-ri* or *tûr-sen-ten'ə-ri*, *adj* of or relating to three hundred years, or to a 300th anniversary or the celebrations for it. — *n* a 300th anniversary, or the celebrations for it. — *adj* **tercentennial** (*tûr-sen-ten'yəl*) of 300 years. — *n* a 300th anniversary. [L *ter* thrice, and **centenary**]

tercet *tûr'sit* (*prosody*), *n* a group of three lines that rhyme together or are associated by rhyme with an adjacent set of three. [Ital *terzetto*]

tercio *tûr'si-ō*, *-shi-ō* (*Scott* **tertia**), (*hist*) *n* an infantry regiment, *orig* Spanish: — *pl* **ter'cios**. [Sp]

terebene *ter'i-bēn*, *n* a light-yellow disinfectant liquid, a mixture of hydrocarbons made from oil of turpentine, used as a solvent for paint. [*terebinth* and sfx *-ene*]

terebinth *ter'i-binth*, *n* the turpentine tree (*Pistacia terebinthus*; family *Anacardiaceae*) yielding turpentine. — *adj* **terebinth'ine** of or relating to the terebinth; of, relating to or resembling turpentine. [Gr *terebinthos*]

terebra *ter'i-brə*, *n* a Roman engine for boring walls; a boring instrument or organ; a piercing ovipositor (*biol*); (with *cap*) a genus of gasteropods with auger-shaped shell: — *pl* **ter'ebras** or **ter'ebrae** (*-e*). — *adj* **ter'ebrant** boring; having a piercing ovipositor. — *n* (*facetious*) a bore. — *vt* and *vi* **ter'ebrate** to bore. — *adj* (*-brət*) having scattered perforations; (eg of insects) having a boring organ, such as a sting. — *n* **terebrā'tion**. — *n* **terebrat'ūla** a member of *Terebratūla*, the lamp-shell genus of brachiopods, with perforated beak: — *pl* **terebrat'ūlas** or **terebrat'ūlae** (*-lē*). [L *terebra*]

teredo *te-rē'dō*, *n* a member of the shipworm genus of molluscs *Teredo*, a bivalvular mollusc that bores into wooden ships: — *pl* **terē'dos** or **terē'dines** (*-di-nēz*). [L *terēdō*, *-inis*, from Gr *terēdōn*, *-onos* a boring worm, from root of *teirein* to wear away]

terefa or **terefah** *tə-rā-fä'*, *-rā'*, *adj* not ritually clean, not kosher. [Heb *tāraph* to tear]

terek *ter'ik*, *n* a sandpiper (*Xenus cinereus*) found at the river *Terek* (Russia) and elsewhere (also **Terek sandpiper**).

Terentian *tə-ren'shən*, *-shyən*, *adj* pertaining to the Roman comic poet *Terence*, Publius Terentius Afer (fl 165BC).

terephthalic acid *ter-əf-thal'ik as'id*, *n* a chemical widely used in the manufacture of synthetic, *esp* polyester, fibres. [*tere*bene, and *phthalic*]

teres *ter-ēz*, (*anatom*) *n* either of two muscles of the shoulder blade, **teres major** and **teres minor**, that rotate the arm inwards and outwards respectively. [L *terēs* smooth]

terete *tə-rēt'*, *ter'ēt*, (*biol*) *adj* smooth and cylindrical. [L *teres*, *teretis* smooth, from *terere* to rub]

terf and **terfe**. Milton's spellings of **turf**.

tergite *tûr'jīt*, *n* the back plate of a somite. [**tergum**]

tergiversate *tûr'ji-vər-sāt*, *vi* to turn one's back; to desert, change sides; to shuffle, shift, use evasions. — *n* **tergiversā'tion**. — *n* **ter'giversātor**. — *adj* **tergiver'-satory**. [L *tergum* the back, and *versārī* to turn]

tergum *tûr'gəm*, *n* the back of an arthropod; the thickened dorsal plate of an arthropod segment: — *pl* **ter'ga**. — *adj* **ter'gal**. [L, back]

teriyaki *ter-i-yä'ki*, *n* and *adj* in Japanese cookery, (a dish of meat or shellfish) marinated in a soy sauce and grilled or broiled. [Jap *teri* sunshine, and *yaki* roast, broiled]

term *tûrm*, *n* an end; the normal duration of a pregnancy, or its completion; any limited period; the time for which anything lasts; a division of the academic or school year, alternating with holiday; a period of sittings (*law*); (in *pl*) conditions, stipulations; (in *pl*) charge, fee; a quantity added to or subtracted from others in an expression (*algebra*); an item in a series; either of the two quantities in a ratio (*math*); that which may be a subject or predicate of a proposition (*logic*); a word used in a specially understood or defined sense; an expression generally; (in *pl*) language generally; a limit, boundary (*archaic*); a term day; (in *pl*) a footing, relation; (in *pl*) respect (*Shakesp*); a bust in continuity with its pedestal (*art* and *archaeol*). — *vt* to call, designate. — *n* **term'er** a person who came to town during a law term (*hist*); a termor (*obs*). — *adj* **term'less** endless; inexpressible (*Shakesp*); unconditional. — *adj* and *adv* **term'ly**. — *n* a publication appearing once a term. — *n* **term'or** or (*obs*) **term'er** a person who holds an estate for a term of years or for life. — **term assurance** a *usu* cheap form of life insurance which pays out only if the insured dies within the period specified; **term day** a day of the year fixed for some purpose, such as payment of rent, the beginning or end of a tenancy, hiring of servants, household removals; **term'-time**. — Also *adj*. — **bring to terms** to compel to the acceptance of conditions; **come to terms** to come to an agreement; to submit; **come to terms with** to find a way of living with (some personal trouble or difficulty); **eat one's terms** see under **eat**; **in terms** in so many words, explicitly; engaged in negotiations; **in terms of** having or using as unit; in the language peculiar to; in respect of, with regard to; **keep a term** to give the regular attendance during a period of study; **long'-** or **short'-termer** a person serving respectively a long or short prison sentence; **make terms** to reach an agreement; **on speaking terms** friendly enough to speak to each other; well enough acquainted to speak; **on terms** in friendly relations; on an equal footing; **stand upon terms** to insist upon conditions; **term of art** a term having a special meaning in a certain art, craft, etc, a technical term; **term of years** an interest or estate in land for a fixed period; **terms of reference** see under **refer**; **terms of trade** relation between export and import prices in national accounts. [Fr *terme* a limit, from L *terminus* a boundary]

termagant *tûr'mə-gənt*, *n* a brawling, scolding woman. — *adj* scolding, shrewish; brawling. — *n* **ter'magancy**. — *adv* **ter'magantly**. [ME *Termagan* or *Tervagant*, a supposed Muslim idol, represented in the old plays and moralities as having a violent character]

termer. See under **term**.

Termes *tûr'mēz*, *n* a genus of termites. [L *termes*, *-itis* a wood-worm]

terminable *tûr'mi-nə-bl*, *adj* that may come or be brought to an end. — *n* **terminabil'ity** or **ter'minableness**. — *adv* **ter'minably**. [L *termināre* to limit, from *terminus* limit, boundary]

terminal *tûr'mi-nəl*, *adj* of, at, forming or marking, an end, boundary or terminus; final; (of a diseased condition) representing the final stages of a fatal illness; (of a disease) ending in death; suffering from a terminal illness; extreme, acute (*colloq*); on the terminal market; of a term; occurring every term. — *n* an end; an ending; a rail or bus terminus; an arrival and departure building for travellers by air; the storage base and distribution centre for raw material, eg at the head of an oil pipeline; a free end in an open electric circuit; a device linked to a computer and at a distance from it, by which the computer can be operated (also **terminal unit**); a patient with a terminal illness. — *adv* **ter'minally**. — **terminal guidance** a system for guiding sub-units of a missile warhead towards multiple targets near the end of the missile's flight; **terminal illness** a fatal disease in its final stages; **terminal market** (*finance*) the central market in London for dealing in general commodities; **terminal platform** (*oil industry*) an off-shore platform used as a base for pumping oil or gas ashore; **terminal unit** see **terminal** above; **terminal velocity** the speed of an object on impact with a target; the greatest speed attained by an object falling or fired through a fluid. [L *terminālis*, from *terminus* limit, boundary]

Terminalia *tûr-mi-nā'li-ə*, *n pl* an annual Roman festival in honour of the god Terminus. — *n sing* the myrobalan genus of Combretaceae. [**terminus**]

terminate *tûr'mi-nāt*, *vt* to bring to an end; to end (a pregnancy) before its term. — *vi* to come to an end; (of eg a word) to end (with *in*). — *n* **terminā'tion** the act of terminating; an end or terminating part; ending or result; the ending of a pregnancy before term (*med*). — *adj* **terminā'tional**. — *adj* **ter'minative** tending to terminate or determine; expressive of completion; definitive; absolute. — *adv* **ter'minatively**. — *n* **ter'minātor** someone who, or something which, terminates; the boundary between the illuminated and dark portions of the moon or of a planet. — *adj* **ter'minatory**. [L *termināre* to set a limit to]

terminer *tûr'mi-nər*, (*law*) *n* the act of determining. [L *termināre* to set a limit to]

termini. See under **terminus**.

terminism *tûr'mi-nizm*, *n* nominalism (*philos*); the doctrine that there is a time limit for the repentance and operation of grace (*theol*). — *n* **ter'minist**. [L *termināre* to set a limit to]

terminology *tûr-mi-nol'ə-ji*, *n* nomenclature; the set of terms used in any art, science, etc; the study of correct terms. — *adj* **terminolog'ical**. — *adv* **terminolog'ically**. — **terminological inexactitude** (*facetious*) a lie. [Med L *terminus* term]

terminus *tûr'mi-nəs*, *n* an end, limit; an end point of a bus or railway route; a station at such a point; a finishing point or goal; a starting-point; a boundary stone; a bust ending in a pedestal (*art* and *archit*); (with *cap*) the Roman god of boundaries; a bust of Terminus: — *pl* **ter'mini** (*-nī*) or **ter'minuses**. [L, boundary, limit]

terminus ad quem *tûr'mi-nəs ad kwem* (*L*) the end or limit to which; a finishing point; point of destination; **terminus ante quem** (*an'ti*) the end limit of a period of time; the established time or date before which the event in question must have occurred; **terminus a quo** (*ä kwō*) the end or limit from which; a starting-point; **terminus post quem** (*pōst*) the starting point, earliest point, or a period of time; the established time or date after which the event in question must have occurred.

termite *tûr'mīt*, *n* a so-called white ant, a pale-coloured insect of the order *Isoptera*, only superficially like an ant, some species feeding on wood and damaging trees, buildings, etc. — *n* **termitarium** (*tûr-mi-tā'ri-əm*) or **ter'mitary** (*-tə-ri-*) a nest or mound of termites. [L *termes*, *termitis* a woodworm]

termless, termly, termor. See under **term**.

tern[1] *tûrn*, *n* a long-winged aquatic bird of the subfamily *Sterninae*, related to the gulls but *usu* smaller and with a long forked tail. [Cf ON *therna*; OE *stearn*, *tearn*]

tern[2] *tûrn*, *n* a three, set of three; a prize for drawing three winning numbers; a three-masted schooner. — *adj* **ter'nal** threefold. — *adj* **ter'nary** in threes; of three components; based on three; to the base three (*math*); of a third order. — *n* (*obs*) a triad. — *adj* **ter'nate** with three leaflets (*bot*); grouped in threes. — *adv* **ter'nately**. — *n* **ter'nion** a triad; a section of paper for a book containing three double leaves or twelve pages. — **ternary form** (*music*) a structure in which a first subject is followed by a second and then a repetition of the first. [L *ternī* three each, from *trēs* three]

terne *tûrn*, *n* an alloy, chiefly of lead and tin, known as **terne metal**; sheet-iron or steel coated with this alloy (also **terne plate**). — *vt* **terne** to cover with terne metal. [Fr *terne* dull]

ternion. See under **tern**[2].

Ternstroemiaceae *tûrn-strē-mi-ā'shi-ē*, *n pl* the Theaceae or tea family of plants. [From a genus *Ternstroemia*, named after Christopher *Ternström*, Swedish naturalist]

terotechnology *ter'ō-tek-nol'ə-ji*, *n* the application of managerial, financial, engineering and other skills to extend the operational life of, and increase the efficiency of, equipment and machinery. [Gr *tereein* to watch, observe, and **technology**]

terpene *tûr'pēn*, (*chem*) *n* any one of a group of hydrocarbons with a composition $C_{10}H_{16}$ found in the essential oils of some plants, *esp* conifers. — *n* **ter'penoid** any of a group of substances having a structure like that of terpene. — *n* **terpin'eol** (*tûr-pin'i-ol*) a terpene alcohol used extensively as a perfume base. [From *terpentin*, old form of **turpentine**]

Terpsichore *tərp-sik'ə-rē*, *n* the Muse of choral song and dance. — *adj* **terpsichorē'an** of or relating to dancing. — Also **terpsichorē'al**. [Gr *Terpsichorē*, from *terpsis* delight, from *terpein* to enjoy, and *choros* dance]

Terr. *abbrev*: Terrace (in street names); Territory.

terra *ter'ə*, *n* the Latin and Italian word for earth, used eg in legal contexts; any area of higher land on the moon's surface: — *pl* **terr'ae** (-*ē*). — *adj* **terraqueous** (*te-rā'kwi-əs*; L *aqua* water) of land and water. — *n* **terrā'rium** a vivarium for land animals or (*usu* in the form of a large, often sealed, bottle or jar) for plants: — *pl* **terrār'iums** or **terrāria**. — **terra alba** (*al'bə*; L, white) any of various white, earthlike substances such as gypsum, kaolin, pipeclay, etc; **terracott'a** (Ital *cotta*, from L *cocta* (feminine) baked) an unglazed earthenware made from a mixture of clay and sand, used for statues, etc, and *esp* formerly, as an ornamental building material for facings, etc; an object of art made of it; its deep reddish-brown colour. — Also *adj*. — **terra firma** (*fûr'mə*) the mainland, solid earth; (*colloq* and erroneously) dry land. — *vt* **ter'raform** to alter the atmosphere and ecology of (a planet) artificially, so as to make plant, animal and human life viable there. — **ter'raforming**; **terra ignota** (*ig-nō'tə*; L *ignota* (feminine) strange, unfamiliar) or **terra incognita** (*in-kog'ni-tə*; L *incognita* (feminine) unknown) an unexplored or unknown country or region; **terra-japon'ica** pale catechu or gambier; **terramara** (*te-rə-mä'rə*; *pl* **-re** *-rā*; Ital dialect for *terra marna* marl-earth) a dark earthy deposit formed under prehistoric pile-dwellings in Italy (also **terramare** *te-rə-mä'ri*, *te-rə-mār*); **terra nullius** (L, nobody's land) land that is not part of the sovereign territory of any country; **terra-rossa** (*te-rə-a-ros'ə*; Ital *rossa* (feminine) red) a ferruginous red earth, the residue of the weathering of limestone; **terra sigillata** (*sij-i-lā'tə*, *sig-i-lä'ta*; L, sealed earth) a reddish-brown astringent clay found eg on the islands of Lemnos and Samos; earthenware pottery made from it; Samian ware.

terrace *ter'is*, *n* a raised level bank or walk; a level stretch along the side or top of a slope; ground or a structure that rises stepwise; a connected row of *usu* identical houses, properly one overlooking a slope; a raised paved area alongside a house; a gallery open at the side; a balcony; a flat rooftop; (*usu* in *pl*) the open areas rising in tiers around a football stadium, where spectators stand; a defective spot in marble. — *vt* to form into a terrace or terraces. — *adj* **terr'aced** in terraces. — *n* **terracette** (-*set'*) a small terrace on a slope resulting from soil creep or erosion (also called **sheeptrack**). — *n* **terr'acing**. — **terraced** (or **terrace**) **house** one of the houses forming a terrace. [Fr *terrasse*, from Ital *terrazza*, from LL *terrācea* an earthen mound, from L *terra* the earth]

terracotta. See under **terra**.

terrae filius *ter'ē fil'i-əs*, *ter'ī fēl'i-o͝os*, (*L*) a son of the soil; a person of humble birth.

terra firma, terraform, terra ignota. See under **terra**.

terrain[1] *te-rān'* or *ter'ān*, *n* ground, a tract, regarded as a field of view or of operations, or as having some sort of unity or prevailing character. [Fr, from a LL form of *terrēnum* terrene]

terrain[2]. See under **terrane**.

terra incognita, terra-japonica, terramara, terramare. See under **terra**.

Terramycin® *ter-ə-mī'sin*, *n* oxytetracycline, an antibiotic effective against a wide range of bacteria and some Rickettsiae viruses, and protozoan parasites. [L *terra* the earth, and Gr *mykēs* fungus]

Terran *ter'ən*, *n* a term sometimes used in science fiction for an inhabitant of the planet earth. [L *terra* earth]

terrane *ter'ān*, (*geol*) *n* a rock formation, or series of connected formations (also **terrain**). [See **terrain**[1]]

terra nullius. See under **terra**.

terrapin *ter'ə-pin*, *n* any of various webfooted pond or river turtles of the family *Emydidae*. — Also called **water tortoise**. [Of Algonquin origin]

terraqueous, terrarium, terra rossa. See **terra**.

terras. See under **trass**.

terra sigillata. See under **terra**.

terrazzo *te-rat'sō*, *-raz'ō*, *n* a mosaic covering (sometimes precast) for concrete floors consisting of marble or other chips set in cement and then polished: — *pl* **terrazz'os**. — Also called **Venetian mosaic**. [Ital, terrace, balcony]

terreen. An older spelling of **tureen**.

terrella *ter-el'ə*, *n* a magnetic model of the earth. [A mod dimin of L *terra* the earth]

terremotive *ter-i-mō'tiv*, *adj* seismic. [L *terrae motus* earthquake]

terrene *ti-rēn'* or *ter'ēn*, *adj* of the earth; earthly, worldly; mundane; earthy; terrestrial. — *n* the world; a region, terrain. — *adv* **terrene'ly**. [L *terrēnus*, from *terra* the earth]

terreplein *tār'plān*, *ter-plẽ*, (*fortif*) *n orig* the talus on the inner side of a rampart; the top of a rampart, or space behind the parapet, where guns are mounted. [Fr, from L *terra* earth, and *plēnus* full]

terrestrial *ti-res'tri-əl*, *adj* of, or existing on, the earth; earthly, worldly; living or growing on land or on the ground (*esp* as opposed to the sea or air); representing the earth; (of a planet) like the earth in size or form; signifying signals sent by a land transmitter as distinct from a satellite (*TV*). — *n* an inhabitant of the earth; a man of the world, layman (*Shakesp*). — *adv* **terres'trially**. — **terrestrial magnetism** the magnetic properties exhibited within, on and outside the earth's surface; **terrestrial poles** (*geol*) the two points diametrically opposite on the earth's surface, as opposed to the *magnetic poles*; **terrestrial radiation** (*meteorol*) the loss of the earth's heat by radiation to the sky, resulting in dew and hoarfrost; **terrestrial telescope** a telescope giving an erect image, used for viewing over distances on the earth's surface rather than astronomically. [L *terrestris*, from *terra* the earth]

terret or **territ** *ter'it*, *n* a swivel-ring; a ring for fastening a chain to, eg on a dog's collar; either of the two rings or loops on a harness through which driving reins pass. — Also **torr'et** or **turr'et**. [OFr *toret*, dimin of *tor*, *tour* a round]

terre verte *ter vert*, *n* green earth (see under **green**[1]). [Fr]

terrible *ter'i-bl*, *adj* inspiring fear, terror or awe; awful; dreadful; very bad; pronounced, extreme, notable (*colloq*). — *n* a terrible thing. — *n* **terribil'ity** (*rare*). — *n* **terr'ibleness**. — *adv* **terr'ibly** in a terrible manner; very (*colloq*). [L *terribilis*, from *terrēre* to frighten]

terricolous *te-rik'ə-ləs*, *adj* living in or on the soil. — *n* **terr'icole** (*-i-kōl*) a land animal or plant; a burrower. — Also *adj*. [L *terricola* a dweller upon earth, from *terra* earth, and *colere* to inhabit]

terrier[1] *ter'i-ər*, *n* a small dog of various breeds, *orig* one that would follow burrowing animals underground; a keen, eager person; (*punningly*) a territorial soldier; a person who hunts after criminals [OFr, (*chien*) *terrier* earth (dog), from LL *terrārius* (adj), from *terra* land]

terrier[2] *ter'i-ər*, (*hist*) *n* a register or roll of a landed estate; an inventory; a rent-roll. [OFr, from LL *terrārius* (adj), from *terra* land]

terrific *tə-rif'ik*, *adj* prodigious, very great, large or intense (*colloq*); marvellous, excellent (*colloq*); very good, enjoyable, attractive, etc (*colloq*); frightening, terrifying; dreadful. — *adv* **terrif'ically**. [L *terrificus* frightful]

terrify *ter'i-fī*, *vt* to cause terror in; to frighten badly: — *pr p* **terr'ifying**; *pa t* and *pa p* **terr'ified**. — *n* **ter'rifier**. —

adj **ter'rifying**. — *adv* **ter'rifyingly**. [L *terrificāre*, from *terrēre* to terrify, and *facere* to make]

terrigenous *te-rij'i-nəs, adj* earth-born; derived from the land. — **terrigenous sediments** sediment derived from the erosion of land deposited either on land or in the sea. [L *terrigenus*, from *terra* earth, and *gignere* to produce]

terrine *tə-rēn', n* a casserole, etc, *orig* of earthenware; a dish of meat or fish, etc, cooked in it, *esp* pâté; an earthenware jar sold containing a table delicacy; a tureen. [Fr; see **tureen**]

territ. See under **terret**.

territory *ter'i-tə-ri, n* possessions in land; the whole, or a portion, of the land belonging to a state; (also with *cap*) part of a confederation with an organized government but not yet admitted to statehood; (also with *cap*) a dependency; a region; a jurisdiction; a field of activity; domain; an area in which an agent, commercial traveller, etc works; an area that an animal or bird treats as its own; the area defended by a team or player (*sport*). — *adj* **territo'rial** constituting, concerned with or relating to territory; limited or restricted to a particular territory; (*esp* of an animal, bird, etc) inclined to establish its own stretch of territory and defend it. — *n* a soldier in the Territorial Army. — *n* **territo'rialism** a social system in which the landowning class is dominant; organization on a territorial basis; the theory of church government according to which the civil power is supreme over the church; territoriality. — *n* **territō'rialist**. — *n* **territorial'ity** territorial status; an animal's or bird's tendency to establish and defend its own territory. — *n* **territorializā'tion** or **-s-**. — *vt* **territo'rialize** or **-ise** to make a territory of; to make territorial; to put on a territorial basis; to enlarge (a country) by adding more territory. — *adv* **territo'rially**. — *adj* **terr'itoried** having territory. — **Territorial Army** the name (1920–67, and from 1980) of the voluntary military force organized on a territorial basis, founded in 1908 as the **Territorial Force**, and known (1967–80) as the **Territorial and Army Volunteer Reserve**; **territorial imperative** the need, in vertebrate animals, to occupy and defend a particular area; **territorial waters** that part of the sea reckoned as part of the adjacent state, *orig* within a three-mile limit. [L *territōrium*, domain of a town, perh not orig connected with *terra*]

terror *ter'ər, n* extreme fear; a time of, or government by, terrorism; a person or thing causing extreme fear or dread; a mischievous or troublesome person (*esp* a child), a rogue (*colloq*). — *n* **terr'orism** an organized system of violence and intimidation, *esp* for political ends; the state of fear and submission caused by this. — *n* and *adj* **terr'orist**. — *adj* **terrorist'ic**. — *n* **terrorīzā'tion** or **-s-**. — *vt* **terr'orize** or **-ise** to terrify; to subject to terrorism. — *n* **terr'orizer** or **-s-**. — *adj* **terr'orful**. — *adj* **terr'orless**. — **terror novel** a novel full of supernatural horrors. — *adj* **terr'or-stricken** or **terr'or-struck** smitten with terror. — **King of Terrors** death; **Reign of Terror** or **the Terror** the period (April 1793 to July 1794) of repression and persecution in the first French Revolution when thousands went to the guillotine. [L *terror*, from *terrēre* to frighten]

terry *ter'i, n* a pile fabric with uncut looped pile, used *esp* for towelling; one of the loops; a baby's towelling nappy. — Also *adj*. [Origin unknown]

tersanctus *tûr-sangk'təs* or *tûr-sang'təs, n* the Sanctus (qv). [L *ter* thrice, and **sanctus**]

terse *tûrs, adj* compact, concise, succinct; crisply brief; abrupt, brusque; smooth, clean-cut (*obs*). — *adv* **terse'ly**. — *n* **terse'ness**. — *n* **tersion** (*tûr'shən*) wiping. [L *tersus*, pa p of *tergēre*, *tersum* to rub clean]

tertia. See under **tercio**.

tertial *tûr'shl, adj* (*ornithol*) of or designating the third rank among flight feathers of a wing. — *n* a tertiary flight feather. — *adj* **ter'tian** (*-shən*) occurring every other day (ie on the *third* day, reckoning both first and last days). — *n* a fever with paroxysms every other day. — *adj* **ter'tiary** (*-shər-i*) of the third degree, order or formation; tertial (*ornithol*); (with *cap*) of the third great division of the geological record and time, *incl* Eocene, Oligocene, Miocene, Pliocene; ranking above secondary (*esp* of education); (of an industry) providing services rather than production or extraction. — *n* the Tertiary period; (without *cap*) a member of a third order of a monastic order, a layman who may continue to live an ordinary life in the world; a tertiary feather; that which is tertiary. — **tertiary amines** (*chem*) amines in which the nitrogen atom is attached to three groups; **tertiary college** a college, *esp* one with vocational courses, for the teaching of sixth-form-level students; **tertiary colours** colours resulting from the mixing of two secondary colours, eg olive produced by mixing orange and green. [L *tertiālis*, *tertiānus*, *tertiārius*, from *tertius* third]

tertium quid *tûr'shəm kwid* (or *ter'ti-ōōm*) (*L*) a third unknown thing related to two specific known things; something intermediate between opposites; the third person in the eternal triangle. [Literally, some third thing]

tertius *tûr'shyəs, -shəs, ter'ti-ōōs,* (*L*) *adj* and *n* third (person). — **tertius gaudens** (*gö'denz, gow'dens*) or **gaudet** (*gö'det, gow'*) the third person (who) takes advantage from a dispute between others.

terts *tûrts, n sing* tetrachlor(o)ethylene.

teru-tero *ter'ōō-ter'ō, n* the Cayenne lapwing: — *pl* **ter'u-ter'os**. [Imit of its cry]

tervalent *tûr-vā'lənt* or *tûr'və-lənt,* (*chem*) *adj* having a valency of three, trivalent. [L *ter* thrice, and **-valent**]

Terylene® *ter'i-lēn, n* a synthetic fabric of polyester fibres, light, strong and crease-resistant.

terza rima *ter'tsə rē'mə, n* an Italian verse-form in triplets, in which the middle line of each triplet rhymes with the first and third lines of the next with an odd line to end off the canto: — *pl* **terze rime** (*ter'tsā rē'mā*). [Ital third rhyme]

terzetta *ter-tset'ə, n* a tercet (qv). — *n* **terzett'o** a trio: — *pl* **terzett'ōs** or **terzett'i** (*-ē*). [Ital]

TES *abbrev*: The Times Educational Supplement.

teschenite *tesh'ə-nīt, n* a coarse-grained basic igneous rock composed essentially of plagioclase and augite, *usu* with much analcime. [Found near *Teschen* in Silesia]

TESL (often *tes'əl*) *abbrev*: Teaching (of) English as a Second Language.

tesla *tes'lə, n* the unit of magnetic flux density, equal to 1 weber per sq metre. — **tesla coil** (*elec eng*) a simple source of high voltage oscillations for rough testing of vacuums and gas (by discharge colour) in vacuum systems. [N *Tesla* (1857–1943), US inventor]

TESOL *tē'sol, abbrev*: Teaching of English to Speakers of Other Languages.

TESSA *tes'ə, abbrev*: Tax-Exempt Special Savings Account.

tessara- or **tessera-** *tes'ə-rə-, combining form* denoting four. — *n* **tess'eract** (*Gr aktis* ray) a figure of a cube within a cube. — *adj* **tess'araglot** (Gr *glōtta* tongue) in four languages. [Gr *tessares* four]

tessella *te-sel'ə, n* a little tessera: — *pl* **tessell'ae** (*-ē, -ī*). — *adj* **tess'ellar**. — *vt* **tessellate** (*tes'i-lāt*) to pave with tesserae; to mark like a mosaic. — *vi* (of a number of identical shapes) to fit together exactly, leaving no spaces. — *adj* marked out in little squarish areas. — *adj* **tess'ellated**. — *n* **tessellā'tion** the act of tessellating; the form of tessellated work; an example of tessellated work. [L *tessella*, dimin of *tessera*; see ety for **tessera**]

tessera *tes'ə-rə, n* one of the small pieces of which a mosaic is made; a token or ticket made *usu* of wood or bone (*classical hist*); a password: — *pl* **tess'erae** (*-ē, -ī*). — *adj* **tess'eral** of tesserae; cubic, isometric (*crystallog*). — See also **tessera-** under **tessara-**. [L *tessera* a die, small cube, from Gr *tessares*, *tesseres*, *-a* four]

tesseract. See under **tessara-**.

tessitura *tes-i-tōō'rə, n* the ordinary range of pitch of a voice or a piece of vocal music. [Ital, texture]

Test. *abbrev*: Testament.

test[1] *test*, *n* any critical trial; a means of trial, a standard for trial, judgement or comparison; a written examination, *esp* a short one; anything used to distinguish or detect substances, a reagent (*chem*); a pot or cupel in which metals are tried and refined; any trial; a trial of fitness for admission, eg to an examination; an oath or other evidence of religious belief required as a condition of office or exercise of rights; a test match. — *vt* to put to proof; to try or examine critically; to examine using a reagent (*chem*); to assay and refine (metal). — *vi* to achieve a stated result in a test. — *adj* **test'able**. — *n* **testee'** a person who undergoes a test. — *n* **test'er** a person who tests or thing used for testing. — *n* and *adj* **test'ing**. — **Test Acts** acts meant to secure that none but members of the established religion shall hold office; *esp* an English act of 1673 designed to exclude Roman Catholics from public office; **test ban** the banning (by mutual agreement between nations (**test-ban treaty**)) of the testing of any or all nuclear weapons; **test'-bed** an iron framework on which a machine is placed for testing; anything with a similar purpose (also *fig*); **test card** see **test pattern**; **test case** a law case that acts as a precedent and may settle similar questions about the same point of law in the future; **test drive** a trial drive of a motor vehicle, *usu* with a view to purchasing the vehicle if it is satisfactory; extended to a trial of any piece of equipment or machinery (*colloq*). — Also *vt* (**test'-drive**). — **test flight** a trial flight of a new aeroplane. — *vt* **test'-fly**. — *vt* **test'-market** to offer (a product) for sale in order to test demand, popularity, etc. — **test match** an international cricket match forming one of a series; **test paper** a bibulous paper saturated with some substance that changes colour when exposed to certain chemicals; a paper or questions to test fitness for a more serious examination; **test pattern**, **card** or **chart** (*image technol*) a transmitted chart with lines and details to indicate particular charcteristics of a transmission system, used in TV for general testing purposes; **test pilot** a pilot whose work is testing new aircraft by flying them; **test tube** a glass cylinder closed at one end, used in chemistry, bacteriology, etc; **test-tube baby** *esp* formerly, a child born as as the result of artificial insemination, now *usu* one born from an ovum implanted in the womb after fertilization in a laboratory. [Orig a pot for treating metals, from OFr *test*, from L *testum* an earthen pot, a potsherd, related to *testa* a shell]

test[2] *test*, (*zool* and *bot*) *n* a testa (qv). [See ety for **testa**]

test[3] *test*, *vt* to attest legally and date; to authenticate by a testing clause. — *n* **test'acy** (*-ə-si*) the state of being testate. — *adj* **test'āte** having made and left a valid will. — *n* **testā'tion** a witnessing; a giving by will. — *n* **testā'tor**, *fem* **testā'trix** a person who leaves a valid will at death. — **testā'tum** one of the clauses of an English deed, enumerating the operative words of transfer, statement of consideration, money, etc. — **testing clause** (in a Scots deed) the last clause which recounts when and where the parties signed the deed, before what witnesses, by whose hand it was written, etc. [L *testārī* to testify, witness, pa p (neuter) *testātum*; partly through OFr *tester* to bequeath, partly aphetic for **attest**]

testa *tes'tə*, *n* a hard shell (*zool*); a seed-coat, derived from the ovule integuments (*bot*). — *adj* **testaceous** (*-ā'shəs*) of or having a hard shell; brick-red. [L *testa* a shell, related to *testum* an earthern pot, a potsherd]

testament *tes'tə-mənt*, *n* that which testifies, or in which an attestation is made; the solemn declaration in writing of one's will; a will; a writing or decree appointing an executor, by the testator (**tes'tament=testament'ar**) or by a court (**tes'tament-dā'tive**) (*Scots law*); (with *cap*) either of the main two divisions (**Old Testament** and **New Testament**, often *abbrev* **OT**, **NT**) of the Bible (a translation of Gr *diathēkē*, disposition, compact, covenant); a covenant between God and man, either that with Moses (as expressed in the *Old Testament*), or that instituted by Christ (as expressed in the *New Testament*); (with *cap*) a copy of the New Testament. — *adj* **testament'al**, **testament'ar** (*Scots law*) or **testamen'tary** pertaining to a testament or will; bequeathed or done by will. — *adv* **testamen'tarily**. [L *testāmentum*]

testamur *tes-tā'mūr*, *n* a certificate of having passed an examination. [L *testāmur*, 1st pers pl of *testārī*, to testify, witness]

testate, etc. See under **test**[3].

teste *tes'ti*, *-te*, (*L*) (so-and-so being) witness, on the testimony of (so-and-so). [Ablative of *testis* witness, in ablative absolute construction]

testee. See under **test**[1].

tester[1] *tes'tər*, *n* a canopy or its support, or both, *esp* over a bed. [OFr *testre*, the vertical part of a bed behind the head, and *testiere*, a head-covering, from *teste* (Fr *tête*) head, from L *testa* an earthen pot, the skull]

tester[2] *tes'tər*, or **testern** *tes'tərn*, (*archaic*) *n* a sixpence. — *vt* **tes'tern** (*Shakesp*) to present or reward with a sixpence. [See **teston**]

tester[3]. See under **test**[1].

testes. See under **testis**.

Testicardines *tes-ti-kär'di-nēz*, *n pl* a class of brachiopods with hinged shell and arm skeleton. [L *testa* shell, and *cardo*, *-inis* hinge]

testicle *tes'ti-kl*, *n* a male reproductive gland producing spermatozoa and testosterone, *usu* one of a pair enclosed in the scrotum of mammals. — *adj* **testic'ūlar** of or like a testicle. — *adj* **testic'ūlate** (*-lət*) or **testic'ūlated** like a testicle *esp* in shape. [L *testiculus*, dimin of *testis* witness (eg of virility), testicle]

testify *tes'ti-fī*, *vi* to bear witness; to make a solemn declaration; to protest or declare a charge (with *against*); to give evidence (eg in a court of law). — *vt* to bear witness to; to be evidence of; to affirm or declare solemnly or on oath; to proclaim, declare: — *pr p* **tes'tifying**; *pa t* and *pa p* **tes'tified**. — *n* **testif'icate** (*Scots law*) a solemn written assertion. — *n* **testificā'tion** the act of testifying or of bearing witness. — *n* **testif'icātor**. — *adj* **testif'icatory**. — *adj* **tes'tified**. — *n* **tes'tifier**. [L *testificārī*, from *testis* a witness, and *facere* to make]

testimony *tes'ti-mə-ni*, *n* evidence; evidence given by a witness, *esp* orally, under oath (*law*); declaration to prove some fact; proof; the two tables of the law on which the Ten Commandments are inscribed (*Bible*); the Ark of the Covenant containing these (*Bible*); divine law; a solemn protestation. — *vt* (*Shakesp*) to test, prove or judge by evidence. — *adj* **testi'mōnial** of, affording or of the nature of testimony. — *n* a written attestation; a writing or certificate bearing testimony to a person's character or abilities or to a product's quality; a gift or memorial as a token of respect, *esp* one presented or taking place in public. — *vt* **testimō'nialize** or **-ise** to present with a testimonial. [L *testimōnium*, from *testārī* to witness]

testis *tes'tis* *n* (a more formal word for) a testicle; a rounded body like it: — *pl* **tes'tes** (*-tēz*). [L, a witness (eg of virility), hence a testicle]

teston *tes'tən*, *n* a name for various silver coins, *orig* bearing a king's or duke's head; a Henry VIII shilling; later a sixpence. — *n* **testoon'** a Portuguese or Italian teston. [Obs Fr *teston*, Port *testão*, Ital *testone*, from Ital *testa* head]

testosterone *tes-tos'tə-rōn*, *n* the chief male sex hormone, a steroid secreted by the testes. [*testo* (combining form for *testis*), *ster*ol, and chem sfx *-one*]

testrill (*Shakesp*), **testril** *tes'tril*, *n* a sixpence. [**tester**[2]]

testudo *tes-tū'dō*, *n* a wheeled shelter used by Roman soldiers under attack from above; a similar shelter made by joining shields; a vaulted roof; an ancient lyre, said to have been first made of a tortoise shell; (with *cap*) the genus comprising the typical land tortoises: — *pl* **testū'dōs** or **testū'dinēs**. — *adj* **testū'dinal**, **testū'dinary** or **testūdin'eous** like a tortoise, tortoise-shell, or a testudo. [L *testūdō*, *-inis* tortoise]

testy *tes'ti, adj* irritable; (of remarks, etc) showing touchiness. — *adv* **tes'tily**. — *n* **tes'tiness**. [OFr *testif* headstrong, from *teste* (Fr *tête*) head, from L *testa* pot]

Tet *tet, n* the Vietnamese lunar new year festival. [Viet]

tetanus *tet'ə-nəs, n* a disease due to a bacillus, marked by painful tonic spasms of the muscles of the jaw and other parts; the state of prolonged contraction of a muscle under quickly repeated stimuli. — *adj* **tet'anal**. — *adj* **tetanic** (*ti-tan'ik*) of, occurring in or causing tetanus or the spasms characteristic of tetanus. — *n* a tetanus-causing agent. — *adv* **tetan'ically**. — *n* **tetanīzā'tion** or **-s-**. — *vt* **tet'anize** or **-ise** to produce tetanus or tetanic spasms in. — *adj* **tet'anoid**. — *n* **tet'any** heightened excitability of the motor nerves resulting in painful muscular cramps, associated with lower than normal levels of calcium in the blood. [L, from Gr *tetanos*, from *teinein* to stretch]

tetartohedral *ti-tär-tō-hē'drəl*, (*crystallog*) *adj* having one-fourth of the number of faces required for full symmetry. [Gr *tetartos* fourth, and *hedrā* seat]

tetchy or **techy** *tech'i, adj* irritable. — *adv* **tetch'ily** or **tech'ily**. — *n* **tetch'iness** or **tech'iness**. [Perh from obs *tecche, tetch, tache* blemish, defect, from OFr *tache* spot]

tête[1] *tet*, (*obs*) *n* an elaborately dressed head of hair; a headdress. [Fr]

tête[2] *tet*, (*Fr*) *n* a head. — **tête-à-tête** (*-a-tet* or *tāt-a-tāt'*) a private confidential interview; an S-shaped sofa for two bringing sitters face to face: — *pl* **tête-à-têtes, têtes-à-têtes**. — *adj* confidential, secret. — *adv* in private conversation; face to face. — *adv* **tête-bêche** (*-besh*; Fr *bêche*, from obs *béchevet* double-headed) head-to-tail; (of a postage stamp) printed in an inverted position in relation to its neighbour. — **tête-de-pont** (*də-pɔ̃*) bridgehead; **tête folle** (*fol*; Fr *folle* feminine of *fou* mad) a scatterbrain.

tether *tedh'ər, n* a rope or chain for confining an animal within certain limits; the extent of one's knowledge, endurance, authority, etc. — *vt* to confine with a tether; to restrain within certain limits. — **at the end of one's tether** desperate, having no further strength, patience, resources, etc. [Appar ON *tjōthr*]

Tethys *tē'this, teth'is, n* a sea nymph, wife of Oceanus; a sea that extended in Mesozoic times from Mexico across the middle Atlantic and the Mediterranean into the centre of Asia (*geol*); the third natural satellite of Saturn. [Gr *Tēthȳs*]

tetra[1] *tet'rə, n* any of various species of tropical freshwater fish of the family *Characidae*. [Short form of *Tetragonopterus*, former name of the genus]

tetra[2] *tet'rə, n* a plant mentioned by Spenser (*The Faerie Queene*, II. 7. 52. 4).

tetra- *tet-rə-, ti-tra'*, or **tetr-**, *combining form* denoting four. — *adj* **tetraba'sic** (*chem*) capable of reacting with four equivalents of an acid; (of acids) having four replaceable hydrogen atoms. — *n* **tetrabasicity** (*tet-rə-bā-sis'i-ti*). — *n pl* **Tetrabranchia** or **Tetrabranchiata** (*-brang'ki-ə, -ki-ā'tə*; Gr *branchia* gills) a former order of the nautilus subclass of cephalopods, with four gills. — *adj* **tetrabranch'iate** four-gilled. — *n* any mollusc belonging to the Tetrabranchia. — *n* **tetrachlō'ride** any compound with four chlorine atoms per molecule. — *n* **tetrachloroeth'ylene** or **tetrachloreth'ylene** C_2Cl_4, a liquid used in dry-cleaning, as a solvent, etc. — *n* **tetrachlōromē'thane** carbon tetrachloride. — *n* **tet'rachord** (*-körd*; Gr *chordē* string) a four-stringed instrument; a series of four sounds, forming a scale of two tones and a half. — *adj* **tetrachord'al**. — *adj* **tetrachot'omous**. — *n* **tetrachotomy** (*-kot'ə-mi*, Gr *tetracha* in four parts, and *-tomia* a cutting) division in fours. — *adj* **tetrac'id** having four replaceable hydrogen atoms; capable of replacing four hydrogen atoms of an acid. — *adj* **tetract** (*tet'rakt*; Gr *aktīs, -īnos* ray) four-rayed. — *n* a four-rayed sponge spicule. — *adj* **tetract'inal** (or *-ī'nəl*) or **tetrac'tine**. — *n pl* **Tetractinell'ida** an order of sponges in which some of the spicules are four-rayed. — *adj* **tetracyclic** (*-sī'klik*; Gr *kyklos* ring, wheel) of, in or with four whorls or rings; (of a compound) having four fused hydrocarbon rings in its molecular structure (*chem*). — *n* **tetracy'cline** a crystalline antibiotic used to treat a wide range of infections, *esp* of the respiratory and urinary tracts. — *n* **tetrad** (*tet'rad*) a group of four; an atom, radical or element having a combining power of four (*chem*). — *adj* **tet'rad** or **tetrad'ic**. — *adj* **tetradactyl** (*-dak'til*; Gr *daktylos* digit; *zool*) four-fingered; four-toed. — *n* a four-toed animal. — *adj* **tetradac'tylous**. — *n* **tetradac'tyly** the condition of being tetradactylous. — *n* **tet'radite** a person who attaches mystic properties to the number four; a believer in a godhead of four persons. — *n* **tet'radrachm** (*-dram*) an ancient Greek coin worth four drachmas. — *n* **tetradymite** (*ti-trad'i-mīt*; Gr *tetradymos* fourfold) a grey metallic mineral, an ore of tellurium, Bi_2Te_2S. — *n pl* **Tetradynamia** (*-di-nā'mi-ə*) (in Linnaeus's system) a class corresponding to the Cruciferae. — *adj* **tetradynamous** (*-din'ə-məs*; Gr *dynamis* power) having four long stamens in pairs and two short, as in the Cruciferae. — *adj* **tetraethyl** (*-eth'il, -ē'thīl*) having four ethyl groups, as **tetraethyl lead** or **lead tetraethyl**, $Pb(C_2H_5)_4$, used in petrol as an antiknock agent. — *n* **tet'ragon** (*-gən, -gon*; see **-gon**) a plane figure of four angles and four sides. — *adj* **tetragonal** (*-rag'ə-nəl*) having the form of a tetragon; referable to three axes at right angles, two of them equal (*crystallog*). — *adv* **tetrag'onally**. — *adj* **tetrag'onous** (*bot*) with four angles and convex faces. — *n* **tetragram** (*-gram*; Gr *gramma* a letter) a word or inscription of four letters; (also with *cap*) the tetragrammaton. — *n* a (complete) quadrilateral (*geom*). — *n* **tetragramm'aton** (also with *cap*) vocalized as the name YaHWeH, JeHoVaH, etc, as written with four Hebrew letters, regarded as a mystic symbol; any other sacred word of four letters, as the Latin *Deus*. — *n pl* **Tetragynia** (*-jin'i-ə*; see **gyn-**) (in the Linnaean system) an order of plants (in various classes) with four pistils. — *adj* **tetragyn'ian** or **tetragynous** (*-raj'i-nəs*). — **tetrahē'dral** of, relating to, like or in the form of a tetrahedron. — *adv* **tetrahē'drally**. — *n* **tetrahē'drite** grey copper ore, sulphide of copper and antimony often occurring in tetrahedral crystals. — *n* **tetrahedron** (*-hē'drən*; Gr *hedrā* a base) a solid figure or body with four plane faces; (in full **regular tetrahedron**) a tetrahedron whose surfaces are equilateral triangles: — *pl* **tetrahē'drons** or **tetrahēdra** (*-drə*). — *n* **tetrahydrocann'abinol** the main intoxicant substance in marijuana. — *n* **tetrahydrofō'late** folic acid, vitamin B_7. — *n* **tetrakishexahē'dron** (Gr *tetrakis* four times) a figure got by erecting equal pyramids on all the faces of a cube. — *n* **tetral'ogy** (Gr *tetralogiā*) (in ancient Greece) a group of four dramas, *usu* three tragic and one satyric; any series of four related dramatic or operatic works or stories. — *adj* **tetram'eral** four-parted. — *n* **tetram'erism** division into four parts. — *adj* **tetram'erous** (Gr *meros* part) having four parts, or parts in fours. — *n* **tetrameter** (*ti-tram'i-tər*; Gr *metron* measure) a line of a verse of four measures (dipodies or feet). — Also *adj*. — *n* **Tet'ramorph** a pictorial representation of the symbolic attributes of the four evangelists combined in a single figure. — *adj* **tetramor'phic** (see **morphic**) having four forms. — *n pl* **Tetran'dria** (in Linnaeus's classification) a class of plants with four stamens. — *adj* **tetran'drian**. — *adj* **tetran'drous** (Gr *anēr, andros* man, in the sense of male) having four stamens. — *n* **tetrapla** (*tet'rə-plə*; Gr neuter pl of *tetraploos* fourfold) an edition of four parallel texts, *esp* Origen's of the Old Testament. — *n* **tetraplē'gia** quadriplegia. — *adj* **tetraplēgic**. — *adj* **tetraploid** (*tet'rə-ploid*; Gr *tetraploos* fourfold, and *eidos* form) of cells, nuclei or organisms, having four times the haploid (twice the normal) number of chromosomes. — *n* **tet'raploidy** the condition of being tetraploid. — *n* **tetrapod** (*-pod*; Gr *tetrapous* four-footed, from *pous, podos* foot) a four-footed animal; any vertebrate above the fishes; a reinforced-concrete block laid against a sea wall to break the force of the waves; a structure with four supporting arms at 120° to each other radiating from a central point, three arms supporting the structure at any one time, with the fourth vertical. — Also *adj*. — *adj* **tetrapod'ic** (of verse, a metrical unit) having four metrical feet. — *adj* **tetrapodous** (*-trap'*). — *n* **tetrap'ody** a group of four metrical feet. — *n* **tetrapolis** (*ti-trap'o-lis*; Gr *polis* a city) a group of four towns. — *adj* **tetrapol'itan** (**Tetrapolitan Confession** the Confession which the four cities of Strasburg, Constance, Memmingen and Lindau presented to the Diet of Augsburg (11 July 1530), and, properly speaking, the first Confession of the Reformed Church). — *adj* **tetrap'teran** (*-rən*) or **tetrap'terous** (see **-pteran**, **-pterous**) four-winged. — *n* **tetraptote** (*tet'rap-tōt*; Gr *ptōsis* a case) a noun with only four cases. — *n* **tetrarch** (*tet'rärk*, or *tē'trärk*; Gr *archē* rule, origin; *hist*) under the Romans, the ruler of the fourth part of a province; a subordinate prince; the commander of a subdivision of a Greek phalanx; one of four joint rulers. — *adj* (*bot*; also **tetrarch'ical**) having four xylem strands. — *adj* **tetrarch'ic**. — *n* **tet'rarchy** the office, rank, period of office or jurisdiction of a tetrarch; the fourth part of a province (also **tet'rarchate**); the condition of being tetrarch (*bot*). — *adj* **tetrasemic** (*-sē'mik*; Gr *sēma* a sign; *prosody*) equivalent to four short syllables, as is a dactyl, anapaest or spondee. — *n* **tet'raspore** (*-spōr*, *-spör*; Gr *sporā* seed) an asexual spore formed in groups of four in red seaweeds. — *n* **tetrasporangium** (*-spə-ran'ji-əm*) the sporangium in which tetraspores are formed. — *adj* **tetrasporic** (*-spor'ik*) or **tetrasporous** (*ti-tras'pə-rəs*, or *tet-rə-spō'rəs*, *-spö'*). — *n* **tet'rastich** (*-stik*; Gr *stichos* a row) a stanza or set of four lines. — *adj* **tetrastichal** (*ti-tras'ti-kl*) or **tetrastichic** (*tet-rə-stik'ik*) of or of the nature of tetrastichs. — *adj* **tetras'tichous** (*bot*) in four rows. — *n* **tet'rastyle** (*-stīl*; Gr *stȳlos* a column) a building or portico with four columns supporting a ceiling in front; a group of four pillars. — Also *adj*. — *n* **tetrasyllable** (*-sil'ə-bl*) a word of four syllables. — *adj* **tetrasyllabic** (*-ab'ik*) or **tetrasyllab'ical**. — *n* **tet'ratheism** (*-thē-izm*; Gr *theos* god) the belief in four elements in the Godhead, ie the three persons of the Trinity and a divine essence out of which each of these originates. — *n* **tetrathlon** (*te-trath'lən*; Gr *athlon* contest) a four-event sporting contest. — *adj* **tetratom'ic** having or composed of four atoms to a molecule. — *n* **tetravalent** (*ti-trav'ə-lənt*, *tet-rə-vā'lənt*) quadrivalent. — *n* **tetraxon** (*ti-trak'son*; Gr *axōn*, *-onos* an axis) a sponge spicule with four axes. — *n* **tetrode** (*tet'rōd*; Gr *hodos* a way) a thermionic valve with four electrodes. — *n* **tetrox'ide** an oxide with four atoms of oxygen in the molecule. — *n* **tetryl** (*tet'ril*) a yellow crystalline explosive compound used as a detonator. [Gr *tetra-*, combining form of *tettares*, *tessares* four]

tetrodotoxin *tet-rə-dō-tok'sin*, or **tetrotoxin** *tet-rō-tok'sin*, *n* a deadly nerve poison ($C_{11}H_{17}N_3O_8$) found in a species of Japanese puffer fish. [New L *Tetrodon* (from Gr *tetra-* four-, and *odous*, *odontos* tooth) a genus of puffer fishes, and **toxin**]

tetronal *tet'rə-nəl*, *n* a hypnotic and sedative drug rarely used because of its high toxicity.

tetroxide, **tetryl**. See under **tetra-**.

tetter *tet'ər*, (*Shakesp*) *n* a skin eruption, eg eczema. — *vt* to affect with a tetter. — *adj* **tett'erous** (*Shakesp*) [OE *teter*]

tettix *tet'iks*, *n* a cicada; a cicada-shaped ornament for the hair (*Gr antiq*). [Gr]

teuch or **teugh** *tūhh*, *adj* a Scots form of **tough**.

teuchat (*Scot*). See under **tewit**.

teuchter *tūhh'tər*, (*Scot*; *derog*) *n* a term used by Lowland Scots for a Highlander, *esp* a Gaelic-speaker. [Origin uncertain]

Teucrian *tū'kri-ən*, *n* and *adj* Trojan. [Gr *Teukros* Teucer, first king of Troy]

Teut. *abbrev*: Teutonic.

Teuton *tū'tən*, *n* any speaker of a Germanic language; a member of an ancient Germanic tribe from Jutland (*hist*); (popularly) a German. — *adj* Teutonic. — *adj* **Teutonic** (*-ton'ik*) Germanic, ie of the linguistic family that includes English, German, Dutch and the Scandinavian languages; of the Teutons; (popularly) German in any sense. — *n* the parent language of the Teutons, primitive Germanic. — *adv* **Teuton'ically**. — *n* **Teuton'icism** (*-i-sizm*) or **Teu'tonism** a Germanism; belief in or enthusiasm for the Teutons; the study of Germanic philology and culture. — *n* **Teu'tonist**. — *n* **Teutonīzā'tion** or **-s-**. — *vt* and *vi* **Teu'tonize** or **-ise** to make or become Teutonic, Germanic or German. — **Teutonic Knights** a military-religious order founded in 1191–98 to tend wounded Christians and to fight unbelievers, active first (during the Third Crusade) in Palestine and later against the Prussians and Lithuanians. [L *Teutonēs*, from the root of OE *thēod* people, nation; cf **Dutch**, Ger *deutsch*]

Tevet. See under **Tebeth**.

tew *tū*, (*obs* or *dialect*) *vt* to work up; to taw. — *vi* to toil, hustle. — *n* worry; excitement. [Cf **taw**[2]]

tewart. Same as **tuart**.

tewel *tū'əl*, *n* the rectum or anus, *esp* of a horse (*dialect*); a flue (*obs*); a tuyère (*dialect*). [OFr *tuel* (Fr *tuyau*) tube]

tewit *tē'wit*, or **tewhit** *tē'hwit*, *-wit* (*Scot* **teuchat** *tūhh'ət*), (*dialect*) *n* a lapwing. [Imit]

Tex. *abbrev*: Texas (US state).

Texas *tek'səs*, *n* a state of the USA; (without *cap*) an upper structure on a river-steamer. — *adj* and *n* **Tex'an** (a native or inhabitant) of Texas. — **Texas fever** a protozoal disease of cattle transmitted by ticks; **Texas Rangers** Texas state police, formed in the 19c; **Texas tower** a radar tower built offshore as part of an early-warning system.

Texel *tek'səl*, *n* a breed of sheep, originating in Holland and first imported in quantity to Britain for breeding purposes in 1974. [*Texel*, one of the Friesian islands of the Netherlands]

Tex-Mex *teks'-meks'*, (*US*) *adj* being an Americanized version of some aspect of Mexican culture or cuisine. [*Tex*as, and *Mex*ico]

text *tekst*, *n* the actual words of a book, poem, etc, in their original form or any form they have been transmitted in or transmuted into; a book of such words; words set to music; the main body of matter in a book, distinguished from notes, commentary or other subsidiary matter; the exact wording of a book or piece of writing as opposed to a translation, paraphrase or revision; words or a piece of writing displayed on a VDU (*comput*); matter commented on; a short passage from the Bible taken as the ostensible subject of a sermon, quoted in authority, displayed as a motto, etc; a theme; a textbook; (in *pl*) books for study; the Bible (*Shakesp*); a copybook heading; text-hand. — *adj* **text'less**. — *n* **text'book** a book containing the main principles of a subject. — *adj* (of an operation, example, etc) exactly as planned, in perfect accordance with theory or calculation. — *adj* **text'bookish**. — **text'-editor** (*comput*) a program or series of programs which allows text to be entered and edited on-screen; **text'-hand** a large hand in writing, *orig* one suitable for the text of a manuscript book; **text'-man** a quoter of texts; a textualist; **text'phone** a telephone specially adapted to convert text into spoken messages and vice versa; **text'-processing** (*comput*) the handling of text by computer, eg converting it from one format to another. [Med L *textus* text, from L *textus* structure, texture, from *texere*, *textum* to weave]

textile *teks'tīl* or (*NAm*) *-il*, *n* a woven fabric; fibre, yarn etc suitable for weaving into fabric; any cloth or fabric. — *adj* woven or capable of being woven. — *adj* **texto'rial** (*archaic*) pertaining to weaving. [L *textilis*, from *texere*, *textum* to weave]

textual *teks'tū-əl*, *adj* pertaining to, or contained in, the text; serving for a text. — *n* **text'ualism** (too) strict adherence to a text, *esp* that of the Bible; textual criticism, *esp* of the Bible. — *n* **text'ualist** a person learned in, or a strict adherer to, the text, *esp* of the Bible; a literal interpreter; a quoter of texts. — Also *adj*. — *adv* **text'ually**. — *n* **tex'tuary** a textualist. — **textual criticism** critical study directed towards determining the true reading of a text. [Med L *textuālis*, from *texere*, *textum* to weave]

texture *teks'tyər*, *n* the quality of a material as conveyed to the touch, for example its roughness, smoothness, etc; the general structure, appearance and feel of something; the general quality, character or tenor of something; structural impression resulting from the way that the different elements are combined or interrelated to form a whole, as in music, art, etc; the manner of weaving or connecting (*archaic*); anything woven, a web (*archaic*); disposition of the parts of a body. — *vt* to give a certain texture to, texturize; to weave. — *adj* **text'ural** pertaining to, in the matter of, texture. — *adv* **textur'ally**. — *adj* **text'ured**. — *adj* **text'ureless**. — *vt* **text'urize** or **-ise** to give a particular texture to (food, fabric), to texture. — **texturized vegetable protein** a vegetable substance, *usu* made from soya beans, prepared to resemble meat in appearance and taste (abbrev **TVP**). [L *textūra* web, from *texere*, *textum* to weave]

textus receptus *teks'təs rə-sep'təs*, *teks'tōōs re-kep'tōōs*, (*L*) the received text (of the Greek New Testament).

TG *abbrev*: Togo (IVR); transformational grammar.

TGV *abbrev*: *Train à Grande Vitesse* (qv).

TGWU *abbrev*: Transport and General Workers' Union.

Th. *abbrev*: Thursday.

Th (*chem*) *symbol*: thorium.

th- (*obs*) or **th'** (*archaic* or *dialect*) forms of **the**, *esp* before a vowel, as in Spenser **thelement**, the element, **thelf**, the elf, **thother**, the other.

-th[1] *sfx* forming nouns (1) from verbs, denoting action or process (*growth*); (2) from adjectives, denoting abstract qualities (*filth*, *width*). [OE *-thu*, *-tho*, *-th*]

-th[2] or **-eth** *sfx* forming ordinal numbers and fractions from cardinal numbers greater than, or ending in a number greater than, three. [OE *-tha*, *-the*]

thack *thak*, *n* a Scots form of **thatch**. — **under thack and rape** safely secured under thatch and rope, snug generally.

thae *dhā* (*Scot*) *pl demonstrative pronoun* and *demonstrative adj* those. [OE *thā*; see **tho**[1]]

thagi. See under **thug**.

Thai *tī*, *tä'ē*, *adj* of Thailand (the Asian country known before 1939 and between 1945 and 1949 as Siam). — *n* a native of Thailand (also **Thai'lander**); the language of Thailand. — **Thai boxing** a form of boxing practised in Thailand, using gloved fists, feet, knees and elbows.

thaim *dhām*. Scots form of **them**.

thairm *thārm*, (*Scot*) *n* an intestine; catgut, a musical string. [OE *tharm*, *thearm*]

thalamencephalon *thal-ə-men-sef'ə-lon*, (*anatom*) *n* an older name for **diencephalon**; that part of the diencephalon *incl* the pineal gland and thalamus. — *adj* **thalamencephal'ic**. [**thalamus** and **encephalon**]

thalamus *thal'ə-məs*, *n* (in ancient Greece) an inner room, chamber; the receptacle of a flower (*bot*); part of the midbrain where the optic nerve emerges (also, *esp* formerly, **optic thalamus**; *anatom*): — *pl* **thal'amī**. — *adj* **thal'amic** (or *tha-lam'ik*) of the thalamus. — *n pl* **Thalamiflorae** (*-i-flō'rē*, *-flö'*; L *flōs*, *flōris* flower) in some systems, a subclass of dicotyledons with petals free and stamens hypogynous. — *adj* **thalamiflo'ral**. [Gr *thalamos* an inner room, bedroom]

thalassian *tha-las'i-ən*, *adj* marine. — *n* a sea turtle. — *n* **thalassaemia** or **thalassemia** (*thal-ə-sē'mi-ə*) a hereditary disorder of the blood causing anaemia, sometimes fatal in children. — *adj* **thalassae'mic** or **thalassē'mic**. — *adj* **thalass'ic** marine; of the seas, *esp* those which are small or inland. — *n* **thalassoc'racy** or **thalattoc'racy** (Gr *kratos* power) sovereignty of the seas. — *n* **thalassog'rapher**. — *adj* **thalassograph'ic**. — *n* **thalassog'raphy** the science of the sea. — *n* **thalassother'apy** therapy, said to bring harmony to and detoxify the body, rid one of stress etc, involving the application of mud and seaweed, seawater baths and massage. [Gr *thalassa*, *thalatta* sea]

thale-cress *thāl'-kres*, *n* a cruciferous wall plant with small white flowers (*Sisymbrium thalianum*). [Named after Johann *Thal* (1542–83), German physician]

thaler or **taler** *tä'lər*, *n* an obsolete German silver coin. [Ger; cf **dollar**]

Thalia *thə-lī'ə*, (*Gr mythol*) *n* the Muse of comedy and pastoral poetry; one of the Graces. — *adj* **thalī'an**. [Gr *Thaleia*, *Thaliā*, from *thallein* to bloom]

thalictrum *thə-lik'trəm*, *n* a plant of the meadow-rue genus *Thalictnum*. [Gr *thaliktron*, from *thallein* to bloom]

thalidomide *thə-lid'ə-mīd*, *tha-*, *n* a non-barbiturate sedative drug, withdrawn in 1961 because found to cause malformation in the foetus if taken during pregnancy. — **thalidomide baby** an infant showing the teratogenic effects of thalidomide.

thalli. See under **thallus**.

thallium *thal'i-əm*, *n* a soft, highly toxic white leadlike metal (symbol **Tl**; atomic no 81) discovered in 1861. — *adj* **thall'ic** of or containing trivalent thallium. — *adj* **thall'ous** of or containing univalent thallium. [Gr *thallos* a young shoot, from the bright green line in its spectrum]

Thallophyta, **thallophyte**. See under **thallus**.

thallus *thal'əs*, *n* a plant body not differentiated into leaf, stem and root: — *pl* **thall'uses** or **thall'ī**. — *adj* **thall'iform**. — *adj* **thall'ine**. — *adj* **thall'oid**. — *n pl* **Thallophȳ'ta** (Gr *phyton* plant) the lowest main division of the plant kingdom, lacking true stems, roots and leaves, *incl* bacteria, fungi and algae. — *n* **thall'ophyte** any plant belonging to the Thallophyta. — *adj* **thallophy'tic**. [Gr *thallos* a young shoot]

thalweg or **talweg** *täl'vähh*, *-veg*, (*geol*) *n* the longitudinal profile of the bottom of a river-bed; the middle of a main navigable waterway, acting as a boundary between states (*law*). [Ger, from *Thal* (now *Tal*) valley, and *Weg* way]

Thammuz *tam'ōōz*, *-uz* (*Milton*). Same as **Tammuz**.

than[1] *dhan*, *dhən*, *conj* used after a comparative, actual or felt, to introduce that which is in the lower degree; used after adverbs such as *rather* to introduce the *usu* less desirable or rejected option in a statement of alternatives; except, other than. — *prep* (popularly, and in some authors, eg Shelley) in comparison with (*esp* with *whom*, as in Milton). [OE *thonne*, *thanne*, *thænne* than, orig then]

than[2] *dhan*, *dhən*. An *obs* or dialect form of **then**[1].

thana, **thanah** and **thanadar**. See under **tana**[1].

thanage. See under **thane**.

thanatism *than'ə-tizm*, *n* belief that the soul dies with the body. — *n* **than'atist**. [Gr *thanatos* death]

thanato- *than-ə-tō-*, *-tə-*, *-to'-* or **thanat-**, *combining form* denoting death. — *adj* **thanatognomon'ic** (see **gnomonic**) indicating or characteristic of death. — *n* **thanatog'raphy** a narrative of a death. — *adj* **than'atoid** apparently dead; deathly; deadly. — *n* **thanatol'ogy** the scientific study of death and the customs and practices associated with it; care or psychological therapy for the dying. — *n* **thanatophō'bia** a morbid dread of death. — *n* **thanatop'sis** a view of, or reflection upon, death. — *n* **thanatō'sis** gangrene. [Gr *thanatos* death]

thane *thān*, *n* (in Anglo-Saxon England) king's companion, a person who held land by service, hence a noble of lower rank than eorl or ealdorman; a hereditary (not military) tenant of the crown, often a clan chief (*Scot hist*). — *n* **thā'nage**, **thane'dom**, **thane'hood** or **thane'ship**. — See also **thegn**. [OE *thegn* servant, follower, courtier, nobleman; cf ON *thegn* a man, warrior, Ger *Degen* a soldier, servant, Gr *teknon* child]

thank *thangk*, *n* (*usu* in *pl*) gratitude; an expression of gratitude. — *vt* to express gratitude to; to blame or hold responsible. — *interj* **thankee** see **thank you** below.

— *n* **thank'er**. — *adj* **thank'ful** grateful; gladly relieved. — *adv* **thank'fully** gratefully, with a thankful feeling; one feels thankful (that); (of eg words) expressing gratitude. — *n* **thank'fulness**. — *n* **thank'ing** (*usu* in *pl*; *Shakesp*) thanks. — *adj* **thank'less** unthankful; not expressing thanks for favours; bringing no thanks, appreciation, pleasure or profit — *adv* **thank'lessly**. — *n* **thank'lessness**. — *interj* **thanks** see **thank you** below. — **thank'-offering** an offering made to express thanks; **thanks'giver**; **thanks'giving** the act of giving thanks; a public acknowledgement of divine goodness and mercy; (with *cap*) a day (**Thanksgiving Day**) set apart for this, *esp* that in the US since the time of the Pilgrim Fathers, now fixed as the fourth Thursday of November, or that in Canada, fixed as the second Monday in October; a form of giving thanks, a grace, that form preceding the last two prayers of morning or evening prayer or of the litany, the *General Thanksgiving*. — Also *adj*. — *adv* **thank'worthily**. — *n* **thank'worthiness**. — *adj* **thank'worthy** worthy of or deserving thanks. — *adj* **thank'you** expressing gratitude. — *n* anything expressing gratitude, *esp* a gift. — **thank'-you-ma'am** (*US*) a ridge or hollow in a road that causes those who drive over it to bob their heads. — **be thankit** (*Scot*) thank God; **have (only) oneself to thank for** to be the cause of (one's own misfortune); **I'll thank you, him**, etc **to** used, *usu* in anger, to introduce a request or command; **no thanks to** not owing to, implying that gratitude is far from being due; **thank God** (or **thank goodness**, **heavens**, etc) an expression of relief; **thanks** or **thank you** (or *old colloq* **thank'ee**) elliptical forms of earlier *thanks be to you, I thank you* and similar expressions, conventional expressions of gratitude; **thanks be** thank God; **thanks to** owing to; **thank you** (or **thanks) for nothing** (*colloq*) an expression implying that no gratitude is due at all. [OE *thanc*, *thonc*; cognate with Ger *Dank*; from the root of **think**]

thanna or **thannah** See under **tana**[1].

thar *t'här, tär*, *n* the serow, a Himalayan goat like an antelope; by confusion applied to the tahr. [Nepali (Indic language of Nepal) *thār*]

tharborough. See under **farborough**.

Thargelia *thär-gē'li-ə*, or *-jē'*, *npl* an ancient Athenian festival, in honour of Apollo, in the month of *Thargēliōn* (May–June).

that *dhat*, *demonstrative pronoun* and *demonstrative adj* (*pl* **those**) used in pointing out a person or thing; indicating the thing, person, idea, event, etc (already) mentioned, specified or understood; the former (of two); the more distant, removed or less obvious (of two); not this but the other (as in contrast); the one to be indicated or defined; the person spoken to on the telephone; such (*obs*); often indicating an accompanying snap of the fingers (as *I don't care that, It wants that*). — *relative pronoun* (*sing* and *pl*; *dhət*, *dhat*) who, whom, or which (*esp* when defining or limiting, not merely linking on an addition). — *adv* (*dhat*) to the degree or extent shown or understood; at which (often omitted); to such a degree or extent, so (*colloq* or *dialect*). — *conj* (*dhət*, *dhat*) used to introduce a noun clause, an adverbial clause showing purpose, reason, result or consequence, or an expression of a wish in the subjunctive; because (*Shakesp*). — *adv* **that'away** (*NAm dialect*, or *facetious*) in that direction. — *n* **that'ness** the quality of being a definite thing, that. — **all that** (*colloq*) (*usu* with a negative) very; **and (all) that** (*colloq*) and all the rest of that sort of thing, used as a summary way of dismissing what is vaguely thought of; **(and) that's that** (and) that is the end of that matter; no more of that; **at that** at that point; moreover (*colloq*); nevertheless (*colloq*); **(just) like that** straight away, without effort; without further ado; **that's more like it** that is better, that is more like what is required. [OE *thæt*, neuter demonstrative pronoun cognate with Ger *das*, *dass*; Gr *to*, Sans *tad*; see **the**]

thatch *thach*, *vt* to cover or roof with straw, reeds, heather, palm-leaves, or any similar material. — *vi* to do thatching. — *n* a covering or covering material of straw, reeds, heather, palm-leaves etc; a roof or covering formed from such material; thick hair; a condition of grass in which a mat of dead vegetative fibre builds up, inhibiting the penetration of air to, and the growth of, the roots. — *adj* **thatched** (or *old* **thatcht**). — *n* **thatch'er**. — *n* **thatch'ing** the act or art of covering with thatch; materials used for thatching; the development of thatch in grass. — Also *adj*. — *adj* **thatch'less**. — **thatch'-board** a building-board made of straw. [OE *thæc* covering, thatch, and *theccan* to cover; cognate with Ger *decken*, L *tegere*, Gr *stegein* to cover]

Thatcherism *thach'ə-rizm*, *n* the policies and style of government associated with Margaret *Thatcher*, British prime minister 1979–1990. — *adj* **Thatch'erite** of, relating to or representing the policies of Margaret Thatcher and her associates. — Also *n*.

thaumato- *thö-mə-to-*, or **thaumat-**, *combining form* denoting wonder or miracle. — *n* **thau'matin** a sweetener extracted from a W African fruit, *Thaumatococcus daniellii*, 2000 to 4000 times sweeter than sucrose. — *n* **thaumatogeny** (*-toj'*) the doctrine of the miraculous origination of life. — *n* **thaumatog'raphy** description of natural wonders. — *n* **thaumatol'atry** (see **-latry**) wonder-worship. — *n* **thaumatol'ogy** the study of, or a written study on, miracles. — *n* **thau'matrope** (Gr *thauma* wonder, and *tropos* a turning) an optical toy in which pictures on both sides of a card are seen to combine when the card is rotated rapidly. — *n* **thaumaturge** (*thö'mə-tûrj*; Gr *thaumatourgos* wonder-worker, from *ergon* work) a wonder-worker, magician. — *adj* **thaumatur'gic** or **thaumatur'gical**. — *n pl* **thaumatur'gics** the performance of magic tricks using sleight-of-hand, etc. — *n* **thaumatur'gism**. — *n* **thaumatur'gist**. — *n* **thaumaturgus** (*-tûr'gəs*) a wonder-worker, a thaumaturge; a worker of miracles, applied eg to certain saints. — *n* **thaumaturgy** the performing of miracles. [Gr *thaumat(o)-*, from *thauma*, *-atos* wonder]

thaumasite *thö'mə-sīt*, *n* a mineral, hydrated silicate, carbonate and sulphate of calcium. [Gr *thaumasios* wonderful]

thaw *thö*, *vi* (of ice, etc) to melt or grow liquid; to become so warm as to melt ice; to become less cold, stiff or reserved in manner. — *vt* to cause to melt. — *n* the melting of ice or snow by heat; the change of weather that causes it; an increase in relaxation, a lessening of control; an increase in friendliness of manner. — *n* **thaw'er** an ice-melting agent or apparatus. — *n* and *adj* **thaw'ing**. — *adj* **thaw'less**. — *adj* **thaw'y** inclined to thaw. — **thaw out** to return from frozen to normal condition. [OE *thawian*]

THC *abbrev*: tetrahydrocannabinol.

ThD *abbrev*: *Theologiae Doctor* (*New L*), Doctor of Theology.

the[1] *dhē* (emphatic), *dhə* or *dhi*, *dhē* (before vowels), *demonstrative adj* called the definite article, used to refer to a particular person or thing, or a group of things, already mentioned, implied or known; used to refer to a unique person or thing; used before a singular noun to refer to all the members of that group or class; used before a singular noun to denote a species; used before certain titles and proper names; used before an adjective or noun describing an identified person; used after a preposition to refer to a unit of time, quantity, etc; used before a noun denoting a profession or activity; (*usu* stressed) the best (*colloq*); my, our (*colloq* or *facetious*); used instead of the pfx *to-*, this (*Scot*; as **the day** today, **the night** tonight, **the morn** tomorrow, **the morn's morn** tomorrow morning, **the year** this year). [OE *the* (supplanting *se*), masc of *thæt* that]

the[2] *dhə*, *adv* (with comparatives) (by) how much; (by) so much; used before superlative adjectives and adverbs to indicate an amount beyond all others. [OE *thȳ* by that, by that much, the instrumental case of the definite article]

Thea *thē'ə*, *n* the tea genus of evergreen plants (sometimes *incl* Camellia), giving name to the family **Theā'ceae**, (*-ā'si-ē*) related to the Guttiferae. — *adj* **theā'ceous**. [From the root of **tea**, but taken as if from Gr *theā* goddess]

theandric *thē-an'drik*, *adj* divine and human at the same time. [Gr *theos* a god, and *anēr*, *andros* man]

theanthropic *thē-ən-throp'ik*, *adj* simultaneously divine and human; embodying deity in human forms. — *n* **thean'thropism** or **thean'thropy** the ascribing of human qualities to deity, or divine qualities to man; a doctrine of union of divine and human. — *n* **thean'thropist**. [Gr *theos* a god, and *anthrōpos* man]

thearchy *thē'ärk-i*, *n* rule or government by a god or gods, theocracy; a body of divine rulers. — *adj* **thear'chic**. [Gr *theos* a god, and *archein* to rule]

theat. *abbrev*: theatre; theatrical.

Theatine *thē'ə-tīn*, *n* a member of a RC religious brotherhood founded in 1524 by John Peter Caraffa, bishop of Chieti (L *Teāte*), afterwards Pope Paul IV, and others, or of a sisterhood modelled on it. — Also *adj*.

theatre or (*NAm*) **theater** *thē'ə-tər*, *n* a structure, *orig* in the open air, for drama or other spectacles; a cinema (*NAm* and *Austr*); any natural land formation backed by a curving hillside or rising by steps like seats of a theatre; a building or room, *usu* with tiered seats, which is adapted for lectures, anatomical or surgical demonstrations, etc; an operating theatre; a scene of action, field of operations; (with *the*) the social unit comprising actors, theatre companies, producers, etc, or its characteristic environment and conditions; an audience, house; (with *the*) plays or a specified group of plays, collectively; the writing and production of plays; material or method judged by its suitability for a dramatic presentation. — *adj* **the'atral**. — *adj* **theatrical** (or *rare* **theat'ric**) relating or suitable to, or savouring of, the stage, actors or acting; stagy; histrionic, melodramatic, exaggerated; aiming at or producing dramatic effects; of, in or for the cinema (*esp NAm*). — *n* **theat'ricalism** or **theatrical'ity** staginess, artificiality. — *vt* **theat'ricalize** or **-ise** to adapt to dramatic representation; to make stagy. — *vi* to act; to attend the theatre. — *adv* **theat'rically**. — *n* **theat'ricalness**. — *n pl* **theat'ricals** dramatic performances; theatrical affairs, properties or people. — *n* **theat'ricism** theatricality, affectation, staginess. — *vi* **theat'ricize** or **-ise** (*-sīz*) to play a part. — *n* **theat'rics** the staging of plays, etc, or the art of doing this; histrionics. — *n* **theatromā'nia** a craze for play-going. — *n* **theat'rophone** (*hist*) a telephone connecting callers to a theatre so they can listen to a live performance there. — **the'atre-goer** a person who regularly goes to the theatre; **theatre-in-the-round'** a theatre with a central stage and the audience on all sides; the style of staging plays in such a theatre; **theatre organ** a cinema-organ; **theatre sister** a sister in charge of the nursing team in an operating theatre; **theatre weapons** weapons for use in a theatre of war (as opposed to intercontinental or strategic weapons), applied *esp* to nuclear weapons intended for use in Central Europe. — **theatre of cruelty** a branch of drama, based on the theories of Antonin Artaud (1896–1948), intended to induce in the audience a feeling of suffering and an awareness of the presence of evil; **theatre of fact** a branch of drama using material closely based on real happenings; **theatre of the absurd** a branch of drama dealing with fantastic deliberately unreal situations, in reaction against the tragedy and irrationality of life. [Gr *theātron*, from *theaesthai* to see]

theave *thēv*, (*dialect*) *n* a young ewe, *esp* in its first year.

thebaine *thē'bā-ēn*, *-īn*, *thē'-bə-ēn*, *n* a poisonous alkaloid ($C_{19}H_{21}NO_3$) obtained from opium. [New L *thebaia* opium, as prepared at **Thebes**, Egypt; chem sfx *-ine*]

Thebes *thēbz*, *n* a city of ancient Boeotia, in Greece; a city of ancient Egypt. — *adj* **Thebaic** (*thē-bā'ik*) of Egyptian Thebes; of opium (as an Egyptian product). — *n* **Thebaid** (*thē'bā-id*) a poem on the Seven against Thebes (such as that by Statius); the district of Thebes (Egyptian or Greek). — *adj* **Thē'ban** of Thebes. — *n* a native of Thebes; a Boeotian. — **Theban year** the Egyptian year of 365¼ days. [Gr *Thēbai* Thebes]

theca *thē'kə*, *n* a sheath, case or sac (*zool*); a spore-case (*bot*); a lobe or loculus of an anther (*bot*): — *pl* **thē'cae** (*-sē*). — *adj* **thē'cal** of a theca. — *adj* **thē'cate** having a theca. [Latinized from Gr *thēkē* case, sheath]

Thecla *thek'lə*, *n* the hair-streak genus of butterflies. [New L]

thecodont *thek'ə-dont*, *n* an extinct reptile of the Triassic period, having teeth set in sockets. — *adj* (of mammals) having teeth set in sockets. [Gr *thēkē* case, and *odous*, *odontis* a tooth]

thé dansant *tā dã-sã*, (*Fr*) *n* a dance held in the afternoon at which tea is served: — *pl* **thés dansants**.

thee[1] *dhē*, (*formal*, *liturgical*, *dialect* or *archaic*) *pronoun* the dative and accusative form of **thou**[1]; the nominative form of **thou**[1], used *esp* formerly by Quakers. — *vt* to use *thee* in speaking to (someone). — *vi* to use *thee*. [OE *thē* the]

thee[2] *thē*, (*Spenser*) *vi* to prosper, to thrive. [OE *thēon*; cf Ger *gedeihen*]

theek *thēk*. A Scots form of **thatch** (*vb*).

theft *theft*, *n* (the or an) act of thieving; a thing stolen. — *adj* **theft'ūous** thievish. — *adv* **theft'ūously**. — **theft'boot** or **theft'-bote** illegal compounding of a theft. [OE *thēofth*, *thīefth*, from *thēof* thief]

thegither *dhə-gidh'ər*, a Scots form of **together**.

thegn *thān*, (*hist*) *n* the older form of **thane**.

theine *thē'īn*, *-in*, *n* an alkaloid found in tea, identical with caffeine. — *n* **thē'ic** a person who drinks too much tea or who suffers from theism. — *n* **thē'ism** a morbid state resulting from too much tea-drinking. [**Thea**]

their *dhār*, *dhər*, *pronoun* (*genitive pl*) and *possessive adj* of or belonging to them; his or her (a use unacceptable to some; see **they**). — *pronoun* **theirs** (a double genitive) used predicatively or absolutely, a person or thing that belongs to them. [ON *theirra*, superseding OE *thǣra*, genitive pl of the definite article]

theism[1] *thē'izm*, *n* belief in the existence of God with or without a belief in a special revelation. — *n* **thē'ist**. — *adj* **thēist'ic** or **thēist'ical**. [Gr *theos* God]

theism[2]. See under **theine**.

thelement, **thelf**. See under **th-**.

Thelemite *thel'ə-mīt*, *n* a monk of Rabelais's imaginary abbey of *Thélème*, of an order whose rule was 'Do as you like'. — Also *adj*. [Gr *thelēma* will]

thelytoky *thi-lit'ə-ki*, *n* parthenogenetic production of female offspring only. — *adj* **thelyt'okous**. [Gr *thēlys* female, and *tokos* birth]

them *dhem*, *dhəm*, *pronoun* the dative and accusative form of **they**; themselves (*archaic*, *colloq* or *US dialect*). — *demonstrative adj* (*dialect* or *colloq*; *dhem*) those. — **them and us** (*colloq*) any of various pairs of groups in society, such as management and workforce, considered to be in opposition to each other. [ON *theim* or OE (Anglian) *thæm* (dative)]

theme *thēm*, *n* a subject set or proposed for discussion, or spoken or written about; a recurrent idea in literature or art; subject, a short melody developed with variations or otherwise (*music*); the stem of a word without its inflexions; a thesis, a brief essay or exercise; a ground for action; an administrative division of the Byzantine empire. — *adj* planned around or having a certain subject — *vt* to decorate or equip (a pub, restaurant, etc) in keeping with a certain subject, eg seafaring or the Wild West. — *n* **thē'ma** (or *them'ə*) a theme: — *pl* **the'mata**. — *adj* **thematic** (*thi-mat'ik*) of or relating to a theme; (of philately) concerned with collection of sets showing flowers, or birds, etc; (of a vowel) not forming part of the root of a word, nor part of any inflection or suffix (as the vowel *o* in *cytoplasm*); (of a word) forming the major constituent of a sentence (*linguistics*). — *adv* **themat'ically**. — *adj* **themed'** having or planned around a single unifying subject or theme. — *adj* **theme'less**. — **thematic catalogue** (*music*) a catalogue giving the names, etc of works and also their opening themes; **theme park** a large area with displays, fairground, rides, etc, all devoted to or based on one subject; **theme song** a melody that is repeated often in a musical drama, film, or radio or television series, and is associated with a certain character, idea, emotion, etc; a signature tune; a person's characteristic, often repeated, complaint, etc. [Gr *thema*, *-atos*, from root of *tithenai* to place, set; partly through OFr *tesme*]

Themis *them'is*, *n* the Greek goddess of law and justice. [Gr *Themis*]

themselves *dhəm-selvz'*, *pronoun*, *pl* of **himself**, **herself** and **itself**; himself or herself (a use unacceptable to some; see **they**). — *pronoun* **themself'** (*colloq*; unrecognized in standard English) introduced as a *singular pronoun* to avoid **himself** or **herself** when the sex of the person is unspecified. [**them** and **self**]

then[1] *dhen*, *dhən*, *adv* at that time; afterward, after that; immediately; at another time; further, again; on the other hand, at the same time; for that reason, therefore; in that case; used to continue a narrative after a break or digression; used *esp* at the end of the questions which ask for an explanation, opinion, etc or which ask for or assume agreement. — *adj* being at that time. — *n* that time. — *adv* **then'about** or **then'abouts** about that time. — **by then** by that time; **then and there** at once and on the spot. [OE *thonne*, *thanne*, *thænne*]

then[2] *dhən*, (*Spenser*, etc) *conj* Same as **than**[1].

thenar *thē'när*, (*anatom*) *n* the palm; the ball of the thumb; the sole. — Also *adj*. [Gr *thenar*, *-aros*]

thence *dhens*, *adv* from that place; from those premises; from that time; from that cause, for that reason. — *adv* **thence'forth** or **thencefor'ward** from that time forward; from that place onward. [ME *thennes*, from *thenne* (OE *thanon* thence), with adverbial genitive ending; cf **hence**, **whence**]

theo- *thē'ō-*, *-ə-*, or *-o'-*, *combining form* denoting god. — *In the following article, strict alphabetical order is not followed; in most cases, the abstract noun in -y precedes adjectives, etc, dependent on it.* — *n* **Theobroma** (*-brō'mə*; *Gr brōma* food) the chocolate or cocoa genus of Sterculiaceae. — *n* **theobrō'mine** (*-mēn*, *-mīn*, *-min*) an alkaloid obtained from the chocolate seed, used in medicine. — *adj* **theocen'tric** having god as its centre. — *n* **theocracy** (*thē-ok'rə-si*; Gr *theokratiā*, from *kra-teein* to rule) that constitution of a state in which God, or a god, is regarded as the sole sovereign, and the laws of the realm as divine commands rather than human ordinances, the priesthood necessarily becoming the officers of the invisible ruler; the state governed in this way. — *n* **theocrat** (*thē'ə-krat*) a divine or deified ruler. — *adj* **theocrat'ic** or **theocrat'ical**. — *adv* **theocrat'-ically**. — *n* **theocrasy** (*thē-ok'rə-si*, *thē-ō-krā'si*; Gr *krāsis* a mixing) a mixture of religions: the identification or equating of one god with another or others; a mystic union of the soul with God reached through profound contemplation. — *n* **theodicy** (*thē-od'i-si*; Gr *dikē* justice) a vindication of the justice of God in establishing a world in which evil exists. — *n* and *adj* **theodicē'an**. — *n* **theogony** (*thē-og'ə-ni*; Gr *theogoniā*, from *-gonia* begetting, generation) the birth and genealogy of the gods; an account of this, eg in poetry. — *adj* **theogonic** (*thē-ə-gon'ik*) or **theogon'ical**. — *n* **theog'-onist** a writer on theogony. — *n* **theologaster** (*-gas'tər*) a shallow theologian. — *n* **theol'ogate** (*-gət*) a seminary for RC priests. — *n* **theol'oger** (*-jər*; sometimes *derog*) a theologian. — *n* **theologian** (*thē-ə-lō'jyən*) a student of, or a person well versed, in theology; a divine, a professor of or writer on divinity, *esp* in RC usage, a theological lecturer attached to a cathedral or collegiate church. — *adj* **theologic** (*thē-ə-loj'ik*) or **theolog'ical**. — *adv* **theolog'ically**. — **theol'ogist** (*rare*) a theologian. — *vt* **theol'ogize** or **-ise** to render theological, to treat theologically. — *vi* to discourse, speculate, etc, on theology. — *n* **theol'ogizer** or **-s-**. — *n* **theologoumenon** (*thē-ə-lə-goo'mə-non*; Gr, from *theologein* to talk about God) theological statement, *esp* as opposed to divine revelation or an inspired doctrine: — *pl* **theologou'mena**. — *n* **thē'ologue** (*-log*) a theologian (*rare*); a theological student (*US*). — *n* **theology** (*thē-ol'ə-ji*; Gr *theologiā*, from *logos* discourse) the study of God, religion and revelation; a system of theological doctrine; a system of principles, *esp* one rigidly adhered to. — *n* **theomachy** (*thē-om'ə-ki*; Gr *theomachiā*, from *machē* a battle) war among or against the gods, as (in Greek mythoogy) by the Titans and giants; opposition to the divine will. — *n* **theom'achist**. — *n* **theomancy** (*thē'ə-man-si*; Gr *theomanteiā* spirit of prophecy, from *manteiā* divination) divination by means of oracles, or of persons directly inspired immediately by some divinity. — *adj* **theoman'tic**. — *n* **theomania** (*-mā'ni-ə*; see **-mania**) religious madness; belief that one is a god oneself. — *n* **theomā'niac**. — *adj* **theomorphic** (*-mör'fik*; Gr *theomorphos* of divine form, from *morphē* form) having the form or likeness of a god; in the image of God. — *n* **theomor'phism**. — *n* **theon'omy** (Gr *nomos* law) government or rule by God; the state of being so ruled. — *adj* **theon'omous**. — *n* **Theopaschite** (*-pas'kīt*; Gr *paschein* to suffer) a Monophysite, believing that God had suffered and been crucified. — *adj* **Theopaschitic** (*-kit'ik*). — *n* **Theopas'chitism** (*-ki-tizm*). — *n* **theopathy** (*thē-op'ə-thi*; Gr *pathos* experience, emotion) a religious emotion aroused by meditation about God. — *adj* **theopathet'ic**. — *n* **theophagy** (*thē-of'ə-ji*; Gr *phagein* to eat) the sacramental eating of a god. — *adj* **theoph'agous** (*-gəs*). — *n* **theophany** (*thē-of'ə-ni*; Gr *theophaneiā* a vision of God, exhibition of gods' statues, from *phainein* to show) a manifestation or appearance of deity to man. — *adj* **theophanic** (*thē-ə-fan'ik*). — *n* **theophilanthropy** (*-fi-lan'thrə-pi*; Fr *théophilanthropie* love to God and man; cf **philanthropy**) a deistical system of religion drawn up under the French Directory in 1796, and designed to take the place of Christianity. — *adj* **theophilanthrop'ic**. — *n* **theophilan'thropism**. — *n* **theophilan'thropist**. — *n* **theophobia** (*-fō'bi-ə*; see **-phobia**) morbid fear of God; hatred of God. — *n* **theophō'biac** or **theophobist** (*-of'ə-bist*). — *adj* **theophor'ic** derived from or bearing the name of a god. — *adj* **theopneust** (*thē'op-nūst*) or **theopneu'stic** (Gr *theopneustos*, from *pneustos* inspired, from *pneein* to breathe) divinely inspired. — *n* **theopneust'y** divine inspiration. — *n* **theosophy** (*thē-os'ə-fi*; Gr *theosophos* wise in things of God, from *sophos* wise) divine wisdom; immediate divine illumination or inspiration claimed to be possessed by specially gifted people, along with abnormal control over natural forces; the system of doctrine expounded by the Theosophical Society. — *n* **theosoph** (*thē'ə-sof*), **theos'opher** or **theos'ophist**. — *adj* **theosoph'ic** or **theosoph'ical**. — *adv* **theosoph'ically**. — *n* **theos'ophism** theosophical tenets. — *adj* **theosophist'ical** theosophical; sophistical in theology. — *vi* **theos'ophize** or **-ise** to practise theosophy. — *n* **theotechny** (*-tek'ni*; Gr *technē* art) the employment of gods as the machinery or moving forces of a poem. — *adj* **theotech'nic**. — *n* **theotokos** (*thē-ot'ə-kos*; Gr *theotokos*, from *-tokos* having given birth to, from *tiktein* to give birth to) the mother of God, a title of the Virgin Mary repudiated by Nestorius, accepted by the Council of Ephesus. — **theological virtues** faith, hope and charity; **Theosophical Society** a religious body founded by Mme Blavatsky and others in 1875, whose doctrines include belief in karma and reincarnation. [Gr *theos* a god]

Theobroma... to ... **theocrasy**. See under **theo-**.

Theocritean *thē-ok-ri-tē'ən*, *adj* after the manner of *Theocritus* (3c BC), the greatest of Greek pastoral poets; pastoral, idyllic.

theodicy, etc. See under **theo-**.

theodolite *thē-od'ə-līt*, *n* a surveying instrument for measuring horizontal and vertical angles, consisting of a small telescope able to move both horizontally and vertically. — *adj* **theodolit'ic**. [Ety unknown]

theol. *abbrev*: theologian; theological; theology.

theologony... to ... **theophoric**. See under **theo-**.

theophylline *thē-ə-fil'ēn, -īn, -in,* (*chem*) *n* an isomer of theobromine found in tea, used in medicine. [**Thea**, and Gr *phyllon* leaf]

theopneust, etc. See under **theo-**.

theorbo *thē-örb'ō, n* a large double-necked bass lute, the second neck carrying bass strings: — *pl* **theorb'os**. — *n* **theorb'ist**. [Ital *tiorba*]

theorem *thē'ə-rəm, n* a demonstrable or established but not self-evident principle; a proposition to be proved. — *adj* **theoremat'ic** or **theoremat'ical**. — *adv* **theoremat'ically**. — *n* **theorematist** (*-rem'ə-tist*). [Gr *theōrēma, -atos* spectacle, speculation, theorem, from *theōreein* to be a spectator, to view]

theory *thē'ə-ri, n* an explanation or system of anything; an exposition of the abstract principles of a science or art; an idea or explanation which has not yet been proved, a conjecture; speculation as opposed to practice; an ideal, hypothetical or abstract situation (*esp* in the phrase *in theory*); ideal, hypothetical or abstract reasoning. — *adj* **theoret'ic** or **theoret'ical** based on, or pertaining, according, or given to, theory; not practical; speculative. — *n* **theoret'ic** (*usu* in *pl*) the speculative parts of a science. — *adv* **theoret'ically**. — *n* **theoretician** (*-ə-tish'ən*) a person who is concerned chiefly with the theoretical aspect of a subject. — *n* **the'oric** or **the'orique** (*Shakesp*) theory, speculation. — *n* **the'orist** a theorizer; a person given to theory and speculation, to the invention of theories; a person who is expert in the abstract principles of a subject. — *vi* **the'orize** or **-ise** to form a theory; to form opinions solely by theories; to speculate. — *n* **the'orizer** or **-s-**. — **theoretical plate** (*chem eng*) a concept, used in distillation design, of a plate in which the vapour and liquid leaving the plate are in equilibrium with each other. — **theory of everything** (*phys*) a comprehensive theory, yet to be satisfactorily formulated, that is believed will explain all known physical phemomena in quantum terms, possible candidates for the designation being the twistor theory and string theory (abbrev **TOE**). [Gr *theōriā* view, theory, from *theōreein* to be a spectator, to view]

theosophy... to ... **theotokos**. See under **theo-**.

theow *thā'ow,* (*hist*) *n* a slave. [OE *thēow*]

theralite *thēr'ə-līt, n* a holocrystalline igneous rock composed essentially of plagioclase, nepheline and augite. [Gr *thēraein* to hunt, seek after, and *lithos* stone, so called because its discovery was expected]

Therapeutae *ther-ə-pū'tē, ther-a-pū'tī, n pl* a traditional ascetic sect, allied to the Essenes, living chiefly near Alexandria in the 1c AD. [L, from Gr *therapeutai* servants, ministers]

therapeutic *ther-ə-pū'tik, adj* pertaining to the healing arts; of or relating to the curing of disease, curative; contributing towards or performed to improve health or general well-being. — *adv* **therapeu'tically**. — *n sing* **therapeu'tics** that part of medicine concerned with the treatment and cure of diseases. — *n* **therapeu'tist** a person skilled in therapeutics. [Gr *therapeutēs* servant, worshipper, medical attendant, from *therapeuein* to take care of, to heal]

therapy *ther'ə-pi, n* the treatment of physical or mental diseases and disorders by means other than surgery; treatment used to combat a disease or an abnormal condition; therapeutics; curative power. — *n* **ther'apist** a person who practises therapy of a particular kind. [Gr *therapeiā* service, treatment, from *therapeuein* to take care of, to heal]

therapsid *thə-rap'sid, n* a member of the *Therapsida*, an order of extinct reptiles of the Permian and Triassic periods, showing many mammal-like features and thought to be the ancestors of the mammals. — Also *adj*. [New L *Therapsida*, from Gr *thēr* wild beast, and *apsis* arch or vault, so-called because of the temporal arch of the skull]

Theravada *ther-ə-väd'ə, n* the doctrines of the Hinayana Buddhists. — *adj* **Theravad'in**. [Pali, doctrine of the elders]

therblig *thûr'blig, n* a unit of work into which an industrial operation may be divided. [Anagram of the name of its inventor, F B *Gilbreth* (1868-1924), US engineer]

there *dher, dhār, adv* in that place; at that point; to that place; in that respect; (also *dhr*) used without any meaning of its own to allow the subject to follow the predicate, and also in corresponding interrogative sentences, etc; used without any meaning to draw or attract attention or for emphasis. — *n* that place. — *interj* expressing reassurance, sympathy, satisfaction, approval, encouragement, finality, accompanying a blow, to comfort, etc. — *n* **there'ness** the property of having relative situation or existence. — *adv* **there'about** or **there'abouts** (also *-bowts'*) about or near that place; near that number, quantity, degree, or time. — *adv* **thereaft'er** after or according to that; accordingly. — *adv* **thereagainst'** against that. — *adv* **thereamong'** among that or those. — *adv* **thereanent'** (*Scot*) concerning that matter. — *adv* **thereat'** at that point, place or occurrence; on that account. — *adv* **there'away** in that direction; thereabout. — *adv* **therebeside'** beside that. — *adv* **thereby'** beside that; about that amount; by that means; in consequence of that. — *adv* **therefor'** (*law*) for that. — *adv* **therefore** (*dher'fər*) for that reason; consequently. — *adv* **therefrom'** (*formal*) from that. — *adv* **therein'** (*formal*) in or into that or it; indoors (*Scot*). — *adv* **thereinaft'er** and **thereinbefore'** (*formal*) later or from this point, and earlier or up to this point in the same document. — *adv* **therein'to** (*formal*) into that place, thing, matter, etc. — *adv* **thereof'** (*formal*) of that; from that. — *adv* **thereon'** (*old*) on that. — *adv* **thereout'** (*old*) out of that; out of doors (*Scot*). — *adv* **therethrough'** (*old*) through that; by that means. — *adv* **thereto'** or **thereun'to** (*formal*) to that; in addition. — *adv* **there'tofore** (*formal*) before that time. — *adv* **thereun'der** (*formal*) under that. — *adv* **thereunto'** (*old*) to that. — *adv* **thereupon'** upon that; immediately; in consequence of that (*Shakesp*). — *adv* **therewith'** with that; thereupon; for that reason (*old*). — *adv* **there'withal** (*old*) with that; immediately after; in addition. — *adv* **therewithin'** (*old*) within that. — **all there** (*colloq*) of normal intelligence; **have been there before** (*slang*) have been in the same, *esp* unpleasant, situation before; **so there** an expression of triumph, defiance, derision, finality, etc; **there and then** forthwith; immediately; **there it is** that is the situation (and nothing can be done about it); **there or thereabouts** somewhere near; **there you are** used to express triumph when something one predicted would occur does occur, or resignation over something that cannot be changed; used to accompany the action of handing something expected or requested to someone; **there you go** (*colloq*) used with the same force as **there you are**, both as a comment and as an accompaniment to the gesture of handing or passing. [OE *thǣr*; related to **the**, **that**, etc]

theriac *thē'ri-ak*, or **theriaca** *thē-rī'ə-kə,* (*archaic*) *n* an antidote to venomous bites, etc. — *adj* **thērī'acal**. [Gr *thēriakē*, from *thērion* a wild beast, *esp* a poisonous snake]

therian *thēr'i-ən,* (*zool*) *adj* of or belonging to the **Thēr'ia** subclass of mammals, comprising marsupials and placentals, and their extinct ancestors. — *n* a therian animal. [Gr *thērion* wild animal]

therio- *thē-ri-o, -ə-, -o'-*, or before a vowel **theri-**, or **thero-** *thē-rō-, -rə-, -ro'*, or before a vowel **ther-**, *combining form* denoting beast, mammal. — *adj* **therianthrop'ic** (Gr *anthrōpos* man) combining human and animal forms (of eg certain gods, mythical figures); of or relating to therianthropic gods or figures. — *n* **therian'thropism** the representation or worship of therianthropic forms or gods. — *n pl* **Theriodontia** (*-ə-don'shyə, -ti-ə*; Gr *odous, odontos* a tooth) an extinct order of reptiles with teeth like mammals. — *n* **theriol'atry** (see **-latry**) animal-worship. — *n* **ther'iomorph** (see **-morph**) an animal form in art. — *adj*

theriomorph'ic (*esp* of gods) having an animal-like form; of theriomorphism. — *n* **theriomorph'ism** belief in or worship of gods of the form of animals. — *n pl* **Theriomor'pha** or **Theromor'pha** an extinct order of reptiles with affinities to the labyrinthodont Amphibia and mammals. — *n* **theriomorphō'sis** (or *-mör'*) transformation into a beast. — *adj* **theriomor'phous** beastlike; mammal-like; of the Theriomorpha. — *n* **therol'ogy** the study of mammals. — *n* **ther'opod** (see **-pod**) any dinosaur of the **Therop'oda**, bipedal, carnivorous, saurischian dinosaurs. [Gr *thēr* and *thērion* a wild beast]

therm *thûrm*, *n* 100 000 British thermal units (used as a unit in reckoning payment for gas); a bathing establishment, public bath or hot bath (often in *pl*; *archaic*). — *adj* **therm'ic** or **therm'ical** of or by heat. — *adv* **therm'ically**. — **thermic lance** a cutting instrument consisting of a steel tube containing metal rods which, with the help of oxygen, are raised to an intense heat. [Gr *thermē* heat]

thermae *thûr'mē*, *n pl* hot springs or baths, *esp* in ancient Greece or Rome. [L, from Gr *thermai*, *pl* of *thermē* heat]

thermal *thûr'məl*, *adj* pertaining to or producing heat; warm; (of clothes) designed to prevent the loss of body heat. — *n* an ascending current of warm air, used eg by birds and gliders to gain height. — *n* **thermaliza'tion** or **-s-**. — *vt* **ther'malize** or **-ise** to reduce the kinetic energy and speed of (fast neutrons) in a nuclear reactor. — *vi* to undergo thermalization — *adv* **therm'ally**. — **thermal agitation** (*phys*) the random movements of free electrons in a conductor, caused by thermal energy and producing noise signals which may be noticeable in some circumstances; **thermal barrier** heat barrier; **thermal capacity** (*phys*) the amount of heat required to raise the temperature of a system through one degree; **thermal dissociation** the splitting of certain molecules into simpler molecules by heat, followed by recombination on cooling; **thermal conductivity** (*phys*) a measure of the rate of flow of thermal energy through a material in the presence of a temperature gradient; **thermal diffusion** (*phys*) a process in which a temperature gradient in a mixture of fluids tends to establish a concentration gradient; **thermal efficiency** (*eng*) of a heat engine, the ratio of the work done by the engine to the mechanical equivalent of the heat supplied in the steam or fuel; **thermal imaging** the visualization of objects, substances, etc by detecting and processing the infrared energy they emit, used in medical thermography and to locate bodies underground; **thermal neutron** (*phys*) a neutron of very low speed and hence very low energy, responsible for various types of nuclear reaction, *incl* fission; **thermal reactor** a nuclear reactor in which fission is induced mainly by low-energy neutrons; **thermal shock** stress, often resulting in fracture, occurring when a body is subjected to sudden changes in temperature; **thermal springs** natural springs of hot water. [Fr *thermal*, from Gr *thermē* heat]

Thermalite® *thûr'mə-līt*, *n* a manufactured material for building-blocks, of light density and high insulation value. [**thermal** and **-ite**]

Thermidor *thûr-mi-dör'*, *n* the eleventh month of the French Revolutionary calendar, 19 July–17 August. — *adj* (*cookery*; without *cap* and postpositive, in *lobster thermidor*) denoting a method of preparation, the flesh being mixed with a cream sauce seasoned with mustard, and served in the shell. — *n* **Thermido'rian** a participator in the fall of Robespierre. [Gr *thermē* heat, and *dōron* gift]

thermion *thûr'mi-ən*, *n* an electrically charged particle, an electron or ion, emitted by an incandescent body. — *adj* **thermion'ic** of or relating to thermions. — *n sing* **thermion'ics** the science of thermions and thermionic emissions. — **thermionic emission** the emission of electrons from incandescent solids or liquids; **thermionic valve** or **tube** a vacuum tube containing a heated cathode from which electrons are emitted, an anode for collecting some or all of these electrons and, generally, additional electrodes for controlling their flow to the anode. [Gr *thermē* heat, and **ion**]

thermistor *thûr-mis'tə*, (*elec eng*) *n* a semiconductor, a mixture of certain oxides with finely divided copper, of which the resistance is very sensitive to change of temperature. [*therm*al res*istor*]

thermite *thûr'mīt* or **Thermit**® *thûr'mit*, *n* a mixture of aluminium powder with oxide of metal (*esp* iron), which when ignited produces great heat, used for local heating, welding and in some incendiary bombs. [Ger *Thermit*, from Gr *thermē* heat]

thermo- *combining form* denoting heat. — *n* **thermobal'ance** a balance for weighing bodies at high temperatures. — *adj* **thermochem'ical**. — *adv* **thermochem'ically**. — *n* **thermochem'ist**. — *n* **thermochem'istry** the study of heat changes accompanying chemical action. — *n* **therm'ocline** (in lakes) a region of rapidly changing temperature, found between the epilimnion and the hypolimnion. — *n* **therm'ocouple** a pair of different metals in contact giving a thermoelectric current. — *adj* **thermodū'ric** resistant to heat. — *adj* **thermodynam'ic** or **thermodynam'ical**. — *n sing* **thermodynam'ics** the science of the relation of heat to mechanical and other forms of energy. — *adj* **thermoelec'tric** or **thermoelec'trical** — *n* **thermoelectric'ity** electricity developed by the unequal heating of bodies, *esp* between a junction of metals and another part of a circuit. — *n* **therm'oform** a three-dimensional representation, or a relief, of a painting in an art gallery, designed to help visitors (*esp* those who are blind) to appreciate the tactile qualities, perspective, etc of the painting. — *n* **thermogenesis** (*-jen'*) production of heat, *esp* in the body by physiological processes. — *adj* **thermogenet'ic** or **thermogen'ic**. — *n* **therm'ogram** a thermograph record of temperature. — *n* **therm'ograph** a self-registering thermometer; the photographic apparatus used in thermography. — *n* **thermog'rapher**. — *adj* **thermograph'ic**. — *n* **thermog'raphy** any process of writing, photographing, etc involving the use of heat; a method of producing embossed text, using a heating process (*printing*); the production of a photographic record or an image on a small picture-tube by using an infrared camera; a pictorial record of heat emission from the patient's body used in medical diagnosis, eg for detecting tumours. — *adj* **thermolā'bile** readily decomposed by heat. — *n* **thermol'ogy** the science of heat. — *n* **thermoluminesc'ence** release of light by irradiated material as a result of heating, used in archaeological dating. — *adj* **thermoluminesc'ent**. — **thermol'ysis** (see **-lysis**) dissociation or dissolution by heat; loss of body heat. — *adj* **thermolyt'ic**. — *n* **thermometer** (*-om'i-tər*) an instrument for measuring temperature depending on any of several properties of a substance that vary linearly with change of temperature, *esp* a graduated sealed tube containing mercury or alcohol. — *adj* **thermometric** (*-ə-met'rik*) or **thermomet'rical**. — *adv* **thermomet'rically**. — *n* **thermomet'rograph** a self-registering thermometer, a thermograph. — *n* **thermom'etry** the branch of physics dealing with the measurement of temperature and the design of thermometers, etc. — *n* **therm'onasty** nastic movement in response to heat or temperature change. — *adj* **thermonuc'lear** exhibiting or dealing with the fusion of nuclei as seen in a **thermonuclear reaction**, a power reaction produced by the fusion of nuclei at extremely high temperatures, as in nuclear weapons; pertaining to the use of such reactions as a source of power or force. — *adj* **therm'ophile** (*-fil*), **therm'ophil**, **thermophil'ic** or **thermoph'ilous** (of eg bacteria, plants) requiring, or thriving best in, high temperatures. — *n* **thermophile** or **thermophil** a bacterium, plant, etc, which requires, or thrives best in, high temperatures. — *adj* **thermoph'yllous** (Gr *phyllon* a leaf) (*bot*) having leaves only in the warmer part of the year, deciduous. — *n* **therm'opīle**

(-*pīl*) an apparatus, *usu* consisting of thermocouples, for the direct conversion of heat into electrical energy. — *adj* **thermoplast'ic** becoming plastic when heated and hardening again when cooled. — *n* any resin that can be melted and cooled repeatedly without appreciable change in properties. — *n* **thermoplastic'ity**. — *n* **therm'oscope** an instrument for detecting changes of temperature. — *adj* **thermoscop'ic** indicating, or sensitive to, temperature changes. — *adv* **thermoscop'ically**. — *adj* **thermosett'ing** (of eg resin or plastic) setting permanently, after melting and moulding. — *n* **thermosiph'on** (*eng*) a method of circulating a cooling liquid through a system by using the slight difference in density between the hot and cool parts. — *n* **therm'osphere** the region of the earth's atmosphere above the mesosphere, in which the temperature rises steadily with height. — *adj* **thermosta'ble** not readily decomposed by heating. — *n* **therm'ostat** a device for keeping temperature steady. — *adj* **thermostat'ic**. — *adv* **thermostat'ically**. — *adj* **thermotact'ic** or **thermotax'ic** of or showing thermotaxis. — *n* **thermotax'is** a movement of an organism towards a position of higher or lower temperature. — *n* **thermother'apy** (*med*) the treatment of a part of the body by heat. — *adj* **thermot'ic** or **thermot'ical** of or due to heat. — *n sing* **thermot'ics** the science of heat. — *adj* **thermotol'erant** (*bot*) able to endure high temperatures but not growing well under such conditions. — *adj* **thermotrop'ic**. — *n* a thermotropic plant. — *n* **thermot'ropism** (Gr *tropos* turning) the tendency of a plant to grow towards, or bend away from, a source of heat. [Gr *thermos* hot, *thermē* heat, *thermotēs* heat]

Thermos® *thûr'məs*, *n* a brand of vacuum flask (Also **Thermos® flask**) [Gr *thermos* hot]

-thermy *combining form* denoting heat, heat generation. — *adj combining form* **-thermic** or **-thermal**. [New L *-thermia*, from Gr *thermē* heat]

thero-. See under **therio-**.

theroid *thēr'oid*, *adj* of, relating to or like a beast or wild animal. [Gr *thēr* wild animal, and **-oid**]

Thersitic *thər-sit'ik*, or **Thersitical** *-kəl*, *adj* like *Thersītēs*, an ill-looking Greek mentioned in the *Iliad*, who was forever vilifying the Greek leaders.

thesaurus *thi-sö'rəs*, *n* a storehouse of knowledge, *esp* of words, quotations, etc, a dictionary; a book with systematically arranged lists of words and their synonyms, antonyms, etc, a word-finder; a treasury: — *pl* **thesau'ri** (*rī*) or **thesau'ruses**. [L, from Gr *thēsauros*]

these *dhēz*, *demonstrative adj* and *demonstrative pronoun pl* of **this**. [OE *thǣs*, a by-form of *thās*, *pl* of *thēs thēos*, *this*, this; cf **those**]

thesis *thē'sis*, or (*prosody*, *music*) *thes'is*, *n* a long dissertation, *esp* one based on original research and presented for a doctorate; a subject dealt with in this way; a position or that which is set down or advanced for argument; an essay on a theme: a down beat in a bar or metrical foot (*Gr prosody* and *music*); hence, the strong position in a bar or foot; understood by the Romans as the weak position; used in English in both senses (*opp* to *arsis*): — *pl* **the'ses** (*sēz*). — *adj* **thetic** (*thet'ik*) or **thet'ical** positively asserting; bearing the thesis (*Gr prosody* and *music*). — *adv* **thet'ically**. — **thesis novel** roman à thèse (see under **roman**). [Gr *thesis*, from the root of *tithenai* to put, set]

Thesmophoria *thes-mə-, -phö'ri-ə, -phō'ri-ə*, *n pl* in ancient Greece, a married women's festival in honour of Demeter *Thesmophoros* (law-giving). [Gr *thesmophoria*]

thesmothete *thes'mə-thēt*, *n* a law-giver, *esp* one of the six junior archons in ancient Athens. [Gr *thesmothetēs*, from *thesmos* law, and *thetēs* a placer, setter]

Thespian *thes'pi-ən*, (also without *cap*) *adj* pertaining to tragedy or to drama in general; tragic. — *n* a tragic actor; an actor (*facetious*). [Gr *Thespis*, founder of Greek tragedy]

Thess. (*Bible*) *abbrev*: (the Letters to the) Thessalonians.

theta *thē'tə*, *thā'tə*, *n* the eighth (*orig* ninth) letter of the Greek alphabet (Θ, θ) transliterated *th*, its sound an aspirated *t*, but in modern Greek like English *th*; as a Greek numeral θ' = 9, ͵θ = 9000; a mark of condemnation (from the θ for *thanatos* death, used in balloting). [Gr *thēta*; Semitic]

thetch *thech*, (*Spenser*) *vi* to thatch. [OE *theccan*]

thete *thēt*, (*Gr hist*) *n orig* a serf; a poor freeman in Athens under Solon's constitution. [Gr *thēs*, *thētos*]

thether. See under **thither**.

thetic. See under **thesis**.

theurgy *thē'ər-ji*, *n* magic or miracles by the agency of good spirits; miraculous divine action; the beneficial magical science of the Egyptian Neoplatonists. — *adj* **theur'gic** or **theur'gical**. — *n* **the'urgist**. [Gr *theourgiā*, from *theos* a god, and *ergon* work]

thew *thū*, (used chiefly in *pl* **thews** or **thewes**; *literary*) *n* custom: trait; manner; moral quality; bodily quality, muscle or strength. — *adj* **thewed** mannered (*Spenser*); muscular. — *adj* **thew'less** (see also **thowless**). — *adj* **thew'y** muscular, strong. [OE *thēaw* manner]

they *dhā*, *pronoun*, *nominative pl* used as plural of **he**, **she**, **it**; people in general, some; used, with a plural verb, instead of **he** or **she**, where the antecedent is a singular common-gender word such as *someone* or *person* (but unacceptable to some, *esp* in written English); people in authority. — **they'd** a contraction of **they had** or **they would**; **they'll** a contraction of **they will** or **they shall**; **they're** a contraction of **they are**; **they've** a contraction of **they have**. [ME *thei*, from ON *theirr*, which supplanted *hi* (OE *hīe*)]

thiamine *thī'ə-mēn*, *-min* or **thiamin** *thī'ə-min*, *n* vitamin B_1, found in seeds, grains, beans and liver, a deficiency of which causes beri-beri. [Gr *theion* sulphur, and **amine**]

thiasus *thī'ə-səs*, *n* a group of worshippers collected together to sing and dance in praise of a god, *esp* Bacchus. [Gr *thiasos*]

thiazide *thī'ə-zīd*, *n* any of a group of drugs used as diuretics and to treat hypertension. [*thio-*, *azo-*, *oxide*]

thiazine *thī'ə-zēn*, (*chem*) *n* any of several organic compounds containing four carbon atoms, one sulphur and one nitrogen atom.

Thibet. See under **Tibet**.

thible *thib'l*, *thīb'l* or **thivel** *thiv'l*, *thīv'l*, (*Northern*) *n* a porridge-stick. [Origin unknown]

thick[1] *thik*, *adj* having a great (or specified) distance in measurement from surface to surface in the lesser dimension; broad; deep; dense; viscous; firm or dense in consistency, close set or packed; crowded; made of thick or warm material; very friendly, intimate, in close confidence (*colloq*); abundant; frequent, in quick succession; aboundingly or completely covered or occupied; foggy; opaque; dull; stupid; gross; husky, muffled; indistinctly articulate; (of an accent) strong, marked; excessive, unfair, approaching the intolerable (*colloq*). — *n* the thickest part of anything; the midst; a stupid person (*slang*); a thicket (*Spenser*). — *adv* thickly; closely; frequently; fast; to a great (or specified) depth. — *vt* and *vi* (*Spenser*, *Shakesp*) to make or become thick. — *vt* and *vi* **thick'en** to make or become thick or thicker. — *vi* to become more complicated. — *n* **thick'ener**. — *n* **thick'ening** a making or becoming thicker; a thickened place; material or a substance added to something (*esp* liquid) to thicken it. — Also *adj*. — *n* **thick'et** (OE *thiccet*) a dense mass of trees or shrubs. — *adj* **thick'eted**. — *adj* **thick'ety**. — *adj* **thick'ish** somewhat thick. — *adv* **thick'ly**. — *n* **thick'ness** the state or quality of being thick; the degree to which something is thick; the space between outer surfaces; a layer. — *n* **thick'o** (*slang*) a stupid person: — *pl* **thick'os** or **thick'oes**. — *adj* **thick-and-thin'** unwavering in devotion to party or principle. — *adj* **thick'-com'ing** (*Shakesp*) coming close upon one another. — **thick ear** (*colloq*) a swollen ear, *usu* a result of a blow administered as punishment. — *adj* **thick'-eyed** dim-sighted. — *adj* **thick'-grown** (*Shakesp*). — **thick'head** a stupid person, a blockhead; any bird of an Australian family (*Pachycephalidae*) related to flycatchers and shrikes. — *adj* **thick-head'ed** having a thick head or skull; stupid; having a feeling of numbness, paralysis and often pain in the head often accompanying eg a cold or a hangover. — *n* **thick-head'edness**. — **thick'-knee** the stone curlew (*Burhinus oedicnemus*), a large plover with thickened knee joints. — *adj* **thick'-lipped** (*Shakesp*) — **thick'-lips** (*Shakesp*) a Negro. — *adj* **thick'-pleached** (*Shakesp*) closely interwoven. — *adj* **thick'-ribbed** (*Shakesp*). — *adj* **thick'-set** having a short thick body; closely set or planted. — *n* a thicket; a stout cotton. — *adj* **thick'-sight'ed** (*Shakesp*) dim-sighted. — **thick'skin** a blockhead. — *adj* **thick-skinned'** having a thick skin; insensitive; indifferent to criticism or insult. — **thick'-skull** a blockhead. — *adj* **thick-skull'ed** having a thick skull; stupid; dull, slow to learn, doltish. — *adj* **thick'-sown** planted closely; close-set. — **thick''un** (*old slang*) a sovereign; a crown. — *adj* **thick-witt'ed** dull, slow to learn, doltish. — *adv* **thick-witt'edly**. — *n* **thick-witt'edness**. — **a bit thick** (*colloq*) more than one can reasonably be expected to put up with; **as thick as a plank** or **as thick as two short planks** very stupid; **as thick as thieves** very friendly; **in the thick of** in the middle of, extremely busy or occupied with; **lay it on thick** to praise something extravagantly; to exaggerate; **through thick and thin** in spite of all obstacles; without any wavering. [OE *thicce*; Ger *dick*]

thick[2], **thicky**. See under **thilk**.

thief *thēf*, *n* someone who takes unlawfully what is not his or her own, *esp* by stealth; a flaw in a candle-wick that causes guttering: — *pl* **thieves** (*thēvz*). — *adj* and *adv* **thief'-like**. — **thief'-catcher** or **-taker** a person whose business is to arrest thieves; a detective. — **thieves' kitchen** a haunt of thieves and other criminals. [OE *thēof*: cf Ger *Dieb*]

thieve *thēv*, *vi* to practise theft; to steal. — *vt* to steal (something). — *n* **thiev'ery** an act or the practice of thieving; what is thieved. — *n* and *adj* **thiev'ing**. — *adj* **thiev'ish** given to, or like, theft; thief-like; furtive; infested by thieves (*Shakesp*). — *adv* **thiev'ishly**. — *n* **thiev'ishness**. [OE *thēofian* to thieve, and *thēof* thief]

thig *thig*, (*Scot*) *vi* to beg; to live on alms. — *vt* to beg; to get by begging: — *pa t* and *pa p* **thigg'it**. — *n* **thigg'er**. — *n* **thigg'ing**. — **thigging and sorning** extortionate begging and sponging. [ON *thiggja*; cf OE *thicgan* to take]

thigh *thī*, *n* the thick fleshy part of the leg from the knee to the hip; a corresponding part in animals. — **thigh'bone** the bone of the leg between the hip-joint and the knee, the femur; **thigh boot** a tall boot covering the thigh. [OE *thēoh* (Anglian *thēh*); ON *thjō*; OHGer *dioh*]

thigmotaxis *thig-mə-tak'sis*, (*biol*) *n* the movement of an organism towards or away from a solid object, in response to contact with it. — *adj* **thigmotac'tic**. — *adv* **thigmotac'tically**. [Gr *thigma*, *-atos* touch, and *taxis*, from *tassein* to arrange]

thigmotropism *thig-mot'trəpizm*, *-mə-trō'*, (*biol*) *n* the turning of an organism (or part of it) towards or away from an object in response to the stimulus of touch. — *adj* **thigmotropic** (*-mə-trop'ik*). [Gr *thigma*, *-atos* touch, and *tropos* a turning]

thilk *dhilk*, (*dialect*) *adj* and *pronoun* the same, that same; this. — Also (*SW England*) **thick** (*dhik*) or **thicky** (*dhik'i*). [**the ilk**]

thill[1] *thil*, *n* the shaft of a cart or carriage. — *n* **thill'er** a thill-horse. — **thill'-horse** a shaft-horse, or the last of a team. [Poss OE *thille* board, plank]

thill[2] *thil*, (*dialect*) *n* underclay or floor of a coal-seam; a bed of fireclay. [Origin unknown]

thimble *thim'bl*, *n* a (metal, ceramic, plastic, etc) cover for the finger, used in sewing; any object of similar form; a metal ring with a grooved or concave outer edge fitted into a rope ring, etc to prevent chafing (*naut*); a thimbleful. — *vi* to use a thimble. — *vt* to use a thimble on. — *n* **thim'bleful** as much as a thimble will hold; a small quantity: — *pl* **thim'blefuls**. — **thim'ble-case**; **thim'blerig** a sleight-of-hand trick in which the performer conceals, or pretends to conceal, a pea or small ball under one of three thimble-like cups. — *vi* to cheat by such means. — *vt* to manipulate in this or a similar way: — *pr t* **thimb'lerigging**; *pa p* and *pa t* **thimb'lerigged**. — **thimb'lerigger**; **thim'blerigging**; **thimb'leweed** any of several plants with a thimble-shaped head, *esp* the N American *Anemone riparia* or *Anemone virginiana*. [OE *thȳmel* thumb covering, from *thūma* thumb]

thimerosal *thī-me'rə-səl*, (*pharmacol*) *n* a cream-coloured, crystalline, water-soluble powder, used eg on the skin to treat minor abrasions.

thin *thin*, *adj* (*compar* **thinn'er**; *superl* **thinn'est**) having little thickness; slim; lean; narrow; freely mobile; watery; dilute, lacking viscosity; of little density; rarefied; not closely packed, covered or occupied; sparse; made of thin material; slight; flimsy; lacking in body or solidity; meagre; poor; tinkling; too much to the left (golf, etc). — *n* that which is thin. — *adv* thinly. — *vt* to make thin or thinner; to make less close, crowded or dense (with *away*, *out*, etc); to hit (the ball) too near the top so that it travels parallel to the ground, but only just above it, thus not travelling very far (*golf*). — *vi* to grow or become thin or thinner: — *pr p* **thinn'ing**; *pa t* and *pa p* **thinned**. — *adv* **thin'ly**. — *n* **thinn'er** a person or thing that thins, *esp* (often in *pl*, sometimes treated as *n sing*) a diluent for paint. — *n* **thin'ness**. — *n* **thinn'ing**. — *adj* **thinn'ish** somewhat thin. — *adj* **thin'-belly** (*Shakesp*) narrow in the belly. — *adj* **thin'-faced** (*Shakesp*). — *adj* **thin-skinned'** having thin skin; sensitive; irritable. — **thin-skinned'ness**. — *adj* **thin'-sown** sparsely sown. — *adj* **thin'-spun** drawn out fine. — **thin''un** (*old slang*) a half sovereign. — *adj* **thin-walled'**. — **a thin time** a time of hardship, misery, etc; **into** (or **out of**) **thin air** into (or out of) nothing or nothingness; **thin blue line** a line of policemen drawn up to quell crowd violence, etc (coined in imitation of **thin red line**); **thin on the ground** present in very small, inadequate quality or numbers; **thin on top** balding; **thin red line** a designation for the British army (*orig* used in reports of the Crimean campaign, when uniforms were still red) conveying an image of indomitability against heavy odds. [OE *thynne*; Ger *dünn*; ON *thunnr*]

thine *dhīn*, (*formal*, *liturgical*, *dialect* or *archaic*) *pronoun*, genitive of **thou**[1], used predicatively or absolutely, belonging to thee; thy people; that which belongs to thee; adjectivally, *esp* before a vowel or *h*, thy. [OE *thīn*]

thing *thing*, *n* a matter, affair, problem, point; a circumstance; a fact; an event, happening, action; an entity; that which exists or can be thought of; an inanimate object; a quality; a living creature (*esp* in pity, tolerant affection, kindly reproach); a possession; that which is wanted or is appropriate (*colloq*); a slight obsession or phobia (*colloq*); a typical example; an unaccountable liking or dislike (*colloq*); (in *pl*) clothes, *esp* a woman's additional outdoor garments; (in *pl*) utensils, *esp* for the table; (in *pl*) personal belongings; an aim; (in *pl*) affairs in general; property (*law*); a piece of writing, composition, etc; an assembly, parliament, court, council (*hist*). — *n* **thing'amy**, **thing'ummy**, **thing'amybob**, **thing'amyjig**, **thing'umabob**, **thing'umajig**, **thing'umbob**, **thing'ummybob** or **thing'ummyjig** (*colloq*) what-d'you-call-him, -her, -it; what's-his-name, etc — used when one cannot or will not recall the name. — *n* **thing'hood** the state or fact of being a thing; substantiality. — *n* **thing'iness** or **thing'liness** reality, objectivity; a materialistic or matter-of-fact turn of mind. — *n* **thing'ness** the character or fact of being a thing; reality. — *adj* **thing'y** real; actual; objective; matter-of-fact. — *n* thingumajig. — **thing-in-itself'** (in the philosophy of Kant) a noumenon, the German *Ding an sich*. — **a good thing** a fortunate circumstance; **and things** and other (similar) things; **a stupid** (or **wise**, etc) **thing to do** a stupid (or wise, etc) action; **be all things to all men** to meet each person on his or her own ground, accommodate oneself to his or her circumstances and outlook (1 Cor. 9, 22); (loosely and disparagingly) to keep changing one's opinions, etc, so as to suit one's company; **be on to a good thing** (*colloq*) to be in a particularly profitable position, job, etc; **do one's (own) thing** (*colloq*) to behave as is natural to or characteristic of oneself; to do something in which one specializes; **do the handsome thing by** to treat generously; **do things to** to affect in some good or bad way; **for one thing . . . for another (thing)** expressions used in enumerating reasons; **have a good thing going** (*colloq*) to be established in a particularly profitable position, etc; **hear things** to hear imaginary noises, voices, etc; **know a thing or two** (*colloq*) to be shrewd; **make a good thing of it** to reap a good advantage from; **make a thing of** to make an issue, point of controversy, etc of; to fuss about; **no such thing** something very different; no, not at all; **not a thing** (*colloq*) nothing; **not quite the thing** (*old colloq*) not in very good health (see also **the thing**); **one of those things** a happening one cannot account for or do anything to prevent; **see things** to see something that is not really there; **the thing** or **the done thing** that which is conventional, fashionable, approved, right or desirable. [OE and ON *thing* parliament, object, etc; Norw, Swed, Dan *ting* parliament; Ger *Ding* thing]

think[1] *thingk*, *vt* to form, conceive or revolve in the mind; to have as a thought; to imagine; to judge; to believe or consider; to expect or intend; to purpose, design; to remember or recollect; to bring into a particular condition by thinking: to believe to exist (*Milton*). — *vi* to exercise the mind (often with *about*, *of*, or (*archaic*) *on*, *upon*); to revolve ideas in the mind; to judge; to be of an opinion; to consider; to call to mind, recollect; to conceive or hit on a thought; to aspire or form designs (with *of* or *about*); to be capable of thinking and reflecting: — *pa t* and *pa p* **thought** (*thöt*). — *n* (*colloq*) a spell of thinking; a thought. — *adj* **think'able** capable of being thought; conceivably possible. — *n* **think'er** a person who thinks, *esp* someone with a powerful mind; a horse which takes care of itself in a race and therefore does not try hard enough (*horse-racing*). — *n* **think'ing** an opinion or judgement; the process of thought. — *adj* using or capable of rational thought. — *adv* **think'ingly**. — **think'-in** (*colloq*) a meeting to discuss ideas, thoughts on a subject, etc; **think'-tank** a person or a group of people, *usu* expert in some field, regarded as a source of ideas and solutions to problems. — **have another think coming** (*colloq*) to be wrong in what one thinks (about future events or actions); **I don't think** I disbelieve; a warning that what was said was ironical (*colloq*); **I shouldn't** (or **wouldn't**) **think of** I would not under any conditions; **just think of it** or **to think of it** an expression of surprise, disapproval, longing, etc; **put on one's thinking-cap** to devote some time to thinking about some problem; **think again** to (be forced) change one's opinion; **think aloud** to utter one's thoughts unintentionally; **think back to** to bring to one's mind the memory of (a past event, etc); **think better of** to change one's mind about (doing something) on reflection; to feel more approval for; **think for** (*archaic*) to expect; **think little of** to have a poor opinion of (*opp* to **think much** or **well of**); **think long** (*archaic*) to yearn; to weary (from deferred hopes or boredom); **think nothing of** not to consider difficult, exceptional, etc; not to hesitate in (doing); **think nothing of it** it does not matter, is not important; **think out** to devise, project completely; to solve by a process of thought; **think over** to reconsider at leisure; **think shame** to be ashamed; **think through** to solve by a process of thought; to project and consider all the possible consequences, problems, etc relating to (some course of action); **think twice** (often with *about*) to hesitate (before doing something); to decide not to do something; **think up** to find by thinking, devise or concoct. [OE *thencan*]

think[2] *thingk*, *vi* (*impers*, *archaic* with dative pronoun prefixed, as in *methinks*; otherwise *obs*) to seem: — *pa t* **thought** (*thöt*). [OE *thyncan* to seem]

thio- *thī'ō-*, *-ə-*, or **thi-**, *combining form* denoting sulphur; indicating in chemistry a compound theoretically derived from another by substituting an atom or more of sulphur for oxygen. — *n* **thi'o-acid** an acid analogous in constitution to an oxy-acid, sulphur taking the place of oxygen. — *n* **thio-al'cohol** mercaptan. — *n* **thiobacill'us** any of several rod-shaped bacteria, genus *Thiobacillus*, that live in soil, sewage, etc and that derive energy from the oxidation of sulphur or sulphur compounds. — *n* **Thiobacillus ferro-oxidans** a thiobacillus which, in the presence of water, converts copper sulphide ores into copper sulphate (see **bacterial leaching** under **leach**[1]). — *n* **thiobarbit'urate** a salt of **thiobarbitu'ric acid** ($C_6H_4N_2O_2S$) similar in effect to a barbiturate. — *n* **thiocar'bamide** thiourea. — *n* **thiocy'anate** a salt of **thiocyan'ic acid**, HSCN. — *n* **thiodiglycol** (*-dī-glī'kol*) a chemical compound soluble in eg water and alcohol used eg as an industrial cleaning agent, and also as an ingredient of mustard gas and nerve gas. — *n* **thio-e'ther** a compound in which the ether oxygen has been replaced by sulphur. — *n* **thī'ol** (or *-ōl*) mercaptan. — *n* **thiopent'one** or (*NAm*) **thiopent'al** see under **Pentothal**. — *n* **thi'ophen** (*-fen*) or **thi'ophene** (*-fēn*) a five-membered heterocyclic compound with sulphur. — *adj* **thi'ophil** (of eg bacteria) having an affinity for sulphur and its compounds. — *n* **thi'o-salt** a salt of a thio-acid. — *n* **thiosul'phate** a salt of **thiosulphuric acid** ($H_2S_2O_3$). — *n* **thiouracil** (*thī-ō-ū'rə-sil*) a derivative of thiourea that interferes with the synthesis of thyroid hormone. — *n* **thiourea** (*thī-ō-ū'ri-ə*) urea with its oxygen replaced by sulphur, a bitter crystalline substance that inhibits thyroid activity and is used eg in photographic fixing. [Gr *theion* sulphur]

thir *dhir*, (*Scot*) *pl demonstrative pronoun* and *demonstrative adj* these. [Origin obscure]

thiram *thīram*, *n* a fungicide. [*thi*our*ea* and carb*am*ic]

third *thûrd*, *adj* the last of three; next after the second in time, place, order, rank, etc; equal to one of three equal parts. — *n* one of three equal parts; a person or thing in third position; an interval of two (conventionally called three) diatonic degrees (*music*); a note separated from another by this interval (*music*); a handicap of a stroke at six holes out of eighteen (*golf*); third gear; (also **third class**) an honours degree of the third, and *usu* lowest, class. — *adv* in the third place; as the third point. — *vt* to divide by three; to support after the seconder. — *n* **third'ing** a third part. — *adv* **third'ly** in the third place; as the third point. — *n* **Third Age** those people aged over 60 (in some cases over 50) collectively seen as a distinct group within society, with opportunities (eg for travel and education), special needs, and a positive contribution to make to society in general; **Third-A'ger**; **third class** the class (of degree, hotel accommodation, travel, etc) next below second class. — *adj* and *adv* **third-class'**. — **third degree** see under **degree**; **third dimension** depth, thickness; the dimension of depth, distinguishing a solid object from a two-dimensional or planar object. — *adj* **third=dimen'sional**. — **third estate** see under **estate**; **third force** a group (eg in a political party) following a middle or uncommitted course between contending extremes; **third gear** the gear which is one faster than second, and *usu* one lower than top, in a gearbox. — *adj* **third-hand'**. — **third man** (*cricket*) a fielder on the offside between point and slip; this position; **Third market** (*stock exchange*, *esp US*) trade in listed stocks done otherwise than on the stock exchange; the market where such trade is done; **third order** the lay members affiliated to a monastic order, who continue to live an ordinary life in the world; **third party** a person other than the principal people involved (eg in the agreement between the insured and insurer). — *adj* **third'-party**. — **third person** see under **person**. — *adj* **third'-programme** highbrow, in allusion to the Third Programme (1946–70) of the BBC. — **third rail** a rail carrying electricity to an electrically-powered train; **third-rail system** (*elec eng*) a system of electric traction supply by which current is fed to the tractor from an insulated conductor rail running parallel with the track. — *adj* **third'-rate** of the third rank, class order, etc; of poor quality. — **third reading** (in a legislative assembly) in Britain the consideration of committee reports on a bill; in the USA the final consideration of a bill; **Third Reich** see under **Reich**; **thirds'man** a mediator. — *adj* **third'-stream** of a style of music, having features of both jazz and classical music. — Also *n* (**third stream**). — **Third World** the developing countries of Africa, Asia and Latin America, not aligned politically with the large power blocks; **Third-Worl'der** a person living in or from the Third World; a believer in or supporter of Third-Worldism; **Third-Worl'dism** an ideology which supports and encourages the development of the Third World. — **Picardy third** tierce de Picardie. [OE *thridda*; cf Ger *dritte*, Gr *tritos*, L *tertius*]

thirdborough *thûrd'bə-rə*, (*hist*) *n* an under-constable. [Supposed to be from OE *frithborh* a surety for peace (see under **frith**[2])]

thirl[1] *thûrl*, (*dialect*) *n* a hole; an opening; a short passage between two headings in a mine. — *vt* to pierce; to thrill. — *vi* to vibrate, tingle, thrill. [OE *thyrel* hole, from *thurh* through; cf **thrill**]

thirl[2] *thûrl*, *n* a serf, a form of **thrall** (*rare*); thirlage. — *vt* to bind or subject; to enslave; to confine, restrict. — *n* **thirl'age** a form of servitude by which the grain produced on certain lands had to be ground (or at least paid for) at a certain mill. [Esp Scot, variant of *thrill* to enslave, variant of **thrall**]

thirst *thûrst*, *n* the discomfort caused by lack of drink; vehement desire for drink; eager desire or craving for anything. — *vi* to feel thirst. — *n* **thirst'er**. — *adj* **thirst'ful**. — *adv* **thirst'ily**. — *n* **thirst'iness**. — *adj* **thirst'less**. — *adj* **thirst'y** suffering from thirst; dry; parched; causing thirst; vehemently desiring. [OE *thurst* (noun), *thyrstan* (verb); cf Ger *Durst*, *dürsten*, Gr *tersesthai*, L *torrēre* to dry]

thirteen *thûr'tēn*, or *-tēn'*, *n* three and ten; a symbol for this number; the age of 13; anything, eg a size, denoted by the number 13; a set of 13 people or things. — *adj* amounting to 13; 13 in age. — *adj* **thir'teenth** (or *-tēnth'*) last of thirteen; next after the twelfth; equal to one of thirteen equal parts. — *n* a thirteenth part; a person or thing in thirteenth position. — *adv* **thir-teenth'ly**. [OE *thrēotīene*, *-tēne*, from *thrēo* three]

thirty *thûr'ti*, *n* three times ten; a symbol for this number; the age of 30; anything denoted by the number 30; a set of 30 people or things. — *adj* amounting to 30; 30 in age. — *n pl* **thir'ties** the numbers from 30 to 39; the years so numbered in life or any century; a range of temperatures from thirty to just under forty degrees. — *adj* **thir'tieth** last of thirty; next after the twenty-ninth; equal to one of thirty equal parts. — *n* a thirtieth part; a person or thing in thirtieth position. — *adj* and *adv* **thir'tyfold**. — *adj* **thir'tyish** somewhere about the age of thirty. — **Thirty-nine Articles** the set of doctrines of the Church of England, formally accepted by those taking orders; **thirty-second note** (*NAm*; *music*) a demisemiquaver; **thir'tysomething** (*colloq*) the ages between 30 and 39; a person aged between 30 and 39, *esp* when considered as part of a social group of similarly aged people with specific desires, aims and needs. — *adj* (*colloq*) of, being or for a person aged between 30 and 39. — *adj* **thirty-two'mo** (for *tricesimo secundo*, 32mo) of a book, in sheets folded to give 32 leaves (64 pages). — *n* a book constructed in this way: — *pl* **thirty-two'mos**. [OE *thrītig*, from *thrēo* three, and *-tig*, sfx denoting ten]

this *dhis*, *sing demonstrative pronoun* denoting a person, animal, thing or idea near, topical, already mentioned or about to be mentioned, or otherwise understood from the context; a person, animal or thing which is nearby, *esp* which is closer to the speaker than something else (often designated by *that*); (up to and including) the present time or place; the place where the speaker is; an action, event or circumstance; (when telephoning) the person speaking, or the person spoken to: — *pl* **these**. — *adj* being the person, animal or thing just mentioned, about to be mentioned, or otherwise understood from the context; being the person, animal or thing which is nearby, *esp* closer than something else; relating to today, or time in the recent past ending today; used sometimes almost with the force of an indefinite or definite article, eg for emphasis or in narrative, as in *I saw this big bright object in the sky* (*colloq*): — *pl* **these**. — *adv* to this (extreme) degree or extent, with adjectives or adverbs *esp* of quantity, eg *this high*, *far*, etc, or (*colloq*) with others, eg *this difficult*, *well*, etc; (*Shakesp*) thus. — *n* **this'ness** the quality of being this, not something else, haecceity. — **this and that** or **this, that and the other** various minor unspecified objects, actions, etc; **this here** (*colloq*) an emphatic form of this; **with this** at that, thereupon. [OE, neuter of *thes*, *thēos*, *this* (instrumental *thīs*, *thȳs*; nominative plural *thās*, *thǣs*)]

thistle *this'l*, *n* a prickly composite plant (*Carduus*, *Cnicus*, *Onopordon*, etc) with pink, white, yellow but *usu* purple flower heads, the national emblem of Scotland. — *adj* **this'tly** like a thistle; overgrown with thistles. — **this'tle-butterfly** the painted lady, *Vanessa cardui*; **this'tledown** the tufted feathery parachutes of thistle seeds. — **Order of the Thistle** a Scottish order of knighthood. [OE *thistel*]

thither *dhidh'ər*, (*Spenser* often **thether**; *literary*, *formal* or *archaic*) *adv* to that place; to that end or result. — *adv* on the far side. — *adv* **thith'erward** or **thith'erwards** toward that place. [OE *thider*]

thivel. See under **thible**.

thixotropy *thik-sot'rə-pi*, *n* (*chem*, *eng*, *paint technology*, etc) the property (of gels) of showing a temporary reduction in viscosity when shaken or stirred. — *n* **thix'otrope** a thixotropic substance. — *adj* **thixotropic** (*-trop'ik*) of or showing, thixotropy; (of paints) non-drip. [Gr *thixis* action of touching, and *tropos* a turn]

thlipsis *thlip'sis*, *n* constriction; compression. [Gr *thlīpsis*, from *thlībein* to press]

tho[1] *dhō*, (*Spenser*) *pl demonstrative adj* those. [OE *thā*, plural of *se*, *sēo*, *thæt* that]

tho[2] *dhō*, (*Spenser*) *adv* then. [OE (and ON) *thā*]

tho' (*US* or *poetic*). Same as **though**.

thoft *thoft*, (*dialect*) *n* a rowing-bench. [OE *thofte*]

thole[1] *thōl*, *n* (also **thole pin**) a pin in the side of a boat to keep the oar in place; a peg. — Also **thowl** or **thowel**. [OE *thol*; Du *dol*, ON *thollr*]

thole[2] *thōl*, (chiefly *Scot*) *vt* and *vi* to endure; to suffer. [OE *tholian* to suffer; Gothic *thulan*, ON *thola*; OHGer *dolên*, Ger *Geduld* patience, *dulden* to suffer, L *tollere*, Gr *tolmaein*]

tholus *thō'ləs*, *n* a round building, dome, cupola, or tomb, *esp* a dome-shaped tomb from the Mycenaean period: — *pl* **thō'li** (*-lī*). — Also **tholos** (*thol'os*): — *pl* **thol'oi** (*-loi*). — *n* **tholobate** (*thol'ə-bāt*; from Gr *-batēs* someone or something that goes, from *bainein* to go) the substructure of a dome or cupola. [Gr *tholos*]

Thomism *tō'mizm*, *n* the theological and philosophical doctrines of *Thomas* Aquinas (born *prob* 1225; died 1274). — *n* and *adj* **Thō'mist**. — *adj* **Thōmist'ic** or **Thōmist'ical**.

Thompson submachine-gun *tom'sən sub-mə-shēn'gun*, a tommy-gun. — Also **Thompson gun**.

thon *dhon*, and **thon'der** *-dər*. Unexplained modern Scots forms of **yon** and **yonder** *prob* influenced by *this* and *that*.

thong *thong*, *n* a strap; a strip; the lash of a whip or crop; a sandal held on by a thong between the toes, a flipflop (*NAm*, *Austr* and *NZ*); a garment, eg for wear on the beach, consisting of a narrow band of material running between the legs and attached to a cord round the waist. — *adj* **thonged** having a thong or thongs. [OE *thwang*]

Thor *thör*, *n* the Scandinavian thunder-god, Old English Thunor. [ON *Thōrr*]

thoraces, **thoracic**. See under **thorax**.

thoraco- *thō-rə-kō-*, *-kə-*, *-ko'*, or *thö-*, or **thorac-** *-rəs*, *-rək-*, *combining form* denoting thorax. — *n* **thoracentesis** or **thoracocentesis** (*-sen-tē'sis*; Gr *kentēsis*, from *kentein* to prick) surgery performed to draw off fluid from the pleural cavity, *usu* using a hollow needle inserted through the wall of the chest. — *n* **tho'racoplasty** (Gr *plassein* to form) surgery to collapse a diseased lung by removing selected portions of the ribs. — *n* **tho'racoscope** an instrument for examining the pleura covering the lung and the chest wall. — *n* **thoracos'tomy** (see **-stomy**) the construction of an artificial opening in the chest, *usu* to draw off fluid or release a build-up of air. — *n* **thoracot'omy** (see **-tomy**) an incision into the wall of the chest, for drawing pus from the pleural cavity or lung. [Gr *thōrāx*, *-ākos* breastplate, chest]

Thorah. See under **Torah**.

thorax *thō'raks*, *thö'*, *n* the part of the body between the head and abdomen, in man the chest, in insects the division that bears legs and wings (*zool*); a corslet or breastplate (*Gr antiq*): — *pl* **tho'raxes** or **tho'races** (*-sēz*). — *adj* **thoracic** (*-ras'ik*) or **tho'racal** (*-rə-kl*). — **thoracic duct** the main trunk of the vessels conveying lymph in the body. [Gr *thōrāx*, *-ākos*]

thoria *thō'ri-ə*, *thö'*, *n* the oxide of thorium. [**thorium**]

thorite *thō'rīt*, *thö'*, *n* a radioactive mineral, thorium silicate, in which thorium was first discovered, by Berzelius. [**thorium**]

thorium *thō'ri-əm*, *thö'*, *n* a radioactive metal (symbol **Th**; atomic no 90) resembling aluminium, used eg as a source of nuclear power. [*Thor*, the god]

thorn *thörn*, *n* a sharp hard part of the leaf, stem or root of a plant; an animal spine; anything prickly; a spiny plant; a thorn-bearing tree or shrub, *esp* the hawthorn; the wood of such a tree or shrub; the Old English and Old Norse letter þ (*th*). — *vt* to set with thorns; to prick. — *adj* **thorned**. — *n* **thorn'iness**. — *adj* **thorn'less**. — *adj* **thorn'set** set or beset with thorns. — *adj* **thorn'y** full of thorns; prickly; troublesome, difficult; harassing. — **thorn apple** a poisonous plant (*Datura stramonium*, or related species) of the potato family, with a prickly capsule; a haw; **thorn'back** the roker, a ray (*Raja clavata*) with large-based thorns in its back; **thorn'bill** any of several Australian warblers of the genus *Acanthiza*; any of several S American humming birds with thorn-like bills, *esp* of the genera *Chalcostigma* and *Ramphomicron*; **thorn'bush** any thorny shrub, *esp* hawthorn; **thorn'hedge** a hedge of hawthorn; **thorn'proofs** trousers made *usu* from thick brushed cotton, typically worn for country pursuits; **thorn'tree** a thorny tree, *esp* a hawthorn; **thorny devil** the Australian moloch lizard. — **thorn in the flesh** any cause of constant irritation (from the Bible: 2 Cor 12. 7). [OE *thorn*; ON *thorn*, Ger *Dorn*]

thoron *thō'ron*, *thö'*, *n* the radioactive isotope of radon given off by the decomposition of thorium. [**thorium**]

thorough *thur'ə*, also (*NAm*) *thur'ō*, *adj* passing or carried through, or to the end; complete; entire; out-and-out; (of a person) assiduous and scrupulous in completing work and attending to every detail; (of a task etc) done with great care and attention to detail. — *prep* (*obs*) through. — *n* that which goes through, a passage; (also with *cap*) the blind and obstinately tyrannical policy of Strafford and Laud in administering civil and ecclesiastical affairs without regard to opposite convictions (*hist*). — *adv* **thor'oughly**. — *n* **thor'oughness**. — **thor'ough-bass** (*music*) (*esp* in baroque music) a bass part underlying a piece, *usu* with figures to indicate the chords, and *usu* played on a keyboard instrument; (loosely) harmony; (erroneously) a deep bass; **thor'oughbrace** (*US*) a leather band supporting the body of certain types of carriage; a stagecoach. — *adj* **thor'oughbraced**. — *adj* **thor'oughbred** thoroughly or completely bred or trained; (of a horse) bred from a dam and sire of the best blood, and having the qualities supposed to depend on such breeding; pure-bred; (with *cap*) pertaining to the Thoroughbred breed of horses; high-spirited. — *n* an animal (*esp* a horse) of pure blood; (with *cap*) a racehorse of a breed descended from any of three Arabian stallions of the early 18c whose ideal gait is the gallop. — **thor'oughfare** a passage or way through; a road open at both ends; a public way or street; right of passing through. — *adj* **thor'oughgoing** going through or to the end; going all lengths; complete; out-and-out. — *adv* **thor'oughgoingly**. — *n* **thor'oughgoingness**. — *adj* **thor'ough-paced** (of a horse) thoroughly or perfectly trained in all paces; complete. — **thor'ough-pin** (*vet*) inflammation of a horse's hock joint; **thor'oughwax** or **thor'ow-wax** the plant hare's-ear, from the stem seeming to *wax* (ie grow) through the leaves. — **post-vintage thoroughbred** a car built between 1 January 1931 and 31 December 1941. [The longer form of **through**]

thorp or **thorpe** *thörp*, (*archaic*; found eg in place names) *n* a hamlet; a village. [OE *thorp*, *throp*; ON *thorp*, Gothic *thaurp*, Ger *Dorf*]

those *dhōz*, *demonstrative pronoun* and *adj*, plural of **that**. [OE *thās*, plural of *thes* this]

Thoth *thōth*, *thoth*, *tōt*, *n* the ancient Egyptian ibis-headed god of art, science, etc. [Gr *Thōth*, from Egyp *Tehuti*]

thother. See under **th-**.

thou[1] *dhow*, (*formal*, *liturgical*, *dialect* or *archaic*) *pronoun* the nominative of the second person singular pronoun, now largely superseded by **you**. — *vt* to apply the pronoun *thou* to: — *pa t* and *pa p* **thou'd**. — See also **thee**, **thine** and **thy**. [OE *thū*; Gothic *thu*, Doric Gr *ty*, L *tū*, Sans *tvam*]

thou[2] *thow*, *n* one thousandth of an inch: — *pl* **thou** or **thous**. — *n* and *adj* (*colloq*) thousand or thousandth.

though *dhō*, *conj* admitting; allowing; if or even if; notwithstanding that. — *adv* nevertheless; however. — **as though** as if. [ON *thauh*, *thō*; OE *thēah*, *thēh*, Ger *doch*]

thought[1] *thöt*, *pa p* and *pa t* of **think**[1] and *pa t* of **think**[2]. [OE *thōhte*, past tense, (*ge*)*thōht*, past participle]

thought[2] *thöt*, *n* the act or process of thinking; mind; consciousness; the faculty or power of reasoning; serious and careful consideration, deliberation; (often in *pl*) that which one thinks; a notion, idea, fancy; consideration, opinion, meditation; design, care, considerateness; purpose, intention; the intellectual ideas which are typical of a particular place, time, group, etc; resolution; a very slight amount, a hint or trace; grief, anxiety (*obs*). — *adj* **thought'ed** having thoughts. — *adj* **thought'en** (*Shakesp*) firm in belief, assured. — *adj* **thought'ful** full of thought; engaged in or fond of meditation, pensive; attentive; considerate; expressive of or favourable to meditation. — *adv* **thought'fully**. — *n* **thought'fulness**. — *adj* **thought'less** inconsiderate; unthinking; incapable of thinking; showing a lack of careful or serious thought; carefree; careless; inattentive. — *adv* **thought'lessly**. — *n* **thought'lessness**. — **thought'cast** a mode of thought. — *adj* **thought-ex'ecuting** carrying out the wishes of someone, *esp* a master (*old*); *perh* acting with the speed of thought (*Shakesp*). — **thought process** a train of thought; a manner of thinking; **thought'-reader**; **thought'-reading** discerning what is passing in another's mind by any means other than the ordinary and obvious, mind-reading. — *adj* **thought'-sick** (*Shakesp*) sick with the thought. — **thought'-transference** telepathy; **thought'-wave** a wavelike progress of a thought among a crowd or the public; a sudden accession of thought in the mind; an impulse in some hypothetical medium assumed to explain telepathy. — **in thought** thinking, reflecting; **on second thoughts** on reconsideration; **take thought** to think things over; to conceive a purpose; to be anxious or troubled (*obs*); **upon** (or **with**) **a thought** (*Shakesp*) in a moment; with the speed of thought. [OE (*ge*)*thōht*]

thous *dhowz*. A Northern contracted form of **thou is**, thou art (*Spenser*) and of **thou sal**, thou shalt.

thousand *thow'zənd*, *n* ten hundred; any symbol for this, eg M; anything having one thousand parts, etc; (*usu* in *pl*) often used vaguely or hyperbolically to indicate a very large, unspecified amount: — *pl* **thousands** or, in the first sense given, **thousand**. — *adj*, *adv* and *n* (**a**) **thou'sandfold** a thousand times as much. — *adj* **thou'sandth** last of a thousand, or in an equivalent position in a greater number; equal to one of a thousand equal parts. — *n* a thousandth part; a person or thing in thousandth position. — **Thousand Island dressing** a salad dressing made with mayonnaise, and flavoured with chopped gherkins, pimentos, etc; **thou'sand-legs** a centipede or millipede. — *adj* **thousand-pound'** weighing, costing, priced at a thousand pounds. — *adj* **thou'sand-year** lasting or coming once in a thousand years. — **a thousand and one** (*colloq*) very many; an overwhelming number; **one in** (or **of**) **a thousand** anything exceedingly rare or excellent. [OE *thūsend*; Ger *tausend*, Gothic *thūsundi*]

thowel, **thowl**. See under **thole**[1].

thowless *thow'lis*, (*Scot*) *adj* pithless; listless; inert. [Appar **thewless**]

thrae *thrā*. Another form of Scots **frae**.

thrall *thröl*, *n* (*literary* or *archaic*) a slave, serf; slavery, servitude, subjugation; a stand for barrels, pans, etc. — *adj* (*archaic*) enslaved. — *vt* to enslave. — *n* **thral'dom** or (*esp NAm*) **thrall'dom** slavery; bondage. — **in thrall** in a state of rapt absorption or immobility, under some powerful influence. [OE *thrǣl*, from ON *thræll*]

thrang *thrang*. A Scots form of **throng**.

thrapple *thrap'l*. A Scots form of **thropple**.

thrash[1] *thrash*, *vt* to thresh; (with *out*) to discuss exhaustively, or arrive at by debate; to beat soundly or severely; to defeat thoroughly. — *vi* to lash out, beat about one, in anger, panic, etc; to move the legs up and down in swimming; to force one's way, *esp* against the wind or tide (*naut*). — *n* an act of threshing or thrashing; a party (*colloq*); (in full **thrash metal**) very fast, loud rock music, often with violent themes and the energy of punk rock (*slang*). — *n* **thrash'er** a thresher; a thresher-shark, a large, long-tailed shark; someone or something that thrashes. — *n* and *adj* **thrash'ing** threshing; beating. — **thrash'ing-floor**, **thrash'ing-machine** and **thrash'ing-mill** same as **threshing-floor**, etc (see under **thresh**[1]). [Orig a dialect form of **thresh**[1]]

thrash[2] *thrash* or **thresh** *thresh*, (*Scot*) *n* a rush (plant). [Obscurely connected with **rush**[2]]

thrasher[1] *thrash'ər*, or **thresher** *thresh'ər*, *n* any of several American birds of the mockingbird family (*Mimidae*). [Perhaps Eng dialect *thresher* thrush]

thrasher[2]. See under **thrash**[1].

thrasonic *thrə-*, *thrā-son'ik*, or **thrason'ical** *-kl*, *adj* like *Thrasōn*, the bragging soldier, a stock character in Greek New Comedy, or *Thrasō* in Terence's *Eunuchus*; boastful, bragging. — *adv* **thrason'ically**.

thrave *thrāv* or **threave** *thrēv*, (*dialect*) *n* two stooks of (*usu*) twelve sheaves each; two dozen; a good number. [Scand; cf Icel *threfi*, Dan *trave*]

thraw *thrö*, a Scots form of **throw**[1] with some old senses preserved; also of **throe**, with senses overlapping **throw**[1]. — *vt* to turn; to twist; to wring; to distort; to wrest; to cross, thwart. — *vi* to turn; to twist; to writhe; to sway; to go counter; to be perverse: — *pa t* **threw**; *pa p* **thrawn**. — *adj* twisted; distorted; wry. — *n* a twist; a fit of perversity; a throe. — *adj* **thrawn** twisted; wry, crooked; stubborn, perverse. — **dead thraw** the agony of death; **heads and thraws** side by side, the head of the one by the feet of another.

thrawart or **thraward** *thrö'ərt*, (*Scot*) *adj* froward, obstinate; crooked. [ME *fraward*; see **froward**; perhaps influenced by **thraw**; cf **thrae**]

thrawn. See under **thraw**.

thread *thred*, *n* a very thin line of any substance, *esp* linen or cotton, twisted or drawn out; several strands of yarn twisted together for sewing; a filament; a fibre; (in *pl*) clothes (*slang*); the prominent spiral part of a screw; a continuous connecting element in a story, argument, etc; a thin seam of coal or vein of ore. — *vt* to pass a thread through; to string on a thread; to pass through, make (one's way) through (a narrow way, a crowd, obstacles, etc); to fit or supply with a thread. — *vi* (of boiling syrup) to form a fine strand when poured. — *adj* made of linen or cotton thread. — *adj* **thread'en** (*Shakesp*) made of thread. — *n* **thread'er**. — *n* **thread'iness**. — *adj* **thread'y** like thread or threads; slender; containing or consisting of thread; (of the pulse) barely perceptible (*med*). — *adj* **thread'bare** worn to the bare thread; having the nap worn off; poor or meagre; shabby; hackneyed; used till its novelty or interest is gone. — **thread'bareness**; **thread'-cell** (in jellyfishes, etc) a stinging cell that throws out a stinging thread; **thread'fin** any small, spiny-finned tropical fish of the family *Polynemidae*, with five threads on its pectoral fins; **thread'-lace** lace made of linen thread; **thread'maker**; **thread mark** a coloured thread incorporated in banknotes to make counterfeiting difficult; **thread'-paper** a piece of thin soft paper for wrapping up a skein of thread; **thread vein** a very fine vein on the surface of the skin, *esp* on the face; **thread'worm** any member of the *Nematoda*, a family of more or less threadlike worms, many of which are parasitic, *esp Oxyuris vermicularis*, parasitic in the human rectum. — **hang by a thread** see under **hang**; **thread and thrum** all, the good and bad together; **thread of life** (*Gr mythol*) the thread imagined to be spun and cut by the Fates. [OE *thrǣd*; cf **throw**[1], **thraw**]

Threadneedle Street *thred'nē-dl strēt*, *n* a street in the city of London. — **Old Lady** (or **Woman**) **of Threadneedle Street** the Bank of England.

threap or **threep** *thrēp*, (*Scot* and *Northern dialect*) *vt* to rebuke; to maintain persistently; to insist on; to urge, to press eagerly; to contradict. — *vi* to dispute: — *pa t* and *pa p* **threap'it** or **threep'it**. — *n* stubborn insistence or assertion; accusation; a traditional belief. [OE *thrēapian* to rebuke]

threat *thret*, *n* a declaration or indication of an intention to inflict harm, punish or hurt; an appearance of impending evil; a source of danger (with *to*). — *vt* and *vi* (*Shakesp*, *Milton*, *Byron*, etc) to threaten. — *vt* **threat'en** to offer a threat of, or against; to intimidate by threats; to seem to impend over; to indicate danger of, or to, to portend. — *vi* to use threats; to give warning that something is likely to happen; to portend evil. — *adj* **threat'ened**. — *n* **threat'ener**. — *n* **threat'ening**. — *adj* menacing; portending danger or evil; (of the sky) heavily clouded over, promising rain, stormy weather, etc. — *adv* **threat'eningly**. — *adj* **threat'ful** menacing. [OE *thrēat* (noun), *thrēatian*, *thrēatnian* (verbs); cf Ger *verdriessen* to tremble, L *trūdere* to thrust]

threave. See under **thrave**.

three *thrē*, *n* two and one; a set of three; a symbol for three; a playing card with three pips; a score of three points, strokes, etc; an article of a size denoted by three; the third hour after midnight or midday; the age of three years. — *adj* amounting to three; three years old. — *n* **three'ness** the state of being three. — *n* **three'some** a group of three people; a game or dance for three. — *adj* for three; triple. — **three balls** the pawnbroker's sign. — *adj* **three-bott'le** able to drink three bottles of wine at a sitting. — *adj* **three'-card** played with three cards. — **three-card trick** a card-sharp's play in which the victim is invited to bet on which of three cards, turned face-down and deftly manipulated, is the queen (also called *find the lady*). — *adj* **three-cen'tred** (of an arch) composed of circular arcs with three different centres. — **three cheers** three shouts of 'hurrah', to show approval, etc (also *fig*). — *adj* **three'-cleft** cut halfway down into three lobes. — *adj* **three'-colour** involving or using three colours as primary. — **three-colour process** the method of producing colour pictures from three primary originals — yellow, red, blue — prepared by photography. — *adj* **three-cor'nered** triangular in form or section; having three competitors or three members. — **three-day event** and **three-day eventer** see under **event**. — *adj* **three'-deck**. — **three-deck'er** a ship with three decks or guns on three decks; a building or structure with three floors or tiers; a pulpit with three levels; a three-volume novel; a double sandwich, with two layers of filling and three layers of bread; any other thing with three layers, levels, etc. — Also *adj*. — *adj* **three-dimen'sional** having, or seeming to have, three dimensions; giving the effect of being seen or heard in an environment of three dimensions (shortened to **three-D** or **3-D**); (of, eg a literary work) developed in detail and thus realistic. — **three'-dimensional'ity**. — *adj* **three-far'thing**. — *n sing* **three-far'things** a silver coin issued under Queen Elizabeth I, distinguished from a penny by a rose behind the queen's head. — *adj* and *adv* **three'fold** in three parts; (by) three times as much. — *n* **three'-foldness**. — *adj* **three'-foot** measuring or having three feet. — *adj* **three-four'** (*music*) with three crotchets to the bar. — **three-four'** or **three-four time** the time signature ($\frac{3}{4}$) indicating three crochets to the bar; **three-halfpence** (*thrē-hā'pəns*) an old penny and a halfpenny; a coin of that value. — *adj* **three-halfpenny** (*thrē-hāp'ni*). — **three-half'pennyworth** or **threeha'porth** (*thrē-hāp'ərth*) an amount of something costing one old penny and a halfpenny. — *adj* **three'-handed** having three hands; played by three players. — **three-jaw chuck** (*eng*) a scroll chuck (qv) with three jaws for holding cylindrical workpieces, materials or tools. — *adj* **three'-leaved** (or **three'-leafed**) having three leaves or leaflets; having leaves in threes. — *adj* **three'-legged** (*-legd*, *-leg'id*) having three legs; (of a race) run by pairs of runners, each with a leg tied to his or her partner's adjacent one. — **three-line whip** see under **whip**. — *adj* **three'-man** (*Shakesp*) worked or performed by three men. — *adj* **three-mast'ed**. — **three-mast'er** a ship with three masts; **three-mile limit** (in international law) the outer limit of the territorial waters around a state, extending to three nautical miles. — *n* and *adj* **three'-monthly** quarterly. — *adj* **three'-nooked** (*Shakesp*) three-cornered. — *adj* **three'-pair** or **three'-pair-of-stairs** on a third floor. — *n* a room so situated. — *adj* **three'-part** composed in three parts or for three voices. — *adj* **three-part'ed** consisting of three parts; parted in three; divided into three nearly to the base. — *adv* **three'-parts** to the extent of three-quarters. — **threepence** (*threp'*, *thrip'*, *thrup'əns*) money, or a coin, of the value of three old pence. — *adj* **threepenny** (*threp'*, *thrip'*, *thrup'ni* or *-ə-ni*) sold or offered at threepence; of little worth; mean, vulgar. — *n* a coin of the value of threepence (also **threepenny bit** or **piece**). — **three-pennyworth** or **threepenn'orth** (*thrē-pen'i-wərth*, *thrē-pen'ərth*), also (chiefly *Scot*) **threep'enceworth** an amount of something costing threepence. — *n pl* **three-per-cents'** bonds or other securities paying three per cent interest, *esp* a portion of the consolidated debt of Great Britain. — *adj* **three'-phase** (*elec eng*) (of an electric supply system) in which the alternating potentials on the three wires differ in phase from each other by 120°. — *adj* **three'-piece** comprising three parts, three matching pieces, etc. — *n* anything with three matching pieces, *esp* a suite of furniture. — *adj* **three'-pile** having loops of three threads. — *n* (*Shakesp*) the finest kind of velvet. — *adj* **three'-piled** three-pile; piled three-high. — *adj* **three'-ply** having three layers or strands. — **three-point landing** (*aeronautics*) a landing with all three wheels touching the ground at the same moment, a perfect landing; **three-point turn** the process of turning a vehicle round to face in the opposite direction by moving it forward, reversing, then moving forward again, turning the steering-wheel appropriately. — *adj* **three'-pound** costing or weighing three pounds. — **three-pound'er** a thing that weighs three pounds; a gun that shoots a three-pound ball; **three'-pricker** (*airmen's slang*) a three-point landing; anything right or perfect. — *adj* and *adv* **three-quar'ter** to the amount of three-fourths; (*adj*) being three quarters of the normal size or length (used of beds, coats, etc). — *n* a three-quarter back. — **three-quarter back** (*Rugby football*) a player between halfbacks and full back; **three-quarter face** an aspect between full face and profile. — *adj* **three-quar'ter-length** (of a coat, sleeve, etc) being three quarters of the full length. — **three quarters** (a part equal to) three fourths of a whole; the greater part of something; **three-ring circus** a circus with three rings in which simultaneous separate performances are given; a showy or extravagant event (*fig*); a confusing or bewildering scene or situation; **the three R's** see under **R**. — *n* and *adj* **three'score** sixty. — *adj* **three-sid'ed** having three sides. — **three-speed gear** a gear-changing device with three gear positions. — *adj* **three'-square** having an equilateral triangle as a cross-section. — *adj* **three-star'** (*esp* of a hotel) of a quality or rank denoted by three in a four- or five-star grading system; of or being a lieutenant general (*US*). — *adj* **three'-suit'ed** (*Shakesp*) allowed three suits of clothes a year as a serving-man. — **three times three** three cheers repeated three times. — *adj* **three'-volume** in three volumes. — *adj* **three'-way** giving connection in three directions from a centre; involving three people or things. — **three-went way** (*dialect*) a place where three roads meet; **three-wheel'er** a vehicle having three wheels, *esp* a motor vehicle with two rear wheels and a single front wheel. [OE *thrēo*, feminine and neuter of *thrī*; Gothic *threis*, Ger *drei*, L *trēs*, *trēs*, *tria*, Gr *treis*, *treis*, *tria*, Sans *tri*]

threep. See under **threap**.

thremmatology *threm-ə-tol'ə-ji*, *n* the science of breeding domestic animals and plants. [Gr *thremma*, *-atos* a nurseling, and *logos* discourse]

threnody *thren'ə-di*, *thrē'nə*, or **threnode** *-ōd*, *n* an ode or song of lamentation, *esp* for the dead. — Also (*Shakesp*) **threne** (*thrēn*) or **thren'os**. — *adj* **threnet'ic** or **threnet'ical**. — *adj* **threnō'dial** or **threnodic** (*-od'*). — *n* **thren'odist**. [Gr *thrēnōidiā*, from *thrēnos* a lament, and *ōidē* song]

threonine *thrē'ə-nīn*, *n* an amino acid essential for bodily growth and health, present in certain proteins. [Gr *erythro-* red, by rearrangement, with *-n-* and *-ine*]

thresh[1] *thresh*, *vt* to beat out, subject to beating out, by trampling, flail or machinery; to thrash. — *vi* to thresh corn, to separate the grain from the husks and straw; to thrash. — *n* an act of threshing. — *n* **thresh'el** a flail; a flail-like weapon, a spiky ball on the end of a chain. — *n* **thresh'er** a person who threshes; a flail; a threshing-machine or a beating part of it; (also **thresh'er-shark**) a large, long-tailed shark of the genus *Alopias*, especially *Alopias vulpinus*. — *n* and *adj* **thresh'ing**. — **thresh'er-whale** a grampus; **thresh'ing-floor** a surface on which grain is threshed; **thresh'ing-machine** or **-mill** one for threshing corn, etc. [OE *therscan*; cf Ger *derschen* to thresh; see **thrash**[1]]

thresh[2]. See under **thrash**[2].

thresher. See under **thrasher**[1] and **thresh**[1].

threshold *thresh'ōld*, *-hōld*, *n* the sill of a house door; the place or point of entering; the outset; the limit of consciousness; the point at which a stimulus begins to bring a response, as in *threshold of pain*, etc; the smallest dose of radiation that will produce a specified result; the point, stage, level, etc, at which something will happen, become true, etc; (in a pay agreement, etc) a point in the rise of the cost of living at which a wage-increase is prescribed. — *adj* at or constituting a threshold. — **threshold dose** (*radiol*) the smallest dose of radiation that will produce a specified result; **threshold lighting** or **lights** a line of lights across the ends of a runway or landing area to indicate the usable limits; **threshold of audibility** or **of sound** the minimum intensity or pressure of sound wave which the normal human listener can just detect at any given frequency. [OE *therscold*, *therscwald*, *threscold*, appar from *therscan* to thrash, thresh, in its older sense of trample, tread]

thretty *thret'i*. A dialect form of **thirty**.

threw *throo͞*, *pa t* of **throw**[1].

thrice *thrīs*, (*formal*) *adv* three times; three times as much; highly, greatly (*archaic*). [ME *thriës*, from OE *thrīwa*, *thrīga* thrice, from *thrī* three, with adverbial genitive ending *-es*]

thrid *thrid*, (*Spenser*) *n* a thread. — *vt* (*obs*) to thread. [**thread**]

thridace *thrid'əs*, *n* inspissated lettuce juice used eg as a sedative. [Gr *thridax* lettuce]

thrift *thrift*, *n* frugality; economy; the sea pink (*Armeria*), a seaside and alpine plant of the Plumbaginaceae family; a savings and loan association similar in function to a building society (*US finance*); the state of thriving (*rare* or *old*); prosperity (*archaic*); increase of wealth (*archaic*); gain (*archaic*); profitable occupation (*dialect*); savings (*archaic*). — *adv* **thrift'ily**. — *n* **thrift'iness**. — *adj* **thrift'less** not thrifty; extravagant; not thriving (*rare* or *old*). — *adv* **thrift'lessly**. — *n* **thrift'lessness**. — *adj* **thrift'y** showing thrift or economy; thriving by frugality; prosperous, in good condition (*US*): — *compar* **thrift'ier**; *superl* **thrift'iest**. — **thrift shop** a shop, *usu* run on behalf of a charity, which sells second-hand clothes and other articles. [**thrive**]

thrill *thril*, *vt* to affect with a strong glow or tingle of sense or emotion, now *esp* a feeling of excitement or extreme pleasure; to pierce (*archaic*). — *vi* to pass tinglingly; to quiver; to feel a sharp, shivering sensation; (of something sharp) to pierce or penetrate (with *through*) (*archaic*). — *n* a sudden feeling of excitement or extreme pleasure; a tingle; a shivering feeling or emotion; a tremor or vibration palpable at the surface of the body, *esp* in valvular disease of the heart (*med*). — *adj* **thrill'ant** (*Spenser*) piercing. — *n* **thrill'er** a sensational or exciting story, *esp* one about crime and detection; any person or thing that thrills. — *adj* **thrill'ing**. — *adv* **thrill'ingly**. — *n* **thrill'ingness**. — *adj* **thrill'y**. [OE *thyrlian* to bore, from *thyrel* a hole; Ger *drillen* to drill a hole]

thrimsa. See under **thrymsa**.

thrips *thrips*, *n* any insect of the order Thysanoptera, *esp* a minute black insect of the genus *Thrips*, common in flowers; popularly extended to leaf-hoppers, and to other small insects: — *pl* **thrips** or **thrip'ses**. [Gr *thrīps*, *thrīpos* a woodworm]

thrissel or **thristle** *thris'l*, *thrus'l*, Scots forms of **thistle**. [Possibly influenced by *thrist* to thrust]

thrist *thrist* and **thrist'y** *-i*. Old forms (*Spenser*) of **thirst** (*n* and *v*) and **thirsty**.

thrive *thrīv*, *vi* to grow; to grow healthily and vigorously; to get on, do well; to be successful, flourish; to prosper; to increase in goods. — *pa t* **thrōve** or **thrīved**; *pa p* **thriven** (*thriv'n*) or **thrīved**. — *adj* **thrīve'less** not thriving or prospering. — *adj* **thriven** (*thriv'n*) grown, developed; successful. — *n* **thrī'ver**. — *n* and *adj* **thrī'ving**. — *adv* **thrī'vingly** (*rare*). — *n* **thrī'vingness**. [ON *thrīfa* to grasp]

thro' or **thro** *throo͞*. Same as **through**.

throat *thrōt*, *n* the passage from the back of the mouth to stomach; the forepart of the neck, in which the gullet and windpipe are located; voice; a sore throat (*informal*); a narrow entrance, aperture or passage; the narrow part, eg of a vase; a corolla (*bot*); a groove under a coping or moulding; the end of a gaff next to the mast (*naut*). — *adj* **throat'ed** with a throat. — *adv* **throat'ily**. — *n* **throat'iness**. — *adj* **throat'y** sounding as from the throat, guttural; hoarse; croaking; deep or full-throated; having a rather sore throat (*colloq*); full or loose-skinned about the throat; potent in swallowing. — **throat'-band**, **-strap**, **-lash** or **-latch** a band about the throat, eg holding a horse's bridle in place. — *adj* **throat'-full** full to the throat. — **throat microphone** one held directly against the speaker's throat and actuated by vibrations of the larynx; **throat'wort** the nettle-leaved bellflower (*Campanula trachelium*) once reputed good for throat ailments; the giant bellflower (*C. latifolium*). — **be at someone's throat** or **at each other's throats** (*colloq*) to be engaged in a fierce, bitter argument with someone or with each other; **cut one's (own) throat** to commit suicide by cutting (*usu*) the jugular vein; to pursue some course ruinous to one's interests; **give someone the lie in his** or **her throat** to accuse someone to his or her face of uttering a lie; **have by the throat** to have at one's mercy; **jump down someone's throat** see under **jump**; **sore throat** an inflamed and painful condition of the tonsils and neighbouring parts; **stick in one's throat** to be more than one can bear, accept or manage; **thrust** (or **ram**) **down someone's throat** to force (eg one's own opinion) upon someone insistently. [OE *throte*; cf **throttle**]

throb *throb*, *vi* to beat strongly, as the heart or pulse does, *esp* in response to some emotion, stimulus, etc; (of an injured or sore part of the body) to be affected by rhythmic waves of pain; (of an engine, etc) to produce a deep regular sound: — *pr p* **throbb'ing**; *pa t* and *pa p* **throbbed**. — *n* a beat or strong pulsation. — *n* and *adj* **throbb'ing**. — *adv* **throbb'ingly**. — *adj* **throb'less**. [ME *throbben*; possibly connected with L *trepidus* trembling]

throe, earlier (*Shakesp*, *Spenser*) **throw** or **throwe**, *thrō*, (*Scot*) **thraw** *thrö*, *n* a spasm; a paroxysm; a pang or pain, *esp* a birth-pang. — *vt* to subject to pangs. — *vi* to suffer pangs. — **in the throes** in the struggle (of), struggling (with); in the thick (of); in travail. [ME *thrahes*, *throwes*, *thrawes*; perh there have been cross-influences between OE *thrawu* pang, *thrāg* paroxysm, *thrōwian* to suffer, *thrāwan* to twist, throw; see also **thraw**]

thrombin *throm'bin*, *n* an enzyme that causes the blood to clot. [*thrombus* and *-in*]

thrombo- *throm-bō-*, *-bə-*, (*med*) *combining form* denoting a blood clot. — *n* **throm'bocyte** (Gr *kytos* vessel, hollow) a platelet. — *n* **thrombocyto'pēnia** (Gr *penia* poverty) an abnormal decrease in the number of platelets in the blood, causing haemorrhage. — *n* **thromboem'bolism** a blockage of a blood vessel caused by an embolus carried by the bloodstream from its point of origin. — *adj* **thrombolyt'ic** (of a drug) dissolving clots in the blood. — *n* a thrombolytic drug. — *n* **thrombokī'nase** an enzyme active in the clotting of blood; thromboplastin. — *n* **thrombophlebī'tis** phlebitis with formation of a thrombus. — *n* **thrombophil'ia** combined inflammation and thrombosis of a vein. — *n* **thromboplas'tin** a substance, found *esp* in platelets, which participates in the clotting of blood. [Gr *thrombos* a clot]

thrombose *throm-bōz'*, *vt* to cause thrombosis in. — *vi* to be affected with thrombosis. [Back-formation from **thrombosis**]

thrombosis *throm-bō'sis*, *n* clotting of blood in a vessel during life; a coronary thrombosis: — *pl* **thrombō'sēs**. — *adj* **thrombot'ic**. [Gr *thrombōsis* curdling, from *thrombos* a clot]

thrombus *throm'bəs*, *n* a clot of blood in a living vessel, obstructing circulation: — *pl* **throm'bī**. [Gr *thrombos* a clot]

throne *thrōn*, *n* a monarch's, pope's, or bishop's chair of state; kingship; the power or duty of a monarch, etc; a lavatory (*colloq*); an angel of the third of the nine orders of angels. — *vt* to enthrone; to exalt. — *vi* to sit in state, to sit on a throne. — *adj* **throned**. — *adj* **throne'less**. — **throne'-room**. — **power behind the throne** a person or group of people who exercise power or influence without having the formal authority to do so. [Gr *thronos* a seat]

throng *throng*, *n* a crowd; a great multitude; crowding. — *vt* to crowd (a place); to press or jostle; to press hard (*Shakesp*). — *vi* to move or gather in a crowd. — *adj* (*colloq*) crowded; busy; intimate. — *adj* **thronged** packed, crowded; (with *up*) overpowered (*Shakesp*). — *adj* **throng'ful** thronged. — *n* and *adj* **throng'ing**. [OE *gethrang*, from *thringan* to press]

thropple *throp'l* (*Scot* **thrapple** *thrap'l*), *n* the throat; the windpipe, *esp* of an animal. — *vt* to throttle; to strangle. [Poss OE *throtbolla* windpipe, gullet, from *throte* throat, and *bolla* boll]

throstle *thros'l*, *n* the song-thrush (see under **thrush**[1]); (in full **throstle frame**) a machine for drawing, twisting and winding fibres (from its sound). — **thros'tle-cock** a male song-thrush or (*dialect*) missel-thrush. [OE *throstle*; Ger *Drossel*, L *turdus* thrush]

throttle *throt'l*, *n* (in full **thrott'le-valve**) a valve regulating the supply of steam or of gas and air in an engine; (in full **thrott'le-lever**) a lever that opens and closes a throttle-valve; the throat or windpipe. — *vt* to choke by pressure on the windpipe; to strangle; to suppress or silence; to check the flow of; to cut down the supply of steam, or of gas and air, to or in, by means of a throttle. — *vi* to breathe hard, as when nearly suffocated. — *n* **thrott'ler**. — *n* and *adj* **thrott'ling**. — **thrott'le-pipe** the vertical pipe between the throttle-valve and the dry-pipe of a locomotive. — **at full throttle** at full speed; **throttle down** to slow down by closing the throttle. [Appar dimin of **throat**]

through *thrōō*, *prep* from end to end, side to side, or boundary to boundary of, by way of the interior; from place to place within; everywhere within; by way of; along the passage of; clear of; among; from beginning to end of; up to and including, to or until the end of (*NAm*); by means of; in consequence of. — *adv* from one end or side to the other; from beginning to end; all the way; clear; into a position of having passed; in connection or communication all the way. — *adj* passing, or serving for passage, all the way without interruption; having completed or come to the end; (in telephoning) connected (*colloq*). — *adv* **through'ly** same as **thoroughly** (*obs*); far through (*archaic*). — *prep* **throughout'** in, into, through or during the whole of. — *adv* in every part; everywhere. — **through ball** (*football*) a ball kicked so as to get past the defence; **through'-bolt** a bolt that passes through from side to side of what it fastens; **through bridge** (*civ eng*) a bridge in which the track is carried by the lower strings. — *adj* **through-compōs'ed** (*music*) (of a song) having different music for each verse. — **through'fare** (*Shakesp*) same as **thoroughfare**. — *adj* **through'-ganging** (*Scot*) thorough-going. — **through'-going** (*Scot* **through'gaun** *-gön*) a scolding. — *adj* passing through; active, energetic. — *adv* **through'-other** (*Scot*) in indiscriminate mixture; higgledy-piggledy, in disorder. — *adj* (*Scot*) confusedly mixed; without orderliness. — **through pass** same as **through ball**; **through'put** the amount of material, etc, put through a process; **through'-stone** (*building*) a bonder or bondstone in building (see also separate entry below); **through ticket** a ticket for the whole of a journey; **through traffic** the traffic between two centres at a distance from each other; traffic passing straight through an area, as opposed to that travelling within the area; **through train** a train that goes the whole length of a long route; **through'way** or **thru'way** (*NAm*) a motorway. — **be through** (*NAm*) to have done (with *with*); to be finished; to have no future (as); to have no more to do (with *with*); **through and through** through the whole thickness; completely; in every point; **through the day** or **through the night** (*Scot*) in the daytime or in the night-time. [OE *thurh*; Ger *durch*]

through-stone *thrōōhh'-*, *throhh'-stōn*, or **through-stane** *-stān*, (*Scot*) *n* a horizontal tombstone on pillars. — See also **through-stone** under **through**. [OE *thrūh* sarcophagus, and **stone**]

throve *thrōv*, *pa t* of **thrive**.

throw[1] *thrō*, *vt* to cast, hurl, fling through the air; to project; to emit; to cause (one's voice) to appear to come from elsewhere; to cause to be in some place or condition, *esp* suddenly; to render suddenly; to put; to put on or take off (clothes etc) quickly, carelessly or violently (with *off*, *on*, *on to*); to execute, perform; to have or suffer (eg a fit or tantrum); to give (a party); to bemuse, perplex, disconcert; to move (a switch) so as to connect or disconnect; to form (pottery) on a wheel; to turn with a lathe; to wind or twist (yarn) together; (of a horse) to dislodge (its rider) from the saddle; to cast (one's opponent) to the ground (*wrestling*); to deliver (a punch) (*boxing*); to bowl (a ball) bending illegally and straightening the arm during delivery (*cricket*); to play (a card); to make a cast of dice amounting to; to cast (dice); to lose (a contest) deliberately, *esp* in return for a bribe (*colloq*); to defeat, get the better of, or discomfit; (of an animal) to give birth to; to produce. — *vi* to cast or hurl; to cast dice; to lay about one (*Spenser*): — *pa t* **threw** (*thrōō*); *pa p* **thrown** (*thrōn*). — *n* an act of throwing; a cast, *esp* of dice or a fishing-line; the distance to which anything may be thrown; a woollen wrap or small rug (*esp NAm*); a turn, go, occasion, etc (*colloq*); a risky venture (*colloq*); the vertical displacement of a particular rock, vein or stratum due to a fault (cf *lateral shift*; *geol*); a deflection caused by a sudden fluctuation (*phys*); amplitude of movement (*phys*); a blow (*Spenser*). — *n* **throw'er**. — *n* and *adj* **throw'ing**. — *adj* **thrown** twisted; cast, flung. — *n* **throw'ster** a person who twists silk thread into yarn; a gambler. — **throw'away** an advertisement brochure or handbill freely distributed to the public (*NAm*); a contest without serious competition; a line, or a joke, that an actor purposely delivers casually or without emphasis, often for the sake of realism. — *adj* (of manner or technique) casual, without attempt at dramatic effect; ridiculously cheap, as if being thrown away; intended to be discarded or not recovered after use. — **throw'back** a reversion (eg to an earlier developmental type); a person, plant, etc showing characteristics of an earlier developmental type; a setback; **throw'-down** a home-made firework, *esp* one that makes a noise when dropped on the ground; **throw'-in** an act of throwing in; a throw to put the ball back into play (*football*, *basketball*, etc); **throw'ing-stick** a grooved stick for giving a spear greater leverage when thrown; a throw-stick; **throw'ing-table** a potter's wheel; **thrown'-silk** organzine; **throw'-out** an act of throwing out; a rejected thing; **throw rug** a throw; **throw'-stick** a weapon thrown whirling from the hand, such as the boomerang; **throw weight** the maximum weight that can be lifted by a ballistic missile, *incl* the weight of the warhead(s) and guidance systems, but not the weight of the rocket itself. — **throw about** or **throw around** to spend (money) extravagantly or recklessly; to throw carelessly in different directions; (**throw about**) to cast about or try expedients (*Spenser*); **throw a fit** (*colloq*) to have a fit, behave wildly; **throw away** to reject, toss aside; to squander; to fail to take advantage of; to discard (a card); (of an actor) to speak (lines) deliberately without emphasis; to bestow or expend on something unworthy; **throw back** to retort, to refuse; to force (someone) to rely (on something); to revert to some ancestral character; **throw down** to demolish; **throw down the gauntlet** see under **gauntlet**; **throw in** to interject; to throw (a football) back into play from the side of the pitch; to add as an extra at no extra cost; **throw in the towel** or **throw in one's hand** to give up, surrender; **throw in one's lot** see under **lot**; **throw mud at** see under **mud**; **throw off** to divest oneself of; to disengage or release oneself from; to tell or compose in an offhand way; to perplex or disconcert; **throw on** to put on hastily; **throw oneself at** to make a determined and obvious attempt to captivate; **throw oneself into** to engage heartily in; **throw oneself on** or **upon** to attack, assault; to entrust oneself to the power of; **throw open** to cause to swing wide open; to make freely accessible; **throw out** to cast out; to reject; to expel; to emit; to utter casually; to cause to project; to build (a projecting extension); to disconcert or distract; to put (the batsman) out by throwing the ball at, and hitting, the wicket (*cricket*); to put (the batter) out by throwing the ball to a fielder to prevent the batter from reaching a base (*baseball*); to distance, leave behind; **throw over** to discard, desert or jilt; **throw together** to put together in a hurry; to bring into contact by chance; **throw (caution**

etc) **to the winds** see under **wind**[1]; **throw up** to erect hastily; to show prominently, to reveal; to give up, to resign; to vomit (*colloq*); **throw up (something) against someone** to reproach someone with (something); **throw up the sponge** see under **sponge**. [OE *thrāwan* to turn, to twist; Ger *drehen* to twist; see also **thraw**, **throe**]

throw[2] *thrō*, (*Spenser*) *n* a while. [OE *thrāg*, *thrāh*]

throw[3], **throwe**. See under **throe**.

thru (*esp NAm*). An informal or commercial spelling of **through**, alone or in compounds.

thrum[1] *thrum*, *n* the end of a weaver's thread; any loose thread or fringe; bits of coarse yarn. — *adj* made of or having thrums. — *vt* to furnish, cover or fringe with thrums: — *pr p* **thrumm'ing**; *pa t* and *pa p* **thrummed**. — *adj* **thrumm'y** made of, or like, thrums. — **thrum'-cap** a cap made of thrums or of coarse, shaggy cloth. — *adj* **thrum'-eyed** (*esp* of primulas) short-styled with the stamens in the throat of the corolla (*opp* to *pin-eyed*). — **thrummed hat** (*Shakesp*) a hat made of, fringed with, or covered with thrums. [OE *thrum* (found in combination); Ger *Trumm*]

thrum[2] *thrum*, *vt* and *vi* to strum rhythmically and monotonously; to hum, drone or repeat monotonously; to drum with the fingers: — *pr p* **thrumm'ing**; *pa t* and *pa p* **thrummed**. — *n* an act or the sound of monotonous strumming; a purring (*dialect*). — *n* **thrumm'er**. — *n* and *adj* **thrumm'ing**. — *adv* **thrumm'ingly**. [Imit]

thruppence or **thruppenny**. Informal variants of **threepence**, **threepenny**.

thrush[1] *thrush*, *n* any member of the *Turdinae* subfamily (family *Muscicapidae*) of songbirds, *esp* those of the genus *Turdus*, particularly those species having a spotted breast, eg the song thrush (*Turdus philomelos*) and missel-thrush (*T. viscivorus*); applied to other birds more or less similar, such as some of the babblers. [OE *thrysce*]

thrush[2] *thrush*, *n* a disease, *esp* of children, causing fungous blisters in the mouth and throat; a similar fungal disease affecting the vagina; an inflammation in the frog of a horse's foot. [Cf Dan and Norw *troske*, Swed *torsk* thrush]

thrust[1] *thrust*, *vt* to push, *esp* with sudden force or violence; to impose or inflict (something on someone); to force; to push one's way; to stab, pierce; to intrude (oneself). — *vi* to make a lunge (with *at*); to force one's way (with *into*, *past*, *through* etc): — *pa t* and *pa p* **thrust**. — *n* a sudden or violent push; a pushing force; a stab; pertinacity, determination, drive; the chief message, gist or direction of an argument, etc; the force produced by a jet or rocket engine that drives an aircraft forward, or the measurement of this; the horizontal force on the abutment of an arch; a thrust plane. — *n* **thrust'er** a person who or thing which thrusts; a small rocket engine used as a booster rocket, or to correct course or altitude; an auxiliary propeller on a ship that may be operated athwartships. — *n* and *adj* **thrust'ing**. — **thrust'-hoe** a hoe worked by pushing; **thrust plane** (*geol*) a plane along which a block of lower rocks has overridden higher rocks almost horizontally, a reversed fault of very low hade; **thrust stage** a stage that extends into the auditorium. [ON *thrȳsta* to press]

thrust[2] *thrust*, (*Spenser*) *vi* to thirst. — *n* thirst.

thrutch *thruch*, (*dialect*) *vt* to thrust, press, shove; to crush, squeeze. — *vi* to make one's way by great effort. — Also *n*. [OE *thrycc(e)an*]

thruway. A NAm spelling of **throughway**.

thrymsa or **thrimsa** *thrim'zə*, *-sə*, *n* an Anglo-Saxon gold coin, or its value. [OE, genitive plural of *trymes*, *trimes*, a coin representing the Roman *tremis*, a third of an aureus; influenced by *thri* three]

Thu. *abbrev*: Thursday.

thud *thud*, *n* a dull sound as of a heavy body falling soft. — *vi* to make a thud; to fall with a thud. — *vt* to beat: — *pr p* **thudd'ing**; *pa t* and *pa p* **thudd'ed**. — *adj* **thudd'ing**. — *adv* **thudd'ingly**. [Perh OE *thyddan* to strike]

thug *thug*, *n* a violent ruffian; a cut-throat; (properly *t'hug*) a member of a religious fraternity in India that murdered stealthily by strangling or poisoning with datura, extirpated 1826–35 (*hist*). — *n* **thuggee'**, **thagi'** or **thugg'ism** the practices of the Indian thugs. — *n* **thugg'ery** thuggism; ruffianly or violent behaviour. — *n* **thugg'o** (*colloq*) a ruffian or thug: — *pl* **thugg'os**. [Hindi *thag* cheat]

thuja *thōō'jə*, *-yə*, or **thuya** *thōō'yə*, *n* an evergreen tree of the arbor vitae genus *Thuja*, with small, scalelike leaves. [Gr *thyiā* a kind of juniper]

Thule *thū'lē*, *n* an island six days N of Orkney discovered by Pytheas (4c BC), variously identified as Shetland, Iceland, Norway, Jutland; hence (*usu ultima Thule*) the extreme limit, northernmost land. — *n* **thu'lia** thulium oxide. — *n* **thu'lite** a red zoisite found in Norway. — *n* **thu'lium** a soft metallic element of the lanthanide series (symbol **Tm**; atomic no 69). [L *Thūlē*, from Gr *Thoulē* (understood by P T Cleve (1840–1905, Swedish chemist) as Scandinavia)]

thumb *thum*, *n* the short, thick digit, consisting of two phalanges, on the radial side of the human hand; the part of a glove that covers it; the corresponding digit in other animals, or that of the hind foot, *esp* when opposable; a thumb's breadth, an inch. — *vt* to play, spread, press, touch, wear or smudge with the thumb; to read intensively; to turn (the pages of a book, etc) rapidly with the thumb (also *vi* with *through*); to signal to with the thumb; to hit (in the eye) with the thumb (*boxing*); to handle awkwardly. — *adj* **thumbed** having thumbs; marked by the thumb, worn. — *n pl* **thumb'ikins** or **thumb'kins** (*Scot*) the thumbscrew. — *adj* **thumb'less**. — *adj* **thumb'like**. — *n* **thumb'ling** a pygmy. — *adj* **thumb'y** grubby with thumb-marks; like thumbs, clumsy, awkward. — **thumb'-hole** a hole to insert the thumb in; **thumb index** one arranged as indentations on the outer margins of the pages of books, to facilitate quick reference to a particular place. — *vt* **thumb-in'dex** to provide with a thumb index. — **thumb knot** an overhand knot; **thumb latch** a latch worked by pressure of the thumb; **thumb'-mark** a mark left by the thumb, eg on a book; a thumbprint. — *adj* **thumb'-marked**. — **thumb'nail** the nail of the thumb; a sketch (more *usu* **thumb'nail sketch**) as small as a thumbnail. — *adj* brief, concise. — **thumb'nut** a butterfly-nut; **thumb piano** an mbira (qv); **thumb'piece** a piece that is pressed by the thumb or receives the thumb; **thumb'pot** a very small flowerpot; **thumb'print** an impression of the markings of the thumb, taken as a means of identification; **thumb'-ring** a ring worn on the thumb (*Shakesp*); a ring to protect an archer's thumb; **thumb'screw** an old instrument of torture for compressing the thumb by means of a screw; **thumbs-down** and **thumbs-up** see **thumbs down** and **thumbs up** below; **thumb'stall** a covering or sheath for the thumb; **thumb'tack** (*NAm*) a drawing-pin. — **be all (fingers and) thumbs, one's fingers are all thumbs** or **have one's fingers all thumbs** to be awkward and fumbling; **bite one's thumb** to make a sign threatening revenge; **keep one's thumb on** to keep secret; **rule of thumb** a rough-and-ready practical method, found by experience to be convenient; **thumb a lift** or **ride** (*colloq*) to beg a lift from passing motorists by signalling from the side of the road with the thumb; **thumb one's nose** to cock a snook (*lit* and *fig*) (see under **snook**[3]); **thumbs down** a sign indicating disapproval, prohibition, failure, etc (also *fig*; see also **pollice verso**; *n* **thumbs-down'**); **thumbs up** a sign indicating approval, success, hope of, or wishes for, success etc (also *fig*; *n* **thumbs-up'**); **under one's thumb** under one's domination. [OE *thūma*; Ger *Daumen*]

Thummim *thum'im*. See under **Urim**.

thump *thump*, *n* a dull heavy blow (*esp* with the hand) or its sound. — *vt* to beat with dull heavy blows; to play (a tune), *esp* on a piano, by pounding heavily on the keys (with *out*); to trounce. — *vi* to throb or beat violently; to deliver dull heavy blows (with *at*, *on*, etc); to move with heavy, pounding steps (with *along*, *around*, etc). — *n* **thump'er** someone who, or that which, thumps; anything very big, a big lie, etc (*colloq*). — *adj* **thump'ing** (*colloq*) unusually big. — Also *intensive adv*. — *adv* **thump'ingly**. [Prob imit]

thunbergia *thŏŏn-bûr'ji-ə, tŏŏn-ber'gi-ə*, *n* any plant of the *Thunbergia* genus of evergreen climbing plants of the acanthus family (Acanthaceae). [After the Swedish botanist Carl *Thunberg*, 1743–1828]

thunder *thun'dər*, *n* the deep rumbling sound after a flash of lightning, caused by the disturbance by electricity of atmospheric gases; any loud noise; a thunderbolt; vehement denunciation. — *vi* (*usu* with *it* as the subject) to make the noise of thunder; to make a noise like thunder; to move very heavily and *usu* quickly; to inveigh or denounce with vehemence (with *against*, etc). — *vt* to utter with noise or violent denunciation; to deal or inflict (blows, etc) like thunder. — *n* **thun'derer** a thunder-god, Zeus, Thor, etc; a thundering denunciator, inveigher, orator, journalist or periodical, especially *The Times* or its leader-writer; a person who operates stage-thunder; a bull-roarer. — *n* **thun'dering**. — *adj* discharging thunder; unusually big, tremendous (*colloq*) — Also *adv*. — *adv* **thun'deringly**. — *adj* **thun'derless**. — *adj* **thun'der-like** (*Shakesp*). — *adj* **thun'derous** or **thun'drous** like, threatening, or suggesting thunder. — *adv* **thun'derously**. — *n* **thun'derousness**. — *adj* **thun'dery** indicative of thunder, or accompanied by it. — *adj* **thun'der-and-light'ning** in glaring colours. — *n* a glaringly coloured woollen cloth. — **thun'der-bearer** (*Shakesp*) Jove; **thun'derbird** a huge mythical bird thought by some of the N American nations to cause thunder and lightning; a representation of such a bird; **thun'derbolt** a clap of thunder accompanied by a flash of lightning; a popularly imagined material body seen as lightning; a stone identified with it, such as a belemnite, a stone axe; anything sudden and overwhelming; a missile of the thunder-god; a fulmination; a violent and irresistible destroyer or hero; **thun'derbox** (*slang*) a chamberpot enclosed in a box or stool; any primitive or portable toilet; **thun'derclap** a sudden crash of thunder; anything unexpected and alarming; **thun'dercloud** a cloud charged with electricity; a black or livid threatening appearance; **thun'der-dart** a thunderbolt; **thun'der-darter** or **thun'der-master** (both *Shakesp*) Jove. — *vt* **thun'der-drive** (*Spenser*) to drive with thunderbolts. — **thun'der-egg** (*Austr* and *US*) an agate-filled cavity within a rock mass, or a fossil, supposed to have been flung to earth by lightning; **thun'derflash** a container, such as a blank shell, filled with explosive powder, which makes a flash and a loud explosion when detonated; **thun'der-god** a god that wields thunder; **thun'derhead** a distinctively rounded mass of cumulus cloud projecting above the general cloud mass, *usu* the precursor of a storm; **thun'der-peal** a resounding noise of thunder; **thun'der-plump** a heavy fall of rain in a thunderstorm; **thun'der-sheet** a large sheet of tin-plate shaken to produce the sound of thunder or similar noises as a theatrical, etc sound-effect; **thun'der-shower** a shower accompanied with thunder, or a short heavy shower from a thundercloud; **thun'der-stone** (*Shakesp*) a thunderbolt; **thun'derstorm** continued discharges of electricity from the clouds, producing lightning and thunder, generally with heavy rain. — *vt* **thun'derstrike** to strike with, or as if with, lightning. — **thun'der-stroke** (*Shakesp*) a stroke or blast by lightning. — *adj* **thun'derstruck** (also **thun'der-stricken**) struck by lightning; struck dumb with astonishment, amazed, shocked. — **steal someone's thunder** see under **steal**[1]. [OE *thunor* thunder, *Thunor* the thunder-god, Thor; Ger *Donner* thunder, L *tonāre* to thunder; cf **Thor, Thursday**]

Thur. *abbrev*: Thursday.

Thurberesque *thûr-bə-resk'*, *adj* similar in style, etc to the work of James *Thurber* (1894–1961), US writer and cartoonist.

thurible *thū'ri-bl*, *n* a censer. — *n* **thū'rifer** an acolyte who carries the thurible during a religious ceremony. — *adj* **thurif'erous** incense-bearing. — *n* **thurificā'tion**. — *vt* **thū'rify** to cense. — *n* **thus** (*thus*, *thūs*) frankincense. [L *t*(*h*)*ūs*, *t*(*h*)*ūris* frankincense, from Gr *thyos* a sacrifice; cf **thyme**]

Thursday *thûrz'di*, *n* the fifth day of the week (*orig* sacred to Thunor, the English thunder-god). [OE *Thunres dæg* Thunor's day; ON *Thōrsdagr* Thor's day; Ger *Donnerstag*]

thus[1] *dhus*, *adv* in this or that manner, in the way mentioned or demonstrated; to this degree or extent; accordingly, therefore. — *n* **thus'ness** (*usu facetious*) the state of being thus. — *adv* **thus'wise** in this manner. — **thus far** so far, up till now. [OE *thus*]

thus[2]. See under **thurible**.

thuya. See under **thuja**.

thwack *thwak*, *vt* to whack, strike loudly, *esp* with something flat. — *n* a loud whack. — *n* **thwack'er**. — *n* and *adj* **thwack'ing**. [Perh **whack**, or OE *thaccian* to smack]

thwaite *thwāt*, *n* a piece of reclaimed wasteland (now only found in place names). [ON *thveit*]

thwart *thwört*, *vt* to cross; to cross the path of; to obstruct; to oppose; to frustrate; to balk; to set crosswise; to plough crosswise. — *vi* to cross; to conflict. — *n* frustration; hindrance; a rower's bench placed across a boat. — *adv* crosswise; from side to side. — *adj* crosswise, transverse; cross, adverse; cross, perverse, cross-grained. — *prep* (*obs*) across, athwart. — *adj* **thwar'ted** prevented, frustrated. — *adv* **thwar'tedly**. — *n* **thwar'ter**. — *n* and *adj* **thwar'ting**. — *adv* **thwar'tingly** perversely. — *adv* **thwart'ly**. — *adv* **thwart'ship** or **thwart'ships** across the ship. — *adj* **thwart'ship**. — *adv* **thwart'ways**. — *adv* **thwart'wise**. — *adj* **thwart'wise**. [ON *thvert*, neuter of *thverr* perverse]

thy *dhī*, (*formal*, *liturgical*, *dialect* or *archaic*) *possessive pronoun* or *adj* of thee. — cf **thine**. **[thine]**

Thyestean *thī-es'ti-ən*, *-ə-stē'ən*, *adj* of *Thyestes* (Gr *Thyestēs*), who was made to eat his own sons (*Gr mythol*); cannibal. — Also **Thyestian**.

thyine *thī'in*, *adj* of a tree supposed to be sandarach (Rev 18. 12). [Gr *thyinos*, from *thyon*, *thyā* thyine tree]

thylacine *thī'lə-sēn*, *-sīn*, *-sin*, *n* the so-called Tasmanian wolf (qv). [Gr *thȳlakos* pouch]

thylose, thylosis. See under **tylosis**.

thyme *tīm*, *n* any member of the labiate genus *Thymus*, low half-shrubby plants with two-lipped corolla and calyx and four diverging stamens, *esp* the fragrant garden thyme (*T. vulgaris*) and wild thyme (*T. serpyllum*). — *n* **thymol** (*thī'mol*) an antiseptic phenol obtained from oil of thyme by distillation. — *adj* **thymy** (*tī'mi*) like, smelling of or abounding in thyme. — **basil thyme** a kind of calamint; **lemon thyme** a species of thyme (*T. citriodorus*) with a lemony flavour and scent; **oil of thyme** a fragrant essential oil got from garden and other thymes; **water thyme** Canadian pondweed. [Fr *thym*, from L *thymum*, from Gr *thymon*, from *thyein* to burn a sacrifice]

thymectomy. See under **thymus**.

thymelaeaceous *thim-ə-li-ā'shəs*, *adj* of the **Thymelaeā'ceae** (*-si-ē*), the family of trees and shrubs with simple leaves and tough bark to which *Daphne* (spurge laurel) belongs. [Gr *thymelaiā*, supposed to be a species of Daphne, from *thymos* thyme, and *elaiā* olive]

thymic, thymidine, thymine, thymocyte. See under **thymus**.

thymus *thī'məs*, (*anatom*) *n* a ductless gland near the root of the neck, producing white blood cells at early ages but vestigial in adult humans, that of veal and lamb being called *neck sweetbread*: — *pl* **thy'mī**. — Also *adj*. — *n* **thymec'tomy** surgical removal of the thymus. — *adj* **thy'mic** of or relating to the thymus. — *n* **thy'midine** (*-dēn*) a nucleoside of thymine, found in DNA. — *n* **thymine** (*thī'mēn*) one of the four bases in deoxyribonucleic acids (DNA), in close association with adenine.

— *n* **thy'mocyte** a lymphocyte found in the thymus. — **thymus-derived cells** (*immunol*) lymphocytes derived from the thymus. [Gr *thymos* thymus gland]

thymy. See under **thyme**.

thyratron *thī'rə-tron*, (*electronics*) *n* a gas-filled valve with heated cathode, able to carry very high currents, *orig* a trademark for one containing mercury vapour. — *n* **thyristor** (*thī-ris'tər*; *thyr*atron and trans*istor*) a thyratron-like solid-state semiconductor device. [Gr *thyrā* door]

thyro- *thī-rō-*, *-rə-*, or **thyreo-** *-ri-ō-*, *-ə-*, or **thyr-**, *combining form* denoting thyroid. — *n* **thyrotoxicō'sis** hyperthyroidism; hyperthyroidism with goitre and exophthalmia, Grave's disease. — *n* **thyrotrō'pin** or **thyrotrō'phin** a hormone, produced in the anterior lobe of the pituitary gland, which stimulates the thyroid gland. — *n* **thyrox'in** or **thyrox'ine** an iodine compound, the hormone forming the active principle of the thyroid gland. [**thyroid, thyreoid**]

thyroid *thī'roid*, more correctly but less commonly **thyreoid** *-ri-oid*, *adj* shield-shaped; pertaining to the thyroid gland or the thyroid cartilage. — *n* the thyroid gland, a ductless gland in the neck which secretes thyroxin, whose overactivity may lead to exophthalmic goitre and swelling of the eyeballs, and whose malfunction may lead to cretinism; the principal cartilage of the larynx, forming the Adam's apple. — *n* **thyroidec'tomy** the surgical removal of the thyroid gland. — *n* **thyroidī'tis** inflammation of the thyroid gland. [Gr *thyreoeidēs* shield-shaped, the thyroid cartilage, from *thyreos* a (door-shaped) shield, from *thyrā* a door, and *eidos* form]

Thyrostraca *thī-ros'trə-kə*, *n pl* the cirripedes. [Gr *thyrā* door, valve, and *ostrakon* shell]

thyrsus *thûr'səs*, *n* the wand of Bacchus, a staff wreathed with ivy; a dense panicle broadest in the middle, eg in the lilac and grape (*bot*); *esp* one whose lateral branches are cymose: — *pl* **thyr'si** (*-sī*). — *n* **thyrse** (*thûrs*) a thyrsus: — *pl* **thyr'ses**. — *adj* **thyr'soid** or **thyr'soidal** having the form of a thyrsus. [Gr *thyrsos*]

Thysanoptera *this-ə-nop'tə-rə*, *n pl* an order of insects with fringed wings, some of which are serious pests to fruit, such as thrips. — *adj* **thysanop'terous**. [Gr *thysanos* fringe, tassel, and *pteron* a wing]

Thysanura *this-ə-nū'rə*, *n pl* the bristle-tails, an order of small wingless insects with abdominal appendages. — *n* **thysanū'ran** a member of this order. — *adj* **thysanū'rous**. [Gr *thysanos* a fringe, tassel, and *ourā* a tail]

thyself *dhī-self'*, (*formal, liturgical, dialect or archaic*) *pronoun* emphatic for (and *usu* in apposition to) **thou** or **thee**; reflexive for **thee**. [**thee** (altered to **thy**), and **self**]

Ti (*chem*) *symbol*: titanium.

ti[1] *tē*, (*music*) *n* in the tonic sol-fa system, the note below *doh*, a substitute for *si*, to avoid the initial sound of *so* (*sol*). — Also, in anglicized spelling, **tē**.

ti[2] *tē*, *n* a small Pacific liliaceous tree of the *Cordyline* genus, *esp C. terminalis*, with edible roots, whose sword-shaped leaves are used for thatching and fodder; sometimes also applied (wrongly) to the Australian **tea tree**. [Polynesian]

tiara *ti-ä'rə*, *n* a richly jewelled semicircular head-ornament worn by women; the Jewish high-priest's mitre; the pope's triple crown; the papal dignity; the high ornamental headdress of the ancient Persian kings. — *n* **tiar** (*tī'ər, tīr*; *poetic*) a tiara. — *adj* **tia'ra'd** or **tia'raed** wearing a tiara. [Gr *tiārā*]

Tib *tib*, *n* used as a typical woman's name (*Shakesp*); the ace of trumps in gleek (*obs*; *Scott*). — **Tib'-cat** a she-cat; **Tib's** or **Tibb's Eve** see under **saint**. [**Isabella**]

Tibert *tib'ərt*, *tī'bərt*, *n* the cat in *Reynard the Fox*; in *Shakesp* identified with Tibalt.

Tibet or **Thibet** *ti-bet'*, *n* an autonomous region in W China, with the Himalayas in the south; (**thibet**) a woollen stuff generally printed in colours; a heavy goat's-hair fabric used instead of fur (also **Tibet cloth**). — *adj* **Tibet'an** (or *tib'*) belonging to or characteristic of Tibet. — *n* the language of Tibet, of the Sino-Tibetan family of languages; a native of Tibet. — **Tibetan apso** same as **lhasa apso**.

tibia *tib'i-ə*, *n* (*anatom* and *zool*) the shinbone, the thicker of the two bones of the leg below the knee in humans; the corresponding bone in other vertebrates; the tibiotarsus in birds; the fourth joint of an insect's leg; an ancient flute or pipe: — *pl* **tib'ias** or **tib'iae** (*-i-ē*). — *adj* **tib'ial**. — *n* **tibiotarsus** (*tib-i-ə-tär'səs*) (in birds) a bone formed by the fusion of the tibia and some of the tarsals: — *pl* **tibiotar'si** (*-sī*). [L *tībia* shinbone, flute]

tibouchina *ti-bə-kī-nə*, *-kē'*, *n* a plant of the *Tibouchina* genus of shrubs and herbs (family *Melastomaceae*) with purple flowers. [From a native name in Guiana]

tic *tik*, *n* a convulsive (*esp* nervous) twitching of certain muscles, *esp* of the face; an involuntary habitual response (*fig*). — **tic douloureux** (*-dol-ə-roo'*, *tēk doo-loo-rø*) a disorder of the fifth cranial nerve causing paroxysms of pain in face and forehead. [Fr; cf **tick**[5]]

tical *ti-käl'*, *tik'l*, *n* an obsolete Siamese silver coin, about equal to a rupee, replaced by the baht in 1928; a unit of weight formerly used in Siam (Thailand), approx 14 gms (½ oz). [Port *tical*]

ticca *tik'ə*, (*Ind*) *adj* hired. [Hindi *thīkā* hire]

tice *tīs*, *vt* (*Shakesp*) to entice. — *n* an enticement (*Shakesp*); a yorker (*cricket*). [Aphetic for **entice**, or from OFr *atisier*]

tich, tichy. See under **titch**.

tichorrhine *tī'kə-rīn*, *adj* having an ossified nasal septum, as the fossil woolly rhinoceros. [Gr *teichos* wall, and *rhīs, rhīnos* nose]

tick[1] *tik*, *n* the sound of a watch, clock, etc; a beat; a moment (*colloq*); a small mark (✓) used to indicate or mark off anything as checked, dealt with, required, correct, etc; a light tap or pat (*obs*); the game of tig. — *vi* to make a sound like a mechanical clock; to beat time; to work, be operated; to tap, pat (*obs*; **tick and toy** to dally). — *vt* to mark with a tick (sometimes with *off*); to measure, record, indicate (eg time) by a ticking sound (sometimes with *out*); to dot. — *adj* **ticked** ticked off; speckled. — *n* **tick'er** anything that ticks, *esp* a telegraph instrument that prints signals on a tape, or (*slang*) a watch; the heart (*slang*). — *n* and *adj* **tick'ing**. — **ticker tape** paper ribbon on which a ticker prints; anything similar, such as a streamer (**ticker-tape welcome**, etc, a welcome, etc *esp* in New York, in which ticker tape, confetti, etc is thrown (through the streets) during the progress of a celebrity); **ticking-off'** (*slang*) a reprimand; **tick'-tack** ticking of a clock, etc; (also **tic'-tac**) bookmakers' telegraphy by arm signals; (see also **trick-track**). — Also *adj*. — *adv* with recurring ticking. — **tick-tack-toe'**, **tick-tack-too'** or **tic-tac-to'** (*NAm*) noughts and crosses; **tick-tick'** a ticking; (**tick'-tick**) a child's word for a watch; **tick-tock'** a ticking, as of a big clock; a tapping; (**tick'-tock**) a child's word for a clock. — **in two ticks** in a moment; **make (someone** or **something) tick** (*colloq*) to cause to operate or function; to be the driving force behind; to cause to behave, think, etc in a certain way; **tick away** (of time, life, etc) to pass away with the regularity of the ticking of a clock; **ticked off** (*US slang*) annoyed, angry; **tick off** to mark with a tick; to reprimand (*slang*); **tick over** (of an engine) to run gently, disconnected from the transmission (*n* **tick'-over**); (of a person) to lead an inactive, uneventful existence; to function, operate (*fig*). [ME *tek*; cf Du *tik*, LGer *tikk*; prob imit]

tick[2] *tik*, *n* any of the larger bloodsucking mites of the *Acarina* order; applied also to the sheep-ked and similar degenerate bloodsucking *Diptera* parasitic on cattle and horses, etc; a small and *usu* objectionable person (*colloq*). — **tick bird** the ox-pecker; **tick fever** Rocky Mountain spotted fever or any similar disease transmitted by ticks; East Coast fever; Texas fever. [OE *ticia* (perh for *tīca* or *ticca*); Du *teek*, Ger *Zecke*]

tick[3] *tik*, *n* the cover of a mattress; ticking. — *n* **tick'en** or **tick'ing** the strong, *usu* striped cloth of which ticks are made. [L *thēca*, from Gr *thēkē* a case; see **theca**]

tick[4] *tik* (*slang*) *n* credit, delayed payment (*esp* in the phrase *on tick*); trust. — *vi* to get or give credit. — **tick'-shop** a shop where goods are given on credit. [**ticket**]

tick[5] *tik*, *n* crib-biting; a whimsy. [**tic**]

ticket *tik'it*, *n* a card, slip, or (formerly) placard bearing a notice or serving as a token of any right or debt, eg for admission, travel by public transport, penalty for some offence (*esp* motoring), etc; a tag or label, *esp* one showing the price, size, etc of the item to which it is attached; a certificate (*slang*); discharge from the army (*slang*); a list of candidates put forward by a party for election (*US*); any or all of the principles associated with a particular political party, *esp* as a basis for its election to government (*US*); a visiting-card (*obs*). — *vt* to label, to designate for a particular use; to issue a ticket to: — *pr p* **tick'eting**; *pa t* and *pa p* **tick'eted**. — **ticket agent** an agent who sells tickets on behalf of a theatre, or a railway, etc; **tick'et-collector**; **ticket day** the day before settling-day on the Stock Exchange, when notes of transactions completed are received; **tick'et-holder** a person possessing a ticket, eg for a concert or other event; **tick'et-office** a place where tickets are sold; **tick'et-porter** a licensed porter; a railway porter who collects tickets; **tick'et-punch** an instrument for punching holes in tickets; **tick'et-writer** an expert in lettering who writes placards for shop windows, etc; **tick'et-writing**. — **have tickets on oneself** (*Austr colloq*) to be conceited; **straight ticket** all the nominees of a political party, and no others; **that's (just) the ticket** (*colloq*) that's exactly the right thing or the thing to be done; **ticket of leave** (formerly) a licence to leave prison before expiry of sentence, but with certain restrictions on one; **ticket-of-leave man**. [OFr *estiquet(te)*, from *estiquer* to stick, from OLGer *stekan*; cf **stick**[1]]

tickety-boo or **tickettyboo** *tik'i-ti-boo'*, (*colloq*) *adj* fine, satisfactory. [Ety uncertain]

tickey or **ticky** *tik'i*, (*SAfr*) *n* a former S African coin, a threepenny-bit; now used of a decimal coin of small denomination. [Origin uncertain]

tickle *tik'l*, *vt* to excite with a pleasant thrill; to produce a disturbing feeling in (someone) by a light touch, *usu* tending to excite involuntary laughter, accompanied by attempts to wriggle free; to amuse (*colloq*); to please (*colloq*); to perplex; to touch lightly, *esp* when catching fish using the hands; to beat. — *vi* to be the site of a tickling or itching feeling; to tingle (*Spenser*). — *adj* unstable, in unstable equilibrium, delicately set, insecure (*Spenser*, *Shakesp*); ticklish, nice (*obs* or *dialect*). — *n* an act or feeling of tickling; a slight touch, eg (*cricket*) of the ball with the bat. — *n* **tick'ler** someone who or something which tickles; a puzzle, a difficult problem (*colloq*); a feather-brush; a poker; a cane; a device for reminding; a dram of spirits. — *n* and *adj* **tick'ling**. — *adj* **tick'lish** easily tickled; difficult, needing careful attention, treatment, etc; unstable, precarious; easily affected; nice; critical. — *adv* **tick'-lishly**. — *n* **tick'lishness**. — *adj* **tick'ly** tickling; easily tickled. — **tick'le-brain** (*Shakesp*) strong liquor; **tickler file** (*esp US*) a file containing memoranda, short notes, etc, to remind the user of facts, things to be done, etc. — *n pl* **tick'ly-bend'ers** thin ice that bends underfoot; a game played on it. — **tickle pink** or **tickle to death** (*slang*) to please or amuse very much. [Perh a frequentative of **tick**[1]; perh by metathesis from **kittle**]

tick-tack-toe, **tick-tack-too**. See under **tick**[1].

ticky. See under **tickey**.

Tico *tē'kō*, (*US* and *Central Am*) *n* a native or inhabitant of Costa Rica: — *pl* **Tī'cos**. — *adj* of or relating to Costa Rica or its inhabitants. [Perh from Sp Am *-itico*, a sfx used to form diminutives]

tic-tac. Same as **tick-tack** (see under **tick**[1]).

tic-tac-to. See under **tick**[1].

tid *tid*, (*Scot*) *n* fit time or condition; a mood.

tid or **t.i.d.** *abbrev*: (in prescriptions) *ter in die* (*L*), three times a day.

tidal. See under **tide**[1].

tidbit. Same as **titbit**.

tiddle[1] *tid'l*, *vi* a child's word for urinate. — Also *n*. [cf **widdle**]

tiddle[2] *tid'l*, *vi* to potter, trifle.

tiddled. See under **tiddly**[1].

tiddleywink, **tiddledywinks**. See under **tiddlywink**.

tiddler *tid'lər*, *n* a small fish, eg a minnow or a stickleback; any very small person or thing. [Perh **tittlebat**, **tiddly**[2] or **tiddy**[2]]

tiddley[1] *tid'li*, (*naval colloq*) *adj* smart and trim. — Also **tidd'ly**. [Perh **tiddly**[2] or **tidy**]

tiddley[2]. See under **tiddly**[1,2].

tiddly[1] *tid'li*, (*slang*) *adj* slightly drunk. — *n* alcoholic drink. — Also **tidd'ley**. — *adj* **tidd'led** (*colloq*) slightly drunk. — **on the tiddly** (*slang*) drunk. [Earlier *titley*]

tiddly[2] *tid'li*, (*colloq* or *dialect*) *adj* small, tiny. — Also **tidd'ley**. [Perhaps a childish form of **little**; cf **tiddy**[2]]

tiddlywink *tid'li-wingk*, *n* (also **tiddledywink**, *tid'l-di-*) any of the discs used in **tiddlywinks**, or **tiddledywinks**, a game in which one attempts to flip a small disc into a cup by pressing its edge with a bigger one; an unlicensed pawnshop or beer-house (*slang*).

tiddy[1] *tid'i*, (*Scott*) *n* the four of trumps at gleek.

tiddy[2] *tid'i*, (*dialect*) *adj* very small. [Origin uncertain]

tide[1] *tīd*, *n* ebb and flow, *esp* of the sea twice daily, caused by the gravitational pull of the sun and moon; a time of ebbing, of flowing, or both; a sudden access or flood of feeling, etc; a time or season (*archaic* or *poetic*); a festival (*archaic* or *poetic*); opportunity (*archaic*); a trend; sea-water (*poetic*); a flow; a river, river water, or current (*poetic*); floodtide. — *combining form* (*archaic* or *poetic*) denoting a time or season (*usu* attached to a church festival, as in *Christmas-tide*, *Easter-tide*). — *vt* (*esp fig*) to carry by, or as if by, the tide; to effect by means of the tide. — *vi* to run like the tides; to make one's way by taking advantage of the tides, to be carried by the tide (also *vt* with *it*). — *adj* **tīd'al** of, depending on or regulated by the tide; flowing and ebbing. — *adj* **tide'less**. — **tidal flow** the regulated movement of traffic in both directions along a multi-laned road, the numbers of lanes for travel in each direction being governed by the amount of traffic travelling in that direction; **tidal power** (the generation of electricity by harnessing) the energy of tidal flows; **tidal wave** a huge wave caused by the tides; improperly, a huge wave started by an earthquake and running on with its own momentum (see **tsunami**); a widespread demonstration of public opinion, feeling, etc; the tidewave; **tide'-gate** a gate that admits water at floodtide and retains it at ebb; **tide'-gauge** an instrument for registering the state of the tide continuously; **tide'land** (*US*) land which is submerged at high tide; **tide'-lock** a lock by which ships may pass out or in at all times of the tide; **tide'mark** a line on the shore made by the tide at the water's highest point; a marker indicating the highest point reached by the tide; a mark of the limit of washing (*jocular fig*); **tide'mill** a mill with a waterwheel moved by tidewater; **tide race** a swift tidal current; **tide'-rip** disturbed sea due to currents; a tidal wave; **tides'man** a customs officer who waited the arrival of ships (*orig* coming in with the tide); **tide table** a table of times of high tide; **tide'-waiter** a tidesman; a person who waits to see how things go before acting; **tide'waitership**; **tide'water** water brought by the tide; river water affected by the tide (*US*); coastal land, seaboard (*US*); **tide'wave** the tide regarded as a wave passing round the earth; **tide'way** a track followed by the tide, *esp* a channel through which there is a strong current or tide. — **tide over** to carry (someone) over, or (*old*) to get over (a critical or difficult period). [OE *tīd*; Du *tijd*, Ger *Zeit*]

tide[2] *tīd*, (*archaic*) *vi* to happen. [OE (*ge*)*tīdan*; cf **betide**]

tide[3]. Spenser's spelling of **tied**.

tidings *tī'dingz*, (*esp literary*) *n pl* news. [Late OE *tīdung*, from OE *tīdan* to tide, happen, or from ON *tīthindi* events, tidings]

tidivate. Same as **titivate**.

tidy *tī'di, adj* trim; orderly; neat; fairly good or big, considerable (*colloq*); seasonable (*obs*); in good condition or order (*dialect*); plump (*dialect*); comely (*dialect*); shapely (*dialect*). — *n* a receptacle for odd scraps; a cover for a chair-back; an act of tidying. — *vt* to make neat and tidy; to clear away for the sake of tidiness: — *pr p* **tī'dying**; *pa t* and *pa p* **tī'died**. — *adv* **tī'dily**. — *n* **tī'diness**. [**tide**[1]; cf Ger *zeitig*]

tie[1] *tī, vt* to bind; to fasten; to knot; to make (a knot, etc); to restrict, restrain; to unite; to mark (two notes of the same pitch) with a curved line indicating that they are to be played as a single sustained, not repeated, note (*music*); to perform in this way (*music*); to limit; to oblige; to equal in competition, etc; to subject to bonds; to confirm (*Shakesp*); to ligature; to make (an artificial fly for angling). — *vi* to be equal in votes, score, etc; (of dogs) to linger on the scent: — *pr p* **ty'ing**; *pa t* and *pa p* **tied** (*tīd*). — *n* a knot, bow, etc; a bond; a string, ribbon, etc, for tying; a band of material passed under the collar of a shirt, etc and tied under the chin, *esp* one having one end wider than the other, tied to hang down the shirt front with the wider end overlying the narrower, worn *esp* by men, or as part of a uniform; a shoe (*US*); a structural member sustaining only a tension; a railway sleeper (*NAm*); a restraint; an obligation; a mode of tying; an equality in score, votes, etc; a match, *esp* one at any stage of a tournament in which the losers are eliminated; a curved line drawn over notes of the same pitch to be performed as one, sustained not repeated (*music*); a tie-wig (*obs*). — *adj* **tied** having been tied; having a draw or equality as a result; (of a public house or garage) denoting one whose tenant is obliged to get his or her supplies from one particular brewer or distiller, or oil- and petrol-producer; (of a house, cottage, etc) denoting one whose tenant may occupy the premises only as long as he or she is employed by the owner. — *adj* **tie'less**. — *n* **tī'er** a person who ties; a child's apron (*US*). — **tie'back** a length of fabric or ribbon used to tie a curtain to one side; **tie beam** a beam connecting the lower ends of rafters to prevent their moving apart; **tie'-break** a number of points played at the end of a tied set to decide the winner (*tennis*); generally, a situation in a contest when a tie-breaker is required to decide the winner; **tie'-breaker** a tie-break; any game(s), question(s) or competition(s) intended to break a tie and decide a winner; **tie clip** an ornamental clip which attaches one's tie to one's shirt; **tie-dye'ing** a method of hand-dyeing textiles in which patterns are produced by binding or knotting parts of the fabric so as to resist the dye (Also **tie'-and-dye'**); **tie'-in** a connection; something, *esp* a book, which ties in with, is connected or promoted with something else, eg a film or TV programme; **tie line** a telephone line used solely for connecting two private branch exchanges (also **inter-switchboard line**); **tie'-neck** a collar terminating in two long pieces that can be tied in a bow, etc under the chin. — *adj* (of a blouse, etc) having a tie-neck. — **tie'pin** an ornamental pin for securing one's tie to one's shirt; **tie'rod** a rod, eg in a vehicle, that prevents parts from moving apart; **tie'tac** or **tie'tack** a tie clip; **tie'-up** a standstill; an entanglement; a connection; a business association; tape for tying a bookbinding or portfolio; an animal tied up for a bait; **tie'-wig** a wig tied with ribbon at the back. — **fit to be tied** (*colloq*) extremely angry; **tie down** to fix (*lit* and *fig*); to bind by conditions, etc; **tie in with** or **tie up with** to agree with; to be closely associated with; to be linked with, as eg a book containing the story of, or a story concerning the characters in, a popular film or TV series; **tie up** to parcel up with string; to tie so as to remain up, hanging, etc; to tether, secure or bind by tying; to moor; to invest, make illiquid (funds, etc); to secure against squandering, alienation, etc, or restrict the use of, by conditions. [OE *tēah* band, string, *tīgan* to tie]

tie[2]. See under **tye**[1].

tie[3]. See under **tye**[2].

tier *tēr, n* a row, level, rank, or layer, *esp* one of several placed one above another; a row of guns; a mountain range (*Tasmania*). — Also in combination. — *vt* and *vi* to pile or be piled in tiers. — *adj* (also in combination) **tiered**. [OFr *tire* sequence]

tierce *tērs, n* a third (*obs*); one-third of a pipe (of wine), *approx* 35 British or 42 US gallons; a cask or vessel of that capacity; (*tûrs*) a sequence of three cards of the same suit; a third (*music*); the note two octaves and a third above a given note (*music*); a parrying position, or the corresponding thrust (*fencing*); the third canonical hour of the day (ending 9 am); the canonical office taking place at that hour, the terce (*eccles*). — *adj* **tiercé** (*tēr'si*; Fr, divided into three parts) or **tierced** (of the surface of a shield) divided into three equal parts, each of a different metal or colour (*heraldry*). — *n* (in horse-racing) a system of betting by which the first, second and third horses must be named in the right order, or a race for which this system obtains. — *n* **tier'ceron** (*-sə-ron*; *archit*) (in vaulting) a subordinate rib springing from the intersection of two other ribs. — **tierce de Picardie** (*tyers də pē-kar-dē*; *music*) a major third closing a piece otherwise in a minor key. [OFr *tiers*, *tierce*, from L *tertia* (*pars*)]

tiercel, tiercelet. See under **tercel**.

tierceron. See under **tierce**.

tiercet. Same as **tercet**.

tiers état *tyer-zā-tä*, (*Fr hist*) *n* the third estate, or commons. [Fr]

TIFF (*comput*) *abbrev*: tagged-image file format, a standard graphics file format.

tiff[1] *tif, n* a slight quarrel; a display of irritation, a pet, huff. — *vi* to be in a huff; to squabble. — Also (*esp Scot*) **tift**. [Prob imit]

tiff[2] *tif, n* stale, sour, or thin liquor; a sip; a dram. — *vi* to sip; to drink; to lunch. — Also (*Scot* and *dialect*) **tift**. — *n* **tiff'ing** sipping; (also **tiff'in**; *esp* as used by the British Raj in colonial India) lunch, a light meal. [Perh orig slang]

tiff[3] *tif*, (*obs*) *vt* and *vi* to dress, trick out. [OFr *tiffer* (Fr *atiffer*), to adorn]

Tiffany *tif'ə-ni, adj* denoting objects designed or produced by C L *Tiffany* (1812–1902), founder of the New York jeweller's, Tiffany and Co., or (*esp*) his son L C Tiffany (1848–1933), Art Nouveau glassmaker and designer. — **Tiffany glass** another name for **favrile** (qv); **Tiffany lamp** a lamp with a distinctive umbrella-shaped shade made of favrile.

tiffany *tif'ə-ni, n* a silk-like gauze. — *adj* of tiffany; transparent. [Gr *theophaneia* theophany, or *diaphaneia* transparency]

tiffin. See under **tiff**[2].

tifosi *ti-fō'zē*, (*Ital*) *n pl* fans, devotees, *esp* of some sport. — *sing* **tifō'sō**. [*tifo* typhus, fanaticism]

tift. See under **tiff**[1,2].

tig[1] *tig, n* a touch; a twitch; a game in which someone who is 'it' chases the others, the person he or she touches then becoming 'it'. — *vt* to touch, *esp* in the game of tig: — *pr p* **tigg'ing**; *pa t* and *pa p* **tigg'ed**. [Poss a form of **tick**[1]]

tig[2] *tig, n* an old drinking-cup with two or more handles.

tige *tēzh, n* the shaft of a column. [Fr, from L *tībia* a pipe]

tiger *tī'gər*, (*fem*) **tigress** *tī'gris, n* a fierce, yellowish, black-striped Asiatic animal, one of the two largest cats (*Panthera tigris*); the leopard (*SAfr*); the jaguar (*American tiger*) (*US*); the puma (*red tiger*); a ferocious or bloodthirsty person; a flashy vulgarian; a formidable opponent or competitor; a boy in livery *usu* perched behind a vehicle; a yell to supplement a cheer (*US*); a tiger beetle, tiger moth, tiger shark, tiger lily, etc. — *adj* **ti'gerish** or **ti'grish** like a tiger in manner, *esp* fierce-tempered; flashy. — *adv* **ti'gerishly** or **tī'grishly**. — *n* **ti'gerishness** or **tī'grishness**. — *n* **ti'gerism** swagger. — *adj* **ti'gerly**. — *adj* **ti'gery, ti'grine** (*-grīn*) or **ti'groid** like a tiger. — **tiger badge** a proficiency badge awarded by the Himalayan Club to Sherpas; **tiger beetle** any flesh-eating beetle of the Cicindelidae, found mainly in warm, dry regions; **tiger cat** a general name for a middle-sized striped or spotted wild cat, such as the margay, ocelot, serval, etc; **tiger country** (*golf slang*) dense rough; **ti'ger-eye** or **ti'ger's-eye** a golden-brown striped pseudomorph of quartz after crocidolite, used eg in jewellery; a pottery glaze resembling this; **tiger fish** a large game fish of African rivers, *Hydrocyenus goliath*; **ti'ger-flower** a Mexican iridaceous plant (genus *Tigridia*) with purple, yellow or white streaked flowers. — *adj* **ti'ger-foot'ed** (*Shakesp*) fiercely swift. — **tiger lily** a lily with black-spotted orange flowers; **tiger moth** any one of the Arctiidae family of moths, with long and *usu* brightly coloured wings; **tiger nut** the edible rhizome of *Cyperus esculentus*, a European sedge; the chufa (*US*); **tiger shark** a voracious striped shark of the Indian Ocean (*Galeocerdo cuvieri*); **tiger snake** the most deadly of Australian snakes (*Notechis scutatus*), brown with black crossbands; **tiger tail** a type of fast-growing hybrid worm; **tiger team** (*US*) a group of counter-intelligence agents who test the security of military bases; a group of computer hackers who are employed to test the secureness of a computer system; **tiger wolf** the spotted hyena; the thylacine; **ti'ger-wood** any of several showy black-striped woods used in cabinet-making. [Fr *tigre*, from L *tigris*, from Gr *tigris*, prob from Zend]

tiggywinkle *tig'i-wink-əl*, (*colloq*) *n* a hedgehog. [Appar coined by Beatrix Potter (1866–1943), English children's author, perh from dialect *tig* little pig]

tight[1] *tīt*, *adj* close; compact; close-fitting; too close-fitting; cramped; (of a schedule, timetable, etc) allowing little space, time or opportunity for deviation from plan; (of a situation) difficult or dangerous; (of a contest) closely fought; (of style) concise; taut, not slack; (of eg control) very firm, strict; precise; under control; firmly fixed; impervious, not leaky, proof; trim; neat; snug; competent; hampered or characterized by lack of money; (of money or a commodity) scarce, hard to obtain; unwilling to part with money, miserly (*colloq*); intoxicated (*colloq*); (of a person, muscle, etc) showing tension, taut, not relaxed (*colloq*); (of a team of people) working or performing well together, well-co-ordinated; denoting play in set scrums and line-outs (*Rugby football*). — *adv* tightly; soundly. — *n* (*Rugby football*) tight play. — (In combination) **-tight** signifying proof against or impervious to the thing specified. — *vt* and *vi* **tight'en** (sometimes with *up*) to make or grow tight or tighter. — *n* **tight'ener** a person or thing that tightens; a tensor (*anatom*); a heavy meal (*slang*). — *adj* **tight'ish**. — *adv* **tight'ishly**. — *adv* **tight'ly**. — *n* **tight'ness**. — *n pl* **tights** a close-fitting garment, often made of nylon, covering the lower part of the body and the legs *esp* as worn by women and girls as an alternative to stockings; close-fitting men's breeches (*hist*). — **tight arse** or (*US*) **tight ass** (*slang*) a mean, tight-fisted person; **tight end** (*Am football*) a player who is positioned at the outside of the offensive line. — *adj* **tight'-fisted** (*colloq*) stingy. — **tight-head prop** (*Rugby football*) the prop forward on the right of the front row of the scrum in either team. — **tight junction** (*biol*) a junction between epithelial cells where the membranes are in close contact, with no intervening intercellular space. — *adj* **tight-knit'** or **tightly-knit'** close-knit; closely integrated; tightly organized. — *vt* and *vi* **tight-lace'** (*adj* **tight'-lace**). — *adj* **tight-laced'** strait-laced. — *n* **tight-lā'cer**. — *n* **tight-lā'cing** compression of the waist by tight clothes. — *adj* **tight'-lipped** uncommunicative. — **tight'rope** a taut rope or wire on which feats of balancing and acrobatics are performed; a middle course between dangerous or undesirable alternatives (*fig*); **tight'wad** (*colloq*; *esp NAm*) a skinflint, miser. — **a tight corner** or **spot** a difficult situation; **run a tight ship** to be in control of an efficient, well-run organization or group; **tighten the screws** to increase pressure (*esp* on someone to do something). [Earlier *thight*, appar from an older form of ON *thēttr*, influenced by various English words of similar meaning; cf Ger *dicht*]

tight[2] *tīt*, (*Spenser*) *pa t* and *pa p* of **tie**.

tight[3]. See under **tite**.

tigon *tī'gon*, *-gən*, *n* the offspring of a tiger and a lioness. — Also **tī'glon**. [*ti*ger and *l*i*on*]

tigress, **tigrine**, **tigrish**, **tigroid**. See under **tiger**.

tika *tē'kə*, *n* a red mark or pendant on the forehead of Hindu women, formerly of religious significance but now worn for ornament. [Hindi]

tike. Same as **tyke**.

tiki *tik'ē*, *n* an image, often in the form of a small greenstone ornament, representing an ancestor, in some Polynesian cultures worn as an amulet or charm. [Maori]

tikka *tik'ə*, (*Ind cookery*) *adj* denoting a dish of meat or vegetables marinated in yogurt and spices and cooked in a *tandoor* or clay oven, eg *chicken tikka*, *lamb tikka*. [Hindi *ṭikka*]

til *til*, *tēl*, *n* sesame. — Also **teel**. — **til'-oil**; **til'-seed**. [Hindi *til*, from Sans *tila*]

tilapia *ti-lap'i-ə*, *-lā'* *n* any member of an African freshwater genus (*Tilapia*) of edible cichlid fishes. [New L]

tilbury *til'bə-ri*, *n* a light, open, two-wheeled, horse-drawn carriage seating two people. [Said to be so named from its first maker]

tilde *til'də*, *-di*, *-də*, *tild*, *n* the diacritical sign over *n* in Spanish to indicate the sound *ny* — thus *ñ* (as in *cañon*); used in Portuguese over *a* and *o* to indicate nasalization. [Sp, from L *titulus* a title]

tile *tīl*, *n* a slab of baked clay (or a substitute) for covering roofs, floors, etc; a tube-shaped piece of baked clay used in pipes for drains; a piece in the boardgame of mah-jongg; tiling, a tiled area; a hat (*slang*); a top hat (*Scot*). — *vt* to cover with tiles; to drain by means of tiles; to secure against intrusion by placing a person at the door; to bind to secrecy. — *adj* **tiled** covered with tiles; imbricated; (of fish) sun-dried (*Scott*). — *n* **ti'ler** a maker or layer of tiles; a freemasons' doorkeeper — also **tyl'er**. — *n* **til'ery** a place where tiles are made. — *n* **til'ing** an area covered with tiles; tiles collectively; the act of laying tiles. — **tile'-hat** (*Scot*) a top hat. — *adj* **tile'-hung** (of a wall) covered with flat roofing tiles as protection against the weather. — **tile'-red** a brownish-red, the colour of baked tiles; **tile'-stone** a flat stone used for roofing, *esp* a thin-bedded sandstone. — **Dutch tiles** enamelled earthenware tiles, *usu* decorated in blue, with scriptural subjects, etc, for chimney-pieces, etc; **have a tile loose** (*slang*) to be a little mad; **hung tiles** tiles hung vertically, covering a wall; **on the tiles** (*colloq*) at play, having a wild time, on a spree. [OE *tigele*, from L *tēgula*, from *tegere* to cover]

tilefish *tīl'fish*, *n* an American Atlantic food fish noted for the sudden changes in its numbers. [Appar from its generic name, Lopholatilus, and perh its tile-like spotted pattern]

tiler, **tilery**. See under **tile**.

Tilia *til'i-ə*, *n* the lime or linden genus of flowering trees and shrubs, giving name to the family **Tiliā'ceae** (*-si-ē*), related to the mallows. — *adj* **tiliā'ceous** belonging to the family. [L *tilia* lime-tree]

tiling. See under **tile**.

till[1] *til*, *n* a drawer or receptacle for money in or behind a counter; a compartment or drawer in a chest, cabinet, etc (*obs*). [Cf ME *tillen* to draw, OE *fortyllan* to draw aside, seduce]

till[2] *til*, *prep* up to the time of; to, towards (*Scot*); to (with the infinitive) (*Scot*). — *conj* up to the time when. [OE (Northumbrian) *til*, from ON *til*; cf OE *till* a fixed point, Ger *Ziel* end, goal]

till[3] *til*, *vt* to work (land), cultivate; to set (*obs* or *dialect*). — *adj* **till'able** arable. — *n* **till'age** the act or practice of tilling; husbandry; a place tilled. — *n* **till'er**. — *n* **till'ing**. [OE *tilian* to aim at, till, from *till* limit; see ety for **till**[2]]

till[4] *til*, *n* a stiff impervious clay (*orig Scot*); boulder-clay (*geol*); shale (*mining*). — *n* **till'ite** indurated till. — *adj* **till'y**. [Cf **thill**[2]]

tillandsia *ti-land'zi-ə*, *n* any plant of the mainly epiphytic tropical American genus (*Tillandsia*) of the pineapple family. [So called from Finno-Swedish botanist, Elias *Tillands* (d. 1693)]

tiller[1] *til'ər*, *n* the handle or lever for turning a rudder. — *adj* **till'erless**. — **till'er-chain** or **-rope** the chain or rope connecting the tiller with the steering-wheel. [ME *tillen* to draw (see **till**[1]), or OFr *telier* crossbow stock, from LL *tēlārium* a weaver's beam, from L *tēla* a web]

tiller[2] *til'ər*, **teller** or **tellar** *tel'ər*, *n* a sapling; a shoot from a tree stump; a sucker from the base of a stem; a side-shoot from the base as in corn, etc. — *vi* to form tillers. [OE *telgor* shoot, twig]

tiller[3]. See under **till**[3].

tillite, **tilly**. See under **till**[4].

tilly-vally *til'i-val'i* or **tilly-fally** *-fal'i*, (*Shakesp*) *interj* expressing impatience at what has been said. — Also **till'ey-vall'ey**.

tilt[1] *tilt*, *n* a cover, awning, for a wagon, boat, etc; a tent; a hut. — *vt* to cover with a tilt. — *adj* **tilt'ed**. — **tilt'-boat** a large rowing-boat with a tilt. [OE *teld*; cf Ger *Zelt*]

tilt[2] *tilt*, *vi* to lean, heel over; to slope; (of a ship) to pitch; to slant, *esp* in a vertical plane; to joust, ride and thrust with a spear; to charge, attack (with *at*; *lit* or *fig*); to take part in a contest with (with *with*); to criticize (with *at*); to thrust. — *vt* to incline, slant; to tip out, by tilting; to move by tilting; to forge using a tilt-hammer. — *n* an act of tilting; a condition of being tilted; a slope; a joust, a charge against an opponent with a lance; an encounter, attack, etc; a dispute; a duel; a thrust; a tilt-yard. — *adj* **tilt'able**. — *n* **tilt'er**. — *n* **tilt'ing**. — **tilt** or **tilting fillet** (*building*) a triangular roofing timber used at eaves to tilt the undereaves course of slates, etc to close off the front edge; **tilt'-hammer** a heavy pivoted hammer lifted by a cam, used in forging; **tilt'-yard** (*hist*) a place for tilting, jousting. — **full tilt** at full speed, headlong. [OE *tealt* tottering]

tilth *tilth*, *n* cultivation; cultivated land; the depth of soil turned up in cultivation. [From **till**[3]]

Tim. (*Bible*) *abbrev*: (the Letters to) Timothy.

timarau. See under **tamarau**.

timariot *ti-mä'ri-ot*, (*hist*) *n* a Turkish feudal militiaman. [Fr, from Turk *timār*]

timbal or **tymbal** *tim'bl*, (*archaic*) *n* a kettledrum. — *n* **timbale** (*tɛ̃-bal*, *tam'bal*, *tim'bl*) a dish of meat, fish, etc cooked in a cup-shaped mould or shell; a mould of pastry. [Fr *timbale*; see **atabal**; appar influenced by L *tympanum*]

timber *tim'bər*, *n* wood suitable for building or carpentry, whether growing or cut; standing trees of oak, ash, elm, or (locally by custom) other kinds suitable for timber, forming part of an inheritance (*English law*); material generally; a beam or large piece of wood in a framework, of eg a house, ship, etc; familiarly, a wooden object or part; a wooden leg; wood (*dialect*); woodland, forest-land (*NAm*). — *adj* of timber; wooden; wooden in tone, unmusical (*Scot*). — *vt* to provide with timber or beams; to build (*obs*). — *interj* a warning given when a tree being felled is about to fall. — *adj* **tim'bered** built, constructed, *esp* of wood; provided with timber; shored up with timber; (of country) wooded; *appar* massive (*Spenser*). — *n* **tim'bering** timber collectively; work in timber. — **half-timbered** see under **half**. — **tim'ber-head** the top of a ship's timber rising above the deck and used as a bollard; a bollard placed in a similar position; **tim'ber-hitch** see under **hitch**; **tim'berland** (*US*) land covered with trees used for timber; **tim'berline** the upper limit of timber-trees on the mountains, etc; **tim'ber-man** a person responsible for the timbers in a mine; **tim'ber-mare** see under **horse**; **tim'ber-toes** a person with a wooden leg; **tim'ber-tree** a tree suitable or grown for timber; **timber wolf** an American variety of the common wolf, the grey wolf; **tim'beryard** a yard or place where timber is stored or sold. [OE *timber* building, wood, *timbrian* to build; Ger *Zimmer* room]

timbó *tim-bō'*, *n* a S American sapindaceous climbing plant (*Paullinia pinnata*); a fish-poison and insecticide obtained from its bark: — *pl* **timbós'**. [Guaraní]

timbre *tɛ̃br'*, *tim'bər*, *tam'bər*, *n* the quality of a sound, tone-colour, as opposed to pitch and loudness. [OFr, bell, from L *tympanum* a drum]

timbrel *tim'brəl*, (*hist*, *esp Bible*) *n* an Oriental tabor or tambourine. — *adj* **tim'brel'd** (*Milton*) sung to the timbrel. [OFr *timbre*, from L *tympanum* drum]

timbrology *tim-brol'ə-ji*, **timbromania** (*-brō-mā'ni-ə*) and **timbrophily** (*-brof'i-li*), *n* old-fashioned words for stamp-collecting. — *n* **timbrol'ogist**, **timbromā'niac** and **timbroph'ilist**. [Fr *timbre* postage-stamp]

Timbuctoo *tim-buk-tōō'*, *n* any distant place. [*Timbuktu*, a town in Mali on the River Niver]

time *tīm*, *n* a concept arising from change experienced and observed, expressed by past, present and future, and often measured by the amount of turning of the earth on its axis; a quantity measured by the angle through which the earth turns on its axis; (with *cap*) any of the clock-settings used as standard times in the various time zones, as in *Pacific Time*, *Central European Time*, etc; a moment at which, or stretch of existence during which, things happen; season; the due, appointed, suitable or usual occasion of occurrence; the hour of death or of birth or coming into existence; a spell, interval, period; the actual occasion or period of being something or somewhere, eg apprenticeship, residence, prison sentence, student days, life, etc; (a given period in) the existence of the world; leisure or opportunity long enough for a purpose; a spell of exciting, *usu* pleasurable, experience; the duration, or shortest duration, of performance, as in a race; rhythm, tempo (*music*); the duration of a note (*music*); rate of speed; a unit of duration in metre, a mora (*prosody*); an occasion; an occasion regarded as one of a recurring series; one of a number of multiplied instances; generalized as an indication of multiplication (eg 3 *times* = multiplied by 3); (the rate of) payment for work by the hour, day, etc; back-pay (also **back time**); a reckoning of time; an interval; past existence; an allotted period, *esp* its completion, as in boxing rounds, permitted drinking hours, etc; the call, bell, whistle, buzzer or other signal announcing this; (in *pl*) the contemporary, obtaining conditions; (in *pl* with *cap*) often the name of a newspaper; (with *cap*) a personification of time, a bald-headed old man with a forelock, a beard, a scythe, and often an hourglass. — *vt* to arrange, fix or choose a time for; to mark, measure, adjust or observe the rhythm or time of; to ascertain the time taken by; to regulate the time of. — *vi* to keep or beat time. — *adj* of or relating to time; reckoned by time; timed; of or for a future time. — *interj* indicating that time is up, or that action is now forbidden or permitted. — *adj* **timed**. — *adj* **time'less** independent of time; unconnected with the passage of time; eternal, unaffected by time; untimely (*archaic*); premature (*Shakesp*); ill-timed; failing to keep time or rhythm. — Also *adv*. — *adv* **time'lessly**. — *n* **time'lessness**. — *n* **time'liness**. — *adj* **time'ly** coming or occurring at a suitable or the correct time; well-timed; in good time, early; seasonable; temporal (*obs*); of the time of day (*Spenser*); in time, keeping time (*Spenser*). — *adv* (*archaic*) early, soon; in due time or in good time. — *adj* **timeous** or **timous** (*tī'məs*; chiefly *Scot*) in good time; seasonable. — *adv* **time'ously** or **ti'mously** in good time. — *n* **tī'mer** a person or thing that times anything; a clocklike device which sets something off or switches something on or off at a pre-set time; (in combination) signifying a person who belongs to, works for, etc, a specified time. — *n* **ti'ming** fixing, choosing, adjusting, ascertaining, or recording of times; (the co-ordination of) departure and arrival times; co-ordination in time; (in an internal-combustion engine) the regulation of the valve-operating mechanism so that the valves open and close in correct relation to the crank. — *n* **ti'mist** a time-server (*obs*); a person who keeps in time; a person who times his or her movements. — **time'-ball** a ball mounted on a vertical pole, eg on top of a high building, that drops at a regular point in each day as an indication of mean time; **time'-bargain** a contract to buy or sell at a certain time in the future. — *adj* **time'-barred** disallowed because out of legal time limits. — *adj* **time-beguil'ing** making time seem to pass quickly. — *adj* **time-bett'ering** (*Shakesp*) in which times are growing better. — *adj* **time-bewast'ed** (*Shakesp*) spent by time. — **time'-bill** a timetable; **time bomb** a bomb that is exploded by a time-fuse; a routine actuated at a particular time or date which destroys data held in a computer program; **time capsule** a capsule containing objects, etc, representative of the current time, buried in the ground or set in the foundations of a building for discovery at a future date; **time'card** a card for use with a time clock; **time charter** a hire agreement valid for a specified period of time; **time clock** a clocklike apparatus which stamps on cards the time of arrival and departure of eg office or factory workers; **time code** a track separate from the main one on a video or audio tape, on which time is recorded digitally, to help editing. — *adj* **time'-consum'ing** requiring much, or too much time; wasting time. — **time deposit** a bank deposit from which withdrawals may be made only after a certain time or with due notice; **time dilation** (*phys*) the principle that the time interval between two events appears to be larger when they occur in a reference frame which is moving relative to the observer's reference frame, than when they occur at rest relative to the observer — a consequence of the special theory of relativity. — *adj* **time'-expired** having completed a term of enlistment. — **time exposure** (*photog*) an exposure for a relatively long time (*usu* seconds) in comparison with one called instantaneous; **time'frame** a limited or restricted period of time, eg as allotted for an event; **time fuse** a fuse preset to act at a definite time; **time gun** a gun fired to indicate a certain hour. — *adj* **time'-honoured** (of a custom) honoured or respected on account of antiquity. — **time immemorial** the distant past no longer remembered; time before legal memory, fixed by statute as before 1189 (*law*); **time'keeper** a clock, watch or other instrument that measures time; a person who keeps account of worker's hours; an employee thought of in terms of his or her punctuality; a person who beats or observes time; **time'-killer** a person or thing that kills time (see **kill**). — *n* and *adj* **time'-killing.** — **time lag** the interval of delay between two connected events or phenomena. — *adj* **time'-lapse** of or relating to **time-lapse photography**, a method of recording and condensing long or slow processes by taking a large number of photographs at regular intervals, the film made from these being projected at normal speed. — **time limit** a time within which something has to be done; **time loan** a loan repayable by a specified date. — *adj* **timely-part'ed** (*Shakesp*) having died at a natural time. — **time machine** a hypothetical machine by which one may travel to the future or past, through time; **time out** a short break during a sporting contest (eg *Am football*) for rest, discussion of tactics, substitution of a player, etc; any similar short suspension of activity; a cancellation action or automatic logoff that takes place if the user does not input data or a command within a given time, or if a terminal fails to make contact with a peripheral device (eg a printer) within a given time (*comput*); **time'piece** a piece of machinery for keeping time, *esp* one that does not strike but is bigger than a watch; **time'-pleaser** (*Shakesp*) a time-server. — *adj* **time'-release** or **timed'-release** slow-release. — *n* and *adj* **time'-saving.** — **time'scale** the time envisaged for the carrying out of (the stages of) a project; a statement of the times of occurrence, completion, etc of a series of processes, stages, etc. — *adj* **time'-served** (of a craftsman) having completed his or her apprenticeship, fully trained. — **time'-server** a person who cynically or servilely suits his or her opinions to the times or those in authority for the time; **time'-service.** — *n* and *adj* **time'-serving.** — **time'-share** the time-sharing of property, etc; such a property. — Also *adj.* — **time'-sharer**; **time'-sharing** the optimum utilization of a computer and its peripheral devices whereby the differential processing-time of each machine is allowed for, and is used accordingly; a scheme by which a person buys the right to use a holiday home for the same specified period of time each year for a specified number of years; **time sheet** a record of the time worked by a person; **time signal** an intimation of the exact time given by radio or otherwise from an observatory; **time signature** (*music*) an indication of rhythm (in the form of two figures placed one over the other, the top one representing the number of beats to the bar, and the bottom, the length of the beat) at the beginning of a line or wherever there is a change; **time slot** a particular period of time in the day or week allocated to a certain radio or television programme; a particular period assigned to a certain purpose, etc; **time spirit** the genius of the age; **time switch** one working automatically at a set time; **time'table** a table of times, eg of classes, events, trains, etc. — *vt* to insert into a timetable; to plan, divide into sessions, etc, according to a timetable. — **time'-thrust** (*fencing*) a thrust made at the moment the opponent draws breath for his or her thrust; **time trial** an event, *esp* in cycling, in which competitors set off one at a time, and attempt to cover a set distance in the shortest time; **time'-trialling**; **time unit**; **time warp** (in science fiction, etc) a hypothetical distortion in the time continuum, allowing one to pass from the present to the past or future, or to stand still in the present; **time work** work paid for by the hour or the day (as opposed to *piece-work*). — *adj* **time'-worn** worn or decayed by time. — **time zone** one of 24 longitudinal divisions of the globe, each 15° wide, having a standard time throughout its area; a similar zone adapted to a particular country. — **against time** with the aim or necessity of finishing by a certain time; **ahead of one's time** having ideas, etc too advanced or progressive to be acceptable at the time; **ahead of time** earlier than expected; **all in good time** in due course; soon enough; **all the time** continuously, constantly; **apparent time** time according to the real sun, ie sundial time without regard to the equation of time; **astronomical time** (till 1925) the time past mean noon, now midnight, reckoned on to twenty-four hours in mean time; **at one time** formerly; simultaneously; **at the same time** simultaneously; notwithstanding; **at the time** at the time stated or under consideration; **at times** at distant intervals; occasionally; **before one's time** ahead of one's time (see above); **behind the times** not abreast of changes; **behind time** late; **between times** in the intervals; **by times** betimes; **common time** (*music*) time with two beats or a multiple of two beats to a bar or other measure (**compound common time** where each beat is of three quavers or crotchets); **do time** (*slang*) to serve a sentence of imprisonment; **for a time** for a while; temporarily; **for the time being** at the present time or the actual time in question; **from time to time** now and then; **gain time** to provide oneself with more time to do something (eg by delaying something else); **half the time** (*colloq*) as often as not, frequently; **have a good time** to enjoy oneself; **have a time of it** (*colloq*) to experience problems, difficulties, etc; **have little** (or **no**) **time for** to have little (or no) interest in or patience with; **in good time** quite early enough; with some time to spare; indeed (*ironic*; *obs*); **in one's own** (or **own good**) **time** at a time, rate, etc of one's own choosing; **in one's own time** in one's spare time, when not at work; **in one's time** at some past time in one's life, *esp* when one was at one's peak; **in the nick of time** see under **nick**[1]; **in time** after a lapse of time; early enough;

eventually; keeping rhythm; **keep time** to run accurately, like a clock (also **keep good time**); to move or perform in the same rhythm; to record times of workers, etc; **know the time of day** to know the state of affairs, what is going on; to know what one is about, or the best way of doing something; **local time** time reckoned from the local meridian; **lose time** (of eg a clock) to run down; to fall behindhand; to let time pass without full advantage; **make good time** to make speedy progress on a journey; **make time** to regain lost time; to find an opportunity; **mark time** see under **mark**[1]; **mean solar time** time reckoned not by the actual but by the mean position of the sun; **not before time** rather tardily; none too soon; about time too!; **no time** or **no time at all** a very short time; **on** (or **upon**) **a time** once; at a time in the past (*usu* imaginary); **on time** punctual, in accordance with time limits; punctually; **out of time** not keeping rhythm; too late (*law*); **sidereal time** the portion of a sidereal day that has elapsed since the transit of the first point of Aries; **solar time** time reckoned by the sun, real or mean; **standard time** a system of time adopted for a wide area instead of local time, *usu* Greenwich mean time or a time differing from it by a whole number of hours; **summer time** see under **summer**; **take one's time** (*colloq*) not to hurry, to dawdle; **take Time by the forelock** to seize an opportunity before it is too late; **take time off** (or in US **out**) to find time to do something, or time for an activity; **the time of one's life** a very enjoyable time; **time after time** repeatedly; **time about** (chiefly *Scot*) in turns, alternately; **time and again** repeatedly; **time and a half** a rate of pay equivalent to one and a half times the usual rate, offered eg for overtime; **time and motion study** an investigation of the motions performed and time taken in industrial, etc, work with a view to increased proficiency and thus production; **time of day** the time by the clock; the point of time reached; a greeting, salutation; **time out** (*comput*) (of a computer) to enter an automatic logoff command (eg from a printer) if data or a command is not input within a given time; **time out of mind** during the whole time within human memory, from time immemorial; **time was** there once was a time (when); **time-zone disease** or **fatigue** jet lag; **triple time** (*music*) three beats, or three times three beats, to a bar or other measure; **up to time** punctual, punctually; not later than the due time; **what time** (*poetic*) when. [OE *tīma*; ON *tīmi*]

timenoguy *tim'ə-nog-i*, *n* a rope stretched from place to place in a ship, *esp* one to prevent the fore-sheet fouling (*naut*); a makeshift; a what's-its-name. [Origin obscure, perh Fr *timon* (see **timon**) and **guy**[1]]

timid *tim'id*, *adj* inclined to fear; lacking courage; faint-hearted. — *n* **timid'ity**. — *adv* **tim'idly**. — *n* **tim'idness**. — *adj* **tim'orous** (*-ə-rəs*) timid. — *adv* **tim'orously**. — *n* **tim'orousness**. — *adj* **tim'orsome** (*dialect*) easily frightened. [L *timidus* timid, *timor*, *-ōris* fear, from *timēre* to fear]

timing, **timist**. See under **time**.

timocracy *tī-mok'rə-si*, *n* a form of government in which property is a qualification for office; a form of government in which ambition or desire of honour is a guiding principle. — *adj* **timocratic** (*-ō-krat'ik*) or **timocrat'ical**. [Gr *tīmokratiā*, from *tīmē* honour, and *krateein* to rule]

Timon *tī'mən*, *n* a famous Athenian misanthrope (5c BC) celebrated by Aristophanes, Lucian, Plutarch and Shakespeare; hence, a misanthrope. — *vi* **Tī'monize** or **-ise** to play the misanthrope. — *n* **Tī'monism**. — *n* **Tī'monist**.

timon *tī'mən*, (*obs*) *n* a helm. — *n* **timoneer'** a helmsman. [Fr, from L *tēmō*, *-ōnis* a beam]

timorous, etc. See under **timid**.

timothy *tim'ə-thi*, *n* (in full **timothy grass**) cat's-tail grass (*Phleum pratense*), a perennial grass used as fodder and pasture. [*Timothy* Hanson, who promoted its cultivation in America about 1720]

timous. Same as **timeous** (see under **time**).

timpano or **tympano** *timp'ə-nō*, *n* an orchestral kettle-drum: — *pl* **tim'pani** or **tym'pani** (*-nē*), often shortened to **timps** (*colloq*). — *n* **timp'anist** or **tympanist** a person who plays timpani. [Ital; see **tympanum**]

tim-whiskey or **tim-whisky** *tim'-(h)wis'ki*, *n* a whisky (gig).

tin *tin*, *n* a silvery-white, easily fusible, malleable metal (symbol **Sn** (for L *stannum*); atomic no 50); money (*slang*); a *usu* airtight container or vessel of tin or tin-plate, a can, etc; a tinful; a rectangular loaf of bread; a strip of tin along the lower boundary of the playable area of the front wall of a squash court. — *adj* made of tin or tin-plate or (*colloq*) of corrugated iron: paltry (*colloq*). — *vt* to coat or overlay with tin or tinfoil; to cover thinly with solder before soldering; to pack (eg food) in tins for preservation: — *pr p* **tinn'ing**; *pa t* and *pa p* **tinned**. — *n* **tin'ful**: — *pl* **tin'fuls**. — *adj* **tinned**. — *n* **tinn'er** a tinsmith; a tin-miner; a canner. — *n* **tinn'ing**. — *adj* **tinn'y** like tin; (of sound) thin and metallic, not rounded and resonant; (of metal goods) cheaply and flimsily made; lucky (*Austr* and *NZ colloq*). — *n* (*slang*) (also **tinn'ie**) a mug made of tin-plate; a can of beer (*Austr*). — **tin can**; **tin fish** (*naut slang*) a torpedo; **tin'foil** tin or (now) tin-lead alloy (or aluminium) in thin sheets, eg for wrapping foodstuffs; **tin god** an overbearing, dictatorial person; someone or something misguidedly revered; **tin hat** (*informal*) a military steel helmet; **tin'horn** (*orig* and *esp US*) a flashy, small-time gambler; a pretentious but worthless person. — Also *adj*. — **tin lizzie** (*colloq*) an old or decrepit motor car; **tin'man** a worker in tin; a dresser of tin ore; a dealer in tinware; **tin'-opener** an instrument for cutting open tins of food, etc; **tin'plate** thin sheet-iron or steel coated with tin. — Also *adj*. — *vt* to coat with tinplate. — **tin'pot** a pot of or for tin or tinplate. — *adj* paltry, rubbishy. — **tin'smith** a worker in tin; **tin'snips** a pair of hand-shears for cutting sheet metal, *esp* tin plate; **tin soldier** a toy soldier made of metal; someone who enjoys playing at being a soldier; **tin'stone** cassiterite, a brown tin dioxide; **tin'-streamer** a person who washes tin from alluvial deposits; **tin'-streaming**; **tin'tack** a tack coated with tin; **tin terne** same as **terne**; **tin'type** a ferrotype; **tin'ware** articles made of tin; **tin whistle** a cheap six-holed metal flageolet; **tin works** a place where tin is prepared for use. — **put the tin hat** (or **lid**) **on** to finish off, bring to an end, suppress; **Tin Pan Alley** *orig* a nickname for 28th Street, New York, the centre of the song-publishing district; the popular-music-publishing district of a city; the realm of popular-music production. [OE *tin*; ON *tin*, Ger *Zinn*]

Tina *tē'na*. An acronym for *t*here *i*s *n*o *a*lternative.

tinaja *ti-na'hha*, *n* a very large full-bellied earthenware jar, used (*esp* for storing and maturing wine) in Spain. [Sp]

tinamou *tin'ə-mōō*, *n* a S American partridge-like bird (*Tinamus*) of or related to the Ratitae. [Fr, from Galibi (Indian language of Fr Guiana) *tinamu*]

tincal *ting'kəl*, *n* crude borax. [Malay *tingkal*]

tinchel *tin'hhyəl*, *ting'kəl*, *n* a circle of men who close in round a herd of deer. [Gaelic *timchioll* a circuit]

tinct *tingkt*, *n* a tint; a tinge; the alchemist's elixir (*Shakesp*). — *adj* (*Spenser*) tinged. — *vt* (*obs*) to tint, tinge, dye; to imbue; to subject to transmutation. — *adj* **tinctō'rial** of or relating to dyeing; giving colour. — *n* **tinct'ure** a tinge or shade of colour; a colouring matter; a metal, colour, or fur (*heraldry*); a quality or slight taste added to anything; an alcoholic solution of a drug (*med*); a *usu* small alcoholic drink (*colloq*); a principle extracted in solution (*old chem*); the transmuting elixir or philosopher's stone (*alchemy*). — *vt* to tinge; to imbue. [L *tingere*, *tinctum* to dye; cf **tint**, **tinge**]

tind *tind*, *tīnd* (now *dialect*), **teend** *tēnd* (*Herrick*), or **tine** *tīn* (*Milton*), *vt* and *vi* to kindle: — *pa t* and *pa p* **tind'ed** or **tined** (*Spenser* **tīnd**, **tȳnd** or **tȳnde**). [OE *tendan*, and prob a lost collateral form; cf **tinder**]

tindal *tin'dəl*, *n* a petty officer of lascars. [Malayalam *tandal*]

tinder *tin'dər*, *n* dry inflammable matter, *esp* that used for kindling fire from a spark. — *adj* **tin'der-like** (*Shakesp*) inflammable as tinder. — *adj* **tin'dery** like tinder; easily angered. — **tin'derbox** a box for tinder, and *usu* flint and steel; a person, thing or situation that is (potentially) explosive. [OE *tynder*; ON *tundr*, Ger *Zunder*; OE *tendan*, Ger *zünden* to kindle]

tine[1] *tīn*, *n* a spike or point, eg of a fork, harrow or deer's horn. — *adj* **tīned**. [OE *tind*]

tine[2] or **tyne** *tīn*, (*Scot*) *vt* to lose. — *vi* to be lost; to be painful (*Spenser*); to perish (*Spenser*): — *pa t* and *pa p* **tint** (*tint*) or (*Spenser*) **tyned**. — *n* (*Spenser*) teen, affliction. — *n* **tinsel** (*tin'sl*; *Scot*) loss. [ON *tȳna* to destroy, lose, perish; cf **teen**]

tine[3] *tīn*, (*dialect*) *vt* to shut; to enclose. [OE *tȳnan* to surround; cf **town**]

tine[4] *tīn*, (*dialect*) *n* a wild vetch or tare.

tine[5] or **tyne** *tīn*, (*Shakesp*) *adj* tiny (always preceded by little).

tine[6]. See under **tind**.

tinea *tin'i-ə*, *n* ringworm; any of several skin diseases caused by fungi, such as **tinea pedis**, athlete's foot; (with *cap*) the clothes-moth genus, giving its name to the **Tineidae** (*ti-nē'i-dē*), a large family of small moths. — *adj* **tin'eal** of, relating to or of the nature of tinea. — *adj* **tineid** (*tin-ē'id*) of or relating to the *Tineidae* family or Tinea genus. — *n* an individual tineid moth. [L *tinea* moth, bookworm, etc]

ting *ting*, *vt* and *vi* to ring. — *n* the sound of a small bell. — *n* **ting'-a-ling** a ringing or tinkling. — Also *adv*. [Imit]

tinge *tinj*, *vt* to tint or colour; to suffuse; to impart a slight modification or trace to. — *vi* to take on a tinge: — *pr p* **tin'ging** or **tinge'ing**. — *n* a slight colouring, modification or trace. [L *tingere*, *tinctum*; connected with Gr *tengein* to wet, to stain]

tingle[1] *ting'gl*, *vi* to feel or be the site of a thrilling or slight stinging sensation; to thrill; to throb; to ring; to vibrate. — *vt* to cause to tingle; to ring. — *n* a tingling sensation. — *n* **ting'ler** a stinging blow. — *n* and *adj* **ting'ling**. — *adj* **ting'lish** thrilling. — *adj* **ting'ly** tingling. [ME *tinglen*, a variant of *tinklen*]

tingle[2] *ting'gl*, *n* a small tack or nail; a clip of lead; a patch over a leak in a boat's planking. [Cf Ger *Zingel*]

tinguaite *ting'gwə-īt*, *n* a fine-grained igneous rock composed essentially of feldspar, nepheline and aegirine. [*Tingua* Mountains in Brazil]

tinhorn. See under **tin**.

tinier, etc. See under **tiny**.

tink *tingk*, *n* a clear high-pitched short bell-like sound; a chime of rhyme; a tinker (*Scot derog*); a quarrelsome, vulgar person (*Scot derog*). — *vt* and *vi* to sound in this way; to tinker. [ME *tinken* to tink]

tinker *tingk'er*, *n* an itinerant mender of kettles, pans, etc; a botcher or bungler; a rascal (*colloq*); a member of a group of travelling people, a gypsy (*esp Scot* and *Ir*; *derog*); a slight, temporary or unskilful patching-up. — *vt* (*archaic*) to repair, *esp* ineffectually. — *vi* to do a tinker's work; (often with *with*) to potter, fiddle, meddle, in trivial, ineffectual ways. — *n* **tink'erer**. — *n* **tink'ering**. — **not give a tinker's curse** or **damn** (*slang*) not to care in the slightest. [ME *tinkere* pert, connected with *tinken* to tink]

tinkle *tingk'el*, *vi* to make small, bell-like sounds; to jingle; to clink repeatedly or continuously; (*esp* of water) to go with tinkling sounds; (used *esp* to or by children) to urinate; to tingle; to make empty sounds or mere sound. — *vt* to cause to tinkle; to ring. — *n* a sound of tinkling; (used *esp* to or by children) an act of urinating. — *n* **tink'ler** a small bell; a tinker, gypsy or vagrant (*Scot derog*). — *n* and *adj* **tink'ling**. — *adv* **tink'lingly**. — *adj* **tink'ly**. — **give someone a tinkle** (*colloq*) to call someone on the telephone. [ME *tinken* to tink; imit]

tinnie, **tinny**. See under **tin**.

tinnitus *ti-nī'təs*, *tin'i-təs*, *n* a medical condition in which there is constant ringing or other noise in the ears. [L *tinnītus*, *-ūs* a jingling, from *tinnīre* to ring]

tinsel[1] *tin'sl*, *n* thin glittering metallic sheets or spangles, used eg to decorate Christmas trees; yarn or fabric with interwoven metallic, glittery threads; anything showy but of little value. — *adj* of or like tinsel; gaudy. — *vt* to adorn with, or as if with, tinsel; to make glittering or gaudy: — *pr p* **tin'selling** or (*US*) **tin'seling**; *pa t* and *pa p* **tin'selled** or (*US*) **tin'seled**. — *adj* **tin'selled**. — *adj* **tin'selly** like tinsel, gaudy, showy. — *n* **tin'selry** glittering and tawdry material. — *n* and *adj* **tin'sey** (*obs dialect*) tinsel. — *adj* **tinsel-slipp'er'd** (*Milton*). — **Tin'seltown** (*colloq*) Hollywood. [OFr *estincelle*, from L *scintilla* a spark]

tinsel[2]. See under **tine**[2].

tinsey. See under **tinsel**[1].

tint[1] *tint*, *n* a colour, shade; a slight tinge distinct from the principal colour; a hue mixed with white; a series of parallel lines or rows of dots in engraving, producing a uniform shading; a faint colour forming a background; hair dye which *usu* washes out after a few weeks. — *vt* to colour slightly, to give a tint to; to tinge. — *vi* to take on a tint. — *adj* **tint'ed**. — *n* **tint'er** a person or thing that tints. — *n* **tint'iness**. — *n* **tint'ing**. — *adj* **tint'less**. — *adj* **tin'ty** unevenly tinted. — *n* **Tintom'eter**® a name for a colorimeter. — **tint'-block** a block for printing a background; **tint'-tool** an implement for producing a tint by parallel lines or rows of dots. [L *tinctus*; cf **tinct**, **tinge**]

tint[2] *tint*. See under **tine**[2].

tintinnabulate *tin-ti-nab'ū-lāt*, *vi* (*esp* of bells) to ring. — *adj* **tintinnab'ulant**, **tintinnab'ular** or **tintinnab'ulary**. — *n* **tintinnabulā'tion** bell-ringing. — *adj* **tintinnab'ulous**. — *n* **tintinnab'ulum** a *usu* high-pitched bell; a bell-rattle: — *pl* **tintinnab'ula**. [L *tintinnabulum* a bell, from *tintinnāre* to jingle, reduplicated from *tinnīre* to jingle]

tiny *tī'ni*, *adj* very small: — *compar* **ti'nier**; *superl* **ti'niest**. — *n* (*usu* in *pl*) a small child. — *adv* **ti'nily**. — *n* **ti'niness**. [Cf **tine**[5]]

-tion *sfx* forming nouns denoting action, condition, result or process. [From OFr, from L *-tiō*, *-tiōnis*]

tip[1] *tip*, *n* a slender, often tapering extremity; a small piece forming an end; the furthest part; a leafbud on tea. — *vt* to put a tip on; to be the tip of; to remove the tip from; (with *in*) to attach (a page) to the inside edge of another page: — *pr p* **tipp'ing**; *pa t* and *pa p* **tipped** or **tipt**. — *adj* **tipped** or **tipt**. — *n* **tipp'ing**. — *adj* (*slang*) topping, ripping, excellent. — *adj* **tipp'y** (*slang*) in the height of fashion; smart. — *adj* **tip'-tilted** (*Tennyson*) turned up at the tip. — **on the tip of one's tongue** almost, but not (yet) quite, remembered; on the very point of being spoken; **tip of the iceberg** see under **ice**. [Cf ON *typpa* to tip, Du, Norw, Dan *tip*, Ger (dimin) *Zipfel*]

tip[2] *tip*, *vt* to strike lightly but definitely; to hit glancingly: — *pr p* **tipp'ing**; *pa t* and *pa p* **tipped**. — *n* a tap; a glancing blow. — *n* **tipp'ing** a way of articulating with the tongue to give staccato effects on the flute, trumpet, etc. — **tip-and-run'** a kind of cricket in which the batsmen must run if they hit at all. — *adj* denoting a raid in which the raiders make off at once. [Cf Du and Ger *tippen*, Swed *tippa* to tip]

tip[3] *tip*, *vt* to give, hand, pass, convey; to give a tip to; to indicate. — *vi* to give tips: — *pr p* **tipp'ing**; *pa p* and *pa t* **tipped**. — *n* a gift of money in return for services, in excess of any charges, a gratuity; a hint or piece of special, *usu* inside information supposed to be useful (eg in betting, examinations, etc); a helpful or casual piece of advice; a trick or dodge. — *n* **tipp'er**. — *n* **tipp'ing**. — *n* **tip'ster** a person who makes a living by providing tips, *esp* about horses on which to bet. — **tip'-off** a hint, warning, a piece of secret information (eg about a crime). — **tip off** to give a tip-off to; **tip someone the wink** to convey a secret hint. [Orig rogues' cant]

tip[4] *tip*, *vt* to throw down; to upset or overturn; to tilt; to shoot, dump, empty (out) by tilting; to toss (off). — *vi* to topple (over); to tilt: — *pr p* **tipp'ing**; *pa p* and *pa t* **tipped**. — *n* a tilt; a place for tipping rubbish, coal, etc; a dump; an extremely untidy place (*colloq*); a staith or shoot; a tram for expeditiously transferring coal. — *adj* **tipp'able**. — *n* **tipp'er** a person or thing that tips; a lorry or truck, the body of which can be tipped up for unloading (also *adj*). — *n* **tipp'ing**. — *adj* **tipp'y** inclined or likely to tip, eg because of being top-heavy. — **tip'-cart** a cart emptied by being tilted up; **tip'cat** a cat or pointed piece of wood tapering at both ends; a game in which the cat is struck with a cat-stick and made to spring up; **tip'-cheese** (*Dickens*) *appar*, tipcat. — *adj* **tip'-up** constructed so as to be able to be tilted. — **tip off liquor** to turn up the glass, bottle, etc till quite empty; **tip one's hat** to raise, tilt or touch the brim of one's hat as a polite greeting; **tip the balance** or **tip the scale** (or **scales**) to make something more, or less, favourable to someone; to be the deciding factor in a result; **tip the scale** or **scales** to depress one end of the scales; to weigh (with *at*). [ME *type*; origin obscure]

tipi. See under **tepee**.

tipper[1] *tip'ər*, *n* a kind of ale — from Thomas *Tipper*, who brewed it in Sussex.

tipper[2]. See under **tip**[3,4].

tippet *tip'it*, *n* a long band of cloth or fur, eg (*hist*) on a hanging part of a garment; a shoulder cape, *esp* of fur; an animal's ruff of hair or feathers; an ecclesiastical scarf; the hangman's rope (*obs*, *facetious*); a moth's patagium. [Prob **tip**[1]]

Tipp-Ex® or (erroneously) **Tippex** *tip'eks*, *n* correcting fluid, *usu* white, for covering over mistakes in typing or writing. — Also *vt* (often with *out*).

tipple[1] *tip'l*, *vt* and *vi* to drink constantly in small quantities; to booze, *esp* habitually. — *n* an alcoholic drink. — *n* **tipp'ler**. — **tipp'ling-house**. [Cf Norw dialect *tipla* to drip slowly]

tipple[2] *tip'l*, *n* a device that overturns freight cars, mine trucks, etc to unload their contents; a place where this is done; an area where coal is cleaned and loaded into freight cars, trucks, etc in a mine. — *n* **tipp'ler** a person who works at a tipple, *esp* in a mine. [From **tip**[4]]

tippy. See under **tip**[1,4].

tipstaff *tip'stäf*, *n* a staff tipped with metal; an officer who carries it, a sheriff's officer: — *pl* **tip'staffs** or **tip'staves** (*-stāvz*). [**tip**[1] and **staff**]

tipster. See under **tip**[3].

tipsy *tip'si*, *adj* partially or slightly intoxicated; askew, awry, *esp* as if slightly intoxicated. — *vt* **tip'sify** to make drunk. — *adv* **tip'sily**. — *n* **tip'siness**. — **tipsy cake** a cake made of pastry and almonds, with wine; **tip'sy-key** a watchkey in which the head is released if an attempt is made to turn it backward. [Prob from **tip**[4]]

tipt. See under **tip**[1].

tiptoe *tip'tō*, *n* the end of the toe or toes, more often merely the toes. — *adv* on tiptoe (*lit* or *fig*), through excitement, expectation, etc. — *vi* to walk on tiptoe, to go lightly and stealthily: — *pr p* **tip'toeing**; *pa t* and *pa p* **tip'toed**. — **on tiptoe** on the tips of one's toes, as if trying to be quiet or stealthy; eagerly or excitedly expecting. [**tip**[1] and **toe**]

tiptop *tip-top'*, *n* the extreme top; the height of excellence. — *adj* of the highest excellence. — Also *adv*. [**tip**[1] and **top**[1]]

tipula *tip'ū-lə*, *n* any fly of the daddy-long-legs genus of flies *Tipula*, giving its name to the family **Tipū'lidae**. [L *tippula* a water-spider]

TIR *abbrev*: *Transports Internationaux Routiers* (*Fr*), International Road Transport, a haulage organization.

tirade *ti-räd'*, *tī-räd'*, *tē-räd'*, *n* a long vehement or angry harangue; a string of invective; a laisse (*prosody*); a run between two notes (*music*). [Fr, from Ital *tirata*, from *tirare* to pull]

tirage à part *tē-räzh a pär*, (*Fr*) *n* an offprint or article reprinted separately from a periodical — the German *Abdruck*.

tirailleur *tē-rä-yœr'*, *n* a skirmisher, sharpshooter. [Fr]

tiramisu *tēr-ə-mē-zōō'*, (*Ital*) *n* a dessert made with pieces of sponge soaked in coffee and marsala, layered with mascarpone and chocolate.

tirasse *ti-ras'*, *n* a pedal-coupler in an organ. [Fr, from *tirer* to pull]

tire[1] *tīr*, *vi* to become weary; to have one's energy exhausted; to have one's interest or patience exhausted or worn down. — *vt* to make weary; to exhaust the energy of; to bore; to wear out. — *adj* **tired** exhausted, fatigued; wearied, bored (with *of*); showing deterioration through time or usage, eg limp, grubby, played out. — *adv* **tired'ly**. — *n* **tired'ness**. — *adj* **tire'less** untiring. — *adv* **tire'lessly**. — *n* **tire'lessness**. — *n* **tire'ling** a tired animal. — Also *adj* (*Spenser*, *tyreling jade*). — *adj* **tire'some** fatiguing; wearisome; boring; tedious; (loosely) irritating, troublesome, irksome (*colloq*). — *adv* **tire'somely**. — *n* **tire'someness**. — *adj* **tir'ing**. — **tired and emotional** (*colloq*, *joc*, *euphem*) drunk; **tire down** to hunt to exhaustion. [Appar OE *tīorian* to be tired]

tire[2] *tīr*, *n* a metal hoop to bind a wheel; an *obs* or *US* spelling of **tyre**. — *vt* to put a tire on. — *adj* **tired**. — *adj* **tire'less**. — *n* **tir'ing**. [Archaic *tire* a headdress, from ME, aphetic for **attire**]

tire[3] *tīr*, (*archaic*) *n* equipment, furniture (*Shakesp*); attire, apparel; a headdress; a pinafore (*US*). — *vt* to attire; to dress (eg the head). — *n* **tir'ing**. — **tire'-val'iant** (*Shakesp*) a kind of fanciful headdress; **tire'-woman** a lady's-maid; **tir'ing-glass**; **tir'ing-house** or **-room** a theatre dressing-room; **tir'ing-woman**. [Aphetic for **attire**]

tire[4] *tīr*, (*Spenser*) *n* a train; a tier of guns. [Variant of **tier**]

tire[5] *tīr*, *n* a volley; a broadside. [Fr *tir*]

tire[6] *tīr*, (*Shakesp*) *vi* to tear and tug or feed greedily, like a bird of prey; to be intent, occupy oneself, feed one's thoughts or desires. — *n* **tir'ing** (in falconry) a bony or tough portion of meat given to a bird to pull at for exercise. [OFr *tirer* to pull]

tired. See **tire**[1,2].

tirl[1] *tirl*, (*Scot*) *vt* and *vi* to turn; to whirl; to rattle. — *n* a turnstile or the like. — **tirlie-wir'lie** a twirl. — *adj* twirled; intricate. — **tirl'ing-pin** the pin of a door-latch, rattled to seek admission (*obs*); now *usu* taken to mean a risp. [**trill**[2]]

tirl[2] *tirl*, (*Scot*) *vt* to strip. [Cf **tirr**]

Tir nan-Og *tēr-na-nōg'*, *n* the Irish Elysium. [Ir, land of the young]

tiro or **tyro** *tī'rō*, *n* a beginner; a novice: — *pl* **ti'ros**, **ti'roes**, **tyros**, **ty'roes** or **tyrones** (*tī-rō'nēz*). — *n* **tirocinium** (*-sin'i-əm*) early training; first experience. [L *tīrō* (LL *tȳrō*), *-ōnis* a recruit, *tīrōcinium* a first campaign]

Tironensian *tī-rō-nen'si-ən*, *n* a Benedictine of a congregation founded (1109) at *Tiron* (Thiron, near Nogent-le-Rotrou), absorbed (in 1627) by that of St Maur. — Also *adj*. — Also **Tyronen'sian**.

Tironian *tī-rō'ni-ən*, *adj* of *Tīrō* (*-ōnis*), Cicero's amanuensis, or of shorthand writing (**Tironian notes**) ascribed to him. — **Tironian sign** an ampersand.

Tiros *tī'rōs*, *n* the name given to one of a series of satellites transmitting meteorological information to the earth from observation of the clouds. [From *t*elevision *i*nfra-*r*ed *o*bservation *s*atellite]

tirr *tir*, (*Scot*) *vt* and *vi* to strip. [ME *tirve*; origin unknown]

tirra-lirra or **tirra-lyra** *tir-ə-lir'ə*, *n* and *interj* an old refrain, ascribed by Shakespeare to the lark.

tirrit *tir'it*, (*Shakesp*) *n* Mistress Quickly's word for alarm, fright.

tirrivee or **tirrivie** *tir'i-vi*, *-vē'*, (*Scot*) *n* a tantrum or fit of passion; a commotion.

'tis *tiz*. A contraction of **it is**.

tisane *ti-zan'*, *n* an infusion of eg herbs or flowers. [See **ptisan**]

Tishah b'Ab or **tisha be'Ab** *tish'ə bə-ab*, *n* (in the Jewish calendar) the ninth day of Ab (qv), observed as a fast day to commemorate the destruction of the first and second temples in Jerusalem. — Also **Tishah B'Av**, **Tisha Be'Av**, **Tisha Baav** or **Tisha Bov**. [Heb, ninth in Ab]

Tishri *tish'ri*. Same as **Tisri**.

tisick *tiz'ik*, (*Shakesp*) *n* a cough. [**phthisic**]

Tisiphone *ti-sif'ə-nē*, (*Gr mythol*) *n* one of the Furies. [Gr *Tīsiphonē*, from *tisis* retribution, and *phonos* murder]

'tisn't *tiz'nt*. A contraction of **it is not**.

Tisri *tiz'ri* or **Tishri** *tish'ri*, *n* (in the Jewish calendar) the first month of the Jewish civil year, seventh of the ecclesiastical, *usu* part of September and October.

tissue *tish'ōō*, *-ū*, *tis'ū*, *n* a collection of cells with a similar structure and particular function in an animal or plant (such as *muscle tissue*) (*biol*); tissue paper; a piece of soft, absorbent paper used as a disposable handkerchief, etc; anything woven, *esp* a rich or gauzy fabric interwoven with gold or silver thread; a complex accumulation (of lies, nonsense, etc); paper coated with gelatine and pigment (*photog*). — *vt* to weave or interweave, *esp* with gold or silver thread; to clothe, cover or decorate with tissue or tissue paper; to variegate. — **tissue culture** the growing of detached pieces of animal or plant tissue in nutritive fluids; a piece so grown; **tissue-equivalent material** (*radiol*) phantom material; **tissue paper** a thin, soft, semi-transparent paper used for tracing, wrapping delicate or breakable objects, decoration, etc (said *orig* to have been put between folds of tissue); **tissue plasminogen activator** (*med*) an anti-clotting enzyme occurring naturally in the blood, manufactured genetically as a drug and used to dissolve blood clots; **tissue-specific antigen** (*immunol*) an antigen present in a certain tissue but not found in other tissues; **tiss'ue-typing** the determination of body tissue types, eg to ensure compatibility between the donor and the recipient in transplant surgery. [Fr *tissu* woven, pa p of *tître* (OFr *tistre*), from L *texere* to weave]

tiswas or **tizwas** *tiz'woz*, (*colloq*) *n* a tizzy, flap, state of excitement, commotion. [Ety unknown; connected with **tizzy**, **tizz**]

Tit. (*Bible*) *abbrev*: (The Letter of Paul to) Titus.

tit[1] *tit*, *n* a variant of **teat**; a nipple (*colloq*); (*usu* in *pl*) a female breast (*vulg*); a contemptible person (*vulg*). — *adj* **titt'ish**.

tit[2] *tit*, *n* (*dialect*) a tap. — **tit for tat** an eye for an eye (a tip for a tap), retaliation in kind (*adj* **tit-for-tat'**); a hat, *usu* shortened to **tit'fer** (*cockney rhyming slang*). [A variant of **tip**[2]]

tit[3] *tit*, *n* any of various kinds of small songbirds of the family *Paridae* (the titmice), *esp* those of the genus *Parus*; a small, inferior, worthless or worn-out horse; a nag; a girl, young woman (*derog*). [Icel *tittr* titmouse]

tit[4] *tit*, (chiefly *Scot*) *n* a twitch; a tug. — *vt* and *vi* to tug.

tit[5]. See under **tite**.

Titan *tī'tən*, *fem* **Titaness** *tī'tə-nes*, (*Gr mythol*) *n* a son, daughter or other descendant of Uranus and Gaea; one of the elder gods and goddesses overthrown by Zeus; the name of one of them, Hyperion; Helios, the sun god; the sun personified; Prometheus; Saturn's largest satellite (*astron*); (without *cap*) anything gigantic; (without *cap*) a man of great intellect but not the highest inspiration. — Also *adj*. — *n* **Titania** (*tī-tā'ni-ə*, *ti-tä'ni-ə*) the queen of fairyland, wife of Oberon; a satellite of Uranus (*astron*). — *adj* **Tītanesque** (*-esk'*). — *adj* **Tītā'nian**. — *adj* **Titanic** or **titanic** (*tī-* or *ti-tan'ik*) of or like the Titans, *esp* in being of enormous size or strength; requiring unusual strength or effort. — *adv* **Titan'ically** or **titan'ically**. — *n* **Tītā'nis** (also without *cap*) an ostrich-like prehistoric N American bird. — *n* **Tī'tanism** (also without *cap*) the spirit of revolt against the universe, the established order, authority, convention. — *n* **Tītanomachy** (*-om'ə-ki*; Gr *machē* fight; *Gr mythol*) the war of the Titans against the Olympian gods. — *n* **Tītanosau'rus** a gigantic Cretaceous dinosaur. — *n* **Tītanothē'rium** a huge rhinoceros-like American Oligocene fossil ungulate. [Gr *Tītān*]

Titanic, **titanic**. See under **Titan** and **titanium**.

titanium *ti-*, *tī-tā'ni-əm*, *n* a strong, light and corrosion-resistant metallic element (symbol **Ti**; atomic no 22) found in ilmenite, sphene, rutile, etc. — *n* **titanate** (*tī'tə-nāt*) a salt of titanic acid. — *adj* (of a mineral) containing titanate. — *adj* **tītanic** (*-tan'ik*) of or containing quadrivalent titanium (**titanic acid** H_2TiO_3; **titanic iron** ilmenite). — *adj* **tītanif'erous** containing titanium. — *n* **tī'tanite** sphene, a brown, green or yellow monoclinic mineral, calcium silicate and titanate. — *adj* **tī'tanous** of or containing trivalent titanium. — **titanium dioxide** a pure white powder (TiO_2) of high opacity occurring naturally used *esp* as a pigment; **titanium white** titanium dioxide used as pigment. [Gr *Tītān* Titan, on the analogy of **uranium**]

titbit *tit'bit*, *n* a choice delicacy or item. — Also *esp* in US **tid'bit**.

titch or **tich** *tich*, (*colloq*) *n* a very small person; often used with *cap* as a nickname. — *adj* **titch'y** or **tich'y**. [From the music-hall artist Harry Relph (1867–1928), known as Little *Tich*]

tite, **tyte**, **tight** *tīt*, **tit** *tit*, or **titely**, etc, *-li*, (*obs*) *adv* promptly; at once. [Cf ON *tītt* often]

titer. See under **titrate**.

titfer *tit'fər*. See under **tit**[2].

tithe, **tythe** *tīdh*, *n* a tenth part, an indefinitely small part; the tenth of the produce of land and stock taken *orig* as a tax for church purposes; rent charged in lieu of this; any levy or fee of one-tenth. — *adj* tenth. — *vt* to take a tithe of or from; to pay a tithe on; to decimate (*obs*). — *vi* to pay a tithe. — *adj* **tith'able** subject to the payment of tithes. — *adj* **tithed**. — *n* **tith'er** a person who collects tithes. — *n* **tith'ing** a tithe; exaction or payment of tithes; a district containing ten householders, each responsible for the behaviour of the rest (*hist*). — **tithe barn** formerly a barn for storing the tithe in corn paid by a parish. — *adj* **tithe'-free** exempt from paying tithes. — **tithe'-gatherer**. — *adj* **tithe'-paying**. — **tithe'-pig** one pig out of ten paid as a tithe; **tithe'-proctor** a collector of tithes; **tith'ingman** (*hist*) the chief man of a tithing. [OE *tēotha* tenth; cf **tenth**, **teind**]

titi[1] or **tee-tee** *tē'tē*, *n* a small S American monkey of the genus *Callicebus* with a long, non-prehensile tail.

titi[2] *tē'tē*, *n* a shrub or small tree of the family *Cyrillaceae* native to the southern US, *esp Cliftonia monophylla*, which has glossy leaves and clusters of fragrant white flowers. [Ety uncertain]

Titian or **titian** *tish'ən*, *-yən*, *n* (in full **Titian red**) a striking red colour used by the Venetian painter *Titian* (Tiziano Vecellio, c. 1490–1576) *esp* for hair. — *adj* (chiefly of hair) red-gold, or (loosely) any other shade of red or reddish-brown. — *adj* **Titianesque** (*-esk'*) in the manner of Titian, a combination of the richest surface and colour.

titillate *tit'il-lāt*, *vt* to stimulate gently, *esp* in a sexual way; to tickle. — *adj* **tit'illāting**. — *adv* **tit'illātingly**. — *n* **titillā'tion**. — *adj* **tit'illātive**. — *n* **tit'illātor**. [L *titillāre*, *-ātum*]

titivate, **tittivate** *tit'i-vāt*, **tidivate** *tid'*, (*slang*) *vi* and *vt* to smarten up or put the finishing touches to (eg one's appearance). — *n* **titivā'tion**, **tittivātion** or **tidivā'tion**. [Poss coined from **tidy**]

titlark *tit'lärk*, *n* any bird of the pipit family, *esp* the meadow pipit. [**tit**[3] and **lark**[1]]

title *tī'tl*, *n* the distinctive name of a book, poem, tale, picture, etc; a chapter-heading; a title-page; a book or publication, as an item in a catalogue (*publishers' jargon*); (often in *pl*) a caption giving credits at the end of a film or television programme; a subtitle; an appellation of rank or distinction or a formal designation; an inscription or descriptive placard; a section of a law-book; a championship (*sport*); a right to possession or ownership (*law*); a basis of a claim (*law*); the evidence supporting a claim or right; a title deed (*law*); a fixed sphere of work, source of maintenance, or a certificate thereof, required as a condition for ordination (*eccles*); a cardinal-priest's parish in Rome. — *vt* to designate; to give or attach a title to. — *adj* **ti'tled** having a title, *esp* an appellation of rank or nobility — *adj* **ti'tleless** untitled; nameless (*Shakesp*). — *n* **ti'tler** a writer of titles; a claimant (*obs*). — *n* **ti'tling** the giving or attaching of a title. — **title deed** a document that proves right to possession; **ti'tle-holder** a person holding a title, *esp* legal, or a championship in some sport; **title leaf** the leaf containing the title of a book; **title page** the page of a book containing its title and the author's (and often publisher's) name; **title poem** the poem which gives its title to a book; **title role** the character in a play after whom the play is named; **title sheet** the first sheet of a book as printed, containing title, abbreviated or short title, etc. [OE *tītul* or *titul* and OFr *title* (Fr *titre*), from L *titulus*]

titling *tit'ling*, *n* a small stockfish; the meadow pipit (*esp Scot*); the hedge-sparrow. [Norw dialect *titling* small stockfish; ON *titlingr* sparrow; cf **tit**[3]]

titmouse *tit'mows* (*Spenser* **titmose** *-mōs*), *n* a tit, any of various kinds of small active acrobatic bird of the *Parus* or related genus: — *pl* **titmice** (*tit'mīs*). [**tit**[3] and ME *mose* titmouse, from OE *māse*; Ger *Meise*; confused with **mouse**]

Titoism *tē'tō-izm*, *n* the variant of communism as practised by Marshal *Tito* (1892–1980) in the former Yugoslavia, adhering to international communism but not at the sacrifice of national independence. — *n* and *adj* **Ti'toist**.

titoki *ti-tok'i*, *tē'*, *n* a New Zealand tree with reddish paniculate flowers. [Maori]

titrate *tī'trāt*, *tī-trāt'*, (*chem*) *vt* to measure the strength of (a solution) by titration. — *n* **titrā'tion** the addition of a solution from a graduated vessel to a known volume of a second solution until the chemical reaction is just completed, the knowledge of the volume of liquid added (the **titre** or *US* **titer**; *tī'tər* or *tē'tər*) and of the concentration of one of the solutions enabling that of the other to be calculated. [Fr *titre* standard]

ti-tree. Same as **ti**[2].

titter[1] *tit'ər*, *vi* to giggle, snicker or laugh furtively or restrainedly. — *n* a stifled laugh. — *n* **titt'erer**. — *n* and *adj* **titt'ering**. [Cf Swed dialect *tittra*]

titter[2] *tit'ər*, *vi* to totter, sway. [ON *titra* to shake]

tittivate. See under **titivate**.

tittle[1] *tit'l*, *n* a dot, stroke, accent, vowel-point, contraction or punctuation mark; the smallest part. [OFr *title*, from L *titulus* a title]

tittle[2] *tit'l*, (*dialect*) *vt* and *vi* to whisper; to tattle. — *n* **titt'le-tatt'le** idle, empty talk, rumour. — *vi* to talk idly, *esp* in relaying rumours of gossip. — **titt'le-tatt'ler**. — *n* **titt'le-tatt'ling**.

tittlebat *tit'l-bat*, *n* a childish form of **stickleback**.

tittup or **titup** *tit'əp*, *vi* to prance, skip about gaily: — *pr p* **titt'upping** or **tit'upping**, or (*US*) **titt'uping** or **tit'uping**; *pa p* and *pa p* **titt'upped** or **tit'upped**, or (*US*) **titt'uped** or **tit'uped**. — *n* a light springy step, a canter. — *adj* **titt'upy** or **tit'upy** gay, lively; unsteady. [Imit]

titty[1] *tit'i*, (*esp vulg* or used by children) *n* a teat; the breast. [Dimin of **tit**[1] or **teat**]

titty[2] *tit'i*, (*Scot*) *n* a sister.

titubate *tit'ū-bāt*, *vi* to stagger, stumble. — *n* **tit'ūbancy** staggering. — *adj* **tit'ūbant**. — *n* **titūbā'tion** (*med*) staggering; unsteadiness; a tremor (*esp* of the head), often a symptom of a cerebral or spinal disease. [L *titubāre*, *-ātum* to stagger]

titular *tit'ū-lər*, *adj* or or relating to title; in name or title only; nominal; having the title without the duties of an office; (of a church) giving a title to a cardinal or bishop. — *n* a titled person; someone who enjoys the title of an office, without actual possession; a person invested with a title in virtue of which he or she holds a benefice, whether or not he or she performs its duties; the holy personage, entity, etc from which a church takes its name (eg Corpus Christi), as opposed to *patron* if it takes its name from a saint or angel (*RC*). — *n* **titularity** (*-ar'i-ti*). — *adv* **tit'ularly**. — *adj* **tit'ulary** titular. — *n* a person holding a title. — **titular bishop** (*RC*) a bishop without a diocese, taking his title from a place where there is no longer a bishop's see (before 1882 bishop in partibus infidelium). — **titular of the teinds** or **tithes** a layman invested with church lands after the Reformation in Scotland. [L *titulus*]

titule *tit'ūl*, *n* and *vt* Same as **title**. [L *titulus*]

titup. See **tittup**.

tityre-tu *tit-*, *tīt-i-ri-too'*, *-tū'*, *n* a member of a 17c fraternity of aristocratic hooligans. [Opening words of Virgil's first eclogue, *Tītyre tū*, Tityrus, thou (lying under the spreading beech), conjectured to indicate the class that had beech trees and leisure to lie under them]

Tiw *tē'w* or **Tiu**, *tē'oo*, *n* the old English war-god. [OE *Tīw*; cf **Tuesday**, **Tyr**]

tizwas. See under **tiswas**.

tizzy *tiz'i*, *n* a state of agitation, nervousness, confusion or dither for little reason (*slang*; also **tizz**); a sixpence (*old slang*). [Ety unknown]

tjanting *chan'ting*, *n* a small tool consisting of a long bamboo handle with a small copper or brass bowl at one end, used for applying hot wax to cloth to form patterns in batik. [Indonesian word]

TKO (*boxing*) *abbrev*: technical knockout.

Tl (*chem*) *symbol*: thallium.

TLC (*facetious*) *abbrev*: tender loving care.

Tlingit *tlin'git*, *n* (a member of) a native N American people living in parts of Alaska and British Columbia; the language spoken by this people. — *adj* of or relating to this people, their language or culture. [Tlingit, person]

TLS *abbrev*: Times Literary Supplement.

TM *abbrev*: transcendental meditation.

Tm (*chem*) *symbol*: thulium.

tmesis *tmē'sis*, (*gram*) *n* the separation or splitting up of a word into parts by one or more intervening words: — *pl* **tmē'sēs**. [Gr *tmēsis*, from *temnein* to cut]

TN *abbrev*: Tennessee (US state); tradename; Tunisia (IVR).

TNT *abbrev*: trinitrotoluene or trinitrotoluol.

TO *abbrev*: Tax Officer: telegraph office; Transport Officer; turn over.

to *too*, *too*, *tə*, *prep* serving as sign of the infinitive (which is sometimes understood) and forming a substitute for the dative case; used to introduce the indirect object of a verb; in the direction of; as far as; all the way in the direction of; until; into the condition of; towards; beside; near; at; in contact with, close against; before, before the hour of; answering, by way of response or reaction; for; of; with the object or result of; against; in accordance, comparison, proportion or relation with; in honour of, or expressing good wishes for; along with, in addition. — *adv* in one direction, forward; in or into a required or fixed position, contact, closed or fastened condition. — **to and fro** alternately this way and that; **toing and froing** going backwards and forwards in an agitated way, or without achieving anything (also *fig*). [OE *tō*; Ger *zu*, Gothic *du*; Gr suffix *-de*]

toad *tōd*, *n* a toothless tailless amphibian (family *Bufonidae*) with a warty skin that walks or crawls instead of jumping like the frog, *esp* one belonging to the *Bufo* or related genus; any of several similar amphibians belonging to different families; a hateful or contemptible person or animal; bufo (*alchemy*). — *n* **toad'y** a sycophant, an obsequious flatterer. — *vt* and *vi* to fawn on and flatter like a sycophant: — *pr p* **toad'ying**; *pa t* and *pa p* **toad'ied**. — *adj* **toad'yish**. — *n* **toad'yism**. — **toad'-eater** (*archaic*) a toady, a fawning sycophant, *orig* a mountebank's assistant, whose duty was to swallow, or pretend to swallow, toads; **toad'-eating** sycophancy. — *adj* sycophantic. — **toad'fish** any of several toadlike fish of the *Batrachoidiae* family, with wide mouths, large heads and tapering bodies; **toad'-flax** any species of *Linaria*, a genus closely related to the snapdragon, with flaxlike leaves; **toad-in-the-hole'** a dish *orig* of beef, now *usu* sausage meat, cooked in batter; **toad'rush** or **toad'grass** a low rush (*Juncus bufonius*) with mostly solitary flowers; **toad'-spit** or **toad'-spittle** cuckoo-spit. — *adj* **toad'-spotted** thickly stained or spotted like a toad. — **toad'stone** a stone formerly believed to be found in a toad's head, and valued as an amulet; a basalt lava found in carboniferous limestone in Derbyshire (so called perhaps because of its toadlike markings, but possibly from German *totes Gestein* dead stone, from the lead-miner's point of view); **toad'stool** any of several spore-producing, poisonous, umbrella-shaped fungi; any capped fungi *incl* the edible mushroom and poisonous toadstool (*old rare*). [OE *tāde*, *tādige*, *tādie*]

toast *tōst*, *vt* to brown (*esp* bread) by exposing it to direct heat, eg under a grill; to half-melt (eg cheese) in this way; to warm, by exposing to heat; to dry and parch; to drink to (someone's health, success, etc). — *vi* to drink toasts; (of *esp* bread) to become brown or be suitable for browning by exposing to direct heat; to become warm by being exposed to heat. — *n* slices of bread toasted on both sides; the person (*orig* a woman) or thing drunk to, as the most admired or celebrated for the moment; a call to drink to an admired person or thing; a wish for someone's continued health; a piece of spiced toasted bread put in liquor (*archaic*). — *adj* **toast'ed**. — *n* **toast'er** an electric device, *usu* with a timer, for toasting bread; a person who toasts; a toasting-fork; that which can be toasted. — *n* **toast'ie** (*colloq*) a toasted sandwich (also **toast'y**). — *n* **toast'ing**. — *adj* (*colloq*) hot. — **toast'ing-fork** or **toast'ing-iron** a long-handled fork for toasting bread; a sword (*facetious*); **toast'master** or **toast'mistress** a person who announces toasts, introduces speakers, at a dinner; **toast rack** a stand with partitions for slices of toast. — **have been had on toast** to have been swindled; **have someone on toast** (*colloq*) to be in a dominant position over someone, to have someone at one's mercy; **on toast** served on a slice of toast. [OFr *toster*, from L *tostus* roasted, pa p of *torrēre*; some senses of the verb and noun reflect the idea that a woman's name (ie as the person whose health is being drunk) would flavour the wine like spiced toast]

toaze *tōz* (*Shakesp*). See under **toze**.

Tob. (*Bible*) *abbrev*: (the Apocryphal Book of) Tobit.

tobacco *tə-bak'ō*, *n* (in full **tobacco plant**) any American solanaceous plant of the genus *Nicotiana*, especially *N. tabacum*, with narcotic leaves; its prepared leaves used for smoking, chewing, or snuff: — *pl* **tobacc'o** or **tobacc'oes**. — *n* **tobaccanā'lian** a smoker (*facetious*, after *bacchanalian*). — *n* **tobacc'onist** a seller or manufacturer of tobacco and cigarettes, a smoker (*obs*). — **tobacc'o-heart** (*old*) a functional disorder of the heart due to excessive use of tobacco; **tobacco mosaic virus** a virus causing mosaic disease in tobacco; **tobacc'o-pipe** a pipe for smoking tobacco; **tobacc'o-pouch** a pouch for holding tobacco; **tobacc'o-stopper** an instrument for pressing down the tobacco in a pipe. [Sp *tabaco*, from Haitian]

Tobagonian *tə-bā-gō'ni-ən*, *adj* of or relating to the island of *Tobago* in the S W Indies. — *n* a native of Tobago.

to-be *tōō-* or *tə-bē'*, *n* the future. — *adj* (now *usu* as a *combining form* **-to-be'**) signifying something in the future, yet to become.

Tobit *tō'bit*, *n* an apocryphal Old Testament book, containing the story of *Tobit*.

toboggan *tə-bog'ən*, *n* a long narrow flat sledge turned up in front, used on snow and ice. — *vi* to slide, coast or travel on, or as if on, a toboggan: — *pr p* **tobogg'aning**; *pa t* and *pa p* **tobogg'aned**. — Earlier also **tobogg'in**, **tabogg'an** or **tarbogg'in**. — *n* **tobogg'aner**. — *n* **tobogg'aning**. — *n* **tobogg'anist**. [Micmac *tobākun*]

to-break *tōō-* or *tə-brāk'*, (*obs*) *vt* to break in pieces: — *pa t* (*Bible*, *Bunyan*) **to-brake'** (*usu* printed *to brake*); *pa p* **to-bro'ken**. [OE *tōbrecan*, from pfx *tō-* asunder, and *brecan* to break]

to-bruise *tə-brōōz'*, (*obs*) *vt* to bruise severely; to break up: — *pa p* (*Spenser*) **to-brusd'**. [OE *tō-brysan*]

Toby *tō'bi*, *n* a beer-mug or other vessel shaped like a man wearing a three-cornered hat (also **To'by-jug**; also without *cap*); Punch's dog.

toby *tō'bi*, *n* the road (*thieves' slang*); robbery on the road; a stop-cock in a gas- or water-main under the road (*Scot*); the cover protecting it (*Scot*). — **high toby** highway robbery on horseback; **low toby** robbery by a highwayman on foot. [Shelta *tōbar*]

toc or **tock** *tok*, *n* telecommunications code for signalling the letter *t*. — **toc emma** (*em'ə*; emma, signallers' code for *m*; *military slang*) a trench mortar; **Toc H** (*āch*; signallers' code for *h*) a society formed after World War I to promote the spirit of comradeship and Christian fellowship, from its first meetings at *T*albot *H*ouse, at Poperinghe in Belgium.

toccata *to-kä'tə*, (*music*) *n* a musical work intended primarily to display the performer's touch, or in which he or she seems to try the touch of an instrument in a series of runs and chords before breaking into a fugue; (loosely) a sort of fantasia or overture. — *n* **toccatel'la** or **toccatina** (*-tē'nə*) a short toccata. [Ital, from *toccare* to touch]

toc emma, **Toc H**. See under **toc**.

Tocharian or **Tokharian** *to-kä'ri-ən*, *-kā'*, *n* an extinct Indo-European language, related to Latin and Celtic, preserved in manuscripts discovered in the 20c in Chinese Turkestan, and divided into two dialects, **Tocharian A** and **Tocharian B**; a member of the people speaking this language, living in central Asia until c.800AD. — Also **Tocha'rish** or **Tokha'rish**. [Gr *Tocharoi*, a people supposed to be its speakers on the strength of the Uigur (language of Chinese Turkestan) name *Tochri*]

tocher *tohh'ər*, (*Scot*) *n* a dowry. — *vt* to dower. — *adj* **toch'erless**. — **toch'er-good** property given as tocher. [Ir *tochar*, Gaelic *tochradh*]

tock[1] *tok*, *n* the sound made by a clock or watch, like a tick but deeper and more resonant. — *vi* (of a clock, etc) to make such a sound. — **tick-tock** see under **tick**[1]. [Prob imit]

tock[2]. See under **toc**.

toco *tō'kō*, (*slang*) *n* punishment: — *pl* **tō'cos**. — Also **tō'kō**: — *pl* **tō'kos**. [Origin uncertain; Gr *tokos* interest, and Hindi *thōkō*, from *thoknā* to thrash, have been suggested]

tocology or **tokology** *tok-ol'ə-ji*, *n* obstetrics. [Gr *tokos* birth, offspring, and *logos* discourse]

tocopherol *tok-of'ə-rol*, *n* vitamin E, a group of fat-soluble substances found in wheatgerm, egg yolk, green leafy vegetables, etc whose deficiency causes sterility in some species. [Gr *tokos* birth, offspring, *pherein* to bring, bear, and **-ol**]

tocsin *tok'sin*, *n* an alarm-bell, or the ringing of it. [Fr *tocsin*, from Provençal *tocasenh*, from *tocar* to touch, strike, and *senh*, from L *signum* sign (LL bell)]

tod[1] *tod*, (*Scot*) *n* a fox; a sly person. — **Tod-low'rie** a nickname for a fox, (ie Laurence) Reynard. [Origin unknown]

tod[2] (*Spenser* **todde**) *tod*, *n* a bush, *esp* of ivy; an old wool weight, about 28 lb; a load. — *vi* to yield a tod. — *vt* to yield a tod for.

tod[3] *tod*: **on one's tod** alone. [Rhyming slang *on one's Tod Sloan* (own)]

today *tōō-*, *tə-dā'*, *n* this; the present times. — *adv* on or during the present day; nowadays. [OE *tōdæg(e)*]

todde. See under **tod**[2].

toddle *tod'l*, *vi* to walk with short feeble steps, as a young child does; to saunter (*colloq*); (with *off*) to go, depart (*facetious*). — *n* a toddling gait; an aimless stroll (*colloq*); a toddling child. — *n* **todd'ler** a person who toddles, *esp* a young child learning to walk. — *adj* of or for a toddler. — *n* **todd'lerhood**. — *adj* **todd'ling**. [Orig Northern dialect]

toddy *tod'i*, *n* the fermented sap of various palm trees; a mixture of spirits, sugar and hot water. — **todd'y-cat**

the palm-civet; **todd'y-ladle** a small ladle for mixing or serving toddy; **todd'y-palm** coconut, palmyra or other species of palm yielding toddy; **todd'y-stick** a stick used in mixing toddy. [Hindi *tāṛī*, from *tāṛ* a palm-tree, prob of Dravidian origin]

to-do *tə-, too-doo'*, *n* a bustle; a stir; a commotion: — *pl* **to-dos'**.

tody *tō'di*, *n* a small W Indian insectivorous bird of the genus *Todus* — the *green sparrow*, *green hummingbird*, etc, related to the kingfishers. [L *todus* a small bird of some kind]

TOE (*phys*) *abbrev*: theory of everything.

toe *tō*, *n* one of the five small projecting members at the front of the human foot; the corresponding part of other animals; the front of a hoof; the corresponding part of a shoe, sock, etc, covering the toes; the corresponding part of the head of a golf club, hockey stick, etc; the lowest part of the front of anything, *esp* if it projects. — *vt* to stand with the toes against (eg a starting-line); to provide (eg a sock or stocking) with a toe; to mend the toe of (a sock, etc); to kick; to strike with the toe of a club; to nail obliquely through the foot; to perform with the toe. — *vi* to walk with the toes pointing in a particular direction: — *pr p* **toe'ing**; *pa t* and *pa p* **toed**. — *adj* **toed** (*tōd*) having toes (of a specified kind or number; also *combining form*); nailed obliquely. — *adj* **toe'less**. — **toe'cap** a (*usu* steel) cap covering the toe of a shoe; **toe'clip** an attachment to a bicycle pedal that holds the toe and thus the foot, firm; **toe dance** a dance performed on tiptoes (also *vi* **toe'-dance**); **toe'hold** a place to anchor the toes in; a first established position, an initial position or advantage; a hold in which the opponent's toes are grasped and the foot is bent back or twisted (*wrestling*); **toe'-in** a slight forward convergence given to the planes of a vehicle's front wheels to promote steering stability and equalize tyre-wear; **toe'-jump** (*ice-skating*) a jump executed by pushing off with the toe of one's free foot; **toe'-loop** (*ice-skating*) a toe-jump and a loop performed in combination; **toe'nail** a nail covering the upper surface of a human or animal toe; an obliquely driven nail. — *vt* to join (eg two pieces of wood) by driving nails obliquely. — **toe'-piece**. — **big** or **great toe** the largest of the toes; **little toe** the smallest of the toes; **on one's toes** poised for a quick start, alert, eager; **take to one's toes** to run away; **toe the line** to stand with toes against a marked line, eg when starting a race; to conform; **toe to toe** (*fig*) in close, direct confrontation (*adj* **toe-to-toe'**); **tread on someone's toes** to offend someone; **turn up one's toes** (*colloq*) to die. [OE *tā* (pl *tān*); ON *tā*, Ger *Zehe*]

toea *tō'ä*, *n* the monetary unit of Papua New Guinea, 1/100th of a kina. [Native name]

toerag *tō'rag*, (*slang*) *n* a beggar, tramp; generally, a ruffian or rascal; a despicable person. — Also **toe-ragg'er**. [Prob from the strips of rag used by tramps to wrap around their toes in place of socks]

toetoe. See under **toitoi**.

toey *tō'i*, (*Austr slang*) *adj* nervous, restless, on edge; apprehensive, eager.

to-fall *too'fōl*, (*archaic*) *n* a beginning, incidence. [**to** and **fall**]

toff *tof*, (*slang*) *n* a person of the upper classes; a swell, dandy; a good sort. — *adj* **toff'ish**. — *n* **toff'ishness**. — *adj* **toff'y**. [Perh **tuft**]

toffee or **toffy** *tof'i*, *n* a hard-baked chewy sweet, made of sugar and butter. — Earlier and *US* **taff'y**. — **toff'ee-apple** a toffee-coated apple on a stick. — *adj* **toff'ee-nose** or **toff'ee-nosed** (*slang*) supercilious, conceited, snobbish. — **for toffee** (*colloq*) (always with a *neg*) at all, as in *he can't dance for toffee*. [Ety unknown]

tofore *too-, tə-fōr', -fōr'*, *adv* (*Shakesp*), *prep*, *conj* (*obs*) before. [OE *tōforan* (prep)]

toft *toft*, *n* a homestead (*hist*); a hillock (*dialect*). [Late OE *toft*, from ON *topt*, *tupt*, *toft*]

tofu *tō'foo*, *n* unfermented soy bean curd, having a pale, creamy colour and a bland flavour. [Jap, from Chin *toufu*, from *tou* beans, and *fu* rotten]

tog[1] *tog*, (*slang*) *n* (*usu* in *pl*) a garment, an item of clothing; a swimming costume (*Austr*). — *vt* to dress: — *pr p* **togg'ing**; *pa t* and *pa p* **togged**. — *n* **togg'ery** clothes. — **long'-togs** (*naut*) shore clothes; **tog up** to dress (oneself) *esp* in one's best clothes. [Prob ultimately L *toga* a robe]

tog[2] *tog*, *n* a unit of measurement of thermal insulation as a property of textile fabrics used eg for quilts. — **tog rating** or **value** the amount of thermal insulation provided by a fabric, measured in togs. [Appar an invention, perh connected with **tog**[1]]

toga *tō'gə*, *n* the outer garment of a Roman citizen, a long piece of cloth wound round and draped over the body. — Also **toge** (*tōg*; *Shakesp* conjectured). — *adj* **tō'ga'd**, **tō'gaed**, **tō'gate**, **tō'gated** or **toged** (*tōgd*; *Shakesp*). — **toga praetexta** (*prē-, prī-teks'tə, -ta*) a toga with a deep border of purple, worn by boys, magistrates, etc; **toga virilis** (*vir-ī'lis, wir-ē'lis*) the garb of manhood. [L *toga*; cf *tegere* to cover; **thatch**]

together *tə-, too-gedh'ər*, *adv* with someone or something else, in company; in or into one place; at the same time; so as to be in contact, joined or united; by action with one or more other people; continuously; into a proper or suitable order or state of being organized (*colloq*). — *adj* (*colloq*, chiefly *US*) well-organized, mentally composed, emotionally stable, etc. — *n* **togeth'erness** unity; closeness; a sense of unity or affection from being with other people. — **get** or **put it (all) together** (*colloq*, chiefly *US*) to perform something successfully, get something right; to become well-organized, stable, etc; to establish a good relationship (with). [OE *tōgædere*, from *tō* to, and *geador* together]

toggle *tog'l*, *n* a crosspiece on a rope, chain, rod, etc, to prevent slipping through a hole, or to allow the rope, etc to be twisted; a short bar acting as a button, passed through a loop for fastening a garment; an appliance for transmitting force at right angles to its direction; a switch or a keyboard command which turns a particular feature (eg bold type or read-only mode) on or off (*comput*). — *vt* to hold or provide with a toggle; to fix fast; (with *on*, *off*) to turn (a particular feature, eg bold type) on or off using a toggle switch or a keyboard command (*comput*). — *vi* (with *between*) to move between (different features, modes, files, etc) using a toggle switch or keyboard command (*comput*). — **togg'leiron** a harpoon with a toggle instead of barbs; **toggle joint** an elbow or knee joint; a mechanism consisting of two levers hinged together, force applied to straighten the hinge producing a considerable force along the levers; **toggle switch** a switch which, in a circuit having two stable or quasi-stable states, produces a transition from one to the other (*telecomm* and *electronics*); a switch or button on a computer keyboard used to turn a particular feature (eg bold type) on or off (*comput*). [Appar connected with **tug** and **tow**[1]]

Togolese *tog-ə-lēz'*, *adj* of or relating to Togo in W Africa, or its inhabitants. — *n* a person born, in or a naturalized inhabitant of, Togo.

togs. See under **tog**[1].

togue *tōg*, *n* the Great Lake char (or trout), a gigantic salmonid of North America. [From Am Ind name]

toheroa *tō-ə-rō'ə*, *n* an edible shellfish found at low tide buried in sandy beaches in New Zealand; a soap made from it. [Maori]

toho *tō-hō'*, *interj* a call to pointers or setters to stop: — *pl* **tohos'**.

tohu bohu *tō'hoo bō'hoo*, *n* chaos. [Heb *thōhū wa-bhōhū* emptiness and desolation (Gen 1. 2)]

tohunga *to'hoong-ə, to-hoong'ə*, (*NZ*) *n* a Maori priest, a wise man with healing powers. [Maori]

toil[1] *toil*, *vi* to struggle hard; to labour hard; to make one's way forwards or progress with great difficulty or effort. — *vt* (*archaic* or *dialect*) to effect or work out with toil; to subject to toil. — *n* a struggle; hard or exhausting labour; contention (*obs*). — *adj* **toiled**. — *n* **toil'er**. — *adj* **toil'ful**. — *n* and *adj* **toil'ing**. — *adj* **toil'less**. — *adj* **toil'some** involving toil, laborious; toiling; owing to toil (*Spenser* **toyl'som** or **toyle'some**). — *adv* **toil'somely**. — *n* **toil'someness**. — *adj* **toil'-worn** worn, weary with toil. [Anglo-Fr *toiler* (Fr *touillier*) said to be from L *tudiculāre* to stir]

toil[2] *toil*, (*usu* in *pl*, often *fig*) *n* a net; a snare or trap. [OFr *toile*, from L *tēla* web]

toile *twäl*, *n* a thin cotton or linen dress material; a sample of a garment made in cheap material so that alterations may be made before the garment is made up in the correct material. [Fr, from L *tēla* web]

toilet *toil'it n* a bowl-like receptacle for the body's waste matter, with a water supply for washing this into a sewer; a dressing-room, bathroom, or lavatory; the act or process of dressing; the whole dress and appearance of a person, any particular costume; the cleansing and dressing of a wound; a dressing-table with a mirror; a toilet-table; the articles used in dressing; a toilet-cover; a cloth for the shoulder during hairdressing (*archaic*). — *vt* to take to the toilet or otherwise assist with toilet procedures. — *adj* (*archaic*) **toil'eted** dressed. — *n* (*usu* in *pl*) **toil'etry** any article, preparation or cosmetic used in washing and dressing oneself: — *pl* **toil'etries**. — **toil'et-cloth** or **-cover** a dressing-table cover; **toil'et-glass** a mirror set on the dressing-table; **toilet paper** or **tissue** thin, absorbent paper for wiping oneself after defecation or urination; **toilet roll** a roll of toilet paper; **toil'et-service** or **-set** the utensils (eg brushes, combs, etc) used in dressing; **toilet soap** soap for personal use; **toil'et-table** a dressing-table; **toilet training** the training of children to control bladder and bowels and to use the lavatory; **toilet water** a lightly perfumed liquid similar to cologne. [Fr *toilette*, dimin of *toile*, from L *tēla* web]

toilette *twä-let'*, *n* the act of washing and dressing oneself. [Fr, dimin of *toile*, from L *tēla* web]

toilinet or **toilinette** *toi-*, *twäl-i-net'*, *n* a kind of woollen cloth, silk and cotton warp with woollen weft, used for waistcoats. [Prob from Fr *toile* linen, cloth, and *-et*, *-ette*, from *satinet*, *satinette*, *sarsanet*, etc]

toing and froing. See under **to**.

toise *toiz*, *n* an old French lineal measure equivalent to 6·395 feet (very nearly 2 metres). [Fr, from L *tendere*, *tēnsum* to stretch]

toiseach or **toisech** *tö'shəhh* (*hist*) *n* a Celtic noble of ancient times ranking below a mormaor. [Gaelic]

toison *twa-zɔ̃*, (*Fr*) *n* a fleece. — **toison d'or** (*dor*) the golden fleece.

toitoi or **toetoe** *toi'toi*, *n* any of several tall reedlike grasses native to New Zealand, *esp* those of the genus *Arundo*, and *esp A. conspicua*. [Maori]

to kalon *to ka'lon*, (*Gr*) *n pl* the beautiful.

tokamak *tō'kə-mak*, (*nuc eng*) *n* in fusion, a toroidal apparatus in which plasma is contained by means of two magnetic fields, a strong toroidal field and a weaker poloidal field generated by an intense electric current through the plasma. — Also *adj*. [Russ, acronym from *to*roidalnaya *ka*mera s *ma*gnitnym polem (toroidal chamber with a magnetic field)]

Tokay *tō-kā'*, *n* a sweetish and heavy wine with an aromatic flavour, produced at *Tokay* (*Hung* **Tokaj**) in Hungary; the grape used to produce this wine. — Also **tokay**.

tokay *tō-kā'*, *n* a geeko (*Gekko gecko*), native to the Malay archipelago and SE Asia. [Malay]

toke *tōk*, (*US slang*) *n* a puff on a cigarette (*esp* one containing marijuana). — Also *vi*. [Poss short for **token**]

token *tō'kn*, *n* a mark, sign or distinctive feature (of something); a symbol; a portent; an indication; something providing evidence; a plague-spot (*obs*); anything serving as evidence of authenticity, proof or a guarantee; anything serving as a reminder or souvenir, a keepsake; a voucher worth a stated amount of money which can be exchanged for goods of the same value; a small coin-like piece of metal or plastic which is used instead of money, eg in slot machines; a unit of computer code representing a word or character used in a program (see **lexical analysis**); (in Presbyterian churches) a metal voucher admitting to communion (superseded by the communion card); a measure of hand-press work, *usu* 250 pulls. — *adj* serving as a symbol; done or given as a token and therefore of no real value, nominal. — *vt* to be a warning or sign of, to betoken. — *adj* **tō'ken'd** (*Shakesp*) indicated by plague-spots. — *n* **tō'kenism** the principle or practice of doing something on a single occasion or with minimum effort, in order to create the impression that a law, code or precept is being properly complied with, eg employing one coloured person or one woman to give the impression of being committed to equal opportunities. — *adj* **tokenist'ic**. — **token money** money worth more than its intrinsic value as metal; private tokens; **token ring** (*comput*) a form of network in which each token or signal controls access to the network; **token vote** a parliamentary vote of money in which the amount stipulated forms a basis for discussion and is not meant to be binding. — **by the same token** in addition, in corroboration, by the way; **more by token** see under **more**[1]; **the Lord's tokens** (*Shakesp*) plague-spots. [OE *tācen*; Ger *Zeichen* a mark]

Tokharian, Tokharish. See **Tocharian**.

toko. See under **toco**.

tokology. See **tocology**.

tokoloshe *tok-o-losh'i*, *n* (in Bantu folklore) a hairy malevolent dwarflike creature with supernatural powers. [Zulu *tikoloshe*]

Tok Pisin *tok piz'in*, *n* Melanesian pidgin, as spoken in Papua New Guinea. [**talk pidgin**]

tola *tō'lə*, *n* an Indian unit of weight equivalent to 180 grains troy (11·66 grammes). [Hindi, from Sans *tulā* weight]

tolbooth. See under **toll**[1].

tolbutamide *tol-būt'əm-īd*, *n* a drug administered orally in the treatment of diabetes. [*tol*uyl, *but*yric acid, and **amide**]

told *tōld*, *pa t* and *pa p* of **tell**[1].

tole[1] or **toll** *tōl*, *vt* (now *US* and *dialect*) to lure, decoy. — *n* **tol'ing** or **toll'ing** (*US*) the use of toll-bait; a method of decoying ducks, etc, by exciting their curiosity. — **toll'-bait** (*US*) chopped bait thrown to attract fish. [ME *tollen*, from root of OE (*for*)*tyllan*; see **till**[1]]

tole[2] *tōl*, *n* painted, lacquered or japanned tinware, popular in the 18c and 19c. — *n* **tole'ware** articles made of tole collectively. [Fr *tôle* sheet metal, from a dialect word for table]

Toledo *tōlē'dō*, *n* a tapering sword or sword-blade made in *Toledo*, Spain: — *pl* **Tolē'dos**.

tolerate *tol'ə-rāt*, *vt* to endure, *esp* with patience or forebearance, to put up with; to treat fairly, to accept (a person with different religious, political, etc beliefs or opinions); to allow to be done or to exist, to permit; to be able to resist the (harmful) effects of (a drug). — *n* **tolerabil'ity**. — *adj* **tol'erable** endurable; passable; fairly good. — *adv* **tol'erably**. — *n* **tol'erance** the ability to resist or endure pain or hardship; the disposition, ability or willingness to be fair towards and accepting of different religious, political, etc beliefs and opinions; the ability to tolerate and hence no longer benefit from the effects of a drug after prolonged use; the permissible range of variation in values when measuring. — *adj* **tol'erant** tolerating the beliefs, opinions, etc of others; enduring; capable of enduring (eg unfavourable conditions, a parasite, a drug) without showing serious effects (*biol* and *med*); indulgent, permissive; favouring toleration. — *adv* **tol'erantly**. — *n* **tolerā'tion** the act of tolerating; the allowance of what is not approved; the freedom of a minority to hold and express political or religious opinions which differ from those of the majority. — *n* **tolerā'tionism**. — *n* **tolerā'tionist**. — *n* **tol'erātor**. — **tolerance dose** (*med*) the maximum dose which can be permitted to a specific tissue during radiotherapy involving irradiation of any other adjacent tissue. [L *tolerāre*, *-ātum*, from *tollere* to lift up]

toll[1] *tōl*, *n* a tax for the privilege of using a bridge or road, selling goods in a market, etc; a portion of grain kept by a miller in payment for grinding; a place where there is or was or might have been a building for collecting road tolls or tollbar, a road junction (*Scot*); the cost in damage, injury or lives; a toll call. — *vi* to take or pay tolls. — *vt* to take toll of; to take as a toll. — *adj* **toll'able** subject to toll. — *n* **toll'age** payment of toll; the right to charge a toll; the amount paid as toll. — *n* **toll'er** a person who collects a toll. — **tolbooth** or **tollbooth** (*tōl'*, *tol'bo͞oth*, *-bo͞odh*; *Scot -bəth*) an office where tolls are or were collected; a town hall (*Scot*); a prison (*Scot*); often a building combining a town hall and a prison (*Scot*); **toll bar** a movable bar across a road, etc, to stop travellers liable to pay a toll; **toll'bridge** or **toll'-gate** a bridge or gate where tolls are collected; **toll call** a short-distance telephone trunk call; a long-distance telephone call at a charge above the local rate (*US*); a long-distance telephone call to a place outside a free-dialling area (*NZ*); **toll'dish** a dish for measuring the toll of grain in a mill; **toll'-gatherer** a person who collects a toll, eg at a tollbridge or tollgate; a person who collects taxes. — *adj* and *adv* **toll-free'**. — **toll'house** a house at a tollbridge, tollgate, etc used by the collector of tolls; **toll'man** a person who collects tolls; a person who collects taxes; **tolsel** (*tōl'sel*), **tolzey** (*-zi*) or **tolsey** (*tol'si*) local names for a tolbooth or exchange (*appar* from OE *seld* seat, or *sæl* hall). — **take (a) toll of** or **take its toll on** to inflict loss, hardship, pain, etc, on; to have a deleterious effect on. [OE *toll*; cf Du *tol*, Ger *Zoll*; supposed to be from LL *tolōneum*, from Gr *telōnion* customs, from *telos* fulfilment, tax, etc; by some connected with **tell, tale**]

toll[2] *tōl*, *vi* to sound, as a large bell does, *esp* with slow, measured strokes. — *vt* to cause (a bell) to sound with slow, measured strokes; to sound, strike, signal, announce, summon, send etc by tolling; to toll for the death of. — *n* an act to tolling; the slow, measured sound of a bell tolling. — *n* **toll'er**. [Prob **tole**[1]]

toll[3] *tōl*, (*law*) *vt* to bar; to take away the right of. [Anglo-Fr *toller*, from L *tollere* to take away]

toll[4]. See **tole**[1].

tol-lol *tol-lol'*, (*old slang*) *adj* pretty good. — *adj* **tol-lol'ish** tolerable. [**tolerable**]

tolsel, tolsey. See under **toll**[1].

tolt *tōlt*, *n* an old English writ removing a court-baron cause to a county court. [Anglo-Fr *tolte*, from LL *tolta*, from L *tollere* to take away]

Toltec *tol'tek*, *n* a member of a central American Indian people who lived in Mexico until overrun by the Aztecs; the language spoken by this people. — Also *adj*. — *adj* **Tol'tecan**. [Nahuatl *tōltēcah*, pl of *tōltēcatl* person from *Tula* (the capital of the Toltec civilization)]

tolter *tol'tər*, (*dialect*) *vi* to flounder about.

Tolu or **tolu** *tō-lo͞o'*, *n* (in full **balsam of Tolu**) a balsam yielded by the S American papilionaceous tree *Myroxylon toluifera* or *M. balsamum*, used in medicine and perfumery. [From Santiago de *Tolú* in Colombia]

toluate *tol'ū-āte*, (*chem*) *n* any salt or ester of toluic acid. [**Tolu** and chem sfx *-ate*]

toluene *tol'ū-ēn* or **toluol** *tol'ū-ol*, (*chem*) *n* methyl benzene, a colourless flammable liquid ($C_6H_5{\cdot}CH_3$) used as a solvent and in the manufacture of other organic chemicals and explosives [**Tolu** and chem sfx *-ene*]

toluic *tol-ū'ik*, (*chem*) *adj* of or containing toluene or toluic acid. — **toluic acid** any of four isomeric acids derived from toluene, all having the formula $CH_3C_6H_4COOH$. [*tol*uene and chem sfx *-ic*]

toluidine *tol-ū-i-dēn*, (*chem*) *n* an amine ($C_6H_4{\cdot}CH_3NH_2$) derived from toluene, used in making dyes. [*tol*uene and chem sfxs *-ide* and *-ine*]

tolzey. See under **toll**[1].

Tom *tom*, *n* short for *Thomas*; (without *cap*) a male of various animals, *esp* a cat; (without *cap*) a name for a big bell; (without *cap*) a prostitute (*police* and *underworld slang*). — **Tom'-and-Jerry** hot rum and eggs, spiced and sweetened; **tom'cat** a male cat; **Tom Collins** a cocktail of gin, lime-juice, soda and sugar or syrup; **Tom-nodd'y** the puffin; a fool; **Tom'-trot** a kind of toffee. — **Long Tom** a long gun, *esp* one carried amidships on a swivelling carriage; **Old Tom** gin; **Tom, Dick, and/or Harry** anybody; people in general (also **Tom and Tib** (*old*); **Tom o' Bedlam** (formerly) a madman let out of an asylum with a licence to beg; **Tom Tidd'ler's ground** a place where wealth is to be had for the picking up; debatable land; no man's land (from a children's game so called).

tom. See **tomfoolery** under **tomfool**.

tom. *abbrev*: *tomus* (*L*), tome or volume.

tomahawk *tom'ə-hök*, *n* a N American Indian war-axe; a hatchet (*Austr*). — *vt* to attack or kill with a tomahawk; to hack, cut up or slate. [Virginian Indian *tämähāk*]

tomalley *to-mal'i*, *n* American lobster fat ('liver'), eaten as a delicacy; extended to tamal (qv). [Perh Caribbean]

toman *tō-män'*, *n* a myriad, or ten thousand; a former Persian gold coin worth 10 000 dinars. [Pers *tumān*]

tomatillo *tom-ə-tē'l-yō*, *tom-ə-tē'ō*, *n* a plant, *Physalis ixocarpa*, of the nightshade family with yellow flowers and sticky edible berries, native to Mexico; a berry from this plant, much used in Mexian cooking: — *pl* **tomati'lloes** or **tomati'llos**. [Sp, dimin of *tomate* tomato]

tomato *tə-mä'tō* (*US -mā'*), *n* a S American plant (*Lycopersicum esculentum* or *Solanum lycopersicum*) related to the potato, formerly called the love-apple; its glossy red or yellow pulpy edible fruit: — *pl* **toma'toes**. — *adj* **toma'toey**. — **gooseberry tomato** or **strawberry tomato** the Cape gooseberry. [Sp *tomate*, from Mex *tomatl*]

tomb *to͞om*, *n* any place serving as a grave; a *usu* underground vault for the disposal of dead bodies; a sepulchral monument; (with *the*) death. — *vt* to entomb; to bury. — *adj* **tombic** (*to͞om'ik*, *-bik*). — *adj* **tomb'less**. — **tomb'stone** a memorial stone over a tomb. [OFr (Fr) *tombe*, from L *tumba*, from Gr *tymbos*]

tombac, **tombak** *tom'bak* or **tambac** *tam'bak*, *n* an alloy of either copper with a little zinc or copper and arsenic, used for making cheap jewellery. [Fr *tombac*, from Malay *tambaga* copper]

tomboc *tom'bok*, *n* a Javanese long-handled weapon.

tombola *tom-bō'lə*, *tom'*, *n* a kind of lottery in which winning tickets are drawn from a revolving drum (at a fête, etc); a type of bingo, played *esp* in the armed services. [Ital, from *tombolare* to tumble]

tombolo *tom'bə-lō*, *n* a bar of sand or gravel connecting an island with another or with the mainland: — *pl* **tom'bolos**. [Ital, from L *tumulus* mound]

tomboy *tom'boi*, *n* a high-spirited romping girl; a girl with boyish looks, dress, habits, etc; (formerly) a hoyden; an immodest woman (*Shakesp*). — *adj* **tom'boyish**. — *adv* **tom'boyishly**. — *n* **tom'boyishness**. [**Tom** and **boy**]

tome *tōm*, *n* a large book or volume. [Fr, from L *tomus*, from Gr *tomos*, from *temnein* to cut]

-tome *combining form* denoting: an instrument for cutting; a segment. [Gr *tomē* a cutting, from *temnein* to cut]

tomentum *tō-men'təm*, (*bot*) *n* a matted cottony down on leaves and stems, etc. — *adj* **tomentose** (*tō-mən-tōs'*, *tō-men'tōs*) or **tomen'tous**. [L]

tomfool *tom'fo͞ol'*, *n* a great fool; a buffoon; a trifling person (*archaic*). — *adj* extremely foolish. — *vi* to play the fool. — *n* **tomfool'ery** foolish behaviour; nonsense, rubbish; buffoonery; trifles, ornaments; jewellery, *esp* stolen jewellery (often shortened to **tom**; *rhyming slang*). — *n* **tomfool'ishness**. [**Tom**]

tomium *tō'mi-əm*, *n* the cutting edge of a bird's bill. — *adj* **tō'mial**. [Latinized from Gr *tomeion* a knife-edge, from *temnein* to cut]

tommy *tom'i*, *n* (sometimes with *cap*) a private in the British army; a penny roll, bread; food; a tommy-shop; the truck system. — *vt* to oppress by the truck system. — **Tommy Atkins** a generic name for the private in the British army; **tommy bar** a rod used as a lever for turning a tubular spanner or the like; **tomm'y-gun** a light machine-gun (after its American inventor, General J T *Thompson*); **tomm'y-rot** absolute nonsense; **tomm'y-shop** a truck-shop. — **soft tommy** soft bread, as opposed to hardtack or sea-biscuit. [From the name **Thomas**]

tomography *tō-mog'rə-fi*, *n* any scanning technique used to obtain a detailed image of a particular section or plane, of or within a solid structure or body, *esp* (*med*) the use of X-rays or ultrasound waves to produce an image, for diagnostic purposes, of a chosen section at a particular depth within the body. — *n* **tom'ogram** a radiogram or other visual record produced by tomography. — *n* **tom'ograph** a machine for producing tomograms. — *adj* **tomograph'ic**. — **positron emission tomography** (*med*) a technique used to evaluate brain function by measuring the emission (by active brain cells) of radioactive particles injected into the patient (*abbrev* **PET**). [Gr *tomos* slice, and *graphein* to draw]

tomorrow *tə-*, *tōō-mor'ō*, *n* the day after today; the future. — *adv* on the day after today; in the future. [OE *tō morgen*]

tompion[1] See under **tampion**.

tompion[2] *tom'pi-ən*, (*obs*) *n* a watch of the kind made by Thomas *Tompion* (1639–1713).

tompon. Same as **tampon**.

Tom Thumb *tom thum'*, *n* a dwarf or midget; a dwarf variety of a plant. [*Tom Thumb* the tiny hero of several folk tales]

tomtit *tom'tit'*, *n* the bluetit or other species of tit. [**Tom** and **tit**[3]]

tom-tom *tom'-tom*, *n* an American Indian or oriental drum played with the hands; a similar drum used in jazz-bands, etc; any primitive drum or substitute; (*esp* formerly) a Chinese gong, tam-tam. — *vi* to beat on or play a tom-tom. — Also (*esp* formerly) **tam'-tam** or **tum'-tum**. [Hindi *tam-tam*, imit]

-tomy *-tə-mi*, *combining form* denoting surgical incision into an organ. [Gr *-tomia* the operation of cutting, from *tomē* a cut, from *temnein* to cut]

ton[1] *tun*, *n* (in full **long ton**) a unit of weight equivalent to 20 cwt (2240 lb or 1016 kg); (in full **short ton**) a unit of weight equivalent to 2000 lb (907·2kg, *US*); (in full **metric ton**, also **tonne**) a unit of weight equal to 1000kg (*approx* 2204.6 lb); (in full **displacement ton**) a unit used to measure the amount of water a ship displaces, equal to 2240 lb or 35 cubic feet of sea water; (in full **register ton**) a unit (*orig* a *tun* of wine) used to measure a ship's internal capacity, equal to 100 cubic feet; (in full **freight ton**) a unit for measuring the space taken up by cargo, equal to 40 cubic feet; 100 (*colloq*); a score, total, etc of 100 (*colloq*); 100 runs (*cricket*; *colloq*); 100 mph (preceded by *a* or *the*; *slang*); a great weight (*colloq*); (in *pl*) many, a great amount (*colloq*). — See also **tournage**. — **-tonn'er** *combining form* denoting a vehicle, vessel, etc weighing a specified number of tons or having a specified amount of tonnage; a load of a specified number of tons. — *adj* **ton'-up** (*slang*) (*orig* of a motorcyclist) travelling or having travelled at more than 100 mph; fond of travelling at fast speed; noisy and reckless. — *n* a speed of 100 mph; a person who habitually travels this fast. [OE *tunne* a vat, tub; see **tun**]

ton[2] *tɔ̃*, *n* fashion; people of fashion. — *adj* **tonish** or **tonnish** (*ton'ish*) modish, having ton. — *adv* **ton'ishly** or **tonn'ishly**. — *n* **ton'ishness** or **tonn'ishness**. [Fr]

tonal *tōn'əl*, *adj* of or relating to tone or tonality; according to key; (of a fugue) having an answer written in the same key but with different melodic invervals. — *adv* **tōn'ally**. — *adj* **tōnal'itive** of tonality. — *n* **tōnal'ity** the melodic and harmonic relationships between the tones of a scale or musical system (*music*); a particular scale, a key (*music*); the scheme of colours, shades and tones in a painting. [Med L *tonālis*, from L *tonus*, from Gr *tonos* pitch, tension]

tonalite *tō'nə-līt*, *n* a coarse-grained igneous rock, quartz-mica-diorite, found at Monte *Tonale*, Tirol.

tonalitive, tonality. See under **tonal**.

to-name *tōō'-nām*, *n* a byname, nickname; an additional name used to distinguish persons whose names are alike. [OE *tōnama*, from pfx *tō-* in addition to, and *nama* name]

tonant *tōn'ənt*, *adj* thundering. [L *tonāns*, *-antis*, pr p of *tonāre* to thunder]

tondo *ton'dō*, *n* a circular painting or circular carving in relief: — *pl* **ton'di** (*-dē*) or **ton'dos**. — *n* **tondi'no** (*-dē'nō*) a circular or semicircular moulding (*archit*); a small tondo: — *pl* **tondi'ni** (*-nē*) or **tondi'nos**. [Ital short for *rotondo* round, from L *rotundus*]

tone[1] *tōn*, *n* the character of a sound; the quality of sound; accent; intonation; vocal inflexion, rise or fall in pitch, *esp* as expressing feeling, mood, etc; rising, falling intonation or pitch, etc used as a way of distinguishing words, eg in Mandarin Chinese (*linguistics*); a musical sound of definite pitch; a major second, one of the larger intervals between successive notes in the scale, as between C and D (*music*); a Gregorian psalm-tune; vocal expression; bodily firmness, elasticity, or tension, *esp* in muscles; the general or prevailing character, quality or style (eg of a piece of writing, speech, etc); a generally high quality, style, character, etc (*esp* in the phrase *lower the tone*); mood; temper; harmony or general effect of colours; depth or brilliance of colour; a tint or shade. — *vt* to give tone or the desired tone to; to alter the tone of; to give (a photograph) a softer or otherwise altered colour using a chemical solution (*photog*); to intone (*archaic*). — *vi* to take a tone; to harmonize (with *in* or *with*). — *adj* **toned** having a tone (in compounds); braced up; treated to give tone; slightly tinted. — **tone'less** soundless; expressionless; dull; relaxed; listless. — *adv* **tone'lessly**. — *n* **tone'lessness**. — *n* **ton'er** a person or thing that tones; a cosmetic lotion for toning the skin; a hair preparation used for toning or tinting; fine powdered pigment used in xerography; a chemical solution used to soften, etc colours or tones in photographic work. — *adj* **tōn'ey** or **tōn'y** (*slang*) high-toned; fashionable. — *n* and *adj* **tōn'ing**. — **tone'-arm** the movable arm that carries an electric pick-up on a gramophone; (*orig*) that part of a gramophone connecting the sound-box to the horn; **tone control** a manual control in a radio set which adjusts the relative amplitude of high, medium and low frequencies. — *adj* **tone'-deaf** unable to appreciate or distinguish differences in musical pitch. — *n* **tone-deaf'ness**. — **tone language** a language (eg Chinese) in which difference of intonation distinguishes words of different meaning that would otherwise sound the same; **tone'pad** an electronic device similar to a remote control handset for a television, video, etc, which allows data to be input into a central computer from a distance, *usu* via a telephone link; **tone picture** a piece of descriptive music; **tone poem** a piece of programme music, not divided into movements, conveying or translating a poetic idea or literary theme; **tone row** (in serial music) the basic set of notes in the chosen order. — **tone down** to make or become lower in tone; to moderate; to soften, to harmonize the colours of (eg a painting) as to light and shade; **tone up** to make or become stronger in tone; to make or become intensified; to make or become healthier, stronger, more vigorous. [Gr *tonos* pitch, tension, partly through Fr *ton* and L *tonus*]

tone[2] *tōn*, (*obs* or *dialect*) *pronoun* and *adj* the one. — *Scot* **tane** (*pronoun*), **tae** (*adj*). [**that one**; cf **tother**]

toneme *tō'nēm* (*linguistics*) *n* (in a tone language) a phoneme which can be distinguished from another only by its particular intonation. — *adj* **tonēmic** [**tone** and phon*eme*]

tonetic *tō-net'ik*, (*linguistics*) *adj* of or relating to linguistic tones, tone languages or intonation. — *adv* **tonet'ically**. [**tone** and phon*etic*]

toney. See under **tone**[1].

tong[1] *tong*, *n* a Chinese guild or secret society, particularly one associated with organized crime. — *n* **tong'ster** (*slang*) a member of a tong. [Chin *t'ang*]

tong[2] *tong*, (*orig* and *esp US*) *vt* to hold, pick up, manipulate, curl (hair), etc using tongs. — *vi* to use tongs. [**tongs**]

tonga[1] *tong'gə*, *n* a light two-wheeled Indian vehicle. [Hindi *tāṅgā*]

tonga[2] *tong'gə*, *n* a Fijian toothache remedy made from an aroid root (*Epipremnum*). [Arbitrary invention]

tongabean. See under **tonka-bean**.

tongs *tongz*, *n pl* a gripping and lifting instrument, consisting of two legs joined by a pivot, hinge, or spring; curling tongs. — **tong-test ammeter** (*elec eng*) an AC ammeter and current transformer combination whose iron core can be opened and closed round a cable. [OE *tang*, *tange*; ON *töng*, Ger *Zange*]

tongue *tung*, *n* the fleshy organ in the mouth, used in tasting, swallowing and speech; the tongue of an ox, etc, as food; the rasping organ in molluscs; the power of speech; the manner of speaking; a language; speech; discourse; voice; utterance; anything like a tongue in shape; a point of land; a bell clapper; the reed of a musical instrument; a flap in the opening of a shoe or boot; the catch of a buckle; the pointer of a balance; any narrow projection; a langue or language (qv) of a religious or military order; a vote (*Shakesp*). — *vt* to utter; to lick; to touch with the tongue; to provide with a tongue; to talk, prate (with *it*); to produce or play by tonguing (*music*); to pronounce (*dialect*); to articulate; to attack with words (*Shakesp*). — *vi* to give tongue; to stick out; to practise tonguing (*music*). — *adj* **tongued** having a tongue. — *adj* **tongue'less** having no tongue; unspoken of (*Shakesp*). — *n* **tongue'let** a little tongue. — *adj* **tongue'like**. — *n* **tongue'ster** a babbler. — *n* **tongu'ing** (*music*) articulation to separate the notes in playing wind instruments (see also **flutter-tonguing** under **flutter**). — **tongue'-and-groove** a system of joining boards by fitting a projection along the side of one into a groove in the next; these boards. — *adj* **tongue-doubt'ie** (ie **doughty**; *Milton*) bragging. — *adj* and *adv* **tongue-in-cheek'** with ironic, insincere or humorous intention. — **tongue'-lashing** a severe verbal reprimand. — *adj* **tongue'-tacked** tongue-tied. — **tongue'-tie** (*med*) a congenital condition in which the tongue's mobility is impeded by an abnormally short frenum. — *adj* **tongue'-tied** unable to speak out, *esp* because of fear or embarrassment; affected with tongue-tie. — **tongue'-twister** a formula or sequence of words difficult to pronounce without blundering; **tongue'-work** babble, chatter. — **give tongue** to give utterance, to voice; to give voice as hounds on a scent do; **hold one's tongue** see under **hold**[1]; **lose one's tongue** to become speechless from emotion; **on the tip of one's tongue** see under **tip**[1]; **speaking in tongues** or **gift of tongues** glossolalia; **with one's tongue hanging out** (*colloq*) eagerly; **with (one's) tongue in (one's) cheek** tongue-in-cheek (*adv*). [OE *tunge*; ON *tunga*, Ger *Zunge* the tongue; L *lingua* (from *dingua*)]

tonic *ton'ik adj* relating to tone or tones; producing tension, eg of the muscles; giving tone and vigour to the system (*med*); giving or increasing strength; of or being the first note of a scale (*music*); of or relating to the main or primary stress on a word. — *n* a medicine which invigorates and strengthens; any person or thing that enlivens or invigorates; the first note of a scale, a keynote (*music*); a key or chord based on the keynote (*music*); tonic water; a stressed syllable in a word. — *n* **tonicity** (*ton-is'i-ti*) the property or condition of having tone; mode of reaction to stimulus; the healthy elasticity of muscular fibres when at rest. — **tonic accent** emphasis given to a particular syllable through a change in pitch; **tonic sol-fa** (*music*) a system of notation and teaching devised by Sarah Glover (1785–1867) and developed by John Curwen, using modified sol-fa syllables and their initial letters for the notes of the scale with *doh* (see **doh**) as the keynote for the major keys and *lah* (see **la**) for the minor, and dividing the bar by colons, dots and inverted commas; **tonic spasm** (*med*) a prolonged uniform muscular spasm (as opposed to *clonic spasm* or *clonus*); **tonic water** aerated quinine water. [Gr *tonikos* relating to stretching or tones]

tonight *tə-*, *tōō-nīt'*, *n* this night; the night of the present day. — *adv* on this night or the night of today; last night (*obs*; *Shakesp*). [OE *tō niht*]

tonish. See under **ton**[2].

tonite *tō'nīt*, *n* a blasting explosive made from guncotton and barium nitrate. [L *tonāre* to thunder]

tonk[1] *tonk*, (*colloq*) *vt* to strike; to defeat; to hit (a cricket ball) into the air; to hit (a ball) with a flat, wooden sound, or with an unenergetic or casual stroke. — *n* **tonk'er**. [Imit]

tonk[2] *tonk*, (*Austr slang*) *n* a penis; a homosexual; an effeminate, weak or ineffectual person. [Ety unknown]

tonka-bean *tong'kə-bēn'*, *n* the coumarin-scented seed of a large papilionaceous tree (*Dipteryx*) of Guiana, used for flavouring snuff, etc; the tree from which it comes. — Also **tonga-bean** (*tong'gə-*), **tonquin-bean** (*tong'kēn-*). [The local Guyana name]

tonker. See under **tonk**[1].

tonlet *tun'lət*, *n* one of a set of overlapping strips that make up the skirt on a suit of armour; a skirt of armour. [MFr *tonnel* a short skirt; also Fr *tonnelet*, dimin of *tonneau* a cask, barrel (similarly made up of strips)]

tonnag *tō'nag*, *n* a shawl with a shaped neck and side fastening. [Gaelic]

tonnage *tun'ij*, *n* the cargo- or freight-carrying capacity of a ship measured in tons (*orig* in *tuns* of wine); the weight of a cargo or freight on a ship; the total cargo-carrying capacity of a country's merchant shipping, measured in tons; a duty on ships, based on their cargo-carrying capacity; a duty on cargo charged per ton; a tax of so much a *tun* on imported wines (sometimes **tunnage**; *hist*). — See also **ton**. — **gross tonnage** the total space capable of carrying cargo in a ship, measured in register tons; **net register tonnage** gross tonnage less deducted spaces (those spaces required in running the ship). [See **ton, tun**]

tonne *tun*, *ton*, *n* the preferred name for a **metric ton**, a unit of weight equal to 1000 kilograms (2204·62 lb, or 0·984 ton). [Fr]

tonneau *ton'ō*, *n* the rear part of a (*usu* open) motorcar body in which passengers sit, *orig* opening at the back; (in full **tonneau cover**) a detachable cover to protect the rear passenger seats in an open car when not in use; a tonne: — *pl* **tonn'eaus** or **tonn'eaux** (*-nō*, *-nōz*). [Fr, cask, tun]

tonnell. *Obs* form of **tunnel**.

-tonner. See under **ton**[1].

tonnish. See under **ton**[2].

tonometer *tōn-om'ə-tər*, *n* a device for determining the frequencies of tones, *esp* one consisting of tuning forks (*music*); an instrument for measuring fluid pressure (eg within the eyeball), blood pressure or vapour pressure. — *n* **tonom'etry**. [Gr *tonos* pitch, tension, and *metron* measure]

tonquin-bean. See under **tonka-bean**.

tonsil *ton'sl*, *-sil*, *n* either of two lymph glands on either side of the root of the tongue in vertebrates (*zool*); any mass of lymphatic tissue (*anatom*). — *adj* **ton'sillar** or **ton'sillary**. — *n* **tonsillec'tomy** surgical removal of one or both of the tonsils. — *adj* **tonsillit'ic**. — *n* **tonsillī'tis** inflammation of the tonsils. — *n* **tonsillot'omy** an incision into, *usu* followed by complete or partial removal of, a tonsil. — Also **tonsilitis**, etc. [L *tōnsillae* (pl)]

tonsor *ton'sər*, *n* a barber. — *adj* **tonso'rial** (*usu facetious*) of or relating to hairdressing or barbering. — *n* **ton'sure**

(-*shər*) the act or mode of clipping the hair, or of shaving the head; (in the RC and Eastern Churches) the shaving or cutting of part of the hair of the head (typically that on the crown) on entering the priesthood or a monastic order; the shaven part; the state of being shaven. — *vt* to give a tonsure to. — *adj* **ton'sured** (of eg a priest) having the crown of the head shaven; shaven; bald; clipped. [L *tōnsor* barber, *tōnsūra* a shearing, from *tondēre*, *tōnsum* to clip]

tontine *ton'tēn*, *ton-tēn'*, *n* an annuity scheme in which several subscribers share a common fund, with their individual benefits increasing as members die until only one member is left alive and receives everything or until a specified date at which the proceeds are divided amongst the survivors. — Also *adj*. — *n* **tontin'er**. [From Lorenzo *Tonti*, a Neapolitan who devised the scheme in 1653]

tonus *tō'nəs*, (*med*) *n* the normal elasticity of healthy muscle at rest, tonicity; atonic spasm. [New L, from L *tonus*, from Gr *tonos* pitch, tension]

Tony *tō'ni*, *n* (in the US) an award for meritorious work in the theatre: — *pl* **Tonys** or **Tonies**. [After US actress *Antoinette* Perry (died 1946)]

tony[1] *tō'ni*, (*obs slang*) *n* a simpleton. [**Antony**]

tony[2]. See under **tone**[1].

too *tōō*, *adv* as well, in addition, also, likewise; to a greater extent than is required, desirable or suitable; so much as to be incompatible with a condition; extremely; used to enforce eg a command (*colloq*). — *adj* **too'-too** or **too too** (*colloq*) exquisite; extravagantly and affectedly sentimental, gushing. — *adv* all too; quite too. — **none too** hardly, barely; not very; **too much** more than is reasonable, tolerable, etc; also used as an *interj* expressing approval, amazement, etc (*slang*, chiefly *US*). [Stressed form of **to**]

tooart. Same as **tuart**.

toodle-oo *tōō'dəl-ōō'* or **toodle-pip** *-pip'*, (*old colloq*) *interj* good-bye. [Perh imit of a motorcar horn, or from Fr (*à*) *toute à l'heure* see you later]

took *tŏŏk*, *pa t* and *obs pa p* of **take**.

tool *tōōl*, *n* a working instrument, *esp* one used by hand; the cutting part of a machine tool; someone who is used as the mere instrument of another; (*esp* in *pl*) anything necessary to the pursuit of a particular activity; any of several devices used to impress a design on a book cover; an impressed design on a book cover; a weapon, *esp* a gun (*slang*); a penis (*vulg slang*); a utility, feature of function available as part of eg a word-processing package or database (*comput*). — *vt* to shape or finish with a tool; to mark with a tool, *esp* to ornament or imprint designs upon (a book cover), or to chisel the face of (stone); to supply with tools, *esp* with machine tools for a particular purpose (also **tool up**); to drive (a car or other vehicle) *esp* smoothly and skilfully, and *usu* at moderate speed (*slang*); to carry or draw in a vehicle. — *vi* to work with a tool; to provide tools (also **tool up**); to travel (along) in a vehicle, *esp* smoothly and skilfully, and *usu* at moderate speed; (of a vehicle, draught animal) to travel (along, etc) in this way. — *n* **tool'er**. — *n* **tool'ing** workmanship done with a tool, eg on stonework or a book cover; the provision and setting up of tools for eg a machining process. — **tool'bag** (or **tool'box**) a bag (or box) for carrying and storing tools; **tool'bar** (*comput*) a bar with a list of utilities, features, functions, etc which appears *usu* at the top of a computer screen when running some word-processing and database packages; **tool'house** a shed or outhouse for keeping tools in; **tool'kit** a set of tools; **tool'maker** a worker who makes or repairs tools, *esp* machine tools; **tool'making**; **tool'man** a man who works with tools or in a toolroom; **tool'pusher** the supervisor of drilling operations at an oil well; **tool'-room** that part of a factory occupied by toolmakers; **tool'-shed**; **tool steel** steel suitable for making tools, hard enough and tough enough to keep a cutting edge. — **tooled up** (*slang*) carrying a weapon, *esp* a gun. [OE *tōl*]

toom *tōōm*, *tüm*, *tim*, (now only *Scot*) *adj* empty. — *n* a rubbish tip. — *vt* to empty. [OE *tōm* clear]

toon[1] *tōōn*, *n* an Indian tree (*Cedrela toona*), of the mahogany family, with aromatic red wood used for furniture, carving, etc and astringent bark. [Hindi *tūn*]

toon[2], **toun** *tōōn*, (*Scot*) *n* same as **town**.

toorie or **tourie** *tōōr'i*, (*Scot*) *n* a small heap; a knob of hair; a tuft or bobble on a bonnet, or (also **toorie bonnet**) the bonnet itself. [Dimin of *toor*, Scots for **tower**]

toot[1] or **tout** *tōōt*, *vi* to make short sharp sounds, eg on a flute or horn. — *vt* to blow (eg a horn, etc) so as to give short sharp sounds; to inhale (a drug, *usu* cocaine) (*US slang*). — *n* a blast, *esp* as of a horn; a drinking binge (*NAm slang*); a snort (qv) of cocaine, or any drug (*esp* cocaine) for snorting (*US slang*); a toilet (*Austr slang*). — *n* **toot'er** a person who toots, or the instrument used. [Prob imit]

toot[2] *tōōt*, *vi* to pry, peer, peep about (*Spenser*); to be prominent (*obs*). — *n* a hill on which a lookout is posted (*SW England*); a lookout place (*obs*). — *n* **toot'er**. [OE *tōtian* to stick out, peep out]

toot[3]. See under **tut**[1].

tooth *tōōth*, *n* one of the hard bonelike enamel-coated structures embedded in the jawbones, used for biting and chewing; a hard projection of similar function in invertebrates; taste, relish or appetite; a toothlike projection, prong, cog, jag, as on the margin of a leaf, on a comb, saw or wheel; (in *pl*) force, sufficient power to be effective: — *pl* **teeth** (*tēth*). — *vt* to provide with teeth; to cut into teeth. — *vi* (of cog-wheels) to interlock. — *adj* **toothed** (*tōōtht*, *tōōdhd*) having teeth; dentate. — *adj* **tooth'ful** full of teeth; toothsome. — *n* a small drink of spirits, etc. — *adv* **tooth'ily**. — *n* **tooth'iness**. — *adj* **tooth'less** lacking teeth; powerless or ineffective. — *adj* **tooth'like**. — *adj* **tooth'some** palatable, appetizing, tasty; attractive, pleasant, agreeable. — *adv* **tooth'somely**. — *n* **tooth'someness**. — *adj* **tooth'y** with prominent teeth; toothsome; biting (*Scot*). — **tooth'ache** an ache or pain in a tooth; **tooth'ache-tree** the prickly ash (*Xanthoxylum*), so-called because its leaves and bark were used formerly to make a concoction to relieve toothache; **tooth'-billed pigeon** same as **manumea**; **tooth'brush** a brush for cleaning the teeth; **toothbrush moustache** a small stiff moustache; **tooth'comb** a fine-tooth(ed) comb (qv under **fine**[1]); **tooth'-drawer** (*Shakesp*) an extractor of teeth. — *n* and *adj* **tooth'-drawing**. — **tooth fairy** a fairy who substitutes a coin for a milk tooth placed under a child's pillow (*orig US*); **tooth'-ornament** dogtooth; **tooth'paste** (or **tooth powder**) a paste (or powder) used with a toothbrush to clean the teeth; **tooth'pick** an instrument for picking shreds of food from between the teeth; a Bowie knife (*US slang*); **tooth'-picker** (*Shakesp*) a toothpick; someone or something that picks teeth, eg the bird trochilus; **tooth'shell** the tusk shell, *Dentalium*; **tooth'-wash** a liquid preparation for cleansing the teeth; **tooth'wort** a pale fleshy plant (*Lathraea squamaria*) of the broomrape family, parasitic on tree-roots, with toothlike scale-leaves; the cruciferous coral-root (*Cardamine*, or *Dentaria*, *bulbifera*). — **a colt's tooth** an addiction to youthful pleasures; **armed to the teeth** armed as completely as possible, from top to toe; **a sweet tooth** a taste for sweet things; **by the skin of one's teeth** see under **skin**; **cast**, **throw** or **fling in someone's teeth** to fling at someone as a taunt or reproach; **get one's teeth into** to tackle, deal with, vigorously, eagerly, etc; **in** or **to someone's teeth** to someone's face; in direct affront; **in spite of someone's teeth** or **in the teeth of** in direct opposition to; **lie through one's teeth** to lie brazenly; **long in the tooth** elderly, like a horse whose gums are receding with age; **set one's teeth on edge** see under **edge**; **take the teeth out of** to render harmless or powerless; **through clenched teeth** reluctantly; **tooth and nail** with all possible vigour and fury. [OE *tōth* (pl *tēth*); Gothic *tunthus*, L *dēns*, *dentis*, Gr *odous*, *odontos*, Sans *danta*]

tootle *tōōt'l*, *vi* to make feeble sounds, as on the flute; to go casually along, *esp* by car (*colloq*). — *n* a soft sound on the flute, etc; a casual trip, a drive (*colloq*). [Frequentative of **toot**[1]]

toots[1]. See under **tut**[1].

toots[2] *tōōts* or **tootsy** *toot'si*, (*colloq*, *esp US*) *n* sweetheart. [Ety obscure]

tootsie, **tootsy** or **tootsy-woodsy** *tōōt'si* (*-wōōt'si*), *n* jocular or childish words for a foot or toe. [Perh a childish pron of **foot**]

top[1] *top*, *n* the highest or uppermost part or place; the highest or most important position (eg in a profession, company, salary scale, scale of authority or privilege, etc); the person occupying this position; the upper edge or surface; a lid or cover; a garment for the upper part of a person's (*esp* a woman's or child's) body; the highest or loudest degree of pitch; (in *pl*; with *the*) the very best person or thing (*colloq*); top gear; (*esp* in *pl*) the part of a root vegetable that is above the ground; a handful or bundle of flax, wool, etc, for spinning; a circus tent (*slang*; **big top** the main tent); a topsail; a small platform at the head of the lower mast; a crest or tuft (*naut*); a trench parapet; a top-boot (*esp* in *pl*); topspin; the earliest part (as *top of the morning* — a conventional Irish greeting); (in *pl*) in oil-refining, the first part of a volatile mixture to come off in the distillation process; a stroke that hits the upper quarter of the ball (*golf*). — *adj* highest; best; most important, able, etc. — *vt* to cover on the top; to tip; to rise above; to surpass; to reach the top of; to surmount; to be on or at the top of; to take off the top of; to hit (the ball) on the upper quarter, so that it only travels a few inches along the ground (*golf*); to kill (*slang*); (eg of a male animal) to cover (*Shakesp*). — *vi* to finish up, round off (with *off* or *up*): — *pr p* **topp'ing**; *pa t* and *pa p* **topped**. — *adj* **top'full** (*Shakesp*) full to the top or brim. — *adj* **top'less** without a top; (of women's clothing) leaving the breasts uncovered; (of a woman) with bare breasts; (of a place, entertainment, etc) that features women with bare breasts; without superior (*Shakesp*). — *n* **top'lessness**. — *adj* **top'most** (*-mōst*, *-məst*) uppermost; highest. — *adj* **topped**. — *n* **topp'er** a person or thing that tops in any sense; a person who excels at anything, a good sort (*colloq*); a top hat (*colloq*). — *n* **topp'ing** the act of a person or thing that tops; (in *pl*) pieces cut from the top; a sauce or dressing to go over food. — *adj* surpassing, pre-eminent; excellent (*old slang*); arrogant (*US*). — *adv* **topp'ingly**. — *adj* **tops** (*colloq*) best, excellent. — *adv* (*colloq*) at most, as a maximum. — **top'-boot** a knee-length boot with a showy band of leather round the top. — *adj* **top'-booted** wearing top-boots. — **top brass** see under **brass**; **top'coat** an overcoat; **top dead-centre** (of a reciprocating engine or pump) the piston position at the beginning of the outstroke, ie when the crank-pin is nearest to the cylinder (also **inner dead-centre**); **top dog** (*colloq*) the winner, leader or dominant person. — *adj* **top-down'** organized or controlled from the top, by the most important or powerful people involved. — **top drawer** the highest level, *esp* of society (**out of the top drawer**, belonging to this social rank). — *adj* **top-draw'er**. — *vt* **top'-dress**. — **top'-dressing** manure or fertilizer applied to the surface of soil and not dug in; the application of it; any superficial covering or treatment (*fig*). — *adj* **top'-flight** excellent, superior, of the highest class or quality. — *adj* **topgallant** (*tə-*, *top-gal'ənt*) above the topmast and topsail and below the royal mast. — *n* a topgallant mast or sail, or the topgallant rigging; **top gear** the highest gear in a motor vehicle or on a bicycle; **top-hamp'er** unnecessary weight on a ship's upper deck; **top hat** a man's tall cylindrical hat with a narrow brim, made of silk plush. — *adj* (with *hyphen*) upper class; designed to benefit high executives, or the rich, as in *top-hat budget*, *top-hat* (*insurance*) *policy*. — *adj* **top-heav'y** having the upper part too heavy or large for the lower; (eg of an organization or company) with too many administrative staff or executives; (of a company) overcapitalized; tipsy. — *adj* **top-hole'** (*old slang*) excellent, first-class (also *interj*). — **top'knot** a crest, tuft of hair, often a piece of added hair, or knot of ribbons, etc, on the top of the head; the head (*slang*); a small fish (of several species) related to the turbot. — *adj* **top'knotted**. — *adj* **top'-level** at the highest level; involving people from this level. — *adj* **top'line** important enough to be mentioned in a headline. — *vi* to feature in a headline; to star, appear as the principal performer. — **toplin'er** a person who is top-line; a principal performer, a star. — *adj* **top'loftical** or **top'lofty** (*facetious*) high and mighty, haughty; stuck-up. — *adv* **top'loftily**. — **top'loftiness**; **top'man** a seaman stationed in the topgallant or topsail rigging; a top-sawyer; **top'mast** (*-məst*, *-mäst*) the second mast, or that immediately above the lower mast; **top'minnow** a small, surface-feeding, soft-rayed fish belonging to any of various species, either viviparous (of the family *Cyprinodontidae*) or egg-laying (of the family *Poeciliidae*) (also called **mosquito fish**; see also **killifish**). — *adj* **top-notch'** (*colloq*) excellent, first-rate. — **top-notch'er**; **topped crude** crude oil after some of its lighter constituents have been removed by distillation; **topping lift** (*naut*) tackle running from the masthead for raising booms; **topp'ing-out** see **top out** below. — *adj* **top'-priority** very urgent. — *adj* **top'-proud** (*Shakesp*) proud in the highest degree. — **top quark** (*phys*) a particle believed to be one of the fundamental constituents of nuclear matter; **top'sail** (*-sl*, *-sāl*) a sail across the topmast; **top-saw'yer** the upper sawyer in a sawpit; a superior, a person of importance (*colloq*). — *adj* **top secret** profoundly secret and of the highest importance. — **top'side** the upper part; the outer part of a round of beef; a lean cut of beef from the rump; the part of an oil rig, etc above the deck; (also in *pl*) the part of the outer surface of a vessel above the waterline. — Also *adv*. — **tops'man** a head drover, a foreman (*Scot*); a hangman (*slang*). — *adj* **top'-shelf** (*Austr*) of the latest design. — **top'soil** the upper part or surface of the soil; **top'soiling** removal of the topsoil; **top'spin** spin imparted to a ball by hitting it sharply on the upper half with a forward and upward stroke to make it travel higher, further, or more quickly; extra, not always reliable or well-attested, information (*journalists' slang*); **top'-stone** a stone placed on the top, or forming the top; **top table** the place assigned to the most important people at a meeting or banquet; **top'-up** an amount added to bring something back up to a reasonable or the original level; **top-up**, **topping-up** see also **top up** below; **top-up loan** a loan to bring a mortgage, grant, etc up to the required amount. — **at the top of one's voice** at one's loudest; **go over the top** to go over the front of a trench and attack the enemy; to take sudden action after hesitation; to exceed the bounds of reason, decorum, etc; **in the top flight** in the highest class; **off the top of one's head** without previous thought or preparation; **on top of the world** near the North Pole; on a high mountain; exuberant, in the very best of spirits; **over the top** (*colloq*) too far, extreme, to an excess, to, at or of an unreasonable or unnecessary degree; **the tops** (*slang*) the very best; **top and tail** to wash (a baby's) face and buttocks; to prepare (fruit or vegetables, eg carrots) by removing the top and bottom parts; **top one's part** (*theat*) to excel in playing one's part; **top out** to finish (a building) by putting on the top or highest course; (of eg prices) to reach the highest level (and go no further) (*n* **topp'ing-out**); **top the bill** to be the most important attraction in a programme of entertainment, etc; **top up** to fill up, eg with fuel oil, alcoholic beverage; to bring (eg a wage) up to a generally accepted or satisfactory level (*n* **top'-up** or **topp'ing-up**); (of a ship's yards) to place at an angle to the deck (*naut*). [OE *top*; Ger *Zopf*]

top[2] *top*, *n* a toy that can be set spinning on its pointed base (also called **spinning top**); a grooved cone held back between the strands in rope-making; a marine gasteropod of the genus *Trochus*, with a pearly flattish-based conical shell (also called **top'-shell**). — *n* **top'-maker**. — *n* **top'making**. — **sleep like a top** to sleep very soundly. [Appar late OE *top* (but the meaning is doubtful)]

toparch *top'ärk*, *n* the ruler of a district. — *n* **top'archy** a toparch's territory. [Gr *toparchēs*, from *topos* a place, and *archein* to rule]

topaz *tō'paz*, *n* a precious stone, silicate of aluminium and fluorine, yellowish, bluish or colourless; a variety of orange and tangerine hybrid; (loosely) a shade of dark yellow; a S American hummingbird of the genus *Topaza*. — *adj* **tō'pazine**. — *n* **topaz'olite** a yellowish or greenish garnet. — **oriental topaz** a yellow corundum. [Gr *topazos* a green gem]

tope[1] *tōp*, *vi* to drink hard regularly. — *interj* (*obs*) used in drinking to someone's health. — *n* **tō'per** a drunkard. [Poss Fr *toper* to accept a wager]

tope[2] *tōp*, *n* a Buddhist stupa or dome for relics. [Hindi *top*, from Sans *stūpa* a heap]

tope[3] *tōp*, *n* any of various small sharks, *esp Galeorhinus galeus*. [Said to be Cornish]

tope[4] *tōp*, *n* in (E) India, a grove (eg of mangoes), a plantation. [Tamil *tōppu*, from Telugu *topu*]

topectomy *top-ek'tə-mi*, (*med*; now *obs*) *n* the excision of a part of the cerebral cortex as treatment for certain mental illnesses. [Gr *topos* place, *ek* from, and **-tomy**]

topee. See under **topi**.

topek. Same as **tupik**.

Tophet *tō'fet*, *n* an ancient place of human sacrifice near Jerusalem, the valley of Hinnom or part of it, later a place of refuse disposal; hence Hell. [Heb *tōpheth*]

tophus *tō'fəs*, (*med*) *n* a gouty deposit, a hard nodule formed of sodium biurate crystals in soft body tissue: — *pl* **tō'phi** (*-fī*). — *adj* **tophā'ceous**. [L *tōphus*, *tōfus* porous stone, tufa]

topi[1] or **topee** *tō-pē'*, *tō'pē*, *n* a hat, *esp* a sola hat, pith helmet, worn *esp* in India. — **to'pi-wallah** a European in India. [Hindi *ṭopī* hat (perh from Port *topo* top)]

topi[2] *tō'pi*, *n* a large African antelope (*Damaliscus korrigum*) with curved horns and long muzzle. [Appar from a native word]

topiary *tō'pi-ə-ri*, *n* a branch of gardening, the clipping of trees into imitative and fantastic shapes; an example of this; mural decoration in fanciful landscape. — Also *adj*. — *adj* **topiā'rian**. — *n* **tō'piarist**. [L *topiārius*, from *topia* (pl), landscape, landscape gardening, from Gr *topos* a place]

topic *top'ik*, *n* a general consideration suitable for argument; a subject or theme of discourse or argument; a matter; a head under which a rhetorician might look up matter for discourse. — *adj* **top'ical** of or relating to current affairs; local; relating to a topic or subject; affecting only part of the body (*med*). — *n* **topical'ity** the quality of being topical; an item or subject possessing this. — *adv* **top'ically**. [Gr *topikos* pertaining to place or to commonplaces, *ta topika* the general principles of argument, from *topos* a place]

to-pinch a false emendation of some Shakespeare editors (*Merry Wives* IV. 4. 59), for *to pinch*, the second of two infinitives having *to* where the first is without *to*.

topography *top-og'rə-fi*, *n* the detailed study, description or features of a limited area, district, etc; the detailed study or description of external features of the body with reference to those underneath. — *n* **topog'rapher**. — *adj* **topographic** (*top-ə-graf'ik*) or **topograph'ical**. — *adv* **topograph'ically**. [Gr *topographiā*, from *topos* a place, and *graphein* to describe]

topoi. See under **topos**.

topology *top-ol'ə-ji*, *n* the topographical study of a particular place; topographical anatomy; a branch of geometry concerned with those properties of a figure which remain unchanged even when the figure is bent, stretched, etc; the study of those properties of sets of points (eg geometrical figures) that are invariant under one-to-one continuous transformations (*math*); the interconnection, organization, etc of computers within a network. — *adj* **topolog'ic** or **topolog'ical**. — *adv* **topolog'ically**. — *n* **topol'ogist**. [Gr *topos* a place, and *logos* a discourse]

toponym *top'ə-nim*, *n* a place name; a descriptive place name, *usu* derived from a geographical feature; a name derived from a place name, eg a place of origin. — *adj* **topon'ymal, toponymic** (*-ə-nim'ik*) or **toponym'ical**. — *n* **toponymy** (*top-on'i-mi*) the study of place names (also *n sing* **toponym'ics**); the nomenclature of regions of the body. [Gr *topos* place, and *onyma* (*onoma*) name]

topophilia *top'ə-fil-iə*, *n* great affection for a particular place. [Gr *topos* place, and *phileein* to love]

topos *top'os*, *n* a stock theme, topic or expression in literature or rhetoric: — *pl* **top'oi** (*-oi*, *-ē*). [Gr, literally, a place]

topotype *top'ə-tīp*, (*zool*) *n* a specimen collected in the same locality as the original specimen of the same species. [Gr *topos* a place, and **type**]

topped, topping, etc. See under **top**[1].

topple *top'l*, *vi* to overbalance and fall headlong; to threaten to fall from top-heaviness, to totter. — *vt* to cause to topple. [**top**[1]]

to prepon *to pre'pon*, (*Gr*) the fitting; the becoming or seemly.

topsy-turvy *top'si-tûr'vi*, *adv* bottom upwards. — *adj* turned upside down. — *n* confusion. — *vt* to turn upside down. — also **top'side-tur'v(e)y**, (*Scot* **tap'-salteer'ie**, as *adj*, *adv*, *n*). — *n* **topsy-turvificā'tion** a turning upside down. — *adv* **topsy-tur'vily**. — *n* **topsy-tur'viness**. — *n* **topsy-tur'vydom**. [**top**, and the obs verbs *terve* to turn (cf OE *tearflian* to roll); **so**, **set**, and **side** are only conjectures]

toque *tōk*, *n* a woman's close-fitting brimless or nearly brimless hat; a 16c form of cap or turban (*hist*); a hair-pad (*obs*); a chef's tall white hat; a macaque (*Macacus pileatus*), of Ceylon. [Fr]

toquilla *tə-kē'yə*, *n* (a fibre obtained from the leaves of) a S American palm-like tree, *Carludovica palmata*. [Sp, dimin of *toca* toque]

tor or **torr** *tör*, *n* a hill, a rocky height. [OE *torr* tor, from L *turris* tower, or perh from Celtic]

Torah or **Thorah** *tō'*, *tö'rə*, (*Judaism*) *n* the Mosaic Law; the book of the law, the Pentateuch; a scroll containing this. [Heb *Tōrāh*]

toran *tör'*, *tör'ən* or **torana** *-'ənə*, *n* (in India) a type of arched gateway; a garland of flowers or leaves hung between two points; a richly embroidered hanging hung above the doorway to the main room of a house. [Hindi]

torbanite *tör'bən-īt*, *n* a shale, almost a coal, once mined for oil at *Torbane* Hill, Bathgate, Scotland.

torbernite *tör'bərn-īt*, *n* a bright green radioactive hydrous phosphate of copper and uranium. [After *Torbern* Bergmann (1735–84), Swed chemist]

torc. See under **torque**.

torch *törch*, *n* a piece of wood or inflammable material dipped in tallow or wax and lighted, carried or mounted on a wall, etc to give light; a large candle; a small, battery-powered portable electric lamp; an appliance producing a hot flame for welding, burning, etc; a source of enlightenment, guidance, etc; an arsonist (*US slang*); a glowing flower or inflorescence, eg mullein; a tall cactaceous plant. — *vt* to light with a torch or torches; to set alight deliberately (*slang*, *esp US*); to sing (a torch-song) (*rare*; *US*) — *n* **torch'er** (*Shakesp*) a light-giver. — *n* **torch'ing** (*slang*, *esp US*); the act of setting something alight, *esp* deliberately. — **torch'bearer** a person who carries a torch; a leading, prominent figure in a cause, etc (*fig*); **torch'-dance**; **torch'light**; **torch'-lily** the red-hot poker (*Kniphofia* or *Tritoma*); **torch'-race** a race in which the runners carried torches and passed them to others; **torch'-singer**; **torch'-song** a popular song of the 1930s giving lugubrious expression to the pangs of unrequited love; a sentimental or melancholy love song; **torch'-staff** (*pl* **torch'-staves**; *Shakesp*) a staff for carrying a torch; **torch'-thistle** a cereus; **torch'wood** any of several resinous woods suitable for making torches; any tree yielding such wood, *esp Amyris balsamifera*, native to Florida and the W Indies. — **carry the** (or **a**) **torch** (**for**) to suffer unrequited love (for); **put to the torch** to burn down. [Fr *torche*, from L *torquēre*, *tortum* to twist]

torchère *tor-sher'*, (*Fr*) *n* a tall ornamental candlestick or lampstand.

torchier or **torchière** *tor-sher'*, (*Fr*) *n* a floor lamp consisting of a bowl for reflecting light upwards mounted on a tall stand.

torchon *tör-shɔ̃*, *n* (*Fr*) a duster or dishcloth; (in full **torchon lace**) peasants' bobbin lace of loose texture and geometrical design, or a machine-made imitation; (in full **torchon paper**) a rough paper for watercolour drawing. [Fr, from *torcher* to wipe]

torcular *tör'kū-lər*, *n* a tourniquet. [L *torcular*, *-āris* a wine-press, oil-press]

tordion *tor-di-ōn'*, *tor'di-ən*, *n* a dance similar to, but less spirited than, a galliard, *esp* common in the 15c and 16c. [Fr, from OFr *tourdion*, from Fr *tordre* to twist]

tore[1] *tōr*, *tör*, *pa t* and *obs pa p* of **tear**[2].

tore[2]. See under **torus**.

toreador *tor'i-ə-dör*, *n* a bullfighter, *esp* on horseback. — *n* **torero** (*tor-ā'rō*) a bullfighter on foot: — *pl* **tore'ros**. — **toreador pants** tight-fitting calf-length trousers for women (resembling those worn by toreadors). [Sp *toro* bull, from L *taurus* bull]

to-rend *tə-*, *tōō-rend'*, (*obs*) *vt* to rend in pieces: — *pa p* (*Spenser*) **to-rent'**.

toreutic *tör-ū'tik*, *-ōō'*, *adj* (of metal) chased or embossed. — *n sing* **toreu'tics** artistic work in metal, producing by chasing and embossing. [Gr *toreutikos*, *-ē*, *-on*, from *toreuein* to bore]

torgoch *tör'gohh*, *n* the red-bellied char. [Welsh]

tori, **toric**. See under **torus**.

torii *tör'ē-ē*, *n* a Japanese Shinto temple gateway: — *pl* **tor'ii**. [Jap]

torment *tör'ment*, *n* physical or mental pain or suffering; a cause of this; torture (*archaic*); an instrument of torture (*archaic*). — *vt* **torment** (*-ment'*) to cause extreme pain or suffering to; to distress; to afflict; to pester or tease; to harass; to torture (*archaic*); to agitate, stir violently; to distort, force violently. — *adj* **tormen'ted**. — *adv* **torment'edly**. — *n* and *adj* **tor-ment'ing**. — *adv* **tormen'tingly**. — *n* **tormen'tor** or **tormen'ter** a person or thing that torments; a torturer, an executioner (*Bible*); a long meat-fork; a wing in the first groove of a stage, screened from the audience eg by a curtain. [L *tormentum*, from *torquēre* to twist]

tormentil *tör'men-til*, *n* a four-petalled potentilla with bright yellow flowers and an astringent woody root, growing on heaths. [OFr *tormentille*, from Med L *tormentilla*, from L *tormentum* torment, in reference to its use as an analgesic]

tormentum *tör-men'təm*, (*hist*) *n* a Roman machine for hurling missiles. [L, from *torquēre* to twist]

tormina *tör'mi-nə*, *n pl* gripes. — *adj* **tor'minal** or **tor'-minous**. [L, from *torquēre* to twist]

torn *törn*, *tōrn*, *adj* and *pa p* of **tear**[2]. — *adj* **torn'-down** (*US*) unruly. — **that's torn it!** (*colloq*) an expression of annoyance indicating that something has spoilt one's plans, etc.

tornado *tör-nā'dō*, *n* (*orig*) a violent tropical Atlantic thunderstorm, occurring eg off the W coast of Africa; a very violent whirling windstorm characterized by a long, funnel-shaped cloud, affecting a narrow strip of country; (loosely) a hurricane: — *pl* **tornā'does** or **tornā'dos**. — *n* (*poetic*) **tornade'**. — *adj* **tornadic** (*-nad'ik*). [Prob Sp *tronada* thunderstorm, altered as if from Sp *tornada* turning]

toroid, **toroidal**. See under **torus**.

torose *tör'ōz* or **torous** *tör'əs*, *adj* cylindrical with swelling or bulges at intervals (*bot*); swelling, bulging, knobby. [L *torōsus* bulging, full of muscle]

torpedo *tör-pē'dō*, *n* a self-propelled submarine weapon (*usu* cigar-shaped), carrying a charge which explodes on impact, launched from aircraft, ships or submarines; a bomb, cartridge, case of explosives, or detonator of various kinds, used in warfare, in boring, as a fog-signal, firework, etc; a member of the genus *Torpedo* of cartilaginous fishes, related to the skates and rays, with organs on the head that give an electric shock, giving name to the family **Torpedinidae** (*-pə-din'i-dē*): — *pl* **torpē'does** or **torpē'dos**. — *vt* to attack, strike, destroy, by torpedo; to wreck (eg a plan). — *adj* **torpē'dinous** numbing. — *n* **torpē'doer**. — *n* **torpē'doist**. — **torpedo boat** a small swift warship discharging torpedoes; **torpe'do-boat destroyer** a swifter, more powerful, type of torpedo boat *orig* used to destroy ordinary torpedo boats; **torpedo boom** a spar for carrying a torpedo, projecting from a boat or anchored in a channel; **torpe'do-net** a steel net hung round a ship to intercept torpedoes; **torpedo tube** a tube from which torpedoes are discharged. [L *torpēdō*, *-inis* numbness, the torpedo (fish), from *torpēre* to be stiff]

torpefy *tör'pi-fī*, *vt* to make numb or torpid, to paralyse. — *n* **torpesc'ence** the process of becoming numb or torpid. — *adj* **torpesc'ent** becoming numb or torpid. [L *torpefacere* to make numb, and *torpescĕre* to grow numb, from *torpēre* to be numb]

torpid *tör'pid*, *adj* numb; lethargic; having lost the power of motion and feeling; sluggish; (of a hibernating animal) dormant. — *n* (at Oxford University) a second boat of a college, or its crew; (in *pl*) the Lent term races of eight-oared clinker-built boats. — *n* **torpid'ity**. — *adv* **tor'pidly**. — *n* **tor'pidness**. — *n* **tor'pitude**. — *n* **tor'por** numbness; inactivity; dullness; stupidity. — *adj* **torporif'ic**. [L *torpidus*, *torpor*, from *torpēre* to be numb]

torquate *tör'kwāt* or **torquated** *-id*, (*zool*) *adj* with a distinctive ring (eg of feathers or a different colour) round the neck. [L *torquātus* wearing a necklace, from *torquēs*, *-is* a necklace]

torque *törk*, *n* the measure of the turning effect of a tangential force; a force or system of forces causing or tending to cause rotation or torsion; a necklace or armband in the form of a twisted metal band (also **torc**). — *adj* **torqued** (*törkt*) twisted. — **torque converter** (*mech*) a device which acts as an infinitely variable gear; **torque'-meter**; **torque spanner** (*eng*) a spanner with a special attachment allowing force to be applied to a bolt through the medium of the nut. [L *torquēre* to twist; *torquēs*, *-is* a necklace]

torr[1]. See under **tor**.

torr[2] *tör*, (*phys*) *n* a unit used in expressing very low pressures, $\frac{1}{760}$ of a standard atmosphere, equal to one millimetre of mercury. [E *Torr*icelli; see **Torricellian**]

torrefy *tor'i-fī*, *vt* to scorch or parch; to dry or roast (ore, drugs, etc) with intense heat: — *pr p* **torr'efying**; *pa t* and *pa p* **torr'efied**. — *n* **torrefac'tion**. [L *torrēre* to parch, roast, and *facere* to make]

torrent *tor'ənt*, *n* a rushing stream; a variable mountain stream; an abounding, strong or turbulent flow. — *adj* rushing in a stream. — *adj* **torrential** (*-en'shl*). — *n* **torrentiality** (*-en-shi-al'i-ti*). — *adv* **torren'tially**. — *adj* **torrent'uous**. — **torr'ent-bow** a bow of prismatic colours formed by the spray of a torrent. [L *torrēns*, *-entis* boiling, pr p of *torrēre* to dry]

torret *tor'it*. See under **terret**.

Torricellian *tor-i-chel'i-ən*, *adj* pertaining to the Italian mathematician Evangelista *Torricelli* (1608–47) who discovered in 1643 the principle of the barometer. — **Torricellian tube** a barometer in which mercury rises and falls in a vacuum; **Torricellian vacuum** the vacuum in this type of barometer.

torrid *tor'id*, *adj* scorching or parching; violently hot; dried with heat; intensely passionate, emotional, etc. — *n* **torrid'ity** or **torr'idness**. — *adv* **torr'idly**. — **torrid zone** the zone between the tropics. [L *torridus*, from *torrēre* to parch, roast]

Torridonian *tor-i-dō'ni-ən*, (*geol*) *n* and *adj* Pre-Cambrian of the NW Highlands of Scotland, as around Loch *Torridon*.

torse[1] *törs*, *n* a heraldic wreath. — *n* **torsade** (*-sād'*) an ornament like a twisted cord, eg on a hat. [Fr, from L *torquēre* to twist]

torse[2]. See under **torso**.

torsel *tör'sl*, *n* a plate in a brick wall to support the end of a beam. — Also **tassel**. [L *taxillus* a die, Ital *tassello*, Fr *tasseau*]

torsi. See under **torso**.

torsion *tör'shən*, *n* twisting; a twist; the strain produced by twisting; the force with which a thread or wire tends to return when twisted; the checking of a haemorrhage by twisting the cut end of the artery (*surg*). — *n* **torsibility** (*-si-bil'i-ti*) the ability to be twisted or subjected to torsion; the degree to which twisting or torsion can be recovered from. — *n* **tor'siograph** an instrument for measuring and recording the frequency and amplitude of torsional vibrations in a shaft. — *adj* **tor'sional**. — *adj* **tor'sive** twisted spirally. — **tor'sion-balance** an instrument for measuring very minute forces by a horizontal needle suspended by a very fine filament; **torsion bar** a metal bar which absorbs force by twisting, used *esp* in vehicle suspension; **torsion meter** a torque-meter. [L *torsiō*, *-ōnis*, from *torquēre*, *tortum* to twist]

torsk *törsk*, *n* a N Atlantic fish (*Brosmius brosme*) of the cod family, with a long single dorsal fin. [Swed, Norw, Dan *torsk*, from ON *thorskr*; cf Ger *Dorsch* haddock]

torso *tör'sō*, *n* the trunk of a statue or human body, without head or limbs; anything incomplete or unfinished: — *pl* **tor'sos** or (*rare*) **tor'si** (*-sē*). — Also **torse** (*Fr*). [Ital, stalk, core, torso, from L *thyrsus*, from Gr *thyrsos*]

tort *tört*, *n* wrong, injury (*Spenser*); any wrong, not arising out of contract, for which an action for compensation or damages may be brought (*law*). — *adj* **tortious** (*tör'shəs*) wrongful; of the nature of a tort (*law*). — *adv* **tor'tiously**. — **tort'feasor** (*-fē-zər*; *law*) a person guilty of tort. [Fr, from LL *tortum*, from L *torquēre*, *tortum* to twist]

torte *tör'tə*, *tört*, *n* a rich sweet cake or pastry, Austrian in origin, often garnished or filled with fruit, nuts, cream, chocolate, etc: — *pl* **tor'ten**, **tor'tes** (*-ez*) or **tortes**. [Ger, perh from LL *torta* a round loaf]

tortellini *tör-tə-lē'ni*, *n pl* small round pasta cases filled with a savoury, *usu* meat, filling and seasoning and boiled in water. [Ital, ult from LL *torta* a round loaf of bread]

tortfeasor. See under **tort**.

torticollis *tör-ti-kol'is*, (*pathol*) *n* wry-neck. [LL, from L *tortus* twisted, and *collum* neck]

tortile *tör'tīl*, *adj* twisted; wreathed; coiled. — *n* **tortility** (*-til'*). — *adj* **tor'tive** (*Shakesp*) turned awry. [L *tortilis*, *tortīvus*, from *torquēre* to twist]

tortilla *tör-tē(l)'ya*, *-yə*, *n* a Mexican round flat cake made from maize or wheat flour cooked on a griddle, *usu* eaten hot with a filling; a thick Spanish omelet made mainly of potato and egg. [Sp, dimin of *torta* cake]

tortious. See under **tort**.

tortive. See under **tortile**.

tortoise *tör'təs*, *n* any land or freshwater (rarely marine) chelonian of the family *Testudinidae*, with a dome-shaped leathery shell (now, in Britain, *usu* restricted to land forms); a testudo (*military*). — **tortoise beetle** any of various beetles (*Cassidinae*) of the family *Chrysomelidae* which resemble the tortoise, having broad, often brightly-coloured or metallic wing-covers; (*specif*) a green leaf-beetle (*Cassida viridis*); **tor'toise-plant** elephant's-foot; **tortoiseshell** (*tör'tə-shel*) the shell of a tortoise; a translucent mottled material, the horny plates (*esp* of the back) of the hawksbill turtle; a similar synthetic material; a tortoiseshell butterfly or cat. — *adj* made of, or mottled like, tortoiseshell. — **tortoiseshell butterfly** any of several species of butterfly with orange or reddish wings marked with black and yellow, edged with blue, etc, *esp Aglais urticae* (small tortoiseshell), and *Nymphalis polychlorus* (large tortoise-shell); **tortoiseshell cat** a domestic cat (nearly always female) mottled in yellow and black. [LL *tortuca*]

tortoni *tör-tō'nē*, *n* a rich ice cream flavoured with dessert or fortified wine and containing chopped fruit, nuts, etc. [Ital, perh from an Italian café owner in Paris in the 18c]

tortrix *tör'triks*, *n* a member of the *Tortrix* genus of moths belonging to the **Tortricidae** (*-tris'i-dē*), a large family of small moths whose caterpillars spin silken webs drawing leaves, flowers, etc into a rolled-up protective covering around themselves: — *pl* **tortrices** (*-trī'sēz*). — *n* **tortrī'cid** any moth of the *Tortricidae* family. — Also *adj*. [Invented L, twister]

tortuous *tör'tū-əs*, *adj* full of twistings and windings; devious; far from straightforward, circuitous. — *n* **tortuos'ity**. — *adv* **tor'tuously**. — *n* **tor'tuousness**. [L *tortuōsus*, from *torquēre*, *tortum* to twist]

torture *tör'chər*, *n* the infliction of severe pain *esp* as a means of punishment or persuasion; extreme physical or mental pain; anguish. — *vt* to subject to torture; to subject to extreme pain; to exact by torture; to distort violently. — *adj* **tor'tured** suffering or entailing torture or anguish; fraught with worries or difficulties, painful (*colloq*); violently distorted. — *adv* **tor'turedly**. — *n* **tor'turer**. — *adj* **tor'turesome**. — *n* and *adj* **tor'turing**. — *adv* **tor'turingly**. — *adj* **tor'turous** causing torture or violent distortion. [Fr, from L *tortūra* torment, from *torquēre*, *tortum* to twist]

toruffled *tə-*, *tōō-ruf'ld*, (*archaic*) *adj* (*Milton* **to ruffl'd**) ruffled up. [Pfx *to-*, intens, and **ruffle**[1]]

torula *tör'ū-lə*, *n* a yeastlike microorganism of the genus *Torula*; a commercially produced yeast used in food and medicine: — *pl* **tor'ulae** (*-lē*). — *n* **tor'ūlin** a vitamin in yeast. — *n* **torūlō'sis** infection with a member of the *Torula* genus affecting the nervous system. [New L, from L *tonus* a bulge, swelling]

torulose *tör'ū-lōz*, (*bot*) *adj* with small swellings at intervals. [L *tonus* a bulge, swelling]

torulus *tör'ū-ləs*, (*zool*) *n* the socket of an insect's antenna: — *pl* **tor'ūli** (*-lī*). [Dimin of L *torus* a bulge, swelling]

torus *tō'*, *tö'rəs*, *n* a large moulding, semicircular or nearly so in section, common at the base of a column (*archit*); a figure generated by the revolution of a circle or other conic section about a straight line in its own plane (*geom*); the receptacle of a flower (*bot*); a ridge or prominence (*zool*, *anatom*); a ring-shaped discharge-tube: — *pl* **to'rī**. — *n* **tore** (*tōr*, *tör*; *archit* and *geom*) a torus. — *adj* **toric** (*tor'*, *tōr'*, *tör'*) of or having the form of a torus or a part of a torus. — *adj* **toroid** (*tor'*, *tōr'*, *tör'*) shaped like an anchor-ring. — *n* a coil or transformer of that shape. — *adj* **toroid'al**. [L *torus* a bulge, swelling, bed, torus moulding]

Tory *tō'*, *tö'ri*, *n* a Conservative (*UK politics*); a bigoted or extreme Conservative; a member of the English political party who opposed the exclusion of James II from the monarchy in the 17c (*hist*); (in Ireland) a Roman Catholic, *esp* an outlaw or robber, who preyed on English settlers in the 17c (*hist*); a person who sided with the British in the Revolution (*US hist*). — *adj* Conservative. — *vt* **Tō'rify** or **Tō'ryfy** to infect with Tory principles. — *adj* **Tō'ryish**. — *n* **Tō'ryism** the principles of the Tories. [Ir *toiridhe* a pursuer, robber; first applied to the Tories in Ireland; next, about 1680, to the most hot-headed asserters of the royal prerogative]

tosa *tō'zə*, *n* (in full **Japanese tosa**) a heavily built, smooth-haired dog, the adult of which weighs *approx* 7 stone, bred for fighting. [Jap]

tose. See under **toze**.

tosh[1] *tosh*, (*Scot*) *adj* neat, trim; comfortable, friendly, intimate. — Also *adv*. — *vt* to trim.

tosh[2] *tosh*, (*slang*) *n* bosh, twaddle. — *adj* **tosh'y**.

tosh[3] *tosh*, (*slang*) *n* (used as a form of address) friend, chum.

toshach *tö'shəhh*, *tosh'əhh*, *n* a phonetic rendering of **toiseach**.

tosher *tosh'ər*, (*university slang*) *n* a non-collegiate student. [From **unattached**]

toss *tos*, *vt* to throw up in the air; to throw lightly and carelessly (with *away*, *aside*, *out*, etc); to fling, jerk (eg the head), eg as a sign of impatience; to roll about or throw from side to side or to and fro, *esp* repeatedly and violently; to throw (a coin) into the air to make a decision, etc based on the side which falls upwards; to settle a dispute with (someone) by doing this; (of a horse) to throw (its rider); (of a bull, etc) to throw (a person, etc) into the air with its horns; to coat (food) by mixing it gently with a dressing; to discuss or consider, *esp* in an informal or light-hearted way; to agitate; to turn the leaves of (*obs*); to tilt in drinking; to drink. — *vi* to be tossed; to be in violent commotion; to be rolled or thrown about from side to side or to and fro, *esp* repeatedly and violently; to fling; to toss up a coin: — *pa t* and *pa p* **tossed** (*tost*), or rarely **tost**. — *infinitive* (*Spenser*) **toss'en**. — *n* an act of throwing upward; a throwing up or back of the head; confusion, commotion; the act of tossing a coin; a fall from a horse. — *n* **toss'er** a person or thing that tosses; an unpleasant or despicable person (*vulg slang*). — *adv* **toss'ily** pertly. — *n* and *adj* **toss'ing**. — *adj* **toss'y** pert, contemptuous. — **toss'pot** (*slang*) a toper, a drunkard (*old*); an incompetent, unpleasant or foolish person (*prob* by confusion with **tosser**); a jocular or hearty term of address, *usu* to a man (*Austr*); **toss'-up** the throwing up of a coin to decide anything; an even chance or risk. — **argue the toss** to dispute a decision; **toss and turn** be wakeful, restless and fidgety in bed; **toss off** to perform or produce quickly or cursorily; to drink off in a single draught; to remark casually; to masturbate (*vulg slang*); **toss out** (*old*) to dress smartly, fancily; **toss up** to toss a coin; to cook and serve up hastily. [Origin unknown]

tostada *tos-tä'də*, *n* a tortilla fried until crisp and served with a savoury topping of eg beans, minced meat and vegetables. [Sp Am, from Sp *tostar* to toast]

tosticated *tos'ti-kā-tid*, (*dialect*), *adj* fuddled; perplexed — also **toss'icāted**. — *n* **tosticā'tion** perplexity. [A corruption of **intoxicated**, associated with **toss**]

tot[1] *tot*, *n* anything little, *esp* a young child, a drinking-cup, or a dram. — *n* **tott'ie** or **tott'y** (*dimin*) a very small child; a woman or young girl, *esp* when considered sexually attractive (*slang*). — *adj* (*dialect*) very small. [Cf Icel *tottr* a dwarf]

tot[2] *tot*, *vt* and *vi* to add or mount up or total (also **tot up**): — *pr p* **tott'ing**; *pa t* and *pa p* **tott'ed**. — *n* an addition of a long column. — *n* **totting-up'** adding up; the cumulation of certain motoring offences, eventually resulting in disqualification. [**total**]

tot[3] *tot*, (*slang*) *n* a bone; anything retrieved from a dustbin, rubbish-heap, etc. — *n* **tott'er** a person who searches through dustbins and rubbish-heaps for reusable or saleable items; a rag-and-bone-man, scrap dealer. — *n* **tott'ing** retrieval of reusable or saleable objects from refuse. [Origin uncertain]

total *tō'tl*, *adj* whole; complete, absolute; including all; co-ordinating everything towards one end. — *n* the whole; the entire amount. — *vt* to bring to a total, add up; to amount to; to kill or destroy completely (*slang*). — *vi* (with *to*, *up to*) to amount to: — *pr p* **tō'talling**; *pa t* and *pa p* **tō'talled**. — *adj* **totalitarian** (*tō-tal-i-tā'ri-ən*) of, relating to, or characteristic of, a form of government that includes control of everything under one authority, and allows no opposition. — *n* a person in favour of such a government. — *n* **totalitā'rianism**. — *n* **totality** (*tō-tal'i-ti*) the condition or fact of being total; an entirety; completeness; the whole; the period during an eclipse when the eclipse is total (*astron*). — *n* **totalizā'tion** or **-s-**. — *n* **tō'talīzātor** or **-z-**, or **tō'talīzer** or **-s-** (familiarly shortened to **tote** *tōt*) a system of betting in which the total amount staked (minus tax, etc) is divided among the winners in proportion to the size of their stake; an automatic betting-machine, the *pari-mutuel*. — *vt* **tō'talize** or **-ise** to find the sum of; to bring to a total. — *vi* to use a totalizator. — *adv* **tō'tally**. — **total abstainer** a person who abstains altogether from all forms of alcohol; **total allergy syndrome** a condition in which a person suffers from a collection of symptoms attributable to accumulated allergies to substances encountered in the modern environment; **total body burden** (*radiol*) the summation of all radioactive materials contained in any person; the maximum total amount of radioactive material any person may be permitted to contain; **total depravity** the theological doctrine that man is totally corrupt and completely dependent on God for spiritual regeneration; **total eclipse** an eclipse in which the eclipsed body appears to be completely hidden; **total internal reflection** (*phys*) the complete reflection of a light ray at the boundary of a medium with a lower refractive index; **total parenteral nutrition** (*med*) hyperalimentation, the supply of essential nutrients intravenously to patients incapable of ingesting food normally (*abbrev* **TPN**); **total recall** see **recall**; **total theatre** dramatic entertainment comprising in one performance all or most of the following: acting, dancing, gymnastic feats, singing and instrumental music of various kinds, elaborate costumes and other visual effects, sometimes poetry; **total war** see under **war**[1]. [LL *tōtālis*, from L *tōtus* whole]

totanus *tot'ə-nəs*, *n* the redshank (*Tringa totanus*), a member of the *Tringidae* subfamily of sandpipers, with toes webbed at the base. [Ital *totano* squid, from its habit of feeding on small crustaceans and invertebrates]

totaquine *tō'tə-kwēn*, *-kwin*, *n* an anti-malarial drug containing alkaloids derived from cinchona bark and quinine. [New L *tōtaquina*, from L *totus* whole, and Sp *quina* cinchona bark]

totara *tō'tə-rə*, *n* a large coniferous New Zealand tree, a variety of *Podocarpus*, valued for its hard reddish timber. [Maori]

tote[1] *tōt*, (*orig US*) *vt* to carry. — *n* **to'te**. — **tote bag** a large bag for shopping, etc. [Origin unknown]

tote[2] *tōt*, (*slang*) *vt* to add (with *up*). [**total**]

tote[3]. See **totalizator** under **total**.

to-tear *tə-*, *tōō-tār'*, *vt* to tear in pieces: — *pa p* (*Spenser*) **to-torne'**. [Pfx *to-* asunder, and **tear**[2]]

totem *tō'təm*, *n* (*esp* in N American Indian society) any species of living or inanimate thing regarded, and often venerated, as an outward symbol of an existing intimate unseen relation, often adopted as an emblem or symbol of a family, clan or tribe; any outward symbol given undue respect. — *adj* **totemic** (*-tem'ik*). — *n* **tō'temism** the use of totems as the foundation of a social system of obligation and restriction; the rituals, customs and taboos associated with this. — *n* **tō'temist** an individual or group designated by a totem. — *adj* **totemist'ic**. — **totem pole** a pole carved and painted with totemic symbols, set up by Indians in the north-west of N America, eg as a tribal symbol. [From Algonquin]

tother or **t'other** *tudh'ər*, (*dialect* or *humorous*) *pronoun* and *adj* the other. — **tell tother from which** tell one from another. [**that other**; cf **tone**[2] and Scot **tae**, **tane**]

totidem verbis *tōt-ī'dəm vûr'bis*, *tot-i'dem ver'-*, *wer'bēs*, (*L*) in just so many words.

totient *tō'shənt*, *n* the number of totitives of a number. [L *totiēs* so many]

toties quoties *tō'shi-ēz kwō'shi-ēz*, *tot'i-ās kwot'i-ās*, (*L*) as often as; on each occasion.

totipalmate *tō-ti-pal'mit*, (*ornithol*) *adj* (of birds) having all four toes fully webbed. — *n* **totipalmā'tion**. [L *tōtus* entire, and **palmate**]

totipotent *tō-tip'ə-tənt*, (*zool*) *adj* capable of development into a complete organ or embryo; capable of differentiation. — *n* **tōtip'ency**. [L *totus* entire, and **potent**]

totitive *tot'i-tiv*, *n* a number less than another and prime to it. [L *tot* so many]

toto caelo *tō'tō sē'*, *kī'lō*, (*L*) literally, by the whole heavens; diametrically opposed.

to-torne. See under **to-tear**.

totter[1] *tot'ər, vi* to stand or walk unsteadily; to sway; to waver; to rock; to threaten to fall; to reel; to be on the verge of ruin. — *n* a tottering movement. — *n* **tott'erer**. — *n* and *adj* **tott'ering**. — *adv* **tott'eringly**. — *adj* **tott'ery** shaky. [Cf Norw dialect *tutra, totra* to quiver, Swed dialect *tuttra*]

totter[2]. See under **tot**[3].

tottered *tot'ərd, adj* a variant of **tattered** (*Shakesp*); later (from association with **totter**) ruinous. — *adj* **tott'ring** (*Shakesp*) hanging in rags.

tottie. See under **tot**[1].

totting. See under **tot**[2,3].

totty[1] *tot'i, adj* unsteady; dazed; tipsy. [Cf **totter**]

totty[2]. See under **tot**[1].

toucan *to͞o'kən, -kan, -kän', n* any of various large tropical American fruit-eating birds of the family *Rhamphastidae*, with large brightly-coloured beaks. — *n* **tou'canet** a smaller kind of toucan. [Fr, from Tupí *tucana*]

touch *tuch, vt* to come or be in contact with; to cause to be in contact; to feel or tap lightly, *esp* with the hand; to get at; to reach as far as; to attain; to equal, rival or compare with; to make a light application to; to begin to eat, eat a little of; to make use of; to affect, *esp* injuriously; to hit, wound or injure; to disturb or harm (*usu* with *neg*); to cope or deal with; to impress; to affect with emotion, *esp* pity; to have to do with; to concern; to strike home to; to mark or modify by light strokes; to tinge; to extract money from (with *for*; *colloq*); to make some reference to, say something about *esp* in passing; to meet without cutting, or meet tangentially (geom); to play (eg an instrument or melody) (*music*); to call at (eg a port); to cause to touch the ground behind the goal line (commonly with *down*; *Rugby football*); to test as with a touchstone; to receive, draw, pocket; to bribe (*obs*); to cheat (*slang*). — *vi* to be or come in contact; to make a passing call at a port; to verge; to make some mention or reference (with *on* or *upon*); to have reference. — *n* the sense by which nature, texture and quality of objects can be perceived through physical contact with the hands, feet, skin, lips, etc; the particular texture and qualities as perceived through such contact; an act of touching or the sense of being touched; a feeling; a slight application, modification, stroke; a small quantity; a slight attack of illness; a tinge; a trace; a smack; ability, skill; a trait; a little; a slight hit, wound, blemish or reproach; the manner or nicety of producing tone on (now *esp*) a keyed instrument; the instrument's response; a characteristic manner, style or trait; a stroke of art; the relation of communication, sympathy, harmony; communication, contact; a game in which one has to pursue and touch others; either side of the field outside the bounds (*football*, etc); a test, eg with a touchstone; a touchstone; a black marble or similar monumental stone (*obs*); an official stamp of fineness on gold, etc; fineness; stamp (*fig*); theft (*slang*); a sum got by theft or by touching (*slang*); a person from whom money can be obtained by touching (*slang*); that which will find buyers at such and such a price (*slang*). — *adj* **touch'able** capable of being touched; fit to be touched. — *n* **touch'ableness**. — *adj* **touched** having been touched; affected with emotion, *esp* pity; slightly unsound mentally. — *n* **touch'er**. — *adv* **touch'ily**. — *n* **touch'iness**. — *n* **touch'ing**. — *adj* affecting; moving; pathetic. — *prep* concerning. — *adv* **touch'ingly**. — *n* **touch'ingness**. — *adj* **touch'less** without a sense of touch; intangible. — *adj* **touch'y** over-sensitive; irascible; risky, requiring careful handling or caution (*esp US*). — **touch-and-go'** a narrow escape; a critical or precariously balanced situation. — *adj* precarious; offhand. — **touch'back** (*Am football*) a play in which the ball is dead on or behind a team's own goal line, having been put across the line by an opponent but actually put down by a member of that team; **touch'-box** a tinderbox for a matchlock; **touch'down** touching of the ball to the ground by a player behind the goal line (*Rugby football*); the possession of the ball by a player behind the opponents' goal line (*Am football*); (of air- or spacecraft) the act of alighting; **touch football** football in which tackling is replaced by touching; **touch'-hole** the small hole of a cannon through which the fire is communicated to the charge; **touch'-in-goal** (*Rugby football*) the areas at each end of the pitch behind the goal lines and outside the touchlines; **touch'-judge** (*Rugby football*) an official who marks when and where the ball goes into touch; **touch'line** either of the lines marking the side boundary in football, etc; **touch'mark** the maker's official stamp on pewter; **touch'-me-not** any of various plants of the genus *Impatiens*, having seed-pods which, when ripe, spring open at a touch; lupus; a forbidden topic. — *adj* standoffish. — **touch-me-not'ishness**; **touch pad** (*comput*) a small portable input device, operated by touching different areas on its surface; **touch'-paper** paper steeped in saltpetre for firing gunpowder, fireworks, etc; **touch'-piece** a coin or medal formerly given by a king to those he touched for king's-evil; **touch'-plate** a plate bearing the pewterers' official stamp; **touch rugby** or **rugger** a modified form of rugby football in which touching takes the place of tackling; **touch'-screen** (*comput*) a visual display unit screen that doubles as an input device, and is operated by being touched. — Also *adj*. — **touch'stone** Lydian stone, a highly siliceous (*usu* black) stone or other stone for testing gold or silver by the colour of the mark each makes on it; any criterion. — *adj* **touch'tone** (of telephones) having push buttons (rather than a dial) that cause distinct tones to sound at the exchange. — *n* **Touch'tone**® telephone equipment using this system. — *vt* and *vi* **touch'-type** to type without looking at the keys of the typewriter. — **touch'-typist**; **touch'wood** decayed wood that can be used as tinder. — **an easy** (or **a soft**) **touch** (*colloq*) a person or institution easily persuaded, *esp* to lend money; **in** (or **out of**) **touch** in (or out of) communication or direct relations; **near touch** a close shave; **touch down** (of an air or spacecraft) to land; to put the ball behind the opposing team's goal line (*Rugby football, Am football*); **touch off** to trigger, to cause to begin (also *fig*); **touch up** to improve by a series of small touches; to stimulate (eg a horse) by a light blow; to caress, touch or molest sexually; **touch wood** or (*US*) **knock on wood** or **knock wood** to touch something wooden as a superstitious guard against bad luck (also used as *interj*, to accompany the gesture or independently). [OFr *tuchier* (Fr *toucher*); origin doubtful]

touché *to͞o'shā, to͞o-shā', interj* claiming or acknowledging a hit in fencing, or a point scored in argument, etc. [Fr, touched, scored against]

tough *tuf, adj* stiff and dense; tenacious; hard to cut, chew, break up or penetrate; resistant; viscous, sticky; capable of or requiring strenuous effort and endurance; unyielding, resolute; intractable; robust; laborious; refractory; criminal, violent; unlucky, unfortunate (*colloq*). — *n* a rough or aggressive person, *esp* a criminal or hooligan (also **tough guy**). — *interj* (*colloq*) tough luck. — *adv* (*colloq*) violently, aggressively. — *vt* or *vi* **tough'en** to make or become tough. — *n* **tough'ener**. — *n* and *adj* **tough'ening**. — *n* **tough'ie** (*colloq*) a tough person, difficult or intractable problem, etc. — *adj* **tough'ish** rather tough. — *adv* **tough'ly**. — *n* **tough'ness**. — **tough luck** see under **luck**. — *adj* **tough-mind'ed** hard-headed, determined, not influenced by sentiment, etc. — **get tough with** (*colloq*) to deal with (more) severely, sternly; **tough out** or **tough it out** (*colloq*) withstand; endure stoically or defiantly. [OE *tōh*]

touk. See under **tuck**[2].

toun *to͞on, n* a Scots spelling of **town**.

toupee *to͞o-pē', -pā', to͞o', n* a wig or hairpiece worn to disguise baldness; a wig with a topknot (*hist*). — Also **toupet** (*to͞o-pā', to͞o'pā*). [Fr *toupet*]

tour *to͞or*, *n* a round; a prolonged journey from place to place, eg for pleasure, or to give entertainment as a performer, or to give lectures, play matches, etc; a pleasure trip or outing; a shift or turn of work; a period of military or diplomatic service in a particular place (also **tour of duty**); a border of false hair (*hist*). — *vi* to make a tour, go on tour. — *vt* to make a tour through or of; to tour with (a play, etc). — *n* **tour'er** a touring car; a tourist. — *n* and *adj* **tour'ing**. — *n* **tour'ism** the activities of tourists and those who cater for them, *esp* when regarded as an industry. — *n* **tour'ist** a person who travels for pleasure, *esp* a sightseeing traveller; a member of a sports team travelling *usu* abroad to play a series of matches. — *adj* **touris'tic**. — *adj* **tour'isty** (*derog*) designed for, or full of, tourists. — **touring car** a large motor car, with ample room for passengers and luggage; **tourist class** the cheapest class of accommodation on a boat or aeroplane; **tour operator** a person or firm organizing (*esp* package-tour) holidays. — **Grand Tour** (*hist*) a journey through Western Europe, once fashionable as completing a youth's education. [Fr; see **turn**]

touraco. Same as **turaco**.

tourbillion *to͞or-bil'yən*, or **tourbillon** *to͞or-bē'yɔ̃*, *n* a swirl; a vortex; a whirlwind; a whirling firework; a whirling or revolving mechanism or system. [Fr *tourbillon* whirlwind, from L *turbō, -inis*]

tour de force *to͞or də fors*, (*Fr*) a feat of strength or skill; an outstanding effort or performance: — *pl* **tours de force**.

tour d'horizon *to͞or dor-ē-zɔ̃*, (*Fr*) a general survey, review.

Tourette's syndrome *to͞orets' sin'drōm*, (*med*) *n* a disorder characterized by a variety of facial tics, muscular jerks and involuntary behaviour, sometimes involving compulsive imitation of others and use of offensive language. — Also **Tourette syndrome**. [Gilles de la *Tourett* (1857–1904), French physician]

tourmaline *to͞or'mə-lēn*, *n* a beautiful mineral of complex and varying composition, *usu* black (schorl) or blackish, strongly pyro-electric and pleochroic. [Fr, from Sinh *tòramalli* carnelian]

tournament *to͞or'nə-mənt*, *n* a series of games to determine a winner or winning team by elimination; a military and athletic display; a military sport of the Middle Ages in which combatants engaged mainly on horseback, either in troops or singly (as in jousts), with spear and sword. [OFr *tournoiement*, from *torner*, from L *tornāre* to turn]

tournedos *to͞or'nə-dō*, *n* a small round thick beef fillet: — *pl* **tour'nedos** (*-dōz*). [Fr]

tourney *to͞or'*, *tûr'*, *tör'ni*, *n* a medieval tournament. — *vi* to take part in a tournament. — *n* **tour'neyer**. [OFr *tornoi*, from *torner*, from L *tornāre* to turn]

tourniquet *to͞or'ni-ket*, *-kā*, *n* any appliance for compressing an artery to stop bleeding; a turnstile (*rare*). [Fr, from L *tornāre* to turn]

tournure *to͞or-nür'*, *n* contour, the characteristic turn of line; a bustle or pad worn at the waist. [Fr]

touse, **touze**, **towse** or **towze** *towz*, *vt* to haul, to pull about; to dishevel, rumple, tumble; to worry; to rack (*obs*); to tease out (*obs*). — *vi* to touse each other; to be toused; to tussle; to rummage. — *n* a tousing. — *n* **tous'er** or **tows'er** someone who touses; (with *cap*) a common name for a big dog. — *n* and *adj* **tous'ing**. — *vt* **tousle** or **touzle** (*towz'l, Scot to͞oz'l*) to disarrange, to tumble; to dishevel. — *vi* to tussle; to touse things. — *n* a tousled mass. — *adj* **tousy**, **touzy**, **towsy** or **towzy** (*towz'i, Scot to͞oz'i*) shaggy, unkempt, tousled; rough. — **tousy tea** (*Scot*) high tea. [Prob from a lost OE word answering to Ger *zausen*]

tous-les-mois *to͞o-lā-mwä'*, *n* a W Indian plant (*Canna edulis*) with bright red flowers, cultivated for the edible starch of its rhizome; its rhizome. [Fr, every month, but perh really from a native name]

toustie *to͞os'ti*, (*Scott*) *adj* irascible. [Perh a mixture of **testy** and **tout**[2]]

tout[1] *towt*, *vi* to solicit for custom in an obtrusive, aggressive or brazen way; to spy on racehorses in training. — *vt* to watch or spy on; to advertise, praise or recommend strongly. — *n* a person who touts; someone who hangs about racing-stables, etc, to pick up profitable information; someone who buys up numbers of tickets for a popular sporting event, etc and sells them at a large profit (also **ticket tout**). — *n* **tout'er**. [Appar related to **toot**[1]]

tout[2] or **towt** *towt*, (*Scot*) *vi* to pout. — *n* a pet, a fit of the sulks; a sudden illness. — *adj* **tout'ie** petulant.

tout[3] *to͞o*, (*Fr*) *adj* all; every; whole. — *adv* quite; entirely. — **tout à fait** (*to͞o ta fe*) entirely; wholly; **tout au contraire** (*to͞o tō kɔ̃-trer*) quite the contrary; **tout à vous** (*to͞o ta vo͞o*) wholly yours; yours truly; **tout court** (*ko͞or*) quite brief(ly), without preface, simply; **tout de même** (*də mem*) all the same; nevertheless; **tout de suite** (*to͞ot swēt*, *to͞od*) at once, immediately; **tout ensemble** see under **ensemble**; **tout le monde** (*lə mɔ̃d*) all the world, everybody.

tout[4]. See under **toot**[1].

touze, **touzle**. See under **touse**.

tovarish *to-vä'rish*, *n* comrade. — Also **tova'risch** or **tova'rich**. [Russ *tovarishch*]

tow[1] *tō* (*Scot tow*), *vt* to pull (eg another car, caravan, etc) behind one with a rope or cable; to pull along. — *vi* to proceed by being towed. — *n* the condition of being towed; an act of towing; a towrope; that which is towed; a rope, *esp* a bell-rope or a hangman's rope (*Scot*). — *adj* **tow'able**. — *n* **tow'age** an act of towing; the condition of being towed; a fee for towing. — *n* **tow'er**. — *n* and *adj* **tow'ing**. — **tow'bar** a metal bar or frame used for towing trailers, etc; **tow'ing-bitts** upright timbers projecting above eg a ship's deck for fastening towlines to; **tow'boat** a tug; **tow'-iron** a toggleiron used in whaling; **tow'line** or **tow'rope** a line, rope or cable used in towing; **tow'-net** or **tow'ing-net** a dragnet for collecting objects of natural history, etc; **tow'path** or **tow'ing-path** a path beside a canal or river for horses towing barges; **tow'-plane** an aircraft which tows gliders; **tow truck** (*NAm*) a breakdown truck, *esp* one able to tow another vehicle. — **have** (or **take**) **in tow** to tow (another vehicle, vessel, etc); to take along with one, be accompanied by; to have or assume charge of; **on tow** (of vehicles) or **under tow** (of vessels) being towed. [OE *togian* to drag]

tow[2] *tō*, *n* prepared fibres of flax, hemp or jute; *esp* separated shorter fibres; fibres of synthetic fabric, eg rayon. — *adj* of or like tow. — *adj* **tow'y**. — *adj* **tow'-coloured** (of hair) very fair, flax-coloured. — **tow'-head** a person with light-coloured or tousled hair. — *adj* **tow'-headed**. [OE *tow-* (in compounds), related to ON *tō* wool]

toward *tō'ərd, tōrd*, *adj* (*archaic*) or (*dialect*) approaching; at hand; impending; getting on; on hand; favourable; well-disposed; apt; ready to do or learn; on the left or near side. — *adv* in the direction facing one, inward. — *prep* towards. — *n* **tow'ardliness**. — *adj* **tow'ardly** (*archaic*) favourable; promising; well-disposed; tractable. — Also *adv*. — *n* **tow'ardness**. — *prep* **towards** (*tə-wördz'*, *to͞o-wörd'z*, *twördz*, *tōrdz*, *tördz*) in the direction of; in relation or regard to; with a tendency to; for, as a help or contribution, to; near, a little short of. [OE *tōweard*, adj, adv, prep, from *tō* to, and sfx *-weard* -ward]

towel *tow'əl*, *n* a piece of absorbent cloth or paper for drying the body; a tea towel; a sanitary towel; (formerly) a cloth for various purposes, eg a table-napkin, an altar-cloth. — *vt* to dry or rub (eg oneself) with a towel; to cudgel (*hist slang*); to thrash (*slang*): — *pr p* **tow'elling** or (*NAm*) **tow'eling**; *pa t* and *pa p* **tow'elled** or (*NAm*) **tow'eled**. — *n* **tow'elling** a rubbing with a towel; an absorbent fabric for towels, sometimes used for bathrobes, curtains, etc; a thrashing (*slang*). — **tow'el-gourd** the loofah; **tow'el-horse**, **tow'el-rack** or **tow'el-rail** a frame or rail for hanging towels on. — **a lead towel** (*hist slang*) a bullet; **an oaken towel** (*hist slang*) a cudgel; **throw in the towel** see under **throw**[1].

[OFr *toaille*, from Gmc; cf OHGer *dwahila*, from *dwahan*, *twahan*, OE *thwēan* to wash]

tower *towr*, *tow'ər*, *n* a tall building, standing alone or forming part of another, eg a church; a fortress, castle, with or formed of a tower; a place of defence or retreat; a medieval war machine consisting of a tall movable structure, which allowed access to a castle's ramparts from outside (*hist*); a control tower; a floor-standing unit containing eg a hard disk, floppy disk drives, etc and serial ports (*comput*); (*esp* in the 17c) a woman's high headdress; the high flight of a bird. — *vi* to rise into the air (above); to be or stand very high or tall; to be superior; (of eg a hawk) to soar up high so as to swoop on quarry. — *vt* (*Milton*) to rise aloft into. — *adj* **tow'ered**. — *adj* **tow'ering** very tall, elevated; (eg of anger, rage) very violent or intense. — *adv* **tow'eringly**. — *adj* **tow'erless**. — *adj* **tow'ery** having towers; very tall. — **tower block** a tall residential or office building; **tower mill** see **smock mill** under **smock**; **tow'er-shell** a gasteropod (*Turritella*) with an elongated many-whorled spiral shell, or its shell. — **tower of strength** a stable, reliable person; **tower over** to be considerably taller than; to be markedly superior to. [OFr *tur*, from L *turris* a tower]

towhee *tow'hē*, *tō'hē*, *n* any of various N American finches of the genera *Pipilo* or *Chlorura*, the chewink, ground-robin, or marsh-robin. [Imit]

towmont, **towmond** or **towmon** *tow'mən(t)*, *-mən(d)*, (*Scot* and *N of England*) *n* forms of **twelvemonth**.

town *town*, *n* an urban area bigger or less rural than a village, with some level of local government and defined boundaries; the principal town of a district, *esp* (in SE England) London; an urban community; the people of a town, *esp* fashionable society, tradesmen (distinguished from academic inhabitants), or immoral classes; the business or shopping centre; urban communities generically; a municipal or political division of a county (which may include villages and towns in the ordinary sense), a township (*US*); *orig*, an enclosure (*obs*); (*Scot tōōn*) in Scotland a farmstead or similar group of houses. — *adj* of a town; urban. — *n* **townee'** or **tow'nie** (often *derog*) an inhabitant of a town, not a member of the university or a country dweller. — *adj* **town'ish** characteristic of town as opposed to country. — *adj* **town'less**. — *n* **town'ling** a town-dweller. — *adj* **town'ly** townish. — *n* **town'ship** an urban settlement of black and coloured Africans (*SAfr*); a subdivision of a county or province (*US*); an administrative district (*US*); a thirty-six square mile block of public land (*US*); a site for a town (*Austr*); a small settlement (*Austr*); the territory or district of a town; the corporation of a town; a village, a community or local division; a parish (*hist*); a farm in joint tenancy (*Scot*); the people living in a township. — *n* **town'y** an inhabitant of a town; a fellow inhabitant. — *adj* townish. — **town clerk** (in Britain until 1974) the secretary and legal adviser of a town; the official responsible for town records (*US*); **town council** the elected governing body in a town; **town councillor**; **town crier** (*hist*) an official who makes public proclamations in a town; **town'-dweller**; **town'-end** the end of the main street; **town** (or **towns**) **gas** *usu* a mixture of coal-gas and carburetted water gas, made and supplied for domestic or industrial use (now largely superseded by *natural gas*); **town hall** a building for the official business of a town, *usu* with public rooms; a town-house; **town'house** (chiefly *Scot*) a town hall; **town house** a house in town belonging to the owner of another in the country; a fashionable, *usu* terraced urban house, *esp* typically with a garage on the ground floor and living-room above; **town'land** (chiefly *hist*) the land forming a manor; (in Ireland) a sub-parochial land division, or a township; (in Scotland) the enclosure round a farm; **town'-meet'ing** (in New England) a meeting of the voters of a town, *esp* to transact public business; **town-plann'er**; **town'-plann'ing** the deliberate designing of the building and growth of towns to avoid haphazard and speculative building; **town's'-bairn** (*Scot*) a native of a town, *esp* one's own; **town'scape** a portion of a town which the eye can view at once; a picture of it; the design or building of all or part of a town. — Also *vt* and *vi*. — **town'scaping**; **towns'folk** the people of a town; **town'skip** (*Dickens*) a city urchin; **towns'man**, *fem* **towns'woman** an inhabitant or fellow-inhabitant of a town; **towns'people** townsfolk; **town'-talk** the general talk of a town; the subject of common conversation. — **go to town** (*colloq*) to act, behave or perform enthusiastically, with thoroughness, without restraint; **on the town** out to amuse oneself in town; **take to town** (*slang*) to mystify, bewilder; **town and gown** the general community and the members of the university. [OE *tūn* an enclosure, town; ON *tūn* enclosure, Ger *Zaun* hedge]

to-worne *tə-wōrn'*, *-wörn'*, *adj* (*Spenser*) worn-out. [Pfx *to-*, intens, and **worn**]

tow-rag. A mistaken spelling of **toe-rag**.

towse, **towsy**. See under **touse**.

towt. See under **tout**².

towy. See under **tow**².

towze, **towzy**. See under **touse**.

tox-, **toxi-**, **toxico-**, or **toxo-**, *combining form* denoting poison, poisonous. [Gr *toxikon* (*pharmacon*) (poison for) the bow, from *toxon* bow]

toxaemia or (*NAm*) **toxemia** *toks-ē'mi-ə*, *n* blood poisoning; a condition in late pregnancy characterized by a sudden rise in blood pressure. — *adj* **toxaem'ic** or (*NAm*) **toxe'mic**. [**tox-** and Gr *haima* blood]

toxaphene *toks'-ə-fēn*, (*chem*) *n* chlorinated camphene used as an insecticide. [**tox-** and cam*phene*]

toxic *toks'ik*, *adj* of poison; poisonous; poisoned; caused by poison. — *adj* **tox'ical**. — *adv* **tox'ically**. — *adj* **tox'icant** poisonous. — *n* a poisonous substance. — *n* **toxicā'tion** or **toxicity** (*-is'*) the state of being toxic; the degree to which a substance is toxic. — *adj* **toxicolog'ic** or **toxicolog'ical**. — *adv* **toxicolog'ically**. — *n* **toxicol'ogist**. — *n* **toxicol'ogy** the science or study of poisons and their antidotes. — **toxic shock syndrome** a potentially fatal condition characterized by high fever, vomiting, and diarrhoea, sometimes occurring in menstruating women using tampons, and attributed to a toxin apparently associated with staphylococcal infection. [Gr *toxon* a bow, *toxikos* for the bow, *toxikon* arrow-poison]

toxicogenic *toks-i-kō-jen'ik*, *adj* producing toxic substances and poisons. [**toxico-** (see under **tox-**), and Gr *-genēs* born]

toxicomania *toks-i-kō-mā'ni-ə*, *n* a morbid craving for poisons. [**toxico-** (see under **tox-**), and **mania**]

toxicophagous *toks-i-kō-fa'gəs* or **toxiphagous** *toks-i-fa'gəs*, *adj* poison-eating. [**toxico-** (see under **tox-**), and Gr *phagein* to eat]

toxicophobia *toks-i-kō-fō'bi-ə* or **toxipho'bia** *toks-i-fō'-bi-ə*, *n* morbid fear of poisoning. — *n* and *adj* **toxiphō'biac**. [**toxico-** (see under **tox-**), and Gr *phobeein* to fear]

toxin *toks'in*, *n* a ptomaine; a specific poison of organic origin, *esp* one stimulating the production of antibodies. [*tox*ic and **-in**]

toxocara *tok-sə-kär'ə*, *n* any of various parasitic worms found in the intestines of dogs and cats and known to cause disease (**toxocarī'asis**) and eye damage in humans. [**toxo-** (see under **tox-**), and Gr *kara* head]

toxoid *toks'oid*, *n* a toxin that has been treated to remove its toxic properties without destroying its ability to stimulate production of antibodies. [*tox*in and **-oid**]

toxophilite *toks-of'i-līt*, *n* a lover of archery; an archer. — *adj* of or relating to archery. — *adj* **toxophilit'ic**. — *n* **toxoph'ily** love of archery; archery. [Gr *toxon* a bow, and *phileein* to love]

toxoplasmosis *toks-ō-plaz-mō'sis*, *n* an infection of animals (*esp* the domestic cat) and humans by microorganisms, *prob* protozoa, of the genus *Toxoplasma*, causing eg spontaneous abortion in pregnant women. — *adj* **toxoplas'mic**. [**toxo-** (see under **tox-**), and **plasma**]

toy *toi, n* a plaything, *esp* for a child; a trifle; anything, *esp* a gadget, intended or thought of as for amusement, appearances or pleasure rather than practical use; a matter of no importance or thing of little value; a dwarf breed; a jest, idle tale (*archaic*); a trivial dance-tune, or the like (*archaic*); a whim, crotchet; an old woman's cap with side flaps (*Scot*); amorous sport (*archaic*). — *adj* made in imitation of something else as a plaything; of, for or being a dwarf breed. — *vi* (*usu* with *with*) to play with in an idle way and without really being interested; to sport; to flirt or amuse oneself amorously (with). — *n* **toy'er**. — *n* and *adj* **toy'ing**. — *adj* **toy'ish** given to toying or trifling; playful; wanton (*obs*). — *adv* **toy'ishly**. — *n* **toy'ishness**. — *adj* **toy'less**. — *adj* **toy'like**. — *adj* **toy'some** sportive; playful; whimsical; disposed to toy; wanton (*obs*). — **toy boy** the young male lover of a much older woman (sometimes *derog*); **toy dog** a very small pet dog; **toy'man** or *fem* **toy'woman** a seller of toys; **toy'shop** a shop where toys are sold; **toy soldier** a miniature model of a soldier; a soldier (*derog slang*). [Poss Du *tuig* tools; Ger *Zeug* stuff]

toylsom, toylesome. See under **toil**[1].

toze or **tose** (*Shakesp* **toaze**) *tōz, vt* to tease out, card, comb; to draw out, elicit. [ME *tosen*, related to **tease**]

tozie *tōz'i*, (*Scott*) *n* a shawl made from a goat's inner coat.

tp *abbrev*: township; troop.

t-pa *abbrev*: tissue plasminogen activator (qv under **tissue**).

TPI *abbrev*: tax and prices index: Town Planning Institute.

Tpr *abbrev*: Trooper.

tpr *abbrev*: teleprinter.

TR *abbrev*: Turkey (IVR).

tr. *abbrev*: transactions; translator; transpose; trustee.

tra- *pfx* signifying: across; beyond; through. [Ety as for **trans-**]

trabeate *trab', trāb'i-āt* or **trabeated** *-id*, (*archit*) *adj* built of horizontal beams, not arches and vaults. — *n* **trabeā'tion** an entablature; a combination of beams in a structure. [L *trabs, trabis* beam]

trabecula *trə-bek'ū-lə*, (*anatom* and *bot*) *n* a cell, row of cells, band, or rodlike structure running across a cavity or forming an internal support to an organ: — *pl* **trabec'ūlae** (*-lē*). — *adj* **trabec'ūlar**. — *adj* **trabec'ūlate** or **trabec'ūlated** having trabeculae; transversely barred. [L, dimin of *trabs, trabis* beam]

tracasserie *tra-kas-(ə)-rē*, (*Fr*) *n* turmoil.

trace[1] *trās, n* an indication, mark of what is or has been; a vestige; a small quantity that can just be detected; a track; a footprint; a beaten path (*US*); a tracing; a line marked by a recording instrument; a line or lines on the screen of a cathode-ray tube forming the display; a mental or neural change caused by learning; an amount of rain- or snowfall that is too small to be measured; an intersection with or projection on a surface; a way, course (*Spenser*); the ground-plan of a work (*fortif*). — *vt* to track; to follow step by step; to detect; to discover the whereabouts of; to follow or mark the outline of (eg a design), *esp* mechanically or on a translucent paper; to outline, delineate, plan or write; to follow to its origins or source (*usu* with *back*); to produce as tracery; to cover with tracery; to take one's way along or through (eg a path), traverse. — *vi* to be traceable or datable (*usu* with *back*); to proceed (*archaic*); to walk (*archaic*); to move (*archaic*); to tread a measure (*obs*). — *n* **traceabil'ity**. — *adj* **trace'able** that may be traced. — *n* **trace'ableness**. — *adv* **trace'ably**. — *adj* **trace'less**. — *adv* **trace'lessly**. — *n* **trā'cer** a person who traces; an instrument for tracing; a probe for tracing a nerve, etc; a device by which a projectile leaves a detectable trail, *usu* of smoke; a projectile equipped with this; (also **tracer element**) a radioactive isotope introduced into the body to study physiological, etc processes by tracking the radiation it produces. — *adj* **trā'ceried**. — *n* **trā'cery** an ornamental, fine, decorative pattern; ornamental openwork in Gothic architecture, *esp* in the upper part of windows. — *n* **trā'cing** the act of someone who traces; a drawing copied mechanically or on translucent paper laid over the original; an instrumental record. — **trace element** a micronutrient, a substance (such as zinc, copper, molybdenum, etc) whose presence in the soil or food in minute quantities is necessary for plant and animal growth; **trace fossil** the fossilized tracks, burrows, etc of an organism (but not the organism itself); **tracer bullet**; **tracer shell**; **tracing paper** translucent paper for tracing on. [Fr *trace*, from L *tractus*, pa p of *trahere* to draw]

trace[2] *trās, n* (*usu* in *pl*) a rope, chain or strap attached to an animal's collar or breast-strap for drawing a vehicle; a bar for transmitting motion; the vascular tissue branching from the cylinder to pass into a leaf or branch (*bot*); a short piece of wire, gut or nylon connecting the hook to the fishing line (*angling*). — *vt* to harness in traces. — *n* **trā'cer** a trace-horse; a person (*orig* a boy) who attends a trace-horse. — **trace'-horse** a horse that draws in traces. — **kick over the traces** see under **kick**. [OFr *trays, trais*, pl of *trait* draught; cf **trait**]

trachea *trə-kē'ə, trā', n* a passage strengthened by cartilaginous rings that carries air from the larynx to the bronchi, the windpipe; the air-tube in air-breathing arthropods; a conducting tube in xylem (*bot*): — *pl* **trachē'ae** (*-ē*). — *adj* **trachē'al**. — *n pl* **Trācheā'ria** *usu* small arachnids such as mites and ticks, with tracheae, but no lung-books. — *n* and *adj* **trācheā'rian**. — *n* and *adj* **trā'cheary**. — *n pl* **Trācheā'ta** arthropods with tracheae. — *adj* **trā'cheate** or **trā'cheated** having a trachea. — *n* **tracheid** or **tracheide** (*trə-kē'īd, -id, trak'i-*) a long tubelike but closed cell in xylem. — *n* **tracheitis** (*trak-i-ī'tis*) inflammation of the trachea. — *n* **trachī'tis** a wrong form of **tracheitis**. [Med L *trāchēa* for L *trāchīa*, from Gr *trācheia* (*artēriā*) rough (artery)]

trachelate *trak'ə-lāt, adj* having a neck. [Gr *trachēlos* neck]

tracheo- *trak-i-ō-* or *trak-i-o'-*, combining form denoting the trachea. — *n* **tra'cheophyte** (*bot*) a plant with a vascular system of xylem and phloem. — *n* **tracheos'copy** inspection of the trachea. — *n* **tracheos'tomy** surgical formation of a temporary or permanent opening into the trachea. — *n* **tracheot'omy** an incision into the trachea, *usu* to relieve an obstruction. [Ety as for **trachea**]

trachinus *tra-kī'nəs, n* a member of the weever genus of fishes *Trachinus*, giving name to the family **Trachinidae** (*-kin'i-dē*). [LL *trachina*, said to be a local name of a fish]

trachitis. See under **trachea**.

trachoma *tra-kō'mə, n* a contagious disease of the eye, characterized by hard pustules on the inner surface of the eyelids. — *adj* **trachomatous** (*-kom'ə-təs, -kō'mə-təs*). [Gr *trāchōma*]

trachypterus *trak-ip'tə-rəs, n* a member of the dealfish genus *Trachypterus*, giving name to the ribbonfish family **Trachypteridae** (*-ter'i-dē*). [Gr *trāchys* rough, and *pteron* fin]

trachyte *trak'īt, n* a fine-grained intermediate igneous rock, *usu* with little or no quartz, consisting largely of alkali-feldspars (eg sanidine) and a small amount of coloured silicates (eg hornblende or mica). — *adj* **trachytic** (*trə-kit'ik*). — *adj* **trach'ytoid**. [Gr *trāchys* rough]

tracing. See under **trace**[1].

track[1] *trak, n* a mark or trail left; a beaten path or road; a made path; a sequence or course of thoughts or actions; the predetermined line of travel of an aircraft; a line of motion or travel; a course, *usu* oval-shaped, on which races are run; a railway line, the rails and the space between; the groove cut in a gramophone record by the recording instrument; one out of several items recorded on a disc or tape; one of several areas or paths on magnetic recording equipment (eg magnetic tape) receiving information from a single input channel; a film's soundtrack; any of several more or less demanding courses of study designed to meet the respective needs of students divided into groups according to ability (*US*); the endless band on which the wheels of a caterpillar vehicle run (*adj* **tracked** equipped with such metal bands); (in a factory, etc) a conveyor carrying goods in process of manufacture; track and field events collectively (*NAm*); the distance between a pair of wheels measured as the distance between their respective points of contact with the ground; a path followed by a particle, *esp* when rendered visible in photographic emulsion by cloud chamber, bubble chamber or spark chamber. — *vt* to follow the track of; to find by so doing; to traverse; to beat, tread (a path, etc); to follow the progress of; to follow the movement of (a satellite, spacecraft, etc) by radar, etc, and record its positions; to follow or move in relation to (a moving object) while filming it; to leave dirty marks on (a floor) (with *on* or *up*; *US*); to make dirty marks on eg a floor with (snow, mud, etc) (*US*). — *vi* to follow a trail; to make one's way (*colloq*); to run in alignment, *esp* (of gramophone needles) to follow the grooves; (of a camera or camera operator) to follow or move in relation to a moving object being filmed; to move a dolly camera in a defined path while taking a shot (**tracking shot**). — *adj* **track'able**. — *n* **track'age** provision of railway tracks. — *n* **track'er**. — *n* **track'ing** the action of the verb; excessive leakage current between two insulated points due eg to moisture (*elec eng*); disposition of the tone-arm on a gramophone so that the stylus remains correctly positioned in the groove; the division of study courses or students into tracks (qv above) (*US*). — *adj* **track'less** without a path; untrodden; leaving no trace; running without rails. — *adv* **track'lessly**. — *n* **track'lessness**. — **track'ball** or **track'erball** (*comput*) a spherical ball mounted in a small boxlike device, that can be rotated with the palm of the hand causing the cursor to move across the screen; **tracker dog** one used for tracking, *esp* in police searches; **track event** (in a sports competition) a race of any kind; **tracking station** a station with radar and radio equipment allowing it to track spacecraft, aircraft and satellites through the atmosphere or space; **track'layer** a tracklaying vehicle; a trackman (*US*). — *adj* **track'laying** (of a vehicle) having caterpillar tracks. — **track'man** (*US*) a platelayer; **track record** a record of past performance, *orig* that of an athlete, now generally that of any individual, company, etc; **track shoe** a lightweight spiked running shoe worn by athletes; **track suit** a loose warm suit worn by athletes before and after competing or when in training; **track'-walker** a person who has charge of a railway track; **track'way** a beaten track; an ancient road. — **across the tracks** or **the wrong side of the tracks** (*colloq*) a slum or other socially disadvantaged area; **in one's tracks** just where one stands; **keep** (or **lose**) **track of** keep (or fail to keep) oneself informed about; **make tracks** (*colloq*) to make off; to go quickly; **make tracks for** (*colloq*) to go towards; **off the beaten track** away from frequented roads; out of the usual, not normal or conventional (*fig*); **off the track** off course, in the wrong direction; **on the right** (or **wrong**) **track** pursuing a correct (or mistaken) course; **track down** to find after intensive search. [Fr *trac*; prob Gmc; cf **track²**]

track² *trak*, *vt* to tow. — *vi* to travel by towing. — *n* **track'age** towing. — *n* **track'er** a person who tows; a tug; a pulling part in the action of any organ. — **track'-boat** a towed boat; **track'road** a towpath; **track'-scout** a trekschuit. [See **trek**]

tracklement *trak'l-mənt*, (*dialect*) *n* a condiment, accompaniment, etc, to food. [Ety uncertain]

tract¹ *trakt*, *n* a stretch or extent of space or time; a region, area; a region of the body occupied by a particular system (eg *the digestive tract*); a trace, track (*Shakesp*, *Spenser*); a psalm sung instead of the Alleluia in Lent (*RC*; also **tract'us**; *perh* as drawn out, *perh* as sung at a stretch without answers). — *vt* (*Spenser*) to trace, track. [L *tractus*, *-ūs* drawing, dragging, from *trahere*, *tractāre* to draw, pull]

tract² *trakt*, *n* a tractate; a pamphlet or leaflet, *esp* political or religious. — *n* **tractā'rian** a writer of tracts, *esp* (with *cap*) of the *Tracts for the Times* (Oxford, 1833–41 — Pusey, Newman, Keble, Hurrell Froude, etc). — Also *adj*. — *n* **Tractār'ianism** the system of religious opinion promulgated in these, its main aim being to assert the authority and dignity of the Anglican Church, the *Oxford movement*. — *n* **tract'ate** a treatise, a tract. — *n* **tractā'tor** a tractarian. [ME *tracte*, appar shortening of Med L *tractātus* tractate, from L *tractāre* to handle]

tractable *trak'tə-bl*, *adj* easily drawn, managed or taught; docile; malleable. — *n* **tractibil'ity** or **tract'ableness**. — *adv* **tract'ably**. [L *tractābilis*, from *tractāre* to draw, handle]

tractile *trak'tīl*, *adj* ductile, capable of being drawn out. — *n* **tractility** (*-il'*). [Ety as for **tract¹**]

traction *trak'shən*, *n* the act of drawing or pulling or state of being drawn or pulled; the pulling on a muscle, organ, etc, by means, eg of weights, to correct an abnormal condition (*med*); the grip of a wheel, tyre, etc on the surface on which it moves; the propulsion of vehicles. — *adj* **trac'tional**. — *adj* **tract'ive** pulling. — **traction engine** a locomotive for hauling heavy loads over roads, fields, etc; **traction load** (*geol*) that part of the solid material carried by a river which is rolled along the river bed; **tractive force** the pull which a locomotive, etc engine is capable of exerting at the draw-bar; the force necessary to detach the armature from an excited electromagnet. [Med L *tractio*, from *tractus*; see also ety for **tract¹**]

tractor *trak'tər*, *n* a motor vehicle used for hauling trailers, agricultural implements, etc; the short front section of an articulated lorry, containing the engine and driver's cab; a traction engine; an aircraft with a screw propeller in front; a screw propeller mounted in front on an aircraft; a motorized plough; (in *pl*) bars of different metals which, drawn over diseased parts of the body, were supposed to give relief (*hist*). — *n* **tractorā'tion** (*hist*) the use of metal bars to give relief to diseased parts of the body. — **tractor feed** a device for feeding and advancing continuous stationery through the platen of a typewriter, printer, etc by use of a toothed wheel or sprocket and perforation in the paper. [LL, that which draws, from *trahere*, *tractāre* to draw, pull]

tractrix *trak'triks* (*math*) *n* a curve such that the intercept of a tangent by a fixed straight line is constant: — *pl* **tractrices** (*trak-trī'sēz*). [New L, from *trahere*, *tractāre* to draw, pull]

trad *trad* or **trad jazz** (*jaz*), *n* a shortened form of *traditional jazz*, a style of early 20c jazz which originated in New Orleans, characterized by improvisation against a regular rhythmical background. — *adj* **trad**.

trade *trād*, *n* an occupation, way of livelihood, *esp* skilled but not learned; shopkeeping; commerce, *esp* as opposed to a profession; buying and selling; people engaged in a specific occupation, *esp* the liquor trade or the book trade; customers, clientele; commercial customers as opposed to the public in general; business at a particular time or for a particular market; a craft, *esp* requiring training; a deal; commodities, *esp* for barter; a practice; (in *pl*) the trade winds; a track, trail, treading (*Spenser*); a way of traffic; resort (*Shakesp*); a way, a course (*obs*); rubbish (*dialect*); medicine. — *vi* to have dealings (with *with*); to engage in commerce (often with *in*); to deal; to traffic; to buy and sell; to take goods to a place (with *to*); to reckon, count, presume (with *on*), *esp* unscrupulously; to tread, go (*obs*); to resort, *esp* for commerce; to ply; to occupy oneself (*obs*). — *vt* to exchange (*esp* commercially), to barter; to buy and sell; to exchange (eg one thing for another, blows, etc); to tread (*obs*). — *adj* **trade'able** or **trad'able**. — *adj* **trād'ed** (*Shakesp*) versed, practised. — *adj* **trade'ful** (*Spenser*) busy in traffic. — *adj* **trade'less**.

— *n* **trād'er** a person who trades; a trading ship; a member of the stock exchange trading privately and not on behalf of clients (*US*). — *n* and *adj* **trād'ing**. — **trade barrier** anything which prevents or hinders international trade, eg tariffs and quotas; **trade board** (*hist*) a council for settling disputes consisting of representatives of both employers and employees in a trade; **trade'craft** skill or expertise in the practice of a trade, *esp* that of espionage; **trade cycle** the recurring series of conditions in trade from prosperity to depression and back to prosperity; **trade discount** a discount offered to others in the same trade; **trade edition** a standard edition of a book rather than a de-luxe or bookclub edition; **traded option** (*stock exchange*) an option that can itself be bought and sold. — *adj* **trade'-fallen (trade'-falne**; *Shakesp*) unsuccessful in trade, bankrupt. — **trade gap** the amount by which a country's visible imports exceed its visible exports in value; **trade'-in** that which is given in part payment; **trade journal** a periodical containing information and comment on a particular trade; **trade-last'** (*US*) a compliment paid to someone which one offers to tell that person in exchange for a compliment heard about oneself; **trade'mark** or **trade mark** any name or distinctive device warranting goods for sale as the production of any individual or firm; **trade'name** a name serving as a trademark; a name in use in the trade; the name under which a company trades; **trade'-off** the giving up of one thing in return for another, *usu* as an act of compromise; **trade-off study** (*aeronautics, space tech*) a logical evaluation, during the preliminary design process, of the pros and cons of alternative approaches and/or parameters which leads to the choice of the preferred ones; **trade paper** a trade journal; **trade paperback** a trade edition (qv) of a paperback book; **trade plate** a temporary number plate attached to a vehicle by dealers, etc prior to its being registered; **trade price** the price at which goods are sold to members of the same trade, or by wholesale to retail dealers; **trade route** a route followed by caravans or trading ships; **trade sale** an auction sale of goods by producers, etc, to persons in the trade; **trade school** a school teaching mainly skilled crafts; **trade secret** a secret and successful formula, process, technique, etc known only to one manufacturer; **trades'folk** tradespeople; **trades'man**, *fem* **trades'woman** a shopkeeper; a skilled worker; a mechanic: — *adj* **trades'manlike**. — **trades'people** people engaged in trade; shopkeepers; mechanics; skilled workers; **trade union** an organized association of workers of an industry for the protection of their common interests; **trade unionism**; **trade unionist**; **trades union** an association of trade unions, such as the **Trades Union Congress** (*abbrev* **TUC**). — *adj* **trade'-weighted** (*econ*) (of exchange rates) weighted according to the significance of the trade carried on with the various countries listed. — **trade wind** a wind blowing toward the thermal equator and deflected westward by the eastward rotation of the earth; **trading estate** an industrial estate; **trading post** a store, etc established in an *esp* remote, thinly-populated or hostile area; **trading stamp** a stamp given by the retailer to a purchaser of goods which, when a specified number have been collected, may be exchanged without payment for articles provided by the trading stamp firm. — **Board of Trade** a department of government for matters of industry and commerce; **trade down** or **up** to deal in lower grade, cheaper or higher grade, dearer goods; to buy a smaller (or larger) house, etc than one sells; **trade in** to give in part payment; **trade off** to exchange, *esp* as a compromise; **trade on** to count on or take advantage of, *esp* unscrupulously. [Prob LGer *trade*; related to **tread**]

tradescantia *trad-is-kan'shi-ə*, *n* any plant of the American *Tradescantia* (spiderwort) genus, with attractive, often variegated foliage. [After the English gardener, naturalist and traveller John *Tradescant* (c. 1567–1637)]

tradition *trə-dish'ən*, *n* the, *esp* oral, passing from generation to generation of tales, beliefs, practices, etc; a tale, belief or practice thus handed down; a collection of these belonging to a specific family, people, country, etc; a long-established belief or custom; anything bound up with or continuing in the life of a family, community, etc; religious teaching, doctrine or laws based on (*usu* early) oral tradition, *esp* (often with *cap*) in Christianity, the teaching of Christ and the Apostles not found in Scripture, in Judaism, the laws believed to have been given to Moses by God, and in Islam, the words and deeds of Mohammed; the continuous development of principles etc of a body of eg literature, music; a handing over (*law*). — *adj* **tradi'tional** or (*rare*) **tradi'tionary**. — *n* **tradi'tionalism**. — *n* and *adj* **tradi'tionalist**. — *adj* **traditionalis'tic**. — *n* **tradition-al'ity**. — *adv* **tradi'tionally** or (*rare*) **tradi'tionarily**. — *n* **tradi'tioner** or **tradi'tionist** a person who adheres to tradition. — *adj* **traditive** (*trad'i-tiv*) traditional. — *n* **trad'itor** a traitor, betrayer (*obs*); a person who under persecution gave up sacred books or objects or the names of his or her coreligionists, *esp* a Christian under Roman persecution (*hist*): — *pl* **trad'itors** or **traditores** (*-tö'rāz*). — **traditional jazz** see under **trad**; **traditional option** (*stock exchange*) an option which, once purchased, cannot be exchanged. [L *trāditiō*, *-ōnis*, *trāditor*, *-ōris*, from *trādere* to give up, from *trāns* over, and *dare* to give]

traduce *trə-dūs'* or (*US*) *-dōōs'*, *vt* to calumniate, to malign; to defame; to translate (*obs*); to propagate or transmit (*obs*). — *n* **traduce'ment**. — *n* **tradū'cer**. — *n* **Tradū'cian** (*-shi-ən*) a person who believes that children receive soul as well as or concomitantly with their body from their parents through natural generation. — Also *adj*. — *n* **Tradū'cianism**. — *n* **Tradū'cianist**. — *adj* **Tradūcianis'tic**. — *adj* **tradū'cible**. — *n* and *adj* **tradū'cing**. — *adv* **tradū'cingly**. — *n* **traduction** (*-duk'shən*). — *adj* **traduc'tive** transmitted. [L *trādūcere*, *trāductum*, from *trāns* across, and *dūcere* to bring]

traffic *traf'ik*, *n* vehicles, pedestrians, etc (collectively), using a thoroughfare; similar movement at sea or in the air; the transportation of goods and people on a railway, air or sea route, etc; the goods or people transported along a route; dishonest or illegal trading; commerce, trade; dealings or communication between groups or individuals; a passing to and fro; the volume of messages transmitted through a communications system; a trading voyage (*obs*); commodities (*obs*). — *vi* to trade; to trade, *esp* dishonestly or illegally (with *in*); to intrigue. — *vt* to trade in or barter; to use, pass to and fro on (a highway, etc): — *pr p* **traff'icking**; *pa t* and *pa p* **traff'icked**. — *n* **traff'icātor** (formerly) a movable pointer raised or lowered by the driver of a vehicle to warn of a change of direction. — *n* **traff'icker**. — *n* and *adj* **traff'icking**. — *adj* **traff'icless**. — **traffic-calming** control of vehicular traffic in built-up, *esp* residential, areas by the use of various devices designed to reduce speed and volume, eg sleeping policemen, ramps, etc; **traffic circle** (*NAm*) a road intersection where traffic circulates in one direction only, a roundabout; **traffic cop** (*colloq*, *esp US*) a policeman supervising road traffic; **traffic island** a raised section in the centre of a road to separate lanes, guide traffic, etc; **traffic jam** congestion, and resultant stoppage, of traffic, eg at a busy junction; **traff'ic-lights** or **traff'ic-signals** coloured lights to regulate street traffic, *esp* at intersections; **traff'ic-manager** the manager of the traffic on a railway, etc; **traffic pattern** the disposition of aircraft in the skies around an airport; **traff'ic-returns** statistics of passengers and goods carried by a transportation service and money received in return; **traffic warden** an official controlling road traffic, *esp* the parking of vehicles. [From a Romance language; cf Fr *trafic*, Ital *traffico*, Sp *tráfico*; origin obscure]

tragacanth *trag'ə-kanth*, *n* a gum (also **gum tragacanth**) used in pharmacy and as a vehicle for dye in calico-printing, obtained from several spiny shrubs of the genus *Astragalus*; the plant yielding it. [Gr *tragakantha*, from *tragos* goat, and *akantha* thorn]

tragedy *traj'i-di*, *n* a type of drama dealing with tragic events and often involving the fall of an honourable, worthy and important protagonist, often with elevated action and language; a play of this type; the art of such drama; any piece of literature, music, etc ending with disaster for the protagonist; a disaster, any sad story or turn of events; any event involving death or killing (*journalism*). — *n* **tragedian** (*trə-jē'di-ən*) a writer or (*usu*) an actor of tragedy. — *n* **tragedienne** (*trə-jē-di-en'*) or (*Fr*) **tragédienne** (*trä-zhā-di-en'*) an actress of tragic rôles. [L *tragoedia*, from Gr *tragōidiā* tragedy, appar literally goat-song, from *tragos* a he-goat, and *ōidē* song (variously explained)]

tragelaph *trag'*, *traj'i-laf*, *n* a fabulous animal, part goat, part stag; any African antelope of the genus *Tragelaphus*. — *adj* **tragel'aphine**. [Gr *tragelaphos*, from *tragos* a goat, and *elaphos* a deer]

tragi. See under **tragus**.

tragic *traj'ik*, *adj* extremely sad or distressing, disastrous; relating to or of the nature of tragedy. — Also **trag'ical**. — *adv* **trag'ically**. — *n* **trag'icalness**. — **tragic irony** a form of irony, *orig* in Greek tragedy, in which the tragic, prophetic meaning of the words is known to the audience but not the character speaking. [L *tragicos*, from Gr *tragōidiā* tragedy; see ety for **tragedy**]

tragicomedy *tra-ji-kom'idi*, *n* a play or story in which grave and comic scenes or themes are blended; a comedy that threatens to be a tragedy; such plays as a genre; any event having both tragic and comic elements. — *adj* **tragicom'ic** or **tragicom'ical**. — *adv* **tragicom'ically**. [LL *tragicōmedia*; see etys for **tragedy** and **comedy**]

tragopan *trag'ō-pan*, *n* a brilliantly coloured Asiatic pheasant with horny process on the bill. [Gr *tragopān* hornbill, from *tragos* goat, and *Pān* the god Pan]

tragus *trā'gəs*, *n* a small fleshy prominence at the entrance of the external ear; any of the hairs growing in the outer ear, *esp* from this part: — *pl* **trā'gi** (*-jī*). — *n* **tragule** (*trag'ūl*) a chevrotain. — *adj* **trag'uline** (*-īn*). [Gr *tragos* goat, tragus]

trahison *tra-ē-zɔ̃*, (*Fr*) *n* treason; treachery. — **trahison des clercs** (*dā kler*) the treason of intellectuals, the entry of academics into politics.

traik *trāk*, (*Scot*) *vi* to make one's way wearily or with effort; to stray; to get lost; to gad; to decline in health. — *n* a loss, *esp* of sheep; the mutton of sheep that have died of disease or accident. — *adj* **traik'it** worn out. — **traik after** to dangle after. [**trek**]

trail[1] *trāl*, *vt* to draw along behind or near the surface; to drag wearily; to drag along; to lag behind; to track, follow or hunt; to make (a path or track) through; to advertise (a forthcoming programme, etc) by trailer; to carry (a weapon) with the butt near the ground, or horizontally; to lead on; to quiz (*colloq*); to cover with a trailing ornament. — *vi* to be drawn out in length; (of eg a garment) to hang, float, or drag loosely behind; (of eg a plant) to sprawl over the ground or a support; to straggle or lag; to drag oneself along; to tail off (with *away* or *off*); to move with slow sweeping motion or with dragging drapery; to be losing in a game or competition. — *n* a track or series of marks left by a person, animal etc moving over a surface; a track or scent, eg of hunted game; a beaten path in the wilds; a path or route; anything drawn out in length or dragging behind; a train or tail; an act or manner of trailing; a television or cinema trailer; the track of a star on a stationary photographic plate; the part of a gun-carriage resting on the ground behind; the distance between the point at which a steered wheel meets the ground and that at which the intersection of a swivel-pin axis meets the ground (*autos*). — *adj* **trail'able**. — *n* **trail'er** a person who trails; a tracker; a creeping plant; an *esp* two-wheeled conveyance, towed or dragged by a car, bicycle or tractor; the rear section of an articulated lorry; a house on wheels, a caravan (*US*); a short film advertising a forthcoming entertainment on television or in the cinema; the blank piece of film at the end of a reel. — *vt* to advertise (a programme, etc) by trailer. — *adj* **trail'ing**. — *adv* **trail'ingly**. — *adj* **trail'-less**. — **trail bike** a motorcycle suitable for riding over rough ground and tracks; **trail'-blazer** a pioneer; a person or thing that leads the way in anything. — *adj* and *n* **trail'-blazing**. — **trailing edge** the rear edge of a wing, aerofoil or propeller; the falling portion of a pulse signal (*telecomm*); **trailing vortex** (*aeronautics*) the vortex passing from the tips of the main surfaces of an aircraft and extending downstream and behind it; **trail mix** a mixture of pieces of dried fruit (eg bananas, dates, pineapple, apricots, etc) nuts and seeds eaten as a snack, *orig* by hikers; **trail'-net** a dragnet. — **trail a pike** (*obs*) to serve as a soldier; **trail away** or **off** (*esp* of a sound) to become fainter; **trail one's coat** to invite a quarrel. [Ety doubtful; OE *træglian* to pluck, pull, and OFr *trailler* to tow, perh from L *tragula* sledge, dragnet, are possibilities]

trail[2] *trāl*, *n* an aphetic form of **entrail**.

trailbaston *trāl'bas-tən*, (*hist*) *n* a ruffian or brigand in 14c England. [Anglo-Fr *traille-baston*, from OFr *traille*, imperative of *trailler* to trail, and *baston* cudgel]

train[1] *trān*, *vt* to instruct and discipline, *esp* in a particular skill; to cause (a plant, etc) to grow in the desired manner; to prepare for a specific purpose (*esp* a competition) by instruction, practice, diet, exercise or otherwise; to bring up; to direct, aim (as a gun or telescope); to draw along (*archaic*); to allure (*obs*); to draw on (*obs*). — *vi* (*Spenser* **trayne**) to undergo instruction, *esp* in a particular skill; to prepare oneself by instruction, exercise, diet or otherwise; to be under drill; to travel by rail; to trail, drag (*rare*). — *n* a string of railway carriages or wagons with a locomotive or other means of propulsion; that which is dragged along or follows behind; a tail; tail-feathers or trailing back-feathers; the part of a dress that trails; a retinue; a series; a sequence; a number of things, animals, etc in a string or succession; a process; a line of combustible material to fire an explosive charge; a set of wheels acting on each other, for transmitting motion; artillery and other equipment for a siege or battle; a lure; a thing dragged on the ground to make a scent; a sledge (*Can*). — *n* **trainabil'ity**. — *adj* **train'able**. — *adj* **trained** having received training; having a train. — *n* **trainee'** a person who is under training. — *n* **trainee'ship** the period of being a trainee; the position of or maintenance provided for a trainee. — *n* **train'er** a person who prepares athletes for competion, horses for a race, or the like; any machine or device used in training, *esp* an aeroplane with duplicated controls for training pilots; a soft running shoe, *usu* laced, with a thick sole, used in training or for general casual wear (*usu* in *pl*). — *n* **train'ing** the process of instructing in a skill, etc; practical education in any profession, art or handicraft; a course of diet and exercise for developing physical strength, endurance or dexterity. — *adj* **train'less**. — **train'band** (*hist*) a band of citizens from the 16c to 18c trained to bear arms; **train'-bearer** a person who holds up the train of a robe or gown; **trainer pants** or (*US*) **training pants** thick cotton briefs with extra padding, used to help toilet-train young children; **train ferry** a ferry that conveys railway trains; **Training Agency** an organization established in 1989 to train and retrain adult workers and operate the Youth Training Scheme; **train'ing-college** former name for a college of education; **train'ing-ship** a ship in which young people are trained for the sea; **train mile** a unit of railway traffic, a run of one mile by one train; **train'-spotter** a person who collects locomotive or carriage numbers as a hobby; **train'-spotting**. — **in train** in progress; **in training** undergoing training; physically fit; **train fine** to bring body or mind to a high pitch of efficiency. [Mainly OFr *traïner*, *trahiner* (Fr *traîner*) to drag (nouns *traïn*, *traïne*); partly with overlap of meanings, from OFr *traïne* guile]

train[2] *trān, n* (*usu* **train'-oil**) whale oil extracted from the blubber by boiling. [Du *traen* (now *traan*) tear, exudation]

Train à Grande Vitesse *trẽn ä grã vi-tes*, (*Fr*) *n* a high-speed French passenger train (*abbrev* **TGV**).

traipse or **trapes** *trāps, vi* to trail; to trudge; to gad; to go in a slatternly way. — *n* a trudge; a slattern. — *n* and *adj* **traips'ing** or **trapes'ing**. — *vi* **trape** to traipse. [Origin unknown]

trait *trā, trāt, n* a characteristic or distinguishing feature; a stroke, touch. [Fr, from L *trahere, tractum* to draw]

traitor *trā'tər, n* a betrayer; a person who commits treason: —*fem* **trait'ress**. — Also *adj*. — *n* **trai'torhood, trait'orism** or **trai'torship**. — *adj* **trait'orly** (*Shakesp*). — *adj* **trait'orous**. — *adv* **trait'orously**. — *n* **trait'orousness**. [Fr *traître*, from L *trāditor*, from *trādere* to give up]

traject *trə-jekt', vt* to take across (*obs*); to transmit or transport (*archaic*). — *n* (*traj'ikt*) a crossing; a ferry; a transference, transmission (*rare*). — *n* **trajec'tion** (*-shən*) a crossing; a transmission; a transposition; a passage (*obs*). — *n* **trajectory** (*traj'ik-tər-i, trə-jekt'ər-i*) the path described by a body under the action of given forces, *esp* the curved path of a projectile; a curve that cuts a system of curves or surfaces at a constant angle (*geom*). [L *trājicere, -jectum*, from *trāns* across, and *jacere* to throw]

tra-la *trä-lä, interj* used to express joy, pleasure, etc, or when humming a song.

tralaticious or **tralatitious** *tral-ə-tish'əs, adj* transmitted; traditional; handed on, second-hand. [L *trālātīcius*, from *trānslātum*, serving as supine to *trānsferre*; see **transfer**]

tram[1] *tram, n* an electrically-powered public vehicle running on rails in the road (also **tram'car** or **tramway car**); a truck used in mines; a tramway; a shaft of a barrow or cart. — Also *adj*. — **tram'-conductor**; **tram'line** the track on which a tram runs; (in *pl*) the lines marking the sides of a tennis or badminton court and the lines parallel to them inside the court; (in *pl*) a rigid set of principles. — *adj* **tram'lined** (*colloq*) running, or as if running, in tramlines, very straight, rigid and inflexible. — **tram'road** a track with sunken wooden, stone or metal rails (legally one not running along a road); **tram'-stop** a stopping-place for tramcars; **tram'way** a track or system of tracks with sunken rails along a road; a tramcar system; a tramroad (*esp US*). [Cf LGer *traam* beam, shaft, etc]

tram[2] *tram, n* silk yarn for weft, of two or more strands. [Fr *trame*, from L *trāma* weft]

tram[3] *tram*. See under **trammel**.

tram[4] *tram, n* a device for adjusting or aligning a piece of machinery. — *vt* to adjust or align using a tram: — *pr p* **tramm'ing**; *pa t* and *pa p* **tramm'ed**. [A short form of **trammel**]

trammel *tram'l, n* anything that confines or hinders (*usu* in *pl*); a net whose inner fine-meshed layer is carried by the fish through the coarse-meshed outer layer, and encloses it in a pocket; a fowling net; a hobble; shackles for making a horse amble; an instrument for describing an ellipse consisting of a metal or wooden beam with two adjustable pegs (also **tram**); a series of adjustable rings or hooks suspended from a crossbeam in the chimney, for hanging kettles, cooking pots, etc above a fireplace; (in *pl*) a tress. — *vt* to shackle; to confine; to impede or hinder; to entangle: — *pr p* **tramm'elling**; *pa t* and *pa p* **tramm'elled**. — *n* **tramm'eller**. — **tramm'el-net** a trammel. [OFr *tramail* a net, from LL *tramacula*, from L *trēs* three, and *macula* a mesh]

tramontane *tra-mon'tān, adj* beyond the mountains (*esp* the Alps from Rome); foreign; uncivilized. — *n* an inhabitant of a region beyond the mountains; a foreigner; a barbarian. — *n* **tramontana** (*trä-mon-tä'na*) (in Italy) a cold north wind. [Ital *tramontana*, from L *trāns* beyond, and *mōns, montis* a mountain]

tramp *tramp, vi* to tread, *esp* heavily or noisily; to walk; to go on a walking tour or long walk; to hike in the bush (*NZ*); to live as a vagrant; to go in a tramp steamer. — *vt* to traverse on foot, *esp* wearily; to trample; to tread in a tub in washing clothes (*Scot*). — *n* a foot-journey; the sound of heavy footsteps or horses hooves; a vagrant; a cargo-boat with no fixed route (also **tramp steamer**); a prostitute, an immoral woman (*slang*); a plate of iron worn on the sole for pressing a spade or for giving a foothold on ice; the footrest of a spade. — *adv* with tramping noise. — *n* **tramp'er**. — *n* **tramp'ing**. — *adj* **tramp'ish**. — **tramp metal** (*eng*) stray metal pieces accidentally entrained in food or other processed materials, which must be removed before the material leaves the process. [ME *trampen*; cf Ger *trampen*]

trampet or **trampette** *tram-pet', n* a small trampoline used for springing off, in gymnastic vaulting. [Dimin of **trampoline**]

trample *tramp'l, vt* to tread roughly under foot; to treat with pride, to insult. — *vi* (*usu* with *on* or *upon*) to tread roughly or in contempt; to tread forcibly and rapidly. — *n* the sound or an act of trampling. — *n* **tramp'ler**. — *n* **tramp'ling**. — Also *adj*. [Frequentative of **tramp**]

trampoline *tram'pə-lin, -lēn, n* a framework supporting a piece of canvas, stretched and attached by springs, for acrobats, gymnasts, diving learners, etc, to jump, somersault, etc on. — *vi* to jump, turn somersaults, etc on a trampoline. — Also **tram'polin**. — *n* **tram'poliner** or **tram'polinist**. [Ital *trampolino* springboard]

tran- *tran-, pfx* signifying: across; beyond; through. [L *trans* across, beyond]

trance[1] *träns, n* a dazed, abstracted, ecstatic or exalted state; a deep sleeplike state, profound and prolonged; catalepsy; a state of being apparently unaware of one's surroundings, as claimed by mediums. — *vt* to throw into a trance; to entrance (*poetic*). — *adv* **tranced** (*tränst, trän'sid*) in a trance. — *adv* **tranc'edly**. [Fr *transe*, from *transir*, from L *trānsīre* to go across, in LL, to die]

trance[2] or **transe** *träns*, (*Scot*) *n* a through passage.

tranche *trãsh, n* a slice; a block, portion, *esp* of money or of an issue of shares. [Fr, slice, from *trancher* to cut]

tranchet *trã'shā, n* a shoemaker's paring knife; a neolithic or mesolithic flint with a chisel-shaped end (*archaeol*). [Fr, from *trancher* to cut]

tranect *tran'ekt*, (*Shakesp*) *n* a ferry. [As if L *trāns* across, and *nectere* to join; but supposed to be a misprint for **traject**]

trangam *trang'gəm, n* a showy, worthless article or knick-knack. [Origin unknown]

trangle *trang'gl*, (*heraldry*) *n* a diminutive of the fesse. [Obs Fr]

trankum *trang'kəm*, (*Scott*) *n* a trinket. **[trinket]**

trannie or **tranny** *tran'i*, (*colloq*) *n* a transistor radio. [Short form of **transistor**]

tranquil *trangk'wil, adj* calm; peaceful. — *n* **tranquillīzā'tion** or **-s-**, or (*NAm*) **tranquilīzā'tion**. — *vt* **tranq'uillize** or **-ise**, or (*NAm*) **tranq'uilize** to make tranquil, *esp* by sedation. — *n* **tranquillī'zer** or **-s-**, or (*NAm*) **tranquil'ī'zer** that which tranquillizes; a sedative drug. — *adv* **tranquillī'zingly** or **-s-**, or (*NAm*) **tranquilī'zingly** — *n* **tranquill'ity** or (*NAm*) **tranquil'ity**. — *adv* **tran'quilly**. — *n* **tran'quilness**. [L *tranquillus*]

trans. *abbrev*: transitive; translated; translation.

trans- *tranz-, tränz-, trənz-, trans-, träns-, trəns-, pfx* signifying: across; beyond; through; (of an isomer) having two identical groups of atoms on opposite sides of a bond (*chem*); having a higher atomic number. — Also **tran-, tra-**. [L *trans* across, beyond]

transact *tranz-akt', tränz-, trənz-, -s-, vt* to conduct (business, etc), negotiate (a deal, etc); to perform; to deal with (*archaic*). — *vi* to negotiate; to have to do. — *n* **transac'tion** the act of transacting; an agreement; a piece of business performed; (*pl*) the reports or publications of certain learned societies. — *adj* **transac'tional**. — *adv* **transac'tionally**. — *n* **transac'tor**. — **transactional analysis** (*psychol*) a form of psychotherapy based on the concept of three 'ego-states' — child, adult and parent — in any one personality, and aimed at adjusting the balance between them, *esp* so as to improve the patient's interpersonal relations. [L *transactum*, pa p of *transigere*, from *agere* to carry on]

transactinide *tranz-ak'ti-nīd*, (*chem*) *adj* of or relating to elements with atomic numbers higher than the actinide series. — *n* such an element. [**trans-**]

transalpine *tranz-al'pīn, tränz-, adj* beyond the *Alps* (*orig* from Rome); crossing the Alps. — *n* an inhabitant of a region or country beyond the Alps. [L *transalpīnus*, from *Alpae* Alps]

transaminase *tranz-a'mi-nāz*, (*biol*) *n* an enzyme which catalyzes amino acids to keto acids. — *n* **transminā'tion**. [**trans**, *amin*(o) and chem sfx *-ase*]

transandine *tranz-an'dīn, tränz-, trənz-, adj* beyond, or crossing, the *Andes*. — Also **transandē'an** (or *-an'di-ən*). [**trans-**]

transatlantic *tranz-ət-lan'tik, tränz-, adj* beyond, from or belonging to the other side of the *Atlantic* Ocean; crossing the Atlantic. [**trans-**]

transaxle *tranz'ak-səl*, (*eng*) *n* (in a motor vehicle) a driving axle and differential gearbox forming an integral unit. [*trans*mission *axle*]

transcalent *tranz-kā'lənt, tränz-, adj* pervious to or allowing the passage of heat. — *n* **transcal'ency**. [**trans-**, and L *calēns, -entis*, from *calēre* to be hot]

transcaucasian *tranz-kö-kā'zhən, tränz-, adj* across or beyond the *Caucasus* mountains in Georgia, Armenia and Azerbaijan; (with *cap*; also *n*) of or relating to the region or the people of *Transcaucasia*, south of the Caucasus mountains. [**trans-**]

transceiver *tran-sē'vər, trän-, n* a piece of radio equipment (eg a walkie-talkie) whose circuitry permits both transmission and reception. [*trans*mitter and re*ceiver*]

transcend *tran-send', trän-, vt* to pass or lie beyond the range or limit of (human understanding, etc); to rise above; to surmount; to surpass; to exceed. — *n* **transcend'ence** or **transcend'ency**. — *adj* **transcend'ent** transcending; superior or supreme in excellence; surpassing others; as applicable to *being*, relating to the absolute, transcending all limitation — as applicable to *knowledge*, relating to what transcends experience, being given *a priori*; beyond human knowledge or consciousness; abstrusely speculative, fantastic. — *adj* **transcenden'tal** transcending; going beyond usual human knowledge or experience; supereminent, excelling, surpassing others; concerned with what is independent of experience; supernatural or mystical; vague; (of a function) not capable of being produced or expressed algebraically (*math*). — *n* (*math*) a transcendental number. — *n* **transcenden'talism** the investigation of what is *a priori* in human knowledge, or independent of experience; that which is vague and illusive in philosophy; the state of being transcendental; transcendental language; the American reaction against Puritan prejudices, humdrum orthodoxy, old-fashioned metaphysics, materialistic philistinism, and materialism — best associated with the name of R W Emerson (1803–82). — *n* **transcenden'talist**. — *n* **transcendental'ity**. — *vt* **transcenden'talize** or **-ise**. — *adv* **transcenden'tally**. — *adv* **transcend'ently**. — *n* **transcend'entness**. — **transcendental function** (*math*) any function which cannot be defined by a finite number of algebraic operations; **transcendental meditation** a system of meditation designed to promote spiritual wellbeing and a relaxed state of consciousness through silent repetition of a mantra; **transcendental number** (*math*) a number that is not a root of any algebraic equation with integral coefficients. [L *transcendere*, from *scandere* to climb]

transcontinental *tranz-kont-i-nent'l, tränz-, adj* extending or passing across or belonging to the farther side of a *continent*. — *adv* **transcontinen'tally**. [**trans-**]

transcribe *tran-skrīb', trän-, vt* to write over from one book into another; to copy; to write out (notes etc) in full; to transliterate; to arrange (a composition) for an instrument, voice or combination other than that for which it was composed (*music*); to record for future broadcasting or the like; to broadcast a transcription of; to transfer (information) from one type of storage system to another (*comput*); to make a phonetic or phonemic transcription of (speech, sounds, etc; *linguistics*); to cause to undergo transcription (qv) (*genetics*). — *adj* **transcrīb'able**. — *n* **transcrīb'er**. — *n* **transcript** (*tran'skript, trän'*) a written or printed copy, *esp* a legal or official copy of (sometimes secret) proceedings, testimony, etc; any copy; a length of RNA transcribed from a DNA template, or of DNA transcribed from a RNA template (*genetics, biochemistry*); an official copy of a school pupil's educational report (*NAm*). — *n* **transcrip'tion** the act of transcribing; any transcribed text; the natural process by which a molecule of RNA is synthesized on the model of a DNA template carrying the necessary genetic information (*genetics*). — *adj* **transcrip'tional**. — *adv* **transcrip'tionally**. — *adj* **transcrip'tive**. — *adv* **transcrip'tively**. [L *transcrībere, -scrīptum*]

transcriptase *tran-skrip'tāz, trän-*, (*genetics*) *n* the enzyme that brings about transcription (qv) (see also **reverse transcriptase** under **reverse**). [*transcript*ion and chem sfx *-ase*]

transcutaneous *trans-kū-tā'ni-əs, träns-, adj* passing or entering through the skin. — **transcutaneous electrical nerve stimulation** (*abbrev* **TENS**) a method of pain relief in which electrodes are placed on the skin near the source of pain and a small electric current passed through, effective eg in childbirth. [**trans-**]

transducer *trans-dū'sər, träns-, -z-*, or (*US*) *-dōōs'ər, n* a device that transfers power from one system to another in the same or in a different form. — *n* **transduc'tion** transfer, *esp* transfer of genetic material from one bacterial cell to another by bacteriophage. — *n* **transduc'tor** an arrangement of windings on a laminated core or cores, part of a device for amplifying current. [L *transdūcere, -ductum* to lead across]

transe. Same as **trance**[2].

transect *trans-ekt', träns-, vt* to cut across transversely. — *n* (*tran'sekt, träns-*) a sample belt of vegetation marked off for study. — *n* **transect'ion**. [**tran**(**s**)- and **sect**[2]]

transenna *tran-sen'ə, n* a screen enclosing a shrine. [L *trānsenna* trellis, lattice-work]

transept *tran'sept, trän-*, (*archit*) *n* part of a church at right angles to the nave, or of another building to the main structure; either wing of such a part where it runs right across. — *adj* **transept'al** of a transept. — *adj* **transept'ate** divided by transverse septa. [L *saeptum* (used in pl) fence, enclosure]

transeunt *tran'zi-ənt, trän'-, -si-*. See under **transient**.

transf. *abbrev*: transfer; transferred; transference.

transfard *trans-färd'*, (*Spenser*) transferred (*pa t*).

transfection *trans-fek'shən, träns-*, (*microbiol*) *n* the introduction of DNA isolated from a cell or virus into another cell. — *vt* **transfect'** to cause transfection in (a cell). [*trans*fer and in*fection*]

transfer *trans-fûr', träns-, vt* to carry or bring over; to convey or move from one place, person, ownership, object, group, school, football club, etc, to another; to change over; to convey (eg a design) to another surface. — *vi* to change over, *esp* (*US*) from one railway, train or station, to another; to move from one school, football club, etc to another: — *pr p* **transferr'ing**; *pa t* and *pa p* **transferred'**. — *n* **trans'fer** the act of transferring; a design to be conveyed from one surface to another; conveyance from one person, place, etc, to another; a person who or thing which is transferred or is to be transferred (eg a football player); a transfer-ticket (*esp NAm*) the passing of property or some other right to another person (*law*); any document attesting to this (*law*). — *n* **transferabil'ity** (also **transferrabil'ity** or **transferribil'ity**). — *adj* **trans'ferable** (*-fûr'-*), **transfer'able**, **transferr'able** or **transferr'ible** (*-fûr'-*). — *n* **transferee'** the person to whom a thing is transferred; a person who is transferred. — *n* **trans'ference** the act of transferring or conveying; passage from place to place; unconscious transferring of one's hopes, desires, fears, etc, from one person or object to another (*psychol*). — *adj* **transferen'tial**. — *n* **trans'feror** (*law*) or **transferr'er** (*general*) a person who transfers. — *n* **transferr'al** an act of transferring. — **transferable vote** a vote which, if the candidate voted for should be out of the running, is to be transferred to another as second or subsequent choice; **transfer book** a register of the transfer of property, shares, etc; **transfer day** a day for registering transfer of bank-stock and government funds at the Bank of England; **transfer fee** a fee paid by one club in return for a transferred player; **transfer list** a list of footballers available for transfer to another club; **transfer machine** (*eng*) a machine in which a workpiece or assembly passes automatically through a number of stations, undergoing one or more production processes at each; **trans'fer-paper** a specially coated paper used for transferring impressions with copying-presses, etc; **transfer RNA** (*biol*) a small RNA molecule which links messenger RNA and protein synthesis, one end of the molecule binding to a specific codon of the mRNA, the other bearing the corresponding amino acid (*abbrev* **tRNA**); **trans'fer-ticket** a ticket for a journey to be resumed on another route. [L *trānsferre*, from *ferre* to carry]

transferase *trans'fə-rāz*, (*biol*) *n* an enzyme which catalyzes the transfer of chemical groups between compounds. [**transfer** and chem sfx *-ase*]

transferrin *trans-fer'in*, *träns-*, (*biochem*) *n* a protein in the blood that transports iron. [Pfx **trans-** and L *ferrum* iron]

transfigure *trans-fig'ər*, *träns-*, *vt* to change the appearance or form of; to glorify. — *n* **transfiguration** (-ə-, *-ū-rā'shən*) a transformation or glorification in appearance or form; (with *cap*) the glorification of Christ's appearance before three of his disciples (from the Bible: Matt. 17. 2); (with *cap*) the Christian festival celebrating this on August 6. — *n* **transfig'urement**. [L *trānsfigūrāre*, from *figūra* form]

transfinite *trans-fī'nīt*, *träns-*, *adj* surpassing what is finite; (of a cardinal or ordinal number) surpassing all finite numbers (*math*). [**trans-**]

transfix *trans-fiks'*, *träns-*, *vt* to pierce through; to paralyse with sudden emotion, horror or shock; to cut through (a limb), as in amputation (*med*). — *n* **transfixion** (*-fik'shən*). [L *trānsfīgere*, *-fīxum*, from *fīgere* to fix]

transform *trans-förm'*, *träns-*, *vt* to change the shape of; to change *esp* radically or thoroughly to another form, appearance, substance or character; to change the form of (an algebraic expression or geometrical figure) (*math*); to change the voltage of (an alternating current) using a transformer. — *vi* to be changed in form or substance. — *n* (*träns'*) an expression or figure derived from another (*math*); any of a group of linguistic constructions related in some way through the application of transformational rules; (in digital computers) a process that alters the form of information without changing its meaning. — *adj* **transform'able**. — *n* **transformā'tion** the act of transforming; a change of form, constitution or substance; metamorphosis (*zool*); transmutation; (in full **transformation scene**) a sudden, dramatic change of scene, *esp* a scene on the stage that changes in presence of the audience or in which the characters of the pantomime were transformed into those of the harlequinade; change from one linguistic transform to another of the group; (also **transformational rule**) any of a number of grammatical rules converting the deep structure of a sentence into its surface structure (*linguistics*); reflection, rotation, translation or dilatation (*geom*); the transfer of genetic information from one cell to another to another, resulting in genetic change in the recipient cell (*genetics*); a transformed person (*Shakesp*); false hair, a wig (*archaic*). — *adj* **transformā'tional**. — *adv* **transformā'tionally**. — *adj* **transform'ative**. — *adj* **transformed'**. — *n* **transform'er** a person who or thing that transforms; an apparatus for obtaining an electric current from another of a different voltage. — *n* and *adj* **transform'ing**. — *n* **transform'ism** the theory of the mutability of species, the theory of evolution. — *n* **transform'ist**. — *adj* **transformis'tic**. — **transformational grammar** a method of studying or describing a language by stating which elements or structures can be derived from or related to others by transformation; a grammatical description which includes transformational rules. — **conformal transformation** (*math*) a change of shape which still preserves a one-to-one matching of points in the original surface with points in the new surface, as in map making. [L *trānsfōrmāre*, from *fōrma* form]

transfuse *trans-fūz'*, *träns-*, *vt* to pour out into another vessel; to transfer (eg blood) to another's veins; to treat (a patient, etc) by transfusion; to cause to pass, enter or diffuse through; to imbue; to instil; to cause to be imbibed. — *n* **transfū'ser**. — *adj* **transfū'sible** or **transfū'sable**. — *n* **transfū'sion** (*-zhən*) transfusing, *esp* of blood into a patient. — *n* **transfū'sionist**. — *adj* **transfū'sive** (*-siv*) tending or having power to transfuse. — *adv* **transfū'sively**. [L *trānsfundere*, from *fundere*, *fūsum* to pour]

transgenic *trans-jen'ik*, (*bot* and *zool*) *adj* (of animals or plants) containing genetic material introduced from another species by techniques of genetic engineering. — *n* a transgenic plant or animal. — *n* **transgen'esis**. [**trans-**]

transgress *trans-gres'*, *träns-*, *-z-*, *vt* to pass beyond the limit of or set by; to overstep, exceed; to infringe; (of the sea) to flood over (the land). — *vi* to offend by violating a law; to sin. — *n* **transgression** (*-gresh'ən*) an overstepping; an infringement; sin. — *adj* **transgress'ional**. — *adj* **transgressive** (*-gres'iv*). — *adv* **transgress'ively**. — *n* **transgress'or**. [L *trānsgredī*, *-gressum*, from *gradī*, *gressum* to step]

tranship or **transship** *tran(s)-ship'*, *trän(s)-*, *trən-*, *vt* to transfer from one ship or other conveyance to another. — *vi* to change ship, etc. — *n* **tranship'ment** or **transship'ment**. — *n* **transhipp'er** or **transshipp'er**. — *n* **transhipp'ing** or **transshipping**. [**tran(s)-**]

transhume *trans-(h)ūm'*, *träns-*, *-z-*, *vt* and *vi* to transfer or pass from summer to winter or from winter to summer pastures. — *n* **transhu'mance**. — *adj* **transhu'mant**. [Sp *trashumar*, from L *trāns* across, beyond, and *humus* ground]

transience, **transiency**. See under **transient**.

transient *tran'zi-ənt*, *trän'*, *-si-*, *adj* passing; of short duration, impermanent; making, or for people making, only a short stay; passing (*music*); (of a mental process) producing an effect outside the mind (also **transeunt**; *philos*). — *n* a temporary resident, worker, etc; a brief alteration in a waveform, etc, as a sudden surge of voltage or current (*phys*). — *n* **tran'sience** or **tran'siency**. — *adv* **tran'siently**. — *n* **tran'sientness**. [L *trānsiēns*, *-euntis*, from pr p of *trānsīre* to cross, from *īre*, *itum* to go]

transilient *tran-sil'i-ənt*, *trän-*, *trən-*, *adj* leaping or passing across. — *n* **transil'iency**. [L *trānsilīre*, from *salīre* to leap]

transilluminate *tranz-i-lū'mi-nāt*, *tränz-*, *-s-*, *-lo͞o'*, (*med*) *vt* to pass a strong light through, *esp* for the purposes of examination. — *n* **transilluminā'tion**. [**trans-**]

transire *tranz-ī'ri*, *tränz-*, *-s-*, *träns-ē're* *n* customs warrant for clearing goods, cargo, etc. [L *trānsīre*; cf **transient**]

transisthmian *tranz-is(th)'mi-ən*, *tränz-*, *-s-*, *adj* across an isthmus. [**trans-**]

transistor *tranz-ist'ər*, *tränz-*, *-s-*, *n* a three-electrode semiconductor device, able to perform many functions of multi-electrode valves; an amplifier with crystal and two cat's whiskers. — *n* **transistorizā'tion** or **-s-**. — *vt* **transist'orize** or **-ise** to fit with or convert to use transistors. — **transistor** or **transistor radio** a small portable radio. [*trans*fer and re*sistor*]

transit *tran'zit, trän', -sit, n* the conveyance or passage of things or people over, across or through a distance; a route; passenger transport (*esp US*); the apparent passage of a heavenly body over the meridian (*astron*); the apparent passage of a smaller planet etc over the disc of a greater (*astron*); the passage of a planet across some particular region or point on the zodiac (*astrol*); a transit-circle, transit-instrument, or transit-theodolite. — *vi* to pass across. — *vt* to pass across; to reverse. — *adj* **trans'itable**. — **transit camp** a camp where eg refugees, immigrants, soldiers, etc are temporarily accommodated before travelling on to a further destination; **tran'sit-circle** a transit-instrument with a graduated circle for declinations; **tran'sit-duty** a duty chargeable on goods passing through a country; **tran'sit-instrument** a telescope mounted in the meridian and turned on a fixed east and west axis; **transit lounge** a lounge for transit passengers at an airport; **transit passenger** a passenger stopping briefly at an airport between flights; **tran'sit-theodolite** (*surveying*) one whose telescope can be reversed; **tran'sit-trade** the trade of carrying foreign goods through a country; **transit visa** one allowing only transit through a country and not residence. — **in transit** (of goods, etc) in the process of being transported from one place to another. [L *trānsitus, -ūs*, from *īre, itum*, to go]

transition *tran'-, trän'sizh'ən, -zish'ən, -sish'ən, n* passage from one place, state, stage, style or subject to another; a change of key, *esp* an abrupt one not using modulation (*music*); the specific passage from Romanesque or Norman to Gothic (*archit*); a change in the structure of an atomic nucleus, accompanied by photon emission or absorption. — *adj* transitional. — *adj* **transi'tional**. — *n* (*archit*) transition. — *adj* **transi'tionary**. — *adv* **transi'tionally**. — **transition element** or **transition metal** (*phys*) one of a group with an incomplete inner electron shell, characterized by the ability to form coloured complexes; **transition point** (*chem*) the temperature at which a crystalline form of a substance is converted into a solid form, ie that at which they can both exist in equilibrium. [L *trānsitiō, -iōnis*, from *trānsitus*; see ety for **transit**]

transitive *trans'i-tiv, träns'-, adj* passing over; having the power of passing; (of a verb) taking a direct object (*gram*); denoting a relation in which if the first element bears a relation to the second, and the second bears the same relation to a third, then the first bears the same relation to the third (*logic*). — *adv* **trans'itively**. — *n* **trans'itiveness**. — *n* **transitiv'ity**. [LL *trānsitīvus*, from L *trānsitus*; see ety for **transit**]

transitory *trans'i-tə-ri, träns'-, adj* lasting or appearing for a short time; going or passing away; vanishing quickly. — *adv* **trans'itorily**. — *n* **trans'itoriness**. — **transitory action** (*law*) an action that can be brought in any country no matter where the action originated. [LL *trānsitōrius*, from L *trānsitus*; see ety for **transit**]

translate *trans-lāt', träns-, trəns-, -z-, vt* to render into another language; to express in another artistic medium; to put in plainer terms, explain; to interpret the significance or meaning of (an action, behaviour, etc); to transfer (a cleric) from one ecclesiastical office to another; to remove or transfer to another place; to remove to heaven, *esp* without death; to transform or convert (often with *into*); to perform a translation on (*mech, math*); to interpret genetic information stored in (RNA) in the synthesis of a protein or polypeptide (*biol*); to enrapture; to renovate, make new from old. — *vi* to practise translation; to be translatable; to be transformed or converted (with *into*). — *adj* **translā'table**. — *n* **translā'tion** the act of translating; rendering into another language; a version; removal to another place, see, ecclesiastical office, etc; motion, change of place, such that every point moves in the same direction at the same speed; similar change of place of a geometrical figure; an algebraic function obtained by adding the same constant to each value of the variable in a given function, thus moving the graph of this function (or moving the rectangular axes parallel to themselves) while preserving its shape; the automatic retransmission of a telegraphic message; the process by which genetic information stored in RNA causes a protein or polypeptide to be synthesized to a particular pattern (*biol*); the working up of new things from old materials. — *adj* **translā'tional**. — *adv* **translā'tionally**. — *adj* **translā'tive** (*gram*) denoting, as in Finnish, 'turning into'. — *n* the translative case. — *n* **translā'tor** a person or machine that translates from one language into another; a program which converts another program from one language to another, *usu* into machine code (*comput*); a relay transmitter. — *adj* **translātor'ial**. — *adj* **trans'latory** (also *-lā'*) of or relating to direct onward motion without rotation. [L *trānslātum*, used as supine of *trānsferre*; see **transfer**]

transleithan *tranz-lī't(h)ən, tränz-, -s-, adj* beyond the river *Leitha*, once in part the boundary between Austria and Hungary; hence, Hungarian. [**trans-**]

transliterate *tranz-lit'ə-rāt, tränz-, -s-, vt* to write (a word) in letters of another alphabet or language. — *n* **transliterā'tion**. — *n* **translit'erātor**. [**trans-** and L *littera* letter]

translocation *tranz-lō-kā'shən, tränz-, -s-, n* transference from place to place, *esp* of materials within the body of a plant; the transfer of a portion of a chromosome to another part of the same chromosome or to a different chromosome, without (*balanced translocation*) or with (*unbalanced translocation*) loss of genetic material (*genetics*). — *vt* **translocate'**. [**trans-** and L *locus* place]

translucent *tranz-lōō'sənt, tränz-, -s-, -lū', adj* shining through; imperfectly transparent; clear. — *n* **translu'cence** or **translu'cency**. — *adv* **translu'cently**. — *adj* **translu'cid** translucent. — *n* **translucid'ity**. [L *trānslūcēns, -entis*, from *lūcēre* to shine, from *lūx, lūcis* light]

translunar *tranz-lōō'nər, tränz-, -s-, adj* of or relating to the region beyond the moon's orbit round the earth. — *adj* **translun'ary** (*tranz'*) beyond the moon; visionary; celestial rather than earthly. [**trans-**]

transmanche *tranz-mãsh', trãz-mãsh', (Fr) adj* of, for or relating to the tunnel under the English Channel. [Fr, from L *trāns* across, and la *Manche* the English Channel]

transmarine *tranz-mə-rēn', tränz-, -s-, adj* across or beyond the sea. [L *trānsmarīnus*, from *mare* sea]

transmew *tranz-mū', tränz-, -s-, (Spenser) vt* to transmute. [OFr *transmuer*, from L *transmūtāre*; see **transmute**]

transmigrate *tranz'mī-grāt, tränz', -s-, -grāt', vi* to remove to another place of abode or state; (of the soul) to pass into another body at death. — *vt* to cause to transmigrate. — *n* **trans'mīgrant** (*-mī'*) a person who transmigrates;. a migrant passing through a country on the way to another in which he or she means to settle. — *adj* passing through; transmigrating. — *n* **transmīgrā'tion**. — *adj* **transmīgrā'tional**. — *n* **transmīgrā'tionism** belief in the transmigration of souls. — *n* **transmīgrā'tionist**. — *adj* **trans'mīgrātive** (*-mī'grə-tiv*). — *n* **trans'mīgrātor**. — *adj* **transmī'gratory** (*-grə-tər-i*). [L *trānsmigrāre, -ātum*, from *migrāre* to migrate]

transmissible, transmission, etc. See under **transmit**.

transmit *tranz-mit', tränz-, -s-, vt* to send on; to pass on; to hand on; to communicate; to hand down to posterity; to send out or broadcast (radio signals, programmes, etc); to transfer (eg power from one part of a machine to another); to allow the passage of, act as a medium for (heat, energy, light, sound, etc). — *vi* to send out a radio signal, etc: — *pr p* **transmitt'ing**; *pa t* and *pa p* **transmitt'ed**. — *n* **transmissibil'ity**. — *adj* **transmiss'ible** (also **transmitt'able**, or, less correctly **transmitt'ible**). — *n* **transmission** (*-mish'ən*) the process of transmitting or state of being transmitted; that which is transmitted; a programme, message, etc sent out by radio, etc; the system of interdependent parts in a motor vehicle, by which power is transferred from the engine to the wheels; transmittance (*phys*). — *adj* **transmiss'ional**. — *adj* **transmiss'ive** having the quality of transmitting or of being transmitted. — *adv* **trans-**

miss'ively. — *n* **transmiss'iveness** or **transmissiv'ity** (*phys*) a measure of the ability of a material or medium to transmit radiation. — *n* **transmitt'al**. — *n* **transmitt'ance** the act of transmitting; the ratio of energy transmitted by a body to that incident on it (*phys*). — *n* **transmitt'er** a person who or thing that transmits; apparatus for producing, modulating and sending out anything, eg signals, messages, etc; a neurotransmitter. — **transmission coefficient** (*phys*) the probability of penetration of a nucleus by a particle striking it; **transmission electron microscope** (*phys*) an electron microscope which produces a two-dimensional image from the diffraction of electrons after passage through the specimen; **transmission line** (*elec eng*) any conductor used to transmit electric or electromagnetic energy, eg a power line or telephone line. [L *transmittere*, *-missum*, from *mittere*, *missum* to send]

transmogrify *tranz-mog'ri-fī, tränz-, -s-*, (*colloq, facetious*) *vt* to transform or transmute, *esp* bizarrely: — *pr p* **transmog'rifying**; *pa t* and *pa p* **transmog'rified**. — *n* **transmogrificā'tion**. [Appar a pseudo-Latinism]

transmontane *tranz-mon'tān, tränz-, -s-*, *adj* another form of **tramontane**.

transmove *tranz-mōōv', tränz-, -s-*, (*Spenser*) *vt* to transmute. [Appar for **transmew**, remodelled on **move**]

transmundane *tranz-mun'dān, tränz-*, *adj* not belonging to this world, out of, beyond, this world. [LL *transmundanus*, from *mundus* world]

transmute *tranz-mūt', tränz-, -s-*, *vt* to change to another form or substance; to change (base metals) into gold or silver (*alchemy*). — *n* **transmūtabil'ity**. — *adj* **transmū'table**. — *n* **transmū'tableness**. — *adv* **transmū'tably**. — *n* **transmūtā'tion** a changing into a different form, nature or substance, *esp* that of one chemical element into another; the process supposed to change base metals into gold or silver (*alchemy*); (in full **atomic transmutation**) the change of one type of atom to another as a result of nuclear radiation (*phys*); the transformation of one species into another (*biol*). — *adj* **transmūtā'tional**. — *n* **transmūtā'tionist**. — *adj* **transmū'tative** serving or tending to transmute. — *n* **transmū'ter**. [L *trānsmūtāre*, from *mūtāre* to change]

transnational *tranz-nash'nəl, tränz-, -s-*, *adj* transcending national boundaries, concerning more than one nation. [**trans-**]

transoceanic *tranz-ō-shi-an'ik, tränz-, -s-*, *adj* crossing the ocean; across or on the other side of the ocean. [**trans-**]

transom *tran'səm*, *n* a structure dividing a window horizontally; a lintel; a small window over the lintel of a door or window; a crosspiece; a crossbeam; any of several crossbeams used to strengthen the stern of a vessel. [OFr *traversin*, from *traverse* crosspiece]

transonic, transonics. See under **trans-sonic**.

transpacific *trans-pə-sif'ik, träns-*, *adj* crossing the Pacific; beyond or on the other side of the Pacific. [**trans-**]

transpadane *trans'pə-dān, träns'-, -z-, -pā'dān*, *adj* beyond or from beyond the Po (viewed from Rome). [L *Padus* the Po]

transparent *trans-pār'ənt, träns-, trəns-, -z-, -par'*, *adj* able to be seen through, clear; pellucid; pervious to rays; easily detected, understood; obvious, evident; ingenuous, frank; shining through (*Shakesp*). — *n* **transpar'ency** the quality of being transparent (also **transpar'ence**); that which is transparent; a picture, photograph, design or device visible, or to be viewed, by transmitted light, eg through a slide projector, a slide; Thackeray's humorous translation of the German title *Durchlaucht*. — *adv* **transpar'ently**. — *n* **transpar'entness**. [Med L *trānspārēns*, *-entis*, from L *pārēre* to appear]

transpersonal *trans-pûr'sə-nəl, träns-* *adj* going beyond or transcending the individual personality; denoting a form of psychology or psychotherapy that utilises mystical, psychical or spiritual experience as a means of increasing human potential. [**trans-**]

transpicuous *tran-spik'ū-əs, trän-, trən-*, *adj* transparent. — *adv* **transpic'ūously**. [L *trānspicere* to see through, from *specere* to look]

transpierce *trans-pērs', träns-*, *vt* to pierce through; to permeate. [**trans-**]

transpire *tran-spīr', trän-*, *vt* to give off as vapour; to exhale; to emit through the skin. — *vi* to exhale; to give off water vapour (as plants do) or waste material through the skin (as some animals do); to become known, come to light; (loosely) to happen; to prove to be the case. — *adj* **transpīr'able**. — *n* **transpiration** (*tran-spi-rā'shən*) the act or process of transpiring; exhalation through the skin; (in plants) emission of water vapour through the stomata, etc. — *adj* **transpīr'atory**. [L *trāns* through, and *spīrāre* to breathe]

transplant *trans-plänt', träns-, -z-*, *vt* to remove (a plant) from the ground where it grows and plant in another place; to transfer (eg an organ or tissue) surgically from one person or animal to another, or to another part of the same; to remove and establish elsewhere. — *vi* to tolerate or withstand transplanting. — *n* **trans'plant** a part or organ removed from its normal position and grafted into another position in the same individual or into another individual; the organ, tissue etc transplanted; the act of transplanting; a plant which has been transplanted. — *adj* **transplan'table**. — *n* **transplantā'tion**. — *n* **transplan'ter**. — *n* **transplan'ting**. [LL *trānsplantāre*, from L *plantāre* to plant]

transponder *tranz-pon'dər, tränz-, -s-*, *n* a radio or radar device which, on receiving a signal, transmits a signal of its own. [*trans*mitter res*ponder*]

transpontine *trans-pon'tīn, träns-, -z-*, *adj* across or on the other side of a bridge; on the Surrey side of the Thames, hence, from the type of theatrical productions there in the 19c, melodramatic (*old*). [L *trāns* across, and *pōns*, *pontis* a bridge]

transport *trans-pört', -pört', träns-, -z-*, *vt* to carry, convey or remove from one place to another; to send overseas to a penal colony (*hist*); to carry away by strong emotion; to throw into an ecstasy; to translate (eg a minister); to put to death (*Shakesp*); *perh* to carry off (as by the fairies) (*Shakesp*). — *n* **trans'port** carriage or conveyance of goods or people from one place to another; the management of or arrangements for such conveyance; means of conveyance for getting from place to place; the conveyance of troops and their equipment; a ship, aircraft, etc, for this purpose; ecstasy, or any strong emotion; someone who has been transported or sentenced to transportation (*hist*). — *n* **transportabil'ity**. — *adj* **transport'able** able to be transported; (eg of an offence) liable, or rendering liable, to transportation (*hist*). — *n* **transport'al**. — *n* **transport'ance** (*Shakesp*) conveyance, transport. — *n* **transportā'tion** removal; the act of transporting or process of being transported; removal of offenders to penal colonies beyond seas (*hist*); the transporting of goods or people; means or system of transport; tickets or passes for transport. — *adj* **transport'ed**. — *adv* **transport'edly**. — *n* **transport'edness**. — *n* **transport'er** someone or something that transports, *esp* a large vehicle for carrying heavy goods. — *n* and *adj* **transport'ing**. — *adv* **transport'ingly**. — *adj* **transport'ive** tending or having power to transport. — **transport café** a roadside café catering mainly for long-distance lorry drivers; **transporter bridge** a bridge for transporting vehicles, consisting of a movable platform suspended from a girder; **trans'port-rider** (*SAfr*) a carrier transporting goods by wagon (*hist*); **trans'port-ship** a ship used for carrying troops, stores, etc. [L *trānsportāre*, from *portāre* to carry]

transpose *trans-pōz', träns-, -z-*, *vt* to transfer; to turn, alter; to change the order or position of, interchange; to write, perform or render in another key (*music*); to transfer (a term) from one side of an equation to the other, with a corresponding reversal of sign (*algebra*); to interchange the rows and columns of (a matrix) (*math*); to transform (*Shakesp*). — *n* (*math*) a matrix resulting from rows and columns being interchanged.

— *adj* **transpōs'able**. — *adv* **transpōsabil'ity**. — *n* **transpōs'al** a change of place or order. — *n* **transpōs'er**. — *n* and *adj* **transpōs'ing**. — *n* **transposition** (*-pō-*, *-pə-zish'ən*). — *adj* **transposi'tional**. — *adj* **transpositive** (*-poz'*). — **transposable element** (*genetics*) a transposon; **transposing instrument** an instrument which, by a mechanical device, transposes music into another key; an instrument, eg a horn, for which music is written in a different key from the key that instrument actually produces. [Fr *transposer*; see **pose**]

transposon *trans-pō'zon*, (*genetics*) *n* a sequence of DNA capable of moving to different sites in a chromosome or to a different chromosome, with a subsequent change in the genetic makeup of the cell. [*transpos*ition and *-on*]

transputer *trans-pū'tər*, *träns-*, (*comput*) *n* a chip capable of all the functions of a microprocessor, *incl* memory, and able to process in parallel rather than sequentially. [*trans*istor and com*puter*]

transsexual or **trans-sexual** *trans-seks'ū-əl*, *träns-*, *n* a person anatomically of one sex but having a strong desire to adopt the physical characteristics and role of a member of the opposite sex; a person who has had medical and surgical treatment to alter the external sexual features so that they resemble those of the opposite sex. — Also *adj*. — *n* **transsex'ualism**. [**trans-**]

trans-shape *trans-shāp'*, *träns-*, (*Shakesp*) *vt* to transform.

trans-ship, **transship**. Same as **tranship**.

trans-sonic *trans-son'ik*, *träns-*, *adj* relating to the range of speeds close to, or equalling, that of sound. — Also **transonic** (*tran-*, *trän-son'ik*). — *n sing* **trans-son'ics** or **transonics** the study of such speeds. — **trans-sonic** (or **transonic**) **barrier** the sound barrier. [L *sonus* sound]

transubstantiate *tran-səb-stan'shi-āt*, *trän-*, *-zəb-*, *vt* to change to another substance. — *adj* **transubstan'tial**. — *adv* **transubstan'tially**. — *n* **transubstantiā'tion** a change into another substance; the doctrine that, or the mystical process by which, in the consecration of the elements of the eucharist, the whole substance of the bread and wine is converted into Christ's body and blood, only the appearances of bread and wine remaining (*Christian relig*, *esp RC*; cf **consubstantiation**). — *n* **transubstantiā'tionalist**, **transubstantiā'tionist** or **transubstan'tiātor** a person who believes in transubstantiation. [L *substantia* substance]

transude *tran-sūd'*, *trän-*, *-zūd'*, *vi* and *vt* to ooze out, eg through pores. — *n* **tran'sūdate** a substance that transudes or has been transuded, eg a fluid that passes through a membrane or the walls of a blood vessel. — *n* **transūdā'tion**. — *adj* **transū'datory**. [L *sūdāre* to sweat]

transume *tran-sūm'*, *trän-*, *-zūm'*, *vt* (*obs*) to transcribe officially. — *n* **transumpt** (*-sumt'*) a copy of a legal document. — *n* **transumption** (*-sum'shən*) transcription; metaphor; transference or translation — *adj* **transumptive** (*-sump'tiv*). [L *trān(s)sūmere* to transcribe, from *sūmere* to take]

transuranic *trans-ū-ran'ik*, *träns-*, *-z-*, *adj* (of an element) having an atomic number greater than that of *uranium*. — Also **transurā'nian** or **transurā'nium**. [**trans-**]

transvalue *trans-val'ū*, *träns-*, *-z-*, *vt* to re-estimate the value of, *esp* on a basis differing from the accepted standards. — *n* **transvaluā'tion**. — *n* **transval'uer**. [**trans-**]

transverse[1] *tranz'vûrs*, *tränz'*, *-vûrs'*, *adj* set, sent, lying, etc crosswise. — *adj* crosswise. — *n* anything set crosswise. — *vt* (*-vûrs'*) to cross; to thwart; to reverse; to transform. — *adj* **transvers'al** transverse. — *n* a line cutting a set of lines. — *n* **transversal'ity**. — *adv* **transvers'ally**. — *adv* **transverse'ly**. — *n* **transver'sion**. — **transverse colon** (*anatom*) the part of the colon lying across the abdominal cavity; **transverse flute** see under **flute**; **transverse wave** (*phys*) a wave motion in which the disturbance of the medium occurs at right angles to the direction of wave propagation. — **by transverse** (*Spenser*) awry. [L *trānsversus*, from *vertere*, *versum* to turn]

transverse[2] *tranz-vûrs'*, *tränz-*, *vt* to turn from prose into verse. — *n* **transver'sion** (*-shən*). [A pun in Buckingham's *Rehearsal*]

transvest *tranz-vest'*, *tränz-*, *vt* and *vi* to dress oneself in the clothes of another person, *esp* of the opposite sex. — *adj* **transvest'ic**. — *n* and *adj* **transvestite** (*-vest'īt*) (of or relating to) a person who gets psychological gratification from wearing clothes typically worn by the opposite sex. — *n* **transvest'ism**. — *n* **transvest'ist**. — *n* **transvest'itism**. [**trans-**, and L *vestis*, from *vestīre*, *vestītum* to dress; cf **travesty**]

tranter *trant'ər*, (*dialect*) *n* a hawker; a carrier. — *vt* and *vi* **trant** (back-formation) to hawk. [Cf LL *trāvetārius*]

trap[1] *trap*, *n* any enclosure or mechanical device, *usu* baited, for catching animals, etc; a snare, gin; a hidden danger; a plan or trick for surprising a person into speech, action, or for catching someone unawares; a pitfall; a trapdoor; a door in a loft, allowing pigeons to enter but not leave; a ventilating door in a mine; a lock; a bend in a pipe, *esp* a drainpipe, to stop the passage of air or foul gases; a light carriage; a device for throwing up or releasing a ball or clay pigeons; a boxlike stall from which a greyhound is released at the beginning of a race; the mouth (*slang*); a person who catches offenders (*slang*); (in *pl*) a police officer (*Austr slang*); trickery (*slang*); a bunker or other hazard (*golf*); (in *pl*) drums or other percussion instruments (*jazz*). — *vt* to catch in a trap; to catch (a person) out with a plan or trick; to provide with a trap or traps; to control (a ball) so that it stops dead (*football*). — *vi* to act as a trapper: — *pr p* **trapp'ing**; *pa t* and *pa p* **trapped**. — *n* **trapp'er** a person who traps animals for their fur; a person, *orig* a boy, who minds a mine trap; a horse for a trap. — *n* **trapp'iness**. — *n* and *adj* **trapp'ing**. — *adj* **trap'like**. — *adj* **trapp'y** full of traps, treacherous. — **trap'-ball** an old game played with a ball, bat, and trap; **trap'door** a door set in a floor, stage or ceiling, *esp* one flush with its surface; **trapdoor spider** one that makes a lair in the ground and covers it with a hinged door composed of earth and silk; **trap'-fall** a trapdoor that gives way beneath the feet; a pitfall; **trap'shooter**; **trap'shooting** clay pigeon shooting; **trap'-stick** a bat for trap-ball. [OE *trappe*, from *træppe*, *treppe*]

trap[2] *trap*, (*geol*; in full **traprock**) *n* any dark fine-grained columnar igneous rock (lying often in steps or terraces), *esp* basalt. — *adj* **trapp'ean** (*-ē'*). [Swed *trapp*, from *trappa* a stair]

trap[3] *trap*, *n* a fault (*mining*); a ladder leading to a loft (*Scot*); a flight of steps (*Scot*). — *adj* **trap'-cut** (of gems) cut in steps, step-cut. — **trap'-ladder**, **trap'-stair**. [Cf Du *trap* step; cf ety for **trap**[2]]

trap[4] *trap*, *n* (in *pl*) personal luggage or belongings; a horsecloth (*obs*). — *vt* to caparison, deck with trappings. — *adj* **trapped**. — *n* **trapp'er** (*hist*) a covering, either protective for use in battle or decorative, worn by a horse. — *n pl* **trapp'ings** characteristic accompaniments, adornments, paraphernalia (of office, etc); ornaments, *esp* ceremonial harnesses, etc for horses; gay, colourful clothes. [Appar connected with Fr *drap*, Sp and Port *trapo*, LL *drappus* (*trapus*) cloth]

trapan. A variant spelling of **trepan**[1].

trape, **trapes**. See under **traipse**.

trapeze *trə-pēz'*, *n* a swinglike apparatus used by acrobats, consisting of one or more crossbars suspended between two ropes; a device attached by a line to the masthead of a light sailing boat, allowing a crew member to sit almost completely out of the boat. — *vi* to perform or go on a trapeze. [From Fr, special use of *trapèze*; see ety for **trapezium**]

trapezium *trə-pē'zi-əm*, *n orig*, any quadrilateral that is not a parallelogram; one with one (and only one) pair of parallel sides (*UK*); one with no sides parallel (*NAm*); a bone of the wrist articulating with the thumb metacarpal: — *pl* **trapē'zia** or **trapē'ziums**. — *adj* **trapē'zial** of or relating to a trapezium. — *adj* **trapē'ziform** having the form of a trapezium. — *n* **trapē'zius** (*anatom*; also **trapezius muscle**) (either of two triangular halves of) a large, flat, quadrilateral-shaped muscle extending up the thoracic spine to the neck, and across the back of the shoulders, that draws the head and shoulders back. — *n* **trapēzohē'dron** a solid figure whose faces are trapezia or trapezoids: — *pl* **trapēzohē'dra** or **trapēzohē'drons**. — *adj* **trapēzohē'dral**. — *n* **trapezoid** (*trap'i-zoid, trə-pē'zoid*) a quadrilateral with no sides parallel; one with two sides parallel (*NAm*); a bone of the wrist next to the trapezium. — Also *adj*. — *adj* **trapezoid'al**. [Latinized from Gr *trapezion*, dimin of *trapeza* a table; literally four-legged, from *tetra-* four, and *peza* a foot]

trappean. See under **trap**[2].

trappings. See under **trap**[4].

Trappist *trap'ist*, *n* a Cistercian monk of the reformed rule established by De Rancé (1626–1700), abbot of La *Trappe* in Normandy, noted for its austerity and rule of silence. — Also *adj*. — *n* **Trapp'istine** (*-tēn, -tin*) a nun of an affiliated order.

trapunto *trə-pun'tō, -pōōn'*, *n* an Italian type of quilting done by stitching the design through two layers of fabric, and inserting wadding between the threads of the back layer. [Ital, quilting]

trash[1] *trash*, *n* anything worthless or of poor quality; scraps; rubbish, refuse (*esp NAm*); a receptacle for rubbish (*NAm*); nonsense; paltry stuff; worthless people; (in full **poor white trash**) poor whites, *esp* in the southern US (*US*); a worthless person (*Shakesp*); broken twigs, hedge-cuttings, splinters; dry sugar-cane refuse, used eg as fuel. — *vt* to remove the outer leaves and branches from (sugar cane); to lop the tops from; to discard, reject, expose or criticize as worthless; to wreck or vandalize (*esp US*) — *n* **trash'ery** trash, rubbish. — *adv* **trash'ily**. — *n* **trash'iness**. — *n* **trash'trie** (*Scot*) trash. — *adj* **trash'y** like trash; worthless, of poor quality. — **trash'can** (*NAm*) a receptacle for refuse; **trash farming** a method of cultivation in arid regions of N America in which waste plant material from crops, etc is left on or near the surface of the soil to inhibit erosion and enrich the soil; **trash'man** (*NAm*) a dustman, refuse collector. [Prob Scand; cf Norw dialect *trask* trash, ON *tros* fallen twigs]

trash[2] *trash*, *vt* to check (*Shakesp*); to restrain with a leash (*obs* or *dialect*). — *n* (*dialect*) a leash or other restraint. [Origin obscure]

trash[3] *trash*, *vt* to wear out, to harass. — *vi* to trudge. [Cf Swed *traska*, Norw *traske*]

trashtrie. See under **trash**[1].

trass *tras*, *n* an earthy volcanic tuff used as a hydraulic cement. — Also **tarras'** or **terras'**. [Du *tras*]

trattoria *trät-tö-rē'ə, tra-tə-rē'ə*, *n* an Italian restaurant: — *pl* **trattō'rias** or **trattō'rie** (*-rē-ā*). — Colloquial short form **trat** or **tratt**. [Ital, from *trattore* restaurateur, from Fr *traiteur*]

trauchle *tröhh'l*, (*Scot*) *vt* to bedraggle; to weary or overburden with drudgery or plodding. — *vi* to drudge; to trail along. — *n* a troublesome task; drudgery. [Cf Flem *tragelen* to go heavily]

trauma *trö'mə, trow'mə*, *n* a wound; an injury (*med*); an emotional shock that may be the origin of a neurosis (*psychiatry*); the state or condition caused by a physical or emotional shock: — *pl* **trau'mas** or **trau'mata**. — *adj* **traumatic** (*-mat'ik*) relating to, resulting from or causing, wounds; of or causing a lasting emotional shock; (loosely) frightening, unpleasant. — *adv* **traumat'ically**. — *n* **trau'matism** (*-mə-tizm*) a condition caused by a wound, shock; an injury or wound. — *n* **traumatizā'tion** or **-s-**. — *vt* **trau'matize** or **-ise** to inflict a mental or physical trauma on. — *n* **traumatol'ogy** the study of wounds and of the effects of injuries. — *adj* **traumatolog'ical**. — *n* **traumatonas'ty** a nastic movement after wounding. — **trauma centre** (*orig US*) a centre or hospital specifically for the treatment of trauma victims. [Gr *trauma, -atos* a wound]

travail[1] *trav'āl, -əl*, (*literary* or *archaic*) *n* excessive labour; toil; labour in childbirth; travel (*obs*). — *vi* to labour; to suffer the pains of childbirth; to travel (*obs*). — *adj* **trav'ailed** toilworn; wearied; experienced; having been in travail. — **trav'ail-pain**; **travail'-pang**. [OFr (and Fr) *travail*]

travail[2]. See **travois**.

trave *trāv*, (*obs* or *dialect*) *n* a beam or shaft (eg of a cart); a frame in which to shoe a fractious horse. [OFr *trave* beam, from L *trabs*]

travel *trav'l*, *vi* to journey; to be capable of withstanding a journey; to go; to go round as a salesman soliciting orders; to go on circuit; to move along a course; to go with impetus; to pass; to move; to walk (*dialect*); to travail (*obs*). — *vt* to journey over or through; to conduct or send on a journey (*archaic*): — *pr p* **trav'elling** or (*NAm*) **trav'eling**; *pa t* and *pa p* **trav'elled** or (*NAm*) **trav'eled**. — *n* journeying; impetus; power of going; range of movement; passage; (in *pl*) an account of journeys; travail (*obs*). — *adj* **trav'elled** or (*NAm*) **trav'eled** having made journeys; experienced; (of a road, etc) beaten, frequented; (of rocks, earth, etc) transported, not in its original place. — *n* **trav'eller** or (*NAm*) **trav'eler** a person who travels or has travelled; a wayfarer; one of the travelling people; a salesman who travels for a company; a ring that slides along a rope or spar; a piece of mechanism that moves on a gantry, etc. — *n* and *adj* **trav'elling** or (*NAm*) **trav'eling**. — *n* **travelogue** or (*NAm*) **travelog** (*trav'ə-log*) a talk, lecture, article, or film on travel. — **travel agency** an agency which provides information, brochures, tickets, etc, relating to travel; **travel agent**; **traveller's cheque** a cheque which can be cashed at any foreign branch or specified agent of the bank issuing it; **traveller's joy** a climbing plant, *Clematis vitalba*, sometimes called old man's beard; **traveller's tale** an amazing account, *esp* an untrue one, about what one professes to have seen abroad; **traveller's tree** a Madagascan tree (*Ravenala*) of the banana family with great leaves on two sides only, accumulating water in the leaf-bases; **travelling folk** or **people**, etc the name by which itinerant people often call themselves, in preference to the derogatory names gipsies or tinkers; **travelling-wave tube** a device used in communications for increasing signal power, amplification being produced by interaction between a wave of radio frequency travelling on a wire helix and an electron beam travelling at roughly the same velocity inside the helix. — *adj* **trav'el-sick** suffering from travel sickness. — **travel sickness** nausea experienced, as a result of motion, by a passenger in a car, ship, aircraft, etc. — *adj* **trav'el-soiled**, **trav'el -stained** or **trav'el-tainted** (*Shakesp*) showing the marks of travel. [Later variant of **travail**]

travelator. Another spelling of **travolator**.

traverse *trav'ûrs*, *adj* cross; oblique. — *n* a crossing or passage across; a straight length in a zigzag course; a passage across the face of a rock (*mountaineering*); the zigzag course of a sailing vessel tacking (*naut*); a survey by measuring straight lines from point to point and the angles between (*surveying*); anything set or lying across, a crosspiece, etc; an obstruction; a parapet; adversity; a curtain, screen, partition (*obs*); a barrier (*obs*); a gallery from one side of a large building to another, a screened-off compartment; a denial or contradiction, *esp* (*law*) the formal denial of a fact alleged by the other side; an opposing, counteracting movement (*fencing*). — *vt* (also *-vûrs'*) to cross; to pass through, across, or over; to move about over; to pass over by traverse; to survey (a road, etc) by traverse; to oppose; to thwart; to dispute; to deny, contradict (*esp law*); to turn sideways. — *vi* to make a traverse; to move to the side; to direct a gun to the right or left. — *adj* **trav'ersable**. — *n* **travers'al** the action of traversing. — *adj* **trav'ersed** crossed, passed over; set crosswise (*Shakesp*). — *n* **trav'erser** a person who traverses; a platform for shifting wagons and carriages sideways. — *n* and *adj* **trav'ersing**. — **traversing bridge** one that can be withdrawn horizontally. [Fr *travers, traverse, traverser*, from L *trāns*, and *vertere, versum* to turn]

travertine *trav'ər-tīn, -tēn, -tin, n* a pale limestone deposited from solution, eg from springs. — Also **travertin**. [Ital *travertino*, from L *tīburtīnus* (*lapis*) stone of Tibur (now Tivoli) in Italy]

travesty *trav'is-ti, n* burlesque, parody; a ridiculously inadequate representation (of something); disguise, *esp* of a man as a woman or vice versa. — *vt* to burlesque; to disguise. — **travesty role** (*theat*) a role intended to be taken by a performer of the opposite sex to that of the character. [Fr *travesti*, pa p of *travestir* to disguise, from L *trāns*, and *vestīre* to clothe; cf **transvest**]

travis. See also **treviss**.

travois *trä-voi'* (*pl* **travois** *trä-voiz'*) or **travail** *trä-vä'i, n* a kind of N American Indian sledge, a pair of trailing poles attached to each side of the saddle, joined by a board or net. [Can Fr pron of Fr *travail*]

travolator *trav'ō-lā-tər*, or **travelator** *trav'l-, n* a moving footpath for the conveyance of pedestrians. [From stem of **travel**, modelled on **escalator**]

trawl *tröl, n* an open-mouthed bag-net for dragging along the sea bed; a trawl-line (qv below); an act of trawling. — *vt* and *vi* to catch or fish with a trawl or (*Scot* and *US*) a seine-net. — *vt* to search over, comb, investigate thoroughly, in order to gather information. — *vi* to look for something (eg a suitable person for a post, etc) by gathering suggestions from various sources (with *for*; strictly, a meaning developed from **troll**[2]). — *n* **trawl'er** a trawling vessel; a person who trawls. — *n* **trawl'ing**. — **trawl'erman** a person who mans a trawler; **trawl'-fish** fish caught with a trawl; **trawl'-line** a buoyed line with baited hooks at intervals; **trawl'-net**. [Cf **trail**[1] and MDu *traghel* drag-net]

tray[1] *trā, n* a flat board, etc with a low rim, used for carrying articles (such as crockery, etc); a tray of food, *esp* instead of a meal at table. — *n* **tray'ful**: — *pl* **tray'fuls**. — **tray'-cloth** a cloth for covering a tray; **tray'mobile** (*Austr*) a household trolley, for serving tea, etc. [OE *trīg*, *trēg* board]

tray[2] *trā*. See under **trey**. — **tray'-trip** (*Shakesp*) a game played with dice.

trayne. See under **train**[1].

treacher or **treachour** *trech'ər, n* (*obs*) a deceiver by trickery; a betrayer; a traitor. — Also **treach'erer**. [OFr *trecheor*, *trecheur* deceiver, from *trechier* to trick; cf **trick**]

treacherous *trech'ər-əs, adj* ready to betray; not to be trusted; misleadingly inviting in appearance. — *adv* **treach'erously**. — *n* **treach'erousness**. — *n* **treach'ery** betrayal; readiness to betray; falseness; treason. — *n* **treach'etour** (*Spenser*) a deceiver; a traitor. [OFr *trecheros*, *trecherie*, from *trecheur* (see **treacher**) and *trechier* to trick]

treacle *trē'kl, n* the dark, viscous uncrystallizable syrup obtained in refining sugar (also called **black treacle**); molasses, the drainings of crude sugar; blandishments, *esp* when suggestive of the cloying and nauseating taste and thickness of treacle; intolerable sentimentality; *orig* an antidote or prophylactic against bites, poisons, etc. — *vt* to dose or smear with treacle. — *vi* to treacle trees in order to collect moths. — *n* **trea'cliness**. — *adj* **trea'cly** of or like treacle; thick and sweet; unctuously blandishing; intolerably sentimental. — **treacle mustard** the cruciferous plant, *Erysimum cheiranthoides*. [OFr *triacle*, from Gr *thēriakē* (*antidotos*, an antidote to the bites) of beasts, from *thērion* a wild beast]

tread *tred, vi* to set the foot down; to step; to walk; to trample; (of a male bird) to copulate. — *vt* to walk on; to press with the foot, eg in threshing or pressing grapes; to trample, crush with the feet; to beat or form (a path, etc); to perform by treading, dance; (of a male bird) to copulate with; to oppress (*fig*): — *pa t* **trod**; *pa p* **trodd'en** or **trod**. — *n* the act or manner of treading; a step or tramp; a thing or part trodden on, eg on a step; the part that touches the ground, eg on a shoe or a wheel; (the thickness of) the moulded ridged rubber surface of a pneumatic tyre, which has contact with the road; a footprint; a track; the distance between wheels or pedals; the cicatricula, or the chalaza, of an egg; business, trade (see also ety below) (*Scot*). — *n* **tread'er**. — *n* **tread'ing**. — *n* **tread'le** or **tredd'le** a foot-lever for working a machine; a pedal; the chalaza of an egg (once thought to be derived from the cock) (*dialect*). — *vi* to work a treadle. — *n* **tread'ler**. — *n* **tread'ling**. — **tread'mill** a machine with a continuously moving surface of adjustable speed used for exercising on by running or walking; a cylinder turned by treading on boards on its outside, as formerly by prisoners; a mill so worked; routine drudgery; **tread'-wheel** a wheel or cylinder turned by treading outside or inside; a treadmill. — **tread water** to float upright by an action as if of climbing a ladder. [OE *tredan*; Ger *treten*; ON *trotha*; cf **trade**]

treague *trēg*, (*Spenser*) *n* a truce. [LL *tregua*, *treuga*, from Gothic *triggwa* treaty]

treas. *abbrev*: treasurer.

treason *trē'zn, n* betraying of the government or an attempt to overthrow it; treachery; disloyalty. — *adj* **trea'sonable** pertaining to, consisting of or involving treason. — *n* **trea'sonableness**. — *adv* **trea'sonably**. — *adj* **trea'sonous**. — **treason felony** any of several offences which ceased to be considered to be a full-blown act of treason in the mid-19c. — **constructive treason** anything that may be interpreted as equivalent to actual treason by leading naturally to it; **high treason** any of several offences against the state or the sovereign; **misprision of treason** knowledge of treason and concealment thereof; **petty treason** (*hist*) the murder of a husband by a wife, a master by a servant, etc. [Anglo-Fr *tresun*, OFr *traïson* (Fr *trahison*), from *traïr* (*trahir*), from L *tradere* to betray]

treasure *trezh'ər, n* wealth stored up; riches; anything much valued; a valued, indispensable servant, helper, etc. — *vt* to hoard up; to collect for future use; to value greatly; to enrich (*obs*). — *n* **treas'urer** a person who is in charge of a treasure or treasury; a person who is in charge of collected funds. — *n* **treas'urership**. — *n* **treas'ury** a place where treasure is deposited; (often with *cap*) a department of a government which has charge of the finances; mistakenly applied to a beehive tomb in Mycenaean Greece. — **treas'ure-chest** a box for keeping articles of value; **treas'ure-city** a city for stores, etc; **treas'ure-house** a house for holding treasures; a treasury; a store of valuable things; **treasure hunt** a hunt for treasure; a game in which competitors attempt to win a prize by being first to complete a course indicated by clues which have to be solved; **treas'ure-trove** (*trové*, pa p of Anglo-Fr *trover* to find) ownerless objects of intrinsic or historical value found hidden (in England gold and silver only), property of the crown; **Treasury bench** the front bench on the Speaker's right in the House of Commons, occupied by the members of the government; **Treasury bill** a security entitling the holder to a stated amount to be paid from the Consolidated Fund at a specified date; **Treasury note** a currency note issued by the Treasury; **treasury tag** a short piece of cord with a metal tag at each end, for holding papers together. [OFr *tresor* (Fr *trésor*), from L *thēsaurus*, from Gr *thēsauros*]

treat *trēt, vt* to deal with; to handle; to discuss; to behave towards; to act upon; to deal with the case of; to deal with (illness or a sick person) by applying remedies; to subject to a process; to stand a drink or other gratification to. — *vi* to negotiate; to deal (with *of*); to stand treat. — *n* a free entertainment, pleasure excursion or feast; a turn or act of providing and paying; a source of great gratification; negotiation, parley (*Spenser*). — *adj* **treat'able** able to be treated; tractable, moderate (*obs*). — *n* **treat'er**. — *n* **treat'ing**. — *n* **treat'ise** (*-iz, -is*) a written composition, *esp* one treating a subject formally or systematically. — *n* **treat'ment** the act or manner, or an instance, of treating; management; behaviour to anyone; a draft of a screenplay, including camera angles, descriptions of sets, etc (*cinematog*). — **Dutch treat** see under **Dutch**; **stand treat** see under **stand**; **the (full) treatment** (*colloq*) the appropriate method (in every detail) of dealing, whether ceremoniously or punitively, with a particular type of person, case, etc. [OFr *traitier*, from L *tractāre* to manage, from *trahere*, *tractum* to draw]

treaty *trē'ti*, *n* negotiation; a formal agreement, *esp* between states; any of several formal agreements between the Canadian government and Indian bands whereby the **treaty Indians** give up their lands (apart from allocated reserves) and receive an annual payment of **treaty money**; entreaty (*Shakesp*). — **treaty port** a port, *esp* in China, etc, opened by treaty to foreign trade. [Anglo-Fr *treté*, OFr *traité*, from Med L *tractātis*, from L *tractāre* (see ety of **treat**)]

treble *treb'l*, *adj* triple; threefold; in the treble (*music*); high-pitched. — *n* that which is triple or threefold; three times as much; the highest part, soprano, now *esp* applied to boys' voices (*music*); a treble singer, voice, instrument, string, sound, etc; high-frequency sound as output from an amplifier, etc; the narrow inner ring on a dartboard, or a hit on this; a bet involving three horse-races, the stake and winnings from the first being bet on the second, and those from the second on the third. — *vt* to make three times as much. — *vi* to become threefold. — *n* **treb'leness**. — *adv* **treb'ly**. — **treble chance** a mode of competing in football pools in which, in a selection of matches made from a list, the aim is to pick all the draws and all the home and away wins; **treble clef** (*music*) the clef in which the G immediately above middle C is placed on the second line. — *adj* **treb'le-dated** living three times as long as man. [OFr, from L *triplus*; see **triple**]

trebuchet *treb'ū-shet*, *trā-bü-shā'*, *n* a medieval engine of war for launching stones, etc. [OFr]

trecento *trā-chen'tō*, *n* and *adj* 14th-century (in Italian art, etc). — *n* **trecen'tist**. [Ital, three (for thirteen) hundred]

treck. Same as **trek** (*vi* and *n*).

tre corde *trā kor'dā*, (*music*) a direction to piano players to release the soft pedal. [Ital, three strings].

treddle. Same as **treadle** (see under **tread**).

tredrille or **tredille** *trə-d(r)il'*, *n* a card game for three. [Modelled on **quadrille**, from L *trēs* three]

tree *trē*, *n* a large plant with a single branched woody trunk (sometimes loosely applied); timber; a wooden structure or part of various kinds; a saddle-tree; a boot- or shoe-tree; a branching figure or structure, such as an arborescent aggregate of crystals (eg *lead tree*), a branching stand (eg *ring-tree*, *mug-tree*), a pedigree, a branching diagram; a gallows (*archaic*); a cross for crucifixion (*archaic*). — *vt* to drive into a tree, to corner (also *fig*); to form on a tree. — *vi* to take refuge in a tree. — *adj* wooden. — *combining form* **tree-** denoting: inhabiting, frequenting or growing on trees; taking the form of a tree; dendritic. — *adj* **tree'less**. — *n* **tree'lessness**. — *n* **tree'ship** existence as a tree. — **tree bicycle** a mechanical device used for climbing trees; **tree-bur'ial** disposal of the dead in the branches of trees; **tree'-calf** a light-brown calf bookbinding, in conventional imitation of a branching tree; **tree'-creeper** any small N hemisphere bird of the family *Certhildae* that runs up tree-trunks in search of insects; **tree farm** a commercially-managed forest or woodland area; **tree fern** a large, tropical fern with a tall woody trunk; **tree frog** an arboreal amphibian, *esp* one of the family *Hylidae*, more akin to toads than to frogs; **tree hopper** any of the homopterous leaping insects of the family *Membracidae*; **tree'-house** a house built in a tree, *esp* as a playhouse; **tree kangaroo** a tree-climbing kangaroo (*Dendrolagus*); **tree lily** a xerophytic treelike plant of the Brazilian campos (*Vellozia*); **tree line** same as **timber-line**. — *adj* **tree'-lined** (of roads, etc) having trees along either side. — **tree mallow** *Lavatera arbarca*, a treelike plant of the *Malvaceae* family, having reddish-purple flowers; **tree moss** moss or lichen growing on a tree; a moss like a tiny tree in shape; **treenail** or **trenail** (*trē'nāl*, *tren'l*) a long wooden pin or nail to fasten the planks of a ship to the timbers; **tree onion** a variety of onion with bulbs instead of flowers; **tree peony** a shrub (*Paeonia suffruticosa*, also called **moutan**) of the family *Ranunculaceae*, native to China and Tibet, with pale pink flowers, from which many garden varieties have been developed; **tree rings** annual rings; **tree shrew** a squirrel-shrew, any insectivorous mammal of the E Indian family *Tupaiidae*, squirrel-like animals related to shrews; **tree'-snake** a tree-dwelling snake; **tree sparrow** a small European bird of the sparrow family, *Passer montanus*; a N American finch, *Spizella arborea*; **tree'-stump**; **tree surgeon** a person who preserves diseased trees by filling cavities, amputating damaged branches, etc; **tree surgery**; **tree toad** a tree frog; **tree tomato** the tamarillo, a S American solanaceous shrub (*Cyphomandra betacea* or *C. crassifolia*) or its tomato-like fruit; **tree'top** the top of a tree; **tree'-trunk**; **tree'-worship**; **tree'-worshipper**. — **at the top of the tree** in the highest position in eg a profession; **family tree** pedigree; **out of one's tree** (*Austr colloq*) crazy; **tree of heaven** ailanthus; **tree of lead** Saturn's tree; **tree of knowledge (of good and evil)** the tree in the Garden of Eden which bore the forbidden fruit eaten by Adam and Eve (Gen. 2.17); **tree of life** arbor vitae; a tree in the Garden of Eden whose fruit gave everlasting life (Gen. 2.9); **tree of silver** or **Diana's tree** an arborescent deposit of silver; **up a tree** (*colloq*, *esp NAm*) in difficulties (cf **up a gum tree** under **gum**[2]). [OE *trēow*, *trēo*; cf Gr *drȳs* oak, and *dory* spear; Sans *dru* tree]

treen *trē'ən*, *adj* of a tree (*Spenser*); wooden. — *n* small articles made of wood, *esp* eating and drinking utensils (**treen'ware**) of past times; the art of craft of making treenware. [See ety for **tree** and sfx *-en*]

tref, **treif** *trāf* or **trefa** *trā'fə*, (*Judaism*) *adj* forbidden as food, not kosher. [Heb *terēphāh* torn flesh, from *taraph* to tear]

trefoil *trē'foil*, *tre'foil*, *n* a three-lobed form, ornament or aperture, as in tracery or heraldry; a leaf of three leaflets; a trifoliate plant, *esp* of the clover genus (*Trifolium*). — *adj* **tre'foiled**. — **bird's-foot trefoil** see under **bird**. [Anglo-Fr *trifoil*, from L *trifolium*, from *trēs* three, and *folium* a leaf]

tregetour *trej'ə-tər*, (*archaic*) *n* a juggler; a trickster; a deceiver. [OFr *tresgetour*, from *tresgeter*, from L *trāns*, and *jactāre* to throw]

trehala *tri-hä'lə*, *n* Turkish manna, a sweet substance obtained from the cocoons of a type of beetle. [Turk *tīqālah*]

treille *trāl*, *n* a trellis. — *n* **treill'age** trelliswork; a trellis. — *adj* **treill'aged**. [Fr, from L *trichila* a bower]

trek *trek*, *vi* to make a long hard journey, *usu* on foot; to tramp and camp, dragging one's equipment; to migrate; to journey by ox-wagon. — *vt* to drag: — *pr p* **trekk'ing**; *pa t* and *pa p* **trekked**. — *n* a journey or stage; a migration. — *n* **trekk'er**. — **trek'-ox**; **trek'-schuit** (*-s'hhoit*, *-skoit*) a towed canal-boat. [Du *trekken* to draw]

trellis *trel'is*, *n* a structure of cross-barred or lattice-work. — *vt* to provide with a trellis; to train on a trellis. — *adj* **trell'ised**. — **trell'is-win'dow** a lattice-window (qv); **trell'is-work** lattice-work. [OFr *treliz*, from L *trilīx*, *-īcis* woven with triple thread, modified by association with **treille**, qv]

trema *trē'mə*, *n* an orifice; a diaeresis, two dots placed as a mark of separate pronunciation over a vowel-letter. — *adj* **trematic** (*tri-mat'ik*; *zool*) of the gill-slits. — *n* **trematode** (*trem'ə-tōd*) any member of the **Trematoda**, a class of parasitic, unsegmented flatworms with adhesive suckers. — *n* and *adj* **trem'atoid**. [Gr *trēma*, *-atos* a hole]

tremble *trem'bl*, *vi* to shake, eg from fear, cold, or weakness; to quiver; to vibrate; to pass tremulously. — *vt* to set trembling. — *n* the act of trembling; tremulousness; a tremulous state; (in *pl*) a morbid trembling; (in *pl*; *specif*) a condition of muscular weakness and trembling in cattle and sheep caused by eating certain plants, *esp* white snakeroot (*Eupatorium rugosum*), also a name for milk sickness (qv) in humans. — *adj* **tremblant** (*trem'blənt*; of jewellery) having the stones set on springs, so as to give a trembling effect. — *n* **trem'blement**. — *n* **trem'bler** a person, animal or thing that trembles; any of a number of W Indian birds of the family *Mimidae*; a vibrating device that makes and breaks a circuit (*elec*). — *adj* (of jewellery) tremblant. — *n* and *adj* **trem'bling**. — *adv* **trem'blingly**. — *adj* **trem'bly** tremulous. — **trembling poplar** the aspen. [OFr (Fr) *trembler*, from L *tremulus* trembling, from *tremere* to shake]

Tremella *tri-mel'ə*, *n* a genus of gelatinous fungi, such as witches' meat, found on decaying wood, etc. [L *tremulus* quivering]

tremendous *tri-men'dəs*, *adj* awe-inspiring, dreadful; huge, extraordinarily great (*colloq*); prodigious, extraordinary, very good (*slang*). — *adv* **tremen'dously**. — *n* **tremen'dousness**. [L *tremendus* to be trembled at]

trémie or **tremie** *trā-mē*, *trem'i*, *n* a hopper-like device for laying concrete under water. [Fr, hopper, from L *trimodia* a three-peck measure]

tremolando, **tremolant**. See under **tremolo**.

tremolite *trem'ə-līt*, *n* a calcium-magnesium amphibole, *usu* in long prisms or fibres, pale or colourless. — *adj* **tremolitic** (*-lit'ik*). [From the Val *Tremola* in the Alps, where the mineral found is not true tremolite]

tremolo *trem'ō-lō*, (*music*) *n* a tremulous effect as by a rapid succession of the same note or of two notes at least a third apart; a tremulant: — *pl* **trem'olos**. — Also *adj*. — *n*, *adj* and *adv* **tremolan'do**: — *pl* **tremolandi** or **tremolan'dos**. — *n* and *adj* **trem'olant** tremolo. [Ital *tremolo*, *tremolando*, *tremolante*]

tremor *trem'ər*, *n* a quiver; a quavering; a thrill; an involuntary agitation; a vibration. — *vi* to quiver. — *adj* **trem'orless**. [L *tremor*, *-ōris*]

tremulous *trem'ū-ləs*, *adj* trembling; quivering. — *adj* **trem'ūlant** tremulous. — *n* a device in an organ or electronic instrument for producing a tremolo effect. — *vi* and *vt* **trem'ūlate**. — *adv* **trem'ūlously**. — *n* **trem'ūlousness**. [L *tremulus* trembling, and LL *tremulāre*, *-ātum* to tremble]

trenail. See under **tree**.

trench *trench*, *trensh*, *n* a long, narrow, deep cut in the earth; a protective ditch dug in warfare, with the excavated earth used as a parapet; a deep furrow or wrinkle in the skin. — *vi* to make trenches; to dig deep with spade or plough; to encroach; to border, verge. — *vt* to cut; to make trenches in; to put in a trench; to provide with a trench; to entrench; to divert by a trench (*Shakesp*). — *n* **trench'ancy** causticity. — *adj* **trench'ant** (*Spenser* **trench'and**) cutting; incisive, forthright; sharply defined, distinct. — *adv* **trench'antly**. — *n* **trench'er**. — **trench coat** or **trench'-coat** a short waterproof coat with belt, for men or women; **trench fever** an infectious disease causing pain in joints and muscles, prevalent among soldiers living in trenches, caused by a *Rickettsia* and transmitted by lice; **trench'=foot** or **-feet** a diseased condition of the feet caused by long exposure to cold and wet, *esp* affecting soldiers in trench warfare; **trench'-knife** a knife with double-sided blade, used by patrols in the Trenches; **trench mortar** a small mortar which throws large shells short distances, useful in trench warfare; **trench'-plough** a plough for ploughing more deeply than usual. — *vt* to plough with a trench-plough. — **trench warfare** warfare in which each side entrenches itself in lines facing the enemy. — **the Trenches** (also without *cap*) the protective ditches dug for the infantry on the Western Front in World War I, or the Western Front itself. [OFr *trenche* cut (Fr *tranche* slice), and *trencher* (Fr *trancher* to cut, to slice) to cut, prob from L *truncāre* (see **truncate**)]

trenchard. See under **trencher**[1].

trencher[1] *tren'chər*, *-shər*, *n* a plate or platter; a board. — *n* **trenchard** (*tren'shərd*) the word used at St Andrews University for a trencher cap. — **trencher cap** a college-cap, mortarboard. — *adj* **tren'cher-fed** (of fox-hounds) kept each by his owner, not in a pack. — **tren'cher=friend** or **-knight** (both *Shakesp*) a person who frequents the table of another, a parasite; **tren'cherman** a hearty eater; a trencher-friend. [Anglo-Fr *trenchour* (Fr *tranchoir*), from *trencher* to cut]

trencher[2]. See under **trench**.

trend *trend*, *vi* to turn, wind; to have a tendency or prevailing direction. — *n* general tendency; a bend (*dialect*). — *adv* **trend'ily**. — *n* **trend'iness**. — *adj* **tren'dy** (*colloq*) in the forefront of fashion in any sphere. — *n* (*usu derog*) a trendy person. — *n* **trend'yism**. — *n* **trend'setter** someone who helps to give a new direction to fashion. — *n* and *adj* **trend'setting**. [OE *trendan*]

trendle-tail. See under **trundle**.

trenise *trə-nēz'*, *n* the fourth movement of a quadrille. — Also **la trenise**. [Fr]

trental *tren'tl*, *n* a series of thirty requiem masses. [LL *trentāle*, from L *trīgintā* thirty]

trente-et-quarante *trât-ā-ka-rât*, *n* the card-game rouge-et-noir. [Fr, thirty and forty]

trepan[1] *tri-pan'*, *n* an obsolete cylindrical saw for perforating the skull; a tool for boring shafts. — *vt* to remove a piece of the skull from (*surg*); to cut a cylindrical disc from; to cut an annular groove in. — *n* **trepanation** (*trep-ə-nā'shən*). — *n* **trepann'er**. — *n* and *adj* **trepann'ing**. [Fr *trépan*, from LL *trepanum*, from Gr *trȳpanon*, from *trȳpaein* to bore]

trepan[2] *tri-pan'*, (*archaic*) *n* a decoy; a snare; an entrapping. — *vt* to ensnare; to lure: — *pr p* **trepann'ing**; *pa t* and *pa p* **trepanned'**. — *n* **trepann'er**. — *n* and *adj* **trepann'ing**. [Earlier *trapan*; prob connected with **trap**]

trepang *tri-pang'*, *n* a sea cucumber, a holothurian eaten by the Chinese. [Malay *trīpang*]

trephine *tri-fēn'*, *-fīn'*, *n* a refined form of trepan. — *vt* to operate on, perforate, or remove a circular section from (eg the skull or cornea) with the trephine. — *n* **trephin'er** a surgeon who uses a trephine. — *n* **trephin'ing**. [Earlier *trafine*, from L *trēs fīnēs* three ends, modified by **trepan**[1]]

trepidation *trep-i-dā'shən*, *n* trembling; alarmed agitation; a libration of the celestial sphere assumed to explain a supposed oscillation of the ecliptic (*old astron*; *Milton*). — *adj* (*rare*) **trep'id** quaking. — *adj* **trep'idant**. — *adj* **trepid'atory**. [L *trepidāre*, *-ātum* to hurry with alarm, from *trepidus* restless]

treponema *trep-ə-nē'mə* or **treponeme** *trep'ə-nēm*, *n* a bacterium of the genus *Treponema* of spirochaetes, one of which, *T. pallidum*, causes syphilis: — *pl* **treponē'mata**, **treponē'mas** or **trep'onemes**. [Gr *trepein* to turn, and *nēma* thread]

très *tre*, *trez*, (*colloq*) *adv* very. [Fr]

trespass *tres'pəs*, *vi* to interfere with another's person or property; to enter unlawfully upon another's land; to encroach (on); to intrude (with *on*); to sin (*liturgical*). — *n* an act of trespassing; any injury to another's person or property; a sin (*liturgical*). — *n* **tres'passer**. [OFr *trespasser*, from L *trāns*, and *passus* a step]

tress[1] *tres*, *n* a plait or braid of the hair of the head; a long lock, braided or not. — *vt* to form into tresses. — *adj* **tressed** braided; in tresses; having tresses. — *combining form* **-tressed** denoting having tresses of a specified kind. — *adj* **tress'y** having or like tresses. [Fr *tresse*, from LL *tricia*, perh from Gr *tricha* threefold, from *treis* three]

tress[2], **tressel**. See under **trestle**.

tressure *tresh'ər*, (*heraldry*) *n* a subordinary, half the breadth of the orle, and *usu* borne double, and flowered and counter-flowered with fleurs-de-lis. — *adj* **tress'ured**. [Fr, from *tresser* to plait]

trest. See under **trestle**.

trestle *tres'l*, *n* a support composed of a horizontal beam on sloping legs; a braced framework. — Also **tress'el**. — *n* (*obs* or *dialect*) **tress** or **trest** (*trest*) a trestle. — **trest'le-bridge** one resting on trestlework; **trest'le-table** one made of boards laid on trestles; **trest'lework** a braced framework. [OFr *trestel* (Fr *tréteau*) and *treste*, *trestre*, from L *trānstrum* cross-beam]

tret *tret*, (*hist*) *n* an allowance to purchasers of 4 lb on every 104 lb for waste. [Poss Anglo-Fr *tret* pull, turn of the scale, or Fr *traite* transport, both from *traire* to draw, from L *trahere*, *tractum*]

trevally *tri-val'i*, (*Austr* and *NZ*) *n* any horse-mackerel of the genus *Caranx*. [Prob a modification of **cavally**]

treviss or **trevis** *trev'is* or **travis** *trav'is*, *trāv'is*, *n* a stall partition; a stall. [Variants of **traverse**]

trew. An old spelling of **true**.

trews *trōōz*, *n pl* (*orig sing*) trousers, *esp* of tartan cloth. — **trews'man** a wearer of trews. [Ir *trius*, Gaelic *triubhas*; cf **trouse**, **trousers**]

trey *trā*, *n* the three in cards and dice; a set of three; the third tine of a deer's horn (in full **trey-ant'ler**, **-tine**; also **tray** or **trez** *trā*, *trāz*); a threepenny bit (also **trey'bit**, **tray** or **tray'bit**; *slang*). [OFr *treis*, *trei*, from L *trēs* three]

trez. See under **trey**.

TRH *abbrev*: Their Royal Highnesses.

tri- *trī-*, *tri-*, *combining form* denoting three, threefold. [L *trēs*, *tria*, and Gr *treis*, *tria*]

triable. See under **try**.

triacid *trī-as'id*, (*chem*) *adj* having three replaceable hydrogen atoms; capable of replacing three hydrogen atoms of an acid. [**tri-**]

triaconter *trī-ə-kon'tər*, *n* an ancient Greek ship, perhaps with thirty men to each group of oars. [Gr *triākontērēs*, from *triākonta* thirty]

triact *trī'akt*, (*zool*) *adj* three-rayed. — *adj* **trīact'inal** (*-i-nəl* or *-ī'nəl*) or **trīact'ine** (*-in*). [**tri-**, and Gr *aktīs*, *-īnos* ray]

triad *trī'ad*, *-əd*, *n* a group, set, or union of three; (in Welsh literature) a group of three sayings, stories, etc, about related subjects; a group of three lines or stanzas in different metres; a chord of three notes, *esp* the common chord (*music*); an atom, element, or radical with a valency of three (*chem*); (with *cap*) any of many Chinese secret societies (*orig* so named from their use of the triangle in their rituals), some founded in the 17c to resist the Manchu regime, some now associated with criminal activities, *esp* heroin trading. — *adj* **trī'ad** or **trīad'ic**. — *n* **trī'adist** a composer of triads. [L *trias*, from Gr *trias*, *triados*, from *treis* three]

triadelphous *trī-ə-del'fəs*, (*bot*) *adj* with three bundles of stamens. [**tri-**, and Gr *adelphos* a brother]

triage. See under **try**.

triakisoctahedron *trī-ə-kis-ok-tə-hē'drən*, *n* a solid figure like an octahedron with a three-faced pyramid on each face. [Gr *triakis* three times]

Trial *tri-al*, (*Fr*) *n* a tenor with special aptitude for comedy parts, often noted more for his acting than for his vocalism. [After the French tenor, Antoine *Trial* (1736-1795), renowned for his comedy rôles at the Opéra-Comique in Paris]

trial¹ *trī'əl*, *n* a trying; examination by a test; a test of the efficacy, safety, etc, of a new product, *esp* a drug before it is marketed, or in order to gain official approval for its general use; examination by a court to determine a question of law or fact, *esp* the guilt or innocence of a prisoner; (often in *pl*) examination, sometimes merely formal, of a candidate; (often in *pl*) a competition, *esp* to select members of a major team; a competition comprising various tests, for sheepdogs or horses; a competition to test vehicles in difficult conditions; suffering; temptation; an attempt; a piece used as a test; a troublesome thing, a nuisance. — *adj* done, taken, etc, for the sake of trial. — *vt* to test (*esp* a new product): — *pr p* **tri'alling**; *pa t* and *pa p* **tri'alled**. — *n* **tri'alist** or **tri'allist** a person taking part in a trial or test; a competitor or player under consideration for a place in a major team (*sport*). — **trial balance** (*book-keeping*) in the double-entry system, a statement drawn up of the credit and debit totals to demonstrate that they are equal; **trial balloon** a ballon d'essai; **tri'al-day** (*Shakesp*) day of trial; **tri'al-fire** (*Shakesp*) a fire for trying or proving; **trial marriage** for a couple intending matrimony, a period of living together with a view to testing their compatibility; **trial run** a test drive in a motor vehicle to ascertain its efficiency; any introductory test, rehearsal, etc; **trial trip** an experimental trip of a new vessel, to test its sailing-powers, etc. — **by trial and error** by trying out several methods and discarding those which prove unsuccessful; **on trial** undergoing proceedings in a court of law; on probation, as an experiment; subject to a prospective purchase proving satisfactory; **stand trial** to undergo trial in a court of law; **trial of strength** a contest to find out who is the stronger (or strongest); a struggle between two irreconcilable parties, prolonged until one of them weakens. [Anglo-Fr, from *trier* to try]

trial² *trī'əl*, *adj* threefold, trinal; expressing or representing three things (*gram*). — *n* a grammatical form expressing or representing three things. — *n* **tri'alism** the doctrine of the existence of body, soul and spirit in man; a scheme for turning the Dual Monarchy into a triple (Austria, Hungary, and a South Slav state; *hist*). — *n* **tri'alist**. — *n* **trīality** (*-al'i-ti*). [Modelled on **dual**, from L *trēs*, *tria* three]

trialogue *trī'ə-log*, *n* a conversation between three people. [On false analogy of **dialogue**, as if *dia-* meant two]

triandrous *trī-an'drəs*, (*bot*) *adj* with three stamens. — *n pl* **Trian'dria** (in Linnaeus's classification) a class of plants with three stamens. — *adj* **trian'drian**. [**tri-**, and Gr *anēr*, *andros* a man, male]

triangle *trī'ang-gl* (also *-ang'*), *n* a plane figure with three angles and three sides (*math*); part of the surface of a sphere bounded by three arcs of great circles (*spherical triangle*); any mark or thing of that shape; a musical instrument of percussion, formed of a steel rod bent in triangle-form, open at one angle; a tripod, *esp* for a pulley for raising weights, or formerly (*usu* in *pl*) for binding soldiers to for flogging. — *adj* **tri'angled**. — *adj* **triang'ūlar** having three angles; (of a number) any of the series of numbers 0, 1, 3, 6, 10, 15, etc, the series being formed by adding 1, 2, 3, 4, 5, consecutively to consecutive members of the series; involving three persons or parties. — *n* **triangūlar'ity**. — *adv* **triang'ūlarly**. — *vt* **triang'ūlate** to survey by means of a series of triangles. — *adj* with, marked with or made up of triangles; triangular. — *adv* **triang'ūlātely**. — *n* **triangūlā'tion** the act or process of triangulating, eg for map-making; the series of triangles so used. — **the eternal triangle** an emotional situation involving two men and a woman or two women and a man. [L *triangulum*, from *angulus* an angle]

triapsidal *trī-aps'i-dəl*, *adj* with three apses. — Also **triaps'al**. [**tri-**]

triarch¹ *trī'ärk*, (*bot*) *adj* having three xylem strands in the stele. [**tri-**, and Gr *archē* origin]

triarch². See under **triarchy**.

triarchy *n* government by three people; a state governed by a triumvirate; a state divided into three parts each having its own ruler; one of three such parts. — *n* **trī'arch** a ruler of a triarchy; a member of a triumvirate. [Gr *triarchiā*, from *archē* rule]

Trias *trī'əs*, (*geol*) *n* the oldest Mesozoic or Secondary system. — *adj* **Triassic** (*trī-as'ik*). [Gr *trias* triad, from its threefold subdivision in Germany into Bunter, Muschelkalk and Keuper]

triathlon *trī-ath'lon*, *n* a sporting contest consisting of three events held without a break between each, *usu* swimming, cycling and running. — *n* **triath'lete**. [**tri-**, and Gr *athlon* a contest]

triatic or **triatic stay** *trī-at'ik* (*stā*), (*naut*) *n* a rope joining adjacent mastheads to which tackle is attached; each of a pair of stays joining the tops of direction-finding masts diagonally and supporting from their points of intersection a vertical aerial. [Origin obscure]

triatomic *trī-ə-tom'ik*, *adj* consisting of three atoms; having three replaceable atoms or groups; trivalent. — *adv* **triatom'ically**. [**tri-**]

triaxial *trī-ak'si-əl*, *adj* having three axes. — *n* a triaxial sponge spicule. — Also **triax'on**. [**tri-**, L *axis*, axle, and Gr *axōn*]

tribade *trib'ad*, *n* a female homosexual, a lesbian. — *adj* **tribad'ic**. — *n* **trib'adism** or **trib'ady** lesbian masturbation simulating heterosexual intercourse in the missionary position. [Fr, through L *tribas*, *-adis*, from Gr *tribas*, *-ados*, from *trībein* to rub]

tribal, etc. See under **tribe**.

tribasic *trī-bā'sik*, (*chem*) *adj* capable of reacting with three equivalents of an acid; (of acids) having three replaceable hydrogen atoms. [**tri-**, and **base**]

tribble *trib'l*, *n* a horizontal frame with wires stretched across it for drying paper. [Origin unknown]

tribe *trīb*, *n* a division of a pre-industrial nation or people for political purposes; a set of people theoretically of common descent; an aggregate of families, forming a community; a race; a breed; a class or set of people; (loosely) a classificatory division. — *adj* **trī'bal**. — *n* **trī'balism** the existence of tribes as a social phenomenon; (loyalty to) the conventions, etc, of one's tribe. — *n* **trī'balist**. — *adj* **trī'balistic**. — *adv* **trī'bally**. — *adj* **tribe'less**. — *n* **tribes'man**: — *fem* **tribes'woman**. — *n pl* **tribes'people**. [L *tribus*, *-ūs* one of the divisions of the ancient Roman people, conjecturally originally three in number, and hence perh related to L *trēs*, *tria* three]

triblet *trib'lit*, *n* a tapering mandrel on which rings, nuts, etc, are forged. [Fr *triboulet*]

tribo- *trī-bo-*, *trib-ō-*, *tri-bo'-*, *combining form* denoting rubbing or friction. — *adj* **triboelec'tric**. — *n* **tribo-electric'ity** electricity generated by friction. — *n* **tribol'ogist**. — *n* **tribol'ogy** the study of friction, wear, lubrication, etc, between surfaces moving in contact with one another. — *n* **triboluminescence** (*-es'əns*) emission of light caused by friction. — *adj* **triboluminesc'cent**. — *n* **tribom'eter** a sled-like apparatus for measuring sliding friction. [Gr *tribein* to rub]

tribrach *trī'brak*, (*prosody*) *n* a foot of three short syllables. — *adj* **tribrach'ic**. [Gr *tribrachys*, from *brachys* short]

tribromo- or **tribrom-** *trī-brōm'(ō)-*, *combining form* denoting (a compound) having three atoms of bromine, *esp* replacing hydrogen.

tribulation *trib-ū-lā'shən*, *n* severe affliction; the state of being in pawn (*obs slang*); a rowdy gang (*Shakesp*). [L *trībulāre*, *-ātum* to afflict, from *trībulum* a sledge for separating grain from chaff by rubbing, from *terere* to rub]

tribune *trib'ūn*, *n* a senior officer in a Roman legion; a magistrate elected by the plebeians in ancient Rome to defend their rights; a champion of popular rights; in this and the following sense, sometimes used as the title of a newspaper; a platform for speaking from; a raised area or stand; bishop's stall or throne. — *n* **tribunal** (*trib-*, *trīb-ū'nl*; *Spenser trib'*) a court of justice or arbitration; a body appointed to adjudicate in some matter or to enquire into some disputed question; a seat or bench in a court from which judgement is pronounced, a judgement-seat; a confessional. — *adj* of, of the nature of or authorized by a tribunal. — *n* **trib'unāte** or **trib'uneship** the office of tribune. — *n* **Trib'unite** a member of the Tribune Group. — *adj* **tribunitial** or **tribunicial** (*-ish'l*) or **tribunitian** or **tribunician** (*-ish'ən*). — **Tribune Group** a left-wing group within the British parliamentary Labour party. [L *tribūnus* tribune, and *tribūnāl* tribunal, from *tribus* a tribe]

tribute *trib'ūt*, *n* a payment in acknowledgement of subjection; an act, gift, words or other expression of approbation; (loosely) a testimony, a credit (to); a percentage of ore or its value received (or paid to the owners) by a miner. — *adv* **trib'utarily**. — *n* **trib'utariness**. — *adj* **trib'utary** paying tribute; contributing; paid in tribute. — *n* a payer of tribute; a stream that runs into another. — *n* **trib'uter** a miner paid by tribute. — **trib'ute-mon'ey** money paid as tribute. [L *tribūtum*, from *tribuere* to assign]

tricameral *trī'kam-ə-rəl*, *-kam'-*, *adj* having three chambers. [**tri-**, and L *camera* chamber]

tricar *trī'kär*, *n* a motor-tricycle with a passenger's seat or luggage carrier in front; a three-wheeled car. [**tri-**]

tricarboxylic *trī-kär-boks-il'ik*, *adj* (of an acid) having three carboxyl groups in each molecule. — **tricarboxylic acid cycle** a cyclical series of metabolic interconversions occurring in aerobic respiration, which produces reducing power that eventually contributes to the generation of ATP. [**tri-**]

tricarpellary *trī-kär'pəl-ər-i* or *-pel'ər-i*, (*bot*) *adj* of or with three carpels. [**tri-**]

trice *trīs*, *vt* (*naut*) to haul; to haul and make fast. — *n* a moment (as if the time of a single tug); a pulley (*obs*). [MDu *trisen* (Du *trijsen*) to hoist]

tricentenary *trī-sen-tē'nə-ri* or *-ten'ə-ri*, *n*. Same as **tercentenary**.

tricephalous *trī-sef'ə-ləs*, *adj* three-headed. [Gr *trikephalos*, from *kephalē* a head]

triceps *trī'seps*, *adj* three-headed. — *n* (*anatom*) a muscle with three separately arising heads, *esp* the muscle at the back of the upper arm that straightens the elbow. [L *trīceps*, *-cipitis*, from *caput* head]

triceratops *trī-ser'ə-tops*, *n* an ornithischian, quadrupedal, herbivorous dinosaur of the Cretaceous period, having a horn over each eye and one on its nose. [**tri-**, and Gr *keras*, *keratos* horn, and *ōps* face]

tricerion *trī-sē'ri-on*, (*Greek Church*) *n* a three-branched candlestick. [Late Gr, from Gr *kēros* wax]

trich- *trik-*, or **tricho-** *-ō-*, *-o'-* *combining form* denoting hair. [Gr *thrix*, genitive *trichos*]

trichiasis *trik-ī'ə-sis*, (*med*) *n* the turning in of hairs around an orifice, *esp* of eyelashes so that they rub against the eye; the presence of hairlike filaments in the urine. [LL, from Gr *thrix*, *trichos* hair]

trichina *trik'i-nə*, *tri-kī'nə*, or **trichinella** *trik-i-nel'ə*, *n* a member of the genus *Trichina* of nematode worms parasitic in rat, pig, and man, the adult in the small intestine, the larva encysted in muscle: — *pl* **trichin(ell)ae** (*-ē*), or **trichin(ell)as**. — *n* **trichiniasis** (*trik-i-nī'ə-sis*) or **trichinō'sis** a disease caused by trichinae. — *n* **trichinīzā'tion** or **-s-** infestation with trichinae. — *vt* **trich'inize**, **-s-** or **trich'inose** (*-nōs*) to infest with trichinae. — *adj* **trichinot'ic** or **trich'inous** pertaining to trichinosis. [Gr *trichinos* of hair, from *thrix*, *trichos* hair]

trichite *trik'īt*, *n* a hairlike crystallite. — *adj* **trichitic** (*-it'ik*). [Gr *thrix*, *trichos* hair]

Trichiurus *trik-i-ū'rəs*, or *-ōō'rəs*, *n* a genus of hair-tails, giving name to the family **Trichiu'ridae**, related to mackerels and tunnies. [**trich-**, and Gr *ourā* tail]

trichloro- or **trichlor-** *trī-klōr'(ō)-*, *-klör'(ō)-*, *combining form* denoting (a compound) having three atoms of chlorine, *esp* replacing hydrogen. — *n* **trichloroethylene** or **trichlorethylene** (*trī-klōr(-ō)-eth'i-lēn*, *-klör*) an acetylene derivative, used as a solvent, in paint manufacture, and as an analgesic and anaesthetic (*colloq abbrev* **trike** *trīk*).

tricho-. See **trich-**.

trichobacteria *trik-ō-bak-tē'ri-ə*, *n pl* filamentous bacteria. [**tricho-**]

trichogyne *trik'ō-jīn*, *-jin*, *n* in red seaweeds, and some fungi, a threadlike prolongation of the female organ. [**tricho-**, and Gr *gynē* woman, female]

trichoid *trik'oid*, *adj* hairlike. [Gr *trichoeidēs*]

trichology *trik-ol'ə-ji*, *n* the scientific study of hair and its disorders. — *adj* **tricholog'ical**. — *n* **trichol'ogist** a person skilled in trichology; a name appropriated by hairdressers. [Gr *thrix*, *trichos* a hair]

trichome *trik'ōm*, *trīk'ōm*, *n* a plant hair or outgrowth from the epidermis. [Gr *trichōma* a growth of hair]

trichomonad *trik-ə-mon'ad*, *n* a parasitic protozoon of the genus **Trichomonas** (*tri-kom'* or *-kə-mon'*). — *n* **trichomoni'asis** (*-mon-ī'*) a sexually transmitted disease caused by trichomonads, found in human beings and in animals. [**tricho-**, and Gr *monas*, *-ados* a unit]

trichophyton *trik-of'i-tən*, *n* any fungus of the genus *Trichophyton*, causing ringworm. — *n* **trichophytō'sis** ringworm caused by *Trichophyton*. [**tricho-**, and Gr *phyton* plant]

Trichoptera *trik-op'tər-ə*, *n pl* an order of insects with hairy wings, caddis-flies. — *n* **trichop'terist** someone who studies the caddis-flies. — *adj* **trichop'terous**. [**tricho-**, and Gr *pteron* wing]

trichord *trī'körd*, *adj* three-stringed; with three strings to one note. — *n* a three-stringed instrument; a triad. [Gr *trichordos*, from *chordē* a string]

trichosis *trik-ō'sis*, *n* arrangement, distribution, or morbid condition of hair. [Gr *trichōsis* hairiness]

trichotillomania *trik-ō-til-ō-mā'ni-ə*, *n* a neurosis in which the patient pulls out tufts of his or her own hair. [**tricho-**, Gr *tillein* to pull, and **mania**]

trichotomous *trī-kot'ə-məs*, *adj* divided into three; forking in threes. — *vt* and *vi* **trichot'omize** or **-ise** to divide in three or threes. — *adv* **trichot'omously**. — *n* **trichot'omy** trichotomous division or forking. [Gr *tricha* threefold, from *treis* three, and *tomē* a cutting, from *temnein* to cut]

trichroic *trī-krō'ik*, *adj* having or exhibiting three colours, *esp* when viewed in different directions. — *n* **trī'chroism**. [Gr *trichroos* three-coloured]

trichromatic *trī-krō-mat'ik*, *adj* characterized by three colours; having normal colour vision. — *n* **trichro'mat** someone who has normal colour vision. — *adj* **tri'-chrome** trichromatic. — *adj* **trichrō'mic** trichromatic. — *n* a trichromat. — *n* **trichrō'matism**. [Gr *trichrōmatos*, from *chrōma* colour]

trichronous *trī'kro-nəs*, *adj* trisemic. [Gr *trichronos*, from *chronos* time]

trick *trik*, *n* an artifice; a deceitful device; a deception; a prank; a performance aimed at astonishing, puzzling, or amusing; an expedient or knack; a characteristic habit, mannerism or trait; a spell or turn, *esp* at the helm; a round of play at cards; the cards so played and taken by the winner, forming a unit in scoring; a trinket or toy; a watch (*slang*); an outline sketch (*heraldry*); the customer of a prostitute (*slang*). — *vt* to deceive, to cheat; to beguile; to dress or decorate fancily (with *out*); to trim; to sketch in outline. — *adj* of the nature of, or for the purpose or performance of, a trick; unreliable, defective (*US colloq*); adroit and trim (*obs*). — *n* **trick'er**. — *n* **trick'ery** the act or practice of playing tricks; artifice; stratagem; imposition. — *adv* **trick'ily**. — *n* **trick'iness**. — *n* and *adj* **trick'ing**. — *adj* **trick'ish** tricky. — *adv* **trick'ishly**. — *n* **trick'ishness**. — *adj* **trick'less**. — *n* **trick'siness**. — *adj* **trick'some**. — *n* **trick'ster** a cheat; someone who practises trickery. — *n* **trick'stering** playing the trickster. — *adj* **tricks'y** given to pranks, mischievous; tricky, crafty; dressed or adorned smartly (*obs*). — *adj* **trick'y** addicted to trickery; clever in tricks; ticklish, difficult to handle; complicated. — **trick cyclist** an acrobat who performs tricks on a unicycle or cycle; a psychiatrist (*slang*). — **do the trick** to bring something about; **how's tricks?** (*slang*) how are you?; **trick or treat** (*esp NAm*) the (children's) practice of dressing up to visit neighbouring houses at Hallowe'en, and threatening to play a trick unless a treat is produced; **turn a trick** (*slang*, *esp US*) to have casual sexual relations with someone, *esp* for money; **up to (one's) tricks** misbehaving. [OFr *trique*, Northern form of *triche* deceit; perh in part of other origin]

trickle[1] *trik'l*, *vi* to run or pass in drops or in a small irregular stream. — *vt* to emit in a trickle. — *n* a succession of drops; a sparse intermittent rivulet; a drop (*obs*). — *n* **trick'let** a little trickle. — *n* and *adj* **trick'ling**. — *adj* **trick'ly** trickling. — *vt* **trick'le-charge** to charge (a battery) over a long period at a low rate. — **trick'le-charger**; **trick'le-down** (*orig* and *esp US*) filtration of benefits, *esp* money, downwards through the social community. — *adj* of or pertaining to the idea that economic benefits received by advantaged sectors, eg large companies, ultimately filter down to benefit the less well off. [ME *triklen*, prob for *striklen*, frequentative of **strike**]

trickle[2] *trik'l*, (*Spenser*) *adj* ticklish, precarious (another reading is **tickle**). [Prob derived from **trick**]

trick-track *trik'-trak*, *n* a form of backgammon in which pegs as well as pieces are used. — Also **tric'-trac** or **tick'-tack**. [Fr *tric trac*; imit of the sound made by the pieces]

triclinic *trī-klin'ik*, (*mineralogy*) *adj* of the crystal system in which three unequal axes are obliquely inclined to each other. [Gr *treis* three, and *klīnein* to bend]

triclinium *trī-klin'i-əm*, (*Roman antiq*) *n* a couch running round three sides of a table for reclining on at meals; a dining-room. [L *triclīnium*, from Gr *triklīnion*, from Gr *treis* three, and *klīnē* a couch]

tricolour or **tricolor** *trī'kul-ər*, *adj* three-coloured. — *n* (*tri'*) a three-coloured flag, *esp* that of France (*trē-kol-or*). — *adj* **trī'coloured**. [L *tricolor* and Fr *tricolore*]

triconsonantal *trī-kon-sə-nant'l*, *adj* having three consonants. — Also **triconsonan'tic**. [**tri-**]

tricorn or **tricorne** *trī'körn*, *adj* three-horned; three-cornered. — *n* a three-cornered hat with the brims turned up. [L *tricornis* three-horned, from *cornū* a horn]

tricorporate *trī-kör'pə-rāt*, *-rit*, or **tricorporated** *-id*, (*esp heraldry*) *adj* three-bodied (with one head). [**tri-**, and L *corpus*, *corporis* body]

tricostate *trī-kos'tāt*, *adj* three-ribbed. [**tri-**, and L *costa* rib]

tricot *trē'kō*, *n* a hand-knitted woollen fabric, or imitation of this; a soft, slightly-ribbed cloth for women's garments. — *n* **tricoteuse** (*trē-kot-øz*) (literally a woman who knits) in the French Revolution, one of the women who enthusiastically attended public meetings and executions, knitting as they sat; a 19c two-tiered work-table for knitters. [Fr *tricot* knitting]

tricrotic *trī-krot'ik*, *adj* (in measuring an arterial pulse) having three waves to one beat of the pulse; triple-beating. — *n* **tri'crotism**. — *adj* **tri'crotous**. [**tri-**, and Gr *krotos* a beat]

tric-trac. See under **trick-track**.

tricuspid or **tricuspidate** *trī-kus'pid*, *-āt*, *adj* having three cusps or points. [L *tricuspis*, *-idis*, from *cuspis* a point]

tricycle *trī'si-kl*, (*colloq abbrev* **trike** *trīk*) *n* a three-wheeled cycle; a light three-wheeled car for the use of a disabled person. — *vi* to ride a tricycle. — *n* **tri'cycler**. — *adj* **tricyclic** (*trī-sī'klik*) having three whorls or rings; (of a chemical compound) having three rings in its molecular structure, some compounds of this type being used as antidepressant drugs. — *n* **tri'cycling** (*-si-*). — *n* **trī'cyclist**. — **tricycle undercarriage** or **landing-gear** an aircraft's undercarriage or landing-gear, which has three wheels. [**tri-**, and Gr *kyklos* circle, wheel]

tridacna *trī-dak'nə*, *n* any clam of the genus *Tridacna*, giant clams of the Indian Ocean, the largest known bivalves (more than 200kg). [Gr *tridaknos* eaten at three bites (applied to a big oyster), from *daknein* to bite]

tridactyl or **tridactylous** *trī-dak'til*, *-əs*, *adj* three-toed; three-fingered. [**tri-**, and Gr *daktylos* finger, toe]

tridarn *trē'därn*, *n* a Welsh dresser having three tiers or stages. [Welsh]

tride. An *obs* spelling (*Spenser*, *Shakesp*) of **tried** (see under **try**).

trident *trī'dənt*, *n* a three-pronged spear, *esp* that of the sea-god Poseidon or Neptune (*classical mythol*); anything of similar shape. — *adj* **tri'dent**, **tridental** (*-dent'*) or **trident'āte** three-pronged. — *adj* **tridented** (*trī-dent'id*) three-pronged; (*trī'dənt-id*) having a trident. [L *tridēns*, *-dentis*, from *dēns* tooth]

Tridentine *trī-*, *tri-dent'īn*, (*hist* or *RC*) *adj* of Trent in Southern Tyrol, or the Council (1545–63) held there. — *n* a native of Trent; a person who accepts the decrees of the Council, an orthodox Roman Catholic. [L *Tridentum* Trent]

tridimensional *trī-dī-men'shən-əl, adj* having three dimensions. **[tri-]**

tridominium *trī-dō-min'i-əm, n* threefold rule. **[tri-**, and L *dominium* lordship]

triduan. See under **triduum**.

triduum *trid'ū-əm* or *trīd'*, (*esp RC*) *n* a space of three days; a period of prayer or religious celebration lasting three days. — *adj* **trid'ūan** lasting three days. [L *trīduum*, from *diēs* day]

tridymite *trid'i-mīt*, (*mineralogy*) *n* an orthorhombic form of silica, in hexagonal scales, often combined in threes. [Gr *tridymos* threefold]

trie. An *obs* spelling of **try**.

triecious. See **trioecious**.

tried. See under **try**.

triennial *trī-en'yəl, adj* continuing for three years; happening every third year. — *adv* **trienn'ially**. [L *triennis*, from *annus* a year]

trier. See under **try**.

trierarch *trī'ər-ärk*, (*Gr hist*) *n* the commander of a trireme; a person required (alone or with others) to fit out a trireme. — *adj* **tri'erarchal**. — *n* **tri'erarchy** the office of trierarch; the obligation of fitting out ships. [Gr *triērarchos*, from *triērēs* a trireme, and *archein* to rule]

tries. See under **try**.

trieteric *trī-i-ter'ik, adj* biennial. [Gr *trietērikos*, from *trietēris* a biennial festival, from *treis* three, and *etos* a year (inclusive reckoning being applied)]

triethyl *trī-eth'il, adj* having three ethyl groups. — *n* **triethylamine** (*-mēn'*) an oily liquid corresponding to ammonia with ethyl replacing all the hydrogen. **[tri-]**

trifacial *trī-fā'shl, adj* threefold and pertaining to the face. — **trifacial nerve** the trigeminal nerve. **[tri-** and **facial]**

trifarious *trī-fā'ri-əs, adj* arranged in three rows; facing three ways. [L *trifārius*]

trifecta *trī-fek'tə*, (*Austr*; *horse-racing*) *n* same as **triple**. **[tri-**, and **per***fecta*]

triff *trif*, (*slang*) *adj* terrific, excellent, highly enjoyable or attractive. — Also **triff'ic**. [Colloq contraction of **terrific**]

triffid *trif'id, n* a monstrous (fictional) stinging plant, mobile and rapidly multiplying, of invasive habit and malign intent. — *adj* **triffid'ian** or **triff'idy** in the nature of or reminiscent of a triffid or triffids. [From John Wyndham's science-fiction novel *The Day of the Triffids* (1951)]

trifid *trif'id, trī'fid, adj* cleft into three parts (*bot*, etc); (of a spoon) having a three-pointed decorative top to its handle. [L *trifidus* cleft into three parts, from *findere* to split]

trifle *trī'fl, n* anything of little importance or value; a small amount; a dessert of sponge cake soaked with sherry and covered with jam or fruit, topped with custard and whipped cream; a kind of pewter or articles made from it. — *vi* (often with *with*) to occupy oneself desultorily; to play, toy, amuse oneself; to behave without seriousness or respect; to meddle irresponsibly. — *vt* to spend, pass or waste (*esp* time) idly; to render trivial in comparison (*Shakesp*). — *n* **tri'fler**. — *adj* **tri'fling** of small value, importance, or amount; trivial. — *adv* **tri'flingly**. — *n* **tri'flingness**. — **a trifle** slightly. [OFr *trufle* mockery, deception]

trifocal *trī-fō'kəl, adj* (of a spectacle lens) giving separately near, intermediate, and far vision. — *n pl* **trifo'cals** spectacles with such lenses. **[tri-]**

trifoliate *trī-fō'li-āt, adj* having three leaves or leaflets. — *n* **trīfō'lium** any plant of the clover or trefoil genus *Trifolium*. — *n* **trifoly** (*trif'ə-li*; *Browning*) trefoil. [L *trifolium*, from *folium* leaf]

triforium *trī-fō'ri-əm, -fö'*, (*archit*) *n* a gallery, storey, or arcade over an aisle: — *pl* **trifo'ria**. [Anglo-L; ety obscure]

triform *trī'förm* or **triformed** *adj* having a triple form. [L *trifōrmis*, from *fōrma* form]

trifurcate *trī'fər-kāt*, or *-fûr'*, *adj* three-forked. — *vi* to divide into three branches. — *adj* **tri'furcated** (or *-fûr'*). — *n* **trifurcā'tion**. [L *trifurcus*, from *furca* a fork]

trig[1] *trig, adj* trim, neat (chiefly *Scot*); tight, sound. — *vt* to make trig; to block or hold back with a wedge; to stuff (*obs* except *dialect*). — *n* a block or wedge to stop a wheel. — *adv* **trig'ly**. — *n* **trig'ness**. [ON *tryggr* faithful, secure; cf **true**]

trig[2] *trig*, (*colloq*) *n* trigonometry. — *adj* trigonometric or trigonometrical. — **trig point** trigonometrical point.

trigamy *trig'ə-mi, n* the having of three legal or supposed wives or husbands at once; a third marriage (*eccles law*). — *n* **trig'amist** a person who has committed trigamy. — *adj* **trig'amous** of the nature of, involving or living in trigamy. [Gr *trigamos* thrice married, from *gamos* marriage]

trigeminal *trī-jem'i-nl, adj* threefold; three-branched. — **trigeminal nerve** (*anatom*) a facial nerve having three branches, supplying the eye, nose, skin, scalp and muscles of mastication (also called **trifacial nerve**); **trigeminal neuralgia** (*med*) another term for **tic douloureux**. [L *trigeminus* born three at a birth, from *geminus* born at the same birth]

trigger *trig'ər, n* a lever that releases a catch so as to fire a gun or set a mechanism going; anything that starts a train of actions. — *vt* (often with *off*) to set in action. — *adj* applied to something activated by or acting as a trigger. — **trigger finger** the finger used to pull the trigger on a gun, ie the forefinger of the dominant hand; a condition in which a finger is subject to involuntary muscular spasm, *esp* where it cannot be straightened when unclenching the fist (*med*); **trigg'er-fish** or **trigg'er-fish** a fish of the family *Balistidae*, having on the first dorsal fin a large front spine which can be locked upright by a second smaller spine; **trigger-happ'iness**. — *adj* **trigg'er-happy** over-ready to shoot (*lit* and *fig*); irresponsibly willing to take the risk of beginning a fight or a war. — **trigg'erman** a gangster's bodyguard; the man who actually fires a shot. [Du *trekker*, from *trekken* to pull]

triglot *trī'glot, adj* in or using three languages, trilingual. — *n* a book which is written in three languages. **[tri-**, and Gr *glōtta* tongue]

triglyceride *trī-glis'ər-īd*, (*chem*) *n* any of a group of commonly occurring fats, those fatty acid esters of glycerol in which all three hydroxyl groups have had their hydrogen atoms replaced by acid radicals. **[tri-]**

triglyph *trī'glif* (*archit*) *n* a three-grooved tablet in the Doric frieze. — *adj* **triglyph'ic**. [Gr *triglyphos*, from *glyphein* to carve]

trigon *trī'gon, n* a triangle; a set of three signs 120° apart, the zodiac being divided into four trigons, *watery* (consisting of Cancer, Scorpio and Pisces), *earthly* (Taurus, Virgo and Capricorn), *airy* (Gemini, Libra and Aquarius) and *fiery* (Aries, Leo and Sagittarius; *astrol*). — *adj* **trigonal** (*trig'ə-nl*) of a trigon; triangular; trigonous; bounded by three planes; (of symmetry about an axis) such that a rotation through 120° gives the same figure. — *adj* **trigonic** (*trī-gon'ik*) of a trigon; triangular. — *adj* **trigonous** (*trig'ə-nəs*; *esp bot*) triangular in section, or nearly so. [Gr *trigōnon*, from *gōniā* an angle]

trigonometry *trig-ə-nom'i-tri. n* the branch of mathematics that deals with the relations between the sides and angles of triangles. — *n* **trigonom'eter** a person skilled in or occupied with trigonometry; an instrument for solving triangles. — *adj* **trigonometric** (*-nə-met'rik*) or **trigonomet'rical**. — *adv* **trigonomet'rically**. — **trigonometrical point** (*geog*, etc) in triangulation, a fixed point whose position as vertex of a triangle is calculated astronomically (often shortened to **trig point**). [Gr *trigōnon* a triangle, and *metron* a measure]

trigram *trī'gram, n* an inscription of three letters; a figure of three lines. — *adj* **trigrammat'ic** or **trigramm'ic**. **[tri-**, and Gr *gramma* a letter]

trigraph *trī'gräf, n* a combination of three letters for one sound. **[tri-**, and Gr *graphē* a writing]

Trigynia *trī-jin'i-ə, n pl* in the Linnaean system, an order of plants (in various classes) with three pistils. — *adj* **trīgyn'ian** or **trigynous** (*trij'i-nəs*). [**tri-**, and Gr *gynē* a woman, female]

trihedral *trī-hed'rəl, -hēd'*, (*geom*, etc) *adj* having three faces. — *n* a figure with a trihedral aspect, formed by three planes meeting at a point. — Also **trīhed'ron** (or *-hēd'*). [**tri-**, and Gr *hedrā* a seat]

trihybrid *trī-hī'brid, n* a hybrid differing from its parents in three independently heritable characteristics. — Also *adj*. [**tri-**]

trihydric *trī-hī'drik*, (*chem*) *adj* having three hydroxyl groups. [**tri-**]

tri-jet *trī'jet n* an aircraft having three jet engines. [**tri-**]

trike[1]. See under **trichloroethylene**.

trike[2]. See under **tricycle**.

trilateral *trī-lat'ər-əl, adj* three-sided; of or having three parties or participants. — *n* a triangle. — *n* **trilat'eralism**. — *n* **trilat'eralist**. — *adv* **trilat'erally**. — *n* **trilatera'tion** a technique involving the measurement of selected sides of a triangulation (qv) network, for map-making, surveying, etc. [**tri-**, and L *latus, lateris* side]

trilby *tril'bi, n* a soft felt hat with an indented crown and narrow brim (also **trilby hat**); (in *pl*) feet (*slang*): — *pl* **tril'bies** or **tril'bys**. [From George du Maurier's novel, *Trilby* (1894)]

trild (*Spenser*). See under **trill**[2].

trilemma *tri-, trī-lem'ə, n* a form of argument or a situation differing from a dilemma in that there is a choice of three instead of two. [Modelled on **dilemma**]

Trilene® *trī'lēn, n* trichlorethylene.

trilinear *trī-lin'i-ər, adj* consisting of, having or referred to three lines. — *adj* **trīlin'eate** marked with three lines. [**tri-**, and L *līnea* line]

trilingual *trī-ling'gwəl, adj* in or using three languages, *esp* as native or habitual languages. — *n* **triling'ualism**. [**tri-**, and L *lingua* tongue]

triliteral *trī-lit'ər-əl, adj* consisting of three letters. — *n* **trilit'eralism** the characteristic (as in Semitic languages) of having roots consisting of three consonants. [**tri-**, and L *littera* a letter]

trilith *trī'lith* or **trilithon** *trī-lith'on, tri'lith-on, n* a form of megalithic monument consisting of two upright stones supporting another lying crosswise. — *adj* **trīlith'ic**. [**tri-**, and Gr *lithos* stone]

trill[1] *tril, n* a trillo; a tremulous sound; a run or roulade of bird-song; a consonant-sound produced by vibration. — *vt* and *vi* to play, sing, pronounce or sound with a trill. — *n* **trill'o** (*music*) a shake (qv): — *pl* **trill'oes**. [Ital *trillo*; imit]

trill[2] *tril, vt* and *vi* to twirl, roll, trundle; to pour in a fine stream: — *pa t* **trilled** (*Spenser* **trild**). [Cf Norw and Swed *trilla* to roll]

trilling *tril'ing, n* a threefold compound of crystals; one child of triplets. [**tri-**, and **-ling**; cf Dan and Swed *trilling*; Ger *Drilling*]

trillion *tril'yən, n* the cube of a million; the cube of ten thousand (*orig US*, and before 1948 in France); (loosely; *esp* in *pl*) an enormous number (*colloq*). — *n* and *adj* **trill'ionth**. [Fr, modelled on *million*]

trillium *tril'i-əm, n* a three-leaved trimerous plant of the *Trillium* genus of the lily family. [L *trēs* three]

trillo. See **trill**[1].

trilobe *trī'lōb, n* something that has three lobes. — Also *adj*. — *adj* **trilobate** (*trī'* or *-lō'*), **tri'lobated** or **trī'lobed** having three lobes. — *n* **trilobite** (*trī'lō-bīt* or *tril'ə-bīt*) any fossil arthropod of the Palaeozoic order **Trilobī'ta**, with broad head-shield and body longitudinally furrowed into three lobes. — *adj* **trilobitic** (*-bit'ik*). [**tri-**, and Gr *lobos* lobe]

trilocular *trī-lok'ū-lər*, (*esp bot*) *adj* three-celled. [**tri-**, and L *loculus*]

trilogy *tril'ə-ji, n* any group of three works, such as novels, plays, etc; a group of three related Greek tragedies, *orig* performed together; a triad. [Gr *trilogiā*, from *logos* discourse]

trim *trim, vt* to put in due condition; to fit out; to make ready for sailing; to adjust the balance of (a boat, submarine or aircraft); to dress, arrange; to set in order; to decorate (clothes, etc) eg with ribbons, lace, contrasting edging, etc; to make tidy or neat; to clip into shape; to make compact; to reduce the size of, by removing excess; to smooth; to rebuke sharply; to thrash; to cheat (*slang*); to adjust the inclination of a plane to the horizontal. — *vi* to balance; to balance or fluctuate between parties, be a trimmer; to adjust one's behaviour as expediency dictates: — *pr p* **trimm'ing**; *pa t* and *pa p* **trimmed**. — *adj* in good order; neat; tidy; well-kept; clean-cut; slim. — *adv* trimly. — *n* condition for sailing or flight; balance; condition, order; a fit, trim condition; humour, disposition, temper, way; array; fittings; the colour-scheme and chrome parts on the outside of a car, etc, or the upholstery, door-handles, etc inside it; decorative additions to clothes, eg contrasting edging, etc; an act of trimming; window-dressing (*US*); parts trimmed off; adjustment of an aircraft's controls to achieve stability in a desired condition of flight. — *adv* **trim'ly**. — *n* **trimm'er** someone who or something that trims; a person who fluctuates between parties, adjusting his or her opinions, etc to match his or her changing loyalties; a time-server; a scold; anything trouncing or redoubtable; a small horizontal beam on a floor into which the ends of joists are framed; a float bearing a baited hook and line, used in fishing for pike; a trimming tab; something fine, excellent, approved of (*Austr* and *NZ colloq*). — *n* **trimm'ing** making trim; balancing; clipping; a sharp rebuke; (*usu* in *pl*) ornamental additions; (in *pl*) accessories; (in *pl*) sauces and other accompaniments for a dish; (in *pl*) fittings; (in *pl*) parts trimmed off. — *adj* that trims. — *adv* **trimm'ingly**. — *n* **trim'ness**. — **trimming tab** or **trim'tab** a tab or aerofoil on an aircraft or boat, that can be adjusted in mid-passage to trim the craft; **trim size** (*printing*) the size of a book once its pages are trimmed. — **trim one's sails** to rule one's conduct, principles, etc, to accord with prevailing circumstances. [OE *trymman, trymian* to strengthen, set in order, from *trum* firm]

trimaran *trī'mə-ran, n* a boat with three hulls. [**tri-**, and cata*maran*]

trimer *trī'mər*, (*chem*) *n* a substance in which molecules are formed from three molecules of a monomer. — *adj* **trīmer'ic** (*chem*) having the same empirical formula but a relative molecular mass three times as great. — *adj* **trim'erous** (*trim'ə-rəs*) (*bot*) having three parts, or parts in three. [**tri-**, and Gr *meros* part]

trimester *tri-mes'tər, n* three months; an academic term. — *adj* **trimes'trial**. [L *trimēstris* of three months, from *mēnsis* a month]

trimeter *trim'i-tər*, (*prosody*) *n* a line of verse of three measures (dipodies or feet). — *adj* **trim'eter**, **trimetric** or **trimetrical** (*trī-met'rik, -l*) consisting of three measures, *esp* iambic. [Gr *trimetros*, from *metron* measure]

trimethyl *trī-meth'il*, (*chem*) *adj* containing three methyl radicals in combination. — *n* **trimeth'ylamine** (*-ə-mēn*) a gas, $(CH_3)_3N$, obtainable from herring-brine, corresponding to ammonia with methyl replacing all the hydrogen. — *n* **trimeth'ylene** (*-ēn*) cyclopropane. [**tri-**]

trimetric. See under **trimeter**.

Trimetrogon *trī-met'rə-gon, n* and *adj* applied to a technique of aerial photography using three cameras, which increases the range and detail of the coverage. [**tri-**, and *metrogon* a type of camera lens]

trimonthly *trī-munth'li, adj* every three months. [**tri-**]

trimorphism *trī-mör'fizm, n* occurrence of three forms in the same species (*biol*); the property of crystallizing in three forms (*chem*). — *adj* **trimor'phic** or **trimor'phous**. [**tri-**, and Gr *morphē* form]

trimtab. See under **trim**.

Trimurti *tri-mōōr'ti, n* the Hindu trinity, Brahma, Vishnu, and Siva. [Sans *tri* three, and *mūrti* shape]

Trin. *abbrev*: Trinity.

trin. See under **trine**[1].

Trinacrian *trī-*, *trī-nā'kri-ən*, *adj* Sicilian; (without *cap*) three-pointed; with three extremities. — *adj* **trinacriform** (*trin-ak'ri-förm*) three-pronged. [L, from Gr *Trīnakriā* Sicily, from *trinax*, *-akos* a three-pronged mattock, or *thrīnax* a trident]

trinal, **trinary**. See under **trine**[1].

trindle *trin'dl*, *n* one of several thin pieces of wood, etc, which hold the spine of a book flat while the front edge is trimmed; a wheel, *esp* of a barrow. — *vt* and *vi* to roll, to trundle. — **trin'dle-tail** a trundle-tail. [**trundle**]

trine[1] *trīn*, *adj* threefold; (of the aspect between two planets) 120° apart (*astrol*); hence, benign (*astrol*). — *n* a triad; the aspect of two planets, as seen from the earth, distant from each other one-third of the zodiac or 120° (*astrol*); a triplet. — *vt* to join in trine aspect. — *n* **trin** (*trin*) a triplet (by birth). — *adj* **trinal** (*trī'nl*) or **trī'nary**. [L *trīnus*, from *trēs*, *tria* three]

trine[2] *trīn*, *vi* to go. — **trine to the (nubbing) cheat** (*cant*) to go the gallows. [Scand]

tringle *tring'gl*, *n* a curtain-rod. [Fr]

Trinidadian *trin-i-dad'i-ən*, *-dād'i-ən*, *adj* of or pertaining to the island of *Trinidad* in the W Indies. — *n* a native of Trinidad.

triniscope *trīn'i-skōp*, *n* a cathode-ray tube for colour television. [L *trīnus* triple, and Gr *skopeein* to view]

trinitro- *trī-nī'trō-*, *combining form* denoting (a compound) having three nitro-groups (NO_2), *esp* replacing hydrogen. — *n* **trinī'trate** a nitrate with three nitrate groups in the molecule. — *n* **trinī'trin** glyceryl trinitrate or nitroglycerine, used to treat angina pectoris. — *n* **trinitroben'zene** $C_6H_3(NO_2)_3$, corresponding to benzene C_6H_6. — *n* **trinitrophē'nol** a similar derivative of phenol, *esp* picric acid. — *n* **trinitrotol'uene** or **-tol'uol** a high explosive (commonly called **TNT**), a trinitro-derivative of toluene. [**tri-**]

trinity *trin'i-ti*, *n* threefoldness; three in one; a triad; *esp* (with *cap*) the triune God of orthodox Christians (Father, Son and Holy Ghost); (with *cap*) any symbolical representation of the Trinity; (with *cap*) Trinity Sunday; (with *cap*) Trinity term. — *adj* **Trinitā'rian** of, in relation to or believing in the Trinity; of the Trinitarians. — *n* someone who adheres to the doctrine of the Trinity; a member of a religious order founded at Rome in 1198 to redeem Christian captives from the Muslims (also called *Mathurins* and *Redemptionists*); a member of Trinity College (eg in Cambridge or Dublin). — *n* **Trinitā'rianism**. — **Trinity House** a lighthouse and pilot authority for England, Wales and the Channel Islands, *orig* chartered at Deptford in 1514; **Trinity Sunday** the Sunday after Whitsunday; **Trinity term** one of the terms of the English law-courts beginning after Trinity Sunday (now **Trinity law sittings**); the university term beginning after Trinity Sunday. [L *trīnitās*, *-ātis*, from *trīnus* threefold]

trinket *tring'kit*, *n* a small ornament or piece of jewellery; any paltry object; a despised religious observance (*hist*); a delicacy (*obs*). — *vi* (*obs*) to have secret or underhand dealings (*with*). — *n* **trink'eter** (*obs*) an intriguer. — *n* **trink'eting**. — *n* **trink'etry** trinkets collectively. [Poss OFr *trenquet* small knife]

trinkum *tring'kəm*. Same as **trankum**. — Also **trink'um-trank'um**.

trinomial *trī-nō'mi-əl*, *adj* consisting of three terms (for genus, species and subspecies or variety; *biol*); consisting of three terms connected by the plus or minus sign (*math*). — *n* a trinomial name or expression. — *n* (*biol*) **trino'mialism** the system of naming by three terms. — *n* **trino'mialist**. [Modelled on **binomial**]

trio *trē'ō*, *n* a set of three; a composition for, or combination of, three performers (*music*); the second section of a minuet, scherzo, or march (said to have been originally for three instruments), followed by a repetition of the first section (*music*): — *pl* **tri'os**. — **trio sonata** a sonata for three parts, often played either by four instruments (ie with an additional harpsichord accompaniment) or by eg an organ alone. [Ital]

triode *trī'ōd*, *adj* with three electrodes. — *n* a three-electrode valve. [**tri-**, and Gr *hodos* a path, way]

Triodion *trī-ō'di-on*, (*Greek church*) *n* a service-book for the ten weeks before Easter. [Mod Gr *triōdion*, from *ōdē* hymn]

trioecious or **triecious** *trī-ē'shəs*, (*bot*) *adj* (of an order of plants) having male, female, and hermaphrodite flowers on different individuals. [**tri-**, and Gr *oikos* house]

triolet *trī'ō-lit*, *trē'ō-lā*, *-let*, *n* an eight-lined poem rhymed *ab aa abab*, lines 4 and 7 repeating 1, and 8 repeating 2. [Fr]

triones *trī-ō'nēz*, *n pl* the seven stars of the Plough. [L *triōnēs* plough-oxen]

trionym *trī'ə-nim*, *n* a trinomial. — *adj* **trionymal** (*-on'i-məl*). [Gr *triōnymos*, from *onyma* (*onoma*) name]

trior. See under **try**.

trioxide *trī-oks'īd*, (*chem*) *n* a compound with three atoms of oxygen. [**tri-**]

trip[1] *trip*, *vi* to move with short, light steps or skips; to stumble or catch one's foot; to make a slip in accuracy, virtue, etc (often with *up*); to tip up, tilt; to make an excursion; to experience the hallucinatory effects of LSD or similar drug (also **trip out**; *slang*). — *vt* to cause to stumble or fall by catching the foot (often with *up*); to catch in a fault; to dance trippingly; to trip or dance upon; to release (an anchor) from the sea bed, by a long rope; to release or operate (a switch or piece of machinery) by striking; to tilt up: — *pr p* **tripp'ing**; *pa t* and *pa p* **tripped**. — *n* a light, short step or skip; a catching of the foot, a stumble; a slip or lapse; a single journey, one way or to and fro; the distance of a race (*horse-racing*); a pleasure excursion, jaunt; a specially arranged journey at a cheap fare; a group of people on an excursion; a striking part that releases a catch; a hallucinatory experience under the influence of a drug such as LSD, or (loosely) a quantity of a drug that will produce such an experience (*slang*); any stimulating experience (good or bad) (*slang*). — *adj* **tripp'ant** (*heraldry*) tripping, with right foot raised. — *n* **tripp'er** someone who trips; an excursionist, *esp* of the disturbing kind (often *derog*); a device that when struck, passed over, etc, operates a switch. — *adj* **tripp'erish** or **tripp'ery** of, like or reminiscent of the vulgar or noisy tripper. — *n* and *adj* **tripp'ing**. — *adv* **tripp'ingly**. — **trip hammer** a tilt hammer; **trip'-hook** (*Browning*) some kind of instrument of torture; **trip recorder** an instrument in a vehicle that can be reset to record distance travelled eg on a specific trip; **trip switch** a circuit-breaker; **trip'wire** a wire which releases some mechanism when pulled, eg by being tripped over. — **trip out** to stop (a machine) working by disconnecting it, *esp* automatically; (of a machine) to become disconnected and therefore stop working. [OFr *triper*; of Gmc origin; cf OE *treppan* to tread, Ger *trappe(l)n*, Du *trippen*, *trappen*, *trippelen*, Swed *trippa*]

trip[2] *trip*, *n* a small flock of sheep, wildfowl, etc. [Perh related to **troop**]

tripartite *trī-pär'tīt*, *adj* in three parts; split in three nearly to the base (*bot*); relating to three parties. — *n* **tripar'tism** an established system of dialogue between three related groups, *specif* government, employers, and unions, for mutually acceptable planning and follow-up; division into three parts, *esp* political parties (*rare*). — *n* **tripartition** (*-tish'ən*). [L *tripartītus*, from *partīrī* to divide, from *pars* a part]

tripe *trīp*, *n* parts of the compound stomach of a ruminant, prepared as food, ie the paunch or rumen (*plain tripe*), and the smaller reticulum (*honeycomb tripe*); rubbish, poor stuff (*colloq*); claptrap (*colloq*); entrails (*archaic*). — *n* **trīp'ery** a place for the preparation or sale of tripe. — *adj* **trip'ey** or **trip'y** (*colloq*) rubbishy, worthless. — **tripe'hound** (*slang*) a newspaper reporter; a dog (*Austr*); **tripe'man**, **tripe'-wife** or **tripe'-woman** a dresser or seller of tripe; **tripe'-shop**. — *adj* **tripe'-visag'd** (*Shakesp*) with a face like tripe. — **tripe de roche** (*trēp də rosh*; Fr) rock-tripe. [OFr (Fr) *tripe*; origin obscure]

tripedal *trip'-, trī'pi-dl, trī-pē'dl, adj* three-footed. [**tri-**, and L *pēs, pedis* foot]

tripersonal *trī-pûr'sən-əl, adj* consisting of three persons. — *n* **triper'sonalism**. — *n* **triper'sonalist** a believer in the Trinity. — *n* **tripersonal'ity**. [**tri-**]

tripetalous *trī-pet'əl-əs, adj* three-petalled. [**tri-**, and Gr *petalon* leaf]

tripey. See under **tripe**.

triphenyl- *trī-fē'nil-*, (*chem*) *combining form* denoting (a compound) containing three phenyl radicals. — *n* **triphenylamine** (*-ə-mēn*) a crystalline compound corresponding to ammonia with all the hydrogen replaced by phenyl; **triphenylmē'thane** a crystalline solid used in the preparation of dyes. [**tri-**]

triphibious *trī-fib'i-əs, adj* (*esp* of military operations) taking place on land, in the water and in the air. [**tri-**, and *-phibious*, modelled on **amphibious** with wrong word-division]

triphone *trī'fōn, n* a shorthand sign representing a triphthongal sound. [**tri-**, and Gr *phōnē* sound]

triphthong *trif'thong, trip', n* a combination of three vowel sounds in one syllable (*phonetics*); (loosely) a trigraph. — *adj* **triphthongal** (*-thong'gl*). [**tri-**, and Gr *phthongos* sound]

triphyllous *trī-fil'əs*, (*bot*) *adj* three-leaved. [**tri-**, and Gr *phyllon* a leaf]

Triphysite *trif'i-zīt, -sīt, n* a believer in the existence of three natures in Christ (human, divine, and a third resulting from the union of these). [**tri-**, and Gr *physis* nature]

tripinnate *trī-pin'āt, -it, adj* pinnate with the pinnae themselves pinnate, and their pinnae again pinnate. [**tri-**]

Tripitaka *trip-i-tä'kə, -pit'ə-kə, n* (also without *cap*) the whole body of the northern Buddhist canonical writings, comprising the *sutras*, or discourses of the Buddha for the laity, *Vinaya*, or discipline for the order, and *Abhidharma*, or metaphysics. [Pali, literally three baskets]

triplane *trī'plān, n* an aeroplane with three sets of wings, one above another. [**tri-**]

triple *trip'l, adj* threefold; consisting of three; three times as much; third (*Shakesp*). — *n* a quantity three times as much; a thing (eg a star) that is triple; a peal of bells interchanging in three sets of two; a betting system requiring that the horses which finish first, second and third in a race are selected in correct order. — *vt* and *vi* to treble. — *n* **trip'leness**. — *n* **trip'let** three of a kind, or three united; three lines rhyming together; a group of three notes occupying the time of two, indicated by a slur and the figure 3 (*music*); one of three (people or animals) born at one birth; a state in which there are two unpaired electrons (*chem*); a cycle for three riders. — *adj* **trip'lex** triple. — *n* (*Shakesp*) triple time. — *adj* **trip'licate** threefold; made thrice as much; equal to the cube of the quantity (*old math*). — *n* a third copy or thing corresponding to two others of the same kind; the third power or cube (*old math*). — *vt* to make threefold. — *n* **triplicā'tion** the act of triplicating; a reply to a duplication. — *n* **triplicity** (*trip-lis'i-ti*) tripleness; a triad; a trigon (*astrol*). — *n* **trip'ling** a making triple; a triplet, trilling or trin. — *adv* **triply** (*trip'li*). — *n* (*tri-plī'*; *Scots law*) a pursuer's reply to a defender's duply. — *vt* and *vi* to reply to a duply. — **Triple Alliance** the league of England, Sweden, and the Netherlands formed against France in 1668; the alliance of Britain, France, and Holland against Spain in 1717; the alliance between Germany, Austria, and Italy, 1883–1915, counterbalanced by the **Triple Entente**, a friendly understanding (developing into an alliance) between Britain, France, and Russia; **triple crown** the pope's tiara; a victory by England, Scotland, Wales or Ireland in all three matches against the others in the series played each season (*Rugby football*, etc). — *adj* **trip'le-crowned** having three crowns or a triple crown, as the pope. — **triple event** the Two Thousand Guineas, St Leger, and Derby; **triple glazing** glazing formed by three layers of glass with the optimum air space between each layer for insulation and/or soundproofing. — *adj* **trip'le-head'ed** three-headed. — **triple jump** an athletic event, formerly called the hop, skip and jump (qv), the object of which is to cover the longest possible distance; **triple point** the temperature and pressure at which solid, liquid, and gaseous phases of a substance can co-exist, *esp* triple point of water, 273.16K and 610N/m^{-2}; **triple time** time or rhythm of three beats, or of three times three beats, in a bar. — *vi* **triple-tongue'**. — **triple-tongu'ing** (*music*) rapid articulation of fast passages by wind-players. — *adj* **trip'le-turned** (*Shakesp*) three times faithless. — **Triplex® glass** a combination of glass and mica in three layers. — *adj* **triplicate-ternate** see under **triternate**. — **in triplicate** in three exact copies. [Fr, from L *triplus*, from Gr *triploos* (*triplous*); and L *triplex*]

triploid *trip'loid*, (*biol*) *adj* having three times the haploid number of chromosomes. — *n* **trip'loidy** the state of being triploid. [Gr *triploos* triple]

triply. See under **triple**.

tripod *trī'pod, trip'od, n* anything on three feet or legs, *esp* a stand for an instrument; the stool on which the priestess at Delphi sat to deliver an oracle. — *adj* three-legged. — *adj* **tripodal** (*trip'əd-əl*). — *n* **tripody** (*trip'ə-di*) a line of verse or group of three feet. [Gr *tripous, tripodos*, from *pous, podos* foot]

tripoli *trip'ə-li, n* diatomite. [Orig brought from *Tripoli* in Africa]

tripos *trī'pos, n* any of the honours examinations for the BA degree at Cambridge; any of the recognized courses leading to the BA at Cambridge; the list of successful candidates in it; a tripod (*obs*). [Prob traceable to the custom by which a BA, known as Mr *Tripos*, sat on a three-legged stool and disputed in the Philosophy School at Cambridge on Ash Wednesday, his speech being called the Tripos speech]

trippant, tripper, tripping, etc. See under **trip**[1].

trippet *trip'it, n* a trivet; in a machine, a piece which projects in order to strike another part of the mechanism regularly. [Cf **trivet** and OFr *trepied*]

tripple *trip'l*, (*SAfr*) *n* a horse's ambling canter, between a fast walk and a slow trot. — Also *vi*. — *n* **tripp'ler**. [Du *trippelen*]

tripsis *trip'sis, n* pulverization; shampooing; massage. [Gr *trīpsis*, from *trībein* to rub]

triptane *trip'tān, n* trimethyl butane, a powerful aviation fuel. [*tri*methyl *butane*, with *b* altered to *p*]

tripterous *trip'tər-əs*, (*bot*) *adj* three-winged. [Gr *tripteros*, from *pteron* wing]

triptote *trip'tōt, adj* used in three cases only. — *n* a triptote word. [Gr *triptōtos*, from *ptōsis* a case, falling]

triptych *trip'tik, n* a set of three tablets, painted panels, etc, hinged together as one work of art. [Gr *triptychos* threefold, from *ptyx, ptychos* a fold, from *ptyssein* to fold]

triptyque *trēp-tēk, n* (*Fr*) an international pass for a motor-car. [**triptych** (because divided in three sections)]

tripudium *trī-pū'di-əm, tri-pŏŏd'i-ŏŏm, n* an ancient Roman religious dance in triple time, or dance generally; divination from the hopping of birds feeding, or from the dropping of scraps from their bills. — *adj* **tripu'diary**. — *vi* **tripu'diate** to dance for joy; to exult; to stamp. — *n* **tripudiā'tion**. [L *tripudium, prob* from *trēs* three, and *pēs, pedis* foot]

tripy. See under **tripe**.

triquetra *trī-kwet'rə, n* an ornament consisting of three interlaced arcs, common in early art in northern Europe. — *adj* **triquet'ral** or **triquet'rous** triangular; three-edged with concave faces (*bot*). — *adv* **triquet'rously**. — *n* **triquet'rum** a Wormian bone: — *pl* **triquet'ra**. [L *triquetrus, -a, -um* triangular, from *trēs* three]

triradiate *trī-rā'di-āt, adj* three-rayed. — Also **trirā'dial**. [**tri-**]

trireme *trī'rēm, n* an ancient Greek galley, *esp* a war-galley, with three banks of rowers. [L *trirēmis*, from *rēmus* an oar]

trisaccharide *trī-sak'ə-rīd, n* a sugar that hydrolyses into three molecules of simple sugars. [**tri-**]

trisagion *tris-ag'i-on, n* an ancient hymn consisting of the words 'O Holy God, holy and mighty, holy and immortal, have mercy on us'; loosely, the Tersanctus. [Gr *tris* thrice, and *hagios* holy]

trisect *trī-sekt', vt* to cut or divide into three (*usu* equal) parts. — *n* **trisec'tion** (*-shən*). — *n* **trisect'or** a person who trisects; *esp* a person who thinks he or she can trisect an angle by Euclidean methods (ie using straight-edge and compasses) which has been proved to be impossible; a line that trisects. — *n* **trisect'rix** a curve of polar equation $r = 1 + 2\cos\theta$, by which an angle can be trisected. [**tri-** and L *secāre*, *sectum* to cut]

triseme *trī'sēm, (prosody) adj* equal to three short syllables. — *n* a trisemic foot, the tribrach, iamb or trochee. — *adj* **trisē'mic**. [Gr *trisēmos*, from *sēma* a sign]

trishaw *trī'shö, n* a three-wheeled light vehicle pedalled by a driver behind the passenger seat. [**tri-** and rick*shaw*]

triskaidekaphobia or **triskaidecaphobia** *tris-kī-dek-ə-fōb'i-ə, n* fear of the number thirteen. — *n* **triskaidek'aphobe** a person who suffers from triskaidekaphobia. [Gr *tr(e)iskaideka* thirteen, and **phobia**]

triskele *tris'kēl, n* a figure consisting of three radiating curves or legs, as in the arms of the Isle of Man. — Also **triskelion** (*tris-kel'i-on*): — *pl* **triskel'ia**. [**tri-** and Gr *skelos* a leg]

Trismegistus *tris-mi-gis'təs, adj* thrice greatest, an epithet of Thoth, the Egyptian moon-god. [Latinized from Gr *trismegistos*]

trismus *triz'məs, n* (*med*) tetanic spasm of the muscles of mastication, causing difficulty in opening the mouth. [Latinized from Gr *trismos* a creaking, grating, from *trizein* to grate, gnash]

trisoctahedron *tris-ok-tə-hē'dron, n* a solid with twenty-four faces, three for every face of an octahedron: — *pl* **trisoctahē'drons** or **trisoctahē'dra**. [Gr *tris* thrice, and **octahedron**]

trisomic *trī-sōm'ik, adj* designating an otherwise normal diploid organism in which one chromosome type is represented thrice instead of twice. — *n* **tri'sōme** a chromosome that occurs three times in a cell instead of twice; a trisomic individual. — *n* **tri'sōmy** a trisomic condition. [**tri-**]

trist or **triste** *trist, (archaic) adj* sorrowful; dismal. — Also **trist'ful** (*Shakesp*). — *n* **tristesse'** sorrow, grief, melancholy. [Fr *triste*, from L *tristis* sad]

tristich *tris'tik, n* a group of three lines of verse: — *pl* **tris'tichs** (*-tiks*). — *adj* **tristich'ic**. — *adj* **tris'tichous** (*biol*) in or having three rows. [Gr *tristichiā* a triple row, tristich, from *stichos* a row]

tristimulus values *trī-stim'ū-ləs val'ūz, n pl* amounts of each of three colour primaries that must be combined to form an objective colour match with a sample. [**tri-**]

trisula *tri-soo'lə, n* the trident of Siva. — Also **trisul'**. [Sans *triśūla*]

trisulcate *trī-sul'kāt, adj* having three forks or furrows. [L *trisulcus*, from *sulcus* a furrow]

trisulphide *trī-sul'fīd, n* a sulphide with three atoms of sulphur to the molecule. [**tri-**]

trisyllable *tri-sil'ə-bl*, also *trī-, n* a word of three syllables. — *adj* **trisyllabic** (*-ab'ik*) or **trisyllabical**. — *adv* **trisyllab'ically**. [**tri-**]

tritagonist *tri-tag'ən-ist, n* the third actor in ancient Greek drama. [Gr *tritagōnistēs*, from *tritos* third, and *agōnistēs* an actor]

tritanopia *trī-tən-ō'pi-ə, n* inability to distinguish the colour blue. — *adj* **trītanop'ic**. [Gr *tritos* a third, and New L *anopia* blindness, ie blindness to a third of the spectrum]

trite[1] *trīt, adj* worn; worn-out; well-trodden; used till novelty and interest are lost; hackneyed. — *adv* **trite'ly**. — *n* **trite'ness**. [L *trītus* rubbed, pa p of *terere* to rub]

trite[2] *trī'tē, (Gr music) n* the third string of the lyre or tone of the tetrachord, reckoned downwards. [Gr *tritē* (fem) third]

triternate *trī-tûr'nāt, adj* thrice ternate, ie ternate with each division ternate, and each again ternate. — Also **trip'licate-ter'nate**. [**tri-**]

tritheism *trī'thē-izm, n* belief in three Gods; belief that the Father, Son and Holy Ghost are actually different beings. — *n* **tri'theist**. — *adj* **tritheis'tic** or **tritheis'tical**. [**tri-** and Gr *theos* a god]

trithionic *trī-thī-on'ik, adj* containing three sulphur atoms (**trithionic acid**, $H_2S_3O_6$). — *n* **trithionate** (*trīthī'ən-āt*) a salt of trithionic acid. [**tri-** and Gr *theion* sulphur]

tritiate. See **tritium**.

tritical *trit'i-kl, adj* trite, common. — *adv* **trit'ically**. — *n* **trit'icalness** or **trit'icism** triteness. [Formed from **trite**[1] in imitation of **critical**, etc]

Triticum *trit'i-kəm, n* the wheat genus of grasses. — *n* **trit'icale** a hybrid cereal grass, a cross between wheat and rye, grown as a food crop. — *adj* **triticeous** (*-ish'əs*) wheatlike. [L *trīticum* wheat, from *terere*, *trītum* to rub]

tritium *trish'i-əm, trit', (chem) n* an isotope of hydrogen of triple mass. — *vt* **tritiate** (*trish'i-āt, trit'i-āt*) to replace normal hydrogen atoms in (a compound) by tritium. — *n* **tritiā'tion**. — *n* **trit'ide** a compound of tritium with another element or radical. — *n* **triton** (*trī'tən*) the nucleus of tritium, composed of one proton and two neutrons. [New L, from Gr *tritos* third]

Tritoma *trit'ō-mə*, wrongly *trī-tō'mə, n* a synonym of *Kniphofia*. [Gr *tritomos* thrice cut, from *tomē* a cut (from the splitting capsule)]

Triton *trī'tən, n* a minor Greek sea-god, son of Poseidon and Amphitrite, represented with a dolphin's tail, and sometimes horse's forelegs, blowing a conch (*Gr mythol*); (in *pl*) the attendants of Poseidon; applied to a sailor or a ship (*fig*); a genus of large gasteropods with shells that can be used like conchs; a disused generic name for newts; the larger of the two satellites of the planet Neptune, the other being Nereid. [Gr *Trītōn, -ōnos*]

triton. See **tritium**.

tritone *trī'tōn, (music) n* an augmented fourth, an interval of three whole tones. [Gr *tritonos*, from *tonos* tone]

tritonia *trī-tō'ni-ə, n* a plant of the genus *Tritonia* of iridaceous S African plants, sometimes called montbretia.

tritubercular *trī-tū-bûr'kū-lər, adj* having three tubercles or cusps. — Also **trituber'culate**. — *n* **trituber'culism**, **trituber'culy**. [**tri-**]

triturate *trit'ū-rāt, vt* to rub or grind to a fine powder. — *n* the fine powder thus obtained. — *n* **triturā'tion**. — *n* **trit'urātor**. [LL *trītūrāre, -ātum*, from L *terere* to rub]

triumph *trī'əmf, n* complete or signal victory or achievement; exultation for success; in ancient Rome, a solemn procession in honour of a victorious general; a pageant; festivity (*obs*); pomp, observance (*obs*); a captive led in triumph (*Milton*); a trump (*cards*; *obs*). — *vi* to celebrate a victory with pomp; to rejoice for victory; to obtain victory, prevail (often with *over*); to exult, insult (often with *over*); to show in glory (*Shakesp*). — *vt* (*Milton*) to triumph over. — *adj* **triumphal** (*trī-umf'l*) relating to triumph; used in celebrating victory. — *n* (*Milton*) a token of victory. — *n* **triumph'alism** an attitude of righteous pride and self-congratulation in the defeat of perceived evil. — *adj* and *n* **triumph'alist**. — *adj* **triumph'ant** celebrating or having achieved a triumph; exultant; transcendent in glory (*Shakesp*); triumphal (*Shakesp*). — *adv* **triumph'antly**. — *n* **tri'umpher**. — *n* **triumph'ery** (*Shakesp*) see under **triumvir**. — *n* and *adj* **tri'umphing**. — **triumphal arch** an arch erected in connection with the triumph of a Roman general; any decorative arch in public rejoicings, etc. — **church triumphant** see under **church**. [L *triumphus*; related to Gr *thriambos* a hymn to Bacchus]

triumvir *trī-um'vər, trē-ŏŏm'vir*, *n* each of three men in the same office or government; each of three sharing supreme power: — *pl* **trium'virī** or **trium'virs**. — *adj* **trium'viral**. — *n* **trium'virate** (*obs* **trium'viry**; *Shakesp* **trium'phery**) an association of three men in office or government, or for any political ends, *specif* that of Pompey, Crassus and Caesar (60 BC), and that of Octavian (Augustus), Mark Antony and Lepidus (43 BC); any trio or triad. [L *triumvir*, from the genitive *pl trium virōrum* of three men]

triune *trī'ūn*, *adj* three in one. — *n* a trinity in unity. — *n* **triū'nity**. [L *trēs*, *tria* three, and *ūnus* one]

trivalent *trī-vā'lənt, triv'ə-lənt*, (*chem*) *adj* having a valency of three. — *n* **trivā'lence** (or *triv'əl-*) or **trivā'lency** (or *triv'əl-*). [**tri-** and **-valent**]

trivalve *trī'valv*, *adj* three-valved. — *n* that which is three-valved. — *adj* **tri'valved** or **trival'vūlar**. [**tri-** and L *valva* a door-leaf]

trivet *triv'it*, *n* a tripod, *esp* one for a pot or kettle; a bracket with three projections for fixing on the top bar of a grate; a three-legged pot; a *usu* metal plate placed in a pressure cooker to raise the food to be cooked off the bottom of the vessel. — **right as a trivet** perfectly right (from its stability). [OE *trefet*, appar from L *tripēs*, *tripedis*, from *pēs* a foot]

trivia *tri'vi-ə*, *n pl* trifles, trivialities, unimportant details. — *adj* **trivial** (*triv'i-əl*) of the trivium; to be found anywhere; of little importance; trifling; vernacular (*biol*); (of a name) specific (as opposed to *generic*) (*biol*); with value zero (*math*). — *n* **triv'ialism** a trivial matter or remark. — *n* **triviality** (*-al'i-ti*) the state or quality of being trivial; that which is trivial, a trifle. — *n* **trivializā'tion** or **-s-**. — *vi* **triv'ialize** or **-ise** to make trivial or unimportant. — *adv* **triv'ially**. — *n* **triv'ialness**. — *n* **triv'ium** in medieval schools, the group of liberal arts first studied, comprising grammar, rhetoric and logic; the three anterior radii of an echinoderm (*zool*). [L *trivium* a place where three ways meet, from *trēs* three, and *via* a way]

tri-weekly *trī-wēk'li*, *adj* occurring or appearing once in three weeks or three times a week. — *adv* once in three weeks; three times a week. — *n* a periodical appearing three times a week. [**tri-**]

-trix *-triks*, *sfx* denoting a feminine agent: — *pl* **-trixes** or **-trices** (*-trī-sēz, -tri-siz*). [L]

trizone *trī'zōn*, *n* a unit or country formed of three zones, *specif* the area of West Germany comprised in the British, French and American zones of occupation after World War II (also called **Trizōn'ia**). — *adj* **trizō'nal**. [**tri-** and **zone**]

tRNA *abbrev*: transfer RNA.

troad or **troade** (*Spenser*). See **trod**[1].

troat *trōt*, *vi* (of a buck) to bellow. — Also *n*. [OFr *trout*, *trut*, interjection used to urge on animals]

trocar *trō'kär*, *n* a surgical perforator used for inserting a cannula, to drain off or introduce liquid, etc; sometimes, a cannula. [Fr *trocart*, from *trois* three, and *carre* side]

trochaic. See under **trochee**.

trochal. See under **trochus**.

trochanter *trō-kan'tər*, *n* a rough eminence on the thigh-bone to which muscles are attached (*anatom*); the second segment of an insect's leg (*entomol*). — *adj* **trochanteric** (*-ter'ik*). [Gr *trochantēr*, from *trechein* to run]

troche and **trocheameter**. See under **trochus**.

trochee *trō'kē*, (*prosody*) *n* a foot of two syllables, a long followed by a short; in English, etc, a stressed followed by an unstressed syllable. — *adj* **trochaic** (*-kā'ik*). — *n* a trochaic verse. [Gr *trochaios* (*pous*) running or tripping (foot), from *trochos* a running, from *trechein* to run]

Trochelminthes and **Trochidae**. See under **trochus**.

trochilus *trok'i-ləs*, *n* a concave moulding; the crocodile bird; any bird of the hummingbird genus *Trochilus*, giving its name to the hummingbird family **Trochil'idae**. — *adj* **trochil'ic** relating to rotatory motion. [Gr *trochilos* a crocodile bird, a wren, a pulley sheaf, from *trechein* to run]

trochiscus, **trochisk** and **trochite**. See under **trochus**.

trochlea *trok'li-ə*, (*zool*) *n* any pulley-like structure, *esp* a foramen through which a tendon passes. — *adj* **troch'lear**. — **trochlear nerve** the fourth cranial nerve. [L *trochlea*, from Gr *trochiliā* a pulley]

trochoid, etc. See under **trochus**.

trochus *trō'kəs*, *n* a wheel or hoop (*Gr antiq*); the inner ring of cilia in a rotifer; (with *cap*) the top genus of molluscs. — *adj* **tro'chal** wheel-like. — *n* **troche** (*trōk*, *trōsh* or *trōch*; *trō'kē* is frowned upon) a round medicinal tablet. — n pl **Trochelminthes** (*trōk-el-min'thēz*; Gr *helmins*, *helminthos* worm) the rotifer phylum of animals. — *n pl* **Troch'idae** the top family of molluscs. — *n* **trochisc'us** or **troch'isk** a troche. — *n* **troch'ite** an encrinite joint. — *n* **troch'oid** the curve traced by a fixed point, not on the circumference, in the plane of a rolling circle. — *adj* wheel-like; like a Trochus; trochoidal. — *adj* **trochoid'al** of the nature of a trochoid. — *n* **trochom'eter** or (*ill-formed*) **trocheam'eter** a hodometer. — *n* **troch'ophore** or **troch'osphere** a free-swimming, pelagic larval form of many invertebrates. — *n* **troch'otron** *troch*oidal magne*tron*, a high-frequency counting tube which deflects a beam on to radially disposed electrodes. [Gr *trochos* a wheel, from *trechein* to run]

trock (*Scot*). See **truck**[1].

trocken *trok'ən*, (*Ger*) *adj* (of wine) dry.

troctolite *trok'tə-līt*, *n* troutstone, a coarse-grained basic igneous rock composed of feldspar spotted with olivine. [Gr *trōktēs* a kind of sea-fish, from *trōgein* to gnaw, nibble, and *lithos* stone]

trod[1] *trod* (*Spenser* **troad**, **troade** or **trode**, *trōd*), (*obs*) *n* a track; path; footing. — **hot trod** (*Scott*) the pursuit of moss-troopers. [OE *trod*, *trodu* track, trace; cf **tread**]

trod[2], and **trodden**. See under **tread**.

trode. See **trod**[1].

troelie and **troely**. See **troolie**.

trog *trog*, (*colloq*) *vi* to walk, *usu* heavily and wearily: — *pr p* **trogg'ing**; *pa t* and *pa p* **trogged**. [Poss from **trudge** and **slog**]

troggs *trogz*, (*Scot*) *n* and *interj* troth.

troglodyte *trog'lə-dīt*, *n* a cave-dweller; an anthropoid ape (*obs* and *erron*). — Also *adj*. — *n* **Troglodytes** (*-lod'i-tēz*) the wren genus. — *adj* **troglodytic** (*-dit'ik*) or **troglodyt'ical** cave-dwelling. — *n* **trog'lodytism** (*-dīt-izm*). [Gr *trōglodytēs*, from *trōglē* a hole, and *dyein* to get into]

trogon *trō'gon*, *n* any member of a family (**Trogon'idae**) of tropical and *esp* S American birds (*incl* the quetzal), with brilliantly-coloured plumage and backward-facing first and second toes. [Appar Gr *trōgōn* nibbling]

Troic *trō'ik*, *adj* Trojan. [Gr *Trōikos*]

troika *troi'kə*, *n* a Russian vehicle drawn by three horses abreast; a team of three horses abreast; a team of three people, etc, acting equally as leaders, a triumvirate. [Russ, from *troe* a set of three]

troilism *troi'lizm*, *n* sexual activity between three people (of two sexes). — *n* **troi'list**. [Origin uncertain; perh Fr *trois* three, influenced by **dualism**]

troilite *trō'il-īt*, *n* native ferrous sulphide, found in meteorites. [After Dominico *Troili*, who observed it in the 18c]

troisième âge *trwä'z-i-em äzh*, (*Fr*) *n* third age (see under **third**).

Trojan *trō'jən*, *adj* of Troy. — *n* a citizen or inhabitant of Troy; a boon companion; a doughty, trusty or hard-working person; a good fellow; a Trojan horse (see below; *comput*). — **Trojan horse** the gigantic wooden horse inside which the Greeks are said to have entered Troy; a person or organization, placed within a country, group, etc with the purpose of destroying it; a concealed insertion of disruptive coded material within a program (*comput jargon*). [L *Trōjānus*, from *Trōja* Troy]

troke (*Scot*). See **truck**[1].

troll[1] *trōl*, (*Scand mythol*) *n* a goblin or supernatural dwarf (earlier, giant). [ON]

troll[2] *trōl*, *vt* to roll (*obs*); to trundle (*archaic*); to spin (*archaic*); to circulate, pass around the table (*archaic*); (*Milton* **troule**) to move nimbly, wag (the tongue); to utter fluently, set rolling off the tongue (*obs*); to sing the parts of (eg a catch or round) in succession (*archaic*); to fish for, or in, with a spinning or otherwise moving bait; to allure (*obs*). — *vi* to roll (*obs*); to move or run about (*obs*); to sing a catch; to stroll, ramble (*obs*); to fish with revolving or trailing lure (see also **trawl**). — *n* an instance of moving round, repetition; a round song; trolling; a lure for trolling. — *n* **troll'er**. — *n* and *adj* **troll'ing**. — **troll'ing-bait** or **troll'ing-spoon** a metallic revolving lure used in trolling. [Cf OFr *troller* (Fr *trôler*) to quest, Ger *trollen* to roll]

trolley[1] or **troly** *trol'i*, *n* lace with the pattern outlined with thicker thread or a flat border: — *pl* **troll'eys** or **troll'ies**. [Cf Flem *tralje* trellis]

trolley[2] *trol'i*, *n* a basket, tray or table (or set of tiered trays) on castors or wheels, used for transporting goods, luggage, etc, or for serving food and drink; a bogie; a bed on wheels used for transporting hospital patients; a pulley, receptacle or car travelling on an overhead wire or rail; a trolley-wheel; a tram-car (*US*): — *pl* **troll'eys**. — Also (*rare*) **troll'y**: — *pl* **troll'ies**. — *vt* to convey by trolley. — *vi* to travel by trolley. — **troll'eybus** a bus that receives power by a trolley-wheel from a pair of overhead wires; **troll'ey-car** (*US*) a tram-car so driven; **troll'ey-man** a man who works a trolley or on a trolley; **troll'ey-table** a tiered trolley for a dining-room; **troll'ey-wheel** a grooved wheel by which a bus, tram-car, etc receives current from an overhead wire. — **off one's trolley** (*slang*) daft, crazy. [Prob **troll**[2]]

trollius *trol'i-əs*, *n* a perennial plant of the genus *Trollius*, family *Ranunculaceae*, with orange or yellow globular flowers. [New L, appar from Ger *Trollblume*, from *trollen* to roll]

troll-my-dame *trōl-mi-dām'* or **troll-my-dames** *-dāmz'*, (*Shakesp*) *n* an old game like bagatelle, in which bullets were trolled into a little arcade. — Also **trou-madame** (*trōō-mä-däm*). [Fr *trou-madame*, from *trou* hole, associated with **troll**[2]]

trollop *trol'əp*, *n* a slatternly or untidy woman; a shameless or promiscuous woman; a prostitute. — *vi* (*Scot*) to draggle; to go, dress or work in a slovenly way. — *n* **trollopee'** (*hist*) a woman's loose dress worn in the 18c. — *adj* **troll'oping**, **troll'opish** or **troll'opy**. [Perh **troll**[2]]

Trollopean or **Trollopian** *tro-lə-pē'ən*, *adj* of or in the style of the novels of Anthony *Trollope* (1815–82). — *n* an admirer or student of his novels.

trolly. See **trolley**[1] and **trolley**[2].

tromba marina *trom'bə mə-rē'nə*, *n* an obsolete viol, generally one-stringed, with an irregular bridge, played in harmonics, giving a trumpet-like tone. [Ital, marine (speaking-)trumpet]

trombiculid *trom-bik'ū-lid*, *adj* of or relating to any of the mite family (*Trombiculidae*). — *n* a trombiculid mite or harvest-bug (qv).

trombone *trom-bōn'*, *n* a brass musical wind instrument, consisting of a tube bent twice on itself, with a slide. — *n* **trombōn'ist**. [Ital; augmentative of *tromba* trumpet]

tromino *trom'in-ō*, *n* a flat, three-sided shape made up of a number of identical squares placed edge to edge: — *pl* **trom'inos** or **trom'inoes**. [**tri-** and (on a false analogy) **domino**]

trommel *trom'əl*, *n* a revolving cylindrical sieve for cleaning or sizing minerals. [Ger *Trommel* drum]

tromometer *trom-om'i-tər*, *n* an instrument for measuring slight earthquake shocks. — *adj* **tromomet'ric**. [Gr *tromos* a trembling, and *metron* a measure]

tromp *tromp*, (*esp US*) *vi* to tramp or trample. [Variant of **tramp**, perh influenced by **stomp**]

trompe or **tromp** *tromp*, *n* an apparatus for producing a blast of air in a furnace by means of falling water. [Fr]

trompe l'œil *trɔ̃p lœ-y'*, (*Fr*) *n* literally 'something that deceives the eye'; appearance of reality achieved by use of minute, often trivial, details or of other effects in painting, architecture, etc.

tron *tron* or **trone** *trōn*, (chiefly *Scot*) *n* a public weighing machine, used also as a place of punishment; the market-place; a system of weights used at the tron. [OFr *trone*, from L *trutina*, from Gr *trȳtanē* a pair of scales]

-tron *-tron*, *sfx* signifying agent or instrument, particularly: (1) thermionic valve, eg *klystron*, (2) elementary particle, eg *positron*, (3) particle accelerator, eg *cyclotron*. [Gr]

trona *trō'nə*, *n* a native combination of acid and normal sodium carbonate. [Swed, from Ar *trōn* for *natrūn*; see **natron**]

tronc *trongk*, Fr *trɔ̃*, *n* a collection of tips to be divided out later, eg among waiters; the system by which this is done. [Fr, collecting box]

trone. See **tron**.

troolie, **troelie** or **troely** *trōō'li*, *n* the bussu palm; its leaf. [Tupí *tururí*]

troop *trōōp*, *n* a body of soldiers; (in *pl*) military forces; a band of people; a flock, herd or swarm of animals; (*esp* in *pl*) a great number; a division of a cavalry squadron; a group of (Boy) Scout patrols; a troupe; the command of a troop of horse; a drum signal for assembling. — *vi* to assemble (*archaic*); to consort (*archaic*); to pass in a body or in rapid succession; to be off. — *vt* to cause to troop; to receive and carry ceremonially along the ranks (as in *troop the colour* or *colours*). — *n* **troop'er** a private cavalry soldier (proverbially a swearer); a private soldier in armoured (tank) units; a mounted policeman (*US* and *Austr*); a cavalry horse; a troop-ship. — **troop'-carrier** a motor vehicle, ship or aeroplane for carrying troops; **troop'-horse** a cavalry horse; **troop'-ship** a ship for transporting troops. [Fr *troupe*, from LL *troppus*; poss Gmc]

troopial. Same as **troupial**.

trop-. See **tropo-**.

tropaeolum *tro-pē'ə-ləm*, *n* the Indian cress and canary-creeper genus, S American trailing or climbing plants constituting a family **Tropaeolā'ceae** related to the geraniums, *esp* the garden nasturtium. — *n* **tropae'olin** any of a group of dyes of complex structure. [Gr *tropaion* a trophy (from the shield-shaped leaves and helmet-like flowers)]

troparion *tro-pä'ri-on* or *-ar'*, (*Greek Ch*) *n* a stanza or short hymn: — *pl* **tropar'ia**. [Dimin of Gr *tropos* trope]

trope *trōp*, *n* a figure of speech, properly one in which a word or expression is used in other than its literal sense, eg metaphor, metonymy, synecdoche or irony ; a short cadence peculiar to Gregorian melodies; a phrase formerly interpolated in different parts of the mass. — *vt* to provide with tropes. — *adj* **trop'ical**. — *n* **trop'ist** a user of tropes; someone who understands the Bible as figurative. — *adj* **tropolog'ic** or **tropolog'ical**. — *adv* **tropolog'ically**. — *n* **tropol'ogy** figurative language; a moral interpretation of the Bible. [Gr *tropos* a turn, from *trepein* to turn]

-trope *-trōp*, *combining form* denoting a tendency towards or affinity for, as in *heliotrope*. — *adj combining form* **-tropic**. — *n combining form* **-tropism**. [Gr *tropos* a turn]

troph- *trof-* or *trəf-*, **tropho-** *-ō-* or *-o'-*, **-troph-** *trəf*, or **-trophy** *-trəf-i*, *combining forms* denoting nutrition. — *n* **trophallax'is** (Gr *allaxis* exchange) or **trophobīō'sis** (Gr *biōsis* way of life) mutual exchange of nutriment in symbiosis. — *adj* **trophallac'tic** or **trophobīot'ic**. — *adj* **trophesial** (*-ē'zi-əl*, *-shl*) relating to trophesy. — *n* **troph'esy** or **trophoneurō'sis** a state of deranged nutrition owing to disorder of the trophic action of the nerves. — *n pl* **trophi** (*trō'fī*) the mouth-parts of an insect; the teeth of the pharynx of a rotifer. — *adj*

troph'ic relating to nutrition. — *n* **troph'oblast** the differentiated outer layer of epiblast in a segmenting mammalian ovum. — *adj* **trophoblast'ic**. — *n* **troph-ol'ogy** the study of nutrition. — *n* **troph'oplasm** protoplasm which is mainly concerned with nutrition. — *n* **trophotax'is** and **trophot'ropism** chemotaxis and chemotropism where the stimulating substance is food. — *adj* **trophotact'ic** or **trophotrop'ic**. — *n* **trophozō'ite** in *Protozoa*, the trophic phase of the adult, which generally reproduces by schizogony. — **trophic level** a division of an ecosystem consisting of all organisms whose food is obtained from plants by the same number of intermediate steps; **trophic structure** a feature of an ecosystem, measured and described in terms of standing crop per unit area or energy fixed per unit area per unit time. [Gr *trophē* food, *trophos* a feeder, from *trephein* to feed]

Trophonian *trō-fō'ni-ən*, *adj* of the deified *Trophōnius* (Gr *Trophōnios*) or the cave in Boeotia where he delivered oracles and conferred solemnizing mystic experiences.

trophy *trō'fi*, *n* a memorial of victory, *orig* arms or other spoils set up on the spot; displayed spoils, such as skulls and antlers; a piece of plate or suchlike awarded as a prize; a memorial of success, glory, etc; an ornamental group of weapons, flags, etc, or a representation of such. — *vt* (*poetic*) to set with trophies; to confer trophies on. — *adj* **trō'phied**. [Fr *trophée*, from L *trophaeum* (classical *tropaeum*), from Gr *tropaion*, from *tropē* a turning, from *trepein* to turn]

tropic *trop'ik*, *n* an imaginary circle on the celestial sphere about 23° 28′ N (*tropic of Cancer*) or S (*of Capricorn*) of the equator, where the sun turns on reaching its greatest declination north or south; a corresponding circle on the terrestrial globe; (in *pl*) the part of the earth between the tropics of Cancer and Capricorn; a turning-point or limit. — *adj* of or relating to the sun's turning; of the tropics; of or of the nature of a tropism (*biol*). — *adj* **trop'ical** of or relating to a tropic or the tropics; found in or characteristic of the tropics; fervidly hot; luxuriant; of the nature of a trope, figurative. — *adv* **trop'ically**. — **tropical month** and **year** see **month** and **year** respectively; **tropic bird** a tropical sea-bird *Phaethon* with long tail-feathers. [Gr *tropos* a turning]

tropism *trō'pizm*, (*biol*) *n* orientation in response to stimulus; a general term for helio*tropism*, geo*tropism*, etc. — *adj* **tropistic** (*trop-ist'ik*) of tropism. [Gr *tropos* a turning]

-tropism. See under **-trope**.

tropist. See under **trope**.

tropo- *trō-pō*, *trop-o-*, *-ō-* or *-ə-*, also **trop-**, *combining form* denoting: turning; change; tropism. — *n* **tropomy'osin** (*biol*) a filamentous protein which controls the interaction of actin and myosin in muscle fibres, and hence muscle contraction. — *n* **trop'opause** (Gr *pausis* a ceasing) the boundary between troposphere and stratosphere. — *adj* **tropoph'ilous** tropophytic. — *n* **trop'ophyte** (*-fīt*; Gr *phyton* plant) a plant adapted to alterations of moisture and drought. — *adj* **tropophytic** (*-fit'ik*). — *n* **trop'oscatter** the propagation of radio waves by using irregularities in the troposphere to scatter the signals beamed up by means of high-powered UHF transmitters and parabolic antennas. — *n* **trop'osphere** the lowest layer of the atmosphere in which temperature falls as height increases. — *adj* **tropospher'ic**. [Gr *tropos* a turning]

tropologic, etc. See **trope**.

troppo *trop'ō*, (*Ital*) *adv* in music, too much; excessively.

trossers *tros'ərz*, *n* an *obs* form of **trousers**.

trot[1] *trot*, *n* a pace between walking and running (of a horse, with legs moving together diagonally); an act or spell of trotting; continual activity in moving about; a toddling child (*colloq*); a trotline (*angling*); any of the single lines attached to a trotline; a crib, literal translation (*US slang*). — *vi* to go, ride or drive at a trot; to jog; to bustle about; to fish using a baited hook which travels downstream just above the bottom. — *vt* to cause to trot; to conduct around; to bring out for exhibition; to draw out so as to make a butt of (*usu* with *out*); to jog on one's knee; to trot upon; to execute at a trot: — *pr p* **trott'ing**; *pa t* and *pa p* **trott'ed**. — *n* **trott'er** a person or thing that trots; a horse trained to trot in harness racing; a foot, *esp* of a sheep or pig. — *n* **trott'ing** the action of the verb; harness racing. — **trot'line** (*angling*) a long line across a waterway to which shorter lines with baited hooks are attached. — **on the trot** (*colloq*) in succession, without a break; busy, bustling about; **the trots** (*slang*) diarrhoea; **trot out** to exhibit the paces of; to bring forward, adduce, produce for show, *esp* repeatedly; to go out with, court (*archaic*). [OFr *trot* (noun), *troter* (verb); perh Gmc; cf OHGer *trottōn*, Eng **tread**]

trot[2] *trot*, (*Shakesp*) *n* an old woman, a crone. [Anglo-Fr *trote*]

Trot *trot*, (*colloq*; *derog*) *n* and *adj* short for **Trotskyist** or **Trotskyite**.

trot-cozy or **trot-cosey** *trot'-kō'zi*, (*Scott*) *n* a riding-hood. [Appar **trot**[1] (Jamieson says **throat**) and **cosy**]

troth *trōth*, *troth*, (*formal* or *archaic*) *n* faith, fidelity. — *vt* (*Shakesp*) to betroth. — *interj* in truth. — *adj* **troth'ful**. — *adj* **troth'less**. — **troth'-plight** a plighting of troth, betrothal. — *vt* (*archaic*) to betroth. — *adj* (*Shakesp*) betrothed. — Also **troth'-plighted**. — **troth'-ring** a betrothal ring. [Variant of **truth**]

Trotskyism *trot'ski-izm*, *n* the form of Communism associated with Leon *Trotsky* (pseudonym of Lev Davidovich Bronstein, 1879–1940), who advocated worldwide revolution. — *n* **Trot'skyist** or **Trot'skyite**. — Also *adj*.

trottoir *trot-wär*, (*Fr*) *n* a pavement. [Fr, from *trotter* to trot]

trotyl *trō'til*, *n* trinitrotoluene. [trini*trot*oluene, and **-yl**]

troubadour *trōō'bə-dōōr*, *-dōr* or *-dör*, *n* any of a class of mostly aristocratic poets composing lyrics on courtly love, who first appeared in Provence, and flourished from the 11c to the 13c; a poet or singer (*usu* one concerned with love). [Fr, from Provençal *trobador*, from *trobar* (Fr *trouver*) to find]

trouble *trub'l*, *vt* to agitate; to disturb; to muddy; to make turbid; to molest; to afflict; to annoy; to busy or engage overmuch; to put to inconvenience. — *vi* to take pains; to put oneself to inconvenience; to be troublesome (*obs*). — *n* disturbance; affliction; distress; a scrape; travail; anything amiss; disease; uneasiness; exertion; the taking of pains; a cause of trouble. — *adj* **troub'led** (*trub'ld*). — *adv* **troub'ledly**. — *n* **troub'ler**. — *adj* **troub'lesome** causing or giving trouble or inconvenience; vexatious; importunate. — *adv* **troub'lesomely**. — *n* **troub'lesomeness**. — *n* and *adj* **troub'ling**. — *adj* **troub'lous** (*archaic* or *poetic*) full of trouble or disorder; agitated; tumultuous; disturbing. — *adv* **troub'lously**. — *n* **troub'lousness**. — *adj* **troub'le-free** easy, not beset with problems. — **troub'le-house**, **trouble-state**, **troub'le-town** or **troub'le-world** (*archaic* or *poetic*) someone who disturbs the peace of a house, state, etc; **troub'lemaker** someone who disturbs the peace and (*usu*) incites others to do so; **troub'le-mirth** a killjoy; **troub'leshooter** an expert detector and mender of any trouble, mechanical or other. — *vt* **troub'leshoot**. — *n* and *adj* **troub'leshooting**. — **trouble spot** a place where trouble, *esp* social or political unrest, occurs. — **ask** or **look for trouble** to behave in such a way as to bring trouble on oneself; **I'll trouble you to** please; **in trouble** (*euphem*) pregnant (when unmarried); **trouble and strife** (*rhyming slang*) wife; **trouble someone for** to ask someone to provide, pass, etc. [OFr *trubler* (Fr *troubler*) from a LL frequentative of L *turbāre* to disturb, from *turba* a crowd]

trou-de-loup *trōō-də-lōō'*, (*hist*) *n* a pit with a vertical stake in the middle, used as a defence against cavalry: — *pl* **trous-de-loup** (*trōō-*). [Fr, wolf-hole]

trough *trof*, *n* a long narrow vessel for watering or feeding animals; a vessel for kneading, brewing, washing, tanning or various domestic and industrial purposes; a vessel for liquid over which gases are collected (*pneumatic trough*); a channel, gutter or conduit; a long narrow depression; a hollow between wave-crests; a low point (*fig*); an elongated area of low atmospheric pressure, *usu* extending from a depression and marking a change of air-mass (*meteorol*). — **trough'-fault** (*geol*) a pair of parallel faults with downthrow between them; **trough'-shell** a lamellibranch with a somewhat triangular shell thought to resemble a kneading-trough (*Mactra*). — **troughing and peaking** ranging between low and high points or levels. [OE *trog*; Ger *Trog*]

troule (*Milton*). See **troll²**.

trou-madame. Same as **troll-my-dame**.

trounce¹ *trowns, vt* to harass (*obs*); to indict (*dialect*); to punish, beat, rebuke or censure severely. — *n* **trounc'er**. — *n* **trounc'ing**. [Origin obscure]

trounce² *trowns*, (*dialect* or *archaic*) *vi* to skip, prance, move briskly. — *vt* to whisk off, make to skip. [Origin obscure]

troupe *tro͞op, n* a company, *esp* of theatrical performers. — *vi* to travel about as a member of a theatrical troupe. — *n* **troup'er** a member of a theatrical troupe; an experienced actor; an experienced person. [Fr; see **troop**]

troupial or **troopial** *tro͞o'pi-əl, n* a bird (*Icterus icterus*) famous for its song; any bird of the *Icteridae*. [Fr *troupiale*, from *troupe* troop]

trouse *tro͞oz, trowz*, (*hist*) *n* Irish close-fitting breeches; trews. — Also in *pl* (now *vulg*) trousers. [See **trews**]

trousers *trow'zərz*, (*obs*) **trossers** *tros'ərz*, (*Shakesp*) **strossers** *stros'*, *n pl* long breeches; a garment worn on the lower part of the body with a loose tubular branch for each leg; (as *sing*, **trou'ser**) a pair or style of these; any other garment of similar form, such as pantalettes. The *sing* is used to form compounds, eg **trou'ser-butt'on**, **trou'ser-clip**, **trou'ser-leg'**, **trou'ser-pock'et**, **trou'ser-stretch'er**, etc. — *vt* **trou'ser** (*slang*) to appropriate (money, etc), to pocket. — *adj* **trou'sered** wearing trousers. — *n* **trou'sering** (*usu* in *pl*) material for trousers. — **trouser suit** a woman's suit, consisting of a jacket and trousers. — **(caught) with one's trousers down** (taken) unawares; **wear the trousers** (of a wife) to be the dominant partner in a marriage. [See **trews**]

trousseau *tro͞o'sō, n* the clothes (and sometimes household linen, etc) collected by a bride for her marriage; a bundle (*archaic* and *rare*): — *pl* **trou'sseaux** or **trou's-seaus** (*-sōz*). [Fr, dimin of *trousse* bundle]

trout *trowt, n* a freshwater fish (*Salmo fario*) of the salmon genus, much sought after by anglers; extended to various fishes related to or superficially resembling this; an unpleasant, interfering old person, *esp* a woman: — *pl* **trout** or (*rare*) **trouts**. — *n* **trout'er** a person who fishes for trout. — *adj* **trout'ful** full of trout. — *n* and *adj* **trout'ing** trout-fishing. — *adj* **trout'less**. — *n* **trout'let** or **trout'ling** a little trout. — *adj* **trout'y**. — **trout'-basket** an osier or willow creel for carrying trout. — *adj* **trout'-coloured** speckled like a trout; white, with spots of black, bay or sorrel. — **trout'-farm** a place where trout are reared artificially; **trout'-rod** a fishing-rod for trout; **trout'-spoon** a small revolving spoon used as a lure for trout; **trout'stone** troctolite; **trout'-stream** a stream in which trout are caught. [OE *truht*, from L *tructa*, *tructus*, from Gr *trōktēs* a sea-fish with sharp teeth, from *trōgein* to gnaw, nibble]

trouvaille *tro͞o-vä'ē, n* a fortunate find. [Fr]

trouvère *tro͞o-ver'* or **trouveur** *tro͞o-vœr', n* any of the medieval narrative or epic poets of northern France. [Fr]

trove. See **treasure-trove** under **treasure**.

trover *trō'vər*, (*law*) *n orig*, finding and keeping; hence, formerly, a legal action brought to recover goods from a person to whom they do not belong. [OFr *trover* (Fr *trouver*) to find]

trow¹ *trō*, (*archaic*) *vt* to trust; to believe (often elliptically for *I trow* or *trow you?*). [OE *trēowan* (*trēowian*, *trūwian*); ON *trūa*, Ger *trauen*]

trow² *trow*, (*Shetland* and *Orkney*) *n* a form of **troll¹**.

trow³ *trow*, (*dialect*) *n* any of various small boats or barges, *usu* flat-bottomed. [**trough**]

trowel *trow'əl, n* a flat or scoop-shaped tool with a short handle, for plastering, gardening, etc. — *vt* to dress, apply or move with or as if with a trowel: — *pr p* **trow'elling**; *pa t* and *pa p* **trow'elled**. — *n* **trow'eller**. — **lay it on with a trowel** to spread something thickly; to say grossly flattering things. [OFr *truelle*, from LL *truella* (L *trulla*, dimin of *trua* a ladle)]

trowsers *trow'zərz*, (*archaic*) *n*. A variant spelling of **trousers**.

troy *troi, n* a system of weights used for precious stones and metals, the pound (no longer in legal use) of 5760 grains being divided into 12 ounces of 20 pennyweight (also **troy weight**). — Also *adj*. [*Troyes*, in France]

Troyan *troi'ən*, (*Shakesp* and *Spenser*) *adj* Trojan.

truant *tro͞o'ənt, n* someone who, idly or without excuse, absents himself or herself from school (also *fig*); an idler (*archaic*); a vagrant (*obs*); a vague term of reproach (*obs*). — Also *adj*. — *vi* to play truant. — *n* **tru'ancy**, **tru'antry** or **tru'antship**. — **play truant** to stay away from school without permission or good reason. [OFr *truant* (Fr *truand*), prob from Celtic]

Trubenize® or **Trubenise** *tro͞o'bən-īz, vt* to stiffen (a fabric) by binding together two layers by an intermediate layer of cellulose acetate.

trucage or **truquage** *trü-käzh*, (*Fr*) *n* the faking of works of art. — *n* **truqueur** (*trü-kœr*) a faker of works of art.

truce *tro͞os, n* a suspension of hostilities; a respite. — *adj* **truce'less**. — *adj* **trucial** (*tro͞o'shl, -syəl, -shi-əl*) bound by a truce. — **truce'-breaker**. — **Trucial States** former name (until 1971) for the United Arab Emirates on the S coast of the Persian Gulf, so called from being in treaty with Britain. — **Truce of God** a cessation of war, decreed by the Church, more or less observed, *esp* in the 11c and 12c, in France, Italy, England, etc, from Saturday (afterwards from Wednesday) evening to Monday morning, also during Advent and Lent and on certain holy days. [ME *trewes*, *treowes*, *pl* of *trewe*, from OE *trēow* truth, pledge, treaty; cf **true**]

truchman *truch'mən*, (*obs*) *n* an interpreter: — *pl* **truch'-men** or **truchmans**. [Ar *turjamān*; cf **dragoman**]

truck¹ *truk, vt* to exchange; to barter; to pay in goods. — *vi* to traffic; to have dealings or intercourse; to barter; to bargain; to potter about; to do nothing (*slang*); to move along, make progress generally (*slang*); to persevere (*slang*). — *Scot* **trock** (*trok*) or **troke** (*trōk*). — *n* exchange of goods; barter; payment in goods; (*Scot* **trock** or **troke**) dealings, intercourse; a small job, chore; small goods (*colloq*); rubbish (*colloq*); fresh vegetables, market-garden produce (*US*). — *n* **truck'-age** barter. — *n* **truck'er** someone who trucks; a market-gardener (*US*). — *n* **truck'ing**. — **truck'-farm** (*US*) a market-garden; **truck'-farmer**; **truck'-farming**; **truck'-shop** (*hist*) a shop operated by employers in which their workers were obliged to buy goods; **truck system** the practice of paying workers in goods instead of money, forbidden by the Truck Acts, 1831, etc. — **have no truck with** (*colloq*) to have nothing to do with. [OFr *troquer* to truck; Sp *trocar* to barter, Ital *truccare* to truck]

truck² *truk, n* a small or solid wheel; an open railway wagon for goods; a trolley; a bogie; a low flat barrow; a small two-wheeled barrow with a turned-up front; a motor vehicle of heavier construction than a car, designed for the transportation of commodities, or often a specific commodity; a lorry (*esp US*); a cap at the top of a mast or flagstaff; a jazz dance, *orig* and *esp* of the 1930s, using a rhythmic strutting walk (*US slang*). — *vi* to drive a truck (chiefly *US*); to dance the truck (see noun above) (*US slang*); to walk in an affectedly lounging style with loping strides, the body laid back from the hips (*US slang*). — *vt* to convey by truck; to put on a truck. — *n* **truck'age** carriage by truck; charge for carriage by truck; supply of trucks. — *n* **truck'er** or **truck'man** (chiefly *US*) a lorry driver.

— *n* **truck'ie** (*Austr* and *NZ colloq*) a lorry driver. — *n* **truck'ing**. — **truck'-load**. [L *trochus* a wheel, from Gr *trochos*, from *trechein* to run]

truckle *truk'l*, *n* a pulley-wheel; a castor (*obs*); a truckle-bed; a barrel-shaped cheese (*dialect*). — *vt* to move on rollers. — *vi* to sleep in a truckle-bed; to behave with servility (*usu* with *to*). — *n* **truck'ler**. — *n* and *adj* **truck'ling**. — **truck'le-bed** a low bed that may be wheeled under another. [Gr *trochileiā*, *-iā*, etc a pulley, from *trochos* a wheel]

truculent *truk'-*, *trōōk'ū-lənt*, *adj* very fierce (*archaic*); cruel (*archaic*); aggressive and discourteous. — *n* **truc'ulence** or **truc'ulency**. — *adv* **truc'ulently**. [L *truculentus*, from *trux* wild, fierce]

trudge *truj*, *vi* to walk with labour or effort; to plod doggedly. — *vt* to plod wearily or doggedly along, over, etc. — *n* a heavy or weary walk; a trudger. — *n* **trudg'er**. — *n* and *adj* **trudg'ing**. [Origin obscure]

trudgen (incorrectly **trudgeon**) *truj'ən*, *n* a swimming stroke in which each hand alternately is raised above the surface, thrust forward, and pulled back through the water. — Also *adj*. [John *Trudgen*, who popularized the stroke in Britain]

true *trōō*, *adj* faithful; constant; trusty; genuine; properly so called; typical; conformable; accurately adjusted or in tune; straight or flat; agreeing with fact; actual; absolute; corrected; accurate; exact; right; rightful; honest; sincere; truthful. — *adv* truly; faithfully; honestly; in accurate adjustment; dead in tune; after the ancestral type. — *vt* to adjust accurately. — *n* that which is true, truth; accurate adjustment. — *n* **true'ness**. — *adv* **tru'ly**. — **true bill** (*law*; *NAm* or *hist*) a bill of indictment endorsed, after investigation, by a grand jury, as containing a case for the court. — *n* **true blue** and *adj* **true-blue'** see under **blue**[1]. — *adj* **true'-born** of genuine birth; pure-bred; true to the qualities of the breed; legitimate. — *adj* **true'-bred** pure-bred; typical; of good breeding. — *adj* **true'-devot'ed** (*Shakesp*) full of honest zeal. — *adj* **true'-dispos'ing** (*Shakesp*) just. — *adj* **true-heart'ed** sincere; faithful. — **true-heart'edness**; **true'-love** someone truly or really beloved; a sweetheart; a faithful lover; a true-love knot; a quatrefoil; a four-leaved clover (also **true'-love grass**; *obs*); herb-Paris. — Also *adj*. — **true'-love knot** or **true'-lov'er's knot** an ornamental or symbolic knot or interlaced design, as a two-looped bow or a knot with two interlaced loops; **true'man** (*archaic*) an honest man; **true'penny** (*Shakesp*) an honest fellow. — *adj* **true-seem'ing** (*Spenser*) seeming (falsely or truly) to be true. — **true time** the time according to the position of the sun, as opposed to mean time. — **out of true** not straight, not properly balanced, adjusted or calibrated. [OE *trēowe*; ON *tryggr*, Ger *treu*]

truffle *truf'l*, *trōōf'l*, *n* any fungus of the genus *Tuber* or the family *Tuberaceae*; its underground edible fructification; a rich confection made with chocolate, butter, etc, *usu* shaped into balls. — *adj* **truff'led** cooked, stuffed or dressed, with truffles. — *n* **truff'ling** the action of gathering truffles. — **truff'le-dog** or **truff'le-pig** a dog or pig trained to find truffles. [OFr *truffle* (Fr *truffe*); poss from L *tūber* lump, swelling]

trug *trug*, (*dialect*) *n* a shallow wooden fruit-basket. [Prob **trough**]

truism *trōō'izm*, *n* a self-evident truth; a commonplace or trite statement. — *adj* **truist'ic**. [**true**]

trull *trul*, (*archaic*) *n* a prostitute. [Cf Ger *Trolle*]

Trullan *trul'ən*, *adj* held in the domed hall of the palace at Constantinople, applied to the Sixth Ecumenical Council (680-1) and *esp* to the Council of 692, which was not accepted by the Western Church. [LL *trullus* a dome, from L *trulla* a ladle]

truly. See under **true**.

trumeau *trōō-mō'*, *n* a piece of wall or pillar between two openings: — *pl* **trumeaux** (*-mōz'*). [Fr]

trump[1] *trump*, (*obs*) *vt* to deceive. — *n* **trump'ery** showy and worthless stuff; rubbish; ritual foolery. — Also *adj*. [Fr *tromper* to deceive]

trump[2] *trump*, (*archaic* or *poetic*) *n* a trumpet; a blast; a Jew's-harp (now *Scot*). — *vt* and *vi* to trumpet. — **trump marine** the tromba marina. [OFr *trompe*]

trump[3] *trump*, *n* a card of a suit that takes any card of any other suit; ruff, an old card-game like whist; a good, trusty person (*colloq*). — Also *adj*. — *vt* to play a trump card upon instead of following suit; to take (a trick, etc) in this way (also *fig*); of an Oxford University college, to gain (a student) by trumping. — *vi* to play trumps on another suit. — *n* **trump'ing** at Oxford University, the system whereby colleges may offer an award and a place (which must be accepted) to other colleges' gifted applicants, so ensuring a more even spread of talented students among the colleges. — **trump'-card** the card turned up to determine the trump suit; any card of that suit; an advantageous or victorious expedient. — **no'-trumps** a declaration in bridge and whist whereby no suit is more powerful than the rest. — *adj* **no'-trump**. — **no'-trump'er** a hand suitable for no-trumps; **turn up trumps** to behave in a very helpful or generous way, *esp* unexpectedly. [**triumph**]

trump[4] *trump*, *n* (*obs*) an obstruction cast in one's way. — *vt* to cast as an obstruction (*obs*); to allege (*obs*); to concoct and put forward unscrupulously (with *up*). — *adj* **trumped'-up**. [**trump**[3], affected by, or partly from, **trump**[1]]

trumpet *trum'pit*, *n* an orchestral, military and signalling wind instrument of powerful and brilliant tone, in its present form a narrow tube bent twice upon itself, with cupped mouthpiece and flaring bell, giving, by action of the lips and breath-pressure, harmonics of its fundamental, the scale filled up by use of crooks, slides, or valves; applied to other instruments more or less resembling this; a speaking-trumpet; an ear-trumpet; a trumpet-shaped object, such as a flared bell or horn, a corolla or corona; a sound of, or as if of, a trumpet; a trumpeter; an organ reed-stop of trumpet-like tone. — *vt* to sound or play on a trumpet or with trumpet-like sound; to proclaim, celebrate, summon, denounce, expel, etc by trumpet. — *vi* to sound a trumpet; to make a sound like a trumpet: — *pr p* **trum'peting**; *pa t* and *pa p* **trum'peted**. — *adj* **trum'peted** sounded on a trumpet; loudly extolled; having a trumpet; funnel-shaped. — *n* **trum'peter** a person who plays or sounds the trumpet; a person who proclaims, praises or denounces; a loud-voiced crane-like S American bird (*Psophia*); a trumpeter swan; a kind of domestic pigeon; a large Australian and New Zealand food-fish (*Latris*) or other fish that trumpets when caught. — *n* and *adj* **trum'peting**. — **trum'pet-call** a conventional phrase or passage played on the trumpet as a signal; any call to action; **trumpeter swan** a black-billed American swan (*Cygnus buccinator*), the largest of the world's swans; **trum'pet-fish** the snipe-fish or bellows-fish (*Macrorhamphosus* or *Centriscus*), a long-snouted fish related to the pipefish; a flute-mouth, a sea-fish with a tubular muzzle; **trum'pet-flower** a name for various bignoniaceous, solanaceous and other plants with large trumpet-shaped flowers; **trum'pet-major** a head-trumpeter in a regiment; **trumpet marine** the tromba marina. — *adj* **trum'pet-shaped** like the bell of a trumpet. — **trum'pet-shell** a shell of the genus *Triton*; **trum'pet-tone** the sound of a trumpet; a loud voice. — *adj* **trum'pet-tongued** (*Shakesp*) proclaiming loud as a trumpet. — **trum'pet-tree** or **trum'pet-wood** a S American *Cecropia* whose hollow branches the Indians use as trumpets. — **blow one's own trumpet** to sound one's own praises; **feast of trumpets** a Jewish feast held at the beginning of Tisri in which trumpets played an important part. [Fr *trompette*, dimin of *trompe* trump]

truncal. See under **trunk**.

truncate *trungk-āt'*, *vt* to cut short; to lop; to delete those digits of a number which are not considered to be significant (*math*); to maim; to replace (an edge or corner where similar faces meet) by a symmetrically placed face (*crystal geom*). — *adj* **trunc'ate** or **trunc'ated**

appearing as if squared off at the tip; ending in a transverse line or plane, *esp* one parallel to the base. — *adv* **trunc'ately**. — *n* **truncā'tion**. — **truncation error** (*math*) one caused by operating with a truncated number or numbers. [L *truncāre*, *-ātum*, from *truncus* (cf **trunk**)]

truncheon *trun'shən*, *-chən*, *n* a broken or cut piece; a length for grafting or planting; a broken spear; a spear-shaft; a short staff; a cudgel (*archaic*); a cudgel or baton carried by a police officer; a staff of authority. — *vt* to carve (an eel); to beat with a truncheon. — *adj* **trun'cheoned** provided with a truncheon; armed with a lance. — *n* **trun'cheoner** (*Shakesp*) a person armed with a truncheon. [OFr *tronchon* (Fr *tronçon*), from *tronc*; see **trunk**]

trundle *trun'dl*, *n* a little wheel, castor; a roller; a hoop; a truck (*obs*); a trundle-bed; a spool of golden thread (*heraldry*). — *vt* and *vi* to wheel, *esp* heavily or clumsily; to roll; to twirl; to spin (*archaic*); to bowl along. — *n* **trun'dler**. — **trun'dle-bed** a truckle-bed; **trun'dle-tail**, **tren'dle-tail** or **trin'dle-tail** a curly-tailed dog. [OE *trendel*]

trunk *trungk*, *n* the stem of a tree; the body of an animal apart from head and limbs; the body generally; a main line of road, railway, telephone, etc; a junction circuit between telephone exchanges (*US*); the main body of anything; the shaft of a column; the body of a pedestal; a chest or box, *esp* for travelling; a box for fish; a boxlike channel, trough, shaft, conduit or chute; a tube; a speaking-tube; a telescope (*obs*); a pea-shooter (*obs*); a large hollow piston; a proboscis; same as **bus** (*comput*); (in *pl*) the game of trou-madame; (in *pl*) trunk-hose, also breeches, *esp* those worn on the stage over tights, or pants worn for sports, swimming, etc; the luggage compartment of an automobile, the boot (*NAm*). — *adj* **trunc'al** relating to the trunk; principal. — *adj* **trunked** having a trunk; truncated, beheaded (*Spenser*); relating to radio trunking. — *n* **trunk'ful** as much as will fill a trunk: — *pl* **trunk'fuls**. — *n* **trunk'ing** casing; a system of sharing a number of radio channels among a number of users of mobile (eg car) radio communication systems, the users being able to use any channel which is free at any given time. — **trunk'-call** the former name for a long-distance telephone call, involving connection between two centres, a **national call**; **trunk dialling** the dialling of trunk telephone calls directly, connections not being made by an operator; **trunk'fish** the coffer-fish; **trunk'-hose** or **trunk'-breech'es** full breeches reaching from waist to mid-thigh, worn in the 16c and early 17c; **trunk'-line** the main line of a railway, canal, gas or oil pipeline, etc; **trunk'-mail** (*obs*) a travelling trunk; **trunk'-maker** a maker of travelling trunks; **trunk'-road** a main road, *esp* one administered by central authority; **trunk'sleeve** (*Shakesp*) a puffed sleeve; **trunk'-work** (*Shakesp*) clandestine visiting in a trunk. [Fr *tronc* and L *truncus* a stock, a torso, from *truncus* maimed; with associations of Fr *trompe* a trump, a proboscis]

trunnion *trun'yən*, *n* either of a pair of side projections on which anything (eg formerly a big gun) is pivoted to move in a vertical plane; a stick, club (*Scott*). — *adj* **trunn'ioned** provided with trunnions. [Fr *trognon* stump]

truquage and **truqueur**. See **trucage**.

truss *trus*, *n* a bundle, *esp* of hay or straw, or a block cut from a stack (*esp* 56 lb of old hay, 60 lb of new, 36 lb of straw); a framed structure for supporting a weight; an attachment for holding a yard to the mast; a tuft of flowers or fruit at the top of the main stalk or stem; a corbel (*archit*); a surgical appliance for retaining a reduced hernia; a close-fitting coat or (in *pl*) breeches (*hist*). — *vt* to bundle up; to muffle up; to tuck up; to lace up, tie the points of (*hist*); to string up, hang (*obs*); to fix for cooking, as with a skewer; to catch in the talons, *esp* in the air, and carry off (*falconry*); to provide with a truss. — *vi* to pack up; to make off. — *adj* **trussed**. — *n* **truss'er**. — *n* **truss'ing**. — **truss'-beam** a wooden beam strengthened by a steel tie-rod; a steel framework acting as a beam. [Fr *trousse* (noun), *trousser* (verb)]

trust *trust*, *n* worthiness of being relied on; fidelity; confidence in the truth of anything; confident expectation; a resting on the integrity, friendship, etc of another; faith; hope; credit (*esp* sale on credit or on promise to pay); ground of confidence; that which is given or received in confidence; charge; responsibility; anything felt to impose moral obligations; an arrangement by which property is handed to or vested in a person, to use and dispose of it for the benefit of another; an estate so managed for another; an arrangement for the control of several companies under one direction, to cheapen expenses, regulate production, beat down competition, and so obtain a maximum return. — *adj* held in trust. — *vt* to place trust in; to believe; to expect confidently; to hope; to give credit to; to commit to trust. — *vi* to have trust; to rely (with *to*). — *n* **trustee'** a person to whom anything is entrusted; someone to whom the management of a property is committed in trust for the benefit of others. — *n* **trustee'ship** the state of being or action of a trustee; a trust territory. — *n* **trust'er**. — *adj* **trust'ful** trusting. — *adv* **trust'fully**. — *n* **trust'fulness**. — *adv* **trust'ily**. — *n* **trust'iness**. — *adj* **trust'ing** confiding. — *adv* **trust'ingly**. — *adj* **trust'less** not to be trusted, untrustworthy; distrustful. — *n* **trust'lessness**. — *adv* **trust'worthily**. — *n* **trust'worthiness**. — *adj* **trust'worthy** worthy of trust or confidence; trusty. — *adj* **trust'y** to be trusted; deserving confidence; faithful; honest; strong; firm; involving trust (*Shakesp*): — *compar* **trust'ier**, *superl* **trust'iest**. — *n* a person who can be trusted; a well-behaved prisoner, often granted special privileges; a greatcoat (*Ir*). — **trust** or **trustee account** a savings account administered by a trustee, the balance of which can be left to a beneficiary; **trust'buster** (*US* and *colloq*) a person who works for or achieves the break-up of business trusts, eg by legislation; **trust company** or **corporation** a commercial enterprise formed to act as a trustee; **trust deed** a deed conveying property to a trustee; **trust estate** an estate held by trustees; **trust fund** a fund of money, etc, held in trust; **trust'-house** a hotel or tavern owned by a trust company, not privately or by liquor manufacturers; **trust** or **trustee stock** that in which a trustee may legally invest trust funds without being personally liable if it should depreciate in value; **trust territory** a territory ruled by an administering country under supervision of the Trusteeship Council of the United Nations (also **trusteeship**). — **active** or **special trust** a trust in which the trustee's power of management depends upon his or her having the right of actual possession; **breach of trust** a violation of duty by a trustee, etc; **in trust** as a charge, for safe-keeping, for management as a trustee; **investment trust** an organization which invests its stockholders' money and distributes the net return among them; **Public Trustee** a government officer (and his or her department) empowered to act for the state as trustee, executor, etc; **on trust** on credit; (accepted) without question; **split investment trust** a trust (which must be wound up at a specified date) offering two classes of shares, income and capital, the former earning dividend but to be repaid at par, the latter without dividend but increasing in capital value; **trustee in bankruptcy** a person, *usu* an accountant, appointed (by the court) to administer the affairs of a bankrupt and to realize assets for the benefit of creditors; **trustee savings bank** a savings bank statutorily controlled under trustees and having its general fund guaranteed by the state; **unit trust** a type of investment trust in which given amounts of different securities form a unit, choice of a number of differently constituted units being available. [ON *traust* trust; Ger *Trost* consolation]

truth *trōōth*, *n* faithfulness; constancy; veracity; agreement with reality; fact of being true; actuality;

accuracy of adjustment or conformity; (in the fine arts) a faithful adherence to nature; that which is true or according to the facts of the case; the true state of things, the facts; a true statement; an established fact; true belief; known facts, knowledge. — *adj* **truth'ful** habitually or actually telling what one believes to be true; put forward in good faith as what one believes to be true; conveying the truth. — *adv* **truth'fully**. — *n* **truth'fulness**. — *adj* **truth'less**. — *n* **truth'lessness**. — *adj* **truth'like**. — *adj* **truth'y** (*rare*) true; truthful. — **truth drug** or **truth serum** any of various drugs, such as scopolamine or thiopentone sodium, which make subjects under questioning less wary in their replies; **truth'-teller**. — *adj* **truth'-telling**. — **truth table** a Boolean logic table in which the binary digits 0 and 1 are assigned values either 'true' or 'false'; **truth'-value** (*logic*) the truth or falsity of a statement. — **God's truth** a thing or statement absolutely true; **in truth** truly, in fact; **moment of truth** see under **moment**; **of a truth** (*Bible*) truly; **tell the truth** to speak truthfully, not to lie. [OE *trēowth*, from *trēowe*, *trīewe* true]

try *trī*, *vt* to separate out (*obs*); to sift (*obs*); to render; to extract (*obs*); to refine (*obs*); to purify (*obs*); to test; to prove by testing (*Shakesp*); to use, treat or resort to experimentally; to put to the test; to strain; to annoy, irritate, afflict; to experience, undergo (*Milton*); to examine critically; (of a judge) to examine and decide the truth, justice, guilt or innocence; (of a lawyer) to conduct in court (*US*); to attempt, endeavour, essay (*usu* with *to*). — *vi* to make an effort; (*Spenser* **trie**) to turn out, prove; to lie to, keep one's head to the wind (*naut*; *Shakesp*): — *3rd pers pr t* **tries**; *pr p* **try'ing**; *pa t* and *pa p* **tried** (*trīd*). — *n* a trial; effort; in Rugby football, the score of three points (Rugby League) or five points (Rugby Union) gained by a player who succeeds in placing the ball with his hand over the opposition's goal line; in American football, an attempt to gain further points after scoring a touchdown. — *adj* (*Spenser* **trye**) choice, purified. — *adj* **trī'able** subject to legal trial; that can be tried. — *n* **trī'age** sorting out; in war, etc, the selection for treatment of those casualties most likely to survive; allocation of resources to where they will have the most effect, rather than to where the need is most urgent or severe; broken coffee-beans. — *n* **trī'al** see separate entry. — *adj* **tried** (*trīd*) proved good by test. — *n* **trī'er** a person who tries in any sense; a test; (formerly also **trī'or**) someone appointed to decide on a challenge to a juror, or a peer who is a juror in the trial of a peer; (also **try'er** (*cricket*) someone who is assiduous in trying to win. — *n* **try'ing**. — *adj* making trial or proof; adapted to try; searching, severe; testing; distressing; causing strain. — *adv* **try'ingly**. — **try'-house** a place in which oil is extracted from blubber, etc; **try'-on** an act of trying on a garment; an attempt at imposition by audacity (*slang*); **try'-out** a test performance; **trysail** (*trī'sl*) a reduced sail used by small craft, instead of the mainsail, in a storm; a small fore-and-aft sail set with a boom and gaff; **try'-square** a tool used in carpentry to check right angles. — **try and** (*colloq*) try to; **try back** to revert, hark back; **try for** make an attempt to reach or gain; **try it on** (*colloq*) to attempt to do something risky or audacious to see how far one can go unscathed; **try on** to put on (a garment, etc) for trial; **try out** to test (see also **try-out** above). [OFr *trier* to pick out]

Trygon *trī'gon*, *n* the sting-ray genus. [Gr *trȳgōn* a sting-ray]

tryp *trip*, *n* short form of **trypanosome**.

trypaflavine *trip-ə-flā'vēn*, *n* acriflavine.

trypanosome *trip'ən-ə-sōm*, *n* a flagellate protozoon (genus **Trypanosō'ma** of various species, family **Trypanosomat'idae**) parasitic in the blood of vertebrates. — *adj* **trypanocidal** (*-sī'dl*). — *n* **tryp'anocide** (*-sīd*; L *caedere* to kill) a drug that kills trypanosomes. — *n* **trypanosomiasis** (*-sō-mī'ə-sis*) disease caused by a trypanosome, *esp* sleeping sickness. [Gr *trȳpanon* a borer, from *trȳpaein* to bore, and *sōma* body]

trypsin *trip'sin*, (*biol*) *n* an enzyme secreted by the pancreas. — *adj* **tryp'tic**. — *n* **tryptophan** (*trip'tō-fan* or **triptophane** (*-fān*) an essential amino-acid obtained eg by the cleavage of casein by pancreatic enzymes. [Gr *trīpsis* rubbing (as first got by rubbing down the pancreas with glycerine), or *trȳein* to wear out, modelled on **pepsin**]

trysail. See under **try**.

tryst *trīst*, (*archaic*; formerly chiefly *Scot*) *n* an appointment to meet; appointed place of meeting; a cattle-fair. — *vt* to make an appointment with. — *vi* to agree to meet. — *n* **tryst'er**. — **tryst'ing-day**; **tryst'ing-place**, **tryst'ing-stile**, **tryst'ing-tree**. — **bide tryst** to wait for a person at the appointed place and time. [OFr *triste* a hunter's station]

Tsabian. See **Sabian**.

tsaddik and **tsaddiq**. See **zaddik**.

tsamba *tsam'bə*, *n* a Tibetan barley dish. [Tibetan]

tsar or **czar**, also (*rare*) **tzar**, *zär*, *tsär*, (*hist*) *n* the title of the emperors of Russia and of the kings of Bulgaria; a great potentate or despot. — *n* **tsar'dom** or **czar'dom**. — *n* **tsar'evich** or **tsar'evitch**, **czar'evich** or **czar'evitch** (Russ *tsär-ye'vēch*) a son of a tsar. — *n* **tsarev'na** or **czarev'na** a daughter of a tsar; a wife of a tsarevitch; **tsarina** or **czarina** (*-ē'nə*; not a Russian form), **tsarit'za** or **czarit'sa** a Russian empress; **tsar'ism** or **czar'ism** the government of the Russian tsars; absolutism. — *n* **tsar'ist** or **czar'ist** an upholder of tsarism (also *adj*). — *n* **tsesar'evich**, **tsesar'evitch**, **cesar'evich**, **cesar'evitch**, **tsesar'ewich**, etc or **tsesar'ewitch**, etc (Russ *-ye'vēch*) the eldest son of a tsar; heir to the tsardom. — *n* **tsesarev'na** or **cesarev'na** the wife of a tsar's eldest son. [Russ *tsar'*, etc, from L *Caesar*, Caesar]

TSB *abbrev*: Trustee Savings Bank.

TSE *abbrev*: transmissible spongiform encephalopathy.

tsessebe *tses'ə-bi*, (*SAfr*) *n* the sassaby. [Tswana *tsêsêbe*]

tsetse or **tzetse** *tset'si*, *n* *Glossina morsitans*, or other species of the African genus *Glossina*, small flies that transmit trypanosome parasites and cause sleeping sickness, nagana (**tsetse-fly disease**). — Also **tsetse fly** or **tzetse fly**. [Tswana]

Tshi *chē* or *chwē*, *n*. Same as **Twi**.

T-shirt. See under **tee**[1].

tsigane. See **tzigany**.

TSO *abbrev*: town sub-office.

tsotsi *tsot'si*, *n* (*SAfr*) a member of a Black African street gang, a young hooligan or thug. — **tsotsi suit** a zoot suit. [Origin uncertain; perh from Nguni *ukutsotsa* to wear exaggerated dress]

tsouris. See **tsuris**.

TSP *abbrev*: textured soya protein.

tsp *abbrev*: teaspoonful (*pl* **tsps**).

TSRB *abbrev*: Top Salaries Review Body.

TSS *abbrev*: toxic shock syndrome.

tsuba *tsōō'bə*, *n* a metal plate at the top of a Japanese scabbard, serving as a sword-guard, often highly ornamental. [Jap]

Tsuga *tsōō'gə*, *n* the hemlock spruce genus. [Jap *tsuga* larch]

tsunami *tsōō-nä'mē*, *n* a very swiftly travelling sea wave that attains great height, caused by an undersea earthquake or similar disturbance. [Jap *tsu* harbour, and *nami* wave]

tsuris or **tsouris** *tsōō'ris*, (*Yiddish*) *n* grief, trouble, woe. [Yiddish *tsures*, *tsores*, pl of *tsure*, *tsore* trouble, from Heb]

tsutsugamushi disease *tsōō-tsōō-gə-mōō'shi diz-ēz'*, *n* any of various rickettsial diseases, *incl* scrub typhus. [Jap *tsutsuga* illness, and *mushi* insect]

tsutsumu *tsōō-tsōō'mōō*, *n* the Japanese art of wrapping articles in a harmonious way. [Jap, to wrap]

Tswana *tswä'nə* or *swä'nə*, *n* a Negroid people of southern Africa; a member of this people; their language, of the Bantu family: — *pl* **Tswan'a** or **Tswan'as**. — Also *adj*.

TT *abbrev*: teetotal; Tourist Trophy; Trinidad and Tobago (IVR); tuberculin tested.

Tu. or **Tues.** *abbrev*: Tuesday.

tuan[1] *to͞o-än'*, *n* sir; lord, master; a title of respect in the Malay Archipelago and Indonesia. [Malay]

tuan[2] *to͞o'ən*, *n* the brush-tailed phascogale or wambenger, an Australian arboreal marsupial (*Phascogale tapoatafa*). [Aboriginal native name]

Tuanku *to͞o-äng'ko͞o*, (*Malay*) *n* majesty, highness (as a title or form of address).

Tuareg *twä'reg*, *n* a nomadic Berber of the Sahara; the language of the Tuaregs. [Ar *tawāriq*]

tuart, **tooart** *to͞o'ərt* or **tewart** *tū'*, *n* a strong-timbered eucalyptus (*Eucalyptus gomphocephala*). [Australian Aboriginal]

tuatara *to͞o-a-tä'rə*, *n* a New Zealand lizard-like reptile (genus *Sphenodon* or *Hatteria*), the sole survivor of the class *Rhynchocephalia*. [Maori, spine on the back]

tuath *to͞o'ə*, (*Ir hist*) *n* a people; an ancient territorial division. [Ir *tūath*]

tub *tub*, *n* an open container, *orig* of wooden staves and hoops, later also of metal, plastic, etc; a small cask or carton for food, etc, *usu* plastic or cardboard; anything like a tub; a tubful; a pulpit (*facetious*); a clumsy ship or boat; a bath, bathtub (*esp NAm*); a pit-shaft casing; a bucket, box or vehicle for bringing up coal from the mine; a tubfish. — *vt* to set, bathe or treat in a tub; to line with a tub. — *vi* to take a bath. — *n* **tubb'er**. — *n* **tubb'iness**. — *n* **tubb'ing** the art of, or material for, making tubs; mine-shaft lining; rowing in clumsy boats; the taking of baths. — *adj* **tubb'ish** round and fat. — *n* **tubb'y** sounding like an empty tub; dull in sound; plump, round like a tub. — *n* **tub'ful** as much as a tub will hold: — *pl* **tub'fuls**. — **tub'fast** (*Shakesp*) treatment of venereal disease by fasting and sweating in a hot tub; **tub'fish** the sapphirine (or other) gurnard. — *vi* **tub'-thump**. — **tub'-thump'er** a declamatory or ranting preacher or public speaker. — *n* **tub'-thumping**. [Cf LGer *tubbe*]

tuba *tū'bə*, *to͞o'bə*, *n* a straight trumpet (*Rom antiq*); the bombardon (**bass tuba**) or (sometimes) other low-pitched brass instrument of the saxhorn class; a person who plays this instrument; a powerful organ reed-stop; a tube (*anatom*): — *pl* **tu'bas** or (*L*) **tu'bae** (*-bē*, *-bī*). [L and Ital *tuba*]

tube *tūb*, *n* a pipe; any long hollow body; a telescope or other optical instrument (also **optic tube**; *archaic*); a collapsible cylinder from which material in the form of paste or viscous liquid can be squeezed out; a thermionic valve; an underground railway running through tube-shaped tunnels, *specif* (with *cap*) the London Underground (*colloq*); the united part of calyx, corolla, etc (*bot*); any vessel in a plant or animal body; an aircraft (*slang*); a television set (*slang*); a can or bottle of beer (*Austr slang*). — *vt* to provide with, fit with or enclose in a tube; to insert a tube in the neck of (a horse) to help breathing. — *vi* to travel by tube. — *n* **tub'age** insertion of a tube. — *adj* **tub'al**, **tub'ar** or **tub'ate** tubular. — *n* **tubec'tomy** (*med*) surgical cutting or removal of the Fallopian tubes. — *adj* **tubed** (*tūbd*). — *n* **tube'ful**: — *pl* **tube'fuls**. — *adj* **tube'less**. — *adj* **tube'like**. — *n* **tub'er** a participant in the sport of tubing (see below). — *adj* **tubic'olar**, **tub'icole** (also *n*), or **tubic'olous** inhabiting a tube. — *adj* **tubiflo'rous** having tubular flowers. — *adj* **tub'iform** shaped like a tube. — *n* **tub'ing** the act of making or supplying tubes; the sport of floating in a river in an inflated inner tube, often for fishing; tubes collectively; material for tubes. — *n* **tub'oplasty** (*med*) surgical repair of a Fallopian tube. — *adj* **tub'ūlar** having the form of a tube; made of or with tubes; having a sound like that made by the passage of air through a tube. — *n* **Tubūlā'ria** a genus of *Hydrozoa*. — *adj* and *n* **tubūlā'rian**. — *n* **tubūlar'ity**. — *vt* **tub'ūlate** to form into a tube; to provide with a tube. — *adj* tubular. — *adj* **tub'ūlated**. — *n* **tubūlā'tion**. — *n* **tub'ūlature**. — *n* **tub'ūle** a small tube. — *n pl* **Tubūliflo'rae** a section of the *Compositae* with tubular disc-flowers. — *adj* **tubūliflo'ral** or **tubūliflo'rous**. — *n* **tub'ulin** (*biol*) a globular protein which forms the basic unit for the contraction of microtubules. — *adj* **tub'ūlous** tubular. — **tubal ligation** the placing of a clip or ligature round a loop in each of the Fallopian tubes as a means of sterilization; **tube foot** in echinoderms, a tube protruding through a pore, used in locomotion and respiration; **tubeless tyre** or **tire** see under **tyre**; **tube'nose** any seabird of the order *Tubinares*, characterized by having extended tubular nostrils (also called **petrel**); **tube skirt** a close-fitting, straight skirt; **tube'well** a pipe used to obtain water from beneath the ground, with perforations just above its sharp point; **tube worm** a worm that makes a tube to dwell in; **tubular bells** an orchestral musical instrument in the percussion section, consisting of a number of metal tubes suspended in a frame, giving the sound of bells when struck. — **to go down the tubes** (*slang*) to fail dismally, to be ruined. [Fr, from L *tubus* a pipe; also (as in *Fallopian* and *Eustachian tubes*) from L *tuba* a trumpet (see **tuba**)]

tuber[1] *tū'bər*, *n* a lump; a rounded swelling (*pathol*); a knob; a protuberance; a swelling, *usu* underground, in a plant, where reserves are stored up, formed either in the stem (as in the potato, Jerusalem artichoke, etc), or sometimes in the root (as in the dahlia); (with *cap*) the truffle genus of fungi, giving its name to the **Tuberā'ceae**, saprophytic Ascomycetes, many with edible underground fructifications (truffles). — *adj* **tuberā'ceous**. — *adj* **tuberif'erous**. — *adj* **tu'beriform**. — *adj* **tuberose** (*tū'bə-rōs*, *-rōz*) tuberous. — *n* (*tū'bə-rōs*, *-rōz*; often, by false association with tube and **rose**, *tūb'rōz*) a Mexican amaryllid (*Polianthes tuberosa*) grown for its fragrant creamy-white flowers, propagated by tubers. — *n* **tuberosity** (*-ros'i-ti*). — *adj* **tub'erous** having tubers; of the nature of, or like, a tuber; knobbed. — **tuberous root** a fleshy root resembling a tuber but not having buds or eyes. [L *tūber* a swelling, from root of L *tumēre* to swell]

tuber[2]. See under **tube**.

tubercle *tū'bər-kl*, *n* a small tuber, protuberance or swelling; a nodule; a nodule or morbid growth in the lung or elsewhere, in cases of tuberculosis (*pathol*). — *adj* **tu'bercled** having tubercles. — *adj* **tubercular** (*-bûr'*) nodular; having tubercles; affected by or suffering from tuberculosis. — *adj* **tuber'culate** or **tuber'culated** having or covered with tubercles. — *n* **tuberculā'tion**. — *n* **tu'bercule** a tubercle. — *n* **tuber'culin** a preparation from a culture of tubercle bacillus used for testing for tuberculosis. — *n* **tuberculīzā'tion** or **-s-**. — *vt* **tuber'culize** or **-ise** to infect with tuberculosis. — *n* **tuberculo'ma** a slow-growing, circumscribed tuberculous lesion. — *adj* **tuber'culose** or **tuber'culosed** tuberculous; tuberculated. — *n* **tuberculō'sis** consumption or phthisis, a disease caused by the **tubercle bacillus** (*Bacillus tuberculosis*), characterized by development of tubercles. — *adj* **tuber'culous** of or affected by tuberculosis; tuberculated (now *rare*). — *n* **tuber'culum** a tubercle. — *adj* **tuber'culin-tested** applied to milk from cows that have been tested for and certified free from tuberculous infection. [L *tūberculum*, dimin of *tūber*]

tuberose. See under **tuber**.

tubfast. See under **tub**.

tubicolar. See under **tube**.

tubifex *tū'bi-feks*, *n* an oligochaete worm of the genus *Tubifex*, *usu* living in riverbeds or lake-beds. [New L]

tubiform, **tubing**, **tubular**, etc. See under **tube**.

Tubigrip® *tū'bi-grip*, *n* a tubular elastic bandage for use on an ankle, knee, etc.

TUC *abbrev*: Trades Union Congress.

tuchun *to͞o-chün'*, *do͞o-jün'*, *n* a Chinese military governor. [Chin]

tuck[1] *tuk*, (*Shakesp*) *n* a rapier. [Fr *estoc*, from Ger *Stock* stick]

tuck[2] *tuk*, *Scot* **touk** *to͝ok*, (*dialect*) *n* a stroke, tap or beat, *esp* of a drum. — Also *vi* and *vt*. [ONFr *toker*, *toquer* (Fr *toucher*) to touch]

tuck[3] *tuk*, *vt* to draw or thrust in or together; to stuff, cram; to fold under; to gather or gird up (often with *up*); to contract (with *up*); to enclose by pressing clothes closely around or under; to put tucks in; to put or stow away; to full, dress, or put on tenters; to hamper; to eat (with *in*; *slang*); to hang (with *up*; *slang*). — *vi* to make an onslaught upon food (*usu* with *in* or *into*). — *n* an act of tucking; a pleat or fold, now one stitched down; the gathering of the bottom planks of a ship at the stern (*naut*); eatables, *esp* delicacies (*slang*). — *n* **tuck'er** someone who or something that tucks; a piece of cloth tucked or drawn over the bosom; a fuller; food (*Austr* and *NZ slang*). — *vt* (*US slang*) to tire exceedingly (often with *out*). — **tuck box** a box of or for tuck, at a boarding school; **tuck'erbag, tuck'erbox** (*Austr*) a bag or box, for carrying food in; **tuck'-in** (*slang*) a hearty feed. — *adj* contrived for tucking in an edge. — **tuck'-mill** or **tuck'ing-mill** a fulling-mill; **tuck'-out** (*slang*) a tuck-in; **tuck shop** (*orig schoolboys'*, etc *slang*) a confectioner's or a pastrycook's shop; now *esp* such a shop or anything similar on school premises. [OE *tūcian* to disturb, afflict; cf Ger *zucken* to twitch]

tuckahoe *tuk'ə-hō*, *n* an edible but tasteless underground fungus of the southern US; the edible rootstock of several American aroids; an inhabitant of eastern Virginia. [From Algonquian]

tucket *tuk'it*, (*archaic*) *n* a flourish on a trumpet. [Cf **tuck**[2] and Ital *toccata* a touch]

tucutuco *tōō-kŏŏ-tōō'kō* or **tucotuco** *tōō-kō-tōō'kō*, *n* a S American rodent of mole-like habits (genus *Ctenomys*): — *pl* **tucutu'cos** or **tucotu'cos**. [Imit, from its cry]

Tudor *tū'dər*, *adj* pertaining to the Welsh family of *Tudor*, the time when it held the English throne (1485–1603), or the style of architecture (Late Perpendicular) that prevailed then. — *adj* **Tudorbē'than** in imitation of Tudor or Elizabethan style. — *adj* **Tudoresque'**. — **Tudor flower** a trefoil ornament frequent in Tudor architecture; **Tudor rose** a red and white rose (combining those of Lancaster and York) adopted as a badge by Henry VII.

Tuesday *tūz'di*, *n* the third day of the week, the day following Monday. — *abbrev* **Tues** or **Tu**. [OE *Tīwes dæg* the day of *Tīw* (the God of war), translating L *diēs Martis* Mars's day; but etymologically, *Tīw*, ON *Tȳr*, corresponds to L *Jūpiter* (for *Djew pater*), Gr *Zeus*]

tufa *tōō'fə*, *tū'fə*, *n* calc-sinter (often *calcareous tufa*); tuff or other porous rock (*obs*). — *adj* **tufā'ceous**. [Ital *tufa*, a variant of *tufo*, from L *tōfus* a soft stone]

tuff *tuf*, *tōōf*, *n* a rock composed of fine volcanic fragments and dust; tufa or other porous rock (*obs*). — *adj* **tuffā'ceous**. [Fr *tuf*, *tuffe*, from Ital *tufo*; see **tufa**]

tuffe *tuf*, *n* (*Shakesp*). Same as **tuft**. — *n* **tuff'et** a tuft; a tussock; a mound.

tuft *tuft*, *n* a bunched cluster; a clump; a crest; a separate lock of hair; any of the cut or uncut loops of wool, etc forming the pile of a carpet or rug; a goatee or imperial beard; a small tassel; a gold tassel formerly worn on a nobleman's cap in the English universities; hence, a titled undergraduate; a person of social consequence. — *vt* to separate into tufts; to make or decorate with tufts; to beat (the ground) in deer-hunting; to dislodge (game). — *adj* **tuft'ed** having or made of tufts; having many short crowded branches all arising at or near the same level (*bot*); (of birds) with a tuft or crest of feathers on the head. — *n* **tuft'er** a hound that drives deer out of cover. — *n* **tuft'ing**. — *adj* **tuft'y**. — **tuft'-hunter** a toady; **tuft'-hunting**. [Supposed to be from OFr *tuffe* (Fr *touffe*), from L *tūfa* crest, from Gmc (cf OLGer *top* top); but there are difficulties]

tuftaffety *tuf-taf'ə-ti* or **tuftaffeta** *-tə*, (*archaic*) *n* a taffeta with tufted pile. — *adj* of or wearing tuftaffety; richly dressed. — Also (*obs*) **tufftaffety** or **tufftaffeta**.

tug *tug*, *vt* to pull forcibly; to haul; to tow; to drag. — *vi* to pull forcibly; to strive; to toil: — *pr p* **tugg'ing**; *pa t* and *pa p* **tugged**. — *n* a forcible or jerking pull; a hard struggle; a rope or chain for pulling; a name for various parts of harness, such as a trace or a loop to receive a shaft; a tug-boat; an aeroplane towing a glider. — *n* **tugg'er** a person who tugs. — *n* and *adj* **tugg'ing**. — *adv* **tugg'ingly**. — **tug'boat** a towing vessel; **tug-of-love'** a dispute over the guardianship of a child, eg between divorced parents, or natural and foster parents (also *adj*); **tug-of-war'** a laborious contest; a contest in which opposing teams tug at a rope and strive to pull one another over a line. [ME *toggen*, intensive, from root of OE *tēon*; cf **tow**[1]]

tugra or **tughra** *tōō'grə*, (*hist*) *n* the ornamental monogram of the Turkish Sultan, used on coins and documents, etc. [Turk *tura*, *tuğra*]

tugrik or **tughrik** *tōō'grēk*, *n* the standard unit of currency of Mongolia, 100 mongos. [Mongolian]

tui *tōō'ē*, *n* a New Zealand honey-guide, *Prosthemadera novaeseelandiae*, with glossy blue-black plumage with tufts of white at the neck, the parson-bird. [Maori]

tuille *twēl*, *n* in plate armour, a steel plate hanging below the tasses. — *n* **tuillette'** (*dimin*). [Fr, from L *tēgula* a tile]

tuilyie or **tuilzie** *tül'i*, *tül'yi*, (*Scot*; *obs*) *n* a fight, brawl, tussle. — *vi* to struggle. [OFr *tooil* (noun), *toillier* (verb)]

tuism *tū'izm*, *n* apostrophe; reference to, or regard to the interests of, a second person. [L *tū* thou]

tuition *tū-ish'ən*, *n* guardianship (*obs*); teaching, instruction. — *adj* **tui'tional** or **tui'tionary**. [L *tuitiō*, *-ōnis*, from *tuērī*, *tuitus* to watch over]

tuk tuk *tuk'tuk*, *n* in Thailand, a motorized rickshaw. [Imit of the engine sound]

tularaemia or **tularemia** *tōō-lə-rē'mi-ə*, *n* a disease of rodents caused by a bacterium (*Bacterium tularense* or *Pasteurella tularensis*) transmitted to humans either by insects or directly, causing fever, etc. — *adj* **tularae'mic** or **tulare'mic**. [*Tulare* county, California, where it was first discovered, and Gr *haima* blood]

tulban. See **turban**.

tulchan *tulhh'ən*, *n* a calf's skin set beside a cow to make her give milk freely. — **tulchan bishop** (*Scot hist*) a titular bishop appointed to transmit most of the revenues of a diocese to the nobles (1572). [Gaelic *tul(a)chan* a hillock]

tule *tōō'lā*, *n* a large American bulrush (genus *Scirpus*). [Sp, from Nahuatl *tollin*]

tulip *tū'lip*, *n* any plant or flower of the bulbous liliaceous genus **Tu'lipa**, with showy, *usu* solitary, flowers; a showy person. — *n* **tulipant'** (*obs*) a turban. — *n* **tulipomā'nia** a craze for tulip-growing. — *adj* **tu'lip-eared** prick-eared, as a dog. — **tu'lip-poplar** the tulip tree; **tu'lip-root** a disease affecting the stem of oats; **tulip-tree** a N American timber tree (*Liriodendron*), of the magnolia family, with tulip-like flowers; **tu'lipwood** its wood. — **African tulip tree** a tree of the genus *Spathodea*, of the Bignoniaceae. [OFr *tulipe*, *tulippe*, *tulipan*, from Turk *tulbend* turban]

tulle *tōōl*, *tūl*, *tül*, *n* a delicate thin silk network fabric. [Fr; from *Tulle*, in the department of Corrèze]

Tullian *tul'i-ən*, *adj* of or like *Tully*, ie Marcus *Tullius* Cicero; Ciceronian.

tulwar *tul'wär*, *n* an Indian sabre, *esp* the curved sabre used by the Sikhs. [Hind *talwār*]

tum. See **tummy**.

tumble *tum'bl*, *vi* to roll, wallow, toss about; to perform as a dancer or acrobat; to turn over in flight or fall; to fall headlong, floundering or revolving; to collapse, fall in a heap; to rush confusedly and hastily; to come by chance (*usu* with *on*); to comprehend (often with *to*; *slang*). — *vt* to send tumbling or headlong; to overthrow; to bundle from one place to another; to jumble; to throw about; to disorder, rumple. — *n* act of tumbling; a fall; a somersault; a tumbled condition or mass. — *n* **tum'bler** a person who tumbles; an acrobat; a large drinking-glass or tall cup, formerly one that could not stand; a tumblerful; a tumbrel; a toy weighted to rock and right itself; a pigeon that turns back-somersaults in the air; a dog that performed antics in catching rabbits (*obs*); a revolving barrel or cage; part of a lock that holds the bolt in place, till it is moved by the key; part of a firearm lock that receives the thrust of the mainspring and forces the hammer forward; a member of a gang of London ruffians in the early 18c who set women on their heads (*hist*); a tumble-drier (see below); a machine consisting of a revolving drum in which (gem)stones are polished (also **tum'bling-barrel** or **tum'bling-box**). — *n* **tum'blerful** as much as will fill a tumbler: — *pl* **tum'blerfuls**. — *n* and *adj* **tum'bling**. — **tum'ble-bug** or **tum'ble-dung** (*US*) a dung-beetle (from its activity of rolling pellets of dung); **tum'ble-car** or **tum'ble-cart** a vehicle with wheels and axle in one piece. — *adj* **tum'bledown** dilapidated, threatening to fall. — **tumble-drī'er** a machine which dries (clothes, etc) by tumbling them in a strong current of hot air (also **tum'bler-drī'er**). — *vt* **tumble-dry'** to dry (clothes, etc) in a tumble-drier. — **tum'bler-switch** a switch that is turned over to put electric current off or on; **tum'bleweed** a type of plant that snaps off above the root, curls into a ball, and rolls about in the wind; **tumbling-barrel** and **tumbling-box** see **tumbler** above. — **tumble in** or **home** (of a ship's sides) to incline inward above the extreme breadth; to fit, as a piece of timber into other work; to go to bed; **tumble over** to toss about carelessly, to upset; to fall over; **tumble up** to get out of bed; to throw into confusion; to scurry up on deck. [Frequentative from OE *tumbian*; cf Ger *tummeln*]

tumbrel *tum'brəl* or **tumbril** *tum'-bril*, *n* an old instrument of punishment, a pillory or cucking-stool (*obs*); a cart, *esp* for dung, that tips over backwards to empty its load; a two-wheeled military cart (*archaic*); the name given to the carts that conveyed victims to the guillotine during the French Revolution. [OFr *tomberel* (Fr *tombereau*), from *tomber* to fall]

tumefy *tū'mi-fī*, *vt* and *vi* to swell: — *pr p* **tu'mefying**; *pa t* and *pa p* **tu'mefied**. — *adj* **tumefacient** (*tū-mi-fā'shənt*). — *n* **tumefac'tion**. — *vi* and *vt* **tumesce'** to (cause to) swell, to tumefy; to (cause to) have an erection (*facetious*). — *n* **tumescence** (*tū-mes'əns*) a tendency to swell; a swelling. — *adj* **tumesc'ent**. — *adj* **tu'mid** swollen or enlarged; inflated; falsely sublime; bombastic. — *n* **tumid'ity**. — *adv* **tu'midly**. — *n* **tu'midness**. [L *tumefacere*, *tumescere*, *tumidus*, from *tumēre* to swell, and *facere* to make]

tummy *tum'i*, (*colloq* or *childish*) *n* a stomach. Also **tum** or **tum'-tum**. — **tumm'y-button** a navel.

tumour or (*NAm*) **tumor** *tū'mər*, *n* swelling; turgidity; a morbid swelling or enlargement, now *esp* a new growth of cells in the body without inflammation. — *n* **tumorigen'esis** (Gr *genesis* creation) the causing or production of tumours. — *adj* **tumorigen'ic** or **tumorgen'ic** causing or producing tumours. — *n* **tumorigenic'ity** or **tumorgenic'ity**. — *adj* **tu'morous**. [L *tumor*, from *tumēre* to swell]

tump[1] *tump*, (*dialect*) *n* a hillock, mound or barrow; a clump. — *vt* to make a mound around. — *adj* **tump'y** hummocky. [Origin unknown]

tump[2] *tump*, (*US*) *vt* to drag. — **tump'-line** a strap across the forehead or chest for carrying burdens or hauling. [Prob from Algonquian]

tumphy *tum'fi*, (*Scot*) *n* a blockhead; coaly fireclay.

tumshie *tum'shi*, *n* (*Scot*, often *humorous*) a turnip.

tum-tum[1]. See **tom-tom**.

tum-tum[2]. See **tummy**.

tumular, **tumulary** and **tumuli**. See **tumulus**.

tumult *tū'mult*, *-məlt*, *n* violent commotion, *usu* with uproar; a riot; a state of violent and confused emotion. — *vi* (*Milton*) to make a tumult. — *vt* (*archaic*) to put in tumult. — *adj* **tumultūary** (*-mult'*) acted or acting in tumult; haphazard; chaotic; tumultuous. — *vi* **tumult'ūate** (*archaic*) to make a tumult. — *vt* (*archaic*) to disturb with tumult; to make a tumult in. — *n* **tumultūā'tion** (*archaic*). — *adj* **tumult'ūous** full of tumult; disorderly; agitated; noisy. — *adv* **tumult'ūously**. — *n* **tumult'ūousness**. [L *tumultus*, *-ūs*, from *tumēre* to swell]

tumulus *tū'mū-ləs*, *too'moo-loos*, *n* a burial mound, a barrow: — *pl* **tu'muli** (*-lī*, *-lē*). — *adj* **tū'mūlar** or **tū'mūlary**. [L, from *tumēre* to swell]

tun *tun*, *n* a large cask; an obsolete liquid measure equivalent to 216 gallons of ale, or 252 of wine; a ton (*obs*). — *vt* to put in a tun. — *n* **tunn'age** see **tonnage**. — *n* **tunn'ing**. — *adj* **tun'bellied**. — **tun'belly** a pot-belly; **tun'-dish** (*Shakesp*) a wooden funnel. [OE *tunne*; cf **ton**[1]]

tuna[1] *too'nə*, *tū'nə*, *n* a prickly-pear (plant or fruit). [Haitian]

tuna[2] *too'nə*, *tū'nə*, *n* any large scombridoid marine fish of the genus *Thunnus*; its flesh as food: — *pl* **tu'na** or **tu'nas**. — Also **tu'na-fish**, **tunn'y** or **tunn'y-fish**. [Sp, from L *tunnus*, from Gr *thynnos*]

tuna[3] *too'nə*, *n* a New Zealand eel. [Maori]

tunable. See under **tune**.

tund *tund*, (*archaic*) *vt* and *vi* to beat, thump. [L *tundere*]

tundra *toon'-*, *tun'drə*, *n* an Arctic plain with permanently frozen subsoil, and lichens, mosses and dwarfed vegetation. [Lapp]

tundun. See **turndun**.

tune *tūn*, *n* tone; a melody or air; melodiousness; accurate adjustment in pitch or frequency; harmonious adjustment (*fig*); frame of mind, temper. — *vt* to adjust the tones of; to put in condition for producing tones in tune; to put in smooth working order; to synchronize; to adjust (a radio receiver) so as to produce the optimum response to an incoming signal; to put in accord, bring to a desired state; to begin to play or sing (*archaic*); to start the singing of (*archaic*); to utter, express or celebrate in music (*archaic*). — *vi* to give forth musical sound. — *adj* **tūn'able** or **tune'able** tuneful; in tune. — *n* **tun'ableness**. — *adv* **tun'ably**. — *adj* **tuned** (*tūnd*). — *adj* **tune'ful** full of tune; melodious; musical. — *adv* **tune'fully**. — *n* **tune'fulness**. — *adj* **tune'less** without tune; not melodious or tuneful; unmusical; without sense of tune; silent (*poetic*). — *n* **tun'er** a person who tunes instruments, engines, etc; someone who makes music, or sings; an apparatus for receiving radio signals; a knob, dial, etc by which a radio or television receiver is adjusted to different wavelengths; in organs, an adjustable flap for altering the pitch of the tone. — *n* **tun'ing**. — *adj* **tun'y** tuneful, *esp* in a superficial, obvious way. — **tuner amplifier** a piece of hi-fi equipment incorporating a radio receiver and an amplifier which can also be used with a record-player, tape deck, etc; **tune'smith** (*facetious*) a song-writer or composer of light music; **tun'ing-fork** a two-pronged instrument giving a sound of known pitch or vibration; **tun'ing-key** or **tun'ing-hammer** a key for turning wrest-pins; **tun'ing-peg** or **tun'ing-pin** a peg around which the end of a string is wound and by which it is tuned. — **call the tune** see **pay the piper** under **pipe**[1]; **change one's tune** or **sing another tune** to alter one's attitude, or way of talking; **in tune** true in pitch; in accord (*fig*); **out of tune** not true in pitch; not agreeing (*fig*); **to the tune of** to the amount of; **tune in** to adjust a wireless receiver for reception (often with *to*); **tune one's pipes** see under **pipe**[1]; **tune out** to adjust a wireless receiver so as to eliminate; to ignore; **tune up** to put instruments into tune for beginning; of engines, etc, to (be) put into smooth working order; to begin to perform, strike up. [A form of **tone**[1]]

tung-oil *tung'-oil*, *n* wood-oil obtained from seeds of the **tung'-tree** or **Chinese varnish tree** (*Aleurites fordii* or other species). [Chin *yu-t'ung* tung-oil]

tungsten *tung'stən*, *n* an element (symbol **W**, atomic no 74), a rare metal also known as wolfram, chiefly obtained from wolframite, used for making lamp filaments and tungsten steel. — *n* **tung'state** a salt of **tung'stic acid** (H_2WO_4). — **tungsten-halogen lamp** a compact high-intensity light source, consisting of a bulb with a tungsten filament, filled with an inert gas, used for car-lamps, cine projectors, etc (also **tungsten lamp**); **tungsten steel** a type of hard steel containing varying amounts of tungsten and small quantities of carbon, used in making tools, etc. [Swed, literally heavy stone, from *tung* heavy, and *sten* stone]

Tungus *tōōng'gōōs* or *tōōng-gōōs'*, *-gōōz'*, *n* a member of an E Siberian people and race, of the type often called Mongol; their language: — *pl* **Tungus** or **Tunguses**. — Also *adj*. — *n* **Tungus'ic** the family of Ural-Altaic languages that includes Tungus and Manchu. — *adj* of or relating to (speakers of) these languages (also **Tungus'ian**). [Russ *Tunguz*; Chin *Tung-hu*]

tunic *tū'nik*, *n* a Roman shirtlike undergarment; applied also to the Greek chiton, and to various similar garments, *usu* a sort of belted coat and gown, or blouse; a close-fitting soldier's or police officer's jacket; a tunicle; an investing layer, membrane or integument (*biol*). — *n pl* **Tunicā'ta** the *Urochorda*, a subphylum of degenerate Chordata, including the ascidians. — *n* **tu'nicate** a member of the Tunicata. — *adj* **tu'nicate** or **tu'nicated** (*bot* and *zool*) having a tunic; formed in concentric coats; of the Tunicata. — *n* **tu'nicin** (*-ni-sin*) a gelatinous substance in the tests of tunicates. — *adj* **tu'nicked**. — *n* **tu'nicle** a little tunic; an ecclesiastical vestment like a dalmatic, worn by a subdeacon or a bishop at mass. [L *tunica*]

Tunker *tungk'ər*, *n*. See **Dunker**.

Tunku *tōōng'kōō* or **Tengku** *teng'kōō* (*Malay*) *n* prince, raja.

tunnage. See under **tun ton**[1].

tunnel *tun'l*, *n* a passage cut underground; any tubular passage; an animal's burrow, in earth, wood, etc; a tunnel-net; a flue, chimney; (with *cap*) the tunnel under the English Channel connecting England and France; see also **snake**. — *vt* to make a passage or passages through; to hollow out; to catch in a tunnel-net. — *vi* to make a tunnel; to pass through, or as if through, a tunnel: — *pr p* **tunn'elling** or (*NAm*) **tunn'eling**; *pa t* and *pa p* **tunn'elled** or (*NAm*) **tunn'eled**. — *n* **tunn'eller** or (*NAm*) **tunn'eler**. — *n* and *adj* **tunn'elling**. — **tunnel diode** (*electronics*) a junction diode, used as a low noise amplifier, oscillator or very low power microwave, in which electrons bypass the potential energy barrier by a phenomenon known in wave mechanics as **tunn'elling**; **tunn'el-net** a funnel-shaped net; **tunnel vault** same as **barrel vault** under **barrel**; **tunnel vision** a medical condition in which one is unable to see objects other than those straight ahead; single-minded concentration on one's own pursuits or viewpoints to the total exclusion of those of others. [OFr *ton(n)el* (Fr *tonneau*) cask, and *tonnelle* vault, tunnel-net, dimin of *tonne* cask]

tunny *tun'i*, *n* a tuna, *esp Thunnus thynnus*. [L *tunnus*, from Gr *thynnos*]

tuny. See under **tune**.

tup *tup*, *n* a ram; a paving rammer; a pile-driving monkey; the striking-face of a steam hammer. — *vt* (of a ram) to copulate with (a ewe); to put to the ram. — *vi* of sheep, to copulate: — *pr p* **tupp'ing**; *pa t* and *pa p* **tupped**. [Origin unknown]

Tupaia *tōō-pī'ə*, *n* a genus of insectivores, giving its name to the tree-shrew family **Tupai'idae**. [Malay *tūpai* (*tānah* ground) squirrel]

tupek. See **tupik**.

tupelo *tōō'pə-lō*, *n* an American gum-tree (*Nyssa*): — *pl* **tu'pelos**. [From Creek]

Tupí or **Tupi** *tōō-pē'*, *tōō'pē*, *n* a S American Indian of a group of peoples inhabiting the Atlantic coast and the Amazon basin; their language, serving as a lingua franca. — Also *adj*. — *adj* **Tupi'an**.

tupik *tū'pik* or **tupek** *-pek*, *n* an Inuit animal-skin tent. [Eskimo]

tuppence and **tuppenny**. Colloquial forms of **twopence** and **twopenny**.

Tupperware® *tup'ər-wār*, *n* a range of plastic storage containers, *esp* for food. [US company name *Tupper*, and **ware**]

tuptowing. See **typto**.

tuque *tūk*, *n* a Canadian cap made by tucking in one tapered end of a long cylindrical bag, closed at both ends. [Fr *toque*]

tu quoque *tū kwō'kwē*, *tōō kwok'we*, (*L*) *interj* you too, you're another.

turacin *tū'rə-sin*, *n* the soluble red pigment of turaco feathers, containing copper and porphyrin, unique in the animal kingdom. (*turaco* and *-in*]

turaco or **touraco** *tōōrə-kō*, *-kō'*, *n* any of various African arboreal birds of the family *Musophagidae*, of the genus *Tauraco* and related genera, with glossy, brightly-coloured plumage and short, stout bills: — *pl* **tu'racos** or **tou'racos**. [Perh a W African name]

turacoverdin *tōō-rə-kō-vûr'din*, *n* an iron-based pigment in turaco feathers, the only pure green pigment found in birds. [**turaco** and *verdin*, from Fr *verd* green]

Turanian *tū-rā'ni-ən*, (*obs philol*) *adj* of Asiatic languages, neither Iranian nor Semitic; latterly almost the same as Ural-Altaic. — *n* a speaker of one of these languages. [Pers *Turān* not Iran, applied to those parts of the Sassanian Persian empire beyond the Oxus]

turban *tûr'bən* (*obs* **tulipant'** or **tul'ban**; *Shakesp* **tur'band** or **tur'bond**; *Spenser* **turribant'**; *Milton* **tur'bant**) *n* a head-covering, *esp* as worn by Muslim or Sikh men, consisting of a long sash wound round the head or round a cap; a woman's headdress similar to this. — *adj* **tur'baned** wearing a turban. [Turk *tulbend*, from Pers *dulband*; cf **tulip**]

turbary *tûr'bə-ri*, *n* the right to take peat from another's ground; a place where peat is dug. [LL *turbāria*, from *turba* turf; of Gmc origin; see **turf**]

Turbellaria *tûr-bə-lā'ri-ə*, *n pl* a class of ciliated flatworms. — *n* and *adj* **turbellā'rian**. [L *turbellae* a disturbance]

turbid *tûr'bid*, *adj* disordered; muddy; thick. — *n* **turbidim'eter** a device for determining the surface area of a powder by measuring the light-scattering properties of a fluid suspension. — *n* **tur'bidite** the sediment deposited by a turbidity current. — *n* **turbid'ity**. — *adv* **tur'bidly**. — *n* **tur'bidness**. — **turbidity current** a volume of sediment-carrying water which flows violently down a slope under water. [L *turbidus*, from *turba* tumult]

turbinacious *tûr-bin-ā'shəs*, (*Scott*) *adj* (of the smell of whisky) peaty. [A blundering form from LL *turba* peat, under the influence of L *turbō*, *-inis* a spinning-top, a swirl]

turbine *tûr'bin* (sometimes *-bīn*), *n* a rotary motor in which a wheel or drum with curved vanes is driven by reaction or impact or both by a fluid (water in the **water-turbine**, steam in the **steam-turbine**, expanding hot air in the **gas-turbine**) admitted to it and allowed to escape. — *adj* **tur'binal** turbinate. — *n* a scroll-like bone of the nose. — *n* **tur'binate** a turbinal; a turbinate shell. — *adj* **tur'binate** or **tur'binated** shaped like a top or inverted cone; spirally coiled; scroll-like; turbinal. — *adj* **tur'bined** having or driven by a turbine or turbines. — **tur'bine-pump** a device for raising water by the inverted action of a turbine wheel; **tur'bine-steamer** a ship driven by steam-turbine. [Fr, from L *turbō*, *-inis* a whirl, a spinning-top]

turbines, *pl* of **turbine** and **turbo'**.

turbit *tûr'bit*, *n* a domestic pigeon having white body, coloured wings, and short beak. [Ety doubtful]

turbith. See **turpeth**.

turbo[1] *tûr'bō*, *n* a member of the tropical genus *Turbo* of turbinate wide-mouthed gasteropods, large specimens of which are often used as ornaments: — *pl* **turbines** (*tûr'bi-nēz*). [L *turbō*, *-inis* a whirl, a spinning-top]

turbo[2] *tûr'bō*, *n* short form of **turbocar** and **turbocharger**: — *pl* **tur'bos**.

turbo- *tûr-bō-*, *combining form* signifying having, connected to or driven by a turbine. — **tur'bocar** or **turbo car** a car propelled by a turbocharged engine. — *adj* **tur'bocharged**. — *n* **tur'bocharger** a turbine operated by the exhaust gases of an engine, thereby boosting its power. — *n* **tur'bocharging**. — *adj* **turbo-elec'tric** using a form of electric drive in which turbine-driven generators supply electric power to motors coupled to propeller, axle shafts, etc. — *n* **tur'bofan** a gas-turbine aero-engine in which part of the power developed is used to drive a fan which blows air out with the exhaust and so increases thrust (also **turbofan engine** or **ducted fan**). — *n* **turbo-gen'erator** a generator of electric power, driven by a steam-turbine. — *n* **tur'bojet** (an aeroplane powered by) an internal-combustion aero-engine in which the gas energy produced by a turbine-driven compressor is directed through a nozzle to produce thrust. — *n* **tur'boprop** a jet-engine in which the turbine is coupled to a propeller; **turbo-ram'-jet** an engine consisting of a turbo-jet mounted within the duct of a ram jet. — *n* **turbo-su'percharger** an aero-engine supercharger operated by a turbine driven by the exhaust gases of the engine. [Ety as **turbine**]

turbond (*Shakesp*). See **turban**.

turbot *tûr'bət*, *n* a large flatfish (*Psetta maxima*) with bony tubercles; its flesh (as a highly valued food); extended to various more or less similar fishes. [OFr *turbot*]

turbulent *tûr'bū-lənt*, *adj* tumultuous, violently disturbed; in violent commotion; producing commotion; stormy; of fluid, showing turbulence; insubordinate, unruly; having an exciting, disturbing effect. — *n* **tur'bulātor** a device which creates turbulence, eg in order to mix or disperse fluids; a device fitted to a ship's funnel to assist the dispersal of smoke, fumes, etc. — *n* **tur'bulence** disturbed state (also, *esp* formerly, **tur'bulency**); unruly character or action; irregular eddying motion of particles in a fluid; irregular movement of large volumes of air (also **atmospheric turbulence**). — *adv* **tur'bulently**. [L *turbulentus*, from *turba* a turmoil]

Turco *tûr'kō*, (*colloq*) *n* an Algerian infantryman in the French service: — *pl* **Tur'cos**. [Ital, Turk]

Turcoman. Same as **Turkoman**.

Turcophil *tûr'kō-fil* or **Turcophile** (*-fīl*), *n* (Gr *phileein* to love) someone who favours the Turks. — Also *adj*. — *n* **Turcophilism** (*-kof'il-izm*). — *n* **Tur'cophobe** (Gr *phobeein* to fear) someone who fears or dislikes the Turks. — Also *adj*. — *n* **Turcophō'bia**. [Gr *Tourkos* Turk]

turcopole *tûr'kō-pōl*, *n* a light-armed soldier of the Knights of St John of Jerusalem. — *n* **tur'copolier** (*-pō-lēr*) their commander, always an Englishman. [Mod Gr *Tourkopoulon* a Turkish boy]

turd *tûrd*, *n* a lump of dung; a despicable person (*vulg slang*). [OE *tord*]

turdion *tûr-di-ōn'*, *tûr'-*. Same as **tordion**.

Turdus *tûr'dəs*, *n* the thrush genus. — *adj* **tur'dine** (*tûr'-dīn*, *-din*) of, resembling or belonging to a thrush or the thrushes. — *adj* **tur'doid** thrush-like. [L]

tureen *tə-rēn'*, *tū-rēn'*, *n* a large dish for holding soup, vegetables, etc at table. [Fr *terrine*, from L *terra* earth]

turf *tûrf*, *n* the surface of land matted with the roots of grass, etc; a slab of turf cut off; a sod; a slab of peat; territory, area of operation or influence, patch (*slang*); horse-racing, the race-course, the racing world: — *pl* **turfs**, sometimes **turves**. — *vt* to cover with turf. — *adj* **turfed**. — *adj* **tur'fen** (*archaic*). — *n* **tur'finess**. — *n* **tur'fing**. — *n* **tur'fite** (*slang*) someone devoted to horse-racing (also **turf'man**; chiefly *US*). — *adj* **tur'fy** of, like or covered in turf; relating to horse-racing. — **turf accountant** (*euphem*) a bookmaker. — *adj* **turf'-clad** covered with turf. — **turf'-drain** one covered with turf; **turf'ing-iron** an implement for cutting turf; **turf'-spade** a long narrow spade for digging turf. — **turf out** (*informal*) to throw out forcibly, to eject. [OE *turf*; ON *torf*]

turgent *tûr'jənt*, *adj* (*obs*) turgid. — *adv* (*obs*) **tur'gently**. — *n* **turgescence** (*-jes'əns*) the act or process of swelling up; swollenness; distension of cells and tissues with water. — *n* **turgesc'ency**. — *adj* **turgesc'ent** swelling; growing big. — *adj* **tur'gid** swollen; extended beyond the natural size; dilated; inflated; pompous; bombastic; firm and tense by distension with water (*bot*). — *n* **turgid'ity** or **tur'gidness**. — *adv* **tur'gidly**. — *n* **turgor** (*tûr'gör*) the state of being full, the normal condition of the capillaries; balance of osmotic pressure and elasticity of cell-wall (*bot*). [L *turgēre* to swell]

Turing machine *tū'ring mə-shēn'*, *n* a hypothetical computer, able to perform an infinite number of calculations. [First described by A M *Turing* (1912–54), British mathematician]

turion *tū'ri-ən*, (*bot*) *n* an underground bud, growing upward into a new stem. [L *turiō*, *-ōnis* a shoot]

Turk *tûrk*, *n* a native or citizen of *Turkey*; a Muslim of the former Ottoman empire; any speaker of a Turkic language; a Muslim (*obs*); anyone with qualities ascribed to Turks, *esp* an unmanageable unruly person (*derog*); a Turkish horse; a Turkish ship. — *adj* Turkish. — *adj* **Turki** (*tōōr'kē*) of the Turkish as distinguished from the Tatar branch of Turko-Tatar languages. — *n* a Turki speaker or language. — *n* **Turkess** (*tûrk'es*; *rare*) a Turkish woman. — *adj* and *n* **Turk'ic** or **Turko-Ta'tar** (of) that branch of the Ural-Altaic languages to which Turkish belongs. — *vt* **Turk'icize** or **-ise**. — *vt* **Turk'ify**. — *adj* **Turk'ish** of Turkey, the Turks, or their language; Turkic. — *n* the language of the Turks. — *n* and *adj* **Turk'man** or **Turk'men** same as **Turkoman**. — **Turkey carpet** a soft thick kind of carpet with a distinctive bright pattern; **Turkey hone** novaculite; **Turkey merchant** one trading with the Near East; **Turkey oak** a Levantine species of oak (*Quercus cerris*); **Turkey red** a fine durable red dye, obtained from madder, but now mostly chemically; **Turkey stone** Turkey hone; the turquoise (*rare*); **Turkish bath** a kind of hot-air bath in which the client is sweated, rubbed down, massaged, and gradually cooled; **Turkish delight** a gelatinous confection, *orig* and *esp* Turkish, variously flavoured and coloured, and coated with powdered sugar; **Turkish manna** trehala; **Turk's cap** or **Turk's cap lily** the martagon lily (*Lilium martagon*), from the appearance of the rolled-back petals of the nodding flower; **Turk's head** a kind of knot; a long broom; a figure set up for practice in swordsmanship. — **Grand Turk** (*hist*) the Ottoman Sultan; **turn Turk** to become Muslim; to be completely reversed; **Young Turk** see under **young**.

turkey *tûrk'i*, *n* formerly, a guinea-fowl (thought to have come from *Turkey*); now, an American genus (*Meleagris*) of the pheasant family; a domestic breed of that genus; its flesh as food (in *US* also a substitute); extended to various big birds, such as bustard, ibis and megapode; a play, film, etc that is a complete failure (*slang*, chiefly *NAm*); a fool, a slow or inept person (*slang*). — **turkey brown** an angler's name for the mayfly *Paraleptophlebia submarginata*, or an artificial imitation of it; **turkey buzzard** or **vulture** an American vulture, *Cathartes aura*; **turk'ey-cock** a male guinea-fowl (*obs*); a male turkey; a strutting, pompous, arrogant blusterer; **turk'ey-hen** a guinea-hen (*obs*); a female turkey; **turk'ey-shoot** (*slang*, *esp US*) a battle involving large-scale killing or destruction of easy targets (*military*); anything easily won or accomplished; **turk'ey-trot** a kind of ragtime dance. — **cold turkey** see under **cold**; **talk turkey** (chiefly *NAm*) to talk bluntly; to talk business.

Turki. See **Turk**.

turkis and **turkies**. See **turquoise**.

Turkoman *tûr'kō-man*, *n* a member of any of the Turkic peoples living mainly in Turkmenistan and NE Iran (*pl* **Turk'omans**); their Turkic language. — Also *adj*. — Also **Tur'coman** or **Turk'man**. — *adj* **Turk'mē'nian**.

turlough *tûr'lohh*, (*Ir*) *n* a pond that dries up in summer. [Ir *turloch*]

turm (*Milton* **turme**) *tûrm*, *n* a troop. [L *turma*]

turmeric *tûr'mər-ik*, *n* a plant (*Curcuma longa*) of the ginger family; its rootstock, or a powder made from it, used in making curry powder and as a dye. — **turmeric paper** a chemical test-paper impregnated with turmeric, changed from yellow to brown by alkali. [Earlier *tarmaret*; cf Fr *terre-mérite*, as if from L *terra merita* deserved earth; origin unknown]

turmoil *tûr'moil* (*Shakesp -moil'*), *n* commotion; disquiet; tumult. — *vt* (formerly *-moil'*; *archaic*) to harass with commotion; to toss about. — *vi* (*dialect*) to toil. [Origin unknown]

turn *tûrn*, *vi* to revolve; to rotate, to spin, whirl; to move round; to hinge; to depend; to issue; to change or reverse direction or tendency; to return; to deviate; to direct oneself, face (with *to* or *towards*); to shape one's course; to betake oneself; to direct one's attention; to change sides, religion or mode of life; to be fickle; to change; to be transformed or converted (often with *into*); to become; to result, prove or lead in the issue; to be shaped on the lathe; to become sour; to change colour; to become giddy; to be nauseated; to bend back, become turned; to tack, beat to windward (*naut*). — *vt* to rotate; to move round; to change the direction of; to deflect; to bend; to bend back the edge of; to reverse; to pass round or beyond; to perform by turning; to wind; to set outside-in, or remake in that form; to set upside-down; to direct; to point; to apply; to send, drive, set; to pour or tumble out; to employ in circulation, pass through one's hands; to translate; to change; to make (milk, cream, etc) sour; to nauseate; to make giddy; to infatuate; to transfer, hand over; to convert, make; to make the subject of (with *to* or *into*); to render; to put by turning; to return, give back; to form in a lathe; to shape; to round off, fashion; to pass, become (a certain age, hour, etc); to cause or persuade (an enemy agent) to work for one's own side. — *n* act, occasion or place of turning; new direction or tendency; a twist; a winding; a complete revolution; a bend; a single traversing of a beat or course; a short walk (or ride or drive); a fit of illness or emotion, *esp* an emotional shock, jar or feeling of faintness; an embellishment in which the principal note is preceded by that next above and followed by that next below (or vice versa in the **inverted turn**), the whole ending (and sometimes beginning) with the principal note (*music*); turning-point; a culmination; a time or moment of change; on a golf course, the halfway point, at which the players turn to begin the return nine holes; a crisis; a spell; a recurring opportunity or spell in rotation or alternation; rotation; a trick; a performer's act or the performer; a shift; a bout; fashion; manner; cast of mind; aptitude; bent; occasion, exigency; a vicissitude; a characteristic quality or effect; act of kindness or malice; an inverted type serving for a temporarily missing letter; a complete financial transaction, covering the buying and selling of a commodity, etc. — *adj* **turned** fashioned; wrought in a lathe; beyond the age (now *usu* without *of*); reversed; outside-in; (*esp* of printing type) upside-down; soured. — *n* **turn'er** a person who or thing that turns; a person who uses a lathe; a member of a gymnastic club (*US*, from *Ger*). — *n* **turn'ery** the art of turning in a lathe; turner's work; a turner's shop. — *n* **turn'ing** rotation; reversal; a bend; the act of making a turn; a winding; deviation; a place where a road strikes off; a shaping, *esp* the art of shaping wood, metal, etc, into forms having a curved (generally circular or oval) transverse section, and also of engraving figures composed of curved lines upon a smooth surface, by means of a turning-lathe; (in *pl*) a shaving from the lathe; in pottery, the shaping of a vase, etc; conversion, transformation. — **turn'-about** or **turn'around** a turning to face the opposite direction; a reversal in opinion, policy, course of action, etc; **turn'again** (*archaic*) a refrain; **turnaround** see **turnabout** and **turnround**; **turn'back** a folded-back part; a person who retreats from or abandons an enterprise. — *adj* **turn'-back** (able to be) folded back. — **turn'broach** a turnspit; **turn'buckle** a coupling with screw-threads for adjusting tension; **turn'coat** a renegade to one's principles or party; **turn'cock** a valve which by turning regulates waterflow; an official who turns off and on the water for the mains, etc. — *adj* **turn'-down** folded down. — *n* a turn-down part; a turn-down collar; a turning down, rejection; **turn-in** see **turn in** below; **turning circle** the smallest possible circle in which a vehicle can turn round; **turn'ing-lathe**; **turn'ing-point** the point at which anything turns in its course; a maximum or minimum point on a graph; a critical point; **turn'ing-saw** a sweep-saw, a thin-bladed saw held taut in a frame, used for cutting in curves; **turn'key** an under-jailer; a turncock; (a contract for) a job in which the contractor is to complete the entire operation, leaving the building, plant, etc ready for use (also *adj*). — *adj* **turn'key** (*comput*) designed and ready for immediate use by the purchaser, as in **turnkey system** or **package** (*comput*) a computer system complete with hardware and software, *usu* designed, installed, tested and maintained by the supplier and ready for immediate use by the purchaser. — **turn'off** or **turn'-off** a smaller road leading from a main one; see also **turn off** below; **turn-on** see **turn on** below; **turn'out** a getting out of bed; a coming on duty; a call to come on duty; a siding, passing-place, or turning-place (*archaic*); a movable tapered rail for changing to another track; a muster or assembly; a carriage and its horses, a team; output; get-up, outfit (of clothes); a display (of goods, equipment, etc); a strike (*archaic*); a striker (*archaic*); **turn'over** a turning over; a transference; a part folded over; a newspaper article begun on the front page and continued overleaf; a small pie made by folding over the crust; a small shawl (*archaic*); an apprentice transferred to a new employer to complete the apprenticeship (*dialect*); the total amount of money changing hands in a business; the number of employees starting or finishing employment at a particular place of work over a given period; the money value of total sales over a period; loss of possession of the ball by a team, due to error or breach of a rule (*Am football* and *basketball*). — *adj* folded over, or made to fold over. — **turnover tax** a tax paid every time goods change hands during manufacture and marketing; **turn'-penny** (*archaic*) someone who is eager for profit; **turn'pike** a spiked barrier (*hist*); a turnstile (*obs*); a toll-gate or road with a toll-gate (*hist*); a motorway on which tolls are paid (*US*); a spiral stair (also **turnpike stair**; *Scot*); **turn'pike-man** (*hist*) a toll-gate keeper; **turn'pike-road** a road on which there are or were tollgates; a main road; **turn'round** or **turn'-around** a turning round; the whole process of a ship, aircraft, etc docking or landing, unloading, taking on cargo, passengers or both, and setting off again; generally, the whole process of dealing with something and passing it on to the next stage; a complete reversal of direction; **turn'-screw** (*archaic*) a screwdriver; **turn'-skin** (*archaic*) a werewolf; **turn'spit** a person who turns a spit; a long-bodied, short-legged dog employed to drive a wheel by which roasting-spits were turned; a spit, roasting-jack; **turn'stile** a revolving frame that allows one person to pass at a time; **turn'stone** a bird (genus *Arenaria*), related to the plover and sandpiper, that turns over pebbles on the beach in search of food; **turn'table** a rotating table, platform, disc or pair of rings, one rotating within another, used for turning a locomotive, carrying a gramophone record, cementing a microscope slide, turning a camera, etc; **turn'-up** (or *tûrn-up'*) a disturbance; a thing or part that is turned up, *esp* the cuff at the bottom of a trouser-leg; an unexpected or fortuitous result or occurrence; a piece of good luck. — *adj* turned up. — **a good** (or **bad**) **turn** a helpful service (or a disservice); **at every turn** everywhere; incessantly; **(take) a turn for the better** or **worse** (to make) an improvement or a deterioration; **by turns** one after another; at intervals; **in turn** one after another, in succession; **in one's turn** when it is one's occasion, opportunity, duty, etc; **not turn a hair** to be quite undisturbed or unaffected; **on the turn** at the turning-point, changing; on the point of turning sour; **serve its** or **one's turn** to answer the purpose; to do well enough; **take a turn** to go for a stroll; to have a go (*colloq*); **take one's turn** or **take turns** to participate in rotation; **to a turn** exactly, perfectly (as if of the spit); **turn about** to face round to the opposite direction; to spin, rotate; **turn about** or **turn and turn about** alternately; in rotation; **turn a deaf ear to** to ignore; **turn adrift** to unmoor and let float away; to cast off; **turn again** to turn back; to revert; **turn against** to use to the injury of; to render hostile to; to rebel against; **turn an enemy's flank, line** or **position** to manoeuvre so as to attack in the rear; to outwit; **turn an honest penny** see under **penny**; **turn around** see **turn round** below; **turn aside** to avert; to deviate; to avert the face; **turn away** to dismiss from service, to discharge; to avert, to turn or look in another direction; to deviate, to depart; to refuse admittance to; to reject, send away; **turn back** to cause to retreat; to return; to fold back; **turn colour** to change colour; **turn down** to bend, double, or fold down; to invert; to lower (a light, volume on a radio, etc); to reject; **turn forth** to expel; **turn in** to bend inward; to enter; to register (a score); to surrender, hand over voluntarily (*n* **turn'-in**); to go to bed (*colloq*); **turn in on oneself** to become introverted; **turn into** to become by a process of change; **turn it up** or **in** stop (saying) it (*imperative*; *colloq*); **turn King's** or **Queen's evidence** see under **evident**; **turn loose** to set at liberty; **turn of events** course or direction of events; **turn off** to deviate; to dismiss; to divert; to complete, achieve by labour; to shut or switch off; to make (someone) lose interest or enthusiasm, to bore, be disliked by or distasteful to (*n* **turn'-off**; *slang*); to give in marriage (*archaic*); to hang (*obs slang*); **turn of speed** a burst of speed; **turn of the century** or **year** the period of the end of one century or year and the beginning of the next; **turn on** to set running (eg the flow of water); to set in operation by switching on (also *fig*); to depend on; to turn towards and attack (physically or verbally); to give (a person) a sense of heightened awareness and vitality as do hallucinogenic drugs (*slang*); to rouse the interest of, excite, *esp* sexually (*n* **turn'-on**; *slang*); **turn one's back on** to abandon or reject; **turn one's hand to** to apply oneself to; **turn out** to bend outwards; to drive out, to expel; to remove the contents of; to dress, groom, take care of the appearance of; to put (cattle, etc) to pasture; to produce and put forth; to prove in the result; to muster; to go on strike; to switch off (a light); to get out of bed (*colloq*); to go out of doors (*colloq*); **turn over** to roll over; to set the other way up; to change sides; to hand over, pass on; to handle or do business to the amount of; to examine by turning the pages; to ponder; to rob (*slang*); to start up (an engine); **turn round** or **around** of a ship, aircraft, etc, to arrive, unload, reload and leave again; to reverse the course or direction of; to reverse the fortunes of (*fig*); **turn tail** see under **tail**[1]; **turn someone round one's little finger** see **twist someone round one's little finger** under **finger**; **turn someone's head** or **brain** to make someone giddy; to infatuate with success; **turn the other cheek** to accept harm, violence, etc without defending oneself; **turn the scale** to decide, determine; **turn the stomach** to nauseate; **turn the tables** see under **table**; **turn to** to have recourse to; to point to; to result in; to change or be changed into; to set to work; **turn turtle** see under **turtle**[2]; **turn up** to point upwards; to fold upwards; to come or bring to light; to appear by chance; to set face up; to invert; to grub up; to disturb; to strengthen or increase (eg the level of light, radio volume, etc); to refer to, look up; to disgust (*colloq*); **turn-up for the book** or **books** a totally unexpected occurrence; **turn upon** to cast back upon, retort; to hinge on. [OE *turnian*, *tyrnan*, and perh partly OFr *torner* (Fr *tourner*); all from L *tornāre* to turn in a lathe, from *tornus* a turner's wheel, from Gr *tornos* lathe, compasses]

Turnbull's blue *tûrn'bəlz blōō*, *n* ferrous ferricyanide (or *poss* ferric ferrocyanide). [From *Turnbull*, a Glasgow manufacturing chemist (18c), not the discoverer]

turndun *tûrn'dun* or **tundun** *tun'*, *n* an Australian bull-roarer. [Aboriginal]

turner[1] *tûr'nər*, *n* a 17c Scots bodle. [Origin doubtful; cf Fr *tournois* coined at *Tours*]

turner[2]. See under **turn**.

Turneresque *tûr-nər-esk'*, *adj* resembling the work of the painter J M W *Turner* (1775–1851). — Also **Turnerian** (*-nē'ri-ən*).

turnip *tûr'nip*, *n* the swollen edible root of *Brassica rapa* or (*Swedish turnip* or *swede*) of *Brassica rutabaga*, cruciferous biennials with respectively white and yellowish flesh; the root as food; the plant producing it; extended to more or less similar roots and plants, such as the American papilionaceous *prairie turnip* (*Psoralea esculenta*); a big watch (*old slang*); a dunderhead. — *vt* to plant with turnips; to feed on turnips. — **turnip cabbage** same as **kohlrabi**; **turnip flea** a leaping beetle that eats young turnip and cabbage plants; **turnip-fly** a fly whose maggots burrow in turnip-roots; the turnip flea; **turnip greens** turnip-tops, *esp* as a vegetable; **turnip lantern** a lantern made (*esp* traditionally at Hallowe'en) by scooping out the flesh of a swede; **tur'nip-top** the green sprout of a turnip in its second year, used as a vegetable. [See **neep**; the first part may be from **turn** or Fr *tour*, implying roundness]

turnkey ... to ... **turnskin**. See under **turn**.

turnsole *tûrn'sōl*, *n* a plant whose flowers are supposed to face the sun, as heliotrope or the euphorbiaceous *Chrozophora tinctoria*; a deep-purple dye obtained from the latter; litmus. [Fr *tournesol*, from L *tornāre* (see **turn**), and *sōl* the sun]

turnspit ... **to** ... **turntable**. See under **turn**.

turpentine *tûr'pən-tīn*, *n* a viscous resin, *orig* that of the terebinth tree (*Chian turpentine*), now generally of conifers; popularly, oil of turpentine; a tree that yields turpentine, *esp* the terebinth. — *vt* to treat or smear with turpentine. — *adj* **tur'pentīny**. — **turpentine tree** a small Mediterranean tree (genus *Pitacia*) that yields a turpentine, the terebinth-tree. — **oil** or **spirit of turpentine** (*colloq* **turps**) an oil distilled from turpentine. [OFr *terbentine*, from L *terebinthina* (*rēsīna*) terebinth (resin); see **terebinth**]

turpeth *tûr'pəth* or **turbith** *-bith*, *n* an Oriental plant (genus *Ipomoea*) or its cathartic root. — **turpeth mineral** basic mercuric sulphate. [LL *turpethum*, *turbithum*, from Pers and Ar *turbed*, *turbid*]

turpitude *tûr'pi-tūd*, *n* baseness; depravity; vileness. [L *turpitūdō*, from *turpis* base]

turps. See under **turpentine**.

turquoise *tûr'kwäz*, *-k(w)oiz*, *-kwöz*, formerly **turkis** (*Milton* and *Tennyson*), **turkies** (*Shakesp*) *tûr'kiz*, *-kis*, *n* a massive opaque sky-blue to pale green mineral or gemstone, a hydrous basic aluminium phosphate, found in Persia; the colour of this stone. — *adj* of turquoise; of the colour of turquoise. — *n* and *adj* **tur'quoise-blue'** turquoise; **tur'quoise-green'** pale bluish green. — **bone** or **fossil turquoise** odontolite. [OFr *turkeis* (later Fr *turquoise*) Turkish, as first brought through *Turkey* or from *Turkestan*]

turret[1] *tur'it*, *n* a small tower, *usu* attached to a building, often containing a spiral stair; a structure, often revolving, carrying a gun; part of a lathe that holds the cutting tool. — *adj* **turr'eted** having turrets; formed like a tower or a long spiral. — **turr'et-clock** a clock for a tower; a large clock with movement quite separate from the dials; **turr'et-gun** one for use in a revolving turret; **turret lathe** a lathe having a number of tools carried on a turret mounted on a saddle which slides on the lathe bed; **turr'et-ship** a warship with gun-turrets. [OFr *tourete*, dimin of *tur*; see **tower**]

turret[2]. Same as **terret**.

turribant. See **turban**.

turriculate *tur-ik'ū-lāt* or **turriculated** *-lāt-id*, *adj* turreted; formed in a long spiral. — *n* **Turritell'a** the tower-shell genus of gasteropods. [L *turris* a tower; dimin *turricula*]

turtle[1] *tûr'tl*, *n* (*archaic*) a turtledove; a constant or demonstrative lover. — **tur'tledove** any dove of the genus *Turtur* or *Streptopelia*, a favourite cage-bird, a type of conjugal affection and constancy; the mourning dove (*US*). [OE *turtla*, *turtle*, from L *turtur*; cf Ger *Turtel*, Fr *tourtereau*, *tourterelle*]

turtle[2] *tûr'tl*, *n* any marine reptile of the order *Chelonia*; *esp* in US, also a terrestrial chelonian; sometimes a freshwater chelonian; the edible flesh of a turtle, *esp* the green turtle; turtle-soup; a drawing device which converts information from a computer into pictures, *orig* a device (*floor turtle*) with a pen or pens, which could be made to move across a flat surface with paper, etc on it, now often simulated by graphics on a screen (a *screen turtle*) (*comput*). — *vi* to hunt or catch turtles. — *n* **tur'tler** a hunter of turtles. — *n* **tur'tling** the hunting of turtles. — **tur'tleback** anything arched like a turtle's back, *esp* a structure over a ship's bows or stern; **turtle graphics** (*comput*) drawing by means of a turtle (qv); **tur'tleneck** (a garment having) a high close-fitting neckline. — *adj* **tur'tle-necked**. — **tur'tle-shell** the shell of the hawk's-bill turtle, commonly called tortoise-shell; **tur'tle-soup** a soup made from the flesh, fat, and gelatinous tissue of the female green turtle (*Chelone mydas*); **tur'tle-stone** a septarium. — **mock turtle** a soup made of calf's head or other meat in lieu of turtle meat; **turn turtle** to render a turtle helpless by turning it on its back; to turn bottom up, capsize. [Fr *tortue*, Sp *tortuga* or Port *tartaruga* tortoise, assimilated to **turtle**[1], all from LL *tortuca*]

turves. See **turf**.

Tuscan *tus'kən*, *adj* of *Tuscany* in Central Italy; Doric as modified by the Romans, with unfluted columns, and without triglyphs (*archit*). — *n* classical Italian as spoken in Tuscany; a native of Tuscany; an ancient Etruscan. [L *Tuscānus* Etruscan]

tusche *tŏŏsh*, *n* a substance used in lithography for drawing the design which then does not take up the printing medium. [Ger *tuschen* to touch up (with paint, etc)]

tush[1], *tush*, (*Shakesp*) *n* a tusk (*archaic*); a small stunted tusk; a horse's canine tooth. [OE *tūsc*; cf **tusk**[2]]

tush[2] *tush*, (*archaic*) *interj* pshaw; pooh. — Also *vi*. — *n* **tush'ery** word coined by R L Stevenson meaning (a style of period novel, etc using) would-be archaic language.

tush[3] *tŏŏsh*, (*slang*; *esp US*) *n* the bottom, buttocks. — Also **tush'ie** or **tush'y**. [Corrupted shortening of Yiddish *tokhes*]

tushkar and **tushker**. See **tuskar**.

tusk[1]. Same as **torsk**.

tusk[2] *tusk*, *n* a long protruding tooth; a tush; a sharp projection. — *vt* to pierce with the tusks. — *adj* **tusked** or **tusk'y**. — *n* **tusk'er** a boar, elephant, etc with tusks. — *n* **tusk'ing** (*archit*) the stubs of walling stones left projecting from a wall for bonding later with another wall or building. — *adj* **tusk'less**. — **tusk'-shell** the mollusc *Dentalium* or its shell. [OE *tūx* (*tūsc*); cf **tush**[1]]

tuskar or **tusker** *tus'kər*, **tushkar** or **tushker** *tush'kər*, or **twiscar** *twis'kər*, (*Orkney* and *Shetland*) *n* a peat-spade. [ON *torfskeri*, from *torf* turf, and *skera* to cut]

tusky. See under **tusk**[2].

tussac-grass. See **tussock**.

tussah *tus'ə* or **tusseh** *-e*, *n*. Faulty forms of **tusser**.

tusser, **tussore** or **tasar** *tus'ər*, *n* a fawn-coloured silk from wild Indian silkworms (also **tuss'er-silk**); its colour; a dress made of it. — [Hind *tasar* shuttle, from Sans *tasara* silkworm]

tussie mussie *tus'i-mus'i*, *n* a small bunch of flowers, a posy.

tussis *tus'is*, (*med*) *n* a cough. — *adj* **tuss'al** or **tuss'ive**. [L]

tussle *tus'l*, *n* a sharp struggle. — *vi* to struggle. [Frequentative of **touse**; cf **tousle**]

tussock *tus'ək*, *n* a tuft; a bunchy clump of grass, rushes, etc; tussock-grass; a tussock-moth. — *adj* **tuss'ocky**. — **tuss'ock-grass** or **tuss'ac-grass** a large grass (*Poa flabellata*) of the Falkland Islands, forming great tufts; **tuss'ock-moth** any moth of the family *Lymantriidae* (related to *Lasiocampidae*), from the tufts of hair on the caterpillars. [Origin obscure]

tussore. Same as **tusser**.

tut[1] *tut*, *interj* an exclamation of rebuke, mild disapprobation, impatience, etc. — *vi* to say 'tut': — *pr p* **tutt'ing**; *pa t* and *pa p* **tutt'ed**. — *n* **tutt'ing**. — Also **tut-tut'** and (*n*) **tut-tutt'ing**; *Scot* **toot**, **toots** or **tuts**.

tut[2] *tut*, (*dialect*) *n* work paid by measurement or piece. — *vi* to do such work. — **tut'work**; **tut'worker**; **tut'-workman** or **tut'man**. [Origin unknown]

tutania *tū-tā'ni-ə*, *n* a kind of Britannia metal. [From W *Tutin* (c.1780), its maker or inventor]

tutee. See under **tutor**.

tutelage *tū'ti-lij*, *n* guardianship; state of being under a guardian; tuition. — *adj* **tu'telar** or **tu'telary** protecting; having the charge of a person or place. — *n* a guardian spirit, god, or saint. [L *tūtēla* guard, from *tūtārī* to guard, from *tuērī* to look to]

tutenag *tū'ti-nag*, *n* an alloy of zinc, copper, etc; loosely, zinc. [Marathi *tuttināg*]

tutiorism *tū'ti-ər-izm*, *n* in RC moral theology, the doctrine that in a case of doubt between right and wrong one should take the safer course, ie the one in verbal accordance with the law. — *n* and *adj* **tū'tiorist**. [L *tūtior*, *-ōris* safer, comparative of *tūtus* safe]

tutor *tū'tər*, *n* a private instructor or coach; a person who helps a boy or girl with lessons; a college officer who has supervision of an undergraduate; a college teacher who instructs by conference with a small group of students; an instruction book; a guardian; a guardian of the person and estate of a boy under fourteen, or girl under twelve (*Scots law*). — *vt* to act as tutor to; to instruct; to coach; to control; to discipline. — *n* **tutee'** a person who is tutored. — *n* **tu'torage** tutorship; tutoring; charge for tutoring; tutelage (*obs*). — *n* **tu'toress** or **tu'tress** (*archaic*; also *obs* **tu'trix**) a female tutor. — *adj* **tutorial** (*tū-tō'ri-əl*, *-tö*) of a tutor. — *n* a study meeting between one or more students and a college tutor. — *adv* **tuto'rially**. — *n* **tu'toring**. — *n* **tu'torism**. — *vt* and *vi* **tu'torize** or **-ise**. — *n* **tu'torship**. [L *tūtor*, *-ōris* a guardian, from *tuērī* to look to]

tuts (*Scot*). See **tut**[1].

tutsan *tut'sən*, *n* parkleaves, a species of St John's wort (*Hypericum androsaemum*) once regarded as a panacea. [OFr *toutesaine*, from *tout*, from L *tōtus* all, and *sain*, from L *sānus* sound]

Tutsi *tŏŏt'si*, *n* a member of a Bantu people inhabiting parts of Rwanda. [Bantu]

tutti *tŏŏt'(t)ē*, (*music*) *pl adj* all (performers). — *n* a passage for the whole orchestra or choir, or its rendering. [Ital, pl of *tutto*, from L *tōtus* all]

tutti-frutti *tŏŏt'(t)ē- frŏŏt'(t)ē*, *n* a confection, *esp* ice-cream, flavoured with different kinds of fruit. [Ital, all fruits]

tut-tut *tut-tut'*. Same as **tut**[1].

tutty *tut'i*, *n* crude zinc oxide. [OFr *tutie*, from LL *tutia*, from Ar *tūtiyā*]

tutu[1] *tōō'tōō*, *n* any of several New Zealand shrubs of the genus *Coriaria*, having poisonous black berries. [Maori]

tutu[2] *tōō'tōō*, *n* a ballerina's short, stiff, spreading skirt. [Fr]

tu-whit tu-whoo *tŏŏ-(h)wit' tŏŏ-(h)wōō'*, *n* an owl's hoot. — *vi* **tu-whoo'** to hoot.

tux *tuks*, (*colloq*; *orig US* and *Austr*) *n* short for **tuxedo**.

tuxedo *tuk-sē'dō*, (*orig US*) *n* a dinner-jacket: — *pl* **tuxe'dos** or **tuxe'does**. [From a fashionable club at *Tuxedo* Park, NY]

tuyère. See **twyer**.

tuzz *tuz*, (*Dryden*) *n* a tuft. — **tuzz'i-muzzy** or **tuzz'y-muzzy** (*obs*) same as **tussie-mussie**.

TV *abbrev*: television. — **TV dinner** a (*usu* pre-processed and easily prepared) meal for eating from a tray, etc while watching TV; **TV game** an electronic game, played on a television; **TV movie** a film made specifically for TV rather than cinema screening.

TVEI *abbrev*: Technical and Vocational Education Initiative, a national scheme, complementary to the National Curriculum, intended to give school students more job-orientated and technological courses.

TVP *abbrev*: textured vegetable protein.

TWA *abbrev*: Trans-World Airlines.

twa *twā, twö, twä*, also **twae** or **tway** *twā, adj* and *n* Scots forms of **two**. — *adj* and *adv* **twa'fald** (*-föld*) twofold; bent double. — *n* and *adj* **twa'some** see **twosome**. — *adj* **twa'-loft'ed** two-storied.

twaddle *twod'l, n* senseless or tedious uninteresting talk; a talker of twaddle (*obs*). — *vi* to talk twaddle. — *n* **twadd'ler**. — *n* and *adj* **twadd'ling**. — *adj* **twadd'ly**. [Perh **twattle**]

twain *twān*, (*archaic*) *adj* two. — *n* a couple, pair. — **in twain** asunder. [OE *twēgen* (masc) two]

twaite *twāt, n* one of the British species of shad. — Also **twaite shad**. [Origin unknown]

twal *twöl, twäl, adj* and *n* a Scots form of **twelve**. — *n* **twal'hours** (*-o͞orz*) a noonday meal or refreshment. — *n* (*hist*) **twal'penny** or **twal'pennies** a shilling in old Scots money, an old penny sterling.

twang[1] *twang*, (*dialect*) *n* a sharp flavour; an aftertaste; a smack, suggestion. [**tang**[3], affected by **twang**[2]]

twang[2] *twang, n* the sound of a plucked string; a nasal tone; a twinge (*dialect*); a local intonation (*colloq*). — *vt* and *vi* to sound with a twang. — *n* and *adj* **twang'ing**. — *adv* **twang'ingly**. — *n* **twangle** (*twang'gl*) a slack or jangly twanging. — *vt* and *vi* to sound with a twangle. — *n* and *adj* **twang'ling** (*-gling*). — *adv* **twang'lingly** (*-gling-li*). — *adj* **twangy** (*twang'i*). — *n* **twank** (*dialect*) a short twang; a slap. [Imit]

twankay *twang'kā, n* a kind of green tea; gin (*slang*). [*Tong-ke* or Tun-chi in China]

'twas *twoz, twəz*, (*archaic* or *dialect*). A contraction of **it was**.

twat *twot, twat, n* the vulva (*vulg slang*); mistakenly, part of a nun's dress (*Browning*); a coarse general term of reproach (*slang*). [Origin obscure]

twattle *twot'l, n* chatter; babble; twaddle. — *vt* and *vi* to babble. — *n* **twatt'ler**. — *n* and *adj* **twatt'ling**. [Perh connected with **tattle**]

tway *twā, adj* and *n* a form of **twain** (*Spenser*); a form of **twain**, or of **two** (**twae**) (*Scot*). — **tway'-blade** an orchid (*Listera*) with small green flowers and one pair of leaves; also an American orchid (*Liparis*).

tweak *twēk, vt* to twitch, to pull; to pull or twist with sudden jerks; to fine-tune (eg a mechanism); to rewrite or alter (editorial or author's copy) (*journalists' slang*). — *n* a sharp pinch or twitch; a fine-tuning adjustment, a slight modification designed to improve anything; rewriting or alteration of copy (*journalists' slang*); agitation, perplexity (*obs*). — *n* **tweak'ing**. [Appar connected with **twitch**[1]]

twee *twē*, (*colloq*) *adj* small and sweet; sentimentally pretty. — *adv* **twee'ly**. — *n* **twee'ness**. [*tweet* for 'sweet', and later *tiny* and *wee*]

tweed *twēd, n* a rough woollen cloth much used for men's suits; (in *pl*) clothes of tweed. — *n* **tweed'iness**. — *adj* **tweed'y** of or resembling tweed; of a predominantly upper-class, hearty, outdoor type. [Said to be from a misreading of **tweel**, the cloth being made in the Tweed basin; or perh a shortening of *tweeled* (twilled)]

tweedle *twē'dl, vi* to play casually (on an instrument), strum, tootle; (of a bird) to pipe or whistle; to swindle, con (*slang*). — *vt* to pipe into acquiescence; to wheedle. — *n* **tweedledee'** (*Burns*) a fiddler. — **Tweedledee and Tweedledum** two almost indistinguishable characters or things (*orig* the proverbial names of two rival musicians). — *vi* **tweedledee'** to tweedle. — *n* **tweed'ler** (*slang*) a con man; a stolen vehicle sold as though legitimate. [Prob imit, influenced by **wheedle**]

tweedy. See under **tweed**.

tweel *twēl*, a Scots form of **twill**[1].

'tween. A contraction of **between**. — *adj* **'tween'-deck** lodging between decks. — *n* **'tween'decks** (*naut*) the space between two decks of a vessel. — *adv* in or into this area. — *n* **tween'y** (*colloq*) a between-maid.

tweer[1]. See **twyer**.

tweer[2]. See **twire**[1].

tweet *twēt*, or **tweet'-tweet'** *n* the note of a small bird. — *vt* and *vi* to chirp as a small bird does. — *n* **tweet'er** a loudspeaker used in high-fidelity sound reproduction for the higher frequencies (also *colloq* **top tweet**). [Imit]

tweezers *twēz'ərz, n pl* small pincers for pulling out hairs, etc. — *vt* **tweeze** (*esp US*) to grasp or pluck with or as if with tweezers. — **tweez'er-case** an étui. [Obs *tweeze* a surgeon's case of instruments, from Fr *étui*]

twelfth *twelfth, adj* last of twelve; immediately following the eleventh in order, position, etc; equal to one of twelve equal parts. — *n* a twelfth part; a person or thing in twelfth position; a tone eleven (conventionally twelve) diatonic degrees above or below a given tone (*music*); an octave and a fifth. — *adv* **twelfth'ly** in the twelfth place. — **Twelfth'-cake** an ornamental cake traditionally eaten on Twelfth-night; **Twelfth'-day** the twelfth day after Christmas, Epiphany, 6 January; **twelfth man** (*cricket*) a player selected beyond the necessary eleven to play if required as a substitute; **Twelfth'-night** the eve of Twelfth-day, 5 January; also the evening of Twelfth-day, 6 January; **Twelfth'-tide** the season of Epiphany. — **the glorious Twelfth** 12 August, opening day of the grouse-shooting season. [OE *twelfta*, from *twelf*]

twelve *twelv, n* the cardinal number next above eleven; a symbol representing that number; a set of that number of things or persons; an article of a size denoted by 12; a score of twelve points; the hour of midday or midnight; the age of twelve years; (in *pl*) duodecimo; (**12**) a certificate designating a film passed as suitable only for people of twelve and over. — *adj* consisting of twelve. — *adj* and *adv* **twelve'fold**. — *n* **twelve'mo** (*pl* **twelve'mos**) duodecimo, written **12mo**. — *n* **twelve'-month** a year. — *adj* of the number twelve; twelve years old. — *adj* **twelve'-penny** shilling. — **twelve score** two hundred and forty (yards); **Twelve Tables** the earliest code of Roman law, civil, criminal and religious, made by the decemvirs in 451–449 BC. — *adj* **twelve'-tone** or **twelve'-note** relating to music based on a pattern formed from the twelve notes of the chromatic scale, *esp* as developed by Arnold Schönberg (1874–1951) and his pupils (**twelve-tone row** or **twelve-note row** being the basic pattern of notes; see also **series** and **serial**). — **the Twelve** (*Bible*) the twelve apostles. [OE *twelf* (Ger *zwölf* and Gothic *twa-lif*) ie prob two left; see **eleven**]

twenty *twen'ti, adj* twice ten; nineteen and one; an indefinite number of. — *n* the number immediately above nineteen; a score; a symbol representing that number; the age of twenty years; a set of twenty things or persons; a score of twenty points; an old English division of infantry. — *n pl* **twen'ties** the numbers twenty to twenty-nine; the years so numbered in life or any century; a range of temperatures from twenty to just less than thirty degrees. — *adj* **twen'tieth** next after the nineteenth; last of twenty; equal to one of twenty equal parts. — *n* a twentieth part; a person or thing in twentieth position. — *n, adj* and *adv* **twen'tyfold** twenty times as many or much. — *adj* **twen'tyish** about twenty. — **twenty-five'** a line on a hockey pitch (and formerly on a rugby pitch) twenty-five yards from the goal-line; **twenty-four'** a sheet folded into twenty-four leaves (forty-eight pages); a form arranged for printing it. — *n* **twenty-four'mo** (written **24mo**, for L *in vīcēsimō quārtō*) a book made up of sheets folded in twenty-four leaves (forty-eight pages). — Also *adj*. — **twenty-pence piece** or **twenty-penny piece** in Britain, a coin worth 20 pence. — *adj* **twenty-twen'ty** (or **20/20**) (of human vision) normal, also (*colloq*) sharp, clear. — **twenty-two'** a line on a rugby pitch twenty-two metres from the goal-line. — **and twenty** (*Shakesp*) supposed to be a mere intensive, as in *good even and twenty* or *sweet and twenty* (see under **sweet**). [OE *twēntig*, prob from *twēgen* twain, and sfx *-tig* (Gothic *tigjus*) ten; Ger *zwanzig*]

'twere. A contraction of **it were**.

twerp *twûrp*, (*slang*) *n* a silly and/or contemptible person. [Origin uncertain; a connection with one T W Earp, once president of the Oxford University Union, has been suggested]

twi- or **twy-** *twī*, *pfx* two; double. — *adj* **twi'fold** or **twy'fold** twofold. — *adj* **twi'forked** or **twy'forked** bifurcate. — *adj* **twi'formed** or **twy'formed** having two forms. — *adj* **twi'-natured** or **twy'-natured** of double nature. [OE pfx *twi-*]

Twi *ch(w)ē*, *n* a dialect, and also a literary language, of Ghana. — Also **Tshi**. — Also *adj*.

twibill *twī'bil*, *n* a double-headed axe. [OE *twibill*, from **twi-** and **bill**[1]]

twice *twīs*, *adv* two times; doubly; for a second time. — *n* **twi'cer** a person who is both compositor and pressman; someone who habitually goes to church twice on Sunday (*eccles slang*). — *adj* **twice'-born** born twice, as Bacchus; of high Hindu caste; regenerate (*theol*); **twice'-laid** made of old yarns twisted together again; **twice'-told** counted twice; told twice; hackneyed. — **at twice** in two stages or operations; **twice over** twice (emphatically). [Late OE *twiges*, from *twiga*, *twiwa*, *tuwa* twice, with adverbial genitive ending]

twichild *twī'chīld*, (now *dialect*) *n* a person in his or her second childhood. [**twi-**]

twiddle *twid'l*, *vt* to twirl idly; to finger idly, play with; to rotate. — *vi* to twirl; to trifle with something. — *n* a twirl; a curly mark, ornament. — *n* **twidd'ler**. — *n* and *adj* **twidd'ling**. — *adj* **twidd'ly**. — **twidd'ling-line** formerly, a line for steadying the steering-wheel; a string for setting the compass-card to play freely. — **twiddle one's thumbs** to rotate the thumbs around each other; to be idle (*fig*). [Prob suggested by **twirl**, **twist** and **fiddle**]

twier. See **twyer**.

twig[1] *twig*, *n* a small thin shoot or branch; a divining-rod. — *adj* made of twigs. — *vt* to birch, switch. — *adj* **twigg'en** (*Shakesp*) covered with or made of wickerwork. — *adj* **twigg'y**. — *adj* **twig'some**. [OE *twig*; cf Ger *Zweig*]

twig[2] *twig*, (*colloq*) *vt* and *vi* to observe, perceive; to realize, comprehend (*esp* suddenly); to understand. [Poss Ir *tuigim* discern; cf Gaelic *tuig* understand]

twig[3] *twig*, (*slang*) *n* fettle; fashion; recognizable condition. — *vi* to act vigorously. — *n* **twigg'er** (*obs*) a vigorous breeder; a wanton. [Origin obscure]

twight *twīt*, *vt* (*Spenser*) for **twit**[1].

twilight *twī'līt*, *n* the faint light after sunset and before sunrise; this time of day; dim light or partial darkness; a period of decay following a period of success, vigour, greatness, etc. — *adj* of or at twilight; *specif* of work, educational classes, etc, taking place after normal daytime hours, between late afternoon and early evening; faintly illuminated; obscure, indefinite; partial, transitional. — *vt* to illuminate faintly. — *adj* **twī'lighted** or **twī'lit**. — **twilight sleep** partial anaesthesia, eg in childbirth, by the use of drugs; **twilight zone** a dilapidated, decaying area of a city or town typically situated between the main business and commercial area and the suburbs; any area or state transitional or indefinite in character. — **twilight of the Gods** see ety for **Ragnarök**. [**twi-** and **light**]

'twill, (*archaic* or *dialect*). A contraction of **it will**.

twill[1] *twil*, or (*Scot*) **tweel** *twēl*, *n* a woven fabric showing diagonal lines, the weft yarns having been worked over one and under two or more warp yarns; the appearance so produced. — *vt* to weave with a twill. — **cavalry twill** a strong woollen twill used *esp* for trousers. [OE *twilic*]

twill[2] *twil* and **twilt** *twilt*. Dialect forms of **quill** and **quilt**.

twilled *twil'id*, (*Shakesp*) *adj prob*, protected against floods by plaited osiers (the word so used still at Stratford); according to some, ridged like twilled cloth; or reedy, from an alleged *obs* word *twill* a reed.

twilly *twil'i*, *n* a willowing-machine. [**willow**]

twin[1] *twin* or **twine** *twīn*, (*obs* and *Scot*) *vt* and *vi* to separate; to part. — *vt* to deprive. [**twin**[2]]

twin[2] *twin*, *n* either of two born at a single birth; one very like, or closely associated with, another; a counterpart; a pair of twins or pair generally (*obs*); a combination of two crystals symmetrically united about a plane that is a possible face of each or an axis that is a possible edge of each, or of more than two by repetition. — *adj* twofold, double; born two at one birth; forming one, or consisting of both, of two identical or very similar parts or counterparts; very like another. — *vt* to couple together, or to produce, like a twin or twins. — *vi* to be born at the same birth; to give birth to two at one birth; to be paired or suited: — *pr p* **twinn'ing**; *pa p* **twinned**. — *n* **twin'er** (*Walter de la Mare*) a double limerick. — *n* **twin'ling** (now *dialect*) a twin. — *adj* **twinned** produced at one birth; constituting a twin; paired, matched. — *n* **twinn'ing**. — *n* **twin'ship** the condition or relation of a twin or twins. — **twin'-ax'is** the axis of symmetry of a twin crystal; **twin bed** either of a matching pair of single beds; **twin'-birth** a birth of twins; a twin; a pair of twins. — *adj* **twin'-born** born at the same birth. — **twin-broth'er** a brother born at the same birth; **twin** (or **twinned**) **crystal** (*crystallog*, *mineralogy*) a crystal composed of two or more individuals in a systematic crystallographic orientation with respect to one another; **twin'flower** a N American plant of the genus *Linnaea* having paired flowers; **twin paradox** a phenomenon suggested by the theory of relativity in which one of a pair of twins lives in the normal way, while the other twin is sent out in a spaceship travelling at great speeds — the travelling twin would theoretically be younger than the other twin on his return after a long time; **twin'-plane'** the plane of symmetry of a twin crystal. — *adj* **twin'-screw** with two propellers on separate shafts. — **twin'set** a cardigan and jumper made more or less to match; **twin=sist'er** a sister born at the same birth; **twin town** a town paired with another foreign town of similar size for the purpose of social, cultural and commercial exchanges. — *adj* **twin'-track** consisting of or split between two simultaneous, complementary or reciprocal elements, activities, jobs, etc. — **twin'-tub** a type of washing-machine with separate drums for washing and spin-drying (also *adj*). — **the Twins** Gemini. [OE *getwinn* (noun) twin, *twinn* (adj) double; cf **twi-**]

twine[1] *twīn*, *n* a twisted cord; string or strong thread; a coil; a twist; a twisted stem or the like; an act of twisting or clasping. — *vt* to wind; to coil; to wreathe; to twist; to twist together; to encircle; to make by twisting. — *vi* to wind; to coil; to twist; to make turns; to rise or grow in spirals; to wriggle. — *adj* **twīned**. — *n* **twī'ner** a person who, or thing which, twines; a twining plant. — *n* and *adj* **twī'ning**. — *adv* **twī'ningly**. — *adj* **twī'ny**. — **twining plant** one that climbs by twining its stem round a support. [OE *twīn* double or twisted thread, linen thread; cf Du *twijn*]

twine[2] *twīn*, *n* a variant of **twin**[1].

twiner[1]. See under **twin**[2].

twiner[2]. See under **twine**[1].

twinge *twinj*, *vt* to tweak or pinch; to affect with a momentary pain. — *vi* to feel or give a momentary pain. — *n* a tweak, a pinch; a sudden short shooting pain; a brief pang. [OE *twengan* to pinch]

twi-night *twī'-nīt*, (*baseball*; *NAm*) *adj* of or designating a double-header in which the first game is played in the late afternoon and the second in the evening. — Also *n*. — *n* **twi'-nighter**. [*twi*light and **night**]

twink *twingk*, *vi* to blink; to twinkle. — *n* a twinkling, a moment. [Root of **twinkle**]

twinkle *twing'kl*, *vi* to blink; to quiver the eyelid; to shine by flashes; to glitter; to sparkle; to flicker, vibrate. — *vt* to guide by twinkling. — *n* a blink; a wink; a glitter; a quiver; a flicker; a sparkle; a twinkling; a dance step. — *n* **twink'ler**. — *n* **twink'ling** a quick motion of the eye; the time occupied by a wink; an instant; the scintillation of the fixed stars. — *adj* scintillating; quivering; blinking (*obs*). [OE *twinclian*]

twinter *twin'tər*, (*Scot*) *adj* two years old. — *n* a two-year-old sheep or other animal. [OE *twiwintre* two-winter]

twire[1] *twīr* or **tweer** *twēr*, (*Shakesp*) *vi* to peer. — *n* (*obs*) a glance, leer. [Cf MHGer *zwieren* to peer]

twire[2]. See **twyer**.

twirl *twûrl*, *vt* and *vi* to spin; to whirl; to twist; to coil. — *n* a twist; a spin; a whirl; a whorl; a curly figure. — *n* **twirl'er**. — *adj* **twirl'y**. — **twirl one's thumbs** to twiddle one's thumbs. [Connection with OE *thwiril* churn handle, whisk, doubtful]

twirp. An alternative spelling of **twerp**.

twiscar. See **tuskar**.

twist *twist*, *vt* to twine; to unite or form by winding together; to form from several threads; to wind spirally; to form into a spiral; to wring; to wrest; to distort; to force, pull out of natural shape, position, etc; to entangle; to impart a spin to; to force round; to eat heartily (often with *down*; *old slang*); to pervert, warp. — *vi* to twine; to coil; to move spirally or tortuously; to turn aside; to revolve; to writhe; in the card-game vingt-et-un (pontoon), to deal or receive a card face upwards. — *n* that which is twisted or formed by twisting; a cord; a strand; thread; silk thread; warp yarn; a twisted part; torsion; an act or manner of twisting; a contortion; a wrench; a wresting; a turning aside; a spin, screw, or break; a distortion; a perverted bent or set; an unexpected event or change of direction *lit* and *fig*); a tangle; a twisted roll of tobacco or bread; a small curled piece of lemon, etc flavouring a drink; a spiral ornament in the stem of a glass; a twig (*obs*); the fork of the body (*obs*); a mixed drink (*slang*); a good appetite (*slang*). — *adj* **twist'able**. — *adj* **twist'ed**. — *n* **twist'er** a person who or thing which twists; a sophistical, slippery, shuffling or dishonest person; a ball sent with a twist; a tornado (*US colloq*). — *n* and *adj* **twist'ing**. — *adj* **twist'y**. — **twist drill** a drill for metal having one or more deep helical grooves round the body; **twisted pair** (*comput* and *telecomm*) a pair of electrically-insulated wires twisted together to form a single cable to improve signal transmission; **round the twist** (*colloq*) crazy, mad; **the twist** a dance which became popular in 1962, in which the dancer constantly twists the body; **twist someone round one's little finger** see under **finger**; **twist someone's arm** to persuade someone, *esp* forcefully. [OE *twist* rope (found in the compound *mæst-twist* a stay)]

twistor *twist'ər*, (*math* and *phys*) *n* one of a number of complex variables representing the space–time co-ordinates, retaining their relevant symmetries. — **twistor theory** (*phys*) a theory, a candidate for the so-called 'theory of everything', which attempts to describe the structure of space as eight-dimensional, using complex numbers and particle spin — the building blocks of this structure being twistors.

twit[1] *twit*, *vt* to upbraid; to taunt: — *pr p* **twitt'ing**; *pa t* and *pa p* **twitt'ed**. — *n* a reproach. — *vt* **twitt'er** (*Fielding*) to twit. — *n* and *adj* **twitt'ing**. — *adv* **twitt'ingly**. [OE *ætwītan* to reproach, from *æt* against, and *wītan* to reproach]

twit[2] *twit*, (*slang*) *n* a fool. [Prob **twit**[1]]

twitch[1] *twich*, *vt* to jerk; to pluck; to snatch; to steal; to pinch or tweak. — *vi* to jerk; to move spasmodically; to carp, sneer. — *n* a sudden, quick pull; a spasmodic contraction of the muscles; a twinge; a noose; the sudden tapering of a vein of ore; the yips (qv) (*golf*). — *n* **twitch'er** a person who or thing which twitches; a bird-watcher whose main interest is the spotting of as many rare species as possible (*colloq*). — *n* and *adj* **twitch'ing**. — *adj* **twitch'y** that twitches; jerky; inclined to twitch; on edge, nervous (*colloq*). [Related to OE *twiccian* to pluck; Ger *zwicken*]

twitch[2] *twich* and **twitch grass**. Forms of **quitch** and **quitch grass** (see **couch grass**).

twite *twīt*, *n* the mountain linnet, *Acanthis flavirostris*, a N European finch with streaked brown plumage. [From its note]

twitten *twit'n*, (*dialect*) *n* a narrow lane between two walls or hedges. — Also **twitt'ing**. [Perh related to LGer *twiete* alley, lane]

twitter[1] *twit'ər*, *n* a tremulous chirping; a flutter of the nerves. — *vi* to make a succession of small tremulous noises; to palpitate. — *vt* to chirp out; to twiddle. — *n* **twitt'erer**. — *n* and *adj* **twitt'ering**. — *adv* **twitt'eringly**. — *adj* **twitt'ery**. [Imit; cf Ger *zwitschern*]

twitter[2] *twit'ər*, or **twitt'er-bone** *-bōn*, *n* an excrescence on a horse's hoof. — *adj* **twitt'er-boned**. [A form of **quitter**]

twitter[3] and **twitting**[1]. See under **twit**[1].

twitting[2]. See **twitten**.

'twixt. A contraction of **betwixt**.

twizzle *twiz'əl*, *vt* to twirl, spin. [Prob formed under influence of **twist** and **twirl**]

two *tōō*, *n* the sum of one and one; a symbol representing two; a pair; a deuce, card with two pips; a score of two points, strokes, etc; an article of a size denoted by two; the second hour after midnight or midday; the age of two years. — *adj* of the number two; two years old. — *n* **two'er** (*colloq*) anything that counts as or for two, or scores two. — *adj* and *adv* **two'fold** in two divisions; twice as much; (*esp Scot* **twafald** *twä, twö-föld*) in a doubled-up position. — *n* **two'foldness**. — *n* **two'ness** the state of being two; duality. — *n* **two'some** (*Scot* **twa'some**) a group of two; a tête-à-tête; a game between two players (*golf*). — *adj* consisting of two; performed by two. — **two bits** (*NAm*) twenty-five cents, a quarter. — *adj* **two'-bit** (*NAm*) cheap, paltry. — *adj* **two'-bottle** able to drink two bottles of wine at a sitting. — **two-by-four'** (a piece of) timber measuring four inches by two inches in cross-section (somewhat less when dressed); **two'-decker** a ship with two decks or with guns on two decks; a bus or tram-car carrying passengers on a roofed top. — *adj* **two'-digit** in double figures. — *adj* **two'-dimensional**. — **two-dimensional'ity** the property of having length and breadth but no depth. — *adj* **two'-edged** having two cutting edges; capable of being turned against the user; **two'-eyed** having two eyes (**two-eyed steak** (*slang*) a bloater); **two'-faced** having two faces; double-dealing, false; **two'-fisted** clumsy; capable of fighting with both fists; holding the racket with both hands (*tennis*); **two'-foot** measuring, or with, two feet; **two'-footed** having two feet; capable of kicking and controlling the ball equally well with either foot (*football*, etc). — **two'-for-his-heels** a knave (from the score for turning up a knave in cribbage). — *adj* **two'-forked** having two prongs or branches. — *adj* **two'-four** (*music*) with two crotchets to the bar. — *adj* **two'-hand** (*Shakesp*) for two hands; **two'-handed** with or for two hands; for two persons; ambidextrous; strapping. — **two-hand'er** anything designed for, written for or requiring both hands or two people (eg actors). — *adj* **two'-headed** having two heads; directed by two authorities; **two'-horse** for two horses (**two-horse race** any contest in which only two of the participants have a genuine chance of winning); **two'-inch** measuring two inches; **two'-leaved** or **two'-leafed** with two leaves or leaflets; with leaves in twos; **two'-legged** with two legs; **two'-line** (*printing*) having double depth of body; **two'-lipped** having two lips; bilabiate; **two'-masted** having two masts. — **two'-mast'er** a two-masted ship. — *adj* **two'-pair** or **two'-pair-of-stairs** on a second floor. — *n* a room so situated. — *adj* **two'-part** composed in two parts or for two voices. — *adj* **two'-parted** bipartite; divided into two nearly to the base. — **twopence** (*tup'əns*) or (decimalized currency) **two pence** (*tōō pens*) the sum of two pennies; a coin worth two pence. — *adj* **twopence-coloured** see under **penny**. — **two-pence piece** or **two-penny piece** (*tōō'*) in Britain, a coin worth 2 pence (also **two'penny-piece**). — *adj* **twopenny** (*tup'ni*) sold, offered at or worth twopence; cheap, worthless. — *n* ale sold at twopence a quart; in leapfrog, the head. — *adj* **twopenny-halfpenny** (*tup'ni-hāp'ni*) or **twopence-halfpenny** paltry, petty. — *n* **two-penn'yworth** or **two-penn'orth** (*tōō-pen'ərth*), also (chiefly *Scot*) **twopenceworth** (*tup'*). — *n* **two'-piece** anything consisting of two separate parts, pieces or members. — Also *adj*. — *adj* **two'-ply** having two layers, or consisting of two strands; woven double. **two-pot screamer** (*Austr slang*) a person who gets drunk on a comparatively small amount of alcohol; **two-power standard** (*hist*) the principle that the strength of the British navy must never be less than the combined strength of the navies of any two other powers. — *adj* **two'-roomed**. — *n* and *adj* **two'-score** forty. — **two'-seater** a vehicle or aeroplane seated for two. — *adj* **two'-sid'ed** having two surfaces, aspects or parties; facing two ways; double-faced; having the two sides different. — **two-sid'edness**; **two-speed gear** a gear-changing contrivance with two possibilities; **two-start thread** see **double-threaded screw** under **double**; **two'-step** a gliding dance in duple time; a tune for it. — *vi* to dance the two-step. — *adj* **two'-storeyed** or **two'-stor'ey**. — *adj* **two'stroke** (of an engine cycle) consisting of two piston strokes; relating to or designed for such an engine. — *vt* **two'-time** to deceive; to double-cross. — **two'-timer** a person who deceives or double-crosses. — *adj* **two'-timing**. — *adj* **two'-tone** having two colours or two shades of the same colour; (of eg a car-horn) having two notes. — **two'-up** an Australian game in which two coins are tossed and bets made on both falling heads up or both tails up. — *adj* **two'-way** permitting passage along either of two ways *esp* in opposite directions; able to receive and send signals (*radio*); of communication between two persons, groups, etc, in which both participate equally; involving shared responsibility; able to be used in two ways; having a double mode of variation or two dimensions (*math*). — *adj* **two'-wheeled** having two wheels. — **two-wheel'er** a two-wheeled vehicle with two wheels, *esp* a motor-cycle, or formerly a hansom cab. — *adj* **two'-year-old**. — *n* a child, colt, etc aged two. — **be two** to be at variance; **in two** asunder, so as to form two pieces; **in two twos** or **two ticks** (*slang*) in a moment; **put two and two together** see under **put**[1]; **that makes two of us** (*colloq*) the same thing applies to me; **two or three** a few; **two-up, two-down** (a small, traditionally built terraced house) having two bedrooms upstairs and two reception rooms downstairs. [OE *twā* (fem and neuter) two (masc *twēgen*); Ger *zwei*, Gothic *twai*; Gr *dyo*, L *duo*, Sans *dva*, Gaelic *dà*]

TWOC *twok*, *abbrev*: taking without owner's consent, the technical name for the offence of stealing a car, etc. — *n* **twocc'er** (*slang*) a person who commits this offence. — *n* **twocc'ing** (*slang*).

'twould *twŏŏd*, (*archaic* or *dialect*). A contraction of **it would**.

twp *tŏŏp*, (*Welsh*) *adj* dim-witted, stupid. [Welsh]

twy-. See **twi-**.

twyer, twyere, tweer, twier, twire or **tuyère** *twēr*, also *twīr*, *twē-yer'*, *n* a nozzle for a blast of air. [Fr *tuyère*]

TX *abbrev*: Texas (US state).

Tyburn *tī'bərn*, *n* the historic place of execution in London. — **Ty'burn-ticket** a certificate of exemption from certain parochial offices formerly granted to the prosecutor of a felon to conviction; **Ty'burn-tippet** a halter; **Ty'burn-tree** the gallows.

Tyche *tī'kē*, (*Gr mythol*) *n* the goddess of fortune. — *n* **ty'chism** a theory that accepts pure chance. [Gr *tychē* chance]

Tychonic *tī-kon'ik*, *adj* relating to the Danish astronomer, *Tycho* Brahe (1546–1601), or his system.

tycoon *tī-kōōn'*, *n* the title by which the Shoguns of Japan were known to foreigners; a business magnate. — *n* **tycoon'ate** the shogunate. — *n* **tycoon'ery**. [Jap *taikun* great prince, from Old Chin *t'ai* great, and *kiun* prince]

tyde. A Spenserian spelling of **tied**, *pa t* and *pa p* of **tie**.

tye[1] or **tie** *tī*, *n* an inclined trough for washing ore. — *vt* to wash in a tye. [OE *tēag* case, chest]

tye[2] or **tie** *tī*, (*local*) *n* an area of common land or pasture. [OE *tēag*, perh same as **tye**[1]; cf ON *teigr* strip of land]

tyg. Same as **tig**[2].

tying *tī'ing*, *pr p* of **tie**.

tyke or **tike** *tīk*, (chiefly *Scot* and *N Eng*) *n* a dog; a cur; a rough-mannered person; a small child (*colloq*); a Yorkshireman; a Roman Catholic (*derog Austr* and *NZ slang*). — *adj* **tyk'ish**. [ON *tīk* bitch]

tylectomy *tī-lek'tə-mi*, *n* the same as lumpectomy. [Gr *tylē* lump, and *ektomē* cutting out]

tyler. See under **tile**.

Tylopoda *tī-lop'ə-də*, *n pl* a section of the ungulates with padded toes, comprising camels and llamas. — *n* and *adj* **ty'lopod**. [Gr *tylos* a knob, callus, and *pous*, *podos* a foot]

tylosis *tī-lō'sis*, *n* an ingrowth from a neighbouring cell through a pit into a vessel (also, *perh orig*, **thylose** *thī'lōs*, or **thylosis** *thī-lō'sis*; *pl* **thylo'sēs**; perh from Gr *thylakos* a pocket; *bot*); an inflammation of the eyelids; a callosity: — *pl* **tylō'sēs**. — *n* **tylote** (*tī'lōt*) a cylindrical sponge spicule, knobbed at both ends. [Gr *tylos* a knob, callus]

tymbal. Same as **timbal**.

tymp *timp*, *n* the plate of a blast-furnace opening. [**tympan**]

tympan *tim'pən*, *n* any drum-like instrument (*archaic*); a tympanum; an ancient Irish stringed instrument played with a bow (Ir *tiompan*); a frame covered with parchment or cloth, on which sheets are placed for printing (*printing*); material placed between the platen and the paper to give an even impression (*printing*). [OFr, or as for **tympanum**]

tympanal. See under **tympanum**.

tympani. See **tympano**.

tympanic ... to ... **tympanitis**. See under **tympanum**.

tympano *tim'pə-nō*, *n*. A variant of **timpano**: — *pl* **tym'pani** (*-ē*).

tympanum *tim'pə-nəm*, *n* a drum; a drumhead; the middle ear; the membrane separating it from the outer ear, the drum (also called the **tympanic membrane**); in insects, a vibratory membrane in various parts of the body, serving as an eardrum; in birds, the resonating sac of the syrinx; an air-sac in the neck in grouse, etc; the recessed face of a pediment (*archit*); a space between a lintel and an arch over it (*archit*); an early type of wheel for scooping up water: — *pl* **tym'pana**. — *adj* **tym'panal** (*anatom* and *zool*) of or relating to the tympanum. — *adj* **tympanic** (*-pan'ik*) of or like a drum or tympanum; tympanitic. — *n* (*anatom*) a bone of the ear, supporting the drum-membrane. — *adj* **tym'paniform** (or *-pan'*) drum-shaped; drum-like. — *n* **tym'panist** a drummer, now *esp* (also **tim'panist**) a player of the timpani. — *n* **tympanī'tēs** flatulent distension of the belly. — *adj* **tympanitic** (*-it'ik*) of or affected with tympanites. — *n* **tympanī'tis** (*med*) inflammation of the membrane of the ear. — *n* **tym'pany** any swelling, *esp* of the abdomen; tympanites; a blowing up as with pride; a drum (*rare*). [L *tympanum*, from Gr *tympanon*, *typanon* a kettledrum, from *typtein* to strike]

tynd, tyn'd, tyned, tynde or **tyne** (also *Scot*), (*Spenser* and *Shakesp*). See **tind** and **tine**[2,5].

Tynwald *tin'wold*, *n* the parliament of the Isle of Man. [ON *thing-völlr*, from *thing* assembly, and *völlr* field]

typ or **typo** *abbrev*: typographer; typography.

type *tīp*, *n* a mark or stamp; the device on a coin or medal; a distinguishing mark; insignia; a designation; an emblem; a foreshadowing; an anticipation; an exemplar; a model or pattern; a kind; the general character of a class; that which well exemplifies the characteristics of a group; a person of well-marked characteristics; (loosely and derogatorily) a person; a simple chemical compound representative of the structure of more complex compounds; the actual specimen on which the description of a new species or genus is based (also called **type specimen**) (*biol*); a rectangular piece of metal or of wood on one end of which is cast or engraved a character, sign, etc used in printing; printing types collectively, letter; print; lettering. — *adj* serving as a type. — *vt* to prefigure, foreshadow, symbolize (*theol*); to be the type of; to determine the type of (*med*); to exemplify; to typewrite; to print (*rare*). — *vi* to typewrite. — *adj* **ty'pal** or **typic** (*tip'*) typical. — *n* **typing** (*tīp'ing*). — *n* **typist** (*tīp'ist*) a person who uses a typewriter; someone whose occupation is typewriting. — **type'-bar** a line of type cast in one piece; in a typewriter, each of the levers on the ends of which are the types; **type'-body** a measurement of breadth of shank for a size of type; **type case** a tray with compartments for storing printing types. — *vt* **type'cast** to cast (someone) in a rôle that accords with what he or she is by nature; to cast continually for the same kind of part. — *adj* **type'cast**. — **type'-cutter** someone who engraves dies for printing types; **type'-cyl'inder** the cylinder of a rotary printing-machine on which plates are fastened for printing; **type'-face** the printing surface of a type; any of a variety of styles in which it is cut; a complete range of type cut in a particular style; **type'-founder** someone who founds or casts printers' type; **type'-founding**; **type'-foundry**; **type'-genus** the genus that gives its name to its family. — *adj* and *adv* **type'-high** of or at the standard type height (*approx* 0.918in; 23.317mm), measured in the direction of the shank; (of a woodcut, etc) at the height required for printing. — **type'-holder** a bookbinder's pallet or holder for use in hand-stamping; **type locality** the area in which a genus or a geological formation occurs most typically or in which it was classified; **type'-metal** metal used for making types; an alloy of lead with antimony and tin, and sometimes copper; **type'script** typewritten matter or copy; type in imitation of handwriting or of typewriting. — *adj* typewritten. — *adj* **type'set**. — **type'setter** a compositor; a machine for setting type; **type'setting**; **type'-species** a species taken as the one to which the generic name is primarily attached; **type specimen** a holotype. — *vt* and *vi* **type'write** to print or copy with a typewriter. — **type'writer** a machine, *usu* with a keyboard, for printing as a substitute for handwriting; a typist (*rare*). — *n* **type'writing**. — *adj* **type'written**. [L *typus*, from Gr *typos* blow, mark, stamp, model, from *typtein* to strike]

-type *-tīp*, *sfx* of the same type as, resembling (eg *pampas-type grass*; *esp colloq*). — *combining form* denoting printing type. [**type**]

Typha *tī'fə*, *n* the reed-mace genus, tall erect herbs growing *esp* in marshy areas, giving its name to a family of monocotyledons, **Typhā'ceae**. — *adj* **typhā'ceous**. [Gr *typhē* reed-mace]

typhlitis *tif-lī'tis*, (*med*) *n* inflammation of the blind-gut. — *adj* **typhlitic** (*-lit'ik*). — *n* **typhlol'ogy** the study of blindness and the blind. [Gr *typhlos* blind]

Typhoeus *tī-fō'yəs*, *tī-fē'əs*, *n* a monster of Greek mythology buried under Etna. — *adj* **Typhoean** (*tī-fō'yən*, *tī-fē'ən*). [Gr *Typhōeus*]

typhoid *tī'foid*, *adj* like typhus. — *n* (for **typhoid fever**) enteric fever caused by the bacillus *Salmonella typhosa*, long confused with typhus, on account of the characteristic rash of rose-coloured spots. — *adj* **typhoid'al**. [Gr *typhōdēs* delirious, from *typhos* a fever, and *eidos* likeness; cf **typhus**]

Typhon *tī'fon*, *-fən*, *n* son of Typhoeus, later identified with him, father of dangerous winds (*Gr mythol*); (without *cap*) a whirlwind (*obs*). — *adj* **Typhonian** (*-fō'ni-ən*) or **Typhonic** (*-fon'ik*; also without *cap*).

typhoon *tī-fōōn'*, *n* a violent cyclonic storm of the China seas and West Pacific area. [Gr *Typhōn* Typhon, *typhōn* a whirlwind; but partly also from Port *tufão*, from Ar, Pers, Hindi *tūfān* a hurricane (perh itself from Gr), and partly from Chin *t'ai fung* a great wind]

typhus *tī'fəs*, *n* a dangerous fever transmitted by lice harbouring a Rickettsia and marked by the eruption of red spots. — *adj* **ty'phoid** (qv). — *adj* **ty'phous**. [Latinized from Gr *typhos* fever, stupor, delusion; cf *typhein* to smoke]

typical *tip'i-kəl*, *adj* relating to, or constituting, a type; emblematic; figurative; characteristic; representative; typographical (*rare*). — *n* **typical'ity**. — *adv* **typ'ically**. — *n* **typ'icalness**. [Med L *typicālis*, from L *typicus*]

typify *tip'i-fī*, *vt* to make or be a type of; to exemplify or symbolize: — *pr p* **typ'ifying**; *pa t* and *pa p* **typ'ified**. — *n* **typificā'tion**. — *n* **typ'ifier**. [L *typus* (see **type**) and sfx *-fy* (ult from L *facere* to make]

typist, etc. See under **type**.

typo[1] *tī'po*, (*colloq*) *n* a typographical error, a literal: — *pl* **ty'pos**.

typo[2]. See **typ**.

typography *tī-pog'rə-fi*, *n* the art or style of printing, or of using type effectively. — *n* **typog'rapher** a compositor; a person engaged in or skilled in typography; a beetle that bores letter-like tunnels in the bark of pine and other trees. — *n pl* **typograph'ia** matter relating to printers and printing. — *adj* **typograph'ic** or **typograph'ical** — *adv* **typograph'ically**. — *n* **typog'raphist** a person who studies or is knowledgeable in the history or art of printing. [New L *typographia* (equivalent to **type** and **-graphy**)]

typology *tī-pol'ə-ji*, *n* the study of types and their succession in biology, archaeology, etc; the doctrine that things in the New Testament are foreshadowed symbolically in the Old. — *adj* **typolog'ical**. — *n* **typol'ogist**. [Gr *typos* type, and **-logy**]

typomania *tī-po-mā'ni-ə*, *n* a craze for printing one's lucubrations; a craze for finding types in the Old Testament. [Gr *typos* type, and **-mania**]

typto *tip'tō*, *vi* to conjugate the Greek verb *typtō* I strike; to work at Greek grammar: — *pr p* (*Scott*) **tup'towing**.

Tyr *tir*, *tür*, *n* the old Norse war-god. [ON *Tȳr*; OE *Tīw*; cf **Tuesday**]

tyramine *tī'rə-mēn*, *n* a colourless crystalline amine found in cheese, ergot, mistletoe and decayed animal tissue or derived from phenol, similar in action to adrenaline. [*tyr*osine and *amine*]

tyrant *tī'rənt*, *obs* **tyran** *tī'rən*, *n* in the *orig* Greek sense, an absolute ruler, or one whose power has not been constitutionally arrived at; now *usu* a ruler who uses power arbitrarily and oppressively; an oppressor; a bully; a tyrant-bird. — *vt* and *vi* (*obs*) **ty'ran**, **tyranne**, **ty'rant**. — *n* **tyr'anness** (*archaic*) a female tyrant. — *adj* **tyrannic** (*ti-ran'ik*; sometimes *tī-*) or **tyrann'ical**. — *adv* **tyrann'ically**. — *n* **tyrann'icalness**. — *adj* **tyrannicī'dal**. — *n* **tyrann'icide** the killing or the killer of a tyrant. — *n pl* **Tyrann'idae** the tyrant-bird family. — *n* **tyrannis** (*ti-ran'is*; Gr) a régime illegally set up. — *vi* **tyrannize** or **-ise** (*tir'*) to act as a tyrant; *esp* to rule with oppressive severity. — *vt* to act the tyrant to. — *adj* **tyrannous** (*tir'*) despotic; domineering; overpowering; oppressive. — *adv* **tyr'annously**. — *n* **tyranny** (*tir'*) absolute or illegally established power; the government or authority of a tyrant; absolute power cruelly administered; oppression; cruelty; harshness. — **ty'rant-bird** or **ty'rant-fly'catcher** any member of an American family of birds related to the pittas and cotingas. [Gr *tyrannos*, partly through OFr *tirant* (Fr *tyran*) and L *tyrannus*]

tyrannosaur *ti-ran'ə-sör*, or **tyrannosaurus** *-sör'əs*, *n* a large bipedal carnivorous lizard-hipped dinosaur of the carnosaur group of theropods, common during the Cretaceous period. [New L *Tyrannosaurus*, from Gr *tyrannos* and dino*saur*]

tyre *tīr*, *n* a variant spelling of **tire**[2]; a rubber cushion or tube round a wheel-rim. — *adj* **tyred**. — *adj* **tyre'less**. — **tyre chain** see under **chain**; **tyre gauge** a device for measuring the air pressure in a pneumatic tyre. — **tubeless tyre** a pneumatic tyre that has no inner tube, and, being self-sealing, deflates only slowly when punctured. [See **tire**[2]]

Tyrian *tir'i-ən*, *adj* of *Tyre*; red or purple, like the dye formerly prepared at the ancient Mediterranean port of Tyre. — *n* a native of Tyre. — **Tyrian cynosure** the north star, a guide to Tyrian mariners.

tyro. See **tiro**.

tyroglyphid *ti-rog'li-fid*, *n* a mite of the genus **Tyrog'lyphus**, including the cheese-mite and the flour-mite. [Gr *tȳros* cheese, and *glyphein* to carve]

Tyrolese *tir-ə-lēz'*, *adj* relating to the mountainous west Austrian province of *Tyrol* (Tirol), or to its people. — *n* a native of Tyrol. — *n* and *adj* **Tyrolē'an** (or *tir-ō'li-*

ən). — *n* **Tyrolienne** (*ti-rō-li-en'*) a Tyrolese peasants' dance, song or tune with yodelling.

Tyronensian. See **Tironensian**.

tyrones. See **tiro**.

tyrosine *tī'rō-sēn*, *n* an amino-acid formed by decomposition of proteins, first obtained from cheese. — *n* **ty'rosinase** an enzyme found in plants and animals that assists in converting tyrosine to melanin. [Gr *tȳros* cheese]

Tyrrhenian *ti-rē'ni-ən*, *n* and *adj* Etruscan. — Also **Tyrrhēne'**. — **Tyrrhenian Sea** that part of the Mediterranean between Tuscany and Sardinia and Corsica. [Gr *Tyrrhēnia* Etruria]

Tyrtaean *tər-tē'ən*, *adj* of or relating to *Tyrtaeus* (Gr *Tyrtaios*), a Greek martial poet of the 7c BC.

tystie *tī'sti*, (*Orkney and Shetland*) *n* the black guillemot. [Scand; cf ON *theist*]

tyte. See **tite**.

tythe. See **tithe**.

tzaddik and **tzaddiq**. See **zaddik**.

tzar. See **tsar**.

tzatziki *tsat-sē'ki*, *n* a Greek dish made of yoghurt and finely sliced or chopped cucumber, flavoured with garlic, mint, etc, eaten as a dip. [Mod Gr]

tzigany *tsig'ä-ni*, *-ə-ni*, *-ny'*, *n* a Hungarian gypsy. — Also *adj*. — Also **tsigane** (*tsi-gän'*). [Hung *cigány* gypsy; cf Ital *zingano*, *zingaro*, Ger *Zigeuner*]

tzimmes *tsi'mis*, *n* a sweetened stew or casserole of vegetables, fruit and sometimes meat: — *pl* **tzimm'es**. [Yiddish]

U

U[1] or **u** *ū*, *n* the twenty-first letter in the modern English alphabet, derived from V, a form of Y which the Romans borrowed from the Greeks. From V, the lapidary and capital form, the uncial and cursive forms U and *u* were developed, gradually V (used until modern times initially) becoming appropriated as the symbol for the consonant sound (see **V**) and the medial form *u* as the symbol for the vowel. In modern English the vowel has the sounds exemplified in *rule*, *put*, *but*, and the diphthongal sound that serves as the name of the letter; something shaped like or into a U shape. — **U'-bend** an air-trap in the form of a U-shaped bend in a pipe; **U'-bolt**, **U'-trap** and **U'-tube** a bolt, drain-trap and tube bent like the letter U. — *adj* **U'-shaped**. — **U'-turn** a turn made by a vehicle which reverses its direction of travel, crossing into the flow of traffic on the other side of the road; any reversal of direction (*fig*).

U[2] *ōō*, *n*. A Burmese title of respect, prefaced to a man's name. [Burmese]

U[3] *ū*, (*colloq*) *adj* (of words, behaviour, etc) as used by or found among the upper classes, hence socially acceptable; upper-class. — *adj* **non'-U** not used or practised by, consciously eschewed or avoided by, the upper classes, hence socially unacceptable. [**upper-class**]

U or **U.** *abbrev*: unionist; united; universal, (a certificate designating) a film which people of any age are allowed to see; university; Uruguay (IVR). — **U'-boat** *abbrev*: *Untersee(boot)* (*Ger*), a German submarine.

U (*chem*) *symbol*: uranium.

UAE *abbrev*: United Arab Emirates.

uakari or **ouakari** *wa-ka'ri*, *n* any of various short-tailed, long-haired S American monkeys of the genus *Cacajao* (family *Cebidae*), related to the saki. [Tupí]

UAR *abbrev*: United Arab Republic.

Übermensch *ü'bər-mensh*, (*Ger*) *n* a superman.

uberous *ū'bə-rəs*, (*rare*) *adj* yielding an abundance of milk; abounding. — *n* **u'berty** fruitfulness; abundant productiveness. [L *ūber* udder, fruitfulness]

uberrima fides *ū-ber'i-mə fī'dēz*, *ōō-be-rē'ma fi'dās*, (*L*) complete faith.

uberty. See **uberous**.

UB 40 *abbrev*: unemployment benefit (form) 40, a registration card issued by the Department of Employment and held by an unemployed person.

ubiety *ū-bī'i-ti*, *n* the state of being in a definite place; location. [L *ubi* where]

ubique *ū-bī'kwē*, *ōō-bē'kwe*, (*L*) *adv* everywhere.

ubiquinone *ū-bik'wi-nōn*, (*biochem*) *n* a quinone involved in the transfer of electrons during cell respiration. [L *ubīque* everywhere, and **quinone**]

ubiquity *ū-bik'wi-ti*, *n* existence everywhere at the same time; omnipresence. — *adj* **ubiquā'rian** found everywhere; ubiquitous. — *n* **ubiquitā'rian** someone who believes that Christ's body is everywhere, in the Eucharist as elsewhere. — Also *adj*. — *adj* **ubiq'uitary** being everywhere at once. — *adj* **ubiq'uitous** to be found everywhere. — *adv* **ubiq'uitously**. [L *ubīque* everywhere, from *ubi* where]

ubi supra *ū'bī sōō'prə*, *ōō'bē sōō'prä*, (*L*) where mentioned above.

UBR *abbrev*: Uniform Business Rate.

UC *abbrev*: University College.

uc (*printing*) *abbrev*: upper-case, ie capital.

UCAR *abbrev*: Union of Central African Republics.

UCATT *ūk'at*, *abbrev*: Union of Construction, Allied Trades and Technicians.

UCCA *uk'ə*, *abbrev*: Universities Central Council on Admissions.

UCI *abbrev*: *Union Cycliste Internationale* (*Fr*), International Cycling Union.

uckers *uk'ərz*, *n* a form of the game ludo, played in the Navy. [Origin uncertain]

UDA *abbrev*: Ulster Defence Association.

udal *ū'dl*, (*Orkney* and *Shetland*) *adj* without feudal superior, allodial. — *n* an estate so held. — *n* **u'daller** a holder of such an estate. [ON *ōthal*]

UDC *abbrev*: Universal Decimal Classification; Urban District Council.

udder *ud'ər*, *n* the organ containing the mammary glands of the cow, mare, etc, having more than one teat; a dug or teat (*rare*). — *adj* **udd'ered**. — *adj* **udd'erful** with full udder. — *adj* **udd'erless** unsuckled. [OE *ūder*; Ger *Euter*, L *ūber*, Gr *outhar*]

UDF *abbrev*: United Democratic Front, a South African organization of anti-apartheid groups.

UDHR *abbrev*: Universal Declaration of Human Rights.

UDI *abbrev*: Unilateral Declaration of Independence.

UDM *abbrev*: Union of Democratic Mineworkers.

udo *ōō'dō*, (*bot*) *n* a Japanese species of Aralia with edible shoots: — *pl* **u'dos**. [Jap]

udometer *ū-dom'i-tər*, *n* a name for a rain-gauge, never included in the official glossary of British meteorological terms. — *adj* **udomet'ric**. [Through Fr, from L *ūdus* wet, and **-meter**]

UDR *abbrev*: Ulster Defence Regiment; *Union des Démocrates pour la République* (*Fr*), the former name for the French Gaullist party, the RPR.

uds *udz*, (*archaic*) *interj* in oaths, for **God's**, or for **God save** (as in *uds my life*).

UDT *abbrev*: United Dominions Trust.

UEFA *ū-ā'fə* or *ū-ē'fə*, *abbrev*: Union of European Football Associations.

uey *ū'i*, (*Austr colloq*; *usu fig*) *n* a U-turn, as in *do a uey*.

UF *abbrev*: United Free Church (of Scotland).

UFC *abbrev*: Universities Funding Council.

UFF *abbrev*: Ulster Freedom Fighters.

UFO or **ufo** *ū'ef-ō'*, *ū'fō*, (*colloq*) *n* an *u*nidentified *f*lying *o*bject, such as a flying saucer: — *pl* **U'FOs** or **u'fos**. — *n* **ufology** (*ū-fol'ə-ji*) the study of UFOs. — *n* **ufol'ogist**.

ug. See under **ugly**.

UGC *abbrev*: University Grants Committee (replaced, 1979, by **UFC**).

ugh *uhh*, *ug*, *ōōh*, *ûh*, *interj* an exclamation of repugnance. — *n* (*old*) used as a representation of a cough or grunt.

ugli® *ug'li*, *n* a name given to a citrus fruit which is a cross between a grapefruit, a Seville orange and a tangerine; the plant producing this fruit. [**ugly**; from the fruit's unprepossessing appearance]

ugly *ug'li*, *adj* offensive to the sight or other sense, or to refined taste or moral feeling; ill-natured; threatening; disquieting; suggesting suspicion of evil; frightful, horrible (*obs*). — *n* an ugly person (*colloq*); a shade attached to a lady's hat (mid-19c). — *vt* (*rare*) to make ugly. — *vt* **ug** (*obs* or *dialect* in all meanings) to arouse loathing in; to loathe. — *vi* to feel loathing: — *pa t* and *pa p* **ugged**. — *n* **uglificā'tion**. — *vt* **ug'lify** to make ugly. — *adv* **ug'lily**. — *n* **ug'liness**. — *adj* **ug'some** (*obs*) disgusting; hideous. — *n* (*obs*) **ug'someness**. — **ugly customer** a dangerous antagonist; **ugly duckling** a despised or overlooked member of a family or group who later proves the most successful, attractive, etc; **ugly man** (*obs*) an actual garrotter, distinguished from his confederates. [ON *uggligr* frightful, *uggr* fear]

Ugrian *ū'gri-ən, ōō'*, *adj* of that division of the Finno-Ugrian languages and peoples that includes the Magyars, Ostyaks and Voguls. — Also *n*. — *adj* **U'gric**. — *adj* **U'gro-Finn'ic** Finno-Ugrian. [Russ *Ugri* the Ugrian peoples]

UHF (*radio*) *abbrev*: ultra-high frequency (see **frequency** under **frequent**).

uh-huh *u'hu, m'hm, interj* a sound used in place of 'yes'.

uhlan *ōō'län, ū'*, (*hist*) *n* a light cavalryman in semi-oriental uniform; a Prussian lancer. [Ger *Uhlan*, from Polish *ulan*, orig a light Tatar horseman, from Turk *oglān* a young man]

UHT *abbrev*: ultra-heat-treated (qv); ultra high temperature.

uhuru *ōō-hōō'rōō*, *n* (*esp* in E Africa) freedom (eg from slavery); national independence. [Swahili, from *huru* free]

uillean (or **uilleann**) **pipes** *ōō'li-ən pīps*, *n pl* Irish bagpipes, worked by squeezing bellows under the arm. — Also **union pipes**. [Ir *piob uilleann*; *piob* pipe, and *uilleann*, genitive sing of *uille* elbow]

uintaite or **uintahite** *ū-int'ä-īt*, *n* a natural tarlike asphalt found in the *Uinta* valley, Utah. — Also **gilsonite** (*gil'sən-īt*). — *n* **uint'athēre** any animal of the genus **Uintathē'rium**, gigantic Eocene fossil ungulates from *Uinta* County, Wyoming.

uitlander *œ'it-, āt', ā'it-land-ər*, (*SAfr*; chiefly *hist*) *n* a foreigner (*orig* a British person in the Transvaal or Orange Free State). [Afrik, outlander, foreigner, from Du *uit* out, and *land* land]

ujamaa *ōō-jə-mä' n* in Tanzania, a form of village community based on collective ownership and work-sharing, resembling the Israeli kibbutz. [Swahili, brotherhood]

UJD *abbrev*: *Utriusque Juris Doctor* (*L*), Doctor of both Laws (Canon and Civil).

UK *abbrev*: United Kingdom.

UKADGE *abbrev*: United Kingdom Air Defence Ground Environment.

UKAEA *abbrev*: United Kingdom Atomic Energy Authority.

ukase *ū-kāz', -kās'*, *n* an edict with force of law in Tsarist Russia; an edict with bearing on existing legislation issued by the Presidium of the Supreme Soviet and subject to later ratification by the Supreme Soviet; any arbitrary decree from any source. [Russ *ukaz*]

uke *ūk*, (*colloq*) *n* a ukulele.

ukelele. A common spelling of **ukulele**.

UKIAS *ū-kī'əs*, *abbrev*: United Kingdom Immigrants' Advisory Service.

ukiyo-e *ōō-kē'yō-yā, yō-ā*, *n* a Japanese style of painting and print-making flourishing between the 17c and 19c, typically depicting scenes from everyday life. [Jap, world, life picture]

Ukrainian *ū-krān'i-ən, ōō-krīn'i-ən*, *n* a native or citizen of (the) *Ukraine*, a republic of the former Soviet Union, a rich agricultural region in SW Russia; its language, Ruthenian. — Also *adj*.

ukulele *ū-kə-lā'li, ōō-kōō-lā'lā*, *n* a small, *usu* four-stringed, guitar, popularized in Hawaii, although *orig* Portuguese. [Hawaiian, jumping flea]

ULA or **ula** (*comput*) *abbrev*: uncommitted logic array.

ULCC *abbrev*: ultra-large crude carrier, a tanker over 320 000 dead-weight tons.

ulcer *ul'sər*, *n* an open sore, on the skin or mucous membrane, often discharging pus; a continuing source of evil, pain or corruption, an unsound element. — *vt* and *vi* to ulcerate. — *vi* **ul'cerate** to form an ulcer. — *vt* to cause an ulcer in; to affect with insidious corruption. — *n* **ulcerā'tion**. — *adj* **ul'cerātive**. — *adj* **ul'cered**. — *adj* **ul'cerous**. — *adv* **ul'cerously**. — *n* **ul'cerousness**. — **ulcerative colitis** (*med*) chronic ulceration of the colon; **ulcerative dermal necrosis** a fungal disease of salmon. [L *ulcus, ulceris*; cf Gr *helkos*]

ule or **hule** *ōō'lā*, *n* a Central American rubber tree (*Castilloa*); its crude rubber. [Sp *hule*, from Nahuatl *ulli*]

ulema *ōō'li-mə*, *n* the body of professional theologians, expounders of the law, in a Muslim country; a member of such a body. [Ar *'ulema*, pl of *'ālim* learned]

ulex *ū'leks*, *n* any plant of the gorse genus *Ulex*. [L *ūlex, -icis* a kind of rosemary or the like]

ULF *abbrev*: ultra-low frequency.

ulicon, ulichon and **ulikon** *ōō'li-kən*. Same as **eulachon**.

uliginose or **uliginous** *ū-lij'i-nəs*, *adj* slimy; oozy; swampy; growing in swampy places. [L *ūlīginōsus*, from *ūlīgō, -inis* moisture]

ulitis *ū-lī'tis*, *n* inflammation of the gums, gingivitis. [Gr *oula* gums, and *-itis*]

ullage *ul'ij*, *n* the quantity by which a vessel is holding less than its full capacity, or sometimes the amount left in the vessel; loss by evaporation or leakage; dregs (*slang*). — *vt* to reckon the ullage of; to affect with ullage; to fill up; to draw off a little from. — *n* **ull'ing** the making good of ullage. [Anglo-Fr *ulliage*, OFr *eullage*, from *œiller* to fill up]

Ulmus *ul'məs*, *n* the elm genus, giving name to the family **Ulmā'ceae**, related to the nettles. — *adj* **ulmā'ceous** of or like an elm; of its family. — *n* **ul'min** a gummy exudation from elms and other trees. [L *ulmus* elm]

ulna *ul'nə*, *n* the inner and larger of the two bones of the forearm; the corresponding bone in an animal's foreleg or a bird's wing (*zool*): — *pl* **ul'nae** (*-nē*). — *adj* **ul'nar**. — *n* **ulnā'rē** the bone of the carpus opposite the ulna: — *pl* **ulnā'ria**. [L *ulna* elbow, arm; cf **ell**, and Gr *ōlenē* forearm]

ulosis *ū-lō'sis*, (*med*) *n* the formation of a scar. [Gr *oulōsis*, from *oulē* a scar]

Ulothrix *ū'lō-thriks*, *n* a genus of filamentous algae, giving name to the **Ulotrichales** (*ū-lot-ri-kā'lēz*), an order of multicellular uninucleate green algae, marine and freshwater. — *adj* **ulotrichous** (*ū-lot'ri-kəs*) woolly-haired. — *n* **ulot'richy** (*-ki*) woolly-hairedness. [Gr *oulos* woolly, and *thrix, trichos* hair]

ulster *ul'stər*, *n* a long loose overcoat, first made in *Ulster*, Northern Ireland. — *adj* **ul'stered** wearing an ulster. — *n* **ulsterette'** a light ulster. — **Ul'sterman** and **Ul'sterwoman** a native or inhabitant of Ulster.

ult. *abbrev*: ultimate; ultimately; see also **ultimo** under **ultimate**.

ulterior *ul-tē'ri-ər*, *adj* on the further side; beyond; in the future; remoter; (of eg a motive) beyond what is stated or apparent. — *adv* **ultē'riorly**. [L *ulterior*, from *ultrā* (adv and prep), *uls* (prep) beyond]

ultima *ul'ti-mə*, *n* the last syllable of a word. — **ultima ratio** (*ul'ti-mə rā'shē-ō, ōōl'ti-ma rä'ti-ō*; *L*) the last argument; **ultima ratio regum** (*rē'gəm, rā'gōōm*; *L*) the last argument of kings (ie war; once inscribed on French cannon). [L, fem of *ultimus* last]

ultimate *ul'ti-māt, -mit*, *adj* furthest; last; final; fundamental; maximum; most important; limiting. — *n* a final point; a fundamental; the greatest (or otherwise most extreme) thing achievable or conceivable of its sort (*colloq*). — *n* **ul'timacy** (*-mə-si*). — *adv* **ul'timately** finally. — *n* **ultimā'tum** final terms; a last offer or demand; a last word; a final point; something fundamental: — *pl* **ultimā'ta**. — *adj* **ul'timo** (*abbrev* **ult.** or **ulto.**) in the last (month). — *n* **ultimogeniture** (*-jen'*; *law*) succession of the youngest, as in borough-English (qv), *opp* to *primogeniture*. — **ultimate load** (*aeronautics*) the maximum load which a structure is designed to withstand without a failure; **ultimate tensile stress** (*eng*) the highest load applied to a metal in the course of a tensile test, divided by the original cross-sectional area. — **the ultimate deterrent** the hydrogen bomb. [L *ultimus* last]

ultima (or **Ultima**) **Thule**. See under **Thule**.

ultimus haeres *ul'ti-məs hē'rēz, ōōl'ti-mōōs hī'rās*, (*L*) in law, the crown or the state, which succeeds to the property of those who die intestate or without next of kin; **ultimus Romanorum** (*rō-mən-ōr'əm, -ör', -ōōm*) last of the Romans.

ultion *ul'shən*, (*obs*) *n* revenge; avengement. [L *ultiō, -ōnis*]

ulto. *abbrev*: ultimo (see under **ultimate**).

Ultonian *ul-tō'ni-ən, adj* of Ulster. — *n* an Ulsterman or -woman. [LL *Ultōnia* Ulster; OIr *Ult-*, stem of *Ulaid* Ulster]

ultra- *ul'trə-, pfx* signifying: (1) beyond in place or position (as in **ultra-Neptu'nian** beyond the planet Neptune); (2) beyond the limit, range, etc, of (as in **ultramicroscop'ic**); (3) beyond the ordinary, or excessive(ly) (as in **ultra-Conserv'ative**, **ultra-Conserv'atism**, **ultra-fash'ionable**, **ultra-mod'ern** and **ultra-Prot'estant**). — *adj* **ul'tra** extreme, *esp* in royalism, fashion, or religious or political opinion. — *n* an extremist. — *n* **ultraism** (*ul'trə-izm*) (an) extreme principle, opinion, or measure; an attempt to pass beyond the limits of the known. — *n* **ul'traist**. [L *ultrā* beyond]

ultrabasic *ul-trə-bā'sik, (petrology) adj* extremely basic, very poor in silica. [**ultra-** (3)]

ultracentrifuge *ul-trə-sen'tri-fūj, n* a very high-speed type of centrifuge. — *vt* to subject to the action of an ultracentrifuge. — *adj* **ultracentrif'ugal** (or *-fū'gəl*). — *n* **ultracentrifugation** (*-gā'shən*). [**ultra-** (2)]

ultracrepidate *ul-trə-krep'i-dāt, vi* to criticize beyond the sphere of one's knowledge. — *n* and *adj* **ultracrepidā'rian**. [From the painter Apelles's answer to the cobbler who went on from criticizing the sandals in a picture to finding fault with the leg, *nē sūtor ultrā crepidam*, the cobbler must not go beyond the sandal]

ultra-distance *ul-trə-dis'təns, (athletics) adj* denoting a distance greater than 30 miles, *esp* as part of a competition, eg a race run over several days. [**ultra-** (3)]

ultrafiche *ul'trə-fēsh, n* a sheet of microfilm the same size as a microfiche but with a greater number of micro-copied records on it. [**ultra-** (3)]

ultrafilter *ul'trə-fil-tər, (biol* and *chem) n* an extremely fine filter which retains particles as fine as large molecules. — *vt* to pass through an ultrafilter. — *n* **ultrafil'trate** a substance that has passed through an ultrafilter. — *n* **ultrafiltrā'tion** the separation of particles by filtration, under suction or pressure. [**ultra-** (2)]

ultra-heat-treated *ul-trə-hēt-trē't-id, adj* (of milk, etc) sterilized by exposing to very high temperatures, increasing shelf-life (*usu abbrev* **UHT**). [**ultra-** (3)]

ultra-high *ul-trə-hī', adj* very high. — **ultra-high frequency** see **frequency** under **frequent**. [**ultra-** (3)]

ultraism, ultraist. See **ultra-**.

ultramarine *ul-trə-mə-rēn', adj* overseas; from overseas; deep blue. — *n* a deep blue pigment, *orig* made from lapis-lazuli brought from beyond the sea; its colour. [L *ultrāmarīnus*, from *ultrā* beyond, and *mare* sea]

ultramicro- *ul-trə-mī-krō, pfx* signifying smaller than, or dealing with smaller quantities than, **micro-**, eg *n* **ultramicrochem'istry** chemistry dealing with minute quantities, sometimes no greater than one-millionth of a gram.

ultramicroscope *ul-trə-mī'krə-skōp, n* a microscope with strong illumination from the side, whereby the presence of ultramicroscopic objects can be observed through the scattering of light from them. — *adj* **ultramicroscopic** (*-skop'ik*) too small to be visible under the ordinary microscope; pertaining to ultramicroscopy. — *n* **ultramicroscopy** (*-kros'kə-pi*). [**ultra-** (2)]

ultramicrotome *ul'trə-mī'krə-tōm, n* a microtome for cutting ultra-thin sections for examination with the electron microscope. — *n* **ultramicrotomy** (*-ot'ə-mi*). [**ultra-** (2)]

ultramontane *ul-trə-mon'tān, adj* beyond the mountains (*esp* the Alps); *orig* used in Italy of the French, Germans, etc; afterwards applied by the northern nations to the Italians; of or pertaining to a faction within the Roman Catholic Church which is extreme in favouring the Pope's supremacy. — *n* a person who lives beyond the mountains, *esp* south of the Alps; a member of the ultramontane faction within the Roman Catholic Church. — *n* **ultramon'tanism** (*-tən-izm*). — *n* **ultramon'tanist**. [Med L *ultrāmontānus*, from L *ultrā* beyond, and *mons, montis* a mountain]

ultramundane *ul-trə-mun'dān, adj* beyond the world, or beyond the limits of our solar system. [LL *ultrāmundānus*, from L *ultrā* beyond, and *mundus* world]

ultra-rapid *ul-trə-rap'id, adj* of a motion-picture film, exposed at much greater speed than that at which it is to be exhibited, giving a slow-motion picture. [**ultra-** (3)]

ultrared *ul'trə-red', (obs) adj* infra-red. [**ultra-** (1)]

ultrasensual *ul'trə-sen'sū-əl, -shōō-əl, adj* beyond the reach of the senses. [**ultra-** (2)]

ultrashort *ul'trə-shört', adj* (of electromagnetic waves) of less than ten metres' wavelength. [**ultra-** (3)]

ultrasonic *ul-trə-son'ik, adj* pertaining to, or (of an instrument or process) using, ultrasound (qv), sound waves of too high a frequency to be audible to the human ear. — *adv* **ultrason'ically**. — *n sing* **ultrason'ics** the study of such vibrations, used medically for diagnostic and therapeutic purposes. — *n* **ultrasonography** (*-sən-og'rə-fi*) the directing of ultrasonic waves through body tissues to detect abnormalities, eg in a foetus. — **ultrasonic communication** underwater communication using ultrasonic waves. [**ultra-** (2)]

ultrasound *ul'trə-sownd, n* sound waves or vibrations too rapid to be audible, useful *esp* in medical diagnosis. — See also **ultrasonic**. [**ultra-** (2)]

ultrastructure *ul'trə-struk'chər, (biol) n* the ultimate structure of protoplasm at a lower level than can be examined microscopically. [**ultra-** (2)]

ultra-tropical *ul'trə-trop'ik-əl, adj* beyond the tropics; hotter than the tropics. [**ultra-** (1) and (3)]

ultraviolet *ul-trə-vī'ə-lit, (phys) adj* beyond the violet end of the visible spectrum; pertaining to, or using, radiations of wavelengths less than those of visible light. — **ultraviolet spectroscopy** (*chem*) the study of material by its absorption of ultraviolet radiation; **ultraviolet star** one of a class of invisible stars giving out intense ultraviolet radiation. [**ultra-** (1)]

ultra vires *ul'trə vī'rēz, ŏŏl'trä wē'rās, (L)* beyond one's powers or authority.

ultra-virtuous *ul'trə-vûr'tū-əs, adj* prudish. [**ultra-** (3)]

ultroneous *ul-trō'ni-əs, adj* spontaneous, voluntary. — *adv* **ultrō'neously**. — *n* **ultrō'neousness**. [L *ultrōneus*, from *ultrō* spontaneously]

ululate *ūl'ū-lāt*, also *ul', vi* to hoot or screech. — *adj* **ul'ulant**. — *n* **ululā'tion** howling, wailing. [L *ululāre, -ātum* to hoot]

ulva *ul'və, (bot) n* a kind of edible seaweed. [L *ulva* sedge]

ulyie and **ulzie** *ül'yi, ül'i, obs* Scots forms of **oil**.

um *əm, um, interj* used by speakers when momentarily hesitating or in doubt.

umbel *um'bəl, (bot) n* a flat-topped inflorescence in which the flower stalks all spring from about the same point in an axis (which in a **compound umbel** is grouped in the same way with other axes). — *adj* **um'bellar** (or *-bel'*). — *adj* **um'bellate** or **um'bellated** constituting an umbel; having umbels. — *adv* **um'bellately**. — *n* **umbellifer** (*um-bel'i-fər*) any plant of the *Umbelliferae* family, the carrot and hemlock family of plants with umbels and divided leaves. — *n pl* **Umbellif'erae** the carrot and hemlock family of plants with (*usu* compound) umbels, schizocarpic fruit, leaves with sheathing bases. — *adj* **umbellif'erous**. — *n* **um'bellule** a partial umbel. [L *umbella* a sunshade, dimin of *umbra* a shade]

umber[1] *um'bər, n* a brown earthy mineral (hydrated oxides of iron and manganese) used as a pigment. — *vt* to colour with umber. — *adj* brown like umber. — *adj* **um'bered** or **um'bery**. — **um'ber-bird** the umbrette. — **burnt umber** umber heated to give a dark reddish-brown colour; **raw umber** untreated umber, a yellowish-brown colour. [Ital *terra d'ombra* shadow earth, or possibly Umbrian earth]

umber[2] *um'bər, n* the grayling. [L *umbra*]

umbilicus *um-bil'i-kəs, um-bi-lī'kəs, n* the navel; a depression at the axial base of a spiral shell; a small depression. — *adj* **umbilical** (*-bil'*; sometimes *-bi-lī'*) relating to the umbilicus or the umbilical cord. — *adj* **umbil'icate** navel-like; having a depression like a navel. — *n* **umbilicā'tion**. — **umbilical cord** a long flexible tube connecting the foetus to the placenta, the navel-string;

an electrical cable or other servicing line attached to a rocket vehicle or spacecraft during preparations for launch; the lifeline outside a vehicle in space by which astronauts receive air and communicate with the vehicle; any similar connection of fundamental importance. [L *umbilīcus* the navel; Gr *omphalos*]

umbles *um'blz, n pl* entrails (liver, heart, etc), *esp* of a deer. — Also **hum'bles** or **num'bles**. — **um'ble-pie'**, **hum'ble-pie'** or **num'ble-pie'** a pie made from the umbles of a deer. [OFr *nombles*, from *lomble* loin, from L *lumbulus*, dimin of *lumbus* loin]

umbo *um'bō, n* the central boss of a shield; a knob; the protuberant oldest part of a bivalve shell; a knob on a toadstool cap; a projection on the inner surface of the eardrum where the malleus is attached: — *pl* **umbō'nēs** or **um'bos**. — *adj* **um'bonal** (*-bən-əl*). — *adj* **um'bonate** (*bot*) having a central boss. — *n* **umbonā'tion**. [L *umbō, -ōnis*]

umbra *um'brə, n* a shadow; the darker part of the shadow or dark inner cone projected in an eclipse (*astron*); the darker part of a sunspot; a shade or ghost; an uninvited guest who comes with an invited one: — *pl* **um'brae** (*-brē*) or **um'bras**. — *adj* **umbraculate** (*um-brak'ū-lāt, -lət*) overshadowed by an umbraculum. — *adj* **umbrac'uliform** umbrella-shaped. — *n* **umbrac'ulum** an umbrella-shaped structure. — *adj* **um'bral** of an umbra. — *adj* **um'brāted** (*heraldry*) faintly traced. — *adj* **umbratic** (*-brat'*; *rare*), **umbrat'ical**, **umbratile** (*um'brə-tīl, -til*) or **umbratilous** (*-brat'i-ləs*) shadowy; shaded; shade-giving; indoor; secluded. — *adj* **umbrif'erous** shade-giving. — *adj* **umbrose** (*-brōs'*) shade-giving; dusky. — *adj* **um'brous** shaded. [L *umbra* shade, shadow, dimin *umbrāculum*, adj *umbrātilis*]

umbrage *um'brij, n* offence, *esp* in the phrases *give* and *take umbrage*; suspicion of injury; shade, shadow, or something which casts a shadow (*archaic* or *poetic*); a shelter (*obs*); a shadowy appearance (*rare*); a pretext, colour (*obs*); an inkling (*obs*). — *vt* to shade; to offend (*rare*). — *adj* **umbrā'geous** shady or forming a shade. — *adv* **umbrā'geously**. — *n* **umbrā'geousness**. [Fr *ombrage*, from L *umbrāticum* (neuter adj), from *umbra* a shadow]

umbral. . . to . . . **umbratilous**. See under **umbra**.

umbre *um'bər*. See under **umbrette**.

umbrel. See under **umbriere**.

umbrella *um-brel'ə, n* a dome-shaped canopy of light fabric mounted on a stick, carried or set up as a protection against rain or sun, that can be collapsed and furled when not in use; anything of similar form, eg a jellyfish disc; a protection; (something, eg an agency, that provides) a general cover or representation; a cover of fighter aircraft for ground forces (*military*). — Also (*obs*) **ombrell'a** or **umbrell'o** (*pl* **umbrell'os** or **umbrell'oes**). — *adj* **umbrella** broadly embracing or including a number or a variety of things. — *adj* **umbrell'aed** or **umbrell'a'd** with an umbrella. — **umbrell'a-ant** the sauba ant; **umbrell'a-bird** any of a number of birds of the *Cotinga* genus with umbrella-like crest and a lappet attached to the throat or breast; **umbrell'a-fir** a Japanese conifer with radiating tufts of needles; **umbrella group**, **organization**, etc a group of representatives of small parties, clubs, etc, which acts for all of them where they have common interests; **umbrella pine** same as **stone-pine**; **umbrell'a-plant** an African sedge with umbrella-like clusters of slender leaves, a common houseplant; **umbrell'a-stand** a rack or receptacle for closed umbrellas and walking-sticks; **umbrell'a-tree** any of various trees or shrubs whose leaves or branches grow in an umbrella-like formation, *esp* a small N American magnolia. [Ital *ombrella, ombrello*, from *ombra* a shade, from L *umbra*]

umbrere. See under **umbriere**.

umbrette *um-bret', n* the hammerhead (*Scopus umbretta*), a brown African bird related to the storks, remarkable for its huge nest. — Also **um'bre** (*-bər*) or **umber-bird**. [Fr *ombrette*, from *ombre* umber]

Umbrian *um'bri-ən, adj* of *Umbria*, in central Italy. — *n* a native of Umbria; an Indo-European language related to Oscan.

umbriere *um'bri-ēr*, (*Spenser*) *n* a visor. — Also **um'brere**, **um'bril** or **um'brel**. [OFr *ombriere*, *ombrel* shade]

umbriferous, **umbrose**, **umbrous**. See under **umbra**.

umbril. See under **umbriere**.

umiak, **oomiak**, **oomiac** or **oomiack** *ōō'mi-ak, ōōm'yak, n* an open boat, made of wood and stretched skins, *usu* crewed by women. [Inuit]

UMIST *ū'mist, abbrev*: University of Manchester Institute of Science and Technology.

umlaut *ōōm'lowt, n* a vowel change in Germanic languages brought about by a vowel or semivowel (*esp i* or *j*, *usu* now lost) in the following syllable; the diacritical sign (¨), dots placed over a vowel, indicating such a modification. — *vt* to modify (a vowel) with an umlaut. [Ger, from *um* around, and *Laut* sound]

umph *hmh, hm, mf*. Same as **humph¹**.

umpire *um'pīr, n* a third person called in to decide a dispute or a deadlock; an arbitrator; an impartial person chosen to supervise the game, enforce the rules, and decide disputes (*cricket*, etc). — Also *vi* and *vt*. — *n* **um'pirage** or **um'pireship**. [ME *noumpere*, *oumper*, from OFr *nomper*, from *non-* not, and *per*, *pair* peer, equal]

umpteen *um'tēn* or *ump'tēn*, or **umpty** *um'ti* or *ump'ti*, (*colloq*) *adj* an indefinitely large number. — *adj* **ump'teenth** or **ump'tieth** latest or last of many. [*Umpty* in Morse, a dash, from its sound on a telegraph key]

umquhile *um'hwīl, adv* and *adj* a Scots form of **um'while** formerly, late, whilom. [OE *ymb(e) hwīle* about or at a time]

UN *abbrev*: United Nations.

un or **'un** *un, ən*, (*dialect*) *pronoun* and *n* for **one**; also for **him**. [OE accusative *hine*]

Only a selection of words beginning with the prefix **un-** is given in the dictionary. They are listed continuously from **unabashed** to **unzoned**, either in the text or in the separate panels. Words beginning with **un-** in which **un-** is not a prefix, such as **uncle** and **union**, follow the prefixed words on pp 1903 and 1907. Words beginning with the prefix **under-** start on pp 1904.

un- *un-, pfx* (1) meaning 'not' (in many cases, the resultant word is more than a mere negation and has a positive force, as in **unkind**, which *usu* means 'cruel' rather than just 'not kind'); (2) indicating a reversal of process, removal or deprivation; (3) merely emphasizing reversal or deprivation already expressed by the simple word, as in **unbare** or **unloose**; sometimes (in *Shakespeare* and *Milton*) added to a present participle with a passive meaning. The meaning is often ambiguous, *esp* in participial adjs. [Partly OE *un-*, negative; cf Ger *un-*, L *in-*, Gr *an-* or *a-* ; partly OE *on-* (or *un-*), the unstressed form of *and-*; cf Ger *ent-*, Gr *anti* against]

Words starting with **a-**, *prefixed by* **un-**.

adj **unaba'ted** not made less in degree. — *adj* **una'ble** not able; not having sufficient strength, power or skill (to do); weak, incompetent (*archaic*); ineffectual (*archaic*). — *adj* **unaccent'ed** without accent or stress in pronunciation; not marked with an accent. — *adj* **unaccomm'odated** unprovided. — *adj* **unaccomm'odating** not compliant. — *adj* **unaccom'panied** not accompanied, escorted or attended; having no instrumental accompaniment (*music*). — *adj* **unaccom'plished** not achieved; lacking accomplishments. — *n* **unaccom'plishment** the fact of not being achieved. — *n* **unaccountabil'ity**. — *adj* **unaccount'able** difficult or impossible to explain; not answerable (to a higher authority); (of a person) puzzling in character. — *n* **unaccount'ableness**. — *adv* **unaccount'ably** inexplicably. — *adj* **unaccount'ed-for** unexplained; not included in an account. — *adj* **unaccus'tomed** not customary; not used (with *to*). — *n* **unaccus'tomedness**. — *adj* **unacknowl'edged** not acknowledged, recognized, confessed or noticed. — *n* **unacquaint'ance** lack of acquaintance (often with *with*). — *adj* **unacquaint'ed** (*Scot* **unacquaint'**) not on terms of acquaintance (with *with*); ignorant of (with *with*, or *Swift*, *in*); uninformed; unknown (*obs*); unusual (*Spenser*). — *n* **unacquaint'edness**. — *adj* **unact'able** unfit for the stage. — *adj* **unact'ed** not performed. — *adj* **unac'tive** inactive. — *adj* **unadop'ted** not adopted (**unadopted road** a road for the repairing, maintenance, etc, of which the Local Authority is not responsible). — *adj* **unadul'terāte** or **unadul'terated** unmixed, pure or genuine; sheer, absolute. — *adj* **unadvīs'able** inadvisable; not prepared to accept advice. — *n* **unadvīs'ableness**. — *adv* **unadvīs'ably**. — *adj* **unadvīsed'** not advised; without advice; not prudent or discreet; ill-judged; inadvertent (*Spenser*). — *adv* **unadvīs'edly**. — *n* **unadvīs'edness**. — *adj* **unaffect'ed** not affected or influenced; untouched by emotion; without affection; not assumed; plain; real; sincere. — *adv* **unaffect'edly**. — *n* **unaffect'edness**. — *adj* **unaffect'ing**. — *adj* **unagree'able** disagreeable (with *to*); inconsistent (with *with*); discordant. — *adj* **unāk'ing** (*Shakesp*) unaching. — *adj* **unā'lienable** inalienable. — *adv* **unā'lienably**. — *adj* **unaligned'** non-aligned. — *adj* **unalive'** not fully aware of (with *to*); lacking in vitality. — *adj* **unallayed'** unmixed, unqualified; not diminished, unquenched. — *adj* **unallied'** not related; without allies. — *adj* **unalloyed'** not alloyed or mixed, pure (*lit* and *fig*). — *adj* **un-Amer'ican** not in accordance with American character, ideas, feeling or traditions; disloyal, against American interests. — *vt* **un-Amer'icanize** or **-ise** to make un-American. — *vt* **unanch'or** to loose from anchorage. — *vi* to become loose or unattached; to weigh anchor. — *adj* **unaneled** or (*Shakesp*) **unnaneld** (*un-ə-nēld'*) without extreme unction. — *adj* **unan'imated** not alive; not animated or lively; not actuated (with *by*). — *adj* **unannealed'** not annealed (but see also **unaneled**). — *adj* **unan'swerable** impossible to answer; not to be refuted, conclusive. — *n* **unan'swerableness**. — *adv* **unan'swerably**. — *adj* **unan'swered** not answered; unrequited. — *adj* **unappeal'able** not allowing or being capable of an appeal to a higher court, conclusive, final. — *adj* **unapplaus'ive** not applauding. — *adj* **unappoint'ed** not appointed; not equipped. — *adj* **unapprehend'ed**. — *adj* **unapprehen'sible**. — *adj* **unapprehen'sive** without fear; without understanding. — *n* **unapprehen'siveness**. — *adj* **unapprised'** not informed. — *adj* **unapproach'able** out of reach, inaccessible; stand-offish; inaccessible to advances or intimacy; beyond rivalry. — *n* **unapproach'ableness**. — *adv* **unapproach'ably**. — *adj* **unapproached'**. — *adj* **unapprō'priate** unappropriated; inappropriate. — *adj* **unapprō'priated** not taken possession of; not applied to some purpose; not granted to any person, corporation, etc. — *adj* **unapproved'** unproved; unsanctioned; not approved of; untested (*obs*). — *adj* **unapprov'ing**. — *adv* **unapprov'ingly**. — *adj* **unapt'** unfitted; unsuitable; not readily inclined or accustomed (with *to*); lacking in aptitude, slow. — *adv* **unapt'ly**. — *n* **unapt'ness**. — *adj* **unar'gūable** that cannot be argued; irrefutable. — *adv* **unar'gūably**. — *adj* **unar'gued** (*Milton*) undisputed; not debated. — *vt* **unarm'** to help (someone) to take off armour; to strip (oneself) of armour; to deprive of arms, to disarm; to make harmless. — *vi* to take off one's armour. — *adj* **unarmed'** without weapons; defenceless; unprotected; unaided or without accessory apparatus; without arms or similar limbs or appendages. — *adj* **unar'moured** without armour or armour-plating. — *adj* **unart'ful** artless, genuine; inartistic; unskilful. — *adv* **unart'fully**. — *adj* **unartic'ūlate** not articulate. — *adj* **unartic'ūlated** not jointed; not in distinct syllables. — *adj* **unartist'ic** not coming within the sphere of art; not concerned with art; inartistic. — *adj* **unasked'** not asked; not asked for; uninvited. — *adj* **unassayed'** not attempted; untested. — *adj* **unassumed'**. — *adj* **unassum'ing** making no assumption; unpretentious, modest. — *adv* **unassum'ingly**. — *n* **unassum'ingness**. — *adj* **unassured'** uncertain (of); doubtfully recognized (*Spenser*); insecure; lacking in self-assurance, diffident; not insured against loss. — *adj* **unatōn'able** that cannot be atoned for; irreconcilable (*archaic*). — *adj* **unattached'** not attached; detached; not arrested; not belonging to a club, party, college, diocese, department, regiment, etc; not married; having no romantic and/or sexual attachment to a particular person. — *adj* **unattaint'ed** not legally attainted; unstained; not blemished by partiality (*Shakesp*). — *adj* **unattempt'ed** not attempted; not made the subject of an attempt or attack. — *adj* **unattend'ed** not accompanied or attended; not listened to or paid attention; not attended to (*archaic*). — *adj* **unatten'tive** inattentive (the latter being the preferred form). — *adj* **unaugment'ed** not augmented;

Some words with **un-** prefix; see **un-** entry for numbered senses.

unabashed' *adj* (1).
unabbrēv'iated *adj* (1).
unabol'ished *adj* (1).
unabridged' *adj* (1).
unab'rogated *adj* (1).
unabsolved' *adj* (1).
unacadem'ic *adj* (1).
unaccen'tūāted *adj* (1).
unaccept'able *adj* (1).
unaccept'ableness *n* (1).
unaccept'ance *n* (1).
unaccred'ited *adj* (1).
unaccūs'able *adj* (1).
unaccūs'ably *adv* (1).
unaccūsed' *adj* (1).
unachiev'able *adj* (1).
unāch'ing *adj* (1).
unac'tuated *adj* (1).
unadapt'able *adj* (1).
unadapt'ed *adj* (1).
unaddressed' *adj* (1).
unadjust'ed *adj* (1).
unadmīred' *adj* (1).
unadmīr'ing *adj* (1).
unadmitt'ed *adj* (1).
unadmon'ished *adj* (1).
unadōred' *adj* (1).
unadorned' *adj* (1).
unadvent'urous (*Milton* **unadvent'rous**) *adj* (1).
unad'vertised *adj* (1).
unaffil'iated *adj* (1).
unafraid' *adj* (1).
unaid'able *adj* (1).
unaid'ed *adj* (1).
unaimed' *adj* (1).
unaired' *adj* (1).
unalike' *adj* (1).
unallott'ed *adj* (1).
unallow'able *adj* (1).
unalterabil'ity *n* (1).
unal'terable *adj* (1).
unal'terableness *n* (1).
unal'terably *adv* (1).
unal'tered *adj* (1).
unal'tering *adj* (1).
unamazed' *adj* (1).
unambig'ūous *adj* (1).
unambig'ūously *adv* (1).
unambi'tious *adj* (1).
unambi'tiously *adv* (1).
unamē'nable *adj* (1).
unamend'able *adj* (1).
unamend'ed *adj* (1).
unamerced' *adj* (1).
unāmiabil'ity *n* (1).
unā'miable *adj* (1).
unā'miableness *n* (1).
unamū'sable *adj* (1).
unamūsed' *adj* (1).
unamū'sing *adj* (1).
unamū'singly *adv* (1).
unanalys'able or **-z-** *adj* (1).
unan'alysed or **-z-** *adj* (1).
unanalyt'ic or **unanalyt'ical** *adj* (1).
unanch'ored *adj* (1).
unann'otated *adj* (1).
unannounced' *adj* (1).
unantic'ipāted *adj* (1).
unanx'ious *adj* (1).
unapologet'ic *adj* (1).
unapostol'ic or **unapostol'ical** *adj* (1).
unapostol'ically *adv* (1).
unappalled' *adj* (1).
unappar'el *vt* (2).
unappar'elled *adj* (1).
unappar'ent *adj* (1).
unappeal'ing *adj* (1).
unappeas'able *adj* (1).
unappeased' *adj* (1).
unapp'etizing or **-s-** *adj* (1).
unapp'licable *adj* (1).
unapplied' *adj* (1).
unapprē'ciated *adj* (1).

without the augment (*gram*). — *adj* **unauspi'cious** (*Shakesp*) inauspicious. — *adj* **unavail'able** not available; of no avail (*archaic*). — *n* **unavail'ableness**. — *adv* **unavail'ably**. — *adj* **unavail'ing** of no avail or effect, useless. — *n* **unavoidabil'ity**. — *adj* **unavoid'able** not to be avoided; inevitable; not voidable (*law*). — *n* **unavoid'ableness**. — *adv* **unavoid'ably**. — *adj* **unavoid'ed** not avoided; unavoidable, inevitable (*Shakesp*). — *adj* **unaware'** not aware; unwary (*Shelley*). — *adv* unawares. — *n* **unaware'ness**. — *adv* **unawares'** without being, or making, aware; without being perceived; unexpectedly. — *n* in the phrase **at unawares**, unexpectedly, at a sudden disadvantage.

Words starting with **b-**, *prefixed by* **un-**.
adj **unbacked'** without a back; without backing or backers; unaided; not moved back; riderless; never yet ridden. — *vt* **unbag'** to let out of a bag. — *adj* **unbaked'** not baked; immature. — *n* **unbal'ance** lack of balance. — *vt* to throw off balance; to derange. — *adj* **unbal'anced** not in a state of equilibrium; without a counterpoise or compensation; without mental balance, erratic or deranged; (of eg a view or judgement) not giving due weight to all features of the situation; not adjusted so as to show balance of debtor and creditor (*book-keeping*). — *adj* **unball'asted** without ballast; unsteady, unstable, flighty. — *adj* **unbanked'** not deposited in, provided with, or having, a bank. — *vt* **unbar'** to remove a bar from or of; to unfasten. — *vi* to become unbarred. — *adj* **unbarbed'** without barb; without bard, caparison or armour (so *prob* in *Shakesp*, *Coriolanus* III. 2. 99); uncropped, untrimmed. — *vt* **unbare'** to bare, lay bare. — *vt* **unbark'** to strip of bark. — *adj* **unbarked'** not deprived of bark; deprived of bark. — *adj* **unbash'ful** free from bashfulness; shameless (*Shakesp*). — *adj* **unba'ted** undiminished; unblunted (*Shakesp*). — *vt* (*obs*) **unbe'** to cause not to be. — *vi* to cease to be, or be non-existent (*Hardy*). — *vt* **unbear'** to free from the bearing-rein. — *adj* **unbear'able** intolerable. — *n* **unbear'ableness**. — *adv* **unbear'ably**. — *adj* **unbear'ing** barren. — *adj* **unbea'vered** without a beaver or hat (*archaic*); having the beaver of the helmet open (*hist*). — *adj* **unbecom'ing** unsuitable; not suited to the wearer, or not showing her or him to advantage; (of behaviour, etc) not befitting, unseemly (with *to* or *in*, or, *archaic*, without preposition or with *of*). — *n* the transition from existence to non-existence. — *adv* **unbecom'ingly**. — *n* **unbecom'ingness**. — *vt* **unbed'** to rouse, remove or dislodge from a bed. — *adj* **unbedd'ed** unstratified; not put to bed. — *adj* **unbedimmed'** (*Wordsworth*). — *adj* **unbedinned'** (*Leigh Hunt*) not made noisy. — *vt* **unbeget'** to undo the begetting of. — *adj* **unbegged'** (of a person) not entreated; not begged for. — *adj* **unbeginn'ing** without beginning. — *adj* **unbegot'** or **unbegott'en** not yet begotten; existing independent of any generating cause. — *vt* **unbeguile'** to undeceive. — *adj* **unbeguiled'** not deceived. — *adj* **unbegun'** not yet begun; without beginning. — *adj* **unbehōl'den** unseen; under no obligation of gratitude. — *adj* **unbe'ing** non-existent. — *n* non-existence. — *adj* **unbeknown'** or **unbeknownst'** unknown. — *adv* (with *to*) without the knowledge of, unobserved by. — *n* **un'belief** (or *-lēf'*) disbelief, or withholding of belief, *esp* in accepted religion. — *adj* **unbeliev'able** incredible; (loosely) astonishing, remarkable. — *adv* **unbeliev'ably**. — *vt* and *vi* **unbelieve'** to disbelieve; to refrain from believing; to cease to believe. — *adj* **unbelieved'**. — *n* **unbeliev'er** a person who does not believe, *esp* in the prevailing religion; a habitually incredulous person. — *adj* **unbeliev'ing**. — *adv* **unbeliev'ingly**. — *vt* **unbelt'** to undo the belt of (a garment). — *adj* **unbelt'ed** without a belt; freed from a belt. — *vt* **unbend'** to relax (eg a bow) from a bending tension; to straighten; to undo, unfasten (*naut*); to relax (the mind); to allow a frown, etc, to disappear from (the brow, etc). — *vi* to become relaxed; to behave with freedom from stiffness, to be affable. — *adj* **unbend'able**. — *adj* **unbend'ed**. — *adj* **unbend'ing** not bending; unyielding; resolute. — *n* a relaxing. — *adv* **unbend'ingly**. — *n* **unbend'ingness**. — *adj* **unbent'** not bent; relaxed; not overcome or vanquished. — *vt* **unbeseem'** to misbecome; to fail to fulfil (*Byron*). — *adj* **unbeseem'ing**. — *adv* **unbeseem'ingly**. — *vt* **unbespeak'** to cancel an order for. — *vt* **unbi'as** to free from bias. — *adj* **unbi'ased** (sometimes **unbi'assed**). — *adv* **unbi'asedly** or **unbi'assedly**. — *n* **unbi'asedness** or **unbi'assedness**. — *adj* **unbib'lical** contrary to or unwarranted by the Bible. — *adj* **unbid'** unbidden; not bid; not prayed for (*Spenser*). — *adj* **unbidd'en** not bid or commanded; uninvited; spontaneous. — *vt* **unbīnd'** to remove a band from; to loose; to set free. — *n*

Some words with **un-** prefix; see **un-** entry for numbered senses.

unapprē'ciative *adj* (1).
unapproved' *adj* (1).
unaris'en *adj* (1).
unarranged' *adj* (1).
unartifi'cial *adj* (1).
unartifi'cially *adv* (1).
unart'istlike *adj* (1).
unascend'able or **unascend'ible** *adj* (1).
unascend'ed *adj* (1).
unascertain'able *adj* (1).
unascertained' *adj* (1).
unashamed' *adj* (1).
unasham'edly *adv* (1).
unas'pirated *adj* (1).
unaspīr'ing *adj* (1).
unaspīr'ingly *adv* (1).
unaspīr'ingness *n* (1).
unassail'able *adj* (1).
unassailed' *adj* (1).
unasser'tive *adj* (1).
unassīgn'able *adj* (1).
unassīgned' *adj* (1).
unassim'ilable *adj* (1).
unassim'ilated *adj* (1).
unassist'ed *adj* (1).
unassist'edly *adv* (1).
unassist'ing *adj* (1).
unassō'ciated *adj* (1).
unassuage'able *adj* (1).
unassuaged' *adj* (1).
unatōned' *adj* (1).
unattain'able *adj* (1).
unattain'ableness *n* (1).
unattain'ably *adv* (1).
unattend'ing *adj* (1).
unattest'ed *adj* (1).
unattīred' *adj* (1).
unattract'ive *adj* (1).
unattract'ively *adv* (1).
unattract'iveness *n* (1).
unauthen'tic *adj* (1).
unauthen'ticated *adj* (1).
unauthentic'ity *n* (1).
unauthor'itative *adj* (1).
unau'thorized or -s- *adj* (1).
unavailabil'ity *n* (1).
unavenged' *adj* (1).
unavert'able or (*rarely*) **unavert'ible** *adj* (1).
unavowed' *adj* (1).
unavow'edly *adv* (1).
unawāk'ened *adj* (1).
unawāk'ening *adj* (1).
unawed' *adj* (1).
unbaff'led *adj* (1).
unbail'able *adj* (1).
unbait'ed *adj* (1).
unband'ed *adj* (1).
unbaptize' or **-ise'** *vt* (2).
unbaptized' or **-s-** *adj* (1).
unbar'bered *adj* (1).
unbarred' *adj* (1).
unbarr'icade *vt* (2).
unbathed' *adj* (1).
unbāthed' *adj* (1).
unbatt'ered *adj* (1).
unbeard'ed *adj* (1).
unbeat'able *adj* (1).
unbeat'en *adj* (1).
unbeaut'iful *adj* (1).
unbefitt'ing *adj* (1).
unbefriend'ed *adj* (1).
unbeloved' (or *-luv'id*) *adj* (1).
unben'eficed *adj* (1).
unbenefi'cial *adj* (1).
unben'efited *adj* (1).
unbenight'ed *adj* (1).
unbenign' *adj* (1).
unbenig'nant *adj* (1).
unbenign'ly *adv* (1).
unbereft' *adj* (1).
unbesought' *adj* (1).
unbespoke' *adj* (1).

unbīnd'ing the removal of a band or bond; a loosing; a setting free. — *adj* loosening; not binding. — *n* and *adj* **unbirth'day** (*Lewis Carroll*) (pertaining to) a day other than one's birthday. — *vt* **unbish'op** to deprive of the status of bishop. — *vt* **unbitt'** (*naut*) to take off from the bitts. — *adj* **unbitt'ed** without a bit; unbridled. — *adj* **unblenched'** (or, *Milton*, *un'*) unflinching; unstained. — *adj* **unblench'ing** unflinching. — *vt* **unbless'** to withhold happiness from; to deprive of blessing. — *adj* **unblessed'** or **unblest'**. — *n* **unbless'edness**. — *adj* **unblind'** not blind. — *vt* to free from blindness or from blindfolding. — *adj* **unblind'ed**. — *vt* **unblind'fold** (*pa p* *Spenser* **unblind'fold**). — *adj* **unblink'ing** without blinking; not wavering; not showing emotion, *esp* fear. — *adv* **unblink'ingly**. — *adj* **unblowed'** (*Shakesp*), **unblown'** (or *un'*) not blown; still in the bud, not yet having bloomed. — *adj* **unblush'ing** not blushing; without shame; impudent. — *adv* **unblush'ingly**. — *adj* **unbod'ied** disembodied; not having a body or a form. — *adj* **unbō'ding** not expecting. — *vt* **unbolt'** to draw back a bolt from. — *vi* to become unbolted; to explain, expound (*Shakesp*). — *adj* **unbolt'ed** unfastened by withdrawing a bolt; not fastened by bolts; not separated by bolting or sifting; coarse. — *vt* **unbonn'et** to remove the bonnet from. — *vi* to uncover the head. — *adj* **unbonn'eted** bare-headed; in *Shakesp Othello*, I. 2. 23, according to some, without taking off the cap, on equal terms. — *adj* **unbooked'** not entered in a book; unreserved; not literary. — *adj* **unbook'ish** unlearned; not given to or depending on reading; not savouring of books. — *adj* **unborn'** not yet born; non-existent; without beginning. — *adj* **unborr'owed** not borrowed; original. — *vt* **unbo'som** to pour out, tell freely (what is in the mind); to reveal to the eye; (*reflexive*) to unburden (oneself) confide freely (also *vi*). — *n* **unbo'somer**. — *adj* **unbott'omed** bottomless; having no foundation or support; not founded (with *in* or *on*). — *adj* **unbought'** obtained without buying; not bribed. — *adj* **unbound'** not bound; loose; without binding (also *pa t* and *pa p* of **unbind**, freed from bonds). — *adj* **unbound'ed** not limited; boundless; having no check or control. — *adv* **unbound'edly**. — *n* **unbound'edness**. — *adj* **unbowed'** not bowed or bent; not vanquished or overcome, free. — *vt* **unbox'** to remove from a box or crate. — *vt* **unbrace'** to undo the braces, points or bands of; to loose or relax. — *adj* **unbraced'** (*Spenser* **unbrāste'**) not braced; with clothing unfastened; (of a drum) with tension released; relaxed (*lit* and *fig*). — *adj* **unbraid'ed** not plaited; untarnished, unfaded (*Shakesp*). — *adj* **unbreath'able** not respirable. — *adj* **unbreathed'** out of breath; not out of breath; not breathed; not even whispered; not exercised or practised (*Shakesp*). — *adj* **unbreathed'-on** untouched by breath, *esp* the breath of detraction. — *adj* **unbreath'ing** not breathing. — *adj* **unbred'** ill-bred; untrained; not yet born (*Shakesp*). — *vt* **unbreech'** to remove the breeches, breech or breeching from. — *adj* **unbreeched'** wearing no breeches. — *vt* **unbrī'dle** to free from the bridle; to free from (*usu* politic) restraint. — *adj* **unbrī'dled** not bridled; unrestrained. — *n* **unbrī'dledness**. — *adj* **un-Brit'ish** not in accordance with British character or traditions. — *adj* **unbrizzed** see **unbruised**. — *adj* **unbroke'** (*archaic*) unbroken. — *adj* **unbrō'ken** not broken; (of a record) not surpassed; uninterrupted; not thrown into disorder; not variegated; not infringed. — *adv* **unbrō'kenly**. — *n* **unbrō'kenness**. — *adj* **unbruised'** (*Shakesp* **un'brused**; *Scott* **unbrizzed'**) not bruised or crushed. — *vt* **unbuck'le** to unfasten the buckle(s) of; to unfasten. — *vi* to undo the buckle(s) of a garment, etc; to unbend (*fig*). — *adj* **unbudd'ed** not yet in bud; not yet having emerged from the bud. — *vt* **unbuild'** to demolish, pull down. — *adj* **unbuilt'** (or *un'*) not built; not built upon. — *adj* **unbuilt'-on**. — *vi* and *vt* **unbun'dle** to price and sell separately the constituents of a larger package of products or services. — *n* **unbun'dling**. — *vt* **unbur'den**, (*archaic*) **unbur'then** to free from a burden; to discharge, cast off (eg a burden); (*reflexive*) to tell one's secrets or anxieties freely, unbosom (oneself). — *adj* **unbur'dened**, (*archaic*) **unbur'thened** not burdened; relieved of a burden. — *vt* and *vi* **unburr'ow** to bring or come out of a burrow. — *vt* **unbur'y** to disinter. — *vt* **unbutt'on** to undo the buttons of. — *vi* to undo one's buttons; to unbend and tell one's thoughts. — *adj* **unbutt'oned** without a button; with buttons undone; in a relaxed confidential state; unrestrained.

Words starting with **c-**, *prefixed by* **un-**.

adj **uncalled'** not called or summoned; not invited; not called up for payment. — *adj* **uncalled'-for** (or, predicatively, **uncalled for**) not required, unnecessary; unprovoked; offensively or aggressively gratuitous. — *adv* **uncann'ily**. — *n* **uncann'iness**. — *adj* **uncann'y** weird, supernatural; (of eg skill) much greater than one

Some words with **un-** prefix; see **un-** entry for numbered senses.

unbespōk'en *adj* (1).
unbestowed' *adj* (1).
unbetrayed' *adj* (1).
unbett'erable *adj* (1).
unbett'ered *adj* (1).
unbewailed' *adj* (1).
unblām'able or
unblame'able *adj* (1).
unblām'ably or
unblame'ably *adv* (1).
unblāmed' *adj* (1).
unbleached' *adj* (1).
unblem'ished *adj* (1).
unblend'ed *adj* (1).
unblent' *adj* (1).
unbliss'ful *adj* (1).
unblock' *vt* (2).
unblood'ed *adj* (1).
unblood'ied *adj* (1).
unblood'y *adj* (1).
unblott'ed *adj* (1).
unblunt'ed *adj* (1).
unboast'ful *adj* (1).
unbone' *vt* (2).
unboot' *vt* and *vi* (2).
unbranched' *adj* (1).
unbreach'able *adj* (1).
unbreached' *adj* (1).
unbreak'able *adj* (1).
unbrīb'able *adj* (1).
unbridged' *adj* (1).
unbroth'erlike *adj* (1).
unbroth'erly *adj* (1).
unbrushed' *adj* (1).
unbudg'eted *adj* (1).
unbur'ied *adj* (1).
unburned' or **unburnt'**, (or *un'*) *adj* (1).
unbur'nished *adj* (1).
unbus'inesslike *adj* (1).
unbus'y *adj* (1).
unbutt'ered *adj* (1).
uncage' *vt* (2).
uncal'culated *adj* (1).
uncal'culating *adj* (1).
uncan'did *adj* (1).
uncan'didly *adv* (1).
uncan'didness *n* (1).
uncan'dour *n* (1).
uncanon'ic or
uncanon'ical *adj* (1).
uncanon'icalness *n* (1).
uncan'onize or **-ise** *vt* (2).
uncan'onized or **-s-** *adj* (1).
uncapsīz'able *adj* (1).
uncar'peted *adj* (1).
uncart' *vt* (2).
uncashed' *adj* (1).
uncat'alogued *adj* (1).
uncaught' *adj* (1).
uncel'ebrated *adj* (1).
uncen'sored *adj* (1).
uncensor'ious *adj* (1).
uncen'sured *adj* (1).
uncer'ebral *adj* (1).
uncertif'icated *adj* (1).
unchall'engeable *adj* (1).
unchall'engeably *adv* (1).
unchall'enged *adj* (1).
unchangeabil'ity *n* (1).
unchange'able *adj* (1).
unchange'ableness *n* (1).
unchange'ably *adv* (1).
unchanged' *adj* (1).
unchang'ing *adj* (1).
unchang'ingly *adv* (1).
unchap'eroned *adj* (1).
uncharacterist'ic *adj* (1).
unchar'itable *adj* (1).
unchar'itableness *n* (1).
unchar'itably *adv* (1).

would expect from an ordinary human being; unsafe to associate with; unpleasantly severe (*Scot*); unsafe (*Scot*). — *vt* **uncap'** to remove a cap from (eg a container); to remove an upper limit from. — *vi* to take off one's cap. — *adj* **uncā'pable** (*Shakesp*) incapable. — *vi* **uncape'** (*Shakesp*) *prob* a misprint for **uncope**; explained by some as to uncouple hounds, to unkennel a fox, etc. — *adj* **uncared'-for** (or, predicatively, **uncared for**) neglected; showing signs of neglect. — *adj* **uncare'ful** careless; care-free. — *adj* **uncar'ing** without anxiety, concern or caution; not caring about (*Burns*). — *vt* **uncase'** to take out of a case; to lay bare; to flay (*obs*); to undress (*Shakesp*). — *vi* to strip (*Shakesp*). — *adj* **uncaused'** without any precedent cause, self-existent. — *adj* **unceas'ing** ceaseless; never-ending. — *adv* **unceas'ingly**. — *adj* **unceremō'nious** informal; off-hand. — *adv* **unceremō'niously**. — *n* **unceremō'niousness**. — *adj* **uncer'tain** not certain (with *of* or *about*); not definitely known or decided; subject to doubt or question (**in no uncertain terms** unambiguously); not to be depended upon; subject to vicissitude; hesitant, lacking confidence. — *adv* **uncer'tainly**. — *n* **uncer'tainness**. — *n* **uncer'tainty** (**uncertainty principle** the principle that there is a limit (a) to the precision with which the position and momentum of a particle can be simultaneously known and (b) to the knowledge of the energy of a particle when it is measured for a finite time. — Also **Heisenberg principle**). — *adj* **uncer'tified** not assured, attested or guaranteed. — *adj* **uncess'ant** (*Milton*) incessant. — *vt* **unchain'** to release from a chain; to remove a chain from; to let loose. — *adj* **unchained'**. — *adj* **unchan'cy** (*Scot*) unlucky; ill-omened; dangerous; ticklish. — *vt* **uncharge'** to unload; to acquit (*Shakesp*). — *adj* **uncharged'** not charged; not attacked (*Shakesp*). — *n* **unchar'ity** lack of charity. — *vt* **uncharm'** to free from a spell; to destroy the magical power of. — *adj* **uncharmed'** not affected by a spell; not charmed. — *adj* **unchar'ming** not charming or attractive. — *vt* **unchar'nel** to take from a charnel. — *adj* **unchart'ed** (*lit* and *fig*) not mapped in detail; not shown in a chart; not yet examined, investigated or visited. — *adj* **unchart'ered** not holding a charter; unauthorized. — *n* **unchas'tity** lack or breach of chastity. — *vt* **uncheck'** (*Shakesp*) to fail to check. — *adj* **uncheck'able**. — *adj* **unchecked'** not checked or verified; not restrained; of squares in a crossword puzzle, holding a letter which forms part of two word-solutions; not contradicted (*Shakesp*). — *vt* **unchild'** (*Shakesp*) to make childless; to change from being a child. — *adj* **unchild'like**. — *adj* **unchris'om** (*Lamb*) unchristened. — *vt* **unchrist'en** to annul the christening of; to deprive of a name; to unchristianize (*Milton*). — *adj* **unchrist'ened** unbaptized; without a name. — *adj* **unchris'tian** against the spirit of Christianity; non-christian (*rare*); uncharitable; unreasonable, outrageous (*colloq*). — *vt* to unchristianize (*obs*). — *vt* **unchris'tianize** or **-ise** to cause to change from the Christian faith or character. — *adj* **unchris'tianlike**. — *adv* **unchris'tianly**. — *adj* unchristianlike. — *vt* **unchurch'** to deprive of church membership or of the possession of a church; to take the status of a church from. — *vt* **unci'pher** (*obs*) to decipher. — *adj* **uncir'cumcised** not circumcised; gentile; unpurified (*fig*). — *n* **uncircumcis'ion** uncircumcised condition; the uncircumcised, the gentiles (*Bible*). — *adj* **unciv'il** discourteous; unseemly; against the civic good; not civilized (*Spenser*). — *adj* **unciv'ilized** or **-s-** not civilized; away from civilized communities. — *adv* **unciv'illy**. — *vt* **unclasp'** to loose from a clasp; to relax from clasping; to open. — *vi* to close in a clasp. — *adj* **unclassed'** without class divisions; unclassified; not placed in a class. — *adj* **unclass'ifīable** (or *-fī'-*) that cannot be classified. — *adj* **unclass'ified** not classified; (of a road) minor, not classified as a motorway, A-road or B-road; (of information) not given a special security classification. — *adj* **unclean** (*-klēn'*) not clean; foul; ceremonially impure; lewd. — *adj* **uncleaned'** not cleaned. — *n* **uncleanliness** (*-klen'*). — *adj* **uncleanly** (*-klen'*). — *adv* (*-klēn'*). — *n* **uncleanness** (*-klēn'nis*). — *adj* **uncleansed** (*-klenzd'*). — *adj* **uncler'ical** not characteristic of, or befitting, a clergyman. — *vt* **unclew** (*archaic*) to unwind, unfold or undo. — *vt* **uncloak'** to divest of a cloak; to show up. — *vi* to take one's cloak off. — *vt* **unclog'** to free from a clog or obstruction. — *adj* **unclogged'** not clogged. — *vt* **unclois'ter** to free or remove from the cloister. — *adj* **unclois'tered** not cloistered; without a cloister; freed or taken from a cloister. — *vt* and *vi* **unclose** (*un-klōz'*) to open. — *adj* **unclose** (*un-klōs'*) not close. — *adj* **unclosed** (*un-klōzd'*) not closed; unenclosed; opened. — *vt* **unclothe'** to take the clothes off; to divest of covering. — *adj* **unclothed'**. — *vt* and *vi* **uncloud'** to clear of clouds or obscurity. — *adj* **uncloud'ed** free from clouds, obscurity or gloom; calm. — *n* **uncloud'edness**. — *adj* **uncloud'y**. — *vt* **unclutch'** to release from a clutch. — *vt* **uncock'** to let

Some words with **un-** prefix; see **un-** entry for numbered senses.

unchā'ry *adj* (1).
unchaste' *adj* (1).
unchaste'ly *adv* (1).
unchast'ened *adj* (1).
unchaste'ness *n* (1).
unchastīz'able or **-s-** *adj* (1).
unchastized' or **-s-** *adj* (1).
uncheered' *adj* (1).
uncheer'ful *adj* (1).
uncheer'fully *adv* (1).
uncheer'fulness *n* (1).
unchewed' *adj* (1).
unchiv'alrous *adj* (1).
unchō'sen *adj* (1).
unchron'icled *adj* (1).
uncir'cumscribed *adj* (1).
uncited *adj* (1).
unclad' *adj* (1).
unclaimed' *adj* (1).
unclass'ical *adj* (1).
unclass'y *adj* (1).
unclear' *adj* (1).
uncleared' *adj* (1).
unclear'ly *adv* (1).
unclear'ness *n* (1).
unclench' *vt* and *vi* (2).
unclipped' or **unclipt'** *adj* (1).
unclō'ven *adj* (1).
unclub'able or **unclubb'able** *adj* (1).
unclutt'ered *adj* (1).
uncoat'ed *adj* (1).
uncollect'ed *adj* (1).
uncol'oured *adj* (1).
uncombed' *adj* (1).
uncommend'able *adj* (1).
uncommend'ably *adv* (1).
uncommend'ed *adj* (1).
uncommer'cial *adj* (1).
uncommū'nicable *adj* (1).
uncommū'nicated *adj* (1).
uncommū'nicative *adj* (1).
uncommū'nicativeness *n* (1).
uncommū'ted *adj* (1).
uncompact'ed *adj* (1).
uncompass'ionate *adj* (1).
uncompelled' *adj* (1).
uncom'pensated *adj* (1).
uncompet'itive *adj* (1).
uncomplain'ing *adj* (1).
uncomplain'ingly *adv* (1).
uncomplais'ant (or *-kom'*) *adj* (1).
uncomplais'antly (or *-kom'*) *adv* (1).
uncomplē'ted *adj* (1).
uncomplī'ant *adj* (1).
uncomply'ing *adj* (1).
uncomprehend'ed *adj* (1).
uncomprehend'ing *adj* (1).
unconceal'able *adj* (1).
unconcealed' *adj* (1).
unconceal'ing *adj* (1).
unconcert'ed *adj* (1).
unconcil'iatory *adj* (1).
unconfed'erated *adj* (1).
unconfessed' *adj* (1).
unconfused' *adj* (1).
unconfus'edly *adv* (1).
uncongē'nial *adj* (1).
uncongēnial'ity *n* (1).
unconject'ured *adj* (1).
unconnect'ed *adj* (1).
unconq'uerable *adj* (1).
unconq'uerableness *n* (1).
unconq'uerably *adv* (1).
unconq'uered *adj* (1).
unconscien'tious *adj* (1).
unconscien'tiously *adv* (1).
unconscien'tiousness *n* (1).
unconsent'ing *adj* (1).
unconsoled' *adj* (1).
unconsol'idated *adj* (1).
unconstitū'tional *adj* (1).

down the hammer of (a gun); to spread out from a haycock. — *adj* **uncoff'ined** not put into a coffin; removed from a coffin. — *vt* and *vi* **uncoil'** to unwind. — *adj* **uncoined'** not coined; (*Shakesp* **uncoyned**) variously explained, but *prob* meaning 'natural', 'not artificial or counterfeit'. — *vt* **uncolt'** (*Shakesp*, punning on Falstaff's use of *colt* to cheat, *Henry IV* 1 II. 2. 42) to deprive of a horse. — *vt* and *vi* **uncombine'** (*Dickens*) to separate. — *adj* **uncomatable** or **uncomeatable** (*un-kum-at'ə-bl*) inaccessible; out of reach. — *n* **uncome'liness**. — *adj* **uncome'ly** not comely; indecent; unseemly. — *adj* **uncom'fortable** feeling, involving or causing discomfort or unease. — *n* **uncom'fortableness**. — *adv* **uncom'fortably**. — *adj* **uncom'forted**. — *adj* **uncommitt'ed** not pledged to support any party, policy or action; impartial; not committed (**uncommitted logic array** (often as *abbrev* **ULA** or **ula**; *comput*) a microchip whose logic circuits are left unconnected during manufacture and completed later to the customer's specification). — *adj* **uncomm'on** not common; unusual; remarkably great; strange. — *adv* (*old slang*) remarkably, very. — *adv* **uncomm'only** rarely (*esp* in *not uncommonly*, frequently); in an unusually great degree. — *n* **uncomm'onness**. — *adj* **uncom'panied** unaccompanied. — *adj* **uncompan'ionable** unsociable. — *adj* **uncompan'ioned** without a companion or an equal. — *adj* **uncom'plicated** straightforward, not made difficult by the variety of factors involved; (of a person) simple in character and outlook. — *adj* **uncompliment'ary** not at all complimentary, derogatory. — *adj* **uncompō'sable** incapable of being composed or reconciled. — *adj* **uncompound'ed** not compounded, unmixed; not worsened or intensified. — *adj* **uncomprehen'sive** not comprehensive; incomprehensible (*Shakesp*). — *adj* **uncom'promising** refusing to compromise; unyielding; out-and-out. — *adv* **uncom'promisingly**. — *n* **uncom'promisingness**. — *adj* **unconceiv'able** inconceivable. — *n* **unconceiv'ableness**. — *adv* **unconceiv'ably**. — *adj* **unconceived'**. — *n* **unconcern'** lack of concern or anxiety; indifference. — *adj* **unconcerned'** not concerned, not involved (in); impartial; uninterested; indifferent; untroubled, carelessly secure; sober, unaffected by liquor (*obs*). — *adv* **unconcern'edly**. — *n* **unconcern'edness**. — *adj* **unconcern'ing**. — *n* **unconcern'ment**. — *adj* **unconclu'sive** inconclusive. — *adj* **unconcoct'ed** not digested; crude; not elaborated or finished (*fig*). — *adj* **uncondi'tional** not conditional; absolute, unlimited. — *n* **unconditional'ity**. — *adv* **uncondi'tionally**. — *n* **uncondi'tionalness**. — *adj* **uncondi'tioned** not subject to condition or limitation; infinite, absolute, unknowable; (of a person, response, etc) not conditioned by learning or experience (**unconditioned stimulus** one provoking an unconditioned response); not put into the required state. — *adj* **unconfī'nable** not to be confined; unbounded (*Shakesp*). — *vt* **unconfine'** to release from restraint; to divulge (*Keats*). — *adj* **unconfined'** not confined; not restricted; unlimited; set free. — *adv* **unconfī'nedly**. — *adj* **unconfirmed'** not confirmed; not yet having received confirmation; uncorroborated; not yet firm or strong; ignorant (*Shakesp*). — *adj* **unconform'** (*Milton*) unlike. — *n* **unconformabil'ity** the state or the quality of being unconformable; an unconformity in stratification (*geol*). — *adj* **unconform'able** not conforming (to eg *hist*, the practices of the Church of England); unwilling to conform; showing an unconformability (*geol*). — *n* **unconform'ableness**. — *adv* **unconform'ably**. — *adj* **unconform'ing** not conforming. — *n* **unconform'ity** lack of conformity (*archaic*); nonconformity (*obs*); a substantial break in the succession of stratified sedimentary rocks, following a period of non-deposition (*geol*). — *vt* and *vi* **uncongeal'** to thaw, melt. — *adj* **uncon'jugal** (*Milton*) not suited to, or fitting in, marriage. — *adj* **unconjunc'tive** (*Milton*) impossible to be joined. — *adj* **unconnī'ving** (*Milton*) refusing indulgence. — *adj* **uncon'scionable** (of a person) unscrupulous; not conformable to conscience; outrageous, inordinate. — *n* **uncon'scionableness**. — *adv* **uncon'scionably**. — *adj* **uncon'scious** without consciousness; unaware (with *of*); not self-conscious. — *n* (with **the**) the deepest, inaccessible level of the psyche in which repressed impulses and memories are present in dynamic state. — *adv* **uncon'sciously**. — *n* **uncon'sciousness**. — *vt* **uncon'secrate** to deprive of the character or state of consecration. — *adj* unconsecrated. — *adj* **uncon'secrated** not consecrated. — *adj* **unconsentā'neous** (*Peacock*) not in agreement. — *adj* **unconsid'ered** not valued or esteemed; done without considering. — *adj* **unconsid'ering**. — *adj* **uncon'stant** (*Shakesp*) inconstant. — *adj* **unconstrain'able**. — *adj* **unconstrained'**. — *adv* **unconstrain'edly**. — *n* **unconstraint'** absence of constraint. — *adj* **uncontemned'** (*Shakesp*) not despised. — *adj* **uncontest'able** incontestable. — *adj* **uncontest'ed**. — *adj* **uncontrōll'able** not capable of being controlled; absolute, not con-

Some words with **un-** prefix; see **un-** entry for numbered senses.

unconstitūtional'ity *n* (1).
unconstitū'tionally *adv* (1).
unconsumed' *adj* (1).
uncon'summated *adj* (1).
uncontain'able *adj* (1).
uncontam'inated *adj* (1).
uncon'templated *adj* (1).
unconten'tious *adj* (1).
uncontradict'ed *adj* (1).
uncontrived' *adj* (1).
uncontrover'sial *adj* (1).
unconvers'ant *adj* (1).
unconvert'ed *adj* (1).
unconvert'ible *adj* (1).
unconvict'ed *adj* (1).
unconvinced' *adj* (1).
unconvinc'ing *adj* (1).
uncooked' *adj* (1).
unco-op'erative or **uncoop'erative** *adj* (1).
unco-op'eratively or **uncoop'eratively** *adv* (1).
uncoquett'ish *adj* (1).
uncor'dial *adj* (1).
uncork' *vt* (2).
uncorrect'ed *adj* (1).
uncorrob'orated *adj* (1).
uncor'seted *adj* (1).
uncount'able *adj* (1).
uncount'ed *adj* (1).
uncourt'liness *n* (1).
uncourt'ly *adj* (1).
uncrate *vt* (2).
uncropped' *adj* (1).
uncrow'ded *adj* (1).
uncrump'le *vt* (2).
uncrush'able *adj* (1).
uncrystallīz'able or **-s-** *adj* (1).
uncrys'tallized or **-s-** *adj* (1).
uncuck'olded *adj* (1).
unculled' *adj* (1).
uncult'ivable or **uncultivāt'able** *adj* (1).
uncult'ivated *adj* (1).
uncum'bered *adj* (1).
uncurb'able *adj* (1).
uncurbed' *adj* (1).
uncurd'led *adj* (1).
uncured' *adj* (1).
uncurr'ent *adj* (1).
uncurtailed' *adj* (1).
uncurved' *adj* (1).
undam' *vt* (2).
undam'aged *adj* (1).
undammed' *adj* (1) and (2).
undamned' *adj* (1).
undamped' *adj* (1).
undaunt'able *adj* (1).
undealt' *adj* (1).
undear' *adj* (1).
undebarred' *adj* (1).
undebased' *adj* (1).
undebauched' *adj* (1).
undecayed' *adj* (1).
undecīd'able *adj* (1).
undeclared' *adj* (1).
undecompōs'able *adj* (1).
undecomposed' *adj* (1).
undefaced' *adj* (1).
undefeat'ed *adj* (1).
undefend'ed *adj* (1).
undefiled' *adj* (1).
undelayed' *adj* (1).
undelay'ing *adj* (1).
undelect'able *adj* (1).
undel'egated *adj* (1).
undelib'erate *adj* (1).
undeliv'erable *adj* (1).
undeliv'ered *adj* (1).
undelud'ed *adj* (1).
undemand'ing *adj* (1).

trolled (*archaic*); indisputable (*obs*). — *n* **uncontrōll'ableness**. — *adv* **uncontrōll'ably**. — *adj* **uncontrolled'** not controlled; not disputed (*obs*). — *adv* **uncontrōll'edly**. — *adj* **uncontrovert'ed** not disputed. — *adj* **uncontrovert'ible**. — *adj* **unconven'tional** not conventional; free in one's ways. — *n* **unconventional'ity**. — *adj* **unconvers'able** not able or not disposed to converse freely. — *adj* **uncool'** (*colloq derog*) not sophisticated or smart, old-fashioned. — *adj* **unco-or'dinated** or **unco-or'dinated** not co-ordinated; having clumsy movements, as if muscles were not co-ordinated. — *vt* **uncope'** to unmuzzle, or unsew the mouth of (a ferret; cf **uncape**). — *vt* **uncord'** to free (eg a trunk) from cords. — *adj* **uncorrupt'** incorrupt. — *adj* **uncorrupt'ed**. — *adj* **uncost'ly** inexpensive. — *adj* **uncoun'selled** not given advice; not advised. — *vt* **uncoup'le** to undo the coupling of; to release. — *vi* to become detached; to uncouple hounds. — *adj* **uncoup'led** not married; detached. — *adj* **uncour'teous** discourteous. — *adj* **uncouth** (*un-kōōth'*; OE *uncūth* unknown or strange, from *un-*, and *cūth*, known) awkward, ungraceful, uncultured, *esp* in manners or language; strange and wild or unattractive; unfamiliar (*archaic*); unknown (*obs*); see also **unco** (separate entry). — *adv* **uncouth'ly**. — *n* **uncouth'ness**. — *adj* **uncov'enanted** not promised or bound by covenant; not included in a covenant; not having subscribed to the Solemn League and Covenant of 1643. — *vt* **uncov'er** to remove the cover of; to lay open; to expose; to drive out of cover. — *vi* to take off one's hat or other head covering. — *adj* **uncov'ered**. — *vt* **uncowl'** to withdraw the cowl from. — *adj* **uncowled'**. — *adj* **uncoyned** see **uncoined**. — *vt* **uncreate'** to deprive of existence. — *adj* **uncreā'ted** not (yet) created; not produced by creation (*Milton*). — *n* **uncreāt'edness**. — *adj* **uncreā'ting**. — *adj* **uncred'ible** (*obs*) incredible. — *adj* **uncred'itable** (*obs*) discreditable. — *adj* **uncrit'ical** not critical, without discrimination; not in accordance with the principles of criticism. — *adv* **uncrit'ically**. — *vt* **uncross'** to change or move from a crossed position. — *adj* **uncrossed'** not crossed; not passed over, marked with a cross, thwarted, etc; not marked off as paid (*Shakesp*). — *vt* **uncrown'** to dethrone; to remove the crown from. — *adj* **uncrowned'** not crowned; not yet formally crowned; possessing kingly power without the actual title (**uncrowned king** or **queen** (*facetious*) a man or woman having supreme influence, or commanding the highest respect, within a particular group); unfulfilled. — *adj* **uncrudd'ed** (*Spenser*) uncurdled. — *adj* **uncul'tured** not cultured; not cultivated. — *adj* **uncūr'able** (*Shakesp*) incurable. — *adj* **uncū'rious** incurious; not strange. — *vt* and *vi* **uncurl'** to take or come out of curl, twist or roll. — *adj* **uncurled'** not curled; unrolled or uncoiled. — *adj* **uncurl'ing**. — *vt* **uncurse'** to free from a curse, unsay a curse upon. — *vt* **uncur'tain** to remove a curtain from. — *adj* **uncur'tained** curtainless. — *adj* **uncus'tomed** (of goods) on which customs duty is unpaid, or not payable; unaccustomed (*archaic*); not customary (*archaic*). — *adj* **uncut'** not cut; not shaped by cutting; not abridged; (of a book) (bibliographically) with margins not cut down by the binder (even though opened with a paper-cutter), (popularly) unopened; (of illegal drugs) not adulterated.

Words starting with **d-**, *prefixed by* **un-**.

adj **undashed'** undismayed. — *adj* **undāt'ed** with no date marked or assigned; unending. — *adj* **undaunt'ed** not daunted; bold, intrepid. — *adv* **undaunt'edly**. — *n* **undaunt'edness**. — *adj* **undawn'ing** not yet dawning or showing light. — *vi* **undazz'le** to recover from a dazed state (*Tennyson*). — *adj* **undazz'led** not dazzled. — *adj* **undead'** (of a ghost, vampire, etc) dead but not at rest. — *n pl* such spirits. — *vt* **undeaf'** (*Shakesp*) to free from deafness. — *adj* **undeceiv'able** incapable of being deceived; incapable of deceiving (*obs*). — *vt* **undeceive'** to free from a mistaken belief, reveal the truth to. — *adj* **undeceived'** not deceived; set free from a delusion. — *adj* **undē'cent** indecent (*dialect*); unfitting (*archaic*); unhandsome (*obs*). — *adj* **undecīd'ed** not decided or settled; uncertain, irresolute. — *adv* **undecīd'edly**. — *adj* **undecī'pherable** indecipherable. — *adj* **undecī'sive** indecisive. — *vt* **undeck'** to divest of ornaments. — *adj* **undecked'** not adorned; having no deck. — *adj* **undeclīn'ing** unbowed, unsubmissive. — *adj* **undeed'ed** (*Shakesp*) unused in any action. — *adj* **undefied'** (or *Spenser* **undefide'**) not defied or challenged. — *adj* **undefīn'able**. — *adj* **undefined'** not defined; indefinite. — *vt* **undē'ify** to deprive of the nature or honour of a god. — *n* **undelight'** lack of delight. — *adj* **undelight'ed**. — *adj* **undelight'ful**. — *adj* **undenī'able** not to be denied, indisputable; not to be refused; obviously true; unexceptionable, excellent (*old*). — *n* **undenī'ableness**. — *adv* **undenī'ably** certainly, one cannot deny it. — *adj*

Some words with **un-** prefix; see **un-** entry for numbered senses.

undemocrat'ic *adj* (1).
undemon'strable *adj* (1).
undemon'strative *adj* (1).
undemon'strativeness *n* (1).
undeplored' *adj* (1).
undepraved' *adj* (1).
undeprē'ciated *adj* (1).
undepressed' *adj* (1).
undeprived' *adj* (1).
undescend'ible or **undescend'able** *adj* (1).
undescried' *adj* (1).
undespair'ing *adj* (1).
undespair'ingly *adv* (1).
undespoiled' *adj* (1).
undestroyed' *adj* (1).
undetect'able *adj* (1).
undetect'ed *adj* (1).
undē'viating *adj* (1).
undē'viatingly *adv* (1).
undevout' *adj* (1).
undiagnosed' *adj* (1).
undigest'ed *adj* (1).
undilut'ed *adj* (1).
undimin'ishable *adj* (1).
undimin'ished *adj* (1).
undimmed' *adj* (1).
undint'ed *adj* (1).
undiplomat'ic *adj* (1).
undirect'ed *adj* (1).
undisappoint'ing *adj* (1).
undisclosed' *adj* (1).
undiscom'fited *adj* (1).
undiscord'ant *adj* (1).
undiscour'aged *adj* (1).
undiscov'erable *adj* (1).
undiscov'erably *adv* (1).
undiscov'ered *adj* (1).
undiscuss'able or **undiscuss'ible** *adj* (1).
undishon'oured *adj* (1).
undismant'led *adj* (1).
undismayed' *adj* (1).
undisor'dered *adj* (1).
undispatched' *adj* (1).
undispensed' *adj* (1).
undispūt'ed *adj* (1).
undispūt'edly *adv* (1).
undissō'ciated *adj* (1).
undissolved' *adj* (1).
undissol'ving *adj* (1).
undistilled' *adj* (1).
undistort'ed *adj* (1).
undistract'ed *adj* (1).
undistract'edly *adv* (1).
undistract'edness *n* (1).
undistract'ing *adj* (1).
undisturbed' *adj* (1).
undistur'bedly *adv* (1).
undistur'bing *adj* (1).
undivers'ified *adj* (1).
undivine' *adj* (1).
undivorced' *adj* (1).
undivulged' *adj* (1).
undoc'umented *adj* (1).
undoomed' *adj* (1).
undrain'able *adj* (1).
undrained' *adj* (1).
undramat'ic *adj* (1).
undread'ed *adj* (1).
undread'ing *adj* (1).
undream'ing *adj* (1).
undried' *adj* (1).
undrilled' *adj* (1).
undrink'able *adj* (1).
undrive'able *adj* (1).
undriv'en *adj* (1).
undroop'ing *adj* (1).
undrowned' *adj* (1).
undrunk' *adj* (1).
undubbed' *adj* (1).

undenominā'tional not confined to or favouring any particular sect. — *n* **undenominā'tionalism**. — *adj* **undepend'able** not to be depended upon. — *n* **undepen'dableness**. — *adj* **undepen'ding** (*obs*) independent. — *adj* **undescen'ded'** (of the testes) remaining in the abdominal cavity, failing to move down into the scrotum. — *adj* **undescrī'bable** indescribable. — *adj* **undescribed'**. — *adj* **undescried'**. — *n* **un'desert** lack of merit, unworthiness. — *vt* **undeserve'** to fail or cease to deserve. — *adj* **undeserved'** not deserved. — *adv* **undeser'vedly**. — *n* **undeser'vedness**. — *n* **undeser'ver** (*Shakesp*) someone who is not deserving or worthy. — *adj* **undeser'ving**. — *adv* **undeser'vingly**. — *adj* **undesigned'**. — *adv* **undesign'edly**. — *n* **undesign'edness**. — *adj* **undesign'ing** not designing; artless; straightforward; sincere. — *n* **undesirabil'ity**. — *adj* **undesīr'able** not to be wished for; not sexually desirable. — *n* an undesirable or objectionable person or thing. — *n* **undesīr'ableness**. — *adv* **undesīr'ably**. — *adj* **undesired'**. — *adj* **undesīr'ing**. — *adj* **undesīr'ous**. — *adj* **undeter'minable** indeterminable. — *adj* **undeter'minate** indeterminate. — *n* **undeter'minateness**. — *n* **undeterminā'tion**. — *adj* **undeter'mined** not settled, not fixed; not ascertained; not limited. — *adj* **undeterred'** not discouraged or prevented (from). — *adj* **undevel'oped** not developed; (of land) not built on or used for public works. — *vt* **undid'** *pa t* of **undo**. — *adj* **undiff'erenced** (*heraldry*) without a modification to distinguish a cadet from the main line. — *adj* **undifferen'tiated** not differentiated. — *vt* **undight** (*un-dīt'*; *Spenser*) to undo, take off, doff (*pa t* and *pa p* **undight'**). — *adj* unadorned; not dressed, (of hair) loose (*Spenser*, etc). — *adj* **undig'nified**. — *vt* **undig'nify** to deprive of dignity. — *adj* **undipped'** not dipped; unbaptized. — *adj* **undiscerned'** unobserved, unperceived. — *adv* **undiscern'edly**. — *adj* **undiscern'ible**. — *adv* **undiscern'ibly**. — *adj* **undiscern'ing** showing lack of discernment or discrimination. — *n* lack of discernment. — *adj* **undischarged'** not paid or settled; (of eg an obligation) not carried out; not released from debt or other liability; (of a gun) not fired. — *adj* **undisc'iplinable**. — *n* **undisc'ipline** lack of discipline. — *adj* **undisc'iplined** untrained; unruly. — *adj* **undiscord'ing** (*Milton*) not discordant. — *adj* **undiscrim'inating** not making distinctions; not showing critical taste or ability. — *adj* **undiscussed'** not discussed; unsettled (*obs*). — *adj* **undisguīs'able**. — *adj* **undisguised'** not disguised; frank, open. — *adv* **undisguīs'edly**. — *adj* **undisposed'** not disposed (*usu* with **-of**); disinclined (*Shakesp*); disinclined (to do, or with *to*). — *adj* **undissem'bled** unfeigned; undisguised, unconcealed. — *adj* **undistemp'ered** not deranged, disturbed, ruffled or in unhealthy condition. — *adj* **undistinc'tive** not distinctive; undistinguishing. — *adj* **undisting'uishable** indistinguishable. — *n* **undisting'uishableness**. — *adv* **undisting'uishably**. — *adj* **undisting'uished** not distinguished or observed; not marked out by conspicuous qualities, not famous; not having an air of distinction. — *adj* **undisting'uishing** not discriminating. — *adj* **undistrib'uted** not distributed (**undistributed middle** the fallacy of reasoning without distributing the middle term, ie without making it universal, in at least one premise). — *adj* **undivert'ed** not turned away; not amused. — *adj* **undivert'ing**. — *adj* **undivest'ed** (*Richardson*) detached. — *adv* **undivest'edly**. — *adj* **undivid'able** indivisible. — *adj* **undivī'ded** not divided; (of one's attention to something) wholly concentrated, not distracted. — *adv* **undivī'dedly**. — *n* **undivī'dedness**. — *vt* **undo** (*un-dōō'*) to reverse the doing of; to cancel or annul; to bring to nothing; to unfasten by unbolting, etc; to open; to unbutton, untie, etc; to unravel; to solve (a problem or riddle) (*archaic*); to bring ruin on (*archaic*); to seduce (*archaic*); to prevent the happening or being of (*Shakesp*). — *vi* to come undone; to reverse what has been done: — *pa t* **undid'**; *pa p* **undone** (*un-dun'*; see also below). — *vt* **undock'** to take (a ship) out of dock; to release (a spacecraft) from its coupling with another spacecraft, station, etc in space. — Also *vi*. — *adj* **undocked'** not docked or cut short. — *adj* **undoc'tored** without a doctor's degree; not patched up, tampered with or sophisticated. — *n* **undoer** (*un-dōō'ər*) someone who undoes; someone who ruins; a seducer (*archaic*). — *n* **undo'ing** the reversal of what has been done; unfastening; opening; ruin or cause of ruin. — *adj* **undomes'tic** not domestic; not content with, adapted to, or relating to, home life; unhomelike (*Coleridge*). — *vt* **undomes'ticate** to make undomestic; to untame. — *adj* **undomes'ticated** not domesticated; not tamed; emancipated from mere domestic interests. — *adj* **undone** (*un-dun'*) not done; annulled; brought to naught; unfastened (**come undone** to become unfastened or detached; to go wrong); opened; ruined; seduced (*archaic*). — *vt* and *vi* **undoub'le** to unfold, open out. — *adj* **undoubt'able** indubitable. — *adj* **undoubt'ed** not doubted; unques-

Some words with **un-** prefix; see **un-** entry for numbered senses.

undug' *adj* (1).
undulled' *adj* (1).
uneat'able *adj* (1).
uneat'ableness *n* (1).
uneat'en *adj* (1).
uneclipsed' *adj* (1).
uned'ucable *adj* (1).
uned'ucated *adj* (1).
uneffaced' *adj* (1).
uneffect'ed *adj* (1).
unelab'orate *adj* (1).
unelab'orated *adj* (1).
unelat'ed *adj* (1).
unelect'ed *adj* (1).
unelect'rified *adj* (1).
unembarr'assed *adj* (1).
unembell'ished *adj* (1).
unembitt'ered *adj* (1).
unembod'ied *adj* (1).
unemphat'ic *adj* (1).
unemp'tied *adj* (1).
unenclosed' *adj* (1).
unencumb'ered *adj* (1).
unendang'ered *adj* (1).
unendowed' *adj* (1).
unendūr'able *adj* (1).
unendūr'ably *adv* (1).
unengaged' *adj* (1).
unenjoy'able *adj* (1).
unenlight'ened *adj* (1).
unenquīr'ing *adj* (1).
unenriched' *adj* (1).
unenslaved' *adj* (1).
unentailed' *adj* (1).
unen'tered *adj* (1).
unen'terprising *adj* (1).
unentertained' *adj* (1).
unentertain'ing *adj* (1).
unenthralled' *adj* (1).
unenthusiast'ic *adj* (1).
unentīt'led *adj* (1).
uneq'uable *adj* (1).
unerā'sable *adj* (1).
unescāp'able *adj* (1).
unescort'ed *adj* (1).
unespied' *adj* (1).
unessayed' *adj* (1).
uneth'ical *adj* (1).
unevangel'ical *adj* (1).
unē'ven *adj* (1).
unē'venly *adv* (1).
unē'venness *n* (1).
unevent'ful *adj* (1).
unevent'fully *adv* (1).
unev'idenced *adj* (1).
unexact'ing *adj* (1).
unexagg'erated *adj* (1).
unexalt'ed *adj* (1).
unexam'ined *adj* (1).
unex'cavated *adj* (1).
unexcelled' *adj* (1).
unexcī'table *adj* (1).
unexcī'ted *adj* (1).
unexcī'ting *adj* (1).
unexclu'ded *adj* (1).
unexclu'sive *adj* (1).
unexclu'sively *adv* (1).
unexem'plified *adj* (1).
unex'ercised *adj* (1).
unexhaus'ted *adj* (1).
unexpan'ded *adj* (1).
unexpec'tant *adj* (1).
unexpec'ted *adj* (1).
unexpec'tedly *adv* (1).
unexpec'tedness *n* (1).
unexpen'sive *adj* (1).
unexpen'sively *adv* (1).
unexpē'rienced *adj* (1).
unex'piated *adj* (1).
unexpired' *adj* (1).
unexplain'able *adj* (1).

tioned; certainly genuine or such as is represented; indubitable. — *adv* **undoubt'edly** without doubt, certainly. — *adj* **undoubt'ful**. — *adj* **undoubt'ing**. — *adv* **undoubt'ingly**. — *adj* **undraped'** without drapery; nude. — *vt* and *vi* **undraw'** to draw back. — *adj* **undreamed'** or **undreamt'** (also with **-of**) not imagined even in a dream. — *vt* **undress'** to remove the clothes or dressing from. — *vi* to take off one's clothes. — *n* (*un'*) scanty or incomplete dress; ordinary, informal dress; uniform for ordinary occasions. — Also *adj*. — *adj* **undressed'** not dressed; not set in order, or made trim, or treated or prepared for use, etc; divested of clothes (**get undressed** to take one's clothes off). — *n* **undress'ing**. — *adj* **undross'y** (*Pope*) pure. — *adj* **undue'** not due or owing; unjustifiable; inappropriate; excessive (**undue influence** (*law*) a strong influence over another person which might prevent the exercise of that person's free will). — *adv* **undū'ly** unjustifiably; more than is right or reasonable, excessively; wrongfully (*archaic*). — *adj* **undū'teous** (*poetic*) undutiful. — *adj* **undū'tiful**. — *adv* **undū'tifully**. — *n* **undū'tifulness**. — *adj* **undyed'** not dyed. — *adj* **undy'ing** not dying, immortal; unceasing. — *adv* **undy'ingly**. — *n* **undy'ingness**.

Words starting with **e-**, *prefixed by* **un-**.

adj **uneared'** not eared; untilled (*Shakesp*). — *adj* **unearned'** not earned by work (**unearned income** income, eg dividends, that is not remuneration for work done; **unearned increment** increase in value of land independent of owner's labour or expenditure); (of something pleasant or unpleasant) unmerited. — *vt* **unearth'** to dig up, disinter; to bring out of obscurity, bring to light; to expel from a burrow. — *adj* **unearthed'** not connected to earth electrically; dug up, brought to light, etc. — *n* **unearth'liness**. — *adj* **unearth'ly** celestial; weird, ghostly; unconscionable, absurd (*esp* of an early hour). — *n* **unease'** lack of ease; discomfort; apprehension. — *adv* **uneas'ily**. — *n* **uneas'iness**. — *adj* **uneas'y** not at ease; disquieted; apprehensive; showing troubled restlessness (*lit* and *fig*); uncomfortable; difficult to do or accomplish (now *rare*); (of roads, etc) difficult because of physical obstacles (*obs*). — *adj* **uneath** (*un-ēth'*; OE *unēathe*; see **eath**; *archaic*) difficult; distressing. — *adv* (*archaic*) with difficulty; in hardship; hardly, scarcely; almost (*Spenser*). — Also (*adv*) **uneath'**, **uneathes'** or **unnethes'**. — *adj* **unecono'mic** not in accordance with sound economics. — *adj* **uneconom'ical** not economical. — *vt* **unedge'** to blunt. — *adj* **uned'ifying** not instructing or uplifting morally or aesthetically; morally degrading or degraded. — *adj* **uned'ited** never edited, never before published. — *adj* **unemo'tional**. — *adv* **unemo'tionally**. — *adj* **unemo'tioned** impassive. — *adj* **unemploy'able**. — *adj* **unemployed'** out of work; not put to use or profit; for or pertaining to those who are out of work. — *n* (with **the**) the number of people out of work in a given period. — *n* **unemploy'ment** (**unemployment benefit** a weekly payment supplied under the national insurance scheme to a person who is unemployed). — *adj* **unenchant'ed** (*Milton* **uninchant'ed**). — *adj* **unendeared'** (*Milton* **unindeared'**) not made precious. — *adj* **unend'ing** endless: everlasting; never ceasing, incessant; thorough-going (*Carlyle*). — *adv* **unend'ingly**. — *n* **unend'ingness**. — *adj* **unenforce'able** that cannot be (*esp* legally) enforced. — *adj* **unenforced'**. — *adj* **un-Eng'lish** not English in character. — *adj* **un-Eng'lished** not translated into English. — *adj* **unen'viable** not to be envied; (of a task, etc) not exciting envy. — *adv* **unen'viably**. — *adj* **unen'vied**. — *adj* **unen'vious**. — *adj* **unen'vying**. — *adj* **unē'qual** not equal; not or adequate or equal (with *to*); varying, not uniform; (of an agreement, etc) not evenly balanced, eg with regard to concessions made or advantages gained; inadequate (*obs*); unjust (*obs*); excessive (*obs*). — Also *adv* (*Shakesp*). — *n* someone who is not equal in rank, ability, etc. — *adj* **unē'qualled** without an equal. — *adv* **unē'qually**. — *adj* **uneq'uitable** inequitable. — *adj* **unequiv'ocal** unambiguous; explicit; clear and emphatic. — *adv* **unequiv'ocally**. — *adj* **unerr'ing** making no error, infallible; not, or never, missing the mark (*lit* and *fig*). — *adv* **unerr'ingly**. — *n* **unerr'ingness**. — *vt* **uness'ence** to deprive of essence or being (*Lamb*). — *adj* **unessen'tial** not of the essence; inessential, not necessary, not important; without being, immaterial (*Milton*, etc). — *adj* **unestab'lished** not established; not on the establishment or permanent staff. — *adj* **uneth** see **uneath** above. — *adj* **unexam'pled** unprecedented, without like or parallel. — *adj* **unexcep'tionable** not liable to objection or criticism; exactly right, excellent; without exception (*Ruskin*). — *n* **unexcep'tionableness**. — *adv* **unexcep'tionably**. — *adj* **unexcep'tional** not admitting or forming an exception; run-of-the-mill; unexceptionable. — *adv* **unexcep'tionally**. — *adj* **unex'ecuted** not executed; not brought into action

Some words with **un-** prefix; see **un-** entry for numbered senses.

unexplained' *adj* (1).
unexploit'ed *adj* (1).
unexplored' *adj* (1).
unexposed' *adj* (1).
unexpressed' *adj* (1).
unexpress'ible *adj* (1).
unex'purgated *adj* (1).
unexten'ded *adj* (1).
unexten'uated *adj* (1).
unexting'uishable *adj* (1).
unexting'uishably *adv* (1).
unexting'uished *adj* (1).
unextreme' *adj* (1).
unfā'dable *adj* (1).
unfā'ded *adj* (1).
unfā'ding *adj* (1).
unfā'dingly *adv* (1).
unfā'dingness *n* (1).
unfall'en *adj* (1).
unfal'tering *adj* (1).
unfal'teringly *adv* (1).
unfamed' *adj* (1).
unfamil'iar *adj* (1).
unfamiliar'ity *n* (1).
unfamil'iarly *adv* (1).
unfanned' *adj* (1).
unfastid'ious *adj* (1).
unfault'y *adj* (1).
unfā'vourable *adj* (1).
unfā'vourableness *n* (1).
unfā'vourably *adv* (1).
unfeas'ible *adj* (1).
unfeath'ered *adj* (1).
unfed' *adj* (1).
unfelled' *adj* (1).
unfem'inine *adj* (1).
unfenced' *adj* (1).
unferment'ed *adj* (1).
unfer'tilized or **-s-** *adj* (1).
unfeued' *adj* (1).
unfig'ured *adj* (1).
unfil'ial *adj* (1).
unfil'ially *adv* (1).
unfill'able *adj* (1).
unfilled' *adj* (1).
unfilmed' *adj* (1).
unfil'tered *adj* (1).
unfired' *adj* (1).
unfirm' *adj* (1).
unfished' *adj* (1).
unflagg'ing *adj* (1).
unflagg'ingly *adv* (1).
unflatt'ering *adj* (1).
unflatt'eringly *adv* (1).
unflā'voured *adj* (1).
unflawed' *adj* (1).
unflinch'ing *adj* (1).
unflinch'ingly *adv* (1).
unfloored' *adj* (1).
unflus'tered *adj* (1).
unfō'cused or **unfō'cussed** *adj* (1).
unford'able *adj* (1).
unforeknow'able *adj* (1).
unforeknown' *adj* (1).
unforesee'able *adj* (1).
unforesee'ing *adj* (1).
unforeseen' *adj* (1).
unforetold' *adj* (1).
unforewarned' *adj* (1).
unfor'feited *adj* (1).
unforged' *adj* (1).
unforgett'able *adj* (1).
unforgett'ably *adv* (1).
unforgiv'able *adj* (1).
unforgiv'en *adj* (1).
unforgive'ness *n* (1).
unforgiv'ing *adj* (1).
unforgiv'ingness *n* (1).
unfor'matted *adj* (1).
unfor'midable *adj* (1).

(*Shakesp*). — *adj* **unexpē'rient** (*Shakesp*) inexperienced. — *adj* **unexpress'ive** not expressive; inexpressible, beyond the power of description (*Shakesp*, *Milton*). — *adj* **unexpug'nable** inexpugnable. — *adj* **unextinct'** not extinguished or dead (*fig*). — *adj* **uneyed'** unseen, unobserved.

Words starting with **f-**, *prefixed by* **un-**.
adj **unfa'bled** not fabled, real. — *n* **un'fact** a fact that must not be acknowledged, or a falsehood that must pass as fact, *esp* in international politics. — *adj* **unfail'ing** never failing or giving up; infallible; constant; inexhaustible. — *adv* **unfail'ingly**. — *adj* **unfair'** not fair, ugly; inequitable, unjust; involving deception or fraud and leading to undue advantage over business rival(s). — *vt* (*Shakesp*) to deprive of beauty. — *adv* **unfair'ly**. — *n* **unfair'ness**. — *n* **unfaith'** lack of faith or trust. — *adj* **unfaith'ful** not of the approved religion; not faithful, violating trust; breaking faith with one's husband, wife or lover, *usu* by having sexual intercourse with someone else; not true to the original. — *adv* **unfaith'fully**. — *n* **unfaith'fulness**. — *adj* **unfall'ible** (*Shakesp*) infallible. — *adj* **unfash'ionable** not fashionable; shapeless (*Shakesp*); incapable of being fashioned (*obs*). — *n* **unfash'ionableness**. — *adv* **unfash'ionably**. — *adj* **unfash'ioned** not formed; not shaped; not made polished, elegant, etc (*obs*). — *vt* **unfasten** (*un-fäs'n*) to release from a fastening; to unfix (*Shakesp*). — *vi* to become loose or open. — *adj* **unfas'tened** released from fastening; not fastened. — *adj* **unfa'thered** without a father or acknowledged father; deprived of a father; of unknown source, origin, etc. — *adj* **unfa'therly** unbefitting a father. — *adj* **unfath'omable** not able to be fathomed (*lit* and *fig*). — *n* **unfath'omableness**. — *adv* **unfath'omably**. — *adj* **unfath'omed** not sounded, of unknown depth; of unascertained meaning (*fig*). — *adj* **unfazed'** not perturbed. — *adj* **unfeared'** not feared; unafraid (*obs*). — *adj* **unfear'ful** not afraid. — *adv* **unfear'fully**. — *adj* **unfear'ing**. — *adj* **unfeat'ured** without marked or well-formed features (*lit* and *fig*). — *adj* **unfeed'** not retained by a fee; unpaid. — *adj* **unfeel'ing** without physical sensation; without kind or sympathetic feelings; hard-hearted. — *adv* **unfeel'ingly**. — *n* **unfeel'ingness**. — *adj* **unfeigned'** not feigned, real; not feigning, sincere. — *adv* **unfeign'edly**. — *n* **unfeign'edness**. — *adj* **unfeign'ing**. — *adj* **unfell'owed** unmatched. — *adj* **unfelt'** not felt; intangible (*Shakesp*). — *vt* **unfett'er** to free from fetters. — *adj* **unfett'ered** unrestrained. — *adj* **unfeu'dal** not marked by social attitudes and assumptions like those under the feudal system. — *vt* **unfeud'alize** or **-ise** to defeudalize. — *adj* **unfiled'** not rubbed with a file (**file**[2]), unpolished (*Spenser* **unfilde'**); undefiled (cf **file**[3]; now *dialect*); not placed on a file (**file**[1]). — *adj* **unfill'eted** not bound with a fillet; not boned. — *adj* **unfil'terable** or **unfil'trable** unable to pass through a filter (or an ordinary filter). — *adj* **unfine'** not fine. — *adj* **unfin'ished**. — *n* **unfin'ishing** (*Milton*) the leaving unfinished. — *adj* **unfit'** not fit; not fitting or suitable; not in fit condition; not meeting required standards. — *n* an unfit person. — *vt* to make unfit; to render or cause to be unsuitable (with *for*); to disqualify. — *adv* **unfit'ly** unsuitably, inappropriately. — *n* **unfit'ness**. — *adj* **unfitt'ed** not provided (with *with*); without fittings; not made to fit, or tested for fit; not adapted, qualified, or having the ability (to do, or with *for*). — *n* **unfitt'edness**. — *adj* **unfitt'ing** unsuitable; unbecoming, indecorous. — *adv* **unfitt'ingly**. — *vt* **unfix'** to unfasten, detach; to unsettle (*fig*). — *vi* to become loose. — *adj* **unfixed'**. — *n* **unfix'edness** or **unfix'ity**. — *adj* **unflapp'able** (*colloq*) imperturbable, never agitated or alarmed. — *n* **unflappabil'ity**. — *adv* **unflapp'ably**. — *adj* **unfledged'** not yet fledged; undeveloped or inexperienced; of early youth. — *vt* **unflesh'** to remove the flesh from. — *adj* **unfleshed'** deprived of flesh, reduced to a skeleton; not fleshed, not having tasted blood, uninitiated. — *adj* **unflesh'ly** spiritual; incorporeal; not carnal. — *vi* **unflush'** (*Arnold*) to lose a flush of colour. — *vt* **unfold'** (cf **fold**[1]) to open the folds of; to spread out; to tell; to disclose, make known; to reveal, display. — *vi* to open out, spread open to the view (*lit* and *fig*). — *vt* **unfold'** (cf **fold**[2]) to let out from a sheep-fold. — *adj* **unfold'ed** not folded; opened out from a folded state. — *adj* **unfold'ed** not enclosed in a sheep-fold. — *n* **unfold'er**. — *n* and *adj* **unfold'ing** opening out from folds: disclosing. — *n* and *adj* **unfold'ing** letting out from a sheep-fold. — *adj* (of a star; *Shakesp*) showing the time for unfolding sheep. — *vt* **unfool'** to undo the fooling of; to undeceive. — *adj* **unfoot'ed** untrodden. — *adj* **unforbid'** (*Milton*) or **unforbidd'en**. — *adj* **unforced'**. — *adv* **unfor'cedly**. — *adj* **unfor'cible** incapable of being forced or (*Milton*) enforced; without strength (*obs*). — *adj* **unforebōd'ing** not giving or feeling foreboding. — *adj* **unfore'skinned** (*Milton*) circumcised. — *adj* **unfor'ested** not wooded;

Some words with **un-** prefix; see **un-** entry for numbered senses.

unform'ulated *adj* (1).
unforsā'ken *adj* (1).
unforthcom'ing *adj* (1).
unfor'tified *adj* (1).
unfossilif'erous *adj* (1).
unfoss'ilized or **-s-** *adj* (1).
unfos'tered *adj* (1).
unfran'chised *adj* (1).
unfranked' *adj* (1).
unfrē'quent *adj* (1).
unfrequen'ted *adj* (1).
unfrequent'edness *n* (1).
unfrē'quently *adv* (1).
unfright'ened *adj* (1).
unfrō'zen *adj* (1).
unfruc'tuous *adj* (1).
unfruit'ful *adj* (1).
unfruit'fully *adv* (1).
unfruit'fulness *n* (1).
unfū'elled *adj* (1).
unfulfilled' *adj* (1).
unfunn'y *adj* (1).
unfurred' *adj* (1).
unfurr'owed *adj* (1).
ungag *vt* (2).
ungainsaid' *adj* (1).
ungainsay'able *adj* (1).
ungall'ant *adj* (1).
ungall'antly *adv* (1).
ungar'bled *adj* (1).
ungar'mented *adj* (1).
ungar'nered *adj* (1).
ungar'nished *adj* (1).
ungar'tered *adj* (1).
ungath'ered *adj* (1).
ungauged' *adj* (1).
ungen'erous *adj* (1).
ungen'erously *adv* (1).
ungenteel' *adj* (1).
ungenteel'ly *adv* (1).
ungen'uine *adj* (1).
ungen'uineness *n* (1).
ungift'ed *adj* (1).
ungild' *vt* (2).
ungild'ed *adj* (1).
ungilt' *adj* (1).
ungiv'ing *adj* (1).
unglad' *adj* (1).
unglazed' *adj* (1).
unglossed' *adj* (1).
unglove' *vt* (2).
ungloved' *adj* (1).
ungraced' *adj* (1).
ungrace'ful *adj* (1).
ungrace'fully *adv* (1).
ungrace'fulness *n* (1).
ungrammat'ic or **ungrammat'ical** *adj* (1).
ungrammat'ically *adv* (1).
ungrat'ified *adj* (1).
ungrave'ly (*Shakesp*) *adv* (1).
ungroomed' *adj* (1).
ungrown' *adj* (1).
ungrudged' *adj* (1).
ungrudg'ing *adj* (1).
ungrudg'ingly *adv* (1).
unguer'doned *adj* (1).
unguessed' *adj* (1).
unguid'ed *adj* (1).
unguilt'y *adj* (1).
ungyve' *vt* (2).
ungyved' *adj* (1).
unhab'itable *adj* (1).
unhabit'uated *adj* (1).
unhacked' *adj* (1).
unhack'neyed *adj* (1).
unhailed' *adj* (1).
unhall'ow *vt* (2).
unhall'owed *adj* (1).
unhamp'ered *adj* (1).
unhand'seled *adj* (1).

not reckoned as deer-forest; deforested. — *adj* **unforgott'en** (*archaic* **unforgot'**). — *vt* **unform'** to unmake. — *adj* **unfor'mal** informal. — *adj* **unfor'malized** or **-s-** not made formal. — *adj* **unformed'** unmade, uncreated; formless, unshaped; immature, undeveloped. — *adj* **unfor'tunate** unlucky; regrettable; of ill omen; (*esp* formerly) living by prostitution. — *n* an unfortunate person. — *adv* **unfor'tunately** in an unlucky way; by bad luck; I'm sorry to say. — *n* **unfor'tunateness.** — *n* **unfor'tune** (*archaic*). — *adj* **unfor'tuned.** — *adj* **unfought'** (*archaic* **unfought'en**). — *adj* **unfound'** not found. — *adj* **unfound'ed** not founded; without foundation, baseless; without bottom, bottomless (*Milton*). — *adv* **unfound'edly.** — *adj* **unframed'** not formed or fashioned (*lit* and *fig*); not set in a frame. — *adj* **unfraught'** not fraught or charged. — *vt* to unload or discharge. — *adj* **unfree'** not free; in servitude; not having the freedom of a corporation (*obs*). — *adj* **unfreed'.** — *n* **unfree'man** someone who does not have the freedom of a corporation (*obs*). — *vt* and *vi* **unfreeze'** to thaw; to (allow to) progress, move, etc after a temporary restriction or stoppage. — *vt* to free (prices, wages, funds) from the control imposed by a government, etc. — *adj* **unfrett'ed** not eaten away or rubbed; not annoyed or worried. — *n* **unfriend'** a person who is not a friend. — *adj* **unfriend'ed** not provided with or supported by friends. — *n* **unfriend'edness.** — *adv* **unfriend'lily.** — *n* **unfriend'liness.** — *adj* **unfriend'ly** ill-disposed; somewhat hostile. — *adv* (*old*) unkindly. — *n* **unfriend'ship** (*archaic*) unfriendliness. — *adj* **unfright'ed** (*archaic*) not frightened. — *vt* **unfrock'** to strip of a frock or gown; to depose from priesthood; to remove from a comparable position in another sphere of activity. — *adj* **unfrocked'.** — *adj* **unfumed'** not fumigated. — *adj* undistilled (*Milton*). — *adj* **unfund'ed** (of a public debt, etc) not funded, floating, in the form of exchequer bills and bonds, to be paid up at certain dates. — *vt* **unfurl'** to release from being rolled up; to unfold or display. — *vi* to spread open. — *vt* **unfur'nish** to deprive of men, defences, furniture; to deprive (*Shakesp*). — *adj* **unfur'nished** not furnished; unsupplied.

Words starting with **g-**, *prefixed by* **un-**.

adj **ungain'** (*obs*, *archaic* or *dialect*; from **gain**[2]) indirect; inconvenient; unpleasant; ungainly, awkward; unskilled. — *adj* **ungain'ful.** — *n* **ungain'liness.** — *adj* **ungain'ly** awkward, clumsy, uncouth. — *adv* (*rare*) awkwardly. — *adj* **ungalled'** not made painful by rubbing; not irritated or inflamed (*fig*). — *adj* **ungazed'** not gazed (with **-at** or **-upon**). — *vt* **ungear'** to disconnect (a part of a system of moving parts) (also *fig*); to unharness (*archaic*). — *adj* **ungeared'** (*econ*; of a business, etc) having its capital in the form of ordinary shares rather than loans requiring fixed interest. — *adj* **ungē'nial** not sympathetically cheerful; not comfortably warm, raw; not congenial; not favourable to natural growth. — *adj* **ungen'itured** (*Shakesp*) without means of generation, or not produced by ordinary generation. — *n* **ungentil'ity.** — *adj* **ungen'tle** not gentle; not of gentle birth; not of or befitting the gentle. — *adj* **ungen'tlemanlike** not like or befitting a gentleman. — Also *adv.* — *n* **ungen'tlemanliness.** — *adj* **ungen'tlemanly** unbecoming a gentleman; not gentlemanlike. — Also *adv.* — *n* **ungen'tleness.** — *adv* **ungent'ly.** — *adj* **ungermane** (*-jər-mān'*) irrelevant. — *vt* **unget'** to deny the begetting of; to disown. — *adj* **ungetat'able** or **unget-at'-able** (*colloq*) inaccessible. — *adj* **unghost'ly** not pertaining to or like a ghost; not spiritual. — *vt* **ungird'** to free from a girdle or band; to undo the fastening of and take off. — *adj* **ungirt'** or **ungird'ed** not girt; freed from a girdle; not tightened up, not strengthened for action (*fig*). — *vt* **ungirth'** to remove a girth from; to free from a girth. — *adj* **ungirthed'.** — *vt* **unglue'** to loosen or detach (something glued). — Also (*rare*) *vi.* — *adj* **unglued'** no longer held or fixed together by glue (**become** or **come unglued** to go awry, become confused, come apart). — *vt* **ungod'** to divest of divinity; to make godless. — *adj* **ungod'like.** — *adv* **ungod'lily** in an ungodly manner. — *n* **ungod'liness.** — *adj* **ungod'ly** not godly; outrageous, unconscionable (*colloq*). — *adj* **ungored'** (*Shakesp* **ungord'**; another reading **ungorg'd'**) unwounded. — *adj* **ungorged'** not gorged or sated. — *adj* **ungot'** or **ungott'en** not got or acquired; unbegotten. — *adj* **ungov'ernable** uncontrollable; unruly. — *n* **ungov'ernableness.** — *adv* **ungov'ernably.** — *adj* **ungov'erned.** — *vt* **ungown'** to deprive or divest of a gown; to unfrock. — *adj* **ungowned'** not wearing a gown; deprived of one's gown. — *adj* **ungrā'cious** without grace; graceless; ungraceful; lacking in courtesy, affability or urbanity; behaving with a bad grace; unmannerly; making offensive or disagreeable. — *adv* **ungrā'ciously.** — *n* **ungrā'ciousness.** — *adj* **ungrād'ed** not classified in

Some words with **un-** prefix; see **un-** entry for numbered senses.

unhang' *vt* (2).
unhanged' *adj* (1).
unhar'dened *adj* (1).
unhar'dy *adj* (1).
unharmed' *adj* (1).
unharm'ful *adj* (1).
unharm'fully *adv* (1).
unharm'ing *adj* (1).
unharmo'nious *adj* (1).
unhar'vested *adj* (1).
unhast'ing *adj* (1).
unhast'y *adj* (1).
unhaunt'ed *adj* (1).
unhaz'arded *adj* (1).
unhaz'ardous *adj* (1).
unheat'ed *adj* (1).
unhedged' *adj* (1).
unheed'ed *adj* (1).
unheed'edly *adv* (1).
unheed'ful *adj* (1).
unheed'fully *adv* (1).
unheed'ing *adj* (1).
unheed'ingly *adv* (1).
unheed'y *adj* (1).
unhelped' *adj* (1).
unhelp'ful *adj* (1).
unher'alded *adj* (1).
unherō'ic or **unherō'ical** *adj* (1).
unherō'ically *adv* (1).
unhewn' *adj* (1).
unhidd'en *adj* (1).
unhind'ered *adj* (1).
unhired' *adj* (1).
unhitch' *vt* (2).
unhome'like *adj* (1).
unhome'ly *adj* (1).
unhon'oured *adj* (1).
unhood' *vt* (2).
unhood'ed *adj* (1) and (2).
unhook' *vt* (2).
unhū'man *adj* (1).
unhū'manize or **-ise** *vt* (2).
unhum'bled *adj* (1).
unhunt'ed *adj* (1).
unhurr'ied *adj* (1).
unhurr'iedly *adv* (1).
unhurr'ying *adj* (1).
unhurt' *adj* (1).
unhurt'ful *adj* (1).
unhurt'fully *adv* (1).
unhurt'fulness *n* (1).
unhygien'ic *adj* (1).
unhy'phenated *adj* (1).
unīdentifī'able *adj* (1).
unīdent'ified *adj* (1).
unidiomat'ic *adj* (1).
unidiomat'ically *adv* (1).
unillumed' *adj* (1).
unillu'minated *adj* (1).
unillu'minating *adj* (1).
unillu'mined *adj* (1).
unill'ustrated *adj* (1).
unimbued' *adj* (1).
unimmor'tal (*Milton*) *adj* (1).
unimpaired' *adj* (1).
unimpart'ed *adj* (1).
unimpēd'ed *adj* (1).
unimpēd'edly *adv* (1).
unimplored' *adj* (1).
unimport'ance *n* (1).
unimport'ant *adj* (1).
unimpreg'nāted (or *-im'*) *adj* (1).
unimpressed' *adj* (1).
unimpress'ible *adj* (1).
unimpress'ionable *adj* (1).
unimpress'ive *adj* (1).
unimpris'oned *adj* (1) and (2).
unimpugnable (*-pūn'*) *adj* (1).
uninaug'urated *adj* (1).
unincit'ed *adj* (1).

grades; not adjusted to easy gradients. — *adj* **un-grassed'** not grown with grass, without grass growing. — *adj* **ungrate'ful** not feeling gratitude; disagreeable, irksome; not repaying one's labour, thankless. — *adv* **ungrate'fully**. — *n* **ungrate'fulness**. — *adj* **ungrazed'** not grazed; (of land) not grazed by livestock. — *adj* **unground'** not ground. — *adj* **unground'ed** not based (with *in*); without basis, unreal or false; without sound fundamental instruction. — *adv* **unground'edly**. — *n* **unground'edness**. — *vt* **unguard'** to make or leave unguarded. — *adj* **unguard'ed** without guard; unprotected; unscreened; incautious; inadvertent. — *adv* **unguard'edly**. — *n* **unguard'edness**. — *vt* **ungum'** to free from gum or gummed condition. — *adj* **ungummed'** not gummed; freed from gum or gumming (**come ungummed** (*colloq*; of a plan) to go amiss).

Words starting with **h-**, *prefixed by* **un-**.

adj **unhā'ble** an obsolete form of **unable**. — *vt* **unhair'** to deprive of hair. — *vi* to become free from hair. — *adj* **unhaired'** freed from hair. — *adj* **unhalsed** (*un-höst'*; *Scott*) unsaluted. — *vt* **unhand'** to take the hands off; to let go. — *adv* **unhand'ily** awkwardly. — *n* **unhand'iness**. — *adj* **unhan'dled** not handled or managed; not broken in. — *adj* **unhand'some** not handsome; unseemly; ungenerous; ungracious; unskilful in action (*obs*); clumsy, inconvenient (*obs*). — Also *adv* (*Spenser*). — *adv* **unhand'somely**. — *n* **unhand'someness**. — *adj* **unhand'y** awkward, not skilful; not convenient. — *adv* **unhapp'ily** in an unhappy manner; unfortunately, regrettably, I'm sorry to say; unsuccessfully; unfavourably (*Shakesp*); shrewdly (*Shakesp*); maliciously (*obs*). — *n* **unhapp'iness**. — *adj* **unhapp'y** bringing misfortune; not fortunate; miserable; infelicitous, inapt; mischievous (*obs*). — *vt* (*Shakesp*) to make unhappy or unfortunate. — *vt* **unhar'bour** to dislodge from shelter. — *adj* **unhar'boured** without a shelter; dislodged from shelter. — *vt* **unhar'ness** to take the harness or the armour off. — *adj* **unhar'nessed** not in, or freed from, harness or armour. — *vt* **unhasp'** to unfasten by undoing a hasp. — *vi* **unhat'** to take off the hat from respect. — *adj* **unhatched'** (*Shakesp* **unhatch'd**) not out of the egg; not developed; not shaded; unhacked. — *adj* **unhatt'ed** hatless. — *n* **unhatt'ing** lifting of the hat. — *vt* **unhead'** to take the head from. — *vt* **unheal'** see **unhele**. — *adj* **unheal'able**. — *adj* **unhealed'**. — *n* **unhealth'** ill-health. — *adj* **unhealth'ful**. — *adv* **unhealth'fully**. — *n* **unhealth'fulness**. — *adv* **unheal'thily**. — *n* **unheal'thiness**. — *adj* **unheal'thy** not healthy; morbid; unfavourable to health; dangerous (*colloq*). — *adj* **unheard'** not heard; not granted a hearing; not heard of, unknown to fame; unprecedented (in *Shakesp*, *King John* V. 2. 133, understood by some as unhaired or beardless). — Also **unheard'-of**. — *vt* **unhearse'** (used by Spenser in the *pa t* **unherst'**) *appar* to remove from a hearse or a stand for candles at a funeral. — *adj* **unhearsed'** without a hearse. — *vt* **unheart'** (*Shakesp*) to dishearten. — *adv* **unheed'ily** unheedfully. — *vt* **unhele'** or **unheal'** (*Spenser*) to uncover, disclose. — *vt* **unhelm'** to divest of helmet. — *adj* **unhelmed'** or **unhel'meted** without or divested of helm or helmet. — *adj* **unhelp'able** incapable of receiving help. — *adj* **unheppen** (*un-ep'n*; *Yorkshire*, *Lincolnshire*, *Tennyson*; ON *heppinn* dexterous) clumsy. — *vt* (*pa t*) **unherst** see **unhearse**. — *adj* **unhes'itating** not hesitating or doubting; prompt; ready. — *adv* **unhes'itatingly**. — *adj* **unhide'bound** (*Milton*) not having a skin confining the body. — *vt* **unhinge'** to take from the hinges; to derange. — *adj* **unhinged'**. — *n* **unhinge'ment**. — *adj* **unhip'** (*slang*) square, not trendy. — *adj* **unhistor'ic** not historic. — **unhistor'ical** not mentioned in history; not in accordance with history; not important historically; not having actually existed or happened. — *vt* **unhive'** to drive from a hive. — *vt* **unhoard'** to take from a hoard. — *adv* **unhō'lily**. — *n* **unhō'liness**. — *adj* **unhōl'pen** (*archaic*) not helped. — *adj* **unhō'ly** not holy; very wicked; unconscionable, outrageous, unearthly (*colloq*). — *adj* **unhon'est** (*obs*) unseemly, indecent, dishonourable; immoral; dishonest. — *vt* **unhoop'** to remove hoops from. — *adj* **unhoped'** beyond what was expected with hope (*archaic*; now **unhoped'-for**); unexpected (*obs*). — *adj* **unhope'ful**. — *adv* **unhope'fully**. — *vt* **unhorse'** to dislodge or throw from a horse; to take a horse or horses from. — *adj* **unhos'pitable** (now *usu* **inhospitable**). — *vt* **unhouse'** to deprive of or drive from a house or shelter. — *adj* **unhoused'** houseless; deprived of a house. — *adj* **unhous'eled** (*Shakesp* **unhouzz'led**) not having received the sacrament. — *adj* **unhung'** not hung; without hangings; unhanged. — *adj* **unhus'banded** uncultivated; without a husband. — *vt* **unhusk'** to strip the husk from. — *adj* **unhyph'enated** without a hyphen or hyphens.

Some words with **un-** prefix; see **un-** entry for numbered senses.

uninclosed' *adj* (1).
unincor'porated *adj* (1).
unin'dexed *adj* (1).
uninfect'ed *adj* (1).
uninflamed' *adj* (1).
uninflamm'able *adj* (1).
uninflāt'ed *adj* (1).
uninflect'ed *adj* (1).
unin'fluenced *adj* (1).
uninfluen'tial *adj* (1).
uninhab'itable *adj* (1).
uninhab'ited *adj* (1).
uninhib'ited *adj* (1).
unini'tiated *adj* (1).
unin'jured *adj* (1).
uninquīr'ing *adj* (1).
uninquis'itive *adj* (1).
uninscribed' *adj* (1).
uninspired' *adj* (1).
uninspīr'ing *adj* (1).
uninstruct'ed *adj* (1).
uninstruct'ive *adj* (1).
uninsured' *adj* (1).
unin'tegrated *adj* (1).
unintellect'ual *adj* (1).
unintell'igent *adj* (1).
unintelligibil'ity *n* (1).
unintell'igible *adj* (1).
unintell'igibly *adv* (1).
unintend'ed *adj* (1).
uninten'tional *adj* (1).
unintentional'ity *n* (1).
uninten'tionally *adv* (1).
unintermitt'ed *adj* (1).
unintermitt'edly *adv* (1).
unintermitt'ing *adj* (1).
unintermitt'ingly *adv* (1).
uninter'pretable *adj* (1).
uninterrup'ted *adj* (1).
uninterrup'tedly *adv* (1).
unintox'icating *adj* (1).
unintroduced' *adj* (1).
uninured' *adj* (1).
uninven'tive *adj* (1).
uninvest'ed *adj* (1).
uninvid'ious *adj* (1).
uninvī'ted *adj* (1).
uninvī'ting *adj* (1).
uninvolved' *adj* (1).
unī'onized or **-s-** *adj* (1).
unī'roned *adj* (1).
unjā'ded *adj* (1).
unjaun'diced *adj* (1).
unjeal'ous *adj* (1).
unjoy'ful *adj* (1).
unjoy'ous *adj* (1).
unjust' *adj* (1).
unjus'tifiable (or *-fī'*) *adj* (1).
unjus'tifiably (or *-fī'*) *adv* (1).
unjus'tified *adj* (1).
unjust'ly *adv* (1).
unjust'ness *n* (1).
unlā'belled *adj* (1).
unlabō'rious *adj* (1).
unlā'dylike *adj* (1).
unlament'ed *adj* (1).
unleased' *adj* (1).
unleav'ened *adj* (1).
unleis'ured *adj* (1).
unleis'urely *adj* (1).
unlet' *adj* (1).
unlibid'inous (*Milton*) *adj* (1).
unlife'like *adj* (1).
unlim'ited *adj* (1).
unlim'itedly *adv* (1).
unlim'itedness *n* (1).
unlin'eal *adj* (1).
unliq'uefied *adj* (1).
unliq'uidated *adj* (1).
unlit' *adj* (1).
unlit'erary *adj* (1).

Words starting with **i-**, **j-** *and* **k-**, *prefixed by* **un-**.
adj **unīdē'a'd** without ideas; with unfurnished mind. — *adj* **unīdē'al** not ideal; not idealistic; without ideals; conveying no idea (*obs*); without ideas (*obs*). — *n* **unīdē'alism**. — *adj* **unīdēalist'ic**. — *adj* **unimag'inable**. — *n* **unimag'inableness**. — *adv* **unimag'inably**. — *adj* **unimag'inative** not imaginative, prosaic. — *adv* **unimag'inatively**. — *n* **unimag'inativeness**. — *adj* **unimag'ined**. — *adj* **unimpass'ioned** not impassioned, calm, tranquil. — *adj* **unimpeach'able** not to be impeached; not liable to be accused; free from fault; blameless. — *adj* **unimpeached'**. — *adj* **unim'portuned** (or *-tūnd'*, *-chōōnd'*; often *-pör'*) not persistently begged (to do something). — *adj* **unimposed'**. — *adj* **unimpōs'ing** unimpressive; not burdensome (*Thomson*). — *adj* **unimproved'** not made better; not cultivated, cleared or built upon; not put to use. — *adj* **uninchanted** see **unenchanted**. — *adj* **unincum'bered** unencumbered. — *adj* **unindeared** see **unendeared**. — *adj* **unin'dexed** not index-linked. — *adj* **uninforce'able** and **uninforced** same as **unenforceable**, **unenforced**. — *adj* **uninform'ative**. — *adj* **uninformed'** not having received information; untaught; uneducated; not imbued with life or activity (*archaic*). — *adj* **uninform'ing**. — *adj* **unin'terested** not personally concerned; not taking an interest; **unin'teresting**. — *adv* **unin'terestingly**. — *vt* **unjoint'** to disjoint. — *adj* **unjoint'ed** disjointed, incoherent; without joints. — *adj* **unked**, **unket** and **unkid** (*ōōngk'id*, *ungk'id*, *-it*; *N and W England*; forms of **uncouth**) strange, uncomfortable, lonely, eerie. — *adj* **unkempt'** (see **kemb**) uncombed; scruffy; unpolished, rough. — *adj* **unkenned'** or **unkent'** unknown. — *vt* **unkenn'el** to dislodge (a fox) from a hole; to let out from a kennel. — *adj* **unkept'** not kept; untended. — *adj* **unket** and **unkid** see **unked**. — *adj* **unkīnd'** lacking in kindness; cruel; unnaturally wicked (*obs*). — *adj* **unkin'dled** not kindled. — *n* **unkīnd'liness** lack of kindliness. — *adj* **unkīnd'ly** unnatural; not kind. — *adv* in an unkindly manner; cruelly; unnaturally (*Milton*); against right feeling (*Shakesp*). — *n* **unkīnd'ness** lack of kindness or affection; cruelty; ill-feeling; a flock of ravens (*obs*). — *vt* **unking'** to deprive of kingship or of a king. — *adj* **unking'like**. — *adj* **unking'ly** unbecoming a king; unlike a king. — *vt* **unkiss'** (*Shakesp*) to annul by means of a kiss. — *adj* **unkissed'** not kissed. — *adj* **unknelled** (*un-neld'*) without tolling. — *vt* **unknight** (*un-nīt'*) to divest of knighthood. — *adj* **unknight'ed** not knighted. — *n* **unknight'liness**. — *adj* **unknightly** (*un-nīt'li*) unlike or unbecoming to a knight. — *adv* in an unknightly manner. — *vt* **unknit** (*un-nit'*) to undo the knitting of; to untie; to smooth out (the eyebrows) from a frown; to relax. — *vi* to become unknitted. — *adj* loose, not closely compacted or united. — *vt* **unknot** (*un-not'*) to free from knots; to untie. — *adj* **unknowable** (*un-nō'ə-bl*) incapable of being known. — *n* an unknowable thing; the first or original cause; that which is cognizable only in its relations. — *n* **unknow'ableness**. — *adj* **unknow'ing** ignorant, unaware; unwitting; unknown (with *to*; *dialect*); ignorant (with *of*; *archaic*); not knowing (*archaic* or *poetic*). — *adv* **unknow'ingly**. — *n* **unknow'ingness**. — *adj* **unknown** (*un-nōn'*) not known. — *n* an unknown person or quantity; (with **the**) that which is unknown. — *n* **unknown'ness**.

Words starting with **l-**, *prefixed by* **un-**.
adj **unlā'boured** showing no traces of labour; unworked; unrestrained, easy; natural, not contrived or forced. — *adj* **unlā'bouring**. — *vt* **unlace'** to free from being laced; to undo the lacing of; to carve (*esp* a rabbit) (*obs*); to undo, destroy (*Shakesp*). — *vt* **unlade'** to unload. — *adj* **unlā'den** not laden. — *n* **unlā'ding**. — *adj* **unlaid'** not laid. — *vt* **unlash'** (*naut*) to loose the lashings of. — *vt* **unlast** or **unlaste** (*un-läst'*, *-lāst'*) Spenserian *pa t* and *pa p* of **unlace**. — *vt* **unlatch'** to lift the latch of. — *n* **un'law** breach of law (*archaic*); a fine, penalty (*Scots law*; *obs*). — *vt* **unlaw'** to annul, repeal; to fine (*obs*). — *adj* **unlaw'ful** forbidden by law; illegitimate; illicit; acting illegally. — *adv* **unlaw'fully**. — *n* **unlaw'fulness**. — *vt* **unlay'** (*naut*) to untwist. — *vt* **unlead** (*un-led'*; *printing*) to take the lead or leads from. — *adj* **unlead'ed** not covered or decorated, etc with lead; (of petrol) with no added lead; (of type) without leading (*printing*). — *adj* **unleal'** (*archaic*) unfaithful. — *vt* **unlearn'** to undo the process of learning; to rid one's mind of, eliminate habit(s) of. — *adj* **unlearned** (*-lûr'nid*; also *poetic -lûrnd'*) having no learning; uneducated; (*-lûrnd'*) not learnt, got up or acquired; eliminated by unlearning. — *adv* **unlear'nedly**. — *n* **unlear'nedness**. — *adj* and *pa p* **unlearnt** (*-lûrnt'*) not learnt; eliminated by unlearning. — *vt* **unleash'** to free from a leash, let go; to release (*lit* and *fig*). — *adj* **unled'** not led, without guidance. — *adj* **unless'oned** not instructed. — *adj* **unlett'able** (of a building) that cannot be let, *usu* because it is in unfit condition. — *adj*

Some words with **un-** prefix; see **un-** entry for numbered senses.

unliv'able or **unlive'able** *adj* (1).
unlive'liness *n* (1).
unlive'ly *adj* (1).
unlopped' *adj* (1).
unlos'able *adj* (1).
unlost' *adj* (1).
unlove'liness *n* (1).
unlove'ly *adj* (1).
unluxur'iant *adj* (1).
unluxur'ious *adj* (1).
unmacad'amized or -s- *adj* (1).
unmaimed' *adj* (1).
unmaintain'able *adj* (1).
unmaintained' *adj* (1).
unmali'cious *adj* (1).
unmalleabil'ity *n* (1).
unmall'eable *adj* (1).
unman'acle *vt* (2).
unman'acled *adj* (1) and (2).
unman'ageable *adj* (1).
unman'ageableness *n* (1).
unman'ageably *adv* (1).
unman'aged *adj* (1).
unmas'culine *adj* (1).
unmā'ted *adj* (1).
unmater'nal *adj* (1).
unmathemat'ical *adj* (1).
unmatric'ulated *adj* (1).
unmatured' *adj* (1).
unmeek' *adj* (1).
unmell'owed *adj* (1).
unmelo'dious *adj* (1).
unmelt'ed *adj* (1).
unmem'orable *adj* (1).
unmer'cenary *adj* (1).
unmer'chantable *adj* (1).
unmet'alled *adj* (1).
unmetaphor'ical *adj* (1).
unmetaphys'ical *adj* (1).
unmethod'ical *adj* (1).
unmeth'odized or -s- *adj* (1).
unmet'rical *adj* (1).
unmil'itary *adj* (1).
unmilked' *adj* (1).
unmilled' *adj* (1).
unming'led *adj* (1).
unministē'rial *adj* (1).
unmirac'ulous *adj* (1).
unmī'ry *adj* (1).
unmissed' *adj* (1).
unmistāk'able or **unmistake'able** *adj* (1).
unmistāk'ably or **unmistake'ably** *adv* (1).
unmistrust'ful *adj* (1).
unmixed' *adj* (1).
unmix'edly *adv* (1).
unmod'ernized or -s- *adj* (1).
unmod'ifīable *adj* (1).
unmod'ifīableness *n* (1).
unmod'ified *adj* (1).
unmod'ulated *adj* (1).
unmois'tened *adj* (1).
unmolest'ed *adj* (1).
unmort'gaged *adj* (1).
unmort'ified *adj* (1).
unmoth'erly *adj* (1).
unmourned' *adj* (1).
unmown' *adj* (1).
unmuni'tioned *adj* (1).
unmur'muring *adj* (1).
unmur'muringly *adv* (1).
unmūs'ical *adj* (1).
unmūs'ically *adv* (1).
unmū'tilated *adj* (1).
unneed'ed *adj* (1).
unneed'ful *adj* (1).
unneed'fully *adv* (1).
unnō'ted *adj* (1).
unnō'ticeable *adj* (1).
unnō'ticed *adj* (1).

unlett'ered unlearned; illiterate; without lettering. — *adj* **unlī'censed** without a licence; unauthorized. — *adj* **unlich** (*un-lich'*; *Spenser*) unlike. — *adj* **unlicked'** not licked; not licked into shape. — *vt* **unlid'** to uncover, open. — *adj* **unlidd'ed** lidless. — *adj* **unlight'ed**. — *adj* **unlight'ened**. — *adj* **unlight'some** (*Milton*) without light. — *adj* and *adv* (tending to become a *prep*) **unlike'** not like; different (from); unlikely (*Spenser* and *Shakesp*). — *n* someone who or something which is unlike. — *adj* **unlik'able** or **unlike'able** not likeable. — *n* **unlike'lihood** or **unlike'liness** improbability. — *adj* **unlike'ly** not likely; improbable; unpromising (*obs*); unprepossessing (*obs* or *dialect*); unsuitable (*obs*). — *adv* in an unlikely manner, improbably. — *n* **unlike'ness** lack of resemblance. — *vt* **unlim'ber** to remove (a gun) from its limber ready for use. — *vt* **unlime'** to free from lime. — *adj* **unlimed'** not limed. — *vt* **unline'** to remove the lining from. — *adj* **unlined'** without lines or lining. — *vt* **unlink'** to undo the linking or links of. — *vi* to become unlinked. — *adj* **unlinked'** not linked. — *adj* **unliq'uored** (*Milton*) not in liquor, sober. — *adj* **unlist'ed** not entered in a list; (of a telephone number) not listed in a directory, ex-directory (*US*); (of companies and securities) not quoted on the Stock Exchange's official list. — *adj* **unlis'tened** not listened to (*poetic*; also **unlis'tened-to**). — *adj* **unlis'tening**. — *vt* **unlive** (*un-liv'*) to undo the living of; to live in the contrary manner to; to live down; (*un-līv'*) to deprive of life (*Shakesp*). — *adj* **unlived'-in** not lived in. — *adj* **unliv'ing**. — *vt* **unload'** to take the load or charge from; to discharge; to disburden; to remove as a load; to get rid of; to dump. — *vi* to discharge freight. — *adj* **unload'ed** not loaded; discharged. — *n* **unload'er**. — *n* **unload'ing**. — *adj* **unlocā'ted** not located; not surveyed or marked off (*US*). — *vt* **unlock'** to undo the locking of; to free from being locked up; to let loose; to open, make accessible, or disclose. — *vi* to become unlocked. — *adj* **unlock'able**. — *adj* **unlocked'**. — *adj* **unlog'ical** not logical; illogical. — *adj* **unlooked'** not looked (with *at* or *into*). — *adj* **unlooked'-for** unexpected. — *vt* **unloose'** or (more *usu*) **unloos'en** to loosen, unfasten, detach; to set free (also *fig*); (**unloose**) to discharge (a debt, etc) (*Scot*). — *vt* **unlord'** to strip of the dignity of a lord. — *adj* **unlor'ded** deprived of, or not raised to, the rank of lord; not lorded over, without a lord. — *adj* **unlord'ly**. — *adj* **unlov'able** or **unlove'able**. — *vt* **unlove'** to cease to love; not to love. — *n* (*un'*) absence of love. — *adj* **unloved'**. — *adj* **unlov'erlike**. — *adj* **unlov'ing**. — *adv* **unlov'ingly**. — *n* **unlov'ingness**. — *adv* **unluck'ily** in an unlucky way; by bad luck; I'm sorry to say, unfortunately. — *n* **unluck'iness**. — *adj* **unluck'y** unfortunate; ill-omened; bringing bad luck; not praiseworthy (*archaic*).

Words starting with **m-**, *prefixed by* **un-**.

adj **unmade'** not made or not yet made; self-existent; subjected to unmaking. — *adj* **unmade-up'** not made up; (of a road) not made (qv); (of a person) not wearing make-up. — *adj* **unmaid'enly** unbecoming a maiden; not like a maiden. — *adj* **unmail'able** (*US*) incapable of being transmitted or delivered by post. — *adj* **unmailed'** not clad in mail (*hist*; **mail**[1]); not sent by post (**mail**[2]). — *adj* **unmā'kable**. — *vt* **unmake'** to undo the making of; to undo, ruin. — *n* **unmā'king**. — *vt* **unman'** to deprive of the nature, attributes or powers of humanity, manhood or maleness: to deprive of fortitude; to deprive of men. — *adv* **unman'fully**. — *adj* **unman'like**. — *n* **unman'liness**. — *adj* **unman'ly** not becoming a man; unworthy of a noble mind; base; cowardly. — *adj* **unmanned'** without a crew; without a garrison; without inhabitants; untamed (*esp* of a hawk); deprived of fortitude. — *adj* **unmann'ered** unmannerly, bad-mannered; not affected or pretentious, free from mannerism. — *n* **unmann'erliness**. — *adj* **unmann'erly** not mannerly; ill-bred. — *adv* in an unmannerly manner. — *vt* **unman'tle** to divest of a mantle; to dismantle (*rare*). — *vi* to take off one's mantle. — *adj* **unmanufac'tured** in a raw state. — *adj* **unmanured'** not manured; untilled (*obs*). — *adj* **unmarked'** bearing no mark; not noticed. — *adj* **unmar'ketable** not suitable for the market, not saleable. — *adj* **unmarred'** (*Spenser* **unmard'**) not marred. — *adj* **unmarr'iable** (*obs*), **unmarr'iageable**. — *n* **unmarr'iageableness**. — *adj* **unmarr'ied** not married, *usu* never having been married; freed from marriage. — *vt* **unmarr'y** to dissolve the marriage of. — *vi* to dissolve one's marriage. — *vt* **unmask'** to take a mask or a disguise from; to discover the identity of (eg a thief; *fig*); to reveal the place of (a gun, battery) by firing; to expose, show up. — *vi* to take off a mask. — *adj* **unmasked'** not wearing a mask; undisguised; divested of mask or disguise; (of eg identity) revealed. — *n* **unmask'er**. — *n* **unmask'ing**. — *adj* **unmas'tered** uncontrolled; not overcome; without a master. — *adj*

Some words with **un-** prefix; see **un-** entry for numbered senses.

unnō'ticing *adj* (1).
unnour'ished *adj* (1).
unnour'ishing *adj* (1).
unobjec'tionable *adj* (1).
unobjec'tionably *adv* (1).
unobnox'ious *adj* (1).
unobscured' *adj* (1).
unobstruc'ted *adj* (1).
unobstruc'tive *adj* (1).
unobtain'able *adj* (1).
unobtained' *adj* (1).
unobtru'sive *adj* (1).
unobtru'sively *adv* (1).
unobtru'siveness *n* (1).
unob'vious *adj* (1).
unocc'upied *adj* (1).
unoff'ered *adj* (1).
unoiled' *adj* (1).
unopposed' *adj* (1).
unoppress'ive *adj* (1).
unordained' *adj* (1).
unor'ganized or **-s-** *adj* (1).
unornamen'tal *adj* (1).
unor'namented (or *-ment'*) *adj* (1).
unor'thodox *adj* (1).
unor'thodoxly *adv* (1).
unor'thodoxy *n* (1).
unoss'ified *adj* (1).
unostentā'tious *adj* (1).
unostentā'tiously *adv* (1).
unostentā'tiousness *n* (1).
unovercome' *adj* (1).
unoverthrown' *adj* (1).
unox'idized or **-s-** *adj* (1).
unpac'ified *adj* (1).
unpaid' *adj* (1).
unpained' *adj* (1).
unpain'ful *adj* (1).
unpal'sied *adj* (1).
unpam'pered *adj* (1).
unpar'donable *adj* (1).
unpar'donableness *n* (1).
unpar'donably *adv* (1).
unpar'doned *adj* (1).
unpar'doning *adj* (1).
unpar'tial *adj* (1).
unpas'teurized or **-s-** *adj* (1).
unpas'toral *adj* (1).
unpas'tured *adj* (1).
unpā'tented *adj* (1).
unpathed (*-pädhd'*) *adj* (1).
unpathet'ic *adj* (1).
unpath'wayed *adj* (1).
unpatriot'ic *adj* (1).
unpatriot'ically *adv* (1).
unpat'ronized or **-s-** *adj* (1).
unpeace'able *adj* (1).
unpeace'ableness *n* (1).
unpeace'ful *adj* (1).
unpeace'fully *adv* (1).
unped'igreed *adj* (1).
unpeg' *vt* (2).
unpen'sioned *adj* (1).
unpepp'ered *adj* (1).
unperceiv'able *adj* (1).
unperceiv'ably *adv* (1).
unperceived' *adj* (1).
unperceiv'edly *adv* (1).
unpercep'tive *adj* (1).
unper'forated *adj* (1).
unperformed' *adj* (1).
unperform'ing *adj* (1).
unperfumed' (or *-pûr'*) *adj* (1).
unper'ilous *adj* (1).
unper'ishable *adj* (1).
unper'ished *adj* (1).
unper'ishing *adj* (1).
unper'jured *adj* (1).
unper'petrated *adj* (1).

unmatch'able. — *adj* **unmatched'** matchless; unequalled. — *adj* **unmatē'rial** not composed of matter. — *adj* **unmatē'rialized** or **-s-**. — *adj* **unmean'ing** meaningless; purposeless; expressionless. — *adv* **unmean'ingly**. — *n* **unmean'ingness**. — *adj* **unmeant** (*un-ment'*). — *adj* **unmeas'urable** immeasurable; too great to measure; inordinate; not capable of being measured. — *adv* **unmeas'urably**. — *adj* **unmeas'ured**. — *adj* **unmechan'ical** (*archaic* **unmechan'ic**). — *vt* **unmech'anize** or **-ise** to disorganize (*Sterne*). — *adj* **unmech'anized** or **-s-** disorganized; not mechanized. — *adj* **unmedicinable** (*un-med'sin-ə-bl*) incurable; unable to cure. — *adj* **unmed'itated** not meditated, unpremeditated. — *adj* **unmeet'** not meet, unfit. — *adv* **unmeet'ly**. — *n* **unmeet'ness**. — *adj* **unmen'tionable** not fit to be mentioned. — *n* **unmen'tionableness**. — *n pl* **unmen'tionables** otherwise *inexpressibles*, a 19c would-be humorous name for trousers; now *usu* humorously used for articles of underclothing. — *adj* **unmer'ciful** merciless; excessively and unpleasantly great. — *adv* **unmer'cifully**. — *n* **unmer'cifulness**. — *adj* **unmer'itable** (*Shakesp*) undeserving. — *adj* **unmer'ited**. — *adv* **unmer'itedly**. — *adj* **unmer'iting**. — *adj* **unmet'** not met; (of a payment, need, etc) not satisfied. — *adj* **unmē'ted** not meted or measured. — *vt* **unmew'** to free, to release as if from a mew or cage. — *adj* **unmind'ed** unheeded. — *adj* **unmind'ful** not keeping in mind, regardless (of). — *adv* **unmind'fully**. — *n* **unmind'fulness**. — *adj* **unmit'igable** that cannot be mitigated. — *adv* **unmit'igably**. — *adj* **unmit'igated** not mitigated; unqualified, out-and-out. — *adv* **unmit'igatedly**. — *adj* **unmoaned'** not lamented. — *adj* **unmō'dish** unfashionable. — *adj* **unmon'eyed** or **unmon'ied** without money; not rich. — *vt* **unmoor'** to loose from moorings. — *vi* to cast off moorings. — *adj* **unmor'al** having no relation to morality; amoral. — *n* **unmoral'ity** detachment from questions of morality. — *adj* **unmor'alized** or **-s-** not moralized upon; having no moral attached; without morality. — *adj* **unmor'alizing** or **-s-**. — *adj* **unmor'tised** disjoined from a mortise (*lit* and *fig*). — *adj* **un-Mosā'ic** not of or according to *Moses* or the Mosaic law. — *adj* **unmō'tivated** having no motive; lacking incentive. — *adj* **unmō'tived** without motive; without an artistic motive. — *vt* **unmould'** to change or destroy the form of. — *adj* **unmould'ed** not moulded. — *vt* **unmount'** to remove from mountings or mount; to dismount. — *vi* to dismount. — *adj* **unmount'ed** not mounted. — *adj* **unmov'able** or **unmove'able** immovable; not movable. — *adv* **unmov'ably** or **unmove'ably**. — *adj* **unmoved'** firm, not moved; not persuaded; not touched by emotion, calm. — *adv* **unmov'edly**. — *adj* **unmov'ing**. — *vt* **unmuff'le** to take a muffle, muffling or covering from. — *vi* to throw off mufflings. — *vt* **unmuzz'le** to take a muzzle off. — *adj* **unmuzz'led**. — *n* **unmuzz'ling**.

Words starting with **n-**, *prefixed by* **un-**.
vt **unnail'** (*un-nāl'*) to free from nails or from being nailed. — *adj* **unnamable** or **unname'able** (*un-nā'mə-bl*) impossible to name; not to be named. — *adj* **unnamed** (*un-nāmd'*). — *adj* **unnaneld** Shakespearian spelling of **unaneled**. — *adj* **unnative** (*un-nā'tiv*) not native. — *adj* **unnatural** (*un-nat'ū-rəl*) not according to nature; without natural affection; monstrous, heinous; (of a sexual act, vice, etc) considered not only immoral but also unacceptably indecent or abnormal. — *vt* **unnat'uralize** or **-ise** to make unnatural; to divest of nationality. — *adj* **unnat'uralized** or **-s-** not naturalized. — *adv* **unnat'urally** in an unnatural or improbable way (*esp* in the phrase **not unnaturally** of course, naturally). — *n* **unnat'uralness**. — *adj* **unnavigable** (*un-nav'*) not navigable. — *adj* **unnav'igated**. — *adv* **unnecessarily** (*un-nes'*). — *n* **unnec'essariness**. — *adj* **unnec'essary** not necessary. — *adj* **unneighboured** (*un-nā'bərd*) without neighbours. — *n* **unneigh'bourliness**. — *adj* **unneigh'bourly** not neighbourly, friendly or social. — *adv* in an unneighbourly manner. — *vt* **unnerve** (*un-nûrv'*) to deprive of nerve, strength or vigour; to weaken; to disconcert. — *adj* **unnerved'**. — *adj* **unnerv'ing**. — *vt* **unnest** (*un-nest'*) to turn out of a nest (*lit* and *fig*). — *adv* **unnethes** see **uneath**. — *adj* **unnett'ed** not enclosed in a net. — *adj* **unnō'ble** not noble; ignoble (*Spenser* and *Shakesp*). — *vt* to deprive of nobility. — *adj* **unnumbered** (*un-num'bərd*) not counted, too many to be numbered; not marked or provided with a number. — *adj* **unnurtured** (*un-nûr'chərd*) not nurtured or educated; ill-bred.

Words starting with **o-**, *prefixed by* **un-**.
adj **unobē'dient** disobedient. — *adj* **unobeyed'** (*Milton*). — *adj* **unobserv'able**. — *n* **unobser'vance** failure to observe rules, etc; failure to notice; lack of observing power; inattention. — *adj* **unobser'vant**. — *adj* **unobserved'**. — *adv* **unobserv'edly**. — *adj* **unobser'ving**. — *adj* **unoffend'ed**. — *adj* **unoffend'ing**. — *adj* **un-**

Some words with **un-** prefix; see **un-** entry for numbered senses.

unperplex' *vt* (2).
unperplexed' *adj* (1).
unper'secuted *adj* (1).
unpersuād'able *adj* (1).
unpersuād'ableness *n* (1).
unpersuād'ed *adj* (1).
unpersuās'ive *adj* (1).
unperturbed' *adj* (1).
unphilosoph'ic or **unphilosoph'ical** *adj* (1).
unphilosoph'ically *adv* (1).
unphonet'ic *adj* (1).
unpierced' *adj* (1).
unpill'owed *adj* (1).
unpī'loted *adj* (1).
unpinned' *adj* (1) and (2).
unpit'ied *adj* (1).
unpit'iful *adj* (1).
unpit'ifully *adv* (1).
unpit'ifulness *n* (1).
unpit'ying *adj* (1).
unpit'yingly *adv* (1).
unplagued' *adj* (1).
unplait' *vt* (2).
unplait'ed *adj* (1) and (2).
unplanked' *adj* (1).
unplanned' *adj* (1).
unplant'ed *adj* (1).
unplast'ered *adj* (1).
unplay'able *adj* (1).
unplayed' *adj* (1).
unpleat'ed *adj* (1).
unpledged' *adj* (1).
unplī'able *adj* (1).
unplī'ably *adv* (1).
unplī'ant *adj* (1).
unploughed' *adj* (1).
unplucked' *adj* (1).
unplug' *vt* (2).
unplugged' *adj* (1) and (2).
unpoet'ic or **unpoetical** *adj* (1).
unpoet'ically *adv* (1).
unpoet'icalness *n* (1).
unpoised' *adj* (1).
unpolarīz'able or **-s-** *adj* (1).
unpo'larized or **-s-** *adj* (1).
unpoliced' *adj* (1).
unpol'ish *vt* (2).
unpol'ishable *adj* (1).
unpol'ished *adj* (1).
unpol'itic *adj* (1).
unpolit'ical *adj* (1).
unpollut'ed *adj* (1).
unpop'ular *adj* (1).
unpopular'ity *n* (1).
unpop'ularly *adv* (1).
unpop'ulated *adj* (1).
unpop'ulous *adj* (1).
unposed' *adj* (1).
unpow'dered *adj* (1).
unprac'tical *adj* (1).
unpractical'ity *n* (1).
unprac'tically *adv* (1).
unprecise' *adj* (1).
unprej'udiced *adj* (1).
unpreocc'upied *adj* (1).
unprescribed' *adj* (1).
unpressed' *adj* (1).
unpresum'ing *adj* (1).
unpresump'tuous *adj* (1).
unpreten'tious *adj* (1).
unpreten'tiousness *n* (1).
unprett'iness *n* (1).
unprett'y *adj* (1).
unprimed' *adj* (1).
unprince'ly *adj* (1).
unpris'on *vt* (2).
unpris'oned *adj* (1) and (2).
unpriv'ileged *adj* (1).
unprō'cessed *adj* (1).
unproclaimed' *adj* (1).

offen'sive inoffensive. — *adj* **unoff'icered**. — *adj* **unoffi'cial** not official. — *adv* **unoffi'cially**. — *adj* **unoffi'cious** not officious. — *adv* **unoften** (*un-of'n*; *rare*) seldom (*usu* as *not unoften*). — *adj* **unō'pened** not opened; of a book, not having the leaves cut apart. — *adj* **unop'erative** inoperative. — *vt* **unor'der** to countermand. — *adj* **unor'dered** disordered; unarranged, not ordered or commanded. — *adj* **unor'derly** not orderly. — *adj* **unor'dinary** not ordinary. — *adj* **unorig'inal** not original; without origin or birth (*Milton*). — *n* **unoriginality** (*-al'*). — *adj* **unorig'inate** or **unorig'inated** not originated. — *adj* **unowed'** not owed or due; unowned (*Shakesp*). — *adj* **unowned'** unavowed, unacknowledged; ownerless; (*un-ō'nid*) lost (*Milton*).

Words starting with **p-**, *prefixed by* **un-**.

adj **unpaced'** (*athletics*, *cycle racing*, etc) without the assistance of a pace-setter. — *vt* **unpack'** to remove packed articles from (a case, etc); to take out of a suitcase or other packed container; to remove from packing materials; to open; to remove a pack from (a pack animal). — *vi* to do unpacking. — *adj* **unpacked'** subjected to unpacking; (*un'pakt'*) not packed. — *n* **unpack'er**. — *n* **unpack'ing**. — *adj* **unpaged'** without numbering of pages. — *vt* **unpaint'** to free from paint; to paint out, obliterate by painting over. — *adj* **unpaint'able**. — *adj* **unpaint'ed** not painted. — *adj* **unpaired'** not paired; not forming one of a pair. — *adj* **unpal'atable** unpleasant to taste, distasteful, disagreeable (*lit* and *fig*). — *adv* **unpal'atably**. — *vt* **unpan'el** (*obs*; also **unpann'el**; from **panel** *n*, a saddle) to unsaddle. — *adj* **unpan'elled** not panelled. — *adj* **unpanged'** without pangs. — *vt* **unpā'per** to remove paper from. — *adj* **unpā'pered** not papered. — *vt* **unpar'adise** to turn out of Paradise; to make no longer a paradise. — *adj* **unpar'agoned** unmatched. — *adj* **unpar'allel** not parallel. — *adj* **unpar'alleled** without parallel or equal. — *adj* **unpared'** (of fruit) not having the skin removed; (of nails) not cut. — *adj* **unparent'al** not befitting a parent. — *adj* **unpā'rented** without parent or acknowledged parent, or parental care. — *adj* **unparliament'ary** contrary to the usages of Parliament. — *adj* not such as may be spoken, or (of language) used, in Parliament. — *adj* **unpass'able** impassable; (of money) not current. — *n* **unpass'ableness**. — *adj* **unpass'ionate** or **unpass'ioned** without passions; calm; dispassionate. — *adj* **unpatt'erned** unexampled, unequalled; without a pattern. — *adj* **unpaved'** without pavement; gelded (*Shakesp*). — *adj* **unpavil'ioned** without a canopy. — *vt* **unpay'** to make good, undo, do away by payment. — *adj* **unpay'able**. — *adj* **unpeeled'** not peeled; (*Shakesp*, *Love's Labour's Lost* II. 2. 88) (according to some) stripped, desolate (others think it a misprint for **unpeopled**, without servants (the folio reading)). — *adj* **unpeer'able** not to be matched. — *adj* **unpeered'** unequalled. — *vt* **unpen'** to let out from a pen or enclosure. — *adj* **unpenned'** unwritten (**pen**[2]); unconfined, let loose (**pen**[1]). — *adj* **unpenn'ied** without pennies. — *adj* **unpent'** not penned in. — *vt* **unpeo'ple** to empty of people. — *adj* **unpeo'pled** uninhabited; without servants; depopulated. — *vt* **unperch'** to drive from a perch. — *adj* **unper'fect** (now *rare*) imperfect; unskilled. — *n* **unperfec'tion** (*obs*). — *adv* **unper'fectly** (*obs*). — *n* **unper'fectness** (*rare*). — *n* **un'person** an individual whose existence is officially denied, ignored, or deleted from record, eg a person who has been politically superseded. — *vt* to make (someone) into an unperson. — *vt* **unpervert'** to reconvert. — *adj* **unpervert'ed** not perverted. — *vt* **unpick'** to pick loose, undo by picking. — *adj* **unpick'able** impossible to pick; able to be unpicked. — *adj* **unpicked'** not gathered; not selected; not having had unwanted material removed by picking; picked loose. — *adj* **unpill'ared** stripped of pillars; without pillars. — *vt* **unpin'** to free from pins or pinning; to unfasten the dress of by removing pins. — *adj* **unpinked'** or **unpinkt'** (*Shakesp*) not pinked, not ornamental with punched holes. — *vt* **unplace'** to displace. — *adj* **unplaced'** not assigned to or set in a place; not inducted to a church; not appointed to an office; not among the first three (horses) in a race. — *adj* **unplained'** (*Spenser*) not lamented. — *adj* **unplau'sible** implausible. — *adv* **unplau'sibly**. — *adj* **unplau'sive** not approving. — *adj* **unpleas'ant** not pleasant; disagreeable. — *adv* **unpleas'antly**. — *n* **unpleas'antness** the state or quality of being unpleasant, disagreeableness; a disagreeable incident; disagreement involving open hostility. — *n* **unpleas'antry** lack of pleasantness; any unpleasant occurrence, any discomfort. — *adj* **unpleased'**. — *adj* **unpleas'ing** not pleasing; displeasing. — *adv* **unpleas'ingly**. — *adj* **unpleas'urable**. — *adv* **unpleas'urably**. — *vt* **unplumb'** to remove the lead from. — *adj* **unplumbed'** unsounded; unfathomed. — *vt* **unplume'** to strip of feathers or plumes (often *fig*). — *adj* **unpoint'ed**

Some words with **un-** prefix; see **un-** entry for numbered senses.

unprocūr'able *adj* (1).
unproduced' *adj* (1).
unproduc'tive *adj* (1).
unproduc'tively *adv* (1).
unproduc'tiveness *n* (1).
unproductiv'ity *n* (1).
unprofaned' *adj* (1).
unprofitabil'ity *n* (1).
unprof'itable *adj* (1).
unprof'itableness *n* (1).
unprof'itably *adv* (1).
unprof'iting *adj* (1).
unprogress'ive *adj* (1).
unprogress'ively *adv* (1).
unprogress'iveness *n* (1).
unprohib'ited *adj* (1).
unprojec'ted *adj* (1).
unprolif'ic *adj* (1).
unprom'ised *adj* (1).
unprom'ising *adj* (1).
unprom'isingly *adv* (1).
unpromp'ted *adj* (1).
unpronounce'able *adj* (1).
unpronounced' *adj* (1).
unprop' *vt* (2).
unprop'ertied *adj* (1).
unprophet'ic or
unprophet'ical *adj* (1).
unpropi'tious *adj* (1).
unpropi'tiously *adv* (1).
unpropi'tiousness *n* (1).
unproposed' *adj* (1).
unpropped' *adj* (1).
unpros'perous *adj* (1).
unpros'perously *adv* (1).
unpros'perousness *n* (1).
unprotec'ted *adj* (1).
unprotec'tedness *n* (1).
unprotest'ing *adj* (1).
unprov'able *adj* (1).
unproved' *adj* (1).
unprō'ven *adj* (1).
unprovis'ioned *adj* (1).
unprovoc'ative *adj* (1).
unpruned' *adj* (1).
unpub'lished *adj* (1).
unpuck'ered *adj* (1).
unpulled' *adj* (1).
unpunct'ual *adj* (1).
unpunctual'ity *n* (1).
unpunct'uated *adj* (1).
unpun'ishable *adj* (1).
unpun'ishably *adv* (1).
unpun'ished *adj* (1).
unpur'chasable or
unpur'chaseable *adj* (1).
unpur'chased *adj* (1).
unpurged' *adj* (1).
unpū'rified *adj* (1).
unpur'posed *adj* (1).
unpursued' *adj* (1).
unqual'ifiable *adj* (1).
unqual'ified *adj* (1).
unqual'ifiedly *adv* (1).
unqual'ifiedness *n* (1).
unqual'ify *vt* (2).
unquanti'fied *adj* (1).
unquant'ized or **-s-** *adj* (1).
unquarr'ied *adj* (1).
unqueen' (*Shakesp*) *vt* (2).
unqueened' *adj* (2).
unqueen'like *adj* (1).
unqueen'ly *adj* (1).
unquelled' *adj* (1).
unquench'able *adj* (1).
unquench'ably *adv* (1).
unquenched' *adj* (1).
unquick'ened *adj* (1).
unraced' *adj* (1).
unraised' *adj* (1).
unran'somed *adj* (1).

not pointed; without point or points; with joints uncemented. — *vt* **unpoi'son** to rid of poison, cure of poisoning. — *adj* **unpoi'soned** not poisoned. — *adj* **unpol'icied** without formal political organization; impolitic. — *adj* **unpolite'** impolite; unpolished (*obs*); inelegant (*obs*). — *adv* **unpolite'ly**. — *n* **unpolite'ness**. — *adj* **unpolled'** not polled; not having voted. — *vt* **unpope'** to divest of popedom. — *adj* **unpor'tioned** without a portion. — *adj* **unpossessed'** not possessed; not in possession; unprejudiced (*obs*). — *adj* **unpossess'ing** (*Shakesp*) without possessions. — *adj* **unposs'ible** (*Shakesp*; *dialect*) impossible. — *adj* **unpost'ed** not posted, in any sense; not posted up; without a post. — *adj* **unpō'table** undrinkable, unfit to drink. — *adj* **unprac'ticable** (formerly common) impracticable. — *adj* **unprac'tised** having little or no practice or experience, inexpert; not carried out in practice; not yet familiar through practice (*obs*). — *n* **unprac'tisedness**. — *vt* **unpraise'** to dispraise; to deprive of praise. — *adj* **unpraised'** not praised. — *adj* **unpraise'worthy**. — *vt* **unpray'** to revoke the praying of. — *adj* **unpreach'** to recant in preaching; to undo the preaching of. — *adj* **unpreach'ing** not preaching. — *adj* **unprec'edented** (*-pres'*, or *-prēs'*) not warranted by judicial, etc, precedent; of which there has been no previous instance. — *adv* **unprec'edentedly**. — *vi* **unpredict'** (*Milton*) to revoke what has been predicted. — *n* **unpredictabil'ity**. — *adj* **unpredict'able** that cannot be foretold; (of a person or thing) liable to behave in a way that cannot be predicted. — *adv* **unpredict'ably**. — *adj* **unpreferred'** without preferment or advancement. — *adj* **unpreg'nant** (*Shakesp*) slow-witted, unready, ineffective; not quickened by a lively sense (with *of*). — *adj* **unprelat'ical** unbecoming in or to a prelate; not episcopal. — *adj* **unpremed'itable** not to be foreseen. — *adj* **unpremed'itated** not studied or purposed beforehand. — *adv* **unpremed'itatedly**. — *n* **unpremed'itatedness**. — *n* **unpremeditā'tion**. — *vt* **unprepare'** to make unprepared. — *adj* **unprepared'** not prepared or ready; not prepared for death; without preparation. — *adv* **unprepā'redly**. — *n* **unprepā'redness**. — *adj* **unprepossessed'** not prepossessed or prejudiced. — *adj* **unprepossess'ing** not predisposing others in one's favour, unpleasing. — *adj* **unpresent'able** not fit to be seen. — *adj* **unpretend'ing** not pretending or making pretence; modest. — *adv* **unpreten'dingly**. — *adj* **unpreten'tious** not pretentious; modest. — *adj* **unprevail'ing** unavailing. — *adj* **unpreven'table**. — *n* **unpreven'tableness**. — *adj* **unpreven'ted** not prevented or obviated; not anticipated or preceded (*obs*). — *adj* **unpriced'** having no fixed or stated price; beyond price, priceless. — *vt* **unpriest'** to divest of priesthood. — *adj* **unpriest'ly** unbecoming, unlike or not of the nature of, a priest. — *adj* **unprin'cipled** without good principles; not based on or in accordance with principles; not restrained by conscience; profligate; uninstructed (*Milton*). — *adj* **unprint'able** not fit to be printed. — *adj* **unprint'ed**. — *adj* **unprīz'able** (*Shakesp*) worthless; beyond price. — *adj* **unprized'** not prized. — *adj* **unprocē'dūral** not in accordance with established or accepted procedures. — *adj* **unprofessed'**. — *adj* **unprofess'ional** not of a profession or the profession in question; beyond the limits of one's profession; unbecoming to a member of a particular profession. — *adv* **unprofess'ionally**. — *adj* **unprof'ited** without profit or advantage. — *adj* **unprop'er** improper; common, not one's own (*Shakesp*). — *adv* **unprop'erly**. — *adj* **unpropor'tionable** out of due proportion. — *adv* **unpropor'tionably**. — *adj* **unpropor'tionate** out of due proportion. — *adv* **unpropor'tionately**. — *adj* **unpropor'tioned** not proportioned. — *vt* **unprot'estantize** or **-ise** to transform from Protestantism; to strip of Protestant character. — *adj* **unprotest'ed** not objected to or protested against. — *vt* **unprovide'** (*Shakesp*) to unfurnish, to deprive of what is necessary. — *adj* **unprovī'ded** not furnished, provided, or provided for (also **unprovī'ded-for**). — *adv* **unprovī'dedly**. — *adj* **unprov'ident** (*Shakesp*) improvident. — *vt* **un'provoke** (*Shakesp*) to counteract provocation of. — *adj* **unprovoked'** not provoked; uncalled for. — *adv* **unprovō'kedly**. — *adj* **unprovō'king**. — *vt* **unpurse'** to relax (the lips) from pursing; to disburse. — *adj* **unpurveyed'** (*Spenser* **unpurvaide'**) not purveyed; not provided with (with *of*; *Spenser*); unprovided or unprepared (*obs*). — *adj* **unputdown'able** (*colloq*) of a book, too absorbing to be set aside, compelling one to read to the end without interruption.

Words starting with **q-**, *and* **r-**, *prefixed by* **un-**.

adj **unqual'itied** or **unqual'ited** (*Shakesp*) bereft of qualities. — *vt* **unqueen'** to deprive of a queen; in bee-keeping, to deprive (a beehive) of a queen bee. — *adj* **unques'tionable** not to be questioned, certain, beyond doubt; averse to conversation, or *perh* impatient of question (*Shakesp*). — *adv* **unques'tionably** in such a

Some words with **un-** prefix; see **un-** entry for numbered senses.

unrat'ed *adj* (1).
unrat'ified *adj* (1).
unrav'ished *adj* (1).
unreach'able *adj* (1).
unreached' *adj* (1).
unreac'tive *adj* (1).
unreaped' *adj* (1).
unrebuked' *adj* (1).
unrecap'turable *adj* (1).
unreceipt'ed *adj* (1).
unreceived' *adj* (1).
unrecep'tive *adj* (1).
unrecip'rocated *adj* (1).
unreck'onable *adj* (1).
unreck'oned *adj* (1).
unreclaim'able *adj* (1).
unreclaim'ably *adv* (1).
unreclaimed' *adj* (1).
unrec'ognīzable or **-s-** (or *-nīz'*) *adj* (1).
unrec'ognīzably or **-s-** (or *-nīz'*) *adv* (1).
unrec'ognized or **-s-** *adj* (1).
unrec'ognizing or **-s-** *adj* (1).
unrecollect'ed *adj* (1).
unrecommend'able *adj* (1).
unrecommend'ed *adj* (1).
unrec'ompensed *adj* (1).
unrec'oncīlable (or *-sīl'*) *adj* (1).
unreconcīl'ableness *n* (1).
unrec'oncīlably (or *-sīl'*) *adv* (1).
unrec'onciled (or *-sīld'*) *adj* (1).
unrecord'ed *adj* (1).
unrecount'ed *adj* (1).
unrecov'erable *adj* (1).
unrecov'erably *adv* (1).
unrecov'ered *adj* (1).
unrect'ified *adj* (1).
unreduced' *adj* (1).
unredūc'ible *adj* (1).
unreel' *vt* and *vi* (2).
unrefined' *adj* (1).
unreflect'ed *adj* (1).
unreflect'ing *adj* (1).
unreflect'ingly *adv* (1).
unreflect'ive *adj* (1).
unreform'able *adj* (1).
unreformed' *adj* (1).
unrefract'ed *adj* (1).
unrefreshed' *adj* (1).
unrefresh'ing *adj* (1).
unrefū'ted *adj* (1).
unregard'ed *adj* (1).
unregard'ing *adj* (1).
unreg'imented *adj* (1).
unreg'istered *adj* (1).
unreg'ulated *adj* (1).
unrehearsed' *adj* (1).
unrejoiced' *adj* (1).
unrejoic'ing *adj* (1).
unrelāt'ed *adj* (1).
unrel'ative *adj* (1).
unrelaxed' *adj* (1).
unreliev'able *adj* (1).
unrelieved' *adj* (1).
unreliev'edly *adv* (1).
unrel'ished *adj* (1).
unreluc'tant *adj* (1).
unremain'ing *adj* (1).
unremark'able *adj* (1).
unremarked' *adj* (1).
unrem'edied *adj* (1).
unremem'bered *adj* (1).
unremem'bering *adj* (1).
unremūn'erative *adj* (1).
unren'dered *adj* (1).
unrenewed' *adj* (1).
unrenowned' *adj* (1).
unrent' *adj* (1).
unrepaid' *adj* (1).
unrepair' *n* (1).

way as to be unquestionable; certainly, without doubt. — *adj* **unques'tioned** not called in question; not subjected to questioning; not examined. — *adj* **unques'tioning**. — *adj* **unquī'et** disturbed; restless; uneasy. — *n* disquiet, inquietude. — *vt* to disquiet. — *adv* **unquī'etly**. — *n* **unquī'etness**. — *adj* **unquōt'able** unsuitable or unfit for quotation. — *vi* **unquote'** to close a quotation; to mark the end of a quoted passage with superscript comma or commas, used as *interj* to indicate that a quotation is finished. — *adj* **unquot'ed** (of a company) not quoted on the Stock Exchange list. — *adj* **unracked'** (of liquor) not drawn off from the lees; not stretched on the rack; not strained. — *vt* **unrake'** to uncover by raking. — *adj* **unraked'** not raked; uncovering by raking; (of a fire) not banked up. — *vt* **unrav'el** to disentangle; to unknit. — *vi* to become disentangled. — *adj* **unrav'elled**. — *n* **unrav'eller**. — *n* **unrav'elling**. — *n* **unrav'elment**. — *adj* **unrā'zored** unshaven. — *n* **unread** (*un-red'*) not informed by reading; not perused. — *adj* **unreadable** (*un-rēd'ə-bl*) indecipherable; too dull or badly-written to be read. — *n* **unread'ableness**. — *adv* **unreadily** (*-red'*). — *n* **unread'iness**. — *adj* **unread'y** not ready, prepared or prompt; hesitating, holding back; (*Shakesp*, etc) undressed or not dressed (**make unready** *obs* to undress); (earlier **unredy**) uncounselled or unwise, redeless (*obs*; from **rede**). — *adj* **unrē'al** not real or like reality; incredible; illusory; amazing, unbelievable (*colloq*); a general expression of appreciation or admiration (*slang*, *orig US*). — *n* **unrē'alism**. — *adj* **unrealist'ic** not like reality; unreasonable or impracticable. — *n* **unreal'ity** absence or lack of reality or existence; an unreal thing. — *vt* **unrē'alize** or **-ise** to divest of reality. — *adj* **unrē'alized** or **-s-**. — *adv* **unrē'ally**. — *n* **unrea'son** lack of reason or reasonableness; nonsense; injustice (*obs*); see also **abbot of unreason** at **abbot**. — *adj* **unrea'sonable** not agreeable to reason; exceeding the bounds of reason, immoderate; not influenced by reason. — *n* **unrea'sonableness**. — *adv* **unrea'sonably**. — *adj* **unrea'soned** not argued or thought out. — *adj* **unrea'soning** not reasoning; showing lack of reason, irrational. — *adv* **unrea'soningly**. — *vt* **unreave'** (from dialect *reeve* or *reave* to wind or unwind) to unweave (*Spenser*); to unwind (*dialect*). — *adj* **unrebā'ted** unblunted; undulled; without rebate. — *adj* **unrecall'able**. — *adj* **unrecalled'**. — *adj* **unrecall'ing** (*Shakesp*; *Milton*) impossible to undo, not to be recalled. — *adj* **unrecked'** not regarded or cared about. — *adj* **unreconcil'iable** (*Shakesp*) unreconcilable. — *adj* **unreconstruct'ed** not reconstructed or rebuilt; not accepting the current situation or opinions; not adjusted or reconciled to reconstruction (*US hist*). — *adj* **unrecūr'ing** (*Shakesp*) incurable. — *adj* **unred'** (*Spenser*) for **unread** (unrecounted, untold). — *adj* **unredeem'able**. — *adj* **unredeemed'** not redeemed, *esp* spiritually or from pawn; without compensatory quality or circumstance, hence unmitigated, unrelieved. — *adj* **unredressed'** or **unredrest'** not redressed; without redress or possibility of escape (*Spenser*). — *adj* **unredy** see **unready** above. — *vt* **unreeve'** to withdraw from being reeved. — *n* **unregen'eracy**. — *adj* **unregen'erate** not regenerate; unrepentant, refusing to be reformed. — *adj* **unregen'erated**. — *vt* **unrein'** to relax the rein of, give rein to. — *adj* **unreined'** unchecked. — *adj* **unrelen'ting**. — *adv* **unrelen'tingly**. — *n* **unrelen'tingness**. — *adj* **unrelen'tor** (*Keats*) someone who does not relent. — *n* **unrelīabil'ity** (see note at **rely**). — *adj* **unrelī'able** not to be relied upon. — *n* **unrelī'ableness**. — *adj* **unrelig'ious** not connected with religion; not religious without being necessarily contrary or hostile to religion; irreligious. — *adj* **unremitt'ed**. — *adv* **unremitt'edly**. — *adj* **unremitt'ent**. — *adv* **unremitt'ently**. — *adj* **unremitt'ing** not remitting or relaxing; continued; incessant. — *adv* **unremitt'ingly**. — *n* **unremitt'ingness**. — *adj* **unremorse'ful** feeling no remorse. — *adv* **unremorse'fully**. — *adj* **unremorse'less** (*obs*) remorseless. — *adj* **unremov'able** not removable; immovable, fixed, constant (*obs*). — *adj* **unremoved'** not removed; fixed, unshaken (*obs*). — *adj* **unrepeat'able** not repeatable; indecent, gross; that cannot be done, etc again. — *adj* **unrepeat'ed**. — *adj* **unreprov'able**. — *adj* **unreproved'** (or *-proo͞'vid*) not reproved; not liable to reproof, blameless (*Spenser* and *Milton*). — *adj* **unreprov'ing**. — *adj* **unrequired'** unasked; unasked-for; unnecessary. — *adj* **unrequīt'ed** not reciprocated or returned. — *adv* **unrequīt'edly**. — *n* **unreserve'** absence of reserve. — *adj* **unreserved'** not reserved; without reserve or reservation; unrestricted, unqualified. — *adv* **unreser'vedly**. — *n* **unreser'vedness**. — *adj* **unresist'ed**. — *adj* **unresist'ible** (*rare*) irresistible. — *adj* **unresist'ing**. — *adv* **unresis'tingly**. — *adj* **unresolv'able**. — *adj* **unresolved'** not resolved, determined, settled or solved; irresolute; undecided; not separated into its constituent parts. — *n* **unresol'vedness** irresolution. — *adj* **unrespect'ed**. —

Some words with **un-** prefix; see **un-** entry for numbered senses.

unrepair'able *adj* (1).
unrepaired' *adj* (1).
unrepeal'able *adj* (1).
unrepealed' *adj* (1).
unrepelled' *adj* (1).
unrepen'tance *n* (1).
unrepen'tant *adj* (1).
unrepen'ted *adj* (1).
unrepen'ting *adj* (1).
unrepen'tingly *adv* (1).
unrepī'ning *adj* (1).
unrepī'ningly *adv* (1).
unreplace'able *adj* (1).
unreplen'ished *adj* (1).
unreport'able *adj* (1).
unreport'ed *adj* (1).
unrepose'ful *adj* (1).
unrepōs'ing *adj* (1).
unrepresent'ative *adj* (1).
unrepresent'ed *adj* (1).
unrepriev'able *adj* (1).
unreprieved' *adj* (1).
unrep'rimanded *adj* (1).
unreproached' *adj* (1).
unreproach'ful *adj* (1).
unreproach'ing *adj* (1).
unreprodūc'ible *adj* (1).
unrepug'nant *adj* (1).
unrepuls'able *adj* (1).
unreq'uisite *adj* (1).
unrescind'ed *adj* (1).
unresent'ed *adj* (1).
unresent'ful *adj* (1).
unresent'ing *adj* (1).
unrespon'sive *adj* (1).
unrespon'sively *adv* (1).
unrespon'siveness *n* (1).
unrestored' *adj* (1).
unrestrain'able *adj* (1).
unrestrained' *adj* (1).
unrestrain'edly *adv* (1).
unrestraint' *n* (1).
unrestric'ted *adj* (1).
unrestric'tedly *adv* (1).
unretard'ed *adj* (1).
unretent'ive *adj* (1).
unretouched' *adj* (1).
unreturn'able *adj* (1).
unreturned' *adj* (1).
unreturn'ing *adj* (1).
unreturn'ingly *adv* (1).
unreveal'able *adj* (1).
unrevealed' *adj* (1).
unreveal'ing *adj* (1).
unrevenged' *adj* (1).
unrevenge'ful *adj* (1).
unreversed' *adj* (1).
unrevised' *adj* (1).
unrevoked' *adj* (1).
unrewar'ded *adj* (1).
unrewar'dedly *adv* (1).
unrewar'ding *adj* (1).
unrhyth'mical *adj* (1).
unrhyth'mically *adv* (1).
unribbed' *adj* (1).
unrid'able or **unride'able** *adj* (1).
unridd'en *adj* (1).
unrī'fled *adj* (1).
unringed' *adj* (1).
unripe' *adj* (1).
unrī'pened *adj* (1).
unripe'ness *n* (1).
unris'en *adj* (1).
unrī'valled *adj* (1).
unriv'en *adj* (1).
unrō'manized or **-s-** *adj* (1).
unroman'tic or **unroman'tical** *adj* (1).
unroman'tically *adv* (1).
unros'ined *adj* (1).

adj **unrespect'ive** indiscriminate; inattentive, unthinking (*Shakesp*); undiscriminating (*Shakesp*). — *adj* **unres'pited** (*Milton*) without respite or pause. — *n* **unrest'** lack of rest; disquiet; disturbance; discontent verging on insurrection. — *adj* **unrest'ful** not restful; uneasy; full of unrest. — *n* **unrest'fulness**. — *adj* **unrest'ing**. — *adv* **unrest'ingly**. — *n* **unrest'ingness**. — *adj* **unrev'erend** not reverend; not reverent, irreverent, unreverent (*Shakesp*). — *adj* **unrev'erent** not reverent. — *adj* **unrevert'ed** not turned back. — *adj* **unrhymed'** not rhymed. — *adj* **unrid'** (*archaic*) unridden. — *vt* **unridd'le** to read the riddle of; to solve. — *adj* **unridd'leable**. — *n* **unridd'ler**. — *vt* **unrig'** to strip of rigging or of clothes, etc. — *adj* **unrigged'** without rigging; stripped of rigging. — *n* **unright'** (*archaic*) wrong; unfairness, injustice. — *adj* (*archaic*) wrong. — *adj* **unrigh'teous** sinful or unjust. — *adv* **unrigh'teously**. — *n* **unrigh'teousness**. — *adj* **unright'ful**. — *adv* **unright'fully**. — *n* **unright'fulness**. — **unrimed'** same as **unrhymed**. — *vt* **unrip'** to rip up or open; to strip, lay bare; to disclose. — *adj* **unripped'** not ripped; ripped up or open. — *n* **unripp'ing**. — *vt* **unriv'et** to loose from being riveted; to detach (*fig*). — *vt* **unrobe'** to strip of a robe, to undress. — *vi* to take off a robe, *esp* of state. — *vt* **unroll'** to open out from a rolled state; to strike off the roll (*Shakesp*). — *vi* to become unrolled. — *vt* **unroof'** to strip the roof from. — *adj* **unroofed'** not roofed; stripped of its roof. — *vt* **unroost'** (*Shakesp*) to drive out of a roost. — *vt* **unroot'** to tear up by the roots. — *adj* **unroot'ed** without root; not uprooted (with *out*); rooted out. — *vt* **unrope'** to loose from a rope. — *adj* **unrough'** not rough; (*Shakesp* **unruffe'**) beardless. — *adj* **unround'ed** not rounded; articulated with spread lips (*phonetics*). — *adj* **unrude'** not rude; also (*obs, prob* by confusion from obsolete *unride*, from OE *ungerȳde* rough, from *gerȳde* smooth, easy) rude, uncouth. — *adj* **unruff'able** (*Dickens*) imperturbable. — *vt* **unruff'le** to restore or recover from ruffling. — *adj* **unruff'led** smooth; calm; not disturbed or flustered. — *n* **unrule'** anarchy. — *adj* **unruled'** not governed; without ruled lines. — *n* **unrul'iment** (*Spenser*) unruliness. — *n* **unrul'iness**. — *adj* **unrul'y** ungovernable; unmanageable; turbulent; stormy.

Words starting with **s-**, *prefixed by* **un-**.

vt **unsadd'le** to take the saddle from; to dislodge from the saddle. — *adj* **unsadd'led**. — *adj* **unsafe'** not safe or secure; (of a conclusion, conviction, etc) based on insufficient or suspect evidence. — *adv* **unsafe'ly**. — *n* **unsafe'ness**. — *n* **unsafe'ty**. — *adj* **unsaid'** not said (see also **unsay**). — *adj* **unsailed'** unnavigated. — *adj* **unsail'orlike**. — *adj* **unsained'** unblessed. — *vt* **unsaint'** to divest of saintliness or of the title of saint. — *n* **unsaint'liness**. — *adj* **unsaint'ly**. — *adj* **unsanc'tified**. — *vt* **unsanc'tify** to undo the sanctification of; to desecrate. — *adj* **unsan'itary** without (regard to) sanitation, unhealthy. — *adj* **unsā'table** (*Browning*) and **unsā'tiable** (now *rare*) insatiable. — *adj* **unsat'urated** not saturated (in all senses; **unsaturated fat** an animal fat (*usu* solid, eg lard or butter) containing a high proportion of saturated fatty acids). — *adv* **unsā'vourily**. — *n* **unsā'vouriness**. — *adj* **unsā'voury** not savoury, tasteless; unpleasant, disagreeable; offensive; disreputable. — *vt* **unsay'** to retract: — *pa t* and *pa p* **unsaid'**. — *adj* **unsay'able** that cannot be said. — *vt* **unscabb'ard** to unsheathe. — *adj* **unscāl'able** that cannot be climbed. — *vt* **unscale'** to remove scales from. — *adj* **unscaled'** unclimbed; cleared of scales; scaleless. — *adj* **unscanned'** not scanned as verse; not scrutinized; (*Shakesp* **un'skan'd**) unconsidered. — *adj* **unscathed'** not harmed or injured. — *adj* **unscav'engered** (*Dickens*) not cleared of rubbish. — *adj* **unscep'tred** without a sceptre; deposed. — *adj* **unsciss'ored** not cut with scissors. — *adj* **unscott'ified** deprived of Scottish qualities or characteristics. — *vt* **unscram'ble** to decode from a scrambled state, or to restore to natural sound; to restore (something in which categories have been deliberately jumbled) to a system of classification and separation. — *adj* **unscreened'** not screened; unsifted. — *vt* **unscrew'** to loose from a state of being screwed; to open, loosen or detach by screwing. — *vi* to be capable of being or becoming unscrewed. — *adj* **unscrip'ted** not using a script; unrehearsed; (of comments, moves, etc) not planned, not in the script (*radio*, *TV*, etc). — *adj* **unscrip'tural** not in accordance with, or not warranted by, the Bible. — *adv* **unscrip'turally**. — *adj* **unscru'pled** unscrupulous; not scrupled at. — *adj* **unscru'pulous** without scruples or principles. — *adv* **unscru'pulously**. — *n* **unscru'pulousness**. — *vt* **unseal'** to remove or break the seal of; to free from sealing or closure; to open (sometimes *prob* for **unseel**). — *adj* **unsealed'** not sealed; freed from a seal; opened. — *vt* **unseam'** to undo a seam of; to rip open (*Shakesp*). — *adj* **unseamed'**

Some words with **un-** prefix; see **un-** entry for numbered senses.

unrott'ed *adj* (1).
unrott'en *adj* (1).
unrouged (-*rōōzhd'*) *adj* (1).
unround' *adj* (1).
unround' *vt* (2).
unround'ed *adj* (1).
unroused' *adj* (1).
unroy'al *adj* (1).
unroy'ally *adv* (1).
unrubbed' *adj* (1).
unrum'pled *adj* (1).
unsalabil'ity or **unsaleabil'ity** *n* (1).
unsal'able or **unsale'able** *adj* (1).
unsal'aried *adj* (1).
unsalt'ed *adj* (1).
unsalu'ted *adj* (1).
unsal'vageable *adj* (1).
unsanc'tioned *adj* (1).
unsan'dalled *adj* (1).
unsapped' *adj* (1).
unsashed' *adj* (1).
unsāt'ed *adj* (1).
unsā'tiate or **unsā'tiated** *adj* (1).
unsā'tiating *adj* (1).
unsāt'ing *adj* (1).
unsatir'ical *adj* (1).
unsatisfac'tion *n* (1).
unsatisfac'torily *adv* (1).
unsatisfac'toriness *n* (1).
unsatisfac'tory *adj* (1).
unsat'isfiable *adj* (1).
unsat'isfied *adj* (1).
unsat'isfiedness *n* (1).
unsat'isfying *adj* (1).
unsat'isfyingness *n* (1).
unsatura'tion *n* (1).
unsaved' *adj* (1).
unscarred' *adj* (1).
unscar'y *adj* (1).
unscent'ed *adj* (1).
unsched'uled *adj* (1).
unschol'arlike *adj* (1).
unschol'arly *adj* (1).
unschooled' *adj* (1).
unscientif'ic *adj* (1).
unscientif'ically *adv* (1).
unscorched' *adj* (1).
unscoured' *adj* (1).
unscratched' *adj* (1).
unscru'tinized or **-s-** *adj* (1).
unsculp'tured *adj* (1).
unscythed' *adj* (1).
unsea'worthiness *n* (1).
unsea'worthy *adj* (1).
unsec'onded *adj* (1).
unsecta'rian *adj* (1).
unsecta'rianism *n* (1).
unsec'ular *adj* (1).
unsecured' *adj* (1).
unseduced' *adj* (1).
unsegment'ed *adj* (1).
unseg'regated *adj* (1).
unsell'able *adj* (1).
unsensā'tional *adj* (1).
unsens'itive *adj* (1).
unsens'itized or **-s-** *adj* (1).
unsent' *adj* (1).
unsent'enced *adj* (1).
unsentiment'al *adj* (1).
unsep'arable (*Shakesp*) *adj* (1).
unsep'arated *adj* (1).
unsep'ulchred *adj* (1).
unsēr'ious *adj* (1).
unser'viceable *adj* (1).
unsev'ered *adj* (1).
unshā'ded *adj* (1).
unshak'able or **unshake'able** *adj* (1).

without seams. — *adj* **unsearch'able** inscrutable, not possible to be searched into; mysterious. — *n* **unsearch'ableness**. — *adv* **unsearch'ably**. — *adj* **unsearched'**. — *vt* **unsea'son** (*Spenser*) to affect disagreeably. — *adj* **unsea'sonable** not in season; ill-timed. — *n* **unsea'sonableness**. — *adv* **unsea'sonably**. — *adj* **unsea'soned** without seasoning; not matured; not inured or habituated; unseasonable (*Shakesp*). — *vt* **unseat'** to remove from a seat; to throw (a horse-rider); to oust from a parliamentary seat. — *adj* **unseat'ed** not seated; ousted, thrown, removed from a seat. — *adj* **unsē'cret** (*Shakesp*) failing to preserve secrecy. — *adj* **unsecu'red** not secured or made safe; (of a loan or creditor) without security. — *adj* **unsee'able** invisible. — *adj* **unseed'ed** not seeded; (in lawn-tennis tournaments, etc) not placed in the draw of top players. — *adj* **unsee'ing** not seeing; unobservant; without insight or understanding. — *vt* **unseel'** (**seel**[1]) to unsew the eyes of, undo the seeling of. — *n* **unseem'ing** (*Shakesp*) not seeming. — *adj* (*obs*) unbecoming, unseemly. — *n* **unseem'liness**. — *adj* **unseem'ly** not seemly, becoming or decent; ill-looking. — *adv* in an unseemly manner. — *adj* **unseen'** not seen; invisible; not previously seen or prepared for; inexperienced, not well up (*obs*). — *n* an unprepared passage for translation. — *adj* **unseiz'able**. — *adj* **unseized'** not seized; not taken or put in possession. — *adv* **unsel'dom** not seldom (*literally* and *rarely*); misused to mean seldom (as in *not unseldom*, frequently). — *n* **un'self** altruism; impersonality. — *vt* **unself'** to divest of personality, individuality, selfhood or selfishness. — *adj* **unselfcon'scious**. — *adv* **unselfcon'sciously**. — *n* **unselfcon'sciousness**. — *adj* **unself'ish** having or showing concern for others; generous. — *adv* **unself'ishly**. — *n* **unself'ishness**. — *adj* **unsem'inar'd** or **unsem'inaried** (*Shakesp*) without means of generation, deprived of semen or seed. — *vt* **unsense'** to deprive of sense or consciousness. — *adj* **unsensed'** meaningless. — *adj* **unsens'ible** (*obs* or *dialect*) insensible. — *adv* **unsens'ibly** (*obs*) insensibly, imperceptibly; without sense. — *vt* **unsens'ualize** or **-ise** to free from the dominion of the senses. — *vt* **unset'** to undo the setting of. — *adj* not set; not yet firm or solid; (of a jewel) not in a setting; unplanted. — *vt* **unsett'le** to change from being settled; to make uncertain, unstable or restless; to unfix. — *vi* to become unsettled. — *adj* **unsett'led** not settled, fixed or determined; changeable; not having the dregs deposited; not yet inhabited and cultivated; turbulent, lawless. — *adv* **unsett'ledly**. — *n* **unsett'ledness**. — *n* **unsett'lement**. — *n* and *adj* **unsett'ling**. — *vt* **unsew'** to undo the stitching of (a garment, etc). — *adj* **unsewn'** (also **unsewed'**) not sewn (**unsewn binding** a bookbinding in which the gathered sections are held in place by a process other than sewing, *esp* perfect binding or burst binding (qqv)). — *vt* **unsex'** to divest of sex; to divest of the characteristics or of the qualities expected of one's own sex. — *adj* **unsexed'** without the characteristics or qualities expected of one's sex. — *adj* **unsex'ist**. — *adj* **unsex'ual**. — *vt* **unshack'le** to loose from shackles; to remove a shackle from. — *adj* **unshack'led**. — *vt* **unshad'ow** to clear of shadow; to reveal. — *adj* **unshad'owable** impossible to shadow. — *adj* **unshad'owed** not darkened. — *vt* **unshale'** to shale or shell, strip the husk from; to reveal. — *adj* **unshamed'** not ashamed; not put to shame. — *vt* **unshape'** to deprive of shape; to undo, destroy or confound. — *adj* **unshaped'**. — *adj* **unshape'ly**. — *adj* **unshāp'en**. — *vt* **unsheathe'** to draw from the sheath; to uncover. — *adj* **unsheathed'** drawn from the sheath; not sheathed. — *adj* **unshed'** not shed; unparted (*Spenser*). — *vt* **unshell'** to shell, remove the shell from. — *adj* **unshent'** (*archaic*) uninjured; not disgraced. — *vt* **unship'** to unload (cargo) from a ship or boat, etc; to remove from a fixed or allotted place (such as oars from the rowlocks); (of a horse) to unseat (the rider). — *vi* to be capable of or undergo unshipping. — *adj* **unshod'** shoeless; with shoe or shoes removed. — *vt* **unshoe'** to strip of a shoe or shoes. — *vt* **unshout'** (*Shakesp* **unshoot'**) to revoke the shouting of by a contrary shout. — *adj* **unshowered** (*unshowrd'* or *unshow'ərd*) not watered by showers. — *vt* **unshroud'** to uncover. — *adj* **unshrubbed'** (*unshrubd' Shakesp*) without shrubs. — *adj* **unshunn'able**. — *adj* **unshunned'** (*unshun'd' Shakesp*) inevitable. — *vt*, *vi* and *adj* **unshut'** open. — *vt* **unshutt'er** to open or remove the shutters of. — *adj* **unsift'ed** not sifted; not critically examined; inexperienced. — *adj* **unsight'ed** not seen (also *obs*, **unsight'**); (of a gun, etc) having no sights; fired without use of sights; prevented from seeing, *esp* by an obstruction. — *n* **unsight'liness**. — *adj* **unsight'ly** displeasing to the eye; ugly. — *vt* **unsin'ew** to take the strength from. — *adj* **unsin'ewed** (*Shakesp* **unsinn'owed**). — *adj* **unsis'tered** without a sister. — *n* **unsis'terliness**. — *adj* **unsis'terly**. — *adj* **unsist'ing** (*Shakesp*, *Measure for Measure* IV. 2. 92) variously

Some words with **un-** prefix; see **un-** entry for numbered senses.

unshak'ably or **unshake'ably** *adv* (1).
unshaked' (*Shakesp*) *adj* (1).
unshāk'en *adj* (1).
unshāk'enly *adv* (1).
unshared' *adj* (1).
unsharp'ened *adj* (1).
unshaved' *adj* (1).
unshā'ven *adj* (1).
unshel'tered *adj* (1).
unshewn' (*archaic*) *adj* (1).
unshield'ed *adj* (1).
unshift'ing *adj* (1).
unshing'led *adj* (1).
unshock'able *adj* (1).
unshocked' *adj* (1).
unshorn' *adj* (1).
unshot' *adj* (1).
unshown' *adj* (1).
unshrink'able *adj* (1).
unshrink'ing *adj* (1).
unshrink'ingly *adv* (1).
unshrived' *adj* (1).
unshriv'en *adj* (1).
unsick'er (*Scot*) *adj* (1).
unsick'led *adj* (1).
unsighed'-for *adj* (1).
unsigh'ing *adj* (1).
unsigned' *adj* (1).
unsink'able *adj* (1).
unskil'ful *adj* (1).
unskil'fully *adv* (1).
unskil'fulness *n* (1).
unskilled' *adj* (1).
unskimmed' *adj* (1).
unslain' *adj* (1).
unslaked' *adj* (1).
unsleep'ing *adj* (1).
unslept'-in *adj* (1).
unsliced' *adj* (1).
unslipp'ing *adj* (1).
unslum'bering *adj* (1).
unslum'brous *adj* (1).
unslung' *adj* (1).
unsmart' *adj* (1).
unsmiled'-on *adj* (1).
unsmil'ing *adj* (1).
unsmil'ingly *adv* (1).
unsmirched' *adj* (1).
unsmitt'en *adj* (1).
unsmoth'erable *adj* (1).
unsnap' *vt* (2).
unsneck' *vt* (2).
unsnuffed' *adj* (1).
unsoftened *adj* (1).
unsoftening *adj* (1).
unsoiled' *adj* (1).
unsol'aced *adj* (1).
unsōld' *adj* (1).
unsōl'dierlike *adj* (1).
unsōl'dierly *adj* (1).
unsolic'ited *adj* (1).
unsolic'itous *adj* (1).
unsol'id *adj* (1).
unsolid'ity *n* (1).
unsol'idly *adv* (1).
unson'sy (*Scot*) *adj* (1).
unsoured' *adj* (1).
unsown' *adj* (1).
unspe'cialized or **-s-** *adj* (1).
unspecif'ic *adj* (1).
unspec'ified *adj* (1).
unspec'tacled *adj* (1).
unspectac'ular *adj* (1).
unspec'ulative *adj* (1).
unspilled' *adj* (1).
unspilt' *adj* (1).
unsplint'erable *adj* (1).
unspoiled' *adj* (1).
unspoilt' *adj* (1).
unspoke' (*Shakesp*) *adj* (1).

explained as unassisting, unresisting, insisting, unresting. — *adj* **unsiz'able** or **unsize'able** (*obs*) extraordinarily big; too little, immature. — *adj* **unsized'** not fitted, adjusted or sorted in respect of size; not treated with size. — *adj* **unskan'd** (*Shakesp*) see **unscanned**. — *adj* **unskinned'** skinned; not skinned. — *vt* **unsling'** to free from slings or from being slung: — *pa t* and *pa p* **unslung'**. — *vt* **unsluice'** to let flow; to open the sluice of. — *adj* **unsmooth'**. — *vt* to roughen; to wrinkle. — *adj* **unsmoothed'**. — *adj* **unsmote'** (*archaic*) unsmitten. — *vt* **unsnarl'** to disentangle. — *adj* **unsoaped'** not soaped; unwashed. — *n* **unsociabil'ity**. — *adj* **unsō'ciable** not wanting to associate with others. — *n* **unsō'ciableness**. — *adv* **unsō'ciably**. — *adj* **unsō'cial** not social; not regarding or contributing to the good of society; not sociable; (of hours of work) not falling within the normal working day. — *n* **unsō'cialism** or **unsocial'ity**. — *adj* **unsō'cialized** or **-s-** not socialized, not aware of one's function in, or lacking attributes for living in, society. — *adv* **unsō'cially**. — *vt* **unsock'et** to take out of the socket. — *adj* **unsod'** or **unsodd'en** unboiled; not soaked or saturated. — *adv* **unsoft'** (*Spenser*) not softly. — *vt* **unsolder** (*un-sod'ər* or *-sol'dər, sōl', -sö', -sō'*) to separate from being soldered. — *adj* **unsol'emn** not solemn; informal. — *adj* **unsolv'able** impossible to solve. — *adj* **unsolved'** not solved. — *adj* **unsoote'** (*Spenser*) unsweet. — *adj* **unsophis'ticate** (now *rare*) or **unsophis'ticated** genuine, unadulterated; unfalsified; free from artificiality; ingenuous; inexperienced in evil. — *n* **unsophis'ticatedness**. — *n* **unsophisticā'tion**. — *adj* **unsort'ed** not sorted or arranged; ill-chosen; unfitting, unsuitable. — *adj* **unsought'** not sought or solicited. — *vt* **unsoul'** to deprive of soul or spirit. — *adj* **unsouled'** deprived of or not endowed with soul. — *adj* **unsound'** unhealthy; injured or damaged; not firm or solid; ill-founded; unreliable. — *adj* **unsound'able** unfathomable. — *adj* **unsound'ed** not sounded, pronounced or made to sound; unfathomed, unplumbed. — *adv* **unsound'ly**. — *n* **unsound'ness**. — *adj* **unsourced'** having no source, or no established or authenticated source. — *vt* **unspar'** to withdraw a spar from. — *adj* **unspared'** not spared; unstinted. — *adj* **unspār'ing** not sparing, liberal, profuse; unmerciful. — *adv* **unspār'ingly**. — *n* **unspār'ingness**. — *vt* **unspeak'** (*Shakesp*) to retract. — *adj* **unspeak'able** unutterable; inexpressible, *esp* indescribably bad. — *n* **unspeak'ableness**. — *adv* **unspeak'ably**. — *adj* **unspeak'ing**. — *adj* **unsped'** (*rare*) without achievement or success; unaccomplished. — *vt* **unspell'** to free from a spell. — *adj* **unspent'** not spent. — *vt* **unsphere'** to draw or remove from its sphere. — *adj* **unspied'** (*Spenser* **unspide'**, *Milton* **unspi'd'**) unobserved. — *adj* **unspir'ited**. — *adj* **unspir'itual**. — *vt* **unspir'itualize** or **-ise** to deprive of spirituality. — *adv* **unspir'itually**. — *adj* **unsprung'** not sprung; without springs. — *vt* **unstack'** to remove from a stack. — *adj* **unstanch'able** or **unstaunch'able**. — *adj* **unstanched'** or **unstaunched'** (or *un'*) not stanched; unsated (*Shakesp*); leaky, hence incontinent (*Shakesp*). — *vt* **unstarch'** to free from starch — *adj* **unstarched'** not starched. — *vt* **unstate'** (*Shakesp*) to deprive of state or dignity. — *adj* **unstat'ed** not stated or declared. — *adj* **unstat'ūtable** contrary to statute. — *adv* **unstat'ūtably**. — *adj* **unstayed'** not stayed or restrained; unsupported; unstable (*Spenser*); without stays. — *adj* **unstay'ing** without stop. — *adv* **unstead'ily**. — *n* **unstead'iness**. — *adj* **unstead'y**. — *vt* to make unsteady. — *vt* **unsteel'** to soften, to disarm. — *vt* **unstep'** to remove (*esp* a mast) from its place. — *adj* **unsterc'orated** not manured. — *vt* **unstick'** to free from sticking. — *vi* to come off from the surface: — *pa t* and *pa p* **unstuck'**. — *adj* detached, loosened from sticking (**come unstuck** of a plan, to go amiss). — *vt* **unstitch'** to take out the stitches of. — *vt* **unstock'** to deplete of stock; to remove the stock from; to launch (*obs*). — *adj* **unstocked'** not stocked; without stock; not wearing a stock. — *adj* **unstock'inged** not wearing a stocking or stockings. — *vt* **unstop'** to free from being stopped; to draw out the stop or stopper of. — *adj* **unstopp'able** not able to be stopped. — *adv* **unstopp'ably**. — *adj* **unstopped'** not stopped; (of a consonant) open; without a pause at the end of the line. — *vt* **unstopp'er** to take the stopper from. — *vt* **unstow'** to empty of contents; to take out of stowage. — *adj* **unstrained'** not strained or purified by straining; not subjected to strain; not forced, natural. — *vt* **unstrap'** to undo the straps of. — *adj* **unstreamed'** (of schoolchildren) not divided into classes according to ability. — *adj* **unstressed'** not subject to stress; not stressed or emphasized. — *adj* **unstrī'ated** not striped. — *vt* **unstring'** to take the strings from; to loose the strings of; to take from a string; to put out of tone; to disorganize. — *vi* to loose the strings of one's purse. — *adj* **unstringed'** not stringed, not provided with strings. — *vt* **unstrip'** (now *dialect*) to strip. — *adj* **unstripped'**

Some words with **un-** prefix; see **un-** entry for numbered senses.

unspō'ken *adj* (1).
unsport'ing *adj* (1).
unsports'manlike *adj* (1).
unspott'ed *adj* (1).
unspott'edness *n* (1).
unsprink'led *adj* (1).
unspun' *adj* (1).
unsquared' *adj* (1).
unstā'ble *adj* (1).
unstā'bleness *n* (1).
unstaid' *adj* (1).
unstaid'ness *n* (1).
unstain'able *adj* (1).
unstained' *adj* (1).
unstamped' *adj* (1).
unstates'manlike *adj* (1).
unstead'fast *adj* (1).
unstead'fastly *adv* (1).
unstead'fastness *n* (1).
unster'ile *adj* (1).
unster'ilized or **-s-** *adj* (1).
unstī'fled *adj* (1).
unstig'matized or **-s-** *adj* (1).
unstilled' *adj* (1).
unstim'ulated *adj* (1).
unstint'ed *adj* (1).
unstint'ing *adj* (1).
unstirred' *adj* (1).
unstoop'ing *adj* (1).
unstrapped' *adj* (1).
unstrat'ified *adj* (1).
unstrength'ened *adj* (1).
unstriped' *adj* (1).
unstruck' *adj* (1).
unstruc'tured *pa p* and *adj* (1).
unstuffed' (*Shakesp* **un'stuft**) *adj* (1).
unsubdū'able *adj* (1).
unsubdued' *adj* (1).
unsub'ject *adj* (1).
unsubject'ed *adj* (1).
unsub'limated *adj* (1).
unsublimed' *adj* (1).
unsubmerged' *adj* (1).
unsubmiss'ive *adj* (1).
unsubmitt'ing *adj* (1).
unsubscribed' *adj* (1).
unsub'sidized or **-s-** *adj* (1).
unsubstan'tiated *adj* (1).
unsubt'le *adj* (1).
unsucc'oured *adj* (1).
unsucked' *adj* (1).
unsued'-for or **unsued-to** *adj* (1).
unsull'ied *adj* (1).
unsumm'oned *adj* (1).
unsuper'fluous (*Milton*) *adj* (1).
unsu'pervised *adj* (1).
unsupp'le *adj* (1).
unsupp'leness *n* (1).
unsupplied' *adj* (1).
unsuppōs'able *adj* (1).
unsuppressed' *adj* (1).
unsur'faced *adj* (1).
unsurmised' *adj* (1).
unsurpass'able *adj* (1).
unsurpass'ably *adv* (1).
unsurpassed' *adj* (1).
unsurprised' *adj* (1).
unsurveyed' *adj* (1).
unsuscept'ible *adj* (1).
unsuspend'ed *adj* (1).
unsustain'able *adj* (1).
unsustained' *adj* (1).
unsustain'ing *adj* (1).
unswall'owed *adj* (1).
unsweet' *adj* (1).
unsweet'ened *adj* (1).
unswept' *adj* (1).
unsympathet'ic *adj* (1).
unsympathet'ically *adv* (1).
unsym'pathizing or **-s-** *adj* (1).
unsym'pathy *n* (1).

not stripped. — *adj* **unstrung'** with strings removed or slackened; not strung; relaxed; disorganized; unnerved. — *adj* **unstuck** see **unstick**. — *adj* **unstud'ied** not studied; not having studied; without premeditation; unlaboured; spontaneous; natural, easy. — *adj* **un'stuffy** (*fig*) not stodgy or strait-laced. — *adj* **unsubstan'tial** not substantial, real, corporeal, solid or strong. — *n* **unsubstantial'ity**. — *n* **unsubstantiā'tion**. — *vt* **unsubstan'tialize** or **-ise**. — *adj* **unsucceed'ed** without a successor. — *n* **unsuccess'** lack of success; failure. — *adj* **unsuccess'ful**. — *adv* **unsuccess'fully**. — *n* **unsuccess'fulness**. — *adj* **unsuccess'ive** not successive; not in or passing by succession. — *adj* **unsuff'erable** (*obs*) insufferable. — *adj* **unsuffi'cient** (*obs*) insufficient. — *vt* **unsuit'** to make unsuitable. — *n* **unsuitabil'ity**. — *adj* **unsuit'able**. — *n* **unsuit'ableness**. — *adv* **unsuit'ably**. — *adj* **unsuit'ed** not suited or adapted. — *adj* **unsuit'ing**. — *adj* **unsummed'** uncounted. — *adj* **unsumm'ered** not possessing the characteristics of summer. — *adj* **unsung'** not sung; not celebrated in song; not honoured, not given due recognition. — *adj* **unsunned'** not exposed to the sun; not lighted, warmed or affected by the sun; not exposed to view. — *adj* **unsunn'y**. — *adj* **unsupport'able** insupportable; indefensible. — *adj* **unsupport'ed**. — *adv* **unsupport'edly**. — *adj* **unsure** (*un-shŏŏr'*) insecure; precarious; uncertain; doubtful; not assured; untrustworthy. — *adj* **unsured'** (*Shakesp*) not made sure. — *adj* **unsurmount'able** insurmountable. — *adj* **unsuspect'** (*Milton*) not subject to suspicion. — *adj* **unsuspec'ted** not suspected; not known or supposed to exist. — *adv* **unsuspec'tedly**. — *n* **unsuspec'tedness**. — *adj* **unsuspec'ting** not suspecting; innocent. — *adv* **unsuspec'tingly**. — *n* **unsuspec'tingness**. — *n* **unsuspi'cion** absence of suspicion. — *adj* **unsuspi'cious** not feeling or arousing suspicion. — *adv* **unsuspi'ciously**. — *n* **unsuspi'ciousness**. — *vt* **unswadd'le** to unswathe. — *vt* **unswathe'** to take swathings or bandages from. — *adj* **unsway'able** (*Shakesp*). — *adj* **unswayed'** (*Shakesp* **unswai'd'**) not wielded; not controlled; uninfluenced; not persuaded. — *vt* **unswear'** to retract the swearing of. — *vi* to recall an oath. — *n* **unswear'ing**. — *adj* **unswerv'ing** not swerving or deviating; steadfast. — *adv* **unswerv'ingly**. — *adj* **unsworn'** not confirmed, or not bound, by oath. — *adj* **unsyll'abled** not syllabled, not articulated. — *adj* **unsymmet'rical**. — *adv* **unsymmet'rically**. — *adj* **unsymm'etrized** or **-s-**. — *n* **unsymm'etry** asymmetry.

Words starting with **t-**, *prefixed by* **un-**.

vt **untack'** to detach from tacking; to unharness. — *vt* **untack'le** to strip of tackle; to free from tackle; to unharness. — *adj* **untaint'ed** not tainted; unblemished; not attainted. — *adv* **untaint'edly**. — *n* **untaint'edness**. — *adj* **untaint'ing**. — *adj* **untām'able** or **untame'able** that cannot be tamed. — *n* **untam'ableness** or **untame'ableness**. — *adv* **untam'ably** or **untame'ably**. — *adj* **untame'** not tame. — *vt* to make untame, undo the taming of. — *adj* **untamed'** not tamed; wild. — *n* **untamed'ness**. — *vt* **untang'le** to disentangle. — *adj* **untang'led**. — *adj* **untaught'** uninstructed; not taught or communicated by teaching; spontaneous, native or inborn. — *vt* **untax'** to remit a tax on. — *adj* **untaxed'** not taxed; not charged with any fault. — *vt* **unteach'** to undo the teaching of. — *adj* **unteach'able** not capable of being instructed; that cannot be imparted by teaching. — *n* **unteach'ableness**. — *vt* **unteam'** to unyoke. — *adj* **untem'per** to destroy the temper of, deprive of suitable temper. — *adj* **untem'pered** not tempered; not regulated. — *adj* **untem'pering** (*Shakesp*) unconciliating. — *n* **untenabil'ity**. — *adj* **unten'able** (or *-tē'*) not tenable, not defensible. — *n* **unten'ableness** untenability. — *vt* **unten'ant** to deprive of a tenant; to dislodge. — *adj* **unten'antable**. — *adj* **unten'anted** not occupied. — *vt* **untent'** to remove from a tent. — *adj* **untent'ed** having no tents; (of a wound) unprobed, undressed or impossible to treat with a tent; unheeded (*Scot*). — *adj* **untent'y** (*Scot*) careless. — *vt* **unteth'er** to release from a tether. — *adj* **unteth'ered** not tethered. — *vt* **unthatch'** to strip of thatch. — *adj* **unthatched'** not thatched. — *vt* and *vi* **unthaw'** to thaw. — *adj* **unthawed'** not thawed. — *vt* and *vi* **unthink'** to think to the contrary, reverse in thought. — *n* **unthinkabil'ity**. — *adj* **unthink'able** that cannot be thought; outside the realm of thought; beyond the power of thought; inconceivable; unimaginable; utterly impossible (often of things impending but too painful to think about). — *adj* **unthink'ing** not thinking; thoughtless. — *adv* **unthink'ingly**. — *n* **unthink'ingness**. — *adj* **unthought'ful**. — *adv* **unthought'fully**. — *n* **unthought'fulness**. — *adj* **unthought'-of**. — *vt* **unthread'** to take a thread from; to unweave; to loosen; to find one's way through. — *adj* **unthread'ed** not threaded. — *n* **un'thrift** unthriftiness; a prodigal; a spendthrift. — *adj* prodigal. — *adv* **unthrift'ily**. — *n* **unthrift'iness**. — *adj* **unthrift'y** not thrifty; wasteful; prodigal; not thriving; unprofit-

Some words with **un-** prefix; see **un-** entry for numbered senses.

unsystemat'ic or **unsystemat'ical** *adj* (1).
unsystemat'ically *adv* (1).
unsys'tematized or **-s-** *adj* (1).
untailed' *adj* (1).
untā'ken *adj* (1).
untal'ented *adj* (1).
untalked'-of *adj* (1).
untan'gible *adj* (1).
untanned' *adj* (1).
untapped' *adj* (1).
untar'nished *adj* (1).
untarred' *adj* (1).
untast'ed *adj* (1).
untaste'ful *adj* (1).
untear'able *adj* (1).
untech'nical *adj* (1).
untell'able *adj* (1).
untemp'ted *adj* (1).
untend'ed *adj* (1).
untend'er *adj* (1).
unten'dered *adj* (1).
unten'derly *adv* (1).
unter'minated *adj* (1).
unterres'trial *adj* (1).
unterr'ified *adj* (1).
unterr'ifying *adj* (1).
untest'ed *adj* (1).
unthanked' *adj* (1).
unthank'ful *adj* (1).
unthank'fully *adv* (1).
unthank'fulness *n* (1).
untheolog'ical *adj* (1).
unthick'ened *adj* (1).
unthor'ough *adj* (1).
unthreat'ened *adj* (1).
untī'dily *adv* (1).
untī'diness *n* (1).
untī'dy *adj* (1).
untī'dy *vt* (2).
untill'able *adj* (1).
untilled' *adj* (1).
untinc'tured *adj* (1).
untinged' *adj* (1).
untīr'able (*Shakesp* **untyre'able**) *adj* (1).
untired' *adj* (1).
untīr'ing *adj* (1).
untīr'ingly *adv* (1).
untoil'ing *adj* (1).
untorment'ed *adj* (1).
untorn' *adj* (1).
untor'tured *adj* (1).
untracked' *adj* (1).
untract'able *adj* (1).
untract'ableness *n* (1).
untrained' *adj* (1).
untramm'elled *adj* (1).
untramp'led *adj* (1).
untran'quil *adj* (1).
untrans'ferable (or *-fûr'*) or **untransferr'able** (*-fûr'*) *adj* (1).
untransformed' *adj* (1).
untranslatabil'ity *n* (1).
untranslā'table *adj* (1).
untranslā'tableness *n* (1).
untranslā'tably *adv* (1).
untranslā'ted *adj* (1).
untransmīgrā'ted *adj* (1).
untransmiss'ible *adj* (1).
untransmitt'ed *adj* (1).
untransmū'table *adj* (1).
untransmū'ted *adj* (1).
untranspa'rent *adj* (1).
untrav'elled *adj* (1).
untrav'ersable *adj* (1).
untrav'ersed *adj* (1).
untrem'bling *adj* (1).
untrem'blingly *adv* (1).
untremen'dous *adj* (1).
untrem'ulous *adj* (1).

able. — *n* **unthrift'yhed** or **unthrift'yhead** (*Spenser*) unthriftiness. — *vt* **unthrone'** to dethrone. — *vt* **untie'** to loose from being tied; to unbind; to solve, resolve. — *vi* to come loose. — *adj* **untied'** not tied; loosed; not loosed, still tied (*Shakesp*). — *vt* **untile'** to strip of tiles. — *adj* **untiled'** not tiled; stripped of tiles. — *adj* **untim'bered** not strongly timbered (*Shakesp*); unwooded. — *n* **untime'liness**. — *adj* **untime'ly** not timely; before the time, premature; immature; unseasonable, ill-timed; inopportune. — *adv* (*archaic*) at an unsuitable time; too early, prematurely; unseasonably; inopportunely. — *adj* **untime'ous** (*untī'məs*) untimely. — *adv* **untime'ously**. — *vt* **untin'** to take the tin from. — *adj* **untinned'** not tinned. — *adj* **untī'tled** having no title; deprived of title; having no legal claim. — *adj* **untoch'ered** (*Scot*) without tocher or dowry. — *adj* **untold'** (or *un'*) not counted; innumerable; not narrated; not communicated; not informed. — *vt* **untomb'** to disentomb, remove from a tomb. — *adj* **untombed'** not entombed. — *adj* **untoned'** not toned; without tones. — *adj* **untouch'able** impossible to touch; not to be equalled or touched. — *n* someone whose excellence in some respect cannot be rivalled; (*esp* formerly) a Hindu of very low caste, a member of one of the scheduled castes. — *adj* **untouched'** not touched; intact; unrivalled. — *adj* **untoward** (*un-tə-wörd'* or *un-tō'ərd*) inconvenient; unlucky; unfavourable; unfitting; not easily guided; froward; awkward. — *n* **untoward'liness** or **unto'wardliness**. — *adv* **untoward'ly** or **unto'wardly**. — *adj* untoward. — *n* **untoward'ness** or **unto'wardness**. — *vt* **untrace'** to loose from traces. — *adj* **untrace'able** impossible to trace. — *adj* **untraced'** not traced or found. — *adj* **untrā'ded** unfrequented, *specif* for trade (*obs*); unhackneyed (*Shakesp*). — *vt* **untread'** (*Shakesp*) to tread back, to retrace. — *vt* **untreas'ure** to despoil (of treasure). — *adj* **untreat'able** that cannot be treated; intractable (*obs*). — *adj* **untreat'ed**. — *adj* **untressed'** not dressed or arranged in tresses. — *adj* **untried'** not tried, tested, attempted, experienced or subjected to trial in court; (*Shakesp*, **untride'**) *prob* not ventured upon, hence not noticed or dealt with. — *vt* **untrim'** to deprive of trimming or trimness. — *adj* **untrimmed'** not trimmed. — *adj* **untrodd'en** or (*archaic*) **untrod'** not trodden upon; unfrequented. — *adj* **untroub'led** not troubled or disturbed; not turbid. — *adv* **untroub'ledly**. — *adj* **untrue'** not true; false; not faithful; dishonest; inexact; not in accordance with a standard. — *adv* (*Shakesp*) untruly, untruthfully. — *n* **untrue'ness**. — *n* **untru'ism** an untrue platitude. — *adv* **untru'ly** falsely. — *vt* **untruss'** to unpack; to unfasten; to untie (*esp* the points or laces on clothes; *hist*); to untie the points of (*hist*). — *adj* **untrussed'** or **untrust'** not trussed; untied; with points untied (*hist*). — *n* **untruss'er**. — *n* **untruss'ing**. — *n* **untrust'** distrust. — *adj* **untrust'ful** not trusting; not trustworthy; not to be trusted. — *n* **untrust'iness** (*obs*). — *adv* **untrust'worthily**. — *n* **untrust'worthiness**. — *adj* **untrust'worthy** not worthy of trust. — *adj* **untrust'y** not trusty, not deserving trust. — *n* **untruth'** falseness; falsity; that which is untrue; a lie; unfaithfulness. — *adj* **untruth'ful** not truthful. — *adv* **untruth'fully**. — *n* **untruth'fulness**. — *vt* **untuck'** to unfold or undo from being tucked up or in; to take out tucks from. — *adj* **untucked'** not tucked up or in. — *adj* **untuck'ered** not having a tucker on. — *adj* **untūn'able** (also **untune'able**) harsh. — *n* **untūn'ableness**. — *adv* **untūn'ably**. — *vt* **untune'** to put out of tune. — *adj* **untuned'** not tuned; put out of tune. — *adj* **untune'ful** not tuneful or melodious. — *adv* **untune'fully**. — *n* **untune'fulness**. — *vt* **unturf'** to strip of turf. — *vt* **unturn'** to turn backwards. — *adj* **unturn'able**. — *adj* **unturned'** not turned. — *adj* **unturn'ing**. — *adj* **untū'tored** untaught; uninstructed. — *vt* and *vi* **untwine'** to untwist; to separate by untwisting. — *vt* and *vi* **untwist'** to twist backwards so as to open out; to straighten out from a twist. — *adj* **untwist'ed** not twisted; subjected to untwisting. — *n* **untwist'ing**. — *adj* **unty'pable** that cannot be defined as a particular type.

Words starting with **u-** *and* **v-**, *prefixed by* **un-**.
adj **unused** (*un-ūzd'*) not used; (also *un-ūst'*) unaccustomed; unusual (*archaic*). — *adj* **unuseful** (*-ūs'*). — *adv* **unuse'fully**. — *n* **unuse'fulness**. — *adj* **unūs'ual** not usual; uncommon; remarkable. — *adv* **unūs'ually** more than usually; in an unusual way. — *n* **unūs'ualness**. — *adj* **unutt'erable** beyond utterance, inexpressible; not to be uttered. — *n* an unutterable thing; (in *pl*) trousers (*old slang*). — *adv* **unutt'erably**. — *adj* **unutt'ered**. — *adj* **unval'uable** not valuable, of little worth; invaluable, priceless (*obs*). — *adj* **unval'ued** not prized or highly esteemed; without having a value assigned; invaluable, priceless (now *rare*). — *adj* **unvar'nished** not varnished; not artfully embellished or sophisticated. — *vt* **unveil'** (*obs* **unvail'** or **unvaile'**) to remove or set aside a veil

Some words with **un-** prefix; see **un-** entry for numbered senses.

untrenched' *adj* (1).
untres'passing *adj* (1).
untum'bled *adj* (1).
untumult'uous *adj* (1).
untur'bid *adj* (1).
unty'ing *n* (2).
untyp'ical *adj* (1).
ununderstand'able *adj* (1).
unuplift'ed *adj* (1).
unurged' *adj* (1).
unū'sable *adj* (1).
unū'sably *adv* (1).
unush'ered *adj* (1).
unū'tilized or **-s-** *adj* (1).
unvac'cinated *adj* (1).
unvan'quishable *adj* (1).
unvan'quished *adj* (1).
unvā'riable *adj* (1).
unvā'ried *adj* (1).
unvā'riegated *adj* (1).
unvā'rying *adj* (1).
unvend'ible *adj* (1).
unven'erable *adj* (1).
unvent'ilated *adj* (1).
unver'ifiable *adj* (1).
unverifiabil'ity *n* (1).
unver'ified *adj* (1).
unvett'ed *adj* (1).
unvexed' *adj* (1).
unvī'able *adj* (1).
unviewed' *adj* (1).
unvī'olated *adj* (1).
unvī'tal *adj* (1).
unvi'tiated *adj* (1).
unvit'rifiable *adj* (1).
unvit'rified *adj* (1).
unvō'cal *adj* (1).
unvō'calized or **-s-** *adj* (1).
unvul'nerable (*Shakesp*) *adj* (1).
unwaked' *adj* (1).
unwāk'ened *adj* (1).
unwalled' *adj* (1).
unwand'ering *adj* (1).
unwant'ed *adj* (1).
unward'ed *adj* (1).
unwar'like *adj* (1).
unwarmed' *adj* (1).
unwarned' *adj* (1).
unwarped' *adj* (1).
unwāst'ed *adj* (1).
unwāst'ing *adj* (1).
unwatched' *adj* (1).
unwatch'ful *adj* (1).
unwatch'fully *adv* (1).
unwatch'fulness *n* (1).
unwā'vering *adj* (1).
unwā'veringly *adv* (1).
unweakened (*-wēk'*) *adj* (1).
unweaned' *adj* (1).
unwearable (*-wār'*) *adj* (1).
unweariable (*-wē'*) *adj* (1).
unwea'riably *adv* (1).
unwea'ried *adj* (1).
unwea'riedly *adv* (1).
unwea'ry *adj* (1).
unwea'rying *adj* (1).
unwea'ryingly *adv* (1).
unwebbed' *adj* (1).
unwed' *adj* (1).
unwedd'ed *adj* (1).
unweed'ed *adj* (1).
unwel'come *adj* (1).
unwel'comed *adj* (1).
unwel'comely *adv* (1).
unwel'comeness *n* (1).
unwet' *adj* (1).
unwett'ed *adj* (1).
unwhipped' (*obs* **unwhipt'**) *adj* (1).
unwhis'tleable *adj* (1).
unwife'like *adj* (1).
unwife'ly *adj* (1).

from; to open to public view by the ceremonial removal of a covering; to disclose or reveal. — *vi* to remove one's veil; to become unveiled, to reveal oneself. — *adj* **unveiled'** without a veil; with veil set aside or removed; unconcealed and undisguised. — *n* **unveil'er**. — *n* **unveil'ing** the ceremonial removal of a covering. — *adj* **unvent'ed** not vented; without a vent. — *adj* **unverā'cious** not truthful. — *n* **unverac'ity**. — *adj* **unversed'** not experienced or skilled; not put in verse. — *n* **unvir'tue** lack of virtue. — *adj* **unvir'tuous**. — *adv* **unvir'tuously**. — *adj* **unvis'itable** unfit to be visited; unsuitable for visiting; unable to visit (*obs*). — *adj* **unvis'ited**. — *vt* **unvīs'or** or **unviz'ard** to remove or open the visor of. — *vi* to unvisor oneself; to unmask. — *vt* **unvoice'** to change to, or utter with, a voiceless sound. — *adj* **unvoiced'** not spoken or expressed; without voice; (of a speech sound) voiceless, uttered with the breath rather than with vibration of the vocal cords (*phonetics*). — *n* **unvoic'ing** change to a voiceless sound. — *adj* **unvoy'ageable** not navigable, impassable. — *adj* **unvul'gar**. — *vt* **unvul'garize** or **-ise** to free from vulgarity.

Words starting with **w-**, **y-** *and* **z-**, *prefixed by* **un-**.
adj **unwaged'** not given wages; unpaid; unemployed. — *adj* **unware'** (OE *unwær*) unwary (*obs*); unaware, without knowing (*Spenser* and *Milton*) unexpected (*obs*). — *adv* unknowingly; unexpectedly. — *adv* **unware'ly** unwarily (*obs*); suddenly, unexpectedly (*Spenser*). — *n* **unware'ness** (*archaic*) unwariness. — *adv* **unwares'** (*archaic*) unawares; unexpectedly, suddenly; unknowingly (*Shakesp*). — *adv* **unwā'rily**. — *n* **unwā'riness**. — *adj* **unwarr'antable** not justifiable. — *adv* **unwarr'antably**. — *adj* **unwarr'anted** not justified or deserved. — *adv* **unwarr'antedly**. — *adj* **unwā'ry** not wary; not aware of danger; (*Spenser* **unwarie**) unexpected. — *adj* **unwashed'** or (*Bible*) **unwash'en** (**the great unwashed** see under **great**). — *vt* **unwa'ter** to drain (*esp* a mine). — *adj* **unwa'tered** freed from water; not watered. — *adj* **unwa'tery**. — *adj* **unwayed'** (*obs*) not accustomed to roads; (hence) intractable. — *n* **unweal'** (*obs*) affliction, ill. — *vt* **unweap'on** to disarm. — *adj* **unweap'oned** unarmed; disarmed. — *adj* **unweath'ered** not worn by the weather or atmospheric agencies. — *vt* **unweave'** to undo from being woven. — *adj* **unwedge'able** (*Shakesp* **unwedg'able**) unable to be split with wedges. — *adj* **unweened'** (*archaic*) unexpected. — *adj* **unweet'ing** (*archaic*) unwitting. — *adv* **unweet'ingly** (*archaic*) unwittingly. — *adj* **unweighed'** not weighed; not pondered; unguarded. — *adj* **unweigh'ing** (*Shakesp*) thoughtless, inconsiderate. — *adj* **unwell'** in poor health; mildly sick, indisposed. — *n* **unwell'ness**. — *adj* **unwept'** not wept for; (of tears) not shed. — *adj* **unwhole'some** not wholesome; unsound; tainted in health, taste or morals. — *adv* **unwhole'somely**. — *n* **unwhole'someness**. — *adv* **unwiel'dily**. — *n* **unwiel'diness**. — *adj* **unwiel'dy** (*Spenser* etc, **unwel'dy**) difficult to wield or move, from bulk or weakness; heavily awkward; unmanageable. — *vt* **unwill'** to will the contrary of; to deprive of will. — *adj* **unwilled'** not willed; involuntary. — *adj* **unwill'ing** reluctant; done reluctantly; not willed, unintentional (*Shakesp*). — *adv* **unwill'ingly**. — *n* **unwill'ingness**. — *vt* **unwind** (*un-wīnd'*) to undo the winding of; to free from being wound; to wind down or off; to slacken; to relax (*colloq*). — *vi* to become unwound; to relax (*colloq*): — *pa t* and *pa p* **unwound** (*un-wownd'*). — *adj* not wound; released from being wound. — *n* and *adj* **unwind'ing** uncoiling. — *adj* not winding. — *vt* **unwire'** to take the wire from. — *n* **unwis'dom** lack of wisdom; foolishness; injudiciousness. — *adj* **unwise'** not wise; injudicious; foolish. — *adv* **unwise'ly**. — *n* **unwise'ness**. — *vt* **unwish'** (*Shakesp*) to wish to be away, not to be, to be unfulfilled or to be undone. — *adj* **unwished'** (or **unwished'-for**) not wished for. — *adj* **unwish'ful**. — *adj* **unwish'ing**. — *adj* **unwist'** not known (*archaic*; *Spenser*, etc); unknowing (*Spenser*). — *vt* **unwit'** (*Shakesp*) to deprive of wits. — *adj* **unwitch'** to free from witchcraft. — *adj* **unwithdraw'ing** liberal, lavish. — *adj* **unwithhold'en** (*Coleridge*) not held back, not restrained. — *adj* **unwithhold'ing** not holding back. — *adv* **unwitt'ily**. — *adj* **unwitt'ing** without knowing; unaware; not cognizant; unintentional. — *adv* **unwitt'ingly**. — *n* **unwitt'ingness**. — *adj* **unwitt'y** foolish; without wit; unskilled (*archaic*). — *vt* **unwive'** to deprive of a wife. — *adj* **unwived'** without a wife. — *vt* **unwo'man** to make unwomanly. — *n* **unwo'manliness**. — *adj* **unwo'manly** not befitting a woman; not such as a woman is expected to be. — *adv* in an unwomanly manner. — *adj* **unwont'** (now *rare*; *Spenser*, etc) or **unwont'ed** unaccustomed; unusual. — *adv* **unwont'edly**. — *n* **unwont'edness**. — *adj* **unword'ed** speechless; not expressed in words. — *vt* **unwork'** to undo. — *adj* **unwork'able** not workable; impracticable. — *adj* **unworked'** not shaped or moulded; not mined, not exploited. — *adj* **unwork'ing**. — *adj* **unwork'manlike** not like or worthy of a good workman. — *n* **unworld'liness**. — *adj* **unworld'ly** not of this world; spiritual; naive; above worldly or self-interested motives. — *adj* **unwormed'** not worm-eaten; (of a dog) not having had the worm or lytta cut out from the tongue. — *n* **unworth'** lack of worth. — *adj* unworthy. — *adv* **unwor'thily**. — *n* **unwor'thiness**. — *adj* **unwor'thy** not worthy; worthless; unbecoming; discreditable; undeserved. — *adj* **unwound** see **unwind**. — *vt* **unwrap** (*un-rap'*) to remove wrappings from; to unroll, unwind. — *vi* to become unwrapped. — *adj* **unwreaked** (*un-rēkt'*) unrevenged. — *vt* **unwreathe** (*un-rēdh'*) to take out of a wreathed condition. — *vt* and *vi* **unwrink'le** to smooth out from a wrinkled state. — *adj* **unwrink'led** not wrinkled, smooth. — *vt* **unwrite'** to undo the writing of. — *adj* **unwrīt'ing** not writing. — *adj* **unwritt'en** not written or reduced to writing, oral; (of a rule, law, etc) traditional, generally accepted; containing no writing. — *adj* **unwrought** (*un-röt'*) not done or worked; not fashioned, formed, composed or worked up; not mined; not tilled; undone, brought back to an original state. — *adj* **unyeaned'** (*dialect*) unborn. — *adj* **unyiel'ding** not yielding; stiff; obstinate. — *adv* **unyiel'dingly**. — *n* **unyiel'dingness**. — *vt* **unyoke'** to loose from a yoke or harness; to set free; to disjoin. — *vi* to unyoke an animal; to cease work. — *adj* **unyoked'** not yoked or harnessed; freed from yoke or harness; unrestrained (*Shakesp*). — *adj* **unzoned'** not in or divided into zones; ungirt.

una corda *ūn'ə kör'də* or *o͞on'ä kör'dä*, (*Ital music*) one string (an indication to pianists to use the soft pedal).

unalist *ū'nəl-ist*, (*eccles*) *n* a holder of one benefice. [L *ūnus* one]

unanimous *ū-nan'i-məs*, *adj* of one mind; without any-one's dissenting. — *n* **unanimity** (*ū-nən-im'i-ti*) agree-

Some words with **un-** prefix; see **un-** entry for numbered senses.

unwigged' *adj* (1).	**unwithheld'** *adj* (1).	**unwor'shipful** *adj* (1).
unwil'ful *adj* (1).	**unwithstood'** *adj* (1).	**unwor'shipped** *adj* (1).
unwinged' *adj* (1).	**unwit'nessed** *adj* (1).	**unwoundable** (*-wo͞ond'*) *adj* (1).
unwink'ing *adj* (1).	**unwon'** *adj* (1).	**unwound'ed** *adj* (1).
unwink'ingly *adv* (1).	**unwood'ed** *adj* (1).	**unwō'ven** *adj* (1).
unwinn'owed *adj* (1).	**unwooed'** *adj* (1).	**unwrung'** *adj* (1).
unwiped' *adj* (1).	**unworn'** *adj* (1).	**unzeal'ous** *adj* (1).
unwith'ered *adj* (1).	**unworr'ied** *adj* (1).	**unzip'** *vt* (2).
unwith'ering *adj* (1).		

ment without anyone's dissenting. — *adj* **unan'imously**. [L *ūnanimus*, from *ūnus* one, and *animus* mind]

unau *ū'nö* or *o͞o'now*, *n* the two-toed sloth. [Fr, from Tupí]

una voce *ūn'ə vō'sē* or *o͞on'ä wō'ke*, (*L*) with one voice, by general consent.

unberufen *o͞on-bə-ro͞of'ən*, (*Ger*) *adj* not called for, used as an exclamation to avert the ill-luck that may possibly follow an over-confident or boastful statement.

uncate. See under **uncus**.

unce *uns*, *n*. Scots form of **ounce**.

uncial *un'shəl* or *-si-əl*, *adj* denoting, or executed in, a form of writing found in Greek and Latin manuscripts of the 3c to the 9c, using majuscule letters of rounded form; pertaining to an inch or an ounce. — *n* an uncial letter; uncial writing; a manuscript written in uncials. [L *unciālis*, from *uncia* a twelfth; meaning with reference to lettering disputed, poss 'an inch high' or perh an error for *uncīnālis* hooked]

UNA *abbrev*: United Nations Association.

unciform, **uncinate**, etc. See under **uncus**.

uncle *ung'kl*, *n* the brother of one's father or mother, or an aunt's husband, or a great-uncle (used with *cap* as a title, either before a man's first name or independently); used as a form of address to an elderly man, *esp* a Black (chiefly *US*); a pawnbroker (*slang*); (with *cap*) a title sometimes used by children for male friends of their parents. — *vt* to address as uncle. — *n* **un'cleship** the state of being an uncle. — *adj* **uncle** (or **Uncle**) **Dick** (*Cockney rhyming slang*) sick. — **Uncle Sam** the United States or its people; **Uncle Tom** (*US derog*) a black American whose co-operative attitude to white people is thought to show disloyalty to Blacks (based on the hero of Harriet Beecher-Stowe's *Uncle Tom's Cabin*). [OFr *uncle* (Fr *oncle*), from L *avunculus* a maternal uncle]

unco *ung'kə*, *-kō*, (*Scot*) *adj* strange, unusual; fearsome; remarkable; great. — *n* a stranger; a piece of news; a remarkable thing: — *pl* **un'cos**. — *adv* remarkably, very. — **unco guid** (*gid*) the obtrusively rigorous in morals. [**uncouth**]

uncouth. See **un-**.

UNCSTD *abbrev*: United Nations Conference on Science and Technology for Development.

UNCTAD *ungk'tad*, *abbrev*: United Nations Conference on Trade and Development.

unction *ungk'shən*, *n* an anointing; that which is used for anointing; ointment; that quality in language which raises emotion or devotion; warmth of address; religious glibness; divine or sanctifying grace; gusto. — *n* **unctūos'ity** unctuousness. — *adj* **unc'tūous** oily; greasy; full of unction; offensively suave and smug. — *adv* **unc'tūously**. — *n* **unc'tūousness**. — **extreme unction** (*RC*) the sacrament of anointing a dying person with consecrated oil. [L *unctiō*, *-ōnis* unction, besmearing, *ūnctum* fat]

uncus *ung'kəs*, *n* a hook or hook-like process: — *pl* **unci** (*un'sī*). — *adj* **unc'ate** hooked. — *adj* **unciform** (*un'si-förm*) hook-shaped. — *adj* **un'cinate** or **un'cinated** unciform; hooked at the end. — *n* **uncī'nus** (*zool*) a hooklet; a marginal tooth of a mollusc's radula; a hooked chaeta in annelids: — *pl* **uncī'nī**. [L *uncus* and *uncinus* hook]

undated[1] *un'dā-tid* or **un'dāte** *adj* wavy. [L *unda* a wave]

undated[2]. See under **un-**.

undé, **unde**. See **undee**.

undecimal *un-des'i-məl*, *adj* based on the number eleven. — *n* **undec'imole** (*music*) a group of eleven notes in the time of eight. [L *undecim* eleven, from *ūnus* one, and *decem* ten]

undee, **undée**, **undé** or **unde** *un'dā*, (*heraldry*) *adj* wavy. [Fr *ondé*; cf **oundy**, **undate**]

under *un'dər*, *prep* beneath; below; in or to a position lower than that of, *esp* vertically lower; at the foot of; within, on the covered side of; short of; in or into subjection, subordination, obligation, liability, etc, to; in course of; in the state of; (of cultivated land) supporting a specified crop; by the authority or attestation of; in accordance with; in the aspect of; referred to the class, heading, name, etc, of; in the reign or administration of; within the influence of (a particular sign of the zodiac). — *adv* in or to a lower (*esp* vertically lower) position; in or into a lower degree or condition; in or into subjection; in or into a covered, submerged or hidden state; in a state of unconsciousness (*colloq*); below; under par (*golf*). — *adj* lower; subordinate; falling short. — *n* **un'derling** a contemptuous word for a subordinate; a weakling (*archaic*). — *adj* **un'dermost** lowest; inmost. — *adv* in or to the undermost place. — **under-and-over** see **over-and-under** under **over**. — **go**, **knock** or **snow under** see **go**[1], **knock**, **snow**[1]; **under age**, **arms**, or **canvas**, etc see **age**, **arm**, **canvas**; **under starter's orders** (of racehorses) about to be released by the starter at the beginning of a race; ready to start (*fig*); **under the counter** see under **count**[2]; **under the lee** to the leeward. [OE *under*; Gothic *undar*, ON *undir*, Ger *unter*, L *infrā*]

Words with the prefix **under-** are listed in the following text or in the separate panel.

under- *un-dər-*, *pfx* signifying: (1) below, beneath; (2) lower in physical position; (3) lower in rank, or subordinate; (4a) too little in quantity, too small, insufficient; (4b) in too small a degree, insufficiently; (5) not coming, or not allowed to come, to the surface or into the open. — *vi* **underachieve'** to achieve less than one's potential or less than expected, *esp* academically. — *n* **underachieve'ment**. — *n* **underachiev'er**. — *vt* and *vi* **underact'** to make too little of (one's part, etc) in acting; to play for the sake of effect, with little emphasis. — *n* **underac'tion** subordinate action; less than normal or adequate action. — *n* **underact'or**. — *adj* **under-age'** (done, participated in, etc, by someone) not yet of full, or the required, age; immature. — *n* **underā'gent** a subordinate agent. — *adj* and *adv* **un'derarm** placed or held under the arm; with the arm kept below the shoulder. — *vt* **underbear'** (*Shakesp*) to sustain; (*pa p* **underborne'** *Shakesp*) *perh* to trim (on the

Some words with **under-** prefix; see **under-** entry for numbered senses.

underbud'get *vt* and *vi* (4b).
undercapitalizā'tion or -s- *n* (4a).
undercap'italized or -s- *adj* (4a).
undercon'sciousness *n* (5).
un'der-constable *n* (3).
un'derdeck *n* (2).
underfish' *vt* (4b).
underfulfil' *vt* (4b).
un'derfloor *adj* (1).
un'dergown *n* (1).
undergrown' *adj* (4b).
un'der-hangman *n* (3).
un'derkeeper *n* (3).
un'derking *n* (3).
un'derkingdom *n* (3).
un'dermeaning *n* (5).
un'dernamed *adj* (1).
underpaid' *adj* (4b).
un'derpart *n* (1).
underpreparā'tion *n* (4b).
underprepared' *adj* (4b).
underprop' *vt* (1).
un'der-shepherd *n* (3).
un'dersheriff *n* (3).
un'dersleeve *n* (1).
un'dersoil *n* (2).
un'dersupply *n* (4a) and *vt* (4b).
un'dersurface *n* (1).
un'derten'ancy *n* (3).
un'dertenant *n* (3).
un'der-tū'nic *n* (1).
underuse (-*ūz'*) *vt* (4b).
underuse (-*ūs'*) *n* (4a).
underutilizā'tion or -s- *n* (4a).
underū'tilize or -ise *vt* (4b).
underū'tilized or -s- *adj* (4b).

lower part), *perh* to line or support by a foundation, *perh* to have sewn underneath or on strips of tinsel. — *n* **un'derbearer** (*dialect*) someone who helps to carry a coffin. — *n* **underbear'ing**. — *adj* unassuming. — *n* **un'derbelly** the under surface of a body or of something suggesting a body; (also **soft underbelly**) the vulnerable part or spot; the hidden or little-known side of something. — *vt* **underbid'** to offer a lower bid than; to offer at a price lower than that of; to outbid; to bid less than the value of (*bridge*). — *vi* to bid unduly low. — *n* (*bridge*) a bid too low to be valid, or less than the hand is worth. — *n* **underbidd'er** someone who underbids; the next below the highest bidder. — *vt* **underbite'** to bite insufficiently with acid, as in etching. — *adj* **underbitt'en**. — **un'derblanket** a blanket of a warm material placed under, rather than over, a person in bed. — *adv* **un'der-board** (*obs*) secretly, under the table, *opp* to *above-board*. — *adj* **un'der-bonnet** relating to the engine of a motor vehicle, generally to be found under the bonnet. — *adj* **underborne** see **underbear** above. — *n* **un'derbough** a lower branch. — *n* **un'der-boy** a boy in the lower or more junior part of a school. — *n* **un'derbreath** a subdued voice; rumour. — *adj* **under-bred'** of inferior breeding or manners; not pure-bred. — *n* **un'derbridge** a bridge carrying a road or railway as opposed to a bridge over one. — *n* **un'derbrush** undergrowth of brushwood or shrubs. — *vt* to clear of underbrush. — *vt* **underbuild'** to build under in support, to underpin; to build too little upon or in. — *n* **un'derbuilder** a subordinate or assistant builder. — *adj* **un'derburnt** insufficiently burnt. — *n* and *vt* **un'derbush** same as **underbrush**. — *vt* **underbuy'** to buy less of than the amount required; to buy at less than the price paid by, or the value of. — *n* **un'dercard** (*boxing*) a programme of matches supporting the main event. — *n* **un'dercarriage** the supporting framework under the body of a carriage or vehicle; the landing-gear of an aircraft, or its main part. — *n* **un'dercart** (*colloq*) an aircraft's landing-gear, the undercarriage. — *n* **un'dercast** an air-passage crossing under a road in a mine. — *n* **un'dercharge** too small a charge. — *vt* **undercharge'** to charge too little, or too little for. — *adj* **underclad'** not wearing enough clothes. — *n* **un'derclay** a bed of clay underlying a coal-seam representing the soil in which the plants grew. — *n* **un'derclass** (*US*) a low, or the lowest, social class. — *n* **underclass'man** (*US*) a sophomore or freshman. — *n* **un'der-clerk** a subordinate clerk. — *n* **un'der-clerk'ship**. — *n* **un'dercliff** a terrace of material that has fallen from a cliff. — *vt* **un'derclothe** (*rare*) to provide with underclothing. — *adj* **un'derclothed** provided with or wearing underclothing; (*-klōdhd'*) underclad, not wearing enough clothing. — *n pl* **un'derclothes** and *n sing* **un'derclothing** clothes worn under others, *esp* those next to the skin. — *vt* **underclub'** (*golf*) to hit with a club which has too great loft to achieve the desired distance. — Also *vi*. — *n* **un'dercoat** a coat worn under another; an underlayer of fur or hair, or of paint; an underskirt (*obs*). — *vt* **undercook'** to cook insufficiently or to a lesser extent than usual. — *vt* **un'dercool** to supercool; to cool insufficiently. — *n* **un'der-countenance** (*Wordsworth*) that which underlies the superficial aspect of the face. — *adj* **un'dercover** working or done in secret (**under cover of** hidden by, using as concealment). — *n* **un'dercovert** a covert of undergrowth. — *n* **un'der-craft** (*Sterne*) a sly trick. — *vt* **undercrest'** (*Shakesp*) to bear like a crest. — *n* **un'dercroft** (cf Du *krocht* crypt) a crypt or vault. — *n* **un'dercurrent** a current under the surface (*lit* and *fig*). — *adj* running below or unseen. — *vt* **undercut'** to cut under; to cut away under the surface, so as to leave part overhanging; to undermine; to strike with a heavy blow upward; to underbid; to offer at a lower price than. — *adj* made so as to cut from the underside; done by undercutting; having the parts in relief cut under. — *n* (*un'*) the act or effect of cutting under; a blow dealt upward; the tenderloin, or fillet, or underside of a sirloin. — *n* **un'derdamper** (*music*) in a type of upright piano, a damper positioned below the hammers. — *vt* **underdevel'op**. — *adj* **underdevel'oped** insufficiently developed; (of a country) with resources inadequately used, having a low standard of living and education. — *n* **underdevel'opment**. — *vt* **underdo'** to do, perform, act or *esp* cook insufficiently or inadequately: — *pa t* **underdid'**; *pa p* **underdone'**. — *n* **underdo'er**. — *n* **un'derdog** the dog that gets the worst of it in a fight; anyone in adversity; a person dominated, or being or likely to be beaten, by another. — *adj* **underdone'** done less than is necessary; insufficiently or slightly cooked. — *vt* **underdrain'** to drain by deep underground ditches. — *vt* **un'derdraw'** to draw or describe with moderation or reticence or short of the truth; to cover the underside of with boards or lath and plaster. — *n* **un'derdrawing** an outline drawing on a canvas, etc, done before paint is applied. — *n* **un'derdress** underclothing; a dress or part of a dress worn or showing under another. — *vt* and *vi* **underdress'** to dress too plainly or simply. — *adj* **underdressed'**. — *n* **un'derdrive** a gear which transmits to the driving shaft a speed less than engine speed. — *adj* **under-driv'en** driven from beneath. — *adj* **un'derearth** underground. — *n* **underemploy'ment** insufficient use (with *of*); the condition of having too large a part of the labour force unemployed; partial employment, or employment on work requiring less skill than the worker has. — *n* **un'der-espi'al** a subordinate spy (*Scott*). — *vt* **underes'timate** to estimate or value too low. — *n* an estimate that falls short of the truth or true quantity. — *n* **underestimā'tion**. — *vt* **underexpose'** to expose too little, *esp* (*photog*) to light. — *n* **underexpōs'ure**. — *adj* **underfed'** insufficiently fed. — *vt* and *vi* **underfeed'** to give too little food. — *n* **un'derfelt** an older term for an underlay, *usu* of felt. — *adj* **underfin'ished** (of cattle and sheep) having too little finish (qv). — *vt* **un'derfire'** to fire or bake insufficiently. — *n* **un'der-five'** a child less than five years old — *n* **un'derflow** an undercurrent. — *adv* **underfoot'** beneath one's feet; in the way; in a downtrodden manner. — *vt* to underpin. — *adj* (*un'*) downtrodden. — *vt* **underfund'** to provide with insufficient funds. — *n* **underfund'ing**. — *n* **un'derfur** short fur hidden by longer hairs. — *n* **un'dergarment** any article of clothing worn under another, *esp* that worn next to the skin, underclothing. — *vt* **undergird'** to brace with ropes under the bottom; to support (*fig*). — *adj* **un'derglaze** applied or done before glazing (such as *underglaze painting* in a vitrifiable pigment before the glaze is applied). — *n* **undergrad'uate** a student who has not taken any degree (*colloq* contraction **un'dergrad**). — *adj* pertaining to such a student. — *n* **undergrad'uateship**. — *n* **undergraduette'** (*old colloq*) a female undergraduate. — *adj* **un'derground** under the surface of the ground; (of a railway) running through underground tunnels; secret; characterized by avant-gardism and experimentation, rejection of current trends or norms, appeal to a minority, anti-establishment tendencies, etc. — *n* the underworld; an underground place; an underground railway; underlying ground; low ground; a secret resistance movement, or body of people; a group whose activities are partly concerned with resisting things they disapprove of in social, artistic and political life. — *adv* **underground'** beneath the surface of the earth; secretly. — *n* **un'dergrove** a grove of low trees under taller trees. — *n* **un'dergrowth** low plants growing under taller ones, *esp* shrubs under trees; stunted growth. — *adv* **underhand'** surreptitiously; with the hand kept below the elbow or shoulder. — *adj* **un'derhand** surreptitious, secret; not straightforward; delivered underhand; unobtrusive (*Shakesp*). — *n* an underhand ball; (with **the**) a subordinate position. — *adj* and *adv* **underhan'ded** underhand; short of workers. — *adv* **underhan'dedly**. — *n* **underhan'dedness**. — *adj* **underhon'est** (*Shakesp*) not quite honest. — *adj* **underhung'** (or *un'*) (of a lower jaw) protruding; having a protruding lower jaw; running on rollers on a rail below. — *n* **under-jaw'** the lower jaw. — *adj* **un'derjawed** with a heavy or underhung under-jaw. — *vt* **underkeep'** (*Spenser*) to keep under or in subjection. — *adj* **underlaid** see **underlay**. — *adj* **underlain** see **underlie**. — *vt* **underlap'** to extend beneath and some way beyond the edge of. — *vt* **underlay'** to support or provide with something laid under; to lay under; to put down, surpass (*Spenser*); often erroneously for **underlie**, of which it is the *pa t*. — *vi* (*mining*) to slope away from the vertical, to hade: — *pa t* and *pa p* **underlaid'**. — *n* (*un'*) something laid under, eg felt or rubber to help preserve a carpet, or (*printing*) a piece of paper, etc, pasted under to bring to type-height. — *n* **underlay'er** someone who underlays; (*un'*) a lower layer, substratum. — *n* **un'derlease** a sublease. — *vt* and *vi* (*-lēs'*) to sublease. — *vt* **underlet'** to let below the full value; (also *vi*) to sublet. — *n* **underlett'er**. — *n* **underlett'ing**. — *vt* **underlie'** to lie beneath (*lit* and *fig*); to undergo; to be subject or liable to: — *pr p* **underly'ing**; *pa t* **underlay'**; *pa p* **underlain'**. — *n* (*mining*) a hade, a slope away from the vertical. — *vt* **underline'** to draw a line under; to stress. — *n* (*un'*) a caption, legend; a line drawn under a word. — *n* **un'derlinen** (*archaic*) underclothing, properly of linen. — *n* **un'derling** see at **under**. — *n* **un'derlip** a lower lip. — *n* **un'derlooker** a mine manager's assistant. — *adj* **underly'ing** lying beneath (*lit* and *fig*); fundamental; present though not immediately obvious. — *n* **un'derman** an inferior; a subordinate; a man subjected to adverse conditions. — *vt* (*-man'*) to supply or man with too few workers. — *adj* **undermanned'**. — *adj* **undermast'ed** with too small masts. — *adj* **undermen'tioned** mentioned underneath or hereafter. — *vt* **undermine'** (*Spenser* **underminde'**) to dig beneath (eg a wall) in order to make it fall; to wash away or remove by burrowing, etc, the ground from under; to weaken gradually or insidiously; to intrigue against; to tamper with the fidelity of. — *n* **undermī'ner**. — *n* **undermī'ning**. — *n* **un'dernice'ness** lack of niceness or delicacy. — *n* **un'dernote** a subdued note; an undertone; a note added below. — *vt* to note below. — *adj* **un'dernoted**. — *adj* **undernour'ished** living on less food than is necessary for satisfactory health and growth (also *fig*). — *n* **undernour'ishment**. — *n* **underpaint'ing** the first layer of painting, when the design is set out. — *n pl* **un'derpants** an undergarment worn by men and boys, covering the buttocks and sometimes the legs. — *n* **un'derpass** a road passing under another road or a railway, etc. — *n* **un'derpassion** an underlying or subconscious passion. — *vt* and *vi* **un'derpay** to pay less than required or deserved. — *n* **underpay'ment**. — *vt* **underpeep'** (*Shakesp*) to peep under. — *adj* **underpeo'pled** not sufficiently populated. — *vi* **underperform'** to do less well than expected or thought possible, etc. — *vt* **underpin'** to support by building underneath, or to prop up (also *fig*); to corroborate. — *n* **underpinn'ing**. — *vt* **underplant'** to plant smaller plants in between (trees or taller plants). — *vi* **underplay'** to play a low card while holding a higher of the same suit. — *vt* to play down, understate. — *vt* and *vi* to underact. — *n* (*un'*) the strategem of underplaying (*cards*). — *n* **un'derplot** a subordinate plot in a play or tale; a secret scheme, a trick. — *adj* **underpop'ulated** having too small a population, insufficient to exploit the land. — *n* **un'der-power** (*Wordsworth*) an auxiliary power. — *adj* **underpow'ered** insufficiently or not fully powered. — *vt* **underpraise'** to praise below what is deserved. — *adj* **underpriced'** having too low a price. — *adj* **under=priv'ileged** not enjoying normal social and economic rights. — Also *n*. — *vt* **underprize'** (*obs* **underprise'**) to value too little; to underpraise (*Shakesp*). — *vt* and *vi* **under-produce'**. — *n* **under-produc'tion** too little production; production short of demand. — *adj* **under-proof'** (of alcohol) lower or weaker than proof. — *vt* **underquote'** to offer at a price lower than. — *vt* **underrate'** to rate too low. — *n* (*un'*) a price less than the worth. — *adj* (*Swift*) inferior. — *n* **under-representā'tion** too little representation; less representation than one is entitled to. — *adj* **under-represent'ed**. — *vt* and *vi* **un'der-ring** to ring up (an amount or total) less than the actual price on a till. — *n* an instance of under-ringing. — *adj* **un'der-ripe'** not quite ripe. — *n* **un'der-roof** (*Tennyson*) a roof under another. — *vt* **underrun'** to run or pass beneath; to take aboard on one side (eg a cable, line, or net for examination, clearing or baiting) and put overboard on the other. — *vi* to move under; to run on the underside. — *n* **underrunn'ing**. — *n* **un'der-saw'yer** a bottom-sawyer; an inferior, an unimportant person. — *vt* **undersay'** (*obs*; *Spenser* **undersaye'**) to say in answer or contradiction. — *n* **un'der-school** (*obs*) the lower or junior school. — *vt* **underscore'** to underline. — *n* **un'derscrub** brushwood. — *adj* and *adv* **undersea'** below the surface of the sea. — *vt* **underseal'** to coat exposed parts of the underside of (a motor vehicle) with corrosion-resisting substance. — Also *n* (*un'*). — *n* **underseal'ing**. — *n* **un'der-sec'retary** a secretary immediately under the principal secretary. — *n* **under-sec'retaryship**. — *n* **un'derself** the subconscious self. — *vt* **undersell'** to sell below the price charged by; to sell too cheap. — *n* **undersell'er**. — *n* **un'dersense** a deeper sense; a secondary sense; a subconscious awareness. — *n* **un'derset** an undercurrent; a lower vein of ore; a set of underclothing. — *vt* (*-set'*) to set under; to prop; to sublet (*obs*). — *adj* **undersexed'** having less than normal interest in sexual relations or sexual activity. — *adj* **un'dershapen** (*Tennyson*) imperfectly formed. — *n* **un'dershirt** (*US*) an undergarment worn under a shirt *usu* made of cotton jersey, a vest. — *vt* **undershoot'** to fail to reach by falling short (also *fig*). — *n* (*aeronautics*) a falling short of the mark in landing. — *n pl* **un'dershorts** (*NAm*) short underpants. — *adj* **un'dershot** driven by water passing under; having the lower jaw projecting, underhung. — *n* **un'dershrub** a shrubby plant or a low shrub. — *n* **un'derside** the lower or under surface. —*vt* **undersign'** to sign below. — *adj* **un'dersigned** (or *-sīnd'*) whose signature is appended. — *adj* **un'dersized** below the usual or desired size. — *n* **un'derskinker** (*Shakesp*) an assistant tapster. — *n* **un'derskirt** a petticoat; a foundation for a dress or skirt. — *n* **un'dersky** (*poetic*) a lower sky. — *adj* **underslung'** suspended, or supported, from above, or hung so as to extend below a part which, in another arrangement, it might be wholly above; (of a vehicle chassis) extending below the axles. — *n* **un'dersong** (*archaic*) a burden or refrain, etc of song or of sound; an undertone less pleasant in quality (*fig*). — *vi* and *vt* **underspend'** to spend less than one could or should of (eg a budget). — *n* the amount left unspent from an allocated budget, etc. — *adj* **understaffed'** having too few members of staff. — *vt* **understate'** to state more moderately than truth would allow or require; to state or describe, or to use artistically, without emphasis. — *adj* **understāt'ed** effective through simplicity, without embellishment or dramatic emphasis. — *n* **understate'ment** (or *un'*). — *n* **un'dersteer** a tendency in a motor vehicle to follow a wider curve than the turning applied by the steering wheel should cause it to follow. — Also *vi*. — *n* **un'derstock** (*archaic*) a stocking. — *vt* **understock'** to supply with an insufficient amount of stock. — *adj* **understood** see **understand** (separate entry). — *n* **un'derstorey** or (*rare*) **un'derstory** the smaller trees and bushes forming a lower level of cover beneath the tallest trees in a forest, etc. — *n* **un'derstrapper** an inferior agent, an underling. — *adj* **un'derstrapping** subordinate. — *n* **un'derstratum** an underlayer: — *pl* **un'derstrata**. — *vt* **un'derstudy** to study (a part), or to study the part of (an actor or other person) in order to take over in an emergency, or in due course. — Also *vi*. — *n* someone who understudies. — *n* **un'derthirst** (*Wordsworth*) an underlying or subconscious thirst. — *n* **un'derthrust** (*geol*) a fault in which one mass of rock is moved under another relatively static layer. — *adj* **undertimed'** (of a photograph) underexposed. — *n* **un'dertint** a subdued tint; a tint showing through. — *n* **un'dertone** a subdued tone of voice, sound, colour, etc; a tone felt as if pervading, underlying, or perceptible through others, including (*fig*) an emotional tone; a difference tone (qv); a low state of body. — *adj* **un'dertoned** in an undertone; (*-tond'*) lacking in tone. — *n* **un'dertow** (*-tō*) an undercurrent opposed to the surface current; the recoil or back-draught of a wave. — *n* **un'der-trick** (*bridge*) a trick short of the number declared. — *n* **under-turn'key** (*hist*) an assistant jailer. — *n* **undervaluā'tion**. — *vt* **underval'ue** to value below the real worth; to reduce the value of; to esteem too lightly; to rate as inferior (with *to*; *Shakesp*). — *n* (*un'*) a value or price under the real worth. — *n* **underval'uer**. — *n* **un'dervest** an undershirt, or a similar garment for a woman. — *n* **un'derviewer** an underlooker. — *n* **un'dervoice** a subdued voice. — *n* **un'derwater** underground water; undertow. — *adj* and (**underwa'ter**) *adv* (existing, acting, carried out, etc) below the surface of the water; below the waterline. — *n* **un'derwear** underclothing. — *n* **un'derweight** shortness of weight; short weight. — *adj* short in weight. — *vt* **underwhelm'** (*facetious*) to fail to impress. — *n* **un'derwing** a wing covered by another, such as an insect's hindwing; a moth (*Catocala*, etc) with conspicuous hindwings. — *adj* and *adv* (**underwing'**; of a bird or aircraft) under the wing. — *adj* **underwir'ed** (of a bra, etc) having shaping provided by a thin strip of light metal, etc, under each cup. — *n* **underwir'ing**. — *n* **un'derwit** inferior wit; a half-wit. — *n* **un'derwood** undergrowth; a coppice. — *vt* **underwork'** to undermine; to employ too little in work; to work for less than the wage of; to work secretly against (*obs*; *Shakesp pa t* **underwrought'**). — *vi* to do less work than is desirable. — *n* (*un'*) a substructure; underhand, inferior or subordinate work. — *n* **un'derworker**. — *n* **un'der-work'man**. — *n* **un'derworld** the world beneath the heavens; the world, or a region, beneath the earth; the place of departed souls; the part of the world below the horizon; the antipodes; a submerged, hidden or secret region or sphere of life, *esp* one given to crime, profligacy or intrigue. — *vt* **un'derwrite** to write (something) beneath; to subscribe to (a statement, etc); to accept the risk of insuring; to guarantee to take, or find others to take (certain shares, under certain conditions); to write too little about; (*reflexive*) to write below the level of which one is capable, not to do (oneself) justice; to sign one's name beneath (*obs*); to subscribe (one's name; *obs*); to agree to (*Shakesp*). — *vi* to practise as an underwriter. — *n* **un'derwriter** someone who practises insurance business, *esp* in ships. — *n* **un'derwriting**. — *vt* **underwrought** see **underwork**.

underachieve... to ... **underflow**. See **under-**.

underfong *un-dər-fong'*, (*Spenser*) *vt* to overcome, entrap; to undertake. [OE *underfangen*, pa p of *underfōn* to receive, take or steal]

underfoot... to ... **underglaze**. See **under-**.

undergo *un-dər-gō'*, *vt* to be subjected to; to endure or suffer; to pass through, experience; to enjoy, partake of (*Shakesp*); to take in hand (*Shakesp*). — *adj* **undergō'ing** (*Shakesp*) enduring. [Late OE *undergān*, from *gān* to go]

undergraduate... to ... **undermining**. See **under-**.

undern *un'dərn*, (*obs*) *n* the third hour, about nine in the morning; terce; the forenoon; the afternoon or early evening; a light meal. — *n* **un'derntime** (*Spenser* **un'dertime**) the time of the midday meal. [OE *undern*]

underneath *un-dər-nēth'*, *adv* and *prep* beneath, below in position; under the control of (*archaic*). — *n* the under part or side. — *adj* lower. [OE *underneothan*]

underniceness... to ... **understaffed**. See **under-**.

understand *un-dər-stand'*, *vt* to comprehend; to grasp with the mind; to be able to follow the working, logic, or meaning, etc, of; to take the meaning of (a sign or a person); to realize; to have a sympathetic, *usu* tacit, perception of the character and aims, etc, of (a person); to know the meaning of; to be expert in; to have knowledge or information (that), to have been informed; to assume, take to be true; to interpret (as), take to mean; to imply; to support; (*reflexive*) to know how to conduct (oneself) (*Shakesp*); to stand under (*Shakesp*). — *vi* to have understanding; to comprehend: — *pa t* and *pa p* **understood'**, *archaic pa p* **understand'ed**. — *adj* **understand'able**. — *n* **understand'er** someone who understands; a supporter (*Browning*); someone who stands in the pit of a theatre (*obs*). — *n* **understand'ing** the act of comprehending; the power to understand; intellect; an informal agreement; an understood condition (eg *on the understanding that*); sympathetic or amicable agreement of minds; (in *pl*) feet, legs, shoes, boots (*old slang*). — *adj* intelligent; discerning; sympathetic. — *adv* **understand'ingly**. — *adj* **understood'** (often *gram*) implied but not expressed. — **understand each other** or **one another** to have reached an agreement, sometimes collusive. [OE *understandan*, from **under** and *standan* to stand]

understate... to ... **understudy**. See **under-**.

undertake *un-dər-tāk'*, *vt* to pledge oneself (that); to take upon oneself; to take upon oneself (to deal with, manage or look after); to set about, engage in; to engage in contest with; to receive (*obs*); to perceive (*Spenser*); to assume (*Shakesp*); to be surety for (*Shakesp*). — *vi* to promise (*archaic*; sometimes with *for*); to become a surety (with *for*); to conduct funerals (*colloq*): — *pa t* **undertook'**; *pa p* **undertā'ken**, (*Shakesp*, etc) **undertā'en'**, (*Spenser*) **undertane'**. — *adj* **undertā'kable**. — *n* **un'dertaker** someone who takes in hand an enterprise, task or encounter; someone who manages funerals; a projector, entrepreneur; a contractor; a publisher (*obs*); a stage producer (*obs*); a compiler or editor (*obs*); a sponsor or surety (*obs*); a tax-farmer (see under **tax**; *obs*); one of the Fife adventurers who tried to colonize the island of Lewis (*c.* 1600); one of those who undertook to manage the House of Commons for the Stewart kings; one of the English and Scottish settlers on forfeited lands in Ireland. — *n* **un'dertaking** that which is undertaken; any business or project engaged in; a task one sets oneself; the business of conducting funerals. — *adj* enterprising, full of initiative. [12c *undertaken* to entrap, from OE *under*, and late OE *tacan*; see **take**]

underthirst, **underthrust**. See **under-**.

undertime. See **underntime** at **undern**.

undertimed... to ... **underwater**. See **under-**.

underway. See under **way**[2] and **weigh**[2].

underwear... to ... **underwrought**. See **under-**.

undies *un'diz*, (*colloq*) *n pl* women's underclothing. [**under**]

undine *un'dēn* or *un-dēn'* (Ger *o͝on-dē'nə*), *n* according to Paracelsus, a water-spirit that can obtain a human soul by bearing a child to a human husband. — **un'dinism** (*psychol*) a preoccupation with water, specifically with urine and the act of urination. [L *unda* a wave]

UNDP *abbrev*: United Nations Development Programme.

UNDRO *abbrev*: United Nations Disaster Relief Organization.

undulate *un'dū-lāt*, *vt* and *vi* to move like or in waves; to make or be wavy; to vibrate. — *adj* wavy; with wavy margin, surface or markings. — Also **un'dulated**. — *n* **un'dulancy**. — *adj* **un'dulant** undulating; rising and falling. — *adv* **un'dulately**. — *adj* **un'dulating**. — *adv* **un'dulatingly**. — *n* **undulā'tion** an undulating, a wave-like motion or form; waviness; a wave. — *n* **undulā'tionist** someone who holds the undulatory theory of light. — *adj* **un'dulatory** of the nature of undulation; undulating; wavy; referring light to waves in a medium. — *adj* **un'dulose** or **un'dulous** (both *rare*) undulating. — **undulant fever** Malta, Mediterranean, Neapolitan, or Rock fever, a remittent fever with swelling of the joints and enlarged spleen, caused by a bacterium (*Brucella*) transmitted by goat's (or cow's) milk. [L *undulātus* undulated, from *unda* a wave]

UNEF *ū'nef*, *abbrev*: United Nations Emergency Force.

UNEP *abbrev*: United Nations Environment Programme.

UNESCO *ū-nes'kō, abbrev*: United Nations Educational, Scientific and Cultural Organization.

UNFPA *abbrev*: United Nations Fund for Population Activities.

unguent *ung'gwənt, n* ointment. — *n* **unguentā'rium** a vessel for holding unguents. — *adj* **ung'uentary** of or for unguents. — *n* an unguentarium; a perfumer, a maker of or dealer in unguents. [L *unguentum*, from *unguere* to anoint]

unguis *ung'gwis, n* a claw or nail (*zool*); the claw of an insect's foot; the base of a petal (*bot*): — *pl* **ung'ues** (*-gwēz*). — *adj* **ung'ual** (*-gwəl*) of or bearing a claw. — *adj* **unguiculate** (*ung-gwik'ū-lāt*) or **unguic'ulated** clawed. — *adj* **unguiform** (*ung'gwi-förm*). [L *unguis* a nail]

ungula *ung'gū-lə, n* a hoof (*zool*); a section of a cylinder, cone, etc, cut off by a plane oblique to the base (*geom*): — *pl* **ung'ulae** (*-lē*). — *adj* **ung'ulate** hoofed. — *n* a hoofed animal, a member of the order **Ungulā'ta**, hoofed digitigrade mammals, such as artiodactyls and perissodactyls. — *adj* **unguled** (*ung'gūld*; *heraldry*) with claws or hoofs tinctured specially. — *adj* **ung'uligrade** walking on hoofs. [L *ungula* claw, hoof, from *unguis* nail]

UNHCR *abbrev*: United Nations High Commission (or Commissioner) for Refugees.

uni *ū'ni*, (*colloq*) *n* university.

uni- *ū-ni-, combining form* denoting one. — *adj* **uniax'ial** having one axis, *esp* (*crystallog*) one optic axis or (*biol*) one main line of growth or unbranched axis. — *adv* **uniax'ially**. — *adj* **unicam'eral** (L *camera* vault; see **chamber**) having or consisting of only one chamber. — *n* **unicam'eralism** the system or principle of having one legislative chamber. — *n* **unicam'eralist**. — *adj* **unicell'ular** of or having only one cell. — *adj* **unicen'tral** having a single centre. — *adj* **ū'nicolor**, **ū'nicolour**, **ū'nicoloured**, (or *-kul'*), **unicol'orate**, or **unicol'orous** of one uniform colour. — *n* **ū'nicorn** (L *cornū* a horn) a fabulous animal mentioned by ancient Greek and Roman authors as a native of India, with a body like a horse and one straight horn; an unfortunate translation of the Hebrew *re'ēm* (Assyrian *rīmu*) anticipated by the *monokerōs* of the Septuagint, variously understood as the rhinoceros, wild ox, or ox-antelope (*Bible*); applied to various animals with the appearance of a single horn, such as the narwhal (also **un'icorn-whale**), a moth (**un'icorn-moth**) whose caterpillar has a long process, an American Pacific gasteropod (*Latirus*, etc) with a spine on the lip of the shell (**un'icorn-shell**); a team of two abreast and one in front, or a carriage drawn by it; an old Scottish gold coin bearing a unicorn, worth 18 shillings Scots; (with *cap*) one of the Scottish pursuivants. — *adj* one-horned. — *adv* with two abreast and one in front. — *adj* **unicos'tāte** (L *costa* rib) one-ribbed. — *n* **ū'nicycle** an acrobat's one-wheeled cycle. — *adj* **unidirec'tional** mainly or wholly in one direction. — *adj* **unifīl'ar** (L *fīlum* thread) with one thread. — *adj* **uniflō'rous** (L *flōs*, *flōris* a flower) one-flowered. — *adj* **unifo'liate** (L *folium* leaf; *bot*) with only one leaf; unifoliolate. — *adj* **unifō'liolāte** (L *foliolum*, dimin of *folium* leaf; *bot*) having a single leaflet, but compound in structure. — *adj* **unilā'biate** (L *labium* lip) one-lipped. — *adj* **unilat'eral** (L *latus*, *lateris* side) one-sided; on one side; affecting or involving, etc, only one person or group, etc, out of several; produced with one side of the tongue only, as a Welsh *ll* (*phonetics*). — *n* **unilat'eralism**. — *n* **unilat'eralist** someone who favours unilateral action, *esp* in abandoning or reducing production of nuclear weapons. — *n* **unilateral'ity**. — *adv* **unilat'erally**. — *adj* **uniling'ual** (L *lingua* tongue) of, in or using, one tongue or language. — *adj* **unilit'eral** (L *littera*, *lītera* letter) of, or involving, one letter or script. — *adj* **unilō'bar** or **unilōbed'** having one lobe. — *adj* **unilob'ular** having one lobule. — *adj* **uniloc'ular** having only one loculus or cavity. — *adj* **unimolec'ular** (**unimolecular layer** same as **monomolecular layer**). — *adj* **uninū'clear** with a single nucleus. — *adj* **uninū'cleate**. — *adj* **unip'arous** (L *parĕre* to bring forth) producing one at a birth. — *adj* monochasial (*bot*). — *adj* **unipar'tite** not divided into parts. — *adj* **u'niped** (see **-ped**) one-footed. — *n* a one-footed person, animal or object. — *adj* **uniper'sonal** existing as only one person. — *adj* **uniplā'nar** lying in one plane. — *n* **ū'nipod** (see **-pod**) a one-legged support, eg for a camera. — *adj* **unipō'lar** of, from or using one pole; (of a nerve cell) having one process only. — *n* **unipolar'ity**. — *adj* **u'niramous** (*zool*) having only one branch, as some Crustacean appendages (cf **biramous**). — *adj* **unisē'rial** in one series or row. — *adv* **unisē'rially**. — *adj* **unisē'riate** uniserial. — *adv* **unisē'riately**. — *adj* **ū'nisex** (of a style, *esp* in clothes) adopted by both sexes; applicable to or usable by, etc, persons of either sex. — *adj* **unisex'ual** of one sex only. — *n* **unisexual'ity**. — *adv* **unisex'ually**. — *n* **ū'nison** (or *-zən*; L *sonus* sound, *sonāre* to sound) identity of pitch; loosely, pitch differing by one or more octaves; a sound of the same pitch; complete agreement. — *adj* in unison. — *adj* **unis'onal**. — *adv* **unis'onally**. — *n* **unis'onance**. — *adj* **unis'onant**. — *adj* **unis'onous**. — *n* **univā'lence** (or *-iv'əl-*) or **univā'lency** (or *-iv'əl-*). — *adj* **univā'lent** (or *-iv-əl-*; *chem*) having a valency of one, capable of combining with one atom of hydrogen or its equivalent. — *adj* and *n* (pertaining to) one of the single chromosomes which separate in the first meiotic division. — *adj* **ū'nivalve** having one valve or shell only. — *n* a shell of one valve only; a mollusc whose shell is composed of a single piece. — *adj* **unival'vular**. — *adj* **univā'riant** having one degree of freedom. — *adj* **univā'riate** (of a distribution) having one variate only. — *adj* **univol'tine** (Ital *volta* a turn, winding) of silkworms, having one brood a year. [L *ūnus* one; Gr *oinē* ace (on dice); OE *ān* one]

Uniat *ū'ni-ət*, or **Uniate** *ū'ni-āt* or *-ət*, *n* a member of any community of Christians, *esp* in eastern Europe and Asia, that acknowledges the papal supremacy but which is allowed to retain its own customs and practices with regard to all else, ie clerical matrimony, communion in both kinds, church discipline, rites and liturgy. [Russ *uniyat*, from *uniya* union, from LL *ūniō*, *-ōnis*, from L *ūnus* one]

uniaxial, **unicameral**. See under **uni-**.

UNICEF *ū'ni-sef, abbrev*: United Nations International Children's Emergency Fund, now United Nations Children's Fund.

unicellular... to ... **unicentral**. See under **uni-**.

unicity *ū-nis'i-ti, n* oneness; uniqueness. [L *ūnicus* unique]

unicolor... to ... **unidirectional**. See under **uni-**.

UNIDO *ū-nē'dō, abbrev*: United Nations Industrial Development Organization.

Unifil *abbrev*: United Nations Interim Force in Lebanon.

unifoliolate. See under **uni-**.

uniform *ū'ni-förm, adj* alike; alike all over, throughout, or at all times; unvarying; of a military or other uniform. — *n* a distinctive garb for members of a body; a suit of it. — *vt* to make uniform; to clothe in uniform. — *adj* **ū'niformed** wearing uniform. — *n* and *adj* **uniformitā'rian**. — *n* **uniformitā'rianism** the doctrine that geological changes were brought about not in the main by great convulsions but by such action as may be seen going on now. — *n* **uniformitā'rianist**. — *n* **uniform'ity** the state or fact of being uniform; agreement with a pattern or rule; sameness; likeness between parts. — *adv* **ū'niformly**. — *n* **ū'niformness**. — **Uniform Business Rate** (*finance*) a system of business rating introduced in 1990. [L *ūniformis*, from *ūnus* one, and *fōrma* form]

unify *ū'ni-fī, vt* to make into one; to consolidate. — *adj* **ū'nifīable**. — *adj* **unif'ic** making one. — *n* **unificā'tion**. — *adj* **ū'nified**. — *n* **ū'nifīer**. — *n* and *adj* **ū'nifying**. — **unified field** an ultimate basis on which the physicist seeks to bring within a single theory the workings of all natural phenomena; **unified scale** the scale of atomic and molecular weights based on the mass of the carbon-12 isotope of carbon being taken as 12 exactly. — **Unification Church** see **Moonies**. [LL *unificāre*, from L *ūnus* one, and *facere* to make]

unigeniture *ū-ni-jen'i-chər*, *n* the state or fact of being the only begotten. — *n* **Unigen'itus** (from its first word) a bull of Clement XI (1713) condemning 101 propositions of the Jansenist Quesnel. [LL *ūnigenitus* only-begotten]

unilabiate... to ... **uninucleate**. See under **uni-**.

Unio *ū'ni-ō*, *n* the pearl-mussel genus of freshwater molluscs, giving name to the family **Unionidae** (*ū-ni-on'i-dē*). — *n* **union** (*ūn'yən*; *Shakesp*) a fine large pearl, a unique or single pearl. [L *ūniō*, *-ōnis*, prob from *ūnus* one; cf **solitaire** as applied to a diamond set by itself]

union[1] *ūn'yən*, *n* a uniting; the state of being united; the state of wedlock; a united whole; combination; a growing together in healing; general concord; the incorporation of states in a federation or in a single state; a single state (or sometimes a federation) formed in this way; an association or league, *esp* a trade union; a students' club; (formerly) a combination of parishes for poor-law purposes; its workhouse or poorhouse; a connecting part for pipes, etc; a device emblematic of union shown on a flag; the same device used separately as a flag, such as the Union Jack; a textile fabric of more than one kind of fibre; the set formed from all the elements present in two (or more) sets (*math*). — *n* **ūn'ionism** (also with *cap*). — *n* **ūn'ionist** an advocate or supporter of or believer in union or trade unions; a member of a trade union; (with *cap*) an opponent of Irish Home Rule, *esp* a Liberal Unionist (see **Liberal**), hence, a Conservative; (with *cap*) a supporter of the federal union of the United States, *esp* at the time of the Civil War. — Also *adj*. — *n* **ūnionīzā'tion** or **-s-**. — *vt* **ūn'ionize** or **-ise** to recruit into a trade union; to organize the workforce of (a body, company or industry) into a trade union. — **union catalogue** a library catalogue combining, *usu* alphabetically, the contents of a number of catalogues or listing the contents of a number of libraries; **union flag** a flag symbolizing union, *esp* the national flag of the United Kingdom, consisting of a union of the crosses of St George, St Andrew, and St Patrick, commonly called the **Union Jack**; **union language** an artifical language formed from related dialects; **union list** a list of materials available on a specific subject, in each case naming the library, and locating the material precisely in it; **union pipes** see **uillean(n) pipes**; **Union Shona** see **Shona**; **union suit** underwear in the form of combinations for man or boy; **union territory** one of the administrative divisions that, along with states, make up the Republic of India. — **art union** an association aiming at promotion of an interest in the fine arts, *esp* by raffling pictures; **the Union** the legislative incorporation of England and Scotland in 1707, or of Ireland with both in 1801; the American Union or United States; the Union of South Africa (1910). [Fr *union*, from LL *ūniō*, *-ōnis*, from L *ūnus* one]

union[2]. See under **Unio**.

unionized[1] *un-ī'ən-īzd*. See **un-**.

unionized[2] or **unionised**, *pa t* and *pa p* of **unionize** or **-ise** (see under **union**[1]).

uniparous... to ... **unipolarity**. See under **uni-**.

unique *ū-nēk'*, *adj* sole; without a like; often used loosely for unusual, pre-eminent; found solely in, belonging solely to, etc (with *to*). — *n* anything that is unique. — *adv* **unique'ly**. — *n* **unique'ness**. [Fr, from L *ūnicus*, from *ūnus*]

uniserial... to ... **unisonous**. See under **uni-**.

Unit *abbrev*: Unitarian.

unit *ū'nit*, *n* one; a single thing or person; a single element, section or item, regarded as the lowest subdivision of a whole; a group of persons forming a subdivision of a larger body; a distinct part within a piece of electrically powered equipment which has its own specific function; a single complete domestic fixture combining what are sometimes separate parts; a *usu* independently owned dwelling apartment, one of several into which a building is divided, a home unit (*Austr*); the least whole number; anything taken as one; a quantity by reference to which others are measured. — *adj* of the character or value of a unit; individual. — *adj* **ū'nital**. — *adj* **ū'nitary** pertaining to unity or to a unit; of the nature of a unit; integral; based on unity. — *n* **unitīzā'tion** or **-s-**. — *vt* **ū'nitize** or **-ise** to convert into unit trusts (*commerce*); to make into, or treat as, a unit. — **unitary taxation** (*US*) the system of taxing multinational companies on their worldwide income rather than merely that received within the area under the taxation authority's jurisdiction; **unit furniture** furniture which may be bought as single items rather than as sets or suites; **u'nitholder** someone holding a unit of securities in a unit trust; **unit-pack'aging** a method of packaging (pills, etc) in which the items are individually encased; **unit price**; **unit-pri'cing** a method of pricing foodstuffs, etc by showing the cost per agreed unit (eg kilogram or pound) as well as, or instead of, the overall price of the item; **unit trust** see under **trust**. — **unit of account** a monetary unit not necessarily corresponding to any actual denomination of currency and in certain cases of variable value, used as a basis of exchange or comparison or as a unit in accounting. [Formed from **unity**, following eg *digit*]

UNITA *ū-nē'tə*, *abbrev*: *União Nacional por Independência Total de Angola* (*Port*), National Union for the Total Liberation of Angola.

unitard *ū'ni-tärd*, *n* a *usu* close-fitting one-piece garment extending from the neck to the feet, worn chiefly by dancers, gymnasts, etc. [**uni-** and leo*tard*]

Unitarian *ū-ni-tā'ri-ən*, *n* someone who asserts the unity of the Godhead as opposed to the Trinity, ascribes divinity to God the father only, and who believes that each congregation should have independent authority; someone who believes in the unity of God, in freedom of, and tolerance of the differences in, religious beliefs, etc; a member of a particular body holding such doctrines; a monotheist generally; (without *cap*) a holder of some belief based on unity or union. — Also *adj*. — *n* **Unitā'rianism** (also without *cap*). [Mod L *unitarius*, from *ūnitās* unity]

unite *ū-nīt'*, *vt* to make one; to join into one; to join; to combine; to clasp; to marry; to have in combination; to make to agree or adhere. — *vi* to become one; to combine; to join; to grow or act together. — *n* (also *ū'*) an English gold coin of James I, worth 20 shillings, later 22 shillings. — *adj* **unī'ted**. — *adv* **unī'tedly**. — *n* **unī'tedness**. — *n* **unī'ter**. — *n* and *adj* **unī'ting**. — *n* **unition** (*ū-nish'ən*) conjunction. — *adj* **unitive** (*ū'ni-tiv*) harmonizing, uniting. — *adv* **u'nitively**. — **United Brethren** see **Moravian**; **United Free Church** see under **free**; **United Irishmen** a radical political organization which, agitating for absolute emancipation, parliamentary reform and universal suffrage, caused the 1798 rising; **United Kingdom (of Great Britain and Ireland**; or from 1922 **Northern Ireland**) the official title adopted in 1801 for the kingdom consisting of England and Wales, Scotland, and (Northern) Ireland; **United Nations** (treated as *n sing* or *n pl*) an association of states formed in 1945 to promote peace and international security and co-operation, taking over many of the functions of the dissolved League of Nations; **United Presbyterian Church** see under **Presbyterian**; **United Provinces** Holland, Zealand (Zeeland), Utrecht, Gelderland, Groningen, Friesland and Overyssel, united in 1579 under the Union of Utrecht; **United Reformed Church** a church formed by the union in 1972 of the Presbyterian Church in England and the Congregational Church in England and Wales; **United States** a federal union of states, *esp* that of (north) America. [L *ūnītus*, pa p of *ūnīre* to unite, from *ūnus* one]

unity *ū'ni-ti*, *n* oneness; the number one; the state or fact of being one or at one; that which has oneness; a single whole; the arrangement of all the parts to one purpose or effect; a unite (*Dickens*). — **unity element** (*math*) an identity element for multiplication. — **the unities** (of *place*, *time*, and *action*) the three canons of the classical drama, ie that the scenes should be at the same place, that all the events should be such as might happen within a single day, and that nothing should be admitted not directly relevant to the development of the plot. [L *ūnitās*, *-ātis*, from *ūnus* one]

Univ *abbrev*: Universalist; University.

univalence... to ... **univariate**. See **uni-**.

universe *ū'ni-vûrs*, *n* the cosmos; a system of stars such as the galactic system; the whole system of things; all that is; the world, everyone. — *adj* **univers'al** of the universe; comprehending, affecting, or for use by the whole world or all people; without exception; comprising all the particulars; all-round; unlimited; capable of being applied to a great variety of uses. — *n* something which is universal; a universal proposition; a general term; a universal concept. — *n* **Univer'salism** the doctrine or belief of universal salvation, or the ultimate salvation of all mankind, and even of the fallen angels. — *n* **Univer'salist** a believer in Universalism. — Also *adj*. — *adj* **universalis'tic**. — *n* **universality** (*-sal'*) the state or quality of being universal. — *n* **universalīzā'tion** or **-s-**. — *vt* **univer'salize** or **-ise-**. — *adv* **univer'sally**. — *n* **univer'salness**. — **universal beam** a beam made in a standard size; **universal donor** a person whose blood can be transfused into persons of the other blood groups without causing destruction of their red blood cells; **universal grinder** a versatile machine tool, able to perform external and internal cylindrical grinding, surface-grinding, etc; **universal joint** a joint capable of turning all ways; **universal second** see **universal time**; **universal time** mean solar time or Greenwich time, in which the value of the second is subject to irregularities which are due to characteristics of the earth's rotation. [L *ūniversum*, neuter singular of *ūniversus* whole, from *ūnus* one, and *vertere*, *versus* to turn]

university *ū-ni-vûr'si-ti*, *n* an institution of higher learning with power to grant degrees, its body of teachers, students, graduates, etc, its college or colleges, or its buildings; a corporate body (*obs*). — *adj* **universitā'rian**. — **university of the air** an earlier name for the **Open University** (qv). [L *ūniversitās -ātis* a whole, in LL a corporation; see **universe**]

univocal *ū-niv'ə-kl* or *ū-ni-vō'kl*, *adj* of one voice; having one meaning only; unmistakable; unambiguous; of things of the same species (*obs*). — *n* a word with only one meaning. — *adv* **univocally**. [L *ūnivocus*, from *ūnus* one, and *vōx*, *vōcis* a voice]

univoltine. See under **uni-**.

unked, **unkempt**, **unket**, **unkid**. See **un-**.

unless *un-les'*, or *ən-les'*, *conj* (tending to pass into a *prep*) if not; except (when or if). [Earlier followed by *than* or *that*; *on lesse than* on a less condition than]

unneath *ə-nēth'*, (*dialect*) *prep* underneath. [Cf **aneath**, **underneath**]

UNO *abbrev*: United Nations Organization.

uno animo *ū'nō* or *ōō'nō an'i-mō*, *adv* with one mind, with one accord. [L]

UNRRA *abbrev*: United Nations Relief and Rehabilitation Administration.

UNRWA *un'rə*, *abbrev*: United Nations Relief and Works Agency.

until *un-til'*, or *ən-til'*, *prep* and *conj* till. [Pfx *und-* as far as, and **till**]

unto *un'tōō*, or *-tōō*, (*archaic* or *formal*) *prep* to. — *conj* (*obs*) until. [Pfx **und-**, as far as, and **to**]

UOM *abbrev*: Union of Myanmar (formerly Burma).

UP *abbrev*: United Presbyterian; United Press.

up *up*, *adv* in, to or toward a higher place, level or state; aloft; on high; towards a centre (such as a capital, great town, or university); in residence, at school or college; northward; to windward; in or to a more erect position or more advanced stage of erection; out of bed; on horseback; in an excited state; in revolt; with (increased) vigour, intensity or loudness; afoot; amiss; into prominence, notice or consideration; forward for sale; in or into court; into custody, keeping or possession; away in a receptacle, place of storage or lodging (such as a sheath, purse or stable); ahead in scoring; into closed or compact state, together; to a total; in, near or towards arrival, overtaking or being abreast; as far as; all the way; to a standstill; at an end; to a finish; thoroughly, completely, fully; well informed, versed. — Also elliptically passing into a verb or interjection by omission of *go*, *come*, *put*, etc, often followed by *with*. — *adj* placed, going or directed up; top; risen; (of time) ended; having gained (so many) more holes than an opponent (*golf*): — *compar* **upp'er**; *superl* **up'most** or **upp'ermost** see below. — *prep* in an ascent along, through or by; to or in a higher position on; to or in an inner or more remote part of; along against the current; along; up into (*NAm*). — *n* a rise; a high place; a success, spell of prosperity; someone who is in prosperity. — *vt* to drive upstream (as swans for owner marking); to lift or haul up; to raise, increase. — *vi* (*colloq*) to set up; to move up; to intervene boldly, start into activity or speech: — *pr p* **upp'ing**; *pa t* and *pa p* **upped** (*upt*). — *adj* **up'most** uppermost. — *adj* **upp'er** (see above) higher; superior; higher in rank. — *n* the part of a boot or shoe above the sole and welt; an upper tooth; a drug producing a stimulant or euphoric effect, or a pill containing such a drug (*slang*). — *adj* **upp'ermost** (see above) highest; first to come into the mind. — *adv* in the highest place, first. — *n* **upp'ing** the action of **up** *vt* (see above). — *adj* **upp'ish** assuming, pretentious, snobbish. — *adv* **upp'ishly**. — *n* **upp'ishness**. — *adj* **upp'ity** uppish; difficult to control, resistant to persuasion. — *adv* **up'ward** (*-wərd*) or **upwards** from lower to higher; from outlet towards source; from modern to more ancient; in the upper part (**upward of** or **upwards of** more than; **and upwards** and higher, and more). — *prep* **up'ward** upwards along. — *adj* **up'ward** directed upward; ascending; placed high. — *n* (*Shakesp*) top. — *adv* **up'wardly**. — *n* **up'wardness** a rising tendency; a state of being high. — *adj* **up'-and-com'ing** alert and pushful; likely to succeed (in a career, etc). — *adj* **up'-and-down'** (see also **up and down** below) undulating; going or working both, or alternately, up and down; downright (*US*). — *adj* **up'-and-o'ver** (of a door, etc) raised to a horizontal position when opened (also **up'-o'ver**). — *n* **up'-and-un'der'** (*Rugby*) a movement in which the ball is kicked high and forward, and the players rush to try to catch it. — *n* **up'-beat** an unaccented beat, at which the conductor raises his baton; an optimistic note or mood; a promising development. — *adj* (**up'beat**; *colloq*) cheerful; optimistic. — *n* **up'-bow** (*music*) a movement of the bow from point towards nut over the strings. — *n* **up'-current** or **up'-draught** a rising current of air. — *adj* **upfront** see **up front** below. — *n* **up'land** inland, hilly or high-lying country; upper or high land, as opposed to meadows, river-sides, etc (*NAm*). — *adj* high-lying; remote; inland; rural; of the uplands. — *n* **up'lander**. — *adj* **upland'ish** (*obs*) rustic; rural; outlandish. — *n* **up'-line** a railway line for upgoing trains (ie those going to, not from, eg a city). — *n* **upper atmosphere** the region of the atmosphere above about 20 miles from the earth. — *adj* **upp'er-brack'et** in an upper grouping in a list, etc. — *adj* **upp'er-case** (*printing*) literally, kept in an upper case, capital as opposed to small (of letters). — *n* **upper class** or **classes** the people of the highest social rank (*adj* **upp'er-class'**). — *n* **upper crust** the top of a loaf; the aristocracy, or the upper class or classes in any society (*adj* **upp'er-crust'**); the head (*slang*); a hat (*slang*). — *n* **upp'ercut** an upward short-arm blow. — *n* **upper hand** mastery, advantage. — *n* **upper house** in a bicameral legislature, the house that is the more restricted in membership, eg House of Lords, Senate of US and other countries. — *n* **Upper Roger** corruption of Hindi *Yuva-rājā*, young prince. — *n* **upper storey** or (*esp* in *NAm*) **story** any storey above the first floor; the brain (*slang*). — *n* **upper ten (thousand)** the richest or most influential class. — *n pl* **upp'erworks** the upper part of a structure (of a ship above the load-line); the head (*slang*). — *n* **upp'ing-block**, **upp'ing-stock**, or **upp'ing-stone** a horse block. — *n* **up'side** the upper side. — *adv* on the upper side. — *adv* **up'side-down'** or **upside down** (earlier **up so down**; *Spenser* **up'sideowne'**) with the upper part undermost; in, or into, complete confusion. — *adj* turned upside down. — *adv* **up'sides** on a par (with *with*); beside. — *n* **up'-train** a railway train proceeding towards the chief terminus. — *n* **upward mobility** the (desired) state of the **upwardly mobile**, those people moving (or attempting to move) to a higher social rank or position of greater status. — **be up in** to have a knowledge of; **have had it up to here** (*colloq*) to have had as much as one can take, to be fed up (*usu* with a gesture towards the throat); **it is all up (with)** there is no hope (for); **not up** (*tennis*) called when the ball bounces twice before the player manages to hit it; **on one's uppers** with soles worn off one's shoes; very short of money; **on the up** (*cricket*) (of a stroke) played as the ball rises from its bounce; **on the up and up** in a state of continuous progress towards ever greater success; honest, on the level; **something is up** something is amiss, something unusual or unexpected is happening or has happened; **up against** face to face with, confronted with (**up against it** in almost desperate straits); **up and doing** bestirring oneself; **up and down** to and fro; here and there through or about; throughout; vertically; out-and-out; **up and running** fully functional; **up at** attending, studying at (a university); **up for** available for or undergoing (some process); standing as a candidate for; **up front** (also as *adj*, **up-front'** or **upfront'**) at the front; to the forefront; foremost; (of money) paid in advance; candidly, openly; **ups and downs** undulations; vicissitudes; **up sticks** (*colloq*) to move one's home, business, etc, decamp; **up to** as far up as; into the immediate neighbourhood or presence of; immersed or embedded as far as; about, meditating or engaged in doing (*colloq*); capable of and ready for (*colloq*); incumbent upon (*orig US*); **up to date** to the present time or time in question; containing all recent facts, statistics, etc; knowing the latest developments of fashion, usage, etc (*adj* **up'-to-date'**); **up top** (*colloq*) in the head, in respect of intelligence; **up to the minute** or **moment** right up to the present time (*adj* **up-to-the-min'ute** or **up-to-the-mo'ment** very up-to-date); **up town** into town; in or to the residential part of a town (*NAm*); **up with** abreast of; even with; to take off or swallow; put, get, etc up (see under **up**), often as an exclamation of approbation and partisanship; **up yours** (*vulg slang*) an expression of refusal, defiance, contempt, etc; **what's up (with you**, etc)? what's the matter, what's wrong (with you, etc)? [OE *ūp*, *upp* up, *uppe* above, *uppian* to rise; Ger *auf*]

Words beginning with the prefix **up-** are listed in the following text or in the separate panels. Other words beginning with **up-** follow the prefixed ones on page 1913.

up- *up-* *pfx* with meanings of *adv*, *prep* (and *adj*; see previous article) **up**. Many of the compounds are archaic or poetic. — *adv* **up'-along** (*dialect*) up the road; homeward. — *vi* **up-anch'or** to weigh anchor. — *vt* **upbear'** to raise aloft; to hold up; to sustain. — *vt* **upbind'** to bind up: — *pa p* **upbound'** (*Spenser* also **upbound'en**). — *vt* and *vi* **upblow'** to blow up or upward; (of the wind) to spring up. — *adj* **upblown'** (or *up'*) inflated. — *vt* **upbraid** see separate article. — *vt* **upbrast'** (*Spenser*) *pa t* of **upburst**. — *vt* **upbray'** (*Spenser*) see separate article. — *n* **up'break** a break-up; an outbreak. — *vt* (*-brāk'*) to break up or open. — *vi* to break out. — *n* **up'bringing** bringing up, rearing, training, education. — *vt* **upbrought'** (*Spenser*) *pa p* of *obs* **upbring'** to bring up. — *vt* **upbuild'** to build up. — *n* **upbuild'ing** (or *up'*) building up; development; edification. — *adj* **upburn'ing** flaming upwards. — *n* **upbuoy'ance** (*rare*) buoying up. — *n* **up'burst** a bursting upwards. — *vt* and *vi* (*-bûrst'*). — *adj* **upburst'ing**. — *adv* **upby'** or **upbye'** (*Scot*) up the way, a little farther on or up; up there; at the big house. — *n* **up'cast** an upward throw; an upthrow; material thrown up; an upward current of air from a mine; a shaft carrying it (**up'cast-shaft**); a chance, accident, fluke or according to some, throw or final throw at bowls (*Shakesp*); a reproach (*Scot*); an upset (*Scot*). — *adj* thrown or turned upward. — *vt* (*-käst'*) to cast up. — *vt* **upcatch'** to catch up: — *pa t* and *pa p* **upcaught'**. — *adv* **up-Chann'el** along the English Channel from west to east (also *adj*). — *vt* **upcheer'** to encourage: — *pa t* **upcheered'** or (*Spenser*) **upcheard'**. — *vi* and *vt* **up'-chuck** (*NAm slang*) to vomit. — *adj* **up'coast** up the coast. — *adv* (*-kōst'*). — *vi* **upcoil'** to coil upwards; to coil up. — *n* **up'come** produce, outcome; outward appearance of promise (*Scot*; *obs*); decisive movement (*Scot*). — *adj* **up'coming** forthcoming, approaching; likely to succeed. — *n* **up'-country** the interior, inland part. — *adj* of or in the interior. — *adv* (*-kun'*) in or to the interior. — *adj* **upcurv'ed**. — *vt* **update'** to bring up to date. — *n* (*up'*) the act of bringing up to date; an updated account or version; a report or bulletin that updates. — *vt* **up-end'** or **upend'** to set on end; to affect or alter greatly, turn upside down. — *vi* to rise on end. — *n* **up'flow** an upward flowing. — *vi* (*-flō'*) to stream up. — *adj* **up'flung** (or *-flung'*). — *vt* **upfoll'ow** to follow (*Keats*). — *n* **up'gang** (*Scot*) ascent. — *vt* **upgath'er** to gather up or together. — *n* **upgradā'tion**. — *n* **up'grade** an upward slope or course; an improved upgraded piece of equipment. — *adj* and *adv* uphill. — *vt* (*-grād'*) to raise in status, quality or value, etc; to improve (equipment or machinery) by replacing an old, out-of-date component with a new one. — *vi* **upgrow'** to grow up: — *pr p* **upgrow'ing**; *pa t* **upgrew'**; *pa p* **upgrown'**. — *n* and *adj* **up'growing**. — *adj* **up'grown**. — *n* **up'growth** the process of growing up, development; that which grows up; a structure that has grown upward. — *adj* **up'hand** lifted by hand. — *vt* **uphaud'** Scots form of **uphold**. — *n* **upheav'al** a profound, thorough or revolutionary change or movement; any large-scale disturbance or disruption; the bodily elevation of tracts of country (*geol*); a heaving up. — *vt* and *vi* **upheave'**. — **upheld**, **uphild** see **uphold** below. — *adj* **up'hill** ascending; difficult. — Also *n*. — Also *adv* (*-hil'*). — *adv* **uphill'ward** (*Milton*). — *vt* **uphoard'** (*Spenser*, *Shakesp* **uphoord'**) to hoard or heap up. — *vt* **uphold'** to hold up; to sustain; to countenance; to defend, give support to; to keep in repair or good condition; (chiefly *Scot*, **uphaud'**) to maintain, warrant: — *pa t*

Some words with **up-** prefix.

upboil' *vi*.	**updrawn'** *adj*.	**up'going** *adj*.
upclimb' *vt* and *vi*.	**upfill'** *vt*.	**upgoing** (*-gō'* or *up'*) *n*.
upclose' *vt* and *vi*.	**up'filling** *n*.	**upgrade'able** or **upgrad'able** *adj*.
upcurl' *vt* and *vi*.	**upflash'ing** *adj*.	**upgrad'er** *n*.
upcurved' *adj*.	**upfurl'** *vt*.	**up'gush** *n*.
updrag' *vt*.	**upgaze'** *vi*.	**upgush'** *vi*.
updraw' *vt*.	**upgo'** *vi*.	**up'gushing** *adj*.

upheld'; *pa p* **upheld'**, (*Spenser*) **uphild'**. — *n* **uphold'er** a support or supporter; a dealer in second-hand clothes and furniture, etc (*obs*); a funeral undertaker (*obs*); an upholsterer (*obs*). — *n* and *adj* **uphold'ing**. — *vi* **upjet'** to spout up. — *n* **up'keep** (the cost of) maintenance. — *vt* **upknit'** to knit up; to bring together, reconcile, or perhaps conclude, explain or sum up (*Spenser*). — *vt* **uplay'** to lay up, to hoard. — *vt* **uplead'** to lead up: — *pa t* and *pa p* **upled'**. — *vi* **uplean'** (*Spenser*) to rest one's weight. — *vt* **uplift'** to lift up, raise; to elevate; to raise to a higher moral or spiritual level; to elate; to collect (eg a parcel or passenger) (*Scot*, *NZ*); draw (money) (*Scot*); to increase (eg an interim dividend) (*commerce*): — *pa p* and *adj* **uplift'ed** or **uplift'** (*archaic*). — *n* **up'lift** a lifting up, raising; upheaval; elevation, *esp* moral or spiritual, or the feeling of it; an increase (*commerce*). — *adj* (*up'*) (of a brassière) designed to raise the breasts higher; providing uplift, eg of a moral or spiritual kind. — *n* **uplift'er**. — *n* and *adj* **uplift'ing**. — *adv* **uplift'ingly**. — *adj* **uplight'ed** lighted up. — *n* **up'lighter** a light-fitting that throws light upwards. — *n* **up'link** a transmitter which sends signals up to a communications satellite. — *n* and *adj* **up'linking**. — *vt* **uplock'** to lock up. — *adj* **uplock'ed** (*Shakesp*). — *vi* **uplook'** to look up. — *n* **up'look** an upward look. — *adj* **up'lying** upland, elevated. — *n* **up'make** the action or mode of making up; constitution (*esp* mental or moral); galley proofs arranged in page form. — *n* **up'maker**. — *n* **up'making** filling-up, *esp* between bilge-ways and ship's bottom before launching; arrangement of lines into columns or pages (*printing*). — *n* **up'manship** same as **one-upmanship** (see under **one**). — *adj* **up-mar'ket** of (buying, selling or using) commodities relatively high in price, quality or prestige. — Also *adv*. — *vt* to make (more) up-market. — *adj* **up-perch'ed** (*Keats*) perched aloft. — *adj* **uppiled'** piled up. — *adj* **up-pricked'** pricked up, erected. — *n* **up'-putting** (*Scot*) lodging and entertainment. — *vt* **upraise'** to raise or lift up; to exalt; to excite, arouse (*Milton*). — *adj* **upraised'**. — *vt* **uprate'** to upgrade; to increase the rate or size of. — *vt* **uprear'** to raise up; to rear up. — *adj* **upreared'**. — *n* **uprest** see **uprist** below. — *adj* **up'right** (also *up'rīt'* or *up-rīt'*) right or straight up; in an erect position (**upright piano** one with the wires in a vertical plane); habitually honourable or righteous; honest; just; supine (eg *lying upright*; *obs*). — *n* **up'right** an upright post, stone, stroke, etc; a vertical member of a structure; an upright piano; verticality; an elevation (*obs*); a basket-maker's tool. — *vt* to set erect or right side up. — *adv* (*up'rīt*, *up'rīt'* or *up-rīt'*) vertically; honestly. — *adv* **upright'eously** (*Shakesp*) with moral right. — *adv* **up'rightly** in an upright manner; honestly; vertically. — *n* **up'rightman** (*obs cant*) a sturdy beggar, leader of a gang. — *n* **up'rightness**. — *n* **uprīs'al**. — *n* **uprise'** (or *up'*) rising. — *vi* (*-rīz'*) to rise up, arise: — *pa t* **uprose'**; *pa p* **upris'en**. — *n* **uprīs'ing** (or *up'*) a rising up; a violent revolt against a ruling power. — *adj* which rises up or is rising up. — *n* **uprist'** (*Shelley* **uprest'**) rising. — *vi* **uprist'** (*Coleridge*) or **upryst'** (*Spenser*) an old form of *upriseth*, mistakenly used for a *pa t* or *pa p* (or *perh* from a misunderstanding of the noun). — *n* **up'roar** see separate entry. — *vt* and *vi* **uproll'** to roll up or close; to roll upward. — *vt* **uproot'** to pull up by the roots; to destroy or eradicate (*fig*); to remove forcibly and completely (from eg native land). — *n* **uproot'al** uprooting. — *n* **uproot'er**. — *n* **uproot'ing**. — *vi* **uprose'** *pa t* of **uprise**. — *vi* **upryst** see **uprist** above. — *adj* **up'scale** up-market. — *vt* **upset'** to overturn, capsize; to spill or tip out; to interfere with, defeat (a plan); to disconcert; to distress; to disorder (a bodily process or organ); to affect the health of (a person) temporarily; to thicken and shorten (metal, eg the end of a bar). — *vi* to be upset: — *pa t* and *pa p* **upset'**. — *n* (*up'set*) the action of upsetting or state of being upset; an upheaval or disturbance. — *adj* (*upset'*) disturbed, anxious, unhappy; (*up'set*) (of a price) the lowest that will be accepted, at which bidding is started. — *n* **upsett'er**. — *adj* **upsett'ing** causing upset; conceited, assuming (*Scot*). — *n* overturning; overthrow; metal-working to produce an increase in the size of part of a component (*eng*); (*up'*) presumption, overweening assumption (*Scot*). — *vt* and *vi* **upshoot'** to shoot upward. — *n* (*up'*) an upshooting; that which shoots up; upshot (*Shakesp*). — *n* **up'shot** the outcome, final result; the conclusion of an argument; the substance, the general effect; the final shot (*archery*); aim (*Spenser*); end (*obs*). — *adj* (*up'shot'*) shot upward. — Also *pa t* and *pa p* of **upshoot**. — *n* **up'sitting** sitting up, *esp* after illness or childbirth (*archaic*); a reception of company on such an occasion (*obs*); sitting up at night as part of courtship (*SAfr*); listlessness (*obs Scot*). — *adj* (*obs Scot*) listless. — *vi* **upspeak'** to begin to speak: — *pa t* **upspoke'**, (*archaic*) **upspake'**. — *vi* **upspear'** (of grass) to shoot up straight like a spear (*Cowper*). — *vi* **upspring'** to spring up; to come into being: — *pa t* **upsprang'**; *pa p* **upsprung'**. — *n* **up'spring** (*Shakesp*) a lively dance (according to others, *adj*, newly introduced). — *adv* **up'stage** towards the back of the stage. — *adj* towards the back of the stage; stand-offish, superior (*slang*). — *vt* (*up-stāj'*) to treat in a supercilious manner; (of an actor) to move upstage and so force (another actor) to face away from the audience, putting him or her at a disadvantage; to divert interest or attention away from (a fellow actor) to oneself; generally, to outshine or draw attention away from (someone or something). — *adv* **upstairs'** in or toward a higher storey, or (*fig*) position; in the head, mentally (*colloq*). — *adj* **up'stairs** or **up'stair** of or in an upper storey or flat. — *n* **upstairs'** the part of a building above the ground floor; (*esp* formerly) (the occupants (*usu* the householder and family) of) the upper part of a house, as opposed to the servants' quarters in the basement. — *vi* **upstand'** (*Milton*) to stand up: — *pa t* **upstood'**. — *n* (*building*) a turned-up edge on a horizontal or sloping plane where it adjoins a vertical plane. — *adj* **upstand'ing** erect; on one's feet (*Scot*); straight and well-built; honest and downright. — *vi* **upstare'** to stare upward; (of hair) to stand up (*Spenser*, *Shakesp*). — *adj* **upstar'ing**. — *n* **up'start** someone who has suddenly risen to wealth, importance or power, a parvenu. — *adj* newly or suddenly come into being; characteristic of a parvenu; pretentious and vulgar; new-fangled; standing on end (*Spenser*). — *vi* **upstart'** to start up. — *adj* **up'state'** (*US*) pertaining to a part of a state away from, and *usu* to the north of, the principal city of the state. — Also *adv*. — *vt* **upstay'** to sustain. — *adv* **up'stream** (or *-strēm'*) against the current. — *adj* further up the stream; going against the current; relating to any of the activities which precede production, eg exploration (*oil industry*). — *vi* (*-strēm'*) to stream up. — *n* **up'stroke** an upward stroke; an upward line in writing. — *vi* **upsurge'** to surge up. — *n* (*up'*) a

Some words with **up-** prefix.

uphang' *vt*.	**uprouse'** *vt*.	**up'swept** *adj*.
upheap' *vt*.	**uprun'** *vi*.	**uptilt'** *vt*.
upheap'ing *n*.	**uprush'** *vi*.	**uptilt'ed** *adj*.
uphoist' *vt*.	**up'rush** *n*.	**upwaft'** *vt*.
uphurl' *vt*.	**upsend'** *vt*.	**upwell'** *vi*.
upleap' *vi*.	**up'sweep** *n*.	**upwhirl'** *vt* and *vi*.
up'river *adj*.	**upswell'** *vt* and *vi*.	

surging up, *esp* of emotion. — *n* **upsur'gence**. — *vt* **upswarm'** (*Shakesp*) to send up in a swarm. — *vt* **upsway'** to swing up. — *n* **up'swing** an upward swing; an economic recovery. — *n* **up'take** the act of lifting up; a pipe or flue with upward current; the act of taking up; understanding, mental apprehension (*orig Scot*; in *Scot usu* **up'tak**; **gleg in** or **at the uptak** quick to understand). — *vt* (*-tāk'*) to take up. — *vt* **uptear'** to pull up or out by the roots, from the base, etc. — *adj* **up-tem'po** played or sung at a fast tempo. — *vt* **upthrow'** to throw up. — *n* (*up'*) an upheaval, uplift; the amount of vertical displacement of the relatively raised strata at a fault (*geol*). — *vt* **upthrust'** to thrust upward. — *n* (*up'*). — *vi* **upthun'der** (*Coleridge*) to send up a noise like thunder. — *vt* **uptie'** to tie up; to conclude, to wind up (*fig*). — *adj* **uptight'** (*colloq*) tense, in a nervy state; angry, irritated; conventional, strait-laced. — *prep* **up-till'** (*obs* and *Scot*) up to. — *adj* **up'torn** (also *up-torn'*, *pa p* of **uptear**). — *adv* **uptown'** or *adj* and *n* (*up'*) (in or toward) the upper part or (*US*) the residential quarters of a town. — *n* **uptown'er** (or *up'*). — *vt* and *vi* **uptrain'** to train up, educate (*obs*). — *n* **up'trend** upward tendency. — *adj* **up'trilled** trilled high (*Coleridge*). — *n* **up'turn** an upheaval; a disturbance; a movement upward or towards improvement, a rise; an upturned part. — *adj* **up'turned**. — *n* and *adj* **upturn'ing**. — *n* **upvaluā'tion**. — *vt* **upval'ue** to increase the value of. — *n* **up'wrap** (*geol*) an anticline. — *n* **upwell'ing** a welling up; the rising to the surface of nutriment-bearing water from the depths of the ocean. — *vt* and *vi* **upwind** (*up-wīnd'*) to wind up: — *pa t* and *pa p* **upwound'**. — *adv* **upwind** or **up-wind** (*up-wind'*) and *adj* (*up'*) against the wind. — *vt* (*pa p*) **upwrought'** wrought up.

upadaisy. Same as **ups-a-daisy**.

upaithric *ū-pī'thrik*, *adj* from the same root as, and identical in meaning with, **hypaethral** (qv).

Upanishad or **Upanisad** *ōō-pan'i-shad* or *ōō-pä'ni-shäd*, *n* any of a number of Sanskrit theosophic or philosophical treatises. [Sans *upa* near, and *ni-ṣad* a sitting down]

upas *ū'pəs*, *n* (in full **u'pas-tree**) a fabulous Javanese tree that poisoned everything for miles around (*mythol*); a Javanese tree (*Antiaris toxicaria*) of the mulberry family, yielding sap used as poison; the poison of its latex. [Malay, poison]

upbraid *up-brād'*, *vt* to reproach or chide; to adduce in reproach (against or to a person; *obs*). — *vi* to utter reproaches. — *n* (*obs*) reproach, reproof. — *n* **up-braid'er**. — *n* and *adj* **upbraid'ing**. [OE *ūpbregdan*]

upbray *up-brā'*, (*Spenser*) *vt* to upbraid; to bring reproach on. — *n* an upbraiding. [From *upbrayd*, obs pa t of **upbraid**]

Up-Helly-Aa *up-hel'i-ä*, *n* a midwinter festival, representing an older Celtic fire festival, held on the last Tuesday of January in Lerwick, Shetland, and now including guisers (qv) and the ceremonial burning of a Viking ship. [**up** at an end, finished, and Scot *haliday* holiday, ie the end of the Yule holiday]

upholster *up-hōl'stər*, *vt* to provide with stuffing, springs, covers, etc; to cushion, be a cover to; to provide with curtains and carpets, etc. — *vi* to do upholstery. — *n* (*obs*) an upholsterer. — *n* **uphōl'sterer**, *fem* **uphōl'stress**, someone who makes or deals in furniture, beds, and curtains, etc. — **uphōl'stery** upholsterer's work or goods. [Back formation from *upholsterer*, from **up-holder** in obs sense (qv under **up-**)]

uphroe *ū'frō*. Same as **euphroe**.

UPI *abbrev*: United Press International.

upmost. See under **up**.

upo' *ə-pō'*, (*archaic* or *dialect*) *prep* upon. [From *up of*]

upon *ə-pon'* or *ə-pən*, *prep* on. — *adv* thereon, on the surface (*Shakesp*); on the person (*archaic*); thereafter (*Shakesp*); close in approach (*Shakesp*). [ME, from **up** and **on**]

upper, **uppermost**. See under **up**.

uproar *up'rōr* or *-rör*, *n* loud outcry, clamour; insurrection, commotion and tumult (now *rare*). — *vt* **uproar'** (*Shakesp*) to throw into uproar or confusion. — *vi* to make an uproar. — *adj* **uproar'ious**. — *adv* **uproar'iously**. — *n* **uproar'iousness**. [Du *oproer*, from *op* up, and *roeren* (Ger *rühren*, OE *hrēran*) to stir; modified by association with **roar**]

ups-a-daisy *ups'ə-dā'zi*, *interj* of encouragement eg when lifting a child or helping someone climb or to get up after falling.

upsey, **upsee** or **upsy** *up'si*, (*obs*) *prep* in the manner of (eg *upsey whore*). — *adv* (in full **upsey Dutch**, **English**, or **Friese** (*frēz*), in the German, English, or Frisian manner of drinking) deeply, heavily, heartily. — *n* a carousal. — *interj* a Bacchanalian exclamation. [Du *op zijn*, in his (ie the; 'manner' understood)]

upsilon *ūp-sī'lon*, *ōōp-*, *ūp'si-* or *up'si-*, or **ypsilon** *ip-sī'lon*, or *ip'si-*, *n* the twentieth letter of the Greek alphabet (Y, υ); as a numeral $\upsilon' = 400$, $\upsilon = 400\,000$. — *adj* **ypsiliform** (*-sil'*) or **ypsiloid** (*ip'sil-oid*) shaped like an ypsilon. [Gr, simple u]

upsy. Same as **upsey**.

upsy-daisy *ups'i-dā-zi*, *interj*. Same as **ups-a-daisy**.

uptrain. See under **up-**; **up-train**. See under **up**.

UPU *abbrev*: Universal Postal Union.

UPW *abbrev*: Union of Post Office Workers.

upward. See under **up**.

UR *abbrev*: Ukraine (IVR; provisional).

ur *ûr*, *interj* used by speakers to fill a gap in speech, when hesitant.

ur- *ōōr-*, *pfx* primitive, original. [Ger]

urachus *ū'rə-kəs*, *n* a ligament connecting the bladder with the umbilicus. [Gr *ourachos*, the fetal structure from which it is formed]

uracil *ūr'ə-sil*, (*biochem*) *n* a form of pyrimidine present in living tissue as a base of RNA. [*ur*ea and *ac*et*i*c]

uraemia or (*US*) **uremia** *ū-rē'mi-ə*, (*med*) *n* retention of waste materials normally excreted in urine in the blood. — *adj* **urae'mic** or (*US*) **ure'mic**. [Gr *ouron* urine, and *haima* blood]

uraeus *ū-rē'əs*, *n* the snake symbol on the headdress of Egyptian gods and kings. [Gr *ouraios* a kind of snake; prob Egyptian]

Ural *ū'rəl*, *n* a river rising in the Urals and flowing through Kazakhstan to the Caspian Sea; (*usu* in *pl*) a mountain range running from the Arctic Ocean through Russia and Kazakhstan to the Caspian Sea. — *adj* **Uralian** (*ū-rā'li-ən*) of the Ural Mountains (**Uralian emerald** a semi-precious green garnet); of or relating to Uralic. — *n* Uralic. — *n* **Uralic** (*ū-ral'ik*) a language group comprising the Finno-Ugric and the Samoyed languages. — *adj* Uralian. — *n* **ū'ralite** an altered mineral, hornblende after augite. — *adj* **uralitic** (*-lit'ik*). — *n* **uralītīzā'tion** or **-s-**. — *vt* **ū'ralitize** or **-ise** to turn into uralite. — *adj* **Ural-Altaic** (*-al-tā'ik*) of the Ural and Altai Mountains; applied to a family of languages (Finno-Ugrian, Turko-Tatar, Mongolian, Manchu, Tungus, etc) and their speakers. — *n* the Ural-Altaic family of languages.

urali. Same as **wourali**.

uranalysis. See under **urine**.

Urania *ū-rā'ni-ə*, (*Gr mythol*) *n* the Muse of astronomy; a name for Aphrodite. — *adj* **Ura'nian**. [L, from Gr *Ourania*, from *ouranos* heaven]

Uranian. See **Urania** and **Uranus**.

uranic *ū-ran'ik*, *n* of uranium in higher valency (*chem*); celestial (*obs*); of the palate. [From Gr *ouranos* heaven, roof of the mouth, palate]

uranide *ū'rən-īd*, *n* a transuranic element. [*uran*ium and chem sfx *-ide*]

uranin *ū'rən-in*, (*chem*) *n* a sodium or potassium salt of fluorescein (from its fluorescence, like that of uranium glass). [**uranium**]

uraninite *ū-ran'i-nīt*, *n* pitchblende. [**uranium**]

uraniscus *ū-rən-isk'əs*, *n* the roof of the mouth. [Gr *ouraniskos*]

uranism *ū'-rə-nism*, (*rare*) *n* homosexuality, *esp* male homosexuality. [Ger *Uranismus*, from Gr *ouranious* heavenly, esp as applied to Aphrodite]

uranite *ū'-rə-nīt*, *n* autunite; torbernite. — *adj* **uranit'ic**. [**uranium**]

uranium *ū-rā'ni-əm*, *n* a radioactive metal (symbol U; atomic no 92) named by Klaproth, 1789, after the recently discovered planet Uranus. — **uranium glass** a yellow fluorescent glass containing uranium compounds; **uranium hexafluoride** a volatile compound of uranium with fluorine, used in the gaseous diffusion process for separating the uranium isotopes; **uranium-lead dating** (*geol*) a method of determining the age in years of geological material, based on the known decay rate of uranium isotopes to lead isotopes.

urano- *ūr-ə-nō-*, *-nə-* or *-no'*, *combining form* denoting: the sky, the heavens; the roof of the mouth, palate (*med*); uranium. — *n* **uranog'rapher**. — *adj* **uranograph'ic** or **uranograph'ical**. — *n* **uranog'raphist**. — *n* **uranog'raphy** (see **-graphy**) descriptive astronomy and mapping, *esp* of the constellations. — *n* **uranol'ogy** astronomy. — *n* **uranom'etry** astronomical measurement. — *n* **ū'ranoplasty** plastic surgery of the palate. [Gr *ouranos* heaven]

Uranoscopus *ūr-ə-nos'ko-pəs*, *n* the star-gazer genus of fishes. [Gr *ouranoskopos* heaven-gazing]

uranous *ūr'ə-nəs*, (*chem*) *adj* of uranium in lower valency. [**uranium**]

Uranus *ū'rə-nəs* or *ū-rā'nəs*, *n* an old Greek god, father of Kronos (Saturn) and the Titans (*Gr mythol*); a planet discovered in 1781 by Herschel. — *adj* **Urā'nian** (also without *cap*) heavenly; of the heavens; astronomical; of the god or planet Uranus. [L, from Gr *Ouranos*]

uranyl *ū'rə-nil*, (*chem*) *n* the group UO_2. — *adj* **ūranyl'ic**. [**uranium**]

urao *ōō-rä'ō*, *n* natron. [Sp *urao*, from Caribbean]

urari. Same as **wourali**.

urate *ū'rāt*. See under **uric**.

urban *ûr'bən*, *adj* of, situated in or belonging to a city. — *adj* **urbane** (*ûr-bān'*) pertaining to or influenced by a city; civilized; elegant, refined; courteous; smooth-mannered. — *adv* **urbane'ly**. — *n* **urbane'ness**. — *adj* **urbanist'ic** pertaining to the planning and development of towns. — *n* **ur'banite** (chiefly *US*) a person who lives in a town or city. — *n* **urbanity** (*-ban'i-ti*) the quality of being urbane; (in *pl*) civilities; townishness, town-life. — *n* **urbanizā'tion** or **-s-**. — *vt* **ur'banize** or **-ise** to make (a district) townlike (as opposed to rural) in character. — *n* **urbanol'ogist** someone who studies urban conditions. — *n* **urbanol'ogy**. — **urban district** a thickly-populated district, a subdivision of a county, administered by an **Urban District Council** (*hist*); **urban guerrilla** a guerrilla engaged in terrorist activities in towns and cities; **urban renewal** (*esp US*) the clearing and/or redevelopment of slums etc. [L *urbānus*, from *urbs* a city]

urbi et orbi *ûr'bi* (or *ōōr'*) *et ör'bi*, (*L*) (of a papal blessing, addressed) to the city and to the world.

URC *abbrev*: United Reformed Church.

urceolus *ûr-sē'ə-ləs*, (*zool* and *bot*) *n* a pitcher-shaped structure, with contracted mouth, such as the sheath of some rotifers. — *adj* **ur'ceolate** having the form of an urceolus. [L *urceolus*, dimin of *urceus* a pitcher]

urchin *ûr'chin*, *n* a mischievous child, *esp* a boy, and *esp* when young and raggedly dressed; a child; a sea-urchin; a hedgehog (*archaic* or *dialect*); a deformed person, a hunchback (*obs* or *dialect*); an elf or imp (*obs*). — *adj* like, of the nature of or due to an urchin. — *n pl* **ur'chin-shows** appearances of elves or goblins. — *adj* **ur'chin-snout'ed** with a snout like a hedgehog. [OFr *herichon*, *heriçon* (Fr *hérisson*), from L *ēricius* a hedgehog]

urd *ûrd*, *n* an Indian plant of the bean family (*Phaseolus mungo*), or its edible blackish seed. — Also **urd bean** or **black gram**. [Hindi]

urdé, **urdée**, **urdee**, or **urdy** *ûr'dā*, *-dē* or *-di*, (*heraldry*) *adj* pointed; having points. [Origin obscure]

Urdu *ōōr'dōō* or *ōōr-dōō'*, *n* and *adj* a form of Hindustani incorporating many Persian and Arabic words, the official literary language of Pakistan. [Hindi *urdū* camp (language); cf **horde**]

ure[1] *ūr*, (*obs*) *n* use, practice, operation. [OFr *uevre* (Fr *œuvre*), from L *opera* work, service]

ure[2] *ūr*, (*obs*) *n* the urus, an extinct wild ox. [L *ūrus*]

ure[3] *ûr*, (*hist*; *Orkney and Shetland*) *n* an eighth of a mark, or an area of land paying so much in feu-duty. [Cf Norw, Swed, Dan *öre*, from L *aureus* a gold solidus]

-ure *sfx* forming nouns denoting: action, process or result; office or function. [L *-ura*]

urea *ū-rē'ə*, or *ū'rē-ə*, *n* carbamide, $CO(NH_2)_2$, a substance found in mammalian urine, the chief form in which nitrogenous waste is excreted. — *adj* **urē'al** (or *ū'ri-əl*) or **ūrē'ic**. — *n* **ureide** (*ū'rē-īd*) (*chem*) any of several organic compounds derived from urea; an acyl derivative of urea, such as urethan. — *n* **ū'ridine** a pyrimidine nucleoside based on uracil and ribose. — **urea resins** thermosetting resins used eg in adhesive, made by heating urea and aldehyde, *usu* formaldehyde. [Gr *ouron* urine]

uredo *ū-rē'dō*, *n* rust in plants; a rust-fungus in its summer stage (also **urē'do-stage**); urticaria: — *pl* **uredines** (*ū-rē'di-nēz*). — *n pl* **Uredinā'lēs** the Uredineae. — *adj* **uredine** (*ū'ri-dīn*). — *n pl* **Uredineae** (*ū-ri-din'i-ē*) the rust-fungi, an order of parasitic Basidiomycetes. — *adj* **uredin'ial** (*US*). — *n* **uredin'iospore** or **urē'diospore** (*US*) a uredospore. — *n* **uredin'ium** or **urē'dium** (*US*) a uredosorus: — *pl* **uredin'ia** or **urē'dia**. — *adj* **urē'dinous**. — *n* **urēdoso'rus** (*-sō'* or *-sö'*) a pustule producing and containing uredospores. — *n* **urē'dospore** a spore produced by rust-fungi in the uredo-stage. [L *ūrēdō*, *-inis* blight, from *ūrere* to burn]

ureide. See under **urea**.

uremia, **uremic**. See **uraemia**, **uraemic**.

urena *ū-rē'nə*, *n* any plant of the tropical genus *Urena* of the mallow family, yielding a jute substitute. [Malayalam *uren*]

urent *ū'rənt*, *adj* burning, stinging. [L *ūrēns*, *-entis*, pr p of *ūrere* to burn]

uresis *ū-rē'sis*, (*med*) *n* urination. [Gr *ourēsis*]

ureter *ū-rē'tər*, (*anatom* and *zool*) *n* a duct that conveys urine from the kidneys to the bladder or cloaca. — *adj* **urē'teral**. — *adj* **ureteric** (*ū-ri-ter'ik*). — *n* **urēterī'tis** (*med*) inflammation of a ureter. [Gr *ourētēr*, *-ēros*, from *ouron* urine]

urethan or **urethane** *ū'ri-than*, *-thān*, or *-than'*, *-thān'*, *n* a crystalline ester, $NH_2{\cdot}COOC_2H_5$, prepared from urea and ethyl alcohol, used eg as an anaesthetic, and in pesticides. [**urea**, **ethyl** and chem sfx *-ane*]

urethra *ū-rē'thrə*, (*anatom* and *zool*) *n* the canal by which the urine is discharged from the bladder: — *pl* **urethras** or **urethrae** (*-thrē*). — *adj* **urē'thral**. — *adj* **urēthrit'ic**. — *n* **urēthrī'tis** (*med*) inflammation of the urethra. — *n* **urē'throscope** (*med*) an instrument for examining the urethra. — *adj* **urēthrosco'pic**. — *n* **urēthros'copy**. — **non-specific urethritis** (*med*) a disease resembling gonorrhoea, not associated with any identifiable virus. [Gr *ourēthrā*, from *ouron* urine]

uretic *ū-ret'ik*, *adj* pertaining to, or occurring in urine. [Gr *ourētikos*, from *ouron* urine]

urge *ûrj*, *vt* to put forward (an argument, etc; or in argument, with *that*); to incite; to allege earnestly; to advise strongly; to drive, impel; to press forward, *esp* with earnestness, or insistence (success, an enterprise, etc; *archaic*); to stimulate, excite (*archaic*); to hasten (*archaic*). — *vi* to press; to be urgent or insistent; to push on. — *n* an impulse; a prompting; a strong desire or drive. — *n* **ur'gence** (*rare*). — *n* **ur'gency**. — *adj* **ur'gent** earnest, persistent; pressing; calling for immediate attention. — *adv* **ur'gently**. — *n* **ur'ger**. — *n* and *adj* **ur'ging**. [L *urgēre*]

-uria *sfx* forming nouns denoting the presence of a substance in, or an abnormal condition of, the urine. — *adj sfx* **-uric**. [Mod L, from Gr *ouron* urine]

urial or **oorial** *ōō'ri-əl*, *n* a Himalayan wild sheep. [Punjabi *hureāl*]

uric *ū'rik*, *adj* of, obtained from or present in urine. — *n*

ū'rate a salt of uric acid. — *n* **ū'ricase** an enzyme occurring in the liver and kidneys, which catalyses the oxidation of uric acid. — **uric acid** an acid, $C_5H_4O_3N_4$, present in urine and blood. [Gr *ouron* urine]

Uriconian *ū-ri-kō'ni-ən, adj* of the Roman station *Uriconium* (*Viroconium*) on the site of Wroxeter in Shropshire; applied to the apparently Pre-Cambrian igneous rocks forming the Wrekin, etc.

uridine. See **urea**.

Urim *ū'rim, n pl* and **Thummim** *thum'im, n pl* first mentioned in Exod. 28. 30, *appar* a pair of objects used as a kind of traditional oracle. [Heb *ūrīm* and *t(h)ummīm*]

urinal. See under **urine**.

urinant *ū'rin-ənt*, (*heraldry*) *adj* diving, head downward. — *n* **ū'rinātor** a diver. [L *ūrīnārī* to plunge]

urine *ū'rin, n* the *usu* amber liquid produced by the kidneys, the chief means of excreting nitrogenous waste. — *vi* (*obs*) to urinate. — *n* **ū'rinal** (or *-rī'*) a vessel for urine, *esp* one for the use of an incontinent or bedridden person; a sanitary fitting *usu* plumbed into a wall, for the use of men when urinating; a room or building having fixed receptacle(s) for use in urination; a chamber-pot (*archaic*). — *n* **urinal'ysis** analysis of urine, eg to detect disease. — Also **uranal'ysis**. — *adj* **ū'rinary** pertaining to or like urine, or the organs producing urine. — *n* (*obs*) a reservoir for the collection of urine eg for manure; a urinal. — *vi* **ū'rinate** to discharge urine. — *n* **urinā'tion**. — *adj* **ū'rinātive**. — *adj* **urinif'erous** conveying urine. — *adj* **urinip'arous** producing urine. — *adj* **urinogen'ital** pertaining jointly to urinary and genital functions or organs. — *n* **urinol'ogy**, **urinos'copy**, etc, variant forms for **urology**, **uroscopy**, etc (qv under **uro-**[1]). — *n* **urinom'eter** a hydrometer for urine. — *adj* **ū'rinous** like or of the nature of urine. — Also **ū'rinose**. [L *ūrīna*; cf Gr *ouron*]

urite *ū'rīt, n* an abdominal segment. [Gr *ourā* a tail]

urman *ōōr-män', n* (swampy) pine forest. [Russ, from Tatar *ūrmān*]

urn *ûrn, n* a vase with rounded body, *usu* a narrowed mouth and often a foot; *esp* such a vase for ashes of the dead; hence, any respository for the dead (*esp poetic*); a monumental imitation of a burial-urn; a river-source (*poetic*); a vessel for water; a closed vessel with a tap and now *usu* with a heating device inside, for making tea or coffee in quantity; a moss-capsule (*bot*); an urn-shaped object; a ballot-box; a container into which to put voting-tablets, etc (*Roman hist*, etc). — *vt* to enclose in an urn. — *adj* **urn'al**. — *adj* **urned**. — *n* **urn'ful** as much as an urn will hold: — *pl* **urn'fuls**. — **urn'field** a late Bronze Age cemetery containing cinerary urns. — *adj* **urn'-shaped** rounded with a narrowed mouth. [L *urna*]

urning *ûr'ning*, (*rare*) *n* a (*esp* male) homosexual. [Ger, irregularly formed; cf **uranism**]

uro-[1] *ū-rō-, -rə-* or *-ro'-, combining form* denoting urine. — *n* **ū'rochrome** the yellow pigment in urine. — *adj* **urogen'ital** urinogenital. — *adj* **urog'enous** producing, or produced in, urine; having a function in the production and excretion of urine. — *adj* **urograph'ic**. — *n* **urog'raphy** radiological examination of the urinary tract. — *n* **urokī'nase** (or *-kin'*) an enzyme, found in human urine, which dissolves blood clots, used in the treatment of pulmonary embolisms. — *n* **urolag'nia** sexual arousal caused by, or associated with, urination or urine. — *n* **ū'rolith** (*med*) a calculus in the urine or the urinary tract. — *n* **urolithī'asis** (*med*) the formation of uroliths; the condition caused by uroliths. — *adj* **ūrolith'ic**. — *adj* **urolog'ic** or **urolog'ical**. — *n* **urol'ogist**. — *n* **urol'ogy** the branch of medicine dealing with diseases and abnormalities of the urinary tract and their treatment; the scientific study of urine (*obs*). — *n* **uropoiē'sis** formation of urine. — *adj* **uroscop'ic**. — *n* **uros'copist**. — *n* **uros'copy** diagnostic examination of urine. — *n* **urō'sis** disease of the urinary organs. — *n* **uros'tomy** an artificial opening made in part of the urinary tract, with a passage constructed out through the skin or to another organ, allowing urine to be drained. [Gr *ouron* urine; cf L *ūrīna*]

uro-[2] *ū-rō-, -rə-* or *-ro'-, combining form* denoting: tail; posterior part. — *n* **ū'rochord** (*-körd*) a notochord confined to the caudal region, as in larval ascidians; any member of the **Urochord'a** or **Urochorda'ta** a subphylum of Chordata having a urochord in the larva, ascidians and related forms. — *adj* **urochor'dal**. — *adj* and *n* **urochor'date**. — *n pl* **Urodē'la** (Gr *dēlos* clear, plain) the (permanently) tailed Amphibia, eg newts and salamanders. — *n* and *adj* **urodē'lan** or **ū'rodele**. — *adj* **urodē'lous**. — *n* **ū'romere** (Gr *meros* part) an abdominal segment of an arthropod. — *n* **ū'ropod** an abdominal appendage of an arthropod, *esp* just before the telson. — *n* **ū'rosome** (see **-some**[2]) the tail region. — *n* **urostege** (*ū'rə-stēj*) or **urostegite** (*ū-ros'ti-jīt*; Gr *stegē* roof, deck) a snake's ventral tail-plate. — *adj* **urosthen'ic** (Gr *sthenos* strength) having a tail developed for propulsion. — *n* **ū'rostyle** (Gr *stȳlos* column) a prolongation of the last vertebra in frogs, toads etc. [Gr *ourā* tail]

uropygium *ū-rō-pij'i-əm, n* (in birds) the rump, which supports the tail feathers. — *adj* **uropyg'ial**. — **uropygial gland** a gland at the base of the tail in most birds, which secretes oil used in preening. [Gr *ouropȳgion* or *orropȳgion*, from *orros* the end of the sacrum, and *pȳgē* buttocks]

Ursa *ûr'sə, n* the Latin name of two constellations, *Ursa Major* and *Ursa Minor*, the Great and the Little Bear. — *adj* **ur'sine** of a bear; bearlike. — *n* **Ur'sus** the bear genus. [L *ursus, ursa* bear]

urson *ûr'sən, n* the Canadian porcupine. [Fr *ourson*, dimin of *ours*, from L *ursus* bear]

Ursuline *ûr'sū-lin* or *-līn, adj* of or relating to St *Ursula*, *esp* of the teaching order of nuns founded by St Angela Merici of Brescia in 1537. — Also *n*.

Ursus. See under **Ursa**.

urtext *ûr'tekst, n* the earliest version of a text, from which extant texts are deemed to be derived; an edition of a musical score showing only the composer's own original work, not altered by subsequent editorial revision. [Ger, from *ur* original, and *Text*]

urtica *ûr-tī'kə* or commonly *ûr'ti-kə, n* any plant of the nettle genus *Urtica*, giving name to the family **Urticaceae** (*ûr-ti-kā'si-ē*), related to (or including) elms and mulberries. — *adj* **urticā'ceous** like or of the nature of a nettle; of the nettle family. — *adj* **ur'ticant** stinging; irritating. — *n* **urticā'ria** (*med*) nettle-rash. — *adj* **urticā'rial**. — *adj* **urticā'rious**. — *vt* **ur'ticate** to sting; to flog with nettles. — *n* **urticā'tion**. [L *urtīca* a nettle, from *ūrere* to burn]

Uru. *abbrev*: Uruguay.

urubu *ōō-rōō-bōō', n* a S American vulture. [Tupí *urubú*]

urus *ū'rəs, n* the aurochs (qv): — *pl* **urusēs'**.

urva *ûr'və, n* the crab-eating mongoose of SE Asia. [Nepali]

US *abbrev*: Under-secretary; United Service(s); United States (of America).

us *us, pronoun* the objective (dative and accusative) case of **we**; (in editorial and royal use) one, oneself; me (*colloq*). — *adv* **us'ward** toward us (also *n*, as in *to usward*). [OE *ūs*]

us *abbrev*: *ut supra* (*L*), as above.

U/S or **u/s** *abbrev*: unserviceable.

USA *abbrev*: United States Army; United States of America (also IVR).

usable. See under **use**[1].

USAF *abbrev*: United States Air Force.

usage *ū'zij* or *-sij, n* use; act or mode of using; treatment; practice; custom; the normal or acceptable speech patterns, vocabulary, etc of a language or dialect; interest on money (*obs*); (in *pl*, with **the**) four ceremonies in the celebration of the eucharist, dispute about which caused a separation of the Nonjurors into two groups (*hist*). — *n* **ū'sager** one of the Nonjurors who maintained 'the usages' (*hist*). — *n* **ū'sance** usage;

interest, or lending at interest (*Shakesp*); time allowed for payment of foreign bills of exchange. [OFr, from L *ūsus* use]

USCL *abbrev*: United Society for Christian Literature.

USDAW *uz'dö, abbrev*: Union of Shop, Distributive and Allied Workers.

USGA *abbrev*: United States Golfing Association.

use[1] *ūz, vt* to put to some purpose; to avail oneself of; to employ habitually, to exercise; to treat or behave towards; to make use of (a person; see under **use**[2]); to take or consume (drugs or alcohol) regularly (*slang*; also as *vi*); to habituate or accustom (*old* except in *pa p*; see **used**); to observe, practise, follow (*archaic*); to resort to (a place) (*archaic*); to behave, comport (oneself) (*archaic*). — *vi* to be accustomed (to do, etc; chiefly in the past tense **used**, pronounced in this sense *ūst*; **usedn't** or **usen't** *ūs'nt*, for *used not*); to accustom oneself (with *to*) (*Scot*); to be in the habit of so doing (*archaic*); to resort (*archaic*). — *adj* **ū'sable**. — *n* **ūs'ableness** or **ūsabil'ity**. — *adv* **ūs'ably**. — *pa p* **used** (*ūst*) accustomed, habituated (with *to*, or (*old Scot*) *in* or *with*). — *adj* (*ūzd*) already made use of; second-hand; experienced, expert (*Scot*); usual, customary (*obs*). — *n* **ū'ser** a person who uses; a person who takes drugs, a drug addict (*colloq*); continual enjoyment of a right (cf **non-user**; Fr *user*); a right established by long use (*law*). — *adj* **used-up'** exhausted. — *adj* **user-friend'ly** (of a computer or software item) designed to be easily understood and operable by non-specialists, guiding the user by means of clear instructions and menus, etc; (generally, of any product, etc) designed with the ease of the user in mind, deliberately not off-putting. — **I could use** (*colloq*) I would feel better for, I want, need; **use up** to consume; to exhaust; to tire out. [Fr *user*, from LL *ūsāre*, from L *ūtī*, *ūsus* to use]

use[2] *ūs, n* the act of using; the state or fact of being used; an advantageous purpose for which a thing can be used; the fact of serving a purpose; usefulness; employment causing wear; a need to use (with *for*); the manner of using; the power of using (eg tongue or limb); the habit of using; custom; ordinary experience (*Shakesp*); a distinctive form of public worship or service peculiar to a church or diocese, etc; the profit derived from property; (in *pl*) a form of equitable ownership peculiar to English law by which one person enjoys the profit of lands, etc, the legal title to which is vested in another in trust; interest for money (*archaic*; also *fig* in *Shakesp*). — *adj* **use'ful** advantageous, serviceable (**useful** or **applied arts** those arts with a utilitarian purpose (eg weaving or pottery) as opposed to the fine arts (see under **art**[2])). — *adv* **use'fully**. — *n* **use'fulness**. — *adj* **use'less** having no use; not answering any good purpose or the end proposed; weak, poor, ineffectual (often with *at*; colloq). — *adv* **use'lessly**. — *n* **use'lessness**. — **useful life** (*elec eng*) the life which can be expected from a component before the chance of failure begins to increase (often *fig*). — **have no use for** to have no need for; to have no liking for; **in use** in employment or practice; **make use of** to use, employ; to take the help, etc, of (a person) in obtaining an end with no intention of repaying him or her, to exploit; **of no use** useless; **of use** useful; **out of use** not being used or employed; **use and wont** the customary practice. [L *ūsus*, from *ūtī* to use]

usher *ush'ər, n* a doorkeeper; someone who escorts people to seats in a hall, etc; an officer who introduces strangers or walks before a person of rank; a minor court official responsible for keeping order (*Eng law*); an under-teacher or assistant (*hist*): — *fem* **ush'eress** or **usherette'** (*esp* in a theatre or cinema). — *vt* to conduct; to show (in or out); to introduce, lead up to (now *usu* with *in*). — *n* **ush'ering**. — *n* **ush'ership**. [Anglo-Fr *usser*, OFr *ussier* (Fr *huissier*), from L *ostiārius* a doorkeeper, from *ostium* a door]

USIA *abbrev*: United States Information Agency.

USM *abbrev*: Unlisted Securities Market.

USN *abbrev*: United States Navy.

usnea *us'ni-ə, n* any member of the *Usnea* genus of lichens, tree-moss. [Pers *ushnah* moss]

USPG *abbrev*: United Society for the Propagation of the Gospel.

usque ad nauseam *us'kwi ad nö'zi-am* or *ōōs'kwe ad now'se-am*, (*L*) *adv* to the point of disgust.

usquebaugh *us'kwi-bö, n* whisky. [Ir and Gaelic *uisge-beatha*, from *uisge* water, and *beatha* life]

USS *abbrev*: United States Ship or Steamer.

USSR or (*Russ*) **CCCP** *abbrev*: Union of Soviet Socialist Republics.

Ustilago *us-ti-lā'gō, n* a genus of basidiomycetous fungi, of the family **Ustilaginaceae** (*-laj-i-nā'si-ē*) and order **Ustilaginales** (*-laj-i-nā'lēz*) or **Ustilagin'eae**, the smut-fungi. — *adj* **ustilagin'eous** or **ustilag'inous**. [L *ustilāgō, -inis* a kind of thistle]

ustion *us'chən*, (*obs*) *n* burning; cauterization by burning. — *n* **ustulation** (*us-tū-lā'shən*) burning; roasting. [L *ūstiō, -ōnis*]

usu. or **usu** *abbrev*: usually.

usual *ū'zhōō-əl, adj* occurring in ordinary use; common; customary. — *n* (*colloq*) one's normal health; one's habitual drink, etc. — *adv* **ū'sually**. — *n* **ū'sualness**. — **as usual** as is or was usual; **the usual** (*colloq*) the drink, etc one regularly orders or takes; anything one customarily experiences or does, eg menstruation. [L *ūsuālis*, from *ūsus* use]

usucapion *ū-zū-kā'pi-ən* or **usucaption** *-kap'shən*, (*Roman* and *Scots law*) *n* the acquisition of property by long possession and enjoyment. — *n* **usucā'pient** a person who claims or holds by usucapion. — *vt* **ū'sucapt** (*-kapt*) to acquire by usucapion. — *adj* **usucapt'ible**. [L *ūsūcapere*, from *ūsus* use, and *capere*, *captum* to take]

usufruct *ū'zū-frukt*, (*Roman* and *Scots law*) *n* the right to use and profit from another's property on the condition that it remains uninjured; life-rent. — *vt* to hold in usufruct. — *adj* **usufruc'tūary**. — *n* someone who has usufruct. [LL *ūsūfrūctus*, from L *ūsus* (*et*) *frūctus* use and enjoyment]

usure, **usurer**, etc. See under **usury**.

usurp *ū-zûrp', vt* to take possession of by force, without right, or unjustly; to assume (the authority or place, etc, of someone or something else); to take possession of (the mind); to take or borrow (a name or a word); to supplant (*archaic*). — *vi* to practise usurpation; to encroach (with *on* or *upon*). — *n* **usurpā'tion**. — *adj* **usur'pative** or **usur'patory**. — *n* **usurpā'ture** (*poetic*) usurpation. — *adj* **usurped'**. — *adv* **usur'pedly**. — *n* **usur'per**. — *n* and *adj* **usur'ping**. — *adv* **usur'pingly**. [Fr *usurper* and L *ūsūrpāre*, perh from *ūsus* use, and *rapere* to seize]

usury *ū'zhə-ri, n* the taking of (now only iniquitous or illegal) interest on a loan; interest (*archaic*); money-lending (*archaic*). — *n* **ū'sure** (*obs*) interest; usury. — *vi* (*obs*) to practise usury. — *n* **ū'surer** a moneylender (now *usu* at excessive rates of interest): — *fem* **ū'suress**. — *adj* **ū'suring** (*Shakesp*) taking or expecting usury. — *adj* **usū'rious**. — *adv* **usū'riously**. — *n* **usū'riousness**. — *adj* **ū'surous** (*obs*). [LL *ūsūria*, L *ūsūra*, from *ūtī*, *ūsus* to use]

usus loquendi *ūz'əs lo-kwen'dī* or *ōōs'ōōs lo-kwen'dē*, (*L*) *n* current usage of speech.

USW *abbrev*: ultrashort waves; ultrasonic waves.

usw *abbrev*: *und so weiter* (*Ger*), and so forth.

usward. See under **us**.

UT *abbrev*: Universal Time; Utah (US state; also **Ut**.).

ut[1] *ōōt* or *ut, n* a syllable representing the first note of the scale, now generally superseded by *doh*. [See **Aretinian** and **gamut**]

ut[2] *ut, ōōt*, (*L*) *adv* and *conj* as. — **ut dictum** (*dik'təm* or *-tōōm*) or *abbrev* **ut dict**. as said; **ut infra** (*in'frə* or *ēn'frä*) as below; **ut supra** (*sū'prə*, *sōō'prä* or *sōō'*) or *abbrev* **ut sup**. as above.

utas *ū'tas*, (*obs*) *n* the octave of a festival. [MFr *huitaves*, from OFr *outaves* (pl), from L *octāva* eight]

UTC *abbrev*: Universal Time Co-ordinates (used in telecommunications for GMT).

ut dict. See under **ut**[2].

Ute *ūt* or *ū'ti*, *n* (a member of) a N American Indian people of Utah, Colorado and New Mexico; the Uto-Aztecan language of this people: — *pl* **Ute** (*ū'te*) or **Utes** (*ū'tes*). — *adj* of this people or language. [Shortening of *Utah*]

ute. See **utility** under **utilize**.

utensil *ū-ten'sil*, formerly *ū'ten-sil*, *n* any useful or ceremonial implement, tool or vessel. [OFr *utensile*, from L *ūtēnsilis* fit for use, from *ūtī* to use]

uterus *ū'tər-əs*, *n* the womb: — *pl* **ū'terī**. — *n* **uterec'tomy** hysterectomy. — *adj* **ū'terine** (*-īn*) of, in or for the uterus; (of siblings) having the same mother but a different father. — *n* **uterī'tis** inflammation of the womb. — *n* **ū'terogestā'tion** gestation in the womb. — *n* **uterot'omy** hysterotomy. [L]

Utgard *ōōt'gärd*, (*Scand mythol*) *n* the abode of the giants. [ON *ūt* out, and *garthr* garth, yard]

utile *ū'tīl*, *adj* (with *to*) useful, profitable. [ME, from OFr, from L *ūtilis* useful, from *ūtī* to use]

utilisation, **utilise** etc. See under **utilize**.

utilitarian *ū-til-i-tā'ri-ən*, *adj* consisting in, based upon or relating to utility or to utilitarianism; concerned with or based on usefulness alone, without regard to or without caring about beauty and pleasantness, etc. — *n* someone believing in utilitarianism; someone who looks to usefulness alone. — *n* **utilitā'rianism** the ethical theory which finds the basis of moral distinctions in the utility of actions, ie their fitness to produce happiness for the majority. — *vt* **utilitā'rianize** or **-ise** to make to serve a utilitarian purpose. [Jeremy Bentham's coinage from **utility**]

utility *ū-til'i-ti*, *n* usefulness; the power to satisfy the wants of people in general (*philos*); a utility program (*comput*); a useful thing; a public utility, public service, or a company providing such (*esp US*); profit (*obs*); (*usu* in *pl*) stock or bond of public utility; a small truck, pick-up or van (in full **utility truck**; short form **ute**; *Austr*). — *adj* produced or supplied primarily for usefulness; provided in order that the public may be supplied in spite of rise of prices; (of a breed of dog) originally bred to be useful, to serve a practical purpose. — **utility man** an actor playing several important parts; a person who can be used to fill any gap, do any job etc; (also **utility player**) a player who can play in any of various positions as required (*sport*); **utility pole** (*US*) a pole supporting power cables, telegraph wires, etc; **utility program** (*comput*) a program in the system software designed to perform a commonplace task such as transferring data from one storage device to another or sorting a set of data; **utility room** a room, *esp* in a private house, where things required for the work of running the house are kept, eg a washing machine. [L *ūtilitās* usefulness]

utilize or **-ise** *ū'ti-līz*, *vt* to make use of, turn to use. — *adj* **ū'tilīzable** or **-s-**. — *n* **utilizā'tion** or **-s-**. — *n* **ū'tilīzer** or **-s-**. — **utilization factor** (*elec eng*) the ratio of the luminous flux reaching a specified plane to the total flux emanating from an electric lamp. [Fr *utiliser*, from *utile* useful, from L *ūtilis*, from *ūtī* to use]

ut infra. See under **ut**[2].

uti possidetis *ū'tī pos-i-dē'tis*, *ōō'tē pos-i-dā'tis*, (*L*) *n* (in international law) the principle under which belligerents keep the territory or property they possess at the close of hostilities unless otherwise agreed. [L, as you possess]

utis *ū'tis*, (*Shakesp*) *n* clamour, din. [ME *ūthēs* hue and cry, appar from OE *ūt* out, and *hæs* hest]

utmost *ut'mōst* or *-məst*, *adj* outmost; last; in the greatest degree, extreme. — *n* the limit; the extreme; the most or greatest possible; the end (*Shakesp*). [OE *ūtemest*, with double superlative suffix *-m-est* from *ūte* out]

Uto-Aztecan *ū'tō-az'tek-ən*, *n* a large linguistic and geographic group of N American Indians, of central and western N America, including Shoshone, Hopi, Ute, Comanche and Nahuatl (Aztec); a person belonging to this group. — *adj* of or relating to any of these peoples or their languages. [**Ute** and **Aztec**]

Utopia *ū-tō'pi-ə*, *n* an imaginary state described in Sir Thomas More's Latin political romance or satire *Utopia* (1516); (often without *cap*) any real or imaginary state or place believed to be ideal, perfect, excellent. — *adj* **Utō'pian** (also without *cap*). — *n* an inhabitant of Utopia; someone who imagines or believes in a Utopia; (often without *cap*) someone who advocates impracticable reforms or who expects an impossible state of perfection in society. — *n* **utō'pianism**. — *vt* and *vi* **utō'pianize** or **-ise**. — *n* **utō'pianizer** or **-s-**. — *n* **utō'piast**. — *n* **ū'topism** (*-təp-izm*). — *n* **ū'topist**. [Literally 'no place', from Gr *ou* not, and *topos* a place; *Eutopia* (Gr *eu* well), 'ideal place' coined, poss by More himself, in a punning reference to *Utopia*]

Utraquist *ū'trə-kwist*, *n* a Calixtine, or asserter of the right of the laity to communicate in both kinds (ie to take the wine as well as the bread). — Also *adj*. — *n* **U'traquism**. [L *utrāque*, from *sub utrāque speciē* under each kind]

utricle *ū'tri-kl*, *n* a little bag, bladder or cell (*biol*); a bladder-like envelope of some fruits (*bot*); a chamber in the inner ear (*zool*). — *adj* **ūtric'ūlar** like or having a utricle. — *n* **utricūlā'ria** any plant of the bladderwort genus *Utricularia* of Lentibulariaceae. — *n* **ūtric'ūlus** a utricle: — *pl* **ūtric'ūlī**. [L *ūtriculus* a small bag, dimin of *ūter*, *ūtris* a bag, a bottle]

ut sup. See under **ut**[2].

utter[1] *ut'ər*, *adj* extreme; total, absolute; out-and-out; outer (*archaic*): — *superl* **utt'erest**. — *adv* **utt'erly**. — *adj* and *n* **utt'ermost** utmost. — *n* **utt'erness**. — **utter barrister** (formerly) a barrister of rank next below a bencher; a person who pleads outside the bar, an ordinary barrister, not a king's or queen's counsel or a serjeant-at-law. [OE *ūtor* outer, from *ūt* out]

utter[2] *ut'ər*, *vt* to speak, pronounce, give voice to; to put (money) in circulation; to (try to) pass off (a forged document, etc) as genuine or put (counterfeit money) into circulation (*law*); to offer for sale (*obs*); to put out, emit, *esp* with force (*lit* and *fig*; *archaic*). — *vi* (*colloq*) to make a remark or express an opinion. — *adj* **utt'erable**. — *n* **utt'erableness**. — *n* **utt'erance** an act of uttering; a manner of or the power of speaking; the expression in speech, or in other sound, of a thought or emotion (eg **give utterance to**); a stretch of speech in some way isolated from, or independent of, what precedes and follows it (*linguistics*). — *n* **utt'erer**. — *n* **utt'ering** the circulation eg of counterfeit notes, etc. — *adj* **utt'erless** that cannot be uttered in words. [ME *uttren*, from OE *ūt* out; and MDu *uteren* to announce]

utterance[1] *ut'ər-əns*, *n* extremity, the bitter end (*Shakesp*); the utmost degree (*obs*); the utmost effort or force (*archaic*). [Fr *outrance*, from *outre*, from L *ultrā* beyond]

utterance[2]. See under **utter**[2].

utu *ōō'tōō*, (*Maori*) *n* settlement (whether monetary or in kind) of a debt; retribution, vengence.

UU *abbrev*: Ulster Unionist.

UV or **uv** *abbrev*: ultraviolet.

UVA or **UV-A** *abbrev*: ultraviolet radiation with a range of 320–380 nanometres.

uva *ū'və*, (*bot*) *n* a grape; a grapelike berry, one formed from a superior ovary. — **u'va-ursi** (*ûr'sī*; *ursī* bear's) bear-berry; an infusion of its leaves. [L *ūva* grape]

uvarovite *ōō-vä'rə-vīt*, *n* a green lime-chrome garnet. [After Count S S *Uvarov*, Russian minister of education]

uvea *ū'vi-ə*, (*zool*) *n* the posterior pigment-bearing layer of the iris of the eye; the iris, ciliary body and choroid. — *adj* **ū'veal** or **ū'veous** of the uvea. — *adj* **ūvei'tic**. — *n* **uveitis** (*ū-vi-ī'tis*) inflammation of the iris, ciliary body and choroid. [Med L, from L *uva* grape]

UVB or **UV-B** *abbrev*: ultraviolet radiation with a range of 280–320 nanometres.

UVF *abbrev*: Ulster Volunteer Force.

UVR *abbrev*: ultraviolet radiation.

uvula *ū'vū-lə*, (*anatom*) *n* the fleshy conical body suspended from the palate over the back part of the tongue: — *pl* **ū'vulas** or **ū'vulae** (*lē*). — *adj* **ū'vular** of or produced by vibration of the uvula (eg the Parisian French *r*). — *adv* **ū'vularly**. — *n* **uvulī'tis** inflammation of the uvula. [Dimin from L *ūva* grape]

UWIST *ū'wist*, *abbrev*: University of Wales Institute of Science and Technology.

UWT. See **NAS/UWT**.

ux. *abbrev*: *uxor* (*L*), wife.

uxorial *uk-sō'ri-əl*, *-sö'*, *-zō'*, or *-zö'*, *adj* of a wife. — *adv* **uxor'ially**. — *adj* **uxoricī'dal**. — *n* **uxo'ricide** (*-sīd*) a wife-killer; wife-killing. — *adj* **uxorilo'cal** (of marriage) matrilocal. — *adj* **uxo'rious** excessively or submissively fond of a wife. — *adv* **uxo'riously**. — *n* **uxo'riousness**. [L *uxor*, *-ōris* a wife]

Uzbeg *uz'beg* or **Uzbek** *uz'bek*, *n* a member of the Turkic people of Turkestan; their language. — Also *adj*.

Uzi *ōō'zi*, *n* an Israeli sub-machinegun: — *pl* **U'zis**. [*Uziel* Gal, Israeli army officer who designed it]

V

V, v *vē*, *n* the twenty-second letter of the modern English alphabet, a differentiated form of U (qv), representing a voiced labiodental sound; an object or mark shaped like the letter; as a Roman numeral V = 5; $\bar{V}$ = 5000. — **V'-neck** the neck of a garment cut in a V shape. — *adj* **V'-necked**. — **V-shape**. — *adj* **V'-shaped**. — **V'-sign** a sign made with the index and middle fingers in the form of a V, with palm turned outwards in token of victory, with palm inwards as a sign of contempt or derision; **V-6** or **V-8** an engine or car with respectively 6 or 8 cylinders arranged in a V-shape.

V *abbrev*: Vatican City (IVR); vatu (currency of Vanuatu; also **VT**); volt. — **V'-agents** poisonous gases, less volatile than G-agents; **V'-day** Victory day, *specif* VE day.

V *symbol*: vanadium (*chem*); (Roman numeral) 5.

V-1 *vee-wun'* and **V-2** *vee-tōō'*, *n* respectively, a robot flying bomb and long-range rocket-powered missile, used by the Germans in World War II *esp* to bomb the southern part of England. [Ger *Vergeltungswaffe* retaliation weapon]

v *abbrev*: velocity; verb; versed; versus; very; *vide* (*L*) see; volume.

VA *abbrev*: Vice-Admiral; (Royal Order of) Victoria and Albert; Virginia (US state; also **Va**).

vac *vak*, (*colloq*) *n* the (*esp* university) vacation; a vacuum-cleaner. — *vt* and *vi* to clean with a vacuum-cleaner: — *pr p* **vack'ing**; *pa t* and *pa p* **vacked**.

vacant *vā'kənt*, *adj* empty; unoccupied; (of a period of time) not assigned to any activity, free; blankly incurious; unthinking; inane, vacuous. — *n* **vacance** (*və-kans'*, *-käns'* or *va'*; *Scot*) vacation. — *n* **vā'cancy** emptiness; empty space; a gap; an unfilled post or situation; a room available (in a motel, boarding-house, etc); idleness, inactivity; emptiness of mind, inanity; blankness; (a period of) leisure (*obs*). — *adv* **vā'cantly**. — *n* **vā'cantness**. — *vt* **vacate** (*və-kāt'*, or *US* *vā'kāt*) to stop occupying, leave empty; to empty out, unload; to quit; to annul, to make useless (*obs*). — *n* **vacā'tion** a vacating; a voiding; the holidays, *esp* of schools, colleges, law-courts; a holiday (*esp NAm*); leisure (*obs*); an intermission (*obs*). — *vi* (*esp NAm*) to take a holiday. — *n* (*NAm*) **vacā'tioner** or **vacā'tionist** a holidaymaker. — *adj* **vacā'tionless**. — *n* **vacā'tur** the act of annulling in law. — **vacant possession** (of property) (the state of being ready for) occupation immediately after purchase, the previous owner or occupier already having left. [L *vacāre*, *-ātum* to be empty; pr p *vacāns*, *-antis*; 3rd pers pr indicative passive *vacātur*]

vaccine *vak'sēn*, *-sin*, *n* any preparation containing dead or attenuated microorganisms, eg viruses or bacteria, used to confer immunity to a disease by inoculation; cowpox virus or lymph containing it, used for inoculation against smallpox (*hist*); a program intended to combat a computer virus. — *adj* of, or derived from, the cow; of vaccinia; of vaccination. — *adj* **vac'cinal** (*-sin-*) of or due to vaccine or vaccination. — *vt* **vac'cinate** to inoculate with a vaccine. — *n* **vaccinā'tion**. — *n* **vac'cinātor**. — *adj* **vac'cinatory**. — *n* **vaccin'ia** cowpox; (in humans) a mild or localized reaction to inoculation with the vaccinia virus against smallpox. — *adj* **vaccin'ial**. [L *vaccīnus*, from *vacca* a cow]

vaccinium *vak-sin'i-əm*, *n* any plant of the genus *Vaccinium* including cranberry, whortleberry, and cowberry, giving name to a family **Vacciniā'ceae**, or a division **Vaccinioid'eae** of Ericaceae. [L *vaccīnium* whortleberry]

vacherin *vash-rɛ̃*, *n* (*cookery*) a dessert made with meringue and whipped cream, *usu* with ice-cream, fruit, nuts, etc. [Fr]

vacillate *vas'i-lāt*, *vi* to sway to and fro; to waver; to be unsteady. — *adj* **vac'illant** vacillating. — *adj* **vac'illāting**. — *adv* **vac'illātingly**. — *n* **vacillā'tion**. — *adj* **vac'illatory** wavering. [L *vacillāre*, *-ātum*]

vacked, vacking. See under **vac**.

vacuate *vak'ū-āt*, (*obs*) *vt* to empty; to evacuate; to annul. — *n* **vacūā'tion**. [L *vacuāre*, *-atum* to empty]

vacuity. See under **vacuous**.

vacuole *vak'ū-ōl*, *n* a small cavity in a cell, containing air, fluid, etc. — *adj* **vac'ūolar** of a vacuole. — *adj* **vac'ūolate** or **vac'ūolated** having vacuoles. — *n* **vacūolā'tion**. — *n* **vacūolīzā'tion** or **-s-** formation of vacuoles. [Fr, little vacuum]

vacuous *vak'ū-əs*, *adj* blank, expressionless; foolish, empty-headed; empty. — *n* **vacū'ity** emptiness; space unoccupied; idleness, listlessness; vacancy of mind. — *adv* **vac'ūously**. — *n* **vac'ūousness**. [L *vacuus* empty]

vacuum *vak'ū-əm*, *n* a space completely empty of matter; a space from which air has been excluded as completely as possible; a space containing gas at a pressure lower than atmospheric; an emptiness or void left where something has ceased or been removed; a condition of isolation or insulation from outside forces and influences; a vacuum-cleaner (*colloq*): — *pl* **vac'ūums** or (not of the cleaner) **vac'ua** (*-ū-ə*). — *vt* and *vi* to clean with a vacuum-cleaner. — *adj* relating to a vacuum; containing a vacuum; operating by means of a vacuum. — *n* **vac'ūist** a person who thinks there are empty spaces in nature. — **vacuum brake** a brake in the working of which suction by vacuum(s) supplements the pressure applied by the operator, *esp* a braking system of this type applied simultaneously throughout a train. — *vt* and *vi* **vac'ūum-clean**. — **vacuum cleaner** an apparatus for removing dust by suction; **vacuum cleaning**; **vacuum concrete** concrete enclosed in special shuttering which enables suction to be applied to remove excess water; **vacuum flask** an insulated flask for keeping substances hot or cold by means of a vacuum lining; **vacuum forming** a method or process of shaping thermoplastic by applying suction to it when warmed and placed over a mould. — *adj* **vac'uum-packed** sealed in a container from which most of the air has been removed. — **vacuum printing frame** a frame from which air can be exhausted to ensure close contact between the film image and plate; **vacuum pump** a general term for apparatus which displaces gas against a pressure; **vacuum tube** a sealed glass tube in which a vacuum has been made, eg a thermionic valve. — **ultra-high vacuum** a very close approach to complete vacuum, important for certain work of scientists and technologists. [L, neuter of *vacuus* empty]

VAD *abbrev*: Voluntary Aid Detachment, an organization of British volunteer nurses who served in the First World War.

vade *vād*, *vi* to fade (*Shakesp*); to pass away (*Spenser*); to depart (*obs*). [Partly a form of **fade**, partly from, or associated with, L *vādere* to go]

vade-mecum *vä'di-mē'kəm*, *n* a useful handbook that one carries about with one for constant reference, a pocket-companion. [L *vāde* go (imperative of *vādere*), and *mēcum* with me]

vadose *vā'dōs*, *adj* of or relating to underground water above the water-table. [L *vadōsus* full of shallows, from *vadum* a shallow piece of water]

vae *vā*. Same as **voe**.

vae victis *vē vik'tēs, vī, wī wik'*, (*L*) woe to the conquered.

vagabond *vag'ə-bond, n* a person who wanders without settled habitation; an idle wanderer; a vagrant; a scamp, a rascal (*humorously*). — *adj* roving; without settled home; unsettled. — *vi* to play the vagabond. — *n* **vag'abondage**. — *adj* **vag'abondish**. — *n* **vag'abondism**. — *vi* **vag'abondize** or **-ise** to wander like a vagabond. [Fr *vagabond* and L *vagābundus*, from *vagāri* to wander]

vagal. See under **vagus**.

vagary *vā'gə-ri, və-gā'ri, n* a devious excursion; a digression or rambling; a freakish prank; a caprice: — *pl* **vagaries**. — *adj* **vagā'rious**. — *adj* **vagā'rish**. [Appar L *vagārī* to wander]

vagi. See **vagus**.

vagile *va'jīl, -jil, adj* having the ability to move about. — *n* **vagility** (*-jil'*) the quality of being vagile; hence the ability to succeed in the struggle for existence. [L *vagus* wandering]

vagina *və-jī'nə, n* the genital passage in women and girls and other female mammals, running from the neck of the womb to the external opening contained within the vulva; a sheath; a sheathing leaf-base: — *pl* **vagī'nas** or **vagī'nae** (*-nē*) — *adj* **vagī'nal** (or *vaj'i-nəl*). — *adv* **vagī'nally**. — *adj* **vag'inant** sheathing. — *adj* **vag'inate** (*-nāt* or *nət*) or **vag'ināted** (*bot*) sheathed; having a sheath. — *adj* **vaginic'oline** or **vaginic'olous** living in a sheath. — *n* **vaginis'mus** spasmodic contraction of the vagina. — *n* **vaginī'tis** inflammation of the vagina. — *n* **vagin'ūla** (or *-jīn'*; *pl* **-lae** *-lē*) or **vag'inule** a little sheath, *esp* one surrounding the base of a moss seta. [L *vāgīna* sheath]

vagitus *vaj-ī'təs, n* a cry or wail, *esp* of a baby. [L *vagīre* to cry]

vagrant *vā'grənt, n* a person who has no settled home or work; a tramp, wanderer. — *adj* wandering, roving, travelling from place to place; having no settled dwelling; unsettled, inconstant; uncertain, erratic; (of plants) of straggling growth. — *n* **vā'grancy**. [Perh Anglo-Fr *wakerant* of Gmc origin (cf **walk**), assimilated to L *vagārī* to wander]

vagrom *vā'grəm, adj* (*Shakesp*) Dogberry's perversion of **vagrant** (*Much Ado* III. 3. 26).

vague *vāg, adj* lacking precision or sharpness of definition; indistinct; blurred; uncertain, indefinite; addicted to, or showing, haziness of thought. — *n* (*obs*) a vague or indefinite state; an indefinite expanse. — *vi* to be vague; to wander (*Scot*; now *rare*). — *adv* **vague'ly**. — *n* **vague'ness**. [L *vagus* wandering, from *vagārī* to wander]

vagus *vā'gus*, (*anatom*) *n* the tenth cranial nerve, concerned in regulating heart beat, rhythm of breathing, etc: — *pl* **vā'gi** (*-jī*). — *adj* **vā'gal** (*-gəl*). [L, wandering]

vahine *vä-hē'nä, n* in Polynesia, a woman or wife. [Tahitian]

vail[1]. An *obs* spelling of **veil**.

vail[2] *vāl*, (*archaic*) *vt* to lower, let down; to doff in salutation or submission. — *vi* to lower a sail; to lift one's hat; to yield; to do homage (*Shakesp*); to go down; to abate. — *n* (*Shakesp*) setting. [OFr *valer*, or aphetic for **avale**]

vail[3] *vāl*, (*archaic*) *vi* and *vt* to profit, avail. — *n* (*usu* in *pl*; also **vales**) a tip, perquisite, dole, or bribe. [OFr *valoir* to be worth]

vain *vān, adj* without real worth; futile; unavailing; thoughtless; empty-headed; pettily self-complacent; priding oneself inordinately on one's appearance, accomplishments or possessions; conceited; empty, devoid (*obs*). — *n* **vain'esse** (*Spenser*) vanity, futility. — *adv* **vain'ly**. — *n* **vain'ness** vanity. — **for vain** (*Shakesp*) in vain, vainly; **in vain** fruitlessly; to no end; **take in vain** to utter (*esp* God's name) with levity. [Fr *vain*, from L *vānus* empty]

vainglory *vān-glō'ri, n* vain or empty glory in one's own performances; idle boastfulness. — *vi* to boast vainly. — *adj* **vainglorious** (*-glō', -glō'*) given to, or proceeding from, vainglory. — *adv* **vainglo'riously**. — *n* **vainglo'riousness**. [OFr *vaine gloire*]

vair *vār, n* a kind of squirrel fur, bluish-grey and white, represented heraldically by rows of blue and white shields or bells. — *adj* **vairé** or **vairy** (*vā'ri*) charged or variegated with vair. [OFr, from L *varius* variegated]

Vaishnava *vīsh'nä-vä, -nə-və, n* a worshipper of Vishnu. — Also *adj*. [Sans]

Vaisya *vīs'yä, vīsh'*, or **Vaishya** *vīsh'yä, n* a member of the third caste among the Hindus. [Sans *vaiśya*]

vaivode. See **voivode**.

vakass *vä'käs, n* an Armenian ephod.

vakil or **vakeel** *vä-kēl', n* an Indian agent, representative, or pleader. [Hindi, from Ar *vakīl*]

valance *val'əns, n* a hanging border of drapery, attached eg along the sides of a bed; a pelmet (*NAm*); a hinged panel on the side of a vehicle allowing access to the engine; a side panel on a vehicle or locomotive which partially covers a wheel or wheels and is designed to reduce drag or catch splashes. — Also **val'ence**. — *adj* **val'anced** trimmed with a valance. [Poss Anglo-Fr *valer* to descend]

Valdenses. See under **Waldenses**.

vale[1] *vāl, n* a valley (chiefly *poetic*); the world (*fig*, as in *vale of tears, earthly vale*). — **vale of years** old age. [Fr *val*, from L *vallis* a vale]

vale[2] *vā'lē, vä'lā* or *wä', n* and *interj* farewell (addressed to one person) or (addressed to more than one person) **valete** (*-lē'tā, -lā'tā*). [L *valē, valēte*, imperative sing and pl of *valēre* to be well]

valediction *val-i-dik'shən*, (*formal*) *n* the act of bidding farewell; a farewell. — *n* **valedicto'rian** (*NAm*) the speaker of a college valedictory address. — *adj* **valedic'tory** saying farewell; in the nature of a farewell; of or for a leave-taking. — *n* (*NAm*) a farewell address given by a graduand. [L *valē* farewell, and *dīcere, dictum* to say]

valence[1] *vā'ləns*, (*chem*) *n* valency (*esp NAm*); chemical bond (*chem*). [L *valentia* capacity, strength]

valence[2]. See under **valance**.

Valenciennes *val-ən-sēnz', -si-en', vä-lā-syen', n* a kind of lace made at *Valenciennes* in France, the design being made at the same time as the ground and with the same thread.

valency *vā'lən-si, n* the combining power of an atom measured by the number of hydrogen (or equivalent) atoms that it can combine with or displace (*chem*); the capacity (expressed numerically) of a verb to combine dependent elements within a sentence (*linguistics*). — **valency electrons** those of the outermost shell of the atom, largely responsible for its chemical and physical properties. [L *valentia* strength, capacity]

-valent *-vā'lent* or *-və-lənt, combining form* denoting: of a stated valency, as in *trivalent*. [L *valens, -entis*, pr p of *valēre* to be strong]

valentine *val'ən-tīn, n* a person chosen on St Valentine's day, 14 Feb, as one's sweetheart; an amatory or humorous card, message or gift sent, often anonymously, that day; (with *cap*) a British heavy tank of World War II. — **Saint Val'entide** (*Spenser*) the season of St Valentine's Day. [L *Valentīnus*, name of two early saints]

Valentinian *val-ən-tin'i-ən, n* a follower of the Gnostic *Valentinus* (died c. AD 160). — Also *adj*.

valerian *və-lē'ri-ən, n* the plant all-heal (*Valeriana officinalis*) or other plant of the genus, which gives name to the family **Valērianā'ceae** (*-si-ē*) related to the teasels; its rhizome and roots which have medicinal properties. — *adj* **valērianā'ceous** of this family. — **valerianic** (*-an'ik*) or **valeric** (*-er'ik*) **acid** a fatty acid $C_5H_{10}O_2$ (in several isomers). — **Greek valerian** Jacob's ladder; **red** or **spur valerian** a plant (*Centranthus*) related to valerian. [Perh from someone called *Valerius*, or from L *valēre* to be strong]

vales. See **vail**[3].

valet *val'it* or *val'ā, n* a male servant who attends to a gentleman's clothes, dressing, grooming, etc. — *vt* (*val'it*) to serve or attend to as valet; to clean *esp* the interior of (a car). — *n* **val'eting**. — **valet parking** (*esp NAm*) a service at a restaurant, airport, etc, whereby a patron's car is taken away to, and fetched back from, a parking place by an attendant. — **valet de chambre** (*val'ā də shãbr'*) an attendant; a footman; **valet de place** (*val'ā də plas*) a person who serves as a guide, messenger, etc, *esp* for strangers. [Fr]

valeta. See under **veleta**.

valetudinarian *val-i-tū-di-nā'ri-ən*, *adj* pertaining to ill-health; sickly; weak; anxious and fanciful about one's own health. — *n* a valetudinarian person. — *n* **valetūdinā'rianism**. — *adj* and *n* **valetūd'inary** (*-ə-ri*) valetudinarian. [L *valētūdinārius*, from *valētūdō* state of health, from *valēre* to be strong]

valgus *val'gəs*, (*pathol*) *adj* displaced from normal alignment so as to deviate away from the midline of the body. — Also **val'gous** (*rare*). — *n* a valgus condition. [L, bow-legged]

Valhalla *val-hal'ə*, (*Scand mythol*) *n* the palace of bliss for the souls of slain heroes. [ON *Valhöll*, from *valr* the slain, and *höll* hall]

vali *vä-lē'*, *n* a governor, *esp* of a vilayet. [Turk]

valiant *val'yənt*, *adj* brave; actively courageous; heroic; strong (*obs*). — *n* (*obs*) a valiant person. — *n* **val'iance** or **val'iancy** valour; a deed of valour. — *adv* **val'iantly**. [Fr *vaillant*, from L *valēre* to be strong]

valid *val'id*, *adj* sound; legally adequate, or efficacious; fulfilling all the necessary conditions; (in logic) well based, applicable; strong (*archaic*). — *vt* **val'idate** to make valid; to ratify; to check (items of) to ensure that they conform to input rules and eg fall within an acceptable range (*comput*); to confirm, substantiate, verify. — *n* **validā'tion** the act of validating. — *n* **valid'ity**. — *adv* **val'idly**. — *n* **val'idness**. [L *validus*, from *valēre* to be strong]

valine *vā'lēn*, *val'*, *n* an amino-acid, $C_5H_{11}NO_2$, essential to health and growth in humans and vertebrate animals. [From *val*eric acid]

valise *və-lēz'* (or *-ēs'*; now *rare* except *US*), *n* an overnight travelling bag; a kit-bag. [Fr; cf Ital *valigia*, Sp *valija*]

Valium® *val'i-əm*, *n* a proprietary name for diazepam, a tranquillizer.

Valkyrie *val'kir-i*, *val-kīr'i*, *-kir'i*, *-kēr'i*, (*Scand mythol*) *n* any one of the minor goddesses who conducted the slain from the battlefield to Valhalla: — *pl* **Valkyries** or **Valkyr'iur**. [ON *Valkyrja*, from *valr* the slain, and the root of *kjōsa* to choose; cf OE *Wælcyrige*, Ger *Walküre*]

vallar, **vallary**. See under **vallum**.

vallecula *va-lek'ū-lə*, *n* a groove or furrow: — *pl* **vallec'ulae** (*-lē*). — *adj* **vallec'ular** or **vallec'ulate**. [LL dimin of L *vallis* valley]

valley *val'i*, *n* an elongated hollow between hills; a stretch of country watered by a river; a trough between ridges; the hollow between two roof-slopes, or between one and a wall: — *pl* **vall'eys**. [OFr *valee* (Fr *vallée*), from *val*, from L *vallis* a valley]

Vallisneria *val-is-nē'ri-ə*, *n* a tropical and subtropical genus of submerged water-plants of the frogbit family. [After Antonio *Vallisnieri* (1661–1730), Italian naturalist]

vallum *val'əm*, (*Roman British archaeol*) *n* a rampart; a wall of sods, earth, or other material, *esp* of that thrown up from a ditch. — *adj* **vall'ar** or **vall'ary** applied to an honorific garland bestowed in ancient Rome on the first to mount an enemy's rampart. [L]

valonia, **vallonia** or **valonea** *və-lō'ni-ə*, *n* a tanning material, acorns of a Levantine oak (valonia oak, *Quercus aegilops*) or similar species. [Ital *vallonea*, from Gr *balanos* an acorn]

Valonia *və-lō'ni-ə*, *n* a genus of marine green algae, forming the family **Valoniā'ceae**.

valour or (now *US*) **valor** *val'ər*, *n* intrepidity; courage; bravery; value, worth (*obs*). — *n* **valorīzā'tion** or **-s-** fixing of price. — *vt* **val'orize** or **-ise** to fix or stabilize the price of (*esp* by a policy imposed by a government or controlling body). — *adj* **val'orous** intrepid; courageous. — *adv* **val'orously**. [OFr *valour*, from LL *valor*, *-ōris*, from L *valēre* to be strong]

valse *väls*, *n*, *vi* and *vt* waltz. [Fr]

value *val'ū*, *n* worth; a fair equivalent; intrinsic worth or goodness; recognition of such worth; that which renders anything useful or estimable; the degree of this quality; relative worth; high worth; esteem; efficacy; excellence; price; precise meaning; relative duration (*music*); relation with reference to light and shade (*painting*); the special determination of a quantity (*math*); the exact amount of a variable quantity in a particular case; the sound represented by a written symbol (*phonetics*); (in *pl*) moral principles, standards, etc. — *vt* to estimate the worth of; to rate at a price; to esteem; to prize. — *vt* or *vi* (*Shakesp*) to be worth. — *adj* **val'uable** having value or worth; of high value. — *n* (*usu* in *pl*) a thing of value, a choice article. — *n* **val'uableness**. — *adv* **val'uably**. — *vt* **val'uate** (*US*) to appraise, value or evaluate. — *n* **valuā'tion** estimation of value; the price at which something is valued. — *adj* **valuā'tional**. — *n* **val'uātor** a person who makes valuations, an appraiser. — *adj* **val'ued** that has a value assigned; priced; highly esteemed; prized. — *adj* **val'ueless**. — *n* **val'uer** a valuator; a person who sets a high value. — **valuable consideration** (*law*) a consideration (qv) having material or monetary value; **valuation roll** a list of properties and their assessed values for local taxation purposes; **value added** the difference between the overall cost of a manufacturing or marketing process and the final value of the goods; **value-added tax** a tax on the rise in value of a product due to the manufacturing and marketing processes (*abbrev* **VAT**); **value judgement** a personal estimate of merit in a particular respect; **value received** a phrase indicating that a bill of exchange, etc, has been accepted for a valuable consideration. — **good value** full worth in exchange; **value in exchange** exchange value; the amount of other commodities for which a thing can be exchanged in the open market (*econ*). [OFr *value*, fem pa p of *valoir* to be worth, from L *valēre*]

valuta *vä-lū'tə*, *-lōō'*, *n* the comparative value of a currency; a standard of money. [Ital]

valvassor. See **vavasour**.

valve *valv*, *n* a single piece forming part or the whole of a shell; one of the parts of a dry fruit separating in dehiscence; a structure or device that regulates flow or passage or allows it in one direction only; one of the three mechanical devices on almost all modern brass musical instruments, pressed down by the player so as to increase the length of the tube and thereby enable a full chromatic scale to be played; a rectifier (*elec*); (loosely) a thermionic device used in electronic apparatus as rectifier, amplifier, oscillator or otherwise; a leaf of a folding door (*archaic*). — *vt* (*rare*) to fit with a valve or valves. — *vt* and (*rare*) *vi* (often with *off*) to release gas through a valve (from eg a vacuum system, hot-air balloon, etc). — *adj* **val'val**. — *adj* **val'var**. — *adj* **val'vate** with or having a valve or valves; meeting at the edges without overlapping (*bot*). — *adj* **valved**. — *adj* **valve'less**. — *n* **valve'let**, **val'vūla** (*pl* **-lae** *-lē*; *combining form* **valvūlo-**) or **val'vule** a little valve. — *adj* **val'vūlar** of or having a valvule or valve. — *n* **valvūlī'tis** inflammation of a valve of the heart. — **valve bounce** the unintended secondary opening of an engine valve due to inadequate rigidity of various parts in the valve gear; **valve gear** the linkage by which the valves of an engine derive their motion and timing from the crankshaft rotation. [L *valva* a folding-door]

vambrace *vam'brās*, (*hist*) *n* armour for the forearm. — Also **vant'brace** or (*Milton*) **vant'-brass**. — *adj* **vam'-braced**. [Anglo-Fr *vantbras* for *avant-bras* forearm]

vamoose *və-mōōs'*, **vamose** *-mōs'*, (*slang*) *vi* to depart, leave in a hurry. — *vt* to leave. [Sp *vamos* let us go]

vamp[1] *vamp*, *n* the part of a boot or shoe covering the front of the foot; anything patched up; a simple and uninspired improvised accompaniment (*music*). — *vt* to provide with a vamp; to repair with a new vamp; to patch up; to give a new face to; to improvise inartistically (*music*). — *vi* to improvise crude accompaniments; to trudge (now *dialect*). — *n* **vam'per**. — *n* and *adj* **vamp'ing**. [OFr *avanpié*, from *avan* (Fr *avant*) before, and *pié* (Fr *pied*), from L *pēs*, *pedis* foot]

vamp[2] *vamp*, (*colloq*) *n* a woman who attracts men sexually, then seduces and exploits them. — *vt* to seduce and/or exploit (a man) in this way. [Short form of **vampire**]

vampire *vam'pīr*, *n* in E European folklore, a dead person that leaves the grave to drink the blood of the living; a blood-sucker, a relentless extortionate parasite or blackmailer; a vampire-bat; a stage trapdoor. — *vt* to prey upon. — *adj* **vampir'ic**. — *n* **vam'pirism** belief in human vampires; the actions of a vampire. — *vi* **vam'pirize** or **-ise** to play the vampire. — *vt* (*lit* and *fig*) to suck the blood of. — *adj* **vamp'ish**. — **vam'pire-bat** a blood-sucking Central and South American bat (eg Desmodus or Diphylla); applied to various bats wrongly supposed to be blood-suckers (eg *Vampyrus*). [Some Slav languages have *vampir*]

vamplate *vam'plāt*, *n* a guard for the hand on a lance. [Anglo-Fr *van-* for *avant* before, and *plate* plate]

van[1] *van*, *n* short for **vanguard** (often *fig*, as in *in the van of fashion*). — Also (*Shakesp*) **vant** or **vaunt**. — *adj* and *adv* **van'ward** towards the van or front.

van[2] *van*, (*tennis*) *n* short for **advantage**.

van[3] *van*, *n* a shovel for testing ore; a test of ore by washing on a shovel; a winnowing basket or shovel; a wing; a windmill sail. — *vt* to winnow or test with a van. — *n* **vann'er** one who vans; an ore-separator. — *n* and *adj* **vann'ing**. [S Eng form of **fan**; perh in part directly from L *vannus* or OFr *van*]

van[4] *van*, *n* a large covered wagon; a light vehicle used in transporting goods; a railway carriage or compartment for luggage, etc; a caravan. — *vt* and *vi* to send, convey, confine, travel, or tour in a van: — *pr p* **vann'ing**; *pa t* and *pa p* **vanned**. — *n* **vann'er** a horse suitable for a van. [Short form of **caravan**]

vanadium *və-nā'di-əm*, *n* a silvery metallic element (symbol **V**; atomic no 23). — *n* **vanadate** (*van'ə-dāt*) a salt of vanadic acid. — *adj* **vanadic** (*və-nad'ik*) of vanadium in higher valency. — *n* **van'adinite** (or *-nad'*) a mineral, lead vanadate and chloride. — *adj* **van'adous** of vanadium in lower valency. [Named by a Swedish chemist Sefström from ON *Vana-dīs*, the goddess Freyja]

Van Allen radiation belts *van al'ən rā-di-ā'shən belts*, *n pl* zones of intense particle radiation surrounding the earth at a distance of above 1200 miles (1930 km) from it. [J A *Van Allen*, American physicist, born 1914]

V and A *vee-ənd-ā'*, (*colloq*) the *V*ictoria *and A*lbert Museum, London.

vandal *van'dəl*, *n* a person who wantonly damages property; a person who destroys what is beautiful; (with *cap*) a member of a NE Germanic people who overran Gaul, Spain, and N Africa, and sacked Rome in 455. — *adj* **Van'dal**. — *adj* **Vandal'ic**. — *n* **van'dalism** (or *van'-*). — *vt* **van'dalize** or **-ise** to inflict wilful and senseless damage on (property, etc).

Van de Graaff generator *van də gräf jen'ər-ā-tər*, (*elec eng*) *n* a very high voltage electrostatic machine, using a high-speed belt to accumulate charge on the surface. [R J Van de Graaff (1901–66), US physicist]

van der Waals' forces *van der wölz fōr'sis*, (*chem*) *n pl* weak attractive forces between molecules, or crystals. [J D van der Waals (1837–1923), Dutch scientist]

vandyke or **Vandyke** *van-dīk'* or *van'-*, *n* a broad collar with the edge cut into deep points (also **Vandyke collar**); (something with) a deep-cut edging; a short pointed beard (also called **Vandyke beard**). — *vt* and *vi* to notch or zig-zag. — *adj* **vandyked'**. — **van'dyke brown** a deep brown colour; a mixture of lampblack or other material and ochre. [Sir Antony *Van Dyke* (or *Vandyke*), 17c painter, of whose portraits these features were characteristic]

vane *vān*, *n* a weathercock or revolving plate, or a streamer, serving to show how the wind blows; a heraldic or ornamental plate fixed on a pinnacle; a blade of a windmill, propeller, revolving fan, etc; a fin on a bomb or a paravane; a sight on an observing or surveying instrument; the web of a feather. — *adj* **vaned** having a vane or vanes. — *adj* **vane'less**. [S Eng variant of **fane**]

vanessa *və-nes'ə*, *n* a butterfly of the red admiral genus *Vanessa*. [Perh for *Phanessa*, from Gr *Phānēs*, a mystic divinity]

vang *vang*, (*naut*) *n* a guy-rope to steady a gaff. [A form of **fang**]

vanguard *van'gärd*, *n* the foremost of an army, etc; the forefront; those who lead the way or anticipate progress. — *n* **van'guardism** the condition of being or practice of positioning oneself as or within the vanguard of a movement (*esp* political). [Fr *avant-garde*, from *avant* before, and *garde* guard]

vanilla *və-nil'ə*, *n* a flavouring substance obtained from the pods of *Vanilla planifolia*, a Mexican climbing orchid, and other species; the plant yielding it. — *adj* flavoured with vanilla or a substitute; ordinary, usual, normal (*orig comput slang*). — *n* **vanill'in** its aromatic principle ($C_8H_8O_3$). [Sp *vainilla*, from *vaina*, from L *vāgīna* a sheath]

vanish *van'ish*, *vi* to disappear; to fade out; to cease to exist; to become zero (*math*); to exhale, emanate (*Shakesp*). — *vt* to cause to disappear. — *n* a vanishing; a glide with which a sound ends. — *n* **van'isher**. — *n* and *adj* **van'ishing**. — *adv* **van'ishingly**. — *n* **van'ishment**. — **vanishing cream** cosmetic cream that, when rubbed over the skin, virtually disappears; **vanishing point** the point at which parallel lines seen in perspective converge; the verge of disappearance of anything. [Aphetic for **evanish**]

vanitas *van'it-as*, *n* a 17c Dutch still-life painting in which motifs such as the hour-glass, skull or candle feature as reminders of the transience and vanity of human life and aspirations; any painting of this genre. [L, vanity]

Vanitory® *van'i-tər-i*, *n* (often without *cap*) a unit consisting of a wash-hand basin built into a dressing-table. — Also **Vanitory unit**. — Also *adj* (*usu* without *cap*).

vanity *van'i-ti*, *n* the priding of oneself on one's personal appearance, accomplishments, etc, conceit; extravagance or ostentation; folly or futility; something vain. — **vanity bag**, **vanity box** or **vanity case** a container for cosmetics and a small mirror, etc, carried by a woman; **Vanity Fair** the world, or any place or society in it where people are wholly devoted to vanity, triviality, and empty ostentation (from the fair at the town of Vanity, in Bunyan's *Pilgrim's Progress*); **vanity publishing** publication by the author, at his or her own expense; **vanity unit** a Vanitory unit or similar piece of furniture. [Fr *vanité*, from L *vānitās*, *-ātis*; see **vain**]

vanner, **vanning**, etc. See **van**[3], **van**[4].

vanquish *vangk'wish*, *vt* to conquer; to overcome. — *vi* to be victor. — *adj* **vanq'uishable**. — *n* **vanq'uisher**. — *n* **vanq'uishment**. [Anglo-Fr *venquir*, *venquiss-* (Fr *vaincre*), from L *vincere* to conquer]

Vansittartism *van-sit'ərt-izm*, *n* extreme anti-Germanism. [From the British diplomat Lord *Vansittart* (1881–1957)]

vant *vant*, (*Shakesp*) *n*. See under **van**[1].

vantage *vän'tij*, *n* advantage; a now less usual short form of advantage (*tennis*); opportunity (*Shakesp*); excess, addition (*Shakesp*). — *vi* (*Spenser*) to benefit, profit. — *adj* **van'tageless**. — **vantage ground** or **point** a favourable or commanding position. [Anglo-Fr *vantage*; cf **advantage**]

vantbrace, **vant-brass**. See under **vambrace**.

vanward. See under **van**[1].

vapid *vap'id*, *adj* insipid; dull; flat. — *n* **vapid'ity**. — *adv* **vap'idly**. — *n* **vap'idness**. [L *vapidus*]

vaporetto *va-po-ret'ō*, *n* a motorboat that serves as a water bus in Venice: — *pl* **vaporett'os** or **vaporett'i** (*-ē*). [Ital, from *vapore* a steamboat]

vapour or (*esp US*) **vapor** *vā'pər*, *n* a substance in the form of a mist, fume, or smoke, *esp* one coming off from a solid or liquid; a gas below its critical temperature, liquefiable by pressure; water in the atmosphere; (in *pl*) exhalations supposed to arise in the stomach or elsewhere in the body, affecting the health (*old med*); (in *pl*, *usu* with **the**) low spirits, boredom, nervous disorder; anything insubstantial, vain, or transitory; a fanciful notion; a boast. — *vi* to pass off in vapour; to emit vapour; to evaporate; to brag, make empty boasts; to swagger, show off. — *vt* to convert into vapour; to affect with the vapours; to boast; to drive (*away*) by bluster. — *adj* **vā'porable** capable of being turned to vapour. — *adj* **vāporif'ic** vaporizing. — *adj* **vā'poriform** existing in the form of vapour. — *n* **vāporim'eter** an instrument for measuring vapour pressure or vapour. — *adj* **vāporīz'able** or **-s-**. — *n* **vāporizā'tion** or **-s-**. — *vt* **vā'porize** or **-ise** to convert into vapour; to make disappear suddenly; to spray; to obliterate (*colloq*). — *vi* to become vapour. — *n* **vāporīz'er** or **-s-** an apparatus for discharging liquid in a fine spray. — *n* **vāporos'ity**. — *adj* **vā'porous** of, in the form of, like, or full of vapour; vain; affected with the vapours; insubstantial; flimsy; vainly fanciful. — *adv* **vā'porously**. — *n* **vā'porousness**. — *adj* **vā'poured** full of vapours; affected with the vapours. — *n* **vā'pourer** a person who vapours; a moth (*Orgyia*) of the tussock family. — *n* and *adj* **vā'pouring**. — *adv* **vā'pouringly**. — *adj* **vā'pourish** vapoury. — *n* **vā'pourishness**. — *adj* **vā'poury** full of vapour; affected with the vapours. — **vā'porware** (*facetious comput slang*) software or hardware loudly heralded but not yet available and possibly never to become so; **va'pour-bath** a bath in vapour; a place or apparatus for the purpose; **vapour density** the density of a gas or vapour relative to that of hydrogen at the same temperature and pressure; **vapour lock** (*eng*) the formation of vapour in a pipe carrying a volatile fluid, resulting in an interruption of the flow; **vapour trail** a white trail of condensed vapour left by high-flying aircraft. [L *vapor*, *-ōris*]

vapulate *vap'ū-lāt*, *vt* to flog. — *vi* to be flogged. — *n* **vapūlā'tion** a flogging. [L *vāpulāre*, *-ātum* to be flogged]

vaquero *vä-kā'rō*, (*US*) *n* a herdsman: — *pl* **vaque'ros**. [Sp, from L *vacca* a cow]

vara *vä'rä*, *n* a Spanish-American linear measure, varying from 33 to 43 in (c. 84–110 cm). [See **vare**]

varactor *var-ak'tər*, (*electronics*) *n* a two-electrode semiconductor device in which capacitance varies with voltage. [*var*ying *re*actor]

varan *var'ən*, *n* a monitor lizard. — *n* **Var'anus** the monitor genus, constituting the family **Varanidae** (*-an'*). [Ar *waran*]

Varangian *va-ran'ji-ən*, *n* a Scandinavian settler in what became Russia; a (*usu* Scandinavian) member of the bodyguard of the Eastern emperors; their Scandinavian language (*Scott*). — Also *adj*. [LL *Varangus*, from Late Gr *Barangos*, from ON *Væringi*]

vardy *vär'di*, *n* an *obs* or dialect variant of **verdict**.

vare *vār*, *n* a vara; a wand of authority. [Sp *vara* a rod, from L *vāra* a trestle, forked stick, from *vārus* crooked]

varec or **varech** *var'ek*, *n* kelp; wrack. [Fr; of Scand origin: cf **wrack**, **wreck**]

vareuse *vä-rœz'*, (*Southern US*) *n* a kind of loose jacket. [Fr]

vargueño *vär-gān'yō*, *n* a cabinet or desk of a kind made at *Vargas* (Bargas) near Toledo: — *pl* **vargue'ños**.

variable *vā'ri-ə-bl*, *adj* that may be varied; changeable; tending or liable to change or vary; showing variations; unsteady; quantitatively indeterminate (*math*); changing in brightness (*astron*). — *n* a quantity subject to continual increase or decrease (*math*); an expression which may have any of a number of values (*math*, *comput*); a symbol referring to a known semantic range, but unspecified as to exact meaning (*logic*); a shifting wind; a variable star. — *n* **variabil'ity**. — *n* **vā'riableness**. — *adv* **vā'riably**. — **variable costs** costs which, unlike fixed costs (qv), vary with the level of production; **variable gear** see under **gear**; **variable-geometry aeroplane** an aeroplane of varying wing, swept-back for flight, but at right angles for take-off and landing, so removing the need for long runways and high landing-speeds; **variable-pitch propeller** (*aeronautics*) a propeller with blades movable by mechanical means during rotation to optimize the pitch for different speeds and engine revs; **variable region** (*immunol*) part of an immunoglobulin molecule which differs in amino acid sequence between different molecules; **variable star** any star with a luminosity not constant with time. — *adj* **va'riable-sweep'** (of an aircraft wing) of which the sweep-back may be varied, as on a variable-geometry aeroplane. — **variable interest rate** a rate of interest on a loan, etc, that varies with the market rate of interest.

variae lectiones *vā'ri-ē lek-shi-ōn'ēz*, *wa'ri-ī lek-ti-ōn'ās*, (*L*) various readings.

variance *vā'ri-əns*, *n* variation; deviation; alteration; an exemption from normal building regulations (*NAm*); a discrepancy; the difference between estimated and actual costs, projects, etc (*commerce*); a disagreement, dispute; the average of the squares of the deviations of a number of observations from the mean (*statistics*). — *n* **vā'riant** a different form of the same thing (*esp* a word); a different reading; a specimen slightly differing from a type or standard. — *adj* changeful; varying; diversified; different; diverging from a type or standard. — **at variance** in disagreement, dissension or dispute (with); not in accordance (with). [OFr, from L *variāre* to vary]

variate *vā'ri-ət*, *n* any one of the observed values of a quantity (*statistics*); the variable quantity which is being studied (*statistics*); a variant. — *vt* and *vi* to change, vary. — *n* **variā'tion** a varying; a change; continuous change; difference in structure or character among offspring of the same parents or among members of a related group; departure from the mean or usual character; the extent to which a thing varies; a variant; declination of the compass; an inequality in the moon's motion discovered by Tycho Brahe; a change in the elements of an orbit by the disturbing force of another body; transformation of a theme by means of new figures in counterpoint, florid treatment, changes in tempo, key, etc (*music*); a solo dance (*ballet*). — *adj* **variā'tional**. — *n* **variā'tionist** a composer of variations; a person who attaches importance to variation. — *adj* **vā'riative** variational. [L *variātus*, pa p of *variāre* to vary]

varicella *var-i-sel'ə*, (*med*) *n* chickenpox. — *adj* **varicell'ar**. — *adj* **varicell'oid** resembling varicella. — *adj* **varicell'ous** pertaining to varicella. [Irreg dimin of **variola**]

varices. *Pl* of **varix**.

varicocele *var'i-kō-sēl*, (*pathol*) *n* an enlargement of the veins of the spermatic cord, or of those of the scrotum. [L *varix*, *varicis* varicose vein, and Gr *kēlē* tumour]

varicoloured *vā'ri-kul'ərd*, *adj* diversified in colour. [L *varius* various, and *color* colour]

varicose *var'i-kōs*, *adj* (of superficial veins, *esp* those of the leg) twisted and dilated so that they produce raised knots on the surface of the skin. — *n* **varicosity** (*var-i-kos'i-ti*) the state of being varicose; a distended place or vein. — **varicose ulcer** an ulcerating knot of varicose veins. [L *varicōsus*, from *varix* varicose vein]

varicotomy. See under **varix**.

Varidase® *vär'i-dāz*, *n* the proprietary name of a drug used to liquefy, for draining away, clotted blood, thick pus, and dead tissue in deep infections.

varied, etc. See **vary**.

variegate *vā'ri-(ə-)gāt*, *vt* to diversify, *esp* with colours in patches. — *adj* **vā'riegated**. — *n* **vāriegā'tion**. — *n* **vā'riegātor**. [L *variegātus*, from *varius*; see **vary**]

variety *və-rī'ə-ti*, *n* the quality of being various; diversity; difference; many-sidedness, versatility; a varied group or collection; a kind differing in minor features or points; a race not sufficiently distinct to be counted a species, a subspecies; an artificially bred strain; music-hall entertainment, a succession of varied turns: — *pl* **varī'eties**. — *adj* of, for, or performing in, music-hall entertainment. — *adj* **varī'etal** of or having the character of a variety (*biol*); (of wine) (named as being) from a single variety of grape. — *n* such a wine. — *adv* **varī'etally**. — **variety meat** offal (*US*); processed meat, sausage, etc (*orig US*). [L *varietās*, *-ātis*, from *varius* various]

variform *var'i-förm*, *adj* of various forms. [L *varius*, and sfx *-form*]

variola *və-rī'ə-lə*, (*med*) *n* smallpox; sheep-pox. — *adj* **varī'olar**. — *vt* **variolate** (*vā'ri-ə-lāt*) to inoculate with smallpox virus. — *n* **vāriolā'tion** inoculation with smallpox virus. — *n* **vā'riolātor** a person who carries out variolation. — *n* **variole** (*vā'ri-ōl*) a pock-like marking; a spherule in variolite. — *n* **vā'riolite** (Gr *lithos* stone) a fine-grained basic igneous rock with spherules of radiating feldspar resembling pock-marks. — *adj* **vāriolitic** (*-lit'-ik*) of or like variolite. — *adj* **vā'rioloid** resembling smallpox. — *n* modified smallpox occurring in the vaccinated or those who have already had the disease. — *adj* **variolous** (*və-rī'ō-ləs*) of, pertaining to, or suffering from, smallpox; covered with varioles. [LL *variola* pustule, pox, from L *varius* various, spotted]

variometer *vā-ri-om'ə-tər*, *n* an instrument for comparing magnetic forces; a variable inductor composed of two connected coils, one rotating inside the other (*electronics*); an instrument that indicates by a needle the rate of climb and descent (*aeronautics*). [L *varius* various, and **meter**[1]]

variorum *vā-ri-ö'rəm*, *adj* (of an edition of a text) including the notes of earlier commentators or editors, or variant readings. — *n* a variorum edition; a succession of changes (*joc*). [L *cum notis variorum* with the notes of various scholars]

various *vā'ri-əs*, *adj* varied, different; several; unlike each other; variegated; changeable, uncertain (*archaic*). — *adv* **vā'riously**. — *n* **vā'riousness**. [L *varius*; see **vary**]

variscite *var'i-sīt*, *n* a greenish mineral, hydrated aluminium phosphate. [L *Variscia*, Vogtland, in Saxony]

varistor *və-ris'tər*, *n* a two-electrode semi-conductor used to short-circuit transient high voltages in delicate electronic devices. [*vari*able resi*stor*]

Varityper® *vā'ri-tī-pər*, *n* a typewriter-like machine which has changeable type. — *n* **vā'ritypist**.

varix *vā'riks* or *wa'riks*, *n* an abnormally dilated, lengthened, and tortuous vein, artery, or lymphatic vessel (*med*); dilatation of a blood vessel (*med*); a ridge marking a former position of the mouth of a shell (*zool*): — *pl* **varices** (*vā'ri-sēz* or *wa'ri-kās*). — *n* **varicot'omy** the surgical removal of a varix or a varicose vein. [L]

var. lect. *abbrev*: *varia lectio* (*L*), a variant reading.

varlet *vär'lit*, (*archaic*) *n* an attendant; a municipal officer; a rascal, rogue, knave. — *fem* (*rare*) **var'letess**. — *n* **var'letry** (*Shakesp*) the rabble, the crowd. — *n* **varlett'o** (*Shakesp*, *sham Ital*) a varlet. [OFr *varlet*; cf **valet**]

varmint or **varment** *vär'mint*, *n* old variants (now *dialect*, *esp US* or *slang*) of **vermin**; a troublesome or mischievous animal or person; (*perh* another word) a skilled amateur sportsman (*obs*). — *adj* natty, dashing; sharp, cunning.

varna *vûr'nə*, *vär'nə*, *n* any of the four great Hindu castes. [Sans, class]

varnish *vär'nish*, *n* a resinous solution used to coat and give a hard, glossy, *usu* transparent surface to woodwork, paintings, etc; any of several other preparations for giving a glossy surface to something, eg *nail varnish*; a gloss or glaze; a superficial lustre, a surface showiness, *esp* with the implication of underlying shoddiness or inadequacy; an application of varnish. — *vt* to coat with varnish; to give a superficial lustre or sheen to. — *n* **var'nisher**. — *n* **var'nishing**. — **var'nishing-day** a day before the opening of a picture exhibition when exhibitors may varnish or retouch their pictures after they have been hung; **var'nish-tree** the tung-tree or other tree whose resinous juice is used for varnishing or for lacquering. [Fr *vernis*; prob from Med L *veronix* sandarac]

varroa *var'ō-ə*, *n* (also with *cap*) an Asiatic mite (*Varroa jacobsoni*) which parasitizes and kills the honey-bee; infection by this mite. [LL]

varsal *vär'səl*, (*illiterate*) *adj* universal.

varsity *vär'si-ti*, (*colloq*; *usu sport*) *n* and *adj* university.

varsovienne *vär-sō-vi-en'*, *n* a dance imitated from the Polish mazurka; a tune for it. [Fr, fem of *Varsovien* from Varsovie, Warsaw]

vartabed *vär'tə-bed*, *n* a member of an Armenian order of clergy. [Armenian *vartabet*]

Varuna *vu'ro͝o-nä*, *var'*, *vär'*, *n* an ancient Indian Vedic god of the heavens, later of the waters. [Sans; cf Gr *Ouranos*]

varus *vā'rəs*, (*pathol*) *adj* displaced from normal alignment so as to deviate towards the midline of the body. — *n* a varus condition. [L *vārus* bent, knock-kneed]

varve *värv*, (*geol*) *n* a seasonal layer of sediment deposited in still water, used in establishing Ice Age chronology. — *adj* **varve** or **varved** stratified in distinct layers of annual deposit. [Swed *varv* layer]

varvel, **varvelled**. See **vervel**, **vervelled**.

vary *vā'ri*, *vt* to make different; to diversify, modify; to alter or embellish (a melody) preserving its identity (*music*); to change to something else; to make of different kinds; to express in other words (*obs*). — *vi* to alter or be altered; to be or become different; to change in succession; to deviate; to disagree; to be subject to continuous increase or decrease (*math*): — *pr p* **vā'rying**; *pa t* and *pa p* **vā'ried**. — *n* a change. — *adj* **vā'ried**. — *adv* **vā'riedly**. — *n* **vā'rier** a person who varies. — *n* and *adj* **vā'rying**. — For **variance**, **variation**, etc, see **variable**. [ME, from (O)Fr *varier* or L *variāre*, from L *varius* various, diverse]

vas *vas*, (*anatom*) *n* a vessel, tube or duct carrying liquid: — *pl* **vasa** (*vā'sə*). — *adj* **vā'sal**. — *n* **vasectomy** (*və-sek'tə-mi*; Gr *ek* out, and *tomē* a cut) the excision of part or all of the vas deferens, *esp* in order to produce sterility. — *adj* **vasiform** (*vā'zi-förm*) duct-shaped; tubular; vase-shaped. — *combining form* **vaso-** (*vā-zō* or *-zə*; *med*) denoting a duct or vessel. — *n* **vasoconstric'tion** narrowing of a blood vessel. — *n* **vasoconstric'tor** a nerve or drug that causes vasoconstriction. — *adj* **vasoconstric'tory**. — *n* **vasodilatā'tion** expansion of a blood vessel. — *adj* **vasodilatā'tory**. — *n* **vasodilā'tor** a nerve or drug that causes vasodilatation. — *adj* **vasodilā'tory**. — *adj* **vasomō'tor** causing constriction or expansion of blood vessels. — *n* **vasopress'in** a pituitary hormone (also prepared synthetically) that raises blood pressure, regulates kidney secretion, etc. — *n* **vasopress'or** a substance that causes a rise of blood pressure. — Also *adj*. — **vas deferens** (*def'ə-renz*) the spermatic duct, carrying spermatozoa from the testis to the urethra: — *pl* **vā'sa deferen'tia** (*-shyə*). [L *vās*, *vāsis* vessel]

vasculum *vas'kū-ləm*, *n* a botanist's collecting case: — *pl* **vas'culums** or **vas'cula**. — *adj* **vas'cular** of, relating to, composed of, or provided with vessels conveying fluids, eg blood, sap. — *n* **vascular'ity**. — *n* **vascularizā'tion** or -s- the formation of blood-vessels in an organ or tissue. — *vt* **vas'cularize** or **-ise** to render vascular. — *adv* **vas'cularly**. — *n* **vas'culature** a vascular system. — *adj* **vas'culiform** shaped like a small vase. — **vascular bundle** a strand of **vascular tissue** in the higher plants, composed of xylem, phloem, and cambium; **vascular cryptogams** the pteridophytes, or ferns and related plants; **vascular disease** any of various diseased conditions of the blood vessels; **vascular plants** seed-plants and pteridophytes. [L *vāsculum*, dimin of *vās* a vessel]

vase *väz*, old-fashioned *vöz*, (*UK* and *US*) *vāz*, (*US*) *vās*, *n* a vessel, usually tall, round in section, and (now) ornamental, now used *esp* for holding cut flowers; the body of the Corinthian capital (*archit*). — **vase'=**

painting the decoration of vases with pigments, *esp* the decoration of the pottery of the ancient Greeks. [Fr, from L *vās*]

vasectomy. See under **vas**.

Vaseline® *vas'i-lēn*, *n* an ointment or lubricant consisting of petroleum jelly. — Also *vt*. [Ger *Wasser* water, and Gr *elaion* oil]

vasiform, **vasomotor**, **vasopressin**, etc. See under **vas**.

vassail. See under **vessel**.

vassal *vas'əl*, *n* a dependant, retainer; a person or nation subject to another; a person holding land from a feudal superior in return for homage and loyalty (*hist*); a person holding land from a superior in return for the payment of feu-duty (*Scots law*); a low wretch (*Shakesp*). — *adj* in the relation or state of a vassal; subordinate; servile; of a vassal. — *vt* to subject. — *n* **vass'alage** the state of being a vassal; dependence; subjection; a fee, fief; vassals collectively; prowess, or deeds of prowess (*obs*). — *n* **vass'aless** a female vassal. — *n* **vass'alry** vassals collectively. [Fr, from LL *vassallus* servant, from Celtic; cf Breton *goaz* man, Welsh *gwas* boy, servant]

vast *väst*, *adj* boundless; huge; exceedingly great; considerable, appreciable (*colloq*). — *n* an immense tract, a boundless or empty expanse of space or time; a huge quantity, vast amount (*dialect* or *colloq*). — *n* **vastid'ity**, **vast'itude** or **vast'ity** vastness; a vast extent. — *adv* **vast'ly**. — *n* **vast'ness**. — *adj* (*archaic*) **vast'y** vast. — **a vast many** (*obs*) a great many. [L *vastus* waste, desolate, huge; cf **waste**]

Vat or **VAT** *vat* or *vē-ā-tē*, *n* (sometimes without *cap*(*s*)) a colloquial acronym for *v*alue-*a*dded *t*ax. — *adj* **vat'able** or **VAT'able** (of goods, etc) liable to VAT. — *n* **Vat'man** or **VAT'man** (*vat'*; sometimes without *cap*(*s*)) an employee of the Customs and Excise Board responsible for administering, assessing, collecting, etc value-added tax.

vat *vat*, *n* a large vessel or tank, *esp* for fermentation, dyeing, or tanning; a liquor containing a reduced, colourless, soluble form of insoluble dye (**vat dye**) in which textiles are soaked, in order afterwards to take up the colour through oxidation when exposed to the air. — *vt* to put, or treat, in a vat: — *pr p* **vatt'ing**; *pa p* **vatt'ed**. — *n* **vat'ful** as much as a vat will hold: — *pl* **vat'fuls**. — *n* **vatt'er**. [S Eng form of **fat**[2], from OE *fæt*; cf Du *vat*, ON *fat*, Ger *Fass*]

vatic *vat'ik*, *adj* prophetic; oracular; inspired. — *n* **vat'icide** (*-sīd*; see **-cide**) the killer or killing of a prophet. — *adj* **vaticinal** (*-is'i-nl*). — *vt* and *vi* **vati'cinate** (*esp ironic*) to prophesy. — *n* **vaticinā'tion** prophecy. — *n* **vati'cinator** a prophet. [L *vātēs* a prophet, and *vāticinārī* to prophesy]

Vatican *vat'i-kən*, *n* an assemblage of buildings on the Vatican Hill in Rome, including one of the pope's palaces; the papal authority. — *n* **Vat'icanism** the system of theology and ecclesiastical government based on absolute papal authority, ultramontanism. — *n* **Vat'icanist**. — *n* **Vaticanol'ogist** (*colloq*) a person who studies Vatican affairs, history, etc. — **Vatican City** a small area on the Vatican Hill set up as an independent papal state in 1929; **Vatican Council** the council that met in St Peter's (1869) and proclaimed papal infallibility (1870), or the similar council (**Vatican II**) held between 1962 and 1965. [L *Mōns Vāticānus* the Vatican Hill]

vaticide, **vaticinate**, etc. See under **vatic**.

vatu *vä'tōō*, *n* the standard monetary unit of Vanuatu (100 centimes).

vau *wow*, *n* the digamma (see **episemon**). [L, from Gr *wau*, from Semitic *wāw*]

vaudeville *vō'də-vil*, *vö'də-vil*, *n* variety entertainment; a play interspersed with dances and songs incidentally introduced and usually comic; *orig* a popular song with topical allusions. — Also *adj*. — *n* **vaudevill'ian** or **vaudevill'ean** a performer or writer of vaudeville. — Also *adj*. — *n* **vau'devillist** a composer of vaudeville. [From *vau* (*val*) *de Vire* the valley of the Vire, in Normandy, where such songs were composed in the 15c]

Vaudois[1] *vō-dwä*, *n* a native of the Swiss Canton *Vaud* (*pl* **Vaudois**); its French. — Also *adj*. [Fr]

Vaudois[2] *vō-dwä*, *n* and *adj* Waldensian. [Fr; same root as **Waldenses**]

vaudoo, **vaudoux**. See **voodoo**.

vault[1] *völt*, or earlier *vöt*, *n* an arched roof or ceiling; a chamber with an arched roof or ceiling, *esp* underground; a cellar; a wine-cellar; a burial-chamber; a cavern; anything vaultlike such as the *vault of heaven*, or the *cranial vault* the dome of the skull. — *vt* to shape as a vault; to roof with an arch or vault; to form vaults in. — *vi* to curve in a vault. — *n* **vaul'tage** an arched cellar (*Shakesp*); a cavern; a range of vaults; vaulted work. — *adj* **vaul'ted** arched; concave overhead; covered with an arch or vault. — *n* **vaul'ting** vaulted work. — *adj* **vaul'ty** (*Shakesp*) vault-like. [OFr *vaute*, *vaulte*, *voute*, *volte* (Fr *voûte*), from L *volvere*, *volūtum* to roll]

vault[2] *völt*, or earlier *vöt*, *vi* to leap, *esp* by springing initially on to one or both hands, or by using a pole, to get extra height; to achieve great heights of success, fame, etc. — *vt* to spring or leap over, *esp* by this means; to cause (someone or something) to attain great success, etc. — *n* an act of vaulting. — *n* **vault'er**. — *n* **vault'ing**. — *adj* relating to or for vaulting; (of eg ambition) inordinate, overweening. — **vault'ing-horse** a piece of gymnastic apparatus for vaulting over; **vault'ing-house** (*obs*) a brothel. [Appar OFr *volter* to leap]

vaunce *vöns*, *vt* and *vi obs* aphetic form of **advance**: — *pr p* (*Spenser*) **vaunc'ing**.

vaunt[1] *vönt*, or (*US*) *vänt*, *vi* to boast; to behave boastfully or exultingly. — *vt* to boast; to boast of; to make known by display (*Spenser*). — *n* a boast; boastful behaviour. — *adj* **vaunt'ed**. — *n* **vaunt'er**. — *n* **vaunt'ery** (*archaic*) vaunting. — *adj* **vaunt'ful**. — *n* and *adj* **vaunt'ing**. — *adv* **vaunt'ingly**. — *adj* (*esp Scot*) **vaunt'y**. [OFr *vanter*, from LL *vānitāre*, from L *vānitās* vanity, from *vānus* vain; partly aphetic for **avaunt**[2]]

vaunt[2] *vönt*, (*Shakesp*) *n* the first part. [Cf **van**[1]]

vauntage *vönt'ij*, (*Spenser*) *n*. Same as **vantage**.

vaunt-courier *vönt-kōō'ri-ər*, (*archaic*) *n* one sent in advance; a forerunner. [Fr *avant-coureur*]

vaurien *vō-ryɛ̃*, (*Fr*) *n* a good-for-nothing.

vaut, **vaute**. Old forms of **vault**[1,2].

vavasour *vav'ə-sōōr* or **valvassor** *val'və-sör*, *n* (in feudal society) a knight, noble, etc, with vassals under him, who is himself the vassal of a greater noble. — *n* **vav'asory** the tenure or the lands of a vavasour. [OFr, appar from LL *vassus vassōrum* vassal of vassals, from *vassus* vassal]

vaward *vö'ərd*, (*Shakesp*) *n* forefront. — *adj* front. [A form of **vanguard**]

vawte. Same as **vaute**.

vb *abbrev*: verb.

VC *abbrev*: Victoria Cross.

VCR *abbrev*: video cassette recorder.

VD *abbrev*: venereal disease.

VDQS *abbrev*: *vins délimités de qualité supérieure* (*Fr*), wines of superior quality from approved vineyards.

VDU *abbrev*: visual display unit.

've *v*. A shortened form of **have**.

Veadar *vē'ə-där*, *n* an intercalary month in the Jewish calendar, following Adar in embolismic years. [Heb *ve* and]

veal *vēl*, *n* calf's flesh as food; a calf (*obs*). — *adj* of veal. — *n* **veal'er** (*esp NAm*, *Austr* and *NZ*) a calf raised to provide veal. — *adj* **veal'y** like veal or like a calf; immature. [OFr *veël* (Provençal *vedel*), from L *vitellus*, dimin of *vitulus*; cf Gr *italos* a calf]

veale *vēl* (*Spenser*). Same as **veil**.

Vectian *vek'tiən*, (*geol*) *adj* of or pertaining to the Isle of Wight or the specific geological formation of which it is a part. [L *Vectis* the Isle of Wight]

vector *vek'tər*, *n* a directed quantity, as a straight line in space, involving both its direction and magnitude (*math*); a carrier of disease or infection; a phage or plasmid that is used to transfer foreign DNA into a cell (*genetic eng*); the course of an aircraft, missile, etc; a one-dimensional sequence of elements within a matrix (*comput*); such a sequence having a single identifying code or symbol, *esp* one acting as an intermediate address (qv) (*comput*); a DNA molecule which can accept DNA sequences and can be used to transfer DNA from one organism to another (*biol*). — *vt* to direct (an aircraft in flight) to the required destination, *esp* by radio; to direct or change the direction of (*esp* the thrust of an aircraft engine). — *adj* **vecto'rial**. — *adv* **vecto'rially**. — *n* **vec'tograph** a picture giving a three-dimensional effect when looked at through special spectacles. — *n* **vec'toring** (*comput*) the process of transferring control (in a program) to an intermediate vector. — *n* **vectorizā'tion** or **-s-**. — *vt* **vec'torize** or **-ise** (*math, comput*). — *n* **vec'torscope** an instrument that displays the phase and amplitude of an applied signal, eg of the chrominance signal in colour television. [L *vector*, *-ōris* bearer, carrier, from *vehere*, *vectum* to convey]

Veda *vā'də* or *vē'*, *n* any one of, or all of, four ancient holy books of the Hindus: — *pl* **Vedas**. — *n* **Vedan'ta** a system of Hindu philosophy based on the Vedas. — *adj* **Vedan'tic** or **Ve'dic**. — *n* **Ve'dism**. — *n* **Ve'dist** a person learned in the Vedas. [Sans *veda* knowledge; cf **wit**, L *vidēre* to see, Gr *oida* I know; Sans *Vedānta*, from *veda* and *anta* end]

vedalia *vi-dā'li-ə*, *n* an *orig* Australian ladybird, *Rodolia cardinalis*, introduced elsewhere to control insect pests.

VE day *vē-ē'dā*, *abbrev*: Victory in Europe day (8 May, the date of the Allied victory in 1945).

Vedda *ved'ə*, *n* (a member of) an aboriginal people of Sri Lanka. — *adj* **Vedd'oid** of, pertaining to, or resembling, the Veddas; of a S Asian race, dark-skinned and curly-haired, to which the Veddas belong. — Also *n*.

vedette *vi-det'*, *n* a mounted sentry stationed to watch an enemy; a small vessel (**vedette'-boat**) for a similar purpose; (*və-det'*) a stage or film star. [Fr, from Ital *vedetta*, from *vedere*, from L *vidēre* to see]

Vedic, Vedism, Vedist. See under **Veda**.

veduta *ve-doo'tə, -tä*, *n* a panoramic view of a town, etc: — *pl* **vedu'te** (*-tā*). — *n* **vedutis'ta** a painter of vedute: — *pl* **vedutis'ti** (*-tē*). [Ital, a view]

vee *vē*, *n* the twenty-second letter of the alphabet (V, v); a mark or object shaped or angled like a V. — *combining form* **vee-** (also **V-**) shaped like the letter V, as in **vee'-gutter**, **vee'-joint**, etc.

veena. Same as **vina**.

veep *vēp*, (*US colloq*) *n* a vice-president. [**VP**]

veer[1] *vēr*, *vi* to change direction, *esp* (of the wind) clockwise; to shift round in direction or in mental attitude; to change course, *esp* away from the wind (*naut*); to turn, wind. — *vt* to turn, shift; to turn away from the wind. — *n* a shifting round. — *n* and *adj* **veer'ing**. — *adv* **veer'ingly**. [Fr *virer*]

veer[2] *vēr*, (*naut*) *vt* to pay out (cable, etc); to slack. [MDu *vieren*]

veery *vēr'i*, *n* the tawny thrush of N America. [Prob imit]

veg *vej*, (*colloq*) *n* short for vegetable or vegetables.

Vega *vē'gə*, *n* the first-magnitude star α Lyrae. [Ar *al wāqi'* (*al nasr*) the falling (vulture)]

vega *vā'gə*, *n* in Spain and S America, a low fertile plain; in Cuba, etc a tobacco-field. [Sp]

Vegan *vē'gən*, *n* (often without *cap*) a member of a subgroup of vegetarians using no animal produce at all. — Also *adj*. — *adj* **vegan'ic** pertaining to manuring with material which is purely *veg*etable org*anic*. — *n* **Vē'ganism** (also without *cap*).

vegeburger or **veggie-burger** *veg'i-bûr-gər*, *n* a hamburger-like creation prepared from vegetables rather than meat products. [*veg*etable or **veggie** and ham*burger*]

Vegemite® *vej'i-mīt*, (*Austr*) *n* a strongly flavoured yeast extract used as a spread, etc.

vegetable *vej'i-tə-bl*, *n* a plant or part of one used for food, other than those considered to be fruits; a person whose capabilities are so low, *esp* because of damage to the brain, that he or she is scarcely human (*colloq*); a dull, uninteresting person (*colloq derog*); an organism belonging to the plant kingdom. — *adj* of, for, derived from, composed of or of the nature of vegetables. — *adv* **veg'etably** in the manner of a vegetable. — **vegetable butter** any of several butter-like vegetable fats; **vegetable ivory** see under **ivory**; **vegetable kingdom** that division of natural objects which consists of vegetables or plants; **vegetable marrow** a variety of pumpkin cooked as a vegetable; the akee fruit; **vegetable mould** mould consisting mostly of humus; **vegetable oil** any of various oils extracted from plants, used eg in cooking; **vegetable oyster** salsify; **vegetable parchment** paper treated with dilute sulphuric acid; **vegetable sheep** in New Zealand, a dense cushion of composite plants (*Raoulia, Haastia*) at a distance resembling a sheep; **vegetable wax** a wax secreted by various plants that protects their surface from moisture loss. [L *vegetābilis* animating, from *vegetāre* to animate; cf **vigour**]

vegetal *vej'i-təl*, *adj* belonging to or characteristic of vegetables or plants in general; vegetative; of a level of life below the sensitive. — *n* (*rare*) a plant, vegetable. — **vegetal pole** (*zool*) the lower portion or pole of an ovum in which cleavage is slow owing to the presence of yolk. [Med L *vegetālis*, from L *vegetāre* to animate]

vegetarian *vej-i-tā'ri-ən*, *n* a person who lives wholly on vegetable food, with or without dairy products, honey, and eggs. — Also *adj*. — *n* **vegetā'rianism** the theory or practice of a vegetarian. [*veget*able and sfx *-arian*]

vegetate *vej'-i-tāt*, *vi* to grow or live as, or like, a vegetable or plant; to increase vegetatively; to live an inactive, almost purely physical, or dull life. — *adj* **veg'etant** vegetating. — *adj* **veg'etāted** covered with vegetation. — *n* and *adj* **veg'etāting**. — *n* **vegetā'tion** the process of vegetating; vegetable growth; a plantlike growth; plants growing in the mass; a plant (*obs*). — *adj* **veg'etātive** growing, as plants; producing growth in plants; concerned with the life of the individual rather than of the race (*biol*); by means of vegetative organs, not special reproductive structures (*biol*); relating to unconscious or involuntary bodily functions as resembling the process of vegetable growth (*biol*); without intellectual activity, unprogressive. — *adv* **veg'etātively**. — *n* **veg'etātiveness**. — **vegetative nervous system** the nervous system regulating involuntary bodily activity, as the secretion of the glands, the beating of the heart, etc; **vegetative organs** leaves, stems, roots; **vegetative reproduction** reproduction by detachment of part of the plant-body; budding. [L *vegetāre*, *vegetātum* to animate]

vegete *vi-jēt'*, *adj* vigorous. [L *vegetus*, from *vegēre* to be vigorous]

vegetive *vej'i-tiv*, *n* (*Shakesp*) a vegetable. — *adj* vegetative. [Back-formation from *vegetative* (see under **vegetate**)]

veggie or **vegie** *vej'i*, (*colloq*) *n* a vegetarian; a vegetable (*esp* in *pl*). — Also *adj*.

veggie-burger. See **vegeburger**.

vehement *vē'(h)ə-mənt*, *adj* marked by, or evincing, an urgency and forcefulness born of strong conviction. — *n* **vē'hemence** or (now *rare*) **vē'hemency**. — *adv* **vē'hemently**. [L *vehemēns*, *-entis* eager, ardent]

vehicle *vē'i-kl*, *n* a means of conveyance or transmission, *esp* a structure with wheels in or on which people or things are transported by land; a medium, eg for the expressing or performing of something; a substance with which a medicine, a pigment, etc, is mixed for administration or application; (**space vehicle**) a structure for carrying burdens through air or space or (also **launch vehicle**) a rocket used to launch a spacecraft. — *adj* **vehicular** (*vi-hik'ū-lər*). — **vehicle-actuated signal** see under **pad**[2]. [L *vehiculum*, from *vehere* to carry]

Vehm or **Fehm** *fām* or **Vehmgericht** or **Fehmgericht** *-gə-rihht*, *n* a medieval German (*esp* Westphalian) court in which initiated persons held of the emperor power to try capital cases in public or in secret, their lower officers executing the guilty on the spot or where they could find them: — *pl* **Vehm'e, Fehm'e, Vehmgerichte** or **Fehmgerichte** (*-ə*). — *adj* **Vehm'ic, Vehm'ique** or **Fehm'ic**. — Forms without **-gericht** also without *cap*. [Ger *Vehm*, *Fehm*, now *Feme* criminal court, and *Gericht* court, judgement]

veil *vāl*, *n* a covering of fine fabric for the head, face, or both, for protection, concealment, adornment or ceremonial purpose, *esp* the white transparent one often worn by a bride; a nun's or novice's head-covering; a disguise or concealment; an obstruction of tone in singing; a velum; a humeral; a curtain, a covering (*archaic*). — *vt* to cover with a veil; to cover; to conceal, disguise or obscure. — *vi* to wear a veil. — *adj* **veiled**. — *n* **veil'ing** the act of concealing with a veil; a veil; material for making veils. — Also *adj*. — *adj* **veil'less** wanting a veil; uncovered. — *adj* **veil'y** like a veil, diaphanous. — **draw a veil over** to conceal discreetly; to refrain from mentioning; **eucharistic** or **sacramental veils** linen or silk covers for eucharistic vessels and elements; **take the veil** to become a nun. [OFr *veile* (Fr *voile*), from L *vēlum* a curtain, veil, sail]

veilleuse *vā-yœz'*, *n* a shaded night-lamp. [Fr, from *veiller* to watch]

vein *vān*, *n* one of the vessels or tubes that convey the blood back to the heart; (loosely) any blood vessel; one of the horny tubes forming the framework of an insect's wing; a vascular bundle forming a rib, *esp* a small rib, in a leaf; a small intrusion, or a seam of a different mineral running through a rock; a fissure or cavity; a streak in wood, stone, etc; a streak running through one's nature, a strain of character or ability; (a recurrent characteristic streak in) manner or style; a mood or humour. — *vt* to form veins or the appearance of veins in. — *adj* **veined** having veins; streaked, variegated. — *n* **vein'ing** formation or disposition of veins; streaking. — *n* **vein'let**. — *adj* **vein'ous** full of veins. — *adj* **vein'y** veined; veinous. — **vein'stone** or **vein'stuff** gangue. [Fr *veine*, from L *vēna*. See **vena**]

Vela *vē'lə*, *n* the Sail, a southern constellation, one of the divisions of Argo. [L, pl of *vēlum* sail]

vela. See under **velum**.

velamen *və-lā'mən*, *n* a multi-layered sheath of dead cells on some aerial roots (*bot*); a velum (*anatom*): — *pl* **velā'mina**. [L, veil]

velar, velarium, velate, etc. See under **velum**.

velatura *vel-ə-tōō'rə*, *n* a method of glazing a painting by rubbing with the hand. [Ital]

Velcro® *vel'krō*, *n* a nylon fastening material for clothes, etc consisting of two facing layers, the one composed of tiny hooks, the other of tiny loops, strips of which, attached one on either side of an opening, form a secure closure when pressed together.

veld or (outside S Africa) **veldt** *felt*, *velt*, *n* in S Africa, open, unforested, or thinly-forested grass-country. [Du *veld* (formerly *veldt*) field]

veldschoen (*old*) or **veldskoen** *felt'skōōn*, *n*. Same as **velskoen**.

vele *vēl*, (*Spenser*) *n*. Same as **veil**.

veleta or **valeta** *və-lē'tə*, *n* a dance or dance tune in quick waltz time. — Also **valē'ta**. [Sp, weather-cock]

veliger. See under **velum**.

velitation *vel-i-tā'shən*, *n* a skirmish. [L *vēlitātiō, -ōnis*, from *vēles, -itis* a light-armed soldier]

vell *vel*, *n* the fourth stomach of a calf, used in making rennet. [Origin unknown]

velleity *ve-lē'i-ti*, *n* volition in its lowest form; mere inclination. [LL *velleitās*, irregularly formed from L *velle* to wish]

vellenage *vel'ən-āj* (*Spenser*). Same as **villeinage**.

vellet *vel'it* (*Spenser*). Same as **velvet**.

vellicate *vel'i-kāt*, *vt* and *vi* to twitch. — *n* **vellicā'tion**. [L *vellicāre, -ātum* to pluck]

vellon *ve-lyōn'*, *n* billon; old Spanish copper money. [Sp *vellon*, from Fr *billon*]

Vellozia *ve-lō'zi-ə*, *n* the Brazilian tree-lily genus, giving name to an African and S American family **Vellozi-ā'ceae**, related to the amaryllids. [José *Vellozo* (1742–1811), Brazilian botanist]

vellum *vel'əm*, *n* a fine kind of parchment prepared by lime-baths and burnishing from the skins of calves, kids, or lambs; a manuscript, etc printed or written on vellum; a superior quality of writing paper. — *adj* made of, printed on, etc vellum. [OFr *velin*, from *vel* calf]

veloce *vā-lō'chā*, (*music*) *adj* and *adv* with great rapidity. [Ital]

velocimeter *vel-ə-sim'ə-tər*, *n* an instrument that measures velocity. — *n* **velocim'etry**. [L *vēlōc*itas, and **-meter**]

velocipede *vi-los'i-pēd*, *n* an early form of bicycle, *orig* one propelled by the feet on the ground; a swift-footed person (*obs*). — *adj* swift of foot. — *vi* to ride a velocipede. — *n* and *adj* **velocipē'dean** or **velocipē'dian**. — *n* **veloc'ipēder** (or *-pēd'*). — *n* and *adj* **velocipedestrian** (*obs*; *-pi-des'tri-ən*). — *n* **veloc'ipēdist** (or *-pēd'*). [Fr *vélocipède*, from L *vēlōx, -ōcis* swift, and *pēs, pedis* foot]

velocity *vi-los'i-ti*, *n* rate of motion (distance per unit of time) in a stated direction; (loosely) speed. — **velocity-distance law** (*astron*) the law that the more distant a nebula the greater is its speed of recession. — **velocity of circulation** (*econ*) the ratio between the value of a country's national product and the money supply within a specified time. [L *vēlōcitās, -ātis*, from *vēlōx* swift]

velodrome *vel'ə-drōm*, *n* a stadium containing a cycle-racing track. [Fr *vélodrome*]

velours or **velour** *və-lōōr'*, *n* a fabric with velvet-like pile; a polishing pad for silk hats. — Also *adj*. — *n* **veloutine** (*vel-ōō-tēn'*) a velvety corded wool fabric. — *n* **velure** (*və-lōōr'*, *-lūr'*; *Shakesp*) velvet; a velours. — *vt* to dress (a hat) with a velours. — *adj* **velutinous** (*-lōō'*, *-lū'*) velvety. [Fr *velours*]

velouté or **velouté sauce** *və-lōō-tā' (sōs)*, *n* a smooth white sauce made with stock. [Fr, velvety]

velskoen *fel'skōōn*, (*SAfr*) *n* a shoe made of rawhide. [Du *vel* skin, and *schoen* shoe]

velt-mareschal (*Scott*) *n* a field marshal. [Ger *Feld-marschall*]

velum *vē'ləm*, *vā'*, *wā'lōōm*, *n* an integument or membrane; the membrane joining the rim of a young toadstool with the stalk; the pendulous soft palate; a ciliated disc, a locomotor organ in some molluscan larvae; an in-turned rim in jellyfishes: — *pl* **vē'la**. — *adj* **vē'lar** of the velum; produced by the back of the tongue brought close to, or in contact with, the soft palate (*phonetics*). — *n* a velar consonant, back consonant. — *adj* **velar'ic** pertaining to a velar. — *n* **velā'rium** (L *vā-lä'ri-ōōm*) an awning over an auditorium; in Scyphozoa, the thin marginal region of the umbrella: — *pl* **velā'ria**. — *n* **velarīzā'tion** or **-s-**. — *vt* **ve'larize** or **-ise** to pronounce (a non-velar sound) with the back of the tongue brought close to the soft palate, *esp* through the influences of a vowel sound. — *adj* **ve'larized** or **-s-**. — *adj* **vē'late** or **vēlā'ted** having a velum. — *n* **vē'liger** (*-jər*) a mollusc larva with a velum. [L *vēlum* veil, sail, *vēlāmen, -āminis* covering, *vēlārium* awning]

velure, velutinous. See **velours**.

velvet *vel'vit*, *n* a silk, cotton, etc fabric with a soft close-cut pile; any of various other velvety fabrics; the velvetlike covering of a growing antler; a velvety surface or skin; gains, winnings (*slang*). — *adj* made of velvet; soft or smooth like velvet. — *n* **vel'veret** a cotton with a silk pile. — *adj* **vel'veted** clad in velvet. — *n* **velveteen'** a cotton, or mixed cotton and silk, fabric similar to velvet. — *n* **vel'vetiness**. — *n* **vel'veting** velvet material. — *adj* **vel'vety** soft and smooth like velvet; deep and soft in colouring. — **velvet ant** a wasp of the family *Mutillidae*; **vel'vet-crab** or **vel'vet-fidd'ler** a swimming crab with velvety pile; **vel'vet-duck** or **vel'vet-sco'ter** a black duck with a white mark on its wing; **vel'vet-guards** (*Shakesp*) velvet trimmings, applied metaphorically to the citizens who wore them; **vel'vet-leaf** false pareira; tree-mallow; **vel'vet-pa'per** flock paper; **vel'vet-pile** material with a soft nap. — **on velvet** in a safe or advantageous position; secure against losing, whatever happens; **the velvet glove** gentleness concealing strength (see **iron hand** under **iron**); **the velvet revolution** the bloodless transition from communism to democracy in Czechoslovakia in 1989. [LL *velvettum*, related to L *villus* a tuft]

vena *vē'nə*, (*anatom*) *n* a vein: — *pl* **ve'nae**. — *adj* **vē'nal** venous. — *n* **venation** (*vi-nā'shən*) a system or arrangement of blood vessels or of the veins of a leaf or an insect's wing. — *adj* **venā'tional**. — *n* **venesec'tion** or **venisec'tion** surgical incision into a vein, phlebotomy; the opening of a vein so as to let blood as a remedial measure. — *adj* **venograph'ic** or **venograph'ical**. — *n* **venog'raphy** radiography of a vein after injection of a contrast medium. — **vena cava** (*kā'və*) either of the two major veins (the **superior** and **inferior vena cava**) taking venous blood to the heart: — *pl* **vēnae cāvae** (*-nē* and *-vē*); **vē'na contrac'ta** the point of minimum cross-sectional area in a jet of fluid discharged from an orifice. [L, vein]

venal[1] *vē'nl*, *adj* open to bribery, able to be bought over; corruptly mercenary. — *n* **venality** (*-nal'i-ti*). — *adv* **vē'nally**. [L *vēnālis*, from *vēnum* goods for sale; cf Gr *ōnē* purchase]

venal[2]. See under **vena**.

venatic or **venatical** *vi-nat'ik*, *-əl*, *adj* relating to hunting. — *adv* **venat'ically**. — *n* **venation** (*vi-nā'shən*; *rare*) hunting; a hunt. — *n* **venā'tor** a huntsman, hunter. — *adj* **venatorial** (*ven-ə-tō'ri-əl*, *-tö'*). [L *vēnārī* to hunt, *vēnātiō* hunting, *vēnātor* a hunter]

venation. See **vena**, **venatic**.

vend *vend*, *vt* to sell or offer for sale, deal in, *esp* in a small way; to utter (*perh* altered from **vent**). — *n* a sale; the amount sold. — *n* **vendee'** a buyer. — *n* **vender** see under **vendor** below. — *n* **vendibil'ity**. — *adj* **vend'ible** that may be sold, offered for sale, or readily sold. — *n* a thing for sale; a possible object of trade. — *n* **ven'dibleness**. — *adv* **ven'dibly**. — *n* **venditā'tion** (*rare*) offering for sale. — *n* **vendi'tion** sale. — *n* **ven'dor** or **ven'der** a seller (*esp law*); a vending machine. — **vending machine** a slot-machine dispensing *esp* food or cigarettes. [Fr *vendre* or L *vendere* to sell, from *vēnum dare* to offer for sale]

vendace *ven'dəs*, *n* a freshwater white fish (*Coregonus vandesius*) formerly found in lochs in SW Scotland; another species (*C. gracilior*) found in lakes in NW England. — Also **ven'dis** or **ven'diss**. [Poss OFr *vendese*, *vendoise* (Fr *vandoise*) dace]

vendange *van'danj*, *n* the grape harvest. — Also **vendage** (*ven'dij*). [ME, from (O)Fr *vendange*; see **vintage**]

Vendean *ven-dē'ən*, *n* an inhabitant of La *Vendée*, in France; one of those who there resisted the French Revolution. — Also *adj*.

vendee. See under **vend**.

Vendémiaire *vâ-dā-myer'*, *n* the first month in the French Revolutionary calendar, about 22 September to 21 October. [Fr, from L *vīndēmia* vintage, from *vīnum* wine, and *dēmere* to take away, from *dē* from, and *emere* to take]

vendetta *ven-det'ə*, *n* a blood-feud; any similarly prolonged, violent, etc feud or quarrel. [Ital, from L *vindicta* revenge, from *vindicāre* to claim]

vendeuse *vā-dœz'*, *n* a saleswoman. [Fr]

vendible, **venditation**, **vendition**, etc. See under **vend**.

vendis, **vendiss**. See under **vendace**.

vendor. See under **vend**.

vendue *ven-dū'*, (*US*) *n* a public auction sale. [Du *vendu*, from Fr *vendue*]

veneer *və-nēr'*, *vt* to overlay or face (coarse wood, etc) with a thin sheet of fine wood or other material; to disguise with superficial refinement. — *n* a thin layer for veneering; a specious outward appearance of good quality, refinement, respectability, etc; a grass-moth, from its markings (also **veneer'-moth**). — *n* **veneer'er**. — *n* **veneer'ing**. [Formerly **fineer**, from Ger *furniren*, from OFr *fornir* (Fr *fournir*), Ital *fornire* to furnish]

venefic or **venefical** *vi-nef'ik*, *-əl*, **veneficious** *ven-i-fish'əs* or **veneficous** *vi-nef'i-kəs*, *adj* acting by poison or potions or by sorcery. — *adv* **venef'ically**, **venefic'iously** or **venefic'ously**. [L *venēficus*, from *venēnum* poison, and *facere* to do]

venepuncture or **venipuncture** *ven'i-* or *vē'ni-pungk-chər*, (*med*) *n* the puncturing of a vein with a hypodermic needle, to draw off a sample of blood or inject a drug. [L *vēna* a vein]

venerable *ven'ə-rə-bl*, *adj* worthy of reverence; hallowed by associations or age; aged-looking; an honorific prefix to the name of an archdeacon, or to a person in process of canonization. — *n* **ven'erableness**. — *adv* **ven'erably**. [L *venerābilis* worthy of reverence]

venerate *ven'ə-rāt*, *vt* to revere. — *n* **venerā'tion** the act of venerating; the state of being venerated; awed respect. — *n* **ven'erātor**. [L *venerārī*, *-ātus*]

venereal *vi-nē'ri-əl*, *adj* relating to sexual desire or intercourse; transmitted by sexual intercourse; relating to or affected by venereal disease. — *adj* (*obs*) **venē'rean** relating to Venus or her service, or to sexual desire or intercourse. — *n* (*obs*) a person addicted to sexual gratification. — *adj* **venē'reous** lustful; venereal; aphrodisiac. — **venereal disease** any of various contagious diseases characteristically transmitted by sexual intercourse. [L *venereus*, from *Venus*, *Veneris* the goddess of love]

venereology *vi-nē-ri-ol'ə-ji*, *n* the study of venereal diseases. — *adj* **venereolog'ical**. — *n* **venereol'ogist**. [L *venereus* relating to sexual love, and **-ology**]

venerer. See under **venery**[2].

venery[1] *ven'ə-ri*, (*archaic*) *n* the pursuit of sexual gratification. [Med L *veneria*, from L *Venus*, *Veneris* the goddess of love]

venery[2] *ven'ər-i*, (*archaic*) *n* hunting; game. — *n* **ven'erer** a gamekeeper; a hunter. [OFr *venerie*, from *vener*, from L *vēnārī* to hunt]

venesection. See under **vena**.

Venetian *vi-nē'shən*, *adj* of Venice. — *n* a native or inhabitant of Venice, in NE Italy; a Venetian blind. — *adj* **Vene'tianed** having Venetian blinds or shutters. — **Venetian blind** a window-blind of horizontal slats adjustable to let in or keep out light; **Venetian glass** very delicate glass made at Murano, near Venice; **Venetian mast** a spirally banded pole for street decoration; **Venetian mosaic** see under **terrazzo**; **Venetian red** ferric oxide as a pigment. [L *Venetiānus*, from *Venetia* Venice]

venewe *ven'ū* or **veney** *ven'i*. Shakespearian forms of **venue**.

venge *venj*, *vt* (*Shakesp*) to avenge. — *adj* **venge'able** revengeful (*Spenser*); destructive (*dialect*); extraordinarily great (*obs*). — *adv* **venge'ably**. — *n* **venge'ment** (*Spenser*) vengeance, penal retribution. — *n* **ven'ger** (*Spenser*) an avenger. [OFr *venger*, from L *vindicāre*]

vengeance *ven'jəns*, *n* the inflicting of injury in punishment or revenge; retribution; harm, mischief (*Shakesp*); a curse (*Shakesp*). — *adv* (*Shakesp*) extremely, exceedingly. — **what a** (or **the**) **vengeance** used to intensify questions; **with a vengeance** (*orig*) with a curse; violently, thoroughly, exceedingly (*colloq*). [OFr, from *venger* to avenge, from L *vindicāre*]

vengeful *venj'fəl*, *adj* eager for revenge; vindictive; retributive, retaliatory. — *adv* **venge'fully**. — *n* **venge'fulness**. [**venge**]

venial *vē'ni-əl*, *adj* pardonable; excusable; permissible (*Milton*). — *n* **veniality** (*-al'i-ti*). — *adv* **vē'nially**. — **venial sin** sin other than mortal. [L *veniālis* pardonable, from *venia* pardon]

Venice *ven'is*, *n* a city and former republic of Italy. — *adj* (*archaic*) Venetian. — **Venice glass** the former name for Venetian glass; **Venice gold** (*Shakesp*) gold thread made in Venice; **Venice talc** steatite; **Venice treacle**

(*archaic*) a supposed antidote for all poisons, of many ingredients; **Venice turpentine** larch turpentine, formerly shipped from Venice. [Fr *Venise*, from L *Venetia*]

venidium *ven-i'di-əm*, (*hortic*) *n* a plant native to S Africa, of the *Venidium* genus (family *Compositae*), having yellow or cream flowers. [New L, from L *vēna* vein]

venin *ven'in*, (*chem*) *n* any of various toxic substances in venom. [*ven*om and **-in**]

venipuncture. See **venepuncture**.

venire *ve-nī'rē, we-nē're* (in full **venire facias** *fā'shi-as, fa'ki-as*; *hist* and *US*) *n* a writ issued to a sheriff requiring him to cause a certain number of qualified persons to appear in court at a specified time so that jurors may be chosen from them; the persons so caused to appear. — **venī'reman** (*US*) a juror. [L, make... come]

venison *ven'i-zn* or (*esp* in Scotland) *-i-sən*, *n* deer's flesh as food; any game animal, *esp* its flesh as food (*obs*). [Anglo-Fr *venison* (Fr *venaison*), from L *vēnātiō, -ōnis* hunting, from *vēnārī* to hunt]

venite *vi-nī'ti, we-nē'te*, *n* the 95th Psalm, beginning *Venīte exultēmus* O come let us rejoice; a musical setting of this.

Venn diagram *ven dī'ə-gram*, (*math*) *n* a diagram in which sets and their relationships are represented, by overlapping circles or other figures. [John *Venn* (1834–1923), mathematician]

vennel *ven'l*, (*Scot*) *n* a lane. [Fr *venelle*, from L *vēna* a vein]

venom *ven'əm*, *n* poisonous fluid secreted by certain snakes and various other creatures, introduced into the victim by a bite or sting; spite. — *adj* (*Shakesp*) poisonous. — *vi* (*obs*) to poison; to envenom. — *adj* **ven'omed** venomous; charged with poison, envenomed. — *adj* **ven'omous** poisonous; having power to poison, *esp* by bite or sting; malignant, full of spite. — *adv* **ven'omously**. — *n* **ven'omousness**. — *adj* **ven'om'd-mouth'd** (*Shakesp*) having a venomous mouth, slanderous. [OFr *venim* (Fr *venin*), from L *venēnum* poison]

venose *vē'nōs, -nōs'*, *adj* veiny; veined; with very marked veins. [L *vēnōsus* veiny]

venous *vē'nəs*, *adj* relating to, or contained in, veins; full of veins; (of blood) deoxygenated, and, in human beings, dark red in colour; veined. — *n* **venosity** (*vē-nos'i-ti*) the state or quality of being venous, or of having or being like venous blood. [L *vēna* vein, and sfx *-ous*]

ven'son. Same as **venison**.

vent[1] *vent*, *n* a slit in a garment, *esp* in the back of a jacket; a crenel (*obs*). [Fr *fente*, from L *findere* to split; cf **fent**]

vent[2] *vent*, *n* an opening, aperture; an airhole; a touch-hole for firing a cannon, etc; an outlet; a volcanic orifice; an animal's or bird's anus; a chimney flue (*Scot*); an outlet; an emission, discharge or escape, *esp* of gas, smoke or a liquid; an otter's rise to the surface for breath; the opening in a parachute canopy through which air escapes at a controlled rate. — *vt* to give a vent or opening to; to let out, as at a vent; to allow to escape; to publish, utter (*archaic*); to discharge, emit, pour forth; to scent; to sniff at; to lift or open so as to admit air (*Spenser*). — *vi* to have or find an outlet; to discharge smoke, to function as a chimney, draw (*Scot*); to sniff or snuff; (of a beaver or otter) to take breath or rise for breath. — *n* **vent'age** or **vent'ige** (*Shakesp*) a finger-hole, as in a flute; a small hole. — *adj* **vent'ed**. — *n* (*obs*) **vent'er** a person who utters or publishes. — *n* **vent'iduct** (L *dūcere, ductum* to lead) a ventilating pipe or passage. — *n* and *adj* **vent'ing**. — **vent'-hole** a hole for admission or escape of air, fumes, etc, or to admit light; **vent'-peg** or **vent'-plug** a plug for stopping the vent of a barrel; **vent'-pipe** an escape-pipe, eg for steam or foul gases. — **give vent to** to allow to escape or break out; to give (*usu* violent) expression to (an emotion). [Fr, from L *ventus* wind; partly Fr *éventer* to expose to air; associated with **vent**[1] and **vent**[3]]

vent[3] *vent*, (*obs*) *n* a sale; a market. — *vt* (*obs* or *dialect*) to sell. [OFr *vente*, from L *vendere, venditum* to sell]

ventail, (*Spenser*) **ventayle** or **ventaile** *ven'tāl*, *n* in medieval armour, the part of a helmet protecting the lower part of the face. [Fr *ventail*, OFr *ventaille*, ult from L *ventus* wind]

ventana *ven-tä'nä*, *n* a window. [Sp]

ventayle. See **ventail**.

venter[1] *ven'tər*, (chiefly *zool* and *bot*) *n* the belly or abdomen; a womb or mother (*law*); a swelling or protuberance; a medial swelling; the dilated basal part of an archegonium; a shallow concave surface of a bone; the upper side or surface of a leaf, etc. — *adj* **ven'tral** of the belly; on the upper side or towards the axis (*bot*); on the side normally turned towards the ground (as opposed to *dorsal* or *neural*; *zool*). — *n* a ventral fin. — *adv* **ven'trally**. — *adj* **ven'tricose** or (*rare*) **ven'tricous** distended or swollen in the middle, at the side, or round the base (*bot, zool*); having a prominent or swollen belly. — *adj* **ventric'ūlar** of or of the nature of a ventricle; abdominal. — *n* **ven'tricule** or **ventric'ūlus** (*pl* **-lī**) a ventricle. — *n* **ventriculog'raphy** (*med*) radiography of the heart or brain after the introduction of a contrast medium (in the latter case *usu* air) into the ventricle(s). — **ventral fin** either of the paired fins on the belly of a fish; **ventral tank** (*aeronautics*) an auxiliary fuel tank, fixed or able to be jettisoned, mounted externally under the fuselage. — Also **belly tank**. [L *venter, -tris* belly, dimin *ventriculus*]

venter[2] *ven'tər*. An old form (*Milton*) of **venture**.

venter[3] See under **vent**[2].

ventiduct. See under **vent**[2].

ventifact *ven'ti-fakt*, (*geol*) *n* a stone shaped and/or polished by wind-blown sand. [L *ventus* wind, and arti*fact*]

ventige. See under **vent**[2].

ventil *ven'til*, (*music*) *n* a valve for giving sounds intermediate between the open harmonics in wind instruments; a valve in an organ for controlling the wind supply to various stops. [Ger, from LL *ventīle* shutter, sluice, from *ventus* wind]

ventilate *ven'ti-lāt*, *vt* to open or expose to the free passage of air; to provide with duct(s) for circulating air or for escape of air; to cause (blood) to take up oxygen, by supply of air; to supply air to (lungs); to expose to examination and discussion, to make public; to fan, winnow, blow upon. — *adj* **ven'tilable**. — *n* **ventilā'tion**. — *adj* **ven'tilātive**. — *n* **ven'tilātor** a device for introducing fresh air; a machine which ventilates the lungs of a person whose respiratory system is not functioning adequately; a person, animal or object that causes ventilation. [L *ventilāre, -ātum* to fan, wave, agitate, from *ventus* wind]

venting. See **vent**[2].

ventose *ven-tōs'* or *ven'*, *adj* windy; flatulent; puffed up with conceit. — *n* **Ventôse** (*vã-tōz*) the sixth month of the French Revolutionary calendar, about 19 February to 20 March. — *n* **ventosity** (*ven-tos'i-ti*) windiness. [L *ventōsus*, from *ventus* wind]

ventouse extraction *vã-tōōz iks-trak'shən*, *n* a method of obstetric delivery using a vacuum suction cup on the crown of the baby's head. [Fr *ventouse* suction cup]

ventral, etc. See under **venter**[1].

ventre *ven'tər*. An old form of **venture**.

ventre à terre *vã-tra-ter*, (*Fr*) belly to the ground; at high speed.

ventricle *ven'tri-kl*, (*anatom*) *n* either of the two lower contractile chambers of the heart, the right ventricle receiving venous blood from the right atrium and pumping it into the pulmonary loop for oxygenation, the left receiving oxygenated blood from the left atrium and pumping it into the arterial system for circulation round the body; any of various other cavities in the body, eg one of the four main cavities of the brain; the stomach (*obs*); the womb (*Shakesp*). — **ventricular fibrillation** unco-ordinated rapid electric activity of a heart ventricle. [L *ventriculus*, dimin of *venter* belly]

ventricose, etc, **ventricule**, etc. See under **venter**[1].

ventriloquism *ven-tril'ə-kwizm*, *n* the art of speaking so as to give the illusion that the sound comes from some other source. — *adj* **ventril'oqual** or **ventriloquial** (*-lō'kwi-əl*). — *adv* **ventrilō'quially**. — *n* **ventril'oquist**. — *adj* **ventriloquis'tic**. — *vi* **ventril'oquize** or **-ise** to practise ventriloquism. — *adj* **ventril'oquous**. — *n* **ventril'oquy** ventriloquism. [L *ventriloquus* a person who speaks by a spirit in the belly, from *venter* the belly, and *loquī* to speak]

ventring. See under **venture**.

ventripotent *ven-trip'ə-tənt*, (*facetious*) *adj* with great capacity or appetite for food. [After Rabelais, from L *venter* belly, and *potēns* powerful, from *posse* to be able]

venture *ven'chər*, *n* an undertaking whose issue is uncertain or dangerous; a commercial enterprise or speculation with a risk of loss; something attempted; chance, luck, hazard (*archaic*); that which is put to hazard (*esp* goods sent by sea at the sender's risk); a prostitute (*Shakesp*). — *vt* to expose to hazard; to risk; to take the risk of; to dare to put forward; to send on a venture. — *vi* to make a venture; to run a risk; to dare; to dare to go. — *n* **ven'turer**. — *adj* **ven'turesome** inclined or willing to take risks; involving the taking of risk; risky. — *adv* **ven'turesomely**. — *n* **ven'turesomeness**. — *n* and *adj* **ven'turing** (*Milton* **ven'tring**). — *adv* **ven'turingly**. — *adj* **ven'turous** (*Spenser*, *Milton*, etc, **ven'trous** or **ven't'rous**) adventurous; daring. — *adv* **ven'turously**. — *n* **ven'turousness**. — **venture capital** money supplied by individual investors or business organizations for a new, *esp* speculative, business enterprise, also called **risk capital**; **venture capitalist** such an investor; **Venture Scout**, **Venture Air Scout** and **Venture Sea Scout** a male or female member of a senior branch of the Scout organization (for 16 to 20-year-olds), formerly called Rover (Scout). — **at a venture** at hazard, random. [For **a venture**, obs variant of **adventure**]

Venturi *ven-tōō'ri* or **Venturi tube** *tūb*, (also without *cap*) *n* a tube or duct, wasp-waisted and expanding at the ends, used in measuring the flow rate of fluids, or as a means of regulating flow, or to provide suction. [G B *Venturi* (1746–1822), Italian physicist]

venue *ven'ū*, (*Shakesp* **venewe** or **veney**) *n* a meeting-place or rendezvous; the chosen location for a sports event, concert, etc; the place where a case is to be tried, or the district from which the jurors are drawn (*usu* the county in which the alleged offence was committed) (*law*, *hist*); a hit or thrust in fencing (*obs*); a bout or match (*obs*). — **change of venue** change of place of trial; **lay the venue** to specify the place where the trial is to be held. [OFr *venue* arrival, from *venir*, from L *venīre* to come]

venule *ven'ūl*, (*anatom* and *zool*) *n* a branch of a vein in an insect's wing; any of the small-calibre blood vessels into which the capillaries empty, and which join up to form veins. [L *vēnula*, dimin of *vēna* vein]

Venus *vē'nəs*, *n* the goddess of love, *orig* of spring, patron of flower-gardens, later identified with the Greek Aphrodite (*Roman mythol*); the most brilliant of the planets, second in order from the sun; copper (*alchemy*); an alluring grace, beauty (*obs*); venery (*obs*); (without *cap*) a mollusc of a genus (*Venus*) of lamellibranch molluscs, including the quahog, or of related genera (**Ve'nus-shell'** a shell, or mollusc, of the genus). — *n* and *adj* **Venusian** (*ven-ōō'zi-ən*, *ven-ū'*), less commonly **Venutian** (*ven-ōō'shi-ən*, *ven-ū'*) (in science fiction, an inhabitant) of the planet Venus. — **Venus's comb** an umbelliferous plant (*Scandix pecten-Veneris*) with long-beaked fruits set like comb teeth; **Venus's flowerbasket** a deep-sea sponge with a skeleton of glassy spicules; **Venus's** (or **Venus**) **fly trap** an insectivorous plant with hinged leaves that snap shut on insects that land on them; **Venus's girdle** a ribbonlike gelatinous sea creature; **Venus's looking-glass** a garden plant (*Specularia*) with small bright flowers. — **girdle of Venus** (*palmistry*) a line on the palm forming a semicircle from between the first and second to between the third and fourth fingers, apparently indicative of a hysterical and desponding temperament; **mount of Venus** the elevation at the base of the thumb; the mons Veneris or mons pubis (qv). [L, orig personified from *venus*, *veneris* desire; related to *venerārī* to worship]

venville *ven'vil*, *n* a form of tenure in parishes around Dartmoor that gives tenants certain rights to the use of land on Dartmoor. [Origin obscure]

Vera *vē'rə*, *n* a machine that records television pictures and sound on magnetic tape for almost immediate reproduction. [*v*ision *e*lectronic *r*ecording *a*pparatus]

veracious *və-rā'shəs*, *adj* truthful. — *adv* **verā'ciously**. — *n* **veracity** (*-ras'i-ti*) truthfulness. [L *vērāx*, *-ācis*, from *vērus* true]

veranda or **verandah** *və-ran'də*, *n* a roofed gallery, terrace, or open portico along the front or side of a building. — *adj* **veran'da'd** or **veran'dahed** having a veranda. [Hindi *varaṇḍā*, prob from Port *varanda* a balcony]

veratrum *və-rā'trəm*, *n* a plant of the white hellebore genus *Veratrum*. — *n* **veratrin** or **veratrine** (*ver'ə-trin*, *-trēn*) an alkaloid or mixture of alkaloids obtained from white hellebore rhizomes, sabadilla, etc. [L *vērātrum* hellebore]

verb *vûrb*, *n* (*gram*) a part of speech consisting of a word or group of words that signify an action, experience, occurrence or state, in sentence analysis constituting or introducing the predicate. [L *verbum* word]

verbal *vûr'bəl*, *adj* of, relating to or derived from a verb or verbs; of, in, of the nature of, in the matter of or concerned with words, or words rather than things; word-for-word, literal; oral; voluble; articulate. — *n* a word, *esp* a noun, derived from a verb; (often in *pl*) an oral statement, *esp* an arrested suspect's confession of guilt, made to the police, or claimed by them to have been made (*slang*); (an) insult, (piece of) abuse or invective (*slang*); (*usu* in *pl*) fast talk, glib patter. — *vt* (*slang*) (of the police) to attribute a statement or admission to, or extract it from, (a suspect, etc): — *pr p* **verb'alling**; *pa t* and *pa p* **verb'alled**. — *n* **ver'balism** an expression; wording; undue attention to words alone; literalism. — *n* **ver'balist** a person skilled in words; a literalist; a person who is concerned with words alone. — *n* **verbal'ity** the quality of being verbal or merely verbal; mere words. — *n* **verbalīzā'tion** or **-s-**. — *vt* **ver'balize** or **-ise** to turn into a verb; to put in words. — *vi* to use too many words, be prolix. — *adv* **ver'bally**. — *n* **verbā'rian** a coiner of words. — *n* and *adj* **verb'icide** (*-sīd*) (the quality of) destroying the meaning of a word. — *n* **verb'id** (*gram*) a non-finite part of a verb, such as a verbal noun or infinitive. — *n* **verbificātion**. — *vt* **verb'ify** to convert into a verb. — *vi* **verbigerate** (*-ij'ə-rāt*). — *n* **verbigerā'tion** the morbid and purposeless repetition of certain words and phrases at short intervals, eg as occurs in schizophrenia. — *adj* **verb'less**. — **verbal inspiration** dictation of every word of a book (*usu* the Bible) by God; **verbal note** in diplomacy, an unsigned reminder of a neglected, though perhaps not urgent, matter; **verbal noun** a form of a verb, eg infinitive or (*esp*) gerund, functioning as a noun. [L *verbum* word]

Verbascum *vər-bas'kəm*, *n* the mullein (qv) genus. [L]

verbatim *vər-bā'tim*, *-ba'tim*, *adv* word for word, using exactly the same words (also *adj*); by word of mouth (*Shakesp*). — **verbatim et literatim** (*-ā'tim*, *-a'tim*) word for word and letter for letter. [L]

verbena *vûr-bē'nə*, *n* a plant of the vervain genus *Verbena*, giving name to the family **Verbenaceae** (*vûr-bi-nā'si-ē*), closely related to the labiates; any plant of similar appearance. — *adj* **verbenā'ceous**. — **verbe'na-oil** an oil obtained from the related plant *Lippia citriodora* (called **lemon-scented verbena**) or from lemon-grass. [L *verbēna* a leafy twig, sacred bough]

verberate *vûr'bər-āt*, (*archaic*) *vt* to beat. — *n* **verberā'tion**. [L *verberāre*, *-ātum* to scourge]

verbiage *vûr'bi-əj, n* superfluity of words, verbosity, prolixity; wording (*rare*). [Fr, from OFr *verbier* to chatter]

verbicide. See under **verb**.

verbose *vûr'bōs, adj* using or containing more words than are desirable; wordy. — *adv* **verbose'ly**. — *n* **verbose'ness** or **verbosity** (*-bos'*). [L *verbōsus* prolix]

verboten *fer-bō'tən,* (*Ger*) *adj* forbidden.

verb. sap., verbum sap. or **verbum sat.** *vûrb* or *vûr'bəm, abbrev*: *verbum sapienti sat est* (*L*), a word is sufficient to the wise, no need for further explanation.

verdant *vûr'dənt, adj* (*esp* of landscape or vegetation) green; covered with fresh green vegetation; green, unsophisticated, raw and gullible. — *n* **ver'dancy**. — *adv* **ver'dantly**. — *n* **ver'det** copper acetate. [OFr *verdeant*, *verdet*, ult from L *vindis* green]

verd-antique *vûrd-an-tēk'* (*obs Fr*) or **verde-antico** *ver'dā-än-tē'kō,* (*Ital*) *n* a breccia of serpentine containing calcite, etc. — **oriental verd-antique** a green porphyry. [Antique green; Fr now *vert*]

verdelho *vər-del'yo͞o, n* (a white Madeira made from) a white grape grown *orig* in Madeira, now also in Portugal, Sicily, Australia and S Africa. [Port]

verderer or **verderor** *vûr'-də-rər,* (*hist*) *n* an officer of the law responsible for order in the royal forests. [Anglo-Fr, from OFr *verdier*, from L *viridis* green]

verdet. See **verdant**.

verdict *vûr'dikt* or formerly (*Spenser, Milton*) **verdit** *-dit, n* the decision of a jury at a trial; judicial decision or decision generally. — **formal verdict** see under **formal**; **open verdict** see **open**; **special verdict** a verdict in which specific facts are found and put on the record. [OFr *verdit* and LL *vērēdictum*, from L *vērē* truly, and *dictum* said]

verdigris *vûr'di-grēs, n* basic cupric acetate; (popularly) the green coating of basic cupric carbonate that forms in the atmosphere on copper, brass, or bronze. — *vt* to coat with verdigris. [OFr *verd de Grece* green of Greece]

verdin *vûr'din, n* a small yellow-headed tit, *Auriparus flaviceps*, from SW N America. [Fr, yellowhammer]

verdit. See **verdict**.

verdite *vûr'dīt, n* a S African green mica, used ornamentally in jewellery and architecture. [*verd*ant and **-ite**]

verditer *vûr'di-tər,* (*archaic*) *n* a blue or green pigment, hydrated cupric carbonate. [OFr *verd-de-terre*, earth green]

verdoy *vûr'doi,* (*heraldry*) *adj* charged with flowers, leaves, or vegetable charges, as a bordure. [Fr *verdoyé*, pa p of *verdoyer* to become green]

verdure *vûr'dyər,* (chiefly *poetic*) *n* fresh greenness; greenery, green vegetation; fresh taste (*obs*); freshness (*fig*). — *adj* **ver'dured** clad with verdure. — *adj* **ver'dureless**. — *adj* **ver'durous**. [OFr, from *verd* (Fr *vert*), from L *viridis* green]

verecund *ver'i-kund, adj* modest. [L *verēcundus*]

Verein *fər-īn',* (*Ger*) *n* union, association.

Verey light. See **Very light**.

verge[1] *vûrj, n* a limit, boundary; a rim; the brink, extreme edge; the horizon (*poetic*); the edge of a roof projecting beyond the gable (*archit*); a grass edging to a road, etc; a rod or rodlike part; the spindle of the balance wheel in early clocks; a rod or staff of office; extent of jurisdiction, *esp* of the Lord High Steward of the royal household (*hist*); a precinct or pale; range or scope; jurisdiction; — *vt* to edge. — *vi* (with *on*) to border, be on the edge of; (with *on*) to come close to, nearly be (a state or condition). — **verge'-board** a barge board. — **on the verge of** on the point of; on the brink of, very close to (a state, condition or situation). [L *virga* a rod; the area of jurisdiction of the holder of the office symbolized by the rod, hence, limit, boundary]

verge[2] *vûrj, vi* to incline; to tend downward; to slope; to tend; to pass gradually, merge. — *n* **ver'gence** (*opthalmol*) the simultaneous motion of both eyes either inwards or outwards when changing focus. — *n* **ver'gency**. [L *vergere* to bend]

verger *vûr'jər, n* in various Episcopal churches, a church official who acts as attendant and caretaker; an official who, on ceremonial occasions, bears the vergé or staff of office before a bishop or other dignitary. — *n* **ver'gership**. [**verge**[1]]

Vergilian. See **Virgilian**.

verglas *ver'glä, n* a film of ice on rock. [Fr (*verre* glass, and *glace* ice), from OFr]

veridical *vi-rid'i-kl, adj* truthful; coinciding with fact; (of a dream or vision) corresponding exactly with what has happened or with what happens later; seemingly true to fact. — *n* **veridicality** (*-kal'i-ti*). — *adv* **verid'ically**. — *adj* **verid'icous** truthful. [L *vēridicus*, from *vērus* true, and *dīcere* to say]

verier, veriest. See **very**.

verify *ver'i-fī, vt* to ascertain, confirm, check or test the truth or accuracy of; to assert or prove to be true; to testify to the truth of, support (a statement; *law*); to check (items of data input) for accuracy eg by having the same data keyed twice, by two separate operators, and then checked by computer for discrepancies (*comput*); to back up or support (*Shakesp*): — *pr p* **ver'ifying**; *pa t* and *pa p* **ver'ified**. — *n* **verifīabil'ity**. — *adj* **ver'ifīable**. — *n* **verificā'tion**. — *adj* **ver'ificātory**. — *n* **ver'ifīer**. [L *vērus* true, and *facere* to make]

verily. See **very**.

verisimilitude *ver-i-si-mil'i-tūd, n* the quality of seeming real or true, an appearance of truth or reality; a statement, etc that merely sounds true. — *adj* **verisim'ilar**. — *adv* **verisim'ilarly**. — *n* **verisimil'ity** (*obs*). — *adj* **verisim'ilous**. [L *vērīsimilitūdō*, from *vērus* true, and *similis* like]

verism *vē'rizm* or *ver'izm, n* use of everyday contemporary material, including what is ugly or sordid, in the arts, *esp* in early 20c Italian opera (Ital **verismo** *vā-rēs'mō*); the theory supporting this. — *adj* and *n* **ver'ist**. — *adj* **verist'ic**. [Ital *verismo* from *vero*, from L *vērus* true]

vérité. See **cinéma vérité** under **cinema**.

verity *ver'i-ti, n* truth; a truth, *esp* a basic or fundamental one; truthfulness; something that exists, a reality. — *pl* **ver'ities**. — *adj* **ver'itable** true; genuine; real, actual; truly or justifiably so called. — *n* **ver'itableness**. — *adv* **ver'itably**. — **of a verity** (*archaic*) assuredly. [L *vēritās*, *-ātis*, from *vērus* true]

verjuice *vûr'jo͞os, n* the juice of unripe fruit; sourness, tartness. — *adj* sour. — *adj* **ver'juiced** soured. [Fr *verjus*, from *vert* (L *viridis*) green, and *jus* juice (L *jūs* broth)]

verkramp *fər-kramp', adj* (used predicatively) in S Africa, narrow-minded, illiberal and rigidly conservative in attitude, *esp* towards black and coloured people. — *adj* (used *attrib*) and *n* **verkrampte** (*-kram(p)'tə*) (a person) of such rigidly conservative political attitudes. [Afrik, restricted]

verlig *fər-lihh', adj* (used predicatively) in S Africa, liberal, politically enlightened, *esp* towards black and coloured people. — *adj* (used *attrib*) and *n* **verligte** (*-lihh'tə,*) (a person) of such enlightened and liberal political attitudes. [Afrik, enlightened]

vermal. See under **vermis**.

vermeil *vûr'mil, -māl, n* and *adj* bright red, scarlet, vermilion; silver-gilt or gilt bronze. — *vt* to colour with vermeil. — Also **ver'mil** or **ver'meille** (*Spenser* **ver'mell** or **ver'mily**). [OFr and Fr, from L *vermiculus* a little worm, kermes, dimin of *vermis* worm; cf **vermilion**]

vermes. See under **vermis**.

vermi- *vûr-mi-, combining form* denoting worm. — *adj* **ver'midical** (*vûr'mi-sī-dl*). — *n* **ver'micide** a worm-killing agent. — *n* **ver'miculture** the farming of earthworms, *esp* as bait for fishing. — *adj* **ver'miform** having the form of a worm (**vermiform appendix** (*anatom*) the appendix, a worm-shaped process projecting from the lower end of the ascending colon). — *adj* **vermifugal** (*vər-mif'ū-gl*) expelling worms. — *n* **ver'mifuge** (*-fūj*) a drug that expels worms. — *adj* **vermiv'orous** worm-eating. [L *vermis*, a worm]

vermian. See under **vermis**.

vermicelli *vûr-mi-sel'i* or *-chel'i*, *n* a very slender type of pasta; (more *usu* **chocolate vermicelli**) short thin pieces of chocolate used for decoration of cakes, sweets, etc. — Also *adj*. [Ital, pl of *vermicello*, dimin of *verme* worm, from L *vermis*]

vermicidal, etc. See under **vermi-**.

vermicular *vûr-mik'ū-lər*, *adj* of, of the nature of or like a worm; relating to or caused by intestinal worms (*pathol*); vermiculate (*archit*). — *adj* **vermic'ulate** (*-lət*) or **vermic'ulated** bearing a decoration reminiscent of a mass of curly worms, rusticated (*archit*); worm-eaten. — *n* **vermiculā'tion** rustication (*archit*); a worm-eaten condition; peristalsis of the intestines (*physiol*) — *n* **ver'micule** a little worm. — *n* **vermic'ūlite** an altered mica that curls before the blowpipe flame and expands greatly at high temperature, forming a water-absorbent substance used in seed-planting, and also used as insulating material. — *adj* **vermic'ūlous** wormy. [L *vermiculus*, dimin of *vermis* worm]

vermiculture, **vermiform**, **vermifugal**, etc. See under **vermi-**.

vermil, etc. See **vermeil**.

vermilion *vər-mil'yən*, *n* a bright-red pigment, mercuric sulphide; its bright scarlet colour. — *adj* bright scarlet. — *vt* to colour vermilion. [OFr *vermillon*, from *vermeil* (see **vermeil**)]

vermin *vûr'min*, *n* a collective name for small animals, insects or birds that are troublesome or destructive to crops, game or domestic stock; obnoxious or despicable people. — *vi* **ver'minate** to breed vermin. — *n* **verminā'tion**. — *adj* **ver'mined** infested with vermin. — *adj* **ver'minous** or **ver'miny** infested with vermin; like vermin. — **ver'min-killer**. [Fr *vermin*, from L *vermis* a worm]

vermis *vûr'mis*, *n* a worm or wormlike structure, eg (*anatom*) the *vermis cerebelli*, the central lobe of the cerebellum: — *pl* **vermes** (*-mēz*) worms; (with *cap*) in old classifications (now abandoned) a subkingdom of animals, according to Linnaeus including all invertebrates except arthropods, later mainly flat-worms, thread-worms and annelids. — *adj* **ver'mal** or **ver'mian**. [L, worm]

vermivorous. See under **vermi-**.

vermouth *vûr'məth* or *vər-mōōth'*, *n* a drink with white wine base, flavoured with wormwood or other aromatic herbs. [Fr, from Ger *Wermut(h)* wormwood (OE *wermōd*)]

vernacular *vər-nak'ū-lər*, *adj* (of language) indigenous, native, spoken by the people of the country or of one's own country; of, in, or using the vernacular language; of the jargon or idiom of a particular group; (of other things) native, local, endemic, *esp* of architecture or general style of building. — *n* a native language or dialect; a class jargon; profane language (*facetious*); a vernacular style of building. — *n* **vernac'ularism** a vernacular expression or idiom; the use of the vernacular. — *n* **vernac'ularist** a user of the vernacular. — *n* **vernacularity** (*-lar'i-ti*). — *n* **vernaculariza'tion** or **-s-**. — *vt* **vernac'ularize** or **-ise** to make vernacular. — *adv* **vernac'ularly**. [L *vernāculus*, from *verna* a home-born slave]

vernal *vûr'nəl*, *adj* of, happening or appearing in spring; springlike; fresh and youthful (*poetic*). — *n* **vernality** (*-nal'i-ti*) springlike quality; freshness. — *n* **vernalīzā'tion** or **-s-**. — *vt* **ver'nalize** or **-ise** to make springlike; to freshen; to hasten the development of (seeds or seedlings) by treating them in various ways before planting, eg by subjecting them to a low temperature. — *adv* **ver'nally**. — *adj* **ver'nant** (*Milton*) flowering or sprouting in spring. — *n* **vernā'tion** the arrangement of leaves in the vegetative bud (rarely that of the individual leaf). — **vernal grass** an early-sprouting meadow grass (*Anthoxanthum odoratum*) that gives its scent of coumarin to hay. [L *vērnālis* vernal, *vērnāre*, *-ātum* to sprout, from *vēr* spring]

Verner's law. See under **law**[1].

vernicle *vûr'ni-kl*, *n* a cloth bearing an impression of the face of Christ, believed to have been miraculously impressed on it when St *Veronica* wiped his face; any representation of this; a medal or badge bearing it, worn by pilgrims who had been at Rome. [OFr *veronicle*, from L *veronica* St Veronica's cloth]

vernier *vûr'ni-ər*, *n* a short scale sliding on a graduated scale to give fractional readings; a small auxiliary device that enables a piece of apparatus to be adjusted very accurately (eg a **vernier condenser** a condenser of small capacitance connected in parallel with one of larger capacitance); a small rocket engine used to make the movement of a booster rocket, or of a ballistic missile, more precisely as required. — Also *adj*. [P *Vernier* (1580–1637), French mathematician, who invented the scale]

vernis martin *ver-nē mär-tɛ̃*, *n* (also with *caps*) a varnish used on 18c furniture, etc, in imitation of oriental lacquer. [Fr *vernis* varnish, and *Martin* surname of the French brothers who were noted as producers of such items]

vernissage *ver-nēs-äzh'*, *n* varnishing-day (qv). [Fr, varnishing]

Veronal® or **veronal** *ver'ə-nal*, *-nəl*, *n* barbitone.

veronica *və-ron'i-kə*, *n* any of several herbs and shrubs of the speedwell genus *Veronica*; (Sp *vā-rō'nē-kä*; in bullfighting) a movement with the cape supposedly reminiscent of St Veronica's in offering her handkerchief to Christ; a vernicle. [St *Veronica*]

véronique *vā-ro-nēk'*, (*Fr*) *adj* (used after the noun) served with white grapes, eg *sole véronique*. [Origin uncertain]

verquere *vər-k(w)ēr'*, *n* an obsolete form of backgammon. — (*Scott*) **verquire'**. [Du *verkeeren* to turn round, to play at backgammon]

verrel *ver'l*, *n* old (now *dialect*) form of **ferrule**.

verrey, **verry** *ver'i*. Same as **vairé**.

verruca *və-rōō'kə*, *n* a wart, *esp* one on the sole of the foot; a wartlike outgrowth: — *pl* **verru'cae** (*-sē*, *-kī*) or **verru'cas**. — *adj* **verru'ciform** (*-si-fōrm*) wartlike. — *adj* **verrucose** (*ver'* or *-rōō'*) or **verru'cous** (or *ver'*) warty. — *n* **verru'ga** (*Sp*; also *pl* **verru'gas**) a fever with warty tumours, endemic in Peru. [L *verrūca* a wart]

vers *ver*, (*Fr*) *n* verse. — *n* **verset** (*vûr'sət*) a short organ interlude or prelude (*music*); a versicle; a little scrap of verse. — **vers de société** (*də so-syā-tā*) light witty verse; **vers d'occasion** (*dok-az-yɔ̃*) occasional verse, produced for a particular event; **vers libre** (*lē'br'*) free verse, hence *n* **verslibrist** (*ver-lē'brist*) or (*Fr*) **verslibriste** (*ver-lē'brēst*) a writer of free verse.

versability *vûr-sə-bil'i-ti*, (*obs*) *n* aptness to be turned round. [L *versābilis*, from *versāre* to turn over]

versal[1] *vûr'səl* or *vär'səl*, (*obs colloq*) *adj* whole; single, individual. [For **universal**]

versal[2] *vûr'səl*, *n* an ornamental letter at the beginning of a section, eg in an illuminated manuscript. [**verse**, and *-al*, noun-forming *sfx*]

versant[1] *vûr'sənt*, *adj* versed, conversant; busied, concerned. [L *versāns*, *-antis*, pr p of *versāre* to turn over, consider]

versant[2] *vûr'sənt*, *n* the general slope of a mountain, or the area over which this extends. [Fr *versant*, from *verser* to turn over, from L *versāre*]

versatile *vûr'sə-tīl* or (*US*) *-təl*, *adj* turning easily from one thing to another; of many-sided ability; capable of many uses; turning freely; dangling, hanging freely, as an anther attached by the middle of the back (*bot*); capable of free movement, reversible, as the toes of some birds (*zool*); changeable; unsteady. — *adv* **ver'satilely**. — *n* **ver'satileness** or **versatility** (*-til'i-ti*). [L *versātilis*, from *versāre*, frequentative of *vertere* to turn]

verse[1] *vûrs*, *n* poetry as opposed to prose; a line of metre; a metrical composition, form, or work; versification; a stanza; a short division of a chapter, *esp* of the Bible; a portion of an anthem to be performed by a single voice to each part; a versicle. — *vt* and *vi* to versify. — *n* **verse'let** a little verse; a short poem. — *n* **ver'ser** a writer of verse. — *n* **ver'sicle** a little verse; in liturgy, the verse said by the officiant. — *adj* **versic'ūlar** of or in verse. — *n* **ver'sing** the composing of verse. — **verse'-maker**; **verse'-making**; **verse'-man** (*archaic*) a writer of verse; **verse'-monger** a scribbler of verses; **verse'-mongering**; **verse'-smith** a writer of verse. — **free verse** see under **free**. [OE *fers*, reinforced by Fr *vers*, both from L *versus*, *vorsus*, *-ūs* a line, row, verse, from *vertere* to turn]

verse[2]. See under **versed**[1].

versed[1] *vûrst*, *adj* thoroughly acquainted, skilled (with *in*). — *vt* **verse** to make conversant (with *in*). [L *versātus*, pa p of *versārī* to busy oneself]

versed[2] *vûrst*, (*math*) *adj* turned, reversed. — **versed sine** a trigonometrical function of an angle, one minus the cosine (short form **versin** or **versine**). [L *versus*, pa p of *vertere* to turn]

verselet, **verser**. See under **verse**[1].

verset. See under **vers**.

versicle, etc. See under **verse**[1].

versicoloured *vûr'si-kul-ərd*, *adj* diversely or changeably coloured. [L *versicolor*, *-ōris*, from *vertere*, *versum* to change, and *color* colour]

versiform *vûr'si-fŏrm*, *adj* varying in form. [L *versus* turned, and **-form**]

versify *vûr'si-fī*, *vi* to compose verse. — *vt* to tell or express in verse; to turn into verse: — *pr p* **ver'sifying**; *pa t* and *pa p* **ver'sified**. — *n* **versificā'tion** the art or process of composing in verse or turning something into verse; the manner of construction, metrical pattern, etc of verse. — *n* **ver'sificātor** or **ver'sifier** a maker of verses. [OFr *versifier*, from L *versificāre*, from *versus* verse, and *facere* to make]

versin *vûr'sin* or **versine** *vûr'sīn*, (*math*) *n* short for versed sine (qv under **versed**[2]).

version *vûr'shən*, *n* a particular form in which something is embodied, as a particular way of telling a story; a variant; a turning (of something), now *esp* (*med*) a manual turning of the foetus shortly before birth to a head-first position; translation; a Latin prose (*Scot*). — *adj* **ver'sional**. — *n* **ver'sioner** or **ver'sionist** the producer of a version. [L *versiō*, *-ōnis*, from *vertere*, *versum* to turn]

verslibrist(e). See under **vers**.

verso *vûr'sō*, *n* the back of a leaf of printed or manuscript material; a left-hand page of an open book (*printing*, etc); the reverse of a coin or medal: — *pl* **ver'sos**. [L *versō* (*foliō*), turned leaf (ablative)]

verst *vûrst*, *n* a Russian measure of length, *approx* 1.07 km (0.66 miles). [Russ *versta*]

versus *vûr'səs*, (*law*, *games*) *prep* against (*abbrev* **v** and **vs**). [L]

versute *vər-sūt'*, *adj* crafty, wily. [L *versūtus*]

vert[1] *vûrt*, *n* in forest law, all greenery in a forest that may serve as cover for deer; the right or power to cut green trees or wood (*archaic*); a green colour, represented by parallel lines sloping diagonally from dexter chief to sinister base (*heraldry*). [Fr *vert*, from L *viridis* green]

vert[2] *vûrt*, *n* a familiar shortening of **convert** or (*hist*) **pervert** (*esp* to Roman Catholicism). — *vi* to become a vert.

vertebra *vûr'ti-brə*, *n* any of the segments that compose the backbone: — *pl* **ver'tebrae** (*-brē*). — *adj* **ver'tebral** relating to vertebrae (**vertebral column** the spinal column). — *adv* **ver'tebrally**. — *adj* **ver'tebrate** backboned; of, belonging or relating to the vertebrates; articulated; firm of character. — *n* a backboned animal, one belonging to the subphylum **Vertebrā'ta**, including fishes, amphibians, reptiles, birds and mammals. — *adj* **ver'tebrated** having a backbone; articulated like a backbone. — *n* **vertebrā'tion** vertebral structure; division into vertebrae or vertebra-like segments; backbone (*fig*). [L, from *vertere* to turn]

vertex *vûr'teks*, *n* the top or summit; the zenith (*astron*); the crown of the head (*anatom*); the point opposite the base (*geom*); the meeting-point of the lines bounding an angle; the intersection of a curve with its axis: — *pl* **ver'texes** or **ver'tices** (*-ti-sēz*). — *n* **vertic'ity** (*-tis'i-ti*) the power of turning. [L *vertex*, *verticis* summit]

vertical *vûr'ti-kl*, *adj* perpendicular to the plane of the horizon; of or at the vertex; in the direction of the axis (*bot*); comprising the various successive stages in the production of the same goods; in strata one above the other; (of a mechanism) in which one part is above another. — *n* a vertical line or position. — *n* **verticality** (*-kal'i-ti*). — *adv* **ver'tically**. — *n* **ver'ticalness**. — *n* **ver'tiport** an airport designed for vertical take-off and landing. — **vertical angles** opposite angles formed by intersecting lines; **vertical circle** a great circle of the heavens passing through the zenith and the nadir; **vertical grouping** in primary schools, the teaching of groups of children of various ages together (also called **family grouping**); **vertical integration** (*econ*) the merging (or takeover) of one company with (or by) another involved in a different stage of production of the same thing; **vertical scanning** (*TV*) scanning in which the lines are vertical, not, as normally, horizontal; **vertical take-off** (*aeronautics*) immediate take-off without preliminary run (also *adj*). [Fr *vertical*, from L *vertex*, *verticis* summit, from *vertere* to turn]

verticil *vûr'ti-sil*, (*bot*) *n* a whorl. — *n* **verticillas'ter** (*bot*) an inflorescence so condensed as to look like a whorl. — *adj* **verticillate** (*vər-tis'i-lət*) or **vertic'illāted** whorled. — *n* **verticill'ium** a fungus some species of which cause plant disease. [L *verticillus*, dimin of *vertex*]

vertigo *vûr'ti-gō*, *n* dizziness, giddiness; a whirling sensation experienced when the sense of balance is disturbed: — *pl* **vertigos**, **vertigoes** or **vertigines** (*-tij'i-nēz*). — *adj* **vertiginous** (*-tij'*) relating to vertigo; dizzy; giddy; whirling; producing dizziness, dizzying. — *adv* **vertig'inously**. — *n* **vertig'inousness**. [L *vertīgō*, *vertiginis*, from *vertere* to turn]

vertiport. See under **vertical**.

Vertoscope® *vûrt'ō-skōp*, *n* a device in which any photographic negative can be viewed immediately as a positive. [L *vertere* to turn, and **-scope**]

vertu[1] *vər-tōō'*, *n* a variant of **virtu**.

vertu[2] or **vertue** *vûr'tū*, *n* old forms of **virtue**. — *adj* **ver'tuous** (*Spenser*) possessing virtue or power.

Verulamian *ver-ōō-lā'mi-ən*, *ver-ū-*, *adj* of or pertaining to St Albans, or Francis Bacon, Baron *Verulam*, Viscount St Albans (1561–1626). [L *Verulāmium*, an ancient British city near the site of St Albans]

verumontanum *ver-ōō-mon'tā'nəm*, (*anatom*) *n* a ridge on the male urethra where the duct conveying prostatic fluid, sperm and other fluids enter it: — *pl* **verumontā'na** or **verumontā'nums**. [L *veru* spit, and *montanus* hilly]

vervain *vûr'vān*, *n* a wild verbena, long believed to have great magical and medicinal powers. [OFr *verveine*, from L *verbēna*]

verve *vûrv*, *n* gusto, spirit, animation, energy; enthusiasm that animates a poet or artist (*archaic*). [Fr]

vervel *vûr'vl* or **varvel** *vär'*, *n* a ring for a hawk's jess. — *adj* **ver'velled** or **var'velled**. [Fr *vervelle*]

verven *vûr'vən*, (*Spenser*) *n* vervain.

vervet *vûr'vit*, *n* an African guenon monkey. [Fr]

very *ver'i*, *adv* in a high degree, extremely; (used for emphasis with a *superl adj* or with *own* or *same*) absolutely, quite, truly, as in *my very own room*, *the very best quality*, *the very same day*. — *adj* used for emphasis, eg with the force of 'absolute' (*the very top*), precise, 'actual' (*this very minute*, *her very words*), 'most suitable' (*the very tool*), 'mere' (*the very thought*); true (*archaic*): — used, chiefly formerly, in *compar* **ver'ier**, and also (oftener) in *superl* **ver'iest**, most truly so called, merest. — *adv* **ver'ily** (*liturgical*, *formal* or *archaic*) truly; really. — **in very deed** of a truth, certainly; **not very** far from, not at all, the opposite of; **the very thing** precisely what is wanted or needed; **very good** or **very well** used in compliance or assent; **very high frequency** (*radio*) a frequency between 30 and 300 megahertz (*abbrev* **VHF**); **very large scale integration** see **VLSI**; **Very Reverend** see under **reverend**. [Older *verray*, *veray*, from Anglo-Fr *ver(r)ai* (Fr *vrai*), from a derivative of L *vērus* true; cf Ger *wahr*]

Very light *ver'i līt* or *vē'ri*, *n* a signalling or illuminating coloured flare fired from a pistol. — Also **Verey light**. [Invented by Edward W *Very*, 1877]

vesica *ves'i-kə*, *vi-sī'*, (*anatom*) *n* a bladder, sac, *esp* the urinary bladder: — *pl* **vesicae** (*ves'i-sē*, *vi-sī'*). — *adj* **vesical** (*ves'i-kl*) of or pertaining to a vesica. — *adj* **ves'icant** blistering. — *n* anything that causes blisters. — *vt* and *vi* **ves'icate** to blister. — *n* **vesicā'tion**. — *n* and *adj* **ves'icatory** (or *-ik'*) vesicant. — *n* **ves'icle** (*med* and *zool*) a small globule, bladder, sac, blister, cavity, or swelling; a primary cavity of the vertebrate brain. — *n* **vesic'ūla** a vesicle: — *pl* **vesic'ūlae** (*-lē*). — *adj* **vesic'ūlar**. — *vi* **vesic'ūlāte** to become vesicular. — *adj* **vesic'ūlate** (*-lət*) or **vesic'ūlāted**. — *n* **vesicūlā'tion** formation of vesicles. — *adj* **vesic'ūlose**. — **vesica piscis** (*pis'is*; L *wā-sē'ka pis'kis*; fish's bladder) a halo in the form of two circular arcs each (properly) passing through the other's centre, enclosing the whole figure. [L *vēsica* bladder, blister]

vespa *ves'pə*, *n* a common wasp of the genus *Vespa*, giving name to the family **Ves'pidae** (*-dē*). — *n* **ves'piary** (modelled on *apiary*) a wasps' nest. — *adj* **ves'pine** of wasps; wasplike. — *adj* **ves'poid** wasplike. [L *vespa* wasp]

vesper *ves'pər*, *n* evening (*poetic*); (*usu* in *pl*) the last but one of the seven canonical hours; (*usu* in *pl*) evensong, evening service generally; a vesper-bell; (with *cap*) Venus as the evening star, Hesperus. — *adj* **ves'peral**. — *adj* and *n* **vespertil'ionid** (a member) of the wide-spread family **Vespertilionidae** of insect-eating bats. — *adj* **vespertī'nal** or **ves'pertine** of or pertaining to the evening; happening, opening, appearing, active, or setting, in the evening. — **ves'per-bell** the bell that summons to vespers. [L *vesper*; cf Gr *hesperos*]

vespiary, **vespine**, **vespoid**. See under **vespa**.

vessel *ves'l*, *n* a utensil for holding something; a craft or structure (*usu* large) for transport by water; an airship; a conducting tube for body-fluids in animals, for water in plants; a person regarded as a receptacle, recipient, or embodiment (*Bible*, etc); vessels collectively, plate (*Scott* **vessail** or **vassail**). — **the weaker vessel** a woman (1 Pet 3. 7). [OFr *vessel* (Fr *vaisseau*), from L *vāscellum*, dimin of *vās*, *vāsis* a vessel]

vest *vest*, *n* an undergarment for the top half of the body, an undershirt; a waistcoat (chiefly *NAm*); an additional facing to the front of a bodice; garb, dress (*obs*); a garment (*obs*); a robe (*obs*); a vestment (*obs*). — *vt* to invest; to settle, secure, or put in fixed right of possession (*law*); to endow (*law*); to clothe, robe, put vestments on (*archaic*); to drape (an altar). — *vi* (of a right, etc) to descend, devolve, or take effect. — *adj* **vest'ed** clad, robed, wearing vestments; not contingent or suspended, hence (*law*) already acquired. — *n* **vest'ing** the act or fact of clothing, investing, securing legally, etc; material for waistcoats. — **vested interest** a particular interest in the continuance of an existing system, institution, etc, for personal reasons, often financial; (in *pl*) interests already established; (in *pl*) the class of persons who have acquired rights or powers in any sphere of a country's activities; **vest pocket** a waistcoat-pocket. — *adj* **vest'-pocket** small enough to go into one (also *fig*). [L *vestis*]

vesta *ves'tə*, *n* a wax-stemmed match; a short match with a wooden stem: — *pl* **ves'tas**. [L *Vesta*, the Roman goddess of the hearth and household]

vestal *ves'təl*, *adj* (often with *cap*) pertaining or consecrated to the Roman goddess Vesta; of or like the vestal virgins; virgin; chaste. — *n* one of the Roman patrician virgins consecrated to Vesta; a woman dedicated to celibacy, a nun; a virgin; a woman of spotless chastity. — **vestal virgin** (*hist*) in ancient Rome, one of the patrician virgins consecrated to Vesta, who kept the sacred fire burning on her altar. [L *vestālis*, from *Vesta*]

vestiary *vest'i-ər-i*, *n* a vestry, robing-room, or cloakroom. — *adj* of or relating to clothes. [L *vestiārium*; see **vestry**]

vestibule *ves'ti-būl*, *n* an entrance-hall; a cavity serving as entrance to another, *esp* that of the inner ear (*anatom*); part of a railway carriage connecting with and giving access to the next (*NAm*); a forecourt (*antiq*). — *vt* to provide with a vestibule. — *adj* **vestib'ūlar**. — *n* **vestibuli'tis** (*med*) inflammation of the labyrinth and cochlea of the inner ear, causing vertigo, ataxia and deafness. — *n* **vestib'ūlum** (*anatom*) a vestibule. [L *vestibulum*]

vestige *ves'tij*, *n* a trace; a surviving trace of what has almost disappeared; a footprint (*rare*); a scrap, shred, the least bit; a reduced and functionless structure, organ, etc, representing what was once useful and developed ((*biol*; also **vestig'ium**: — *pl* **vestig'ia**). — *adj* **vestig'ial**. [Fr, from L *vestīgium* footprint]

vestiment *ves'ti-mənt*, (*obs*) *n* vestment, garb, garment. — *adj* **vestimental** (*-men'tl*) or **vestiment'ary**. [L *vestīmentum*]

vestiture *ves'ti-chər*, (*rare*) *n* investiture; clothes; covering, such as hair, feathers, scales. [LL *vestītūra*, from L *vestis*]

vestment *vest'mənt*, *n* a ceremonial garment, *esp* one worn in religious ceremonies; an official or state robe; a garment as covering. — *adj* **vestment'al**. — *adj* **vest'-mented**. [L *vestīmentum*, from *vestīre* to clothe, *vestis* a garment]

vestry *ves'tri*, *n* a room in a church in which vestments are kept and parochial meetings held; a small room attached to a church; in Anglican and Episcopalian parishes, a meeting of church members or their elected representatives; the group who meet thus for parish business; a robing-room; a cloakroom; apparel (*obs*). — *adj* **ves'tral**. — **ves'try-clerk** an officer chosen by the vestry to keep the parish accounts and books; **ves'-tryman** a member of a vestry; **ves'try-room** a vestry; the meeting-place of a vestry. — **common vestry** an assembly of all the ratepayers; **select vestry** a board of representatives of the ratepayers. [Prob through OFr, from L *vestiārium*, from *vestis* a garment]

vesture *ves'chər*, *n* garb, clothing (*archaic*); a garment (*archaic*); vegetation covering the soil (*law*). — *vt* (*archaic*) to cover or clothe. — *adj* **vest'ural**. — *adj* **vest'ured**. — *n* **vest'urer** a keeper of vestments. [OFr, from LL *vestītūra*, from *vestis* garment]

Vesuvian *vi-sōō'vi-ən*, *-sū'* or *-zōō'*, *adj* of or like the volcano *Vesuvius*. — *n* **vesu'vian** a smoker's slow-burning match (*archaic*); vesuvianite. — *n* **vesu'vianite** the mineral idocrase, silicate of aluminium and calcium, found in blocks ejected by Vesuvius.

vet[1] *vet*, *n* a *vet*erinary surgeon. — *vt* to treat, or examine, medically (an animal, or *facetiously*, a person); to examine (eg a document or candidate) thoroughly and critically (and pass as sound or correct): — *pr p* **vett'ing**; *pa t* and *pa p* **vett'ed**.

vet[2]. See under **veteran**.

vetch *vech*, *n* any of various climbing plants of the pea family, *usu* with blue or purple flowers, often used as fodder. — *n* **vetch'ling** any plant of the sweet-pea genus (*Lathyrus*). — *adj* **vetch'y** covered with vetches. — **bitter vetch** various species of the *Vicia* and Lathyrus genera; **kidney vetch** see under **kidney**; **milk vetch** a plant of the *Astragalus* genus. [ONFr *veche* (Fr *vesce*), from L *vicia*]

veteran *vet'ə-rən*, *n* a person who has seen long service in any activity; an experienced soldier; an ex-serviceman (*NAm*; *colloq abbrev* **vet**). — *adj* old, experienced; experienced in military service. — **veteran car** an early motor-car, *specif* one made before 1905. [L *veterānus*, from *vetus*, *veteris* old]

veterinary *vet'ə-rin-ər-i*, *adj* concerned with the treatment of diseases of animals. — *n* a person trained in the treatment of diseases of domestic animals. — Also **veterinā'rian** (*NAm*) and **veterinary surgeon**. [L *veterīnārius*, from *veterīnae* cattle, beasts of burden]

vetiver *vet'i-vər*, *n* cuscus grass and root. [Fr *vétiver*, from Tamil *veltivēru*]

vetkoek *fet'kōōk*, (*S Afr*) *n* a deep-fried cake, *usu* unsweetened, but otherwise similar to a doughnut. [Afrik, from Du *vet* fat, and *koek* cake]

veto *vē'tō*, *n* any authoritative prohibition; the power of rejecting or forbidding; the right to reject or forbid a proposed measure, *esp* in a legislative assembly or the UN Security Council: — *pl* **vetoes** (*vē'tōz*). — *vt* to reject by a veto; to withhold assent to; to forbid. — **local veto** the power of a local area to prohibit the liquor trade within its bounds. [L *vetō* I forbid]

Vet. Surg. *abbrev*: Veterinary Surgeon.

vettura *vet-tōō'rə*, *n* in Italy, a carriage, cab, or car. — *n* **vetturino** (*-rē'nō*) its driver or proprietor: — *pl* **vetturi'ni** (*-nē*). [Ital, from L *vectūra* a carrying, from *vehere* to convey]

vex *veks*, *vt* to harass; to distress; to annoy; to trouble, agitate, disturb; to discuss to excess. — *vi* (now *rare*) to grieve, fret. — *n* (*Scot*) a grief. — *n* **vexā'tion** a vexing; the state or feeling of being vexed; a source of grief or annoyance. — *adj* **vexā'tious** vexing; troublesome; (of a law action) brought on insufficient grounds, with the intention merely of annoying the defendant. — *adv* **vexā'tiously**. — *n* **vexātiousness**. — *adj* **vex'atory**. — *adj* **vexed** or (*obs*) **vext** (*vekst*). — *adv* **vex'edly**. — *n* **vex'edness**. — *n* **vex'er**. — *n* and *adj* **vex'ing**. — *adv* **vex'ingly**. — *n* **vex'ingness**. — **vexed question** a matter greatly debated. [Fr *vexer*, from L *vexāre* to shake, annoy]

vexata quaestio *vek-sā'tə kwēs'ti-ō, wek-sä'ta kwīs'ti-ō*, (*L*) *n* a disputed question.

vexillum *vek-sil'əm*, *n* the series of barbs on the sides of the shaft of a feather (*zool*); a standard (*bot*); a Roman standard; a vexillation; a scarf on a pastoral staff: — *pl* **vexill'a**. — *n* **vex'illary** a standard-bearer; one of a company of Roman veterans serving under a special standard. — *adj* of, relating to or under a vexillum. — *n* **vexillā'tion** a company under one vexillum. — *n* **vexillol'ogist**. — *n* **vexillol'ogy** the study of flags. [L *vehere* to carry]

vezir. See **vizier**.

VF *abbrev*: video frequency; voice frequency.

VG *abbrev*: Vicar-General.

vg *abbrev*: very good.

VGA *abbrev*: video-graphics array, a computer monitor screen display system with the ability to display many colours, and resolution of 640 x 480 pixels.

VHF *abbrev*: very high frequency.

VHS *abbrev*: video home system, a video cassette system for use in domestic video recorders.

vi *abbrev*: verb intransitive.

via[1] or **viâ** *vī'ə, vē'ə* or *wē'ä*, *prep* by way of; through. [L *viā*, ablative of *via* way]

via[2] *vī'ə, vē'ə* or *wē'a*, (*L*) *n* a way, road. — **via crucis** (*krōō'sis, -kis*) the way of the Cross, the succession of stations of the Cross (see under **station**); **via dolorosa** (*dol-ə-rō'sə, do-lō-rō'sa*) the way to Calvary (literally mournful way); an upsetting or daunting course of action; **Via Lactea** (*lak'ti-ə* or *-te-a*) the Milky Way; **via media** (*mē'di-ə* or *me'di-a*) a middle course; **via trita, via tuta** (*trī'tə* or *trē'ta, tūt'ə* or *tōō'ta*) a beaten path is a safe path.

via[3] *vē'ə*, (*obs*) *interj* of incitement or dismissal: come on; be off; enough of that. [Ital, from L *via* way]

viable *vī'ə-bl*, *adj* capable of living, surviving, germinating, or hatching; (of a plan or project) of such a kind that it has a prospect of success; practicable. — *n* **viabil'ity**. [Fr, from *vie*, from L *vīta* life]

viaduct *vī'ə-dukt*, *n* a structure carrying a road or railway over a valley, etc. [Modelled on **aqueduct**, from L *via* a way]

vial *vī'əl*, *n* same as **phial**; a spirit-level. — *n* **vī'alful**. — *adj* **vī'alled** put or contained in a vial. — **pour out vials of wrath** to inflict judgement (Rev 16. 1); to storm, rage.

viameter *vī-am'i-tər*, (*archaic*) *n* a hodometer; a cyclometer. [L *via* road, and **-meter**]

viand *vī'ənd*, *n* (*formal*) an article of food; (*usu* in *pl*) food. [Fr *viande*, from L *vīvenda* food necessary for life, from *vīvere* to live]

viaticum *vī-at'ik-əm* or *wē-ä'ti-kōōm*, *n* money, provisions, etc, for a journey; the eucharist given to people in danger of dying (*RC Church*): — *pl* **viat'icums** or **viat'ica** — *n pl* **viat'icals** baggage. [L *viāticum*, from *via* way]

viator *vī-ā'tər* or *wē-ä'tör*, *n* traveller, wayfarer. — *adj* **viatorial** (*vī-ə-tö'ri-əl* or *-tö'*). [L *viātor, -ōris*, from *via* a way]

vibes *vībz*, (*colloq*) *n pl* feelings, sensations, etc, experienced or communicated (shortening of **vibrations**). — *n sing* or *n pl colloq* shortening of **vibraphone**. — *n* **vī'bist** (*colloq*) a person who plays the vibraphone.

vibex *vī'beks*, (*med*) *n* a streak under the skin due to the leakage of blood: — *pl* **vibices** (*vī-* or *vi-bī'sēz*). [L *vībex, vībīcis* a weal]

vibraculum *vī-brak'ū-ləm*, *n* a long bristle, a modified zooid, in some Polyzoa: — *pl* **vibrac'ula**. — Also **vibraculā'rium**: — *pl* **vibraculā'ria**. [Coined from L *vibrāre* to shake]

vibra-. Variant of **vibro-**.

vibraharp. See under **vibraphone**.

Vibram® *vē'brəm*, *n* tough heavily-patterned rubber used, without nails, for the soles of climbing and walking boots. — *n pl* **vibs** (*vibz*; *colloq*) shoes with Vibram soles. [*Vi*tale *Bram*ini, inventor]

vibrant *vī'brənt*, *adj* vibrating; thrilling; resonant; (of colours) very bright. — *n* **vibrancy** (*vī'brən-si*). — *adv* **vī'brantly**. [L *vibrans, -antis*, pr p of *vibrāre* to vibrate]

vibraphone *vī'brə-fōn*, *n* an instrument having metal bars under which are electrically-operated resonators, played by striking the bars with small hammers. — Also **vī'braharp** (*US*). — *n* **vī'braphōnist**. [L *vibrāre* to shake, and Gr *phōnē* voice]

vibrate *vī'brāt* or *-brāt'*, *vi* to shake, to tremble; to oscillate, to swing; to change to and fro, *esp* rapidly; to resound, ring; to tingle, thrill. — *vt* to cause to vibrate; to give off (sound, light, etc) in vibrations; to measure by single vibrations; to brandish (*obs*). — *adj* **vī'bratile** (*-brə-tīl*, or *NAm -til* or *-təl*) vibratory; having or capable of vibratory motion. — *n* **vibratility** (*-til'i-ti*). — *n* **vibrā'tion** a vibrating; the state of being vibrated; tremulousness; quivering motion; a whole period or movement to and fro of anything vibrating; sometimes a half period or movement one way; (in *pl*, often *abbrev* **vibes**) feelings communicated from person to person (*colloq*); (in *pl*, often *abbrev* **vibes**) feelings aroused in one by a person, place, etc (*colloq*). — *adj* **vibrā'tional**. — *adj* **vibrā'tionless**. — *n* **vibratiuncle** (*vī-brā-shi-ung'kl*) a small vibration. — *adj* **vī'brative** (*-brə-tiv*) vibrating; consisting in vibrations; causing vibrations. — *n* **vi'brātor** that which vibrates; a vibrating part in many appliances; a vibrating tool; a type of dildo that can be made to vibrate mechanically. — *adj* **vibratory** (*vī'brə-tər-i*) of, of the nature of, causing, or capable of, vibration. — **vibrational energy** (*chem*) energy due to the relative oscillation of two contiguous atoms in a molecule. [L *vibrāre, -ātum* to tremble]

vibrato *vē-brä'tō* or *vi-*, (*music*) *n* a throbbing effect, without perceptible change of pitch, in singing and in stringed and wind instrument playing, obtained by varying breath pressure or by the shaking movement of the finger on a string: — *pl* **vibra'tos**. [Ital]

vibrio *vib'ri-ō* or *vīb'*, *n* a bacterium of the genus *Vibrio*, with a slight spiral curve and *usu* one flagellum, eg that of cholera: — *pl* **vib'rios**. — *n* **vibriō'sis** infection with these bacteria. [New L, from L *vibrāre* to shake]

vibrissa *vī-bris'ə*, *n* a tactile bristle, such as a cat's whisker; a vaneless rictal feather; a bristle, hair, as in the nostril: — *pl* **vibriss'ae** (*-ē*). [L, a hair in the nostril]

vibro- *vī-brō-* or *-bro-*, *combining form* denoting vibration. — *n* **vī'broflotation** a process for compacting sand. — *n* **vī'brograph** or **vibrom'eter** an instrument for recording vibrations. [L *vibrāre, -ātum* to tremble, shake]

vibronic *vī-bron'ik*, (*phys*) *adj* of, relating to, caused by, etc, electronic vibration. [*vib*ration, and elect*ronic*]

vibs. See **Vibram**.

viburnum *vī-bûr'nəm*, *n* any plant of the guelder-rose and wayfaring-tree genus (*Viburnum*) of Caprifoliaceae. [L *vīburnum* the wayfaring tree]

Vic. *abbrev*: Vicar; Vicarage; Victoria (Australian state).

vicar *vik'ər*, *n* a parson of a parish (who formerly received only the smaller tithes or a salary) (*Ch of Eng*); a bishop's deputy (*RC*); a person who holds authority as the delegate or substitute of another, *esp* in the performance of a religious function; a deputy or substitute. — *n* **vic'arage** the residence or benefice of a vicar. — *n* **vic'arate** vicariate. — *n* **vic'aress** an abbess's deputy; a vicar's wife. — *adj* **vicarial** (*vī-* or *vi-kā'ri-əl*) delegated; of a vicar or vicars. — *adj* **vicā'riate** delegated. — *n* the office, authority, time of office, or sphere of a vicar, in any sense. — *n* **vic'arship** the (time of) office of a vicar. — *n* **vic'ary** (*obs*) a vicarship. — **vicar-apostol'ic** (formerly) one to whom the pope delegated some remote portion of his jurisdiction; (now *usu*) a titular bishop appointed to a country where there are no sees; a titular bishop exercising authority in a vacant see or during the bishop's incapacity; **vicar-cho'ral** a cleric or layman appointed to sing in an English cathedral choir; **vic'ar-forane** (*for-ān'*; a variant of **foreign**) a rural dean; **vicar-gen'eral** an official performing the work of an archdeacon under the bishop (*RC*); a lay official representing the bishop, the chancellor of the diocese. — **Vicar of Bray** a person who changes allegiance to suit the times (from Simon Aleyn, vicar of *Bray*, Berkshire, from 1540 to 1588); **Vicar** or (*obs*) **vicar-general of Christ** (*RC*) the pope, as representative of Christ on earth. [OFr *vicaire*, from L *vicārius* substitute; see **vicarious** and **vice-**]

vicarious *vi-kā'ri-əs*, *adj* (loosely) not experienced personally but imagined through the experience of others; exercised, performed or suffered by one person or thing instead of another; filling the place of another. — *adv* **vicā'riously**. — *n* **vicā'riousness**. — **vicarious sacrifice** the suffering and death of Christ held by orthodox Christians to be accepted by God in lieu of the punishment to which guilty man is liable. [L *vicarius*, from *vicis* a recurring turn, a rôle or function]

vice[1] or (*NAm*) **vise** *vīs*, *n* a tool with movable jaws for gripping an object that is being worked on; a grip (*Shakesp*); a screw (*obs*); a winding stair or its newel (*obs*). — *vt* to grip, force, jam or strain as with a vice. [OFr (and Fr) *vis* screw, from L *vītis* a vine]

vice[2] *vīs*, *n* a blemish or fault; immorality, depravity; an immoral habit; a bad trick or habit, eg in a horse; (with *cap*) the personification of a vice in a morality play, *usu* a farcical part (*hist*); hence, a buffoon (*hist*). — *adj* **vice'less**. — **vice squad** a police squad whose task is to see that the laws dealing with gambling, prostitution, etc, are observed. [OFr, from L *vitium* defect]

vice[3] *vī'si*, *vī'sē* or *vīs*, *prep* in place of; in succession to. — *combining form* **vice-** (*vīs-*) in place of. — *n* **vice** (*vīs*) place, stead (*rare*); short for **vice-president**, **vice-chancellor**, etc (*colloq*). — *n* **vice-ad'miral** a navy officer ranking next under an admiral. — *n* **vice-ad'miralty** the office or jurisdiction of a vice-admiral. — *n* **vice-chair'** a vice-chairman. — *n* **vice-chair'man** a deputy chairman. — *n* **vice-chair'manship**. — *n* **vice-cham'berlain** the Lord Chamberlain's deputy and assistant. — *n* **vice-chan'cellor** a person acting for a chancellor; (in certain British universities) the head of administration, the chancellor being titular head only. — *n* **vice-chan'cellorship**. — *n* **vice-con'sul** a consul's deputy; an official who acts as consul in a less important district. — *n* **vice-con'sulate**. — *n* **vice-con'sulship**. — *n* **vice-count'y** part of a county divided for floristic purposes. — *n* **vice'-dean** a canon chosen to represent an absent dean. — *n* **vicegerency** (*-jer'* or *-jēr'ən-si*). — *adj* **vicegerent** (*-jer'* or *-jēr'*; L *vicem gerēns*, *-entis* wielding office) acting in place of another, having delegated authority. — *n* a person ruling or acting in place of a superior. — *n* **vice-gov'ernor** deputy governor. — *n* **vice'-king** a person who acts in place of a king. — *n* **vice-mar'shal** same as **air-vice-marshal**. — *n* **vice-pres'idency**. — *n* **vice-pres'ident** (*abbrev* **VP**) a president's deputy or assistant; an officer next below the president. — *adj* **vice-presiden'tial**. — *n* **vice-princ'ipal** assistant principal. — *n* **vice'-queen** a female viceroy; a viceroy's wife, vicereine. — *adj* **vice-re'gal** of a viceroy; of a governor-general (*Austr*, *NZ*). — *n* **vicere'gent** properly, a substitute for a regent; often used mistakenly for vicegerent. — *n* **vicereine** (*vīs'ren'* or *-rān'*) a viceroy's wife; a female viceroy (*rare*). — *n* **vice'roy** a governor acting in the name of the sovereign. — *n* **viceroy'alty** or **vice'royship**. [L ablative, in the turn or place, from *vicis* a turn]

vice anglais *vēs ā-gle n* the English vice, most often applied to flagellation or corporal punishment, but also to eg sodomy. [Fr]

vicenary *vis'i-nər-i*, *adj* based on the number twenty. [L *vīcēnārius*, from *vīcēnī* twenty each, from *vīgintī* twenty]

vicennial *vī-sen'yəl*, *adj* lasting, or coming at the end of, twenty years; occurring every twenty years. [L *vīcennium*, from *vīciēs* twenty times, and *annus* a year]

vicesimal, etc. See **vigesimal**.

vice versa *vī'si*, *vī'sē* or *vīs vûrsə*, *adv* the other way round. [L ablative absolute, the position having been turned, from *vicis* position, and *verto*, *versum* to turn, change]

Vichyite *vē'shē-īt* or *vish'i-īt*, *n* an adherent of the French Government (1940–42) ruling the unoccupied part of France from *Vichy*, and collaborating with the Germans. — Also *adj*. — *adj* **vichyssois** (*vē-shē-swä'*) of the Vichyite government: — *fem* **vichyssoise** (*-swäz'*). — *n* **vichyssoise'** a cream soup *usu* served chilled, with ingredients such as potatoes and leeks. — **Vichy** (or **vichy**) **water** (*vē'shē*) mineral water from Vichy springs, containing sodium bicarbonate, etc, or a natural or artificial water resembling it. — Also **vichy**. [*Vichy*, town in central France]

viciate. See under **vitiate**.

vicinage *vis'i-nij*, *n* a neighbourhood; the residents in such. — *adj* **vic'inal** (or *-īn'əl*) neighbouring; local; denoting or relating to positions on adjacent carbon atoms in a molecule (*organic chem*); of crystal faces, very nearly in the plane of a normal face. — *n* **vicin'ity** neighbourhood; nearness. [L *vīcīnus* neighbour, from *vīcus* street, village, district]

viciosity. See **vitiosity** under **vitiate**.

vicious *vish'əs*, *adj* malignant, spiteful; bad-tempered; addicted to vice or bad habits; immoral, depraved; bad; faulty; impaired, nullified by a flaw, unlawful (*law*); mistaken (*Shakesp*); foul, impure, morbid (*obs med*, etc). — *adv* **vic'iously**. — *n* **vic'iousness**. — **vicious circle** reasoning in a circle, seeking to prove a proposition by means of a conclusion drawn from it; a process in which an evil is aggravated by its own consequences; **vicious intromission** see under **intromit**. [OFr *vicieus*, from L *vitiōsus* faulty, vicious]

vicissitude *vi-sis'i-tūd*, *n* change; alternation; mutation; change of fortune (*colloq*, for the worse). — *adj* **vicissitū'dinous**. [L *vicissitūdō*, *-tūdinis*; see **vice**[3]]

vicomte *vē-kɔ̃*, (*Fr*) *n* in France, a noble equal in rank to a viscount: — *fem* **vicomtesse** (*-es*).

victim *vik'tim*, *n* a living being offered as a sacrifice; a living being subjected to death, suffering, or ill-treatment; a prey; a sufferer. — *n* **victimīzā'tion** or **-s-**. — *vt* **vic'timize** or **-ise** to make a victim of; to single out for oppressive treatment; to cheat. — *n* **vic'timizer** or **-s-**. — *adj* **vic'timless** (of crimes) involving no injured party, such as loitering, drunkenness, etc. — *n* **victimol'ogist**. — *n* **victimol'ogy** the behavioural study of victims of crime, to discover the psychological effects on them, and their role in its commission. [L *victima* a beast for sacrifice]

victor *vik'tər*, *n* a winner or winning side in a contest of any kind: — *fem* **vic'toress** (*obs*), **vic'tress** or **vic'trix**. — *adj* **vic'tor** (*archaic*) or **victo'rious** (*-tō'* or *-tö'*) having gained a victory; winning in a contest; of, with or marking victory. — *adv* **victo'riously**. — *n* **victo'riousness**. — *n* **victory** (*vik'tər-i*) a contest won; success against an opponent; (with *cap*) (a statue of) the Roman goddess Victoria or the Greek goddess Nikē. — *adj* **vic'toryless**. — **victory ship** a successor to the liberty ship. [L *victor*, *-ōris*, from *vincere*, *victum* to conquer]

victoria *vik-tō'ri-ə* or *-tö'*, *n* a gigantic water-lily of the Brazilian genus *Victoria*; a low, light, four-wheeled carriage with a folding hood; (also with *cap*) a large red and yellow oval plum (also **victoria plum**). — *adj* **Victo'rian** of, contemporary with or typical of the reign of Queen Victoria; strict but somewhat conventional in morals, with connotations of prudery, solemnity and sometimes hypocrisy; of or relating to the state (colony 1851–1901) of Victoria in Australia. — *n* a contemporary of Queen Victoria; a person of Victorian morality or outlook; a native or inhabitant of Victoria. — *npl* **Victoriana** (*vik-tō-ri-ä'nə*, *-tö-* or *-ā'nə*; also without *cap*) bric-à-brac and other characteristic possessions or creations of the Victorian age. — *n* **Victo'rianism**. — **Victoria Cross** a bronze Maltese cross, the highest British military decoration, founded by Queen Victoria (1856); **Victoria Day** Empire Day, a day on or near Queen Victoria's birthday (24 May), observed as a holiday in Canada. [Victoria, queen of the United Kingdom (1837–1901)]

victorine *vik-tə-rēn'*, *n* a fur tippet with long ends; a variety of peach. [Woman's name]

victor ludorum *vik'tər lōō-dō'rəm* or *vik'tör lōō-dō'rōōm*, (*L*) *n* in school sports, etc, the most outstanding athlete.

victress, victrix. See under **victor**.

Victrolla® *vik-trō'lə*, *n* (also without *cap*) an early variety of gramophone. [From the company producing it, *Vic*tor Talking Machine Co]

victual *vit'l*, *n* (*usu* in *pl*) food, *esp* food for humans; (in *sing*) grain crops, cut or ready for cutting (*Scot*). — *vt* to supply or store with provisions. — *vi* to lay in victuals; (*esp* of animals) to feed: — *pr p* **victualling** (*vit'l-ing*); *pa t* and *pa p* **victualled** (*vit'ld*). — *n* **vict'uallage** provisions. — *n* **victualler** (*vit'l-ər*) a purveyor of provisions; a victualling-ship. — *adj* **vict'ualless**. — **vict'ualling-bill** a customs document warranting the captain of an outward-bound vessel to ship bonded stores for the voyage; **vict'ualling-off'ice** or **vict'ualling-ship** an office supplying, or a ship conveying, provisions to the navy; **vict'ualling-yard'** a public establishment for the collection and supply of provisions to the navy. — **licensed victualler** see under **licence**. [OFr *vitaille*, from LL *victuālia*, from L *victuālis*, from *victus* food, from *vivere*, *victum* to live]

vicuä *vi-kōō'nyə*, *n* a wild species of the llama genus; (cloth made of) its fine soft wool, or an imitation. [Sp, from Quechua]

vid *vid*, (*colloq*) *n* short form of **video**.

vidame *vē-däm'*, *n* in French feudal jurisprudence, the deputy of a bishop in temporal affairs; a minor noble. [Fr, from LL *vicedominus*]

vide *vī'dē*, *vē'* or *wi'dā*, (*L*) see, consult, refer to. — **vide infra** (*in'frə* or *ēn'frä*) see below; **vide supra** (*sū'prə* or *sōō'prä*) see above.

videlicet *vi-del'i-sit*, *vi-* or *wi-dā'li-ket*, (*L*) to wit, namely (*usu abbrev* **viz**).

videndum *vī-den'dəm*, *vi-* or *wi-den'dōōm* (*pl* **videnda** *-də* or *-da*; *L*) thing(s) to be seen.

video *vid'i-ō*, *n* (*abbrev* **vid**) a videocassette or videocassette recorder; video recording; television as a medium (*US colloq*); the visual aspect or elements of TV, etc (cf **audio**): — *pl* **vid'eos**. — *adj* pertaining to the bandwidth and spectrum position of the signal arising from TV scanning, or to the signal, or to the resultant image, or to television; using, used for, relating to, etc, the system of video recording. — *vt* and *vi* to make a video recording (of): — *pr p* **vid'eoing**; *pa p* **vid'eoed**. — **video camera** a camera which records its (moving) film on to videotape; **videocassette'** a cassette containing videotape; **videocassette recorder** a video recorder in which videocassettes are used; **videocon'ference**; **videocon'ferencing** live discussion between people in different places using electronically linked telephones and video screens; **vid'eodisc** a compact disc on which visual images and sound are prerecorded for playing back on a CD player linked to hi-fi and TV; **vid'eofit** a type of identikit picture put together on television; **video frequency** a frequency in the range required for a video signal; **video game** an electronically-operated game played on visual display unit; **vid'eogram** a commercial video film; a prerecorded videocassette or videodisc; **video nasty** a pornographic or horror video film; **vid'eophone** or **videotel'ephone** a telephone with accompanying means of transmitting a picture of each speaker; **video recorder** a machine for recording and playing back television broadcasts or films made on videotape, using videotape or videodiscs; **video signal** that part of a TV signal which conveys all the information required for establishing the visual image; **vid'eotape** magnetic tape for recording visual images (as well as sound), *esp* television programmes or film for later transmission. — *vt* to record on videotape. — **videotape recorder** a tape recorder that records visual images on magnetic tape; **vid'eotex** or **vid'eotext** a system used to display pages of information on a television screen, eg teletext or viewdata (qv); **video tube** a television tube. [Modelled on **audio**, from L *vidēre* to see]

vidette. A variant of **vedette**.

Vidicon® *vid'i-kon*, *n* a small television camera tube operating on the photoconducting principle. [*Vid*eo *icon*(oscope)]

vidimus *vī'di-məs*, *vē'* or *wē'di-mōōs*, *n* an attested copy; an inspection, eg of accounts. [L *vīdimus* we have seen, from *vidēre* to see]

viduous *vid'ū-əs*, *adj* widowed; empty. — *n* **vid'ūage** widowhood; widows collectively. — *adj* **vid'ūal**. — *n* **vidū'ity** widowhood. [L *vidua* a widow, *viduus* deprived, bereaved]

vie *vī*, *vi* to contend in rivalry; to make a vie (*obs*). — *vt* (*obs*) to stake; to declare, bid (*cards*); to put forward in competition or emulation, or (*Shakesp*) repeatedly: — *pr p* **vy'ing**; *pa t* and *pa p* **vied** (*vīd*). — *n* (*obs*) a bid, challenge, stake. — *n* **vī'er**. — *adv* **vy'ingly**. [Fr *envier*, from L *invitāre* to challenge, invite]

vielle *vē-el'*, *n* a hurdy-gurdy, a stringed instrument played by a wheel; a medieval stringed and bowed instrument resembling a viol. [Fr]

Viennese *vē-e-nēz'*, *adj* of *Vienna*, the capital of Austria. — *n sing* and *n pl* an inhabitant or the inhabitants of Vienna. — **vienna** (or **Vienna**) **loaf** a long, round-ended loaf of white bread; **vienna steak** a meat rissole.

vi et armis *vī et är'mis*, *vē* or *wē et är'mēs* (*L*) forcibly. [Literally, by force and arms]

Viet Cong or **Vietcong** *vyet-kong'*, *n* a member of the South Vietnamese Communist guerrilla army in the Vietnam war. — Also *adj*. [Vietnamese *Viet Nam Cong San* Vietnamese Communist]

Vietnam *vyet-nam'*, *n* a war or conflict which sucks in to an ever-increasing extent, and then exhausts, the resources of an apparently overwhelmingly superior participant. [From the experience of the US in the Vietnam war of the 1960s and 1970s]

Vietnamese *vyet-nəm-ēz'*, *n* a native or inhabitant, or the language, of *Vietnam*: — *pl* **Vietnamese'**. — Also *adj*.

vieux jeu *vyōō zhōō*, *adj* old-fashioned; old hat. [Fr, literally old game or joke]

view *vū*, *n* an act, possibility or opportunity of looking; range or field of sight; whole extent seen; a prospect, wide or distant extent seen; that which is seen; an inspection; appearance; an aspect or scene; the picture of a scene; general survey of a subject; mode of thinking of something; opinion; intention, purpose; expectation; (with *cap*) used in street names, etc. — *vt* to see; to look at; to look at on television; to inspect (a house) as a prospective purchaser; to observe; to consider; to examine intellectually. — *vi* to watch television. — *adj* **view'able** able to be seen; sufficiently interesting to be looked at or watched. — *n* **view'er** a person who views; a television watcher; an apparatus used to project film for purposes of editing and cutting; a device with magnifying lens, etc, for viewing transparencies; an inspector, a person appointed to examine and report; a colliery superintendent. — *n* **view'ership** the estimated number of viewers of a television programme. — *n* **view'iness** the condition or quality of being viewy. — *n* **view'ing**. — *adj* **view'less** (*poetic*) invisible. — *adv* **view'lessly**. — *adj* **view'ly** (*dialect*) pleasing to look at. — *adj* **view'y** showy; having views that are considered odd or fanciful by most. — **view'data** a communications system by which information can be received and requested via a telephone line and presented through a television or video display unit; **view'finder** a camera attachment or part for determining the field of view; **view'-halloo'** the huntsman's cry when the fox breaks cover (also *interj*); **view'phone** another name for **videophone**; **view'point** point of view; standpoint; a selected position for admiring scenery. — **dissolving views** pictures thrown on a screen and made to pass one into another; **in view** in sight; in mind; as an aim or prospect; **in view of** in a position to see or to be seen by; having regard to; **on view** open to general inspection; **take a dim view of** to regard unfavourably; **view away** to see breaking cover; **with a view to** having in mind; with the aim of. [Fr *vue*, from *vu*, pa p of *voir*, from L *vidēre* to see]

vifda See under **vivda**.

vigesimal *vī-jes'i-məl* or **vicesimal** *vī-ses'-i-məl*, *adj* based on the number twenty. — *adj* **viges'imo-** (or **vices'imo-**) **quar'to** twenty-fourmo (*printing*). [L *vigēsimus* (or *vīcēsimus*) twentieth, from *vīgintī* twenty]

vigia *vi-jē'ə* or *vi-hhē'ä*, *n* a danger warning on a chart. [Sp *vigía* look-out, from L *vigilia*]

vigil *vij'il*, *n* watching, *esp* by night, *usu* on guard or in prayer; the eve of a holy day; a religious service by night; a keeping awake, wakefulness. — *n* **vig'ilance** watchfulness; wakefulness; a guard, watch (*Milton*); a planned effort to uncover and punish corruption and bribery (*Ind*). — *adj* **vig'ilant** watchful. — *n* **vigilante** (*-an'ti*; *orig US*, from *Sp*) a member of an organization formed to look after the interests, threatened in some way, of a group, *esp* a self-appointed and unofficial policeman; a member of a vigilance committee. — *n* **vigilan'tism** behaviour associated with vigilantes, *esp* militarism and bellicosity. — *adv* **vig'ilantly**. — **vigilance committee** (*US*) an unauthorized body which, in the absence or inefficiency of regular government, exercises powers of arrest, punishment, etc; any self-appointed association for the compulsory improvement of local morals according to its own standards. [L *vigilia*, from *vigil* awake, watchful; cf *vigēre* to be lively]

vigneron *vēn-yə-rɔ̃*, *n* a vine-grower. [Fr]

vignette *vēn-yet'*, *n* a character sketch, a word-picture; a small embellishment without a border, *esp* on a title-page or as a headpiece or tailpiece; a photographic portrait shading off around the head; the illustration on a bank-note; *orig* a design of vine-leaves and tendrils. — *vt* to make a vignette of. — *n* **vignett'er** or **vignett'ist**. [Fr, from *vigne*, from L *vīnea* a vine, a vineyard]

vigorish *vig'ə-rish*, (*US slang*) *n* a percentage of a gambler's winnings taken by the bookmaker, organizers of a game, etc; excessive interest charged on a loan. [Prob Yiddish, from Russ *vȳigrȳsh* profit, winnings]

vigoro *vig'ə-rō*, (*Austr*) *n* a 12-a-side game (played by women) having similarities to cricket and baseball. [Poss from **vigour**]

vigour or (*NAm*) **vigor** *vig'ər*, *n* active strength; vital power; healthy growth (in plants etc); forcefulness; activity; energy; legal validity (now *esp US law*). — *adj* **vig'orous**. — *adv* **vig'orously**. — *n* **vig'orousness**. [Anglo-Fr *vigour* (Fr *vigueur*), and L *vigor*, *-ōris*, from *vigēre* to be strong]

vihara *vē-hä'rə*, *n* a Buddhist or Jain precinct, temple, or monastery. [Sans *vihāra*]

vihuela *vi-wā'lə*, *n* an old Spanish musical instrument, related to the guitar. [Sp]

viking *vī'king*, *n* (also with *cap*) any of the Scandinavian adventurers who raided, traded with, and settled in, many parts of Europe between the eighth and eleventh centuries; any aggressive sea-raider, a pirate. — Also *adj*. — *n* **vī'kingism**. [ON *vīkingr*, prob from OE *wīcing* pirate]

vil. or **vill.** *abbrev*: village.

vilayet *vil-ä'yet*, *n* a Turkish province. [Turk *vilāyet*, from Ar *welāyeh*]

vild or **vilde** *vīld*, *adj* an old variant (*Spenser*, *Shakesp*) of **vile**. — *adv* **vild'ly**. — *n* **vild'ness**.

vile *vīl*, *adj* detestable, loathsome; foul; depraved; very bad; base; worthless, mean, paltry. — *adv* (*archaic*) vilely. — *adv* **vile'ly**. — *n* **vile'ness**. — *n* **vilificā'tion** (*vil-*) the act of vilifying; defamatory speech; abuse. — *n* **vilifīer** (*vil'*). — *vt* **vilify** (*vil'*) to make vile; to disparage; to defame: — *pr p* **vil'ifying**; *pa t* and *pa p* **vil'ified**. — *vt* **vilipend** (*vil'*; L *vīlipendere*, from *pendere* to weigh) to despise, make light of; to disparage; to slander, vilify. — *vi* to use vilification. [OFr *vil* and L *vīlis* worthless]

viliaco *vil-yä'kō* or **viliago**, (*Shakesp*) **villiago** *-gō*, (*obs*) *n* a coward. — Also (*Scott*, *prob erron*) **villagio**: — *pl* **-oes** or **-os**. [Ital *vigliacco*, from L *vīlis* worthless]

vilification, etc. See under **vile**.

vill *vil*, *n* a township, or feudal territorial unit (*hist*); a manor (*hist*); a village (*poetic*). — *adj* **vill'ar** of a vill. [OFr *ville* farm, village (Fr, town), from L *villa* (see **villa**)]

vill. See **vil**.

villa *vil'ə*, *n orig*, a country house or farmhouse with subsidiary buildings; a country seat, in Italy often a castle; a detached house of some size; a superior middle-class house. — *n* **vill'adom** villas collectively; the villa-dwelling world. — *adj* **villatic** (*-at'ik*; *Milton*) farmyard-; village-. — **villa home** or **unit** (*Austr*) a terraced, *esp* single-storey house, typically joined to the next house by a garage. [L *villa* a country house, through Ital]

village *vil'ij*, *n* an assemblage of houses, shops, etc smaller than a town, *usu* in or close to the countryside; a small municipality (*NAm*); a residential complex temporarily housing participants at a particular event, *esp* the athletes and officials taking part in international games; the people of a village. — *adj* of or dwelling in a village. — *n* **vill'ager** an inhabitant of a village. — *n* **villagery** (*vil'ij-ri*; *Shakesp* **villagree**) villages collectively or *perh* village people. — *n* **villagizā'tion** or **-s-** the organization of land, *esp* in Africa and Asia, so that it is under the control of villages (as opposed to nationalization); the removal of scattered groups of population into large new villages, *esp* in Africa and Asia. — **the Village** Greenwich Village in New York; **village cart** see under **cart**; **village college** an adult educational and recreational centre serving a rural area (also **community college**). [Fr *village*, L *villāticus*]

villagio. See under **viliaco**.

villagree. See under **village**.

villain *vil'ən*, *n* a violent, malevolent or unscrupulous evil-doer; the wicked enemy of the hero or heroine in a story or play; playfully, a wretch; a criminal (*slang*); (*orig*) a villein. — *adj* villainous; low-born (*archaic*); base (*obs*). — *n* **vill'ainage** or **vill'anage** villeinage. — *n* **vill'ainess** a female villain. — *adj* **vill'ainous** or **vill'anous** of the nature of, like, or suited to a villain; detestable, vile. — *adv* (*Shakesp*) villainously. — *adv* **vill'ainously** or **vill'anously**. — *n* **vill'ainy** or **vill'any** the act or (*obs*) the words of a villain; extreme wickedness; an atrocious crime; disgrace (*obs*). — *n* **vill'an** a villein. [OFr *villain*, from LL *villānus*, from L *villa* a country house]

villanelle *vil-ə-nel'*, *n* a poem, on two rhymes, in five tercets and a quatrain, the first line repeated as sixth, twelfth, and eighteenth, the third as ninth, fifteenth, and last. [Fr, from Ital *villanella*, from *villano* rustic]

villanous(ly). See under **villain**.

Villanovan *vil-ə-nō'vən*, *adj* of an early Iron Age culture of which remains occur at *Villanova*, near Bologna.

villany. See under **villain**.

villar. See under **vill**.

villatic. See under **villa**.

-ville *-vil*, (*slang*) *combining form* denoting a supposed world, milieu, etc, frequented by a specified type of person, or characterized by a specified quality, etc, as in *squaresville*, *dullsville*. [The suffix *-ville* in names of towns, esp in US, from Fr *ville* town]

villeggiatura *vi-lej-ə-to͞o'rə*, *n* a stay in the country. [Ital]

villein *vil'ən* or *vil'in*, (*hist*) *n orig appar* a free villager; *later* (13c) a serf, free in relation to all but his lord, and not absolutely a slave; *later* a copyholder. — *n* **vill'einage** or **vill'enage** a villein's tenure or status. [Anglo-Fr; cf **villain**]

villenage. See under **villein**.

villi, villiform. See under **villus**.

villiago. See **viliaco**.

villication *vil-i-kā'shən*, (*Smollett*) *n appar* intended as a Scots pronunciation of **vellication**.

villus *vil'əs*, (*bot* and *anatom*) *n* a long soft hair; a hairlike process, *esp* one of the frond-like extensions of the lining of the small intestine: — *pl* **vill'i** (*-ī*). — *adj* **vill'iform** having the form of villi. — *adj* **vill'ose** or **vill'ous** covered with or formed of villi; like the pile of velvet. — *n* **villos'ity**. [L, wool]

vim *vim*, (*slang*) *n* energy, vigour. [Appar L *vim*, accusative of *vīs* force]

vimana *vi-män'ə*, *n* the central shrine of an Indian temple with pyramidal roof; a temple gate; a heavenly chariot, chariot of the gods. [Sans *vimāna* literally a marking out]

vimineous *vim-in'i-əs*, (*bot*) *adj* with long flexible shoots. [L *vīmineus*, from *vīmen*, *-inis* osier, switch]

Vimule® *vim'ūl*, *adj* and *n* (denoting) a type of contraceptive cap for the cervix with a two-tiered dome.

vin *vɛ̃*, (*Fr*) *n* wine. — **vin blanc** (*blɑ̃*) white wine; **vin ordinaire** (*ör-di-nār'*) inexpensive table wine for ordinary use; **vin rosé** rosé wine. — **les grands vins** wines from famous vineyards; **vin du** (or **de**) **pays** (*dü* or *də pā-ē*) country or local wine.

vina *vē'nə*, *n* an Indian stringed instrument with fretted fingerboard over two gourds. [Sans *vīṇā*]

vinaceous. See under **vine**.

vinaigrette *vin-ā-gret'*, *n* a mixture of oil, vinegar, seasoning and herbs, used as a salad dressing (also **vinaigrette dressing** or **sauce**); a box or bottle for aromatic vinegar or smelling-salts. — *adj* (*esp* placed after its noun) of a dish, served with this dressing. [Fr, from *vinaigre* vinegar]

vinal, Vinalia. See under **vine**.

vinasse *vi-nas'*, *n* residue in alcoholic distillation, *esp* in beet-sugar-making, a source of potash salts. [Fr]

vinblastine *vin-blas'tēn*, *n* a drug derived from the Madagascar or rosy periwinkle (*Vinca rosea*), used in the treatment of cancer, *esp* leukaemias and lymphomas. [Contraction of *vincaleucoblastine*, from **vinca** and **leucoblast**]

vinca *ving'kə*, *n* any plant of the periwinkle genus *Vinca*. [New L, from L *vinca pervinca*]

Vincentian *vin-sen'shən* or *-shyən*, *adj* pertaining to St *Vincent* de Paul (1576–1660) or to the charitable associations founded by him, or to St Vincent of Lérins (died 450), or other Vincent.

Vincent's angina *vin'sənts an-jī'nə*, *n* a bacterial infection of the tonsils, mouth and gums. [J K *Vincent* (1862–1950), French physician]

vincible *vin'si-bl*, *adj* that may be overcome. — *n* **vincibil'ity**. [L *vincibilis*, from *vincere*, *victum* to conquer]

vincristine *vin-kris'tēn*, *n* an alkaloid substance derived from the madagascar or rosy periwinkle, *Vinca rosea*, used in the treatment of certain types of leukaemia. [New L *vinca* a periwinkle, and *crista* fold]

vinculum *ving'kū-ləm*, *n* a horizontal line placed above a part of an equation, etc, equivalent to brackets (*math*); a tendinous band (*anatom*); a bond: — *pl* **vinc'ula**. [L, from *vincīre* to bind]

vindaloo *vin'də-lo͞o*, *n* a type of very hot Indian curry. [Prob Port *vin d'alho* wine with garlic sauce]

vindemial *vin-dē'mi-əl*, (*archaic*) *adj* pertaining to the vintage. — *vi* (*archaic*) **vindē'miate** to gather grapes or other fruit. [L *vīndēmia* vintage; see **vintage**]

vindicate *vin'di-kāt*, *vt* to justify; to clear from criticism, etc; to defend with success; to make good a claim to; to lay claim to; to maintain (a point of view, cause, etc); to avenge (*obs*); to free (*obs*). — *n* **vindicability** (*-kə-bil'i-ti*). — *adj* **vin'dicable**. — *n* **vindicā'tion** act of vindicating; defence; justification; support. — *adj* **vin'dicātive** (or *vin-dik'ə-tiv*) vindicating; tending to vindicate; revengeful, vindictive (*Shakesp*). — *n* **vindic'ativeness** vindictiveness. — *n* **vin'dicātor** a person who vindicates (*fem* **vin'dicātress**). — *adv* **vin'dicatorily**. — *adj* **vin'dicatory** (*-ə-tər-i* or *-ā-tər-i*) serving or tending to vindicate; punitive; retributive; avenging. [L *vindicāre*, *-ātum*]

vindictive *vin-dik'tiv*, *adj* revengeful or spiteful; pursuing revenge; punitive (as in *vindictive damages*); retributive (as in *vindictive justice*). — *adv* **vindic'tively**. — *n* **vindic'tiveness**. [L *vindicta* revenge; see **vindicate**]

vine *vīn*, *n* a woody climbing plant (*Vitis vinifera* or other of the genus) that produces grapes; a climbing or trailing stem or (*US*) plant (*hortic*). — *vt* to remove vines from, eg vines and pods from (peas). — *adj* **vīnā'ceous** wine-coloured. — *adj* **vī'nal** of or due to wine. — *n pl* **Vīnā'lia** (*vē-nä'li-a*) an ancient Roman wine festival celebrated on 23 April, when the previous year's vintage was tasted and offered to Jupiter; an ancient Roman vintage festival on 19 August. — *n* **vī'ner** a vine-grower. — *n* **vinery** (*vī'nə-ri*) a hot-house for rearing vines; a vineyard (*obs*). — *combining form* **vini-** or **vin-** (*vin(-i)* or *vīn-(i-)*) denoting wine. — *adj* **vinicul'tural** (*vin-* or *vīn-*). — *n* **vin'iculture** cultivation of the vine for wine-making, and often also the making of the wine. — *n* **vinicul'turist**. — *n* **vinificā'tion** (*vin-*) the process of converting grape-juice, etc, into wine. — *n* **vinificā'tor** a condensing device that collects the alcoholic vapour produced by the fermentation. — *adj* (*obs*) **vī'nolent** addicted to wine. — *n* **vinol'ogist** (*vīn-* or *vin-*). — *n* **vinol'ogy** the scientific study of vines, *esp* the grapevine. — *n* **vīnos'ity** vinous character; the characteristic qualities of a particular wine; addiction to wine. — *adj* **vī'nous** pertaining to wine; like wine; wine-coloured; caused by or indicative of wine. — *adj* **vī'ny** pertaining to, like, consisting of or bearing vines; entwining. — **vine'-branch** a branch of a vine; a Roman centurion's badge. — *adj* **vine'-clad** covered with vines. — **vine'-disease** a disease affecting the vine; **vine'-dresser** a person who trims and cultivates vines; **vine'-fretter** a small insect that infests vines, *esp* Phylloxera or other greenfly; **vine fruit** the fruit of the vine in any form, ie as grape or raisin, etc; **vine'-gall** a gall on a vine, *esp* one made by a weevil; **vine'-leaf** the leaf of a vine; **vine'-mildew** a disease of vines due to the oidium stage of a mildew fungus, *Uncinula*; **vine'-prop** a support for a vine; **vine'-rod** a Roman centurion's badge; **vine'-stock** the stock on which a vine of another kind is grafted; **vineyard** (*vin'yərd* or *-yärd*) a plantation of vines, *esp* grape-bearing vines; a particular sphere of labour, *esp* of an intellectual, academic or spiritual kind. — **dwell under one's vine and fig-tree** to live at peace on one's own land. [OFr *vine*, *vigne*, from L *vīnea* a vineyard, a vine, from *vīnum* wine; Gr *oinos* wine]

vinegar *vin'i-gər*, *n* a condiment and pickling medium, a dilute impure acetic acid, made from beer, weak wine, etc; bad temper or mood; energy or vigour (*NAm colloq*). — *vt* to apply vinegar to. — *n* **vinegarrette'** a vinaigrette, the container. — *adj* **vin'egarish** sourish. —

adj **vin'egary** like or flavoured with vinegar; sour (also *fig*). — **vin'egar-eel** a minute threadworm that breeds in vinegar; **vin'egar-fly** a fruit-fly; **vin'egar-plant** a bacterium causing acetic fermentation. [Fr *vinaigre*, from *vin* (L *vīnum*) wine, and *aigre* sour (L *ācer* keen, sharp, pungent)]

vinew *vin'ū, vt* and *vi* to make or become mouldy. — *n* mouldiness. — *adj* **vin'ewed** mouldy; musty. [OE *fynegian* to become mouldy, from *fynig* mouldy, from *fyne* mould]

vingt-et-un *vɛ̃-tā-œ̃* or **vingt-un** *vɛ̃-tœ̃, n* a card game with the aim of acquiring cards to the value of exactly (or the nearest below) twenty-one, pontoon. [Fr, twenty-one]

vinho verde *vēn'yō ver'de, n* a light, sharp, immature Portuguese wine. [Port, literally, green wine]

viniculture. See under **vine**.

vino *vē'nō,* (*slang*) *n* wine. — *pl* **vi'nos**. [Ital and Sp]

vinolent, vinology, vinous, etc. See under **vine**.

vint[1] *vint, n* a card game like contract bridge. [Russ]

vint[2]. See under **vintage**.

vintage *vint'ij, n* the gathering of grapes and preparation for wine-making; a season's yield of grapes or wine; the time of gathering grapes; wine, *esp* of a good year; the product of a particular period; a period of origin. — *adj* pertaining to the grape vintage; (of wine) of a specified year and of good quality; generally (eg of a play by an author or of a period) among the (best and) most characteristic; out of date and no longer admired. — *vt* to strip of grapes; to gather (grapes); to make (wine), *esp* of a good year. — *n* and *vt* **vint** (back-formation from **vintage**). — *n* **vint'ager** a worker at the vintage. — *n* **vint'aging**. — **vintage car** an old-fashioned car (*specif* one built between 1919 and 1930; **post-vintage thoroughbred** see under **thorough**); **vintage year** one in which a particular product (*usu* wine) reaches an exceptionally high standard. [Anglo-Fr *vintage*, OFr (Fr) *vendange*, from L *vīndēmia*, from *vīnum* wine, grapes, and *dēmere* to remove (from *dē* out of or away, and *emere* to take); modified by influence of **vintner**]

vintner *vint'nər, n* a person who sells wine. — *n* **vint'ry** a wine-store; a wine-shop. [OFr *vinetier*, from LL *vīnetārius*, from L *vīnum* wine]

viny. See **vine**.

vinyl *vīn'il, n* an organic radical $CH_2{=}CH$-, the equivalent of a molecule of ethylene with a hydrogen atom removed; any vinyl polymer, plastic or resin; gramophone records collectively (*colloq*). — *adj* of, consisting of, containing or made of vinyl. — *n* **vinylidene** (*vīn-il'i-dēn*) the bivalent radical $CH_2{:}C{=}$; **Vinylite** (*vīn'il-īt*) proprietary name for a series of vinyl resins. — **vinyl resins** and **plastics** thermoplastic resins, polymers or co-polymers of vinyl compounds, eg polymers of **vinyl chloride** ($CH_2C{:}HCl$) a gaseous compound with various industrial applications, and **vinyl acetate** ($CH_3COOCH{:}CH_2$) a colourless liquid used to make polyvinyl acetate (see under **poly-**). [L *vīnum* wine, and **-yl**]

viol *vī'əl, n* any member of a class of stringed instruments, tuned in fourths and thirds, forerunners of the violin class, of which the double-bass is perhaps the closest modern relative. — *n* **viola** (*vi-ō'lə*) a tenor fiddle, slightly bigger than the violin, tuned a fifth lower. — *n* **violer** (*vī'ə-lər*) a viol player; a fiddler. — *n* **violin** (*vī-ə-lin'* or *vī'*) the smallest of the modern stringed instruments with four strings tuned in fifths (G, D, A, E), held under the chin and played with a bow; a violinist. — *n* **vī'olinist** (or *-lin'*) a player on the violin. — *adj* **violinist'ic**. — *adv* **violinist'ically**. — *n* **violist** (*vī'əl-ist*) a player on the viol; (*vē-ō'list*) a player on the viola. — *n* **violoncellist** (*vē-* or *vī-ə-lən-chel'ist*) a cello-player. — *n* **violoncell'o** a bass instrument of the violin class, commonly called **cello**: — *pl* **violoncell'os**. — *n* **violone** (*vē-ō-lō'nā* or *vī'ə-lōn*) a double-bass viol, bigger than the viola da gamba, perhaps the ancestor of the modern double-bass. — **vi'ol-de-gam'boys** (*Shakesp*) the viola de gamba; **violin'-bow**; **violin spider** a very small brown and orange spotted spider of S America, whose bite can be fatal to humans; **violin'-string**. — **viola da braccio** (*dä brät'chō*; Ital, viol for the arm) a tenor viol, held along the arm; **viola da gamba** (*gäm'ba*; Ital, viol for the leg) a bass viol, resembling the cello; **viola d'amore** (*dä-mō'rā*; Ital, of love) a tenor viol with sympathetic strings under the finger-board; **viola da spalla** (*späl'la*; Ital, for the shoulder) a bigger form of tenor viol. [Partly **vielle**; partly Fr *viole* and Ital *viola*, dimin *violino*, augmentative *violone*, and its dimin *violoncello*; origin uncertain; cf LL *vitula*, and **fiddle**]

viola[1]. See under **viol**.

viola[2] *vī'ə-lə, n* any plant of the violet and pansy genus *Viola*, giving name to the family **Violā'ceae**, with spurred zygomorphic flowers. — *adj* **violā'ceous** of the Violaceae; violet-coloured. [L]

violate *vī'ə-lāt, vt* to fail to observe duly; to abuse; to rape or submit to sexual abuse of any kind; to profane; to do violence to (*obs*). — *adj* violated; defiled. — *adj* **vī'olable** that may be violated. — *adv* **vī'olably**. — *n* **vī'olāter**. — *n* **violā'tion**. — *adj* **vī'olātive** causing, tending towards or involving violation. — *n* **vī'olātor**. [L *violāre*, *-ātum*, from *vīs* strength]

viold (*Milton*). Same as **vialled**.

violent *vī'ə-lənt, adj* intensely forcible; impetuous and unrestrained in action; overmasteringly vehement; due to violence; perverting or distorting the meaning, etc; expressing violence. — *vt* (*obs*) to force. — *vi* (*Shakesp*) to rage. — *n* **vi'olence** the state or quality of being violent; excessive, unrestrained, or unjustifiable force; outrage; profanation; injury; distortion of the meaning, etc; rape. — *adv* **vi'olently**. [L *violentus* or *violēns*, *-entis*, from *vīs*]

violer. See **viol**.

violet *vī'ə-lit, n* any plant or flower of the genus *Viola*; extended to unrelated plants, such as **African violet** or **water-violet** (see under **Africa** and **water**); a bluish purple. — *adj* bluish purple. — **shrinking violet** (*facetious*) a shy, hesitant person. [Fr *violette*, from L *viola*]

violin, violist, violoncello, etc. See under **viol**.

VIP *abbrev*: very important person.

viper *vī'pər, n* any of the small venomous snakes of the family **Viperidae** (*vī-per'i-dē*), including the **common viper** or adder, Britain's only venomous snake; extended to some other snakes, eg the pit-vipers and horned vipers; an ungrateful or treacherous, malignant person. — *adj* **viperiform** (*-per'*) resembling the viper. — *adj* **vī'perine** (*-pər-īn*) related to or resembling the viper. — *adj* **vī'perish** venomous; spiteful; like a viper. — *adj* **vī'perous** having the qualities of a viper; venomous; malignant. — *adv* **vī'perously**. — **viper's bugloss** a stiff bristly boraginaceous plant (*Echium*) of dry places, with intensely blue flowers, once thought to be a remedy or prophylactic for snake-bite; **viper's grass** black salsify. [L *vīpera*, from *vīvus* living, and *parere* to bring forth]

VIR *abbrev*: *Victoria Imperatrix Regina* (*L*), Victoria, Empress and Queen.

viraemia. See under **virus**.

virago *vi-rä'gō* or *vi-rā'gō, n* a violent or bad-tempered woman; a heroic or manlike woman; an amazon: — *pl* **vira'goes** or **vira'gos**. — *adj* **viraginian** (*vi-rə-jin'i-ən*), **viraginous** (*vi-raj'*) or **vira'goish**. [L *virāgō*, *virāginis*, from *vir* a man]

viral. See under **virus**.

viranda, virando (*pl* **viran'dos**). *Obs* forms of **veranda**.

vire. See under **virement**.

virelay *vir'ə-lā, n* an old French lyric form in two-rhymed stanzas of short lines, linked by recurrent lines. [Fr *virelai*, appar from meaningless refrain *vireli*, but associated with *virer* to turn, and *lai* a song]

virement *vē-rə-mã* or *vīr'mənt,* (*accountancy*) *n* authorized transference of a surplus to balance a deficit under another heading; authorized redirection of funds for one purpose to a more urgent occasion. — *vt* **vire** (*vīr*) to transfer (funds) in this way. [Fr *virement*]

virent *vīr'ənt, adj* verdant (*archaic*); fresh (*obs*); green (*archaic*). — *n* **virescence** (*vir-* or *vīr-es'əns*). — *adj* **viresc'ent** turning green; inclining to green; fresh; green; abnormally green. [L *virēns, -entis*, pr p of *virēre* to be green; *virēscēns*, pr p of *virēscere* to become green]

vireo *vir'i-ō, n* any American singing bird of the genus *Vireo*, the greenlets, giving name to the family **Vireonidae** (*-on'i-dē*): — *pl* **vir'eos**. [L *vireō, -ōnis* perh greenfinch]

vires. See under **vis**.

virescence, virescent. See under **virent**.

viretot *vir'i-tot*, (*Scott* after *Chaucer*) *n* rush, dash, gad. [Origin obscure]

virga *vûr'gə*, (*meteorol*) *n* (also *n pl*) trails of water, drops, or ice particles coming from a cloud but not reaching the ground as precipitation. [L, a twig, streak in the sky]

virgate *vûr'gāt, adj* rodlike; twiggy. — *n* an old land measure, commonly 30 acres. [L *virga* rod]

virge *vûrj, n obs* Latinized spelling of **verge**[1]. — *n* **virg'er** (*obs* except in certain cathedrals, *esp* St Paul's) verger.

Virgilian or **Vergilian** *vər-jil'i-ən, adj* of or in the manner of *Virgil* (*Publius Vergilius Maro*), the Roman poet (70–19 BC).

virgin *vûr'jin, n* a person (*esp* a woman) who has had no sexual intercourse; a member of a religious order of women who have undertaken to remain virgins; a maiden; (*usu* with *cap*) a Madonna, a figure of the Virgin; (with *cap*) Virgo, a sign, and a constellation, of the zodiac. — *adj* in a state of virginity; of a virgin; maidenly; pure; chaste; undefiled; in the original condition, unattained, untouched, unexploited, never scaled, felled, captured, wrought, used, etc; never having previously undergone or been affected by the thing mentioned; (of *esp* olive oil) obtained at the first pressing; (of silver, etc) mined in a pure, unmixed state. — *vt* (with *it*; *Shakesp*) to continue chaste. — *adj* **vir'ginal** of or appropriate to a virgin or virginity; in a state of virginity; like a virgin; parthenogenetic. — *adv* **vir'ginally**. — *n* **vir'ginhood** or **virgin'ity** the state or fact of being a virgin. — *adj* **vir'ginly** pure. — *adv* chastely. — **virgin birth** or **generation** parthenogenesis; **Virgin Birth** (*Christian theol*) (the doctrine of) the birth of Christ, His mother being a virgin. — *adj* **virg'in-born** born of a virgin. — **virgin gold** gold in the condition in which it is found; **virgin knot** the fastening of a Greek or Roman woman's girdle, loosed at marriage; **virgin neutron** a neutron which has not yet experienced a collision and therefore retains its energy at birth; **vir'gin's-bow'er** traveller's-joy (*Clematis vitalba*); **virgin soil** soil never previously tilled or cultivated; material as yet untried or unaffected. — **the Blessed Virgin** or **the Virgin** Mary the mother of Christ; **the Virgin Queen** Elizabeth I of England. [Partly through Fr, from L *virgō, virginis*]

virginal[1] *vûr'jin-əl, n* (often in *pl*, also *pair of virginals*) an old keyboard instrument like a small single-manual harpsichord. — *vi* (*Shakesp*) to finger, as on a virginal. [Perh because it was played by young ladies (see **virgin** above), or perh from L *virga* rod, which formed part of the instrument's action]

virginal[2], **virginhood**, etc. See **virgin**.

Virginia *vər-jin'yə, n* a tobacco grown and manufactured in *Virginia*. — *adj* **Virgin'ian**. — *n* a native or citizen of Virginia. — *n* **virgin'ium** (*chem*) a name proposed for the element of atomic no 87 (see **francium**). — **Virginia creeper** an American climbing-plant closely related to the vine, bright red in autumn; **Virginia stock** see under **stock**[1]. [The US state, named after Elizabeth, the *virgin* queen]

virginity, etc. See **virgin**.

Virgo *vûr'gō, n* the Virgin in the Zodiac; a person born between 23 August and 22 September, under the sign of the Virgin. — *n* **Virgō'an** a person born under the sign of the Virgin. — Also *adj*. — **virgo intacta** (*in-tak'tə* or *-tä*; L, untouched) a woman who has not had sexual intercourse. [L]

virgule *vûr'gūl, n* a slanting line, an old form of comma, a solidus. — *adj* **vir'gulate** shaped like a rod. [Fr, comma, from L *virgula*, dimin of *virga* a twig, rod]

viricide, etc. See under **virus**.

virid *vir'id, adj* green. — *n* **viridesc'ence**. — *adj* **viridesc'ent** greenish. — *n* **virid'ian** a green pigment, hydrated chromium sesquioxide. — *n* **vir'idite** an indeterminate green decomposition product in rocks. — *n* **virid'ity** verdure; greenness. [L *viridis* green, from *virēre* to be green]

virile *vir'īl* or (*esp NAm*) *vir'il, adj* having the qualities of a mature male human being; robustly masculine; manly; (of a man) sexually potent or with a particularly high sexual drive. — *n* **virilescence** (*vir-il-es'əns*) development of male character in the female. — *adj* **virilesc'ent**. — *n* **vir'ilism** (*med*) the presence of male sexual characteristics in a female. — *n* **viril'ity** the state or quality of being a mature male; the power (*esp* sexual) of a mature male; manhood; masculinity; vigour, energy. — *n* **virilizā'tion** or **-s-** the development of male sexual characteristics in the female. — *adj* **vir'ilized** or **-ised**. — *adj* **vir'ilizing** or **-s-**. [L *virīlis*, from *vir* a man; cf OE *wer* man]

virion. See **virus**.

virl *virl*, (now *Scot*) *n* See under **ferrule**.

virogene, virology, virose, etc. See under **virus**.

virtu *vûr-tōō', n* a love of the fine arts; a taste for curiosities; objects of art or antiquity collectively. — *adj* **virtuose** (*-tū-ōs'*) or **virtuō'sic** exhibiting the qualities of a virtuoso. — *n* **virtuosity** (*-os'*) the character of a virtuoso; exceptional technical skill in music or other fine art; interest in or knowledge of articles of virtu. — *n* **virtuoso** (*vûr-tū-ō'sō* or *-zō*; also *adj*) a person with a good deal of knowledge of or interest in works of art, antiquities, curiosities and the like; a musician (or other artist) of the highest technical skill: — *pl* **virtuō'sōs** or **virtuō'si** (*-sē*): — *fem* **virtuō'sa**, *pl* **virtuō'se** (*-sā*). — *n* **virtuō'sōship**. — **article** (or **object**) **of virtu** an object of artistic or antiquarian interest, a curio. [Ital *virtù*, from L *virtūs, -ūtis* (see **virtue**)]

virtual *vûr'tū-əl, adj* in effect, though not in fact; not such in fact but capable of being considered as such for some purposes; (of memory or storage) appearing to be internal but actually transferred a segment at a time as required from (and to) back-up storage into (and out of) the smaller internal memory (*comput*); computer-simulated in virtual reality (qv below); having virtue or efficacy (*archaic*); virtuous (*obs*). — *n* **vir'tualism** the doctrine of Christ's virtual presence in the eucharist. — *n* **vir'tualist**. — *n* **virtual'ity** essential nature; potentiality; virtual reality. — *adv* **vir'tually** in effect, though not in fact; (loosely) almost, nearly. — **virtual image** see under **image**; **virtual reality** (often *abbrev* **VR**) a computer-simulated environment (used, eg for training astronauts, and for video games) which gives the operator the impression of actually being in the environment, interacting with it and causing things to happen, by means of goggles, a joystick or other special equipment. [Med L *virtūalis*, from L *virtus* virtue]

virtue *vûr'tū, n* excellence; worth; moral excellence; inherent power; efficacy; the practice of duty; a good quality, *esp* moral; sexual purity; (loosely) virginity; one of the orders of the medieval celestial hierarchy; an accomplishment (*rare*); valour (now *rare*). — *adj* **vir'tueless**. — *adj* **vir'tuous** having virtue; morally good; blameless; righteous; practising duty; according to moral law; chaste. — *adv* **vir'tuously**. — *n* **vir'tuousness**. — *adj* **vir'tue-proof** (*Milton* **vertue-**) impregnable in virtue. — **by** (or **in**) **virtue of** through the power, force, or efficacy of; because of; on account of; **make a virtue of necessity** to do as if from a sense of duty (or with a sense of duty called in for the occasion) something unpleasant one is forced to do; **seven principal virtues** faith, hope, charity, justice, prudence, temperance, and fortitude, the first three being the *theological*, the last four the *moral* virtues; **the cardinal virtues** see under **cardinal**. [OFr *vertu* and L *virtus* bravery, moral excellence, from *vir* a man; cf Gr *hērōs*, Sans *vīra* a hero, OE *wer* man]

virtuose, virtuoso, etc. See **virtu**.

virtute officii *vûr-tū'ti of-is'i-ī* or *wir-tōō-te of-ik'i-ē*, (*L*) by virtue of office.

virucidal, etc. See under **virus**.

virulent *vir'ū-lənt* or *-ōō-*, *adj* extremely infectious; highly poisonous or malignant; venomous; acrimonious. — *n* **vir'ulence** or **vir'ulency**. — *adv* **vir'ulently**. — **virulent phage** a bacteriophage which always kills its host. [L *vīrulentus*, from *vīrus* (see **virus**)]

virus *vī'rəs*, *n* a pathogenic agent, *usu* a protein-coated particle of RNA or DNA, capable of increasing rapidly inside a living cell; an illness caused by a virus (*colloq*); (**computer virus**) a piece of computer code inserted into an apparently innocent program in order to corrupt or destroy other data and unknowingly passed on from one user to another; the transmitted cause of infection; contagious or poisonous matter (as of ulcers, etc); venom; any corrupting influence. — *n* **viraemia** (*vī-rē'mi-ə*) the presence of viruses in the bloodstream. — *adj* **vīrae'mic**. — *adj* **vī'ral** pertaining to or caused by a virus. — *adj* **vī'ricidal** (or *vir'*). — *n* **vī'ricide** (or *vir'*) a substance that destroys or eliminates a virus. — *n* **virino** (*vi-rē'nō*) a hypothetical organism suggested as the cause of BSE, said to be a tiny piece of nucleic acid coated with protective protein taken from the host. — *n* **vī'rion** (or *vir'*) a virus particle in its mature, infectious state. — *n* **vī'rogene** a virus-forming gene. — *n* **vī'roid** a particle of RNA, uncoated by protein, that can cause some diseases in plants. — *adj* **virolog'ical**. — *n* **virol'ogist**. — *n* **virol'ogy** the study of virus, viruses and virus diseases. — *adj* **vī'rose** poisonous; foul. — *n* **virō'sis** a disease caused by a virus. — *adj* **vī'rous** virose. — *adj* **vī'rucidal**. — *n* **vī'rucide** same as **viricide** above. — **virus disease** a disease caused by a virus. [L *vīrus* venom; Gr *īos*, Sans *viṣa* poison]

vis *vis*, *vēs*, *wēs*, (*L*) *n* force, power: — *pl* **vires** (*vī'rēz*, *wē'rāz*). — **vis comica** (*kom'ik-ə*, *kōm'ik-a*) comic power; **vis inertiae** (*in-ûr'shi-ē*, *in-ert'i-ī*) the power of inertia; passive resistance; **vis major** (*mā'jər*, *mä'yor*) superior force; **vis mortua** (*mör'tū-ə*, *mor'tōō-a*) force of pressure, dead force; **vis viva** (*vī'və*, *vē'va* or *wē'wa*) living force, equal to the mass of a moving body multiplied by the square of its velocity. — **vis a tergo** (*ā tûr'gō* or *ä ter'gō*) compulsion from behind.

visa *vē'zə* or (*archaic*) **visé** *vē'zā*, *n* an authenticating endorsement on a passport, etc, allowing the holder to enter or leave the country issuing it. — *vt* to put a visa on: — *pa t* and *pa p* **vi'saed** or **vi'séed**. [L *vīsa*, pa p fem of *vidēre* to see, and Fr *visé*, pa p masc of *viser* to examine]

visage *viz'ij*, *n* (*literary*) the face; an outward appearance (*archaic*). — *adj* **vis'aged**. — *n* **visagiste** (*vē-zazh-ēst*) or **visagist** (*viz'ə-jist*) an expert in facial make-up. [Fr *visage*, from L *vīsus* look]

vis-à-vis *vē-za-vē*, *adv* face-to-face. — *prep* face-to-face with; in relation to, with regard to. — *n* a person who faces, or is opposite to, another; an opposite number; a light carriage with seats facing each other; an S-shaped couch. [Fr *vis* face (from L *vīsus* look), and *à* to]

Visc. *abbrev*: Viscount.

viscacha *vis-kä'chə*, *n* a S American burrowing rodent of heavy build. — Also **vizca'cha**, **bisca'cha** and **bizca'cha**. — *n* **viscachera** (*-chā'rə*) a settlement of viscachas. [Sp, from Quechua *huiscacha*]

viscera, visceral, viscerate, visceri-, viscero-, etc. See under **viscus**.

viscid *vis'id*, *adj* semi-fluid, sticky, glutinous, viscous; (of a surface) clammy and covered with a sticky secretion (*bot*). — *n* **viscid'ity**. — *n* **viscin** (*vis'in*) the sticky substance present in the fruits of mistletoe. [LL *viscidus*, from L *viscum* (see **viscous**)]

visco-, viscometer, etc. See under **viscous**.

viscose *vis'kōs*, *n* the sodium salt of cellulose xanthate, used in the manufacture of **viscose rayon**. — *adj* viscous. [Ety as for **viscous**]

viscosimeter, viscosity. See under **viscous**.

viscount *vī'kownt*, *n* a British title of nobility next below an earl (first granted in 1440); the son or young brother of a count; an officer who acted as administrative deputy to an earl, a sheriff (*hist*); (*esp* with *cap*) a similar official in Jersey: — *fem* **viscountess** (*vī'kownt-es*) the wife of a viscount; a woman holding a viscounty in her own right; a size of roofing slate, 18 × 10 inches (457 × 254 mm). — *n* **vi'scountcy** or **vi'scountship** a viscounty. — *n* **vi'scounty** the rank or dignity of a viscount; the jurisdiction of, or territory under, a viscount (*hist*); a viscount (*obs*). [OFr *visconte* (Fr *vicomte*), from *vis-* (L *vice* in place of), and *conte* count, after LL *vicecomes*, from L *comes* a companion]

viscous *vis'kəs*, *adj* resistant, or highly resistant, to flow owing to forces acting between the molecules; sticky; viscid. — *n* **viscos'ity** the quality of being viscous. — *n* **vis'cousness**. — **vis'cō-** *combining form* denoting viscous or viscosity. — *adj* **viscōelas'tic** having both viscous and elastic properties. — *n* **viscoelastic'ity** — *n* **viscom'eter** or **viscōsim'eter** an instrument for measuring viscosity. — *adj* **viscōmet'ric, viscōmet'rical, viscōsimet'ric** or **viscosimet'rical**. — *n* **viscom'etry** or **viscōsimetry**. — **viscous damping** (*phys*) an opposing force proportional to velocity, eg that resulting from viscosity of oil; **viscous flow** a type of fluid flow in which there is a continuous steady motion of the particles, the motion at a fixed point always remaining constant; **viscous water** water thickened by addition of chemicals, used in fighting forest fires. [LL *viscōsus* sticky, from L *viscum* bird-lime, mistletoe; cognate with Gr *ixos* mistletoe]

viscum *vis'kəm*, *n* bird-lime; (with *cap*) a genus of parasitic plants including the common mistletoe. [L]

viscus *vis'kəs*, (*med* and *zool*) *n* any one of the organs situated within the chest and the abdomen, heart, lungs, liver, etc: — *pl* **viscera** (*vis'ər-ə*; in common general use, *esp* the abdominal organs). — *adj* **visc'eral** of or relating to the viscera; instinctive or intuitive, not cerebral or rational (*colloq*); having to do with the more earthy feelings and emotions (*colloq*). — *vt* **visc'erate** to disembowel. — *combining form* **visc'erō-** or **visc'eri-** denoting of or pertaining to the viscera or to a viscus. — *n* **viscerōptō'sis** (Gr *ptōsis* a falling) an abnormally low position of the intestines in the abdominal cavity. — *n* **viscerōtōn'ia** a pattern of temperament associated with the endomorphic body type, extravert, sociable and fond of bodily comforts. — *adj* **viscerōton'ic**. [L *vīscus*, pl *vīscera*]

vise[1] *vīz* (*obs*), *vt* to advise; to look at. — *vi* to look (with *on*); to consider (with *on*). [Partly **advise**; partly Fr *viser*, from L *vidēre*, *vīsum* to see]

vise[2]. *NAm* spelling of **vice**[1].

visé, viséed. See **visa**.

Vishnu *vish'nōō*, (*Hinduism*) *n* the second god of the Hindu triad, believed to appear in many incarnations, regarded by some worshippers as the saviour. — *n* **Vish'nuism**. — *n* and *adj* **Vish'nuite**. [Sans]

visible *viz'i-bl*, *adj* that may be seen; in sight; obvious; (of supplies of a commodity) actually in store, known to be available; relating to goods rather than services (*econ*); applied to indexing systems in which the edge of each card etc (containing key information) is immediately visible, in order to make it easier to identify the correct card, etc (*commerce*); ready or willing to receive a visitor or visitors. — *n* a visible thing (often in *pl*). — *n* **visibil'ity** the state or quality of being visible, or perceivable by the eye; the clearness of the atmosphere; clarity and range of vision in the atmospheric conditions, seeing; a visible thing (*usu* in *pl*); a sight, showplace (*obs*); appearance (*obs*); the power of seeing, sight (*obs*). — *n* **vis'ibleness**. — *adv* **vis'ibly**. — **Visible Church** the body of professing Christians on earth at any specific moment; **visible exports** or **imports** see under **exports** or **imports**; **visible horizon** see under **horizon**; **visible means** means or resources which are apparent to or ascertainable by others; **visible radiation** electromagnetic radiation which can be detected by the eye, light; **visible speech** a system of phonetic characters each of which suggests the configuration of the organs in producing the sound. [Through OFr or direct from L *vīsibilis*, from *vidēre*; see **vision**]

visie. See **vision**.

visier. See **vizier**.

Visigoth *viz'i-goth*, (*hist*) *n* one of the Western Goths (as distinguished from the Ostrogoths or Eastern Goths) who formed settlements in the south of France and in Spain, their kingdom in the latter lasting into the 8c. — *adj* **Visigoth'ic**. [LL *Visigothī*, from Gmc word meaning perh noble Goths, perh west Goths]

visile *viz'īl* or *-il*, *adj* of or pertaining to sight; learning by means of visual images and recalling such images readily. — *n* a person who learns and remembers best by visual images. [Modelled on **audile**, from L *vidēre*, *vīsum* to see]

visiogenic *viz-i-ō-jen'ik*, *adj* suitable artistically for television transmission. [Tele*vision* and **-genic**]

vision *vizh'ən*, *n* the act of seeing; the faculty of sight; anything seen; television, *esp* as opposed to sound radio; a look, glance; a vivid concept or mental picture; a person or scene of great beauty (sometimes ironically); a pleasing imaginative plan for, or anticipation of, future events; an apparition; a revelation, *esp* divine, in sleep or a trance (sometimes without article); the act or power of perceiving imaginative mental images; imaginative perception; foresight; mystical awareness of the supernatural. — *vt* to see as a vision, to imagine; to present, or to call up, as in a vision. — *n* **visie**, **viz'y** or **vizz'ie** (*Scot*; *viz'i*) a close or careful look; aim; a sight on the muzzle of a gun. — *vt* and *vi* (*Scot*) to look (at) closely; to aim. — *adj* **vis'ional** of or pertaining to a vision; derived from a vision; visionary, not real; pertaining to sight. — *adv* **vis'ionally**. — *n* **vis'ionariness**. — *adj* **vis'ionary** capable of seeing visions; apt to see visions; given to reverie or fantasy; showing or marked by imagination or foresight; out of touch with reality, unpractical; of the nature of, or seen in, a vision, visional; fanciful, not real; impracticable; characterized by visions or fantasy; pertaining to physical or mental vision. — *n* a person who sees visions; a person who forms impracticable schemes. — *adj* **vis'ioned** inspired so as to see visions; seen in a vision; produced by or associated with a vision. — *n* **vis'ioner** a visionary. — *n* **vis'ioning** seeing visions. — *n* **vis'ionist** a person who professes to be a visionary; a person who believes that the Biblical details of creation were revealed in vision. — *adj* **vis'ionless** destitute of vision. — **vision mix**; **vision mixer** a technician who blends or combines different camera shots in television or films. — **beatific vision** see under **beatify**. [Fr, from L *visiō*, *visiōnis*, from *vidēre*, *vīsum* to see; cf Gr *idein*, Eng *wit*]

visiophone *viz'i-ə-fōn*, *n* a videophone (qv under **video**). [*visio*n and tele*phone*]

visit *viz'it*, *vt* to pay a call upon, or to be in the habit of doing so; to go to for sight-seeing, recreation, or religious purposes; to go to stay with; to make a stay in, eg of migratory birds; (of a professional or his or her client, patient, etc) to go to see professionally; to examine or inspect (a place), *esp* officially; to come to, or to go to see, in order to give comfort or aid; to go to with intention of injuring; to inflict (punishment, etc) (with *on*); to punish (a person) (with *with*; *archaic*); to punish (eg wrong-doing) (*archaic*); (of an idea) to take temporary hold on the mind of; to afflict or trouble, eg with disease (*archaic*). — *vi* to be in the habit of seeing or meeting each other at home; to make a visit or visits. — *n* an act of visiting; a short stay; a sightseeing excursion; an official or a professional call; a chat (*NAm colloq*). — *adj* **vis'itable** subject to official visitation; attractive to visitors. — *adj* **vis'itant** paying visits, visiting. — *n* a person who visits; a person who is a guest in the house of another; a supernatural visitor; a migratory bird; (with *cap*) one of an order of nuns founded by St Francis de Sales in 1610, also called *Salesians*, *Order* (or *Nuns*) *of the Visitation*. — *n* **visitā'tion** the act of visiting; a long and wearisome visit; a formal or official visit by a superior, *esp* ecclesiastical; an examination by authority; the act of a naval commander in boarding a merchant vessel of another state to ascertain her character and object; a visit of God, or of a good (or evil) supernatural being; a dispensation of divine favour or displeasure; a sore affliction; the operation of a destructive power, or an instance of it; an influence acting on the mind; an unusual and extensive influx of a species of animals into a region; (with *cap*) a Christian festival to commemorate the visit of the Virgin Mary to Elizabeth, observed by the Roman and Greek Churches on 2 July. — *adj* **visitā'tional** or **vis'itātive**. — *n* **vis'itātor** an official visitor. — *adj* **visitatō'rial**. — *n* **visitee'** the person to whom a visit is paid. — *n* **vis'iting** the act, or an instance, of paying a visit; a visitation, in the senses of divine dispensation, heavy affliction, or influence operating on the mind. — *adj* that visits (often *opp* to *resident*); pertaining to visiting. — *n* **vis'itor** (now rarely **vis'iter**; *fem* **vis'itress**) a person who visits, calls on, or makes a stay with another person; a person authorized to visit for purposes of inspection or supervision; a migratory bird. — *adj* **visitō'rial**. — **vis'iting-book** a book recording the names of persons who have called or are to be called on; a visitors' book (*Thackeray*); **vis'iting-card** a small card bearing the name and address, or title, left in paying visits, and sometimes (*esp* formerly) sent as an act of courtesy or in token of sympathy; **vis'iting-day** a day on which one is at home and ready to receive callers; **visitor general** (*hist*) a personal representative of the King of Spain appointed to investigate affairs, *esp* in Spanish America; **visitors' book** a book in which visitors write their names and sometimes comments; **visitors' passport** (also **British Visitors' Passport**) a simplified form of passport, valid for one year for visits not exceeding three months to certain countries, obtainable at post offices. — **visitation of the sick** an Anglican form of service for use by clergy visiting the sick; **visit with** (*NAm*) to visit; to be a guest with; to chat with. [Fr *visiter*, from L *vīsitāre*, frequentative of *vīsere* to go to see, visit, from *vidēre* to see]

visite *vi-zēt'*, *n* a woman's light short cloak worn in the mid 19c. [Fr]

visive *viz'iv*, (*rare*) *adj* of or pertaining to sight, visual; able to see; able to be seen. [LL *vīsīvus*, from L *vīsus* sight]

visne *vē'ni*, (*law*) *n* a venue. [OFr *visné* neighbourhood, from L *vīcīnus* neighbour]

visnomy *viz'nə-mi*, (*archaic* and *dialect*) *n* physiognomy. — Also **vis'nomie**. [Variant of **physiognomy**]

vison *vī'sən*, *n* the American mink. [Fr; origin unknown]

visor or **vizor** *vīz'ər*, *n* a movable part of a helmet covering the face, or the upper part of the face, with holes or slits for the eyes and mouth; a mask or other means of disguise (*archaic*); the peak of a cap; a movable flap on a motor-car windscreen, used as a shade against the sun; a hood placed over a signal light; face, aspect, outward appearance (*obs*). — *vt* to disguise or cover with a visor. — *adj* **vis'ored** or **viz'ored**. — **vis'or-mask** a vizard-mask. [Anglo-Fr *viser* (Fr *visière*), from *vis* countenance]

vista *vis'tə*, *n* a view or prospect, *esp* as seen through an avenue; an avenue or other long narrow opening or passage; the trees, etc that form the avenue; a mental view or vision extending far into the past or future, or into any subject engaging the thoughts. — Also (*obs*) **vis'to** (*pl* **vis'tos**). — *vt* (*rare*) to make into, or see in, vistas. — *adj* **vista'd** or **vis'taed** (*-təd*) having or forming a vista or vistas (*lit* and *fig*). — *adj* **vis'tal**. — *adj*

vis'taless (*-tə-les*). [Ital *vista* sight, view, from L *vidēre*, *vīsum* to see]

visual *vizh'ū-əl* or *viz'ū-əl*, *adj* of or pertaining to sight; concerned with seeing, or (*fig*) with mental vision; attained by, or received through, sight, now often as contrasted with a mechanical or other means of observation; of the nature of, or conveying, a mental vision; visible, having visibility; optic, as in **visual axis** (see **optic axis** under **optic**); of the eye (*poetic*); (of beams) coming from the eye (*obs*). — *n* something visible; a rough sketch of the layout of an advertisement; (often in *pl*) a drawing, piece of film, etc, as distinct from the words or sound accompanying it. — *n* **vis'ualist** a visualizer; a visile. — *n* **visual'ity** (*Carlyle*) the quality or state of being visible to the mind; a mental picture. — *n* **visualīzā'tion** or **-s-**. — *vt* **vis'ualize** or **-ise** to make visible, externalise to the eye; to call up a clear visual image of. — *vi* to call up a clear visual image; to become visible (*med*). — *n* **vis'ualīzer** or **-s-**. — *adv* **vis'ually**. — **visual acuity** the spatial resolving power of the eye; **visual aid** a picture, photograph, film, diagram, etc, used as an aid to teaching; **visual arts** painting, sculpture, films, etc as opposed to literature, music, etc; **visual purple** see under **purple**. — **visual display unit** (*comput*; often *abbrev* **VDU**) a cathode ray tube which displays data, entered by keyboard or light pen, from a computer's memory. [LL *vīsuālis*, from L *vīsus* sight]

visuo- *vizh'ū-ō* or *viz'ū-ō*, *combining form* denoting sight. [L *vīsus*]

vita *vī'tə*, *vē'* or *wē'ta*, (*L*) *n* life; a CV (*NAm*; also **vitae** *-tī* or *-tē*): — *pl* **vi'tas** (or *vē'*). — **vita patris** (*-tä pat'ris*) in the father's lifetime.

Vitaceae. See under **Vitis**.

Vita glass® *vī'tə gläs*, *n* a type of glass that transmits ultraviolet rays.

vital *vī'tl*, *adj* characteristic of life, or of living things; supporting or necessary to life; essential; extremely important; pertaining to life, birth, and death; fatal to life (*obs*); full of life, lively, energetic; being a manifestation of organic life (*biol*); life-giving, invigorating (*poetic*); animate, living (*archaic*); capable of living (*obs*). — *n* **vi'talism** the doctrine that there is a vital force (qv). — *n* **vi'talist** a person who holds this doctrine. — *adj* **vitalis'tic**. — *adv* **vitalis'tically**. — *n* **vitality** (*-tal'*) the state or quality of being vital; the quality of being fully or intensely alive; the capacity to endure and flourish; animation, liveliness; the principle of life, power of living; the state of being alive; a living or vital thing or quality: — *pl* **vital'ities**. — *n* **vitalizā'tion** or **-s-**. — *vt* **vi'talize** or **-ise** to give life to; to stimulate activity in; to give vigour to; to make lifelike. — *n* **vi'talizer** or **-s-**. — *adj* **vi'talizing** or **-s-**. — *adv* **vi'tally**. — *n pl* **vi'tals** (rarely in *sing*) the interior organs essential for life; the part of any whole necessary for its existence (*obs*). — *n* **vi'tascope** an early form of motion-picture projector. — *adj* **vi'tative** concerned with the preservation of life. — *n* **vi'tativeness** love of life, assigned by the phrenologists to a protuberance under the ear. — **vital air** (*obs*) oxygen; **vital force** the force on which the phenomena of life in animals and plants were thought to depend, distinct from chemical and mechanical forces operating in them; **vital functions** the bodily functions that are essential to life, such as the circulation of the blood; **vital principle** the principle (the *anima mundi*) which according to the doctrine of vitalism, gives life to all nature; a principle that directs all the actions and functions of living bodies; **vital signs** (the level or rate of) breathing, heartbeat, etc; **vital spark** or **flame** life or a trace of life; the principle of life in man; **vital stain** (*bot*, *zool*) a stain that can be used on living cells without killing them; **vital statistics** statistics dealing with the facts of population, ie births, deaths, etc; a woman's bust, waist and hip measurements (*colloq*). [L *vītālis*, from *vīta* life, from *vīvere* to live; cognate with Gr *bios* life]

vitamin *vit'ə-min* or (*esp NAm*) *vīt'* (*orig* **vitamine** *-mēn*), *n* any of numerous organic substances, 'accessory food factors', present in minute quantities in nutritive foods and essential for the health of the animal organism, designated provisionally vitamin A, B_1, B_2, B_6, B_{12}, C, D, D_2, D_3, E, F (*obs*), G (another name for B_2; *esp NAm*), H, K, K_1, K_2, K_3, L, P (previously called X), PP (a vitamin effective against pellagra, as nicotinic acid): later these were analysed and given names indicating something of their nature, such as: **retinol**; **aneurin** (**thiamine**), **riboflavin**, **pantothenic acid**, **nicotinic acid** (**niacin**), **pyridoxine** (**adermin**), **cyanocobalamin**, **folic acid**, **pteroic acid**; **ascorbic acid**; **calciferol**, *esp cholecalciferol* and *ergocalciferol*; **tocopherol**; **linoleic** and **linolenic acid**; **biotin**; **phylloquinone** (or **phytonadione**), **menadione**, menaquinone; **bioflavonoid** (also called **citrin**). — *vt* **vi'taminize** or **-ise** to add vitamins to (a food). — **vitamin B complex** a group of vitamins formerly regarded as being a single vitamin. [Coined in 1906 from L *vīta* life, and (inappropriately) **amine**]

vitascope, **vitative**, etc. See under **vital**.

vite *vĕt*, (*music*) *adv* quickly. [Fr]

vitellus *vi-* or *vī-tel'əs*, *n* the yolk of an egg: — *pl* **vitell'ī**. — *adj* **vit'ellary** pertaining to the vitellus; yellow like the yolk of an egg. — *n* **vitell'icle** a yolk-sac. — *adj* **vitelligenous** (*-ij'*) producing yolk. — *n* **vitell'in** a phosphoprotein present in yolks of eggs. — *n* **vitell'ine** a vitellus. — *adj* vitellary. [L, a yolk; a transferred use of *vitellus*, from *vitulus* a calf]

vitex *vī'teks*, *n* any plant of the genus *Vitex* of trees or shrubs, chiefly tropical, of the family Verbenaceae, having a drupe with a four-celled stone, some species of which yield valuable timber. [L]

vitiate *vish'i-āt*, *vt* to render faulty or defective; to spoil; to make impure; to deprave, corrupt, pervert, debase; to make ineffectual, invalid or inconclusive; to violate or rape (*obs*); to adulterate (*obs*). — Also (*obs*) **vi'ciate**. — *adj* (*archaic*) vitiated. — *adj* **vi'tiable**. — *n* **vitiā'tion**. — *n* **vi'tiātor**. — *n* **vitios'ity** (also **vicios'ity**) the state or quality of being vicious, or (*Scots law*) faulty. [L *vitiāre*, *-ātum*, from *vitium* (see **vice**[2])]

viticetum, **viticide**, **viticulture**, etc. See under **Vitis**.

vitiligo *vit-i-lī'gō* or *-ə-lē'gō*, (*med*) *n* a skin abnormality in which irregular patches of the skin lose colour and turn white. [L *vitilīgo* a skin eruption]

vitilitigation *vit-i-lit-i-gā'shən*, (*rare*) *n* vexatious wrangling. — *vi* (*rare*) **vitilit'igate**. [Formed from L *vitilītigāre*, *-ātum* to quarrel disgracefully, from *vitium* a blemish, and *lītigāre* to quarrel]

vitiosity. See under **vitiate**.

Vitis *vī'tis*, *n* the grapevine genus of woody climbing plants of the family **Vitaceae** (*vī-tā'sē-ē*) or *Ampelidaceae*. — *n* **viticetum** (*vīt-* or *vit-i-sē'təm*) a plantation of vines. — *n* **vit'icide** a vine pest. — *adj* **vitic'olous** living on vines. — *n* **vit'iculture** cultivation of the vine. — *n* **viticul'turist**. — *adj* **vitif'erous** bearing vines. [L *vītis* a vine, from *viēre* to twist]

vitrage *vē-träzh* or *vit'rij*, *n* (used also adjectivally) a kind of thin curtain for windows or glazed doors. [Fr, glass window]

vitrail *vit'rāl* or *vē-trä'ē*, *n* stained glass: — *pl* **vitraux** (*vē-trō'* or *vit'*). — *adj* **vitrailled** (*vit'rāld*). — *n* **vit'raillist** a maker of glass, *esp* stained glass. [Fr]

vitrain *vit'rān*, *n* a separable constituent of bright coal, of vitreous appearance. [L *vitrum* glass, and sfx *-ain*]

vitraux. See under **vitrail**.

Vitreosil®. See under **vitreous**.

vitreous *vit'ri-əs*, *adj* glassy; pertaining to, consisting of or like glass; glass-green in colour; resembling glass in absence of crystalline structure, in lustre, etc (*geol*). — *n* **Vit'reosil®** vitreous silica used for apparatus which is subject to large temperature variations. — *n* **vitreos'ity** or **vit'reousness**. — *n* **vitresc'ence**. — *adj* **vitresc'ent** tending to become glass; capable of being turned into glass. — *n* **vitrescibil'ity**. — *adj* **vitresc'ible**. — *n* **vit'reum** the vitreous humour of the eye. — *adj* **vit'ric**. — *n pl* **vit'rics** glassy materials; glassware. — *n sing* the study of glass and its manufacture. — *n* **vitrifac'tion** or

vitrificā'tion the act, process, or operation of vitrifying, or converting into glass; the state of being vitrified; a vitrified substance. — *n* **vitrifac'ture** the manufacture of glass. — *adj* **vit'rifiable**. — *adj* **vit'rified**. — *adj* **vit'riform** having the form or appearance of glass. — *vt* and *vi* **vit'rify** to make into or become glass or a glassy substance. — *n* **Vitrī'na** a genus of thin-shelled land molluscs, between slugs and true snails, the glass-snails. — *n* **vit'rine** (*-rēn* or *-rin*) a glass display case used to protect delicate articles, exhibit specimens, etc. — **vitreous electricity** an old name for positive electricity, because glass becomes positively charged when rubbed with silk; **vitreous enamel** a glazed coating fused on to a steel surface for protection and/or decoration; **vitreous humour** the jellylike substance filling the posterior chamber of the eye of a vertebrate, between the lens and the retina; **vitrified fort** a hill fort in (*esp*) Scotland, in which the siliceous stone has been vitrified by fire, whether by intention or accident is uncertain. [L *vitrum* glass]

vitriol *vit'ri-əl*, *n* oil of vitriol (qv below); a hydrous sulphate of a metal, eg *blue*, *green* and *white vitriol*, respectively that of copper (cupric), iron (ferrous), and zinc; rancorous or caustic criticism, etc. — *vt* **vit'riolāte** to convert into or treat with vitriol. — *n* **vitriolā'tion**. — *adj* **vitriolic** (*-ol'*) pertaining to, or having the qualities of, vitriol; biting, scathing, expressing intense ill-will. — *n* **vitriolizā'tion** or **-s-**. — *vt* **vit'riolize** or **-ise** to vitriolate; to injure with vitriol. — **elixir of vitriol** aromatic sulphuric acid (ie sulphuric acid mixed with certain other substances for use in medicine); **oil of vitriol** concentrated sulphuric acid (because formerly prepared from green vitriol). [Fr, from LL *vitriolum*, from L *vitreus* of glass]

vitro- *vit'rō-*, *combining form* denoting glass. — *n* **Vit'rolite®** (*-līt*) a kind of opaque glass with a fire-finished surface. [L *vitrum* glass]

vitro-di-trina *vit'rō-di-trē'nä*, *n* a Venetian white glass in which fine threads of cane form a lace-like pattern. [Ital, glass of lace]

Vitruvian *vi-trōō'vi-ən*, *adj* of or in the style of *Vitruvius* Pollio, a Roman architect under Augustus; denoting a kind of convoluted scrollwork.

vitta *vit'ə*, *n* a stripe of colour (*bot* and *zool*); a thin, elongated cavity containing oil, found in the pericarps of some fruits (*bot*): — *pl* **vitt'ae** (*-ē*). — *adj* **vitt'ate** having vittae; striped lengthwise. [L, a fillet or band for the head]

vittle or **vittles** *vit'l(z)*, a variant (*esp dialect*) form of **victual** or **victuals**.

vitular *vit'ū-lər*, *adj* pertaining to a calf or to calving. — *adj* **vituline** (*vit'ū-līn*) pertaining to a calf or to veal. [L *vitulus* a calf]

vituperate *vi-tū'pə-rāt* or *vī-*, *vt* to attack with violently abusive criticism or disapproval. — *vi* to use violently abusive language. — *adj* **vitū'perable** deserving vituperation. — *n* **vitūperā'tion**. — *adj* **vitū'perative** (*-rət-* or *-rāt-*) containing vituperation; uttering, or prone to utter, abuse. — *adv* **vitū'peratively**. — *n* **vitū'perātor**. — *adj* **vitū'peratory** vituperative. [L *vituperāre*, *-ātum*, from *vitium* a fault, and *parāre* to set in order, prepare]

Vitus: **St Vitus's dance**. See **chorea**.

viva[1] *vē'vä*, (*Ital* and *Sp*) *interj* long live.

viva[2]. See under **viva voce**.

vivace *vē-vä'che*, (*music*) *adj* and *adv* lively; in a lively manner: — *superl* **vivacis'simo**. [Ital]

vivacious *vi-vā'shəs* or *vī-*, *adj* lively, full of vitality; sprightly, sportive; long-lived, or tenacious of life (*obs*). — *adv* **vivā'ciously**. — *n* **vivā'ciousness** or **vivac'ity** the state of being vivacious; vigour; animation; liveliness or sprightliness of temper or behaviour; a vivacious act or saying (*rare*); vitality (*obs*); tenacity of life, or longevity (*archaic*). [L *vīvāx*, *vīvācis*, from *vīvere* to live]

vivamente. See under **vivo**.

vivandière *vē-vã-dyer*, (*hist*) *n* in the French and some other Continental armies, a female attendant in a regiment, who sold spirits and provisions: — *masc* **vivandier** (*-dyā*). [Fr, fem of *vivandier*, from Ital *vivandiere* a sutler, from assumed LL *vivanda* food]

vivarium *vī-vā'ri-əm*, *n* an artificial enclosure for keeping or raising living animals, such as a park, a fish-pond; a glass-sided box, etc: — *pl* **vīvā'ria** or **vīvāriums**. — Also **vī'vary** (*archaic*). [L *vīvārium*, from *vīvus* alive, from *vīvere* to live]

vivat *vī'vat* or *vē'vat*, (*L*) *interj* long live. — *n* an expression of applause or enthusiastic approval.

viva voce. *vī'və vō'sē* or *vō'chi*, *adv* by oral testimony. — *n* (*usu* **viva** alone) an oral examination. — *vt* (*usu* **viva**) to examine orally. [L]

vivda *viv'dä* or *vev'dä*, *n* in Shetland, meat hung and dried without salt. — Also **vif'da**. [Perh ON *vöthvi* muscle]

vive[1] *vīv*, (*Scot* and *obs*) *adj* lively, forcible; vivid. — *adv* **vive'ly**. — *n* **vīv'ency** (*rare*) vitality. [Fr, or L *vīvus* alive]

vive[2] *vēv*, (*Fr*) *interj* long live.

viver[1] *vē'vər*, (*obs* and *dialect*) *n* a fish-pond. [Anglo-Fr, from L *vīvārium*; see **vivarium**]

viver[2] *vī'vər*, (*dialect*) *n* a fibre, rootlet. [Variant of **fibre**]

Viverra *vi-* or *vī-ver'ə*, *n* the civet genus, giving name to the family **Viverr'idae** (*-i-dē*), and the subfamily **Viverrinae** (*-ī'nē*); (*usu* without *cap*) any of the Viverridae, *esp* one of the Viverrinae. — *adj* **viverr'ine** of or like the ferret or the civet family. [L *viverra* a ferret]

vivers *vī'vərz* or *vē'vərz*, (*Scot* and *literary*) *n pl* food, eatables. [Fr *vivres*, from L *vīvere* to live]

vives *vīvz*, *n sing* a disease of horses, swelling of the submaxillary glands. [OFr *avives*, *vives*, from Sp *avivas*, from Ar *addhība*, from *al* the, and *dhība* she-wolf]

vivi- *vi'vi-*, *combining form* denoting alive, living. — *adj* **viviparous** (*vī-vip'ə-rəs* or *vi-*; L *parere* to produce) producing living young that have already reached an advanced stage of development before delivery (opposite to *oviparous*; *zool*); germinating from a seed still on the parent plant (*bot*); producing bulbils or young plants in the flower clusters, etc (*bot*). — *n* **vivip'arism** viviparous reproduction. — *n* **viviparity** (*viv-i-par'i-ti*) or **vivip'arousness** the quality of being viviparous. — *adv* **vivip'arously**. — *n* **vivip'ary** viviparity in plants. — *vt* **vivisect'** to practise vivisection on. — Also *vi*. — *n* **vivisection** (*-sek'shən*; L *sectiō* the act of cutting, from *secāre* to cut) the act or practice, or an instance, of making surgical operations on living animals for the purposes of physiological research or demonstration; merciless and minute examination or criticism. — *adj* **vivisec'tional**. — *n* **vivisec'tionist** a person who practises or defends vivisection. — *adj* **vivisec'tive** practising vivisection. — *n* **vivisec'tor** someone who practises vivisection. — *n* **vivisectō'rium** a place for vivisection. — *n* **vivisepulture** (*-sep'l-chər*; *rare*) burial alive. [L *vīvus*]

vivianite *viv'yə-nīt*, *n* ferrous phosphate, blue by oxidation, often found coating fossil fishes and bones. [After J G *Vivian*, 19c English mineralogist, who first found it crystallized]

vivid *viv'id*, *adj* (of a colour) very bright; presenting a clear and striking picture; forming brilliant mental images; lively, intense; full of life, vigorous. — *adv* **viv'idly**. — *n* **viv'idness** or (*rare*) **vivid'ity**. — *adj* **vivif'ic** vivifying. — *n* **vivificā'tion**. — *n* **viv'ifier**. — *vt* **viv'ify** to endue with life; to make vivid; to assimilate or convert into living tissue. — *adj* **viv'ifying**. [L *vīvidus*, from *vīvere* to live]

viviparous, **vivisection**, etc. See under **vivi-**.

vivo *vē'vō*, (*music*) *adj* lively. — *adv* **vivamente** (*vē-vä-men'tä*) in a lively manner. [Ital]

vivres. Same as **vivers**.

vixen *vik'sn*, *n* a female fox; a bad-tempered woman. — *adj* **vix'en**, **vix'enish** or **vix'enly** bad-tempered, snarling. [S Eng dialect form of *fixen*, from OE *fyxen*, fem of *fox*]

Viyella® *vī-el'ə*, *n* a fine soft woven fabric made of cotton and wool. — Also *adj*.

viz. See **videlicet**.

vizament *viz'ə-mənt*, (*Shakesp*) *n* for **advisement**.

vizard *viz'ərd*, *n* a mask (*lit* and *fig*). — *vt* (*obs*) to mask; to disguise, conceal. — *adj* **viz'arded** masked; pretended. — **viz'ard-mask** a mask; a masked woman; a prostitute. [Variant of **visor**]

vizcacha. See **viscacha**.

vizier or **vizir** *vi-zēr'*, *viz'yər* or *viz'i-ər*, *n* a minister or councillor of state in various Muslim states. — Also **visier'**, **vezir'** or **wizier'**. — *n* **vizier'ate**, **vizir'ate**, **vizier'ship** or **vizir'ship** the office of a vizier. — *adj* **vizier'ial** or **vizir'ial**. — **Grand Vizier** in pre-Republican Turkey, the prime minister, and at one time also commander of the army. [Ar *wazīr* a porter, from *wazara* to bear a burden]

vizor. See **visor**.

vizsla *viz'lə* or *vizh'lə*, *n* a Hungarian breed of hunting dog with smooth red or rust-coloured coat. [*Vizsla*, a town in Hungary]

vizy, **vizzie**. See **visie** under **vision**.

VJ day *vē-jā'dā*, *abbrev*: Victory over Japan day (15 Aug, 1945, the date of the surrender of Japan to the Allies).

vl *abbrev*: *varia lectio* (*L*), variant reading (*pl* **vvll**).

Vlach *vlak*, *n* one of a non-Slav people of SE Europe, found chiefly in Romania, a Walachian. [OSlav *Vlachu*, from OHGer *walh* a foreigner, esp a Slav or a Latin]

VLCD *abbrev*: very low calorie diet.

vlei *flā*, *n* low-lying ground where a shallow lake forms in the wet season (*Afrik*); a swamp (local *US*). — Also **vly**. [Dialect Du, from Du *wallei* valley]

VLF *abbrev*: very low frequency.

VLSI (*comput*) *abbrev*: very large scale integration, a technological process by which 100 000 or more circuits are integrated on to a single silicon chip.

VMD *abbrev*: *Veterināriae Medicinae Doctor* (*L*), Doctor of Veterinary Medicine.

VMH *abbrev*: Victoria Medal of Honour.

VN *abbrev*: Vietnam (IVR).

vo *abbrev*: verso (qv).

voar *vōr* or *vör*, *n* in Orkney and Shetland, spring, seed-time. [ON *vār* spring; cf **ware**[3]]

voc. *abbrev*: vocative.

vocab *vō'kab* or *və-kab'*, (*colloq*) *n* vocabulary.

vocable *vō'kə-bl*, *n* that which is sounded with the voice, a word, or a single sound of a word; a term, name (*obs*). — *adj* capable of being uttered. — *adj* **vocab'ūlar** (*vō-* or *və-kab'*) of or concerning words. — *adj* **vocabūlār'ian** of or pertaining to vocabulary. — *n* a person much, or too much, concerned with words. — *adj* **vocab'ūlaried**. — *n* **vocab'ūlary** a list of words explained in alphabetical order; a dictionary; any list of words; the words of a language; the words known to and used by eg a particular person; the words used in a (particular) science or art; the signs or symbols used in any non-verbal type of communication, eg in computer technology; a collection of forms used in an art or by a particular practitioner of an art. — *n* **vocab'ūlist** the maker of a vocabulary; a lexicographer. [L *vocābulum* a name or term, from *vōx*, *vōcis* voice]

vocal *vō'kəl*, *adj* having a voice; uttered by the voice; oral; sung, or for singing (opposite to *instrumental*); resounding; talkative; outspoken; eloquent; concerned in the production of speech; of or pertaining to a vowel; having a vowel function; voiced. — *n* (often in *pl*) singing, or that which is sung, *esp* in a piece of popular music. — *n* (*jazz*) **vōcalese'** a type of singing in which the singer improvises words to familiar instrumental solos. — *adj* **vōcal'ic** containing (*esp* many) vowels; of, pertaining to, or of the nature of a vowel or vowels. — *n* **vocalise** (*vō-kə-lēz'*; *music*) a wordless composition or exercise for solo voice. — *n* **vō'calism** exercise of the vocal organs; the art of using the voice in singing; a vocal sound; a system of vowels. — *n* **vō'calist** a singer (*esp* opposite of *instrumentalist*). — *n* **vōcal'ity**. — *n* **vōcalizā'tion** or **-s-**. — *vt* **vō'calize** or **-ise** to form into voice, to articulate; to sing; to give expression to; to make vocal, endow with power of expression; to convert into a vowel; to utter with voice (*phonetics*); to insert the vowel points eg in Hebrew. — *vi* to sing; to sing *esp* exercises on a vowel or vowels. — *n* **vō'calizer** or **-s-**. — *adv* **vō'cally**. — *n* **vō'calness**. — *adj* **vocicul'tūral** (*vō-si-*) pertaining to voice-training. — *adj* **vocūlar** (*vok'*; *rare*) vocal. — *n* **vocule** (*vok'ūl*) a slight vowel sound completing the articulation of certain consonants. — **vocal cords** in air-breathing vertebrates, folds of the lining membrane of the larynx, by the vibration of the edges of which, under the influence of the breath, the voice is produced; **vocal music** music produced by the human voice alone (opposite of *instrumental music*); **vocal score** a musical score showing the singing parts in full and the instrumental parts as a piano accompaniment. [L *vōcālis*, from *vōx*, *vōcis* voice]

vocalion *vō-kā'li-ən*, *n* a musical instrument resembling a harmonium, with broad reeds. [**vocal**, and sfx *-ion*, as in **accordion**]

vocation *vō-kā'shən*, *n* a calling by God to his service in special work or in a special position, or to a state of salvation; a fitness for God's or other specified work; a way of living or sphere of activity to which one has been called by God, or for which one has a special fitness or inclination; one's occupation, business, or profession. — *adj* **vocā'tional** pertaining to, concerned with, or in preparation for a trade or occupation. — *n* **vocā'tionalism** the giving of an important place in education to vocational training. — *adv* **vocā'tionally**. [L *vocātiō*, *-ōnis*, from *vocāre* to call]

vocative *vok'ə-tiv*, *adj* pertaining to the act of calling; applied to the grammatical case used in some inflected languages in direct personal address. — *n* the case of a word when a person or thing is addressed; a word in that case. [L *vocātīvus*, from *vocāre* to call]

voces. See under **vox**.

vocicultural. See under **vocal**.

vociferate *vō-sif'ə-rāt*, *vi* to cry out with a loud voice, to bawl. — *vt* to utter in a loud voice. — *n* **vocif'erance** clamour. — *adj* **vocif'erant** clamorous. — *n* **vociferā'tion** the act of vociferating; a violent or loud outcry. — *n* **vocif'erātor**. — *n* **vociferos'ity** (*rare*). — *adj* **vocif'erous** making a loud outcry; noisy. — *adv* **vocif'erously**. — *n* **vocif'erousness**. [L *vōciferāt-*, pa p stem of *vōciferārī*, from *vōx*, *vōcis* voice, and *ferre* to carry]

vocoder *vō-kō'dər*, *n* an electronic device, similar to a synthesizer, for producing synthetic speech. [*vo*cal *cod*ifier]

vocular, **vocule**. See under **vocal**.

Vodafone® or **Vodaphone** *vō'də-fōn*, *n* a UK cellular phone system; a cellular phone. [*vo*ice, *da*ta and *phone*]

vodka *vod'kə*, *n* a Russian spirit, properly distilled from rye, but sometimes from potatoes, etc. [Russ, dimin of *voda* water]

voe *vō*, *n* in Orkney and Shetland, a bay, creek. [ON *vāgr* a creek]

voetganger *fŏŏt'hhäng-ər* or *fŏŏt'gäng-ər*, (*SAfr*) *n* a locust before its wings grow; a pedestrian; an infantryman. [Du *voet* foot, and *gang* walk]

voetstoots *fŏŏt'stōō(ə)ts*, (*S Afr*) *adj* (of something sold) as it stands, with any defects it has, visible or not. — Also *adv*. [Afrik]

vogie *vō'gi*, (*Scot*) *adj* vain; merry. [Origin obscure]

vogue[1] *vōg*, *n* the mode or fashion at any particular time; a place in popular favour, or the period of it; popularity; the chief place in popular esteem (*obs*). — *adj* in vogue, fashionable. — *vt* (*archaic* or *obs*) to give vogue to, or to repute, reckon. — *adj* **vog'uey** or **vog'uish**. — **vogue word** a word much used at a particular time. [Fr *vogue* (orig the trim of a rowing vessel), from *voguer* to row, from Ital *vogare*; ety uncertain]

vogue[2] *vōg*, (*colloq*, *orig US*) *vi* to perform to pop music a stylized dance imitative of the poses of fashion models.

— *n* **vōg'uer**. — *n* **vōg'uing** (or **vog'ueing**). [From *Vogue*, the fashion magazine]

voice *vois*, *n* sound produced by the vocal organs of living beings, *esp* of human beings in speech or song; sound given out by anything; the faculty or power of speech or song; the ability to sing, *esp* well; a mode of utterance; the quality and range of musical sounds produced by a singer; a singer; a part for a singer, or one of the parts in an instrumental composition; utterance, expression; someone who speaks; sound uttered with resonance of the vocal cords (*phonetics*); a mode of inflecting verbs to indicate their relationship with the subject (*gram*; see **active**, **passive**, and **middle**); an expressed wish or opinion; a vote, approval; a medium of expression; something said (*obs*); rumour, report, reputation (*obs*). — *vt* to utter (*rare*); to give utterance or expression to; to regulate the tone of (*music*); to write the voice parts of; to utter with vibration of the vocal cords (*phonetics*); to endow with voice; to act as mouthpiece of (*rare*); to rumour or *esp* (in *impers* construction) to be rumoured or commonly stated (*obs*); to speak of (*obs*); to acclaim (*obs*); to nominate, appoint, elect (*obs*). — *adj* **voiced** endowed with voice; having a voice of a specified kind; uttered with voice (*phonetics*). — *adj* **voice'ful** having a voice; vocal (with *with*); full of sound. — *n* **voice'fulness**. — *adj* **voice'less** having no voice; speechless, silent; unspoken; failing to, or unable to, express one's opinion or desire, or to make this felt; having no vote; not voiced (*phonetics*). — *n* **voice'lessness**. — *n* **voic'er**. — *n* **voic'ing** the regulation of the tone of organ pipes, ensuring proper power, pitch, and quality. — **voice'= box** the larynx; **voice mail** (*telecomm*) a system by which telephone messages can be stored in a central location and picked up by the addressee at their convenience. — Also *adj* **voice'-mail**; **voice'-over** the background voice of an unseen narrator in a film, etc; **voice'print** an electronically recorded visual representation of speech indicating frequency, amplitude and duration; **voice recognition** the identification of a human speaker by a computer (which compares their voice with sounds stored in its memory) before it carries out an instruction, allows access, etc; **voice response** output from a computer in the form of synthesized speech rather than a visual display; **voice synthesis** the ability of a computer to produce simulated speech from sounds stored in its memory; **voice vote** a vote judged on the relative strengths of the shouted ayes and noes. — **give voice to** to express; **in good voice** or **in voice** in good condition for singing or speaking; **in my voice** (*Shakesp*) in my name; **with one voice** unanimously. [Anglo-Fr *voiz*, *voice* (Fr *voix*), from L *vōx*, *vōcis*; related to Gr *epos* a word]

void *void*, *adj* containing nothing, empty, deserted; unoccupied, unutilized; having no holder, vacant; devoid, destitute, free (with *of*); ineffectual, useless; not binding in law, null, invalid; worthless (*obs*). — *n* an empty space; (with *the*) the expanse of space; emptiness; a lack, *esp* an emotional lack strongly felt; an unfilled space (*archit*); the total absence of cards of a particular suit (*bridge*, etc). — *vt* to make vacant, to empty, clear; to empty (the bladder or bowels); to send out, discharge, emit; to make of no effect, to nullify; to send away, dismiss (*obs*); to remove, clear away (*obs*); to go away from, withdraw from, quit (*obs*); to avoid (*obs*); to lay aside, divest oneself of (*obs*). — *adj* **void'able** that may be voided; that may be either voided or confirmed (*law*). — *n* **void'ance** the act of voiding or emptying; the state of being void; (of a benefice) the fact or state of being vacant. — *adj* **void'ed** (*heraldry*) (of a charge) having the inner part cut away and showing the tincture of the field. — *n* **void'ee** (*hist*) wine and light food taken before going to bed, or before the departure of guests. — *n* **void'er** (*lit* and *fig*) a person who empties or (*hist*) who clears a table; a tray for carrying away dirty dishes, crumbs, etc, or a tray, etc, for carrying sweetmeats (*obs*); a piece of armour covering an unprotected part of the body. — *n* **void'ing** the act of voiding; that which is voided (often in *pl*). — *n* **void'ness**. — **void'ing-lobby** (*obs*) an anteroom. [OFr *voide* empty, from popular L *vocitus*, from *vocitāre* to empty, from *vocuus*, for L *vacuus* empty]

voilà *vwä-lä*, *interj* behold; there you are. — **voilà tout** (*to͞o*) that is all. [Fr, behold, there is, there are]

voile *voil*, *n* any of several kinds of thin semitransparent material. [Fr, veil]

voir dire *vwär dēr*, (*law*) *n* an oath administered to a witness; an investigation, in the course of a trial, into the truth or admissibility of evidence about to be given. [OFr *voir* true, truth, and *dire* to say]

voisinage *voi'si-nij*, (*obs*) *n* neighbourhood, or the neighbourhood. [Fr]

voiture *vwä-tür*, *n* a carriage. — *n* **voiturier** (*vwä-tür-yā*) the driver of a carriage or coach. [Fr]

voivode *voi'vōd* or **vaivode** *vā'vōd*, *n orig*, the leader of an army; later, in SE Europe, the title of the head of an administrative division, a provincial governor; in Moldavia and Walachia, the former title of the princes; in Turkey, an inferior administrative official. — *n* **voi'vodeship** or **vai'vodeship**. [Russ *voevoda* (Serb *vojvoda*, Pol *wojewoda*)]

voix céleste *vwä sā-lest*, *n* an organ stop producing a soft, tremulous sound. [Fr, heavenly voice]

vol *vol*, (*heraldry*) *n* two wings displayed and conjoined in base. [Fr]

vol. *abbrev*: volume; volunteer.

vola *vō'lə*, (*anatom*) *n* the hollow of the hand or foot: — *pl* **volae** (*vō'lē*). — *adj* **vo'lar** pertaining to the palm or to the sole. [L]

volable *vol'ə-bl*, (*Shakesp*) *adj* nimble-witted. [L *volāre* to fly]

volage *vō'läzh*, *adj* giddy, flighty; fickle. — Also **volageous** (*vō-lā'jəs*). [Fr]

Volans *vō'lanz*, *n* the Flying Fish, a southern constellation. [L pr p of *volāre* to fly]

volant *vō'lənt*, *adj* flying; passing lightly through the air; flying or pertaining to flight (*zool*); nimble; represented as flying (*heraldry*); (of armed forces, etc) organized for rapid movement (*obs*). — *adj* **volante** (*vō-län'tā*; *music*) moving lightly and rapidly. — *n* **vo'lary** an aviary. — *adj* **volat'ic** (now *rare*) flying about. — *n* **vol'ery** a volary; a place for repair, etc, of aircraft. [L *volāre* to fly]

volante[1] *vō-lan'tā*, *n* a two-wheeled covered vehicle with long shafts, with a chaise-body hung before the axle, and the horse, or one of the horses, being ridden by a postillion. [Sp]

volante[2]. See under **volant**.

Volapük *vol'*, *vōl'ə-pük*, *-puk* or *-pük'*, *n* an early international language invented about 1879 by Johann Schleyer of Constance, Baden. — *n* **Volapük'ist** one versed in Volapük; one who advocates the adoption of Volapük. [Literally world-speech, from *vol* world, and *pük* speak]

volar. See under **vola**.

volary, etc. See under **volant**.

volatile *vol'ə-tīl* or (*NAm*) *-til* or *-təl*, *adj* evaporating very quickly; explosive; flighty, apt to change; (of stock markets, etc) showing rapid changes in prices; transient, short-lived, fleeting; not retaining information after the power supply is turned off (*comput*); capable of flying; moving lightly and rapidly about. — *n* a volatile substance; a creature capable of flying (*obs*). — *n* **vol'atileness** or **volatility** (*-til'*). — *adj* **vol'atilīzable** or **-s-** (or *-at'-*). — *n* **volatilīzā'tion** or **-s-**. — *vt* and *vi* **vol'atilize** or **-ise** (or *-at'-*) to make or become volatile. — *vt* to cause to evaporate; to make light, unsubstantial or delicate (*fig*). — **volatile alkali** (*obs*) ammonia; **volatile memory** (*comput*) stored information that can be destroyed by a power failure (cf **non-volatile memory**); **volatile oils** see **essential oils**. [L *volātīlis* able to fly, fleeting, from *volāre* to fly]

vol-au-vent *vol-ō-vã*, *n* a kind of small pie of light puff pastry filled with meat, or fish, etc in a sauce. [Fr, literally flight in the wind]

volcano *vol-kā'nō*, *n* a centre of eruption of subterranean matter, typically a more or less conical hill or mountain, built of ash and lava, with a central crater and pipe; a state of affairs, emotional condition, etc, suggestive of a volcano because an upheaval or outburst seems imminent; a form of firework: — *pl* **volcan'oes**. — *adj* **volca'nian** (*Keats*). — *adj* **volcanic** (*vol-kan'ik*) pertaining to, of the nature of, produced or caused by a volcano; characterized by the presence of volcanoes. — *adv* **volcan'ically**. — *n* **volcanicity** (*-kə-nis'i-ti*) volcanic action or phenomena. — *n* **volcanism** and **volcanist** (also with *caps*) see **vulcanism** and **vulcanist**. — *n* **volcanizā'tion** or **-s-**. — *vt* **vol'canize** or **-ise** to subject to the action of volcanic heat. — *adj* **vol'canized** or **-s-**. — *adj* **volcanolog'ical**. — *n* **volcanol'ogist** a vulcanologist. — *n* **volcanol'ogy** vulcanology. — **volcanic ash** or **ashes**, and **volcanic bomb** see under **ash** and **bomb**; **volcanic dust** fine particles of powdered rock blown out from a volcano; **volcanic glass** rock without a crystalline structure, as obsidian, pumice, etc, produced by rapid cooling of molten lava; **volcanic mud** or **sand** volcanic ash which has been deposited under water and sorted and stratified; **volcanic rocks** those formed by volcanic agency. [Ital *volcano*, from L *Volcānus*, *Vulcānus* Vulcan, god of fire]

vole[1] *vōl*, *n* any of numerous blunt-nosed, short-eared, mouselike or ratlike rodents, including the so-called water-rat and some fieldmice. [For *vole-mouse*, ie fieldmouse, of Scand origin]

vole[2] *vōl*, *n* in certain card games, (the winning of) all the tricks in one deal. — *vi* to win all the tricks in one deal. — **go the vole** to risk all for great gain; to try everything. [Fr, from L *volāre* to fly]

volens *vō'lenz*, (*law*) *adj* consenting to a course of action which involves a risk of some sort (therefore unable to sue if injury occurs). — Also *n*. — **volenti non fit injuria** (*vō-len'ti nōn fit in-jōō'ri-a*) no injury is done to a consenting party. [Pr p of L *velle* to be willing]

volente Deo *və-len'tē dē'ō*, *vō-*, *wō-len'te de'ō*, (*L*) God willing.

volery. See under **volant**.

volet *vol'ā*, *n* one of the wings of a triptych picture; a short veil worn at the back of the head (*hist*). [OFr (Fr, a shutter), from L *volāre* to fly]

Volga-Baltaic *vol'gä-böl-tā'ik*, *adj* of or pertaining to the group of languages to which Estonian, Finnish and Lapp belong. [*Volga* river, and *Baltic* Sea]

volitant *vol'ə-tant*, *adj* flying; flitting; fluttering; moving about; able to fly. — *vi* **vol'itate** to flutter, fly. — *n* **volitā'tion** flight; the power of flying. — *adj* **volitā'-tional**. — *adj* **volitorial** (*-tō'ri-*) having the power of flight. [L *volitāre* to flit, flutter]

volition *vō-lish'ən*, *n* the act of willing or choosing; the exercise of the will, or the result of this; the power of determining. — *adj* **voli'tient** (*rare*) willing. — *adj* **voli'tional** or **voli'tionary**. — *adv* **voli'tionally**. — *adj* **voli'tionless**. — *adj* **vol'itive** of or pertaining to the will; originating in the will; willed, deliberate; expressing a wish (*gram*). — *n* a desiderative verb, etc. [Fr, from LL *volitiō*, from L *volō*, pr indicative of *velle* to will, be willing]

volk *folk*, (*SAfr*) *n* the Afrikaner people. [Du, people, nation]

Völkerwanderung *fœlk-ər-vän'dər-ōōng*, (*Ger*) *n* the migration of Germanic and other peoples, chiefly in the 4c to 6c.

Volkskammer *folks'käm-ər*, *n* the parliament of the former German Democratic Republic (the new Bundestag now serves united Germany). [Ger *Volk* people, and *Kammer* chamber]

Volkslied *folks'lēt*, *n* a German folk-song: — *pl* **Volkslieder** (*-lē-dər*). [Ger]

volksraad *folks'rät*, *n* a legislative assembly, *esp* (with *cap*) that of the Transvaal or the Orange Free State before 1900. [Du *volk* people, and *raad* council]

volley *vol'i*, *n* a flight of missiles; the discharge of many weapons (*esp* small arms) at once; a round fired by every gun in a battery; an outburst of many words, etc at once; (in tennis, cricket, etc) a return of the ball before it reaches the ground (a **half-volley** is a return by striking the ball immediately after it bounces); a ball returned in this way: — *pl* **voll'eys**. — *vt* to discharge in a volley; to return (a ball) before it bounces; to fire a volley or volleys at. — *vi* to fly or be discharged in a volley; to sound or produce sounds like a volley; to roll, move or be emitted like a volley; to produce a volley in tennis, etc. — *adj* **voll'eyed**. — *n* **voll'eyer**. — **voll'eyball** a team game in which a large ball is volleyed by the hand over a high net; the ball used in the game. [Fr *volée* a flight, from L *volāre* to fly]

volost *vō'lost*, *n* a division for local government in tsarist Russia (*hist*); a soviet of a rural district. [Russ *volost*]

volpino *vol-pē'nō*, *n* a small Italian dog with long, straight hair and foxlike appearance: — *pl* **volpin'os**. [Ital, foxy, from *volpe* fox, from L *vulpēs*]

volplane *vol'plān*, (*aeronautics*) *vi* to glide down to earth in an aeroplane with the engine shut off; to glide to earth. — *n* a descent of this kind. [Fr *vol plané*, from *vol* flight, and *plané*, pa p of *planer* to glide]

Volscian *vol'shən*, *n* one of the *Volscī*, an ancient Italian people incessantly at war with the Romans for 200 years previous to 338 BC; their Italic language. — *adj* of or pertaining to the Volsci.

Volsungs *vol'sōōngz*, *n pl* a famous heroic race in old German legend, its founder *Volsung* being the grandson of Woden or Odin.

volt[1] or **volte** *volt*, *n* a sudden movement or leap to avoid a thrust (*fencing*); the gait of a horse going sideways round a centre; a track made by a horse executing this movement. — *n* **vol'tage**. [Fr *volte*, from Ital *volta*, from L *volvere*, *volūtum* to turn]

volt[2] *vōlt*, *n* the MKSA and SI unit of electromotive force, electric potential, or potential difference, the difference of potential between two points in a conductor carrying a current of one ampere when the power dissipated between them is one watt. — *combining form* **volta-** (*vol'tə-*) denoting voltaic, as in **volta-electric'ity** and **volta-elec'tric**. — *n* **voltage** (*volt'* or *vōlt'ij*) electromotive force in volts; power, intensity (*fig*). — *adj* **voltaic** (*vol-tā'ik*) pertaining to Alessandro *Volta*, who constructed the first electrical battery, a **voltaic pile**, and established the science of current electricity; (of electricity) generated by chemical action; used in producing such electricity; of, pertaining to or caused by voltaic electricity. — *n* **vol'taism** the branch of electricity concerning the production of an electric current from the chemical interaction of two immersed dissimilar metals. — *n* **voltameter** (*vol-tam'i-tər*) an instrument for measuring an electric current by means of the amount of metal deposited, or gas liberated, from an electrolyte in a given time by the passage of the current. — *n* **vōlt'meter** an instrument for measuring electromotive force directly, calibrated in volts. — **voltaic cell** a primary cell; **volt-amp'eres** the product of actual voltage (in volts) and actual current (in amperes) in a circuit. [Alessandro *Volta* (1745–1827), Italian scientist]

volta *vol'tə*, *n* an old dance, the lavolta; turn, time (*music*): — *pl* **vol'te** (*-tā*). [Ital]

voltage[1,2]. See under **volt**[1,2].

voltaic. See under **volt**[2].

Voltairian or **Voltairean** *vol-tār'i-ən*, *adj* pertaining to *Voltaire* (1694–1778), French poet, dramatist, historian, and sceptic. — *n* a person who advocates the views and principles of Voltaire. — *n* **Voltair'ianism**, **Voltair'eanism** or **Voltair'ism** the spirit of Voltaire, ie a sceptical and sarcastic attitude, *esp* towards Christianity, or an instance of this, or adherence to his doctrines.

voltameter. See under **volt**^{2}.

volte. See **volt**^{1}, **volta**.

volte-face *volt-fäs*, *n* a turning round; a sudden and complete change in opinion or in views expressed. [Fr]

voltigeur *vol-ti-zhœr'*, (*hist*) *n* in the French army, one of a light-armed company of picked men for skirmishing. [Fr, from *voltiger* to flutter, vault]

voltinism *vol'tin-izm*, *n* breeding rhythm, brood frequency (*esp* of insects). [Ital *volta*]

voluble *vol'ū-bl*, *adj* fluent in speech; too fluent or glib; talkative, verbose; twining (*bot*); changeable (*rare*); easy to roll, revolving readily or smoothly (*rare*; *Milton* **volubil**); flowing smoothly. — *n* **volubil'ity** or **vol'ubleness**. — *adv* **vol'ubly**. [L *volūbilis*, from *volvere*, *volūtum* to roll]

volucrine *vol'ū-krin* or *-krīn*, *adj* pertaining to birds, bird-like. [L *volucris* a bird, from *volāre* to fly]

volume *vol'ūm*, *n* quantity, bulk; cubic capacity; a large quantity; a quantity considered in terms of its bulk; fullness of tone; loudness, or the control for adjusting it on a radio, etc; a book, whether complete in itself or part of a larger work; a roll or scroll, which was the form of ancient books; anything (*esp* in the natural world) that may be studied like a book (*archaic*). — *vi* (*archaic*) to swell, rise, roll. — *vt* (*archaic*) to send out in volumes, or in great quantity; to make into or bind into a volume. — *adj* of or concerned with large volumes or amounts. — *adj* **vol'umed** having the form of a volume or roll; bulky. — *combining form* **-vol'umed** denoting consisting of (*esp* a specified number of) volumes. — *n* **volumenom'eter** or **volumom'eter** an instrument for measuring the volume of a solid body by the quantity of fluid it displaces. — *n* **volu'meter** an instrument for measuring the volumes of gases and liquids. — *adj* **volumet'ric** or **volumet'rical**. — *adv* **volumet'rically**. — *adj* **volu'minal** pertaining to cubic capacity. — *n* **voluminos'ity** extensiveness of writing. — *adj* **volu'minous** bulky, filling much space; in many volumes; capable of filling many volumes; having written much, as an author; consisting of many coils, windings or folds. — *adv* **volu'minously**. — *n* **volu'minousness**. — *n* **vol'umist** (*rare*) an author. — **volumetric analysis** the estimation of the amount of a particular constituent present in a compound by determining the quantity of a standard solution required to satisfy a reaction in a known quantity of the compound. — **speak** or **express**, etc **volumes** to mean much, to be very significant. [Fr, from L *volūmen*, *-inis* a roll, from *volvere*, *volūtum* to roll]

voluntary *vol'ən-tər-i*, *adj* spontaneous, free; done or made without compulsion or legal obligation; acting by choice, able to will; freely given, or supported by contributions freely given; done without expectation of payment or recompense of any kind, *esp* monetary; free from state control; proceeding from the will; designed, intentional; subject to the will; of or pertaining to voluntaryism. — *n* a person who does anything of his or her own free will; a piece of music played at will; a voluntary or extempore composition of any kind; a piece of music played before, during, or after a church service; an unwarranted fall from a horse; an upholder of voluntaryism; a volunteer (*obs*). — *adv* **vol'untarily**. — *n* **vol'untariness**. — *n* **vol'untarism** the philosophical doctrine that the will dominates the intellect; voluntaryism. — *n* **vol'untarist**. — *adj* **voluntaris'tic**. — *n* **vol'untaryism** the principle or practice of reliance on voluntary action, not coercion; the principle or system of maintaining the church by voluntary offerings, instead of by the aid of the state; the principle or system of maintaining voluntary schools (qv below). — *n* **vol'untaryist**. — *adj* **vol'untātive** voluntary. — **voluntary chain** or **retailers** a group of independent retailers who combine to buy their stock so as to increase profits; **voluntary muscle** a muscle, or muscular tissue, that is controlled by the will; **voluntary school** in England, a school supported by voluntary subscriptions, in many cases controlled by a religious body. — **Voluntary Service Overseas** (often *abbrev* **VSO**) a British organization which promotes voluntary work, mainly by young people, in developing countries; the work itself. [L *voluntārius*, from *voluntās* choice, from *volō*, pres indicative of *velle* to will]

volunteer *vol-ən-tēr'*, *n* a person offers to do something voluntarily; a person who enters military service, of his or her own free choice; a soldier belonging to any body other than the regular army; someone who acts of his or her own free will, *esp* (*law*) in a transaction, without either legal obligation to do so or promise of remuneration; a person to whom property is transferred without their giving valuable consideration (*law*). — *adj* consisting of or pertaining to volunteers; giving voluntary service; given voluntarily; (of a plant or plants) growing spontaneously, from seed not deliberately sown. — *vt* to offer voluntarily to give, supply or perform; to give (information) unasked. — *vi* to offer to do something of one's own free will or without being asked; to enter military service voluntarily. [Fr *volontaire*, from L *voluntārius*]

voluptuary *və-lup'tū-ər-i*, *n* a person excessively fond of or devoted to bodily enjoyments or luxury, a sensualist. — *adj* promoting or characterized by sensual pleasure. [LL *voluptuārius*, from L *voluptās* pleasure]

voluptuous *və-lup'tū-əs*, *adj* full of or suggestive of pleasure, *esp* sensuous; pertaining to, consisting of, derived from or ministering to sensual pleasure; shapely and sexually attractive; given to excess of pleasure, *esp* sensual. — *adv* **volup'tuously**. — *n* **volup'tuousness** or (*obs*) **voluptuos'ity**. [L *voluptuōsus*, from *voluptās* pleasure]

Völuspa *vol-us-pa'* or *vœl'ōōs-pa*, *n* one of the poems of the Elder Edda; (without *cap*) a sibyl or prophetess (a wrong use, found in Scott's *Pirate*). [ON *Völuspā* the song of the sibyl, from *völva* a wise woman]

volutation *vol-ū-tā'shən*, (*rare* or *obs*; *lit* and *fig*) *n* the action of rolling, turning, wallowing. [L *volūtātiō*, *-ōnis*, from *volūtāre*, from *volvere*, *volūtum* to roll]

volute *və-lūt'* or *vol'ūt*, *n* a spiral scroll used *esp* in Ionic capitals; a spiral form; a thing or part having such a shape; any marine shell of the genus *Voluta* or related genera, allied to the whelks, or the animal itself; a whorl of a spiral shell. — *adj* rolled up in any direction, having a spiral form. — *adj* **volū'ted** in spiral form; having a volute or volutes. — *n* **vol'ūtin** a substance found in granular form (**volutin granules**) in the cytoplasm of various cells, believed to contribute to the formation of chromatin. — *n* **volū'tion** a revolving movement; a convolution; a whorl. — *adj* **vol'ūtoid** like a volute. [L *volvere*, *volūtum* to roll]

volva *vol'və*, (*bot*) *n* a sheath enclosing the whole of the fruit body of some agarics. — *adj* **vol'vate** having a volva. [L; see **vulva**]

volve *volv*, (*obs*) *vt* and *vi* to turn over; to ponder. [L *volvere*]

volvox *vol'voks*, (*bot*) *n* any member of the genus *Volvox* of simple organisms found in ponds, canals, etc, commonly regarded as algae, consisting of green flagellate cells united by protoplasmic bridges in a hollow spherical colony. [New L, from L *volvere*]

volvulus *vol'vū-ləs*, (*med*) *n* the twisting of an abdominal viscus causing internal obstruction. [New L, from L *volvere*]

vomer *vō'mər*, (*anatom* and *zool*) *n* a bone of the skull in most vertebrates, in man a thin flat bone, shaped like a wedge or ploughshare, forming part of the middle partition of the nose. — *adj* **vomerine** (*vō'* or *vo'mə-rīn* or *-rin*). — *combining form* **vo'mero-** denoting the vomer, as in **vomeronas'al**, pertaining to the vomer and the nasal cavity. [L *vōmer* a ploughshare]

vomica. See under **vomit**.

vomit *vom'it*, *vi* to throw up the contents of the stomach through the mouth, to spew; (of an emetic) to cause vomiting; to be ejected with violence. — *vt* to spew; to throw out with violence; to cause to vomit: — *pr p*

vom'iting; *pa t* and *pa p* **vom'ited**. — *n* the act of vomiting; matter ejected from the stomach; vile people or things; something that induces vomiting, an emetic. — *n* **vom'ica** a cavity in the lung containing pus. — *n* **vom'iting**. — *adj* **vom'itive** causing vomiting. — *n* an emetic. — *n* **vom'ito** the worst form of yellow fever, *usu* accompanied by black vomit. — *n* **vom'itory** an opening in a large building by which the crowd is let out (also, *Roman hist*, **vomitō'rium**); a vent (*lit* and *fig*); an emetic (*archaic*). — *adj* emetic. — *n* **vomituri'tion** violent retching. — *n* **vom'itus** matter vomited. [L *vomere*, *-itum* to vomit; Gr *emeein*]

voodoo or **voudou** *vōō'dōō* or *-dōō'*, *n* religious beliefs and practices of African origin found among the Black peoples of the W Indies and southern US, formerly including serpent-worship, human sacrifice and cannibalism, but now largely confined to sorcery; any form of magic-working; a person who practises this kind of religious sorcery. — *adj* of, pertaining to or carrying out voodoo practices. — *vt* to bewitch by voodoo charms. — Also **vaudoux** or **vaudo** (*vō-dōō'*). — *n* **voo'dooism** (or *-dōō'*) voodoo practices or beliefs. — *n* **voo'dooist** (or *-dōō'*). — *adj* **voodooist'ic**. [W Afr *vodu* a spirit]

voortrekker *fōr-trek'ər*, *fōōr'* or *vōr-*, *n* (*usu* with *cap*) one of the Dutch farmers from Cape Colony who took part in the Great Trek into the Transvaal in 1836 and following years; a member of an Afrikaner Scout-type youth movement; a pioneer. [Cape Du, from Du *voor-* before, and **trek**]

vor *vör*, (*Shakesp*, King Lear IV. 6. 247, in dialect passage) *vt* (*perh*) to warn.

Vor *vör*, *n* an American aid to aircraft navigation. [*V*ery-High-Frequency *O*mni-Directional-*R*ange]

voracious *və-rā'shəs*, *vö-* or *vō-*, *adj* eating greedily or in large quantities; taking in or engulfing a great deal; very eager, or insatiable; characterized by greediness (*lit* and *fig*). — *adv* **vorā'ciously**. — *n* **voracity** (*-ras'*) or **vorā'ciousness**. [L *vorāx*, *vorācis*, from *vorāre* to devour]

voraginous *vō-raj'i-nəs* or *vö-*, (*obs* or *rare*) *adj* pertaining to a whirlpool; voracious. — *n* **vorā'go** (*-gō*) a gulf: — *pl* **vorā'goes**. [L *vorāgo*, from *vorāre* to devour]

vorant *vō'rənt* or *vö'*, (*heraldry*) *adj* devouring. [L *vorāns*, *-antis*, pr p of *vorāre* to devour]

vorpal *vör'pəl*, *adj* a nonsense word coined by Lewis Carroll to describe a sword, later used to mean sharp-edged.

vortex *vör'teks*, *n* a whirling motion of a liquid, gas or fire forming a cavity in the centre, a whirlpool, an eddy, a whirlwind; a pursuit, way of life, situation, etc, that engulfs one irresistibly or remorselessly, taking up all one's attention or energies; according to a hypothesis of Descartes, etc, a rotary movement of atoms or particles of subtle matter round an axis, or the matter itself in rotation, such phenomena accounting for the formation of the universe and the relative motion of its parts: — *pl* **vor'tices** (*-ti-sēz*) or **vor'texes**. — *adj* **vor'tical** of or pertaining to a vortex; whirling. — *adv* **vor'tically**. — *n* **vor'ticism** (*-tis-izm*) a British movement in the arts, a development from futurism, blending cubism and expressionism, and emphasizing the complications of machinery that characterize modern life. — *n* **vor'ticist** a person who supports or practises vorticism. — *n* **vortic'ity** the amount of vortical motion in a fluid. — *adj* **vor'ticose**, **vortic'ūlar** or **vortiginous** (*-ij'*) vortical. — **vortex street** (*aerodynamics*) the regular procession of vortices forming behind a bluff or rectangle body in two parallel rows; **vortex theory** a theory (by Kelvin) that the material atom consists of a vortically moving frictionless fluid. [L *vortex*, variant of *vertex*, *-icis*, from *vortere*, variant of *vertere* to turn]

vorticella *vör-ti-sel'ə*, *n* any organism of the genus *Vorticella* of ciliated infusorians belonging to the order *Peritricha*, in which the cilia are restricted to a fringe round the mouth: — *pl* **-ae** (*-ē*). [New L dimin, from L *vortex*]

Vosgian or **Vosgean** *vōzh'i-ən*, *adj* of or pertaining to the *Vosges* Mts.

votary *vō'tə-ri*, *n* a person dedicated by or as if by a vow to some service, worship or way of life; someone enthusiastically addicted to a pursuit, study, etc; a devoted worshipper or adherent: — *fem* **vō'taress** or **vō'tress**. — *adj* (*obs*) consecrated by, or of the nature of, vows; of the nature of a vow. — *n* **vō'tarist** a votary. — *adj* **vōt'ive** given, erected, etc, by vow; undertaken or observed in fulfilment of a vow; consisting of or expressing a vow or a wish; voluntary, not obligatory (*relig*, *esp RC*). — **votive picture** or **tablet** one dedicated in fulfilment of a vow. [LL *vōtārius*, from L *vovēre*, *vōtum* to vow]

vote *vōt*, *n* an expression of a wish or opinion in an authorized formal way; collective opinion, decision by a majority; a group or votes or voters collectively; a voter; the right to vote; a means by which a choice is expressed, such as a ballot; a ballot-paper; the total number of votes cast; an earnest desire (*obs*). — *vi* to express choice, *esp* at an election, by vote; to declare oneself in favour of, or against (with *for* or *against*), *esp* by vote. — *vt* to determine by vote; to grant by vote; to bring about (a specified result or change) by vote; to elect to an office; to declare by general consent, to pronounce, adjudge to be (*colloq*); to propose, suggest (*colloq*); to present for voting, to record the votes of (*US*). — *adj* **vote'less**. — *n* **vō'ter**. — **voting machine** (*esp US*) a machine on which to register votes. — **split one's vote** or **votes** to divide one's votes among two or more candidates; **split the vote** to injure a cause by influencing a body of possible supporters to vote in some other way (*n* **vote'-splitt'ing**); **vote Conservative**, **Labour**, etc, to give one's vote, on a particular occasion or habitually, to the Conservative, Labour, etc, candidate or party; **vote down** to defeat or suppress by vote, or by some other means; **vote in** to elect; **vote of no confidence** the legal method of forcing the resignation of a government or governing body; **vote straight** to give one's vote honestly; **vote with one's feet** to indicate one's dissatisfaction with a situation or conditions by leaving. [L *vōtum* a wish, from *vovēre*, *vōtum* to vow]

voteen *vō-tēn'*, (*Ir*) *n* a devotee. [Perh **devote**]

votive. See under **votary**.

vouch *vowch*, *vi* to bear witness, or be surety (with *for*). — *vt* to support by evidence; to testify (that); to be sponsor for (*rare*); to guarantee legal possession of (*Shakesp*); to vouchsafe, condescend to grant (*archaic*); to second, support (*Milton*); to call upon to witness, *esp* to a title to real estate (*archaic*; also **vouch to warrant**, **vouch to warranty**); to cite as authority (*obs*); to assert, declare (*obs*); to assert or guarantee to be true (*obs*). — *n* an assertion; an attestation. — *n* **vouchee'** the person summoned to witness to a title to real estate; a person quoted as authority or appealed to as witness. — *n* **vouch'er** (partly Anglo-Fr *voucher*, infinitive; partly sfx *-er*) a piece of evidence, or a written document serving as proof; a paper which confirms the truth of anything, such as a receipt, a certificate of correctness; a ticket, etc, substituting or exchangeable for cash or goods; a person who vouches or gives witness; the act of vouching to warrant (*obs law*). [OFr *voucher*, *vocher* to call to defend, from L *vocāre* to call]

vouchsafe *vowch-sāf'*, formerly also (*Milton*) **voutsafe** *vowt'sāf*, *vt* to condescend to grant; to condescend to allow, to accept, or to engage in; to condescend, be graciously willing to tell, etc; to warrant safe, guarantee (*obs*). — *vi* to condescend: — *pr p* **vouchsāf'ing**; *pa t* and *pa p* **vouchsafed'**. — *n* **vouchsafe'ment**. — *n* **vouchsāf'ing**. [Orig two words, **vouch** and **safe**]

voudou. See **voodoo**.

vouge or **voulge** *vōōzh*, *n* a weapon carried by foot-soldiers in the 14c, having a blade fixed on a long staff. [Fr]

voulu *vōō-lü*, (*Fr*) *adj* deliberate, studied.

voussoir *vōō-swär'*, (*archit*) *n* one of the wedge-like stones that form part of an arch. — *vt* to form with voussoirs. [Fr, through LL, from L *volūtus*, from *volvere* to roll]

voutsafe. See **vouchsafe**.

vow *vow*, *n* a voluntary promise made to God, or to a saint, or to a god or gods; a binding undertaking or resolve; a solemn or formal promise of fidelity or affection; a firm assertion; an earnest wish or prayer. — *vt* to give or dedicate by solemn promise; to promise or threaten solemnly; to maintain solemnly. — *vi* to make vows. — *adj* **vowed** devoted, confirmed, undertaken, etc, by vow, or as if by vow; bound by religious vows (*obs*). — *n* **vow'er**. — *n* **vow'ess** (*hist*) a woman who has taken a vow; a nun. — **vow'-fellow** (*Shakesp*) a person bound by the same vow. — **baptismal vows** the promises made at baptism by the person baptized, or by their sponsors or parents; **simple vow** a more limited, less permanent vow than a solemn vow; **solemn vow** a vow made on entering a religious order (such as those of poverty, obedience, and chastity), involving complete and irrevocable commitment. [OFr *vou* (Fr *vœu*), from L *vōtum*, from *vovēre* to vow]

vowel *vow'əl*, *n* a speech-sound produced by the unimpeded passage of the breath (modified by the vocal cords into voice) through the mouth, different vowel sounds being made by altering the form and position of the tongue and the lips; a letter (usually *a*, *e*, *i*, *o* or *u*) used alone or in combination to represent a vowel sound; (in *pl*) an IOU (*old slang*). — *adj* of, representing or of the nature of a vowel. — *vt* (also **vow'elize** or **-ise**) to insert vowel signs in (words written primarily with consonants only); to use as a vowel; to modify by vowel sounds; (only **vowel**) to promise to pay, offer an IOU to (*old slang*). — *adj* **vow'elled** having vowels, *esp* to a marked degree; having a vowel or vowels of a specified kind. — *adj* **vow'elless** without vowels. — *adj* **vow'elly** full of vowels. — **vowel gradation** ablaut; **vowel mutation** umlaut; **vowel point** a mark inserted, eg in Hebrew, to indicate a vowel; **vowel'-rhyme** assonance. [Fr *voyelle*, from L *vōcālis*, from *vōx*, *vōcis* voice]

vox *voks*, *vōks* or *wōks*, *n* voice: — *pl* **voces** (*vō'sēz*, *-kēs* or *wō'kās*). — **vox angelica** (*an-jel'i-kə*, *an-gel'i-ka*), **vox caelestis** (*sē-les'tis*, *kī-*) voix céleste; **vox humana** (*hū-mā'nə*, *hū-mä'nə* or *hōō-mä'na*) in organ-building, a reed-stop producing tones resembling those of the human voice. — **vox populi vox Dei** (*pop'ū-lī*, *dē'ī*, *po'pōō-lē*, *de'ē* or *dā'ē*) the voice of the people is the voice of God, hence **vox populi** (often shortened to **vox pop**) public or popular opinion, **vox pop** now *esp* applied to brief street interviews with members of the public on radio or TV (also *adj*). [L *vōx*]

voyage *voi'ij*, *n* a passage by water or by air to some place at a considerable distance; a round trip; a cruise; an account of such a journey; a journey of any kind (*archaic*); travel (*obs*); a military expedition (*obs*); an enterprise (*obs*). — *vi* to make a voyage, cruise or journey. — *vt* to traverse, pass over. — *adj* **voy'ageable** navigable. — *n* **voy'ager**. — *n* **voyageur** (*vwä-yä-zhœr'*) in Canada a person who kept up communication by canoe between trading-posts; a boatman; a trapper. [OFr *veage*, *voiage*, etc, from L *viāticum* (see **viaticum**)]

voyeur *vwä-yœr'*, *n* a person who derives gratification from surreptitiously watching sexual acts or objects; a peeping Tom; a person who takes a morbid interest in sordid sights. — *n* **voy'eurism**. — *adj* **voyeuris'tic**. [Fr, one who sees]

vozhd *vozhd*, *n* a supreme leader in Russia, often applied to Stalin. [Russ, chief]

VP *abbrev*: Vice-President.

VR *abbrev*: *Victoria Regina* (*L*), Queen Victoria; virtual reality.

vraic *vrāk*, *n* a Channel Islands name for seaweed, used for fuel and manure. — *n* **vraick'er** a gatherer of vraic. — *n* **vraick'ing** the gathering of vraic. [Dialect Fr; see **varec**]

vraisemblance *vrā-* or *vre-sā-blās'*, *n* verisimilitude; a picture. [Fr *vrai* true, and *semblance* appearance]

V. Rev. *abbrev*: Very Reverend.

VRI *abbrev*: *Victoria Regina et Imperatrix* (*L*), Victoria, Queen and Empress.

vril *vril*, *n* electric fluid represented as the common origin of the forces in matter, in E G L Bulwer-Lytton's *The Coming Race*, 1871.

vroom *vrōōm* or *vrŏŏm*, (*colloq*) *interj* denoting the sound of an engine revving or of a car travelling at high speed. — *vi* to travel speedily. — *vt* to rev (an engine).

vrouw or **vrow** *vrow* or *frow*, *n* (*esp* of Afrikaners in S Africa) a woman, goodwife, housewife. [Du]

VS *abbrev*: Veterinary Surgeon.

vs *abbrev*: versus (also **v**).

VSO *abbrev*: Voluntary Service Overseas.

VSOP *abbrev*: very special old pale.

VT *abbrev*: vatu (currency of Vanuatu; also **V**); Vermont (US state; also **Vt**).

vt *abbrev*: verb transitive.

VTOL *vē'tol*, *n* a system enabling aircraft to land and take off vertically; an aircraft operating by this system. [*V*ertical *t*ake-*o*ff and *l*anding]

VTR *abbrev*: videotape recorder.

vug *vug*, *n* a Cornish miner's name for a cavity in a rock, *usu* lined with crystals. — *adj* **vugg'y**.

Vul. or **Vulg.** *abbrev*: Vulgate.

Vulcan *vul'kən*, *n* the god of fire and metal-working (*Roman mythol*); a planet (*intramercurial planet*) once postulated between the sun and Mercury; (without *cap*) a blacksmith or an iron-worker (*poetic*). — *n* **Vulcanā'lia** an ancient Roman festival in honour of Vulcan, held on 23 August. — *adj* **Vulcā'nian** of, pertaining to, like, related to, sprung from or made by Vulcan; (without *cap*) volcanic; (without *cap*) of a volcanic eruption which discharges gases and ash but little or no lava. — *adj* **vulcanic** (*-kan'ik*) volcanic; (with *cap*) of Vulcan. — *n* **vulcanicity** (*-is'i-ti*) volcanic action or phenomena, volcanicity. — *n* **vul'canism** volcanic activity (also **vol'canism**); (with *cap*) the teaching of the Vulcanists. — *n* **Vul'canist** or **Vol'canist** (*old geol*) a Plutonist, a follower of James Hutton (1726–97), who asserted the geological importance of subterranean heat and the igneous origin of such rocks as basalt (opposed to *Neptunist*); (without *cap*) a vulcanologist. — *n* **vul'canite** the harder of the two kinds of vulcanized rubber, the softer kind being called *soft rubber*; a general name for any igneous rock of fine grain-size. — *adj* **vulcanī'zable** or **-s-**. — *n* **vulcanīzā'tion** or **-s-**. — *vt* **vul'canize** or **-ise** to treat (rubber, etc) with sulphur or sulphur compounds, etc to improve its strength or otherwise modify its properties. — *vi* to undergo such treatment. — *adj* **vulcanolog'ical** or **volcanolog'ical**. — *n* **vulcanol'ogist** or **volcanol'ogist**. — *n* **vulcanol'ogy** the scientific study of volcanoes and volcanic phenomena. — **vulcanized fibre** a fibre obtained by treating paper pulp with zinc chloride solution, used for low-voltage insulation; **Vulcan's badge** a cuckold's horns. [L *Vulcānus*]

vulg. *abbrev*: vulgar.

vulgar *vul'gər*, *adj* unrefined; (of language, etc) coarse; lacking in taste, manners, delicacy, etc; spiritually paltry, ignoble, debased, or pretentious; pertaining to the common people; plebeian; vernacular; public; common, usual, customary; common to all; prevalent; commonplace. — *n* the common people; one of the unrefined, of the uneducated, or of those not in good society; the common language of a country, the vernacular; a class of inferior persons (*obs*). — *n* **vulgā'rian** a vulgar person; a rich unrefined person. — Also *adj*. — *n* **vul'garism** a vulgar phrase; coarseness; an instance of this. — *n* **vulgarity** (*-gar'*). — *n* **vulgarizā'tion** or **-s-**. — *vt* **vul'garize** or **-ise** to make common or ordinary; to popularize (and therefore spoil to some extent); to make unrefined or coarse. — *adv* **vul'garly**. — **Vulgar era** the Christian era; **vulgar fraction** a fraction written in the usual way (one number above another, separated by a line), as opposed to a *decimal fraction*; **Vulgar Latin** any of the spoken varieties of Latin in the Common Era (as opposed to literary Classical Latin) *esp* when considered as the precursors of the Romance languages; **vulgar tongue** the vernacular. [L *vulgāris*, from *vulgus* the people]

Vulgate *vul'gāt* or *-git*, *n* a Latin version of the Scriptures, made by St Jerome and others in the 4c, and later twice revised, so called from its common use in the RC church; (without *cap*) a comparable accepted text of any other book or author. — *adj* of or pertaining to the Vulgate; (without *cap*; of speech, etc) commonly used or accepted. [L *vulgāta* (*editio*) popular edition (of the Bible); see **vulgar**]

vulgo *vul'gō*, *vo͝ol'* or *wo͝ol'gō*, *adv* commonly, popularly. [L]

vulgus *vul'gəs*, *n* the common people; in some public schools, a short verse task in Latin. [L; see **vulgar**]

vulnerable *vul'nər-ə-bl*, *adj* capable of being physically or emotionally wounded or injured; open to successful attack; capable of being persuaded or tempted; (in contract bridge, of a side that has won a game towards the rubber) liable to increased penalties (or bonuses) accordingly. — *vt* **vuln** (*vuln*; *heraldry*) to wound. — *adj* **vulned** (*heraldry*). — *n* **vulnerabil'ity** or **vul'nerableness**. — *adj* **vul'nerary** pertaining to wounds; useful in healing wounds. — *n* anything useful in curing wounds. — *vt* **vul'nerate** (*obs*) to wound. — *n* **vulnerā'tion** (*obs*). [L *vulnerāre* to wound, from *vulnus*, *vulneris* a wound]

Vulpes *vul'pēz*, *n* the genus of animals which includes the common fox. — *n* **vul'picīde** the killing of a fox, except in hunting; a fox-killer. — *adj* **vulpine** (*vul'pin* or *-pīn*) of, pertaining to or like a fox; cunning. — *n* **vul'pinism** craftiness. — **vulpine opossum** or **phalanger** the common Australian opossum (*Trichosurus vulpecula*). [L *vulpēs* a fox]

vulpinite *vul'pin-īt*, *n* a granular scaly form of the mineral anhydrite. [*Vulpino* in Lombardy]

vulsella *vul-sel'ə*, *n* a forceps with toothed or clawed blades: — *pl* **vulsell'ae** (*-ē*). — Also **vulsell'um**: — *pl* **-a**. [L]

vulture *vul'chər*, *n* any of a number of large rapacious birds of prey, feeding chiefly on carrion, belonging to the families *Accipitridae* (Old World) and *Cathartidae* (New World); someone or something that resembles a vulture. — Also *adj*. — *adj* **vul'turīne**, **vul'turish** or **vul'turous** of, pertaining to or like a vulture; rapacious. — *n* **vul'turism** (*Carlyle*) rapacity. — *n* **vul'turn** (*-tûrn*; *obs*) the Australian brush turkey. [OFr *voutour*, *voltour*, etc (Fr *vautour*), from L *vulturius*, from *vultur*]

vulva *vul'və*, (*anatom* and *zool*) *n* the external genitals of the female mammal, *esp* the orifice of the vagina. — *adj* **vul'val**, **vul'var** or **vul'vate**. — *adj* **vul'viform** oval; like a cleft with projecting edges. — *n* **vulvī'tis** (*med*) inflammation of the vulva. — *combining form* **vul'vo-** denoting the vulva, as **vul'vo-ū'terine**, pertaining to the vulva and the uterus. [L *vulva*, *volva* wrapping, womb]

vum *vum*, (*US dialect*) *vt* and *vi* a corruption of **vow**, in the phrase *I vum*.

vv *abbrev*: verses; vice versa.

vvll. See **vl**.

VW *abbrev*: Very Worshipful; Volkswagen.

Vw *abbrev*: View (in addresses, etc).

vying *vī'ing*, *pr p* of **vie**.

W

W or **w** *dub'l-ū*, *n* the twenty-third letter of the modern English alphabet, a 5c addition to the Roman alphabet, a doubled u or v used to express the voiced consonantal sound heard eg in English *way*, *weak*, *warrant*; from the 13c it was regularly used in writing English, superseding the letter wyn (qv). In modern English *w* is found as a consonant and also as the second component in certain vowel and diphthong digraphs, ie those in *law*, *few*, *now*. The unvoiced form of the consonant is written *wh* (corresponding to OE *hw*), as in *what*, *when*, but many English people substitute the voiced sound in pronouncing words spelt *wh*, and Northern speakers insist upon sounding *hw*. *W* is no longer pronounced in *write*, *two*, etc, or in *whole* (which represents a dialectal variation of OE *hāl*). OE *cw* has become *qu*, as in *queen*, from OE *cwēn*.

W or **W.** *abbrev*: watt or watts; weak (*phys*; in particle physics a **W particle** or **W boson** is a hypothetical positively or negatively charged subatomic particle of large mass, responsible in theory for weak interaction between particles); Welsh; West; Western; winter; women or women's; won (Korean currency).

W (*chem*) *symbol*: tungsten (*wolframium*, Latinized form of *wolfram*, an earlier name).

w *abbrev*: week; wife; with.

WA *abbrev*: Washington (US state); West Africa; Western Australia.

wa' *wö*, Scots form of **wall**.

WAAC or **Waac** *wak*, *n* the Women's Army Auxiliary Corps (founded 1917), or a member of it, now **WRAC**.

WAAF or **Waaf** *waf*, *n* the Women's Auxiliary Air Force (founded 1939), or a member, now **WRAF**. [From the initial letters]

wabain. See under **ouabain**.

wabbit *wab'it*, (*Scot*) *adj* exhausted, tired out. [Scot *wobart* feeble]

wabble, **wabbler**, etc. See under **wobble**.

waboom. See under **wagenboom**.

wabster. See under **webster**.

WAC *abbrev*: (in US) Women's Army Corps.

wack[1] *wak*, (*US slang*) *n* an eccentric person. — *adj* bad; extreme. [Poss back-formation from **wacky**]

wack[2] *wak*, (*dialect*, *esp Liverpool*) *n* (also **wack'er**) a familiar term of address for a companion, pal, mate. [Origin uncertain]

wacke *wak'ə*, *n* an old name for a decomposed basalt. [Ger, from OHGer *wagge* a pebble; cf **greywacke**]

wacko or **whacko** *wak'ō*, *adj* mad; eccentric. [Cf **wacky**]

wacky *wak'i*, (*slang*) *adj* crazy. — *n* **wack'iness**. [Perh connected with *whack*, or with dialect *whacky* left-handed, a fool]

wad[1] *wod*, *n* a pad of loose material such as hay, tow, etc, thrust in to aid packing, etc; a disc of felt or paper (formerly a small plug of paper or tow, etc) to keep the charge in a gun; a sandwich, cake or bun (*slang*); a bundle eg of hay; a roll or bundle, eg of bank notes; a large quantity, *esp* of money (*slang*); a compact mass, often small; a lump of a soft substance (*rare*). — *vt* to form into a mass; to pad, stuff out; to stuff a wad into: — *pr p* **wadd'ing**; *pa t* and *pa p* **wadd'ed**. — *n* **wadd'ing** a wad or the materials for wads; sheets of carded cotton for stuffing garments, etc; cotton-wool. [Origin uncertain; cf Swed *vadd* wadding; Ger *Watte*, Fr *ouate*]

wad[2], **wadd** or **wadt** *wod*, *n* an earthy ore of manganese, mainly hydrated oxide of manganese; plumbago or black lead (*dialect*). [Ety doubtful]

wad[3]. See under **wed**.

waddle *wod'l*, *vi* to take short steps and sway from side to side in walking, as a duck does; to move in a way suggestive of this; to become a defaulter (*stock exchange slang*). — *n* the act of waddling; a clumsy, rocking gait. — *n* **wadd'ler**. — *adj* **wadd'ling**. [Frequentative of **wade**]

waddy *wod'i*, *n* an Australian Aboriginal wooden club used in warfare; a cowboy; a walking stick. — Also **wadd'ie**. — *vt* to strike with a waddy. [Perh from Eng **wood**[1]]

wade *wād*, *vi* to walk through a substance that yields with difficulty to the feet, *esp* water; (with *through*) to make one's way through laboriously; to go (*obs*). — *vt* to cross by wading; to cause to cross thus. — *n* the act of wading; a ford (*colloq*). — *n* **wā'der** someone who wades; a bird that wades in search of food, eg the snipe, sandpiper, etc, and sometimes larger birds such as the heron, etc; a high waterproof boot; (in *pl*) a waterproof garment for the feet, legs and lower body. — *n* and *adj* **wā'ding**. — **wade in** to make a very vigorous attack; **wade into** to tackle (eg a job) energetically; to attack or criticize fiercely. [OE *wadan* to go; Ger *waten*]

wadi or **wady** *wod'i*, *n* the dry bed of a torrent; a river valley. [Ar *wādī*]

wadmal *wäd'* or *wud'məl*, (*hist*) *n* a thick or coarse woollen cloth, woven *esp* in Orkney and Shetland. — Also **wad'maal**, **wad'mol** or **wad'moll**. [ON *vathmāl*, from *vāth* cloth, and *māl* measure]

wadset *wod'set*, (*Scot*) *n* a mortgage; something pledged or pawned. — Also **wad'sett**. — *vt* to mortgage; to pawn. — *n* **wad'setter** a mortgagee. [**wad**, qv under **wed**, and **set**]

wadt. See **wad**[2].

wady. See **wadi**.

wae *wā*, *n* (*Scot*, *Spenser*) woe. — *adj* (*Scot*) sorrowful. — *adj* **wae'ful** (sometimes **wae'fu'**) or **wae'some** (*Scot*) woeful, pitiful. — *n* **wae'ness** sadness. — *interj* (*Scot*) **waesucks'** alas. [Dialect form of **woe**]

Wafd *woft*, *n* a Nationalist party in Egypt founded in 1918, dissolved in 1953.

wafer *wā'fər*, *n* a very thin crisp cake or biscuit baked in **wafer irons** or **wafer tongs**, formerly eaten with wine; a similar biscuit eaten with ice cream, etc; a thin round cake of unleavened bread, *usu* stamped with a cross, an Agnus Dei or the letters IHS, etc, used in the Eucharist; a leaf of adhesive material for sealing letters, etc; a piece of edible material used to enclose a medicinal powder, etc to be swallowed; a thin slice of silicon from which chips are cut; a thin slice of anything. — *vt* to close, fasten, stick (eg on a wall), with a wafer. — *adj* **wā'fery** like a wafer. — **wafer cake** a wafer. [ONFr *waufre* (OFr and Fr *gaufre*), from MLGer *wafel* cake of wax]

waff[1] *waf* or *wöf*, (*Scot*) *adj* wandering, stray; worthless, paltry; listless. — *n* a worthless person. [Variant of **waif**[1]]

waff[2] *waf*, *n* (*Scot*) a waving, or a slight, hasty motion; a signal; a quick light blow; a puff or blast; a sudden ailment; a faint, *usu* disagreeable odour; a glimpse; a ghost. — *vt* and *vi* (*dialect* or *obs*) to wave, flap, flutter, wave away. [Noun from verb, which is a variant of **wave**]

waff[3] *waf*, (*dialect*) *vi* to bark. — Also **waugh**. [Imit]

waffle[1] *wof'l*, *n* a kind of cake made from batter, baked in an iron utensil of hinged halves called a **waffle iron**. [Du *wafel* wafer]

waffle[2] *wof'l*, (*dialect*) *vi* to wave. [Frequentative of **waff**[2]]

waffle[3] *wof'l*, (*colloq*) *vi* to talk or write in an imprecise and wordy manner, to go on and on, to talk or write nonsense (often with *on*); to waver, vacillate. — *n* such talk or writing. — *n* **waff'ler**. — *n* and *adj* **waff'ling**. — *adj* **waff'ly**. [Frequentative of **waff**[3]]

waft *wäft*, *woft* or *waft*, *vt* to bear, convey, transport or propel safely or lightly on the surface of or through a fluid medium such as air or water (*poetic*; also *fig*); to signal to, beckon (*perh* for **waff**[2]); to turn (one's eyes; *Shakesp*). — *vi* to float, sail, pass through the air: — *pa t* and *pa p* **waft'ed** (*Spenser* **weft**). — *n* a scent or sound, or puff of smoke or vapour carried by the air; a rush of air (also *fig*); a slight taste, *esp* an unpleasant one; an act of wafting or waving; a waving movement; a passage across the sea or other water (*obs*); a flag or substitute hoisted as a signal, *esp* an ensign, stopped together at the head and middle portions, slightly rolled up lengthwise, and hoisted at different positions at the after-part of a ship (also **weft** or **wheft**); the act of displaying such a signal. — *n* **waft'age** the act of wafting; transportation through air or across water. — *n* **waft'er**. — *n* **waft'ing**. — *n* **waft'ure** (*Shakesp*; Rowe's emendation, *Julius Caesar*, II.1.246) the act of wafting or of waving; a waving motion; a beckoning; something wafted. [From obs *wafter* a convoying vessel, prob from LGer or Du *wachter* guard]

WAG *abbrev*: (West Africa) Gambia (IVR); Writers and Artists Guild.

wag *wag*, *vi* to move or be moved from side to side, or to shake to and fro; to oscillate; to move, or to move one's limbs; to move on, get on one's way (*archaic*); to play truant (*slang*); (of the tongue, chin, beard, etc) to move in light, gossiping or indiscreet talk; (of the world, etc, in the sense of human affairs) to go (in respect of good fortune and bad). — *vt* to move, shake or wave to and fro or up and down; to move (the tongue, chin, etc) in chatter or indiscreet talk; to move (the head or *esp* the finger) so as to express reproof or derision, etc; to brandish (*obs*); (*usu* with *neg*) to move, stir (a limb, etc) (*obs*): — *pr p* **wagg'ing**; *pa t* and *pa p* **wagged**. — *n* a shake; an act of wagging; ability to wag; truant (in **play the wag**); an amusing, mischievous person, a habitual joker, a wit (*perh* from obsolete **wag'halter**, someone who deserves hanging); a fellow (*obs*). — *n* **wagg'ery** mischievous merriment or jesting; an instance of this. — *adj* **wagg'ish** amusing or mischievous. — *adv* **wagg'ishly**. — *n* **wagg'ishness**. — **wag'-at-the-wa'** or **wag'-at** (or **-by)-the-wall'** (*Scot* and *N Eng*) a hanging clock with exposed pendulum and weights. [ME *waggen*, from same root as OE *wagian* to shake]

WAGBI *abbrev*: Wildfowl Association of Great Britain and Ireland.

wage *wāj*, *vt* to engage in or carry on, *esp* war; (*esp* in *pa p*) to pay wages to; to pledge, offer as a pledge (*obs*); to wager (*obs*); to hazard (*obs*); to hire for pay (*obs*); to bribe (*obs*); to let out for pay (*Spenser*). — *vi* (*Shakesp*) to be equal in value; to contend, battle. — *n* payment for services, *esp* a regular payment made by an employer to an (unskilled or semi-skilled) employee, or (*fig*) reward (both often **wages**, *pl* in form, but sometimes construed as *sing*); a gage or pledge (*obs*). — *adj* and *n pl* **wage'less**. — **wage differential** the difference in the wages paid to different classes of workers (eg skilled and unskilled) in an industry, or to workers doing similar jobs in different industries or areas; **wage'-earner** anyone who works for wages; the person who earns the money that supports, or money that helps to support, the household; **wage'-earning**; **wage freeze** a fixing of wages at a certain level for some time ahead; **wage fund, wages fund** or **wages-fund theory** the former theory that there is at any given time in a country a determinate amount of capital available for the payment of labour, therefore the average wage depends on the proportion of this fund to the number of people who have to share in it; **wage packet** a small envelope in which a worker's wages are issued; (loosely) one's wages; **wage plug** (*Austr colloq*) a wage-earner or wage slave; **wage-push inflation** inflation caused by wage increases; **wages council** a body that settles wages, consisting of employers' and workers' representatives; **wage slave** a person dependent on a (*usu* low) wage or salary; **wage slip** or **wages slip** a pay slip; **wage work** work done for wages. — **living wage** see under **living**. [ME *wagen*, from ONFr *wagier* (OFr *gagier*) to pledge (through popular L from a Gmc word)]

wagenboom *vä'gən-bōm*, *-bo͞om* or (*Afrik*) **waboom** *vä'bo͞om*, *n* a S African tree (*Protea grandiflora*) whose wood is used in making wagon wheels. [Du, wagon-tree]

wager *wā'jər*, *n* something staked on an outcome not yet known; a bet; the act of making a bet; that on which bets are laid; a hazard (*rare*); a contest for a prize (*rare*); a pledge (*obs*); the act of giving a pledge (*obs*). — *vt* to bet (money, etc) on the outcome of anything. — *vi* to lay a wager, make a bet. — *n* **wā'gerer**. — **wager boat** a light boat for a race between single scullers. — **wager of battle** (*law*; *hist*) trial by combat, a usage which permitted the accused and accuser, in cases where direct evidence was lacking, to challenge each other to mortal combat; **wager of law** (*hist*) compurgation, ie the act, by several witnesses, of swearing jointly to the character of a defendant or accused person, so as to clear him or her. [Anglo-Fr *wageure* a pledge, from ONFr *wagier*; see **wage**]

wagger-pagger *wag'ər-pag'ər*, or **wagg'er-pagg'er-bagg'er** *-bag'ər*, (*colloq*, *esp facetious*) *n* a wastepaper basket.

waggle *wag'l*, *vi* and *vt* to wag, *esp* in an unsteady manner. — *n* an act or the action of waggling. — *adj* **wagg'ly**. — **waggle dance** (*behav*) the sequence of movements by which hive bees communicate the distance and location of new nest sites and food sources. [Frequentative of **wag**]

waggon, etc. See **wagon**.

wagmoire *wag'moir*, (*Spenser*) *n* a quagmire.

wag-'n-bietjie. See under **wait**[1].

Wagnerian *väg-nē'ri-ən*, *adj* relating to or characterized by the ideas or style of Richard *Wagner* (1813–83), German composer of music dramas (qv); relating to Rudolf *Wagner* (1805–1864), physiologist. — *n* a follower or admirer of Richard Wagner. — *adj* **Wagneresque'**. — *n* **Wag'nerism** or **Wagne'rianism** the art theory of Richard Wagner, its main object being the freeing of opera from traditional and conventional forms, and its one canon, dramatic fitness. — *n* **Wag'nerist** or **Wag'nerite** an adherent of Wagner's musical methods.

wagon or **waggon** *wag'ən*, *n* a four-wheeled vehicle, *esp* one for carrying heavy goods; an open railway truck or a closed railway van; a car, *esp* an estate car (*colloq*); a movable piece of furniture with shelves (see **dinner-wagon**); a chariot (*obs*). — *vt* to transport by wagon. — *vi* to travel in a wagon. — *n* **wag'onage** conveyance by wagon, or money paid for it; a collection of wagons (*Carlyle*). — *n* **wag'oner** or **wagg'oner** someone who drives a wagon; a charioteer (*obs*). — *n* **wagonette'** a kind of carriage with one or two seats crosswise in front, and two back seats arranged lengthways and facing inwards. — *n* **wag'onful**. — **wagon box** or **bed** the carrying part of a wagon; **wag'onload** the load carried by a wagon; a great amount; **wagon lock** a kind of iron shoe or other device placed on the rear wheel of a wagon to retard motion in going downhill; **wagon roof** or **vault** a barrel vault; **wagon train** a collection or service of army vehicles for the conveyance of ammunition, provisions, the sick, etc; a train of *usu* horse-drawn wagons used by pioneer settlers to travel into new territory; **wag'onwright** a maker of wagons. — **on** (or **off**) **the wagon** (*slang*) abstaining (or no longer abstaining) from alcohol; **the Wagon** Charles's Wain, the seven brightest stars in the constellation Ursa Major; **the Wagoner** or **Waggoner** the constellation Auriga. [Du *wagen*; cf OE *wægn*, Eng **wain**]

wagon-lit *vä-gɔ̃-lē'*, *n* a sleeping-carriage on a continental train: — *pl* **wagons-lit** (pronounced as *sing*; sometimes **wagon-lits**). [Fr *wagon* (from Eng **wagon**), and *lit* bed]

wagtail *wag'tāl*, *n* any bird of the *Motacilla* and *Dendronanthus* genera, forming with the pipits the family *Motacillidae*, so named from their constant wagging of the tail; applied also to other birds, such as an American water thrush and an Australian fly-catcher; (contemptuously) a pert or obsequious person (*obs*); a harlot (*obs*).

Wahabi or **Wahabee** *wä-hä'bē*, *n* a member of a sect of Muslims founded in Central Arabia about 1760 by Abd-el-*Wahhab* (1691–1787), whose aim was to restore primitive Islam. — Also **Waha'bite** or **Waha'biite**. — *n* **Waha'bism** or **Waha'biism** the doctrine and practices of the Wahabis.

Wahiguru *wä-hē-gōō'rōō*, (*Sikh religion*) *n* Wonderful Lord, a popular designation for God. [Hindi *wahi* great one, and *guru* teacher]

wahine *wä-hē'ne*, *n* a Maori woman. [Maori]

wahoo[1] *wa-hōō'*, *n* the burning bush (genus *Euonymus* or *Evonymus*), an ornamental shrub with scarlet-coated seeds. [Dakota Indian *wanhu*]

wahoo[2] *wa-hōō'*, *n* a Californian buckthorn (*Rhamnus purshiana*) which yields cascara sagrada; the winged elm, with hard-grained wood; also the rock-elm. [Creek Indian *ûhawhu*]

wahoo[3] *wa-hōō'*, *n* a large fast-moving marine food and game fish, *Acanthocybium solandri*, related to the mackerel. [Origin unknown]

wah-wah *wä'wä*, (*music*) *n* the sound produced on a brass instrument by inserting and removing the mute, imitated on an electric guitar by varying the level of amplification. [Imit]

waid or **waide**. Old spellings of **weighed**, *pa t* and *pa p* of **weigh**[1] (but in *Shakesp*, *Taming of the Shrew*, III.2.56 or 57 probably for **swayed**; see **sway**).

waif[1] *wāf*, *n* a neglected ownerless child; a homeless wanderer; a piece of property found ownerless, eg a strayed animal, or goods cast up by the tide (*Spenser* **waift** or **weft**; also *fig*); stolen goods abandoned by the thief (*obs*). — *adj* (*Scot*) wandering, neglected. — *vt* (*rare*; in *pa p*) to cast up as a waif. — **waif and stray** strayed property, same as **waif**; **waifs and strays** homeless, destitute people. [OFr *waif*; prob from Scand; cf ON *veif* any flapping or waving thing]

waif[2] *wāf*, *n* a streak, puff, same as **waff**[2].

waift. See **waif**[1].

wail *wāl*, *vi* to lament or express sorrow or pain audibly, *esp* with prolonged high-pitched mournful cries; (of eyes) to weep (*Shakesp*). — *vt* to bemoan; to grieve over. — *n* the activity, or a spell, of wailing; a cry of woe; an animal cry or mechanical sound suggesting this. — *n* **wail'er**. — *adj* **wail'ful** (*poetic*) sorrowful; expressing woe. — *n* and *adj* **wail'ing**. — *adv* **wail'ingly**. — **Wailing Wall** a wall in Jerusalem, 18m (59ft) high, a remnant of the western wall of the temple dating back to before the destruction of the city in AD66, where Jews traditionally pray and from which they were excluded for a time. [ME *weilen*, *wailen*; cf ON *væla*]

wain *wān*, *n* a wagon, *esp* for hay or other agricultural produce (now *usu poetic*); a chariot (*obs*). — *vt* (*obs*) to carry, convey. — **wain'wright** a maker of wagons. — **the Lesser Wain** the constellation Ursa Minor, or the seven brightest stars in it; **the Wain** Charles's Wain; the Lesser Wain. [OE *wægn*, *wægen*, *wǣn*, from *wegen*, to carry; cf Du *wagen*, Ger *Wagen*, Eng **wagon**]

wainage *wā'nij*, (*hist*) *n* the team and implements necessary for the cultivation of land; land under cultivation. [ONFr *waaignage*, from OFr *gaaigner* to till, earn, gain]

wainscot *wān'skot*, *-skət*, or *wen'*, *n* fine oak for panelling, etc; woodwork, *esp* panelled, on an interior wall; similar lining of other material; the lower part of an interior wall when lined with material different from that on the upper part; a collector's name for certain noctuid moths. — *vt* to line with, or as if with, boards or panels; to grain in imitation of oak: — *pr p* **wain'scoting** or **wain'scotting**; *pa t* and *pa p* **wain'scoted** or **wain'scotted**. — *n* **wain'scoting** or **wain'scotting** the process of lining with boards or panels; materials for making a wainscot; wainscots collectively. — **wainscot chair** a heavy oak chair with a panelled back, seat, etc. [Orig perh wood used for a partition in a wagon, from Du *wagen-schot*, oak-wood, from *wagen* wagon, or MDu *waeghe* wave (from the appearance of the grain of the wood), and *schot* partition]

wainwright. See under **wain**.

waist *wāst*, *n* the *usu* narrowest part of the human trunk, between the ribs and the hips; a narrow middle part of an insect; the part of a garment that lies round the waist of the body; a woman's blouse or bodice (*US*); any narrow middle part, eg of a musical instrument; the middle part of a ship; the middle (of the day or night) (*obs*); something that surrounds, a girdle (*obs*). — *adj* **waist'ed** having a waist, often of specified type as in *high-waisted*. — *n* **waist'er** a seaman stationed in the waist, performing menial duties, *esp* a greenhand on a whaler. — **waist anchor** an anchor stowed in the waist of a ship; **waist apron** an apron covering the body only from the waist down; **waist bag** a small bag worn on a belt round the waist, a bum bag; **waist'band** the strip of fabric in a garment that fits round the waist; a belt or sash; **waist'belt** a belt for the waist; **waist'boat** a boat carried in the waist of a vessel; **waist'cloth** a loin cloth; (in *pl*) coloured cloths hung about a ship's waist as ceremonial decoration or to conceal the men in a naval action (*obs*); **waist'coat** (*wās'* or *wāst'kōt*; *archaic*, now *dialect*, *wes'kət*) a garment, plain or ornamental, reaching to or below the waist and now sleeveless, worn by men at different periods under doublet, coat, jacket, etc (and intended to be partly visible), and now often without any other garment over it; a woman's similar garment or front; **waistcoateer'** (*obs*) a strumpet; **waist'coating** material for men's waistcoats, *esp* of a fancy pattern. — *adj* **waist'-deep** or **-high** deep or high enough to reach up to the waist. — **waist'line** a line thought of as marking the waist, but not fixed by anatomy in women's fashions; the measurement of a waist. [ME *wast*, from presumed OE *wæst* growth, size; cf Icel *vöxtr*, OE *wæstm* growth, Eng **wax**[2]]

wait[1] *wāt*, *vi* to be or remain in expectation or readiness (with *for*); to be or remain in a place in readiness (also **wait about** or **around**); to delay action; to be delayed; to remain temporarily undealt with; to be in attendance, or in readiness to carry out orders; to bring food to the table and clear away used dishes; to keep watch, be on guard (*Spenser* **waite**; *obs*); to be on the watch for someone, lie in ambush (*obs*). — *vt* to postpone (eg a meal) for some purpose (*colloq*); to watch, watch for, or lie in ambush for (*obs*); to be or remain in expectation of, await (*obs*); to attend on, attend or escort (*obs*). — *n* the act of waiting or of expecting; a delay; ambush (as in *lie in wait*); the period of attendance of a lord- or lady-in-waiting; (in *pl*) musicians employed by a town to play on ceremonial occasions (*hist*); (in *pl*) people who welcome in Christmas by playing or singing out of doors at night; a member of a Christmas band or town band of waits; a watchman, sentinel or spy (*obs*). — *n* **wait'er** someone who waits; a man whose job is to wait, *esp* at table in a hotel or restaurant, etc; an attending servant (*obs*); a salver or tray; a dumb-waiter; a uniformed attendant at the London Stock Exchange; a watchman (*obs*); a customs officer (*obs*). — *n* **wait'erage** (*rare*) service. — *n* **wait'erhood** (*rare*) or **wait'ering** the occupation of a waiter. — *n* **wait'ing** the act of remaining in expectation, delaying, etc; attendance, service, eg at table. — Also *adj*. — *adv* (*rare*) **wait'ingly**. — *n* **wait'ress** a woman whose job is to wait at table in a hotel or restaurant, etc. — *n* **wait'ressing** the occupation of a waitress. — **wait'-a-bit** (also often *adj*) a name given to various plants, *esp* S African (*Afrik* **wag-'n-bietjie** *vuhh'ə(n)-bē-kē*), with thorns that catch the clothing of the passer-by; **wait'-a-while** a wait-a-bit; an Australian wattle growing in dense thickets; **wait'ing-list** or **wait'-list** a list of people waiting, eg candidates awaiting a vacancy, etc; **wait'ing-maid** or **wait'ing-woman** (*archaic*) a female attendant; **wait'ing-room** a room for the use of people waiting; **wait'ing-vassal** (*obs*) an attendant; **wait'-list** see **waiting-list**. — *vt* to add the name of (a person) to a waiting-list, *esp* for a seat on an aircraft. — **wait-on** see **wait on** below; **wait'person** (*US*) a waiter or waitress. — **lay wait** (*archaic*) to lie in wait; **lie in wait** to be in hiding ready to attack or surprise (*lit* and *fig*); **lords** and **grooms in waiting** certain officers in the Lord Chamberlain's department of the royal household; **minority waiter** (*Sheridan*) meaning uncertain (*perh* a waiter, or a tide-waiter, out of employment); **play a waiting game** to avoid action as far as possible in the hope of having an opportunity later to use one's energies with maximum effect; **wait attendance** (*Shakesp*) to remain in attendance; **wait for it!** (*colloq*) an expression injected into a narrative to prepare listeners for something impressive; **wait off** (*racing*) to allow oneself to be temporarily outdistanced by other competitors, reserving one's energies for the final stretch; **wait on** to wait for (*dialect*); to continue to wait (*Scot*); see **wait upon**; (of a hawk) to circle or hover in the air above the falconer's head (*falconry*; *n* **wait'-on**); **wait table** to wait at table during a meal; **wait up** to stay out of bed waiting (with *for*); **wait upon** or **on** to call on, visit formally; to accompany; to attend and serve; to be connected with or follow as a consequence; to carry out the duties of (an office; *Bible*); to gaze at, keep under observation (*obs*); **you wait!** (*colloq*) an expression of warning. [ONFr *waitier* (OFr *guaitier*, Fr *guetter*) to watch, attend; of Gmc origin; cf OHGer *wahta* (Ger *Wacht*) a watchman; cognate with OE *wacan* to watch]

wait[2]. See under **wit**[1].

waitress. See under **wait**[1].

waive *wāv*, *vt* to give up voluntarily (eg a claim or a contention) (*law*); to refrain from claiming, demanding, taking or enforcing; to forgo; to evade, avoid (*archaic*); to defer, postpone; to leave out of consideration, disregard (*obs*); to put away, reject, abandon, forsake, vacate, or resign (*obs*); to outlaw (a woman) (her status in the eyes of the law being such that the usual term was not applicable to her) (*hist*); to abandon (stolen goods) (*obs*). — *n* **wai'ver** the act, or an act, of waiving, or a written statement formally indicating this. [Anglo-Fr *weyver*, from OFr *guesver* to abandon; from same root as **waif**[1]]

waivode *wā'vōd*, and **waiwode** *wā'wōd*, *n* variants of **voivode**.

waka *wa'ka*, *n* a Japanese 31-syllable poem, a tanka, precursor of the haiku, used exclusively by members of the Japanese imperial family; a form of Japanese poetry derived from ancient ballads, lyrical in style. [Jap]

wakane *wa'ka-ne*, *n* an edible seaweed that can be soaked and used as a salad vegetable. [Jap]

wake[1] *wāk*, *vi* to be or remain awake, or active or vigilant; to keep watch or vigil, or pass the night in prayer; to hold a wake; to awake or be roused from sleep or from indifference, day-dreaming, etc (often with *up*); to become animated or lively; to be stirred up, aroused; to hold a late revel (*obs*). — *vt* to rouse from sleep; to keep vigil over (*obs* or *dialect*); to excite, stir up (eg feelings, echoes); to disturb (eg the night or silence) with noise; to animate; to reanimate, revive: — *pa t* **woke** or (*archaic*) **waked** (*wākt*); *pa p* **wo'ken** or (*archaic*) **waked**, (*rare*) **woke**. — *n* the feast of the dedication of a church, formerly kept by watching all night; a festival; (*usu* in *pl*) an annual holiday *esp* in N England, as in *Wakes Week* (*dialect*); a watch or vigil beside a corpse, sometimes with revelry; the act or state of waking (*obs* except in *sleep and/or wake, wake and/or dream*); a serenade (*James Hogg*). — *adj* **wake'ful** not asleep; unable or indisposed to sleep; vigilant; waking; awakening or rousing (*Milton*). — *adv* **wake'fully**. — *n* **wake'fulness**. — *adj* **wake'less** (of sleep) sound, undisturbed. — *n* **wā'ker** someone who wakes. — *n* **wā'king**. — *adj* that wakes, keeps watch, or is vigilant; that rouses or becomes awake; passed, or experienced, in the waking state. — **wake'-man** (*archaic*) a watchman. — *adj* **wake'rife** (*-rif* or *-rīf*; *Scot*) wakeful; vigilant. — **wake'-robin** the cuckoo-pint, *Arum maculatum*; the spotted orchis, *Orchis maculata*; applied to various other flowers, *esp*, in US, to any of the genus *Trillium*; **wake'-up** (*Austr colloq*) a wide-awake person, *esp* in **be a wake-up to** to be alert to; **waking hours** the period of the day during which one is normally awake. — **wake a** (or **the**) **night** to remain awake, or be up and about, all night; **wake to** or **wake up to** to become conscious of, alive to. [A combination of an OE strong verb *wacan* to be born, to awake, and an OE weak verb *wacian* to be awake, to watch; cf **watch**]

wake[2] *wāk*, *n* the streak of smooth-looking or foamy water left in the track of a ship; disturbed air behind a flying body; a track on land (*rare*); a trail of light behind a moving body; the area behind someone or something passing through. — **in the wake of** close behind; immediately after (*usu* implying consequence). [Of Scand origin; cf ON *vök* an ice hole, *vökr* moist]

waken[1] *wā'kən*, *vi* to be or become awake; to become active or lively; to remain awake, keep watch (*obs*). — *vt* to rouse from sleep, unconsciousness or inaction; to excite, stir up, evoke. — *adj* **wā'kened**. — *n* **wā'kener** someone who or something that wakens. — *adj* **wā'kening**. — *n* the act of waking; the revival of an action (*Scots law*). — **waken to** to make or become aware of. [OE *wæcnan*; cf ON *vakna* to awake]

waken[2] *wā'kən*, (*Scot*) *adj* waking, awake.

wakf. See **waqf**.

wakiki *wä'kē-kē*, *n* shell money. [Melanesian]

WAL *abbrev*: (West Africa) Sierra Leone (IVR).

Wal. *abbrev*: Walloon.

Walachian. See **Wallachian**.

wald. See **weld**[2].

Waldenses *wol-den'sēz*, *n pl* a Christian community of austere morality and devotion to the simplicity of the Gospel, *orig* followers of Peter *Waldo*, a merchant of Lyons and preacher in the second half of the 12c; their chief centre was, and is, the Alps in SE France and Piedmont (also **Valdenses** *val-*). — *adj* and *n* **Walden'sian**.

waldflute *wöld'flo͞ot*, *n* an organ flute stop *usu* of 4-foot pitch. [Formed after Ger *Waldflöte*, literally forest flute]

waldgrave *wöld'grāv*, *n* in medieval Germany, a head forest-ranger; an old German title of nobility. — *n* **waldgravine** (*wöld'grä-vēn*) the wife of a waldgrave. [Ger *Waldgraf*, from *Wald* forest, and *Graf* count]

waldhorn *wöld'hörn*, *n* a hunting-horn, a French horn without valves; an organ reed-stop. [Ger]

waldrapp *wöld'rap*, *n* the hermit ibis (*Geronticus eremita*) of N Africa and the Middle East, with black plumage, red face and a crest of feathers on the back of the head. [Ger *Wald* forest, and *Rapp* (variant of *Rabe*) crow]

Waldsterben *vald'shter-bən*, (*ecol*) *n* the dying-off of trees and other forest vegetation as a result of air pollution, observed since the 1970s (also without *cap*). [Ger, forest death, from *Wald* forest, and *sterben* to die]

wale[1] *wāl*, *n* same as **weal**[2], a ridge raised on the flesh by the stroke of a whip, etc; a ridge on the surface of cloth; texture; a vertical ridge in knitted fabrics; a horizontal timber used to bind together piles driven in a row; (in *pl*) planks all along the outer timbers on a ship's side, bends. — *vt* to mark with wales; to make, provide or secure with wales. — **wale knot** see **wall knot** under **wall**. [OE *walu*; cf ON *völr* a rod]

wale[2] *wāl*, (*Scot* and *N Eng*) *n* the act of choosing; choice; the scope of choice; the pick or best. — *vt* and *vi* to choose, pick. [ON *val* choice; Ger *Wahl* choice; from the root of **will**[1]]

waler *wä'lər*, *n* in India, a horse imported from New South *Wales*, or from Australia generally.

Walhalla *val-hal'ə*, *n*. Same as **Valhalla**.

wali *wä'lē*, *n*. Same as **vali**.

Walian *wā'li-ən*, *adj* of or pertaining to (North or South) *Wales* (as *North Walian* or *South Walian*). — *n* a native or inhabitant of (North or South) Wales.

walise (*obs*; *Scot*) *n*. A variant of **valise**.

walk[1] *wök*, *vi* (of a biped) to move along on foot with alternate steps, the walker always having at least one foot on the ground; (of a quadruped) to move along in such a way that there are always at least two feet on the ground; to pace; to journey on foot; to ramble, go on foot for pleasure, etc; (of an inanimate object) to be in motion (*obs*); to make progress (*naut*); (of the tongue) to wag (*obs*); to make slow progress; to circulate, spread, be rife (*obs*); (of a ghost) to go restlessly about; to move; to behave in a certain way, follow a certain course; to move off, depart, withdraw; to conduct oneself, behave; to be in harmonious association (*obs*); to go to first base after receiving four pitches (*baseball*); to leave the cricket pitch or playing-field when out or dismissed; (of an object) to disappear (*usu* with implications of unauthorized removal) (*colloq*, *esp facetious*). — *vt* to pass through or over, perambulate, traverse; to follow or trace out on foot; to measure out by walking; to wear (eg through, to shreds) by walking; to go through (a dance) at a slow pace; to circulate (*obs*); to cause to walk, or to move as if walking; to lead or accompany by walking. — *n* the action or an act of walking; a spell of walking, *esp* for pleasure; a perambulation in procession; a walking race; a gait; that in or through which one walks; a possible or suitable route or course for walking; a path or place for walking; a tree-bordered avenue; a place for animals, eg young hounds, to train or to exercise; a run for fowl; a place where a game cock is kept; high pasture-ground (*obs*); a division of a forest; a distance walked, or a distance as measured by the time taken to walk it; conduct; one's course of life, sphere of action or profession, *esp* in **walk of life**; a hawker's district or round; a hunting-ground (*obs*); (in *pl*) grounds or a park (*obs*); a flock (of snipe or of wagtails). — *adj* **walk'able**. — *n* **walk'er** someone who walks or takes part in walking races; a colporteur or (*dialect*) a vagrant; a forester (*hist*); a person who trains and walks young hounds; any bird that walks rather than hops; a stick insect; any device which helps *esp* babies or elderly people to walk; a man of good social standing who accompanies a woman VIP on official engagements in the absence of her husband (*US slang*). — *interj* (with *cap*; also **Hookey Walker**; *archaic slang*) an exclamation of incredulity (also, as *n*, humbug). — *n* **walk'ing** the verbal noun of walk; pedestrianism; the sport of racing using a walking rather than running gait; the condition of a surface from the point of view of someone who walks on it. — *adj* that walks, or that moves as if walking; that oscillates; used in or for walking; performed by walking; worked by a person or animal who walks; in human form, eg in *walking dictionary*, *walking encyclopedia* a person of vast knowledge. — *adv* **walk'about** on the move, as in *go walkabout*, *esp* temporarily back into the bush (of Australian Aborigines), or meeting the public on foot (of royalty, politicians, etc). — *n* a wandering, a journey; a walk by royalty, etc in order to meet the public. — **walk'-around'** (*esp* formerly) a dancing performance by Negroes or black-faced minstrels in which a large circle is described; a march in procession about the stage (*theat*); the music for either of these; **walk'-away** (*colloq*) an effortless victory; **walk'er-on'** a performer who plays parts non-speaking roles; **walk'ie-talk'ie** or **walk'y-talk'y** a portable transmitting and receiving radiotelephone; **walk'-in** a person who enters premises to make enquiries or offer services without previously making contact; a theft committed by a walk-in thief. — *adj* (of a thief) who gains entrance without breaking in; (of a cupboard, etc) big enough to walk into and move around in. — **walking bass** (*jazz piano*) a bass part in 4/4 rhythm using a simple repetitive tune moving up and down the octave; **walk'ing-beam** a beam or oscillating lever for transmitting power, eg that actuating the cable in cable-drilling for oil; **walking case** a patient not confined to bed; **walking fern** an American fern of the genus *Camptosorus*, whose frond tips take root when touching the ground; **walking fish** any of various fishes, mainly Asiatic, which are able to move about on land; **walk'ing-frame** a *usu* metal frame for giving an infirm person support while walking; **walking gentleman** or **lady** an actor or actress playing very small non-speaking parts for which a good appearance is required; **walking leaf** a leaf-insect; **walk'ing-orders**, **walk'ing-papers** or **walk'ing-ticket** (*slang*) dismissal; **walking part** one in which the actor has nothing to say; **walking race** a race in which competitors must walk rather than run; **walk'ing-stick**, **walk'ing-cane** or **walk'ing-staff** a stick, cane or staff used for support in walking; **walking stick**, **walking straw** or **walking twig** a stick insect; **walking toad** a natterjack; **walk'-mill** a machine operated by the walking of a horse; see also **waulk**; **walk'-on** a walking part. — *adj* (of an air service or aeroplane) for which one does not have to purchase a ticket in advance, the seats being non-bookable; (of a part in a play, etc) non-speaking. — **walk'-out** the act of walking out, *usu* to indicate disapproval; a sudden industrial strike; **walk'-over** a race where only one competitor appears, and has merely to cover the course to win; an easy or unopposed victory, *usu* in sport. — *adj* **walk'-up** (*US*) reached by means of stairs; (of a building) with upper storeys accessible only by stairs. — *n* a walk-up building, apartment, etc; **walk'way** a road or path, etc constructed for pedestrians only; a country track for walkers; **walky-talky** see **walkie-talkie** above. — **charity walk** or **sponsored walk** an organized walk in aid of charity, each participator having obtained from a sponsor or sponsors an agreement to contribute according to distance covered; **walk a tightrope** to follow a narrow and difficult route beset with dangers, as if on a tightrope; **walk away from** to outdistance or outdo easily; to have nothing more to do with; to emerge from (an accident, etc) with no or only minor injuries; **walk away with** to win (a prize, etc) with ease; **walking wounded** (of troops) wounded but not requiring stretchers, not bedridden; (used as *n pl*) such casualties; a person or people handicapped by mental or emotional problems (*colloq*); **walk into** to beat (*archaic*); to storm at (*archaic*); to eat a hearty quantity of (*archaic*); to collide or meet with unexpectedly; to involve oneself in (eg difficulties) *esp* without due circumspection; to enter without effort or opposition; **walk it** to go on foot; to succeed, win easily (*colloq*); **walk off** to leave; to depart; to get rid of (eg disagreeable feelings or effects) by walking; **walk off with** to take surreptitiously or feloniously; to win easily; **walk on** to walk ahead; to continue to walk; to have a walking part; **walk on air** to be exultant or light-hearted; **walk one's chalks** to quit, go away without ceremony; **walk out** to leave, *esp* as a gesture of disapproval; to strike; **walk out on** (*colloq*) to desert, leave in the lurch; **walk out with** to go for walks with as a stage of courtship (also **walk with**; *archaic*); **walk over** to cross or traverse; to win an uncontested race; to have an easy victory or easy success (*colloq*); to beat easily (*colloq*); (also **walk all over**) to disregard the rights or feelings of (*colloq*); **walk tall** (*colloq*) to be proud, have self-respect; **walk the chalk** or **chalkmark** to walk along a chalked line as a test of sobriety; to keep a correct course in manners or morals; **walk the hospitals** to be a student under clinical instruction at a general hospital or infirmary; **walk the plank** see under **plank**; **walk the streets** to wander about in search of work, or simply aimlessly; to be a prostitute. [ME *walken*, *walkien* to walk, to full, from OE *wealcan* to roll, toss, revolve, *wealcian* to roll up, curl; cognate with Ger *walken* to full cloth]

walk[2], etc. See **waulk**.

walkathon *wök'ə-thon*, *n* a long-distance walk, either as a race or in aid of charity. [*walk* and mar*athon*]

Walkman® *wök'mən*, *n* a small portable cassette recorder or radio with headphones, designed for personal use whilst walking, travelling, etc: — *pl* **Walk'mans**.

walkmill. See under **waulk**.

Walkyrie *vol'kir-i*, *-kir'*, also *wol-*, *val-* or *wal-*. Same as **Valkyrie**. [OE *wælcyri(g)e*]

wall *wöl*, *n* an erection of brick, stone, etc, for security or to enclose a space such as a piece of land; the side of a building or of a room; a very steep smooth rock face (*mountaineering*); (in *pl*) fortifications; any bounding or encasing surface suggestive of a wall, eg the membranous covering or lining of an organ of the body or of a plant or animal cell; the side next to the wall; a defence, means of security (*fig*); a psychological and physiological barrier to further effort, encountered eg by long-distance runners (*fig*); (in mah-jongg) the arrangement of the tiles before the hands are drawn; one of the surfaces of rock enclosing the lode (*mining*). — *vt* to enclose with, or as if with, a wall; to fortify with, or as if with, walls; to divide as if by a wall. — *combining form* **wall-** growing on, living in, for hanging on, or otherwise relating to a wall. — *adj* **walled** enclosed with a wall; fortified. — *n* **wall'er** a builder of walls. — *n* **wall'ing** walls collectively; materials for walls. — *adj* **wall'-less**. — **wall bars** horizontal bars fixed to a wall, used by gymnasts; **wall'board** building-board, board for lining walls, consisting of plaster or wood fibre compressed between layers of thick paper; **wall'climber** (*colloq*) a glass-walled elevator whose shaft is on the exterior wall of a building; **wall'covering** wallpaper, or anything used in the same way; **wall cress** rockcress, or any species of Arabis; **wall-eye** see separate entry; **wall'-facing** a facing for a wall; **wall'fish** a snail; **wall'flower** a plant (*Cheiranthus cheiri*) with yellow, orange or orange-brown flowers, found *esp* on old walls; any of various cultivars of this, with various-coloured flowers; a person who remains a spectator at a dance, typically a woman who cannot obtain partners (*colloq*); a yellowish-red colour (also **wallflower brown**); **wall fruit** a fruit tree growing against a wall; its fruit; **wall game** (also **Eton wall game**) a variety of football played at Eton against a wall ('at the wall' instead of 'in the field'); **wall gillyflower** a wallflower; **wall knot** or (properly) **wale knot** a nautical method of tying the strands at the end of a rope; **wall lizard** or **wall newt** a common lizard living in the chinks of walls; **wall moss** a yellow lichen; the common stonecrop; **wall mustard** or **wall rocket** a yellow-flowered cruciferous plant (*Diplotaxis*) of walls, quarries, etc; **wall painting** the decoration of walls with ornamental painted designs; a work of art painted on a wall; **wall'paper** paper, *usu* coloured or decorated, for pasting on the walls of a room; something of a bland or background nature, lacking originality or noteworthiness, etc (*fig*; *colloq*); **wall pass** (*football*) a one-two; **wall pepper** the common stonecrop; **wall plate** a horizontal piece of timber or of rolled steel on a wall, etc, to bear the ends of joists, etc; **wall rue** a small fern growing on walls, etc, one of the spleenworts; **wall space** space on a wall, eg on which to hang a picture; **Wall Street** a street in New York, the chief financial centre in the United States; hence, American financial interests; **Wall'-Streeter** a financier based in Wall Street. — *adj* **wall'-to-wall'** (of carpets, etc) covering the entire floor; widespread, ubiquitous or uninterrupted (*fig*; *colloq*). — **wall tree** a tree trained against a wall; **wall unit** a piece of furniture attached to or standing against a wall; **wall'-washer** a light designed to give overall illumination to a wall or other vertical surface; **wall'wort** a name applied to various plants growing on walls, eg pellitory (*Parietaria officinalis*), wall pepper, etc; see also separate article. — **drive to the wall** to push to extremities; **go to the wall** (or *obs* **walls**) to be hard pressed; to be forced to give way; to fail, go under; to give precedence to something else; **hang by the wall** to remain unused; **off the wall** (*US slang*) off the cuff, unofficially, without preparation; unorthodox, strange; **push** or **thrust to the wall** to force to give way; **the wall** the right of taking the side of the road near the wall when encountering another person, as in the phrase **give** or **take the wall**; **turn one's face to the wall** to resign oneself to death or despair; **up the wall** (*colloq*) mad, distracted; **wall a rope** to make a wall knot on the end of a rope; **wall of death** a fairground show in which a stunt-performer rides a motorcycle, at right angles to the ground, round the interior walls of a cylindrical enclosure; **walls have ears** see under **ear**[3]; **wall up** to block with a wall; to entomb in or behind a wall; **with one's back to the wall** in desperate straits; at bay. [OE *wall* (WSax *weall*), from L *vallum* a rampart]

walla. See **wallah**.

wallaba *wol'ə-bə*, *n* a caesalpiniaceous tree of the Guianas and Brazil, valuable for the medicinal properties of its resin and oil, and for its durable streaked reddish wood. [Native name]

wallaby *wol'əb-i*, *n* any of a number of small marsupials of the family Macropodidae. — **on the wallaby** or **on the wallaby track** (*colloq*; *Austr*) travelling through the bush with one's swag, *esp* looking for work; **the Wallabies** the Australian national Rugby Union football team. [Aboriginal *wolabā*]

Wallace's line *wol'is-iz līn*, *n* a line passing through the East Indian group of islands between Bali and Lombok, roughly separating the very different faunas of the Oriental region and the Australian region, or rather a transitional region. [Alfred Russel *Wallace* (1823–1913), naturalist]

Wallachian or **Walachian** *wol-ā'ki-ən*, *n* a Vlach. — *adj* of or pertaining to the region of Romania which was formerly the principality of *Wal(l)achia*, or to the Vlach people.

wallah *wol'a* or *wol'ə*, *n* (often as *combining form*) someone employed in, or concerned with, a specific type of work; someone who occupies an eminent position in an organization, etc. — Also **wall'a**. — **competition wallah** a member of the Indian Civil Service who obtained appointment by the competitive system instituted in 1856. [Hindi *-wālā*, properly an adjectival suffix, in one sense comparable to L *-ārius* or Eng *-ar*, *-er*, *-or*]

wallaroo *wol-ə-rōō'*, *n* a large kangaroo (*Macropus robustus*). — Also known as **euro**. [Aboriginal *wolarū*]

wallet *wol'it*, *n* a small folding case for holding money, papers, etc, a pocket-book; a bag for tools; a bag for carrying necessaries on a journey; a bag with the opening at the middle and a pouch at each end; anything protuberant and hanging loosely (*Shakesp*). [ME *walet*, poss from *watel* a bag of woven material; cf **wattle**[1]]

wall-eye *wöl'ī*, *n* an eye in which the iris is pale or whitish, particoloured or a different colour from the other, or in which the white part is large or noticeable (as in a divergent squint); glaucoma; any of various fishes, *esp* the pike-perch (*Stizostedion vitreum*; also **wall-eyed pike**) (*NAm*). — *adj* **wall'-eyed** having pale irises, or a whitish or particoloured iris in one eye, or irises of different colours; having a divergent squint; having a staring, glazed or blank expression or (*fig*) appearance; glaring, fierce (*Shakesp*). [The adj *wall-eyed* is the earlier, representing ON *vagleygr*, of which the first element is perh connected with mod Icel *vagl* a film over the eye, and the second is from *auga* eye]

wallie. See **wally**[2].

wallies. See **wally**[1].

Walloon *wol-ōōn'*, *adj* of or pertaining to a French-speaking people living chiefly in southern Belgium and adjacent parts of eastern France, or to their language. — *n* a man or woman of this people; their language, a dialect of French. [Fr *Wallon*; of Gmc origin, cognate with **Welsh**, **Walachian**]

wallop *wol'əp*, *vi* to move with noisy lumbering haste; to flounder; to gallop (*obs*); to bubble and boil (*perh* a different word); to flap about (*Scot*). — *vt* (*colloq*) to beat soundly, thrash; to strike with force. — *n* a plunging movement (*colloq*); a heavy blow (*colloq*); physical or financial power (*colloq*); a gallop (*obs*); a flapping rag (*Scot*); beer (*slang*). — *adv* with a wallop; heavily or noisily. — *n* **wall'oper** someone or something that wallops; something enormous (*colloq*). — *n* **wall'oping**. — *adj* that wallops; enormous, bouncing, whopping (*colloq*; also *intensive adv*). — **wallop in a tow** or **tether** (*Scot*) to be hanged. [ONFr *waloper* (Fr *galoper*); cf **gallop**]

wallow[1] *wol'ō*, *vi* to roll about enjoyably in mud, etc, as an animal does; to immerse or indulge oneself (in emotion, etc); to flounder; (of a ship) to roll from side to side making little progress; in a bad sense, to live in filth or vice; to surge, heave, blow, well up, etc. — *vt* (*obs*) to cause to wallow. — *n* the act of wallowing; the place, or the filth, an animal wallows in; a hollow or depression suggestive of a wallowing-place; a rolling gait (*obs*); the swell of the sea (*poetic*). — *n* **wall'ower**. — *n* **wall'owing**. — *adj* that wallows; very rich (*slang*). [OE *wealwian*, from L *volvere*]

wallow[2] *wol'ō*, (*dialect*) *vi* to fade away. — *adj* **wall'owed** withered, faded. [OE *wealwian*]

wallsend *wölz'end*, *n orig* coal dug at *Wallsend* (at the *end* of the Roman *Wall*) in Northumberland; later, coal of a certain quality and size.

wallwort *wöl'wərt*, *n* dwarf elder (also called Danewort, Dane's blood, etc), a plant with an offensive smell and taste; see also under **wall**. [OE *wealhwyrt* from *wealh* a foreigner, or *wǣlwyrt*, (from the belief that it grew on battlefields), from *wǣl* slaughter, and *wyrt* a root, a plant]

wally[1] *wö'li* or *wa'li*, (*Scot*) *adj* excellent, fine-looking, ample (a general term of commendation); made of china or glazed earthenware, etc; (of a tenement close) tiled. — *adv* (*obs*) finely, well. — *n* an ornament; (in *pl*) finery; a showy trifle; china, glazed earthenware, etc, also (in *pl*) fragments of this used as children's playthings; (in *pl*) dentures (*slang*): — *pl* **wall'ies**. — Also **wa'ly**. [Ety uncertain; perh **wale**[2]]

wally[2] or **wallie** *wo'li*, (also with *cap*; *slang*) *n* a stupid, inept or despised person; generally, a fool. [Ety uncertain; cf **wallydrag**; perh connected with the short form of the name *Walter*]

wallydrag *wol'i-drag*, or **wallydraigle** *wol'i-drā-gl*, (*Scot*) *n* a person or animal that is feeble, worthless or slovenly; the youngest of a family. [Poss **waly**[2], and **drag**, *draigle* (Scots form of **draggle**)]

walnut *wöl'nut*, *n* a genus (Juglans) of beautiful trees, some yielding valuable furniture wood; one of these trees; their wood; the nut of the common or English walnut; walnut juice. — *adj* made from walnutwood; light brown in colour. — **walnut juice** juice from the husk of walnuts, used to stain the skin; **wal'nutwood**. — **black walnut** a N American walnut, the timber of which is more valuable than that of the common walnut, though the fruit is inferior. [OE *walhhnutu*, from *w(e)alh* foreigner, and *hnutu* a nut]

Walpurgis night *val-pûr'gis nīt*, or *-pŏŏr'*, *n* the eve of the first of May, when witches, according to German popular superstition, rode on broomsticks and he-goats to revel with their master the devil, *esp* on the Brocken in the Harz Mountains. [So called because 1 May is the day of St *Walpurga*, abbess of Heidenheim, who died about 778]

walrus *wöl'rəs*, *wol'rəs*, *n* an aquatic, web-footed, carnivorous animal, also called the morse or seahorse, related to the seals, having the upper canine teeth developed into enormous tusks; a walrus moustache (*colloq*). — **walrus moustache** a thick moustache with long drooping ends. [Du *walrus*, *walros* literally whale horse; of Scand origin]

Walter Mitty. See under **Mitty**.

Waltonian *wol-tō'ni-ən*, *adj* of or pertaining to Izaak *Walton* (1593–1683), who wrote *The Compleat Angler*. — *n* a disciple of Walton; an angler.

walty *wol'ti*, (*naut*) *adj* inclined to lean or roll over. [Obs adj *walt* unsteady (from OE *wealt*, found only in *unwealt* steady), and sfx *-y*]

waltz *wölts* or *wöls*, *n orig* a German dance in triple time performed by couples with a rapid whirling motion; a slower circling dance, also in triple time; the music for either dance; a piece of instrumental music in 3–4 time (**concert waltz**). — *vi* to dance a waltz; to move or trip lightly, to whirl (*colloq*); to walk with arrogant assurance (*colloq*); to progress with carefree ease (*colloq*). — *vt* to guide or partner in a waltz; to convey lightly and easily (*colloq*). — *n* **waltz'er** someone who waltzes; a waltzing mouse; a type of fairground roundabout in which customers are spun while revolving. — *n* **waltz'ing**. — **waltzing mouse** a mouse of a breed that moves forward in small circles, rather than a straight line. — **waltz into** (*colloq*) to storm at; **waltz Matilda** see under **Matilda**. [Ger *Walzer* a waltz, from *walzen* to roll, dance]

waly[1]. See **wally**[1].

waly[2] *wā'li*, (*Scot*) *interj* alas. [**wellaway**]

wambenger *wom-beng'ər*, (*Austr*) *n* a small marsupial, same as **tuan**[2]. [Aboriginal]

wamble *wom'bl*, (*dialect*) *vi* (of the intestines or stomach) to give the feeling of working or rolling; to quake; to twist or wriggle; to move unsteadily. — *vt* to turn round, or upside down, or over and over. — *n* a rolling in the stomach; a feeling of nausea; an unsteady, rolling or staggering movement. — *n* **wam'bliness**. — *n* **wam'bling**. — Also *adj*. — *adv* **wam'blingly**. — *adj* **wam'bly** affected with, or causing, sickness; unsteady. — *adj* **wam'ble-cropped** sick at stomach. [Perh two or more verbs; cf Dan *vamle* to feel sick, connected with L *vomere* to vomit; also Norw *vamla*, *vamra* to stagger]

wame *wām*, (*dialect*) *n* the womb or (more frequently) the belly; a protuberant part or a hollow enclosed part. — Also (in 17c literature) **wem**, **wemb** and **weamb**. — *adj* **wamed** having a wame (*usu* of a specified kind). — *n* **wame'ful** a bellyful. [Variant of **womb**]

wammus. See **wamus**.

wampee *wom-pē'*, *n* an edible Asiatic fruit (*Clausena*; family Rutaceae) about the size of a large grape, with a hard yellow rind. [Chin *hwang-pī*, literally yellow skin]

wampish *wom'pish*, (*Scott*) *vt* to brandish, flourish, wave about. — Also *vi*. [Origin uncertain]

wampum *wom'pəm*, *wöm'pəm*, *n* a shortened form of the N American Indian (Algonquian) name for beads made from shells, used as money, etc. — *n* **wam'pumpeag** (*-pēg*) the word of which wampum is a shortened form, literally white string of beads. — **wampum belt** a belt consisting of shell beads so arranged as to convey a message or record a treaty, etc.

wampus. See **wamus**.

wamus *wöm'əs* or *wom'əs*, (*US*) *n* a kind of cardigan or strong jacket buttoned at neck and wrists. — Also **wamm'us** or **wamp'us**. [Du *wammes*, from OFr *wambais* a military tunic orig worn under armour]

WAN *abbrev*: (West Africa) Nigeria (IVR); wide-area network (*comput*).

wan[1] *won*, *adj* lacking colour; pale and sickly; faint; dark, gloomy (*obs*). — *n* (*rare*) wanness. — *vt* and *vi* to make or to become wan. — **wan'd** (*Shakesp*, *Antony and Cleopatra*, II.1.21) *perh* for *pa p* **wanned**. — *adv* **wan'ly**. — *n* **wan'ness**. — *adj* **wann'ish** somewhat wan. [OE *wann* dark, lurid; not found in other Gmc languages]

wan[2] *wan*, old *pa t* of **win**[1]; gained or took (*Spenser*).

wanchancy or **wanchancie** *won-chan'si*, (*Scot*) *adj* unlucky, dangerous or uncanny. [OE privative or negative pfx *wan-* (of Gmc origin; seen in mod Du and in Eng **wanton**), **chance**, and sfx *-y*]

wand *wond*, *n orig* something slender and supple, eg a twig, thin stem, branch or young shoot of a willow used in basketmaking (now *poetic* and *dialect*); something slender and rigid, eg a light walking-cane (*obs*); a rod of authority, a caduceus, a rod used by a fairy, magician, conjurer, conductor or diviner; a measuring rod; a mark in archery. [ON *vöndr* a shoot of a tree; Dan *vånd*]

wander *won'dər*, *vi* to ramble or move with no definite object, or with no fixed course, or by a roundabout way (*lit* and *fig*); to go astray, deviate from the right path or course, the subject of discussion, the object of attention, etc; to lose one's way (*colloq*); to be incoherent in talk, disordered in mind, or delirious. — *vt* to traverse; to lead astray, or to bewilder (*colloq*). — *n* a ramble, stroll. — *adj* **wan'dered** astray; incoherent; bewildered. — *n* **wan'derer** a person or animal that wanders, *esp* habitually or from inclination; (with *cap*) a Covenanter who left his or her home to follow a dispossessed minister (*hist*). — *adj* and *n* **wan'dering**. — *adv* **wan'deringly**. — **Wandering Jew** a legendary Jew in the folklore *esp* of north-western Europe who cannot die but must wander till the end of the world or until Christ's second coming, as a punishment for taunting Christ on the way to the Crucifixion, his name occurring variously as *Cartaphilus*, *Ahasuerus*, *Buttadeus*, etc; **wandering Jew** any of several trailing or creeping plants, *esp* a species of tradescantia (*Tradescantia fluminensis*) with variegated leaves; **wandering nerve** the vagus, the tenth cranial nerve; **wandering sailor** a popular trailing house plant, *Tradescantia blossfeldiana*, with leaves that are maroon on the underside; **wander plug** an electrical plug on a flexible wire capable of being inserted in any appropriate socket; **wander year** a year spent in travel to complete training or broaden experience before settling down to a trade or profession. [OE *wandrian*; cf Ger *wandern*; related to **wend**, and to **wind**[2]]

Wanderjahr *van'dər-yär*, (*Ger*) *n* a year of journeymanship or wandering, a wander year: — *pl* **Wanderjahre**.

wanderlust *won'dər-lust*, *n* an urge to travel or move from place to place. [Ger, wander-longing]

wanderoo *won-də-roo'*, *n* a name *usu* applied to the lion-tailed macaque, a native of the Malabar coast of India; properly, a langur of Sri Lanka. [Sinhalese *wanderu* monkey]

wandle *won'dl*, (*dialect*) *adj* supple, pliant, nimble. — Also **wanle** or **wannel**. [Ety uncertain]

wandoo *won'doo*, *n* a W Australian eucalyptus (*Eucalyptus redunca*) having white bark and durable brown wood. [Aboriginal]

wane *wān*, *vi* (*esp* of the moon) to decrease in size (*opp* to *wax*); to decrease in volume (*obs*); to decline in power, prosperity, intensity, brightness, etc; to draw to a close. — *n* gradual decrease or decline, as in **on the wane**, **in wane** or **in the**, **her** or **its wane**; the time when this is taking place; a defective edge or corner on a plank of wood. — *adj* **waned** diminished; dying or dead. — *adj* **wan'ey** or **wan'y**. — *adj* and *n* **wan'ing**. [OE *wanian*, *wonian* to lessen (ON *vana*), from *wana*, *wona* (also *wan*, *won*) deficient, lacking]

wang[1] *wang*, (*obs*) *n* the cheek; a wang tooth. — **wang tooth** a molar. [OE *wange*]

wang[2]. See **whang**[1].

wangan and **wangun**. See **wanigan**.

wangle *wang'gl*, (*colloq*) *vt* to obtain or accomplish by craft; to manipulate or falsify. — *vi* to get one's way by guile. — *n* an exercise of such methods. — *n* **wang'ler**. — *n* **wang'ling**. [Origin uncertain]

wanhope *won'hōp*, (*obs*) *n* despair. [OE privative or negative pfx *wan-* (see **wanchancy**), and **hope**]

wanigan *won'i-gən*, *n* in a lumber camp, a chest for supplies or a kind of houseboat for loggers and their supplies; also the pay office. — Also **wan'gan** and **wan'gun**. [Algonquian]

wanion *won'yən*, (*Shakesp*, *Scott*) *n* found in the phrases **with a (wild) wanion** with a vengeance, vehemently; **with a (wild) wanion to him** bad luck to him, a curse on him. [Earlier (*in the*) *waniand* (in the) waning (of the moon), ie in an unlucky time]

wank *wangk*, (*vulg slang*) *vi* (of a man) to masturbate. — *vt* to masturbate (a man). — *n* an act or instance of masturbation. — *n* **wank'er** someone who masturbates; a worthless, contemptible person. — *adj* **wank'y** objectionable, contemptible. [Origin unknown]

Wankel engine *wang'kəl en'jin*, *n* a rotary automobile engine having an approximately triangular central rotor turning in a close-fitting oval-shaped chamber rather than conventional pistons and cylinders. [F *Wankel* (1902–1988), the German engineer who invented it]

wankle *wong'kl*, (*dialect*) *adj* unstable, unsteady; changeable; not to be depended on. [OE *wancol*; of Gmc origin]

wanle and **wannel**. See under **wandle**.

wanly. See under **wan**[1].

wanna *won'ə*, a spelling of **want to** representing colloquial, *esp NAm* pronunciation.

wannabe or **wannabee** *won'ə-bē*, (*colloq*, *esp US*) *n* someone who aspires to be associated with an admired person or set of people, and accordingly tries, *esp* ineffectually, to imitate them; a vain fantasist. [(*I*) *want to be*]

wanness. See under **wan**[1].

wannion. Same as **wanion**.

wannish. See under **wan**[1].

wanrestful *won-rest'fool* or *-fl*, (*Scot*) *adj* restless. [OE privative or negative pfx *wan-* (see **wanchancy**), and **restful**]

want[1] *wont*, *n* the state or fact of being without something or of having an insufficient quantity; absence or deficiency of necessities; poverty; (in *pl*) difficult or straitened circumstances (*obs*); a lack, deficiency; a blemish (*obs*); a defect, feebleness, in intelligence (as in **have a want**; *Scot*); (in *pl*) requirements or desires. — *vt* to be destitute of or deficient in; to lack, be without (*Shakesp*, *Macbeth*, III.6.8, *who cannot want*, for *who can want*, *the thought*?); to feel need of, desire; to require, need; to fall short of something by (a specified amount); to dispense with, do without (now *dialect*). — *vi* to be deficient, entirely lacking (*archaic*); to be in need or destitution (*old*); to lack (with *for*; *old*). — *n* **want'age** (*US*) deficiency, shortage. — *adj* **want'ed** lacking; needed; desired; searched for, *esp* by the police. — *n* **want'er** someone who wants. — *adj* **want'ing** absent, missing, lacking; deficient (with *in*, or, *obs*, with *of*); failing to help, do justice to, come up to (with *to*; *old*); slow to (with *infinitive*; *obs*); below the desired or expected standard (in the phrase **found wanting**); mentally defective (*dialect*); poor, needy (*obs*). — Also *n*. — *prep* without, lacking, less. — **want ad** (chiefly *US*) a small advertisement, *esp* in a newspaper, specifying goods, property, employment, etc required by the advertiser; **want'-wit** a fool, someone lacking common sense. — Also *adj*. — **want in**, **out**, **up**, **down**, etc (*colloq*) to want to get in, out, etc. [ON *vant*, neuter of *vanr* lacking, and *vanta* to lack]

want[2] *wont*, (*dialect*) *n* a mole. — **want'-catcher**; **want'hill**. [OE *wand*; cf Norw *vand*; prob same root as **wind**[2] and **wend**]

wanthriven *won-thriv'n*, (*Scot*) *adj* stunted; ill-grown; emaciated. [Privative or negative pfx *wan-* (see **wanchancy**), and **thriven**]

wanton *won'tən*, *adj* thoughtlessly cruel; unprovoked, unjust, merciless; capricious (*archaic*); self-indulgent, given to luxury (*obs*); lascivious, or (*obs*) amorous; undisciplined, unruly, unmanageable (*obs*); immoral, licentious, lewd; insolent, arrogant, merciless in power or prosperity (*obs*); (of people) jovial (*obs*); (of animals and inanimate things) frisky, gay, moving freely or capriciously (*poetic*); growing luxuriantly (*poetic*); unrestrained, prodigal. — *n* an immoral person, *esp* female; a trifler (*old*); a spoilt child or pampered, effeminate person (*obs*); a roguish, playful child, animal, etc (*obs*). — *vi* to frolic; to play lasciviously or amorously; to idle, go idly; to trifle; to indulge oneself, run into excesses; to grow luxuriantly, ramble unchecked. — *vt* to use wastefully, dissipate (also with *away*; *old*). — *vi* **wan'tonize** or **-ise** (*archaic*) to play the wanton. — *adv* **wan'tonly**. — *n* **wan'tonness**. — **play the wanton** to trifle or (*obs*) to behave lewdly. [ME *wantowen*, from privative or negative pfx *wan-* (see **wanchancy**), and OE *togen*, pa p of *tēon* to draw, lead, educate; cf Ger *ungezogen* ill-bred, rude]

wanty *won'ti*, *n* a belt used to secure a load on a pack-horse's back (*obs*); the belly-band of a shaft-horse (*dialect*); a short rope, *esp* one used for binding hay on a cart (*dialect*). [**wame** and **tie**[1]]

wanworth *won'wûrth*, (*Scot*) *n* a very low price; a bargain. — *adj* **wanword'y** worthless; unworthy. [Privative or negative pfx *wan-* (see **wanchancy**), and **worth**[1]]

wanze *wonz*, (*obs*) *vi* to decrease, waste away. [OE *wansian*]

wap[1] *wop*, *vt* to throw or pull quickly or roughly (*dialect*); to strike or drub (*colloq*); to flap (*Scot*): — *pr p* **wapp'ing**; *pa t* and *pa p* **wapped**. — *n* a smart blow; a shake or flap (*Scot*); a blast, storm (*Scot*); a fight or quarrel (*Scot*). [Cf **whop**]

wap[2] *wop*, *vt* (*obs*) to wrap or bind. — *n* (*dialect*) a turn of a string with which anything is tied; a bundle of hay. [Ety uncertain]

wapenshaw and **wapenschaw**. See **wappenshaw**.

wapentake *wop'n-tāk*, (*esp hist*) *n* a name given in Yorkshire and certain other shires to a territorial division of the county similar to the *hundred* of southern counties. [Late OE *wǣpen(ge)tæc*, ON *vāpnatak*, literally weapon-taking, assent at a meeting being signified by brandishing a weapon]

wapinshaw and **wapinschaw**. See **wappenshaw**.

wapiti *wop'i-ti*, *n* a species (*Cervus canadensis*) of deer of large size, native to N America. [Algonquian]

wappend *wop'nd*, *adj* (*Shakesp*, *Timon*, IV.2.38) *perh* for *wappered* (now *dialect*), fatigued, tired; *perh* meaning incontinent, unchaste, and connected with *obs* sense of **wap**[1], to copulate.

wappenshaw, **wapenshaw**, **wapinshaw**, **wappenschaw**, **wapenschaw** or **wapinschaw** *wop'n-shö* or *wap'*, *n* a periodical gathering of the people within an area for the purpose of seeing that each man was armed in accordance with his rank, and ready to take the field when required (*Scot hist*); a rifle-shooting competition (in *SAfr* equivalent to Du *wapenschouwing*). — Also **weap'on-shaw** or **weap'on-schaw**. — *n* **wapp'enshawing**, etc an older form, from which *wappenshaw* is a back-formation. [Scot *wappen* weapon, and *schaw* show]

wapper *wop'ər*, (*dialect*) *vi* to blink; to move tremulously. — *adj* **wapp'er-eyed** blinking. — **wapp'er-jaw** a projecting under-jaw. — *adj* **wapp'er-jawed**. [Cf Du *wapperen* to oscillate]

waqf or **wakf** *wäkf*, (*Islam*) *n* the donation of land, property or money for charitable or pious purposes; such an endowment; (with *cap*) in Jerusalem the authority administering the holy sites. [Ar *waqf*]

War. *abbrev*: Warwickshire.

war[1] *wör*, *n* a state of conflict; a contest between states, or between parties within a state (**civil war**) carried on by arms; any long-continued struggle, often against or between impersonal forces (*fig*); fighting (*poetic*); open hostility; the profession of arms; an army, or war equipment (*rare*; *poetic*); a contest, conflict. — *vi* to make war; to carry on war; to contend: — *pr p* **warr'ing**; *pa t* and *pa p* **warred**. — *adj* of, characteristic of, resulting from, or relating to war. — *adj* **war'like** of or pertaining to war; martial, military; equipped for fighting (*obs*); intended for use in war (*obs*); fond of war; bellicose. — *n* **war'likeness**. — **war baby** a baby born during a war, *esp* a serviceman's illegitimate child; any discreditable or troublesome result of war; **war bonnet** a headdress, often with long trailing chains of feathers, worn by members of certain N American Indian tribes; **war bride** a soldier's bride, met as a result of wartime movements or postings; **war chest** funds set aside to pay for a war, political campaign, etc; **war cloud** a cloud of smoke and dust over a battlefield; a sign that war is threatening or impending (*fig*); **war correspondent** a journalist or other person assigned to a seat of war so as to give first-hand reports of events; **war crime** a crime connected with war, *esp* one that violates the code of war; **war criminal**; **war cry** a cry used in battle for encouragement or as a signal; a slogan (*fig*); **war dance** a dance engaged in by some tribes before going to war; a dance imitating the actions of a battle; **War Department** the name borne 1784–1857 by what became the War Office, still used in speaking of property such as stores or land; **war'dog** a dog used in war; an old warrior; a war hawk; **war drum** a drum beaten as a summons to war, or during a battle; a rumbling or threat of impending war (*fig*); **war'fare** (from **fare** *n*) the activity of engaging in, waging, or carrying on war; armed conflict; conflict, struggle or feuding of any kind. — *vi* (*obs*; *lit* and *fig*) to wage war. — **war'farer**. — *adj* and *n* **war'faring**. — **war game** a mock or imaginary battle or military exercise used to train personnel in tactics, a kriegspiel; a game, *esp* with detailed rules and using models, in which players enact historical or imaginary battles, etc; **war'-gamer** a player of or participant in war games; **war gas** (*chem*) any poisonous or irritant gaseous chemical substance used in warfare or riot control deliberately to harm or temporarily disable those exposed to it; **war god** or **goddess** a deity who presides over war, assigning victory or defeat, etc; **war hawk** someone eager for war; **war'head** the section of a torpedo or other missile containing the explosive material; **war'horse** a charger, a horse used in battle; an old warrior in any field of conflict; any standard, familiar, reliable, much-performed piece of music, play, etc; **war kettle** among N American Indians, a kettle set on the fire as part of the ceremony of going to war; **war loan** a loan raised to pay for a war; **war'lord** a commander or commander-in-chief, *esp* where and when the military power is great (now *usu derog*); **war machine** a machine used in warfare; the combined technical and administrative military resources mobilized by a country, alliance, etc in order to engage in war; **war'man** (*rare*) a warrior; **war memorial** a monument erected to the memory of those (*esp* from a particular locality) who died in a war; **war'monger** a mercenary soldier (*Spenser*); someone who encourages war, *esp* for personal gain; **war'-mongering**; **war neurosis** a more accurate term for shellshock; **war note** (*poetic*) a summons to war; **War Office** a department of the civil government, formerly headed by the Secretary of State for War, since 1964 absorbed in the Ministry of Defence; premises of the department in Whitehall; **war paint** paint applied to the face and body by primitive peoples, indicating that they are going to war; full dress, or finery, *esp* a woman's make-up (*colloq*); **war'path** among the N American Indians, the path followed on a military expedition, or the expedition itself (**on the warpath** engaged in conflict, in a mood for battle); **war'plane** any aircraft designed or intended for use in warfare; **war'-proof** (*rare*) a valour proved in war. — *adj* able to withstand attack. — **war'ship** an armed vessel for use in war; **war song** a song sung by men about to fight; a song celebrating brave deeds in war; **war'time** a period during which a war is being fought. — *adj* of, pertaining to or characteristic of a time of war. — **war trial** the trial of a person accused of war crimes. — *adj* **war'-wast'ed** ravaged by war. — *adj* **war'-wea'ried** or **-wea'ry** tired of or exhausted by war. — **war whoop** a cry uttered on going into battle; **war widow** a woman whose husband has been killed in war; **war'wolf** a medieval siege engine; a fierce warrior (*Scott*); see also **werewolf**. — *adj* **war'-worn** wearied, worn, wasted, ravaged or marked by war. — **carry the war into the enemy's camp** or **country** to take the offensive boldly (*lit* and *fig*); **civil war** see under **civil**; **cold war** see under **cold**; **declare war** (with *on* or *against*) to announce formally that one is about to begin hostilities; to set oneself to get rid of (*fig*); **go to the wars** (*archaic*) to go to fight in a foreign country; **go to war** to resort to armed conflict; **have been in the wars** (*fig*) to show signs of having been knocked about; **holy war** see under **holy**; **make** or **wage war** to carry on hostilities; **private war** warfare between people in their individual capacity, eg by duelling, family feuds, etc; **total war** war with every weapon at the combatant's disposal, sticking at nothing and sparing no one; **war of attrition** a conflict in which both sides are worn down over a long period, with no decisive battles; **war of nerves** systematic attempts to undermine morale by means of threats, rumours and counter-rumours, etc. [Late OE and ONFr *werre* (OFr and Fr *guerre*), from OHGer *werra* quarrel]

war[2] *wär* or *wör*, (*obs* except *dialect*; *Spenser* also **warre**; *Scot* and *N Eng* also **waur** *wör*) *adj* and *adv* worse: — *superl* **warst** or **waurst**. — *vt* (*Scot*) to defeat, worst; to excel: — *pr p* **warr'ing** or **waur'ing**; *pa t* and *pa p* **warred** or **waured**. [ON *verre*]

waratah *wor'ə-tä*, *n* any of a genus (*Telopea*) of Australian proteaceous shrubs with very showy flowers. [Aboriginal]

warble[1] *wör'bl*, *vi* to sing in a vibrating treble or soprano, to trill (sometimes *facetious* or *derog*); to sing with elaborations such as runs and trills; to sing sweetly as birds do; to make or be produced as a sweet quavering sound; to yodel (*US*). — *vt* to sing in a vibratory manner; to sing sweetly; to express or extol in poetry or song; to cause (eg a stringed instrument) to vibrate or sound musically. — *n* the activity, or a spell, of warbling; a quavering modulation of the voice; a song. — *n* **war'bler** someone who warbles; a songster; a singing-bird; any bird of the subfamily *Sylviinae* of the family *Muscicapidae* (willow warbler, reed warbler, whitethroat, blackcap, etc); any of numerous small, brightly coloured American birds of the family *Parulidae*; a whistle used in infant classes, etc; (in bagpipe music) an ornamental group of grace notes. — *n* and *adj* **war'bling**. — *adv* **war'blingly**. [ONFr *werbler* (OFr *guerbler*); of Gmc origin]

warble[2] *wör'bl*, *n* a small hard swelling on a horse's back, caused by the galling of the saddle, etc; a swelling caused by a warble fly or a botfly. — **warble fly** any of several flies of the same family as botflies whose larvae cause painful swellings that spoil the hides of horses and cattle, etc. [Ety uncertain]

warby *wör'bi*, (*Austr colloq*) *adj* worn-out, decrepit, unattractive; unwell, unsteady. [Poss from Eng dialect *warbie* a maggot]

ward *wörd*, *vt* to parry or keep away (now *usu* **ward off**); to watch over, guard (*archaic*); to protect (with *from*; *archaic*); to enclose (eg machinery) in order to prevent accidents (*rare*); to place in a ward. — *vi* to act on the defensive. — *n* a room with several beds in a hospital, etc; the patients in a ward collectively; a division or department of a prison; the activity or a spell of watching or guarding; the state of being guarded; a lookout or watch; care, protection; guardianship; custody; (in feudal times) control of the lands of a minor; a minor or other person under a guardian; a body of guards; a guarded place, eg a courtyard of a castle (**inner** and **outer ward**); a means of protection, such as a bolt or bar; a part of a lock of special configuration to prevent its being turned by any except a particular key, or the part of the key of corresponding configuration; a defensive motion or position (*fencing*; also *fig*); a division of a county (*Scot* and *N Eng*); an administrative, electoral or other division of a town, etc; a division of an army (*obs*; as in *van(t)ward* (vanguard), *middle ward* and *rearward* (rearguard)). — *adj* **ward'ed** (of a lock or key) having a ward or wards. — *n* **ward'er** someone who guards or supervises; a prison officer in charge of prisoners in a jail (*old*); a staff or baton of authority (*hist*). — *vt* to guard as a warder. — *n* and *adj* **ward'ing**. — *n* **war'dress** a female prison officer. — *n* **ward'ship** the office of, or the state of being under, a guardian; protection, custody (*fig*); the state of being in guardianship (*fig*); in English feudal law, the guardianship which the feudal lord had of the land of his vassal while the latter was a minor. — **ward'corn** (*hist*) a payment in corn in lieu of military service; misunderstood as the duty of keeping watch in order to give the alarm by blowing a horn; **ward'mote** a meeting of a ward, or of a court of a ward; **ward'room** the mess room of the officers of a warship; the officers collectively. — **Warden of the Cinque Ports** or **Lord Warden (of the Cinque Ports)** the governor of the Cinque Ports, having the authority of an admiral and the power to hold a court of admiralty; **Wardens of the Marches** officers formerly appointed to keep order in the marches or border districts of England and Scotland; **ward in Chancery** a minor under the protection of the Court of Chancery. [OE *weardian*; cf Ger *warten* to wait, attend, take care of]

-ward *-wərd*, *-wörd* or **-wards** *-wərdz*, *-wördz*, *sfx* forming adjectives and adverbs with the sense of motion towards. [OE *-weard* (genitive *-weardes*), cognate with Ger *-wärts*; connected with OE *weorthan* to become and L *vertere* to turn]

warden[1] *wör'dn*, *n* someone who guards or keeps under supervision people, animals, buildings, precious objects, etc; a gatekeeper or sentinel (*rare*); a regent (*hist*); the governor of a town, district, etc (*hist*); a title of certain officers of the Crown; a member of certain governing bodies; a superintendent; the head of certain institutions, such as schools, colleges, hostels, etc; someone appointed for duties among the civil population in cases of fire or air raids; (*usu* **traffic warden**) an official controlling traffic circulation and parking of motor vehicles. — *vt* (*rare*) to guard as a warden. — *n* **ward'enry** (*rare*) the office of, or district in the charge of, a warden; guardianship (*Thomas Hardy*). — *n* **ward'enship** the office of warden. [ONFr *wardein* (OFr *g(u)arden*) guardian]

warden[2] *wör'dn*, *n* a kind of pear used *esp* in cooking. — **warden pie** a pie made of warden pears. [Origin uncertain; perh from Anglo-Fr *warder* (Fr *garder*) to keep]

warder. See under **ward**.

Wardian *wör'di-ən*, *adj* denoting a kind of glass case for transporting delicate ferns and other such plants or for growing them in indoors. [Nathaniel Bagshaw *Ward* (1791–1868), the inventor]

wardmote. See under **ward**.

Wardour Street English *wör'dər strēt ing'glish*, *n* sham-antique diction as found in some historical novels, from *Wardour Street*, London, once noted for antique and imitation-antique furniture, now given over to the business side of entertainment, *esp* films.

wardress. See under **ward**.

wardrobe *wörd'rōb*, *n* a room or a piece of furniture for containing clothes or theatrical costumes; one's stock of wearing apparel; bright or multicoloured raiment, eg that of flowers (*fig* and *poetic*; *Milton* **ward'rop**); a ship's complement of sails (*naut*); a department of a royal or noble household having charge of robes, wearing apparel, jewels, etc. — *n* **ward'rober** (*hist*) a household official in charge of a royal or noble wardrobe. — **wardrobe mistress** or **master** a person who looks after the theatrical costumes of a company or of an individual actor or actress; **wardrobe trunk** a trunk in which clothing may be hung as in a wardrobe. [ONFr *wardrobe* (OFr *garderobe*); see **guard** and **robe**]

wardrop. See under **wardrobe**.

ware[1] *wār*, *n* (now *usu* in *pl*) articles of merchandise or produce collectively; an article of merchandise (*rare*); pottery, as in *Delftware*, *Wedgwood ware* (qv at **delf**[1], **Wedgwood**); articles of fine workmanship, as in *Benares ware*, ornamental metalwork from India. — *combining form* **-ware** articles of a specified type or material, as in *hardware*, *earthenware*; used to denote categories of material made use of in computer-processing, as in *hardware*, *software*. — **ware'house** a building or room for storing goods; a shop; the music and dancing typical at a warehouse party (qv below) (*pop culture*). — *vt* (*-howz*) to deposit in a warehouse, *esp* a bonded warehouse; to store up (*fig*). — **ware'housing** the act of depositing goods in a warehouse; the practice of covertly building up a block of company shares, using one or more front companies, etc, to obtain shares on behalf of the true purchaser (*stock exchange slang*); **ware'houseman** a man who keeps, or is employed in, a warehouse or a wholesale store; **warehouse party** an acid-house party (qv) held in a large unused building away from main residential areas; **warehousing system** the plan of allowing importers of dutiable goods to store them in a government warehouse without payment of duties until ready to bring the goods into market; **ware potatoes** large potatoes sold to the public for consumption, as distinct from seed potatoes (qv). [OE *waru*; cf Ger *Ware*]

ware[2] *wār*, *adj* aware (*archaic*); wary, cautious (*archaic*; sometimes with *of*); prudent (*archaic*; *esp* in phrase **ware and wise**). — *vi* and *vt* (*archaic*; *usu* in *imperative*) to beware, beware of; (in hunting) to avoid, refrain from riding over, etc (sometimes *wör*). — *adj* **ware'less** (*archaic*) incautious; unaware (with *of*). [OE *wær*; cf ON *varr*; see **aware**]

ware[3] *wār*, (*Scot* and *dialect*) *n* springtime. [ON *vār*]

ware[4] *wār*, (*Scot* and *dialect*) *n* (also **seaware**) seaweed. [OE *wār*; cf **ore**[2]]

ware[5] *wār*, archaic *pa t* of **wear**[1].

ware[6] *wār*, (*Scot*) *vt* to spend. [ON *verja* to clothe, hence to invest: cf **wear**[1]]

warehouse, etc. See under **ware**[1].

wareless. See under **ware**[2].

warfare, etc. See under **war**[1].

warfarin *wör'fə-rin*, *n* a crystalline insoluble substance ($C_{19}H_{16}O_4$) used as a rodenticide and medically (in the form of its sodium salt) as an anticoagulant. [*W*isconsin *A*lumni *R*esearch *F*oundation (the patent owners) and coum*arin*]

warhable *wör-hā'bl*, (*Spenser*) *adj* fit for war. [**war** and **able**]

warhead, warhorse. See under **war**[1].

waribashi *wä-ri-bash'i*, *n* a pair of chopsticks in the form of a single sliver of wood ready scored for splitting into two. [Jap]

warily, wariment, wariness, etc. See under **wary**.

warison or **warrison** *wor'* or *war'i-sən*, (*obs*) *n* wealth; reward or punishment; a note sounding the assault (*Scott*, *erron*). [ONFr (OFr *guarison*), from *warir* to guard; cf **garrison**]

wark *wörk*, Scots form of **work** (*n*).

warlike, etc. See under **war**[1].

warling *wör'ling*, (*obs*) *n* someone disliked, in the proverb 'It is better to be an old man's darling than a young man's warling'. [Prob formed to rhyme with 'darling']

warlock *wör'lok*, *n* a wizard; a magician (*Scot*); a demon; a warrior who cannot be wounded with metals (*Dryden*, *erron*). — *n* **war'lockry** sorcery. [OE *wǣrloga* a breaker of an agreement, from *wǣr* a compact, and *lēogan* to lie; the ending -(*c*)*k* appears earliest in Scots]

warlord. See under **war**[1].

warm *wörm*, *adj* having moderate heat; hot; imparting heat or a sensation of heat; retaining heat; affecting one (pleasantly or unpleasantly) as heat does (*fig*); (of work) making one hot, strenuous; harassing; characterized by danger or difficulty; passionate; vehement; angry; excited; ardent, enthusiastic; lively, glowing; kind-hearted; affectionate; amorous; indelicate (*colloq*); comfortable, well-to-do (*colloq*); (of a colour) containing red or, sometimes, yellow; *esp* in a game, close to discovery or attainment; (of a scent or trail) fresh; denoting a call on a potential customer or supporter made on the strength of a previous referral or contact already established (*business* or *politics*). — *vt* to make warmer; to interest; to excite; to impart brightness or a suggestion of life to; to beat (*colloq*). — *vi* to become warm or ardent; (with *to*) to begin to enjoy, approve of, feel enthusiastic about or fond of. — *n* a beating (*colloq*); an officer's thick overcoat (also **British warm**); a warm area or environment (*colloq*); an act or instance of warming up or being warmed up (*colloq*). — *adv* warmly. — *adj* **warmed**. — *n* **warm'er**. — *n* **warm'ing** the action of making or becoming warm; a beating (*slang*). — *adj* **warm'ish**. — *adv* **warm'ly**. — *n* **warm'ness**. — *n* **warmth**. — **Warm'blood** a race of horse developed from pedigree bloodlines from native European mares for competition jumping and dressage; (also without *cap*) a horse of this type. — Also *adj*. — *adj* **warm'-blood'ed** homothermous or idiothermous, ie having bodily temperature constantly maintained at a point *usu* above the environmental temperature; ardent, passionate. — *vt* **warm-boot'** to re-boot (a computer) without switching it off, eg when changing programs. — *adj* **warmed-o'ver** (*US*) or **warmed-up'** heated anew. — **warm front** (*meteorol*) the advancing front of a mass of warm air. — *adj* **warm'-heart'ed** affectionate; hearty; sympathetic; generous. — **warm'-heart'edness**; **warm'ing-pan** (*hist*) a covered pan with a long handle, for holding live coals to warm a bed; someone temporarily holding a post or position until the person intended for it is able to take it (*old*); **warm'-up** a practice exercise before an event; a preliminary entertainment, etc intended to increase the excitement or enthusiasm of the audience. — **a warm reception** (*fig*) display of hostility; a vigorous resistance or attack; **keep warm** to occupy (a post or position) for someone until he or she is ready to fill it; **warm up** to make or become warm; to heat (already cooked food); to become lively or animated; to grow interested or eager; to limber up prior to an athletic event, contest, etc. [OE *wearm*; cf Ger *warm*]

warman, warmonger, etc. See under **war**[1].

warn[1] *wörn*, *vt* to give notice of danger or evil to; to notify in advance; to caution (with *against*); to admonish; to instruct, command; to summon; to bid or instruct to go or to keep away (with *off*, *away*, etc; *lit* and *fig*); to ban (someone) from all race meetings or from a particular course (with *off*; *horse-racing*); to forbid (*obs*). — *vi* to give notice or warning (with *of*); (of a clock) to make a whirring sound before striking, to 'give warning'. — *n* **warn'er**. — *n* **warn'ing** a caution against danger, etc; something that gives this; an admonition; previous notice; notice to quit, of the termination of an engagement, etc; a summons, call; the sound accompanying the partial unlocking of the striking train in a clock, just before it strikes. — Also *adj*. — *adv* **warn'ingly**. — **warning coloration** conspicuous or gaudy coloration on certain creatures, eg some stinging insects, that deters potential attackers. [OE *warnian*, *warenian* or *wearnian* to caution (cf Ger *warnen*) and perh in part *wiernan* to refuse, forbid]

warn[2] *wörn*, (*Shakesp* and *dialect*) *vt* to warrant.

warp *wörp*, *vt* to twist out of shape; to turn from the right course; to distort; to cause to contract or wrinkle (*Shakesp*); to pervert (eg the mind or character); to misinterpret or give a deliberately false meaning to; to arrange (threads) so as to form a warp; to entwine (*obs*); to move (a vessel) by hauling on ropes attached to posts on a wharf, etc; to improve (land) by flooding so that it is covered by a deposit of alluvial mud; to choke (eg a channel) with alluvial mud; in rope-making, to stretch into lengths for tarring; to cast, throw (*obs*); to lay (eggs) or to bring forth (young), *esp* prematurely (*dialect*). — *vi* to be twisted out of shape; to become perverted or distorted (*fig*); to swerve; to move with effort, or on a zigzag course; (of cattle, sheep, etc) to miscarry. — *n* the state or fact of being warped; the permanent distortion of a timber, etc; a mental twist or bias; the threads stretched out lengthways in a loom to be crossed by a woof (also *fig*); a twist, shift or displacement to a different or parallel position within a (*usu* conceptual) framework or scale, etc (as in *time-warp*); a rope used in towing, one end being fastened to a fixed object; alluvial sediment; a reckoning of four (herrings, oysters, etc), thirty-three warps making a long hundred, and five long hundreds a mease or maze. — *adj* **warped** twisted by shrinking; distorted; perverted; covered or filled with a deposit of alluvial sediment. — *n* **war'per**. — *n* **war'ping**. [OE *weorpan*, *werpan* to throw, cast; cf Ger *werfen*, ON *verpa*]

warpath. See under **war**[1].

warragal, warragle, warragul. See under **warrigal**.

warran and **warrand**. Obsolete forms of **warrant**[1].

warrandice *wör'ən-dis*, (*Scot*; *archaic*) *n* a guarantee; a clause in a deed by which the grantor binds himself or herself to make good to the grantee the right conveyed. [Anglo-Fr *warandise*, *warantise*, from *warantir* to warrant]

warrant[1] *wor'ənt*, *vt* to authorize; to justify, be adequate grounds for; to guarantee to be as specified or alleged; to attest or guarantee the truth of, (*old colloq*) equivalent to 'be sure', 'be convinced' and 'be bound' (also in phrases **I** (or **I'll**) **warrant you** and **I warrant me**); to predict or to presage (*obs*); to secure, or guarantee the possession of, to; to protect, defend, keep (*obs*); to give assurance against danger, etc (*rare*; with *against*, *from*). — *n* someone or something that vouches, a guaranty; a pledge, assurance; a proof; that which authorizes; a writ for arresting a person or for carrying a judgement into execution, or for seizing or searching property; (in the services) an official certificate inferior to a commission, ie appointing a non-commissioned officer; authorization; justification; a written form authorizing the payment of money or certifying payment due, etc; a form of warehouse receipt for goods; a voucher (*obs*); a document issued to a stockholder permitting the purchase of further stock at a stated price; a defender (*obs*); a defence (*obs*). — *adj* **warr'antable** that may be permitted; justifiable; of good warrant, estimable (*obs*); of sufficient age to be hunted. — *n* **warr'antableness**. — *adv* **warr'antably**. — *adj* **warr'anted**. — *n* **warrantee'** the person to whom a warranty is given. — *n* **warr'anter** someone who authorizes or guarantees; a warrantor. — *n* **warr'anting**. — *n* **warr'antise** (*-tīz*; *obs* or *archaic*) an act of guaranteeing; a guarantee; assurance; authorization. — *n* **warr'antor** (*law*) someone who gives warranty; a warranter. — *n* **warr'anty** (*law*) an act of warranting, *esp* in feudal times the covenant by which the grantor of land warranted the security of the title to the recipient (**general warranty** against the claims of all and every person; **special warranty** against the claims of the grantor, or others claiming through or by him or her); an undertaking or assurance expressed or implied in certain contracts; a guarantee; authorization; justification; evidence. — **warrant officer** (in the services) an officer holding a warrant (see also **branch-officer**); a police officer whose duty it is to serve warrants; **warrant sale** (*Scot*; *law*) a public auction of poinded or seized household goods and personal property, authorized by a sheriff for the recuperation of unpaid debt and *usu* held at the house of the debtor. — **of good warrant** (*obs*) esteemed, important; **of warrant** (*obs*) allowed, warranted; esteemed, important; **out of warrant** (*obs*) not allowed; **take warrant on oneself** (*archaic*) to make oneself responsible; **warrant of attachment** a writ authorizing the seizure of property; **warrant of attorney** see under **attorney**. [OFr *warantir* (variant of *guarantir*); of Gmc origin]

warrant[2] *wor'ənt*, or **warren** *wor'ən*, *n* underclay (*coal-mining*). [Perh a use of **warrant**[1]]

warray *wör-ā'*, (*obs*) *vt* to make war on. — *vi* to make war. — Also **warrey'**. [OFr *werreier* (variant of *guerreier*), from Gmc *werra* strife]

warre. See under **war**[2].

warred. See under **war**[1,2].

warren[1] *wor'ən*, *n* a series of interconnected rabbit burrows; the rabbits living there; a densely populated slum dwelling or district; a maze of narrow passages; a piece of ground kept for breeding game, *esp* hares, rabbits, partridges, etc (**beasts** or **fowls of warren**; *hist*); the right of keeping or of hunting such game (*hist*). — *n* **warr'ener** the keeper or owner of a warren (*hist*); an inhabitant of a warren. [Anglo-Fr *warenne* (OFr *garenne*), of Gmc origin]

warren[2]. See **warrant**[2].

warrey. See **warray**.

warrigal *wor'i-gal* or *wor'ə-gl*, *n* the Australian wild dog, the dingo; a wild Australian horse. — *adj* wild, savage. — Also **warr'agal**, **warr'agle** or **warr'agul**. [Aboriginal]

warring. See under **war**[1,2].

warrior *wo'ri-ər*, *n* a skilled fighting man (in the early stages of civilization, or *poetic*); a veteran or distinguished fighter; a redoubtable person. — *n* **warrioress'** (*rare*) a female warrior. [ME and ONFr *werreior*, from Gmc *werra* strife]

warrison. See **warison**.

Warsaw Convention *wör'sō kən-ven'shən*, *n* the set of rules agreed to at the international convention held in *Warsaw*, Poland in 1929, establishing, in principle and within limits, the liability of the airline or carrier for damage to passengers, baggage or cargo in international accidents; **Warsaw Pact** an alliance of E European countries (including the Soviet Union, Bulgaria, Czechoslovakia, E Germany, Hungary, Poland and Romania) formed in 1955 and disbanded in 1991; the military treaty signed by these countries in *Warsaw* in 1955.

warship. See under **war**[1].

warsle *wörs'l*. Scots form of **wrestle**.

warst. See under **war**[2].

wart *wört*, *n* a small hard excrescence on the skin caused by a virus; a small protuberance on a plant surface or on an animal's skin; an abusive term for a disliked person (*slang*). — *adj* **wart'ed**. — *adj* **wart'less**. — *adj* **wart'like**. — *adj* **wart'y** like a wart; covered with warts. — **wart'-biter** (also **wart-biter cricket**) a large grasshopper native to southern England, formerly prized by country people for its ability to bite off warts; **wart cress** swine's cress; **wart'hog** or **wart hog** any of a genus of wild hogs found in Africa, with large wartlike excrescences on their cheeks; **wart'weed** a kind of spurge (its caustic juice thought to cure warts); **wart'wort** any of a family of lichens having a warty thallus; a wartweed. — **warts and all** with blemishes or shortcomings frankly revealed or consciously taken into account. [OE *wearte*; Ger *Warze*; prob related to L *verrūca* wart]

wartime. See under **war**[1].

warwolf. See under **war**[1] and **werewolf**.

wary *wā'ri*, *adj* on one's guard against deception or danger; cautious; circumspect; thrifty (*obs*). — *adv* **war'ily**. — *n* **war'iment** (*Spenser*) wariness. — *n* **war'iness**. — **be wary of** to be cautious with regard to. [**ware**[2]]

was *woz*, used as the 1*st* and 3*rd pers sing* of the *pa t* of the verb **be**. [OE *wæs*, from *wesan* to be; see **wast**[1], **were**, **wert**]

wase *wāz*, (*dialect*) *n* a wisp of hay, straw, etc; a pad on the head to ease the pressure of a burden. [Gmc word; perh Scand]

wasegoose. See **wayzgoose**.

Wash. *abbrev*: Washington (US state).

wash *wosh*, *vt* to cleanse, or to free from impurities, etc, with water or other liquid; to wet, moisten; (of an animal) to clean by licking; to flow over, past or against; to sweep along, down, etc; to form or erode by flowing over; to cover with a thin coat of metal or paint; to separate (ore, etc) from earth by means of water (*mining*); to launder (money, goods, etc) (*colloq*). — *vt* and *vi* (of water, etc) to have the property of cleansing. — *vi* to clean oneself, clothes, etc with water; to wash clothes, etc as one's employment; to stand cleaning (with *well*, *badly*, etc); to be swept or carried by water; to stand the test, bear investigation (*colloq*): — *pa p* **washed**, *archaic* **wash'en**. — *n* a washing; the process of washing; a collection of articles for washing;

that with which anything is washed; a lotion; the break of waves on the shore; the sound of water breaking, lapping, etc; the rough water left behind by a boat, etc, or the disturbed air behind an aerofoil, etc (also *fig*); the shallow part of a river or arm of the sea; a marsh or fen; erosion by flowing water; alluvial matter; a liquor of fermented malt prior to distillation; waste liquor, refuse of food, etc; a watery mixture; a thin, tasteless drink; insipid discourse in speech or writing; a broad but thin layer of colour put on with a long sweep of the brush; a thin coat of paint, metal, etc; the blade of an oar; the material from which valuable minerals may be extracted by washing (*mining*). — *adj* **wash'able** that may be washed without damage. — *n* **wash'er** someone who washes; a washing-machine; a face-cloth (*Austr*); a ring, *usu* flat, of metal, rubber, etc, to keep joints or nuts secure, etc (*perh* a different word); hence derisively (in *pl*) small change (*slang*). — *vt* to fit with a washer or washers. — *n* **wash'ery** a washhouse (*archaic*); a place in which an industrial washing process takes place (eg of coal, ore or wool). — *n* **wash'iness** the state of being watery; feebleness. — *n* **wash'ing** the act of cleansing, wetting or coating, with liquid; clothes or other articles washed or to be washed; a thin coating; the action of breaking, lapping, etc (of waves, etc); (*usu* in *pl*) liquid that has been used to wash something, or matter separated or carried away by water or other liquid. — *adj* that washes; used for washing; washable. — *adj* **wash'y** watery, moist; thin, feeble. — *adj* **wash'-and-wear'** (of garments or dressmaking fabrics) easily washed, quick-drying, and requiring no ironing. — **wash'-away** (*esp Austr*) the destruction of part of a road, railway, etc by flooding; the breach so caused; an erosion of the earth by the action of water; the channel so made; **wash'ball** a ball of toilet-soap; **wash'basin**, **wash'bowl** or **washhand basin** a basin to wash one's face and hands, etc in; **wash'board** a corrugated metal board for rubbing clothes on in washing (also **wash'ing-board**), utilized as a percussion instrument in certain types of music, eg skiffle or Country and Western; a thin plank on a boat's gunwale to prevent the sea from breaking over; a skirting-board (*dialect*); **wash'-bott'le** or **wash'ing-bott'le** a bottle containing liquid used for purifying gases; a bottle with tubes through the stopper, enabling a stream of cleansing liquid to be directed on to a chemical or a piece of apparatus; **wash'cloth** a piece of cloth used in washing, *esp* a dishcloth; a face-cloth or flannel (*NAm*); **wash'day** a day (or the regular day) when one washes one's clothes and linen (also **wash'ing-day**); **wash'-dirt** earth to be washed for gold; **wash drawing** a drawing in pencil or pen and ink over which a transparent wash is applied by brush. — *adj* **washed'-out'** deprived of colour, *esp* by washing; deprived of energy or animation (*colloq*). — *adj* **washed'-up'** deprived of energy or animation (*colloq*); done for, at the end of one's resources (*slang*); finished (with *with*; *slang*). — **wash'erman** or **wash'er-woman** a man or woman who washes clothes, *esp* for a living; **wash'-gild'ing** a gilding made with an amalgam of gold from which the mercury is driven off by heat, leaving a coating of gold; **wash'house** or **wash'ing-house** a house or room for washing clothes in; **wash'-in** (or **-out**) an increase (or decrease) in the angle of incidence, ie the angle between the chord of a wing and the wind relative to the aeroplane, in approaching the wing-tip along the camber; **washing-blue** see under **blue**; **wash'ing-line** a clothes-line; **wash'ing-machine** a machine for washing clothes; **wash'ing-powder** or **-liquid** a powdered or liquid preparation used in washing clothes; **washing-soda** see under **soda**; **wash'ing-up'** the washing of dishes and cutlery after a meal; the crockery, cutlery, etc to be washed after use; **washing-up machine** a dishwasher; **wash'land** an area of land periodically flooded by overflow water from a river, stream, or from the sea; **wash'-leather** split sheepskin prepared with oil in imitation of chamois; a piece of this for washing windows; buff leather for regimental belts; **wash'-out** or **wash'out** an erosion of earth by the action of water; the hole or channel so made; an event spoilt or cancelled because of rain; a complete failure (*colloq*); a useless person (*colloq*); see also **wash-in**; **wash'pot** a vessel for washing one's hands, etc, or for boiling clothes in; **wash'rag** (*NAm*) a face-cloth, a flannel; a servant who washes dishes (*obs*); **wash'room** a room containing lavatories and facilities for washing; a lavatory (chiefly *NAm*); **wash sale** (*US*) the dishonest practice of buying and immediately re-selling large quantities of a stock at an inflated price, so as to create a false impression of strong market interest in it; **wash'stand** or **washhand stand** a piece of furniture for holding jug, basin and other requisites for washing oneself; **wash'tub** *orig* a tub for washing clothes in; a washing-machine; **wash'-up** a washing-up; a washing-up place; anything cast up by the sea, etc; the washing of ore; a quantity of gold obtained by washing; an outcome or result (*Austr slang*); **wash'wipe** (in a motor vehicle) a mechanism for spraying the front or (*esp*) the rear windscreen with washing fluid, which is distributed and wiped off by the windscreen-wiper. — **come out in the wash** (of a stain, etc) to disappear on washing; to become intelligible, work out satisfactorily (*fig*; *colloq*); **wash away** to obliterate; **wash down** (of liquid) to carry downward; to wash from top to bottom; to help the swallowing or digestion of (a solid food) with a drink; **wash its face** (*slang*) (of an undertaking) to just pay its way; **wash one's hands of** to disclaim responsibility for; **wash out** to remove by washing; to wash free from dirt or soap, etc; (of colours or design) to disappear or become fainter as a result of washing; to rain off; to cancel (*colloq*); to exhaust (*colloq*; *esp* in *passive*); to bring the blade of an oar not cleanly out of the water (*rowing*); **wash up** to wash the dishes and cutlery after a meal; to wash one's hands and face (*esp US*); to sweep up on to the shore; to spoil (*colloq*; *esp* in *passive*). [OE *wæscan*, *wascan*; found in other Gmc languages eg OHGer *wascan* (Ger *waschen*); same root as **water**]

washeteria or **washateria** *wosh-ə-tē'ri-ə*, (*esp US*) *n* a launderette. [**wash** and sfx *-teria* from **cafeteria**]

washing *wosh'ing*, (*Shakesp*, *Romeo and Juliet*, I.1.69) *adj* for **swashing**.

Washingtonia *wosh-ing-tō'ni-ə*, *n* a genus of ornamental fan palms of California and Mexico; (also without *cap*) used as a name for the sequoia. [Named after George *Washington* (1732–99)]

wasm *woz'm* (*colloq*) *n* an outmoded policy, belief, theory, doctrine or enthusiasm, an ism of the past. [*was* and is*m*]

WASP or **wasp** *wosp*, (*US*, *usu derog*) *n* an acronym for *W*hite *A*nglo-*S*axon *P*rotestant, an individual qualifying for such a description supposedly representing the most privileged class in US society.

wasp[1] *wosp*, *n* any of a large number of insects belonging to the order Hymenoptera and constituting many families, including the *Vespidae*, to which the common wasp (*Vespa vulgaris*) and the European hornet (*Vespa crabro*) belong, having black-and-yellow-striped bodies, and, in the case of the female, a stinging organ; a petulant and spiteful person. — *n* **was'pie** a ladies' corset which is laced or fitted tightly to draw the waist in; a similarly cinched belt. — *adj* **was'pish** like a wasp; having a slender waist, like a wasp; quick to resent an injury; spiteful, virulent. — *adv* **was'pishly**. — *n* **was'pishness**. — *adj* **was'py** waspish. — *adj* **was'pish-head'ed** (*Shakesp*) hotheaded, passionate. — **wasp'nest**, **wasp's nest** or **wasps' nest** the nest of a wasp or of a community of wasps; a place full of enemies or angry people (*fig*); circumstances in which one is assailed indignantly from all sides (*fig*). — *adj* **wasp'-tongu'd** (*Shakesp*, 1 *Henry IV*, I.3.236; 1st quarto **wasp'-stung**, others **wasp'-tongue**) having a biting tongue, shrewish. — **wasp waist** a very slender waist reminiscent of a wasp's, *esp* contrasting with more substantial proportions above and below it. — *adj* **wasp'-waist'ed**

slender-waisted; laced tightly. [OE *wæsp*, *wæps*; cf Ger *Wespe*, L *vespa*]

wasp[2]. See **WASP**.

wassail *wos'(ā)l* or *was'l*, (*hist*) *n* the salutation uttered in drinking a person's health (*hist*); a liquor in which such healths were drunk, *esp* ale with roasted apples, sugar, nutmeg and toast (*hist*); a festive occasion; revelry; a drinking bout; a drinking or festive song. — *vi* to hold a wassail, to carouse; to sing good wishes, carols, etc from house to house at Christmas. — *vt* to drink to or pour libations for (eg fruit trees) to ensure that they thrive. — *n* **wass'ailer** someone who wassails; a reveller. — *n* **wass'ailing**. — *n* **wass'ailry**. — **wassail bout** a carouse; **wassail bowl** or **cup** a bowl or cup used in wassailing. [ON *ves heill* 'be in health']

wasserman *wos'ər-mən*, (*obs*) *n* a sea monster shaped like a man. [Ger *Wassermann*, from *Wasser* water, and *Mann* man]

Wassermann reaction *väs'ər-man rē-ak'shən*, or **test** *test*, *n* a test for syphilis made on the blood serum or cerebrospinal fluid. [A von *Wassermann* (1866–1925), German bacteriologist]

wast[1] *wost* used (*archaic* or *dialect*) as *2nd pers sing pa t* of the verb **be**. [See **was**]

wast[2], **wastfull**, **wastness**. Obsolete spellings of **waste**, **wasteful**, **wasteness**.

wast[3]. An obsolete spelling of **waist**.

waste *wāst*, *adj* rejected, superfluous; uncultivated, and at most sparsely inhabited; desolate; lying unused; unproductive; devastated, ruinous (*obs*); in a devastated condition (as in **lay waste**); empty, unoccupied; useless, vain (*obs*). — *vt* to spend, use or occupy unprofitably; to use, consume or spend too lavishly; to use or bestow where due appreciation is lacking (often in *passive*); to fail to take advantage of; to treat as waste material; to injure (an estate or property) (*law*); to devastate; to consume, wear out or impair gradually; to cause to decline, shrink physically, to enfeeble; to put an end to, kill (*obs* or *slang*); to impoverish (*obs*); to expend, spend, consume or pass (*obs*). — *vi* to be diminished, used up or impaired by degrees; to lose strength or flesh or weight (often **waste away**); (of time) to be spent (*obs*); to be used to no, or little, purpose or effect; to be guilty of waste. — *n* the act or process of wasting; superfluous, refuse or rejected material; too lavish, or useless, expenditure, or an example of it; squandering; consumption or expenditure (*obs*); a profusion (*archaic*); a waste pipe; gradual decay; destruction; loss; injury done to an estate or property by the tenant (*law*); an uncultivated, unproductive or devastated region; a vast expanse, as of ocean or air; the darkness of midnight (*Shakesp*, *Hamlet*, I.2.198, quartos 2, 3, 4; others have 'vast'); a disused working; (in *pl*) ravages (*obs*). — *adj* **wast'able**. — *n* **wāst'age** loss by use or natural decay, etc; (*esp* in the phrase **natural wastage**) loss of employees through retirement, voluntary resignation, etc rather than by forced dismissal; useless or unprofitable spending; loss, or amount of loss, through this; a devastated or ruined place (*Scot*); waste ground (*Scot*). — *adj* **wāst'ed** unexploited or squandered; exhausted, worn out; shrunken, emaciated; extremely drunk or high on drugs (*slang*; *esp US*). — *adj* **waste'ful** causing waste; extravagant, over-lavish; causing devastation, consuming, destructive (*obs* or *rare*); causing wasting of the body (*rare*); lavish (*obs*); uninhabited, unfrequented, desolate (*poetic*); vain, profitless (*obs*). — *adv* **waste'fully**. — *n* **waste'fulness**. — *n* **waste'ness** the state of being waste; a waste place (*obs*); devastation (*Bible*). — *n* **wast'er** someone or something that wastes; a spendthrift; a good-for-nothing (*colloq*); used with uncertain significance to denote a class of thief (*hist*); an inferior article, *esp* one spoilt in the making; an animal that is not thriving, or that is not suitable for breeding purposes. — *vt* (*Scot*) to use, spend extravagantly (whence *adj* **wāst'erful**, *adv* **wāst'erfully**, *n* **wāst'erfulness**). — *adj* **waste'rife** or **wast'rife** (*-rif* or *-rīf*; *Scot*) wasteful. — *n* wastefulness. — *n* **wast'ery** or **wast'ry** (*Scot*) prodigality. — *adj* improvident. — *n* **wāst'ing**. — *adj* undergoing waste; destroying, devastating; (of an illness, etc) causing emaciation, destructive of body tissues, enfeebling. — *n* **wāst'rel** a profligate, ne'er-do-well, idler; a waif (*old*); refuse (*obs*). — *adj* spendthrift; (of an animal) feeble; waste, refuse (*obs*); going to waste (*obs*). — **waste basket** (*NAm*), **waste bin**, **wastepaper basket** or **wastepaper bin** a basket or bin for holding discarded paper and other rubbish; **waste book** a daybook or journal, or a rougher record preliminary to it; **waste gate** a gate for discharging surplus water from a dam, etc; **waste ground** or (*Can*) **waste'lot** a piece of land lying unused in a built-up area; **waste'land** a desolate, barren area; a culturally or intellectually empty place or time; **waste paper** used paper no longer required for its original purpose; paper rejected as spoiled; **waste pipe** a pipe for carrying off waste or surplus water; **waste product** material produced in a process and discarded on the completion of that process; **wasting asset** any asset (*esp* a natural resource, such as a mine) whose value decreases with its depletion and which cannot be replaced or renewed. — **go to waste** to be wasted; **grow to waste** (*obs*) (of a time) to come near an end; **in waste** (*obs*) to no effect, in vain; **lay waste** to devastate; **run to waste** (*orig* of liquids) to be wasted or lost. [OFr *wast* (variant of *guast*), from L *vāstus* waste]

wastel *wos'tl*, or **wastel bread** (*bred*), (*hist*) *n* bread made from the finest flour. [OFr *wastel*, variant of *guastel*, *gastel* (Fr *gâteau* cake); of Gmc origin]

waster[1] *wās'tər*, (*hist*) *n* a wooden sword for practising fencing with; a cudgel; practice or play with a waster. — **play at waster** or **wasters** to practise fencing. [Ety uncertain]

waster[2]. See under **waste**.

waster[3] *wās'tər*, (*Scot*) *n* a four-pronged or five-pronged salmon-spear. [Earlier *wa(w)sper*, from **spear**, with spelling influenced by **leister**; ety otherwise obscure]

wasterful, **wasterife**, **wastery**, **wasting**, **wastrel**, **wastrife**, **wastry**. See under **waste**.

wat[1] *wot*, (*obs*) *n* a hare. [Prob *Wat*, for Walter]

wat[2] *wät*, (*Scot*) *adj* wet; drunken. [Variant of **wet**]

wat[3] *wät*. Scots form of **wot** (qv under **wit**[1]).

wat[4] *wät*, *n* a Thai Buddhist temple or monastery. [Sans *vātā* enclosed ground]

watap *wa'tap*, *n* fibre from conifer roots used by N American Indians for weaving or as sewing-thread. [Cree *watapiy*]

watch *woch*, *vt* to keep in view, to follow the motions of with the eyes; to observe the progress of, maintain an interest in, follow; to look at or observe attentively; (of a barrister) to attend the trial of (a case) on behalf of a client not directly involved in it; to have in one's care, to look after; to guard; to tend; to beware of danger to or from, to be on the alert to guard or guard against; to be on the alert to take advantage of (an opportunity, etc); to wait for (*obs*); to catch in an act (*Shakesp*); to keep (a hawk) from sleep, in order to tame it (*Shakesp*). — *vi* to be on the alert; to look out (with *for*); to look with attention; to keep guard; (with *over*) to keep guard over; to remain awake; to keep vigil; to attend the sick by night (*old*). — *n* a small timepiece for wearing on a strap round the wrist (also **wristwatch**), or carrying in a pocket; the state of being, or act of staying, awake (*old*); a religious vigil (*old* except in *watch night*, qv below); a vigil beside a corpse, a wake; a flock (of nightingales); a division of the night, of fixed length (*hist*); (in *pl*) the dark hours (of the night) (*poetic*); the state of remaining on the alert, being on the lookout or observing vigilantly; close observation; the activity of guarding, surveillance; the office or duty of keeping guard or of being a sentinel (**stand upon one's watch** (*Bible*) to fulfil the duty of watchman); the activity of lying in wait or in ambush; a watchman or body of watchmen; the body of men who, before the institution of a police force, patrolled the streets at night (*hist*); a sentinel, or the military guard of a place (*old*); in early 18c, a name applied to certain companies of irregular troops in the Highlands; a *usu* four-hour period of duty on deck (but see **dog-watch**) (*naut*); those members (*usu* half) of a ship's officers and crew who are on duty at the same time (the *port* or (*orig*) *larboard watch* and the *starboard watch*); a sailor's or firefighter's turn or period of duty; something that measures or marks time or the passage of time, such as a marked candle, the cry of a watchman, a clock (*obs*); the dial of a clock (*obs*). — *combining form* **-watch** denoting vigilance exercised by a community over some aspect of the environment, *esp* as the professed brief of a television programme, as in *crimewatch*. — *adj* **watch'able** that may be watched; (of an entertainment, *esp* a TV programme) having enjoyment or interest value (*colloq*). — *n* **watch'er** someone who watches; a name used for an angel or for a class of angels. — *adj* **watch'ful** habitually on the alert or cautious; watching or observing carefully; characterized by vigilance; requiring vigilance, or in which one must be on the alert; wakeful (*archaic*); spent in watching (*archaic*). — *adv* **watch'fully**. — *n* **watch'-fulness**. — *adj* **watch'ing** (*naut*; of a buoy) fully afloat. — **watch bill** a list of the officers and crew of a ship, as divided into watches, with their several stations; **watch'box** a sentry box; **watch cap** a close-fitting navy-blue cap worn by sailors in cold weather; **watch'case** the outer case of a watch; a sentry box (*Shakesp*); **watch chain** a chain for securing a watch to one's clothing; **watch clock** a watchman's clock; **watch committee** a committee of a local governing body exercising supervision over police services, etc; **watch crystal** see **watchglass** below; **watch'dog** a dog kept to guard premises and property; any person or organization closely monitoring governmental or commercial operations, etc to guard against inefficiency and illegality (also *adj*); **watch fire** a fire lit at night as a signal; a fire for the use of a watching party, sentinels, scouts, etc; **watch'glass** a sandglass; a glass covering for the face of a watch (also **watch crystal**); a small curved glass dish used in laboratories to hold small quantities of a solution, etc; **watch'guard** a chain or strap, etc used to attach a watch to the clothing; **watch house** a house in which a guard is placed; a police station or lock-up (*old*); **watching brief** instructions to a counsel to watch a legal case; (loosely) responsibility for observing developments, etc in a specific area; **watch key** a key for winding a watch; **watch light** a light used for watching or sitting up in the night; **watch'-maker** a maker or repairer of watches; **watch'making**; **watch'man** a man who watches or guards a building (or, formerly, the streets of a city) at night; **watch'man's clock** a clock recording the times of a watchman's visits; **watch night** (*relig*) in some Protestant churches, the night of Christmas Eve (24 December) or New Year's Eve (31 December); (also **watch-night service**) a service lasting through midnight held on these nights; **watch officer** the officer in charge of the ship during a watch, also called **officer of the watch**; **watch'-out** a lookout; **watch paper** a round piece of paper, often decorated, formerly put inside the outer case of a watch to prevent rubbing; **watch pocket** a small pocket for holding a watch; **watch'spring** the mainspring of a watch; **watch'strap** a strap for fastening a watch round the wrist; **watch'tower** a tower on which a sentinel is placed to look out for the approach of danger; **watch'word** the password to be given to a watch or sentry (*obs*); any word used as a signal; a maxim, slogan or rallying-cry. — **Black Watch** the 42nd and 73rd Regiments, now the 1st and 2nd Battalions of the Black Watch or Royal Highland Regiment; **on the watch** vigilant, looking out (for danger, etc); **watch after** (*Thackeray*) to follow the movements of (with one's eyes); **watch and ward** the old custom of watching by night and by day in towns and cities; uninterrupted vigilance; **watch in** to keep awake to welcome (the New Year); **watch it!** (*colloq*, *esp* admonitory) be careful!; **watch one's back** (*colloq*) to be on the alert for treacherous moves against one; **watch one's step** to step with care; to act warily, be careful not to arouse opposition, give offence, etc (*colloq*); **watch out** (*colloq*; *orig US*) to look out, be careful; **watch over** to guard, take care of; **watch up** (*Thackeray*) to sit up at night. [OE *wæcce* (noun), *wæccan*, *wacian* (verb); cognate with *wacan* to wake]

watchet *woch'it*, (*archaic*) *n* a pale blue; a material of this colour; an angling fly. — *adj* pale blue. [OFr *wachet*; perh orig a material]

wate. See under **wit**[1].

water *wö'tər*, *n* (in a state of purity, at ordinary temperatures) a clear transparent colourless liquid, perfectly neutral in its reaction, and devoid of taste or smell; extended to the same substance (H_2O) in solid or gaseous state (ice or steam); any body of this (in varying degrees of impurity), such as an ocean, lake, river, etc; the surface of a body of water; (in *pl*) waves, moving water, a body of water; a river valley (*Scot*); the position of the tide, as in *high* or *low water*; one of the four elements recognized by early natural philosophers; a quantity of the liquid used in any one stage of a washing operation; a liquid resembling or containing water; mineral water (*usu* in *pl* if at a spa); saliva; (*usu* in *pl*) the amniotic fluid, filling the space between the embryo and the amnion; applied to the fluids secreted by the body, tears, urine, sweat; rain; transparency, lustre, eg of a diamond; class, quality, excellence (*esp* in the phrase **of the first** or **purest water**); an increase in a company's stock issue without an increase in assets to back it up (*econ*). — *vt* to wet, overflow or irrigate with water; to supply (a plant) with water; to give (an animal) water to drink; to dilute or adulterate with water; to soften by soaking (*obs*); (of a river, etc) to surround (a city, etc) (*obs*; also **water about**); to wet and press (eg silk) so as to give a wavy appearance to; to increase (the debt of a company) by issuing new stock without a corresponding increase in assets. — *vi* to fill with, or shed, water; (of the mouth; also, *obs* and *Scot*, the teeth) to secrete saliva at the sight or thought of food, or (*fig*) in anticipation of anything delightful; (of an animal) to drink; to take in water. — *adj* pertaining to or used in the storage or distribution of water; worked by water; used, living or operating on or in water; by way of or across water; made with or formed by water. — *n* **wa'terage** conveyance (eg of cargo or passengers) by water; money paid for this. — *adj* **wa'tered** (of eg silk) marked with a wavy pattern by watering; (of capital or stock) increased in nominal value without any corresponding increase in assets. — *n* **wa'terer** someone or something that waters; a vessel for watering with. — *n* **wa'teriness**. — *n* **wa'tering** the process of giving, irrigating, filling, etc with water; the act of drinking (*obs*); dilution with water; the art or process of giving fabric, etc a wavy, ornamental appearance; such an appearance. — *adj* **wa'terish** resembling, abounding in or filled with water; dilute, thin, poor, insipid. — *n* **wa'terishness**. — *adj* **wa'terless**. — *adj* **wa'tery** full of water; (of eyes) moist, secreting water noticeably; pertaining to, consisting of or containing water; like water; thin or transparent; tasteless; weak, vapid; (of the sky or sun) having a rainy appearance; associated with or controlling the sea, tides, rain, etc; (of the palate) watering, eager (*Shakesp*, *Troilus and Cressida*, III.2.20). — **water bag** a bag for holding water; a camel's reticulum; **water bailiff** a custom-house officer who inspects ships on reaching or leaving port (*obs*); an official whose duty is to enforce bylaws relating to fishing, or to prevent poaching in protected waters (also, now *Scot*, **water bailie**); **water ballast** water carried by a ship to balance or redress the change of draught due to consumption of fuel or provisions or discharge of cargo; water carried for purposes of stability; **water barometer** a barometer in which water is substituted for mercury; **water barrel** or **water cask** a barrel or cask for holding water; **water**

bath a bath composed of water; a vessel of water in which other vessels can be immersed, eg in chemical work; **water battery** a voltaic battery in which the electrolyte is water; a battery nearly on a level with the water (*fortif*); **water bear** the tardigrade, a tiny invertebrate with eight legs; **Wa'ter-bearer** see **Wa'ter=carrier**; **water bed** (a bed with) a rubber or plastic mattress filled with water, sometimes used to prevent bedsores; **water beetle** any of a large number of beetles living on or in water, having fringed legs by means of which they swim easily; **water bellows** a form of blower worked eg by a column of water falling through a vertical tube, formerly used to supply a blast for furnaces; **water bird** a swimming or wading bird; **water biscuit** a thin plain biscuit made with water; **water blink** in Arctic regions, a patch of sky reflecting the colour, and hence indicating the presence, of open water; (in *pl*) the plant blinks (qv); **water blister** a blister containing watery fluid, not blood or pus; **water bloom** or **flowers** large masses of algae, chiefly blue-green, which sometimes develop very suddenly in bodies of fresh water; **water boa** the anaconda (*Eunectes murinus*); **water boatman** any of a number of aquatic leathery-winged insects one pair of whose legs is suggestive of sculls. — *adj* **wa'ter-borne** or **wa'terborne** floating on water; conveyed by water, *esp* in a boat; (of infection, etc) transmitted by means of water. — **water bottle** a leather, glass or plastic bottle for holding drinking water, carried eg by hikers; **water bouget** (*bōō'jət*; *hist*) a skin or leather bottle used to carry water, *usu* one of a pair hung on opposite ends of a yoke. — *adj* **wa'ter=bound** detained by floods; (of a macadam road or road surfacing) formed of broken stone, rolled and covered with a thin layer of hoggin, which is watered in and binds the stones together. — **water box** a water jacket; **wa'ter-brain** gid, a disease of sheep; **water brash** pyrosis, a sudden gush into the mouth of acid fluids from the stomach, accompanied by a burning sensation (heartburn) in the gullet; **water break** a piece of broken water; **wa'ter-breather** any creature that breathes by means of gills. — *adj* **wa'ter-breathing**. — **water brose** (*Scot*) brose made of meal and water alone; **water buck** any of several antelopes, *esp Cobus ellipsiprymnus*; **water buffalo** the common domestic buffalo (Bubalus) of India, etc; **water bug** any of a large variety of hemipterous insects, including water boatmen, etc, found in or beside ponds, etc; **water bull** a mythical amphibious animal like a bull; **water bus** a passenger-carrying boat plying a regular route across a lake, river, etc; **water butt** a large barrel for collecting rainwater, standing out of doors; **water cannon** a high-pressure hosepipe used to disperse crowds; **wa'ter-carriage** conveyance by water; facilities for it; **Wa'ter-carrier** or **Wa'ter-bearer** Aquarius, a constellation and the eleventh sign of the zodiac; **water cart** a cart for conveying water, *esp* for the purpose of watering streets or roads; **water cell** one of several cells in a camel's stomach used for storing water; **water cement** hydraulic cement; **water chestnut** a water plant (*Trapa natans*, or other species) of or related to the Onagraceae; its edible seed; a Chinese sedge (*Eleocharis tuberosa*), or its edible tuber; **water chute** (*shōōt* or *shōōt*) an artificial cascade or slope leading to water, down which people (sometimes in boats or toboggans) slide for sport; **water clerk** (*old*) an employee of a ship's chandler, who sails about the harbour to seek custom from the ships about to dock; **water clock** a clock that works by means of flowing water; a clepsydra; **water closet** (*abbrev* **WC**) a lavatory of which the pan is flushed by water; a small room containing such a lavatory; **water cock** the kora, a large E Indian gallinule; **wa'tercolour** or (*US*) **wa'ter-color** a pigment diluted with water and gum (or other substance) instead of oil; a painting in such a colour or colours; **wa'tercolourist** or (*US*) **wa'tercolorist** a painter in watercolours. — *vt* **wa'ter-cool** to cool (eg an engine) by means of water, *esp* circulating water. — *adj* **wa'ter-cooled**. — **wa'ter-cooler** a machine for cooling by means of water or for keeping water cool. — *adj* and *n* **wa'ter-cooling**. — **wa'ter-core** (in an apple or other fruit) an abnormality consisting of water-soaked tissue, *esp* close to the core; (**water core**) (in founding) a hollow core through which water may be passed; **wa'tercourse** a channel through which water flows or has flowed; an artificial water channel; a stream or river; **water cow** a female water buffalo or water bull; **wa'tercraft** a boat; boats collectively; skill in swimming, etc, or in managing boats; **water crane** an apparatus for supplying water from an elevated tank, *esp* to a locomotive tender; a hydraulic crane; **wa'ter-cress** (often, *esp* formerly, in *pl*) a perennial cress (*Nasturtium officinale*) growing in watery places, used as a salad; **water culture** a method of cultivation, often an experimental means of determining the mineral requirements of a plant, the plant being grown with its roots dipping into solutions of known composition; **water cure** medical treatment by means of water, hydrotherapy; **water cycle** the cycle in which water from the sea evaporates into the atmosphere, later condenses and falls to earth as rain or snow, then evaporates directly back into the atmosphere or returns to the sea by rivers; **water deck** a decorated canvas cover for a dragoon's saddle; **water deer** a small Chinese musk deer of aquatic habits; in Africa, one of the chevrotains; **wa'ter-diviner** a person who, *usu* with the help of a divining-rod, detects or tries to detect the presence of underground water; **water doctor** a hydropathist; (formerly) a doctor who divined diseases from the urine; **water dog** any variety of dog (formerly a specific variety, a small poodle) valuable to sportsmen in hunting waterfowl on account of its aquatic habits; a water vole; an otter (*obs*); any of various other animals; an experienced sailor (*colloq*); a good swimmer; a small irregular floating cloud supposed to indicate rain; **wa'ter-drinker** a drinker of water; a teetotaller; **wa'terdrive** the use of water pressure, either occurring naturally or by waterflood (qv), to drive oil, gas, etc from a reservoir; **water drop** a drop of water; a tear; **water dropwort** a genus (*Oenanthe*) of umbelliferous plants, including the common water dropwort (*Oenanthe fistulosa*) and hemlock water dropwort, or water hemlock (*Oenanthe crocata*). — *adj* **wa'tered=down** much diluted; reduced in vigour, modified, attenuated. — **water elder** the guelder rose; **water engine** an engine for raising water; an engine worked by water; an engine for extinguishing fires (*obs*); **water equivalent** thermal capacity, the product of the specific heat of a body and its mass; **wa'terfall** a fall or perpendicular descent of a body of water, a cataract or cascade; a necktie (*obs*); a chignon (*obs*); **water fern** any of the Hydropterideae or rhizocarps, water or marsh plants differing from ferns in the narrower sense in being heterosporous, classified in two families, Marsileaceae and Salviniaceae; **wa'ter-finder** a water-diviner; **water flag** the yellow iris; **water flea** the common name for any of numerous minute aquatic crustaceans; **water flood** an inundation; (**wa'terflood**) the process or an instance of **wa'terflooding**, the practice, in oil, gas or petroleum production, of injecting water to maintain pressure in a reservoir and to drive the oil, etc towards the production wells; **water flow** a current of water. — *adj* **wa'ter-flowing** streaming. — **water fly** an aquatic insect; an insignificant, troublesome person (*Shakesp*); **wa'terfowl** a fowl that frequents water; swimming game birds collectively; **water frame** Arkwright's spinning-machine, which was driven by water; **wa'terfront** the buildings or part of a town along the edge of and facing the sea, a river, etc; **water gall** (*obs* and *dialect*) a watery appearance in the sky accompanying the rainbow; a secondary rainbow; **water gap** a gap in a mountain range containing a stream; **water gas** a mixed gas obtained by passing steam (**blue water gas**) or steam and air (**semiwater gas**) over incandescent coke, or other source of carbon; **water gate** a floodgate; a gate admitting to a river or other body of water; a street leading to the water (*Scot*); see also separate article for **Watergate**; **water gauge** or **gage** an instrument for measuring the quantity or height of water; water pressure expressed in inches, in terms of the height of the head of water; an instrument for measuring differences in pressure (*mining*); **wa'ter-gilding** wash-gilding; **water glass** a water clock; an instrument for making observations beneath the surface of water; a glass vessel for containing water, eg one for holding plants; a finger bowl (*obs*); a tumbler; (**wa'terglass**) a concentrated and viscous solution of sodium or potassium silicate in water, used as adhesive, protective covering, etc, and (*esp* formerly) for preserving eggs; **water god** a deity presiding over a tract of water; **water gong** (*music*) the effect of dipping a vibrating gong into and raising it out of water to produce upward and downward glissandos; **water gruel** gruel made with water; anything insipid; **water guard** river, harbour or coast police; **water hammer** a wave of increased pressure travelling through water in a pipe caused by a sudden stoppage or change in the water flow; the concussion and noise so caused; **water head** the source, eg of a stream; the region where this is found; a dammed-up body of water, or its quantity, height or pressure; **wa'ter-heater** an apparatus for heating domestic water; **water hemlock** a poisonous plant, *Cicuta virosa*; any other plant of the same genus; water dropwort (qv); **wa'terhen** the gallinule or moorhen, or other bird of the rail genus; **water hole** a pool in which water has collected, eg a spring in a desert or a pool in the dried-up course of a river; **water horse** a water spirit like a horse; a kelpie; **water hyacinth** a tropical floating aquatic plant (*Eichhornia crassipes*) with bluish flowers, that grows in thick masses in ponds, etc; **water ice** sweetened fruit juice or purée diluted with water, frozen and served as a kind of ice cream, a sorbet; **wa'tering-call** a cavalry trumpet signal to water horses; **wa'tering-can** or **-pot** a vessel used for watering plants; **wa'tering-cap** (*obs*) a cavalryman's fatigue cap; **wa'tering-hole** a water hole, where animals go to drink; a place where humans seek (*esp* alcoholic) refreshment, a pub (*facetious*); **wa'tering-house** (*obs*) an inn or other place where horses are watered; **wa'tering-place** a place where water may be obtained; a place to which people resort to drink mineral water, or for bathing, etc; **wa'tering-trough** a trough from which horses and cattle drink; a trough between the rails containing water to be scooped up by locomotives; **water jacket** a casing containing water placed round eg the cylinder block of an internal-combustion engine to keep it cool (also **water box**); **water jet**. — *adj* (**wa'ter-jet**) operated by a jet of water. — **water joint** a joint in a pavement that is raised to prevent water lying in it; a joint in sheet-metal roofing forming a channel for rainwater; **water jump** a place where a jump across a stream, pool, ditch, etc, has to be made, eg in a steeplechase; **water key** (*music*) in brass instruments, a sprung lever that allows drainage of accumulated moisture; **water leaf** any plant of the genus *Hydrophyllum* or the family *Hydrophyllaceae*, N American herbs with sharply toothed leaves and cymose flowers; an ornament used in the capitals of columns, probably representing the leaf of some water plant (*archit*); **water lemon** a species of passion-flower, or its edible fruit; **water lens** a simple lens formed by placing a few drops of water in a vessel, eg a small brass cell with blackened sides and a glass bottom; **water level** the level formed by the surface of still water; an instrument in which water is used for establishing a horizontal line of sight; a water table (*geol*); a slightly inclined road to carry off water (*mining*); **wa'terlily** a name commonly given to the different species of Nymphaea and Nuphar, and also to other members of the family Nymphaeaceae (the three British species are the white waterlily *Nymphaea alba*, and the yellow waterlilies *Nuphar luteum* and *Nuphar minimum*, the latter being rare); **wa'terline** any of several lines on a ship to which it is submerged under different conditions of loading, eg the *light waterline* marking the depth when it is without cargo; any of certain lines on a vessel parallel with the water showing the contour of the hull at various heights (*shipbuilding*); the water level; the outline of a coast; a chain line in laid paper, one of the wider-spaced of the two sets of lines intersecting at right angles, visible by transmitted light (vertical in a folio or octavo page and horizontal in a quarto one). — *vt* **wa'terlog** to make (a boat, etc) unmanageable by flooding with water; to saturate with water so as to make heavy, inert or unfit for use, or so as to impede life or growth (also *fig*). — *adj* **wa'terlogged**. — **water lot** a piece or lot of ground that is under water; **water main** a large subterranean pipe supplying water; **wa'terman** a man who plies a boat for hire, a boatman, a ferryman; a good oarsman; a person whose job is to supply water, eg (*hist*) to cab horses or coach horses; an imaginary being living in water; **wa'termanship** oarsmanship; **wa'termark** the line of the greatest height to which water has risen; a tidemark; a ship's waterline; a distinguishing mark in paper, a design visible by transmitted light, made by the mould or the dandy roll. — *vt* to mark with a watermark; to impress as a watermark. — **water meadow** a meadow kept fertile by flooding from a stream; **water measure** a measurement used for goods such as coal, salt, etc sold on board ship, the bushel, etc being larger than the standard bushel, etc (*hist*); **wa'termelon** a plant (*Citrullus vulgaris*) of the cucumber family, of African origin, having a large, pulpy, pleasantly flavoured fruit; the fruit itself; **water meter** an instrument for measuring the quantity of water passing through a particular outlet; **water milfoil** see under **milfoil**; **water mill** a mill driven by water; **water mocassin** a poisonous snake of the southern United States; **water mole** the desman, a shrew-like aquatic animal; the duckbill or platypus; **water monkey** a round, narrow-necked, porous earthenware jar for holding drinking-water, used in hot climates (also **monkey jar**); **water motor** any water wheel or turbine, *esp* any small motor driven by water under pressure; **water mouse** the water vole; any mouse of the genus Hydromys (*Austr*); **water music** (*hist*) music performed, or composed for performance, during an excursion by water; **water nixie** a nixie; **water nymph** a nymph inhabiting water, *esp* a naiad of Greek mythology; **water opossum** the yapok, an amphibious opossum of S America; **water ouzel** the dipper, an aquatic songbird of the genus *Cinclus*; **water parsnip** any plant of the aquatic umbelliferous genus Sium, *esp* the skirret; **wa'ter-parting** a watershed or divide; **water pepper** a very acrid persicaria (*Polygonum hydropiper*) of wet places; **water pipe** a pipe for conveying water; a hookah; **water pistol** a weapon or toy for shooting a jet of water or other liquid; **water plane** a plane passing through any waterline of a ship; the plane of the surface of water; a canal on the level without locks (*hist*); a seaplane; **water plant** a plant that grows in water; **water plantain** a plant (*Alisma plantago*) having plantain-like leaves and clustered white or pink flowers; any other plant of the Alisma genus; **water plate** a plate having a double bottom enclosing a space for hot water, used to keep food warm; **water poet** a writer of doggerel verse (after John Taylor, 1580–1653, a writer of jingling verses, etc, who was for a time a Thames waterman and called himself 'the Water-poet'); **water polo** an aquatic ball game played by swimmers, seven a side; a similar game played by contestants in canoes; **water pore** (*bot*) a hydathode, a water-secreting organ; a madreporite, a sieve-like calcareous plate in certain echinoderms; **water pot** a pot or vessel for holding water; **water potential** (*bot*) a measure of the free energy of water in a solution, eg in a cell or soil sample, and hence of its tendency to move by diffusion, osmosis or in vapour form; **water power** the power of water, employed to move machinery, etc; a flow or fall of water which may be so used; **wa'terpox** varicella, ie chickenpox; **water privilege** the right to the use of water, *esp* for driving machinery; a place where this right may be exercised. — *adj* **wa'terproof** coated eg with rubber or plastic, so as to be impervious to water; so constructed as to exclude water. — *n* a material or an outer garment made impervious to water. — *vt* and *vi* to make or become impervious to water, *esp* through the process of coating with a solution. — **wa'terproofing** the process of making any substance impervious to water; the material with which this is done; **water pump** a pump for raising water; the eye (*humorous*); **water purpie** the plant brooklime; **wa'terquake** a seismic disturbance affecting the sea; **water rail** the common rail (*Rallus aquaticus*) of Europe, a long-beaked wading marsh bird; **water ram** a hydraulic ram; **water rat** the popular name of the water vole; the American muskrat; a pirate; a sailor or boatman; **water rate** a rate or tax for the supply of water; **water reactor** a water-cooled nuclear reactor. — *adj* **wa'ter-repell'ent** (of a fabric, etc) treated so as not to absorb water. — *adj* **wa'ter-resis'tant** (treated so as to be) resistant to penetration by water. — **water rice** a tall aquatic grass, genus *Zizania*; **water rug** a kind of water dog, *perh* from **rug**[1] (*Shakesp*, *Macbeth*, III.1.94); **water sail** (*naut*) on square rigged ships, a fine-weather sail set below a lower studding-sail, almost touching the water; **water sapphire** (translating Fr *saphir d'eau*) an intense blue variety of cordierite used as a gemstone; **water seal** a seal formed by water in a trap; **wa'tershed** the line of high ground separating two river basins; a drainage or a catchment area (*erron*); a slope or structure down which water flows; a crucial point or dividing line between two phases, conditions, etc; **water shoot** a channel for the overflow of water; a water chute. — *adj* **wa'ter-shot** (*rare*) crossed by streams. — **wa'terside** the edge of a sea, lake, etc, a shore. — Also *adj*. — **wa'ter-ski** a water-planing ski used in **wa'ter-skiing**, the sport of being towed at speed on skis behind a motorboat. — Also *vi*: — *pr p* **wa'ter-skiing**; *pa t* and *pa p* **wa'ter-skied** or **wa'ter-ski'd**. — **wa'ter-skier**; **wa'tersmeet** the confluence of two streams; **water smoke** water evaporating as visible mist; **water snail** (*esp US*) a name for the Archimedean screw (qv); **water snake** any of various kinds of snake (*esp* of genus *Natrix*) frequenting fresh water; **wa'ter-softener** a device or substance for removing the causes of hardness in water; **water soldier** an aquatic plant (*Stratiotes aloides*) with sword-like leaves and white flowers reminiscent of plumes of feathers, common in lakes and ditches in the east of England. — *adj* **wa'ter-soluble** soluble in water. — **water souchy** (*sōō'chi* or *sōō'shi*) fish served in the water in which it is boiled (Du *waterzootje*, from *zootje* boiling); **water spaniel** a spaniel bred to retrieve waterfowl, the **Irish water spaniel** having a liver-coloured coat; **water spider** an aquatic spider, *esp* *Argyroneta aquatica*, which has an underwater bell-shaped web inflated with air carried down in bubbles; **water spirit** a water sprite; **water splash** a shallow stream running across a road; **water sports** sports practised on or in the water; sexual arousal or gratification associated with urination (*colloq*); **wa'terspout** a pipe, etc from which water spouts; the spout of water; a torrential downpour of rain; a disturbance like a very small tornado, a revolving column of cloud, mist or spray; **water spring** (*Bible*) a spring; **wa'ter-sprin'kle** (*Spenser*) a spray of water; a sprinkle; **water sprite** a spirit inhabiting water. — *adj* **wa'ter-standing** (*Shakesp*) brimming with tears. — **water starwort** a water plant, genus *Callitriche*; **wa'ter-strider** any long-legged aquatic insect of the family *Hydrobatidae*; **water supply** the obtaining and distribution of water, eg to a community; the amount of water thus distributed; **water table** a moulding, *esp* in the string course of a building, designed to throw rainwater outwards so that it does not flow down the wall below (*archit*); the level below which fissures and pores in the strata are saturated with water (*geol*); **water tap** a tap or cock used for letting out water; **water thermometer** a thermometer filled with water instead of mercury, and used for showing the point at which water has its greatest density; **water thief** (*Shakesp*) a pirate; **water thrush** either of two species of American warbler (*Seiurus motacilla* or *S. noveboracensis*) with brownish backs and striped underparts, living near water; **water thyme** the waterweed anacharis. — *adj* **wa'tertight** so well-seated as not to admit water or let it escape; (of an argument, etc) such that no flaw, weakness or source of misinterpretation can be found in it. — **watertight compartment** a section of a ship's hull or other underwater structure so formed that water cannot enter it from any other part; a part, *esp* of one's thoughts or beliefs, shut off from the influence of other parts; **wa'tertightness**; **water tortoise** a terrapin or other aquatic tortoise, eg *Pelomedusa subrufa*; **water torture** torture using water, *esp* dripping it slowly on to the victim's forehead; **water tower** a tower containing tanks in which water is stored so that it may be delivered at sufficient pressure for distribution to an area; a vertical pipe supplied with water under high pressure, used in fire-fighting; **water tunnel** (*aeronautics*) a tunnel in which water is circulated instead of air to obtain a visual representation of flow; **water twist** a kind of cotton yarn, first made by the water frame; in spinning, more than the usual amount of twist; **water vapour** water in gaseous form, *esp* when evaporation has occurred at a temperature below boiling-point. — *adj* **wa'ter-vas'cular** relating to vessels in certain invertebrates which contain a mixture of water and a nutritive fluid; in echinoderms, relating to the system of coelomic canals (**water-vascular system**) associated with the tube feet and supplying fluid for their movement. — **water vine** a name for various plants yielding a refreshing watery sap; **water violet** a plant of the genus *Hottonia* of aquatic herbs with racemose flowers and crowded submerged leaves; **water vole** a large British vole, *Arvicola amphibius*, commonly known as the water rat; **water wagon** a wagon used to convey water; abstinence from alcohol, as in *be* or *go on the water wagon* (*colloq*); **water wagtail** a wagtail, *esp* the pied wagtail; **water wave** a wave of water; a wave in the hair made by setting it when wet. — *vt* (**wa'ter-wave**) to make such a wave in (hair). — **wa'terway** a series of pieces of timber, extending round a ship at the junction of the decks with the sides, having a groove connecting with the scuppers to carry off water; any channel for water; a stretch of navigable water; a route over, or by, water; **wa'terweed** any plant with very small flowers and leaves growing in ponds, etc, *esp* anacharis (qv); **water wheel** a wheel moved by water; an engine for raising water; **water wings** a wing-like inflated device that fits across the chest, or a pair of inflatable armbands, for keeping a non-swimmer, *esp* a child learning to swim, afloat in water; **water witch** a dowser; **wa'terwork** (*usu* in *pl*) any apparatus or plant by which water is supplied, eg to a town; (*usu* in *pl*) an ornamental fountain, cascade, etc (*obs*); fabric painted to look like and be used like tapestry (*hist*); tear-shedding, weeping (*humorous*); the urinary system (*euphem*). — *adj* **wa'ter-worn** worn by the action of water. — **water yam** a plant with farinaceous rootstock, the lattice leaf. — **above water** out of difficulties, *esp* financial; **by water** using water transport, by ship, boat, etc; **cast someone's water** (*obs*) to examine someone's urine to aid in the diagnosis of disease; **high water** and **high-watermark** see under **high**; **hold water** (of an argument, etc) to be correct or well-grounded, to bear examination; **in deep water** or **waters** in water too deep for safety; in trouble, difficulty or distress, *esp* of the financial kind; **keep one's head above water** to keep solvent; **like water** copiously; extravagantly, recklessly; **like water off a duck's back** (of a scolding, etc) having no effect, making no impression; **low water** and **low-watermark** see under **low**; **make a hole in the water** (*slang*) to drown oneself; **make the mouth water** to arouse a delightful feeling of anticipation or desire; **make water** (of a boat) to leak, take in water; **make** or **pass water** to urinate; **of the first** or **purest water** see **water** (*n*); **pour oil on troubled waters** to take measures to calm down a stormy state of affairs, from the effect of pouring oil on rough water; **pour** or **throw cold water on** or **over** to discourage by one's indifference or dismissiveness; **still waters run deep** a quiet exterior often conceals strong emotions, resolution, cunning, etc; **test the water** or **waters** to try to ascertain probable reaction or response before making a proposal, selling a product, etc; **under water** below the surface; **water down** (*lit* and *fig*) to dilute, make less strong, attenuate; **water of crystallization** or **hydration** the water present in hydrated compounds, which, when crystallized from solution in water, retain a definite amount of water; **water of life** spiritual refreshment; whisky, brandy, etc; **water on the brain** hydrocephalus; **water on the knee** an accumulation of serous fluid in the knee joint; **water under the bridge** experiences that are over and done with; past problems that have been forgotten or put down to experience. [OE *wæter*; cf Du *water*, Ger *Wasser*; cognate with Gr *hydōr*, L *ūdus* wet, *unda* a wave, Sans *udan* water]

Watergate *wö'tər-gāt*, *n* the US political scandal involving an attempted break-in at the Democratic Party headquarters (the *Watergate* building, Washington D.C.) in 1972 by agents employed by President Richard Nixon's re-election organization, and the subsequent attempted cover-up by senior White House officials who had approved the break-in; hence any similar political or public scandal, *esp* one involving corruption, or misuse of power; see also **-gate**.

Waterloo *wö-tər-lōō'*, or *wö'*, *n* a final defeat. — **Waterloo cracker** (*obs*) a kind of firework. — **meet one's Waterloo** to be finally and decisively defeated. [*Waterloo*, near Brussels, where Napoleon was finally defeated in 1815]

waterman ... to ... **watery**. See under **water**.

Watling Street *wot'ling strēt*, *n* one of the great Roman highways of Britain, running from near London through St Albans to Wroxeter; often extended at either end to include the roads to Dover and Chester; loosely applied to other Roman roads; the Milky Way (*obs*). [OE *Wæclinga strǣt* the street of Wæcel's people (of whom nothing is known); the OE name of St Albans was *Wæclinga ceaster*]

wats. See under **wit**[1].

watt *wot*, *n* the practical and MKS unit of power, equal to a rate of working of one joule per second. — *n* **watt'age** an amount of power expressed in watts. — **watt'-hour'** a common unit of electrical energy, being the work done by one watt acting for one hour; **watt'meter** an instrument containing a series (*current*) and a shunt (*voltage*) coil whose combined torque produces a deflection of the needle that is a direct measure of the circuit power in watts. [James *Watt* (1736–1819)]

Watteau *wot'ō*, *adj* applied to articles or features of women's dress resembling those seen in the paintings of Antoine *Watteau* (1684–1721), as in **Watteau bodice**, one with a square opening at the neck and short sleeves. — *adj* **Watt'eauish**.

wattle[1] *wot'l*, *n* (collective *sing* or in *pl*) material for fences, roofs, etc, in the form of rods and branches, etc, either interwoven to form a network or loose; a hurdle (*dialect*); a twig or flexible rod (*dialect*); any of various Australian acacias; (*perh* a word of separate origin) the coloured fleshy excrescence under the throat of some birds, or a similar excrescence or process on any part of the head of a bird, fish, etc. — *vt* to bind with wattle or twigs; to form by plaiting twigs. — *adj* **watt'led**. — *n* **watt'ling** the act of making wattles by interweaving twigs, etc; wattlework, or the material for it. — **watt'lebark** the bark of various acacias, used for tanning; **wattle bird** or **watt'lebird** any of a number of honey-eaters of Australia that have ear wattles; **watt'lework** wickerwork. — **wattle and daub** or **dab** wattlework plastered with mud and used as a building material. [OE *watul*, *watel*; origin uncertain]

wattle[2] *wot'l*, (*hist*; *Orkney* and *Shetland*) *n* the obligation to entertain the foud on his annual journey, or a tax for which it was later commuted. [Perh Norw dialect *veitla*, from ON *veizla* entertainment]

waucht. See **waught**.

wauff. Variant of **waff**[1,2].

waugh[1] *wö*, *interj* expressing sorrow, anger, etc, *usu* attributed to N American Indians.

waugh[2]. See **waff**[3].

waught or **waucht** *wöhht*, (*Scot*) *n* a large draught. — *vt* and *vi* to drink in large draughts. [Perh connected with **quaff**]

wauk and **wauk-mill**. See **waulk**.

waukrife. Same as **wakerife** (see under **wake**[1]).

waul[1] or **wawl** *wöl*, *vi* to cry like a cat or a newborn baby. — Also *n*. — *n* and *adj* **waul'ing** or **wawl'ing**. [Imit]

waul[2] or **wawl** *wöl*, (*Scot*; *obs*) *vi* to roll the eyes; (of the eyes) to roll. [OE *wealwian* to roll, wallow]

waulk, walk or **wauk** *wök*, *vt* to full (cloth). — *n* **waulk'er, walk'er** or **wauk'er** a fuller of cloth. — **waulk'ing-, walk'ing-** or **wauk'ing-song** a song for singing while fulling cloth, *specif* one sung in Gaelic by Hebridean women, its beat setting or reflecting the work rhythm; **waulk'mill, walk'mill** or **wauk'mill** a fulling-mill. [Orig the same verb as **walk**[1] (qv)]

waur, waurst. See **war**[2].

wave *wāv*, *n* a ridge on the surface of a liquid, *esp* of the sea; a surge, consisting of vibrating particles of liquid, moving across the surface of a body of liquid such as the sea (*transverse wave*), the vibrations of the individual particles being at right angles to the line of advance; a unit disturbance in any travelling system of vibrating particles such as a light wave (*transverse wave*) or a sound wave (*longitudinal wave*, the vibrations of the particles being in the direction of advance); an undulating or vibratory motion (eg as a signal), or sound; the sea, or other body of water (*poetic*); curved inequality of surface; a line or streak like a wave; an undulation; an undulating succession of curves in hair, or one of these; a movement of the raised hand expressing greeting, farewell etc; a swell or increase, normally followed by a subsidence or decline; any movement suggestive of a surge, *esp* one of a series or progression. — *vi* to move like a wave; to move backwards and forwards; to float or hover (*obs*); to flutter; to make a signal in this way; to move the raised hand in greeting, farewell, etc or as a signal or sign; to undulate; (of hair) to have a wave or waves, be full of waves; to waver, vacillate (*obs*). — *vt* to move backwards and forwards; to brandish; to flutter; to waft or beckon; to express by a wave; to direct, signal an instruction to, by a wave; to raise into inequalities of surface; to give an undulating appearance to (hair). — *adj* **waved** showing a wavelike form or outline; undulating; (of hair) artificially made to undulate; indented (*heraldry*); having on the margin a succession of curved segments or incisions. — *adj* **wave'less**. — *n* **wave'let** a little wave. — *adj* **wave'like**. — *n* and *adj* **wā'ving**. — **wave'band** (*radio*) a range of wavelengths occupied by transmission of a particular type; **wave energy** or **power** energy or power derived, by some means of conversion, from the movement of sea waves; **wave equation** (*phys*) a differential equation that describes the passage of harmonic waves through a medium; **wave'form** or **wave'shape** (*phys*) a graph showing variation of amplitude of electrical signal, or other wave, against time; **wave'front** (*phys*) in a propagating vibratory disturbance, the continuous locus of points which are in the same phase of vibration; **wave function** (*phys*) a mathematical equation representing the space and time variations in amplitude for a wave system; **wave'guide** (*electronics*) a hollow metal conductor, *usu* rectangular, within which very high-frequency energy can be transmitted efficiently; **wave'length** the distance between two successive similar points on an alternating wave, eg between successive maxima or between successive minima; the distance, measured radially from the source, between two successive points in free space at which an electromagnetic wave has the same phase; such a distance serving to identify radio waves from a particular transmitter (*radio*); **wave mechanics** (*phys*) the part of quantum mechanics dealing with the wave aspect of the behaviour of radiations; **wave'meter** an instrument for measuring wavelengths, directly or indirectly; **wave motion** undulatory movement; motion in waves, or according to the same laws; **wave number** (*phys*) in an electromagnetic wave, the reciprocal of the wavelength, ie the number of waves in unit distance; **wave offering** an ancient Jewish custom of moving the hands in succession towards the four points of the compass in presenting certain offerings, *opp* to the *heave offering*, in which the hands were only lifted up and lowered; **wave-particle duality** the circumstance that light and other electromagnetic radiation behave like a wave motion when being propagated and like particles when interacting with matter; **wave power** see **wave energy**; **waveshape** see **waveform**; **wave theory** (*phys*; *esp hist*) the theory that light or other radiation is transmitted in the form of waves; **wave train** a group of similar waves, of limited duration, produced by a single disturbance. — **make waves** to create a disturbance, make trouble; **on the same wavelength as** in tune with, having the same attitude of mind, background knowledge, etc; **wave aside** to dismiss (a suggestion, etc) as irrelevant or unimportant; **wave down** to signal to stop by waving; **wave off** to wave to (someone moving out of sight on departure) by way of farewell. [OE *wafian* to wave; cf ON *vafra* to waver; noun also an alteration of ME *wage*, *wawe* flood, wave]

waveband ... to ... **wavelike**. See under **wave**.

wavellite *wā'və-līt*, *n* hydrated phosphate of aluminium, occurring commonly in flattened globular aggregates, showing a strongly developed internal radiating structure. [Dr William *Wavel* or *Wavell*, (died 1829) who discovered the mineral near Barnstaple]

wavemeter. See under **wave**.

waver *wā'vər*, *vi* to move to and fro; to shake, be unsteady, be in danger of falling; to falter, show signs of giving way; to vacillate; to vary, change. — *n* **wā'verer**. — *n* and *adj* **wā'vering**. — *adv* **wā'veringly** in a wavering or irresolute manner. — *n* **wā'veringness**. — *adj* **wā'very** or **wā'verous** unsteady. [ON *vafra* to flicker]

WAVES or **waves** *wāvz*, *n pl* or *sing* (*US*) the women's reserve of the US navy. [*W*omen *A*ccepted for *V*oluntary *E*mergency *S*ervice]

waveshape. See under **wave**.

waveson *wāv'sən*, (*rare*) *n* goods floating on the sea after a shipwreck. [Poss by analogy from Anglo-Fr *floteson* flotsam]

wavey or **wavy** *wā'vi*, *n* the snow goose. [Cree]

waving. See under **wave**.

wavy[1] *wāvi adj* (of hair) forming undulations, full of waves; (of a line, etc) describing a series of curves in alternating directions; like waves in shape or movement; curving, undulating; fluctuating, wavering. — *adv* **wā'vily**. — *n* **wā'viness** the state or quality of being wavy. — **Wavy Navy** the Royal Naval Volunteer Reserve, so called from the undulating gold braid on officers' sleeves. [**wave**]

wavy[2]. See **wavey**.

waw (*Scott*) or **wawe** (*Spenser*) *wö*, *n* a wave. [ME *wage*, *wawe* prob from a lost OE form akin to *wæg* wave]

wawl. See **waul**[1,2].

wax[1] *waks*, *n* any of a class of substances of plant or animal origin, *usu* consisting of esters of monohydric alcohols, eg beeswax, $C_{30}H_{61}O{\cdot}CO{\cdot}C_{15}H_{31}$; any of certain hydrocarbons of mineral origin, eg ozokerite; any substance like a wax in some respect, such as ear wax or cerumen; sealing-wax, prepared from shellac and turpentine; a resinous material used by shoemakers to rub their thread; puddled clay (*mining*); a thick sugary substance made by boiling down the sap of the sugar maple, and cooling by exposure to the air; a person found to be readily impressionable or easily influenced; in *Shakesp*, *Timon*, I.1.48, explanation uncertain (according to some, wax tablets; others have thought expansive growth, ie properly from **wax**[2]). — *vt* to coat or treat with wax, *esp* so as to render waterproof; to smear, rub or (*obs*) join with wax. — *adj* **waxed** (of a fabric or garment) made waterproof by being treated with wax. — *adj* **wax'en** made of wax; like wax; easily impressed, penetrated, effaced. — *n* **wax'er** someone or something that waxes. — *adv* **wax'ily**. — *n* **wax'iness**. — *n* **wax'ing**. — *adj* **wax'y** resembling wax in texture or appearance; soft; impressible; impressionable; pallid, pasty. — **wax'berry** the wax myrtle or its waxy-surfaced fruit; **wax'bill** any of various small seed-eating birds of the weaverfinch family with coloured bills like sealing-wax; **wax'chandler** a maker of, or dealer in, wax candles; **wax'cloth** (*old*) another name for both oilcloth and linoleum; **wax doll** a child's doll having the head and bust made of hardened beeswax; **waxed leather** leather finished with a high wax polish on the flesh side; **wax end** or (better) **waxed end** a strong thread having its end stiffened by shoemakers' wax, so as to go easily through the hole made by the awl; **wax flower** an artificial flower made of wax; any of several plants, eg a white-flowered climbing plant of Madagascar, an epiphyte of British Guiana, and plants of the genus *Eriostemon* of Australia; **wax insect** an insect that secretes wax, eg any of several of the Coccidae, etc; **wax light** a candle or taper made of wax; **wax moth** a bee moth (qv), destructive to young bees; **wax myrtle** the US candleberry tree; **wax painting** encaustic (qv) painting; **wax palm** either of two S American palms yielding wax; **wax paper** paper spread with a thin coating of white wax and other materials; **wax plant** any of several plants of the genus Hoya, *esp Hoya carnosa* of Australia and E Asia, an asclepiadaceous climbing plant, with clusters of waxy white or pink star-shaped flowers, and succulent leaves; **wax pocket** in bees, a ventral abdominal pouch that secretes wax. — *adj* **wax'-proofed** made waterproof with a coating of wax. — *adj* **wax'-red** (*Shakesp*) bright red like sealing-wax. — **wax tablet** (*hist*) a wax-coated wooden writing-tablet, for use with a stylus; **wax tree** a tree from which wax is obtained, eg a Japanese sumac (*Rhus succedanea*), the wax myrtle, a privet (*Ligustrum lucidum*), etc; **wax'wing** a member of a genus of passerine birds (*Bombycilla*) with small red horny appendages, resembling red sealing-wax, on their wings; **wax'work** work done in wax; a figure or object modelled in wax; (in *pl*) an exhibition of wax figures; **wax'worker**; **waxy degeneration** a morbid process by which the healthy tissue of various organs is transformed into a peculiar waxy albuminous substance. — **lost wax** see **cire perdue**; **wax up** (of a mare about to foal) to develop a sticky covering over the teats. [OE *weax*; ON *vax*, Du *was*, Ger *Wachs*]

wax[2] *waks*, *vi* to grow or increase; (of the moon as it passes through its phases from new moon to full moon) to show, night by night, an increasing area of illuminated surface (*opp* to *wane*); to pass into another state, become, as in *wax lyrical*: — *pa p* (*archaic*) **wax'en** grown — also (*obs*) *pa t pl* (as in *Shakesp*, *Midsummer Night's Dream*, II.1.56) and *infinitive*. — **wax and wane** to increase and decrease in alternating sequence. [OE *weaxan*; ON *vaxa*, Ger *wachsen*, related to L *augēre* to increase, Gr *auxanein*]

wax[3] *waks*, (*colloq*) *n* a passion, a fit of anger. — *adj* **wax'y** (*colloq*) irate, incensed. [Origin uncertain]

waxberry ... to ... **waxcloth**. See under **wax**[1].

waxen. See **wax**[1,2].

waxer ... to ... **waxwork**. See under **wax**[1].

waxy. See **wax**[1,3].

way[1] *wā*, *n* passage; a road, street, track; (with *cap*) used in street names; direction of motion; the correct or desired route or path; length of space, distance (also in *pl* (*colloq*, *esp US*)); district; room or opportunity to advance; freedom of action, scope; manner of life; established routine; position, as in *wrong way up*, *other way round*, etc; condition, state; advance in life; normal or habitual course or conduct; (in *pl*) a characteristic feature of behaviour, an idiosyncrasy; manner, style; method; means; course; respect; will; progress, forward motion, as in *edge one's way*, *eat one's way through*, etc; progress or motion through the water, headway (*naut*); the direction of the weave, grain, etc; (in *pl*) the machined surfaces of the top of a lathe bed on which the carriage slides, shears (*eng*); (in *pl*) the framework of timbers on which a ship slides when being launched. — *vi* (*Spenser*) to journey. — *adj* **way'less** without a path. — **way baggage** (*US*) baggage to be laid down at a way station; **way'bill** a list of passengers and goods carried by a public vehicle; a document giving details regarding goods sent by rail or road vehicle, etc; a list of places to be visited on a journey; **way'board** or **weigh'board** a thin stratum or seam separating thicker strata (*geol*); **way'bread** (*dialect*; OE *wegbræde*, from *brād* broad, flat) the common plantain. — *vi* **way'fare** (*archaic*) to travel, *esp* on foot. — *n* (*archaic*) travel, *esp* on foot; **way'farer** a traveller, *esp* on foot. — *n* and *adj* **way'faring**. — **way'faring-tree** *Viburnum lantana*, a large shrub with white flowers and berries that turn red and finally black, common in hedges; **way freight** freight for a way station. — *n* and *adj* **way'-going** (*Scot*) departing. — *adj* **way'gone** exhausted by travelling. — *vt* **waylay'** to lie in ambush for; to attack or seize on the way; to lie in wait for in order to converse with; to obstruct or intercept (*obs*): — *pr p* **waylay'ing**; *pa t* and *pa p* **waylaid'**. — **waylay'er**; **way'leave** permission to pass over another's ground or property; **way'-maker** a pioneer; a precursor; **way'mark** a guidepost; something which serves as a guide to a traveller. — *vt* to mark out (a path, etc) with guideposts, signs, etc. — **way passenger** one picked up or set down at a way station or an intermediate point on a coach or bus route; **way point** a point for stopping, changing course, etc, on a journey; **way'post** a guidepost; **way'side** the border of a way, path or highway. — *adj* growing, situated or lying near the wayside. — **way station** (*US*) an intermediate station between principal stations; **way traffic** (*US*) local traffic, as distinguished from through or express traffic; **way train** (*US*) a train stopping at most of the stations on a line; **way warden** a person elected to supervise the upkeep of roads in a district; **way'wiser** an instrument for measuring distance travelled. — *adj* **way'worn** worn out by travel. — **across** or **over the way** on the other side of the street, etc; **be by way of** to be supposed or alleged to be or be (doing, being, etc); **by** or **with someone's way of it** (*Scot*) according to someone's belief or assertion; **by the way** incidentally; while travelling; beside one's path; **by way of** travelling through, via; as if for the purpose of; in character of, as a substitute for; **come someone's way** to come within someone's experience or reach, to become attainable by someone; **come** or **go someone's way** to come or go in the same direction as someone; **divide three**, etc, **ways** to divide into three, etc portions; **get one's** (or **one's own**) **way** to get what one wants; **give way (to)** see under **give**; **go one's way** to depart; **go one's own way** to act independently; **go out of the** (or **one's**) **way** to give oneself trouble; to make a special effort (to do something); **go someone's way** (of circumstances, etc) to favour someone; **go the way of all flesh** or **all the earth** to die; **have a way with** to be good at dealing with or managing (people, etc); **have a way with one** to have a fascinating personality or persuasive manner; **have it both ways** (*usu* with a *neg*) to benefit from two actions, situations, arguments, etc, each of which excludes the possibility, validity, etc of the other; **have it one's** (or **one's own**) **way** to do, think, etc what one pleases, with no regard for others' advice or opinions; **have one's way** to carry one's point, get what one wants; **have way** (*naut*) (of a vessel) to be in motion; **in a bad way** in a serious condition; very upset; **in a fair way to** likely to succeed in; **in a small** (or **big** or **large**) **way** on a petty (or a large or grandiose) scale; **in a way** to some extent; from one point of view; in a state of agitation or distress (*old*); **in his**, etc **way** (or **own way**) as far as his, etc individual merits go, leaving aside the disadvantageous aspects; **in no way** not at all; **in the family way** see under **family**; **in the way** in one's path, impeding one's progress, creating an obstruction; on the way; **in the way of** in a good position for effecting or attaining; in the habit of (*colloq*); in respect of; **lead the way** to act as a guide in any movement; **look the other way** to look away, sometimes deliberately in order not to see someone or something; to take no notice *esp* of something calling for attention; **lose the** (or **one's**) **way** to leave one's intended route by mistake and become lost; **make one's way** to move forward, sometimes with difficulty, to proceed; to make good progress, achieve success; **make way** to give place; to advance; **no way** (*colloq*) under no circumstances, absolutely not; **one way and another** considering various aspects; **one way or the other** by any means possible; **on the** (or **one's**) **way** moving towards a destination or event; in progress; at a point on one's journey; **on the way out** becoming unpopular, unfashionable, etc; **out of the way** so as not to hinder or obstruct; away from main routes, remote (*adj* **out-of-the-way'**); dealt with, finished with; in prison or dead and gone; (*usu* with *neg*) out of the ordinary, unusual; lost, hidden (*Shakesp*); **put someone in the way of** to contrive to make available to someone; **take one's way** to set out, proceed; to follow one's own inclination or plan; **the Way** the Christian Religion (from the Bible, Acts 9.2, etc); **under way** (of a vessel) in motion (also **underway**); **Way of the Cross** a series of pictorial representations of the stages of Christ's progress to Calvary; devotions practised in connection with these stages; **ways and means** resources; methods eg of raising money for the carrying on of government (**Committee of Ways and Means** the House of Commons sitting in the character of a committee to consider methods of raising money supplies; (in the US) a permanent committee of the House of Representatives to which bills concerned with revenue are referred). [OE *weg*; Ger *Weg*; related to Sans *vahati* he carries and to L *vehere* to carry, draw]

way[2] or **'way** *wā*, (*esp* and *orig US*) *adv* far; by a substantial distance or length of time. — *adj* **way-out'** (*slang*) excellent, very satisfying, exceptional; eccentric, unconventional, avant-garde, exotic; rapt, lost, carried away, *orig* in performing avant-garde jazz. — **way back** long ago; the distant past; far into the past. [Shortened from **away**]

way[3] *wā*, (*Spenser*) *vt* to weigh, esteem. [Variant of **weigh**[1]]

way baggage ... to ... **waygone**. See under **way**[1].

waygoose. See **wayzgoose**.

wayless ... to ... **waymark**. See under **way**[1].

wayment *wā-ment'*, (*Spenser*) *vt* and *vi* to lament, grieve. — *n* lamentation, grief. [OFr *waimenter*, from *wai* alas]

way-out. See **way**[2].

waypost. See under **way**[1].

-ways *-wāz*, *sfx* forming adverbs and adjectives of direction and manner, as in *sideways*, *edgeways*. [**way**[1]]

wayward *wā'wərd*, *adj* wilful; capricious; irregular. — *adv* **way'wardly**. — *n* **way'wardness**. [For **awayward**, from **away** and sfx **-ward**]

waywiser. See under **way**[1].

waywode *wā'wōd*, *n* a variant of **voivode**.

wayworn. See under **way**[1].

wayzgoose or **wasegoose** *wāz'gōōs*, *n* a printers' annual dinner or picnic. — Earlier **way'goose**. [Origin obscure]

waza-ari *wä-zə-ä'ri*, *n* (in judo) a score of seven points or 'almost ippon', awarded for a throw not quite worthy of a maximum score (ippon). [Jap]

wazir *wä-zēr'*, *n* a vizier. [Ar *wazīr*]

Wb *abbrev*: weber, the unit of magnetic flux.

WBA *abbrev*: World Boxing Association.

WBC *abbrev*: World Boxing Council.

WC *abbrev*: water closet; West(ern) Central.

wc *abbrev*: water closet; without charge.

WCC *abbrev*: World Council of Churches.

W/Cdr *abbrev*: Wing-Commander.

WD *abbrev*: Dominica, Windward Islands (IVR); War Department; Works Department.

(**2-** or **4-**)**w/d** *abbrev*: (two- or four-)wheel drive.

WDA *abbrev*: Welsh Development Agency.

we *wē*, *pronoun*, *pl* of I; I and others; used for I by monarchs; also used by editors, etc; used when speaking patronizingly, *esp* to children, to mean 'you'. [OE *wē*; cognate with Gothic *weis*, Ger *wir*]

WEA *abbrev*: Workers' Educational Association.

weak *wēk*, *adj* soft (*obs*); lacking strength; not able to sustain a great weight; easily overcome; frail; having poor health; feeble; lacking moral or mental force; impressible, easily led; lacking artistic force; unconvincing; inconclusive; inconsiderable (*Shakesp*); having little of the important ingredient; (with *in*) deficient in respect of; (of a verb) inflected by regular syllabic addition rather than by change of main vowel; (of a Germanic noun or adjective) having inflexions in *-n*; (of a sound or accent) having little force; (of a verse line) having the accent on a normally unstressed syllable; (of a syllable) unstressed; tending downward in price (*stock exchange*); (of an interaction between nuclear particles) having a decay time of *approx* 10^{-10} seconds. — *vt* **weak'en** to make weaker; to reduce in strength or spirit. — *vi* to grow weak or weaker; to become less resolute or determined, show signs of giving in. — *n* **weak'ener**. — *n* **weak'liness**. — *n* **weak'ling** a weak or feeble creature. — *adv* **weak'ly**. — *adj* sickly; not robust; feeble. — *n* **weak'ness** the state of being weak; a flaw, shortcoming; a liking or fondness (with *for*). — **weaker sex** (*usu facetious*) women; **weaker vessel** a woman (from the Bible, 1 Peter 3.7). — *adj* **weak'-eyed** having weak eyes or sight. — **weak'fish** any of a group of weak-mouthed food-fish of the genus *Cynoscion* (family *Sciaenidae*), *esp Cynoscion regalis*. — *adj* **weak'-hand'ed** powerless. — *adj* **weak'-head'ed** having a feeble intellect; easily affected by alcoholic liquor. — *adj* **weak'-heart'ed** of weak spirit; soft-hearted. — *adj* **weak'-hinged'** ill-balanced. — **weak interaction** or **force** (*phys*) an interaction between particles complete in about 10^{-10} seconds, such interactions involving neutrinos and antineutrinos and being responsible for radioactive β-ray decay. — *adj* **weak'-kneed'** having weak knees or a feeling of faintness; weak-willed, feeble, pusillanimous. — *adv* **weak'-kneed'ly**. — *adj* **weak'-mind'ed** having feeble intelligence; having, or showing, lack of resolution; too easily convinced or persuaded. — *adv* **weak'-mind'edly**. — **weak'-mind'edness**; **weak moment** a moment when one is over-easily persuaded or tempted; **weak side** or **point** that side or point in which a person is most easily influenced or most liable to temptation. — *adj* **weak'-sight'ed**. — **weak sister** (*colloq*; *esp US*) a weak, unreliable member of a group. — *adj* **weak'-spir'ited** bearing wrong tamely, cowardly. — *adj* **weak'-will'ed** lacking strength of will, irresolute. [ON *veikr*; related to OE *wāc* pliant, from *wīcan* to yield; Du *week*, Ger *weich*]

weal[1] *wēl*, *n* the state of being well (*literary* or *archaic*); a sound or prosperous state; welfare; commonwealth (*obs*). — *adj* **weal'-balanced** (*Shakesp*, *Measure for Measure*, IV. 3. 108) *perh* kept in a state of just proportion by reasons of state, *perh* for well-balanced. — **weals'man** (*Shakesp*) a statesman. — **the public**, **general** or **common weal** the wellbeing, interest and prosperity of the country. [OE *wela*, *weola* wealth, bliss; related to **well**[2]]

weal[2] *wēl*, *n* a raised streak left on the skin by a blow with a lash, etc. [Variant of **wale**[1]]

weal[3]. Same as **weel**[1].

weald *wēld*, (*poetic*) *n* open country or wooded country. — *adj* **Weald'en** pertaining to the Weald; denoting a series of freshwater beds at the base of the Cretaceous, seen in the Weald. — Also *n*. — **the Weald** a district, once forested, between the North and South Downs. [OE (WSax) *weald* a forest, wold; cf **wold**]

wealk'd. See **welkt**.

wealth *welth*, *n* valuable possessions of any kind; riches; the condition of being rich; prosperity, wellbeing (*archaic*); an abundance or plenitude (with *of*). — *adv* **wealth'ily**. — *n* **wealth'iness**. — *adj* **wealth'y** rich; prosperous. — **wealth tax** a tax on personal property and capital. [ME *welthe*, from *wele*, from OE *wela* prosperity; see **weal**[1]]

weamb. See **wame**.

wean[1] *wēn*, *vt* to accustom (a baby or young animal) to nourishment other than the mother's milk; to reconcile to doing without any accustomed thing, eschewing a former habit, etc (with *from*). — *n* **wean'el** (*Spenser*) a weanling. — *n* **wean'er** a young animal, *esp* a pig, that has recently been weaned. — *n* **wean'ling** a child or animal newly weaned. — Also *adj*. — **weaning brash** a severe form of diarrhoea that sometimes occurs on weaning. [OE *wenian* to accustom; ON *venja*, Ger *gewöhnen* to accustom, *entwöhnen* to disuse, wean]

wean[2] *wān*, (*Scot*) *n* a child. [**wee ane**, ie little one]

weapon *wep'n*, *n* any instrument of offence or defence. — *adj* **weap'oned**. — *adj* **weap'onless** having no weapons. — *n* **weap'onry** weapons collectively; armament. — **weapon salve** a salve supposed to cure a wound by being applied to the weapon that made it. [OE *wǣpen*; Gothic *wēpna* arms, Ger *Waffe*]

weapon-schaw, **weapon-shaw**. See **wappenshaw**.

wear[1] *wār*, *vt* to be dressed in; to carry on the body; to arrange (one's clothes, etc) in a specified way; to display, show; (of eg the face) to exhibit (an expression, etc); to carry the burden of (one's age, years, experience, etc) eg lightly; (of a ship) to fly (a flag); to consume, waste or damage by use, time or exposure; to make or render by friction or constant use; to exhaust, to weary; to bring gradually (into a frame of mind, etc; *old*); to introduce (an idea) little by little (into someone's mind; *old*); to enable to last, endure (*Scot*; *wēr*); to spend (a period of time; *poetic*); to traverse (*Spenser*); to edge, guide or conduct, eg sheep into a fold (*Scot*); to tolerate, accept or believe (*colloq*). — *vi* to waste away by use or time; to be reduced or impaired little by little; (of time) to be spent or pass, *esp* tediously; to last under use; to resist the ravages of age; to stand the test of time; to be in fashion (*Shakesp*); to pass (into a next stage or phase); to become (*obs*); to go, move or progress slowly (*Scot*): — *pa t* **wore** (*wör* or *wōr*), *archaic* **ware** (*wār*); *pa p* **worn** (*wörn* or *wōrn*). — *n* the act of wearing or state of being worn; reduction or impairment of by use or friction; durability; fitness for wearing; articles worn (*usu* in combination, as in *menswear*); fashion. — *n* **wearabil'ity**. — *adj* **wear'able** fit to be worn; good for wearing. — *n* **wear'er**. — *adj* **wear'ing** made or designed for wear; exhausting; consuming. — *n* the process of wasting by attrition or time; the fact of carrying on the body, or displaying, flying, etc; durability; the process of passing; that which is worn, clothes (*obs*). — *adv* **wear'ingly**. — **wear'ing-apparel** dress; **wear iron** an iron plate to take the wear due to friction. — **the worse for wear** showing signs of wear, worn; showing signs of exhaustion, intoxication, etc (*colloq*); **wear and tear** or **tear and wear** damage by wear or use; **wear away** to impair or consume, or be reduced or impaired, by wear; to decay or fade out; to pass off; **wear down** to reduce or impair, or be reduced or impaired, by constant use or friction; to diminish or overcome (eg resistance) gradually by persistence; **wear off** to rub off by friction; to diminish by decay; to pass away by degrees; **wear on** (of time) to pass by, *esp* tediously; **wear out** to impair by use; to render or become useless through age, use or decay; to exhaust or consume; to harass or tire utterly; **wear thin** to become thin or threadbare through use; (of patience) to diminish with excessive calls on it; (of excuses) to become less convincing through over-use; **wear through** to develop a hole through friction or intensive use; **(win and) wear** to (win and) enjoy possession of (eg a wife; *old*). [OE *werian* to wear; ON *verja* to clothe, Gothic *wasian*]

wear[2] *wār*, (*naut*) *vt* and *vi* to alter the course of (a ship) or (of a ship) to alter course by turning the stern to windward in a manoeuvre *opp* to *tacking*: — *pa t* and *pa p* **wore**. [Origin uncertain; apparently unconnected with **veer**[1]]

wear[3] *wēr*, *n* another spelling of **weir**[1].

wear[4] or **weir** *wēr*, (*Scot*) *vt* to guard; to ward off. [OE *werian*]

wearability, wearable, wearer. See under **wear**[1].

weariful, weariless, wearily, weariness. See under **weary**[1].

wearish *wēr'ish*, *adj* tasteless, savourless, insipid (*obs*); feeble, withered, shrunk (*dialect*). [Late ME *werische*; cf **wersh**]

wearisome. See under **weary**[1].

weary[1] *wē'ri*, *adj* having one's strength or patience exhausted; very tired; causing weariness; tiresome, tedious; puny (*dialect*). — *vt* to make weary; to reduce the strength or patience of; to harass. — *vi* to become weary or impatient; to long (with *for*; *Scot*). — *adj* **wea'ried** tired. — *adj* **wea'riful** (*old*) wearisome. — *adv* **wea'rifully**. — *adj* **wea'riless** (*old*) unwearying; incessant. — *adv* **wear'ilessly**. — *adv* **wea'rily**. — *n* **wea'riness**. — *adj* **wea'risome** causing weariness; tedious. — *adv* **wea'risomely**. — *n* **wea'risomeness**. — *adj* **wear'ying**. — *adv* **wear'yingly**. — **Weary Willie** (*colloq*) a tramp or workshy person (*old*); a person habitually lackadaisical or deficient in energy or spirits. — **weary out** (*old*) to exhaust; to get tediously through (a period of time). [OE *wērig* weary]

weary[2] *wē'ri*, (*Scot*) *n* a curse, as in **weary on you, weary fall you**. [**weary**[1], prob with some association with obs *wary* (OE *wiergan*) to curse]

weasand *wē'zənd*, (*old* or *dialect*) *n* the gullet; the windpipe; the throat. — **wea'sand-pipe** (*Spenser*). [OE *wǣsand*; OSax *wāsend*, OHGer *weisant*]

weasel *wē'zl*, *n* a small carnivore (*Mustela nivalis*) with long slender body, active, furtive and bloodthirsty, eating frogs, birds, mice, etc; any of various related species; a furtive, treacherous or sly person; a small amphibious military vehicle for carrying personnel or supplies. — *vi* to equivocate; (with *out of*, *on*, *round*, etc) to extricate oneself from or circumvent (an obligation, etc), *esp* indefensibly (*colloq*). — *n* **wea'seller** or **wea'seler**. — *adj* **wea'selly**. — **weasel cat** a civet-like animal of Borneo and Java, the linsang; **weasel coot** the female or young male of the smew, a sea bird. — *adj* **wea'sel-faced** with a lean sharp face. — **weasel word** (*colloq*) a word that makes a statement evasive or misleading, *orig* a word used illegitimately in conjunction with another word rendering it meaningless or sucking its meaning from it as a weasel sucks out the contents of an egg. — **weasel out** (*colloq*) to evade obligation. [OE *wesle*]

weather *wedh'ər*, *n* atmospheric conditions in terms of heat or cold, wetness, cloudiness, etc; type of atmospheric conditions; vicissitude of fortune; formerly, a storm or adverse weather; the direction in which the wind is blowing (*naut*); the angle the sail of a windmill makes with the perpendicular to its axis. — *vt* to affect by exposing to the air; to put (a hawk) out of doors on a perch in fine weather (*falconry*); to sail to the windward of; to gain or pass (eg a cape); to come safely through (a storm or stormy situation); to shelter from (*obs*); to set (the sails of a windmill); to slope (a roof, etc; *archit*). — *vi* to become discoloured, disintegrated, etc, by exposure; (of a hawk) to be weathered. — *adj* (*naut*) toward the wind, windward. — *adj* **weath'erable**. — *adj* **weath'ered** having the surface altered in colour, form, texture or composition by the action of the elements (*geol*); seasoned by exposure to weather; made slightly sloping so as to throw off water (*archit*); (of boards or tiles) downward-sloping and overlapped so as to keep water out. — *n* **weath'ering** the action of the elements in altering the form, colour, texture or composition of rocks (*geol*); seasoning by weather; a slight inclination given to the top of a cornice or moulding to prevent water from lodging on it (*archit*); the act of passing to windward of a coastal feature, obstacle or other vessel (*naut*); weather conditions (*obs*). — *vt* **weath'erize** or **-ise** to make (a fabric) weatherproof. — *adj* **weath'erly** (*naut*) making little leeway when close-hauled. — *adj* **weath'ermost** (*naut*) furthest to windward. — *n* **weatherom'eter** an instrument for determining the weather-resisting properties of paints or other surfaces. — **weather anchor** the anchor lying to windward. — *adj* **weath'er-beaten** damaged, worn away or seasoned by the weather; (of someone's skin or face) tanned or lined from prolonged exposure. — *adj* **weath'er-bitten** worn or defaced by exposure to the winds. — **weath'erboard** the windward side of a ship; a plank in the porthole, etc of a vessel placed so as to keep off rain, without preventing air from circulating; a board shaped so as to shed water from a building. — *vt* to fit with such planks or boards. — **weath'erboarding** thin boards placed overlapping to keep out rain; the exterior covering of a wall or roof. — *adj* **weath'er-bound** detained by bad weather. — **weather bow** the windward side of the bow; **weather box** see **weather house**; **weather chart** a weather map; **weath'ercloth** a protecting tarpaulin on deck; **weath'ercock** a vane in the form of a cock to show the direction of the wind; someone who changes his or her opinions, allegiance, etc easily and often. — *vt* to serve as a weathercock for; to supply with a weathercock; (with *it*) to behave like a weathercock. — *adj* **weath'er-driven** driven by winds or storms. — **weather eye** the eye considered as the means by which one forecasts the weather; an eye watchful for developments, as in *keep one's weather eye open*. — *vt* **weath'er-fend** (*Shakesp*) to defend from the weather, to shelter. — **weather forecast** a forecast of the weather based on meteorological observations; **weather forecaster**; **weather gage** or **gauge** the position of a ship to the windward of another; advantage of position; **weather gall** (*Scot* **gaw**) an imperfect rainbow or other supposed sign of coming weather; **weather glass** a glass or instrument that indicates the changes of the weather; a barometer; **weather gleam** (*dialect*) a bright aspect of the sky at the horizon. — *adj* **weath'er-headed** (*Scott*) flighty. — **weather helm** a keeping of the helm somewhat to the weather side when a vessel shows a tendency to come into the wind; **weather house** or **weather box** a toy house containing two figures, the emergence of one presaging dry weather, and of the other, rain; **weath'erman** a person who prepares weather forecasts or delivers such forecasts on radio or television; **weather map** a map indicating meteorological conditions over a large tract of country; **weather notation** a system of abbreviation for meteorological phenomena. — *adj* **weath'erproof** proof against rough weather. — *n* weatherproof material or a weatherproof garment. — *vt* to make weatherproof. — **weather prophet** someone who foretells weather; a device for foretelling the weather; **weather roll** the lurch of a vessel to windward when in the trough of the sea; **weather report** loosely, a weather forecast; **weather satellite** a satellite used for the study of cloud formations and other meteorological conditions; **weather ship** a ship engaged in meteorological work; **weather side** the windward side; **weather sign** a phenomenon indicating change of weather; any prognostic; **weather stain** discoloration produced by exposure; **weather station** a station where phenomena of weather are observed; **weather strip** a thin piece of some material fixed along the edge of a window or door, to keep out wind and cold; **weather symbol** a conventional sign indicating a meteorological phenomenon; **weather vane** a weathercock; **weather window** a period of time in which the weather is suitable for a particular purpose, eg oil-drilling; any restricted period during which the opportunity should be seized for getting something done. — *adj* **weath'er-wise** skilful in foreseeing the changes of the weather; quick to sense what turn events will take. — *adv* with regard to weather conditions. — *adj* **weath'er-worn** worn away or damaged by wind, storms, etc. — **above the weather** too high in the air to experience the weather conditions on the ground; not, or no longer, under the weather; **keep one's weather eye open** to be alert; to keep a sharp lookout; **keep** or **have the weather of** to be to the windward of; to have the advantage of; **make fair weather** (*Shakesp*) to be conciliatory, to use flattery (with *to* or *with*); **make good** or **bad weather of it** to behave well or badly in a storm (*lit* and *fig*); **make heavy weather of** to find excessive difficulty in; **stress of weather** violent and unfavourable winds; **under the weather** indisposed, seedy; drunk (*colloq*); **weather along** to make headway against adverse weather; **weather a point** (*fig*) to gain an advantage or accomplish a purpose against opposition; **weather on** to gain on (another vessel) in a windward direction (*lit* and *fig*); **weather out** to hold out against or ride out (a storm or stormy situation) till the end; **weather the storm** to come safely through a period of difficulty, etc. [OE *weder*; ON *vedhr*, Ger *Wetter*]

weave[1] *wēv*, *vt* to make (cloth, tapestry, basketwork, etc) by crossing threads, strands, strips, etc above and below one another; to interlace (eg threads in a loom to form cloth); to depict (figures, a story, etc) in woven work; to combine, mingle or work together into a whole; to introduce (an ingredient or element) subtly (into something); to construct, fabricate or contrive. — *vi* to practise weaving: — *pa t* **wōve**, *rarely* **weaved**; *pa p* **wō'ven**; see also **wove**. — *n* the texture of a woven fabric. — *n* **weav'er** someone who weaves; any bird of a passerine family (*Ploceidae*) resembling the finches, so called from their remarkable woven nests. — *n* **weav'ing** the act or art of making cloth or a 'web' by the intersecting of two distinct sets of fibres, threads or yarns, those passing longitudinally from end to end of the web forming the *warp*, those crossing and intersecting the warp at right angles forming the *weft*. — **weaver bird** a weaver or, less commonly, a weaver finch; **weaver finch** any member of a family of small finch-like birds (*Estrildidae*) which includes the waxbills; **weaver's knot** or **hitch** the sheet bend. [OE *wefan*; ON *vefa*, Ger *weben*; cognate with Gr *hyphē* a web, and *hyphainein* to weave]

weave[2] *wēv*, *vi* to move to and fro; to wind in and out; to move back or forward with sinuous movements of the body (*boxing*); to fly a winding course (*aeronautics*). — *vt* to move to and fro or up and down; to make a signal to by waving something: — *pa t* and *pa p* **weaved**. — *n* and *adj* **weav'ing**. — **get weaving** (*colloq*) to get busy, get on the move. [ME *weve*; of uncertain origin]

weazand *wē'zənd*, *n* same as **weasand**.

weazen *wē'zn*, variant of **wizen**.

web *web*, *n* the fine structure of gossamer threads spun by a spider to entrap insects; that which is woven; a whole piece of cloth as woven in the loom; a kind of cloth or weave; a thin metal plate or sheet; (in paper-making) an endless wire mesh working on rollers; a large sheet or roll of paper; the skin between the toes of waterfowl, etc; in birds, the vexillum of a feather; any connective tissue (*anatom*); the surface between the ribs of a vaulted roof (*archit*); a narrow connecting section between two stouter parts (*machinery*); a film over the eye (*obs*); anything like a cloth web in its complication or a spider's web in its flimsiness or power to entangle; a plot, snare, intrigue or fabrication. — *vt* to envelop or to connect with a web. — *adj* **webbed** having a web; (of the toes or fingers) partially joined together by a membrane of skin. — *n* **webb'ing** a woven strip of hemp, used for belts, etc, for various purposes in upholstery, and as tapes conducting webs of paper in a printing-machine; the condition of being palmate or hand-shaped, palmation (*zool*); the webs of webbed hands or feet. — *adj* **webb'y**. — *adj* **web'-fing'ered**. — **web'foot** a foot the toes of which are united with a web or membrane. — *adj* **web'footed**. — **web offset** a method of offset printing using a reel of paper. — *adj* **web'-toed**. — **web'wheel** a wheel in which the rim, spokes and centre are formed from one single piece of material; a wheel with a web or plate instead of spokes; **web'worm** (*US*) any of a number of caterpillars that spin webs in which they feed or rest. — **web and pin** or **pin and web** (*Shakesp*) see under **pin**. [OE *webb*; ON *vefr*, Ger *Gewebe*; from root of **weave**[1]]

weber *vā'bər* or *wē'bər*, *n* the MKS unit of magnetic flux. [Wilhelm *Weber*, German physicist (1804–91)]

webster *web'stər*, (*obs*) *n* a weaver. — Also (*Scot*) **wab'ster**. [OE *webbestre* a female weaver, from *webban* to weave]

wecht *wehht*, (*Scot*) *n* an instrument for winnowing or for measuring grain. [Perh connected with **weigh**[1]]

Wed. *abbrev*: Wednesday.

wed *wed* (*Scot* **wad** *wöd*) *vt* to marry; to join in marriage; to unite closely; to wager (*obs*). — *vi* to marry: — *pr p* **wedd'ing**; *pa t* **wedd'ed** or (*dialect*) **wed**; *pa p* **wedd'ed** or (*dialect* and *poetic*) **wed**. — *n* (*obs*; Scot **wad**) a pledge, security. — *adj* **wedd'ed** married; of or pertaining to marriage; closely joined; persistently devoted. — *n* **wedd'ing** marriage; marriage ceremony. — **wedding anniversary** the anniversary of one's wedding day; **wedding band** (*US*) a wedding ring; **wedding bed** the bridal bed; **wedding breakfast** a meal served after a wedding; **wedding cake** a highly decorated cake served at a wedding, and also divided among absent friends; **wedding cards** cards announcing a wedding, sent to friends; **wedding day** the day of marriage; its anniversary; **wedding dower** the marriage portion; **wedding dress** a bride's dress; **wedding favour** a white rosette worn by men at a wedding; **wedding finger** the ring-finger; **wedding garment** a garment worn at a wedding; **wedding march** music in march time played as the bride's party enters the church and at the close of a marriage ceremony; **wedding ring** a *usu* plain, gold ring given by the groom to the bride at a wedding; a ring of the same or similar type given reciprocally by the bride to the groom. — **penny-wedding** see under **penny**; **silver, ruby, golden** or **diamond wedding** or **wedding anniversary** the celebrations of the 25th, 40th, 50th and 60th anniversaries of a wedding respectively. [OE *weddian* to promise, to marry (Ger *wetten* to wager), from *wedd* a pledge; Gothic *wadi*, Ger *Wette* a bet]

we'd *wēd*, a contraction of **we had** or **we would**.

Weddell seal *wed'əl sēl*, *n* a large brown seal of Antarctic waters (first described by James *Weddell*, Scottish navigator, 1787–1834), that winters under the ice, gnawing through it to create breathing holes.

wedder *wed'ər*, (*obs* or *dialect*, *esp Scot* and *N Eng*) a form of **wether** or **weather**.

wedding. See **wed**.

wedeln *vā'dəln*, (also with *cap*) *n* a style of downhill skiing in which the skis, kept parallel and close together, are swivelled rapidly from side to side. — *n pl* such swivelling movements. — *vi* (also with *cap*) to execute wedeln on a downhill run. [Ger, orig to wag one's tail]

wedge *wej*, *n* a piece of wood or metal, thick at one end and sloping to a thin edge at the other, used in splitting, or fixing tightly, etc; anything shaped more or less like a wedge, eg a formation of troops, the flying formation of geese and other wildfowl, a piece cut from a circular cake, a stroke in cuneiform characters or (*obs*) an ingot of gold or silver; any v-shaped sign used in notation or as a diacritic; an iron-headed golf club with much loft, used for approaching; a stroke with such a club; a shoe in which the heel and sole together form a wedge with no gap under the instep (also **wedge-heeled shoe**).— *vt* to force (open) or drive (apart) with, or as if with, a wedge; to thrust in tightly; to crowd closely; to fasten or fix with a wedge or wedges; to cleave with a wedge; to make into a wedge. — *vi* to force one's way like a wedge; to become fixed or jammed by, or as if by, a wedge; to make a stroke with a wedge (*golf*). — *adj* **wedged**. — *adv* **wedge'wise** in the manner of a wedge. — *n* **wedg'ie** (*colloq*) a wedge-heeled shoe. — *n* **wedg'ing** a method of joining timbers. — *adj* **wedg'y**. — *adj* **wedge'-shaped** shaped like a wedge. — *adj* **wedge'-tailed** having a tail in which the rectrices form the shape of a wedge, the central pair being longest, the outer pair shortest. — **the thin** or **small end of the wedge** a small beginning that is bound to be followed by a large or significant (and *usu* unwelcome) development; **the wedge** or **wooden wedge** at Cambridge, the student lowest on the classical tripos list (on the analogy of wooden spoon (qv), from *Wedg*wood, a student at Christ's College, whose name was last on the first list, of 1824). [OE *wecg*; ON *veggr*, Ger dialect *weck* a wedge]

Wedgwood® *wej'wŏŏd*, *n* pottery made by Josiah *Wedgwood* (1730–95) and his successors, including a distinctive type with cameo reliefs in white on a coloured ground. — Also **Wedgwood ware**. — **Wedgwood blue** a greyish-blue colour much used in Wedgwood pottery.

wedlock *wed'lok*, *n* matrimony; the married state, *esp* in the phrase **born in** (or **out of**) **wedlock**, ie legitimate (or illegitimate). — **break wedlock** (*old*) to commit adultery. [OE *wedlāc*, from *wedd* a pledge, and sfx *-lāc* implying action of some kind]

Wednesday *wenz'di*, *wed'nz-di*, *n* the fourth day of the week. [OE *Wōdnes dæg* Woden's day]

wee[1] *wē*, (*Scot*) *adj* little, tiny. — *n* a short distance, a short time. — **Wee Free** a member of the minority of the Free Church that refused to join with the United Presbyterian Church in 1900. [ME *we*, *wei* a bit, time or space, as in phrase *a little wei*]

wee[2] *wē*, *interj* imitating the squeal of a young pig. — Also *vi* and *n*.

wee[3] *wē* or **wee-wee** *wē'wē*, (*colloq*; *esp childish*) the act of urinating; urine. — *vi* to urinate: — *pa t* and *pa p* **weed** or **wee'-weed**. [Origin uncertain]

weed[1] *wēd*, *n* any useless plant of small growth; any plant growing where it is not wanted, *esp* amongst cultivated plants; any wild herb (often in combination, as in *bindweed*, *hogweed*, *knapweed*); a thick growth of wild herbs; a plant growing in fresh or salt water (*usu* in combination, as in *pondweed*, *seaweed*); anything useless, troublesome or obnoxious; a worthless animal; a weak, ineffectual or unmanly man (*derog*); (often with **the**) tobacco or a cigar or cigarette (*colloq*); marijuana (*slang*). — *vt* to clear (a garden, etc) of weeds; to remove, uproot (weeds, etc) (often with *out*); to identify and remove (something or someone inferior, unwanted, etc) from a group or collection (*usu* with *out*). — *vi* to uproot weeds. — *adj* **weed'ed**. — *n* **weed'er**. — *n* **weed'ery** a place full of weeds. — *n* **weedicide** (*wē'di-sīd*) a chemical weedkiller. — *n* **weed'iness**. — *n* **weed'ing** the task or process of clearing ground of weeds; what is weeded out. — *adj* **weed'less**. — *adj* **weed'y** weed-like; full of weeds; lanky, ungainly or weakly in appearance; of insipid character. — *adj* **weed'-grown** overgrown with weeds. — **weed'ing-chisel**, **-forceps**, **-fork**, **-hook** and **-tongs** garden implements of varying forms for destroying weeds; **weed'killer** a chemical preparation or other substance for killing weeds. [OE *wēod* a herb]

weed[2] *wēd*, *n* a garment, clothing or outfit (*archaic*); armour (*archaic*); (in *pl*) a widow's mourning apparel (also **widow's weeds**). — *adj* **weed'y** clad in widow's mourning. [OE *wæd*, *wēde* clothing; OHGer *wāt* cloth]

weed[3] or **weid** *wēd*, (*Scot*) *n* any sudden illness, cold or relapse with febrile symptoms, *esp* in women after confinement or nursing; a fever in horses, etc. [From *wedenonfa*, from OE *wēden-* (in combination) mad, and Scot *onfa* **onfall**]

weed[4]. See under **wee**[3].

week *wēk*, *n* the space of seven days, *esp* from Sunday to Saturday (inclusive); the working days of the week; (in *pl*) an indefinite period. — *adj* **week'ly** coming, happening or done once a week. — *adv* once a week; every week. — *n* a publication appearing once a week. — **week'day** any day of the week except Sunday, and now *usu* also excluding Saturday; **week'end** (or *-end'*) the non-working period from Friday evening to Sunday evening (a **long week-end** *usu* incorporating Friday and Monday or yet more liberally extended). — *vi* to spend a weekend holiday. — **weekend'er**; **weekend'ing**; **week'-night** the evening or night of a weekday. — **a prophetic week** (*Bible*) seven years; **a week of Sundays** (*colloq*) seven weeks; a long time; **a week** (or **two weeks**, etc) **today** one week (or two weeks, etc) from today; **Feast of Weeks** a Jewish festival seven weeks after the Passover (also **Shabuoth**, **Shavuot** or **Pentecost**); **Great Week**, **Holy Week** or **Passion Week** the week preceding Easter Sunday; **in by the week** (*obs*) trapped, caught; **this day week** a week from today; **week about** in alternate periods of seven days; **week in, week out** continuously without a break. [OE *wice*; Du *week*, Ger *Woche*]

weeke *wēk*, (*Spenser*) *n*. Same as **wick**[1].

weel[1] or **weil** (*Scot* and *N Eng*) *wēl*, *n* a whirlpool. [OE *wǣl*]

weel[2] *wēl*, *n* a trap or snare for fish (*dialect*); a bearing resembling this (*heraldry*). [OE *wile-* (in combination), from *wilige*; cf **willy**[1]]

weel[3] *wēl*, *adv* Scots form of **well**[2], as in *weel-faur'd*, *-far'd*, etc, well-favoured (qv under **well**[2]).

weeldlesse. See under **wield**.

weem *wēm*, (*Scot*) *n* a subterranean dwelling. [Early Gaelic *uaim* cavern]

ween *wēn*, (*archaic* or *obs*) *vt* to think or fancy; to believe; to expect. — *vi* (*Shakesp*) to imagine expectantly. [OE *wēnan*; cognate with *wēn* expectation, hope]

weeny[1] *wē'ni*, (*colloq*; *esp childish*) *adj* very small, tiny. — **wee'ny-bopper** (*colloq*) a child of up to about 12 years old, *usu* female, who shows a keen interest in pop music and associated fashions and trends (cf **teeny-bopper** under **teen**). [*wee* and *tiny* or *teeny*]

weeny[2]. See under **Wiener**.

weep *wēp*, *vi* to express grief by shedding tears; to wail or lament; to drip, rain; to ooze; to leak; to exude; to droop or be pendent. — *vt* to lament; to pour forth; to express while, or by, weeping; to exude: — *pa t* and *pa p* **wept**. — *n* **weep'er** someone who weeps; a mourning figure carved on a tombstone; a hired mourner; a white border round the sleeve of a mourning dress; a crape hatband; a widow's crape veil; anything drooping or pendent; a weephole. — *n* **weep'ie** or **weep'y** (*colloq*) a highly emotional film, play or book. — *n* **weep'ing**. — *adj* (of a tree or plant variety) having slender drooping branches. — *adv* **weep'ingly**. — *adj* **weep'y** tearful (*colloq*); oozy (*dialect*). — **weep'hole** a hole in a wall, etc to allow water to escape from behind it; **weeping ash** a variety of the common European ash, with drooping branches; **weeping birch** a variety of the white birch, with drooping branches; **Weeping Cross** or **weep'ing-cross** (a former site of) a wayside cross where penitents might pray; in phrases such as **come home by Weeping Cross** to experience bitter regret, disappointment or failure; **weeping elm** a variety of wych-elm, with drooping branches. — *adj* **weep'ing-ripe** (*Shakesp*) ripe or ready for tears. — **weeping rock** a rock through which water percolates slowly; **weeping spring** a spring from which water escapes slowly; **weeping willow** an ornamental Chinese willow (*Salix babylonica*), with pendent branches. [OE *wēpan*; related to *wōp* clamour; Gothic *wōpjan*]

weet[1] *wēt*, (*dialect* and *Spenser*) *adj*, *vt* and *n* a form of **wet**.

weet[2], **weete**, **weeten**, **weeting**. See under **wit**[1].
weetingly. Obsolete form of **wittingly** (qv under **wit**[1]).
weetless. Obsolete form of **witless** (qv under **wit**[2]).
weever *wē'vər*, *n* a genus of fishes (*Trachinus*), of which two species are British, with sharp dorsal and opercular spines capable of inflicting serious wounds. [Prob OFr *wivre* serpent, weever, from L *vīpera*; cf **wivern** and **viper**]
weevil *wēv'l*, *n* a popular name for a large number of beetles (the group Rhynchophora, *esp* the family *Curculionidae*) with the anterior part of the head prolonged into a beak or proboscis, which, either in the larval or the adult form, damage fruit, nuts, grain, trees, etc; any insect injurious to stored grain, etc. — *adj* **weev'illed**, **weev'iled**, **weev'illy** or **weev'ily** infested by weevils. [OE *wifel*]
wee-wee. See under **wee**[3].
wef *abbrev*: with effect from.
weft[1] *weft*, *n* the threads woven into and crossing the warp; the thread carried by the shuttle (also **woof** *wōōf*); a web; a film or cloud. — *vi* (*rare*) to form a weft. — *n* **weft'age** texture. [OE *weft*, *wefta*; related to *wefan*; see **weave**[1]]
weft[2] *weft*, (*Spenser*) *n* a waif, a castaway. — Also **wefte**. [Variant of **waif**[1]]
weft[3] *weft*, (*Spenser*) *pa p* of **waive** and *pa t* of **waft**. — Also **wefte**.
Wehrmacht *vār'mähht*, *n* the German armed forces (1935–45). [Ger, from *Wehr* defence, and *Macht* force]
weid. See **weed**[3].
weigela *wī'gi-lə* or *-gel'*, *n* a plant of a genus (*Weigela*) of deciduous shrubs with large showy pink, purplish or white flowers. [C E von *Weigel* (1748–1831), German botanist]
weigh[1] *wā*, *vt* to find out the heaviness of; to be equal to in heaviness (as in *weigh* 3 *kilos*); to compare or counterbalance on or as if on scales (with *against* or *with*); to raise (a ship's anchor); to apportion or measure a specific weight of; to hold in the hand(s) in order to, or as if to, estimate the weight; to estimate the value of; to ponder in the mind, consider carefully; to consider worthy of notice; to keep evenly outspread (*Milton*). — *vi* to have weight; to be considered of importance; to balance evenly (*Shakesp*); to have value (*Shakesp*); to press heavily (with *on*); to weigh anchor. — *adj* **weigh'able** capable of being weighed. — *n* **weigh'age** the rate paid for the weighing of goods. — *adj* **weighed** experienced; considered, balanced. — *n* **weigh'er** an official who weighs articles or tests weights. — *n* **weigh'ing**. — **weigh'-bauk** (*Scot*) the beam of a balance; (in *pl*) a pair of scales; **weigh'board** see **wayboard** under **way**[1]; **weigh'bridge** a machine for weighing vehicles with their loads; **weigh'-house** a public building for weighing goods, ascertaining the tonnage of boats, etc; **weigh-in** see **weigh in**; **weigh'ing-bottle** (*chem*) a thin-walled cylindrical glass container with a tightly fitting lid, used for accurate weighing of hygroscopic and other materials; **weigh'ing-machine** a machine or apparatus for weighing; **weigh-out** see **weigh out**. — **weigh down** to force down; to depress or oppress; to preponderate over, outweigh; **weigh in** to ascertain one's weight before a boxing match or other sports competition, or after a horse race (*n* **weigh'-in**); to join in a project (*slang*); **weigh into** (*colloq*) to attack; **weigh in with** to produce (a new argument, etc) in a discussion; **weigh off** (*slang*) to sentence (a criminal) *esp* to a term of imprisonment; **weigh out** to weigh and dispense in portions accordingly; to ascertain one's weight before a horse race (*n* **weigh'-out**); **weigh to the beam** (*Shakesp*) to outweigh completely; **weigh up** to force up (*lit* and *fig*); to consider carefully and assess the quality of (eg a person) (*colloq*); **weigh with** to appear important to, to influence. [OE *wegan* to carry; Ger *wiegen*; L *vehere* to carry]
weigh[2] *wā*, *n* a variant of **way**[1] in the phrase 'under way', through confusion with the phrase 'weigh anchor'.
weight[1] *wāt*, *n* the heaviness of a thing, *esp* as determined by weighing; quantity as determined in this way; the force with which a body is attracted to the earth, measured by the product of the mass and the acceleration; a mass of metal adjusted to a standard and used for finding weight; a method of estimating, or a unit of, weight; the amount something ought to weigh; a standard amount that a boxer, etc, should weigh; (in *pl*) weight-lifting or weight-training; scales (*Spenser*); a heavy object; anything heavy or oppressive; a ponderous mass; pressure; importance; power; impressiveness; preponderance or bulk (eg of evidence); the frequency of an item in a frequency distribution or a number indicating this. — *vt* to make heavier; to attach or add a weight or weights to; to hold down in this way; to add substance or solidity to; to increase the weight of (a fabric) by adding chemicals; to assign a handicap weight to (a horse; also *fig*); to oppress, burden; to give (a law or administrative arrangement) a bias *against* or *in favour of* a certain group, etc; to assign greater value to (one factor) than to another; to attach numbers indicating their relative frequency to (items in a frequency distribution) (*statistics*). — *adv* **weigh'tily**. — *n* **weigh'tiness**. — *n* **weight'ing** a weighting allowance. — *adj* **weight'less**. — *n* **weight'lessness** the condition of a freely falling body at the beginning of the fall when its inertia exactly balances the gravitational force, or that of a space traveller and his or her unpowered spacecraft in orbit beyond the earth's atmosphere. — *adj* **weigh'ty** heavy; important; having great influence; being the fruit of judicious consideration and hence worthy of attention; severe (*Shakesp*, *Timon*, III.5.104). — **weighted average** (*statistics*) the average reached when some factor of special importance relating to the variable is included in the calculation along with the frequency factor; **weighting allowance** a salary differential to balance the higher cost of living in a particular area; **weight'-lifter**; **weight'-lifting** a sport in which competitors (attempt to) lift and hold above their heads a barbell made increasingly heavy as the competition progresses; **weight of metal** (*rare* or *old*) the total weight of the projectiles thrown at one discharge from a ship's guns. — *vi* **weight'-train**. — **weight'-training** physical training by means of a series of pulleys, levers, etc with adjustable weights, for building up individual muscle groups; **weight'-watcher** a person, typically female, who is attempting to reduce weight by careful dieting, *esp* one who attends meetings of an association of people similarly engaged; **weight'-watching**. — **by**, **in** or **with weight** (*Shakesp*) fully; **gain** (or **put on**) **weight** to increase one's body weight, get fatter; **lose weight** to decrease one's body weight, get thinner; **throw one's weight about** to over-exercise one's authority; to domineer. [OE *wiht*]
weight[2] *wāt* or (*Scot*) *wehht*, *n*. Same as **wecht**.
weil. See **weel**[1].
Weil's disease *vīlz diz-ēz'*, *n* a severe type of jaundice caused by a spirochaete carried by the urine of rats. [H A *Weil* (1848–1916), German physician]
Weimar Republic *vī'mär ri-pub'lik*, *n* the federal republic in Germany that was founded in 1919 and lasted until 1933, its constitution having been established at *Weimar*. — *n* **Weimaraner** (*vī-mə-rä'nər*, *wī-*, *vī'* or *wī'*) (any one of) a breed of grey short-haired gun dogs with docked tails, *orig* developed at *Weimar*.
weir[1] or **wear** *wēr*, *n* a dam across a river; a fence of stakes set in a stream for catching fish. [OE *wer* an enclosure, related to *werian* to protect; cf Ger *Wehr* a dam, *wehren* to ward]
weir[2]. Another spelling of **wear**[4].
weird *wērd*, *adj* unearthly, uncanny; peculiar, odd (*colloq*); concerned with or controlling fate (*old*). — *n* (*old* and *Scot*) fate; (with *cap*; in *pl*) the Fates; a witch; one's lot, *esp* if evil; a happening, *esp* uncanny; a tale of fate; a spell or charm. — *vt* (*Scot*) to destine or doom; to hand over to as one's fate; to forewarn. — *n* **weird'ie** or **weird'ō** (*pl* **weird'os**) an eccentric; someone uncon-

ventional in dress, etc. — *adv* **weird'ly**. — *n* **weird'ness**. — **dree one's weird** see **dree**; **the Weird Sisters** the Fates; applied by some also to the Norns, the Fates of Scandinavian mythology; the witches in Shakespeare's *Macbeth*. [OE *wyrd* fate; related to *weorthan* to become; Ger *werden*]

weise. See under **wise**[2].

Weismannism *vīs'man-izm*, *n* the doctrine in biology of August *Weismann* (1834–1914), whose central teaching is that acquired characteristics are not transmitted.

weize. See under **wise**[2].

weka *we'kə*, *n* any of the flightless rails of the genus *Ocydromus* or *Gallirallus* of New Zealand. [Maori, imit]

welaway. See **wellaway**.

Welch and **welch** *welsh*, old forms of **Welsh** and **welsh**.

welcher. See under **welsh**.

welcome *wel'kəm*, *adj* received with gladness; admitted willingly; causing gladness; free (to); (with *to*) free to take or enjoy (sometimes *ironic*). — *n* the act of welcoming; a kindly reception; a reception. — *vt* to greet; to receive with kindness or pleasure; to accept or undergo gladly. — *interj* expressing pleasure, *esp* to guests on their arrival. — *n* **wel'comeness**. — *n* **wel'comer**. — *adj* **wel'coming**. — *adv* **wel'comingly**. — **bid a welcome** to receive with professions of kindness; **make someone welcome** to welcome someone, make someone feel welcome; **outstay one's welcome** to stay too long; **wear out one's welcome** to stay too long or visit too often; **you're welcome** it is (or was) no trouble, no thanks are needed. [OE *wilcuma*, from *wil-* (*willa* will, pleasure), and *cuma* guest, with later alteration suggesting a connection with **well**[2] and **come**, prob under the influence of eg OFr *bien venuz*; cf ON *velkominn*]

weld[1] *weld*, *vt* to join (two pieces of metal) by fusing, forging or applying pressure, using any of several methods, eg raising the temperature at the joint by means of external heat or (**resistance welding**) of a heavy electric current or (**arc welding**) of an electric arc, or (**cold welding**) using pressure alone; to join closely. — *vi* to undergo welding; to be capable of being welded. — *n* a welded joint. — *n* **weldabil'ity**. — *adj* **weld'able**. — *n* **weld'er** or **weld'or**. — *n* and *adj* **weld'ing**. — *adj* **weld'less** having no welds. — *n* **weld'ment** the action or process of welding; a welded assembly. [Same as obs or dialect verb *well*, meaning melt, weld; prob from pa p]

weld[2] *weld*, or (*Scot*) **wald** *wäld*, *n* a scentless species of mignonette, also known as dyer's rocket, yielding a yellow dye; the dye itself. [Cf Ger *Wau*]

weld[3] *weld*, (*obs* and *dialect*) *vt* a variant of **wield**.

Weldmesh® *weld'mesh*, *n* (also without *cap*) a type of fencing formed of two sets of parallel lengths of wire welded together at right angles to each other.

welfare *wel'fār*, *n* the state of faring or doing well; freedom from calamity, etc; enjoyment of health, etc; prosperity; welfare work. — *n* **wel'farism** the social policies characteristic of a welfare state. — *n* **wel'farist**. — *adj* **welfaris'tic**. — **welfare state** a social system or state in which socialist principles have been put into effect with the purpose of ensuring the welfare of all who live in it, eg by paying unemployment benefit, old-age pensions, etc and by providing other social services; **welfare work** efforts to improve conditions of living for a class, eg the very poor, or a group, eg employees or workers; **welfare worker**. [**well**[2] and **fare**]

welk[1] *welk*, (*obs*) *vi* to wither or shrivel; to wane or decline (*Spenser* **welke**). — Also *vt*. [ME *welken*; cf Ger *welk* withered]

welk[2]. See under **welkt**.

welkin *wel'kin*, *n* the sky or region of clouds. — *adj* (*Shakesp*) sky-blue. [OE *wolcnu*, plural of *wolcen* cloud, air, sky; Ger *Wolke* cloud]

welkt or **wealk'd** *welkt*, *adj* (*Shakesp*) twisted (in some modern editions written **whelk'd**). — *vi* **welk** (*Scott*, by inference from *Shakesp*) *appar* to twist about. [**whelk**[1]]

well[1] *wel*, *n* a spring; a mineral spring; a source; a lined shaft sunk in the earth whence a supply of water, oil, etc is obtained; an enclosure in a ship's hold round the pumps; a cockpit (*naut*); the vertical opening enclosed between the outer ends of the flights in a winding stair; a lift-shaft; a deep vertical space open to the sky within a block of tall buildings, admitting light and air; the open space in the middle of a courtroom; a cavity; a vessel serving as a reservoir, as in *inkwell*; an eddy. — *vi* to issue forth, as water does from the earth (with *out*, *forth* or *up*). — *vt* (*old*) to pour forth (with *out*, *forth* or *up*). — *n* **well'ing** an outpouring. — **well boat** or **well smack** a fishing-boat having a well for holding live fish; **well'-borer** a person or machine employed in well-boring; **well'-boring** sinking wells by drilling through rock; **well curb** the stone ring built round the mouth of a well; **well deck** a part of the upper deck of a ship enclosed fore and aft by the bulkheads supporting higher decks; **well drain** a pit drawing the water from wet land; **well'-dressing** the festal decoration of wells and springs, as in Derbyshire on Ascension day, etc; **well'head** the source of a spring; a fountainhead, origin or source; a spring in a marsh (*Scot*); the top of a well, or a structure built over it; **well hole** a hole for a well of any kind; the shaft of a well; a shaft for machinery; the vertical opening up through the middle of a winding stair, enclosed by the ends of the flights; **well'house** or **well room** a room built over a well; **well'-sinker** someone employed in digging wells; **well'-sinking**; **well'spring** a fountain. — **the wells** any place where mineral wells are situated; **well over** to overflow. [OE *wella*; cf *weallan* to boil, ON *vella* to boil]

well[2] *wel* (*compar* **bett'er**; *superl* **best**), *adj* (*usu* predicative) in good condition; in good health; fortunate; advisable; satisfactory; comfortable. — *n* (*Spenser*) good health or fortune. — *adv* rightly; skilfully; thoroughly; intimately; favourably, successfully; abundantly; with some degree of luxury; with reason or propriety; conveniently; to a considerable extent; clearly; easily; very possibly; used as an intensifier, *esp* as combining form (eg (*Shakesp*) 'a well-accomplish'd youth' and (*modern slang*) 'well safe', ie absolutely reliable); so be it (said in assent; *archaic*). — *interj* expressing surprise, hesitation, resignation, etc, or introducing resumed narrative. — *n* **well'ness**. — *adj* **well-acquaint'ed** having intimate personal knowledge, familiar (with *with*). — *adj* **well-advised'** prudent; in one's right mind (*Shakesp*). — *adj* **well-affec'ted** well or favourably disposed (with *to* or *towards*); loyal. — *adj* **well-aimed'**. — *adj* **well-appoint'ed** well-equipped. — **well-appoint'edness**. — *adj* **well-bal'anced** having the parts properly adjusted for smooth working; sane and sensible. — *adj* **well-becom'ing** befitting, appropriate to; proper or suitable. — *adj* **well-behaved'** behaving or acting in accordance with propriety or with requirements. — **well'being** welfare. — *adj* **well-beloved** (*-luvd'* or *-luv'id*) very dear. — *adj* **well-beseem'ing** befitting. — *adj* **well-beseen'** (*obs*) showy in appearance. — *adj* **well-born'** born of a good family, not of humble birth. — *adj* **well-breathed** (*-brēdhd'* or *-bretht'*) having strong lungs; exercised; not out of breath. — *adj* **well-bred'** having polite manners and good breeding; of good stock. — *adj* **well-built'** (of a building, a person, a garment, etc) of strong or well-proportioned make or form. — *adj* **well-cho'sen** (now *esp* of words in a speech) carefully assembled, felicitously chosen. — *adj* **well-condi'tioned** in good condition. — *adj* **well-conduct'ed** properly managed; acting properly. — *adj* **well-connec'ted** having friends or relatives in positions of importance or in the upper social strata. — *adj* **well-cov'ered** plump. — *adj* **well-defined'** clearly and precisely determined. — *adj* **well-derived'** (*Shakesp*) of good stock or antecedents. — *adj* **well-deserved'** properly merited or earned; condign. — *adj* **well-desired'** (*Shakesp*) much sought after. — *adj* **well-devel'oped** having developed to an advanced, elaborate, good, desirable, etc state. — *adj* **well-direct'ed** skilfully aimed. — *adj*

well-disposed' well placed or well arranged; inclined to be friendly (with *to* or *towards*); favourable; healthy (*obs*). — **well'-doer** someone who lives uprightly or does good; someone who thrives and is prosperous (*dialect*). — *n* and *adj* **well'-doing**. — *adj* **well-done'** (of food, *esp* meat) thoroughly cooked (see also **well done** below). — *adj* **well-dressed'** wearing stylish clothes. — *adj* **well-earned'** thoroughly deserved. — *adj* **well-ed'ucated** having had a good education. — *adj* **well-endowed'** (*colloq, facetious*) (of a man) having a large penis; (of a woman) having large breasts. — *adj* **well-en'tered** (*Shakesp*) instructed, initiated. — *adj* **well-famed'** (*Shakesp*) very famous. — *adj* **well-fa'voured** (*Scot* **weel-faird** (*wēl-fārd'*), **weel-faur'd, weel-far'd** (*-förd'*), **weel-far't'** or **weel-faurt'** (*-fört'*)) good-looking. — *adj* **well-fed'** plump; given nutritious food. — *adj* **well-formed'** shapely, well-proportioned; correct according to the established rules of grammar (*linguistics*). — *adj* **well-found'** adequately provided, fully equipped; commendable (*obs*). — *adj* **well-found'ed** built on secure foundations; based on solid evidence or sound reasoning. — *adj* **well-giv'en** (*obs*) well-disposed. — *adj* **well-got'ten** obtained honestly. — *adj* **well-graced'** (*Shakesp*) popular. — *adj* **well-groomed'** neat and smart in appearance, with carefully tended hair, hands, etc. — *adj* **well-ground'ed** thoroughly instructed in the fundamentals; firmly founded. — *adj* **well-heeled'** prosperous, rich. — *adj* **well-hung'** hung skilfully; (of meat) hung long enough to mature; (of a man) having sizeable genitals (*colloq*). — *adj* **well-informed'** having sound and sufficient information on a particular subject; full of varied information. — *adj* **well-inten'tioned** having, or arising from, good intentions or purpose. — *adj* **well-judged'** correctly calculated, judicious. — *adj* **well-judg'ing**. — *adj* **well-kept'** carefully looked after, kept in good condition or order. — *adj* **well-knit'** (of a person) strongly built; closely and firmly connected, compact. — *adj* **well-known'** fully known; celebrated; notorious. — *adj* **well-li'king** (*archaic*) in good condition, plump (see also **liking** under **like**[2]). — *n* (*obs*) approbation, fondness. — *adj* **well-lined'** with a good lining; full of money. — *adj* **well-look'ing** good-looking. — *adj* **well-made'**. — *adj* **well-mann'ered** polite. — *adj* **well-marked'** obvious, decided. — *adj* **well-mean'ing** well-intentioned (though unwise). — *adj* **well-meant'** rightly or kindly intended (if misguided). — *adj* **well-mind'ed** favourably inclined; well-disposed. — *adv* **well'-nigh** nearly, almost. — *adj* **well-off'** moderately wealthy (see also **well off** below). — *adj* **well-oiled'** drunk (*facetious*); smoothly mechanical from much practice. — *adj* **well-ord'ered** correctly governed; properly arranged. — *adj* **well-padd'ed** (*colloq*) plump. — *adj* **well-placed'** in a good position (for some purpose); in a position senior enough or intimate enough to gain information, etc. — *adj* **well-pleas'ing** (*old*) acceptable. — *adj* **well-plight'ed** folded, plaited or pleated well (see **plight**[2]). — *adj* **well-preserved'** in good condition, not decayed; looking youthful or younger than one's age. — *adj* **well-propor'tioned** having correct or pleasing proportions. — *adj* **well-read'** (*-red'*) having read widely, well-informed on literature. — *adj* **well-reg'ulated** well-ordered. — *adj* **well-respect'ed** highly esteemed; given due consideration (*Shakesp*, 1 *Henry IV*, IV.3.10). — *adj* **well-round'ed** suitably curved; symmetrical; well constructed and complete; satisfactorily developed in all essentials. — *adj* **well-seen'** (*archaic*) experienced, skilful. — *adj* **well-set'** properly arranged, or well placed; properly put together; firmly fixed; strongly built. — *adj* **well-set-up'** (*colloq*; of a person) well-built, shapely. — *adj* **well-spent'** spent usefully or profitably. — *adj* **well-spo'ken** spoken well or fittingly; ready, graceful or courteous in speech. — *adj* **well-stacked'** (*colloq*; of a woman) having large breasts (see also **stack**[1]). — *adj* **well-tem'pered** good-tempered; having a good bodily or mental constitution (*obs*); (of steel, mortar, etc) tempered satisfactorily; tuned in equal temperament (*music*). — *adj* **well-thewed'** (*obs*) well-mannered, of good disposition; abounding in moral wisdom. — *adj* **well-thought'-of** esteemed. — *adj* **well-thought-out'** reasoned soundly and arranged with skill. — *adj* **well-thumbed'** (of a book) showing marks of much handling or repeated use. — *adj* **well-tim'bered** strongly built of wood; well-built; abounding in growing timber. — *adj* **well-timed'** opportune, timely, judicious; keeping regular time; done at the right moment. — *adj* **well-to-do'**, or (*Scot* and *Shakesp*) **well-to-live'** prosperous, well-off. — *adj* **well-tried'** tried often before, with satisfactory results. — *adj* **well-trodd'en** frequently followed or walked along, much used or frequented. — *adj* **well-turned'** accurately rounded; shapely; felicitously expressed. — *adj* **well-uphol'stered** (*facetious*; of a person) plump, fat. — *adj* **well-warr'anted** having good credit. — **well'-willer** a well-wisher; **well'-wish** (*rare*) an expression of good wishes. — *adj* **well'-wished** (*Shakesp*) being the object of good wishes. — **well'-wisher** someone who is concerned for one's welfare. — *adj* and *n* **well'-wishing**. — **well woman** a woman attending, and pronounced fit at, a **well-woman clinic**, set up to check women for gynaecological disorders and advise them on health matters. — *adj* **well-won'** gained honestly or by hard endeavour. — *adj* **well-worked-out'** thoroughly or logically planned or developed. — *adj* **well-worn'** much worn; trite; becomingly worn (*rare*). — **all very well** an ironic phrase used to introduce an objection to what has gone before; **as well** in addition; also; equally satisfactorily; **as well as** in addition to; no less than; **be as well** (or **just as well**) **to** to be sensible to (do something); **do well** to prosper; to be wise (to do something); **just as well** fortunate, lucky; **leave well alone** not to interfere in a situation that can be tolerated as it is; **very well** a phrase signifying assent, sometimes ironic; **well and good** a phrase signifying acceptance of facts or a situation; **well and truly** completely, thoroughly; **well away** progressing rapidly; far away; drunk (*slang*); **well done** an expression of praise to someone who has accomplished something; **well enough** in a moderate but sufficient degree; **well in** (*colloq*) on good or friendly terms (with *with*); prosperous (*Austr*); **well met** see under **meet**[2]; **well now** or **well then** phrases used to preface questions, conclusions, comments, or requests for such, or other remarks; **well off** in satisfactory circumstances; moderately wealthy; **well up in** (*colloq*) well versed in, well acquainted with, knowledgeable on the subject of; **well, well** an expression of surprise; **wish someone well** to wish someone success or good fortune; to bear someone no ill will. [OE *wel*; cognate with Gothic *waila*, Ger *wohl*; from the root of **will**[1]]

we'll *wēl*, a contraction of **we will** or **we shall**.

welladay *wel'ə-dā*, (*archaic*) *interj* alas. [Alteration of **wellaway**]

wellanear *wel-ə-nēr'*, (*archaic*) *interj* alas. [Variation on **wellaway**]

wellaway or **welaway** *wel-ə-wā'*, (*archaic*) *interj* alas. [OE *weg la weg*, *wei la wei*, replacing *wa la wa* from *wa* woe]

wellie. See **welly**[1].

wellington *wel'ing-tən* or **wellington boot** (*bo͞ot*), *n* a loose-fitting rubber or plastic waterproof boot covering the calf; a riding-boot covering the knee in front but cut away behind (*hist*); a shorter closely-fitting boot, worn under the trousers (**half'-wellington**) (*hist*). [From boots worn by the Duke of *Wellington* (1769–1852)]

Wellingtonia *wel-ing-tō'ni-ə*, *n* a popular name for the genus *Sequoia* of giant conifers; (without *cap*) a tree of the genus. [Named after the Duke of *Wellington* (1769–1852)]

Wellsian *wel'zi-ən*, *adj* of, relating to or characteristic of H G *Wells* (1866–1946), historian and writer of stories and novels with scientific or social interest.

welly[1] or **wellie** *wel'i*, (*colloq*) *n* a wellington of the loose rubber or plastic kind (also **well'y-boot** or **well'ie-boot**); (also **green welly**; often in *pl* and with *cap*) a student or other (young) person, typically of the landed class, whose noticeably preferred footwear is wellingtons, *esp* of a sturdy green variety, suggesting recent arrival from or imminent departure for a rural property (*orig university slang*; *derog*). — **give it welly** or **wellie** (*slang*) to put one's foot down heavily on the accelerator; to put all one's efforts and energy into what one is doing.

welly[2] *wel'i*, (*dialect*) *adv* a corrupted form of **well-nigh**.

Welsh or (*obs*) **Welch** *welsh*, *adj* relating to *Wales* or its inhabitants. — *n pl* the inhabitants of Wales. — *n sing* their P-Celtic or Brythonic language, a development of the ancient British language, related to Cornish and Breton. — **Welsh aunt** or **uncle** (*dialect*) a first cousin of one's father or mother; **Welsh dresser** a dresser *usu* with open shelves above cupboards and drawers; **Welsh harp** a large harp with three rows of strings, two tuned in unison and in the diatonic scale, the third in the sharps and flats of the chromatic; **Welsh hook** an old weapon, a billhook or something similar; **Welsh'man** or **Welsh'woman** a native of Wales; **Welsh onion** the cibol; **Welsh rabbit** or **Welsh rarebit** see **rarebit** under **rare**[1]. [OE (Anglian and Kentish) *welisc*, from *wealh* foreigner, the Anglo-Saxons' word for Briton, Welshman, foreigner; from L *Volcae*, orig the Narbonese Gauls]

welsh or (*obs*) **welch** *welsh*, *vi* to run off from a race course without settling or paying one's bets (*horse-racing*); (with *on*) to fail to pay (one's debts, *esp* in gambling); (with *on*) to avoid fulfilling (an obligation) or fail to keep faith with (a person). — *vt* to cheat in such a way. — *n* **welsh'er** or **welch'er**. [Of uncertain origin]

Welsummer *wel'sum-ər*, *n* a breed of large poultry with golden plumage, prolific egg-layers. [After the Dutch village of *Welsum*, where it was first bred]

Welt *velt*, (*Ger*) *n* world. — **Weltanschauung** (*velt'an-show-ŏŏng*) outlook on the world, world philosophy; **Weltgeist** (*velt'gīst*) the world spirit; **Weltpolitik** (*velt'-pol-i-tēk*) world politics; the policy of taking a forceful part in international affairs; **Weltschmerz** (*velt'-shmerts*) world sorrow; sympathy with universal misery; sadness for the human lot; world-weariness; thoroughgoing pessimism; **Weltstadt** (*velt'shtat*) a cosmopolitan city.

welt[1] *welt*, *n* a band, strip or ribbed border fastened to an edge to give strength or for ornament; a narrow strip of leather used in one method of sewing the upper to the sole of a shoe; a weal; a lash, blow. — *vt* to fit with a welt; to lash, beat. [Origin obscure]

welt[2] *welt*, *vt* and *vi* to wither, dry. [Perh **welk**[1]]

welter *wel'tər*, *vi* to roll or tumble about (*rare* or *dialect*); to wallow about in dirt or moral degradation, etc (*rare*); to be or lie soaked, eg in blood (*poetic*); to be sunk (with *in*); to roll or toss about in the waves; (of the sea) to roll or surge (*poetic*). — *vt* (*rare*) to make (one's way) in a weltering manner. — *n* a state of turmoil, agitation or confusion; a confused mass; a surging mass. — *adj* **wel'tering**. [MDu *welteren*; cf OE *gewæltan* to roll]

welterweight *wel'tər-wāt*, *n* a boxer over 61kg (9st 9lb), amateur 63.5kg (10st), and not over 66.7kg (10st 7lb), amateur 67kg (10st 8lb); a wrestler over 68kg (10st 10 lb) and not over 74kg (11st 8lb); an unusually heavy weight, carried mostly in steeplechases and hurdle races. — **welter race** a race in which such weights are carried; **welter stakes** the stakes in a welter race. — **light welterweight** a boxer, amateur only, whose weight is between 60kg (9st 6lb) and 63.5kg (10st). [Origin obscure]

Weltgeist ... to ... **Weltstadt**. See under **Welt**.

Welwitschia *wel-wich'i-ə*, *n* a plant of a SW African genus (*Welwitschia*) of one species, belonging to the Gnetaceae, with one pair of leaves that grow indefinitely. [After F *Welwitsch* (1806–72), Austrian traveller]

wem or **wemb**. See **wame**.

Wemyss ware *wēmz' wār*, *n* a type of pottery produced between 1882 and 1930 in Kirkcaldy, Fife, named after the *Wemyss* family of Wemyss Castle, and characterized by lively colourful painted decoration, *esp* representing fruit and flowers.

wen[1] *wen*, *n* a sebaceous cyst, *esp* on the scalp; an enormous congested city as in *the great wen*, ie London. — *adj* **wenn'ish** or **wenn'y** wen-like. [OE *wen(n)* a swelling or a wart; Du *wen*; origin obscure]

wen[2] *wen*, *n* a former name for the runic and OE letter **wyn** (qv).

wench *wench* or *wensh*, (*archaic* or *facetious*) *n* a girl or young woman; a servant girl; a child (*obs*); a mistress (*obs*); a prostitute, whore (*obs*). — *vi* to frequent the company of whores; to associate with girls (*Scot* **winch**); to go courting (*dialect*). — *n* **wench'er** (*old*) a man who associates with prostitutes. [OE *wencel* a child]

Wend *wend*, *n* a member of a branch of the Slavs that once occupied the north and east of Germany; a member of the Slavic population of Lusatia (part of Brandenburg, Saxony and Silesia) who still speak the Wendish language. — *adj* **Wend'ic** or **Wend'ish**. — *n* the Wendish language. [Ger *Wende*; origin obscure]

wend *wend*, *vt* to turn (*obs*); to turn to the opposite tack (*naut*); to alter the course of (a person, or a person's thoughts; *obs*); (*reflexive*) to betake (oneself; *obs*); to change (*obs*). — *vi* to turn (*obs*); to change (*obs*); to depart (*archaic*); to make one's way (*archaic*); to move, flow, wander (*archaic*): — *pa t* and *pa p* **wend'ed** or (*obs*) **went** (now used as *pa t* of **go**). — **wend one's way** to make one's way, follow the road, *esp* in a leisurely fashion. [OE *wendan*, a common Gmc verb]

wendigo. See under **windigo**.

Wendy House® *wen'di hows*, *n* a structure of cloth or plastic sheeting, decorated to simulate a little house, stretched over a rigid frame, erected *usu* indoors for children to play in. [From the house built for *Wendy* in J M Barrie's *Peter Pan*]

Wenlock *wen'lok*, (*geol*) *adj* denoting a group or series of rocks of the Upper Silurian period consisting of limestone and shale and largely developed in the neighbourhood of *Wenlock* in Shropshire.

wennish and **wenny**. See under **wen**[1].

Wensleydale *wenz'li-dāl*, *n* a breed of long-woolled sheep; a white crumbly variety of cheese. [*Wensleydale* in the North Riding of Yorkshire]

went *went*, *orig pa t* of **wend**, but now used as *pa t* of **go**. — *n* (*Spenser*) a path; a journey; a way; a course.

wentletrap *wen'tl-trap*, *n* any member of a genus (*Scalaria*) of gasteropod molluscs, having a spiral shell with many deep whorls, crossed by elevated ribs. [Du *wenteltrap* (Ger *Wendeltreppe*) a winding staircase, a spiral shell]

wept *wept*, *pa t* and *pa p* of **weep**.

were *wûr*, *vi* the *pl* of **was**, used as *pa t* (*pl*) and *past subjunctive* (*sing* and *pl*) of **be**. [OE *wǣron*, subjunctive *wǣre*; Ger *waren*, *wäre*]

we're *wēr*, a contraction of **we are**.

werewolf *wēr'wŏŏlf*, or **werwolf** *wûr'wŏŏlf*, *n* a person supposed to be able to change for a time into a wolf (*Scot* **war'wolf**); a member of an underground Nazi organization (also *adj*): — *pl* **were'wolves**, etc. — *adj* **were'wolfish** or **wer'wolfish**. — *n* **were'wolfism** and **were'wolfery** lycanthropy. [OE *werwulf*, from *wer* man, and *wulf* wolf]

wergild *wûr'gild* or **weregild** *wēr'gild*, (*hist*) *n* among Teutonic peoples, a fine by which homicide and other heinous crimes against the person were expiated. [OE *wergield*, from *wer* man, and *gield* tribute, compensation, from *gieldan* to pay]

Wernerian *vûr-nē'ri-ən*, *adj* relating or according to the opinions or system of A G *Werner* (1750–1817), who attributed all geological phenomena to the action of water; Neptunian. — *n* an upholder of Werner's theories. — *n* **wer'nerite** scapolite.

Wernicke's encephalopathy *ver'ni-kəz* (or *wûr'ni-kəz*) *en-sef-ə-lop'ə-thi*, *n* a degenerative brain disease of haemorrhagic type caused by a deficiency of thiamine (vitamin B_1), in many cases the result of chronic alcoholism, characterized by paralysis of the eye muscles, double vision, nystagmus and impaired muscular control, frequently in association with Korsakoff's psychosis (qv). [Karl *Wernicke*, German neuropsychiatrist, (1848–1905)]

wersh *wersh*, (*Scot*) *adj* tasteless, insipid, unsalted; sour or bitter in taste; sickly, feeble; (of weather) raw. [**wearish**]

wert *wûrt*, used (*archaic* or *dialect*) as the *2nd pers sing* of the *past indicative* (for **wast**) and *subjunctive* of **be**. [**were**, and sfx *-t*]

Wertherian *vûr-tē'ri-ən*, *adj* relating to or resembling the character of *Werther* in Goethe's romance *The Sorrows of Young Werther*, ie morbidly sentimental. — *n* **Wer'therism**.

werwolf. See **werewolf**.

wesand *wē'zənd*, *n* (*Spenser*). Same as **weasand**.

Wesleyan *wez'li-ən* or *wes'li-ən*, *adj* relating to John *Wesley* (1703–1791), or to Methodism, the name given to his system of religious doctrine and church organization, or to the Protestant denomination founded by him. — *n* an adherent of Wesley or Methodism. — *n* **Wes'leyanism** Arminian (qv) Methodism, the doctrinal stance of the Wesleyan Methodists; their system of church organization.

west *west*, *n* the quarter of the sky where the sun sets; one of the four chief points of the compass; the direction faced when one stands with one's back to the high altar of a church; the regions in the west of any country, *esp* (with *cap*; *US*) those beyond the Appalachian Mountains (see also **Middle West** under **middle**) or beyond the Mississippi or the Rocky Mountains (see also **Far West** under **far**); (with *cap*) the western part of the world as distinct from the East or Orient; (with *cap*) in mid- to late-20c politics, the non-communist countries of Europe and N America; (with *cap*) the western part of the Roman Empire or Holy Roman Empire (*hist*). — *adj* situated towards, or (of wind) coming from, the west; opposite the high altar of a church. — *adv* towards the west. — *vi* to move towards the west. — *vi* **west'er** to turn westward; to change into the west. — *n* and *adj* **west'ering**. — *adj* **west'erly** lying or moving towards the west; from the west. — *adv* towards the west; from the west. — *n* a westerly wind. — *adj* **west'ern** situated in the west; belonging to the west or (with *cap*) the West; moving towards or (*old*, of wind) coming from the west. — *n* an inhabitant of a western or (with *cap*) Western region or country; a film or novel whose scene is the western United States, *esp* the former Wild West. — *n* **west'erner** a person belonging to the west or (with *cap*) the West. — *n* **west'ernism** an idiom or other characteristic of a western people. — *n* **westernizā'tion** or **-s-**. — *vt* and *vi* **west'ernize** or **-ise** to make or become like the people of Europe and America in customs, or like their institutions, practices or ideas. — *adj* **west'ernmost** furthest to the west. — *n* **west'ing** space or distance westward; departure westward; direction or course towards the west. — *adj* **west'most** most westerly. — *adj* and *adv* **west'ward** towards the west. — *adv* **west'wardly** and **west'wards** towards the west. — *adv* **west'-about** towards the west. — **West Bank** the Jordanian territory to the west of the river Jordan and the Dead Sea, annexed by Israel in 1967; **West-Bank'er** an inhabitant of the West Bank. — *adj* **west'bound** heading or travelling westwards. — **west'-by-north'** (or **-south'**) $11\frac{1}{4}$ degrees north (or south) from due west; **West Country** the south-western part of England; **West-country whipping** (*naut*) a rope-whipping method where a half knot is made alternately on each side, finished off with a reef knot; **West End** the fashionable quarter in the west of London; a similar district in other large towns; **western blotting** (*immunol*) see **immunoblot**; **Western Church** the Latin Church, having its doctrine and ritual from Rome, as distinguished from the Eastern or Greek Church; **Western Empire** the western division of the later Roman Empire; **Western Front** the belt of land, running SE from the coast of Belgium through Rheims to Verdun, which lay between the German and Allied Forces in World War I; **Western hemisphere** the hemisphere of the world containing the Americas; **Western Isles** the Hebrides; **western roll** (*athletics*) a style of high-jumping, taking off from the inside foot and clearing the bar face downwards; **western saddle** a stock saddle as used by cowboys, with a high pommel behind, and wide leather leg-protecting flaps; **Western Wall** the Wailing Wall (qv under **wail**); **West Highland (white) terrier** a breed of small white terrier with a short stiff coat and small pointed ears; **West Indian** and **West Indies** see under **Indian**; **west'-north** (or **south**)**-west'** $22\frac{1}{2}$ degrees north (or south) from the west; **West Saxon** a southern dialect of Old English, the chief literary dialect before the Norman Conquest. — **go west** to go to America; to go to the western states or western frontier; to die (with reference to the setting sun, the Islands of the Blest, or Tyburn), or to be destroyed or completely dissipated; **westward ho!** to the west!, an old cry of London watermen plying westwards. [OE; a common Gmc word; cf L *vesper*]

Westie *wes'ti*, *n* a West Highland terrier.

westlin *wes'lin* or *west'lin*, (*Scot*) *adj* western. — *adv* **west'lins** to or in the west.

Westminster *west'min-stər*, *n* the British Parliament, from the London borough where the Houses of Parliament are situated; Westminster Hall, a court of justice; Westminster School, or a past or present pupil of it. — *adj* denoting the presbyterian-dominated assembly of clerics and laymen convened by the English Long Parliament of 1643 to arrange a religious settlement to replace the Church of England, and the *Confession of Faith*, a statement of Calvinistic principles adopted by it.

Westphalian *west-fā'li-ən*, *adj* relating to *Westphalia*, a duchy, a kingdom, a province of Prussia and, since 1946, part of the German land of Nordrhein-Westfalen. — *n* a native of Westphalia.

wet *wet*, *adj* containing, soaked with or covered with water or other liquid; rainy; bringing or foreboding moisture; tearful; grown in damp soil; (of a method) using liquid (*chem*, etc); (of natural gas) containing large amounts of liquid constituents; given to drinking, or tipsy (*slang*); allowing the sale of intoxicating liquors; ineffectual or feeble (*colloq*); crazily mistaken (*US slang*); in politics, moderately conservative (*derog*). — *n* water, moisture, wetness; the rain; an act of wetting; a dram, a debauch; a weak, ineffectual, wavering person (*colloq*); in politics, a moderate conservative (*derog*). — *vt* to make wet; to soak with water; to urinate, *esp* involuntarily, on or in; (*reflexive*) to make (oneself) wet by urinating inadvertently; to make (tea) by pouring water on the leaves (*dialect*); to celebrate by drinking (*slang*): — *pr p* **wett'ing**; *pa t* and *pa p* **wet** or **wett'ed**. — *adv* **wet'ly**. — *n* **wet'ness**. — *adj* **wett'ish** somewhat wet. — **wet-and-dry paper** a stiff paper coated with powdered silicon carbide, like a fine sandpaper, used either wet or dry for smoothing surfaces; **wet-and-dry-bulb thermometer** a hygrometer consisting of two thermometers, one with a dry bulb, the other with the bulb kept moist; **wet assay** the use of the processes of solution, flotation, or other liquid means to determine a given constituent in ores, metallurgical residues and alloys; **wet'back** (*esp US*) someone illegally entering the USA from Mexico by wading or swimming the Rio Grande; an illegal immigrant generally; **wet bar** (*US*) a bar from which to serve alcoholic drinks in a private house or hotel suite, equipped with a sink and running water; **wet bike** a vehicle like a motorbike that travels over water on skis; **wet blanket** (*colloq*) a dismal person inclined to damp other peoples' spirits, a killjoy; **wet bob** (*public school slang*) a schoolboy at Eton or other school who goes in for rowing in the summer term in preference to cricket; **wet cell** an electric cell with a liquid electrolyte; **wet dock** a dock maintaining a level nearly uniform with that of high water; **wet dream** an erotic dream resulting in ejaculation of semen; **wet fish** fresh fish, as contrasted with frozen or dried fish. — *adj* **wet'-fly** (*angling*) with the fly under water. — **wet'land** (also in *pl*) marshy land; **wet lease** (*air travel*) the leasing of aircraft complete with crew. — Also *vt* (**wet'-lease**). — *adj* **wet'-look** made of a glossy material, *usu* PVC, which gives the appearance of being wet. — **wet meter** a gas meter in which the gas to be measured passes through water; **wet nurse** a nurse who suckles a child for its mother. — *vt* (**wet'-nurse**) to be a wet nurse to, to suckle (another woman's baby); to treat like a helpless child, to nanny. — **wet pack** (the wrapping of a person in) blankets or the like dampened with warm or cold water as a medical treatment; the dampened material used; **wet plate** (*photog*) a plate coated with collodion and sensitized with a salt of silver; **wet rot** a form of decay in timber caused by certain fungi which develop in wood that is alternately wet and dry. — *adj* **wet'-shod** (*dialect wet'shəd*) having wet shoes or feet. — **wet suit** a suit for wearing in water, which allows water to pass through but retains body heat; **wetting** (or **wetting-out**) **agent** any chemical that, added to a liquid, reduces its surface tension so that it is more readily spread over or absorbed by the materials it is applied to; **wet'ware** (*comput*; *facetious*) the living human brain. — **wet behind the ears** very young, immature, gullible; **wet one's whistle** (*colloq*) see under **whistle**; **wet out** to wet thoroughly (*old*); to cleanse (eg raw material in textile manufacture) by so doing; **wet the baby's head** (*colloq*) to celebrate the baby's birth with (alcoholic) drinks; **wet the bed** to urinate accidentally in bed; **wet through** with one's clothes completely soaked. [OE *wǣt* (noun and adj), *wǣtan* (verb); the short vowel is from the ME pa t and pa p of the verb]

weta *wet'ə*, *n* a large horned wingless grasshopper of New Zealand, its bite reported by some to be venomous. [Maori]

wether *wedh'ər*, *n* a castrated ram. [OE; cf Ger *Widder*]

wetted, wetting, wettish. See under **wet**.

WEU *abbrev*: Western European Union.

we've *wēv*, a contraction of **we have**.

wex and **wexe**. Obsolete forms of **wax**[1,2,3].

wey *wā*, *n* a measure or weight for dry goods differing with different commodities (eg, for salt, corn, etc 40 bushels). [Variant of **weigh**]

weyard and **weyward**. Obsolete spellings of **weird**, found in older editions of Shakespeare's *Macbeth*.

wezand. Obsolete form of **weasand**.

wf (*printing*) *abbrev*: wrong fount.

WFA *abbrev*: White Fish Authority.

WFTU *abbrev*: World Federation of Trade Unions.

WG *abbrev*: Grenada, Windward Islands (IVR).

wg *abbrev*: water gauge; wire gauge.

wha *hwä* or *hwö*, (*Scot*) form of **who**.

whack *wak* or *hwak*, (*colloq*) *vt* to strike hard and smartly; to put or take with violence; to beat decisively; to parcel out, share. — *vi* to strike; to settle accounts. — *n* a blow; the sound of a blow; a share; an attempt. — *adj* **whacked** (*colloq*) exhausted. — *n* **whack'er** (*colloq*) something big of its kind; a blatant lie. — *adj* or *intensifying adv* **whack'ing** (*colloq*) enormous. — *n* a beating or thrashing. — *interj* **whack'ō** (*colloq*) an expression of pleasure or enthusiasm: — *pl* **whack'oes** or **whack'os**. — **out of whack** (*colloq*) out of order, not straight. [Imit of the sound]

whacko[1]. See **wacko**.

whacko[2]. See under **whack**.

whacky *wak'i* or *hwak'i*, *adj* same as **wacky**.

whaisle or **whaizle** *wā'zl* or *hwā'zl*, (*Scot*) *vi* to wheeze. [A form of **wheezle**; see **wheeze**]

whale[1] *wāl* or *hwāl*, *n* any of an order of cetaceous mammals, including the *toothed* whales, such as the sperm whales and the dolphins, and the *whalebone* whales, such as the right whales and the rorquals, in which the teeth are only embryonic; a person with a large appetite (*slang*); something very large of its kind (*slang*); (with *cap*) the constellation Cetus. — *vi* to catch whales. — *n* **whāl'er** a whaleboat; a whaleman; something very large of its kind (*slang*). — *n* **whāl'ery** whaling. — *adj* **whāl'ing** concerned with or used in whale-catching. — *n* the business of catching whales. — **whale'back** a turtleback; a kind of steamboat used on the Great Lakes to carry grain, etc having a rounded upper deck, etc; a mound shaped like the back of a whale; **whale'boat** a long, narrow boat sharp at both ends once used in the pursuit of whales; a similar boat carried on a large vessel as a life-boat; **whale'bone** a light flexible substance consisting of the baleen plates of whales; an article made of this. — *adj* made of whalebone. — **whale calf** (also **calf whale**) a young whale; **whale'-fisher**; **whale'-fishery**; **whale'-fishing**; **whale'-head** the shoebill (also **whale-headed stork**); **whale line** strong rope used for harpoon lines in whale-fishing; **whale louse** a genus (*Cyamus*) of amphipod Crustacea parasitic on the skin of cetaceans; **whale'man** a person or ship employed in whale-fishing; **whale oil** oil got from the blubber of a whale; **whale's bone** (*obs*) ivory eg from the walrus; **whale's food** or **whale food** small animals eaten by whales, *esp* the *Clio* genus of shell-less pteropods; **whale shark** a huge but harmless shark of tropical seas; **whal'ing-gun** a harpoon gun, a contrivance that fires a harpoon attached to a line; **whal'ing-master** the captain of a whaler; **whal'ing-port** a port where whalers are registered. — **bull** and **cow whale** an adult male and female whale respectively; **whale of a time** (*colloq*) a hugely enjoyable time. [OE *hwæl*; cf ON *hvalr*, Ger *Walfisch*]

whale[2] *wāl* or *hwāl*, (*slang*) *vt* to thrash; to strike violently. — *n* **whāl'ing** a thrashing. — *adj* or *intensifying adv* enormous. [Perh **wale**[1]; perh from *whale*bone whip]

whally *wöl'i* or *hwöl'i*, (*Spenser*) *adj* wall-eyed; (of the eye) showing much white. [From **wall-eye**]

wham *wam* or *hwam*, *n* a resounding noise caused by a hard blow. — *vi* to crash or bang (with *into*, etc). — *vt* to hit or bang: — *prp* **whamm'ing**; *pa t* and *pa p* **whammed**. — Also *adv* and *interj*. — *interj* **whamm'o** (or *wa-mō'* or *hwa-mō'*) descriptive of violent impact. — *n* impressive verve and energy. — Also *adj*. — *n* **whamm'y** (*colloq*, *orig US*) a malevolent spell or influence cast by someone's evil eye, such a spell cast by both eyes being a **double whammy**; now, generally, a stunning blow, the winning punch (*colloq*). — **put the whammy on** to put the evil eye on, cast an evil spell on; **wham bam thank you ma'am** (*vulg slang*) quick impersonal sexual intercourse that brings speedy gratification to the male. [Imit]

whample *hwöm'pl* or *hwam'pl*, (*Scot*) *n* a stroke or blow.

whang[1] *wang* or *hwang*, *n* a leather thong; a thick slice; a penis (*vulg*; also **wang**). — *vt* to flog; to throw, push or pull violently; to cut in great slices. [*thwang*, obs form of **thong**]

whang[2] *wang* or *hwang*, *n* a resounding noise; a blow. — *vi* to career or go headlong, with a resounding impact. — *vt* to (cause to) hit with a whang. — Also *adv* and *interj*. [Imit]

whangam *wang'gəm* or *hwang'gəm*, (*Goldsmith*) *n* an imaginary animal.

whangee *wang-ē'* or *hwang-ē'*, *n* any of several grasses of a genus (*Phyllostachys*) related to the bamboos, found in China and Japan; a cane made from the stem of one. [Prob Chin *huang* yellow, and *li* bamboo]

whap, **whapped**, **whapping**. See under **whop**.

whare *wor'i*, *hwor'i*, *hwär'ā* or *fär'ā*, (*New Zealand*) *n* a house. [Maori]

wharf *wörf* or *hwörf*, *n* a landing-stage, built *esp* along the shore, for loading or unloading vessels; the bank of a river (*Shakesp*): — *pl* **wharfs** or **wharves**. — *vt* to strengthen or secure by means of a wharf (*obs*); to place on, or bring to, a wharf. — *n* **wharf'age** the dues paid for using a wharf; accommodation at a wharf. — *n* **wharf'ing** material for making a wharf; wharfs. — *n* **wharfinger** (*wör'fin-jər* or *hwör'fin-jər*) the owner or keeper of a wharf. — **wharf rat** the common brown rat;

a loafer who hangs about a wharf. [Late OE *hwearf* bank, shore; related to *hweorfan* to turn]

wharve. See **whorl** (*spinning*).

wharves. See **wharf**.

what *wot* or *hwot*, *interrog pronoun* neuter of **who**, used to form questions regarding identity, selection from an indefinite number, nature, value, etc (also used elliptically (as in *what did you say*?, *what do you think*?, *what is it*?); who (*obs*). — Also *interrog adj*. — *rel pronoun* and *adj* that which; such ... as; which (*dialect*); any or anything whatever; whoever (*Shakesp*). — *indefinite pronoun* (or *n*) something; a portion, bit (*Spenser*); fare (in the phrase *such homely what*; *Spenser*, *Faerie Queene* VI.9.7.4). — *adv* why? (*obs*); in what way, how? to what degree? — *conj* as much as (*dialect*); that (as in **but what** that ... not). — *interj* used in summoning, calling attention, expressing surprise, disapprobation, protest, etc. — *adj* **what'en** or **whatt'en** (*dialect*; from *whatkin* what kind) what; what kind of. — *adj* **what'na** (from *whatkin a*) same as **whaten**. — *n* **what'ness** what a thing is; essence; quiddity. — **what'abouts** the things one is occupied about; **what'd'you** (or **ye**)**-call-it**, **-'em**, etc, a word substituted for the name of a thing or person in forgetfulness or contempt. — Also **what'-you-may-call-it**, etc. — *pronoun* **whatev'er** or (*literary*) **whate'er** (*wot-ār'* or *hwot-ār'*) anything that; no matter what; what? (*colloq*). — *adj* any or all that, no matter what. — **what's'-his-(her-, its-, etc) name** (*colloq*) someone or something indicated or understood whose name one cannot, or cannot be bothered to, recall. — Also **what'sit** and (*US*) **what'sis**. — *adj* **what'-like** (*dialect*) of what kind, character or appearance. — **what'not** see separate article and **what not** below. — *adj* **what'so** (*archaic*) of whatever kind. — *pronoun* whatever (*archaic*); whoever (*obs*); whosoever (*obs*). — *adj* and *pronoun* **whatsoev'er** or (*old*) **whatsoe'er** (*wot-sō-ār'* or *hwot-sō-ār'*) whatever. — *adj* and *pronoun* **whatsomev'er** (*dialect*) whatsoever. — **what-you-may-call-it** see **what-d'you-call-it**. — **and what all** and so on, and suchlike things; **know what it is** to know what is involved in an action or experience; to have experienced or suffered it; **or whatever** (*colloq*) or some such thing; **so what**? what of it?; **what about** do you fancy (something, or doing something)?; what is your opinion of (someone or something)?; aren't you forgetting (someone or something)?; **what an if** (*Shakesp*) what if, or though; **what else**? could anything else be the case?; **what ... for**? for what reason, or with what purpose in mind? (also *dialect* **what for** ...?); **what for** (*colloq*) punishment, chastisement, as in *I'll give you what for*!; **what for a** (*obs*) what kind of; **what have you** (*colloq*) what not; anything else of the kind; **what ho** a loud hail or summons; **what if** what would it matter if? (also **what matter if**); what would happen if?; **what ... like**? a common form of request for a description or opinion of something or someone, as in *what is she like*?, *what does this look*, *sound*, *like*?; **what next**? what is to be done next?; what will happen next? (often said in despair or trepidation); **what not** (elliptical for 'what may I not say?') (and) other such things, (and) so forth; (and) anything and everything else (*old*); **what now**? what is the meaning of this latest interruption?; what is to be done now?; what's wrong now?; **what of** what comes of or follows from?; what do you think of?; what is the news of? **what of it**? does it matter? (with the implication that it does not); **what's more** and, more importantly; **what's new**? see under **new**; **what's with** (*colloq*; *esp US*) what's the matter with?, what's up with?; what do you mean by (doing something)?; **what's what** the true position of affairs; the proper, conventional or profitable way to behave or proceed; what really counts or matters; **what the hell, the dickens, the devil**, etc (*colloq*) whatever; **what then**? what would come of it?, what would be the consequence?; what happened after that?; **what though** what does it matter though; notwithstanding the fact that; **what time** (*archaic*) at the very time when; **what with** because of. [OE *hwæt*, neuter of *hwā* who; Ger *was*, L *quod*]

Whatman paper® *wot'mən* or *hwot'mən pā'pər*, *n* fine-quality paper used for drawings, engravings, filtering, etc. [Name of manufacturing firm]

whatna. See under **what**.

whatnot *wot'not* or *hwot'not*, *n* a light piece of furniture with shelves for bric-à-brac, etc; a nondescript article. [**what** and **not**]

whatsis, **whaten**, **whatten**, etc. See under **what**.

whaup *hwöp* or *wop*, (*Scot*) *n* a curlew, sometimes *great whaup* as distinct from *little whaup*, the whimbrel. [Primarily imit; history uncertain]

whaur *hwör* or *wör*, a Scots form of **where**.

wheal[1]. Variant of **weal**[2].

wheal[2] *wēl* or *hwēl*, *n* a Cornish name for a mine. [Cornish *hwel*]

whear or **wheare**. Obsolete spelling of **where**.

wheat *wēt* or *hwēt*, *n* any cereal grass of the genus Triticum, or its grain, from which a white or brown flour for bread, etc is produced; known as *bearded*, *beardless* or *bald*, according to the presence or absence of awns or beard; as *white*, *red* or *amber* according to colour; and as *winter* or *spring* (also *summer*) according to whether it is a type normally sown in autumn or spring. — *adj* **wheat'en** made of wheat; wholemeal; of the colour of ripe wheat. — **wheat berry** and **wheat corn** the grain of wheat; **wheat bird** the chaffinch; **wheat crop**; **wheat ear** an ear of wheat; **wheat-ear stitch** a fancy stitch in embroidery; **wheat eel** (also **wheat'worm**) a small nematode worm that makes its way up wheat stems to the ears; the disease it causes (also *ear-cockle*); **wheat'field**; **wheat fly** the name of several flies that destroy wheat, eg the Hessian fly; **wheat germ** the vitamin-rich germ or embryo of wheat, part of a grain of wheat; **wheat'meal** wheat flour with some of the bran and germ removed; **wheat midge** a dipterous insect that lays its eggs in the flowers of wheat heads, and whose reddish larvae devour the kernels; **wheat mildew** either of two fungus diseases of wheat; **wheat moth** any of several small moths whose larvae devour stored wheat; **wheat'sheaf** a sheaf of wheat; **wheatworm** see **wheat eel**. [OE *hwǣte*; Ger *Weizen*; related to **white**; named from its colour]

wheatear *wē'tēr* or *hwē'tēr*, *n* any of various songbirds of the genus *Oenanthe*, *esp Oenanthe oenanthe*, having a white belly and rump. [Prob a corruption of *white arse*]

Wheatstone *wēt'stən* or **Wheatstone's bridge** *wēt'stənz brij* (or *hwēt'stən* or *hwēt'stənz*) *n* an apparatus for measuring electrical resistance, much used, but not invented, by Sir Charles *Wheatstone* (1802–75).

whee *wē* or *hwē*, *interj* an expression of delight, exuberance, etc.

wheech *hwēhh* or *wēhh*, (*Scot*) *vi* to move rapidly with a whizzing sound; to dart; (with *through*) to do, deal with, etc rapidly. — *vt* to carry, remove rapidly; to throw. — *n* a rapid movement or throw; a whizzing sound. [Imit]

wheedle *wēd'l* or *hwē'dl*, *vt* and *vi* to entice by soft words, flatter, cajole; to obtain by coaxing (with *out of*); to cheat by cajolery (with *out of*); to winkle (with *out*). — *n* a piece of wheedling; a person giving to coaxing (*obs*). — *n* **wheed'ler**. — *adj* **wheed'lesome** coaxing. — *n* **wheed'ling**. [Perh from OE *wǣdlian* (orig) to be in want, to beg]

wheel *wēl* or *hwēl*, *n* a circular frame turning on an axle; a steering-wheel; a potter's wheel; a spinning-wheel; an old instrument of torture; a rotating firework; a bicycle or tricycle (*colloq*); (in *pl*) personal transport (*colloq*); the wheel by which a spit is turned (*Shakesp*); the wheel attributed to Fortune personified, the emblem of mutability; hence, the course of events; a celestial sphere (*obs*); a disc; a circular design; a circular motion; (in *pl*) the parts of a machine; the intricate workings of something; one or more short lines following a bob at the end of a stanza; a refrain; a dollar (*slang*). — *vt* to cause (a body of troops) to turn or revolve, *esp* round an axis or pivot; to cause to move in a circular course; to put a wheel or wheels on; to form or treat on the wheel; to convey on wheels; to propel on wheels; to encircle (*Milton*); to make wheel-shaped (*rare*); (with *out, forward,* etc; *colloq*) to bring out, forward, etc, to produce. — *vi* to turn round or on an axis; to change direction; to move in a circle; to reel, be giddy; to roll forward; to wander, roam (*Shakesp*); to travel in a wheeled vehicle; to ride a bicycle or tricycle (*colloq*); to be provided with wheels on which to be propelled. — *adj* **wheeled** having wheels; moving on wheels; (in combination) having a specified kind or number of wheels, as in *solid-wheeled, three-wheeled*; formed into a wheel (*rare*). — *n* **wheel'er** someone who wheels; a cyclist (*colloq*); a maker of wheels (*dialect*); (in combination) something that wheels, or that has a specified kind or number of wheels, as in *two-wheeler*; a wheelhorse. — *n* **wheel'ie** (*colloq*) a manoeuvre, eg on a bicycle, motorbike or skateboard, involving travelling for a short distance with the front wheel or wheels off the ground; a U-turn accomplished at speed with a loud skidding noise (*Austr*); a wheelie bin (*colloq*). — *n* **wheel'ing** the act of moving or conveying on wheels; a turning or circular movement; a rather coarse woollen yarn. — *adj* **wheel'y** like a wheel. — **wheel animal** or **animalcule** a rotifer (qv), a tiny aquatic animal; **wheel'barrow** a barrow with one wheel in front and two handles and legs behind; (loosely) any other handcart; **wheel'base** the distance between the front and rear axles of a vehicle; the area enclosed by lines joining the points at which the wheels of a locomotive, etc touch the rails or the ground, or the length of this area; **wheel carriage** any kind of carriage moved on wheels; **wheel'chair** a chair moving on wheels, *esp* an invalid's chair. — *adj* provided, designed, adapted or arranged for people confined to wheelchairs, as *wheelchair housing, wheelchair Olympics*, etc. — **wheel clamp** a device used by traffic authorities, etc to immobilize an illegally parked vehicle until it is removed after payment of a fine. — Also *vt* (**wheel'-clamp**). — *adj* **wheel'-cut** (of glass) cut, or ground and polished, on a wheel. — **wheel'-cutter** a machine for cutting teeth on wheels; **wheel'er-deal'er**; **wheel'er-deal'ing** (*colloq*; *orig US*) shrewd dealing or bargaining to one's maximum advantage in business, politics, etc, *esp* without regard for others' interests; **wheel'horse** one of the horses next to the wheels in a team; **wheel'house** a shelter in which a ship's steering-wheel is placed; a paddle box; a prehistoric wheel-shaped dwelling; **wheelie bin** a large dustbin in a wheeled frame; **wheel lock** (a gun having) a lock in which sparks are struck off a flint by a small steel wheel (*hist*); **wheel'man** a steersman; a cyclist; **wheel plough** a plough running on wheels, or one the depth of whose furrow is regulated by a wheel; **wheel race** the part of a race in which the water wheel is fixed; **wheel spin** rotation of the wheels of a vehicle without the purchase required for forward or backward movement; **wheel window** a circular window with radiating tracery, a rose window; **wheel'work** a combination of wheels and their connection in machinery; **wheel'-wright** a maker of wheels and wheeled carriages. — **at the wheel** driving a vehicle or steering a boat; **big wheel** a Ferris wheel (qv); a person of importance or self-importance; **break a butterfly** (or **fly**, etc) **on the wheel** to inflict a punishment out of all proportion to the offence; to employ great exertions for insignificant ends; **go on wheels** to move swiftly, smoothly, and hence pleasantly; **left** (or **right**) **wheel** (a command to perform) a swing to the left (or right); **put a spoke in someone's wheel** see under **spoke**; **put one's shoulder to the wheel** see under **shoulder**; **take the wheel** to take charge or control; **wheel and axle** one of the mechanical powers, in its primitive form a cylindrical axle, on which a wheel, concentric with the axle, is firmly fastened, the power being applied to the wheel, and the weight attached to the axle; **wheel and deal** (*colloq*; *orig US*) to engage in wheeler-dealing; **wheeling and dealing** (*colloq*; *orig US*) same as **wheeler-dealing**; **wheel of fortune** Fortune's wheel (see **wheel** above); a gambling device; **wheel of life** an optical toy giving an illusion of animation, a zoetrope (qv); **wheels within wheels** said of a situation in which a complication of influences is at work. [OE *hwēol*; ON *hjōl*]

wheen *hwēn* or *wēn*, (*Scot*) *n* a few. — *adj* (*obs*) few. — **a wheen** a few; a good many; (used adverbially) a little. [OE *hwǣne*, from *hwōn*, adv, a little]

wheenge. See under **whinge**.

wheeple *hwē'pl* or *wē'pl*, (*Scot*) *vi* to make a long-drawn-out cry such as that of the curlew; to whistle feebly. — Also *vt* and *n*. [Imit]

wheesh. See under **whish**[2].

wheesht. See **whisht**.

Wheeson (*Shakesp*; 2 *Henry IV*, II.1.99) Whitsun.

wheeze *wēz* or *hwēz*, *vi* to breathe with a hissing sound; to breathe audibly or with difficulty. — *vt* to utter with such a sound. — *n* the act or sound of wheezing; a gag (*theat slang*); a catch-phrase (*slang*); a standard joke (*slang*); a cunning plan (*colloq*). — *adv* **wheez'ily**. — *n* **wheez'iness**. — *n* **wheez'ing**. — *vi* **wheez'le** (*Scot*) to make wheezy sounds. — *adj* **wheez'y**. [Prob ON *hvæsa* to hiss]

wheft. See **waft**.

whelk[1] *wilk*, *welk* or *hwelk*, *n* a popular name for a number of marine gasteropods, *esp* applied to species of the genus *Buccinum* common on the coasts of northern seas. — *adj* **whelked** ridged like a whelk. — *adj* **whelk'y** knobby, rounded; formed in a shell (*Spenser*, *Virgil's Gnat*, 105). [Wrong form of older *welk*, from OE *wiloc*, *weoluc*; origin obscure]

whelk[2] *welk* or *hwelk*, *n* a pimple; by confusion with **wale**[1], the mark of a stripe on the body, a wrinkle, an inequality or protuberance. [Late OE (WSaxon) *hwylca*, from *hwelian* to suppurate]

whelk'd. See **welkt**.

whelm *welm* or *hwelm*, (*archaic*) *vt* to turn (eg a hollow vessel) upside down, *esp* so as to cover something else (now *dialect*); to cover completely in such a way (*obs*), or with eg water, etc; to overturn, overthrow; to plunge deep; to submerge; to overpower; to overburden; to ruin, destroy; to pass over in such a way as to submerge. — *n* the overwhelming surge of waves (*poetic*); a watercourse constructed from hollowed, inverted tree trunks. [ME *whelmen* to turn over]

whelp *welp* or *hwelp*, *n* a young dog, a puppy; the cub of a bear, wolf, lion or tiger (*archaic*); (contemptuously) a young man; a ridge running longitudinally on the barrel or drum of a capstan or windlass to control the cable; a sprocket on a wheel. — *vi* and *vt* to bring forth (young). [OE *hwelp*; ON *hvelpr*]

whemmle *wem'l* or *hwem'l*, **whomble**, **whommle** *wom'l* or *hwom'l*, or **whummle** *wum'l* or *hwum'l*, (*dialect*) *n* an overthrow, overturn; confusion. — *vt* to overturn; to turn upside down; to throw into a state of disorder or agitation; to move from side to side; to cover eg with an inverted dish. — *vi* to capsize. [By metathesis from **whelm**]

when *wen* or *hwen*, *adv* (*interrog* and *rel*) and *conj* at what time?; at which time; at or after the time that; upon or after which; while; although; at which (or *rel pronoun*). — *n* the (question of) the time at which something happened or is to happen. — *interj* (*Shakesp*) an exclamation of impatience, like *what!* — *conj* **whenas'** (*archaic*) when; in as much as; whereas. — *conj* **whenev'er** or (*literary*) **whene'er'** (*wen-ār'*, *hwen-ār'*) at every time when; as soon as (*Scot*). — *conj* **whensoev'er** or (*literary*) **whensoe'er** (*wen-sō-ār'* or *hwen-sō-ār'*) at whatsoever time. — **or whenever** (*colloq*) or at any comparable time; **say when** (*colloq*) tell me when to stop, *specif* when pouring a drink; **seldom when** (*Shakesp*) seldom that. [OE *hwanne*, *hwonne* (Ger *wann*, *wenn*); from the stem of interrog pronoun *hwā* who]

whence *wens* or *hwens*, *adv* and *conj* (also **from whence**) from what place; from which place?; from which things; wherefore. — *n* a place of origin; a source. — *adv* **whenceforth'** (*Spenser*) whence. — *conj* **whencesoev'er** or **whencev'er** from whatsoever place, cause or source. [ME *whennes*, *whannes*]

whe'r. See under **whether**.

where *wār* or *hwār*, *adv* (*interrog* and *rel*) and *conj* at or to which place; at what place?; to what place?; from what source; to a, or the, place in or from which (*archaic*); in what circumstances or condition; at what point; whereas; wherever; (a or the place) in, at or to which (or *rel pronoun*). — *n* the (question of) the location or destination of something. — *n* **where'ness** the state of having place or position; position, situation. — *adv* and *conj* **whereabout'** or **whereabouts'** near what?; approximately where?; about which, about where; on what errand (*Shakesp*; *n* what one is about). — **where'about** or, more *usu*, *n sing* or *n pl* **where'abouts** one's (*esp* approximate) location. — *conj* **whereaf'ter** after which. — *adv* and *conj* **whereagainst'** (*archaic*) against which. — *adv* and *conj* **whereas'** when in fact; but on the contrary; taking into consideration, in view of, the fact that; where (*obs*). — *adv* and *conj* **whereat'** at which; at what? — *adv* and *conj* **whereby'** by which. — *adv* and *conj* **wherefor'** (*formal*) for which. — *adv* and *conj* **where'fore** (*-fər*) for which, or what, reason; why? — *n* the cause. — *adv* and *conj* **wherefrom'** (*archaic*) whence. — *adv* and *conj* **wherein'** (*formal*) in which place or respect; in what? — *adv* and *conj* **whereinsoev'er** (*archaic*) in whatsoever place or respect. — *adv* and *conj* **wherein'to** (or *-in-tōō'*; *archaic*) into which; into what? — *adv* and *conj* **whereof'** (*formal*) of which; wherewith (*Shakesp*); of what? — *adv* and *conj* **whereon'** (*archaic*) on which; on what? — *adv* and *conj* **whereout'** (*archaic*) out of which. — *adv* and *conj* **wheresoev'er** or (*old*) **where'so** and **wheresoe'er** (*wār-sō-ār'*, *hwar-sō-ar'*; *literary*) in or to whatsoever place; whencesoever (*archaic*). — *adv* and *conj* **wherethrough'** (*archaic*) through which; through the agency of which. — *adv* and *conj* **whereto'** (*formal*) to which; to what? — *adv* and *conj* **whereun'der** (*formal*) under which. — *adv* and *conj* **whereuntil'** (*Shakesp*) to what. — *adv* and *conj* whereunto. — *adv* and *conj* **whereun'to** (or *-un-tōō'*; *archaic*) whereto; for what purpose? — *adv* and *conj* **whereupon'** upon or in consequence of which; on what grounds (*Shakesp*). — *adv* and *conj* **wherev'er** or (*literary*) **where'er** (*war-ār'*, *hwār-ār'*) at whatever place. — *adv* and *conj* with which?; with what. — *adv* and *conj* **wherewithal** (*wār-wi-dhöl'*, *hwār-wi-dhöl'*) with which?; with what. — *n* (**where'withal**) the means. — **from where** whence; from the, or a, place where; **or wherever** (*colloq*) or in (or towards) any comparable place; **see, look**, etc **where** behold; **tell someone where to get off** (*colloq*) to tell someone that his or her behaviour will not be tolerated; **where away**? a query as to the direction of an object sighted by the lookout (*naut*); where are you going? (*dialect*); **where it is** (*colloq*) the real situation, point or explanation; **where it's at** (*slang*) (the scene of) whatever is considered to be the most important, exciting, trendy, etc; **where you are** (*colloq*) what you are saying or getting at. [OE *hwǣr*, *hwār*; from stem of **who**; cf **there**]

wherret. See under **whirret**.

wherry *wer'i* or *hwer'i*, *n* a light shallow boat, sharp at both ends for speed; a kind of barge: — *pl* **wherr'ies**. — **wherr'yman** a man employed in a wherry, *esp* one who rows a wherry. [Ety dubious]

whet *wet* or *hwet*, *vt* to sharpen by rubbing; to make keen; to excite; to incite (*obs*); to preen (*obs*; *rare*): — *pr p* **whett'ing**; *pa t* and *pa p* **whett'ed**. — *n* an act of sharpening; sharpness; a time, occasion (*dialect*); an incitement or stimulus; something that sharpens the appetite; an appetizer. — *n* **whett'er**. — **whet'-slate** novaculite; **whet'stone** a stone for sharpening edged instruments; a stimulant. — **whet on** or **forward** (*Shakesp*) to urge on. [OE *hwettan*, cognate with *hwæt* sharp; Ger *wetzen*]

whether *wedh'ər* or *hwedh'ər*, (in *Shakesp* often scanned as one syllable; also spelt **whe'r**) *conj* introducing the first of two alternative words, phrases or clauses, the second being introduced by *or*, or (in the case of clauses) sometimes by *or whether*; introducing a single dependent question. — *interrog* and *rel pronoun* (*archaic*) which (of two). — **whether or no** (or **not**) whether so or not so; in any case, in any event. [OE *hwæther*, from stem of *hwā* who, with the old compar sfx *-ther*; cognate with Gothic *hwathar*, Ger *weder*; also with L *uter*, Ionic Gr *koteros*, Sans *katara*]

whetstone, **whetted**, **whetter**, **whetting**. See under **whet**.

whew[1] or **wheugh** *hū*, *wū* or *hwū*, *interj* expressing wonder, relief or dismay. — *n* a whistling sound, *esp* one expressing astonishment. — *vi* to utter such a sound. [Imit]

whew[2] *wū* or *hwū*, (*dialect*) *vi* to bustle about. [Perh **whew**[1]]

whewellite *hū'əl-īt*, *n* calcium oxalate. [Named after William *Whewell* (1794–1866)]

whey *wā* or *hwā*, *n* the watery part of milk, separated from the curd, *esp* in making cheese. — *adj* of or containing whey; like whey; whey-coloured. — *adj* **whey'ey** and **whey'ish** of whey; like whey. — *n* **whey'ishness**. — **whey'-face** a pale or white face. — *adj* **whey'-faced** pale, *esp* with terror. — **whey tub**. [OE *hwǣg*; LGer *wey*]

which *wich* or *hwich*, *interrog pronoun* and *adj* what (thing(s) or person(s)) of a number? — *interrog pronoun* (*obs* or *dialect*) what? — *interrog adj* (*obs*) of what sort or kind? — *rel pronoun* (used chiefly in reference to things or ideas, etc rather than people) that; who or whom (*obs*); used after a comma to add a clause commenting on something, the antecedent sometimes being a circumstance or statement, and 'which' the equivalent of 'and that' or 'but that'. — *pronoun* and *adj* **whichev'er** and **whichsoev'er** every one that; any one, no matter which. — **the which** (*archaic*) which; **which . . . he** (*obs*) who; **which . . . his** (*obs*) whose; **which is which**? which is the one and which is the other? [OE *hwilc*, *hwelc*, from the stem of *hwā* who, and *līc* (from a word meaning body, form) like; Gothic *hweileiks*, Ger *welch*, *welcher*; L *qualis*; cf **such** and **each**]

whicker *wik'ər* or *hwik'ər*, (*dialect*) *vi* to neigh; to bleat; to snigger, titter. — *n* a neigh, bleat or titter. [Imit]

whid[1] *hwid* or *wid*, (*Scot*) *n* a rapid noiseless movement. — *vi* to move quickly, to whisk. — *vi* **whidd'er** to whiz. [Perh connected with ON *hvitha* a squall, OE *hwitha* a breeze]

whid[2] *wid* or *hwid*, *n* a lie (*Scot*); a word (*obs slang*); a quarrel (*dialect*). — *vi* to lie: — *pr p* **whidd'ing**; *pa t* and *pa p* **whidd'ed**. — **cut boon whids** to speak good words. [Poss OE *cwide* a word, from *cwethan* to say]

whidah. See **whydah**.

whidder. See **whid**[1].

Whieldon *wēl'dən* or *hwēl'dən*, *adj* denoting a type of pottery with a mottled underglaze in green, yellow and brown, made in the factory of Thomas *Whieldon* of Staffordshire (1719–1795).

whiff[1] *wif* or *hwif*, *n* a sudden puff of air or smoke from the mouth; a slight inhalation; a puff of smell, often an unpleasant one; a slight blast; a small amount, *esp* of something causing or associated with a transient sensation; a slight trace or suggestion; a discharge of shot; a cigarette (*slang*); a small cigar; a jiffy (*colloq*); a failure to hit the bell, etc (*US*); a light kind of outrigger boat; a small signal flag (*naut*); a glimpse (*dialect*). — *vt* to throw out in whiffs; to puff; to drive or convey by, or as if by, a whiff; to inhale, smell. — *vi* to go out or off in a whiff; to move with, or as if with, a puff of air; to blow slightly; to aim at, and fail to hit, a ball, etc (*US*); to smell. — *n* **whiff'er**. — *adj* **whiff'y**. [Prob partly ME *weffe*; imit]

whiff[2] *wif* or *hwif*, *n* a fish related to the turbot. [Ety dubious]

whiff[3] *wif* or *hwif*, *vi* to fish with a hand line towed behind a boat. — *n* **whiff'ing**. [Perh **whiff**[1]]

whiffet *wif'ət* or *hwif'ət*, *n* a paltry person, a whipper-snapper; a little dog. [**whiff**[1]]

whiffle *wif'l* or *hwif'l*, *vi* to blow in puffs; to move as if blown by a puff; to talk idly; to make a slight whistling or puffing sound; to veer; to vacillate; to prevaricate. — Also *vt*. — *adj* **whiff'led** (*slang*) drunk. — *n* **whiff'ler** someone who whiffles; a swaggerer; a contemptible person. — *n* **whiff'lery** levity; trifling. — *n* and *adj* **whiff'ling**. [Frequentative of **whiff**[1]]

whiffler[1] *wif'lər* or *hwif'lər*, (*hist*) *n* an official who clears the way for a procession. [Perh *wifel* (obs) javelin, battle-axe; affected by **whiff**[1] and **whiffle**]

whiffler[2]. See under **whiffle**.

whiffletree *wif'l-trē* or *hwif'l-trē*, *n*. Same as **whippletree**.

whift *wift* or *hwift*, (*obs* or *dialect*) *n* a slight puff or blast; a snatch of music or song; a small signal flag (*naut*). [Variant of **whiff**[1]]

Whig *wig* or *hwig*, (*hist*) *n* a name applied to members of one of the great English political parties, in the late 17c applied to those upholding popular rights and opposed to the King; after 1830 almost superseded by 'Liberal'; a Scottish Presbyterian, first so called in the middle of the 17c; one of those who in the colonial period were opposed to British rule (*US*); one of the party formed from the survivors of the old National Republican party and other elements, which disintegrated in the 1850s, first called by the name in 1834 (*US*). — *adj* of, relating to or composed of Whigs. — *n* **Whigg'archy** government by Whigs. — *adj* **Whigg'ish**. — *adv* **Whigg'ishly**. — *n* **Whigg'ism, Whigg'ery, Whigg'ishness** or **Whig'ship** Whig principles. [Prob short for **whiggamore** a 17c Scottish Presbyterian rebel]

whig[1] *hwig* or *wig*, (*Scot*) *vi* to jog along. — *vt* to urge forward: — *pr p* **whigg'ing**; *pa t* and *pa p* **whigged**. [Origin uncertain]

whig[2] *wig* or *hwig*, (*dialect*) *n* sour milk; whey; buttermilk. — *vt* and *vi* to curdle: — *pr p* **whigg'ing**; pa t and *pa p* **whigged**. [Prob related to **whey**]

whiggamore *wig'ə-mör* or *-mōr*, or *hwig'*, *n* one of the 7000 Western Covenanters who marched on Edinburgh in 1648, sealing the doom of Charles I; a Scottish Presbyterian, a Whig. [Origin disputed; most prob *whig* to urge forward, and *mere* mare]

Whiggery, etc. See under **Whig**.

whigmaleerie or **whigmaleery** *hwig-mə-lē'ri* or *wig-mə-lē'ri*, (*Scot*) *n* a trinket or knick-knack; a fantastic ornamentation; a whim. [Origin uncertain]

while *wīl* or *hwīl*, *n* a space of time; time and trouble spent. — *conj* (also **whilst** *wīlst* or *hwīlst*) during the time that; at the same time that; as long as; whereas; although; notwithstanding the admitted fact that; until (*Northern dialect*). — *prep* (*Shakesp*; *Northern dialect*) until. — *vt* to pass (time) without irksomeness (with *away*). — *conj* **whiles** (*Bible*) while, at the same time that; until (*Shakesp*). — *adv* (*Scot*) at times (*orig* genitive of OE *hwīl*). — *adv* **while-ere** or **whilere** (*wī-lār'* or *hwī-lār'*; *archaic*) a little while ago, formerly. — **all the while** during all the time (that); **in between whiles** during the intervals; **make it worth someone's while** (*colloq*) to pay someone well for his or her trouble; **once** (or **every once**) **in a while** now and then; **the while** (*Shakesp*) at the present time, in the meantime; **the whilst** (*obs*) while; in the meantime; **worth one's while** worth taking time and trouble over. [OE *hwīl*; Gothic *hweila*, Ger *Weile*]

whilk *wilk* or *hwilk*, *pronoun* obsolete and dialect form of **which**.

whilly *hwil'i* or *wil'i*, (*Scot*) *vt* to wheedle, cajole. [Prob shortened from **whillywha**]

whillywha or **whillywhaw** *hwil'i-hwö* or *wil'i-wö*, (*Scot*) *vt* to coax, wheedle or cajole. — *n* cajolery; a coaxing, insinuating person. — *adj* smooth-tongued, wheedling. [Origin obscure; poss imit of equivocation]

whilom *wī'ləm* or *hwī'ləm*, (*archaic*) *adv* formerly, once. — *adj* former. [Orig dative plural of OE *hwīl* time]

whilst. See under **while**.

whim *wim* or *hwim*, *n* a caprice; a fancy; a fantastic creation of brain or hand (*obs*); a whimsical person (*obs*); a vertical rope drum revolved by a horse, used for hoisting from shallow shafts. — *vi* (*obs*) (of the head) to turn round, swim; to be whimsical. — *vt* to desire capriciously; to turn aside or put off by a whim (with *off*; *obs*): — *pr p* **whimm'ing**; *pa t* and *pa p* **whimmed**. — *adj* **whimm'y** full of whims. [Poss from **whim-wham**]

whimberry *wim'bə-ri* or *hwim'bə-ri*, *n* a localized name for the bilberry or whortleberry. [Assimilated form of **whinberry** (qv)]

whimbrel *wim'brəl*, *hwim'brəl*, or **wimbrel** *wim'brəl*, *n* a species of small curlew. [Prob imit of bird's cry; dimin sfx *-rel*]

whimmy. See **whim**.

whimper *wim'pər* or *hwim'pər*, *vi* to cry feebly or plaintively. — *vt* to utter plaintively or in a whimper. — *n* a feebly plaintive cry. — *n* **whim'perer**. — *n* and *adj* **whim'pering**. — *adv* **whim'peringly**. [Imit; cf Ger *wimmern*]

whimple *wim'pl* or *hwim'pl*, *n*. Same as **wimple**.

whimsy or **whimsey** *wim'zi* or *hwim'zi*, *n* delicately fanciful behaviour; gentle fantasy; a whim or freak of fancy; something odd or quaint. — *adj* full of whims, changeable; quaint, odd. — *adj* **whim'sical** full of whims; odd, fantastical; delicately fanciful; (loosely) expressing gently humorous tolerance. — *n* **whimsical'ity** or **whim'sicalness**. — *adv* **whim'sically**. — *adv* **whim'sily**. — *n* **whim'siness**. [**whim**]

whim-wham *wim'wam* or *hwim'hwam*, *n* a ridiculous notion; an odd device; a fanciful trifle. [Origin uncertain; cf ON *hvima* to have the eyes wandering]

whin[1] *win* or *hwin*, *n* gorse, furze. — *adj* **whinn'y** abounding in whins. — **whin'chat** a bird that frequents whins, very similar in appearance, *esp* when it assumes its duller autumn plumage, to the stonechat, to which it is related. [Prob Scand]

whin[2]. See under **whinstone**.

whinberry *win'bə-ri* or *hwin'bə-ri*, *n* an older form of **whimberry**. [Orig *winberry* or *wineberry*, from OE *winberige* grape]

whinchat. See under **whin**[1].

whine *wīn* or *hwīn*, *vi* to utter a plaintive cry, whimper; to complain peevishly; to cry fretfully; to speak in a thin, ingratiating or servile tone; (of eg machinery) to make a continuous high-pitched noise. — *vt* to express or utter in a whine; to say peevishly; to cause to make a whining noise. — *n* a plaintive cry; a thin, ingratiating, nasal tone of utterance; a continuous shrill noise. — *n* **whī'ner**. — *n* **whī'niness**. — *n* and *adj* **whī'ning**. — *adv* **whī'ningly**. — *adj* **whī'ny**. [OE *hwīnan* to whine; ON *hvīna* to whistle through the air]

whinge *winj* or *hwinj*, also (*Scot*) **wheenge** *wēnj* or *hwēnj*, (*colloq*; *orig dialect*) *vi* to complain peevishly (also *Austr*); to whine; to cry fretfully. — *n* a peevish complaint. — *adj* and *n* **whinge'ing**. — *n* **whing'er**. [OE *hwinsian*, from root of *hwīnan*; see **whine**]

whinger *wing'ər* or *hwing'ər*, also (*h*)*win'jər* and (*h*)*wing'gər*, (*hist*) *n* a dirk or short sword. [Origin obscure; related to **whinyard**]

whiniard. See **whinyard**.

whinid'st (*Shakesp*, *Troilus and Cressida*, II.1.15) folio reading for which Johnson conjectured *vinewd'st* mouldy.

whinny[1] *win'i* or *hwin'i*, *vi* to neigh: — *pr p* **whinn'ying**; *pa t* and *pa p* **whinn'ied**. — *n* a neigh. [Imit]

whinny[2]. See under **whin**[1].

whinstone *win'stōn*, *hwin'stōn*, or *-stən*, *n* any hard and compact kind of rock, *usu* basalt or the like; a piece of this. — Also **whin**. — **Whin Sill** a sheet of intrusive quartz-dolerite or quartz-basalt exposed almost continuously for nearly 200 miles from the Farne Islands to Middleton-in-Teesdale. [*whin* (origin obscure), and **stone**]

whiny. See **whine**.

whinyard or **whiniard** *win'yərd* or *hwin'yərd*, (*hist*) *n* a short sword or dirk. [Origin uncertain; related to **whinger**]

whip *wip* or *hwip*, *n* a lash with a handle for punishing or driving; a stroke administered by a whip or similar implement; an act of whipping or a whipping motion; a driver, a coachman; someone who enforces the attendance and discipline of a political party; a call made on members of parliament to be in their places in readiness for an important division (called, according to number of times the message is underlined as indication of urgency, **three-line whip**, etc; **five-line whip** is no longer used); a whipper-in, the person who manages the hounds; a simple form of hoisting apparatus, a small tackle consisting of a single rope and block; a preparation of whipped cream, eggs, etc; a whipping or overcasting; (also, more *usu*, **whip'-round**) a collection of cash contributions made hastily among a group of people; an individual share in money collected in equal amounts; an instant (*Scot*); an arm carrying a sail of a windmill; a long twig, slender branch or shoot; a fairground ride featuring cars that move with sudden jerks. — *vt* to strike with a lash; to drive, or make to move, with lashes; to punish with lashes, or (loosely) by spanking; to strike in a manner suggesting a lash; to lash with sarcasm; to lash (eg a crowd) into an emotional state; to defeat, outdo (*colloq*); to stiffen (eg cream or white of egg) or make (eggs, etc) frothy, by rapid agitation with a whisk or similar utensil; to keep (eg a party) together; to fly-fish; to overlay (eg one cord with another); to bind round; to sew lightly; to overcast (eg a seam); to move quickly, snatch (with *up*, *away*, *out*, etc); to steal (*colloq*); to rouse (support, enthusiasm, etc; with *up*). — *vi* to move nimbly; to move in the manner of a whiplash; to make a cast in fly-fishing: — *pr p* **whipp'ing**; *pa t* and *pa p* **whipped** or (*old*) **whipt**. — *adj* **whip'like**. — *n* **whipp'er** someone or something that whips; an official who inflicts the penalty of whipping. — *n* **whipp'iness**. — *n* **whipp'ing** the action of lashing; corporal punishment, *esp* with a whip or lash; a defeat; a binding of twine, eg at the end of a rope; material for binding in this way; overcasting. — *adj* **whipp'y** whip-like; pliant; supple. — **whip'-and-derr'y** a hoisting apparatus consisting of a whip (qv) and a derrick; **whip'bird** the coachwhip-bird; **whip'cat** a tailor; **whip'-cord** cord for making whips; a fabric with a bold steep warp twill, used chiefly for dresses, suitings and coatings; a whiplike seaweed such as *Chorda filum* or *Chordaria flagelliformis*. — *adj* **whip'cord** or **whip'cordy** like whipcord. — *vt* **whip'-graft** to graft by fitting a tongue cut on the scion to a slit cut slopingly in the stock. — Also *n* (**whip graft**). — **whip'-grafting**; **whip hand** the hand that holds the whip; the advantage; **whip handle** the handle or stock of a whip; an advantage; **whip'jack** a whining beggar who pretends to be a sailor; **whip'lash** the lash of a whip; something resembling or suggesting the lash of a whip or its action; (also **whiplash injury**) an injury to the neck caused by the sharp forwards-and-backwards wrenching it suffers in a vehicle collision. — *vi* to move like a whiplash. — **whipp'er-in** an assistant to a huntsman, who controls the hounds; an official whose job is to enforce the discipline of a political party, a whip (*obs*); at any moment in a race, the horse in the last place (*slang*); a little or young insignificant but pretentious or irritating person; **whipp'ing-boy** a boy educated along with a prince and punished for the royal pupil's faults (*hist*); anyone on whom falls the odium of, or blame and punishment for, the shortcomings of others; **whipp'ing-cheer** (*obs*; *humorous*) flogging; **whipp'ing-cream** cream with enough butterfat in it to allow it to be beaten stiff; **whipp'ing-post** a post to which offenders are tied to be whipped; the punishment itself; **whipp'ing-top** (or **whip'-top**) a top kept spinning by means of a whip; **whip-round** see **whip** above; **whip'saw** a narrow saw for dividing timber lengthways, *usu* set in a frame and often worked by two people. — *vt* to cut with a whipsaw; to have the advantage of at every point, defeat at every turn (*slang*). — **whip scorpion** any arachnid of the order Pedipalpida, slightly resembling true scorpions but being without sting and *usu* having a whiplike appendage at the rear of the body; **whip snake** any of various snakes resembling a whiplash, as *Masticophis flagelliformis* (the coachwhip snake) and species of Philodryas, etc; **whip socket** a socket to hold the butt of a whip; **whip'staff** a former steering device, a vertical wooden lever controlling a ship's rudder; **whip'stall** (*aeronautics*) a stall as the result of which the nose of the aircraft whips forward and down. — *vi* and *vt* to go or put, into such a stall. — **whip'-stitch** a small overcasting stitch; a hasty composition; a tailor; a kind of half-ploughing or raftering (qv; *dialect*). — Also *vt* and *vi*. — **whip'stock** the rod or handle of a whip; in an oil well, a tapered steel wedge used to deflect the drill bit from a straight line. — *adj* **whip'tail** or **whip'tailed** having a long, slender tail. — **whip-top** see **whipping-top**; **whip'worm** a worm of the genus *Trichocephalus*, with posterior end thick and anterior long and thin, found parasitic in human intestines. — **fair crack of the whip** a reasonable or fair chance given to one to do something properly; **whip and spur** with great haste; **whip in** to act as a whipper-in; **whip into shape** to get (a person or group) into a condition ready for action, etc by force or rigorous training; generally, to reshape vigorously to one's satisfaction; **whip the cat** to practise small economies; to work by the day as a dressmaker, tailor, etc, going from house to house; to idle; to play a practical joke. [ME *whippen*; cf Du *wippen* to shake]

whippersnapper *wip'ər-snap-ər* or *hwip'ər-snap-ər*, (*old colloq*) *n* a cheeky young lad; any lowly person who behaves impudently. [Perh jinglingly extended from *whip-snapper* a cracker of whips]

whippet *wip'it* or *hwip'it*, *n* a breed of dog developed from a cross between a greyhound and spaniel or terrier; a racing-dog; a small speedy tank. — *n* **whipp'eting** the training and racing of whippets. [Partly **whip**, and partly obsolete *whippet* to move briskly]

whippletree *wip'l-trē* or *hwip'l-trē*, *n* the crosspiece of a carriage, plough, etc, which is made so as to swing on a pivot and to which the traces of a harnessed animal are fixed (often used in conjunction with a doubletree). [From **whip**]

whippoorwill *wip'pōōr-wil* or *hwip'pōōr-wil*, or *-wil'* or *-pər-*, *n* a species of nightjar native to N America. [Imit of its call]

whippy. See **whip**.

whipster *wip'stər* or *hwip'stər*, (*obs*) *n* a term of contempt formerly with various meanings, notably (*Shakesp*, *Othello*, V.2.242) a whippersnapper. [**whip**]

whir. See **whirr**.

whirl *wûrl* or *hwûrl*, *n* a rapid turning; any of various devices that revolve rapidly, eg the whorl or flywheel of a spindle; another name for whorl in other senses; a brief trip (*colloq*); a quick turn on the dance floor (*colloq*); a round of intense activity; a giddy degree of emotion or excitement; a commotion or tumult; a circling or spiralling pattern. — *vi* to revolve or circle rapidly; to move rapidly, *esp* in an agitated manner; to turn swiftly round or aside. — *vt* to turn round rapidly; to carry or move rapidly, on or as if on wheels (often with *away*, *off*, etc); to throw violently. — *n* **whirl'er**. — *n* and *adj* **whirl'ing**. — *adj* **whirl'y** characterized by whirls or whirling. — **whirl'-about** the act of whirling about; anything that turns round rapidly; **whirl'bat** (also **whorl'bat** and **hurl'bat**) (*obs*) translating L *caestus* (see **cestus**[2]); **whirl'blast** a whirling blast of wind; **whirl bone** the round head of a bone turning in a socket; the knee-cap; **whirling dervish** one of an order of Muslim devotees who dance or spin round, the dancing dervishes, founded in 1273; **whirl'ing-table** a machine exhibiting the effects of centripetal and centrifugal forces (also **whirl'ing-machine**); a potter's wheel; **whirl'pool** a circular current in a river or sea, produced by opposing tides, winds or currents; an eddy; a huge whale-like sea monster (*obs*); **whirlpool bath** same as **Jacuzzi®**; **whirl'wind** a small rotating windstorm, which may extend upwards to a height of many hundred feet, a miniature cyclone; something which moves in a similarly rapid and *usu* destructive way. — *adj* describing anything that develops rapidly or violently. — **whir'lybird** (*slang*) a helicopter. — **give something a whirl** (*colloq*) to try something out. [ME *whirlen*, from ON *hvirfla*, frequentative of *hverfa* to turn round; Ger *wirbeln*]

whirligig *wûr'li-gig* or *hwûr'li-gig*, *n* a toy that spins or whirls round, eg a top or paper windmill; a merry-go-round; any device, etc that revolves rapidly; an ancient instrument of punishment consisting of a pivoted wooden cage in which the prisoner was spun round; (also **whirligig beetle**) any water beetle of the family *Gyrinidae* (*esp Gyrinus natator*), from their habit of whirling round on the surface of ponds, etc. [**whirl** and obsolete *gig* whipping-top]

whirlybird. See under **whirl**.

whirr or **whir** *wûr* or *hwûr*, *n* the sound of a rapid whirling or vibratory motion. — Also *adv*. — *vi* to turn or spin with a humming noise; to fly or move with such a sound. — *vt* to hurry away with, or as if with, a whirring or whizzing sound: — *pr p* **whirr'ing**; *pa t* and *pa p* **whirred**. — *n* **whirr'ing**. [Imit; cf Dan *hvirre* to whirl]

whirret *wir'it* or *hwir'it*, (*obs*) *n* a blow. — *vt* to give a sharp blow to. — Also **wherr'et**. [Poss imit]

whirry *hwûr'i* or *wûr'i*, (*Scot*) *vi* and *vt* to move rapidly. [Prob from **whirr**]

whirtle. See **wortle**.

whish[1] *wish* or *hwish*, (*dialect*) *vi* to move with the whizzing sound of rapid motion; to call 'whish'. — *vt* to drive (animals, etc) with calls of 'whish'. — *n* the rushing or swishing sound of rapid movement through the air, etc. — *interj* imitative of a rushing sound or movement. [Imit]

whish[2] *wish* or *hwish*, (*dialect*) *interj* (also *Scot* **wheesh** *hwēsh* or *wēsh*) calling for silence, hush! — *vt* and *vi* to silence, fall silent or be silent. [Cf **hush, whisht**]

whisht *wisht* or *hwisht*, *Scot* **wheesht** *hwēsht* or *wēsht*, (*old* or *dialect*) *interj* calling for silence, hush! — *n* silence; a whisper. — *adj* silent. — *vi* and *vt* to keep silent. — **hold one's whisht** or (*Scot*) **haud one's wheesht** to keep silence. [Cf **whist**[2], **hush**]

whisk[1] *wisk* or *hwisk*, *vt* to move quickly and lightly; to sweep rapidly; to beat (egg whites, cream, etc) with a quick, light movement. — *vi* to move nimbly and rapidly. — *n* a light rapid sweeping motion; a small bundle or tuft of anything used as a brush; a small hand-held utensil for beating or whisking eggs, etc; (also **fly whisk**) a flexible implement for swatting flies; a type of women's neckerchief or large collar worn in the later 17c (*hist*); a hairlike appendage, eg on an insect; a tuft; a panicle *esp* of millet; the common millet. — *n* **whis'ker** someone or something that whisks. — *adj* **whis'king** moving briskly. — *adj* **whis'ky-fris'ky** flighty. [Orig Scot, related to ON *visk* wisp]

whisk[2] *wisk* or *hwisk*, *n* the earlier name for **whist**[1]. [Said to be from **whisk**[1], from the rapid action of sweeping the cards off the table]

whisker[1] *wis'kər* or *hwis'kər*, *n* any of the long coarse sensory hairs growing round the mouth of a cat, mouse, etc; a coarse hair growing on a human face, *usu* a man's; (in *pl*) a man's moustache (*esp* formerly) or beard, *esp* the parts growing on the cheeks; a hair's breadth, a very narrow margin; a very thin strong fibre or filament made by growing a crystal, eg of silicon carbide, silicon nitride or sapphire; either of two bars extending on each side of the bowsprit (*naut*). — *adj* **whis'kered** and **whis'kery** having whiskers. [Related to ON *visk* wisp]

whisker[2]. See under **whisk**[1].

whiskerando *wis-kə-ran'dō* or *hwis-kə-ran'dō*, *n* a whiskered person, in allusion to Don Ferolo *Whiskerandos* in Sheridan's *Critic*: — *pl* **whiskeran'dos**. — *adj* **whiskeran'doed** having whiskers.

whisket *wis'kit* or *hwis'kit*, *n*. Variant of **wisket**.

whisky[1] (*Ir* and *US* **whiskey**) *wis'ki* or *hwis'ki*, *n* as legally defined, a spirit obtained by distillation from a mash of cereal grains saccharified by the diastase of malt (see also **malt whisky**); formerly applied also to a spirit obtained from potatoes, beetroot, or any starch-yielding material; a glass of any of such spirits. — *adj* **whis'keyfied** or **whis'kified** intoxicated. — **Whisky Insurrection** an outbreak against the excise regulations which occurred in Western Pennsylvania in 1794; **whis'ky-liver** cirrhosis of the liver, from too much whisky; **whisky mac** a mixed drink of whisky and ginger wine; **whisky** (or **whiskey**) **sour** a sour (qv) having whisky as its chief ingredient; **whisky toddy** toddy having whisky for its chief ingredient. [Gaelic *uisgebeatha*, from *uisge* water, and *beatha* life; cf L *vita* life]

whisky[2] or **whiskey** *wis'ki* or *hwis'ki*, *n* a light gig. [**whisk**[1]]

whisky john *wis'ki-* or *hwis'ki jon*, *n* the grey or Canada jay (also **whisky jack**). [From an Am Ind name of similar sound]

whisper *wis'pər* or *hwis'pər*, *vi* to speak by breathing rather than voicing one's words; to speak in a low voice; to speak covertly, spread rumours; to plot secretly; to make a rustling sound, or a sound like soft speech. — *vt* to utter in a low voice or under the breath, or covertly, or by way of gossip. — *n* a low hissing voice or sound; a sound uttered with the breath rather than the voice; voiceless speech with narrowed glottis (*phonetics*); a hissing or rustling sound; cautious or timorous speaking; a secret hint; a rumour. — *n* **whis'perer** someone who whispers; a secret informer. — *n* and *adj* **whis'pering**. — *adv* **whis'peringly** in a whisper or low voice. — *adv* **whis'perously** in a whisper. — *adj* **whis'pery**. — **whispering campaign** an attack by means of furtively spread rumours; **whispering gallery** or **dome** a gallery or dome so constructed that a whisper or slight sound is carried to an unusual distance. [OE *hwisprian*; Ger *wispern*, ON *hviskra*; related to **whistle**]

whiss *wis* or *hwis*, *vi* to hiss, whistle, wheeze, etc. [Imit]

whist[1] *wist* or *hwist*, *n* a card game played by two against two, in which the object is to take a majority of the thirteen tricks, each trick over six scoring one point. — **whist drive** a progressive whist party; **whist'-player**. — **dummy whist** whist played with a dummy hand; **long whist** a game of ten points; **short whist** a game of five points. [**whisk**[2]; said to be assimilated to **whist**[1] because of the silence during play]

whist[2] *wist* or *hwist*, *interj* hush; silence; be still. — *adj* (*archaic*) hushed, silent; attentive. — *vi* to become silent. — *vt* (*Spenser*) to hush or silence. [Imit]

whistle *wis'l* or *hwis'l*, *vi* to make a shrill sound by forcing the breath through the pursed lips or the teeth; to make this sound in derision, etc; to make this sound as a call or signal; (of a bird) to pipe, sing; to make a similar sound with a wind instrument or other device; (of eg the wind) to make a shrill sound; to whizz through the air; to become an informer (*colloq*); to give a landlord information that leads to raising rent (*Scott*). — *vt* to perform, utter or express by whistling; to summon with a whistle (often with *up*); to send with a whistling sound. — *n* an act of whistling; the sound made in whistling, or any similar sound; any of many devices producing a similar sound, eg one operated by steam on a railway locomotive or a kettle, or one blown by a referee to regulate play on the pitch; a simple wind instrument consisting of a wooden or metal pipe with finger holes; a summons; the throat (*slang*). — *adj* **whis'tleable**. — *adj* **whis'tled** (*slang*) drunk. — *n* **whis'tler** someone or something that whistles; a large kind of marmot; a broken-winded horse; a mythical bird whose whistle is fatal to the hearer (*Spenser*). — *n*

whis'tling. — *adv* **whis'tlingly**. — **whis'tle-blower** (*slang*) someone who blows the whistle on someone or something; **whis'tle-blowing** (*slang*). — Also *adj*. — *adj* **whis'tle-** (or **whis'tled-)drunk** (*obs*) too drunk to whistle. — **whistle fish** a rockling; **whistle stop** (*colloq*) a small town or railway station, where trains stop only by signal; hence **whistle-stop speech** an electioneering speech made on tour (*orig* at railway stations), and **whistle-stop tour** *orig* such an electioneering tour, now any rapid tour involving brief stops at many places. — *vi* (**whis'tle-stop**) (of a political candidate) to make an electioneering tour with many brief personal appearances. — **whistling kettle** a kettle whose spout is fitted with a device that gives a whistling sound when steam escapes through it, indicating that the water in it is boiling; **whis'tling-shop** (*slang*) somewhere such as a room in a prison, where liquor was sold without a licence; **whistling swan** an American swan with a melodious whistling call. — **blow the whistle** (with *on*; *slang*) to expose or give information *usu* to the authorities about (illegal or underhand practices); to declare (something) illegal, underhand or otherwise unacceptable; **boatswain's whistle** (also **pipe**, **call**) a whistle of special shape used by a boatswain or boatswain's-mate to summon sailors to various duties; **go whistle** (*Shakesp*) to go to the deuce; **pay for one's whistle** to pay highly for one's caprice (from Benjamin Franklin's story of a whistle he, as a boy, bought at an exorbitant price); **pigs and whistles** see **pig**[2]; **wet one's whistle** (*colloq*) to take an alcoholic drink; **whistle away** see **whistle off**; **whistle down the wind** (from the practice of casting a hawk off down the wind when turning it loose) to abandon or let go; to talk to no purpose; **whistle for** to summon by whistling; to ask for or expect in vain (*colloq*); **whistle for a wind** a superstitious practice of old sailors during a calm; **whistle in the dark** to do something to quell one's fear; **whistle off** or **whistle away** to send off or dismiss by, or as if by, a whistle (*hawking*); to turn loose; to abandon; **worth the whistle** worth the trouble of calling for. [OE *hwistlian*]

Whit *wit* or *hwit*, *n* Whitsuntide. — *adj* of or belonging to Whitsuntide.

whit *wit* or *hwit n* the smallest particle imaginable; the least bit. [By-form of **wight** creature]

white *wīt* or *hwīt*, *adj* of the colour of snow, the colour that reflects the maximum and absorbs the minimum of light rays; snowy or snow-covered; (sometimes *cap*) belonging to one of the pale-skinned, *specif* European races; relating to or characteristic of these; abnormally pale, pallid, bloodless; colourless; (of eg a rabbit or mouse) albino; (of hair) lacking pigment, as in old age; (of the soul, etc) innocent, pure, unblemished, purified from sin (*poetic*); bright; (of steel) burnished; (of silver) unburnished; (of a variety of anything, eg grapes) pale-coloured, as distinct from darker types; (of wine) made from white grapes or skinned black grapes; (of flour) having had the bran and wheat germ removed; (of bread) made with white flour; (of coffee or tea) with milk or cream added; clothed in white; pertaining to the Carmelite monks; in continental Europe, anti-revolutionary (*politics*); auspicious, favourable; reliable, honest, upright, honourable; (of a witch) not malevolent, using her power for good purposes; (of eg war) without bloodshed. — *n* the colour of snow; white colouring matter, eg paint; white clothes, as in *dressed in white*; (often *cap*) a White person; (also **egg white**) the clear fluid surrounding the yolk of an egg, albumen; the white part of the eyeball surrounding the iris; a white butterfly; in games, a white playing-piece in chess or draughts (or the player of the white pieces), a white ball in snooker, a white ring on an archery target; (in *pl*) household linen, or white clothes worn eg for cricket or tennis; (in *pl*) leucorrhoea (qv), a white discharge from the vagina; a member of a white political party. — *vt* to make white. — *adj* **white'ly** (*obs* except *Scot*) whitish, pale. — *vt* **whīt'en** to make white; to bleach; to free from guilt, or to make to appear guiltless. — *vi* to become or turn white. — *n* **whīt'ener** someone or something that whitens; artificial milk for coffee or tea. — *n* **white'ness**. — *n* **whīt'ening** the act or process of making or becoming white; a substance used to make white, whiting. — *n* **Whīt'ey** or **Whīt'y** (also without *cap*; *colloq*, often *derog*) a white person; white people as a race. — *n* **whīt'ing** ground chalk free from stony matter and other impurities, extensively used as a size, colour, etc (also **whīte'ning**, **Spanish white** and, as the finest quality, **Paris white**). — *adj* **whīt'ish** somewhat white. — *n* **whīt'ishness**. — *adj* **whīt'y** whitish. — *n* (also with *cap*) see **Whitey** above. — **white admiral** any of a genus of butterflies of the same family as the red admiral, having white bands on the wings; **white ale** (*dialect*) ale brewed or mixed with ingredients such as flour, eggs, etc that give it a whitish colour; **white ant** a termite (Isoptera); **white arm** a sword, bayonet or lance, translating Fr *arme blanche*; **white arsenic** see **arsenic**; **white'bait** the fry of various species of herring, sprat, etc; **white'bass** a silvery food fish of the American Great Lake region; **white'beam** a small tree (*Sorbus aria* or *Pyrus aria*) with leaves white and downy on the underside; **white bear** the polar bear; **white'beard** an old man. — *adj* **white'-bearded**. — *adj* **white'-bellied**. — *adj* **white'-billed**. — **white bonnet** someone employed to bid at an auction to raise prices; **white bottle** bladder campion; **white boy** a favourite boy, a white-headed boy; **White'boy** a member of an association of Irish peasants first formed in County Tipperary about 1761 for the purpose of redressing grievances, who, wearing white shirts, committed agrarian outrages by night; **White'boyism** (also without *cap*) the principles of the Whiteboys; **white brass** an inferior alloy of copper and zinc. — *adj* **white'-breasted**. — **white bryony** see **bryony**; **white'cap** the male redstart or other bird with light-coloured head; a crested wave; a member of a self-constituted vigilance committee who, under the guise of purifying the morals of the community, deal violently with persons of whom they disapprove (*esp US hist*); **white cell** or **white blood cell** (*biol*) a colourless blood cell involved in the protection of the body from infection, a leucocyte; **white coal** water power (Fr *houille blanche*); **white'coat** a wearer of a white coat, eg a hospital doctor or (*esp hist*) a soldier; a seal pup in its first furry white pelt. — *adj* **white'-collar** relating to or designating the class of workers, such as clerks, etc, who are not engaged in manual labour. — **white-collar crime** crimes entailing intellectual effort (as distinct from violent crimes, larceny, etc) such as computer fraud, embezzlement, etc; **white copper** a light-coloured alloy of copper; **white corpuscle** a white blood cell (qv above), a leucocyte. — *adj* **white'-crested** or **white'-crowned** (of birds) having a white crest or crown. — **white crops** grain crops such as barley, rye and wheat that lighten to a pale gold as they ripen; **white damp** a poisonous mixture of gases with carbon monoxide predominating, occurring in coal mines; **whited sepulchre** someone professedly righteous but inwardly wicked, a hypocrite (Matt 23.27); **White Dwarf** (also without *caps*) the name given to a class of small dim stars outside the normal spectral sequence, because their luminosities are extremely low for their spectral type, such stars being in the final stages of their evolution; **white elephant** see **elephant**; **White Ensign** a flag with a white field and St George's cross, with the Union Jack in the canton, till 1864 the flag of the White Squadron, now flown by the Royal Navy and the Royal Yacht Squadron; **white'-eye** any bird of the genus *Zosterops* or of related genera of the family *Zosteropidae*, most species of which have a conspicuous ring of minute white feathers round the eye; **white-eyelid monkey** any of the mangabeys, monkeys with white upper eyelids; **white'-face** white make-up, *esp* as worn by a traditional type of clown. — *adj* **white'-faced** having a face pale with fear or from illness; wearing white make-up, eg as a clown; (of animals) having the face, or part of it, white; with white front (also **white'=fronted**). — *adj* **white'-favoured** wearing white favours. — **white feather** a sign of cowardice, as in **show the white feather**; **white fish** a general name for such fish as the whiting, haddock, plaice, cod, sole, menhaden, etc; any species of Coregonus (qv); **white flag** an emblem of truce or surrender; **white'fly** any of several insect pests belonging to the family *Aleurodidae*; **white-footed mouse** the deer mouse; **White Friar** (also without *caps*) one of the Carmelite order of friars, so called from their white clothing. — *adj* **white-fronted** see **white-faced**. — **white frost** hoarfrost; **white gold** gold alloyed with nickel or palladium to give it a white colour; **white goods** household linen; refrigerators, washing machines, dish-washers, freezers and similar appliances, *usu* painted with white enamel. — *adj* **white'=haired** having white hair; white-headed, darling. — **Whitehall** see separate entry. — *adj* **white'-hand'ed** having white hands or paws; having hands unstained with guilt. — **white hass, hause** or **hawse** (*Scot*) an oatmeal pudding made with sheep's gullet; **white'head** the blue-winged snow goose; a breed of domestic pigeons; a pimple or pustule with a white top. — *adj* **white'-headed** (of an animal) with a wholly or partly white head; having white or flaxen hair. — **white=headed boy** a favourite, a protégé; **white-headed eagle** the N American bald eagle. **white'-heart** or **white-heart cherry** a cultivated cherry, related to the gean, with soft, tender flesh and pale skin; **white heat** the degree of heat at which metals, etc emit white light; an intense degree of emotion, passion, activity, keenness, etc (*adj* **white-hot'**); **white herring** a fresh or uncured herring; **white hole** a suggested source of the matter and energy observed flowing into the universe (cf **black hole**); **white honeysuckle** an azalea known also as the *clammy* or *swamp azalea*; **white hope** a person on whom hopes for success, honour, etc are grounded (also **great white hope**); **white horse** a white-topped wave; a figure of a horse on a hillside, formed by removing the turf from the underlying chalk, the most famous being in Oxfordshire, at Uffington. — *adj* **white-hot** see **white heat** above. — **White House** the official residence in Washington of the President of the USA; **white hunter** a white man who is a professional hunter of big game; a white man who acts as guide to hunting parties and safaris; **white iron** pig iron or cast iron in which all the carbon is in chemical combination with the iron; **white knight** (*stock exchange slang*) a person who rescues a company from an unwanted takeover bid (cf **white squire**). — *adj* **white'-knuckle** (*colloq*) giving rise to extreme anxiety, alarm or terror, *esp* in **white-knuckle ride** a fairground roller-coaster or any similarly terrifying ride. — **white lady** a spectral figure said to be associated with the fortunes of a family, as in some German castles; a cocktail made of gin, orange liqueur and lemon juice; methylated spirits as a drink, sometimes mixed with similar substances (*Austr slang*); **white lead** basic lead carbonate used in paint and putty; **white leather** supple skins from deer, sheep and goats, tawed (ie soaked in alum, stretched and scraped) and kept in their natural colour, used for gloves, purses, etc; **white'-leg** *phlegmasia alba dolens*, a form of phlebitis occurring after parturition (also called **milk=leg**); **white lie** a forgivable lie, *esp* one told out of tactfulness; **white light** light containing all wavelengths in the visible range at the same intensity (the term is used, however, to cover a wide range of intensity distribution in the spectrum); **white lime** (*obs*) whitewash; **white line** a longitudinal continuous or broken line painted on a highway as a line demarcation for traffic. — *adj* **white'-listed** having white stripes on a darker ground. — *adj* **white'-livered** having a pale look (once thought to be caused by a white liver); cowardly. — **white man** a member of the white race; someone assumed to deal fairly with others (*colloq*); **white man's burden** (*Kipling*) the white man's (formerly) perceived obligation to govern and educate backward coloured peoples; **white matter** (*anatom*) pale-coloured fibrous nerve tissue in the brain and spinal cord; **white meat** food made of milk, butter, eggs, etc; the flesh of poultry, rabbits, calves, etc; the lighter parts of the cooked flesh of poultry (eg the breast), as opposed to the darker meat of the leg; **white metal** a tin-base alloy with over 50 per cent of tin; also, an alloy in which lead is the principal metal; **white meter** a meter that records off-peak consumption of electricity; **white night** a sleepless night; in northern latitudes, a summer night that never becomes completely dark; **white noise** a noise in which there are a large number of frequencies of roughly equal intensity; **white'-out** a phenomenon in snow-covered regions in fog or overcast conditions in which earth and sky merge in a single whiteness; a dense blizzard; see also **white out** below; **white paper** a statement, printed on white paper, issued by government for the information of parliament; **white pepper** light-coloured pepper made from peppercorns from which the dark outer husk has been removed; **white'pot** a Devonshire dish of sliced rolls, milk, eggs, sugar, etc, baked; **white precipitate** a white mercurial substance used in ointments for treating worm-infestations, etc; **white pudding** an oatmeal and suet pudding in a sausage skin; **white pyrites** marcasite; **white race** one of the main divisions of mankind, distinguished generally by light complexion and certain types of hair and skull, also known as Caucasian; **white rat** an albino strain of the brown rat, much used in laboratory experiments; **white rent** (*hist*) the tinner's poll tax of eightpence to the Duke of Cornwall; rent paid in silver; **white rhinoceros** a large African two-horned grazing rhinoceros, *Ceratotherium simum* (also **square-lipped rhinoceros**); **white rose** (*hist*) in the Wars of the Roses, the emblem of the House of York. — *adj* **white'-rumped**. — **White Russian** a Byelorussian; **white sale** a sale of linen goods at reduced prices; **white salt** salt dried and calcined; **white sauce** a sauce made with roux thinned with milk or stock eg from chicken or veal, and flavoured as desired; **white seam** (*Scot*) plain needlework. — *vi* (**white'-seam**) to do plain needlework. — **white settler** (*derog*) a *usu* wealthy outsider who moves into a district and makes use of its amenities without blending sympathetically into the local community; **white sheet** (*relig*; *hist*) the garb symbolically worn by a penitent. — *adj* **white'=shoe** (*slang*; *orig US*) namby-pamby. — **white slave** a girl procured for prostitution purposes (*esp* when exported), whence **white slaver**, **white slavery** and **white=slave traffic**; **white'smith** a worker in tinned or white iron; a tinsmith; a polisher or finisher of metals; **white spirit** a petroleum distillate used as a substitute for turpentine in mixing paints, and in paint and varnish manufacture; **White Squadron** one of three divisions of the British Navy in former times; white-painted vessels built in 1883 and following years as part of a strong US Navy; **white squall** a sudden tropical whirlwind or windstorm heralded by little more than a choppiness of the sea or the appearance of a small white cloud; **white squire** (*stock exchange slang*) a friendly party to whom a company chooses to transfer the bulk of its shares as a defence against a takeover move; **white stick** a walking-stick used by a blind person to feel his or her way, painted white as an indication of the user's blindness; **white stuff** (*slang*) heroin, morphine or cocaine; **white sugar** refined sugar; **white-suprem'acist** an advocate of **white supremacy** the philosophy or policy of giving dominance to white people on the grounds of their alleged superiority. — *adj* **white'=tailed**. — **white'thorn** the common hawthorn; **white'-throat** either of two warblers of the same genus (Sylvia) as the blackcap, having white throat feathers; a species of American sparrow; any of several species of humming-bird; **white tie** a white bow tie, part of formal evening dress; hence, formal evening dress (*adj* **white'=tie**); **white vitriol** zinc sulphate; **white voice** a singing voice of pure, neutral tone, expressing no emotion. — *adj* **white'wall** (of pneumatic tyres) having a broad white band around the side walls. — Also *n*. — **white'ware** articles made of white porcelain, pottery or other ceramic material; **white'wash** a mixture of lime and water, or whiting, size and water, used for coating walls; a wash for the skin; false colouring; statements made or measures taken to rehabilitate a reputation, cover up official misdemeanours, etc; a glass of sherry after other wines; an act of whitewashing. — *vt* to cover with whitewash; to give a fair appearance to; to take steps to clear the stain from (a reputation), cover up (an official misdemeanour) or rehabilitate (a person) in the public eye; to beat (an opponent) so decisively in a game that he or she fails to score at all (*colloq*). — **white'washer** someone who whitewashes; **white water** shoal water near the shore, breakers; the foaming water in rapids, etc (*adj* **white'-water** as in *white-water canoeing*, *rafting*, etc); **white wax** bleached beeswax; Chinese wax; **white whale** the beluga; **white'wing** the velvet scoter, or an American scoter closely related to it; the chaffinch. — *adj* **white'-winged**. — **white'wood** a name applied to a large number of trees or their light-coloured timber, eg the American tulip tree, whitewood cedar (*Tecoma*, or *Tabebuia*, *leucoxylon*; Bignoniaceae), etc; unstained wood or wood prepared for staining (as in *whitewood furniture*); **whīt'ing-time** (*Shakesp*) bleaching-time. — *adj* **whīt'y-brown** white with a tinge of brown. — **bleed white** to drain completely of resources; **China white** a very pure variety of white lead (also **silver white** and **French white**); **mark with a white stone** see **stone**; **white out** to delete (written or typed material) with (white) correcting fluid, over which a corrected version may be written; to omit or cover up (secret or sensitive material in a report, transcript, etc) so leaving blank spaces; to (cause to) lose definition in conditions of white-out (qv above); to subject (an audience) to a blinding glare or flash (*theatre*); **whiter than white** extremely white; very pure, very law-abiding. [OE *hwīt*; ON *hvītr*, Ger *weiss*]

Whitechapel *wīt'chap-l* or *hwīt'chap-l*, *n* a lead from a one-card suit, straightforward leading out of winning cards, or other type of unskilful play (*whist*); the intentional pocketing of an opponent's ball (*billiards*). — **Whitechapel cart** see **cart**. [*Whitechapel* in London]

Whitehall *wīt'höl* or *hwīt'höl*, *n* a street with government offices, in London; the British government or its policy.

whither[1] *widh'ər* or *hwidh'ər*, *adv* and *conj* to what place?; in which direction?; towards what state?; to which place; (used relatively) to which; to what; whithersoever. — *adv* **whithersoev'er** to whatsoever place. — *adv* **whith'erward** or **whith'erwards** in what direction, to what point. — **no whither** to no place. [OE *hwider*, related to **who**]

whither[2]. See under **wuther**.

whiting[1] *wī'ting* or *hwī'ting*, *n* a small edible white-fleshed sea fish related to the cod. — **whiting pout** the bib or pout (qv). [**white**]

whiting[2]. See under **white**.

whitleather *wit'ledh-ər* or *hwit'ledh-ər*, *n* leather dressed with alum, white leather; the paxwax of the ox. [**white leather**]

Whitley Council *wit'li* (or *hwit'li*) *kown'səl*, *n* a joint standing industrial council (national or local), composed of representatives of employers and workpeople in an organized trade, to consider and settle conditions of employment, etc. — Also called **industrial council**. [Recommended (1917) in the 'Whitley Report', the report of a Reconstruction Subcommittee presided over by Rt Hon J H *Whitley*]

whitling *wit'ling* or *hwit'ling*, *n* a kind of trout, probably a young bull trout. [**white**, and sfx **-ling**]

whitlow *wit'lō* or *hwit'lō*, *n* a painful inflammation of a finger or toe, *esp* near the nail, paronychia. — **whitlow grass** any of several plants alleged to cure whitlows, eg a small British saxifrage (*Saxifraga tridactylites*), or a small crucifer (*Draba verna*); whitlow-wort; **whit'low-wort** any of a number of plants of the genus Paronychia. [Perh a corruption of *whick-flaw*, quick-flaw (cf **quick** and **flaw**) or of *whitflaw*, from **white** and **flaw**]

Whit Monday *wit* or *hwit mun'dā*, *n* the Monday following Whitsunday.

whitret. See **whittret**.

whitster *wit'stər* or *hwit'stər*, (*archaic*) *n* a bleacher of clothes or cloth. [**white**, and female agent sfx *-ster*]

Whitsun *wit'sən* or *hwit'sən*, *adj* relating to or observed at Whitsuntide. — *n* Whitsuntide. — **Whitsun ale** a festival formerly held at Whitsuntide; **Whit'sunday** the seventh Sunday after Easter, commemorating the day of Pentecost, when the converts in the primitive Church wore white robes; in Scotland, one of the term-days (May 15) on which rents, annuities, etc are payable, the Whitsunday removal terms in towns being fixed as May 28; **Whit'suntide** the season of Pentecost, comprising **Whitsun week**, **Whit week**, the week beginning with Whitsunday. [**white** and **Sunday**]

whittawer *wit'ö-ər* or *hwit'ö-ər*, *n* a saddler or harness-maker (*dialect*); a maker of white leather, a tawer (*hist* or *dialect*). — Also **whitt'aw** (*wit'ö* or *hwit'ö*). [**white** and **tawer**]

whitter. Another spelling of **witter**.

whitterick. See **whittret**.

whittie-whattie *hwit'i-hwot'i* or *wit'i-wot'i*, (*Scot*) *vi* to mutter, whisper; to shilly-shally. — *n* vague language intended to deceive; a frivolous excuse. [Perh formed from **what**]

whittle[1] *wit'l* or *hwit'l*, *vt* to pare or cut with a knife; to shape with a knife; to diminish gradually (often with *down*, *away*); to lessen the force or scope of (with *down*, *away*). — *vi* to cut wood aimlessly; to peach, or to confess at the gallows (*obs slang*); to fret (*dialect*). — *n* a clasp knife, sheath knife or other large knife. — *n* **whitt'ler**. — *n* **whitt'ling**. — **whittle away at** to pare or whittle; to reduce, curtail or circumscribe little by little. [ME *thwitel*, from OE *thwītan* to cut]

whittle[2] *wit'l* or *hwit'l*, (*dialect*) *n* a woollen shawl; a blanket. [OE *hwītel* a white mantle, from *hwīt* white]

whittret or **whitret** *hwit'rət*, *hwut'rət*, *wit'rət* or *wut'rət*, or **whitterick** *hwit'rik*, *wit'rik*, *hwit'ə-rik* or *wit'ə-rik*, (*Scot*) *n* a weasel.

Whitworth *wit'wərth* or *hwit'wərth*, (*eng*) *adj* denoting the standard British pre-metric screw thread, cut with an inter-pitch angle of 55°, first proposed by Sir J *Whitworth* (1803–87) in 1841.

Whity, whity. See **white**.

whizz or **whiz** *wiz* or *hwiz*, *vi* to fly through the air with or as if with a whistling noise; to move rapidly (*colloq*); to make a hissing, rustling or sizzling noise (*dialect* or *old*). — *vt* to cause to whizz: — *pr p* **whizz'ing**; *pa t* and *pa p* **whizzed**. — *n* a person remarkably talented or skilful at something (*colloq*); a hissing sound; a bargain, agreement (*US slang*, eg *Twain*). — Also *adv* and *interj*. — *n* **whizz'er** something that whizzes; a pickpocket (*slang*). — *n* and *adv* **whizz'ing**. — *adv* **whizz'ingly**. — **whizz'-bang** or **whiz'bang** (*World War I slang*) a light shell of high velocity which is heard arriving before the sound of a gun's report; a firework reminiscent of this; **whizz kid**, **whiz kid** or (suggesting influence by **wizard**) **wiz kid** (*colloq*) someone who achieves success rapidly and early, through ability, inventiveness, dynamism and ambition. [Imit; cf **wheeze, hiss**]

WHO *abbrev*: World Health Organization.

who *hōō*, *interrog* and *rel pronoun* what person or people?; which person or people (replaceable by **that**); used after a comma to add a clause commenting on a person or people; he or she or they that, the person or people that, anyone that; whoever; of what name, standing, etc: — *objective case* **whom** (OE *hwām*, *orig* the dative of *hwā* who, in the 12c and 13c replaced the older accusative *hwone*; *possessive case* **whose** (ME *hwas*, from OE *hwæs*, genitive of *hwā*). — *pronoun* **whoev'er**, **whosoev'er** and **who'so** (*archaic*) every one who; whatever person: — *objective case* **whom'ever** and **whomsoev'er**; *possessive case* **whosev'er** and **whose-**

soev'er. — **who's who** a directory listing names and biographical details of prominent people. — **as who should say** (*Shakesp*) like someone saying; **know who's who** to know the position and influence of everyone; **the who** (*Shakesp*) who; **who but he** or **she**, etc who else?, he or she, etc only. [OE *hwā*; cognate with Gothic *hwas*, OHGer *hwer*, Ger *wer*; also with Sans *ka*, L *quis*]

whoa *wō* or *hwō*, *interj* stop. — *interj* **whoa-ho-ho'** or **-hoa'** (*obs*) used to hail a person from a distance.

who'd *hōōd*, contracted form of **who would** and **who had**.

who-dun-it or **whodunnit** *hōō-dun'it*, (*colloq*) *n* a story or play concerned with the elucidation of a crime mystery. — *n* **whodun'itry** or **whodunn'itry** this genre of writing; over-zealous culprit-seeking. [**who** and **done** (non-standard past tense of **do**), and **it**]

whole *hōl*, *adj* not broken; undamaged; not broken up, or ground, or deprived of any part; containing the total amount, number, etc; complete; (of a sister or brother) full-blooded, related through both parents; as yet unworked (*mining*); from which no constituents have been removed, as in *whole blood*, *milk*, etc; processed as little as possible; sound in health (*archaic*); uninjured; restored to health; healed. — *n* the entire thing; not less than, all (with *of*); something complete in itself, *esp* if an integrated system or combination of parts. — *adv* completely, altogether; in one unbroken piece, as in *swallowed it whole*. — *n* **whole'ness**. — *adj* **whole'some** healthy in body, taste, morals or (*Shakesp*) condition; indicating health; conducive to bodily or spiritual health; remedial (*obs*); propitious (*Shakesp*); reasonable, sensible (*Shakesp*). — *adv* **whole'somely**. — *n* **whole'someness**. — *n* **whō'lism** an alteration of **holism**. — *n* **whō'list**. — *adj* **whōlist'ic**. — *adv* **wholly** (*hōl'li* or *hō'li*) completely, altogether. — **whole blood** donor blood for use in transfusions, from which no constituents have been extracted; **whole-body monitor** (*nuc eng*) an assembly of large scintillometers, heavily shielded against background radiation, used to identify and measure the gamma radiation emitted by the human body; **whole cloth** cloth in its full manufactured size (**cut out of whole cloth** (*NAm colloq*) wholly fabricated, utterly false). — *adj* **whole'-coloured** all of one colour. — **whole'food** food, unprocessed or processed as little as possible, produced without any artificial fertilizers or pesticides, etc. — *adj* **whole'=foot'ed** (*colloq*) unreserved. — *adj* **whole'grain** (of bread, flour, etc) made from the complete grain, with no parts discarded during manufacture. — *adj* **whole'=heart'ed** hearty, generous, zealous and sincere. — *adv* **whole'-heart'edly**. — *adj* **whole'-hog** (*slang*) out-and-out, complete. — **whole'-hogg'er** someone who is inclined to go the whole hog. — *adj* **whole'-hoofed** having an undivided hoof. — *adj* **whole'-length** giving the whole figure; full-length. — *n* a portrait or statue showing the whole figure. — **whole-life insurance** a life-insurance policy on which premiums are payable up to the death of the insured person; **whole'meal** meal made from entire grains of wheat (also *adj*); **whole milk** milk from which nothing has been extracted, as distinct from skimmed or semi-skimmed milk; **whole note** (*US*) a semibreve; **whole number** a unit, or a number composed of units, an integral number; **whole'sale** sale of goods, *usu* by the whole piece or large quantity, to a retailer. — *adj* buying and selling, or concerned with buying and selling, thus; extensive and indiscriminate. — *adv* by wholesale; extensively and indiscriminately. — **whole'saler** someone who sells by wholesale. — *adj* **whole'-skinned** unhurt; safe in reputation. — *adj* **whole'-souled'** whole-hearted. — **whole step** (*US*) a whole tone; **whole'stitch** a weaving stitch used to fill in a pattern, cloth stitch (*lace-making*); **whole tone** (*music*) an interval of two semitones. — *adj* **whole'wheat** wholemeal. — *adj* **wholl'y-owned** describing a company all of whose shares are owned by another company. — **go the whole hog** to do what one is doing thoroughly or completely; to commit oneself to anything unreservedly; **out of whole cloth** see **whole cloth** above; **upon** or **on the whole** generally speaking; all things considered; **with whole skin** safe, unscathed. [OE *hāl* healthy; ON *heill*, Ger *heil*; see **hale**[1]]

who'll *hōōl*, contracted form of **who will** and **who shall**.

wholly. See under **whole**.

whom, whomever, whomsoever. See under **who**.

whommle or **whomble**. See **whemmle**.

whoobub *hōō'bub*, (*obs*) *n*. See **hubbub**.

whoop *wōōp*, *hwōōp* or *hōōp*, also **hoop** *hōōp*, *n* a loud eager cry; a N American Indian war cry; a form of hide-and-seek; (*ōōp* or *hōōp*) the long noisy inspiration heard in whooping-cough. — *vi* to give a loud cry of triumph, eagerness, scorn, etc; to hoot. — *vt* to cheer or insult with shouts; to summon, or to urge on, by whooping. — *interj* (*Shakesp*) ho! — *n* **whoop'er** someone or something that whoops; a whooping swan or whooping crane (also **hoop'er**). — *n* and *adj* **whoop'ing**. — **whooper swan** a swan (*Cygnus cygnus*) with a whooping call, common in N Europe and Asia; **whooping cough** or **hooping cough** pertussis, an infectious and epidemic disease, mostly attacking children, characterized by catarrh of the respiratory tract with bouts of violent coughing that end in a long gasping inspiration; **whooping crane** an American crane (*Grus americana*), on the brink of extinction; **whooping swan** a whooper swan. — **whoop it up** (*colloq*) to indulge in noisy boisterous amusements or celebrations. [OFr *houper* to shout]

whoopee *wōō-pē'* or *hwōō-pē'*, *interj* and *n* an exclamation of delight. — **whoopee cushion** a rubber cushion that makes a noise like the breaking of wind when sat on. — **make whoopee** (*wōō'pē* or *hwōō'pē*; *colloq*) to indulge in hilarious fun or frivolity. [**whoop**]

whoops *wōōps*, *interj* an exclamation of surprise or concern made when one has a slight accident, makes an error, etc, or sees someone else do so. — *n* **whoop'sie** (*colloq*) a mess, *specif* of the excretory kind, made by a baby, animal, etc. [Variant of **oops**]

whoosh *wōōsh* or *hwōōsh*, or **woosh** *wōōsh*, *n* the sound of, or like that of, something large passing rapidly through the air. — *vi* and *vt* to move or cause to move with, or as if with, such a sound. — Also *adv* and *interj*. [Imit]

whoot. Obsolete variant of **hoot**.

whop or **whap** *wop* or *hwop*, (*colloq* or *dialect*) *vt* to whip, thrash; to defeat or surpass; to throw or pull suddenly or violently. — *vi* to fall, thump or move suddenly; to flop down: — *pr p* **whopp'ing** or **whapp'ing**; *pa t* and *pa p* **whopped** or **whapped**. — *n* a blow; a bump; the noise made by either of these. — *n* **whopp'er** someone or something that whops; anything very large; a lie. — *adj* or *intensifying adv* **whopp'ing** very large. — *n* a thrashing. [Variant of **wap**[1]; origin obscure, prob partly imit]

whore *hōr* or *hör*, *n* a prostitute; any unchaste woman; an allegedly corrupt religious community or practice. — *vi* to be, or associate with, a whore or whores. — *vt* to make a whore of, debauch; to spend in whoring. — *n* **whore'dom** whoring; any illicit sexual intercourse; idolatry. — *adj* **whō'rish**. — *adv* **whō'rishly**. — *n* **whō'rishness**. — **whore'house** a brothel; **whore'master** (*archaic*) a whoremonger. — *adj* **whore'masterly** libidinous. — **whore'mistress** (*archaic*) a woman who runs a brothel; **whore'monger** a lecher; a pander; **whore's bird** a whore's child; used as a vulgar term of abuse; **whore's egg** a sea-urchin; **whore'son** (*-sən*; *archaic*) son of a whore; a bastard; a term of coarse contempt or familiarity. — *adj* mean, scurvy. — **whore after** to pursue (an unworthy, dishonest or selfish goal). [Late OE *hōre*, prob from ON *hōra* adulteress]

whorl *wörl*, *hwörl*, *wûrl* or *hwûrl*, *n* a group of similar members arising from the same level on a stem, and forming a circle around it (*bot*); a single turn in a spiral shell; a convolution, eg in the ear; a disc on the lower part of a spindle serving as a flywheel (also **wharve** *wörv* or *hwörv*; *spinning*); in a fingerprint, a ridge forming a complete circle; a type of fingerprint having such ridges. — *adj* **whorled** having whorls; arranged in the form of a whorl or whorls. [Late ME *wharwyl*, etc, variants of **whirl**]

whorlbat. See **whirlbat**.

whortleberry *wûr'tl-ber-i* or *hwûr'tl-ber-i*, also *-bə-ri*, *n* a widely spread heath plant with a dark blue edible berry, the bilberry, blaeberry or whimberry, sometimes contracted to **whort**; extended to certain other plants of the same genus (*Vaccinium*). [Orig a SW variant of **hurtleberry**]

who's *hōōz*, contracted form of **who is** and **who has**.

whose *hōōz*, *pronoun* the possessive case of **who** (qv) and also **which**. — **whosesoever**, **whosever**, **whoso**, **whosoever** see under **who**.

whot *wot* or *hwot*, (*Spenser*) *adj* variant of **hot**[1].

who've *hōōv*, contracted form of **who have**.

whow *hwow* or *wow*, (*Scot*) *interj* of deploration. — Often **eh whow** (or **aich** (*āhh*) **wow**).

whummle. See **whemmle**.

whunstane. Scots form of **whinstone**.

why *wī* or *hwī*, *adv* and *conj* for what cause or reason?; wherefore; (used relatively) on account of which. — *interj* expressing sudden realization or protest, or marking resumption after a question or a slight pause, or (*Shakesp*) used to call a person. — *adv* **whyev'er** (*colloq*) for whatever reason. — **why'-not** a challenge for reasons (*old*); a dilemma (*obs*; **at a why-not** at a disadvantage). — **for why** (*archaic* and *dialect*) for what reason; because; **the why and wherefore** the whole reason; **why, so** (*Shakesp*) so let it be. [OE *hwī*, *hwȳ*, instrumental case of *hwā* who, and *hwæt* what]

whydah or **whidah** *wī'də* or *hwī'də*, *n* (also **whidah bird** or **whydah bird**) any of a group of African birds belonging or related to the weaver finch family, with much black in their plumage; any of various birds of a related family (*Ploceidae*). [**widow bird**, from the widow's black clothing; spelling altered in the belief that the bird was named from *Whydah* (Ouidah) in Dahomey (now Benin)]

WI *abbrev*: West Indies; Wisconsin (US state); Women's Institute.

wicca *wik'ə*, *n* witchcraft, *esp* as a revived practice; (with *cap*) an organization or cult of people practising or involved in witchcraft. — *n* **wicc'an** a member of this cult, or a practiser of witchcraft. — Also *adj*. [Re-use of OE *wicca* a (male) witch]

wice *wīs*, (*Scot*) *adj* wise, canny; sane, rational. [**wise**]

wich. See **wych**.

-wich. See **wick**[3].

wick[1] *wik*, *n* the twisted threads of cotton or other substance in a candle, lamp or lighter, which draw up the inflammable liquid to the flame; any strip of material that draws up liquid by capillary action. — *vt* to draw up (liquid) in this way. — **dip one's wick** (*vulg slang*; of a man) to have sexual intercourse; **get on someone's wick** (*colloq*) to irritate someone. [OE *wēoce*, *wēoc*; allied to Du *wick* a roll of lint, Ger *Wieche*]

wick[2] *wik*, (*dialect*) *n* a creek. [ON *vīk* a bay]

wick[3] *wik*, *n* a village or town (*dialect*); a farm (*dialect*); as sfx (*-ik* or *-wik*; also **-wich** *-ij*, *-ich* or *-wich*) in Ber*wick*, Green*wich*, etc. [OE *wīc*, prob an old Gmc borrowing from L *vīcus* a village]

wick[4] *wik*, (*curling*) *vt* and *vi* to strike (a stone) in an oblique direction. [Perh OE *wīcan* to bend, yield, give way]

wick[5] *wik*, (*obs* or *dialect*) *adj* wicked. [OE *wicca* wizard, *wicce* witch]

wicked *wik'id*, *adj* evil in principle or practice; sinful; ungodly; (of an animal) vicious; cruel; mischievous, spiteful; very bad, harmful, or offensive; roguish (*colloq*); unlucky (*Shakesp*); excellent, admirable (*slang*). — *n* a wicked person (*Bible*); (with *the*) wicked people. — *adv* **wick'edly**. — *n* **wick'edness**. — **the wicked one** the devil. [ME *wicked*, *wikked*, prob from *wicke*, *wikke* wicked, from OE *wicca*, wizard]

wicken. See **quicken**[1].

wicker *wik'ər*, *n* a small pliant twig or osier; wickerwork. — *adj* made of twigs or osiers; encased in wickerwork. — *adj* **wick'ered** made of wicker; covered with wickerwork. — **wick'erwork** basketwork of any kind. [ME *wiker*, of Scand origin; cf OE *wīcan* to bend]

wicket *wik'it*, *n* a small gate; a small door in or near a larger one; a grill or loophole (*obs*); an opening or a window with a grille, eg at a ticket office, bank, etc (*US*); (the following meanings all *cricket*) the upright arrangement of three stumps with two bails on top which the batsman defends against the bowling; a stump; the pitch, *esp* in respect of its condition; a batsman's stay at the wicket, or his joint stay there with another; a batsman's innings. — **wicket door** or **gate** a wicket; **wick'et-keeper** the fieldsman who stands immediately behind the striker's wicket (*cricket*). — **get**, **take**, etc **a wicket** to bowl a batsman or have him or her put out in any way as a result of one's bowling; **keep wicket** to be wicket-keeper; **over** (or **round**) **the wicket** (of bowling) delivered with the hand nearer (or farther away from) the wicket; **sticky wicket** see under **stick**[1]; **throw down the wicket** (of a fielder) to bring down the wicket with a throw of the ball; **win by so many wickets** to win with so many wickets still to fall. [ONFr *wiket* (Fr *guichet*); of Gmc origin]

wickiup *wik'i-up*, *n* a N American Indian hut constructed with an oval frame and covered with grass or mats. [Fox (Am Indian language) *wikiyapi*]

wicky. See **quicken**[1].

widdershins, **widershins**, etc. Variants of **withershins**.

widdle *wid'l*, (*hypocoristic*) *vi* to urinate. [Poss from **wee**[3] and **piddle**]

widdy[1] *wid'i*, (*dialect*) *n* a rope, *esp* one made of osiers; a halter for hanging. [Variant of **withy**]

widdy[2] *wid'i*. Dialect form of **widow**.

wide *wīd*, *adj* extending far; having a considerable distance between the sides; broad; of a specified breadth; roomy; expanded or extended; opened as far as possible; far apart; far from the point aimed at, or (*rare*) place mentioned (with *of*); very different (with *of*; *old*); of large scope, including or considering much; astute, wily (*slang*); lax in morals (*slang*); broad, the reverse of *narrow* (*phonetics*). — *n* wideness; a ball bowled out of reach of the batsman (*cricket*); a penalty run allowed for this. — *adv* (also **far and wide**) to a great distance, over a large region; at a distance (*Spenser*); far from the point aimed at, the subject under discussion, the truth, etc; far to one side (with *of*); so that there is a large space or distance between. — *combining form* **-wide** extending throughout a specified area, etc as in *nationwide*, *countrywide*, *worldwide*. — *adv* **wide'ly**. — *vt* and *vi* **wī'den** to make or grow wide or wider; to throw open (*Shakesp*). — *n* **wī'dener** someone or something that widens; a kind of tool for widening something. — *n* **wide'ness**. — *adj* **wī'dish**. — *adj* **wide'-angle** (*photog*; of a lens) having an angle of view of 60° or more and a short focal length. — **wide-area network** (*comput*) a computer network operating nationally or internationally, using telecommunications links, microwaves and satellites (*abbrev* **WAN**); **wide'awake** a low wide-brimmed soft felt hat; **wide'-awake'ness** the condition of being wide awake. — *adj* **wide'body** or **wide'-bod'ied** (of aircraft) having a wide fuselage. — **wide boy** (*slang*) an astute or wily person, *esp* one prone to sharp practice. — *adj* **wide'chapped** (*Shakesp*) open-mouthed. — *adj* **wide'-eyed** showing great surprise; naive, credulous. — **wide'-gab** (*Scot*) the angler, a wide-mouthed fish. — *adj* **wide'-rang'ing** covering a wide range of topics, interests, cases, etc. — **wide receiver** (*Am football*) a member of the offence whose task is to catch and run with the ball; **wide screen** a wide curved cinema screen designed to give the viewer a greater sense of actuality in the picture (*adj* **wide'screen**; also *fig*). — *adj* **wide'-spec'trum** (of antibiotic, etc) effective against a wide range of micro-organisms. — *adj* **wide'spread** extended or extending widely; found, operative, etc in many places. — *adj* **wide'-stretched** (*Shakesp*) large. — *adj* **wide'-watered** (eg *Milton*) bordered or covered by wide waters, having a great extent of water. — **to the wide** completely; utterly; **wide awake** fully awake; on the alert; keen and knowing (*colloq*); **wide of** (*Shakesp*) indifferent to, far from observing; **wide of the mark** far out, astray from the truth; **wide open** opened wide; open to attack (*colloq*); (also as *adj* **wide-o'pen**) lax in enforcing laws and regulations (*US*). [OE *wīd*; ON *vīthr*, Ger *weit*]

widgeon. See **wigeon**.

widget *wij'it*, *n* a gadget; any small manufactured item or component. [Ety obscure; perh an alteration of **gadget**]

widgie *wij'i*, (*Austr* and *NZ*) *n* an Australian Teddy girl of the 1950s, the female counterpart of a bodgie (qv). [Formed after **bodgie**]

widow *wid'ō*, *n* a woman whose husband is dead and who has not remarried; a woman whose husband spends much time away from her on some (*esp* sporting) pursuit, as in *golf widow* (*colloq*); in the early Church, one of a special class of pious women; an extra hand in some card games; a short last line at the end of a paragraph which stands at the top of a page or column of print (*printing*). — *vt* to leave (someone) a widow or widower; to strip of anything valued; to endow with a widow's right (*Shakesp*); to be a widow to (*Shakesp*). — *n* **wid'ower**, or (*dialect*) **wid'owman** a man whose wife is dead. — *n* **wid'owerhood**. — *n* **wid'owhood** the state of being a widow or (*rarely*) a widower; a widow's right (*Shakesp*). — **widow bird** see **whydah**; **widow's bench** (*hist*) a widow's share of her husband's estate besides her jointure; **widow's chamber** the apparel and bedroom furniture of the widow of a London freeman, to which she was entitled; **widow's cruse** a source of supply that never fails (from the story in the Bible, 1 Kings 17.10–16); **widow's man** (*naut*) any of a number of fictitious persons formerly entered as a part of a ship's company in order that the pay allotted to them might be set aside for widows' pensions; **widow's mite** a small offering generously given (Mark 12.42; see also **mite**); **widow's peak** a point of hair over the forehead, like the cusped front of the widow's cap formerly worn; **widow's weeds** the mourning apparel formerly worn by all widows; **widow wail** a dwarf shrub (*Cneorum*) with pink scented flowers, native to Spain and south France; daphne or mezereon (*Daphne mezereum*). — **a widow bewitched** a woman deserted by or separated from her husband, a grass widow; **the Widow** Veuve (Fr, widow) Clicquot, a famous brand of champagne. [OE *widewe*; Ger *Witwe*, L *vidua* bereft of a husband, Sans *vidhavā*]

width *width*, *n* extent from side to side, breadth; wideness; the distance from side to side across a swimming-pool. — *adv* **width'ways** or **width'wise** in the direction of the width, across the width. [A 17c formation on the analogy of **breadth**, replacing **wideness**]

wiel. Same as **weel**[1].

wield *wēld*, *vt* to use, or lift ready to use (a tool, weapon, etc); to have or exert (power, authority, influence, etc); to use (eg one's pen, wit, etc) in the manner of a tool or weapon; to rule (*obs*); to possess, enjoy, gain (*obs*); to control, manage (eg lands; *obs*). — *adj* **wield'able** capable of being wielded. — *n* **wield'er**. — *n* **wield'iness**. — *adj* **wield'less** (*Spenser* **weeldlesse**) unmanageable. — *adj* **wield'y** easy to wield; manageable; dexterous, active (*obs*). — **wield the sceptre** to have supreme command or control. [OE *weldan* (not recorded; WSax *wealdan*); Gothic *waldan*, Ger *walten*]

Wiener *wē'nər* or (*colloq*) **wienie** or **weeny** *wē'ni*, (*NAm*) *n* short for **Wienerwurst** (*wē'ner-wûrst*) a small smoked beef, pork or veal sausage. — **Wiener schnitzel** (*vē'nər shnit'səl*) a veal cutlet dressed with breadcrumbs and eggs; **Wiener Werkstätte** (*vē'nər verk'shtet-ə*; *Ger*, Viennese workshops) an association of craftspeople and designers founded in Vienna in 1903 whose main influences were the English Arts and Crafts movement and Art Nouveau. [Ger *Wiener* of *Wien*, ie Vienna]

wife *wīf*, *n* the woman to whom one is married; a married woman; a woman (*archaic* or *dialect*); (also **goodwife** (qv)) the mistress of a house, a hostess (*obs*); (as *combining form*) a woman engaged in some particular work or purveyance, as in *housewife*, *midwife*, *fishwife*, *alewife*; the passive or subservient partner in a homosexual relationship (*slang*): — *pl* **wīves**. — *n* **wife'hood** the state of being a wife. — *adj* **wife'less** without a wife. — *adj* **wife'like**. — *n* **wife'liness**. — *adj* **wife'ly**. — *n* **wī'fie** (*Scot colloq*) a woman. — **wife'-swapping** (*colloq*) a form of sexual activity in which married couples exchange partners temporarily. — **take to wife** (*archaic*) to marry (a woman). [OE *wīf*; ON *vīf*, Ger *Weib*]

wig[1] *wig*, *n* an artificial covering of hair for the head worn to conceal baldness, to disguise the appearance or as part of stage costume, cosmetically, or for fashion's sake, as in the full-dress **full-bottomed wig** of Queen Anne's time, still worn in an official capacity by the Speaker of the House of Commons and by judges, and the smaller **tie-wig**, still represented by the judge's undress wig and the barrister's or advocate's frizzed wig; a judge (*slang*). — *adj* **wigged** wearing a wig. — *n* **wigg'ery** false hair; excess of formality (*Carlyle*). — *adj* **wig'less** without a wig. — *adj* **wig'like**. — **wig block** a block or shaped piece of wood for fitting a wig on; **wig'-maker** a maker of wigs. — **wigs on the green** a fray. [Short for **periwig**]

wig[2] *wig*, (*colloq*) *vt* to scold: — *pr p* **wigg'ing**; *pa t* and *pa p* **wigged**. — *n* **wigg'ing** (*colloq*) a scolding. — **wig out** (*US slang*) to go crazy, freak out. [**wig**[1]]

wigan *wig'ən*, *n* a stiff canvas-like fabric for stiffening garments; a plain grey cloth for boot-linings, etc. [*Wigan*, the town]

wigeon or (now rarely) **widgeon** *wij'ən*, *n* any of various ducks of the genus *Anas*, with a bill shorter than the head, short legs, rather small feet, long pointed wings and a wedge-shaped tail; in the UK, *specif Anas penelope*; a fool (*obs*). [Of uncertain origin]

wigged[1], **wiggery**. See under **wig**[1].

wigged[2], **wigging**. See under **wig**[2].

wiggle *wig'l*, *vi* and *vt* to waggle, wriggle. — *n* a wiggling motion. — Also *vi*, *vt* and *n* **wigg'le-wagg'le**. — *n* **wigg'ler** someone who wriggles. — *adj* **wigg'ly** wriggly; wavy, *esp* irregularly so. — **get a wiggle on** (*slang*) to hurry. [Frequentative of verb from which is derived dialect *wig* to wag; connected with MLGer *wiggelen*]

wight[1] *wīt*, *n* a creature or a person (*archaic*, *dialect* or *ironic*); a supernatural being (*obs*). [OE *wiht* a creature, thing; Ger *Wicht*; cf **whit**]

wight[2] *wīt*, (*archaic* and *dialect*) *adj* swift, nimble; courageous, strong. — *adv* **wight'ly**. [ON *vīgr* warlike, from *vīg* war (OE *wīg*)]

wight[3]. See **wite**[1].

Wigorn. *abbrev*: *Wigorniensis* (*L*), of Worcester.

wigwag *wig'wag*, *vi* to twist about; to signal by means of flags. — *n* the act of wigwagging; a level-crossing signal which gives its indication, with or without a red light, by swinging about a fixed axis. — *adj* twisting. — *adv* to and fro. [Dialect *wig* (from same root as **wiggle**) and **wag**]

wigwam *wig'wom* or *wig'wam*, *n* a domed tent-like N American Indian dwelling made of arched poles covered with skins, bark or mats; often applied to the cone-shaped dwelling more correctly known as a tepee. [Abenaki and Massachuset *wikewam*]

wilco *wil'kō*, *interj* (in signalling, telecommunications, etc) an *abbrev* of 'I *will* comply' (with instructions); used generally to signify compliance (*colloq*).

wild[1] *wīld*, *adj* being in a state of nature, not tamed or cultivated; of an undomesticated or uncultivated kind; uncivilized, savage; desolate, rugged, inhospitable, uninhabitable or uninhabited; tempestuous; violent; fierce; passionate; frantically excited; unrestrained, uncontrolled, out of control; licentious; agitated; shy; distracted, distraught; furious; intensely enthusiastic, eager, keen (with *about*); strong and irrational; fantastic; crazy, impracticable; enjoyable, terrific (*slang*); disordered, dishevelled; unconsidered, rough, random, approximate; wide of the mark; fresh and natural;

(with *cap*) applied to the extreme Evangelical party in the Church of Scotland (*hist*); (of a playing-card) having any value desired. — Also *adv*. — *n* (also in *pl*) an uncultivated region; a wilderness or desert (also *fig*); an empty region of air or water (*poetic*); (in *sing*) a wild animal's or plant's natural environment or life in it. — *n* **wīld'ing** that which grows wild or without cultivation; a wild crab-apple; a garden plant self-sown, an escape; see **go wilding** below. — *adj* uncultivated or wild. — *adj* **wild'ish** somewhat wild. — *adv* **wild'ly**. — *n* **wild'ness**. — **wild animals** undomesticated animals; **wild ass** any of several Asiatic or African asses, such as the onager, living naturally in a wild state; **wild birds** birds not domesticated, *esp* those protected at certain seasons under the Acts of 1880 onwards; **wild boar** a wild pig, *esp Sus scrofa*, from which most domestic pigs are derived. — *adj* **wild'-born** born in the wild. — **wild card** a person allowed to compete in a sports event even though lacking the stipulated qualifications, etc; (the offering of) such a chance to compete; a character which can stand for any other character or group of characters in a file, etc (*comput*); **wild'cat** an undomesticated species of cat (*Felis sylvestris*) native to Europe; any of various small wild animals of the cat family; the skins of these; a quick-tempered, fierce person; a speculative or unsound financial scheme (*US*); someone who takes part in such a scheme (*US*); an exploratory well (*US*). — *adj* (of a business scheme, etc) haphazard, reckless, unsound financially; (of a strike) unauthorized by union officials; (of an oil well) exploratory (*US*). — *vt* and *vi* (*US*) to drill an experimental well in an area of unknown productivity in search of oil, gas, ore, etc. — **wild'catter** (*US*); **wild cherry** any uncultivated tree bearing cherries, such as the gean (*Prunus avium*), or its fruit; **wild dog** any wild species of the dog genus or family, such as the dhole, the dingo, etc; **wild duck** any duck excepting the domesticated duck; *specif*, the mallard. — *adj* **wild-eyed'** looking angrily distressed or distracted; of an idea or plan, unrealistic, impracticable. — **wild'fire** a sweeping, destructive fire; a need-fire; any of various inflammable materials used in warfare, such as Greek fire (*hist*) (**like wildfire** extremely fast); lightning without thunder; a disease of sheep; will-o'-the-wisp; **wild'fowl** the birds of the duck tribe; game birds; **wild'fowler**; **wild'fowling** the pursuit of wildfowl; **wild goose** a wild or feral bird of the goose kind; a flighty or foolish person; (in *pl*, **Wild Geese**; *hist*) Irish Jacobites who migrated to the Continent after the abdication of James II, *esp* those who joined the French army; **wild-goose chase** a search that is doomed, *esp* for reasons unknown to the searcher, to be unsuccessful; *orig* a chase hither and thither of the follow-my-leader kind; **wild grape** a grapevine (*Vitis* or *Muscadinia*) in the wild state, or its fruit; Coccoloba (see **grapetree**); **wild honey** the honey of wild bees; **Wild Hunt** in Germanic legend, a host of phantoms rushing along, accompanied by the shouting of huntsmen and the baying of dogs; **Wild Huntsman** their leader; **wild hyacinth** (*esp Scot*) the bluebell, *Endymion* or *Scilla nonscriptus*; **wild indigo** any of several plants of different genera belonging to the same family (*Papilionaceae*) as indigo, such as an American tumbleweed (*Baptisia tinctoria*); **wild'land** land completely uncultivated; **wild'life** wild animals, birds, etc collectively; FCB wildlife park a safari park containing native or non-native animals; **wild man** someone uncivilized, a savage (*old*); a man of extreme or radical views in politics; **wild mare** a seesaw; an instrument of punishment, the horse; **wild oat** any of several tall perennial weeds related to the cultivated oat, eg *Avena fatua*; **wild olive** the oleaster (qv); **wild rice** a tall aquatic grass, Zizania; **wild service** a tree, *Sorbus torminalis*, of the same genus as the service tree (qv); **wild silk** silk from wild silkworms; short-fibred silk imitating this; **wild thyme** see **thyme**; **wild track** a soundtrack recorded independently of a photographic track, but used in editing; **wild type** (*biol*) the form of a species typically occurring under natural breeding conditions, as distinct from mutant types; **wild water** the foaming water in rapids, etc; **Wild West** the western United States in the days of the first settlers, chiefly cattlemen and goldminers, before the establishment of law and order; **Wild-West Show** a performance of roping or riding of steers, shooting, etc by (people dressed as) cowboys; **wild Williams** (*dialect*) ragged-Robin; **wild'wood** wild uncultivated, or unfrequented, woodland. — Also *adj*. — **go wilding** (*US*) of a gang of youths, or as a member of such a gang, to attack violently, by beating, robbing and raping; **run wild** to take to loose living; to live or grow in freedom from constraint or control; to revert to the wild or uncultivated state; **sow one's wild oats** see under **oat**; **wild and woolly** unpolished; unrestrained; suggestive of the Wild West, lawless. [OE *wilde*; common Gmc word]

wild[2] *wīld*, obsolete variant of **weald** or **wield**.

wildcat. See under **wild**[1].

wildebeest *vild'i-bāst*, *wild'i-bēst* or *vild'ə-bēst*, (*SAfr*) *n* a gnu. [Du *wilde* wild, and *beest* ox]

wilder *wil'dər*, (*poetic*) *vt* to cause to stray; to bewilder. — *vi* to wander wildly or widely. — *adj* **wil'dered**. — *adj* **wil'dering**. — *n* **wil'derment**. [Origin uncertain, perh formed from **wilderness**]

wilderness *wil'dər-nəs*, *n* a region uncultivated and uninhabited; a pathless, unfrequented or unexplored region; such a region deliberately preserved from the inroads of tourism; a desolate waste of any kind, eg an extent of open sea (*poetic*); a part of a garden or estate allowed to run wild, or cultivated in imitation of natural woodland; an overgrown tangle of weeds, etc; conditions of life, or a place, in which the spirit feels desolate; the situation of being without public office or influence, or of being forgotten by the public, after playing a leading role; the present world; a large confused or confusing assemblage; wildness (*obs*). — **crying in the wilderness** see under **cry**. [ME, from *wilderne* wild, wilderness, from OE *wilddēoren*, from *wild* wild, and *dēor* animal]

wildfowl, etc. See under **wild**[1].

wildgrave *wīld'grāv*, (*obs*) *n* a waldgrave. [Ger *Wildgraf*, from *Wild* game, and *Graf* count]

wilding, **wildish**, **wildland**, **wildlife**, **wildly**, **wildness**. See under **wild**[1].

wile *wīl*, *n* a pleasing artifice; a trick; deceit (*rare*); (in *pl*) cajolery. — *vt* to beguile, inveigle; to coax, cajole; to make to pass easily or pleasantly (with *away*; confused with **while**). — *adj* **wile'ful** full of wiles. [OE *wīl*; cf **guile**]

wilful or (*US*) **willful** *wil'fŏŏl*, *adj* self-willed, obstinate, headstrong; deliberate, intentional; willing (*Shakesp*). — *adv* (*Shakesp*) wilfully. — *adv* **wil'fully**. — *n* **wil'fulness**. [**will**[1]]

wilga *wil'gə*, (*Austr*) *n* a small white-flowered tree of the genus *Geijera*, able to withstand drought. [Aboriginal]

Wilhelmine *vil'həl-mīn*, *adj* relating to Kaiser *Wilhelm II* of Germany (1888–1918) or his reign.

Wilhelmstrasse *vil'helm-shträ-sə*, *n* a street in Berlin; formerly, the German Foreign Office.

wili *vē'lē*, *n* in the ballet *Giselle* (based on a legendary theme from Heinrich Heine) the spirit of a maiden who dies before her wedding day. [Of Slav origin; cf Czech *víla* fairy]

wilily, **wiliness**. See **wily**.

wilja. Same as **wiltja**.

will[1] *wil*, *v* used with an infinitive or absolutely: *esp* in 2*nd* and 3*rd pers* to form a future tense (**shall** often being used in 1*st pers*); in 1*st pers* to express intention or determination; to make requests, issue commands, or invite; to indicate capacity, as in *the car will seat six*; to suggest willingness or readiness on the part of someone or something, as in *the car will not start*; to express assumptions; to wish, desire or want, as in *say what you will*; to express resignation or frustration at events, another's perversity, etc: — 2*nd pers sing present* *indicative* (with *thou*; *archaic*) **wilt**; *3rd pers* **will**; *pa t* **would** (*wŏŏd*); *2nd pers sing* (with *thou*; *archaic*) **wouldst**; no *pa p*. [OE *wyllan*, *willan* to wish, to be willing]

will[2] *wil*, *n* the power or faculty of choosing or determining; the act of using this power; volition; choice or determination; pleasure, wish or desire; inclination, preference; lust; command; arbitrary disposal; (in combination) feeling towards others, as in *goodwill* or *ill-will* (qv under **good** and **ill**); the disposition of one's effects at death; the written document containing this. — *vt* to decree; to seek to force, influence (oneself or another to perform a specified action) by silent exertion of the will; to dispose of by will, to bequeath; to wish, desire or want, as in *what you will*; to wish for (*archaic*); to command, order, require (*obs*): — *pa t* and *pa p* **willed**; *2nd pers present indicative* **will'est**; *3rd pers* **wills**. — *vi* to exercise choice, choose, decree; to be willing. — *adj* **will'able**. — *adj* **willed** having a will; voluntary; given or disposed of by will; brought under another's will, as in hypnotism; (in combination) having a will of a particular kind, as in *weak-willed*, *strong-willed*, etc. — *n* **will'er** someone who wills. — *adj* **will'-less** having no will of one's own. — *adv* **will'-lessly**. — *n* **will'-lessness**. — **will'power** the ability to control one's actions, emotions, impulses, etc; **will'-worship** (*Bible*) worship after one's own will or fancy, superstitious observance without divine authority. — **at will** when or as one chooses; **a will of one's own** a strong, self-assertive will; **by my will** (*Shakesp*) voluntarily; with my consent; **conjoint** or **joint will** a testamentary act by two persons jointly in the same instrument; **have one's will** to obtain what one desires; **living will** see under **living**; **tenant at will** someone who holds lands only so long as the owner pleases; **with a will** heartily and energetically; **with the best will in the world** no matter how willing or persevering one is; **work one's will** to do exactly what one chooses. [OE *willa* will, determination, whence the weak verb *willian*]

will[3] or **wull** *wil* or *wul*, (*Scot*) *adj* and *adv* at a loss; astray; bewildered. [ON *villr* astray; cf **wild**[1]]

willemite *wil'əm-īt*, *n* orthosilicate of zinc, Zn_2SiO_4, white when pure but commonly red, brown, or green through the presence of manganese or iron, noteworthy as exhibiting an intense bright yellow fluorescence in ultraviolet light. [*Willem* (William) I of the Netherlands]

Willesden paper *wilz'dən pā'pər*, *n* a specially treated paper which keeps out wet and acts as a sound and heat insulator, placed under slates in roofing. [*Willesden*, orig place of manufacture]

willet *wil'it*, *n* a large N American wading bird of the sandpiper family (*Catoptrophus semipalmatus*), grey with black and white wings. [Imit]

willey. See **willy**[1].

willful. See **wilful**.

Williamite *wil'yə-mīt*, (*hist*) *n* during the political upheavals of 1688–9, a supporter of *William* of Orange (William III, 1688–1702). — *adj* relating to or supporting the cause of William of Orange against the Jacobites (supporters of James II).

willie. See **willy**[2].

willies *wil'iz*, (*slang*) *n pl* the creeps.

williewaught *wil'i-wöhht*, (*Scot*) *n* a deep draught. [From misunderstanding of Burns, *Auld Lang Syne*, 4.3, 'a right guid willie (or guid-willie) waught' (where 'guid willie' means 'good will'), a generous and friendly draught]

willing *wil'ing*, *adj* ready, glad or not disinclined (to do something); eager, cooperative; ready and prompt to act; voluntary; chosen; intentional (*rare*); of or relating to the will. — *adv* **will'ingly**. — *n* **will'ingness**. — *adj* **will'ing-heart'ed** heartily consenting. — **willing horse** a person or animal always prepared to work hard at any task. [**will**[2]]

williwaw *wil'i-wö*, *n* a gust of cold wind blowing seawards from a mountainous coast, eg in the Straits of Magellan; a sudden squall; a tumult or disturbance. [Origin uncertain]

will-o'-the-wisp *wil'-ə-dhə-wisp'*, *n* the ignis fatuus (qv); any elusive and deceptive person or thing: — *pl* **wills'-o'-the-wisp'** or **will'-o'-the-wisps'**. [Orig *Will-with-the-wisp*, from *Will*, *abbrev* of William, and **wisp** (qv)]

willow *wil'ō*, *n* any tree or shrub of the genus *Salix*, having slender pliant branches; any of several plants resembling it; the wood of the willow; a cricket bat, traditionally made of willow; a willowing-machine. — *vt* to clean in a willowing-machine. — *adj* **will'owed** abounding with, or grown with, willows. — *adj* **will'owish** like a willow; of the colour of willow leaves; slender and supple. — *adj* **will'owy** abounding in willows; flexible; slender and graceful. — **willow grouse** a European species of grouse (*Lagopus lagopus*) with brown plumage; **will'owherb** a perennial herb (*Epilobium* or *Chamaenerion*) of the evening primrose family (including rose-bay, bay willow, French or Persian willow) with willow-like leaves and seeds; **will'owing-machine** a machine in which a spiked revolving cylinder, *usu* contained in a spiked box, loosens or cleans cotton, wool, rags for paper, etc; **willow pattern** a blue design of Chinese character but English origin used on china from the late 18c onwards; **willow warbler** or **willow wren** a small European sylviine bird (*Phylloscopus trochilus*); **willow weed** one of various species of Polygonum or knotweed; the purple loosestrife. [OE *welig*; LGer *wilge*, Du *wilg*]

willpower. See under **will**[2].

willy[1] or **willey** *wil'i*, (*dialect*) *n* a willow basket; a willowing-machine. — *vt* to clean in a willowing-machine. [OE *wilige*; related to **willow**]

willy[2] or **willie** *wil'i*, *n* hypocoristic for the penis.

willyard *wil'ərd* or *wil'yərd*, or **willyart** *wil'ərt* or *wil'yərt*, *adj* (*Scot*) wilful; shy. [**will**[3]]

willy-nilly *wil'i-nil'i*, *adv* willing or unwilling, whether one wishes or not; compulsorily, inevitably. — *adj* having no choice; being so, or occurring, willy-nilly; vacillating (*erron*). [**will**[1] and **nill**]

willy-willy *wil'i-wil'i*, (*Austr*) *n* a cyclone. [Aboriginal]

Wilms' tumour *wilmz tū'mər*, (*pathol*) *n* a malignant kidney tumour *usu* occurring in early childhood, composed of embryonal structures. [M *Wilms*, German surgeon (1867–1918)]

Wilson's disease *wil'sənz diz-ēz'*, *n* a hereditary degenerative disease of the nervous system and liver, in which there is an accumulation of copper in the tissues. [Samuel *Wilson* (1878–1937), English neurologist]

wilt[1] *wilt*, *vi* (of flowers) to droop, become limp or wither, from heat or lack of water; to lose energy, to droop from fatigue or too much heat; to lose self-confidence or courage. — *vt* to render limp, cause to droop or wither; to cause to lose spirit, self-confidence or courage. — *n* the process of wilting; any of various diseases that cause wilting of plants. [Orig dialect; perh from **welk**[1]]

wilt[2] *wilt*, *2nd pers sing* of **will**[1].

wiltja *wil'chə*, (*Austr*) *n* an Aboriginal shelter or hut. [Aboriginal]

Wilton *wil'tən*, *n* (in full **Wilton carpet**) a carpet with a velvety cut-loop pile and a woven pattern, typically of a simple, three-colour kind, long made at *Wilton*, in Wilts.

Wilts. *abbrev*: Wiltshire.

wily *wī'li*, *adj* full of wiles, crafty, cunning, astute. — *adv* **wī'lily**. — *n* **wī'liness**. [**wile**]

wimble[1] *wim'bl*, *n* an instrument for boring holes, turned by a handle; a gimlet; an auger; a kind of brace; an instrument for boring in soft ground. — *vt* to bore through with a wimble. [Through ONFr, from MDu *wimpel*]

wimble[2] *wim'bl*, (*Spenser*) *adj* active, nimble. [Northern word of Scand origin, now dialect]

wimbrel. See **whimbrel**.

WIMP *wimp*, *abbrev*: an acronym for *w*indows, *i*cons, *m*ouse (or *m*enus) and *p*ointer, user-friendly computer interface (*comput*); an acronym for *w*eakly *i*nteracting *m*assive *p*articles (*particle phys*).

wimp[1] *wimp*, (*slang*) *n* an ineffectual or pusillanimous person. — *adj* **wim'pish**. — *adv* **wim'pishly**. — *n* **wim'pishness**. — *adj* **wim'py**. — **wimp out** to funk something, to chicken out. [Orig US; variously explained]

wimp[2] *wimp*, (*old slang*) a young woman. [Perh from *women*]

wimple *wim'pl*, or **whimple** *wim'pl* or *hwim'pl*, *n* a veil folded so as to cover the head and neck and closely frame the cheeks, a fashion of the Middle Ages that remained part of a nun's dress; a fold, wrinkle or ripple; a turn or bend; a crafty twist (*Scot*). — *vt* to wrap in or hide with a wimple; to enwrap, enfold; to blindfold (*Shakesp*; in *pa p*); to lay in folds. — *vi* to meander; to ripple; to lie in folds (*Spenser*). [OE *wimpel* neck-covering; cf OHGer *wimpal* a light robe, Ger *Wimpel* a pennon, Fr *guimpe* a nun's veil, Eng *gimp* a thin cloth for trimming]

Wimpy® *wim'pi*, *n* a kind of hamburger served in a bread roll. [Orig the name of a hamburger-loving character in a comic strip]

win[1] *win*, *vt* to get by labour; to gain in contest; to secure; to achieve, effect; to reach; to be the victor in; to allure, persuade or prevail upon; to gain influence over; to obtain the favour of; to mine (an ore); to open up (a new portion of a coal seam). — *vi* to gain the victory; to make one's way, betake oneself (*dialect*); to get oneself (into a desired place or state, etc): — *pr p* **winn'ing**; *pa t* and *pa p* **won** (*wun*). — *n* (*colloq*) a victory, success. — *n* **winnabil'ity**. — *adj* **winn'able**. — *n* **winn'er** someone who wins; something very good, impressive or successful (*slang*). — *n* **winn'ing** the achieving of victory; (*usu* in *pl*) that which is won; a shaft or pit to open a bed of coal. — *adj* that wins; of or relating to the achievement of victory; attractive, prepossessing; persuasive. — *adv* **winn'ingly**. — *n* **winn'ingness**. — **winn'ing-gallery** in real tennis, the gallery furthest away from the net at either end of the court, any shot played into this winning a point; **winn'ing-post** the goal of a race-course. — **win by a head** or **short head** to win very narrowly; **win in a canter** to win easily; **win of** (*obs*) to get the better of; **win on** or **upon** to gain on; to get the better of; to obtain favour with or influence over; **win** or **gain one's spurs** to earn one's knighthood by valour on the field, hence to gain recognition or reputation by merit of any kind; **win out** to get out; to succeed or prevail, *esp* with a struggle (*colloq*; also **win through**); **win over** or **round** to bring over to one's opinion or party; **you can't win** (*colloq*) nothing you do will be satisfactory, find favour, etc. [OE *winnan* to struggle, suffer; ON *vinna*, Ger *gewinnen* to win]

win[2] *win*, (*Scot*) *vt* to dry by exposure to the wind: — *pr p* **winn'ing**; *pa t* and *pa p* **won** (*wun*). [**win**[1] influenced by **wind**[1]]

win[3] or **winn** *win*, or **wing** *wing*, (*slang*) *n* a penny.

wince[1] *wins*, *vi* to shrink or start back; to make an involuntary movement, as in sudden pain; to register sudden mental pain or acute embarrassment; to kick (*obs* or *dialect*); to be restive, like a horse uneasy with its rider. — *n* an involuntary start back or shrinking; a kick (*obs*). — *n* **win'cer**. — *n* and *adj* **win'cing**. [Cf OFr *guinchir*, *ganchir* to wince, from a Gmc word; cf OHGer *wenkan* (Ger *wanken*) to wince]

wince[2]. See **winch**[1].

wincey or **winsey** *win'si*, *n* a cloth, plain or twilled, *usu* with a linen or cotton warp and woollen filling. — *n* **winceyette'** a plain cotton cloth of light weight, raised slightly on both sides. [Orig Scot, from **linsey-woolsey**]

winch[1] *winch* or *winsh*, or **wince** *wins*, *n* a reel or roller; the crank of a wheel or axle; a powerful type of hauling or hoisting machine. — *vt* to haul, hoist, etc using such a machine (with *up*, *in*, etc). — **winch'man** someone who operates a winch or takes part in winching operations, eg aboard a helicopter. [OE *wince*, from a Gmc and Indo-European root]

winch[2]. See under **wench**.

Winchester[1] *win'chəs-tər*, *adj* formerly used of various measures (eg 'Winchester bushel'), the standards of which were kept at *Winchester*. — *n* a narrow-necked bottle for liquid chemicals, *orig* so called because it contained a 'Winchester quart' (*approx* 80 fluid ounces, or 2.25 litres).

Winchester[2]® *win'chəs-tər* or **Winchester rifle** *n orig* a tradename for a repeating rifle made by Oliver F *Winchester*, American manufacturer; now a tradename for firearms, etc, produced by the makers of the rifle.

Winchester disc *win'chə-stər disk*, (*comput*) *n*. Same as **hard disk**. [After the 3030 *Winchester rifle*, the IBM number of the disk being 3030]

wincopipe. Obsolete form of **wink-a-peep** (qv under **wink**[1]).

wind[1] *wind* (*poetic wīnd*), *n* air in motion; a current of air, usually horizontal, either natural or produced by artificial means; any of the directions from which the wind may blow; breath; power of breathing; flatulence; conceit; empty, insignificant words; the wind instruments in an orchestra; their players; air impregnated with scent of game; a hint or suggestion, as of something secret; part of the body covering the stomach (*slang*); a disease of sheep in which the inflamed intestines are distended by gases. — *vt* to perceive by the scent; to expose to wind; to drive or punch hard, so as to put out of breath; to allow to recover wind; to burp (a baby); (*wīnd*) to sound or signal by blowing (*archaic*): — *pr p* **wind'ing** or (of a horn) **wīnd'ing**; *pa t* and *pa p* **wind'ed** or (of a horn) **wound** (*wownd*). — *n* **wind'age** the difference between the size of the bore of a gun and that of the ball or shell; the influence of the wind in deflecting a missile, the amount of deflection due to wind, or the allowance made for it; air friction on a moving, *esp* revolving, part of a machine. — *n* **wind'er** (*slang*) a blow that takes one's breath away; (*wīnd'er*) someone who sounds a horn. — *adv* **wind'ily**. — *n* **wind'iness**. — *adj* **wind'less** without wind. — *adv*, *adj* and *n* **wind'ward** (towards or on) the side the wind blows from. — *adv* **wind'wards**. — *adj* **wind'y** like, characterized by or exposed to the wind; moved, played or produced by wind (*poetic*); controlling the winds (*poetic*); suffering from, producing or produced by flatulence; suggestive of wind, in being eg insubstantial, changeable, boastful, conceited or wordy; frightened, nervous (*colloq*). — **wind'bag** a person of mere words, an excessively talkative person communicating little of interest or value (*colloq*); the bellows of a bagpipe, or (*obs*) organ; the lungs or chest (*old facetious*); an inflated bag as a charm to procure a favourable wind; **wind'baggery** (*colloq*) the output of a windbag or empty talker; **wind band** a musical ensemble made up of wind instruments; **wind'blow** windthrow (qv below). — *adj* **wind'blown** blown along or blown about by the wind; windswept. — *adj* **wind'borne** (of pollen, seeds, etc) carried by the wind. — *adj* **wind'bound** hindered from sailing by contrary wind. — **wind'break** something serving as a protection against the force of the wind, such as a fence or line of trees; **Wind'breaker**® (*US*) a type of windproof jacket with elasticated cuffs and waistband. — *adj* **wind'-broken** (of a horse) broken-winded. — **wind'burn** inflammation of the skin due to over-exposure to the wind. — *adj* **wind'-changing** fickle. — **wind chart** a chart showing the direction of the wind; **wind'cheater** a close-knitted pullover; a windproof jacket, an anorak; **wind chest** the box or reservoir that supplies compressed air to the pipes or reeds of an organ; **wind chill** the cooling effect that wind has as it blows on a surface; the combined chilling effect *esp* on a human body of low temperature, wind speed and relative humidity; **wind-chill factor** a measurement of this; **wind chimes** a hanging decoration composed of pieces of shell, etc that tinkle against one another as the breeze catches them; **wind cone** a sleeve floating from the top of a mast eg at an airport, its angle with the ground giving a rough conception of the velocity of the wind, and its angle in a horizontal plane the wind direction; **wind dispersal** (*bot*) the dispersal of spores, seeds and fruits by the wind; **wind dropsy** flatulent distension, tympanites; **wind egg** an addled egg; a soft-shelled or imperfectly formed egg; **wind energy** wind power (qv below); **wind'fall** a piece of fruit blown off a tree by the wind; a sum of money that comes to one unexpectedly or suddenly, or any other piece of good fortune; **windfall tax** a tax levied on **windfall profits**, profits arising, *esp* suddenly and unexpectedly, as a result of events not directly connected with the company, etc concerned, such as changes in currency exchange rates. — *adj* **wind'fallen** blown down by wind. — **wind farm** a concentration of wind-driven electricity-generating turbines, *usu* sited on agricultural land; **wind'flower** an anemone, *esp* the wood-anemone; **wind furnace** any form of furnace using the natural draught of a chimney without aid of a bellows; **wind'gall** a puffy swelling around the fetlock joints of a horse; **wind gap** a dried-up river valley in the mountains; **wind gauge** an instrument for measuring the velocity of the wind; a gauge for measuring pressure of wind in an organ; an appliance fixed to a rifle by means of which the force of the wind is ascertained so that allowance may be made for it in sighting; **wind'gun** an air-gun; **wind harp** the aeolian harp (qv); **wind'hover** (*-hov'ər* or *-huv'ər*) the kestrel; **wind instrument** a musical instrument sounded by means of a current of air, *esp* a woodwind or brass instrument sounded by the breath; **wind'jammer** a large sailing vessel; a windproof jacket, a windcheater or anorak; **wind machine** a machine which produces wind or the sound of wind (*theat*, etc); **wind'mill** a mill, eg for grinding grain, in which the motive power is the wind acting on a set of vanes or sails; a wind-driven set of vanes used to pump water, generate electricity, etc; any device which is caused to rotate by reason of its being carried through the air, and so develops power (*aerodynamics*); a toy with a set of plastic or paper vanes mounted on a stick, that revolve in the wind. — *vt* and *vi* (to cause) to move like the vanes of a windmill. — **wind park** a wind farm (qv above); **wind'pipe** the passage running from the back of the throat to the lungs, through which air is drawn into and expelled from the lungs, the trachea; **wind power** wind considered as an energy source, eg for the generation of electricity by means of windmills, etc. — *adj* **wind'proof** (of garments or fabrics) resistant to or impenetrable by wind. — **wind pump** a windmill-driven pump; **wind rock** the loosening effect on plant roots and tree roots of violent wind. — *adj* **wind'-rode** (*naut*) riding at anchor with head to the wind. — **wind'rose** a rosette-like diagram showing the relative frequency and strength of winds in a locality for given periods of the year; **wind'row** hay raked together into a line to be made into cocks; a row of peats, etc, set up for drying. — *vt* to arrange in windrows. — **wind'sail** (*naut*) a wide funnel of canvas used to convey a stream of air below deck; a vane of a windmill; **wind'screen** a shelter against wind; the sheet of glass constituting the window of a motor vehicle, *esp* the front window; **wind'shake** a flaw in wood said to be due to the bending of the tree in the wind. — *adj* **wind'-shak'd** or **-shaken** agitated by the wind. — **wind shear** (*meteorol*) a sudden change in wind velocity at right angles (horizontally or vertically) to its direction; the rate of such change; conditions in which there are sudden changes of wind velocity and direction, constituting a danger to aircraft; **wind'shield** a windscreen (*NAm*); a device to protect eg a microphone from the wind; **wind'ship** a wind-powered ship, a sailing ship; **wind side** the side exposed to the wind; **wind sleeve** or **wind'sock** a wind cone; **wind'storm** a storm consisting of very strong winds; **wind'-sucker**; **wind'-sucking** (in horses) a harmful habit of swallowing air, in many cases associated with crib-biting. — *vi* **wind'surf** to sail on a sailboard (qv). — **wind'surfer**; **wind'surfing** (also called **sail-boarding**) the sport of riding the waves on a sailboard. — *adj* **wind'swept** exposed to, or swept by, the wind; dishevelled by the wind. — *adj* **wind'-swift** swift as the wind. — **wind synthesizer** (*music*) a synthesizer designed with fingering like that of a wind instrument and played using the power of the player's breath, whose technique with the mouthpiece modulates the sound produced; **wind'throw** the blowing-down of trees by the wind. — *adj* **wind'tight** airtight. — **wind tunnel** an experimental apparatus for producing a uniform steady airstream past a model for aerodynamic investigation work; **wind turbine** a wind-driven electricity generator, a tall slim structure with propeller-like vanes; **Windy City** (*US colloq*) Chicago. — **a capful of wind** a slight breeze; **before the wind** carried along by the wind; **between wind and water** that part of a ship's side which is now in, now out of, the water owing to the fluctuation of the waves; in a vulnerable or precarious place or position; **break wind** to release flatus from the anus; **cast** or **lay an anchor to windward** to make prudent provision for the future; **cast, fling** or **throw to the winds** to scatter or throw away recklessly; to abandon (restraint, prudence, caution, discretion, etc); **down the wind** moving with the wind; towards decay (*obs*); **fight windmills** to tilt at windmills (qv below); **get one's wind** to recover one's breath; **get the wind of** to get on the windward side of; **get the wind up** (*slang*) to become nervous, apprehensive, agitated; **get to windward of** to secure an advantage over; **get wind of** to get a hint or intimation of; **hang in the wind** to remain in suspense or uncertainty; **have the wind of** to be on the trail of; **how the wind blows** or **lies** the state of the wind; the position of affairs; **in the wind** astir, afoot; **in the wind's eye** or **in the teeth of the wind** right against the wind; **like the wind** rapidly; **on the windy side** (*Shakesp*) on the windward side, from which one cannot be attacked, hence safe, at an advantage; **put the wind up someone** (*slang*) to make someone apprehensive or agitated; **raise the wind** (*colloq*) to raise the funds one needs; **sail close to** or **near the wind** to keep the boat's head so near to the wind as to fill but not shake the sails; to be in danger of transgressing an approved limit; **second wind** power of respiration recovered after breathlessness; the energy necessary for a renewal of effort; **sow the wind and reap the whirlwind** to act wrongly and receive a crushing retribution; **take the wind out of someone's sails** to deprive someone of an advantage, to frustrate or discomfit someone; **tilt at windmills** to struggle with imaginary opposition, from the story of Don Quixote who charged at windmills under the misapprehension that they were giants; **wind** or **winds of change** a pervasive influence bringing change, immortalized as a phrase by Harold Macmillan, speaking as Prime Minister in 1960 of the inevitability of African independence, but previously used by the poet A C Swinburne in *Tiresias*. [OE; related to ON *vindr*, Ger *Wind*, L *ventus*]

wind[2] *wīnd*, *vt* to turn, to twist or coil; to (cause to) encircle or enfold; to coil the spring of (a watch, etc) or draw up the weights of (a clock) by turning a screw, to start, or keep, it going; to make or direct (one's way) or (*archaic*) to traverse, by turning and twisting; to insinuate (oneself; *archaic*); to change the course of, deflect, control (*rare* or *obs*); to turn (a horse) to the left; to swing (a ship) round so as to head in another direction; to bring in, involve (*obs*), or to extricate, stealthily; to wind up or sum up (a discussion, etc; *archaic*); to weave (*Spenser*); to wield (*obs* or *dialect*); to haul or hoist, eg with a winch (*esp naut*). — *vi* to turn round something (with *round*, etc); to twist; to move or go by turns and twists, or deviously; to meander; to go (*obs*); to writhe, wriggle (*obs* or *dialect*); to extricate oneself (with *out*; *obs*); to be twisted or warped (*dialect*); (of a horse) to turn to the left: — *pr p* **wīnd'ing**; *pa t* and *pa p* **wound** (*wownd*); chiefly *naut* **wīnd'ed**; *Burns pa t* **win't**. — *n* a turn, coil or twist; a turning; a twisted or warped condition. — *n* **wīnd'er** someone who winds; an instrument for winding; a clock or watch key; an electrically driven winding-engine for hoisting a cage or cages up a vertical mineshaft; the person who operates such an engine; a twisting plant; a triangular step at the turn of a stair or in a spiral staircase. — *adj* and *n* **wīnd'ing**. — *adv* **wind'ingly**. — **wind'ing-engine** a machine for hoisting; **wind'ing-sheet** a sheet for wrapping a corpse in; a shroud; the dripping grease that clings to the side of a candle (*dialect*); **winding stair** a spiral stair constructed round a solid newel; a stair with an open well hole, constructed on a geometric (ie circular or elliptical) plan; **wind'ing-strips** two pieces of wood with parallel edges, used for testing the trueness of timber, etc; **wind'-up** the close, finish; an instance of winding up. — **turn the wind** (now *rare*) to go, move or cause to move from side to side or on a winding course; **wind down** to relax or become quiet after a period of activity; to lose strength; to reduce the strength or scope of; to open (the window of a vehicle) by turning a handle; **wind up** to bring or come to a conclusion; to adjust for final settlement; to terminate the activities of, liquidate (a commercial firm, etc); to excite or agitate (*esp* in *pa p* **wound up**); to coil completely; to wind the spring or the mechanism of tightly; to close (the window of a vehicle) by turning a handle; to furl (*obs*); to tighten; to hoist, eg by a winch; to restore to harmony (*Shakesp*); to tease; to irritate, annoy or anger (*colloq*); **wind up and down** (*obs*) to revolve in the mind. [OE *windan*; cf Ger *winden*, ON *vinda*, Gothic *windan*; cf **wend**, **wander**]

windac. See **windas**.

windage. See **wind**[1].

windas *wind'as*, (*obs*) *n* a windlass; (*R L Stevenson*, **wind'ac**) an instrument for bending a crossbow (*hist*). [Anglo-Fr *windas*; cf ON *vindāss*, from *vinda* to wind, and *āss* pole]

windbag ... to ... **windcheater**. See under **wind**[1].

winded, winder. See under **wind**[1,2].

windfall ... to ... **windhover**. See under **wind**[1].

Windies *win'diz*, (*cricketing slang*) *n pl* the West Indies.

windigo *win'di-gō*, or **wendigo** *wen'di-gō*, *n* a mythical monster among some N American Indian tribes, which eats human flesh. [Ojibwa *wintiko*]

windily, windiness. See under **wind**[1].

winding. See under **wind**[1,2].

windjammer. See under **wind**[1].

windlass[1] *wind'ləs*, *n* any of various modifications of the wheel and axle employing a revolving cylinder, used for hauling or hoisting; a windas for a crossbow (*hist*). — *vi* to use a windlass. — *vt* to hoist by means of a windlass. [Prob from **windas**]

windlass[2] *wind'ləs*, (*obs*) *n* a circuitous movement, *esp* to intercept game; an indirect, crafty action. — *vi* to take a roundabout course. [Prob from *wanlace*, an earlier Anglo-Fr form, of unknown origin]

windle *win'dl*, *n* an appliance for winding yarn. — Also (*Scot*) **winn'le**. [**wind**[2]]

windless. See under **wind**[1].

windlestraw *win'dl-strö*, *n* a thin dry stalk of grass; any of various long-stalked species of grass, eg rye grass; anything light or insubstantial; a lanky or feeble person. — Also (*Scot*) **windlestrae** (*win'l-strā*). [OE *windelstrēaw*, from *windel* a woven basket, and *strēaw* straw]

windmill. See under **wind**[1].

windock. See **winnock**.

windore *win'dör* or *-dōr*, (*Ben Jonson*, etc; *obs*) *n* a form of **window**. [For *wind-door*, a popular derivation of **window**]

window *win'dō*, *n* an opening in the wall of a building, etc, to look out through, or to let in air and light; a wooden or metal frame fitted with panes of glass for placing in such an opening; the space immediately behind the opening; a windowpane; a glass-covered aperture eg at a theatre or railway station, at which one purchases one's ticket; any opening suggesting a window; (in *pl*) the eyes, or (*Shakesp*) the eyelids; (*esp* with *cap*) *orig* the code-name for strips of metallic foil which when scattered from aircraft derange radar reception; a closed outcrop of strata lying beneath a thrust plane and exposed by denudation (*geol*); a weather window (qv); in various technical uses designating a part that is clear, free of a particular type of obstruction, etc; a period of time when conditions are suitable for a particular activity and constitute an opportunity for it, as with **launch window** (planetary positions, weather conditions, etc, for the launch of a spacecraft), **re-entry window** (for the re-entry of a spacecraft), etc; a rectangular section of a screen which can be used independently of the rest of the screen (*comput*). — *vt* to fit with windows; to make tears or holes in (*Shakesp*). — *adj* **win'dowed** having a window or windows, or openings or holes resembling these; placed in a window (*Shakesp*). — *n* **win'dowing** (*comput*) the displaying of an image or data from a file in a window. — *adj* **win'dowless** having no windows. — **window bar** a wooden or iron bar between the panes of a window; a bar fitted into a window for security; (*Shakesp* **window-barne**, emended *bars*, *Timon*, IV.3.116) lattice-work across a woman's stomacher; **window blind** a blind or screen for a window; **window-bole** see **bole**[3]; **window box** a box for growing plants in on a windowsill; **window curtain** a curtain hung over a window, inside a room; **win'dow-dressing** the arranging of goods in a shop window; the art of doing so effectively; the art or practice of giving something superficial appeal by skilful presentation; **window envelope** an envelope with a transparent panel through which the address of the recipient on the enclosed letter can be read; **window frame** a frame that surrounds a window; **window gardening** the cultivation of plants indoors along a window ledge, or in boxes fitted on the outside sill; **window glass** glass suitable or used for windows; **window ledge** a windowsill; **win'dowpane** a sheet of glass set in a window; **window sash** a frame in which panes of glass are set; **window screen** any ornamental device for filling the opening of a window; **window seat** a seat in the recess of a window; a seat beside a window in a bus, aeroplane, etc. — *vi* **win'dow-shop**. — **win'dow-shopping** the activity of eyeing goods in shop windows as the next-best thing to buying them; **win'dowsill** an interior or exterior ledge running along the bottom of a window; **window tax** a tax levied on windows of houses (repealed 1851). — **out of** (or **out**) **the window** (*colloq*) finished with, done for or abandoned. [ME *windowe*, *windoge*, from ON *vindauga*, from *vindr* wind, and *auga* eye]

windpipe, windproof. See under **wind**[1].

windring *wīnd'ring*, *adj* (*Shakesp*) *perh* for **winding** or **wandering**.

windrose. **windrow**. See under **wind**[1].

winds. See under **winze**[2].

windsail ... to ... **windship**. See under **wind**[1].

Windsor *win'zər*, *adj* relating to *Windsor*, in Berkshire. — **Windsor chair** a chair with a solid wooden seat that has sockets into which the legs and the (*usu* slender spindle-shaped) uprights of the back are fitted; **Windsor knot** a type of wide triangular knot used in tying a tie; **Windsor soap** a kind of perfumed toilet soap (*usu* brown).

windsurf ... to ... **windy**. See under **wind**[1].

wine *wīn*, *n* an alcoholic drink made from the fermented juice of grapes or from other fruits or plants; a wine-drinking or wine party (*obs*); the rich dark red colour of red wine. — Also *adj*. — *vt* to supply with wine; to treat or entertain with wine. — *vi* to take wine. — *n* **wī'nery** (*orig US*) a place where wine is prepared. — *adj* **wī'ny** or **wī'ney** tasting of or looking like wine; affected by wine-drinking, intoxicated (*obs*). — **wine bag** a wine skin; a tippler; **wine bar** a bar that specializes in serving wines and *usu* food; **wine'berry** a grape (*obs*); a redcurrant, gooseberry or bilberry (*dialect*; see also **whinberry**); a raspberry (*Rubus phoenicolasius*) of

China and Japan; the tutu, or another New Zealand tree, the makomako; **wine'-bibber** a continual drinker of wine; a drunkard; **wine'-bibbing**; **wine biscuit** a biscuit *orig* intended to be served with wine; **wine bottle** a glass bottle of a standard size for wine, holding 75cl ($26\frac{2}{3}$fl oz); **wine box** a foil-lined cardboard carton of wine fitted with a tap for dispensing it; **wine cask** a cask for holding wine; **wine cellar** a cellar for storing wine; the wines stored there, or one's stock of wines generally. — *adj* **wine'-coloured** of the colour of red wine. — **wine'-cooler** a receptacle for cooling wine in bottles about to be served at table; **wine funnel** a type of funnel, *usu* made of silver or pewter, used for decanting wine from the bottle; **wine'glass** a small glass used for drinking wine; **wine'glassful**; **wine'-grower** someone who cultivates a vineyard and makes wine. — *n* and *adj* **wine'-growing**. — **wine lake** a surplus of wine bought up by an economic community to prevent a fall in prices; **wine list**; **wine measure** an old English liquid measure, its gallon $\frac{5}{6}$ of the gallon in beer measure; **wine merchant** a dealer in wine, *esp* wholesale; **wine palm** any palm yielding palm-wine (eg *Borassus*, *Raphia*); **wine party** a drinking-party; **wine'press** a machine in which grapes are pressed in the manufacture of wine; **wine'-sap** a variety of deep-red winter apple; **wine'skin** a bag for holding wine, made out of a skin; **wine'-stone** crude argol, the crust that forms on the walls of wine casks; **wine'-taster** someone whose business is to sample wines; **wine'-tasting** (a gathering for) sampling wines; **wine vat** or (*old*) **wine fat** a vat in which grapes are pressed in wine-making; **wine vault** or **vaults** a vaulted wine cellar; a place where wine is tasted or drunk; **wine vinegar** vinegar made from wine rather than malt; **wine waiter** a waiter in charge of serving the wine in a restaurant, etc. — **in wine** (*archaic*) drunk, intoxicated; **red wine** see under **red**; **spirit of wine** alcohol; **white wine** see under **white**; **wine and dine** to partake of, or entertain to, a meal accompanied by wine. [OE *wīn*; Gothic *wein*, Ger *Wein*; all from L *vīnum*; cognate with Gr *oinos*]

wing[1] *wing*, *n* one of the arm-like limbs of a bird or bat that are adapted for flying; an insect's similar flying-organ; an animal organ resembling a wing; one of the structures projecting from either side of an aircraft body, the plane of an aeroplane; flight; means of flying; anything resembling a wing; a fan or vane; (*usu* in *pl*) a sail; a part of a building projecting from the central or main section; (*usu* in *pl*) the area at each side of a stage, where performers wait to enter, out of sight of the audience; a piece of side scenery; a plane of an aeroplane; any of the corner sections of a motor-vehicle body, forming covers for the wheels; a similar part of a carriage; a side piece projecting forward from the back of an armchair; one of the longer sides of crownworks or hornworks (*fortif*); the flank corps or division of an army on either side; the ships on either extremity of a fleet ranged in line; (a player on) either the extreme left or extreme right of the forward line in football, etc; either edge of a football, etc pitch, along which such a player moves; a section of a political party or other body, with its own distinct views and character; a group of several squadrons in the Royal Air Force; (in *pl*) a qualified pilot's badge; (formerly) the badge of any member of an air-crew other than the pilot; a flock (of plovers); (*usu* in *pl*) means or power of rapid movement, a sudden access of speed; protection, as in *under someone's wing* (qv below). — *vt* to provide or transport with wings; to lend speed to; to supply with side pieces; to bear in flight, to waft; to effect on wings; to traverse by flying; to wound in the wing; to wound in the arm or shoulder; to improvise one's way through (a speech of theatrical part that one has not fully rehearsed) (*colloq*, *esp US*; see also **wing it** below). — *vi* to soar on the wing; to move or travel with speed. — *adj* **winged** (*wingd* or *wing'id*) having wings; (*wingd*; of a stem) bearing the thin flattened bases of decurrent leaves, or (of a fruit or seed) having a flattened appendage; (*wingd*) wounded in the wing, shoulder or arm; swift; lofty, sublime; (in **winged words**, rendering Homer's *epea pteroenta*) spoken, uttered, flying from one person to another; full of flying birds (*Milton*). — *adv* **wing'edly** on or by wings. — *n* **wing'er** a player in a position on the wing in football, etc; a pal, colleague or favourite (*forces slang*); (as *combining form* in *left-winger* or *right-winger*) a person to the side of centre in a party, etc. — *adj* **wing'less** without wings. — *n* **wing'let** a small wing; a bastard wing (qv); a wing-like appendage; a small vertical wing attached to the tip of an aeroplane wing to improve lift. — *adj* **wing'y** having, resembling or soaring on wings; lofty. — *adv* **wing'-and-wing'** in the condition of a ship sailing before the wind with the foresail at one side and the mainsail at the other. — **wing chair** a high-backed armchair with forward-projecting lugs; **wing'beat** a beat or flap of a bird's or insect's wing; **wing case** the horny case or cover over the wings of some insects, such as the beetles; **wing collar** a man's stiff collar, worn upright with the points turned down; **wing commander** a Royal Air Force officer of the rank below group captain, corresponding in rank to a naval commander or to a lieutenant-colonel; **winged bean** a legume *orig* from SE Asia (*Psophocarpus tetragonolobus*), of special value for its high protein content; **winged bull** a common form in Assyrian sculpture, symbolic of domination; **winged elm** an elm tree of N America, its young branches having corky projections; **winged words** see **winged** above. — *adj* **wing'-footed** having wings attached to the feet (*mythol*, etc); fast-moving, swift (*poetic*); aliped (*zool*). — **wing forward** one of the two outside players of the second row of the scrum, a flanker (*Rugby football*). — *adj* **wing'-led'** (*Shakesp*) *prob* led in wings or divisions. — **wing loading** (*aerodynamics*) the maximum flying weight of an aeroplane divided by the total area of the main planes, including the ailerons; **wing mirror** a rear-view mirror projecting from the side of a vehicle; **wing nut** a nut with flattened projections for easy turning by finger and thumb, a butterfly-nut; **wing sheath** a wing case; **wing shell** a mollusc of the genus *Strombus*; a mollusc of genus *Malleus* or a related genus, or its shell; a wing snail; **wing'-shoot'ing** the act or practice of shooting flying birds; **wing shot** a shot at a bird on the wing; a marksman who shoots birds in flight. — *adj* (**wing'-shot**) shot in the wing, or while on the wing. — **wing snail** a swimming gasteropod, the pteropod (qv); **wing'span** or **wing'spread** the distance from tip to tip of a bird's extended wings, or of the wings of an aircraft; **wing'-walker** an acrobat who performs stunts on the wing of an airborne aeroplane; **wing'-walking**. — **birds of one wing** (*obs*) birds of the same kind; **flying wing** see under **fly**; **in the wings** (*colloq*) waiting in reserve; **lend wings to** to give speed to; **make** or **take wing** to begin flight; to depart; **on a wing and a prayer** with no more than a slight hope of succeeding; **on** or **upon the wing** flying; in motion; departing; **on the wings of the wind** with the highest speed; **on wings** speedily; **spread** or **stretch one's wings** to explore one's potential; **under someone's wing** under someone's protection; **wing it** (*colloq*, *esp US*) to extemporize in public speaking or ad-lib in a theatrical performance. [ON *vængr* a wing]

wing[2]. See **win**[3].

wingding *wing'ding*, (chiefly *NAm*) *n* a wild party; a lavish social function; a drug-addict's seizure; a pretended seizure. [Origin uncertain]

winge *winj*, (*colloq*). Non-Scottish (*esp Austr*) variant of **whinge**.

winged, **winger**, **wingless**, **winglet**, **wingy**. See under **wing**[1].

wink[1] *wingk*, *vi* to shut an eye briefly; to do this as a sign, hint or communication, eg to convey an amused understanding; to shut the eyes (*obs*); to blink; to seem not to see; to connive (*usu* with *at*); to flicker, twinkle. — *vt* to close and open (an eye) quickly; to flicker; to express by flashlights. — *n* the act of winking; a hint conveyed, or as if conveyed, by winking; a blink; a closing of the eyes for sleep, or a short spell of sleep, as in *forty winks, not sleep a wink*; a very small time or distance. — *n* **wink'er** someone who winks; (*usu* in *pl*) a horse's blinker; an eye, eyelid or eyelash (*dialect* and *NAm colloq*); the nictitating membrane of a bird's eye; a small bellows in an organ, regulated by a spring, controlling variations of wind pressure; either of the flashing direction indicators on a motor vehicle (*colloq*). — *n* **wink'ing** the act of giving a wink. — *adj* (*Shakesp*) closed, or with eyes shut, or blind. — *adv* **wink'ingly**. — **wink'-a-peep** (*dialect*) the scarlet pimpernel. — **easy as winking** very easily indeed; **forty winks** (*colloq*) a short nap; **like winking** (*slang*) very rapidly; **tip someone the wink** (*colloq*) to give someone a useful hint. [OE *wincian*; Ger *winken*]

wink[2] *wingk*, *n* one of the small coloured discs used in the game of tiddlywinks. [Short for **tiddlywink**]

winkle *wing'kl*, *n* a small edible snail-shaped shellfish, the periwinkle (see **periwinkle**[2]); the penis (*slang* or *hypocoristic*). — *vt* (with *out*) to extract or force out little by little and with difficulty. — *n* **wink'ler** someone or something that winkles out; a person who evicts tenants on behalf of the property owner (*colloq*). — **wink'le-pickers** shoes with long pointed toes, *esp* popular in the early 1960s. [Short for **periwinkle**[2]]

winn. See **win**[3].

winna *win'ə* or *wun'ə*. A Scots form of **will not**.

winnability, **winnable**, **winner**, **winning**[1], **winningly**, **winningness**. See under **win**[1].

winning[2]. See under **win**[2].

winnle. See **windle**.

winnock *win'ək*, or **windock** *win'dək*, (*Scot*) *n* a window. [Scot development of ME *windoge*; see **window**; cf ety of **warlock**]

winnow *win'ō*, *vt* to separate the chaff from (grain) by blowing a current of air through it; to fan; to sift; to separate; to blow on; to waft; to diffuse; to set in motion (*Milton*); to flap, flutter (*rare*). — *vi* to separate chaff from grain; to fly; to blow in gusts. — *n* a fan for winnowing. — *adj* **winn'owed** *perh* wise (*Shakesp*). — *n* **winn'ower**. — *n* **winn'owing**. — **winn'owing-fan** or **-machine** a fan or machine for winnowing. [OE *windwian* to winnow, from *wind*; see **wind**[1]]

wino *wī'nō* (*slang*) *n* someone, *esp* a down-and-out, addicted to cheap wine: — *pl* **wī'nos**. [**wine**]

winsey. Same as **wincey**.

winsome *win'səm*, *adj* charming, captivating, attractive; cheerful; pleasant. — *adv* **win'somely**. — *n* **win'someness**. [OE *wynsum* pleasant, from *wyn* joy (Ger *Wonne*), and *-sum* (see sfx **-some**)]

win't (*Burns*) See **wind**[2].

winter *win'tər*, *n* the cold season of the year, in northern temperate regions, from November or December to January or February; astronomically, from the winter solstice to the vernal equinox; (*usu* in *pl*) a year (*literary*); any season of cheerlessness. — *adj* wintry; suitable for wear or use in winter; sown in autumn, as eg **winter wheat**, **winter barley**, **winter crop**, etc. — *vi* to pass the winter somewhere, *esp* somewhere warm. — *vt* to feed and keep through winter. — *adj* **win'tered** having seen many winters, aged (*obs*); exposed to winter; worn in winter (*Shakesp*). — *n* **winterizā'tion** or **-s-**. — *vt* **win'terize** or **-ise** (*esp NAm*) to make suitable for use under wintry conditions. — *adj* **win'terly** cheerless. — *n* **win'triness**. — *adj* **win'try** or **win'tery** resembling, belonging to or characteristic of winter; stormy; cheerless, unfriendly, cold or hostile. — **winter aconite** see **aconite**; **winter apple** an apple that keeps well in winter, or that does not ripen till winter. — *adj* **win'ter-beaten** (*Spenser*) beaten or injured by the cold of winter. — **win'terberry** a name given to several shrubs of the genus *Ilex*, growing in the eastern parts of N America; **win'ter-bloom** the witch-hazel; a species of azalea; **win'terbourne** an intermittent spring of water, as found in the chalk districts; **winter bud** a bud protected by scales in which next year's shoot passes the winter; **winter cherry** any species of Physalis, *esp Physalis alkekengi*; its edible fruit; the balloon vine, or its fruit. — *adj* **win'ter-clad** warmly clad. — **winter clover** the partridge-berry; **winter cress** a cruciferous plant (*Barbarea*) formerly cultivated for winter salad; **winter garden** an ornamental garden of evergreens, etc, or a conservatory with flowers, for winter; (in *pl*, with *cap*) used sometimes as the name of a theatre, concert-hall, etc; **win'tergreen** a plant of the genus Pyrola, also of *Chimaphila*; a plant of the genus *Gaultheria*, whose oil is an aromatic stimulant, used in flavouring confectionery and in medicine (**chickweed wintergreen** either of two plants, *Trientalis europaea* or *Trientalis americana*, belonging to the Primulaceae, having white starlike flowers). — *vt* **win'ter-ground** (*Shakesp*, *Cymbeline*, IV.2.229) assumed to mean protect (a plant) from the inclemency of winter. — *vt* **win'terkill** (*NAm*) to kill (a plant or crop) by exposure to the winter's cold. — **winter quarters** the quarters of an army during winter; a winter residence; **winter solstice** the time of year when, in the northern hemisphere, the sun reaches its southernmost point, or, in the southern hemisphere, its northermost, respectively 21 December and 21 June; the point on the celestial sphere at which, in the northern hemisphere, the ecliptic is furthest south of the celestial equator, or in the southern hemisphere, furthest north (*astron*); **winter sports** open-air sports practised on snow and ice, such as skiing, etc; **win'ter-sweet** a Japanese shrub (*Chimonanthus praecox*) of the family *Calycanthaceae* whose fragrant yellow flowers appear before the leaves; another name for marjoram; **win'tertide** (*archaic*) wintertime; **win'tertime** the season of winter. — *adj* **win'ter-weight** (of clothes) heavy enough or thick enough to be suitable for cold weather. [OE; cf ON *vetr*, Ger *Winter*; from the Indo-European root seen in **wet** and **water**]

winter's bark *win'tərz bärk*, *n* a stimulant, aromatic and tonic bark, named after Captain *Winter*, who first brought it from the Strait of Magellan in 1579.

wintle *win'tl*, (*Scot*) *vi* to stagger. — *n* a stagger. [Flem *windtelen*, from *winden* to wind]

Winton. *abbrev*: *Wintoniensis* (*L*), of Winchester.

wintriness, **wintry**. See under **winter**.

winy. See under **wine**.

winze[1] *winz*, (*Scot*) *n* a curse. [Flem *wensch*; from root of **wish**[1]]

winze[2] *winz*, *n* a small ventilating shaft between two levels (*mining*). — Also **winds**. [Perh **wind**[2]]

wipe *wīp*, *vt* to clean or dry by rubbing with a cloth, on a mat, etc; to remove by wiping (with *away*, *off*, *out*, *up*); to pass (eg a cloth) across something to clean or dry it, etc; to rub (a liquid, etc) on to a surface; to apply solder to (eg a joint between two lengths of lead piping) with a piece of cloth or leather; to strike (*colloq*); to clear (magnetic tape) of its content or erase (the content) from magnetic tape; to eradicate or eliminate; to cancel, forget, scrub (*colloq*); to reject (a person; *Austr*). — *n* the act of cleaning by rubbing; a blow, a swipe; a brand, a scar (*Shakesp*); a sarcasm, a jibe (*obs*); a handkerchief (*old slang*); a piece of (*esp* specially treated) fabric or tissue for wiping and cleaning; a style of film editing in which the picture on the screen appears to be pushed or wiped off the screen by the following one. — *n* **wī'per** someone who wipes, *esp* a cleaner in certain industrial jobs; something that wipes or is used for wiping; a mechanism attached to a rotating or oscillating part that causes forwards-and-backwards motion in another part (*weaving*); a moving arm or other conducting device for making a selected contact out of a number of possible connections (*elec*); (also **wind'screen-wiper**) a mechanical arm that swings to and fro across a windscreen to clear it of rain, etc. — *n* **wī'ping** the act of cleaning, rubbing, erasing, etc; a thrashing. — *adj* **wipe'-clean** (of a plastic, etc surface) easily cleaned by wiping. — **wipeout** (*wī'powt*) a fall from a surfboard, skateboard or skis, etc, *esp* a spectacular one (*slang*); a complete failure or disaster (*colloq*). — **wipe out** to obliterate, annihilate or abolish;

to fall from a surfboard, skis, etc (*slang*); (in *pa p* **wiped out**) exhausted, weary, dead-beat (*colloq*, *esp US*). [OE *wīpian*; OHGer *wīfan* to wind round, *waif* bandage, Gothic *weipan* to crown]

WIPO *wī'pō*, *abbrev*: World Intellectual Property Organization.

wippen *wip'ən*, (*music*) *n* a part of the hammer mechanism in a piano, raised as the note is played. [Poss Ger *Wippe* seesaw or dialect *wippen* whippletree]

wire *wīr*, *n* metal drawn out to a narrow flexible strand or thread; a length of this for any of various purposes; a length of this *usu* enclosed in insulating material, used for carrying an electric current; (sometimes in *pl*) the cable connecting point with point in a telecommunications system; the telephone (*old colloq*); a telegram or telegraph (*colloq*, *esp US*); information (*slang*, *esp US*); a warning or tip-off (*slang*, *esp US*); a portable recording device (*slang*, *esp US*); a metallic string of a musical instrument; a metal knitting-needle (*Scot*); a pickpocket (*slang*); a lash made of wire (*Shakesp*); a fence made of wire; a wire stretched over or across the starting and finishing line on a racetrack, hence *esp* the finishing line itself (*orig US*). — *adj* formed of or using wire; running on wire; relating to wiredrawing. — *vt* to bind, support, protect, snare or fit with wire; to supply (a building) with wires for carrying electricity; to connect up (an electrical apparatus) with wires, ready for use (with *up*); to supply (an area) with fibre-optic cables for the reception of cable television; to send a telegram to, or send (a message) by telegram; to place (a croquet ball) where a hoop hampers it. — *vi* to send a telegram. — *adj* **wired** supplied or secured with wire; (also **wired up**) taking drugs (*slang*); in a tense, nervous state (*slang*). — *adj* **wire'less** without, or lacking, a wire or wires; of or relating to telegraphy or telephony without wires. — *n* (*old*) short for **wireless telegraphy** or **telephony**, signalling through space without the use of conducting wires between transmitter and receiver, by means of electromagnetic waves generated by high-frequency alternating currents; a receiving or transmitting set used for this purpose; a message or broadcast so transmitted in this way (**wireless station** a station used for such transmission); broadcast programmes or broadcasting generally. — *vt* and *vi* (*old*) to communicate by radio. — *n* **wī'rer** someone who wires, or who uses wire, eg to snare animals. — *adv* **wī'rily**. — *n* **wī'riness**. — *n* **wī'ring** the complex of wires in an electrical system or installation; the act of securing with, equipping with, or communicating by, wire. — *adj* **wī'ry** made of or resembling wire; flexible and strong; (of hair) coarse and wavy; (of a person) of slight build but strong and agile. — **wire bar** (*metallurgy*) copper of a high purity cast into a tapered ingot and used to produce copper wire; **wire bird** the St Helena plover, named from the wire grass that is its habitat; **wire bridge** a suspension bridge; **wire brush** a brush with wire bristles, for cleaning rust off metal, dirt off suede shoes, etc; **wire cloth** closely woven wire mesh; **wire'-dancer** a performer on a tight wire; **wire'-dancing**; **wired glass** glass in which a wire mesh has been incorporated during rolling as a resistance against fire and explosion blast. — *vt* **wire'draw** to draw into wire by pulling through successively smaller holes in a hard steel dieblock; to throttle a fluid by passing it through a small orifice, thus reducing the pressure; to draw or spin out to a great length; to strain the meaning of. — **wire'drawer**; **wire'drawing**. — *adj* **wire'drawn** spun out into needless fine distinctions. — **wired wireless** the transmission of signals by means of electromagnetic waves guided by conductors, the frequencies being of the same order as those used for radio communication; **wire gauge** a disc or plate with graded indents representing standard sizes, in which to measure the diameter of wire; any system for designating the diameter of wires by means of a set of numbers; the diameter of a particular piece of wire; **wire gauze** a kind of stiff close fabric made of fine wire; **wire glass** glass reinforced with an embedded sheet or wire mesh; **wire grass** a kind of fine meadow grass (*Poa compressa*); any of various other grasses with wiry stems; **wire guard** a guard made of wire netting for placing in front of a fire; **wire'-hair** a wire-haired terrier. — *adj* **wire'-haired** (of an animal) having a coat of rather rough, hard hair. — **wire-haired terrier** a fox terrier with this kind of coat; **wire'-heel** in horses and cattle, a defect or disease of the foot; **wire line** one of the close-set lines in laid paper, perpendicular to the water lines or chain lines, visible by transmitted light; **wire'man** a telegraph fitter or electrician who installs or maintains wires; an expert at wiretapping (*colloq*); a journalist sending wires for a telegraphic news agency (*colloq*); **wire nail** a common type of nail, round or elliptical in cross-section, cut from steel wire; **wire netting** a texture of galvanized wire woven in the form of a net; **wire'photo** a photograph sent over a wire circuit by electrical means; **wire'-puller** someone who exercises an influence felt but not seen; an intriguer or manipulator; **wire'-pulling**; **wire rope** a rope made of twisted wire. — *adj* **wire'-sewn** or **wire'-stitched** (of booklets, etc) stapled with wire rather than sewn with thread. — *adj* **wire'-stringed**. — *vt* **wire'tap** to tap (a telephone) or the telephone of. — **wire'-walker** a wire-dancer; **wire'way** an enclosed channel, duct or conduit for wires; channelling of wires thus; **wire wheel** a wheel, *esp* on a sports car, etc, in which the rim is connected to the hub by wire spokes; **wire wool** a mass of very fine wire for scouring; **wire'work** the making of wire or of objects of wire; articles or fabric made of wire; **wire'worker**; **wire'working**; **wire'worm** a hard-bodied worm-like larva of the click beetle, destructive to plant roots. — *adj* **wire'wove** denoting a fine quality of writing-paper (see **wove**). — **down to the wire** (*colloq*) as far as the finishing post, up till the very last moment; **give (someone) the wire** (chiefly *military*) to give advance information; **pull the wires** to pull strings, be a wire-puller (qv above); **wire away** or **in** (*old colloq*) to act or work with vigour; **wire into** (*old colloq*) to eat vigorously and assiduously. [OE *wīr*; ON *vīrr* (combining form)]

wirricow. See **worricow**.

Wirtschaftswunder *virt'shafts-vŏŏn-dər*, (*Ger*) *n* an economic miracle, *specif* that of Germany's speedy recovery after the 1939–45 war.

Wis. or **Wisc**. *abbrev*: Wisconsin (US state).

wis *wis*, also **wist** *wist*, *Shakesp* **wish** *wish*, (all *sham archaic*) *vt* to know; to believe. [Partly from misunderstanding of the adv **iwis** (qv) as *I wis*, partly a new present from the past tense **wist** (see **wit**[1])]

wisard *wiz'ərd*, *n* an old spelling of **wizard**.

Wisd. (*Bible*) *abbrev*: Wisdom of Solomon (apocryphal book).

wisdom *wiz'dəm*, *n* the quality of being wise; judgement; the ability to make right use of knowledge; prudence, common sense; learning, knowledge; the weight of informed opinion; a wise discourse, saying or teaching, or wise sayings generally (*archaic*); skilfulness, speculation, spiritual perception (*Bible*); sanity (*Shakesp*); (with *cap*) the apocryphal Book of the Wisdom of Solomon; (with *cap*) Jesus Christ (*theol*). — **Wisdom literature** writings of the ancient Middle East which consist of philosophical reflections on life or maxims and precepts about the right conduct of one's life; Jewish pre-Christian literature of this type as contained in the book of Job, Proverbs, Ecclesiastes, Wisdom of Solomon, Ecclesiasticus, and certain Psalms, to which list some add the New Testament Epistle of James; **wisdom tooth** any of four double back teeth cut after childhood, *usu* from the late teens. — **in his, her** etc **wisdom** (*ironic*) for reasons best known to himself, herself, etc. [OE *wīsdōm*; from **wise** and **-dom**]

wise[1] *wīz*, *adj* having knowledge; learned; able to make good use of knowledge; judging rightly, prudent, sensible; astute, shrewd, sagacious; discreet; skilful, proficient (*obs*); dictated by wisdom; containing wisdom; pious, godly; skilled in magic (*dialect*); normal mentally (*dialect*); (as *combining form*) knowing the ways of, as in *streetwise*, *worldly-wise*. — *adj* **wise'-like** (*Scot*; *wīs'līk*) sensible, judicious; decent; fitting; looking as if capable of playing one's part well. — *n* **wise'ling** (*old*) someone who pretends to be wise. — *adv* **wise'ly**. — *n* **wise'ness**. — **wise'crack** a pungent retort or comment, a gibe or joke. — *vi* to make wisecracks. — *adj* **wise'cracking** making, or addicted to making, wisecracks. — **wise guy** a conceited, over-confident person; a smart alec. — *adj* **wise'-heart'ed** having wisdom; prudent. — **wise man** a sage or elder; a wizard, magician or seer (*dialect*); **wise woman** a witch or seeress; a midwife (*Scot*). — **be** (or **get**) **wise to** (*esp US slang*) to be or become aware of; **never, no, none** (or **not much**) **the wiser** still in ignorance; **put someone wise** (*esp US slang*) to put someone in possession of essential information, make someone aware (with *to*); **the Wise Men (of the East), the Three Wise Men** the three Magi (in some traditions kings) who according to St Matthew's Gospel (Matt 2) came to worship the baby Jesus at Bethlehem; **the wiser for** having learnt sense from (some salutary experience); **wise after the event** only too aware of how something could have been avoided, done better, etc, when it has already occurred; **wise up** (*esp US slang*) to make or become aware, informed, etc. [OE *wīs*; Ger *Weise*; from root of **wit**]

wise[2], **weise** or **weize** *wīz*, (*Scot*) *vt* to guide in a certain direction. [OE *wīsian*, from *wīs*; **wise**[1]]

wise[3] *wīz*, (*archaic*) *n* way, manner, now chiefly in the phrases **in any wise**, **in no wise** in any way, in no way, **on this wise** in this way, and as a *sfx*, denoting direction or manner, as in *lengthwise*, *clockwise*, *likewise*, *otherwise* or (*colloq*) meaning as regards, as in *money-wise*, *business-wise*. [OE *wīse*; Ger *Weise*; related to **wise**[1] and **wit**; doublet **guise**]

wiseacre *wīz'ā-kər*, *n* someone who unduly assumes an air of superior wisdom; a wise guy; a simpleton quite unconscious of being one. [MDu *wijssegger*, from OHGer *wīzago* a prophet]

wisecrack, **wiseling**, **wisely**, **wiseness**. See under **wise**[1].

wisent *wē'zənt*, *vē'*, *n* another name for the European bison. [Ger]

wish[1] *wish*, *vt* to want or require, as in *anything you wish*, or (*dialect*) *wish a cup of tea*; to desire, *esp* vainly or helplessly, as in *wish you'd told me*; to express a desire for (luck, happiness, etc) to come to; to say (good afternoon, etc) to; (with a *neg* and *on*) to desire (something to be inflicted on), to invoke, as in *wouldn't wish it on my worst enemy*; to impose, inflict or foist (with *on*; *colloq*); to bid or request; to hope (*archaic*); to recommend (*obs*); to bewitch (*dialect*); to greet, wish (someone) well (*SAfr*); to state (a wish) in superstitious hope of its being magically fulfilled. — *vi* to have a desire (with *for*); to long (with *for*); to state a desire in superstitious hope of its being magically fulfilled. — *n* a desire, longing; a thing desired; an expression of desire; (*usu* in *pl*) an expression of desire for good fortune for another; the stating of a desire in superstitious hope of its being magically fulfilled; a malediction (*obs*). — *n* **wish'er**. — *adj* **wish'ful** having a wish or desire; eager; desirable, desired (*obs*). — *adv* **wish'fully**. — *n* **wish'fulness**. — *n* and *adj* **wish'ing**. — **wish fulfilment** (*psychol*) the satisfaction of a desire in dreams, daydreams, etc; **wishful thinking** (*psychol*) a type of thinking in which the individual substitutes the fantasy of the fulfilment of the wish for the actual achievement; a belief that a particular thing will happen, or is so, engendered by desire that it should happen, or be so; (loosely) thinking about and wishing for an event or turn of fortune that may not take place; **wish'ing-bone** or **wish'bone** the V-shaped bone formed by the fused clavicles of a bird's breast, by tradition pulled apart by two people in playful divination, the longer part indicating the first to be married or the one whose wish will be fulfilled; a V-shaped member used in independent suspension systems (*autos*); **wish'ing-cap** a cap by wearing which one obtains everything one wishes; **wish'ing-stone**, **-tree**, **-well**, etc a stone, tree, well, etc supposed to have the power of making a wish expressed at it come true; **wish list** a mental list of desiderata. — **wish someone further** (*slang*) to wish someone was in some other place, not present; **wish someone joy of something** (*usu ironic*) to hope that the possession of something (*usu* that one is glad not to have, or glad to be rid of) will be of benefit to someone; **wish to God** to wish earnestly. [OE *wȳscan* to wish; Ger *wünschen*, Swed *önska*]

wish[2]. See **wis**.

wishtonwish *wish'tən-wish*, *n* the N American prairie-dog; the whip-poor-will (*Fenimore Cooper*). [Am Ind]

wish-wash *wish'-wosh*, (*colloq*) *n* anything wishy-washy. — *adj* **wish'y-wash'y** thin and weak; diluted; feeble; of poor quality. [Formed from **wash**]

wisket *wis'kit*, (*dialect*) *n* a basket. [Scand, from the same root as **whisk**[1]]

wisp *wisp*, *n* a small bundle of straw or hay; a tuft, a shred; a thin strand or band; a small broom; a twisted bunch used as a torch; the will-o'-the-wisp; something slight or insubstantial; a flock (of snipe). — *vt* to make into a wisp or bundle; to rub down with a wisp. — *vi* to fall, drift or otherwise move in wisps or like a wisp. — *adj* **wis'py** wisp-like, light and fine in texture; slight, flimsy, insubstantial. [Origin uncertain]

wist *wist*, (*sham archaic*) *vt* and *vi* to know. [See **wis**, **iwis**, **wit**[1]]

wistaria *wis-tā'ri-ə*, *n* a plant of a genus (*Wistaria*) of papilionaceous plants, some of the species among the most magnificent ornamental climbers known in English gardens, named after the American anatomist Caspar *Wistar* (1761–1818). — Also, wrongly, **Wistē'ria** (so spelt by Thomas Nuttall, who named it).

wistful *wist'fo͝ol* or *-fl*, *adj* longing; yearning with little hope; pensive; intent (*obs*); earnest (*obs*). — *adv* **wist'fully**. — *n* **wist'fulness**. [Poss from **wistly** or its back-formation *wist* intent, with meaning altered through association with **wishful**]

wistiti *wis'ti-ti*, *n* a marmoset. [Fr *ouistiti*; from its cry]

wistly *wist'li*, (*Shakesp*) *adv* longingly, earnestly. [Prob for *whistly* silently; see **whist**[2]]

wit[1] *wit*, *vt* and *vi* (*archaic* except in *legal* use) to know; to be aware (with *of*); to recognize, discern; to know how: — *infinitive* **wit**, *Spenser*, *Shakesp* and others **weet** or **weete** (*wēt*), *Spenser* **weet'en**, also **wot** (*wot*); *pr t 1st pers sing* **wot**, *Scot* **wat** (*wöt*), **wite** or **wyte** (*wīt*); *2nd* **wost** (**wott'est**); *3rd* **wot** (**wots**, **wott'eth**), *Scot* **wate**, **wait**, **wats**; *pl 1st, 2nd, 3rd* **wot**; *pa t* **wist** (**wott'ed**); *pr p* **witt'ing** or **weet'ing** (**wott'ing**); *pa p* **wist**. — *n* **witt'ing** (*obs* and *dialect*) knowledge; information. — *adj* cognisant; conscious; deliberate. — *adv* **witt'ingly** knowingly; by design. — **do to wit** to cause to know; **to wit** that is to say, namely (the OE gerund *tō witanne*). [OE *witan* to know (pr t *wāt*, *wāst*, *wāt*, pl *witon*; pa t *wiste*, or *wisse*, pl *wiston*, pa p *wist*); Gothic *witan* to observe, Ger *wissen*; cf L *vidēre* to see; Gr *idein*]

wit[2] *wit*, *n* the mind (*obs*); the understanding (*archaic*); imagination or invention (*archaic*); ingenuity; intelligence, sense (as in **have the wit to**); (*usu* in *pl*) any of the five bodily senses, or a mental faculty generally (*archaic*); the power of combining ideas with a pointed verbal effect; the product of this power; humour, wittiness; a person endowed with wit; information (*obs*; as in **to get wit of**). — *adj* **wit'less** lacking wit, wisdom or sense; without intellectual faculties (*obs*); out of one's mind; stupid, unintelligent; unaware, unconscious. — *adv* **wit'lessly**. — *n* **wit'lessness**. — *n* **wit'ling** someone with little wit; a pretender to wit. — *adj* **witt'ed** (*usu* as *combining form*) having wit or understanding (of a specified type, as in *quick-witted*, *slow-witted*). — *n* **witticism** (*wit'i-sizm*) a witty remark; a sentence or phrase affectedly witty; (formerly) a jibe. — *adv* **witt'ily**. — *n* **witt'iness**. — *adj* **witt'y** possessed of wit; amusing, droll; sarcastic; ingenious (*Bible*); wise, discreet, sensible (*obs*). — **wit'-cracker** someone who makes witty remarks in a crisp style; **wit'-monger** a poor would-be wit; **wit'-snapper** (*Shakesp*) someone who affects wit or repartee. — *vt* **wit'wanton** (with *it*; *obs*) to indulge in irreverent wit. — **at one's wits'** (or **wit's**) **end** utterly perplexed; in a state of desperation; **have one's wits about one** to be alert and resourceful; **live by one's wits** to gain a livelihood by ingenious expedients rather than by honest labour; **the five wits** (*archaic*) the five senses. [OE (*ge*)*wit*, from **wit**[1]]

witan *wit'an*, *n pl* members of the Anglo-Saxon council, the witenagemot (qv); the witenagemot itself. [Pl of OE *wita* a man of knowledge; cf **wit**[1,2]]

witblits *vit'blits*, (*SAfr*) *n* a strong home-distilled alcoholic spirit. [Afrik *wit* white, and *blits* lightning]

witch[1] *wich*, *n* a person, *esp* a woman, supposed to have supernatural or magical power and knowledge *esp* through compact with the devil or a minor evil spirit; a hag, crone; a dangerously or irresistibly fascinating woman (*colloq*); a wizard (now *rare*); a flatfish, the craigfluke; a curve whose equation is $x^2y = 4a^2(2a - y)$ (*math*). — *vt* to bewitch; to effect, change, transport, etc by means of witchcraft; to fascinate. — *vi* to practise witchcraft or fascination. — *n* **witch'ery** witchcraft; fascination. — *n* **witch'ing** sorcery; enchantment. — *adj* suited to witchcraft; weird; fascinating. — *adv* **witch'ingly**. — *adj* **witch'like**. — *adj* **wit'chy** witchlike, suggestive of witches. — **witch'craft** the craft or practice of witches; the black art, sorcery; supernatural power; **witch doctor** in tribal societies, a magician who detects witches and counteracts evil magical influences; someone who professes to heal by means of magic; **witches' brew** (*fig*) a heady concoction of disparate elements, a confused or mysterious mixture; **witches' broom** a dense tuft of poorly developed branches formed on a woody plant attacked by a parasite (chiefly fungi and mites); **witches' butter** Nostoc and other gelatinous blue-green algae; **witches' meat** Tremella; **witches' Sabbath** a witches' midnight gathering (see also **Sabbath**); **witches' thimble** a name for various plants with thimble-like flowers, eg the foxglove; **witch'-finder** (*hist*) a person whose business was to detect witches; a witch doctor; **witch hunt** (*orig US*) the searching out of political opponents for exposure on grounds of alleged disloyalty to the state, etc; any comparable hunting-down or persecution of a group or an individual alleged to be behaving in a dangerously heretical manner; **witching hour** the hour when witches are supposed to stir into activity, midnight; **witch'knot** a knot, *esp* in the hair, supposed to be tied by means of witchcraft; **witch'meal** the inflammable pollen of the club-moss, lycopodium. — *adj* **witch'-ridden** ridden by witches. — **witch's hat** a tall black conical brimmed hat, the traditional wear of fairytale witches; **witch'-wife** (*Scot*) a woman who practises witchcraft. [ME *wicche* (both masc and fem), from OE *wicca* (masc), *wicce* (fem), wizard, witch, and verb *wiccian* to practise witchcraft; ety doubtful]

witch[2] or **witch-**. See **wych**.

witchen *wich'ən*, *n* the mountain ash; the wych-elm. [**witch**[2]]

witchetty *wich'ə-ti*, *n* (also **witchetty grub**) any of the edible grubs of species of certain moths (*Cossus*) and of longicorn beetles. [Aboriginal]

witch-hazel *wich'hā-zl*, *n* any of a number of trees, such as the wych-elm, the hornbeam, or a N American shrub (*Hamamelis virginiana*) a distillate of whose bark and leaves is dissolved in alcohol to make an astringent lotion; this lotion, used for treating bruises, etc. [**witch**[2]]

wite[1], **wyte** or **wight** *wīt*, *vt* (*obs* or *Scot*) to blame; to lay the blame on. — *n* (now *dialect*) blame, reproach. — *adj* **wite'less** (now *dialect*) blameless. [OE *wītan* to see, blame; related to **wit**]

wite[2]. See **wit**[1].

witenagemot *wit'ə-nə-gə-mōt*, popularly *wit-ə-nag'ə-mōt*, *n* the supreme council of England in Anglo-Saxon times, composed of the bishops, the ealdormen of shires, and a number of the king's friends and dependents. [OE *witena*, genitive pl of *wita* wise man, councillor, and *gemōt* meeting; cf **witan**, **wit**[1,2]]

witgat *vit'hhat* or **witgatboom** *vit'hhat-bo͝om*, *n* a S African evergreen tree (*Boscia albitrunca*) with pale bark, hard coarse-grained white wood, and edible roots used *esp* as a coffee substitute when roasted; any of various species of the genus *Boscia*. [Afrik, from *wit* white, *gat* hole, and *boom* tree]

with[1] *widh* or *with*, *prep* denoting nearness, association or connection; by, beside; among; on the side of; in the company of; in the possession or care of; having or containing; supplemented by (as in *With the tip, it cost* £10.50); possessing; characterized by; in the same direction as; at the time of; at the same time or rate as (*rise with the birds*; *Discretion increases with age*); immediately after; in competition or contest against; in respect of, in regard of (*What's wrong with it*?); by, by means of, through; as a result of (*shaking with fear*); because of having (*With her talents, she'll go far*); in spite of having (*With all his money he's still unhappy*); using; denoting separation, from (*dispense with*); denoting manner (*answered with a nod*); denoting accompanying circumstances (*fall asleep with the light on*); in (the specified circumstances, as *I can't go abroad with my mother so ill*); expressing agreement, disagreement or comparison (*correspond with*, *inconsistent with*, *compared with*); featuring, starring; used in exclamations after adverbs (*Down with the tyrant*!); understanding (*Are you with me*?; *colloq*); supporting (*with you all the way*). — **feel** or **think with** to feel as, or be of the same opinion as; **in with** (*colloq*) friendly with; enjoying the favour of; **what's with** see under **what**; **with it** (*colloq*) following current trends in popular taste (*adj* **with'-it**); **with that** thereupon. [OE *with* against; ON *vith*, Ger *wider*. It ousted the OE *mid* with (Ger *mit*)]

with[2] *n*. See **withe**[1].

with[3] *with*, (*building*) *n* a partition between chimney flues. — Also **withe**. [Poss corruption of **width**]

withal *wi-dhöl'*, (*literary* or *archaic*) *adv* with all or the rest; besides; therewith; thereupon; nevertheless, for all that. — *prep* an emphatic form of *with*, used after its object. [ME, from **with**[1] and **all**]

withdraw *widh-drö'* or *with-drö'*, *vt* to draw back or away; to take back or away; to cause (troops) to retire; to take (money, savings, etc) from deposit or investment; to remove (with *from*); to cancel or discontinue (a service, offer, etc); to deflect, turn aside (*rare*); to recall, retract, unsay. — *vi* to retire; to go away; to back out of a contest or other activity; (with *from*) to stop oneself taking (a drug to which one is addicted); to become uncommunicative or unresponsive; to take back what one has said, or to recall a motion one has proposed: — *pa t* **withdrew** (*-dro͞o'*); *pa p* **withdrawn'**. — *n* **withdraw'al** an act or gradual process of withdrawing; retreat, *esp* if unforced; the removal of money from a bank account; the breaking of a drug addiction, with associated discomfort; a retreat into silence and self-absorption; (also **withdrawal method**) coitus interruptus, interruption of sexual intercourse before ejaculation of semen, as a means of contraception. — *n* **withdraw'er**. — *n* **withdraw'ment** (*rare*). — *adj* **withdrawn'** (of a place) secluded; remote; (of a person, manner, etc) detached; uncommunicative, unresponsive, shy or reserved; introverted. — **withdrawal symptom** any of a number of symptoms such as pain, nausea or sweating, experienced by someone being deprived of a drug to which he or she is addicted; **withdraw'ing-room** a room used to retire into; a drawing room. [Pfx *with-* against, back, and **draw**]

withe[1] or **with** *widh*, *with* or *wīdh*, *n* a flexible twig, *esp* of willow; a band of twisted twigs; a halter (*obs*); an elastic handle to a tool to save the hand from the shock of blows; a boom-iron. — *vt* to bind with a withe or withes; to capture with a noose of withes. — *adj* **with'y** made of withes; like withes, flexible; wiry and agile. [OE *withthe*; ON *vīthir*, Ger *Weide* willow; cf **withy**[1]]

withe[2]. See **with**[3].

wither *widh'ər*, *vi* to fade or become dry; to lose freshness; to languish, decline; to decay, waste. — *vt* to cause to dry up, fade or decay; to blight, destroy; to humiliate, mortify or cause to feel very unimportant or despicable; to dry (eg tea). — *adj* **with'ered** dried, faded, shrivelled; (of a limb) stunted or shrivelled through illness or injury. — *n* **with'eredness**. — *n* **with'ering**. — *adj* fading, becoming dry, etc, or causing to do so; used for drying or curing; blasting, blighting, scorching, destructive; snubbing, humiliating, destructive. — *adv* **with'eringly**. — **with'ering-floor** the drying-floor of a malthouse. [ME *wederen* to expose to weather]

witherite *widh'ər-īt*, *n* the chief source of barium compounds, barium carbonate, occurring as orthorhombic crystals in pseudohexagonal pyramids. [Dr W *Withering*, who first discriminated it from barytes, 1784]

withers *widh'ərz*, *n pl* the ridge between the shoulder blades of a horse. — *adj* **with'er-wrung** injured in the withers. — **wring someone's withers** to wound someone by a snub, etc; to cause someone anguish. [OE *wither* against, an extension of *with* against]

withershins *widh'ər-shinz* or *wid'ər-shinz*, (*Scot*) *adv* in the contrary direction, contrary to the course of the sun (*opp* to **deasil**); in the wrong way. [LGer *weddersins*; cf OE *wither* against, LGer *sind* direction, OE *sīth* journey]

withhault. Pseudo-archaic *pa t* of **withhold**.

withhold *widh-hōld'* or *with-hōld'*, *vt* to hold back, restrain; to keep back; to refuse to give; to keep in bondage or custody (*obs*). — *vi* to refrain (with *from* or infinitive; *obs*); to postpone (*Pope*): — *pa t* and *pa p* **withheld'** (*archaic pa p* **withhold'en**). — *n* **withhold'er**. — *n* **withhold'ment**. — **withholding tax** (*US*) income tax deducted at source, *incl* tax levied by a country on dividends, etc paid to a non-resident. [Pfx *with-* against, and **hold**]

within *wi-dhin'* or *wi-thin'*, *prep* in or to the inner part of (*archaic*); inside; in the limits of; not going beyond; in less than (a certain time or distance, as in *within the hour*, *within a hair's breadth of death*); on the inner side of (*obs*); entered from; into. — *adv* inside; in the inner part; inwardly; in the mind, soul, heart; behind the scenes; at home (*archaic*); indoors; in or to an inner room (*archaic*); herein. — **within land** (*obs*) inland; **within reach** so positioned as to be obtainable or attainable without much difficulty, effort or loss of time. [OE *withinnan*, from *with* against, with, and *innan* in]

without *wi-dhowt'* or *wi-thowt'*, *prep* not having the company of; deprived of; not having; lacking; free from; not (behaving as expected or in a particular way), as in *answered without smiling*; not giving, showing, etc (*complied without a murmur*); not encountering (some expected circumstance), as in *got there without anyone getting hurt*; in neglect of (a usual procedure), as in *imprisoned without trial*; not using, not having the help of; if it had not been for (*would have died without their help*); outside or out of (*archaic*); outside the limits of (*archaic*); beyond (*archaic*). — *adv* on the outside; outwardly; outside, not members of, a particular group or society; out of doors (*archaic*). — *conj* (*archaic* or *dialect*) unless, except. — *adj* **without'-door** (*Shakesp*) outward. — *prep* **without'en** (*archaic*) without. — **from without** from the outside; **without distinction** indiscriminately; **without doors** out of doors; outside the family, nation, etc; outside Parliament. [OE *withūtan*, from *with* against, and *ūtan* outside]

withstand *widh-stand'* or *with-stand'*, *vt* to oppose, brave or resist; to hinder (*obs*). — *vi* to stand one's ground, offer resistance: — *pa t* and *pa p* **withstood'**. — *n* **withstand'er**. [OE *withstandan*, from *with* against; see **stand**]

withwind *with'wīnd*, or **withywind** *widh'i-wīnd*, (*dialect*) *n* bindweed, or other climbing plant. [OE *withewinde*; cf **withy**[1] and **wind**[2]]

withy[1] *widh'i*, *n* the osier willow; any willow; a flexible twig or branch, *esp* one used for binding. [OE *wīthig* willow; cf **widdy**[1], **withe**[1]]

withy[2]. See **withe**[1].

witless, witling. See **wit**[2].

witloof *wit'lōf*, *n* a kind of chicory with large leaves. [Du, literally white leaf]

witness *wit'nis*, *n* someone who sees or has personal knowledge of an event, etc; someone who gives evidence; someone whose signature confirms the genuineness of a document, or of a signature already added; a remnant of original surface or scribed line, left during machining or hand-working to prove that a minimum quantity of material has been removed or an outline accurately preserved (*eng*); (something that is) proof or evidence of anything; knowledge brought in proof; testimony of a fact. — *vt* to have direct knowledge of; (loosely) to see; (of a place or period) to be the scene or setting of; (of a person) to live through; to give testimony to; to attest; to act as legal witness of; to sign, to add one's signature in confirmation of the genuineness of (a document, another's signature, etc); to show; to evince (*archaic*). — *vi* to give evidence; (with *to*) to confirm, attest to. — *n* **wit'nesser**. — **witness box** or (*US*) **stand** the enclosure in which a witness stands when giving evidence in a court of law. — **bear witness** to give or be evidence (*esp* with *to*); **with a witness** (*Shakesp*) with a vengeance; **witness (such and such)** let (such and such) serve as evidence. [OE (*ge*)*witnes*, from (*ge*)*wit*; see **wit**[2]]

witter *wit'ər*, or **whitter** *wit'ər* or *hwit'ər*, (chiefly *Scot*) *vi* to talk or mutter peevishly or ineffectually (*esp* with *on*). [Ety doubtful]

witticism, wittily, wittiness. See under **wit**[2].

witting. See under **wit**[1].

wittol *wit'əl*, (*archaic*) *n* a man who knows his wife's faithlessness, and submits to it. — *adj* **witt'olly** (*Shakesp*) like a wittol or contented cuckold. [ME *wetewold*; associated with **cuckold** (qv), and perh from **witwall**, or from **wit**[1]]

witty. See under **wit**[2].

witwall *wit'wöl*, (*dialect*) *n* the green woodpecker or the greater spotted woodpecker. [Cf Ger *Wittewal*, *Wiedewall*; cf also **woodwale**]

witwanton. See under **wit**[2].

WIVAB *abbrev*: Women's Inter-Varsity Athletic Board.

wive *wīv*, (*archaic*) *vt* to take for a wife; to provide with a wife; to become the wife of. — *vi* to marry a wife. — *n* **wive'hood** (*Spenser*) wifehood. [OE *wīfian*, from *wīf* wife]

wivern *wī'vərn*, (*heraldry*) *n* a fictitious monster, winged and two-legged, combining characteristics of the dragon and the griffin. [ONFr *wivre* a viper, from L *vīpera*]

wives *wīvz*, *pl* of **wife**.

wizard *wiz'ərd*, *n* a man who practises witchcraft or magic, a sorcerer or magician; someone who works wonders, an expert, a genius; a wise man (*obs*). — *adj* with magical powers (*old* or *poetic*); wonderful, delightful (*old colloq*). — *adv* **wiz'ardly** like a wizard. — *n* **wiz'ardry** sorcery, magic. [ME *wysar*(*d*), from *wys* wise, and noun sfx *-ard*]

wizen *wiz'n*, *vt* and *vi* to make or become dry and shrivelled. — *adj* (*old*) wizened. — *adj* **wiz'ened** dried up, thin, shrivelled, wrinkled. — **wiz'en-faced** having a thin, shrivelled face. — Also **weazen** (*wē'zn*), etc. [OE *wisnian*, to wither; cognate with ON *visna* to wither]

wizier. Same as **vizier**.

wiz kid. See under **whizz**.

wk *abbrev*: week.

WL *abbrev*: St Lucia, Windward Islands (IVR).

WLA *abbrev*: Women's Land Army (disbanded 1950).

WLF *abbrev*: Women's Liberal Federation.

Wm *abbrev*: William.

WMO *abbrev*: World Meteorological Organization.

WNP *abbrev*: Welsh National Party.

WNW *abbrev*: west-north-west.
WO *abbrev*: (formerly) War Office; warrant officer; walk-over.
wo. Older variant of **woe**, or **whoa**.
w/o *abbrev*: without.
woad *wōd*, *n* a genus (Isatis) of cruciferous plants, mostly natives of countries round the Mediterranean, a species of it, *Isatis tinctoria* or *dyer's woad*, yielding a good and very permanent blue dye, largely superseded by indigo; the dye itself. — *adj* **woad'ed** dyed blue with woad. [OE *wād*; Ger *Waid*]
wobbegong *wob'i-gong*, *n* a carpet shark. [Aboriginal]
wobble *wob'l*, *vi* to move unsteadily or uncertainly from side to side; to progress thus; to shake or rock, be unstable or unsteady; to quiver; (of the voice) to quaver, be unsteady; to vacillate, waver. — Also *vt*. — *n* an unsteady, unequal motion or movement. — *n* **wobb'ler**. — *n* **wobb'liness**. — *n* **wobb'ling**. — *adj* **wobb'ly** shaky; unsteady through illness; inclined to wobble. — *n* (*colloq*) a fit of nerves. — Also **wabb'le**, **wabb'ler**, etc. — **wobble board** a sheet of hardboard shaken to obtain certain sound effects. — **throw a wobbly** (*colloq*) to have a fit of hysterics or a tantrum, or behave otherwise unnervingly. [LGer *wabbeln*]
wobegone. See under **woe**.
wock. See **wok**.
Woden or **Wodan** *wō'dən*, (*mythol*) *n* the chief god of the ancient Germanic peoples. — *n* **Wō'denism** the worship of Woden. [OE *Wōden*; OHGer *Wuotan*; cf **Odin**]
wodge *woj*, (*colloq*) *n* a large or roughly-cut portion; a lump, chunk or wad. [**wedge**]
woe or (*archaic*) **wo** *wō*, *n* grief (*archaic*); misery; (often in *pl*) a misfortune or calamity; a physical pain (*obs*); a curse (*obs*); (often **wō**, *pl* **wōs**) an exclamation of grief. — *adj* (*archaic* and *dialect*) sad, wretched, sorry. — *adj* **woe'ful** or **wō'ful** sorrowful or afflicted; bringing misery or calamity; deplorable; wretched, paltry. — *adv* **woe'fully** or **wō'fully**. — *n* **woe'fulness or wō'fulness**. — *adj* **woe'begone** or **wō'begone** (see **bego**) beset with woe; dismal-looking, manifesting misery. — *adj* **woe'some** (*Scot* **wae'some**) woeful. — *adj* **woe'-wea'ried** or **woe'-worn** wearied, worn with woe. — **in weal and woe** in prosperity and adversity; **woe betide** (*old* or *facetious*) misfortune will be (or may misfortune be) the lot of (whoever offends in some specified way); **woe is me** (*archaic*) unhappy that I am!; cursed am I; **woe unto** calamity will befall; may calamity befall; **woe worth the day** cursed be the day (see **worth**[2]). [OE (interj) *wā*; Ger *Weh*; L *vae*; cf **wail**]
wog[1] *wog*, (*offensive*) *n* any non-white foreigner, *orig* used only of Arabs. [Perh from **(golly)wog**; popularly thought to be an acronym, of which several expansions are propounded]
wog[2] *wog*, (*Austr colloq*) *n* an insect or grub; a germ, bug, infection, illness. [Origin uncertain]
woggle *wog'l*, *n* the ring of leather, plastic or other material through which Scouts and Guides, etc thread their neckerchiefs. [Origin uncertain]
wo ha ho *wō-hä-hō'*, (*falconry*) *interj* a call for summoning a bird.
woiwode *woi'wōd*. A variant of **voivode**.
wok or **wock** *wok*, *n* a hemispherical pan used in Chinese cookery. [Chin]
woke, woken. See **wake**[1].
wold *wōld*, *n* an open tract of country, now chiefly upland country. [OE (Anglian) *wald* forest, applied orig to wooded parts of the country; cf **weald**]
wolf *wo͝olf*, *n* the common name of certain predatory species of the genus *Canis* that hunt in packs, including the common wolf (*Canis lupus*), the grey or timber wolf, and the coyote; anything symbolically seen as a cruelly rapacious or ravenous creature; a greedy and cunning person; a tuberculous excrescence or cancerous growth (*obs*); a dissonance heard in a keyed instrument tuned by unequal temperament (*music*); an extraneous non-harmonic note made by the bow on a string of a violin, etc (*music*); a man who insatiably pursues and seduces women (*colloq*): — *pl* **wolves** (*wo͝olvz*). — *vi* (also **wolve** *wo͝olv*) to hunt for wolves. — *vt* (often with *down* or *up*; *colloq*) to devour ravenously. — *n* **wolf'er** or **wolv'er** a hunter of wolves. — *n* **wolf'ing** or **wolv'ing** the hunting of wolves for their skins. — *adj* **wolf'ish** or **wolv'ish** like a wolf; rapacious; ravenous. — *adv* **wolf'ishly** or **wolv'ishly**. — *n* **wolf'kin** and **wolf'ling** a young wolf. — **wolf'berry** a N American shrub (*Symphoricarpus occidentalis*) of the honeysuckle family, with white berries, hairy leaves and pink flowers; **wolf cub** a young wolf; (with *caps*) a member of the former Wolf Cubs (now Cub Scouts), a junior division of the Scout Association; **wolf dog** a dog of a large breed formerly used in hunting wolves and guarding sheep from attack by wolves; (**wolf'-dog**) a cross between a wolf and a domestic dog; **wolf'-fish** (also **sea-wolf** and **catfish**) any genus of fierce and voracious salt-water fishes; **wolf'hound** any of several breeds of large domestic dog, such as the Irish wolfhound, formerly used to hunt wolves; **wolf note** (*music*) a wolf; **wolf pack** a pack of wolves; a flotilla of submarines surfacing together for attack; **wolfs'bane** or **wolf's bane** an aconite, *esp Aconitum lycoctonum*; **wolf's foot** or **wolf's claw** the club moss (Lycopodium); **wolf'skin** the skin or pelt of a wolf; **wolf's peach** the tomato; **wolf spīder** any spider of the genus (*Lycosa*) to which the true tarantula belongs, or of the family Lycosidae; **wolf tooth** a small supernumerary premolar in a horse; **wolf whistle** a two-note whistle uttered as a coarse expression of admiration, typically by a man at the sight of a woman. — **cry wolf** to give a false alarm, from the story of the boy who cried 'Wolf' when there was none, and was not believed when there was one; **have a wolf by the ears** to be in a desperately difficult situation; **have a wolf in the stomach** to be ravenously hungry; **keep the wolf from the door** to keep away poverty or hunger; **see a wolf** to be tongue-tied (in allusion to an old superstition); **throw** or **fling to the wolves** to abandon to certain destruction; **wolf in sheep's clothing** someone who behind a kindly and inoffensive exterior is dangerous and unscrupulous. [OE *wulf*; Ger *Wolf*; L *vulpēs* fox, *lupus* wolf; Gr *lykos* wolf]
Wolffian *wo͝ol'fi-ən* or *vol'fi-ən*, *adj* relating to, or associated with the German embryologist K F *Wolff* (1733–94); designating the renal organs in the embryo of vertebrates. — **Wolffian body** the organ of excretion in the embryo, the primitive kidney or mesonephros; **Wolffian duct** the excretory duct of the mesonephros.
Wolfian[1] or **Wolffian** *wo͝ol'fi-ən* or *vol'fi-ən*, *adj* relating to the philosophy of Christian *Wolf* (1679–1754), who systematized and popularized the philosophy of Leibniz, and gave a strong impulse to that development of natural theology and rationalism. — *n* **Wolf'ianism**.
Wolfian[2] *wo͝ol'fi-ən* or *vol'fi-ən*, *adj* relating to, or associated with Friedrich August *Wolf* (1759–1824), applied *esp* to his theory that the *Odyssey* and *Iliad* consist of numerous ballads by a variety of minstrels, strung together in the course of time by editors.
wolfram *wo͝olf'rəm*, *n* (also **wolf'ramite**) a native compound of tungstate of iron and manganese; tungsten. [Ger; origin uncertain]
Wolf-Rayet star *wo͝olf'-rā'ət stär*, *n* one of a rare class of very hot stars, whose spectra are similar to those of novae, broad bright lines predominating, indicating violent motion in the stellar atmosphere. [C J E *Wolf* (1827–1918) and G A P *Rayet* (1839–1906), French astronomers]
wolfsbane, wolfskin. See under **wolf**.
wollastonite *wo͝ol'əs-tə-nīt*, or *wo͝o-las'tə-nīt*, *n* a pyroxene of relatively simple composition, silicate of calcium, $CaSiO_3$, also called **tabular spar**. [After the scientist W H *Wollaston* (1766–1828)]
wolly[1] *wol'i*, (*slang*) a uniformed policeman, *esp* a raw young constable. [Ety uncertain; cf **wally**[2]]
wolly[2] *wol'i*, (*Cockney slang*) *n* a pickled olive or cucumber. [Origin uncertain; the street cry 'Oh! olives!' suggested]

Wolof *wō'lof*, *n* a tribe living near the Senegal River in western Africa; a member of the tribe; its language. — Also *adj*.

wolve, **wolver**. See under **wolf**.

wolverine or **wolverene** *wo͝ol'və-rēn*, *n* a large solitary carnivorous mammal of the weasel family, found in forests in N America and Eurasia; its fur. [Extension of **wolf**]

wolves, **wolving**, **wolvish**. See under **wolf**.

woman *wo͝om'ən*, *n* an adult female of the human race; a wife (now *dialect*); a mistress; the female sex, women collectively; (with **the**) the natural urges specific to a woman; a man over-concerned with domestic niceties (*derog*); a female attendant (*hist* or *archaic*); a charwoman or daily domestic help (*colloq*); (as *combining form*) a woman of a specified occupation, skill or nationality, as in *policewoman*, *markswoman*, *Manxwoman*; the reverse or Britannia side of a coin: — *pl* **women** (*wim'in*). — *adj* female, as in *woman doctor*. — *vt* to cause to act like a woman (*obs*); (with *it*) to play the part of a woman; to provide or staff with a woman or women; to call a person 'woman' abusively. — *adj* **wo'man'd** (*Shakesp*) accompanied by a woman. — *adv* **wom'anfully** like a woman of spirit. — *n* **wom'anhood** the state, character or qualities of a woman; womenkind. — *adj* **wom'anish** (of a man, his behaviour or appearance) effeminate, unmanly; associated with women, feminine. — *adv* **wom'anishly**. — *n* **wom'anishness**. — *vt* and *vi* **wom'anize** or **-ise** to make or become effeminate. — *vi* (*derog*; of a man) to pursue women with a view to amorous adventures. — *n* **wom'anizer** or **-s-**. — *n* **wom'ankind** women generally, the female sex (also **wom'enkind**); a woman (*obs*). — *adj* **wom'anless**. — *adj* and *adv* **wom'anlike**. — *n* **wom'anliness**. — *adj* **wom'anly** like or becoming to a woman; feminine. — *adv* in the manner of a woman. — **wom'an-bod'y** (*Scot*) a woman. — *adj* **wom'an-born** born of woman. — *adj* **wom'an-built** built by women. — **wom'an-child** a female child: — *pl* **wom'en-children**; **wom'enfolk** or **wom'enfolks** the women of a household, family or other community or group; women generally, womankind. — *adj* **wom'an-grown** grown to womanhood. — **wom'an-hater** a man who hates women, a misogynist; **woman post** (*Shakesp*) a female messenger; **wom'an-quell'er** a killer of women; **wom'an-suffrage** women's suffrage. — *adj* **wom'an-tired** (*Shakesp*) hen-pecked (**tire**[6]). — *adj* **wom'an-vested** wearing women's clothes. — **Women's Institute** an organization for women *esp* of rural areas, with regular meetings for social and cultural activities, demonstrations of craftwork, etc; **women's liberation** (also with *caps*) a movement of active feminists forming part of the women's movement (*colloq* contraction **women's lib**); **women's liberationist** (*colloq* contraction **women's libber**); **women's movement** (also with *caps*) the movement amongst women to try to achieve equality with men, with regard to eg job opportunities, pay, legal status, etc; **women's rights** equal rights with men thus sought by women; **women's suffrage** possession of the electoral franchise by women; **wom'enswear** clothes for women. — **kept woman** a mistress; **play the woman** to give way to weakness; **the little woman** (*facetious* or *patronizing*) one's wife; **woman of the town** or **streets** a prostitute; **woman of the world** a woman of fashion or of worldly wisdom; a woman who knows and makes allowance for, or accepts, the ways of the world; a married woman (*obs*); **Women's Royal Voluntary Service** (from its formation in 1938 until 1966 the **Women's Voluntary Service**) a nationwide service assisting government departments, local authorities and other voluntary bodies in organizing and carrying out welfare and emergency work for the community. [OE *wimman*, from *wīfman*, from *wīf* a woman, and *man* man, human being]

womb *wo͞om*, *n* the uterus, the organ in the female mammal in which the young develop after conception and stay till birth; the abdomen, the stomach or the bowels (*obs*); the place where anything is conceived, originated, developed or produced; any deep cavity; any warm, sheltering, enclosing environment. — *vt* (*Shakesp*) to enclose. — *adj* **wombed**. — *adj* **womb'like**. — *adj* **womb'y** (*Shakesp*) hollow, capacious. — **womb'-leasing** (*colloq*) surrogate motherhood (qv) undertaken in return for a fee. [OE *wamb*, *womb*; Ger *Wamme* paunch]

wombat *wom'bat*, *n* an animal belonging to any of several species of heavy, short-legged, herbivorous, burrowing marsupials of the family *Vombatidae*. [Aboriginal]

women. See under **woman**.

womera. Same as **woomera**.

won[1] *wun*, *pa t* and *pa p* of **win**[1,2].

won[2] *wun*, *wo͝on* or *wŏn*, *n* the standard monetary unit of North and South Korea (100 *chon*): — *pl* **won**. [Korean *wån*]

won[3] *wun* or *wōn*, *vi* to dwell, abide (*archaic* and *dialect*); to be, or become, accustomed (*obs*): — *pa t* **wonned**; *pa p* **wont** (qv). — *n* (*obs*) a dwelling, an abode; habit, custom. — *n* **won'ing** or **wonn'ing** the state of dwelling; a dwelling-place. — **did won** (*Spenser*) was accustomed. [OE *wunian*, Du *wonen*, Ger *wohnen* to dwell]

wonder *wun'dər*, *n* the state of mind produced by something new, unexpected or extraordinary, amazement, awe or bafflement; admiration (*obs*); the quality of being strange, unexpected or awesome; a strange, astonishing or admirable thing or happening, a marvel; a prodigy; a miracle; a sweet friedcake, a cruller (*US*). — *adj* and *combining form* notable for accomplishing marvels, as in *wonder drug*, *wonderwoman*, *wonderboy*. — *vi* to feel wonder; to be surprised, as in *shouldn't wonder if she won*; to be amazed (with *at*); to speculate (with *about*); to feel doubt. — *vt* to speculate, to ask oneself (with noun clause or direct quotation); used to introduce polite requests or inquiries. — *adj* **won'dered** or **wond'red** (*obs*) marvellous; having performed, or able to perform, wonders (*Shakesp*). — *n* **won'derer**. — *adj* **won'derful** causing wonder; strange, extraordinary; expressing vague commendation, admirable, splendid (*colloq*). — *adv* (*archaic* or *dialect*) wonderfully. — *adv* **won'derfully**. — *n* **won'derfulness**. — *n* and *adj* **won'dering**. — *adv* **won'deringly**. — *n* **won'derment** surprise; an expression of wonder; a wonderful thing; the quality of being wonderful. — *adj* **won'drous**, also (*old*) **won'derous**, such as to cause wonder, wonderful, strange or awesome. — Also *adv* (*archaic*) strangely, wonderfully; exceedingly. — *adv* **won'drously**. — *n* **won'drousness**. — **won'derland** an imaginary place full of marvels, fairyland; a scene of strange unearthly beauty; **won'dermonger** a wonder-worker; someone who talks garrulously of wonders, *esp* incredible ones; **won'dermongering**. — *adj* **won'der-struck** or **won'der-stricken** struck with wonder or astonishment, thunderstruck. — **won'derwork** a prodigy, miracle; thaumaturgy, the performing of miracles; **won'der-worker**; **won'der-working**. — Also *adj*. — *adj* **won'der-wounded** (*Shakesp*) wonder-stricken. — **bird of wonder** the phoenix; **do** or **work wonders** to achieve marvellous results; **for a wonder** by way of an unexpected but pleasant change; **nine days' wonder** something that astonishes everybody for the moment; **no wonder** or **small wonder** it isn't surprising; **seven wonders of the world** see **seven**; **to a wonder** (*archaic*) marvellously; extremely well; **wonders never** (or **will never**) **cease** (*colloq*) an expression of surprise at some unexpected but welcome development. [OE *wundor*; Ger *Wunder*, ON *undr*]

wondred, **wondrous**. See under **wonder**.

wonga *wong'gə*, (*slang*) *n* money. [Origin uncertain]

wonga-wonga *wong'ə-wong'ə* or *wong'gə-wong'ge*, *n* the large Australian white-faced pigeon (also **wong'a**); any of several varieties of hardy evergreen climbing vine of the family *Bignoniaceae*. [Aboriginal]

wongi *wong'gi*, (*Austr colloq*) *n* a talk, chat, conversation. — *vi* to converse, chat, talk: — *pa t* **wong'ied**. [Aboriginal]

woning. See under **won**³.

wonky *wongk'i*, (*colloq*) *adj* unsound; shaky; amiss; awry. [Cf **wankle**]

wonned, wonning. See under **won**³.

wont historically *wunt*, commonly *wōnt*, *adj* (*literary* or *archaic*) used or accustomed. — *n* (*literary* or *facetious*) habit. — *vi* to be accustomed. — *adj* **wont'ed** accustomed, habituated; usual, customary. — *n* **wont'edness**. — *adj* **wont'less** (*archaic*) unaccustomed. [Orig pa p of **won**³]

won't *wōnt*, will not. [Contracted form of ME *wol not*]

won ton *won ton*, (*Chin cuisine*) *n* a spicy dumpling containing minced pork, *esp* served in soup. [Cantonese Chin *wan tan* pastry]

WoO (*music*) *abbrev*: *Werke ohne Opuszahl* (*Ger*), works (by Beethoven) without an opus number (prefixed to assigned number).

woo *wōō*, *vt* (of a man) to try to win the affection of, to court (a woman; *esp old*); to invite or court (eg destruction); to solicit eagerly, seek the support of (eg voters); to seek to gain (success, fame, etc). — Also *vi*: — *pa t* and *pa p* **wooed** (*wōōd*). — *n* **woo'er**. — *n* and *adj* **woo'ing**. — *adv* **woo'ingly**. [OE *wōgian* to woo; origin obscure]

woobut. See **woubit**.

wood¹ *wŏŏd*, *n* (often in *pl*) a collection of more or less densely growing trees; a stretch of country supporting such growth; the hard substance composing the trunks and branches of trees and shrubs, xylem; trees cut or sawn, timber; a kind of timber or wood; firewood; a tree (*obs*); the Cross (*obs*); the cask or barrel as storage for wine, etc, as distinguished from the bottle; a woodblock (*printing*); (commonly in *pl*) the woodwind instruments of an orchestra; a golf club with a bulky curved head, traditionally made of wood though now often of metal, used for hitting the ball long distances; a bowl (*bowls*); the outer rim of a tennis racquet if, as traditionally, of wood; an idol made of wood; the pulpit (*old slang*). — *adj* made of or using wood. — *vt* (chiefly in *pa p*) to cover with trees; to supply or load (a ship) with wood. — *vi* to take in a supply of wood (sometimes with *up*). — *adj* **wood'ed** supplied with wood; covered with trees. — *adj* **wood'less** without wood. — *n* **wood'lessness**. — *adj* **wood'sy** (*wŏŏd-zi*; *NAm colloq*) characteristic of or relating to woods. — **wood acid** wood vinegar; **wood alcohol** wood spirit; **wood anemone** any anemone growing in woods, *esp Anemone nemorosa*, which has a single whorl of leaves and a white flower; **wood ant** a large forest-dwelling ant; a termite infesting the wood of old buildings; **wood ash** (often in *pl*) ash obtained by burning wood or plants, a source of potassium salts; **wood'block** a die cut in relief on wood and ready to produce ink impressions; a woodcut; **wood'-borer** any of a number of insect larvae, molluscs or Crustacea, that bore into wood. — *adj* **wood'-boring**. — *adj* **wood'-born** born in the woods. — **wood'carver**; **wood'carving** the process of carving in wood; an object or decoration carved in wood; **wood'chat** a species of shrike, with grey, black and white plumage but a red-brown crown; **wood'chip** a chip of wood; woodchip board or paper; **woodchip board** reconstituted wooden board, chipboard; **woodchip paper** paper for decorating walls, etc, incorporating chips of wood for texture; **wood coal** coal like wood in texture, lignite or brown coal; charcoal; **wood'cock** a genus (*Scolopax*) of birds related to the snipes, but bulkier in the body and shorter and stronger in the leg; a stupid person, a simpleton (*archaic*); **wood'cock's-head** (*obs*) a tobacco-pipe; **wood'craft** skill in working or carving wood; skill in hunting and everything relating to life in the woods; forestry generally; **wood'cut** a design for printing incised into the surface of a block of wood cut along the grain; an impression taken from this; **wood'-cutter** someone who cuts wood; a maker of woodcuts; **wood'cutting**; **wood'-engraver** a maker of wood-engravings; any of certain beetles that make a pattern of furrows in the wood of trees; **wood'-engraving** a design for printing, incised into the surface of a block of hard wood cut across the grain; an impression taken from this; the art of cutting such designs; **wood'-evil** diarrhoea of herbivorous animals; **wood fibre** a thick-walled, elongated, dead element found in wood, developed by the elongation and lignification of the wall of a single cell, differing from a tracheide in its inability to conduct water; **wood flour** or **wood'meal** a fine powder, made from sawdust and wood waste, used as a filler in many industries, in the manufacture of guncotton and dynamite, and as an absorbent in surgical dressings; **wood'-fretter** a wood-borer; **wood germander** *Teucrium scorodonia*, which has racemes of yellow flowers; **wood'grouse** the capercailzie; **wood'hole** a place where wood is stored; **wood honey** wild honey; **wood'horse** a sawhorse; **wood'house** a house or shed in which wood for fuel is deposited; a variant of **woodwose** (qv); **wood hyacinth** the wild hyacinth or English bluebell, of the genus *Endymion* (or *Scilla*); **wood ibis** any bird of the genera *Mycteria* (or *Tantalus*) and *Ibis* of the subfamily *Mycteriinae* of storks; **wood'land** land covered with wood (also *adj*); **wood'lander** an inhabitant of woodland; **wood'lark** a species of lark that perches on trees but sings chiefly on the wing; **wood lot** a piece of land reserved entirely for the growing of timber; **wood'louse** (*pl* **wood'lice**) any of numerous isopod crustaceans of family *Oniscidae*, found in damp places, under stones and bark, in woodwork, among moss, etc; a booklouse; a termite (*US*); **wood'man** a man who fells trees for timber; a forest officer; a huntsman; **woodmeal** see **wood flour**; **wood mite** any of numerous small mites found in woods; **wood'mouse** a type of fieldmouse, *Apodemus sylvaticus*, with large ears and a long tail; **wood naphtha** wood spirit, methanol; **wood nightshade** another name for **woody nightshade** (qv under **woody**); **wood'note** (*Milton*) a wild musical note, like that of a songbird; **wood nymph** a nymph of the woods; **wood'-offering** (*Bible*) wood burned on the altar; **wood oil** gurjun balsam; tung oil; also various other oils obtained from trees; **wood opal** a form of common opal which has replaced pieces of wood entombed as fossils in sediments, in some cases retaining the original structure; **wood owl** the European brown or tawny owl, or other owl living in woods; **wood paper** paper made from wood pulp; **wood'pecker** any of a family (*Picidae*) of birds in the order Picariae, remarkable for modification of the skull and bill enabling the latter to be used to drill holes, and for the long flexible tongue, used to extract insects from crevices; **wood'pigeon** the ring-dove, a common species of pigeon (*Columba palumbus*) living in woods; in New Zealand, the kuku (qv); **wood'pile** a pile of wood, *esp* firewood; **wood pulp** wood mechanically or chemically pulped for paper-making; **wood'reeve** the overseer of a wood; **wood'rush** any plant of the genus Luzula, of the same family as the true rushes, growing in woods; **wood sage** wood germander; **wood sandpiper** a common European sandpiper; **wood sanicle** see **sanicle**; **wood'screw** a tapered screw for fastening pieces of wood or wood and metal, etc; **wood'shed** a shed for storing firewood (**something nasty in the woodshed** (*facetious*) an unpleasant or shocking experience from one's past, *esp* if kept hushed up); an intensive, *esp* private, practice or rehearsal (*music slang*; *orig US*). — *vt* and *vi* to practise (a piece of music), *esp* intensively and alone. — **wood'shedding** such intensive practice; spontaneous barber-shop singing; **wood'shrike** the woodchat (qv above); **wood'skin** an Indian canoe made of bark, or the bark itself; **woods'man** someone familiar with the lore of the woods; a forester or woodcutter; a huntsman; **wood sorrel** any plant of the genus Oxalis, *esp Oxalis acetosella*, with trifoliate leaves and white or rose-tinted flowers, which yields potassium binoxalate,

$KHC_2O_4{\cdot}H_2O$; **wood spirit** a spirit living among trees; methyl alcohol, wood naphtha or methanol; **wood'spite** the green woodpecker; **wood stamp** a stamp made of wood, as for stamping fabrics in colours; **wood'stone** petrified wood; **wood sugar** xylose; **wood swallow** any of the fly-catching *Artamidae*, also called swallow-shrikes, the resemblance to shrikes being more fundamental than that to swallows; **wood tar** a product of destructive distillation of wood, containing paraffins, naphthalene and phenols; **wood'thrush** a thrush common in the woods of the eastern United States, reddish-brown above, olive on the rump, white spotted with black on the breast; locally in Britain, the missel thrush or the song thrush; **wood tick** any tick of the family *Ixodidae*, the young of which are transferred to man and animals from bushes; **wood tin** a botryoidal or reniform variety of the tin ore cassiterite showing a concentric structure of radiating brown, wood-like fibres; **wood vinegar** crude acetic acid obtained from wood, pyroligneous acid; **wood warbler** a yellowish-green European warbler, *Phylloscopus sibilatrix*; any bird of the genera *Dendroica*, *Vermivora*, etc of the American family *Parulidae*; **wood'ward** an officer who guards or has charge of the woods; **wood wasp** a large hymenopterous insect (*Sirex*) that bores wood with its ovipositor, the horntail; **wood'wax** or **wood'waxen** dyer's greenweed; **wood'wind** any orchestral wind instrument other than the brass instruments, made, or formerly made, of wood, some now being made of metals such as silver, including the flute, oboe, bassoon, clarinet, etc; (collectively) the section of an orchestra comprising these; **wood wool** fine wood shavings; **wood-wool slabs** slabs made from long wood shavings with a cementing material, used for linings, partitions, etc; **wood'work** the wooden parts of any structure; carpentry or joinery; goalposts, etc (*football, etc*; *colloq*); **wood'worker** a craftsman or worker in wood; **wood'-worm** the larva of any of several beetles, that bores into wood; **wood wren** the willow warbler (*Phylloscopus trochilus*); the wood warbler (*Phylloscopus sibilatrix*); **wood'yard** a yard in which wood is cut and stored. — **Commissioners of Woods and Forests** a department (1810–1924) having charge of the Crown woods and forests; **not see the wood for the trees** to fail to grasp the whole because of the superabundance of, or one's over-concentration on, detail; **out of the wood** or **woods** out of difficulty or danger; **touch wood** or (*US*) **knock** (or **knock on**) **wood** (*usu* as *interj*) to touch something wooden as a superstitious protection against bad luck. [OE *wudu*; cognate with ON *vithr* wood, OIr *fid* timber]

wood[2] *wo͝od*, (*Shakesp*; *Scot* **wud** *wud*) *adj* mad; fierce, furious. — *n* **wood'ness**. [OE *wōd*; ON *ōthr*, Ger *Wut* madness]

woodbine *wo͝od'bīn*, or **woodbind** *wo͝od'bind*, *n* the honeysuckle; applied also to other climbers, such as some kinds of ivy, the Virginia creeper, etc; *perh* bindweed (*Shakesp*); (also with *cap*) someone English, *esp* a soldier (*Austr slang*; from the brand name of a popular and inexpensive cigarette). [OE *wudubind*, from *wudu* wood, and *bind* binding]

woodburytype *wo͝od'bər-i-tīp*, *n* a photo-mechanical process in which an exposed and developed bichromated film is forced into a metal plate by great pressure, and so forms a matrix for subsequent printing. [Named from the inventor]

woodchat, **woodchip**. See under **wood[1]**.

woodchuck *wo͝od'chuk*, *n* a N American species of marmot (*Marmota* or *Arctomys monax*). [Corruption of an Am Indian name]

woodcock ... to ... **wood-engraving**. See under **wood[1]**.

wooden *wo͝od'ən*, *adj* made of or like wood; (of a golf club) having a head made of wood; hard; dull, insensible; heavy, stupid; lacking animation or grace of manner or execution, unnatural, inhibited; clumsy. — *adv* **wood'enly**. — *n* **wood'enness** wooden quality; lack of spirit or expression. — **wood'enhead** (*colloq*) a blockhead, stupid person. — *adj* **woodenhead'ed** having a head made of wood; stupid. — **woodenhead'edness**; **wooden horse** the Trojan horse (qv); a former instrument of punishment in the army (see **horse**); a ship (*archaic*); **wooden kimono** or **overcoat** (*US slang*) a coffin; **wooden leg** an artificial leg made of wood; **wooden pear** an Australian tree whose pear-shaped seed vessels have a woody outside; **wooden spoon** a spoon made of wood presented to the person coming bottom in the mathematical tripos list at Cambridge; hence, a booby prize; **wooden tongue** woody tongue (qv under **woody**); **wood'entop** (*derog slang*) a uniformed policeman; a guardsman; **wooden type** large type cut in wood; **wooden walls** (*literary*) warships (in allusion to Gr *xylinon teichos*, Herodotus 7. 141). [**wood[1]**]

wood-evil ... to ... **woodhouse**. See under **wood[1]**.

woodie *wo͝od'i* or *-ē*, (*Scot*) *n* the gallows. [**widdy[1]**]

woodiness. See under **woody**.

woodland ... to ... **woodreeve**. See under **wood[1]**.

woodruff *wo͝od'ruf*, or (*obs*) **woodroof** *wo͝od'ro͞of*, *n* a plant of the genus *Asperula* of rubiaceous plants with whorled leaves and a funnel-shaped corolla, *esp* **sweet woodruff**, which has small white flowers and a pleasant scent. [OE *wuduroffe*, from *wudu* wood, with unexplained 2nd element]

woodrush ... to ... **woodshed**. See under **wood[1]**.

woodsia *wo͝od'zi-ə*, *n* a fern of a genus of ferns (*Woodsia*; family *Polypodiaceae*) of cool or mountainous regions, with tufted rhizomes. [James *Woods* (1776–1864), botanist]

woodskin ... to ... **woodstone**. See under **wood[1]**.

woodsy. See under **wood[1]**.

woodwale *wo͞o'wāl*, *n* the woodpecker, *esp* the green woodpecker. [ME *wudewale*, from OE *wudu* wood, and an unexplained 2nd element; cf **witwall**]

woodwind... to ... **woodworm**. See under **wood[1]**.

woodwose *wo͝od'wōs* or **woodhouse** *wo͝od'hows*, (*obs* or *heraldry*) *n* a wild man of the woods, a figure sometimes found as a supporter in heraldry; a satyr, faun. [OE *wuduwāsa*, from *wudu* wood, with unexplained 2nd element]

woody *wo͝od'i*, *adj* abounding with woods; inhabiting woods (*Spenser*); situated in a wood; relating to wood; consisting wholly or largely of wood; ligneous; like wood in texture, smell, taste, etc. — *n* **wood'iness**. — **woody nightshade** bittersweet (*Solanum dulcamara*), a purple-flowered climbing plant with poisonous red berries; **wood'y-tongue** actinobacillosis, a chronic inflammation of cattle, rare in sheep and pigs, occasionally transmitted to man, due to infection, *usu* of the tongue, by the fungus *Actinobacillus ligniersi*. [**wood[1]**]

woodyard. See under **wood[1]**.

wooer, **wooing**, etc. See under **woo**.

woof[1] *wo͞of*, *n* weft; thread for a weft; texture. — *adj* **woofed** (*wo͞oft* or *wo͞of'id*) woven. — *adj* **woof'y** dense in texture. [ME *oof*, with *w* added by association with **warp**, etc (*oof* being the normal development of OE *ōwef*, from *on* and *wefan* to weave)]

woof[2] *wo͞of*, (*N Eng*) *n* a catfish. [Origin obscure]

woof[3] *wo͝of*, *n* (an approximate rendering of the sound of a dog's bark. — *vi* (of a dog) to bark; to imitate a dog's bark. — *n* **woof'er** a large loudspeaker used to reproduce low-frequency sounds only (cf **tweeter**). [Imit]

woofter *wo͝of'tər*, (*slang*) *n*. Same as **poofter**.

woofy. See under **woof[1]**.

wool *wo͝ol*, *n* the fleece of sheep, goats, yaks, etc, a modified kind of hair of which the fibres are soft, fine and curly, with an imbricated surface that makes for felting; this spun into yarn or thread for knitting or weaving; fabric or clothing woven or knitted from such yarn; downy hair under the coat of any of various furry animals; short crisply curling human hair, or (*facetious*) one's hair generally; short, thick human hair; any light, fleecy substance like wool, eg the fine soft fibres of some plants; any substance with a fibrous texture, resembling wool, eg steel wool, glass wool, wood wool. — *adj* made of or relating to wool. — *adj* **woolled** (*wŏŏld*) bearing wool. — *adv* **wool'ward** (*obs*) with wool next the skin, *esp* as a penance. — **wool ball** a ball of wool, such as is sometimes found in a sheep's stomach. — *adj* **wool'-bearing** bearing or yielding wool. — **wool card** or **wool comb** a machine for **wool'-carding** or **wool'-combing**, separating the fibres of wool preparatory to spinning; **wool'-carder** or **wool'-comber**; **wool church** an English, *esp* E Anglian, church built or converted using funds accrued during the Tudor wool-trade boom, many seeming of inappropriate size and grandeur for their setting; **wool clip** a crop of wool from a particular flock of sheep, *esp* that gathered in one season; **wool'-driver** a buyer-up of wool. — *adj* **wool'-dyed** dyed before spinning or weaving. — **wool'-fat** lanolin; **wool'fell** (*archaic*) the skin with the wool still on it; **wool'-gathering** absent-minded dreaming. — *adj* dreamy; absent-minded. — **wool'-grower** a breeder of sheep for the production of wool; **wool'-growing**; **wool'man** a dealer in wool; **wool mill** a woollen mill; **wool oil** any oil obtained from woolfat; an oil used to oil wool before spinning; **wool'pack** the bag in which wool was formerly packed for sale, or the fabric of which it was made; a bale or bundle of wool, *esp* formerly weighing 240 lb; cirrocumulus cloud; the woolsack (*obs*); **wool'-packer**; **wool'-picker** a machine for cleaning wool; **wool'sack** (also with *cap*) the seat of the Lord Chancellor in the House of Lords, being a large square sack of wool covered with scarlet; the office of Lord Chancellor; **wool shears** shears used in shearing sheep; **wool'shed** (*Austr* and *NZ*) a large shed for shearing sheep and baling wool; **wool'sorter** a person who sorts wool according to quality, etc; **woolsorter's disease** anthrax; **wool staple** the fibre or pile of wool; a market where wool was sold; **wool'-stapler** a dealer in wool; a woolsorter; **wool'-winder** a person who packs fleeces; **wool'work** needlework done in wool, *usu* in canvas, imitative of tapestry. — **against the wool** against the texture of the wool, the wrong way; **dye in the wool** to dye (wool) before spinning; see also **dye**; **great** or **much cry and little wool** much palaver and little result; **keep one's wool on** (*colloq*) to keep one's hair on, stay calm; **pull** or **draw the wool over someone's eyes** to hoodwink or deceive someone. [OE *wull*; Gothic *wulla*, Ger *Wolle*, L *vellus*]

woold *wŏŏld*, *vt* to wind a rope or chain round. — *adj* **woold'ed**. — *n* **woold'er** a stick used in woolding a mast or yard; a pin in a ropemaker's top. — *n* **woold'ing**. [Du *woelen*; Ger (*be*)*wuhlen*]

woolen. See **woollen**.

woolfat ... to ... **woolled**. See under **wool**.

woollen or (*US*) **woolen** *wŏŏl'ən*, *adj* made of wool; relating to wool; covered of clad in wool; rustic, simple (*obs fig*). — *n* a garment made of wool, *esp* a knitted one; a fabric made from wool. — **wooll'en-draper** a dealer in woollen goods; **wooll'en-drapery**; **woollen mill** a mill where wool is spun and woven into fabric. [**wool**]

woolly *wŏŏl'i*, *adj* made of or consisting of wool; resembling wool in texture or appearance; downy, fleecy; covered or clad in wool or a substance resembling it; (of language, thinking or argument) lacking clarity and logic; hazy, not firm, definite or distinct; (*esp* in *wild and woolly*) having the atmosphere or quality of the Wild West (*colloq*). — *n* (*colloq*) a woollen garment, *esp* a knitted sweater, cardigan, etc; a sheep, *esp* (*Austr*) before shearing (*Austr* and *US colloq*): — *pl* **wooll'ies**. — **woolly aphis** a plant louse (*Eriosoma lanigerum*), covered with hair resembling cotton-wool, that infests *esp* apple trees; **wooll'yback** (*colloq*) a sheep; an unsophisticated person from out of town (*esp Liverpool dialect*): **woolly bear** the hairy caterpillar of a number of moths, including the tiger moths; the larva of the carpet beetle; **wooll'ybutt** (*Austr*) any of a number of eucalyptus trees, eg *Eucalyptus longifolia*, with fibrous bark. — *adj* **wooll'y-haired** having thick soft curly hair; woolly-headed. — **woolly-hand crab** the mitten-crab (qv). — *adj* **wooll'y-headed** having short, crisply-curling hair; woolly-minded. — *adj* **woolly-min'ded** vague, illogical or muddled in thought. — **woolly-min'dedness**. [**wool**]

woolman ... to ... **woolsack**. See under **wool**.

woolsey *wŏŏl'zi*, (*obs rare*) *n* a fabric composed of cotton and wool. [Shortened from **linsey-woolsey**]

woolshed ... to ... **woolwork**. See under **wool**.

woomera *wōō'mə-rə*, **womera** *wom'ə-rə*, or **woomerang** *wōō'mə-rang*, (*Austr*) *n* a stick for launching a spear with greater force. [Aboriginal]

woon *wōōn*, (*Spenser*) *vi*. Same as **won**[3].

woorali, **woorara**. See **wourali**.

woosel, **woosell**. See **ouzel**.

woosh. See **whoosh**.

woot or **woo't** *wōōt*, (*Shakesp*) wilt (thou)? — Also **wot**.

wootz *wōōts*, *n* steel made in India, from ancient times, by fusing iron with carbonaceous matter. [For *wook*, from Kanarese *ukku* steel]

woozy *wōō'zi*, (*colloq*) *adj* fuddled eg with drink or drugs, etc; dazed, dizzy; blurred, woolly, vague. — *adv* **wooz'ily**. — *n* **wooz'iness**. [Origin obscure]

wop[1] *wop*, (*offensive slang*) *n* a member of a Mediterranean or Latin race, eg an Italian, *esp* as an immigrant or visitor. [Perh Ital (dialect) *guappo* swaggerer, from Sp *guapo* lady's man, pimp, ruffian]

wop[2] *wop*, *vt* variant of **whop**: — *pr p* **wopp'ing**; *pa t* and *pa p* **wopped**.

worcester *wŏŏs'tər*, *n* fine woollen material made at *Worcester* (*hist*); (with *cap*; in full **Worcester china**) fine china made there in the mid 18c. — **worces'terberry** a N American species of gooseberry (*Ribes divaricatum*), not a hybrid; **Worcester** (or **Worcestershire** *wŏŏs'tər-shər*) **sauce** a pungent sauce *orig* made in Worcestershire.

Worcs. *abbrev*: Worcestershire.

word *wûrd*, *n* the smallest unit of language that can be used independently; such a unit represented in writing or printing, *usu* separated off by spaces; (in *pl*) language as a means of communication; a saying or expression; a brief conversation; a rumour; a hint; a signal or sign, as in *say the word*; a message, as in *send word*; one's solemn promise; one's expressed will or wishes; a declaration; news or information; a password; a watchword; a war cry; (in *pl*) verbal contention; (in *pl*) discussion in contrast to action; (in *pl*) the lyrics of a song, etc; (in *pl*) the text of an actor's part in a play; used as *combining form* after a letter, to mean 'that (*esp* unmentionable or taboo) word beginning with', eg *m-word* for 'marriage' (*colloq*); a set of bits stored and transferred as a single unit of meaning (*comput*). — *vt* to express in (*esp* carefully chosen) words; to speak to, or of, in words (*obs*; *rare*); to flatter (*Shakesp*). — *vi* (*obs*) to speak, talk. — *n* **word'age** words generally, *esp* text as opposed to pictures, etc; verbiage, wordiness; quantity of words, length of text; choice of words, wording. — *adj* **word'ed** expressed in words. — *adv* **word'ily**. — *n* **word'iness** the quality of being wordy. — *n* **word'ing** the process of expressing in words; choice of words, phrasing; speaking, utterance (*archaic*). — *adj* **word'ish** (*obs*) verbose. — *n* **word'ishness**. — *adj* **word'less** unspoken; silent. — *adj* **word'y** using too many words to say something, long-winded, *esp* pompously so; conducted in words. — **word'-association** (*psychiatry*) the psychoanalytic practice of giving patients a word to which they have to respond with the first word that occurs to them, a technique believed to afford insights into the unconscious; **word bite** (*colloq*) any brief quotable item from a speech, etc, sounding as if it carries an important message. — *adj* **word'-blind**. — **word'-blindness** the lack or loss of the ability to read, a non-technical name for both **alexia** and **dyslexia**; **word'book** a book with a collection of words; a dictionary or vocabulary. — *adj* **word'bound** unable to find expression in words; bound by a promise. — **word'break** (*printing*) the point of division in a word that runs on to the following line; **word'-building** the formation of words from letters or from root words and affixes. — *adj* **word'-deaf** affected by **word'-deafness**, inability to distinguish words, resulting from damage to the auditory part of the brain. — **word-finder** a book designed as a tool for finding a required word; a thesaurus; **word'game** any game or puzzle in which words have to be constructed, deciphered, etc; **word'lore** information about the history, use, etc of words; **word memory** the power of recalling words to the mind; **word order** the sequence in which words are arranged in a sentence, relevant to the sense in many languages, including English; **word'-painter**; **word'-painting** the act or art of describing vividly in words. — *adj* **word'-per'fect** having memorized (words to be repeated, recited, etc) exactly. — **word picture** a description in words that presents an object, scene, etc, to the mind as if in a picture; **word'play** punning or witty repartee exploiting verbal ambiguity, etc; **word'-processing** the arranging and storing of text with the aid of a word-processor; **word'-processor** any of several types of machine that perform electronically the tasks of typing, data-recording, dictating, transcribing, etc, *usu* incorporating screens for visual display; **word'-puzzler** a person who engages in puzzles or games involving words; **word salad** (*psychol*) a confused outpouring of speech consisting of real and non-existent words, typically occurring in severe cases of schizophrenia; **word'smith** an accomplished user of words (sometimes *ironic*); a coiner of words; **word'-smithery**; **word'-splitting** hair-splitting, quibbling; **word square** a square grid composed of a set of words that read the same down as they do across; **word'-wrapping** (*comput*) (on a visual-display unit) the automatic placing of the word being input on to a new line when the last character space on the line the word was keyed into is filled before the word is completed, wraparound. — **at a word** without more ado, at once; to be brief, in short (*obs*); **a word in someone's ear** a confidential conversation; **be as good as one's word** to keep one's promise; **break one's word** to fail to keep one's promise; **by word of mouth** orally, through the spoken word (*adj* **word'-of-mouth'**); **eat one's words** to retract what one has said, or apologize for it, *usu* under compulsion; **fair words** (*archaic*) pleasant, conciliatory words, *usu* implying flattery or deceit; **get a word in edgeways** to interpose what one needs to say with difficulty into a conversation dominated by others or another; **have a word with** to speak to, *usu* for some specific purpose; **have no words for** to be at a loss to describe or express; **have words** to quarrel, dispute (with *with*); **in a** (or **one**) **word** in short, to sum up; **in other words** saying the same thing in a different way; **in so many words** explicitly; bluntly; **in word** in one's speech or professions only, in contrast to one's deeds; **keep one's word** to fulfil one's promise; **my word** or (*old*) **upon my word** a mild interjection expressing surprise, dismay, etc; **not the word for it** not a strong enough word to express or describe it; **of few** (or **many**) **words** taciturn (or verbose); **of one's word** (in *a man of his word*, etc) having a reputation for keeping one's promises; **on my word** on my honour, truly; **pass one's word** to make a promise; **put in a good word for** to make commendatory mention of (someone) in a quarter where it will do him or her good; **put words into someone's mouth** to attribute or supply to someone words that he or she did not, or does not intend to, use; **take someone at his** (or **her**) **word** to take someone's offer, etc literally; **take someone's word for it** to accept what someone says as true, when one has no means of knowing personally; **take the words out of someone's mouth** to say exactly what someone else was about to say; **take** (or **take up**) **the word** to begin speaking or continue a discourse begun by someone else; **the last word** the closing remark in an argument, *esp* if having an appearance of conclusiveness; the conclusive statement; the ultimate authority; (also **the latest word**) the most up-to-date design or model, the most recent advance in something or a consummate example of it; **the Word** (*Christian relig*) the Scriptures; the gospel message; the second person in the Trinity, the Logos; **too funny**, **stupid**, etc **for words** (*colloq*) exceptionally funny, stupid, etc; **word for word** literally, verbatim. [OE; Gothic *waurd*, ON *orth*, Ger *Wort*; L *verbum* word, Gr *eirein* to say, speak]

Wordsworthian *wûrdz-wûr'thi-ən*, *adj* pertaining to the poet William *Wordsworth* (1770–1850) or his style. — *n* an admirer or imitator of Wordsworth.

wore *wōr* or *wör*, *pa t* of **wear**[1,2].

work *wûrk*, *n* physical or mental effort directed towards making or achieving something; employment; one's place of employment; tasks to be accomplished; that on which one is labouring, one's task or workpiece; the product of mental or physical labour, anything made or done; materials for accomplishing one's task; needlework, embroidery (*old*); a deed; doings; the result of action; the manner of performing or completing a task, quality of working, workmanship; (*usu* in *pl*) an action in its moral aspect, *esp* as tending to justification (*theol*); a literary, artistic, musical or dramatic composition or creation; a book; (as *combining form*) things made, or ornamentation executed, in the material or with the tools specified, as in *basketwork*, *woolwork*, *crewelwork*; (as *combining form*) the parts of a building, etc in a specified material, as in *brickwork*, *stonework*, *woodwork*, *paintwork*; (in *pl*) building or repair operations, as in *roadworks*, *clerk of works*; (in *pl*) a factory, workshop (as *adj*, of a racing-car, entered officially in a race by the manufacturer); (in *pl*) walls, ramparts, trenches, etc (*fortif* or *archaeol*); (in *pl*) the mechanism or operating parts, eg of a watch; (in *pl*) the syringe and associated drug-injecting equipment (*drug-taking slang*); the act of producing an effect by means of a force (F) whose point of application moves through a distance (s) in its own line of action, measured by the product of the force and the distance (W = Fs; *phys*); the spin given to a ball by a bowler to cause it to break on pitching (*cricket*); (by confusion with OE *wærc*) ache, trouble, fuss (*dialect*). — *adj* relating to, suitable for, etc work, as in *work clothes*. — *vi* to exert oneself mentally or physically to achieve or attain anything, to toil, labour or study; to perform the tasks and duties involved in a job; to be occupied in business or labour; to move, or make one's way, slowly and laboriously; to move or shift gradually out of position, as in *work loose*; (of a ship's timbers) to shift and gape through the action of wind and water; to be in action; to operate, function; to produce effects; to behave in the desired way when operated; to prove practicable; (of a craftsperson; with *in*) to fashion things in (a certain material); to ache, be painful (*dialect*); to ferment; (of eg features) to be agitated, move convulsively; to strain, labour; to sail in a course, *esp* to beat to windward (*naut*); to contrive, plan (*archaic*). — *vt* to impose tasks on, to cause to labour; to put in motion or operate (a machine, etc); to shape or fashion (material or an artefact); to cultivate (land); to extract materials from (a mine); to knead or manipulate (dough); to cause to ferment; to sew or embroider (*old*); to cover (an area) as a sales representative, etc; to achieve (miracles, wonders, etc) to effect or seek to effect (one's revenge); to manipulate (a system, rules, etc) to one's advantage (*colloq*); to influence, cajole or trick (*colloq*; *reflexive*) to get (oneself into an emotional state, rage, etc); to make (one's way); to cause to shift little by little, by persistent manipulation; to exercise (a part of the body); to purge (*dialect*); to solve by mathematical calculation (*NAm*); to earn (one's sea passage) by unpaid work on board; to finance (one's way through university, etc) by doing paid work: — *pa t* and *pa p* **worked** or (*archaic*) **wrought** (qv as separate article). — *n* **workabil'ity** or **work'-ableness**. — *adj* **work'able** that may be worked; practicable. — *adj* **workaholic** (*wûr-kə-hol'ik*) addicted to work (coined facetiously in imitation of *alcoholic*;

see **-aholic**). — Also *n*. — *n* **work'aholism**. — *adj* **worked** that has been treated or fashioned in some way; embroidered; ornamented. — *n* **work'er** someone who works; a toiler; someone employed in manual work; (among social insects) one of a caste of sterile individuals that do all the work of the colony. — *n* **work'erist** (*old*) a supporter of proletarian rights and values, *esp* (*derog*) one of upper or middle class. — Also *adj*. — *adj* **work'ful** industrious. — *n* **work'ing** the act or process of shaping, making, effecting, solving, fermenting, etc; an exposition of the process of calculation (*math*, etc); manner of operating or functioning; (in *pl*) internal processes; endeavour (*obs*); (in *pl*) deeds (*obs*); mental or emotional activity (*obs*); contortion due to agitation; slow and laborious progress; (in *pl*) the parts of a mine, etc where work is, or has been, carried on. — *adj* active; operational; labouring; having a job or employment; relating to labour, a job or employment; (of a period of time) devoted to, or denoting that part that is devoted to, work; adequate for one's purposes, as in *working knowledge*; stirring the emotions (*obs*). — *adj* **work'less** having no job, unemployed. — Also *n pl*. — *adj* **work'some** (*Carlyle*) industrious. — *adj* **work'aday** suitable for a work day, plain and practical; toiling; dull, prosaic. — *n* (*obs* or *dialect*) a working day. — **work'bag** and **work'basket** respectively a bag and basket for holding materials for work, *esp* needlework; **work'bench** a bench, often purpose-built, at which a craftsman, mechanic, etc works; **work'boat** one used for work such as fishing, harbour maintenance, carrying industrial supplies, etc rather than for naval or passenger service; **work'book** a book of exercises, often with spaces for the answers, to accompany another book; a record book of jobs undertaken, in progress or completed; **work'box** a box for holding instruments or materials for work; **work camp** a camp attended by *esp* young people who work voluntarily, and *usu* manually, on projects of benefit to the community; **work'day** a day for work, a weekday. — *adj* relating to a workday. — **worker director** a worker appointed to the board of a firm so as to represent its employees in policy-making discussions; **worker participation** the involvement of workers in decision-making; see also **participate**; **worker priest** a priest in the Roman Catholic Church who also works full-time or part-time in a secular job in order to understand better the problems of lay people; **workers' co-operative** a business or other enterprise jointly owned and run by its members, who share the profits; **work ethic** the general attitude of a group towards work, *esp* one (**Protestant work ethic**) which places a high moral value on (hard) work; **work'fare** an unemployment benefit scheme under which recipients are required to do work of some kind, *usu* some kind of public service; **work'fellow** someone engaged on the same job as oneself, a workmate; **work'folk** or **work'folks** workers; **work'force** the number of workers engaged in a particular industry, factory, etc; the total number of workers potentially available; **work function** (*phys*) the minimum energy that must be supplied to eject an electron from a material in a vacuum, such energy being produced by heating the material or by illuminating it with radiation; **work'girl** a girl or young woman employed in manual labour. — *vt* **work'=harden** (*eng*) to harden and strengthen (metals) by working (*esp* cold-working) them, subjecting them to processes such as hammering and rolling. — **work'=hardening**; **work'horse** a horse used in a labouring capacity rather than for recreation, racing, etc; a person, machine or anything else heavily depended on to do arduous work, give intensive service, etc; **work'house** (*hist*) a house where any work or manufacture is carried on; a house of shelter for the poor, who are given work to do; **work-in** see **work in** below; **work'ing-beam** a walking-beam (qv); **working breakfast, lunch**, etc one arranged as an alternative to a formal meeting, for the discussion of diplomatic or other business; **working capital** see under **capital**[1]; **working class** (often in *pl*) the class in society that comprises manual workers and wage-earners (*adj* **work'ing-class**); **working day** a day on which work is done; the period of actual work each day. — *adj* (**wor'king-day**) laborious; plodding; ordinary. — **working drawing** a drawing of the details of the construction or assembly of something by which the builders are guided in their work; **working edge** an edge of a piece of wood trued square with the working face to assist in truing the other surfaces square; **working face** that face of a piece of wood which is first trued and then used as a basis for truing the other surfaces; **working girl** (*colloq*; *orig US*) a prostitute; **working hours** the period of the day during which work is normally done, and offices, shops, etc are open; **working house** (*obs*) a workshop; **working hypothesis** an assumption on the basis of which to make plans or take action; **working lunch** see **working breakfast**; **working majority** a majority sufficient to enable the party in office to carry on without accidental defeats; **working man** or **woman** a worker, *esp* a manual one; **working model** a model of a machine that can do, on a smaller scale, the same work as the machine; **working paper** a paper produced as a basis for discussion, to report on progress made, etc, rather than as a final statement; **working** (or **work**) **party** a group of people who carry out a specially assigned task; a group appointed to investigate a subject, such as methods of attaining maximum efficiency in an industry; **working week** or (*NAm*) **work'week** that part of the week in which work is normally done, *esp* Monday to Friday; any week in which such work is done, as opposed eg to holidays; **work'load** the amount of work assigned to an individual, machine, etc for completion within a certain time; **work'man** a man who works, *esp* manually; a skilful artificer or craftsman. — *adj* **work'manlike** like a workman; befitting a skilful workman; well performed. — *adj* **work'manly** befitting a skilful workman, workmanlike. — *adv* (*old*) in a workmanlike manner. — **work'manship** the skill of a workman; manner of making; the degree of expertise shown in making something, or of refinement of finish in the completed product; that which is made or produced by one's hands (also *fig*); **work'master** or **work'mistress** an expert worker or craftsperson, overseer or employer; **work'mate** a companion at work, a workfellow; **work=out** see **work out** below; **work'people** people engaged in manual labour, workers; **work'piece** a piece of work in progress, being manufactured; something on which a tool or machine is working; **work'place** the office, factory, etc where one works; **work'room** a room for working in; **works committee** or **council** a body on which both employer and employees meet to handle labour relations within a business; **work'-sharing** job-sharing (qv); **work'sheet** a paper or form on which to detail work planned or performed; **work'shop** a room or shop where work is done; a group of people working on a creative or experimental project; such a project. — *adj* **work'shy** hating or avoiding work, lazy. — Also *n pl*. — **work station** (in a production line) a position at which a particular job is done; (in an office or other workplace) a computer terminal having a keyboard, screen and processor, or the location of this; **work study** a time and motion study; **work'table** a table on which work is done, *esp*, formerly, a small table used by ladies at their needlework; **work'top** a surface designed for working on, fitted eg along the top of kitchen units, etc; **work'watcher** (*horse-racing*; *euphem*) a tout; **work'wear** overalls or other clothing for work, issued to factory workers, etc; **workweek** see **working week**; **work'woman** a woman who makes her living by manual labour. — *adj* and *n* **work'y-day** (*obs*) workaday. — **a work of time** a change, achievement, etc requiring or brought about by time; **give someone the works** (*slang*) to give someone the full punitive, coercive, ceremonial, etc treatment considered appropriate to his or her case;

have one's work cut out to have one's work prescribed; to be faced with a difficult task; **in working order** functioning properly; **make short work of** to accomplish, dispose of or consume speedily; **Ministry** (previously **Office) of Works** (formerly) the body having the management and control of public works and buildings, the expenses of which are defrayed from public money; **out of work** without employment (*adj* and *n pl* **out'-of-work'** unemployed (people)); **place of work** one's workplace (qv); **set to work** to employ in, or to engage energetically in, a piece of work; **Seven Works of Corporal Mercy** to feed the hungry, give drink to the thirsty, clothe the naked, visit prisoners, visit the sick, harbour strangers, bury the dead; **Seven Works of Spiritual Mercy** to convert sinners, instruct the ignorant, counsel the doubtful, console the afflicted, bear wrongs patiently, forgive injuries, pray for the living and the dead; **shoot the works** see under **shoot**[1]; **the works** (*colloq*) everything possible, available or going, the lot; **work at** to apply oneself to; **work back** (*Austr*) to work overtime; **work double tides** (*naut*) to work night and day; **work for** (or **against**) to exert oneself in support of (or in opposition to); **work in** to intermix; to introduce carefully and deliberately; to cause to penetrate; (of workers) to continue at work, *esp* by occupying the premises and taking over the running of the business, as a protest against proposed factory closure, dismissal, etc (*n* **work'-in**); **work into** to make way gradually into; to insinuate; to change or alter into; **work of art** a painting, sculpture or other production in the fine arts, *esp* one of high quality; anything constructed or composed with manifest skill; **work off** to separate and throw off; to get rid of by effort and exertion, or little by little; to repay (a debt, etc) with one's labour rather than with money; to print ready for circulation; to pass or palm off (*colloq*); to dispose of by hanging (*old slang*); **work on** or **upon** to act or operate on; to try to perfect or improve; to use one's powers of persuasion on; to use (an assumption, hypothesis, etc) as a basis for planning, etc; **work out** to solve or calculate; to develop in detail, elaborate; to study fully (*rare*); to loosen or come out little by little; to turn out in the end; to reach a final (satisfactory) result; (of an athlete, etc) to train, exercise (*n* **work'-out**); to effect by continued labour; to expiate, to discharge (a debt or obligation) with one's labour (*old*); to make by cutting, digging, etc (*obs*); to exhaust (a mine); **work over** to do or work at thoroughly or elaborately; to examine in detail; to beat up, thrash (*slang*; *n* **work'-over** or **work'ing-over**); **work through** to deal with (a problem, *esp* an emotional one) in one's own way, *esp* by absorption in it for some time; **work to rule** (of workers) to observe all the regulations scrupulously for the express purpose of slowing down work, as a form of industrial action (*n* **work'-to-rule'**); **work up** (often in *pa p*) to excite, agitate or rouse; to create by slow degrees; to summon up (an appetite, enthusiasm, energy, etc); to expand, elaborate; to use up (eg material); to give an irksome or needless task to (*naut*); to move upwards little by little; (with *to*) to reach or achieve, by effort and gradually; **work with** to strive to influence by appeals, etc. [OE *weorc*; ON *verk*, Ger *Werk*; further connected with Gr *ergon*]

world *wûrld*, *n* the earth; the earth and its inhabitants; the universe; the system of things; the present state of existence; any analogous state; any planet or heavenly body; public life or society; a sphere of interest or activity; environment; the public; the materialistically minded; mundane interests; a secular life; the course of life; one of the three kingdoms of nature; a class or division; a part, or a related group of parts, of the world, historically, sociologically or geographically speaking, as in *Ancient World, Third World, Old World*; a great deal, as in *did her a world of good*; a large quantity, as in *a world of ills*; time, as in *world without end*; the realm of possibility, as in *nothing in the world*; the ungodly (*Bible*). — *adj* **world'ed** containing worlds. — *n* **world'liness**. — *n* **world'ling** someone who is devoted to worldly pursuits and temporal possessions; a mortal (*obs*). — *adj* **world'ly** relating to the world, *esp* as distinguished from the world to come; devoted to this life and its enjoyments; bent on gain; having knowledge and experience of the ways of the world; mortal (*obs*). — Also *adv*. — **World Bank** the popular name of the International Bank for Reconstruction and Development, an agency of the United Nations set up in 1945 to make loans to poorer countries; **world'-beater** (*colloq*) a person, product, enterprise, etc that is supreme in its class. — *adj* **world'-beating**. — *adj* **world'-class** good enough to be classed with or compete with the best in the world. — **World Court** the popular name of the Permanent Court of International Justice at the Hague, set up under the League of Nations in 1921 to settle or advise on disputes between states; **World Cup** an international competition in some sport, notably football, participating teams *usu* having qualified in preliminary rounds. — *adj* **world-fa'mous** known or renowned throughout the world. — **world language** a language either widely used internationally or designed for international use; **world line** (*phys*) a curving line in space-time representing the path of a particle during its existence. — *adj* **world'ly-mind'ed** having one's mind set on the present world, material possessions, etc. — **world'ly-mind'edness**. — *adj* **worldly-wise'** having the wisdom of those experienced in, and affected by, the ways of the world, knowing, cynical. — *adj* **world'-old** exceedingly ancient. — **world music** popular folk music with its origins in non-western cultures, particularly African culture, *esp* as produced by non-Western artists; **world power** a state, group of states, etc, strong enough to make its influence felt in world politics; **world'scale** the scale of freight rates for oil-tankers; **World Series** (*baseball*) a set of championship matches played annually in the US. — *adj* **world'-shaking** or **world'-shattering** (*usu ironic*) devastatingly important. — **world sheet** (*phys*) the 2-dimensional space occupied by a string in its space-time history; **world'-view** outlook on or attitude to the world or life; **World War** a war of worldwide scope, *esp* the Great War of 1914–1918 (First World War, World War I) and that of 1939–45 (Second World War, World War II). — *adj* **world'-wearied** or **world'-weary** tired of the world, bored with life. — *adj* and *adv* **world'wide** (extending) over, or (found) everywhere in, the world. — **all the world** everybody; everything; **all the world and his wife** (*colloq*) everybody; an ill-assorted assembly; **best** (or **worst) of both worlds** the advantage (or disadvantage) of both alternatives in a choice; **bring into the world** to give birth to; to attend the birth of, deliver; **carry the world before one** to pass through every obstacle to success; **come into the world** to be born; **come up** (or **down) in the world** to rise (or fall) in social status; **dead to the world** (*colloq*) deeply asleep; in a drunken stupor; **for all the world** (*colloq*) precisely or entirely (as if); **Fourth World** see under **fourth**; **go to the world** (*Shakesp*) to get married; **in the world** used intensively, *esp* after an interrogative pronoun or adverb; **next world** life after death; **not for the world** not for any reward, not under any circumstances; **on top of the world** (*colloq*) in a state of great elation or happiness; **out of this world** wonderful, delightful, good beyond all experience; **set the world on fire** to create a sensation, have spectacular success; **the New World** the western hemisphere, the Americas; **the Old World** the eastern hemisphere, comprising Europe, Africa and Asia; **the other world** the non-material sphere, the spiritual world; **the whole world** the sum of what is contained in the world; **the world is one's oyster** see **oyster**; **the world over** throughout the world, worldwide; **the world's end** the most distant point possible; **the world, the flesh and the devil** temptations of the kind that notoriously distract one from the path of virtue; **the world to come** the next world, the life after death; **think the world of** to be very fond of; **Third World** see under **third**; **world without end** eternally (*adj* **world'-without-end'**). [OE *woruld*, *world*, *weorold*, orig meaning age or life of man, from *wer* man, and the root of **old**; ON *veröld*, OHGer *weralt* (Ger *Welt*)]

WORM *wûrm*, (*comput*) *abbrev*: write once read many times, denoting an optical disk used for read-only storage of data.

worm *wûrm*, *n* a small long slender cylindrical animal without backbone or limbs, *esp* one of the Chaetopoda, including the earthworm and marine worm; any superficially similar but unrelated animal, such as the flatworms (Platyhelminthes) and the roundworms (Nematoda); a grub; a maggot; a snake or a dragon (*archaic*); any creeping or crawling animal (*obs*); anything spiral; the thread of a screw; the lytta or vermiform cartilage of the tongue of a dog or other carnivorous mammal; a spiral pipe for condensation in distilling; anything that corrupts, gnaws or torments; remorse; a mean, grovelling or in any way contemptible creature; (in *pl*) any intestinal disease characterized by the presence of parasitic worms; any ailment supposed to be caused by a worm, eg toothache (*obs*); a tick or mite in the hand, etc, *esp* one alleged humorously to infest the hands of idlers (*obs*); a piece of software designed, like a virus, for sabotage, differing from a virus in being an independent program rather than a piece of coding, which, once inserted into a network, reproduces itself like a parasitic worm throughout it (*comput*). — *vi* to seek for or catch worms; to move or make one's way like a worm, to squirm; to work slowly or secretly. — *vt* to treat for or rid of worms; to cause to be eaten by worms; (*reflexive*) to work (oneself) slowly or secretly; to elicit by slow and indirect means (with *out* or *from*); to remove the lytta or vermiform cartilage from the tongue of; to fill the interstices in (a rope or cable) with spirally wound cord or packing (*orig naut*). — *adj* **wormed** bored through or damaged by worms. — *n* **worm'er**. — *n* **worm'ery** a place, apparatus, etc in which worms are bred, eg as fishing bait. — *adj* **worm'y** like a worm; grovelling; containing a worm; abounding in worms; relating to worms; dank-smelling; dismal, like the grave. — **worm'cast** a little spiral heap of earth voided by an earthworm or lugworm as it burrows; **worm conveyor** the Archimedes screw (qv). — *adj* **worm'-eaten** eaten into by worms; old; worn-out. — *adj* **worm'-eating** living habitually on worms. — **worm fence** a zigzag fence formed of stakes crossing at their ends; **worm fever** a feverish condition in children ascribed to intestinal worms; **worm gear** a gear connecting shafts whose axes are at right angles but do not intersect, consisting of a core carrying a single- or multi-start helical thread of special form (the *worm*), meshing in sliding contact with a concave-face gear-wheel (the *worm wheel*); **worm gearing**; **worm grass** pinkroot, any of several types of pink, whose roots are used as a vermifuge; a kind of stonecrop (*Sedum album*); **worm'hole** the hole made by a woodworm, earthworm, etc; a hypothetical tunnel in space-time, serving as a short cut between widely distant parts of it (*phys*). — *adj* **worm'holed** perforated by wormholes. — **worm powder** a drug that expels intestinal worms, a vermifuge; **worm'seed** any of a number of plants that (are said to) have anthelmintic properties, ie expel or destroy intestinal worms, such as certain species of Artemisia (eg *Artemisia santonica*), *Erysimum cheiranthoides* (**treacle wormseed** or **treacle mustard**), *Chenopodium anthelminticum*, etc; the drug santonica; **worm tube** the twisted shell or tube produced by several marine worms; **worm wheel** see **worm gear** above. — **the worm may turn** the most abject of victims may be goaded into retaliating. [OE *wyrm* dragon, snake, creeping animal; cognate with Gothic *waurms* a serpent, ON *ormr*, Ger *Wurm*; also with L *vermis*]

Wormian *wûrm'i-ən*, *adj* associated with the name of the Danish anatomist Olaus *Worm* (1588–1654), applied *esp* to the supernumerary bones developed in the sutures of the skull.

wormwood *wûrm'wŏŏd*, *n* the bitter plant *Artemisia absinthium*, formerly used as a vermifuge, with which absinthe is flavoured (see also **absinthe**); (a source of) acute chagrin or bitterness. [OE *wermōd* (Ger *Wermuth*) wormwood; of doubtful origin, but influenced by **worm** and **wood**[1]]

worn *wōrn* or *wörn*, *pa p* of **wear**[1]. — *adj* that has been worn; showing effects of wear, or (*fig*) of work, worry, illness, age, etc; (of land) exhausted; hackneyed, trite. — *adj* **worn'-out** extensively damaged or rendered useless by wear; (of expressions, language, etc) ineffective from overuse; wearied; exhausted; (of time) past, gone (*obs*).

worral or **worrel** *wor'əl*, *n* a monitor lizard. [Ar *waral* lizard]

worricow, **worrycow** or **wirricow** *wur'i-kow*, (*Scot*) *n* a hobgoblin; the devil; anything frightful or even only grotesque. [**worry** (verb), and *cow* a hobgoblin]

worrit *wur'it*, *vt*, *vi* and *n*. Dialect form of **worry**.

worry *wur'i*, *vt* to cause to be anxious; to harass; to pester; to tease; to tear with the teeth; to devour ravenously (*Scot*); to make, get, etc by persistent methods; to choke (*Scot*). — *vi* to trouble oneself; to be unduly anxious; to fret: — *pa t* and *pa p* **worr'ied**. — *n* trouble, perplexity; anxiety; a cause of this; a spell or bout of worrying; an act of biting and shaking by a dog, etc. — *adj* **worr'ied**. — *adv* **worr'iedly**. — *n* **worr'ier**. — *n* **worr'iment** (*colloq*; *esp NAm*) worry, anxiety; the cause of this. — *adj* **worr'isome** (*old*) inclined to worry; causing worry, vexatious. — *n* and *adj* **worr'ying**. — *adv* **worr'yingly**. — **worry beads** a string of beads serving as an object for the hands to play with, as a means of relieving mental tension, *esp* popular in Greece; **worr'yguts** (*colloq*) and **worr'ywart** (*wur'i-wört*; *colloq*, *esp US*) a person who worries unnecessarily or to excess. — **I should worry!** (*colloq ironic*) I'm the last person who should worry; **not to worry** (*colloq*, *esp NAm*) there's no cause for alarm; **worry down** to swallow with a strong effort; **worry out** to find a solution to by intense or anxious effort. [OE *wyrgan*, found in compound *āwyrgan* to harm; cf Du *worgen*, Ger *würgen* to strangle]

worrycow. Same as **worricow**.

worse *wûrs*, *adj* (used as *compar* of **bad** and **ill**) more bad; more ill; more grave, serious or acute; inferior in standard. — *n* something worse, as in *worse was to come*. — *adv* less well; more badly or severely. — *vt* (*obs*) to worst. — *vi* and *vt* **wors'en** to grow or make worse. — *n* **worse'ness**. — *adj* and *adv* **wors'er** a redundant comparative of *worse*. — **could do worse than** would be well-advised to (do something); **for better or for worse** whatever may befall of good fortune or bad; **for the worse** to a worse state; **go by** or **with the worse** (*obs*) to lose, be defeated; **go from bad to worse** to get even worse, to deteriorate further; **have the worse** to be at a disadvantage; to be defeated; **none the worse for** not harmed by; **put to the worse** (*Bible*) to defeat; **the worse for** harmed or impaired by; **the worse for wear** worn or shabby from use; in a poor state of health, drunk (*colloq*); **worse off** financially poorer. [OE *wyrsa* (Gothic *wairsiza*), formed with compar sfx from a Gmc root *wers*, found in Ger (*ver*)*wirren* to confuse, entangle]

worship *wûr'ship*, *n* adoration paid to a deity, etc; religious service; profound admiration and affection; glorification, exaltation, idolization; the act of revering or adoring; dignity, reputation, high standing (*archaic*); a position of honour (*obs*); (with *cap* preceded by *Your*, *His*, etc) a title of honour in addressing or referring to certain magistrates, etc. — *vt* to pay divine honours to; to adore or idolize; to glorify or exalt (something unworthy, eg money); to honour, respect, treat with signs of honour (*obs*). — *vi* to perform acts of adoration; to take part in religious service: — *pr p* **wor'shipping**; *pa t* and *pa p* **wor'shipped**. — *adj* **wor'shipable** capable of being worshipped. — *adj* **wor'shipful** worthy of worship or honour; used as a term of respect in addressing certain dignitaries, eg mayors; worshipping, adoring. — *adv* **wor'shipfully**. — *n* **wor'shipfulness**. — *adj* **wor'shipless** without worship or worshippers. — *n* **wor'shipper**. — **house** or **place of worship** a church or chapel, synagogue, mosque or temple; **win one's worship** (*obs*) to gain honour or fame. [OE *weorthscipe*, from *weorth*, *wurth* worth, and sfx *-scipe* -ship]

worst *wûrst*, *adj* (used as *superl* of **bad** and **ill**) most bad, evil, unpleasant, etc; most grave, severe, acute or dire; most inferior, lowest in standard. — *adv* most badly; most gravely, acutely or severely. — *n* the most advanced degree of badness; the most bad, or least good, thing, part, state, effect or possibility. — *vt* to get the better of in a contest; to defeat; to damage or make worse (*obs*). — *vi* (*obs*) to grow worse. — **worst case** the most unfavourable circumstances possible (*adj* **worst'-case**). — **at** (or **at the**) **worst** in the worst possible circumstances, taking the most negative view possible; **at its**, etc **worst** in the worst state or severest degree; **do one's worst** to do one's utmost in evil or mischief; to produce one's worst possible effort, whether deliberately or not; **get the worst of it** or **come off worst** to be defeated in a contest, be the loser in a given situation; to produce one's worst possible effort, whether deliberately or not; **if the worst comes to the worst** if the worst or least desirable possibility occurs; if all else fails. [OE *wyrst*, *wyrrest*, *wyrresta*, from the same source as **worse**]

worsted[1] *wŏŏst'id*, or *wōōrst'id*, *n orig* a fine wool fabric; twisted thread or yarn spun out of long, combed wool; smooth, closely-woven material made from this; woollen yarn for ornamental needlework. — *adj* made of worsted yarn. — **worst'ed-work** needlework done with worsted. [*Worstead*, village near Norwich, England]

worsted[2] *wûrst'id*, *pa t* and *pa p* of **worst**.

wort[1] *wûrt*, *n* any herb or vegetable (now *rare* except as *combining form*); *specif* a plant of the cabbage kind (*obs*). [OE *wyrt* a root, herb; Ger *Wurz*, *Wurzel* a root]

wort[2] *wûrt*, *n* malt unfermented or in the process of fermentation (*sweetwort*); such liquor boiled with hops (*hopped-wort*); malt extract used as a medium for the culture of micro-organisms. [OE *wyrt*;cf Ger *Würze* spice; related to **wort**[1]]

worth[1] *wûrth*, *n* value; price; an amount of something (the value of) which is expressed in money or otherwise, as in *a thousand pounds' worth of equipment*, *three days' worth of work*; that quality which renders a thing valuable; moral excellence; merit; importance; possessions (*obs*). — *adj* equal in value to; having possessions to the value of; deserving, justifying, meriting, repaying or warranting (consideration, attention, the effort, the journey, taking some action, etc); valuable (*archaic*); worth while (*obs*). — *adj* (*archaic*) **worth'ful** honourable; meritorious; valuable. — *adj* **worth'less** having no value, virtue, excellence, etc; useless; unworthy (*obs*). — *adv* **worth'lessly**. — *n* **worth'lessness**. — *adj* **worthwhile'** such as to repay trouble and time spent on it (predicatively also, strictly, **worth while**; see **while**); good; estimable; useful, beneficial or rewarding. — **for all it's**, etc **worth** to the utmost; **for all one is worth** with all one's might or energy; **for what it is worth** a phrase implying that one is doubtful of the truth of what one has to report or unwilling to be responsible for its accuracy, or aware that one's proposal or suggestion may be of minimal worth; **well worth** amply repaying the effort of; **worth it** worth while. [OE *weorth*, *wurth* (Ger *Wert*) value]

worth[2] *wûrth*, *vi* to be, become, happen, as in the phrase **woe worth** woe be (to). [OE *weorthan* to become; cf Ger *werden*]

worthy *wûr'dhi*, *adj* having worth; valuable; estimable (*esp patronizing*); (with *of*) deserving; fit (to be or do something); deserving of (*archaic*); (with *of*) suited or appropriate to, in keeping with, proper for; of sufficient merit, fit, adequate, as in *a worthy successor*; of high social position (*obs*). — *n* a person of eminent worth; a notability, *esp* local (sometimes *ironic*); anything of value, an excellence (*Shakesp*): — *pl* **wor'thies**. — *vt* (*obs*) to make worthy, to honour. — *adv* **wor'thily**. — *n* **wor'thiness**. — *adj sfx* **-worthy** fit, in good condition for, as in *roadworthy*; deserving of, as in *trustworthy*, *noteworthy*. — **nine worthies** *usu* listed as Hector, Alexander the Great, Julius Caesar: Joshua, David, Judas Maccabaeus: Arthur, Charlemagne, Godfrey of Bouillon; **worthiest of blood** (in questions of succession) male as opposed to female. [**worth**[1]]

wortle *wûr'tl*, or **whirtle** *wûr'tl*, *hwûr'tl*, *n* a perforated plate through which wire or tubing is drawn to make it thinner. [Ety uncertain]

wos. See under **woe**.

wosbird *wōz'bûrd*, (*dialect*) *n* a variant of **whore's bird**.

wost. See under **wit**[1].

wot[1], **wottest**, **wotteth**, etc. See under **wit**[1].

wot[2]. See under **woot**.

wot[3]. A facetious spelling of **what**.

Wotan *wō'tan* or *vō'tan*, (*mythol*) *n* the German name for the god Woden (qv).

wotcher *wot'chər*, (*slang*) *interj* a greeting, developed from *archaic* **what cheer**? how are you?

wotted, **wotting**. See under **wit**[1].

woubit *wōō'bit*, *n* (*usu* **hairy woubit**) a hairy caterpillar, *esp* one of a tiger moth; applied derogatorily to a person, often implying smallness and shabbiness. — Also **woo'but**, **ou'bit** or **oo'bit**. [ME *wolbode*, *wolbede*; prob from *wol* wool, with unexplained second element]

would *wŏŏd* (formerly, eg in *Spenser*, *wōld*) *pa t* of **will**[1], used: in reported speech; to suggest willingness or readiness on the part of someone or something, as in *the car would not start*; to express probability and condition; to express lack of surprise or indicate frustration at events, another's perversity, etc; to formulate invitations, suggestions, offers, requests and desires: — *2nd pers sing* (*archaic*; with *thou*) **wouldst** (*wŏŏdst*). — *n* the desired or intended, as distinct from *could*, or *should*. — *adj* **would'-be** aspiring, or merely professing, to be; meant to be. — *n* a vain pretender. — **would (that)**, also **would to God** (or **to heaven**, etc) **(that)** (*literary* or *archaic*) used to express (*esp* vain) desires. [OE *wolde*, pa t of *wyllan* to wish, will]

Woulfe bottle *wŏŏlf bot'l*, *n* a *usu* three-necked bottle used for purifying gases, or dissolving them in suitable solvents, from the London chemist Peter *Woulfe* (*c*.1727–1803).

wound[1] *wownd*, *pa t* and *pa p* of **wind**[1,2].

wound[2] *wōōnd*, *n* any open injury to living animal or plant tissue externally caused by eg cutting, piercing, striking, crushing, tearing or poisoning; a surgeon's incision; an injury caused to the pride, feelings, reputation, etc. — *vt* to make a wound in, inflict a wound on; to injure (feelings, etc). — Also *vi*. — *adj* **wound'able** capable of being wounded. — *n* **wound'er**. — *adv* **wound'ily** (*archaic*) excessively. — *n* and *adj* **wound'ing**. — *adv* **wound'ingly**. — *adj* **wound'less** unwounded; invulnerable (*obs*); harmless. — *adj* and *adv* **wound'y** (*archaic*) excessive(ly). — **wound tissue** (*bot*) protective tissue that forms in response to wounding; **wound'wort** any of several plants popularly held to have wound-healing properties, such as the kidney-vetch, and a number of plants of genus *Stachys* (*marsh* or *clown's woundwort*). [OE *wund* (Ger *Wunde*, ON *und*); also OE *wund* wounded]

wourali or **woorali** *wōō-rä'li*, **woorara** (*wōō-rä'rə*), **ourali** or **ourari** (*ōō-rä'ri*), **urali** (*ōō-rä'li*) or **urari** (*ōō-rä'ri*), *n* the plant yielding curare (qv). [Caribbean variants of *kurari*; see **curare**]

wou-wou. See **wow-wow**.

wove and **woven** *pa t* and *pa p* of **weave**[1]. — **wove paper** paper with a fine, uniformly smooth surface, as distinct from *laid paper* with its impressed pattern of chain lines and wire lines.

WOW (*oil industry*) *abbrev*: waiting on weather.

wow[1] *wow*, *interj* an exclamation of wonder, mingled with other emotions such as aversion, sorrow, admiration or pleasure (see **whow**). — *vt* (*slang*) to impress (an audience, etc) considerably, to amaze, bowl over. — *n* (*slang*) anything thrillingly good, successful, or according to one's wishes. — *interj* **wowee'** an intensification of **wow**. [Perh orig Scot]

wow[2] *wow*, *vi* to howl. — *n* a bark; a howl; rhythmic or arrhythmic changes in reproduced sound, fundamentally arising from fluctuations in speed, of comparatively long cycle, in the operation of either reproducer or recorder. [Imit]

wow[3] *wow*, (*Spenser*) *vt* to woo.

wowf *wowf*, (*Scot*) *adj* crazy. [Origin unknown]

wowser *wow'zər* (*esp Austr slang*) *n* a puritanical person who tries to interfere with the pleasures of others, a spoilsport. [Origin uncertain]

wow-wow or **wou-wou** *wow'-wow*, *n* the name for two types of gibbon found in Indonesia, the *silver gibbon* of Java and the *agile gibbon* of Sumatra. [Imit of its cry]

wox and **woxen** (*obs*) *pa t* and *pa p* of **wax**[2].

WP or **wp** *abbrev*: weather permitting; word-processing or word-processor; (**WP**) Warsaw Pact.

Wp *abbrev*: Worship or Worshipful.

wpb (*colloq*) *abbrev*: wastepaper basket.

WPBSA *abbrev*: World Professional Billiards and Snooker Association.

WPC *abbrev*: Woman Police Constable.

Wpfl *abbrev*: Worshipful.

wpm *abbrev*: words per minute.

WR *abbrev*: Western Region.

WRAAC *abbrev*: Women's Royal Australian Army Corps.

WRAAF *abbrev*: Women's Royal Australian Air Force.

WRAC *rak*, *abbrev*: Women's Royal Army Corps.

wrack[1] *rak*, *n* vengeance, punishment (*obs*); destruction, devastation (cf **rack**[2]); what remains after devastation, a remnant (in *Shakesp*, *Tempest*, IV.1.156 a misalteration of *rack*; see **rack**[2]). — *adj* **wrack'ful** (*rare*) destructive. [OE *wræc*, from *wrecan* to drive; connected, and confused, with **wrack**[2]]

wrack[2] *rak*, *n* a wreck (*dialect*); wreckage; seaweed cast ashore, or growing where it is exposed by the tide (*archaic*); any of the *Fucaceae*, the bladderwrack family of seaweeds. [MDu or MLGer *wrak*; cf **wrack**[1]]

wrack[3] *rak*, *vt* to torture, torment. [An erroneous spelling of **rack**[1]]

WRAF *raf*, *abbrev*: Women's Royal Air Force.

wraith *rāth*, *n* a spectre; an apparition, *esp* of a living person; a person of spectral thinness and pallor. [Orig Scot; perh ON *vörthr* a guardian]

wrangle *rang'gl*, *vi* to dispute noisily or peevishly; to argue, debate, dispute (*archaic*). — *vt* to obtain, persuade or tire by, or spend (time) in, wrangling; to debate; to herd (cattle; *NAm*). — *n* a noisy dispute; the activity of disputing, *esp* noisily (*rare*). — *n* **wrang'ler** someone who wrangles; a cattle-herder, a cowboy (*NAm*); (also **horse'-wrangler**) a horseman in charge of or escorting saddle horses or racers (*NAm*); a stubborn foe (*Shakesp*); at Cambridge University, a student gaining first-class honours in the final mathematics examinations, the **senior wrangler** being the student with the highest marks and (formerly) the **second wrangler** the one in second place, and so on. — *n* **wrang'lership**. — *adj* **wrang'lesome** given to wrangling. — *n* and *adj* **wrang'ling**. [ME *wranglen*, a frequentative verb related to **wring**]

WRANS *abbrev*: Women's Royal Australian Naval Service.

wrap[1] *rap*, *vt* to fold (something) round something; to enfold, envelop, clothe, cover or swathe (in something; often with *up*); to pack in paper for posting or presentation; to roll or fold together (*old*); to embrace (*literary*); to hide, obscure; to involve or entangle (*obs*); (with *in*) to absorb or engross; (with *round*) to crash (a vehicle) into (a tree, lamp post, etc; *colloq*). — *vi* to wind, twine or lap (with *round*, etc); (with *up*) to put on a wrap, cloak, etc; to dress warmly: — *pr p* **wrapp'ing**; *pa t* and *pa p* **wrapped**. — *n* a shawl or stole for the shoulders; an outdoor garment (*old*); a light dressing-gown or bathrobe; a protective covering or material for this, a wrapper, wrapping; a wraparound (*printing*); a single turn or fold round (*old*); (in *pl*) secrecy, concealment (*colloq*). — *n* **wrapp'age** the act of wrapping; covering; wrapping materials. — *n* **wrapp'er** someone or something that wraps; formerly, a loose outer garment for a woman; a loose paper book cover, a dust jacket; a paper band, eg put round a newspaper for posting; a paper or cellophane cover for a sweet, packet, etc. — *vt* to cover with a wrapper. — *n* **wrapp'ing** (often in *pl*) any of various types of cover, wrapper or packing material. — **wrap'around** a wraparound skirt, blouse, dress, etc (also **wrap'round**); on a visual display unit, the automatic division of input into lines, whereby a new line is started as the last character position on the previous line is occupied; (also **wrap'-round**) a plate of flexible material, such as plastic, rubber or metal that wraps round a cylindrical plate (*printing*); (also **wrap'round**) a separately printed sheet that is wrapped round a gathering for binding (*printing*); (also **wrap'round**) a strip advertising a special offer, etc, wrapped round the dust cover of a book, etc. — *adj* (of a blouse, skirt, dress, etc) designed so as to be wrapped round the body with one edge overlapping the other, and tied, tucked in, etc rather than fastened by a zip, row of buttons, etc (also **wrap'over** or **wrap'round**); (of a windscreen, bumper, etc) curving round from the front to the sides (also **wrap'round**). — **wrap'over** a wraparound skirt or other garment; **wrapp'ing-paper** paper, either strong and coarse, or decorative, for parcels; **wrap'-ras'cal** a loose greatcoat worn in the 18c (*humorous*); **wrapround** see **wraparound** above. — **keep under wraps** (*colloq*) to keep secret, conceal; **take the wraps off** (*colloq*) to reveal, disclose; **wrapped up in** bound up in; comprised in; engrossed in, devoted to; **wrap up** (*slang*) to settle completely; to have completely in hand; (as *interj*) be quiet! (*offensive*). [ME *wrappen*, also *wlappen*]

wrap[2], **wrapt**. Erroneous forms of **rap**[2], **rapt**.

wrap[3], **wrap up**. See under **rap**[5].

wrasse *ras*, *n* any of several brightly coloured bony fishes of the family *Labridae* including many species on European and N African coasts. [Cornish *wrach*, related to Welsh *gwrach* old woman]

wrast. Obsolete Northern form of **wrest** directly from Old Norse.

wrate. Obsolete and Scot *pa t* of **write**.

wrath *röth*, *roth*, or (*Scot*) *räth*, *n* violent anger; an instance, or fit, of anger (*obs*); divine indignation, the righteous anger of God; violence or severity (of eg a storm); ardour (*Shakesp*). — *adj* (*archaic*) angry, wroth. — *vt* and *vi* (*obs*) to make or become angry. — *adj* **wrath'ful** very angry; springing from, expressing or characterized by wrath. — *adv* **wrath'fully**. — *n* **wrath'fulness**. — *adv* **wrath'ily**. — *n* **wrath'iness**. — *adj* **wrath'less**. — *adj* **wrath'y** (chiefly *US*) inclined to wrath; expressing or characterized by wrath; fierce, tempestuous. [OE *wrǣththu*, from *wrāth*, adj; cf **wroth**]

wrawl *röl*, (*Spenser*) *vi* (of a cat) to caterwaul. [Imit]

wraxle *rak'sl*, (*dialect*; *SW England*) *vi* to wrestle. — *n* **wrax'ling**. [OE *wraxlian*; cf **wrestle**]

wreak[1] *rēk*, *vt* to effect, bring about or cause (harm, havoc, damage, etc); to inflict (vengeance, one's revenge, etc; with *on*); to give expression, vent, free play to (anger, etc); (*reflexive*; of a feeling, quality, etc) to find expression or outlet for (itself); to bestow; to punish (*obs*); to harm (*obs*); to avenge (*archaic*); to take vengeance on (*obs*); to revenge (with *of*) (*obs*); to drive out (*obs*): — *pa t* **wreaked**, *archaic* **wrōke**; *pa p* **wreaked**, *archaic* **wrōk'en**, *Spenser* **wrōke** or **ywrōke**. — *n* punishment, vengeance (*archaic*); damage (*obs*). — *n* **wreak'er** (*archaic*). — *adj* **wreak'ful** revengeful; avenging. — *adj* **wreak'less** unpunished. [OE *wrecan* to drive, push; ON *reka* to drive, pursue, avenge; Ger *rächen*; connected with L *urgēre*]

wreak[2] *rēk*, (*Spenser* and *Shakesp*) for **reak**[2], variant of **reck**. — Also (*Milton*) **wreck**.

wreath *rēth*, *n* a circlet or ring of flowers or foliage, eg for wearing on the head as a symbol of honour, or laying on a grave as a tribute; a circlet of other intertwined materials; a representation of such a circlet beneath a crest (*heraldry*); a carved representation of a wreath of foliage (*archit*); a single twist or coil in a helical object; a drift or curl of vapour or smoke; a snowdrift; a defect in glass: — *pl* **wreaths** (*rēdhz*). — *vt* **wreathe** (*rēdh*) to form by twisting; to twist together; to form into a wreath; to twine about or encircle; to twist or contort (limbs); to cause (the face) to crease or pucker (in smiles); (of snow) to cover by drifting (*Scot*); to encircle, decorate, etc with a wreath or wreaths. — *vi* to be interwoven; to twine; to twist; to form coils; (of snow) to form a drift or wreath (*Scot*); to turn (*obs*). — *adj* **wreathed** (*rēdhd* or *rēdh'id*). — *adj* **wreath'en** (*rē'dhən*; *archaic pa p*) wreathed. — *n* **wreath'er** (*rē'dhər*). — *adj* **wreath'less**. — *adj* **wreath'y** (*rē'thi* or *rē'dhi*). — **wreathed string** (*building*) the continuous curved outer string round the well hole of a wooden stair; **wreath filament** the usual type of filament in large gas-filled electric lamps, the filament wire being festooned from a horizontal supporting spider. [OE *writha*; related to *wrīthan* to writhe]

wreck[1] *rek*, *n* destruction; the act of wrecking or destroying; the destruction of a ship; a badly damaged ship; shipwrecked property; anything found underwater and brought ashore; the death of a large number of oceanic birds, eg during a storm; the remains of anything ruined; a person ruined mentally or physically; a dilapidated or unserviceable vessel or vehicle (*colloq*). — *vt* to destroy or disable; to cause the wreck of (a ship); to involve in a wreck; to cast up, eg on the shore; to ruin. — *vi* to suffer wreck or ruin. — *n* **wreck'age** the process of wrecking; wrecked material; a person whose life is, or people whose lives are, ruined. — *n* **wreck'er** a person who purposely causes a wreck or who plunders wreckage; someone who criminally ruins anything; a person who (or machine which) demolishes or destroys; a person or ship employed in recovering disabled vessels or their cargo; a person, vehicle or train employed in removing wreckage; a vehicle equipped with a hoisting device, used to tow wrecked or disabled motor vehicles (*US*); a person who is employed in demolishing buildings, etc. — *adj* **wreck'ful** (*poetic*) causing ruin. — *n* and *adj* **wreck'ing**. — **wreck buoy** a buoy, *usu* green, marking the position of a wrecked vessel; **wreck commissioners** a tribunal that inquires into shipping disasters; **wreck'fish** the stone bass, a large perch of the Atlantic, Mediterranean and Tasman Sea, *Polyprion americanus*, having the reputation of frequenting wrecked ships; **wreck'master** a person taking charge of a disabled ship or train and its cargo or freight. — **receivers of wrecks** wreckmasters. [Anglo-Fr *wrec*, *wrek*, etc, of Scand origin; related to **wreak**]

wreck[2]. See **wreak**[2].

Wren *ren*, *n* a member of the WRNS.

wren *ren*, *n* a member of a genus (*Troglodytes*) of small songbirds, having very short and rounded wings, and a short tail carried erect, or of any of several related genera, together forming the family *Troglodytidae*; *specif* in the UK, *Troglodytes troglodytes*; extended to various very small birds, such as the **golden-crested wren** (goldcrest) and the **willow wren** (willow warbler). — **wren tit** a Californian bird (*Chamaea fasciata*) resembling the wren and the titmouse. [OE *wrenna*, *wrænna*]

wrench *rench* or *rensh*, *vt* to pull (something from someone or something) *esp* with a twisting or wringing action; to force or wrest violently; to shift with the help of a wrench; to sprain; to distort. — *vi* to turn or twist suddenly or violently. — *n* an act or instance of wrenching; a violent twist; a sprain; an instrument for turning nuts, etc, an adjustable spanner; a separation or change that is difficult to bear, or the pain of this; (in coursing) bringing the hare round at less than a right angle. [OE *wrencan* to deceive, twist, *wrenc* deceit, twisting; cf Ger *renken* to twist, *Rank* trick, intrigue]

wrenching *rensh'ing*, (*Shakesp*) *n* for *renching*, from dialect verb *rench* to rinse.

wrest *rest*, *vt* to turn, twist, or (*obs*) screw; to twist, extract or take away, by force or unlawfully; to get by toil (eg a living from an unpromising environment); to twist from truth or natural meaning, to distort; to misinterpret; to pervert; to derive improperly (*Spenser*); to sprain (*Scot*). — *vi* (*Spenser*) to force a way. — *n* the act of wresting; violent pulling and twisting; distortion; a wrench-like key for tuning a piano, etc (*archaic*). — *n* **wrest'er**. — **wrest block** or **wrest plank** (in a piano, etc) the board fitted with the wrest pins; **wrest pin** a pin round which the end of a wire (eg a piano wire) is wound, turned by the wrest. [OE *wrǣstan*; Dan *vriste*]

wrestle *res'l*, *vi* to contend with another person by grappling, each trying to throw and then pinion the other; to struggle or tussle (with *with*); to apply oneself keenly to mastering something (with *with*); to pray earnestly (*with* God; *old*); to strive (*with* one's conscience, etc); to dispute, debate, argue, wrangle; to writhe, wriggle; to proceed laboriously. — *vt* to contend with in wrestling; to push or force with a wriggling or wrestling motion; (with *out*) to go through, carry out, with a great struggle. — *n* a bout, or the activity, of wrestling; a struggle. — *n* **wrest'ler**. — *n* **wrest'ling** a sport or exercise in which two people struggle to throw and pin each other to the ground, governed by certain fixed rules; the activity of struggling, grappling, striving, contending, etc. [OE *wrǣstan* to wrest]

wretch *rech*, *n* a most miserable, unfortunate or pitiable person; a worthless or despicable person; a being, a creature (in pity or sometimes admiration); an exile or outcast (*obs*). — *adj* (*Spenser*) wretched. — *adj* **wretched** (*re'chid*) very miserable, distraught; unfortunate, pitiable; distressingly bad, pitiful; despicable; worthless; used to intensify, as in *wretched nuisance*, *bore*, etc. — *adv* **wretch'edly**. — *n* **wretch'edness**. [OE *wrecca* an outcast, from *wrecan*; see **wreak**[1]]

wrethe *rēth*, (*Spenser*) *vt* and *vi*. Same as **wreathe**.

WRI *abbrev*: Women's Rural Institute.

wrick or **rick** *rik*, *vt* to twist, sprain or strain. — *n* a sprain or strain. [Related to LGer *wrikken* to turn]

wrier, **wriest**. See **wry**.

wriggle *rig'l*, *vi* and *vt* to twist to and fro; to move, advance or make (one's way) sinuously or deviously. — *vi* to use evasive tricks; (with *out of*) to evade or shirk (responsibilities, etc). — *n* an act or the motion of wriggling; a sinuous or wavy marking, a turn or bend. — *n* **wrigg'ler**. — *n* **wrigg'ling**. — *adj* **wrigg'ly**. [LGer *wriggeln*; cf Du *wriggelen* to wriggle]

wright *rīt* (*Scot rihht*), *n* (*esp* as *combining form*) a maker, deviser or repairer, as in *shipwright*, *playwright*, *wainwright*, etc); a carpenter or joiner (*Scot*). [OE *wyrhta*, *wryhta*, related to *wyrht* a work, from *wyrcan* to work]

wring *ring*, *vt* to twist; to expel moisture from (cloth, etc) by squeezing between rollers or twisting by hand; to force out (moisture) from cloth, etc by twisting; to force (eg tears) from someone, to extract *esp* with difficulty; to clasp and shake (someone's hand) fervently; to clasp or twist (the hands) together convulsively in grief or agitation; to break (the neck) of a bird, etc by twisting; (of a shoe) to pinch (*old*); to harrow or rend (the heart); to hurt or injure (*old*); to extort or exact (a consent, admission or money) from someone; to bend or strain out of position; to distort; to wreathe, coil (*rare*). — *vi* to twist or writhe (*rare*); to feel pain (*rare*): — *pa t* and *pa p* **wrung**, *obs* **wringed**. — *n* an act or instance of wringing; a cider press, wine press or cheese press. — *n* **wring'er** someone who wrings; a machine for forcing water from wet clothes (also **wring'ing-machine**). — *n* **wring'ing**. — **wring bolt**

(*naut*) a bolt with a ring or eye, used to secure a ship's planks against the frame till they are permanently fixed in place, a ring bolt. — *n pl* **wring staves** (*sing* **wring staff**) strong pieces of wood used in applying wring bolts. — **wringing wet** so wet that water can be wrung out; **wring off** to force off by wringing; **wring out** to squeeze (moisture) out by twisting; to twist (a wet garment, cloth, etc) so as to expel the drops of liquid. [OE *wringan* to twist; Du *wringen*, Ger *ringen*]

wrinkle[1] *ring'kl*, *n* a small crease or furrow on a surface; a crease or ridge in the skin (*esp* as a result of ageing); an unevenness; a minor problem or difficulty to be smoothed out. — *vt* to contract into wrinkles or furrows; to make rough. — *vi* to shrink into ridges. — *adj* **wrink'led**. — *adj* **wrink'ly** full of wrinkles; liable to get wrinkled. — *n* (*esp* in *pl*; *colloq derog*) an elderly person. [History obscure; noun and verb may be back-formations from adj **wrinkled**]

wrinkle[2] *ring'kl*, (*colloq*) *n* a tip, valuable hint; a handy dodge or trick; an idea, notion, suggestion. [Perh from OE *wrenc* a trick; perh same as **wrinkle**[1]]

wrist *rist*, *n* the joint by which the hand is connected to the arm, the carpus; the part of the forearm where this joint is, or the part of a garment covering it; a corresponding part of an animal; a wrist pin. — *n* **wrist'let** a band or strap for the wrist; a bracelet; a watch for wearing on the wrist (also **wristlet watch**); a handcuff (*slang*). — *adj* **wrist'y** making extensive use of the wrist or wrists, as in a golf shot, etc. — **wrist'band** a band or part of a sleeve covering the wrist; **wrist drop** inability to extend the hand, often caused by lead poisoning; **wrist pin** a pin joining the end of a connecting rod to the end of a piston rod; **wrist shot** a short stroke using power mainly from the wrist, *usu* played with an iron club (*golf*); **wrist'watch** a watch worn on a strap round the wrist, a wristlet watch. — **a slap** or **smack on the wrist** (*colloq*) a slight but *usu* formal punishment or reprimand. [OE; allied to *wrīthan* to twist; Ger *Rist*]

writ[1] *rit*, *archaic pa t* and *pa p* of **write**. — **writ large** written in large letters, hence on a large scale or very obvious.

writ[2] *rit*, *n* a legal or formal document; a written document by which one is summoned or required to do, or refrain from doing, something (*law*); a writing (*rare*). — **Holy Writ** (also without *caps*) the Scriptures; **serve a writ on** (*law*) to deliver a summons to; **writ of execution** (*law*) a written order for the execution of a judgement. [OE (*ge*)*writ*; ON *rit*, Gothic *writs*]

write *rīt*, *vt* to form (letters, symbols, numbers, words, sentences) with a pen, pencil, etc on a surface, *esp* paper; to express in writing; to compose, be the composer or author of; to inscribe, carve or engrave (a surface); to record, state or communicate in a letter, book, article, etc; to decree or foretell; to make out or fill in (a prescription, cheque, etc); to transfer (data) to a memory or storage device (*comput*); to display (a quality, condition, etc) all too clearly, as in *guilt written all over her face*; to communicate with by letter; to underwrite (an insurance policy). — *vi* to perform or practise the art of writing; to be employed as a clerk; to compose articles, novels, etc; to work as an author; to compose or send a letter; to communicate with a person by letter: — *pr p* **wrīt'ing**; *pa t* **wrōte**, (*archaic*) **writ** (*rit*); *pa p* **written** (*rit'n*), (*archaic*) **writ**. — *adj* **wrīt'able** capable of being expressed or described in writing; suitable for writing with. — *adj* **wrīt'ative** (*rare*) inclined, or characterized by an inclination, to write. — *n* **wrīt'er** someone who writes; a professional scribe or clerk; an ordinary legal practitioner in a Scottish country town; an author or his or her works; someone who paints lettering for signs; a seller (of options) (*stock exchange*): — *fem* **wrīt'eress** (*rare*). — *adj* **wrīt'erly** having or showing an accomplished literary style. — *n* **wrīt'ership** the office of a writer. — *n* **wrīt'ing** the act or activity of recording, expressing or communicating by inscribing words, letters, etc; that which is written; (often in *pl*) a literary production or composition; (in *pl* with *cap*) the Old Testament books known as the Hagiographa (qv; *relig*); handwriting, penmanship; the state of being written. — *adj* **writt'en** reduced to or expressed in writing (*opp* of *oral*). — **write'-back** an amount restored to a company's accounts because the size of an earlier liability had been overestimated; **write-down** see **write down** below. — *adj* **write'-in** (*NAm*) of or relating to a candidate not listed in the ballot paper, but whose name is written in by the voter. — *n* such a candidate or vote. — **write'-off** a car so badly damaged that the cost of repair would exceed the car's value; a crashed aircraft (*airmen's slang*); a total loss; see also **write off** below; **writer's cramp** see under **cramp**; **write-up** see under **write up** below; **writ'ing-book** a book of paper for practising penmanship; **writ'ing-case** a portable case containing materials for writing; **writ'ing-desk** a desk with a sloping top for writing on; a portable writing-case; **writ'ing-ink** ink suited for writing with; **writ'ing-master** a master who teaches the art of penmanship; the yellow-bunting; **writ'ing-pad** a pad of writing-paper; **writ'ing-paper** paper finished with a smooth surface, for writing on; **writ'ing-school** (*hist*) a school for penmanship; **writ'ing-table** a table designed or used for writing on; **written law** statute law as distinguished from common law. — **nothing to write home about** see **home**; **write away** see **write off** below; **write down** to put down in written characters; to write in disparagement of; to write so as to be intelligible or attractive to people of lower intelligence or inferior taste; to reduce the book value of an asset (*n* **write'-down**); **write in** to write a letter to an organization, etc; (with *for*) to apply for or request in such a letter, send away for; to insert (extra matter) in writing into a document, etc; to add (the name of an extra candidate) to a ballot paper (*US*; *adj* and *n* **write'-in**); **write off** to cancel, *esp* in book-keeping, to take (eg a bad debt) off the books; to regard or accept as an irredeemable loss; to destroy or damage irredeemably (a car, etc) (*n* **write'-off**); (*reflexive*) to get (oneself) killed (*airmen's slang*); (also **write away**; with *for*) to apply for or request in a letter to an organization, etc; to compose (eg a letter) with fluent ease; **write out** to transcribe; to write in full; (*reflexive*) to exhaust one's mental resources by too much writing; to remove (a character or scene) from the script of a film, broadcast, etc; **write protect** (*comput*) protecting of data on disk from alteration or erasure, eg by software command or a mechanical device on the disk (*adj* and *vt* **write-protect'**); **Writer to the Signet** a member of an ancient society of solicitors in Scotland who formerly had the exclusive right to prepare all summonses and other writs pertaining to the supreme court of justice, and still have the exclusive privilege of preparing crown writs; **write to** (*comput*) to record (data) on to (magnetic disk); **write up** to put a full description of in writing; to write a report or review of; to write in praise of, *esp* to praise above its merits; to bring the writing of (one's diary, etc) up to date; to increase the book value of an asset (*n* **write'-up**); **writing** (also, *esp US*, **handwriting**) **on the wall** a happening or sign foreshowing downfall and disaster (Daniel 5.5 *ff*); **written off** (of a car) damaged beyond reasonable repair; completely ruined; (of a person) killed (*airmen's slang*); (of an aircraft) wrecked (*airmen's slang*); see also **write off** above. [OE *wrītan*, orig meaning to scratch; ON *rīta*]

writhe *rīdh*, *vi* to move the body sinuously; to twist and contort oneself in agony; to feel acute shame or embarrassment (*colloq*). — *vt* to twist or coil; to intertwine (*obs*); to contort or distort (*obs*). — *n* a twist or a contortion. — *adj* **writhen** or **wrythen** (*ridh'ən*; *archaic*) twisted, convoluted, contorted. — *n* and *adj* **wrīth'ing**. — *adv* **wrīth'ingly**. [OE *wrīthan* to twist; ON *rītha*; cf **wreath**, **wrest**, **wrist**]

writhled *rith'ld*, (*archaic*) *adj* wrinkled, shrivelled. [Perh **writhe**]

writing, **written**, etc. See under **write**.

wrizled *riz'ld*, (*Spenser*) *adj* wrinkled. [Perh **writhled**]

WRNS *renz*, *abbrev*: Women's Royal Naval Service.

wroath *rōth*, (*Shakesp*) *n* misfortune. [Prob from **ruth**]

wroke, **wroken**. See under **wreak**[1].

wrong *rong*, *adj* incorrect; erroneous; morally unacceptable, immoral, wicked, sinful; unacceptable according to some other recognized or imposed standard eg of taste or judgement; not that (thing or person) which is required, intended, advisable or suitable; amiss, unsatisfactory; defective, faulty; mistaken, misinformed; (of one side of a garment, fabric, etc) intended to be turned inward or under, not intended to be on view, under, inner, reverse; crooked, curved, twisted, bent (*obs*). — *n* whatever is not right or just; any injury done to another; wrongdoing; damage, harm (*rare*). — *adv* incorrectly; not in the right way, improperly, badly; away from the right direction, astray. — *vt* to treat unjustly, do wrong to; to judge unfairly, impute fault to unjustly; to deprive of some right; to defraud; to dishonour; to seduce (*old*); to harm physically (*obs* and *Scot*); to impair, spoil (*obs*). — *n* **wrong'er** a person who wrongs another. — *adj* **wrong'ful** wrong; unjust; unlawful; not legitimate; unjustly held (*Spenser*). — *adv* **wrong'fully**. — *n* **wrong'fulness**. — *adv* **wrong'ly**. — *n* **wrong'ness**. — *adj* **wrong'ous** (*rong'gəs* or *rong'əs*; *old*) unjust, illegal, wrongful. — *adv* **wrong'ously**. — **wrong'doer** an offender or transgressor; **wrong'doing** evil or wicked action or conduct. — *vt* **wrong-foot'** to cause to be (physically or mentally) off balance, or at a disadvantage. — *adj* **wrong-head'ed** obstinate and perverse, adhering stubbornly to wrong principles or policy. — *adv* **wrong-head'edly**. — **wrong-head'edness**. — *adj* **wrong-mind'ed** having erroneous views. — **wrong number** a telephone number with which a caller is connected in error, *esp* through misdialling; a call involving such a misconnection. — *adj* **wrong'-timed'** (*old*) inopportune. — **wrong 'un** (*colloq*) a dishonest character, a rogue; a googly (*cricket*). — **do wrong** to act immorally or illegally; **do wrong to (someone)** or **do (someone) wrong** to treat (someone) unjustly; (with *oneself*) to be mistaken (*obs*); **get hold of the wrong end of the stick** to misunderstand something totally; **get in wrong with** (*colloq*) to get on the wrong side of; **get off on the wrong foot** see under **foot**; **get on the wrong side of** to arouse dislike or antagonism in; **get out of bed on the wrong side** to get up in the morning in a bad mood; **get wrong** to misunderstand; to misinterpret (a person) as in (*colloq*) **don't get me wrong**; to get the wrong answer to (a sum, puzzle, question, etc); **go down the wrong way** (of food) to enter the trachea instead of the oesophagus; **go wrong** (of plans, etc) to fail to go as intended; to make a mistake or mistakes; to stray morally; to stop functioning properly; **have wrong** (*obs*) to suffer injustice or injury; **in the wrong** holding an erroneous view or unjust position; guilty of error or injustice; **private wrong** a violation of the civil or personal rights of an individual; **public wrong** a crime which affects the community; **put in the wrong** to cause to appear in error, guilty of injustice, etc; **wrong in the head** (*colloq*) mentally unbalanced, mad; **wrong side out** inside out; **wrong way round** or **up** respectively back to front and upside down. [OE *wrang* a wrong; most prob ON *rangr* unjust; related to OE *wringan* to wring (like Fr *tort* from L *tortus* twisted)]

wroot. Obsolete form of **root**[2] and **wrote**.

wrote *rōt*, *pa t* of **write**.

wroth *rōth* or *roth*, (*literary* or *poetic*) *adj* wrathful; in commotion, stormy. [OE *wrāth* angry; cf ON *reithr*]

wrought *röt*, *archaic pa t* and *pa p* of **work**. — *adj* made, formed, fashioned or manufactured; decorated or ornamented; (of metal) beaten into shape as distinct from being cast. — **wrought iron** malleable iron, iron containing only a very small amount of other elements, but containing slag in the form of particles elongated in one direction, more rust-resistant than steel and welding more easily (*adj* **wrought'-iron**). — *adj* **wrought'-up** in an agitated condition, over-excited. [OE *worhte*, *geworht*, pa t and pa p of *wyrcan*, *wircan* to work]

WRP *abbrev*: Workers' Revolutionary Party.

wrung *rung*, *pa t* and *pa p* of **wring**.

WRVS *abbrev*: Women's Royal Voluntary Service (previously **WVS**).

wry *rī*, *adj* (of a facial expression) with the features twisted into a grimace; (of a remark, sense of humour, etc) mocking, bitter, ironic or sardonic; twisted or turned to one side or in the wrong direction; perverse, cross, ill-natured (*old*): — *compar* **wry'er** or **wri'er**; *superl* **wry'est** or **wri'est**. — *n* (*rare*) distortion. — *vi* to swerve, to go astray (*obs*); to be deflected, undergo deflection (*obs*); to writhe (*obs*). — *vt* to give a twist to, contort (*archaic*); to avert (the face, head, etc; *obs*); to pervert (*obs*). — *adv* wryly. — *adv* **wry'ly**. — *n* **wry'ness**. — **wry'bill** a New Zealand bird (*Anarhynchus frontalis*), related to the plovers, having a sideways-curving bill with which it gets food from under stones. — *adj* **wry'-mouthed** having a crooked mouth; (of criticism, etc) mocking, bitter (*old*). — **wry'neck** a twisted position of the head on the neck due to spasm, with torsion of the cervical muscles, or to congenital injury to a neck muscle; a member of a genus of small birds (Jynx) related to the woodpecker, which twist round their heads strangely when surprised. — *adj* **wry'-necked** having wryneck, or a twisted neck; denoting a kind of fife, either as having a twisted neck or played with the head on one side (*Shakesp*). — **make** or **pull a wry face** or **mouth** to pucker up the face or mouth in reaction to a bitter or astringent taste, or to pain, or to express disgust or distaste. [OE *wrīgian* to strive, move, turn]

wrythen. See under **writhe**.

WS *abbrev*: Western Samoa (IVR); Writer to the Signet.

WSW *abbrev*: west-south-west.

wt *abbrev*: weight.

WTO *abbrev*: Warsaw Treaty Organization.

Wu *wōō*, *n* a group of Chinese dialects, spoken in the coastal provinces of Kiangsu and Chekiang. [Chin]

wud. Scots form of **wood**[1,2].

wulfenite *wōōl'fən-īt*, *n* a molybdate of lead, $PbMoO_4$, occurring commonly as yellow crystals in veins with other lead ores, named after F X von *Wulfen* (1728–1805), an Austrian mineralogist.

wull[1] *wul*, (*Spenser* and *dialect*) *vi*. Same as **will**[1].

wull[2]. See **will**[3].

wunderkind *vōōn'dər-kint*, *n* a child prodigy; someone who achieves remarkable success early in life: — *pl* **wun'derkinder** (*-kin-dər*). [Ger, literally wonder child]

wunner. See **oner** under **one**.

wurley *wûr'li*, (*Austr*) *n* an Aborigine's hut, traditionally made of branches, bark, leaves and plaited grass; a nest, *esp* a rat's nest: — *pl* **wur'leys** or **wur'lies**. [Aboriginal]

Würm *vürm*, *n* the fourth stage of glaciation in the Alps. — Also *adj*. — *adj* **Würm'ian**. [From a river of Upper Bavaria]

wurst *vōōrst* or *wûrst*, *n* a large German sausage of several types. [Ger, literally something rolled; cf L *vertere*, to turn]

wurtzite *wûrts'īt*, *n* sulphide of zinc, ZnS, of the same composition as sphalerite, but crystallizing in the hexagonal system, in black hemimorphic pyramidal crystals. [From the French chemist C A *Wurtz* (1817–84)]

wus or **wuss** *wus*, (*S Welsh dialect*) *n* a term used to address a companion, mate, pal. [Welsh *gwas* servant]

wushu, **Wushu**, **wu shu** or **Wu Shu** *wōō'shōō*, *n* the Chinese martial arts, kung fu. [Chin, from *wu* military, and *shu* art]

wuther *wudh'ər*, (*dialect*) *vi* to move swiftly or with force; (of the wind) to make a sullen roaring. — *vt* to throw or beat violently. — *n* a blow or blast, or the sound of these; a tremble. — *adj* **wuth'ering** (of the wind) blowing strongly with a roaring sound; (of a place) characterized by windy weather of this kind. — Also **whither** (*widh'ər* or *hwidh'ər*). [From ON]

wuzzle *wuz'l*, (*US*) *vt* to jumble.

WV *abbrev*: St Vincent, Windward Islands (IVR); West Virginia (US state; also **W.Va.**).

WVS. See **WRVS**.

WWF *abbrev*: Worldwide Fund for Nature (formerly World Wildlife Fund); World Wrestling Federation.

WWI or **II** *abbrev*: World War I or II.

WX *abbrev*: women's extra.

WY or **Wy**. *abbrev*: Wyoming (US state).

Wy *abbrev*: Way (in street names).

wyandotte *wī'ən-dot*, *n* a useful breed of the domestic fowl, of American origin. [From the name of a N American tribe]

wych, **wich** or **witch** *wich*, *n* and *combining form* a tree with pliant branches, such as the rowan. — **wych'-alder** any of a genus of N American shrubs related to the witch-hazel; **wych'-elm** a common wild elm, also called Scotch elm or witch-hazel; **wych'-hazel** a less common spelling of **witch-hazel**. [OE *wice*, related to *wīcan* to give way]

Wyclifite or **Wycliffite** *wik'lif-īt*, *adj* relating to the English reformer and translator of the Bible, John *Wyclif* or *Wycliffe* (*c*.1329–84). — *n* a follower of Wyclif; a Lollard.

wye *wī*, *n* the letter Y (qv) or anything shaped like it. — **wye level** see **Y**.

Wykehamist *wik'əm-ist*, *n* a pupil or former pupil of Winchester College, which was founded by William of *Wykeham*, Bishop of Winchester (1324–1404).

wyliecoat *wī'li-kōt*, (*Scot*) *n* a flannel undervest or petticoat; a nightdress. [Unexplained first element, and prob **coat**]

wyn or **wynn** *win*, *n* a rune ᚹ, having the value of modern English *w*, adopted into the OE alphabet as Ƿ ƿ. — Also formerly **wen** (*wen*). [(Initial letter of) OE *wynn* joy]

wynd *wīnd*, (*Scot*) *n* a narrow alley or lane in a town. [From the stem of **wind**[2]]

Wyo. *abbrev*: Wyoming (US state).

wysiwyg *wiz'i-wig*, (*comput*) an acronym for *w*hat *y*ou *s*ee (ie on the screen) *i*s *w*hat *y*ou *g*et (on the print-out).

wyte. See **wit**[1], **wite**[1].

wyvern. Same as **wivern**.

X

X or **x** *eks*, *n* the twenty-fourth letter in the modern English alphabet, and twenty-first of the Roman alphabet, taken from the Chalcidian alphabet, and of the same form, though perhaps not the same origin, as Ionic and classical Greek chi (*X*, *χ*; pronounced *k-h*, and later *hh*); an object or symbol in the shape of the letter X. (X was used in Old English medially and finally as a variant for *cs*. In modern English, medially and finally, it has the value of *ks*, as in *extinct* and *axe*, and, medially only, of *gz*, as in *exist*, or *ksh*, as *usu* in *luxury*, or *gzh*, as in *luxurious*; (at the beginning of a word it is *usu* pronounced *z*, or, rarely, *gz*).

X *symbol*: (also **x** or *x*) the first variable, unknown or yet to be ascertained quantity or factor (*algebra*, etc); (as a Roman numeral) ten (X representing a thousand, X̄ ten thousand); Christ (see also **chi**[1]), also used as an abbreviation, as in **Xmas** and **Xian** (Christian); a former category of cinema film to which persons under eighteen were not admitted (superseded by the designation **18**); used to indicate various other things, such as a choice on a ballot paper, an error on an examination paper, etc, or a kiss. — **X'-body** (*bot*) an inclusion in a plant-cell suffering from a virus disease; **X'-chromosome** a chromosome associated with sex-determination, *usu* occurring paired in the female zygote and cell, and alone in the male zygote and cell; **X'-craft** (*hist*) a British midget submarine; **X'-factor** that part of a serviceman's or servicewoman's pay intended as compensation for the disruptions and disadvantages of life in the armed forces; **x'-height** (*printing*) the height of a lower-case x, used as a measure of the height of a typeface; **X-inactivā'tion** (*biol*) the inactivation of one or other X-chromosome in female mammalian cells, with repression of most of the genes on the chromosome; **X'-particle** a meson. — *adj* **X'-rated** of a film, in the former X category; graphically violent or sexually explicit in content, language, etc. — **X-ray** see separate entry.

x *abbrev*: *ex* (*L*, without), as in **xd**, ex dividend.

xanth- *zanth-* or **xantho-** *zan'thō-* or *-tho'-*, *combining form* denoting yellow. — *n* **xant'han** (*zan'than*) or **xan'tham** (also **xanthan**, or **xantham**, **gum**) a substance used as a thickening agent in food preparation. — *n* **xan'thate** a salt of xanthic acid. — *n* **xanthein** (*zan'thē-in*) a soluble yellow colouring matter present in flowers. — *n* **xanthene** (*zan'thēn*) a white crystalline compound of carbon, hydrogen and oxygen, from which are derived **xanthene dyestuffs**. — *adj* **xan'thic** of a yellow tint, *esp* as a description of flowers (*esp bot*); relating to xanthin or xanthine; designating **xanthic acid**, any of a series of addition compounds of an alcohol with carbon disulphide, *esp* ethyl-xanthic acid. — *n* **xan'thin** a name given to the insoluble yellow colouring matter found in various flowers; a yellow colouring-matter obtained from madder; (*usu* **xan'thine**) a white substance, structurally related to uric acid, found in muscle tissue, the liver and other organs, urine, etc, which leaves a lemon-yellow residue when evaporated with nitric acid. — *n* **Xan'thium** (Gr *xanthion* a plant used for dyeing the hair yellow) any of a small but widely distributed genus of composite plants whose fruits bear hooked prickles very troublesome to sheep and other animals. — *n pl* **Xanthochroi** (*zan-thok'rō-ī*; Gr *chroā* or *chroiā* skin) according to Huxley and other ethnologists, one of the five groups of human races, comprising those with fair hair and pale skin. — *n* **xanthochroia** (*-thō-kroi'ə*) yellowness of the skin. — *adj* **xanthochrō'ic** or **xan'thochroid** (*-kroid*; also used as *n*). — *n* **xanthochroism** (*-thok'rō-izm*) a condition in which all pigments other than yellows disappear, as in goldfish, or in which normal colouring is replaced by yellow. — *adj* **xanthochroous** (*-thok'rō-əs*) xanthochroic. — *n* **xanthochrō'mia** (*med*) any yellowish discoloration, *esp* of the cerebrospinal fluid. — *n* **xanthoma** (*zan-thō'mə*) a yellow tumour composed of fibrous tissue and of cells containing cholesterol ester, occurring on the skin (eg in diabetes) or on the sheaths of tendons, or in any tissue of the body: — *pl* **xanthō'mas** or **xanthom'ata**. — *adj* **xanthom'atous**. — *adj* **xanthomelanous** (*zan-thō-mel'ə-nəs*; Gr *melas*, *-anos* black) applied by Huxley to members of the human race with black hair and yellow or olive skins. — *n* **xanthophyll** (*zan'thō-fil*) $C_{40}H_{56}O_2$, one of the two yellow pigments present in the normal chlorophyll mixture of green plants. — *n* **xanthop'sia** the condition in which objects appear yellow to the observer, as in jaundice or after taking santonin. — *n* **xanthop'terin** or (*rare*) **xanthop'terine** (*-in*) a yellow pigment obtainable from the wings of yellow butterflies and the urine of mammals. — *adj* **xanthous** (*zan'thəs*) yellow. — *n* **xanthoxyl** (*zan-thok'sil*; Gr *xylon* wood) a plant of the genus *Xanthoxylum* of the *Rutaceae*, comprising over one hundred species, of which many are found in Brazil and the W Indies; in particular, either of two species known respectively as the prickly-ash and Hercules club; the dried bark of either of these two species. — *n* **Xanthura** (*-thū'rə*) or **Xanthoura** (*-thōō'rə*; Gr *ourā* tail) the former name of a genus of yellow-tailed American jays, now *Cyanocorax*. [Gr *xanthos* yellow]

Xanthian *zan'thi-ən*, *adj* relating to *Xanthus*, the capital of ancient Lycia in Asia Minor.

xanthic, **xanthin**, **Xanthium**, **xantho-**, etc. See under **xanth-**.

Xantippe *zan-tip'i*, *n* a scold or shrew. — Also **Xanthippe** (*-thip'i*). — (*Shakesp* in older editions, **Zan'tippe** or **Zen'tippe**). [Gr *Xanthippē* the wife of Socrates]

X-body, **X-chromosome** and **X-craft**. See under **X** (symbol).

xd *abbrev*: *ex dividend* (*L*), of a share price, etc, not including the next dividend to be paid.

Xe (*chem*) *symbol*: xenon.

xebec *zē'bek*, *n* a small three-masted ship used *esp* by the former pirates of Algiers. [Fr *chebec*, influenced by the Spanish spelling; perh from Turkish or Arabic]

Xema *zē'mə*, *n* a genus or subgenus of gulls. [Arbitrarily invented by Leach in 1819]

Xenarthra ... to ... **xenium**. See under **xeno-**.

xeno- *zen-ō-* or *zi-no'-*, or before a vowel **xen-** *zen-* or *zēn-*, *combining form* denoting: strange, foreign; a guest. — *n* **Xenar'thra** (Gr *arthron* a joint) a group of American edentates, including ant-eaters, sloths and armadillos, the dorsolumbar vertebrae of which are jointed in an unusual manner. — *adj* **xenar'thral** having additional facets on the dorsolumbar vertebrae. — *n* **xē'nia** (*bot*) the direct influence of pollen upon endosperm (explained by double fertilization) or upon the mother-plant of the embryo. — *adj* **xenial** (*zē'ni-əl*) of or concerning hospitality or relations with guests. — *n* **xenium** (*zē'ni-əm*) a present made to a guest or an ambassador; an offering, or a compulsory gift, to a ruler, the Church, etc: — *pl* **xē'nia**. — *adj* **xenobiotic** (*-bī-ot'ik*; *biol*, etc) denoting or relating to a substance foreign to or not rightly found in a body, biological system, etc. — *n* a xenobiotic substance. — *n* **xen'ocryst** (*-krist*) a crystal or mineral grain which has been taken in by magma during its upward flow. — *n* **xenodochium** (*zen-ō-do-kī'əm*; Gr *docheion* a receptacle) a building for the reception of strangers, eg a guest-house in a monastery. — *n* **xenogamy** (*zen-og'ə-mi*; Gr *gamos* marriage; *bot*) cross-fertilization. — *n* **xenogenesis** (*zen-ō-jen'ə-sis*; Gr *genesis* birth) the (imagined) generation of something altogether and permanently unlike the parent. — *adj* **xenogenet'ic**. — *adj* **xenogenous** (*zi-noj'i-nəs*) due to an outside cause. — *n* **xenogloss'ia** (Gr *glōssa* tongue) in psychical research, a person's knowledge of a language which he or she has never learned. — *n* **xen'ograft** (*biol*) a graft from a member of a different species. — *n* **xen'olith** a fragment of rock of extraneous origin which has been incorporated in magma. — *n* **xenomania** (*-mā'ni-ə*; Gr *maniā* madness) an inordinate attachment to foreign things. — *n* **xenomenia** (*-mē'ni-ə*; Gr *mēniaia* menses) vicarious menstruation, in which, in the absence of normal menstruation, bleeding occurs at regular monthly intervals from other parts of the body (eg the nose). — *adj* **xenomorphic** (*-mör'fik*; Gr *morphē* form; *geol*) allotriomorphic. — *n* **xen'ophile** a person who likes foreigners or foreign things. — *n* **xen'ophobe** (*-fōb*; Gr *phobos* fear) a person who fears or hates foreigners or foreign things. — *n* **xenophobia** (*-fō'bi-ə*) or (*rare*) **xen'ophoby** fear or hatred of foreigners and foreign things. — *n pl* **xenophya** (*zen-of'i-ə*; Gr *xenophyēs* strange in shape or nature; *biol*) elements of a shell or skeleton not secreted by the organism itself. — *adj* **xenoplas'tic** in experimental zoology, of or denoting transplantation in which transplant and host belong to the young germs of different species or genera. — *n* **Xen'opus** a genus of African aquatic frogs (see **platanna**). — *n* **xenotime** (*zen'ō-tīm*; Gr *xenos* strange, in error for *kenos* empty, vain, and *timē* honour, in reference to the fact that the mineral was at first thought to contain a new metal) yttrium phosphate, often containing small quantities of cerium, erbium and thorium, and an important source of these rare elements. — *n* **Xenurus** (*zē-nū'rəs*; Gr *ourā* tail) a genus of armadillos in which the tail is almost without plates. — *adj* **xenū'rine**. [Gr *xenos* (n) guest, host, stranger, (adj) strange, foreign]

xenon *zen'on* or *zē'non*, *n* an element of zero valency (symbol **Xe**; atomic no 54), a heavy gas present in the atmosphere in the proportion of 1 : 17 x 10^7 by volume, and also a fission product. — **xenon lamp** a high-pressure lamp, containing traces of xenon, used in film projectors, high-speed photography, etc. [Ety as for **xeno-**]

Xenurus and **xenurine**. See under **xeno-**.

xerafin *sher'ə-fēn* or **xeraphim** *-fēm*, *n* a former silver coin of Goa. [Port]

xeransis ... to ... **xerasia**. See under **xero-**.

Xeres *hher'es*, (*obs*) *n* sherry. [Sp, wine of Jerez (formerly Xeres)]

xeric. See under **xero-**.

xero- *zē-rō-*, or before a vowel **xer-** *zēr-*, *combining form* denoting dry. — *n* **xeran'sis** a drying up. — *n* **xeranthemum** (*-an'thi-məm*; Gr *anthemon* flower) any plant of the *Xeranthemum* genus of plants of southern Europe, belonging to the thistle family; one species of these, also called **everlasting**. — *adj* **xeran'tic** drying up. — *adj* **xerarch** (*zē'rärk*; *bot*; Gr *archē* beginning) of a plant succession, starting on land where conditions are very dry. — *n* **xerasia** (*zi-rā'si-ə*) an abnormal or unhealthy dryness of the hair. — *adj* **xē'ric** dry, lacking in moisture; xerophytic. — *n* **xerochasy** (*zi-rok'ə-si*; *bot*, etc) dehiscence on drying. — *n* **xeroderma** (*zē-rō-dûr'mə*; Gr *derma* skin) or **xeroder'mia** a disease characterized by abnormal dryness of the skin and by abnormal, excessive growth of its horny layer. — *adj* **xerodermat'ic**, **xeroder'matous** or **xeroder'mic**. — *adj* **xerograph'ic**. — *n* **xerog'raphy** a non-chemical photographic process in which the plate is sensitized electrically and developed by dusting with electrically-charged fine powder. — *n* **xeroma** (*-rō'*) xerophthalmia: — *pl* **xerō'mas** or **xerom'ata**. — *n* **xē'romorph** (*-mörf*; Gr *morphē* form) a xerophyte. — *adj* **xeromor'phic** or **xeromor'phous** of parts of a plant, protected against excessive loss of water by thick cuticles, coatings of hairs and similar structural features. — *n* **xerophagy** (*zi-rof'ə-ji*; Gr *phagein* to eat) the eating of dry food, or of bread, vegetables and water, as a form of fast. — *adj* **xerophilous** (*-of'il-əs*; Gr *philos* loving) of a plant, tolerant of a very dry habitat. — *n* **xeroph'ily** adaptation to dry conditions. — *n* **xērophthalmia** (*-of-thal'mi-ə*; Gr *ophthalmos* eye) a dry lustreless condition of the conjunctiva due to deficiency of vitamin A in the diet. — *n* **xē'rophyte** (*-fīt*; Gr *phyton* plant) a plant able to inhabit places where the water supply is scanty, or where conditions, eg excess of salts, make it difficult to take in water. — *adj* **xerophytic** (*-fit'*) able to withstand drought. — *n* **xeroradiog'raphy** X-ray photography by xerography. — *n* **xerō'sis** abnormal dryness, eg of the skin, mouth, eyes, etc. — *n* **xerostoma** (*-os'tom-ə*; Gr *stoma* mouth) or **xerostō'mia** excessive dryness of the mouth due to insufficient secretions. — *n* **xerotes** (*zē'rō-tēz*) xerosis. — *adj* **xerotic** (*-rot'*) of bodily tissues, abnormally dry. — *n* **xerotripsis** (*-trip'sis*; Gr *trīpsis*, from *trībein* to rub) dry friction. [Gr *xēros* dry]

Xerox® *zē'roks*, *n* a registered trademark used in respect of copying machines operating a xerographic method of reproduction; a copy so produced. — *vt* to produce a copy by this method. [Ety as for **xero-**]

X-factor, **X-height**. See under **X** (symbol).

Xhosa *kō'sə*, *-zə* or *hhō'sə*, *n* a group of Bantu-speaking tribes from the Cape district of S Africa, formerly often known as Kaffirs; a member of one of these tribes; the language of these tribes. — Also **Xo'sa**. — *adj* **Xho'san**.

xi *zī*, *ksī* or *ksē*, *n* the fourteenth letter of the Greek alphabet (Ξ or ξ), corresponding to X; as a numeral ξ' = 60, ͵ξ = 60 000.

Xian, short for **Christian**. See also under **X** (symbol).

xiph- *zif-* or **xipho-** *zif-o-* or *-ō-*, *combining form* denoting sword. — *n* **xiphihumeralis** (*-i-hū-mər-ā'lis*) in vertebrates, a muscle leading from the xiphoid cartilage to the humerus. — *adj* and *n* **xiphiplas'tral**. — *n* **xiphiplas'tron** in chelonians, one of the plates forming the plastron, lying posterior to the hypoplastron. — *n* **xiphister'num** a posterior element of the sternum. — *adj* **xiph'oid** (*anatom*) sword-shaped; relating to or designating the **xiphoid process** or xiphisternum (also, when cartilaginous, known as **xiphoid cartilage**). — *adj* **xiphoid'al**. — *n* **xiphop'agus** (Gr *pēgnynai* to fix or fasten together) Siamese twins joined in the region of the xiphoid cartilage. — *adj* **xiphopagic** (*-paj'ik*) or **xiphop'agous**. — *adj* **xiphophyllous** (*-ə-fil'əs*; Gr *phyllon* leaf) with sword-shaped leaves. — *n* **Xiphosura** (*-ō-sū'rə*; formed irregularly from Gr *ourā* tail) an order of *Arthropoda* of which the only survivors are the king-crabs. — *adj* and *n* **xiphosu'ran**. [Gr *xiphos* a sword]

Xiphias *zif'i-as*, *n* the common swordfish genus, from which the family **Xiphī'idae** is named. [Gr *xiphias* swordfish, from *xiphos* sword]

Xm *abbrev*: Christmas (see also **X** (symbol)).

Xmas *eks'məs* or *kris'məs*, *n* short form of **Christmas** (see also **X** (symbol)).

Xn *abbrev*: Christian (see also **X** (symbol)).

xoanon *zō'ə-non*, *n* a primitive statue, said to have fallen from heaven, *orig* of wood, later overlaid with ivory and gold: — *pl* **xō'ana**. [Gr *xoanon*, from *xeein* to carve]

Xosa. See **Xhosa**.

X-particle. See under **X** (symbol).

X-ray *eks'-rā*, *n* an electromagnetic ray of very short wavelength which can penetrate matter opaque to light-rays, produced when cathode rays impinge on matter, discovered by Röntgen in 1895. — Also *adj* — *n* a photograph taken by X-rays. — *vt* to photograph or treat by, or otherwise expose to, X-rays. — **characteristic X-rays** secondary X-rays emitted when X-rays fall on matter, which contain monochromatic radiations that vary in wavelength according to the atoms from which they are scattered; **X-ray astronomy** a branch of astronomy using satellites or rockets to detect and measure X-ray emissions from stars, etc; **X-ray crystallography** the study of crystal structures as shown by their diffraction of X-rays; **X-ray micrography** the preparation, and study through the microscope, of radiographs obtained by means of X-rays; **X-ray spectrum** a wavelength or frequency diagram in which a series of lines indicate by their positions the particular X-rays emitted by a body as the result of cathode-ray bombardment; **X-ray telescope** a telescope designed to investigate the emission of X-rays from stars, etc; **X-ray therapy** the use of X-rays for medical treatment; **X-ray tube** a tube enclosing a vacuum, in which X-rays are emitted from a metal target placed obliquely opposite to an incandescent cathode whose rays impinge on the target. [**X** (symbol) after its unknown nature on discovery; translated from orig Ger term *X-Strahlen* (pl), *Strahl* a ray]

Xt *abbrev*: Christ (see also **X** (symbol)).

Xtian *abbrev*: Christian (see also **X** (symbol)).

xu *so͞o*, *n* in the currency of Vietnam, (a coin of the value of) one-hundredth of a dong: — *pl* **xu**. [Viet, from Fr *sou* sou]

xylo- *zī-lō-*, or before a vowel **xyl-** *zīl-*, *combining form* denoting wood. — *n* **xylem** (*zī'ləm*; *bot*) woody tissue in trees and plants, *usu* consisting of vessels, tracheides and fibres, all with lignified walls, with some more or less lignified parenchyma, concerned in the conduction of aqueous solutions, with storage and with mechanical support of the plant. — *n* **xy'lene** $C_6H_4(CH_3)_2$, any of three dimethyl-benzenes, occurring in coal-tar but not separable by fractional distillation. — *n* **xy'lenol** a synthetic resin, $(CH_3)_2{\cdot}C_6H_3{\cdot}OH$, any of six monohydric phenols derived from xylenes. — *adj* **xy'lic** relating to xylem; designating any of six acids, derivatives of xylene. — *n* **xy'litol** a sweet crystalline alcohol obtained from xylose, that can be used as a sugar substitute. — *n* **xylobal'samum** (Gr *balsamon* the balsam tree) the dried twigs, or the wood, of the balm of Gilead tree. — *n* **xy'locarp** a hard and woody fruit, such as a coconut. — *adj* **xylocarp'ous**. — *n* **xy'lochrome** (Gr *chrōma* colour) a mixture of substances to which the colour of heartwood is due, including tannins, gums, and resins. — *n* **xy'logen** (*-jen*) xylem. — *adj* **xylogenous** (*-loj'ən-əs*; *bot*) growing on wood. — *n* **xylography** (*zī-log'rə-fi*) the art of engraving on wood. — *n* **xyl'ograph** an impression or print from a wood block; an impression of the grain of wood for surface decoration. — *n* **xylog'rapher**. — *adj* **xylograph'ic** or **-al**. — *adj* **xy'loid** woody, ligneous. — *n* **xyloidin** or **xyloidine** (*zi-loi'din*; Gr *eidos* form, appearance) an explosive like gun-cotton, prepared by the action of strong nitric acid on starch or woody fibre — pyroxylin, or a similar substance. — *n* **xy'lol** (L *oleum* oil) xylene. — *n* **xylol'ogy** the study of the structure of wood. — *n* **xylō'ma** in fungi, a sclerotium-like body which forms spores internally and does not put out branches which develop into sporophores: — *pl* **xylō'mas** or **xylom'ata**. — *n* **xylom'eter** an instrument for determining the specific gravity of wood. — *adj* **xylon'ic** designating an acid obtained by oxidizing xylose. — *n* **xy'lonite** or **Xy'lonite®** a non-thermosetting plastic of the nitrocellulose type. — *n* **xylophagan** (*-lof'ə-gən*; Gr *phagein* to eat) one of the **Xyloph'aga**, a genus of boring bivalves. — *n* **xy'lophage** (*-fāj*) an insect larva, mollusc, etc that eats or bores into wood. — *adj* **xylophagous** (*-lof'ə-gəs*) wood-eating. — *adj* **xyloph'ilous** fond of wood, living on wood. — *n* **xy'lophone** (Gr *phōnē* voice) a musical instrument consisting of a graduated series of wooden, or sometimes metal, bars, which are struck with wooden hammers; an instrument used to measure the elastic properties of wood. — *adj* **xylophon'ic**. — *n* **xyloph'onist**. — *n* **Xylopia** (*-lō'pi-ə*; Gr *pikros* bitter) a genus of trees and shrubs of the custard-apple family, natives of the tropics, chiefly in America. — *n* **xylopyrog'raphy** designs engraved on wood with a hot poker; the act of making such designs. — *n* **xylorim'ba** an extended xylophone combining the ranges of the *xylo*phone and the ma*rimba*. — *n* **xy'lose** a pentose found in many plants, also known as wood-sugar ($C_5H_{10}O_5$). — *adj* **xylot'omous** (Gr *tomē* a cut) of insects, wood-boring or wood-cutting. — *adj* **xylotypograph'ic** pertaining to, or printed from, wooden type. — *n* **xylotypog'raphy**. — *n* **xy'lyl** (*-lil*) any of the univalent radicals, C_8H_9, of the xylenes or their derivatives. [Gr *xylon* wood]

Xyris *zī'ris*, *n* a genus of sedge-like plants, *usu* with yellow flowers, of the family **Xyridaceae** (*zir-i-dā'si-ē*) and order **Xyridales** (*-dā'lēz*). — *adj* **xyridā'ceous** (*-shəs*) of the Xyridaceae. [Gr *xyris* a kind of iris]

xyst. See **xystus**.

xyster *zis'tər*, *n* a surgeon's instrument for scraping bones. [Gr *xystēr* an engraving tool]

xystus *zis'təs*, (*antiq*) *n* a covered portico used by athletes for their exercises; an open colonnade; a tree-planted walk: — *pl* **xys'tī**. — Also **xys'tos** (*pl* **xys'toi**) and **xyst**. [L, from Gr *xystos* or *-on*, perh orig a cleared or raked place, from *xyein* to scrape; cf **xyster**]

XYY syndrome *eks-wī-wī' sin'drōm*, (*biol*) *n* a condition in which the human male has an extra Y chromosome, resulting in reduced growth and sometimes minor behavioural abnormalities.

Y

Y or **y** *wī*, *n* the twenty-fifth letter of the modern English alphabet, twenty-third of the Roman alphabet, derived, as are also U and V, from Greek upsilon (*Y*, *υ*); an object or figure in the shape of the letter Y. (**Y** is used to represent a consonant sound as in *year* (*y* = OE ʒ; ME ʒ, yogh), and the diphthongal sounds, *i*, as in *hymn* and *folly*; *ī*, as in *my* and *pyre*; *ə*, as in *satyr*; *û*, as in *myrrh*; it is also used in digraphs, such as *oy* instead of *oi* when word-final, eg in *toy*. Early printers used y as a substitute for thorn (þ), which their founts lacked; hence it came to be so used in manuscripts and inscriptions, as in *yat* or y^t for *that*, or *ye* for *the*; cf **ye**[2]). — **Y'-alloy** an aluminium-based alloy of the duralumin type, containing copper 4%, magnesium 1·5%, silicon 0·7%, nickel 2%, iron 0·6%, and titanium 0·2%; **Y'-fronts** underpants for men or boys, with a front seamed opening in the shape of an inverted **Y**; **Y'-level** a type of engineers' level whose essential characteristic is the support of the telescope, namely, Y-shaped rests in which it may be rotated or reversed end-for-end (also called **wye'-level**); **Y'-moth** any of a genus of destructive noctuid moths with a silvery Y-shaped mark on the forewings; **Y'-track** a short track laid at right angles to a railway-line, connected with it by two switches resembling a Y, used for reversing engines.

Y or **Y**. *abbrev*: yen (Japanese currency).

Y *symbol*: (also **y** or *y*) a variable, unknown or yet to be ascertained quantity or factor, used as distinct from and in addition to **X** (or **x** or *x*) (*algebra*, etc); ythrium (*chem*); as a medieval numeral Y = 150, $\bar{Y}$ = 150,000. — **Y'-chromosome** one of a pair of chromosomes associated with sex-determination (the other being the **X-chromosome**).

y or **y**. *abbrev*: yard; year.

y- *i-*, *pfx* derived from OE pfx *ge-* (*ʒe-*), *orig* a preposition meaning 'with, together', seen in OE nouns and adjectives, eg *gefēra* companion, *getheaht* counsel, *gelīc* alike, and in verbs such as *getheōdan* to join together, *gerinnan* to congeal, but even in OE times often used with no very definite meaning; in primitive Germanic *gi-* imparted a perfective meaning to past participles; in OE (as *ge-*) and in ME (as *ʒe-*, *y-*, *i-*, etc) it was prefixed to past participles indiscriminately, and it was used freely in this way by Spenser and other archaizers.

-y[1] *-i*, *sfx* forming adjectives with the senses 'characterized by', 'full of', 'having the quality of' or 'inclined to', as in *icy*, *sandy*, *slangy*, *shiny*, etc. [OE *-ig*]

-y[2] *-i*, *sfx* forming nouns denoting (1) a diminutive, or a term of affection, as in *doggy* or *daddy*; (2) a person or thing having a certain specified characteristic, as in *fatty*. [Orig Scot **-ie** in names, etc]

-y[3] *-i*, *sfx* forming nouns denoting a quality, state, action or entity, as in *fury*, *jealousy*, *subsidy*, *society*, etc. [OFr *-ie*, from L *-ia*]

yabber *yab'ər*, (*Austr*) *n* talk, conversation, jabber. — *vi* to talk or jabber. [Aboriginal word *yabba* language, perh modified by **jabber**]

yabby or **yabbie** *yab'i*, (*Austr*) *n* a small freshwater crayfish, often used as bait. [Aboriginal]

ya-boo. See **yah-boo** under **yah**[2].

yacca *yak'ə*, *n* either of two evergreens (*Podocarpus coriacea* or *Podocarpus Purdieana*) of the W Indies, or their wood. [Sp *yaca*, from Taino]

yacht *yot*, *n orig* a light fast-sailing vessel; a sailing, steam-powered, etc vessel elegantly fitted out for pleasure-trips or racing. — *vi* to sail or race in a yacht. — *n* **yacht'er** a person sailing a yacht. — *n* **yacht'ie** (*colloq*; *esp Austr* and *NZ*) a yachtsman, yachtswoman or yachting enthusiast. — *n* and *adj* **yacht'ing**. — *adj* **yacht'-built** built in the style of a yacht. — **yacht'-club** a club for yachtsmen and yachtswomen; **yachts'man** or **yachts'woman** a person who owns or sails a yacht; **yachts'manship** the art of sailing a yacht. — **land'-yacht** or **sand'-yacht** a wheeled boat with sails, for running on land, *usu* along sea-beaches; **land'-yachting** or **sand'-yachting**. [Du *jacht* (formerly *jagt*), from *jagen* to chase; Ger *jagen* to hunt]

yack or **yak** *yak*, (*slang*) *n* persistent, and often idle or stupid, talk. — *vi* to talk persistently, *esp* in a foolish or gossiping manner. — Also **yack'ety-yack'**, **yak'ety-yak'** and **yak'ity-yak'**. [Imit]

yacker. Same as **yakka**.

yaff *yaf*, (*Scot*) *vi* to bark like a snarling dog; to scold or nag. [Imit]

yaffle *yaf'l*, or (*dialect*) **yaffingale** *yaf'ing-gāl*, (*Tennyson*) *n* the green woodpecker. [From its call; influenced by **nightingale**]

yager *yä'gər*, *n*. Same as **jäger**.

yagger *yag'ər*, (*Scot*) *n* a pedlar. [Variant of **jagger** (see under **jag**[2])]

Yagi *yä'gi* or *yag'i*, *adj* denoting a type of highly directional television or radio astronomy aerial, with several elements in a close parallel arrangement, fixed at right angles to a central support that points in the direction of strongest reception. [Hidetsugu *Yagi* (1886–1976), Japanese electrical engineer]

yah[1] *yä*. Variant of **yea**.

yah[2] *yä*, *interj* an exclamation of derision, contemptuous defiance (also **ya(h)'-boo'** and **ya(h)-boo sucks'**) or disgust.

Yahoo *yä'hōō* or *yä-hōō'*, *n* a name given by Swift in *Gulliver's Travels* to a class of animals which are human in form but which have the understanding and passions of brutes; (without *cap*) a brutal or boorish lout.

Yahweh or **Yahwe** *yä'wā*, *n* Jehovah (qv). — *n* **Yah'wist** Jehovist. — Also **Yah've(h)** and **Yah'vist**.

Yajurveda *yuj'ōōr-vā-də*, or *-ve-*, *n* one of the four Vedas, the Veda of prayers. [Sans]

yak[1] *yak*, *n* a species of ox found in Tibet, and domesticated there, with a thick coat of long silky hair, the lower parts of which hang down almost to the ground. [Tibetan]

yak[2], **yakety-yak**, etc. See **yack**.

yakhdan *yak'dän*, *n* a box used for carrying ice, strapped on to the back of an animal. [Pers *yakh* ice and *dān* box]

yakimona *ya-ki-mō'nō*, *n* in Japanese cookery, grilled food, a grilled dish. [Jap, from *yaki* grill, and *mono* thing]

yakitori *ya-ki-tō'ri* or *ya-ki-tö'ri*, *n* a Japanese dish of boneless chicken pieces, grilled on skewers and basted with a thick, sweet sauce (**yakitori sauce**) containing sake, mirin and soy sauce. [Jap, from *yaki* grill, and *tori* bird]

yakka *yak'ə*, (*Austr*) *n* hard toil. — Also **yacker** or **yakker**. [Aboriginal (Queensland) word]

yakow *yak'ow*, *n* an animal crossbred from a male yak and a domestic cow. [**yak** and **cow**]

Yakut *yä-kōōt'*, *n* a member of a mixed Turkic race living in NE Siberia; their language.

yakuza *yə-kōō'za*, *n* a Japanese gangster, typically involved in drug-dealing, gambling, extortion, gun-running or prostitution: — *pl* **yaku'za**. [Jap, from *ya* eight, *ku* nine, and *za* or *sa* three, this being the worst hand of cards in gambling]

yald. See **yauld**.

Yale® *yāl* or **Yale lock** (*lok*), *n* a trademark for a type of cylinder lock operated by a flat key with a notched upper edge. [Linus *Yale* (1821–68), American locksmith]

yale *yāl*, *n* a mythical animal, depicted in heraldry as resembling a horse with tusks, horns and an elephant's tail. [L *ealē* an unidentified Ethiopian animal mentioned by Pliny]

y'all *yöl*, (*US*; *esp Southern*) a contraction of **you-all** (see under **you**).

Y-alloy. See under **Y** (noun).

yam *yam*, *n* a large tuberous edible root like the potato, grown in tropical countries; any plant of the genus *Dioscorea*, some species of which yield these tubers; a variety of potato (*obs Scot*); a sweet potato (*Southern US*). [Port *inhame*]

Yama *yum'ə* or *yam'ə*, *n* in Hindu mythology, the first mortal. [Sans]

yamen *yä'men*, (*hist*) *n* the offices and residence of a mandarin. [Chin]

yammer *yam'ər*, (*dialect* and *colloq*) *vi* to lament or wail; to whine; to make an outcry; to express yearning. — Also *n*. — *n* and *adj* **yamm'ering**. [OE *gēom(e)rian*, from *gēomor* sad; influenced in ME by Du *jammeren*]

yamulka *yä'məl-kə*. Same as **yarmulka**.

yang[1] *yang*, *n* (also with *cap*) one of the two opposing and complementary principles of Chinese philosophy, religion, medicine, etc influencing destiny and governing nature, seen as the positive, masculine, light, warm, active element (cf **yin**[2]). [Chin, bright]

yang[2] *yang*, *n* any of various species of *Dipterocarpus*, all valuable timber trees. [Thai]

Yank *yank*, (*colloq*) *n*. See **Yankee**.

yank *yangk*, *vt* (*colloq*) to carry, move or pull with a jerk. — *vi* to pull or jerk vigorously (*colloq*); to move actively (*obs* or *dialect*). — *n* a blow or slap (*Scot*); a strong jerk (*colloq*). — *n* **yank'er** (*Scot*) a rap; a big lie. — *n* **yank'ie** (*Scot*) a scold; an impudent woman. — *adj* **yank'ing** active (*Scot*); pulling, jerking (*colloq*). [Ety doubtful]

Yankee *yang'ki*, *n* (also *colloq* **Yank**) in America, a citizen of the New England States, or an inhabitant of the northern United States, as opposed to the southern; (also *colloq* **Yank**) in British usage, generally an inhabitant of the United States; (also **Yankee bet**) a multiple bet on four horses in four races, consisting of six doubles, four trebles and one accumulator. — Also *adj*. — *n* **Yank'eedom** the land of Yankees; Yankees generally. — Also *adj*. — *adj* **Yank'eefied**. — *n* **Yank'eeism** Yankee characteristics. — **Yankee bet** see **Yankee** above; **Yankee-Doo'dle** a Yankee (from a popular song). [Prob Du *Jantje* Johnnie, or *Jan Kees* John Cheese, both said to be used by the Dutch settlers as nicknames for British settlers]

yanqui *yang'kē*, (*Sp*) *n* in Latin America, a N American, *esp* from the United States. [Sp form of **Yankee**]

yaourt. See **yoghurt**.

yap *yap*, *vi* of eg a small dog, to bark sharply or constantly; to speak constantly, *esp* in a noisy or foolish manner (*colloq*); to scold (*colloq*). — *n* a yelp; a cur (*dialect*); incessant, foolish chatter (*colloq*); a fool or bumpkin (*US*); the mouth (*slang*). — *n* **yapp'er** or **yap'ster** a dog. — *adj* **yap'py**. [Imit]

yapok or **yapock** *yap'ək*, *n* the S American amphibious opossum (*Chironectes minimus*), which feeds on shrimps, etc. [From the river *Oyapok* in French Guiana]

yapon. See **yaupon**.

yapp *yap*, *n* a limp leather binding in which the cover overlaps the edges of the book. [*Yapp*, a bookseller]

yapper and **yapster**. See under **yap**.

yappy[1]. See under **yap**.

yappy[2] or **yappie** *yap'i*, (*colloq*) *n* a *y*oung *a*spiring *p*rofessional, or (more recently) *y*oung *a*ffluent *p*arent. [Acronymic]

yaqona *yə-kō'nə*, *n* the Fijian name for kava (qv).

Yarborough *yär'bər-ə*, *n* a hand containing no card above a nine. [From an Earl of *Yarborough*, said to have bet against its occurrence]

yard[1] *yärd*, *n* a straight thin branch, a rod of authority, a stick for beating as punishment, or a rod for measuring (*obs*); in English-speaking countries, a measure of 3 feet or 36 inches and equivalent to 0·9144 metre; a piece of material this length; a long beam on a mast for spreading square sails; the penis (*obs*). — *n* **yard'age** the aggregate number of yards; the length, area or volume measured or estimated in linear, square or cubic yards; the cutting of coal at so much a yard. — **yard'-arm** the outer tapering end of either half of a ship's yard; **yard'land** or **yard of land** (*hist*) a measure of land, a virgate (30 acres); **yard'stick** a stick 3 feet long; any standard of measurement (*fig*). — Also (*obs*) **yard'wand**. — **by the yard** sold or measured in yard lengths; in large quantities (*fig*); **yard of ale**, etc a tall slender glass for beer, etc, or the amount it holds. [OE *gyrd* or *gierd* a rod or measure; Du *garde*, Ger *Gerte*; connected with Gothic *gazds* a prickle or sting; and prob with L *hasta* a spear]

yard[2] *yärd*, *n* an enclosed place, *esp* near a building, often in compounds such as 'backyard', 'courtyard', 'farmyard' and 'prison-yard', or a place where any special work is carried on, as in 'brickyard', 'wood-yard' and 'dockyard'; a garden. — *vt* to enclose in a yard. — *n* **yard'age** the use of a yard, or the charge made for such. — **yard'bird** (*US slang*) a convict; a recruit; a soldier confined to camp or required to carry out some menial task as a punishment; **yard-long bean** the asparagus bean; **yard'man** a person in charge of a farmyard; a person employed in a marshalling yard in making up trains, etc; **yard'-master** a person in charge of a marshalling yard. — **the Yard** New Scotland Yard, the London Metropolitan Police headquarters. [OE *geard* fence, dwelling, enclosure; Ger *Garten*; connected with L *hortus* and Gr *chortos*]

yardang *yär'däng*, *n* a ridge formed by wind erosion from sand, silt, etc, *usu* lying parallel to the prevailing wind direction. [Turk, ablative of *yar* steep bank, precipice]

Yardie *yär'di*, (*slang*; *orig* W Indies) *n* a member of a W Indian gang or Mafia-like syndicate involved in drug-dealing and related crime. — Also *adj*. — **Yardie squad** a special police squad set up to tackle Yardie activities. [Jamaican dialect *yard* a dwelling, home or (by Jamaicans abroad) Jamaica]

yare *yär*, *adj* (*archaic* and *dialect*) ready, prepared; quick, brisk; easily handled, manageable. — *interj* (*Shakesp*) quick. — *adv* **yare'ly** (*archaic* and *dialect*) promptly; skilfully. [OE *gearu* or *gearo*, ready, prompt; Du *gaar*, done, cooked sufficiently, Ger *gar* wholly]

yarfa. See **yarpha**.

yarmulka or **yarmulke** *yär'məl-kə*, *n* the skullcap worn by Jewish males, *esp* during prayers or ceremonial occasions. [Yiddish, from Pol *yarmulka* small cap]

yarn *yärn*, *n* spun thread; one of the threads of a rope, or these collectively; a sailor's story, spun out to some length, and often having incredible elements; a story generally (*colloq*). — *vi* (*colloq*) to tell stories. [OE *gearn* thread; ON *garn*, Ger *Garn*]

yarpha or **yarfa** *yär'fə*, (*Scot*) *n* peaty soil in Shetland; clayey, sandy or fibrous peat; a peat-bog. [ON *jörfi* gravel]

yarr *yär*, (*dialect*) *n* the corn spurrey, *Spergula arvensis*. [Cf Fris *jīr*]

yarraman *ya'rə-mən*, (*Austr*) *n* a horse. [Aboriginal]

yarrow *yar'ō*, *n* a strong-scented plant, *Achillea millefolium*, or any similar species of milfoil. [OE *gearwe*; Ger *Garbe*]

yarta or **yarto**. See **jarta**.

yashmak *yash'mak* or *-mak'*, *n* the double veil worn by Muslim women in public, leaving only the eyes uncovered. [Ar *yashmaq*]

yatagan or **yataghan** *yat'ə-gan*, *n* a long Turkish dagger, without a guard and *usu* curved. [Turk *yātāghan*]

yate *yāt*, (*Spenser*) *n* a gate. [Variant of **gate**[1]]

yatter *yat'ər*, (*Scot*) *n* tiresome, irritatingly demanding or persistent chatter. — *vi* to jabber incessantly. — *n* and *adj* **yatt'ering**. — *adv* **yatt'eringly**. [Imit]

yaud *yöd* or *yäd*, (*Scot*) *n* a mare; an old mare; an old horse generally. [ON *jalda*. Cf **jade**[1]]

yauld or **yald** *yöld* or *yäld*, (*Scot*) *adj* active, nimble or strong. [Ety unknown]

yaup *yöp*, (*Scot*) *adj* hungry. [OE *gēap* shrewd]

yaupon *yö'pən*, *n* a bushy evergreen shrub (*Ilex vomitoria*) of the holly genus, native to the SE coasts of the US, its leaves used to brew an emetic or purgative tea, the so-called 'black drink' of the American Indians. — Also **yapon** (*yö'*) or **yupon** (*yōō'*). [Catawba]

yaw *yö*, *vi* of a ship, to deviate temporarily from, or turn out of the line of, its course; to move unsteadily or zigzag (*fig*); of an aircraft, to deviate in a horizontal direction from the line of flight. — *vt* to cause to deviate from course, cause to zigzag, etc. — *n* a deviation from the course; the angular motion of an aircraft in a horizontal plane about the normally vertical axis. [Origin uncertain; cf ON *jaga* to move to and fro, eg as a door does on its hinges]

yawey. See under **yaws**.

yawl[1] *yöl*, *vi* to howl. — *n* a howl. [Variant of **yowl**]

yawl[2] *yöl*, *n* a ship's small boat, generally with four or six oars; a small fishing-boat; a small sailing-boat with a jigger and a shortened mainboom. [Du *jol*]

yawn *yön*, *vi* to take a deep involuntary breath because of drowsiness, boredom, etc; to gape; to gape with astonishment (*Shakesp*); of eg a chasm, to be wide or wide open. — *vt* to make or produce, or cause to be or become, by yawning; to utter with a yawn. — *n* an involuntary deep breath caused by weariness or boredom; a chasm or opening; dullness (*Shelley*); a boring event, person, etc (*colloq*). — *adj* **yawn'ing** gaping or wide open; drowsy; causing drowsiness or sleep (*Shakesp*). — *n* the act of producing a yawn. — *adv* **yawn'ingly**. — *adj* **yawn'y**. [OE *gānian* to yawn and *geonian* or *ginian* (combining form *gīnan*, pa t *gān*), to gape widely; ON *gīna* to gape]

yawp *yöp*, (chiefly *US*) *vi* to utter or cry harshly or hoarsely and noisily; to yelp or bark. — *n* a harsh, hoarse, etc cry. — *n* **yawp'er**. [Imit; cf **yap** and **yelp**]

yaws *yöz*, *n* a tropical epidemic and contagious disease of the skin (also known as *framboesia*, *button scurvy*, *verruga Peruviana*, *buba* or *boba*, etc). — *adj* **yaw'ey** or **yaw'y**. [Origin uncertain; perh Am Ind]

Yb (*chem*) *symbol*: ytterbium.

ybet *i-bet'*, *obs pa p* of **beat**.

yblent *i-blent'*, *obs pa p* of **blend**[2] and **blind**.

ybore *i-bör'*, *obs pa p* of **bear**[1].

ybound *i-bownd'* and **ybounden** *i-bownd'ən*, *obs pa p* of **bind**.

ybrent *i-brent'*, *obs pa p* of **burn**.

Y-chromosome. See under **Y** (symbol).

yclad *i-klad'* and **ycled** *i-kled'*, *obs* forms of **clad**, *pa p* of **clothe**.

ycleepe *i-klēp'*, (*Spenser*) *vt* to clepe. [Back-formation from **yclept**]

yclept *i-klept*, and **ycleped** (or *Milton* **ycleap'd**). See **clepe**.

ycond *i-kond'*, *obs pa p* of **con**[2].

yd *abbrev*: yard: — *pl* **yd** or **yds**.

ydrad *i-drad'* or **ydred** *i-dred'*, *obs pa p* of **dread**.

ye[1] *yē* or *yi*, (now *archaic*, *dialect* or *poetic*) *pronoun* the second person *pl* (sometimes *sing*) pronoun; cf **you**. Formerly, eg in the Authorized Version of the English Bible, *ye* was always used as a nominative, and *you* as a dative or accusative; later *ye* was sometimes used for all these cases. [ME *ye*, nominative; *your*, genitive; *you*, *yow*, dative and accusative pl, from OE *gē*, nominative; *ēower*, genitive; *ēow*, dative and accusative]

ye[2] *thē*, *thi* or (reflecting the spelling) *yē*, *demonstrative adj* an archaic spelling for 'the', arising from printers' use of y for the letter thorn, þ. See **Y** (noun).

yea *yā*, (*archaic*) *adv* yes (now *esp* in the phrase *say yea or nay*; for the former distinction between *yea* and *yes*, see the note at **yes**); indeed; indeed more than that. — *n* (*formal* or *archaic*) an affirmative vote or voter. — **yea'-sayer** a person who agrees or assents, *esp* one who does so habitually and in a positive, enthusiastic manner. [OE *gēa*; Du and Ger *ja*, ON *jā*; cf **yes**]

yead, **yede** or **yeed** *yēd*, (*Spenser*) *vi* to go or proceed: — *pa t* **yod** (*yod*) or **yode** (*yōd*). [OE *ēode* went, used as the pa t of *gān* to go]

yeah *ye*, *yä* or *ye'ə* (*colloq*) *adv* yes.

yealdon *yel'dən*, (*Scott*, as an imitation of Cumberland dialect) *n*. Same as **eldin**.

yealm. See **yelm**.

yean *yēn*, (*archaic* and *dialect*) *vt* and *vi esp* of a sheep, to give birth to (young). — *n* **yean'ling** a lamb or a kid. — Also *adj*. [OE *ge-* (see **y-**) and *eanian* to give birth to (see **ean**)]

year *yēr* or *yûr*, *n* the time taken by the earth to orbit the sun, *approx* 365 days 6 hours but varying slightly according to the method of measurement (see **anomalistic year**, **astronomical year**, etc below); the time taken by any specified planet to revolve round the sun or, eg in science fiction, round any star; the period of time beginning on 1 January and ending on 31 December, consisting of 365 days (except in a **leap year**, when one day is added to February, making the number 366), the present *legal*, *civil* or *calendar year* (see below); a space of twelve calendar months, or a period within each twelve-month space characterized by a particular activity, etc; students, etc as a group at the same stage of their education; (in *pl*) a period of time or a person's life; (in *pl*) a person's age; (in *pl*) old age (*archaic* or *poetic*); (in *pl*) a very long time: — *pl* **years** or, used adjectivally with a preceding numeral, **year**, (eg *a three-year period*). — *n* **year'ling** an animal a year old; a racehorse one year old, as calculated from 1 January of its year of foaling; a bond maturing after one year (*finance*). — *adj* a year old; maturing after one year (*finance*). — *adj* **year'ly** happening every year; lasting a year; for a year. — *adv* once a year; from year to year. — *n* a publication appearing, an event occurring, etc, once a year. — **year'book** a book published annually, reviewing the events of the past year; **year-end'** the end of the (*esp* financial) year. — Also *adj*. — *adj* **year'long** lasting a year. — *adj* **year'-round** existing, lasting, open, etc throughout the year. — *adj* **year-on-year'** (*econ*) of figures, set against figures for the equivalent period in the previous year. — **anomalistic year** a year as measured by the earth's time of passage from perihelion to perihelion, ie 365 days, 6 hours, 13 minutes, 49 seconds; **astronomical year** a year as measured by the time between two occurrences of the same equinox or solstice, ie the time taken for one complete mean apparent circuit of the ecliptic by the sun, ie 365 days, 5 hours, 48 minutes, 46 seconds (also called the **equinoctial**, **natural**, **solar** or **tropical year**); **calendar year** see **legal year** below; **canicular year** the Sothic year (see under **Sothic**); **civil year** see **legal year** below; **ecclesiastical year** the year as arranged in the ecclesiastical calendar, with the saints' days, festivals, etc; **embolismic year** a year of thirteen lunar months (384 days) occurring in a lunisolar calendar such as that of the Jews; **equinoctial year** see **astronomical year** above; **financial year** see under **finance**; **fiscal year** see under **fiscal**; **great year** see **Platonic year** below; **Hebrew year** a lunisolar year, of 12 or 13 months of 29 or 30 days (in every cycle of nineteen years the 6th, 8th, 11th, 14th, 17th and 19th having thirteen months instead of twelve); **Julian year** the year according to the Julian calendar (introduced by Julius Caesar, modified by Augustus; superseded by the Gregorian calendar), a period of $365\frac{1}{4}$ days, longer than an astronomical year by about 11 minutes (see also **style**); **leap year** see **year** above; **legal**, **civil** or **calendar year** the year by which dates are reckoned (it has begun on different dates at different periods in history, and for six centuries before 1752 it began in England on 25 March since when (earlier in Scotland) it has begun on 1 January); **lunar year** a period of twelve lunar months or 354 days; **natural year** see **astronomical year** above; **Platonic year** a cycle of years at the end of which the heavenly bodies were supposed to be again in the same place as at the Creation (also called **great** or **perfect year**); **sabbatical year** see under **Sabbath**; **sidereal year** the period required by the sun to move from a given star to the same star again, having a mean value of 365 days, 6 hours, 9 minutes, 9·6 seconds; **solar** or **tropical year** see **astronomical year** above. — **the year dot** see under **dot**; **year in, year out** (happening, done, etc) every year; with monotonous regularity; **the Year of Grace**, or **of our Lord** a formula used in stating any particular year since Christ's birth. [OE *gēar*; Ger *Jahr*, ON *ār*, Gr *hōrā* season]

yeard and **yeard-hunger**, etc. See **yird**.

yearn[1] *yûrn*, *vt* to desire strongly or feel longing for (*obs*; also **earn**); to express a desire for or ask for (*obs*); to cause to mourn (*Shakesp*). — *vi* to feel great desire; to feel compassion, tenderness or grief (also used impersonally, as 'it yearns me'; *obs*, *Spenser* and *Shakesp*; also **earn**); to express longing, eg by sound or appearance. — *n* a yearning. — *n* **yearn'er**. — *n* and *adj* **yearn'ing**. — *adv* **yearn'ingly**. [OE *geornan* (WSax *giernan*) to desire; related to *georn* desirous, eager; cf Ger *gern* willingly]

yearn[2] *yûrn*, (*obs* and *dialect*) *vt* to earn. [**earn**[1]]

yearn[3]. See **earn**[2].

yeast *yēst*, *n* one of a group of simple unicellular fungi, with features making them highly suitable for genetic and biochemical studies, and for use in brewing, baking, etc; the froth on beer (*obs*); spume or foam on water (*Shakesp*); leaven (*fig*). — *vi* (*lit* and *fig*) to ferment or be covered with froth. — *n* **yeast'iness**. — *adj* **yeast'like**. — *adj* **yeast'y** like yeast; frothy or foamy; insubstantial. — **yeast plant** any of a group of tiny, one-celled fungi (*Saccharomyces*) that produce alcoholic fermentation in saccharine fluids; **yeast powder** dry powdered yeast used in baking; baking-powder. [OE *gist* or *gyst*; Ger *Gäscht*, *Gischt*]

yech *yehh*, *yuhh*, *yuk*, *yûhh*, etc *interj* an expression of distaste or disgust. [Imit; cf **yuk** and **ugh**]

yede and **yeed**. See **yead**.

yegg *yeg*, (*US*) *n* a burglar, *esp* a burglar of safes. — Also **yegg'man**. [Origin unknown]

yeld *yeld* or **yell** *yel*, (*Scot*) *adj* barren; not giving milk; unproductive. [Late OE *gelde*; cf **geld**[2]]

yeldring *yeld'ring*, *n*. Same as **yoldring**. — Also **yeld'rock**.

yelk. See **yolk**[1].

yell[1] *yel*, *vi* to howl or cry out with a sharp noise; to scream in pain or terror. — *vt* to utter with a yell. — *n* a sharp cry or loud shout, whether of words or inarticulate sounds; a rhythmic cheer or chant, often including nonsense words or syllables, used eg to encourage sports teams, *esp* in N American colleges (*esp NAm*); an extremely funny person or thing, a scream (*old slang*). — *n* **yell'ing**. — *vi* **yell'och** (*-əhh*; *Scot*) to yell. — *n* a yell. [OE (Anglian) *gellan*; Ger *gellen*; connected with OE *galan* to sing]

yell[2]. See **yeld**.

yellow *yel'ō*, *adj* of the colour of sulphur, egg-yolk, gold, a ripe lemon, a primrose, etc; of Mongolic or Oriental race (Chinese, Japanese, etc) (now often considered *derog*); of mixed black and white race (*US*); of skin, sallow, sickly-looking; cowardly (*colloq*); sensational (*colloq*). — *n* the colour of the rainbow between the orange and the green or of sulphur, egg-yolk, gold, a ripe lemon, a primrose, etc; any dye or pigment producing such a colour; a yolk; (in *pl*) peach-yellows (see **peach**[2]), or other plant disease in which the foliage turns yellow; (in *pl*) jaundice in horses, etc. — *vt* and *vi* to make or become yellow. — *adj* **yell'owish** somewhat yellow. — *n* **yell'owishness**. — *n* **yell'owness** the quality or state of being yellow; jealousy (*obs*; *fig*). — *adj* **yell'owy** yellowish. — **yellow alert** an alarm, etc one stage less serious than a red alert; **yellow-ammer** see **yellowhammer** below; **yell'owback** a cheap, sensational novel, *specif* one with yellow board or paper covers, common in the 19c; **yell'ow-belly** (*slang*) a coward (*adj* **yell'ow-bellied**); **yellow berries** Persian berries, the fruit of various species of buckthorn; **yell'owbird** any of various, *esp* N American, birds of a yellow colour such as the American goldfinch; **yell'ow-boy** (*obs slang*) a gold coin; a mulatto or dark quadroon (*fem* **yell'ow-girl**); **yellow brick road** a path to fame, wealth, etc; **yellow bunting** the yellowhammer; **yell'owcake** uranium oxide, obtained in the form of a yellow precipitate during the processing of uranium ore; **yellow card** an official warning to a football, etc player (signalled by the showing of a yellow card), typically following an infringement (not used in English domestic football matches since 1981); any similar warning, or a symbol of it (*fig*); **yellow dog** a mongrel; a cur; a contemptible or cowardly person (also used adjectivally, *esp US*, as in **yellow-dog contract**, *orig* one requiring an employee not to be a member of a trade union, now, in a more general sense, one which gives acceptable advantages to an employee); **yellow earth** yellow ochre; **yellow-eyed grass** any plant of the genus *Xyris*, growing abundantly in the pine-barrens of the southern US; **yellow fever** an acute disease occurring in tropical America and W Africa, caused by infection with a virus transmitted to humans by the bite of a mosquito and characterized by high fever, acute nephritis, jaundice and haemorrhages; **yellow flag** a flag of a yellow colour, displayed by a vessel in quarantine or over a military hospital or ambulance; **yellow-girl** see **yellow-boy** above; **yell'owhammer** or (*obs*) **yell'ow-ammer** a bunting (*Emberiza citrinella*), so named from the yellow colour of the male (also called **yellow bunting**); **yell'ow-head** a species of fly catcher (*Mohoua ochrocephala*) found in New Zealand; **Yellow Jack** (*slang*) yellow fever; **yellow jacket** (*NAm*) a small common wasp or hornet (genus *Vespa*) with yellow markings; **yellow jersey** (Fr *maillot jaune*) the jersey worn each day in the Tour de France cycle race by the winner of the previous day's stage of the race; **yellow line** a line of yellow paint, or other substance, on a road indicating parking restrictions; **yellow metal** a brass consisting of sixty parts copper and forty parts zinc; **Yellow Pages**® a telephone directory, printed on yellow paper, which classifies participating subscribers alphabetically according to trades, professions, services, etc; **yellow pepper** see under **pepper**; **yellow peril** (also *caps*; *derog* or *facetious*) the supposed danger that the Oriental races, *esp* the Chinese, might overthrow the white or Western races and overrun the world; the Chinese or Japanese; **yellow poplar** the American tulip-tree, or its wood; **yellow press** (also with *cap*) newspapers abounding in exaggerated, sensational articles; **yellow rattle** see under **rattle**; **yellow ribbon** (*US*) a symbol of welcome for those returning home after having undergone some danger, *orig* a decoration on US cavalrymen's tunics, given to sweethearts as favours; **yell'ow-root** golden-seal; **yellow rust** a fungus damaging to wheat; **yellow snow** snow sometimes observed in the Alps and in the Antarctic regions, coloured yellow by the growth on it of certain algae; **yellow soap** common soap composed of tallow, resin and soda; **yellow spot** the macula lutea, the small area at the centre of the retina in vertebrates at which vision is most distinct; **yellow streak** a tendency to cowardly behaviour; **yellow wash** a lotion consisting of a mixture of mercuric chloride and lime water; **yell'ow-weed** the common ragwort; goldenrod; weld (the plant) (*dialect*); **yell'ow-wood** any of various woods that are light in colour, such as satinwood, or which yield yellow dye, such as *Cladrastis lutea* (American yellow-wood) of the southern US; any of the trees that yield these woods; a tree, such as a sumach, that yields yellow dye from a part other than the wood; **yell'ow-wort** an annual of the gentian family (also **yellow centaury**); **yell'ow-yite**, **yellow yoldring**, **yellow yorling** or **yellow-yow'ley** same as **yoldring**. [OE *geolu*; Ger *gelb*; cognate with L *helvus* light bay]

yelm or **yealm** *yelm*, (*dialect*) *n* a bundle of straw laid straight, ready for thatching. — *vt* to straighten and arrange (straw) for thatching. [OE *glim* a handful of reaped corn, a bundle]

yelp *yelp*, *vi* to boast (*obs*); to utter a sharp cry or bark. — *n* a sharp cry or bark. — *n* **yelp'er**. — *n* and *adj* **yelp'ing**. [OE *gielpan* to boast or exult; ON *gjālpa* to yelp]

yelt *yelt*, (*dialect*) *n* a young sow. [OE *gilte*, from MLGer *gelte* a spayed sow]

Yemeni *ye'mə-ni*, *adj* of or relating to the Republic of Yemen, its inhabitants or language. — Also *n*.

yen[1] *yen*, *n* formerly a Japanese gold or silver coin; the Japanese monetary unit since 1871: — *pl* **yen**. [Jap, from Chin *yüan* round, a dollar]

yen[2] *yen*, (*colloq*) *n* an intense desire, longing or urge. — *vi* to desire or yearn. [Chin dialect *yeen*, craving or addiction]

Yenglish. See **Yinglish**.

yenta *yen'tə*, (*US*) *n* a gossip; a shrewish woman. [From the Yiddish personal name]

Yeo. *abbrev*: Yeomanry.

yeoman *yō'mən*, *n* a gentleman serving in a royal or noble household, ranking between a sergeant and a groom (*hist*); after the 15c, a member of a class of small farmers, *usu* freeholders, the next grade below gentlemen (often serving as foot soldiers; *hist*); any small farmer or countryman above the grade of labourer; an assistant to an official; a member of the yeomanry cavalry or of the yeomen of the guard; a petty officer on a warship whose duties are clerical: — *pl* **yeo'men**. — *adj* **yeo'manly** of yeoman's rank; humble and honest; staunch; brave. — *adv* staunchly or bravely. — *n* **yeo'manry** the collective body of smaller freeholders; a cavalry volunteer force in Great Britain formed during the wars of the French Revolution, later mechanized as part of the Territorial Army. — **yeoman** or **yeoman's service** powerful aid, such as came from the yeomen in the English armies of early times. — **Yeomen of the Guard** a veteran company of picked soldiers, employed on special occasions in conjunction with the gentlemen-at-arms as the sovereign's bodyguard (constituted a corps in 1485 by Henry VII, and still wearing the costume of that period). [ME *yòman* or *yeman*; perh for *young man*]

yep *yep*, (*esp US*) *dialect* and *colloq* variant of **yes**.

yerba *yûr'bə*, *n* a herb, *esp* (also **yerba mate** or **yerba de maté**) Paraguay tea or maté (qv). [Sp, from L *herba*]

yerd and **yerd-hunger**. See **yird**.

yerk *yûrk*, (all meanings now *dialect*) *vt* of a shoemaker, to draw (stitches) tight; to bind or tie with a jerk; to throw or thrust with a sudden, quick motion; to move with a jerk; to lash out with; to utter jerkily; to beat; to rouse or excite (*fig*). — *vi* to draw tight, bind, strike, move or rise with a jerk; to kick; to engage in with energy or eagerness; to gibe or carp. [Origin obscure; earlier than **jerk**]

yersinia *yər-sin'i-ə*, *n* a bacterium of the genus *Yersinia* spread by animals or birds, one of which (*Yersinia pestis*) causes plague and others **yersinio'sis**, an acute infection of the small intestine: — *pl* **yersin'ias** or **yersin'iae** (*-i-ē*). [A E J *Yersin*, French bacteriologist, 1863–1943]

yes *yes*, *adv* a word of affirmation, agreement or consent; a word used to indicate that the speaker is present, or (often said interrogatively) to signal someone to act or to speak; in fact, indeed, or on the contrary (formerly used *esp* in answer to a negative question or to express disagreement with a previous negative statement, in contradistinction to *yea* which was used for simple agreement or affirmation until it became obsolete in the early 17c, its functions then being taken over by *yes*). — *n* a vote or answer of yes; a person who votes or answers yes: — *pl* **yess'es**, **yes'es** or **yes's**. — **yes-but'** (*colloq*) a qualified consent or agreement; **yes'-man** (*colloq*) someone who agrees with everything that is suggested; an obedient follower with no initiative. [OE *gēse* or *gīse*, from *gēa* or *gē* yea, and *sī* let it be]

yeshiva or **yeshivah** *yə-shē'və*, *n* a school for the study of the Jewish Scripture, the Talmud; a seminary for the training of rabbis; an orthodox Jewish elementary school: — *pl* **yeshi'vas**, **yeshi'vahs**, **yeshi'vōt** or **yeshi'vōth**. [Heb *yeshībhāh* a sitting]

yesk. See **yex**.

yest and **yesty**. *Obs* forms of **yeast** and **yeasty**.

yester *yes'tər*, *adj* (*dialect* and *archaic* **yes'tern**) and *combining form* relating to yesterday; last. — *adv* **yestreen'** (contraction of **yestereven**; *Scot* and *poetic*) yesterday evening. — **yes'terday** the day immediately before today; (often in *pl*) the (recent) past. — *adv* on the day immediately before today; formerly; in the (recent) past. — **yestereve'**, **yestere'ven**, **yestereve'ning**, **yestermorn'** and **yestermorn'ing** (*archaic*, *dialect* or *poetic*) yesterday evening, or morning; **yesternight'** (*archaic*, *dialect* or *poetic*) last night; **yes'teryear** (*orig D G Rossetti*) last year, or the past in general. [OE *geostran* or *giestran* (always followed by *dæg*, etc); Ger *gestern*; cf L *hesternus*, Gr *chthes*]

yet *yet*, *adv* in addition, besides; up to the present time; still; hitherto; at the same time; even; before the affair is finished. — *conj* nevertheless; however. — **as yet** up to the time under consideration. [OE *gīet gīeta*; Ger *jetzt*]

yeti *yet'i*, *n* the abominable snowman. [Tibetan *yeh-teh*]

yett *yet*, (*Scot*) *n* a gate or door. [Variant of **gate**[1]]

yeuk. See **yuke**.

yeve *yēv*, (*obs*) *vt* to give: — *pa p* (*Spenser*) **yeven** (*yev'ən*). [OE *giefan*; cf **give**]

yew *ū*, *n* any tree of the genus *Taxus* (family *Taxaceae*, itself a division of the group *Coniferae*) widely diffused over the northern parts of the world, with narrow lanceolate or linear leaves, *esp Taxus baccata* which yields an elastic wood good for bows; its wood; a bow made of its wood; yew twigs regarded as emblematic of grief (yew trees having traditionally been planted in graveyards throughout Europe). — *adj* **yew'en** (*archaic*) made of yew. — **yew tree**. [OE *īw* or *ēow*; Ger *Eibe*]

yex *yeks*, (now *Scot* and *dialect*) *vi* to hiccup, belch or spit. — *n* a hiccup, etc. — Also **yesk** (*yesk*). [OE *geocsian* to sob]

Yezidi *ye'zi-di*, *n* a member of a sect in Armenia and the Caucasus who believe in a Supreme God but also pay respect to the devil, believing him to have been reinstated as chief angel (called by them *Yazid*), and other minor gods. — Also **Yez'di**, **Yez'idee**, **Zez'idee**, etc.

yfere *i-fēr'*, (*obs*) *adv* together, in company. [See **fere**[1] and **infere**]

Y-fronts. See under **Y** (noun).

Yggdrasil, **yggdrasill** or **ygdrasil** *ig'drə-sil*, (*Scand mythol*) *n* the ash tree binding together heaven, earth and hell, and extending its branches over the whole world and above the heavens. [ON; perh from *Yggr* a surname of Odin, and *drasil* horse]

yglaunst *i-glönst'*, (*Spenser*) *pa p* of **glance**.

ygo or **ygoe** *i-gō'*, (*Spenser*) *pa p* of **go**; ago. [**go**]

YHA *abbrev*: Youth Hostels Association.

yibbles. See **able**.

yicker. Same as **yikker**.

Yiddish *yid'ish*, *n* a language spoken by Jews, based on medieval German dialects with Hebrew and Slavonic additions, *usu* written in the Hebrew alphabet. — *n* **Yid** (*offensive*) a Jew. — *adj* **Yidd'isher** in or relating to Yiddish; Jewish. — *n* a Jew, a speaker of Yiddish. — *n* **Yidd'ishism** an idiom or other speech characteristic derived from Yiddish. [Ger *jüdisch* Jewish]

yield *yēld*, *vt* to pay or repay, or to reward (*obs*); to render as due or appropriate (*archaic*); to grant or accord; to admit or concede; to give out; to furnish or afford; to produce; to deliver, surrender, relinquish or resign. — *vi* to submit; to cease fighting or contesting; to give way under pressure; to give place; to concede; to give way (in traffic) (*US*). — *n* an amount yielded; a product; the return of a financial investment, *usu* calculated with reference to the cost and dividend. — *adj* **yield'able** that may be yielded; inclined to yield. — *n* **yield'ableness**. — *n* **yield'er**. — *adj* **yield'ing** giving, or inclined to give, way; compliant. — *n* a giving way; compliance. — *adv* **yield'ingly**. — *n* **yield'ingness**. — **yield point** in iron and annealed steels, the stress at which a substantial amount of plastic deformation takes place suddenly; **yield strength** in materials which do not exhibit a sudden plastic deformation under stress (cf **yield point** above), the level of stress at which a given amount of deformation takes place. — **yield up the ghost** (*archaic*) to give up the ghost (see under **ghost**). [OE (WSax) *gieldan* to pay; OHGer *gelten*, ON *gjalda*]

yike *yīk* or **yikes** *yīks*, (*colloq*) *interj* expressing alarm or astonishment. — *n* (*Austr*) an argument, fight.

yikker *yik'ər*, *vi* of an animal, to utter sharp little cries. — Also *n*. [Imit]

yill *yil*, *n* Scots form of **ale**.

yin[1] *yin* and **yince** *yins*. Scots forms of **one** and **once** generally written **ane** and **ance**.

yin[2] *yin*, *n* (also with *cap*) one of the two opposing and complementary principles of Chinese philosophy, religion, medicine, etc influencing destiny and governing nature, seen as the negative, feminine, dark, cold, passive element (cf **yang**[1]). [Chin, dark]

yince-errand. See under **errand**.

Yinglish *ying'glish*, (*facetious orig US*) *n* a mixture of *Y*iddish and E*nglish* spoken by US Jews; a dialect of English containing a large number of Yiddishisms. — Also **Yeng'lish**.

yip *yip*, *vt esp* of a dog, to give a short, sudden cry. Also *n*. [Imit]

yippee *yip-ē'*, *interj* expressing delight, exultation, etc.

yipper. See under **yips**.

yippy *yip'i*, *n* any of a group of young people with ideals based on those of the hippies. [From the *Y*outh *I*nternational *P*arty of 1968]

yips *yips*, (*sport*, *esp* and *orig golf*) *n pl* (*usu* with *the*) an attack of nervous trembling caused by tension before making a shot, etc. — *n* **yipp'er** a golfer, etc suffering from the yips.

yird *yûrd*, *n* a Scots form of **earth**. — Also **eard** (*ûrd* or *erd*), **yeard** or **yerd**. — *vt* to bury. — **eard'-house**, **yird'-house**, etc an earth-house (see under **earth**); **eard'-hunger**, **yird'-hunger**, etc earth-hunger, a hunger for land; the hunger sometimes felt by persons approaching death; voracious hunger. — *adj* **eard'-hungry**, **yird'-hungry**, etc. [**earth**]

yirk. Same as **yerk**.

yite *yīt*, (*dialect*) *n* the yellowhammer. [Origin obscure]

-yl *-il*, (*chem*) *sfx* forming nouns denoting a radical, eg carbon*yl*, carbox*yl*, etc. [Gr *hȳlē* matter]

ylang-ylang *ē'lang-ē'lang*, *n* a tree (*Canangium odoratum*) of the Malay Archipelago and Peninsula, the Philippines, etc; an essence (also **ylang-ylang oil**) distilled from its flowers. [Tagálog]

ylem *ī'ləm*, *n* the original substance from which, according to some theories, the elements developed. [OFr *ilem*, from L *hȳlem*, accusative of *hȳlē*, from Gr *hȳlē* matter]

Y-level and **Y-moth**. See under **Y** (letter).

ylike (*Spenser*). Same as **alike**.

ylke. *Obs* spelling of **ilk**[1].

YMCA *abbrev*: Young Mens' Christian Association.

ymolt *i-mōlt'* (*Spenser*) or **ymolten** *i-mōl'tən*, (*obs*) *pa p* of **melt**[1].

ympe and **ympt** (*Spenser*). Same as **imp** and **imped**.

Yn *abbrev*: yen (Japanese currency).

ynambu *ē-näm-bo͞o'*, *n* a very large tinamou. [Port *inambu*; of Tupí origin, related to **tinamou**]

Ynd (*Spenser*). Same as **Ind**.

yo *yō*, *interj* calling for or accompanying effort, calling for attention or used in greeting, etc; used to indicate one's presence (eg at a roll-call), to acknowledge an order or request, etc (*esp US*): — *pl* **yos**. — *interj* **yo-hō'** or **yo-hō-hō'** calling for attention; (also **yo-heave-hō'**) formerly, a sailors' chant while hauling on ropes.

yob *yob*, (*slang*) *n* a raw recruit; a teenage loafer; a lout. — *n* **yobb'ery** yobbish behaviour. — *adj* **yobb'ish**. — *adv* **yobb'ishly**. — *n* **yobb'ism** yobbish behaviour. — *n* (*slang*) **yobb'o** a yob: — *pl* **yobb'os** or **yobb'oes**. [Back-slang for **boy**]

yock. See **yok**.

yod or **yode**. See **yead**.

yodel or **yodle** *yō'dl*, *vt* and *vi* to sing or shout, changing frequently from the ordinary voice to falsetto and back again. — *n* a song or phrase sung, or a cry made, in this fashion. — Also **jodel** (*yō'dl*). — *n* **yō'deller** or **yō'dler**. [Ger dialect *jodeln*]

yoga *yō'gə*, *n* a system of Hindu philosophy showing the means of emancipating the soul from further reincarnations and uniting it with the supreme being; any of a number of systems of physical and mental disciplines based on this, such as hatha yoga (see below) or raja yoga (qv); the practice of yogic exercises prescribed in such a system. — *n* **yō'gi** (*-gē*) or **yō'gin** a Hindu ascetic who practises the yoga system, consisting in the withdrawal of the senses from external objects, the holding of special postures or asanas for long periods of time, etc: — *fem* **yōgi'ni**. — *adj* **yō'gic**. — *n* **yō'gism**. — **yogic flying** in transcendental meditation, a form of levitation. — **hatha yoga** (*hath'ə* or *hut'ə*; Sans *haṭha* force) a form of yoga (the most common in the Western hemisphere) stressing the importance of physical exercises and positions and breathing-control in promoting physical and mental wellbeing. [Sans, union]

yogh *yohh*, *n* the ME letter ȝ, derived from OE ȝ, representing especially *y* and *hh* sounds. [Origin uncertain, but appropriate as exemplifying the two chief sounds of the letter]

yoghurt, **yoghourt** or **yogurt** *yog'ərt* or *yō'gərt*, *n* a semi-liquid food made from fermented milk. — Also **yaourt** (*yä'o͞ort*). [Turk *yōghurt*]

yogi, **yogin**, etc. See under **yoga**.

yohimbine *yo-him'bēn*, *n* an alkaloid obtained from the bark of *Corynanthe johimbe*, a W African rubiaceous tree. [Of Bantu origin]

yoicks *yoiks*, *interj* an old fox-hunting cry. — *vi* or *vt* **yoick** or **yoicks** to make, or urge on by, this cry.

yojan *yō'jan* or **yojana** *yō'ja-nə*, *n* an Indian measure of distance, *usu* about five miles. [Hindi *yojan*, from Sans *yojana* (distance covered in one) yoking]

yok or **yock** *yok*, (*theat slang*) *n* a laugh. — Also *vi*. [Imit]

yoke *yōk*, *n* something that joins together; a frame of wood joining draught oxen at the necks; any similar frame, such as one for carrying pails; a part of a garment that fits the shoulders (or the hips); a period of work, eg from mealtime to mealtime (*dialect*); a mark of servitude; slavery; an oppressive burden; a bond or union; a pair or couple, eg of oxen; a set of current coils for deflecting the electron beam in a TV or VDU cathode-ray tube; part of a magnetic circuit not enclosed by a current-carrying coil; an object, a thing, a tool, etc (*Ir*). — *vt* to put a yoke on; to join together; to attach a draught-animal to; to enslave; to set to work (*fig*). — *vi* to be joined; to go together; to set to work (*Scot*). — *n* **yōk'ing** (*dialect*) as much work as is done at one time. — **yoke'-devil** (*Shakesp*) a companion devil; **yoke'-fellow** or **yoke'-mate** an associate, partner or fellow-worker. — *adj* **yoke'-toed** zygodactyl. [OE *geoc*; Ger *Joch*; L *jugum*, Gr *zygon*]

yokel *yō'kl*, *n* a country bumpkin. — *adj* **yō'kelish**. [Ety doubtful]

yokozuna *yō-kə-zo͞o'nə*, *n* in sumo wrestling, a grand champion. [Jap, from *yoko* across, and *tsuma* rope, from the garland orig presented to a champion]

yokul. See **jokol**.

yold. *Obs pa t* and *pa p* of **yield**.

yoldring *yōld'ring, n* a yellowhammer. [Variant of dialect *yowlring*, from OE *geolu*; see **yellowhammer** under **yellow**]

yolk[1] *yōk*, or (*obs* or *dialect*) **yelk** *yelk, n* the yellow part of the egg of a bird or reptile; the nutritive non-living material contained by an ovum. — *adj* **yolked** or **yolk'y** like yolk. — **yolk'-sac** (*zool*) the yolk-containing sac which is attached to the embryo by the **yolk'-stalk**, a short stalk by means of which yolk substance may pass into the alimentary canal of the embryo. [OE *geolca* or *geoleca*, from *geolu* yellow]

yolk[2] *yōk, n* wool-oil, lanolin. — *adj* **yolk'y**. — Cf **suint**. [OE *ēowocig* yolky]

Yom Kippur *yōm kip'o͞or, n* the Day of Atonement, a Jewish fast day. — **Yom Tob** (*tōb*) or **Tov** (*tōv*) any Jewish religious festival. [Heb *yōm* day, and *kippūr* atonement, or *tōbh* good]

yomp *yomp*, (*esp military colloq*) *vi* to carry heavy equipment on foot over difficult terrain; (loosely, often *facetious*) to walk or trek in a determined, dogged or laboured manner, *esp* heavily laden. — Also *n*. [Poss imit]

yon *yon*, (now *poetic, Scot* or *dialect*) *adj* that; those; yonder. — *pronoun* that; the thing you know of. — *adv* yonder. — *prep* **yond** (*Scot usu* **yont**) across or through (*obs*); to, or in, a position beyond. — *adj* and *pronoun* yon. — *adv* yonder. — *adv* **yon'der** to, or at, a distance but within view. — *adj* that or those at a distance within view (actually or theoretically); (with *the*) farther, more distant. — *pronoun* that one, yon. — *n* (with *the*) the distance, distant places. — *adj* **yon'derly** (*dialect*) mentally or emotionally distant, vague, absent-minded; mentally or physically weak or low (*archaic*). — **hither and yon**, or **yond** (*dialect*) hither and thither; **hither**, or **here**, **and yonder** hither and thither. [OE *geon* (*adj, pronoun*), *geond* (*prep* and *adv*), and ME *yonder*]

yond *yond*, (*Spenser*) *adj* furious, mad. [Said to be due to misunderstanding of a passage in an earlier writer; Chaucer's *Clerk's Tale* 1143 has been suggested, but 16c black-letter Chaucers do not have the word in this line]

yonder. See under **yon**.

yongthly. Same as **youngthly** (see under **young**).

yoni *yō'nē, n* a representation of the female genitals, the symbol under which the Hindu goddess Sakti is worshipped. [Sans]

yonker. *Obs* form of **younker**.

yonks *yongks*, (*colloq*) *n* ages, a long time. [Poss *y*ears, m*on*ths and wee*ks*; or perh compressed from *donkey's years*]

yont. See **yon**.

yoof *yo͞of*, (*colloq*; *usu derog*) *n* youth, young people. — *adj* (*esp* of magazines, TV or radio programmes, etc) relating to, specifically aimed at, pandering to, or dealing with topics (thought to be) of interest to modern youth. [**youth**, with *f* substituted for *th* as in certain forms of London speech]

yoo-hoo *yo͞o'-ho͞o, interj* a call to attract someone's attention.

yoop *yo͞op, n* and *interj* (representing) a sobbing sound.

YOP *yop, abbrev*: Youth Opportunities Programme. — *n* **yopp'er** a young person employed on this programme.

yore *yōr* or *yör*, (*obs* or *poetic*) *adv* long ago. — *n* time long ago or long past. — Also *adj*. — **days of yore** times past; **of yore** in times past. [OE *gēara* formerly; appar connected with *gēar* a year]

yorker *yörk'ər*, (*cricket*) *n* a ball pitched to a point directly under the bat (formerly called a tice). — *vt* **york** to bowl (or attempt to bowl) someone out with a yorker. [Prob from *Yorkshire*, but history quite unknown]

Yorkie *yör'ki*, (*colloq*) *n* (also without *cap*) a Yorkshire terrier.

Yorkish *yörk'ish, adj* of, from or relating to the city of *York*; Yorkshire (*adj*; *archaic*); supporting the House of York in the Wars of the Roses (*hist*). — *n* **York'ist** (*hist*) a supporter of the House of York. — Also *adj*. — *adj* **York'shire** of or from the area comprising the former county of Yorkshire (now divided into N, W and S Yorkshire: — *abbrev* **Yorks**. — *n* any of a breed of animal, *esp* pigs, originating in Yorkshire. — **Yorkshire fog** a tall grass, *Holcus lanatus*; **Yorkshire grit** a grit from Yorkshire used for polishing; **Yorkshire pudding** a pudding made of unsweetened batter, and baked along with meat or in meat dripping (*orig* under the spit so as to catch the drippings); **Yorkshire terrier** a small long-haired kind of terrier.

Yorks. *abbrev*: Yorkshire.

Yoruba *yo'ro͞o-bə* or *yō', n sing* and *n pl* a linguistic group of coastal W Africa; a member of the group; the language of the group. — *adj* **Yo'ruba** or **Yo'ruban**.

you *ū, pronoun* the second person pronoun, *orig* only plural (cf **thou**), now both singular and plural; (*indefinite pronoun*) anyone; the personality (or something in tune with the personality) of the person addressed (*colloq*). — **you-all'** (*US*; *esp Southern*) you (*esp* in addressing two or more people); **you'-know-what'** and **you'-know-who'** some unspecified but well-understood or well-known thing or person. [OE *ēow* (perh through a later form *eōw*), orig only dative and accusative; cf **ye**[1]]

you'd *yo͞od* or *yo͝od*, a contraction of **you had** or **you would**.

youk. See **yuke**.

you'll *yo͞ol* or *yo͝ol*, a contraction of **you will** or **you shall**.

young *yung, adj* (*compar* **younger** *yung'gər, superl* **youngest** *yung'gist*) born recently; in early life; in the first part of growth; youthful; vigorous; relating to youth; junior, the younger of two persons having the same name; inexperienced; newly arrived; miniature (*colloq*). — *n* the offspring of animals; (with *the*) those who are young. — *adj* **youngish** (*yung'ish* or *yung'gish*) fairly young. — *n* **young'ling** (*archaic*) a young person or animal. — *adj* youthful, young. — *adv* **young'ly** (*rare*) in youth; in the manner of youth. — *n* **young'ness**. — *n* **young'ster** a young person, *esp* a young man, or (formerly) a lively young man; a child (*colloq*). — *n* **youngth** (*Spenser*) youth. — *adj* **youngth'ly** (*Spenser*) youthful. — **young blood** a fresh accession of strength, personnel, ideas, etc; **Young England** during the corn-laws struggle (1842–45), a small band of young Tory politicians who hated Free Trade and Radicalism, and professed a sentimental attachment to earlier forms of social life in England; **Young England, America**, etc the rising generation in England, America, etc. — *adj* **young'-eyed** (*Shakesp*) with the bright eyes of youth. — **young fogy** or **fogey** a young person with (*esp* vociferously proffered) conservative or reactionary opinions. — *adj* **young fō'gyish** or **fō'geyish**. — **Young Ireland** a group of Irish nationalists who broke away from O'Connell about 1844, because of his strong objection to the use of physical force; **Young Italy** an association of Italian republican agitators, active about 1834, under the lead of Mazzini; **young lady** or **young man** a girlfriend or boyfriend, a sweetheart; **young offender** a law-breaker aged between 17 and 21 (**young-offender institution** an establishment, replacing the borstal, for the detention of young offenders who are given custodial sentences); **young person** someone aged fourteen and over, but under seventeen (*law*); in Factory Acts, etc, a person who is under eighteen years of age but no longer a child; **Young Turk** any of a body of Turkish reformers who brought about the revolution of 1908; (also without *caps*) a progressive, rebellious, impetuous, etc member of an organization. — **with young** (of an animal) pregnant. [OE *geong*; Ger *jung*; also connected with L *juvenis*, Sans *yuvan* young]

youngberry *yung'ber-i* or *-bər-i, n* a large reddish-black fruit, a cross between a variety of blackberry and a variety of dewberry. [B M *Young*, an American fruitgrower, and **berry**]

Young modulus *yung mod'ū-ləs* or **Young's modulus** (*yungz*), *n* the coefficient of elasticity of stretching, ie for a stretched wire, the ratio of the stretching force per unit cross-sectional area to the elongation per unit length. [Thomas *Young* (1773–1829), English physicist]

younker *yung'kər*, *n* a young person (*old*); a young gentleman or knight (*Spenser*). [ODu *jonckher* (Du *jonker*), from *jong heer* young master or lord; Ger *Junker*]

your *yör* or *ūr*, *pronoun* (*genitive pl*) or *possessive adj* of or belonging to you; used to denote a person or thing of a particular well-known class or type, the typical or ordinary (*usu* implying some contempt; *colloq*); of or relating to an unspecified person or people in general. — *pronoun* **yourn** (*dialect*) yours. — *pronoun* **yours** (a double genitive) used predicatively or absolutely; short for 'your letter'. — **you and yours** you and your family or property; **yours faithfully**, **sincerely**, **truly**, etc, **yours to command**, etc, forms used conventionally in letters just before the signature; **yours truly** also sometimes used by a speaker to mean himself or herself (*colloq*). [OE *ēower*, genitive of *gē* ye]

you're *yör* or *ūr*, a contraction of **you are**.

yourself *ūr-self'* or *yör-*, *pronoun* the emphatic form of **you**; in your real character; having command of your faculties; sane; in good form; the reflexive form of **you** (objective); often used *colloq* and incorrectly instead of **you** (unreflexive second person singular): — *pl* **yourselves'**.

yourt. See **yurt**.

youth *yōōth*, *n* the state of being young; early life, the period immediately following childhood; an early period of existence; a young person, *esp* a young man (*pl* **youths** *yōōdhz*); young persons collectively; recentness, freshness (*Shakesp*). — *adj* **youth'ful** relating to youth or early life; young; suitable to youth; fresh; buoyant, vigorous. — *adv* **youth'fully**. — *n* **youth'fulness**. — *n* **youth'head** or **youth'hood** (*obs*) youth. — *adj* **youth'ly** (*Spenser*) young, youthful (also *adv*). — *adj* **youth'some** (*obs*) youthful. — *adj* **youth'y** (*Scot*) young. — **youth club** a place or organization providing leisure activities for young people; **youth custody** a custodial sentence of between four and eighteen months passed on a person aged between 15 and 21; **youth hostel** a hostel where hikers, etc who are members of the Youth Hostels Association or a related organization find inexpensive and simple accommodation. — *vi* to stay in youth hostels. — **youth hosteller**; **youth leader** a social worker who works with the young people of a particular community or area. — **Youth Opportunities Programme** or **YOP** between 1978 and 1983, a government-sponsored scheme giving work experience to unemployed young people, replaced in 1983 by the **Youth Training Scheme** (or **YTS**) a similar government-sponsored scheme to give training and job experience to unemployed school-leavers. [OE *geoguth*, from *geong* young; Ger *Jugend*]

you've *yōōv* or *yōōv*, a contraction of **you have**.

yow or **yowe** *yow*, (*Scot* and *dialect*) *n* a variant of **ewe**.

yowie¹ *yow'i*, (*Scot*) *n* a little ewe.

yowie² *yow'i*, (*Austr folklore*) *n* a tall, ape-like monster of SE Australia. [Aboriginal *yuwi*]

yowl *yowl*, *vi* (of eg a dog) to cry mournfully; to yell or bawl. — *n* a cry of distress. — *n* **yowl'ing** a howling. [ME *youlen*; cf ON *gaula* to howl]

yowley. Same as **yoldring**.

yo-yo *yō'-yō*, *n* a toy consisting of a reel wound with an attached length of string which is held in the hand while the reel is let drop to fall and rise under its own weight, similar to the 18c bandalore or quiz; any person or thing resembling a yo-yo in movement or ease of manipulation; an indecisive or useless person, a fool (*slang*; *orig US*). — *vi* to operate a yo-yo; to move rapidly up and down; to fluctuate rapidly or be very unsettled. — *adj* of or resembling a yo-yo; rising and falling, or fluctuating from one position or extreme to the other, *esp* rapidly or without due control (as in *yo-yo economy*, *yo-yo dieting*). [Manufacturer's trademark, appar from a Filipino word]

ypight *i-pīt'*, *obs pa p* of **pitch**².

yplast *i-plāst'*, *obs pa p* of **place**.

yplight *i-plīt'*, *obs pa p* of **plight**.

ypsilon *ip-sī'lon*, *-sē'* or *ip'si-*, *n* (*rare*). Same as **upsilon**. — *adj* **ypsiliform** (*-sil'*) or **ypsiloid** (*ip'sil-oid*) shaped like an upsilon. [Ety as for **upsilon**]

yr *abbrev*: year; younger; your.

yrapt *i-rapt'*, (*Spenser*). Same as **rapt**.

yravished *i-rav'ish-id*, (Malone's emendation of Shakespeare's *iranyshed*) *obs pa t* of **ravish**.

yrent *i-rent'*, *obs pa p* of **rend**.

yrivd *i-rīvd'*, *obs pa p* of **rive**.

yrneh *yûr'ni*, *n* unit of reciprocal inductance. [*henry*, the unit of inductance, spelled backwards]

ysame *i-sām'*, (*Spenser*) *adv* together. [Perh **in** and **same** (*n*)]

yshend *i-shend'*, (*Spenser*). Same as **shend**.

yslaked *i-slākt'*, *obs pa p* of **slake**¹; quenched or relaxed the energies of (*Shakesp*).

ythundered *i-thun'də-rid*, (*Spenser*) *pa p* struck by a thunderbolt.

ytost *i-tost'*, (*Spenser*) *pa p* of **toss**.

Y-track. See under **Y** (noun).

YT *abbrev*: Yukon Territory (Canada).

yt (*obs*) *abbrev*: that (see **Y** (noun)).

YTS *abbrev*: Youth Training Scheme.

ytterbium *i-tûr'bi-əm*, *n* a metallic element (symbol **Yb**, atomic no 70) a member of the rare-earth group; the name *orig* given to a substance later shown to consist of a mixture of this and lutetium. — *n* **ytter'bia** ytterbium oxide (Yb_2O_3). [*Ytterby*, a Swedish quarry]

yttrium *it'ri-əm*, *n* a metallic element (symbol **Y**, atomic no 39) in the third group of the periodic system, *usu* classed with the rare earths. — *n* **ytt'ria** its oxide (Y_2O_3), a yellowish-white powder. — *adj* **ytt'ric** or **ytt'rious**. — *adj* **yttrif'erous**. — *n* **ytt'ro-cē'rite** a mineral, *usu* violet in colour, found embedded in quartz, a fluoride of yttrium, cerium, etc; **yttro-col'umbite** or **yttro-tan'talite** a brownish mineral found at Ytterby, a tantalate of yttrium, iron, calcium, etc. [From *Ytterby*; see ety for **ytterbium**]

YTV *abbrev*: Yorkshire Television.

YU *abbrev*: (the former) Yugoslavia (IVR).

yu *yü* or *ū*, *n* precious jade (nephrite or jadeite). — Also **yu'-stone**. [Chin *yü* jade, *yü-shih* jade-stone]

yuan *yü-än'*, *n* the monetary unit of the People's Republic of China: — *pl* **yuan**. [Chin]

yuca or **yucca** *yuk'ə*, *n* (*usu* **yuca**) cassava; any plant of the genus *Yucca* of plants of the family *Liliaceae*, native to Mexico, New Mexico, etc, some (such as *Yuca gloriosa*, the Spanish dagger) cultivated in gardens on account of their splendid appearance. [Of Carib origin]

yuck¹ or **yuk** *yuk*, (*slang*) *n* unpleasantly messy or disgusting material; sickly sweet sentimentality. — *interj* expressing extreme distaste or disgust. — *adj* **yucky** or **yukky** (*yuk'i*) unpleasantly messy or disgusting; sickly sentimental. [Imit]

yuck². See **yuke**.

yucker *yuk'ər*, *n* the American flicker or golden-winged woodpecker. [Imit of its note]

yucky¹. See under **yuck**¹.

yucky². See under **yuke**.

yuft *yuft*, *n* Russia leather. [Russ]

yuga *yōō'gə*, *n* any of the four Hindu ages of the world. — Also **yug**. [Sans]

Yugoslav (also *obs* **Yugo-slav**) *yōō'gō-släv* or *-släv'*, *n* a native, citizen or inhabitant of the former state of Yugoslavia; one of the southern group of Slavs consisting of Serbs, Croats and Slovenes; the Serbo-Croat language (see under **Serb**; *rare*). — Also *adj*. — *adj* and *n* **Yugoslav'ian** and **Yugoslav'ic**. — Also (*old*) **Jugo-Slav**, **Jugoslav**, etc. [Serbo-Croat *jugo-*, from *jug* the south, and **Slav**]

yuk and **yukky**. See **yuck**¹.

yukata *yōō-ka'tə*, *n* a light kimono, *usu* of printed cotton, worn as a bathrobe or housecoat. [Jap, from *yu* hot water, bath, and *kata*(*bira*) light kimono]

yuke *yo͞ok* or **yuck** *yuk*, (*dialect*) *vi* to itch. — *n* itching; the itch. — Also **youk**, **yeuk**, **euk** or **ewk**. — *adj* **yuk'y** or **yuck'y** itchy. [Same as **itch**; prob influenced by the MDu form *jeuken*]

yuko *yo͞o'kō*, *n* an award of five points in judo. [Jap]

yulan *yo͞o'lan*, *n* a Chinese magnolia, producing large white flowers. [Chin]

Yule *yo͞ol*, (*old-fashioned* or *dialect*) *n* the season or feast of Christmas. — **Yule log** a cake shaped and decorated to resemble a log, eaten at Christmas time; *orig* a log cut down in the forest, dragged to the house, and set alight in celebration of Christmas; **Yule'tide** the time or season of Yule or Christmas. — Also **yule** or **yule'tide**. [OE *gēol*, Yule, *se ǣrra gēola*, December; ON *jōl*]

yummy. See under **yum-yum**.

yump[1] *yump*, (*slang*) *vi* in rally-driving, to leave the ground (in one's vehicle) when going over a ridge or crest. — *n* an instance of this. [Norw *jump* jump (as pronounced)]

yump[2]. See **yumpie**.

yumpie or **Yumpie**, *yum'pi*, (*colloq*) *n* one of the *y*oung *u*pwardly-*m*obile *p*eople, a dismissive designation for young rising or ambitious professionals. — Also **yump**. — See also **yuppie**.

yum-yum *yum'-yum'*, (*colloq*) *interj* expressing delighted or pleasant anticipation, *esp* of delicious food. — *interj* **yumm'y** yum-yum. — *adj* delicious, attractive, etc. [Imit]

yunx *yungks*, *n* a variant of **Jynx**.

yup *yup* or *yəp*. Same as **yep**.

Yupik *yo͞o'pik*, *n sing* and *n pl* a people inhabiting the W Alaskan coast and parts of Siberia, speaking an Eskimo-Aleut language; a member of this people; their language. — Also *adj*. [From the root of *juk* a person, the Yupik equivalent of *inuk* (see ety of **Innuit**)]

yupon. See **yaupon**.

yuppie or **yuppy** *yup'i*, *n* (also with *cap*) a *y*oung *u*rban *p*rofessional, a dismissive designation for the young city careerist, the word now being commoner than **yumpie** (qv) and even explained by some as derived acronymically from *y*oung *u*pwardly-mobile *p*eople. — *n* **yupp'iedom** the state of being a yuppie; the world or circles which yuppies frequent. — *n* **yuppificā'tion**. — *vt* **yupp'ify** to adapt (*esp* a locality or a particular venue) to suit the taste of yuppies; to be frequented by or suitable for yuppies. — **yuppie flu** (*colloq*) myalgic encephalomyelitis.

yurt or **yourt** *yo͞ort*, *n* a light tent of skins, etc used by nomads in Siberia. [From Russ]

YV *abbrev*: Venezuela (IVR).

YWCA *abbrev*: Young Women's Christian Association.

Z

Z or **z** *zed*, *n* the twenty-sixth and last letter in the modern English alphabet, derived through the Greek *zeta* (Z, ζ), from *zayin*, the seventh letter of the Semitic alphabet. Its sound is a voiced sibilant, either voiced *s* as in 'zeal', or a voiced *sh* as in 'azure'; used in Scots to represent ME ȝ (the letter yogh), as in *capercailzie*, but now sometimes pronounced as a Z, as in the English pronunciation of the Scottish family name *Menzies* (*men'ziz, Scot ming'iz*); something similar to the letter Z in shape, as in **Z'-bend** a series of sharp bends in a road. — **Z-DNA** a form of duplex DNA, in which purines and pyrimidines alternate in a strand, resulting in a left-handed helix. See also under **cedilla**, **zed** and **zeta**[1].
Z or **Z.** *abbrev*: zaire (Zaïrean currency); Zambia (IVR).
Z *symbol*: (also **z** or *z*) the third variable, unknown or yet to be ascertained quantity or factor in a series, after X and Y (or **x**, **y** or *x*, *y*) (*algebra*, etc); as a medieval Roman numeral, Z = 2 000.
Z *symbol*: atomic number (*chem*); impedance (*phys*).
z or **z.** *abbrev*: zenith; zero; zone.
z *symbol*: used as a contraction-mark, as in *viz*, *oz*, etc.
ZA *abbrev*: *Zuid Afrika*, (*Afrik*) South Africa (IVR).
zabaglione *zä-bäl-yō'ni*, *n* a frothy custard made from egg yolks, marsala and sugar. — Also **zabaione** (*-bə-yō'ni*). [Ital]
zabeta *za-bē'ta*, (*Ar*) *n* a stated tariff.
Zabian *zā'bi-ən*, *adj* and *n*. Same as **Sabian**.
zabra *zä'brä*, (*hist*) *n* a small vessel used off the Spanish coast. [Sp]
zabtieh. See **zaptieh**.
zack *zak*, (*Austr slang*) *n* formerly a sixpenny, now a five-cent, piece.
zaddik, **tsaddik**, **tsaddiq**, **tzaddik** or **tzaddiq**, *tsad'ik*, *n* in Judaism, a Hasidic leader, or person of extraordinary piety: — *pl* **zaddikim**, etc or **zadd'iks**, etc. [Heb *saddīq* righteous or just]
Zadkiel *zad'ki-əl*, *n* the name assumed by Richard James Morrison (1794–1874), compiler of a popular astrological almanac.
zaffre or **zaffer** *zaf'ər*, *n* the impure oxide (used as a pigment) obtained by partially roasting cobalt ore previously mixed with two or three times its weight of fine sand. [Fr *zafre*, of Ar origin]
zag *zag* *n* a new line, or sharp change, of direction on a zigzag course. — Also *vi*: — *pr p* **zagg'ing**; *pa t* and *pa p* **zagged**. [*-zag* extracted from **zigzag**]
zaire *zä-ēr'*, *n* the standard unit of currency of *Zaire*, a republic of central Africa: — *pl* **zaire'**. — *adj* **Zairean** (*-ē'ri-ən*) of or relating to Zaire. — *n* a native or citizen of Zaire.
zakat *za-kät'*, *n* in Islam, a tax of $2\frac{1}{2}$ per cent payable by Muslims on certain kinds of property, the money so raised being devoted to religious and charitable purposes. [Pers, from Ar *zakāh*]
zakuska *zä-kōōs'ka*, *n* an hors-d'œuvre; a snack: — *pl* **zakuski** (*-kē*). [Russ]
zalambdodont *za-lam'dō-dont*, *adj* having molar teeth with V-shaped ridges, as some Insectivora do. — Also *n*. [Gr *za-* very, *lambda* the letter Λ (= L) and *odous*, *odontos* a tooth]
Zalophus *zal'ō-fəs*, *n* a genus of eared seals. [Gr *za-* (intensive), and *lophos* a crest]
zaman *zə-män'* or **zamang** *zə-mäng'*, *n* the saman or rain-tree. [Carib]
zamarra *thä-mär'ä* or **zamarro** *-ō*, (*Sp*) *n* a shepherd's sheepskin coat: — *pl* **zamarr'as** or **zamarr'os**.
Zambian *zam'bi-ən*, *adj* of or relating to the republic of *Zambia* (formerly Northern Rhodesia) in central Africa. — *n* a native or citizen of Zambia.
zambo *zam'bō*, *n*. Same as **sambo'**: — *pl* **zam'bos**. [Sp; see **sambo**]
zambomba *thäm-bom'bä*, *n* a simple Spanish musical instrument, made by stretching a piece of parchment over a wide-mouthed jar and inserting a stick in it, sounded by rubbing the stick with the fingers. [Sp]
zamboorak. See **zumbooruk**.
zambuk or **zambuck** (*NZ* and *Austr colloq*; also with *cap*) a member of the St John's Ambulance Brigade, *esp* one on duty at a sporting event. [The proprietary name of an antiseptic ointment]
zamia *zā'mi-ə*, *n* a plant of the *Zamia* genus of palm-like trees or low shrubs of the family *Cycadaceae*, some species of which yield an edible starchy pith. [Named through misreading in Pliny *azaniae nuces*, pine cones that open on the tree, from Gr *azanein* or *azainein* to dry]
zamindar, **zamindari** and **zamindary**. See under **zemindar**.
zamouse *za-mōōs'*, *n* the short-horned buffalo of W Africa. [Ar *jāmūs*]
zampogna *tsam-pō'nyä*, *n* the Italian bagpipe. [Ital]
zampone *tsam-pō'nē*, *n* a stuffed pig's trotter sausage: — *pl* **zampō'ni**. [Ital]
zander *zan'dər*, *n* a species of pike-perch, *Lucioperca sandra*, a food fish. [Ger]
zanella *zə-nel'ə*, *n* a mixed twilled fabric for covering umbrellas. [Origin uncertain]
zanja *thäng'hhä*, *n* in Latin America, an irrigating canal. — *n* **zanjero** (*-hhā'rō*) someone who superintends the distribution of water in irrigation canals: — *pl* **zanje'ros**. [Am Sp, from Sp, ditch, trench]
zante *zan'tē*, *n* (also **zan'te-wood**) the wood of the European smoke-tree, from *Zante*, one of the principal Ionian Islands; satinwood. — *n* **Zan'tiot** (*-ot*) or **Zan'tiote** (*-ōt*) a native or citizen of Zante. — **Zante currant** the small seedless fruit of a Zante grape.
zantedeschia *zan-ti-des'ki-ə*, *n* a plant of the *Zantedeschia* genus of the arum family (*Araceae*), including *Zantedeschia aethiopica*, known as the calla lily. [Francesco *Zantedeschi*, Italian botanist]
zanthoxyl. Same as **xanthoxyl**.
Zantiot or **Zantiote**. See under **zante**.
Zantippe. See **Xantippe**.
ZANU *zä'nōō*, *abbrev*: Zimbabwe African National Union. — Also **Za'nu**.
zany *zā'ni*, *n* an assistant clown or buffoon (*hist*); a toady (*obs*); a simpleton (*dialect*); someone who plays the fool (*colloq*). — *adj* of or relating to a zany; crazy, clownish, endearingly amusing (*colloq*). — *vt* (*obs*) to play the zany to. — *n* **zā'niness**. — *n* **zā'nyism** the state of being, or the behaviour of, a buffoon. [Fr *zani*, from Ital *zanni*, the Venetian form of *Gianni*, *Giovanni* John, a name given to comic servant characters in the commedia dell'arte]
zanze *zän'ze*, *n* an African musical instrument. [Ar *sanj* castanets or cymbals]
Zanzibari *zan-zi-bär'i*, *n* a native or inhabitant of Zanzibar. — Also *adj*.
zap *zap*, (*colloq*) *vt* to hit, strike, destroy, shoot, etc (*lit* and *fig*); to erase or correct (a fault) (*comput*); to cause to move or pass by quickly. — *vi* to go speedily or suddenly (often with *off* or *along*); to keep changing television channels, using a remote-control device (*colloq*). — *n* vitality or force. — *interj* expressing suddenness. — *n* **zapp'er** (*colloq*) a person who or thing which zaps, *esp* a remote-control device for a TV or

video recorder. — *adj* **zapp'y** (*slang*) full of verve or punch, lively, energetic; speedy. — **zap (it) up** to make (things) livelier. [Imit]

zapata *zə-pä'tə*, *adj* denoting a type of flowing moustache drooping down on each side of the mouth. [Emilio *Zapata*, Mexican revolutionary (1879–1919), who wore a moustache of this shape]

zapateado *thä-pä-te-ädh'ō*, *n* a lively Spanish dance for a solo performer, with a great deal of clicking and stamping of the heels: — *pl* **zapatead'os**. [Sp]

Zapodidae *za-pod'i-dē*, *n pl* the jumping-mouse family. [Formed from Gr *za-* very, *pous*, *podos* foot, and sfx *-idae*]

Zaporogian *zā-pō-rō'ji-ən*, *adj* relating to or designating the Ukraine Cossacks dwelling near the Porogi or falls of the Dnieper. — *n* a member of this people. [Russ *za* beyond, and *porogi* rapids]

zapotilla *zap-ō-til'ə*, *n*. Same as **sapodilla**.

zaptieh *zap'ti-e*, *n* a Turkish policeman. — Also **zap'tiah** or **zab'tieh**. [From Turk]

ZAPU *zä'pōō*, *abbrev*: Zimbabwe African People's Union. — Also **Za'pu**.

zarape *sä-rä'pe*, *n*. Same as **serape**.

Zarathustrian *zar-ə-thōōs'tri-ən*, *adj* and *n* Zoroastrian. — *n* **Zarathus'trianism** or **Zarathus'trism** Zoroastrianism. — *adj* and *n* **Zarathus'tric** Zoroastrian. [*Zarathustra*, Avestan name for the founder of the religion]

zaratite *zä'rə-tīt*, *n* a hydrous carbonate of nickel, found *usu* as an incrustation on chromite. [From *Zárate*, a Spaniard]

zareba *zə-rē'bä*, *n* in the Sudan, a stockade, thorn-hedge, etc protecting against wild animals or enemies; a fortified camp generally. — Also **zaree'ba**, **zari'ba**, **zere'ba** or **zeri'ba**. [Ar *zarībah* a pen or enclosure for cattle]

zarf *zärf* or **zurf** *zûrf*, *n* an ornamental holder for a hot coffee-cup. [Ar *ẓarf* a vessel]

zarnich *zär'nik*, *n* a naturally occurring sulphide of arsenic, such as orpiment (arsenic trisulphide) or realgar (arsenic monosulphide). — Also **zar'nec**. [Ar *zarnīkh*]

zarzuela *thär-thōō-ā'lä*, or *-thwā'*, *n* a traditional Spanish form of operetta or vaudeville; a Spanish fish and shellfish stew. [The royal residence of La *Zarzuela*, Madrid, where first performed]

zastruga *zas-trōō'gä*, *n*: — *pl* **zastru'gi** (*-gē*). Same as **sastruga**.

zati *zä'ti*, *n* the bonnet-monkey.

zax. A variant of **sax**[1].

z.B. *abbrev*: *zum Beispiel* (*Ger*), for example.

'zbud. See **'sblood**.

Zea *zē'ə*, *n* a genus of cereals having monoecious flowers, the only species being *Zea mays*, maize; (without *cap*) the fresh styles and stigmas of this plant, formerly used as a diuretic. [Gr *zeā* or *zeia* one-seeded wheat]

zeal *zēl*, *n* strong feeling, such as love, anger, etc, or passionate ardour (*archaic*); intense (sometimes fanatical) enthusiasm; activity arising from warm support or enthusiasm; a zealot (*obs*). — *n* **zeal'ant** or **zel'ant** (*Bacon*) a zealot. — *adj* **zeal'ful**. — *adj* **zeal'less**. — *n* **zealot** (*zel'ət*) an enthusiast; a fanatic; (with *cap*) a member of a militant Jewish sect vigorously opposing the Roman domination of Palestine until the ruin of Jerusalem in AD 70. — *n* **zealotism** (*zel'*) the character or actions of a zealot. — *n* **zealotry** (*zel'*). — *adj* **zealous** (*zel'*) full of zeal; keenly engaged in, or ardent in support of, anything; devoted. — *adv* **zealously** (*zel'*). — *n* **zealousness** (*zel'*). [OFr *zele*, from L *zēlus*, from Gr *zēlos*, from *zeein* to boil]

zebec and **zebeck**. Variants of **xebec**.

zebra *zē'brə* or *ze'brə*, *n* any of a group of striped animals of the genus *Equus*, all of which are peculiar to the African continent; (used, *esp* as *adj* in names, to denote) any animal, fish, plant or mineral having stripes reminiscent of a zebra's, such as the *zebra duiker* (a striped W African antelope), the *zebra finch* (see below), etc; a referee (having a striped shirt) in American football (*US slang*). — *n* **ze'brass** the offspring of a male zebra and a female ass. — *adj* **zē'brine** or **zē'broid**. — *n* **zebrinn'y** (cf **hinny**') the offspring of a male horse and a female zebra. — *n* **ze'brule** or **ze'brula** the offspring of a male zebra and a female horse. — **zebra crossing** a street crossing (marked with black and white stripes) where pedestrians have priority; **zebra finch** an Australian weaver bird with black and white striped markings; **zebra parakeet** the budgerigar; **zebra spider** any of several striped spiders of the *Salticidae*; **ze'bra-wood** the hard and beautifully striped wood of a Guianan tree, *Connarus guianensis*; the tree itself; applied also to various other trees or their wood. [African]

zebrina *zeb-rī'nə*, *n* a trailing or creeping herbaceous plant of the Central American genus *Zebrina*, with pointed, ovate, striped leaves. [New L]

zebu *zē'bū* or *zē'bōō*, *n* a humped domestic ox (*Bos indicus*) closely related to the common ox, found throughout the Indian subcontinent, China, the east coast of Africa, etc. [Fr *zébu*, the name taken by Buffon from the exhibitors of one at a French fair in 1752]

zebub *zē'bub*, *n* the zimb. [Ar (dialect) *zubāb* a fly]

zecchino *tsek-kē'nō*, *n* a former Italian gold coin (also called **sequin**): — *pl* **zecchi'nos** or **zecchi'ni** (*-ē*). — Also **zecchine** (*zek'in*). [See **sequin**]

Zech. (*Bible*) *abbrev*: (the Book of) Zechariah.

Zechstein *zek'stīn*, (*geol*) *n* a deposit of calcareous rock, the higher of the two series into which the Permian system of Germany is divided. [Ger, from *Zeche* mine, and *Stein* stone]

zed *zed*, (*US*) **zee** *zē*, *n* the twenty-sixth letter of the English alphabet (Z, z); a bar of metal shaped like the letter Z. [Fr *zède*, from L and Gr *zēta*]

zedoary *zed'ō-ə-ri*, *n* certain species of curcuma, native to the Indian subcontinent, China, etc, whose rootstocks are aromatic, bitter and pungent. [Through medieval L, from Ar *zedwār*]

zee *zē*. See **zed**.

Zeeman effect *zā'män if-ekt'*, (*phys*) *n* the splitting of a spectral line into several symmetrically disposed components which occurs when the source of light is placed in a strong magnetic field. [Named from Dutch physicist Pieter *Zeeman* (1865–1943)]

zein *zē'in*, *n* a protein found in maize. [**Zea**]

zeitgeist *tsīt'gīst*, *n* (also with *cap*) the spirit of the age. [Ger]

Zeitvertreib *tsīt'fər-trīp*, (*Ger*) *n* a pastime.

zek *zek*, *n* an inmate of a prison or labour camp in the former USSR. [Russ slang, poss from abbrev *zk* for *zaklyuchënnyi* prisoner]

zel *zel*, *n* a form of Oriental cymbal. [Turk *zīl*]

Zelanian *zə-lā'ni-ən*, *adj* in zoogeography, of or relating to New *Zealand*.

zelant. See under **zeal**.

zelatriks *zel'ə-triks*, **zelatrice** *-tris*, or **zelator** *-tər*, *n* a nun whose duty is to keep watch on the behaviour of the younger nuns in the convent, or on that of the mother superior. [L *zelator* and *zelatrix*, Fr *zélatrice*, from L *zelus*, from Gr *zelos* zeal, from *zeein* to boil]

zelophobia *zel-ō-fō'bi-ə*, *n* an irrational or morbid aversion to or fear of jealousy. — *adj* and *n* **zelophō'bic**. [**zelotypia** and **-phobia**]

zeloso *zel-ō'sō*, (*music*) *adv* with fervour. [Ital]

zelotypia *zel-ō-tip'i-ə*, (*obs*) *n* jealousy; unhealthily excessive zeal in the carrying-out of any project or cause. [Gr *zēlotypiā* jealousy, from *zēlos* zeal, and *typtein* to strike]

zemindar *zem-in-där'* or *zem'*, *n* under the Mogul emperors of India, a tax-farmer responsible for collecting revenue from land held in common by the cultivators; later, the actual native proprietor paying revenue direct, and not to any intermediate superior. — Also **zamindar**. — *n* **zem'indari** or **zem'indary** the jurisdiction of a zemindar; the system of land-tenure and taxation involving zemindars. — Also **zam'indari** or **zam'indary**.

[Hindi *zamīndār*, from Pers *zamīn* land, and *-dar* holder]

zemstvo *zems'tvō*, *n* in Russia, from 1864 until 1917, a district and provincial assembly to which the administration of certain of the affairs of the district and the province was committed: — *pl* **zems'tvos** or **zems'tva**. [Russ]

Zen *zen*, *n* an *orig* Japanese branch of Buddhism (with various sects) which holds that the truth is not in scriptures but in a person's own heart if they will only strive to find it by meditation and self-mastery. — Also *adj*. — *adj* **Zen'ic**. — *n* **Zen'ist** or **Zenn'ist**. [Jap, from Chin *ch'an*, from Pali *jhāna* and Sans *dhyāna* religious contemplation]

zenana *ze-nä'nə*, *n* in India and Iran, etc, a part of a house in which women and girls are secluded, corresponding to the harem in Arabic-speaking Muslim countries. — **zenana mission** a mission to women of the zenanas, necessarily conducted by women. [Pers *zanāna*, from *zan* a woman]

Zend *zend*, *n* the Avesta or Zend-Avesta; Avestan, the ancient East-Iranian Indo-European language in which the Zend-Avesta was orally preserved and finally written down, closely related to Vedic Sanskrit. — **Zend-Aves'ta** (properly meaning the Avesta with the commentary on it), the ancient sacred writings of the Parsees, including works of widely differing character and age, collected into their present canon under Shahpuhar or Shah-pur II (AD 309–338). [Pers *zend* or *zand* commentary]

zendik *zen'dik*, (*hist*) *n* in Middle-Eastern countries, an unbeliever in revealed religion, a heretic; someone who practises magic. [Ar *zendīq*]

Zener cards *zē'nər kärdz*, *n pl* a set of 25 cards, consisting of five sets of five, each set having one symbol, used in parapsychological experimentation. [Invented by K E *Zener*, 1903–61, US psychologist]

Zener diode *zē'nər dī'ōd*, (*electronics*) *n* a type of semiconductor device, a diode whose sudden increase in reverse current makes it useful in voltage-limiting circuits. [C M *Zener*, US physicist, born 1905]

zenith *zen'ith*, *US zēn'*, *n* the point on the celestial sphere vertically above the observer's head, one of the two poles of the horizon, the other being the nadir; the greatest height (*lit* and *fig*). — *adj* **zen'ithal**. — **zenithal projection** (*geog*) a type of map projection in which the plane of projection is tangential to the sphere: **zenith distance** the angular distance of a heavenly body from the zenith; **zenith sector** formerly, any of several instruments used for measuring zenith-distances. [OFr *cenit* or *cenith*, ultimately from Ar *samt*, short for *samt-ar-ras*, literally way or direction of the head]

Zeno's paradoxes *zē'nōz par'ə-doks-is*, (*math*) *n pl* four paradoxes (including that of Achilles and the tortoise) designed to demonstrate that either of the hypotheses that space and time consist of indivisible quanta or that space and time are infinitely divisible leads to a dilemma. [*Zeno* of Elea (c.430–c.490 BC), Greek philosopher and mathematician]

Zentippe. See **Xantippe**.

zeolite *zē'ō-līt*, *n* any of a large group of alumino-silicates of sodium, potassium, calcium and barium, containing very loosely held water which can be removed by heating and regained by exposure to a damp atmosphere. — *adj* **zeolitic** (*-lit'*). — *adj* **zeolit'iform**. — **zeolite process** a water-softening process using zeolites (formerly zeolites occurring naturally, now synthetic ones). [Gr *zeein* to boil (in allusion to the fact that many swell up when heated with a blowpipe), and *lithos* a stone]

Zeph. (*Bible*) *abbrev*: (Book of) Zephaniah.

zephyr *zef'ər*, *n* the west wind; a soft, gentle breeze (*poetic*); thin light worsted or woollen yarn; a shawl, jersey, or other garment made of such; any of various types of lightweight material, such as a gingham, a flannel with a silk warp, a thin woollen cloth, etc; anything very light and fine of its kind; (with *cap*) the god of the west wind. — **zephyr lily** a lily-like plant of the genus *Zephyranthes* (family *Amaryllidaceae*), *orig* from the warmer parts of N and S America. [Gr *Zephyros*; related to *zophos* darkness, the west]

zeppelin *zep'əl-in*, *n* a dirigible, cigar-shaped airship of the type designed by Count *Zeppelin* (c.1900).

zerda *zûr'də*, *n* a fennec. [Ar *zardawa*]

zereba and **zeriba**. See **zareba**.

Zernebock *zûr'nə-bok*, *n* Czerni Bog, an evil god of the Slavs, wrongly described by Scott in *Ivanhoe* as a god 'of the ancient Saxons'.

zero *zē'rō*, *n* a cipher; nothing; the point from which the reckoning begins on scales, such as those of the barometer, etc; the lowest point (*fig*); zero hour: — *pl* **zē'ros**. — *vt* to set at or adjust to zero: — *pr p* **zē'roing**; *pa t* and *pa p* **zē'roed**. — *adj* having no measurable size, amount, etc; not any (*colloq*). — *adj* **zē'rōth** denoting a term in a series regarded as preceding the 'first' term. — **zero-base** (or **zero-based**) **budgeting** a system in which the budget of an organization, department, etc is drawn up anew each year without reference to any previous budget; **zero-coupon bond** or **zero-dividend share** (*stock exchange*) a bond, or share, that carries no interest, but has a redemption price higher than its issue price; **zero fuel weight** the weight of a loaded aircraft after all usable fuel has been consumed; **ze'ro-grazing** a system of dairy farming in which the cattle are kept indoors and cut grass is brought to them, thus avoiding the wastage caused by conventional grazing; **zero hour** the exact time (hour, minute and second) fixed for launching an attack or beginning an operation; **zero option** a proposal, *orig* made by President Reagan of the United States, to limit or abandon the deployment of (medium range) nuclear missiles if the opposing side does likewise; (loosely) a proposal to abandon or eliminate a particular range, category, division, etc; **zero-point energy** (*phys*) total energy at the absolute zero of temperature; **zero-power reactor** a nuclear reactor, used for experimental purposes, in which there is no significant build-up of fission products and no cooling is required. — *vt* **zē'ro-rate** to assess at a zero rate of value-added tax. — *adj* **ze'ro-ra'ted** used of goods on which the purchaser pays no value-added tax and on which the seller can claim back any value-added tax already paid by him or her. — **ze'ro-ra'ting**. — *adj* **ze'ro-sum** of a game, etc, in which the total cumulative gains equal the total cumulative losses. — *adj* **ze'ro-valent** (*chem*) incapable of combining with other atoms. — *adj* **ze'ro-ze'ro** (*meteorol* and *aeronautics*) of conditions in which cloud ceiling and horizontal visibility are both zero. — **zero-zero** (or sometimes **double zero**) **option** a proposal which extends the zero option (qv above) to include also intermediate (300–600 mile) range missiles. — **absolute zero** see under **absolute**; **zero in** (**on**) (*colloq*) to direct oneself straight towards (a target); to focus one's attention or energies on, as if on a target; to aim for or move towards. [Fr *zéro*, from Ar *sifr*; cf **cipher**]

zerumbet *zə-rum'bet*, or *ze'*, *n* an E Indian drug, related to cassumunar and zedoary. [Pers *zerunbād*]

zest *zest*, *n* the thin outer layer of orange or lemon peel; orange or lemon peel, or the oil squeezed from it, used as a flavouring; anything that gives a relish; piquancy; relish; enthusiasm. — *vt* to give zest to. — *n* **zest'er** a utensil scraped across the surface of an orange or lemon to remove the zest. — *adj* **zest'ful**. — *adv* **zest'fully**. — *n* **zest'fulness**. — *adj* **zest'y**. [Fr *zeste*, orig the woody thick skin quartering a walnut; origin obscure]

ZETA or **Zeta** *zē'tə*, *abbrev*: zero-energy thermonuclear apparatus (formerly used in the study of controlled thermonuclear reactions), toroid in shape.

zeta[1] *zē'tə*, *n* the Greek z (Z, ζ); as a numeral $\zeta' = 7$; $_{,}\zeta = 7000$.

zeta[2] *zē'tə*, (*hist*) *n* a small room or closet of some kind, as *perh* the sexton's room over a church porch. [Gr *diaita* a dwelling]

zetetic *zē-tet'ik*, *adj* proceeding by inquiry. — *n* a search or investigation; a seeker, *specif* a Pyrrhonist. [Gr *zētētikos*, from *zēteein* to seek]

Zeuglodon *zū'glō-don*, *n* a genus of fossil whales, so named from the yoke-like double-rooted formation of their cheek teeth. — *adj* and *n* **zeug'lodont**. — *n pl* **Zeuglodon'tia** a suborder of *Cetacea*, represented by the zeuglodonts. [Gr *zeuglē* the strap or loop of the yoke, and *odous*, *-ontos* a tooth]

zeugma *zūg'mə*, *n* a figure of speech by which an adjective or verb is applied to two nouns, though strictly appropriate to only one of them. — *adj* **zeugmat'ic**. [Gr, from *zeugnynai* to yoke]

Zeus *zūs*, *n* the greatest of the ancient Greek gods, son of Kronos (Saturn) and Rhea, and consort of Hera, his supreme seat being Mount Olympus in Thessaly. [Gr]

Zeuxian *zūk'si-ən*, *adj* relating to Zeuxis, styled 'of Heraclea' and 'of Ephesus' (fl. c.420–400 BC), a Greek painter who excelled in accuracy of imitation of natural objects and in rendering types of sensuous beauty.

zeuxite *zūk'sīt*, *n* a ferriferous tourmaline. [Gr *zeuxis* joining, from *zeugnynai* to join]

zex *zeks*, (*dialect*) *n* a variant of **zax** or **sax**[1].

zeze *zā'zā*, *n* a stringed musical instrument resembling a zither, played in eastern and central Africa. [Swahili]

Zezidee. See **Yezidi**.

zho *zhō*, *n* a kind of hybrid domestic cattle found in parts of the Himalayas, said to be a cross between the male yak and the common horned cow; the male of this cross. — Also **zo**, **dso**, **dzho** or **dzo** (*dzō*). — *n* **zhomo** (*zhō'mō*) the female of this cross. — Also **dsō'mo** or **jō'mo**. — *n* **zō'bō** the male of this cross. — Also **zō'bu** or **dsō'bō**. — *Pl* in all cases **-s**. [Tibetan *mdzo*]

zibeline or **zibelline** *zib'ə-lin* or *-līn*, *adj* of or relating to the sable. — *n* the fur of the sable; (*zib'ə-lēn*) a soft woollen material with a lustrous pile. [Fr, from Ital *zibellino*, prob from Slav; cf **sable**]

zibet *zib'it*, *n* an Asiatic civet. [Ital *zibetto*, from Ar *zabād*; cf **civet**]

zidovudine *zi-dō'vū-dēn*, *n* the manufacturer's name for the drug, AZT. [From the chemical name, *azidothymidine*]

Ziegler catalyst *zē'glər kat'ə-list*, (*chem*) *n* a catalyst which induces specific steric orientation in polymer production. [Karl *Ziegler* (1898–1973), German chemist]

ziff *zif*, (*Austr slang*) *n* a beard. [Ety unknown]

ziffius *zif'i-əs*, (*Spenser*) *n* a sea-monster, *perh* a swordfish. [Cf **Xiphias** and **Ziphius**]

ZIFT or **Zift** *abbrev*: zygote intra fallopian transfer, a technique in which a fertilized egg is inserted into the recipient's fallopian tube.

zig *zig*, *n* a new line or sharp change of direction on a zigzag course. — Also *vi*: — *pr p* **zigg'ing**; *pa t* and *pa p* **zigged**. [*zig-* extracted from **zigzag**]

zigan *zi-gan'*, *n*. A variant of **tzigany**.

ziganka *zi-gang'kə*, *n* a Russian country-dance; the music for this, *usu* quick and with a drone bass. [Russ *tsyganka* a gypsy woman]

Zigeuner *tsi-goi'nər*, (*Ger*) *n* a gypsy: — *pl* **Zigeu'ner**.

ziggurat *zig'ōō-rat*, *n* a Babylonian temple-tower, much like a pyramid in shape, consisting of a number of storeys each successive one of which was smaller than the one below it. — Also **zikkurat** (*zik'*). [Assyrian *ziqquratu* a pinnacle, the top of a mountain]

zigzag *zig'zag*, *n* a short, sharp turning; a line, road, fence, moulding, etc with sharp angles to right and left alternately. — *adj* having short, sharp alternate turns; bent from side to side alternately. — *vt* to form with short, alternate turns. — *vi* to move forward making an alternation of short, sharp turns: — *pr p* **zig'zagging**; *pa t* and *pa p* **zig'zagged**. — *adv* with frequent sharp turns. — Also **zig'zaggy**. — *n* **zigzagg'ery** angular crookedness. — *adj* **zig'zaggy** zigzag. — **zigzag stitch** (*sewing*) a machine stitch worked in a zigzag line, used to prevent fraying, etc. [Fr *zigzag*; Ger *Zickzack*]

zikkurat. Same as **ziggurat**.

zilch *zilch*, (*slang*) *n* zero, nothing. [Origin unknown]

zillah or **zila** *zil'a*, (*hist*) *n* an administrative district in British India. [Ar *dila* (in Hindi pronunciation, *zila*) a rib, a side, a district]

zillion *zil'yən*, (*colloq*) *n* an extremely large but unspecified number, many millions (analogous in formation and use to *million* and *billion*). — *n* and *adj* **zill'ionth**.

zimb *zimb*, *n* an Ethiopian dipterous insect, like the tsetse, harmful to cattle. [Amharic, a fly]

Zimbabwean *zim-bä'bwi-ən*, *adj* of or relating to the Republic of Zimbabwe (formerly Rhodesia) in southern Africa. — *n* a native or citizen of Zimbabwe.

zimbi *zim'bi*, *n* a kind of cowrie used as money. [Port *zimbo*; of African origin]

Zimmer® *zim'ər*, *n* (also without *cap*) a metal frame held in front of one, used as an aid to walking. [Name of the original manufacturer]

zimocca *zi-mok'ə*, *n* a type of bath sponge. [New L]

zinc *zingk*, *n* a bluish-white metallic element (symbol **Zn**; atomic no 30), resistant to atmospheric corrosion, a constituent of several alloys (eg brass) and used in galvanizing, battery electrodes, etc. — Also *adj*. — *vt* to coat with zinc: — *pr p* **zincing** (*zingk'ing*), **zinck'ing** or **zink'ing**; *pa t* and *pa p* **zinced** (*zingkt*), **zincked** or **zinked**. — *adj* **zincif'erous** (*zingk-*) or **zinkif'erous** containing or producing zinc. — *n* **zincificā'tion**, **zinckificā'tion** or **zinkificā'tion** the process of coating or impregnating an object with zinc. — *vt* **zinc'ify**, **zinck'ify** or **zink'ify** to cover or impregnate with zinc. — *n* **zincite** (*zingk'īt*) a naturally occurring oxide of zinc, brittle, translucent and deep red. — *adj* **zinc'y**, **zinck'y** or **zink'y** relating to, containing, or looking like zinc. — *n* **zinco** (*zing'kō*) a zincographic block or picture: — *pl* **zinc'os**. — *n* **zinc'ode** (*obs*) an anode. — *n* **zinc'ograph** a plate or picture produced by zincography. — *n* **zincographer** (*-kog'rə-fər*). — *adj* **zincograph'ic** and **zincograph'ical**. — *n* **zincography** (*-kog'rə-fi*) an engraving process in which zinc is covered with wax and etched; any process in which designs for printing are made on zinc plates. — *adj* **zinc'oid** like zinc. — *n* **zincol'ysis** (*obs*) electrolysis. — *adj* **zinc'ous** relating to or like zinc. — **zinc'-blende** sphalerite, naturally occurring sulphide of zinc; **zinc'-bloom** basic zinc carbonate, hydrozincite; **zinc colic** a colic caused by the slow poisoning effect of zinc oxide; **zinc ointment** a mixture of zinc oxide and a suitable ointment base (lanolin, petroleum jelly, etc); **zinc oxide** a whitish solid, much used as a paint pigment in the rubber and other industries, and also medicinally as an antiseptic and astringent (also called **flowers of zinc**); **zinc white** zinc oxide used as a pigment; **zinc'-worker**. [Ger *Zink*; origin unknown]

Zincalo *zing'kə-lō*, (*Sp*) *n* a gypsy: — *fem* **Zin'cala**, *pl* **Zin'cali**. [Sp Romany name]

zineb *zin'əb*, *n* an organic fungicide and insecticide sprayed on cereal grasses, fruit trees, etc. [*Zinc* *e*thylene *b*isdithiocarbamate, its chemical name]

Zinfandel or **zinfandel** *zin'fən-dəl*, *n* a black wine-grape of California; the red or white dry wine produced from it. [Origin obscure]

zing *zing*, *n* a short shrill humming sound, such as that made by a bullet or vibrating string; zest, spirit, vitality, etc (*colloq*). — *vi* to move very swiftly, *esp* with a high-pitched hum. — *vt* to make (something) zing; to criticize or scorn (*US slang*). — *n* **zing'er** (*colloq*; *esp US*) something or someone with zing, *esp* a sharp, lively quip, punchline or retort. — *adj* **zing'y** (*colloq*) full of zest, etc. [Imit]

Zingaro *zing'gə-rō*, (*Ital*) *n* a gypsy: — *pl* **Zing'ari**; *fem* **Zing'ara**, *pl* **Zing'are**. — Also **Zing'ano**, etc. [Cf **Zincalo** and **Zigeuner**]

zingel *tsing'əl* or *zing'əl*, *n* a fish of the *Aspro* genus of the perch family, *esp Aspro zingel* found in the Danube. [Ger]

zingiber *zin'ji-bər*, *n* any plant of the *Zingiber* genus (*Zingiber officinale* being the common ginger), belonging to the family **Zingiberaceae** (*zin-ji-bə-rā'sē-ē*) of perennial tropical monocotyledonous herbs, with horizontal thickened rootstock and cone-like inflorescence. — *adj* **zingiberā'ceous** or **zinziberā'ceous**. [L *zingiber*, from Gr *zingiberis* ginger]

zingy. See under **zing**.

Zinjanthropus. See **nutcracker man** under **nut**.

zinke *tsing'kə*, *n* an old wind instrument like the cornet. [Ger]

zinked, **zinkify**, etc. See under **zinc**.

zinkenite *zingk'ən-īt*, *n* a steel-grey mineral, essentially sulphide of lead and antimony. [J K L *Zincken*, a mine director]

zinnia *zin'i-ə*, *n* any plant of the *Zinnia* genus of American composite plants, popular for their bright showy flowers. [From J G *Zinn*, botanist (1727–59)]

zinziberaceous. See under **zingiber**.

Zion *zī'ən*, *n* Jerusalem; the Israelite theocracy; the Jewish people; a place ruled over by God; the Christian Church; heaven. — *n* **Zī'onism** the movement which secured national privileges and territory in Palestine for the Jews and which now helps to maintain and develop the state of Israel. — *n* **Zī'onist** a supporter of Zionism. — *adv* **Zī'onward** heavenward. [Heb *tsīyōn*, orig the name of a part of one of the hills of Jerusalem]

zip[1] *zip*, *n* the ping or sound of a bullet striking an object or whizzing through the air; a whizzing sound; a zip-fastener; energy, vigour (*colloq*). — *vi* and *vt* to whizz; to fasten with a zip; to be full of, act with, proceed with, or (*usu* **zip up**) infuse with, life and energy (*colloq*): — *pr p* **zipp'ing**; *pa t* and *pa p* **zipped**. — *n* **zipp'er** (*esp NAm*) a zip-fastener. — *adj* **zipp'ered** provided with a zip-fastener. — *adj* **zipp'y** (*colloq*) quick, energetic or lively. — **zip-fastener** (*zip-fäs'nər*) a fastening device for clothes, etc, on which two sets of teeth can be opened or interlocked by pulling a slide along them. — *adj* **zip'-front**, **zip'-neck**, **zip'top**, etc having the front-, neck- or top-opening, etc fastened with a zip. — *adj* **zip'-on**, **zip'-off**, **zip'-in**, etc able to be added, removed, inserted, etc by means of a zip. — *adj* **zip'lock** (*US*) of a plastic bag, having ridged strips at the opening which may be pressed together to interlock, so sealing the bag. [Imit]

zip[2] *zip* or **zippo** *zip'ō*, (*slang*; *orig US*) *n* nothing, zero.

zip code *zip kōd*, (*US*) *n* the US postal code. [*zone improvement plan*]

Ziphius *zif'i-əs*, *n* a genus of whales, giving its name to the family **Ziphī'idae**, the beaked whales. [Gr *xiphios* swordfish, from *xiphos* sword]

zircon *zûr'kən*, *n* a tetragonal mineral, zirconium silicate, of which jacinth and jargoon are varieties. — *n* **zir'caloy** (also **Zir'coloy**®) an alloy of zirconium with tin, chromium and nickel, widely used (*esp* in the nuclear power industry) for its heat- and corrosion-resistant properties. — *n* **zircō'nia** oxide of zirconium. — *adj* **zirconic** (*-kon'*) of zirconium. — *n* **zircō'nium** a metallic element (symbol **Zr**; atomic no 40), highly resistant to corrosion. — **cubic zirconia** a synthetic stone used as a diamond substitute, produced from zirconia heated with any of various stabilizing metallic oxides. [Ar *zarqūn*, from Pers *zargūn* gold-coloured; cf **jargoon**]

zit *zit*, (*slang*; *orig NAm*) *n* a spot or pimple. [Origin obscure]

zither *zidh'ər* or *zith'ər*, *n* a stringed instrument consisting of a wooden frame and flat soundbox with from twenty-nine to forty-two metal or sometimes gut strings, placed on a table or on the knees, some strings being played by a plectrum on the right thumb, others being played with the fingers; used generically for other instruments of this type and shape. — Also **zith'ern**. [Ger]

ziti *zē'tē*, *n pl* a type of pasta like large, short-cut macaroni. — Also **zi'te**. [Ital, *pls* of *zito* and *zita*]

ziz. See **zizz**.

zizania *zi-* or *zī-zā'ni-ə*, *n* any tall aquatic grass of the genus *Zizania*, also known as *wild*, *water*, *Indian* or *Canada rice* (ordinary cultivated rice belongs to the genus *Oryza*). [Gr *zizanion* darnel]

zizel *ziz'əl*, *n* the chipmunk. [Ger *Ziesel*]

zizyphus *ziz'i-fəs*, *n* a shrub or tree of the genus *Zizyphus* of the buckthorn family, the jujube trees. [L, jujube tree]

zizz or **ziz** *ziz*, (*slang*) *n* a nap or sleep. — Also *vi*. [Representation of *z-z-z-z-...*, the conventional phoneticization of snoring used in strip cartoons, etc]

Zl. *abbrev*: zloty.

zloty *zlot'i* or *zwot'ü*, *n* the monetary unit of Poland: — *pl* **zloty** or **zlotys**. [Pol *zloty*, literally golden]

Zn (*chem*) *symbol*: zinc.

zo. See **zho**.

zo-. See **zoo-**.

zoa. See **zoon**.

Zoantharia *zō-an-thā'ri-ə*, *n pl* an order of Anthozoa, including sea-anemones and many corals, the members of which may be either solitary or colonial and possess either six, or more than eight, simple tentacles. — *adj* and *n* **zoanthā'rian**. [New L, from Gr *zōion* animal, and *anthos* flower]

zoanthropy *zō-an'thrə-pi*, *n* a form of mental delusion in which a person believes himself or herself to be an animal. — *adj* **zōanthropic** (*-throp'*). [Gr *zōion* animal, and *anthrōpos* man]

Zoanthus *zō-an'thəs*, *n* the typical genus of the **Zoan'thidae** (*-ē*), a family of *Anthozoa* permanently attached by their bases and having no solid skeleton. [Gr *zōion* animal, and *anthos* flower]

zoarium *zō-ā'ri-əm*, *n* the zooids of a polyzoan colony collectively. [Gr *zōarion*, dimin of *zōion* animal]

zobo and **zobu**. See **zho**.

zocco *zok'ō*, *n* a socle: — *pl* **zocc'os**. — Also **zocc'olo**: — *pl* **zocc'olos**. [Ital *zocco*, *zoccolo*; see **socle**]

zodiac *zō'di-ak*, *n* an imaginary belt in the heavens, about 18° wide, through which the ecliptic passes centrally, and which forms the background of the motions of the sun, moon and planets. It is divided into twelve equal parts of 30° called **signs of the zodiac**, named from the constellations that once corresponded to them but no longer do so. The constellations, with the symbols of the corresponding signs, are as follows: Aries (*Ram*), ♈; Taurus (*Bull*), ♉; Gemini (*Twins*), ♊; Cancer (*Crab*), ♋; Leo (*Lion*), ♌; Virgo (*Virgin*), ♍; Libra (*Balance*), ♎; Scorpio (*Scorpion*), ♏; Sagittarius (*Archer*), ♐; Capricorn (*Goat*), ♑; Aquarius (*Water-bearer*), ♒; Pisces (*Fishes*), ♓; a set or diagram of these; a year (*obs*); a set of twelve, or a recurrent series or course (*fig*). — *adj* **zodī'acal**. — **zodiacal light** a faint illumination of the sky, lenticular in form and elongated in the direction of the ecliptic on either side of the sun, fading away at about 90° from it (best seen after sunset or before sunrise in the tropics). [Fr *zodiaque*, from L *zōdiacus*, from Gr *zōidiakos* of figures, from *zōidion* a small carved or painted figure, from *zōion* an animal]

zoea *zō-ē'ə*, *n* a larval stage of certain decapod crustaceans, eg of crabs: — *pl* **zoē'ae** (also **zoē'as**). — Also **zooea** (*zō-ē'ə*). — *adj* **zoē'al** or **zooē'al**. — *adj* **zō'eform**. [Gr *zōē* life]

zoechrome. See **zoetrope**.

zoetic *zō-et'ik*, *adj* relating to life, vital. [Gr *zōē* life]

zoetrope *zō'i-trōp*, *n* the 'wheel of life', an instrument in which figures on the inside of a rotating cylinder are made visible through slots and provide an illusion of animated motion; (also **zō'echrome**) any of several early processes for colour cinematography, using rapidly repeated images of the selected colours in sequence on a screen, the synthesis arising from persistence of vision in the eye. — *adj* **zoetropic** (*-trop'ik*). [Gr *zōē* life, *tropos* a turning, and *chrōma* colour]

Zohar *zō'här*, *n* one of the most important cabbalistic texts, being an allegorical interpretation of the Pentateuch. [Heb, brightness, splendour]

zoiatria *zō-i-at'ri-ə* or *zō-ī-ə-trī'ə*, *n* and **zoiatrics** *zō-i-at'riks*, *n sing* veterinary surgery. [Gr *zōion* an animal, and *iātreiā* healing]

zoic *zō'ik*, *adj* pertaining to animals; of rocks, containing evidences of life, in the form of fossils (*geol*). [Gr *zōikos* of animals, from *zōion* an animal]

Zoilism *zō'i-lizm*, *n* carping and unjust criticism. — *adj* **Zoil'ean** characteristic of *Zoilus*, a Greek grammarian who flourished in the time of Philip of Macedon, and criticized Homer with such asperity that his name became proverbial for a captious and malignant critic. — *n* **Zō'ilist** a carping critic.

zoisite *zois'īt* or *zō'is-īt*, *n* an orthorhombic mineral closely related to epidote. [Baron S *Zois* von Edelstein (1747–1819), Slovenian nobleman]

zoism *zō'izm*, *n* the doctrine that life originates from a specific vital principle. — *n* **zō'ist** a person who maintains this theory. [Gr *zōē* life]

Zolaism *zō'lä-izm*, *n* the literary principles and practice of the French novelist Émile *Zola* (1840–1902), who aimed at what he called 'naturalism' (qv).

Zöllner's lines *tsœl'nərz līnz*, *n pl* rows of parallel lines appearing to be not parallel through the optical effect of oblique lines intersecting them in something like a herring-bone pattern. — Also **Zöllner's illusion** or **pattern**. [J K F *Zöllner* (1834–82), German physicist]

Zollverein *tsol'fər-īn*, *n* a customs union; a union of the German states, under the leadership of Prussia, to enable them to act as one state in their commercial relations with other countries (*hist*). [Ger *Zoll* duty, and *Verein* union]

zombi or **zombie** *zom'bi*, *n* (with *cap*) *orig* in W African voodooism, the python god; (with *cap*) in W Indian and American voodooism, the snake god; a corpse reanimated by sorcery; the power supposed to enter such a body; a stupid or useless person; a very slow-moving, lethargic person. — *vt* **zom'bify** to reduce to the state of a zombie. — *n* **zom'biism** belief in a zombie, or practice of rites associated with this belief. [Kongo (W African language) *zumbi* fetish, and *nzambi* god]

zomboruk. See **zumbooruk**.

zona *zō'nə*, *n* a girdle or belt; an area, patch, strip or band (*zool*); a zone; a zona pellucida; herpes zoster: — *pl* **zonae** (*zō'nē*). — **zona pellucida** (*pe-lōō'si-də*; *zool*) a thick, transparent membrane around the mature mammalian ovum. [L, girdle]

zonal, **zonary**, etc. See under **zone**.

zonda *son'də*, *n* a dry, hot, dusty wind blowing from the Andes across the Argentine pampas during July and August. [Sp; perh from Am Indian]

zone *zōn*, *n* a girdle, belt, or encircling band (chiefly *poetic*); an encircling stripe of different colour or substance; any of the five great belts into which the surface of the earth is divided by the tropics and arctic and antarctic circles; any continuous tract with particular characteristics; a region; a group of strata characterized by a distinctive fauna or flora, and bearing the name of one fossil, called the **zonal index** (*geol*); a set of crystal faces all parallel to the same line (the **zonal** or **zone axis**); that part of the surface of a sphere between two parallel planes, intersecting the sphere (*math*). — *vt* to surround with, or as with, a zone, to encircle, with a zone; to divide into, or assign to, zones; (*esp* with *off*) to mark as a zone. — *adj* **zō'nal** or **zō'nary** like a zone; arranged in zones; pertaining to a zone. — *adj* **zō'nate** or **zō'nated** marked with zones, belted. — *n* **zonā'tion** (*bot*) the formation of bands differentiated by colour or other characteristics, or the arrangement of such bands; the occurrence of vegetation in well-marked bands, each band having its characteristic dominant species. — *adj* **zoned** wearing a zone; having zones. — *adj* **zone'less**. — *n* **zō'ning** division into zones; assignment according to zones. — *adj* **zō'noid** like a zone. — *n* **Zonotrichia** (*zō-nō-trik'i-ə*; Gr *thrix*, *trichos* hair) a genus of American sparrows, some with white or golden crowns. — *n* **zō'nula** a small zone. — *adj* **zō'nular** like a zone or zonule. — *n* **zon'ule** a small zone or band. — *n* **zon'ulet** (*poetic*) a small belt or girdle. — *n* **zonure** (*zō'nūr*; Gr *ourā* tail) a lizard of the tropical African genus *Zonurus* of lizards whose tails are ringed with spiny scales, giving its name to the family **Zonu'ridae**. — **zonal defence** (*football*, etc) a method of defending in which a player patrols a particular area of the field rather than marking a specific opponent; **zone'-ticket** a railway ticket usable for a time between any stations of a group. [L *zōna*, from Gr *zōnē* a girdle, from *zōnnynai* to gird]

zonk *zonk*, (*colloq*) *n* a sharp blow; the sound of a swift, sharp or firm impact. — *vt* to hit sharply, or with a zonk; to blast. — Also *adv*. — *adj* **zonked** (*zongkt*) or **zonked out** (*slang*) utterly exhausted; in a deep sleep; intoxicated; under the influence of drugs. [Imit]

zonula, **zonule**, **zonure**, etc. See under **zone**.

zoo *zōō*, *n* a zoological garden or park; *orig* (with *cap*) the Zoological Gardens in London; a place, group of people, etc characterized by noise and unruly behaviour (*fig*; *colloq*). — **zoo'-keeper**. [*zoo*logical garden]

zoo- *zō-ō-* or *zō-o'-*, or **zo-** *zō-*, *combining form* denoting (*esp* in zoological terms, etc) animal. — *adj* **zoobiotic** (*zō-ō-bī-ot'ik*; *biol*) parasitic on, or living in association with, an animal. — *n* **zooblast** (*zō'ō-blast*; *zool*; Gr *blastos* a germ) an animal cell. — *adj* **zoocephalic** (*-si-fal'ik*) animal-headed. — *adj* **zōochem'ical**. — *n* **zōochem'istry** the chemistry of the animal body. — *adj* **zoochorous** (*zō-ō-kör'əs*; *bot*; Gr *chōreein* to spread) of spores or seeds, dispersed by animals. — *n* **zō'ochore**. — *n* **zō'ochory** (*bot*) the condition of being dispersed by animals. — *n* **zō'oculture** (*US*) the domestication and control of animals. — *n* **zōocytium** (*-sish'i-əm*; Gr *kytos* a hollow vessel; *zool*) a zoothecium: — *pl* **zōocyt'ia**. — *n* **zōoden'drium** (*zool*) the branched stalk connecting the members of the colony in certain colonial Infusoria. — *n* **zooecium** (*zō-ē'shi-əm*; Gr *oikiā* a house; *zool*) the body-wall or enclosing chamber of a polyzoan individual: — *pl* **zooe'cia**. — *n* **zō'ogamete** a motile gamete. — *adj* **zoogamous** (*zō-og'ə-məs*; Gr *gamos* marriage) relating to zoogamy. — *n* **zōog'amy** sexual reproduction of animals. — *adj* **zōogenic** (*-jen'*) or **zōog'enous** produced from animals. — *n* **zoogeny** (*zō-oj'ə-ni*; Gr *-geneia*, sfx denoting production) the doctrine, or the process, of the origination of living beings. — *n* **zōogeog'rapher**. — *adj* **zōogeograph'ic** or **zōogeograph'ical**. — *n* **zōogeog'raphy** the science of the distribution of animals on the surface of the globe. — *n* **zōogloea** (*-glē'ə*; Gr *gloiā* glue; *bacteriol*) a mucilaginous mass of bacteria embedded in slimy material derived from swollen cell walls. — *adj* **zōogloe'ic**. — *adj* **zōogloe'oid**. — *n* **zōogonid'ium** (*bot* and *zool*) a swarm-spore: — *pl* **zōogonid'ia**. — *adj* **zōog'onous** (*zool*) viviparous. — *n* **zoogony** (*zō-og'ə-ni*; L *-gonia*, from Gr *-goneia*, sfx denoting origin or production) zoogeny. — *n* **zō'ograft** (*-gräft*) a piece of tissue from the living body of an animal grafted on to the human body. — *n* **zō'ografting**. — *n* **zōog'rapher** or **zōog'raphist**. — *adj* **zōograph'ic** or **zōograph'ical**. — *n* **zoog'raphy** the study or description of animals and their habits; the painting of animals. — *n* **zōol'ater** (Gr *latreiā* worship) someone who worships animals. — *n* **zōolatrī'a** or **zōol'atry** worship of animals. — *adj* **zōol'atrous**. — *n* **zoolite** (*zō'ō-līt*; Gr *lithos* a stone) a fossil animal. — Also **zō'olith**. — *adj* **zōolith'ic** or **zōolit'ic**. — *adj* **zōomagnet'ic**. — *n* **zōomag'netism** animal magnetism. — *n* **zoomancy** (*zō'ō-man-si*; Gr *manteiā* divination) divination by observation of animals. — *adj* **zōōman'tic**. — *adj* **zōōmet'ric**. — *n* **zōometry** (*-om'ə-tri*; Gr *metron* a measure) comparative measurement of the parts of animals. — *n* **zō'omorph** (*-mörf*; Gr *morphē* form) in art, a representation of an animal form; an image or symbol of a god, etc who is conceived as having an animal form. — *adj* **zōomor'phic** relating to zoomorphism; representing animals in art. — *n* **zōomor'phism** the representation, or the conception, of a god or a man in an animal form. — Also **zōomor'phy**. — *adj* **zōon'ic** relating to animals. — *n* **zō'onite** any of the segments of an articulated animal. — *adj* **zōonit'ic**. — *adj* **zōonom'ic**. — *n* **zōon'omist**. — *n* **zoonomy** (*zō-on'ə-mi*; Gr *nomos* law) animal physiology. — Also **zōonō'mia**. — *n* **zōopathol'ogy** the study of disease in animals. — *n* **zoopathy** (*zō-op'ə-thi*; Gr *pathos* suffering) animal pathology. — *adj* **zōop'eral**. — *n* **zōop'erist**. — *n* **zōop'ery** (Gr *peirā* experiment) experimentation on animals. — *n pl* **Zoophaga** (*zō-of'ə-gə*; Gr *phagein* to eat; *zool*) the carnivorous animals collectively. — *n* **zōoph'agan** a carnivorous animal. — *adj* **zōoph'agous** of or relating to the Zoophaga; feeding on animals. — *n* **zōoph'agy** the practice of feeding on animals. — *n* **zō'ophile** (*-fīl*; Gr *philos* loving) a zoophilist; a zoophilous plant (*bot*). — *n* **zōophil'ia**, **zōoph'ilism** or **zōoph'ily** love of animals; erotic fondness for animals. — *n* **zoophilist** (*zō-of'il-ist*) a lover of animals; someone who has or suffers from zoophilia. — *adj* **zōoph'ilous** loving animals; experiencing or suffering from zoophilia; pollinated by animals other than insects (*bot*); of insects, feeding on animals (*zool*). — *n* **zōophōb'ia** (Gr *phobos* fear) abnormal fear of animals; fear of animal ghosts. — *adj* **zōoph'obous**. — *adj* **zōophoric** (*-för'*). — *n* **zōophorus** (*-of'ə-rəs*; Gr *pherein* to bear) a continuous frieze sculptured in relief with figures of people and animals. — *n* **zōophysiol'ogist**. — *n* **zōophysiol'ogy** animal physiology. — *n pl* **Zoophyta** (*zō-of'it-ə*; Gr *phyton* plant) in older classifications, a group of invertebrates which lack the ability to move from place to place, such as sponges, corals, etc. — *n* **zō'ophyte** (*-fīt*) any plant supposed to resemble an animal (*obs*); any of numerous invertebrates resembling plants, such as sponges, corals, sea-anemones, etc, *esp* hydroid colonies of a branched form. — *adj* **zōophytic** (*-fit'*) or **zōophyt'ical**. — *adj* **zōoph'ytoid**. — *adj* **zōophytolog'ical** (*-fīt-*). — *n* **zōophytol'ogist**. — *n* **zōophytol'ogy**. — *n* **zōoplank'ton** floating and drifting animal life. — *adj* **zōoplas'tic** (Gr *plassein* to form) relating to **zō'oplasty**, the operation of transplanting living tissue from one of the lower animals to humans. — *n* **zōopsychol'ogy** the psychology of the lower animals. — *adj* **zōoscop'ic**. — *n* **zōoscopy** (*-os'kop-i*; Gr *skopeein* to look at) a form of mental delusion in which one sees imaginary animals, *esp* snakes. — *n* **zō'osperm** (Gr *sperma* seed; *biol*) a spermatozoid; a zoospore. — Also **zōosper'mium**. — *adj* **zōospermat'ic**. — *n* **zōosporan'gium** (*bot*) a sporangium in which zoospores are formed. — *n* **zō'ospore** (Gr *sporos* a seed) a swarm-spore; an asexual reproductive cell that can swim by means of flagella. — *adj* **zōospor'ic** or **zōos'porous**. — *n* **zō'otaxy** (Gr *taxis* arrangement) the science of the classification of animals, systematic zoology. — *n* **zōotechnics** (*-tek'niks*; Gr *technē* art) or **zō'otechny** the science of the breeding and domestication of animals. — *n* **zōothap'sis** (Gr *thaptein* to bury) premature burial: — *pl* **zōothap'sēs** (*-sēz*). — *adj* **zōothē'cial** (*-shi-əl*). — *n* **zōothecium** (*-thē'shi-əm*, or *-si-*; Gr *thēkion* casket, dimin of *thēkē* box; *zool*) the tubular sheath of certain social infusorians: — *pl* **zōothē'cia**. — *n* **zōothē'ism** the attribution of divine qualities to an animal. — *adj* **zōotheis'tic**. — *n* **zōother'apy** (Gr *therapeiā* treatment) veterinary therapeutics. — *n* **zō'othome** (Gr *thōmos* heap; *biol*) a group of zooids, such as a mass of coral. — *adj* **zōotom'ic** or **zōotom'ical**. — *adv* **zōotom'ically**. — *n* **zōot'omist** (Gr *tomē* a cut) someone who dissects the bodies of animals, an anatomist. — *n* **zōot'omy** the dissection of animals; comparative anatomy. — *n* **zōotox'in** a toxin produced by an animal such as a snake. — *n* **zō'otrope** a zoetrope. — *adj* **zōotrophic** (*-trof'ik*; Gr *trophos* food) relating to the nourishment of animals. — *n* **zōot'rophy**. — *n* **zō'otype** (*zool*) an animal serving as a type. — *adj* **zōotypic** (*-tip'ik*). [Gr *zōion* animal]

zooea. See **zoea**.

zooid *zō'oid*, (*zool*) *n* formerly, a free-moving cell, such as a sperm-cell; in alternation of generations, an individual of an asexually-produced form; *usu*, an individual forming part of a colonial organism. — *adj* **zōoid'al**. [**zoo-** and **-oid**]

zooks *zo͞oks*, *interj*. Same as **gadzooks**.

zoolatry, etc. See under **zoo-**.

zoology *zo͞o-ol'ə-ji*, or *zō-ol'*, *n* the science of animal life, included along with botany in the science of biology; the animal life of a region, etc. — *adj* **zoological** (*zo͞o-ō-loj'i-kl* or *zō-ō-*) relating to zoology. — *adv* **zoolog'ically**. — *n* **zool'ogist** (*zo͞o-*, or *zō-*) a specialist in or student of zoology. — **zoological garden** or **park** a garden or park where animals are kept, studied and *usu* on show to the public. [New L *zoolōgia*; see **zoo-** and **-logy**]

zoom *zo͞om*, *vi* to make a loud, deep, persistent buzzing noise; to move with this sound; to move very quickly; to use the stored energy of the forward motion of an aircraft in order to gain height (*aeronautics*); to soar (*fig*); to change focus rapidly, eg with a zoom lens; (*usu* with *in*) to enlarge a section of text, part of a diagram, a window, etc on a VDU screen, so as to make it easier to work. — *vt* to cause to zoom; to enlarge (a section of text, part of a diagram, a window, etc) on a VDU screen. — *n* the act of zooming; a zooming noise. — **zoom lens** a lens of variable focal length used, eg, for bringing television, cinematographic or cine-camera pictures from distance to close-up without moving the camera; a similar lens used in still cameras and in microscopes. [Imit]

zoomagnetic ... to ... **zoomorphy**. See under **zoo-**.

zoon *zō'on*, (*zool*) *n* a structurally unified individual creature, either the total product of a fertilized ovum or a group of zooids constituting a compound animal: — *pl* **zō'a** or **zō'ons**. — *adj* **zō'onal** like a zoon.

zoonic ... to ... **zoonomy**. See under **zoo-**.

zoonosis *zō-ən-ō'sis* or *zō-on'ə-sis*, *n* a disease of animals which can be transmitted to humans, such as rabies, etc; a disease due to animal parasites: — *pl* **zoonō'ses** (*-sēz*). — *adj* **zoonot'ic**. [Gr *zōion* an animal, and *nosos* disease]

zoon politikon *zō'on po-lit'i-kon*, (*Gr*) *n* (said of a human being) a political animal.

zoopathology ... to ... **zootrophy**. See under **zoo-**.

zoot suit *zo͞ot so͞ot* or *sūt*, *n* a flashy type of man's suit with padded shoulders, fitted waist, knee-length jacket, and trousers narrow at the ankles (introduced in the late 1940s). — *n* **zoot'suiter** someone who wears a zoot suit. [Origin unknown; prob **zoot** to rhyme with **suit**]

zootype, etc. See under **zoo-**.

zoozoo *zo͞o'zo͞o*, (*dialect*) *n* the wood-pigeon. [From the sound made by it]

zopilote *sō-pi-lō'te* or *zō'pi-lōt*, *n* any of the smaller American vultures of the family *Cathartidae*, *esp* the turkey buzzard, or the urubu. [Mexican Sp, from Nahuatl *pilotl*]

zopp *tsop'pə* or (*esp* formerly) **zoppo** *tsop'pō*, (*music*) *adj* syncopated, *usu* in phrase *alla zoppa*, with syncopation. [Ital, limping]

zorgite *zör'gīt*, *n* a metallic copper-lead selenide, found at *Zorge*, in the Harz Mountains, Germany.

zoril, **zorille**, **zorillo** and **zorino**. See under **zorro**.

Zoroastrianism *zor-ō-as'tri-ən-izm*, *n* an ancient dualistic religion founded or reformed by *Zoroaster* (Gr *Zoroastrēs*, Avestan *Zarathustra*), whose scriptures are the Zend-Avesta, and which is still adhered to by the Guebres in Iran and Parsees in India. — *n* and *adj* **Zoroas'trian**. [L *Zōroastrēs*, from Gr]

zorro *sor'ō*, *n* a S American fox or fox-like wild dog: — *pl* **zorr'os**. — *n* **zoril** or **zorille** (*zor'il* or *-il'*) an African skunk-like musteline animal (genus *Zorilla*). — *n* **zorillo** (*sor-ē'yō* or *zor-il'ō*) a S American skunk: — *pl* **zorill'os**. — *n* **zorino** (*zor-ēn'ō*) a euphemism for skunk fur used to make garments: — *pl* **zorin'os**. [Sp *zorro* or *zorra* fox, and dimin *zorilla*, *zorillo* (Fr *zorille*) skunk]

zoster *zos'tər*, *n* an ancient Greek waist-belt for men; herpes zoster or shingles (*med*). [Gr *zōstēr* a girdle]

Zostera *zos-tē'rə*, *n* the eelgrass or grasswrack genus. [Gr *zōstēr* a kind of grasswrack]

Zouave *zo͞o-äv'* or *zwäv*, (*hist*) *n* a soldier belonging to a body of French infantry, *orig* Algerians, wearing a quasi-Moorish uniform; any of a number of volunteer regiments, modelling themselves on the Zouaves, who fought on the side of the North in the American Civil War; a woman's short embroidered jacket. [From the *Zouaoua*, an Algerian tribe]

zouk *zōōk*, *n* a style of dance music, *orig* from the French Antilles, combining Latin American, African and Western disco rhythms. [Perh from W Indian creole *zouk* to enjoy oneself]

zounds *zowndz* or *zōōndz*, (*archaic*) *interj* an exclamation of anger and astonishment. [A corruption of *God's wounds*]

zowie *zow'i*, (*US*) *interj* expressing surprise and pleasure. — *n* (with *cap*) a former name for the slang in use among hippies.

ZPG *abbrev*: zero population growth.

Zr (*chem*) *symbol*: zirconium.

ZRE *abbrev*: Zaire (IVR).

ZST *abbrev*: Zone Standard Time.

zucchetto *tsōō-ket'ō*, *n* the skullcap worn by a RC priest, etc, covering the tonsure: — *pl* **zucchett'os**. — Also **zuchett'a** or **zuchett'o** (*pl* **zuchett'as** or **zuchett'os**). [Ital, dimin of *zucca* a gourd]

zucchini *zōō-kē'nē*, (*esp US* and *Austr*) *n* a courgette: — *pl* **zucchi'ni** or **zucchi'nis**. [Ital]

zufolo *tsōō'fō-lō*, *n* a small flute or flageolet used in training songbirds: — *pl* **zuf'oli**. — Also **zuff'olo**. — *pl* **zuff'oli** (-*ē*). [Ital]

zugzwang *tsōōhh'tsväng*, (*chess*) *n* a blockade position in which any move is disadvantageous to the blockaded player. [Ger]

Zulu *zōō'lōō*, *n* a people of the Nguni branch of the Bantu family, inhabiting mainly Natal in S Africa; a member of this people; the Bantu language of the Zulus. — *adj* relating to the Zulus, their language, etc; (without *cap*) in communications, used for zero. — **zulu time** (*telecomm*) Greenwich Mean Time. [Zulu *amazulu* people of heaven]

zulu *zōō'lōō*, *n* a type of two-masted fishing vessel formerly used in N E Scotland. [Said to have been introduced during the *Zulu* war of 1878–79]

zum Beispiel *tsōōm bī'shpēl*, (*Ger*) for example: — *abbrev* **z.B.**

zumbooruk *zum'bōō-ruk* or *-bōō'*, *n* a small cannon mounted on a swivel, carried on the back of a camel. — Also **zum'booruck**, **zom'boruk** or **zam'boorak**. [Hindustani *zambūrak*; from Pers]

Zuñi *zōō'nyē* or *sōō'nyē*, or **Zuni** *zōō'nē*, *n* a member of a Pueblo Indian people traditionally living in large communal houses near the *Zuñi* river in Western New Mexico; the language of the Zuni. — Also *adj*. — *adj* and *n* **Zu'ñian** or **Zun'ian**. [Am Sp, from Keresan]

zupa *zū'pə*, *n* a confederation of village communities governed by a **zū'pan**, in the early history of Serbia, etc. [Serbian]

zurf. See **zarf**.

zuz *zōōz*, *n* a silver coin of ancient Palestine. [Heb]

ZW *abbrev*: Zimbabwe (IVR).

Zwanziger *tsvan'tsi-gər*, *n* an old Austrian silver coin, equivalent to twenty kreutzers. [Ger, from *zwanzig* twenty]

Zwieback *tsvē'bäk* or *tswē'*, *n* biscuit rusk, or a sweet spiced bread toasted. [Ger]

Zwinglian *zwing'gli-ən* or *tsving'li-ən*, *adj* relating to the Swiss reformer Huldreich *Zwingli* (1484–1531), or his doctrines, *esp* his divergence from Luther in the doctrine of the Eucharist (Zwingli rejecting every form of local or corporeal presence, whether by transubstantiation, impanation or consubstantiation). — *n* a follower of Zwingli. — *n* **Zwing'lianism**. — *n* **Zwing'lianist**.

zwischenzug *zvish'ən-zōōg* or *tsvish'ən-tsōōk*, (*chess*) *n* an interim move, made to play for time. [Ger, from *zwischen* between, and *Zug* move]

zwitterion *tsvit'ər-ī-ən*, (*chem*) *n* an ion carrying both a positive and a negative charge. [Ger *Zwitter* a hybrid, and **ion**]

Zygaena *zī-jē'nə*, *n* the burnet moth genus, the typical genus of the family **Zygae'nidae**; the former name of the hammerhead genus of sharks, now called *Sphyrna*. — *adj* **zygae'nid**, **zygae'nine** or **zygae'noid**. [Gr *zygaina* a shark]

zygo- *zī'gō-* or *zig'ō-*, or before a vowel **zyg-** *zīg-* or *zig-*, *combining form* denoting a yoke, union or the presence of two similar things. — *adj* **zy'gal** relating to a zygon; formed like a letter H. — *n* **zygan'trum** (*zool*; Gr *antron* a cave) in snakes and some lizards, an additional vertebral articulation, consisting of a fossa on the posterior surface of the neural arch, into which the zygosphene fits. — *adj* **zygapophyseal** or **zygapophysial** (*-fiz'i-əl*). — *n* **zygapophysis** (*-pof'i-sis*; Gr *apophysis* process; *zool*) any of the yoke-pieces or articulations of the vertebrae: — *pl* **zygapoph'ysēs**. — *adj* **zygobranchiate** (*-brangk'i-āt*; *zool*; Gr *branchia* gills) having paired, symmetrically placed, gills; belonging to the **Zygobranchiā'ta**, a division of the *Gastropoda*. — *n* and *adj* **zy'gobranch** and **zygobranch'iate**. — *n* **zy'gocactus** a cactus of the Brazilian genus *Zygocactus* of jointed, branching cactuses with zygomorphic flowers, also known as the Christmas cactus. — *adj* **zygocardiac** (*-kär'di-ak*; *zool*; Gr *kardiā* heart) a term used to describe certain paired lateral ossicles in the gastric mill of Crustacea. — *adj* **zygodactyl** (*-dak'til*; *zool*; Gr *daktylos* toe) having two toes in front and two behind, as parrots have. — Also **zygodactyl'ic** or **zygodac'tylous**. — *n* **zygodac'tylism**. — *adj* **zy'godont** (Gr *odous*, *odontos* tooth) relating to molar teeth whose cusps are paired; possessing such molars. — *adj* **zygomor'phic** or **zygomorphous** (*-mör'fəs*; Gr *morphē* form) yoke-shaped; designating flowers symmetrical about one plane only. — *n* **zygomor'phism** or **zy'gomorphy**. — *n pl* **Zygomycetes** (*-mī-sē'tēz*; Gr *mykēs*, *mykētos* a mushroom) a group of fungi (moulds, etc), a division of the *Phycomycetes*, marked by the production of zygospores. — *n* **zygomycete'**. — Also *adj*. — *adj* **zygomycē'tous**. — *n* **zy'gon** a connecting bar; an H-shaped fissure of the brain (*anatom*). — *n pl* **Zygophyllaceae** (*-fil-ā'sē-ē*; Gr *phyllon* a leaf) the bean caper family, desert and steppe plants related to the *Rutaceae*, the typical genus being **Zygophyll'um**. — *adj* **zygophyllā'ceous**. — *n* **zy'gophyte** (*-fīt*; Gr *phyton* a plant) a plant in which reproduction takes place by means of zygospores. — *adj* **zygopleural** (*-plōō'rəl*; *biol*; Gr *pleurā* side) bilaterally symmetrical. — *adj* **zy'gose** relating to zygosis. — *n* **zygosis** (*-gō'sis*; *biol*) conjugation. — *n* **zy'gosphene** (*-sfēn*; Gr *sphēn* wedge; *zool*) in snakes and some lizards, an additional vertebral articulation, consisting of a process on the anterior surface of the neural arch, which fits into the zygantrum. — *n* **zy'gospore** (Gr *sporā* a seed; *bot*) a spore produced by the union of buds from two adjacent hyphae in the process of conjugation by which some fungi multiply. — Also **zy'gosperm**. [Gr *zygon* yoke]

zygoma *zī-gō'mə*, or *zi-*, (*anatom*) *n* the arch formed by the malar bone and the zygomatic process of the temporal bone of the skull: — *pl* **zygo'mas** or **zygo'mata**. — *adj* **zygomat'ic** relating to, or in the region of, the zygoma. — **zygomatic arch**; **zygomatic fossa** the lower part of the fossa bridged over by the zygomatic arch; **zygomatic muscles** two muscles, *major* and *minor*, extending from the zygomatic arch. [New L, from Gr *zȳgōma*, from *zygon* yoke]

zygote *zī'gōt*, or *zig'*, *n* (*bot* and *zool*) the product of the union of two gametes; by extension, the individual developing from that product. — *adj* **zygotic** (*-got'*). — **zygotic number** (*bot*) the diploid chromosome number. [Gr *zygōtos* yoked, from *zygon* yoke]

zylonite. Erroneous spelling of **xylonite**.

zymase *zī'māz* or *-mās*, *n* any of a group of enzymes inducing the alcoholic fermentation of carbohydrates. [Fr, from Gr *zȳmē* leaven, and sfx *-ase* denoting an enzyme]

zyme *zīm*, *n* a ferment; a disease germ. — *adj* **zy'mic** relating to fermentation. — *n* **zy'mite** a priest who uses leavened bread in the Eucharist. [Gr *zȳmē* leaven, *zȳmōsis* fermentation]

zymo- *zī-mō-*, or before a vowel **zym-** *zīm-*, *combining form* relating to fermentation. — *n* **zy'mogen** (*biol*) a non-catalytic substance formed by plants and animals as a stage in the development of an enzyme. — *adj* **zymogen'ic**. — *adj* **zy'moid** like a ferment. — *adj* **zymolog'ic** or **zymolog'ical** relating to zymology. — *n* **zymol'ogist** a specialist in zymology. — *n* **zymol'ogy** the science of fermentation. — *n* **zymol'ysis** the action of enzymes. — *adj* **zymolyt'ic**. — *n* **zymom'eter** or **zymosim'eter** an instrument for measuring the degree of fermentation. — *n* **zymō'sis** fermentation; the course, process or condition, thought to be analogous to fermentation, constituting a zymotic disease. — *adj* **zymotech'nic** or **zymotech'nical** producing and utilizing fermentation. — *n sing* **zymotech'nics** the art of managing fermentation. — *adj* **zymot'ic** relating to fermentation; of the nature of, relating to or causing an infectious disease. — *n* an infectious disease. — *adv* **zymot'ically**. [Ety as for **zyme**]

zymome *zī'mōm*, *n* an old name for the part of gluten insoluble in alcohol. [Gr *zȳmōma* a fermented mixture]

zymurgy *zī'mûr-ji*, *n* the branch of chemistry that deals with wine-making, brewing, distilling, and similar processes involving fermentation. [Gr *zȳmē* leaven, and *ergon* work]

Zyrian *zir'i-ən*, *n* a member of a people of north-eastern Russia; their Finno-Ugric language. — Also *adj.*

zythum *zī'thəm*, *n* a kind of beer made by the ancient Egyptians, highly commended by Diodorus Siculus, a writer of the first century BC. [Gr *zȳthos*]

Some first names

Masculine names are marked *m*, feminine names *f*

Aaron *ā'rən*, *m* (*Heb*) lofty, mountaineer.

Abigail *ab'i-gāl*, *f* (*Heb*) father rejoiced, or father of exaltation.—Dimins **Abby**, **Nabby**, **Gail**.

Abraham *ā'brə-həm*, **Abram** *ā'brəm*, *m* (*Heb*) *perh* father of a multitude, high father.—Dimins **Abe**, **Bram**.

Ada *ā'də*, *f prob* for **Adelaide** or other Germanic name beginning with *Adel-*, *Adal-* (noble).

Adam *ad'əm*, *m* (*Heb*) man, earth, red earth.

Adela *ad'i-lə*, **Adèle** *-del'*, **Adella** *-del'ə*, *f* (*Gmc*) noble.

Adelaide *ad'i-lād*, *f* from French *Adélaïde*, from German *Adelheid* (from *Adelheidis*), noble kind or sort.—Dimins **Addie**, **Addy**.

Adrian *ā'dri-ən*, *m* (*L*) of Adria (in Italy).—Fem **Adrianne** (*-an'*), **Adrienne** (*-en'*).

Agatha *ag'ə-thə*, *f* (*Gr*) good.—Dimin **Aggie**.

Agnes *ag'nis*, *f* (*Gr*) chaste.—Dimins **Aggie**, **Aggy**, **Annis**, **Annot**, **Nance**, **Nancy**, **Nessa**, **Nessie**, **Nesta**.

Aidan, **Aiden** *ā'dən* *m* (*Ir*) a diminutive form from *aodh*, fire.

Aileen *ā'lēn*, *ī'lēn*, *f* (*Ir* and *Scot*) *prob* a form of **Evelyn** and **Helen**, a variant of **Eileen**.

Ailsa *āl'sə*, *f* from the Scottish island rock, Ailsa Craig.

Alan, **Allan**, **Allen** *al'ən*, *m* (*prob Celtic*) harmony.

Alasdair, **Alastair**, **Alistair**, **Alister** *al'is-tər*, *m* (*Gaelic*) forms of **Alexander**.

Albert *al'bərt*, *m* (*Gmc*) nobly bright.—Dimins **Al**, **Bert**, **Bertie**.—Fem **Albertina** (*-ē'nə*), **Albertine** (*-ēn*).

Alexander *al-ig-zan'dər*, *-zän'*, *m* (*Gr*) defender of men.—Dimins **Alec**, **Alex** (*-lik*, *-lix*), **Sandy**.—Fem **Alexandra**.—Dimins **Alex**, **Alexa**, **Sandra**.

Alexis *ə-lek'sis*, *m* and *f* (*Gr*) helper.—Fem **Alexia**.

Alfred *al'frid*, *m* (*Gmc*) elf counsel (good counsellor).—Dimins **Alf**, **Alfie**.

Algernon *al'jər-nən*, *m* (*OFr*) moustached.—Dimin **Algy**.

Alice, *al'is*, **Alicia** *ə-lish'i-ə*, *-lis'i-ə*, *f* (*Gmc*) from Old French *Aliz* for *Adelheidis* (see **Adelaide**).—Dimins **Ailie**, **Ali**, **Allie**, **Ally**, **Ellie**, **Elsie**. See also **Alison**.

Alison, **Allison** *al'i-sən*, *f* a Norman French pet form of **Alice**, latterly used *esp* in Scotland.—Dimins **Ailie**, **Ali**, **Elsie**.

Alistair. See **Alasdair**.

Allan, **Allen**. See **Alan**.

Alma *al'mə*, *f* (*L*) fostering, nourishing, loving.

Althea *al-thē'ə*, *al'*, *f* (*Gr*) a healer, or wholesome.

Alun *al'ən*, *m poss* from the name of a Welsh river, but thought of as a variant of **Alan**.

Alwin, **Alwyn** *al'win*, *m* (*Gmc*) elf (good or noble) friend.

Amabel *am'ə-bel*, *f* (*L*, *amabilis*) lovable.—Deriv **Mabel**.

Amanda *ə-man'də*, *f* (*L*) lovable.—Dimin **Mandy**.

Amber *am'bər*, *f* (*Eng*) from the precious material.

Ambrose *am'brōz*, *m* (*Gr*) of the immortals, divine.

Amelia *ə-mē'li-ə*, *f* (*Gmc*) struggling, labour.—Dimin **Millie**.

Amy *ā'mi*, *f* (*Fr*) beloved.

Anastasia *an-ə-stā'zhə*, *-zi-ə*, *f* (*Gr*) resurrection.—Dimin **Stacey**, **Stacy** (*stā'si*).

Andrew *an'drōō*, *m* (*Gr*) manly.—Dimins **Andie**, **Andy**, **Drew** (*drōō*).—Fem **Andrea** (*-dri-ə*), **Andrina** (*-drē'nə*).

Aneurin, **Aneirin** *a-nā'rin*, *-nī*, *-noi'*, *m* (*Welsh*) of uncertain meaning, *perh* noble, seemly.—Dimin **Nye** (*nī*).

Angela *an'ji-lə*, *f* **Angel** *ān'jəl*, *m* and *f* (*Gr*) angel, messenger.—Fem deriv **Angelica** (*-jel'ik-ə*).—Dimins **Angelina** (*an-ji-lē'nə*, *-lī'nə*), **Angie**, **Angy** (*an'ji*).

Angharad *an-gar'ad*, *-hhar'ad*, *f* (*Welsh*) much loved.

Angus *ang'gəs*, *m* (*Celtic*) *perh* one choice.

Ann, **Anne** *an*, **Anna** *an'ə*, **Hannah** *han'ə*, *f* (*Heb*) God has favoured me.—Dimins **Anita** (*ə-nē'tə*, Sp), **Anneka**, **Annika** (*an'ə-kə*, Swed), **Annette** (*a-net'*, Fr), **Annie**, **Anushka** (*a-nōō'shkə*, Russ), **Nan**, **Nance**, **Nancy**, **Nanette**, **Nina** (*nē'nə*, *nī'nə*), **Ninette** (*nē-net'*, *ni-*, Fr).

Annabel, **Annabelle** *an'ə-bel*, **Annabella** *-bel'ə*, *f poss* an alteration of **Amabel**.—Dimins **Bel**, **Bell**, **Bella**, **Belle**.

Annis *an'is*, **Annot** *an'ət*. Diminutives of **Agnes**.

Anthea *an'thi-ə*, *-thē'*, *f* (*Gr*) flowery.

Anthony *an'tə-ni*, (*US*) *an'thə-*, **Antony** *an'tə-ni*, *m* (*L*) from Roman family name, meaning unknown.—Dimin **Tony** (*tō'ni*).—Fem **Antonia**.

Antoinette *an-twə-net'*, *f* (*Fr*) a diminutive feminine of *Antoine*, French form of **Anthony**.—Dimins **Net**, **Nettie**, **Netty**.

April *ā'pril*, *f* (*L*) from the name of the month.

Arabella *ar-ə-bel'ə*, *f* origin and meaning uncertain: *perh* an alteration of **Amabel**, or *perh* (L *orabilis*) easily entreated.—Dimins as for **Annabel**.

Archibald *är'chi-bld*, *-böld*, *m* (*Gmc*) genuine and bold.—Dimins **Arch**, **Archie**, **Archy**.

Ariadne *a-ri-ad'ni*, *f* (*Gr*) *perh* very holy.

Arnold *är'nld*, *-nold*, *m* (*Gmc*) eagle rule or power.

Arthur *är'thər*, *m* (*Celtic*) *perh* bear, or (*Ir*) stone; or from a Roman family name *Artorius*.

Asa *ā'sə*, *-zə*, *m* (*Heb*) healer.

Ashley, **Ashleigh** *ash'li*, *m* and *f* (*Gmc*) from the surname derived from common place name, meaning ash wood.

Astrid *as'trid*, *f* (*Scand*) divinely beautiful.

Aubrey *ö'bri*, *m* (*Gmc*) elf rule.—Dimin **Auberon**.

Audrey *ö'dri*, *f* (*Gmc*) noble power.

Augustine *ö'gəs-tēn*, *ö-gus'tin*, *m* (*L*) belonging to Augustus.

Augustus *ö-gus'təs*, *m* (*L*) venerable, exalted.—Dimins **Gus**, **Gussie**.—Fem **Augusta**.

Auriel, **Auriol** *ör'i-əl*, *f* derivatives of Latin *aurum*, gold.

Aurora *ö-rō'rə*, *-rö'rə*, **Aurore** *-rōr'*, *-rör'*, *f* (*L*) dawn.

Austin *ö'stin*, *m* a contraction of **Augustine**.

Averil *av'ə-ril*, *m* and *f* (*Gmc*) *perh* boar-battle.

Avril *av'ril*, *m* and *f* (*Fr*) April.

Barbara *bär'bə-rə*, *f* (*Gr*) foreign woman.—Dimins **Bab**, **Babs**, **Babbie**, **Barbie**.

Barnabas *bär'nə-bəs*, **Barnaby** *-bi*, *m* (*Heb*) son of exhortation.—Dimin **Barney**.

Barney *bär'ni*, *m*. See **Bernard**, **Barnabas**.

Barry *bar'i*, *m* (*Ir*) spear, or short for Irish *Finbarr*, fairhead, or from the surname and place name.—Dimins (*esp Austr*) **Baz**, **Bazza**.

Bartholomew *bär-thol'ə-mū*, *m* (*Heb*) son of Talmi.—Dimins **Bart**, **Bat**.

Basil *baz'il*, *m* (*Gr*) kingly.

Beatrice *bē'ə-tris*, **Beatrix** *-triks*, *bē-ā'*, *f* (*L*) making happy (*perh* an alteration of early Christian *Viatrix* (female voyager, pilgrim) by association with *beatus*, blessed).—Dimins **Bea**, **Bee**, **Beatty**, **Trix**, **Trixie**.

Becky *bek'i*, *f*. See **Rebecca**.

Belinda *bə-lin'də*, *f* of uncertain origin, *perh* Germanic, *perh* formed from Italian *bella*, beautiful.

Bell, **Belle** *bel*, **Bella** *bel'ə*, *f*. See **Isabella**, **Annabel**, **Arabella**.

Benedict *ben'i-dikt*, **Benedick** *-dik*, *m* (*L*) blessed.

Benjamin *ben'jə-min*, *m* (*Heb*) son of the right hand (ie of good fortune).—Dimins **Ben**, **Benjie**, **Benny**.

Berenice *ber'i-nēs*, **Bernice** *bûr-nēs'*, *f* (*Gr*) from the Macedonian form of *Pherenīkē*, victory-bringer.

Bernard *bûr'nərd*, *m* (*Gmc*) bear-hard.—Dimins **Bernie**, **Barney**.—Fem **Bernadette**.

Bert *bûrt*, **Bertie** *bûr'ti*, *m* diminutives of **Albert**, **Herbert** or other name ending in *-bert*, and of **Bertram** and (*f*) **Bertha**.

Bertha *bûr'thə*, *f* (*Gmc*) bright.—Dimins **Bert**, **Bertie**.

Bertram *bûr'trəm*, *m* (*Gmc*) bright raven.—Variant (or independent name meaning 'bright shield') **Bertrand** *bûr'trənd*.—Dimins **Bertie**, **Bert**.

Beryl *ber'il*, *f* (*Gr*) from the precious stone.

Bess, **Bessie**, **Beth**. See **Elizabeth**.

Bethany *beth'ə-ni, f* (*Biblical*) from the name of the village near Jerusalem.
Betsy, **Bettina**, **Betty**. See **Elizabeth**.
Beverley *bev'ər-li, m* and *f* (*Gmc*) from the surname and place name, meaning beaver meadow or stream.
Bianca *bi-ang'kə, f* the Italian form of **Blanche**.
Biddie, **Biddy** *bid'i, f*. See **Bridget**.
Bill *bil*, **Billie**, **Billy** *bil'i, m* diminutives of **William**.
Blaise *blāz, m* (*Fr* from *L*) *perh* stuttering.
Blanche, **Blanch** *blänsh, f* (*Fr*, from *Gmc*) white.
Bob. See **Robert**.
Bonnie *bon'i, f* (*Scot*) pretty (used *esp* in US).
Boris *bor'is, bö', m* (*Russ*) *perh* Tatar, small, but associated with *bor*, fight.
Bram. See **Abraham**.
Brenda *bren'də, f perh* a feminine form of the Norse name *Brand*, brand or sword, or of **Brendan**.
Brendan *bren'dən, m* (*Ir*) meaning uncertain.
Brent *brent, m* from the surname, itself *orig* a place name.
Brett *bret, m* (*Eng*) from Latin *Brit(t)o*, Briton.
Brian, **Bryan** *brī'ən, m* (*Celtic*) meaning uncertain.
Bridget, **Brigid**, **Brigit** *brij'it*, **Bride** *brīd, f* (*Celtic*) of uncertain meaning; name of a Celtic fire-goddess and an Irish saint.—Dimins **Biddie**, **Biddy**, **Bridie** (*brī'di*) .
Briony, **Bryony** *brī'ə-ni, f* (*Eng*) from the plant name.
Bronwen *bron'win, f* (*Welsh*) white breast.
Bruce *broos, m* from the surname, *orig* from Normandy, and the place name *Brieuse*.
Bruno *broo'nō, m* (*Gmc*) brown.
Bryan. See **Brian**.
Brynmor *brin'mör, m* (*Welsh*) from the place name formed from *bryn*, hill and *mawr*, great.—Dimin **Bryn**.
Bryony. See **Briony**.
Bunnie, **Bunny** *bun'i, m* and *f* (*Eng*) a pet name.
Bunty *bun'ti, f* (*Eng*) a pet name.

Caitlín *kat'lin, kāt', -lēn', f* Irish form of **Catherine**, anglicized as **Kathleen**.
Calum, **Callum** *kal'əm, m* Gaelic form of the saint's name *Columba* (*L*, dove).
Camilla *kə-mil'ə, f* (*L*) *perh* a free-born attendant at a sacrifice; in Virgil, name of a queen of the Volsci.
Candice *kan'dis, f* meaning uncertain; dynastic name of the queens of ancient Ethiopia.—Dimin **Candy**.
Candida *kan'di-də, f* (*L*) white.
Cara *kä'rə, f* (*L* and *Ital*) dear one.—Dimin **Carina** (*kə-rē'nə*).
Carl, **Karl** *karl, m* Germanic forms of **Charles**.—Fem **Carla**, **Karla** (*kär'lə*).—Fem derivs **Carleen**, **Carlene** (*kär-lēn'*).—Dimins **Carlie**, **Carly**.
Carmel *kär'məl* (*Heb*), **Carmen** *kär'men* (Sp, altered by association with Latin *carmen*, a poem, song), *f* garden.
Carol *kar'əl*, formerly *m* from *Carolus*, Latin form of **Charles**.—Fem **Carol** (*perh* a diminutive of **Caroline**), **Carola** (*kar'ə-lə*), **Carole** (*kar'əl*).
Caroline *kar'ə-līn*, **Carolyn** *-lin, f* derivatives of *Carolus*, Latin form of **Charles**.—Dimins **Caddie**, **Caro**, **Carrie**, **Lina** (*lē'nə*).
Carys *kar'is, f* (*Welsh*) modern invention, from *car*, love.
Caspar *kas'pər, m*. See **Jasper**.
Cassandra *kə-san'drə, -sän', f* (*Gr, mythol*) a daughter of Priam of Troy, a prophetess whom no-one heeded.—Dimins **Cass**, **Cassie**.
Catherine, **Catharine**, **Katharine**, **Katherine** *kath'ə-rin, kath'rin*, **Kathryn** *kath'rin*, **Catherina** *-ə-rē'nə*, **Katrine** *kat'rin*, **Katerina** *kat-ə-rē'nə*, **Katrina** *kə-trē'nə, f* from Greek *Aikaterinē*, of uncertain origin, later assimilated to *katharos*, pure.—Dimins **Casey**, **Cathie**, **Cathy**, **Kate**, **Katie**, **Katy**, **Kath**, **Kathie**, **Kathy**, **Kay**, **Kit**, **Kittie**, **Kitty**.
Catriona *kə-trē'ə-nə, kat-ri-ō'nə, f* the Gaelic form of **Catherine**.
Cecil *ses'il, m* (*L*) the Roman family name *Caecilius* (literally, blind).—Fem **Cecilia** (*si-sil'yə, -sēl'yə*), **Cecily** (*ses'i-li*), **Cicely** (*sis'i-li*).—Dimins **Cis**, **Cissy**, **Cissie**.
Cedric *sed'rik, m prob* a mistake of Scott's for *Cerdic* (name of the first king of the West Saxons).
Celia *sē'li-ə, f* feminine of the Roman family name *Caelius* (*poss* heavenly).
Charles *chärlz, m* (*Gmc*) manly.—Dimins **Charlie**, **Charley**, **Chae**, **Chay** (*chā*), (*US*) **Chuck**.—Fem deriv **Charlene** (*shär'lēn, -lēn'*).
Charlotte *shär'lət, f* (*Fr*) diminutive of **Charles**.—Dimins **Charley**, **Lottie**.
Charmaine, **Sharmaine** *shär-mān', f prob* a 20c invention.
Charmian *shär'mi-ən, chär', kär', f* (*Gr*) joy.
Cher, **Chère** *shār*, **Cherie**, **Sherry** *sher'i, f* (*Fr*) dear one.
Cherry *cher'i, f* from the fruit or blossom; also a variant of **Cherie**.—Deriv **Cheryl** (*cher'il, sher'il*), **Sheryl** (*sher'*).
Chloe *klō'i, f* (*Gr*) a green shoot, verdure.
Christabel *kris'tə-bel, f* (*Gr*) 'anointed' (or 'Christ') and (*L*) 'fair'.
Christian *kris'ti-ən, -chən, m* and *f*, belonging to, follower of, Christ.—Dimins **Chris**, **Christie**, **Christy**.—Fem **Christiana** (*-ti-ä'nə*), **Christina** (*-tē'nə*), **Christine** (*kris'tēn* or *-tēn'*), (*Scot*) **Kirsteen** (*kûr'stēn*), **Kirstin**.—Dimins **Chris**, **Chrissie**, **Kirsty**, **Kirstie**, **Teenie**, **Tina** (*tē'nə*).
Christopher *kris'tə-fər, m* (*Gr*) carrying Christ.—Dimins **Chris**, **Kit**.
Chrystal. See **Crystal**.
Chuck *chuk, m*. See **Charles**.
Ciara, **Ciaran**. See **Kieran**.
Cicely. See **Cecil**.
Cindy, **Sindy** *sin'di, f* diminutives of **Cynthia**, **Lucinda**.
Clara *klā'rə*, **Clare**, **Claire** *klār, f* (*L*) bright.—Derivs **Clarice** (*klar'is*), **Clarinda** (*klə-rin'də*), **Clarissa** (*-ris'ə*).
Clarence *klar'əns, m* from the dukedom held by royal princes, from a place name.
Claud, **Claude** *klöd, m* (*L*) lame.—Fem **Claudia**.
Clement *klem'ənt, m* (*L*) mild, merciful.—Dimin **Clem**.—Fem **Clementina** (*-ē'nə*), **Clementine** (*-ēn, -īn*).
Cleopatra *kli-ə-pat'ra, -pä'trə, f* (*Gr*) glory of her father.—Dimin **Cleo** (*klē'ō*).
Clifford *klif'ərd, m* from the surname.
Clive *klīv, m* from the surname, *orig* honouring Robert Clive of India (1725–74).
Colette *ko-let', f*. See **Nicholas**.
Colin *kol'in, kō', m orig* a diminutive of **Nicholas**; also an anglicization of Gaelic *Cailean*, follower of Columba.
Colm, **Colum** *kol'əm, m* Irish forms of Latin *Columba*. See **Calum** and **Malcolm**.
Conor, **Connor** *kon'ər, m* (*Ir*) an anglicized form of *Conchobhar*, *perh* high desire.
Conrad *kon'rad, m* (*Ger*) bold in counsel.
Constance *kon'stəns, f* (*L*) steadfast, or constancy.—Dimins **Con**, **Connie**.—Deriv **Constantine** (*kon'stən-tīn*), *m*.
Cora *kō'rə, kö'rə, f poss* (*Gr*) girl, used also as a diminutive eg of Sp *Corazon*, heart.
Coral *kor'əl, f* from the precious material.
Cordelia *kör-dē'li-ə, f perh* (*L*) warm-hearted.
Corin *kor'in, m* (*L*) from *Quirinus*, a designation of Romulus, Rome's founder, of uncertain meaning.
Corinne *ko-rin', -rēn'*, **Corinna** *-rin'ə, f* (*Gr*) diminutive of *korē*, maiden.
Craig *krāg, m* from the surname, itself from Gaelic *creag*, rock, found in place names.
Cressida *kres'i-də, f* (*Gr*) English form of *Chryseis*, accusative *Chryseida*, daughter of *Chryseis*.
Crispin *kris'pin*, **Crispian** *-pi-ən, m* (*L*) from the Roman family name *Crispinus*, from *crispus*, curly-headed.
Crystal, **Chrystal**, **Krystal**, **Krystle** *kris'təl, f* crystal, the precious material, itself from Greek, ice .
Cuthbert *kuth'bərt, kudh', m* (*OE*) well-known, bright.
Cynthia *sin'thi-ə, f* (*Gr*) of Mount Cynthus in Delos, an epithet of the goddess Artemis (Diana).—Dimins **Cindy**, **Sindy**.
Cyril *sir'il, m* (*Gr*) lordly.
Cyrus *sī'rəs, m* (*Pers*) of uncertain meaning.—Dimin **Cy**.

Dai *dī, m* regarded as a Welsh diminutive of **David**, but *orig* a distinct Celtic name, *perh* 'bright'.
Daisy *dā'zi, f* (*Eng*) a translation of Fr *Marguerite*.

Damian, **Damien** *dā'mi-ən*, **Damon** *-mən*, *m* (*Gr*) *perh* connected with *damaein*, to tame.

Daniel *dan'yəl*, *m* (*Heb*) the Lord is judge.—Dimins **Dan**, **Danny**.—Fem **Daniela** (*-i-ä'lə*), **Daniella**, **Danielle** (*-el'*).

Daphne *daf'ni*, *f* (*Gr*) laurel.

Darren *dar'ən*, *m* from the Irish surname.

David *dā'vid*, *m* (*Heb*) beloved.—Dimins **Dave**, **Davie**, **Davy**.

Dawn *dön*, *f* (*Eng*) dawn.

Dean *dēn*, *m* from the surname.

Deanna. See **Diana**.

Deborah *deb'ə-rə*, *di-bō'rə*, *-bö'*, **Debra** *deb'rə*, *f* (*Heb*) bee.—Dimins **Deb**, **Debbie**, **Debby**.

Dee *dē*, *m* and *f* from the surname, the river name, or a shortening of any name with the initial *D*.

Deirdre *dēr'dri*, *f* (*Ir*) meaning doubtful.

Delia *dē'li-ə*, *f* (*Gr*) of the island of Delos.

Della *del'ə*, *f* a diminutive of **Adela**, alteration of **Delia**, or a 19c invention.

Delyth *del'ith*, *f* (*Welsh*) pretty.

Denis, **Dennis**, **Denys** *den'is*, *m* (*Fr*) a medieval contraction of Latin *Dionysius*, belonging to Dionysus or Bacchus.—Dimins **Den**, **Denny**.—Fem **Denise** (*də-nēz'*).

Derek, **Derrick**, **Deryck** *der'ik*, *m* (*Gmc*) a medieval form of *Theodoric*, people-rule.—Dimin **Del**.

Dermot *dûr'mət*, (*Celtic*) free of envy.

Désirée *dā-zē'rā*, *-rā'*, *f* (*Fr*, from *L*) longed-for.—Masc **Désiré**.

Desmond *dez'mənd*, *m* (*Ir*) from the surname or the district.

Diana *dī-an'ə*, **Dian** *dī-an'*, **Diane** *dē-än'*, *dī-an'*, **Dianne** *dē-an'*, *dī-an'*, **Deanne** *dē-an'*, **Deanna** *-an'ə*, *f* (*L*) the Roman goddess Diana.—Dimins **Di**, **Die** (*dī*).

Dick, **Dickie**, **Dickon**. See **Richard**.

Dilwyn *dil'in*, *m* (*Welsh*) steadfast and fair.

Dilys *dil'is*, *f* (*Welsh*) sure, constant, genuine.

Dinah *dī'nə*, *f* (*Heb*) judged, or dedicated.

Dionne *dē-on'*, *f* (*Gr*) feminine diminutive formed from *Dionysius* (see **Denis**).

Dirk *dûrk*, *m* Dutch form of **Derek**.

Dolores *də-lō'rēz*, *-lö'*, *f* (*Sp*) sorrows.—Dimin **Lola**, **Lolita**.

Dolly. See **Dorothy**.

Dominic, **Dominick** *dom'i-nik*, *m* (*L*) Sunday.—Fem **Dominica** (*də-min'i-kə*).

Donald *don'əld*, **Donal** *dō'nəl*, *don'*, *m* (*Celtic*) world chief.—Dimins **Don**, **Donnie**.

Donna *don'ə*, *f* (*Ital*) mistress, lady; sometimes used as feminine of **Donald**.

Dora *dō'rə*, *dö'rə*, *f prob* a diminutive of **Dorothy**; used also for **Theodora** and other names ending in *-dora*.

Doreen *dō'rēn*, *dö'*, *dō-rēn'*, *dö-*, *f* a derivative of **Dora** or of **Dorothy**.

Doris *dor'is*, *f* (*Gr*) the name of a sea-nymph.

Dorothy *dor'ə-thi*, **Dorothea** *-thē'ə*, *f* (*Gr*) gift of God.—Dimins **Dolly**, **Dora**, **Dorrie**, **Do**, **Dot**, **Dottie**.

Dougal *doo͞'gəl*, **Dugald** *doo͞'gəld*, *m* (*Celtic*) dark stranger.

Douglas *dug'ləs*, *m* (*orig Scot*) from the surname, or the river.—Dimins **Doug** (*dug*), **Duggie**.

Drew. See **Andrew**.

Duane, **Dwane** *dwān*, *m* (*Ir*) from the surname *Ó Dubháin*, from *dubh*, black.

Dugald. See **Dougal**.

Dulcie *dul'si*, *f* (*L*) sweet — a 19c invention.

Duncan *dung'kən*, *m* (*Celtic*) brown, brown warrior.

Dylan *dil'ən*, *m* (*Welsh*) *perh* wave, the name of a sea-god.

Eamonn, **Eamunn** *ā'mən*, *m* Irish form of **Edmund**.

Eartha *ûr'thə*, *f* from the word 'earth'.

Edgar *ed'gər*, *m* (*OE*) happy spear.—Dimins **Ed**, **Eddie**, **Eddy**, **Ned**, **Neddie**, **Neddy**.

Edith *ē'dith*, *f* (*OE*) happy or rich war.—Dimins **Edie**, **Edy**.

Edmund *ed'mənd*, *m* (*OE*) happy protection.—Dimins **Ed**, **Eddie**, **Eddy**, **Ned**, **Neddie**, **Neddy**.

Edna *ed'nə*, *f* an anglicized form of Irish **Eithna**, or (*Heb*) pleasure, delight.

Edward *ed'wərd*, *m* (*OE*) rich guard.—Dimins **Ed**, **Eddie**, **Eddy**, **Ned**, **Neddie**, **Ted**, **Teddie**, **Teddy**.

Edwin *ed'win*, *m* (*OE*) prosperity or riches, friend.—Dimins as for **Edmund**.—Fem **Edwina** (*-wē'nə*).

Eileen *ī'lēn*, *ī-lēn'*, *f* (*Ir*) *prob* a form of **Evelyn**, also used for **Helen**. See also **Aileen**.

Eiluned, **Eluned** *i-lin'əd*, *f* (*Welsh*) idol, image.

Eithne, **Ethne** *eth'ni*, **Eithna**, **Ethna** *-nə*, *f* (*Ir*) from *aodhnait*, diminutive of *aodh*, fire. See also **Aidan**.

Elaine *i-lān'*, *f* an Old French form of **Helen**; some suggest a Celtic origin, with meaning 'fawn'.

Eleanor, **Eleanore**, **Elinor** *el'i-nər*, *f perh* forms of **Helen**, or from a Germanic root meaning 'foreign'.—Dimins **Ella**, **Ellen**, **Nell**, **Nellie**, **Nelly**, **Nora**.

Elizabeth, **Elisabeth** *i-liz'ə-beth*, *f* (*Heb*) God is satisfaction.—Dimins **Bess**, **Bessie**, **Bessy**, **Bet**, **Beth**, **Betsy**, **Bettina**, **Betty**, **Eliza**, **Elsie**, **Libby**, **Lisa** (*lī'zə*, *lē'*, *lē'sə*), **Liza**, **Lise** (*lēz*), **Lisbet**, **Lisbeth**, **Lizbeth**, **Liz**, **Lizzie**, **Lisette** (*li-zet'*).

Ella *el'ə*, *f* (*Gmc*) all.—Also a diminutive of **Eleanor** and **Ellen** or of **Isabella** or other name ending in *-ella*.

Ellen *el'in*, *f* a form of **Helen**, also used for **Eleanor**.—Dimin **Ellie**.

Elma *el'mə*, *f* a diminutive of **Wilhelmina**, or a combination of eg **Elizabeth Marjory**, **Elizabeth Mary**.

Elsie *el'si*. See **Elizabeth**, **Alison**, **Alice**.

Elspeth *el'spəth*, **Elspet** *el'spət*, *f* (*Scot*) forms of **Elizabeth**.

Eluned. See **Eiluned**.

Elvis *el'vis*, *m* (*Ir*) *perh* from *Ailbhe*, the name of an Irish saint.—Fem **Elva**.

Elwyn *el'win*, *m* (*Welsh*) *perh* fair face.

Emerald *em'ə-rəld*, *f* from the precious stone.

Emily *em'-i-li*, *em'li*, *f* (*L*) from the Roman family name *Aemilius*.—Dimin **Millie**.

Emlyn *em'lin*, *m* (*Welsh*) origin uncertain.—Latin *Aemilianus*, a Roman family name, has been suggested.

Emma *em'ə*, *f* (*Gmc*) *orig* a diminutive of various names beginning *Ermin-*, *Irmin-*, an element denoting 'whole', 'universal'.—Dimins **Emm**, **Emmie**, **Emmy**.

Emmanuel *i-man'ū-əl*, *m* (*Heb*) God with us.—Dimin **Manny**.

Emmeline *em'i-lēn*, *f prob* a derivative of **Amelia**.

Emrys *em'ris*, *m* Welsh form of **Ambrose**.

Ena *ē'nə*, *f* (*Ir*) fire; or a shortened form of **Eugenia** or other name of similar sound.

Enid *ē'nid*, *f* (*Welsh*) of uncertain origin.

Enoch *ē'nək*, *m* (*Heb*) *poss* consecrated, or teaching, skilled.

Eric *er'ik*, *m* (*Gmc*, *ON Eirikr*) *perh* sole ruler.—Fem **Erica** (*er'i-kə*), associated with Gr *ereikē*, L *erica*, heather.

Erin *er'in*, *ā'rin*, *f* Ireland, from Irish *Éirinn*, dative of *Éire*.

Ernest *ûr'nist*, *m* (*Gmc*) earnest.—Dimin **Ernie**.

Errol *er'əl*, *m* of obscure origin, *perh* from the Scottish place name, *perh* a variant of **Eryl**.

Eryl *er'il*, *m* and *f* (*Welsh*) watcher.

Esmond *ez'mənd*, *m* (*OE*) 'grace' and 'protection'.

Estelle *e-stel'*, *f* (*OFr*) star.—Deriv **Estella** (*-stel'ə*).

Esther *es'tər*, **Hester** *hes'tər*, *f poss* Persian, 'star' or 'turtle'.—Dimins **Essie**, **Hetty**.

Ethel *eth'l*, *f* (*OE*) noble.

Ethne, **Ethna**. See **Eithne**.

Eugene *ū'jēn*, *m* (*Gr*) well-born.—Dimin **Gene**.—Fem **Eugenia**, **Eugénie** (*ū-zhā'ni*).—Dimins **Ena**, **Gene**.

Eunice *ū'nis*, *f* (*Gr*) happy victory.

Euphemia *ū-fē'mi-ə*, *f* (*Gr*) of good report.—Dimins **Effie**, **Phemie**.

Eustace *ū'stəs*, *m* (*Gr*) rich in corn (*eustachys*, confused with *eustathēs*, stable).—Fem **Eustacia** (*ū-stā'si-ə*, *-shə*).

Eva *ē'və*, **Eve** *ēv*, *f* (*Heb*) life.—Dimin **Evie**.

Evan *ev'ən*, *m* (*Welsh*) an anglicization of *Ifan* and *Ieuan*, forms of **John**.

Evelyn *ēv'lin*, *ev'lin*, *ev'i-lin*, *f* partly diminutive of **Eve**, partly Germanic; (*m*) *prob* from the surname, derived from the female name.

Ewan, **Ewen** *ū'ən*, *m* (*Ir* and *Gaelic*) anglicizations of *Eóghan*, of uncertain meaning. See also **Owen**.

Ezra *ez'rə*, *m* (*Heb*) help.

Faith *fāth*, *f* from the Christian virtue.

Fanny *fan'i*, *f*. See **Francis**.
Fay, **Faye** *fā*, *f* (*OFr*) either fairy, or faith; also a shortening of **Faith**.
Feargal *fûr'gəl*, *m* (*Ir*) *perh* man of courage.
Felicity *fi-lis'i-ti*, *f* (*L*) happiness.
Felix *fē'liks*, *m* (*L*) happy.—Fem **Felicia** (*fi-lish'i-ə, -lis'i-ə*), **Felice** (*fi-lēs'*).
Fenella *fi-nel'ə*, *f* anglicization of Gaelic *Fionnghuala*, white shoulder.—Ir **Finola** (*fi-nō'lə*), **Fionnuala** (*fi-noo'lə*).—Dimins **Nola** (*nō'lə*), **Nuala** (*noo'lə*).
Ferdinand *fûr'di-nənd*, *m* (*Gmc*) *perh* journey-risk.
Fergus *fûr'gəs*, *m* (*Gaelic*) an anglicization of *Fearghas*, *perh* manly vigour, or supremely choice.
Fingal *fing'gəl*, *m* (*Gaelic*) an anglicization of *Fionnghall*, fair stranger.
Finlay, **Finley** *fin'li*, *m* (*Gaelic*) *prob* fair warrior.
Finn *fin*, **Fionn** *fyun, fūn*, *m* (*Ir* and *Gaelic*) fair.
Fiona *fē-ō'nə, fē'ə-nə*, *f* from Gaelic *fionn*, fair.
Fleur *flûr*, *f* (*Fr*) flower.
Flora *flö'rə, flō'*, *f* (*L*) name of the Roman flower goddess.—Dimins **Flo**, **Florrie** (*flor'i*).
Florence *flor'əns*, *f* (*L*) blooming; also, born in Florence.—Dimins **Flo**, **Florrie**, **Flossie**, **Floy**.
Francis *frän'sis*, *m* (*Fr*) French.—Fem **Frances** (*frän'sis*).—Dimins **Fanny**, **Francie**, **Francine**, **Frankie**.
Frank *frangk*, *m* either (*Gmc*) a Frank, a Frenchman, or a diminutive of **Francis**.—Dimin **Frankie**.
Freda *frē'də*, *f* diminutive of **Winifred**, or a variant of **Frieda**.
Frederick, **Frederic** *fred'ə-rik, fred'rik*, *m* (*Gmc*) peace-rule.—Fem **Frederica** (*fred-ə-rē'kə*).—Dimins (*m* and *f*) **Fred**, **Freddie**, **Freddy**.
Frieda *frē'də*, *f* (*Gmc*) peace.

Gabriel *gā'bri-əl, gab'*, *m*, formerly also *f* (*Heb*) God is mighty, or man of God.—Fem **Gabrielle** (*gā'bri-əl, gab'*).—Dimins (*m* and *f*) **Gabi**, **Gabby**.
Gaia, **Gaea** *gī'ə*, *f* (*Gr; mythol*) the goddess Earth.
Gail, **Gale**, **Gayle** *gāl*, *f orig* diminutive of **Abigail**.
Gareth *gar'ith*, *m* Malory's remodelling of Old French *Gahariet*, *prob* from a Welsh name.
Gary, **Garry** *gar'i*, *m* from the place name and surname, used also as a diminutive of **Gareth**.
Gavin *gav'in*, *m* (*Welsh*) *perh* white hawk.
Gay, **Gaye** *gā*, *m* and *f* (*Eng*) cheerful.
Gaynor *gā'nər*, *f* (*Welsh*) a form of **Guinevere**.
Gemma, **Jemma** *jem'ə*, *f* (*Ital*) a gem.
Gene *jēn*, for **Eugene**, **Eugenia**.
Genevieve *jen'i-vēv*, *f* (*Fr*, from *Celtic*) meaning obscure.
Geoffrey, **Jeffrey** *jef'ri*, *m* (*OHGer*) *prob* a conflation of two names, *Gaufrid*, district peace, and *Walahfrid*, traveller peace.—Dimins **Geoff**, **Jeff**.
George *jörj'*, *m* (*Gr*) farmer, husbandman.—Dimins **Geordie**, **Georgie**, **Georgy**.—Fem **Georgia** (*jör'jə*), **Georgiana** (*-ji-ä'nə*), **Georgette** (*-jet'*), **Georgina** (*-jē'nə*).—Dimin **Georgie**.
Geraint *ge-rīnt'*, *m* (*Welsh*) of uncertain origin.
Gerald *jer'əld*, *m* (*Gmc*) spear-wielding.—Fem **Geraldine** (*-ēn*).
Gerard *jer'ärd, -ərd, jə-rärd'*, *m* (*Gmc*) spear-hard.
Gerda *gûr'də*, *f* (*ON*) in Norse mythology, the name of the wife of the god Frey.
Germaine *jûr-mān', jər-, zher-men'*, *f* (*Fr*, from *L*) German.
Gerrie, **Gerry** *jer'i*, *m* diminutive of **Gerald**, **Gerard**, or (*f*) of **Geraldine**.
Gertrude *gûr'trood*, *f* (*Gmc*) spear-might.—Dimins **Gert**, **Gertie**, **Trudy**.
Gilbert *gil'bərt*, *m* (*Gmc*) bright pledge.—Dimin **Gil**.
Giles *jīlz*, *m* (*Fr*, from *Gr*) kid.
Gillespie *gi-les'pi*, *m* (*Gaelic*) servant of the bishop.
Gillian *jil'i-ən*, *f orig* a variant of **Julian** (qv).—Dimin **Gill**.
Gina *jē'nə*, *f* diminutive of **Georgina** or **Regina**.
Ginny. See **Virginia**.
Giselle *ji-'zel', zhi-*, *f* (*Fr*, from *Gmc*) pledge.
Gladys *glad'is*, *f* a simplified form of Welsh *Gwladys*, of uncertain origin.
Glen, **Glenn** *glen*, *m*, also *f*, from the surname, or directly from the Gaelic place-name element *gleann*, glen, valley.
Glenda *glen'də*, *f* (*Welsh*) a combination of *glan*, pure, and *da*, good.
Glenys *glen'is*, *f* (*Welsh*) pure, holy, clean.
Gloria *glō'ri-ə, glö'*, *f* (*L*) glory.
Glyn *glin*, *m* (*Welsh*) valley.
Glynis *glin'is*, *f* (*Welsh*) *prob* pure, a variant of **Glenys**, but taken as a feminine of **Glyn**.
Godfrey *god'fri*, *m* (*Gmc*) God's peace.
Golda, **Golde** *gōl'də*, **Goldie** *gōl'di*, *f* (*Yiddish*) gold.
Gordon *gör'dən*, *m* from the Scottish surname.
Grace *grās*, *f* (*Fr*) grace, *orig esp* in its religious sense.—Dimin **Gracie**.
Graham, **Grahame**, **Graeme** *grā'əm*, *m* from the surname.
Gráinne, **Granya** *grä'nyə*, **Grania** *-ni-ə*, *f* (*Ir*) of uncertain origin, in Irish myth the name of the hero Finn's beloved.
Gregory *greg'ə-ri*, (*Scot*) **Gregor** *greg'ər*, *m* (*Gr*) watcher.—Dimin **Greg**.
Greta *grē'tə, gret'ə*, *f* diminutive of **Margaret**.
Griselda, **Grizelda** *gri-zel'də*, *f* (*Gmc*) *perh* grey war, *perh* Christ war.—Dimin **Zelda**.
Gudrun *good'rən*, *f* (*Gmc*) war-counsel.
Guinevere *gwin'ə-vēr*, *f* (*OFr*, from *Welsh*) 'fair' and 'soft'.
Guy *gī*, *m* (*Gmc*) *perh* wood, *perh* wide.
Gwendolen *gwen'də-lin*, *f* (*Welsh*) white (second element obscure).—Dimins **Gwen**, **Gwenda**, **Gwennie**.
Gwillym, **Gwilym** *gwil'im*, *m* Welsh forms of William.
Gwyn *gwin*, *m* (*Welsh*) white, fair.
Gwyneth *gwin'ith*, *f* (*Welsh*) blessed.

Hal *hal*, *m* a diminutive of **Henry**.
Haley. See **Hayley**.
Hamish *hā'mish*, *m* (*Gaelic*) anglicization of *Sheumais*, vocative of *Seumas*, **James**.
Hank *hangk*, *m orig* a back-formation from *Hankin*, a diminutive of **John**, now used as a diminutive of **Henry**.
Hannah *han'ə*, *f*. See **Ann**.
Harold *har'əld*, *m* (*Gmc*) army rule.
Harriet *har'i-ət*, feminine form of **Henry**.
Harry. See **Henry**.
Harvey, **Hervey** *här'vi*, *m* (*Celtic*) from *Haerveu*, name of a Breton saint, *perh* worthy in battle; or from the surname.
Hatty. See **Henry**.
Haydn, **Hayden**, **Haydon** *hā'dən*, *m* (*esp* in Welsh use) from the surnames, the first spelling honouring the composer.
Hayley, **Haley** *hā'li*, *f* from the surname.
Hazel *hā'zəl*, *f* from the plant.
Heather *hedh'ər*, *f* from the plant. See also **Erica**.
Hector *hek'tər*, *m* (*Gr*) holding fast.
Heidi *hī'di*, *f* (*Ger*) diminutive of *Adelheid* (see **Adelaide**).
Helen *hel'ən, -in*, **Helena** *hel'i-nə, hə-lā'nə*, **Ellen** *el'ən*, *f* (*Gr*) bright.—Dimins **Lena** (*lē'nə*), **Nell**, **Nellie**, **Nelly**.
Helga *hel'gə*, *f* (*Gmc, Norse*) holy.
Henry *hen'ri*, **Harry** *har'i*, *m* (*Gmc*) house ruler.—Dimin **Hal**.—Fem **Henrietta**, **Harriet**.—Dimins **Hatty**, **Hetty**.
Herbert *hûr'bərt*, *m* (*Gmc*) army-bright.—Dimins **Bert**, **Bertie**, **Herbie**.
Hermione *hər-mī'ə-nē*, *f* (*Gr*) derivative of *Hermes* (Greek god).
Hervey. See **Harvey**.
Hester. See **Esther**.
Hetty *het'i*, *f* diminutive of **Hester** and **Henrietta**.
Hew. See **Hugh**.
Hilary *hil'ə-ri*, *m* and (more recently) *f* (*L*, from *Gr*) cheerful.
Hilda *hil'də*, *f* (*Gmc*) *orig* a short form of names containing the element *hild*, battle.
Holly *hol'i*, *f* (*Eng*) from the plant.
Homer *hō'mər*, *m* (*US*) from the name of the Greek poet.
Honor, **Honour** *on'ər*, **Honora** *ho-nō'rə, -nö'rə*, *f* (*L*) honour, honourable.—Dimins **Nora**, **Norah**, (*Ir*) **Noreen**.
Hope *hōp*, *m* and *f* (*Eng*) hope, *orig* as a Christian virtue.
Horace *hor'is*, *m* (*L*) from the Roman family name *Horatius*.

Howard *how'ərd, m* from the surname, *perh* meaning high guardian.
Howell, Howell. See **Hywel**.
Hubert *hū'bərt, m* (*Gmc*) mind-bright.
Hugh, Hew *hū,* **Hugo** *hū'gō, m* (*Gmc*) mind.—Dimins **Huey, Hughie**.
Humphrey, Humphry *hum'fri, m* (*Gmc*) *perh* bear-, warrior- or giant-peace.—Dimin **Humph**.
Huw *hū, m* Welsh form of **Hugh**.
Hywel, Howel, Howell *how'əl, m* (*Welsh*) eminent.

Iain, Ian *ē'ən, m* (*Gaelic*) forms of **John**.
Ida *ī'də, f* (*Gmc*) labour.
Idris *id'ris, m* (*Welsh*) fiery lord.
Ifor *ē'vor, m* (*Welsh*) of uncertain origin; anglicized as **Ivor**.
Ike. See **Isaac**.
Ilana *i-lä'nə, f* (*Heb*) tree.—Masc **Ilan** (*-lan'*).
Ilona *i-lō'nə, f* (*Hung*) form of **Helen**.
Imelda *i-mel'də, f* (*Gmc*) *prob* a combination of words meaning 'whole' and 'battle'.
Imogen *im'-ə-jən, f prob* a misprint for *Innogen* (*Celtic*, daughter, girl) in Shakespeare's *Cymbeline*.
Ina *ī'nə, ē'nə, f orig* a diminutive of any of several names ending in *-ina*.
Ines, Inez *ī'nez, ē', f* (*Sp*) forms of **Agnes**.
Inga *ing'ə, ing'gə,* **Inge** *ing'ə, f* (*Scand, Ger*) *orig* a short form of names containing the god Ing's name, eg *Ingeborg*.
Ingrid *ing'grid, f* (*Scand*) ride of Ing (the god Frey), or a combination of 'Ing' and 'beautiful'.
Inigo *in'i-gō, m* (*Sp*) a form of the Roman family name *Ignatius* or *Egnatius*.
Iona *ī-ō'nə, f* from the place name.
Ira *ī'rə, m* (*Heb*) watchful.
Irene *ī-rē'nē,* also *ī'rēn, ī-rēn',* **Irena** *i-rē'nə, f* (*Gr*) peace.—Dimin **Rene** (*rē'ni*).
Iris *ī'ris, f* (*Gr*) rainbow, iris (plant).
Irma *ûr'mə, f* (*Gmc*) *orig* a short form of *Irmintrude* and other names beginning with the same element. See **Emma**.
Isaac *ī'zək, m* (*Heb*) laugh.—Dimins **Ik, Ike, Iky**.
Isabella *iz-ə-bel'ə,* **Isabel, Isobel** *iz'ə-bəl, -bel,* or (*Gaelic*) **Iseabail, Iseabal, Ishbel,** *ish'bəl,* (*Scot*) **Isbel** *iz'bəl, f orig* the Spanish form of **Elizabeth**.—Dimins **Bel, Bell, Belle, Bella, Ella, Ib, Ibby, Isa** (*ī'zə*), **Tib, Tibbie, Tibby**.
Isaiah *ī-zī'ə,* or *-zā', m* (*Heb*) Yahweh helps.
Isidore *iz'i-dōr, -dör,* **Isadore, Isodore** *iz'ə-, m* (*Gr*) *perh* gift of Isis.—Fem **Isidora, Isadora**.
Isla *ī'lə, f* from the river name.
Ivan *ī'vən, ē-vän', m* (*Russ*) form of **John**.—Fem **Ivana** (*ē-vä'nə*).
Ivor *ī'vər, m* (*ON*) of uncertain meaning, *perh* bow-warrior.
Ivy *ī'vi, f* (*Eng*) from the plant; also (*masc, Scot*) a diminutive of **Ivor**.

Jacinth, Jacinthe *ja-sinth',* **Jacintha** *-sin'thə,* **Jacinta** *-sin'tə, f* forms of the flower-name hyacinth (*Gr hyakinthos*, larkspur); also from the precious stone jacinth (OFr *jacinte*).
Jack *jak, m orig* a diminutive of **John**, from *Jankin*, its Middle English pet form. See also **Jake, Jock**.
Jacob *jā'kəb, m* (*Heb*) follower, supplanter, or deceiver.—Dimin **Jake**,
Jacqueline, Jaqueline *zhak'ə-lēn, jak'ə-lin, -lēn,* **Jackeline** *jak'ə-lēn, -lin,* **Jacquelyn** *jak'ə-lin,* **Jacquetta** *jə-ket'ə,* feminine derivatives of French *Jacques* (**James**).
Jade *jād, f* from the precious stone.
Jake *jāk, m* a form of **Jack** or a diminutive of **Jacob**.
James *jāmz, m orig* a form of **Jacob** through Latin *Jacobus* (later *Jacomus*, whence the forms with *m*).—Dimins **Jim, Jimmie, Jimmy, Jem, Jemmie, Jamie**.
Jamie *jā'mi, m* a diminutive of, or *f* (*esp US*) a feminine of, **James**.
Jan *jan, f* a shortening of **Janet, Janice**.
Jane, Jayne *jān, orig* a feminine of **John**.—Dimins **Janey, Janie**.—See also **Jean, Joan, Joanna**.
Janet *jan'it, f orig* a diminutive of **Jane**.—Dimins **Jan**, (*Scot*) **Jess, Jessie, Jessy, Netta, Nettie, Nita** (*nē'tə*).—Derivs **Janetta, Jannetta** (*jə-net'ə*), **Janette** (*-net'*).
Janice, Janis *jan'is, f orig* a diminutive of **Jane**.
Janine *jə-nēn',* **Janina** *-nē'nə, f* diminutives of **Jan**, or from French *Jeannine*, diminutive of *Jeanne* (**Jane**).
Jasmine *jas'min,* **Yasmin** *yaz', f* (*Pers*) the flower jasmine.
Jason *jā'sən, m* (*Gr*) *poss* a rendering of **Joshua**, or simply 'healer'.
Jasper *jas'pər,* **Caspar** *kas', m prob* Persian, treasure-bringer.
Jay *jā, m* and *f* a diminutive of names begining with *J*, or (*OFr*) from the bird.
Jean *jēn, f orig* a feminine of **John**.—Dimins **Jeanie, Jeannie**.
Jeffrey *jef'ri, m*. See **Geoffrey**.
Jem, Jemmie. Diminutives of **James**.
Jemima *ji-mī'mə, f* (*Heb*) meaning unknown (day, dove, pure, fortunate, have been suggested).
Jemma. See **Gemma**.
Jennifer, Jenifer *jen'i-fər, f* the *orig* Cornish form of Welsh *Guinevere*, 'fair' and 'soft'.—Dimins **Jen, Jenna, Jennie, Jenny**.
Jeremy *jer'i-mi, m* (*Heb*) Yah is high, or heals, or founds.
Jerome *jer'ōm, ji-rōm', m* (*Gr*) holy name.
Jerry *jer'i, m* diminutive of **Jeremy, Gerald, Gerard, Jerome**.
Jess *jes,* **Jessie, Jessy** *jes'i, f* diminutives of **Janet** (*esp Scot*), or of **Jessica**; **Jess** (*m*) a shortening of **Jesse**.
Jesse *jes'i, m* (*Heb*) Yah is.
Jessica *jes'i-kə, f* (*appar Heb*) *perh* Yah is looking.
Jillian *jil'i-ən, f orig* a variant of **Julian**.—Dimin **Jill**.
Jim, Jimmie. See **James**.
Jinny. See **Virginia**.
Jo *jō, m* and *f* diminutive of **Joanna, Joseph, Josepha, Josephine**.
Joan *jōn, f orig* a contraction of Old French *Joanne* (see **Joanna**).—Dimins **Joanie, Joni**.
Joanna, Johanna *jō-an'ə,* **Joanne** *jō-an', f* respectively the Latin and Old French feminines of *Joannes, Johannes*, Latin forms of **John**.
Jocelyn, Jocelin, Joscelin *jos'lin, -ə-lin, m* and *f perh* (*Gmc*) one of the Geats (a people of southern Sweden), or (*L*) connected with **Justin**.—Fem also **Joceline**.
Jock *jok, m* (*Scot*) a form of **Jack**.—Dimin **Jockie**.
Jodie, Jodi, Jody *jō'di, f* diminutives of **Judith** or derivatives of **Jo**.
Joe *jo,* **Joey** *jō'i, m* and *f* diminutives of **Joseph, Josepha, Josephine**.
Joel *jō'əl, m* (*Heb*) Yah is the Lord.—Fem **Joelle** (*jō-el'*).
John *jon, m* (*Heb*) *poss* Yah is gracious.—Dimin **Johnnie**.—See also **Jack**.—Fem see **Jane, Jean, Joanna**.
Jolyon *jō'li-ən, m* a variant of **Julian**.
Jon *jon, m* a diminutive of **Jonathan** or a variant of **John**.
Jonathan, Jonathon *jon'ə-thən, m* (*Heb*) Yah has given.
Joni. See **Joan**.
Joseph *jō'zif, m* (*Heb*) Yah increases.—Dimins **Jo, Joe, Joey, Jos** (*jos*).—Fem **Josepha** (*-zē'fə, -ze'fə*), **Josephine** (*jō'zi-fēn*).—Dimins **Jo, Joe, Josie, Jozy**.
Josette *jō-zet', f* (*Fr*) a diminutive of **Josephine**.
Joshua *josh'ū-ə, m* (*Heb*) Yah saves.—Dimin **Josh**.
Joy *joi, f* (*Eng*) joy, *esp orig* in a religious sense.
Joyce *jois, f*, formerly *m* (*Celtic*) lord.
Jude *jo͞od, m* short form of *Judas* (for Hebrew *Judah, perh* 'praise'); also (*f*) a diminutive of **Judith**.
Judith *jo͞o'dith, f* (*Heb*) Jewess.—Dimins **Judy, Judie, Jude, Jodie**.
Julia. See **Julius**.
Julian *jo͞o'lyən, -li-ən, m*, formerly also *f* (*L*) derived from, belonging to Julius.—Dimins **Jule, Jools**.—Fem **Juliana** (*-ä'nə*).—Dimin **Julie**.
Julie *jo͞o'li, f* the French form of **Julia** or a diminutive of **Julia** or **Juliana**.
Juliet *jo͞o'li-et, f* English form of French *Juliette*, diminutive of **Julie**.
Julius *jo͞o'li-əs, m* (*L*) a Roman family name, *perh* downy-bearded.—Dimin **Jule**.—Fem **Julia**.—Dimin **Julie**.
June *jo͞on, f* (*L*) from the month.

Justin *jus'tin, m* (*L*) a derivative of *Justus*, just.—Fem **Justina** (*-tē'nə, -tī'nə*), **Justine** (*jus'tēn*).

Karen, **Karin** *kä'rin, kar'in, f* respectively the Danish and Swedish forms of **Catherine**.

Karina, **Karena** *kə-rē'nə, f* variants of **Karin**, **Karen**, or of **Carina** (see **Cara**).

Karl, **Karla**. See **Carl**.

Kate, **Katharine**, **Katrine**, **Katrina**. See **Catherine**.

Kathleen *kath'lēn, f* (*Ir*) *orig* an anglicization of **Caitlín** (qv).—Dimin **Kath**.

Kay, **Kaye** *kā, f* a diminutive of names beginning with *K*, *esp* **Katharine**, or (*m, L*) a form of *Gaius*, *perh* joyful.

Keith *kēth, m* from the surname or place name.

Kelly *kel'i, m* and *f* (*Ir*) from the surname.

Kenneth *ken'ith, m* (*Gaelic*) handsome, or born of fire.—Dimins **Ken**, **Kennie**, **Kenny**.—Fem **Kenna**.

Kerry *ker'i, m* and *f* (*Ir*) from the name of the Irish county.

Kevin *kev'in*, **Kevan** *-ən, m* (*Ir*) comely birth.

Kieran, **Kieron**, **Ciaran** *kē'ə-rən, m* (*Ir*) an Irish saint's name, from *cíar*, dark.—Fem **Ciara**, **Kiera**, **Kyra** (*kē'ə-rə*).

Kim *kim, m* and *f* shortening (as in Kipling's *Kim*) of Irish **Kimball** (*kim'bəl*), *orig* a surname, or of **Kimberley**.

Kimberly, **Kimberley** *kim'bər-li, f, orig m*, from the S African town.

Kirsty *kûr'sti*, **Kirsteen** *-stēn, f*. See **Christian**.

Kit. See **Christopher**, **Catherine**.

Kitty. See **Catherine**.

Kylie *kī'li, f* (*orig Austr*) said to be an Aboriginal word for 'curl' or 'boomerang', *perh* used also as a variant of **Kelly**.

Lachlan *lahh'lən, m* (*Gaelic*) warlike.—Dimin **Lachie**.

Lalage *lal'ə-jē, f* (*L*, from *Gr*) talkative, prattling.—Dimins **Lallie**, **Lally**, **Lala**, **Lalla**.

Lance *läns, m* (*Gmc*) land.—Dimins **Lancelot**, **Launcelot** (*-ə-lot*).

Lara *lä'rə, f* (*Ital*) explained as from *Larunda* (*Roman mythol*), a nymph, or *Larissa*, a Greek martyr.

Laraine, **Larraine**. See **Lorraine**.

Larry. See **Laurence**.

Laura *lö'rə, f* (*L*) laurel.—Dimins **Lauren** (thought of also as feminine of **Laurence**), **Lauretta**, **Laurie**, **Loretta**.

Laurel *lor'əl, f* from the tree, or *perh* used as a diminutive of **Laura**.

Laurence, **Lawrence** *lor'əns, m* (*L*) of Laurentum, a town in Italy.—Dimins **Larry**, **Laurie**, **Lawrie**.

Lavinia *lə-vin'i-ə, f* (*L*) origin unknown (second wife of Aeneas).

Lea, **Leah** *lē'ə, f* (*Heb*) a cow.

Leanne, **Lian**, **Lianne** *lē-an'*, **Liane** *-än'*, **Liana** *-ä'nə*, **Lianna** *-an'ə, f perh* a form of French *Éliane* (from the Roman family name *Aelianus*), or a combination of **Lee** and **Anne**, or a diminutive of **Julian**.

Lee, **Leigh** *lē, m* and *f* from the surname.

Leila *lā', lē', lī'lə, f* (*Pers*) night.

Leo *lē'ō, m* (*L*) lion.—Fem **Leonie** (*lē'ə-ni*).

Leonard *len'ərd, m* (*Gmc*) lion-hard.—Dimins **Len**, **Lennie**, **Lenny**.

Leonora *lē-ə-nō'rə, -nö'rə, f* a form of **Eleanor** (qv).

Leopold *lē'ə-pōld, m* (*Gmc*) people-bold.

Leslie *m*, **Lesley** *f*, *lez'li*, from the surname or place name.

Lewis *loo'is*, **Louis** *loo'is, loo'i*, **Ludovic**, **Ludovick** *loo'də-vik, m* (*Gmc*) famous warrior.—Dimins **Lewie**, **Louie**, **Lew**.—Fem **Louisa** (*loo-ē'zə*), **Louise** (*-ēz'*).—Dimins **Lou**, **Louie**.

Liam *lē'əm, m* Irish form of **William**.

Lian, **Liana**, **Lianne**, etc. See **Leanne**.

Libby *lib'i, f* a diminutive of **Elizabeth**.

Lilian, **Lillian** *lil'i-ən*, (*Scot*) **Lilias**, **Lillias** *-əs, f prob orig* forms of **Elizabeth**, but associated with **Lily**.

Lily *lil'i, f* from the flower.

Linda, **Lynda** *lin'də, f* of uncertain evolution, *perh orig* a diminutive of Germanic names ending in *-lind*, an element of disputed meaning, *perh* soft, gentle.—Dimin **Lindy**.

Lindsay, **Lindsey** *lind'zi*, **Lynsey** *lin'zi, m* and *f* from the surname.

Linnette, **Linette**, **Linnet**, **Lynette** *li-net', f* (*Fr*) medieval French forms of Welsh **Eluned**.

Linus *lī'nəs, m* (*Gr*; *mythol*) the name of a minstrel, of uncertain origin; also a New Testament name.

Lionel *lī'ə-nəl, m* (*L*) young lion.

Lisa, **Lisbeth**, **Lise**, **Lisette**, **Liz**, etc. See **Elizabeth**.

Llewelyn *(h)lē-wel'in, loo-el'in, m* (*Welsh*) meaning doubtful.

Lloyd *loid, m* (*Welsh*) grey.

Lois *lō'is, f* (*Gr*) good.

Lola *lō'lə, f* a diminutive of **Dolores**.—Dimin **Lolita** (*lo-lē'tə*).

Loretta *lo-ret'ə, f*. See **Laura**.

Lorna *lör'nə, f* popularized, if not invented, by R D Blackmore as the name of the heroine of his novel *Lorna Doone*.

Lorraine, **Larraine**, **Laraine** *lə-rān', f* (*Fr*) from the region of France.

Lottie *lot'i, f* a diminutive of **Charlotte**.

Louis *m*, **Louisa**, **Louise** *f*. See **Lewis**.

Lucius *loo'si-əs, -shəs, m* (*L*) a Roman given name *prob* connected with *lux*, light.—Fem **Lucia** (*loo'si-ə, -shə, -chē'ə*), **Lucy** (*loo'si*).—Derivs **Lucinda** (*loo-sin'də*), **Lucilla** (*-sil'ə*), **Lucille** (*-sēl'*).

Ludovic, **Ludovick**. See **Lewis**.

Luke *look, m* (*L*) of Lucania (in Italy).

Lydia *lid'i-ə, f* (*Gr*) Lydian woman.

Lynda. See **Linda**.

Lynette. See **Linnette**.

Lynn, **Lynne** *lin, f* diminutives of **Linda** or **Linnette**.

Mabel *mā'bl, f orig* an aphetic form of **Amabel**.

Madeleine, **Madeline**. See **Magdalen**.

Madge *maj, f*. See **Margaret**.

Madonna *mə-don'ə, f* (*Ital*) my lady, a title of the Virgin Mary.

Mae *mā, f* a variant of **May**.

Maeve, **Maev** *māv, f* (*Ir*) anglicizations of *Meadhbh*, name of a legendary queen of Connaught.

Mag *mag*, **Maggie** *mag'i, f* diminutives of **Margaret**.

Magdalen *mag'də-lin*, **Magdalene** *-lin, -lēn*, **Madeline** *mad'lin, -lēn, -līn, mad'ə-*, **Madeleine** *-len, -lēn, -lin, f* of Magdala on the Sea of Galilee.—Dimins **Lena** (*lē'nə*), **Magda**.

Magnus *mag'nəs, m* (*L*) great.

Máire *moi'rə*, **Màiri** *mä'ri, f*, respectively Irish and Gaelic forms of **Mary**.

Mairead *mī'rad* (*Gaelic*), **Mairéad** *mə-rād'* (*Ir*), *f* forms of **Margaret**.

Maisie *mā'zi, f orig* a diminutive of **Margaret**.

Malcolm *mal'kəm, möl', m* (*Gaelic*) Columba's servant.

Mandy. See **Amanda**.

Marcel *mär-sel', m* (*Fr*, from *L*), a diminutive of **Marcus**.—Fem **Marcelle** (*-sel'*), **Marcella** (*-sel'ə*).

Marcia, **Marsha** *mär'shə, f* (*L*) from the Roman family name *Marcius*, derived from **Marcus**.

Marcus. See **Mark**.

Margaret *mär'gə-rit, f* (*Gr*) pearl.—Dimins **Madge**, **Mag**, **Maggie**, **Margery**, **Marjory**, **Meg**, **Megan** (*meg'ən, Welsh*), **Meta** (*mē'tə*), **Maisie**, **Peg**, **Peggy**, **Greta**, **Rita**.

Margot *mär'gō, f* (*Fr*) *orig* a diminutive of *Marguerite* (**Margaret**).

Maria, **Marie**. See **Mary**.

Marian, **Marion** *mar'i-ən, mā'ri-ən*, **Marianne** *mar-i-an'*, (*Fr*) *orig* diminutives of **Mary**; used also for the combination **Mary Ann**.

Marigold *mar'i-gōld, f* from the flower.

Marilyn. See **Mary**.

Marina *mə-rē'nə, f* (*L*) *prob* from *Marcus*, but *usu* explained as from *marinus*, of the sea.

Marjory, **Marjorie**, **Margery** *mär'jə-ri, f orig* a diminutive of **Margaret**.

Mark *märk*, **Marcus** *mär'kəs, m* (*L*) a Roman given name *prob* derived from Mars (the god).

Marlene *mär'lēn, f* (*Ger*) a combination of *Maria* and *Magdalena*.

Marsha. See **Marcia**.

Martha *mär'thə, f* (*Aramaic*) lady, mistress.—Dimins **Mat**, **Mattie**, **Matty**, **Pat**, **Pattie**, **Patty**.

Martin, **Martyn** *mär'tin, m* (*L*) *prob* warlike, of Mars.—Fem **Martina** (*-tē'nə*), **Martine** (*-tēn'*).

Marvin *mär'vin m* a variant of **Mervyn**.

Mary *mā'ri*, **Maria** *mə-rī'ə, -rē'ə*, **Marie** *mä'ri, mə-rē', f* (*Heb*) from the New Testament form (*Mariam*) of **Miriam** (qv), of uncertain meaning.—Dimins **May**, **Moll**, **Molly**, **Mamie**, **Minnie**, **Poll**, **Polly**.—Deriv **Marilyn**.

Mat, **Matty**. See **Martha**, **Matilda**, **Matthew**.

Matilda, **Mathilda** *mə-til'də, f* (*Gmc*) battle-might.—Dimins **Mat**, **Matty**, **Maud**, **Maude**, **Patty**, **Tilly**, **Tilda**.

Matthew *math'ū*, **Matthias** *mə-thī'əs, m* (*Heb*) gift of Yah.—Dimin **Mat**.

Maud, **Maude** *möd, f orig* a diminutive of **Matilda** or **Magdalen**.

Maureen *mö'rēn, mö-rēn', f* (*Ir*) an anglicization of *Máirín*, a diminutive of *Máire* (**Mary**).

Maurice, **Morris** *mor'is, m* (*L*) Moorish, dark-coloured.

Mavis *mā'vis, f* (*Eng*, from *OFr*) thrush.

Maximilian *mak-si-mil'yən, m* (*L*) a derivative of the Roman name *Maximus*, greatest.—Dimin **Max**.

Maxine *mak'sēn, f* a 20c feminine of **Max**.

May *mā, f* partly a diminutive of **Mary**, partly from the month.—Dimin **Minnie**.

Meg, **Megan**. See **Margaret**.

Melanie *mel'ə-ni, f* (*Gr*) black.

Melissa *mə-lis'ə, f* (*Gr*) bee.

Melvin, **Melvyn** *mel'vin, m* from the surname, or a masculine of *Malvina*, from Macpherson's Ossianic poems.

Mercy *mûr'si, f* (*Eng*) mercy, *orig esp* that of God.

Meredith *mer'i-dith, mə-red'ith, m* and *f* (*Welsh*) an anglicization of *Maredudd*, of uncertain meaning, or from the surname.

Meriel, **Merriel** *mer'i-əl, f* forms of **Muriel**.

Mervyn *mûr'vin, m* (*Welsh*) of uncertain derivation.

Meryl *mer'il, f poss* a variant of **Meriel**.

Meta. See **Margaret**.

Mia *mē'ə, f* an *orig* Scandinavian diminutive of **Maria**.

Michael *mī'kl, m* (*Heb*) who is like the Lord?—Dimins **Mick**, **Micky**, **Mike**.—Fem **Michaela** (*mi-kī'lə, -kā'*).

Michelle *mē-shel', f* (*Fr*) a variant of *Michèle*, feminine of *Michel* (**Michael**).

Mildred *mil'drid, f* (*Gmc*; *OE Mildthryth*) mild power.—Dimin **Millie**.

Miles *mīlz, m* of uncertain origin, *perh* Slavonic 'merciful'.

Millicent *mil'i-sənt, f* (*Gmc*) work-strong.—Dimin **Millie**.

Millie *mil'i, f* a diminutive of **Mildred**, **Millicent**, **Amelia**, **Emily**.

Minnie *min'i, f* a diminutive of **Mary**, **May**, or **Wilhelmina**.

Miranda *mi-ran'də, f* (*L*) to be admired or wondered at.

Miriam, **Myriam** *mir'iəm, f* (*Heb*) *perh* wished-for child.

Moira, **Moyra** *moi'rə, f* (*Ir*) an anglicization of Irish *Máire* and Gaelic *Moire*, forms of **Mary**.

Moll, **Molly** *mol'i, f orig* diminutives of **Mary**.

Mona *mō'nə, f* (*Ir*) noble.

Monica *mon'i-kə, f* the name, possibly African, of St Augustine's mother.

Morag *mō'rag, mö', f* (*Gaelic*) a diminutive of *Mór*, great.

Moray. See **Murray**.

Morgan *mör'gən, m* (*Welsh*) variously thought to contain elements meaning 'sea', 'rim', 'great' and 'bright'.

Morna *mör'nə, f* (*Gaelic*) beloved.

Morris. See **Maurice**.

Morven *mör'vən, f* (*Gaelic*) *perh* the Argyllshire district *Morvern* or 'great mountain'.

Mungo *mung'gō, m* (*Gaelic*) amiable.

Murdo *mûr'dō*, **Murdoch** *mûr'dəhh, -dək, m* (*Gaelic*) seaman.

Muriel *mū'ri-əl, f* (*Celtic*) *perh* sea-bright.

Murray, **Moray** *mur'i, m* from the surnames.

Myfanwy *mi-van'wi, f* (*Welsh*) *perh my-banwy*, my fine one.

Myles *mīlz, m* a variant of **Miles**, .

Myra *mī'rə, f* an arbitrary invention; sometimes used as an anagram of **Mary** or a substitute for **Mairead**.

Myrtle *mûr'tl, f* from the shrub.

Nadia *nä'di-ə, nā', f* from Russian *Nadya*, diminutive of *Nadezhda*, hope.

Nadine *nä'dēn, nā', f* a French derivative of **Nadia** (qv).

Nan, *nan, f* diminutive of **Ann**.

Nance *nans*, **Nancy** *-si, f orig* diminutives of **Ann**, **Agnes**.

Nanette *nə-net', f* a diminutive variation of **Nan**.

Naomi *nā-ō'mi, -mī*, or *nā', f* (*Heb*) pleasant.

Nat *nat, m* a diminutive of **Nathaniel**, **Nathan**.

Natalie *nat'ə-li*, **Natalia** *-tä'li-ə, f* (*L*) (Christ's) birthday, Christmas.—Dimin **Natasha** (*nə-tash'ə, Russ*).

Nathan *nā'thən, m* (*Heb*) gift.—Dimin **Nat**.

Nathaniel *nə-than'yəl, m* (*Heb*) gift of God.—Dimin **Nat**.

Neal, **Neale**. See **Neil**.

Ned *ned*, **Neddie**, **Neddy** *ned'i, m* diminutives of **Edward**, **Edgar**, **Edmund**, **Edwin**.

Neil, **Neal**, **Neale**, **Niall** *nēl, m* (*Ir*) *perh* champion.

Nell *nel*, **Nellie**, **Nelly** *nel'i, f* diminutives of **Helen**, **Ellen**, **Eleanor**.

Nerys *ner'is, f* (*Welsh*) *perh* based on *ner*, lord.

Neville *nev'il, m* from the surname.

Niall *nēl*. See **Neil**.

Niamh *nē'əv, f* (*Ir*) brightness, brilliance.

Nicholas, **Nicolas** *nik'ə-ləs, m*, formerly also *f* (*Gr*) victory of the people.—Dimins (*m*) **Nick**, **Nicky**, **Colin** (qv), **Colley**, **Nicol**, **Nichol**.—Fem **Nicola**, **Nichola** (*nik'ə-lə*), **Nicole** (*ni-kōl'*).—Dimins **Nicolette**, **Colette**, **Nicky**.

Nigel *nī'jl, m* anglicized form of *Nigellus*, Latinized form of **Neil**, but understood as diminutive of Latin *niger*, black.

Nina, **Ninette**. See **Ann**.

Ninian *nin'yən, m* (*Celtic*) meaning unknown.

Noel *nō'əl, m* and *f* (*Fr*, from Latin *natalis*) (Christ's) birthday, Christmas.—Fem also **Noele**, **Noelle** (*nō-el'*).

Nola. See **Fenella**.

Nona *nō'nə, f* (*L*) ninth.

Nora, **Norah** *nō'rə, nö', f orig* a diminutive of **Honora**, **Leonora**, **Eleanor**.—Deriv (*Ir*) **Noreen** (*-rēn'*).

Norma *nör'mə, f* (*L*) a rule, precept; used as a feminine of **Norman**.

Norman *nör'mən, m* (*Gmc*) Northman.

Nuala. See **Fenella**.

Nye. See **Aneurin**.

Odette *ō-det', f*. See **Ottilie**.

Olga *ol'gə, f* (*Russ*, from *Norse*) holy.

Olive *ol'iv*, **Olivia** *ə-liv'i-ə, f* (*L*) olive.—Dimin **Livy** (*liv'i*).

Oliver *ol'i-vər, m* (*Fr*) olive-tree, or an alteration of *Olaf* or other Germanic name.

Olwen, **Olwin**, **Olwyn**, **Olwyne** *ol'wən, f* (*Welsh*) white track.

Oona, **Oonagh** *o͞o'nə*. See **Una**.

Ophelia *ə-fē'li-ə, ō-, f prob* (*Gr*) help.

Orlando *ör-lan'dō, m* (*Ital*) form of **Roland**.

Osbert *oz'bərt, m* (*Gmc*) god-bright.

Oscar *os'kər, m* of disputed origin, *perh* (*Gmc*) god-spear or (*Ir* and *Gaelic*) champion.

Oswald *oz'wəld, m* (*Gmc*) god-power.

Ottilie *ot'i-li, f* (*Gmc*) heritage.—Dimin **Odette** (*ō-det'*).

Owen *ō'ən, m* (*Welsh*) said to mean youth; (*Ir*) used as a substitute for *Eóghan* (see **Ewan**).

Paddy *pad'i, m* and *f* a diminutive of **Patrick**, **Patricia**.

Pamela *pam'i-lə, f prob* an invention (as *pa-mē'lə*) of Sir Philip Sidney's.

Pandora *pan-dö'rə, -dō', f* (*Gr*) every gift.

Pansy *pan'zi, f* (*Fr*) thought; or from the name of the flower.

Pat *pat, m* and *f* a diminutive of **Patrick**, **Patricia**, **Martha**.

Patience *pā'shəns, f* patience, *orig* in the sense of longsuffering.

Patrick *pat'rik, m* (*L*) nobleman, patrician.—Dimins **Pat**, **Paddy**.—Fem **Patricia** (*pə-trish'ə*).—Dimins **Pat**, **Paddy**, **Patsy**, **Patty**, **Tricia**, **Trisha**.

Paul *pöl, m* (*L*) little.—Fem **Paula** (*pö'lə*).—Deriv **Paulina** (*pö-lī'nə, -lē'nə*), **Pauline** (*pö'lēn*).—Dimin **Paulette** (*-let'*).

Pearl *pûrl, f* from the gem.

Peg *peg*, **Peggy** *peg'i, f* diminutives of **Margaret**.

Penelope *pi-nel'ə-pi*, *f* (*Gr*) *perh* weaver.—Dimins **Pen**, **Penny**.
Percival *pûr'si-vl*, *m* (*Fr*) *appar* penetrate the valley, but *perh* an alteration of a Celtic name.
Percy *pûr'si*, *m* from the surname.
Peregrine *per'i-grin*, *m* (*L*) wanderer, traveller, pilgrim.—Dimin **Perry**.
Peter *pē'tər*, *m* (*Gr*) rock.—Dimin **Pete** (*pēt*).
Petula *pi-tū'lə*, *f* of uncertain origin, *perh* an invention based on the endearment 'pet'.
Philip, **Phillip** *fil'ip*, *m* (*Gr*) lover of horses.—Dimins **Phil**, **Pip**.—Fem **Philippa**.—Dimin **Pippa**.
Phoebe *fē'bi*, *f* (*Gr*) shining, a name of Artemis as moon-goddess.
Phyllis *fil'is*, *f* (*Gr*) foliage, leafy branch.—Variant **Phyllida** (*fil'i-də*).—Dimin **Phyl**.
Piers *pērz*, *m* (*OFr*) the Middle English form of **Peter**.
Pip *pip*, *m*, and **Pippa** *pip'ə*, *f*, diminutives of **Philip**.
Polly *pol'i*, *f orig* a variant of **Molly** as a diminutive of **Mary**.
Primrose *prim'rōz*, *f* from the flower.
Priscilla *pri-sil'ə*, *f* (*L*) diminutive of the Roman name *Priscus*, former, ancient.
Prudence *proo'dəns*, *f* from the virtue.—Dimin **Prue**.
Prunella *proo-nel'ə*, *f* (*L*) little plum.

Queenie *kwē'ni*, *f* from *queen*.
Quintin *kwin'tin*, **Quinton** *-tən*, **Quentin** *kwen'*, *m* (*L*) fifth.

Rachel, **Rachael** *rā'chl*, *f* (*Heb*) ewe.—Dimins **Ray**, **Rae**.
Rae *rā*, *f* diminutive of **Rachel**, used (*esp Scot*) independently.—Deriv **Raelene** (*rā'lēn*).
Ralph *rāf*, *ralf*, *m* (*Gmc*) counsel-wolf.
Randal, **Randall** *ran'dl*, **Randolph**, **Randolf** *ran'dolf*, *m* (*Gmc*) shield-wolf.—Dimin **Randy**.
Ranulf, **Ranulph** *ran'əlf*, *m* either (*ON*) counsel-wolf, or a variant of **Randolph**.
Ray *rā*, *m* and *f* a diminutive of **Raymond** or **Rachel**, but also used independently.
Raymond *rā'mənd*, *m* (*Gmc*) counsel (or might) protector.—Dimins **Ray**, **Rae**.
Rebecca *ri-bek'ə*, *f perh* (*Heb*) noose.—Dimin **Becky**.
Regina *ri-jī'nə*, *-jē'*, *f* (*L*) queen.—Dimin **Gina** (*jē'nə*).
Reginald *rej'i-nəld*, *m* (*Gmc*) counsel rule, from *Reginaldus*, Latin respelling of **Reynold**.—Dimins **Reg** (*rej*), **Reggie**.
Rene. See **Irene**.
René *ren'i*, *rə-nā'*, *m* (*Fr*) born again.—Fem **Renée** (*Fr*), **Renata** (*ri-nä'tə*, *L*).
Reuben *roo'bən*, *m* (*Heb*) behold a son, or renewer.
Rex *reks*, *m* (*L*) king; also a diminutive of **Reginald**.
Reynold *ren'əld*, *m* (*Gmc*) the original Norman form of **Reginald**.
Rhian *rē-an'*, *f* (*Welsh*) maiden.
Rhiannon *rē-an'ən*, *f* (*Welsh*) goddess or nymph.
Rhoda *rō'də*, *f* (*Gr*) rose.
Rhona *rō'nə*, *f* origin and meaning obscure, *poss* connected with **Rowena**.
Rhonda *ron'də*, *f prob* a combination of **Rhoda** and **Rhona**.
Rhys *rēs*, *m* (*Welsh*) *perh* impetuous man.
Ria *rē'ə*, *f* a diminutive of **Maria**.
Richard *rich'ərd*, *m* (*Gmc*) rule-hard.—Dimins **Dick**, **Dickie**, **Dicky**, **Dicken**, **Dickon**, **Rick**, **Ricky**, **Richie** (*rich'i*).
Rita *rē'tə*, *f orig* a diminutive of **Margaret**.
Robert *rob'ərt*, *m* (*Gmc*) fame-bright.—Dimins **Bert**, **Bertie**, **Bob**, **Bobbie**, **Bobby**, **Dob**, **Dobbin**, **Rob**, **Robbie**, (*Scot*) **Rab**, **Rabbie**.—Fem **Roberta** (*-bûr'tə*).
Robin *rob'in*, *m* and (also **Robyn**) *f orig* a diminutive of **Robert**.—Fem **Robina** (*ro-bē'nə*).
Roderick *rod'ə-rik*, *m* (*Gmc*) fame-rule.—Dimins **Rod**, **Roddy**.
Rodney *rod'ni*, *m* and *f* from the surname or place name.—Dimins **Rod**, **Roddy**.
Roger *roj'er*, *m* (*Gmc*) fame-spear.
Roland, **Rowland** *rō'lənd*, *m* (*Gmc*) fame of the land.
Rolf *rolf*, *m* (*Gmc*) fame-wolf.
Romy *rō'mi*, *f* a diminutive of **Rosemary** or (*Ger*) *Rosemarie*.
Rona *rō'nə*, *f* from the island name, derived from Gaelic *ron*, seal, but used as a variant of **Rhona**.
Ronald *ron'əld*, (*Gaelic*) **Ranald** *ran'*, *m* (*ON*) counsel-ruler.
Rory *rō'ri*, *rö'*, (*Ir*) **Ruaidhri**, (*Gaelic*) **Ruairidh**, **Ruaraidh**, **Ruairi** *roo'ə-ri*, *m* red.
Rosalind *roz'ə-lind*, *f* (*Gmc*) *perh* gentle horse, but associated with **Rose**.—Dimins **Ros**, **Roz**.
Rosamund, **Rosamond** *roz'ə-mənd*, *f* (*Gmc*) horse protection; reinterpteted as Latin *rosa munda*, fine rose, or *rosa mundi*, rose of the world.—Dimins **Ros**, **Roz**.
Rose *rōz*, **Rosa** *rō'zə*, *f* (*L*) rose, the flower; also (*Gmc*), horse.—Derivs **Rosabel** (*roz'ə-bel*), **Rosalie** (*roz'* or *rō'zə-li*) (L *rosalia*, the hanging of rose garlands on tombs).—Dimins **Rosetta**, **Rosie**.
Roseanna, **Rosanna** *rō-zan'ə*, **Roseanne** *-zan'*, **Rosemarie** *-mə-rē'*, *f* compounds of **Rose** with **Anna**, **Anne**, **Marie**.
Rosemary *rōz'mə-ri*, *f* from the plant; also for **Rose Mary**.
Rosie *rō'zi*, *f* a diminutive of **Rose** and **Rosemary**.
Ross *ros*, *m* from the surname and place name, *prob* from Gaelic *ros*, headland, peninsula.
Rowan *rō'ən*, *row'ən*, *m* from the Irish surname, derived from *ruadh*, red, or from the tree.
Rowena *rō-ē'nə*, *f perh* Geoffrey of Monmouth's mistake for Welsh *Rhonwen*, white skirt.
Rowland. See **Roland**.
Roxane *rok-sän'*, **Roxanne** *-san'*, **Roxana** *-sä'nə*, *f* (*prob Pers*) *perh* dawn.
Roy *roi*, *m* (*Gaelic*) red.
Ruaidhri, **Ruairidh**. See **Rory**.
Ruby *roo'bi*, *f* from the stone.—Deriv **Rubina** (*-bē'nə*).
Rudolf, **Rudolph** *roo'dolf*, *m* (*Gmc*) fame-wolf, from *Rudolphus*, Latinized form of **Rolf**.
Rufus *roo'fəs*, *m* (*L*) red.
Rupert *roo'pərt*, *m* (*LGer*) form of **Robert**.
Russell *rus'əl*, *m* from the surname.
Ruth *rooth*, *f* (*Heb*) meaning obscure; associated with English *ruth*, pity.

Sabrina *sə-brē'nə*, *f* the Latin name for the River Severn.
Sacha, **Sasha** *sash'ə*, *m* and *f* (*Russ*) diminutives of **Alexander** and **Alexandra**.
Sadie *sā'di*, *f* a diminutive of **Sarah**.
Sal *sal*, **Sally** *sal'i*, *f* diminutives of **Sarah**.
Salome *sə-lō'mi*, *f* (*Heb*) perfect, or peace.
Samantha *sə-man'thə*, *f* of uncertain but *prob* American origin, *perh* devised as a feminine of **Samuel**.
Samuel *sam'ū-əl*, *m* (*Heb*) heard by God, or name of God.—Dimins **Sam**, **Sammy**.
Sandra *san'drə*, *sän'*, *f orig* Italian diminutive of **Alessandra**; used as a diminutive of **Alexandra**.
Sandy *san'di*, *m*. See **Alexander**.
Sarah, **Sara** *sā'rə* or *sä'rə*, *f* (*Heb*) princess, queen.—Dimins **Sadie**, **Sal**, **Sally**.
Sasha. See **Sacha**.
Saskia *sas'ki-ə*, *f* (*Du*) of uncertain origin.
Saul *söl*, *m* (*Heb*) asked for.
Scarlett *skär'lit*, *f* from the surname.
Scott *skot*, *m* from the surname.
Seamas, **Seamus** *shā'məs*, *m* Irish forms of **James**.
Sean *shön*, *m* Irish form of **John**.
Sebastian *si-bas'ti-ən*, *m* (*Gr*) man of Sebasteia (in Pontus).
Selina *si-lē'nə*, *f poss* connected with **Celia**, but associated with Greek *selēnē*, moon.
Senga *seng'gə*, *f* backward spelling of **Agnes**.
Serena *si-rē'nə*, *f* (*L*) calm, serene.
Seth *seth*, *m* (*Heb*) substitute, or compensation.
Seumas *shā'məs*, *m* the Gaelic form of **James**.
Shamus *shā'məs*, *m* (*Ir*) anglicization of **Seamas**.
Shane *shān*, **Shaun**, **Shawn** *shön*, *m* (*Ir*) anglicizations of **Sean**.
Sharmaine. See **Charmaine**.
Sharon *shā'rən*, *shar'ən*, *f* (*Heb*) a Biblical place name.
Sheena *shē'nə*, *f* an anglicization of **Síne**, **Sìne**.
Sheila, **Shelagh** *shē'lə*, *f orig* anglicizations of *Síle*, Irish form of **Celia**.

Shelley *shel'i, m* from the surname, or (*f*) *perh* a variant of **Shirley**.
Sherry. See **Cher**.
Sheryl. A variant of **Cheryl** (see **Cherry**).
Shirley *shûr'li, f* (formerly *m*) from the surname or place name.
Shona *shō'nə, f* (*Gaelic*) *perh* ultimately a diminutive of **Catriona**, but thought of as an anglicization of *Seonaid* (**Janet**) or *Seonag* (**Joan**).
Shula *shoo'lə, f* (*Heb*) peace.
Sian *shän, f* Welsh form of **Jane**.
Sibyl, now **Sybil** *sib'il*, **Sibylla** *si-bil'ə, f* (*L*) a Sibyl.
Sidney, **Sydney** *sid'ni, m* and *f* from the surname.
Siegfried *sēg'frēd, m* (*Gmc*) victory-peace.
Silas *sī'ləs*, **Silvester**, **Sylvester** *sil-ves'tər, m* (*L*) living in the woods.—Fem **Silvia**, **Sylvia**.
Simon *sī'mən, m* (*Heb*) *perh* hearing; *perh* (*Gr*) snub-nosed.—Dimin **Sim**.—Fem **Simone** (*-mōn'*).
Sindy. See **Cindy**.
Síne, **Sìne** *shē'nə, f* respectively Irish and Gaelic forms of **Jane**.
Sinéad *shi-nād', f* Irish form of **Janet**.
Siobhán *shə-vön', f* Irish form of **Jane**.
Siôn *shon, m* Welsh form of **John**.
Solomon *sol'ə-mən, m* (*Heb*) peaceable.—Dimins **Sol**, **Solly**.
Somhairle. See **Sorley**.
Sonia, **Sonya** *son'yə, f* (*Russ*) *orig* a diminutive of **Sophia**.
Sophia *sə-fī'ə, -fē'*, **Sophie**, **Sophy** *sō'fi, f* (*Gr*) wisdom.
Sorley, **Somhairle** *sör'li, m* (*Gaelic*) a form of Scandinavian *Somerled*, viking, literally summer wanderer.
Stacey, **Stacy**. See **Anastasia**.
Stanley *stan'li, m* from the surname or place name.
Stella *stel'ə, f* (*L*) star. See also **Estelle**.
Stephen, **Steven** *stē'vən, m* (*Gr*) crown, wreath.—Dimins **Steve**, **Stevie**.—Fem **Stephanie** (*stef'ə-ni*).
Stewart, **Steuart**, **Stuart** *stū'ərt, m* from the surname.
Susan *soo'zən, sū'zən*, **Susanna**, **Susannah** *-zan'ə, f* (*Heb*) lily.—Dimins **Sue**, **Suke**, **Sukie**, **Suky**, **Susie**, **Susy**.
Sybil. See **Sibyl**.
Sydney. See **Sidney**.
Sylvester, **Sylvia**. See **Silas**.

Tabitha *tab'i-thə, f* (*Aramaic*) gazelle.
Taffy *taf'i, m* an anglicized form of *Dafydd*, the Welsh form of **David**.
Tamara *tə-mä'rə, f* (*Russ*) a Caucasian name, *perh* (*Heb*) date palm.
Tammy, **Tammie** *tam'i, f* diminutives of **Tamara** and **Tamsin**.
Tamsin *tam'sin, f orig* a Cornish diminutive of **Thomasina**.
Tania, **Tanya** *tän'yə, tan', f* diminutives of Russian *Tatiana*.
Tara *tä'rə*, from the place name in County Meath, Ireland.
Ted *ted*, **Teddie**, **Teddy** *-di, m* diminutives of **Edward**.
Terence, **Terrance** *ter'əns, m* (*L*) the Roman family name *Terentius*.—Dimin **Terry**.
Teresa, **Theresa** *tə-rē'zə*, **Theresia** *-zi-ə, f* (*Gr*); *perh* relating to the island *Thera*.—Dimins **Terry**, **Tessa**, **Tracy**.
Terry *ter'i, m* and *f* a diminutive of **Terence**, **Teresa**; also (*m*) from the surname.
Tessa *tes'ə*, **Tess**, *f orig* diminutives of **Teresa**.
Thea *thē'ə, f* (*Gr*) goddess, or a diminutive of **Dorothea**.
Thelma *thel'mə, f poss* (*Gr*) will.
Theodore *thē'ə-dōr, -dör, m* (*Gr*) gift of God.—Fem **Theodora** (*-dō'rə, -dö'rə*).
Theresa, **Theresia**. See **Teresa**.
Thomas *tom'əs, m* (*Heb*) twin.—Dimins **Tom**, **Tommy**, (*Scot*) **Tam**.—Fem **Thomasina**, **Tomasina** (*-sē'nə*).
Thora *thö'rə, thō', f* (*Scand*) *perh* Thor's battle.
Tiffany *tif'ə-ni, f* (*Gr*) from *theophania*, revelation of God.
Tilda *til'də*, **Tilly** *til'i, f* diminutives of **Matilda**.
Timothy *tim'ə-thi, m* (*Gr*) honoured of God.—Dimins **Tim**, **Timmie**.
Tina *tē'nə, f* a diminutive of **Christina** (see **Christian**).
Toby *tō'bi*, **Tobias** *tə-bī'əs, m* (*Heb*) Yah is good.
Tom, **Tommy**. See **Thomas**.
Tony *tō'ni, m* diminutive of **Anthony**.
Torquil *tör'kwil, m* (*Gaelic*, from *ON*) *perh* Thor-cauldron.
Tracy, **Tracey** *trā'si, f orig* a diminutive of **Teresa**, or (*m*) *perh* from the surname.
Trevor *trev'ər, m* from the surname.
Tricia, **Trisha** *trish'ə*, **Trish** *trish, f* diminutives of **Patricia**.
Tristram *tris'trəm*, **Tristan** *-tən, m* (*Celtic*) *perh* tumult.
Trix *triks*, **Trixy**, **Trixie** *-i, f* diminutives of **Beatrix**.
Trudy *troo'di, f orig* a diminutive of names ending in *-trude*, eg **Gertrude**.
Tyrone *ti-rōn', m* (*Ir*) from the name of the Irish county.

Ulric *ul'rik, ool', m* (*Gmc*) wolf-rule.—Fem **Ulrica** (*-rē'kə*).
Una *ū'nə, f* (*Ir*) of uncertain meaning, interpreted as Latin 'one' (anglicized as **Oona** or **Oonagh**).
Unity *ū'ni-ti, f* from the noun.
Ursula *ûr'sū-lə, f* (*L*) little she-bear.

Valentine *val'ən-tīn, m* and *f* (*L*) healthy.—Dimin **Val**.
Valerie *val'ə-ri, f* (*L*) from the Roman family name *Valerius*.—Dimin **Val**.
Vanessa *və-nes'ə, f* a name invented by Swift from *Es*ther *Van*homrigh.
Vaughan *vön, m* (*Welsh*) small one.
Venetia *və-nē'shə, f* (*L*) Venetian.
Vera *vē'rə, f* (*Russ*) faith, but understood as Latin 'true'.
Verity *ver'i-ti, f* (*L*) truth.
Vernon *vûr'nən, m* from the surname.
Veronica *vi-ron'i-kə, f* (*Gr*) a form of **Berenice**, but seen as an anagrammatic form of Latin *vera icon*, true image.
Victor *vik'tər, m* (*L*) conqueror.—Dimin **Vic**.
Victoria *vik-tō'ri-ə, -tö', f* (*L*) victory.
Vincent *vin'sənt, m* (*L*) conquering.
Viola *vī'ə-lə*, **Violet** *-lit, f* (*L*) violet (the flower).
Virgil *vûr'jil, m* (*L*) from the Roman family name *Vergilius*, *esp* honouring the poet Publius *Vergilius* Maro.
Virginia *vər-jin'i-ə, f* (*L*) from the Roman family name *Virginius*.—Dimin **Ginny**, **Jinny** (*jin'i*).
Vita *vē'tə, f perh* (*L*) a feminine of the saint's name *Vitus*, or from *vita*, life; also a diminutive of **Victoria**.
Vivian, **Vyvyan**, **Vyvian** *viv'i-ən, m* and (*usu* **Vivien**) *f* (*L*) lively.—Dimin (*m* and *f*) **Viv**.

Walter *wöl'tər, m* (*Gmc*) rule-people (or -army).—Dimins **Wat** (*wot*), **Watty** (*-i*), **Wally** (*wol'i*), **Walt** (*wölt*).
Wanda *won'də, f* (*Gmc* or *Slavic*) *perh* 'Wendish'.
Wendy *wen'di, f* an invention of J M Barrie's.
Wilfrid, **Wilfred** *wil'frid, m* (*Gmc*) will-peace.
Wilhelmina *wil-həl-mē'nə, wil-əl-, f* (*Gmc*) a feminine formed from *Wilhelm* (German form of **William**).—Dimins **Elma**, **Wilma**, **Mina**, **Minnie**.
William *wil'yəm, m* (*Gmc*) will-helmet.—Dimins **Bill**, **Billie**, **Billy**, **Will**, **Willie**, **Willy**.
Winifred *win'i-frid, f prob orig* Welsh 'holy reconciliation'.—Dimins **Win**, **Winnie**, **Freda** (*frē'də*).
Winston *win'stən, m* from the place name.
Wyn *win, m* (*Welsh*) fair, white.
Wynne *win, m* (*OE*) from the surname, itself meaning 'friend'.

Xanthe *zan'thi, f* (*Gr*) fair, golden.
Xavier *zav'i-ər, m* (*Sp*) *prob* from a Basque place name.

Yasmin. See **Jasmine**.
Yolanda *yō-lan'də, f appar* a medieval form of *Violante*, a derivative of **Viola**.
Yvonne *ē-von'*, **Yvette** *ē-vet', f* (*Fr*) feminines respectively of *Yvon* and *Yves*, from Germanic *Ivo*, yew.

Zachary *zak'ə-ri, m* (*Heb*) Yah is renowned.—Dimins **Zach**, **Zack**.
Zara *zä'rə, f* (*Ar*) *perh* flower, blossom, or bright as the dawn.
Zena *zē'nə, f perh* (*Pers*) a woman.
Zoe, **Zoë**, **Zowie** *zō'ē, f* (*Gr*) life.
Zola *zō'lə, f* from the Italian surname, or *perh* a derivative of **Zoe**.
Zuleika *zoo-lē'kə, -lī'kə, f* (*Pers*) *perh* brilliance, beauty.

Phrases and quotations from Latin, Greek and modern foreign languages

Single foreign words, and certain phrases often used in an English context, are given in the main dictionary

abiit, excessit, evasit, erupit (L) he is gone, he is off, he has escaped, he has broken away.—Cicero, *In Catilinam* II.i.1.
ab imo pectore (L) from the bottom of the heart.
à bon chat, bon rat (Fr) to a good cat, a good rat—well matched: set a thief to catch a thief.
ab ovo usque ad mala (L) from the egg to the apples—of a Roman banquet: from the beginning to the end.
à chaque saint sa chandelle (Fr) to every saint his candle: to every patron his meed of service.
actum est de republica (L) it is all up with the state.
ad majorem Dei gloriam (L) for the greater glory of God—the Jesuit motto.
ad vitam aut culpam (L) for life or till fault: of appointments, for life unless misconduct necessitates dismissal.
aide-toi, le ciel t'aidera (Fr) help yourself and heaven will help you.
aliquid haeret (L) something sticks.
Allah il Allah a corruption of Arabic *lā ilāha illā 'llāh* = there is no god but God.
alter ipse amicus (L) a friend is another self.
amare et sapere vix deo conceditur (L) to be in love and to be wise is scarce granted even to a god.—Laberius.
a mensa et toro (L) from bed and board.
à nos moutons. See **revenons**.
après moi (nous) le déluge (Fr) after me (us) the deluge: then the deluge may come when it likes—attributed to Mme de Pompadour and to Louis XV.
aquila non capit muscas (L) an eagle does not catch flies.
Arcades ambo (L) Arcadians both: two of the same stamp.—Virgil, *Ecl.*, VII. 4.—Rendered by Byron blackguards both, *Don Juan*, IV. xciii.
ariston men hydōr (Gr) water is best.—Pindar, *Olympian Odes*, i.1.
ars est celare artem (L) true art is to conceal art.
ars longa, vita brevis (L) art is long, life is short.—Seneca, *De Brevitate Vitae*, 1. Cf **ho bios brachys**.
atra cura (L) black care. See **post equitem**.
at spes non fracta (L) but hope is not yet crushed.
au bout de son latin (Fr) at the end of his Latin, at the end of his knowledge, at his wits' end.
audentes fortuna juvat (L) fortune favours the daring.—Virgil, *Aen.*, X.284.
audi alteram partem (L) hear the other side.—St Augustine, *De Duabus Animabus*, XIV.2.
aufgeschoben ist nicht aufgehoben (Ger) put off is not given up.
aujourd'hui roi, demain rien (Fr) king today, nothing tomorrow.
auri sacra fames (L) accursed hunger for gold.—Virgil, *Aen.*, III.57.
au royaume des aveugles les borgnes sont rois (Fr) in the kingdom of the blind the one-eyed are kings.—As a Latin proverb, *beati monoculi in regione caecorum*.
aussitôt dit, aussitôt fait (Fr) no sooner said than done.
Austriae est imperare orbi universo (L) it is Austria's part to command the whole world—often AEIOU.
aut amat aut odit mulier, nihil est tertium (L) a woman either loves or hates, there is no third course.—Syrus, 42.
autant d'hommes (or de têtes), autant d'avis (Fr) so many men, so many minds. Cf **quot homines.**
aut insanit homo aut versus facit (L) either the man is mad or he is making verses.—Horace, *Sat.*, II.vii.117.
aut non tentaris aut perfice (L) either do not attempt or else achieve.—Ovid, *A.A.*, I.389.
aut regem aut fatuum nasci oportet (L) one should be born either king or fool.—Proverb; quoted by Seneca.
aut vincere aut mori (L) to conquer or die.
aux absents les os (Fr) the bones to the absent.
aux grands maux les grands remèdes (Fr) to desperate evils desperate remedies.
ave, Caesar (or **imperator**), **morituri te salutant** (L) hail, Caesar, men doomed to die salute thee (said by gladiators).
a verbis ad verbera (L) from words to blows.
à vieux comptes nouvelles disputes (Fr) old accounts breed new disputes.
avise la fin (Fr) weigh well the end.

barba tenus sapientes (L) sages as far as the beard—ie with an appearance of wisdom only.
bella, horrida bella (L) wars, horrid wars.—Virgil, *Aen.*, VI.86.
bellaque matribus detestata (L) and wars abhorred by mothers.—Horace, *Od.*, I.i.24–5.
belua multorum capitum (L) monster with many heads—the irrational mob.—Horace, *Epistolae*, I.i.76.
beneficium accipere libertatem est vendere (L) to accept a favour is to sell one's liberty.—Syrus, 49.
bene qui latuit bene vixit (L) he has lived well who has lived obscure.—Ovid, *Trist.*, III.iv.25.
bibere venenum in auro (L) to drink poison from a cup of gold.
bis dat qui cito dat (L) he gives twice who gives promptly.—Proverb; by Bacon.
bis peccare in bello non licet (L) in war one may not blunder twice.
bis pueri senes (L) old men are twice boys.
bon avocat, mauvais voisin (Fr) a good lawyer is a bad neighbour.
bon jour, bonne oeuvre (Fr) better day, better deed.
bonnes nouvelles adoucissent le sang (Fr) good news sweetens the blood.
Borgen macht Sorgen (Ger) borrowing makes sorrowing.
brevis esse laboro, obscurus fio (L) I labour to be brief, and I become obscure.—Horace, *A.P.*, 25–26.
briller par son absence (Fr) to be conspicuous by its absence.
buen principio, la mitad es hecha (Sp) well begun is half-done.

caeca invidia est (L) envy is blind.—Livy, xxxviii.49.
caelum non animum mutant qui trans mare currunt (L) they change their sky, not their mind, who scour across the sea.—Horace, *Epist.*, I.xi.27.
Caesar non supra grammaticos (L) Caesar has no authority over the grammarians.
ça ira (Fr) it will go— refrain of a famous song of the French Revolution.
candida Pax (L) white-robed Peace.—Tibullus, I.x.45.
carpe diem, quam minimum credula postero (L) enjoy the present day, trust the least possible to the future.—Horace, *Od.*, I.xi.8.
cedant arma togae (L) let arms yield to the gown: let military authority yield to civil.—Cicero, *De Officiis*, I.xxii.77, *in Pisonem*, xxx.73.
cela va sans dire (Fr) that goes without saying: of course.
celui qui veut, peut (Fr) who will, can.
ce monde est plein de fous (Fr) this world is full of madmen.
c'en est fait de lui (Fr) it is all up with him.
ce n'est que le premier pas qui coûte (Fr). See **il n'y a**.
c'est égal (Fr) it's all one (to me): it makes no odds.
c'est le commencement de la fin (Fr) it is the beginning of the end.—*Attrib* to Talleyrand.
c'est magnifique, mais ce n'est pas la guerre (Fr) it is

magnificent, but it is not war (said at Balaklava by a French general watching the charge of the Light Brigade).
c'est pire (or **plus) qu'un crime, c'est une faute** (Fr) it is worse than a crime, it is a blunder (on the execution of the Duc d'Enghien; attributed to various persons, incl. Boulay de la Meurthe).
ceterum censeo (L) but I think (said of persistent obstruction like that of Cato).
chapeaux bas (Fr) hats off.
cherchez la femme (Fr) look for the woman: there's a woman at the bottom of it.—Dumas *père*.
che sarà sarà (Ital) what will be will be.
chiesa libera in libero stato (Ital) a free church in a free state (Cavour's ideal for Italy).
chi tace confessa (Ital) who keeps silence, confesses.
circulus in probando (L) arguing in a circle, using the conclusion as one of the arguments.
civis Romanus sum (L) I am a Roman citizen.—Cicero, *In Verrem*, VI.57.
conscia mens recti (L) a mind conscious of rectitude.—Ovid, *Fast.*, IV.311. Cf **mens sibi**.
consensus facit legem (L) consent makes law or rule.
consuetudo pro lege servatur (L) custom is held as a law.
contraria contrariis curantur (L) opposites are cured by opposites.
corruptio optimi pessima (L) the corruption of the best is the worst of all.
coûte que coûte (Fr) cost what it may.
crambe repetita (L) cauld kale het again—cold cabbage warmed up.—Juvenal, VII.154.
cucullus non facit monachum (L) the cowl does not make the monk.
curiosa felicitas (L) studied felicity of expression—said by Petronius Arbiter, *Saturae (Satyricon)*, 118, 5 of Horace's style: (*loosely*) curious felicity.

damnosa haereditas (L) an inheritance of debts (*Roman Law*): any hurtful inheritance.—Gaius, *Institutes*, ii.163.
damnum absque injuria (L) loss without legal injury.
das Ewig-Weibliche zieht uns hinan (Ger) the eternal feminine draws us upward.—Goethe, *Faust*, at end.
data et accepta (L) expenditures and receipts.
decus et tutamen (L) an ornament and a protection (inscription round the milled edge of the one-pound coin, earlier used on a coin of Charles II, at John Evelyn's suggestion).—Virgil, *Aen.*, V.262.
de l'audace, encore de l'audace, et toujours de l'audace (Fr) to dare, still to dare, and ever to dare (Danton's famous phrase).
delenda est Carthago (L) Carthage must be wiped out (a saying constantly repeated by Cato).
de minimis non curat lex (L) the law does not concern itself about very small matters.—Bacon, Letter cclxxxii.
de mortuis nil nisi bonum (L) say nothing but good of the dead.
desipere in loco. See **dulce**.
de te fabula narratur (L) the story is about you.—Horace, *Sat.*, I.i.69–70. See also **quid rides**.
Dichtung und Wahrheit (Ger) poetry and truth.
dictum de dicto (L) hearsay report.
dictum sapienti sat est (L) a word to the wise is enough (*usu* quoted as **verbum**).—Plautus, *Persa*, IV.vii.19.
diem perdidi (L) I have lost a day (said by the Emperor Titus).
di grado in grado (Ital) by degrees.
dis aliter visum (L) the gods have adjudged otherwise.—Virgil, *Aen.*, II.428.
disjecta membra (L) scattered limbs (after Ovid, *Met.*, III.724); **disjecti membra poetae** limbs of the dismembered poet.—Horace, *Sat.*, I.iv.62.
divide et impera (L) divide and rule.
docendo discimus (L) we learn by teaching.
doli capax (L) capable of committing a wrong—*opp* to *doli incapax*.
Domine, dirige nos (L) Lord, direct us (the motto of London).
Dominus illuminatio mea (L) the Lord is my light.
domus et placens uxor (L) a home and a pleasing wife.—Horace, *Od.*, II.xiv.21–22.
dorer la pilule (Fr) to gild the pill.
dos moi pou stō kai tēn gēn kinēsō (Gr) give me where to stand, and I will move the earth (attributed to Archimedes).
do ut des (L) I give that you may give.
dulce est desipere in loco it is pleasant to play the fool on occasion.—Horace, *Od.*, IV.xii.28.

écrasez l'infâme (Fr) crush the vile thing.—Voltaire against the Roman Catholic Church of his time.
ego et rex meus (L) I and my king.—Cardinal Wolsey.
eheu fugaces . . . labuntur anni (L) alas! the fleeting years slip away.—Horace, *Od.*, II,xiv.1–2.
eile mit Weile (Ger) make speed with leisure.
ein Mal, kein Mal (Ger) just once counts nothing.
Ēli, Ēli, lama sabachthani (Matt. 27.46), **Eloi, Eloi, lamma sabachthani** (Mark 15.34) (Gr transliterations of Aramaic my God, my God, why hast thou forsaken me?
epea pteroenta (Gr) winged words.—Homer (*Iliad*, 1.201, etc). See also Dictionary under **wing**[1].
ephphatha (Aramaic) be opened (Mark 7.34).
e pluribus unum (L) one out of many—before 1956 regarded as motto of the United States.
ergo bibamus (L) therefore let us drink.
Erin go bragh (Ir) Erin forever.
errare est humanum (L) to err is human.
est modus in rebus (L) there is a mean in (all) things.—Horace, *Sat.*, I.i.106.
et tu, Brute (L) you too, Brutus. (Caesar's alleged exclamation when he saw Brutus amongst his assassins.)
euphemeite (Gr) hush! (shouted at the start of a Greek drama).
eventus stultorum magister (L) the outcome is the schoolmaster of fools.—Livy, XXII,39.
exegi monumentum aere perennius (L) I have reared a monument more lasting than brass.—Horace, *Od.*, III.xxx.1.
exempla sunt odiosa (L) examples are hateful.
ex nihilo (or **nilo) nihil** (or **nil) fit** (L) out of nothing nothing comes.
ex pede Herculem (L) (we recognize) Hercules from his foot.
experientia docet stultos (L) experience teaches fools.
experto crede, or (Virgil, *Aen.*, XI.283) **credite** (L) trust one who has tried, or had experience.
expertus metuet, or **metuit** (L) he who has experienced it will fear (or fears).—Horace, *Epist.*, I.xviii.87.
ex ungue leonem (L) (judge, or infer) the lion from his claws.

fable convenue (Fr) fable agreed upon—Voltaire's name for history.
facile est inventis addere (L) it is easy to add to things invented already.
facilis descensus Averno, or **Averni** (L) descent to Avernus is easy.—Virgil, *Aen.*, VI.126.
facta non verba (L) deeds, not words.
factum est (L) it is done.
faire bonne mine (Fr) to put a good face on the matter.
falsus in uno, falsus in omnibus (L) false in one thing, false in all.
fama nihil est celerius (L) nothing is swifter than rumour.—Livy.
fama semper vivat (L) may his (or her) fame live for ever.
far niente (Ital) doing nothing.
fas est et ab hoste doceri (L) it is right to learn even from an enemy.—Ovid, *Met.*, IV.428.
Fata obstant (L) the Fates oppose.—Virgil, *Aen.*, IV.440.
Fata viam invenient (L) the Fates will find out a way.—Virgil, *Aen.*, X.113.
felicitas multos habet amicos (L) prosperity has many friends.
fiat justitia, ruat caelum (L) let justice be done, though the heavens should fall.
fiat lux (L) let there be light.
fide, sed cui vide (L) trust, but take care in whom.
finem respice (L). See **respice finem**.
finis coronat opus (L) the end crowns the work.
fin mot de l'affaire (Fr) the bottom of the matter, the explanation.
flecti non frangi (L) to be bent, not broken.

forsan et haec olim meminisse juvabit (L) perhaps some day we shall like to remember even these things.—Virgil, *Aen.*, I.203.
Fors Clavigera (L) Fortune the club-bearer (used as a title by Ruskin).
fortes Fortuna adjuvat (L) Fortune helps the brave (Terence, *Phormio*, I.iv.26).
fortiter in re, suaviter in modo (L). See **suaviter**.
frangas, non flectes (L) you may break, you shall not bend.
fraus est celare fraudem (L) it is a fraud to conceal a fraud.
fugit hora (L) the hour flies.—Persius, V.153.
fulmen brutum (L) a harmless thunderbolt.

geflügelte Worte (Ger) winged words. See **epea**.
genus irritabile vatum (L) the irritable tribe of poets.—Horace, *Epist.*, II.ii.102.
giovine santo, diavolo vecchio (Ital) young saint, old devil.
gli assenti hanno torto (Ital) the absent are in the wrong.
glückliche Reise (Ger) prosperous journey to you.
gnōthi seauton (Gr) know thyself.—Inscribed on the temple of Apollo at Delphi. See also **nosce teipsum**.
Gott mit uns (Ger) God with us—Hohenzollern motto.
gradu diverso, via una (L) with different step on the one way.
gradus ad Parnassum (L) a step, or stairs, to Parnassus, a Latin or Greek poetical dictionary.
Graecum est: non legitur (L) this is Greek; it is not read (placed against a Greek word in medieval MSS, a permission to skip the hard words).
gratia placendi (L) the delight of pleasing.
gravis ira regum est semper (L) the anger of kings is always serious.
grosse Seelen dulden still (Ger) great souls suffer in silence.—Schiller, *Don Carlos*, I.iv., end of scene.
grosse tête et peu de sens (Fr) big head and little wit.
gutta cavat lapidem (L) the drop wears away the stone.—Ovid, *Pont.*, IV.x.5.

habendum et tenendum (L) to have and to hold.
habent sua fata libelli (L) books have their destinies.—Maurus, *De Litteris, Syllabis et Metris*.
Hannibal ad portas (L) Hannibal at the gates.—Cicero, *Philippica*, I.v.11.
heu pietas! heu prisca fides! (L) alas for piety! alas for the ancient faith!—Virgil, *Aen.*, VI.879.
hiatus valde deflendus (L) a gap deeply to be deplored.
hic finis fandi (L) here (was, or let there be) an end of the speaking.
hinc illae lacrumae (L) hence [came] those tears.—Terence, *Andria*, I.i.99; also Horace, *Epist.*, I.xix.41.
ho bios brachys, hē de technē makrē (Gr) life is short and art is long.—Attributed to Hippocrates.
hoc age (L) this do.
hoc saxum posuit (L) placed this stone.
hodie mihi, cras tibi (L) me today, you tomorrow.
hominis est errare (L) it belongs to man to err.
homo alieni juris (L) one under control of another; **homo sui juris** one who is his own master; **homo sum: humani nihil a me alienum puto** I am a man: I count nothing human indifferent to me (Terence, *Heaut.*, I.i.25); **homo trium litterarum** man of three letters—ie *fur* = thief; **homo unius libri** a man of one book.
hon hoi theoi philousi apothnēskei neos (Gr) whom the gods love dies young.—Menander. Cf **quem di diligunt . . .**
honi soit qui mal y pense (OFr) the shame be his who thinks ill of it—the motto of the Order of the Garter.
honneur et patrie (Fr) honour and native land.
honor virtutis praemium (L) honour is the reward of virtue.
hora fugit (L) the hour flies.
horas non numero nisi serenas (L) I number none but shining hours. (Common on sundials.)
horresco referens (L) I shudder in relating.—Virgil, *Aen.*, II.204.
horribile dictu (L) horrible to relate.
humanum est errare (L) to err is human.
hurtar para dar por Dios (Sp) to steal in order to give to God.
hypage Satana (Gr) away Satan.—Matt.4.10.
hypotheses non fingo (L) I do not frame hypotheses (ie unverifiable speculations).—Newton.

ici on parle francais (Fr) here French is spoken.
Iesus Hominum Salvator (L) Jesus, Saviour of men.
ignorantia juris neminem excusat (L) ignorance of the law excuses nobody.
ignotum per ignotius (L) the unknown by the still more unknown.
i gran dolori sono muti (Ital) great griefs are mute.
il a inventé l'histoire (Fr) he has invented history.
il a les défauts de ses qualités (Fr) he has the defects that answer to his good qualities.
il gran rifiuto (Ital) the great refusal (the abdication of Pope Celestine V).—Dante, *Inferno*, III.60.
il n'y a pas à dire (Fr) there is nothing to be said.
il n'y a que le premier pas qui coûte (Fr) it is only the first step that counts. (Mme du Deffand on St Denis walking after decapitation.)
ils n'ont rien appris ni rien oublié (Fr) they have learned nothing and forgotten nothing (said of the French *Émigrés*, often of the Bourbons).
incidis in Scyllam cupiens vitare Charybdim (L) you fall into Scylla trying to avoid Charybdis.—Philip Gaultier de Lille.
incredulus odi (L) I hate and disbelieve.—Horace, *A.P.*, 188.
in meditatione fugae (L) in contemplation of flight.
integer vitae scelerisque purus (L) blameless in life and clear of offence.—Horace, *Od.*, I.xxii.1.
inter arma silent leges (L) amid wars laws are silent (Cicero).
interdum stultus bene loquitur (L) sometimes a fool speaks aright.
invita Minerva (L) against the will of Minerva: uninspired.—Horace, *A.P.*., 385.
ira furor brevis est (L) rage is a brief madness.—Horace, *Epist.*, I.ii.62.
Italia irredenta (Ital) unredeemed Italy—the parts of Italy still under foreign domination after the war of 1866—South Tirol, etc.

jacta est alea (L) the die is cast (quoted as said by Caesar at the crossing of the Rubicon).
je n'en vois pas la nécessité (Fr) I don't see the necessity for that (said by the Comte d'Argental in reply to a man who pleaded, 'But one must live somehow').
joci causa (L) for the joke.
j'y suis, j'y reste (Fr) here I am, here I stay (said by Macmahon at the Malakoff).

kai ta leipomena, kai ta loipa (Gr) and the rest: and so on.
kat' exochēn (Gr) pre-eminently: *par excellence*.
keine Antwort ist auch eine Antwort (Ger) no answer is still an answer: silence gives consent.
Kirche, Küche, Kinder (Ger) church, kitchen, children—said, eg during the Nazi period, to be the proper interests of a German woman.

laborare est orare (L) work is prayer.
labore et honore (L) by labour and honour.
labuntur et imputantur (L) [the moments] slip away and are laid to our account (inscription on sundials). Also **pereunt et imputantur** (qv).
la donna è mobile (Ital) woman is changeable.
la garde meurt et ne se rend pas (Fr) the guard dies, it does not surrender.
lā ilāha illā 'llāh (Ar) there is no god but God.
l'appétit vient en mangeant (Fr) appetite comes as you eat.
lasciate ogni speranza, voi ch'entrate (Ital) abandon all hope ye who enter.—Dante, *Inferno*, III.9. From the inscription over the gate of hell.
le génie n'est qu'une grande aptitude à la patience (Fr) genius is merely a great aptitude for patience (attributed to Buffon).
l'empire c'est la paix (Fr) the empire means peace (said by Louis Napoleon in 1852).
l'état, c'est moi (Fr) I am the state (alleged to have been said by Louis XIV).

liberté, égalité, fraternité (Fr) liberty, equality, fraternity—a slogan of the French Revolution.
littera scripta manet (L) what is written down is permanent. See **vox audita**.
l'union fait la force (Fr) union makes strength.
lupus in fabula (L) the wolf in the fable: talk of the devil.—Terence, *Adelphi*, IV.i.21.

magni nominis umbra (L) the mere shadow of a mighty name.—Lucan, I.135.
man spricht Deutsch (Ger) German spoken here.
mea virtute me involvo (L) I wrap myself in my virtue.—Horace, *Od.*, III,xxix.54–55.
mēden agan (Gr) [let there be] nothing in excess.
medio tutissimus ibis (L) thou wilt go safest in the middle.—Ovid, *Met.*, II.137.
mega biblion, mega kakon (Gr) big book, great evil.
mē kinei Kamarinan (Gr) do not stir up Kamarina (a pestilent marsh in Sicily): let well alone.
mens sibi conscia recti (L) a mind conscious of rectitude.—Virgil, *Aen.*, I.604. Cf **conscia mens recti**.
monstrum horrendum, informe, ingens (L) a frightful monster, ill-shapen, huge.—Virgil, *Aen.*, III.658.
morituri te salutant. See **ave**.

natura abhorret vacuum (L) nature abhors a vacuum.
naviget Anticyram (L) let him sail to Anticyra [where hellebore could be had, to cure madness].—Horace, *Sat.*, II.iii.166.
nec cupias, nec metuas (L) neither desire nor fear.
ne cede malis (L) yield not to misfortune.—Virgil, *Aen.*, VI.95.
necessitas non habet legem (L) necessity has no law.
nec scire fas est omnia (L) it is not permitted to know all things—Horace, *Od.*, IV.iv.22.
nemo me impune lacessit (L) no one provokes me with impunity—the motto of the kings of Scotland and of the Order of the Thistle; **nemo repente fuit turpissimus** no one ever became utterly bad all at once.—Juvenal, II.83.
ne obliviscaris (L) do not forget.
neque semper arcum tendit Apollo (L) Apollo does not always bend his bow.—Horace, *Od.*, II.x.19–20.
ne quid nimis (L) [let there be] nothing in excess.
nescit vox missa reverti (L) a word published cannot be recalled.—Horace, *A.P.*, 390.
n'est-ce pas? (Fr) is it not so?
ne sutor ultra (or supra) crepidam (L) a cobbler should not criticize (a work of art) beyond (or above) the sandal—let the cobbler stick to his last. See also **ultracrepidate** in Dictionary).
ne temere (L) not rashly—a papal decree of 1907 denying recognition to the marriage of a Catholic unless contracted before a priest.
nicht wahr? (Ger) is it not true? isn't that so?
nisi Dominus frustra (L) except the Lord (keep the city, the watchman waketh but) in vain.—Ps.127—the motto of Edinburgh.
nitor in adversum (L) I strive in opposition.—Ovid, *Met.*, II.72.
non est inventus (L) he has not been found (he has absconded).
non multa, sed multum (L) not many, but much.
non nobis, Domine (L) not unto us, O Lord.—Psalm 115.
non possumus (L) we cannot—a form of refusal.
non ut edam vivo sed ut vivam edo (L) I do not live to eat, but eat to live.—Quintilian.
nosce teipsum (L) know thyself—a translation of **gnōthi seauton** (qv).
nous avons changé tout cela (Fr) we have changed all that.—Molière, *Le Médecin malgré lui*, II.iv.
nous verrons (ce que nous verrons) (Fr) we shall see (what we shall see).
nulla nuova, buona nuova (Ital) no news is good news.
nunc est bibendum (L) now is the time to drink.—Horace, *Od.*, I.xxxvii.1.

obscurum per obscurius (L) (explaining) the obscure by means of the more obscure.
odi profanum vulgus et arceo (L) I loathe and shun the profane rabble.—Horace, *Od.*, iii.i.1.
O fortunatos nimium, sua si bona norint, agricolas (L) Oh too happy farmers, if they but knew their luck.—Virgil, *Georg.*, II.458.
ohe! jam satis (L) hold! enough now (a common phrase).
ohne Hast, ohne Rast (Ger) without haste, without rest.—Goethe's motto.
olim meminisse juvabit. See **forsan**.
omnem crede diem tibi diluxisse supremum (L) believe each day to have dawned as your last.—Horace, *Epist.*, I.iv.13.
omne tulit punctum qui miscuit utile dulci (L) he has carried every vote who has combined the useful with the pleasing.—Horace, *A.P.*, 343.
omne vivum ex ovo (L) every living thing comes from an egg.—Attributed to Harvey.
omnia mutantur. See **tempora mutantur**.
omnia vincit amor, et nos cedamus amori (L) love overcomes all things, let us too yield to love.—Virgil, *Ecl.*, X.69.
O si sic omnia! (L) Oh that he had done all things thus, or Oh that all things were thus!
O tempora! O mores! (L) O the times! O the manners! Occurs in Cicero's first speech against Catiline.
otium cum dignitate (L) dignified leisure.
ouk esti? (Gr) is it not so?
ovem lupo committere (L) to entrust the sheep to the wolf.

pace tua (L) by your leave.
pallida Mors aequo pulsat pede pauperum tabernas regumque turres (L) pale Death knocks with impartial foot at poor men's huts and kings' castles.—Horace, *Od.*, I.iv.13–14.
palmam qui meruit ferat (L) let him who has won the palm wear it.—Dr Jortin, *Lusus Poetici*, viii.20.
panem et circenses (L) bread and (Roman) circus-games—food and amusements at public expense.—Juvenal, X.81.
panta rhei (Gr) all things are in a flux (a saying of Heraclitus).
parturiunt montes, nascetur ridiculus mus (L) the mountains are in travail, an absurd mouse will be born.—Horace, *A.P.*, 139.
pas op (Afrik) look out.
pathēmata mathēmata (Gr) sufferings [are] lessons.
peccavi (L) I have sinned.
pereunt et imputantur (L) [the moments, hours] pass away and are reckoned to our account.
pleidiol wyf i'm gwlad (W) loyal am I to my country (inscription round the edge of a Welsh one-pound coin).
pleon hēmisy pantos (Gr) the half is more than the whole.—Hesiod, *Erga*, 40.
plus ça change, plus c'est la même chose (Fr) the more that changes the more it is the same thing (no superficial or apparent change alters its essential nature).
poeta nascitur, non fit (L) the poet is born, not made.
pollōn onomatōn mia morphē (Gr) one shape of many names.—Aeschylus, *Prometheus*, 210.
polyphloisboio thalassēs (Gr) of the much-sounding sea.—Homer, *Il.*, I.34; also Hesiod, *Erga*, 648.
populus vult decipi, ergo decipiatur (L) the public wishes to be fooled, therefore let it be fooled.—Ascribed to Cardinal Caraffa.
post equitem sedet atra cura (L) behind the horseman sits black care.—Horace, *Od.*, III.i.40.
post hoc, ergo propter hoc (L) after this, therefore because of this (a fallacious reasoning).
pour encourager les autres (Fr) to encourage the others (Voltaire, *Candide*, on the shooting of Admiral Byng).
purpureus pannus (L) a purple patch.—From Horace, *A.P.*, 15–16.

que diable allait-il faire dans cette galère? (Fr) what the devil was he doing in that galley?—Molière, *Les Fourberies de Scapin*, II.vii.
quem di diligunt adolescens moritur (L) whom the gods love dies young.—Plautus's translation of **hon hoi theoi** . . .
quem Iupiter vult perdere dementat prius, or quem deus

perdere vult, prius dementat (L) whom Jupiter (a god) wishes to destroy, he first makes mad.
que sais-je (sçai-je)? (Fr) what do I know?—Montaigne's motto.
quicunque vult salvus esse (L) whosoever will be saved (the beginning of the Athanasian creed).
quid rides? mutato nomine de te fabula narratur (L) why do you laugh? with change of name the story is about you.—Horace, *Sat.*, I.i.69–70.
quién sabe? (Sp) who knows?
quieta non movere (L) not to move things that are at rest—to let sleeping dogs lie.
quis custodiet ipsos custodes? (L) who will guard the guards themselves?—Juvenal, VI.347–8.
quis desiderio sit pudor aut modus tam cari capitis? (L) what shame or stint should there be in mourning for one so dear?—Horace, *Od.*, I.xxiv.1.
qui s'excuse s'accuse (Fr) he who excuses himself accuses himself.
qui tacet consentit (L) who keeps silence consents.
qui va là? (Fr) who goes there?
quod ubique, quod semper, quod ab omnibus (L) what everywhere, what always, what by all (has been believed).—St Vincent of Lérin's definition of orthodoxy.
quot homines, tot sententiae (L) as many men, so many minds or opinions.—Terence, *Phormio*, II.iv.14 (or 1.454).

redolet lucerna (L) it smells of the lamp.
re galantuomo (Ital) the honest king—king and gentleman (said of Victor Emmanuel II).
religio loci (L) the religious spirit of the place.—Virgil, *Aen.*, VIII.349.
rem acu tetigisti (L) you have touched the thing with a needle, hit it exactly.—Proverbial expression used by Plautus.
res ipsa loquitur (L) the thing speaks for itself: the accident as in itself evidence of negligence.
respice finem (L) look to the end.—Playfully perverted into **respice funem**, beware of the (hangman's) rope.
retro me, satana (L) in Vulgate, **vade retro me, satana**, get thee behind me, Satan (Matt.16.23, Mark 8.33, Luke 4.8): stop trying to tempt me.
revenons à nos moutons (Fr) let us return to our sheep, ie our subject.—From the medieval farce *Maître Pathelin*.
rhododaktylos Eōs (Gr) rosy-fingered Dawn.—Homer, *Odyssey*, II.1.
Roma locuta, causa finita (L) Rome has spoken, the cause is ended.
ruat caelum. See **fiat justitia**.
rus in urbe (L) the country in town.—Martial, XII.57.21.

salus populi suprema lex esto (L) let the welfare of the people be the final law (Cicero, *De Legibus*, III.iii: **suprema est lex**).
sans peur et sans reproche (Fr) without fear and without reproach.
sapere aude (L) dare to be wise.—Horace, *Epist.*, I.ii.40.
sartor resartus (L) the tailor retailored.
se non è vero, è ben trovato (Ital) if it is not true, it is cleverly invented.
sero venientibus ossa (L) the bones to the late-comers.
sic itur ad astra (L) such is the way to the stars.—Virgil, *Aen.*, IX.641.
sic transit gloria mundi (L) so passes away earthly glory.
si jeunesse savait, si vieillesse pouvait (Fr) if youth but knew, if age but could.
s'il vous plait (Fr) if you please.
similia similibus curantur (L) likes are cured by likes—a hair of the dog that bit one.
si monumentum requiris, circumspice (L) if you seek (his) monument, look round you (inscription for the architect Christopher Wren's tomb in St Paul's).
simplex munditiis (L) elegant in simplicity.—Horace, *Od.*, I.v.5.
si parla Italiano (Ital) Italian spoken.
siste, viator (L) stop, traveller.
si vis pacem, para bellum (L) if you would have peace, be ready for war.
spero meliora (L) I hope for better things.
stet fortuna domus (L) may the fortune of the house last long.
sua si bona. See **O fortunatos**, etc.
suaviter in modo, fortiter in re (L) gentle in manner, resolute in deed.
suggestio falsi. See **suppressio veri**, etc.
sunt lacrimae rerum (L) there are tears for things (unhappy).—Virgil, *Aen.*, I.462.
suo motu (L) on one's own initiative.
suppressio veri suggestio falsi (L) suppression of truth is suggestion of the false. (In law, **suppressio veri** is passive, **suggestio falsi** active, misrepresentation.)
sursum corda (L) lift up your hearts.
surtout, pas de zèle (Fr) above all, no zeal.
sutor ne ultra (or **supra**) **crepidam**. See **ne sutor . . .**

tempora (*orig* **omnia) mutantur, nos et mutamur in illis** (L) the times (all things) change, and we with them.
tempus edax rerum (L) time, consumer of things.—Ovid, *Met.*, XV.234.
thalassa, thalassa! or **thalatta, thalatta!** (Gr) the sea, the sea! (the exulting cry of Xenophon's men on beholding the sea). Xenophon, *Anabasis*, IV.7.
timeo Danaos et dona ferentes (L) I fear the Greeks, even when bringing gifts.—Virgil, *Aen.*, II.49.
toujours perdrix (Fr) partridge every day—too much of a good thing.
tria juncta in uno (L) three things in one.

ubi bene, ibi patria (L) where it goes well with me, there is my fatherland.
und so weiter (Ger), or **usw**, and so forth.

vade in pace (L) go in peace.
vade retro me, satana. See **retro**.
varium et mutabile semper femina (L) woman is ever a fickle and changeable thing.—Virgil, *Aen.*, IV.569.
vedi Napoli, e poi muori (Ital) see Naples, and die.
veni Creator Spiritus (L) come, Creator Spirit—the beginning of an early Latin hymn.
veritas odium parit (L) truth begets hatred.—Terence, *Andria*, I.i.41.
vestigia . . . nulla retrorsum (L) no footprints backwards (at the lion's den): sometimes used to mean no going back.—Horace, *Epist.*, I.i.74–75.
vigilate et orate (L) watch and pray.
virginibus puerisque canto (L) I sing for maidens and boys—for the young person.—Horace, *Od.*, III.i.4.
vita brevis, ars longa (L) life is short, art is long (see **ho bios**, etc); **vita sine litteris mors est** life without literature is death.
vive la bagatelle (quasi-Fr) long live folly.
vive ut vivas (L) live that you may live.
vivit post funera virtus (L) virtue lives beyond the grave.
vogue la galère! (Fr) row the boat: row on: come what may!
volto sciolto e pensieri stretti (Ital) open face, close thoughts.
vous l'avez voulu, George Dandin (Fr) you would have it so.—Molière, *George Dandin*, Act I.
vox audita perit, littera scripta manet (L) the heard word is lost, the written letter abides.

Wahrheit und Dichtung (Ger) truth and poetry.
Wein, Weib und Gesang (Ger) wine, women and song.
wer da? (Ger) who is there?
wie geht's? (Ger) how are you?

zonam perdidit (L) he has lost his money-belt: he is in needy circumstances; **zonam solvere** to loose the virgin zone, ie to marry.

The Greek alphabet

Α	α	alpha	=	a
Β	β	bēta	=	b
Γ	γ	gamma	=	g
Δ	δ	delta	=	d
Ε	ε	epsīlon	=	e
Ζ	ζ	zēta	=	z
Η	η	ēta	=	ē
Θ	θ ϑ	thēta	=	th (*th*)
Ι	ι	iōta	=	i
Κ	κ	kappa	=	k
Λ	λ	lambda	=	l
Μ	μ	mū	=	m
Ν	ν	nū	=	n
Ξ	ξ	xī	=	x (*ks*)
Ο	ο	omicron	=	o
Π	π	pī	=	p
Ρ	ρ	rhō	=	r
Σ	σ ς	sigma	=	s
Τ	τ	tau	=	t
Υ	υ	upsīlon (often transcribed *y*)	=	u (*o͞o*, *ü*)
Φ	φ	phī	=	ph (*f*)
Χ	χ	chī (often transcribed *ch*, as in Latin)	=	kh (*hh*)
Ψ	ψ	psī	=	ps
Ω	ω	ōmega	=	ō

The Greek alphabet, apart from its use as the official script in Greek-speaking areas, is of worldwide importance as a source of symbols used in all branches of science and mathematics. The equivalents in our alphabet given above are intended as a guide to transliteration and as an indication of the anglicized pronunciation of ancient Greek. We have not attempted to describe modern Greek pronunciation. See also Dictionary under **digamma**, **episemon**, **koppa**, **sampi**, **san**.

The Russian alphabet

А	а	=	a (*ä*)
Б	б	=	b
В	в	=	v
Г	г	=	g
Д	д	=	d
Е	е	=	e (*ye*)
Ё	ё	=	(*yö*) (often printed as E, e)
Ж	ж	=	zh (*zh*)
З	з	=	z
И	и	=	i (*ē*)
Й	й		(consonantal *y* sound; only used as the second letter of a diphthong)
К	к	=	k
Л	л	=	l
М	м	=	m
Н	н	=	n
О	о	=	o (*ö*)
П	п	=	p
Р	р	=	r
С	с	=	s
Т	т	=	t
У	у	=	u (*o͞o*)
Ф	ф	=	f
Х	х	=	kh (*hh*)
Ц	ц	=	ts
Ч	ч	=	ch (*ch*)
Ш	ш	=	sh
Щ	щ	=	shch (often pronounced rather as *sh* followed by consonantal *y*)
	ъ	=	hard sign (sign used to separate in pronunciation a following palatalized vowel from a preceding consonant either palatalized or unpalatalized)
	ы	=	ı (a sound similar to *i*)
	ь	=	soft sign (sign used after a consonant to indicate palatalization, a sound like consonantal *y*)
Э	э	=	e (*e*)
Ю	ю	=	u (*yo͞o*)
Я	я	=	ya (*yä*)

Roman numerals

I = 1 V = 5 X = 10 L = 50 C = 100 D = 500 M = 1000

From the above symbols the numbers are made up as follows:—

I	=	1	L	=	50
II	=	2	LI	=	51
III	=	3	LII, etc.	=	52, etc.
IV (or IIII, e.g. on clocks)	=	4	LX	=	60
V	=	5	LXI	=	61
VI	=	6	LXII, etc.	=	62, etc.
VII	=	7	LXX	=	70
VIII	=	8	LXXI	=	71
IX	=	9	LXXII, etc.	=	72, etc.
X	=	10	LXXX	=	80
XI	=	11	LXXXI	=	81
XII	=	12	LXXXII, etc.	=	82, etc.
XIII	=	13	XC	=	90
XIV	=	14	XCI	=	91
XV	=	15	XCII, etc.	=	92, etc.
XVI	=	16			
XVII	=	17	C	=	100
XVIII	=	18	CC	=	200
XIX	=	19	CCC	=	300
XX	=	20	CCCC or CD	=	400
XXI	=	21	D (or IↃ)	=	500
XXII, etc.	=	22, etc.	DC (or IↃC)	=	600
XXX	=	30	DCC (or IↃCC)	=	700
XXXI	=	31	DCCC (or IↃCCC)	=	800
XXXII, etc.	=	32, etc.	CM (or DCCCC or IↃCCCC)	=	900
XL	=	40	M	=	1000
XLI	=	41	MM	=	2000
XLII, etc.	=	42, etc.	$\overline{\text{V}}$[3] (or IↃↃ)[1]	=	5000

Other letters also were used as numerals in medieval times (see Dictionary). For additional information about medieval methods of writing numerals, see below.

1. The symbol Ↄ, known as the *apostrophus*, might be repeated one or more times after IↃ, each Ↄ making the number ten times greater, as IↃↃ = 5000, IↃↃↃↃ = 500000. A number of this type might be multiplied by two by adding (in front) as many C's as there were Ↄ's in the number, e.g. CCIↃↃ = 10000, CCCCIↃↃↃↃ = 1000000.

2. The symbols I,V,X,L,C,D,M are still used today. In the Middle Ages, and also in much later times, methods of writing numerals were common which are found neither in the Roman period nor in the present century. Some are noted below.

3. In the Middle Ages and later, a line was placed above a symbol representing a number 1000 times greater, as $\overline{\text{X}}$ = 10000. $|\overline{\text{X}}|$ and |X| were variant methods of expressing 1000000.

4. In the Middle Ages and later, and still in medical usage, numerals could be written lower case, and j was often substituted for final i.

5. In the Middle Ages and later, Ꮷ appears with the same meaning as D, and there is sometimes a small version of the apostrophus. To take at random an example of the latter, the third volume of John Ray's *Historia Plantarum*, is dated cIↄ Iↄ CCIV—that is 1704.

Books of the Bible

Old Testament

Books of the Law

Genesis
Exodus
Leviticus
Numbers
Deuteronomy

Historical Books

Joshua
Judges
Ruth
1 Samuel
2 Samuel
1 Kings
2 Kings
1 Chronicles
2 Chronicles
Ezra
Nehemiah
Esther

Books of Poetry and Wisdom

Job
Psalms
Proverbs
Ecclesiastes
Song of Solomon

Books of the Prophets

Isaiah
Jeremiah
Lamentations
Ezekiel
Daniel
Hosea
Joel
Amos
Obadiah
Jonah
Micah
Nahum
Habakkuk
Zephaniah
Haggai
Zechariah
Malachi

New Testament

The Gospels and Acts

Matthew
Mark
Luke
John
Acts of the Apostles

The Epistles or Letters

Romans
1 Corinthians
2 Corinthians
Galatians
Ephesians
Philippians
Colossians
1 Thessalonians
2 Thessalonians
1 Timothy
2 Timothy
Titus
Philemon
Hebrews
James
1 Peter
2 Peter
1 John
2 John
3 John
Jude

Book of Revelation, or Apocalypse of St John

Apocrypha

1 Esdras
2 Esdras
Tobit
Judith
Additions to Esther
Wisdom of Solomon
Ecclesiasticus
Baruch
Epistle of Jeremiah
Prayer of Azariah
Song of the Three Young Men
History of Susanna
Bel and the Dragon
Prayer of the Manasseh
1 Maccabees
2 Maccabees

The Roman Catholic Church includes Tobit, Judith, all of Esther, Maccabees 1 and 2, Wisdom of Solomon, Ecclesiasticus and Baruch in its canon.

Plays of Shakespeare

The Two Gentlemen of Verona, *1590–1*
Henry VI Part One, *1592*
Henry VI Part Two, *1592*
Henry VI Part Three, *1592*
Titus Andronicus, *1592*
Richard III, *1592–3*
The Taming of the Shrew, *1593*
The Comedy of Errors, *1594*
Love's Labours Lost, *1594–5*
Richard II, *1595*
Romeo and Juliet, *1595*
A Midsummer Night's Dream, *1595*
King John, *1596*
The Merchant of Venice, *1596–7*
Henry IV Part One, *1596–7*
The Merry Wives of Windsor, *1597–8*
Henry IV Part Two, *1597–8*
Much Ado About Nothing, *1598*
Henry V, *1598–9*
Julius Caesar, *1599*
As You Like It, *1599–1600*
Hamlet, Prince of Denmark, *1600–1*
Twelfth Night, or What You Will, *1601*
Troilus and Cressida, *1602*
Measure for Measure, *1603*
Othello, *1603–4*
All's Well That Ends Well, *1604–5*
Timon of Athens, *1605*
The Tragedy of King Lear, *1605–6*
Macbeth, *1606*
Antony and Cleopatra, *1606*
Pericles, *1607*
Coriolanus, *1608*
The Winter's Tale, *1609*
Cymbeline, *1610*
The Tempest, *1611*
Henry VIII, *1613*

Chemical elements

symbol	element	derived from	atomic no
Ac	actinium	Greek *aktis* = ray	89
Ag	silver	Anglo-Saxon *seolfor*	47
Al	aluminium	Latin *alumen* = alum	13
Am	americium	America	95
Ar	argon	Greek *argos* = inactive	18
As	arsenic	Latin *arsenicum*	33
At	astatine	Greek *astatos* = unstable	85
Au	gold	Anglo-Saxon *gold*	79
B	boron	Persian *būrah*	5
Ba	barium	Greek *barys* = heavy	56
Be	beryllium	Greek *beryllion* = beryl	4
Bi	bismuth	German (origin unknown)	83
Bk	berkelium	Berkeley, California	97
Br	bromine	Greek *bromos* = stench	35
C	carbon	Latin *carbo* = charcoal	6
Ca	calcium	Latin *calx* = lime	20
Cd	cadmium	Greek *kadmeia* = calamine	48
Ce	cerium	planet Ceres	58
Cf	californium	California	98
Cl	chlorine	Greek *chloros* = green	17
Cm	curium	Pierre and Marie Curie	96
Co	cobalt	German *Kobold* = goblin	27
Cr	chromium	Greek *chroma* = colour	24
Cs	caesium	Latin *caesium* = bluish-grey	55
Cu	copper	Cyprus	29
Dy	dysprosium	Greek *dysprositos*	66
Er	erbium	Ytterby, a Swedish town	68
Es	einsteinium	Einstein	99
Eu	europium	Europe	63
F	fluorine	Latin *fluo* = flow	9
Fe	iron	Anglo-Saxon *iren*	26
Fm	fermium	Fermi	100
Fr	francium	France	87
Ga	gallium	Latin *gallia* = France	31
Gd	gadolinium	Gadolin, a Finnish chemist	64
Ge	germanium	Latin *Germania*	32
H	hydrogen	Greek *hydro* = water + *gen*	1
He	helium	Greek *helos* = sun	2
Hf	hafnium	Hafnia = Copenhagen	72
Hg	mercury	Mercury (myth)	80
Ho	holmium	*Holmia* = Stockholm	67
I	iodine	Greek *iodes* = violet	53
In	indium	its indigo spectrum	49
Ir	iridium	Latin *iris* = a rainbow	77
K	potassium	English potash	19
Kr	krypton	Greek *kryptos* = hidden	36
La	lanthanum	Greek *lanthan* = conceal	57
Li	lithium	Greek *lithos* = stone	3
Lu	lutetium	Lutetia, ancient name of Paris	71
Lw	lawrencium	Lawrence, US physicist	103
Md	mendelevium	Mendeléev, Russian chemist	101
Mg	magnesium	Magnesia, district in Thessaly	12
Mn	manganese	Latin *magnes* = magnet	25
Mo	molybdenum	Greek *molybdos* = lead	42
N	nitrogen	Greek *nitron* = saltpetre	7
Na	sodium	English *soda*	11
Nb	niobium	Niobe (Greek myth)	41
Nd	neodymium	Greek *neos* = new and *didymos* = twin	60
Ne	neon	Greek *neos* = new	10
Ni	nickel	German, abbreviation of *Kupfernickel*	28
No	nobelium	Nobel	102
Np	neptunium	planet Neptune	93
O	oxygen	Greek *oxys* = acid + *gen*	8
Os	osmium	Greek *osme* = odour	76
P	phosphorus	Latin, from Greek 'light-bearing'	15
Pa	protactinium	Greek *protos* = first + *actinium*	91
Pb	lead	Anglo-Saxon *lead*	82
Pd	palladium	planet Pallas	46
Pm	promethium	Prometheus, stealer of fire from heaven (Greek myth)	61
Po	polonium	Poland	84
Pr	praseodymium	Greek *prasios* = green and *dydymos* = twin	59
Pt	platinum	Spanish *platina* = silver	78
Pu	plutonium	planet Pluto	94
Ra	radium	Latin *radius* = ray	88
Rb	rubidium	Latin *rubidus* = red	37
Re	rhenium	German *Rhein*	75
Rh	rhodium	Greek *rhodon* = rose	45
Rn	radon	radium emanation	86
Ru	ruthenium	Ruthenia	44
S	sulphur	Latin *sulfur*	16
Sb	antimony	L Latin *antimonium*	51
Sc	scandium	Scandinavia	21
Se	selenium	Greek *selene* = moon	34
Si	silicon	Latin *silex* = flint	14
Sm	samarium	Samarski, a Russian savant	62
Sn	tin	Anglo-Saxon *tin*	50
Sr	strontium	Strontian, a Scottish village	38
Ta	tantalum	Tantalus (Greek myth)	73
Tb	terbium	Ytterby, a Swedish town	65
Tc	technetium	Greek *technetos* = artificial	43
Te	tellurium	Latin *tellus* = earth	52
Th	thorium	god Thor	90
Ti	titanium	Latin *Titanes* = sons of the earth	22
Tl	thallium	Greek *thallos* = budding twig	81
Tm	thulium	Greek and Roman Thule = Northland	69
U	uranium	planet Uranus	92
Une	unnilennium		109
Unh	unnilhexium		106
Unp	unnilpentium		105
Unq	unnilquadium		104
Uns	unnilseptium		107
V	vanadium	goddess Vanadis (Freya)	23
W	tungsten	Swedish, heavy stone	74
Xe	xenon	Greek *xenos* = stranger	54
Y	yttrium	Ytterby, a Swedish town	39
Yb	ytterbium	Ytterby, a Swedish town	70
Zn	zinc	German *zink*	30
Zr	zirconium	Persian *zargun* = gold-coloured	40

Quantities, conversions and sizes

Physical constants

c speed of light in vacuo, $2{\cdot}997\,925 \times 10^{8}$ metres per second ($m{\cdot}s^{-1}$).

e electron charge, $1{\cdot}602\,192 \times 10^{-19}$ coulomb.

g standard acceleration of gravity, 9·806 65 metres per second per second ($m{\cdot}s^{-2}$). (At Greenwich, $g = 9{\cdot}811\,83$ metres per second per second.)

G gravitational constant, $6{\cdot}664 \times 10^{-11}\ N{\cdot}m^2{\cdot}kg^{-2}$.

h Planck('s) constant, the constant in the expression for the quantum of energy, $6{\cdot}626\,196 \times 10^{-34}$ J·s.

$\hbar$ *h*-bar, Dirac's constant, $\frac{h}{2\pi}$ (Planck's constant divided by 2π), the unit in which electron spin is measured.

m_e the mass of an electron at rest, $9{\cdot}109\,558 \times 10^{-31}$ kg.

m_p the mass of a proton at rest, $1{\cdot}672\,614 \times 10^{-27}$ kg.

m_n the mass of a neutron at rest, $1{\cdot}674\,92 \times 10^{-27}$ kg.

N_A Avogadro('s) number, constant, number of molecules in a mole of any substance, $6{\cdot}022\,52 \times 10^{23}$ per mole.

Speed of sound at sea level at 0°C, 331·7 metres per second.

Standard temperature and pressure (stp), 0°C and 101 325 $N{\cdot}m^{-2}$.

Standard volume of ideal gas, $2{\cdot}241\,36 \times 10^{-2}\ m^3{\cdot}mol^{-1}$ at stp.

Melting point of ice, 0°C or 273·15 K.

Temperature conversion

between degrees Celsius and Fahrenheit

°C	°F	°C	°F	°C	°F	°C	°F
1	33.8	26	78.8	51	123.8	76	168.8
2	35.6	27	80.6	52	125.6	77	170.6
3	37.4	28	82.4	53	127.4	78	172.4
4	39.2	29	84.2	54	129.2	79	174.2
5	**41.0**	**30**	**86.0**	**55**	**131.0**	**80**	**176.0**
6	42.8	31	87.8	56	132.8	81	177.8
7	44.6	32	89.6	57	134.6	82	179.6
8	46.4	33	91.4	58	136.4	83	181.4
9	48.2	34	93.2	59	138.2	84	183.2
10	**50.0**	**35**	**95.0**	**60**	**140.0**	**85**	**185.0**
11	51.8	36	96.8	61	141.8	86	186.8
12	53.6	37	98.6	62	143.6	87	188.6
13	55.4	38	100.4	63	145.4	88	190.4
14	57.2	39	102.2	64	147.2	89	192.2
15	**59.0**	**40**	**104.0**	**65**	**149.0**	**90**	**194.0**
16	60.8	41	105.8	66	150.8	91	195.8
17	62.6	42	107.6	67	152.6	92	197.6
18	64.4	43	119.4	68	154.4	93	199.4
19	66.2	44	111.2	69	156.2	94	201.2
20	**68.0**	**45**	**113.0**	**70**	**158.0**	**95**	**203.0**
21	69.8	46	114.8	71	159.8	96	204.8
22	71.6	47	116.6	72	161.6	97	206.6
23	73.4	48	118.4	73	163.4	98	208.4
24	75.2	49	120.2	74	165.2	99	210.2
25	**77.0**	**50**	**122.0**	**75**	**167.0**	**100**	**212.0**

The table reads in both directions, showing equivalent Celsius and Fahrenheit temperatures; it is based on whole number Celsius temperatures.

Where whole number Fahrenheit temperatures occur, they and their Celsius equivalents are shown in bold type. Approximate Celsius equivalents for other whole number Fahrenheit temperatures can be worked out – eg 54°F will be between 12°C and 13°C, but nearer 12°C. It is in fact 12.2°C.

Exact Celsius equivalents for Fahrenheit temperatures can be found by using the equation: – 32, × 5, ÷ 9. For example 54°F – 32 = 22 × 5 = 110 ÷ 9 = 12.2°C.

Conversion factors

Imperial to metric

Length		*Multiply by*
inches	→ millimetres	25.4
inches	→ centimetres	2.54
feet	→ metres	0.3048
yards	→ metres	0.9144
statute miles	→ kilometres	1.6093
nautical miles	→ kilometres	1.852

Area		*Multiply by*
square inches	→ square centimetres	6.4516
square feet	→ square metres	0.0929
square yards	→ square metres	0.8361
acres	→ hectares	0.4047
square miles	→ square kilometres	2.5899

Volume		*Multiply by*
cubic inches	→ cubic centimetres	16.3871
cubic feet	→ cubic metres	0.0283
cubic yards	→ cubic metres	0.7646

Capacity		*Multiply by*
UK fluid ounces	→ litres	0.0284
US fluid ounces	→ litres	0.0296
UK pints	→ litres	0.5682
US pints	→ litres	0.4732
UK gallons	→ litres	4.546
US gallons	→ litres	3.7854

Weight		*Multiply by*
ounces (avoirdupois)	→ grams	28.3495
ounces (troy)	→ grams	31.1035
pounds	→ kilograms	0.4536
tons (long)	→ tonnes	1.016

Metric to imperial

Length		*Multiply by*
millimetres	→ inches	0.0394
centimetres	→ inches	0.3937
metres	→ feet	3.2808
metres	→ yards	1.0936
kilometres	→ statute miles	0.6214
kilometres	→ nautical miles	0.54

Area		*Multiply by*
square centimetres	→ square inches	0.155
square metres	→ square feet	10.764
square metres	→ square yards	1.196
hectares	→ acres	2.471
square kilometres	→ square miles	0.386

Volume		*Multiply by*
cubic centimetres	→ cubic inches	0.061
cubic metres	→ cubic feet	35.315
cubic metres	→ cubic yards	1.308

Capacity		*Multiply by*
litres	→ UK fluid ounces	35.1961
litres	→ US fluid ounces	33.8150
litres	→ UK pints	1.7598
litres	→ US pints	2.1134
litres	→ UK gallons	0.2199
litres	→ US gallons	0.2642

Weight		*Multiply by*
grams	→ ounces (avoirdupois)	0.0353
grams	→ ounces (troy)	0.0322
kilograms	→ pounds	2.2046
tonnes	→ tons (long)	0.9842

International paper sizes

A series

	mm	*in*
A0	841 × 1189	33.11 × 46.81
A1	594 × 841	23.39 × 33.1
A2	420 × 594	16.54 × 23.39
A3	297 × 420	11.69 × 16.54
A4	210 × 297	8.27 × 11.69
A5	148 × 210	5.83 × 8.27
A6	105 × 148	4.13 × 5.83
A7	74 × 105	2.91 × 4.13
A8	52 × 74	2.05 × 2.91
A9	37 × 52	1.46 × 2.05
A10	26 × 37	1.02 × 1.46

A series is used for writing paper, books and magazines.

B series

	mm	*in*
B0	1000 × 1414	39.37 × 55.67
B1	707 × 1000	27.83 × 39.37
B2	500 × 707	19.68 × 27.83
B3	353 × 500	13.90 × 19.68
B4	250 × 353	9.84 × 13.90
B5	176 × 250	6.93 × 9.84
B6	125 × 176	4.92 × 6.93
B7	88 × 125	3.46 × 4.92
B8	62 × 88	2.44 × 3.46
B9	44 × 62	1.73 × 2.44
B10	31 × 44	1.22 × 1.73

B series for posters.

C series

	mm	*in*
C0	917 × 1297	36.00 × 51.20
C1	648 × 917	25.60 × 36.00
C2	458 × 648	18.00 × 25.60
C3	324 × 458	12.80 × 18.00
C4	229 × 324	9.00 × 12.80
C5	162 × 229	6.40 × 9.00
C6	114 × 162	4.50 × 6.40
C7	81 × 114	3.20 × 4.50
DL	110 × 220	4.33 × 8.66
C7/6	81 × 162	3.19 × 6.38

C series for envelopes.

All sizes in these series have sides in the proportion of $1:\sqrt{2}$.

Detailed chart of pronunciation

Vowels and diphthongs in accented syllables

Symbol		Examples	Pronunciation
ā	as in	name, aid, rein, tare, wear, hair, heir, fairy	*nām, ād, rān, tār, wār, hār, ār, fār'i*
ä	,,	grass, path, palm, harm, heart	*gräs, päth, päm, härm, härt*
a	,,	sat, bad, have, marry	*sat, bad, hav, mar'i*
ē	,,	lean, keel, dene, chief, seize, gear, sheer, here, bier, query	*lēn, kēl, dēn, chēf, sēz, gēr, shēr, hēr, bēr, kwē'ri*
e	,,	red, thread, said, bury	*red, thred, sed, ber'i*
ī	,,	side, shy, dye, height, hire, byre, fiery	*sīd, shī, dī, hīt, hīr, bīr, fīr'i*
i	,,	pin, busy, hymn	*pin, biz'i, him*
ō	,,	bone, road, foe, low, dough, more, soar, floor, port, Tory	*bōn, rōd, fō, lō, dō, mōr, sōr, flōr, pōrt, tō'ri*
		(For alternative pronunciation of port, more, etc, see *ö*)	
ö	,,	haul, lawn, fall, bought, swarm, more, soar, floor, port, Tory	*höl, lön, föl, böt, swörm, mör, sör, flör, pört, tö'ri*
		(For alternative pronunciation of port, more, etc, see *ō*)	
o	,,	got, shot, shone	*got, shot, shon*
o͞o	,,	fool, sou, boor, tour	*fo͞ol, so͞o, bo͞or, to͞or*
o͝o	,,	good, full, would	*go͝od, fo͝ol, wo͝od*
ū	,,	tune, due, newt, view, endure, fury	*tūn, dū, nūt, vū, in-dūr', fū'ri*
u	,,	bud, run, love	*bud, run, luv*
û	,,	heard, bird, word, absurd	*hûrd, bûrd, wûrld, ab-sûrd'*
ow	,,	mount, frown, sour	*mownt, frown, sowr*
oi	,,	toy, buoy, soil	*toi, boi, soil*

Stress

In words of more than one syllable, the syllable with the main accent is shown by a stress mark ' following that syllable, both in the respellings (eg *äf'tər, bi-gin'*) and in entries in bold-faced type (eg **af'ters**, **beginn'er**).

Note the difference in pronunciation, as shown by the position of the stress mark, between **blessed'** (*blest*) and **bless'ed** (*bles'id*), **refined'** (*ri-fīnd'*) and **refin'edly** (*ri-fīn'id-li*).

Vowels in unaccented syllables

Neutral vowels in unaccented syllables are usually shown by ə (schwa)
eg *el'ə-mənt, in'fənt, ran'dəm, pre'shəs* (precious), *nā'chər* (nature).

In certain cases, they are more exactly represented by *i*
eg *ē'vil, bi-hōld', bles'id, man'ij, di-ment'*.

Vowels followed by *r*

In certain accents, for example in Scots, Irish, General American, **r** is pronounced wherever it occurs in the spelling and this is the form adopted in the dictionary.

In certain other accents, for example Received Pronunciation or what is sometimes called the BBC accent, it is pronounced only when it occurs before a vowel. Elsewhere the following rules apply:

ār	is pronounced as	*eə*	*ör*	is pronounced as	*ö* or *öə*
är	,, ,, ,,	*ä*	*o͞or*	,, ,, ,,	*o͞oə*
ēr	,, ,, ,,	*iə*	*ūr*	,, ,, ,,	*ūə*
er	,, ,, ,,	*eə*	*ûr*	,, ,, ,,	*û*
īr	,, ,, ,,	*īə*	*owr*	,, ,, ,,	*owə*

See also page x